国家出版基金项目
NATIONAL PUBLICATION FOUNDATION

# 海上絲綢之路文獻集成

總主編 陳支平 陳春聲

## 科技與文化編 93

主編 王揚宗 葉農

海峽出版發行集團
THE STRAITS PUBLISHING & DISTRIBUTING GROUP
福建人民出版社

# 本册目次

# 中文會話及凡例

（*Dialogues and Detached Sentences in the Chinese Language; With a Free and Verbal Translation in English*）

〔英〕馬禮遜（Robert Morrison）編

《中文會話及凡例》，英國馬禮遜編。馬禮遜（Robert Morrison，一七八二—一八三四），首位基督教新教來華傳教士。生於英國布勒古林，一八〇七年來華，在華前後達二十五年，曾創辦英華書院。編撰有《英華字典》、《中國一覽》、《廣東省土話字彙》等。此書係漢語對話學習資料，正文首列會話三十一段，涉及諸多西人來華活動場景；後爲中國古代經典名言及民間俗語；末附度量、花甲子、拜帖、告示等，皆爲中英文對照。據一八一六年澳門版影印。

# DIALOGUES

AND

*DETACHED SENTENCES*

IN THE

# CHINESE LANGUAGE;

WITH A FREE AND VERBAL

## TRANSLATION IN ENGLISH.

COLLECTED FROM VARIOUS SOURCES.

DESIGNED AS AN INITIATORY WORK FOR THE USE OF STUDENTS OF CHINESE.

MACAO:

PRINTED AT THE HONORABLE EAST INDIA COMPANY'S PRESS,

*BY P. P. THOMS.*

1816.

TO

*THE HONORABLE THE COURT OF DIRECTORS*

OF

THE UNITED EAST INDIA COMPANY,

*THE FOLLOWING WORK*

IS MOST RESPECTFULLY DEDICATED

*BY THIR MOST OBEDIENT, AND*

VERY MUCH OBLIGED HUMBLE SERVANT,

THE COMPILER.

# PREFACE.

*THE Translation of the following Papers was made by the REV. ROBERT MORRISON, at the commencement of his Chinese Studies. The Text (somewhat altered) of the Pieces marked with a Dagger, were supplied by a Gentleman of the Honorable East India Company's Establishment, at China;* and the whole Printed under the inspection of James Bannerman, Esq. of the same Establishment. The Honorable the Court of Directors, who have already Printed at their sole expense, a Chinese Grammar, composed in 1812, by the Compiler of these Dialogues, and have undertaken in the same liberal manner a Chinese Dictionary, also Print at their own expense, the following little Work.*

---

* See Contents.

*The verbal rendering must not be considered as giving the invariable sense of each Word, but as containing an approximation to it's import in the connexion in which it stands in the sentence explained. A perfect verbal rendering is impracticable. Acquaintance with the Language will enable the mind to feel much more of the sense of Characters, than can be conveyed by the words of another Language, in a close verbal translation. The Dialogues being collected from different sources, exhibit a considerable variety of style.*

*Macao, July* 1, 1816.

# CONTENTS.

# DIALOGUES.

## DIALOGUE I. WITH A SHOPMAN AND VISITOR.

S. Pray sit down.

Ts'hing 請 Pray
tso. 坐。 sit

V. (It is the custom of the Chinese to echo the same and say,)

Ts'hing 請 Pray
tso. 坐。 sit.

S. (To the Servant) Bring Tea.

Taou 倒 Invert, i. e. pour out
ch'ha 茶 tea
lae. 來。 come.

S. (To the Guest) Will you take Tea?

Ts'hing 請 Pray (take)
ch'ha. 茶。 tea?

V. (The Guest echos the compliment, and assents by saying,)

Ts'hing 請 Pray (take)
ch'ha. 茶。 tea.

S. I have not seen you for a long time. I hope you have been very well?

Kew 久 Long time
wei 違。 opposed, i.e. separated
ne 你 you
yĭh 一 one
hëang 向 while past
tĭh 得 obtain
e 意 wish
tĭh 得 } in a high degree?*
hăn. 狠。

* In Chinese, though it be a general rule, that each Character and Syllable, has a determinate sense affixed to it; yet, cases are numerous, in which two or more

B

V. You are very polite; I hope your concerns have been prosperous. For sometime, I have not called on you.

| | | |
|---|---|---|
| Haou | 好 | Well |
| shwŏ, | 說。 | said, |
| tŏ | 托 | (I have) engaged * |
| pe | 庇 | (your) protection, |
| ne | 你 | your |
| paou | 寶 | valuable |
| hang | 行 | hong |
| săng | 生 | trade † |
| e | 意 | |
| haou | 好 | good |
| tĭh | 得 | very ? |
| hăn | 狠。 | |
| wo | 我 | I |
| yĭh | 一 | one |
| hëang | 向 | while past |
| shaou | 少 | seldom |
| lae | 來 | come |
| wăn | 問 | to inquire and |
| how. | 候。 | wait (on you). |

S. How could I expect it. My business has been rather limited; the present are our leisure months; besides, the European ships have not yet arrived, and therefore, we have not much to do.

| | | |
|---|---|---|
| K'he | 豈 | How ‡ |
| kan. | 敢。 | dare (I). |

Characters are joined in the apprehension of the reader, and form in fact, a compound word, similar to the Polysyllabic Languages of the West. Generally the sense of the compound arises naturally from the several component Characters; at other times, the sense of each is much obscured, or entirely lost. 得 Tĭh, "To obtain," 狠 Hăn, or 很 Hăn, "The noise of dogs fighting, or people wrangling," taken together, make the Superlative degree, and affords an instance of an obscure compound.

* "I have engaged your protection," i. e. by your kind assistance; or by the prosperous fortunes which ever accompany you, and all those whom you countenance, I have been well.

† 生意 Săng e, "Living intention; i. e. whatever is done to obtain a livelihood in the inferior departments of the community, as trade, mechanical employments, &c

‡ 豈敢 K'he kan, "How dare! or how presume!" i. e. I presume not to think

| | | |
|---|---|---|
| săng | 生 | Trade |
| e | 意 | |
| chay | 這 | this |
| seay | 些 | little |
| she | 時 | time |
| too | 都 | all |
| yew | 有 | have |
| hëen | 限。 | limit, |
| wei | 爲 | because |
| tsae | 在 | the present |
| she | 是 | are |
| hëen | 閒、 | leisure |
| yuĕ, | 月。 | months, |
| hwang | 況 | besides |
| ts'heay | 且 | |
| yang | 洋 | ocean |
| chuen | 船 | ships |
| yĭh | 亦 | also |

| | | |
|---|---|---|
| we | 未 | not |
| tsang | 曾 | yet |
| taou | 到 | arrived; |
| tĭh | 得。 | |
| so | 所 | therefore |
| e | 以 | |
| mŭh | 沒 | not |
| yew | 有 | have |
| shin | 甚 | any of consequence* |
| mo | 麽 | |
| săng | 生 | trade. |
| e. | 意。 | |

V. Very true. Why are the European ships so late? of late years they arrived sooner. What is the cause of this?

| | | |
|---|---|---|
| She | 是 | Yes. |
| ya, | 呀。 | |

myself entitled to such civility; implying, you treat me as a superior. This mode of expression, is in constant use, as a reply to any civil compliment, or mark of polite attention. The same is otherwise expressed by 不敢當 Pŭh kan t'hang, I "presume not to appropriate to myself, or deem myself worthy" of such polite treatment. The Tartars for K'he kan, use much 那裡 Na le, "How! where!" is there any foundation for your compliment!

甚麽 Shin mo, commonly denote "What;" they possess in this sentence a qualifying sense, and preceded by a negative, denote "Not any thing to speak of; not any of consequence." 未有甚麽事 We yew shin mo sze, "There is nothing particular occurring; or I have nothing particular to do," is a common expression.

| | | |
|---|---|---|
| kin | 今 | This |
| nëen | 年 | year |
| yang | 洋 | ocean |
| chuen | 船 | ships |
| joo | 如 | how |
| ho | 何 | |
| lae | 來 | come |
| tĭh | 得 | |
| che? | 遲。 | late? |
| wang | 往 | gone |
| nëen | 年 | years |
| e | 已 | have |
| king | 經 | |
| tsaou | 早 | earlier |
| taou | 到 | arrived. |
| leaou, | 了。 | |
| chay | 這 | This |
| she | 是 | is |
| shin | 甚 | what |
| mo | 麽 | |
| yuen | 緣 | cause? |
| koo | 故。 | |

S. I have heard that things are in an unsettled state at sea; that the foreigners are always fighting, and hence they arrive late.

| | | |
|---|---|---|
| Wo | 我 | I, (or my) |
| urh | 耳 | ear |
| wăn, | 聞 | heard |
| shwŏ, | 說。 | say, |
| hae | 海 | sea |
| mëen | 面 | surface |
| pŭh | 不 | not |
| hăn | 狠 | very |
| tae | 太 | peaceable; |
| ping; | 平。 | |
| chang | 常 | constantly |
| yew | 有 | have |
| e | 夷 | foreign |
| jin | 人 | men |
| ta | 打 | fight; |
| ch'hang | 仗 | |
| so | 所 | therefore |
| e | 以 | |
| lae | 來 | come |
| tĭh | 得 | |
| che. | 遲。 | late. |

V. As the European ships do not arrive, I am apprehensive, that the foreign commodities will be high this year.

| | | |
|---|---|---|
| She. | 是 | (Is) true, or, so. |
| kin | 今 | This |
| nëen | 年 | year |

| | | |
|---|---|---|
| yang | 洋 | European ships |
| chuen | 船 | |
| puh | 不 | not |
| taou, | 到。 | come, |
| chĭh | 只 | only |
| pa | 怕 | fear |
| yang | 洋 | foreign commodities |
| ho | 貨 | |
| yaou | 要 | (want) will |
| k'he | 起 | rise |
| kea. | 價。 | price. |

S. True. If the ships do not now arrive, all foreign articles will be dear; and more, it will be difficult to do business.

| | | |
|---|---|---|
| She | 是 | True. |
| ya. | 呀。 | |
| Joo | 如 | If |
| jŏ | 若 | |
| chay | 這 | this |
| ko | 個 | |
| she | 時 | time |
| how | 候 | |
| chuen | 船 | ships |
| pŭh | 不 | not |
| taou | 到。 | come; |
| kŏ | 各 | every |
| yang | 様 | sort |
| yang | 洋 | foreign |
| ho | 貨 | article, |
| too | 都 | all |
| she | 是 | will be |
| yaou | 要 | |
| kwei | 貴 | dear. |
| tĕĭh | 的 | |
| tsae | 再 | Again |
| chay | 者 | |
| mae | 買 | buying |
| mae | 賣 | selling |
| săng | 生 | trade |
| e | 意 | |
| yĭh | 亦 | also |
| nan | 難 | difficult |
| tso. | 做。 | to do. |

V. Yes. If the ships arrive soon it will be well, I also think of buying a few small things for presents; as the price is now high, I shall wait till the ships have arrived, when I will call again, and afford you some little assistance.

| | | |
|---|---|---|
| She | 是 | True. |
| ya. | 呀。 | |
| Jŏ | 若 | If |

chuen 船 ship
tsaou 早 soon
taou 到 arrive
tsew 就 then
haou 好 } well,
leaou, 了。 }
wo 我 I
yĭh 亦 also
seang 想 think
mae 買 buy
seay 些 little (a few)
ling 零 } odd things
wŭh 物 }
sung 送 to present
jin, 人。 to persons,
tan 但 but
mŭh 目 } now
hea 下 }
kea 價 } the price
tsëen 錢 }
tae 太 very
kwei 貴。 dear;
sze 俟 wait
chuen 船 ship
taou 到 } have arrived,
leaou 了。 }
tsae 再 then
lae 來 come
pang 幇 } assist a little.
chin. 趂 }

S. I am much obliged to you. If the ships arrive, I will send a person to let you know, Sir, and beg your countenance.

Haou 好 Well
shwŏ. 說。 said.
Jŏ 若 If
chuen 船 ship
taou 到。 arrive,
wo 我 I
ta 打 } send
fă 發 }
jin 人 a man
lae 來 (come) go
fung 奉 present
ts'hing 請 request
ta 大 } to (you) Sir,
kea; 駕。 }
tsze 賜 to confer
koo, 顧, regard,
tsze 賜 to confer
koo. 顧。 regard.

V. Very good, I will bid you good bye.

Haou 好 Well

shwŏ. 說。 said.

Joo 如 } Thus
tsze 此 }

kaou 告 announce

tsze 辭 } leave,
leaou. 了 }

S. Pray sit a little.

Tsae 再 Again

ts'hing 請 pray

tso 坐 sit,

tso. 坐 sit.

V. No. I have a little business at home.

Pŭh, 不 No,

shay 舍 } at home
hea 下 }

hwan 還 still

yew 有 have

seay 些 little

wei 微 trifling

seaou 小 small

sze. 事 business.

S. In that case, I will not detain you.

Joo 如 } Thus
tsze 此 }

pŭh 不 not

kan 敢 dare

fung 奉 present (or offer)

lew. 留。 detention.

V. You are very polite. I have paid you a short visit.

Haou 好 Well

shwŏ. 說。 said.

Shaou 少 Little

pei. 陪。 wait upon (you).

S. Forgive my not accompanying you far.

Shoo 恕 Excuse

pŭh 不 not

yuen 遠 far

sung. 送。 accompany.

I do not expect it. Good bye.

K'he 豈 How

kan, 敢。 dare!

ts'hing. 請。 Good bye.

S. Good bye.

Ts'hing. 請。 Good bye.

The above was composed by a Native Chinese.

# DIALOGUE II.

*WITH A TEA MERCHANT,*

ON HIS ARRIVAL IN CANTON FROM A DISTANT PROVINCE.

A. How do you do?

| | | |
|---|---|---|
| Laou | 老 | Venerable |
| yay | 爺 | father |
| haou. | 好。 | well? |

B. I hope you are well.

| | | |
|---|---|---|
| Ne | 你 | You |
| haou | 好 | well, |
| ya? | 呀。 | ?* |

—I wish to see you about business.

| | | |
|---|---|---|
| Wo | 我 | I |
| yaou | 要 | want |
| k'han | 看 | to see |
| ne, | 你。 | you, |
| kwan | 歡 | wish |
| he | 喜 | |
| pan | 辦 | to do |
| sze. | 事。 | business. |

A. When did you come to Canton.

| | | |
|---|---|---|
| Ne | 你 | You |
| ke | 幾 | what |
| she | 時 | time |
| taou | 到 | come to |
| laou | 了 | |
| Kwan-tung. | 廣東。 | Canton. |

B. I arrived about a fortnight ago.

| | | |
|---|---|---|
| Wo | 我 | I |
| taou | 到 | arrived |
| leaou | 了 | |
| yew | 有 | have |
| pan | 半 | half |
| ko | 個 | |
| too | 多 | more |
| yuĕ. | 月。 | moon. |

* 呀 Ya, or A broad, is a mere tone.

A. Indeed! I heard but to-day that you had come; if I had known sooner I would have gone to see you.

| | | |
|---|---|---|
| Kwo | 果 | Indeed |
| jen | 然 | |
| she! | 是。 | is so! |
| wo | 我 | I |
| kin | 今 | to- |
| jĭh | 日 | day |
| tsae | 纔 | only |
| t'hing | 聽 | heard |
| shwŏ | 說 | say |
| ne | 你 | you |
| taou | 到 | had arrived. |
| leaou, | 了。 | |
| jŏ | 若 | If |
| wo | 我 | I |
| sëen | 先 | before |
| che | 知 | know, |
| taou, | 道。 | |
| tsaou | 早 | early |
| ts'hëen | 前 | before |
| pae | 拜 | visit |
| ne | 你 | you |
| k'heu. | 去。 | gone. |

B. I am much obliged to you—thank you

| | | |
|---|---|---|
| Wo | 我 | I |
| to | 多 | much |
| seay | 謝 | thank |
| ne | 你 | you |
| tĭh | 得 | very. |
| hăn. | 狠。 | |

A. Had you a pleasant journey?

| | | |
|---|---|---|
| Yĭh | 一 | The road |
| loo | 路 | |
| ping | 平 | pleasant |
| gan | 安 | |
| mo? | 麽。 | ? |

B. Not pleasant; it was difficult travelling.

| | | |
|---|---|---|
| Pŭh | 不 | Not |
| ping | 平 | pleasant: |
| gan: | 安 | |
| loo | 路 | road |
| shang | 上 | upon |
| nan | 難 | difficult |
| hing. | 行。 | travel. |

— The road being narrow I travelled in a chair.

| | | |
|---|---|---|
| We | 未 | Not |
| to | 多 | very |
| kwan | 寬 | broad |
| loo; | 路。 | road, |
| wo | 我 | I |

| | | |
|---|---|---|
| tso | 坐 | sat |
| keaou | 轎 | chair |
| tsze | 子 | |
| hing. | 行。 | travelled. |

A. I thought, Sir, you came in a boat all the way.

| | | |
|---|---|---|
| Wo | 我 | I |
| sëang | 想 | thought, |
| tsun | 尊 | Sir, |
| kea, | 駕 | |
| yĭh | 一 | the road |
| loo, | 路 | |
| too | 都 | all |
| she | 是 | was |
| tso | 坐 | sit |
| chuen | 船 | boat |
| lae | 來 | come. |
| tëĭh. | 的。 | |

B. Indeed, yes, but this year the water is all dried up in consequence of the drought.

| | | |
|---|---|---|
| Kwo | 果 | Indeed |
| jen | 然 | |
| she ; | 是。 | is ; |
| wei, | 惟 | but |
| kin | 今 | this |
| nëen, | 年 | year |
| yin | 因 | because |
| jŏ | 熱 | hot |
| tĭh | 得 | very, |
| hăn, | 狠。 | |
| so | 所 | therefore |
| e | 以 | |
| ho | 河 | river |
| taou | 道 | road |
| too | 都 | all |
| kan | 乾 | dried. |
| leaou. | 了。 | |

A. Though it was so, I yet perceive you look very well.

| | | |
|---|---|---|
| Sŭy | 雖 | Although |
| jen | 然 | |
| joo | 如 | thus, |
| tsze, | 此。 | |
| taou | 到 | yet |
| te | 底 | |
| wo | 我 | I |
| k'han | 看 | see |
| tsun | 尊 | your honor's |
| yung | 容 | countenance |
| yew | 有 | has |
| seay | 些 | a little |
| fung | 風 | colour. |
| sĭh. | 色。 | |

— When do you return to Nanking.

| | | |
|---|---|---|
| Ne | 你 | You |
| ke | 幾 | what |
| she | 時 | time |
| hwŭy | 回 | return |
| Nan- | 南 | Nan- |
| king | 京 | king |
| k'heu. | 去。 | go. |

B. I cannot go before the next year.

| | | |
|---|---|---|
| Sin | 新 | New |
| nëen | 年 | year |
| che | 之 | 's, |
| ts'hëen | 前 | before |
| wo | 我 | I |
| pŭh | 不 | not |
| năng | 能 | can |
| k'he | 起 | raise |
| shin. | 身。 | body. |

A. As you will be in Canton some time, we shall have constant opportunities of seeing each other.

| | | |
|---|---|---|
| Ke | 既 | Since |
| jen | 然 | |
| ne | 你 | you |
| hwan | 還 | still |
| tsae | 在 | be in |
| Săng- | 省 | Canton |
| ching | 城 | |
| jĭh | 日 | day |
| tsze | 子 | |
| ch'hang | 長。 | long, |
| wo | 我 | we |
| mun | 們 | |
| pëĕ | 必 | must |
| yew | 有 | have |
| ke | 機 | opportunity |
| hwuy | 會 | |
| chang | 常 | constantly |
| chang | 常 | |
| këen | 見 | to see |
| mëen. | 面。 | face. |

B. You are very kind. I thought of going to your house to day, but was afraid you might not be at home.

| | | |
|---|---|---|
| Haou | 好 | Well |
| shwo, | 說。 | said, |
| wo | 我 | I |
| sëang | 想 | think |
| kin | 今 | to- |
| jĭh | 日 | day |
| taou | 到 | to go to |
| foo | 府 | your house |
| shang | 上 | |

| | | |
|---|---|---|
| fung | 奉 | to present |
| pae, | 拜 | respects, |
| tan | 但 | but |
| kung | 恐 | apprehend |
| pa | 怕 | |
| ne | 你 | you |
| pŭh | 不 | not |
| tsae | 在 | be at |
| foo, | 府。 | home, |
| joo | 如 | now, |
| kin | 今 | |
| wo | 我 | I |
| yay | 也 | also |
| yaou | 要 | want |
| k'heu | 去 | to go |
| pae | 拜 | to visit |
| pëĕ | 別 | other |
| tëĭh | 的 | |
| Laou | 老 | Gentlemen. |
| yay | 爺 | |
| mun. | 們。 | |

A. I shall be at home to receive you; — if I should have a little business to call me from home, you can wait a little; for I cannot remain long abroad, having business at home.

| | | |
|---|---|---|
| Wo | 我 | I |
| tsae | 在 | be at |
| shay | 舍 | home * |
| hea | 下 | |
| fung | 奉 | to wait. |
| how, | 候。 | |
| Hwŏ | 或 | Perhaps |
| chay | 者 | |
| wo | 我 | I |
| yew | 有 | have |
| sŭh | 俗 | vulgar |
| sze | 事 | business |
| pŭh | 不 | not |
| tsae | 在 | be at |
| kea | 家 | home |
| ne | 你 | you |
| k'ho | 可 | may |
| e | 以 | |
| tăng | 等 | wait |
| yĭh | 一 | a |

* 舍 Shay, denotes A cottage, 府 Foo, A superior mansion. 舍下 Shay hea, "Cottage below," is, My house. 府上 Foo shang, "Mansion above," is, Your house. The Pronouns My and Your are omitted, as Foo-shang is never applied to one's own house; nor Shay-hea to the house of another person.

| | | |
|---|---|---|
| hwŭy, | 會。 | while, |
| wo | 我 | I |
| pŭh | 不 | not |
| năng | 能 | can |
| ch'ang | 長 | long |
| tsae | 在 | be |
| wae, | 外。 | without, |
| yin | 因 | because |
| shay | 舍 | at home |
| hea | 下 | |
| yew | 有 | have |
| sŭh | 俗 | vulgar |
| sze | 事 | business |
| po | 頗 | rather |
| to. | 多。 | much. |

B. When I come, should you not be at home, I will take a walk and return.

| | | |
|---|---|---|
| Wo | 我 | I |
| lae | 來 | come |
| she | 時 | time |
| jŏ | 若 | if |
| ne | 你 | you |
| pŭh | 不 | not |
| tsae | 在 | at |
| foo | 府 | home, |
| shang, | 上 | |
| wo | 我 | I |
| kwang | 逛 | walk |
| yĭh | 一 | a |
| hwŭy | 會 | while |
| tsew | 就 | soon |
| hwŭy | 回 | return |
| lae. | 來 | come. |

A. (Very well,) if you have not yet visited the Chief, you had better wait on him first.

| | | |
|---|---|---|
| Ne | 你 | You |
| jŏ | 若 | if |
| we | 未 | not |
| tsăng | 曾 | yet |
| pae | 拜 | visit |
| Ta- | 大 | the Chief, * |
| pan, | 班 | |
| pŭh | 不 | not } better† |
| joo | 如 | as |

* 班 Pan, denotes A series of Persons who perform a certain duty in rotation, 大班 Ta-pan, denotes "The first of the series, the Chief."

† 不如 Pŭh joo, "Not as;" i. e. not so good as. That way not so good as this; or, better do so.

urh 而 } now
kin 今
sëen 先 first
taou 到 to
ta 他 his
kea 家 house
k'heu. 去。 go.

B. I ought, and also wish it, but fear that I cannot visit so many in one morning.

Kae 該 } Ought,
tang, 當。
wo 我 I
yay 也 also
yuen 願 } wish (it),
e, 意。
tan 但 but
pa 怕 fear
yĭh 一 one
taou 早 morning
pŭh 不 not
năng 能 can
pae 拜 visit
to 多 many
jin. 人。 persons.

A. If you wish it, it is better; it is not necessary to remain long at each Gentleman's house to hinder yourself. It will be more convenient to visit them all in one day.

Jŏ 若 If
she 是 it be
ne 你 } your
tĕĭh 的
e 意 } wish,
sze 思
hăn 狠 very
haou, 好。 good,
che 只 } only
she 是
pŭh 不 no
yung 用 use
tsae 在 to remain
kŏ 各 every
jin 人 persons
kea 家 house
tan 躭 } impeding
woo 悮
kung 工 } the work,
foo, 夫
jŏ 若 if
she 是 it be
yĭh 一 one
jĭh 日 day

| | | |
|---|---|---|
| tsuen | 全 | altogether |
| pae | 拜 | visit |
| ta | 他 | them |
| mun | 們 | |
| kăng | 更 | more |
| haou. | 好。 | good. |

B. Very well, I shall just do so.

| | | |
|---|---|---|
| Haou | 好 | Good, |
| ya, | 呀。 | |
| tsew | 就 | just |
| she | 是 | |
| chay | 這 | thus |
| yang | 樣 | |
| tso. | 做。 | do. |

—I will bid you good morning. Should you have any business, I will thank you to send your servant to my boat to call me.

| | | |
|---|---|---|
| Wo | 我 | I |
| urh | 而 | now |
| kin | 今 | |
| taou | 告 | take leave, * |
| tsze, | 辭。 | |
| kung | 恐 | (I) fear |
| fang | 防 | |
| yew | 有 | have |
| sze, | 事。 | business, |
| ts'hing | 請 | beg |
| ne | 你 | you |
| keaou | 叫 | to call |
| ne | 你 | your |
| tëĭh | 的 | |
| kăn | 跟 | servant † |
| pan | 班 | |
| taou | 到 | to go to |
| wo | 我 | my |
| chuen | 船 | boat |
| shang | 上 | |
| chaou | 找 | seek |
| wo | 我 | me |
| lae. | 來。 | come. |

* 告辭 Kaou tsze, "Announce taking leave." This expression is made use of by the Chinese when about to leave a person; q. d. "I shall now go." In formal language, 告坐 Kaou tso, "I announce my sitting down," is said by inferiors when they sit down; q. d. "I shall sit down with your permission."

† 跟班 Kăn pan, "Heel pan," or one who takes his place at the heels, or behind another person; a footman, a servant.

A. Very good.

| | | |
|---|---|---|
| Hăn | 狠 | Very |
| haou. | 好。 | good. |

B. I should like to go. May I trouble you to send your servant to go to my boat and call for a man to come here.

| | | |
|---|---|---|
| Wo | 我 | I |
| yaou | 要 | want |
| kaou | 告 | to take leave, |
| tsze, | 辭。 | |
| tsae | 再 | again |
| chay | 者 | |
| urh | 而 | now |
| kin | 今 | |
| ts'hing | 請 | beg |
| ne | 你 | your |
| kea | 家 | servant |
| jin | 人 | |
| tsae | 在 | at |
| wo | 我 | my |
| chuen | 船 | boat |
| shang | 上 | |
| keaou | 呌 | call |
| ko | 個 | a |
| jin | 人 | man |
| lae. | 來。 | come. |

# DIALOGUE III.

## *MANDARIN AND VISITORS.*

Mandarin calling his Servant, says,

Kwăn 官 } Servant.
urh. 兒 }

Servant answers by

Yew. 有 Have.

M. Go to the gate, and wait there, if Visitors from the different offices come to pay their respects, say, My Master has been much fatigued at the Examinations for several days, and feels indisposed to receive any one. Leave your card, that he may return the visit in a few days.

Ne 你 You
taou 到 go to
mun 門 } door
shang 上 }

sze 伺 } and wait,
how 候 }
t'hang 倘 if
yew 有 have
kŏ 各 every
Ya- 衙 } office
mun 門 }
pae 拜 } pay respects,
ho, 賀 }
shwŏ, 說 say,
wo 我 My
laou 老 } Master,
yay, 爺 }
lëen 連 successive
jĭh 日 day
ko 科 } at the Examination*
chang 塲 }

* 科塲 Ko-chang, A triennial examination of the Literati.

sin 辛 } fagged,
koo 苦。}
lan 懶 lazy
yu 於 in
tsëĕ 接 receiving and
këen, 見。 seeing,
che 止 only
lew 留 leave
tëĕ, 帖。 a card
yung 容 allow
jïh 日 days
tă 答 answer
pae. 拜。 visit.

S. Yes, Sir.

Ah. 吓。 (A tone.)*

(Servants without say), This is the place.

Chay 這 } Here
le 裡 }
she 是 } it is.
leaou. 了。}

Seaou-săng. Announce a Visitor.

T'hung 通 } Communicate report.
paou. 報。}

S. Yes.

Ah. 吓。 Yes.

S. (To the Porter,) I will trouble you to announce a recently made Tsin-sze, who pays his respects.

Seang 相 Mutually
fan 煩 trouble
t'hung 通 } to announce
paou 報 }
sin 新 New
Tsin- 進 } Tsin-sze,†
sze 士 }
pae. 拜。 pays respects.

S. My Master is fatigued by Examining the exercises; he is indisposed to see any one. Leave your card, and he will return your visit in a few days.

Kea 家 Family‡

* 吓 Ah, is a mere sound, enunciated by servants, and implying That they understand the commands given them.

† 進士 Tsin-sze, 'An advanced scholar.' A literary title of considerable respectability.

‡ 家 Kea, 'House family,' as on several other occasions, is used for the Pronoun My.

yay, 爺 father
yuĕ 閱 looking over
keuen 卷 papers
sin 辛 } fagged,
koo, 苦。
lan 懶 lazy
yu 於 in
tsëĕ 接 receiving and
këen; 見。 seeing;
che 止 only
lew 留 retain
tëĕ 帖 } card,
urh, 兒。
yung 容 allow
jĭh 日 days
tă 答 to answer
pae. 拜。 visit.

V. My good man, go and say that Hwang-foo-yin, the distressed scholar, begs an interview.

Tsun 尊 Honorable
kwăn, 官。 officer,
ne 你 you
k'heu 去 go
pin 稟 petition and
shwŏ, 說。 say,
nan 難 the distressed
săng 生 pupil
Hwang- 皇 }
foo- 甫 } Hwang-foo-yin,
yin, 吟 }
k'hew 求 begs
këen. 見。 to see him.

(Chow, A servant of the house, to another servant inquires,) May I announce it?

Paou 報 Announce
tĭh 得 } can?
tëĭh 的。

(Who assents by echoing the question,) It may be announced.

Paou 報 Announce
tĭh 得 } can?
tëĭh. 的。

Chow. Very good.

She. 是。 Be it so.

S. Sir, A newly made Tsin-sze, pays his respects.

Ke 啟 (I) begin,
yay, 爺。 Sir,
Sin 新 New
Tsin- 進 } Tsin-sze
sze 士
pae. 拜。 visits.

M. Tush. What did I tell you! You still come to announce people.

| | | |
|---|---|---|
| Woo! | 嘸 | Tush! |
| wo | 我 | I |
| tsăng | 怎 | what |
| mo | 麽 | |
| yang | 樣 | manner |
| fun | 吩 | command, |
| foo, | 咐 | |
| ne | 你 | you |
| yew | 又 | still |
| lae | 來 | come |
| pin. | 稟 | to petition. |

S. I answered him according to your order; but he said, that he must beg to see you.

| | | |
|---|---|---|
| Seaou | 小 | I |
| kwăn | 官 | |
| yay | 也 | also |
| she | 是 | did |
| chay | 這 | thus |
| tăng | 等 | |
| hwŭy | 回 | answer |
| t'ha; | 他 | him; |
| t'ha | 他 | he |
| shwŏ | 說 | said |
| nan | 難 | distressed |
| săng | 生 | pupil |
| yih | 一 | positively |
| ting | 定 | |
| yaou | 要 | wanted |
| k'hew | 求 | to beg |
| këen. | 見 | to see. |

M. A distressed scholar! O, the distressed scholar, Hwang-foo-yin! it is he,—Say I will come out.

| | | |
|---|---|---|
| Na | 那 | That |
| ko | 個 | |
| nan | 難 | distressed |
| săng! | 生 | pupil! |
| woo, | 嘸 | O, |
| nan | 難 | the distressed |
| mun | 門 | scholar |
| săng | 生 | |
| hwang | 皇 | Hwang-foo-yin. |
| foo- | 甫 | |
| yin, | 吟 | |
| yuen | 原 | origin } it proves |
| lae | 來 | come |
| she | 是 | is } to be, |
| t'ha, | 他 | he |
| shwŏ | 說 | Say |
| wo | 我 | I |

ch'hŭh 出 } will go out.
lae. 來。

S. Very well.

Ah. 吓。 Yes.

S. (To the Visitor,) My Master is coming out.

Laou 老 } Master
yay 爺
ch'hŭh 出 } will come out.
lae. 來。

M. My worthy friend.

Hëen 賢 Virtuous
ke. 契。 bond.

V. My benefactor, (kneeling).

Găn 恩 Gracious
sze. 師。 teacher.

M. (Smiling,) Indeed, it is my worthy friend. Pray rise, pray rise up.

Kwo 果 } In truth,
jen, 然。
she 是 it is
hëen 賢 } my worthy friend,
ke, 契。
Ah- 阿 } Ah-ya!
ya! 呀。
ts'hing 請 beg (you)
k'he! 起。 rise!
ts'hing 請 beg (you)
k'he! 起。 rise!

V. I ought not, (rising).

Pŭh 不 Not
kan. 敢。 dare.

M. My worthy friend, pray (enter).

Hëen 賢 } My worthy friend
ke 契
ts'hing. 請。 pray.

V. My benefactor, precede me.

Pŭh 不 Not
kan, 敢 dare,
găn 恩 } Benefactor
sze 師
ts'hing. 請。 pray.

M. My worthy friend, you must indeed precede.

Tsze 自 } Indeed
jen 然
she 是 is
hëen 賢 } worthy friend
ke 契
ts'hing. 請。 pray.

V. I cannot presume, pray precede me.

Pŭh 不 Not
kan 敢 dare
ts'hing. 請。 pray.

M. My good friend, as you are so determined, I will desist. I can only shew you the way.

Ah, 吓 Ah,
hëen 賢 } my worthy friend
ke 契
chǐh 执 holds fast
e 意 idea
pŭh 不 not
hing, 行 walk,
pa, 罷 well,
laou 老 } the old fellow
foo 夫
chǐh 只 only
tang 當 must
yin 引 lead
taou. 道 the way.

V. My Benefactor, pray take the higher place, till your distressed pupil kneels in your presence.

Găn 恩 } Benefactor
sze 師
ts'hing 請 pray
shang, 上 go high,
tae 待 till
nan 難 distressed
mun 門 } scholar
săng 生
pae 拜 bows
këen. 見 and sees.

M. It is not necessary.

Pŭh 不 Not
seaou. 消 necessary.

V. I was in distress, but happily by your aid, benevolent Sir, my life was saved, and I obtained my liberty. Now again, I have to thank you for my promotion. Goodness and virtue like this, cannot be recompensed by the sacrifice of my life.

Nan 難 (1) distressed
săng 生 scholar
hing 幸 happily
lae, 賴 relied,
găn 恩 benevolent
sze, 師 Sir,
shǐh 釋 } and was set at liberty,
fang, 放
tǐh 得 obtained
e 以 thereby
săng 生 life
tsuen. 全 complete.
Kin- 今 To
jǐh 日 day
yew 又 again

| | | |
|---|---|---|
| mung | 蒙 | give thanks |
| te | 提 | being raised, |
| pă, | 拔 | |
| tsze | 此 | this |
| găn | 恩 | benevolence, |
| tsze | 此 | this |
| tĭh | 德 | virtue! |
| keuen | 捐 | giving up |
| keu | 軀 | my person (to death) |
| nan | 難 | impossible |
| paou. | 報 | to recompense. |

M. On a former day, your acquittal was a part of my duty; and my worthy friend, your promotion to day, is owing to your own progress in learning.—What merit attaches to me! It is the appointment of heaven, not from man.

| | | |
|---|---|---|
| Ts'hëen | 前 | Former |
| jĭh | 日 | day |
| shĭh | 釋 | set you at liberty, |
| fang, | 放 | |
| she | 是 | was |
| hea | 下 | my* |
| kwăn. | 官 | |

| | | |
|---|---|---|
| fun | 分 | part |
| nuy | 內 | within |
| che | 之 | 's |
| sze, | 事 | business, |
| kin | 今 | to- |
| jĭh | 日 | day |
| kaou | 高 | high |
| chŏ, | 擢 | exaltation, |
| she | 是 | is |
| hëen | 賢 | worthy friend's |
| ke | 契 | |
| wăn | 文 | literature |
| tsae | 才 | |
| so | 所 | that which |
| tseu, | 取 | obtain, |
| yu | 與 | to |
| hea | 下 | me |
| kwăn | 官 | |
| ho | 何 | what |
| kung | 功 | merit |
| che | 之 | 's |
| yew, | 有 | have, |
| tsze | 此 | this |
| nae | 乃 | is |
| t'hëen | 天 | heaven |

* 下官 Hea-kwăn, 'Inferior officer;' 下職 Hea-chĭh, 'Inferior office;' and 卑職 Pei-chĭh, 'Mean office,' are periphrases used for the Personal Pronouns I, me, my, mine.

ting, 定 fix,
k'he 豈 how
yew 由 from
jin 人 men
wei. 爲 effected.

V. Your goodness, lofty as the mountain, and immense as the ocean, forms part of myself, and will never be forgotten.

Shan 山 Hill
hae 海 seas
che 之 's
găn 恩 favor
lun 淪 has entered
yu 于 to (my)
kwŏ 骨 bones and
suy; 髓 marrow;
k'he 豈 how
kan 敢 dare
wang 忘 forget
yu 于 either
tan 旦 morning
seĕh. 夕 evening.

M. Pray sit down.

Ts'hing 請 Pray
tso. 坐 sit.

V. My benefactor pray be exalted; how should I dare to sit in his presence.

Găn 恩 } Benefactor
sze 師 }
tsae 在 be
shang, 上 exalted,
nan 難 distressed
mun 門 } scholar
săng 生 }
tsăng 怎 how
kan 敢 dare
tso. 坐 sit.

M. We must have a little conversation together. Why should you not sit down? Do, do sit down.

We 未 Not
mëen 免 avoid
yew 有 have
ke 幾 few
keu 句 }
hwa 話 } words
urh 兒 }
tan 談 } conversation or fa-
tan, 談 } miliar chat.
na 那 where
yew 有 have
pŭh 不 not

tso 坐 sit
che 之 the
le, 理。 reason,
ts'hing 請 pray
ts hing 請 pray
tso. 坐。 sit.

V. Well, I will sit down.

Kaou 告 Announce
tso 坐 } sit.
leaou. 了。 }

(Servants without,) This is the place.

Chay 這 } Here
le 理 }
she 是 } it is.
leaou. 了。 }

Visitor, Announce me.

T'hung 通 } Announce.
paou. 報。 }

(Servant call out,) Is there any one at the gate?

Mun 門 } At the door
shang 上 }
yew 有 have
jin 人 man
mo? 麽。

(Servant of the house,) Who is there?

Shĕ 什 } What
mo 麽 }
jin? 人。 man?

S. Announce Mr. Ch'hang the Yu-she.

T'hung 通 } Announce
paou 報 }
Yu- 御 } the Yu-she
she 史 }
Ch'hang 張 } Mr. Ch'hang
laou 老 }
yay 爺 }
pae. 拜。 visits.

S. My Master is fagged by examining the exercises, and is indisposed to see any one. Leave your card that he may return the visit in a few days.

Kea 家 } My master
yay 爺 }
yuĕ 閱 looking over
keuen 卷 papers
sin 辛 } is fagged,
koo, 苦。 }
lan 懶 lazy
yu 于 in
tsëĕ 接 meeting
keën, 見。 seeing,

| | | |
|---|---|---|
| che | 止 | only |
| lew | 留 | leave |
| tëĕ | 帖 | a card |
| urh | 兒 | |
| yung | 容 | in a few days |
| jĭh | 日 | |
| tă | 答 | return |
| pae. | 拜 | visit. |

2nd. V. Very well,—leave a card.

| | | |
|---|---|---|
| Woo, | 唔 | Well, |
| lew | 留 | leave |
| hea | 下 | |
| tëĕ | 帖 | a card. |
| urh. | 兒 | |

S. Yes, Sir.

| | | |
|---|---|---|
| Ah. | 吓 | Yes. |

2nd. V. Come here.

| | | |
|---|---|---|
| Lae. | 來 | Come. |

S. Here.

| | | |
|---|---|---|
| Yew. | 有 | Have. |

2nd. V. Whose is this small chair?

| | | |
|---|---|---|
| Chay | 這 | This (mean) |
| shing | 乘 | |
| seaou | 小 | small |
| keaou | 轎 | chair |
| she | 是 | is |
| shwŭy | 誰 | whose? |
| tëĭh? | 的 | |

S. A newly made Tsin-sze's.

| | | |
|---|---|---|
| Sin | 新 | New |
| Tsin | 進 | Tsin-sze |
| sze | 士 | |
| tëĭh. | 的 | 's. |

2nd. V. Ah, a New made Tsin-sze, can I see him; and shall it be said that I cannot see him, stand back.

| | | |
|---|---|---|
| Ah, | 吓 | What, |
| sin | 新 | New |
| Tsin- | 進 | Tsin-sze |
| sze | 士 | |
| këen | 見 | see |
| tĭh | 得 | can? |
| nan | 難 | hard |
| taou | 道 | to say |
| wo | 我 | I |
| taou | 到 | then |
| pŭh | 不 | not |
| këen | 見 | see |
| tĭh | 得 | can |
| mo? | 麽 | ? |
| hwŭy | 廻 | stand back. |
| pe. | 避 | |

(A servant orders the chair to be put

down, and one goes in to announce him.) Master, Mr. Ch'hang the Yu-she has called.

Ke 啟 (I) begin,
yay 爺 Sir, (to speak)
Yu- 御 } the Yu-she
she 史 }
Ch'hang 張 Ch'hang
laou 老 } Mr.
yay 爺 }
pae. 拜。 visits.

M. O, Ch'hang, the Yu-she.—My good friend, have you visited him yet?

O, 哦。 O,
Ch'hang 張 Ch'hang
Yu- 御 } the Yu-she;
she; 史。 }
hēen 賢 } my worthy friend
ke 契 }
k'ho 可 } have you yet
tsăng 曾 }
pae 拜 } visited him.
kwo. 過。 }

V. Not yet.

Kwan 還 Still
we. 未。 not.

M. In that case, I will thank you to step into the library and sit a little.

Joo 如 } Thus
tsze 此 }
ts'hing 請 pray
taou 到 go to
shoo 書 the book
fang 房 room
shaou 少 little
tso. 坐。 sit.

V. Very well.

She. 是。 Yes.

M. (To the Servant,) Say, I beg him to walk in.

Taou 道 Say
yew 有 have
ts'hing. 請。 request.

S. My Master is coming out.

Kea 家 } My Master*
yay 爺 }
ch'hŭh 出 out
lae. 來。 come.

M. Ah! His Excellency Ch'hang.

Ah! 吓 Ah!

* 家 Kea, 'House family,' is often used for My; 家父 Kea-foo, 'My father,' and the phrase in the text, Kea-yay.

| | | |
|---|---|---|
| Ch'hang, | 張 | Ch'hang, |
| Ta | 大 | great |
| jin. | 人。 | man. |

V. Mr. Le, Mr. Le.

| | | |
|---|---|---|
| Le | 李 | Le |
| ta | 大 | great* |
| jin. | 人。 | man. |

M. Pray walk on up to the place of honor.

| | | |
|---|---|---|
| Ta | 大 | Sir |
| jin | 人 | |
| ts'hing. | 請。 | pray. |

2nd. V. Pray Sir, take the higher place, and allow me to make my bow.

| | | |
|---|---|---|
| Ts'hing, | 請 | Pray, |
| ta | 大 | Sir, |
| jin | 人 | |
| ts'hing | 請 | pray |
| shang, | 上 | go high, |
| hea | 下 | inferior |
| kwăn | 官 | officer |
| yew | 有 | have |
| yĭh | 一 | a |
| pae. | 拜。 | bow.† |

M. I also make my bow.

| | | |
|---|---|---|
| Heŏ | 學 | Pupil‡ |
| săng | 生 | |
| yay | 也 | also |
| yew | 有 | have |
| yĭh | 一 | a |
| pae. | 拜。 | bow. |

2d. V. I congratulate you, Sir, on being the Superintendant at the literary examination. We also are honored by it.

| | | |
|---|---|---|
| Kung | 恭 | Congratulate, |
| he | 喜 | |
| ta | 大 | (you) Sir, |
| jin, | 人 | |
| choo | 主 | controuling |
| sze | 事 | the business |
| wăn | 文 | of the literary |
| chang, | 場。 | arena. |

* 大人 Ta jin, 'Great man,' is a title applicable to officers of the first and second rank, and by courtesy to those of the third.

† 拜 Pae, 'To bow, to worship,' said either of acts of obeisance to fellow creatures; or of solemn acts of adoration to departed spirits and the gods.

‡ 學生 Heŏ săng, 'A scholar, a pupil;' a common phrase amongst literary Persons for I, &c.

woo 吾 }We
pei 輩 }
yew 有 have
kwang. 光。 light or glory.

M. I have to thank his Majesty for his unmerited goodness, in granting me the charge of the Examination; I am really anxious about, and ashamed of my defects. Pray sit down, Sir.

Hea 下 }I
kwăn 官 }
taou 叨 }thank
mung 蒙 }
shing 聖 (His Majesty's) sacred
găn, 恩 goodness,
mew 謬 erroneously (giving)
chang 掌 the care of the silk's
Sze 絲 }unfolding;
lun, 綸。 }
shih 實 }very much
ts'hëě 切 }
hwang 惶 agitated and
kwei. 愧。 ashamed.
Ta 大 }Sir,
jin 人 }
ts'hing 請 pray
tso. 坐。 sit.

2nd. V. I will sit down, Sir.

有 Have
tso, 坐 sit,
ta 大 great
jin, 人。 man.

M. Sir.

Ta 大 Great
jin. 人。 man.

2nd. V. I heard there was some visitor with you:—why do you not request him to come out a little?

Wăn 聞 }Heard
tih 得 }
shĕ 什 }some
mo 麼 }
kwei 貴 honorable
kŏ 客 visitor

* 絲綸 Sze-lun, Sze denotes 'Silk;' Lun, 'The careful and orderly folding up from the ball.' Here used to express Drawing forth, and describing on the merits of, the elegant compositions of the Candidates for literary honors. By a like metaphor, the Imperial Mandates and Official Declarations are called 綸音 Lun-yin, 'Silken sounds envolved with consummate order and harmony.'

| | | |
|---|---|---|
| tsae | 在 | here; |
| tsze; | 此 | |
| ho | 何 | why |
| pŭh | 不 | not |
| ts'hing | 請 | beg |
| ch'hŭh | 出 | out |
| lae | 來 | come |
| yĭh | 一 | a |
| hwŭy. | 會 | while. |

M. There is no person —

| | | |
|---|---|---|
| Mŭh | 沒 | Not |
| yew, | 有 | have, |
| ah. | 吓 | |

2d.V. The little chair without side, is—?

| | | |
|---|---|---|
| Wae | 外 | Outside |
| pëen | 邊 | |
| chay | 這 | this |
| shing | 乘 | |
| seaou | 小 | small |
| keaou | 轎 | chair |
| she. | 是 | is? |

M. Oh, he is not a visitor, he is a pupil of mine.

| | | |
|---|---|---|
| Ah, | 吓 | O, |
| fei | 非 | not |
| kŏ, | 客 | a visitor, |
| yay | 也 | also (only) |
| she | 是 | is |
| pe | 敝 | worthless |
| mun | 門 | pupil. |
| săng. | 生 | |

2nd. V. He is a pupil of your's, why not invite him to come out a little?

| | | |
|---|---|---|
| She | 是 | Is |
| kwei | 貴 | noble |
| mun | 門 | pupil, |
| săng, | 生 | |
| ho | 何 | why |
| pŭh | 不 | not |
| ts'hing | 請 | request |
| ch'hŭh | 出 | out |
| lae | 來 | come |
| yĭh | 一 | a |
| hwŭy. | 會 | while. |

M. When here, just now, the was saying that he wanted to visit Mr. Ch'hang. (To the Servant,) Come here.

| | | |
|---|---|---|
| Fang | 方 | Just now |
| tsae | 纔 | |
| ching | 正 | whilst, when here, |
| tsae | 在 | |
| tsze | 此 | |
| taou | 道 | speaking |
| k'heĭh | 及 | about |

ching 正* just
yaou 要 wanting
pae 拜 to visit
Ch'hang 張 Ch'hang,
ta 大 Great
jin. 人。 man. (To the ser.)
Kwo 過 Across
lae. 來。 come

S. Yes.

Yew. 有。 Here

M. Request Mr. Hwang-foo, to come out.

Ts'hing 請 Request
Hwang-foo 皇甫 } Hwang-foo,
yay 爺 Mr.
ch'hŭh 出 out
lae. 來 come.

S. Yes, Sir; (goes in,) Mr. Ch'hang-foo, you are requested to come out.

Ah, 吓。 Yes,
Hwang-foo 皇甫 } Hwang-foo,
yay 爺 Mr.
yew 有 there is
ts'hing. 請。 an invitation.

V. (Comes out,) My Benefactor.

Găn 恩 Gracious
sze. 師。 Master.

M. My worthy friend, you just now said that you wanted to go and visit Mr. Ch'hang. He is now here, you may as well see him. (To Mr. Ch'hang) Sir, my pupil begs to pay his respects to you.

Hëen ke 賢契 } My worthy friend,
ne 你 you
fang tsae 方纔 } just now
shwŏ, 說 said,
yaou 要 wanted
k'heu 去 to go
pae 拜 to visit
Ch'hang 張 Ch'hang,
ta jin, 大人 } Mr.
na, na, na, 哪哪哪 } Ah, ah, ah,

* 正 Ching, 'Right; straight; in the exact point of time; just whilst,

joo 如 } now
kin 今
ta 大 } His Excellency
jin 人
tsae 在 } is here,
tsze, 此。
k he 豈 how
pŭh 不 not
tsew 就 forthwith
mëen 面 face
pae 拜 } bow
leaou ? 了
lae, 來 come
lae, 來 come,
lae. 來。 come,

(To the second visitor.)

Ta 大 } Sir,
jin, 人
pe 敝 (my) worthless
num 門 } pupil
săng 生
k'hew 求 begs
këen. 見。 to see.

2nd. V. Oh, this is your worthy pupil.

Ah, 吓。 Oh,
chay 這 this
tsew 就 then
she 是 is
kwei 貴 noble
mun 門 } pupil.
săng. 生。

V. Sir.

Ta 大 Great
jin. 人。 man.

2nd. V. Mr. Tsin-sze.

Tsin 進 } Tsin-sze
sze 士
kung. 公。 Mr.

M. Bow to the ground, make a prostration.

Kow 叩 Head to the ground
hea 下 down
h'heu 去 go
hea 下 down
ko 個 a
tseuen 全 complete
le. 禮。 ceremony.

V. There is no occasion for that, a common bow is enough.

Pŭh 不 No
seaou, 消 occasion,
chang 常 common
le 禮 ceremony
pa. 罷。 enough

M. In this case obey.

| | | |
|---|---|---|
| Joo | 如 | Thus |
| tsze | 此 | |
| tsung | 從 | comply with |
| ming | 命 | orders |
| pa. | 罷。 | well. |

2nd. V. Mr. Tsin-sze, pray sit down.

| | | |
|---|---|---|
| Tsin- | 進 | Tsin-sze, |
| sze | 士 | |
| kung | 公 | Mr. |
| ts'hing | 請 | pray |
| tso. | 坐。 | sit. * |

V. How shall I dare to sit in your presence.

| | | |
|---|---|---|
| Ta | 大 | Sir, |
| jin | 人 | |
| tsae | 在 | here |
| tsze | 此 | |
| tsăng | 怎 | how |
| kan | 敢 | dare |
| tso. | 坐。 | sit. |

M. My Pupil ougnt not to sit, Sir, in your presence.

| | | |
|---|---|---|
| Ta | 大 | Sir, (you) |
| jin, | 人。 | |
| tsae | 在 | being |
| tsze, | 此。 | here, |
| pe | 敝 | worthless |
| mun | 門 | Pupil |
| săng | 生 | |
| yen | 焉 | how |
| kan | 敢 | dare |
| tso. | 坐。 | sit. |

2nd. V. Why not sit down ?

| | | |
|---|---|---|
| Na | 那 | Where |
| yew | 有 | have |
| pŭh | 不 | not |
| tso | 坐 | sit |
| che | 之 | the |
| le. | 理。 | reason. |

M. Well, my worthy friend.

| | | |
|---|---|---|
| Ah, | 吓 | So, |
| yay | 也 | also |
| pa, | 罷 | well, |
| hëen | 賢 | my worthy friend. |
| ke. | 契。 | |

V. My benefactor.

| | | |
|---|---|---|
| Găn | 師 | Gracious master. |
| sze. | 恩。 | |

* Excessive and tiresome as all this ceremony is, it appears a true representation of what prevails amongst such Persons as are delineated in the Story.

F

M. Bow and sit down; bow and sit down.

Na, 哪 Oh,
kaou 告 announce
ko 個 a
tso 坐 } sit,
urh, 兒。
kaou 告 announce
ko 個 a
tso 坐 } sit.*
urh. 兒。

2nd. V. It is unnecessary.

Pŭh 不 No
seaou. 消。 occasion.

V. Sir, I shall sit down.

Ta 大 } Sir,
jin 人
kaou 告 announce
tso 坐 } sitting down.
leaou. 了。

2nd. V. Mr. Tsin-sze, sit down.

Tsin- 進 } Tsin-sze,
sze 士
kung 公 Mr.
tso 坐 } sit down.
leaou. 了。

M. As he requires you to be seated, sit down.

Ta 大 } The Gentleman
jin 人
ming 命 orders
tso, 坐。 to sit,
tso 坐 } sit down.
leaou. 了。

V. Yes.

She. 是。 Is.

2nd. V. Pray, Mr. Tsin-sze, is not your eminent name —

Ts'hing 請 Beg
wăn 問 to ask
Tsin- 進 } Tsin-sze,
sze 士
kung 公 Mr.
kaou 高 eminent
sing 姓 surname
she. 是。 is —

V. Sir, I have a double surname, Hwang, foo, my name is Yin.

Fŭh 覆 Double

* To anounnce that one is going to sit, seems to imply an acknowledgment that it is by favor a seat is granted.

| | | |
|---|---|---|
| sing | 姓 | surname |
| Hwang- | 皇 | Hwang |
| foo, | 甫 | foo, |
| ming | 名 | name |
| Yin. | 吟。 | Yin. |

2nd. V. Your native place is Chin-chow, is it not?

| | | |
|---|---|---|
| Kwei | 貴 | Noble |
| choo | 處 | place |
| mŭh | 莫 | not |
| fei | 非 | not |
| she | 是 | is |
| Chin- | 眞 | Chin-chow? |
| chow. | 州。 | |

V. How do you happen to know it, Sir?

| | | |
|---|---|---|
| Ta | 大 | Sir, |
| jin | 人 | |
| ho | 何 | how |
| e | 以 | |
| che | 知 | know |
| che? | 之 | it? |

2nd. V. I have heard, for along time, that at Chin-chow, there was a Person of great learning, whose name was Hwang-foo-yin. I presume you are the person.

| | | |
|---|---|---|
| Hea | 下 | I |
| kwăn | 官 | |
| k'hew | 久 | long |
| wăn | 聞 | heard |
| Chin- | 眞 | Chin-chow |
| chow | 州 | |
| yew | 有 | had |
| ko | 個 | a |
| paou | 飽 | satiated |
| heŏ | 學 | scholar |
| kaou | 叫 | called |
| tso | 做 | |
| Hwang- | 皇 | Hwang-foo-yin; |
| foo- | 甫 | |
| yin; | 吟。 | |
| tsew | 就 | just |
| she | 是 | is |
| Tsin- | 進 | Tsin-sze, |
| sze | 士 | |
| kung | 公 | Mr. |
| mo? | 麽。 | ? |

M. It is no other than my Pupil.

| | | |
|---|---|---|
| Tsew | 就 | Just |
| she | 是 | is |
| pe | 敝 | worthless |
| num | 門 | Pupil. |
| săng. | 生。 | |

2nd. V. I have long admired you.

K'hew 久 Long
yang 仰 looked up
ah! 吓。 ah!

2nd. V. I dare not presume to appropriate to myself your compliment.

Pŭh 不 Not
kan. 敢。 dare presume.

2nd. V. Pray, Sir, have many of the Tsin-sze come to see you?

Ts'hing 請 Beg
wăn 問 to ask
ta 大 } Sir,
jin, 人。}
choo 諸 all
Tsin- 進 } Tsin-sze
sze 士 }
to 多 many
lae 來 come
tsan 叅 } to see (you)
këen 見 }
kwo 過 } have
leaou 了 }
mo? 麼。 ?

M. Not yet.

Hwan 還 Yet
we. 未。 not.

2nd. V. As they have not all come, what is the reason of this Gentleman alone coming.

Choo 諸 All
Tsin- 進 } Tsin-sze
sze 士 }
we 未 not
lae 來 come,
wei 惟 only
kung 公 Mr.
tŭh 獨 alone
che, 至 come,
ho 何 why
yay? 也。 ?

M. Ah! there is a reason.

Ah! 吓 Oh!
yew 有 have
ko 個 a
yuen 緣 } reason.
koo. 故。}

2nd. V. What reason?

Shĕ 什 } What
mo 麽 }
yuen 緣 } reason.
koo. 故。}

M. This pupil is different from others.

| | | |
|---|---|---|
| Chay | 這 | This |
| ko | 個 | |
| pe | 敝 | worthless |
| mun | 門 | Pupil |
| săng | 生 | |
| yu | 與 | with |
| pëĕ | 別 | others |
| ko | 個 | |
| pŭh | 不 | not |
| t'hung. | 同。 | same. |

2nd. V. Why?

| | | |
|---|---|---|
| Wei | 爲 | Why? |
| ho. | 何。 | |

M. At first he was in prison, I pitied and liberated him; his promotion at present is also owing to me. He is grateful for these two circumstances, and hence has come first to see me.

| | | |
|---|---|---|
| T'ha | 他 | He |
| t'hang | 當 | at |
| ch'hoo | 初 | the beginning, |
| wei | 爲 | because of |
| sze | 事 | an affair, |
| tsae | 在 | was in |
| yŭh, | 獄。 | prison, |
| she | 是 | was |
| hea | 下 | I |
| kwăn | 官 | |
| seŭ | 恤 | commiserated |
| hing | 刑 | punishment |
| shĭh | 釋 | liberated (him), |
| fang, | 放。 | |
| kin | 今 | now |
| ko | 科 | examination |
| kaou | 高 | high |
| chuĕ; | 掇。 | raised; |
| yew | 又 | also |
| she | 是 | is |
| hea | 下 | I |
| kwăn | 官 | |
| so | 所 | that which |
| tseu; | 取 | obtained; |
| t'ha | 他 | he |
| kan | 感 | moved gratefully |
| tsze | 此 | (by) these |
| urh | 二 | two |
| tsëĕ, | 節 | circumstances, |
| so | 所 | therefore |
| e | 以 | |
| sëen | 先 | first |
| lae | 來 | come |
| k'han | 看 | see |

laou 老 the old
foo. 夫 fellow.

2nd. V. So,—I am thinking, that as the Gentleman present was of the literati, what offence he could commit.

Ah, 吓 Oh,
seang 想 think
Tsin- 進 } Tsin-sze,
sze 士
kung 公 Mr.
ke 旣 since
tsae 在 in
Hung- 黌 } the College-gate,
mun, 門
so 所 that which
fan 犯 } committed
tëĭh 的
she 是 is
ho 何 what
tsuy. 罪. crime.

M. It would take a long time to detail the affair.

Shwŏ 說 To speak,
yay 也 also
hwa 話 words
ch'hang. 長. long.

2nd. V. Though its should, I will thank you to let me know.

Taou 到 Still
yaou 要 want
ts'hing 請 to beg
keaou. 教. instruction.

M. My Pupil's affair. Was it not respecting marriage.

Pe 敝 Worthless
mun 門 } Pupil,
săng, 生.
oh 呵 ah,
wei 爲 because of
këĭh. 結. knotting?

V. My benefactor.

Găn 恩 Gracious
sze. 師. teacher.

M. Though Mr. Ch'hang be here, there is no objection to your mentioning it. Mention it,—do mention it.

Ah, 吓 Oh,
ne 你 you
këen 見 seeing
Ch'hang, 張 Ch'hang,

* 黌門 Hung-mun, 'The gate of learning;' a disciple of the school of Confucius.

| | | |
|---|---|---|
| ta | 大 | Mr. |
| jin, | 人。 | |
| tsae | 在 | is |
| tsze | 此 | here, |
| pŭh | 不 | no |
| fang | 妨 | obstacle |
| shwŏ | 說 | to speak out; |
| tĭh | 得 | |
| tëĭh; | 的。 | |
| shwŏ | 說 | can speak' |
| tĭh | 得 | |
| pa, | 罷 | well, |
| shwŏ | 說 | speak can. |
| tĭh. | 得。" | |

2nd. V. I beg to be informed.

| | | |
|---|---|---|
| Ts'hing | 請 | Pray |
| keaou. | 教。 | inform. |

M. What was the name of his father-in-law.

| | | |
|---|---|---|
| T'ha | 他 | His |
| ling | 令 | honored |
| yŏ | 岳 | father-in-law* |
| keaou | 呌 | called |
| shĕ | 什 | what? |
| mo? | 麼。 | |

M. His father-in-law's name was She-chĭh, he rejected a poor man, for the sake of a rich person.

| | | |
|---|---|---|
| T'ha | 他 | His |
| tëĭh | 的 | |
| nae | 奶 | Wife' |
| yŏ | 岳 | Father's |
| ming | 名 | name |
| hwan | 喚 | call |
| She- | 史 | She-chĭh. |
| chĭh. | 直。 | |
| T'ha | 他 | He |
| hëen | 嫌 | rejected |
| pin | 貧 | poor, |
| gae | 愛 | loved |
| foo | 富 | riches |
| che | 之 | 's |
| mun. | 門。 | door. |

2nd. V. Did this Lady accord with her father's wishes?

| | | |
|---|---|---|
| Tsze | 此 | This |
| neu | 女 | woman |
| k'ho | 可 | could |
| tsung? | 從。 | accord? |

M. This Lady was firm and virtuous,

* 岳 Yŏ, 'The father of his espoused wife.'

she made an appointment to meet in the garden.

Sze 斯 This
neu 女 woman
këen 堅 firm
ching 貞 chaste
seang 相 mutually
ke 期 agreed
hwŭy 會 to meet
tsae 在 in
yuen 園 } the garden.
ting. 亭。

2nd. V. Did Mr. Tsin-sze* go at the time.

K'he 其 The
she 時 time
Tsin- 進 } Tsin-sze,
sze 士
kung 公 Mr.
k'ho 可 } already
tsăng 曾
k'heu. 去。 go?

M. Had my Pupil gone it would have been well.

Pe 敝 Worthless
mun 門 } Pupil
săng 生
jŏ 若 if
k'heu, 去。 go,
taou 到 then
she 是 had been
yĭh 一 a
toàn 段 section
haou 好 good
sze. 事。 business.

2nd. V. Why did he not go?

Wei 爲 } Why
ho 何
pŭh 不 not
k'heu? 去。 go?

M. He had some suspicions, and consulted with a friend.

T'ha 他 His
sin 心 heart
shang 上 upon
hoo 狐 } doubted,
e, 疑
yu 與 with,
yĭh 一 } a.
ko 個

* Though Tsin-sze be not a proper name, it is used as such to prevent circumlocution.

| | | |
|---|---|---|
| pŭng | 朋 | friend |
| yew | 友 | |
| shang | 商 | consulted. |
| e. | 議。 | |

2nd. V. What was that Person's name?

| | | |
|---|---|---|
| Na | 那 | That |
| jin | 人 | man |
| keaou | 叫 | called |
| shin | 甚 | what? |
| mo? | 麽。 | |

M. That Person's name was —, was —?

| | | |
|---|---|---|
| Na | 那 | That |
| jin | 人 | man |
| keaou | 叫 | called |
| keaou. | 叫。 | called —. |

V. Han-she-chung.

| | | |
|---|---|---|
| Han- | 韓 | Han-she-chung. |
| she- | 時 | |
| chung. | 中。 | |

M. Yes, Han-she-chung.

| | | |
|---|---|---|
| Ah, | 吓。 | Yes, |
| Han- | 韓 | Han-she-chung. |
| she- | 時 | |
| chung. | 中。 | |

2nd. V. Han-she-chung, how then.

| | | |
|---|---|---|
| Han- | 韓 | Han-she-chung, |
| she- | 時 | |
| chung, | 中。 | |
| pëen | 便 | then |
| tsăng | 怎 | what |
| mo | 麽 | |
| yang. | 樣。 | manner. |

M. He falsely exaggerated the danger, and hindered him from keeping the appointment.—That detested She-chung, assumed a false dress and went and deceived her.

| | | |
|---|---|---|
| T'ha | 他 | He |
| kea | 假 | falsely |
| yen | 言 | spoke of |
| le | 利 | danger, |
| hae | 害。 | |
| tsoo | 阻 | prevented |
| t'ha | 他 | his |
| tëïh | 的 | |
| hing | 行 | going to |
| ke, | 期。 | the appointment; |
| kan | 堪 | deserving of |
| han | 恨 | indignation |
| She- | 時 | She-chung, |
| chung, | 中。 | |
| kea | 假 | falsely |

| | | |
|---|---|---|
| pan | 扮 | dressed |
| k'heu | 去 | went (and) |
| tŭh | 脫 | escaped by |
| pëen | 騙 | deception. |
| yay. | 也。 | |

2nd. V. Sir, Did this Lady discover it?

| | | |
|---|---|---|
| Ta | 大 | Sir, |
| jin, | 人 | |
| tsze | 此 | this |
| neu | 女 | woman |
| k'ho | 可 | could |
| jin | 認 | discover |
| tĭh | 得 | |
| ch'hŭh | 出 | |
| fow. | 否。 | not? |

M. Sir, (you are there are you,) Miss She-pëĭh-taou, was a Lady who had not yet been out of the female apartments, how was she to know whether it was her real husband, or a false one?

| | | |
|---|---|---|
| Ta | 大 | Sir, |
| jin, | 人。 | |
| yew | 又 | further |
| lae | 來 | come. |
| leaou.* | 了。 | |
| na | 那 | That |
| She- | 史 | She-pëĭh-taou, |
| pëĭh- | 碧 | |
| taou, | 桃。 | |
| she | 是 | was |
| ko | 個 | a |
| pŭh | 不 | not |
| ch'hŭh | 出 | gone out |
| kwei | 閨 | female apartments |
| mun | 門 | |
| tëĭh | 的 | 's |
| neu | 女 | Woman; |
| tsze; | 子。 | |
| na | 那 | how |
| le | 裡 | |
| she | 是 | was |
| jin | 認 | to be discovered |
| tĭh | 得 | |
| ch'hŭh | 出 | |
| she | 是 | was |
| chin | 眞 | true |
| ch'hang | 丈 | husband |
| foo | 夫 | |
| kea | 假 | false |
| ch'hang | 丈 | husband. |
| foo. | 夫。 | |

* Yew-lae-leaou, 'Again coming,' is generally pronounced aside, and denotes being pressed to a topic that one wishes to avoid.

2nd. V. Mr. Tsin-sze, what did you do after that?

| | | |
|---|---|---|
| Tsin- | 進 | } Ts n-sze, |
| sze, | 士 | |
| kung, | 公 | Mr. |
| e | 以 | } afterwards |
| how | 後 | |
| pëen | 便 | then |
| tsăng | 怎 | } how |
| mo | 麽 | |
| yang? | 樣。 | manner? |

The Visitor being asked, ere he spoke, shed tears.

| | | |
|---|---|---|
| Chŭy | 垂 | Stooping (when) |
| wăn, | 問 | asked, |
| we | 未 | re he |
| yu | 語 | spoke |
| sëen | 先 | first |
| nli. | 淋。 | wept. |

2nd. V. Why do you weep?

| | | |
|---|---|---|
| We | 爲 | } Wherefore |
| ho | 何 | |
| chaou | 掉 | bring |
| hea | 下 | down |
| lŭy | 泪 | tears |
| lae? | 來 | come? |

M. My Pupil's affair is a painful one; being introduced, it makes him weep.

| | | |
|---|---|---|
| Pe | 敝 | Worthless |
| mun | 門 | } Pupil's |
| săng | 生 | |
| sze | 事 | affair |
| tsae | 在 | is |
| shang | 傷 | wounding |
| sin, | 心。 | heart, |
| te | 提 | } raising it up |
| k'he | 起 | |
| chaou | 掉 | brings |
| hea | 下 | down |
| lŭy | 泪 | tears |
| lae. | 來。 | come. |

V. Alas!—my family was poor; but contented in our station, with pure minds we bore our distress. My wife's father seeing my circumstances, wanted to take my (espoused wife) and marry her to another.

| | | |
|---|---|---|
| K'ho | 可 | Worthy of |
| lëen | 憐 | pity, |
| kea | 家 | family |
| pin | 貧 | poor |
| show | 守 | held |
| fun, | 分。 | station, |

| | | |
|---|---|---|
| soo | 素 | pure |
| sin | 心 | heart |
| ying | 映 | (studied by) reflection |
| seŭ | 雪 | snow and * |
| nang | 囊 | (glow-worm in) a bag's |
| ying. | 螢。 | light. |
| Wo | 我 | My |
| tse | 妻 | wife's |
| foo | 父 | father |
| këen | 見 | seeing |
| wan | 晚 | my † |
| săng | 生 | |
| kea | 家 | family |
| han, | 寒。 | cold (distressed), |
| yaou | 要 | wanted |
| tseang | 將 | to take |
| han | 寒 | poor wife |
| king | 荆 | |
| kae | 改 | change |
| kea. | 嫁。 | marriage. |

2nd. V. Marry her to another! to whom?

| | | |
|---|---|---|
| Kae | 改 | Change |
| kea! | 嫁 | marriage! |
| na | 那 | which? |
| ko? | 個。 | |

M. To Wei, the Keu-mëĭh.

| | | |
|---|---|---|
| Wei, | 魏 | Wei, |
| Keu- | 樞 | the Keu-mëĭh. ‡ |
| mëĭh. | 密。 | |

2nd. V. I suppose Wei-kung-lëen.

| | | |
|---|---|---|
| K'ho | 可 | Was it |
| she | 是 | |
| Wei- | 魏 | Wei-kung-lëen. |
| kung- | 公 | |
| lëen. | 廉。 | |

M. It is that old dog.

| | | |
|---|---|---|
| Tsew | 就 | Just |
| she | 是 | is |
| chay | 這 | this |
| laou | 老 | old |
| k'how | 狗 | dog. |
| tsae. | 才。 | |

* Reference to an Ancient Story of a poor Person, who, for want of other means in Winter, read at night by the light reflected from snow; and in Summer, by the light of the glow-worm.

† 晚生 Wăn-sang, 'Evening born,' is used by a younger Person, for the Pronoun I, me, or my.

‡ 樞密 Keu-mëĭh, A certain office.

2nd. V. Do not rail, Sir. He was promoted the same year with me.

Ta 大 } Sir,
jin, 人
pŭh 不 not
yaou 要 want
ma, 罵。 to rail, —
she 是 (He) is
heŏ 學 } my *
săng 生
tëĭh 的
pe 僘 worthless
t'hung 同 same
nëen. 年。 year.

M. Oh, he was your fellow Student.

Ah, 吓。 Oh,
she 是 he is
ta 大 } Your Excellency
jin 人
tëĭh 的 's
kwei 貴 noble
t'hung 同 same +
nëen. 年。 year.

2nd. V. He was my fellow Student.

She 是 Is
pe 僘 worthless
t'hung 同 same
nëen. 年。 year.

M. Sir.

Ta 大 } Sir.
jin. 人。

2nd. V. Sir.

Ta 大 } Sir.
jin. 人。

M. I apprehend, Sir, your fellow Student was not very bright.

Kwei 貴 Noble
t'hung 同 same
nëen, 年 year,
chĭh 只 only
p'ha 怕 fear
k'hëen 欠 defective in
t'hung 通 intelligence.
ah. 吓。

2nd. V. Not very bright.

K'hëen 欠 Defective in
t'hung. 通。 intelligence.

* 學生 Heŏ-săng, 'A scholar,' used for the Personal Pronoun.

+ 同年 T'hung nëen, 'The same year;' i. e. obtained a degree of rank in the same year, such Persons profess a kind of friendship for each other.

V. Not very bright; not very bright.

K'hëen 欠 Defective in
t'hung. 通 intelligence.
K'hëen 欠 Defective in
t'hung. 通 intelligence.

(The Mandarin and 2nd. Visitor smiled)

2nd. V. Did your Lady comply?

Ling 令 } Your wife *
ching 正 }
k'ho 可 } comply?
tsung. 從 }

V. This Lady would not comply.

Tsze 此 This
neu 女 woman
püh 不 not
tsung. 從 comply.

2nd. V. That was good.

Püh 不 Not
tsung 從 comply
haou. 好 good.

M. She, being indignant, threw herself into the river, and was never heard of more.

Han 含 Not disclosing
yuen 冤 resentment, (she)
nëïh 溺 sunk in
shwŭy, 水 the water,
keang 江 river's
sin 心 heart
woo 無 no
ping. 憑 proof.

2nd. V. Oh, Sir! I suppose they took this affair and wanted to ruin Mr. Tsin-sze by it.

Ah, 吓 Oh,
ta 大 } Sir,
jin, 人 }
seang 想 suppose
tsew 就 then
pa 把 take
tsze 此 this
sze 事 affair
lae. 來 come

* 令正 Ling chin, 'Your wife.' Ling, Honorable, commanding and dignified,' is employed for Your. Ching, Right, principal, is used to denote a Person's wife, in contradistinction from those called by courtesy, 如夫人 Joo-joo-jin, 'As a wife;' or 令寵 Ling-chung, 'Your beloved;' i. e. A concubine; in plain language is called 妾氏 Tsëĕ-she.

| | | |
|---|---|---|
| hëen | 陷 | involove * |
| hae | 害 | injure |
| Tsin- | 進 | Tsin-sze, |
| sze | 士 | |
| kung, | 公 | Mr. |
| leaou. | 了。 | |

M. Yes, they wanted to ruin my Pupil.

| | | |
|---|---|---|
| She | 是 | Yes! |
| ah! | 吓。 | |
| lae | 來 | came |
| hëen | 陷 | to involve and |
| hae | 害 | injure |
| pe | 敝 | worthless |
| mun | 門 | Pupil. |
| săng | 生 | |
| leaou. | 了。 | |

V. They charged me with having violated her Person, and consequently occasioning her death, and insisted on the charge.

| | | |
|---|---|---|
| Kaou | 告 | Accused |
| wo | 我 | me |
| yin | 因 | because of |
| këen | 奸 | rape |
| che | 致 | leading |
| sze, | 死, | to death, |
| keŭ | 屈 | stooping under |
| wăn | 問 | investigation. |
| yay. | 也。 | |

2nd. V. Why did you not state the matter fully to the Judge?

| | | |
|---|---|---|
| Tsin- | 進 | Tsin-sze, |
| sze, | 士 | |
| kung, | 公。 | Mr. |
| tsăng | 怎 | why |
| pŭh | 不 | not |
| heang | 向 | before |
| wăn | 問 | the inquiring |
| kwăn | 官 | Magistrate |
| chĭh | 質 | fully, or with witnesses |
| pëen | 辯 | discusts |
| mo? | 麼。 | ? |

V. Sir, at that time they would not suffer me to debate my cause.

| | | |
|---|---|---|
| Ta | 大 | Sir, |
| jin | 人 | |
| na | 那 | that |
| she | 時 | time |

*陷 Hëen, denotes 'To cause to sink in a pit, to involve in ruin.'

tsăng 怎 how
yung 容 allow
wan 晚 } me
săng 生 }
chĭh 質 with witnesses
pëen 辯 discuss.
ah. 吓。

M. Yes, indeed.

She 是 } Just so.
ah. 吓。 }

V. They tortured me in every possible way to confess.

Pĭh 百 Hundred
pan 般 ways
tëĭh 的 of
kaou 敲 knocking
ta 打 beating
chaou 招 to induce
ching. 成。 to perfect.

M. Sir, My Pupil is a thin and weak scholar; unable to go through the three tortures and six interrogatories. He could not bear the punishment, and was beaten till he confessed.

Ta 大 } Sir,
jin, 人 }
pe 敝 my
mun 門 } Pupil
săng 生 }
she 是 is (a)
sow 瘦 thin
këĭh 怯 }
këĭh 怯 } weak
tëĭh 的 }
shoo 書 } scholar,
săng, 生。 }
tsăng 怎 how
king 經 } could pass through
tĭh 得 }
san 三 three
kaou 拷 tortures
lŭh 六 six
wăn, 問 interrogations,
show 受 receiving
hing 刑 punishment.
pŭh 不 not
k'he ; 起。 bear up ;
keŭ 屈 stooping under
ta 打 beating
ching 成 made
chaou 招 }
tëĭh 的 } to bring the crime on himself.
ah. 吓。 }

2nd. V. Did the Judge not understand that his life was unjustly sought for?

| | | |
|---|---|---|
| Wăn | 問 | Judge |
| kwăn | 官 | |
| Pŭh | 不 | not |
| ming | 明 | understand |
| wang | 枉 | falsely accused |
| suy | 遂 | following with |
| sing | 性 | life. |
| ming. | 命。 | |

M. The Judge did not understand; the Judge did not understand.

| | | |
|---|---|---|
| Wăn | 問 | Judge |
| kwăn | 官 | |
| pŭh | 不 | not |
| ming; | 明， | understand; |
| wăn | 問 | Judge |
| kwăn | 官 | |
| pŭh | 不 | not |
| ming. | 明。 | understand. |

V. I am indebted to you, my benefactor, for clearing up the false accusation, liberating me, and saving my life.

| | | |
|---|---|---|
| Lae | 賴 | Depended on |
| găn | 恩 | my benefactor |
| sze | 師 | |
| ming | 明 | clearing up |
| yuen | 冤 | false accusation |
| shĭh | 釋 | and setting at liberty |
| fang | 放。 | |
| chaou | 超 | raising up |
| woo | 吾 | my |
| k'heu | 軀 | body's |
| ming. | 命。 | life. |

2nd. V. Sir, allow me to ask, how you found out the proofs of this affair?

| | | |
|---|---|---|
| Ts'hing | 請 | Beg |
| wăn, | 問 | to ask, |
| ta | 大 | Sir, |
| jin, | 人。 | |
| e | 以 | afterwards |
| how | 後 | |
| pëen | 便 | then |
| tsăng | 怎 | what |
| mo | 麽 | |
| yang | 樣 | manner |
| wăn | 問 | inquire |
| ming | 明 | clearly |
| tsze | 此 | this |
| sze. | 事。 | affair? |

M. I felt for him suffering so much punishment and torture, and examined into the business.

Hea 下 } I,
kwǎn, 官 }
ah, 呵 ah,
seŭh 恤 pitied
hing 刑 punishment
keŭ, 鞫 torture,
shin 審 judged of
k'he 其 the
tsing. 情。 business.

M. I then thought of a scheme, and took She-chung into my house.

Wo 我 I
tsew 就 then
sin 心 heart
sǎng 生 produced
yǐh 一 a
ke, 計。 plan,
pa 把 took
She- 時 } She-chung
chung 中 }
lew 留 detained
tsae 在 in
foo 府 house
chung. 中。 midst.

M. Still there was no proof.

Woo 無 No
ping. 憑。 proof.

M. I could do nothing but dissemble, (smiling).

Chǐh 只 Only
tǐh 得 could
cha. 詐。 deceive.

—. Sir, I tremble as I relate it.

Ta 大 } Sir,
jin, 人 }
shwǒ 說 } speaking
yay 也 }
hwang 惶 agitated
kung. 恐。 fear.

2nd. V. Pray go on, Sir.

Ta 大 } Sir,
jin, 人 }
ts'hing 請 pray
keaou. 教。 inform.

M. I could only affect to receive him as my Son-in-law, and sent a Person to demand the pledge of espousals, (a pin for the headdress, &c.)

Chǐh 只 Only
tǐh 得 could
cha 詐 dissemble
nǎ 納 receive

| | | |
|---|---|---|
| tung | 東 | eastern bed; |
| chwang; | 床 | |
| këen | 遣 | sent |
| jin | 人 | a man |
| chwang | 賺 | to obtain |
| tseu | 取 | |
| chae | 釵 | pin, (&c.) |
| king. | 荆 | |

—. Happily, the villain was enticed out of the Lady's bracelets and pin for the headdress.

| | | |
|---|---|---|
| To | 多 | Much |
| hing, | 幸 | good luck, |
| këen | 奸 | the villain |
| jin | 人 | |
| chae | 釵 | pin |
| chuen | 釧 | bracelets was |
| yew | 誘 | deceived |
| ch'hŭh | 出 | out of. |
| yay. | 也 | |

2nd. V. When you found out the retainer of the things stolen, you ought at one flogging, to have beaten to death that brute.

| | | |
|---|---|---|
| Ta | 大 | Sir, |
| jin, | 人 | |
| ke | 旣 | when |
| chwang | 賺 | obtain |
| ch'hŭh | 出 | |
| yuen | 原 | originally |
| tsang | 賍 | things stolen |
| tsew | 就 | then |
| kae | 該 | ought |
| yĭh | 一 | one |
| tun | 頓 | |
| pan | 板 | beating |
| tsze | 子 | |
| hwŏ | 活 | alive |
| hwŏ | 活 | alive |
| kaou | 敲 | knocked |
| sze | 死 | to death |
| chay | 這 | this |
| chŭh | 畜 | brute. |
| sang. | 生 | |

M. You may be sure I did not spare him.

| | | |
|---|---|---|
| Na | 那 | That |
| she | 時 | time |
| wo | 我 | I |
| tsăng | 怎 | how |
| kăng | 肯 | could |
| jaou | 饒 | spare |

t'ha. 他。 him.

M. I fixed the crime on him, and cleared my Pupil.

T'hang 當 }
she 時 } At that time (he)
tëĭh 的 }
jŭh 入 entered
tsuy, 罪。 crime,
woo 吾 I
shun 伸 exonerated
pe 敝 my
mun 門 }
săng. 生。 } Pupil.

—. And now he has been successful (in obtaining literary rank), and rejoices in the favour his Sovereign.

T'ha 他 He
fŭh 復 again in
Kin 芹 }
kung, 宮。 } Kin-hall, *
yu 於 at
kin 今 this time
tĭh 得 obtain
chung, 中。 hit,
he 喜 rejoices
mŭh 沐 gratefully for
hwang 皇 Imperial
găn. 恩。 goodness.

—. Pray sit down, Sir; why, Sir, have you become pensive?

Ta 大 }
jin, 人 } Sir,
ts'hing 請 pray
tso; 坐。 sit;
ta 大 }
jin, 人 } Sir,
wei 爲 }
ho 何 } why
chin 沉 sunk in
yin 吟 silence
k'he 起 up
lae. 來。 come.

2nd. V. I am not pensive.—Mr. Tsin-sze, now that you have been successful in your literary pursuits, do you think of your Lady who was drowned?

Pŭh 不 Not

* Kin, is the name of an Aquatic Plant, which grows around the Kung, or College of a certain rank. Kin-kung, is the name of a College.

| | | |
|---|---|---|
| she | 是 | is |
| hea | 下 | I |
| kwăn | 官 | |
| chin | 沉 | pensive. |
| yin. | 吟。 | |
| Ts'hing | 請 | Pray |
| wăn | 問 | ask |
| Tsin- | 進 | Tsin-sze, |
| sze, | 士 | |
| kung, | 公。 | Mr. |
| joo | 如 | now |
| kin | 今 | |
| kaou | 高 | highly raised, |
| chuĕ | 掇 | |
| leaou, | 了。 | |
| k'ho | 可 | why |
| sze | 思 | think of |
| seang | 想 | |
| na | 那 | that |
| nĕĭh | 溺 | drowned |
| shwŭy | 水 | |
| tĕĭh | 的 | |
| foo | 夫 | Lady |
| jin | 人 | |
| mo ? | 麽。 | ? |

V. My heart is wounded, I feel the deepest regret for my wife.

| | | |
|---|---|---|
| Chay | 這 | This |
| shang | 傷 | wounds |
| sin | 心 | heart |
| tse | 妻 | (for my) wife |
| shĭh | 室 | |
| han | 含 | cherish |
| yuen. | 寃。 | resentment. |

2nd. V. Do not be grieved.

| | | |
|---|---|---|
| Pŭh | 不 | Do not be |
| yaou | 要 | |
| pei | 悲 | grieved. |
| shang. | 傷。 | |

M. You must not be grieved,—avoid sorrow.

| | | |
|---|---|---|
| Pŭh | 不 | Not |
| pĕĭh | 必 | necessary |
| pei | 悲 | to be grieved; |
| shang; | 傷。 | |
| ts'heay | 且 | therefore |
| mëen | 免 | avoid |
| tsow | 愁 | sorrow. |
| fan. | 煩。 | |

V. After the bonds which I have suffered, how can I but think of it.

| | | |
|---|---|---|
| Foo, | 夫。 | Ah, |
| tsaou | 遭 | me |

luy 縲 } bonds
sëĭh 絏 }
keaou 叫 call
jin 人 Persons
tsăng 怎 how
pŭh 不 not
sze 思 } think.
seang. 想。}

2nd. V. You may indeed think of it.

K'ho 可 May
sze 思 } think.
seang. 想。}

M. Indeed you may think of it.

Ching 正 Just
she 是 so
ne 你 you
k'ho 可 may
sze 思 } think.
seang. 想。}

2nd. V. You are yet young, you may marry again.

Chay 這 } Thus
tăng 等 }
ts'hing 青 azure
nëen 年 year
hwan 還 still
kae 該 should
tsae 再 again
tseu 娶 marry
yĭh 一 } one.
wei. 位。}

V. I carry about with me her bracelets and broach, and can never withdraw my thoughts from her. How shall I ever espouse another!

Wo 我 I
tei 帶 bear about
chae 釵 pin
chuen, 釧。 bracelets,
heuen 懸 suspense
heuen 懸 suspense
seang 想 think
nëen. 念。 muse.
Tsăng 怎 How
kan 敢 dare
pëĕ 別 another
tseu 娶 } marry!
ping 娉 }
ting! 婷。}

M. Do you keep the broach and bracelets about your person morning and evening.

| | | |
|---|---|---|
| Na | 那 | That |
| chae | 釵 | pin |
| chuen | 釧 | bracelets |
| she | 是 | is |
| chaou | 朝 | morning |
| sëĭh | 夕 | evening |
| pei | 佩 | carry |
| tae | 帶 | |
| tsae | 在 | at |
| shin | 身 | body |
| tëĭh | 的 | |
| mo ? | 麽 | ?. |

V. I always keep them about me.

| | | |
|---|---|---|
| Chaou | 朝 | Morning |
| sëĭh | 夕 | evening |
| pei | 佩 | attached to my Person |
| tae | 帶 | |
| tëĭh. | 的。 | they are. |

# DIALOGUE IV.

## *A TRADESMAN AND SCHOLAR.*

T. I have not seen you for a long time.

Wei 違 (I have been) separate
keaou 教. from instruction.

S. How do you do. I have not seen you for a very long time. I hope you have been very well.

Ts'hing 請 } Hail!
leaou! 了. }
wei 違 separated from
keaou 教 instruction
tĭh 得 } very (much),
hăn 狠 }
kin 近 } recently
lae 來 }
shih 實 } (you) very
tsae 在 }
nă 納 } well
fŭh 福. }

T. I am much obliged to you, I have come on purpose to see you.

Tŏ 托 } Depending on you,
lae, 賴 }
tĭh 特 purposely
lae 來 come
wăn 問 } to compliment you.
how. 候. }

B. I could not expect this. We are happy in each other. When did you arrive, Sir.

K'he 豈 (I) how
kan, 敢 presume,
pe 彼 you (and)
tsze 此 I
tsëĕ 藉 } happy in each other,
fŭh, 福 }

tsun 尊 } you, Sir,
kea 駕 }
ho 何 what
she 時 time
taou 到 } arrive.
leaou. 了。 }

A. I arrived yesterday.

Tsŏ 昨 } Yesterday
jĭh 日 }
tsae 纔 then
taou. 到。 arrive.

B. We have long been separated. Two years have passed unheeded. Have you lately made great progress in your studies.

Pëĕ 別 Separated
keŏ, 却 indeed,
to 多 much
she 時 time
leaou, 了。 have been,
pŭh 不 not
keŏ 覺 adverting
tseang 將 it will
yew 有 be
eang 兩 two
tsae. 載。 years.

Kin 近 } Lately
lae 來。 }
wăn 文 literary
sze 思 thoughts
ta 大 greatly
tsin. 進。 advanced.

A. You are very good. I am ashamed to see you. At my window I have toiled in vain, I have merely spent the days and months.

Haou 好 Well
shwŏ, 說。 said,
këen 見 } I feel ashamed,
kwei, 愧。 }
chwang 窓 window
hea 下 below
t'hoo 徒 in vain
laou, 勞。 labored,
pŭh 不 not
kwo 過 more than
kung 空 } idly pass
yen 延 }
jĭh 日 days (and)
yuĕ. 月。 months.

B. The Examination is at hand. You will be then full of engagements.

I shall this year have to congratulate you.

Ko 科 }The examination
chang 場 }
tsae 在 is
tsëĕ, 卽 instantly,
tsun 尊 }(you) Sir,
kea 駕 }
man 滿 full
fŭh 腹 belly
king 經 }of Literature.
lun, 綸 }
Kin 今 This
nëen 年 year
yĭh 一 (to) a
ting 定 certainty
kung 恭 }congratulate (you).
he. 喜 }

A. You are very kind. I am not so well engaged as you, Sir, transacting business with a circle of friends, and extremely happy.

Haou 好 Well
shwŏ, 說 said,
pŭh 不 not
joo 如 as
tsun 尊 }(you), Sir,
kea, 駕 }
king 經 }trading (to the)
kung 營 }
sze 四 four
hae, 海 seas,
kăng 更 more
wei 爲 make
kwae 快 }pleasant
chang 暢 }
che 之 in the
che. 至 extreme.

B. To do business is now very difficult. Lately Shĭh-san hang has had a name, but it is nothing in reality, in consequence of the foreigners being engaged in war; hence, the ships of different countries do not arrive, and there is little sale for the articles of Commerce. Trade is very trifling, and the foreign trade worth nothing. The old saying is true, That the profession of a scholar is best.

Mow 貿 }Trade
yĭh 易 }
yĭh 亦 also
shin 甚 very

| | | |
|---|---|---|
| këen | 艱 | difficult, |
| nan, | 難. | |
| kin | 近 | near |
| she | 時 | time |
| Shĭh- | 十 | Shĭh-san |
| san | 三 | |
| hang | 行 | hang's |
| săng | 生 | trade |
| e | 意 | |
| yew | 有 | had |
| ming | 名 | name |
| woo | 無 | not |
| shĭh, | 實. | reality, |
| yin | 因 | because |
| fan | 番 | foreign |
| jin | 人 | men |
| ta | 打 | are fighting |
| ch'hang | 仗 | |
| shin | 甚 | very keenly; |
| kin; | 緊. | |
| koo | 故 | therefore, |
| tsze | 此 | |
| ping | 並 | moreover |
| woo | 無 | no |
| pëĕ | 別 | other |
| keang | 港 | port's |
| chuen | 船 | ships |
| taou, | 到. | arrive, |
| ho | 貨 | merchandize |
| wŭh | 物 | |
| pŭh | 不 | not |
| shin | 甚 | much |
| seaou | 消 | consumption; |
| lew; | 流. | |
| so | 所 | hence, |
| e | 以 | |
| săng | 生 | trade |
| e | 意 | |
| tan | 淡 | (insipid and thin) trifling. |
| pŏ. | 薄. | |
| Joo | 如 | Now |
| kin | 今 | |
| yang | 洋 | foreign |
| hang | 行 | |
| săng | 生 | trade |
| e | 意 | |
| pŭh | 不 | not |
| chung | 中 | hit |
| yung | 用 | use. |
| leaou. | 了. | |
| Koo | 古 | Ancient |
| yun | 云 | saying |
| chin | 真 | is true, |
| she, | 是 | |

Tùh 讀 To read
shoo 書 book
haou. 好。 is good.

A. Very true. I have always heard People say so: but your abilities, Sir, are superior; you are not to be compared with men in general. At a future day, you must succeed.

She 是 } True,
ya, 呀。 }
wo 我 I
yĭh 亦 also
chang 常 always
ting 聽 hear
jin 人 } every body
jin 人 }
shwŏ 說 say
joo 如 } so;
tsze; 此。 }
tan 但 but
Tsun 尊 } Sir's
kea 駕 }
nang 能 } abilities
kan 幹 }
kwo 過 pass
jin 人 (other) men's
pe 比 compare
pŭh 不 not
joo 如 (as) to
tsin 尋 the seeking
chang 常 common
che 之 the
pei. 輩。 class.
Jĭh 日 Day
how 後 after
pëĕ 必 } must
jen 然 }
tĭh 得 obtain
le. 利。 profit.

B. You are very flattering. I remember our young days, what happiness we had in learning together; but now hurried by business, I seldom see my friends, for which I am extremely sorry.

Haou 好 Well
shwŏ, 說 said,
hwŭy 回 returning
seang 想 think of
shaou 少 few } youth
nëen 年 years }
t'hung 同 (together) same
chwang 窗 window
che 之 the

| | | |
|---|---|---|
| she, | 時。 | time, |
| ho | 何 | what |
| tăng | 等 | |
| kwae | 快 | pleasure, |
| chang, | 暢。 | |
| kin | 今 | now |
| wei | 爲 | doing |
| săng | 生 | business |
| e | 意 | |
| pun | 奔 | hurried; |
| che; | 馳。 | |
| shaou | 少 | seldom |
| tĭh | 得 | obtain |
| tsin | 親 | personal |
| how | 候 | waiting |
| păng | 朋 | friends, |
| yew, | 友。 | |
| shĭh | 實 | really |
| tsae | 在 | |
| fan | 煩 | sorry |
| mun | 悶 | |
| che | 之 | in the |
| che. | 至。 | extreme. |

A. True. Honor and profit drag us along. We both have our difficulties.

| | | |
|---|---|---|
| She | 是 | True, |
| ya, | 呀。 | |
| ming | 名 | a name and |
| le | 利 | profit (are) |
| so | 所 | the things which |
| këen; | 牽。 | drag (us); |
| pe | 彼 | you (and) |
| tsze | 此 | I |
| kŏ | 各 | (every) each |
| yew | 有 | have |
| nan | 難 | difficult |
| choo. | 處。 | circumstances. |

B. To-day, now that we have met, my old friend, I must detain you to converse a little.

| | | |
|---|---|---|
| Kin- | 今 | To- |
| jĭh | 日 | day |
| koo | 故 | old |
| jin | 人 | friends |
| sëang | 相 | mutually |
| hwŭy; | 會。 | met; |
| keŭ | 屈 | stoop |
| kea, | 駕 | Sir, |
| tsze | 此 | this |
| choo, | 處。 | place, |
| tan | 談 | chat |
| tan | 談 | |
| sin | 心 | heart |

| | | |
|---|---|---|
| sze | 事 | business |
| joo | 如 | how. |
| ho. | 何。 | |

A. I am much obliged to you, but I have to see some other friends. Another day I will accept of your invitation. Good morning.

| | | |
|---|---|---|
| To | 多 | Many |
| seay | 謝 | thanks, |
| leaou, | 了。 | |
| wo | 我 | I |
| joo | 如 | now |
| kin | 今 | |
| yaou | 要 | want |
| pae | 拜 | to visit |
| pëë | 別 | other |
| yew, | 友。 | friends, |
| kae | 改 | another day |
| jïh | 日 | |
| tsae | 再 | again |
| lae | 來 | come |
| ling | 領 | receive |
| keaou. | 教。 | instruction. |
| Kaou | 告 | Good bye. |
| tsze | 辭 | |
| leaou. | 了。 | |

B. As it so, I will not urge you to remain. I will call to-morrow and return your visit.

| | | |
|---|---|---|
| Ke | 旣 | Since |
| joo | 如 | thus, |
| tsze, | 此。 | |
| pŭh | 不 | not |
| kan | 敢 | dare |
| keang | 強 | violently |
| lew, | 留。 | detain, |
| ming | 明 | to-morrow |
| jïh | 日 | |
| wo | 我 | I |
| taou | 到 | to |
| lae | 來 | come |
| hwuy | 回 | return |
| pae. | 拜。 | visit. |

A. I cannot expect it, I will send a chair for you.— Pray return.

| | | |
|---|---|---|
| Pŭh | 不 | Not |
| kan, | 敢。 | dare, |
| wo | 我 | I |
| ta | 打 | send |
| fă | 發 | |
| keaou | 轎 | a chair |
| tsze | 子 | |

ts'hing 請 request
ne 你 you
ts'hing 請 pray
hwŭy. 回。 return.

B. Excuse my not accompanying you far.

Shoo 恕 Excuse
pŭh 不 not
yuen 遠 far
sung. 送。 accompany.

A. I cannot expect it. Pray go no further.

K'he 豈 How
kan, 敢。 dare,
ts'hing, 請。 good bye,
lew 留 stop
poo. 步。 step.

B. I do not follow you any further.

Pŭh 不 Not
sung 送 accompany.
leaou. 了。

A. Good bye.

Ts'hing. 請。 Good bye.

# DIALOGUE V.

## *WITH AN ASSISTANT IN LEARNING THE LANGUAGE.*

Student. Master, I will thank you to sit down and read with me a little.

| | | |
|---|---|---|
| Sëen | 先 | Before } Master, |
| săng, | 生 | born } |
| ts'hing | 請 | pray |
| tso | 坐 | sit |
| t'hung | 同 | with |
| wo | 我 | me |
| k'han | 看 | look |
| shoo | 書 | book |
| yĭh | 一 | a |
| hwŭy. | 會。 | while. |

Tutor. I am at your service.

| | | |
|---|---|---|
| Ts'hing | 請 | Pray |
| keaou. | 教。 | direct (me). |

S. Pray, what is tl e best book for beginners to read?

| | | |
|---|---|---|
| Ts'hing | 請 | Beg |
| wăn | 問 | to ask |
| ch'hoo | 初 | begin |
| hëŏ | 學 | to learn |
| k'han | 看 | look |
| shin | 甚 | } what |
| mo | 麽 | } |
| shoo | 書 | book |
| wei | 爲 | is |
| haou? | 好。 | good? |

T. It is of importance to learn the Ta-hëŏ first.

| | | |
|---|---|---|
| Sëen | 先 | First |
| hëŏ | 學 | learn |
| Ta- | 大 | } the Ta-hëo, |
| hëŏ, | 學 | } |
| yaou | 要 | } is important. |
| kin. | 緊。 | } |

S. I apprehend the Ta-hëŏ is difficult, is it not?

| | | |
|---|---|---|
| Kung | 恐 | Apprehend |
| pa | 怕 | |
| Ta- | 大 | the Ta-hëŏ |
| hëŏ | 學 | |
| nan | 難 | difficult |
| ming | 明 | to be understood, |
| pĭh, | 白 | |
| she | 是 | is it |
| fow? | 否 | or not? |

T. Next to it, to read the Hung-low-mung, will do very well.

| | | |
|---|---|---|
| K'he | 其 | It's |
| t'hsze | 次 | next |
| nëen | 念 | read |
| Hung- | 紅 | Hung-low-mung, |
| low- | 樓 | |
| mung | 夢 | |
| shin | 甚 | very |
| haou. | 好 | good. |

S. I have not seen the Hung-low-mung, have you seen it?

| | | |
|---|---|---|
| Hung- | 紅 | Hung-low-mung, |
| low- | 樓 | |
| mung, | 夢 | |
| yĭh | 一 | first volume |
| pun | 本 | |
| shoo, | 書 | book, |
| wo | 我 | I |
| we | 未 | not |
| tsăng | 曾 | yet |
| këen; | 見 | seen; |
| Sëen | 先 | Master |
| săng | 生 | |
| këen | 見 | seen it |
| kwo | 過 | |
| mo? | 麽 | not? |

T. I have not brought it with me, but if you wish to see it, I will write to Canton, and present it to you.

| | | |
|---|---|---|
| Wo | 我 | I |
| mŭh | 没 | not |
| tae | 帶 | bring |
| lae, | 來 | come, |
| joo | 如 | if |
| yaou | 要 | want |
| k'han, | 看 | look, |
| wo | 我 | I |
| ke | 寄 | send |
| sin | 信 | letter |
| taou | 到 | to |
| Săng | 省 | Canton |
| tseu | 取 | obtain |
| lae, | 來 | come, |
| sung | 送 | present |

bang 上 up
ne 你 you
k'han. 看. look.

S. Very good, I will trouble you to write for it.

Hăn 狠 Very
hsou, 好 good,
wo 我 I
to 多 much
fan 煩 trouble
ne 你 you
ke 寄 send
sin 信 letter
tseu 取 obtain
lae. 來. come.

T. I will do so.

Ling 領 Receive
ming. 命. order.

S. How many volumes are there in the Hung-low-mung?

Hung- 紅 }
low- 樓 } Hung-low-mung
mung 夢 }
shoo, 書. book,
yew 有 have
to 多 } how many
shaou 少 }
pun. 本. volumes.

T. Twenty volumes in all. In this book the phraseology is entirely that of Peking.

Kung 共 In all
urh 二 } Twenty
shĭh 十 }
pun 本 volumes
shoo. 書. book.
Tsze 此 This
shoo 書 book
shwŏ 說 } speaks
tĕĭh 的 }
tseuen 全 all
she 是 is
King 京 (Pe) king
hwa. 話. dialect.

S. How is this Character 者 pronounced?

者
Tsze 字 Character
she 是 is
shin 甚 } what
mo 麽 }
yin? 音. sound?

T. 者 Character is pronounced the same as 這 Chay.

| | | |
|---|---|---|
| | 者 | |
| Tsze | 字 | Character |
| yu | 與 | with |
| chay | 這。 | |
| tsze | 字 | character |
| t'hung | 同 | same |
| yin. | 音。 | sound. |

S. What is the meaning of 者 Chay?

| | | |
|---|---|---|
| Chay | 者 | |
| tsze | 字 | Character |
| yew | 有 | has |
| shin | 甚 | } what |
| mo | 麼 | |
| keae | 解 | explanation |
| fă? | 法。 | rule? |

T. It is an Auxiliary.

| | | |
|---|---|---|
| Tsoo | 助 | Assisting |
| yu | 語 | words |
| tsze. | 辭。 | expression. |

S. I will thank you to repeat the sentence which you now pronounced.

| | | |
|---|---|---|
| Tsae | 纔 | } Just now |
| kang | 剛 | |
| shwŏ | 說 | } pronounced |
| tëĭh | 的 | |
| na | 那 | } that |
| yĭh | 一 | |
| keu | 句 | } sentence |
| kwa | 話 | |
| ts'hing | 請 | beg |
| tsae | 再 | again |
| shwŏ. | 說。 | pronounce. |

S. Was the sentence which I uttered correct.

| | | |
|---|---|---|
| Wo | 我 | I |
| tsae | 纔 | just now |
| so | 所 | which |
| shwŏ | 說 | uttered |
| na | 那 | } that |
| yĭh | 一 | |
| keu | 句 | } sentence |
| hwa | 話 | |
| chŏ, | 着 | right, |
| pŭh | 不 | not |
| chŏ. | 着。 | right? |

T. It was very correct.

| | | |
|---|---|---|
| Chay | 這 | This |
| hwa | 話 | sentence |
| shwŏ | 說 | } pronounce |
| tĭh | 得 | |
| shin | 甚 | very |
| chŏ. | 着。 | right. |

# DIALOGUE VI.

## *WITH A SERVANT.*

Master. A-fŭh, go to Pwan-k'he-qua's, and see whether he be at home or not.

| | | |
|---|---|---|
| A- | 亞 | A-fŭh, |
| fŭh, | 福 | |
| ne | 你 | you |
| taou | 到 | go to |
| Pwan- | 潘 | Pwan-k'he-qua's |
| k'he | 啟 | |
| kwăn | 官 | |
| kea | 家 | house |
| le, | 裡 | within, |
| k'han | 看 | see |
| t'ha | 他 | ho |
| tsae | 在 | is in |
| kea, | 家 | house, |
| pŭh | 不 | not |
| tsae | 在 | in |
| kea. | 家 | house. |

S. Pwan-k'he-qua, is in his Factory, Sir.

| | | |
|---|---|---|
| Laou | 老 | Sir, |
| yay, | 爺 | |
| Pwan- | 潘 | Pwan-k'he-qua |
| k'he- | 啟 | |
| kwăn | 官 | |
| tsae | 在 | is |
| hang | 行 | hong |
| le. | 裡 | within. |

M. What is he doing?

| | | |
|---|---|---|
| T'ha | 他 | He |
| urh | 而 | now |
| kin | 今 | |
| tsae | 在 | in (his) |
| hang | 行 | Factory |
| le | 裡 | |
| tso | 做 | do |
| shin | 甚 | what? |
| mo? | 麼 | |

S. He is now at leisure.

| | | |
|---|---|---|
| T'ha | 他 | He |
| urh | 而 | now |
| kin | 今 | |
| tsae | 在 | is |
| hang | 行 | Factory |
| le | 裡 | within |
| hëen | 閒 | at leisure. |
| chŏ. | 着。 | |

M. Ask him if the Tea be ready, I want to go and examine it.

| | | |
|---|---|---|
| Ne | 你 | You |
| k'heu | 去 | go |
| wăn | 問 | ask |
| t'ha | 他 | him |
| ch'ha | 茶 | tea |
| yĭh | 葉 | leaf |
| yu | 預 | be prepared |
| pei | 備 | |
| leaou | 了 | |
| mo ? | 麼。 | ? |
| Wo | 我 | I |
| urh | 而 | now |
| kin | 今 | |
| yaou | 要 | want |
| k'heu | 去 | go |
| k'han | 看 | look |
| ch'ha | 茶。 | tea. |

S. He says, that it is all ready, Sir, you can go immediately and see it.

| | | |
|---|---|---|
| T'ha | 他 | He |
| shwŏ, | 說 | says, |
| ch'ha | 茶 | tea |
| yĭh | 葉 | leaf |
| too | 都 | all |
| yu | 預 | prepared, |
| pei | 備 | |
| leaou, | 了。 | |
| ts'hing | 請 | request |
| Laou | 老 | Sir, |
| yay, | 爺 | |
| tsze | 此 | this |
| k'hĭh | 刻 | moment |
| k'ho | 可 | may |
| e | 以 | |
| k'heu | 去 | go |
| k'han. | 看。 | look. |

M. Turn out this Tea into another chest.

| | | |
|---|---|---|
| Ne | 你 | You |
| tseang | 將 | take |
| chay | 這 | this |
| ko | 個 | |
| ch'ha | 茶 | tea |
| taou | 倒 | invert |
| kwo | 過 | pass |

| | | |
|---|---|---|
| pëĕ | 別 | another |
| tëïh | 的 | |
| seang | 箱 | chest |
| k'heu. | 去。 | go. |

S. All the chests are emptied, Sir.

| | | |
|---|---|---|
| Laou | 老 | Sir, |
| yay, | 爺。 | |
| kŏ | 各 | every |
| seang | 箱 | chest |
| too | 都 | all |
| taou | 倒 | invert |
| kwo | 過 | passed. |
| leaou. | 了。 | |

# DIALOGUE VII.

## EXAMPLE OF THE DEGREES OF COMPARISON.

This year's Tea is pretty good.

| | | |
|---|---|---|
| Kin | 今 | This |
| nëen | 年 | year |
| tëïh | 的 | 's |
| ch'ha | 茶 | tea |
| hwan | 還 | still |
| haou | 好 | good. |
| ma. | 嗎。 | |

Last year's Tea was BETTER than that of this year.

| | | |
|---|---|---|
| K'hew | 舊 | Last |
| nëen | 年 | year |
| tëïh | 的 | 's |
| ch'ha | 茶 | tea |
| haou | 好 | better than |
| kwo | 過 | |
| kin | 今 | this |
| nëen | 年 | year |
| tëïh. | 的。 | 's. |

The Tea three year's since, was STILL BETTER.

| | | |
|---|---|---|
| San | 三 | Three |
| nëen | 年 | year |
| ts'hëen | 前 | before |
| tëïh | 的 | 's |
| ch'ha | 茶 | tea |

hwan 還 still
kăng 更 more
haou. 好。 good.

I see the Green Tea this year is not EQUAL to the Black.

Kin 今 This
nëen 年 year
tëĭh 的 's
lŏ 綠 green
ch'ha 茶 tea
wo 我 I
k'han 看 see
pŭh 不 not
joo 如 as
hĭh 黑 black
ch'ha 茶 tea
haou. 好。 good.

The Congou is EXTREMELY GOOD.

Kung-foo 工夫 Congou
ch'ha 茶 tea
she 是 is
këĭh 極 extremely
haou. 好。 good.

Bohea, connot be SURPASSED.

Woo-e 武夷 Bohea
ch'ha 茶 tea
haou 好 good
pŭh 不 not
kwo tëĭh. 過的。 passed.

However, the Hyson is SUPERIOR TO EVERY other kind.

Taou te 到底 However,
He-chun 熙春 Hyson
ch'ha 茶 tea
kwo 過 passes
yu 于 by
kŏ 各 every
yang 樣 kind
tëĭh 的 of
ch'ha 茶 tea
yĭh. 葉。 leaf.

Other Tea is but common.

Pëĕ tëĭh 別的 Other
ch'ha 茶 tea
too 都 all
ping 平 even
chang. 常。 common.

The word Dialogue appears a misnomer for the above Piece.

# DIALOGUE VIII.

## *RESPECTING A SHIP.*

A. What nation does the Ship belong to, which arrived yesterday?

| | | |
|---|---|---|
| Tsŏ | 昨 | Yesterday |
| t'hëen | 天 | |
| lae | 來 | come |
| taou | 到 | to |
| tëĭh | 的 | the |
| chuen | 船 | ship |
| she | 是 | is |
| na | 那 | what |
| yĭh | 一 | one |
| kwŏ | 國 | nations. |
| tëĭh. | 的。 | |

B. She is an English Ship.

| | | |
|---|---|---|
| She | 是 | Is |
| Ying- | 英 | English |
| këĭh- | 吉 | |
| le | 利 | |
| kwŏ | 國 | nation. |
| tëĭh. | 的。 | |

A. Where is she anchored.

| | | |
|---|---|---|
| Tsae | 在 | Is |
| na | 那 | where |
| le | 裡 | |
| wan | 灣 | anchored |
| pŏ. | 泊。 | |

B. She is anchored at Cross Harbour.

| | | |
|---|---|---|
| Tsae | 在 | Is at |
| shĭh | 十 | Cross |
| tsze | 字 | |
| mun | 門 | door |
| wan | 灣 | anchored. |
| pŏ. | 泊。 | |

A. I perceive that she is a very large ship

| | | |
|---|---|---|
| Wo | 我 | I |
| këen | 見 | see |

| | | | |
|---|---|---|---|
| na | 那 | that | |
| yǐh | 一 | one | |
| chǐh | 隻 | | |
| chuen | 船 | ship | |
| she | 是 | is | |
| ta | 大 | large | |
| tǐh | 得 | very. | |
| hăn. | 狠。 | | |

B. And the larger the better appearance.

| | | | |
|---|---|---|---|
| Urh | 而 | And | |
| ts'heay | 且 | | |
| yew | 又 | more | |
| ta | 大 | large | |
| yew | 又 | more | |
| haou | 好 | good | |
| k'han. | 看。 | look. | |

A. Only, I do not know if she sails well.

| | | | |
|---|---|---|---|
| Tan | 但 | But | |
| pŭh | 不 | not | |
| che | 知 | know | |
| t'ha | 他 | she | |
| tsow | 走 | go (sail) | |
| tǐh | 得 | can | |
| kwae | 快 | fast. | |
| mo. | 麽。 | | |

B. I hear that she sails badly.

| | | | |
|---|---|---|---|
| Wo | 我 | I | |
| ting | 聽 | hear | |
| shwŏ | 說 | say | |
| t'ha | 他 | she | |
| tsow | 走 | goes | |
| tǐh | 得 | | |
| man. | 慢。 | slowly. | |

A. I observe that ship's dimensions are not in proportion.

| | | | |
|---|---|---|---|
| Wo | 我 | I | |
| k'han | 看 | see | |
| na | 那 | that | |
| yǐh | 一 | one | |
| chǐh | 隻 | | |
| chuen | 船 | ship's | |
| teǐh | 的 | | |
| chǐh | 尺 | cubit | dimensions |
| tsun | 寸 | points | |
| pŭh | 不 | not | |
| tüy. | 對。 | uniform. | |

B. Why?

| | | | |
|---|---|---|---|
| Wei | 爲 | For | |
| shin | 甚 | what | |
| mo | 麽 | | |
| yuen | 緣 | cause. | |
| koo. | 故。 | | |

A. Because she is too broad.

| | | |
|---|---|---|
| Yin | 爲 | Because |
| wei | 因 | |
| na | 那 | that |
| chĭh | 隻 | |
| chuen | 船 | ship (is) |
| kwăn | 寬 | broad |
| kwo | 過 | past |
| fun. | 分。 | part. |

B. Indeed, the broader a vessel is the better.

| | | |
|---|---|---|
| Kwo | 果 | Indeed, |
| jen, | 然 | |
| chuen | 船 | a vessel |
| chĭh | 隻 | |
| yuĕ | 越 | more |
| she | 是 | it is |
| kwăn | 寬 | broad |
| yuĕ | 越 | more |
| haou. | 好。 | good. |

A. That is not enough, it should be in proportion.

| | | |
|---|---|---|
| Chay | 這 | This |
| ko | 個 | |
| pŭh | 不 | not |
| năng | 能 | can |
| kow, | 彀、 | enough, |
| yĭh | 亦 | also |
| yaou | 要 | want |
| tso | 做 | made |
| tĭh | 得 | |
| tŭy. | 對。 | uniform. |

B. I tell you that that vessel is a first rate.

| | | |
|---|---|---|
| Wo | 我 | I |
| yu | 與 | to |
| ne | 你 | you |
| shwŏ | 說 | say |
| na | 那 | that |
| chĭh | 隻 | |
| chuen | 船 | ship |
| she | 是 | is |
| te | 第 | number |
| yĭh | 一 | one |
| tăng | 等 | class. |
| tëĭh. | 的。 | |

A. On what account.

| | | |
|---|---|---|
| Wei | 爲 | For |
| shin | 甚 | what. |
| mo. | 麽。 | |

B. Because that fore and aft, all round her, she is all in proportion.

| | | |
|---|---|---|
| Yin | 因 | Because |
| wei | 爲 | |

| | | |
|---|---|---|
| t'ha | 他 | her |
| tĕĭh | 的 | |
| chĭh | 尺 | dimensions |
| tsun | 寸 | |
| ts'hëen | 前 | before |
| how | 後 | behind |
| ke | 幾 | all around |
| chow | 週 | |
| wei | 圍 | |
| too | 都 | all |
| tŭy. | 對。 | uniform. |

A. If it be so, you say very right.

| | | |
|---|---|---|
| Jŏ | 若 | If |
| she | 是 | is |
| chay | 這 | thus |
| yang | 樣 | |
| ne | 你 | you |
| shwŏ | 說 | say |
| tĭh | 得 | |
| hăn | 狠 | very |
| she. | 是。 | right. |

B. Beside, she has an excellent Pilot.

| | | |
|---|---|---|
| Choo | 除 | Exclusive of |
| leaou | 了 | |
| chay | 這 | this, |
| ko, | 個 | |
| t'ha | 他 | she |
| hwan | 還 | beside |
| yew | 有 | have |
| shang | 上 | superior |
| haou | 好 | |
| yĭh | 一 | a |
| ko | 個 | |
| to | 舵 | helm — Pilot. |
| kung. | 工。 | workman |

A. What is his name?

| | | |
|---|---|---|
| T'ha | 他 | His |
| tĕĭh | 的 | |
| sing | 姓 | surname |
| shin | 甚 | what? |
| mo? | 麽 | |

B. His name is Hamilton.

| | | |
|---|---|---|
| T'ha | 他 | His |
| sing | 姓 | surname |
| Hea- | 吓 | Hamilton. |
| me- | 咪 | |
| le- | 喇 | |
| tun. | 噋。 | |

A. When will she return?

| | | |
|---|---|---|
| Ke | 幾 | When |
| she | 時 | |
| tsae | 纔 | then |

hwŭy 回 return
pun 本 original
kwŏ. 國。 country?

B. At the close of the year.

Nëen 年 Year
hea. 下。 below.

# DIALOGUE IX.

## *RESPECTING COTTON.*

Master. Go and ask the price of a bale of Cotton.

Ne 你 You
k'heu 去 go
wăn 問 ask
yĭh 一 one
paou 包 bale
mëen 棉 } cotton
hwa 花 }
tëĭh 的 's
kea 價 } price
tsëen 錢 }
to 多 } how much.
shaou. 少。 }

—. How long is a piece of white cloth.

Yĭh 一 One
pëĭh 疋 piece
pĭh 白 white
poo 布 cloth
yew 有 have
ke 幾 } how much
to 多 }
ch'hang. 長。 long.

Servant. It is fifteen cubits long, and three broad.

Yew 有 Have
ch'hang 長 long
yĭh 一 one } ten cubits
ch'hang 丈 ch'hang }
woo 五 five
chĭh, 尺 cubits,
kwăn 寬 broad
san 三 three
chĭh. 尺。 cubits.

—. The price is ten tales seven mace·

| | | |
|---|---|---|
| Kea | 價 | } Price |
| tsëen | 錢 | |
| shĭh | 十 | ten |
| leang | 両 | tales |
| ling | 零 | odd |
| ts'hĭh | 七 | seven |
| tsëen. | 錢。 | mace.* |

M. That is not dear, I will have a piece·

| | | |
|---|---|---|
| Pŭh | 不 | Not |
| kwei, | 貴 | dear, |
| wo | 我 | I |
| yaou | 要 | want |
| yĭh | 一 | a |
| pëĭh. | 疋。 | piece. |

S. It is said, this year's Cotton is very dear.

| | | |
|---|---|---|
| Yew | 有 | Have |
| shwŏ, | 說 | say, |
| kin | 今 | this |
| nëen | 年 | year |
| tëĭh | 的 | 's |
| mëen | 棉 | } Cotton |
| hwa | 花 | |
| shin | 甚 | very |
| kwei. | 貴 | dear. |

M. I suspect sixteen tales per pecul will be wanted.

| | | |
|---|---|---|
| Kung | 恐 | } Apprehend |
| pa | 怕 | |
| mei | 每 | each |
| t'han | 擔 | pecul |
| yaou | 要 | want |
| mae | 賣 | to sell |
| shĭh | 十 | } sixteen |
| lŭh | 六 | |
| leang | 両 | tales |
| yin | 銀 | } money. |
| tsze. | 子。 | |

—. Tell the Compradore to get a Chop-boat to take this Tea to the ship.

| | | |
|---|---|---|
| Ne | 你 | You |
| shwŏ | 說 | } tell |
| che | 知 | |
| Mae- | 買 | } Compradore |
| pan- | 辦 | |
| chaou | 找 | } seek |
| tĭh | 得 | |
| yĭh | 一 | } one |
| chĭh | 隻 | |

* See Table of Weights and Monies at the close of the volume.

Se- 西
kwa- 瓜
pëen- 扁
chuen 船 } Chop-boat, *
tae 帶 take
chay 這 this
ch'ha 茶
yih 葉 } tea
taou 到 to
chuen 船 ship
shang 上 upon
k'heu. 去。 go.

S. Yes, Sir, but must it not be first marked?

She, 是。 Yes,
tan, 但 but,
Laou 老
yay, 爺 } Sir,
chay 這 this
ch'ha 茶
yih 葉 } tea
pŭh 不 no
yung 用 use
sëen 先 first
kwa 掛 put (suspend)
haou 號 mark
mo? 麽。 ?

M. I forgot;—to be sure it must first be marked.

Wo 我 I
wang 忘
ke 記
leaou, 了。 } forgot,
kwo 果
jen 然 } indeed
woo 務
pĕih 必 } must
sëen 先 first
kwa 掛 put
haou. 號。 mark.

— Better put the chests into their cases.

Chwang 裝 Put
tsae 在 in
taou 套
seang 箱
tsze 子 } cases
kăng 更 more
haou. 好。 good.

* 西瓜 Se-kwa, is the name of a species of melon, which bears some resemblance to the boat alluded to. It is a large boat employed to take ships' cargo to and from Canton. In the jargon of Canton, 'Chop,' denotes any written document, a Custom-house Permit, and so on. From the boats or lighters mentioned, having always a Permit from the Custom-house, they are probably called Chop-boats.

# DIALOGUE X.

## *WITH THE COMPRADORE.*

European. Call the Compradore.

| | | |
|---|---|---|
| Ne | 你 | You |
| keaou | 叫 | call the |
| Mae- | 買 | Compradore |
| pan | 辦 | |
| lae. | 來。 | come. |

Compradore. What do you wish, Sir ?

| | | |
|---|---|---|
| Laou | 老 | Sir, |
| yay, | 爺 | |
| yaou | 要 | want |
| shin | 甚 | what? |
| mo ? | 麽 | |

E. Compradore, you must go a shopping.

| | | |
|---|---|---|
| Mae- | 買 | Compradore |
| pan | 辦 | |
| ne | 你 | you |
| taou | 到 | to |
| poo | 舖 | shop |
| sze | 子 | |
| le | 裡 | within |
| k'heu | 去 | go |
| mae | 買 | buy |
| tung | 東 | things. |
| se. | 西。 | |

C. What things do you want, Sir.

| | | |
|---|---|---|
| Laou | 老 | Sir, |
| yay, | 爺 | |
| yaou | 要 | want |
| shin | 甚 | what |
| mo | 麽 | |
| tung | 東 | things. |
| se. | 西。 | |

E. I want three pieces of white cloth.

| | | |
|---|---|---|
| Yaou | 要 | Want |
| san | 三 | three |

| | | |
|---|---|---|
| pĕĭh | 疋 | pieces |
| pĭh | 白 | white |
| poo. | 布。 | cloth. |

C. Of what quality.

| | | |
|---|---|---|
| Yaou | 要 | Want |
| na | 那 | what |
| yĭh | 一 | one |
| tang | 等 | class |
| tĕĭh | 的 | of |
| poo. | 布。 | cloth? |

E. The finer the better.

| | | |
|---|---|---|
| Yuĕ | 越 | More |
| se | 細 | fine |
| yuĕ | 越 | more |
| haou. | 好。 | good. |

C. What other articles do you wish, Sir?

| | | |
|---|---|---|
| Hwan | 還 | Beside |
| yaou | 要 | want |
| shin | 甚 | what? |
| mo? | 麽。 | |

E. I want a piece of Nankeen better than this; I want also some of the best snuff.

| | | |
|---|---|---|
| Hwan | 還 | Beside |
| yaou | 要 | want |
| yĭh | 一 | one |
| pĕĭh | 疋 | piece |
| Tsze- | 紫 | Nankeen, |
| hwa- | 花 | |
| poo, | 布。 | |
| pe | 比 | compared with |
| chay | 這 | this |
| ko | 個 | |
| haou; | 好。 | good; |
| hwan | 還 | beside |
| yaou | 要 | want |
| shang | 上 | superior |
| tăng | 等 | class |
| tĕĭh | 的 | of |
| pe | 鼻 | snuff. |
| yen. | 烟。 | |

C. How many pounds do you want.

| | | |
|---|---|---|
| Pe | 鼻 | Snuff |
| yen | 烟 | |
| yaou | 要 | want? |
| to | 多 | how many |
| shaou | 少 | |
| kin. | 斤。 | catty |

E. I want six pounds; I want too, some of the best wine; I want a pair of very good stockings.

| | | |
|---|---|---|
| Yaou | 要 | Want |
| ŭh | 六 | six |

| | | |
|---|---|---|
| kin; | 斤。 | catty; |
| yew | 又 | also |
| yaou | 要 | want |
| shang | 上 | best |
| haou | 好 | |
| tëĭh | 的 | |
| tsew; | 酒。 | wine; |
| yew | 又 | also |
| yaou | 要 | want |
| yĭh | 一 | one |
| shwang | 雙 | pair |
| këĭh | 極 | extremely |
| haou | 好 | good |
| tëĭh | 的 | |
| ~~mă~~ wă | 襪 | stockings. |
| tsze. | 子。 | |

C. This piece of Cloth is extremely good; the Snuff is better than yesterday's; the Stockings cannot be surpassed.

| | | |
|---|---|---|
| Chay | 這 | This |
| pëĭh | 疋 | piece |
| poo | 布 | cloth |
| she | 是 | is |
| hăn | 狠 | very |
| haou | 好 | good; |
| tëĭh; | 的。 | |
| chay | 這 | this |
| ko | 個 | |
| pe | 鼻 | snuff |
| yen | 烟 | |
| tsŏ | 昨 | yesterday |
| t'hëen | 天 | |
| tëĭh | 的 | 's |
| pŭh | 不 | not |
| joo | 如 | as |
| kin- | 今 | to- |
| t'hëen | 天 | day |
| tëĭh | 的 | 's |
| haou; | 好。 | good; |
| chay | 這 | this |
| shwang | 雙 | pair |
| ~~mă~~ wă | 襪 | stockings |
| tsze | 子 | |
| haou | 好 | good |
| pŭh | 不 | not |
| kwo | 過 | passed. |
| tëĭh. | 的。 | |

E. Very good.

| | | |
|---|---|---|
| Shĭh | 實 | Really |
| tsae | 在 | |
| she | 是 | is |
| haou | 好 | good. |
| tëĭh. | 的。 | |

# DIALOGUE XI.

## *WITH A LINGUIST.*

European. Linguist, what ship was it which arrived yesterday?

| | | | |
|---|---|---|---|
| T'hung | 通 | Communicate | Linguist |
| sze, | 事。 | business | |
| tsŏ | 昨 | yesterday | |
| t'hëen | 天 | | |
| yew | 有 | have | |
| shin | 甚 | what | |
| mo | 麽 | | |
| chuen | 船 | ship | |
| taou? | 到。 | arrive? | |

Linguist. An American ship arrived.

| | | | |
|---|---|---|---|
| Tsŏ | 昨 | Yesterday | |
| t'hëen | 天 | | |
| yew | 有 | have | |
| Hwa- | 花 | flower | American |
| ke | 旗 | flag | |
| chuen | 船 | ship | |
| yĭh | 一 | one | |
| chĭh | 隻 | | |
| taou | 到 | arrived. | |
| leaou. | 了。 | | |

E. Has that Country ship got her Grand Chop (clearance) yet?

| | | | |
|---|---|---|---|
| Na | 那 | That | |
| chĭh | 隻 | | |
| keang | 港 | Bay | Country |
| k'heŏ | 脚 | foot | |
| chuen | 船 | ship | |
| yew | 有 | have | |
| hung | 紅 | red | clearance |
| pae | 牌 | document | |
| ch'hŭh | 出 | issued | |
| mŭh | 没 | not | |
| yew? | 有。 | have? | |

L. Not yet, in consequence of the Hoppo being absent from the office.

| | | |
|---|---|---|
| We | 未 | Not |
| yew, | 有 | have, |
| yin | 因 | because |
| Hae- | 海 | Hoppo's |
| kwăn | 關 | |
| Ta | 大 | Excellency |
| jin | 人 | |
| pŭh | 不 | not |
| tsae | 在 | is |
| ya | 衙 | office |
| nŭy. | 內 | within. |

E. When will he return to the office?

| | | |
|---|---|---|
| Ta | 大 | Excellency |
| jin | 人 | |
| ke | 幾 | when |
| she | 時 | |
| hwŭy | 回 | return |
| ya | 衙 | to office? |
| mun? | 門 | |

L. After supping this evening at the Commander of the Forces, he will return; and the Clearance may be signed to-morrow.

| | | |
|---|---|---|
| Kin | 今 | This |
| wăn | 晚 | evening |
| tsae | 在 | at |
| Tsëang- | 將 | Tsëang-keun, |
| keun, | 軍 | |
| na | 那 | that |
| le | 裡 | place |
| yin | 飲 | drink |
| wan | 完 | finish |
| pĕïh | 必 | must |
| ting | 定 | |
| hwŭy | 回 | return |
| lae, | 來 | come, |
| ta | 大 | Clearance |
| pae | 牌 | |
| k'ho | 可 | may |
| e | 以 | |
| ming | 明 | to-morrow morning |
| tsaou | 早 | |
| ch'hŭh. | 出 | be issued. |

E. Very well. Have our ships delivered all their cargo, or not?

| | | |
|---|---|---|
| Pa | 罷 | Enough, |
| leaou, | 了 | |
| wo | 我 | my |
| pun | 本 | original |
| kwŏ | 國 | nation |
| chuen | 船 | ship |
| k'he | 起 | take up |

ho 貨 cargo
wan 完 了 finished,
leaou, 
mŭh 没 not
yew? 有。 have?

L. The Company's goods are all up there are yet two boats of the Captain's things not brought up.

Kung-sze 公司 Company's
ho 貨 cargo
k'he 起 take up
wan; 完。 finish;
hwan 還 still
yew 有 have
leang 兩 two
ting 艇 boats
chuen choo 船主 Ship-lord Captain's
ho 貨 goods
we 未 not
k'he. 起。 taken up.

E. When these two boats come up, let me know.

Na 那 Those
leang chĭh 兩隻 two
ting 艇 boats
taou leaou 到了 arrive at
ching, 城。 the city,
ne 你 you
tsëĕ 卽 immediately
keaou soo 告訴 inform
wo 我 me
che taou, 知道。 to know,
tsew she leaou. 就是了。 just so.

L. Very well. These two boats are to go to Mowqua's. I will now request him to send two boats, and by the day after to-morrow, they will be up at Canton.

She, 是 Yes,
she, 是。 yes,
na 那 those
leang 兩 two
ting 艇 boats
he 係 are (by)
Kwang-le 廣利 Mowqua's

| | | |
|---|---|---|
| hang | 行 | hong |
| show | 受 | received. |
| leaou. | 了 | |
| Wo | 我 | I |
| joo | 如 | now |
| kin | 今 | |
| ts'hing | 請 | request |
| na | 那 | that |
| hang | 行 | hong |
| fă | 發 | to send |
| ting | 艇 | boats |
| k'heu | 去 | to go |
| k'he; | 起 | take up |
| how | 後 | the day after to morrow |
| t'hëen | 天 | |
| na | 那 | those |
| leang | 兩 | two |
| ting | 艇 | boat's |
| ho | 貨 | goods |
| pëĭh | 必 | must |
| taou | 到 | reach |
| Săng- | 省 | Canton. |
| ching. | 城 | |
| leaou. | 了。 | |

E. That will do. Has the Country Ship sent down her Chow-chow Chop yet?

| | | | |
|---|---|---|---|
| Chay | 這 | This (is) | |
| ko | 個 | | |
| haou, | 好。 | good, | |
| na | 那 | that | |
| keang | 港 | Country | |
| k'heŏ | 脚 | | |
| chuen | 船 | ship | |
| chĭh | 隻 | | |
| hea | 下 | sent down | |
| leaou | 了 | | |
| saou | 掃 | sweep | last boat |
| tsăng | 艙 | hold | load (of) |
| ho | 貨 | goods | |
| mŭh | 沒 | not | |
| yew? | 有。 | have? | |

L. There are still two boats of the regular goods to go down; if they were gone down, the Captain will certainly take down his Chow-chow Chop.

| | | |
|---|---|---|
| Hwan | 還 | Still |
| leang | 兩 | two |
| ting | 艇 | boats |
| ching | 正 | regular |
| tan | 單 | document |
| ho | 貨 | cargo |
| we | 未 | not |
| hea, | 下。 | gone down, |

| | | | |
|---|---|---|---|
| jŏ | 若 | If | |
| leang | 兩 | two | |
| ting | 艇 | boats | |
| ching | 正 | ship's cargo | |
| tan | 單 | | |
| hea | 下 | go down, | |
| leaou, | 了 | | |
| chuen | 船 | Ship | Captain |
| choo | 主 | lord | |
| pëĭh | 必 | must | |
| ting | 定 | | |
| saou | 掃 | send down the last boat. | |
| tsăng | 艙 | | |
| leaou. | 了。 | | |

E. Very good. I have no further business:—you may go.

| | | |
|---|---|---|
| Haou, | 好。 | Good, |
| hwan | 還 | beside |
| we | 未 | not |
| yew | 有 | have |
| shin | 甚 | (what) any |
| mo | 麽 | |
| sze | 事 | business |
| ne | 你 | you |
| k'ho | 可 | may |
| e | 以 | |
| k'heu. | 去。 | go. |

# DIALOGUE XII.

## *RESPECTING THE SEISURE OF A THIEF.*

Yesterday, when I was in the streets, I met a soldier dragging along a thief.

| | | |
|---|---|---|
| Tsŏ | 昨 | Yesterday |
| t'hëen | 天 | |
| tsae | 在 | being |
| keae | 街 | the street |
| shang | 上 | upon |
| fung | 逢 | met |
| chŏ | 着 | |
| yĭh | 一 | a |
| ko | 個 | |
| ping | 兵 | soldier |
| na | 拿 | seizing (and) |
| la | 拉 | dragging |
| yĭh | 一 | a |
| ko | 個 | |
| tsĭh. | 賊。 | thief. |

Behind were a great number of Persons, who wished to rescue the thief.

| | | |
|---|---|---|
| How | 後 | After |
| yew | 有 | there where |
| heu | 許 | a great many |
| to | 多 | |
| jin | 人 | persons |
| yaou | 要 | wanted |
| k'hew | 救 | to rescue |
| keae | 解 | |
| na | 那 | that |
| ko | 個 | |
| tsĭh. | 賊。 | thief. |

Then the soldier threatened them, saying, if you sit at liberty a thief taken by the Mandarin, you will all be guilty.

| | | |
|---|---|---|
| Na | 那 | That |

| | | |
|---|---|---|
| she | 時 | time |
| keae | 解 | the soldier |
| ping | 兵 | |
| hĭh | 嚇 | threatened |
| hoo | 呼 | |
| t'ha | 他 | them |
| mun | 們 | |
| shwŏ, | 說. | saying, |
| kwăn | 官 | Mandarin |
| foo | 府 | |
| na | 拿 | seized |
| tëĭh | 的 | the |
| tsĭh | 賊 | thief, |
| jin, | 人. | |
| joo | 如 | if |
| jŏ | 若 | |
| fang | 放 | let |
| k'heu | 去 | go |
| ne | 你 | you |
| tăng | 等 | |
| too | 都 | all |
| she | 是 | will |
| yew | 有 | have |
| tsŭy | 罪 | crime. |
| tëĭh. | 的. | |

They did not regard his threatening, but set at liberty the thief. The soldier not assenting, they wrangled and at last killed the soldier.

| | | |
|---|---|---|
| T'ha | 他 | They |
| mun | 們 | |
| pŭh | 不 | not |
| le | 理 | regard |
| t'ha | 他 | his |
| hĭh | 嚇 | threatening |
| hoo | 呼 | |
| tëĭh | 的 | 's |
| hwa, | 話. | words, |
| tseang | 將 | took |
| tsĭh | 賊 | the thief |
| jin | 人 | |
| fang | 放 | let (him) |
| k'heu. | 去. | go. |
| Keae | 解 | The soldier* |
| ping | 兵 | |
| puh | 不 | not |
| e; | 依 | comply; |
| leang | 兩 | both parties |
| kea | 家 | |
| seang | 相 | mutually |

* 解 Keae, denotes 'To deliver to a Magistrate.' 解兵 Keae ping, is the soldier who was carrying the thief to a Magistrate.

| | | |
|---|---|---|
| tsăng | 爭 | wrangled |
| king | 竟 | at last |
| tseang | 將 | took |
| keae | 解 | the soldier (and) |
| ping | 兵 | |
| ta | 打 | struck (him) |
| sze. | 死 | dead. |

Those that were looking on, were all thrown into confusion and fled on every side, the murderer also got off, without the least trace of him.

| | | |
|---|---|---|
| Tsëĕ | 卽 | Then |
| she | 時 | |
| na | 那 | those |
| seay | 些 | |
| k'han | 看 | looking, |
| tëĭh | 的 | the |
| chung | 衆 | multitude |
| jin | 人 | |
| too | 都 | all |
| lwan | 亂 | confusion |
| k'he | 起 | up |
| lae, | 來 | rose, |
| sze | 四 | four |
| choo | 處 | places |
| paou | 跑 | run |
| k'hae, | 開 | apart, |
| lëen | 連 | including |
| na | 那 | that |
| ko | 個 | |
| heung | 兇 | murderous |
| show | 手 | hand |
| too | 都 | all |
| e | 已 | already |
| tŭh | 脫 | escaped (and) |
| taou | 逃 | run |
| woo | 無 | no |
| tsung. | 蹤 | trace. |

The Constable immediately informed the officer of the district; and he instantly sent messengers to search and apprehend the murderer.

| | | |
|---|---|---|
| Tsëĕ | 卽 | Then |
| she | 時 | |
| te | 地 | district |
| paou | 保 | surety |
| lëĭh | 立 | instantly |
| k'hĭh | 刻 | |
| paou | 報 | reported it to |
| te | 地 | the district |
| fang | 方 | |
| kwăn. | 官 | Mandarin. |
| Kwăn | 官 | The Mandarin |
| foo | 府 | |

N

| | | |
|---|---|---|
| suy | 隨 | forthwith |
| tsëĕ | 卽 | |
| tsew | 就 | soon |
| pae | 派 | despatched |
| chae | 差 | messengers |
| jin | 人 | |
| sze | 四 | every where |
| choo | 處 | |
| cha | 查 | to search (and) |
| na | 拿 | take |
| heung | 兇 | the murderer. |
| show. | 手。 | |

The messengers sought every where and could not find him. After three days, they apprehended the murderer, and brought him to the court of the district.

| | | |
|---|---|---|
| Chae | 差 | The messengers |
| jin | 人 | |
| kŏ | 各 | every |
| choo | 處 | place |
| seun | 巡 | went round |
| mëĕ | 覔 | to seek |
| tsëĭh | 緝 | and seize, (but) |
| na | 拿 | |
| pŭh | 不 | (did) not |
| këen; | 見。 | see (him); |
| kwo | 過 | Past had |
| leaou | 了 | |
| san | 三 | three |
| t'hëen | 天 | day |
| tsae | 纔 | then |
| na | 拿 | seized |
| hwŏ | 獲 | |
| heung | 兇 | the murderer |
| show | 手 | |
| keae | 解 | and brought (him) |
| taou | 到 | to |
| Hëen | 縣 | within the Hëen |
| le | 裡 | |
| ya | 衙 | court. |
| mun. | 門。 | |

The Magistrate tried the murderer, but he would not confess.

| | | |
|---|---|---|
| Kwăn | 官 | The Magistrate |
| foo | 府 | |
| shin | 審 | judged and |
| wăn | 問 | asked. |
| heung | 兇 | the murderer, |
| show, | 手。 | |
| t'ha | 他 | He |
| king | 竟 | yet |
| pŭh | 不 | not |
| kăng | 肯 | would |

| | | |
|---|---|---|
| jin | 認 | confess |
| tsŭy | 罪。 | the crime. |

The Magistrate set in motion severe punishment, and tortured him. Doing this again, and a third time, he confessed.

| | | |
|---|---|---|
| Na | 那 | That |
| she | 時 | time |
| how | 候 | |
| kwăn | 官 | the Magistrate |
| foo | 府 | |
| tsew | 就 | forthwith |
| tung | 動 | moved |
| ta | 大 | great |
| hing | 刑 | punishment |
| kaou | 拷 | torture |
| wăn, | 問。 | asked, |
| tsae | 再 | again and |
| san | 三 | a third time |
| sin | 訊 | questioned and |
| kew, | 究。 | scrutinized, |
| tsae | 纔 | then |
| chaou. | 招。 | took it to himself. |

The Magistrate having finished the trial, wrote out his confession, and put him in prison.

| | | |
|---|---|---|
| Kwăn | 官 | The magistrate |
| foo | 府 | |
| shin | 審 | judged |
| ming, | 明。 | clearly, |
| sŭy | 隨 | forthwith |
| tsëĕ | 即 | immediately |
| hwă | 畫 | drew out (his) |
| kung | 供 | declaration (and) |
| show | 收 | received (him to) |
| këen | 監 | prison. |
| nuy. | 內。 | |

As there was sufficient proof, the Magistrate proceeded to condemn him. The next day, they sent the murderer to Canton, to be executed.

| | | |
|---|---|---|
| Taou | 到 | At last |
| te | 底 | |
| yin | 因 | because |
| chay | 這 | this |
| ko | 個 | |
| sze | 事 | business |
| yew | 有 | had |
| ping | 凴 | proof |
| k'heu | 據 | |
| so | 所 | therefore |
| e | 以 | |

| | | |
|---|---|---|
| te | 地 | the district |
| fang | 方 | |
| kwăn | 官 | Magistrate |
| tsae | 纔 | then |
| küng | 肯 | agreed |
| ting | 定 | to fix |
| leaou | 了 | |
| t'ha | 他 | his |
| tĕĭh | 的 | |
| sze | 死 | death |
| tsüy. | 罪 | crime. |
| Taou | 到 | On |
| ts'hze | 次 | next |
| jĭh | 日 | day (he) |
| tseang | 將 | took |
| heung | 兇 | the murderer |
| show | 手 | |
| keae | 解 | conveyed (him) |
| taou | 到 | to |
| Sang | 省 | Canton |
| ching | 城 | |
| chang | 償 | to forfeit |
| ming. | 命。 | life. |

There are a great many idle Persons in China; when I was in Canton, I daily saw messengers going along the streets to take thieves.

| | | |
|---|---|---|
| Chung | 中 | Chinese |
| kwŏ | 國 | |
| te | 地 | country |
| fang | 方 | |
| lan | 爛 | vagrant people |
| tsae | 崽 | |
| to | 多 | many |
| tĭh | 得 | very, |
| hăn, | 狠 | |
| wo | 我 | I |
| tsae | 在 | at |
| Săng | 省 | Canton |
| ching | 城 | |
| tĕĭh | 的 | the |
| she | 時 | time, |
| how, | 候。 | |
| mei | 每 | each |
| jĭh | 日 | day |
| chang | 常 | constantly |
| k'han | 看 | saw |
| kēen | 見 | |
| chae | 差 | runners |
| jin | 人 | |
| kwo | 過 | passing along the streets |
| tsae | 在 | |
| keae | 街 | |
| shang | 上 | |

| | | |
|---|---|---|
| na | 拿 | taking |
| leaou | 了 | |
| tsĭh. | 賊。 | thieves. |

Carrying them to the court, to put the cangue on, or to beat them. Though it be constantly thus, yet they steal and do not fear the laws.

| | | |
|---|---|---|
| Keae | 解 | Carrying (them) |
| taou | 到 | to |
| ya | 衙 | the court to be |
| mun | 門 | |
| kea | 枷 | cangued (and) |
| ta. | 打。 | beaten. |
| Sŭy | 雖 | Though |
| jen | 然 | |
| joo | 如 | thus, |
| tsze, | 此。 | |
| chang | 常 | constantly |
| yew | 有 | have |
| jin | 人 | people |
| t'how | 偷 | stealing |
| tung | 東 | things |
| se | 西 | |
| pŭh | 不 | not |
| kung | 恐 | fearing |
| pa | 怕 | |
| wang | 王 | royal |
| fa. | 法。 | law. |

These bad People are extremely foolish. If the Magistrates be not vigilant in taking them, it will be impossible to live in this place.

| | | |
|---|---|---|
| Chay | 這 | These |
| seay | 些 | |
| gŏ | 惡 | bad |
| jin | 人 | people |
| shĭh | 實 | really |
| tsae | 在 | |
| hoo | 糊 | stupid |
| joo | 塗 | |
| tĭh | 得 | very, |
| hăn, | 狠。 | |
| jŏ | 若 | if |
| she | 是 | (it) be (that) |
| te | 地 | district |
| fang | 方 | |
| kwăn | 官 | officers |
| pŭh | 不 | not |
| kin | 勤 | diligent |
| na | 拿 | take |
| t'ha | 他 | them, |
| mun, | 們。 | |

| | | |
|---|---|---|
| chay | 這 | this |
| ko | 個 | |
| te | 地 | place (to) |
| fang | 方 | |
| yĭh | 一 | a certainty |
| ting | 定 | |
| choo | 住 | dwell |
| pŭh | 不 | not |
| tĭh. | 得。 | can. |

I now perceive, that to live in this place, is not very pleasant.

| | | | |
|---|---|---|---|
| Joo | 如 | Now | |
| kin | 今 | | |
| wo | 我 | I | It occurs to me. |
| k'han | 看 | see | |
| tseang | 將 | take | |
| k'he | 起 | up | |
| lae, | 來。 | come, | |
| choo | 住 | dwell | |
| chay | 這 | this | |
| ko | 個 | | |
| te | 地 | place | |
| fang | 方 | | |
| pŭh | 不 | not | |
| to | 多 | very | |
| haou. | 好。 | good. | |

# DIALOGUE XIII.

## *RESPECTING COTTON.*

Tradesman. How many Catty is there in a bale of Cotton?

| | | |
|---|---|---|
| Yih | 一 | One |
| paou | 包 | bale |
| mëen | 棉 | Cotton |
| hwa | 花 | |
| yew | 有 | have |
| to | 多 | how many |
| shaou | 少 | |
| kin | 斤 | catty |
| chung? | 重。 | heavy? |

Merchant. It weighs a hundred Catty.

| | | |
|---|---|---|
| Yew | 有 | Have |
| yih | 一 | one |
| pih | 百 | hundred |
| kin | 斤 | catty |
| chung. | 重。 | heavy. |

T. Is it dear or cheap?

| | | |
|---|---|---|
| She | 是 | Is |
| kwei | 貴 | dear |
| she | 是 | is |
| tsëen? | 賤。 | cheap? |

M. It is uncertain, not knowing how much has come.

| | | |
|---|---|---|
| Joo | 如 | Now |
| kin | 今 | |
| we | 未 | not |
| ting, | 定。 | certain, |
| pŭh | 不 | not |
| che | 知 | know |
| lae | 來 | come |
| leaou | 了 | has |
| to | 多 | how much? |
| shaou? | 少。 | |

— If much comes it will of course be cheap; if little, I fear it will be high.

| | | | |
|---|---|---|---|
| Lae | 來 | Come | |
| tĭh | 得 | | |
| to | 多 | much | |
| tsew | 就 | then | |
| tsëen, | 賤. | cheap, | |
| lae | 來 | come | |
| tĭh | 得 | | |
| shaou | 少 | little | |
| chĭh | 只 | only | |
| pa | 怕 | fear | |
| tsew | 就 | then | |
| yaou | 要 | will be | |
| kwei. | 貴. | dear. | |

M. What is it bought for at present?

| | | |
|---|---|---|
| Joo | 如 | Now |
| kin | 今 | |
| yaou | 要 | want |
| mae | 買 | to buy |
| shin | 甚 | what |
| mo | 麽 | |
| kea | 價 | price? |
| tsëen? | 錢 | |

T. Now, I think it is sold at fourteen tales.

| | | | |
|---|---|---|---|
| Joo | 如 | Now | |
| kin | 今 | | |
| chĭh | 只 | only | I apprehend |
| pa | 怕 | fear | |
| yaou | 要 | want | |
| mae | 賣 | to sell at | |
| shĭh | 十 | fourteen | |
| sze | 四 | | |
| leang | 両 | tales | |
| yin | 銀 | silver. | |
| tsze. | 子. | | |

T. It is high, I cannot give so much.

| | | |
|---|---|---|
| Kwei | 貴 | Dear |
| leaou | 了 | |
| wo | 我 | I |
| ch'hùh | 出 | produce |
| pùh | 不 | not |
| tĭh | 得 | can |
| chay | 這 | so |
| mo | 麽 | |
| ta | 大 | great |
| kea | 價 | price. |
| tsëen. | 錢 | |

—. I will wait till it be a little cheaper, and then buy.

| | | |
|---|---|---|
| Wo | 我 | I |
| tăng | 等 | wait |
| tsëen | 賤 | cheap |
| leaou | 了 | |

| | | |
|---|---|---|
| tsae | 纔 | then |
| mae. | 買。 | buy. |

— If I buy dear, I shall loose instead of making any thing by it.

| | | |
|---|---|---|
| Jŏ | 若 | If |
| she | 是 | it be |
| mae | 買 | bought |
| tĭh | 得 | |
| kwei, | 貴。 | dear, |
| she | 是 | it |
| yaou | 要 | will |
| chĭh | 折 | break |
| pun, | 本。 | the prime (cost), |
| we | 未 | not |
| yew | 有 | have |
| tsëen | 錢 | money |
| chwan. | 賺。 | profit. |

— When the Cotton arrives, I will thank you to let me know.

| | | |
|---|---|---|
| Yew | 有 | Have |
| Mëen | 棉 | Cotton |
| hwa | 花 | |
| taou | 到 | arrive, |
| leaou, | 了。 | |
| ts'hing | 請 | thank |
| ne | 你 | you |
| chŏ | 着 | to order |
| jin | 人 | a man |
| yu | 與 | to give |
| wo | 我 | me |
| ko | 個 | a |
| sin. | 信。 | letter (a word). |

M. Very well, I will send a Person to let you know.

| | | |
|---|---|---|
| She, | 是。 | Yes, |
| jŏ | 若 | if |
| lae | 來 | come, |
| leaou, | 了。 | |
| wo | 我 | I |
| ta | 打 | send |
| fa | 發 | |
| jin | 人 | a man |
| ts'hing | 請 | to request |
| ne. | 你。 | you. |

# DIALOGUE XIV.

## *ON PURCHASING SILK.*

A. Shopman, I want a piece of Blue Silk.

| | | | |
|---|---|---|---|
| Sze | 事 | Business | Shopman, |
| t'how | 頭 | head | |
| kung, | 公。 | man, | |
| wo | 我 | I | |
| yaou | 要 | want | |
| mae | 買 | to buy | |
| yǐh | 一 | a | |
| pĕǐh | 疋 | piece of | |
| lan | 藍 | blue | |
| töan | 緞 | | silk. |
| tsze. | 子。 | | |

B. We have Silk of every sort and price; the goods are superior and inferior; the prices are hig h and low.

| | | | |
|---|---|---|---|
| Wo | 我 | | We |
| mun | 們 | | |
| yew | 有 | have | |
| töan | 緞 | | silk; |
| tsze; | 子。 | | |
| kŏ | 各 | every | |
| tăng | 等 | degree | |
| kea | 價 | | price |
| tsëen | 錢 | | |
| ho | 貨 | the goods | |
| yew | 有 | are | |
| kaou | 高 | high | |
| te; | 低。 | low; | |
| kea | 價 | price | |
| yew | 有 | is | |
| kwei | 貴 | dear | |
| tsëen. | 賤。 | cheap. | |

A. I will thank you to give me some to look at.

| | | |
|---|---|---|
| Ts'hing | 請 | Beg |

ne 你 you
na 拿 take
seay 些 a little
yu 與 give
wo 我 me
k'han. 看。 look.

B. This piece of Silk is of the first quality.

Chay 這 This
pëĭh 疋 piece
töan 緞 } silk
tsze 子 }
she 是 is
ting 頂 vertex
haou 好 } good.
tëĭh. 的。 }

A. How long and broad is it?

Yew 有 Have
to 多 (how) much
ch'hang, 長。 long,
yew 有 have
to 多 (how) much
kwŏ? 濶。 broad?

B. The length is thirty cubits, the breadth three cubits and a half, the price thirty dollars.

Ch'hang 長 Long
san 三 three
ch'hang, 丈。 ch'hang,
kwăn 寬 broad
san 三 three
chĭh 尺 cubits (and)
pwan, 半。 half,
kea 價 } price
tsëen 錢 }
san 三 } thirty
shĭh 十 }
yuen. 員。 dollars.

A. I will give you twenty dollars.

Wo 我 I
chĭh 只 only
haou 好 like
ch'hŭh 出 } to produce
tĭh 得 }
urh 二 } twenty
shĭh 十 }
yuen. 員。 dollars.

B. If you like, Sir, I will abate you five dollars, I cannot do more.

Jŏ 若 If
laou 老 } Sir,
yay, 爺 }
chung 中 } likes,
e, 意。 }

wo 我 I
tsew 就 then will
këen 減 lessen
woo 五 five
yuen 員 dollars
mae 賣 sell
yu 與 to
ne, 你 you,
to 多 more
këen 減 lessen
pŭh 不 not
năng. 能 can.

A. Very well, I will thank you to send it to my house. I have no money on me, you must enter it on the book.

Pa 罷 } Enough,
leaou 了 }
ts'hing 請 beg
ne 你 you
chŏ 着 send (order)
jin 人 man
na 拿 take
k'heu 去 go
wo 我 my
kea 家 } house;
le; 裡 }

wo 我 I
we 未 not
yew 有 have
yin 銀 silver
tae 帶 bring
lae, 來 come,
ts'hing 請 beg
ne 你 you
shang 上 } put it on the account.
ch'hang. 賬 }

B. Very well.

Haou 好 Well
shwŏ, 說 said,
she 是 } yes.
leaou. 了 }

A. I forgot:—I will trouble you to open it out. I am afraid that it is damaged.

Wo 我 I
wang 忘 } forgot,
leaou, 了 }
ts'hing 請 beg
ne 你 you
ta 打 strike
k'hae 開 open
wo 我 I
k'han; 看 look;

| | | |
|---|---|---|
| chay | 這 | this |
| pĕĭh | 疋 | piece |
| töan | 緞 | silk |
| tsze | 子 | |
| pa | 怕 | fear |
| k'he | 其 | it's |
| chung | 中 | midst |
| k'ho | 可 | may be |
| maou | 毛 | damaged. |
| ping, | 病。 | |

B. It is unnecessary to open it, I was at the Weaver's and chose it. You may be quite easy.

| | | |
|---|---|---|
| Pŭh | 不 | No |
| yung | 用 | use |
| ta | 打 | strike |
| k'hae | 開 | open |
| k'han, | 看。 | look, |
| wo | 我 | I |
| tsae | 在 | at |
| Ke | 機 | Weaver's |
| fang | 房 | room |
| këen | 揀 | chose |
| seuen | 選 | |
| lae | 來 | come, |
| tëĭh, | 的。 | |
| k'ho | 可 | (you) may |
| e | 以 | |
| fang | 放 | compose |
| sin. | 心。 | heart. |

A. Very well;—I think I do not owe you for any thing beside.

| | | |
|---|---|---|
| Joo | 如 | Thus |
| tsze | 此 | |
| pa | 罷 | enough, |
| leaou, | 了。 | |
| wo | 我 | I |
| chae | 猜 | think |
| pŭh | 不 | not |
| k'hëen | 欠 | owe |
| ne | 你 | you |
| pëĕ | 別 | other |
| hëang | 項 | kind |
| tëĭh | 的 | of |
| ho | 貨 | goods |
| kea | 價 | price. |
| tsëen. | 錢。 | |

B. No, you always pay me ready money.

| | | |
|---|---|---|
| Ne | 你 | You |
| we | 未 | not |
| yew, | 有。 | have, |
| ne | 你 | you |
| kea, | 駕。 | Sir, |

hwüy 回 } always
hwüy 回
chaou 照 } countenance (me)
koo 顧
mae 買 buy
ho 貨 goods
too 都 all
she 是 are
hëen 現 present time
yin. 銀. money.

A. You are very right. I do not like to be in People's books.

Pùh 不 Not
tso, 錯, mistake,
wo 我 I
pùh 不 not
hwan 歡 } like
he 喜
k'hëen 欠 owe
pëĕ 別 other
jin 人 } men's
tëih 的
ch'hang 賬 } accounts.
mùh. 目.

B. I shall certainly send the amount to-morrow: but if I do not come, I will thank you to send the bill and a receipt to me. If the money is not at hand, I will send the receipt back again.

Wo 我 I
ming 明 } to-morrow
t'hëen 天
tsze 自 } indeed
jen 然
ts'hing 清 clear
sung 送 present
lae 來 come
ch'hang. 賬. the account.
Jŏ 若 If
wo 我 I
ming 明 } to-morrow
yĭh 日
pùh 不 not
lae, 來. come,
ts'hing 請 beg
na 你 you
k'hae 開 open (on)
che 紙 paper
ch'hang 賬 } account
mùh 目
tan, 單. bill,
këih 及 and
show 收 receive

| | | |
|---|---|---|
| tan | 單 | bill (send) |
| yu | 與 | to |
| wo | 我 | my |
| shay | 舍 | house; |
| hea; | 下 | |
| jŏ | 若 | if |
| wo | 我 | my |
| yin | 銀 | money |
| tsze | 子 | |
| pŭh | 不 | not |
| pëen, | 便 | convenient, |
| wo | 我 | I |
| tsew | 就 | will then |
| ta | 打 | strike |
| hwŭy | 回 | back |
| show | 收 | the receipt |
| tan | 單 | |
| yu | 與 | to |
| ne. | 你 | you. |

A. I again forgot, I want a piece of Black Silk if you can cut it, about three cubits long

| | | |
|---|---|---|
| Wo | 我 | I |
| yew | 又 | again |
| wang | 忘 | forgot, |
| leaou, | 了 | |
| hwan | 還 | still |
| yaou | 要 | want. |
| yĭh | 一 | a |
| kwae | 塊 | fragment |
| hĭh | 黑 | black |
| töan | 緞 | silk, |
| tsze, | 子 | |
| jŏ | 若 | if |
| ne | 你 | you |
| k'ho | 可 | can |
| e | 以 | |
| ts'hëen | 剪 | cut |
| tĭh | 得 | |
| ta | 大 | about |
| yŏ | 約 | |
| san | 三 | three |
| chĭh | 尺 | cubits |
| yu | 與 | for |
| wo. | 我 | me. |

B. That can be done; I will put up this Black Silk with the Blue, and send it to your house.

| | | |
|---|---|---|
| Tso | 做 | Can do it, |
| tĭh, | 得 | |
| chay | 這 | this |
| hĭh | 黑 | black |
| töan | 緞 | silk |
| tsze | 子 | |

yǐh 一 one
tsung 總 whole
paou 包 bundle up
tsae 在 be
lan 藍 blue
töan 緞 } silk
tsze 子 }

nuy, 內 within,
chŏ 着 order
jin 人 man
sung 送 present
taou 到 to
foo 府 } your house.
shang. 上 }

# DIALOGUE XV.

## *WITH A TEACHER OF CHINESE.*

Student. I will thank you to read this page.

Ts'hing 請 Thank
ne 你 you
nëen 念 to read
chay 這 this
yǐh 一 one
pëen 篇 page
shoo. 書 book.

— Speak slowly.

Ts'hing 請 Pray
man 慢 } slowly
man 慢 }
shwŏ. 說 speak.

Teacher. Write the plain hand, and not the contractions.

Ts'hing 請 Pray
seay 寫 write
ching 正 the proper
tsze, 字 character,
pŭh 不 not
yaou 要 want

këen 減 lessened
pëih 筆 pencil
seay 寫 } writing.
tëih. 的 }

— How is that Character written.

Na 那 } That
ko 個 }
tsze 字 character
she 是 is
shin 甚 } what
mo 麼 }
seay 寫 writing
fă? 法 rule?

— What is the Radical of the Character 慢 Man?

Man 慢 Man
tsze 字 character
tsae 在 is in
ho 何 what
poo? 部 Radical?

— Are there any Books to be bought in Macao?

Gaou- 澳 } Macao
mun 門 }
yew 有 have
shoo 書 books
mae 買 to buy
mŭh 沒 not
yew? 有 have?

— What is the difference between these two Characters?

Chay 這 These
leang 兩 } two
ko 個 }
tsze 字 characters
yew 有 have
ho 何 what
fun 分 } difference?
pëĕ? 別 }

— Who wrote the Four-books?

Ts'hing 請 Beg
wăn 問 to ask,
Sze- 四 } Four-books
shoo 書 }
she 是 were
ho 何 whose
tsŏ 作 } making?
tëih? 的 }

B. The Four-books were written by four Persons.

Sze- 四 } Four-books
shoo 書 }
she 是 were

sze 四 } four
ko 個 }
jin 人 Person's
tsŏ 作 } making.
tëĭh. 的 }

— Shang-lun, Hea-lun, were written by Confucius.

Shang- 上 } Shang-lun, and
lun 論 }
Hea- 下 } Hea-lun,
lun 論 }
she 是 were
Kung- 孔 } Confucius
foo- 夫 }
tsze 子 }
tsŏ 作 } making *
tëĭh. 的 }

— The Ta-hëŏ, was compiled by Tsăng-tsze.

Ta- 大 } The Ta-hëŏ
hëŏ 學 }
she 是 was
Tsăng- 曾 } Tsăng-tsze's
tsze 子 }
tsŏ 作 } making.
tëĭh. 的 }

— The Chung-yung was compiled by Tsze-sze.

Chung- 中 } Chung-yung
yung 庸 }
she 是 was
Tsze- 子 } Tsze-sze
sze 思 }
so 所 that which
tsŏ. 作 made.

— Shang-mung and Hea-mung, were written by Măng-tsze.

Shang- 上 } Shang-mung
mung 孟 }
Hea- 下 } Hea-mung
mung 孟 }
she 是 was
Măng- 孟 } Măng-tsze
tsze 子 }
so 所 that which
tsŏ. 作 made.

A. With which should a Learner begin?

Ts'hoo 初 Begin } A learner
hëŏ 學 to learn }
k'he 起 } at first
t'how 頭 }

* They merely contain his sayings, which were taken down by his Pupils.

| | | |
|---|---|---|
| she | 是 | should |
| k'ho | 可 | |
| tŭh | 讀 | read |
| na | 那 | which |
| yĭh | 一 | one |
| pun? | 本。 | volume? |

B. He ought to begin with the Ta-hëŏ; but as the style and doctrines of the Ta-hëŏ and Chung-yung, are more abstruse than the others, it is better to begin with Shang-lun.

| | | |
|---|---|---|
| Ying | 應 | (He) should |
| tang | 當 | |
| tsung | 從 | from |
| Ta- | 大 | the Ta-hëŏ |
| hëŏ | 學 | |
| k'he | 起 | begin; |
| t'how; | 頭。 | |
| tan | 但 | but |
| Ta- | 大 | Ta-hëŏ |
| hëŏ | 學 | |
| k'heĭh | 及 | and |
| Chung- | 中 | Chung-yung, |
| yung, | 庸 | |
| wăn | 文 | style |
| le | 理 | doctrines |
| yuĕ | 越 | more |
| fă | 發 | |
| shin | 深 | deep and |
| gaou, | 奧。 | profound, |
| pŭh | 不 | not as |
| joo | 如 | |
| tsung | 從 | from |
| Shang- | 上 | Shang-lun |
| lun | 論 | |
| k'he | 起 | begin |
| tŭh | 讀 | to read |
| wei | 爲 | is |
| haou. | 好。 | good. |

A. What is the meaning of Shang-lun?

| | | |
|---|---|---|
| Shang- | 上 | Shang-lun |
| lun | 論 | |
| leang | 兩 | two |
| ko | 個 | |
| tsze | 字 | characters |
| yew | 有 | have |
| ho | 何 | what |
| e? | 意。 | meaning? |

B. The word Lun, refers to the book Lun-yu. But this book has two parts; Shang, points out the first part, and Hea, the second.

| | | |
|---|---|---|
| Lun | 論 | Lun |

| | | |
|---|---|---|
| tsze | 字 | character |
| tsëĕ | 卽 | does |
| che | 指 | point to |
| Lun- | 論 | Lun-yu |
| yu | 語 | |
| yĭh | 一 | one |
| pun | 本 | |
| shoo; | 書。 | book; |
| wei | 惟 | but |
| k'he | 其 | that |
| shoo | 書 | book |
| yew | 有 | has |
| leang | 兩 | two |
| keuen, | 卷。 | parts, |
| Shang | 上 | Shang |
| tsze | 字 | character |

| | | |
|---|---|---|
| che | 指 | points to |
| k'he | 其 | it's |
| te | 第 | first |
| yĭh | 一 | |
| keuen, | 卷。 | part, |
| Hea | 下 | Hea |
| tsze | 字 | character |
| che | 指 | points to |
| k'he | 其 | it's |
| te | 第 | second |
| urh | 二 | |
| keuen, | 卷。 | part, |
| tsew | 就 | just so. |
| she | 是 | |
| leaou. | 了。 | |

# DIALOGUE XVI.

## *RESPECTING THE RELIGIONS OF CHINA.*

A. How many Religions are there in China?

| | | |
|---|---|---|
| Chung | 中 | Middle |
| kwŏ | 國 | Nation |
| yew | 有 | have |
| to | 多 | how many |
| shaou | 少 | |
| keaou | 教 | religions? |
| mun? | 門。 | |

B. There are three.

| | | |
|---|---|---|
| Yew | 有 | Has |
| san | 三 | three |
| ko | 個 | |
| keaou | 教 | religions. |
| mun. | 門。 | |

A. What are these three Religions called?

| | | |
|---|---|---|
| Na | 那 | Those |
| san | 三 | three |
| keaou | 教 | religions |
| mun | 門 | |
| keaou | 呌 | called |
| tĭh | 得 | |
| shin | 甚 | what |
| mo | 麽 | |
| ming? | 名。 | name? |

B. They are called Joo, Shĭh, and Taou.

| | | |
|---|---|---|
| She | 是 | They are, |
| Joo, | 儒 | Literati, |
| Shĭh, | 釋 | Fŭh, (and) |
| Taou. | 道。 | Taou. |

A. What is the Religion Joo?

| | | |
|---|---|---|
| Joo | 儒 | Joo |
| keaou | 教 | religion |
| ho | 何 | what |
| ne? | 呢。 | ? |

B. It contains the doctrines of Confucius, in which he taught men Benevolence, Justice, Propriety, Wisdom, and Truth, five constant virtues.

She 是 It is
Kung- 孔
foo- 夫 } Confucius
tsze, 子
e 以 by
jin, 仁 benevolence,
e, 義 justice,
le, 禮 propriety,
che, 智 wisdom,
sin, 信 truth,
woo 五 } five constant (virtues)
chang 常
che 之 the
taou 道 } doctrines
le 理
keaou 教 taught
jin. 人。 men.

A. The Religion Shĭh, is only another name for that of Fŭh, is it not so?

Shĭh 釋 Shĭh
keaou 教 religion
tsew 就 just
she 是 is
Fŭh 佛 Fŭh
keaou 教 religion
tëĭh 的 's
pëĕ 别 other
ming, 名 name,
she 是 is
pŭh 不 not
she? 是。 is?

B. Yes. The ancestor was Joo-lae-fŭh. At first, he uttered the sacred books and pronounced laws, for rescuing the flock of mankind.—He advised them to regulate their conduct and be good.

Jen 然 } Yes, indeed,
yay, 也
nae 乃 and
Joo- 如
lae- 來 } Joo-lae-fŭh's
fŭh 佛
tsoo 祖 ancestor
tang 當 } at that day
jĭh 日
keang 講 discoursed on
king 經 the Sacred books and
shwŏ 說 pronounced

| | | |
|---|---|---|
| fă, | 法 | laws, |
| poo | 普 | universally |
| t'hoo | 度 | to rescue |
| keun | 羣 | the flock (of) |
| săng; | 生 | living; |
| keuen | 勸 | advised |
| jin | 人 | men |
| sew | 修 | to adorn |
| hing | 行 | conduct (and) |
| wei | 爲 | practice |
| shen. | 善 | goodness. |

**A.** Is not the religion of Taou also called Taou-sze?

| | | |
|---|---|---|
| Taou | 道 | Taou |
| keaou | 敎 | religion |
| yay | 也 | also |
| she | 是 | is |
| keaou | 叫 | called |
| tĭh | 得 | |
| Taou | 道 | Taou-sze, |
| sze, | 士 | |
| she | 是 | is |
| fow? | 否 | not? |

**B.** Just so, at first Yuen-che-t'hëen-tsun delivered wonderful rules to induce men to perfect truth, cherish nature, restrain their breath, and mould their figure.*

| | | |
|---|---|---|
| Tsëĕ | 卽 | It is so; |
| she; | 是 | |
| tang | 當 | at that day, |
| jĭh | 日 | |
| Yuen- | 元 | Origin |
| che- | 始 | beginning |
| t'hëen- | 天 | heaven's |
| tsun, | 尊 | honorable, |
| chuen | 傳 | delivered down |
| lew | 流 | |
| meaou | 妙 | wonderful |
| fă, | 法 | laws, |
| taou | 導 | to induce |
| jin | 人 | men |
| tseun | 全 | to complete |
| chin | 眞 | truth, |
| yang | 養 | cherish |
| sing | 性 | nature, |
| fŭh | 服 | to repress |
| k'he | 氣 | breath (and) |
| lëen | 煉 | mould |
| hing. | 形 | figure. |

* This doubtless is obscure, and is inserted merely to shew the phraseology of the Sect.

A. Does the Sect Joo, of the learned, (a very self conceited class of men) worship images or not?

| | | |
|---|---|---|
| Joo | 儒 | In the religion of |
| keaou | 教 | the learned |
| yew | 有 | have |
| pae | 拜 | worship |
| shin | 神 | god |
| seang | 像 | image |
| mŭh | 没 | not |
| yew? | 有。 | have? |

B. Sometimes they kneel down towards heaven and worship; sometimes they worship in their hearts; and sometimes they are in the habit of going to the temples to worship.

| | | |
|---|---|---|
| Yew | 有 | Sometimes |
| she | 時 | |
| kwei | 跪 | kneel |
| hea | 下 | down |
| hëang | 向 | towards |
| t'hëen | 天 | heaven |
| pae; | 拜 | to worship; |
| yew | 有 | sometimes |
| she | 時 | |
| tsae | 在 | in |
| sin | 心 | the heart |
| shang | 上 | upon |
| pae; | 拜 | worship; |
| yew | 又 | and |
| yew | 有 | sometimes |
| she | 時 | |
| chang | 常 | in the habit of |
| wang | 往 | going to |
| meaou | 廟 | the temple |
| le | 裡 | within |
| pae. | 拜。 | to worship. |

A. What temples do they go to?

| | | |
|---|---|---|
| T'ha | 他 | They |
| mun | 們 | |
| wang | 往 | go to |
| ho | 何 | what |
| meaou | 廟 | temples |
| pae? | 拜。 | to worship? |

B. They go to the temple of (the goddess) Kwan-yin; or to the temple of Pih-chang; or to the temple of Ching-hwang, (the god of the Province of Canton.)

| | | |
|---|---|---|
| Wang | 往 | Go to |
| Kwan- | 觀 | Kwan-yin |
| yin | 音 | |
| meaou | 廟 | temple |
| pae | 拜。 | worship, |

| | | |
|---|---|---|
| hwŏ | 或 | or |
| Pĭh-chang | 北帝 | Pĭh-chang |
| meaou; | 廟。 | temple; (or) |
| Ching-hwang | 城隍 | Ching-hwang |
| meaou. | 廟。 | temple. |

A. Do these three temples belong to Fŭh or to Taou?

| | | |
|---|---|---|
| Chay | 這 | These |
| san | 三 | three |
| meaou | 廟 | temples |
| shŭh | 屬 | belong to |
| Fŭh keaou, | 佛教。 | Fŭh religion, |
| hwan | 還 | or |
| shŭh | 屬 | belong to |
| Taou keaou? | 道教。 | the religion of Taou? |

B. Some of them belong to Taou, and others to Fŭh.

| | | |
|---|---|---|
| Yew | 有 | Some |
| shŭh | 屬 | belong to |
| Taou keaou, | 道教。 | the religion of Taou, |
| yĭh | 亦 | also |
| yew | 有 | some |
| shŭh | 屬 | belong to |
| Fŭh keaou. | 佛教。 | the religion of Fŭh. |

A. Do Joo, Shĭh, and Taou, all believe that heaven will reward the good and punish the bad.

| | | |
|---|---|---|
| Joo, | 儒 | Joo, |
| Shĭh, | 釋 | Shĭh, |
| Taou, | 道。 | Taou, |
| too | 都 | all |
| sin | 信 | believe |
| t'hëen | 天 | heaven |
| how lae | 後來 | afterward |
| pëĭh | 必 | must |
| shang | 賞 | reward |
| shen | 善 | the good (and) |
| fă | 罰 | punish |
| gŏ. | 惡。 | the bad. |

B. At heart, the doctrine of the three religions is the same; they firmly believe that heaven will do justice, by rewarding and punishing both good and bad.

| | | |
|---|---|---|
| San | 三 | Three |
| keaou | 教 | religion |
| che | 之 | 's |

| | | |
|---|---|---|
| sin | 心 | heart |
| t'hung | 同 | same |
| yĭh | 一 | one |
| le, | 理。 | reason, |
| woo | 無 | not |
| fei | 非 | not |
| sin | 信 | believe |
| t'hëen | 天 | heaven |
| hing | 行 | do |
| taou | 道 | justice |
| e | 以 | by |
| kung | 公 | justly |
| ping | 平 | |
| shang | 賞 | rewarding |
| fă | 罰 | punishing |
| shen | 善 | good |
| gŏ | 惡 | bad. |
| yen. | 焉。 | |

A. But, are these rewards and punishments in this life, or after death? or are rewards and punishments both in this life, and in that to come.

| | | |
|---|---|---|
| Wei | 惟 | But |
| she | 是 | is it |
| tsae | 在 | being |
| she | 世 | the world |
| këen | 間 | in |
| shang | 賞 | reward |
| fă, | 罰。 | punish, |
| hwan | 還 | or |
| she | 是 | is it |
| tsae | 在 | being |
| sze | 死 | dead |
| leaou | 了 | |
| che | 之 | the |
| how? | 後。 | after? |
| hwŏ | 或 | or |
| she | 是 | is it |
| tsae | 在 | being |
| she | 世 | the world |
| këen | 間 | in |
| yew | 有 | have |
| shang | 賞 | reward |
| fă; | 罰。 | punishment; |
| ping | 並 | moreover |
| lae | 來 | coming |
| săng | 生 | life |
| yĭh | 亦 | also |
| yew | 有 | have |
| shang | 賞 | reward |
| fă. | 罰。 | punishment. |

B. Both in this life, and in the life to come, there are rewards and punishments; but there is regard to the offences of men, whether heinous or not. Speedy punishments are in this life; those that are more remote, in the world to come.

| | | |
|---|---|---|
| She | 世 | The world |
| këen | 間 | in |
| yu | 與 | with |
| lae | 來 | coming |
| săng | 生 | life |
| too | 都 | all |
| yew | 有 | have |
| shang | 賞 | reward |
| fă. | 罰 | punishment. |
| Tan | 但 | But |
| chă | 察 | examine |
| k'he | 其 | the |
| jin | 人 | man's |
| shen | 善 | goodness |
| gŏ | 惡 | wickedness |
| kan, | 根 | root, |
| shin | 深 | deep |
| tsëen; | 淺 | shallow; |
| kin | 近 | near |
| shang | 賞 | reward |
| fă | 罰 | punishment |
| tsĭh | 則 | of course are |
| tsae | 在 | in |
| kin | 今 | this |
| she, | 世 | world, |
| yuen | 遠 | remote |
| shang | 賞 | reward |
| fă | 罰 | punishment |
| tsĭh | 則 | of course |
| tsae | 在 | in |
| lae | 來 | coming |
| săng | 生 | life. |

A. Do the three Sects all believe in a metempsychosis?

| | | |
|---|---|---|
| San | 三 | Three |
| keaou | 教 | religions |
| keae | 皆 | all |
| sin | 信 | believe |
| yew | 有 | have |
| lun | 輪 | circle |
| hwŭy, | 回 | return, |
| she | 是 | is |
| fow? | 否 | not? |

B. This is a mysterious subject; but those, who in this life are good, in the next life will be again men; if in this life they be very bad, they will in the next life sink into hell, and suffer everlasting punishment, or will be changed into beasts.

| | | |
|---|---|---|
| Chay | 這 | This |
| ko | 個 | |
| teaou | 條 | section |
| shŭh | 屬 | belongs to |
| meaou | 杳 | mysterious |
| ming | 冥 | |
| che | 之 | 's |
| sze; | 事 | business; |
| tan | 但 | but |
| kin | 今 | this |
| she | 世 | world |
| tso | 做 | make |
| jin | 人 | man |
| haou, | 好 | good, |
| lae | 來 | coming |
| săng | 生 | life |
| fŭh | 復 | again |
| chuen | 轉 | turned |
| wei | 爲 | to be |
| jin; | 人 | man; |
| jŏ | 若 | if |
| kin | 今 | this |
| she | 世 | life |
| tso | 做 | make |
| jin | 人 | man |
| pŭh | 不 | not |
| haou | 好 | good |
| tĭh | 得 | very, |
| hăn, | 狠 | |
| pŭh | 不 | not |
| tĭh | 得 | can |
| lae | 來 | coming |
| săng | 生 | life |
| chuen | 轉 | be turned to |
| she; | 世 | the world; |
| hwŏ | 或 | perhaps |
| këen | 陷 | fall |
| lŏ | 落 | down to |
| te | 地 | earth's |
| yŭh | 獄 | prison |
| show | 受 | receive |
| yung | 永 | eternal |
| koo | 苦 | misery |
| e! | 矣 | ! |
| hwŏ | 或 | or |
| pëen | 變 | be changed to |
| tsŭh | 畜 | beast |
| săng | 生 | |
| che | 之 | 's |
| lŭy. | 類 | species. |

A. Are there any Athiests in China?

| | | |
|---|---|---|
| Chung | 中 | China |
| kwŏ | 國 | |
| yew | 有 | have |

| | | |
|---|---|---|
| jin | 人 | men |
| shwŏ | 說 | say |
| tsung | 總 | altogether |
| woo | 無 | no |
| Shin ? | 神。 | God ? |

B. No. God made the heavens, earth, and all things; is every where present. How can it be said, that there is no God!

| | | |
|---|---|---|
| Fei | 非 | No.* |
| yay. | 也。 | |
| Shin | 神 | God |
| pun | 本 | originally |
| lae | 來 | |
| chwang | 創 | created |
| tsaou | 造 | |
| t'hëen | 天 | heaven, |
| te | 地 | earth, (and) |
| wăn | 萬 | ten thousand |
| wŭh, | 物。 | things, |
| woo | 無 | no |
| so | 所 | place |
| pŭh | 不 | not |
| tsae; | 在。 | in; |
| ho | 何 | how |
| tĭh | 得 | can |
| yen | 言 | say |
| woo | 無 | no |
| Shin | 神 | God |
| hoo. | 乎。 | ! |

A. Do the three Sects believe that all things are appointed by Heaven?

| | | |
|---|---|---|
| San | 三 | Three |
| keaou | 教 | religions |
| shwŏ | 說 | say |
| fan | 凡 | all |
| sze | 事 | affairs |
| yew | 有 | have |
| t'hëen | 天 | heaven's |
| ming, | 命。 | decree, |
| she | 是 | is |
| fow ? | 否。 | not ? |

B. They all say that they are.

| | | |
|---|---|---|
| San | 三 | Three |
| keaou | 教 | religions |
| keae | 皆 | all |
| yen | 言 | say |
| yew | 有 | have. |
| yay. | 也。 | |

* This was the reply of a Native, who had often heard the doctrine of One True God inculcated. They do not usually express themselves thus.

# DIALOGUE XVII.

## *AN EMBASSADOR INTRODUCED.—A NARRATIVE.*

A. The true Sovereign ascended the throne, and changed the Imperial designation to Tang-tae-tsung-ching kwan.

| | | |
|---|---|---|
| Tsze-wei, | 紫微 | Tsze-wei, |
| chin | 眞 | the true |
| choo | 主 | Lord |
| tăng leaou | 登了 | ascended |
| Lung | 龍 | the Dragon's |
| wei, | 位。 | seat, |
| keae | 改 | changed (the title to) |
| Tang-tae-tsung-ching-kwan | 唐太宗貞觀 | Tang-tae-tsung-ching-kwan's |
| t'hëen tsze. | 天子。 | Emperor. |

B. In truth, the winds were moderate, and the rains in season. The nation was extensive, and the People at peace. All around was profound tranquillity. The People enjoyed the smile of (royal) favor. Prince and People had enjŏyed repose three years.

| | | |
|---|---|---|
| Chin ko | 眞箇 | Truly, |
| fung | 風 | winds |
| teaou | 調 | moderate |
| yu | 雨 | rain |
| shin; | 順。 | seasonable; |
| kwŏ | 國 | nation |
| tae | 泰 | great |

min 民 people
găn, 安 composed,
sze 四 four
fang 方 quarters
ning 寧 } at peace and quiet
ts'hing 靖 }
pĭh 百 } the people
sing 姓 }
che 沾 received
găn. 恩 favor.
Keun 君 Prince (and)
min 民 people
găn 安 peace
hëang 享 enjoyed
san 三 three
nëen. 年 years.

A. It happened one day, that the Emperor, Ching-kwan, descended to give audience.

Hwŭh 忽 Unexpectedly
yĭh 一 one
jĭh 日 day
Ching- 貞 } Ching-kwan,
kwan 觀 }
t'hëen 天 heaven's } Emperor
tsze, 子 són, }
lin 臨 descended
chaou. 朝 to give audience.

B. All the Civil and Military Officers having had an interview, the Officer of the Yellow-gate, announced, saying,

Wăn 文 Civil
Woo 武 military
pĭh 百 a hundred
kwăn 官 officers
chaou 朝 audience
këen 見 see
e 已 now
pëĭh; 畢 finished;
yew 有 there was
Hwang- 黃 Yellow-
mun 門 gate
kwăn 官 officer
k'he 啟 commenced
tsow 奏 official report, and
taou. 道 said.

A. I the Officer of the Yellow-gate, have an affair to announce to your Majesty.

Chin 臣 Minister
Hwang- 黃 } Yellow-gate
mun 門 }
kwăn 官 Officer

| | | |
|---|---|---|
| yew | 有 | have |
| sze | 事 | business |
| tsow | 奏 | to report (to the) |
| wăn | 聞 | hearing of |
| pe | 陛 | } your Majesty. |
| hea. | 下。 | |

A. (The Emperor said,) Say on.

| | | |
|---|---|---|
| Tsow | 奏 | Report |
| lae. | 來。 | come. |

B. There is now a foreign Embassador from the north, who wishes to see your Majesty.—He is without the Southern gate, waiting to receive your pleasure.

| | | |
|---|---|---|
| Kin | 今 | Now |
| yew | 有 | have |
| pĭh | 北 | north |
| fan | 番 | foreign |
| sze | 使 | send |
| chin | 臣 | minister |
| kwăn | 官 | officer |
| yaou | 要 | wants |
| kēen | 見 | to see |
| pe | 陛 | } your Majesty, |
| hea, | 下 | |
| hēen | 現 | he now |
| tsae | 在 | is at |
| woo | 午 | south |
| mun | 門 | door |
| wae | 外 | withoutside |
| how | 候 | waiting |
| che. | 旨。 | (your) pleasure. |

A. His Majesty said, Since he is the Embassador of a foreign country, hasten to summons him into the hall to see me.

| | | |
|---|---|---|
| Chaou | 朝 | } His Majesty |
| ting | 廷 | |
| shwŏ, | 說 | said, |
| ke | 旣 | since |
| yew | 有 | have |
| wae | 外 | external |
| pang | 邦 | country |
| sze | 使 | sent |
| chin, | 臣 | minister, |
| kwae | 快 | hasten |
| seun | 宣 | to summons (him) |
| shang | 上 | up |
| tēen | 殿 | temple |
| lae | 來 | come |
| kēen | 見 | to see |
| kwa | 寡 | the alone |
| jin. | 人。 | man. |

B. His Majesty having uttered this

the Officer of the Yellow-gate, received the Imperial pleasure, and tranferred the summons.

| | | |
|---|---|---|
| Wang | 王 | The king |
| keang | 降 | sent down |
| yĭh | 一 | a |
| shing, | 聲 | sound, |
| Hwang- | 黃 | the Yellow |
| mun | 門 | door |
| kwăn | 官 | officer |
| ling | 領 | received |
| che | 旨 | the pleasure, and |
| chuen | 傳 | communicated |
| seun. | 宣。 | the summons. |

A. (Reader,) Will you look at the appearance of this Embassador? Well, then see him.

| | | |
|---|---|---|
| Ne | 你 | Would you |
| k'han | 看 | see |
| chay | 這 | this |
| ko | 個 | (this) |
| sze | 使 | sent |
| chin | 臣 | minister |
| tsăng | 怎 | what |
| săng | 生 | born |
| mo | 模 | fashion? |
| yang? | 樣 | (fashion?) |
| chĭh | 只 | then |
| këen | 見 | see |
| t'ha. | 他。 | him. |

B. On his head were round fins of black silk, covered with fox skin.

| | | |
|---|---|---|
| T'how | 頭 | Head was |
| tae | 戴 | covered with |
| yuen | 圓 | round |
| che | 翅 | fins (of) |
| woo | 烏 | black |
| sha | 紗 | silk |
| hoo | 狐 | fox (skin) |
| le | 狸 | (fox (skin)) |
| kae | 蓋 | covered |
| ting. | 頂。 | the top. |

— A large red dress, with figures on a square, at the breast and back.

| | | |
|---|---|---|
| Ta | 大 | Large |
| hung | 紅 | red |
| Poo | 補 | Poo-tsze, and |
| tsze | 子 | (Poo-tsze, and) |
| Kung | 宮 | Kung-paou. |
| paou. | 袍。 | (Kung-paou.) |

— Round his loins was a golden girdle.

| | | |
|---|---|---|
| Yaou | 腰 | Loins |
| wei | 圍 | were surround |
| kin | 金 | (with) golden |

R

tae. 帶 girdle.

— He had a round face; short jaws; and a stiff beard.

Yuen 圓 Round
mëen; 面 face;
twan 短 short
sae; 腮 jaw;
ying 硬 stiff
seu. 鬚 beard.

— He ascended the hall with the letter in his hand.

Show 手 Hands
fung 捧 held up
pun 本 } official document
chang 章 } (and he)
shang 上 ascended
tëen. 殿 the hall.

— He fell prostrate on the golden floor, and said,

Foo 俯 } Fell prostrate on
fŭh 伏 }
kin 金 the golden
lwan 鑾 floor (and)
shwŏ. 說 said.

— The Holy Sovereign of the Southern Empire be exalted. A foreign Ambassador, Chow-kang, seeing him who rides in a chariot and four, wishes that he may live forever.

Nan 南 Southern
Chaou 朝 Empire's
Shing 聖 Holy
Choo 主 Lord
tsae 在 be
shang. 上 high.
Yew 有 There is
wae 外 a foreign
pang 邦 nation's
sze 使 sent
chin 臣 minister,
Chow- 周 } Chow-kang,
kang, 綱 }
këen 見 seeing
kea 駕 your Majesty, (he)
yuen 願 wishes
pe 陛 } your Majesty
hea 下 }
shing 聖 sacred
show 壽 age
woo 無 not
keang. 疆 limited.

A. Beloved Minister, in coming into my presence,—is it not to introduce tribute?

| | | |
|---|---|---|
| Gae | 愛 | Beloved |
| king | 卿 | minister |
| taou | 到 | come |
| chin | 朕 | me |
| kea | 駕 | |
| ts'hëen ; | 前。 | before ; |
| k'ho | 可 | is it |
| she | 是 | |
| tsin | 進 | to introduce |
| kung | 貢 | tribute |
| yu | 與 | to |
| kwa | 寡 | me |
| jin | 人 | |
| mo ? | 麽。 | ? |

B. The Embassador replying, said.

| | | |
|---|---|---|
| Sze | 使 | Sent |
| chin | 臣 | Minister |
| hwüy | 回 | returned |
| tsow | 奏 | report (and) |
| taou. | 道。 | said. |

— I have received the order of Lang-choo, and the Ta-yuen-shwae, to repair hither. I have a writing to exhibit for your Majesty's inspection.

| | | |
|---|---|---|
| Chin | 臣 | I |
| fung | 奉 | have received |
| Lang- | 狼 | Lang-choo |
| choo | 主 | |
| yu | 與 | and |
| Ta- | 大 | Ta-yuen-shwae |
| yuen- | 元 | |
| shwae | 帥 | |
| che | 之 | 's |
| che, | 旨 | will, |
| ling | 令 | ordering |
| taou | 到 | to (this place) |
| lae, | 來。 | to come, |
| yew | 有 | have |
| pun | 本 | an official document |
| chang | 章 | |
| hëen | 獻 | to offer |
| yu | 與 | to |
| wan | 萬 | ten thousand |
| süy | 歲 | years' |
| lung | 龍 | dragon |
| müh | 目 | eye |
| tsin | 親 | itself |
| kwan. | 觀。 | to look. |

A. His Majesty communicated his pleasure ;—What writing ? hasten to offer it.

| | | |
|---|---|---|
| Chaou | 朝 | His Majesty |
| ting | 廷 | |

| | | |
|---|---|---|
| chuen | 傳 | communicated |
| che ; | 旨。 | will ; |
| shin | 甚 | what |
| mo | 麽 | |
| peaou | 表 | document, |
| chang, | 章。 | |
| kwae | 快 | hasten |
| hëen | 獻 | offer (it) |
| shang | 上 | up |
| lae. | 來。 | come. |

B. Chow-kang, took the writing, and presented it with both his hands.

| | | |
|---|---|---|
| Chow- | 周 | Chow-kang |
| kang | 綱 | |
| pa | 把 | took |
| peaou | 表 | the document in |
| chang | 章 | |
| shwang | 雙 | both |
| show | 手 | hands |
| ching | 呈 | offered it up. |
| hëen. | 獻。 | |

— The Officers standing by, received it, and handed it up to his Majesty's table.

| | | |
|---|---|---|
| Pang | 傍 | By the side |
| pëen | 邊 | |
| she | 侍 | standing |
| chin | 臣 | officers |
| tsëĕ | 接 | received (and) |
| shang | 上 | handed it up to |
| lung | 龍 | the dragon's |
| găn. | 案。 | table. |

# DIALOGUE XVIII.

## *ON THE MODE OF VISITING IN CHINA.*

A. Suppose, in China, there be a Person, a Sew-tsae, (the lowest literary title); a Këen-săng, (one who has purchased rank); or a Keu-yin, (one eligible to public offices); or one who is already an officer of Government; go to visit a Person resident at Peking.

| | | |
|---|---|---|
| Pe | 比 | Suppose, |
| joo, | 如。 | |
| Chung | 中 | the Middle |
| kwŏ | 國 | nation |
| yew | 有 | have |
| yĭh | 一 | a |
| ko | 個 | |
| jin, | 人。 | man, |
| hwŏ | 或 | either |
| she | 是 | is |
| Sew- | 秀 | Sew-tsae; |
| tsae; | 才。 | |
| Këen- | 監 | Këen-săng; |
| săng; | 生。 | |
| Keu- | 舉 | Keu-jin; |
| jin; | 人。 | |
| hwŏ | 或 | or |
| she | 是 | is |
| yew | 有 | having |
| chĭh | 職 | office |
| kwăn | 官 | an officer, |
| yuen, | 員。 | |
| lae | 來 | comes |
| pae | 拜 | to visit |
| tsae | 在 | living at |
| King | 京 | Peking |
| tëĭh | 的 | 's |
| kŏ. | 客。 | stranger |

— When he first enters the gate, his Servant having in his hand a card, asks whether such a Person be at home or not?

| | | |
|---|---|---|
| Ts'hoo | 初 | First |
| tsin | 進 | enter |
| mun, | 門 | door, |
| ch'hang | 長 | the servant |
| pan | 班 | |
| show | 手 | hand |
| na | 拿 | taking |
| yew | 有 | has |
| yĭh | 一 | a |
| tëĭh | 帖 | card |
| tsze | 子 | |
| wǎn | 問 | asks |
| mow | 某 | such a |
| laou | 老 | Gentleman |
| yay | 爺 | |
| tsae | 在 | is |
| kea | 家 | house |
| le, | 裡 | within, |
| pŭh | 不 | not |
| tsae? | 在 | is? |

— If the Person keeping the house say, He is not at home; the Servant again asks, whither he has gone.

| | | | |
|---|---|---|---|
| Kwǎn | 管 | Rule | Servant, |
| kea | 家 | the house, | |
| jŏ | 若 | if | |
| shwŏ | 說 | say | |
| pŭh | 不 | not | |
| tsae | 在 | is | |
| kea | 家 | house | |
| le; | 裡 | within; | |
| ch'hang | 長 | the servant | |
| pan | 班 | | |
| yew | 又 | again | |
| wǎn | 問 | asks | |
| wang | 往 | proceed | |
| na | 那 | what | |
| le | 裡 | place | |
| k'heu | 去 | gone. | |
| leaou. | 了 | | |

— The People of the house will perhaps say, This morning early at the fourth beat of the drum, he went into the palace to regulaté a clock; after which he will go and visit a number of Persons;—we do not know when he will return.

| | | |
|---|---|---|
| Kwǎn | 管 | House-keeper |
| kea | 家 | |

| | | |
|---|---|---|
| hwŏ | 或 | either |
| shwŏ, | 說 | say, |
| kin | 今 | this |
| tsaou | 早 | morning |
| sze | 四 | four |
| koo | 皷 | drum |
| she | 時 | time, |
| pëen | 便 | then |
| tsin | 進 | enter |
| chaou | 朝 | palace |
| le | 裡 | within |
| k'heu | 去 | go |
| sew | 修 | to adjust and |
| le | 理 | regulate |
| tsze | 自 | itself |
| ming | 鳴 | sound |
| chung; | 鐘 | the bell; |
| how | 後 | afterwards |
| yew | 又 | also |
| yaou | 要 | wants |
| k'heu | 去 | to go |
| pae | 拜 | to visit |
| heu | 許 | a great many |
| to | 多 | |
| kŏ; | 客 | persons; |
| pŭh | 不 | not |
| che | 知 | know |
| ke | 幾 | what |
| she | 時 | time |
| hwŭy | 回 | back |
| lae. | 來 | come. |

— They reply, hitherto, he has been in the habit of coming back at noon; to-day, as he has a great deal to do, he will be later. He may come at one or two.

| | | |
|---|---|---|
| Tă | 答 | Answer |
| shwŏ, | 說 | say, |
| wang | 往 | going |
| chang | 常 | constantly |
| woo | 午 | noon |
| she | 時 | time |
| ts'hoo | 初 | begin |
| hwŭy; | 回 | to return |
| kin- | 今 | to- |
| jĭh | 日 | day |
| sze | 事 | business |
| to, | 多 | much, |
| pëĭh | 必 | must |
| king | 竟 | lead to |
| lae | 來 | come |
| che | 遲 | late |
| seay, | 些 | a little, |
| tsae | 在 | at |

| | | |
|---|---|---|
| we | 未 | one or two |
| she | 時 | time |
| lae | 來 | come |
| tĭh. | 得。 | can. |

— The Servant will then leave a card and say, such a Gentleman came to return a visit.

| | | |
|---|---|---|
| Chay | 這 | This |
| ch'hang | 長 | } servant |
| pan | 班 | |
| lew | 留 | will leave |
| hea | 下 | down |
| yĭh | 一 | a |
| pae | 拜 | visiting |
| tëĭh, | 帖 | card, |
| shwŏ, | 說 | saying, |
| mow | 某 | such a |
| seang | 相 | } Gentleman |
| kung | 公 | |
| hwŭy | 回 | back |
| lae | 來 | come |
| to | 多 | many |
| pae. | 拜。 | respects to pay. |

— The Servant of the house will not dare to receive a large card, or a double folded card; a single leaf will be enough.

| | | |
|---|---|---|
| Kwăn | 管 | } The servant of the house |
| hea | 家 | |
| pŭh | 不 | not |
| kan | 敢 | dare |
| ling | 領 | receive |
| tseun | 全 | large |
| tëĭh, | 帖 | card, |
| ling | 領 | receive |
| koo | 古 | ancient |
| tëĭh | 帖 | } card; |
| këen; | 柬。 | |
| hwŏ | 或 | or |
| tan | 單 | a single |
| tëĭh | 帖 | card |
| pa. | 罷。 | enough. |

— He will also take a pencil, asking, write down the place, in order that the visit may be returned.

| | | |
|---|---|---|
| Yew | 又 | Also |
| tseu | 取 | take |
| pëĭh | 筆 | pencil |
| wăn | 問 | ask |
| sëay | 寫 | to write |
| hea | 下 | down |
| choo | 處 | place, |
| haou | 好 | good |
| lae | 來 | come |

| | | |
|---|---|---|
| hwuy | 回 | back |
| pae. | 拜. | visit. |

— The Servant says, He lives in Smith's lane.

| | | |
|---|---|---|
| Ch'hang | 長 | Servant |
| pan | 班 | |
| shwŏ, | 說. | says, |
| choo | 住 | dwells |
| tsae | 在 | at |
| Tëĭh- | 鐵 | Iron |
| tsëang | 匠 | workman's |
| hoo | 衚 | lane. |
| tung. | 衕. | |

— When you have passed twenty or thirty houses, you will see another house fronting the south, with the name above the door.

| | | |
|---|---|---|
| T'hung | 通 | Having passed |
| kwo | 過 | |
| leaou | 了 | |
| urh | 二 | twenty |
| san | 三 | thirty |
| shĭh | 十 | |
| kea | 家 | house |
| mun | 門 | door |
| mëen, | 面 | face, |
| tsew | 就 | then |
| k'han | 看 | see |
| këen | 見 | |
| pëĕ | 別 | another |
| mun, | 門 | door, |
| shang | 上 | above |
| yew | 有 | have |
| ko | 個 | a |
| pae | 牌 | board with writing on it, |
| pëen | 扁 | |
| tso | 坐 | sitting to the |
| pĭh | 北 | north |
| chaou | 朝 | fronting |
| nan. | 南. | the south. |

— If there be no Person at the door, take the card and put it in at the crevice of the door.

| | | |
|---|---|---|
| Jŏ | 若 | If |
| mun | 門 | door |
| shang | 上 | upon |
| yu | 遇 | meet |
| pŭh | 不 | not |
| chŏ | 着 | do |
| jin, | 人. | people, |
| pa | 把 | take |
| tëĭh | 帖 | the card |
| tsze | 子 | |

| | | |
|---|---|---|
| fang | 放 | place |
| tsae | 在 | |
| mun | 門 | door |
| fung | 縫 | aperture |
| le | 裡 | within |
| chă | 插 | put |
| tsin | 進 | in |
| k'heu. | 去。 | go. |

— Or if you put the card into the Chandler's shop, on the west side, it will do.

| | | |
|---|---|---|
| Hwŏ | 或 | Or |
| yĭh | 亦 | also |
| k'ho | 可 | may |
| tseang | 將 | take |
| tëĭh | 帖 | the card |
| fang | 放 | place in |
| tsae | 在 | |
| se | 西 | west |
| pëen | 邊 | side |
| hëang | 香 | fragrant |
| lă | 蠟 | wax |
| poo | 鋪 | shop |
| yay | 也 | also |
| pa. | 罷。 | enough. |

B. The Gentleman visiting, will perhaps say,—How is it, your Master is always going out; what recompense can be made to a Visitor, troubled in this manner incessantly. I apprehend he is at home, do not deceive me; for I have come on purpose to see your Master.

| | | |
|---|---|---|
| Chay | 這 | This |
| ko | 個 | |
| pae | 拜 | visiting |
| kĭh | 客 | |
| tëĭh | 的 | |
| Seang | 相 | Gentleman |
| kung | 公 | |
| hwŏ | 或 | perhaps |
| yew | 又 | also |
| shwŏ, | 說， | say, |
| ne | 你 | your |
| Seang | 相 | Gentleman (Master) |
| kung | 公 | |
| joo | 如 | why |
| ho | 何 | |
| chang | 常 | always |
| ch'hŭh | 出 | go out |
| mun | 門 | door, |
| pŭh | 不 | not |
| tsae | 在 | remain in |
| kea; | 家 | house; |

| | | |
|---|---|---|
| joo | 如 | how |
| ho | 何 | |
| ying | 應 | recompense |
| chow | 酬 | |
| chay | 這 | such |
| tăng | 等 | |
| fan | 煩 | trouble |
| pae | 拜 | visiting |
| kĭh | 客 | a person |
| pŭh | 不 | incessantly. |
| tseuĕ. | 絕 | |
| Wo | 我 | I |
| kung | 恐 | apprehend |
| pa | 怕 | |
| tsae | 在 | he is |
| kea | 家 | house |
| le, | 裡 | within; |
| pŭh | 不 | do not |
| yaou | 要 | wish |
| hung | 哄 | to deceive |
| wo, | 我 | me, |
| wo | 我 | I |
| she | 是 | am |
| tĭh | 特 | purposely |
| lae | 來 | come |
| pae | 拜 | to visit |
| ne | 你 | your |

| | | |
|---|---|---|
| Seang | 相 | Master. |
| kung. | 公 | |

A. The Servant of the house then replies.

| | | |
|---|---|---|
| Chay | 這 | This |
| kwăn | 管 | servant of the house |
| kea | 家 | |
| yew | 又 | further |
| hwŭy | 回 | returns |
| yen | 言 | words (and) |
| shwŏ. | 說 | says. |

— I would not dare to tell a lie. My Master is indeed from home; when he was at home, and indisposed, heretofore, he has not denied himself.

| | | |
|---|---|---|
| Seaou | 小 | I |
| tëĭh | 的 | |
| pŭh | 不 | not |
| kan | 敢 | dare |
| shwŏ | 說 | to speak |
| hwang. | 謊 | a lie. |
| Wo | 我 | My |
| Seang | 相 | Master |
| kung | 公 | |
| shĭh | 實 | really |
| pŭh | 不 | not |

tsae 在 is in
kea; 家. the house;
jŏ 若 if
tsae 在 in
kea 家 the house
she 時 } time,
tsëĕ, 節 }
tsew 就 then
hwŏ 或 suppose
yew 有 have
seay 些 little
ping, 病. sick,
yay 也 also
tsung 從 } hitherto
lae 來 }
pŭh 不 not
kăng 肯 would
shwŏ 說 say
pŭh 不 not
tsae 在 in
kea 家 house
le. 裡. within.

— When my Master returns, and knows that you called; he will certainly wish to see you.

Wo 我 My
Seang 相 } Master
kung 公 }
hwŭy 回 back
lae, 來 come,
jŏ 若 if
heaou 曉 } know
tĭh 得 }
Seang 相 } Sir, (you)
kung 公 }
lae, 來 come,
pëĭh 必 must
jen 然 indeed
yaou 要 want
seang 相 } to meet (you).
hwŭy. 會. }

— Perhaps he will say, I will not trouble you to call again, Sir, these few days he is extremely busy. He has not a moments leisure; he is not a day at home.

Hwŏ 或 Or
shwŏ 說 say
tsae, 再 again,
pŭh 不 not
kan 敢 dare
leaou 勞 trouble,

| | | |
|---|---|---|
| Seang | 相 | Sir, |
| kung | 公 | |
| lae; | 來。 | come; |
| chay | 這 | these |
| ke | 幾 | few |
| jĭh | 日 | days |
| kĕĭh | 極 | very |
| mang, | 忙。 | hurried |
| mŭh | 沒 | not |
| yew | 有 | have |
| kung | 空 | leisure, |
| hëen, | 閒。 | |
| mŭh | 沒 | not |
| yew | 有 | have |
| yĭh | 一 | one |
| jĭh | 日 | day |
| tĭh | 得 | obtain |
| tsae | 在 | house |
| kea | 家 | |
| le. | 裡。 | within. |

— Few days will be requisite for him to return his visits, after that he will be at leisure.

| | | |
|---|---|---|
| Hwan | 還 | Still |
| yaou | 要 | want |
| kwo | 過 | to pass |
| ke | 幾 | few |
| jĭh | 日 | days |
| pae | 拜 | visit |
| hwan | 還 | back |
| leaou | 了 | |
| kĭh | 客 | persons |
| fang | 方 | then |
| hëen. | 閒。 | at leisure. |

— The Servant of the house will perhaps himself say.

| | | |
|---|---|---|
| Kwăn | 管 | Servant of the house |
| kea | 家 | |
| jŏ | 若 | if |
| tsze | 自 | himself |
| ke | 己 | |
| shwŏ. | 說。 | say. |

— If, Sir, you are very desirous of returning, you had better send a Person before, to see whether or not my Master be gone out, to prevent your having your journey for nothing. If you should come again, and he be gone abroad; on hearing it, my Master will be very uneasy.

| | | |
|---|---|---|
| Jŏ | 若 | If |
| Seang | 相 | Master |
| kung | 公 | |
| shĭh | 十 | ten |

| | | |
|---|---|---|
| fun | 分 | parts |
| tsae | 再 | again |
| yaou | 要 | want |
| lae, | 來 | to come, |
| k'hae | 該 | should |
| sëen | 先 | first |
| chae | 差 | send |
| yĭh | 一 | a |
| ko | 個 | |
| jin | 人 | man |
| lae | 來 | come |
| k'han | 看 | see |
| wo | 我 | my |
| Seang | 相 | Master, |
| kung | 公 | |
| gow | 偶 | happen |
| jin | 然。 | |
| pŭh | 不 | not |
| tsăng | 曾 | yet |
| ch'hŭh | 出 | go out |
| mun | 門 | door |
| fang | 方 | then |
| haou; | 好 | well; |
| mŭh | 沒 | not |
| kung | 空 | in vain |
| tsow; | 走。 | walk; |
| jŏ | 若 | if |
| hea | 下 | below next time |
| ts'hze | 次 | time |
| lae | 來 | come |
| yew | 又 | and |
| yu | 遇 | find (him) |
| ch'hŭh | 出 | gone out |
| leaou | 了 | |
| mun, | 門 | door, |
| wo | 我 | my |
| Seang | 相 | Master |
| kung | 公 | |
| wăn | 聞 | hearing it |
| tĭh | 得 | |
| pĕĭh | 必 | must (certainly) |
| pŭh | 不 | not |
| seang | 相 | feel comfortable. |
| gan. | 安。 | |

B. Perhaps the Master of this house may be at home.

| | | |
|---|---|---|
| Hwŏ | 或 | Perhaps |
| chay | 者 | |
| chay | 這 | this |
| choo | 主 | Master of the house |
| jin | 人 | |
| tsae | 在 | is at |
| kea. | 家。 | home. |

A. The Servant of the house, called also, Ta-kwăn, will say,

| | | |
|---|---|---|
| Kwăn | 管 | The servant of the house |
| kea | 家 | house |
| yĭh | 一 | one (by another) |
| ming | 名 | name (called) |
| Ta- | 大 | Ta-kwăn, |
| kwăn | 官 | |
| wăn | 問 | asks |
| shwŏ. | 說。 | says. |

— My Master is at home, but he has a Visitor with him; and when that Person goes, he has to write a letter to be ready for the man who carries the family letters, and who sets off to-morrow morning at the fifth beat of the drum. My Master has not yet taken breakfast.

| | | |
|---|---|---|
| Seaou | 小 | My |
| tëĭh | 的 | |
| laou | 老 | Master |
| yay | 爺 | |
| she | 是 | is |
| tsae | 在 | at |
| kea | 家 | home |
| le, | 裡。 | within, |
| chĭh | 只 | only |
| le | 裡 | within |
| mëen | 面 | |
| yew | 有 | have |
| kĭh; | 客。 | visitor; |
| kĭh | 客 | visitor |
| k'heu | 去 | go |
| leaou, | 了 | does, |
| hwan | 還 | still |
| yaou | 要 | want |
| seay | 寫 | to write |
| kea | 家 | family |
| shoo, | 書。 | letter, |
| wei | 爲 | to be |
| pëen | 便 | ready for |
| tae | 帶 | carry |
| kea | 家 | family |
| shoo | 書 | letter |
| tëĭh | 的 | the |
| jin | 人 | man |
| ming | 明 | to-morrow morning |
| tsaou | 早 | |
| woo | 五 | five |
| koo, | 皷 | drum, |
| tsew | 就 | then |
| yaou | 要 | want |
| k'he | 起 | to raise |

| | | |
|---|---|---|
| shin, | 身。 | body, * |
| che | 至 | till |
| kin | 今 | now |
| laou | 老 | Master |
| yay | 爺 | |
| we | 未 | not |
| yung | 用 | use (take) |
| tsaou | 早 | morning |
| fan. | 飯。 | meal. |

B. The Visitor says, if it be indeed thus, I will go, and come again to-morrow. I will not leave my card to-day.

| | | |
|---|---|---|
| Chay | 這 | This |
| pae | 拜 | visitor |
| kih | 客 | |
| teih | 的 | |
| shwŏ, | 說。 | says, |
| jŏ | 若 | if |
| chin | 眞 | true |
| she | 是 | is |
| jin | 如 | as |
| tsze, | 此。 | this, |
| wo | 我 | I |
| tsew | 就 | then |
| k'heu, | 去。 | go, |
| ming | 明 | to-morrow |
| jih | 日 | |
| tsae | 再 | again |
| lae. | 來。 | come. |
| Kin | 今 | This |
| jih | 日 | day |
| tseay | 且 | therefore |
| pŭh | 不 | not |
| lew | 留 | leave |
| teih. | 帖。 | card. |

— This Gentleman's Servant then announces to him, such a Person who carries letters, came for one, and said,

| | | |
|---|---|---|
| Chay | 這 | This |
| Choo | 主 | Master |
| jin | 人 | |
| teih | 的 | 's |
| ta | 大 | servant |
| kwăn | 官 | |
| yew | 又 | further |
| pin | 禀 | announce to |
| kea | 家 | house |
| Choo | 主 | Master |
| yun, | 云。 | saying, |
| mow | 某 | such |

* To set off on a journey.

| | | |
|---|---|---|
| jin | 人 | a person |
| tae | 帶 | carry |
| kea | 家 | family |
| shoo | 書 | letter |
| tëĭh | 的 | who does |
| lae | 來 | has come |
| taou | 討 | to obtain |
| shoo | 書 | a letter (and) |
| shwŏ | 說 | says. |
| taou. | 道。 | |

— That he wants to set off; and that he will come to-morrow afternoon for the letter.

| | | |
|---|---|---|
| Tsew | 就 | Soon |
| yaou | 要 | wants |
| k'he | 起 | to raise |
| shin; | 身。 | body; |
| ming | 明 | to-morrow |
| jĭh | 日 | |
| hea | 下 | below |
| woo | 午 | noon |
| lae | 來 | come |
| ling | 領 | to receive |
| shoo. | 書。 | letter. |

— Or he may say, to-morrow he wants to pack up and set off. He is very much hurried; he is afraid he shall not have time to come and receive the letter, it will be better to send it to him.

| | | |
|---|---|---|
| Hwŏ | 或 | Or |
| yew | 又 | further |
| shwŏ, | 說 | say, |
| t'ha | 他 | he |
| ming | 明 | to-morrow |
| jĭh | 日 | |
| yaou | 要 | wants |
| show | 收 | to prepare |
| shĭh | 拾 | |
| k'he | 起 | to set off, |
| shin, | 身。 | |
| mang | 忙 | hurried |
| tĭh | 得 | |
| kin, | 緊 | exceedingly, |
| kung | 恐 | apprehend |
| pa | 怕 | |
| pŭh | 不 | not |
| tĭh | 得 | obtain |
| hëen | 閒 | leisure |
| lae | 來 | come |
| ling | 領 | to receive |
| shoo | 書 | letter, |
| sin, | 信。 | |

| | | |
|---|---|---|
| pŭh | 不 | not } better |
| joo | 如 | as |
| ta | 打 | } send |
| fă | 發 | |
| jin | 人 | a man |
| sung | 送 | to present it. |
| k'heu | 去 | go |
| pa. | 罷。 | well. |

# DIALOGUE XIX.

## *MODE OF VISITING IN CHINA. (CONTINUED.)*

A. When an officer of Government goes to visit a Person, his Servant first goes and asks.

| | | |
|---|---|---|
| Yĭh | 一 | } An |
| wei | 位 | |
| kwăn | 官 | } officer |
| yuen | 員 | |
| lae | 來 | coming |
| pae | 拜 | to visit |
| yĭh | 一 | a |
| kĭh, | 客。 | person, |
| ch'hang | 長 | } the servant |
| pan | 班 | |
| sëen | 先 | first |
| lae | 來 | comes |
| wăn | 問 | asks |
| shwŏ. | 說。 | saying, |

— Is such a Person at home? such a Gentleman is just about to call, with him there are three or four Persons: he requests that the Master of the house will not go abroad.

| | | |
|---|---|---|
| Mow | 某 | Such a |
| Laou | 老 | } Gentleman |
| yay | 爺 | |
| tsae | 在 | is at |
| kea | 家 | home |
| pŭh | 不 | not |

| | | |
|---|---|---|
| tsae? | 在 | is? |
| mow | 某 | such a |
| Laou | 老 | Gentleman |
| yay | 爺 | |
| ting | 停 | stop |
| hwŭy | 會 | a while |
| tsew | 就 | soon |
| yaou | 要 | wants |
| lae | 來 | to come |
| pae; | 拜 | to visit; |
| hwan | 還 | also |
| yew | 有 | have |
| san | 三 | three |
| sze | 四 | four persons |
| wei | 位 | |
| t'hung | 同 | with (him) |
| lae; | 來 | come; |
| ts'hing | 請 | beg, |
| Laou | 老 | Sir, |
| yay | 爺 | |
| mŭh | 没 | not |
| ch'hŭh | 出 | go out |
| mun. | 門 | door. |

B. Perhaps it will be replied, He will wait till the officer of Government comes.

| | | |
|---|---|---|
| Hwŏ | 或 | Perhaps |
| tă | 答 | answer |
| shwŏ, | 說 | say, |
| tsae | 再 | again |
| tăng | 等 | wait |
| how | 候 | |
| che | 至 | till |
| kwăn | 官 | officer |
| yuen | 員 | |
| lae | 來 | come |
| pae | 拜 | visit |
| she. | 時 | time. |

— Perhaps the Master will say, I have not yet dressed; beg him to sit down, I will come out immediately.

| | | |
|---|---|---|
| Chay | 這 | This |
| Choo | 主 | Master of the house |
| jin | 人 | |
| hwŏ | 或 | perhaps |
| shwŏ, | 說 | say, |
| pŭh | 不 | not |
| tsăng | 曾 | yet |
| shoo | 梳 | comb |
| tĭh | 得 | |
| t'how | 頭 | head |
| wan, | 完 | finish, |
| Ts'hing | 請 | Pray |
| tso, | 坐 | sit, |

tsew 就 soon
ch'hŭh 出 out
lae. 來 come.

A. When the Gentleman comes out, each says, I have been long looking for you, or I have been long thinking of you.

Ke 旣 When
ch'hŭh 出 out
lae 來 come
seang 相 mutually
kēen, 見 see,
pe 彼 that } You and I, or the
tsze 此 this } one and the other
pēen 便 then
shwŏ 說 say,
kew 久 long time
yang; 仰 look up;
hwŏ 或 or
kew 久 long time [ately.
moo. 慕 thinking affection-

— They then make a low bow to each other.

Tsew 就 Then
tsŏ 作 make
yih 揖 a bow
pae 拜 worship
yih 一 one
pae. 拜 worship.

B. The Master of the house says, Pray step to the other (more honorable side), I ought not to trouble you (to bow).

Choo 主 } The Master of the
jin 人 } house
shwŏ, 說 says,
ts'hing 請 Pray [side
chuen 轉 turn (to the honorable
pŭh 不 not
kan 敢 dare
laou. 勞 trouble.

— They then bow together, and the Master says, Pray sit in the higher place.

Pēen 便 Then
t'hung 同 together
pae, 拜 worship,
Choo 主 } Master of the house
jin 人 }
shwŏ 說 says,
ts'hing 請 pray
shang 上 high (place)
tso. 坐 sit.

A. The Visitor says, let us sit on each

side (the mode of equals). The Master again says, at our first meeting, you must sit in the highest place.

| | | |
|---|---|---|
| Kĭh | 客 | Visitor |
| shwŏ, | 說 | says, |
| leang | 兩 | each |
| pëen | 邊 | side |
| tso | 坐 | sit |
| pa. | 罷。 | well. |
| Choo | 主 | Master |
| jin | 人 | |
| yew | 又 | again |
| shwŏ, | 說 | says, |
| ts'hoo | 初 | first |
| hwŭy | 會 | meeting |
| tsze | 自 | indeed |
| jen | 然 | |
| shang | 上 | high |
| tso. | 坐。 | sit. |

— The Visitor says, we will sit on each side.

| | | |
|---|---|---|
| Kĭh | 客 | Visitor |
| shwŏ | 說 | says |
| leang | 兩 | each |
| pëen | 邊 | side |
| tso. | 坐。 | sit. |

B. The Master says, when your Servant came the other day, I was not at home; I offend in having lost the opportunity of meeting you. [In our idiom, I am sorry I was not at home].

| | | |
|---|---|---|
| Choo | 主 | Master |
| jin | 人 | |
| shwŏ, | 說 | says, |
| Laou | 老 | venerable |
| sëen | 先 | Tutor |
| săng | 生 | |
| ts'hëen | 前 | before |
| jĭh | 日 | day |
| sze | 使 | send |
| lae, | 來。 | come, |
| hëŏ | 學 | Pupil (I) |
| săng | 生 | |
| kwo | 果 | indeed |
| she | 是 | was |
| pŭh | 不 | not |
| tsae | 在 | at |
| kea; | 家。 | home; |
| shĭh | 失 | lose |
| ying | 迎 | meeting |
| yew | 有 | have |
| tsŭy. | 罪。 | crime. |

A. The Visitor says, I pay my respects;

I have not yet seen you to make my inquiries.

| | | |
|---|---|---|
| Kĭh | 客 | Visitor |
| shwŏ, | 說 | says, |
| hëŏ | 學 | I |
| săng | 生 | |
| fung | 奉 | offer |
| pae | 拜 | respects |
| pŭh | 不 | not |
| tsăng | 曾 | yet |
| tĭh | 特 | purposely |
| mëen | 面 | face (to face) |
| ts'hing | 請 | beg |
| keaou. | 教。 | teaching. |

They ask each other their names.

| | | |
|---|---|---|
| Pe | 彼 | That |
| tsze | 此 | this |
| seang | 相 | mutually |
| wăn | 問 | ask |
| ta | 大 | great |
| haou | 號。 | mark. |

B. Pray what is your age?

| | | |
|---|---|---|
| Ts'hing | 請 | Beg |
| wăn | 問 | to ask |
| kwei | 貴 | noble. |
| kang. | 庚。 | |

— The Master will perhaps ask the Visitor, how many years it is since he came to Peking?

| | | |
|---|---|---|
| Choo | 主 | Master |
| jin | 人 | |
| hwŏ | 或 | perhaps |
| ts'hing | 請 | beg |
| wăn | 問 | to ask |
| kĭh | 客 | the Visitor |
| taou | 到 | come to |
| King- | 京 | Peking |
| sze | 師 | |
| ke | 幾 | how many |
| nëen? | 年。 | years? |

A. The Visitor will perhaps say, It is now ten years since I came. I had before heard your name.

| | | |
|---|---|---|
| Kĭh | 客 | Visitor |
| hwŏ | 或 | perhaps |
| shwŏ, | 說 | say, |
| tsze | 自 | from |
| mow | 某 | such a |
| nëen | 年 | year |
| taou | 到 | arrived |
| yew | 有 | have |
| shĭh | 十 | ten |
| nëen; | 年。 | years; |
| ts'hëen | 前 | before |

wăn 聞 heard
sëen 先 } Teacher's
săng 生 }
kaou 高 eminent
ming. 名. name.

— Perhaps he will say, since I was made a Sew-tsae, I have constantly heard of your great work, (perhaps mention what book); and have constantly thought of you; I am now very happy to see you.

Hwŏ 或 Or
shwŏ, 說 say
tsze 自 from
hëŏ 學 } Pupil's
săng 生 }
tso 做 being made
Sew- 秀 } Sew-tsae
tsae 才 }
she; 時. time;
chang 常 constantly
këen 見 } heard of
ting 聽 }
Laou 老 Venerable
sëen 先 } Teacher's
săng 生 }
ta 大 great
tso, 做 work,
hwŏ 或 or
mow 某 such a
shoo. 書. book.
Këih 極 Extremely
yang 仰 look up to and
moo 慕 think upon
Laou 老 Venerable
sëen 先 } Teacher;
săng; 生. }
kin- 今 to-
jĭh 日 day
tĭh 得 obtaining
këen, 見 a sight,
këŏ 學 } Pupil
săng 生 }
ta 大 greatly
hing. 幸. happy.

B. The Master will perhaps say, I can not retain your card. (Your visit is more than I could expect.)

Choo 主 } Master
jin 人 }
hwŏ 或 perhaps
shwŏ 說 say,
pŭh 不 not
kan 敢 dare

| | | |
|---|---|---|
| ting | 領 | receive |
| tsun | 尊 | honorable |
| tëĭh. | 帖。 | card. |

— He will perhaps say, these several days I have been a little unwell.

| | | |
|---|---|---|
| Hwŏ | 或 | Or |
| shwŏ | 說 | say, |
| hëŏ | 學 | Pupil |
| săng | 生 | |
| chay | 這 | these |
| ke | 幾 | few |
| t'hëen | 天 | days |
| yew | 有 | have |
| seay | 些 | a little |
| tsëen | 賤 | ignoble |
| yang | 恙 | disease |
| tsae | 在 | on |
| shin. | 身。 | body. |

— Perhaps he will say, I am not quite myself; I dare not go from home, I fear I shall not be able to visit you so early as I would.

| | | |
|---|---|---|
| Hwŏ | 或 | Or |
| shwŏ | 說 | say, |
| pŭh | 不 | not |
| tsze | 自 | myself |
| tsae, | 在 | am, |
| pŭh | 不 | not |
| kan | 敢 | dare |
| ch'hŭh | 出 | go out of |
| mun; | 門。 | doors; |
| kung | 恐 | Apprehend |
| pa | 怕 | |
| pae | 拜 | visit |
| che | 遲 | late |
| tĭh | 得 | incur |
| tsŭy. | 罪。 | offence. |

A. The Guest says, at our first meeting, I indeed ought to leave my name.

| | | |
|---|---|---|
| Kĭh | 客 | Visitor |
| shwŏ | 說 | say |
| ts'hoo | 初 | first |
| hwŭy | 會 | meeting |
| tsze | 自 | indeed |
| jen | 然 | |
| k'hae | 該 | should |
| lew | 留 | leave |
| tsëen | 賤 | ignoble |
| ming. | 名。 | name. |

# DIALOGUE XX.

*MODE OF VISITING IN CHINA. (Continued.)*

A. If the Master asks of what Province? what Foo or Hëen are you? or where do you live?

| | | |
|---|---|---|
| Choo | 主 | Master |
| jin | 人 | |
| wăn, | 問 | asking, |
| kwei | 貴 | noble |
| săng, | 省 | province, |
| kwei | 貴 | noble |
| foo, | 府 | foo, * |
| kwei | 貴 | noble |
| hëen, | 縣 | hëen, * |
| kwei | 貴 | noble |
| yu | 寓 | lodging |
| tsae | 在 | is |
| ho | 何 | what |
| choo. | 處 | place. |

B. The Visitor replies, I am of such a Hëen, or such a village.

| | | |
|---|---|---|
| Kĭh | 客 | Visitor |
| tă | 答 | answer |
| shwŏ, | 說 | says, |
| tsae | 在 | is at |
| mow | 某 | such a |
| hëen | 縣 | Hëen, |
| mow | 某 | such a |
| heang. | 鄉 | village. |

— Or he says, We have been separated ten years; I have heard that you were well.

| | | |
|---|---|---|
| Hwŏ | 或 | Or |
| shwŏ, | 說 | say, |
| fung | 奉 | separated |
| pëĕ | 別 | |

* District of a certain extent.

v

| | | |
|---|---|---|
| shĭh | 十 | ten |
| nëen | 年 | years |
| ting | 聽 | heard |
| yĭh | 一 | one |
| hëang | 向 | while past |
| nă | 納 | obtain |
| fŭh. | 福。 | happiness. |

— Perhaps he will say, My family being poor,—having to marry my two daughters, getting a teacher for my son, and attending to all the concerns of the family, my time has been all spent in these things.

| | | |
|---|---|---|
| Hwŏ | 或 | Or |
| shwŏ | 說 | say, |
| yuen | 原 | originally |
| pun | 本 | |
| kea | 家 | family |
| han | 寒 | cold |
| pin, | 貧。 | poor, |
| wei | 爲 | because of |
| kea | 嫁 | marrying |
| leang | 兩 | two |
| seaou | 小 | little |
| neu ; | 女。 | daughters ; |
| yu | 預 | previously |
| ts'hing | 請 | requesting |
| sëen | 先 | Tutor |
| săng | 生 | |
| keaou | 教 | to teach |
| seaou | 小 | little |
| urh ; | 兒。 | boy ; |
| leaou | 料 | managing |
| le | 理 | |
| kŏ | 各 | every |
| yang | 樣 | sort |
| kea | 家 | family |
| sze | 事 | business |
| she | 時 | time |
| how | 候 | |
| too | 都 | all |
| fei | 費 | wasted |
| leaou | 了 | |
| tsae | 在 | at |
| chay | 這 | this |
| yĭh | 一 | one |
| pëen. | 邊。 | side. |

They ask each other, How many boys have you ?

| | | |
|---|---|---|
| Yew | 又 | Further |
| pe | 彼 | that |
| tsze | 此 | this |
| seang | 相 | mutually |
| wăn | 問 | ask |

| | | |
|---|---|---|
| Laou | 老 | Venerable |
| Sëen | 先 | Teacher |
| săng | 生 | |
| yew | 有 | has |
| ke | 幾 | how many |
| wei | 位 | |
| ling | 令 | sons? |
| lang? | 郎。 | |

B. It is replied, I have two sons, one of them is good for nothing—he will not study—he is a debauchee and a gambler. The second has a pretty good disposition; something may be hoped from him; and that his behaviour will be good.

| | | |
|---|---|---|
| Tă | 答 | Answer |
| shwŏ, | 說 | say, |
| yew | 有 | have |
| leang | 兩 | two |
| ko | 個 | |
| seaou | 小 | little |
| urh; | 兒。 | boys; |
| yĭh | 一 | one |
| ko | 個 | |
| pŭh | 不 | not |
| ching | 成 | perfect |
| ke, | 器。 | utensil, |
| haou | 好 | loves |
| peaou, | 嫖。 | whoring, |
| haou | 好 | loves |
| too; | 賭。 | gambling; |
| pŭh | 不 | not |
| tŭh | 讀 | read |
| shoo; | 書。 | book; |
| chĭh | 只 | only |
| te | 第 | number |
| urh | 二 | two |
| ko | 個 | |
| seaou | 小 | little |
| tsze | 子 | son |
| tsze | 姿 | disposition |
| chĭh | 質 | |
| haou | 好 | good |
| seay; | 些。 | a little; |
| hwan | 還 | still |
| k'ho | 可 | may |
| wang | 望 | hope |
| chung | 重 | that he will consolidate and |
| wan | 完 | perfect |
| leaou | 了 | |
| chay | 這 | this |
| ko | 個 | |
| le | 禮 | polite |
| maou. | 貌。 | appearance. |

# DIALOGUE XXI.

## *MODE OF VISITING IN CHINA.* (*Continued.*)

A. A Person from Soo-chow, of the literary rank called Keu-jin, or Sew-tsae, or an officer of Government, going in his chair to visit a Canton Gentleman, on arriving at the door stops his chair, and orders his footman to deliver his card, and announce him, asking whether the Master of the house be at home or not; and saying, that a Person from Soo-chow has come on purpose to visit him.

| | | |
|---|---|---|
| Soo-chow | 蘇州 | Soo-chow |
| yew | 有 | having |
| ko | 個 | a |
| Keu-jin, | 舉人 | Keu-jin, |
| hwŏ | 或 | or |
| Sew-tsae, | 秀才 | Sew-tsae, |
| hwŏ | 或 | or |
| yĭh ko | 一個 | a |
| chĭh | 職 | bearing rule |
| yuen, | 員 | officer, |
| tso | 坐 | sitting |
| keaou | 轎 | chair |
| lae | 來 | come |
| pae | 拜 | to worship |
| Kwang-tung | 廣東 | Canton |
| tĕĭh | 的 | 's |
| jin, | 人 | man, |
| taou | 到 | at |
| mun | 門 | door |
| ts'hēen | 前 | before |

| | | | |
|---|---|---|---|
| tsew | 就 | then | |
| choo | 住 | | stops |
| leaou | 了 | | |
| keaou; | 轎 | chair; | |
| fun | 吩 | | orders |
| foo | 咐 | | |
| Ch'hang- | 長 | senior | |
| pan | 班 | servant | |
| sëen | 先 | before | |
| tow | 投 | throw in | |
| ming | 名 | name | |
| tëĭh | 帖 | card | |
| tsin | 進 | enter | |
| k'heu | 去 | go | |
| tung | 通 | to communicate | |
| paou, | 報 | to announce, | |
| wăn | 問 | ask | |
| Laou | 老 | venerable | |
| yay | 爺 | father | |
| tsae | 在 | in | |
| kea, | 家 | house, | |
| pŭh | 不 | not | |
| tsae | 在 | in | |
| kea? | 家 | house? | |
| Shwŏ | 說 | Say | |
| Soo- | 蘇 | | Soo-chow |
| chow | 州 | | |
| mow | 某 | such a | |
| jin | 人 | man | |
| tĭh | 特 | special | |
| te | 地 | ground | |
| taou | 到 | to | |
| lae | 來 | come | |
| pae | 拜 | visit | |
| how. | 候 | to wait. | |

The Steward comes hastily out to give an answer, (and says) Our Master has but just now left home.

| | | | |
|---|---|---|---|
| Kwăn | 管 | Rule | Steward |
| kea | 家 | the house | |
| mang | 忙 | hastily | |
| tsow | 走 | walk | |
| ch'hŭh | 出 | out | |
| lae | 來 | come | |
| tă | 答 | answer | |
| ying, | 應 | reply, | |
| joo | 如 | | now |
| kin | 今 | | |
| wo | 我 | | our |
| mun | 們 | | |
| laou | 老 | aged | |
| teay | 爹 | father | |
| kang | 剛 | | just |
| kang | 剛 | | |

| | | |
|---|---|---|
| pŭh | 不 | not |
| tsae | 在 | at |
| kea. | 家。 | home. |

— The Servant forthwith inquires, whither has he gone, Do you know? Did he say when he would return?

| | | |
|---|---|---|
| Ch'hang | 長 | Senior |
| pan | 班 | servant |
| shun | 順 | obeying |
| k'how | 口 | mouth |
| tsew | 就 | then |
| wăn, | 問。 | ask, |
| k'heu | 去 | go |
| na | 那 | what |
| le, | 裡。 | place, |
| k'ho | 可 | can |
| che | 知 | know |
| taou | 道 | |
| pŭh | 不 | not |
| che | 知 | know? |
| taou? | 道。 | |
| yew | 有 | have |
| shwŏ | 說 | speak |
| hea | 下 | down |
| ke | 幾 | what |
| she | 時 | time |
| hwŭy | 回 | return |
| lae, | 來 | come, |
| mŭh | 沒 | not |
| yew? | 有。 | have? |

— The Steward further replies, and says, He did not say whither he was going. I suppose no great length of time will elapse ere his return. If your Master have pressing business on which he wishes to see him, I beg that he will step in and sit down, whilst I send a Person to search for my Master.

| | | |
|---|---|---|
| Kwăn | 管 | Rule |
| kea | 家 | house |
| yew | 又 | further |
| tă | 答 | answers |
| shwŏ, | 說。 | saying, |
| we | 未 | not |
| tsăng | 曾 | yet |
| shwŏ | 說 | say |
| hea | 下 | down |
| k'heu | 去 | go |
| hëang; | 向。 | towards, |
| wo | 我 | I |
| seang | 想 | think |
| pŭh | 不 | no |
| yung | 用 | use |

| | | |
|---|---|---|
| ke | 幾 | any |
| kew, | 久 | long time, |
| yay | 也 | also |
| k'hae | 該 | ought |
| hwŭy | 回 | return |
| lae | 來 | come. |
| leaou. | 了 | |
| Joo | 如 | If |
| tsun | 尊 | honored |
| laou | 老 | Venerable |
| yay | 爺 | Father |
| yew | 有 | have |
| kin | 緊 | pressing |
| sze | 事 | business |
| yaou | 要 | wants |
| hwŭy, | 會 | to meet, |
| ts'hing | 請 | pray |
| shang | 上 | ascend |
| ting | 廳 | the hall |
| tang | 堂 | |
| tso | 坐 | sit |
| tso; | 坐 | sit; |
| tae | 待 | wait |
| wo | 我 | we |
| mun | 們 | |
| ta | 打 | issue |
| fă | 發 | |

| | | |
|---|---|---|
| yĭh | 一 | a |
| jin | 人 | man |
| kwae | 快 | fast |
| k'heu | 去 | go |
| chaou | 找 | to inquire |
| tsin. | 尋 | to search. |

— Boys! come hither, and prepare tea, tobacco and areca nut. Make haste also to request your young Master to come out and wait upon this Gentleman.

| | | |
|---|---|---|
| Seaou | 小 | Little |
| hae | 孩 | boys |
| mun | 們 | |
| ah! | 吓 | ! |
| ch'hŭh | 出 | out |
| lae | 來 | come |
| taou | 倒 | pour out |
| ch'ha, | 茶 | tea, |
| chwang | 裝 | put up |
| yen, | 烟 | tobacco, |
| na | 拿 | bring |
| pin | 檳 | areca nut. |
| lang. | 榔 | |
| Kwae | 快 | Hasten |
| ts'hing | 請 | to request |
| urh | 二 | the second |

Seang 相 } Young Gentleman
kung 公 }
pei 陪 to attend on
chay 這 } this
wei 位 }
laou 老 Venerable
yay 爺 Father
tso 坐 sit
tso. 坐。 sit.

— The Steward having called a Person to call home the Master. (He returned). The Guest and Master having seen each other made their bow.

Na 那 That
kwăn 管 rule
kea 家 family
keaou 叫 call
jin 人 man
chaou 找 search
laou 老 aged
teay 爹 father
hwüy 回 return
lae; 來。 come;
pe 彼 that
tsze 此 this
seang 相 mutually
këen 見 see
tuy 對 opposite
yĭh. 揖。 bow.

— The Guest says, We have long been absent from each other. I trust you have been perfectly happy.

Kĭh 客 Guest
shwŏ, 說。 said,
kew 久 long
wei 違 } absent from;
leaou; 了。 }
Laou 老 Venerable
ko 哥 brother
yĭh 一 } of late
hëang 向 }
nă 納 receive
fŭh 福 happiness
ah! 呀 !

— The Master of the house replies, By your kind auspicies I have been well. When you now condescended to visit me, I was very deficient in not being prepared to receive you. I hope you will excuse me.

Choo 主 Lord
jin 人 man
tă, 答 reply,

| | | |
|---|---|---|
| tŏ | 托 | engage |
| pe ; | 庇 | protection ; |
| fang | 方 | just now |
| tsae | 纔 | |
| tsun | 尊 | honored |
| heung | 兄 | brother |
| kwang | 光 | light |
| keang, | 降 | descend, |
| shĭh | 失 | lose |
| ying | 迎 | meeting |
| tĭh | 得 | extremely |
| hăn, | 狠 | |
| këen | 見 | see |
| shoo, | 恕 | excuse, |
| këen | 見 | see |
| shoo. | 恕 | excuse. |

— These two Persons having seated themselves in the order of Master and Guest, discoursed on different subjects.

| | | |
|---|---|---|
| Urh | 二 | Two |
| jin | 人 | persons |
| fun | 分 | separate |
| pin | 賓 | Guest |
| choo | 主 | Host |
| tso | 坐 | sit |
| hea | 下 | down |
| kŏ | 各 | each |
| seu | 敘 | narrate |
| hëen | 閒 | leisure |
| hwa. | 話 | talk. |

B. The Master of the house said, two years ago I had the pleasure to see you at Soo-chow, and was much obliged by your kind attention, whilst I conversed on every subject with you. After that, having some business of my own, I returned to Canton, and have in consequence been long separated from you. Although complimentary letters passed between us, I had not the pleasure of conversing with you face to face, which made me very uncomfortable. I am particularly happy to have the unexpected pleasure of seeing you once again.

| | | |
|---|---|---|
| Choo | 主 | Host |
| shwŏ, | 說 | said, |
| wo | 我 | I |
| ts'hëen | 前 | before |
| leang | 兩 | two |
| nëen | 年 | years |
| wang | 往 | go |

x

| | | |
|---|---|---|
| Soo- | 蘇 | Soo-chow, |
| chow, | 州 | |
| tĭh | 得 | obtain |
| këen | 見 | to see |
| tsun | 尊 | honored |
| yen ; | 顏 | countenance ; |
| pwan | 盤 | platter |
| suen | 旋 | going round |
| shoo | 數 | several |
| jĭh | 日 | days |
| to | 多 | much |
| mung | 蒙 | thank |
| yew | 優 | kind |
| tae ; | 待 | treatment ; |
| how | 後 | after |
| yin | 因 | because |
| tsëen | 賤 | mean |
| sze | 事 | business |
| hwüy | 回 | return |
| yuĕ ; | 粵 | Canton ; |
| tsew | 就 | hence |
| kĭh | 隔 | partitioned |
| pëĕ | 別 | separated |
| chay | 這 | so |
| mo | 麼 | |
| kew ; | 久 | long ; |
| suy | 雖 | although |

| | | |
|---|---|---|
| yew | 有 | have |
| she | 時 | season |
| shoo | 書 | letter |
| sin | 信 | |
| wăn | 問 | asking |
| how | 候 | writing |
| ke | 幾 | few |
| keu ; | 句 | words ; |
| ke | 究 | investigate to the limit — still |
| king | 竟 | |
| woo | 無 | not |
| tĭh | 得 | obtain |
| mëen | 面 | face |
| tan, | 談 | converse, |
| sin | 心 | heart |
| chung | 中 | midst |
| tsung | 總 | altogether |
| pŭh | 不 | not |
| gan | 安 | repose |
| wei. | 慰 | console. |
| Hwŭh | 忽 | Unexpectedly |
| jen | 然 | |
| kin | 今 | this |
| jĭh | 日 | day |
| yĭh | 一 | once |
| këen | 見 | see |
| shĭh | 十 | ten |

| | | |
|---|---|---|
| fun | 分 | parts |
| hwan | 歡 | rejoice |
| he | 喜 | glad |
| che | 之 | the |
| che. | 至。 | extreme. |

A. Guest answers, I know, Sir, that your thoughts have been directed to me, by the valuable presents which you have conferred upon me, for which my mother also feels grateful.

| | | |
|---|---|---|
| Kĭh | 客 | Guest |
| tă, | 答， | replies, |
| che | 知 | know |
| laou | 老 | Venerable |
| ko | 哥 | brother |
| sin | 心 | heart |
| fŭh | 腹 | belly |
| choo | 注 | flowing |
| nëen, | 念 | thoughts, |
| she | 時 | time |
| tsze | 賜 | confer |
| kea | 佳 | excellent |
| wŭh; | 物。 | things; |
| kea | 家 | family |
| moo | 母 | mother |
| yĭh | 亦 | also |
| kan | 感 | moved |
| seay. | 謝。 | thanks. |

B. The Master says, they were mere trifles, not worth speaking about; my view was only like sending a thousand miles a goose's feather, to present to your honored Mother. I fear the present was so trifling as to excite a laugh.

| | | | |
|---|---|---|---|
| Choo | 主 | Host | |
| shwŏ, | 說。 | say, | |
| king | 輕 | light | |
| we | 微 | trivial | |
| che | 之 | a | |
| wŭh, | 物 | thing, | |
| ho | 何 | how | |
| tsŭh | 足 | sufficient to | |
| kwa | 掛 | hang upon | speak |
| che, | 齒。 | the teeth, | about |
| pŭh | 不 | not | |
| kwo | 過 | more than | |
| tsëen | 千 | a thousand | |
| le | 里 | miles | |
| ke | 寄 | sending | |
| go | 鵝 | goose | |
| maou | 毛 | feather | |
| tëĭh | 的 | 's | |
| e | 意 | intention | |

| | | | |
|---|---|---|---|
| sze, | 思 | thought, | |
| fung | 奉 | present | |
| hëen | 獻 | offer | |
| tsun | 尊 | honored | a person's |
| tang, | 堂 | temple, | mother |
| ching | 誠 | sincerely | |
| kung | 恐 | apprehend | |
| këen | 見 | see | |
| seaou. | 笑 | laugh. | |

A. The Guest replied, How dare I presume to accept of your compliment. I constantly look up with regard to, and admiration of your eminent talents. I many times wished to come to Canton and converse with you, but having at my native place opened an Academy, I had no leisure, and hence I have been long in coming to pay my respects to you. You are still looking very well—you have taken good care of yourself, and are the same as formerly. Doubtless every thing is agreeable to you; and I presume your family are all well. Pray present my respects to your honored father (whom I beg to denominate) my venerable Uncle.

| | | | |
|---|---|---|---|
| Kĭh | 客 | The Guest | |
| tă, | 答 | replies, | |
| k'he | 豈 | how | |
| kan, | 敢 | dare, | |
| k'he | 豈 | how | |
| kan! | 敢 | dare! | |
| Wo | 我 | I | |
| yĭh | 亦 | also | |
| she | 時 | time | |
| chang | 常 | constant | |
| yang | 仰 | look up | |
| moo | 慕 | affectionately | |
| laou | 老 | Venerable | |
| ko | 哥 | Brother | |
| wei | 爲 | is | possessing |
| jin | 人 | man | an enlarged |
| sze | 四 | four | and liberal |
| hae, | 海 | seas, | mind, |
| e | 擬 | determined | |
| yŏ | 欲 | wished | |
| ke | 幾 | several | |
| ts'hze | 次 | times | |
| lae | 來 | come | |
| Kwang | 廣 | Canton | |
| seu | 敘 | converse | |
| tan; | 談 | chat; | |
| yin | 因 | because | |

| | | |
|---|---|---|
| wei | 爲 | that |
| tsae | 在 | at |
| pe | 僻 | vile |
| choo | 處 | place |
| k'hae | 開 | opened |
| leaou | 了 | |
| kwăn, | 館 | academy, |
| tsung | 總 | altogether |
| woo | 無 | not |
| hëen | 閒 | leisure |
| kung; | 空 | void; |
| koo | 故 | because |
| tsze | 此 | this |
| che | 遲 | late |
| lae | 來 | come |
| pae | 拜 | to visit |
| how. | 候 | to wait. |
| K'ho | 可 | Still |
| she | 是 | |
| leaou | 老 | Venerable |
| ko | 哥 | Brother |
| yen | 顏 | countenance |
| yung | 容 | |
| kwang | 光 | clear |
| tsae; | 彩 | good-looking; |
| haou | 好 | good |
| yang | 養 | nurse and |

| | | |
|---|---|---|
| show; | 守 | keep; |
| chaou | 照 | as |
| kew | 舊 | formerly |
| yĭh | 一 | one |
| yang | 樣 | fashion; |
| urh; | 兒 | |
| pĕĭh | 必 | must |
| ting | 定 | positively |
| ta | 大 | greatly |
| yew | 有 | have |
| haou | 好 | pleasant |
| e; | 意 | thoughts; |
| hŏ | 合 | united |
| kea | 家 | family |
| leaou | 料 | suppose |
| woo | 無 | no |
| ping | 病 | sickness. |
| ah. | 呀 | |
| Ts'hing | 請 | Request |
| ling | 令 | honored father |
| tsun | 尊 | |
| laou | 老 | old uncle |
| pĭh | 伯 | |
| ta | 大 | great |
| jin | 人 | man |
| tëĭh | 的 | 's |
| gan. | 安 | repose. |

B. The Host said, I dare not to appropriate your expressions of civility. My father is now advanced in years, his hearing and sight fail him. He is not able to do himself the honor of attending on you. I give you great trouble in expending your thoughts on those related to me. [To the Steward] Call a man to fill the pipes and make a pot of good tea.

| | | |
|---|---|---|
| Choo | 主 | Host |
| shwŏ, | 說 | says, |
| pŭh | 不 | not |
| kan | 敢 | dare |
| tang, | 當 | sustain, |
| kea | 家 | family |
| foo | 父 | father |
| hëen | 現 | now |
| yew | 有 | has |
| ke | 幾 | several |
| suy | 歲 | years |
| nëen | 年 | year |
| ke; | 紀 | record; |
| urh | 耳 | ear |
| mŭh | 目 | eye |
| pŭh | 不 | not |
| peën, | 便 | convenient, |
| we | 未 | not |
| tĭh | 得 | obtain |
| fung | 奉 | to offer |
| pei, | 陪 | attendance, |
| laou | 勞 | trouble |
| heung | 兄 | brother |
| fei | 費 | spend |
| sin | 心 | heart. |
| leaou. | 了 | |
| Keaou | 呌 | Call |
| ko | 個 | a |
| jin | 人 | man |
| tsang | 裝 | to fill |
| yen, | 烟 | tobacco, |
| ling | 另 | beside |
| păng | 烹 | boil |
| kwo | 過 | more |
| yĭh | 一 | a |
| hoo | 壺 | pot |
| se | 細 | fine |
| ch'ha. | 茶 | tea. |

A. The Guest replies, it is not necessary; at present we will part, and another day we shall meet again. I am lodging at the house of the Han-lin-yuen, whose name is Le-tan-ching, and who lives at Shĭh-pa-poo.

| | | |
|---|---|---|
| Kĭh | 客 | The Guest |
| tă, | 答。 | replies, |
| pŭh | 不 | no |
| yung; | 用。 | use; |
| kin | 今 | now |
| ts'heay | 且 | then |
| tsan | 暫 | for the present |
| pëĕ, | 別 | separate, |
| yung | 容 | allow |
| jĭh | 日 | day |
| tsae | 再 | again |
| hwŭy | 會 | meet. |
| pa. | 罷。 | |
| Wo | 我 | I |
| tsae | 在 | am at |
| Shih- | 十 | Shĭh-pa-poo, |
| pă- | 八 | |
| poo, | 舖 | |
| Han- | 翰 | the Han-lin-yuen,* |
| lin- | 林 | |
| yuen, | 院。 | |
| Le- | 李 | Le-tan-ching, |
| tan- | 丹 | |
| ching | 誠。 | |
| kea | 家 | house |
| yu, | 寓 | lodging, |
| pëen | 便 | convenient |
| chung | 中 | midst |
| kwo | 過 | come over |
| wo | 我 | my |
| choo | 處 | place |
| tso | 坐 | sit. |
| oh. | 呵。 | |

B. The Host answers, Strange! having taken the trouble to come to my cottage to go away in such a hurry! Do lengthen your visit, I will order wine to be brought out, and we will take a few cups to shew in some degree my good will.

| | | |
|---|---|---|
| Choo | 主 | The Host |
| tă, | 答。 | answers, |
| Ae | 噯 | Ah! |
| ya! | 呀。 | |
| laou | 老 | Venerable |
| heung | 兄 | Brother |
| yĭh | 一 | one |
| chang | 塲 | task |
| taou | 到 | coming to |

* Title of high literary rank.

| | | |
|---|---|---|
| shay | 舍 | cottage |
| hea, | 下 | below, |
| ho | 何 | what |
| pëĭh | 必 | necessity |
| sŏ | 速 | hastily |
| hwüy. | 回 | to return. |
| Ts'hing | 請 | Pray |
| kwan | 寬 | extend |
| tso | 坐 | sit (I will) |
| chŏ | 着 | order |
| jin | 人 | people |
| pan | 辦 | to make ready |
| seay | 些 | a little |
| tsew | 酒 | wine |
| hŏ | 嗑 | to drink |
| pei, | 杯 | a cup, |
| leŏ | 畧 | a little |
| peaou | 表 | manifest |
| tsun | 寸 | an inch |
| sin. | 心 | heart. |

A. The Guest replies, Many thanks to you. I will accept of your invitation for some other day.

| | | |
|---|---|---|
| Kĭh | 客 | Guest |
| tă, | 答 | replies, |
| to | 多 | many |
| seay | 謝 | thanks, |
| leaou, | 了 | |
| kae | 改 | different |
| jĭh | 日 | day |
| tsae | 纔 | then |
| ling | 領 | accept. |
| oh. | 喲 | |

B. The Host says, I must detain you, Sir, to take a family dinner. Do not reject it. And I had better first send away your chair. When evening comes I will procure a chair to carry you to Dr. Le's. That will be just the thing.

| | | |
|---|---|---|
| Choo | 主 | Host |
| shwŏ, | 說 | says, |
| woo | 務 | must |
| seu | 須 | necessarily |
| lew | 留 | detain |
| kea | 駕 | (you) Sir, |
| kĕĭh | 吃 | to eat |
| ko | 個 | a |
| pëen | 便 | convenient |
| fan, | 飯 | meal, |
| pŭh | 不 | not |
| yaou | 要 | want |
| hëen | 嫌 | dislike |

| | | |
|---|---|---|
| ke | 棄。 | eject. |
| Ning | 寧 | Better |
| k'ho | 可 | |
| sëen | 先 | first |
| ta | 打 | send away |
| fă | 發 | |
| keaou | 轎 | chair |
| tsze | 子 | |
| k'heu; | 去、 | go; |
| tae | 待 | till |
| kin | 今 | this |
| wan | 晚 | evening |
| wo | 我 | we |
| mun | 們 | |
| tseu | 取 | get |
| keaou | 轎 | a chair |
| tsze | 子 | |
| sung | 送 | to convey |
| ne | 你 | you |
| hwüy | 回 | back to |
| Le- | 李 | Le, the Han-lin's |
| han- | 翰 | |
| lin- | 林 | |
| kea; | 家。 | house; |
| tsew | 就 | just |
| she. | 是。 | so. |

A. The Guest said, Since I have to thank you, my Brother, for the pleasure you feel in detaining me, I must comply with your request.

| | | |
|---|---|---|
| Kĭh | 客 | Guest |
| shwŏ, | 說。 | says, |
| ke | 旣 | Since |
| jen | 然 | |
| mung | 蒙 | to thank |
| laou | 老 | Venerable |
| ko | 哥 | Brother |
| he | 喜 | rejoice |
| lew, | 留。 | to detain, |
| wo | 我 | I |
| tsew | 就 | then |
| tsung | 從 | obey |
| ming; | 命。 | order; |
| ch'hĭh | 只 | only |
| she | 是 | is |
| pŭh | 不 | not |
| yaou | 要 | want |
| fei | 費 | waste |
| tsae, | 財。 | wealth, |
| suy | 隨 | follow |
| pëen | 便 | convenience |
| tsae | 纔 | then |
| haou. | 好。 | well. |

B. The Host said, Be it so, and ordered

the Steward to hasten to prepare a set out of wine, vegetables, fruit, plates, &c.

| | | |
|---|---|---|
| Choo | 主 | Host |
| shwŏ, | 說。 | said, |
| she, | 是。 | Be it so, |
| fun | 吩 | ordered |
| foo | 咐 | |
| kwăn | 管 | the Steward |
| kea | 家 | |
| kwae | 快 | to hasten |
| pan | 辦 | to prepare |
| yĭh | 一 | a |
| sëĭh | 席 | table |
| tsew, | 酒。 | wine, |
| tsae, | 菜。 | vegetables, |
| kwo, | 菓。 | fruit, |
| tëĕ, | 碟。 | plates, |
| tăng | 等 | &c. |
| luy. | 類。 | |

In a short time the Steward returned and said, Sir, all is ready.

| | | |
|---|---|---|
| Shă | 霎 | Shower of rain |
| she | 時 | time |
| këen, | 間 | midst, |
| na | 那 | that |
| kwăn | 管 | Steward |
| kea | 家 | |
| hwŭy | 回 | returned |
| hwa, | 話。 | said, |
| laou | 老 | venerable |
| teăy | 爹 | Father |
| tsew | 酒 | wine |
| sëĭh | 席 | table |
| pëen | 便 | convenient. |
| leaou. | 了。 | |

B. The Master said, lay the table immediately.

| | | |
|---|---|---|
| Choo | 主 | Host |
| shwŏ, | 說。 | said, |
| pëen | 便 | then |
| tsew | 就 | forthwith |
| fang | 放 | lay |
| chŏ | 棹 | the table. |
| tsze. | 了。 | |

The Steward then laid out the Chopsticks, spoons, small plates for soy, vegetables, &c.

| | | |
|---|---|---|
| Na | 那 | That |
| ko | 個 | |
| kwăn | 管 | Steward |
| kea | 家 | |
| pa | 把 | took |

kwae 快 } Chop-sticks,*
tsze, 子 }
tsew 酒 wine
pei, 杯 cups,
teaou 調 stirring
kăng, 羹 spoons,
tseang 醬 } soy
yew 油 }
tëĕ, 碟 plates,
seaou 小 small
tsae 菜 vegetable
tëĕ, 碟 plates,
ko 各 every
yang 樣 sort
pae 擺 spread
k'hae. 開 open.

B. The Master fixed the seats, and gave to the Guest the chief place. He himself sat opposite, and his son at the lower end.

Choo 主 Host
jin 人 man
ting 定 } fixed
leaou 了 }
wei, 位 the seats,
jang 讓 yielded
kĭh 客 the Guest
show 首 head
wei, 位 seat,
tsze 自 } he himself
ke 己 }
tuy 對 opposite
tso, 坐 sat,
urh 二 second
seaou 小 little
urh 兒 boys
tso 坐 sat
hea 下 low
pēen. 邊 side.

A. The Guest declined, and walking apart from the table, made a low bow, saying, Thank you; I beg that my Venerable Uncle (your Father) take the chief place, and then it will be well; where is your worthy son, Sir? Pray let all come out to converse.

Kĭh 客 Guest
tsze, 辭 refused,

* Kwae-tsze, are small sticks of wood or ivory, sometimes pointed with silver, about nine inches long, and the thickness of a quill, which the Chinese use to lift their food to their mouths. The English call them Chop-sticks.

| | | | |
|---|---|---|---|
| le | 離 | leaving | |
| sëĭh | 席 | the table | |
| tsow | 走 | walked | |
| k'hae, | 開 | open, | |
| shun | 深 | deep | |
| shun | 深 | deep | |
| tsŏ | 作 | made | |
| yĭh | 揖 | a bow | |
| ching | 稱 | expressed | |
| seay, | 謝 | thanks, | |
| ts'hing | 請 | requested | |
| laou | 老 | old | |
| pĭh | 伯 | uncle | |
| tso | 坐 | sit | |
| show | 首 | head | |
| wei | 位 | seat | |
| tsae | 纔 | then | |
| she, | 是 | right, | |
| ta | 大 | great | |
| ling | 令 | honored | |
| lang | 郎 | worthy } | eldest son |
| ne? | 呢 | now? } | where is he? |
| too | 都 | all | |
| ts'hing | 請 | request | |
| lae | 來 | come | |
| seang | 相 | mutually | |
| seu. | 敘 | converse. | |

B. The Host replied, my Father ought by rights to come and attend upon you, but his sight and hearing being bad, it will be as well that he remain withinside. My eldest son is not yet returned from his studies.

| | | |
|---|---|---|
| Choo | 主 | Host |
| tă, | 答 | replied, |
| kea | 家 | family |
| foo | 父 | father |
| pun | 本 | originally |
| ying | 應 | ought |
| fung | 奉 | to offer |
| pei; | 陪 | attendance; |
| yin | 因 | } because |
| wei | 爲 | } |
| urh | 耳 | ear |
| mŭh | 目 | eye |
| pŭh | 不 | not |
| pëen, | 便 | convenient, |
| ping | 凭 | let |
| t'ha | 他 | him |
| tsae | 在 | be |
| le | 裡 | within |
| t'how | 頭 | head |
| këĭh | 吃 | eat |
| fan | 飯 | rice |

| | | |
|---|---|---|
| yay | 也 | also |
| pa. | 罷 | well. |
| Ta | 大 | Great |
| seaou | 小 | little } my son |
| urh | 兒 | son } |
| wae | 外 | outside |
| kwăn | 館 | school-room |
| tŭh | 讀 | reading |
| shoo | 書 | book |
| we | 未 | not |
| hwŭy. | 回 | return. |

B. The Host called the Steward to prepare wine, and to place the dishes on the table in order; also pointed the Guest to his seat, and directed the Servants to attend and serve the wine.

| | | |
|---|---|---|
| Choo | 主 | Host |
| jin | 人 | man |
| keaou | 呌 | called |
| kwăn | 管 | } Steward |
| kea | 家 | } |
| yu | 預 | } to prepare |
| pe | 偹 | } |
| tsew, | 酒 | wine, |
| pa | 把 | to take |
| yĭh | 一 | a |
| wan | 碗 | bowl |
| yĭh | 一 | a |
| wan | 碗 | bowl |
| teĭh | 的 | 's |
| tsae | 菜 | vegetables |
| ts'hze | 次 | next |
| te | 第 | order |
| twan | 端 | right |
| fang, | 放 | place, |
| jang | 讓 | yield |
| kĭh | 客 | the Guest |
| tso | 坐 | to sit |
| hea. | 下 | down. |
| Yew | 又 | Further |
| keaou | 呌 | called |
| kan | 跟 | heel |
| pan | 班 | waiters |
| tsae | 在 | at |
| pang | 傍 | the side |
| she | 侍 | to attend on |
| tsew. | 酒 | wine. |

A. The Guest said, what occasion to go to so much expense. I really cannot get over it.

| | | |
|---|---|---|
| Kĭh | 客 | Guest |
| shwŏ, | 說 | said, |
| ho | 何 | what |

| | | |
|---|---|---|
| pëĭh | 必 | necessity |
| po | 破 | to break upon |
| fei | 費 | expense |
| pan | 辦 | to prepare |
| chay | 這 | so |
| mo | 麽 | |
| to | 多 | much |
| tsae, | 菜 | vegetables, * |
| wo | 我 | I |
| shĭh | 實 | really |
| kwo | 過 | pass |
| e | 意 | thought |
| pŭh | 不 | not |
| k'heu. | 去 | go. |

B. The Host replied, You are very polite; I have merely prepared a little wine that we may chat over it. It is insufficient to shew my respectful intention. Pray take wine.

| | | |
|---|---|---|
| Choo | 主 | Host |
| tă, | 答 | reply, |
| haou | 好 | well |
| shwŏ, | 說 | said, |
| pŭh | 不 | not |
| kwo | 過 | more than |
| lung | 弄 | prepare |
| seay | 些 | a little |
| pŏ | 薄 | thin |
| tsew | 酒 | wine |
| seu | 叙 | to narrate |
| hwa. | 話 | talk. |
| Yay | 也 | Also |
| pŭh | 不 | not |
| ching | 成 | perfect |
| king | 敬 | respectful |
| e. | 意 | intention. |
| Ts'hing | 請 | Pray |
| k'he | 起 | raise |
| pei. | 杯 | the cup. † |

A. Guest says, I request you to precede me.

| | | |
|---|---|---|
| Kĭh | 客 | Guest |
| shwŏ, | 說 | says, |
| ts'hing. | 請 | request. |

B. Pray precede me.

| | | |
|---|---|---|
| Ts'hing. | 請 | Request. |

A. I wish you joy.

| | | |
|---|---|---|
| Kung | 恭 | Reverently(wish you) |
| he | 喜 | joy |
| ah! | 吓 | ! |

* Provisions generally are called vegetables. † The Chinese begin an entertainment by drinking wine.

B. Host says, I wish you joy. Let me recommend some of these dishes.

| | | |
|---|---|---|
| Choo | 主 | Host |
| shwŏ, | 說 | says, |
| kung | 恭 | reverently (wish you) |
| he; | 喜 | joy; |
| tsëen | 薦 | recommend |
| tsae. | 菜 | vegetables. |

A. Guest says, pray precede me.

| | | |
|---|---|---|
| Kĭh | 客 | Guest |
| shwŏ, | 說 | says, |
| ts'hing. | 請 | request. |

B. Boys, fill a bumper!—The Host then pledges his Guest, and the Guest pledges his Host. All eat. The son of the Host pours out a cup with his own hand, carries it to the Guest who drinks it, after which the Son returns to his seat. All again eat. The Guest and Host exchange cups.

| | | |
|---|---|---|
| Seaou | 小 | Little |
| hae | 孩 | boys, |
| tsze, | 子 | |
| chin | 斟 | pour out |
| mwan | 滿 | fill |
| tsew! | 酒 | wine! |
| Choo | 主 | Master |
| jin | 人 | man |
| king | 敬 | honors |
| kĭh | 客 | Guest |
| yĭh | 一 | one |
| pei, | 杯 | cup, |
| kĭh | 客 | Guest |
| king | 敬 | honors |
| hwŭy | 回 | in return |
| choo | 主 | Host |
| jin | 人 | man |
| yĭh | 一 | one |
| pei. | 杯 | cup. |
| Këĭh | 吃 | Eat |
| tsae. | 菜 | vegetables. |
| Keaou | 叫 | Call |
| urh | 二 | second |
| seaou | 小 | little |
| urh | 兒 | boy |
| tsin | 親 | own |
| show, | 手 | hand,† |
| chin | 斟 | pour out |
| leaou | 了 | |

* The Master of the house sometimes puts on the first dish, and brings himself the first cup of wine.

| | | |
|---|---|---|
| yĭh | 一 | a |
| pei | 杯 | cup |
| tsew, | 酒 | wine, |
| tsow | 走 | walk |
| taou | 到 | to |
| kĭh | 客 | Guest |
| wei | 位 | seat |
| king | 敬 | honor |
| tsew; | 酒 | wine; |
| kĭh | 客 | Guest |
| yin | 飲 | drinks |
| fŭh | 復 | returns to |
| wei. | 位 | seat. |
| Ta | 大 | Great * |
| chung | 衆 | company |
| kĕĭh | 吃 | eat |
| tsae. | 菜 | vegetables. |
| Choo | 主 | Host |
| kĭh | 客 | Guest |
| keaou | 交 | exchange |
| pei, | 杯 | cups,† |
| hwan | 歡 | rejoice |
| yin. | 飲 | to drink. |

A. The Guest says, what age is your worthy second son this year. Has he read a great deal.

| | | |
|---|---|---|
| Kĭh | 客 | Guest |
| wăn, | 問 | asks, |
| urh | 二 | second |
| ling | 令 | honored |
| lang | 郎 | worthy |
| kin | 今 | this |
| nëen | 年 | year |
| ke | 幾 | how |
| to | 多 | many |
| suy; | 歲 | years; |
| tŭh | 讀 | read |
| heu | 許 | great |
| to | 多 | many |
| shoo | 書 | books |
| mo? | 麽 | ? |

B. Host replies, He is now sixteen years of age. He is good for nothing. He has but just finished the Commentary on the Four-books.

| | | |
|---|---|---|
| Choo | 主 | Host |
| ta, | 答 | replies, |
| kin | 今 | this |

* The Chinese at an entertainment, all eat at the same time, and pause to drink at the same time.

† One holds his cup to the other's mouth to drink, which is a profession of great respect.

| | | |
|---|---|---|
| nëen | 年 | year |
| shĭh | 十 | ten and |
| lŭh] | 六 | six |
| suy | 歲 | years |
| pŭh | 不 | not |
| chung | 中 | hit |
| yung | 用 | use |
| Sze- | 四 | Four-books |
| shoo | 書 | |
| choo | 註 | commentating |
| kin | 僅 | just |
| k'ho | 可 | can |
| tŭh | 讀 | read |
| wan. | 完。 | finish. |

A. Guest further asks, Your eldest son?

| | | |
|---|---|---|
| Kĭh | 客 | Guest |
| yew | 又 | further |
| wăn, | 問。 | asks, |
| ta | 大 | honored |
| ling | 令 | |
| lang | 郎 | worthy |
| ne? | 呢。 | ? |

B. The Host replies, My eldest Son is now twenty years of age. He attends at Dr. Le's Lectures, at Wan-chang temple, in the City. He boards and lodges there.

| | | |
|---|---|---|
| Choo | 主 | Host |
| tă, | 答。 | replies, |
| ta | 大 | great |
| s'aou | 小 | little |
| urh | 兒 | boy |
| kin | 今 | this |
| nëen | 年 | year |
| urh | 二 | two |
| shĭh | 十 | tens |
| suy, | 歲。 | years, |
| tsae | 在 | at |
| ching | 城 | city |
| nuy | 內 | within |
| wăn | 文 | literary |
| chang | 昌 | splendid |
| meaou; | 廟。 | temple; |
| Le | 李 | Le |
| laou | 老 | old |
| sze | 師 | tutor |
| choo | 處 | place |
| ting | 聽 | hearing |
| shoo, | 書。 | book, |
| këih | 吃 | eat |
| shwüy | 睡 | sleep |
| yay | 也 | also |
| tsae | 在 | at |
| na | 那 | that |

z

choo. 處. place.

A. The Guest said, My worthy, Sir, these, your two sons, being so intelligent and diligent in there studies, they will doubtless obtain promotion, and you will obtain Imperial honors.

| | | |
|---|---|---|
| Kĭh | 客 | Guest |
| shwŏ, | 說. | says, |
| laou | 老 | Venerable |
| ko | 哥 | Brother |
| haou | 好 | good |
| ah! | 吓. | ! |
| ne | 你 | your |
| chay | 這 | these |
| leang | 兩 | two |
| wei | 位 | (two) |
| ling | 令 | worthy sons |
| lang | 郎 | (worthy sons) |
| chay | 這 | so |
| mo | 麽 | (so) |
| tsung | 聰 | hearing well |
| ming | 明 | bright |
| yew | 又 | also |
| kin | 勤 | diligent in the |
| kung, | 功. | noble work, |
| yĭh | 一 | to a |
| ting | 定 | certainty |
| tsin | 進 | enter |
| heŏ | 學 | learning |
| tĕĭh, | 的. | those who, |
| ne | 你 | you |
| tseang | 將 | taking |
| lae | 來 | come |
| laou | 老 | old |
| fung | 封 | Imperial appointed |
| keun | 君 | Prince * |
| yew | 有 | have |
| tĭh | 得 | obtain |
| tso | 做 | make. |
| tĕĭh. | 的. | |

B. Host says, How should I have such good fortune. Is your son, my friend, of late still well.

| | | |
|---|---|---|
| Choo | 主 | Host |
| tă, | 答. | answers, |
| na | 那 | where |
| le | 裡 | (where) |
| yew | 有 | have |
| chay | 這 | this |
| yang | 樣 | manner |

* The Parents of those who obtain official rank, receive some kind of honor from the state.

| | | |
|---|---|---|
| tëĭh | 的 | of |
| tsaou | 造 | good fortune. |
| hwa. | 化。 | |
| Laou | 老 | Venerable |
| heung | 兄 | Brother |
| tëĭh | 的 | 's |
| kung | 公 | son |
| tsze | 子 | |
| kin | 近 | recently |
| hwang | 況 | still more |
| haou | 好 | good. |
| ah. | 吓。 | |

A. The Guest replies, My Son is now twenty-four years of age. He was married last year; and I perceive he is fond of his studies.

| | | |
|---|---|---|
| Kĭh | 客 | Guest |
| tă, | 答。 | replies, |
| seaou | 小 | Little |
| urh | 兒 | boy |
| kin | 今 | this |
| nëen | 年 | year |
| urh | 二 | twice |
| shĭh | 十 | ten |
| sze | 四 | four |
| suy; | 歲。 | years; |
| kew | 舊 | old |
| nëen | 年 | year |
| tseu | 娶 | married |
| leaou | 了 | did |
| tse; | 妻。 | a wife; |
| wo | 我 | I |
| k'han | 看 | observe |
| t'ha | 他 | he |
| gae | 愛 | likes to |
| tùh | 讀 | read |
| shoo. | 書。 | book. |

B. The Host called for more wine.

| | | |
|---|---|---|
| Choo | 主 | Host |
| jin | 人 | |
| keaou | 叫 | called |
| chin | 斟 | to pour out |
| tsew. | 酒。 | wine. |

A. The Guest said, Enough. I feel intoxicated.

| | | |
|---|---|---|
| Kĭh | 客 | Guest |
| shwŏ, | 說。 | said, |
| pa | 罷 | enough, |
| leaou, | 了。 | |
| wo | 我 | I |
| hŏ | 嗑 | have drunk to |
| tsuy | 醉 | intoxication. |
| leaou. | 了。 | |

B. The Host said, My brother, you

can bear a great deal of wine; you must take a few cups more.

Choo 主 Host
shwŏ, 說 said,
laou 老 Venerable
heung 兄 Brother
leang 量 measure
kwang, 廣 wide, *
hwan 還 still
kae 該 must
hŏ 嗑 } drink
tĭh 得 }
ke 幾 a few
pei. 杯 cups.

A. Guest replied, I am not able to drink so much; indeed I feel intoxicated.

Kĭh 客 Guest
tă, 答 replied,
leang 量 measure
pŭh 不 not
shing 勝 } adequate; †
leaou; 了 }
kwo 果 indeed
chin 眞 truly
tsuy 醉 } intoxicated.
leaou. 了 }

B. The Host called, Bring up rice. The attendants presented rice, which having eaten, they rose from table, and the Host led his Guest to the library, where they sat down.

Choo 主 Host
jin 人 man
keaou 叫 called
k'he 起 bring up
fan, 飯 rice, ‡
tso 左 left
yew 右 right §
te 遞 present
fan 飯 rice
shang 上 up
lae 來 come
këĭh 吃 eating
wan, 完 finished,
san 散 dispersed

* The Chinese at convivial parties, mention it as a compliment, that a Person has a large measure; i. e. that he can drink much.

† Shing, commonly denotes To overcome. ‡ At entertainments a bowl of rice finishes the repast. § Attendants on the right and left.

| | | |
|---|---|---|
| seĭh; | 席。 | the table; |
| Choo | 主 | Host |
| jin | 人 | |
| jang | 讓 | yielded |
| kĭh | 客 | Guest |
| jŭh | 入 | to enter |
| shoo | 書 | book |
| fang | 房 | room |
| tso. | 坐。 | sit. |

The boys poured out tea, which when they had drunk, the pipes were filled; water was poured into the washhand basins, and areca nut again brought.

| | | |
|---|---|---|
| Seaou | 小 | Little |
| hae | 孩 | boys |
| tsze | 子 | |
| taou | 倒 | pour out |
| ch'ha, | 茶。 | tea, |
| hŏ | 喥 | drink |
| leaou | 了 | |
| ch'ha, | 茶 | tea, |
| chwang | 裝 | fill |
| yen; | 烟。 | tobacco; |
| taou | 倒 | pour out |
| shwŭy | 水 | water |
| se | 洗 | wash |
| lëen, | 臉 | face, |
| tsae | 再 | again |
| na | 拿 | bring |
| pin | 檳 | areca nut. |
| lang. | 榔。 | |

A. Guest said, I have not brought any thing with me, except a few Keang-nan peas, which are now at Hung-fă's warehouse. I will to-morrow send a few tubs of them for the use of my Venerable Uncle (your Father.)

| | | |
|---|---|---|
| Kĭh | 客 | Guest |
| shwŏ, | 說。 | said, |
| yu | 愚 | Simple younger brother } I |
| te | 弟 | |
| mŭh | 沒 | not |
| yew | 有 | have |
| shin | 甚 | any |
| mo | 麽 | |
| tung | 東 | thing |
| se | 西 | |
| tae | 帶 | bring |
| lae. | 來。 | come. |
| chĭh | 只 | Only |
| she | 是 | is |
| tsŏ | 昨 | yesterday |
| jĭh | 日 | |

| | | |
|---|---|---|
| tae | 帶 | bring |
| leaou | 了 | |
| seay | 些 | a little |
| Keang- | 江 | Keang-nan |
| nan | 南 | |
| pĭh- | 白 | peas |
| pëen- | 扁 | |
| tow- | 豆 | |
| jin | 仁 | |
| tsae | 在 | are at |
| Hung- | 洪 | Hung-fă |
| fă | 發 | |
| hang, | 行 | warehouse, |
| ming | 明 | to-morrow |
| t'hëen | 天 | |
| chŏ | 着 | send |
| jin | 人 | man |
| sung | 送 | present |
| ke | 幾 | a few |
| tung | 桶 | tubs |
| lae | 來 | come |
| këĭh | 給 | give |
| laou | 老 | old |
| pĭh | 伯 | uncle |
| yung. | 用 | use. |

B. The Host said, Keang-nan peas are most excellent.

| | | |
|---|---|---|
| Choo | 主 | Host |
| shwŏ, | 說 | said, |
| K ang- | 江 | Keang-nan |
| nan | 南 | |
| pĭh- | 白 | peas |
| pëen- | 扁 | |
| tow | 豆 | |
| he | 係 | are |
| ting | 頂 | top |
| haou | 好 | good. |
| tëĭh. | 的 | |

A. The Guest rose, and said, I am going. Say good bye, for me to your Father.

| | | |
|---|---|---|
| Kĭh | 客 | Guest |
| k'he | 起 | raised |
| shin | 身 | body |
| kaou | 告 | announced |
| tsze. | 辭 | taking leave. |
| Te | 替 | For |
| wo | 我 | me |
| tsae | 在 | at |
| laou | 老 | old |
| pĭh | 伯 | uncle |
| kăn | 跟 | heel |
| tsëen | 前 | before |
| kaou | 告 | announce |

tsze. 辭 taking leave.

B. The Host said, Excuse my father in not walking to the gate with you. [To the Servant] Bring the chair.

Choo 主 Host
shwŏ, 說 said,
kea 家 House
foo 父 Father
pŭh 不 not
sung 送 } walk out (with you).
leaou. 了 }
keaou 叫 Call
tseu 取 bring
keaou 轎 } chair.
tsze. 子 }

— The Host walked with him to the gate. Each made a bow. The Host stood till the Guest got into the chair

Kĭh 客 Guest
tsŏ 作 made
yĭh 揖 a bow *
pae 拜 worshipped
tsze. 辭 took leave.
Choo 主 } Host
jin 人 }
sung 送 presented
ch'hŭh 出 out
mun, 門 gate,
pe 彼 that
tsze 此 this
yĭh 一 one
yĭh. 揖 bow.
Choo 主 Host
lëĭh 立 erect
how 候 waited
Kĭh 客 Guest
shang 上 ascended the
keaou. 轎 chair.

A. Guest joined his hands, as an act of reverence, and said, Good bye.

Pa 把 Took
show 手 hands
yĭh 一 one
kung, 拱 join before the breast,
ts'hing. 請 good bye.

B. The Host also said, Good bye.

Choo 主 Host
yĭh 亦 also
shwŏ, 說 said,
ts'hing. 請 good bye.

* Yĭh, denotes joining the hands and bending down till the back and head are horizontal

# DIALOGUE XXII.

## *A FIRE AT CANTON.*

On the Twenty-second day of the tenth moon, of the twelfth year of Kea-king, a fire broke out in the suburbs of Canton, and burnt upwards of three hundred houses.

| | | |
|---|---|---|
| Kea- | 嘉 | Kea-king |
| king | 慶 | |
| shĭh | 十 | twelfth |
| urh | 二 | |
| nëen, | 年· | year, |
| shĭh | 十 | tenth |
| yuĕ, | 月· | moon, |
| urh | 二 | twentieth |
| shĭh | 十 | |
| jĭh, | 日· | day, |
| Kwang- | 廣 | Canton |
| chow | 州 | |
| ching | 城 | city |
| wae | 外 | withoutside |
| keae | 街 | street |
| fang | 坊 | |
| k'he | 起 | rise |
| ho, | 火· | fire, |
| shaou | 燒 | burnt |
| k'heu | 去 | away |
| fang | 房 | rooms |
| tsze | 子 | |
| san | 三 | three |
| pĭh | 百 | hundred |
| yu | 餘 | odd |
| këen. | 間 | number. |

The Viceroy, Foo-yuen, and all the Mandarins came out of the City to put a stop to the fire.

| | | |
|---|---|---|
| Ching | 城 | City |
| nuy | 內 | within |

| | | |
|---|---|---|
| Tŭh- | 督 | (the) Viceroy, |
| tae, | 臺。 | |
| Foo- | 撫 | Foo-yuen, |
| tae, | 臺。 | |
| kŏ | 各 | all the |
| kwăn | 官 | officers |
| too | 都 | all |
| ch'hŭh | 出 | out of |
| ching | 城 | city |
| lae | 來 | came to |
| kew | 救 | rescue the |
| ho. | 火。 | fire. |

The water engines from every place, all went to extinguish the fire. After six hours it was put out.

| | | |
|---|---|---|
| Kŏ | 各 | Every |
| choo | 處 | place |
| shwŭy | 水 | water |
| chay | 車 | wheel carriage |
| keae | 皆 | all |
| k'heu | 去 | went out to |
| kew | 救 | rescue |
| ho. | 火。 | fire. |
| How | 後 | After |
| che | 至 | to |
| san | 三 | three |
| ko | 個 | |
| she | 時 | hours* |
| shin | 辰 | |
| kew | 救 | rescued and |
| sëĭh. | 息。 | ceased. |

A great many houses, and a large quantity of goods were destroyed. Fortunately no lives were lost.

| | | |
|---|---|---|
| Shaou | 燒 | Burnt |
| k'heu | 去 | away |
| fang | 房 | houses |
| ŏ | 屋 | |
| ho | 貨 | goods |
| wŭh | 物 | |
| shin | 甚 | very |
| to; | 多。 | many; |
| hing | 幸 | happily |
| mŭh | 沒 | not |
| yew | 有 | have |
| shaou | 燒 | burnt and |
| hwae | 壞 | destroy |
| jin. | 人。 | men. |

* One She-shin, is equal to two European hours.

2 A

# DIALOGUE XXIII.

## *BURNING OF A SHIP.*

In the Ninth Moon of the Twelfth year of Kea-king, the English Company's Servants sent an address to the Hoppo of Canton, saying.

| | | |
|---|---|---|
| Kea- | 嘉 | Kea-king |
| king | 慶 | |
| shĭh | 十 | twelfth |
| urh | 二 | |
| nëen, | 年。 | year, |
| kew | 九 | ninth |
| yuĕ, | 月， | moon, |
| Ying- | 嘆 | (the) English |
| kĕih- | 咭 | |
| le | 唎 | |
| kwŏ | 國 | nation's |
| Kung- | 公 | Company |
| sze | 司 | |
| Pan- | 班 | Supercargoes |
| shang | 上 | |
| keu | 具 | presented |
| pin | 稟 | address |
| yĭh | 一 | one |
| fung | 封 | |
| yu | 與 | to |
| Yuĕ | 粤 | Canton's |
| Hae- | 海 | Hoppo, |
| kwăn, | 關， | |
| shwŏ. | 說。 | saying. |

That the Company had a great quantity of money here, which they did not require for the purchase of goods, and that they wished to send some of it away to another Port.

| | | |
|---|---|---|
| Kung- | 公 | The Company's |
| sze | 司 | |

| | | |
|---|---|---|
| yin | 銀 | treasure |
| tsze | 子 | |
| shin | 甚 | very |
| to | 多 | much |
| che | 置 | purchasing |
| ho | 貨 | cargo |
| yung | 用 | use |
| pŭh | 不 | not |
| wan, | 完。 | entirely, |
| yaou | 要 | want |
| chwang | 裝 | put on |
| seay | 些 | a little |
| hwŭy | 回 | return |
| k'heu | 去 | go |
| pëĕ | 別 | other |
| fow | 埠 | port. |
| t'how. | 頭。 | |

Afterwards the Hoppo granted permission to put it on board the Ship of War.

| | | |
|---|---|---|
| How- | 後 | Afterwards |
| lae | 來 | |
| Hae- | 海 | Hoppo |
| kwăn | 關 | |
| chun | 准 | allowed |
| k'he | 其 | it |
| ch'ŭh | 出 | go out |
| k'how | 口 | mouth |
| tsae | 在 | in |
| ping | 兵 | soldier |
| chuen | 船 | ship |
| chwang | 裝 | put on board |
| hwŭy. | 回。 | go back. |

But heretofore, the Ships of War could not by law, enter the harbour, therefore the Committee consulted about it.

| | | |
|---|---|---|
| Tan | 但 | But |
| ping | 兵 | soldier |
| chuen | 船 | ship |
| le | 例 | regulations |
| hëang | 向 | heretofore |
| pŭh | 不 | not |
| năng | 能 | can |
| tsin | 進 | enter |
| k'how, | 口， | mouth, |
| so | 所 | therefore |
| e | 以 | |
| Ta- | 大 | the Chief |
| pan | 班 | |
| yu | 與 | with |
| kŏ | 各 | all |
| Pan | 班 | the Supercargoes |
| shang | 上 | |

| | | |
|---|---|---|
| kung | 公 | consulted together. |
| e. | 議。 | |

It was found that in a few days, there would be two Country Ships going, and that it would be better to put it on board them, to take it without the Bogue, and deliver it to the Ship of War to take it away.

| | | |
|---|---|---|
| Cha | 查 | It was found |
| tĭh | 得 | |
| kin | 近 | near |
| jĭh | 日 | day |
| yew | 有 | have |
| leang | 兩 | two |
| chĭh | 隻 | |
| keang | 港 | Country |
| kĕŏ | 脚 | |
| chuen | 船 | ships |
| tseang | 將 | will |
| yaou | 要 | want |
| k'hae | 開 | to commence |
| hang, | 行。 | going, |
| pŭh | 不 | better |
| joo | 如 | |
| ke | 寄 | send |
| tsae | 在 | by |
| t'ha | 他 | those |
| chuen | 船 | ships |
| shang | 上 | upon be |
| chwang | 裝 | put in |
| ch'hŭh | 出 | go out the |
| Hoo- | 虎 | Bogue |
| mun | 門 | |
| wae, | 外。 | outside, |
| keaou | 交 | delivered over |
| yu | 與 | to the |
| ping | 兵 | soldier |
| chuen | 船 | ship |
| Choo | 主 | Captain to |
| tae | 帶 | carry |
| hwŭy. | 回。 | back. |

Having all determined on it, they took five hundred chests of Silver, and sent them down to the two Country Ships, and put it on board.

| | | |
|---|---|---|
| Ta | 大 | All |
| kea | 家 | |
| e | 議 | consulted and |
| ting, | 定。 | settled, |
| tsew | 就 | then |
| tseang | 將 | took |
| yin | 銀 | the silver |
| tsze | 子 | |
| woo | 五 | five |

| | | |
|---|---|---|
| pĭh | 百 | hundred |
| seang, | 箱 | chests, |
| hea | 下 | down went |
| leaou | 了 | |
| leang | 兩 | two |
| chĭh | 隻 | |
| keang | 港 | country |
| keŏ | 脚 | |
| chuen | 船 | ships |
| le | 裡 | within. |
| mëen. | 面。 | |

It happened one day, that that Ship took fire by accident.

| | | |
|---|---|---|
| Hwŏ | 忽 | Suddenly |
| yĭh | 一 | one |
| jĭh | 日 | day |
| na | 那 | that |
| chĭh | 隻 | |
| keang | 港 | country |
| keŏ | 脚 | |
| chuen | 船 | ship |
| shĭh | 失 | slipped |
| ho | 火 | fire, |
| leaou, | 了 | |
| tseang | 將 | took the |
| chuen | 船 | ship and |
| shaou | 燒 | burnt. |
| chŏ. | 着。 | |

In the Ship there was raised a cry of fire. The Person hăving the Command, hastened to send a man to Canton to inform the Chief, and to request that the large fire engine might be sent down to Hwang-poo, to extinguish the fire.

| | | |
|---|---|---|
| Chuen | 船 | Ship |
| nŭy, | 內 | within, |
| keaou | 呌 | called out |
| han | 喊 | |
| kew | 救 | save the |
| ho, | 火。 | fire, |
| sze | 司 | take care |
| sze | 事 | business the |
| jin | 人 | man |
| sŏ | 速 | hastened |
| tsëĕ | 即 | immediately to |
| sze | 使 | send a |
| jin | 人 | person |
| shang | 上 | up to |
| Săng | 省 | Canton |
| che | 知 | to tell |
| Ta- | 大 | the Chief, and |
| pan, | 班 | |

| | | |
|---|---|---|
| ts'hing | 請 | request |
| ta | 大 | large |
| ching | 城 | city |
| shwüy | 水 | water |
| chay | 車 | carriage |
| hea | 下 | go down to |
| Hwang- | 黃 | Hwang-poo |
| poo | 埔 | |
| kew | 救 | to save the |
| ho. | 火. | fire. |

The Chiefs, and every Person went down with them to oversee and assist.

| | | |
|---|---|---|
| Ta- | 大 | The Chief |
| pan | 班 | |
| kŏ | 各 | every |
| jin | 人 | man |
| yay | 也 | also |
| süy | 隨 | forthwith |
| tsëĕ | 卽 | |
| hea | 下 | went down to |
| Hwang- | 黃 | Hwang-poo to |
| poo | 埔 | |
| chaou | 照 | oversee and assist. |
| ying. | 應. | |

After five or six hours, the fire was extinguished.

| | | |
|---|---|---|
| How | 後 | After |
| che | 至 | till |
| leang | 兩 | two |
| san | 三 | three |
| ko | 個 | |
| she | 時 | hours |
| shin | 辰 | |
| tseang | 將 | took the |
| ho | 火 | fire |
| kew | 救 | saved |
| sëĭh. | 息. | stopped. |

The greater half of the Ship was already burnt. There only remained the bottom in the water, a small part of that was not consumed.

| | | |
|---|---|---|
| Chuen | 船 | Ship |
| e | 已 | already |
| shaou | 燒 | burnt |
| k'heu | 去 | gone |
| leaou | 了 | |
| ta | 大 | greater |
| pan, | 半, | half, |
| chĭh | 只 | only |
| shing | 剩 | remained |
| chuen | 船 | ship |
| te | 底 | bottom |
| tsae | 在 | remaining |

| | | |
|---|---|---|
| shwŭy | 水 | water |
| le | 裡 | within, |
| mëen, | 面 | |
| yew | 有 | have |
| seay | 些 | a little |
| we | 未 | not |
| tsăng | 曾 | yet |
| shaou | 燒 | burnt (and) |
| hwae. | 壞 | destroyed. |

The Captain sent People to watch, so that not the least thing was stolen.

| | | | |
|---|---|---|---|
| Chuen | 船 | Ship | |
| Choo | 主 | Master | |
| sze | 使 | sent | |
| shwŭy | 水 | water | sailors |
| show | 手 | hand | |
| jin | 人 | men | |
| seun | 巡 | to go round | |
| cha | 查 | examine | |
| k'han | 看 | look and | |
| show, | 守 | keep, | |
| mŭh | 沒 | not | |
| yew | 有 | have | |
| pei | 被 | receive | |
| jin | 人 | men | |
| t'how | 偷 | steal | |
| k'heu | 去 | go | |

| | | |
|---|---|---|
| yih | 一 | one |
| tëen | 點 | Little |
| tung | 東 | thing. |
| se. | 西 | |

The next day, the Chief called for three Chop-boats, and removed the specie, there was some at the bottom of the water melted into pieces of silver.

| | | |
|---|---|---|
| Te | 第 | Second |
| urh | 二 | |
| jih | 日 | day |
| Ta- | 大 | Chief |
| pan | 班 | |
| tsëĕ | 即 | immediately |
| keaou | 叫 | called |
| pëen- | 扁 | chop-boats |
| ting | 艇 | |
| san | 三 | three, |
| chih, | 隻 | |
| tseang | 將 | to take the |
| yin | 銀 | silver |
| pan | 搬 | remove |
| k'he, | 起 | up, |
| yew | 有 | have |
| seay | 些 | a little |
| tsae | 在 | remain |

| | | |
|---|---|---|
| shwǔy | 水 | water |
| le | 裡 | within |
| mëen | 面 | |
| shaou | 燒 | burnt |
| ching | 成 | formed |
| yin | 銀 | silver |
| ping | 餅 | cakes |
| yǐh | 一 | the |
| pan. | 般。 | same. |

In two or three days it was all taken up; and of the whole amount, there were only wanting two or three chests.

| | | |
|---|---|---|
| Leang | 兩 | Two |
| san | 三 | three |
| t'hëen | 天 | days |
| tsae | 纔 | then |
| leaou | 撈 | take up |
| tsing, | 清。 | entirely, |
| tsung | 總 | whole |
| swan | 算 | account |
| che | 止 | only |
| shaou | 少 | defect |
| k'heu | 去 | go |
| yin | 銀 | silver |
| tsze | 子 | |
| leang | 兩 | two |
| san | 三 | three |
| seang. | 箱。 | boxes, |

# DIALOGUE XXIV.

## *A SPRING RAMBLE.*

Wang-yun having looked at it (the letter), said to (Ch'hang-shing), thank your Master for his kind intentions, which overpower me.

| | | |
|---|---|---|
| Wang- | 王 | Wang-yun |
| yun | 雲 | |
| k'han | 看 | look |
| wan, | 完 | finished, |
| hëang | 向 | towards |
| Ch'hang- | 張 | Ch'hang-shing |
| shing | 盛 | |
| taou, | 道 | said, |
| ching | 承 | thank |
| ne | 你 | your |
| Seang | 相 | Master's |
| kung | 公 | |
| mei | 美 | good |
| tsing | 情 | disposition |
| ho | 何 | how |
| e | 以 | |
| kĭh | 克 | able |
| tang. | 當 | to sustain it. |

You may go back and tell your Master, that to-morrow, I shall certainly accept of his invitation.

| | | |
|---|---|---|
| K'ho | 可 | May |
| shang | 上 | up (answer) |
| fŭh | 復 | back |
| ne | 你 | your |
| kea | 家 | family |
| Seang | 相 | Master |
| kung | 公 | |
| shwŏ, | 說 | say, |
| wo | 我 | I |
| ming | 明 | to-morrow |
| jĭh | 日 | |

jen 然 indeed
lae 來 come
ling 領 receive
tsing. 情。 kind feeling.

Ch'hang-shing received the message, and went back to tell his Master.

Ch'hang- 張 } Ch'hang-shing
shing 盛 }
ling 領 receiving the
ming 命 order
hwüy 回 returned (answer)
fŭh 復 back
Choo 主 } Master.
jin. 人。}

Wang-yun returned home, and went to the inner apartments. Mrs. Seu said, where have you been all this time.

Wang- 王 } Wang-yun
yun 雲 }
hwüy 回 returned to
nüy 內 inner
shĭh, 室 appartments,
Seu, 徐 Seu,
Foo 夫 } Mrs.
jin 人 }
taou, 道。 said,

wo 我 my
urh 兒 son
chay 這 this
yĭh 一 one
hwüy 會 time
taou 到 to
na 那 what
seang 廂 (room) place
k'heu 去 go
lae. 來。 come,

Wang-yun said, I will tell you Mother, as I happened to be sauntering before the door, Ch'hang-sew-che, sent a Person with a letter inviting me to-morrow.

Wang- 王 } Wang-yun
yun 雲 }
taou, 道。 said,
kaou 告 tell
moo 母 } mother
tsin 親 }
tĭh 得 obtain
che, 知。 know,
hae 孩 } child
urh 兒 }
shĭh 適 happened
wang 往 to go

中文會話及凡例



| | | |
|---|---|---|
| mun | 門 | door |
| ts'hëen | 前 | before |
| hëen | 閒 | leisure |
| poo, | 步。 | walk, |
| yew | 有 | have |
| Ch'hang- | 張 | Ch'hang-sew-che |
| sew- | 秀 | |
| che | 芝 | |
| chŏ | 着 | send |
| jin | 人 | man |
| sung | 送 | present |
| shoo | 書 | book |
| lae, | 來。 | come, |
| ming | 明 | to-morrow |
| jïh | 日 | |
| ts'hing | 請 | invite |
| hae | 孩 | child. |
| urh. | 兒。 | |

Mrs. Seu said, Where is the letter?

| | | |
|---|---|---|
| Foo | 夫 | Mrs. |
| jin | 人 | |
| taou, | 道。 | said, |
| shoo | 書 | letter |
| tsae | 在 | is |
| na | 那 | what |
| le? | 裡。 | place? |

Wang-yun took it from his sleeve, and presented it to Mrs. Seu.

| | | |
|---|---|---|
| Wang- | 王 | Wang-yun, |
| yun | 雲。 | |
| tsae | 在 | at |
| sew | 袖 | sleeve * |
| chung | 中 | middle |
| tseu | 取 | took |
| ch'hùh | 出 | out |
| te | 遞 | presented |
| yu | 與 | to |
| Foo | 夫 | Mrs. |
| jin. | 人。 | |

Having looked at it, she said, as a friend has invited you, you must not refuse him; only do not impede your studies.

| | | |
|---|---|---|
| K'han | 看 | Looking |
| taou, | 道。 | said, |
| ke | 既 | since |
| ching | 承 | receive |
| păng | 朋 | friend |
| yew | 友 | |
| che | 之 | 's |

* The Chinese have not a convenient place about them for letters, &c. they invariably put them up their sleeve.

tsing, 情. kind regard,
yay 也 also
pŭh 不 not
haou 好 good
keŏ 却 refuse
t'ha, 他. him,
chĭh 只 only
she 是 is
pŭh 不 not
yaou 要 want
hwang 荒 starve
joo 儒 literary
nëĕ. 業. occupation.

Wang-yun said, I understand; it is not necessary to enjoin me.

Wang- 王 } Wang-yun
yun 雲 }
taou, 道. said,
heaou 曉 } understand,
tĭh, 得. }
pŭh 不 not
seaou 消 necessary
moo 母 } mother
tsin 親 }
fun 吩 } direct.
foo. 咐. }

Next morning, having dressed himself, went to ask his Mother how she did.

Tsze 次 Next
tsaou, 早. morning,
Wang- 王 } Wang-yun
yun 雲 }
shoo 梳 comb
se 洗 wash
e 已 now
pĕĭh, 畢. finished,
k'heu 去 go
wăn 問 ask (wish)
Foo 夫 } Mrs.
jin. 人 }
gan. 安. repose.

When they had just done breakfast, a Servant came in and announced that Ch'hang-shing, (Servant of Mr. Ch'hang) was without, requesting Mr. Wang to go.

Tsae 纔 Then
yung 用 use
kwo 過 pass
tsaou 早 morning
fan, 飯. rice,
kea 家 family
jin 人 man

| | | |
|---|---|---|
| tsin | 進 | in |
| lae | 來 | come |
| pin | 稟 | report |
| taou | 道 | say (of) |
| Ch'hang- | 張 | Ch'hang |
| Seang | 相 | Mr. |
| kung | 公 | |
| kea, | 家 | family, |
| Ch'hang- | 張 | Ch'hang-shing |
| shing | 盛 | |
| tsae | 在 | is |
| wae | 外 | outside |
| ts'hing | 請 | requesting |
| Ta | 大 | (you,) Sir. |
| seang | 相 | |
| kung. | 公 | |

Wang-yun, hearing this, rose immediately, changed his cap and clothes.

| | | |
|---|---|---|
| Wang- | 王 | Wang-yun |
| yun | 雲 | |
| wăn | 聞 | hearing |
| yen, | 言 | words, |
| tsëĕ | 卽 | then |
| k'he | 起 | up |
| shin | 身 | body |
| hwan | 換 | changed |
| leaou | 了 | |
| kin | 巾 | cap (and) |
| fŭh. | 服 | clothes. |

Went into the interior apartment, and addressing his Mother said, I am now going to leave you.

| | | |
|---|---|---|
| Tsin | 進 | Entered |
| nüy | 內 | interior |
| tang | 堂 | hall |
| pin | 稟 | announced to |
| Foo- | 夫 | Mrs. |
| jin | 人 | |
| taou, | 道 | said, |
| hae | 孩 | child |
| urh | 兒 | |
| k'heu, | 去 | go, |
| pei | 陪 | turn back upon |
| leaou | 了 | |
| moo | 母 | mother |
| tsin | 親 | |
| lae. | 來 | go. |

Mrs. Seu said, From your Spring ramble, you should return rather soon, to prevent my being uneasy.

| | | |
|---|---|---|
| Foo | 夫 | Mrs. |
| jin | 人 | |
| taou, | 道 | said, |
| wo | 我 | My |

urh, 兒 child,
yew 遊 rambling in
Ch'hun 春 Spring
k'ho 可 should
tsaou 早 soon
seay 些 a little
hwŭy 回 return
lae, 來 come,
mëen 免 prevent
wo 我 me
kwa 掛 } suspense.
hwae. 懷 }

Wang-yun said, I understand.

Wang- 王 } Wang-yun
yun 雲 }
taou, 道 said,
hae 孩 } child
urh 兒 }
heaou 曉 } know.
tĭh. 得 }

He came out and told Kin-che, to follow with Ch'hang-shing.

Ch'hŭh 出 Out
lae 來 go
keaou 叫 call
Kin- 錦 } Kin-che
che 芝 }
kăn 跟 } follow
sŭy 隨 }
t'hung 同 } with
leaou 了 }
Ch'hang- 張 } Ch'hang-shing.
shing. 盛 }

Before he reached the boat, he saw that there were already three or four Persons sitting in it.

We 未 Not
taou 到 reach
chuen 船 boat
pëen, 邊 side,
këen 見 see
yew 有 have
san 三 three
sze 四 four
kĭh 客 Persons
e 已 already
tsae 在 were in
tso 座 } boat
chuen 船 }
chung. 中 midst.

All of them, seeing Wang-yun coming, hastened out of the boat to meet him, and said,

Choo 諸 All

yew 友 the friends
k'han 看 looking
këen 見 saw
Wang- 王 } Wang-yun
yun, 雲 }
măng 忙 hastily
ch'hŭh 出 out
tsang 艙 hole
shang 上 up
lae 來 come
ying 迎 to meet
taou. 道。 said.

Brother Tsing-ne, (another epithet of Wang-yun) Why are you so late in coming.

Tsing- 清 } Tsing-ne,
ne 霓 }
heung, 兄。 brother,
wei 爲 } why
ho 何 }
lae 來 come
che? 遲。 late?

They called to the boatmen to lay a pole across for their hands

Keaou 叫 Called
chuen 船 } boatmen
kea 家 }
tă 搭 } to place
leaou 了 }
foo 扶 support
show. 手。 hands.

Wang-yun went on board, entered the cabin, and having made his bow to all the friends, said, I have arrived very soon—how can you say that I am late!

Wang- 王 } Wang-yun
yun 雲 }
shang 上 ascend
chuen 船 boat
tsin 進 enter
tsang 艙 cabin
yu 與 with
chung 衆 all
yew 友 friends
yĭh 揖 bow
pa 罷 finished
taou, 道。 said,
te 弟 I
che 至 come
shin 甚 very
sŏ, 速 fast,
ho 何 how
yen 言 say

lae 來 come
che! 遲。 late!

Addressing himself to Ch'hang-lan, he said, Thank you my brother for your letter yesterday inviting me. I have had repeatedly to thank you for your kindness, it completely overpowers me.

Hëang 向 Towards
Ch'hang-lan 張蘭 Ch'hang-lan
taou, 道。 said,
ching 承 receive
ch'hang 長 elder
heung 兄 brother
jĭh tsŏ 日昨 yesterday
tsze 賜 conferred the
hwa 華 elegant
han 翰 letter
këen 見 see
chaou, 招。 invitation,
te 弟 I
pŭh 不 not
shing 勝 overcome
tseŏ yŏ, 雀躍 leaping for joy,
chĭh 只 only
she 是 is
lŭy 屢 repeatedly
taou 叨 received
how 厚 (thick) kind
gae 愛 love
ho e 何以 how
kĭh 克 can
tang. 當。 sustain.

Ch'hang-lan said, amusing ourselves with a Spring Ramble, why utter the language of ceremony.

Ch'hang lan 張蘭 Ch'hang-lan
taou, 道。 said,
yew 遊 ramble
Ch'hun 春 Spring
seaou këen, 消遣 to amuse,
ho 何 why
ch'hŭh 出 utter
kĭh 客 visitor's
yen. 言。 words.

Wang-yun said, are there any other friends.

| | | |
|---|---|---|
| Wang- | 王 | Wang-yun |
| yun | 雲 | |
| taou, | 道 | said, |
| hwang | 還 | besides. |
| yew | 有 | have |
| ho | 何 | what |
| kïh? | 客。 | person? |

Chang-lan said, there is no other friend, we were only waiting for your arrival that we might set off.

| | | |
|---|---|---|
| Ch'hang- | 張 | Ch'hang-lan |
| lan | 蘭 | |
| taou, | 道 | said, |
| ping | 並 | further |
| woo | 無 | not |
| t'ha | 他 | other |
| kïh, | 客。 | person, |
| chïh | 只 | only |
| how | 候 | wait |
| heung | 兄 | elder brother |
| che | 至 | come |
| tsew | 就 | then |
| k'hae | 開 | open } set off |
| chuen | 船 | boat. |
| e. | 矣。 | |

He then ordered the boatmen to set off. The boatmen cast off the painter, and proceeded to Hoo-kew.

| | | |
|---|---|---|
| Sŭy | 遂 | Forthwith |
| fun | 吩 | ordered |
| foo | 咐 | |
| k'hae | 開 | to set off. |
| chuen. | 船。 | |
| Chuen | 船 | Boat |
| kea | 家 | family |
| keae | 解 | loosened the |
| lan | 纜 | rope |
| wang | 望 | towards |
| Hoo- | 虎 | Hoo-kew |
| kew | 邱 | |
| tsin | 進 | proceeded. |
| fă. | 發。 | |

# DIALOGUE XXV.

## *A PERSON ILL.*

Sëĭh-jin, seeing that she vomited blood on the ground, became half cold.

| | | |
|---|---|---|
| Sëĭh- | 襲 | Sëĭh-jin |
| jin | 人 | |
| këen | 見 | seeing |
| leaou | 了 | |
| tsze | 自 | herself |
| ke | 己 | |
| t'hoo | 吐 | vomiting |
| tëĭh | 的 | |
| sëen | 鮮 | fresh |
| heuĕ | 血 | blood |
| tsae | 在 | on the |
| te | 地 | ground |
| yay | 也 | also |
| tsew | 就 | then |
| lăng | 冷 | became cold |
| leaou | 了 | |
| pan | 半 | half. |
| tsëĭh. | 截. | |

She recollected what she had formerly heard People say, that if a young Person spit blood, their lives could not be ensured for a month or a year.

| | | |
|---|---|---|
| Seang | 想 | Thought of |
| chŏ | 着 | |
| wang | 往 | former |
| jĭh | 日 | day |
| chang | 常 | always |
| ting | 聽 | hear |
| jin | 人 | people |
| shwŏ, | 說. | say, |
| shaou | 少 | young person |
| nëen | 年 | |
| t'hoo | 吐 | vomit |

heuĕ, 血 blood,
nëen 年 year
yuĕ 月 month
pŭh 不 not
paou. 保。 secure.

Though life should be prolonged, a Person was rendered useless.

Tsung 縱 } Although
jen 然 }
ming 命 life
ch'hang, 長。 lengthened,
chung 終 end
she 是 is to
fei 廢 waste
jin 人 } a person.
leaou. 了。 }

When this occurred to her, she suddenly recollected her former thoughts of future grandour; and seeing them blasted, ere she was aware, the tears started from her eyes.

Seang 想 Thinking
k'he 起 up
tsze 此 these
yen, 言。 words,
pŭh 不 not
keŏ 覺 adverting
tseang 將 took
soo 素 former
jĭh 日 days
seang 想 } thought of
chŏ 着 }
how 後 } future
lae 來 }
tsăng 爭 striving for
yung, 榮。 glory,
kwa 誇 boasting of
yaou, 耀 splendour,
che 之 the
sin 心 heart
tsin 盡 entirely
keae 皆 all
hwŭy 灰 } consumed.
leaou. 了。 }
Yen 眼 Eye
chung 中 midst
pŭh 不 not
keŏ 覺 } adverting
tëĭh 的 }
tëĕ 滴 drop
hea 下 down
lŭy 泪 tears
lae. 來。 come.

Paou-yŭh seeing her weep, also felt himself very uneasy.

| | | |
|---|---|---|
| Paou- | 寶 | Paou-yŭh |
| yŭh | 玉 | |
| këen | 見 | seeing |
| t'ha | 他 | her |
| kŭh | 哭 | weep, |
| leaou, | 了 | |
| yay | 也 | also |
| pŭh | 不 | not |
| keŏ | 覺 | aware |
| sin | 心 | heart |
| söan | 酸 | sour |
| k'he | 起 | became. |
| lae. | 來 | |

He therefore said to her, What are you thinking of?

| | | |
|---|---|---|
| Yin | 因 | Therefore |
| wăn | 問 | asking |
| taou, | 道 | said, |
| ne | 你 | your |
| sin | 心 | heart |
| le | 裡 | within |
| keŏ | 覺 | feel |
| tĭh | 得 | |
| tsăng | 怎 | what |
| mo | 麽 | |
| yang? | 樣 | manner? |

Sëĭh-jin forced a smile and said, that which is good,—What should I be thinking of!

| | | |
|---|---|---|
| Sëĭh- | 襲 | Sëĭh-jin |
| jin | 人 | |
| mëen | 勉 | by force |
| keang | 強 | |
| seaou | 笑 | laughing |
| taou, | 道 | said, |
| haou | 好 | well |
| haou | 好 | well, |
| tëĭh, | 的 | |
| keŏ | 覺 | feel |
| tsăng | 怎 | what |
| mo | 麽 | |
| ne! | 呢 | now! |

Paou-yŭh wanted immediately to call a Person to warm some wine, to get some goat's blood, and some Le-tung pills.

| | | |
|---|---|---|
| Paou- | 寶 | Paou-yŭh |
| yŭh | 玉 | |
| tëĭh | 的 | 's |
| e | 意 | wish was |
| sze | 思 | |

tsëĕ 即 } immediately
kĭh 刻 }
pëen 便 forthwith
yaou 要 wanted
keaou 叫 to call a
jin 人 person
tang 盪 to boil
hwang 黃 yellow
tsew, 酒。 wine,
yaou 要 wanted
shan 山 hill
yang 羊 sheep
heuĕ, 血。 blood,
Le- 黎 } Le-tung
tung 峒 }
wan 丸 pills
lae. 來。 come.

Sëĭh-jin shook her hand, and smiling said.

Sëĭh- 襲 } Sëĭh-jin
jin 人 }
chow 抽 snatched
t'ha 他 } her
tëĭh 的 }
show, 手 hand,
seaou 笑 laughing
taou. 道。 said.

What you are alarmed about, is not of much importanee; if you call a number of People, they will feel indignant at my misconduct.

Ne 你 You
chay 這 this
yĭh 一 one
naou 鬧 bother
pŭh 不 not
ta 大 greatly
kin; 緊。 required;
wăn 問 ask
k'he 起 up
to 多 } how many
shaou 少 }
jin 人 people
lae, 來。 come,
taou 倒 reversed
paou 抱 embrace
yuen 怨 resentment (at)
wo 我 my
king 輕 lightness and
kwang. 狂。 folly (madness).

It will not be well either for you or me,—the right way is to send a boy to Mr. Wang, the Surgeon, and make a request to him to prepare a little medicine to take, and I shall soon be well. No Person will know,—no not the devil himself. Won't that be well?

| | | |
|---|---|---|
| Ne | 你 | You |
| yay | 也 | also |
| pŭh | 不 | not |
| haou, | 好。 | well, |
| wo | 我 | I |
| yay | 也 | also |
| pŭh | 不 | not |
| haou, | 好。 | well, |
| ching | 正 | rightly |
| king | 經 | |
| ming- | 明 | to-morrow |
| jĭh | 日 | |
| ne | 你 | you |
| ta | 打 | send |
| fă | 發 | |
| seaou | 小 | little |
| tsze | 子 | boy |
| wăn | 問 | ask |
| wăn | 問 | ask |
| Wang, | 王 | Wang, |
| Ta | 太 | the great Surgeon |
| E | 醫 | |
| k'heu | 去 | to go |
| lung | 弄 | prepare |
| tëen | 點 | a little |
| tsze | 子 | |
| yŭh | 藥 | medicine |
| kĕĭh, | 吃。 | to eat, |
| kĕĭh | 吃 | eat |
| tsew | 就 | soon |
| haou | 好 | well. |
| leaou. | 了。 | |
| Jin | 人 | Man |
| pŭh | 不 | not |
| che, | 知。 | know, |
| kwei | 鬼 | devil |
| pŭh | 不 | not |
| keŏ | 覺 | observe. |
| tëĭh. | 的。 | |
| K'ho | 可 | How |
| pŭh | 不 | not |
| haou? | 好。 | well? |

Paou-yŭh seeing that it was reasonable, could not help being satisfied.

| | | |
|---|---|---|
| Paou- | 寶 | Paou-yŭh |
| yŭh | 玉 | |
| kēen | 見 | saw (it) |
| leaou | 了 | |
| yew | 有 | had |
| le, | 理。 | reason, |

yay 也 also
chĭh 只 } only could
tĭh 得 }
pa 罷 } cease.
leaou. 了。}

He went towards the table to pour out some tea, to give Sëĭh-jin to wash her mouth.

Hëang 向 Towards
găn 案 table
shang 上 upon
chin 斟 } poured out
leaou 了 }
ch'ha 茶 tea
lae 來 come
kĕĭh 給 gave
Sëĭh- 襲 } Sëĭh-jin
jin 人 }
sew 漱 } to wash
leaou 了 }
k'how. 口。 mouth.

Sëĭh-jin, saw that Paou-yŭh was uneasy, forebore telling him not to serve her, for he would not comply; and another thing, she would alarm other People,—it was better to let him go.

Sëĭh- 襲 } Sëĭh-jin
jin 人 }
che 知 knew
Paou- 寶 } Paou-yŭh
yŭh 玉 }
sin 心 heart
nŭy 內 within
yay 也 also
pŭh 不 not
gan 安 reposed
wăn 穩 } settled,
tëĭh, 的。}
tae 待 still
yaou 要 wanted
pŭh 不 not to
keaou 叫 call
t'ha 他 him to
fŭh 伏 } serve,
she, 侍。}
t'ha 他 he
yew 又 further
pëĭh 必 certainly
pŭh 不 not
e; 依。 agree;
urh 二 second
tsĭh 則 consequence
ting 定 certainly

| | | |
|---|---|---|
| yaou | 要 | would |
| king | 驚 | alarm |
| tung | 動 | |
| pëĕ | 別 | other |
| tëĭh | 的 | |
| jin, | 人。 | people, |
| pŭh | 不 | better |
| joo | 如 | |
| yew | 由 | allow |
| t'ha | 他 | him |
| k'heu | 去 | to go |
| pa. | 罷。 | enough. |

# DIALOGUE XXVI.

## *MASTER AND BEGGARS.*

Master. If any Poor People come, let me know immediately.

| | | |
|---|---|---|
| T'hang | 倘 | If |
| yew | 有 | have |
| koo | 孤 | orphans or |
| pin | 貧 | poor |
| taou | 到 | to |
| lae, | 來。 | come, |
| tsëĕ | 即 | immediately |
| pëen | 便 | then |
| paou | 報 | report (that) |
| wo | 我 | I |
| che | 知 | know. |
| taou. | 道。 | |

Servant. Very well.

| | | |
|---|---|---|
| Heaou | 曉 | Understand. |
| tĭh. | 得。 | |

Beggars. My friends, there is now here one Pang-keu-sze, who lends extensively to be paid in the life to come, he opens wide the Door of Community of Goods; let us go and beg his assistance. Is there any reason why not?

| | | |
|---|---|---|
| Lëĭh | 列 | Constituted |
| wei | 位 | persons |
| ah! | 吓。 | ! |
| Kin | 今 | Now |
| yew | 有 | have |
| Pang- | 龎 | Pang-keu-sze |
| keu- | 居 | |
| sze | 士。 | |
| kwang | 廣 | extensively |
| fang | 放 | places |
| lae | 來 | coming |
| săng | 生 | life |
| chae, | 債。 | debts, |
| ta | 大 | wide |
| k'hae | 開 | opens |
| Fang- | 方 | square and |
| pëen | 便 | convenient * |
| che | 之 | 's |
| mun, | 門。 | door, |
| wo | 我 | we |
| mun | 們 | |
| tsëen | 前 | proceed |
| k'heu | 去 | go |
| kew | 求 | beg |
| t'ha | 他 | him |
| chow | 週 | to supply our wants, |
| tse, | 濟、 | |
| chow | 週 | to supply our wants, |
| tse, | 濟 | |
| yew | 有 | have |
| ho | 何 | what |
| pŭh | 不 | not |
| k'ho? | 可。 | ought? |

— Very good, let us all go and beg alms.

| | | |
|---|---|---|
| Haou | 好 | Good |
| ah, | 吓。 | Ah, |
| ta | 大 | great } all |
| kea | 家 | family |
| tsëen | 前 | proceed |
| k'heu | 去 | go |
| kew | 求 | beg |
| t'ha | 他 | him |
| chow | 週 | to supply our wants. |
| tse. | 濟。 | |

— In what way shall we go and beg?

| | | |
|---|---|---|
| Tsăng | 怎 | What |
| mo | 麽 | |
| yang | 樣 | manner |
| k'heu | 去 | go |

* Fang-peen, denotes liberal regard to the interest of fellow creatures.

2 D

kew 求 to supplicate
t'ha. 他。 him.

— We have a plan; where is your brother and his wife.

Ah! 吓 Ah!
Yew 有 } (We) have it.
leaou. 了。
Joo 如 } Now
kin 今
ne 你 your
k'ho 哥 brother's
saou 嫂 wife
tsae 在 at
na 那 what
le? 裡。 place?

— I do not know.

Pùh 不 Not
che 知 } know.
taou. 道。

— Make haste; go seek your brother and sister, and let us go to sing the four Songs, advising the practice of Integrity, Filial Duty, Brotherly Affection, and Conjugal Harmony, to induce him to give us something.

Kwae 快 Haste
k'heu 去 go
tsin 尋 } find
leaou 了
ne 你 your
ko 哥 brother
saou 嫂 wife
lae 來 come
k'heu 去 go
ch'hang 唱 sing
Chung, 忠。 Fidelity,
Heaou, 孝。 Filial Piety,
E, 義。 Friendly Affection,
Ho, 和 Harmony,
sze 四 } four
taou 套
keuen 勸 advising
tsze 詞 discourses
k'heu 去 go
hwa 化 to induce
t'ha. 他。 him.

— You say what is reasonable;—do you wait at the head of Cross-street till I bring them.

Shwŏ 說 } Said
tĭh 得
yew 有 have
le; 理 reason;
ne 你 you

tsae 在 be at
shih 十 } cross
tsze 字 }
keae 街 street
t'how 頭 head
tăng 等 } wait,
chŏ, 着。 }
wo 我 I
k'heu 去 go
tsin 尋 } seek
leaou 了 }
t'ha 他 them
lae. 來。 come.

— Make haste; make haste.

Kwae 快 Haste
k'heu, 去, go,
kwae 快 haste
k'heu. 去。 go.

— Sister, sister! the more I call you, the faster you go.

Saou, 嫂 Sister,
saou, 匕* sister,
wo 我 I
yuĕ 越 more

keaou 叫 call
ne, 你。 you,
ne 你 you
yuĕ 越 more
tsow 走 walk
haou 好 good
kwae. 快。 fast.

— Calling at such a distance, how can she hear. Why do you come calling so?

Ne 你 You
yuen 遠 distant
yuen 遠 } distant
tĕih 的 }
keaou 叫 call
t'ha, 他。 her,
t'ha 他 she
na 那 } how
le 裡 }
ting 聽 } hear,
këen, 見。 }
ne 你 you
wei 爲 } wherefore
ho 何 }

* The above mark is retained to shew the manner in which the Chinese notice the repetition of a Character. In most of their Novels, and Works of that nature, when a Character is to be repeated, the above is generally inserted, and read as the preceding Character.

| | | |
|---|---|---|
| han | 喊 | call aloud |
| keaou | 叫 | |
| urh | 而 | and |
| lae. | 來。 | come. |

I will tell you, there is one Pang-keu-sze, you may go and sing. All our Comrades are there; if you sing well, he must give us something.

| | | |
|---|---|---|
| Wo | 我 | I |
| kaou | 告 | tell |
| soo | 訴 | |
| ne, | 你。 | you, |
| kin | 今 | now |
| yew | 有 | have |
| Pang- | 龐 | Pang-kew-sze, |
| keu- | 居 | |
| sze, | 士。 | |
| ne | 你 | you |
| k'ho | 可 | may |
| k'heu | 去 | go |
| ch'hang, | 唱 | sing, |
| chung | 衆 | all |
| ho | 夥 | associates |
| ke | 計 | |
| too | 都 | all |
| tsae | 在 | are |
| na | 那 | there; |
| le; | 裡。 | |
| ch'hang | 唱 | sing |
| tĭh | 得 | |
| haou, | 好。 | well, |
| sze | 自 | indeed |
| jen | 然 | |
| chow | 週 | supply our wants. |
| tse. | 濟。 | |

— Since it is thus, let us make haste.

| | | |
|---|---|---|
| Ke | 旣 | Since |
| joo | 如 | thus, |
| tsze, | 此。 | |
| kwae | 快 | haste |
| tsow. | 走。 | to go. |

— This is the place. Is there any Porter at the gate?

| | | | |
|---|---|---|---|
| Chay | 這 | Here | |
| le | 裡 | | |
| she | 是 | is it. | |
| leaou. | 了。 | | |
| Mun | 門 | At the door | |
| shang | 上 | | |
| ta | 大 | great | Porter, |
| shŭh | 叔 | uncle | |
| yew | 有 | have (any) | |
| mo? | 麽。 | ? | |

Servant. Who is there?

| | | |
|---|---|---|
| Shĕ | 什 | What |
| mo | 麽 | |
| jin? | 人。 | man? |

B. Mr. Porter, we are poor People belonging to the Asylum; we have come on purpose to beg an alms from the Squire.

| | | | |
|---|---|---|---|
| Ta | 大 | Great | |
| shŭh, | 叔。 | uncle, | |
| wo | 我 | we | |
| mun | 們 | | |
| she | 是 | are | |
| Yang- | 養 | Nourish | Asylum |
| tse- | 濟 | relieve | |
| yuen | 院 | hall | |
| tëĭh | 的 | 's | |
| pin | 貧 | poor, | |
| keung, | 窮。 | | |
| tĭh | 特 | purposely | |
| lae | 來 | come | |
| kew | 求 | to crave | |
| Yuen | 員 | Squire's | |
| wae | 外 | | |
| chow | 週 | alms, | |
| tse, | 濟 | | |
| chow | 週 | alms. | |
| tse. | 濟。 | | |

S. Master, I have a request to make.

| | | |
|---|---|---|
| Yuen | 員 | Squire |
| wae | 外 | |
| yew | 有 | have a |
| ts'hing. | 請。 | request. |

M. What have you to say?

| | | |
|---|---|---|
| Tsăng | 怎 | What |
| mo | 麽 | |
| shwŏ? | 說。 | say? |

S. Withoutside, there are four poor People. Amongst them, there is an old man carrying on his back a young woman, they have come on purpose to beg of you, Sir, an alms.

| | | |
|---|---|---|
| Wae | 外 | Withoutside |
| mëen | 面 | |
| yew | 有 | have |
| koo | 孤 | destitute |
| pin | 貧 | poor |
| sze | 四 | four |
| ming | 名 | names |
| nuy | 內 | amongst |
| yew | 有 | have |
| yĭh | 一 | an |
| ko | 個 | |

| | | |
|---|---|---|
| leaou | 老 | old man |
| urh | 兒 | |
| pei | 背 | carrying on his back |
| chŏ | 着 | |
| yĭh | 一 | a |
| ko | 個 | |
| nëen | 年 | young |
| shaou | 少 | |
| foo | 婦 | woman, |
| jin, | 人。 | |
| tĭh | 特 | purpose |
| lae | 來 | come |
| kew | 求 | beg |
| Yueu | 員 | Squire's |
| wae | 外 | |
| chow | 週 | alms. |
| tse | 濟 | |
| tëĭh. | 的。 | |

M. Tell them to come in.

| | | |
|---|---|---|
| Chŏ | 着 | Order |
| t'ha | 他 | them |
| mun | 們 | |
| tsin | 進 | to come in. |
| lae. | 來。 | |

S. [To the beggars.] Come here. The Squire orders you to come in.

| | | |
|---|---|---|
| Ah. | 吓 | Yes. |
| Yuen | 員 | Squire |
| wae | 外 | |
| chŏ | 着 | orders |
| ne | 你 | you |
| tsin | 進 | in go. |
| k'heu. | 去。 | |

B. All reply, Yes.

| | | |
|---|---|---|
| Ah. | 吓 | Yes. |

B. [They enter.] Let the Squire be exalted. We prostrate ourselves before him.

| | | |
|---|---|---|
| Yuen | 員 | Squire |
| wae | 外 | |
| tsae | 在 | be |
| shang, | 上。 | exalted, |
| koo | 孤 | destitute |
| pin | 貧 | poor [to the ground |
| kow | 叩 | kneel with foreheads |
| këen. | 見。 | to see. |

M. Rise up.

| | | |
|---|---|---|
| K'he | 起 | Up |
| lae. | 來。 | come. |

B. Pardon our rudeness.

| | | |
|---|---|---|
| Shoo | 恕 | Excuse |
| pŭh | 不 | not |
| këen | 見 | seeing |

le 禮 } politeness.
leaou. 了

M. Why does an old man carry on his back a young woman?

Wei 爲 } Why
ho 何
yĭh 一 } an
ko 個
laou 老 } old man
urh 兒
to 跎 } carrying on his back
chŏ 着
yĭh 一 } a
ko 個
shaou 少 } young
nëen 年
foo 婦 } woman.
jin. 人。

B. It is husband and wife.

She 是 It is
fōo 夫 husband and
fóo. 婦。 wife.

— The husband with grey hairs was born dumb; the wife, who is pretty, has been a leper from a child.

Ch'hang 丈 } The husband
foo 夫
pĭh 白 white
show 首 head
săng 生 born
lae 來 come
ya, 啞。 dumb, the
tse 妻 } wife
tsze 子
hung 紅 red
yen 顏 colour
tsze 自 from
yew 幼 youth a
fung. 瘋。 leper,

M. What do they do for alivelihood?

Ho 何 } How
e 以
wei 爲 make
hwŏ? 活。 live?

B. We have no provision made for food or raiment, we get over the morning and evening by singing of songs.

K'how 口 Mouth
shĭh, 食。 eat,
shin 身 body
chuen, 穿。 put on,
mŭh 沒 no

pae 擺 }
poo, 佈 } provision,
koo 歌 odes
ch'hang 唱 songs
tsze 詞 speeches
keŏ 曲 ballads
too 度 pass
chaou 朝 morning
hwan. 昏 evening.

M. What Songs do you sing?

Ch'hang 唱 Sing
shĕ 什 }
mo 麽 } what
ko 歌 odes
tsze? 詞 speeches?

B. We sing the songs Chung, Heaou, E, and Ho.

Ch'hang 唱 Sing
Chung, 忠 Fidelity,
Heaou, 孝 Filial Piety,
E, 義 Friendly Affection,
Ho 和 Harmony
ko 歌 }
tsze. 詞 } odes.

M. What is Chung?

Ho 何 What
wei 爲 is
Chung? 忠 Chung?

B. It is the fidelity of an officer of State.

Wei 爲 It is a
chin 臣 Minister
tsin 盡 entirely
Chung. 忠 faithful.

M. What is Heaou?

Ho 何 What
wei 爲 is
Heaou? 孝 Heaou?

B. It is a child fulfiling it's duty to it's parents.

Wei 爲 It is a
tsze 子 Son
tsin 盡 entirely
heaou. 孝 dutiful.

M. What is E?

Ho 何 What
wei 爲 is
E? 義 E?

B. Brothers must agree.

Heung 兄 }
te 弟 } Brothers
seu 須 must
e. 義 agree.

M. What is Ho?

Ho 何 What
wei 爲 is
ho? 和。 Ho?

B. Husband and wife should live in harmony.

Fōo 夫 Husband
fóo 婦 wife
tang 當 must
ho. 和。 harmonize.

M. That will pass. You may sing,—if you sing well, I will give you a little more.

Yay 也 Also
pa, 罷。 well,
ne 你 } you
mun 們 }
ts'heay 且 then
ch'hang 唱 sing
lae. 來。 come.
Jŏ 若 If
she 是 be
ch'hang 唱 } sung
tĭh 得 }
haou, 好。 well,
to 多 much
to 多 much

chow 週 } supply
tse 濟 }
ne 你 } you.
mun. 們。 }

B. All reply, Very well.

Ah. 吓。 Well.

B. Old man, the Squire orders us to sing the songs Chung, Heaou, E, and Ho, four hortatory songs. Though you are deaf and dumb, I will stand by your ear and sing loud, and do you move your head and feet to the timbrel.

Laou 老 } Old fellow
t'how 頭 }
urh 兒 }
Yuen 員 } the Squire
wae 外 }
fun 吩 } orders
foo 咐 }
hea 下 down
lae, 來 come,
keaou 叫 call
wo 我 } us
mun 們 }
ch'hang 唱 sing

| | | |
|---|---|---|
| Chung, | 忠 | Chung, |
| Heaou, | 孝 | Heaou, |
| E, | 義 | E, |
| Ho, | 和 | Ho, |
| sze | 四 | four |
| taou | 套 | |
| keuen | 勸 | hortatory |
| tsze; | 詞 | discourses; |
| ne | 你 | you |
| süy | 雖 | though |
| urh | 耳 | deaf, |
| lung, | 聾 | |
| shing | 聲 | dumb, |
| ya, | 啞 | |
| wo | 我 | I |
| tsae | 在 | at |
| ne | 你 | your |
| tëïh | 的 | |
| urh | 耳 | ear |
| pang | 傍 | side |
| kaou | 高 | loud |
| ch'hang, | 唱 | sing, |
| ne | 你 | you |
| k'ho | 可 | may |
| tseang | 將 | take |
| t'how | 頭 | head |
| keŏ | 脚 | feet |

| | | |
|---|---|---|
| gan | 接 | play the |
| pan, | 板 | boards, |
| tsew | 就 | just so. |
| she | 是 | |
| leaou. | 了 | |

M. Very well sung. Take five measures of white rice, and five tales of silver; give it to them, and let them go.

| | | |
|---|---|---|
| Ch'hang | 唱 | Sung |
| tïh | 得 | |
| haou. | 好 | well. |
| Tseang | 將 | Take |
| pïh | 白 | white |
| me | 米 | rice |
| woo | 五 | five |
| tow, | 斗 | tow, |
| yin | 銀 | money |
| tsze | 子 | |
| woo | 五 | five |
| leang, | 兩 | tales, |
| yu | 與 | give |
| t'ha | 他 | them |
| mun | 們 | |
| k'heu | 去 | go |
| pa. | 罷 | enough. |

S. Very well.

| | | |
|---|---|---|
| Ah. | 吓 | Yes. |

S. This is the Squire's gift to you. He gives you five measures of fine rice, and five tales in money.

| | | |
|---|---|---|
| Chay | 這 | This |
| she | 是 | is the |
| Yuen | 員 | Squire |
| wae | 外 | |
| yu | 與 | give |
| ne | 你 | you, |
| mun | 們 | |
| tëĭh, | 的 | |
| pĭh | 白 | white |
| me | 米 | rice |
| woo | 五 | five |
| tow, | 斗。 | tow, |
| yin | 銀 | money |
| tsze | 子 | |
| woo | 五 | five |
| leang, | 両 | tales, |
| yu | 與 | give |
| ne | 你 | you. |
| mun. | 們 | |

B. Many thanks to the Squire. Old Comrade, it is going to rain.

| | | |
|---|---|---|
| To | 多 | Many |
| seay | 謝 | thanks |
| Yuen- | 員 | Squire. |
| wae. | 外。 | |
| Laou | 老 | Old |
| ho | 夥 | companion |
| ke, | 計 | |
| t'hëen | 天 | heaven |
| yaou | 要 | wants to |
| hea | 下 | rain. |
| yu | 雨 | |
| leaou. | 了。 | |

— Many thanks to the Squire. Ah-ya! old man it is going to rain. Let us walk faster a little.

| | | |
|---|---|---|
| To | 多 | Many |
| seay | 謝 | thanks |
| Yuen | 員 | Squire. |
| wae. | 外。 | |
| Ah- | 阿 | Ah-ya! |
| ya! | 呀 | |
| laou | 老 | old fellow, |
| t'how | 頭 | |
| urh, | 兒。 | |
| t'hëen | 天 | heaven |
| yaou | 要 | wants |
| hea | 下 | down |
| yu | 雨 | rain, |
| leaou, | 了。 | |

| | | |
|---|---|---|
| kwae | 快 | faster |
| seay | 些 | a little |
| tsow | 走 | go |
| pa. | 罷。 | well. |

B. Let us walk faster a little.

| | | |
|---|---|---|
| Wo | 我 | We |
| tsow | 走 | walk |
| kwae | 快 | faster |
| seay | 些 | a little |
| pa. | 罷。 | well. |

# DIALOGUE XXVII.

## *TALE OF A COVETOUS MANDARIN ILLUSTRATED.*

A husbandman planted vegetables which died.

| | | |
|---|---|---|
| Yew | 有 | There was |
| nung-foo | 農夫 | a husbandman (who) |
| chung | 種 | planted |
| kay | 茄 | (the vegetable) kay |
| pŭh | 不 | not |
| hwă. | 活。 | live. |

He consulted with an old Gardener.

| | | |
|---|---|---|
| Kew | 求 | Begged |
| ke | 計 | a plan |
| yu | 于 | from |
| laou | 老 | an old |
| Poo. | 圃。 | Gardener. |

The Gardener said, this is an easy affair

| | | |
|---|---|---|
| Poo | 圃 | The Gardener |
| yuĕ, | 曰， | said, |
| tsze | 此 | this (is) |
| pŭh | 不 | not |
| nan. | 難。 | difficult. |

With every vegetable put down a piece of money, they will then live.

| | | |
|---|---|---|
| Mei | 每 | Each |

| | | |
|---|---|---|
| kay | 茄 | kay |
| shoo | 樹 | plant |
| hea | 下 | below |
| mae | 埋 | place |
| tsëen | 錢 | cash |
| yih | 一 | one number |
| wăn | 文 | |
| tsëĕ | 即 | then they (will) |
| hwă, | 活。 | live. |

He was asked the reason, he replied, (it is now the case, that) those who have money live; but those who have none are put to death.

| | | |
|---|---|---|
| Wan | 問 | Asked |
| k'he | 其 | the |
| koo, | 故。 | reason, |
| tă | 答 | answer |
| yew | 有 | have |
| tsëen | 錢 | money |
| chay | 者 | those who |
| săng, | 生。 | live, |
| woo | 無 | not have |
| tsëen | 錢 | money |
| chay | 者 | those who |
| sze. | 死。 | die. |

# DIALOGUE XXVIII.

## *MANDARIN RECEIVING BRIBE.*

A Mandarin extremely covetous, called before him one day, two Clients to examine them.

| | | |
|---|---|---|
| Yĭh | 一 | A |
| Kwăn | 官 | Mandarin |
| tsŭy | 最 | extremely |
| tan | 貪 | avaricious |
| yĭh | 一 | one |
| jĭh | 日 | day |
| keu | 拘 | brought |
| leang | 兩 | two |
| tsaou | 造 | Clients |
| tüy | 對 | opposite to |
| keü. | 鞫。 | examine. |

The Prosecutor bribed the Mandarin with fifty pieces of money.

| | | |
|---|---|---|
| Yuen-keaou | 原告 | The Prosecutor |
| kwei | 餽 | bribed |
| e | 以 | by |
| woo shĭh | 五十 | fifty (pieces of) |
| kin. | 金。 | gold. |

The Defendant hearing this, doubled the bribe.

| | | |
|---|---|---|
| Pei kaou | 被告 | The Defendant |
| wăn | 聞 | hearing |
| che | 之 | it |
| kea | 加 | added |
| pei | 倍 | a double |
| hwüy | 賄 | bribe |
| tŏ. | 托。 | to engage him on his [side. |

Till the moment that the trial came on, he made no inquiry.

| | | |
|---|---|---|
| Këĭh | 及 | At |

| | | |
|---|---|---|
| shin | 審 | trial |
| she | 時 | time |
| pŭh | 不 | not |
| wăn | 問 | ask the |
| tsing | 情 | circumstances. |
| yew. | 由。 | |

He made a signal, (drew out slips of wood, and threw them down) to beat the Prosecutor.

| | | |
|---|---|---|
| Chow | 抽 | Drew out the |
| tsëen | 籤 | Tsëen |
| king | 竟 | that (they) |
| ta | 打 | beat |
| yuen | 原 | the Plaintiff. |
| kaou. | 告。 | |

The Prosecutor held out his hand, and made a sign, saying, I have reason on my side.

| | | |
|---|---|---|
| Yuen | 原 | The Plaintiff |
| kaou | 告 | |
| tseang | 將 | took |
| show | 手 | hand |
| tsŏ | 作 | made |
| woo | 五 | five |
| shoo | 數 | number |
| she | 勢 | form |
| yuĕ, | 曰 | saying, |
| seaou | 小 | I |
| tëĭh | 的 | |
| she | 是 | am (he who) |
| yew | 有 | has |
| le | 理 | reason. |
| tëĭh. | 的。 | |

The Mandarin, also putting down his hand, said, You slave, you say *you* have reason!

| | | |
|---|---|---|
| Kwăn | 官 | The Mandarin |
| yĭh | 亦 | also |
| e | 以 | with |
| show | 手 | hand |
| fŭh | 覆 | put with the palm on [the table |
| yuĕ, | 曰。 | said, |
| noo | 奴 | you slave |
| tsae | 才 | |
| ne | 你 | you |
| keang | 講 | say |
| yew | 有 | have |
| le! | 理。 | reason! |

Then raising his hand, and turning the palm upwards, he said, He has more reason than you.

| | | |
|---|---|---|
| Yew | 又 | Further |
| e | 以 | with |
| show | 手 | hand |

| | | |
|---|---|---|
| yĭh | 一 | a |
| yang | 仰 | palm turned up |
| yuĕ, | 曰 | said, |
| t'ha | 他 | he |
| pe | 比 | compared with |
| ne | 你 | you |
| kăng | 更 | more |
| yew | 有 | has |
| le | 理 | reason. |
| loh. | 哩。 | |

# DIALOGUE XXIX.

## *THE MANDARIN AND GOLDSMITH.*

A Mandarin issued an advertisement for two pieces of virgin gold.

| | | |
|---|---|---|
| Yĭh | 一 | A |
| kwăn | 官 | Mandarin |
| ch'hŭh | 出 | issued |
| choo | 硃 | } an advertisement |
| peaou | 票 | |
| tseu | 取 | to obtain |
| chĭh | 赤 | carnation |
| kin | 金 | gold |
| urh | 二 | two |
| ting. | 錠。 | pieces. |

A shopman brought it, and was present in the hall to receive the price of it.

| | | |
|---|---|---|
| Poo | 鋪 | } Shopman |
| hoo | 戶 | |
| sung | 送 | } having presented it |
| këĕ | 訖 | |
| tang | 當 | was in the |
| tang | 堂 | hall to |
| ling | 領 | receive the |
| kea. | 價。 | price. |

The Mandarin asked how much was the price.

| | | |
|---|---|---|
| Kwăn | 官 | Mandarin |

wăn 問 asked
kea 價 price
chĭh 値 value
ke 幾 } how much?
ho? 何。

The Shopman said, the fair price is so much; but as you, Sir, want it, I will only take half the price.

Poo 舖 } Shopman
kea 家
yuĕ, 曰。 said,
ping 平 level
kea 價 price
keae 該 ought to be
jŏ 若 } so much,
kan, 干。
kĭn 今 } now
joo 如
he 係 it is
Laou 老 } You, Sir,
yay 爺
tseu 取 obtain it to
yung, 用。 use,
chĭh 只 only
ling 領 receive
pan 半 half the
kea 價 price

k'ho 可 } will do.
yay. 也。

The Mandarin, looking at those on his left and right, said, As it is thus, give him a piece back again in payment.

Kwăn 官 Mandarin
koo 顧 looking
tso 左 left
yew 右 right
yuĕ, 曰。 said,
chay 這 } as it is thus,
tăng 等
fă 發 throw back
yĭh 一 one
ting 錠 piece and
hwan 還 pay
t'ha. 他。 him.

They gave him the gold.

Fă 發 Gave back
kin. 金。 the gold.

After this, the Shopman yet waited to receive the price.

How 後 afterwards the
Poo- 舖 } Shopman
hoo 戶
ying 仍 still

2 F

how 候 waited to
ling 領 receive the
kea. 價。 price.

The Mandarin said, I have already given you the price.

Kwǎn 官 Mandarin
yuě, 曰。 said,
kea 價 price
e 已 already
fǎ 發 } have given over to you.
kwo 過 }
leaou. 了。 }

The Shopman said, It has not yet been given.

Poo 舖 } Shopman
kea 家 }
yuě, 曰。 said,
ping 並 still
we 未 not
tsǎng 曾 yet
fǎ. 發。 issued.

The Mandarin in a passion said, You villain,—you said you would take only half the price, and hence I gave you a piece back again, and thereby paid you half the price. I have nót injured you, what do you bother about.—Make haste and turn him out.

Kwǎn 官 Mandarin
noo 怒 in anger
yuě, 曰。 said,
teaou 刁 you rascally
noo 奴 } slave;
tsae; 才。 }
ne 你 you
shwǒ 說 said
chǐh 只 only
ling 領 receive
pan 半 half
kea, 價 price,
koo 故 therefore
fǎ 發 threw back
yǐh 一 a
ting 錠 piece to
hwan 還 pay
ne, 你。 you,
te 抵 } it answers
leaou 了 }
yǐh 一 one
pan 半 half
kea 價 } the price.
tsëen. 錢。 }

| | | | | | |
|---|---|---|---|---|---|
| Pun | 本 | } I | hoo | 胡 | } bother. |
| hëen | 縣 | | chen. | 纏 | |
| pŭh | 不 | not | Kwae | 快 | Haste |
| tsăng | 會 | yet | kwae | 快 | haste |
| kwei | 虧 | injured | nëen | 攆 | drive (him) |
| ne. | 你。 | you. | ch'hŭh | 出 | out |
| Joo | 如 | } Why | k'heu. | 去。 | go. |
| ho | 何 | | | | |

# DIALOGUE XXX.

## *A DOCTOR TAKING LEAVE OF HIS NEIGHBOURS.*

A Surgeon who was going to remove, said to his neighbours, I have hitherto given you much trouble, and now on parting, have nothing to give in token of respect. I will present to each of you a patch of medicine.

| | | | | | |
|---|---|---|---|---|---|
| Yĭh | 一 | A | keu | 居 | dwelling |
| E | 醫 | Doctor | wei | 謂 | addressed |
| tsëen | 遷 | moving | sze | 四 | four * |
| | | | lin | 鄰 | neighbours |
| | | | yuĕ, | 曰。 | saying, |
| | | | hëang | 向 | } hitherto |
| | | | lae | 來 | |
| | | | ta | 打 | } given you much trouble, |
| | | | keaou, | 攪。 | |

* Four, denotes four sides, it often occurs all around.

| | | |
|---|---|---|
| woo | 無 | no- |
| wŭh | 物 | thing |
| k'ho | 可 | can |
| tso | 做 | make |
| pëĭh | 別 | seperating |
| king, | 敬。 | respect, |
| mei | 每 | each |
| wei | 位 | person |
| fung | 奉 | present |
| yŏ | 藥 | medicine |
| yĭh | 一 | one paper. |
| tëĭh. | 帖。 | |

The neighbours excused themselves by saying, that they had no complaint.

| | | |
|---|---|---|
| Lin | 鄰 | The neighbours |
| shay | 舍 | |
| tsze | 辭 | declined |
| e | 以 | by |
| woo | 無 | not |
| ping. | 病。 | sick. |

The Doctor said, only take my physic, and I will warrant you will soon be ill enough.

| | | |
|---|---|---|
| E | 醫 | The Doctor |
| yuĕ, | 曰。 | said, |
| tan | 但 | but |
| këĭh | 吃 | take (eat) |
| leaou | 了 | |
| wo | 我 | my |
| tëĭh | 的 | |
| yŏ, | 藥。 | physic, |
| tsze | 自 | indeed |
| jen | 然 | |
| hwŭy | 會 | happen |
| săng | 生 | produce |
| k'he | 起 | up |
| ping | 病 | disease |
| lae. | 來。 | come. |

# DIALOGUE XXXI.

## POOR WOMAN INVITING A PERSON TO DINNER.

This is already the library door.—
Open the door, open the door.

| | | |
|---|---|---|
| Tsze | 此 | This |
| këen | 間 | |
| e | 已 | already |
| she | 是 | is |
| shoo | 書 | book |
| fang | 房 | room |
| mun | 門 | door |
| show | 首 | head. |
| leaou. | 了。 | |
| k'hae | 開 | Open |
| mun, | 門。 | door, |
| k'hae | 開 | open |
| mun. | 門。 | door. |

Who is there?

| | | |
|---|---|---|
| She | 是 | Is |
| na | 那 | which |
| ko | 個 | |
| lae | 來 | comes? |
| leaou? | 了。 | |

Open the door.

| | | |
|---|---|---|
| K'hae | 開 | Open |
| mun. | 門。 | door. |

Mr. Ch'hang.

| | | |
|---|---|---|
| Ch'hang | 張 | Ch'hang |
| Sëen | 先 | Mr. |
| sǎng. | 生。 | |

Oh! it is Hung-neang-tseay, walk in and sit down.

| | | |
|---|---|---|
| Ah, | 吓。 | Oh, |
| yuen | 原 | proves |
| lae | 來 | |
| she | 是 | to be |
| Hung- | 紅 | Hung-neang-tseay, |
| neang- | 娘 | |
| tseay, | 姐 | |
| ts'hing | 請 | pray |

taou 到 go to
le 裡 } inside
mëen 面 }
tso. 坐。 sit.

Master, my respects.

Sëen 先 } Master,
săng, 生 }
ts'hing. 請。 pray.

Hung-neang-tseay, my respects.

Hung- 紅 }
neang- 娘 } Hung-neang-tseay,
tseay, 姐 }
ts'hing. 請。 pray.

Master, ten thousand blessings.

Sëen 先 } Master
săng 生 }
wan 萬 ten thousand
fŭh. 福。 happiness.

Hung-neang-tseay, on what business have you come here?

Hung- 紅 }
neang- 娘 } Hung-neang-tseay,
tseay, 姐。 }
taou 到 to
tsze 此 this
ho 何 what
kan? 幹。 business?

I have received my husband's order to come and invite you to dinner.

Fung 奉 Received
laou 老 old
foo 夫 } husband
jin 人 }
che 之 's
ming, 命。 order,
chŏ 着 sending
wo 我 me to
lae 來 come to
ts'hing 請 invite
Sëen 先 } Master.
săng 生 }
foo 赴 to go
sëĭh. 席。 table.

Oh, to invite me to dinner.—As it is so, I will go.

Ah, 吓。 Oh,
ts'hing 請 invite
wo 我 me
foo 赴 to go to
sëĭh, 席。 table,
joo 如 } thus
tsze 此 }
tsew 就 then
k'heu. 去。 go.

Pray sit down.

Ts'hing 請 Pray
tso. 坐。 sit.

I will sit down.

Yew 有 Have
tso. 坐。 sit.

Pray Hung-neang-tseay, on what account is this entertainment made?

Ts'hing 請 Beg to
wăn 問 ask
Hung-neang-tseay, 紅娘姐。 Hung-neang-tseay,
tsze 此 this
tsew 酒 wine
wei ho 爲何 why
urh 而 and
shĕ? 設。 appointed?

As an acknowledgement.

Yin 因 Because
seay ching. 謝承。 giving thanks.

What have you for dinner?

Pae 擺 Arranged
shĕ mo 什麽 what
yen seĭh? 筵席。 feast?

We have killed a sheep, have tea and rice.

Shă 殺 Killed
yang, 羊 sheep,
ch'ha 茶 tea
fan. 飯。 rice.

What other Guests have you?

Hwan 還 Besides
ts'hing 請 invite
ho 何 what
kĭh? 客。 guest?

No relations nor neighbours.

Pŭh 不 Not
hwŭy 會 meet
tsin 親 relations
lin. 鄰。 neighbours.

What have you invited me by myself?

Nan 難 Hard to
taou, 道。 say,
keaou 叫 call
wo 我 me
tŏ 獨 alone
chŏ 酌 to pour out
mo? 麽。 ?

I find I am called to make up a match, I am extremely glad.

| | | |
|---|---|---|
| Yuen | 原 | Original first |
| lae | 來 | |
| ts'hing | 請 | invite |
| wo | 我 | me |
| k'heu | 去 | to go to |
| tso | 做 | make |
| tsin, | 親 | relations, |
| wo | 我 | I |
| haou | 好 | will |
| kwae | 快 | prompt |
| hwă | 活 | alive. |
| yay. | 也 | |

Master, Why are you looking on the ground, and going backwards and forwards?

| | | |
|---|---|---|
| Sëen | 先 | Master |
| săng | 生 | |
| wei | 爲 | why |
| ho | 何 | |
| k'han | 看 | look |
| leaou | 了 | |
| te | 地 | ground |
| hea, | 下 | below, |
| chĭh | 只 | trying to |
| kwăn | 管 | |
| tsow | 走 | walk |
| lae | 來 | come |
| tsow | 走 | walk |
| k'heu. | 去 | go. |

Where I am, there is no looking glass I am only borrowing the light of the sun to reflect my shadow.

| | | |
|---|---|---|
| Kĭh | 客 | Guest |
| pëen | 邊 | side |
| fă | 乏 | wants a |
| king, | 鏡 | glass, |
| leaou | 聊 | merely |
| tseay | 借 | borrowing |
| t'hëen | 天 | heaven's |
| kwang | 光 | light |
| e | 以 | to |
| chaou | 照 | reflect |
| wo | 我 | my |
| ying. | 影 | shadow. |

# SENTENCES.

IT is better to educate a Son than accumulate riches for him.

| | | |
|---|---|---|
| Kwang | 廣 | Extensively |
| tsëĭh | 積 | accumulate |
| pŭh | 不 | not |
| joo | 如 | so good as to |
| keaou | 教 | teach |
| tsze. | 子。 | a son. |

—

To examine one's errors, is better than to (flee from, or) avoid being injured.

| | | |
|---|---|---|
| Pëĭh | 避 | Elude |
| ho | 禍 | misery |
| pŭh | 不 | not |
| joo | 如 | so good as to |
| sing | 省 | examine |
| fei. | 非。 | errors. |

What is easily obtained is easily lost: what is obtained with difficulty, is with difficulty parted with.

| | | |
|---|---|---|
| Tĭh | 得 | Obtain |
| che | 之 | it |
| e, | 易。 | easy, |
| shĭh | 失 | lose |
| che | 之 | it |
| e; | 易。 | easy; |
| tĭh | 得 | obtain |
| che | 之 | it |
| nan, | 難。 | difficult, |
| shĭh | 失 | lose |
| che | 之 | it |
| nan. | 難。 | difficult. |

—

A fool dreads his wife: a good wife respects her husband.

| | | |
|---|---|---|
| Che | 痴 | Foolish |
| jin | 人 | man |
| wei | 畏 | dreads |
| foo : | 婦 | wife : |
| hëen | 賢 | virtuous |
| neu | 女 | woman |
| king | 敬 | respects |
| foo. | 夫。 | husband. |

---

He who is ungrateful, is not a man.

| | | |
|---|---|---|
| Yew | 有 | Have |
| găn | 恩 | favor |
| pùh | 不 | not |
| paou, | 報。 | recompensed, |
| fei | 非 | not |
| wei | 爲 | is |
| jin | 人 | man. |
| yay. | 也。 | |

---

When a word is uttered, four horses cannot overtake it.

| | | |
|---|---|---|
| Yĭh | 一 | One |
| yen | 言 | word |
| ke | 旣 | when |
| ch'hŭh, | 出。 | uttered, |
| sze | 四 | four |
| ma | 馬 | horses |
| nan | 難 | cannot |
| chuy. | 追。 | overtake it. |

---

(Confucius said,) The Mechanic that would perfect his work, must first sharpen his tools.

| | | |
|---|---|---|
| Kung | 工 | Workman |
| yŏ | 欲 | wishing |
| shen | 善 | to do well |
| k'he | 其 | his |
| sze, | 事。 | business, |
| pĕĭh | 必 | must |
| seen | 先 | first |
| le | 利 | sharpen |
| k'he | 其 | his |
| ke. | 器。 | tools. |

---

Confucius said, The expectations of life depend on diligence; the hopes of the year depend on the Spring; the hopes of a day on the morning.

| | | |
|---|---|---|
| Tsze | 子 | Confucius |
| yuĕ, | 曰。 | said, |
| yĭh | 一 | a |
| săng | 生 | life |
| che | 之 | 's |
| ke | 計 | plans |

| | | |
|---|---|---|
| tsae | 在 | rest |
| yu | 於 | on |
| kin; | 勤 | diligence; |
| yĭh | 一 | a |
| nëen | 年 | year |
| che | 之 | ' |
| ke | 計 | scheme |
| tsae | 在 | rests |
| yu | 於 | on |
| Chun; | 春 | Spring; |
| yĭh | 一 | a |
| jĭh | 日 | day |
| che | 之 | 's |
| ke | 計 | work |
| tsae | 在 | rests |
| yu | 於 | on |
| yin. | 寅 | morning, (from 3 to 5) |

---

If youth be without learning, old age will know nothing; he that does not plough in Spring, can hope for nothing in Autumn; he that does not rise early will do little all day.

| | | |
|---|---|---|
| Yew | 幼 | Young |
| urh | 而 | and |
| pŭh | 不 | not |
| heŏ, | 學 | learn, |
| laou | 老 | old |
| woo | 無 | not |
| so | 所 | any thing |
| che; | 知 | know; |
| Chun | 春 | Spring |
| jŏ | 若 | if |
| pŭh | 不 | not |
| kăng, | 耕 | plough, |
| Tsew | 秋 | Autumn |
| woo | 無 | not |
| so | 所 | any thing to |
| wăng; | 望 | hope; |
| yin | 寅 | early |
| jŏ | 若 | if |
| pŭh | 不 | not |
| k'he, | 起 | rise, |
| jĭh | 日 | day |
| woo | 無 | not |
| so | 所 | any thing |
| pan. | 辦 | accomplish. |

---

To bring up a child without education is the crime of a father: to educate without due severity is thought the sloth of a master.

| | | |
|---|---|---|
| Yang | 養 | Feed a |
| tsze | 子 | child |

| | | |
|---|---|---|
| pŭh | 不 | not |
| keaou, | 教 | teach, |
| foo | 父 | father |
| che | 之 | 's |
| kwo: | 過 | error: |
| heun | 訓 | teach |
| taou | 導 | |
| pŭh | 不 | not |
| yen, | 嚴 | duly severe, |
| sze | 師 | master |
| che | 之 | 's |
| to. | 惰 | sloth. |

Every thing is from heaven, do not seek to obtain by violence.

| | | |
|---|---|---|
| Wan | 萬 | Ten thousand |
| sze | 事 | affairs |
| yew | 由 | from |
| t'hëen, | 天 | heaven, |
| mŏ | 莫 | not |
| keang | 強 | violently |
| kew. | 求 | to be sought. |

With peace in a family, poverty is good:—without justice, what is the use of riches!

| | | |
|---|---|---|
| Kea | 家 | Family at |
| ho | 和 | peace |
| pin | 貧 | poverty |
| yay | 也 | is |
| haou: | 好 | good: |
| pŭh | 不 | not |
| e | 義 | just |
| foo | 富 | riches |
| ho | 何 | what? |
| joo? | 如 | |

He who wishes to know the future, must examine the past.

| | | |
|---|---|---|
| Yŏ | 欲 | Desire to |
| che | 知 | know |
| we | 未 | not |
| lae, | 來 | come, |
| sëen | 先 | first |
| chă | 察 | examine |
| e | 已 | already |
| wang. | 往 | past. |

Propriety bounds the good man: laws the mean one.

| | | |
|---|---|---|
| Le | 禮 | Propriety |
| fang | 防 | guards or bounds |
| keun | 君 | the good man: |
| tsze: | 子 | |

| | | |
|---|---|---|
| leŭ | 律 | laws |
| fang | 防 | bound |
| seaou | 小 | the worthless man. |
| jin. | 人 | |

—

Confucius said, Do not be in too much haste,—do not regard a trifling advantage. If you be in too much haste you cannot understand,—if you regard a trifling advantage you will effect nothing great.

| | | |
|---|---|---|
| Tsze | 子 | Confucius |
| yuĕ, | 曰 | said, |
| woo | 無 | not |
| yŏ | 欲 | desire |
| sŏ, | 速 | haste, |
| woo | 無 | not |
| këen | 見 | look at |
| seaou | 小 | little |
| le. | 利 | gain. |
| Yŏ | 欲 | Desire |
| sŏ | 速 | haste |
| tsĭh | 則 | then |
| pŭh | 不 | not |
| tă, | 達 | understand, |
| këen | 見 | look at |
| seaou | 小 | little |
| le, | 利 | gain, |
| tsĭh | 則 | then |
| ta | 大 | great |
| sze | 事 | affairs |
| pŭh | 不 | not |
| ching. | 成 | effect. |

—

Specious words destroy Virtue: not to bear with little things, will ruin great affairs.

| | | |
|---|---|---|
| Keaou | 巧 | Artful |
| yen | 言 | words |
| lwan | 亂 | throw into confusion |
| tĭh: | 德 | virtue: |
| seaou | 小 | little |
| pŭh | 不 | not |
| jin, | 忍 | bear, |
| tsĭh | 則 | then |
| lwan | 亂 | confuse |
| ta | 大 | great |
| mow. | 謀 | affairs. |

—

Men's passions are like water,—when water is spilled it cannot be taken up again: when the passions are let loose, they cannot be restrained.

| | | |
|---|---|---|
| Jin | 人 | Man's |

sing 性 passions
joo 如 as
shwŭy, 水 water,
shwŭy 水 water
yĭh 一 once
king, 傾 thrown out,
tsĭh 則 then
pùh 不 not
k'ho 可 can be
fùh: 復 restored.
sing 性 passions
yĭh 一 once
tsung, 縱 let loose,
tsĭh 則 then
pùh 不 not
k'ho 可 can
fan. 反 turned back.

---

He who can bend himself, will be able to deal with every body: he who delights to conquer will meet with an enemy.

Keuĕ 屈 Bend
ke 己 himself
chay 者 who does
năng 能 able
choo 處 manage
chung: 衆 all:
haou 好 love to
shing 勝 overcome
chay 者 who does
pëĭh 必 must
yu 遇 meet
tëĕ. 敵 an enemy.

---

Laou-tsze said, A superior man does not wrangle: an inferior Person delights in it.

Laou- 老 } Laou-tsze
tsze 子 }
yuĕ, 曰 said,
shang 上 Superior
sze 士 scholar
woo 無 not
tsăng: 爭 wrangle:
hea 下 inferior
sze 士 scholar
haou 好 likes to
tsăng. 爭 wrangle.

---

It is said in the Le-ke, A stone not cut, forms no gem: the man who does not learn, is ignorant of good principles.

| | | |
|---|---|---|
| Le- | 禮 | Le-king |
| ke | 記 | |
| yun, | 云。 | says, |
| yŭh | 玉 | gem |
| pŭh | 不 | not |
| chŭh, | 琢。 | cut, |
| pŭh | 不 | not |
| ching | 成 | form |
| ke: | 器。 | utensil: |
| jin | 人 | man |
| pŭh | 不 | not |
| heŏ, | 學。 | learn, |
| pŭh | 不 | not |
| che | 知 | know |
| taou. | 道。 | reason. |

---

Han-wăn-kung said, A man without knowledge, differs from a brute only in being clothed.

| | | |
|---|---|---|
| Han- | 韓 | Han-wăn-kung |
| wăn- | 文 | |
| kung | 公 | |
| yuĕ, | 曰。 | said, |
| jin | 人 | a man |
| pŭh | 不 | not |
| t'hung | 通 | know the |
| koo | 古 | past the |
| kin, | 今。 | present, (is a) |
| ma | 馬 | horse or |
| new | 牛 | cow |
| urh | 而 | and |
| kin | 襟 | breeched. |
| keu. | 裾。 | |

---

Wăn-kung said, He who wishes to measure (judge) another man, should first measure himself. Language that hurts another man, will hurt one's self. He that takes blood into his mouth to spurt at another Person, first defiles his own mouth.

| | | |
|---|---|---|
| Wăn- | 文 | Wăn-kung |
| kung | 公 | |
| yuĕ, | 曰。 | said, |
| yŏ | 欲 | desire |
| leang | 量 | to measure |
| t'ha | 他 | other |
| jin, | 人。 | man, |
| sëen | 先 | first |
| seu | 須 | must |
| tsze | 自 | himself |
| leang. | 量。 | measure. |
| Shang | 傷 | Hurt |
| jin | 人 | men |

| | | |
|---|---|---|
| che | 之 | the |
| yu, | 語. | words, |
| hwan | 還 | revert |
| she | 是 | will |
| tsze | 自 | self |
| shang. | 傷. | hurt. |
| Han | 含 | To hold in the mouth |
| heuĕ | 血 | blood to |
| pun | 噴 | spurt at |
| jin, | 人. | men, |
| sëen | 先 | first |
| woo | 污 | dirties |
| tsze | 自 | own |
| k'how. | 口. | mouth. |

—

Cease to regret that the ground before you is narrow: retire or recede a step, and you will find it broad enough.

| | | |
|---|---|---|
| Hew | 休 | Cease |
| hăn | 恨 | to be indignant |
| yen | 眼 | eye |
| ts'hëen | 前 | before |
| tëen | 田 | ground |
| te | 地 | (ground) |
| tsĕ: | 窄. | narrow: |
| sŭy | 退 | retire |
| how | 後 | back |
| yĭh | 一 | a |
| poo | 步 | step |
| tsze | 自 | indeed |
| jen | 然 | (indeed) |
| kwăn. | 寬. | broad. |

—

With the heart at rest, a shed-cot is good: with the mind composed, the roots of vegetables are fragrant.

| | | |
|---|---|---|
| Sin | 心 | Heart |
| gan | 安 | at ease |
| maou | 茅 | mat-shed |
| ŏ | 屋 | (mat-shed) |
| wăn: | 穩. | is safe: |
| sing | 性 | mind |
| ting | 定 | settled, |
| tsae | 菜 | vegetables |
| kan | 根 | roots |
| heang. | 香. | fragrant. |

—

Long or short life are unquestionably decreed: poverty or sickness, both have their times.

| | | |
|---|---|---|
| Show | 壽 | Long life |
| yaou | 夭 | short life |
| mŏ | 莫 | not |

| | | |
|---|---|---|
| fei | 非 | not |
| ming; | 命。 | decreed; |
| keung | 窮 | poverty |
| t'hung | 通 | success |
| kŏ | 各 | all |
| yew | 有 | have |
| she. | 時。 | time. |

Confucius said, Let your thoughts be pure.

| | | |
|---|---|---|
| Tsze | 子 | Confucius said, |
| yuĕ, | 曰。 | |
| sze | 思 | thought |
| woo | 無 | not |
| seay. | 邪。 | licentious.* |

Choo-foo-tsze said, Keep your mouth like a bottle; guard your thougths like a city. Stories of right and wrong arise from too frequently opening the mouth; uneasiness and anger are all from being too forward.

| | | |
|---|---|---|
| Choo- | 朱 | Choo-tsze |
| tsze | 子 | |
| yuĕ, | 曰。 | said, |
| show | 守 | keep |
| k'how | 口 | mouth |
| joo | 如 | as |
| ping, | 瓶。 | bottle, |
| fang | 防 | guard |
| e | 意 | thought |
| joo | 如 | as |
| ching. | 城。 | city. |
| She | 是 | Right |
| fei | 非 | wrong |
| chĭh | 只 | only |
| wei | 爲 | because |
| to | 多 | often |
| k'hae | 開 | open |
| k'how, | 口。 | mouth, |
| fan | 煩 | trouble |
| naou | 惱 | anger |
| keae | 皆 | all |
| yin | 因 | because |
| keang | 強 | force |
| ch'hŭh | 出 | out |
| t'how. | 頭。 | head. |

Cover men's bad actions, and proclaim their good ones.

* This is quite a standard quotation. It was applied by Confucius to the Odes which he collected; some of which are of a rather dubious character; and hence the Philosopher's caution.

2 H

| | | |
|---|---|---|
| Yen | 掩 | Shade |
| gŏ | 惡 | evil |
| yang | 揚 | promulge |
| shen. | 善。 | good. |

---

He who deceives others, deceives his own heart

| | | |
|---|---|---|
| Ke | 欺 | Deceive |
| jin | 人 | men |
| pëĭh | 必 | must |
| tsze | 自 | himself |
| ke | 己 | |
| ke | 欺 | deceive |
| sin. | 心。 | heart. |

---

Men may be deceived, Heaven cannot be deceived: things may be hid from men, they cannot be hid from Heaven.

| | | |
|---|---|---|
| Jin | 人 | Man |
| k'ho | 可 | may |
| ke, | 欺。 | be deceived, |
| T'hëen | 天 | Heaven |
| pŭh | 不 | not |
| k'ho | 可 | can |
| ke: | 欺。 | be deceived; |
| jin | 人 | man |
| k'ho | 可 | may |
| mwan, | 瞞。 | be kept ignorant of, |
| T'hëen | 天 | heaven |
| pŭh | 不 | not |
| k'ho | 可 | can |
| mwan. | 瞞。 | be kept ignorant of. |

---

When the heart of man conceives a thought, Heaven and Earth fully know it.

| | | |
|---|---|---|
| Jin | 人 | Man's |
| sin | 心 | heart |
| săng | 生 | produce |
| yĭh | 一 | a |
| nëen, | 念。 | thought, |
| T'hëen | 天 | Heaven |
| te | 地 | earth * |
| sëĭh | 悉 | fully |
| keae | 皆 | both |
| che. | 知。 | know. |

---

Bring up a child, and you will then know the goodness of parents.

* Their introducing Earth together with Heaven, causes a strange confusion of ideas.

| | | |
|---|---|---|
| Yang | 養 | Bring up |
| tsze | 子 | a child |
| fang | 方 | then |
| che | 知 | know |
| foo | 父 | father |
| moo | 母 | mother's |
| găn. | 恩 | goodness. |

———

Confucius said, Under the five modes of Punishment, there are three thousand crimes; but there is no crime greater than undutifulness to Parents.

| | | |
|---|---|---|
| Tsze | 子 | Confucius |
| yuĕ, | 曰 | said, |
| woo | 五 | five |
| hing | 刑 | punishment |
| che | 之 | 's [ed under) are |
| shŏ | 屬 | related to (i. e. includ- |
| san | 三 | three |
| tsëen: | 千 | thousand: |
| urh | 而 | and |
| tsŏy | 罪 | crime |
| mŏ | 莫 | not |
| ta | 大 | greater |
| yu | 於 | than |
| pŭh | 不 | undutifulness to |
| heaou. | 孝 | parents. |

Măng-tsze said, He who subjects People by force, does not subject the heart: he who subjects People by goodness, delights their hearts,—this is real subjection.

| | | |
|---|---|---|
| Măng- | 孟 | Mencius |
| tsze | 子 | |
| yuĕ, | 曰 | said, |
| e | 以 | by |
| lëih | 力 | force |
| fŭh | 服 | to subject |
| jin | 人 | men, |
| chay, | 者 | |
| fei | 非 | is not |
| sin | 心 | heart |
| fŭh | 服 | subjected: |
| yay: | 也 | |
| e | 以 | by |
| tĭh | 德 | virtue |
| fŭh | 服 | to subject |
| jin | 人 | men, |
| chay, | 者 | |
| chung | 中 | middle |
| sin | 心 | heart |
| yuĕ, | 悅 | pleased, |
| urh | 而 | and |
| ching | 誠 | in truth |

fŭh 服 } subjected.
yay. 也。

—

Laou-tsze* said, Many desires wound the soul: much wealth involves the body.

Laou-tsze 老子 } Leaou-tsze
yuĕ, 曰、 said,
yŏ 慾 desires
to 多 many
shang 傷 wound
shin: 神。 the spirit:
tsae 財 wealth
to 多 much
lŭy 累 involves
shin. 身。 the body

—

Contentment is a continual feast.

Che 知 To know (one has)
tsŭh 足 sufficient, is †
chang 常 constant
lŏ. 樂。 joy.

Confucius said, He that does good, Heaven will reward him with happiness: he that does evil, Heaven will recompense him with misery.

Kung-Tsze 孔子 } Confucius
yüe, 曰。 said,
wei 爲 do
shen 善 good
chay 者 he who
t'hëen 天 heaven
paou 報 recompense
che 之 him
e 以 with
fŭh: 福。 happiness,
wei 爲 do
pŭh 不 not
shen 善 good
chay 者 he who
t'hëen 天 heaven
paou 報 recompense
che 之 him
e 以 with
ho. 禍。 misery.

* Laou-tsze, the well-known founder of the Sect called Taou-tsze. He lived in the time of Confucius. He said of himself, or others said for him, that he had a pre-existence.

† The two first words denote feeling satisfied.

Goodness has a good recompense, evil an evil recompense: if there be no recompense, the time is not yet arrived.

| | | |
|---|---|---|
| Shen | 善 | Goodness |
| yew | 有 | has |
| shen | 善 | good |
| paou, | 報。 | recompense, |
| gŏ | 惡 | wickedness |
| yew | 有 | have |
| gŏ | 惡 | bad |
| paou: | 報。 | recompense: |
| jŏ | 若 | if |
| hwan | 還 | still |
| pŭh | 不 | not |
| paou, | 報。 | recompensed |
| she | 時 | the time |
| shin | 辰 | (the time) |
| we | 未 | is not |
| taou. | 到。 | arrived. |

———

When goodness or sin have come to an issue, they will finally be recompensed: though you fly high or travel far, it will be difficult to elude it, (the recompense).

| | | |
|---|---|---|
| Shen | 善 | Goodness |
| gŏ | 惡 | evil |
| taou | 到 | brought to |
| t'how, | 頭。 | a head, |
| chung | 終 | at last |
| yew | 有 | have |
| paou: | 報。 | recompense: |
| kaou | 高 | high |
| fei | 飛 | fly |
| yuen | 遠 | remote |
| tsow, | 走。 | go, |
| yay | 也 | yet |
| nan | 難 | difficult |
| taou. | 逃。 | to escape. |

———

Măng-tsze said, He who obeys Heaven will be recompensed; he who opposes Heaven will be destroyed.

| | | |
|---|---|---|
| Măng- | 孟 | Mencius |
| tsze | 子 | (Mencius) |
| yun, | 云 | said, |
| shun | 順。 | obey |
| t'hëen | 天 | heaven |
| chay | 者 | they who |
| tsun: | 存。 | preserved: |
| yĭh | 逆 | oppose |
| t'hëen | 天 | heaven |
| chay | 者 | they who |

wang. 亡。 perish.

---

Confucius said, He who sins against Heaven, has nothing to plead (by which he can obtain forgiveness.)

Tsze 子 Confucius
yuĕ, 曰。 said,
hwŏ 獲 incur
tsŭy 罪 offence
yu 於 towards
t'hëen, 天。 Heaven:
woo 無 (there are) not
so 所 those who
taou 禱 plead.
yay. 也。

---

Tsze-hea said, Whether death or life, it is appointed. Riches and honors depend on the will of Heaven.

Tsze-hea 子夏 Tsze-hea
yuĕ, 曰 said,
sze 死 death
săng 生 life
yew 有 have
ming 命。 decree.
Foo 富 Riches
kwei 貴 honors
tsae 在 are with
t'hëen. 天。 Heaven.

---

Choo-ko, the Woo-how, said, To plan is man's, to accomplish, Heaven's; man wishes thus, and thus, but the will of Heaven is not so.

Choo-kŏ, 諸葛。 Choo-kŏ,
Woo-how, 武侯。 the Woo-how,
yuĕ, 曰 said,
mow 謀 to plan
sze 事 affairs
tsae 在 is with
jin, 人。 man:
ching 成 to perfect
sze 事 affairs
tsae 在 is with
t'hëen: 天。 heaven:
jin 人 man
yuen 願 wishes
joo tsze, 如此。 thus,
joo tsze, 如此 thus,

| | | |
|---|---|---|
| T'hëen | 天 | Heaven's |
| le | 理 | government |
| we | 未 | not so, |
| jen, | 然。 | |
| we | 未 | not so. |
| jen. | 然。 | |

Full of diabolical schemes.

| | | |
|---|---|---|
| Mwan | 滿 | Full |
| too | 肚 | belly |
| pe | 皮 | skin |
| hwae | 懷 | cherishing |
| chŏ | 着 | |
| kwei | 鬼 | devil's |
| tae. | 胎。 | womb. |

Better the first in a village, than the second at Rome.

| | | |
|---|---|---|
| Ning | 寧 | Better |
| wei | 爲 | be a |
| ke | 雞 | fowl's |
| k'how, | 口。 | beak, |
| wŭh | 勿 | not |
| wei | 爲 | be |
| new | 牛 | a cow |
| how. | 後。 | behind. |

Do you twist and I will tie. *

| | | |
|---|---|---|
| Ne | 你 | You |
| new | 扭 | twist |
| wo | 我 | I |
| këĭh. | 結。 | tie. |

If it be uneven shave it level, if even let it alone.

| | | |
|---|---|---|
| Pŭh | 不 | Not |
| ping | 平 | level |
| tsĭh | 則 | then |
| seŏ, | 削。 | pare it: |
| ping | 平 | level |
| tsĭh | 則 | then |
| shay | 舍 | let it alone. |
| che. | 之。 | |

Disobeys the laws of the king, and does not dread the remarks of the village.

| | | |
|---|---|---|
| Pŭh | 不 | Not |
| tsun | 遵 | obey |
| wang | 王 | king's |
| fă, | 法。 | laws: |
| pŭh | 不 | not |
| wei | 畏 | fear |
| heang | 鄉 | village |

* This is a kind of threat, My conduct shall be as yours.

ping. 評 remarks.

—

A man will die for his friend.

Sze 士 A scholar
wei 爲 for (him)
che 知 know
ke 己 himself (friend)
chay 者 who
sze. 死 dies.

—

The pitcher goes down to the well once too often.

Wa 瓦 Earthen
kwan 礶 pitcher
pŭh 不 not
le 離 far removed from
sun 傷 } injury (at any time).
shang. 損 }

—

The eye of God is like the lightning's flash.

Shin 神 God's
mŭh 目 eye
joo 如 as
tëen 電 lightning's
kwang 光 } splendour.
yung. 熒 }

As the shadow follows the substance.

Joo 如 As
ying 影 shadow
sŭy 隨 follows
hing. 形 substance.

—

Persecute the wind and catch at a shadow.

Poo 捕 Persecute the
fung 風 wind
chŏ 捉 catch
ying. 影 a shadow.

—

Is it in this life or the next?

Hwan 還 Whether
she 是 is (it in)
kin 今 this
she, 世 age,
hwan 還 whether
she 是 is (it in)
lae 來 coming
săng? 生 life?

—

Adherence to trifles will injure great affairs.

Keu 拘 } To stick to
ne 泥 }

| | | |
|---|---|---|
| seaou | 小 | little |
| le | 禮 | ceremony |
| shang | 傷 | will wound |
| leaou | 了 | |
| ta | 大 | great |
| e. | 義。 | justice. |

---

If the drum be not beaten, it will not sound; if the bell be not struck, it will not ring.

| | | |
|---|---|---|
| Koo | 鼓 | Drum |
| pŭh | 不 | not |
| ta | 打 | struck |
| pŭh | 不 | not |
| hëang: | 响。 | sound: |
| chung | 鐘 | bell |
| pŭh | 不 | not |
| chwang | 撞 | knocked |
| pŭh | 不 | not |
| ming. | 鳴。 | ring. |

---

This sword is a match for your distaff; i. e. you are well suited.

| | | |
|---|---|---|
| K'he | 其 | His, or the |
| ke | 機 | pointed |
| fung | 鋒 | weapon |
| tsŏ | 作 | made |
| yung, | 用。 | use of, |
| chin | 眞 | truly |
| k'ho | 可 | may |
| yu | 與 | with |
| ne | 你 | your |
| chin | 針 | needle and |
| keae | 芥 | thorn |
| seang | 相 | mutually |
| tow. | 投。 | meet. |

---

Though that man be wrong, what he says is right.

| | | |
|---|---|---|
| K'he | 其 | That |
| jin | 人 | man |
| sŭy | 雖 | though |
| fei, | 非。 | wrong, |
| k'he | 其 | those |
| yen | 言 | words |
| tsĭh | 則 | are |
| she. | 是。 | right. |

# WEIGHTS AND MEASURES.

Parts of the Chinese Pound or Catty, called 斤 Kin.

| | | |
|---|---|---|
| Shĭh | 十 | Ten |
| hwŏ | 忽 | how |
| wei | 爲 | make |
| sze, | 絲 | a sze, |
| shĭh | 十 | ten |
| sze | 絲 | sze |
| haou, | 毫 | a haou, |
| shĭh | 十 | ten |
| haou | 毫 | haou |
| le, | 釐 | a le—a cash * |
| shĭh | 十 | ten |
| le | 厘 | le—cash |
| yĭh | 一 | a |
| fun, | 分 | fun—candareen, |
| shĭh | 十 | ten |
| fun | 分 | fun—candareens |
| yĭh | 一 | a |
| tsëen, | 錢 | tsëen—mace, |
| shĭh | 十 | ten |
| tsëen | 錢 | tsëen—mace |
| yĭh | 一 | a |
| leang, | 兩 | leang—tale. |
| shĭh | 十 | sixteen |
| lŭh | 六 | |
| leang | 兩 | tales |
| yĭh | 一 | a |
| kin, | 斤 | catty, |
| yĭh | 一 | a hundred |
| pĭh | 百 | |
| kin | 斤 | catty |
| yĭh | 一 | a |
| tan. | 担 | pecul. |

* Money is expressed by the same terms as the Weights; hence in the above, the usual epithets applied to Money are inserted opposite the Chinese Character.

**Parts of the 尺 Chĭh, or Cubit.**

Ten 分 Fun, make a 寸 Tsun.

Ten 寸 Tsun, make a 尺 Chĭh,

Ten 尺 Chĭh, make a 丈 Ch'hang,

Ten 丈 Ch'hang, make a 引 Yin.

---

MEASURE OF CONTENTS.

Ten 勺 Chŏ, make a 合 Hŏ,

Ten 合 Hŏ, make a 升 Shing, *

Ten 升 Shing, make a 斗 Tow.

Ten 斗 Tow, make a 斛 Hwŏ.

---

LAND MEASURE.

A 步 Poo, or Pace, is five 尺 Chĭh, or Cubits. One 步 Poo broad, and 440 Poo in length, make a 畝 Mow, or Acre. 360 Poo make a 里 Le, commonly called the Chinese mile.

## THE FORM OF AN ACCOUNT. †

初七日

魚十二両 艮[illegible]

鷄旦八只 艮[illegible]

賀蘭荳一斤艮[illegible]

牛油四両 艮[illegible]

共艮三錢〇五

| | | | M. | C. | C. |
|---|---|---|---|---|---|
| 7th. | | | | | |
| | To twelve Tales of Fish, | —— —— —— | 0 | 7 | 5 |
| | To eight Eggs, | —— —— —— | 0 | 4 | 0 |
| | To a catty of Peas, | —— —— —— | 0 | 7 | 0 |
| | To four tales of Butter, | —— —— | 1 | 2 | 0 |
| | | Total, | 3 | 0 | 5 |

* About a pint.

† In keeping Accounts they use numerous contractions. Below the Article they every time repeat the word Money, as if they would say, 'Amounting to,' &c. The Character is 銀 Yin, 'Silver, money; but the right hand part of the Character only is put down.

## OF TIME.

The Chinese divide the Twenty-four hours into twelve parts, beginning their reckoning at midnight. The Twelve Horary Characters are called 地支 Te che, and are as follows:

| | | | | | |
|---|---|---|---|---|---|
| Tsze 子 | 11 till 1 o'clock | | Woo, 午 | 11 — 1 Noon |
| Chow, 丑 | 1 — 3, | | We, 未 | 1 — 3, |
| Yin, 寅 | 3 — 5, | | Shin, 申 | 3 — 5, |
| Maou, 夘 | 5 — 7, | | Yew, 酉 | 5 — 7, |
| Shin, 辰 | 7 — 9, | | Seŏ, 戌 | 7 — 9, |
| Sze. 巳 | 9 — 11. | | Hae. 亥 | — 11. |

The word 正 Ching is applied to the even numbers, as 正午 Ching-woo, Twelve o'clock in the day. Ching-woo, extends forward to One o'clock. The word 交 Keaou is applied to make it extend backwards, thus 交午 Keaou-woo, is Eleven o'clock. 正未 Ching-we, is Two o'clock; 交未 Keaou-we, One o'clock. The word 刻 K'hĭh, they use to denote a Quarter of an hour. Thus 正夘一刻 Ching maou yĭh k'hĭh, is a Quarter past six in the morning.

With the above Twelve Horary Characters, they use ten others to form the Cycle of Sixty Years. They are called 天干 T'hëen kan, and 十干 Shĭh kan, or 幹 Kan. They are, 甲.乙.丙.丁.戊.巳.庚.辛.壬.癸. Keă, yĭh, ping, ting, woo, ke, kang, sin, jin, kwei. (See the Hwa-keă-tsze, on the following page.)

### THE MONTH

They divide into Decades. The first they call 上旬 Shang-seun; second 中旬 Chung-seun; and third 下旬 Hea-seun.

Every fifteen days they call 節令 Tsëĕ-ling. To each of these Twenty-four Tsëĕ-ling they give a name. 孟 Măng, 仲 Chung, and 季 Ke, are applied to the First, Second, and Third months in each Season of the Year.

# 花甲子

## TABLE OF THE CYCLE OF SIXTY YEARS.

This Table is inserted because this mode of reckoning the year, occurs both in Books and Manuscripts, not unfrequently. The first Year of the present Cycle was 1804—Chinese, Keă-tsze. Two Characters been taken to express the Year.

| | | | | | |
|---|---|---|---|---|---|
| 1804 甲子 | 1814 甲戌 | 1824 甲申 | 1834 甲午 | 1844 甲辰 | 1854 甲寅 |
| 1805 乙丑 | 1815 乙亥 | 1825 乙酉 | 1835 乙未 | 1845 乙巳 | 1855 乙夘 |
| 1806 丙寅 | 1816 丙子 | 1826 丙戌 | 1836 丙申 | 1846 丙午 | 1856 丙辰 |
| 1807 丁夘 | 1817 丁丑 | 1827 丁亥 | 1837 丁酉 | 1847 丁未 | 1857 丁巳 |
| 1808 戊辰 | 1818 戊寅 | 1828 戊子 | 1838 戊戌 | 1848 戊申 | 1858 戊午 |
| 1809 己巳 | 1819 己夘 | 1829 己丑 | 1839 己亥 | 1849 己酉 | 1859 己未 |
| 1810 庚午 | 1820 庚辰 | 1830 庚寅 | 1840 庚子 | 1850 庚戌 | 1860 庚申 |
| 1811 辛未 | 1821 辛巳 | 1831 辛夘 | 1841 辛丑 | 1851 辛亥 | 1861 辛酉 |
| 1812 壬申 | 1822 壬午 | 1832 壬辰 | 1842 壬寅 | 1852 壬子 | 1862 壬戌 |
| 1813 癸酉 | 1823 癸未 | 1833 癸巳 | 1843 癸夘 | 1853 癸丑 | 1863 癸亥 |

They not only denominate the Year by these Characters, but also the Months and the days, In the Callender they are always inserted.

# 九九合數

## FORM OF THE CHINESE MULTIPLICATION TABLE.

(Carried only to Nine times Nine.)

| | |
|---|---|
| | 八十一 |
| | 四　七九六十三　八九七十二　九九 |
| | 四九三十六　五九四十五　六九五十 |
| 九 | 一九如九　二九一十八　三九二十七 |
| | 八　七八五十六　八八六十四 |
| | 四八三十二　五八得四十　六八四十 |
| 八 | 一八如八　二八一十六　三八二十四 |
| | 二　七七四十九 |
| | 四七二十八　五七三十五　六七四十 |
| 七 | 一七如七　二七一十四　三七二十一 |
| | 六 |
| | 四六二十四　五六得三十　六六三十 |
| 六 | 一六如六　二六一十二　三六一十八 |
| | 四五得二十　五五二十五 |
| 五 | 一五如五　二五得一十　三五一十五 |
| | 四四一十六 |
| 四 | 一四如四　二四如八　三四一十二 |
| 三 | 一三如三　二三如六　三三如九 |
| | Yih 一 Once, yih 一 one, joo 如 as, yih. 一 one.　Yih 一 Once, urh 二 two, joo 如 as, urh. 二 two.　Urh 二 Twice, urh 二 two, joo 如 as, sze. 四 four. |

## FORM OF CARDS.

An Invitation Card they call 請酒帖 Ts'hing-tsew-tēĭh.

翌日菲酌候

光

眷教弟馬四明拜訂

'To-morrow I shall prepare a little wine, and wait to be illumined by your presence. Your friend and pupil Ma-sze-ming bows, and appoints the day.'

A VISITING CARD.*

Tseun Tēĭh.

侍教弟馬四明拜

'Your younger brother, who stands to receive instruction, bows.'

---

* A Visiting Card is sometimes single, and called 單帖 Tan-tēĭh, or consisting of many folds, and called 全帖 Tseun-tēĭh. The Cards which they make use of are red, except on funeral occasions.

**Tan Tëĭh.**

| |
|---|
| 馬四明 |

If contains merely the name Ma-sze-ming.

**Card at the New Year.**

| |
|---|
| 新禧賀 馬四明拜 |

'Ma-sze-ming bows, congratulates and wishes happiness this New Year.'

**Form of an Address on Letters.**

| |
|---|
| 煩帶此信至省城交 馬三德老爺開拆 自前山付 |

'I will trouble you to take this Letter to Canton, and deliver it to Mr. Ma-san-tĭh, to open.

Sent from Tsëen-shan.'

On the back where it is pasted, they write

吉 or 護

封

'A happy or private Letter.'

## FORM OF A LETTER.

不親霽宇。每依德頌。回憶。 老兄大人輿居禔福。慰我五中。茲者。弟於是月上旬動身下墨。因俗冗怱怱。未暇赴晤面申鄙意。但沿途叨庇。托賴平安。每叨教誨。無不神馳。遐想吾兄華堂頤養。欣頌班衣。似弟碌碌奔馳。蓬萍無定。何以教我。諺云。鷹飛不到名利所牵。此之謂也。今乘鴻便。肅候福祺。謹此不戩。

上

明兄老兄大人 電

弟馬明德頓首拜

七月初二日冲

2 K

## A FREE TRANSLATION OF THE PRECEDING LETTER.

I am removed from your countenance, which is pleasing as the unclouded sky. Every day I enthusiastically praise your virtue. Imagination returns to you, venerable brother, eminent man! Rising or at rest may you enjoy felicity. It will be an inward source of comfort to me. I would now mention, that in the first decade of this month, I removed to Macao. I have been much engaged, and had not leisure to address you before, nor repair to you, to make known my poor thoughts. On the whole of the passage, being favored with your assistance, I enjoyed peace. I have always to be thankful for your instructions. My spirit ever flies to your presence. I contemplate my brother in his delightful abode, where are plenty, and peace, and joy.

As for me, I am a poor distressed wandering creature, unsettled as a leaf driven by the wind. Tell me what I shall do. As the Proverb says, 'Fame and advantage drag us further than the eagle flies.' This expresses my case. I embrace a favorable opportunity to compliment you, and wish you happiness. Thus far respectfully, though much be left unsaid.

Above,

Ming, my venerable brother, eminent man, whose glance is as lightning.

Your younger brother Ma-ming-tih, bows to the earth and worships.

Despatched 7th month, 2nd day.

## FORM OF A PETITION TO GOVERNMENT.

具稟洋行商人稟爲據情代稟事。竊商等昨據嘆
咭唎國夷商大班哆啉吱寄信投稱伊國嘁啉𠹭
啞船出口。馳至老萬山外洋面。被風打壞。現駛回
澳修葺等語。業經商等據情報明在案。茲本日復
據該大班由澳寄信到省內稱該嘁啉𠹭啞船現
泊十字門外。果係被風打壞。船中十分滲漏。必須
將貨物起駁。方能修葺。再四酌議。無奈只得浼懇
壆門。兵頭將船駕駛入壆內灣泊。並將貨物起貯
司打夷館。然後修船。今已蒙兵頭等應允。夷等未
敢擅便。理合星飛寄信到省。浼商等據情稟懇。
憲恩。俯念出口。夷船遭風打壞。恩准進壆。並借墺門
司打夷館起貯船中貨物。俾得趕緊修葺完固。仍
將原貨運回本船。刻卽揚帆歸國。遠夷沾感各

## FREE TRANSLATION OF THE PRECEDING PETITION TO GOVERNMENT.

A DULY prepared Address. The Hong Merchants make this statement in behalf of others. We humbly mention, that yesterday we received a letter from the English Chief Tolamman, saying, that Wei-lam-keen-shun's Ship proceeded outward bound, as far as the islands without side, when she met with a gale of wind that injured her much. She has returned to Macao to refit, &c. We have already stated this as is on record. We have to day again received a letter from the Chief, from Macao, in which it is said, that Wei-lam-keen-shun's vessel is anchored at Cross harbour, without side, that indeed she is much injured by the gale, that she is very leaky, that she must be unloaded before she can be repaired; that they had consulted a third and a fourth time, and they had no alternative but to request the Governor of Macao to allow her to go into the harbour, and to take out the Cargo and put it into the warehouses of the Senate. After this they will be able to repair her. They have to thank the Governor for complying; but they would not presume to do it, because convenient, without giving proper intimation; therefore they hastened to write to Canton, and requested that we would lay it before your Excellency, that you would be graciously pleased to grant to this Vessel, which has been injured in going out, to go into Macao, and that they may land the goods at the warehouses of the Senate; thereby to be enabled to refit her with the greater expedition. They will undoubtedly take on board the same goods, and hasten to set sail to return home. The Remote Foreigners will be grateful to all the

憲等語．商等理合據情代稟．伏候
憲示飭遵．爲此稟赴
大人臺前察奪施行
嘉慶七年五月　　日稟

批該夷船既因遭風滲漏．准其駛進嶴門修葺．將貨物
起駁司打夷館以示體恤．候飭知嶴門口就近稽查是
否實在情形．刻即稟覆外．並咨明
閣督部堂
巡撫部院查照．該商等仍傳諭該大班嚴行約束催令赶
緊修竣開行．如有乘機夾帶．一經查出．惟商等是問．毋
忽

Superior Officers, &c. In their stead, we state these things and prostrate beg that your Excellency will declare your pleasure; for this we wait, that we may act in obedience to it. For this we lay these circumstances before your Excellency, to examine and grant that it may be done.

Kea-king, 7th year, 5th moon, — day.

Reply.—As the said Foreign Vessel has met with a gale, and is leaky, we allow her to go into Macao to refit; to take out her Cargo and put it into the warehouses of the Senate, and thus manifest compassion. Let them wait till I order the Custom-house, at Macao, to go and examine whether things be really so or not, and immediately give a reply. It will also be stated to the Viceroy and Foo-yuen to be examined. Let the Hong Merchants communicate the Edict to the Chief, and rigorously require that he exercise a strict control, and cause the utmost haste to be made to finish the repairs, and set sail. If an opportunity be seized to take on board other goods, the moment that it is discovered, it will be required of the Merchants only. Do not slight this.

## FORM OF A PROCLAMATION.

特調香山縣正堂加三級又加四級。隨帶加三級紀錄五次彭。爲曉諭事。照得夷人喓嗲嚧嘶戳傷陳亞連身死。屍親匿不稟報。業經拘獲屍親陳寄燕。及拿獲兇夷之李五等到案訊明。起出屍身。驗明傷痕。扎飭該夷目唩嚟哆將喓嗲嚧嘶交出究辦在案。乃該夷等狡詐包匿。不將兇夷送出。查夷人住居澳門。仰蒙

天朝厚恩。食毛踐土。等諸齊民。自應凜遵。

天朝國法。早爲送出以憑查辦。乃該夷等包匿如故。殊屬刁抗。本應逼稟

大憲。將澳門查封。但念該處民夷雜處。一經封澳。則

## FREE TRANSLATION OF THE PRECEDING PROCLAMATION.

PUNG, by special appointment the Hëen of Hëang-shan, raised three degees; again promoted four degrees, and in succession raised three steps, and enrolled five times, proclaims for the information of all, that it is found that the foreigner An-tëĕ-le-she murdered Chin-a-lëen. The relations of the deceased concealed the affair, and did not give due notice to Government. Chin-ke-yen, the relation of the deceased, has been apprehended, and also the foreign murderer Le-woo, &c. They have been brought up and examined, and have discovered the body, the wounds on which have been examined. A letter has been sent to the Head of the Foreigners, Wei-le-to, enjoining him to deliver up to trial the murderer An-tëĕ-le-she. This is on record. But the said Foreigners artfully and wickedly conceal the murderer, and will not deliver him up. It is found that the Foreigners living in Macao are indebted to the immense bounty of the Celestial Empire for the herbs which they eat, and the ground on which they tread, the same as our own People. Indeed, they ought implicitly to obey the laws of the Celestial Empire, and speedily make a delivery of this Person for trial. But these Foreigners still continue to conceal him. They are extremely wicked and obstinate. I ought to Report the affair to the Superior Officers of the Province, that they may examine and shut up Macao completely. But I consider that at that place, Natives and Foreigners dwell together mixed; if the place be shut up at, then the Natives living there will

在澳民諸多不便。合行出示。曉諭。為此示諭澳門商民及工匠人等知悉。所有一切與夷人交易貨物及工匠。坭水。匠人等暫行停止。俟夷目將兇夷送出方許買賣交易工作。如有不遵。一經拿獲。從嚴究辦。決不姑寬。各宜凛遵。毋違特示

嘉慶十年七月二十六日示

experience many inconveniencies. I form and issue this Proclamation. I proclaim to all the Tradesmen and Mechanics in Macao, for their full information, that they shall for the present, put a stop to all dealings with the Foreigners in any commodities whatever; that the Workmen and Bricklayers, &c., are included in this. They must wait till the Head of the Foreigners deliver up the murderer. When that is done, they will be allowed to buy and sell, and do business. If any disobey this, they will be apprehended and severely dealt with. Decidedly no indulgence will be shown. It is proper that all implicitly obey this and not oppose. A special proclamation.

Kea-king, 10th year, 7th moon, 26th day's Proclamation.

## A HAND BILL.

出謝帖人．𠸄咭唎國公司喇咧哐船現泊黃埔海面．于五月下旬．船內水手夷人六名逃匿不見回船．尋覔無踪．想來夷人不能走入內地．恐有躲匿黃埔左近．或別船收留．均未可定．如有四方君子知其下落．煩到省會隆行．或行後咈囒哂頭樓報信．即謝花紅銀壹百大員．決不食言．此帖是實

嘉慶十三年．閏五月初四日　會隆行帖

尋水手六名

## TRANSLATION OF THE PRECEDING BILL.

A Bill of thanks. Captain Robinson of the English Company's ship, now anchored at Whampoa, between the 20th and 30th of the 5th moon, had six Seamen run from his Ship. They have not been seen to return, nor can any trace of them be found. It is remembered that Foreigners cannot enter the interior. It is apprehended that they are secreted on the left side of Whampoa, somewhere near, or on board some other Ship; nothing is certainly known. If any good Person, all around, knows their retreat, he is requested to repair to Hwuy-lung Hong, or to No. 1, of the French Factory, to give information. He will then receive a hundred dollars reward. There will be no retracting. It is a true bill.

Kea-king, 13th year, 5th moon, being intercalary month, 4th day.

Bill issued by Hwuy-lung Hong.

In search of Six Seamen.

## FORMS OF CONGRATULATION AT THE NEW YEAR.

### TO A SCHOLAR.

I wish you joy. May you this year rise to the golden button.

| | | |
|---|---|---|
| Kung | 恭 | Congratulate you, |
| he | 喜 | |
| Laou | 老 | Sir, |
| yay, | 爺 | |
| kin | 今 | this |
| nëen | 年 | year |
| kaou | 高 | high |
| tăng | 登 | ascend to the |
| kin | 金 | golden |
| pang. | 榜 | button. |

### TO A FARMER.

I wish you joy. May every species of grain this year spring forth abundantly.

| | | |
|---|---|---|
| Kung | 恭 | Congratulate |
| he | 喜 | |
| ne, | 你 | you, |
| kin | 今 | this |
| nëen | 年 | year |
| woo | 五 | the five |
| kŭh | 穀 | grains |
| fung | 豐 | abundant |
| tăng. | 登 | rise. |

### TO A MERCHANT.

I wish you joy. May your property this year produce ten thousand pieces of gold.

| | | |
|---|---|---|
| Kung | 恭 | Congratulate |
| he | 喜 | |
| ne, | 你 | you, |
| kin | 今 | this |
| nëen | 年 | year |
| tsae | 財 | wealth |
| fă | 發 | produce |

| | | |
|---|---|---|
| wan | 萬 | ten thousand |
| kin. | 金。 | gold. |

—

TO AN OLD PERSON.

I wish your joy. May your strength be this year much increased.

| | | |
|---|---|---|
| Kung | 恭 | Congratulate |
| he | 喜 | |
| ne, | 你。 | you, |
| kin | 今 | this |
| nëen | 年 | year |
| shin | 身 | body |
| chwang | 壯 | stout |
| lëĭh | 力 | strong |
| këen. | 健 | firm. |

TO A BOY AT SCHOOL.

I wish you joy. May you this year, make rapid progress in learning.

| | | |
|---|---|---|
| Kung | 恭 | Congratulate |
| he | 喜 | |
| ne, | 你。 | you, |
| kin | 今 | this |
| nëen | 年 | year |
| tŭh | 讀 | read |
| shoo | 書 | book |
| tsung | 聰 | intelligently (and |
| ming | 明 | with) |
| kwae | 乖 | nice discernment. |
| heŏ. | 覺。 | |

# 中文對話

（*Chinese Dialogues, Questions, and Familiar Sentences, Literally Rendered into English, with a View to Promote Commercial Intercourse, and to Assist Beginners in the Language*）

〔英〕麥都思（Walter Henry Medhurst）編

《中文對話》，英國麥都思編。麥都思（Walter Henry Medhurst，一七九六—一八五七），英國倫敦會傳教士。一八一六年入倫敦會所屬印刷廠，被派往馬六甲，在此習得馬來語及多種漢語方言。一八三四年抵穗，一八四三年赴滬，創建墨海書館。此書係初級商用官話會話課本，參考馬禮遜《中文會話及凡例》（*Dialogues and Detached Sentences in the Chinese Language*）及裨治文《廣東方言讀本》（*A Chinese Chrestomathy in the Canton Dialect*）二書頗多，後由其子麥華陀加以增訂，一八六三年於上海出版。全書以羅馬字逐字注音英譯，含數目、稱法、丈量、量地、量糧食、銀錢、雜句、通商條款、問答等內容，涉及商業交易等方面。據一八六三年上海版影印。

中外對話

# CHINESE DIALOGUES,

## QUESTIONS,

AND

## FAMILIAR SENTENCES,

LITERALLY RENDERED INTO ENGLISH,

WITH A VIEW TO PROMOTE

## COMMERCIAL INTERCOURSE,

AND TO ASSIST

*BEGINNERS IN THE LANGUAGE.*

BY THE LATE REVD. DR. MEDHURST.

REVISED BY HIS SON.

SHANGHAE:

PRINTED AT THE LONDON MISSION PRESS.

1863.

## NUMERALS

### 數目 SOO MUH.

| | Small text. 小寫 *Seaou sëay.* | Large text. 大寫 *Ta sëay.* | Weighing character. 碼字 *Ma tsze.* | |
|---|---|---|---|---|
| Yih | 一 | 壹 | 〡 | 1 |
| urh | 二 | 貳 | 〢 | 2 |
| san | 三 | 叁 | 〣 | 3 |
| sze | 四 | 肆 | 〤 | 4 |
| woo | 五 | 伍 | 〥 | 5 |
| lëuh | 六 | 陸 | 〦 | 6 |
| ts'eih | 七 | 柒 | 〧 | 7 |
| pah | 八 | 捌 | 〨 | 8 |
| kew | 九 | 玖 | 〩 | 9 |
| shih | 十 | 拾 | 十 | 10 |

*Note.* The "small text" is used in common, as our 1, 2, 3, &c.; the "large text," when accuracy or security is an object, as in filling the blank in a *cheque.* The "weighing characters" are employed in keeping accounts, and then used exactly as figures are by us. The word *two* is also expressed by 兩 *lëang,* when applied to persons, animals, or things, and often to money: Ex. 兩個人 *lëang ko jin,* two men; 兩隻猪子 *lëang chih choo tsze,* two pigs; 兩百塊錢 *lëang pih k'wae ts'ëen,* two hundred dollars.

11.

Shih 十 Ten
yih 一 one

12.

Shih 十 Ten
urh 二 two

20.

Urh 二 Two
shih 十 ten

30.

San 三 Three
shih 十 ten

50.

Woo 五 Five
shih 十 ten

100.

Yih 一 One
pih* 百 hundred

110.

Yih 一 One
pih 百 hundred
yih 一 one
shih 十 ten

150.

Yih 一 One
pih 百 hundred
woo 五 five
shih 十 ten

1,000.

Yih 一 One
ts'ëen 千 thousand

1,100.

Yih 一 One
ts'ëen 千 thousand
yih 一 one
pih 百 hundred

1,220.

Yih 一 One
ts'ëen 千 thousand
urh 二 two
pih 百 hundred
urh 二 two
shih 十 ten

10,000.

Yih 一 One
wan 萬 myriad

12,556.

Yih 一 One
wan 萬 myriad
urh 二 two
ts'ëen 千 thousand
woo 五 five
pih 百 hundred
woo 五 five
shih 十 ten
lëuh 六 six

20,000.

Urh 二 Two
wan 萬 myriad

100,000.

Shih 十 Ten
wan 萬 myriad

1,000,000.

Pih 百 Hundred
wan 萬 myriad

5,000,000.

Woo 五 Five
pih 百 hundred
wan 萬 myriad

5,555,555.

Woo 五 Five
pih 百 hundred
woo 五 five
shih 十 ten
woo 五 five
wan 萬 myriad
woo 五 five
ts'ëen 千 thousand
woo 五 five
pih 百 hundred
woo 五 five
shih 十 ten
woo 五 five

6,789,234.

Lëuh 六 Six
pih 百 hundred
ts'eih 七 seven
shih 十 ten
pah 八 eight
wan 萬 myriad
kew 九 nine
ts'ëen 千 thousand
urh 二 two
pih 百 hundred
san 三 three
shih 十 ten
sze. 四 four.

* Often sounded *paih* or *poh.*

# WEIGHTS.

## 稱法 CH'ING FAH.

Ten atoms equal one filament.

Shih 十 Ten
hwuh 忽 atom
wei 爲 make
yih 一 one
sze. 絲 filament.

Ten filaments equal one hair.

Shih 十 Ten
sze 絲 filament
wei 爲 make
yih 一 one
haou. 毫 hair.

Ten hairs equal one cash.

Shih 十 Ten
haou 毫 hair
wei 爲 make
yih 一 one
le. 釐 cash.

Ten cash equal one candareen.

Shih 十 Ten
le 釐 cash
wei 爲 make
yih 一 one
făn. 分 candareen.

Ten candareens equal one mace.

Shih 十 ten
făn 分 candareen
wei 爲 make
yih 一 one
ts'ëen. 錢 mace.

Ten mace equal one tael.

Shih 十 Ten
ts'ëen 錢 mace
wei 爲 make
yih 一 one
lëang. 兩 tael.

Sixteen taels equal one catty.

Shih 十 Ten
lëuh 六 six
lëang 兩 tael
wei 爲 make
yih 一 one
kin. 斤 catty.

One hundred catties equal one pecul.

Yih 一 One
pih 百 hundred
kin 斤 catty *
wei 爲 make
yih 一 one
tan. 担 pecul.

Sixty five peculs.

Lëuh 六 Six

* The number of taels in a catty and of catties in a pecul differ at times. The Chinese tael or ounce exceeds the corresponding English standard by one-third, and so with the other weights.

shih 十 ten
woo 五 five
tan. 担 pecul.

Nine catties,

Kew 九 Nine
kin, 斤 catty,

Ten taels,

Shih 十 Ten
lëang, 兩 tael,

Six mace,

Lëuh 六 Six
ts'ëen, 錢 mace,

Five candareens,

Woo 五 Five
făn, 分 candareen,

Three cash,

San 三 Three
le, 釐 cash,

Eight hairs,

Pah 八 Eight
haou, 毫 hair,

Two filaments.

Urh 二 Two
sze. 絲 filament.

---

## LONG MEASURE.

### 丈量 CHANG LËANG.

Ten lines equal one inch.

Shih 十 Ten
făn 分 line
wei 爲 make
yih 一 one
ts'ăn. 寸 inch.

Ten inches equal one foot.

Shih 十 Ten
ts'ăn 寸 inch
wei 爲 make
yih 一 one
ch'e.h 尺 foot.

Ten feet equal one pole.

Shih 十 Ten
ch'eh 尺 foot
wei 爲 make
yih 一 one
chang. 丈 pole.

Five feet equal one pace.

Woo 五 Five
ch'eh 尺 foot
wei 爲 make
yih 一 one
poo. 步 pace.

Three hundred and sixty paces equal one furlong (Chinese).

San 三 Three
pih 百 hundred
lëuh 六 six
shih 十 ten
poo 步 pace
wei 爲 make
yih 一 one
le. 里 furlong.

Two hundred and fifty furlongs equal one degree.

Urh 二 Two
pih 百 hundred
woo 五 five
shih 十 ten
le 里 furlong
wei 爲 make
yih 一 one
too. 度 degree.

## LAND MEASURE.

## 量地 LËANG TE.

Five feet equal one pace.

Woo 五 Five
ch'eh 尺 foot
wei 爲 make
yih 一 one
poo. 步 pace.

Two hundred and forty paces of length with one of breadth equal one acre (Chinese).

Urh 二 Two
pih 百 hundred
sze 四 four
shih 十 ten
poo 步 pace
chang 長 long
yih 一 one
poo 步 pace
k'wan 寬 broad
wei 爲 make
yih 一 one
mow. 畝 acre.

## DRY MEASURE.

## 量糧食 LËANG LËANG SHIH.

Ten gills equal one pint (31⅝ cubic punts).

Shih 十 Ten
hoh 合 gill
wei 爲 make
yih 一 one
shing. 升 pint.

Ten pints equal one peck (316 cubic punts).

Shih 十 Ten
shing 升 pints
wei 爲 make
yih 一 one
tow. 斗 peck.

Ten pecks equal one pecul (3,160 cubic punts).

Shih 十 Ten
tow 斗 peck
wei 爲 make
yih 一 one
sheh.* 石 stone.

* Often read *tan.*

# MONIES.

## 銀錢 YIN TS'ËEN.

Dollar.

Yang 洋 Ocean
ts'ëen. 錢 money.

Dollar.

Hwa 華 Flower
pëen. 邊 edge.

One dollar.

Yih 一 One
yuen. 元 round.

Ferdinand dollar.

Shwang 雙 Double
chuh. 燭 candle.

Carolus dollar.

Ta 大 Large
t'ow. 頭 head.

Carolus IIII. dollar.

Sze 四 Four
kung.* 工 workman.

Rupee.

Seaou 小 Small
yang 洋 ocean
ts'ëen. 錢 money.

Half a dollar.

Pan 半 Half
k'wae 塊 piece
ts'ëen. 錢 money.

Half a dollar.

Tuy 對 Opposite
k'ae. 開 open.

¼ of a dollar.

Sze 四 Four
k'ae. 開 open.

⅛ of a dollar.

Pah 八 Eight
k'ae. 開 open.

Sycee.

Wăn 紋 Fine
yin. 銀 silver.

Round ingot sycee.

Yuen 元 Round
paou. 寶 precious.

Square ingot sycee.

Fang 方 Square
paou. 寶 precious.

Refined sycee.

Se 細 Delicate
sze 絲 silk thread.

Globe sycee.

Yuen 元 Round
sze. 絲 silk thread.

Five tael ingot.

Chung 中 Medium
ting. 錠 ingot.

Bank note.

Ts'ëen 錢 Money
pëaou. 票 draft.

Circular note.

Hwuy 滙 Circulate
tan. 單 note.

* Called so because of the four Is in it.

# MISCELLANEOUS SENTENCES.

## 雜句 TSAH KEU.

What's this?

| | | |
|---|---|---|
| Chay | 這 | This |
| she | 是 | is |
| shin | 甚 | what |
| mo | 麼 | |
| tung | 東 | thing? |
| se. | 西 | |

An eatable.

| | | |
|---|---|---|
| Ch'ih | 喫 | Eatable |
| teih | 的 | |
| tung | 東 | thing. |
| se. | 西 | |

What do you call this?

| | | |
|---|---|---|
| Chay | 這 | This |
| ko | 個 | |
| keaou | 叫 | call |
| shin | 甚 | what |
| mo | 麼 | |
| ming | 名 | name? |
| urh. | 兒 | |

It is called shark's fin.

| | | |
|---|---|---|
| Keaou | 叫 | Called |
| yû | 魚 | fish |
| ch'e. | 翅 | fin. |

Where does it come from?

| | | |
|---|---|---|
| She | 是 | Is |
| na | 那 | where |
| urh | 兒 | |
| lae | 來 | come? |
| teih. | 的 | |

Out of the sea.

| | | |
|---|---|---|
| Hae | 海 | Sea |
| le | 裡 | in |
| lae | 來 | come. |
| teih. | 的 | |

What is its use?

| | | |
|---|---|---|
| Chay | 這 | This |
| yew | 有 | have |
| shin | 甚 | what |
| mo | 麼 | |
| yung | 用 | use |
| choo. | 處 | place? |

It is used for food.

| | | |
|---|---|---|
| Tso | 做 | Make |
| ts'ae | 菜 | food |
| ch'ih | 喫 | eating. |
| teih. | 的 | |

Is it good eating?

| | | |
|---|---|---|
| Haou | 好 | Good |
| ch'ih | 喫 | eat |
| puh | 不 | not |
| haou | 好 | good |
| ch'ih. | 喫 | eat? |

Uncommonly good eating.

| | | |
|---|---|---|
| Hăng | 狠 | Very |
| haou | 好 | good |
| ch'ih. | 喫 | eat. |

Will you sell it?

| | | |
|---|---|---|
| Mai | 賣 | Sell |
| puh | 不 | not |
| mai. | 賣 | sell |

I will sell it.

Mai. 賣 Sell.

How much do you want for it?

Yaóu 要 Want
to 多 } how much
shaou 少 }
ts'ëên. 錢 money?

That is too dear.

Chay 這 This
she 是 is
t'aé 太 over
kwuy. 貴 dear.

It is not dear.

Puh 不 not
kwuy. 貴 dear.

Is that its true price?

She 是 Is
shih 實 actual
këa 價 } price
urh 兒 }
mo 麼 ?

Very well, send it to my house.

Haou 好 Good
sung 送 send
taou 到 to
wo 我 I
këa 家 } house
le 裡 }
lae. 來 come.

I will immediately come.

Tsew 就 Immediately
lai. 來 come.

I want to eat rice.

Wo 我 I
yau 要 want
ch'ih 吃 eat
fan. 飯 rice.

It is not cooked yet.

Han 還 Yet
muh 沒 not
yew 有 have
lung 弄 prepare
haou 好 good
ne. 呢 —

When will it be ready?

Shin 甚 } What
mo 麼 }
she 時 } time
how 候 }
urh 兒 —
haou. 好 good?

It will be ready in a few moments.

Tăng 等 Wait
yih 一 one
hwuy 會 turn
urh 兒 —
tsew 就 forthwith
haou 好 good
leaou. 了 finish.

Give me a cup of water.

Kay 給 Give
wo 我 I
yih 一 one
wan 碗 bowl
shuy. 水 water.

Surely cold water is not a good thing to drink.

中外對話

Lëang 凉 Cold
shuy 水 water
p'a 怕 fear
puh 不 not
haou 好 good
hoh 喝 drink
pa 罷 —

Then bring me some tea.

Tsew 就 Then
na 拿 bring
ch'a 茶 tea
lae. 來 come.

When I have had some tea, I will talk to you.

Hoh 喝 } Having drunk
leaou 了 }
ch'a 茶 tea
tsae 再 further
shwoh 說 } talk
hwa 話 }
urh. 兒 —

I want some one to carry my things.

Yaou 要 Want
jin 人 man
t'ëaou 挑 carry
tung 東 } thing.
se. 西 }

Where do you wish them carried to?

T'ëaou 挑 Carry
taou 到 to
na 那 } where
urh 兒 }
k'heu. 去 go.

I want them carried to my lodgings.

T'ëaou 挑 Carry
taou 到 to
wo 我 I
yû 寓 lodging
le 裡 in
k'heu. 去 go.

How much will you give?

Kay 給 Give
to 多 } how much
shaou 少 }
ts'ëen. 錢 money.

I will say when they get there.

T'ëaou 挑 Carry
taou 到 } arrived
leaou 了 }
tsae 再 then
shwoh. 說 say.

Are you well?

Haou 好 Good.
ah. 阿 —

Are *you* well?

Ne 你 You
haou 好 Good.
ah. 阿 —

Where have you come from?

Na 那 } Where
urh 兒 }
lae. 來 come.

From the provincial capital.

Săng 省 Province
ch'ing 城 city

lae. 來 come.

When did you arrive?

Ke 幾 } When
urh 兒 }
taou 到 } arrive.
teih. 的 }

I arrived yesterday.

Wo 我 I
tsoh 昨 } yesterday
urh 兒 }
taou 到 } arrive.
teih. 的 }

What have you come here for?

Taou 到 To
chay 這 } here
urh 兒 }
lae 來 come
tso 做 do
shin 甚 } what.
mo. 麽 }

Merely for a roam.

Hëen 閒 Leisure
kwang 逛 } saunter.
kwang 逛 }
urh. 兒 —

Let us walk out together.

Tung 同 With
wo 我 I
yih 一 } together
kh'wae 塊 }
urh 兒 —
tsow. 走 walk.

I have no time.

Puh 不 Not
tih 得 obtain
hëen 閒 } leisure.
urh. 兒 }

I have something to do.

Wo 我 I
yew 有 have
sze 事 } business.
ts'ing. 情 }

I have no spare time.

Muh 沒 Not
yew 有 have
kh'ung 空 vacant
urh. 兒 —

Come and look at the shops.

Lae 來 Come
kh'an 看 } look at
kh'an 看 }
p'oo 鋪 } shop.
tsze. 子 }

There are some nice things for sale.

Yew 有 Have
haou 好 good
tung 東 } thing
se 西 }
jin 人 } people
këa 家 }
yaou 要 want
mae. 賣 sell.

I cannot buy anything, I have no money.

Wo 我 I

muh 沒 not
yew 有 have
ts'ëen 錢 money
puh 不 not
năng 能 can
mae. 買 buy.

A ship came in to-day.

Kin 今 } To-day
urh 兒 }
yew 有 have
ch'üen 船 ship
taou. 到 arrive.

Where from?

She 是 Is
na 那 } where
urh 兒 }
lae 來 } come.
teih. 的 }

From sea.

Wae 外 Outside
yang 洋 sea
lae 來 } come.
teih. 的 }

What cargo does she bring?

Chwang 裝 } Laden
teih 的 }
she 是 is
shin 甚 } what
mo 麼 }
ho. 貨 goods.

She has cottons, hardware, & a variety of other goods.

Yew 有 Have
yang 洋 ocean
poo, 布 cottons,
yew 有 have
t'ëeh 鐵 iron
kh'e, 器 utensil,
han 還 yet
yew 有 have
koh 各 every
yang 樣 } sort
urh 兒 }
teih 的 of
yang 洋 ocean
ho. 貨 goods.

Where is the store at which they will be offered for sale.

Hang 行 Store
kh'ae 開 open
tsae 在 at
na 那 } where.
urh. 兒 }

Outside the East gate.

Tsae 在 At
tung 東 east
mun 門 gate
wae 外 } outside
t'ow. 頭 }

When do they open shop?

Ke 幾 } When
urh 兒 }
kh'ae 開 } open
chang. 張 }

To-morrow.

Ming 明 } To-morrow.
urh. 兒 }

I wish to go and see, will you go with me?

| | | |
|---|---|---|
| Wo | 我 | I |
| yaou | 要 | want |
| kh'eu | 去 | go |
| kh'an | 看 | look |
| kh'an | 看 | |
| tung | 同 | with |
| choh | 着 | |
| yih | 一 | together |
| kh'wae | 塊 | |
| urh | 兒 | |
| kh'eu | 去 | go |
| haou | 好 | good |
| puh | 不 | not |
| haou. | 好 | good. |

In which direction does this road go?

| | | |
|---|---|---|
| Chay | 這 | This |
| t'eaou | 條 | line |
| loo | 路 | road |
| urh | 兒 | — |
| she | 是 | is |
| wang | 往 | lead |
| na | 那 | where |
| urh | 兒 | |
| kh'eu | 去 | go |
| teih. | 的 | — |

It goes to the south of the city.

| | | |
|---|---|---|
| She | 是 | Is |
| wang | 往 | lead |
| ch'ing | 城 | city |
| nan | 南 | south |
| kh'eu | 去 | go |
| teih. | 的 | — |

How do you get to the East gate?

| | | |
|---|---|---|
| Tung | 東 | East |
| mun | 門 | gate |
| yew | 由 | by |
| na | 那 | where |
| urh | 兒 | |
| tsow. | 走 | walk. |

You get to it this way.

| | | |
|---|---|---|
| Yew | 由 | By |
| chay | 這 | this |
| pëen | 邊 | side |
| urh | 兒 | — |
| tsow. | 走 | walk. |

When you have crossed the bridge, turn to your right, and go straight on for half a furlong, when you will find it.

| | | |
|---|---|---|
| Kwo | 過 | Crossed |
| leaou | 了 | |
| kh'eaou | 橋 | bridge |
| wang | 往 | go |
| yew | 右 | right |
| chüen | 轉 | circuit |
| yih | 一 | straight |
| chih | 直 | |
| teih | 的 | |
| tsow | 走 | walk |
| pan | 半 | half |
| le | 里 | furlong |
| loo | 路 | road |
| tsew | 就 | then |
| she | 是 | is |

| | | |
|---|---|---|
| leaou. | 了 | — |

Thank you! thank you!

| | | |
|---|---|---|
| To | 多 | many |
| sëay | 謝 | thank |
| to | 多 | many |
| sëay | 謝 | thank |

It looks like rain, pray borrow an umbrella.

| | | |
|---|---|---|
| T'ëen | 天 | Heaven |
| yaou | 要 | want |
| hëa | 下 | let fall |
| yû | 雨 | rain |
| ts'ing | 請 | beg |
| ne | 你 | you |
| tsëay | 借 | borrow |
| yih | 一 | one |
| pa | 把 | stick |
| yû | 雨 | rain |
| san | 傘 | shade |
| lae. | 來 | come. |

There are none. Better go to a shop and buy one.

| | | |
|---|---|---|
| Muh | 沒 | Not |
| yew | 有 | have |
| yû | 雨 | rain |
| san | 傘 | shade |
| p'oo | 鋪 | } shop |
| tsze | 子 | } |
| le | 裡 | in |
| mae | 買 | buy |
| p'a. | 罷 | enough. |

What character is this?

| | | |
|---|---|---|
| Chay | 這 | } This |
| ko | 個 | } |
| she | 是 | is |
| shin | 甚 | } what |
| mo | 麼 | } |
| tsze. | 字 | character. |

This is the character "Hae."

| | | |
|---|---|---|
| Chay | 這 | This |
| she | 是 | is |
| ko | 個 | the |
| hae | 海 | Hae |
| tsze. | 字 | character. |

Under what radical is it ranged?

| | | |
|---|---|---|
| Tsae | 在 | In |
| shin | 甚 | } what |
| mo | 麼 | } |
| tsze | 字 | character |
| poo | 部 | radical |
| le. | 裡 | within. |

Under the "Shuy" radical.

| | | |
|---|---|---|
| Tsae | 在 | In |
| shuy | 水 | water |
| tsze | 字 | character |
| poo | 部 | radical |
| le | 裡 | } within. |
| t'ow. | 頭 | } |

How many strokes has it?

| | | |
|---|---|---|
| Yew | 有 | Have |
| to | 多 | } how many |
| shaou | 少 | } |
| peih. | 筆 | strokes. |

What is its meaning?

| | | |
|---|---|---|
| Yew | 有 | Have |
| shin | 甚 | } what |
| mo | 麼 | } |

këae 解 explain
fah 法 rule
urh. 兒 —

Including the radical it has ten strokes.

Lëen 連 With
poo 部 radical
yew 有 have
shih 十 ten
peih. 筆 strokes.

All on the globe which is not land is "Hae."

T'ëen 天 Heaven
hëa 下 below
ch'oo 除 } excepted
leaou 了 }
te 地 land
tsew 就 then
she 是 is
hae. 海 sea.

With what character does it correspond in sense?

Chay 這 } This
ko 個 }
tsze 字 character
teih 的 's
e 意 } meaning
sze 思 }
ho 和 harmony
shin 甚 } what
mo 麼 }
tsze 字 character
yih 一 } one
ko 個 }
yang. 樣 kind.

It corresponds with the character "Yang."

Ho 和 Harmony
yang 洋 Yang
tsze 字 character
yih 一 } one
ko 個 }
yang. 樣 kind.

Pray write it nicely for me.

Ts'ing 請 Beg
ne 你 you
sëay 寫 write
haou 好 good
leaou 了 done
kay 給 give
wo 我 me
kh'an. 看 look.

Say that sentence once more for me to hear.

Tsae 再 Again
shwoh 說 say
na 那 that
keu 句 sentence
hwa 話 word
kay 給 give
wo 我 me
t'ing. 聽 hear.

Say it loudly and slowly for me to hear.

Kaou 高 High
shing 聲 voice
urh 兒 —

man 慢 } slowly
man 慢
teih 的
shwoh 說 say
ch'uh 出 out
lae 來 come
kay 給 give
wo 我 me
t'ing. 聽 hear.

I cannot catch it, if you say it so fast.

Chay 這 This
mo 麽 kind
k'wai 快 quick
shwoh 說 say
ch'uh 出 out
lae, 來 come,
wo 我 I
t'ing 聽 hear
choh 着 get
puh 不 not
ts'ing 清 } clear
ts'oo. 楚

Do you understand me now?

Wo 我 I
shwoh 說 say
ne 你 you
tung 懂 understand
puh 不 not
tung. 懂 understand.

I now understand you distinctly.

Wo 我 I
t'ing 聽 hear
choh 着 get
han 狠 very
tung 懂 } understand.
teih. 的

How would you say it in the *patois*?

Joh 若 If
she 是 is
t'oo 土 native
hwa 話 speech
tsăng 怎 } whatlike
mo 麽
shwoh. 說 say.

Had I best speak in the *patois* or in the official dialect?

Shwoh 說 Say
t'oo 土 native
hwa 話 speech
haou 好 good
hwoh 或 or
she 是 is
kwan 官 official
hwa 話 speech
haou. 好 good.

Better speak the official dialect, as you will then be understood throughout China.

Kwan 官 Official
hwa 話 speech
haou 好 good
shih 十 ten
pah 八 eight
săng 省 provinces
too 都 all

hëaou 曉 } comprehend.
teih. 的 }

Every place has its own *patois.*

Koh 各 Every
ch'oo 處 place
urh 兒 —
yew 有 have
koh 各 every
ch'oo 處 place
urh 兒 —
teih 的 's
t'oo 土 native
hwa. 話 speech.

Hence the difficulty of acquiring the Chinese language.

So 所 } Therefore
e 以 }
chung 中 middle
kwoh 國 kingdom
hwa 話 speech
han 狠 very
nan 難 difficult
hëoh. 學 learn.

The written character is the same throughout the empire.

Sëay 寫 Write
tsze 字 character
t'ung 通 throughout
t'ëen 天 heaven
hëa 下 under
too 都 all
she 是 is
yih 一 one
ko 個 —
yang. 樣 sort.

How long does it take to become proficient in the Chinese language?

Chung 中 Middle
kwoh 國 kingdom
hwa 話 speech
tih 得 take up
to 多 } how many
shaou 少 }
jih 日 } days
tsze 子 }
hëoh 學 learn
teih 的 obtain
hwuy. 會 proficient.

One year's study will suffice to make you proficient in common conversation.

Chih 只 Merely
shwoh 說 speak
këa 家 domestic
ch'ang 常 constant
hwa 話 speech
yih 一 one
nëen 年 year
tsew 就 then
hëoh 學 learn
teih 的 obtain
hwuy. 會 proficient.

But it will need years of application to enable you to master the written language.

Yaou 要 Want

hëoh 學 learn
seih 習 practice
tsze 字 character
wăn 文 composition
ke 幾 several
shih 十 ten
nëen 年 years
yay 也 even
hëoh 學 learn
puh 不 not
tsin. 盡 exhaust.

How many sorts of characters are there?

Tsze 字 Characters
yew 有 have
to 多 } how many
shaou 少 }
yang 様 sorts
urh. 兒 —

There are four or five sorts.

Yew 有 Have
sze 四 four
woo 五 five
yang 様 sorts
urh. 兒 —

How many meanings has each character?

Yih 一 } One
ko 個 }
tsze 字 character
yew 有 have
ke 幾 } how many
ko 個 }
këae 解 explain
fah 法 law
urh. 兒 —

The meanings are not definite in number.

Këae 解 Explain
fah 法 law
puh 不 } uncertain.
ting 定 }
teih. 的 —

How many tones are there?

Yew 有 Have
ke 幾 how many
yang 様 kind
shing 聲 tone
urh. 兒 —

There are four, the even, ascending, receding, and entering.

Yew 有 Have
p'ing 平 even
shang 上 ascending
kh'eu 去 receding
juh 入 entering
sze 四 four
shing. 聲 tone.

I will see about learning them bye and bye.

Tăng 等 Wait
wo 我 I
hëoh 學 } learn
hëoh 學 }
kh'an. 看 see.

Pray come and take a quiet dinner with me to-morrow

Ts'ing 請 Beg

C

| | | |
|---|---|---|
| ne | 你 | you |
| ming | 明 | to-morrow |
| t'ëen | 天 | |
| taou | 到 | to |
| wo | 我 | my |
| shay | 舍 | cottage |
| hëa | 下 | below |
| ch'ih | 吃 | eat |
| fan. | 飯 | rice. |

At what hour?

| | | |
|---|---|---|
| Shin | 甚 | What |
| mo | 麼 | |
| she | 時 | time |
| how | 候 | |
| urh. | 兒 | — |

At noon.

| | | |
|---|---|---|
| Woo | 午 | Noon |
| she. | 時 | hour. |

Thank you; you are really most wasteful in my favour.

| | | |
|---|---|---|
| To | 多 | Many |
| sëay, | 謝 | thank |
| shih | 實 | really |
| tsae | 在 | |
| yew | 又 | more |
| p'o | 破 | waste |
| fei | 費 | expense |
| lëaou. | 了 | — |

By no means, I shall only have a slight spread, at which you must be good enough not to laugh.

| | | |
|---|---|---|
| Puh | 不 | Only |
| kwo | 過 | |
| she | 是 | is |
| pëen | 便 | common |
| fan, | 飯 | rice, |
| ts'ing | 請 | beg |
| puh | 不 | not |
| yaou | 要 | must |
| këen | 見 | look |
| sëaou. | 笑 | laugh. |

How can you say so? I am sure it will be very good.

| | | |
|---|---|---|
| Na | 那 | What |
| le | 裡 | |
| teih | 的 | kind |
| hwa | 話 | speech |
| ne | 呢 | ? |
| haou | 好 | good |
| teih | 的 | very. |
| hăn. | 狠 | |

Pray take some wine.

| | | |
|---|---|---|
| Ts'ing | 請 | Beg |
| hoh | 喝 | drink |
| tsew. | 酒 | wine. |

I can't take wine; pray excuse me, do.

| | | |
|---|---|---|
| Wo | 我 | I |
| muh | 沒 | not |
| yew | 有 | have |
| lëang, | 量 | capacity, |
| ts'ing | 請 | beg |
| shoo | 恕 | excuse |
| wo | 我 | me |
| pa. | 罷 | do. |

Drink as you list, I won't urge you.

Suy 隨 Follow
pëen 便 convenience
hoh 喝 drink
puh 不 not
yaou 要 want
mëen 勉
kh'ëang 强 force.

What meat is this?

Chay 這 This
she 是 is
shin 甚
mo 麽 what
jow. 肉 meat.

It is mutton.

Chay 這 This
she 是 is
yang 羊 goat
jow. 肉 meat.

Is it sheep or goat?

She 是 Is
mëen 綿 wool
yang 羊 goat
she 是 is
shan 山 hill
yang. 羊 goat.

It is sheep.

She 是 Is
mëen 綿 wool
yang. 羊 goat.

You will find this broth very nice. Use a soup spoon, and you will more easily spoon it up.

Chay 這
ko 個 This
t'ang 湯 broth
hǎn 狠 very
haou 好 good
yung 用 use
kăng 羹 soup
she 匙 spoon
yung 容
e 易 easy
ch'ing. 盛 spoon up.

You are not accustomed to chopsticks, I fear.

P'a 怕 Fear
ne 你
mun 們 you
yung 用 use
puh 不 not
kwan 慣 practised
kh'wae 筷
tsze. 子 chopsticks

Try this bowl of vegetables once more.

Tsae 再 Again
ch'ang 嘗
ch'ang 嘗 taste
chay 這 this
wan 碗 bowl
ts'ae. 菜 vegetable.

It is doubtless very nice, but I have really had enough, thank you.

Haou 好 Good
she 是 is
haou 好 good
to 多 many

| | | |
|---|---|---|
| sëay | 謝 | thank |
| wo | 我 | I |
| shih | 實 | truly |
| tsae | 在 | |
| ch'ih | 吃 | eat |
| paou | 飽 | satiety |
| lëaou. | 了 | done. |

I don't feel well.

| | | |
|---|---|---|
| Wo | 我 | My |
| shin | 身 | body |
| shang | 上 | on |
| yew | 有 | have |
| ping. | 病 | sickness. |

What ails you?

| | | |
|---|---|---|
| Shin | 甚 | What |
| mo | 麼 | |
| ping. | 病 | sickness. |

Stomach-ache.

| | | |
|---|---|---|
| Too | 肚 | Stomach |
| le | 裏 | in |
| t'ung. | 疼 | ache. |

Why not ask a doctor to come and look at you?

| | | |
|---|---|---|
| Ts'ing | 請 | Invite |
| ko | 個 | a |
| e | 醫 | doctor |
| săng | 生 | |
| lae | 來 | come |
| kh'an | 看 | look |
| kh'an | 看 | |
| haou | 好 | good |
| puh | 不 | not |
| haou. | 好 | good. |

Which doctor is reckoned the most famous?

| | | |
|---|---|---|
| Na | 那 | Which |
| yih | 一 | one |
| ko | 個 | |
| e | 醫 | doctor |
| săng | 生 | |
| swan | 算 | reckon |
| she | 是 | is |
| tsuy | 最 | very |
| ch'uh | 出 | out |
| ming | 名 | name |
| teih. | 的 | of. |

Outside the west gate there is a doctor surnamed Hwang, who has a great name.

| | | |
|---|---|---|
| Se | 西 | West |
| măn | 門 | gate |
| wae | 外 | outside |
| sing | 姓 | surname |
| Hwang | 黃 | Hwang |
| teih | 的 | of |
| she | 是 | is |
| ko | 個 | one |
| ch'uh | 出 | out |
| ming | 名 | name |
| teih. | 的 | of. |

How much will it cost to ask him round?

| | | |
|---|---|---|
| Ts'ing | 請 | Invite |
| t'a | 他 | him |
| lae | 來 | come |
| yaou | 要 | require |
| hwa | 化 | spend |

to 多 } how much
shaou 少 }
ts'ëen. 錢 money.

Two hundred cash, besides one hundred cash for his sedan.

Urh 二 Two
pih 百 hundred
ts'ëen, 錢 cash,
ling 另 besides
yew 有 have
yih 一 one
pih 百 hundred
keaou 轎 } sedan
tsze 子 }
ts'ëen. 錢 cash.

Yesterday there was a fire on the opposite side of the street.

Tsoh 昨 } Yesterday
t'ëen 天 }
tuy 對 opposite
mëen 面 side
urh 兒 —
këae 街 street
shang 上 on
shih 失 } lost
lëaou 了 }
ho. 火 fire.

The fire commenced at three in the morning.

She 是 Is
tsaou 早 early
shin 晨 mornir
san 三 three
tëen 點 stroke
chung 鐘 clock
k'he 起 } commenced
teih 的 }
ho. 火 fire.

At five o'clock it was put out.

Woo 五 Five
tëen 點 stroke
chung 鐘 clock
tsew 就 then
mëeh 滅 } extinguished.
lëaou. 了 }

Six houses were burnt in all.

T'ung 通 } Altogether
kung 共 }
shaou 燒 burn
hwae 壞 } destroyed
lëaou 了 }
lëuh 六 six
këen 間 lot
fang 房 } houses
tsze. 子 }

No one was hurt.

Muh 沒 Not
yew 有 have
shang 傷 hurt
jin. 人 man.

A quantity of merchandize with the houses was utterly destroyed.

Heu 許 Very
to 多 many
ho 貨 goods
lëen 連 with

fang 房 } houses
tsze 子 }
too 都 all
shaou 燒 burn
kan 乾 } clean
tsin 盡 }
lëaou. 了 complete.

The people are much to be pitied; having neither food to eat nor houses to live in.

Hăn 狠 Very
k'o 可 may
lëen 憐 pity
muh 沒 not
yew 有 have
fan 飯 rice
ch'ih 吃 eat
yew 又 and
muh 沒 not
yew 有 have
fang 房 } houses
tsze 子 }
choo. 住 live.

They should by all means be assisted.

Tsung 總 By all means
yaou 要 ought
chow 賙 bestow
tse 濟 supply
t'a. 他 them.

What is the price of this?

Chay 這 This
she 是 is
shin 甚 } what
mo 麼 }
këa 價 } price.
ts'ëen. 錢 }

How many dollars?

To 多 } How much
shaou 少 }
yang 洋 ocean
ts'ëen. 錢 money.

How many cash?

Ke 幾 How
ko 個 many
t'ung 銅 copper
ts'ëen. 錢 cash.

What price per piece?

Yih 一 One
peih 疋 piece
to 多 } how much
shaou 少 }
ts'ëen. 錢 money.

What price per ten feet?

May 每 Each
chang 丈 10 feet
to 多 } how much
shaou 少 }
ts'ëen. 錢 money.

How many cash per foot?

Yih 一 One
ch'eh 尺 foot
ke 幾 how
ko 個 many
ts'ëen. 錢 cash.

For how much silver will you sell a hundred?

| | | |
|---|---|---|
| Yih | 一 | One |
| pih | 百 | hundred |
| ko | 個 | in number |
| mae | 賣 | sell |
| to / shaou | 多少 | how much |
| yin / tsze. | 銀子 | silver. |

How many will one dollar buy?

| | | |
|---|---|---|
| Yih / ko | 一個 | One |
| yang | 洋 | ocean |
| ts'ëen | 錢 | money |
| mae | 買 | buy |
| ke | 幾 | how |
| ko. | 個 | many. |

How many men have you here?

| | | |
|---|---|---|
| Yew | 有 | Have |
| to / shaou | 多少 | how many |
| jin | 人 | man |
| tsae | 在 | at |
| chay / le. | 這裏 | here. |

How many persons are there to each family?

| | | |
|---|---|---|
| Yih | 一 | One |
| këa / tsze | 家子 | family |
| yew | 有 | have |
| to / shaou | 多少 | how many |
| k'ow / tsze. | 口子 | individual. |

What do you want?

| | | |
|---|---|---|
| Ne | 你 | You |
| yaou | 要 | want |
| shin / mo. | 甚麼 | what. |

What are you doing?

| | | |
|---|---|---|
| Ne | 你 | You |
| tso | 做 | do |
| shin / mo. | 甚麼 | what. |

What is his business?

| | | |
|---|---|---|
| T'a | 他 | He |
| yew | 有 | have |
| shin / mo | 甚麼 | what |
| sze / ts'ing. | 事情 | business. |

What is your profession?

| | | |
|---|---|---|
| Ne | 你 | You |
| yew | 有 | have |
| shin / mo | 甚麼 | what |
| ying / săng. | 營生 | profession. |

What are you doing here?

| | | |
|---|---|---|
| Ne | 你 | You |
| tsae | 在 | at |
| chay / le | 這裏 | here |
| tso | 做 | do |
| shin | 甚 | what |

mo. 麽 ?

What trade do you follow?

Ne 你 You
tso 做 do
shin 甚 } what
mo 麽 }
săng 生 } trade.
e. 意 }

What work do you do?

Ne 你 You
tso 做 do
shin 甚 } what
mo 麽 }
kung 工 } work.
foo. 夫 }

What is your idea in coming?

Ne 你 You
lae 來 come
yew 有 have
shin 甚 } what
mo 麽 }
e 意 } idea.
sze. 思 }

Why did you not come yesterday?

Wei 爲 Do
shin 甚 } what
mo 麽 }
tsoh 昨 } yesterday
t'ëen 天 }
puh 不 not
lae. 來 come.

Why did you not come earlier?

Ne 你 You
ho 何 why
puh 不 not
tsaou 早 early
lae. 來 come.

Why do you not do as I say?

Wei 爲 Do
shin 甚 } what
mo 麽 }
puh 不 not
chaou 照 } according to
choh 着 }
wo 我 I
shwoh 說 say
teih 的 which
hwa 話 words
tso. 做 do.

When are you coming to my house?

Na 那 Which
t'ëen 天 day
yaou 要 intend
taou 到 to
wo 我 my
këa 家 house
le 裡 in
lae. 來 come.

When are you going to the provincial city?

Ne 你 You
ke 幾 } when
she 時 }
yaou 要 intend
wang 往 go

中外對話



săng 省 province
ch'ing 城 city
kh'eu. 去 go.

When do you start?

Shin 甚 } What
mo 麽 }
she 時 } time
how 候 }
urh 兒 —
kh'e 起 } start.
ch'ing. 程 }

When did you arrive here?

Ne 你 You
ke 幾 } when
she 時 }
taou 到 arrive
chay 這 } here.
le. 裡 }

Starting from here, how many days will it take to reach home?

Chay 這 } Here
le 裡 }
kh'e 起 } start
shin 身 }
to 多 } how many
shaou 少 }
jih 日 } days
tsze 子 }
kh'o 可 } may
e 以 }
taou 到 arrive
këa. 家 home.

When may you be returning here?

Ne 你 You
ke 幾 } when
she 時 }
kh'o 可 } may
e 以 }
hwuy 回 return
taou 到 to
chay 這 } here.
le. 裡 }

Where is the Master?

Tung 東 } Master
këa 家 }
tsae 在 at
na 那 } where.
le. 裡 }

Take me to see him.

Tae 帶 Take
wo 我 me
kh'eu 去 go
këen 見 } see
këen 見 }
t'a 他 him.

Where do you live?

Ne 你 You
tsae 在 at
na 那 } where
le 裡 }
choo. 住 live.

Where is the shop?

P'oo 鋪 } Shop
tsze 子 }
tsae 在 at

na 那 } where.
le. 裡 }

Have you seen my little knife?

Wo 我 } My
teih 的 }
sëaou 小 small
taou 刀 } knife
tsze 子 }
ne 你 you
yew 有 have
kh'an 看 } see
këen 見 }
muh 沒 not
yew. 有 have.

Hand me your little knife that I may see whether it is mine or not?

Pa 把 Take
ne 你 } your
teih 的 }
sëaou 小 small
taou 刀 } knife
tsze 子 }
na 拿 hand
ch'uh 出 out
lae 來 come
kay 給 give
wo 我 me
kh'an 看 } look
kh'an 看 }
she 是 is
puh 不 not
she. 是 is.

Is it black, or white? Has it a handle or not?

She 是 Is
pih 白 } white
teih 的 }
she 是 is
hih 黑 } black
teih 的 }
yew 有 have
pa 把 } handle
urh 兒 }
muh 沒 not
yew. 有 have.

Is it native made or foreign?

She 是 Is
păn 本 } native
te 地 }
tso 做 } made
teih 的 }
she 是 is
wae 外 outer
yang 洋 ocean
lae 來 } come.
teih. 的 }

The road to Peking, is it by land or by water?

Wang 往 Proceed
king 京 } capital
le 裡 }
kh'eu 去 go
she 是 is
han 旱 dry
loo 路 route
she 是 is
shuy 水 water
loo. 路 route.

Is the road walkable? Is it smooth?

| | | |
|---|---|---|
| Loo | 路 | Road |
| haou | 好 | walkable |
| tsow | 走 | |
| puh | 不 | not |
| haou | 好 | walkable |
| tsow | 走 | |
| p'ing | 平 | even |
| puh | 不 | not |
| p'ing. | 平 | even. |

Is it a broad road or a path?

| | | |
|---|---|---|
| She | 是 | Is |
| ta | 大 | large |
| loo | 路 | road |
| she | 是 | is |
| sëaou | 小 | little |
| loo. | 路 | road. |

Is it a frequented road?

| | | |
|---|---|---|
| Tsow | 走 | Walk |
| teih | 的 | who |
| jin | 人 | people |
| to | 多 | many |
| puh | 不 | not |
| to. | 多 | many. |

How do you know this is the road?

| | | |
|---|---|---|
| Ne | 你 | You |
| tsăng | 怎 | how |
| mo | 麽 | |
| che | 知 | know |
| taou | 道 | |
| she | 是 | is |
| chay | 這 | this |
| t'ëaou | 條 | line |
| loo. | 路 | road. |

Is the road straight or crooked?

| | | |
|---|---|---|
| Loo | 路 | Road |
| she | 是 | is |
| chih | 直 | straight |
| teih | 的 | |
| she | 是 | is |
| wan | 灣 | crooked. |
| teih. | 的 | |

Is the hill road steep?

| | | |
|---|---|---|
| Shan | 山 | Hill |
| loo | 路 | road |
| tow | 陡 | steep |
| puh | 不 | not |
| tow. | 陡 | steep. |

How many feet broad is the road?

| | | |
|---|---|---|
| Loo | 路 | Road |
| yew | 有 | have |
| ke | 幾 | how many |
| ch'eh | 尺 | foot |
| kh'wan | 寬 | wide. |

What is the distance from this place to that?

| | | |
|---|---|---|
| Chay | 這 | This |
| ko | 個 | |
| te | 地 | place |
| fang | 方 | |
| taou | 到 | to |
| na | 那 | that |
| ko | 個 | |
| te | 地 | place |
| fang | 方 | |

yew 有 have
to 多 how much
yüen. 遠 far.

And will it be necessary to cross rivers?

Han 還 Yet
yaou 要 require
kwo 過 pass
ho 河 river
mo. 麽 ?

How many hills or rivers must be passed?

Yaou 要 Require
kwo 過 pass
to 多 } how many
shaou 少 }
shan 山 hills
to 多 } how many
shaou 少 }
shuy. 水 streams

Where is the Grand Canal?

Yün 運 Transport
lĕang 糧 grain
ho 河 stream
tsae 在 at
na 那 } where
le 裡 }
ne. 呢 ?

In what way is the river to be passed?

Kh'o 可 May
tsăng 怎 } what
mo 麽 }
yang 樣 manner
urh 兒 —
too 渡 ford
kwo 過 pass
ho 河 river
kh'eu 去 go
ne. 呢 ?

Do the hill streams dry up in winter?

Shan 山 Hill
shuy 水 streams
tung 冬 winter
t'ëen 天 weather
hwuy 會 apt to
kan 乾 dry up
mo. 麽 ?

Are there many canals to be met with on the road?

Loo 路 Road
shang 上 on
yew 有 have
kwo 過 } pass
choh 着 }
heu 許 very
to 多 many
sĕaou 小 } canal
ho 河 }
muh 沒 not
yew. 有 have.

How deep is the lake?

Hoo 湖 Lake
shuy 水 water
yew 有 have
to 多 } how many
shaou 少 }

ch'eh 尺 foot
shin. 深 deep.

Is it navigable for vessels?

Kh'o 可 May
she 駛 }
teih 的 } navigate
ch'üen 船 vessel
mo. 麽 ?

Are there bridges over the streams?

Kwo 過 Pass
shuy 水 streams
yew 有 have
kh'ëaou 橋 bridge
mo. 麽 ?

What are the bridges made of?

Kh'ëaou 橋 Bridge
she 是 is
shin 甚 }
mo 麽 } what
tso 做 made
teih. 的 —

Are they of stone, or of wood?

She 是 Is
sheh 石 }
t'ow 頭 } stone
teih 的 of
she 是 is
muh 木 }
t'ow 頭 } wood
teih. 的 —

Are there any floating bridges?

Yew 有 Have
foo 浮 float
kh'ëaou 橋 bridge
muh 沒 not
yew. 有 have.

Are there jetties at every ford?

Koh 各 Every
too 渡 ford
too 都 all
yew 有 have
ma 馬 }
t'ow 頭 } jetty
mo. 麽 ?

Are the jetties made of wood or of stone?

Ma 馬 }
t'ow 頭 } Jetty
she 是 is
sheh 石 }
t'ow 頭 } stone
tsaou 造 made
teih 的 —
she 是 is
muh 木 }
t'ow 頭 } wood
tsaou 造 made
teih. 的 —

Does the tide flow as far as this?

Ch'aou 潮 }
shuy 水 } Tide
chang 漲 }
teih 的 } flow
taou 到 to
chay 這 }
le. 裡 } here

mo. 麽 —

Does this tide make fast or slow?

Chay 這 } This
ko 個 }
ch'aou 潮 tide
she 是 is
kin 緊 fast
lew 流 run
man 漫 slow
lew. 流 run.

The tide flows slowly, but ebbs fast.

Chang 漲 Flow
ch'aou 潮 tide
man 漫 slow
t'uy 退 retire
ch'aou 潮 tide
kin. 緊 fast.

Is there any ferry boat at the jetty?

Ma 馬 } Jetty
t'ow 頭 }
pang 傍 } side
pëen 邊 }
yew 有 have
too 渡 ferry
ch'üen 船 boat
muh 沒 not
yew. 有 have.

How large is the ferry boat?

Too 渡 Ferry
ch'üen 船 boat
yew 有 have
to 多 how much
ta. 大 large.

How many men scull the boat?

Yaou 搖 Scull
ch'üen 船 boat
yew 有 have
ke 幾 how
ko 個 many
jin. 人 man.

How many persons will the ferry boat carry?

Too 渡 Ferry
ch'üen 船 boat
tsae 載 carry
tih 得 can
to 多 } how many
shaou 少 }
jin. 人 man.

How much does each passenger pay?

May 每 Each
jin 人 man
ch'uh 出 pay out
ke 幾 how
ko 個 many
ts'ëen. 錢 cash.

What time does it take to cross the ferry?

To 多 How much
ta 大 great
kung 工 } work
foo 夫 }
too 渡 ferry
teih 的 can

中外對話

kwo 過 pass
kh'eu. 去 go.

Is there any official about here?

Chay 這 This
ko 個
te 地 place
fang 方
yew 有 have
kwan 官 official
muh 沒 not
yew. 有 have.

What is the official's name?

Kwan 官 Official
sing 姓 surname
shin 甚 what.
mo. 麽

Where does he live?

Choo 住 Live
tsae 在 at
na 那 where.
le. 裡

What office does he hold?

She 是 Is
shin 甚 what
mo 麽
kwan. 官 official.

What rank of button does he wear?

She 是 Is
ke 幾 what
p'in 品 rank
ting 頂 button.
tae. 戴

What is the man like in appearance?

Jin 人 Man
teih 的 of
sëang 相 appearance
maou 貌
shin 甚 what
mo 麽
yang. 様 kind.

Is his reputation good?

Ming 名 Reputation
shing 聲
haou 好 good
puh 不 not
haou. 好 good.

How many years has he been in office here?

Tsae 在 At
chay 這 here
le 裏
tso 做 acted
lëaou 了
ke 幾 how many
nëen 年 years
kwan 官 official
lëaou. 了 —

Is he pure, or is he corrupt?

She 是 Is
ts'ing 清 pure
teih 的
she 是 is
t'an 貪 covetous.
teih. 的

Do the people talk of him as good?

| | | |
|---|---|---|
| Pih | 百 | People |
| sing | 姓 | |
| shwoh | 說 | say |
| t'a | 他 | he |
| haou | 好 | good |
| puh | 不 | not |
| haou. | 好 | good. |

Does he receive bribes?

| | | |
|---|---|---|
| Show | 受 | Receive |
| hwuy | 賄 | bribe |
| puh | 不 | not |
| show. | 受 | receive. |

I want to go and call on him.

| | | |
|---|---|---|
| Wo | 我 | I |
| yaou | 要 | want |
| tsin | 進 | enter |
| kh'eu | 去 | go |
| këen | 見 | see |
| t'a. | 他 | him. |

Do the people of this neighbourhood like foreigners?

| | | |
|---|---|---|
| Chay | 這 | This place |
| le | 裡 | |
| teih | 的 | of |
| jin | 人 | men |
| he | 喜 | like |
| hwan | 歡 | |
| wae | 外 | outside |
| kwoh | 國 | nation |
| jin | 人 | men |
| puh | 不 | not |
| he | 喜 | like. |
| hwan. | 歡 | |

Is there any demand for foreign goods?

| | | |
|---|---|---|
| Yew | 有 | Have |
| jin | 人 | man |
| yaou | 要 | want |
| yang | 洋 | ocean |
| ho | 貨 | goods |
| muh | 沒 | not |
| yew. | 有 | have. |

Why don't the people fancy strangers?

| | | |
|---|---|---|
| Pih | 百 | People |
| sing | 姓 | |
| puh | 不 | not |
| he | 喜 | like |
| hwan | 歡 | |
| wae | 外 | outside |
| kwoh | 國 | nation |
| jin | 人 | man |
| she | 是 | is |
| shin | 甚 | what |
| mo | 麼 | |
| yüen | 緣 | reason. |
| koo. | 故 | |

Are the people of this place quiet or violent?

| | | |
|---|---|---|
| Tsze | 此 | This |
| te | 地 | place |
| jin | 人 | man |
| she | 是 | is |
| wăn | 温 | soft |
| jow | 柔 | gentle |
| teih | 的 | — |
| she | 是 | is |

kang 剛 hard
kh'ëang 强 rough.
teih. 的 —

Are the people here in the habit of drinking?

Tsae 在 At
chay 這 } here
le 裡 }
yew 有 have
jin 人 man
hoh 喝 drink
tsuy 醉 drunk
tsew 酒 wine
muh 沒 not
yew. 有 have.

Are there any opium-smokers here?

Yew 有 Have
jin 人 man
tsae 在 at
chay 這 } here
le 裡 }
ch'ih 吃 eat
ya 鴉 } opium
p'ëen 片 }
yen 烟 smoke
mo. 麽 ?

Are the people of this place mostly rich or mostly poor?

Tsze 此 This
ch'oo 處 place
teih 的 of
jin 人 } people
min 民 }
she 是 is
foo 富 } wealthy
kwei 貴 }
teih 的 }
to 多 many
hwoh 或 or
she 是 is
p'in 貧 } poor
kh'ëung 窮 }
teih 的 }
to. 多 many.

How do they earn their money, and how spend it?

T'a 他 } They
mun 們 }
she 是 is
tsăng 怎 } what
mo 麽 }
yang 様 manner
chüen 賺 earn
ts'ëen 錢 money
tsăng 怎 } what
mo 麽 }
yang 様 manner
yung. 用 use.

What are the houses about here made of?

Chay 這 } Here
le 裡 }
teih 的 of
fang 房 } houses
tsze 子 }
she 是 is

yung 用 use
shin 甚 } what
mo 麽 }
tung 東 } thing
se 西 }
tso 做 } made.
teih. 的 }

Is material good here?

Ts'ae 材 } Material
lëaou 料 }
haou 好 good
puh 不 not
haou. 好 good.

What is the cost of each house?

Yih 一 One
këen 間 lot
chih 値 worth
to 多 } how much
shaou 少 }
ts'ëen. 錢 money.

What cotton fabric do the people usually wear?

Min 民 } People
jin 人 }
măn 們 generally
ch'ang 常 usually
ch'üen 穿 } wear
teih 的 }
she 是 is
shin 甚 } what
mo 麽 }
poo. 布 cotton fabric.

What do they wear in summer, and what in winter?

Hëa 夏 Summer
t'ëen 天 time
ch'üen 穿 wear
shin 甚 } what
mo 麽 }
tung 冬 winter
t'ëen 天 time
ch'üen 穿 wear
shin 甚 } what
mo. 麽 }

What is the mode of transporting goods?

Pan 搬 Remove
yun 運 transport
ho 貨 } merchandize
wuh 物 }
she 是 is
tsăng 怎 } what
mo 麽 }
yang 樣 manner
pan 搬 remove
fah. 法 mode.

Are they conveyed by boat, or on horses, or by men?

She 是 Is
ch'üen 船 boat
tsae 載 } convey
teih 的 }
she 是 is
ma 馬 horse
t'o 駝 } carry
teih 的 }
hwoh 或 or
she 是 is

jin 人 man
t'ëaou 挑 } carry.
teih 的 }

Are the people about here a diligent race? Do the women labour?

Chay 這 } Here
le 裡 }
jin 人 man
kh'in 勤 diligent
puh 不 not
kh'in 勤 diligent
neu 女 } woman
jin 人 }
tso 做 do
kung 工 } work
foo 夫 }
puh 不 not
tso. 做 do.

Have any famous men been born here?

Tsze 此 This
ch'oo 處 place
yew 有 have
ch'uh 出 produce
ta 大 great
ming 名 } fame
shing 聲 }
jin 人 man
muh 沒 not
yew. 有 have.

What is the proportion of educated people in every hundred men?

Yih 一 One
pih 百 hundred
jin 人 man
che 之 of
chung 中 middle
yew 有 have
to 多 } how many
shaou 少 }
jin 人 man
tuh 讀 read
shoo. 書 book.

Are there many sick about here?

Chay 這 } This
ko 個 }
te 地 } place
fang 方 }
yew 有 have
ping 病 disease
teih 的 of
jin 人 man
to 多 many
puh 不 not
to. 多 many.

At what time of the year is sickness most general?

She 是 Is
shin 甚 } what
mo 麽 }
she 時 } time
how 候 }
kăng 更 more
hwuy 會 apt
fah 發 produce
ping. 病 disease.

What occasions the sickness?

| | | |
|---|---|---|
| Ping | 病 | Disease |
| she | 是 | is |
| yin | 因 | because |
| shin mo | 甚麽 | what |
| yüen koo | 緣故 | reason |
| kh'e teih. | 起的 | arise. |

Is it occasioned by damp, or by heat, or by cold?

| | | |
|---|---|---|
| Hwoh | 或 | Whether |
| she | 是 | is |
| yin wei | 因爲 | because |
| shih | 濕 | damp |
| kh'e | 氣 | vapour |
| hwoh | 或 | or |
| she | 是 | is |
| yin wei | 因爲 | because |
| show | 受 | receive |
| jeh | 熱 | hot |
| hwoh | 或 | or |
| she | 是 | is |
| yin wei | 因爲 | because |
| show | 受 | receive |
| fung. | 風 | cold. |

Is small-pox prevalent here?

| | | |
|---|---|---|
| Tsze | 此 | This |
| te | 地 | place |
| ch'uh | 出 | come out |
| tow tsze | 痘子 | small-pox |
| teih | 的 | of |
| jin | 人 | man |
| to | 多 | many |
| puh | 不 | not |
| to. | 多 | many. |

Is the foreign mode of vaccination at all sought after?

| | | |
|---|---|---|
| Chung | 種 | Plant |
| yang | 洋 | ocean |
| tow | 痘 | small-pox |
| teih | 的 | of |
| fah tsze | 法子 | mode |
| yew | 有 | have |
| jin | 人 | man |
| yaou | 要 | want |
| yung | 用 | use |
| muh | 沒 | not |
| yew. | 有 | have. |

Are any sold as slaves here?

| | | |
|---|---|---|
| Tsze | 此 | This |
| te | 地 | place |
| yew | 有 | have |
| jin | 人 | man |
| mae | 賣 | sell |
| shin | 身 | body |
| tso | 做 | make |
| noo ts'ae | 奴才 | slave |
| muh | 沒 | not |
| yew. | 有 | have. |

Is the condition of the slaves hard to bear?

| | | |
|---|---|---|
| Tso | 做 | Become |
| noo | 奴 | slave |
| ts'ae | 才 | |
| teih | 的 | of |
| ts'ing | 情 | condition |
| hing | 形 | |
| nan | 難 | difficult |
| tang | 當 | bear |
| puh | 不 | not |
| nan | 難 | difficult |
| tang. | 當 | bear. |

How do persons become slaves?

| | | |
|---|---|---|
| She | 是 | Is |
| tsăng | 怎 | how |
| mo | 麽 | |
| wei | 爲 | become |
| noo | 奴 | slave |
| teih. | 的 | — |

Children are sold by parents.

| | | |
|---|---|---|
| She | 是 | Is |
| foo | 父 | father |
| moo | 母 | mother |
| mae | 賣 | sell |
| teih. | 的 | |

Or is it because people in debt pledge themselves, or felons suffer slavery as a penalty of the law?

| | | |
|---|---|---|
| Hwoh | 或 | Or |
| she | 是 | is |
| yin | 因 | because |
| wei | 爲 | |
| tsze | 自 | self |
| ke | 己 | |
| kh'ëen | 欠 | owe |
| ts'ëen | 錢 | money |
| tang | 當 | pledge |
| shin | 身 | body |
| teih | 的 | — |
| hwoh | 或 | or |
| she | 是 | is |
| fan | 犯 | commit |
| tsuy | 罪 | crime |
| teih. | 的 | — |

Or do people kidnap children from other places, and bring them here for sale?

| | | |
|---|---|---|
| Hwoh | 或 | Or |
| she | 是 | is |
| pëeh | 別 | other |
| ch'oo | 處 | place |
| kwae | 拐 | kidnap |
| sëaou | 小 | little |
| hae | 孩 | child |
| tsze | 子 | |
| tae | 帶 | bring |
| lae | 來 | come |
| mae | 賣 | sell |
| teih. | 的 | — |

Or do poor people sell themselves?

| | | |
|---|---|---|
| Hwoh | 或 | Or |
| she | 是 | is |
| kh'eung | 窮 | poor |
| jin | 人 | man |
| tsze | 自 | self |
| ke | 己 | |

mae 賣 sell
shin 身 body
teih. 的 —

Do the people of this district ever desert their female children?

Păn 本 This
hëen 縣 district
yew 有 have
jin 人 } people
këa 家 }
puh 不 not
yang 養 bring up
hwoh 活 alive
neu 女 female
hae 孩 } child
urh 兒 }
mo. 麽 ?

Do the people drown their daughters?

Yew 有 Have
jin 人 man
neih 溺 } drown
sze 死 }
neu 女 } girl
urh 兒 }
muh 沒 not
yew. 有 have.

Do any persons cast away their daughters in the hope of their being cared for by somebody else?

Yew 有 Have
jin 人 man
p'aou 拋 throw
kh'e 棄 reject
neu 女 } girl
urh 兒 }
sëang 想 think
yaou 要 want
pëeh 別 other
jin 人 man
show 收 take
yang 養 bring up
mo 麽 ?

How many girls are yearly rescued by the foundling hospital?

Yuh 育 Nourish
ying 嬰 infant
t'ang 堂 hall
may 每 each
nëen 年 year
kew 救 rescue
yew 有 have
to 多 } how many
shaou 少 }
neu 女 } girl.
urh. 兒 }

What is the proportion of families in every hundred that drown their girls?

Yih 一 One
pih 百 hundred
këa 家 family
che 之 of
chung 中 middle
yew 有 have
to 多 } how many
shaou 少 }

këa 家 family
neih 溺
sze 死 drown
neu 女
urh 兒 girl
teih. 的 —

Are you acquainted with any persons who drown girls?

Ne 你 You
yew 有 have
jin 認
shih 識 acquainted
neih 溺
sze 死 drown
neu 女
urh 兒 girl
teih 的 who
jin 人 man
mo. 麽 ?

What sect do the people of your part of the country belong to?

Kwei 貴 Honoured
ch'oo 處 place
pih 百
sing 姓 people
tsun 遵
fung 奉 venerate
shin 甚
mo 麽 what
këaou. 教 doctrine.

Are there any disciples of Confucius?

Yew 有 Have
jin 人 man
tsun 遵
fung 奉 venerate
kh'ung 孔
foo 夫 Confucius
tsze 子
teih 的 of
taou 道
le 理 doctrine
muh 沒 not
yew. 有 have

Are the larger half followers of Buddha?

Tsun 遵
fung 奉 Venerate
fuh 佛 Buddha
këaou 教 doctrine
teih 的 who
yew 有 have
yih 一 one
ta 大 large
pan 半 half
jin 人
këa 家 people
mo. 麽 ?

How many men out of every thousand are priests?

Yih 一 One
ts'ëen 千 thousand
jin 人 man
che 之 of
chung 中 middle
yew 有 have
ke 幾 how

ko 個 many
jin 人 man
tso 做 make
ho 和 } priest.
shang. 尚 }

Are there any believers in the Taouist priesthood?

Yew 有 Have
jin 人 man
sin 信 believe
taou 道 Taou
sze 士 priest
muh 沒 not
yew. 有 have.

Which of the three sects, the Literati, Buddhist, and Taouist, has the largest number of temples?

Joo 儒 Literati
shih 釋 Buddhism
taou 道 Taouism
san 三 three
këaou 教 sects
na 那 which
këaou 教 sect
teih 的 of
mëaou 廟 temple
tsuy 最 most
to. 多 many.

Is there any history of China?

Chung 中 } China
kwoh 國 }
yew 有 have
she 史 history
ke 記 record
muh 沒 not
yew. 有 have.

Are the general mirrors of history considered trustworthy?

Kang 綱 General
këen 鑑 mirror
kh'o 可 may
sin 信 believe
puh 不 not
kh'o 可 may
sin. 信 believe.

Who composed them?

She 是 Is
shuy 誰 who
tso 做 } make.
teih. 的 }

How many years have passed since the founding of the nation?

Tsze 自 From
kh'ae 開 open
kwoh 國 nation
che 至 till
kin 今 now
kung 共 } altogether
tsung 總 }
yew 有 have
to 多 } how many
shaou 少 }
nëen. 年 year.

What are the dynasties downward from Yaou and Shun?

Tsze 自 From
yaou 堯 Yaou

shun 舜 Shun
e 以 and
lae 來 downward
too 都 all
she 是 is
shin 甚 } what
mo 麽 }
ch'aou 朝 } dynasty.
tae. 代 }

Which dynasty ruled the country for the longest space of time?

She 是 Is
na 那 } which
ko 個 }
ch'aou 朝 } dynasty
tae 代 }
tso 做 do
t'ëen 天 } empire
hëa 下 }
teih 的 of
nëen 年 } years
suy 歲 }
tsuy 最 most
kew. 久 long.

Which dynasty was the most famous?

She 是 Is
na 那 } which
ko 個 }
ch'aou 朝 } dynasty
tae 代 }
tsuy 最 most
yew 有 have
ming 名 } fame.
shing. 聲 }

What great sages appeared in ancient times?

Tsze 自 From
koo 古 ancient time
e 以 and
lae 來 downward
yew 有 have
shin 甚 } what
mo 麽 }
ch'uh 出 come out
chung 衆 multitude
teih 的 who
shing 聖 } sage.
jin. 人 }

When did that sage flourish?

Na 那 } That
ko 個 }
shing 聖 } sage
jin 人 }
shin 甚 } what
mo 麽 }
she 時 } time
how 候 }
ch'uh 出 come out
she. 世 age.

What great general appeared in ancient times?

Koo 古 Ancient
she 時 } time
how 候 }
yew 有 have

F

| | | |
|---|---|---|
| na | 那 | what |
| ko | 個 | |
| ch'uh | 出 | come out |
| ming | 名 | name |
| teih | 的 | who |
| ta | 大 | great |
| tsëang. | 將 | general. |

Where did he gain a victory, and what were his tactics?

| | | |
|---|---|---|
| Tsae | 在 | At |
| na | 那 | where |
| le | 裡 | |
| ta | 打 | fight |
| shing | 勝 | victory |
| chang | 仗 | battle |
| yew | 有 | have |
| shin | 甚 | what |
| mo | 麼 | |
| t'aou | 韜 | tactics. |
| lëoh. | 畧 | |

Were there also any poets or talented men?

| | | |
|---|---|---|
| Han | 還 | Also |
| yew | 有 | have |
| she | 詩 | poet |
| jin | 人 | |
| ts'ae | 才 | talented men |
| tsze | 子 | |
| muh | 沒 | not |
| yew. | 有 | have. |

When did Le T'ae-pih* flourish?

| | | |
|---|---|---|
| Le | 李 | Le T'ae-pih |
| t'ae | 太 | |
| pih | 白 | |
| she | 是 | is |
| shin | 甚 | what |
| mo | 麼 | |
| she | 時 | time |
| how | 候 | |
| ch'uh | 出 | come out |
| teih | 的 | |
| ming. | 名 | name. |

How many poems did he write?

| | | |
|---|---|---|
| Tso | 做 | Made |
| kwo | 過 | |
| yew | 有 | have |
| to | 多 | how many |
| shaou | 少 | |
| she. | 詩 | poems. |

Are there any manufacturers of cloth here?

| | | |
|---|---|---|
| Păn | 本 | This |
| te | 地 | place |
| yew | 有 | have |
| jin | 人 | man |
| chih | 織 | weave |
| poo | 布 | cloth |
| muh | 沒 | not |
| yew. | 有 | have. |

Is weaving done in families, or in establishments set up for the purpose?

| | | |
|---|---|---|
| Hwoh | 或 | Whether |
| she | 是 | is |
| koh | 各 | every |
| këa | 家 | family |
| tsze | 自 | self |

* A famous poet.

chih 織 weave
hwoh 或 or
she 是 is
sheh 設 set up
ke 機 machine
fang 坊 establishment
tae 代 for
chih 織 weave
ne. 呢 ?

Are there any weaving establishments here?

Chay 這 } Here
le 裡 }
yew 有 have
ke 機 machine
fang 坊 establishments
muh 沒 not
yew. 有 have.

Are the looms worked by hand only, or also by water and cattle power?

She 使 Work
ke 機 machine
tan 單 only
she 是 is
yung 用 employ
jin 人 men
hwoh 或 or
she 是 is
han 還 likewise
yung 用 employ
shuy 水 water
leih 力 power
new 牛 ox
leih. 力 power.

In the weaving establishments, do they also manufacture silks or crapes?

Ke 機 Machine
fang 坊 establishment
le 裡 in
han 還 yet
yew 有 have
chih 織 weave
ch'ow 紬 } silk stuff
twan 緞 }
chow 縐 } crape
sha 紗 }
muh 沒 not
yew. 有 have.

Are there yet any other manufactories?

Han 還 Yet
yew 有 have
pëeh 別 } other
teih 的 }
tsoh 作 } manufactories
fang 坊 }
muh 沒 not
yew. 有 have.

In this city are there any powder manufactories or mints?

Păn 本 This
ch'ing 城 city
le 裡 in
yew 有 have
ho 火 } gunpowder
yoh 藥 }

| | | |
|---|---|---|
| këuh | 局 | establishment |
| choo | 鑄 | melt |
| ts'ëen | 錢 | money |
| këuh | 局 | establishment |
| muh | 沒 | not |
| yew. | 有 | have. |

Is it a government establishment or not?

| | | |
|---|---|---|
| She | 是 | Is |
| kwan | 官 | government |
| sheh | 設 | establish |
| teih | 的 | |
| puh | 不 | not |
| she. | 是 | is. |

Is there any famous manufactory in this place?

| | | |
|---|---|---|
| Tsz'e | 此 | This |
| ch'oo | 處 | place |
| yew | 有 | have |
| ch'uh | 出 | come out |
| ming | 名 | name |
| teih | 的 | of |
| tsoh | 作 | manufactory |
| fang | 坊 | |
| muh | 沒 | not |
| yew. | 有 | have. |

Is it of shoes, or of caps, or of iron, or of wood, or of bamboo, or of needles?

| | | |
|---|---|---|
| Hwoh | 或 | Either |
| she | 是 | |
| hëae | 鞋 | shoe |
| tsoh | 作 | make |
| maou | 帽 | cap |
| tsoh | 作 | make |
| t'ëeh | 鐵 | iron |
| tsoh | 作 | make |
| muh | 木 | wood |
| tsoh | 作 | make |
| chuh | 竹 | bamboo |
| tsoh | 作 | make |
| chin | 針 | needle |
| tsoh. | 作 | make. |

Is there a cotton establishment here?

| | | |
|---|---|---|
| Tsz'e | 此 | This |
| ch'oo | 處 | place |
| yew | 有 | have |
| mëen | 棉 | cotton |
| hwa | 花 | |
| këuh | 局 | establishment |
| mo. | 麽 | ? |

Is the establishment for making cotton stuff, or entirely for carding cotton?

| | | |
|---|---|---|
| Këuh | 局 | Establishment |
| le | 裡 | in |
| she | 是 | is |
| tso | 做 | make |
| mëen | 棉 | cotton |
| poo | 布 | cloth |
| ne | 呢 | ? |
| hwoh | 或 | or |
| she | 是 | is |
| tsin | 盡 | entirely |
| tan | 彈 | card |
| mëen | 棉 | cotton |
| hwa | 花 | |

ne. 呢 ?

Are there any salt manufactories here? Are they official or illicit?

Yew 有 Have
jin 人 man
tso 做 make
yen 鹽 salt
muh 沒 not
yew 有 have
she 是 is
kwan 官 } official
teih 的 }
she 是 is
sze 私 } private.
teih. 的 }

Is the salt boiled or sun-dried?

Yen 鹽 Salt
she 是 is
choo 煮 } boil
teih 的 }
she 是 is
shae 曬 } dry.
teih. 的 }

Are there any porcelain kilns here?

Yew 有 Have
tsz'e 磁 } porcelain
kh'e 器 }
yaou 窰 furnace
mo. 麽 ?

Is porcelain made here?

Chay 這 } Here
le 裡 }
tso 做 } made
teih 的 }
tsz'e 磁 } porcelain.
kh'e. 器 }

Is it better than what is produced at King-teh-chin?*

Pe 比 Compare
king 景 }
teh 德 } King-teh-chin
chin 鎮 }
tso 做 } make
teih 的 }
kăng 更 more
haou 好 good
mo. 麽 ?

What is used for dyeing cloth?

Poo 布 Cloth
yung 用 use
shin 甚 } what
mo 麽 }
jen 染 } dye.
teih. 的 }

Is indigo produced here?

Tsz'e 此 This
ch'oo 處 place
ch'uh 出 produce
lan 藍 blue
tëen 靛 indigo
mo. 麽 ?

Where do saffron and brazil-wood come from?

Hung 紅 } Saffron
hwa 花 }

* The porcelain district of China.

soo 蘇 } brazil-wood
muh 木 }
she 是 is
na 那 } where
le 裡 }
lae 來 } come.
teih. 的 }

What goods are exported hence?

Tsz'e 此 This
ch'oo 處 place
ch'uh 出 leave
kh'ow 口 port
teih 的 which
yew 有 have
shin 甚 } what
mo 麽 }
ho. 貨 goods.

How many peculs of brass-ware are yearly exported?

Yih 一 One
nëen 年 year
tsae 載 carry
ch'uh 出 out
to 多 } how many
shaou 少 }
tan 担 pecul
t'ung 銅 brass
kh'e 器 vessel
kh'eu. 去 go.

Where is plaster* made?

Kaou 膏 } Plaster
yoh 藥 }
she 是 is
tsae 在 at
na 那 } where
le 裡 }
tso 做 } make.
teih. 的 }

What price is rhubarb of the best quality?

Shang 上 Superior
tăng 等 class
ta 大 } rhubarb
hwang 黃 }
mae 賣 sell
shin 甚 } what
mo 麽 }
këa 價 } price.
ts'ëen. 錢 }

In what month does cotton ripen here?

Chung 種 Plant
mëen 棉 } cotton
hwa 花 }
she 是 is
na 那 } which
ko 個 }
yüeh 月 month
ts'ae 纔 then
shuh. 熟 ripe.

Is quick-silver produced here, or is it brought from foreign parts?

Shuy 水 } Quicksilver
yin 銀 }

* Kaou yoh is a general name for all ointments whether intended to soothe, irritate, draw, or heal.

中外對話

| | | |
|---|---|---|
| she | 是 | is |
| păn | 本 | this |
| te | 地 | country |
| ch'uh | 出 | produce |
| teih | 的 | |
| hwoh | 或 | or |
| she | 是 | is |
| wae | 外 | outside |
| kwoh | 國 | nation |
| tae | 帶 | bring |
| lae | 來 | come. |
| teih. | 的 | |

What weights do the natives of this place use in buying and selling?

| | | |
|---|---|---|
| Păn | 本 | This |
| te | 地 | place |
| jin | 人 | man |
| mae | 買 | buy |
| mae | 賣 | sell |
| tung | 東 | things |
| se | 西 | |
| yung | 用 | use |
| shin | 甚 | what |
| mo | 麼 | |
| ch'ing. | 秤 | weights. |

How many taels per catty has the weight in common use?

| | | |
|---|---|---|
| Ch'ang | 常 | Constant |
| yung | 用 | use |
| teih | 的 | of |
| ch'ing | 秤 | weight |
| yih | 一 | one |
| kin | 斤 | catty |
| she | 是 | is |
| to | 多 | how many |
| shaou | 少 | |
| lëang. | 兩 | tael. |

Are the standard weights heavier or lighter as compared with those in common use?

| | | |
|---|---|---|
| Sze | 司 | Government standard |
| ma | 碼 | |
| ch'ing | 秤 | weight |
| pe | 比 | compare |
| ch'ang | 常 | common |
| yung | 用 | use |
| teih | 的 | of |
| ch'ing | 秤 | weight |
| she | 是 | is |
| ta | 大 | large |
| she | 是 | is |
| sëaou. | 小 | small. |

How much lighter are the common weights per hundred catties?

| | | |
|---|---|---|
| Ch'ang | 常 | Common |
| yung | 用 | use |
| teih | 的 | of |
| ch'ing | 秤 | weight |
| yih | 一 | one |
| pih | 百 | hundred |
| kin | 斤 | catty |
| sëaou | 小 | small |
| to | 多 | how much. |
| shaou. | 少 | |

Compared with foreign weights, what is the difference?

| | | |
|---|---|---|
| Pe | 比 | Compare |
| wae | 外 | outside |

kwoh 國 nation
ch'ing 秤 weight
yih 一 one
pih 百 hundred
kin 斤 catty
ch'a 差 differ
to 多 } how much
shaou. 少 }

Are the Custom-house weights used in the English and Chinese trade?

Hwa 華 Chinese
ying 英 English
t'ung 通 intercourse
shang 商 commerce
she 是 is
yung 用 use
hae 海 } Custom-house
kwan 關 }
ch'ing 秤 weight
mo. 麼 ?

How many cash is rice here per pecul?

Chay 這 } Here
le 裡 }
yih 一 one
tan 石 pecul
me 米 rice
swan 算 reckon
to 多 } how many
shaou 少 }
ts'ëen. 錢 cash.

Is rice bought here by the catty or by the peck?

Tsz'e 此 This
te 地 place
mae 買 buy
me 米 rice
she 是 is
lun 論 reckon
kin 斤 catty
she 是 is
lun 論 reckon
tow. 斗 peck.

What is the difference between the four terms, taou, kuh, me, and fan?

Taou 稻 Paddy
kuh 穀 grain
me 米 rice
fan 飯 cooked rice
sze 四 four
yang 樣 sorts
yew 有 have
shin 甚 } what
mo 麼 }
făn 分 } difference.
pëeh. 別 }

Rice whilst growing in the water is called "taou."

Tsae 在 At
shuy 水 water
le 裡 in
chang 長 } grow
teih 的 }
ch'ing 稱 call
wei 爲 is
taou. 稻 paddy.

Rice in the ear is called "kuh."

中外對話

Taou 稻 Paddy
shang 上 on
këeh 結 form
teih 的 which
tsze 子 seed
leih 粒 grain
ch'ing 稱 call
wei 爲 is
kuh. 穀 grain.

The grain of rice unhusked is called "me."

Kuh 穀 Grain
kh'eu 去 remove
lëaou 了 off
p'e 皮 skin
ch'ing 稱 call
wei 爲 is
me. 米 rice.

The unhusked rice boiled is called "fan."

Me 米 Rice
choo 煮 boil
shuh 熟 } cooked
lëaou 了 }
ch'ing 稱 call
wei 爲 is
fan. 飯 rice boiled.

Are the same weights used in buying rice as in buying beans?

Mae 買 Buy
me 米 rice
t'ung 同 with
mae 買 buy
tow 豆 } beans
tsze 子 }
she 是 is
yih 一 one
yang 樣 kind
teih 的 of
ch'ing 秤 weight
mo. 麽 ?

Is oil sold by weight or measurement?

Yew 油 Oil
she 是 is
lăn 論 reckon
ch'ing 稱 weigh
hwoh 或 or
she 是 is
lăn 論 reckon
lëang. 量 measure.

What things are reckoned by weight?

Shin 甚 } What
mo 麽 }
tung 東 } thing
se 西 }
she 是 is
lăn 論 reckon
chung 重 heavy
teih. 的 by.

What things are reckoned by quantity?

Shin 甚 } What
mo 麽 }
tung 東 } thing
se 西 }
she 是 is
lăn 論 reckon
to 多 much

teih. 的 by.

What things are reckoned by number?

Shin 甚 }
mo 麼 } What
tung 東 }
se 西 } thing
she 是 is
lăn 論 reckon
këen 件 article
teih. 的 by.

What things are reckoned by length?

Shin 甚 }
mo 麼 } What
tung 東 }
se 西 } thing
she 是 is
lăn 論 reckon
ch'ang 長 length
teih. 的 by.

What goods are traded in to and fro inland?

Nuy 內 }
te 地 } Inland
le 裡 within
lae 來 come
wang 往 go
yün 運 carry
mae 賣 sell
teih 的 which
she 是 is
shin 麼 }
mo 甚 } what

ho. 貨 goods.

What goods are exported seawards?

Tsae 載 Carry
ch'uh 出 out
hae 海 sea
kh'ow 口 port
teih 的 which
yew 有 have
shin 甚 }
mo 麼 } what
ho 貨 goods.

What goods are most largely exported hence?

Tsz'e 此 This
te 地 place
ch'uh 出 go out
kh'ow 口 port
teih 的 which
shin 甚 }
mo 麼 } what
ho 貨 goods
tsuy 最 most
to. 多 much.

Where are these goods principally carried to?

Chay 這 }
ko 個 } This
ho 貨 goods
ta 大 }
kae 概 } mainly
tsae 載 carry
taou 到 to
na 那 }
le 裡 } where

kh'eu. 去 go.

Is there much fishing along the coast?

Yüen 沿 Along
hae 海 sea
te 地 } place
fang 方 }
yew 有 have
heu 許 very
to 多 many
jin 人 man
ta 打 catch
yü 魚 fish
mo. 麽 ?

Is fish put up with ice or with salt?

Fang 放 Place
yü 魚 fish
she 是 is
yung 用 use
ping 冰 ice
ne 呢 ?
she 是 is
yung 用 use
yen 鹽 salt
ne. 呢 ?

What boats do the natives of this place use?

Păn 本 This
te 地 place
jin 人 man
yung 用 use
shin 甚 what
mo 麽 —
ch'üen. 船 boat.

How many kinds of boats have they here?

Tsz'e 此 This
ch'oo 處 place
yew 有 have
ke 幾 how many
yang 樣 sort
ch'üen. 船 boat.

Can the boats go out to sea?

Ch'üen 船 Boat
kh'o 可 may
năng 能 can
ch'uh 出 go out
hae 海 sea
mo. 麽 ?

How many peculs can the sea-going boats carry?

Kwo 過 Pass
hae 海 sea
ch'üen 船 boat
năng 能 can
tsae 載 carry
to 多 } how many
shaou 少 }
tan. 担 pecul.

How much would a boat of 5,000 peculs burthen cost?

Tsae 載 Carry
woo 五 five
ts'ëen 千 thousand
tan 担 pecul
teih 的 which

ch'üen 船 boat
chih 値 cost
to 多 } how much
shaou 少 }
yin 銀 } money.
tsze. 子 }

How many vessels come and go at this port during the year?

Chay 這 This
hae 海 sea
kh'ow 口 port
may 每 each
nëen 年 year
lae 來 come
wang 往 go
yew 有 have
to 多 } how many
shaou 少 }
ch'üen. 船 boat.

How many people ply boats for a livelihood here?

She 駛 Run
ch'üen 船 boat
wei 爲 for
săng 生 livelihood
teih 的 of
yew 有 have
to 多 } how many
shaou 少 }
jin. 人 man.

How large is the trade at this port?

Chay 這 } This
ko 個 }
ma 馬 } wharf
t'ow 頭 }
yew 有 have
to 多 how much
ta 大 large
săng 生 } trade.
e. 意 }

How many myriads of taels' worth of goods go in and out yearly?

May 每 Each
nëen 年 year
ch'uh 出 go out
juh 入 enter
teih 的 which
ho 貨 } goods
wuh 物 }
chih 値 worth
ke 幾 how many
wan 萬 myriad
yin 銀 } money.
tsze. 子 }

Is the trade of this year larger than that of last year?

Kin 今 This
nëen 年 year
săng 生 } trade
e 意 }
pe 比 compare
wang 往 gone
nëen 年 year
săng 生 } trade
e 意 }
ta 大 large

mo. 麽 —

How much revenue does the Customs receive *per annum*.

May 每 Each
nëen 年 year
hae 海 Maritime
kwan 關 Customs
show 收 receive
to 多 } how much
shaou 少 }
hëang. 餉 duty.

Is there any smuggling here?

Tsz'*e* 此 This
ch'oo 處 place
yew 有 have
t'ow 偷 } smuggling
low 漏 }
teih 的 of
pe 弊 irregularity
mo. 麽 ?

What goods are usually smuggled?

Jin 人 } People
këa 家 }
p'ing 平 } usually
ch'ang 常 }
t'ow 偷 } smuggle
low 漏 }
teih 的 which
sh*e* 是 is
shin 甚 } what
mo 麽 }
ho. 貨 goods.

Are eatables and necessaries of life dear or cheap?

Jin 人 } People
këa 家 }
sin 尋 } commonly
ch'ang 常 }
ch'ih 吃 eat
yung 用 use
teih 的 which
tung 東 } thing
se 西 }
tsz'*e* 此 this
te 地 place
kwei 貴 dear
tsëen. 賤 cheap.

Do the people find a livelihood with ease?

Pih 百 } People
sing 姓 }
măn 們 }
kwo 過 pass
jih 日 } day
tsze 子 }
yung 容 } easy
e 易 }
puh 不 not
yung 容 } easy.
e. 易 }

How do the people here earn their money?

Păn 本 This
te 地 place
jin 人 people
she 是 is
tso 做 do

shin 甚 } what
mo 麽 }
sze 事 business
chüen 賺 earn
ts'ëen. 錢 money.

Do they cultivate, or work, or trade?

She 是 Is
chung 種 plant
t'ëen 田 field
she 是 is
tso 做 do
kung 工 work
hwoh 或 or
she 是 is
tso 做 do
mae 買 buy
mae 賣 sell
teih. 的 —

Are the people here well to do, or poor and wretched?

Tsz'e 此 This
ch'oo 處 place
teih 的 of
pih 百 } people
sing 姓 }
she 是 is
foo 富 rich
tsuh 足 sufficient
teih 的 —
hwoh 或 or
she 是 is
kh'eung 窮 poor
kh'oo 苦 wretched
teih. 的 —

Do more people come in than go away?

Jin 人 People
hwoh 或 either
she 是 are
ch'uh 出 go
wae 外 outside
teih 的 which
to 多 many
hwoh 或 or
she 是 is
wae 外 outside
lae 來 come
teih 的 which
to. 多 many.

In business both sycee and dollars are used.

Mae 買 } Business
mae 賣 }
yew 有 have
yung 用 use
yüen 元 } sycee
paou 寶 }
yew 有 have
yung 用 use
yang 洋 } dollar
ts'ëen 錢 }
teih. 的 —

But dollars, to be exchanged in sycee, must be reckoned according to their intrinsic purity.

Tan 但 But

中外對話



| | | |
|---|---|---|
| yang | 洋 | Dollar |
| ts'ëen | 錢 | |
| tuy | 兌 | exchange |
| hwan | 換 | |
| yin | 銀 | silver |
| tsze | 子 | |
| yaou | 要 | must |
| ngan | 按 | according to |
| ch'ing | 成 | purity |
| sih | 色 | |
| chaou | 照 | proportionately |
| swan | 筭 | reckon |

What rate of purity are dollars reckoned at?

| | | |
|---|---|---|
| Yang | 洋 | Dollars |
| ts'ëen | 錢 | |
| swan | 筭 | reckon |
| shin | 甚 | what |
| mo | 麽 | |
| ch'ing | 成 | purity |
| sih | 色 | |

As a general rule 72 taels of sycee equal 100 dollars?

| | | |
|---|---|---|
| Ta | 大 | Generally |
| kae | 槪 | |
| she | 是 | is |
| ts'eih | 七 | seven |
| shih | 十 | ten |
| urh | 二 | two |
| lëang | 兩 | taels |
| yin | 銀 | silver |
| tsze | 子 | |
| tuy | 兌 | exchange |
| hwan | 換 | |
| yih | 一 | one |
| pih | 百 | hundred |
| yüen | 元 | pieces |
| yang | 洋 | dollars |
| ts'ëen | 錢 | |

But some dollars are purer than others; and they differ in market value.

| | | |
|---|---|---|
| Tan | 但 | But |
| yang | 洋 | dollars |
| ts'ëen | 錢 | |
| yew | 有 | have |
| haou | 好 | good |
| tae | 歹 | bad |
| she | 市 | market |
| këa | 價 | price |
| yay | 也 | also |
| yew | 有 | have |
| puh | 不 | not |
| t'ung. | 同 | similar |

Sycee differs in the purity of its touch.

| | | |
|---|---|---|
| Yin | 銀 | Silver |
| tsze | 子 | |
| teih | 的 | of |
| ch'ing | 成 | purity |
| sih | 色 | |
| yew | 有 | have |
| tsuh | 足 | sufficient |
| puh | 不 | not |
| tsuh. | 足 | sufficient |

If it fails in purity, the deficiency whatever it is, is made up.

Joo 如 If
kwo 果 indeed
puh 不 not
tsuh 足 sufficient
chaou 照 according
soo 數 amount
poo 補 make up
swan 算 reckon

When money is paid as government duty, melting expences must be added.

Joh 若 If
wan 完 pay
kwan 官 government
shuy 稅 duty
wae 外 besides
këa 加 add
ho 火 fire
haou 耗 lessen

The "Ho haou" is properly meltage.

Ho 火 Ho
haou 耗 haou
păn 本 originally
she 是 is
kh'ăng 傾 waste
sëaou 銷 melt
fei 費 expence

But expences of transmission, food of workmen, and other items, are also included.

Tan 但 But
këa 解 transmit
fei 費 expence
fan 飯 rice
'shih 食 eat
koh 各 every
hëang 項 item
yay 也 also
swan 算 reckon
tsae 在 at
nuy 內 within

But the rates and modes of use of dollars and sycee silver differ everywhere.

Tan 但 But
yin 銀 } silver
tsze 子 }
yang 洋 } dollars
ts'ëen 錢 }
koh 各 every
ch'oo 處 place
teih 的 of
hang 行 store
ts'ing 情 circumstances
yung 用 use
fah 法 mode
puh 不 not
t'ung 同 similar

Every place has its own particular mode of weighing silver.

Ch'ing 稱 Weigh
yin 銀 } silver
tsze 子 }
koh 各 every
ch'oo 處 place
yew 有 have
koh 各 every

ch'oo 處 place
teih 的 of
t'ëen 天 } scales.
p'ing. 平 }

The *sze-ma* scales, issued by the Board of Revenue, are accepted as standard throughout China.

T'ung 通 Throughout
t'ëen 天 } empire
hëa 下 }
e 以 take
sze 司 Board
ma 碼 weight
p'ing 平 scale
wei 爲 as
chun 準 standard
she 是 is
hoo 戶 revenue
poo 部 board
pan 頒 } issued.
teih. 的 }

In foreign commerce the Canton Customs scales are the standard.

Wae 外 Outside
kwoh 國 nation
t'ung 通 } commercial intercourse
shang 商 }
e 以 take
yüeh 粤 Canton
hae 海 sea
kwan 關 customs
p'ing 平 scale
wei 爲 as
ch'ang 常 } standard.
tsih. 則 }

There are bankers everywhere who take deposit of money and issue notes as a business.

Koh 各 } Everywhere
ch'oo 處 }
too 都 all
yew 有 have
yin 銀 } banker
haou 號 }
tso 做 do
ts'un 存 deposit
yin 銀 silver
ch'uh 出 issue
p'eaou 票 note
teih 的 of
săng 生 } business.
e. 意 }

In some places there are public valuing establishments set up for valuing silver at.

Yew 有 Have
te 地 } place
fang 方 }
yew 有 have
kung 公 public
koo 估 value
këuh 局 establishment
wei 爲 for
koo 估 value
kh'an 看 look
yin 銀 } silver
tsze 子 }

sheh 設 } set up.
teih. 的 }

For examining each ingot of sycee a certain amount of value money is by rule payable.

Koo 估 Value
kh'an 看 look
may 每 each
ting 錠 ingot
yüen 元 } sycee
paou 寶 }
chaou 照 by
leih 例 rule
foo 付 } pay
kay 給 }
koo 估 value
ts'ëen. 錢 money.

If a mistake is made in valuation, they willingly undertake to make it good.

Joh 若 If
kh'an 看 look
ts'o 錯 wrong
lëaou 了 —
kan 甘 } willing
yüen 願 }
paou 包 undertake
p'ay. 賠 make good.

In buying goods, when the bargain has been struck, a few taels per cent are given as earnest money.

Mae 買 Buy
ho 貨 goods
këa 價 } price
ts'ëen 錢 }
e 議 negotiate
ting 定 } settled
lëaou 了 }
may 每 each
pih 百 hundred
lëang 兩 taels
nuy 內 inside
sëen 先 first
këaou 交 hand
ke 幾 few
lëang 兩 taels
wei 爲 as
ting 定 } earnest money.
yin. 銀 }

If after receiving earnest money, a party withdraws from his bargain, a penalty must be exacted of him.

Show 收 Receive
ting 定 earnest
che 之 of
how 後 after
joo 如 if
yew 有 have
fan 反 } withdraw
hwuy 悔 }
teih 的 —
tsung 總 certainly
yaou 要 must
e 議 agree
fah. 罰 penalty.

When paying the price, only the sum agreed on should be given.

| | | |
|---|---|---|
| Këaou | 交 | Pay |
| këa | 價 | price |
| she | 時 | time |
| how | 候 | |
| chih | 只 | only |
| yaou | 要 | must |
| chaou | 照 | according to |
| yüen | 原 | original |
| e | 議 | agree |
| teih | 的 | — |
| chaou | 找 | make up |
| tsuh. | 足 | sufficient. |

And no further amount need be handed to compradore, servants, &c. as commission.

| | | |
|---|---|---|
| Puh | 不 | Not |
| peih | 必 | must |
| wae | 外 | further |
| këa | 加 | add |
| yung | 用 | commission |
| ts'ëen | 錢 | |
| kay | 給 | give |
| mae | 買 | compradore |
| pan | 辦 | |
| yung | 用 | servant |
| jin | 人 | |
| măn | 們 | such like |
| show | 收 | receive |
| yung. | 用 | use. |

If the compradore, &c. insist on having commission, go to the master and let him know it.

| | | |
|---|---|---|
| Joo | 如 | If |
| yew | 有 | have |
| mae | 買 | compradore |
| pan | 辦 | |
| măn | 們 | such like |
| ying | 硬 | insist |
| yaou | 要 | want |
| yung | 用 | commission |
| ts'ëen | 錢 | |
| teih | 的 | — |
| hëang | 向 | go to |
| tung | 東 | master |
| këa | 家 | |
| shwoh | 說 | tell |
| ming. | 明 | clearly. |

When goods are to be landed from sea-going vessels, their description, number, and weight should first be reported at the Custom-house, and a permit applied for.

| | | |
|---|---|---|
| Yang | 洋 | Sea |
| ch'üen | 船 | vessels |
| hëa | 下 | discharge |
| ho | 貨 | goods |
| ying | 應 | must |
| kae | 該 | |
| sëen | 先 | first |
| taou | 到 | go to |
| hae | 海 | Custom-house |
| kwan | 關 | |
| paou | 報 | report |
| ming | 明 | clearly |
| ho | 貨 | goods |
| sih | 色 | description |
| këen | 件 | piece |

soo 數 number
kin 斤 } weight
lëang 兩 }
ts'ing 請 beg
kay 給 give
yen 驗 examine
tan. 單 paper.

When the permit has been received, the goods may be discharged and carried to the Custom-house jetty for examination.

Ling 領 } Received
lëaou 了 }
yen 驗 examine
tan 單 paper
ts'ae 纔 then
năng 能 can
kh'e 起 } discharge
poh 駁 }
tae 帶 carry
taou 到 to
hae 海 } Custom-house
kwan 關 }
ma 馬 } jetty
t'ow 頭 }
ts'ing 請 ask
yen. 驗 examine.

Merchants may hire any boats they please for removal of the goods, and other people may not interfere.

Koo 僱 Hire
ch'üen 船 boat
poh 駁 remove
ho 貨 goods
jin 任 } at liberty
p'ing 憑 }
shang 商 } merchant
jin 人 }
tsze 自 self
pëen 便 convenient
puh 不 not
chun 准 allow
pëeh 別 other
jin 人 man
ts'ung 從 } between
chung 中 }
pa 把 } monopolize.
che. 持 }

The person in charge of the goods may assist the Custom-house attendants in examining, by particularising to them the number, value, weight, and measurement of the goods named in the permit.

Kwan 管 Have charge
ho 貨 goods
teih 的 who
jin 人 man
kh'o 可 } may
e 已 }
pang 帮 } assist
choh 着 }
kwan 關 Custom-house
yih 役 attendants
ch'a 查 } examine
yen 驗 }
pa 把 take

| | | |
|---|---|---|
| tan | 單 | permit |
| nuy | 內 | inside |
| teih | 的 | which |
| ho | 貨 | goods |
| soo | 數 | number |
| këa | 價 | price |
| chih | 値 | |
| kin | 斤 | weight |
| lëang | 兩 | |
| chang | 丈 | measurement |
| ch'eh | 尺 | |
| sëang | 詳 | detail |
| se | 細 | |
| shwoh | 說 | declare |
| ming. | 明 | clearly. |

He may also point out whether the goods agree with the list contained in the permit or not?

| | | |
|---|---|---|
| Han | 還 | Also |
| kh'o | 可 | may |
| e | 已 | |
| che | 指 | point |
| shwoh | 說 | say |
| ho | 貨 | goods |
| wuh | 物 | |
| yû | 與 | with |
| tan | 單 | permit |
| le | 裡 | in |
| so | 所 | which |
| kh'ae | 開 | contain |
| teih | 的 | |
| tuy | 對 | agree |
| puh | 不 | not |
| tuy. | 對 | agree. |

He also may select out a few bales for the Custom-house attendants to open and look carefully into.

| | | |
|---|---|---|
| Yay | 也 | Also |
| kh'o | 可 | may |
| e | 已 | |
| ch'ow | 抽 | select |
| ch'uh | 出 | out |
| ke | 幾 | several |
| këen | 件 | pieces |
| cheh | 拆 | break |
| kh'ae | 開 | open |
| kay | 給 | allow |
| kwan | 關 | Custom-house |
| yih | 役 | attendants |
| se | 細 | carefully |
| kh'an. | 看 | look. |

If the Custom-house attendants insist on opening the entire lot of bales, then beg the owner of the goods to come and remonstrate with them.

| | | |
|---|---|---|
| T'ang | 倘 | If |
| kwan | 關 | Custom-house |
| yih | 役 | attendants |
| ting | 定 | insist |
| yaou | 要 | |
| pa | 把 | take |
| koh | 各 | every |
| paou | 包 | bale |
| ts'eüen | 全 | entire |
| soo | 數 | number |
| cheh | 拆 | break |
| kh'ae | 開 | open |

tsew 就 then
ts'ing 請 beg
ho 貨 goods
choo 主 master
kwo 過 pass
lae 來 come
tang 當 } face to face
mëen 面 }
le 理 reason
lun. 論 talk.

If they wholly refuse to listen, then have the bales carefully opened.

Joo 如 If
kwo 果 indeed
twan 斷 } on no account
puh 不 }
kh'ăng 肯 consent
t'ing 聽 listen
tsew 就 then
sëaou 小 } carefully
sin 心 }
cheh 拆 break
kh'ae. 開 open.

And when the scrutiny is complete, have them carefully fastened up again, so as to avoid damage or loss.

Kh'an 看 Look
wan 完 complete
tsae 再 again
lew 留 } carefully
sin 心 }
kh'wăn 捆 fasten
t'o 妥 secure
mëen 免 avoid
tih 得 get
shang 傷 hurt
sun 損 injury
e 遺 } loss.
shih. 失 }

If, when discharging the goods, any are found deficient or sea-damaged, a report of the circumstance may be made to the Custom-house, with a request that a memorandum may be inserted in the permit.

Joh 若 If
kh'e 起 discharge
ho 貨 goods
she 時 } time
how 候 }
kh'an 看 see
yew 有 have
twan 短 } deficient
shaou 少 }
shuy 水 } damp
shih 濕 }
tsew 就 then
kh'o 可 } may
e 以 }
paou 報 report
kwan 關 Custom-house
ts'ing 請 beg
tsae 在 in
tan 單 permit
shang 上 on
choo 註 insert
ming. 明 clear.

After the examination is over, the "let pass" memorandum given must be carefully retained, to be compared with the Custom-house books when paying duty.

| | | |
|---|---|---|
| Ch'a | 查 | Examine |
| peih | 畢 | finish |
| so | 所 | which |
| kay | 給 | give |
| teih | 的 | — |
| fang | 放 | let pass |
| hing | 行 | |
| tan | 單 | permit |
| ying | 應 | must |
| kae | 該 | |
| sëaou | 小 | carefully |
| sin | 心 | |
| show | 收 | keep by |
| ts'un | 存 | |
| tăng | 等 | wait |
| choh | 着 | |
| nah | 納 | pay |
| shuy | 稅 | duty |
| she | 時 | time |
| yu | 與 | with |
| kwan | 關 | Custom-house |
| poo | 簿 | books |
| hoh | 覈 | reckon |
| tuy. | 對 | compare. |

Goods must not be examined in warehouse, as it may be inconvenient for the attendants to be away from their Custom-house, and they may receive bribes.

| | | |
|---|---|---|
| Ho | 貨 | Goods |
| wuh | 物 | |
| puh | 不 | not |
| ying | 應 | must |
| tsae | 在 | in |
| chan | 棧 | warehouse |
| le | 裏 | inside |
| ch'a | 查 | examine |
| yen | 驗 | |
| yin | 因 | because |
| p'a | 怕 | fear |
| kwan | 關 | Custom-house |
| yih | 役 | attendants |
| le | 離 | away from |
| kwan | 關 | Custom-house |
| puh | 不 | not |
| pëen | 便 | convenient |
| yew | 又 | also |
| p'a | 怕 | fear |
| yew | 有 | have |
| show | 受 | receive |
| hwuy | 賄 | bribe |
| teih | 的 | of |
| ts'ing | 情 | irregularity. |
| pe. | 弊 | |

# ERRATA.

| | | | | | |
|---|---|---|---|---|---|
| Page | 5. | 長 chang | read | ch'ang. |
| „ | „ | 寬 kwan | „ | kh'wan. |
| „ | 6. | 票 peaou | „ | p'eaou. |
| „ | 10. | 同 tung | „ | t'ung. |
| „ | 12. | „ | „ | „ |

# TRADE REGULATIONS.

## 通商條欵 T'UNG SHANG T'ËAOU KH'WAN.

England was the first of all the nations that entered into Treaty with China for trading purposes.

| | | |
|---|---|---|
| Koh | 各 | Every |
| kwoh | 國 | nation |
| t'ung | 同 | with |
| chung | 中 | China |
| kwoh | 國 | |
| leih | 立 | make |
| yoh | 約 | treaty |
| t'ung | 通 | trade |
| shang | 商 | |
| te | 第 | No. |
| yih | 一 | one |
| tsew | 就 | then |
| she | 是 | is |
| ying | 英 | England |
| kwoh | 國 | |
| kh'e. | 起 | begin. |

In the 22nd year of Taou-kwang (1842) they made the Treaty of perpetual peace.

| | | |
|---|---|---|
| Tsze | 自 | From |
| ts'ung | 從 | |
| taou | 道 | Taou-kwang |
| kwang | 光 | |
| urh | 二 | two |
| shih | 十 | ten |
| urh | 二 | two |
| nëen | 年 | year |
| tsae | 在 | at |
| nan | 南 | Nanking |
| king | 京 | |
| leih | 立 | made |
| lëaou | 了 | |
| wan | 萬 | myriad |
| nëen | 年 | year |
| ho | 和 | amity |
| yoh. | 約 | treaty. |

In the following year they further made at Canton the Supplementary treaty and Commercial Regulations.

| | | |
|---|---|---|
| Tsz'e | 次 | Next |
| nëen | 年 | year |
| tsae | 在 | at |
| yüeh | 粤 | Canton |
| tung | 東 | |
| yew | 又 | further |
| leih | 立 | made |
| shen | 善 | adjust |
| how | 後 | after |
| t'ëaou | 條 | treaty |
| yoh | 約 | |
| t'ung | 通 | commercial |
| shang | 商 | |
| chang | 章 | regulations. |
| ch'ing. | 程 | |

These three instruments together constituted the rules under which the English trade had been carried on since 1842.

I

| | | |
|---|---|---|
| Chay | 這 | This |
| san | 三 | three |
| kh'wan | 欵 | instrument |
| hoh | 合 | join |
| t'ung | 同 | together |
| tsew | 就 | just |
| she | 是 | is |
| tsze | 自 | from |
| urh | 二 | two |
| shih | 十 | ten |
| urh | 二 | two |
| nëen | 年 | year |
| e | 以 | and |
| how | 後 | after |
| tso | 做 | become |
| ying | 英 | England |
| kwoh | 國 | |
| mae | 買 | trade |
| mae | 賣 | |
| teih | 的 | of |
| tsih | 則 | rule. |
| le. | 例 | |

In the 24th year (1844), the United States of America also made a Treaty at Wang-hëa in Canton.

| | | |
|---|---|---|
| Urh | 二 | Two |
| shih | 十 | ten |
| sze | 四 | four |
| nëen | 年 | year |
| may | 美 | America |
| kwoh | 國 | |
| yew | 又 | also |
| tsae | 在 | at |
| kwang | 廣 | Canton |
| tung | 東 | |
| wang | 望 | Wang-hëa |
| hëa | 夏 | |
| leih | 立 | made |
| lëaou | 了 | |
| ho | 和 | amity |
| yoh. | 約 | treaty. |

France likewise made a Treaty that year at Whampoa in Canton.

| | | |
|---|---|---|
| Chay | 這 | That |
| nëen | 年 | year |
| fah | 法 | France |
| lan | 蘭 | |
| se | 西 | |
| yay | 也 | likewise |
| tsae | 在 | at |
| kwang | 廣 | Canton |
| tung | 東 | |
| hwang | 黃 | Whampoa |
| p'oo | 浦 | |
| leih | 立 | made |
| yoh. | 約 | treaty. |

Their treaties in the main resembled that made by England.

| | | |
|---|---|---|
| Ta | 大 | Generally |
| lëoh | 畧 | |
| ho | 和 | with |
| ying | 英 | England |
| kwoh | 國 | |
| teih | 的 | 's |
| sëang | 相 | similar. |
| t'ung. | 同 | |

In the 8th year of Hëen-fung (1858), in consequence of disagreements between England and China having gradually accumulated in the course of several years, the old treaty was revised at Tëentsin.

| | | |
|---|---|---|
| Taou | 到 | Until |
| lëaou | 了 | |
| hëen | 咸 | Hëen-fung |
| fung | 豐 | |
| pah | 八 | eight |
| nëen | 年 | year |
| yin | 因 | because |
| wei | 爲 | |
| ying | 英 | England |
| hwa | 華 | China |
| lëang | 兩 | two |
| kwoh | 國 | nations |
| soo | 數 | several |
| nëen | 年 | year |
| che | 之 | of |
| këen | 間 | course |
| tsëen | 漸 | gradually |
| tsëen | 漸 | |
| puh | 不 | not |
| hoh | 合 | agree |
| yew | 又 | again |
| tsae | 在 | at |
| t'ëen | 天 | Tëentsin |
| tsin | 津 | |
| ch'ung | 重 | revise |
| sew | 修 | |
| kew | 舊 | old |
| yoh. | 約 | treaty. |

And it was not till the tenth year of Hëen-fung, that ratifications were exchanged at the capital.

| | | |
|---|---|---|
| Tan | 躭 | Delay |
| koh | 擱 | |
| taou | 到 | till |
| hëen | 咸 | Hëen-fung |
| fung | 豐 | |
| shih | 十 | ten |
| nëen | 年 | year |
| ts'ae | 纔 | then |
| tsae | 在 | at |
| king | 京 | Capital |
| le | 裡 | |
| lëang | 兩 | two |
| sëang | 相 | mutual |
| woo | 互 | exchanged. |
| hwan. | 換 | |

A supplementary convention was likewise entered into.

| | | |
|---|---|---|
| Yew | 又 | Also |
| ling | 另 | further |
| leih | 立 | made |
| lëaou | 了 | |
| suh | 續 | supplementary |
| tsăng | 增 | added |
| t'ëaou | 條 | treaty. |
| yoh. | 約 | |

And now trade will always be carried on under the provisions of these instruments.

| | | |
|---|---|---|
| Hëen | 現 | Now |
| tsae | 在 | |

| | | |
|---|---|---|
| t'ung | 通 | trade |
| shang | 商 | |
| too | 都 | entirely |
| yaou | 要 | require |
| chaou | 照 | according |
| chay | 這 | this |
| ko | 個 | |
| le | 例 | law |
| hing. | 行 | carried on. |

America and France also revised their Treaties at Tëentsin about the same time.

| | | |
|---|---|---|
| Mei | 美 | America |
| kwoh | 國 | |
| fah | 法 | France |
| lan | 蘭 | |
| se | 西 | |
| kwoh | 國 | |
| yay | 也 | also |
| tsew | 就 | then |
| t'ung | 同 | same |
| she | 時 | time, |
| tsae | 在 | at |
| t'ëen | 天 | Tëen-tsin |
| tsin | 津 | |
| ch'ung | 重 | revise |
| sew | 修 | |
| ho | 和 | treaty. |
| yoh. | 約 | |

Russia likewise made a new treaty.

| | | |
|---|---|---|
| Wo | 俄 | Russia |
| lo | 羅 | |
| sze | 斯 | |
| kwoh | 國 | |
| yay | 也 | also |
| yew | 有 | have |
| sin | 新 | new |
| leih | 立 | made |
| t'ëaou | 條 | treaty. |
| yoh. | 約 | |

At present there are altogether four nations who have treaties.

| | | |
|---|---|---|
| Hëen | 現 | Now |
| tsae | 在 | |
| t'ung | 通 | trade |
| shang | 商 | |
| teih | 的 | which |
| kung | 共 | altogether |
| yew | 有 | have |
| sze | 四 | four |
| kwoh | 國 | nation |
| she | 是 | is |
| yew | 有 | have |
| ho | 和 | treaty |
| yoh | 約 | |
| teih. | 的 | — |

The English treaty has altogether 56 articles.

| | | |
|---|---|---|
| Ying | 英 | England |
| kwoh | 國 | |
| t'ëaou | 條 | treaty |
| yoh | 約 | |
| le | 裡 | inside |
| t'ow | 頭 | |
| kung | 共 | altogether |
| yew | 有 | have |
| woo | 五 | five |
| shih | 十 | ten |

lëuh 六 six
kh'wan. 欵 article.

The matters treated of in it are very numerous, and it gives advantages to both contracting parties.

Nuy 內 } Within
chung 中 }
so 所 which
seu 叙 } treat of
teih 的 }
sze 事 } matters
ts'ing 情 }
hăn 狠 very
to 多 many
pe 彼 that
ts'ze 此 this
lëang 兩 two
kwoh 國 nation
too 都 both
yew 有 have
haou 好 } advantage.
ch'oo. 處 }

The Treaty formerly made at Nanking is to remain in force, but the supplementary and Regulations of trade made at Canton are abrogated.

Ts'ung 從 } Formerly
ts'ëen 前 }
tsae 在 at
nan 南 } Nanking
king 京 }
leih 立 made
teih 的 which
wan 萬 myriad
nëen 年 year
ho 和 amity
yoh 約 treaty
jing 仍 as
kew 舊 of old
tsun 遵 } obey
hing 行 }
pa 把 take
tsae 在 at
kwang 廣 } Canton
tung 東 }
leih 立 made
teih 的 which
t'ung 通 } commercial
shang 商 }
chang 章 } regulations
ch'ing 程 }
shen 善 adjust
how 後 after
t'ëaou 條 } treaty
yoh 約 }
lëang 兩 two
yang 樣 kind
ch'oo 除 } abrogate.
sëaou. 銷 }

England and China may each appoint a high officer to reside at the other's capital city.

Ying 英 England
hwa 華 China
lëang 兩 two
kwoh 國 nation
pe 彼 that

| | | |
|---|---|---|
| ts'ze | 此 | this |
| too | 都 | both |
| chun | 准 | allow |
| koh | 各 | each |
| p'ae | 派 | appoint |
| ta | 大 | great |
| yüen | 員 | officer |
| woo | 互 | mutual |
| hwan | 換 | exchange |
| choo | 駐 | reside |
| chah | 劄 | |
| lëang | 兩 | two |
| kwoh | 國 | nation |
| king | 京 | capital |
| chung. | 中 | in. |

All particulars relating to the mode of receiving the high officers appointed by either nation to reside at the Capitals,—to their treatment,—to the rules for their going and staying, and passing to and fro,—to the mode of sending their official correspondence, &c. are clearly set forth in the 3rd, 4th, 5th and 6th articles of the Treaty.

| | | |
|---|---|---|
| Choo | 駐 | Reside |
| chah | 劄 | |
| king | 京 | capital |
| chung | 中 | in |
| teih | 的 | who |
| lëang | 兩 | two |
| kwoh | 國 | nation |
| ta | 大 | great |
| yüen | 員 | officer |
| tsëeh | 接 | receive |
| këen | 見 | see |
| kh'wan | 欵 | treat |
| tae | 待 | |
| hing | 行 | travel |
| choo | 住 | reside |
| lae | 來 | come |
| wang | 往 | go |
| kh'e | 寄 | send |
| sung | 送 | |
| kung | 公 | public |
| wăn | 文 | documents |
| koh | 各 | every |
| yang | 樣 | kind |
| teih | 的 | of |
| ts'ing | 情 | particulars |
| tsëeh | 節 | |
| too | 都 | all |
| tsae | 在 | at |
| te | 第 | number |
| san | 三 | three |
| sze | 四 | four |
| woo | 五 | five |
| lëuh | 六 | six |
| t'ëaou | 條 | article |
| le | 裡 | in |
| shwoh | 說 | state |
| ming | 明 | clearly |
| lëaou. | 了 | — |

England will appoint English officers to reside at the ports of China as Consuls, and the Chinese officers must treat them with consideration.

| | | |
|---|---|---|
| Ying | 英 | England |
| kwoh | 國 | |
| p'ae | 派 | appoint |
| ying | 英 | English |
| kwan | 官 | officers |
| choo | 駐 | reside |
| chah | 劄 | |
| chung | 中 | China |
| kwoh | 國 | |
| këang | 港 | port |
| kh'ow | 口 | |
| tso | 做 | be |
| ling | 領 | Consul |
| sze | 事 | |
| teih | 的 | — |
| chung | 中 | China |
| kwoh | 國 | |
| kwan | 官 | officers |
| ying | 應 | must |
| tang | 當 | |
| ts'ung | 從 | liberal |
| yew | 優 | |
| sëang | 相 | treat. |
| tae. | 待 | |

The comparative rank, modes of visiting, and styles of correspondence of English and Chinese officers are all clearly defined, so that neither party need be wanting in courtesy, or make a mistake.

| | | |
|---|---|---|
| Ling | 領 | Consul |
| sze | 事 | |
| kwan | 官 | officer |
| t'ung | 同 | with |
| chung | 中 | China |
| kwoh | 國 | |
| kwan | 官 | officer |
| pe | 彼 | that |
| tsz'e | 此 | this |
| teih | 的 | of |
| p'in | 品 | grade |
| keih | 級 | |
| tsëeh | 接 | receive |
| këen | 見 | see |
| kung | 公 | public |
| wăn | 文 | document |
| lae | 來 | come |
| wang | 往 | go |
| koh | 各 | every |
| le | 禮 | ceremony |
| too | 都 | all |
| e | 已 | already |
| ting | 定 | settle |
| ming | 明 | clearly |
| lëang | 兩 | both |
| pëen | 邊 | side |
| tsung | 總 | certainly |
| puh | 不 | not |
| che | 致 | occasion |
| yew | 有 | have |
| kh'ëen | 欠 | fail |
| le | 禮 | courtesy |
| ts'o | 錯 | mistake. |
| woo. | 悞 | |

Englishmen originally resided at five ports for trading purposes, namely, Canton, Amoy, Foochow, Ningpo and Shanghae; but now six new ones have been opened, namely, Newchwang, Tëen-tsin, Tăng-chow, Tae-wan, Swatow, and Haenin, which are to be resided at on the same terms as the five old ones.

| | | |
|---|---|---|
| Ying | 英 | English |
| jin | 人 | man |
| yüen | 原 | originally |
| tsae | 在 | at |
| kwang | 廣 | Canton |
| tung | 東 | |
| hëa | 廈 | Amoy |
| măn | 門 | |
| fuh | 福 | Foochow |
| chow | 州 | |
| ning | 寗 | Ningpo |
| po | 波 | |
| shang | 上 | Shanghae |
| hae | 海 | |
| woo | 五 | five |
| ch'oo | 處 | place |
| keu | 居 | dwell |
| choo | 住 | |
| mae | 買 | trade |
| mae | 賣 | |
| hëen | 現 | now |
| tsae | 在 | |
| yew | 又 | further |
| ling | 另 | besides |
| kh'ae | 開 | opened |
| lëaou | 了 | |
| sin | 新 | new |
| këang | 港 | port |
| lëuh | 六 | six |
| ch'oo | 處 | place |
| tsew | 就 | just |
| she | 是 | is |
| new | 牛 | Newchwang |
| chwang | 庄 | |
| t'ëen | 天 | Tëentsin |
| tsin | 津 | |
| tăng | 登 | Tăngchow |
| chow | 州 | |
| t'ae | 臺 | Formosa |
| wan | 灣 | |
| ch'aou | 潮 | Swatow |
| chow | 州 | |
| kh'ëung | 瓊 | Haenan |
| chow | 州 | |
| yay | 也 | also |
| chaou | 照 | according to |
| ts'ung | 從 | formerly |
| ts'ëen | 前 | |
| woo | 五 | five |
| kh'ow | 口 | ports |
| yih | 一 | one |
| lëuh | 律 | category |
| pan | 辦 | arrange. |
| le. | 理 | |

Englishmen may rent land or buy houses at all the ports new and old, either for purposes of residence or trade, just as they please.

| | | |
|---|---|---|
| Sin | 新 | New |
| kew | 舊 | old |
| koh | 各 | every |
| këang | 港 | port |
| kh'ow | 口 | |
| too | 都 | all |

chun 准 allow
ying 英 English
jin 人 man
tsoo 租 rent
te 地 land
mae 買 buy
fang 房 houses
keu 居 } dwell
choo 住 }
mow 貿 } trade
yih 易 }
jin 任 allow
ts'ung 從 follow
tsze 自 self
pëen. 便 convenience.

The Protestant and Roman Catholic creeds hold the practice of virtue as the basis of their faith: should Englishmen teach the doctrines of either, or the Chinese learn them, the local officers must protect them, and on no account offer the slightest hindrance.

Yay 耶 } Jesus
soo 穌 }
këaou 教 doctrine
t'ëen 天 Heaven
choo 主 Lord
këaou 教 doctrine
yüen 原 originally
she 是 is
hing 行 do
shen 善 right
wei 爲 as
păn 本 basis
ying 英 English
jin 人 man
ch'üen 傳 disseminate
këaou 教 doctrine
hwa 華 Chinese
jin 人 man
tsin 進 enter
këaou 教 doctrine
te 地 } local
fang 方 }
kwan 官 officers
too 都 all
ying 應 } must
kae 該 }
paou 保 } protect
hoo 護 }
twan 斷 } on no account
puh 不 }
chun 准 allow
yew 有 have
sze 絲 filament
haou 毫 hair
kin 禁 } prohibit.
che. 止 }

Englishmen are at liberty to travel in the interior for trade or recreation, only they must have passports; if they be found without passports, or if they offend the laws, the local officers may send them for punishment to the nearest Consul: the local officers must not take on themselves to punish such persons, neither may they oppress or insult them.

J

| | | |
|---|---|---|
| Ying | 英 | English |
| jin | 人 | man |
| too | 都 | all |
| chun | 准 | allow |
| tsin | 進 | enter |
| nuy | 內 | interior |
| te | 地 | |
| hing | 行 | travel |
| tsow | 走 | |
| yew | 遊 | recreation |
| wan | 玩 | |
| mae | 買 | trade |
| mae | 賣 | |
| tsung | 總 | only |
| yaou | 要 | require |
| yew | 有 | have |
| chih | 執 | passport |
| chaou | 照 | |
| joh | 若 | if |
| woo | 無 | no |
| chih | 執 | passport |
| chaou | 照 | |
| hwoh | 或 | or |
| yew | 有 | have |
| fan | 犯 | offend |
| tsuy | 罪 | crime |
| tsew | 就 | then |
| chun | 准 | allow |
| te | 地 | local |
| fang | 方 | |
| kwan | 官 | officers |
| keae | 解 | send |
| sung | 送 | |
| foo | 附 | neighbouring |
| kin | 近 | |
| ling | 領 | Consul |
| sze | 事 | |
| kwan | 官 | |
| pan | 辦 | adjudicate |
| le | 理 | |
| puh | 不 | not |
| chun | 准 | allow |
| te | 地 | local |
| fang | 方 | |
| kwan | 官 | officers |
| shen | 擅 | presume |
| hing | 行 | act |
| tsze | 自 | self |
| pan | 辦 | adjudicate |
| yay | 也 | moreover |
| puh | 不 | not |
| năng | 能 | can |
| tsaou | 蹂 | oppress |
| t'ah | 塌 | |
| ling | 凌 | insult. |
| juh. | 辱 | |

English ships may enter the Yangtsze River, as far as Hankow, and trade backwards and forwards throughout its course.

| | | |
|---|---|---|
| Ying | 英 | England |
| kwoh | 國 | |
| ch'üen | 船 | vessel |
| chun | 准 | allow |
| tsin | 進 | enter |
| yang | 揚 | Yangtsze |
| tsze | 子 | |

këang 江 river
yih 一 } all along
tae 帶
taou 到 to
han 漢 } Hankow
kh'ow 口
wei 爲 as
che 止 limit
lae 來 come
wang 往 go
mae 買 } trade.
mae. 賣

On the river will be established three Custom-house ports for facilitating examination.

Tsae 在 At
këang 江 river
le 裡 in
yaou 要 will
sheh 設 establish
san 三 three
ch'oo 處 places
kwan 關 Custom-house
kh'ow 口 ports
e 以 for
pëen 便 convenience
ke 稽 } examime.
ch'a. 查

Englishmen buying land or hiring houses at the ports or in the interior must do so at the market rate of the place, in which the transaction occurs, and neither party will be allowed to extort.

Ying 英 English
jin 人 man
hwoh 或 either
tsae 在 at
këang 港 } port
kh'ow 口
hwoh 或 or
tsae 在 at.
nuy 內 } interior
te 地
tsoo 租 rent
te 地 land
tsaou 造 build
fang 房 house
ying 應 must
chaou 照 according
păn 本 that
ch'oo 處 place
she 市 market
këa 價 price
e 議 negotiate
ting 定 settle
pe 彼 that
tsz'e 此 this
too 都 both
puh 不 not
chun 准 allow
leh 勒 } extort.
kh'ăng. 掯

If Englishmen hire Chinese, no matter for what object, so long as it is not against the law, the Chinese officials may not prohibit their so doing.

Ying 英 English
jin 人 man

| | | |
|---|---|---|
| koo | 僱 | hire |
| yung | 用 | employ |
| hwa | 華 | Chinese |
| jin | 人 | man |
| woo | 無 | no matter |
| lun | 論 | |
| tso | 做 | do |
| shin | 甚 | what |
| mo | 麽 | |
| sze | 事 | business |
| ts'ing | 情 | |
| joh | 若 | if |
| muh | 沒 | not |
| yew | 有 | have |
| wei | 違 | break |
| le | 例 | law |
| chung | 中 | China |
| kwoh | 國 | |
| kwan | 官 | officers |
| yüen | 員 | |
| puh | 不 | not |
| chun | 准 | allow |
| kin | 禁 | prohibit. |
| che. | 止 | |

Englishmen are at liberty to hire coolies and boats for the conveyance of their merchandize at their option, and if there be no smuggling or evasion of duty, the Chinese officers must not offer the slightest interference.

| | | |
|---|---|---|
| Ying | 英 | English |
| jin | 人 | man |
| koo | 僱 | hire |
| foo | 夫 | coolie |
| koo | 僱 | hire |
| ch'üen | 船 | boat |
| t'ëaou | 挑 | carry |
| poh | 剝 | convey |
| ho | 貨 | merchandize |
| wuh | 物 | |
| too | 都 | all |
| jin | 任 | at liberty |
| p'ing | 憑 | |
| tsze | 自 | self |
| pëen, | 便 | convenience |
| joo | 如 | if |
| kwo | 果 | indeed |
| muh | 沒 | not |
| yew | 有 | have |
| t'ow | 偷 | evade |
| low | 漏 | |
| tsow | 走 | smuggle |
| sze | 私 | |
| hwa | 華 | Chinese |
| kwan | 官 | officer |
| puh | 不 | not |
| chun | 准 | permit |
| sze | 絲 | filament |
| haou | 毫 | hair |
| kan | 干 | interfere. |
| yu. | 預 | |

All matters affecting the persons or property of Englishmen come under the cognizance of the Consul.

| | | |
|---|---|---|
| Ying | 英 | English |
| min | 民 | people |
| fan | 凡 | all |

yew 有 have
kwan 關 } concern
sheh 涉 }
sze 事 } affair
ts'ing 情 }
puh 不 not
lun 論 matter
jin 人 man
ch'an 產 property
too 都 all
kwuy 歸 revert
ling 領 }
sze 事 } Consul
kwan 官 }
kwan 管 see to
pan. 辦 arrange.

If Englishmen break the law in China, their trial and punishment must be conducted by the Consul, according to the law of his own country.

Joh 若 If
ying 英 English
jin 人 man
tsae 在 at
chung 中 } China
kwoh 國 }
fan 犯 break
fah 法 law
kwuy 歸 revert
ying 英 } England
kwoh 國 }
ling 領 } Consul
sze 事 }
chaou 照 according to
păn 本 his own
kwoh 國 nation
le 例 law
ch'a 查 examine
pan. 辦 adjudicate.

If Chinese trespass against Englishmen, then it devolves upon the Chinese authorities to adjudicate the matter.

Joh 若 If
hwa 華 Chinese
jin 人 man
kan 干 } trespass
fan 犯 }
ying 英 English
jin 人 man
ying 應 must
kwuy 歸 revert
hwa 華 Chinese
kwan 官 officer
pan 辦 } arrange.
le. 理 }

If an Englishman is injured by a Chinese, he must apply to the Consul for redress; if a Chinese is injured by an Englishmen, he too may petition the Consul to look into the case, whereupon the Consul must give him proper justice; should the Consul be unable to settle the case satisfactorily, he may request the Chinese authorities to go into it with him in order to arrive at a just decision.

Joh 若 If
ying 英 English

| | | |
|---|---|---|
| jin | 人 | man |
| show | 受 | receive |
| hwa | 華 | Chinese |
| jin | 人 | man |
| ts'an | 殘 | injury |
| hae | 害 | |
| ying | 應 | must |
| tang | 當 | |
| pin | 稟 | petition |
| ling | 領 | Consul |
| sze | 事 | |
| kwan | 官 | |
| pan | 辦 | arrange, |
| le, | 理 | |
| joh | 若 | if |
| hwa | 華 | Chinese |
| jin | 人 | man |
| show | 受 | receive |
| ying | 英 | English |
| jin | 人 | man |
| teih | 的 | of |
| ts'an | 殘 | injury |
| hae | 害 | |
| yay | 也 | also |
| chun | 准 | permit |
| pin | 稟 | petition |
| ling | 領 | Consul |
| sze | 事 | |
| kwan | 官 | |
| ch'a | 查 | examine |
| pan | 辦 | arrange |
| ling | 領 | Consul |
| sze | 事 | |
| kwan | 官 | |

| | | |
|---|---|---|
| ying | 應 | must |
| tang | 當 | |
| ping | 秉 | equitably |
| kung | 公 | |
| tae | 代 | for |
| pan | 辦 | arrange |
| joo | 如 | if |
| joh | 若 | |
| puh | 不 | not |
| năng | 能 | can |
| lëaou | 了 | terminate |
| këeh | 結 | |
| chun | 准 | allow |
| kh'e | 其 | him |
| ts'ing | 請 | request |
| t'ung | 同 | with |
| hwa | 華 | Chinese |
| kwan | 官 | officer |
| kung | 公 | equitably |
| p'ing | 平 | |
| pan | 辦 | arrange. |
| le. | 理 | |

If Chinese criminals escape to the shore, or on board ship at Hongkong, Chinese officers are permitted to write officially to the English authorities to find and seize them, and, if they be really guilty, they must be delivered up forthwith. If criminals escape to English houses or vessels at the trading ports, application must also be made to the Consul to deliver them back to their own authorities for punishment.

| | | |
|---|---|---|
| Chung | 中 | China |
| kwoh | 國 | |
| fan | 犯 | criminal |
| jin | 人 | |
| hwoh | 或 | if |
| yew | 有 | have |
| t'aou | 逃 | run |
| tsae | 在 | to |
| hëang | 香 | Hongkong |
| këang | 港 | |
| ngan | 岸 | shore |
| shang | 上 | on |
| ch'üen | 船 | ship |
| shang | 上 | on |
| teih | 的 | — |
| chun | 准 | allow |
| hwa | 華 | Chinese |
| kwan | 官 | officer |
| chaou | 照 | address |
| hwuy | 會 | |
| ying | 英 | English |
| kwan | 官 | officer |
| ch'a | 查 | find |
| na, | 拏 | seize |
| joo | 如 | if |
| kwo | 果 | indeed |
| shih | 實 | truly |
| she | 是 | is |
| yew | 有 | have |
| tsuy | 罪 | crime |
| ying | 應 | must |
| tang | 當 | |
| leih | 立 | instantly |
| kh'ih | 刻 | |

| | | |
|---|---|---|
| këaou | 交 | deliver |
| ch'uh, | 出 | out |
| joh | 若 | if |
| she | 是 | is |
| ta'ou | 逃 | run |
| tsae | 在 | at |
| t'ung | 通 | trade |
| shang | 商 | |
| këang | 港 | port |
| kh'ow | 口 | |
| ying | 英 | English |
| ch'üen | 船 | vessel |
| ying | 英 | English |
| fang | 房 | house |
| teih | 的 | — |
| yay | 也 | also |
| yaou | 要 | must |
| ts'ing | 請 | beg |
| ling | 領 | Consul |
| sze | 事 | |
| kwan | 官 | |
| këaou | 交 | deliver |
| ch'uh | 出 | out |
| hwan | 還 | back |
| pǎn | 本 | own |
| kwan | 官 | officer |
| sin | 訊 | examine |
| pan. | 辦 | punish. |

If the subjects of either nation become indebted to or defraud those of the other, the officer having jurisdiction over the defaulter, must diligently sue for and recover the property.

| | | |
|---|---|---|
| Lëang | 兩 | Two |
| kwoh | 國 | nation |
| jin | 人 | man |
| pe | 彼 | that |
| tsz'e | 此 | this |
| joo | 如 | if |
| kwo | 果 | indeed |
| yew | 有 | have |
| kh'ëen | 欠 | owe |
| chang | 賬 | account |
| kh'wang | 誆 | defraud |
| p'ëen | 騙 | |
| teih | 的 | of |
| sze | 事 | matter |
| păn | 本 | own |
| kwan | 管 | jurisdiction |
| teih | 的 | of |
| kwan | 官 | officer |
| ying | 應 | must |
| tang | 當 | |
| jin | 認 | diligently |
| chin | 眞 | |
| ch'a | 查 | examine |
| ch'uh | 出 | out |
| lae | 來 | come |
| chuy | 追 | recover |
| hwan. | 還 | restore. |

If Chinese get into debt at Hongkong, the recovery of such debt will devolve on the Hongkong authorities; and if the debtor should escape to Chinese territory, and he be ascertained to possess property there, the Chinese officers and Consul together will take steps to arrange the matter equitably.

| | | |
|---|---|---|
| Chung | 中 | China |
| kwoh | 國 | |
| jin | 人 | man |
| tsae | 在 | at |
| hëang | 香 | Hongkong |
| këang | 港 | |
| kae | 該 | owing |
| lëaou | 了 | |
| chang | 賬 | accounts |
| ying | 應 | must |
| kwuy | 歸 | revert |
| hëang | 香 | Hongkong |
| këang | 港 | |
| te | 地 | local |
| fang | 方 | |
| kwan | 官 | officers |
| ch'a | 查 | examine |
| chuy | 追 | recover |
| joh | 若 | if |
| she | 是 | is |
| kae | 該 | owe |
| chang | 賬 | accounts |
| teih | 的 | who |
| jin | 人 | man |
| t'aou | 逃 | run |
| tsae | 在 | in |
| nuy | 內 | inner |
| te | 地 | land |
| che | 知 | know |
| taou | 道 | |
| t'a | 他 | he |
| yew | 有 | have |

| | | |
|---|---|---|
| ch'an | 產 | property |
| nëeh | 業 | |
| hwa | 華 | Chinese |
| kwan | 官 | officer |
| ling | 領 | Consul |
| sze | 事 | |
| kwan | 官 | |
| hwuy | 會 | together |
| t'ung | 同 | |
| sheh | 設 | adopt |
| fah | 法 | measure |
| kung | 公 | equitably |
| p'ing | 平 | |
| pan | 辦 | manage. |
| le. | 理 | |

The persons, families, and property of Englishmen living in China, must have the constant protection of the Chinese authorities, so as to prevent them from suffering any kind of harm. If incendiarism, wholesale plunder, and such like. take place, the Chinese authorities must use their utmost effort to suppress the out-break, and punish the offenders most severely.

| | | |
|---|---|---|
| Ying | 英 | English |
| jin | 人 | man |
| choo | 住 | live |
| tsae | 在 | in |
| chung | 中 | China |
| kwoh | 國 | |
| teih | 的 | who |
| so | 所 | that which |
| yew | 有 | have |
| shin | 身 | person |
| këa | 家 | family |
| ch'an | 產 | property |
| nëeh | 業 | |
| te | 地 | local |
| fang | 方 | |
| kwan | 官 | officer |
| ying | 應 | must |
| kae | 該 | |
| she | 時 | constantly |
| she | 時 | |
| paou | 保 | protect |
| hoo | 護 | |
| puh | 不 | not |
| che | 致 | come about |
| show | 受 | receive |
| jin | 人 | man |
| teih | 的 | of |
| ts'an | 殘 | destroy |
| hae | 害 | injure |
| joo | 如 | if |
| kwo | 果 | indeed |
| ch'uh | 出 | happen |
| lëaou | 了 | |
| fang | 放 | set |
| ho | 火 | fire |
| ts'ëang | 搶 | plunder |
| këeh | 刼 | |
| teih | 的 | of |
| sze | 事 | matter |
| ts'ing | 情 | |
| hwa | 華 | Chinese |
| kwan | 官 | officer |

| | | |
|---|---|---|
| noo | 努 | exert |
| leih | 力 | strength |
| t'an | 彈 | suppress |
| yah | 壓 | |
| yen | 嚴 | very severely |
| yen | 嚴 | |
| teih | 的 | |
| chung | 重 | heavy |
| pan. | 辦 | punish. |

In all cases where English vessels are plundered by pirates in the China seas, the local authorities must also in like manner discover and punish the robbers.

| | | |
|---|---|---|
| Fan | 凡 | All |
| she | 是 | is |
| ying | 英 | English |
| ch'üen | 船 | vessel |
| tsae | 在 | in |
| chung | 中 | China |
| kwoh | 國 | |
| yang | 洋 | seas |
| mëen | 面 | |
| yu | 遇 | meet |
| taou | 盜 | pirate |
| ts'ëang | 搶 | plunder |
| këeh | 刼 | |
| chung | 中 | China |
| kwoh | 國 | |
| te | 地 | local |
| fang | 方 | |
| kwan | 官 | officer |
| yay | 也 | also |
| ying | 應 | must |

| | | |
|---|---|---|
| yih | 一 | same rule |
| lëuh | 律 | |
| t'e | 替 | for |
| t'a | 他 | him |
| ch'a | 查 | examine |
| pan. | 辦 | punish. |

If an English vessel is wrecked or stranded in the Chinese seas, or runs in to any part of the coast in distress, the local authorities must in every case afford ample protection and relief, and send the ship-wrecked crews to the nearest port, where there is a Consul.

| | | |
|---|---|---|
| Joh | 若 | If |
| she | 是 | is |
| ying | 英 | English |
| ch'üen | 船 | vessel |
| tsae | 在 | at |
| chung | 中 | China |
| kwoh | 國 | |
| yang | 洋 | seas |
| mëen | 面 | |
| t'ang | 倘 | if |
| yew | 有 | have |
| sun | 損 | break |
| hwae | 壞 | |
| koh | 擱 | strand |
| ts'ëen | 淺 | |
| hwoh | 或 | or |
| she | 是 | is |
| yin | 因 | because |
| tsaou | 遭 | meet |
| nan | 難 | difficulty |

| | | |
|---|---|---|
| teih | 的 | of |
| yüen | 緣 | cause |
| koo | 故 | |
| she | 駛 | sail |
| tsin | 進 | enter |
| yüen | 沿 | sea coast |
| hae | 海 | |
| puh | 不 | no |
| lun | 論 | matter |
| shin | 甚 | what |
| mo | 麽 | |
| te | 地 | place |
| fang | 方 | |
| hwa | 華 | Chinese |
| kwan | 官 | officers |
| ying | 應 | must |
| kae | 該 | |
| t'o | 妥 | safely |
| tang | 當 | |
| paou | 保 | protect |
| hoo | 護 | |
| chow | 賙 | relieve |
| tse | 濟 | |
| këaen | 解 | send |
| sung | 送 | |
| foo | 附 | neighbouring |
| kin | 近 | |
| yew | 有 | have |
| ling | 領 | Consul |
| sze | 事 | |
| kwan | 官 | |
| teih | 的 | which |
| këang | 港 | port. |
| kh'ow. | 口 | |

Englishmen who import and export merchandise must in every case pay duty as per tariff. If merchants of other nations enjoy any exemption from or diminution of a fixed duty, Englishmen cannot be called on to pay any more than they.

| | | |
|---|---|---|
| Ying | 英 | English |
| jin | 人 | men |
| fan | 販 | convey |
| yün | 運 | |
| ho | 貨 | goods |
| wuh | 物 | |
| tsin | 進 | enter |
| kh'ow | 口 | port |
| ch'uh | 出 | leave |
| kh'ow | 口 | port |
| too | 都 | all |
| yaou | 要 | require |
| chaou | 照 | according |
| shuy | 稅 | tariff |
| tsih | 則 | |
| nah | 納 | pay |
| shuy | 稅 | duty |
| joh | 若 | if |
| she | 是 | is |
| pëeh | 別 | other |
| kwoh | 國 | nation |
| shang | 商 | merchants |
| jin | 人 | |
| yew | 有 | have |
| mëen | 免 | exempt |
| këen | 減 | diminish |

shuy 稅 } duties
hëang 餉 }
teih 的 of
yang 様 } kind
tsze 子 }
puh 不 not
nǎng 能 may
këaou 叫 call on
ying 英 English
jin 人 man
pe 比 compare
t'a 他 him
to 多 more
ch'uh. 出 pay.

There is a settled period when duties on goods become due; in the case of import goods, they are considered as due on landing, and in the case of export goods on shipment.

Kae 該 Owing
shuy 稅 duty
yew 有 have
yih 一 }
ting 定 } fixed
teih 的 }
hëen 限 } time,
kh'e, 期 }
tsin 進 } import
kh'ow 口 }
ho 貨 goods
shang 上 ascend
ngan 岸 shore
teih 的 of
she 時 } time
how 候 }
swan 算 reckon
kae 該 owing
wan 完 pay
lëaou 了 —
ch'uh 出 } export
kh'ow 口 }
ho 貨 goods
hëa 下 descend
ts'ang 艙 hold
she 時 } time
how 候 }
swan 算 reckon
kae 該 ought
wan 完 pay
lëaou 了 —

According to the tariff formerly fixed under the treaty of Nanking, duties on import and export goods were imposed, as a general rule, at the rate of five per cent *ad valorem;* now however, owing to the decrease in value of many articles of merchandise, the old established tariff of duties is revised and corrected.

Ts'ung 從 } Formerly
ts'ëen 前 }
tsae 在 at
këang 江 } Nanking
ning 寧 }
leih 立 establish
yoh 約 treaty

| | | |
|---|---|---|
| teih | 的 | of |
| shuy | 稅 | tariff |
| tsih | 則 | |
| ch'uh | 出 | export |
| kh'ow | 口 | |
| tsin | 進 | import |
| kh'ow | 口 | |
| teih | 的 | of |
| koh | 各 | every |
| ho | 貨 | goods |
| ta | 大 | generally |
| kae | 概 | |
| chaou | 照 | according to |
| she | 市 | market |
| këa | 價 | price |
| mei | 每 | each |
| pih | 百 | hundred |
| lëang | 兩 | tael |
| ch'ow | 抽 | tax |
| yin | 銀 | money |
| woo | 五 | five |
| lëang | 兩 | tael |
| how | 後 | afterwards |
| lae | 來 | |
| yin | 因 | because |
| wei | 爲 | |
| yang | 樣 | every sort |
| yang | 樣 | |
| ho | 貨 | goods |
| këa | 價 | price |
| to | 多 | much |
| yew | 有 | have |
| këen | 減 | diminish |
| shaou | 少 | less |
| so | 所 | therefore |
| e | 以 | |
| pa | 把 | take |
| kew | 舊 | old |
| leih | 立 | establish |
| teih | 的 | which |
| shuy | 稅 | tariff |
| tsih | 則 | |
| ch'ung | 重 | again |
| sin | 新 | new |
| kae | 改 | alter |
| ching | 正 | correct |
| lëaou. | 了 | — |

At the end of ten years after the conclusion of the treaty, either of the contracting parties may demand a further revision of the tariff and commercial articles. If no demand be made within six months of the expiration of the term of ten years, the tariff shall be regarded as good for ten years more, and so it shall go on for every future term of ten years.

| | | |
|---|---|---|
| Leih | 立 | Conclude |
| yoh | 約 | treaty |
| che | 之 | of |
| how | 後 | after |
| e | 以 | take |
| shih | 十 | ten |
| nëen | 年 | year |
| wei | 爲 | be |
| kh'e | 期 | term |
| lëang | 兩 | two |
| kwoh | 國 | nation |

| | | |
|---|---|---|
| pe | 彼 | that |
| ts'ze | 此 | this |
| too | 都 | either |
| chun | 准 | may |
| tsae | 再 | again |
| ts'ing | 請 | beg |
| pa | 把 | take |
| shuy | 稅 | tariff |
| tsih | 則 | |
| lëen | 連 | with |
| t'ung | 通 | commercial |
| shang | 商 | |
| koh | 各 | every |
| kh'wan | 欵 | article |
| ch'ung | 重 | again |
| sin | 新 | new |
| kae | 改 | alter |
| ching | 正 | correct |
| hëen | 限 | term |
| mwan | 滿 | complete |
| che | 之 | of |
| how | 後 | after |
| joh | 若 | if |
| she | 是 | is |
| kwo | 過 | pass |
| kh'e | 期 | term |
| lëuh | 六 | six |
| ko | 個 | |
| yüeh | 月 | month |
| puh | 不 | not |
| ts'ing | 請 | beg |
| kae | 改 | alter |
| ching | 正 | correct |
| tsew | 就 | then |

| | | |
|---|---|---|
| swan | 筭 | reckon |
| she | 是 | is |
| yew | 又 | further |
| shih | 十 | ten |
| nëen | 年 | year |
| haou | 好 | good |
| yung | 用 | use |
| e | 以 | afterwards |
| how | 後 | |
| too | 都 | ever |
| yaou | 要 | require |
| chaou | 照 | according to |
| chay | 這 | this |
| hëen | 限 | term |
| kh'e | 期 | |
| wei | 爲 | be |
| shwae. | 率 | model. |

Hitherto in the payment of transit duties, there has been no settled rule as to the place of levy, the amount of duty taken, and the persons entitled to impose it, and in consequence the trade has suffered much damage. For the future, if English merchants when purchasing goods in the interior, or conveying them for sale up country, contemplate paying the total amount of transit duties leviable on any merchandize in one payment, so as to avoid separate payments at every several station, they will be at liberty to suit themselves, and do so.

中外對話

| | | |
|---|---|---|
| Yih | 一 | Hitherto |
| hëang | 向 | |
| nuy | 內 | interior |
| te | 地 | |
| nah | 納 | take |
| shuy | 稅 | duty |
| so | 所 | that |
| nah | 納 | take |
| teih | 的 | which |
| te | 地 | place |
| fang | 方 | |
| so | 所 | that |
| nah | 納 | take |
| teih | 的 | which |
| soo | 數 | amount |
| muh | 目 | |
| so | 所 | that |
| nah | 納 | take |
| teih | 的 | which |
| jin | 人 | man |
| too | 都 | all |
| muh | 沒 | not |
| yew | 有 | have |
| yih | 一 | certain |
| ting | 定 | |
| koo | 故 | on account of |
| ts'ze | 此 | this |
| mae | 買 | trade |
| mae | 賣 | |
| hăn | 狠 | very |
| ch'ih | 吃 | received |
| lëaou | 了 | |
| ta | 大 | great |
| k'wuy | 虧 | damage |

| | | |
|---|---|---|
| tsëang | 將 | hereafter |
| lae | 來 | |
| ying | 英 | English |
| shang | 商 | merchant |
| tsae | 在 | at |
| nuy | 內 | interior |
| te | 地 | |
| mae | 買 | buy |
| ho | 貨 | goods |
| hwoh | 或 | or |
| she | 是 | is |
| yün | 運 | carry |
| ho | 貨 | goods |
| tsin | 進 | enter |
| nuy | 內 | interior |
| te | 地 | |
| mae | 賣 | sell |
| yaou | 要 | wish |
| sëang | 想 | contemplate |
| pa | 把 | take |
| kung | 共 | total |
| tsung | 總 | |
| teih | 的 | of |
| shuy | 稅 | duty |
| hëang | 餉 | |
| tsoh | 作 | make |
| yih | 一 | one |
| hwuy | 回 | time |
| wan | 完 | pay |
| lëaou | 了 | |
| mëen | 免 | avoid |
| tih | 得 | obtain |
| tsae | 在 | at |
| koh | 各 | every |

| | | |
|---|---|---|
| tsze | 子 | station |
| kh'ow | 口 | |
| yih | 一 | one |
| fun | 分 | part |
| yih | 一 | one |
| fun | 分 | part |
| teih | 的 | — |
| wan | 完 | pay |
| nah | 納 | |
| t'ing | 聽 | allow |
| kh'e | 其 | them |
| tsze | 自 | own |
| pëen. | 便 | convenience. |

Every vessel entering a port must pay tonnage dues. If her burthen be above 150 tons, she must pay dues at the rate of 4 mace per ton. If her burthen be 150 tons or under, she must pay at the rate of one mace per ton. Vessels which pass to and fro between the ports including Hongkong, may on receipt of a certificate from the Customs, pay their dues only once in four months, the term of exemption to commence from the date of the certificate.

| | | |
|---|---|---|
| Koh | 各 | Every |
| ying | 英 | English |
| ch'üen | 船 | vessel |
| tsin | 進 | enter |
| kh'ow | 口 | port |
| ying | 應 | must |
| tang | 當 | |
| këaou | 交 | deliver |
| nah | 納 | pay |
| ch'üen | 船 | ship |
| ch'aou | 鈔 | dues |
| joh | 若 | if |
| chwang | 裝 | carry |
| yih | 一 | one |
| pih | 百 | hundred |
| woo | 五 | five |
| shih | 十 | ten |
| tun | 噸 | ton |
| e | 以 | above |
| shang | 上 | |
| teih | 的 | which |
| ch'üen | 船 | ship |
| mei | 每 | each |
| tun | 噸 | ton |
| këaou | 交 | deliver |
| ch'aou | 鈔 | dues |
| yin | 銀 | money |
| sze | 四 | four |
| ts'ëen | 錢 | mace |
| joh | 若 | if |
| she | 是 | is |
| chwang | 裝 | carry |
| yih | 一 | one |
| pih | 百 | hundred |
| woo | 五 | five |
| shih | 十 | ten |
| tun | 噸 | ton |
| ching | 整 | exactly |
| ping | 並 | and |
| yih | 一 | one |
| pih | 百 | hundred |

| | | |
|---|---|---|
| woo | 五 | five |
| shih | 十 | ten |
| tun | 噸 | ton |
| e | 以 | below |
| hëa | 下 | |
| may | 每 | each |
| tun | 噸 | ton |
| këaou | 交 | deliver |
| ch'aou | 鈔 | dues |
| yin | 銀 | money |
| yih | 一 | one |
| ts'ëen | 錢 | mace |
| joh | 若 | if |
| ch'üen | 船 | ship |
| tsae | 在 | at |
| t'ung | 通 | commercial |
| shang | 商 | |
| koh | 各 | all |
| kh'ow | 口 | port |
| e | 以 | and |
| keih | 及 | |
| hëang | 香 | Hongkong |
| këang | 港 | |
| lae | 來 | come |
| wang | 往 | go |
| chun | 准 | allow |
| kh'e | 其 | then |
| paou | 報 | report |
| kwan | 關 | Custom-house |
| ling | 領 | receive |
| chaou | 照 | certificate |
| e | 以 | take |
| sze | 四 | four |
| ko | 個 | |
| yüeh | 月 | month |
| wei | 爲 | be |
| kh'e | 期 | term |
| wan | 完 | pay |
| ch'üen | 船 | ship |
| ch'aou | 鈔 | dues |
| yih | 一 | one |
| ts'ze | 次 | time |
| sze | 四 | four |
| ko | 個 | |
| yüeh | 月 | month |
| teih | 的 | of |
| kh'e | 期 | term |
| she | 是 | is |
| kay | 給 | give |
| chaou | 照 | certificate |
| teih | 的 | of |
| jih | 日 | day |
| tsze | 子 | |
| kh'e | 起 | begin |
| swan. | 算 | reckon. |

All boats which carry passengers, baggage, letters, eatables, or articles not subjects to duty, need pay no tonnage dues. But cargo boats which convey any goods properly subject to duty, must pay tonnage dues at the rate of four mace per ton once in every four months.

| | | |
|---|---|---|
| Tae | 帶 | Carry |
| kh'ih | 客 | passenger |
| teih | 的 | which |
| tae | 帶 | carry |

L

| | | |
|---|---|---|
| hing | 行 | baggage |
| le | 李 | |
| teih | 的 | which |
| tae | 帶 | carry |
| shoo | 書 | letter |
| sin | 信 | |
| teih | 的 | which |
| tae | 帶 | carry |
| ch'ih | 吃 | eatable |
| shih | 食 | |
| teih | 的 | which |
| tae | 帶 | carry |
| mëen | 免 | exempt |
| shuy | 稅 | duty |
| ho | 貨 | goods |
| teih | 的 | which |
| koh | 各 | every |
| yang | 樣 | sort |
| t'ing | 艇 | boat |
| ch'üen | 船 | vessel |
| too | 都 | all |
| puh | 不 | not |
| yung | 用 | require |
| wan | 完 | pay |
| ch'üen | 船 | ship |
| ch'aou | 鈔 | due |
| joh | 若 | if |
| she | 是 | is |
| poh | 剝 | cargo boat |
| ch'üen | 船 | |
| chwang | 裝 | carry |
| yün | 運 | |
| ying | 應 | should |
| wan | 完 | pay |

| | | |
|---|---|---|
| shuy | 稅 | duty |
| hëang | 餉 | |
| koh | 各 | any |
| ho | 貨 | goods |
| teih | 的 | which |
| ying | 應 | must |
| tang | 當 | |
| sze | 四 | four |
| ko | 個 | |
| yüeh | 月 | month |
| wan | 完 | pay |
| ch'aou | 鈔 | dues |
| yin | 銀 | money |
| yih | 一 | one |
| ts'ze | 次 | time |
| she | 是 | is |
| mei | 每 | each |
| tun | 墩 | ton |
| yih | 一 | one |
| ts'ëen. | 錢 | mace. |

After the entry of a vessel into port, if it is contemplated before opening of the hatches to send her elsewhere to trade, she need not pay tonnage dues for the space of two days. On the expiration of the two days, she cannot be allowed any further exemption, no matter whether her hatches are opened or not. Besides tonnage dues no other fees of any kind whatever may be taken.

| | | |
|---|---|---|
| Ying | 英 | English |
| ch'üen | 船 | ship |

| | | |
|---|---|---|
| tsin | 進 | enter |
| kh'ow | 口 | port |
| che | 之 | of |
| how | 後 | after |
| joh | 若 | if |
| muh | 沒 | not |
| yew | 有 | have |
| kh'ae | 開 | open |
| ts'ang | 艙 | hold |
| sëang | 想 | contemplate |
| taou | 到 | go to |
| pëeh | 別 | other |
| ch'oo | 處 | place |
| mae | 買 | } trade |
| mae | 賣 | |
| teih | 的 | — |
| chun | 准 | allow |
| tsae | 在 | at |
| lëang | 兩 | two |
| t'ëen | 天 | day |
| che | 之 | of |
| nuy | 內 | inside |
| puh | 不 | no |
| yung | 用 | need |
| wan | 完 | pay |
| ch'aou | 鈔 | dues |
| joh | 若 | if |
| she | 是 | is |
| kwo | 過 | } passed |
| lëaou | 了 | |
| lëang | 兩 | two |
| t'ëen | 天 | day |
| che | 之 | of |
| how | 後 | after |
| woo | 無 | no |
| lun | 論 | matter |
| kh'ae | 開 | open |
| ts'ang | 艙 | hold |
| puh | 不 | not |
| kh'ae | 開 | open |
| ts'ang | 艙 | hold |
| puh | 不 | not |
| năng | 能 | may |
| tsae | 再 | further |
| mëen | 免 | exempt |
| ch'oo | 除 | besides |
| ch'aou | 鈔 | dues |
| yin | 銀 | money |
| che | 之 | of |
| wae | 外 | outside |
| shin | 甚 | } what |
| mo | 麼 | |
| she | 使 | } fees |
| fei | 費 | |
| yih | 一 | } all |
| kae | 概 | |
| puh | 不 | not |
| chun | 准 | allow |
| tsae | 再 | again |
| yaou. | 要 | demand. |

The channels at the entrance and exit of the several ports are all beset with hidden dangers, which render them difficult of navigation. The Consuls will in consultation with the local authorities adopt measures for the erection of beacons, light houses, buoys, &c. on the shoal and rocky places, so that, be it light or dark, vessels which are on the move may see the danger and avoid falling into difficulty.

| | | |
|---|---|---|
| Koh | 各 | Every |
| kh'ow | 口 | port |
| ch'uh | 出 | go out |
| tsin | 進 | enter |
| teih | 的 | which |
| shuy | 水 | water |
| loo | 路 | channel |
| to | 多 | many |
| yew | 有 | have |
| wei | 危 | dangerous |
| hëen | 險 | |
| nan | 難 | difficult |
| tsow | 走 | pass |
| teih | 的 | which |
| ngan | 暗 | secret |
| hae | 害 | injure |
| ling | 領 | |
| sze | 事 | Consul |
| kwan | 官 | |
| ping | 並 | and |
| te | 地 | local |
| fang | 方 | |
| kwan | 官 | officer |
| hwuy | 會 | together |
| t'ung | 同 | |
| sheh | 設 | adopt |
| fah | 法 | measure |
| tsae | 在 | at |
| yew | 有 | have |
| sha | 砂 | sand |
| ts'ëen | 淺 | shallow |
| ts'ëaou | 礁 | reef |
| sheh | 石 | rock |
| teih | 的 | of |
| te | 地 | place |
| fang | 方 | |
| t'ëen | 添 | add |
| sheh | 設 | establish |
| pëaou | 標 | beacon |
| kan | 杆 | |
| tăng | 燈 | light-tower |
| low | 樓 | |
| ping | 並 | and |
| foo | 浮 | buoy |
| pëaou | 標 | |
| tăng | 等 | such like |
| luy | 類 | kind |
| yü | 預 | prepare |
| pay | 備 | |
| jih | 日 | day |
| yay | 夜 | night |
| hing | 行 | move |
| ch'üen | 船 | ship |
| ts'ëaou | 瞧 | look |
| kh'an | 看 | see |
| mëen | 免 | avoid |
| che | 致 | occasion |
| yew | 有 | have |
| woo. | 悞 | mistake. |

English vessels going in and out of port are at liberty to engage pilots to conduct them in or out; it shall be at the option of the captain to hire whom he likes.

| | | |
|---|---|---|
| Ying | 英 | English |
| ch'üen | 船 | vessel |
| tsin | 進 | enter |
| ch'uh | 出 | go out |
| koh | 各 | every |
| kh'ow | 口 | port |
| too | 都 | all |
| chun | 准 | allow |
| koo | 僱 | hire |
| yin | 引 | pilot |
| shuy | 水 | |
| tae | 帶 | lead |
| loo | 路 | way |
| jin | 任 | allow |
| p'ing | 憑 | |
| ch'üen | 船 | captain |
| choo | 主 | |
| tsze | 自 | self |
| pëen. | 便 | convenience. |

When an English vessel has entered port, the Custom house may depute an officer or subordinate to keep guard, who may consult his own convenience as to living on board the vessel, or in his own boat; his expences must be defrayed by the Custom-house, and he may not demand the smallest fee from the captain.

| | | |
|---|---|---|
| Ying | 英 | English |
| ch'üen | 船 | vessel |
| tsin | 進 | entered |
| lëaou | 了 | |
| këang | 港 | port |
| kh'ow | 口 | |

| | | |
|---|---|---|
| chun | 准 | allow |
| hae | 海 | Custom-house |
| kwan | 關 | |
| wei | 委 | depute |
| p'ae | 派 | |
| yüen | 員 | officer |
| yih | 役 | subordinate |
| kh'an | 看 | watch |
| show | 守 | guard |
| hwoh | 或 | either |
| choo | 住 | reside |
| tsae | 在 | on |
| ch'üen | 船 | vessel |
| shang | 上 | upon |
| hwoh | 或 | or |
| choo | 住 | reside |
| tsae | 在 | at |
| păn | 本 | own |
| t'ing | 艇 | boat |
| jin | 任 | allow |
| ts'ung | 從 | follow |
| kh'e | 其 | he |
| pëen | 便 | convenience |
| yih | 一 | all |
| ts'ëeh | 切 | |
| yung | 用 | expences |
| too | 度 | |
| yew | 由 | by |
| kwan | 關 | Custom-house |
| che | 支 | pay |
| fah | 發 | |
| puh | 不 | no |
| năng | 能 | can |
| yaou | 要 | demand |

| | | |
|---|---|---|
| ch'üen | 船 | captain |
| choo | 主 | |
| haou | 毫 | hair |
| le | 釐 | cash |
| sze | 私 | private |
| fei. | 費 | fee. |

After the entry of a vessel into port, the captain must within one day's time carry her register, manifest, &c. to the Consul, who will on the following day report her tonnage and lading to the Custom-house. Should the Captain delay in reporting himself and thus break the law, he will at once be fined. The longer the delay, the heavier will be the penalty, but it must not exceed two hundred taels. If the manifest is erroneously drawn up, the Captain alone will be held responsible.

| | | |
|---|---|---|
| Ying | 英 | English |
| ch'üen | 船 | vessel |
| tsin | 進 | entered |
| lëaou | 了 | |
| kh'ow | 口 | port |
| hëen | 限 | limit |
| yih | 一 | one |
| jih | 日 | day |
| nuy | 內 | inside |
| ch'üen | 船 | Captain |
| choo | 主 | |
| pa | 把 | take |
| ch'üen | 船 | vessel |
| p'ae | 牌 | register |
| ping | 並 | and |
| ts'ang | 艙 | hold |
| kh'ow | 口 | |
| tan | 單 | memorandum |
| tăng | 等 | such like |
| luy | 類 | kind |
| sung | 送 | send |
| këaou | 交 | deliver |
| ling | 領 | Consul |
| sze | 事 | |
| kwan | 官 | |
| ling | 領 | Consul |
| sze | 事 | |
| kwan | 官 | |
| tsz'e | 次 | next |
| jih | 日 | day |
| pa | 把 | take |
| tun | 噸 | ton |
| ho | 貨 | goods |
| teih | 的 | of |
| soo | 數 | list |
| muh | 目 | |
| t'ung | 通 | report |
| che | 知 | |
| hae | 海 | Custom-house |
| kwan | 關 | |
| joh | 若 | if |
| ch'üen | 船 | Captain |
| choo | 主 | |
| tan | 躭 | delay |
| koh | 擱 | |
| wei | 違 | break |
| le | 例 | law |

| | | |
|---|---|---|
| tsew | 就 | forthwith |
| fah | 罸 | fine |
| jih tsze | 日子 | day |
| yu | 逾 | more |
| kew | 久 | long |
| fah | 罸 | fine |
| yin | 銀 | money |
| yu | 逾 | more |
| to | 多 | much |
| tan | 但 | but |
| puh | 不 | not |
| năng | 能 | can |
| kwo | 過 | exceed |
| urh | 二 | two |
| pih | 百 | hundred |
| lëang | 兩 | taels |
| ts'ang kh'ow | 艙口 | hold |
| tan | 單 | memorandum |
| t'ang | 倘 | if |
| yew | 有 | have |
| kh'ae | 開 | draw up |
| ts'o | 錯 | wrong |
| lëaou | 了 | — |
| wei | 惟 | only |
| ch'üen choo | 船主 | captain |
| she | 是 | is |
| wăn. | 問 | responsible. |

After a vessel has been reported on arrival by the Consul to the Custom-house, her hatches may be opened. Should the captain presume of his own accord to open hatches, before such report has been made, he will be forthwith fined, and all the goods discharged will be confiscated.

| | | |
|---|---|---|
| Fan | 凡 | Every |
| ch'üen | 船 | vessel |
| taou | 到 | arrive |
| ling sze kwan | 領事官 | Consul |
| t'ung che | 通知 | report |
| hae kwan | 海關 | Custom-house |
| che | 之 | of |
| how | 後 | after |
| ts'ae | 纔 | then |
| chun | 准 | allow |
| kh'ae | 開 | open |
| ts'ang | 艙 | hold |
| joh | 若 | if |
| she | 是 | is |
| ch'üen choo | 船主 | captain |
| shan | 擅 | presume |
| tsze | 自 | self |
| sëen | 先 | first |
| kh'ae | 開 | open |
| tsew | 就 | forthwith |
| fah | 罰 | fine |
| pa | 把 | take |
| so | 所 | that |
| kh'e | 起 | discharge |

| | | |
|---|---|---|
| teih | 的 | which |
| koh | 各 | every |
| po | 貨 | goods |
| t'ung | 通 | all |
| kung | 共 | |
| juh | 入 | confiscate. |
| kwan. | 官 | |

English merchants who want to land or ship goods must also apply for a permit, on receiving which they may proceed to land or ship. Should any landing or shipping of goods be made without a permit, the goods will be in danger of confiscation.

| | | |
|---|---|---|
| Ying | 英 | English |
| shang | 商 | merchant |
| shang | 上 | discharge |
| hëa | 下 | ship |
| ho | 貨 | goods |
| wuh | 物 | |
| yay | 也 | also |
| yaou | 要 | need |
| ts'ing | 請 | ask |
| ling | 領 | receive |
| chun | 准 | permit |
| tan | 單 | |
| ts'ae | 纔 | then |
| năng | 能 | may |
| kow | 彀 | |
| shang | 上 | discharge |
| hëa | 下 | ship |
| joh | 若 | if |
| muh | 沒 | not |
| yew | 有 | have |
| chun | 准 | permit |
| tan | 單 | |
| sze | 私 | stealthily |
| tsze | 自 | |
| shang | 上 | discharge |
| hëa | 下 | ship |
| tsew | 就 | then |
| p'a | 怕 | fear |
| show | 受 | receive |
| luy | 累 | involve |
| juh | 入 | confiscate. |
| kwan. | 官 | |

If any vessel tranship goods without having first received a permit, the Custom-house may confiscate the goods on seizure.

| | | |
|---|---|---|
| Joo | 如 | If |
| kwo | 果 | indeed |
| koh | 各 | every |
| ch'üen | 船 | vessel |
| poh | 剝 | tranship |
| kwo | 過 | |
| ho | 貨 | goods |
| wuh | 物 | |
| muh | 沒 | not |
| yew | 有 | have |
| sëen | 先 | first |
| ling | 領 | receive |
| chun | 准 | permit |
| tan | 單 | |
| hae | 海 | Custom-house |
| kwan | 關 | |

na 拿 } seize
choh 着 }
t'ing 聽 allow
kh'e 其 them
juh 入 } confiscate.
kwan. 官 }

When the duties on import and export goods have all been paid, the Custom-house will issue a grand chop, on sight of which the Consul will restore the ship's papers to the Captain, and allow him to set sail.

Tsin 進 Enter
ch'uh 出 go out
kh'ow 口 port
teih 的 of
ho 貨 goods
shuy 稅 duty
too 都 all
wan 完 pay
ts'ing 清 clear
how, 後 after,
yew 由 by
hae 海 } Custom-house
kwan 關 }
fah 發 } issue
kay 給 }
hung 紅 red
tan, 單 permit,
ling 領 }
sze 事 } Consul
kwan 官 }
këen 見 } seen,
lëaou, 了 }
tsew 就 then
pa 把 take
ch'üen 船 ship
p'ae 牌 register
këaou 交 deliver
hwan 還 back
ch'üen 船 } Captain,
choo, 主 }
chun 准 allow
t'a 他 him
she 駛 } sail.
hing. 行 }

In all cases where goods have to pay duty *ad valorem*, should the merchant and the examiner of the goods disagree as to their value, both parties may severally call in merchants to value the goods once more in public together, and the highest sum at which they rate the value shall be considered the amount on which to levy the duty.

Fan 凡 All
yew 有 have
ngan 按 according to
koo 估 value
këa 價 price
ch'ow 抽 levy
shuy 稅 duty
teih 的 which
ho 貨 } goods,
wuh, 物 }
t'ang 倘 if

| | | |
|---|---|---|
| shang | 商 | merchant |
| jin | 人 | |
| t'ung | 同 | and |
| yen | 驗 | examine |
| ho | 貨 | goods |
| jin | 人 | man |
| so | 所 | that which |
| koo | 估 | value |
| teih | 的 | of |
| këa | 價 | price |
| ts'ëen | 錢 | |
| puh | 不 | not |
| tuy, | 對 | agree, |
| pe | 彼 | that |
| ts'ze | 此 | this |
| too | 都 | both |
| chun | 准 | allow |
| koh | 各 | each |
| ts'ing | 請 | ask |
| shang | 商 | merchant |
| jin | 人 | |
| t'ung | 同 | together |
| kung | 公 | publicly |
| tsae | 再 | again |
| koo, | 估 | value, |
| chaou | 照 | according to |
| t'a | 他 | they |
| măn | 們 | |
| so | 所 | that which |
| koo | 估 | value |
| teih | 的 | of |
| tsuy | 最 | most |
| to | 多 | much |
| teih | 的 | of |

| | | |
|---|---|---|
| këa | 價 | price, |
| ts'ëen, | 錢 | |
| wei | 爲 | become |
| ngih | 額 | fixed amount |
| kh'o | 科 | calculate |
| shuy. | 稅 | duty. |

In the case of goods whose net weight has to be ascertained, both parties are allowed to select a few cases, break them open, and weigh the contents and casing separately; and duty will be taken on the actual weight of the goods minus the weight of the casing.

| | | |
|---|---|---|
| Joh | 若 | If |
| yew | 有 | have |
| ch'oo | 除 | remove |
| p'e | 皮 | casing |
| swan | 筭 | reckon |
| kh'ing | 輕 | light |
| chung | 重 | heavy |
| teih | 的 | which |
| ho | 貨 | goods, |
| wuh, | 物 | |
| pe | 彼 | that |
| ts'ze | 此 | this |
| too | 都 | both |
| chun | 准 | allow |
| koh | 各 | each |
| këen | 揀 | choose |
| ke | 幾 | few |
| sëang | 箱 | box |
| ch'eh | 拆 | break |

| | | |
|---|---|---|
| kh'ae | 開 | open |
| făn | 分 | separate |
| ch'ing, | 秤 | weigh, |
| ch'oo | 除 | remove |
| kh'eu | 去 | go |
| p'e | 皮 | casing |
| teih | 的 | of |
| kh'ing | 輕 | light |
| chung, | 重 | heavy, |
| shih | 實 | truly |
| chung | 重 | heavy |
| to | 多 | much |
| shaou, | 少 | little, |
| chaou | 照 | according to |
| soo | 數 | amount |
| swan | 算 | reckon |
| shuy. | 稅 | duty. |

If they disagree in opinion, the merchant will be at liberty within one day's time to apply to the Consul, and beg him to arrange the matter equitably with the Custom-house.

| | | |
|---|---|---|
| Joo | 如 | If |
| kwo | 果 | indeed |
| pe | 彼 | that |
| ts'ze | 此 | this |
| e | 意 | opinion |
| këen | 見 | |
| puh | 不 | not |
| t'ung, | 同 | same, |
| hëen | 限 | limit |
| tsae | 在 | at |
| yih | 一 | one |
| t'ëen | 天 | day |
| che | 之 | of |
| nuy, | 內 | inside, |
| jin | 任 | allow |
| p'ing | 憑 | |
| shang | 商 | merchant |
| jin | 人 | |
| pin | 稟 | petition |
| ts'ing | 請 | request |
| ling | 領 | Consul, |
| sze | 事 | |
| kwan, | 官 | |
| hwuy | 會 | with |
| t'ung | 同 | |
| hae | 海 | Custom-house |
| kwan | 關 | |
| ping | 秉 | equitably |
| kung | 公 | |
| lëaou | 料 | arrange. |
| le. | 理 | |

If goods are damp or damaged, duty must be reckoned on them according to their value in their deteriorated condition.

| | | |
|---|---|---|
| T'ang | 倘 | If |
| she | 是 | is |
| ho | 貨 | goods |
| wuh | 物 | |
| yew | 有 | have |
| ch'aou | 潮 | damp |
| shih | 濕 | |
| sun | 損 | damaged, |
| hwae, | 壞 | |

ying 應 } must
kae 該 }
chaou 照 } according to
choh 着 }
hwae 壞 damaged
ho 貨 goods
so 所 that
chih 値 value
teih 的 which
këa 價 } price,
ts'ëen, 錢 }
e 議 } reckon
lun 論 }
ch'ow 抽 levy
shuy. 稅 duty.

Should an English merchant, after having taken any goods into port and paid duties thereon, find them unsaleable, and in consequence wish to carry them to some other port for sale, he must in the first instance report them to the Custom-house, who will examine their books to see that the goods agree with former entries, and that there is no falsification, and, if satisfied on these points, they will make an entry of the goods on the grand chop. This they will deliver to the merchant, and at the same time notify the fact to the other ports, so that when the goods are entered elsewhere they may not be subjected to a second duty.

Ying 英 English
shang 商 merchant
yün 運 carry
ho 貨 goods
tsin 進 enter
kh'ow, 口 port,
wan 完 pay
ts'ing 清 complete
shuy 稅 } duty
hëang 餉 }
how, 後 after,
yin 因 } because
wei 爲 }
puh 不 not
năng 能 can
fah 發 } sell,
mae, 賣 }
yaou 要 want
tae 帶 take
taou 到 to
pëeh 別 other
kh'ow 口 port
mae 買 } trade
mae 賣 }
teih, 的 —,
ying 應 must
sëen 先 first
paou 報 report
hae 海 } Custom-house
kwan 關 }
ch'a 查 examine
ming 明 clearly
te 底 original
poo 簿 book
sëang 相 mutually

| | | |
|---|---|---|
| foo, | 符 | agree, |
| muh | 沒 | not |
| yew | 有 | have |
| ts'o | 錯 | falsification, |
| woo, | 悞 | |
| tsew | 就 | then |
| pa | 把 | take |
| ho | 貨 | goods |
| shuy | 稅 | duty |
| soo | 數 | amount, |
| muh, | 目 | |
| tsae | 在 | at |
| hung | 紅 | grand chop |
| p'ae | 牌 | |
| le | 裡 | in |
| choo | 註 | enter |
| ming, | 明 | clearly, |
| fah | 發 | deliver |
| kay | 給 | |
| shang | 商 | merchant |
| jin | 人 | |
| show | 收 | receive |
| chih, | 執 | hold, |
| yih | 一 | at the same time |
| mëen | 面 | |
| chaou | 照 | write officially |
| hwuy | 會 | |
| pëeh | 別 | other |
| kh'ow, | 口 | port, |
| tăng | 等 | wait |
| yuen | 原 | original |
| ho | 貨 | goods |
| tsin | 進 | enter |
| kh'ow, | 口 | port, |
| puh | 不 | not |
| peih | 必 | must |
| chung | 重 | repeat |
| ching. | 征 | charge. |

When a merchant wishes to convey import goods which are unsaleable, and on which duty has been paid, to another country for sale, he may apply to the Custom-house for a receipt for the duty that he has paid, and for any after lot of import or export goods he may use this receipt in payment of duty.

| | | |
|---|---|---|
| Joh | 若 | If |
| shang | 商 | merchant |
| jin | 人 | |
| yew | 有 | have |
| tsin | 進 | enter |
| kh'ow | 口 | port |
| ho, | 貨 | goods, |
| puh | 不 | not |
| năng | 能 | can |
| fah | 發 | sell, |
| mae, | 賣 | |
| wan | 完 | pay |
| shuy | 稅 | duty |
| how, | 後 | after, |
| yew | 又 | again |
| yaou | 要 | wish |
| tae | 帶 | carry |
| taou | 到 | to |
| pëeh | 別 | other |
| kwoh | 國 | country |

| | | |
|---|---|---|
| fah | 發 | sell |
| mae | 賣 | |
| teih, | 的 | 一, |
| chun | 准 | allow |
| paou | 報 | report |
| hae | 海 | Custom-house, |
| kwan, | 關 | |
| ts'ing | 請 | beg |
| ling | 領 | receive |
| so | 所 | that which |
| nah | 納 | levy |
| teih | 的 | of |
| shuy | 稅 | duty |
| hëang | 餉 | |
| show | 收 | receipt, |
| tan, | 單 | |
| tsëang | 將 | in future |
| lae | 來 | |
| yew | 有 | have |
| tsin | 進 | enter |
| ch'uh | 出 | go out |
| kh'ow | 口 | port |
| teih | 的 | which |
| pëeh | 別 | other |
| ho, | 貨 | goods, |
| tsew | 就 | then |
| pa | 把 | take |
| chay | 這 | this |
| show | 收 | receipt |
| tan | 單 | |
| te | 抵 | make up |
| shuy. | 稅 | duty. |

All foreign-grown grain that has entered port, but has not yet been discharged, may, if it be wished, be carried out again to some other port.

| | | |
|---|---|---|
| Koh | 各 | Every |
| wae | 外 | outside |
| kwoh | 國 | nation |
| so | 所 | which |
| ch'an | 產 | produce |
| teih | 的 | of |
| lëang | 粮 | grain, |
| shih, | 食 | |
| yün | 運 | carry |
| tsin | 進 | enter |
| kh'ow | 口 | port |
| che | 之 | of |
| how, | 後 | after, |
| joh | 若 | if |
| muh | 沒 | not |
| yew | 有 | have |
| kh'e | 起 | discharge, |
| sëay, | 卸 | |
| jing | 仍 | yet |
| yaou | 要 | wish |
| tae | 帶 | convey |
| wang | 往 | go |
| pëeh | 別 | other |
| ch'oo | 處 | place |
| fah | 發 | sell, |
| mae, | 賣 | |
| yay | 也 | also |
| woo | 無 | no |
| puh | 不 | not |
| kh'o. | 可 | may. |

The Chinese authorities who

receive duties at the ports may adopt what measures they think fit for the rigorous prevention of smuggling, and English officers must not interfere.

| | | |
|---|---|---|
| Chung | 中 | China |
| kwoh | 國 | |
| koh | 各 | every |
| kh'ow | 口 | port |
| show | 收 | receive |
| shuy | 稅 | duty |
| teih | 的 | which |
| kwan, | 官 | officer, |
| sheh | 設 | adopt |
| fah | 法 | measure |
| yen | 嚴 | rigorous |
| fang | 防 | prevent |
| t'ow | 偷 | smuggle, |
| low, | 漏 | |
| ying | 應 | must |
| t'ing | 聽 | follow |
| kh'e | 其 | his |
| pëen, | 便 | convenience, |
| ying | 英 | English |
| kwan | 官 | officer |
| puh | 不 | not |
| tih | 得 | can |
| kwo | 過 | pass |
| wăn. | 問 | enquire. |

English ships may only resort for trading purposes to the ports determined on under treaty. If a vessel goes to any other places along the coast than the ports laid down, the local authorities will be at liberty to confiscate both vessel and cargo.

| | | |
|---|---|---|
| Ying | 英 | English |
| ch'üen | 船 | ship |
| chih | 只 | only |
| chun | 准 | allow |
| tsae | 在 | at |
| ho | 和 | treaty |
| yoh | 約 | |
| nuy, | 內 | in, |
| so | 所 | which |
| e | 擬 | determine |
| teih | 的 | of |
| koh | 各 | every |
| kh'ow | 口 | port |
| lae | 來 | come |
| wang | 往 | go |
| mae | 買 | trade, |
| mae, | 賣 | |
| joo | 如 | if |
| joh | 若 | |
| taou | 到 | to |
| yüen | 沿 | sea coast |
| hae | 海 | |
| pëeh | 別 | other |
| ch'oo | 處 | places |
| tsin | 進 | enter |
| ch'uh | 出 | go out |
| t'ung | 通 | trade, |
| shang, | 商 | |
| chun | 准 | permit |
| te | 地 | local |
| fang | 方 | |
| kwan | 官 | officer |

pa 把 take
ch'üen 船 vessel
lëen 連 include
ho, 貨 goods,
t'ung 統 } all
kung 共 }
juh 入 } confiscate.
kwan. 官 }

If an English vessel is guilty of smuggling or evasion, no matter what the goods smuggling are, or what their value may be, they may all be seized and confiscated, and the local authorities will also be at liberty to drive her from the port as soon as her accounts have been settled, and prohibit her from trading further.

Ying 英 English
ch'üen 船 uessel
joo 如 if
yew 有 have
tsow 走 } smuggle
sze 私 }
t'ow 偷 } evade,
low, 漏 }
woo 無 no
lun 論 matter
so 所 that which
tsow 走 smuggle
teih 的 of
she 是 is
shin 甚 } what
mo 麽 }
ho 貨 } goods,
wuh, 物 }
shin 甚 } what
mo 麽 }
këa 價 } price,
ts'ëen, 錢 }
too 都 all
chun 准 allow
na 拿 seize
choo 住 detain
juh 入 } confiscate,
kwan, 官 }
han 還 also
chun 准 permit
te 地 } local
fang 方 }
kwan 官 officer
tăng 等 wait
t'a 他 her
chang 帳 } accounts
muh 目 }
ts'ing 清 } settled
ts'oo 楚 }
how, 後 after,
pa 把 take
ch'uen 船 vessel
kh'eu 驅 } drive away
choh 逐 }
ch'uh 出 go out
kh'ow, 口 port,
kin 禁 } prohibit
che 止 }
tsae 再 } again
hing 行 }

mow 貿 } trade.
yih. 易 }

All fines imposed and confiscations made under the Treaty, will revert to the national treasury of China, to be appropriated for the public service.

Fan 凡 All
yew 有 have
chaou 照 according to
ho 和 } treaty
yoh 約 }
fah 罰 fine
yin 銀 } money
tsze 子 }
teih 的 of
juh 入 } confiscate
kwan 官 }
teih 的 of
koh 各 every
kh'wan 欵 item,
too 都 all
kwuy 歸 revert
chung 中 } China
kwoh 國 }
kwoh 國 national
t'ang 帑 treasury
kung 公 public
yung. 用 use.

Hereafter the English characters shall be employed by English officers in their official communications to the Chinese authorities, but for the present each letter shall be accompanied by a supplementary copy in Chinese text, for the more easy comprehension of the Chinese officials; should any dispute arise as to meaning, the English text shall be held to be the criterion. This rule will apply to the Treaty now made.

E 以 } Hereafter
how 後 }
ying 英 English
kwan 官 officer
tsze 咨 } address
hwuy 會 }
hwa 華 Chinese
kwan 官 officer,
too 都 always
yung 用 employ
ying 英 } England
kwoh 國 }
wăn 文 } character
tsze 字 }
shoo 書 } write,
sëay 寫 }
tan 但 but
hëen 現 } now
tsae 在 }
tsan 暫 } for awhile
ts'ëay 且 }
koh 各 every
wăn 文 letter
foo 附 annex
sung 送 send
han 漢 Chinese

N

| | | |
|---|---|---|
| tsze | 字 | character |
| teih | 的 | of |
| foo | 副 | supplementary |
| wăn | 文 | copy, |
| she | 使 | cause |
| hwa | 華 | Chinese |
| kwan | 官 | officer |
| yung | 容 | easy |
| e | 易 | |
| tung | 懂 | understand, |
| teih | 的 | |
| t'ang | 倘 | if |
| yew | 有 | have |
| pëen | 辯 | dispute |
| lun | 論 | |
| so | 所 | that which |
| sëay | 寫 | write |
| teih | 的 | of |
| e | 意 | meaning, |
| sze | 思 | |
| tsung | 總 | always |
| e | 以 | take |
| ying | 英 | English |
| wăn | 文 | text |
| wei | 爲 | be |
| chun | 準 | criterion, |
| muh | 目 | now |
| kin | 今 | |
| so | 所 | that which |
| leih | 立 | establish |
| teih | 的 | of |
| ho | 和 | treaty, |
| yoh, | 約 | |
| yay | 也 | also |

| | | |
|---|---|---|
| she | 是 | is |
| chaou | 照 | according |
| choh | 着 | |
| ying | 英 | English |
| wăn | 文 | text |
| wei | 爲 | be |
| chun | 準 | criterion |
| teih | 的 | of |
| le | 例 | rule, |
| chay | 這 | this |
| yang | 樣 | way |
| pan | 辦 | manage. |
| le. | 理 | |

The use of the word 夷 *e* in designating Englishmen, will not be allowed in public documents throughout China.

| | | |
|---|---|---|
| Chung | 中 | China |
| kwoh | 國 | |
| shih | 十 | eighteen |
| pah | 八 | |
| săng | 省 | provinces, |
| shoo | 書 | write |
| sëay | 寫 | |
| koh | 各 | every |
| yang | 樣 | kind |
| teih | 的 | of |
| kung | 公 | public |
| wăn | 文 | documents, |
| too | 都 | all |
| puh | 不 | not |
| chun | 准 | allow |
| yung | 用 | employ |
| e | 夷 | E |

| | | |
|---|---|---|
| tsze | 字 | character |
| ch'ing | 稱 | designate |
| hoo | 呼 | |
| ying | 英 | English |
| jin. | 人 | man. |

When an English man-of-war enters any place on the sea-coast, it matters not where, without ill intent, or for the purpose of catching pirates, the local officers must give her every facility for purchasing or procuring fresh water, provisions, and means of repair; and they must likewise treat her officers with all courtesy.

| | | |
|---|---|---|
| Ying | 英 | England |
| kwoh | 國 | |
| ping | 兵 | man-of-war |
| ch'üen | 船 | |
| joo | 如 | if |
| woo | 無 | no |
| tae | 歹 | wrong |
| e | 意 | intention, |
| hwoh | 或 | or |
| yin | 因 | for |
| poo | 捕 | seize |
| taou | 盜 | pirate, |
| she | 駛 | enters |
| tsin | 進 | |
| yüen | 沿 | sea coast, |
| hae | 海 | |
| puh | 不 | no matter |
| lun | 論 | |
| na | 那 | which |
| ch'oo | 處 | place, |
| so | 所 | that which |
| yew | 有 | have |
| mae | 買 | purchase |
| pan | 辦 | procure |
| t'ëen | 甜 | fresh |
| shuy | 水 | water |
| shih | 食 | provision |
| wuh | 物 | |
| sew | 修 | repair |
| ch'üen | 船 | ship, |
| yih | 一 | altogether |
| ts'ëeh | 切 | |
| te | 地 | local |
| fang | 方 | |
| kwan | 官 | officer |
| tsung | 總 | always |
| yaou | 要 | must |
| t'o | 妥 | properly |
| tang | 當 | |
| chaou | 照 | assist, |
| ying | 應 | |
| ch'üen | 船 | vessel |
| shang | 上 | in |
| kwan | 官 | officers |
| yüen | 員 | |
| hwa | 華 | Chinese |
| kwan | 官 | officer |
| yay | 也 | also |
| ying | 應 | must |
| e | 以 | with |
| le | 禮 | courtesy |
| sëang | 相 | treat. |
| tae | 待 | |

The plundering by pirates everywhere throughout the Chinese seas has a prejudicial effect on both native and foreign trade; the two nations will therefore adopt measures for their entire suppression.

| | | |
|---|---|---|
| Chung | 中 | China |
| kwoh | 國 | |
| hae | 海 | seas |
| mëen | 面 | |
| teih | 的 | of |
| kh'ëang | 强 | pirates |
| taou | 盜 | |
| koh | 各 | every |
| ch'oo | 處 | place |
| ts'ëang | 搶 | plunder |
| këeh | 刼 | |
| yu | 與 | to |
| nuy | 內 | native |
| wae | 外 | foreign |
| teih | 的 | of |
| mae | 買 | trade |
| mae | 賣 | |
| ta | 大 | great |
| yew | 有 | have |
| kwan | 關 | prejudice, |
| ngae | 碍 | |
| so | 所 | therefore |
| e | 以 | |
| lëang | 兩 | two |
| kwoh | 國 | nation |
| tsew | 就 | forthwith |
| yaou | 要 | want |
| sheh | 設 | adopt |
| fah | 法 | measure |
| tsëaou | 剿 | exterminate |
| ch'oo | 除 | |
| lëaou | 了 | finish. |

All the advantages to which Englishmen were entitled under the treaty formerly made are now retained to them; and if hereafter further advantages are accorded by treaty to other nations, Englishmen shall enjoy them in like manner.

| | | |
|---|---|---|
| Shang | 上 | Former |
| nëen | 年 | year |
| so | 所 | that which |
| leih | 立 | establish |
| teih | 的 | of |
| ho | 和 | treaty |
| yoh | 約 | |
| fan | 凡 | all |
| she | 是 | is |
| ying | 英 | English |
| jin | 人 | man |
| ying | 應 | must |
| tih | 得 | obtain |
| teih | 的 | which |
| haou | 好 | advantage, |
| ch'oo | 處 | |
| hëen | 現 | now |
| tsae | 在 | |
| jing | 仍 | as before |
| kew | 舊 | old |

| | | |
|---|---|---|
| lew | 留 | retain, |
| choh | 着 | |
| tsëang | 將 | hereafter |
| lae | 來 | |
| pëeh | 別 | other |
| kwoh | 國 | nation |
| leih | 立 | establish |
| yoh | 約 | treaty |
| tih | 得 | obtained |
| lëaou | 了 | |
| pëeh | 別 | other |
| teih | 的 | |
| haou | 好 | advantage, |
| ch'oo | 處 | |
| ying | 英 | English |
| jin | 人 | man |
| yay | 也 | also |
| ying | 應 | must |
| yih | 一 | in like manner |
| lëuh | 律 | |
| chen | 沾 | enjoy |
| show | 受 | receive |

A special article shall be separately agreed to, defining clearly how the payment of the sums due as compensation to English merchants at the provincial city of the Canton province shall be arranged, in order to show friendly feeling.

| | | |
|---|---|---|
| Tsae | 在 | At |
| kwang | 廣 | Canton |
| tung | 東 | |
| săng | 省 | provincial city |
| ch'ing | 城 | |
| ying | 應 | ought |
| kae | 該 | |
| p'ay | 賠 | compensate |
| poo | 補 | |
| shang | 商 | merchant |
| jin | 人 | |
| teih | 的 | which |
| kh'wan | 欵 | sums, |
| hëang | 項 | |
| ling | 另 | separate |
| leih | 立 | establish |
| chüen | 專 | special |
| t'ëaou | 條 | article |
| ting | 定 | define |
| ming | 明 | clearly |
| joo | 如 | how |
| ho | 何 | |
| pan | 辦 | arrange |
| le | 理 | |
| e | 以 | in order to |
| chaou | 昭 | show |
| yew | 友 | friendliness |
| muh | 睦 | |

After this Treaty shall have been ratified by the two contracting parties, each shall, within the term of one year from the date of signature, appoint high officers to exchange copies at Peking.

| | | |
|---|---|---|
| Păn | 本 | This |
| yoh | 約 | treaty |
| tăng | 等 | wait |
| pe | 彼 | that |
| tsze | 此 | this |

| | | |
|---|---|---|
| lëang | 兩 | two |
| pëen | 邊 | side |
| p'e | 批 | declare |
| chun | 准 | allow |
| che | 之 | of |
| how | 後 | after, |
| tsze | 自 | from |
| leih | 立 | made |
| yoh | 約 | treaty |
| jih | 日 | day |
| kh'e | 起 | begin, |
| e | 以 | take |
| yih | 一 | one |
| nëen | 年 | year |
| nuy | 內 | inside |
| wei | 爲 | be |
| kh'e | 期 | term, |
| tsae | 在 | at |
| king | 京 | Peking |
| le | 裡 | |
| koh | 各 | each |
| p'ae | 派 | appoint |
| ta | 大 | great |
| yüen | 員 | officers |
| hoo | 互 | mutually |
| sëang | 相 | |
| këaou | 交 | exchange. |
| hwan | 換 | |

What is above set forth is the general tenor of the several articles of the English treaty; besides these 56 articles a tariff of duties is annexed, together with ten regulations, all which were agreed to at Shanghae on the third day of the 10th month of the 8th year of Hëen-fung's reign.

| | | |
|---|---|---|
| E | 以 | Above |
| shang | 上 | |
| so | 所 | that which |
| seu | 叙 | set forth |
| too | 都 | all |
| she | 是 | is |
| ying | 英 | English |
| kwoh | 國 | nation |
| ho | 和 | treaty |
| yoh | 約 | |
| koh | 各 | every |
| t'ëaou | 條 | article |
| teih | 的 | of |
| ta | 大 | general |
| e | 意 | idea, |
| ch'oo | 除 | besides |
| woo | 五 | fifty |
| shih | 十 | |
| lëuh | 六 | six |
| t'ëaou | 條 | article |
| che | 之 | of |
| wae | 外 | outside, |
| han | 還 | yet |
| yew | 有 | have |
| how | 後 | after |
| foo | 附 | annex |
| teih | 的 | which |
| shuy | 稅 | tariff, |
| tsih | 則 | |
| e | 以 | and |
| keih | 及 | |

| | | |
|---|---|---|
| chang | 章 | regulations |
| ch'ing | 程 | |
| shih | 十 | ten |
| t'ëaou | 條 | articles |
| she | 是 | is |
| yû | 於 | in |
| Hëen | 咸 | Hëen-fung |
| fung | 豐 | |
| pah | 八 | eight |
| nëen | 年 | year |
| shih | 十 | ten |
| yüeh | 月 | month |
| ch'oo | 初 | third |
| san | 三 | |
| jih | 日 | day |
| tsae | 在 | at |
| shang | 上 | Shanghae |
| yang | 洋 | |
| e | 議 | agree to |
| ting | 定 | |
| teih | 的 | — |

# DIALOGUES

## 問答 WĂN TAH.

### WITH A SHOPMAN.

It is long since I have seen you.

Kew 久 Long
wei 違 separate
kew 久 long
wei. 違 separate.

Pray sit down.

Ts'ing 請 Pray
tso. 坐 sit.

Pray sit on the upper seat.

Ts'ing 請 Pray
shang 上 up
tso. 坐 sit.

You are too polite.

Puh 不 Not
kan 敢 dare
puh 不 not
kan. 敢 dare.

Pray have some tea.

Ts'ing 請 Pray
ch'a. 茶 tea.

Thank you.

Ts'ing 請 Pray
ah. 阿 —

Have you been well?

Yih 一 } Hitherto
hëang 向 }
haou 好 well
ah. 阿 ?

Yes, thanks to your auspices.

T'oh 托 Rely
fuh. 福 good fortune.

Has your worthy firm driven a good trade of late?

Paou 寶 Worthy
hang 行 firm
săng 生 } trade
e 意 }
yih 一 } hitherto
hëang 向 }
fah 發 earn
ts'ai 財 wealth
ah. 阿 ?

You are too complimentary.

Haou 好 Good
shwoh 說 word.

I have been remiss in calling to ask after you.

Shaou 少 Little
lae 來 come
wăn 問 ask
how 候 wait
ne. 你 you.

I am unworthy of the compliment.

Kh'e 豈 How
kan. 敢 dare.

Is this year's trade good?

Kin 今 This
nëen 年 year
teih 的 of
săng 生 } trade
e 意
haou 好 good
ah. 阿 ?

Trade is quite dull just now.

Chay 這 This
she 時 } time
how 候
urh 兒 —
săng 生 } trade
e 意
too 都 quite
lăng 冷 } dull.
tan. 淡

Why dull?

Wei 爲 For
shin 甚 } what
mo 麽
lăng 冷 } dull
tan 淡
ne. 呢 ?

Because the foreign ships have not come in, and there is no business doing.

Yin 因 } Because
wei 爲
yang 洋 foreign
ch'üen 船 ship
han 還 yet
muh 沒 not
yew 有 have
taou 到 arrive
yah 也 also
muh 沒 not
yew 有 have
săng 生 } business
e 意
tso. 做 do.

When are they likely to arrive?

Shin 甚 } What
mo 麽
she 時 } time
how 候
ts'ae 纔 then
năng 能 can
taou 到 arrive
ne 呢 ?

They always arrive every year about the fifth or sixth month.

May 每 Every
nëen 年 year
ch'ang 常 always
she 是 is
woo 五 five
lëuh 六 six
yueh 月 month
le 裡 in
taou. 到 arrive.

All kinds of foreign goods not having yet arrived, they have increased in price.

Joo 如 } Now
kin 今
muh 沒 not

| | | |
|---|---|---|
| yew | 有 | have |
| taou | 到 | arrive |
| koh | 各 | every |
| yang | 樣 | sort |
| teih | 的 | of |
| yang | 洋 | foreign |
| ho | 貨 | goods |
| too | 都 | all |
| chang | 長 | increased |
| lëaou | 了 | |
| këa | 價 | price |
| lëaou. | 了 | — |

And every other business it is difficult to do.

| | | |
|---|---|---|
| Lëen | 連 | Include |
| pëĕh | 別 | other |
| teih | 的 | |
| săng | 生 | business |
| e | 意 | |
| too | 都 | all |
| nan | 難 | difficult |
| tso. | 做 | do. |

When the ships do arrive, I think of buying some little things to give away to people.

| | | |
|---|---|---|
| Ch'üen | 船 | Ship |
| taou | 到 | arrived |
| lëaou | 了 | |
| wo | 我 | I |
| sëang | 想 | think |
| mae | 買 | buy |
| tëen | 點 | little |
| tung | 東 | thing |
| se | 西 | |
| sung | 送 | give |
| sung | 送 | |
| jin. | 人 | people. |

Prices are now so dear, that I will not buy.

| | | |
|---|---|---|
| Hëen | 現 | Now |
| tsae | 在 | |
| këa | 價 | price |
| ts'ëen | 錢 | |
| kwuy | 貴 | dear |
| wo | 我 | I |
| tsew | 就 | then |
| puh | 不 | not |
| mae | 買 | buy |
| lëaou. | 了 | — |

Very good; when the ships arrive, I will send some one to your lodgings, and ask you to come and see them.

| | | |
|---|---|---|
| Haou | 好 | Good |
| lëaou | 了 | |
| tăng | 等 | wait |
| ch'üen | 船 | ship |
| taou | 到 | arrived |
| lëaou | 了 | |
| wo | 我 | I |
| tsew | 就 | then |
| ta | 打 | send |
| fah | 發 | |
| jin | 人 | man |
| taou | 到 | to |
| tsun | 尊 | honorable |
| yü | 寓 | lodging |
| ts'ing | 請 | request |

ne 你 you
lae 來 come
kh'an. 看 see.

Your civility is more than I can presume to.

Kh'e 豈 How
kan. 敢 dare.

Some other day, I will come again and look you up.

Kae 改 Another
t'ëen 天 day
wo 我 I
tsae 再 again
lae 來 come
chaou 照 according
koo 顧 look
ne 你 you
pa. 罷 —

Pray be seated; I must go.

Ne 你 You
ts'ing 請 pray
tso 坐 sit
wo 我 I
tsow 走 } go.
lëaou. 了 }

Sit awhile more before going.

Tsae 再 More
tso 坐 } sit
tso 坐 }
kh'eu. 去 go.

I will not stay. I have some business at home.

Puh 不 Not
tso 坐 sit
lëaou 了 —
shay 舍 } at home
hëa 下 }
han 還 yet
yew 有 have
sze 事 business
ne. 呢 —

Such being the case, I will not presume to offer to detain you.

Chay 這 } This case
mo 麼 }
tsew 就 then
puh 不 not
kan 敢 dare
fung 奉 offer
lew. 留 detain.

You compliment me. Pardon my having been such poor company.

Haou 好 Good
shwoh 說 word
shaou 少 little
p'ay. 陪 company.

## WITH A TEA MERCHANT.

What is the name of this chop of tea?

Chay 這 This
haou 號 chop
ch'a 茶 tea
këaou 叫 call
shin 甚 } what
mo 麽 }
ming 名 } name.
tsze. 字 }

Its name is *Le-ke*, and it contains altogether 620 chests.

Chay 這 } This
ko 個 }
këaou 叫 call
tso 做 make
le 利 } *Le-ke*
ke 記 }
t'ung 通 } altogether
kung 共 }
yew 有 have
lëuh 六 six
pih 百 hundred
urh 二 two
shih 十 ten
sëang. 箱 chest.

What price will you sell it for ?

Yaou 要 Wish
mae 賣 sell
shin 甚 } what
mo 麽 }
këa 價 } price.
ts'ëen. 錢 }

I want 22 taels per pecul, duty not included.

May 每 Each
tan 担 pecul
yaou 要 want
urh 二 two
shih 十 ten
urh 二 two
lëang 兩 tael
shuy 稅 } duty
hëang 餉 }
tsae 在 at
wae. 外 outside.

That price is too dear, the tea moreover is not well made.

Na 那 } that
ke 個 }
këa 價 } price
ts'ëen 錢 }
t'ae 太 too
kwuy 貴 dear
lëaou 了 —
chay 這 this
ch'a 茶 tea
tso 做 } made
teih 的 }
yay 也 also
puh 不 not
haou. 好 good.

It contains very many coarse

leaves.

Yew 有 Have
heu 許 very
to 多 many
teih 的 —
ts'oo 粗 coarse
yeh 葉 } leaf.
tsze. 子 }

If these few coarse large leaves are picked clean out.

Joo 如 If
kwo 果 indeed
pa 把 take
chay 這 this
sëay 些 few
ts'oo 粗 coarse
ta 大 large
teih 的 —
yeh 葉 } leaves
tsze 子 }
këen 揀 pick
kan 乾 } clean.
tsing. 淨 }

It may then be worth about 22 or 23 taels the pecul.

May 每 Each
tan 担 pecul
tsew 就 then
kh'o 可 } may
e 以 }
chih 值 worth
tih 得 obtain
urh 二 two
shih 拾 ten
urh 二 two
san 三 three
lëang 兩 tael
teih 的 of
kwang 光 } about.
king. 景 }

This tea cannot be called dear.

Chay 這 This
ch'a 茶 tea
puh 不 not
swan 算 reckon
kwuy. 貴 dear.

This tea was picked before the "grain rain" term of this spring.

Chay 這 This
ch'a 茶 tea
she 是 is
kin 今 this
ch'un 春 spring
kuh 穀 grain
yu 雨 rain
ts'ëen 前 before
ts'ae 採 } pick
chae 摘 }
teih. 的 —

It was moreover produced in the locality of Ho-kh'ow.

Yew 又 Also
she 是 is
ho 河 } Ho-kh'ow
kh'ow 口 }
te 地 } locality
fang 方 }
ch'uh 出 produced

teih 的 —

The tea from Ho-kh'ow and thereabouts is always best when small leaved, and has a Pekoe flavour.

Ho 河 } Ho-kh'ow
kh'ow 口
na 那 } there
le 裡
teih 的 of
ch'a 茶 tea
wang 往 } constantly
ch'ang 常
too 都 all
she 是 is
sëaou 小 small
yeh 葉 leaf
ting 頂 first
haou 好 good
teih 的 —
yew 又 also
yew 有 have
pih 白 } Pekoe
haou 毫
teih 的 of
wei 味 } flavour.
taou. 道

Is the tea grown in the Bohea hills better than the Ho-kh'ow tea?

Woo 武 } Bohea
e 彝
shan 山 hill
ch'uh 出 produce
teih 的 which
ch'a 茶 tea
pe 比 compare
ho 河 } Ho-kh'ow
kh'ow 口
ch'a 茶 tea
han 還 more
haou 好 good
mo. 麽 ?

It is good enough. Pekoes, Souchongs, Boheas, and those sorts of tea are all reckoned to be of superior quality, only they contain a good deal of dust and stalks.

Haou 好 Good
she 是 is
haou 好 good
pih 白 } Pekoe
haou 毫
sëaou 小 } Souchong
chung 種
woo 武 } Bohea
e 彝
koh 各 every
chung 種 sort
teih 的 —
ch'a 茶 tea
too 都 all
swan 算 reckon
t'ow 頭 superior
tăng 等 quality
teih 的 —
chih 只 only

| | | |
|---|---|---|
| she | 是 | is |
| moh | 末 | dust |
| tsze | 子 | |
| to | 多 | much |
| kăng | 梗 | stalk |
| tsze | 子 | |
| to. | 多 | much. |

What teas have you got for sale?

| | | |
|---|---|---|
| Ne | 你 | You |
| yew | 有 | have |
| shin | 甚 | what |
| mo | 麽 | |
| ch'a | 茶 | tea |
| yaou | 要 | want |
| mae. | 賣 | sale. |

I have cargo, Souchong, Pekoe, Hungmay, Campoy, and other sorts.

| | | |
|---|---|---|
| Wo | 我 | I |
| yew | 有 | have |
| kung | 工 | Congo |
| foo | 夫 | |
| sëaou | 小 | Souchong |
| chung | 種 | |
| pih | 白 | Pekoe |
| haou | 毫 | |
| hung | 紅 | Hung-may |
| may | 梅 | |
| këen | 揀 | Campoy |
| pei | 焙 | |
| tăng | 等 | other |
| luy. | 類 | sort. |

I have also Hyson Skin, Twankay, Sunglo, Hyson, Young Hyson, Gunpowder, Imperial, and every kind of green tea.

| | | |
|---|---|---|
| Han | 還 | Also |
| yew | 有 | have |
| he | 熙 | Hyson |
| ch'un | 春 | |
| p'e | 皮 | skin |
| t'un | 屯 | Twankay |
| kh'e | 溪 | |
| sung | 松 | Sung lo |
| lo | 蘿 | |
| he | 熙 | Hyson |
| ch'un | 春 | |
| may | 梅 | Young Hyson |
| pëen | 片 | |
| ma | 蔴 | Gunpowder |
| choo | 珠 | |
| ta | 大 | Imperial |
| choo | 珠 | |
| koh | 各 | every |
| yang | 樣 | sort |
| luh | 緑 | green |
| ch'a. | 茶 | tea. |

I beg you will give me a few sorts of green tea to look at.

| | | |
|---|---|---|
| Ts'ing | 請 | Beg |
| ne | 你 | you |
| na | 拏 | take |
| ke | 幾 | few |
| yang | 樣 | sorts |
| luh | 緑 | green |
| ch'a | 茶 | tea |

| | | |
|---|---|---|
| kay | 給 | give |
| wo | 我 | me |
| kh'an | 看 | look. |
| kh'an. | 看 | |

Here are two sorts, of Hyson and Hyson Skin.

| | | |
|---|---|---|
| Tsae | 在 | At |
| chay | 這 | here |
| le | 裡 | |
| yew | 有 | have |
| He | 熙 | Hyson |
| ch'un | 春 | |
| he | 熙 | Hyson |
| ch'un | 春 | |
| p'e | 皮 | skin |
| lëang | 兩 | two |
| yang. | 様 | sort. |

This Hyson tea is of first rate quality; you may get some water and pour out a cup of it, and you will see how green it is.

| | | |
|---|---|---|
| Chay | 這 | This |
| ko | 個 | |
| He | 熙 | Hyson |
| ch'un | 春 | |
| she | 是 | is |
| ting | 頂 | first |
| haou | 好 | good |
| teih | 的 | — |
| kh'o | 可 | may |
| na | 拏 | take |
| shwuy | 水 | water |
| lae | 來 | come |
| ch'ung | 冲 | pour |
| yih | 一 | one |
| wan | 碗 | cup |
| kh'an | 看 | look |
| t'a | 他 | it |
| teih | 的 | of |
| yen | 顏 | colour |
| sih | 色 | |
| she | 是 | is |
| ts'ing | 青 | green |
| ts'ing | 青 | |
| teih. | 的 | — |

But the leaves seem yellowish, and too open.

| | | |
|---|---|---|
| Tan | 但 | But |
| she | 是 | is |
| yeh | 葉 | leaves |
| tsze | 子 | |
| yen | 顏 | colour |
| sih | 色 | |
| tae | 帶 | carry |
| hwang | 黃 | yellow |
| yew | 又 | also |
| t'ae | 太 | too |
| kh'ae | 開 | open. |
| chen. | 展 | |

Hyson tea should always be tightly rolled up, and azure green in colour: all sorts of green tea are only good when they are like that.

| | | |
|---|---|---|
| He | 熙 | Hyson |
| ch'un | 春 | |
| ch'a | 茶 | tea |
| tsung | 總 | always |

中外對話

yaou 要 require
kh'euen 拳 roll
tih 得 obtain
kin 緊 tight
yaou 要 require
yen 顏 } colour
sih 色 }
pih 碧 azure
luh 綠 green
koh 各 every
yang 樣 sort
luh 綠 green
ch'a 茶 tea
too 都 all
sëang 像 like
chay 這 this
yang 樣 kind
ts'ae 纔 then
haou 好 good
ne. 呢 ?

The price of this Hyson is 14 taels per pecul, reckoning at the Canton standard weight.

Chay 這 This
He 熙 } Hyson
ch'un 春 }
këa 價 } price
ts'ëen 錢 }
may 每 each
pih 百 hundred
kin 觔 catty
shih 十 ten
sze 四 four
lëang 兩 tael
chaou 照 according
Kwang 廣 } Canton
tung 東 }
sze 司 } standard
ma 碼 }
ch'ing 秤 weight
swan. 算 reckon.

At Canton they weigh two chests at once, only reckoning the catties and not counting fractions. When the casing has been removed, and the nett weight correctly ascertained, then they require to add the fraction, whatever it may be per chest, whether half a catty, or four taels, and reckon the weight of the entire lot accordingly.

Tsae 在 At
Kwang 廣 } Canton
tung 東 }
na 拏 take
lëang 兩 two
sëang 箱 chests
yih 一 one
hwuy 回 while
kwo 過 past
ch'ing 秤 scales
chih 只 only
swan 算 reckon
kin 觔 catty
soo 數 account
ling 零 } fraction
t'ow 頭 }
puh 不 not

P

| | | |
|---|---|---|
| ke | 計 | count |
| kae | 該 | must |
| tang | 當 | |
| ch'oo | 除 | remove |
| lëaou | 了 | finish |
| p'e | 皮 | casing |
| che | 知 | know |
| taou | 道 | |
| shih | 實 | true |
| tsae | 在 | |
| kh'ing | 輕 | light |
| chung | 重 | heavy |
| joh | 若 | how much |
| kan | 干 | |
| tsae | 再 | then |
| may | 每 | each |
| sëang | 箱 | chest |
| ling | 零 | fraction |
| yew | 有 | have |
| joh | 若 | how much |
| kan | 干 | |
| hwoh | 或 | whether |
| pan | 半 | half |
| kin | 斤 | catty |
| hwoh | 或 | or |
| sze | 四 | four |
| lëang | 兩 | taels |
| yih | 一 | altogether |
| kae | 概 | |
| chaou | 照 | accordingly |
| këa | 加 | add |
| t'uy | 推 | extend |
| swan. | 筭 | reckon. |

I will give you for this chop of Hyson 40 taels, I paying duty, and the seller defraying all expence of carriage and lighterage on board the ship. Say no more, settle it so, and have done with it.

| | | |
|---|---|---|
| Chay | 這 | This |
| haou | 號 | chop |
| He | 熙 | Hyson |
| ch'un | 春 | |
| wo | 我 | I |
| kay | 給 | give |
| ne | 你 | you |
| sze | 四 | four |
| shih | 十 | ten |
| lëang | 兩 | taels |
| shuy | 稅 | duty |
| hëang | 餉 | |
| wo | 我 | I |
| nah | 納 | pay |
| sung | 送 | send |
| taou | 到 | to |
| ch'üen | 船 | ship |
| shang | 上 | on |
| teih | 的 | — |
| poh | 駁 | lighter |
| t'ing | 艇 | |
| t'ëaou | 挑 | carriage |
| këoh | 脚 | |
| koh | 各 | every |
| fei | 費 | expence |
| too | 都 | all |
| she | 是 | is |
| mae | 賣 | seller |
| choo | 主 | |

| | | |
|---|---|---|
| ch'uh | 出 | defray |
| puh | 不 | not |
| yung | 用 | need |
| to | 多 | much |
| këang | 講 | say |
| tsew | 就 | just |
| she | 是 | is |
| chay | 這 | this |
| yang | 樣 | way |
| ting | 定 | settle |
| kwuy | 規 | |
| lëaou | 了 | finish |
| pa | 罷 | enough. |
| lëaou. | 了 | |

Be it so. I will sell it to you for 40 taels, but I must have Sycee in payment, weighed at Custom-house weight, and, as is the custom, I must beg your worthy firm to give me a note of agreement, whereupon you may send people to weigh the teas, and to-morrow or the day after, you must ship them.

| | | |
|---|---|---|
| Tsew | 就 | Then |
| she | 是 | is |
| lëaou | 了 | — |
| sze | 四 | four |
| shih | 十 | ten |
| lëang | 兩 | taels |
| mae | 賣 | sell |
| kay | 給 | give |
| ne | 你 | you |
| kh'o | 可 | must |
| yaou | 要 | want |
| wăn | 紋 | sycee |
| yin | 銀 | |
| këaou | 交 | give |
| tuy | 兌 | weigh |
| chaou | 照 | according to |
| hae | 海 | Custom-house |
| kwan | 關 | |
| teih | 的 | of |
| p'ing | 平 | scale |
| ma | 碼 | weight |
| yay | 也 | also |
| yaou | 要 | want |
| chaou | 照 | according to |
| chay | 這 | here |
| le | 裡 | |
| teih | 的 | of |
| kwuy | 規 | custom |
| keu | 矩 | |
| ts'ing | 請 | beg |
| paou | 寶 | worthy |
| hang | 行 | hong |
| ch'uh | 出 | give |
| ch'ing | 承 | engage |
| tan | 單 | note |
| lae | 來 | come |
| tsew | 就 | then |
| kh'o | 可 | may |
| e | 以 | |
| këaou | 叫 | direct |
| jin | 人 | man |
| kwo | 過 | weigh |
| ch'ing | 秤 | |
| ming | 明 | to-morrow |
| t'ëen | 天 | |

hwoh 或 or
how 後 } day after
t'ëen 天 }
tsew 就 then
yaou 要 want
hëa 下 lower
ch'üen 船 ship.

Do you yet wish to buy any teas?

Han 還 Yet
yaou 要 want
mae 買 buy
ch'a 茶 tea
mo. 麽 ?

I will buy more, if you have any good, but there are no good teas in the market at all just now.

T'ang 倘 If
yew 有 have
haou 好 good
ch'a 茶 tea
tsew 就 then
mae 買 buy
tan 但 but
ts'*ze* 此 this
sh*e* 時 time
sh*e* 市 market
shang 上 on
tsung 總 all
muh 沒 not
yew 有 have
haou 好 good
ch'a. 茶 tea.

Yes, but in another 50 or 60 day's time, the new black teas will be almost about arriving, and in 70 or 80 days after that, the new green teas will also be here.

She 是 Yes
ah 阿 —
tsae 再 again
kwo 過 pass
woo 五 five
lëuh 六 six
shih 十 ten
t'ëen 天 day
sin 新 new
hih 黑 black
ch'a 茶 tea
ch'a 差 miss
puh 不 not
to 多 much
yaou 要 want
taou 到 arrive
lëaou 了 —
tsae 再 further
tăng 等 wait
ts'eih 七 seven
pah 八 eight
shih 十 ten
t'ëen 天 day
sin 新 new
luh 綠 green
ch'a 茶 tea
yay 也 also
too 都 all
lae 來 come

lëaou. 了 —

Is this year's crop of tea a good one and is it large?

Kin 今 This
nëen 年 year
ts'ae 採 pick
teih 的 which
ch'a 茶 tea
haou 好 good
puh 不 not
haou 好 good
show 收 receive
teih 的 which
to 多 much
puh 不 not
to. 多 much.

This year's tea is rather good than otherwise, and the crop is a very abundant one too.

Păn 本 This
nëen 年 year
teih 的 of
ch'a 茶 tea
taou 倒 still
han 還 yet
haou 好 good
yew 又 also
hăn 狠 very
fung 豐 } abundant.
shing. 盛 }

What price is it selling at on the hills.

Tsae 在 At
păn 本 native
shan 山 hill
mae 賣 sell
shin 甚 } what
mo 麽 }
këa 價 } price.
ts'ëen 錢 }

The price on the hills is dearer than last year's by five or six taels.

Păn 本 Native
shan 山 hill
teih 的 of
këa 價 } price
ts'ëen 錢 }
pe 比 compare
kew 舊 last
nëen 年 year
kăng 更 more
kwuy 貴 dear
lëaou 了 —
woo 五 five
lëuh 六 six
lëang. 兩 tael.

The reason is that silver being plentiful in the Canton market, and the tea merchants being therefore anxious to sell for ready money, without grudging their goods, it follows that every body competes to buy. Every year some 6 or 7 hundred chops are sold to the English merchants, each chop containing 640 chests, and each chest 60 catties.

| | | |
|---|---|---|
| Yin | 因 | Because |
| wei | 爲 | |
| Kwang | 廣 | Canton |
| tung | 東 | |
| she | 市 | market |
| kh'ow | 口 | |
| yin | 銀 | silver |
| tsze | 子 | |
| to | 多 | plenty |
| ch'a | 茶 | tea |
| shang | 商 | merchant |
| she | 是 | is |
| chih | 只 | only |
| yaou | 要 | want |
| mae | 賣 | sell |
| hëen | 現 | ready |
| yin | 銀 | money |
| tsze | 子 | |
| puh | 不 | not |
| seih | 惜 | grudge |
| ho | 貨 | goods |
| so | 所 | therefore |
| e | 以 | |
| too | 都 | all |
| she | 是 | is |
| tsăng | 爭 | compete |
| choh | 着 | — |

| | | |
|---|---|---|
| mae | 買 | buy |
| may | 每 | each |
| nëen | 年 | year |
| mae | 賣 | sell |
| kay | 給 | give |
| ying | 英 | English |
| shang | 商 | merchant |
| teih | 的 | which |
| ch'a | 茶 | tea |
| yew | 有 | have |
| lëuh | 六 | six |
| ts'eih | 七 | seven |
| pih | 百 | hundred |
| haou | 號 | chop |
| may | 每 | each |
| haou | 號 | chop |
| she | 是 | is |
| lëuh | 六 | six |
| pih | 百 | hundred |
| sze | 四 | four |
| shih | 十 | ten |
| sëang | 箱 | chest |
| may | 每 | each |
| sëang | 箱 | chest |
| lëuh | 六 | six |
| shih | 十 | ten |
| kin. | 觔 | catty. |

## WITH A SILK MERCHANT.

I want to buy a piece of blue satin.

| | | |
|---|---|---|
| Wo | 我 | I |
| yaou | 要 | want |
| mae | 買 | buy |
| yih | 一 | one |
| peih | 疋 | piece |
| lan | 藍 | blue |

| | | |
|---|---|---|
| twan | 緞 | satin. |
| tsze. | 子 | |

I have some; but satins differ in quality; some being good, others indifferent; they also differ in price, some are dear and others cheap.

| | | |
|---|---|---|
| Yew | 有 | Have |
| tan | 但 | but |
| she | 是 | is |
| twan | 緞 | satin |
| tsze | 子 | |
| yew | 有 | have |
| haou | 好 | good |
| tae | 歹 | bad |
| teih | 的 | — |
| këa | 價 | price |
| ts'ëen | 錢 | |
| yay | 也 | also |
| yew | 有 | have |
| kaou | 高 | high |
| te | 低 | low |
| puh | 不 | not |
| t'ung. | 同 | same. |

I beg you will bring me a piece to see.

| | | |
|---|---|---|
| Ts'ing | 請 | Beg |
| ne | 你 | you |
| na | 拿 | take |
| yih | 一 | one |
| peih | 疋 | piece |
| lae | 來 | come |
| kay | 給 | give |
| wo | 我 | me |
| kh'an. | 看 | see. |

Here is a piece of superfine quality.

| | | |
|---|---|---|
| Chay | 這 | This |
| she | 是 | is |
| peih | 疋 | piece |
| ting | 頂 | superfine |
| haou | 好 | good |
| teih. | 的 | — |

How long, and how broad is it?

| | | |
|---|---|---|
| Yew | 有 | Have |
| to | 多 | how |
| shaou | 少 | |
| ch'ang | 長 | long |
| to | 多 | how |
| shaou | 少 | |
| kh'wan | 寬 | broad. |

It is thirty feet long, and two feet five inches wide, and my price for it is 20 dollars.

| | | |
|---|---|---|
| Yew | 有 | Have |
| san | 三 | three |
| chang | 丈 | ten foot |
| ch'ang | 長 | long |
| urh | 二 | two |
| ch'eh | 尺 | foot |
| woo | 五 | five |
| tsun | 寸 | inch |
| kh'wan | 寬 | wide |
| këa | 價 | price |
| ts'ëen | 錢 | |
| yaou | 要 | want |
| urh | 二 | two |
| shih | 十 | ten |

| | | |
|---|---|---|
| yüen. | 元 | dollar. |

What are you talking about? It is only worth 15 or 16 dollars.

| | | |
|---|---|---|
| Na | 那 | What |
| le | 裡 | |
| hwa | 話 | talk |
| chih | 只 | only |
| chih | 値 | worth |
| tih | 得 | obtain |
| shih | 十 | ten |
| woo | 五 | five |
| lëuh | 六 | six |
| yüen. | 元 | dollar. |

I can only reduce from two to three dollars. More I cannot.

| | | |
|---|---|---|
| Chih | 只 | Only |
| kh'o | 可 | can |
| këen | 減 | reduce |
| tih | 得 | obtain |
| san | 三 | three |
| lëang | 兩 | two |
| yüen | 元 | dollar |
| to | 多 | more |
| tsew | 就 | then |
| puh | 不 | not |
| năng | 能 | can |
| lëaou. | 了 | — |

Very good. Pray send it to my house, I have forgotten, however, to ask you to open it out for me to look at, as there may be some defect inside.

| | | |
|---|---|---|
| Haou | 好 | Good |
| lëaou | 了 | — |
| ts'ing | 請 | beg |
| ne | 你 | you |
| sung | 送 | send |
| taou | 到 | to |
| wo | 我 | my |
| këa | 家 | house |
| le | 裡 | inside |
| kh'eu | 去 | go |
| wo | 我 | I |
| han | 還 | however |
| wang | 忘 | forget |
| ke | 記 | |
| lëaou | 了 | have |
| ts'ing | 請 | ask |
| ne | 你 | you |
| ta | 打 | open |
| kh'ae | 開 | |
| lae | 來 | come |
| kh'an | 看 | look |
| yih | 一 | a |
| kh'an | 看 | look |
| kh'ung | 恐 | fear |
| p'a | 怕 | |
| nuy | 內 | within |
| le | 裏 | inside |
| t'ow | 頭 | |
| yew | 有 | have |
| shin | 甚 | some |
| mo | 麽 | |
| maou | 毛 | defect |
| ping | 病 | |

There is no need to open it out; it has been selected by our firm at the manufactory, and you may make your mind quite easy on the subject.

| | | |
|---|---|---|
| Puh | 不 | Not |
| yung | 用 | use |
| ta | 打 | open |
| kh'ae | 開 | |
| lëaou | 了 | — |
| too | 都 | all |
| she | 是 | is |
| tsae | 在 | at |
| ke | 機 | manufactory |
| fang | 房 | |
| le | 裏 | in |
| pǎn | 本 | our |
| hang | 行 | firm |
| t'ëaou | 挑 | select |
| këen | 揀 | |
| kwo | 過 | have |
| teih | 的 | — |
| chih | 只 | only |
| kwan | 管 | care |
| fang | 放 | easy |
| sin | 心 | mind |
| pa. | 罷 | — |

If so, enough. I have not brought any cash with me, and I must beg you to put it down to my account.

| | | |
|---|---|---|
| Chay | 這 | So |
| mo | 麼 | |
| pa | 罷 | enough |
| lëaou | 了 | — |
| wo | 我 | I |
| muh | 沒 | not |
| tae | 帶 | bring |
| hëen | 現 | ready |
| yin | 銀 | money |
| tsze | 子 | |
| lae | 來 | come |
| ts'ing | 請 | beg |
| ne | 你 | you |
| shang | 上 | put |
| wo | 我 | my |
| teih | 的 | |
| chang | 賬 | account |
| pa. | 罷 | — |

I fancy, I do not owe you any other sums, do I?

| | | |
|---|---|---|
| Wo | 我 | I |
| sëang | 想 | fancy |
| yay | 也 | also |
| puh | 不 | not |
| kae | 該 | owe |
| ne | 你 | you |
| pëeh | 別 | other |
| teih | 的 | |
| ts'ëen | 錢 | money |
| pa. | 罷 | ? |

Not at all. In all your patronage of me, honored Sir, you have ever paid ready money for goods received.

| | | |
|---|---|---|
| Muh | 沒 | Not |
| yew | 有 | have |
| tsun | 尊 | honored |
| këa | 駕 | sir |
| ch'ang | 常 | always |
| lae | 來 | come |

| | | |
|---|---|---|
| chaou | 照 | patronage |
| koo | 顧 | |
| too | 都 | all |
| she | 是 | is |
| hëen | 現 | ready |
| ts'ëen | 錢 | money |
| këaou | 交 | give |
| yih. | 易 | exchange. |

You are right. I do not like taking credit. I will send you the money to-morrow, and if not, pray have a bill made out, and forwarded to my house with the goods, when I will pay it forthwith.

| | | |
|---|---|---|
| Puh | 不 | Not |
| ts'o | 錯 | wrong |
| wo | 我 | I |
| puh | 不 | not |
| yaou | 要 | want |
| shay | 賒 | credit |
| chang | 賬 | account |
| wo | 我 | I |
| ming | 明 | to-morrow |
| t'ëen | 天 | |
| sung | 送 | send |
| ts'ëen | 錢 | money |
| lae | 來 | come |
| puh | 不 | not |
| jen | 然 | so |
| tsew | 就 | then |
| ts'ing | 請 | beg |
| ne | 你 | you |
| kh'ae | 開 | make out |
| chang | 張 | a |
| tan | 單 | bill |
| tsze | 子 | |
| lëen | 連 | with |
| ho | 貨 | goods |
| sung | 送 | send |
| taou | 到 | to |
| shay | 舍 | my house |
| hëa | 下 | |
| wo | 我 | I |
| ma | 馬 | forthwith |
| shang | 上 | |
| tsew | 就 | at once |
| kay | 給 | give |
| ts'ëen. | 錢 | money. |

I also want a piece of black satin; if you will cut me off about three feet, it will be enough.

| | | |
|---|---|---|
| Wo | 我 | I |
| han | 還 | also |
| yaou | 要 | want |
| kh'wae | 塊 | piece |
| ts'ing | 青 | black |
| twan | 緞 | satin |
| tsze | 子 | |
| ta | 大 | about |
| yoh | 約 | |
| tsëen | 剪 | cut |
| ko | 個 | — |
| san | 三 | three |
| ch'eh | 尺 | foot |
| tsew | 就 | then |
| kow | 彀 | enough |
| lëaou. | 了 | — |

I can do so.

Kh'o 可 Can
e. 以 do.

May I ask whether you have any lustrings.

Ts'ing 請 Pray
wăn 問 ask
yew 有 have
këuen 絹 lustring
muh 沒 not
yew. 有 have.

I have first quality plain lustrings, checked lustrings. flowered lustrings, and also variegated lustrings.

Yew 有 Have
t'ow 頭 first
tăng 等 quality
soo 素 plain
këuen 絹 lustring
pan 斑 check
këuen 絹 lustring
tsae 彩 flower
këuen 絹 lustring
han 還 also
yew 有 have
woo 五 various
sih 色 color
këuen 絹 lustring.

Have you also got satins?

Han 還 Also
yew 有 have
twan 緞 } satins
tsze 子 }
mo. 麼 ?

I have plain and striped satin, fashionable changing satin, and all sorts of 5 thread, and 8 thread tribute satin.

Yew 有 Have
soo 素 plain
twan 緞 satin
lew 柳 willow
t'ëaou 條 twig
twan 緞 satin
she 時 season
yang 樣 sort
teih 的 of
shen 閃 change
twan 緞 satin
woo 五 five
sze 絲 thread
pah 八 eight
sze 絲 thread
koh 各 every
yang 樣 sort
kung 貢 tribute
twan. 緞 satin.

What pongees have you?

Ne 你 You
yew 有 have
shin 甚 } what
mo 麼 }
ch'ow 綢 } pongee
tsze 子 }
ne. 呢 ?

I have Hangchow reeled pongee, very thick, close, bright and smooth; I have tribute and Nanking pongees, plain and flowered; I have stiff pongee, which is made with raw silk; and I have soft pongee, which is soft; and I have reeled pongee, which is woven with silk reeled into threads.

Yew 有 Have
Hang 杭 Hang-chow
fang 紡 reel
ch'ow 綢 pongee
yew 又 very
how 厚 thick
shih 實 close
yew 又 very
kwang 光 bright
hwah 滑 smooth
yew 有 have
kung 貢 tribute
ch'ow 綢 pongee
yew 有 have
Ning 甯 Ningpo
ch'ow 綢 pongee
yew 有 have
soo 素 } plain
teih 的 }
yew 有 have
hwa 花 } flowered
teih 的 }
yew 有 have
săng 生 stiff
ch'ow 綢 pongee
she 是 is
săng 生 raw
sze 絲 silk
chih 織 } weave
teih 的 }
yew 有 have
shuh 熟 soft
ch'ow 綢 pongee
she 是 is
jüen 軟 } soft
teih 的 }
yew 有 have
fang 紡 reel
ch'ow 綢 pongee
yung 用 use
sze 絲 silk
fang 紡 reel
ch'ing 成 make
sëen 線 thread
chih 織 } weave.
teih. 的 }

Have you yet any other sorts of pongees?

Han 還 Yet
yew 有 have
pëeh 別 other
yang 樣 sorts
teih 的 of
ch'ow 綢 pongee
mo 麼 ?

I have gambier colored pongee, black jelly pongee, and cotton pongee, which is made of silk and cotton interwoven together.

Yew 有 Have

| | | |
|---|---|---|
| shoo | 薯 | gambier |
| lëang | 莨 | |
| ch'ow | 綢 | pongee |
| hih | 黑 | black |
| këaou | 膠 | jelly |
| ch'ow | 綢 | pongee |
| mëen | 棉 | cotton |
| ch'ow | 綢 | pongee |
| she | 是 | is |
| yung | 用 | use |
| mëen | 棉 | cotton |
| hwa | 花 | |
| këah | 夾 | mix |
| sze | 絲 | silk |
| chih | 織 | weave |
| ch'ing | 成 | made. |
| teih. | 的 | |

These few pongees all do not suit me. Have you any crapes also?

| | | |
|---|---|---|
| Chay | 這 | These |
| sëay | 些 | few |
| ch'ow | 綢 | silk |
| twan | 緞 | |
| too | 都 | all |
| puh | 不 | not |
| hoh | 合 | suit |
| shih | 式 | |
| han | 還 | also |
| yew | 有 | have |
| chow | 縐 | crapes |
| sha | 紗 | |
| mo | 麽 | ? |

I have thread, Hoo-chow, sea, and knotted crapes, figured and plain, light and heavy, and of various colors. If these do not hit your fancy, I have also got hard *laws*, and soft *laws*, tribute damask, Hangchow damask, and plank damask, very bright and smooth, and exceedingly handsome.

| | | |
|---|---|---|
| Yew | 有 | Have |
| sëen | 線 | thread |
| chow | 縐 | crape |
| yew | 有 | have |
| Hoo | 湖 | Hoo-chow |
| chow | 縐 | crape |
| yew | 有 | have |
| yang | 洋 | sea |
| chow | 縐 | crape |
| yew | 有 | have |
| kh'ow | 扣 | knot |
| chow | 縐 | crape |
| yew | 有 | have |
| hwa | 花 | figured |
| teih | 的 | |
| yew | 有 | have |
| soo | 素 | plain |
| teih | 的 | |
| kh'ing | 輕 | light |
| chung | 重 | heavy |
| yen | 顏 | color |
| sih | 色 | |
| koh | 各 | all |
| yew | 有 | have |
| puh | 不 | not |
| t'ung | 同 | same |

| | | |
|---|---|---|
| joo | 如 | if |
| puh | 不 | not |
| chung | 中 | hit |
| e | 意 | fancy |
| han | 還 | yet |
| yew | 有 | have |
| săng | 生 | hard |
| lo | 羅 | *law* |
| shuh | 熟 | soft |
| lo | 羅 | *law* |
| kung | 貢 | tribute |
| ling | 綾 | damask |
| Hang | 杭 | Hang-chow |
| ling | 綾 | damask |
| pan | 板 | plank |
| ling | 綾 | damask |
| yay | 也 | and |
| kwang | 光 | bright |
| hwah | 滑 | smooth |
| yew | 又 | also |
| hăn | 狠 | very |
| haou | 好 | good |
| kh'an. | 看 | see. |

How many kinds of gauze have you?

| | | |
|---|---|---|
| Sha | 紗 | Gauze |
| yew | 有 | have |
| ke | 幾 | how many |
| yang | 様 | kind |
| ne. | 呢 | ? |

I have close ground gauze, hemp gauze, transparent gauze, lucky cloud gauze, mandarin gauze, sieve gauze, and all such sorts.

| | | |
|---|---|---|
| Yew | 有 | Have |
| shih | 實 | close |
| te | 地 | ground |
| sha | 紗 | gauze |
| yew | 有 | have |
| che | 芝 | hemp |
| ma | 蔴 | |
| sha | 紗 | gauze |
| yew | 有 | have |
| lëang | 亮 | transparent |
| sha | 紗 | gauze |
| yew | 有 | have |
| sëang | 湘 | lucky |
| yun | 雲 | clouds |
| sha | 紗 | gauze |
| yew | 有 | have |
| kwan | 官 | mandarin |
| sha | 紗 | gauze |
| lo | 羅 | sieve |
| te | 底 | bottom |
| sha | 紗 | gauze |
| koh | 各 | every |
| yang. | 様 | sort. |

I beg you will cut me a small slip off each of the kinds and colors of damasks, *laws* and silks, which you have just enumerated, and paste them on paper as samples, and, having made out a list of the really lowest prices, under which you will not sell them, send the list with the samples to my lodging. I will then select several tens of pieces of such as I wish to buy, and take them of you.

| | | |
|---|---|---|
| Ts'ing | 請 | Beg |
| ne | 你 | you |
| fang | 方 | just now |
| ts'ae | 纔 | |
| so | 所 | to |
| shwoh | 說 | say |
| teih | 的 | — |
| ling | 綾 | damask |
| lo | 羅 | *law* |
| ch'ow | 綢 | silk |
| twan | 緞 | satin |
| koh | 各 | each |
| yang | 樣 | kind |
| koh | 各 | each |
| sih | 色 | color |
| too | 都 | all |
| tsëen | 剪 | cut |
| yih | 一 | a |
| sëaou | 小 | small |
| kh'wae | 塊 | piece |
| t'ëeh | 帖 | paste |
| tsae | 在 | on |
| che | 紙 | paper |
| shang | 上 | on |
| tso | 做 | made |
| yang | 樣 | sample |
| tsze | 子 | |
| kh'ae | 開 | open |
| yih | 一 | one |
| ko | 個 | |
| shaou | 少 | few |
| lëaou | 了 | — |
| puh | 不 | not |
| mae | 賣 | sell |
| teih | 的 | — |
| shih | 實 | really |
| tsae | 在 | |
| këa | 價 | price |
| ts'ëen | 錢 | |
| lëen | 連 | with |
| yüen | 原 | original |
| yang | 樣 | pattern |
| sung | 送 | send |
| taou | 到 | to |
| wo | 我 | my |
| yü | 寓 | lodging |
| so | 所 | |
| le | 裏 | in |
| lae | 來 | come |
| yaou | 要 | want |
| mae | 買 | buy |
| teih | 的 | — |
| wo | 我 | I |
| tsew | 就 | then |
| këen | 揀 | select |
| ch'uh | 出 | out |
| ke | 幾 | several |
| shih | 十 | ten |
| p'eih | 疋 | piece |
| lae | 來 | come |
| t'ung | 同 | with |
| ne | 你 | you |
| mae | 買 | buy |
| tsew | 就 | then |
| she | 是 | is |
| lëaou | 了 | — |

## ON COTTON.

**How many catties weight is a bale of cotton?**

| | | |
|---|---|---|
| Yih | 一 | One |
| paou | 包 | bale |
| mëen | 棉 | cotton |
| hwa | 花 | |
| yew | 有 | have |
| to | 多 | how many |
| shaou | 少 | |
| kin | 斤 | catty |
| chung | 重 | heavy. |

**Some weigh a hundred catties, some fifty.**

| | | |
|---|---|---|
| Yew | 有 | Have |
| teih | 的 | |
| yih | 壹 | one |
| pih | 百 | hundred |
| kin | 觔 | catty |
| yew | 有 | have |
| teih | 的 | |
| woo | 五 | fifty |
| shih | 十 | |
| kin | 觔 | catty |

**Where does all the cotton come from?**

| | | |
|---|---|---|
| Mëen | 棉 | Cotton |
| hwa | 花 | |
| too | 都 | all |
| she | 是 | is |
| na | 那 | where |
| le | 裡 | |
| lae | 來 | come |
| teih | 的 | |
| ne. | 呢 | ? |

**It all comes from Bombay. Some also comes from America.**

| | | |
|---|---|---|
| Too | 都 | All |
| she | 是 | is |
| Măng | 孟 | Bombay |
| mae | 買 | |
| lae | 來 | come |
| teih | 的 | |
| yay | 也 | also |
| yew | 有 | have |
| Hwa | 花 | Flower |
| kh'e | 旗 | flag |
| kwoh | 國 | nation |
| lae | 來 | come. |
| teih. | 的 | |

**In China also cotton is grown. Near Nanking a purple flower is produced, with which nankeen cloth is made.**

| | | |
|---|---|---|
| Nuy | 内 | Inner |
| te | 地 | land |
| yay | 也 | also |
| yew | 有 | have |
| tsae | 栽 | grow |
| chung | 種 | |
| mëen | 棉 | cotton |
| hwa | 花 | |
| teih | 的 | — |
| kin | 近 | near |
| Nan | 南 | Nanking |
| king | 京 | |
| ch'uh | 出 | produce |

| | | |
|---|---|---|
| *tsze* | 紫 | purple |
| hwa | 花 | flower |
| kh'o | 可 | can |
| e | 以 | |
| chih | 織 | weave |
| tsze | 紫 | purple |
| hwa | 花 | cotton |
| poo. | 布 | cloth. |

In China, we have two crops in the year. In the first half of the year, wheat is grown. In the second half, autumn rice and cotton.

| | | |
|---|---|---|
| Chung | 中 | Central |
| kwoh | 國 | kingdom |
| she | 是 | is |
| yih | 一 | one |
| nëen | 年 | year |
| lëang | 兩 | two |
| ts'ew | 秋 | crop |
| shang | 上 | first |
| pan | 半 | half |
| nëen | 年 | year |
| chung | 種 | grow |
| mih | 麥 | wheat |
| tsze | 子 | |
| hëa | 下 | second |
| pan | 半 | half |
| nëen | 年 | year |
| chung | 種 | grow |
| ts'ew | 秋 | autumn |
| taou | 稻 | rice |
| ho | 和 | with |
| mëen | 棉 | cotton. |
| hwa. | 花 | |

The cotton produced about Shanghae is all shipped to Fuh-këen, Canton, and other places for sale. Chinese prefer native cotton, and do not much care to use imported cotton, because the native cotton is longer in thread, and not so liable to break.

| | | |
|---|---|---|
| Shang | 上 | Shanghae |
| hae | 海 | |
| te | 地 | place |
| fang | 方 | |
| ch'uh | 出 | produce |
| teih | 的 | which |
| mëen | 棉 | cotton |
| hwa | 花 | |
| too | 都 | all |
| she | 是 | is |
| chwang | 裝 | ship |
| taou | 到 | to |
| Fuh | 福 | Fuh-këen |
| këen | 建 | |
| Kwang | 廣 | Canton |
| tung | 東 | |
| koh | 各 | other |
| ch'oo | 處 | places |
| kh'eu | 去 | go |
| mae | 賣 | sell |
| Chung | 中 | China |
| kwoh | 國 | |
| jin | 人 | man |
| he | 喜 | like |
| hwan | 歡 | |
| păn | 本 | native |
| te | 地 | |

R

| | | |
|---|---|---|
| mëen | 棉 | cotton |
| hwa | 花 | |
| wae | 外 | outside |
| yang | 洋 | sea |
| lae | 來 | come |
| teih | 的 | which |
| puh | 不 | not |
| ta | 大 | much |
| yaou | 要 | want |
| yung | 用 | use |
| yin | 因 | because |
| wei | 爲 | |
| pǎn | 本 | native |
| te | 地 | |
| hwa | 花 | cotton |
| sze | 絲 | thread |
| lew | 絡 | |
| kǎng | 更 | more |
| ch'ang | 長 | long |
| puh | 不 | not |
| hwuy | 會 | liable |
| twan. | 斷 | break. |

The native cotton, for instance, sells at 20 dollars the hundred catties, whereas imported cotton only fetches 12 to 13 dollars the pecul.

| | | |
|---|---|---|
| Pe | 比 | If |
| joo | 如 | |
| pǎn | 本 | native |
| te | 地 | |
| mëen | 棉 | cotton |
| hwa | 花 | |
| may | 每 | each |
| pih | 百 | hundred |
| kin | 斤 | catties |
| mae | 賣 | sell |
| teih | 的 | |
| urh | 二 | twenty |
| shih | 十 | |
| yüen | 員 | dollars |
| wae | 外 | outside |
| yang | 洋 | sea |
| teih | 的 | of |
| may | 每 | each |
| tan | 担 | pecul |
| chih | 只 | only |
| mae | 賣 | sell |
| shih | 十 | ten |
| urh | 二 | two |
| san | 三 | three |
| yüen. | 員 | dollars. |

But seasons differ, and prices cannot rule always at same rates. If the importation be large, prices are reasonable; if small, then they rise.

| | | |
|---|---|---|
| Tan | 但 | But |
| she | 時 | season |
| how | 候 | |
| puh | 不 | not |
| t'ung | 同 | same |
| kwuy | 貴 | dear |
| tsëen | 賤 | cheap |
| yay | 也 | also |
| puh | 不 | not |
| nǎng | 能 | can |
| yih | 一 | one |
| ting | 定 | certain |

| | | |
|---|---|---|
| lae | 來 | come |
| tih | 得 | obtain |
| to | 多 | much |
| tsew | 就 | then |
| p'ëen | 便 | reasonable |
| e | 宜 | |
| taou | 到 | arrive |
| tih | 得 | obtain |
| shaou | 少 | little |
| tsew | 就 | then |
| hwuy | 會 | become |
| kwuy | 貴 | dear |
| lëaou. | 了 | — |

If you buy dear, there is danger of your afterwards losing capital and making no money, therefore it is safe to wait, till prices are reasonable and then to buy.

| | | |
|---|---|---|
| Mae | 買 | Buy |
| tih | 得 | obtain |
| kwuy | 貴 | dear |
| kh'ung | 恐 | fear |
| p'a | 怕 | |
| tsëang | 將 | afterwards |
| lae | 來 | |
| kh'wuy | 虧 | lose |
| păn | 本 | capital |
| muh | 沒 | not |
| ts'ëen | 錢 | money |
| chüen | 賺 | make |
| so | 所 | therefore |
| e | 以 | |
| tăng | 等 | wait |
| taou | 到 | till |
| këa | 價 | price |
| ts'ëen | 錢 | |
| p'ëen | 便 | reasonable |
| e | 宜 | |
| tsae | 再 | then |
| mae | 買 | buy |
| ts'ae | 纔 | then |
| wăn | 穩 | safe. |
| tang. | 當 | |

## ON WOOLLENS.

What cargo has the foreign vessel just arrived brought?

| | | |
|---|---|---|
| Sin | 新 | New |
| lae | 來 | come |
| teih | 的 | which |
| yang | 洋 | foreign |
| ch'üen | 船 | ship |
| too | 都 | all |
| she | 是 | is |
| chwang | 裝 | carry |
| shin | 甚 | what |
| mo | 麼 | |
| ho. | 貨 | cargo. |

The ship which came in yesterday has broad cloths and long ells.

| | | |
|---|---|---|
| Tsoh | 昨 | Yesterday |
| t'ëen | 天 | |

lae 來 come
teih 的 which
ch'üen 船 ship
too 都 all
she 是 is
ta 大 } broad cloths
ne 呢 }
sëaou 小 } long ells.
ne. 呢 }

It being summer just now, surely these woollens will be difficult of sale?

Hëen 現 } Now
tsae 在 }
hëa 夏 summer
t'ëen 天 time
teih 的 of
she 時 } season
how 候 }
kh'ung 恐 } fear
p'a 怕 }
chay 這 this
ne 呢 woollens
nan 難 difficult
sëaou 消 sell off
pa. 罷 ?

At this moment, all kinds of white cottons are rather sought after. But if you buy woollens, and keep them till autumn and winter time, or take them up to the North, where the climate is cold, they will easily be got rid of.

Ts'ze 此 } This
kh'ih 刻 }
koh 各 every
yang 樣 kind
pih 白 white
poo 布 cotton
taou 倒 rather
hing 行 go
she 時 market
yaou 要 want
mae 買 buy
ta 大 } woollens
ne 呢 }
lew 留 keep
taou 到 till
ts'ew 秋 autumn
tung 冬 winter
t'ëen 天 weather
hwoh 或 or
tae 帶 take
taou 到 to
pih 北 north
pëen 邊 side
kh'eu 去 go
na 那 } where
le 裡 }
t'ëen 天 } climate
kh'e 氣 }
han 寒 } cold
lëang 凉 }
tsung 總 must
yung 容 } easy
e 易 }
sëaou. 消 sell.

That is also a good plan, but it needs to have a large capital, to send goods to distant places in other provinces for sale, and it is only large firms and concerns that can do it.

| | | |
|---|---|---|
| Chay | 這 | This |
| yang | 樣 | way |
| yay | 也 | also |
| haou | 好 | good |
| tsung | 總 | only |
| yaou | 要 | need |
| yew | 有 | have |
| ta | 大 | large |
| pǎn | 本 | capital |
| ts'ëen | 錢 | |
| tsae | 載 | send |
| taou | 到 | to |
| pëeh | 別 | other |
| sǎng | 省 | province |
| yüen | 遠 | distant |
| ch'oo | 處 | places |
| kh'eu | 去 | go |
| mae | 賣 | sell |
| ch'oo | 除 | except |
| fei | 非 | not |
| she | 是 | is |
| kh'ae | 開 | open |
| ta | 大 | large |
| hang | 行 | firm |
| ta | 大 | large |
| tëen | 店 | shop |
| ts'ae | 纔 | then |
| kh'o | 可 | can. |
| e. | 以 | |

In the North too there is the cloth which comes from Russia, and which is thicker and closer than these woollens; the price moreover is more moderate.

| | | |
|---|---|---|
| Pih | 北 | North |
| pëen | 邊 | side |
| yew | 又 | also |
| yew | 有 | have |
| Ngo | 哦 | Russia |
| lo | 囉 | |
| sze | 嘶 | |
| kwoh | 國 | nation |
| lae | 來 | come |
| teih | 的 | which |
| hoh | 哈 | cloth |
| lah | 喇 | |
| pe | 比 | compare |
| chay | 這 | this |
| ne | 呢 | woollens |
| kǎng | 更 | more |
| how | 厚 | thick |
| shih | 實 | close |
| këa | 價 | price |
| ts'ëen | 錢 | |
| yew | 又 | moreover |
| sëang | 相 | moderate. |
| ying. | 應 | |

What price is broad cloth selling at just now?

| | | |
|---|---|---|
| Ts'ze | 此 | Just now |
| kh'ih | 刻 | |
| ta | 大 | broad cloth |
| ne | 呢 | |
| mae | 賣 | sell |
| shin | 甚 | what |
| mo | 麽 | |

| | | |
|---|---|---|
| këa | 價 | price. |
| ts'ëen. | 錢 | |

Broad cloth is selling at 26 dollars; long ells are still more valueless.

| | | |
|---|---|---|
| Ta | 大 | Broad cloth |
| ne | 呢 | |
| chih | 只 | only |
| mae | 賣 | sell |
| urh | 二 | twenty |
| shih | 十 | |
| lëuh | 六 | six |
| yüen | 員 | dollar |
| sëaou | 小 | long ells |
| ne | 呢 | |
| kăng | 更 | still more |
| puh | 不 | not |
| chih | 值 | worth |
| ts'ëen | 錢 | money |
| lëaou. | 了 | — |

What colors of woollens are most bought by the Chinese?

| | | |
|---|---|---|
| Chung | 中 | China |
| kwoh | 國 | |
| jin | 人 | man |
| mae | 買 | buy |
| ne | 呢 | woollens |
| shin | 甚 | what |
| mo | 麽 | |
| yen | 顏 | color |
| sih | 色 | |
| yung | 用 | use |
| teih | 的 | |
| to. | 多 | much. |

They buy mostly blue, red, purple, and black colors; but yellow may only be used by the Imperial family, and royal relatives, or on the stage, or by priests of Buddha and Taou when worshipping; none other but these dare to wear the color. Scarlet, and bright green are principally used on felicitous occasions, and at weddings, either giving or taking in marriage. White and gray are required in the event of funerals, and when mourning is worn. They are not worn by any one, on other occasions than these.

| | | |
|---|---|---|
| Lan | 藍 | Blue |
| sih | 色 | color |
| hung | 紅 | red |
| sih | 色 | color |
| tsze | 紫 | purple |
| sih | 色 | color |
| hih | 黑 | black |
| sih | 色 | color |
| keu | 居 | mostly |
| to | 多 | |
| tan | 但 | but |
| hwang | 黄 | yellow |
| yen | 顏 | color |
| sih | 色 | |
| chih | 只 | only |
| yew | 有 | have |
| hwang | 皇 | imperial |
| ts'in | 親 | family |
| kwoh | 國 | national |

| | | |
|---|---|---|
| ts'eih | 戚 | relative |
| hwoh | 或 | or |
| she | 是 | is |
| tso | 做 | make |
| he | 戲 | play |
| săng | 僧 | Buddhist priest |
| taou | 道 | Taouist priest |
| pae | 拜 | worship |
| shin | 神 | gods |
| kh'o | 可 | may |
| e | 以 | |
| yung | 用 | use |
| kh'e | 其 | the |
| yü | 餘 | remainder |
| muh | 沒 | no |
| jin | 人 | man |
| kan | 敢 | dare |
| ch'üen | 穿 | wear |
| ta | 大 | scarlet |
| hung | 紅 | |
| ta | 大 | bright |
| luh | 綠 | green |
| teih | 的 | — |
| she | 是 | is |
| hwăn | 婚 | marriage |
| yin | 姻 | |
| këa | 嫁 | give in marriage |
| ts'eu | 娶 | take to wife |
| he | 喜 | felicitous |
| kh'ing | 慶 | |
| sze | 事 | matter |
| yung | 用 | use |
| tih | 得 | obtain |
| to | 多 | much |
| pih | 白 | white |
| sih | 色 | color |
| hwuy | 灰 | gray |
| sih | 色 | color |
| hwoh | 或 | in case |
| yew | 有 | have |
| sang | 喪 | funeral |
| sze | 事 | matter |
| ch'üen | 穿 | wear |
| soo | 素 | plain |
| fuh | 服 | clothes |
| yaou | 要 | want |
| yung | 用 | use |
| yü | 餘 | remainder |
| wae | 外 | besides |
| muh | 沒 | not |
| yew | 有 | have |
| shin | 甚 | any |
| mo | 麽 | |
| jin | 人 | man |
| ch'üen | 穿 | put on |
| lëaou | 了 | — |

May I ask, if you have any long cloths?

| | | |
|---|---|---|
| Ts'ing | 請 | Beg |
| wăn | 問 | ask |
| yew | 有 | have |
| yang | 洋 | long cloth |
| poo | 布 | |
| muh | 沒 | not |
| yew. | 有 | have. |

I have bleached and gray long cloth and twills, all of different qualities and kinds. Of loom ends there are six or seven gold thread ends, three red thread ends, and twelve red thread ends; also plain ends, and ends lined with red and gold threads alternating, as well as horse and rider ends. But these last few sorts are slow of sale.

| | | |
|---|---|---|
| Yew | 有 | Have |
| p'ëaou | 漂 | bleach |
| pih | 白 | white |
| poo | 布 | long cloth |
| păn | 本 | original |
| sih | 色 | color |
| poo | 布 | long cloth |
| sëay | 斜 | slant |
| wăn | 紋 | |
| poo | 布 | long cloth |
| kh'o | 可 | can |
| yew | 有 | have |
| ke | 幾 | several |
| tăng | 等 | quality |
| ke | 幾 | several |
| yang | 樣 | kind |
| teih | 的 | — |
| na | 那 | it |
| ke | 機 | loom |
| t'ow | 頭 | end |
| shang | 上 | on |
| yew | 有 | have |
| lëuh | 六 | six |
| ts'eih | 七 | seven |
| t'ëaou | 條 | line |
| kin | 金 | gold |
| sëen | 線 | thread |

| | | |
|---|---|---|
| teih | 的 | of |
| yew | 有 | have |
| san | 三 | three |
| t'ëaou | 條 | line |
| hung | 紅 | red |
| sëen | 線 | thread |
| teih | 的 | of |
| yew | 有 | have |
| shih | 十 | twelve |
| urh | 二 | |
| t'ëaou | 條 | line |
| hung | 紅 | red |
| sëen | 線 | thread |
| teih | 的 | of |
| han | 還 | also |
| yew | 有 | have |
| ke | 機 | loom |
| t'ow | 頭 | end |
| she | 是 | is |
| soo | 素 | plain |
| teih | 的 | |
| yew | 有 | have |
| yih | 一 | one |
| t'ëaou | 條 | line |
| kin | 金 | gold |
| sëen | 線 | thread |
| këah | 夾 | alternate |
| yih | 一 | one |
| t'ëaou | 條 | line |
| hung | 紅 | red |
| sëen | 線 | thread |
| teih | 的 | of |
| yew | 又 | besides |
| yew | 有 | have |

| | | |
|---|---|---|
| jin | 人 | man |
| ma | 馬 | horse |
| yin | 印 | stamp |
| haou | 號 | mark |
| teih | 的 | of |
| chay | 這 | this |
| how | 後 | last |
| t'ow | 頭 | |
| ke | 幾 | few |
| yang | 樣 | sort |
| too | 都 | all |
| nan | 難 | difficult |
| sëaou. | 消 | sell. |

In buying long cloths, it is specially necessary to examine whether the texture is fine or coarse, by counting how many threads are comprised within one square inch; then it should be rubbed together between the hands, so as to discover whether it has starch in it or not. This done, the length and breadth of the cloth should be ascertained, after which the negociation for a purchase may go on.

| | | |
|---|---|---|
| Mae | 買 | Buy |
| pih | 白 | white |
| yang | 洋 | long cloth |
| poo | 布 | |
| chih | 只 | specially |
| yaou | 要 | want |
| kh'an | 看 | look |
| sze | 絲 | thread |
| wăn | 紋 | |
| hwoh | 或 | whether |
| ts'oo | 粗 | coarse |
| hwoh | 或 | or |
| se | 細 | fine |
| fang | 方 | square |
| fang | 方 | square |
| yih | 一 | one |
| ts'un | 寸 | inch |
| che | 之 | of |
| chung | 中 | within |
| soo | 數 | count |
| yew | 有 | have |
| to | 多 | how many |
| shaou | 少 | |
| sze | 絲 | thread |
| tsae | 再 | then |
| na | 拿 | take |
| tsae | 在 | in |
| show | 手 | hand |
| le | 裏 | within |
| jow | 揉 | rub together |
| ts'o | 搓 | |
| yih | 一 | one |
| hëa | 下 | while |
| tsew | 就 | then |
| che | 知 | know |
| taou | 道 | |
| na | 那 | the |
| poo | 布 | cloth |
| yew | 有 | have |
| făn | 粉 | starch |
| tsëang | 漿 | |
| muh | 沒 | not |
| yew | 有 | have |

S

tsae 再 again
wăn 問 ask
na 那 the
poo 布 cloth
yew 有 have
to 多 how
ch'ang 長 long
to 多 how
kh'wan 寬 broad
jen 然 } after
how 後 }
tsae 再 again
këang 講 talk
këa 價 } price
ts'ëen 錢 }
ts'ae 纔 then
haou. 好 good.

For what purpose do the Chinese buy white long cloth?

Chung 中 } China
kwoh 國 }
jin 人 man
mae 買 buy
pih 白 white
yang 洋 } long cloth
poo 布 }
tso 做 make
shin 甚 } what
mo 麽 }
yung. 用 use.

They buy it to make linings for clothes, inner short shirts, trowsers, and so on.

Mae 買 Buy
tso 做 make
e 衣 } clothes
shang 裳 }
le 裏 lining
twan 短 short
shan 衫 inside shirt
kh'oo 褲 trowsers
koh 各 all
yang 樣 kind
teih. 的 of.

For what purpose is gray long cloth bought?

Yüen 原 Original
sih 色 color
poo 布 cloth
mae 買 } buy
lëaou 了 }
tso 做 make
shin 甚 } what
mo 麽 }
ne. 呢 ?

It is bought for the purpose of being dyed various colors, or printed with flowers. Sapan-wood is used to dye it red, gamboge to dye it yellow, verdigris to dye it green, and foreign indigo to dye it blue.

Mae 買 Buy
lae 來 come
jen 染 dye
koh 各 every
yang 樣 sort
yen 顏 } color
sih 色 }

| | | |
|---|---|---|
| hwoh | 或 | or |
| she | 是 | is |
| yin | 印 | print |
| hwa | 花 | flower |
| jen | 染 | dye |
| hung | 紅 | red |
| sih | 色 | color |
| yung | 用 | use |
| soo | 蘇 | sapan-wood |
| muh | 木 | |
| jen | 染 | dye |
| hwang | 黃 | yellow |
| sih | 色 | color |
| yung | 用 | use |
| t'ăng | 籐 | gamboge |
| hwang | 黃 | |
| jen | 染 | dye |
| luh | 綠 | green |
| teih | 的 | |
| yung | 用 | use |
| t'ung | 銅 | verdigris |
| luh | 綠 | |
| jen | 染 | dye |
| lan | 藍 | blue |
| teih | 的 | |
| tsew | 就 | then |
| she | 是 | is |
| yung | 用 | use |
| yang | 洋 | foreign |
| tëen. | 靛 | indigo. |

In what way do the natives print upon cloth?

| | | |
|---|---|---|
| Păn | 本 | Native |
| te | 地 | |
| jin | 人 | man |
| poo | 布 | cloth |
| shang | 上 | upon |
| yin | 印 | print |
| hwa | 花 | flower |
| tsăng | 怎 | what |
| mo | 麽 | |
| yin | 印 | print |
| fah. | 法 | mode. |

They first engrave a wooden-block with flowers, then brush the coloring material on, and afterwards print off.

| | | |
|---|---|---|
| Sëen | 先 | First |
| tëaou | 雕 | engrave |
| kh'ih | 刻 | |
| yih | 一 | one |
| kh'wae | 塊 | piece |
| hwa | 花 | flower |
| teih | 的 | of |
| pan | 板 | wooden-block |
| how | 後 | afterwards |
| shwah | 刷 | brush |
| yen | 顏 | coloring |
| lëaou | 料 | material |
| lae | 來 | come |
| yin. | 印 | print. |

What flowers are fashionable for printing cloth with?

| | | |
|---|---|---|
| Yin | 印 | Print |
| hwa | 花 | flower |
| poo | 布 | cloth |
| too | 都 | all |
| she | 時 | season |

sin 新 novelty
shin 甚 } what
mo 麽 }
hwa 花 flower
ne. 呢 ?

The foreign epidendrum, the Mow-tan pæony, the rose, the water-nymph (narcissus), and such like.

Yang 洋 Foreign
lan 蘭 } epidendrum
hwa 花 }
mow 牡 } mowtan
tan 丹 }
hwa 花 flower
may 玫 } rose
kwuy 瑰 }
hwa 花 flower
shwuy 水 water
sëen 仙 nymph
hwa 花 flower
chay 這 this
ke 幾 few
yang. 樣 kind.

To what uses is printed cloth put.

Yin 印 Print
hwa 花 flower
poo 布 cloth
too 都 all
she 是 is
tso 做 make
sëay 些 that
shin 甚 } what
mo 麽 }
yung. 用 use.

Prints are bought to make into coverlets, mattrasses, pillows, wrappers, sedan linings, children's jackets, trowsers, and so on.

Mae 買 } Buy
lëaou 了 }
tso 做 make
pe 被 coverlet
juh 褥 mattrass
chin 枕 pillow
fuh 袱 wrapper
këaou 轎 sedan
le 裏 lining
sëaou 小 small
hae 孩 } child
tsze 子 }
teih 的 of
shan 衫 jacket
kh'oo 褲 trowser
koh 各 every
yang. 樣 kind.

The Chinese prefer buying native printed cottons to foreign chintzes, because the price is more moderate, and the patterns are more to their taste.

Chung 中 } China
kwoh 國 }
jin 人 man
ngae 愛 prefer
mae 買 buy

| | | |
|---|---|---|
| pǎn | 本 | native |
| te | 地 | |
| teih | 的 | of |
| yin | 印 | printed |
| hwa | 花 | |
| poo | 布 | long cloth |
| pe | 比 | rather than |
| yang | 洋 | foreign |
| hwa | 花 | printed |
| poo | 布 | cottons |
| mae | 買 | buy |
| tih | 得 | |
| to | 多 | more |
| yin | 因 | because |
| wei | 爲 | |
| këa | 價 | price |
| ts'ëen | 錢 | |
| p'ëen | 便 | moderate |
| e | 宜 | |
| hwa | 花 | flower |
| yang | 樣 | pattern |
| yay | 也 | moreover |
| hoh | 合 | suit |
| e. | 意 | idea. |

But the colors in native printed cottons are not lasting, and they will not bear much washing, lest they fade away. The lines of the patterns on the blocks are also coarsely engraved.

| | | |
|---|---|---|
| Tan | 但 | But |
| pǎn | 本 | native |
| te | 地 | |
| hwa | 花 | printed |
| poo | 布 | cottons |
| yen | 顏 | color |
| sih | 色 | |
| puh | 不 | not |
| nae | 耐 | lasting |
| kew | 久 | |
| yew | 又 | also |
| puh | 不 | not |
| nǎng | 能 | can |
| to | 多 | much |
| se | 洗 | wash |
| p'a | 怕 | lest |
| t'uy | 退 | fade |
| lëaou | 了 | |
| sih | 色 | color |
| yin | 印 | block |
| pan | 板 | |
| hwa | 花 | flower |
| wǎn | 紋 | line |
| yay | 也 | also |
| tëaou | 雕 | engrave |
| tih | 得 | obtain |
| ts'oo. | 粗 | coarse. |

If the manufacturers of cottons in foreign countries only knew the Chinese fashions and patterns, and could possibly dye their cottons the colors, and print them the flowers suited to Chinamen's fancies, the price being at the same time reasonable, no matter how many thousands, or how many myriads of pieces came, they would all be easily sold off.

| | | |
|---|---|---|
| Tsae | 在 | In |
| wae | 外 | foreign |
| kwoh | 國 | country |
| tso | 做 | make |
| teih | 的 | which |
| yang | 洋 | foreign |
| poo | 布 | cottons |
| joo | 如 | if |
| kwo | 果 | indeed |
| tung | 懂 | know |
| tih | 得 | obtain |
| Chung | 中 | China |
| kwoh | 國 | |
| teih | 的 | of |
| she | 時 | fashion |
| sin | 新 | |
| kh'wan | 欵 | pattern |
| shih | 式 | |
| năng | 能 | possible |
| kow | 彀 | |
| jen | 染 | dye |
| teih | 的 | which |
| yen | 顏 | color |
| sih | 色 | |
| yin | 印 | print |
| teih | 的 | which |
| hwa | 花 | flower |
| too | 都 | all |
| hoh | 合 | suit |
| Chung | 中 | China |
| kwoh | 國 | |
| jĭn | 人 | man |
| che | 之 | of |
| e | 意 | fancy |

| | | |
|---|---|---|
| urh | 而 | at the same time |
| tsëay | 且 | |
| këa | 價 | price |
| ts'ëen | 錢 | |
| tsae | 再 | again |
| p'ëen | 便 | reasonable |
| e | 宜 | |
| puh | 不 | no |
| lun | 論 | matter |
| ke | 幾 | how many |
| ts'ëen | 千 | thousand |
| p'eih | 疋 | piece |
| ke | 幾 | how many |
| wan | 萬 | myriad |
| p'eih | 疋 | piece |
| yay | 也 | yet |
| yung | 容 | easy |
| e | 易 | |
| sëaou. | 消 | sell off. |

What do the Chinese buy silk handkerchiefs for?

| | | |
|---|---|---|
| Chung | 中 | China |
| kwoh | 國 | |
| jin | 人 | man |
| mae | 買 | buy |
| sze | 絲 | silk |
| kin | 巾 | handkerchief |
| tso | 做 | do |
| shin | 甚 | what. |
| mo. | 麽 | |

To make wrappers of, or to tie up presents sent to friends in. Large handkerchiefs may be converted into coverlets, curtains, front aprons for tables, chair-cushions, turbans, girdles, and such like. But for cleansing the nose, drying the perspiration, wiping the hands, brushing tables, clearing away dust, and purposes of that description, coarse gray long cloths only should be used.

| | | |
|---|---|---|
| Mae | 買 | Buy |
| lëaou | 了 | finish |
| tso | 做 | make |
| paou | 包 | wrapper |
| fuh | 袱 | |
| hwoh | 或 | or |
| kae | 蓋 | cover |
| sung | 送 | send |
| jin | 人 | man |
| teih | 的 | which |
| le | 禮 | presents |
| wuh | 物 | |
| ta | 大 | large |
| show | 手 | handkerchief |
| kin | 巾 | |
| kh'o | 可 | may |
| e | 以 | |
| tso | 做 | convert |
| pe | 被 | coverlets |
| mëen | 面 | |
| wei | 幃 | curtain |
| man | 幔 | |
| choh | 桌 | table |
| wei | 圍 | apron |
| e | 椅 | chair |
| tëen | 墊 | cushion |
| paou | 包 | envelope |
| t'ow | 頭 | |
| wei | 圍 | gird |
| yaou | 腰 | loins |
| chay | 這 | such |
| sëay | 些 | like |
| yung | 用 | use |
| ch'oo | 處 | |
| tan | 但 | but |
| she | 是 | is |
| shih | 拭 | cleanse |
| pe | 鼻 | nose |
| t'e | 涕 | mucus |
| ma | 抹 | dry |
| han | 汗 | perspiration |
| ts'ah | 擦 | wipe |
| show | 手 | hand |
| shih | 拭 | brush |
| choh | 桌 | table |
| tsze | 子 | |
| tan | 撣 | clear away |
| hwuy | 灰 | dust |
| ch'in | 塵 | |
| chay | 這 | that |
| sëay | 些 | kind |
| sze | 事 | purpose |
| ts'ing | 情 | |
| chih | 只 | only |
| yung | 用 | use |
| yüen | 原 | original |
| sih | 色 | color |
| ts'oo | 粗 | coarse |
| poo | 布 | cloth |
| tsew | 就 | then |

| | | |
|---|---|---|
| haou | 好 | proper. |
| lëaou. | 了 | |

What other piece goods have you?

| | | |
|---|---|---|
| Han | 還 | Yet |
| yew | 有 | have |
| shin | 甚 | what |
| mo | 麽 | |
| yang | 洋 | piece goods. |
| poo. | 布 | |

I have checks and stripes, and red and blue bands.

| | | |
|---|---|---|
| Han | 還 | Yet |
| yew | 有 | have |
| kh'e | 棋 | chess |
| p'an | 盤 | board |
| kih | 格 | line |
| teih | 的 | |
| yew | 有 | have |
| lew | 柳 | willow |
| t'ëaou | 條 | twig |
| teih | 的 | |
| yew | 有 | have |
| yih | 一 | one |
| taou | 道 | line |
| hung | 紅 | red |
| yih | 一 | one |
| taou | 道 | line |
| lan | 藍 | blue |
| teih. | 的 | — |

The squares of the checks must not be too small, nor the stripes too open, otherwise they will not suit people's fancy. Turkey red cloth has a color which is fast, and will not wash out; hence the Chinese are fond of buying it.

| | | |
|---|---|---|
| Tan | 但 | But |
| kh'e | 棋 | chess |
| p'an | 盤 | board |
| yen | 眼 | square |
| puh | 不 | not |
| yaou | 要 | must |
| t'ae | 太 | too |
| sëaou | 小 | small |
| lew | 柳 | willow |
| t'ëaou | 條 | twig |
| teih | 的 | — |
| puh | 不 | not |
| haou | 好 | good |
| t'ae | 太 | too |
| soo | 疎 | open |
| kh'ung | 恐 | fear |
| p'a | 怕 | |
| jin | 人 | people |
| puh | 不 | not |
| chung | 中 | hit |
| e | 意 | fancy |
| yang | 洋 | foreign |
| hung | 紅 | red |
| poo | 布 | cloth |
| na | 那 | that |
| yen | 顏 | color |
| sih | 色 | |
| tsew | 就 | then |
| nae | 耐 | lasting |
| kew | 久 | |

| | | |
|---|---|---|
| se | 洗 | wash |
| puh | 不 | not |
| t'oh | 脫 | fade |
| Chung | 中 | China |
| kwoh | 國 | |
| jin | 人 | man |
| so | 所 | therefore |
| e | 以 | |
| too | 都 | all |
| he | 喜 | like |
| hwan | 歡 | |
| mae. | 買 | buy. |

## ON COTTON YARN.

How many kinds of cotton yarn have you?

| | | |
|---|---|---|
| Mëen | 棉 | Cotton |
| sha | 紗 | yarn |
| yew | 有 | have |
| ke | 幾 | how many |
| yang. | 樣 | kinds. |

I have two kinds, water twist, and mule twist.

| | | |
|---|---|---|
| Yew | 有 | Have |
| shuy | 水 | water |
| fang | 紡 | twist |
| teih | 的 | |
| yew | 有 | have |
| ho | 火 | fire |
| fang | 紡 | twist |
| teih | 的 | |
| lëang | 兩 | two |
| yang. | 樣 | kinds. |

Do the natives also use foreign yarn?

| | | |
|---|---|---|
| Yang | 洋 | Foreign |
| mëen | 棉 | cotton |
| sha | 紗 | yarn |
| păn | 本 | native |
| te | 地 | |
| jin | 人 | man |
| yay | 也 | also |
| yung | 用 | use |
| mo. | 麽 | ? |

The natives dislike foreign yarn, because it easily breaks, and is not strong; it is sometimes also liable to unravel, or has numerous knots, or carries fragments of seed from insufficient carding, or is spoilt by soaking in salt water.

| | | |
|---|---|---|
| Yang | 洋 | Foreign |
| mëen | 棉 | cotton |
| sha | 紗 | yarn |
| păn | 本 | native |
| te | 地 | |
| jin | 人 | man |
| hëen | 嫌 | dislike |
| t'a | 他 | it |
| yung | 容 | easy |
| e | 易 | |
| twan | 斷 | break |
| puh | 不 | not |
| këeh | 結 | strong |
| shih | 實 | |

yew 有 } have
teih 的 }
hwuy 會 liable
sung 鬆 loose
san 散 open
keh 肐 } knot
tah 䐛 }
yew 又 also
to 多 much
t'an 彈 } card
teih 的 }
hwa 花 cotton
yew 又 also

puh 不 not
tsing 淨 clean
tae 帶 have
hwa 花 cotton
tsze 子 seed
urh 兒 —
yay 也 also
yew 有 have
hëen 鹹 salt
shuy 水 water
tsin 浸 soak
lan 爛 spoil
teih. 的 —

## ON RENTING HOUSES.

I want to rent a set of premises for a ware-house. Are there any houses to rent hereabouts?

Wo 我 I
yaou 要 want
tsoo 租 rent
yih 一 one
so 所 set
fang 房 } premises
tsze 子 }
tso 做 make
chan 棧 } ware-house
fang 房 }
chay 這 } hereabouts
le 裏 }
yew 有 have
fang 房 } houses
tsze 子 }
tsoo 租 rent
mo. 麽 ?

About how many rooms would you want in such a house, and able to hold how many peculs of goods?

Ne 你 You
tsoo 租 rent
chay 這 such
fang 房 } house
tsze 子 }
ta 大 } about
yoh 約 }
tih 得 contain
to 多 } how many
shaou 少 }
këen 間 room
yaou 要 wish

chwang 裝 hold
to 多 } how many
shaou 少 }
tan 担 pecul
ho 貨 goods
teih 的 —

To suit me, it must have 30 rooms or thereabouts, and it must be a storied house with two flats, one above and another below, and it must be capable of containing 6 to 7 thousand peculs of merchandize.

Tsung 總 Must
yaou 要 want
san 三 } thirty
shih 十 }
këen 間 room
kwang 光 } thereabouts
king 景 }
yaou 要 want
low 樓 story
fang 房 house
shang 上 above
hëa 下 below
lëang 兩 two
ts'ăng 層 flat
kh'o 可 } capable
e 以 }
t'un 囤 hold
tih 得 obtain
lëuh 六 six
ts'eih 七 seven
ts'ëen 千 thousand
tan 担 pecul
ho 貨 } merchandize
wuh 物 }
ts'ae 纔 then
haou. 好 well.

So large a house as that will I fear be difficult to find, and when found I suspect a very high rent will be demanded for it.

Chay 這 } Such
mo 麽 }
ta 大 large
fang 房 } house
uh 屋 }
kh'ung 恐 } fear
p'a 怕 }
nan 難 difficult
chaou 找 find
tsew 就 if
she 是 is
chaou 找 } find
teih 的 }
choh 着 reach
lëang 諒 think
peih 必 must
fang 房 house
tsoo 租 rent
yay 也 also
kwuy 貴 dear
teih 的 } very.
hăn. 狠 }

No matter. To do a large business, we must have large warehouses, otherwise goods may arrive, and there would be no place to store them in, besides which, one's capital would still more be wasted.

| | | |
|---|---|---|
| Puh | 不 | No |
| yaou | 要 | matter |
| kin | 緊 | |
| săng | 生 | trade |
| e | 意 | |
| tso | 做 | do |
| teih | 的 | — |
| ta | 大 | large |
| tsung | 總 | must |
| yaou | 要 | require |
| yew | 有 | have |
| ta | 大 | large |
| chan | 棧 | ware-house |
| fang | 房 | |
| puh | 不 | not |
| jen | 然 | indeed |
| ho | 貨 | goods |
| taou | 到 | come |
| lëaou | 了 | — |
| woo | 無 | no |
| ch'oo | 處 | place |
| t'un | 囤 | store |
| kăng | 更 | still more |
| yaou | 要 | want |
| cheh | 折 | waste |
| păn | 本 | capital |
| lëaou. | 了 | — |

Outside the East gate lives a man named Choo, behind whose premises there is a ware-house. It is moreover near the bank of the canal, so as to be convenient for the landing of goods. But the price is too dear.

| | | |
|---|---|---|
| Tung | 東 | East |
| măn | 門 | gate |
| wae | 外 | outside |
| yew | 有 | have |
| yih | 一 | one |
| ko | 個 | piece |
| sing | 姓 | surname |
| Choo | 朱 | Choo |
| teih | 的 | of |
| t'a | 他 | he |
| how | 後 | behind |
| t'ow | 頭 | side |
| yew | 有 | have |
| chan | 棧 | ware-house |
| fang | 房 | |
| yew | 又 | also |
| kin | 近 | near |
| ho | 河 | canal |
| pëen | 邊 | bank |
| shang | 上 | land |
| ho | 貨 | goods |
| yay | 也 | also |
| pëen | 便 | conveniently |
| tang | 當 | |
| tan | 但 | but |
| këa | 價 | price |
| ts'ëen | 錢 | |
| t'ae | 太 | too |
| kwuy. | 貴 | dear. |

How much does he want for it?

| | | |
|---|---|---|
| Yaou | 要 | Want |
| to | 多 | how much |
| shaou | 少 | |

ts'ëen 錢 money
ne. 呢 ?

He wants 600 strings of cash a year, besides 600 strings earnest money.

May 每 Each
nëen 年 year
tsoo 租 rent
ts'ëen 錢 money
yaou 要 want
lëuh 六 six
pih 百 hundred
tëaou 吊 string
yah 押 earnest
tsoo 租 rent
yay 也 also
yaou 要 want
lëuh 六 six
pih 百 hundred
tëaou. 吊 strings.

What is earnest money?

Yah 押 Earnest
tsoo 租 rent
she 是 is
shin 甚 } what.
mo. 麽 }

Earnest money is payment in advance to the land-lord, as the pledge of faith, that the rent shall not fall into arrear, and hereafter when you no longer require the premises and restore them to him, he will give you back your earnest money.

Yah 押 Earnest
tsoo 租 rent
she 是 is
sëen 先 advance
foo 付 pay
fang 房 } land-lord
choo 主 }
tso 做 do
p'ing 憑 proof
sin 信 faith
puh 不 not
che 致 lead
yü 於 to
shaou 少 } owe
kh'ëen 欠 }
t'a 他 } his
teih 的 }
fang 房 house
ts'ëen 錢 money
tsëang 將 } hereafter
lae 來 }
ne 你 you
puh 不 not
choo 住 reside
lëaou 了 —
t'uy 退 } restore
hwan 還 }
t'a 他 } his
teih 的 }
fang 房 } house
tsze 子 }
t'a 他 he
na 那 that
she 時 } time
how 候 }

| | | |
|---|---|---|
| kay | 給 | give |
| hwuy | 囘 | back |
| ne | 你 | your |
| teih | 的 | |
| yah | 押 | earnest |
| tsoo. | 租 | money. |

Reckoning at that rate, the yearly rent 600 strings, the interest on the earnest money, say, 60 strings. Why surely it makes altogether 660 strings, to say nothing of the chance of its being difficult to get back the earnest money, when the time comes for giving up the house.

| | | |
|---|---|---|
| Chay | 這 | This |
| yang | 樣 | way |
| swan | 筭 | reckon |
| kh'e | 起 | up |
| lae | 來 | come |
| fang | 房 | house |
| tsoo | 租 | rent |
| lëuh | 六 | six |
| pih | 百 | hundred |
| tëaou | 吊 | string |
| yah | 押 | earnest |
| tsoo | 租 | rent |
| le | 利 | interest |
| ts'ëen | 錢 | money |
| tsew | 就 | then |
| swan | 筭 | count |
| she | 是 | is |
| lëuh | 六 | sixty |
| shih | 十 | |
| tëaou | 吊 | string |
| yih | 一 | altogether |
| kung | 共 | |
| kh'e | 豈 | how |
| puh | 不 | not |
| she | 是 | is |
| lëuh | 六 | six |
| pih | 百 | hundred |
| lëuh | 六 | sixty |
| shih | 十 | |
| tëaou | 吊 | string |
| lëaou | 了 | — |
| han | 還 | besides |
| kh'ung | 恐 | fear |
| p'a | 怕 | |
| tsëang | 將 | hereafter |
| lae | 來 | |
| hwan | 還 | restore |
| t'a | 他 | him |
| fang | 房 | house |
| tsze | 子 | |
| teih | 的 | of |
| she | 時 | time |
| how | 候 | |
| t'aou | 討 | get |
| hwuy | 囘 | back |
| yah | 押 | earnest |
| tsoo | 租 | rent |
| tsew | 就 | then |
| nan | 難 | difficult |
| lëaou. | 了 | — |

There is no fear of that, for you have the house as security. I would rather pay a little more rent, and not pay any earnest money.

| | | |
|---|---|---|
| Puh | 不 | Not |
| p'a | 怕 | fear |
| yew | 有 | have |
| fang | 房 | house |
| tsze | 子 | |
| tso | 做 | do |
| tang | 當 | security |
| wo | 我 | I |
| puh | 不 | not |
| ch'uh | 出 | give |
| yah | 押 | earnest |
| tsoo | 租 | rent |
| ning | 寧 | rather |
| kh'o | 可 | can |
| këa | 加 | add |
| to | 多 | most |
| tëen | 點 | little |
| fang | 房 | house |
| tsoo | 租 | rent |
| pa. | 罷 | — |

I do not know, whether he will consent to that. He said that it was always the custom of the place to make the arrangement, and if this matter could not be settled in accordance with previous custom, he would not be willing to lease you the house.

| | | |
|---|---|---|
| Puh | 不 | Not |
| che | 知 | know |
| taou | 道 | |
| t'a | 他 | he |
| kh'ăng | 肯 | consent |
| puh | 不 | not |
| kh'ăng | 肯 | consent |
| ne | 呢 | — |
| t'a | 他 | he |
| shwoh | 說 | say |
| kwo | 過 | has |
| ts'ze | 此 | this |
| ch'oo | 處 | place |
| kwuy | 規 | custom |
| keu | 矩 | |
| too | 都 | all |
| she | 是 | is |
| chay | 這 | this |
| yang | 樣 | way |
| puh | 不 | not |
| chaou | 照 | according to |
| choh | 着 | |
| hëang | 向 | hitherto |
| lae | 來 | |
| teih | 的 | of |
| kwuy | 規 | custom |
| keu | 矩 | |
| t'a | 他 | he |
| yay | 也 | also |
| puh | 不 | not |
| kh'ăng | 肯 | willing |
| tsoo | 租 | rent |
| kay | 給 | give |
| ne | 你 | you |
| pa. | 罷 | — |

How many rooms has this house?

| | | |
|---|---|---|
| Na | 那 | That |
| fang | 房 | house |
| tsze | 子 | |
| yew | 有 | have |

to 多 } how much
shaou 少 }
këen. 間 room.

In the upper story it has ten; in the lower story ten, and in the godown fifteen rooms.

Low 樓 Story
shang 上 above
shih 十 ten
këen 間 room
low 樓 story
hëa 下 below
shih 十 ten
këen 間 room
chan 棧 store
fang 房 house
yew 有 have
shih 十 } fifteen
woo 五 }
këen. 間 room.

In what direction does the door way face?

Măn 門 Door
mëen 面 face
tso 坐 place
hëang 向 towards
tsăng 怎 } what
mo 麽 }
yang. 樣 kind.

The premises are situated northerly, and the house has a southern aspect. They are also surrounded by a high wall, which renders them safe from wind or fire. Inside there are two courts, and behind there is a good large yard, round which is a wall which may be used for putting up any number of coarse or heavy articles.

She 是 Is
tso 坐 place
pih 北 north
chaou 朝 aspect
nan 南 south
chow 週 } all round
wei 圍 }
yew 有 have
kaou 高 high
ts'ëang 墻 wall
tsew 就 which
she 是 is
fung 風 wind
ho 火 fire
too 都 all
puh 不 no
yaou 要 } matter
kin 緊 }
le 裡 } inside
t'ow 頭 }
yew 有 have
lëang 兩 } two
ko 個 }
t'ëen 天 } court
tsing 井 }
how 後 } behind
t'ow 頭 }
yew 有 have
ko 個 a

| | | |
|---|---|---|
| haou | 好 | good |
| ta | 大 | large |
| teih | 的 | |
| yuen | 院 | yard |
| tsze | 子 | |
| yew | 又 | also |
| yew | 有 | have |
| wei | 圍 | enclosure |
| ts'ëang | 墻 | wall |
| kh'o | 可 | may |
| e | 以 | |
| tuy | 堆 | heap |
| fang | 放 | place |
| haou | 好 | great |
| to | 多 | many |
| teih | 的 | of |
| ts'oo | 粗 | coarse |
| chung | 重 | heavy |
| tung | 東 | articles. |
| se. | 西 | |

| | | |
|---|---|---|
| yay | 也 | also |
| taou | 倒 | tumble |
| t'ah | 塌 | |
| lëaou | 了 | down |
| fang | 房 | house |
| măn | 門 | door |
| ch'wang | 窗 | window |
| hoo | 戶 | |
| too | 都 | all |
| she | 是 | is |
| p'o | 破 | broken |
| lan | 爛 | |
| teih | 的 | that which |
| na | 那 | how |
| le | 裏 | |
| năng | 能 | possible |
| kow | 彀 | |
| choo | 住 | live |
| teh | 得 | |
| ne. | 呢 | ? |

This house seems to be very dirty, its walls tumbling down and doors and windows all coming to pieces. However will it be possible to live in it?

| | | |
|---|---|---|
| Kh'an | 看 | Look at |
| chay | 這 | this |
| fang | 房 | house |
| tsze | 子 | |
| shih | 十 | extremely |
| făn | 分 | |
| ngang | 骯 | dirty |
| tsang | 髒 | |
| ts'ëang | 牆 | walls |
| peih | 壁 | |

It is the business of the landlord to make repairs. You should lose no time in furnishing the funds, and commencing to repair the house.

| | | |
|---|---|---|
| Sew | 修 | Repair |
| ching | 整 | |
| fang | 房 | house |
| tsze | 子 | |
| păn | 本 | originally |
| lae | 來 | |
| she | 是 | is |
| fang | 房 | landlord |
| tung | 東 | |
| teih | 的 | of |

U

| | | |
|---|---|---|
| sze | 事 | business |
| ne | 你 | you |
| yaou | 要 | want |
| kh'wae | 快 | quickly |
| tang | 當 | |
| tsew | 就 | immediately |
| na | 拿 | take |
| ch'uh | 出 | out |
| ts'ëen | 錢 | money |
| lae | 來 | come |
| sew | 修 | repair. |
| le. | 理 | |

And by and by you may deduct the amount from the earnest money. Should you wish any additions beyond the repairs, or to make alterations of any kind, you will have to pay for such yourself, and when you come to leave the house, you will be allowed to remove them away.

| | | |
|---|---|---|
| How | 後 | Afterwards |
| lae | 來 | |
| yay | 也 | also |
| haou | 好 | good |
| kh'ow | 扣 | deduct |
| t'a | 他 | his |
| teih | 的 | |
| yah | 押 | earnest |
| tsoo | 租 | rent |
| sew | 修 | repair |
| ching | 整 | |
| che | 之 | of |
| wae | 外 | outside |
| joh | 若 | if |
| yaou | 要 | wish |
| chwang | 裝 | additions |
| sew | 修 | |
| kae | 改 | change |
| tsaou | 造 | make |
| shin | 甚 | any |
| mo | 麼 | |
| yang | 樣 | pattern |
| shih | 式 | |
| tsew | 就 | then |
| she | 是 | is |
| ne | 你 | you |
| tsze | 自 | self |
| ke | 己 | |
| hwa | 化 | pay |
| ts'ëen | 錢 | money |
| lëaou | 了 | — |
| tsëang | 將 | hereafter |
| lae | 來 | |
| puh | 不 | not |
| choo | 住 | reside |
| lëaou | 了 | |
| teih | 的 | that which |
| she | 時 | time |
| how | 候 | |
| chun | 准 | allow |
| ne | 你 | you |
| tsze | 自 | self |
| ke | 己 | |
| ch'eh | 拆 | remove |
| hwuy. | 回 | away. |

## ON BUILDING HOUSES.

I am thinking of leasing a plot of ground, and building myself a house on it according to my own ideas, adopting such model as I may fancy.

| | | |
|---|---|---|
| Wo | 我 | I |
| sëang | 想 | think |
| tsoo | 租 | rent |
| yih | 一 | one |
| kh'wae | 塊 | plot |
| te | 地 | ground |
| tsze | 自 | self |
| ke | 己 | |
| tsaou | 造 | build |
| fang | 房 | house |
| tsze | 子 | |
| suy | 隨 | according to |
| wo | 我 | my |
| teih | 的 | that which |
| e | 意 | idea |
| sze | 思 | |
| ngae | 愛 | wish |
| tsaou | 造 | build |
| shin | 甚 | what |
| mo | 麽 | |
| yang | 樣 | model |
| shih | 式 | |
| tsew | 就 | then |
| tsaou | 造 | build |
| shin | 甚 | what |
| mo | 麽 | |
| yang | 樣 | model. |
| shih. | 式 | |

This could be done; only it is to be feared that when the house comes to be built, the native workmen will not understand how to go about it. You should have a plan drawn out of a style of house after the custom of your honorable country, and I will hand the plan to the workmen to look at. You can then with them on the spot point out their mode of proceeding, and who knows but that they may yet be able to accomplish it.

| | | |
|---|---|---|
| She | 使 | Do |
| teh | 得 | can |
| chih | 只 | only |
| p'a | 怕 | fear |
| kae | 蓋 | build |
| fang | 房 | house |
| tsze | 子 | |
| she | 時 | time |
| how | 候 | |
| pǎn | 本 | native |
| te | 地 | |
| tsëang | 匠 | workman |
| jin | 人 | |
| puh | 不 | not |
| tung | 懂 | understand |
| teh | 得 | can |
| tsǎng | 怎 | what |
| mo | 麽 | |
| tsaou | 造 | build |
| fah | 法 | mode |
| yaou | 要 | want |
| chaou | 照 | according to |

| | | |
|---|---|---|
| kwuy | 貴 | honorable |
| kwoh | 國 | country |
| tsaou | 造 | build |
| teih | 的 | that which |
| yang | 樣 | style |
| shih | 式 | |
| yaou | 要 | want |
| hwa | 畫 | paint |
| yih | 一 | one |
| chang | 張 | sheet |
| too | 圖 | plan |
| yang | 樣 | |
| wo | 我 | I |
| na | 拿 | take |
| kay | 給 | give |
| t'a | 他 | him |
| kh'an | 看 | look |
| ne | 你 | you |
| tsze | 自 | self |
| ke | 己 | |
| t'ung | 同 | with |
| tsae | 在 | at |
| na | 那 | there |
| le | 裏 | |
| che | 指 | point out |
| tëen | 點 | |
| t'a | 他 | him |
| lëang | 諒 | think |
| peih | 必 | must |
| yay | 也 | also |
| tsaou | 造 | build |
| teih | 的 | |
| lae | 來 | able |
| too | 都 | all |
| lun | 論 | say |
| puh | 不 | not |
| ting. | 定 | certain. |

At what price are bricks, tiles, and wooden material selling just now?

| | | |
|---|---|---|
| Joo | 如 | Now |
| kin | 今 | |
| teih | 的 | that which |
| chüen | 甎 | brick |
| wa | 瓦 | tile |
| muh | 木 | wood |
| lëaou | 料 | material |
| mae | 賣 | sell |
| shin | 甚 | what |
| mo | 麽 | |
| këa | 價 | price |
| ts'ëen | 錢 | |

Lime is selling at about 500 cash per pecul.

| | | |
|---|---|---|
| Sheh | 石 | Lime |
| hwuy | 灰 | |
| may | 每 | each |
| tan | 担 | pecul |
| ta | 大 | about |
| yoh | 約 | |
| woo | 五 | five |
| peh | 百 | hundred |
| ts'ëen. | 錢 | cash. |

Bricks and tiles are judged by their size, the smaller ones cost from 2,000 and more cash to 3,000 cash or thereabouts. The larger are estimated by their length and superficial area, and are sold by the foot and inch.

| | | |
|---|---|---|
| Chuën | 甎 | Brick |
| wa | 瓦 | tile |
| she | 是 | is |
| kh'an | 看 | look |
| ta | 大 | large |
| sëaou | 小 | small |
| na | 那 | the |
| sëaou | 小 | small |
| teih | 的 | that which |
| yaou | 要 | want |
| mae | 賣 | sell |
| lëang | 兩 | two |
| ts'ëen | 千 | thousand |
| to | 多 | more |
| ts'ëen | 錢 | cash |
| san | 三 | three |
| ts'ëen | 千 | thousand |
| teih | 的 | of |
| kwang king | 光景 | thereabouts |
| ta | 大 | large |
| kh'wae | 塊 | piece |
| teih | 的 | that which |
| hwoh | 或 | either |
| lun | 論 | reckon |
| ch'ang | 長 | long |
| fang | 方 | square |
| ngan | 按 | according to |
| ch'eh | 尺 | foot |
| ts'un | 寸 | inch |
| këang | 講 | tell |
| këa. | 價 | price. |

Wooden planks are sold at two thousand or more cash the square chang of one inch in thickness.

| | | |
|---|---|---|
| Muh | 木 | Wood |
| pan | 板 | plank |
| she | 是 | is |
| yih | 一 | one |
| chang | 丈 | chang |
| ch'ang | 長 | long |
| yih | 一 | one |
| chang | 丈 | chang |
| kh'wan | 寬 | broad |
| yih | 一 | one |
| ts'un | 寸 | inch |
| how | 厚 | thick |
| yaou | 要 | want |
| mae | 賣 | sell |
| urh | 二 | two |
| ts'ëen | 千 | thousand |
| to | 多 | more |
| ts'ëen. | 錢 | cash. |

Beams of five inches in diameter, and one chang in length, fetch 500 or more cash per stick. If wanted larger and longer, more will of course be charged.

| | | |
|---|---|---|
| Muh t'ow | 木頭 | Beams |
| may | 每 | each |
| t'ëaou | 條 | stick |
| king | 徑 | diameter |
| woo | 五 | five |
| ts'un | 寸 | inch |
| yih | 一 | one |
| chang | 丈 | chang |

| | | |
|---|---|---|
| ch'ang | 長 | long |
| teih | 的 | that which |
| teh | 得 | obtain |
| woo | 五 | five |
| peh | 百 | hundred |
| to | 多 | more |
| ts'ëen | 錢 | cash |
| joo | 如 | if |
| kwo | 果 | indeed |
| yaou | 要 | want |

| | | |
|---|---|---|
| ch'ang | 長 | long |
| teih | 的 | that which |
| ta | 大 | large |
| t'eaou | 條 | stick |
| teih | 的 | that which |
| ts'ëen | 錢 | cash |
| tsew | 就 | then |
| to | 多 | more |
| lëaou | 了 | — |

## DIALOGUE BETWEEN FRIENDS.

Long since I have seen you! Long since I have seen you! (Eng. How do you do?)

| | | |
|---|---|---|
| Kew | 久 | Long |
| wei | 違 | separate |
| kew | 久 | long |
| wei. | 違 | separate. |

Pray sit down. Have you been well and enjoying yourself? Where have you been making money?

| | | |
|---|---|---|
| Ts'ing | 請 | Pray |
| tso | 坐 | sit |
| ts'ing | 請 | pray |
| tso | 坐 | sit |
| yih | 一 | hitherto |
| hëang | 向 | |
| haou | 好 | well |
| ah | 阿 | ? |
| nah | 納 | enjoy |
| fuh | 福 | happiness |
| ah | 阿 | ? |
| tsae | 在 | at |
| na | 那 | where |
| le | 裏 | |
| fah | 發 | make |
| tsae | 財 | money |
| ah. | 阿 | ? |

You are too polite! Yes, I have enjoyed myself somewhat, thanks to you, and I have come on purpose to wait upon you, and ask after your welfare.

| | | |
|---|---|---|
| Haou | 好 | Good |
| shwoh | 說 | words |
| too | 都 | always |
| han | 還 | yet |
| t'oh | 托 | partake |
| fuh | 福 | happiness |
| t'eh | 特 | special |
| e | 意 | idea |
| lae | 來 | come |
| how | 候 | wait |
| how | 候 | wait |

ne 你 you
ts'ing 請 ask
ts'ing 請 ask
ngan. 安 welfare.

I am highly complimented. When did your worthy person arrive?

Kh'e 豈 How
kan 敢 presume
puh 不 not
kan 敢 presume
tang 當 bear
tsun 尊 worthy
këa 駕 person
ke 幾 } when
she 時 }
taou 到 } arrive
teih 的 }
ne. 呢 ?

I only arrived yesterday, and that is why I have come to ask after you.

Tsoh 昨 } Yesterday
t'ëen 天 }
ts'ae 纔 only
taou 到 arrive
koo 故 for
ts'ze 此 this
lae 來 come
ts'ing 請 ask
ts'ing 請 ask
ngan. 安 welfare.

It is long since we have met; who would have thought it was two years ago? You must have made vast progress in your literary occupations and researches.

Kew 久 Long
puh 不 not
sëang 相 mutually
këen 見 meet
puh 不 not
këoh 覺 perceive
tsew 就 then
she 是 is
lëang 兩 two
nëen 年 year
lëaou 了 finish
kin 近 } lately
lae 來 }
tuh 讀 read
shoo 書 book
yung 用 occupy
kung 功 literary
hëoh 學 learn
wăn 問 enquire
peih 必 } must
ting 定 }
ta 大 great
tsin 進 progress
lëaou. 了 —

I am really ashamed to hear you praise me so.

Ching 承 Receive
ne 你 you
kwo 過 too much
tsëang 奬 praise

| | | |
|---|---|---|
| shih | 實 | truly |
| tsae | 在 | |
| ts'an | 慚 | shame |
| kh'wuy | 愧 | |
| teih | 的 | very |
| hăn. | 狠 | |

For whole days, I have applied my mind and strength in my little study without a single result, beyond wasting so much valuable time, and I am ashamed to say, dolt that I am, I cannot equal any of my fellow students.

| | | |
|---|---|---|
| Chung | 終 | Whole |
| jih | 日 | day |
| tsae | 在 | at |
| ch'wang | 窗 | window |
| hëa | 下 | under |
| too | 徒 | vainly |
| laou | 勞 | labour |
| sin | 心 | heart |
| leih | 力 | strength |
| puh | 不 | merely |
| kwo | 過 | |
| she | 是 | is |
| heu | 虛 | empty |
| too | 度 | pass |
| kwang | 光 | light |
| yin | 陰 | dark |
| urh | 而 | and |
| e | 已 | all |
| tsew | 就 | even |
| she | 是 | is |
| t'ung | 同 | same |
| ch'wang | 窗 | window |
| che | 之 | of |
| chung | 中 | in |
| tsze | 自 | self |
| kh'wuy | 愧 | shame |
| woo | 無 | no |
| ts'ae | 才 | talent |
| pe | 比 | compare |
| jin | 人 | others |
| puh | 不 | not |
| shang. | 上 | excel. |

You are too polite and self-depreciating.

| | | |
|---|---|---|
| Haou | 好 | Good |
| shwoh | 說 | words |
| t'ae | 太 | too |
| kh'ëen | 謙 | depreciate |
| lëaou | 了 | — |

The literary examinations are just coming on, and I am certain that, with such a style of man, talents, and acquisition as you possess, I shall have to congratulate you this year on your accession to high honor.

| | | |
|---|---|---|
| Kh'o | 科 | Examination |
| ch'ang | 場 | arena |
| tsëang | 將 | about |
| kin | 近 | near |
| sëang | 像 | such as |
| koh | 閣 | you |
| hëa | 下 | |
| jin | 人 | man |
| p'in | 品 | style |

ts'ae 才 talent
hëoh 學 acquisition
kin 今 this
nëen 年 year
yih 一 } certainly
ting 定 }
kung 恭 } congratulate
he 喜 }
kaou 高 high
chung 中 success
teih. 的 —

You are too polite! No; you merchants have the advantage over us, worthy Sir; you traverse the world in search of a livelihood, and ensure your million per cent profit on your outlay. How many are your sources of delight!

Haou 好 Good
shwoh 說 words
puh 不 not
joo 如 like
tsun 尊 worthy
këa 駕 sir
mae 買 } trade
mae 賣 }
jin 人 man
king 經 } roam in search of livelihood
ying 營 }
sze 四 four
hae 海 seas
chin 眞 truly
she 是 is
yih 一 one
păn 本 principal
wan 萬 myriad
le 利 profit
ho 何 what
tăng 等 kind
teih 的 of
ch'ang 暢 } delight
kh'wae 快 }
ne 呢 ?

Yes, but trade has its difficulties. Business has been dull of late, all is rather show than reality, goods will not go off, and the interest gained on one's principal is but trifling. Trade with the West and East moreover now amounts to nothing. The ancients were right when they said, "No pursuit so noble as that of books."

Mow 貿 } Trade
yih 易 }
teih 的 that which
yay 也 also
hăn 狠 very
nan 難 difficult
kin 近 } lately
lae 來 }
săng 生 } business
e 意 }
tan 淡 } dull
poh 泊 }
too 都 all
she 是 is

| | | |
|---|---|---|
| yew | 有 | have |
| ming | 名 | name |
| woo | 無 | no |
| shih | 實 | reality |
| ho | 貨 | goods |
| wuh | 物 | |
| nan | 難 | difficult |
| sëaou | 消 | sell off |
| le | 利 | interest |
| seih | 息 | |
| yew | 有 | has |
| hëen | 限 | limit |
| joo | 如 | now |
| kin | 今 | |
| tung | 東 | east |
| se | 西 | west |
| lëang | 兩 | two |
| yang | 洋 | oceans |
| teih | 的 | of |
| săng | 生 | trade |
| e | 意 | |
| yay | 也 | also |
| puh | 不 | no |
| chung | 中 | use |
| yung | 用 | |
| lëaou | 了 | — |
| koo | 古 | ancients |
| jin | 人 | |
| ch'ang | 常 | always |
| shwoh | 說 | say |
| wei | 惟 | only |
| yew | 有 | have |
| tuh | 讀 | read |
| shoo | 書 | book |
| kaou. | 高 | noble. |

Worthy sir, you are a man clear headed and able beyond the common run of men, and you are certain ere long to amass great wealth.

| | | |
|---|---|---|
| Tsun | 尊 | Worthy |
| këa | 駕 | sir |
| she | 是 | is |
| tsing | 精 | clearheaded |
| ming | 明 | |
| kh'ëang | 强 | able |
| kan | 幹 | |
| teih | 的 | that which |
| pe | 比 | compare |
| puh | 不 | not |
| teh | 得 | can |
| tsin | 尋 | common |
| ch'ang | 常 | |
| che | 之 | of |
| pay | 輩 | class |
| tsëang | 將 | hereafter |
| lae | 來 | |
| peih | 必 | must |
| ting | 定 | |
| hwuy | 會 | able |
| fah | 發 | amass |
| ta | 大 | great |
| ts'ae | 財 | wealth |
| teih. | 的 | — |

I recollect when in former days we sat in the same study, our feelings harmonised, our hearts were one, and we were ever together; now that we are both roaming the world in search of gain, it is difficult to get a sight of each other.

| | | |
|---|---|---|
| Sëang | 想 | Recall |
| ts'ung | 從 | formerly |
| ts'ëen | 前 | |
| t'ung | 同 | same |
| ch'wang | 窗 | window |
| teih | 的 | of |
| she | 時 | time |
| how | 候 | |
| ts'ing | 情 | mind |
| tow | 投 | suit |
| e | 意 | idea |
| hoh | 合 | agree |
| tsaou | 早 | morning |
| wan | 晚 | evening |
| sëang | 相 | together |
| tseu | 聚 | meet |
| joo | 如 | now |
| kin | 今 | |
| wei | 爲 | for |
| le | 利 | gain |
| păn | 奔 | run |
| she | 馳 | ride |
| nan | 難 | hard |
| teh | 得 | get |
| sëang | 相 | mutual |
| këen. | 見 | sight. |

You are striving for profit, I for fame; and both of us are impelled by the ambition to get gain and name. Truly each has his difficulties.

| | | |
|---|---|---|
| Ne | 你 | You |
| she | 是 | is |
| wei | 爲 | make |
| le | 利 | money |
| wo | 我 | I |
| wei | 爲 | is |
| kung | 功 | merit |
| ming | 名 | name |
| too | 都 | all |
| she | 是 | is |
| wei | 爲 | by |
| ming | 名 | name |
| le | 利 | profit |
| so | 所 | that which |
| kh'ëen | 牽 | drag |
| pe | 彼 | that |
| ts'ze | 此 | this |
| koh | 各 | each |
| yew | 有 | have |
| so | 所 | that which |
| nan. | 難 | difficult. |

Now that intimate brethren like us have met after so long a separation, I think I must beg you sir to stay here awhile, and let us have a quiet talk. What say you?

| | | |
|---|---|---|
| Kin | 今 | To-day |
| t'ëen | 天 | |
| che | 知 | know |
| ke | 己 | selves |
| te | 弟 | brethren |
| heung | 兄 | |
| măn | 們 | we |

| | | |
|---|---|---|
| kew | 久 | long |
| peëh | 別 | hinder |
| sëang | 相 | mutual |
| fung | 逢 | meet |
| sëang | 想 | think |
| kh'eüh | 屈 | ask |
| këa | 駕 | sir |
| tsae | 在 | at |
| chay | 這 | here |
| le | 裡 | |
| ta | 大 | we |
| këa | 家 | |
| t'an | 談 | converse |
| t'an | 談 | |
| haou | 好 | well |
| puh | 不 | not |
| haou | 好 | well |
| ne. | 呢 | ? |

I am much obliged to you; but to-day I wish to go on and look up other friends. Some other day, I will come over and put myself under your guidance.

| | | |
|---|---|---|
| To | 多 | Many |
| sëay | 謝 | thank |
| lëaou | 了 | — |
| wo | 我 | I |
| joo | 如 | now |
| kin | 今 | |
| han | 還 | yet |
| yaou | 要 | wish |
| kh'eu | 去 | go |
| kh'an | 看 | look |
| kh'an | 看 | |
| pëeh | 別 | other |
| teih | 的 | |
| p'ăng | 朋 | friend |
| yew | 友 | |
| kae | 改 | another |
| t'ëen | 天 | day |
| tsae | 再 | again |
| kwo | 過 | pass |
| lae | 來 | over |
| ling | 領 | receive |
| këaou | 教 | teach |
| pa. | 罷 | — |

If so I must not attempt to detain you. To-morrow I will certainly call at your mansion to ask after your welfare, and thank you for coming to see me.

| | | |
|---|---|---|
| Ke | 旣 | Since |
| she | 是 | is |
| chay | 這 | thus |
| yang | 樣 | |
| puh | 不 | not |
| kan | 敢 | dare |
| kh'ëang | 强 | compel |
| lew | 留 | keep |
| wo | 我 | I |
| ming | 明 | to-morrow |
| t'ëen | 天 | |
| peih | 必 | must |
| taou | 到 | to |
| foo | 府 | mansion |
| shang | 上 | above |
| kh'eu | 去 | go |
| ts'ing | 請 | ask |

| | | |
|---|---|---|
| ngan | 安 | welfare |
| sëay | 謝 | thank |
| poo. | 步 | step. |

I cannot think of your doing so. Pray wait until I send a sedan to invite you round.

| | | |
|---|---|---|
| Puh | 不 | Not |
| kan | 敢 | dare |
| tang | 當 | support |
| tăng | 等 | wait |
| wo | 我 | I |
| ta | 打 | send |
| fah | 發 | |
| këaou | 轎 | sedan |
| tsze | 子 | |
| lae | 來 | come |
| ts'ing | 請 | invite |
| ne. | 你 | you. |

Pardon my not accompanying you out any distance.

| | | |
|---|---|---|
| Shoo | 恕 | Pardon |
| puh | 不 | not |
| yüen | 遠 | far |
| sung. | 送 | accompany. |

How can you think of such a thing. Do stop.

| | | |
|---|---|---|
| Kh'e | 豈 | How |
| kan | 敢 | dare |
| ts'ing | 請 | beg |
| lew | 留 | stop |
| poo. | 步 | step. |

I wish you well.

| | | |
|---|---|---|
| Ts'ing | 請 | Beg |
| lëaou. | 了 | — |

## DIALOGUE WITH A SERVANT.

Come here.

| | | |
|---|---|---|
| Lae. | 來 | Come. |

Here I am.

| | | |
|---|---|---|
| Yew. | 有 | Have. |

How comes it that there is no one here looking to the door?

| | | |
|---|---|---|
| Wei | 爲 | For |
| shin | 甚 | what. |
| mo | 麽 | |
| muh | 沒 | not |
| yew | 有 | have |
| jin | 人 | man |
| tsae | 在 | at |
| chay | 這 | here |
| le | 裡 | |
| kh'an | 看 | look to |
| măn. | 門 | door. |

We were not aware Master had come home.

| | | |
|---|---|---|
| Puh | 不 | Not |
| che | 知 | know |
| taou | 道 | |
| laou | 老 | venerable |
| yay | 爺 | sir |
| lae. | 來 | come. |

It does not matter whether a visitor arrives or no: in any case a man must be stationed in the doorway; moreover, who knows what idlers or disorderly fellows might not rush in and steal something.

Puh 不 Not
lun 論 matter
yew 有 have
kh'ih 客 visitor
taou 到 come
muh 沒 not
yew 有 have
tsung 總 must
yaou 要 want
yew 有 have
yih 一 } one
ko 個 }
jin 人 man
tsae 在 at
măn 門 } doorway
kh'ow 口 }
sze 伺 } wait
how 候 }
yew 又 also
p'a 怕 fear
yew 有 have
hëen 閒 idle
tsah 雜 disorderly
jin 人 people
ch'wang 闖 rush
tsin 進 enter
lae 來 come
t'ow 偷 steal
tung 東 } things.
se. 西 }

Is the large hall arranged and cleaned?

Ta 大 Large
t'ing 廳 hall
shang 上 in
yew 有 have
show 收 } arrange
shih 拾 }
kan 乾 } clean
tsing 淨 }
mo. 麽 ?

We have been so busy this morning, that we have not swept it out.

Kin 今 This
tsaou 早 morning
teih 的 of
sze 事 } business
ts'ing 情 }
to 多 much
puh 不 not
teh 得 obtain
hëen 閒 leisure
muh 沒 not
yew 有 have
ta 打 } sweep.
saou. 掃 }

Have not I always given orders, that in every part of the house no matter where, everything must be set in order, and swept clean, and that if you found you had not time enough to do so, I had no objection to your calling in another person to assist you.

Wo 我 I
chang 常 always

| | | |
|---|---|---|
| făn | 吩 | order |
| foo | 咐 | |
| ne | 你 | you |
| măn | 們 | |
| puh | 不 | no |
| lun | 論 | matter |
| na | 那 | where |
| le | 裡 | |
| too | 都 | all |
| yaou | 要 | want |
| ngan | 安 | place |
| p'ae | 排 | |
| t'o | 妥 | properly |
| tang | 當 | |
| ta | 打 | sweep |
| saou | 掃 | |
| këeh | 潔 | clean |
| tsing | 凈 | |
| joo | 如 | if |
| kwo | 果 | indeed |
| puh | 不 | not |
| teh | 得 | obtain |
| hëen | 閒 | leisure |
| kh'ung | 空 | |
| kh'o | 可 | may |
| e | 以 | |
| tsae | 再 | further |
| këaou | 叫 | call |
| yih | 一 | one |
| ko | 個 | |
| jin | 人 | person |
| sëang | 相 | mutual |
| pang | 帮 | help |
| yay | 也 | also |
| she | 使 | do. |
| teh. | 得 | |

Every day you must wash the floors, wipe the tables and chairs, dust the dust off, and sweep the rooms. I will not have a particle of dirt about.

| | | |
|---|---|---|
| T'ëen | 天 | Daily |
| t'ëen | 天 | |
| too | 都 | all |
| yaou | 要 | want |
| se | 洗 | wash |
| low | 樓 | floor |
| pan | 板 | |
| shih | 拭 | wipe down |
| choh | 桌 | table |
| e | 椅 | chair |
| tan | 撣 | dust |
| hwuy | 灰 | dust |
| ch'in | 塵 | |
| ta | 打 | sweep |
| saou | 掃 | |
| fang | 房 | house |
| uh | 屋 | |
| puh | 不 | not |
| yaou | 要 | must |
| yew | 有 | have |
| yih | 一 | one |
| tëen | 點 | particle |
| urh | 兒 | — |
| ngang | 骯 | dirt. |
| tsang. | 髒 | |

After meals you should forthwith take the dishes and cups,

wash them clean, and wipe them dry. The silver spoons, knives, and forks should also be rubbed bright and put by, and they will be the more ready when wanted.

| | | |
|---|---|---|
| Ch'ih | 吃 | Eat |
| fan | 飯 | rice |
| how | 後 | after |
| suy | 隨 | forthwith |
| she | 時 | |
| tsew | 就 | then |
| pa | 把 | take |
| p'an | 盤 | dish |
| wan | 碗 | cup |
| se | 洗 | wash |
| tsing | 净 | clean |
| ma | 抹 | wipe |
| kan | 乾 | dry |
| yin | 銀 | silver |
| ch'*e* | 匙 | spoon |
| taou | 刀 | knife |
| ch'a | 叉 | fork |
| too | 都 | all |
| yaou | 要 | want |
| mo | 磨 | rub |
| kwang | 光 | bright |
| show | 收 | put by |
| kh'e | 起 | |
| lae | 來 | come |
| yung | 用 | use— |
| she | 時 | time |
| yay | 也 | also |
| fang | 方 | convenient. |
| pëen. | 便 | |

The silver and other household furniture in use must daily be arranged, and taken count of with care, and in the event of any being missing, they should forthwith be enquired for and searched after; so as to prevent their being entirely lost.

| | | |
|---|---|---|
| So | 所 | That which |
| yung | 用 | use |
| teih | 的 | of |
| yin | 銀 | silver |
| kh'e | 器 | utensils |
| këa | 傢 | household furniture |
| ho | 伙 | |
| jih | 日 | daily |
| jih | 日 | |
| yaou | 要 | must |
| lew | 留 | use |
| sin | 心 | care |
| këen | 檢 | arrange |
| tëen | 點 | count |
| joo | 如 | if |
| kwo | 果 | indeed |
| puh | 不 | not |
| këen | 見 | see |
| leaou | 了 | — |
| suy | 隨 | forthwith |
| she | 時 | |
| tsew | 就 | then |
| yaou | 要 | must |
| ch'a | 查 | enquire |
| wăn | 問 | |
| chaou | 找 | seek for |
| tsin | 尋 | |

| | | |
|---|---|---|
| ts'ae | 纔 | so as |
| puh | 不 | not |
| che | 致 | lead to |
| shih | 失 | lose. |
| loh. | 落 | |

When any thing is lost, the master should forthwith be told of it, lest with lapse of time there be less and less trace of the lost article, and more difficulty in looking for it.

| | | |
|---|---|---|
| T'ang | 倘 | If |
| jen | 然 | |
| puh | 不 | not |
| këen | 見 | seen |
| lëaou | 了 | |
| tung | 東 | thing |
| se | 西 | |
| leih | 立 | at once |
| she | 時 | |
| tsew | 就 | then |
| kaou | 告 | tell |
| soo | 訴 | |
| tung | 東 | master |
| këa | 家 | |
| kh'ung | 恐 | fear |
| p'a | 怕 | |
| jih | 日 | day |
| kew | 久 | lapse |
| yüeh | 越 | more |
| fah | 發 | |
| muh | 沒 | not |
| yew | 有 | have |
| tsung | 踪 | trace |
| tseih | 跡 | |

| | | |
|---|---|---|
| kăng | 更 | still more |
| këa | 加 | add |
| nan | 難 | difficulty |
| chaou | 找 | seek. |
| lëaou. | 了 | |

In the event of dishes, cups, or anything else being broken, you must instantly tell of it, otherwise, you will have to make good every thing you lose or destroy.

| | | |
|---|---|---|
| Joh | 若 | If |
| she | 是 | is |
| p'an | 盤 | dish |
| wan | 碗 | cup |
| koh | 各 | each |
| yang | 樣 | kind |
| teih | 的 | of |
| tung | 東 | thing |
| se | 西 | |
| ta | 打 | break |
| p'o | 破 | |
| lëaou | 了 | — |
| ying | 應 | ought |
| kae | 該 | |
| leih | 立 | instantly |
| kh'eh | 刻 | |
| kaou | 告 | tell |
| soo | 訴 | |
| puh | 不 | not |
| jen | 然 | indeed |
| lung | 弄 | destroy |
| hwae | 壞 | |
| hwoh | 或 | or |

| | | |
|---|---|---|
| shih | 失 | } lose |
| loh | 落 | |
| lëaou | 了 | have |
| too | 都 | all |
| yaou | 要 | require |
| ne | 你 | } you |
| măn | 們 | |
| p'ay | 賠 | } make good. |
| teih. | 的 | |

After, a meal is over, fold up all table cloths and napkins nicely, and put them away in the press ready for to-morrow's use.

| | | |
|---|---|---|
| Ch'ih | 吃 | Eat |
| wan | 完 | finish |
| lëaou | 了 | have |
| fan | 飯 | rice |
| pa | 把 | take |
| choh | 桌 | table |
| poo | 布 | cloth |
| show | 手 | hand |
| kin | 巾 | napkin |
| cheh | 摺 | fold |
| haou | 好 | nicely |
| show | 收 | put away |
| tsae | 在 | into |
| kwuy | 櫃 | press |
| le | 裡 | inside |
| ming | 明 | } to-morrow |
| t'ëen | 天 | |
| tsae | 再 | again |
| yung. | 用 | use. |

When you wish to wipe the plates and cups, coarse cloths may be used; you must on no account use table cloths and napkins, for the purpose.

| | | |
|---|---|---|
| Yaou | 要 | Wish |
| shih | 拭 | wipe |
| p'an | 盤 | plate |
| wan | 碗 | cup |
| chih | 只 | only |
| kh'o | 可 | may |
| yung | 用 | use |
| ts'oo | 粗 | coarse |
| poo | 布 | cloth |
| twan | 斷 | } on no account |
| puh | 不 | |
| haou | 好 | well |
| yung | 用 | use |
| choh | 桌 | table |
| poo | 布 | cloth |
| ho | 和 | and |
| show | 手 | hand |
| kin | 巾 | napkin |
| shih | 拭 | } wipe |
| ma | 抹 | |
| p'an | 盤 | plate |
| wan. | 碗 | cup. |

Of table cloths, napkins, and coarse cloths, I have changes for once or twice in the week, and I will give them to you.

| | | |
|---|---|---|
| Choh | 桌 | Table |
| poo | 布 | cloth |
| t'ung | 同 | with |
| show | 手 | hand |
| kin | 巾 | napkin |

ts'oo 粗 coarse
poo 布 cloths
wo 我 I
too 都 all
yew 有 have
may 每 each
yih 一 } one
ko 個 }
le 禮 } week
pae 拜 }
hwan 換 change
yih 一 one
hwuy 囘 time
hwoh 或 or
lëang 兩 two
hwuy 囘 time
tăng 等 wait
wo 我 I
na 拿 take
kay 給 give
ne. 你 you.

The glass lamps require to be carefully attended to, and filled with wicks; after which their oil should be replenished, and they should be rubbed clean.

Po 玻 } Glass
le 璃 }
teih 的 of
tăng 燈 lamp
t'ae 臺 stand
yaou 要 want
sëaou 小 } careful
sin 心 }
show 收 } attention
shih 拾 }
lung 弄 fix
haou 好 proper
tăng 燈 lamp
sin 心 wick
jen 然 } afterwards
how 後 }
tsae 再 further
t'ëen 添 add
yew 油 oil
ts'ah 擦 rub
kan 乾 } clean.
tsing. 净 }

The hanging and bracket lamps must all have their oil replenished and be rubbed clean, and of course they will be ready by evening when the lighting times comes.

Kwa 掛 Hanging
tăng 燈 lamp
t'ung 同 and
peih 壁 wall
tăng 燈 lamp
too 都 all
yaou 要 want
t'ëen 添 add
mwan 滿 full
yew 油 oil
ts'ah 擦 rub
kan 乾 } clean
tsing 净 }
tăng 等 wait

| | | |
|---|---|---|
| taou | 到 | till |
| wan | 晚 | evening |
| shang | 上 | |
| tëen | 點 | light |
| teih | 的 | that which |
| she | 時 | time |
| how | 候 | |
| kh'e | 豈 | how |
| puh | 不 | not |
| fang | 方 | convenient |
| pëen | 便 | |
| mo | 麽 | ? |

When the guests are departed, and the house-hold are about to retire for the night, it is important that all lights should be blown out or extinguished thro-out the house, and then having securely barred the front and back doors, you may go up to bed and sleep.

| | | |
|---|---|---|
| Kh'eh | 客 | Guest |
| san | 散 | departed |
| lëaou | 了 | |
| këa | 家 | house |
| jin | 人 | people |
| măn | 們 | |
| yaou | 要 | want |
| shuy | 睡 | sleep |
| teih | 的 | that which |
| she | 時 | time |
| how | 候 | |
| yaou | 要 | important |
| kin | 緊 | |

| | | |
|---|---|---|
| ch'uy | 吹 | blow |
| mëeh | 滅 | extinguish |
| koh | 各 | every |
| ch'oo | 處 | place |
| teih | 的 | of |
| tăng | 燈 | light |
| ho | 火 | fire |
| shen | 閂 | bar |
| haou | 好 | complete |
| lëaou | 了 | finish |
| tsëen | 前 | front |
| how | 後 | back |
| teih | 的 | of |
| măn | 門 | door |
| tsae | 再 | then |
| shang | 上 | go up |
| ch'wang | 床 | bed |
| kh'eu | 去 | go |
| shuy | 睡 | sleep. |
| këaou. | 覺 | |

Find out some bread making establishment, and order them to sent two loaves daily, for which payment shall be made at the end of the month.

| | | |
|---|---|---|
| Chaou | 找 | Seek |
| yih | 一 | one |
| këa | 家 | house |
| tso | 做 | make |
| mëen | 麵 | bread |
| paou | 飽 | |
| teih | 的 | that which |
| këaou | 叫 | tell |
| t'a | 他 | them |

| | | |
|---|---|---|
| t'ëen | 天 | daily |
| t'ëen | 天 | |
| sung | 送 | send |
| lëang | 兩 | two |
| ko | 個 | piece |
| man | 饅 | bread |
| t'ow | 頭 | loaf |
| lae | 來 | come |
| taou | 到 | come to |
| lëaou | 了 | |
| yüeh | 月 | month |
| te | 底 | close |
| kay | 給 | give |
| ts'ëen. | 錢 | money. |

Also order the milk man every day to bring one catty of milk, and to sent in his account monthly.

| | | |
|---|---|---|
| Tsae | 再 | Also |
| făn | 吩 | order |
| foo | 咐 | |
| mae | 賣 | sell |
| new | 牛 | cow |
| nae | 奶 | milk |
| teih | 的 | that which |
| këaou | 叫 | tell |
| t'a | 他 | him |
| may | 每 | every |
| jih | 日 | day |
| tae | 帶 | bring |
| yih | 一 | one |
| kin | 斤 | catty |
| new | 牛 | cow |
| nae | 奶 | milk |
| lae | 來 | come |
| ngan | 按 | by |
| yüeh | 月 | month |
| swan | 算 | reckon |
| chang. | 賬 | account. |

Tell the vegetable man also to bring daily several sorts of vegetables for me to choose from, settling for them at the end of the month.

| | | |
|---|---|---|
| Këaou | 叫 | Tell |
| mae | 賣 | sell |
| ts'ae | 菜 | vegetable |
| teih | 的 | that which |
| yay | 也 | also |
| t'ëen | 天 | daily |
| t'ëen | 天 | |
| tan | 擔 | carry |
| ke | 幾 | several |
| yang | 樣 | kinds |
| lae | 來 | come |
| suy | 隨 | follow |
| wo | 我 | I |
| këen | 揀 | choose |
| shin | 甚 | what |
| mo | 麽 | |
| taou | 到 | arrive at |
| yüeh | 月 | month |
| te | 底 | end |
| swan | 算 | reckon |
| chang. | 賬 | account. |

Every day after breakfast, bring your account to me of all money spent on the previous day, and when I have looked over it with you, the account shall be paid. I will at the same time tell you what I want prepared for that day, or what I wish to have to eat.

| | | |
|---|---|---|
| T'ëen | 天 | Daily |
| t'ëen | 天 | |
| tsaou | 早 | morning |
| fan | 飯 | meal |
| how | 後 | after |
| pa | 把 | take |
| ne | 你 | you |
| t'ow | 頭 | previous |
| yih | 一 | |
| t'ëen | 天 | day |
| so | 所 | that which |
| yung | 用 | use |
| teih | 的 | of |
| ts'ëen | 錢 | cash |
| chang | 賬 | account book |
| poo | 簿 | |
| na | 拿 | bring |
| lae | 來 | come |
| t'ung | 同 | with |
| ne | 你 | you |
| swan | 算 | count |
| kwo | 過 | have |
| kay | 給 | give |
| ts'ëen | 錢 | money |
| na | 那 | that |
| she | 時 | time |
| wo | 我 | I |
| tsew | 就 | then |
| kaou | 告 | tell |
| soo | 訴 | |
| ne | 你 | you |
| jih | 日 | day |
| le | 裡 | in |
| yaou | 要 | want |
| yü | 預 | prepare |
| pe | 備 | |
| shin | 甚 | what |
| mo | 麽 | |
| yaou | 要 | want |
| ch'ih | 吃 | eat |
| shin | 甚 | what |
| mo | 麽 | |
| tung | 東 | thing. |
| se. | 西 | |

If you do not tell me day by day what you may have expended on the previous day, and if you take on yourself to purchase anything without my authority, I will not recognize the expenditure, and will order you to make it good.

| | | |
|---|---|---|
| Kin | 今 | To-day |
| t'ëen | 天 | |
| yung | 用 | use |
| teih | 的 | that which |
| ts'ëen | 錢 | cash |
| ming | 明 | to-morrow |
| t'ëen | 天 | |
| puh | 不 | not |
| kaou | 告 | tell |
| soo | 訴 | |

wo 我 me
che 知 } know
taou 道 }
hwoh 或 or
ne 你 you
tsze 自 } yourself
ke 已 }
teih 的 of
choo 主 } responsibility
e 意 }
yaou 要 want
mae 買 buy
shin 甚 } what
mo 麽 }
wuh 物 } thing
këen 件 }
wo 我 I
puh 不 not
năng 能 can
jin 認 recognize
chang 賬 account
këaou 叫 make
ne 你 you
p'ay. 賠 make good.

Go and look out for cook and a coolie for me, and, if anything is wrong, I shall only hold you responsible.

Ne 你 You
kh'eu 去 go
t'e 替 for
wo 我 me
chaou 找 look out
yih 一 } one
ko 個 }
ch'oo 廚 } cook
tsze 子 }
t'ung 同 and
yih 一 } one
ko 個 }
sëaou 小 small
kung 工 work
jin 人 man
joh 若 if
yew 有 have
shin 甚 } any
mo 麽 }
ch'a 差 } wrong
ts'o 錯 }
yaou 要 want
wei 惟 only
ne 你 you
she 試 } enquire.
wăn. 問 }

In buying things be sure to weigh them carefully; for when you bring them home, I will re-weigh them, and if there is any deficiency in the weight, I will call on you to make it good.

Mae 買 Buy
tung 東 } things
se 西 }
tsung 總 certainly
yaou 要 must
ch'ing 稱 weigh
kow 彀 sufficient
na 拿 bring
hwuy 回 return
këa 家 house

| | | |
|---|---|---|
| le | 裡 | inside |
| wo | 我 | I |
| tsae | 再 | again |
| ch'ing | 稱 | weigh |
| kwo | 過 | |
| joo | 如 | if |
| joh | 若 | |
| shaou | 少 | deficient |
| lëaou | 了 | have |
| puh | 不 | not |
| kow | 彀 | up to |
| făn | 分 | weight |
| lëang | 兩 | |
| tsew | 就 | then |
| yaou | 要 | want |
| këaou | 叫 | call upon |
| ne | 你 | you |
| p'ay. | 賠 | make good. |

In purchasing anything you must always state its true price, should I find out in the street that you have been cheating me, I shall be displeased with you and fine you.

| | | |
|---|---|---|
| Mae | 買 | Buy |
| shin | 甚 | any |
| mo | 麽 | |
| tung | 西 | thing |
| se | 東 | |
| too | 都 | all |
| yaou | 要 | want |
| shwoh | 說 | tell |
| shih | 實 | true |
| tsae | 在 | |
| teih | 的 | that which |
| këa | 價 | price |
| ts'ëen | 錢 | |
| wo | 我 | I |
| taou | 到 | go to |
| keae | 街 | street |
| shang | 上 | upon |
| t'ang | 倘 | if |
| jen | 然 | |
| wăn | 問 | find |
| ch'uh | 出 | out |
| lae | 來 | come |
| she | 是 | is |
| mwan | 瞞 | blind |
| p'ëen | 騙 | deceive |
| wo | 我 | I |
| tsew | 就 | then |
| puh | 不 | not |
| e | 依 | approve |
| ne | 你 | you |
| fah | 罰 | mulct |
| ne. | 你 | you. |

If other people cheat me, you should tell me of it at once, so as to prevent my losing by it. I can thereupon abuse them, and admonish them to amend their ways, and that as men they should be honest.

| | | |
|---|---|---|
| Joh | 若 | If |
| yew | 有 | have |
| pëeh | 別 | other |
| jin | 人 | man |
| p'ëen | 騙 | cheat |
| wo | 我 | me |
| ne | 你 | you |

| | | |
|---|---|---|
| tsew | 就 | then |
| ma | 馬 | forthwith |
| shang | 上 | |
| kaou | 告 | tell |
| soo | 訴 | |
| wo | 我 | me |
| mëen | 免 | prevent |
| teh | 得 | obtain |
| wo | 我 | I |
| ch'ih | 吃 | receive |
| kh'wuy | 虧 | loss |
| wo | 我 | I |
| hwoh | 或 | perhaps |
| she | 是 | is |
| shwoh | 說 | abuse |
| t'a | 他 | him |
| kh'euen | 勸 | admonish |
| t'a | 他 | him |
| kae | 改 | alter |
| kwo | 過 | pass |
| wei | 爲 | be |
| jin | 人 | man |
| tsung | 總 | certainly |
| yaou | 要 | should |
| laou | 老 | honest |
| shih | 實 | |
| ts'ae | 纔 | then |
| haou. | 好 | well. |

You must not be afraid of other people's injuring you, nor covet gain for yourself. If you be honest, faithful, and sincere, your good character will be raised, and your master will be pleased with you.

| | | |
|---|---|---|
| Ne | 你 | You |
| puh | 不 | not |
| yaou | 要 | must |
| p'a | 怕 | fear |
| show | 受 | receive |
| jin | 人 | people |
| teih | 的 | of |
| kh'e | 欺 | injure |
| puh | 不 | not |
| haou | 好 | well |
| t'an | 貪 | covet |
| le | 利 | gain |
| ne | 你 | you |
| joh | 若 | if |
| chung | 忠 | honest |
| how | 厚 | faithful |
| laou | 老 | sincere |
| shih | 實 | |
| ming | 名 | character |
| shing | 聲 | |
| yay | 也 | also |
| haou | 好 | good |
| tung | 東 | master |
| këa | 家 | |
| yay | 也 | also |
| hwan | 歡 | approve. |
| he. | 喜 | |

I will by and by give you an addition to your wages, and when you go to some other family, I will write you a testimonial, which will be sure to be of advantage to you.

| | | |
|---|---|---|
| Wo | 我 | I |

| | | |
|---|---|---|
| tsëang | 將 | by and by |
| lae | 來 | |
| kay | 給 | give |
| ne | 你 | you |
| këa | 加 | add |
| kung | 工 | wages |
| ts'ëen | 錢 | |
| tsew | 就 | when |
| she | 是 | is |
| taou | 到 | go to |
| pëeh | 別 | other |
| këa | 家 | family |
| wo | 我 | I |
| kh'o | 可 | can |
| e | 以 | |
| sëay | 寫 | write |
| chang | 張 | slip |
| p'ing | 憑 | testimonial |
| keu | 據 | |
| paou | 保 | insure |
| ne | 你 | you |
| tsung | 總 | certain |
| yew | 有 | have |
| haou | 好 | advantage. |
| ch'oo. | 處 | |

I am asking some friends to dinner to-day. You must have the reception hall and other rooms swept clean and put in order within and without, and go quickly into the street to buy a leg of mutton if you can find one. You must choose a fat delicate hind leg, weighing somewhere about ten catties.

| | | |
|---|---|---|
| Kin | 今 | To-day |
| t'ëen | 天 | |
| wo | 我 | I |
| yaou | 要 | want |
| ts'ing | 請 | invite |
| p'ăng | 朋 | friends |
| yew | 友 | |
| ch'ih | 吃 | eat |
| fan | 飯 | rice |
| t'ing | 廳 | hall |
| fang | 房 | room |
| le | 裏 | inside |
| wae | 外 | outside |
| too | 都 | all |
| yaou | 要 | want |
| ta | 打 | sweep |
| saou | 掃 | |
| këeh | 潔 | clean |
| tsing | 净 | |
| show | 收 | arrange |
| shih | 拾 | |
| ts'e | 齊 | in order |
| ching | 整 | |
| kh'wae | 快 | quickly |
| taou | 到 | go to |
| keae | 街 | street |
| shang | 上 | upon |
| kh'an | 看 | look out |
| yew | 有 | have |
| yang | 羊 | sheep |
| t'uy | 腿 | leg |
| mae | 買 | buy |
| yih | 一 | one |
| t'ëaou | 條 | |

hwuy 囘 come
lae 來 back
yaou 要 must
këen 揀 select
na 那 a
fei 肥 fat
năn 嫩 delicate
teih 的 that which
how 後 hind
t'uy 腿 leg
yoh 約 } about
moh 摸 }
yew 有 have
shih 拾 ten
kin 觔 catty
chung 重 heavy
teih. 的 that which.

See too if you can get a turkey or a capon, and if you can find a fat large one, roast it, and have a dish of ham to go with it. Buy also six chickens, of which take one and make soup of it; one, chop up into force-meat balls; one, convert into cutlets; one, make curry of; one, cut into pieces, and having strung them on a bamboo and added pepper and salt, fry them in lard.

Tsae 再 Also
kh'an 看 look
yew 有 have
ho 火 } turkey
ke 雞 }
hwoh 或 or
sëen 鮮 } capon
ke 雞 }
yaou 要 want
t'ëaou 挑 } choose
sëen 選 }
fei 肥 fat
ta 大 large
teih 的 that which
ts'ae 纔 then
haou 好 well
shaou 燒 } roast
kh'aou 烤 }
tsae 再 and
p'ay 配 add
yih 一 one
yang 樣 kind
ho 火 } ham
t'uy 腿 }
ling 另 besides
mae 買 buy
lëuh 六 } six
chih 隻 }
sëaou 小 } chicken
ke 雞 }
na 拏 take
yih 一 } one
chih 隻 }
tso 做 make
t'ang 湯 soup
yih 一 } one
chih 隻 }
toh 剁 chop
jow 肉 meat
wan 丸 ball

yih 一 } one
chih 隻 }
tso 做 make
jow 肉 } cutlets
p'ëen 片 }
yih 一 } one
chih 隻 }
tso 做 make
hwang 黃 } curry
këang 羌 }
yih 一 } one
chih 隻 }
ts'ëeh 切 cut
kh'wae 塊 piece
yung 用 use
chuh 竹 bamboo
ch'üen 串 } string
haou 好 }
sëen 先 first
sa 撒 spread
hoo 胡 } pepper
tsëaou 椒 }
yen 鹽 salt
tsae 再 then
yung 用 use
yew 油 lard
tsëen. 煎 fry.

The chicken which yet remains have chopped up into a force-meat ball, and having hollowed out some cucumbers, stuff them with it, and serve them when cooked.

Han 還 Yet
yew 有 have
yih 一 one
chih 隻 more
toh 剁 chop
ch'ing 成 make
lëaou 了 have
jow 肉 meat
ping 餅 ball
pa 把 take
hwang 黃 } cucumber
kwa 瓜 }
wah 挖 hollow out
kh'ung 空 empty
jang 鑲 stuff
tsae 在 in
le 裏 } inside
t'ow 頭 }
choo 煮 boil
shuh 熟 done
na 拿 bring
lae. 來 come.

I shall want besides a number of vegetables, such as potatoes, peas, carrots, turnips, Corean cabbage, broad-beans, beans, greens, mustard, brinjal, yams, and parsley: these vegetables are all to be had in the market, and when you have procured them, you may please yourself as to how you dress them, whether by boiling or by frying, only let them be properly cooked.

Han 還 Yet
yaou 要 want

| | | |
|---|---|---|
| koh | 各 | every |
| yang | 樣 | kind |
| ts'ae | 菜 | vegetable |
| soo | 蔬 | |
| tsew | 就 | such as |
| she | 是 | |
| ho | 荷 | Dutch |
| lan | 蘭 | |
| shoo | 薯 | potatoes |
| ho | 荷 | Dutch |
| lan | 蘭 | |
| tow | 荳 | peas |
| hung | 紅 | red |
| lo | 蘿 | carrot |
| poh | 蔔 | |
| peh | 白 | white |
| lo | 蘿 | carrot |
| poh | 蔔 | |
| kaou | 高 | Corea |
| le | 麗 | |
| ts'ae | 菜 | greens |
| pëen | 扁 | broad beans |
| tow | 荳 | |
| ts'an | 蠶 | kidney beans |
| tow | 荳 | |
| peh | 白 | greens |
| ts'ae | 菜 | |
| keae | 芥 | mustard |
| ts'ae | 菜 | |
| keae | 茄 | brinjal |
| tsze | 子 | |
| yü | 芋 | taro |
| t'ow | 頭 | |
| shan | 山 | yams |
| shoo | 薯 | |

| | | |
|---|---|---|
| t'ung | 同 | and |
| kh'in | 芹 | parsley |
| ts'ae | 菜 | |
| chay | 這 | this |
| sëay | 些 | few |
| yang | 樣 | kind |
| ts'ae | 菜 | vegetables |
| keae | 街 | market |
| she | 市 | |
| shang | 上 | upon |
| too | 都 | all |
| yew | 有 | have |
| teih | 的 | that which |
| mae | 買 | buy |
| lëaou | 了 | have |
| hwuy | 回 | return |
| lae | 來 | come |
| kae | 該 | must |
| choo | 煮 | boil |
| teih | 的 | that which |
| kae | 該 | must |
| tsëen | 煎 | fry |
| teih | 的 | that which |
| suy | 隨 | follow |
| ne | 你 | you |
| kh'eu | 去 | go |
| lung | 弄 | dress |
| tsung | 總 | only |
| yaou | 要 | must |
| hoh | 合 | proper. |
| shih. | 式 | |

Besides I want you to buy all sorts of fruit to be used after the meal; such as apples, plums, peaches, dates, pears, arbutus, cherries, apricots, loquats, sugar-cane, lotus-roots, grapes, and so on.

| | | |
|---|---|---|
| Ling | 另 | Besides |
| wae | 外 | |
| han | 還 | yet |
| yaou | 要 | want |
| mae | 買 | buy |
| shuy | 水 | fruit |
| kwo | 菓 | |
| ch'ih | 吃 | eat |
| kwo | 過 | have |
| fan | 飯 | rice |
| yung | 用 | use |
| teih | 的 | that which |
| hwoh | 或 | such as |
| p'ing | 平 | apple |
| kwo | 菓 | |
| le | 李 | plum |
| tsze | 子 | |
| t'aou | 桃 | peach |
| tsze | 子 | |
| tsaou | 棗 | date |
| tsze | 子 | |
| sëueh | 雪 | pear |
| le | 梨 | |
| yang | 楊 | arbutus |
| may | 梅 | |
| ying | 櫻 | cherry |
| t'aou | 桃 | |
| may | 梅 | apricot |
| tsze | 子 | |
| p'e | 枇 | loquat |
| p'a | 杷 | |
| kan | 甘 | sugar cane |
| chay | 蔗 | |
| lëen | 蓮 | lotus root |
| ngow | 藕 | |
| p'oo | 葡 | grape |
| t'aou | 萄 | |
| koh | 各 | every |
| yang. | 樣 | kind. |

I also want preserved dates, raisins, candied oranges, Kumquats, Buddhist fist lemon, candied ginger, and all sorts of candied fruits.

| | | |
|---|---|---|
| Han | 還 | Also |
| yaou | 要 | want |
| meih | 蜜 | sugared |
| tsaou | 棗 | dates |
| p'oo | 葡 | grape |
| t'aou | 萄 | |
| kan | 乾 | dry |
| meih | 蜜 | candied |
| kan | 柑 | orange |
| kin | 金 | kumquat |
| këuh | 橘 | |
| fuh | 佛 | Buddha |
| show | 手 | fist |
| t'ang | 糖 | candied |
| këang | 薑 | ginger |
| t'ung | 同 | and |
| koh | 各 | every |
| yang | 樣 | sort |
| t'ang | 糖 | candied |
| kwo. | 菓 | fruits. |

When the guests have all arrived at six o'clock in the evening, then set on the dishes and bring in the dinner. All the different dishes and dessert fruit must be properly prepared beforehand, so that when the time comes there may be no mistake.

| | | |
|---|---|---|
| Wan | 晚 | Evening |
| shang | 上 | |
| lëuh | 六 | six |
| tëen | 點 | strike |
| chung | 鐘 | clock |
| jin | 人 | guest |
| kh'eh | 客 | |
| lae | 來 | come |
| ts'e | 齊 | collected |
| lëaou | 了 | have |
| tsew | 就 | then |
| yaou | 要 | must |
| shang | 上 | set |
| ts'ae | 菜 | dishes |
| kh'ae | 開 | begin |
| fan | 飯 | meal |
| so | 所 | that which |
| yew | 有 | have |
| ts'ae | 菜 | dishes |
| soo | 蔬 | |
| kwo | 菓 | fruits |
| p'in | 品 | |
| too | 都 | all |
| yaou | 要 | want |
| yü | 預 | beforehand |
| pay | 備 | |
| t'o | 妥 | proper |
| tang | 當 | |
| taou | 到 | arrive |
| na | 那 | that |
| she | 時 | time |
| how | 候 | |
| ts'eeh | 切 | on no account |
| puh | 不 | |
| kh'o | 可 | may |
| woo | 悞 | mistake |
| lëaou. | 了 | — |

First take the table and place it in the centre of the great hall; then set seats for twenty people together, with knives, forks, large and small plates, wine-glasses, and so on.

| | | |
|---|---|---|
| Sëen | 先 | First |
| pa | 把 | take |
| choh | 桌 | table |
| tsze | 子 | |
| pae | 擺 | place |
| tsae | 在 | in |
| ta | 大 | large |
| t'ing | 廳 | hall |
| chung | 中 | centre |
| këen | 間 | |
| tsae | 再 | then |
| pae | 擺 | set |
| urh | 二 | twenty |
| shih | 十 | |
| jin | 人 | man |
| teih | 的 | — |
| tso | 坐 | seat |
| wei | 位 | |
| ho | 和 | together with |
| na | 那 | the |

| | | |
|---|---|---|
| taou | 刀 | knife |
| ch'a | 叉 | fork |
| p'an | 盤 | plate |
| t'eeh | 碟 | small plate |
| tsew | 酒 | wine |
| pay | 盃 | glass |
| koh | 各 | every |
| yang. | 様 | kind. |

These transparent glass decanters are for holding Sherry, the black bottles for Port. The Claret, Rhemish wine and Champagne, place on the side table, and when any visitor wishes to partake of them, then offer him some.

| | | |
|---|---|---|
| Chay | 這 | This |
| t'ow | 透 | transparent |
| lëang | 亮 | |
| teih | 的 | that which |
| peh | 白 | white |
| po | 玻 | glass |
| le | 璃 | |
| p'ing | 瓶 | bottle |
| she | 是 | is |
| chwang | 裝 | hold |
| p'oo | 葡 | grape |
| t'aou | 萄 | |
| tan | 淡 | light |
| hung | 紅 | red |
| tsew | 酒 | wine |
| teih | 的 | that which |
| heh | 黑 | black |
| po | 玻 | glass |
| le | 璃 | |
| p'ing | 瓶 | bottle |
| she | 是 | is |
| chwang | 裝 | hold |
| p'oo | 葡 | grape |
| t'aou | 萄 | |
| ts'ing | 青 | purple |
| tsew | 酒 | wine |
| teih | 的 | that which |
| na | 那 | that |
| heh | 黑 | black |
| tsew | 酒 | wine |
| swan | 酸 | sour |
| tsew | 酒 | wine |
| t'ung | 同 | and |
| na | 那 | that |
| san | 三 | champagne |
| pëen | 變 | |
| tsew | 酒 | wine |
| too | 都 | all |
| fang | 放 | place |
| pae | 在 | on |
| p'ang | 旁 | side |
| pëen | 邊 | |
| choh | 桌 | table |
| tsze | 子 | |
| shang | 上 | upon |
| jin | 人 | visitors |
| kh'eh | 客 | |
| yaou | 要 | want |
| hoh | 喝 | drink |
| tsew | 就 | then |
| te | 遞 | offer |
| kay | 給 | give |
| t'a. | 他 | him. |

You must wait alongside, and watch when any guest wants wine, pour him out some at once, giving him whatever wine he may like.

| | | |
|---|---|---|
| Ne | 你 | You |
| tsae | 在 | at |
| p'ang | 旁 | side |
| pëen | 邊 | |
| sze | 伺 | wait |
| how | 候 | |
| kh'an | 看 | look |
| na | 那 | which |
| wei | 位 | gentleman |
| kh'eh | 客 | guest |
| yaou | 要 | want |
| hoh | 喝 | drink |
| tsew | 酒 | wine |
| tsew | 就 | immediately |
| chin | 斟 | pour |
| kay | 給 | give |
| t'a | 他 | him |
| yew | 由 | according to |
| t'a | 他 | he |
| ngae | 愛 | like |
| hoh | 喝 | drink |
| shin | 甚 | what |
| mo | 麽 | |
| tsew | 酒 | wine |
| suy | 隨 | follow |
| t'a | 他 | his |
| teih | 的 | |
| pëen. | 便 | convenience. |

And when the guests have finished eating one kind of dish, you must give them a change of clean plates, knives and forks.

| | | |
|---|---|---|
| Jin | 人 | Guests |
| kh'eh | 客 | |
| măn | 們 | |
| ch'ih | 吃 | eat |
| wan | 完 | finish |
| lëaou | 了 | have |
| yih | 一 | one |
| yang | 樣 | kind |
| tung | 東 | thing |
| se | 西 | |
| tsew | 就 | then |
| yaou | 要 | must |
| ling | 另 | other |
| hwan | 換 | change |
| kan | 乾 | clean |
| tsing | 淨 | |
| teih | 的 | that which |
| tëeh | 碟 | plate |
| tsze | 子 | |
| taou | 刀 | knife |
| ch'a. | 叉 | fork. |

When dinner is ready, and everything is quite prepared, you must come and tell me, that I may invite the guests to go in with me to the feast.

| | | |
|---|---|---|
| Ta | 大 | Dinner |
| ts'an | 飡 | |
| tso | 作 | make |
| haou | 好 | ready |
| lëaou | 了 | have |

| | | |
|---|---|---|
| yang | 樣 | everything |
| yang | 樣 | |
| pay | 備 | prepare |
| pan | 辦 | |
| ts'e | 齊 | complete |
| ts'euen | 全 | |
| ne | 你 | you |
| tsew | 就 | then |
| lae | 來 | come |
| kaou | 告 | tell |
| soo | 訴 | |
| wo | 我 | me |
| che | 知 | know |
| taou | 道 | |
| wo | 我 | I |
| haou | 好 | well |
| yaou | 邀 | invite |
| kh'eh | 客 | guest |
| lae | 來 | come |
| foo | 赴 | go |
| seih. | 席 | banquet. |

When we sit down to dinner, you must stand aside, and watch whether your master or a guest says grace; then when grace is over, take off the cover from the soup tureen, and as your master ladles the soup out into the soup plates, you must distribute these to the several guests, removing all when the guests have finished.

| | | |
|---|---|---|
| Shang | 上 | Go up |
| seih | 席 | feast |
| teih | 的 | that which |
| she | 時 | time |
| how | 候 | |
| ne | 你 | you |
| chen | 站 | stand |
| tsae | 在 | at |
| p'ang | 旁 | side |
| pëen | 邊 | |
| sëen | 先 | first |
| kh'an | 看 | observe |
| tung | 東 | master |
| këa | 家 | |
| hwoh | 或 | or |
| she | 是 | is |
| kh'eh | 客 | guest |
| nëen | 念 | say |
| king | 經 | prayer |
| puh | 不 | not |
| nëen | 念 | say |
| joh | 若 | if |
| she | 是 | is |
| nëen | 念 | say |
| king | 經 | prayer |
| wan | 完 | finish |
| lëaou | 了 | have |
| ne | 你 | you |
| tsew | 就 | then |
| tsëeh | 接 | take off |
| kh'ae | 開 | |
| t'ang | 湯 | soup |
| tow | 斗 | tureen |
| kae | 蓋 | cover |
| tăng | 等 | wait |
| tung | 東 | master |
| këa | 家 | |

yaou 舀 ladle
t'ang 湯 soup
tsae 在 into
t'ang 湯 soup
p'ăn 盆 plate
le 裡 inside
făn 分 distribute
sung 送 give
koh 各 every
kh'eh 客 guest
ch'ih 吃 eat
wan 完 finish
too 都 all
ch'eh 撤 } remove
lëaou 了 }
kh'eu. 去 go.

After the soup tureen has been removed, put the fish on the table with potatoes, bringing with them the ketchup and fish sauce likewise.

Ch'eh 撤 Remove
lëaou 了 have
t'ang 湯 soup
tow 斗 tureen
tsew 就 then
p'ăng 捧 bring
shang 上 up
yü 魚 fish
t'ung 同 and
ho 荷 } Dutch
lan 蘭 }
shoo 薯 potatoe
lae 來 come
pa 把 take
tsëang 醬 } ketchup
yew 油 }
yü 魚 fish
chih 汁 sauce
yay 也 also
na 拿 bring
lae. 來 come.

When fish has been eaten, change the plates, knives, and forks once more, and then bring on the mutton, poultry, and all kinds of vegetables, after which take the rice and curry, and hand it to each guest to see whether or not he will partake of some.

Ch'ih 吃 Eat
kwo 過 have
lëaou 了 finish
yü 魚 fish
yew 又 then
hwan 換 change
yih 一 one
foo 副 set
taou 刀 knife
ch'a 叉 fork
tëeh 碟 } plate
tsze 子 }
tsew 就 then
p'ăng 捧 offer
yang 羊 } mutton
jow 肉 }
ke 鷄 fowl
yah 鴨 duck

| | | |
|---|---|---|
| ts'ae | 菜 | vegetable |
| soo | 蔬 | |
| koh | 各 | every |
| yang | 樣 | kind |
| pae | 擺 | arrange |
| tsae | 在 | on |
| choh | 桌 | table |
| shang | 上 | upon |
| suy | 隨 | afterwards |
| how | 後 | |
| pa | 把 | take |
| fan | 飯 | rice |
| t'ung | 同 | and |
| hwang | 黃 | curry |
| këang | 薑 | |
| făn | 分 | severally |
| p'ăng | 捧 | hand to |
| koh | 各 | every |
| kh'eh | 客 | guest |
| kh'an | 看 | see |
| t'a | 他 | he |
| yaou | 要 | want |
| puh | 不 | not |
| yaou. | 要 | want. |

After rice has been eaten, have the plates changed for smaller ones, and place on the table the tarts, puddings, custards, pancakes, and all that sort of pastry; and if you happen to have pheasants, wild duck, hare, or any such game delicacies these should be served at this time likewise.

| | | |
|---|---|---|
| Ch'ih | 吃 | Eat |
| kwo | 過 | have |
| lëaou | 了 | finish |
| fan | 飯 | rice |
| hwan | 換 | change |
| sëaou | 小 | small |
| tëeh | 碟 | plate |
| tsze | 子 | |
| tsew | 就 | then |
| pa | 把 | take |
| kwo | 菓 | fruit |
| le | 裡 | inside |
| ping | 餅 | cake |
| paou | 包 | envelope |
| mëen | 麵 | flour |
| kwo | 菓 | fruit |
| new | 牛 | cow |
| nae | 奶 | milk |
| ping | 餅 | cake |
| ke | 鷄 | fowl |
| tan | 蛋 | egg |
| ping | 餅 | cake |
| koh | 各 | every |
| seh | 色 | kind |
| mëen | 麵 | pastry |
| shih | 食 | |
| pae | 擺 | place |
| shang | 上 | on |
| kh'eu | 去 | go |
| joh | 若 | if |
| yew | 有 | have |
| shan | 山 | hill |
| ke | 鷄 | fowl |
| yay | 野 | wild |
| yah | 鴨 | duck |

| | | |
|---|---|---|
| t'oo | 兎 | hare |
| tsze | 子 | |
| chay | 這 | this |
| sëay | 些 | sort |
| yay | 野 | wild |
| we | 味 | delicacy |
| na | 那 | that |
| she | 時 | time |
| how | 候 | |
| yay | 也 | also |
| p'ăng | 棒 | serve |
| shang | 上 | up |
| kh'eu. | 去 | go. |

When the guests have finished eating, have every kind of eatable removed from the table, and take off the table cloth, leaving the decanters and wine-glasses; then serve the dessert, and give the servants whom the guests may have brought with them a hearty meal, but do not allow them to carry anything away with them.

| | | |
|---|---|---|
| Jin | 人 | Guests |
| kh'eh | 客 | |
| măn | 們 | |
| ch'ih | 吃 | eat |
| kwo | 過 | finish |
| che | 之 | of |
| how | 後 | after |
| pa | 把 | take |
| koh | 各 | all |
| yang | 樣 | sort |
| teih | 的 | of |
| ch'ih | 吃 | eatables |
| shih | 食 | |
| ch'eh | 撤 | remove |
| lëaou | 了 | |
| kh'eu | 去 | go |
| na | 拿 | take |
| kh'ae | 開 | off |
| choh | 桌 | table |
| poo | 布 | cloth |
| chih | 只 | only |
| lew | 留 | leave |
| tsew | 酒 | wine |
| p'ing | 瓶 | bottle |
| tsew | 酒 | wine |
| pay | 盃 | glass |
| tsae | 再 | again |
| pa | 把 | take |
| kwo | 菓 | dessert |
| p'in | 品 | |
| na | 拿 | bring |
| lae | 來 | come |
| jin | 人 | guests |
| kh'eh | 客 | |
| tae | 帶 | bring |
| lae | 來 | come |
| teih | 的 | that which |
| kăn | 跟 | serving |
| jin | 人 | man |
| yaou | 要 | want |
| kay | 給 | give |
| t'a | 他 | them |
| măn | 們 | |
| ch'ih | 吃 | eat |
| paou | 飽 | hearty |

| | | |
|---|---|---|
| kh'o | 可 | may |
| puh | 不 | not |
| chun | 准 | allow |
| t'a | 他 | them |
| măn | 們 | |
| tae | 帶 | take |
| hwuy | 回 | back |
| këa | 家 | home |
| kh'eu. | 去 | go. |

When the meal is over, you must count the silver spoons, knives, forks, dishes and plates to see whether they are correct or not, and having done so put them away into the safe. When the guests have left, bar the house door carefully, and having examined every corner, and extinguished the lights in every room, you may then go to bed.

| | | |
|---|---|---|
| Fan | 飯 | Meal |
| how | 後 | after |
| ne | 你 | you |
| tsew | 就 | then |
| këen | 撿 | count |
| tëen | 點 | |
| yin | 銀 | silver |
| che | 匙 | spoon |
| taou | 刀 | knife |
| ch'a | 义 | fork |
| p'ăn | 盤 | dish |
| tëeh | 碟 | plate |
| chaou | 照 | according |
| soo | 數 | number |
| ts'o | 錯 | wrong |
| puh | 不 | not |
| ts'o | 錯 | wrong |
| tsae | 再 | then |
| show | 收 | put away |
| tsae | 在 | into |
| kwuy | 櫃 | safe |
| le | 裡 | inside |
| jin | 人 | guests |
| kh'eh | 客 | |
| măn | 們 | |
| hwuy | 回 | return |
| kh'eu | 去 | go |
| che | 之 | of |
| how | 後 | after |
| yaou | 要 | want |
| shan | 閂 | bar |
| haou | 好 | well |
| ta | 大 | great |
| măn | 門 | door |
| sze | 四 | four |
| ch'oo | 處 | places |
| chaou | 照 | look |
| kwo | 過 | pass |
| pa | 把 | take |
| koh | 各 | every |
| fang | 房 | room |
| tăng | 燈 | light |
| ho | 火 | fire |
| ch'uy | 吹 | blow |
| mëeh | 滅 | extinguish |
| lëaou | 了 | have |
| ts'ae | 纔 | then |
| kh'o | 可 | may |
| e | 以 | |

shang 上 mount
ch'wang 床 bed

shuy 睡
këaou. 覺 } sleep.

## SHOP SIGNS.

Famous teas out of every province.

Koh 各 Every
săng 省 province
ming 名 famous
ch'a. 茶 tea.

Grain from every quarter.

Koh 各 Every
loo 路 quarter
lëang 糧
shih. 食 } grains.

Finest Soochow and Ningpo mats.

Soo 蘇 Soochow
ning 寧 Ningpo
se 細 fine
seih. 蓆 mat.

Fukien, Chapoo and Hangchow tobacco, imported by ourselves.

Tsze 自 Self
yün 運 imported
këen 建 Fukien
p'oo 浦 Chapoo
hang 杭 Hangchow
yen. 烟 tobacco.

Autumn drawn oil. Summer made soy.

Ts'ew 秋 Autumn
yew 油 oil
fuh 伏 mid-summer
tsëang 醬 soy.

Mustard and bean oil thoroughly steeped.

Ts'ae 菜 Mustand
tow 豆 bean
yin 窨 vat
yew. 油 oil.

Steel-yards, duly matched by government standard.

Këaou 較 Compare
chun 準 determine
kwan 官 official
ch'ing. 秤 steel-yard.

Famous incense for honoring Heaven, earth, and the gods.

King 敬 Honor
shin 神 god
san 三 three
sin 信 faith
ming 名 famous
hëang. 香 incense.

Wine manufactory.

Tsew 酒 Wine
fang. 坊 manufactory.

Foochow orange and virgin purity wines.

Fuh 福 Foochow
këuh 橘 orange

neu 女 female
ching. 貞 chastity.

Kwantung millet wine distilled in our own coppers.

Păn 本 Own
kwo 鍋 copper
tsaou 糟 grain
shaou 燒 distil
kwan 關 } Kwantung
tung 東 }
kaou 高 } millet.
lëang. 粱 }

Famous wine from over the seas.

Kwo 過 Beyond
yang 洋 sea
ming 名 famous
tsew. 酒 wine.

Broad-cloth and Long ells.

To 哆 } Broad-cloth
ne 呢 }
peih 嗶 } long-ells
ke. 吱 }

Camlets and foreign goods.

Yü 羽 } Camlet
maou 毛 }
yang 洋 foreign
ho. 貨 goods.

Fukien and Canton hempen sacks.

Min 閩 Fukien
kwang 廣 Kwangtung
ma 蔴 hempen
tae. 袋 sack.

Silks and Satins sprinkled with dye, and foreign printed.

T'an 彈 Sprinkle
jen 染 dye
yang 洋 foreign
yin 印 print
ch'ow 綢 silk
twan. 緞 satin.

Mould-made tribute candles.

Keaou 澆 Pour
tsaou 造 make
tsin 進 enter
ch'ing 呈 present
kung 貢 tribute
chuh 燭 candle.

Double dipped, extra material, finest wick candles.

Chung 重 Double
chen 占 dip
këa 加 add
lëaou 料 material
se 細 fine
sin. 芯 wick.

Incense sticks of Aloes wood, Sandal-wood, *Suh* wood, *Këang* wood, and *Këangnan* wood.

Ch'in 沉 Aloes wood
t'an 檀 sandal-wood
suh 速 suh
këang 降 këang
nan 楠 nan
t'ëaou. 條 stick.

Grass-cloth from every province dealt to customers.

Koh 各 Every
săng 省 province
hëa 夏 summer
poo 布 cloth
fah 發 deal to
kh'eh. 客 customer.

Tobacco pipes of Yün-nan white copper manufactured by ourselves.

Tsze 自 Self
tsaou 造 manufacture
Yün 雲 Yun-nan
peh 白 white
yen 烟 tobacco
tae. 袋 pipe.

Beautiful bamboos selected from famous hill side.

Ming 名 Famous
shan 山 hill
t'eih 剔 choose
sëuen 選 select
sew 秀 elegant
chuh. 竹 bamboo.

Silk and satin shop.

Ch'ow 綢 Silk
twan 緞 satin
p'oo. 舖 shop.

Gauze, *laws*, pongees, and satins.

Sha 紗 Gauze
lo 羅 law
ch'ow 綢 pongee
twan. 緞 satin.

Nanking satin, Canton gauze.

King 京 Nanking
twan 緞 satin
kwang 廣 Kwang-tung
sha. 紗 gauze.

Hang-chow reeled silk, Hoo-chow crape.

Hang 杭 Hang-chow
fang 紡 reeled
hoo 湖 Hoo-chow
chow. 縐 crape.

Hoo-chow cotton mixed silk, Ning-chow pongee.

Hoo 湖 Hoo-chow
mëen 綿 cotton mixture
ning 寧 Ning-chow
ch'ow. 綢 pongee.

Medicine shop.

Yoh 藥 } Medicine
ts'ae 材 }
p'oo. 舖 shop.

Decoctions accurately prepared from the most fragrant material.

Tsing 精 Accurately
che 製 prepared
hëang 香 fragrant
lëaou 料 material
yin 飲 } decoction.
p'ëen. 片 }

Boluses, powders, unguents, and pills carefully mixed.

Kh'ëen 虔 Carefully
sew 脩 mixed
wan 丸 bolus

san 散 powder
kaou 膏 unguent
tan. 丹 pill.

Drugs from every province.

Koh 各 Every
săng 省 province
yoh 藥 } drug.
ts'ae. 材 }

Brass and spelter shop.

T'ung 銅 Brass
seih 錫 spelter
p'oo. 舖 shop.

Brass and tin sounding instrument.

T'ung 銅 Copper
seih 錫 spelter
hëang 响 sound
kh'e. 器 intrument.

Organs, flutes, theatrical drums, guitars, violins, and all sort of musical instruments complete.

Săng 笙 Organ
t'eih 笛 flute
pan 班 theatre
koo 鼓 drum
p'e 琵 } guitar
p'a 琶 }
hëen 絃 } violin
tsze 子 }
yoh 樂 musical
kh'e 器 instrument
keu 俱 all
ts'ëuen. 全 complete.

Cloth shop.

Poo 布 Cloth
p'oo. 舖 shop.

Cloths selected of all kinds of fabric.

Këen 揀 } Selected
sëuen 選 }
koh 各 every
ke. 機 loom.

Robe stuffs purple and white, double lengthed, twilled, and plain, and cloths for summer or winter wear.

Tsze 紫 Purple
peh 白 white
shwang 雙 double
lëen 連 join
sëay 斜 twilled
ching 正 plain
paou 袍 robe
lëaou 料 stuff
tung 冬 winter
hëa 夏 summer
poo 布 cloth
p'eih. 疋 stuff.

Silk thread shop.

Sze 絲 Silk
sëen 線 thread
p'oo. 舖 shop.

We have our own mart, and selecting the finest of silk, sparing neither pains nor labour, we manufacture every kind of bright, beautiful and pure silk thread, and floss silk for embreidery, bowstring, tassels and cords: we make it our special business to weave and plait variegated girdles, and make court caps of newest fashion and Peking style; also cap fringes pearly and straight, perspiration napkins, handkerchiefs, damask and crape, head-bands, gauze and satin collars.

| | | |
|---|---|---|
| Tsze | 自 | Self |
| kh'ae | 開 | open |
| măn | 門 | mart |
| chwang | 庄 | |
| t'eih | 剔 | selected |
| sëuen | 選 | |
| tsëen | 尖 | finest |
| sze | 絲 | silk |
| puh | 不 | not |
| seih | 惜 | guide |
| kung | 工 | labor |
| păn | 本 | expense |
| che | 製 | manufacture |
| tsaou | 造 | |
| koh | 各 | every |
| seh | 色 | color |
| sëen | 鮮 | bright |
| yen | 艷 | beautiful |
| ts'ing | 清 | pure |
| shuy | 水 | |
| sze | 絲 | silk |
| sëen | 綫 | thread |
| sew | 繡 | embroider |
| jung | 絨 | floss silk |
| kung | 弓 | bow-string |
| hëen | 弦 | |
| seu | 鬚 | tassel |
| t'aou | 縧 | cord |
| chuen | 專 | special |
| pan | 辦 | business |
| te | 提 | weave |
| hwa | 花 | flower |
| choh | 琢 | plait |
| tae | 帶 | girdle |
| she | 時 | day |
| shih | 式 | fashion |
| king | 京 | Peking |
| kh'wan | 欵 | style |
| ch'aou | 朝 | court |
| kwan | 冠 | cap |
| wăn | 紋 | silken |
| choo | 珠 | pearl |
| kang | 摃 | stick |
| wei | 緯 | silk |
| han | 汗 | perspiration |
| kin | 巾 | napkin |
| show | 手 | hand |
| p'a | 帕 | kerchief |
| ling | 綾 | damask |
| chow | 縐 | crape |
| paou | 包 | band |
| t'ow | 頭 | head |
| sha | 紗 | gauze |
| twan | 緞 | satin |
| jung | 絨 | velvet |
| ling. | 領 | collars. |

Tartar and Chinese feasts prepared: eatables according to the season: vermicelli smothered with sliced meat ham and sea-slug; meat-puffs of boiled flour;

rice meals plain or with meats always ready.

| | | |
|---|---|---|
| Mwan | 滿 | Tartar |
| han | 漢 | Chinese |
| yen | 筵 | feast |
| seih | 席 | table |
| ngan | 按 | according |
| she | 時 | season |
| p'ăn | 盆 | bowl |
| ts'ae | 菜 | eatables |
| san | 三 | three |
| sëen | 鮮 | fresh |
| ta | 大 | large |
| mëen | 麵 | vermicelli |
| t'ang | 湯 | boil |
| mëen | 麵 | flour |
| jow | 肉 | meat |
| këaou | 餃 | puff |
| hwăn | 葷 | with meat |
| soo | 素 | without meat |
| pëen | 便 | ready |
| fan. | 飯 | rice. |

Sunglo and Bohea teas: also flag and lance, sparrow's tongue, prince's eyebrow, old man's eyebrow, Souchong, silver needle, early spring and bitter clove teas.

| | | |
|---|---|---|
| sung | 松 | Sunglo |
| lo | 羅 | |
| woo | 武 | Bohea |
| e | 彝 | |
| kh'e | 旗 | flag |
| ts'ëang | 鎗 | lance |
| ts'ëaou | 雀 | sparrow |
| sheh | 舌 | tongue |
| keun | 君 | prince |
| may | 眉 | eyebrow |
| show | 壽 | old man |
| may | 眉 | eyebrow |
| sëaou | 小 | Souchong |
| chung | 種 | |
| yin | 銀 | silver |
| chin | 針 | needle |
| tsaou | 早 | early |
| ch'un | 春 | spring |
| kh'oo | 苦 | bitter |
| ting. | 丁 | clove. |

Fashionable head ornaments; court cap-buttons, girdles; Tartar and Chinese head ornaments; antique wine cups; phœnix caps; variegated waist-coats.

| | | |
|---|---|---|
| She | 時 | Fashionable |
| shih | 式 | style |
| show | 首 | head |
| shih | 飾 | ornaments |
| ch'aou | 朝 | court |
| ting | 頂 | button |
| shuh | 束 | bind |
| tae | 帶 | girdle |
| mwan | 滿 | Tartar |
| han | 漢 | Chinese |
| t'ow | 頭 | head |
| mëen | 面 | ornaments |
| poh | 博 | ancient |
| koo | 古 | |
| tsew | 酒 | wine |
| kh'e | 器 | vessel |

海上絲綢之路文獻集成　科技與文化編

fung 鳳 phœnix
kwan 冠 cap
hëa 霞 variegated
p'e. 帔 waist-coat.

We deal in Hangchow tobacco. The fame of it has travelled to Kechow in the North, and its flavour pervades Kiangnan in the South. Our workmanship is of the best, and the manipulation excellent. Famous Sheh-ma tobacco.

Fah 發 } Deal out
tuy 兌 }
hang 杭 Hang-chow
yen 烟 tobacco
ming 名 fame
ch'e 馳 gallop
ke 冀 Ke-chow
peh 北 north
we 味 flavour
chen 占 pervade
këang 江 } Këang-nan
nan 南 }
tsing 精 careful
kung 工 workmanship
këa 佳 excellent
che 製 manipulation
sheh 石 } Sheh-ma
ma 馬 }
ming 名 famous
yen. 烟 tobacco.

Candle shop. Double cased, fine wick, dip candles. "At even tide the mandate came, from courts of Han, that mighty name. They hastened to the tower white, and studied there by midnight light."

Chuh 燭 Candle
haou 號 shop
shwang 雙 double
kae 蓋 case
se 細 fine
sin 心 wick
chen 占 dip
chuh 燭 candle
jih 日 day
moo 暮 decline
han 漢 Han
kung 宫 palace
ch'üen 傳 issue
ling 令 order
yay 夜 night
shin 深 depth
sëueh 雪 snow
koh 閣 gallery
kung 攻 attack
shoo. 書 book.

Dye house. Kingfisher and wove blues. Double black. We rival in our workmanship celestial manufactures.

Jen 染 Dye
fang 坊 house
ts'uy 翠 kingfisher blue
paou 寶 dark blue
shwang 雙 double
meh 墨 black

kh'eaou 巧 skill
toh 奪 rival
t'ëen 天 celestial
kung. 工 work.

Ginger store.

Këang 薑 Ginger
hang. 行 store.

Bean store.

Tow 豆 Bean
hang. 行 store.

Foreign goods store.

Yang 洋 Foreign
ho 貨 goods
hang. 行 store.

Grain store.

Lëang 糧 } Grain
shih 食 }
hang. 行 store.

Bean-cake store.

Tow 豆 Bean
ping 餅 cake
hang. 行 store.

Rice store.

Me 米 Rice
hang. 行 store.

Store for the six preserved articles.

Lëuh 六 Six
ch'in 陳 old
hang. 行 shop.

Store for the eight fresh things.

Pah 八 Eight
sëen 鮮 fresh
hang. 行 shop.

Famous tobacco from Fukëen, and Chapoo; and Lanchow hookah tobacco.

Këen 建 Fuhkëen
p'oo 浦 Chapoo
ming 名 famous
yen 烟 tobacco
Lan 蘭 } Lanchow
chow 州 }
shuy 水 water
yen. 菸 tobacco.

Black coal from the upper rivers dealt in.

Fah 發 } Deal out
tuy 兌 }
shang 上 upper
këang 江 river
ts'ing 青 black
may. 煤 coal.

Summer dried charcoal balls.

Fuh 伏 Summer
t'ëen 天 weather
t'an 炭 charcoal
ke. 基 balls.

Coarse and fine rush hats.

Ts'oo 粗 Coarse
se 細 fine
p'oo 蒲 rush
maou. 帽 hat.

Tea garden.

Ch'a 茶 Tea
yüen. 園 garden.

North and South fruits: tea-cakes spiced and plain.

Nan 南 South
peh 北 north
kwo 菓 } fruits
p'in 品 }
hwăn 葷 spiced
soo 素 plain
ch'a 茶 tea
ping. 餅 cake.

Charcoal factory.

T'an 炭 Charcoal
yüen. 園 factory.

Soy factory.

Tsëang 醬 Soy
yüen. 園 factory.

Tartar and Chinese whole feasts, and eatables for all seasons.

Sze 四 Four
she 時 season
p'ăn 盆 bowls
ts'ae 菜 edibles
mwan 滿 Tartar
han 漢 Chinese
ts'ëen 全 entire
seih. 席 feast.

Tëte-a-tëte meals at pleasure.

Suy 隨 At
e 意 pleasure
sëaou 小 small
choh. 酌 meals.

Tea.

Ming 茗 } Tea.
ch'a. 茶 }

Compasses from Japan.

Tung 東 } Japan
yang 洋 }
p'an 盤 } compass.
chin. 針 }

Sundries from the Western world.

Se 西 } Foreign
yang 洋 }
sze 事 } sundries.
këen. 件 }

Satin store.

Twan 緞 Satin
këuh. 局 store.

Caps made to suit the season.

Ngan 按 According
she 時 season
maou 帽 cap
tsoh. 作 make.

Bat embroidered boots of newest fashions.

She 時 Fashion
yang 樣 sort
fuh 福 bat
leu. 履 boot.

The sign of myriad productions.

Wan 萬 Myriad
săng 生 produce
haou. 號 sign.

Delicacies from both seas.

Lëang 兩 Two
yang 洋 ocean
hae 海 sea

we. 味 delicacy.

Sugar of Fuhkëen, Canton and Foreign parts.

Min 閩 Fuhkëen
kwang 廣 Kwangtung
yang 洋 foreign
t'ang. 糖 sugar.

Dates and walnuts from Kwantung and Shantung.

Kwan 關 Kwantung
shan 山 Shantung
t'aou 桃 walnut
tsaou. 棗 date.

Hard candles with fine wicks.

Se 細 fine
sin 心 wick
këen 堅 firm
chuh. 燭 candle.

Goods sold exactly by label attached.

Chaou 照 According to
ma 碼 label
hwah 劃 draw
yih. 一 line.

Persons favoring us with their patronage are requested to notice carefully our sign, that of the double-headed phœnix, which is the right one.

Mung 蒙 Favor
shang 商 merchant
sze 賜 } patronage
koo 顧 }
jin 認 look
ming 明 well
păn 本 our
haou 號 sign
shwang 雙 double
fung 鳳 phœnix
chaou 招 } sign board
p'ae 牌 }
wei 為 as
ke 記 mark
pëen 便 then
she. 是 right.

Celestial gems a Silversmith.

T'ëen 天 Celestial
paou 寶 gem
yin 銀 silver
low. 樓 gallery.

Quarterly lists of the civil and military belted gentry.

Ngan 按 According to
ke 季 quarter
wăn 文 civil
woo 武 military
tsin 縉 girdle
shin. 紳 belt.

Fashionable gold buttons of metropolitan manufacture.

Nuy 內 Metropolis
këuh 局 manufacture
she 時 } fashionable
kh'wan 款 }
kin 金 gold
ting. 頂 button.

Couplet mottoes hung up.

Peaou 裱 Hang

tuy 對 pair
tëen. 店 shop.

Tartar and Chinese head ornaments.

Mwan 滿 Tartar
han 漢 Chinese
show 首 head
shih. 飾 ornament.

A galloping fame for Hangchow scissors.

Ch'e 馳 Gallop
ming 名 name
Hang 杭 Hangchow
tsëen. 剪 scissors.

Store for satins and crapes at label prices.

Sha 紗 Crape
twan 緞 satin
ch'aou 抄 copy
chwang. 莊 warehouse.

Especial manufacturer of figures of men and things in raised lutestring.

Chuen 專 Special
pan 辦 prepared
tuy 堆 raised
këuen 絹 lutestring
jin 人 man
wuh. 物 thing.

Tartar and Chinese artificial court flowers in rice paper or velvet.

Mwan 滿 Tartar
han 漢 Chinese
jung 絨 velvet
ts'aou 草 rice paper
kung 宮 palace
hwa. 花 flower.

Antique curios fitted with frames and cases for presents.

Tsin 進 Send
ch'ing 呈 present
chwang 裝 } fit with case
hwang 潢 }
koo 古 antique
wan. 玩 curio.

Tables and hangings laid out at weddings.

Hing 行 } Wedding
p'ing 聘 }
ch'in 陳 spread
sheh 設 lay
t'ae 臺 table
ts'ae. 彩 hangings.

Crystal spectacles for old and young.

Shuy 水 } Crystal
tsing 晶 }
laou 老 old
shaou 少 young
yen 眼 } spectacles.
king. 鏡 }

Jadestone vessels and antique curios.

Yuh 玉 Jadestone
kh'e 器 vessel
koo 古 antique
wan. 玩 curio.

Musquitoe antidote suited to the market specially manufactured and dealt out to customers.

| | | |
|---|---|---|
| Chüen | 專 | Special |
| tso | 做 | make |
| she | 市 | market |
| ho | 貨 | goods |
| wăn | 蚊 | musquitoe |
| yen | 烟 | tobacco |
| fah | 發 | deal to |
| kh'eh. | 客 | customers. |

# 六十花甲子

## CYCLE OF SIXTY YEARS.

| | | |
|---|---|---|
| Këah ch'in | 甲辰 | 1844 |
| Yih sze | 乙巳 | 1845 |
| Ping woo | 丙午 | 1846 |
| Ting we | 丁未 | 1847 |
| Woo shin | 戊申 | 1848 |
| Ke yew | 己酉 | 1849 |
| Kăng sëuh | 庚戌 | 1850 |
| Sin hae | 辛亥 | 1851 |
| Jin tsze | 壬子 | 1852 |
| Kwuy ch'ow | 癸丑 | 1853 |
| Këah yin | 甲寅 | 1854 |
| Yih maou | 乙卯 | 1855 |
| Ping ch'in | 丙辰 | 1856 |
| Ting sze | 丁巳 | 1857 |
| Woo woo | 戊午 | 1858 |
| Ke we | 己未 | 1859 |
| Kăng shin | 庚申 | 1860 |
| Sin yew | 辛酉 | 1861 |
| Jin sëuh | 壬戌 | 1862 |
| Kwuy hae | 癸亥 | 1863 |
| Këah tsze | 甲子 | 1864 |
| Yih ch'ow | 乙丑 | 1865 |
| Ping yin | 丙寅 | 1866 |
| Ting maou | 丁卯 | 1867 |
| Woo ch'in | 戊辰 | 1868 |
| Ke sze | 己巳 | 1869 |
| Kăng woo | 庚午 | 1870 |
| Sin we | 辛未 | 1871 |
| Jin shin | 壬申 | 1872 |
| Kwuy yew | 癸酉 | 1873 |
| Këah sëuh | 甲戌 | 1874 |
| Yih hae | 乙亥 | 1875 |
| Ping tsze | 丙子 | 1876 |
| Ting ch'ow | 丁丑 | 1877 |
| Woo yin | 戊寅 | 1878 |
| Ke maou | 己卯 | 1879 |
| Kăng ch'in | 庚辰 | 1880 |
| Sin sze | 辛巳 | 1881 |
| Jin woo | 壬午 | 1882 |
| Kwuy we | 癸未 | 1883 |
| Këah shin | 甲申 | 1884 |
| Yih yew | 乙酉 | 1885 |
| Ping sëuh | 丙戌 | 1886 |
| Ting hae | 丁亥 | 1887 |

中外對話

| | | | | | |
|---|---|---|---|---|---|
| Woo *tsze* | 戊子 | 1888 | Ping shin | 丙申 | 1896 |
| Ke ch'ow | 己丑 | 1889 | Ting yew | 丁酉 | 1897 |
| Kăng yin | 庚寅 | 1890 | Woo sëuh | 戊戌 | 1898 |
| Sin maou | 辛卯 | 1891 | Ke hae | 己亥 | 1899 |
| Jin ch'in | 壬辰 | 1892 | Kăng *tsze* | 庚子 | 1900 |
| Kwuy *sze* | 癸巳 | 1893 | Sin ch'ow | 辛丑 | 1901 |
| Këah woo | 甲午 | 1894 | Jin yin | 壬寅 | 1902 |
| Yih we | 乙未 | 1895 | Kwuy maou | 癸卯 | 1903 |

## TIME OF THE DAY.

The day has twelve hours, named after the "twelve branch" terms.

| | | |
|---|---|---|
| Yih | 一 | One |
| jih | 日 | day |
| yew | 有 | have |
| shih | 十 | ten |
| urh | 二 | two |
| ko | 個 | piece |
| she | 時 | hour |
| ch'in | 辰 | (hour) |
| e | 以 | with |
| te | 地 | earth |
| che | 支 | branch |
| wei | 爲 | make |
| ming. | 名 | name. |

Beginning with 12 o'clock at night, that is mid-night, the hour is called mid "*tsze.*"

| | | |
|---|---|---|
| Yay | 夜 | Night |
| shih | 十 | ten |
| urh | 二 | two |
| tëen | 點 | stroke |
| chung | 鐘 | clock |
| tseih | 卽 | that is |
| pan | 半 | mid |
| yay | 夜 | night |
| kh'e | 起 | begin |
| ch'ing | 稱 | call |
| wei | 爲 | is |
| tsze | 子 | *Tsze* |
| ching. | 正 | middle. |

One o'clock is "opening *ch'ow;*" two o'clock or cock crowing is "mid *ch'ow.*"

| | | |
|---|---|---|
| Yih | 一 | One |
| tëen | 點 | stroke |
| chung | 鐘 | clock |
| ch'ow | 丑 | ch'ow |
| ts'oo | 初 | begin |
| lëang | 兩 | two |
| tëen | 點 | stroke |
| chung | 鐘 | clock |
| tseih | 卽 | that is |
| ke | 鷄 | cock |
| ming | 鳴 | crow |

ch'ow 丑 ch'ow
ching. 正 middle.

Three o'clock is "opening *yin;*" four o'clock, or day-break, is "mid *yin.*"

San 三 Three
tëen 點 stroke
chung 鐘 clock
yin 寅 yin
ts'oo 初 begin
sze 四 four
tëen 點 stroke
chung 鐘 clock
tseih 卽 that is
le 黎 } day-break
ming 明 }
yin 寅 yin
ching. 正 middle.

Five o'clock is "opening *maou;*" six o'clock, or sun-rise is "mid *maou.*"

Woo 五 Five
tëen 點 stroke
chung 鐘 clock
maou 卯 maou
ts'oo 初 begin
lëuh 六 six
tëen 點 stroke
chung 鐘 clock
tseih 卽 that is
jih 日 day
ch'uh 出 exit
maou 卯 maou
ching. 正 middle.

Seven o'clock is "opening *ch'in;*" eight o'clock is "mid *ch'in.*"

Ts'eih 七 Seven
tëen 點 stroke
chung 鐘 clock
ch'in 辰 ch'in
ts'oo 初 begin
pah 八 eight
tëen 點 stroke
chung 鐘 clock
ch'in 辰 ch'in
ching. 正 middle.

Nine o'clock is "opening *sze;*" ten o'clock, or forenoon, is "mid *sze.*"

Kew 九 Nine
tëen 點 stroke
chung 鐘 clock
sze 巳 sze
ts'oo 初 begin
shih 十 ten
tëen 點 stroke
chung 鐘 clock
tseih 卽 that is
tsaou 早 early
pan 半 half
shang 晌 noon
sze 巳 sze
ching. 正 middle.

Eleven o'clock, or little noon, is "opening *woo;*" twelve o'clock, or full noon, is "mid *woo.*"

Shih 十 Ten

yih 一 one
tëen 點 stroke
chung 鐘 clock
tseih 卽 that is
sëaou 小 small
shang 晌 } noon
woo 午 }
woo 午 woo
ts'oo 初 begin
shih 十 ten
urh 二 two
tëen 點 stroke
chung 鐘 clock
tseih 卽 that is
ching 正 exact
shang 晌 } noon
woo 午 }
woo 午 woo
ching. 正 middle.

One o'clock declining noon is "opening *we*;" two o' clock is "mid *we*."

Yih 一 One
tëen 點 stroke
chung 鐘 clock
tseih 卽 that is
shang 晌 } noon
woo 午 }
ts'o 錯 decline
we 未 we
ts'oo 初 begin
urh 二 two
tëen 點 stroke
chung 鐘 clock
we 未 we
ching. 正 middle.

Three o'clock is "opening *shin*;" four o'clock, or afternoon.

San 三 Three
tëen 點 stroke
chung 鐘 clock
shin 申 shin
ts'oo 初 begin
sze 四 four
tëen 點 stroke
chung 鐘 clock
tseih 卽 that is
hëa 下 down
pan 半 half
wan 晚 evening
shin 申 shin
ching. 正 middle.

Five o'clock is "opening *yew*;" six o'clock, or sun-down is "mid *yew*."

Woo 五 Five
tëen 點 stroke
chung 鐘 clock
yew 酉 yew
ts'oo 初 begin
lëuh 六 six
tëen 點 stroke
chung 鐘 clock
tseih 卽 that is
jih 日 sun
muh 沒 sunk
yew 酉 yew
ching. 正 middle.

Seven o' clock is "opening *sëuh;*" eight o'clock, or twilight, is "mid *sëuh.*"

| | | |
|---|---|---|
| Ts'eih | 七 | Seven |
| tëen | 點 | stroke |
| chung | 鐘 | clock |
| sëuh | 戌 | sëuh |
| ts'oo | 初 | begin |
| pah | 八 | eight |
| tëen | 點 | stroke |
| chung | 鐘 | clock |
| tseih | 卽 | that is |
| hwang | 黃 | twilight |
| hwăn | 昏 | |
| sëuh | 戌 | sëuh |
| ching. | 正 | middle. |

Nine o'clock is "opening *hae;*" ten o'clock, or bed time, is "mid *hae.*"

| | | |
|---|---|---|
| Kew | 九 | Nine |
| tëen | 點 | stroke |
| chung | 鐘 | clock |
| hae | 亥 | hae |
| ts'oo | 初 | opening |
| shih | 十 | ten |
| tëen | 點 | stroke |
| chung | 鐘 | clock |
| tseih | 卽 | that is |
| jin | 人 | man |
| ting | 定 | rest |
| hae | 亥 | hae |
| ching. | 正 | middle. |

Eleven o'clock is "opening *tsze,*" and here comes "mid *tsze,*" when all goes over again as before.

| | | |
|---|---|---|
| Shih | 十 | Ten |
| yih | 一 | one |
| tëen | 點 | stroke |
| chung | 鐘 | clock |
| tsze | 子 | tsze |
| ts'oo | 初 | opening |
| che | 至 | up to |
| tsze | 子 | tsze |
| ching | 正 | middle |
| yew | 又 | also |
| chow | 週 | revolve |
| urh | 而 | and |
| fuh | 復 | again |
| she. | 始 | begin. |

## DIALOGUE ON RAW SILK.

What is the name of this silk?

| | | |
|---|---|---|
| Chay | 這 | This |
| ko | 個 | |
| sze | 絲 | silk |
| këaou | 叫 | call |
| shin | 甚 | what |
| mo | 麼 | |
| ming | 名 | name. |
| tsze. | 字 | |

This is called Tsatlee.

| | | |
|---|---|---|
| Këaou | 叫 | Call |
| tso | 做 | make |
| ts'eih | 七 | Tsatlee |
| le | 里 | |

sze. 絲 silk.

Where is it come from?

She 是 Is
na 那
le 裡 } whence
lae 來 come
teih 的 that which
ne. 呢 ?

It comes from Hoochow.

She 是 Is
Hoo 湖
chow 州 } Hoochow
lae 來 come
teih. 的 that which.

How many le is Hoochow from Shanghae?

Hoo 湖
chow 州 } Hoochow
le 離 distant from
Shang 上
hae 海 } Shanghae
yew 有 have
to 多
shaou 少 } how many
le 里 le
loo 路 road
ne 呢 ?

The city of Hoochow is 450 le distant from Shanghae?

Hoo 湖
chow 州
foo 府 } Hoo-chow-foo
ch'ing 城 city
le 離 distant from
Shang 上
hae 海 } Shanghae
she 是 is
sze 四 four
peh 百 hundred
woo 五 five
shih 十 ten
le. 里 le.

Whence comes the silk of Shanghae?

Shang 上
hae 海 } Shanghae
teih 的 of
sze 絲 silk
she 是 is
na 那
le 裡 } whence
teih 的 that which
ne 呢 ?

It all comes from the townships of Nanzing and Shwanglin in the department of Hoo-chow.

Too 都 all
she 是 is
Hoo 湖
chow 州 } Hoo-chow
foo 府 department
Nan 南
tsin 潯 } Nanzing
Shwang 雙
lin 林 } Shwanglin
lëang 兩 two
chin 鎮 town

| | | |
|---|---|---|
| lae | 來 | come |
| teih. | 的 | that which. |

What is the cost of conveying silk from Hoo-chow to Shanghae by boat per bale.

| | | |
|---|---|---|
| Yew | 由 | From |
| Hoo | 湖 | Hoo-chow |
| chow | 州 | |
| chwang | 裝 | load |
| sze | 絲 | silk |
| taou | 到 | to |
| Shang | 上 | Shanghae |
| hae | 海 | |
| may | 每 | each |
| paou | 包 | bale |
| teh | 得 | obtain |
| to | 多 | how much |
| shaou | 少 | |
| ch'üen | 船 | boat |
| ts'ëen | 錢 | money |
| ne. | 呢 | ? |

It costs somewhere about six hundred cash per bale.

| | | |
|---|---|---|
| Ta | 大 | About |
| yoh | 約 | |
| may | 每 | each |
| paou | 包 | bale |
| yaou | 要 | want |
| lëuh | 六 | six |
| peh | 百 | hundred |
| ts'ëen | 錢 | cash |
| ts'ae | 纔 | then |
| kh'o | 可 | can. |
| e. | 以 | |

What is the expence of transporting it per bale by water to Canton?

| | | |
|---|---|---|
| Tsze | 自 | From |
| Hoo | 湖 | Hoochow |
| chow | 州 | |
| tsae | 載 | convey |
| taou | 到 | to |
| Kwang | 廣 | Canton |
| tung | 東 | |
| may | 每 | each |
| paou | 包 | bale |
| yaou | 要 | want |
| yung | 用 | use |
| to | 多 | how much |
| shaou | 少 | |
| shuy | 水 | water |
| këoh | 脚 | leg |
| ne. | 呢 | ? |

Formerly it cost from ten to twenty dollars per bale; but now-a-days it is always purchased at the port nearest the place of production, and never carried to Canton.

| | | |
|---|---|---|
| Ts'ung | 從 | Formerly |
| ts'ëen | 前 | |
| tsew | 就 | then |
| shih | 十 | ten |
| yüen | 元 | dollar |
| che | 至 | to |
| urh | 二 | two |
| shih | 十 | ten |
| yüen | 元 | dollar |

| | | |
|---|---|---|
| puh | 不 | not |
| tăng | 等 | fix |
| hëen | 現 | now |
| kin | 今 | |
| tsung | 總 | all |
| she | 是 | is |
| tsae | 在 | at |
| koh | 各 | every |
| kh'ow | 口 | port |
| tsew | 就 | near neighbourhood |
| kin | 近 | |
| ts'ae | 採 | collect |
| mae | 買 | buy |
| too | 都 | all |
| puh | 不 | not |
| chwang | 裝 | load |
| taou | 到 | to |
| Kwang | 廣 | Canton |
| tung | 東 | |
| kh'eu | 去 | go |
| lëaou. | 了 | — |

This silk is not good. Its colour is not bright and lustrous; it is dirty moreover, and coarse and fine are intermixed in it. The outer part of the bale is good, but the inner part bad.

| | | |
|---|---|---|
| Chay | 這 | This |
| sze | 絲 | silk |
| puh | 不 | not |
| haou | 好 | good |
| yen | 顏 | colour |
| seh | 色 | |
| puh | 不 | not |
| kwang | 光 | bright |
| lëang | 亮 | lustrous |
| yay | 也 | also |
| ngang | 骯 | dirty |
| tsang | 髒 | |
| ts'oo | 粗 | coarse |
| se | 細 | fine |
| këah | 夾 | intermix |
| tsah | 雜 | |
| wae | 外 | outside |
| mëen | 面 | |
| haou | 好 | good |
| le | 裡 | inside |
| t'ow | 頭 | |
| puh | 不 | not |
| haou | 好 | good |
| lëaou. | 了 | — |

If inside of the bale one faulty skein is concealed, it leads people to doubt the entire lot of silk, and reject it as bad also.

| | | |
|---|---|---|
| T'ang | 倘 | If |
| yih | 一 | one |
| paou | 包 | bale |
| le | 裡 | inside |
| t'ow | 頭 | |
| ts'ang | 藏 | conceal |
| yih | 一 | one |
| ch'ay | 車 | skein |
| tsze | 子 | |
| puh | 不 | not |
| haou | 好 | good |
| teih | 的 | of |
| sze | 絲 | silk |

tsew 就 then
këaou 叫 cause
jin 人 man
e 疑 doubt
sin 心 heart
hëen 嫌 } reject
kh'e 棄 }
ts'ëuen 全 whole
too 都 all
she 是 is
puh 不 not
haou 好 good
teih 的 that which
lëaou. 了 —

An English merchant seeing this defect would suspect that the whole was the same, and as it would be impossible to open up each skein, the only plan would be for him to claim to purchase at a lower rate, and decline to give the high price asked.

Ying 英 English
shang 商 merchant
kh'an 看 see
yew 有 have
chay 這 this
ko 個 piece
maou 毛 } defect
ping 病 }
tsew 就 then
e 疑 } doubt
hwoh 惑 }

t'ung 通 whole
she 是 is
yih 一 one
yang 樣 sort
yew 又 also
puh 不 not
năng 能 can
koh 各 every
pa 把 skein
ta 打 break
kh'ae 開 open
chih 只 only
kh'o 可 can
t'an 貪 } claim
t'oo 圖 }
p'ëen 便 } low
e 宜 }
ts'ae 纔 then
mae 買 buy
puh 不 not
kh'ăng 肯 consent
ch'uh 出 give
kaou 高 high
këa 價 price
lëaou. 了 —

It constantly happens that bad silk is covered round and wrapped over by good, or that whilst the upper silk is good, bad is concealed underneath it, or that silk cut short and smoke-soiled silk are interposed amongst good silk in a bale.

Ch'ang 常 Constant

中外對話

| | | |
|---|---|---|
| yew | 有 | have |
| jin | 人 | man |
| na | 拿 | take |
| hwae | 壞 | bad |
| sze | 絲 | silk |
| wae | 外 | outside |
| mëen | 面 | face |
| paou | 包 | envelope |
| kwo | 裹 | wrap |
| haou | 好 | good |
| sze | 絲 | silk |
| hwoh | 或 | or |
| shang | 上 | upper |
| pëen | 邊 | side |
| she | 是 | is |
| haou | 好 | good |
| sze | 絲 | silk |
| hëa | 下 | below |
| ts'ang | 藏 | conceal |
| hwae | 壞 | bad |
| sze | 絲 | silk |
| hwoh | 或 | or |
| këah | 夾 | interpose |
| twan | 斷 | short |
| sze | 絲 | silk |
| yen | 烟 | smoke |
| ho | 火 | fire |
| heung | 燻 | burning |
| hwae | 壞 | destroy |
| teih | 的 | that which |
| chah | 紮 | skein |
| pa | 把 | |
| tsae | 在 | in |
| haou | 好 | good |
| paou | 包 | bale |
| le | 裡 | inside. |
| t'ow. | 頭 | |

This sort of attempts to make money, when discovered it leads to the rejection of the entire lot, or it is only accepted at a valuation, as for soiled silk.

| | | |
|---|---|---|
| Chay | 這 | This |
| yang | 樣 | sort |
| sëang | 想 | attempt |
| chüen | 賺 | make |
| ts'ëen | 錢 | money |
| kay | 給 | by |
| jin | 人 | man |
| ch'a | 查 | discover |
| ch'uh | 出 | |
| lae | 來 | come |
| ts'ëuen | 全 | all |
| too | 都 | entire |
| puh | 不 | not |
| yaou | 要 | what |
| lëaou | 了 | — |
| hwoh | 或 | or |
| koo | 估 | value |
| chaou | 照 | according to |
| hwae | 壞 | soiled |
| sze | 絲 | silk |
| teih | 的 | of |
| këa | 價 | price |
| ts'ëen | 錢 | |
| ts'ae | 纔 | then |
| kh'ăng | 肯 | consent |

mae 買 buy
ne. 呢 ?

Thus it is that to gain a petty advantage, the greater profit is lost.

Kh'e 豈 How
puh 不 not
yin 因 for
sëaou 小 small
shih 失 lose
ta 大 large
mo. 麽 ?

What Silk is this?

Chay 這 This
she 是 is
shin 甚 } what
mo 麽 }
sze. 絲 silk.

This is called Taysaam.

Chay 這 This
këaou 叫 call
ta 大 } Taysaam.
ts'an. 蠶 }

Whence does it come?

Na 那 } Whence
le 裡 }
lae 來 come
teih 的 that which
ne. 呢 ?

Like Tsatlee it comes likewise from Hoo-chow.

T'ung 同 Same as
tseih 七 } Tsatlee
le 里 }
too 都 also
she 是 is
Hoo 湖 } Hoochow
chow 州 }
lae 來 come
teih. 的 that which.

Off how many cocoons is each thread of it spun?

Chay 這 This
sze 絲 silk
may 每 each
t'ëaou 條 thread
yung 用 use
ke 幾 how many
ko 個 piece
këen. 繭 cocoon.

Off eight cocoons.

She 是 Is
pah 八 eight
ko 個 piece
këen 繭 cocoon
teih. 的 that which.

It is new or old?

She 是 Is
sin 新 new
teih 的 that which
ne 呢 ?
she 是 is
kew 舊 old
teih 的 that which
ne. 呢 ?

It is new.

She 是 Is
sin 新 new

teih. 的 that which.

I am afraid this silk is damp and rotten, or perhaps it has broken threads?

Kh'ung 恐 } Fear
p'a 怕 }
chay 這 this
sze 絲 silk
yew 有 have
may 霉 damp
lan 爛 rotten
teih 的 that which
hwoh 或 or
she 是 is
ch'ay 扯 pull
twan 斷 apart
teih 的 that which
pa. 罷 —

Nothing of the kind. It is all good silk.

Too 都 All
muh 沒 not
yew 有 have
too 都 all
she 是 is
haou 好 good
sze. 絲 silk.

How many bales of silk does England consume in a year?

Ying 英 English
kwoh 國 nation
may 每 each
nëen 年 year
kh'o 可 can
sëaou 消 consume
teh 得 obtain
to 多 } how much
shaou 少 }
paou 包 bale
sze 絲 silk
ne. 呢 ?

Formerly when Shanghae was first opened as a port, about eight to nine thousand bales were yearly purchased. But of late years it has already increased to 80 or 90 thousand bales, and hereafter even more than that may be exported.

Ts'ung 從 } Formerly
ts'ëen 前 }
Shang 上 } Shanghae
hae 海 }
ts'oo 初 first
kh'ae 開 open
kh'ow. 口 port
teih 的 that which
she 時 } time
how 候 }
may 每 each
nëen 年 year
mae 買 buy
teh 得 obtain
pah 八 eight
kew 九 nine
ts'ëen 千 thousand
paou 包 bale
teih 的 of

| | | |
|---|---|---|
| kwang | 光 | thereabouts |
| king | 景 | |
| kin | 近 | late |
| nëen | 年 | years |
| e | 已 | already |
| king | 經 | |
| këa | 加 | increase |
| tsăng | 增 | |
| taou | 到 | to |
| pah | 八 | eight |
| kew | 九 | nine |
| wan | 萬 | myriad |
| paou | 包 | bale |
| lëaou | 了 | — |
| tsëang | 將 | hereafter |
| lae | 來 | |
| han | 還 | yet |
| hwuy | 會 | capable |
| ch'uh | 出 | export |
| teh | 得 | obtain |
| to. | 多 | much. |

Do they use any other sorts of silk besides Tsatlee and Taysaam?

| | | |
|---|---|---|
| Ch'oo | 除 | Besides |
| ts'eih | 七 | Tsatlee |
| le | 里 | |
| ta | 大 | Taysaam |
| ts'an | 蠶 | |
| che | 之 | of |
| wae | 外 | outside |
| han | 還 | yet |
| yung | 用 | use |
| pëeh | 別 | other |
| yang | 様 | sort |
| sze | 絲 | silk |
| mo. | 麽 | ? |

They also use yellow and coarse silk.

| | | |
|---|---|---|
| Hwang | 黄 | Yellow |
| sze | 絲 | silk |
| ts'oo | 粗 | coarse |
| sze | 絲 | silk |
| yay | 也 | also |
| too | 都 | both |
| yung. | 用 | use. |

Do English merchants buy the Sze-chuen native silk?

| | | |
|---|---|---|
| Sze | 四 | Sze-chuen |
| ch'üen | 川 | |
| t'oo | 土 | native |
| sze | 絲 | silk |
| Ying | 英 | English |
| shang | 商 | merchant |
| mae | 買 | buy |
| puh | 不 | not |
| mae | 買 | buy |
| ne. | 呢 | ? |

They buy every sort of native silk, no matter what the colour, yellow, white or gray.

| | | |
|---|---|---|
| Koh | 各 | Every |
| yang | 様 | sort |
| teih | 的 | of |
| t'oo | 土 | native |
| sze | 絲 | silk |
| puh | 不 | no |
| lun | 論 | matter |

hwang 黃 yellow
peh 白 white
hwuy 灰 gray
seh 色 color
yay 也 also
too 都 all
mae. 買 buy.

Will English merchants take Tsatlee and Taysaam unpacked in bales?

Ts'eih 七 } Tsatlee
le 里 }
ta 大 } Taysaam
ts'an 蠶 }
muh 沒 not yet
ch'ing 成 make of
paou 包 bale
teih 的 that which
Ying 英 English
shang 商 merchant
yaou 要 want
puh 不 not
yaou 要 want
ne. 呢 ?

This they would prefer, for it would prevent the possibility of counterfeit silk within the bales.

Chay 這 This
yang 樣 kind
kăng 更 more
haou 好 good
lëaou 了 —
mëen 免 prevent
teh 得 obtain
paou 包 bale
le 裡 inside
yew 有 have
këa. 假 counterfeit.

Is this year's crop of Hoochow silk a large one?

Kin 今 This
nëen 年 year
Hoo 湖 Hoochow
sze 絲 silk
show 收 receive
teh 得 obtain
to 多 much
mo. 麽 ?

A large quantity of silk has arrived, but the quantity is not of the best; nevertheless the price is high.

Sze 絲 Silk
taou 到 arrive
hăn 狠 very
to 多 much
tan 但 but
she 是 is
puh 不 not
ta 大 over
haou 好 good
suy 雖 } although
jen 然 }
puh 不 not
haou 好 good
këa 價 } price
ts'ëen 錢 }
han 還 yet

kwuy. 貴 dear.

Could the culture of Hoochow silk be increased?

Hoo 湖 Hoo-chow
sze 絲 silk
kh'o 可 } can
năng 能 }
këa 加 increase
chung 種 culture
mo. 麽 ?

When the mulberry leaf is abundant, and the silk-worms can be strongly reared the silk is also plentiful. But too much culture of the mulberry is liable to interfere with that of all grains.

Sang 桑 Mulberry
yeh 葉 leaf
mow 茂 } abundant
shing 盛 }
ts'an 蠶 silk-worm
yang 養 rear
teih 的 that which
chwang 壯 strong
sze 絲 silk
tsew 就 then
to 多 plentiful
chung 種 plant
teih 的 that which
sang 桑 mulberry
to 多 much
yew 又 also
kh'ung 恐 } fear
p'a 怕 }
yew 有 have
ngae 碍 interfere
woo 五 five
kuh. 穀 grain.

What is "*T'ëen tsan*" wild silk?

Shin 甚 } What
mo 麽 }
wei 爲 constitute
t'ëen 天 heaven
ts'an 蠶 silk-worm
ne. 呢 ?

The silkworms which produce that silk are self-reared, and weave their own cocoons on the trees amongst the hills. Hence they are called "*T'ëen-tsan*" Heaven's worms.

Na 那 That
ts'an 蠶 silk-worm
she 是 is
tsae 在 at
shan 山 hill
le 裡 } inside
t'ow 頭 }
shoo 樹 tree
shang 上 upon
tsze 自 } self
ke 己 }
săng 生 produce
teih 的 that which
chih 織 weave
teih 的 that which
këen 繭 cocoon

| | | |
|---|---|---|
| so | 所 | therefore |
| e | 以 | |
| këaou | 叫 | call |
| tso | 做 | |
| t'ëen | 天 | heaven |
| ts'an | 蠶 | silk-worm |

Where does it come from?

| | | |
|---|---|---|
| She | 是 | Is |
| na | 那 | where |
| le | 裡 | |
| lae | 來 | come |
| teih | 的 | that which |
| ne. | 呢 | ? |

It comes from Shan-tung, Kwan-tung, and other places.

| | | |
|---|---|---|
| She | 是 | Is |
| Shan | 山 | Shan-tung |
| tung | 東 | |
| Kwan | 關 | Kwan-tung |
| tung | 東 | |
| koh | 各 | every |
| ch'oo | 處 | place |
| lae | 來 | come |
| teih. | 的 | that which. |

What price does it sell for?

| | | |
|---|---|---|
| Mae | 賣 | Sell |
| shin | 甚 | what |
| mo | 麼 | |
| këa | 價 | price |
| ts'ëen | 錢 | |
| ne. | 呢 | ? |

Not above a hundred dollars or so per pecul.

| | | |
|---|---|---|
| May | 每 | Each |
| tan | 擔 | pecul |
| puh | 不 | not |
| kwo | 過 | above |
| yih | 壹 | one |
| peh | 百 | hundred |
| to | 多 | more |
| yüen. | 員 | dollar. |

How much duty does it pay on export?

| | | |
|---|---|---|
| Ch'uh | 出 | Export |
| kh'ow | 口 | |
| nah | 納 | pay |
| to | 多 | how much |
| shaou | 少 | |
| shuy | 稅 | duty |
| ne. | 呢 | ? |

Wild silk only pays on passing the Customs two taels five mace duty.

| | | |
|---|---|---|
| T'ëen | 天 | Heaven |
| ts'an | 蠶 | worm |
| sze | 絲 | silk |
| kwo | 過 | pass |
| kwan | 關 | customs |
| may | 每 | each |
| tan | 擔 | pecul |
| chih | 只 | only |
| wan | 完 | pay |
| shuy | 稅 | duty |
| hëang | 餉 | |
| urh | 二 | two |
| lëang | 兩 | tael |
| woo | 五 | five |
| ts'ëen. | 錢 | mace. |

THE END.

国家出版基金项目
NATIONAL PUBLICATION FOUNDATION

# 海上絲綢之路文獻集成

總主編　陳支平　陳春聲

## 科技與文化編 94

主編　王揚宗　葉　農

海峽出版發行集團
THE STRAITS PUBLISHING & DISTRIBUTING GROUP
福建人民出版社

# 本册目次

# 速成漢語

（*The Analytical Reader: A Short Method for Learning to Read and Write Chinese*）

〔美〕丁韙良（William Alexander Parsons Martin）编

《速成漢語》，美國丁韙良編。丁韙良（William Alexander Parsons Martin，一八二七—一九一六），字冠西，美北長老會傳教士。生於美國印地安納州，一八五〇年至寧波，期間推行拉丁字母拼音方案，以羅馬拼音標注寧波方言，對近現代中國漢字改革運動産生一定影響。曾任京師同文館總教習，清政府國際法顧問，京師大學堂西學總教習等。撰有《花甲憶記》、《漢學菁華》，譯有《萬國公法》、《公法便覽》等。此書第一部分爲「方法」，凡五節，含擇字、析字、譯字、學習方法、學校中之應用；第二部分爲「文本與翻譯」，凡四章；第三部分爲「分析」，含析字、偏旁表、各類字體書寫練習；後附部首檢字表與詞彙表。據一八九七年上海版影印。

常字雙千

認字新法

# THE ANALYTICAL READER:

A

## SHORT METHOD

FOR

## LEARNING TO READ AND WRITE CHINESE,

BY

W. A. P. Martin, D.D., LL.D.,

*President Emeritus of the Imperial Tung-wen College.*

Shanghai:

PRINTED AT THE PRESBYTERIAN MISSION PRESS.

1897.

# PREFACE.

A new edition of this little manual has long been called for; but the author has not been willing to have it re-issued without a thorough revision.

In undertaking the task of preparing it for the press, he has been encouraged by the assurances that to those who have given it a trial, it has fulfilled its promise of shortening a weary road and lightening a heavy burden.

Improvements have been effected in several particulars.

1. Many errors have been corrected—*quos aut incuria fudit, aut humana parum cavit natura.*

2. The pronunciation, originally in current Mandarin, has been modified, so as to bring it into conformity with the dialect of Peking.

3. In the first edition no tones were marked except in the vocabulary. In this the Peking tonal system is introduced into the text as well.

4. The number of explanatory notes has been considerably increased.

The Chinese text, I may here state, is printed in a separate form for the use of schools.

As a selection of characters it has met with much favor; but I regret to say that its utility as a spelling book has not often been put to the test. This new edition will, I trust, lead missionaries to renew the experiment in the schools under their care.

I conclude with an extract from the Preface to the first edition, published in 1863 :—

"This book makes no pretension to superseding other manuals. It occupies a field of its own, and proposes to supply beginners with an additional help, the nature of which is explained in the following pages.

"In reference to one of its features I may adopt the words in which Professor Pauli speaks of the key to his Analecta Hebraica, 'It contains a literal translation of all the words *according to their order*; and the author hopes it will greatly assist the beginner, particularly as the finding of words in the lexicon is not only a tedious operation, but a very discouraging task, at the first setting out in the study of the language.'"

W. A. P. M.

Andubon Park,
New York City,
February 24th, 1896.

速成漢語

# CONTENTS.

## PART I—THE METHOD.



## PART II—TEXT AND TRANSLATION.

Containing characters for treating the following subjects:—



## PART III—ANALYSIS.



## APPENDIX.

# PART I.—THE METHOD.

For euphony's sake I have called it *Short*, though in strictness the adjective ought to have been placed in the comparative degree. There is no *positively* short road to an acquaintance with Chinese. But the method explained and illustrated in the following pages proposes, in some measure, to abridge the labor.

This it effects in two ways—

*First*, by furnishing the student with precisely those characters which he needs to know ;

*Secondly*, by laying them open to the eye and impressing them on the memory.

In neither of these respects does it lay claim to entire originality, nor is it a doubtful experiment. It treads in a safe path, at the entrance of which the natives have planted finger-boards, though they have not pursued it quite as far as we propose to venture.

They discovered the magnetic needle ; it was reserved for others to use it in crossing the ocean. They analyze with beautiful simplicity a few scores of family names—we seize the hint and launch into the sea of words, confident that it shows us the *way* to the further shore. They select a thousand characters as a capital for beginners ; and with a view to aiding the memory combine them into verse. We borrow the idea, and duly acknowledging our obligation, proceed, as we believe, to improve upon it. Their thousand were taken at random ; we take twice the number and select them by a regular process, which required years of painstaking. They govern the distribution by no laws but those of metre. We too arrange them in verse ; but dispose them in such a manner that they are presented to the learner in a steady gradation, according to the frequency of their occurrence. These, and other leading features, require further elucidation.

### I. *The Selection of Characters.*

Many years ago, while residing at Ningpo, I commenced a volume on a plan somewhat similar to that of the present work. Its progress was interrupted by a voyage to America ; but when I returned I was enabled to resume the task on a better basis. At first I had been guided in the selection of characters by no surer rule than the judgment of a Chinese scribe, who culled them

from the pages of K'ang-hi's Dictionary. I was now favored with a list, formed on scientific principles, in which every character was placed with numerical precision according to the frequency of its use.

For this I was indebted to Mr. Wm. Gamble, Superintendent of the Presbyterian Mission Press.

Mr. Gamble prepared it for a purpose very different from mine, viz., to ascertain the proportion in which the several letters would be required in casting a font of metallic type and to determine in what order the types should be arranged, so as to bring those in most common use nearest to the hand of the compositor. Both of these ends it succeeded in effecting—preventing a waste of metal in casting useless type, and increasing the rapidity of "composition." It occurred to me that a collection arranged with such elaborate care might be adapted to a higher end—to save the time expended in learning rare or useless characters, and abbreviate for foreign students, or Chinese pupils, the tedious task of acquiring the written language. The process by which these tables were constructed is well stated by Mr. Gamble in an "Introduction," the greater part of which I take the liberty of transcribing for the sake of the information it contains.

"In order to the better understanding of the following lists of selected characters it is necessary to give some explanation of the manner in which they have been prepared and of the object which has been kept in view in their preparation.

"When the art of printing first sprung up in the Western world, printers found it necessary to compute the relative frequency with which each letter of the alphabet occurred in order to ascertain how many type of each sort it would be necessary to cast, so that there should not be too many of one letter and too few of another. Thus for ordinary English book work the proportion of each letter in a font are: of *e* 12,000, of *t* 9,000, of *a* 8,500, of *i n o* and *s* each 8,000, of *r* 6,200; while *k* only occurs 800 times, *q* 500, *j* and *x* 400 and *z* but 200. They also in arranging them in cases, placed those that occurred most frequently in adjoining compartments and near the hand of the compositor, for the purpose of thereby promoting rapidity in the composition or *setting up* of the type.

"But in China the use of metallic type has been of such modern date that little has as yet been done towards ascertaining the relative frequency with which characters occur in the general literature of this peculiar language. This remark holds good even with reference to its Christian literature, which is now becoming pretty extensive and in which those who are engaged in missionary operations are more particularly interested. In conse-

速成漢語

quence therefore of the want of correct data on which to form a *scale*, as printers call it, of the characters in the written language, the method hitherto in use of arranging fonts of Chinese metallic type, has been such that not only have the type themselves taken up much room, but the compositor in going from case to case for each type has unavoidably consumed so much time as thereby to render composition both expensive and tedious.

"With the view therefore of making some improvement upon the former method of arrangement, as well as of ascertaining how many of the 40,919 characters contained in K'ang-hi's Dictionary are in common use, especially in the class of books used and published by those engaged in the missionary work, an examination was made of 4,166 octavo pages, including the whole Bible, together with twenty-seven other publications printed at our press, and embracing in the aggregate nearly one million two hundred thousand characters. In conducting this examination two Chinese scholars were employed for two years each, and it was carried on in such a manner as to secure as much accuracy as possible. The result is shown in the two following lists.

"The FIRST LIST, which is arranged in the usual manner by Radicals and Strokes, contains every character which occurs in the above mentioned books, amounting in number only to 5,150 different characters. The number of times each of these characters occurred is placed opposite to it in figures which, when added together, show an aggregate of 1,166,473 characters. It may here be proper to add that in the Scriptures containing the total number of 676,827 characters there were found 4,141 different ones. In the Old Testament there are in all 503,663 characters and 3,946 different ones; the version used being that printed at the London Mission Press. In the New Testament there are in all 173,164 characters and 2,713 different ones; the version used being that printed at the Presbyterian Mission Press.

"That so few characters are of general use, as is shown by this statement, may seem somewhat incredible to those who have not examined the subject, and who, having been accustomed to hear the number of characters in the Chinese language stated to be forty to eighty thousand, suppose that in order to be able to read or translate Chinese books a knowledge of some tens of thousands of characters is absolutely necessary. Our calculations are, however, corroborated by the author of the Chinese work called the 十三經集字 *Shih san king tsih ts*, who states that the 四書 *Four Books* contain 2,328 different characters; the 五經 *Five Classics* contain 2,426 different characters which do not occur in the *Four Books*, and that the whole number of different characters in the *Thirteen Classics* is 6,544. This

includes 928 rare or obsolete characters occurring in the 爾雅 *Ready Guide*, almost all of which might be omitted, thus leaving less than 6,000 characters.

"The SECOND LIST, like the first one, consists of all the characters different from each other that are to be found in the total number examined, but here it is intended to exhibit them arranged according to their numerical use, or the relative frequency with which they occur. For this purpose they are divided into *fifteen groups*, in each of which is contained all the characters occurring between a certain number of times each, as between 1,000 and 10,000 times each, between 900 and 1,000 times each, between 800 and 900 times each, and so on of the others. The first group, however, has all those that occurred over 10,000 times each; and the fifteenth group includes the 850 mentioned above as taken from another list, which ought properly to be placed in a group by themselves.

"The group—the number of different characters in each group—their minimum and maximum numbers—together with the total number of times that the characters of each group occurred, is shown in the following table:—

| Group. | No. Different Cha. | Min. & Max. Nos. | Totals. |
|---|---|---|---|
| 1st. | 13 | 10,000 | 214,156 |
| 2nd. | 224 | 1,000-10,000 | 563,126 |
| 3rd. | 16 | 900- 1,000 | 15,150 |
| 4th. | 19 | 800- 900 | 16,344 |
| 5th. | 44 | 700- 800 | 32,757 |
| 6th. | 47 | 600- 700 | 31,167 |
| 7th. | 59 | 500- 600 | 32,116 |
| 8th. | 99 | 400- 500 | 44,258 |
| 9th. | 112 | 300- 400 | 38,024 |
| 10th. | 197 | 200- 300 | 47,932 |
| 11th. | 400 | 100- 200 | 56,627 |
| 12th. | 207 | 75- 100 | 17,637 |
| 13th. | 301 | 50- 75 | 18,508 |
| 14th. | 547 | 25- 50 | 19,497 |
| 15th. | 3,715 | 1- 25 | 19,036 |
| | 6,000 | | 1,166,335 |

"As the result of this investigation two most important facts to the printer are established. FIRST: *that five or six thousand well selected characters are sufficient for all practical purposes;* which is about *one-seventh* of what is in the language. This has been long known in China, but appears to have been overlooked by those interested in such matters in Europe. SECOND:

速成漢語

*that a very few characters, from the great frequency with which they occur, constitute the great body of those in a book, and that the great majority occur exceedingly seldom.* Thus, as already stated, the first group has 13 characters, which were found to occur in the whole number examined 214,156 times, which is more than *one-sixth* of the whole. Again, putting the two first groups together there are 237 characters, whose sum is 777,282, which is considerably more than *one-half* of the whole. And again, putting the first eight groups together we have 521 characters, whose sum is 949,074, or nearly *nine-elevenths* of the whole. On the other hand, the last or fifteenth group has (after deducting the 850 which should not be in this group) 2,865 characters, which were found to occur in the whole number examined 19,036 times, or less than *one-sixtieth* of the whole. And again, if we add the fourteenth and fifteenth groups together we have 3,410 characters, whose sum is 38,533, or only about *one-thirtieth* of the whole. The character 之 *Che* alone occurs 42,068 times, which is oftener than the sum total of these 3,410 characters.

"From a knowledge of these facts we have been enabled to arrange a large font of Chinese metallic type in so compact a manner that the compositor can reach any type he wants without moving more than a step in any direction; and by having placed, say five hundred, of the most numerous characters together he has more than *three-fourths* of all he uses just under his hand, almost as conveniently as a font of Roman type are arranged in an English printing office. The result of this arrangement has been to render the work of the compositor at least three times as rapid and cheap as it could be done under the old arrangement of the font."

It is certain that the proportions of Mr. Gamble's list will hold good, with very little alteration, for the entire range of classical Chinese, all the works examined in preparing them having been based on classic models; but they would undergo considerable modification if applied to the mandarin dialects. Besides a change in the ratio of frequency, a dozen characters peculiar to the mandarin would require to be added. They not only confirm the observation of that early sinologue, Premare, that "a good knowledge of four or five thousand characters is sufficient for all ordinary purposes," but furnish us with a safe guide in *selecting* that limited number.

A word as to the form in which these characters are marshalled. Solon published his laws in verse; and for the same reason a judicious mother makes rhyme the vehicle of her nursery lessons. We thus remember the length of the months,

long lines of kings, and many detached facts, which might long since have been given to the winds but for the jingling chain that binds them together. Two senseless syllables imprint on the brain the colors of the solar spectrum; and longer but equally senseless words serve to fix in memory the classifications of Grammar and the formulas of Logic. How much more powerful the association when sense, sound and rythm are all combined! We have then a "three-fold cord not easily broken." With such a bond I have sought to connect these pearls, collected as it were from the ocean sands. When securely stored in memory they will prove of inestimable value for future reference.

The credit of executing the plan is due, in no small degree, to my Chinese scribe, 何師孟 *Ho Sien-sheng*, a bachelor of Nanking, and whatever defects attach to mine, I am sure competent judges will agree that he has performed his part with admirable skill.

He was placed under more embarrassing restrictions than those imposed on themselves by the monkish triflers of the middle ages, or by our own acrostic and alliterative poets of the last two centuries.

The first law of the composition, as of its native model, the 千字文 *Ts'ien ts wen*, was that each word should occur but once. Two or three duplicates do occur, and it will be an interesting exercise to search for them.

The second, that he should confine himself to two thousand characters previously collected.

The third, that this limited number was to be subdivided into parcels of a few hundreds each, beyond which he was not at liberty to expatiate.

With all these disadvantages to contend against, in addition to the restraints of verse, *Ho Sien-sheng* has succeeded in producing a *poem*, the first half of which is almost as lucid and free as it could have been, if the treasures of the Lexicon had been placed at his disposal. The latter part, from the nature of the case, is a little more obscure, but it reflects no less credit on the ingenuity of the composer, though there is a perceptible want of coherence.

Even to these detached phrases Ho has striven to impart a religious tinge in keeping with the primary object of the book, which was to serve as a lesson book for children in schools. This will explain the abrupt intrusion of solemn thoughts in places where they are obviously out of joint.

The author of the *Ts'ien ts wen*, if tradition is to be believed, might have adopted the language of the Prisoner of Chillon:

"My hair is grey; but not with years,
Nor grew it white
In a single night
As men's have grown from sudden fears".

His also "grew white in a single night", but it was in consequence of the exertion required in arranging in a poetical form a thousand arbitrary words—a task imposed on him by a despotic master. Ho Sien-sheng and I, who only *fungor vice cotis*, may not exhibit the same outward demonstration of our labors, but we have experienced enough to believe the story of our predecessor in the thorny path.*

## II. *The Analysis of Characters.*

The object of this part is two-fold, viz., to introduce the foreign learner to the orthography of the language, and to supply the Chinese with what they have never had—a *Spelling Book.*

The want of that elementary manual may excite surprise, but the reason is obvious. Their written language is not, as ours, essentially phonetic; and the analysis of its sounds affords no clue to the composition of its characters. With us orthoepy and orthography are intimately connected, and mutually aid each other, though they are far from coinciding. In China they altogether part company; one speaks wholly to the ear, the other addresses itself entirely to the eye. The system of *fan ch'ie* 反切 relates to the former; the latter, which is incomparably more difficult, has to be learned without the aid of any system. The dictionary presents each character as a whole, and sometimes gives its component parts by way of conjecture as to its origin; but a simple manual, which proceeds from the parts to the whole, presenting first the elements, and then the words resulting from their combination, is still a desideratum.

There is proof too that the want has been felt, at least in one small class of words; and in the same contracted corner an expedient has sprung up which is worthy of being employed on a more extended scale. Custom requires the Chinese, on meeting, to ask each other for their family names; but many of them being similar in sound, as among ourselves, Lee, Lea, McLean, McLain, MacLane, &c., it was found difficult to understand the answers without some further description. Thus:

---

* A native author thus relates the origin of that curious work:

太平廣記云梁武帝於大王書中搨一千字不重者每字片紙雜碎無序召周興嗣謂之曰卿有才思爲我韻之興嗣一夕編綴進上鬢髮皆白

According to the Tai-ping-kwang-ki, the Emperor Wu, of the Liang dynasty, having selected from the manuscript of the elder Wang a thousand characters each on a separate slip with no duplicates, and having purposely mixed them in disorder, called for Cheo Hing-sze and said to him, "You are a man of talent; now turn these into verse for me." Cheo completed the versification in one evening and presented it to His Majesty, but his hair and beard had turned white.

Q. What is the name of your illustrious family?

Ans. The name of my ignoble line is *Chang*.

Q. How is it written?

Ans. It is *Stand up early chang*, not *long bow chang*, *i. e.*, it is the *chang* composed of 立 and 早 not that composed of 弓 and 長: it is 章 not 張.

The *Chings* and *Changs* are by this means distinguished into numerous clans, each wearing its own livery.

The following surnames and others are thus familiarly analyzed:—

FAMILY NAMES ANALYZED.

姓氏俗解

| | | | | | |
|---|---|---|---|---|---|
| 人 | 可 | 何 | 古 | 月 | 胡 |
| 弓 | 長 | 張 | 子 | 系 | 孫 |
| 耳 | 東 | 陳 | 二 | 馬 | 馮 |
| 立 | 早 | 章 | 水 | 王 | 汪 |
| 言 | 午 | 許 | 圈 | 吉 | 周 |
| 人 | 未 | 余 | 人 | 專 | 傅 |
| 走 | 肖 | 趙 | 求 | 衣 | 裘 |
| 木 | 子 | 李 | 西 | 貝 | 賈 |
| 立 | 里 | 童 | 禾 | 呈 | 程 |
| 魚 | 包 | 鮑 | 魚 | 日 | 魯 |
| 木 | 昜 | 楊 | 由 | 共 | 黃 |
| 水 | 工 | 江 | 雙 | 木 | 林 |
| 艸 | 曷 | 葛 | 言 | 甚 | 諶 |
| 成 | 皿 | 盛 | 心 | 眞 | 愼 |

| | | | | | |
|---|---|---|---|---|---|
| 人 | 兒 | 倪 | 未 | 撇 | 朱 |
| 八 | 木 | 米 | 區 | 欠 | 歐 |
| 言 | 者 | 諸 | 木 | 土 | 杜 |
| 享 | 耳 | 郭 | 艸 | 祭 | 蔡 |
| 門 | 耳 | 聞 | 木 | 每 | 梅 |
| 丘 | 山 | 岳 | 龍 | 共 | 龔 |
| 口 | 天 | 吳 | 卯 | 金刀 | 劉 |
| 曲 | 日 | 曹 | 方 | 人也 | 施 |
| 美 | 女 | 姜 | 言 | 身寸 | 謝 |

This is *Spelling;* and if *names* are thus spelled out, in order to enable the hearer to write them properly, why may not other characters be subjected to the same treatment? * The majority are capable of a neat division into two or three elements, each of which is a distinct whole having its own sound and sense. In this case there can hardly be a doubt as to the advantage of applying the solvent.

But there are cases in which its expediency is less clear. Where an element is neither an integer nor a radical, I have sometimes thought it worthy of separate attention, on account of its frequent occurrence in other combinations. And again where these imperfect elements closely resemble certain characters; as the parts of 民 differ but slightly from 口 *K'eu* and 氏 *Shü,* I have thought it safe to borrow the names of those characters for the sake of preserving the recollection of that resemblance, leaving the difference to be learned by observation. It is better to run the risk of learning them with a trifling error than not to learn them at all. So the natives have thought, who

* In fact many of them are analyzed by the natives. Take the following as an instance: The Chinese ministers being disinclined to make treaties with certain minor states some one expostulated with Chung-how, who was at that time a member of the Tsung-li Yamên. He disclaimed any such feeling, adding: "Do you know that the two characters 自 大 (haughty) when put together make 臭 (a stench)?"

As another example take this little rhyme,

而字加女念日耍
丁字加手念日打

give 耳東 as the components of 陳。, 口天 as those of 吳。, and 美女 as those of 姜。.

I may as well remark here, that the whole design of this manual is to aid the student in getting the characters as they are now written; not to serve him as a guide to their etymology. For that, he must penetrate deeper than the forms of the living present, exhume fossils, pursue them through successive ages, and divers metamorphoses; and then become acquainted, not with groups of words, as in the languages of Western Asia, but with individuals, an employment certainly not the most edifying for a beginner. The native dictionary 說文 and Dr. Edkins' Study of the Chinese Characters may help him in that task. Our analysis will familiarize him with the composition of characters; but it will be for the vulgar end of enabling him to read and write, not for the gratification of philological curiosity. It agrees in the main, with the distinction of radicals and primitives; but it does not proceed on it as a basis, because that would be fatal in the end in view, which be it remembered, is *orthography*—not etymology. This compels us to place the upper element before the lower, and the left before the right, irrespective of the position of the radical, *because this is the order which the natives observe in writing.*

To begin with the radical, would be like spelling an English word by beginning with the root or suffix. Again, in dissecting characters with this view, it is of less moment to hit the joints than to divide them in such a manner that they may readily be recomposed. It is easier to spell *cy-clops*, than *cycl-ops*, though the latter shows the roots.

The analysis is accompanied by a commentary giving the sense of the composition, and explaining some of the characters. This will be highly profitable to the foreign student, though specially designed for Chinese readers.

### III. *The Translation.*

A translation injurious to a lad, may be highly beneficial to a person of mature judgment. It is for such only that the present is made; and for so terse a composition, something of the kind is not merely a convenience, but a necessity. The style, like that of its model the 千字文, is exceedingly elliptical, and with all the aid of native teachers, and dictionaries, the learner would be liable to lose the meaning of many a sentence. This translation, though not superseding those indispensable auxiliaries, is so constructed as, in a degree, to perform the office of

both. It will be specially useful to students of Chinese not in China.

The mode of rendering is determined by the end proposed. If that were to introduce the reader to a Chinese poem, I should choose those expressions best suited to represent its thoughts and spirit. But the end is the study of words; and this obliges me *reddere verbum verbo*.

As far as the sense would admit, I have given only the fundamental significations, leaving the reader to infer those that are collateral and derivative. For instance, 生 is rendered *life;* and this places him in possession of its other meanings, such as *live, alive, beget, bear, be born* &c. Each character, in general, may thus play several parts—owing to the absence of inflection, appearing without any change of form, as a substantive, adjective, verb, or adverb, according to its position in a sentence—a feature of the language, which makes the knowledge of two thousand an important acquisition.

Words introduced to complete the sense, excepting particles and pronouns, are printed in italics.

The *order* of the text has been strictly adhered to, and each line represented by a verse in the translation; so that the reader can easily ascertain what words and characters correspond—an arrangement which renders it equally available for a student of either language.

This rule, which in any language would be fatal to the elegance of a translation, is peculiarly embarrassing in Chinese; and while endeavoring to make it strictly literal it has sometimes been necessary to violate a grammatical rule in order to give due relief to the idea of each particular character.

## IV. *The mode of study.*

The student may learn the characters from the simple text by the help of the translation, marking opposite to each its sound as given by a Chinese teacher according to the dialect which he desires to cultivate. When the first chapter is completed, some book, say the Christian 三字經 which is much easier than the native work of the same name, or one of the Gospels, may be taken up by way of practice. The student will be surprised to find himself already in possession of more than one half of the characters. On completing the second chapter, he would have more than nine tenths, and on arriving at the end of the fourth chapter, he will make the pleasing discovery that in any ordinary book the unknown characters are few.

The reading of native tracts on moral subjects* will then prove an agreeable pastime; and the Confucian Classics, with this preparation, will be found less arduous than they are usually regarded.

In order to acquire a thorough mastery of these staple characters, it would be well for the student to proceed to Part III, and apply himself to their orthography. For this purpose he should prepare a blank book ruled in columns answering to the vertical lines of the Chinese. In this the sounds and sense of the characters, and of their elements, should be written down; placing the elements first. Thus:—

| | | |
|---|---|---|
| Yih | Muh | We |
| One | Wood | Not-yet &c. |

One or two lines might be taken at a lesson; the sounds committed to memory precisely as a column in an English spelling book; and the characters recomposed by combining the elements. It should not be regarded as learned until all the characters can be reproduced from the written sounds, without reference to the printed text.

To aid in fixing these select characters in the mind, at once and forever, a kind of mnemonics will be found of service. The student should invent them for himself; seizing on any association, however absurd, which may happen to strike his fancy. The following may serve as specimens.

MNEMONICS.

| | | |
|---|---|---|
| 惟 | 心隹 | The ONLY needful—an *excellent heart.* |
| 大 | 一人 | GREAT—*one man,* the Emperor. |
| 天 | 一大 | HEAVEN—the *one great.* |
| | 旨 | A DECREE—what the *highest said.* |
| 地 | 土也 | The EARTH is *earth.* |
| 池 | 水也 | A POND is *water.* |
| 海 | 水每 | The SEA—*water everywhere.* |
| 秋 | 火禾 | AUTUMN—*fire* in the *rice* fields. |

* The following are some of the most elegant and popular.

朱子家訓 *Chu-ts' Family Monitor*
關帝覺世經 *Kwan-ti's Classic of Wakening the World.*
文昌陰騭文 *Wen-chang's Essay on Providence.*
太上感應篇 *T'ai-shang's Tract on Retribution.*
戒溺女文 *A Dissuasive from the Drowning of Daughters.*

善 羊口 GOOD—a *lamb*-like *mouth*.

惡 亞心 EVIL—an *inferior heart*.

禁 林示 PROHIBITION—*showing* two *trees* and forbidding one.

性 心生 NATURE—the *heart born* with us.

煙 火西土 SMOKE—the *fire* of the *western dirt* (opium).

獄 犭言犬 A LAWSUIT—*words* between two *dogs*.

聖 耳口王 The SAGE—a *prince* with *ear* and *mouth* *i.e.* a great teacher: (王 being sufficiently near to 壬).

The Chinese see in 爲 a resemblance to 馬 and describe it as 馬爲 *ma we;* why may not we, in 來 to COME, see 从人十 three men coming to a cross road? In 從 to FOLLOW, why may we not find 从 卜 *five men* following an *augur*, &c.?

Associations arbitrary and ludicrous are sanctioned by native usage; and the foreign student would do well not to despise them.

When the two thousand characters are thoroughly mastered, or one or two chapters, it will be of great advantage to go over them, writing under each such others as may be connected with it, by regular derivation, or casual resemblance. Thus:

未 Suggests 木末本昧抹妹 &c.
生 ...... 性姓星醒腥笙產 &c.
民 ........................ 氏岷泯 &c.
來 ........................ 徠萊賚 &c.
前 ..................... 箭剪翦煎 &c.
有 ........................ 宥囿賄 &c.
上 ........................ 止正旨 &c.
帝 ............... 禘締蹄蒂諦 &c.

The habit of thus grouping, on a familiar basis, all the characters the student may be able to recall, will augment the amount of his treasures, and confirm him in their possession. In this manner, the original number may easily be tripled or

quadrupled. In this work of expansion such dictionaries as Goodrich or Williams may be referred to for characters, as well as for definitions.

An appropriate sequel to the study of these common characters will be that of the several styles in which they are written, though the foreign student will do well not to burden himself with writing more than one. These are six in number.

1. 宋書 The clear square letter usually preferred in books, and so called from the dynasty of Sung, under which it came in vogue in connexion with the art of printing, at that time a new invention.

2. 楷書 The Pattern style—the happy mean between the stiff sharp angles of the foregoing, and the wavy, flowing, but uncertain lines of the two following The most important documents are always engrossed in *K'ai-shu;* and large works are frequently printed in it.

3. 行書 Running-hand—that employed in ordinary business.

4. 草書 The grass letter—running hand run wild, so as to resemble entangled grass. Though courtesy requires the scholar to apply the name of *ts'au ts* as a depreciative epithet to any specimen of his own chirography, to attain grace and ease in the management of this style is an object of ambition.

5. 隸書 an ornamental hand formerly employed in engrossing official documents, whence the name; though for that purpose it has now given place to the *K'ai-shu.* It is still much used, however, for scrolls, monumental inscriptions, and book-prefaces.

6. 篆書 by foreigners called the Seal character on account of its most frequent use. It is also much used for inscriptions on monuments and in adorning the title pages of books.

The 1st., 2nd., and 5th. stand related to each other somewhat as the Roman, Italic, and Black-letter of our letter press.

The 3rd., 4th., and 6th., may be compared to the Round hand, Running hand, and German text of our chirography. But while, in our own printing and penmanship, all the varieties may be made familiar to the eye, by a little attention to the comparison of a few forms; to acquire a reading knowledge of the different styles in Chinese, is a labor of more difficulty. It requires the careful comparison of some hundreds of leading forms, and, in addition to this, the aid of constant practice. The

acquisition of the 5th. and 6th. is an accomplishment, but an acquaintance with the 2nd., 3rd., and 4th. forms is of great utility.

This is a task which the student will hardly feel himself at liberty to decline. For without it, he is liable to be confounded, not merely confused, by constantly meeting his old friends in new disguises. Not only will he be perplexed by inscriptions on monuments, which he meets in travelling, and the prefaces or title-pages of elegant works; but the proclamation of a mandarin, the bill of a shop-keeper, or the letter of a native friend, will prove an annoying puzzle. The foreign student of German may indulge his literary tastes, without troubling himself to decipher reams of *handschrift;* but if resident on the banks of the Rhine he would find it somewhat inconvenient not to be able to learn for himself the contents of a familiar note. For a resident in China, the styles of business and correspondence are equally indispensable.

The six styles are here mentioned in the order of their importance. The first is that used in the text and analysis; and the reader will have the advantage of seeing it in at least two sizes of type.

Of the others, specimens are included in Part II., and for materials to practise on the learner need be at no loss. Monuments, sign-boards, prefaces, and letters—old ones which a native friend may submit to his perusal—will all come to his aid and further his progress. The 四體千字文 will be found helpful.

## V. *Use in Schools.*

With us the first stages in climbing the hill of knowledge are so gentle that the young scholar saunters unconscious of effort. In China they are so precipitous, that a large proportion of those who attempt the ascent, fall back in despair. To grade the steep, facilitate the acquisition of the elements of education, and promote the efficiency of Christian schools was my prime object in preparing the Chinese portion of this work.

*Via trita via tuta* is a good maxim; but it should not prevent us mending the "old paths." That they have been trodden by the feet of millions is no evidence that they are incapable of improvement. Foreigners in China have not felt compelled to use wooden blocks in printing their books, just because the Chinese have done so ever since the invention of printing. If metallic types and revolving presses are improvements on the native mode of manufacturing books,—acknowledged to be so by the natives who are rapidly adopting them, —why

should it be taken as a foregone conclusion that the foreigner can suggest no better method for acquiring a knowledge of their contents?

Is it not a fact that the majority of pupils in Chinese schools never succeed in learning to read and write? And is it not an equally significant fact, that the man who can read fluently, and write correctly, is regarded as a scholar? The apparatus for obtaining knowledge passes for learning, and rudiments are esteemed accomplishments.

To a certain extent this is owing to the difficulty of the written language, which is not much easier for the native than it is for the foreign student; but it is due in part to imperfections in the method of teaching.

A boy of eight summers attired for the occasion in robes of ceremony, selecting a lucky day, enters on the career of a scholar by doing obeisance to his teacher, and kneeling before the picture of Confucius. A book is placed in his hands, and he is taught the *sounds* of some half a dozen characters. These learned, he hands the book to the teacher, and turning his back recites his lesson in a sing-song tone, keeping time like a pendulum by the vibrations of his body. Day after day he goes on cramming his memory with sounds and forms until he can patter off the Four Books and the Book of Odes as glibly as a breviary. But all this time he has not obtained the glimmering of an idea. He has got the symbols of thought, but not the thoughts.

This ordeal passed, he is deemed worthy of initiation into higher mysteries. The veil is gradually withdrawn, and a ray of light shed on each of those dull figures, kindling them into life, and transforming empty sounds into the articulate voices of human language.

The intellect of the lad feels the stimulus, and wakes as from a hibernation; while his faculties unfold like the buds of Spring. Reading becomes a pleasure; and he delights to employ these signs—not till now significant—for the expression of his own thoughts.

But how many youth are compelled by poverty to quit school before the dawn of this cheering period! How many more toil on for years in unalleviated darkness because they are too dull to complete the preliminary process to the satisfaction of their teachers! What would be thought of a school-master who should compel his pupils to commit the Iliad to memory before translating a line? Yet this is precisely the time-honored system of the Chinese; and it is doing it no wrong to charge it with perpetrating the crime of mental infanticide on an enormous scale.

A partial remedy applied in many mission schools is to require the teacher to deviate so far from the beaten track as to connect the sense of each character with its form and sound in the very commencement of his instructions. A further melioration would be to furnish the student with a selection of characters in common use (*i.e.*, with the Chinese text of this Manual), as the readiest way to the treasures of knowledge; and to teach him from the first to *spell* each one as an aid to memory and a preparation for writing.

How far the first of these conditions will be met by this collection may be inferred from the account already given of the principles on which it is formed; and whether the second will be answered by the analytical method, may also be inferred from the explanation on a previous page. It only remains, therefore, to add an observation or two in regard to the mode of teaching.

Who of us does not remember the young emulation which impelled us to learn pages of words before we had any appreciation of their value, merely from the hope of standing at the head of a spelling-class? How intense the feeling grew when the school was divided into parties and the combatants entered the lists two and two; the victorious boy wearing his honors as proudly as a champion of the ring!

The Chinese system of education is not destitute of this stimulus. The more advanced students contend for academic and civil honors with an ardor unsurpassed in any country. But it is wanting at that stage at which an incentive is most needed. In the early portion of his course each pupil pursues a solitary path, receives instruction alone and recites alone, knowing little and caring less as to the progress of his fellows. In most primary schools the class organization is wholly unknown, and the teacher repeats for each individual an amount of toil which would suffice for a whole form. By this mode of spelling these inconveniences may be obviated—the spur applied to the pupil and labor saved to the teacher: classes may be formed and recitations conducted precisely as in an English school, though in learning their lessons pupils will require an amount of oral instruction which is not called for in a language whose orthography is more purely phonetic.

An experiment made in a mission school while the first edition was passing through the press proved highly satisfactory. In the morning the teacher called a class before him and gave them the sound and sense of the characters and their elements. He then required them to copy the lesson into a book provided for the purpose in order to impress it on the memory and accustom them to writing. In the afternoon he summoned

them to recite. He pronounced a character of the text, and the first pupil responded by giving its elements. The next character was analyzed by the second boy, and so on, until some one made a mistake; when the character was passed on, and the boy who succeeded in spelling it correctly was promoted to the place of him who failed.

The exercise proved novel and exciting; and some of the boys who previously appeared indifferent as to progress began to apply themselves with diligence. Memoriter recitation, definition of characters, translation into the Mandarin or the vernacular dialect, and writing on the black-board, were additional exercises in which it was sought to inspire the pupils with the same emulation, and so render their progress pleasant as well as thorough.

I conclude this introduction with a statement of *Ching Sien-sheng*, a Nanking *Siu ts'ai*, who was in charge of the school. "Since having the care of a school I have often grieved over the difficulty experienced by young pupils in learning the points and strokes of our letters. Lately, however, a work has been prepared, entitled *Jin-ts-sin-fah*, 'A New Method for Learning Characters'. The method consists in resolving one character into several, and combining several into one. The most frequent characters in the Four Books and Five Classics are thus elucidated, so that the student not only learns them with little trouble, but gets at the ideas which gave birth to the characters. Moreover, in learning one he obtains a knowledge of three. I have employed this method in the instruction of my pupils, and found it both expeditious and thorough." *

* The author thought of adding here a sketch of grammar, but abandoned it as foreign to the design of this work. In a language destitute of inflection, grammar is obviously not the thing to begin with, though the study is both interesting and helpful at a more advanced stage. When that is reached the foreign student may take up Dr. Edkins' Mandarin Grammar with advantage. The native student, unless at home in English, has to dispense with such aid. The only branch of grammar to which native writers pay attention is syntax 句 法, which is studied in connexion with first efforts in composition. The student's further progress belongs to 文 法, which may properly be described as rhetoric.

# PART II.

# THE TEXT AND TRANSLATION.

## 常字雙千

## CONSTANT CHARACTERS, A COUPLE OF THOUSANDS.

### NOTE.

Chap. I. contains 237 characters, which occur from 1000 to 10,000 times in the books examined, and the three following from the next group. 羣溫昭

Chap. II. contains 587 characters, which occur from 200 to 1,000 times, with the addition of the five following from the next groups. 欺邀僭恭讓

Chap. III. contains 570 characters, which occur from 75 to 200 times, and six additional from the next groups. 稽均肇袍綻珍

Chap. IV. contains the most frequent characters in the remaining groups, with an intermixture of useful characters compiled from other sources—in all 608. See page 4.

The sum total of the four chapters is 2,016.

The sounds originally given in the current Mandarin have been slightly altered to conform them to the court dialect, though the 入聲, which disappears at Peking, is still marked with a final *h*. The Pekinese tones are indicated by numbers, but it is not possible to learn them without a teacher, nor are they of any value at a distance from the capital.

The vowels are those of the German, except that *i* and *e*, before *n* and *ng*, have the force of *i* in *fin*, and *u fun*; *s*, *ts*, *ch* and *sh* standing alone, have a strong sibillation, as in *rats*, *church*, *pass*, *hush*, when the sound is prolonged.

The Greek aspirate represents a breathing, which can only be learned from the living voice.

第 ti 一 yih 章 chang 論 len 古 ku 始 sh

造物

1

未 4we 生 1sheng 民 2min 來 2lai

前 2tsʻien 有 3yiu 上 4shang 帝 4ti

惟 1we 一 4yih 眞 1chen 神 1shen

無 2wu 聖 4sheng 能 2neng 比 3pi

2

六 4luh 日 4jih 力 4lih 作 4tsoh

先 1sien 闢 4pʻih 天 1tʻien 地 4ti

萬 4wan 物 4wuh 多 1to 焉 1yien

既 4ki 希 1hi 且 3tsʻie 異 4yi

3

遂 4sue 亦 4yih 和 2ho 土 3tʻu

將 1tsiang 爲 2we 靈 2ling 矣 3i

命 4ming 處 3chʻu 賜 4tsʻ 基 1ki

千 1tsʻien 百 4poh 皆 1kie 與 3yü

4

復 3fuh 使 3sh 宜 2i 家 1kia

女 3nü 兮 1hi 往 3wang 事 4sh

謂 4we 之 1ch 日 1yuih 夫 1fu

爾 3r 我 3wo 如 2ju 自 4ts

# CHAPTER I.

## DISCOURSES OF THE ANCIENT BEGINNINGS.

### *Creation.*

1.

Not-yet to life *were* people come,
Before existed the Supreme Ruler,
Only One True God,
No holy *one* can compare *with him.*

2.

Six days *he* mightily wrought,
First divided Heaven and Earth,
Myriads of things multiplied (o),
Both rare AND strange.

3.

Then also tempered clay,
Intending to make a spiritual *being* (o),
Decreed *his* place in the bestowed possession,
By thousands and hundreds all *things* gave.

4.

Again *he* sent *one* to order the family,
Woman (o) went to serve *him*,
And calling him, said, "Husband,
Thou and I *are* as *one* self".

墮惡

5

凡 2 fan
所 3 so
求 2 ch'iu
者 3 che

毋 1 wu
不 4 puh
立 4 lih
予 3 yü

然 2 jan
欲 4 yuh
善 4 shan
惡 4 oh

勿 4 wuh
聽 1 t'ing
手 3 sheu
取 3 ch'ü

6

告 4 kau
云 2 yuin
可 3 k'o
食 2 shih

或 4 hwoh
當 1 tang
見 4 kien
耳 3 r

聞 2 wen
言 2 yien
摩 2 mo
拿 2 na

得 4 toh
罪 4 tsue
因 1 yin
此 3 ts'

7

中 1 chung
傳 2 chuan
亞 4 ya
伯 4 poh

羊 2 yang
祭 4 tsi
信 4 sin
心 1 sin

長 3 chang
子 3 ts
若 4 joh
兄 1 hiung

敵 2 tih
殺 1 shah
及 2 kih
今 1 kin

8

以 3 i
致 4 ch
彼 3 pe
族 2 ts'uh

但 4 tan
安 1 an
利 4 li
名 2 ming

愛 4 ai
身 1 shin
尼 1 niih
色 4 seh

列 4 lih
馬 3 ma
羅 2 lo
金 1 kin

9

父 4 fu
意 4 i
非 1 fe
昔 1 sih

其 2 ch'i
僕 2 p'uh
已 3 i
明 2 ming

即 2 tsih
由 2 yiu
是 4 sh
時 2 sh

大 4 ta
水 3 shue
四 4 s
行 2 hing

速成漢語

## *The Fall.*

5.

Of all the (which) desired things,
*There was* nothing not instantly granted,
Yet wished *they* the good and evil *fruit*,
*They* must-not listen to the hand's taking *it.*

6.

*One* informed *them* saying "Can eat,
Perhaps *you* ought to see" (0),
*They* heard the words, felt and took,
Getting sin *was* because-of this.

7.

*Their* middle progeny Abel (2)
Sheep offered, with a believing heart,
*Their* elder (longer) son, as elder-brother,
Vengefully killed *him; thus it is* till now.

8.

So caused that race,
Solely to rest in gain and name,
To love the body and dote-on beauty (color),
Array horses *for battle*, and gather gold.

9.

The Father's mind was-not as formerly,
His servant already clearly-*saw*,
Then from that time,
The great waters to the four *quarters* went.

| 10 | 11 | 12 降救 | 13 | 14 |
|---|---|---|---|---|
| 卷[2]küin | 居[1]kü | 故[4]ku | 等[3]teng | 相[1]siang |
| 撒[3]sah | 八[1]pah | 又[4]yiu | 間[1]kien | 約[1]yoh |
| 全[2]ts'üin | 從[2]ts'ung | 督[1]tuh | 于[2]yü | 衆[4]chung |
| 死[3]s | 七[1]ts'ih | 教[4]kiau | 三[1]san | 士[4]sh |
| 何[2]ho | 各[4]koh | 甚[4]shen | 倫[2]lun | 必[4]pih |
| 問[4]wen | 拉[1]la | 加[1]kia | 出[1]ch'uh | 知[1]ch |
| 儕[1]ch'ai | 入[4]juh | 世[4]sh | 於[2]yü | 理[3]li |
| 羣[2]k'üin | 門[1]men | 福[2]fuh | 五[3]wu | 數[4]shu |
| 第[4]ti | | 降[4]kiang | 華[2]hwa | 節[2]tsih |
| 歸[1]kwe | | 下[4]hia | 年[2]nien | 禮[3]li |
| 方[1]fang | | 耶[2]ye | 至[4]ch | 守[3]sheu |
| 蓋[4]kai | | 穌[1]su | 殿[4]tien | 法[3]fah |
| 則[2]tsah | | 斯[1]s | 在[4]tsai | 司[1]s |
| 同[2]t'ung | | 實[1]shih | 會[4]hwe | 十[1]shih |
| 義[4]i | | 救[4]kiu | 受[4]sheu | 二[4]r |
| 人[2]jen | | 主[3]chu | 書[1]shu | 徒[2]t'u |

10.

Whirled, scattered, the whole *world* died—
Why ask for classes and companies!
But *those who* turned to the square shelter,
Then *were* the same-with righteous men.

11.

The dwellers eight; the animals followed by sevens,
Each drew *them* into the gate.

## *Redemption.*

12.

Therefore again, God guided and taught *men;*
And greatly adding to the world's happiness,
Sent down Jesus, (2)
He *is* really the Saving Lord.

13.

In rank, the midst OF Three,
In relations *he* came-out OF the Five,
In the flower of *his* years, came-to the temple,
In the assembly, *he* received the books.

14.

*He* joined in covenant many scholars,
Certainly understood principles and numbers,
Regulated rites, observed laws,
And controlled *his* twelve disciples.

15

冷 3 leng
迦 1 kia
城 2 ch'eng
邑 4 yih

巴 1 pa
米 3 mi
道 4 tau
路 4 lu

猶 2 yiu
太 4 t'ai
國 1 kwoh
也 3 ye

西 1 si
乃 3 nai
山 1 shan
乎 1 hu

16

王 2 wang
而 2 r
溫 1 wen
雅 2 ya

後 4 heu
章 1 chang
昭 1 chau
諸 1 chu

凡二百四十字

## 15.

Jerusalem and Capernaum, a city and town,
To Babylon and Media *were* ways and roads,
Judea (2) *was* a kingdom (0),
Sinai (2) a mountain (0).

## 16.

A King, yet (and) meek and gentle,
The after chapter illustrates these.

---

### Notes.

(0) Marks the place of an expletive, which is untranslatable.

(2) indicates that two characters are rendered by one word. In names they stand for syllables, and seldom give the correct pronunciation, 亞 *secondary;* 伯 *lord* or *uncle (verse 7).*

( ) indicates that the word enclosed is another rendering, or an explanation.

Verse 5. Things or persons. 者 is the complement of the relative pronoun 所.

Verse 6. As a substantive 耳 means **ear.**

Verse 8. 列 means a rank; it is also a sign of the plural as 列國 the nations.

Verse 13. The 五倫 five social relations.

君臣, 父子, 夫婦, 兄弟, 朋友,

Assembly, the Synagogue, Luke IV. 16.

Verse 14. 數 numbers, also *destiny.*

Verse 15. In names, the first or last character is frequently taken for the whole. The following are the significations of those in the verse:—

冷 *cold,* 釋迦 name of *Buddha,* 巴 a *handful, grip* or *blow,* 米 *rice,* 猶 *like, yet,* 太 *great, huge,* 西 *west,* 乃 *to be.*

## 第 ti 二 r 章 chang 論 lŭn 耶 ye 穌 su 興 hing 教 kiau

**1** 綱領

親[1]ch'in 營[2]ying 皮[2]p'i 幕[4]mu

赦[4]sheh 過[4]kwo 拯[3]ch'eng 逃[2]t'au

蒙[2]mung 選[3]süen 代[4]tai 贖[2]shuh

聲[1]sheng 稱[1]ch'eng 益[4]yih 高[1]kau

**2**

備[4]pe 歷[4]lih 苦[3]k'u 難[4]nan

顯[3]hien 成[2]ch'eng 功[1]kung 勞[2]lau

追[1]chue 厥[1]küih 本[3]pen 初[1]ch'u

垂[2]chu'e 訓[4]hüin 汝[3]ju 曹[2]ts'au

**3** 出世

母[1]mu 氏[4]sh 瑟[4]soh 妻[1]ch'i

少[4]shau 小[3]siau 待[4]tai 字[4]ts

蓮[2]lien 容[2]yung 素[4]su 端[1]tuan

蘭[2]lan 性[4]sing 較[3]kiau 細[4]si

**4**

曾[2]ts'eng 緣[2]yuen 夢[4]mung 感[3]kan

忽[1]hwuh 產[3]ch'an 男[2]nan 嗣[4]s

# CHAPTER II.

## TREATS OF JESUS STARTING HIS RELIGION.

### *Leading Topics.*

1.

Himself formed a skin tabernacle,
Pardoned transgression, succored refugees,
In the chosen's (2) stead ***paid*** ransom—
His fame and praise ***become*** more high.

2.

He fully passed-through bitter hardships,
Displayed complete his meritorious toil,
Pursuing HIS (its) original beginning,
***We will*** condescendingly instruct you (2).

### *Christ's Advent.*

3.

His mother (2) Joseph's wife,
Of few ***years*** and small, waiting marriage,
***Was*** of lily face and habitually correct,
Her fragrant nature incomparably fine.

4.

Having ***from*** a dream conceived,
She suddenly gave-birth to a male heir.

嬰時

5

東 1 tung
界 4 kie
友 3 yiu
師 1 sh

軍 1 küin
光 1 kwang
詳 2 siang
視 4 sh

造 4 tsau
室 2 shih
辱 3 juh
臨 2 lin

伏 2 fuh
拜 4 pai
依 1 i
次 4 ts'

6

后 4 heu
皇 2 hwang
最 4 tsue
忍 3 jeh

按 4 an
戶 4 hu
戮 4 luh
刑 2 hing

夜 4 ye
深 1 sheng
投 2 t'eu
遠 3 yuen

避 4 pi
境 4 king
藏 2 ts'ang
形 2 hing

7

迨 4 tai
君 1 küin
卒 2 tsuh
沒 4 moh

率 4 soh shuai
眷 4 küen
返 3 fan
止 3 ch

仍 2 jeng
恐 3 k'ung
勒 1 loh
召 4 chau

挪 2 no
負 4 fu
脫 1 t'oh
去 4 k'ü

8

畜 4 ch'uh
老 3 lau
革 2 keh
荒 1 hwang

龍 2 lung
現 4 hien
首 3 sheu
舉 3 kü

免 3 mien
歟 2 yü
幸 4 hing
哉 1 tsai

原 2 yuen
靡 2 mi
終 1 chung
始 3 sh

受洗

9

向 4 hiang
野 3 ye
翰 4 han
呼 1 hu

悔 3 hwe
改 3 kai
務 4 wu
切 4 ch'ieh

就 4 tsiu
洗 4 si
河 2 ho
旁 2 p'ang

循 2 süin
儀 2 i
莫 4 moh
越 4 yüih

速成漢語

## *His Infancy.*

5.

From the Eastern border, friendly Masters,
The host of lights minutely beholding,
Approach the room, humbly arrive,
Bow-down and worship according-to order.

6.

The king (2) was most unfeeling,
Each door he cruelly punished,
At night late (deep) *Joseph* dashed afar,
And flying the region hid his person.

7.

Waiting till the prince deceased (2),
He led his relations and returning stopped,
Yet afraid-of a compulsory summons,
Escaping bore away *the child* and went.

8.

*When* a beast is old, his hide is bare,
*When* a dragon appears, his head is raised,
Escaped (avoided) (0)! *how* fortunate (0)!
Originally he *has* no end or beginning.

## *His Baptism.*

9.

Towards the desert John cried,
Repent, reform, take-care *to be* earnest.
*Christ* came to baptism at the river's brink,
Observed the rite, and did not transgress.

| 10 | 11 見試 | 12 | 13 | 14 宣道 |
|---|---|---|---|---|
| 譬 [4]pi | 嘗 [2]ch'ang | 幷 [4]ping | 修 [1]siu | 乘 [1]ch'eng |
| 樹 [4]shu | 遇 [4]yu | 令 [1]ling | 德 [1]teh | 驢 [2]lü |
| 結 [2]kieh | 魔 [2]mo | 俯 [3]fu | 圖 [2]t'u | 歡 [1]hwan |
| 果 [3]kwo | 試 [4]sh | 望 [4]wang | 報 [4]pau | 樂 [4]loh |
| 適 [2]shih | 指 [3]ch | 尊 [1]tsun | 正 [4]cheng | 總 [3]tsung |
| 口 [3]k'eu | 餅 [3]ping | 榮 [2]yung | 直 [2]chih | 集 [4]tsih |
| 維 [2]we | 爭 [1]ch'eng | 強 [3]ch'iang | 兩 [3]liang | 智 [4]ch |
| 悅 [4]yüih | 遺 [1]i | 施 [1]sh | 虛 [1]hü | 愚 [1]yü |
| 否 [3]feu | 押 [1]yah | | 奉 [4]fung | 條 [2]t'iau |
| 悉 [4]sih | 登 [1]teng | | 諭 [4]yü | 誡 [4]kie |
| 刃 [4]jen | 宮 [1]kung | | 遵 [1]tsun | 張 [1]chang |
| 斷 [4]tuan | 屋 [1]uh | | 譴 [3]ch'ien | 布 [4]pu |
| 便 [4]pien | 崇 [2]ch'ung | | 烏 [1]u | 宰 [3]tsai |
| 付 [4]fu | 垣 [1]yuan | | 敢 [3]kan | 治 [4]ch |
| 焚 [2]fen | 被 [4]pe | | 惑 [4]hwoh | 屬 [3]shuh |
| 烈 [4]lieh | 攜 [2]hi | | 余 [2]yü | 吾 [2]wu |

10.

*John* used the parable of a tree bearing fruit;
Suiting the mouth it *only* gives pleasure,
Otherwise, totally the blade will-cut *it down*,
Thereon *to be* handed-over to burning fierce.

## *His Temptation.*

11.

He once met the Devil's trying,
*Who* pointing to loaves, strove to bestow them,
And carrying him ascended a palatial house,
To a lofty wall WAS he led-up.

12.

Also bidding him bend-down and look *abroad*,
Exalted glory he forcibly offered (gave).

13.

"To cultivate virtue planning for rewards,
*Makes* honesty and rectitude both void.
*I* obey orders, and fulfill my mission,
How dare you tempt me"!

## *His preaching.*

14.

He rode an ass when he rejoiced (2),
Together gathered the wise and stupid,
The lines of command, spread-out (2),
*Saying* "To rule and govern belongs to me.

| 15 | 16 | 17 | 18 | 19 |
|---|---|---|---|---|
| 攻 $^{1}$kung | 陷 $^{4}$hien | 花 $^{1}$hwa | 懼 $^{4}$kü | 孰 $^{2}$shuh |
| 擊 $^{1}$kih | 謀 $^{2}$mo | 嫩 $^{4}$nun | 失 $^{1}$sh | 忘 $^{2}$wang |
| 違 $^{2}$we | 亡 $^{2}$wang | 易 $^{4}$yi | 災 $^{1}$tsai | 足 $^{2}$tsuh |
| 逆 $^{4}$niih | 獄 $^{1}$yuh | 敗 $^{4}$pai | 絕 $^{2}$küih | 畏 $^{4}$we |
| 常 $^{2}$chʻang | 遭 $^{1}$tsau | 麥 $^{4}$maih | 好 $^{4}$hau | 頓 $^{4}$tŭn |
| 聚 $^{4}$chü | 患 $^{4}$hwan | 掃 $^{3}$sau | 甲 $^{3}$kiah | 害 $^{4}$hai |
| 俊 $^{4}$chüing | 沙 $^{1}$sha | 定 $^{4}$ting | 亂 $^{4}$luan | 體 $^{3}$tʻi |
| 英 $^{1}$ying | 洲 $^{1}$cheu | 留 $^{2}$liu | 俱 $^{1}$kü | 魂 $^{2}$hwen |
| 旨 $^{1}$ch | 統 $^{3}$tʻung | 類 $^{4}$le | 仇 $^{2}$chʻeu | 該 $^{1}$kai |
| 斥 $^{4}$chʻih | 轄 $^{2}$hiah | 反 $^{3}$fan | 怒 $^{4}$nu | 恃 $^{3}$sh |
| 氣 $^{4}$chʻi | 的 $^{1}$tih | 鳥 $^{3}$niau | 財 $^{2}$tsʻai | 庇 $^{3}$pi |
| 責 $^{2}$tsah | 裔 $^{2}$i | 獸 $^{4}$sheu | 據 $^{4}$kü | 釋 $^{1}$shih |
| 隱 $^{1}$yin | 征 $^{1}$cheng | 穀 $^{3}$kuh | 兵 $^{1}$ping | 藉 $^{4}$tsieh |
| 暗 $^{4}$an | 途 $^{2}$tʻu | 養 $^{3}$yang | 奪 $^{2}$toh | 謝 $^{4}$sie |
| 畢 $^{4}$pih | 遍 $^{4}$pien | 弗 $^{4}$fuh | 車 $^{1}$chʻe | 恩 $^{1}$en |
| 陳 $^{2}$chʻen | 周 $^{1}$cheu | 憂 $^{1}$yiu | 驅 $^{1}$kʻü | 仁 $^{2}$jen |

15.

I attack and smite disobedient opposers,
Constantly collect the excellent and brave,
Self-will reprove, passion (vapor) rebuke,
The secret and dark, to the utmost display."

16.

He fell-into plots, and fled imprisonment,
Encountered affliction in the sandy isles,
Generally swayed the lineal descendants,
In progressive journeys everywhere circulated.

17.

The flower tender easily wastes,
Wheat in sweeping is certainly retained.
*Our* race is contrary to birds and beasts,
*Which for* grain to nourish do-not grieve.

18.

Dread loss, and calamity will-cease,
Love war, and confusion comes-with it,
If hatred rages, and riches are clutched,
Soldiers seize and chariots drive *them away*.

19.

Who *can* forget *him who is* to be feared?
*Such* at-once injure body and soul.
You ought to rest-on his protection for release,
Dependently thank his grace and goodness.

| 20 | 21 立教 | 22 | 23 | 24 定例 |
|---|---|---|---|---|
| 學[1] hioh | 海[3] hai | 目[4] muh | 邦[1] pang | 燔[2] fan |
| 別[2] pih | 干[1] kan | 紀[4] ki | 都[1] tu | 牡[3] meu |
| 派[4] p‘ai | 哥[1] ko | 矜[1] ch‘in | 省[3] sheng | 割[1] koh |
| 支[1] ch | 弟[4] ti | 恤[1] süih | 京[1] king | 肉[4] juh |
| 埃[2] ye | 棄[4] ch‘i | 志[4] ch | 南[2] nan | 舊[4] kiu |
| 田[2] t‘ien | 業[4] yeh | 揚[2] yang | 北[3] peh | 例[4] li |
| 許[3] hü | 速[2] suh | 讚[4] tsan | 半[4] pan | 雖[1] sue |
| 置[4] ch | 起[3] ch‘i | 美[3] me | 經[1] king | 存[2] ts‘un |
| 敬[4] king | 履[3] lü | 默[4] muh | 每[3] me | 羔[1] kau |
| 妄[4] wang | 武[3] wu | 記[4] ki | 念[4] nian | 牛[2] niu |
| 良[2] liang | 請[3] ts‘ing | 祈[2] ch‘i | 僭[4] tsien | 特[4] t‘ah |
| 分[1] fen | 隨[2] sue | 文[2] wen | 僞[3] we | 犢[2] tuh |
| 詛[2] tsu | 願[4] yuen | 通[1] t‘ung | 化[4] hwa | 錫[2] sih |
| 禁[4] kin | 離[2] li | 達[2] tah | 導[4] tau | 獻[4] hien |
| 祝[4] chuh | 鄉[1] hiang | 古[3] ku | 平[2] p‘ing | 豈[3] k‘i |
| 極[2] kih | 里[3] li | 史[3] sh | 情[2] ts‘ing | 欣[1] hing |

20.

The doctrine distinguishes classes (2),
*Some* in Eden (2), it promises to place,
Reverence and deceit, it well divides,
To curse forbids, in blessing *is* extreme.

## *His Disciples.*

21.

By the sea shore the brothers[g] (2),
Cast-aside their business, hasten to rise,
His sandal steps beg to follow,
Willing to forsake their neighborhood (2).

22.

Their eyes recorded his compassions (2),
With a will they spread his praise,
Silently memorised the prayer-form,
Opened (2) *their minds* to ancient history.

23.

Kingdom, capital, province, metropolis,
South and North, they half traversed,
Ever thinking on the blasphemous and false,
Reformed, led them, calmed their passions.

## *His Ordinances.*

24.

Burning of victims (males) and cutting of
the flesh,
By the old usage, though retained,
*Yet* lamb, cow, ox, and calf,
*As* gifts, and offerings, how *can they* please?

行奇

| 25 | 26 | 27 | 28 | 29 |
|---|---|---|---|---|
| 私 1s | 著 4chu | 鬼 3kwe | 詣 4i | 助 4chu |
| 籲 4yü | 語 3yü | 逐 4chuh | 船 2ch'uan | 罕 3han |
| 公 1kung | 貴 4kwe | 病 4ping | 波 1po | 賴 4lai |
| 禱 3tau | 喻 4yü | 醫 1i | 面 mien | 他 1t'a |
| 葡 2p'u | 奇 2ch'i | 污 1wu | 息 2sih | 審 3shen |
| 萄 2t'au | 畧 4lioh | 解 3kie | 風 1fung | 判 4p'an |
| 飲 3yin | 更 4keng | 禍 4hwo | 舟 1cheu | 咸 2hien |
| 傾 1ch'ing | 捷 2tsieh | 滅 4mieh | 底 3ti | 已 3ki |
| 開 1k'ai | 顧 4ku | 葬 tsang | 愈 4yü | 罰 2fah |
| 堂 2t'ang | 種 4chung | 墓 4mu | 疾 2tsih | 犯 4fan |
| 誠 2ch'eng | 牧 4muh | 寢 3ch'in | 環 2hwan | 廣 3kwang |
| 勸 4k'üen | 傷 1shang | 興 1hing | 觀 1kwan | 援 2yuen |
| 引 3yin | 夕 1sih | 捫 1men | 活 1hwoh | 重 4chung |
| 證 4cheng | 朝 1chau | 衣 1i | 喪 1sang | 權 2k'üen |
| 宣 1süen | 歲 4sue | 婦 4fu | 侍 4sh | 獨 2tuh |
| 音 1yin | 月 4yüih | 潔 2kieh | 喜 3hi | 任 4jin |

25.

*Instead* private supplication, public prayer,
The grape (2), to drink and pour,
To open the hall, and sincerely exhort,
Adduce evidence, and proclaim the sound—

## *His Miracles.*

26.

Publishing ***Christ's*** words, we value parables,
His miracles briefly in-turn succeed,
He watched the ***tender*** plant, shepherded
the bruised
Evening and morning, for years and months;

27.

Devils expelled, sickness healed,
The unclean released, misery extinguished,
The buried in the grave, from slumber rose,
Touching his clothes, a woman was cleansed.

28.

He visited a boat, on the wave's face
And stilled the wind, in the bark's bottom,
Restored sick, around looked-on *him*,
Revived dead, standing-by rejoiced.

29.

For help little ***did he*** depend-on another,
***Even*** the judgment (2) is all his own,
He punishes offenders, widely rescues,
And weighty authority alone sustains.

| 30 | 31 預言 | 32 | 33 臨終 | 34 |
|---|---|---|---|---|
| 固 4 ku | 散 3 san | 廢 4 fe | 工 1 kung | 動 1 tung |
| 保 3 pau | 編 1 pien | 園 2 yuen | 役 4 yi | 偕 2 hie |
| 盛 4 sheng | 賽 4 sai | 吉 2 kih | 貧 2 p'in | 新 1 sin |
| 盈 2 ying | 說 1 shoh | 壤 3 jang | 富 4 fu | 娶 3 ch'ü |
| 恒 2 heng | 錄 4 luh | 頌 4 sung | 左 3 tso | 香 1 hiang |
| 懷 2 hwai | 久 3 kiu | 對 4 tue | 右 4 yiu | 供 1 kung |
| 恭 1 kung | 兆 4 chau | 誰 2 sue | 近 4 chin | 酒 3 tsiu |
| 順 4 shun | 伊 1 i | 欺 1 ch'i | 交 1 kiau | 邀 1 yau |
| 外 4 wai | 毀 3 hwe | 街 1 kie | 餘 2 yü | 執 2 chih |
| 暴 4 pau | 宇 3 yü | 歌 1 ko | 論 4 lün | 油 2 yiu |
| 內 4 ne | 再 4 tsai | 谷 3 kuh | 尤 2 yiu | 膏 1 kau |
| 愆 1 ch'ien | 建 4 kien | 應 4 ing | 服 2 fuh | 坐 4 tso |
| 庶 4 shu | 預 4 yü | 俾 3 pe | 班 1 pan | 流 1 liu |
| 幾 1 ki | 計 4 ki | 讓 4 jang | 旅 3 lü | 血 3 hüih |
| 戰 4 chan | 末 4 moh | 九 3 kiu | 盡 4 tsin | 憫 2 min |
| 勝 4 sheng | 期 1 ch'i | 思 1 s | 招 1 chau | 號 2 hau |

速成漢語

30.

Firmly guard abundance full;
Ever cherish respectful obedience,
And outward violence, inward depravity,
*You* almost-certainly (2) fight victoriously.

## *Prophecies.*

31.

In scattered essays, Isaiah spoke,
And the record long fore-tokened IT,
The demolished temple ***should*** again be-built,
He fore-reckoned (2) the final period.

32.

Waste gardens turn to happy ground;
On comparing (2) who (what) deceives?
In the streets songs, in the vallies answers,
Must yield to mature thought.

## *His Last Days.*

33.

Artisans, officials, poor and rich,
Left and right held near intercourse,
*To his* casual discourses heartily submitted,
Their class companions all summoned.

34.

Moved together-with the Bridegroom (2),
Odours offered, to wine invited,
Held oil and anointed him sitting *at meat.*
*When* flowed his blood, they pityingly cried.

勸世

| 35 | 36 | 37 | 38 |
|---|---|---|---|
| 慧 4 hwe | 察 2 ch'ah | 宗 1 tsung | 偶 3 eu |
| 雨 3 yü | 貨 4 hwo | 姓 4 sing | 像 4 siang |
| 慈 2 ts' | 度 4 toh / tu | 單 1 tan | 阿 1 o |
| 雲 2 yüin | 銀 2 yin | 微 1 we | 回 2 hwe |
| 震 4 chen | 赤 4 ch'ih | 祖 3 tsu | 銅 2 t'ung |
| 角 2 kioh | 白 2 peh / pai | 孫 1 sun | 鐵 3 t'ieh |
| 播 1 po | 用 4 yung | 答 1 tah | 石 2 sh |
| 示 4 sh | 給 3 keh | 述 4 shuh | 木 4 muh |
| 背 4 pe | 提 2 t'i | 共 4 kung | 創 4 ch'uang |
| 架 4 kia | 要 4 yau | 獲 4 hwoh | 識 2 sh |
| 築 4 chuh | 發 1 fah | 濟 4 tsi | 破 4 p'o |
| 壇 2 t'an | 綱 1 kang | 進 4 tsin | 淫 2 yin |
| 納 4 nah | 合 1 hoh | 誓 4 sh | 尚 4 shang |
| 匱 4 kwe | 享 3 hiang | 乏 2 fah | 議 4 i |
| 載 4 tsai | 永 3 yung | 哀 1 ai | 變 4 pien |
| 器 4 ch'i | 位 4 we | 哭 1 k'uh | 俗 2 suh |

凡五百七十六字

## *Exhortation.*

35.

Wisdom as the rain, mercy as the clouds,
With thundering horn disseminate, show forth,
He bore the cross, ***and of it*** built an altar,
***As*** priests took the ark, and bore the vessels.

36.

Inspect the goods, estimate the silver,
The red and white, you must give—
***We have*** handled important, taken-up leading-topics—
***He is*** fit to enjoy an ever-lasting throne.

37.

His family (2), ***is*** solitary and insignificant,
***Yet*** grandfather, grandson answer the record—
Together obtain conveyance to enter,
***Where*** it-is-sworn ***is*** no sorrow or weeping.

38.

Image likenesses, ***why*** dote-on (2)?
Brass, iron, stone, and wood,
Begin ***to be*** intelligent, burst adulterous ***wiles***,
Uppermost consider a change of customs.

## Notes.*

1. 親 usually signifies a near relation, but the usage in this place, which is a frequent one, suggests the idea that one's nearest relation is *himself*.
   This first line contains a natural, though inelegant figure for the incarnation.
3. 字 *letters*, referring to the marriage *contract*.
8. The disclosure of Herod's real character and that of the fugitive. The "dragon," an emblem of the divine, refers to Christ.
16. 亡 usually means to *perish*.
   "Sandy isles"—oases.
   Though the following lines are not exact citations of Scripture, the reader will readily recall passages in which the ideas occur.
21. Lit. *Elder brother* and *Younger brother*, 干 here put for 岸 signifies armor, and to offend.
25. Sound, a contraction for 福音, the Happy Sound, the Gospel.
   There is here an ellipsis, which is readily supplied.
30. Guard it, lest it diminish, according to the saying, "That which is full invites decrease."
32. Mature thought, lit. *nine times thinking*.
35. Lit. *Chest*, 約匱, ark of the covenant.
36. "Red and white," *Gold* and *Silver*.

* Hereafter pronouns will not be italicised where they are implied. In looking out corresponding words in text and translation they are not therefore to be counted, unless in capitals.

---

# CHAPTER III.

# 第三章論人事

| 字 | 聲 | 音 |
| --- | --- | --- |
| 第 | | ti |
| 三 | | san |
| 章 | | chang |
| 論 | | lŭn |
| 人 | | jin |
| 事 | | sh |

## 1 待鞫 萬事

| 字 | 聲 | 音 |
| --- | --- | --- |
| 啓 | 3 | chʻi |
| 穴 | 4 | hüih |
| 屍 | 1 | sh |
| 遡 | 3 | su |
| 淩 | 2 | ling |
| 空 | 1 | kʻung |
| 升 | 1 | sheng |
| 舁 | 4 | kü |
| 寶 | 3 | pau |
| 座 | 4 | tso |
| 式 | 4 | sh |
| 憑 | 2 | pʻing |
| 訟 | 4 | sung |
| 詞 | 2 | tsʻ |
| 迫 | 1 | pʻeh |
| 具 | 4 | kü |

## 2

| 字 | 聲 | 音 |
| --- | --- | --- |
| 辜 | 1 | ku |
| 咎 | 1 | kiu |
| 疑 | 2 | i |
| 輕 | 1 | kʻing |
| 雪 | 3 | süih |
| 冤 | 1 | yüen |
| 艱 | 1 | kien |
| 巨 | 4 | kü |
| 覺 | 2 | kioh |
| 昧 | 4 | me |
| 醒 | 3 | sing |
| 迷 | 3 | mi |
| 陰 | 1 | yin |
| 府 | 3 | fu |
| 抵 | 3 | ti |
| 拒 | 4 | kü |

## 3 勤學

| 字 | 聲 | 音 |
| --- | --- | --- |
| 量 | 2 | liang |
| 才 | 2 | tsʻai |
| 託 | 1 | tʻoh |
| 授 | 4 | sheu |
| 衛 | 4 | we |
| 翼 | 4 | yih |
| 扶 | 2 | fu |
| 持 | 2 | chʻ |
| 詔 | 4 | chau |
| 戒 | 4 | kia |
| 誘 | 4 | yiu |
| 誨 | 4 | hwe |
| 晝 | 4 | cheu |
| 晚 | 3 | wan |
| 鑑 | 4 | kien |
| 茲 | 1 | ts |

## 4

| 字 | 聲 | 音 |
| --- | --- | --- |
| 兒 | 2 | r |
| 輩 | 4 | pe |
| 謳 | 1 | eu |
| 誦 | 4 | sung |
| 賦 | 4 | fu |
| 擇 | 2 | tseh |
| 詩 | 1 | sh |
| 稽 | 1 | ki |
| 齒 | 3 | chʻ |
| 牙 | 2 | ya |
| 申 | 1 | shen |
| 講 | 3 | kiang |
| 遐 | 1 | hia |
| 邇 | 3 | r |
| 均 | 1 | küin |
| 推 | 1 | tʻüe |

# CHAPTER III.

## HUMAN AFFAIRS.

### *Accountability.*

1.

Opening the cave, his corpse revived,
Spurned the empty *air*, and rose aloft,
The jewelled throne, he rested-on (2),
Trial words, he will-speedily complete.

2.

Offences and faults, he judges lightly,
Redresses wrongs difficult and huge,
Arouses the blinded, awakes the deluded,
And the gloomy palace withstands (2).

### *Diligence.*

3.

Measuring talents, he commits (2), ***trusts;***
With protecting wings, supports, holds *us*,
With edicts, prohibitions, persuades instructs,
Morning and evening mirror yourself in these.

4.

The boy's class should-read and recite,
Songs select, poems search,
With front-teeth and molars, repeat, expound,
Remote and near equally generalize.

| 5 幼年 | 6 | 7 壯歲 | 8 | 9 士業 |
|---|---|---|---|---|
| 爰 2 yüen | 秉 3 ping | 幼 4 yiu | 克 1 k‘eh | 博 2 poh |
| 監 4 kien | 質 4 chih | 丁 1 ting | 伐 1 fah | 嗜 4 sh |
| 嬰 1 ing | 清 1 ts‘ing | 漸 4 tsien | 驕 1 kiau | 簡 3 kien |
| 孩 2 hai | 聰 1 ts‘ung | 壯 4 chŭang | 縱 4 tsung | 篇 1 p‘ien |
| 胎 1 t‘ai | 概 4 kai | 習 2 sih | 窘 3 k‘iung | 几 1 ki |
| 元 2 yüen | 除 2 ch‘u | 染 3 jan | 抑 4 ih | 筵 2 yien |
| 誕 2 tan | 雜 2 tsah | 殊 1 shu | 困 4 kw‘en | 勤 2 ch‘in |
| 育 4 yuh | 慾 4 yuh | 童 2 t‘ung | 窮 2 k‘iung | 讀 2 tuh |
| 急 2 kih | 夙 4 suh | 詭 3 kwe | 倘 3 t‘ang | 琴 2 ch‘in |
| 乳 3 ju | 譴 3 ch‘ien | 謙 1 ch‘ien | 憾 4 han | 劍 4 kien |
| 泣 4 ch‘ih | 洪 2 hung | 襲 2 sih | 墮 4 to | 遄 2 ch‘uan |
| 饑 1 ki | 沾 1 chan | 貌 4 mau | 落 4 loh | 遊 2 yiu |
| 席 2 sih | 盍 2 hoh | 駭 2 hai | 機 1 ki | 專 1 chuan |
| 卧 4 wo | 早 3 tsau | 笑 4 siau | 術 4 shuh | 侮 3 wu |
| 綿 2 mien | 濯 2 choh | 匿 4 niih | 奚 1 hi | 愼 4 shen |
| 束 4 shuh | 沐 4 muh | 衷 1 chung | 庸 1 yung | 篤 3 tuh |

## *Childhood.*

5.

Do-but contemplate infant children,
*From* the womb first born and nourished,
Impatient for milk, they weep for hunger,
On matting sleep, in cotton wrapped.

6.

Endowed with talents pure and intelligent,
*They should* altogether exclude mixed desires.
*With* the primitive offence greatly tainted,
Why-not early wash (2) *it away?*

## *Youth.*

7.

Tender youth gradually strengthening,
Acquire stains diverse-from lads.
Deceit and modesty lurk in the countenance,
Terror and laughter hide in the bosom.

## *Bad men.*

8.

Overbearing, boastful proud *they* let-loose,
To persecute and oppress the helpless poor.
If you abhor falling (2), *into this sin*,
The instrument and art *of escape* how simple!

## *Scholars.*

9.

*Some* learnedly voracious of brief essays,
On bench, or at feast, diligently read,
*Some* with harp and sabre restlessly rove,
Intent on insulting the careful and solid.

| 10 | 11 農田 | 12 | 13 工匠 | 14 |
|---|---|---|---|---|
| 尸$^{1}$ sh | 泥$^{2}$ ni | 郊$^{1}$ kiau | 操$^{1}$ ts'au | 酬$^{2}$ ch'eu |
| 爵$^{2}$ tsioh | 塗$^{2}$ t'u | 場$^{2}$ ch'ang | 尺$^{3}$ ch'ih | 值$^{2}$ chih |
| 曠$^{4}$ kw'ang | 奔$^{1}$ pen | 收$^{1}$ sheu | 運$^{4}$ yüin | 竭$^{2}$ kieh |
| 官$^{1}$ kwan | 走$^{3}$ tseu | 積$^{1}$ tsih | 斤$^{1}$ chin | 償$^{2}$ ch'ang |
| 貪$^{1}$ t'an | 竊$^{4}$ ts'ieh | 繼$^{4}$ ki | 係$^{4}$ hi | 泉$^{2}$ ts'üen |
| 祜$^{4}$ hu | 認$^{4}$ jin | 蹟$^{1}$ tsih | 誇$^{1}$ kw'a | 刀$^{1}$ tau |
| 祀$^{4}$ s | 農$^{2}$ nung | 厚$^{4}$ heu | 傑$^{2}$ kieh | 還$^{2}$ hwan |
| 佛$^{2}$ foh | 耕$^{1}$ keng | 豐$^{1}$ fung | 步$^{4}$ pu | 互$^{4}$ hu |
| [口法]$^{3}$ fah | 澤$^{2}$ tseh | 疇$^{2}$ ch'eu | 弓$^{1}$ kung | 苟$^{3}$ keu |
| 唎$^{4}$ li | 灌$^{4}$ kwan | 想$^{3}$ siang | 矢$^{1}$ sh | 悟$^{4}$ wu |
| [口賽]$^{4}$ sai | 烟$^{1}$ yien | 寅$^{2}$ yin | 皿$^{3}$ min | 了$^{3}$ liau |
| 朋$^{2}$ p'ung | 植$^{4}$ chih | 鞫$^{2}$ küih | 料$^{4}$ liau | 休$^{1}$ hiu |
| 輪$^{2}$ lün | 抹$^{3}$ moh | 曲$^{1}$ k'üih | 精$^{1}$ tsing | 連$^{2}$ lien |
| 須$^{1}$ sü | 露$^{4}$ lu | 跪$^{4}$ kwe | 粗$^{1}$ ts'u | 番$^{1}$ fan |
| 鑒$^{4}$ kien | 踐$^{4}$ tsien | 虔$^{2}$ ch'ien | 製$^{4}$ ch | 趨$^{1}$ ch'ü |
| 覆$^{3}$ fuh | 塵$^{2}$ ch'en | 尋$^{2}$ süin | 鑄$^{4}$ chu | 赴$^{4}$ fu |

速成漢語

10.

*Some are* corpses in office, barren mandarins,
*Some* covet bliss and sacrifice to Buddha.
*Of their* Pharisee (3) friends,
The wheel, they should look-at, upturned.

*Husbandmen.*

11.

In clay and mud running and walking,
I stealthy recognize the farmer ploughman,
At the pools irrigating, in the mists planting,
Brushing-off the dews, and trampling the dust.

12.

In suburban grounds, he gathers and stores,
The *fruits* of successive (2) thick abundance,
In the field thinks of solemn judgment,
Bending kneels, and piously seeks.

*Artisans.*

13.

They wield the foot-*rule*, whirl the pound-*axe*,
Are boastful of heroic steps,
Bows, arrows, vessels, materials,
Fine and coarse, they manufacture or cast.

*Merchants.*

14.

They refund prices, exhaust payments,
Coins *like* knives surround on-either-hand,
If they should-reflect on the final end,
With connected steps, they would run and go.

| 15 商客 | 16 | 17 居家 | 18 | 19 服官 |
|---|---|---|---|---|
| 市$^{4}$ sh | 倍$^{4}$ pe | 嘉$^{1}$ kia | 刻$^{4}$ k'eh | 卜$^{3}$ puh |
| 隅$^{2}$ yü | 億$^{4}$ yih | 戚$^{4}$ ts'ih | 薄$^{2}$ poh | 賢$^{2}$ hien |
| 井$^{3}$ tsing | 典$^{3}$ tien | 看$^{1}$ k'an | 肇$^{4}$ chau | 徵$^{1}$ cheng |
| 際$^{4}$ tsi | 掌$^{3}$ chang | 承$^{2}$ ch'eng | 衰$^{1}$ shwai | 哲$^{2}$ cheh |
| 買$^{3}$ mai | 貢$^{4}$ kung | 昆$^{1}$ kwen | 憐$^{2}$ lien | 荷$^{4}$ ho |
| 賣$^{4}$ mai | 稅$^{4}$ shŭe | 玉$^{4}$ yü | 惜$^{1}$ sih | 政$^{4}$ cheng |
| 客$^{4}$ k'eh | 殷$^{1}$ yin | 姊$^{3}$ ts | 奴$^{2}$ nu | 輸$^{1}$ shu |
| 商$^{1}$ shang | 繁$^{1}$ fan | 妹$^{4}$ me | 婢$^{4}$ pe | 忠$^{1}$ chung |
| 却$^{4}$ k'ioh | 錢$^{2}$ ch'ien | 純$^{2}$ ch'un | 普$^{3}$ p'u | 俘$^{2}$ fu |
| 迎$^{2}$ ying | 滿$^{3}$ man | 孝$^{4}$ hiau | 護$^{4}$ hu | 叛$^{4}$ p'an |
| 巖$^{2}$ yen | 慮$^{4}$ lü | 爺$^{2}$ ye | 根$^{1}$ keng | 禦$^{4}$ yü |
| 島$^{3}$ tau | 攘$^{3}$ jang | 懽$^{1}$ hwan | 源$^{2}$ yüen | 盜$^{4}$ tau |
| 坦$^{3}$ t'an | 駐$^{4}$ chu | 卑$^{1}$ pe | 康$^{1}$ k'ang | 驗$^{4}$ yien |
| 坷$^{1}$ k'o | 庫$^{4}$ k'u | 弱$^{4}$ joh | 寧$^{2}$ ning | 印$^{4}$ yin |
| 江$^{1}$ kiang | 穹$^{2}$ k'iung | 佑$^{4}$ yiu | 允$^{3}$ yüin | 頒$^{1}$ pan |
| 洋$^{1}$ yang | 蒼$^{1}$ ts'ang | 惠$^{4}$ hwe | 慰$^{4}$ we | 封$^{1}$ fung |

15.

At the market corner at the well's brink,
Buying and selling is the stranger merchant,
He rejects (leaves) or welcomes precipitous islands,
The smooth or rough of rivers or oceans.

16.

Double ten-myriads, holds in his palm,
Tributes and duties are vast and numerous,
*Of* money full, he dreads (thinks-of) theft—
Locate ***your*** treasury in the concave azure.

## *The Family.*

17.

Worthy relatives, see acceptance,
Brother gems, elder-sister and younger,
Pure filial piety, a father delights-in,
The humble and weak, protects, comforts.

18.

Meanness (2) begins decay,
Be-kind and sparing to slaves and maids,
Widely defend the root and fountain,
Tranquility and peace will certainly comfort you.

## *Officers.*

19.

*They* divine the virtuous, test the worthy,
Bearing government, repay fidelity,
*They* capture the rebel, restrain the robber,
Examine the stamp, distribute the seals.

## 20

賓 1 pin
吏 4 li
阻 3 tsu
蔽 4 pi

釁 4 hing
詰 2 kieh
藐 3 miau
躬 1 kung

俟 4 s
駕 4 kia
奏 4 tseu
職 2 chih

曷 2 hoh
厭 4 yen
寬 1 kw'an
宏 2 hung

## 21 行善

崗 1 kang
磐 4 p'an
晨 2 ch'en
屆 4 kie

湖 2 hu
漢 4 han
星 1 sing
遷 1 ts'ien

延 2 yien
暇 4 hu
藥 4 yoh
送 4 sung

需 2 sü
飢 1 ki
糧 2 liang
捐 1 küen

## 22

偏 1 p'ien
側 4 tseh
陸 4 luh
奠 4 tien

圮 3 ch'i
壞 4 hwai
岸 4 an
堅 1 kien

那 3 na
肯 3 k'en
鬭 4 teu
隙 4 hih

蕪 2 wu
穢 4 hwe
侵 1 ch'in
牽 1 ch'ien

## 23 悔罪

謹 3 kin
恪 4 ch'ioh
密 4 mih
盟 1 meng

譽 2 yü
賞 3 shang
似 4 s
赫 4 hoh

轉 3 chŭan
眼 3 yien
崩 1 peng
薨 1 hung

驚 1 king
覩 3 tu
幽 1 yiu
黑 4 heh

## 24

戾 4 li
網 3 wang
橫 2 heng
罹 2 li

昌 1 ch'ang
衢 1 k'ü
閉 4 pi
塞 4 seh

抱 4 pau
恨 4 hen
沉 1 ch'en
淪 1 lŭn

況 4 kw'ang
兼 1 kien
殘 2 ts'an
賊 4 tseh

20.

If guests or subordinates hinder and obstruct
"The fault seek in *my* unworthy person"
*They* wait the chariot report *their* office,
How too-many broad, capacious *minds ?*

## *Good Works.*

21.

Hill and cliff, *with* dawn *they* arrive-at,
The Lake and Han, by star-*light* pass-over,
To prolong happy-life, medicine present,
For needy hunger, provision contribute.

22.

Uneven sideling ground *they* settle,
Tumbling decaying banks they strengthen,
Whence WOULD they fight and quarrel
Dirt and filth provoke and draw ?

## *Retribution.*

23.

The cautious, dignified, scrupulous in covenant.
*Whose* praises and rewards seem dazzling,
In the turning of an eye, fall and die,
And dread to behold gloom and darkness.

24.

Guilt's net *some* perversely encounter,
The prosperous road is closed, stopped-up,
Hugging vain regrets they sink-down (2),
Much-more those *who* combine cruelty and theft.

僞教

**25**

| Character | Tone | Romanization |
|---|---|---|
| 邪 | 2 | sie |
| 黨 | 3 | tang |
| 毒 | 2 | tuh |
| 蛇 | 2 | she |
| 領 | 3 | ling |
| 部 | 4 | pu |
| 呑 | 1 | t'un |
| 噬 | 1 | sh |
| 舌 | 2 | sheh |
| 蜜 | 4 | mih |
| 售 | 4 | sheu |
| 甘 | 1 | kan |
| 燬 | 3 | hwe |
| 虜 | 3 | lo |
| 倚 | 3 | i |
| 勢 | 4 | sh |

**26**

| Character | Tone | Romanization |
|---|---|---|
| 嫁 | 4 | kia |
| 怨 | 4 | yüen |
| 仗 | 4 | chang |
| 威 | 2 | we |
| 鳴 | 2 | ming |
| 鼓 | 3 | ku |
| 暮 | 4 | mo |
| 季 | 4 | ki |
| 濱 | 1 | ping |
| 退 | 4 | t'e |
| 崙 | 2 | lŭn |
| 逾 | 2 | yü |
| 奈 | 4 | nai |
| 寡 | 3 | kwa |
| 頂 | 3 | ting |
| 替 | 4 | t'i |

設譬

**27**

| Character | Tone | Romanization |
|---|---|---|
| 板 | 3 | pan |
| 柱 | 4 | chu |
| 瓦 | 3 | wa |
| 塔 | 3 | t'ah |
| 僅 | 3 | chin |
| 彰 | 1 | chang |
| 樣 | 4 | yang |
| 制 | 4 | ch |
| 帶 | 4 | tai |
| 繫 | 4 | hi |
| 帕 | 4 | p'a |
| 懸 | 2 | hüen |
| 零 | 2 | ling |
| 珍 | 1 | chen |
| 表 | 3 | piau |
| 餙 | 4 | shih |

**28**

| Character | Tone | Romanization |
|---|---|---|
| 狂 | 2 | kw'ang |
| 犬 | 3 | k'üen |
| 虐 | 4 | nioh |
| 鄰 | 2 | lin |
| 剛 | 1 | kang |
| 忿 | 4 | fen |
| 姑 | 1 | ku |
| 遜 | 4 | süin |
| 放 | 4 | fang |
| 膽 | 3 | tan |
| 裸 | 3 | lo |
| 腹 | 3 | fuh |
| 毛 | 2 | mau |
| 髮 | 3 | fah |
| 謗 | 4 | pang |
| 刺 | 4 | ts' |

**29**

| Character | Tone | Romanization |
|---|---|---|
| 房 | 2 | fang |
| 舍 | 4 | she |
| 樓 | 2 | leu |
| 臺 | 2 | t'ai |
| 只 | 4 | ch |
| 堪 | 1 | k'an |
| 住 | 4 | chu |
| 宿 | 4 | suh |
| 牲 | 1 | sheng |
| 駝 | 2 | t'o |
| 犀 | 1 | si |
| 象 | 4 | siang |
| 禽 | 2 | ch'ing |
| 閃 | 3 | shan |
| 獅 | 1 | sh |
| 突 | 4 | t'uh |

## *The Malicious.*

25.

Corrupt cliques, venemous serpents,
Lead companies to swallow, and devour,
Their tongues honey, *they* sell sweet *words,*
Destroy capture, and rest on force.

26.

They vent spleen and rely on power,
*He shall* sound the drum at evening season—
From the brink retire, the mountain overleap,
(0) Few *will* bear *the duty in your* stead.

## *Detached Images.*

27.

Board pillars, and tile towers,
Merely exhibit the pattern decreed;
The belt to bind, the kerchief to suspend,
*Have* scattered pearls for outside ornaments.

28.

Rabid dogs oppress their neighbors—
To their hard rage, gently yield,
They let-out gall and bare their bellies,
*But* a hair (2) *out of place* they slander and pierce.

29.

House cottage, loft or terrace,
*We* only can dwell-in for a night's-lodging,
Cattle *with* camels, unicorns *with* elephants;
Birds dart; lions *spring* suddenly.

耶穌回憶

| 30 | 31 | 32 | 33 | 34 |
|---|---|---|---|---|
| 移 $^{2}$ i | 屢 $^{3}$ lü | 翦 $^{3}$ tsien | 嚴 $^{2}$ yien | 囊 $^{2}$ nang |
| 磨 $^{2}$ mo | 憶 $^{4}$ i | 枝 $^{1}$ ch | 防 $^{2}$ fang | 綻 $^{4}$ chan |
| 蘇 $^{1}$ su | 釘 $^{1}$ ting | 撻 $^{3}$ t'ah | 假 $^{3}$ kia | 麻 $^{2}$ ma |
| 蟲 $^{2}$ ch'ung | 痛 $^{4}$ t'ung | 打 $^{3}$ ta | 酵 $^{4}$ kiau | 補 $^{3}$ pu |
| 燃 $^{2}$ jan | 竟 $^{4}$ king | 渴 $^{3}$ k'oh | 暫 $^{4}$ chan | 菓 $^{3}$ kwo |
| 燈 $^{1}$ teng | 殲 $^{1}$ sien | 擬 $^{3}$ i | 辭 $^{2}$ ts' | 咒 $^{4}$ cheu |
| 照 $^{4}$ chau | 戈 $^{1}$ ko | 鹽 $^{2}$ yien | 慄 $^{4}$ lih | 葉 $^{4}$ yeh |
| 瞽 $^{3}$ ku | 鋒 $^{1}$ fung | 充 $^{1}$ ch'ung | 杯 $^{1}$ pe | 肥 $^{2}$ fe |
| 忙 $^{2}$ mang | 棘 $^{1}$ kih | 腓 $^{1}$ fe | 鬻 $^{4}$ yuh | 索 $^{4}$ soh |
| 愧 $^{4}$ kwe | 冠 $^{1}$ kwan | 骨 $^{3}$ kuh | 鴿 $^{1}$ koh | 騎 $^{1}$ ch'i |
| 錯 $^{4}$ ts'oh | 頭 $^{2}$ t'eu | 慢 $^{4}$ man | 遁 $^{4}$ tun | 橄 $^{3}$ kan |
| 差 $^{1}$ ch'a | 戴 $^{4}$ tai | 折 $^{2}$ cheh | 院 $^{4}$ yuen | 欖 $^{3}$ lan |
| 仰 $^{3}$ yang | 袍 $^{2}$ pau | 寵 $^{3}$ ch'ung | 捕 $^{3}$ pu | 到 $^{4}$ tau |
| 慕 $^{4}$ mo | 片 $^{4}$ p'ien | 壽 $^{4}$ sheu | 魚 $^{2}$ yü | 郇 $^{1}$ süin |
| 覲 $^{3}$ chin | 搖 $^{2}$ yau | 旋 $^{2}$ süin | 射 $^{4}$ she | 管 $^{3}$ kwan |
| 附 $^{3}$ fu | 紅 $^{2}$ hung | 增 $^{1}$ tseng | 圍 $^{2}$ we | 吹 $^{1}$ ch'üe |

30.

Move a millstone, and you wake insects,
Kindle a lamp, you enlighten the blind.
Make-haste *to be* ashamed of faults (2)
Look up, long to see and be-united *with God.*

*Remembrance of Christ.*

31.

Oft remember the nail's pain—
*Christ* at-last expired *at the* weapon's point,
The thorny crown, his head bore,
His robe skirts waved red.

32.

*They* clipped a branch to scourge and strike,
Thirsty, decreed him the briny *cup*-full,
His leg bones, *they were* slow to break—
Favor and age in-turn were added.

33.

He sternly cautioned against false leaven,
For-a-short-time declined the trembling cup,
Sellers of doves fled the court.
*Also* catchers of fish, shooters of game.

34.

The sack rent, flax must mend,
The fruit-tree cursed *had* leaves fat,
They sought *a beast* to ride to Olivet (2)
Coming-to Zion trumpets (tubes) were-blown.

正教傳宣

35

振⁴chin 枯¹k'u 拔²pah 草³ts'au

宥⁴yiu 勇³yung 伸¹shen 囚²ch'iu

苗²miau 系⁴hi 齊²ch'i 魯³lu

品³p'in 格²keh 呂³lü 歐¹eu

36

朔⁴soh 夏⁴hia 盤²p'an 蹈⁴tau

核²heh 斗³teu 辨⁴pien 州¹cheu

暨⁴ki 寒²han 迄³ch'ieh 熱⁴jeh

曳⁴yeh 杖⁴chang 緯³we 球²ch'iu

凡五百七十六字

35.

He revives the withered, plucks the grass,
Pardons the brave, enlarges the prisoner.
The *ab*-original tribes, as well as Ch'i and Lu;
***All*** classes shall come ***to him*** military or civil.

## *Apostles of the Faith.*

36.

North and South, by the compass they tread,
Compare the pole-star to distinguish lands,
Through extreme cold, and extreme heat,
They drag the staff and girdle the globe.

---

NOTES.

2. Judges, lit. *doubts*, according to classic precedent used here for 擬, *to decide a doubt; to purpose.*
   Redresses, lit. *puts snow on*, allays the burning wrongs.
   Gloomy *palace*, the Powers of Darkness.
4. Generalize, lit. *push*, i.e., push the comparison, 類推.
6. 質 lit. matter, substance. Wash *feet* and *head;* or from foot to head.
   The Chinese commentary says, "by baptism."
10. i.e., take warning by their fate.
13. Heroic steps=lofty climbing.
14. 泉, a fountain is often used as a synonym for 錢 money; which anciently was knife-shaped.
16. 典, a rule or canon; to hold as mortgage.
19. Repay favor with fidelity. 輸 alsomeans defeat.
20. The language of a good officer, who makes himself responsible. Guests, retainers.
26. Denounce them at the evening of time, the end of the world. Reformation is a personal affair.
28 Gall, also used for courage or audacity.

29. It is not easy to discover the pertinence of several expressions in this part of the chapter, but let it be remembered, they were put together merely for the purpose of using up a residuum of characters for which no place could be found elsewhere.

32. See Isaiah 53.10 for explanation of last line.

33. 圍 An enclosure; hence game enclosed for a battue; 打圍 to hunt.

35. All nations, savage or civilized, shall alike submit; and all classes be numbered among his followers. Lü, the family name of Kiang T'ai-kung, Eu, Euyang-siu; the one celebrated for military, the other for literary genius, here employed to represent two grand divisions of society.

# CHAPTER IV.

第ti 四s 章chang 論lŭn 儔ch'eu 類le

總冒

1
緬[3]mien 迹[1]tsih 溯[4]shoh 勳[1]hüin
儘[3]tsin 鮮[3]sien 缺[1]k'üih 漏[4]leu
擲[4]chih 畀[4]pi 某[3]mo 儔[2]ch'eu
搴[1]ch'ien 裳[2]shang 參[1]ts'an 叩[4]k'eu

2
模[2]mu 楷[3]ch'ie k'ai 秘[4]pi mi 探[1]t'an
煩[1]fan 劇[4]kü 暢[4]ch'ang 茂[4]meu
殆[4]tai 冀[4]ki 聵[4]kw'e 聾[2]lung
僉[1]ts'ien 懺[4]ch'an 誤[4]wu 謬[4]miu

天文

3
晴[2]ts'ing 嵐[2]lan 繚[3]liau 繞[3]jau
瞻[1]chan 矚[3]chuh 層[2]ts'eng 霄[1]siau
霞[2]hia 輝[1]hwe 林[2]lin 豔[4]yien
霓[2]ni 彩[3]ts'ai 渡[4]tu 消[1]siau

4
迅[4]süin 雷[2]le 奮[4]fen 響[3]hiang
疏[1]su 霜[1]shŭang 催[1]ch'ŭe 凋[1]tiau
暘[2]yang 霪[2]yin 旱[4]han 潦[4]lau
竚[4]chu 覿[3]tih 燮[2]sheh 調[2]t'iau

# CHAPTER IV.

## MISCELLANEOUS TOPICS.

### *The Voice of Nature.*

1.

In connected steps trace *the Creator's* merit,
Very few are its defects (2),
He cast-forth and gave each-*thing its* class,
Tuck-up *your* clothes, together worship.

2.

Of model forms, the mystery if you *would* fathom,
Perplexing sorely *is* their full abundance,
*You* would almost expect the blind and deaf,
All to repent their mistakes and errors.

### *Meteorology.*

3.

The clear air encircles *us*,
We gaze attentive on the storied vault,
The sunset's lustre *has* a forest of beauties,
The rainbow splendor passes-over and melts.

4.

Swift thunder fiercely echoes,
The herb, frost hastens to wither,
In bright and cloudy, drought and flood,
*We* wistfully behold *Nature's* Alchemist (2).

| 地理 5 | 6 | 時令 7 | 8 | 山水 9 |
|---|---|---|---|---|
| 攷 1k'au | 悞 4wu | 辯 4pien | 靜 4tsing | 岱 4tai |
| 究 1kiu | 歧 2ch'i | 辰 2ch'cn | 占 1chan | 嶽 4yoh |
| 寰 2hwan | 徑 4king | 訝 4yia | 晏 4yien | 嶔 1ch'ing |
| 區 1k'ü | 抄 1ch'au | 午 3wu | 曉 3hiau | 嶷 1i |
| 長 2ch'ang | 併 4ping | 驟 4tseu | 熾 4ch | 渭 4we |
| 短 3toan | 程 2ch'eng | 閱 4yüih | 燄 4yien | 川 1ch'ŭan |
| 闊 4kw'oh | 塹 3chan | 春 1ch'ün | 爍 4sheh | 迢 1t'iau |
| 狹 1hiah | 劃 4hwah | 秋 1ch'iu | 硫 2liu | 遞 4ti |
| 凸 3ku | 盪 4tang | 雙 1shwang | 璣 1ki | 鑿 2tsoh tsao |
| 凹 1wa | 疆 1kiang | 丸 2wan | 衡 2heng | 險 3hien |
| 崎 2ch'i | 拓 4t'oh | 躑 4chih | 驗 4yien | 覓 4mih |
| 嶇 1ch'ü | 輿 2yü | 躅 4chuh | 算 4sŭan | 津 1tsin |
| 豳 1ping | 蠻 2man | 晷 3kwe | 怱 1ts'ung | 陟 3chih |
| 燕 1yien | 貊 4moh | 逝 4sh | 遽 4kü | 涉 4sheh |
| 崖 2yai | 包 1pau | 影 3ing | 躇 1ch'u | 攀 2p'an |
| 峽 4hiah | 刮 4kwoh | 浮 2feu | 躊 1ch'eu | 躋 2tsi |

## *Geography.*

5.

Search, explore, the circle of space,
The long and short, broad and narrow,
Bulged and sunken, rough and uneven,
Ping's and Yien's, cliffs and passes.

6.

*If you* mistake the cross road; *take* a path
for a short-cut:
An urgent journey, a precipice interrupts,
Extending boundaries, and opening territories,
Barbarous and savage *are* embraced (2).

## *Time.*

7.

*We* talk a morning, and are startled by noon,
Passing *in review* spring and autumn;
The twin orbs gallop-on (2),
*On the* dial, the departing shadow floats.

8.

Quietly observe evening and morning,
Kindling flame ignites sulphur,
Globe and transverse verify calculation.
Rapidly, suddenly *Time* rushes-on (2).

## *Hills and Waters.*

9.

The Tai Mountains *are* lofty and eminent,
The We stream *is* a distant reach,
*They* chisel steeps and look for fords;
They mount, wade, cling, and climb.

| 10 | 11 人品 | 12 | 13 宮室 | 14 |
|---|---|---|---|---|
| 嶂 $^{1}$chang | 髫 $^{2}$t'iau | 顢 $^{2}$man | 畫 $^{4}$hwa | 齋 $^{1}$chai |
| 翠 $^{4}$ts'üe | 僮 $^{2}$t'ung | 頇 $^{1}$han | 榭 $^{4}$sie | 塾 $^{2}$shuh |
| 排 $^{2}$p'ai | 耆 $^{2}$ch'i | 伶 $^{2}$ling | 雕 $^{1}$tiau | 序 $^{4}$sü |
| 螺 $^{2}$lo | 耇 $^{1}$keu | 俐 $^{4}$li | 廊 $^{2}$lang | 庠 $^{2}$siang |
| | | | | |
| 潮 $^{2}$ch'au | 倜 $^{2}$t'ih | 縷 $^{3}$lu | 複 $^{3}$fuh | 廩 $^{3}$lin |
| 黃 $^{2}$hwang | 儻 $^{3}$t'ang | 晰 $^{1}$sih | 堦 $^{1}$kie | 廚 $^{2}$ch'u |
| 駛 $^{4}$sh | 俠 $^{4}$hiah | 膚 $^{2}$fu | 夾 $^{1}$kiah | 廁 $^{4}$s |
| 驥 $^{4}$ki | 豪 $^{1}$hau | 毫 $^{2}$hau | 牖 $^{4}$yiu | 廄 $^{4}$kiu |
| | | | | |
| 玄 $^{2}$hüin | 遴 $^{2}$lin | 胞 $^{1}$pau | 斐 $^{3}$fe | 衍 $^{3}$yien |
| 幻 $^{4}$hwan | 薦 $^{4}$tsien | 胚 $^{1}$p'e | 檻 $^{4}$ch'ien | 慶 $^{4}$ch'ing |
| 巧 $^{3}$ch'iau | 勵 $^{4}$li | 配 $^{4}$p'e | 聯 $^{2}$lien | 迓 $^{1}$yia |
| 臻 $^{1}$chen | 奬 $^{3}$tsiang | 綈 $^{4}$t'i | 緜 $^{2}$mien | 休 $^{1}$hiu |
| | | | | |
| 佳 $^{1}$kia | 諂 $^{3}$ch'an | 妙 $^{4}$miau | 綺 $^{3}$ch'i | 恥 $^{3}$ch' |
| 玩 $^{4}$wan | 傲 $^{4}$au | 奧 $^{4}$au | 窓 $^{1}$chw'ang | 玷 $^{4}$tien |
| 攸 $^{1}$yiu | 譏 $^{1}$ki | 頗 $^{1}$p'o | 輻 $^{2}$fuh | 楣 $^{2}$me |
| 寄 $^{4}$ki | 嘲 $^{2}$ch'au | 饒 $^{2}$jau | 輳 $^{4}$ts'eu | 構 $^{4}$keu |

速成漢語

10.

Summits green *are* ranged *like* sea-shells,
In the tide yellow *ships* sail *like* race-horses.
Mysterious changes! skill extreme!
Noble enjoyments *are* therein conveyed.

## *Classes of Men.*

11.

The uncombed lad *serves* the aged greybeard.
The courteous (2) the daring, the generous,
*Are* selected for promotion, stimulated by praise:
Flatterers, and proud, *are butts for* ridicule (2).

12.

*Some are* stupid (2) *some* sprightly (2),
Explain (2) to the skin and hair *(to a nicety)*.
From the womb (2) paired and joined,
Admirable mysteries *are* very abundant.

## *Palaces and Houses.*

13.

*Houses have* painted arbors, carved verandahs,
Double stair-ways, opposite windows,
Elegant railings joined together,
Gauze window-panes in clusters, (2).

14.

Studio, school, academy and college,
Garner, kitchen, privy, stable—*these*
Prolong felicity, *and* welcome good-fortune.
A shameful *act* will stain the door-post (2).

**15 服飾**

葛 2 koh
裘 2 ch'iu
絺 2 ch'
綌 1 hih

簪 1 tsan
珥 3 r
鐲 2 choh
鐶 2 hwan

錦 3 kin
披 1 p'i
繡 4 siu
佩 4 p'e

燦 3 ts'an
爛 4 lan
煇 1 hwe
煌 2 hwang

**16**

衒 4 hüin
耀 4 yau
襟 1 kin
袖 4 siu

掩 3 yien
映 4 ing
副 4 fu
鑲 1 siang

耄 2 mau
齡 2 ling
限 4 hien
促 4 ts'uh

遑 2 hwang
戀 4 loan
裝 2 chwang
潢 2 hwang

**17 器用**

斝 2 hoh
觚 1 ku
評 2 p'ing
材 2 ts'ai

借 4 tsie
筋 1 ts
佐 3 tso
輔 3 fu

睡 4 shwe
眠 2 mien
榻 4 t'ah
牀 2 chw'ang

饔 1 yung
飧 1 sün
匕 3 pi
筋 4 chu

**18**

揮 1 hwe
麈 3 chu
挽 3 wan
韁 3 kiang

吮 3 yüin
筆 3 pih
裁 2 ts'ai
楮 3 ch'u

妥 3 t'o
貯 4 chu
穩 3 wen
儲 2 ch'u

般 1 pan
件 4 kien
臚 2 lu
署 3 shu

**19 珍寶**

寸 4 ts'un
珠 1 chu
咫 4 ch
璧 4 pih

青 1 ts'ing
珩 2 heng
丹 1 tan
瑚 2 hu

洛 4 loh
鐘 1 chung
泗 4 s
磬 4 ch'ing

秦 2 ch'in
鼎 3 ting
唐 2 t'ang
鑪 2 lu

## *Clothes and Ornaments.*

15.

Linen, fur, silk, and hemp,
Hair-pin, pendant, bracelet, ring,
Brocade cloak, embroidered side-piece,
Sparkling, bright, brilliant, splendid.

16.

Dazzling radiant skirts and sleeves,
Veil the image with borders and fringes;
When even the aged's years are limited and brief,
What-leisure ***is there*** to dote-on ornament (2)!

## *Vessels and Utensils.*

17.

***We*** examine the square ***vessel,*** and criticise materials,
***We*** borrow means to aid and assist,
***We*** slumber and sleep on couch and bed,
Breakfast and sup with spoon and chopstick.

18.

Flourish the fly-brush, grasp the rein,
Lick the pen, trim the paper.
Safely store, securely provide,
***Each*** kind and piece record in-order.

## *Precious Stones.*

19.

***Such are the*** inch pearl, the span gem,
Green emerald, red coral,
***Also*** the Loh's bell, the Sze's harp-stone,
Ch'in's tripod, Tang's censer.

20

琳$^{2}$ ling
瑯$^{2}$ lang
琥$^{3}$ hu
玖$^{3}$ kiu

瑪$^{3}$ ma
瑙$^{3}$ nau
碔$^{3}$ wu
砆$^{1}$ fu

崢$^{1}$ chang
嶸$^{2}$ yung
璀$^{1}$ ts'ŭe
璨$^{3}$ ts'an

韞$^{4}$ wen
孕$^{4}$ yüin
含$^{2}$ han
娛$^{2}$ yü

21 音樂

噓$^{1}$ hü
竹$^{2}$ chuh
彈$^{2}$ t'an
絲$^{1}$ s

簫$^{1}$ siau
韶$^{2}$ shau
拊$^{3}$ fu
拍$^{4}$ p'oh p'ai

逸$^{4}$ yih
韻$^{4}$ yüin
鏗$^{1}$ k'en
鏘$^{1}$ ts'iang

淋$^{2}$ lin
鈴$^{2}$ ling
裂$^{4}$ lieh
帛$^{4}$ poh

22

湍$^{1}$ t'ŭan
激$^{1}$ kih
峯$^{1}$ fung
迴$^{2}$ hwe

霆$^{2}$ t'ing
轟$^{1}$ hung
電$^{4}$ tien
掣$^{4}$ ch'eh

賡$^{1}$ keng
詠$^{4}$ yung
翕$^{1}$ hih
諧$^{1}$ hie

濫$^{4}$ lan
竽$^{2}$ yü
羞$^{1}$ siu
測$^{4}$ ts'eh

23 花木

脂$^{1}$ ch
妍$^{2}$ yien
粉$^{3}$ fen
媚$^{4}$ me

秀$^{4}$ siu
麗$^{4}$ li
耑$^{1}$ chŭan
鍾$^{1}$ chung

黛$^{4}$ tai
痕$^{2}$ heng
楊$^{2}$ yang
柳$^{3}$ liu

綠$^{4}$ luh
蔭$^{4}$ yin
梧$^{2}$ wu
桐$^{2}$ t'ung

24

桃$^{2}$ t'au
李$^{3}$ li
競$^{4}$ chin
暖$^{3}$ noan

松$^{1}$ sung
栢$^{1}$ poh
耐$^{4}$ nai
冬$^{1}$ tung

趁$^{4}$ ch'en
候$^{4}$ heu
釀$^{4}$ niang
景$^{3}$ king

苑$^{4}$ yüen
囿$^{4}$ yiu
酣$^{1}$ han
融$^{2}$ yung

速成漢語

20.

Ling and lang, amber and ebony,
Cornelian (2) and agate (2),
Magnificent (2) and sparkling (2) —
Treasured (2) they contain enjoyment.

## *Sounds and Music.*

21.

Blow the bamboo *flute*, beat the silken *chord*,
*Play* the Siao and Shau, press *holes*, touch *keys*—
Pleasure's rhymes *softly* jingle (2),
The Lin-ling (2) *sounds like* tearing silk.

22.

The Billow's dash, the cliff turns-back,
Thunder booms, lightning flashes—
Concert singing *must be* harmonious (2),
The seeming piper *is* ashamed-of discovery[1].

## *Flowers and Trees.*

23.

As the rouged beauty or starched belle,
Blooming, elegant, specially favored,
*Are* the dark shadowed willow (2),
And the green shaded wut'ung (2).

24.

The peach and plum contend for warmth,
The fir and cypress endure winter.
Profiting-by the season, ripening into beauty,
Garden and park intoxicate with harmony.

| 25 蔬菜 | 26 | 27 鳥獸 | 28 | 29 鱗介 |
|---|---|---|---|---|
| 飽 $^{3}$pau | 掇 $^{1}$chŭch | 騰 $^{2}$t'eng | 雞 $^{1}$ki | 鱗 $^{2}$lin |
| 飫 $^{3}$yü | 擷 $^{1}$kih | 祥 $^{2}$siang | 塒 $^{1}$sh | 介 $^{4}$kie |
| 芳 $^{1}$fang | 鬱 $^{4}$yuh | 毓 $^{4}$yuh | 豚 $^{1}$t'un | 蕃 $^{1}$fan |
| 馨 $^{1}$hing | 芬 $^{1}$fen | 瑞 $^{4}$jue | 柵 $^{4}$chah | 滋 $^{1}$ts |
| 蓺 $^{4}$i | 咀 $^{2}$tsu | 鳳 $^{4}$fung | 鴻 $^{2}$hung | 譜 $^{3}$p'u |
| 畝 $^{3}$mu | 嚼 $^{2}$kioh | 翥 $^{3}$tu | 渚 $^{3}$tu | 題 $^{2}$t'i |
| 蓄 $^{1}$hiuh | 彌 $^{2}$mi | 麟 $^{2}$lin | 鵲 $^{4}$ts'ioh | 麤 $^{2}$ts'u |
| 菜 $^{4}$ts'ai | 快 $^{4}$kw'ai | 遨 $^{2}$au | 巢 $^{1}$ch'au | 確 $^{4}$ch'ioh |
| 剖 $^{1}$p'o | 胡 $^{2}$hu | 驊 $^{2}$hwa | 饈 $^{1}$siu | 龜 $^{1}$kwe |
| 瓜 $^{1}$kwa | 羨 $^{4}$sien | 騮 $^{2}$liu | 餌 $^{3}$r | 鼈 $^{1}$pih |
| 採 $^{3}$ts'ai | 腥 $^{1}$sing | 馳 $^{2}$ch' | 敷 $^{1}$fu | 黿 $^{2}$yüen |
| 薇 $^{1}$we | 羶 $^{1}$shan | 騁 $^{3}$ch'eng | 豫 $^{4}$yü | 鼉 $^{2}$t'o |
| 煮 $^{3}$chu | 饌 $^{4}$chŭan | 鸞 $^{2}$lŭan | 詎 $^{4}$kü | 鯤 $^{1}$kw'en |
| 葵 $^{2}$kw'e | 肴 $^{2}$yao | 鶴 $^{2}$hoh hao | 亟 $^{4}$kih | 鰲 $^{2}$ao |
| 拾 $^{2}$shih | 侈 $^{1}$ch' | 翔 $^{2}$siang | 烹 $^{1}$p'eng | 鯨 $^{1}$king |
| 芥 $^{4}$kie | 泰 $^{4}$t'ai | 翱 $^{2}$au | 庖 $^{2}$p'au | 鱷 $^{4}$oh |

## *Herbs and Vegetables.*

25.

Full fed on fragrant aroma,
Work your acres, store your herbs,
Divide the melon, pluck the pot-plant,
Boil the sun-flower, gather mustard.

26.

Pick and break, the confined fragrance,
Chewing (2) increases pleasure,
Why long for stenches and odors,
Meats and viands, profuse, extravagant?

## *Birds and Beasts.*

27.

Mounting, *bodes* prosperity; brooding, good-luck,
The phœnix soars. The kilin roams:
The horse (2) runs and gallops,
The lûan and stork gyrate and hover.

28.

Chickens *live in* coops, pigs *in* lattice *styes;*
Wild-geese on sand-banks, magpies in nests;
*Their* food (2) *is* spread ready—
Who *is* anxious *what* to bake in kitchen?

## *Fishes.*

29.

The scaly-tribe (2) numerous swarms,
The record themes *are* plain and reliable,
Tortoise, terrapin, turtle, water-lizzard,
Leviathan (2) whale and crocodile.

| 30 | 31 昆蟲 | 32 | 33 預終 | 34 |
|---|---|---|---|---|
| 淬 1 süe | 蠶 2 ts'an | 拋 1 p'au | 黽 3 min | 涕 4 t'i |
| 蝗 2 hwang | 織 1 chih | 臠 1 lüan | 勉 3 mien | 淚 4 le |
| 掬 2 küih | 蛛 1 chu | 獵 4 lieh | 肅 4 suh | 悚 3 sung |
| 鰕 1 hia | 組 1 tsu | 蟻 4 i | 雍 1 yung | 惶 2 hwang |
| 泅 1 ts'iu | 蚓 3 yin | 摶 2 t'üan | 慌 1 hwang | 頻 2 p'ing |
| 雀 4 ts'ioh | 唱 4 ch'ang | 飯 4 fan | 逢 2 fung | 挈 2 ch'ieh |
| 撈 1 lau | 蟬 2 ch'an | 鬨 4 hung | 殤 1 shang | 伴 4 pan |
| 蛤 3 koh | 吟 2 yin | 蠅 2 ing | 殂 1 tsu | 侶 3 lü |
| 卵 3 lüan | 徜 1 shang chang | 么 1 yau | 軀 1 k'ü | 旦 4 tan |
| 濕 1 sh | 徉 2 yang | 麼 2 mo | 殼 4 k'uh | 肄 4 i |
| 累 3 le | 邃 4 süe | 瞬 3 shun | 匪 3 fe | 旬 4 süin |
| 孳 1 ts | 閣 2 koh | 盼 4 p'an | 牢 2 lau | 諏 1 tseu |
| 俄 1 o | 紬 1 ch'eu | 罔 3 wang | 眚 3 sheng | 警 3 king |
| 頃 1 k'ing | 繹 4 yih | 忖 3 ts'un | 慝 4 t'eh | 惕 4 t'ih |
| 跳 4 t'iau | 閒 2 hien | 凄 1 ch'i | 酸 1 san | 臭 4 hiu |
| 躍 4 yoh | 庭 2 t'ing | 辛 1 sin | 楚 3 ch'u | 腐 3 fu |

It plunges a locust, and you pick-up a crab,
It swims a sparrow, you clutch an oyster.
Their eggs in moisture frequent multiply,
For-a-moment (2) they leap and spring.

### *Insects.*

31.

The silk-worm weaves, the spider knits,
The earth-worm sings, the locust hums,
They loiter (2) in suites of galleries,
Interwoven (2) in vacant halls.

32.

Throw-down meat, you catch ants,
Knead boiled-rice, then buz the flies—
Little-things! a moment they look-about,
*But* do-not think-of grief and bitterness.

### *Memento Mori.*

33.

*Be* earnest, (2) grave, dignified,
Suddenly to meet early-death or late-death,
This corporeal shell is-not firm,
Faults and offences are sour and painful.

34.

With trickling tears and anxious dread:
Often lead *your* associates (2),
*Each* morning labor, *each* ten-days debate—
Warn *them to be* in awe of dissolution (2).

**35** 旼格

矧 ³shen
窺 ²kw'e
浩 ⁴hau
蕩 ⁴tang

喧 ¹hüin
奕 ⁴yih
无 ²wu
邊 ¹pien

緝 ⁴ch'ih
熙 ¹hi
淵 ¹yüen
穆 ⁴muh

翹 ²ch'iau
睇 ⁴t'i
鈞 ¹küin
顏 ²yien

**36**

匍 ²fu
匐 ²fuh
跣 ³sien
跽 ⁴ki

慙 ¹ch'an
懟 ⁴te
胥 ¹sü
刪 ¹shan

傴 ¹eu
僂 ¹leu
踧 ⁴ts'uh
蹐 ⁴tsih

冥 ²ming
頑 ²wan
徐 ²sü
悛 ²ch'ün

**37** 效德

策 ⁴ts'eh
絜 ²hih
臣 ²ch'en
僚 ²liau

禹 ³yü
湯 ¹t'ang
堯 ²yau
舜 ⁴shun

箴 ¹chen
規 ¹kwe
紳 ¹shen
儒 ²ju

仲 ⁴chung
閔 ³min
孔 ³k'ung
孟 ⁴mung

**38**

斟 ¹chen
酌 ²choh
奢 ¹she
淳 ²ch'un

雙 ¹shŭang
甄 ¹chen
標 ¹piau
準 ³chŭn

炎 ²yien
火 ¹ho
怖 ⁴pu
燒 ¹shau

撫 ³fu
膺 ¹ing
敏 ³min
懇 ³k'en

凡六百八字

## *Exhortation.*

35.

Much-more pry-into the vast grand *mystery*,
Its noise is great without bound,
Brilliant (2) profound, sublime,
Upward look-to the venerable face.

36.

Stooping, creeping, bare-foot, kneeling,
Ashamed, vexed, wholly purging-away *evil.*
Bowing down, (2) with reverence (2),
The dark and stupid gradually reform.

## *Virtue and Vice.*

37.

To spur and lead the official class,
*Point-to* Yu, T'ang, Yau and Shun;
As maxims and rules, for the belted scholar,
*Take* Tslu, Mingts, Confucius, Mencius.

38.

Reflect-on (2) excess and purity,
Of the twain distinguish mark and aim,
Flaming fire *will* consume (2) *the vicious*—
Beating the breast, earnestly entreat.

海上絲綢之路文獻集成　科技與文化編

NOTES.

1. Defects, gaps and leaks. Worship, knock the head. 叩 knock.
2. Forms designed by the Creator, each the model of a class.
3. 嵐 Air of the hills, from 山 and 風, mist or haze.
霞 The evening aurora, the *abendrothe* of the Germans.
4. 燮 To temper with heat, and 調 to change, transform or stir, taken together express the operations of the chemist.
6. 抄 To copy, hence to correct in copying, also to take or attain by a more direct road.
8. 衡 Transverse, a balance, but in connexion with 璣 an astronomical instrument of whose form we are not very certain.
15. 佩 To carry at the side; anything worn at the side.
16. 副 Secondary or subordinate, used for the border of a garment.
17. There was a vessel called 'the square.' "If the square be not square is it a square," said Confucius, in reference to some standard of judgment.
18. 吮 To touch with the tongue, as a Chinese scribe does, to adjust the point of his pen.
19. 寶石 The Chinese title of this verse comprehends two classes. The antique articles named in the last two lines belong to the first class.
洛泗 Names of rivers, 秦唐 Names of dynasties.
20. In uncertainty as to some of these stones, it seems preferable to retain their native names.
21. *Shau* and *Linling* are names of musical compositions.
22. The sounds of nature are represented as imitated in music. The "seeming piper" was one who sought to pass for a musician, by imitating the motions of others in the band, but without hazarding a note.
28. Mat. vi. 26.
29. As *kwen* and *au* are fabulous monsters, it will hardly be admitted that the ichthyology of the Chinese is "plain and reliable."
30. 累 "frequent" has the double sense of the Latin *frequens*. Locusts are believed to turn to crabs, and sparrows to oysters.
31. The musical powers of the earthworm are confidently asserted.
35. "Noise" in a good sense, for fame. Face, the face of God.
37. Yu, T'ang, Yao, Shun, ancient Kings.
38. 標 An object aimed at, 準 a line to guide by.

# PART. III.

## ANALYSIS OF CHARACTERS.

## 常字雙千合釋

### CONSTANT CHARACTERS, A COUPLE OF THOUSANDS—ANALYZED.

*With a Commentary in Chinese.*

NOTE.

The "elements" are of two kinds—perfect and imperfect. Of the former, many are found in the table of radicals, and others occur in the text. The rest, together with the imperfect elements, are arranged in a list at the end of this Part, according to the chapters in which they occur.

# 常字雙千

常字雙千編韻　一名認字新法

## 第一章論古始

造物

逐口一　夅爲巫矢　一卩処易土　十白白八

八　禾十　爿爪霝厶　人虍貝其　𠂉一比皿

遂亦和土　將爲靈矣　命處賜基　千百皆與

八口　乍　兀辟大也　禺勿夕与　旡布一共

十一　亻　丿十門一土　廿牛夕正　白匕乂月田

六日力作　先闢天地　萬物多焉　既希且異

木一氏木　刖月一巾　隹　八申　𡈼𠤎匕

一牛口从　𦍌ナ卜产　忄　直示　耳肖匕

未生民來　前有上帝　惟一眞神　無聖能比

呼 丂考同口音圍

其禁令、而自取罪戾哉、

疾羊切㝵音律靁同靈厶音私虍音

自音怨亠音頭亠音暋乂五古文丮

右第一節、記上主造物之多、所以備人之用也、人奈何犯

口厶口㫗 一田儿 耳口手手 㝵非大匕

牛二丁人 戈口尚目 門言麻合 彳四口止

告云可食 或當見耳 聞言摩拿 得罪因此

丶斤日 个一 火欠口心 惪又

几戶耂 一六 犬谷止亞 耳王

 匀羊 耳

凡所求者 毋不立予 然欲善惡 勿聽手取

复吏且豕 丂生 胃一人 找口目

彳亻宀宀 八彳 言口二 一女一

復使宜家 女兮往事 謂之曰夫 爾我如自

卷 八夫巳
撒 扌散
全 人王
死 一外

父 八乂
意 音心
非
昔 廾一日

以
致 至攵
彼 彳皮
族 方人矢

墮惡
中 口丨
傳 亻專
亞
伯 亻白

何 亻可
問 門口
儕 亻齊
羣 君羊

其 二共
僕 亻菐
己
明 日月

但 亻旦
安 宀女
利 禾刂
名 夕口

羊
祭 癶示
信 亻言
心

第 竹弟
歸 𠂤止帚
方 丶万
蓋 艹盍

即 白匕卩
由 十口
是 日疋
時 日寺

愛 受必
身
尼 尸匕
色 刀巴

長
子 了一
若 艹右
兄 口儿

則 貝刂
同 冂一口
義 羊我
人

大 一人
水
四 八口
行 彳亍

列 歹刂
馬
羅 四維
金 余一

敵 啇攵
殺 杀殳
及
今

救降

攵 古 故　目 叔 又　攵 孝 督 教

四 甘 甚　口 力 加　一 卄 世　畐 示 福

夅 阝 降　卜 一 下　阝 耳 耶　禾 魚 穌

斤 其 斯　貫 宀 實　攵 求 救　王 、 主

同弔自堆本字门音扃 有八人從七者、所携潔畜牝牡各七也、事見創世記、衰弔｜音

矣、尼瞎也、僕、謂挪亞也、方蓋、方舟也、居八者、挪亞眷屬、共

洪水横行、上主實惡其汚穢也、非有義人、則人類幾絕滅

右第二節、記世人之犯禁墮惡、殘殺貪暴、造孽日深、所以

古 尸 居　辵 从 彳 八 從 七　口 夂 各　立 扌 拉 入 門

# 千雙字常



土　𥁕隹　夋早召者
一　氵牙　彳立日言
王而溫雅　後章昭諸

令辶成巴　木辶各　酋丶或
冫加土口　八首足　犭大口
泠迦城邑　巴米道路　猶太國也　西乃山乎

目勹𠂉一　心口里攵　即豊寸去　口一走
木糸四十　一矢王婁　竹示宀氵　𠃌一彳
相約衆士　必知理數　節禮守法　司十二徒

寺日　侖山令二　𠦒土殳　土胄又曰
竹門　亻山方力　廾一厶展　亻人一罒聿
等間于三　倫出於五　華年至殿　在會受書

凡二百四十字

宀音綿丣音必乑音吟夋音逡

出世誕育於人也、事載新約福音書、後章即詳其事、古文夅降在三位之中、居於第二也、倫出於五者、耶穌雖爲神子、而自救、故特降下愛子、爲萬世之救主也、等間于三者、耶穌

右第三節、記上主降救之故、蓋深憫世人、迷於惡途、不能

# 常字雙千

書、同古迴字着備本字厤曆本字𠂤音堆厂音漢㬎音蜆殸音磬

右第一節、總冒下文、此章之綱領也、幕、喻身也、見彼得後

綱領

| 備歷苦難 | 顯成功勞 | 追厥本初 | 垂訓汝曹 |
| --- | --- | --- | --- |
| 䔿止古隹 | 頁力力力 | 辶欠一刀 | 一川女日 |
| 亻厤廿堇 | 㬎戈工𤇾 | 𠂤屰木衣 | 垂言氵一曲 |

| 親營皮幕 | 赦過拯逃 | 蒙選代贖 | 聲稱益高 |
| --- | --- | --- | --- |
| 見呂巾 | 攵辶丞辶 | 冢辶弋賣 | 耳爯血冋 |
| 亲𤇾莫 | 赤咼扌兆 | 廿巽亻貝 | 殸禾亼八古 |

## 第二章論教化

常字雙千編韻（一名認字新法）

軍光、星光也、玨音確 糸音覓

右第二節、記耶穌出世之初、天即垂象、而先顯示於人也、

辶 至 寸 品
告 宀 辰 臣人
造室辱臨

犬 衣 欠
亻 亻 冫
伏拜依次

日 彖 夕 心
八罒 糸 苎 咸
曾緣夢感

心 生 力 司
勿 立丿 田 口冊
忽產男嗣

木 介 又 巾
日 田 𠂇 𠂤一
東界友師

車 兀 羊 見
冖 小 言 示
軍光詳視

出世

必 女
玨 一ヨ
母氏瑟妻

丿 寺 子
小 彳 宀
少小待字

連 谷 系 耑
艹 宀 主 立
蓮容素端

闌 生 交 田
艹 忄 車 糸
蘭性較細

穌也、瘳音六幵音堅彡音衫㐬音留巩 音拱
空也、畜老則毛脫而皮空、喻希律既髦而行惡也、龍、謂耶
穌、右第三節、記耶穌嬰時遭害、備極苦難、而始得安全也、荒、

田匕十㐬
玄耂廿口卄
畜老革荒

龍見自手
音王亠與
龍現首舉

免欠羊戈
刀與土吉
免歎幸哉

小非冬台
厂白麻糸女
原靡終始

辶口十殳
台尹卒氵
追君卒沒

十目辶丨
卒八夫反上
卒眷返止

乃心力口
亻巩革刀
仍恐勸召

夕罙兌厶
衣氵月土
夜深脫去

口王取心
時尸白日刃
嬰后皇最忍

安尸戈刂
扌一翏幵
按戶戮刑

那貝殳辶
扌刀扌袁
挪負投遠

辶竟臧彡
辟土卄幵
避境藏形

速成漢語

## 試見

| | |
|---|---|
| 幷 | 八 幵 |
| 令 | 人 一卩 |
| 俯 | 亻 府 |
| 望 | 亡 月王 |
| 尊 | 酋 寸 |
| 榮 | 𤇾 木 |
| 強 | 弓 虽 |
| 施 | 方 𠂉也 |
| 修 | 亻攵 彡 |
| 德 | 彳 悳 |
| 圖 | 啚 口 |
| 報 | 幸 𠬝 |
| 正 | 一 止 |
| 直 | 自 匸 |
| 兩 | |
| 虛 | 虍 业 |

| | |
|---|---|
| 嘗 | 尚 旨 |
| 遇 | 禺 辶 |
| 魔 | 麻 鬼 |
| 試 | 言 式 |
| 指 | 扌 旨 |
| 餅 | 食 并 |
| 爭 | 爪 尹 |
| 遺 | 貴 辶 |
| 押 | 扌 甲 |
| 登 | 癶 豆 |
| 宮 | 宀 呂 |
| 屋 | 尸 至 |
| 崇 | 山 宗 |
| 垣 | 土 亘 |
| 被 | 衣 皮 |
| 攜 | 扌 巂 |

右第四節、記耶穌受洗之事、河約但河也、越過也、

㡭音繼 壴音紵

## 洗受

| | |
|---|---|
| 譬 | 辟 言 |
| 樹 | 村 壴 |
| 結 | 糸 吉 |
| 果 | 田 木 |
| 適 | 啇 辶 |
| 口 | |
| 維 | 糸 隹 |
| 悅 | 忄 兌 |
| 否 | 不 口 |
| 悉 | 釆 心 |
| 刃 | 刀 丶 |
| 斷 | 㡭 斤 |
| 便 | 亻 更 |
| 付 | 亻 寸 |
| 焚 | 林 火 |
| 烈 | 列 火 |

| | |
|---|---|
| 向 | 丿 冋 |
| 野 | 里 予 |
| 翰 | 𠦝 人 羽 |
| 呼 | 口 乎 |
| 悔 | 忄 每 |
| 改 | 己 攵 |
| 務 | 矛攵 力 |
| 切 | 七 刀 |
| 就 | 京 尤 |
| 洗 | 氵 先 |
| 河 | 氵 可 |
| 旁 | 产 方 |
| 循 | 彳 盾 |
| 儀 | 亻 義 |
| 莫 | 艹日 大 |
| 越 | 走 戉 |

# 常字雙千

## 宣道

攵手辶辶　巾㣺夌央　日丶米貝　㥯音𠦝東

工殳韋𢀖　尚取亻廿　匕斤气主　阝日田阝

攻擊違逆　常聚俊英　旨斥氣責　隱暗畢陳

北盧欠木　囪木日心　条戒長巾　辛台水蜀口

禾馬雚𢆶　糸隹知禺　亻言弓𠂇　宀氵尸五

乘驢歡樂　總集智愚　條誡張布　宰治屬吾

卒離之而去也、舊音俊啚音鄙𠬝音伏

右第五節、記耶穌見試之日、爲魔所逼、而守正不阿、故魔

千俞辶辶　攵心未

三人言尊貴　耳或人

奉諭遵遣　烏敢惑余

速成漢語

| | | |
|---|---|---|
| 患 | 串 | 心 |
| 遭 | 曹 | 辶 |
| 獄 | 狺 | 犬 |
| 陷 | 阝 | 臽 |
| 謀 | 言 | 某 |
| 亡 | | |
| 沙 | 氵 | 少 |
| 洲 | 氵 | 州 |
| 統 | 糸 | 充 |
| 轄 | 車 | 害 |
| 的 | 白 | 勺 |
| 裔 | 衣 | 冏 |
| 征 | 彳 | 正 |
| 途 | 余 | 辶 |
| 遍 | 扁 | 辶 |
| 周 | 冂 | 吉 |

| | | |
|---|---|---|
| 花 | 艹 | 化 |
| 嫩 | 女 | 敕 |
| 易 | 日 | 勿 |
| 敗 | 貝 | 攵 |
| 麥 | 朩 | 人 夂 |
| 掃 | 扌 | 帚 |
| 定 | 宀 | 疋 |
| 留 | 丣 | 田 |
| 類 | 米 | 大 頁 |
| 反 | 厂 | 又 |
| 鳥 | 一 | 烏 |
| 獸 | 嘼 | 犬 |
| 穀 | 壳 | 禾 殳 |
| 養 | 羊 | 食 |
| 弗 | 弓 | 八 |
| 憂 | 亘 | 夊 |

| | | |
|---|---|---|
| 失 | 丿 | 夫 |
| 懼 | 忄 | 瞿 |
| 災 | 巛 | 火 |
| 絕 | 糸 | 色 |
| 好 | 女 | 子 |
| 甲 | 曰 | 丨 |
| 亂 | 𤔔 | 乙 |
| 俱 | 亻 | 具 |
| 仇 | 亻 | 九 |
| 怒 | 奴 | 心 |
| 財 | 貝 | 才 |
| 據 | 扌 | 豦 |
| 兵 | 丘 | 八 |
| 奪 | 大隹 | 寸 |
| 車 | 亘 | 丨 |
| 驅 | 馬 | 區 |

| | | |
|---|---|---|
| 孰 | 享 | 丸 |
| 忘 | 亡 | 心 |
| 足 | 口 | 止 |
| 畏 | 田 | 𧘇 |
| 頓 | 屯 | 頁 |
| 害 | 宀 | 𠀎 |
| 體 | 骨 | 豊 |
| 魂 | 云 | 鬼 |
| 該 | 言 | 亥 |
| 恃 | 忄 | 寺 |
| 庇 | 广 | 比 |
| 釋 | 釆 | 睪 |
| 藉 | 艹耒 | 昔 |
| 謝 | 言 | 射 |
| 恩 | 因 | 心 |
| 仁 | 亻 | 二 |

# 常字雙千

## 立教

每十可弟 業未辶己 復戈青辶 頁隹郎土
氵一可八 云业业束走 尸止言隋 原离乡田
海干哥弟 棄業速起 履武請隨 願離鄉里

子刂𠂢又 矣口午直 夂女艮刀 且示兄亟
𦥑另氵十 土十言四 苟亡一八 言林示木
學別派支 埃田許置 敬妄艮分 詛禁祝極

聲畱畜古文巛川本字乙古文隱字𤔔同亂䖒音渠广醜上聲
气氣本字㥯同隱舀遙上
藋音灌悤音聰屰逆本字
嬌好也、類人類也、好甲、猶好兵也、
悖教者謀訟耶穌、而耶穌避去也、的裔、以色列之民也、嫩、
右第六節、記耶穌宣道之時、多言譬喻以教人也、獄訟也、

厶頁厶壽
禾龠八示
私龥公禱

番土刂人
火牛害内
燔牡割肉

阝阝目小
手者少亠口
邦都省京

一巳今血
日糸矛忄
目紀矜恤

匍匋欠頃
艹艹食亻
葡萄飲傾

臼列隹子
萑亻虽才
舊例雖存

羊匕丶巠
十冂斗牛糸
南北半經

心昜贊大
土扌言羊
志揚讚美

开土成力
門尚言雚
開堂誠勸

火十寺賣
羊𠂉牛牛
羔牛特犢

母心朁爲
𠂉人二亻亻
每念僭僞

犬巳斤又
黑言示丶
默記祈文

丨登亘日
弓言宀立
引證宣音

易犬豆欠
金鬳山斤
錫獻豈欣

匕寸干青
亻道八忄
化導平情

辶辶口乂
甬幸十口
通達古史

# 千雙字常

旨谷皮三 心虫丹氏 心矢睘見 舌寺口
言舟氵而 自凡丿广 俞疒王雚 氵亻吉廿
詣船波面 息風舟底 愈疾環觀 活喪侍喜

允辶丙酉 亏罕咼威 死廾土𠬶廾與 門帚絜
田家疒殹 氵角示氵 廾莫巛同 扌女氵
鬼逐病醫 污解禍滅 葬墓寢興 捫衣婦潔

者吾貝俞 可各又妾 頁重夂昜 月少戌
廿言中一口 大田曰扌 雇禾牛亻 卓止
著語貴喩 奇罯更接 顧種牧傷 夕朝歲月

奇行

也、割肉、割禮也、手音拜 羊音茬 鬳音絭 𠂢派本字 𠫓音突 業音葉

右第七節、記耶穌立教之正、改舊禮而用新禮也、武、足跡

預言

攵扁貝兌 彔 尹 殳于冉廴 頁十木月

昔糸寒言 金 亻 臼土宀一聿 予言一其

散編賽說 錄久兆伊 毀宇再建 預計末期

喻耶穌也、亐今作于咼音跬戚滅本字疒音牀丝音幽

右第八節、記耶穌行奇之多、所以表其權能也、種、種類、牧、

古呆皿皿 亘褱小頁 卜恭入心 灬人戈券

口亻成乃又 忄忄共川 夕日冂衍 庐丝戈單月

固保盛盈 恒懷恭順 外暴內慾 庶幾戰勝

力干頁也 田刂口乙 訁刂巳黃爰 里雚蜀王

且穴東亻 采半戌工 四犭广扌 千木犭亻

助罕頼他 審判咸己 罰犯廣援 重權獨任

力皆斤女　日共酉辶　丸由月土　㐬皿門虎
重亻來取　禾亻氵敫　幸氵高从　氵丿忄号
動偕新娶　香供酒邀　執油膏坐　流血憫號

終臨

殳貝畐　工口辶父　余侖　艮　珏飠皿召
彳分宀　𠂇𠂇斤六　食言　月　刂方聿灬扌
工役貧富　左右近交　餘論尤服　班旅盡招

語、引之以譽耶穌也、又音引雁音因
賽亞、古之預言者也、末期、末日也、九思、君子之成德、見論
右第九節、記耶穌預言之確、卽可信其無所不知矣、賽以

癶袁口褱　頁寸隹欠　行欠口心　卑褱心
广口士土　公丵言其　圭哥八人雁　亻言田
廢園吉壞　頌對誰欺　街歌谷應　俾讓九思

勸世

示生畢散　且系合辶　八獲齊辶　言之口犬
宀女吅彳　示子竹术　丗廾犭氵隹　折一衣吅
宗姓單微　祖孫答述　共獲濟進　誓之哀哭

祭貝又艮　亦曰扌合　是女殳岡　一口子水立
宀化广金　一丿冂糸　扌西癶弓糸　人一ㄙ口二亻
察貨度銀　赤白用給　提要發綱　合享永位

心雨心云　辰用番小　月木木亶　內貴車吅
彗一茲雨　雨刀扌二　北加筑土　糸匚𢦏哭
慧雨慈雲　震角播示　背架築壇　納匱載器

音聶敫音僥

右第十節、記耶穌臨終之慘、皆所以救萬世之人也、福聿畐音

凡五百九十二字

淫、淫祀也、吅音萱 𢼸音薇 戜音秩 戠音職

像、而不變易夫風俗哉、角、箛也、匱、耶和華之約匱、見舊約、

救萬世、人自當心悅誠服、盡其分以待審判、奈何崇事偶

右第十一節、記設教勸世之切、言耶穌既已捨身爲人、以

| | | |
|---|---|---|
| 偶 | 亻 | 禺 |
| 像 | 亻 | 象 |
| 阿 | 阝 | 可 |
| 囘 | 冂 | 已 |
| 銅 | 金 | 同 |
| 鐵 | 金 | 戜 |
| 石 | 厂 | 口 |
| 木 | 十 | 人 |
| 創 | 倉 | 刂 |
| 識 | 言 | 戠 |
| 破 | 石 | 皮 |
| 淫 | 氵 | 全 |
| 尙 | 小 | 冋 |
| 議 | 言 | 義 |
| 變 | 䜌 | 又 |
| 俗 | 亻 | 谷 |

昇、與舉同、疑、擬也、與尚書罪疑惟輕同義、会古陰字吳音疑夌音菱窑寶古文

右第一節、言耶穌升天之後、萬事皆待之而鞫也、淩騰也、

辛口走亞　彐兔艮　見未星辶　会付氏巨
古处吳車　雨宀菓　𦥯日酉米　阝广扌扌
辜咎疑輕　雪寃艱巨　覺昧醒迷　陰府抵拒

攵八死生　夌工卅廾　貝坐工心　公司辶八
戶口宀尸更　冫穴一臼　窑广弋馮　言言白目一
啟穴屍甦　淩空升昇　寶座式憑　訟詞追具

待鞫
萬事

## 第三章論人事

常字雙千編韻 字新法一名認

幼年

秉 ヨ 禾
質 貝 所
清 青 氵
聰 悤 耳

概 既 木
除 余 阝
雜 隹 木 亽
慾 心 欲

夙 万 几
譴 遣 言
洪 共 氵
沾 占 氵

盍 皿 去
早 十 曰
濯 翟 氵
沐 木 氵

爰 叏 爪
監 皿 臣𠂉
嬰 女 賏
孩 亥 子

胎 台 月
元 兀 一
誕 延 言
育 月 云

急 心 刍
乳 乙 孚
泣 立 氵
饑 幾 食

席 巾 广
臥 人 臣
綿 帛 糸
束 木 口

右第二節、言人當勤學以求正道也、稽、考求也、毛幽 音磔 丝音

兒 儿 臼
輩 車 非
謳 區 言
誦 甬 言

賦 武 貝
擇 睪 扌
詩 寺 言
稽 旨 禾尤

齒 凵 止从
牙
申 丨 曰
講 冓 言

遐 辶 叚
邇 辶 爾
均 勻 土
推 隹 扌

正道 勤學

量 里 旦
才
託 乇 言
授 受 扌

衛 行 韋
翼 異 羽
扶 夫 扌
持 寺 扌

詔 召 言
戒 廾 戈
誘 秀 言
誨 每 言

晝 一 書
晚 免 日
鑑 監 金
茲 丝 艹

誇大、縱放肆、窘抑、窘迫而屈抑也、憾恨也、機、機變、術、權術、

而求救者、詭詐也、駭驚也、飾外爲襲、中藏爲匿、克能也、伐、

右第四節、言人年齒既長、習染漸深、易墮惡途、故當謹防

兄 戈 喬 從　君 卬 木 躬　尙 感 土 洛　幾 行 大 用

十 亻 馬 糸　穴 扌 口 穴　亻 忄 隋 艹　木 朮 爫 庚

克伐驕縱　窘抑困窮　倘憾墮落　機術奚庸

力 斬 士　白 木 朱 里　危 兼 衣 兒　亥 夭 若 衣

幺 氵 爿　羽 氿 歹 立　言 言 龍 豸　馬 竹 匸 中

歲壯

幼丁漸壯　習染殊童　詭謙襲貌　駭笑匿衷

欲、夙譴、原罪也、洪、大也、濯沐、洗禮也、字所音垠 叐音跋 䁆音映 乙古隱

右第三節、言人初生之時、惡孽未萌、惟早當洗滌耳慾私

盡其職曰尸爵、曠、虛也、祐、福也、尃音敷 斿音由 叀同專 彡音衫 則永爲罪人矣、嗜、好也、侮、慢也、愼、篤、誠篤之人也、莅官不右第五節、讀書之人、琴劍遨遊、任情妄作、苟不求慕正道、

尸爵曠官　貪祐祀佛　呿唎嚷朋　輪須鑒覆

尉廣吕　貝古巳弗　法利賽月　侖頁金復

爪四日宀　今示示亻　口口口月　車彡臣西

士業

博嗜僐篇　几筵勤讀　琴劍遨遊　專侮愼篤

尃者閒扁　延力賣　今刂辶辶　寸每眞馬

十口竹竹　竹堇言　玨僉嵩斿　叀亻忄竹

庸、用也、幺音邀 匚音方 卭抑古字

## 工匠

操 扌 喿
尺 尸 乀
運 軍 辶
斤

係 亻 系
誇 言 夸
傑 亻 桀
步 止 少

弓
矢 丿 天
皿
料 米 斗

精 米 青
粗 米 且
製 制 衣
鑄 金 壽

審判、卨音薛雚音灌𢇍音繼訇音轟

則永爲罪人矣、以水沃田曰灌、植、種也、抹、摸也、寅、敬惕、鞫、

右第六節、農家者流、三時辛苦、希冀豐收、苟不求慕正道、

郊 交 阝
場 土 昜
收 丩 攵
積 禾 責

繼 糸 𢇍
蹟 足 責
厚 厂 白 子
豐 山 丰 豆

疇 田 壽
想 相 心
寅 西 八 宀
鞫 革 訇

曲 由 丨
跪 足 危
虔 虍 文
尋 ⺕ 寸

## 農田

泥 氵 尼
塗 氵 余 土
奔 大 卉
走 十 疋

竊 穴 釆 卨
認 言 忍
農 曲 辰
耕 耒 井

澤 氵 睪
灌 氵 雚
烟 火 因
植 木 直

抹 扌 末
露 雨 路
踐 足 戔
塵 鹿 土

# 常字雙千

右第八節、行商居賈、跋涉山川、權營子母、苟不求慕正道、

音意八手　貝兌殳糸　戔𦬸思襄　主車弓倉

亻亻曲尙　工禾月敏　金氵虍扌　馬广穴卄

倍億典掌　貢稅般繁　錢滿慮攘　駐庫穹蒼

## 客商

巾禺　祭　貝買各冏　阝辶嚴山　旦可工羊

亠阝　阝　四士宀六　去卬山鳥　土土氵氵

市隅井際　買賣客商　却迎巖島　坦坷江洋

則永爲罪人矣、斤、斧斤也、泉刀、錢也、喿音搔睘音瓊

右第七節、工匠之儔、鉤心鬬角、作爲奇巧、苟不求慕正道、

州直曷賞　水辶　睘　句吾木　辶田芻卜

酉亻立亻　白　睘　卄忄亻　車釆走走

酬值竭償　泉刀還互　苟悟了休　連番趨赴

官服

貝數口　何攵俞心　孚反示皿　念冂頁寸

臤彳折　卄正車中　亻半御次　馬㔾分圭

卜賢徵哲　荷政輸忠　俘叛禦盜　驗印頒封

矣、戚、眷屬也、昆玉、兄弟也、尗菽同尗音淬隶音代

右第九節、一室之內、和氣致祥、能如此者、其孝友誠可嘉

刂寸聿衣　粦昔又卑　日言艮原　隶丁儿心

亥蒲戶攵口一　忄忄女女　並卄隻木氵　广宓而厶尉

刻薄肇衰　憐惜奴婢　普護根源　康寧允慰

家居

加戊目　比、𠂔未　屯子耶雚　十弓右心

一吉尗龵　日王女女　糸耂父一忄　甶弓亻叀

嘉戚看承　昆玉姊妹　純孝爺懽　卑弱佑惠

則永爲罪人矣、却退也、迎進也、坦、平路、坷、險途、門卬音昂吾音透㒼音

義行

偏側陸奠（扁則坴大　亻亻阝八酋）

圮壞岸堅（巳襄厈土　土土山臤）

那肯闞隙（卩月敢㡀　刖止門阝）

蕪穢侵牽（無歲𠬶牛　艹禾亻玄冖）

崗磐晨屆（岡石辰由　山般日尸）

湖漢星遷（胡𦰩生辶　氵氵日䙴）

延蝦藥送（叐叚樂辶　正古艹关）

需飢糧捐（而几量肙　雨食米扌）

職勾音葛厷音肱

小之躬、自喻也、俟駕俟主之駕、奏職、盡己之分、同徵哉同臤音賢數

矣卜、枚卜、徵、聘也、賓、幕中之客、吏、書役也、舋、隙也、藐躬、藐

右第十節、任君之事、鞠躬盡瘁、能如此者、其忠藎誠可嘉

賓吏阻蔽（八省宀　史一且阝　敝艹）

舋詰藐躬（分酉興　吉言貌艹　弓身）

俟駕奏職（矣亻馬加　天夫　戠耳）

曷厭寬宏（匃日　犬厂昌　莧宀　厷宀）

右第十二節、此三等人、能盡其分、誠合於正道矣、惟不求

犬罔黃惟　曰行才土　包艮冗侖　兄秉戔戎

戶糸木四　日瞿門寒　扌忄氵氵　冫八歹貝

戾綱橫羅　昌衢閉塞　抱恨沉淪　况秉殘賊

堇各山皿　言貝以赤　專艮朋死　馬見幺火

言忄宓明　與尚亻赤　車目山芇　敬者山里

謹恪密盟　譽賞似赫　轉眼崩薨　驚覩幽黑

勉勸

不正也、蕪、汚也、凷音塊　坴音六　厈音漢　貟同隙　叐音引

則壽可延、需、急也、捐糧以急饑、則荒可濟、偏側、物將壞而

嘉矣、崗磐、山之高者、湖漢、水之廣者、遐、壽也、送藥以却病、

右第十一節、爲善之人、不存歧視、能如此者、其慈惠誠可

罪也、暮季末世也、濱、水之涯也、崙山之巔也、進善退惡、皆
穌必討其罪也、部、黨類也、售甘、甜言以誘人也、鳴鼓、聲其
右第十三節、今之邪黨橫行、荼毒善類、至末日之審判耶

家心丈女　鳥支日子　賓辶侖辶　示分頁日
百夫
女死亻戌　口壴莫禾　氵艮山俞　大宀丁夫
嫁怨仗威　鳴鼓暮季　濱退崙逾　奈寡頂替

僞姦

阝黑母它　頁阝口筮　口虫口　毀男奇力
牙尙主虫　令音天口　千突隹　火虍亻執
邪黨毒蛇　領部吞噬　舌蜜售甘　燬虜倚勢

橫、罹無辜而蹈禍也、沉淪、陷溺也、殘賊、凶暴之人、宓音伏
慕正道、則不能自救其靈魂、密盟、盟之於心也、赫顯、赫赫也、

多石穌蚰　然登火目　亡鬼昔工　卬小見付
禾麻卄虫　火火昭鼓　忄忄金羊丿　亻莫堇阝
移磨蘇蟲　燃燈照瞽　忙愧錯差　仰慕覲附

方舌婁室　八甚主伯　生它牛豕　离人師犬
戶人木吉　口土亻宀一　牛馬尸勿　人門犭穴
房舍樓臺　只堪住宿　牲駝犀象　禽閃獅突

王丶巳阝　刂心古辶　攵詹果复　犮旁刂
犭大虍粦　岡分女孫　方月衣月　髟言朿
狂犬虐鄰　剛忿姑遜　放膽裸腹　毛髮謗刺

反主荅　堇彡羕刂　巾系白心　令彡衣巾
木木土　亻章木制　帶毄巾縣　雨王主食𠂉
板柱瓦塔　僅彰樣制　帶繫帕懸　零珍表飾

譬設

己自主無預替者也壹音紵百

古百字

敢方段孝 日辛栗不 鬲鳥辶完 甫火寸韋

厂叩阝亻酉 斬匋忄木 粥合盾阝 扌畕身口

嚴防假酵 暫辭慄杯 鬻鴿遁院 捕魚射圍

羽支達丁 曷疑盧儿 非月曼斤 龍疋曾

前木扌扌 氵扌臥厶 月冎忄扌 宀人方土

翦枝撻打 渴擬鹽充 腓骨慢折 寵壽旋增

婁意丁甬 儿韱丿夆 朿寸頁異 包䍃工

尸忄金疒 音歹弋金 朿完豆十戈 衣扌糸

耶穌

回憶

屢憶釘痛 竟殲戈鋒 棘冠頭戴 袍片搖紅

狀怪異也、蘇活也、羕音樣彡音鬚髟音猋䖵音昆

無靈之物、不思得救也、塔高屋也、放縱也、裸露也、閃突形、

右第十四節、借譬以喻耶穌之道、人人皆當遵行不可若

月夂皿舀　亥十辛　旦冫辶火　戈丈韋求
屰𦣻般足　木冫辛刂　既𡨄乞執　口木糸王
朔夏盤蹈　核斗辨州　暨寒迄熱　曳杖緯球

辰古犮早　有力申人　田糸　日　吅各丿口欠
扌木扌艹　宀甬亻口　艹丿　魚　口木口區
振枯拔草　宥勇伸四　苗系齊魯　品格呂歐

正道
傳宣

吹籛也、鑯同簽夆音逢䍃音由鹵同鹽
遁、避去也、射圍、矢魚之戲、見春秋隱公傳、橄欖、山名、吹管、
之言行、固在在可堅信心也、被害而死曰殲、腓骨、脛骨也、
右第十五節、常憶耶穌受害之酷、升天之榮、而稽其生平

裝定林甫　果几枼巴　糸奇敢覽　刂阝官欠
声叩糸广衣　艹吅艹月　声馬木木　至旬竹口
囊綻麻補　菓咒葉肥　索騎橄欖　到郇管吹

凡五百七十六字

體也、夂音撴

知所向、則鑒北斗以辨之、緯象緯、天之度也、球、地球、地之陽修、能文善武者也、極北曰朔、中華曰夏、斗、北斗、夜行不悔改者也、囚、知罪而未伸也、苗系、猶苗裔也、呂、呂尚、歐、歐寒暑不間、固欲普救世人、同享永福也、振、起落也、勇猛於

右第十六節、此言傳道之教師、伸說耶穌之道、險阻不辭、

多也、冀望也、懺悔也、

以起下文也、迹、迹象、勳、功勞、楷模、制之有定者也、煩劇、繁

右第一節、鑒上主創造之迹、以啟世人誠信之心、承上章

總冒

| | | | | |
|---|---|---|---|---|
| 皆莫必罙 | 頁刂昜戊 | 台異貴耳 | 从韱吳翏 |
| 木木禾扌 | 火豦申廾 | 歹北目龍 | 亼忄言言 |
| 楷模秘探 | 煩劇暢茂 | 殆冀贖聾 | 僉懺誤謬 |
| 面辶朔力 | 盡羊夬雨 | 鄭丌木壽 | 手衣彡卩 |
| 糸亦氵熏 | 亻魚缶氵尸 | 扌田甘亻 | 寒尚厽口 |
| 緬迹溯勳 | 儘鮮缺漏 | 擲畀某儔 | 搴裳參叩 |

第四章論儔類

常字雙千編韻 字新法一名認

## 天文

晴嵐繚繞 日山糸糸 青風尞堯

瞻矚層霄 目目尸雨 詹屬曾肖

霞輝林豔 雨光木豐 叚軍木盍

霓彩渡消 雨采氵氵 兒彡度肖

迅雷奮響 凡雨雀鄉 辶田田音

疏霜催凋 疋雨亻冫 㐬相崔周

暘霪旱潦 日雨日氵 昜淫干尞

竚覯燮調 立賣言言 宁見炏又周

右第二節、就天之可見者、以驗上主之功有如此、嵐、天之氣也、繚繞、廻環也、迅、疾也、久晴曰暘、久雨曰霪、不雨而災爲旱、多雨而災爲潦、燮、和燮、調、調理、去聲

凡音信 雀音窺 炏音開

## 地理

攷究寰區 丂穴宀匚 攵九睘品

長短闊狹 矢門犭 豆活夾

凸凹崎嶇 山山 奇區

幽燕崖峽 豖豖山 山山 厓夾

爭口安堯　戠炎樂㐬　幾行僉廾　心辶著壽
青卜日日　火畓火石　王奥馬竹目　匆虍足足
靜占晏曉　熾餤爍硫　璣衡驗算　怱遽躇躊

## 時令

辛言辛牙干　聚兌日火　隹隹又、鄭蜀　咎辶彡孚
辛言丿　馬門夫禾　隹九足足　日折景氵
辯辰訝午　驟閱春秋　雙丸躑躅　晷逝影浮

也、塹、坑也、江爲天塹、丂音考勹音苞
究察也、寰區、四海之內、高出爲凸、低下爲凹、崎嶇、路不平
右第三節、就地之廣大者、以驗上主之功有如此、攷考同、

吳支巠少　并呈土刂　皿畺石車　虫百巳刂
忄止彳扌　亻禾斬畫　湯弓土扌與　言絲豸勹舌
悞歧徑抄　倂程塹劃　盪疆拓輿　蠻貊包刮

右第五節、山川之奇幻、具見匠心、人當推上主之功能、勿

章卒非累　朝由史冀　玄丂秦　圭元攵奇
山羽扌虫　氵共馬馬　亠幺工至　亻王亻宀

嶂翠排螺　潮黃駛驥　玄幻巧臻　佳玩攸寄

## 山水

山獄欽疑　胃辶辶　金僉見聿　步步手齊
代山山山　氵召虒　𣫞阝爪氵　阝氵樊足

岱嶽嶔嶷　渭川迢遞　鑿險覓津　陟涉攀躋

躊躇、猶豫不決之貌、彡音衫　戠音熾　豦音據

時過之速也、璣衡、璇璣玉衡、所以占測者也、忽遽、促迫也、忽促、而急求永福也、雙丸、日月也、躑躅、行貌、熾燄爍硫、喻

右第四節、時序運行不息、少縱卽歷春秋、人宜知光陰之

非人之所能測也、倜儻卓立也、遴選也、薦進也、順人而阿

右第六節、上主生人、靈蠢不一、而締造之苦心、實有奧妙、

| | | | |
|---|---|---|---|
| 頁頁令利 | 婁析胃毛 | 包丕己帝 | 少大頁堯 |
| 㒼干亻亻 | 糸日虍亭 | 月月酉糸 | 女白采皮食 |
| 顢頇伶俐 | 縷晰膚毫 | 胞胚配締 | 妙奧頗饒 |

人品

| | | | |
|---|---|---|---|
| 召童日口 | 周黨夾豕 | 辶薦力大 | 臽敖幾朝 |
| 髟亻老考 | 亻亻亻亭 | 粦廾厲將 | 言亻言口 |
| 髫僮耆耈 | 倜儻俠豪 | 遴薦勵獎 | 諂傲譏嘲 |

如螺也、駛驥、潮來迅急、如驥之駛也、臻至也、字幺音邀 虒音斯 齒殳鑿本

水名、迢遞、遼闊也、登山曰陟、履水曰涉、排螺、言諸山排列

徒羨佳玩之寄也、岱嶽、泰山名、山之宗也、嶔巇、聳立貌、渭、

之清潔哉、複重也、聯緜、連接不斷也、輻輳、聚集也、衍、延也、

右第七節宮室華美承門祚者猶恥玷汚、人奈何不求心

宮室

| | | | |
|---|---|---|---|
| 齋塾序庠 | 廩廚廁廐 | 衍慶迓休 | 恥玷楣構 |
| 小土子羊 | 禾㐭則既 | 行夊辶木 | 心占眉冓 |
| 齊孰广广 | 广广厂广 | 氵声牙亻 | 耳王木木 |
| 畫榭雕廊 | 複堦夾牖 | 斐檻聯緜 | 綺窗輻輳 |
| 一射隹郎 | 复皆从甫 | 文監𦀚系 | 奇囱畐奏 |
| 聿田木周广 | 衣土大片戶 | 非木耳帛 | 糸穴車車 |

分也、締、造也、饒、多也、廌音荐蔄音門

笑人曰嘲、顢頇、言愚蠢之人、辦事無眉目也、縷、細絲也、晰、

附之曰諂、淩人而蔑視之曰傲、微諷以刺人曰譏、曲言以

器用

敫瓜平才　昔貝左甫　垂民羽木　食食肋
西角言木　亻次亻車　目目木日爿　雍夕竹
覈瓠評材　借資佐輔　睡眠榻牀　饔飧匕筋

裝潢、而不急在內之寶貴乎、瞀音騖　瞏音瓊　毄音激

右第八節、服飾僅美外觀、救靈必享永福、何以戀在外之

服飾

行翟禁由　奄央刂裏　毛令艮足　辶心衣黃
玄光衣衣　扌日畐金　老齒卩亻　皇䜌壯氵
衒耀襟袖　掩映副鑲　耄齡限促　遑戀裝潢
曷衣希谷　瞀耳蜀瞏　帛皮肅風　粲闌軍皇
廿求糸糸　竹王金金　金扌糸亻　火火火火
葛裘絺綌　簪珥鐲環　錦披繡佩　燦爛煇煌

迓、迎也、休、吉祥也、玷、汚也、楣、門楣、構、堂構、嫛音愛　复音伏　鬬音鬭

# 常字雙千

## 珍寶

林郎虎久　馬卤武夫　爭桊崔粲　盈子口吳

王王王王　石石石石　山山王王　韋乃令女

琳瑯琥玖　碼碯碔砆　崢嶸璀璨　韞孕含娛

朱只玉　冄行胡　各童四石　禾口盧

王尺辟　主王　王　氵金氵殸　夫丑广金

寸珠咫璧　青珩丹瑚　洛鐘泗磬　秦鼎唐鑪

也、

哉、[illegible]、驗也、觚、器之有棱者也、麈、拂麈也、楮、紙也、臚、署、次序

右第九節人造器物以適己用何不修德爲上主之重器

軍主免畐　允聿衣者　女宁㥯諸　殳牛盧者

扌鹿扌革　口𥫗戈木　爪貝禾亻　舟亻月四

揮麈挽韁　吮筆裁楮　妥貯穩儲　般件臚署

右第十一節、五音迭奏、宮商克諧、不知樂者、不能和聲也、

耑 敫 夆 叉　廷 車車 电 手　貝 永 羽 皆　監 于 丑 則
氵 氵 山 回　雨 車車 雨 制　庚 言 合 言　氵 竹 羊丿 氵
湍 激 峯 廻　霆 轟 電 掣　賡 詠 翕 諧　濫 竽 羞 測

樂音

虛 个 單 糸　肅 召 付 白　辶 員 堅 將　林 令 衣 巾
口 个 弓 糸　竹 音 扌 扌　免 音 金 金　氵 金 列 白
嘘 竹 彈 絲　簫 韶 拊 拍　逸 韻 鏗 鏘　淋 鈴 裂 帛

石也、峥嶸、高峻貌、璀璨、玉光也、韞、藏也、音錄 昷音溫 殸音磬 翏音聊 糸

泗磬、石磬之能浮者、琳、瑯、琥、玖、美玉之名、碼、磂、碔、砆、皆寶

人心含孕韞藏、尙其永寶、八寸曰咫、洛鐘、銅鐘之寶貴者、

右第十節、珍奇之物、猶聖道也、珍奇秘於庫藏、聖道寓於

聖教廣播、遠近交孚、不知道者、不能行善也、簫韶、古樂名、掯撫、同、鏗鏘、樂之節奏、淋鈴、曲名、裂帛、樂聲也、湍激、水流之疾、峯迴、山勢之紆、譬樂聲之徐速也、濫竽、有竽之名、而不能吹者也、夆音逢

## 花木

脂妍粉媚　秀麗耑鍾　黛痕楊柳　綠蔭梧桐

月女米女　禾丽山金　代疒木木　糸卄木木

旨开分眉　乃鹿而重　黑艮昜卯　录陰吾同

桃李競暖　松栢耐冬　趁候釀景　苑圃酣融

木木竝日　木木而夂　走亻酉日　卄口酉鬲

兆子䚕爰　公百寸夂　㐱工矢襄京　夗有甘虫

右第十二節、花木秀於一時、上主猶畀以景色、衆人生於

種也、腥羶、鳥獸之肉、音 音透 叕音輟 氷同水 乂俗四字

滅罪而救靈、不必妄拜他神、徒尚偶像之多、飫饜足也、藝

更求腥羶、徒侈肴饌之盛、猶之聖教爲古今之正道、足以

右第十三節、蔬菜爲天地之正味、足以衛生而悅口、不必

叕 頡 彡 分　且 爵 爾 夬　月 次 星 亶　巽 有 多 氺

扌 扌 鬯林 卄　口 口 弓 忄　古 羊 月 羊　食 乂 亻 夫

掇擷鬱芬　咀嚼彌快　胡羡腥羶　饌肴侈泰

## 蔬菜

包 天 方 香　埶 攵 畜 釆　刂 釆 微　火 癸 合 介

食 食 卄 殸　卄 亠田 卄 卄　音 扌 卄　者 卄 扌 卄

飽飫芳馨　藝畝蓄菜　剖瓜採薇　煮葵拾芥

一世、上主更望其復新、酣暢也、丽古麗字 䍐同昆

## 鱗介

鱗介蕃滋　粦川番茲　魚人卄氵

譜題麤確　普頁鹿隺　言是鹿鹿石

龜鼈黿鼉　黽黽黽　敝元單

鯤鰲鯨鱷　昆魚京噩　魚敖魚魚

衣食之不足、而徒烹庖之爲亟哉、翥飛也、遨遊也、敷豫足也、⿱灷馬俗騰字粤音⿰女屏尃敷古文

右第十四節、鳥獸之微、上主猶備饈餌、以養其生、人何憂

雞塒豚柵　隹時豕冊　奚土月木

鴻渚鵲巢　鳥者鳥果　江氵昔巛

饈餌敷豫　羞耳攵象　食食尃子

詎亟烹庖　巨二火包　言句又亨广

## 鳥獸

騰祥毓瑞　⿱灷馬羊㐬耑　月示每王

鳳翥麟遨　鳥羽粦辶　凡者鹿敖

驊騮馳騁　華留也甹　馬馬馬馬

鸞鶴翔翱　鳥鳥羽羽　䜌隺羊皐

淬蝗掬蝦　泅雀撈蛤　卵濕累孳　俄頃跳躍

氵虫扌虫　氵小扌虫　卵氵田茲　亻匕足足

卒皇匊叚　四隹勞合　八㬎糸子　我頁兆翟

右第十五節、鱗介之族雖多、然中無靈魂、其跳躍不過少頃耳、可見人生甚爲貴重、奈何竟等於鱗介、而不思救其靈哉、蕃滋、言衆多也、淬、泅、沒水之貌、蝗落水則化蝦、又雀入大水爲蛤、見禮記月令、俄頃、少頃也、㬎音顯

## 昆蟲

蠶織蛛組　蚓唱蟬吟　徜徉邃閣　紬繹閒庭

兓日糸虫糸　虫口虫口　彳彳穴門　糸糸門广

蚰戠朱且　引昌單今　尙羊遂各　由睪月廷

終預

黽勉肅雍　慌逢殤殂　軀殼匪牢　胥慝酸楚

力黽隹　荒辶昜且　區殳匚牛　月心夋疋

免聿彡　忄夆歹歹　身殼非宀　生匿酉林

閒也、么麼、渺小也、忖、思也、淒、淒楚、辛、艱辛、巤音獵　兟音莘　䖵音昆

得免淒楚也、組、亦織也、臠、肉屑也、蟻攢肉屑、有如獵然、鬭、

艱辛之事、人則生命甚重、失救甚苦、其當如何信心、而始

右第十六節、么麼小蟲、暫有生命、所以絕無思慮、不知有

力肉巤義　專反共黽　厶么舜分　芒寸妻十

扌九䜌犭虫　扌食門虫　丿麻目目　冂忄冫立

拋臠獵蟻　摶飯鬭蠅　么麼瞬盼　罔忖淒辛

引規告湯　宣大辶　咠火𣶒㣎　羽弟勻頁

矢穴氵卄　口亦自旁　糸臣巳氵禾　堯目金彥

矧窺浩蕩　喧奕无邊　緝熙淵穆　翹睇鈞顏

恐懼之貌、𣶒淵古文

順天死曰殤、壽死曰殂、軀殼、肉身也、眚、小罪、慝、隱惡、悚惶、

惕臭腐之期、靈魂之失於救耳、黽勉、勤求也、肅、誠敬、雍、和

而知肉體之不牢、罪惡之未免、邀結同志、恐懼祈求、蓋深

右第十七節、言人當勤求於道、致敬盡禮、畏死亡之日近、

弟戾束皇　頁手半呂　一聿日取　言易犬肉

氵氵忄忄　步㓞亻亻　日镸勹言　敬忄自府

涕淚悚惶　頻挈伴侶　旦肆句諏　警惕臭腐

束刀糸祭　昜兀舛　咸見申需　中文乚皿
⺮主亻　氵垚⺫　⺮夫糹亻　亻門子子
策絜臣僚　禹湯堯舜　箴規紳儒　仲閔孔孟
緝彡同穆

除也、傴僂、鞠躬也、踧踖、恭敬也、冥頑、不靈者也、悛、改也、同
奕、宣著盛大之貌、緝熙、光明也、淵穆、深遠之意、懟、怨也、刪、畀
謹恭順、感受聖靈、自改其前日之冥頑矣、浩蕩、廣大貌、喧
當沉思邈慮、若或見之、則跪拜禱祝、化其不善之心、而敬
右第十八節、上主之德、廣大無名、上主之功、光明可見、人

甫畐先忌　心心月刂　區婁叔昔　六頁余夋
勹勹足足　斬對疋冊　亻亻足足　冖日元彳忄
匍匐跣跽　慙懟胥刪　傴僂踧踖　冥頑徐悛

四章統計二千十六字

凡六百八字

浮華曰奢、樸實曰淳、甄、別也、膺、心胷之間、豈怖永火之無救、始盡心以昭事上帝哉、策勉也、絜、領、也、當斟酌於眞僞之途、甄別其信從之準、以循當然之則、而

右第十九節、言耶穌之道、其教人致君澤民、正心誠意、人

斗勺者享　又瓦票十　火人布堯　無月攵心

甚酉大氵　雔垔木隹　火八忄火　扌雁每豸艮

斟酌奢淳　雙甄標準　炎火怖燒　撫膺敏懇

From this table those characters are excluded, which are found either in the text or among the radicals. The more useful are marked by a cipher; but many of those contained in the list are obsolete, except as *elements*. The imperfect elements have no fixed sounds, but a Chinese teacher will find no difficulty in giving them names.

## CHAPTER I.

从 *Ts'ung*, Same as 從 from.

刖° *Yüih*, To cut off the feet.

𠂇° *Tso*, Ancient form of 左.

肙 *Yuen*, A small worm.

乍° *Cha*, Just now, anon.

辟° *Pih*, A prince.

禺 *Ü*, A kind of ape.

㐅 *Wu*, Ancient form of 五.

寽 *Lo*, To draw with the hand.

霝 *Ling*, Same as 靈.

巫° *Wu*, A sorcerer.

処° *Ch'u*, Same as 處.

复 *Fuh*, Same as 復.

胃° *We*, Stomach.

找° *Chau*, Seek, pay balance.

个° *Ko*, An individual.

悳 *Tah*, Virtue 德.

㝵 *Ai*, Impede.

啇 *Yih*, Original.

杀 *Shah*, for 煞 baleful.

乂° *I*, Tranquil.

寺° *S*, A monastery.

亍 *Ch'uh*, Step of the left foot.

弔° *Tiau*, Suspend, sympathize. 弔.

帚° *Cheu*, A broom.

𠂤 *Tüe*, Heap.

叔° *Shuh*, Father's younger brother.

匹° *P'ih*, Equal, fellow.

卅° *Sah*, *Sah-shih*, } Thirty.

畐 *Fuh*, High, thick.

夅 *Kiang*, Descend, 降.

貫° *Kwan*, To pierce, string together, a string of cash.

侖 *Lün*, Narrate.

𠦒 *Pih*, Shovel.

𡱂 *T'un*, The buttocks.

冑° *Cheu*, Helmet.

勺° *Shoh*, A spoon.

婁 *Leu*, Name of a star.

豐 *Li*, A sacrificial vessel.

刁° *Tiau*, Perverse, malignant.

酋° *Ts'iu*, To ferment; a chief.

昷 *Wen*, Kind, compassionate.

IMPERFECT ELEMENTS.

亽 夋 〇 亍 羙 辵 羊 土 手 烏 爲 老 亡 無

## CHAPTER II.

咼 *Kwe*, Mouth awry.

丞° *Ch'eng*, To succeed, to be second or lieutenant.

巽 *Süen*, To enter.

再 *Ch'eng*, Altogether.

葡 *Pe*, Complete ready, 備、

厤° *Lih*, A form of 曆 almanac.

縣 *Hien*, Minute.

頁° *Yih*, A leaf.

玨 *K'ioh*, A pair of gems.

闌 *Lan*, A vail.

彖 *T'üan*, Notes on the Book of Changes.

咸° *Hien*, All.

冊° *Ts'ah*, Volume, set of books.

帀° *Tsah*, Twelve months or years' 匝、

翏 *Luh*, Fly high.

袁° *Yüen*, Family name.

臧° *Tsang*, Virtuous, prosperous.

台° *T'ai*, Term of respect, form of 臺、

尹° *Yin*, Mayor.

亦 *Yih*, 亦 Also.

兌° *Tùe*, Exchange.

㐬 *Liu*, A tassel, for 旒、

幵 *Kien*, Equal.

芊 *Yang*, Sheep, goat, for 羊、

卓° *Choh*, Firm, stable, eminent.

盾 *Tun*, Shield.

氏 *Yüih*, Fasces, emblems of power.

壴 *Chu*, Display of music.

亘° *Keng*, Continuous, perpetual.

𢇍 *Ki*, Successive, 繼.

巂° *Süe*, Name of a place.

蚩 *Ch'*, Simple, stupid.

啚 *Pi*, Close, narrow, for 鄙.

𠬝 *Fuh*, Govern, order.

俞 *Yü*, Yes, a girl's answer.

𠳋 *K'ien*, A fragment.

乖° *Kwai*, To differ, distorted.

盧 *Lu*, A fire vessel.

雚 *Hwan*, A small bird.

悤 *Ts'ung*, Quick of hearing, intelligent.

毄 *Kih*, for 擊 to attack.

屰 *Nih*, for 逆 to oppose.

夋 *Ch'üen*, To walk slowly.

央° *Yang*, Middle, invite.

舀° *Yau*, To dip water.

串° *Ch'üan*, Pierce through, string together.

狺 *Yin*, A quarrel between dogs.

囧 *Kiung*, Open windows.

扁 *Pien*, Flat. 匾.

敕° *Ch'ih*, Command.

卯° *Mau*, The 4*th* hour.

嘼 *Hiuh*, Cattle, for 畜.

瞿 *Kü*, An eagle glance.

奴° *Nu*, Slave.

𤔔 *Lüan*, Disorder, for 亂.

豦 *Chü*, Strife, conflict.

丘° *Ch'iu*, A hillock.

屯° *T'un*, Store up, accumulate.

亥° *Hai*, The 12*th* hour.

睪 *Yih*, Espionage.

另° *Ling*, Besides, other.

𠂢 *P'ai*, flow apart, appoint 派.

隋 *Süe*, Name of a dynasty.

离 *Ch'*, A goblin, for 離.

郎 *Long*, Gentleman, a title of honor.

昜 *Yang*, For 陽, the bright or male principle.

贊° *Tsan*, Praise, associate.

甬 *Yung*, A covered way.

巠 *King*, Straight, waves.

朁 *Ts'an*, A particle.

萑 *Chüe*, *wan*, Grassy.

仔 *Ts*, Able, sustain, energetic.

鬳 *Hüen*, A kind of furnace.

匋 *T'au*, Pottery.

臾 *Yü*, A moment.

妾° *Ts'ih*, Concubine.

雇° *Ku*, To hire.

丙° *Ping*, The 3*rd* of the 10 stems.

亐 *Yü*, For 于.

| | |
|---|---|
| 威 *Mih*, Consume, destroy. | 虎° *Hu*, Tiger. |
| 討° *T'au*, Beg, assail. | 筑° *Chuh*, To build. |
| 蜀 *Chuh*, A name of Szechuen. | 亶 *T'an*, T'an-fu, a name. |
| 壬° *Jin*, 9th of the 10 stems. | 吅 *Hüen*, A cry, noise, for 喧. |
| 呆° *Yai*, *Tai*, } Stupid. | 岡 *Kang*, A hill, for 崗. |
| 褱 *Hwai*, Bosom. | 敳 *Cheng*, To test, for 徵. |
| 劵 *Ch'uen*, A document, bond. | 朮 *Chuh*, A medicine. |
| 冉。 *Jan*, A name. | 戴 *T'i*, Name of a place. |
| 襄。 *Siang*, Assist, praise. | 倉° *Ts'ang*, Granary. |
| 圭 *Kwe*, A badge of office, a baton. | 諳° *An*, Understand. |
| 敫 *Kiau*, A stream of light, music. | 垩 *Yin*, To beg. |
| 雁 *Ing*, A kind of bird. | 彗° *Hwe*, A comet. |
| 号° *Hau*, Sign, cry, for 號. | |

IMPERFECT ELEMENTS.

| | | | | |
|---|---|---|---|---|
| 冓 | 业 | 厺 | 寅 | 尹 |
| 尸 | 亲 | 乡 | 丵 | ○ |
| 㠯 | 氏 | 囲 | 衣 | ○ |
| 缶 | 㐫 | 冗 | 巛 | ○ |

## CHAPTER III.

夌 *Ling*, A tomb for 陵、

寚 *Pau*, Precious for 寶、

馮 *Fung*, A name.

侌 *Yin*, The female principle, for 陰、

乇 *Kih*, The root of a tree.

冓 *Keu*, To interlock.

段。 *Tuan*, A section, ball.

賏 *Ing*, Necklace.

孚。 *Fu*, Faith.

芾 *Fuh*, Luxuriant.

翟 *Tih*, A kind of pheasant.

斬。 *Chan*, To cut off.

汍 *Wan*, Flowing tears.

朱。 *Chu*, Scarlet.

危。 *We*, High, perilous.

皃。 *Mau*, for 貌、

喬。 *Ch'iau*, Lofty.

感。 *Kan*, To feel, or excite feeling.

尃 *Fu*, Diffuse, for 敷、

堇 *Chin*, Loam, loess.

叀 *Chüan*, Special, for 專、

㠯 *I*, By, for 以、

涂， *T'u*, Road, a name.

卉 *Hwe*, Flowers.

戔 *Sien*, Minute, small.

丩 *Kiu*, A vine.

訇 *Hung*, Loud noise.

夸 *Kw'a*, Vaunt, boast.

桀。 *Kie*, Oppressive, courageous.

句 *Kü*, Sentence, clause, crooked.

芻 *Ch'u*, Grass.

㒼 *Man*, Equal.

卡 *Ch'a*, A customs' barrier.

戊。 *Meu*, *Wu*, } *5th* of the 10 stems.

朿 *Ts*, To stop.

溥。 *P'u*, Abundant.

粦 *Lin*, Ignis fatuus.

隻。 *Ch*, Single, a classifier.

尉。 *We*, Soothe, comfort.

御。 *Yü*, Royal, drive a chariot.

敝。 *Pi*, Spoiled.

匄 *Kai*, Beg.

莧 *Hien*, Spinach.

厷 *Kung*, Arms, for 肱、

斲 *Choh*, To cut down.

| | |
|---|---|
| 䙴 | *Sien*, Ascend high. |
| 𥬇 | *Siau*, To laugh, for 笑、 |
| 肙 | *Yuen*, Small insect. |
| 坴 | *Luh*, Lump of earth 陸、 |
| 厈 | *An*, Shore, 岸、 |
| 𡭴° | *Hih*, Hole in a wall. |
| 牟 | *Meu*, Lowing of a cow. |
| 冗 | *Jung*, Hurried. |
| 戎° | *Jung*, A weapon; a barbarian. |
| 韱° | *Ts'ien*, A bamboo tally. |
| 夆 | *Fung*, To butt, push. |
| 䀋° | *Yien*, Salt, for 鹽、 |
| 曼 | *Man*, Long. |
| 栗° | *Lih*, Tremble, chestnut. |
| 粥° | *Chuh*, Soft boiled rice. |
| 完° | *Wan*, Finish. |
| 甫° | *Fu*, Just now. |
| 覽° | *Lan*, See, read. |
| 它 | *T'o*, Snake, used for 蛇、*she*. |
| 筮 | *Sh*, Grass used in divination. |
| 咅 | *T'eu*, To spit. |
| 蚤° | *Tsau*, A flea, also for 早 early. |
| 廿° | *Nien*, Twenty. |
| 夗 | *Yün*, unrest. |
| 丈° | *Chang*, 10 ft., Chinese. |
| 戌° | *Suih*, 11*th* hour. |
| 羕 | *Yang*, A long stream. |
| 縣° | *Hien*, A district. |
| 㐱 | *Chen*, Long black hair. |
| 詹 | *Chan*, Oversee, direct. |
| 犮 | *Pah*, To drag. |
| 旁° | *P'ang*, The side. |
| 佰 | *Peh*, 100, A centurion. |
| 乞 | *Ch'i*, Beg. |

IMPERFECT ELEMENTS.

| | | | | |
|---|---|---|---|---|
| 丞 | 曲 | 月 | 丮 | 帀 |
| 臤 | 更 | 𦣝 | 壴 | 冊 |
| 肅 | 烏 | 步 | 寡 | 壬 |

## CHAPTER IV.

面° *Mien*, Face.
熏° *Hüin*, To smoke, to cure meat.
夬 *Kuih*, Different, certain.
鄭 *Cheng*, Dignity, name of a kingdom.
吳 *Wu*, A name.
尞 *Liau*, Bright, clear.
肖° *Siau*, Like, good.
崔 *Ch'ue*, Lofty.
宁 *Chu*, A vestibule.
厓 *Yai*, Shore.
呈° *Ch'eng*, Hand up.
戠 *Ch*, A sort of earth.
匆 *Ts'ung*, Haste, for 怱、
欽° *Ch'in*, Respect, imperial.
虒 *S*, A horned tiger.
斲 *Chuh*, Chisel, for 鑿、
樊 *Fan*, A fence, lattice.
考° *K'au*, Investigate.
廌 *Hie*, A one horned goat.
敖 *Au*, Ramble, for 遨、
析° *Sih*, Separate, explain.
丕° *P'e*, Great.
䜌 *Kwan*, Weave.
眉° *Me*, Eyebrow.

粲° *Ts'an*, A meal.
奄° *Yien*, Detain, conceal.
昜 *T'uh*, Buoyant.
畺 *Kiang*, Boundary, for 疆、
彔 *Luh*, Wood carving.
員° *Yuen*, Round, dollar, officer.
堅° *Kien*, Firm.
廷° *T'ing*, Palace.
庚° *Keng*, 7th of the stems.
丑° *Ch'eu*, 2nd hour.
癸° *Kwe*, 10th of the stems.
丽 *Li*, Beautiful, for 麗、
叕 *Chüeh*, Join.
頡 *Kih*, Neck erect.
甹 *P'in*, Rapid, utterance.
隺° *Hoh*, Crane.
皐 *Kau*, Call, high, a name.
尃 *Fu*, Diffuse, for 敷、
亨° *Heng*, Good luck.
余 *Yu*, A family name.
咢 *Oh*, Fright.
匊 *Küih*, Handful, for 掬、
巤 *Lih*, Hairy.
芒° *Mang*, Beard of grain.

壳° *K'uh* Shell, for 殼、
規° *Kwe,* A rule.
咠 *Ts'ih,* Satire; blame.
毚 *Ts'an,* A hare.

𣶒 *Yuen,* Abyss, for 淵、
匀 *Yüin,* Equal, for 均、
彥 *Yien,* Virtuous, excellent.
忌° *Ki,* Envy, hate.

IMPERFECT ELEMENTS.

| | | | |
|---|---|---|---|
| 㱿 | 囟 | 声 | 电 |
| 丁 | 㡀 | 由 | ○ |

Chapter I. In Five Forms.*

*Pattern, Business, Grass, Old Official, Seal.*

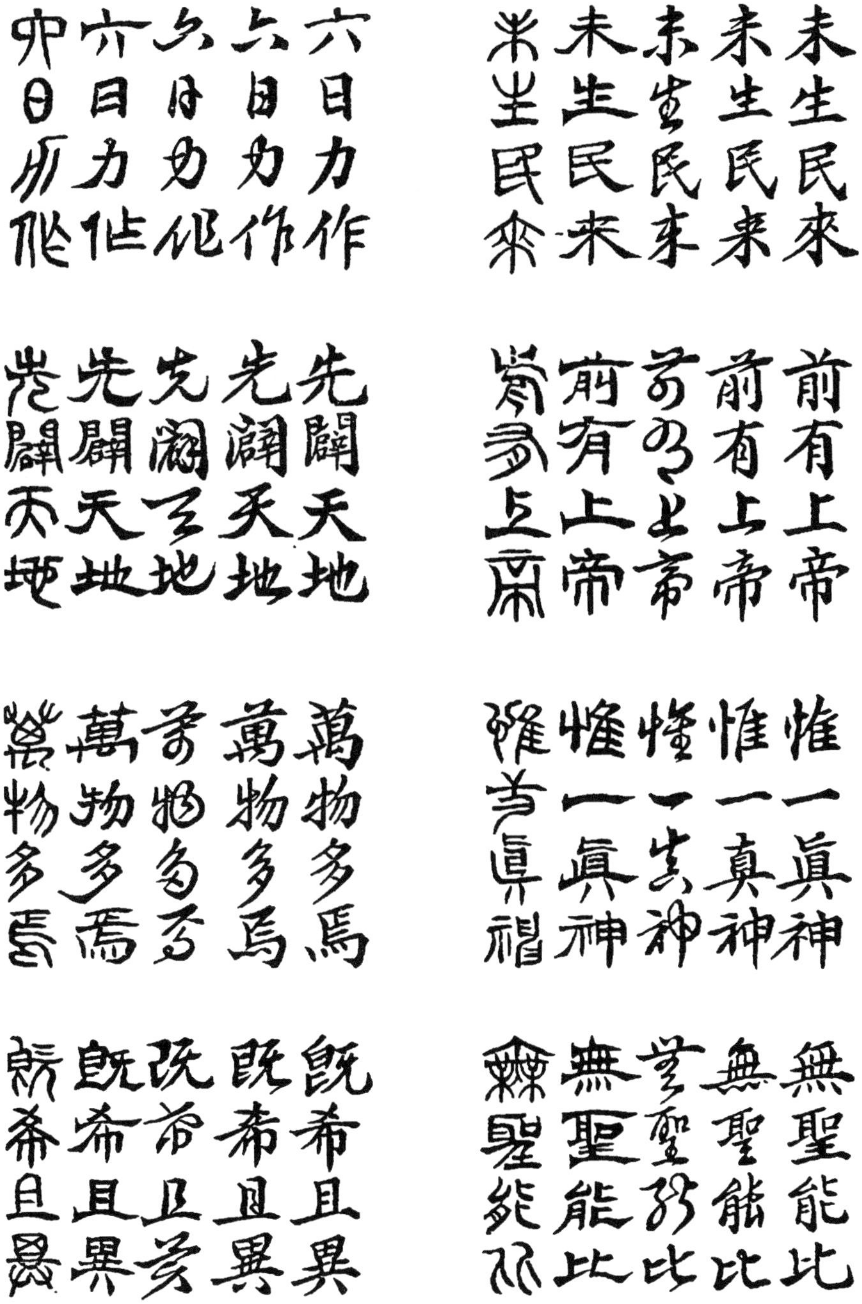

*The Sung-t'i, or book style which completes the 六書, or six forms of writing, may be seen in the text.

遂亦和土
遂亦和土
遂亦和土
遂亦和土
遂亦和土

復使宜家
復使宜家
復使宜家
復使宜家
復使宜家

將為靈矣
將為靈矣
將為靈矣
將為靈矣
將為靈矣

女兮往事
女兮往事
女兮往事
女兮往事
女兮往事

命處賜基
命處賜基
命處賜基
命處賜基
命處賜基

謂之曰夫
謂之曰夫
謂之曰夫
謂之曰夫
謂之曰夫

千百皆與
千百皆與
千百皆與
千百皆與
千百皆與

爾我如自
爾我如自
爾我如自
爾我如自
爾我如自

凡所求者
凡所求者
凡所求者
凡所求者
凡所求者

告云可食
告云可食
告云可食
告云可食
告云可食

毋不立予
毋不立予
毋不立予
毋不立予
毋不立予

或當見耳
或當見耳
或當見耳
或當見耳
或當見耳

然欲善惡
然欲善惡
然欲善惡
然欲善惡
然欲善惡

聞言摩拿
聞言摩拿
聞言摩拿
聞言摩拿
聞言摩拿

勿聽手取
勿聽手取
勿聽手取
勿聽手取
勿聽手取

得罪因此
得罪因此
得罪因此
得罪因此
得罪因此

中中中中中
傳傳傳傳傳
亞亞亞亞亞
伯伯伯伯伯

以以以以以
致致致致致
彼彼彼彼彼
族族族族族

羊羊羊羊羊
祭祭祭祭祭
信信信信信
心心心心心

但但但但但
安安安安安
利利利利利
名名名名名

長長長長長
子子子子子
若若若若若
兄兄兄兄兄

愛愛愛愛愛
身身身身身
尼尼尼尼尼
色色色色色

敵敵敵敵敵
殺殺殺殺殺
及及及及及
今今今今今

列列列列列
馬馬馬馬馬
羅羅羅羅羅
金金金金金

| | | | | |
|---|---|---|---|---|
| 卷 | 卷 | 卷 | 卷 | 卷 |
| 撒 | 撒 | 撒 | 撒 | 撒 |
| 全 | 全 | 全 | 全 | 全 |
| 死 | 死 | 死 | 死 | 死 |

| | | | | |
|---|---|---|---|---|
| 父 | 父 | 父 | 父 | 父 |
| 意 | 意 | 意 | 意 | 意 |
| 非 | 非 | 非 | 非 | 非 |
| 昔 | 昔 | 昔 | 昔 | 昔 |

| | | | | |
|---|---|---|---|---|
| 何 | 何 | 何 | 何 | 何 |
| 問 | 問 | 問 | 問 | 問 |
| 儕 | 儕 | 儕 | 儕 | 儕 |
| 羣 | 羣 | 羣 | 羣 | 羣 |

| | | | | |
|---|---|---|---|---|
| 其 | 其 | 其 | 其 | 其 |
| 僕 | 僕 | 仆 | 僕 | 僕 |
| 已 | 已 | 已 | 已 | 已 |
| 明 | 明 | 明 | 明 | 明 |

| | | | | |
|---|---|---|---|---|
| 第 | 第 | 第 | 第 | 第 |
| 歸 | 歸 | 歸 | 歸 | 歸 |
| 方 | 方 | 方 | 方 | 方 |
| 蓋 | 蓋 | 蓋 | 蓋 | 蓋 |

| | | | | |
|---|---|---|---|---|
| 即 | 即 | 即 | 即 | 即 |
| 由 | 由 | 由 | 由 | 由 |
| 是 | 是 | 是 | 是 | 是 |
| 時 | 時 | 时 | 時 | 時 |

| | | | | |
|---|---|---|---|---|
| 則 | 則 | 則 | 則 | 則 |
| 同 | 同 | 同 | 同 | 同 |
| 義 | 義 | 義 | 義 | 義 |
| 人 | 人 | 人 | 人 | 人 |

| | | | | |
|---|---|---|---|---|
| 大 | 大 | 大 | 大 | 大 |
| 水 | 水 | 水 | 水 | 水 |
| 四 | 四 | 四 | 四 | 四 |
| 行 | 行 | 行 | 行 | 行 |

故故故故故
又又又又又
督督督督督
教教教教教

居居居居居
八八八八八
從從從從從
七七七七七

甚甚甚甚甚
加加加加加
世世世世世
福福福福福

各各各各各
拉拉拉拉拉
入入入入入
門門門門門

降降降降降
下下下下下
耶耶耶耶耶
穌穌穌穌穌

斯斯斯斯斯
實實實實實
救救救救救
主主主主主

等閒于三
等閒于三
等閒于三
等閒于三
等閒于三

相約衆士
相約衆士
相約衆士
相約衆士
相約衆士

倫出於五
倫出於五
倫出於五
倫出於五
倫出於五

必知理數
必知理數
必知理數
必知理數
必知理數

華年至殿
華年至殿
華年至殿
華年至殿
華年至殿

節禮守法
節禮守法
節禮守法
節禮守法
節禮守法

在會受書
在會受書
在會受書
在會受書
在會受書

司十二徒
司十二徒
司十二徒
司十二徒
司十二徒

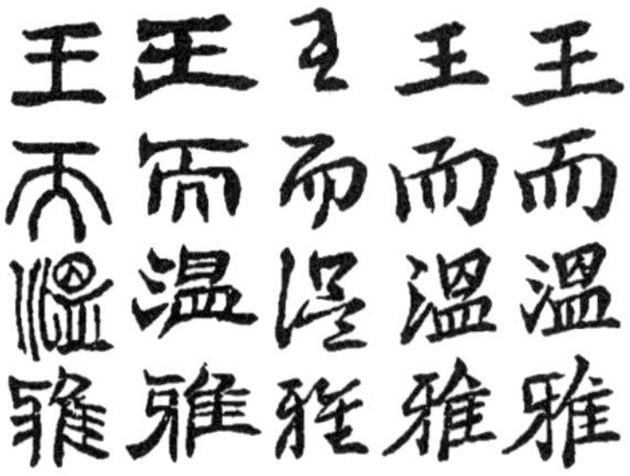

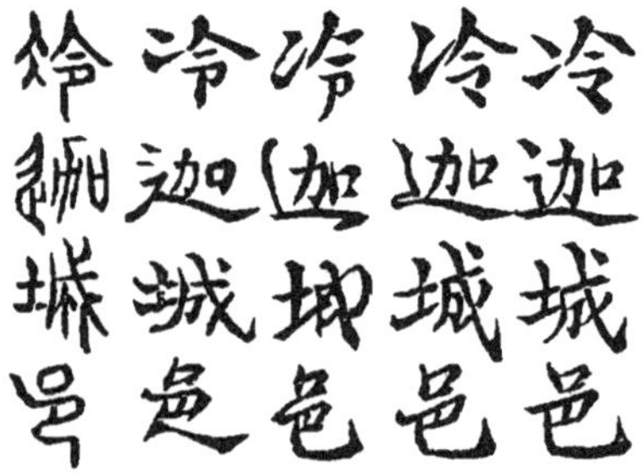

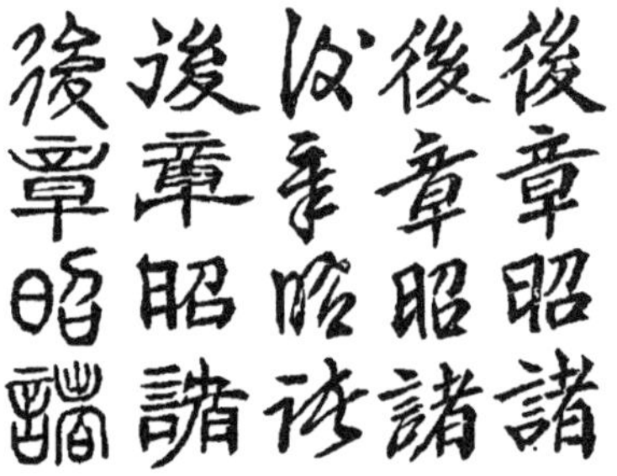

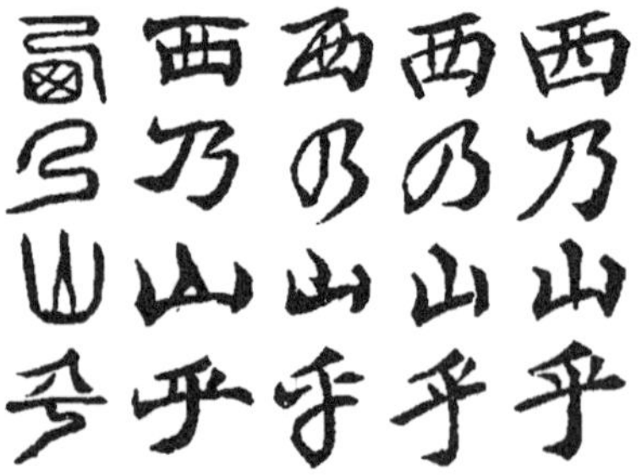

# 常字雙千釋義

A

# VOCABULARY

OF

TWO THOUSAND FREQUENT CHARACTERS,

*Arranged according to Radicals.*

WITH

THEIR MOST COMMON SIGNIFICATIONS,

AND

THE SOUNDS OF THE PEKING DIALECT.

# NOTE.

The student while studying the first two chapters should make himself familiar with the radicals as a preparation for using this vocabulary, or native dictionaries. On completing the four chapters he would find it profitable to read the vocabulary from beginning to end, even though he may have consulted it from time to time.

For the sake of brevity those significations which are most easily deducible, have been omitted ; and the student is expected to bear in mind that feature of the language which admits of the same *words* being employed without alteration in different parts of speech Thus after giving 生 as *life* it would be superfluous to define it further as to *live, alive,* &c.

The mode of transliteration answers in the main to that in general use. The chief departure from it is in the non-use of *hs*. The two classes of words, which in current Mandarin begin with *h* and *s*, are in Peking combined, or rather confused so as to be utterly undistinguishable. In this vocabulary it has been thought best to preserve the distinction. The student can hardly go wrong, if he always sees *h* alongside of *s* and *vice versâ*. The combination is foreign to English, and like the tones, must be learned by ear.

The tone marks are here attached to the transliteration—not to the characters as in the text—the first and second being placed at the lower left; the third at the upper left, and the fourth at the upper right. They are all indicated by ↄ, except the second, which is distinguished by ↄ̲. In case of discrepancy of tone between text and vocabulary the one represents the tone as read; the other as spoken. Where two pronunciations are given for one character they usually indicate a difference of meaning. The student who has not access to a Peking teacher will do well to confine himself to one sound, unencumbered by tones.

# THE 214 RADICALS

WITH THEIR

## SOUNDS AND SIGNIFICATIONS.

### 1 Stroke.

1. 一 Yih. One.
2. 丨 Kwen. Pass through.
3. 丶 Chu. A point.
4. 丿 P'ih. A left stroke.
5. 乙 Yih. One, curved.
6. 亅 Küih. Hooked.

### 2 Strokes.

7. 二 Er. Two.
8. 亠 T'eu. A cover.
9. 人 亻 Jin. A man.
10. 儿 Jin. A man.
11. 入 Juh. To enter.
12. 八 Pah. Eight.
13. 冂 Kiung. A limit.
14. 冖 Mi. To cover.
15. 冫 Ping. Ice.
16. 几 Ki. A bench.
17. 凵 K'ang. A receptacle.
18. 刀 刂 Tau. A Knife.
19. 力 Lih. Strength.
20. 勹 Pau. To infold.
21. 匕 Pi. A spoon.
22. 匚 Fang. A chest.
23. 匸 Hi. To conceal.
24. 十 Shih. Ten.
25. 卜 Poh. To divine.
26. 卩 㔾 Tsih. A seal.
27. 厂 Han. A shelter.
28. 厶 S. Deflected.
29. 又 Yiu. Moreover.

### 3 Strokes.

30. 口 K'eu. The Mouth.
31. 囗 We. To enclose.
32. 土 T'u. Ground, earth.
33. 士 Sh. A scholar.
34. 夂 Ch. To follow.
35. 夊 Shŭai. Walk slowly.
36. 夕 Sih. Evening.
37. 大 Ta. Large.
38. 女 Nü. Female.
39. 子 Ts. A child.
40. 宀 Mien. A cover.
41. 寸 Ts'un. An inch.
42. 小 Siau. Small.
43. 尢 尣 允 Yiu. Distorted.

44. 尸 Sh. A corpse.
45. 屮 Ch'eh. A sprout.
46. 山 Shan. A hill.
47. 巛 川 巜 Ch'üan. A stream.
48. 工 Kung. Work.
49. 己 Ki. Self.
50. 巾 Kin. A napkin.
51. 干 Kan. A shield.
52. 幺 Yau. Small.
53. 广 Yien. A roof.
54. 廴 Ying. A journey.
55. 廾 Kung. To join hands.
56. 弋 Yih. An arrow.
57. 弓 Kung. A bow.
58. 彐 彑 Ki. A swine's head.
59. 彡 Shan. Feathers, hair.
60. 彳 Ch'ih. A short step.

4 Strokes.

61. 心 忄 㣺 Sin. The heart.
62. 戈 Ko. A spear.
63. 戶 Hu. A door.
64. 手 扌 Sheu. A hand.
65. 支 Ch. A branch.
66. 攴 攵 P'ah. A blow.
67. 文 Wen. Literature.
68. 斗 Teu. A measure.
69. 斤 Kin. A catty, a pound.
70. 方 Fang. A Square.
71. 无 Wu. Without.
72. 日 Jih. The sun, a day.
73. 曰 Yüih. To speak.
74. 月 Yüih. The moon.
75. 木 Muh. Wood, timber.
76. 欠 Ch'ien. To owe.
77. 止 Ch. To stop.
78. 歹 歺 Tai. Evil.
79. 殳 Ch'u. Weapons.
80. 毋 Wu. Do not.
81. 比 Pi. To compare.
82. 毛 Mau. Hair.
83. 氏 Sh. The family name.
84. 气 Ch'i. Breath.
85. 水 氵 氺 Shüe. Water.
86. 火 灬 Ho. Fire.
87. 爪 爫 Chau. Claws.
88. 父 Fu. Father.
89. 爻 Hiau. To imitate.
90. 爿 Ch'üang. A bed.
91. 片 P'ien. A splinter.
92. 牙 Ya. Teeth
93. 牛 Niu. A cow.
94. 犬 犭 K'üin. A dog.

5 Strokes.

95. 玄 Hüin. Dark, sombre.
96. 玉 王 Yuh. A gem.
97. 瓜 Kwa. A melon.
98. 瓦 Wa. A tile.
99. 甘 Kan. Sweet.

100. 生 Sheng. Life.
101. 用 Yung. To use.
102. 田 T'ien. A field.
103. 疋 P'ih. A piece of cloth.
104. 疒 Nih. Sick.
105. 癶 Poh. To separate.
106. 白 Peh. White.
107. 皮 P'i. Skin.
108. 皿 Min. A vessel.
109. 目 罒 Muh. The eyes.
110. 矛 Meu. A spear.
111. 矢 Sh. An arrow.
112. 石 Shih. A stone.
113. 示 礻 Sh. To show.
114. 禸 Jeu. To creep.
115. 禾 Ho. Growing rice.
116. 穴 Huih. A cave.
117. 立 Lih. To stand.

## 6 Strokes.

118. 竹 Chuh. Bamboo.
119. 米 Mi. Hulled rice.
120. 糸 S. Silk.
121. 缶 Feu. Earthenware.
122. 网 罒 冗 Wang. A net.
123. 羊 Yang. A sheep.
124. 羽 Yü. Wings.
125. 老 Lau. Aged.
126. 而 Er. And, still.
127. 耒 Le. A plough.
128. 耳 Er. The ear.
129. 聿 Lüh. A pencil.
130. 肉 月 Juh. Flesh.
131. 臣 Ch'eng. A minister.
132. 自 Ts. Self, from.
133. 至 Ch. To, most.
134. 臼 Kiu. A mortar.
135. 舌 Sheh. The tougne.
136. 舛 Ch'üan. Error.
137. 舟 Cheu. A boat.
138. 艮 Ken. Perverse.
139. 色 Seh. Color.
140. 艸 艹 Ts'au. Grass.
141. 虍 Hu. A tiger.
142. 虫 Ch'ung. Reptiles.
143. 血 Hüih. Blood.
144. 行 Hing. Walk, work.
145. 衣 衤 I. Clothes.
146. 西 襾 Si. West.

## 7 Strokes.

147. 見 Kien. To see.
148. 角 Kioh. Horn.
149. 言 Yien. Words.
150. 谷 Kuh. A valley.
151. 豆 Teu. Beans.
152. 豕 Sh. Swine.
153. 豸 Hie. Reptiles, wild beasts.
154. 貝 Pe. Pearls.
155. 赤 Ch'ih. Scarlet.
156. 走 Tseu. To walk.
157. 足 Tsuh. The foot.
158. 身 Shen. The body.
159. 車 Kü, ch'e. A chariot.
160. 辛 Sin. Acrid.
161. 辰 Ch'en. Hour.

162. 辵 辶 Tseu. Motion.

163. 邑 阝 Yih. A city.

164. 酉 Yiu. Liquors.

165. 釆 Ts'ai. Splendor, to select.

166. 里 Li. A mile.

### 8 Strokes.

167. 金 Kin. Metal.

168. 長 镸 Ch'ang. Long.

169. 門 Men. A gate.

170. 阜 阝 Feu. A mound.

171. 隶 Ti. To extend to.

172. 隹 Chŭe. Fowls.

173. 雨 Yü. Rain.

174. 青 Ts'ing. Green.

175. 非 Fe. Wrong, not?

### 9 Strokes.

176. 面 Mien. The face.

177. 革 Keh. Skin, change.

178. 韋 We. Leather.

179. 韭 Kiu. Leeks.

180. 音 Yin. Sound.

181. 頁 Yih. Head, a leaf.

182. 風 Fung. Wind, a custom.

183. 飛 Fe. To fly.

184. 食 Shih. To eat.

185. 首 Sheu. The head.

186. 香 Hiang. Incense.

### 10 Strokes.

187. 馬 Ma. A horse.

188. 骨 Kuh. Bones.

189. 高 Kau. High.

190. 髟 Piau. Long hair.

191. 鬥 Teu. To quarrel.

192. 鬯 Ch'ang. A fragrant liquor.

193. 鬲 Keh, li. A tripod, urn.

194. 鬼 Kwe. A ghost, a devil.

### 11 Strokes.

195. 魚 Yü. Fish.

196. 鳥 Niau. A bird.

197. 鹵 Lu. Brine.

198. 鹿 Luh. A deer.

199. 麥 Meh. Wheat.

200. 麻 Ma. Hemp.

### 12 Strokes.

201. 黃 Hwang. Yellow.

202. 黍 Shu. Millet.

203. 黑 Heh. Black.

204. 黹 Ch'. Embroidery.

### 13 Strokes.

205. 黽 Min. A frog.

206. 鼎 Ting. A tripod.

207. 鼓 Ku. A drum.

208. 鼠 Shu. A rat.

### 14 Strokes.

209. 鼻 Pih. The nose.

210. 齊 Ch'i. Even, orderly.

### 15 Strokes.

211. 齒 Ch'. The teeth.

212. 龍 Lung. A Dragon.

### 16 Strokes.

213. 龜 Kwe. A tortoise.

### 17 Strokes.

214. 龠 Yuh. A flute.

速成漢語

1. 一

一 *i'* One.

上 *Shang'*, Above, up, upper, to go up.

且 *'Ch'ie*, Moreover.

不 *Pu'*, Not.

七 *,Ch'i*, Seven.

世 *Sh'*, The world, a generation.

下 *Hia'*, Below, lower, to go down.

三 *,San*, Three.

丁 *'Ting*, A sting, a nail, an individual, to sustain.

2. 丨

中 *'Chung*, Middle, to hit the centre.

3. 丶

主 *'Chu*, Lord, to control.

丸 *,Wan*, A ball, a pill.

丹 *,Tan*, Pale red, a sovereign remedy.

4. 丿

之 *,Ch*, Sign of possessive case, Pronoun of the *3rd* person.

乃 *,Nai*, But, may-be, it is used as, i.e., or *viz.*

乎 *,Hu*, A sign of doubt, admiration, inquiry; also of the vocative.

乘 *,Ch'eng*, To ride, avail of, a war chariot.

久 *'Kiu*, A long time.

乏 *Fa'*, To want, lack.

么 *,Yau* 么麼 dwarfish, diminutive.

5. 乙

乙 *'I*, One, curved.

也 *,Ye*, Euphonic particle, even, also.

亂 *Loan'*, Confusion, disorder.

九 *'Kiu*, Nine.

乳 *'Ju*, Milk; a suckling.

6. 亅

事 *Sh'*, An act, affair, to serve.

予 *,Ü* Pronoun of *1st* person; to give.

了 *'Liau*, Finished, a sign of the past tense.

7. 二

二 *Er'*, Two.

云 *,Yün*, Speak, say.

亞 *Ya'*, Secondary. A diminutive prefix.

于 *,Ü*, In, in respect to.

五 *'Wu*, Five.

互 *Hu*ʿ, Reciprocal; in turn.

況 *K'wang*ʿ, Much more, *a fortiori.*

亟 *Chi*ʿ, Haste, urgency.

8. 亠

六 *Lu*ʿ, Six.

亦 *I*ʿ, Also.

亡 ˓*Wang*, Perish, lose, flee.

京 ˏ*Ching*, Great, the capital.

交 ˏ*Chiau*, Intercourse, alternate, reciprocal.

享 ʾ*Hiang*, Enjoy.

9. 人

人 ˓*Jen*, Man.

來 ˓*Lai*, Come.

作 *Tso*ʿ, Make, start, arise.

使 ʾ*Sh*, Send, cause, messenger.

傳 ˓*Ch'uen*, Propagate, narrate.

伯 *Po*ʿ, An uncle, a father's brother, a lord.

信 *Sin*ʿ, Belief, faithfulness, a letter.

今 ˏ*Chin*, Now, modern.

以 ʾ*I*, To take, because, by means of.

但 *Tan*ʿ, But, only.

僕 ʾ*P'u*, Slave, servant.

何 ˓*Ho*, Which? why? how?

儕 *Ch'ai*, Class. a plural suffix.

倫 ˓*Lun*, A category, social relations.

代 *Tai*ʿ, A generation, instead of.

備 *Pe*ʿ, Complete, prepared.

伏 *Fu*ʿ, Prostrate, abject, to subject.

依 ˏ*I*, Depend on, according to.

仍 ˏ*Jeng*, As before, still, yet.

儀 ˓*I*, Ceremony, form, manner.

便 *Pien*ʿ, Convenient, ready.

付 *Fu*ʿ, Impart, intrust, pay, commit to.

令 *Ling*ʿ, Command.

俯 ʾ*Fu*, To bow the head; nod assent.

修 ˏ*Siu*, Improve, cultivate: repair, long and slender.

余 ˓*Ü*, Pron. *1st* pers.

俊 *Chiün*ʿ, Superior, fine-looking.

俱 ˏ*Chü*, Together, all.

仇 *Ch'eu*ʿ, Enmity.

仁 ˓*Jen*, Humanity, charity, goodness.

僭 *Chien*ʿ, False assumption, blasphemy.

僞 *Wei*, False, deceitful.

例 *Li*ʿ, A custom, law, example.

傾 ,*Ch'ing*, Overturn, a moment.

傷 ,*Shang*, Wound, bruise; feel.

侍 *Sh*ʿ, Wait on, wait in presence.

他 ,*T'a*, other, pronoun *3rd* pers.

任 *Jen*ʿ, ,*jen*, Bear office or burden, *ad libitum;* let.

保 '*Pau*, Protect, secure.

伊 ,*I*, Pronoun *3rd* pers.

俾 *Pi*ʿ, To cause, so that.

偕 ,*Hie*, Together with.

供 ,*Kung*, Serve, minister.

位 *Wei*ʿ, Seat, position, person.

偶 '*Eu*, Likeness, companion, pair.

像 *Siang*ʿ, Like, *simulacrum*.

俗 *Su*ʿ, Customary, common, coarse, usage.

伐 *Fa*ʿ, Boast, cut, invade.

倘 *T'ang*, If, should.

侮 *Wu*, To insult.

佛 '*Fo*, Buddha.

係 *Hi*ʿ, To be, to concern.

傑 *Chie*ʿ, A hero.

値 *Ch*ʿ, Price, to meet, to manage, to take in turn.

償 ,*Ch'ang*, Pay, recompense.

休 ,*Hiu*, Stop, good fortune.

倍 *Pe*ʿ, Double, 三倍 three-fold, &c., to multiply.

億 *I*ʿ, Ten myriads, quiet, repose; to guess.

佑 *Yiu*ʿ, Divine protection.

俘 ,*Fu*, A captive.

俟 *S*ʿ, To wait for, until.

偏 ,*Pien*, Uneven, partial.

側 *Ts'o*ʿ, Sloping, oblique, at the side.

侵 ,*Ch'in*, Usurp, oppress.

似 *S*ʿ, Like, resemble.

假 '*Chia*, False, to borrow, suppose.

倚 '*I*, Rely, lean on.

仗 *Chang*ʿ, Rely on, weapon, fight.

僅 '*Chin*, Exactly, only, scarcely.

舍 *She*ʿ, A cottage, to bestow, cast away.

住 *Chu*ʿ, Stop, dwell.

仰 '*Yang*, To look up.

伸 ,*Shen*, Extend, explain.

儘 *Chin*ʿ, Altogether, empty, as you please.

儔 ,Ch'eu, A class, a mate.

僉 ,Ch'ien, All.

催 ,Ts'ue, Urge, expedite.

併 Ping, Unite, combine energies.

佳 ,Chia, Excellent.

僮 ,T'ung, Lad, urchin; page.

倜 T'i, Courteous, generous.

儻 'T'ang, If, should; 倜儻 free, noble.

俠 Hia', generous, careless, brave, soldier of fortune.

傲 Au', Proud, insolent.

伶 ,Ling, A play actor, clever.

俐 Li', Smart, 伶俐 clever.

佩 Pe', Side ornaments, to gird, wear at the side.

促 Ts'u', Hasten, shorten.

借 Chie', Borrow.

佐 'Tso, Help.

儲 ,Ch'u, Provide, store, to second, to be second.

件 Chien', A piece, or article.

候 Heu', Wait, inquire for, time.

侈 Ch', Wasteful.

介 Chie', Attendant, usher, shield, shellfish.

俄 ,O, Sudden, lofty.

伴 Pan', A comrade.

侶 'Lü, An associate.

傴 Eu', stooping,

僂 ,Leu, Crooked, bent.

## 10. 儿

先 Jien, Before, first.

兄 ,Hiung, Elder brother.

光 ,Kwang, Light, bright, lustre.

免 'Mien, Avoid, forgive.

兆 Chau', An omen, a million.

兒 ,Er, A boy, child, a euphonic.

元 ,Yuen, Primary, chief.

克 K'o', Overbearing, to overcome.

允 'Yün, Promise, secure.

充 ,Ch'ung, Fill, pretend.

## 11. 入

入 Ju', To enter.

全 ,Ch'iuen, Complete, perfect; all.

兩 'Liang, Two, both, a tael or ounce.

內 'Nei, Inside.

## 12. 八

八 Pa', Eight.

兮 ,Hi, A euphonic expletive.

其 ˏChi, Pron. 3rd pers.

兵 ˏPing, A soldier, weapon.

公 ˏKung, Public, just, duke.

共 Kung', Together, in common.

具 Chü', Complete, instruments.

典 'Tien, A rule, to manage, to mortgage.

兼 ˏChien, To combine.

冀 Chi', Expect, desire.

## 13. 冂

再 Tsai', Again, the second time.

## 14. 冖

冠 ˏKwan', kwan, A cap, crown.

冥 ˏMing, Dark, obscure.

## 15. 冫

冷 ˏLeng, Cold.

凌 ˏLing, Insult, spurn, abandon.

凋 ˏTiau, Wither.

冬 ˏTung, Winter, to freeze.

凄 ˏCh'i, Chilly, grievous.

## 16. 几

凡 ˏFan, All, the world.

几 Chi', Bench, table.

## 17. 凵

出 Ch'u', Out.

凸 ˏKu, Protuberance, a tenon, convex.

凹 ˏWa, A pit, valley, concave.

## 18. 刀

前 ˏCh'ien, Before, formerly.

利 Li', Gain, advantage, sharp.

列 Lie', Numerous, several, classified.

則 Tse', So, then, item.

刑 ˏHing, Punishment.

切 Ch'ie, Divide, cut.

刃 Jen', A blade, a sharp edge.

別 Pie', Distinguish, other, don't.

分 ˏFen, A part, duty.

割 Ko', (c) ˏko, To cut.

判 P'an', Divide, decide.

創 Ch'uang', Originate, create, wound.

劍 Chien', A sabre.

刀 ˏTau, A knife, sword.

刻 K'o', (c) ˏk'o, Carve, cut, griping, close, quarter of an hour, a moment.

制 Ch', Control, appoint, costume, mourning habit.

剛 ˏKang, Hard, steel.

刺 Ts', la, } Pierce, satirize, to cut.
劇 Chü', Excessive, violent increase, a farce, play.
劃 Hwa', carve, scratch, mark, rend asunder.
刮 Kwa', Scrape, include, embrace.
剖 ,P'eu, Divide.
删 ,Shan, To expurgate, amend.

19. 力

力 Li', Strength, force.
加 ,Chia, Add, increase.
功 ,Kung, Merit.
勞 ,Lau, Toil, to reward.
勒 Le', Extort, compel, curb, engrave.
勸 Ch'iuen', Persuade, exhort.
助 Chu', Help.
動 Tung', Move.
勤 ,Ch'in, Industry, diligence.
勢 Sh', Force, power, posture of affairs.
勇 'Yung, Valor, brave.
勵 Li', Stimulate.
勉 'Mien, Encourage, earnest.

20. 勹

勿 Wu', Must not.
包 ,Pau, Wrap up, comprehend.
匍 ,P'u, Creep.
匐 'Fu, Crouch.

21. 匕

北 Po', 'Pe, } North.
化 Hwa', Transform, reform, waste, flower.
匕 'Pi, A spoon.

22. 匚

匱 Kwei', A Chest.
匪 'Fei, Worthless, is not.

23. 匸

匿 Ni', Conceal, hide.
區 ,Ch'ü, Place, space, room, empty,

24. 十

十 ,Sh, Ten.
千 ,Ch'ien, A thousand.
卒 Tsu', End, die, a soldier.
南 ,Nan, South.
半 Pan', Half.
升 ,Sheng, Ascend.
博 Po', Erudite.
井 'Ching, A well, market.

卑 ,*Pe*, Mean, lowly.

午 '*Wu*, Noon, the first hour.

### 25. 卜

卜 '*Pu*, To divine.

占 ,*Chan*, Observe auguries, usurp.

### 26. 卩

卽 *Chi'*, Then, even, *i.e.*

卷 *Chiuen'*, A roll, part of a book.

印 *Yin'*, Print, seal.

卵 '*Loan*, Eggs.

### 27. 厂

厥 *Ch'iue'*, Pron. of 3rd person, also impersonal.

原 ,*Yuen*, Original, of course.

厚 *Heu'*, Thick, generous.

厭 *Yen'*, Satiate, disgust.

### 28. 厶

矣 '*I*, An emphatic particle.

去 *Ch'ü'*, Go, reject.

參 ,*Ts'an*, ,*shen*, A trine, together, examine, accuse.

### 29. 又

又 *Yiu'*, Also, again.

取 '*Ch'ü*, To take.

及 *Chi'* Also, in addition.

受 *Sheu'*, To receive.

友 '*Yiu*, A friend.

反 '*Fan*, Turn, contrary.

叛 *P'an'*, To rebel.

### 30. 口

口 '*K'eu*, Mouth.

和 ,*Ho*, Harmony, mix, together with.

命 *Ming'*, Decree, fate, life.

善 *Shan'*, Good.

告 *Kau'*, Inform, proclaim, accuse.

可 '*K'o*, Can, may.

名 ,*Ming*, Name, fame, nominal.

問 *Wen'*, Ask.

同 ,*T'ung*, Together, like.

各 *Ko'*, Each, every.

司 ,*S*, Control, manage.

嗣 *S'*, To inherit, succeed to.

后 *Heu'*, A sovereign, an empress.

君 ,*Chiün*, A king, a chief.

召 *Chau'*, To summon.

哉 ,*Tsai*, A note of admiration.

向 *Hiang'*, Direction, towards.

呼 ,*Hu*, To call, to breathe.

否 'Feu, If not, or not, otherwise.
嘗 ˏCh'ang, Taste, a sign of the past tense.
吾 ˏWu, Pron. 1st pers. sing.
周 ˏCheu, Circumference, complete.
哥 ˏKo, Elder brother.
古 'Ku, Ancient.
史 'Sh, History, recorder, censor.
喻 Ü', Comparison, to inform.
喪 ˏSang, Decease, loss.
喜 'Hi, Pleasure, joy.
咸 ˏHien, All, entire.
吉 Chi', Good luck.
右 Yiu', The right hand.
器 Ch'i, Vessel, instrument.
合 Ho', To join, agree.
單 ˏTan, Single, a list.
哭 ˏK'u, To weep, cry.
咎 Chiu', Fault, sin, harm.
嗜 Sh, Greedy, vicious indulgence.
啡 'Fa, Pha. } Pharisee.
唎 Li', Ri. } Pharisee.
嚽 Sai', See. } Pharisee.
商 ˏShang, Merchant, to consult.

嘉 ˏChia, Excellent, auspicious.
哲 Che', Wise, worthy.
吏 Li', Officials.
嘏 'Ku, Prosperity, bliss.
嚴 ˏYen, Severe, strict.
呪 Cheu', To curse, incantation.
吹 ˏCh'ue, To blow.
吞 ˏT'un, To swallow.
噬 Sh', To devour.
舌 ˏShe, The tongue.
售 Sheu', To sell.
只 'Ch, Only.
品 'P'in, Class, grade, offerings.
呂 'Lü, A family name, a musical scale.
叩 K'eu', Kot'o, knock the head, knock at a door.
嘲 ˏCh'au, Ridicule.
吮 ˏYün, Lick with the tongue.
咫 ˏCh, A span.
唐 ˏT'ang, Name of a dynasty.
含 ˏHan, To contain, hold in the mouth.
嘘 ˏHü, Blow, puff.
咀 'Tsu, To chew.

嚼 *Chio'* (*c*) *chiau*, To masticate.

唱 *Ch'ang'*, To sing.

吟 *,Yin*, To hum, cantillate.

喧 *,Hiuen*, Noise.

啓 *'Ch'i*, To open, begin.

## 31. 口

四 *Si'*, Four.

因 *,Yin*, Because, from.

國 *Kwo'*, Kingdom, nation.

回 *,Kwei*, Turn, return.

圖 *,T'u*, A map, to plot.

固 *Ku'*, Firm, of course.

園 *,Yuen*, A garden.

困 *Kw'en'*, Press, oppress.

圍 *,Wei*, Enclose, besiege, surround.

囚 *,Ch'iu*, A prisoner.

囿 *Yiu'*, A park, garden.

## 32. 土

土 *'T'u*, Ground, earth, opium.

地 *Ti'*, The earth, ground, a place.

基 *,Chi*, Foundation, estate.

在 *Tsai'*, In, on, at.

城 *,Ch'eng*, A city, a wall.

垂 *,Ch'ue*, To condescend, let down.

境 *Ching'*, Place, region.

垣 *,Yuen*, A wall.

執 *Ch'*, To hold, control, take.

報 *Pau'*, To report, recompense.

埃 *,Yai*, The soil, dust.

堂 *,T'ang*, A hall.

墓 *Mu'*, A tomb, grave.

壤 *'Jang*, Ground, soil.

坐 *Tso'*, To sit.

壇 *,T'an*, An altar.

墮 *To'*, To fall.

塗 *,T'u*, To daub, mortar.

塵 *,Ch'en*, Dust, earth.

場 *,Ch'ang*, An open ground.

坦 *'T'an*, Level ground.

坷 *,K'o*, Uneven ground.

圮 *'Ch'i*, Crumbling, shattered.

壞 *Hwai'*, Spoiled, ruined.

堅 *,Chien*, Firm, solid.

塞 *Se', sai'*, To stop up, boundary.

增 *,Tseng*, To add, increase.

塔 *'T'a*, A tower.

均 *,Chiün*, All, equal.

堪 ,*K'an*, May, can, endure.
塹 *Chan'*, A pit, a ravine.
階 ,*Chie*, Stairway.
塾 *Shu'*, A school.
塒 ,*Shï*, A coop for fowls.

33. 士

士 *Shï'*, A scholar.
壯 *Chwang'*, A bed.
壽 *Sheu'*, Age, longevity.

34. 夂

夏 *Hia'*, Summer, name of a dynasty of China.

36. 夕

多 ,*To*, Much, many.
夕 *Hi'* (c) ,*hi*, Evening.
夢 *Mong'*, A dream.
夜 *Ye'*, Night.
外 *Wai'*, Outside.
夙 *Su'*, Early, north.

37. 大

大 *Ta'*, Great.
天 ,*T'ien*, Heaven.
夫 ,*Fu* A man, husband, *fu-ts*, a teacher, *fu-jin*, a lady, *fu*, a euphonic particle.
太 *T'ai'*, Grand, vast.
奠 *Tien'*, Fix, establish, to make a libation.
奈 *Nai'*, How!
奮 *Fen'*, Earnest, energetic.
奬 '*Chiang*, To praise, exhort.
奧 *Au'*, Mysterious.
夾 *Chia'*, To approach from both sides; to press.
奕 *I'*, Vast, to gamble.
奉 *Feng'*, Obey, receive orders; carry in both hands.
失 *Sh'*, To lose.
奪 *To'*, Snatch, seize.
奇 ,*Ch'i*, Rare, wonderful.
奚 ,*Hi*, How? why?
奔 ,*Pen*, To run.
奏 *Tseu'*, A report or memorial to the sovereign, to strike up music.

38. 女

女 '*Nü*, A woman, a daughter.
如 ,*Ju*, As, like, if.
妻 ,*C'hi*, A wife, the chief wife.
始 '*Shi*, Beginning.
嫩 *Nun'*, Tender, fresh.
好 '*Hau*, Good.
妄 *Wang'*, False, deceitful.

婦 *Fu'*, Woman, wife.

娶 *'Ch'ü*, To marry.

姓 *Hing'*, The family name, the family.

嬰 *,Ying*, An infant.

姊 *'Tsï*, *'chie*, *'chi*, Elder sister.

妹 *Mie'*, Younger sister.

奴 *,Nu*, A slave.

婢 *Pi'*, A maid servant.

嫁 *Chia'*, To give in marriage.

威 *,Wei*, Dignity, majesty, prowess.

姑 *,Ku*, A maiden, an aunt, a wife's mother-in-law.

妙 *Miau'*, Admirable.

妥 *'T'o*, Complete, satisfactory.

娱 *,Ü*, Delight.

妍 *,Yen*, Elegant, refined, delicate.

媚 *Mie'*, To smirk, flatter.

## 39. 子

子 *'Ts*, Son, child, doctor, sir.

字 *Tsï'*, Letters, the marriage name, to love, nourish.

孰 *Shu*, Who? which?

存 *,Tsun*, To retain, preserve, continue.

孫 *,Sun*, A grandson; gentle, yielding.

孩 *,Hai*, A child.

孝 *Hiau'*, Filial piety.

季 *Chi'*, A season, the last of three.

孕 *Yün'*, Pregnant.

孳 *,Tsï*, To multiply, to swarm.

## 40. 宀

宜 *,I*, Proper, fitting, to set in order.

家 *,Chia*, A family.

安 *'An*, Rest, quiet.

守 *'Sheu*, To hold, maintain.

實 *,Sh*, Solid, real.

容 *,Yung*, The face, to tolerate.

室 *Sh'*, A chamber, a house.

宮 *,Kung*, A palace.

宰 *'Tsai*, A ruler, to slay.

定 *Ting'*, Certain, to fix, determine.

害 *Hai'*, To harm, injure.

宣 *,Hiuen*, To proclaim, publish.

寢 *,Ch'in*, To go to bed, sleep.

審 *'Shen*, To examine, judge.

宇 'Ü, A roof, house, the canopy of heaven.

富 Fu', Rich.

宗 ,Tsung, Ancestor, chief, oracle, standard.

察 Ch'a', Search, examine, investigate.

寶 'Pau, Precious.

寃 ,Yuen, Injury, spleen, blame.

官 ,Kwan, Officer, mandarin, to govern.

寅 ,Yin, To reverence; the 3rd of the 12 hours.

客 K'o, A guest, stranger, merchant, customer.

寧 ,Ning, Tranquil, rather.

寬 ,Kw'an, Large, generous, indulgent.

宏 ,Hung, Great, vast.

密 Mi', Close, secret, intimate.

寵 'Ch'ung, Favor, affection.

寡 'Kwa, Destitute, few, a widow.

宿 Su', A constellation, to pass a night, lodge.

宥 Yiu', Indulge, pardon.

寒 ,Han, Cold, frigid.

寰 ,Hwan, The globe, a circuit.

寄 Chi', To lodge, convey, a remainder.

## 41. 寸

寸 Ts'un', An inch.

將 ,Chiang, Take command, intend, will be or do.

導 Tau', To lead.

尊 ,Tsun, To respect, reverence.

對 Tui', Opposite, a pair, to compare.

專 ,Chwen, Special, sole.

尋 ,Hiün, To seek, afterwards.

封 ,Feng, To seal, appoint.

射 She', To shoot.

## 42. 小

小 'Siau, Small.

少 'Shau, Few, young.

尚 Shang', Ch'ang, Above, to exalt, yet.

## 43. 尢

就 Chiu', Then, thereon, come to.

尤 ,Yiu, Blame, fault, more.

## 44. 尸

尼 ,Ni, Near, familiar.

居 ,Chü, To dwell, locate.

屋 Wu' (c) ,wu, A house.
屬 'Shu, To belong to, to enjoin.
履 'Lü, Sandals, to walk, an income.
尸 ,Sh, A corpse, an effigy.
屍 ,Sh, A dead body.
尺 'Ch', A foot, a rule.
屆 Chie', To reach, arrive at.
屢 ,Lü, Often, repeatedly.
層 ,Ts'eng, A story, or stratum.

## 46. 山

山 ,Shan, Hill, mountain.
崇 ,Ch'ung, Lofty, to reverence.
巖 ,Yien, A cliff, precipice.
島 'Tau, An island.
崗 ,Kang, A steep high hill.
岸 Ngan', A shore, bank.
崩 ,Peng, To fall, death of a prince.
崙 ,Lun, A peak, summit.
嵐 ,Lan, Mountain mist; a blue tinge.
崎 ,Ch'i, Rough, uneven.
嶇 ,Ch'ü, Rugged.
崖 ,Yai, A steep bank, a cliff.
峽 Chia', A mountain pass, a strait.
岱 Tai', The Taishan mts.
嶽 Yo', A mountain.
嶔 ,Ch'in, Lofty, sublime.
嶷 I', A dizzy height.
嶂 Chang', A chain of hills.
崢 ,Cheng, Eminent.
嶸 ,Yung, Conspicuous.
峰 ,Feng, A peak.

## 47. 川

州 ,Cheu, An island, continent, district.
川 ,Ch'wen, A stream.
巢 ,Chau, A nest, a lair.

## 48. 工

工 ,Kung, Work, mechanism.
左 'Tso, The left hand, wrong, to aid.
巨 Chü', Huge, chief.
差 ,Ch'a, ,ch'ai, Difference, error, send.
巧 'Ch'iau, Skilful, cunning.

## 49. 已

已 'I, Already, to stop, a euphonic final.
巴 ,Pa, A grip, handful, blow, name of a place, sign of the optative,

己 'Chi, Self, reflex pron.

## 50. 巾

巾 ,Chin, A turban, cap, kerchief.

帝 Ti', A ruler, supreme majesty.

希 ,Hi, To expect, rare.

幕 Mu', Tent, tabernacle.

師 ,Sh, A master, army, multitude.

布 Pu', Cotton cloth, to spread abroad.

常 ,Ch'ang, Constant, always, common.

市 Sh', A market.

席 Si', Matting, feast, meal; professor's chair.

帶 Tai', A belt, draw, convey.

帕 P'a', A veil, a kerchief.

帛 Pé, Silk stuff, wealth, money.

## 51. 干

年 ,Nien, A year.

干 ,Kan, A shield, to offend, serious consequences.

并 Ping', United, also, even.

平 ,Ping, Level, just.

## 52. 幺

幾 ,Chi, 'chi, How, almost.

幼 Yiu', Tender, youth, young.

幽 Yiu', Gloomy, dismal.

幻 Hwan', Transform, sleight of hand.

## 53. 广

庇 'P'i, To protect.

底 'Ti, Bottom.

廣 'Hwang, Broad.

庶 Shu', All, almost.

廢 Fe', To set aside, waste.

度 Tu', A degree, to measure, estimate.

座 Tso', A seat, throne.

府 'Fu, A mansion.

庸 ,Yung, Constant, common, simple, to hire.

庫 K'u', Treasury.

康 ,K'ang, Tranquil, opulent.

廊 ,Lang, Portico, verandah.

序 Hu', Preface, order, a college.

庠 ,Siang, Academy, asylum.

廚 ,Ch'u, A kitchen.

廁 *S*‘, A privy, to cleanse.

廐 *Chiu*‘, Stable.

庥 ,*Hiu*, To protect, shelter.

庖 ꜀*P‘au*, Kitchen, butcher's stall.

庭 ꜀*T‘ing*, A hall.

## 54. 廴

建 *Chien*‘, To build, lay a foundation.

延 ꜀*Yen*, To prolong, to invite.

廻 ꜀*Hwe*, To turn back.

## 55. 弋

弋 *I*‘, An arrow.

式 *Sh*‘, A model, a prop, to lean on.

## 57. 弓

強 ,*Ch‘iang*, ʼ*ch‘iang*, Strong, violent.

張 ,*Chang*, Extend, stretch, bend.

弗 *Fu*‘, Not.

弟 *Ti*‘, Younger brother, disciple.

引 ʼ*Yin*, To lead, introduction.

弓 ,*Kung*, A bow.

弱 *Jo*‘, Weak, feeble.

彈 ꜀*T‘an*, Beat a harp, a ball.

彌 ꜀*Mi*, More, to stop.

## 59. 彡

形 ꜀*Hing*, Form, body.

彰 ,*Chang*, Display, illustrate.

彩 ʼ*Ts‘ai*, Brilliant, ornate.

影 ʼ*Ying*, Shadow.

## 60. 彳

復 *Fu*‘, Return, again.

往 ʼ*Wang*, To go.

得 *Te*‘ (*c*) ꜀*tei*, Obtain, get, can.

彼 ʼ*Pi*, That, adj. pron.

從 ,*Ts‘ung*, Follow, from.

徒 ꜀*T‘u*, Disciple, in vain, only.

後 *Heu*‘, After, posterity.

役 *I*‘, To serve, a low official, police runner.

微 ꜀*Wei*, Minute, subtile.

待 *Tai*‘, Treat, wait.

循 ꜀*Hiün*, Comply, according to.

德 *Te*‘, Virtue.

征 ,*Cheng*, Advance, invade, conquer.

徵 ,*Cheng*, Test, examine, act.

徑 *Ching*‘, A path.

徜 'T'ang, Loll, stroll, lounge.
徉 ꜁Yang, Roving, straying.
徐 ꜁Hü, Gradual, at leisure.

## 61. 心

心 ꜀Sin, Heart.
惟 ꜁We, Only, but, think.
惡 Ngo', wu', Evil, hate.
愛 Ai', Love.
意 I', Thought, intention.
必 Pi', Certainly, must.
性 Ping', Nature.
感 'Kan, Feel, excite feeling.
忽 Hu', Sudden.
忍 'Jen, Unfeeling, patient.
恐 'K'ung, Apprehension, lest.
悔 'Hwe, Regret, repent.
悅 Yue', Please, be pleased.
悉 Si', All, to investigate.
惑 How', hu', Tempt, doubt, waver.
愚 ꜁Ü, Dull, stupid.
患 Huan', Affliction.
憂 ꜀Yiu, Sorrow, grief.
懼 Chü', Dread.
怒 Nu', Anger.

忘 ꜁Wang, Forget.
恃 Sh', To rely on.
恩 ꜀En, ngen, Grace.
恤 Hü', Compassion, pity.
志 Chi', Inclination, will, history, to record.
念 Nien', Thought, to read.
情 ꜁Ch'ing, Passions, affairs, natural feelings.
息 Si', Rest, cease.
愈 Ü', Better, to heal.
恒 ꜁Heng, Persevering, permanent.
懷 ꜁Hwai, Bosom, to feel, cherish.
恭 ꜀Kung, Respect.
暴 Pau', Violent, sudden.
愆 ꜀Ch'ien, Guilt.
應 ꜀Ying, ying', Answer, ought.
思 ꜀S, To think.
憫 'Min, Compassion.
慧 Hwe', Smartness, wisdom.
慈 ꜁Ts'ï, Mercy, tenderness.
憑 ꜁P'ing, Proof, to rest on.
憾 Han', Hate, dislike.
急 Chi', (c) ꜀chi, Haste, urgency.

速成漢語

慾 Ü', Passion, desire, appetite.
愼 *Shen*ʿ, Cautious, precise.
想 *'Hiang*, To think, desire.
悟 *Wu*ʿ, Conscious, awake, to understand.
慮 *Lü*ʿ, To care, be anxious, think about.
懽 *,Hwan*, Pleasure.
惠 *Hwe*ʿ, Comfort, kindness.
憐 *ˏLien*, Pity, love.
惜 *Si*ʿ, Regret, spare, love.
慰 *We*ʿ, Soothe, comfort, support.
忠 *,Chung*, Loyal, faithful.
恪 *C'hio*', Dignified.
恨 *Hen*', Hate, abhor.
憶 *I*ʿ, Think of, remember, conjecture.
慢 *Man*ʿ, Slow, disrespect.
慄 *Li*', Tremble, dread.
怨 *Yuen*ʿ, Blame, resent, discontent.
懸 *ˏHiuen*, Suspend.
忿 *,Fen*ʿ, Anger, rage.
忙 *ˏMang*, Hurried, busy.
慕 *Mu*ʿ, Desire, admire.
懺 *ˏChien, ,chan*, Repent, a penitential prayer.

悞 *ˏÜ*, Mistake, error.
怱 *,Ts'ung*, Haste.
忻 *,Hin*, Delight.
慶 *Ch'ing*ʿ, Felicity.
恥 *'Ch'i*, Shame.
戀 *Lien*ʿ, To dote.
快 *Kw'ai*ʿ, Quick, joyous.
忖 *,Ts'un*, Think, suspect.
悚 *'Sung*, Awe.
惶 *,Hwang*, Dread, apprehension.
慌 *,Hwang*, Hurry, confused.
慝 *T'e*ʿ, Fault, evil, badness.
惕 *T'i*', Reverence.
慙 *ˏTsan*, Shame.
懟 *Tui*ʿ, Vexation, hate.
悛 *ˏCh'iuen*, Reform.

## 62. 戈

或 *Hwo*ʿ, Or, either, suppose, some one.
我 *'Wo*, I, pron. 1*st* pers.
成 *ˏCh'eng*, Make complete.
戮 *Lu*ʿ, Cut to pieces.
戰 *Chan*ʿ, Fight, battle.
戈 *,Ko*, A pike, a weapon.

戒 *Chie'*, To caution, forbid, renounce.
戚 *Chi'*, A relative, sorrow.
戴 *Tai'*, Wear, or bear on the head.
戛 *Chia'*, A lance, jolting, stammering.

## 63. 戶

戶 *Hu'*, A door, family, owner.
戾 *Le'*, Offend, perverse.
房 *,Fang*, House, room.

## 64. 手

手 *'Sheu*, Hand.
摩 *,Mo*, (c) *,mo*, Feel with the hand.
拿 *,Na*, Take, seize.
撒 *Sa'*, Scatter.
拉 *,La*, Draw.
拯 *'Cheng*, Save, succor.
拜 *Pai'*, Worship, bow down.
按 *An'*, According to.
挪 *,No*, Remove, change place of.
投 *,T'eu*, Plunge, cast.
舉 *'Chü*, Elevate, all.
指 *'Chï*, Finger, to point.
押 *Ya'*, Pawn, seal, escort.
携 *,Hi*, *,hie*, Convey, carry.
擊 *Chi'*, Strike.
掃 *,Sau*, Sweep.
據 *Chü'*, Hold, proof.
揚 *,Yang*, Spread, display.
接 *Chie'*, Receive, connect.
捫 *,Men*, Handle, feel with the hand.
援 *,Yuen*, Rescue, succor.
招 *,Chau*, To beckon, call together.
播 *Po'*, Scatter, winnow.
提 *,T'i*, Handle, take up.
抵 *,Ti*, Oppose, balance.
拒 *Chü'*, Resist.
才 *,Ts'ai*, Talent, ability.
授 *Sheu'*, Entrust, impart.
扶 *,Fu*, Sustain.
持 *,Ch'*, Hold, control.
擇 *Cho'*, (c) *,chai*, Choose, select.
推 *,T'ui*, Push.
抑 *I'*, Or, either, repress.
抹 *'Mo*, Wipe, blot, paint.
操 *,Ts'au*, Hold fast, manage.

掌 ,*Chang*, The palm, hold, control.

攘 '*Jang*, Rob, lay bare, oppose.

承 ꜀*Ch'eng*, Receive, thanks, succeed.

捐 ,*Chiuen*, Contribute, offer.

抱 *Pau'*, Nurse, embrace, hug.

搖 ꜀*Yau*, Shake, rock, scull a boat.

撻 '*Ta*, Whip, scourge.

打 '*Ta*, Strike, beat.

擬 '*Ni*, Propose, decide.

折 *Cho'* (*c*) ꜀*cho*, Break open, take apart.

捕 '*P'u*, Capture, seize.

振 *Chen'*, Arouse, stir up.

擲 *C'h'*, Cast, throw.

搴 ,*Ch'ien*, Take hold, seize.

探 *T'an'*, ,*t'an*, Test, try, sound, inquire.

抄 ,*Ch'au*, Transcribe, confiscate, short-cut.

拓 *To'*, Open, inaugurate.

攀 ,*P'an*, Cling, hold to.

排 ꜀*P'ai*, Arrange, spread out.

披 ,*P'i*, Cover, cloak.

掩 '*Yen*, Veil, conceal.

挽 '*Wan*, Draw back.

揮 ,*Hwe*, Wield, manage.

拊 '*Fu*, Beat, play on a harp.

拍 ,*P'ai*, *p'o'*, Pat, tap.

掣 *Ch'e*, Check, hinder, draw lots.

採 '*Ts'ai*, Pick up, cull.

拔 *Pa'*, Pluck up, follow, assist.

拾 *Sh'*, Gather, pick up.

掇 *Ch'o'*, Break, snap.

擷 *Chie'*, Strip, break.

掬 *Chü'*, Handful, to take with both hands.

撈 ꜀*Lau*, (*c*) ,*lau*, Grasp, seize.

拋 ,*P'au*, Cast, throw away.

摶 ,*T'oan*, Knead, compress.

挈 *Sie*, Carry in the hand.

## 65. 支

支 ,*Ch*, Diverge, prop, succor, advance money.

## 66. 攴

敵 *Ti'*, (*c*) ꜀*ti*, Rival, enemy.

致 *Ch'*, To cause, so that, investigate.

故 *Ku'*, A cause, reason, therefore.

教 *Kiau'*, Teach, train, doctrine, religion.
救 *Kiu'*, Save.
數 *Shu'*, Number, destiny.
改 *'Kai*, Change, reform.
敢 *'Kan*, Dare.
攻 *,Kung*, Attack, work at.
敬 *Ching'*, Respect, reverence.
敗 *Pai'*, Defeat, waste, decay.
散 *San'*, *'san*, Scatter.
政 *Cheng'*, Government, politics.
收 *,Sheu*, Receive, collect.
放 *Fang'*, Release, let loose.
攷 *'K'au*, Examine, search.
敷 *,Fu*, Spread, diffuse.

## 67. 文

文 *,Wen*, Literature, figures.
斐 *'Fe*, Elegant.

## 68. 斗

斗 *'Teu*, A peck measure, the Great Bear.
料 *Liau'*, Materials to conjecture.

## 69. 斤

所 *'So*, Which, what, where.
斯 *,S*, This.
斷 *Toan'*, Cut, break, by all means.
斥 *C'h'*, Rebuke.
新 *,Sin*, New, renew.
斤 *,Chin*, A catty, an axe.

## 70. 方

方 *,Fang*, Square, place, method, just before.
族 *Tsu'*, Family clan.
於 *,Ü*, In, on, pertaining to.
旁 *,P'ang*, Side.
施 *,Sh*, Give, bestow.
旅 *'Lü*, Stranger, company, batallion.
旋 *,Hiuen*, Revolve, in turn.

## 71. 旡

既 *Chi'*, Since, already.
旡 *,Wu*, Without, privative.

## 72. 日

日 *Ji'*, Sun, a day.
昔 *Si'*, Formerly, anciently.
明 *,Ming*, Bright, understand; *Ming ji*, to-morrow; *ming nien*, next year.
是 *Shi'*, To be, right.
時 *,Sh*, Time, hour.

昭 ˏ*Chau*, Shine, display.
智 *Chʻ*, Wisdom.
旨 ʼ*Ch*, Will, decree, taste.
暗 *Anʻ*, Dark, obscure.
易 *Iʻ*, Change, easy.
昧 *Meʻ*, Obscure, blinded.
晝 *Cheuʻ*, Noon, daytime.
晚 ʼ*Wan*, Evening, night.
早 ʼ*Tsau*, Early.
曠 *Kwangʻ*, Barren; desert.
昆 ˏ*Kwʻun*, Elder brother, a worm.
普 ʼ*Pʻu*, Far and wide.
晨 ˏ*Chʻen*, Morning, early.
星 ˏ*Hing*, A star.
昌 ˏ*Chʻang*, Prosperous.
暫 *Chanʻ*, Brief, temporary.
暮 *Muʻ*, Evening, twilight.
替 *Tʻiʻ*, Instead, fail.
曁 *Chiʻ*, Also; more, end.
暢 *Chʻangʻ*, Comfortable, copious, expansive.
晴 ˏ*Chʻing*, Clear.
暘 ˏ*Yang*, Bright, fair.
旱 *Hanʻ*, Dry weather.

春 ˏ*Chʻun*, Spring.
晷 ʼ*Kwe*, Sun-dial.
晏 *Yenʻ*, Evening.
曉 ʼ*Hiau*, Morning, to know, make known.
晰 *Siʻ*, Bright, discriminate.
映 *Yingʻ*, Shine on, image.
暖 ʼ*Noan*, Warm; mild.
景 ʼ*Ching*, Admirable, picturesque.
旦 *Tanʻ*, Morning.
旬 ˏ*Hiün*, Ten days.

## 73. 曰

曰 *Yueʻ*, Speak, said, called.
會 *Hweʻ*, Meet, can.
書 ˏ*Shu*, Write, book.
曹 ˏ*Tsʻau*, Class, sign of plural.
曾 ˏ*Tsʻeng* ˏ*tseng*, Sign of past tense, a family name.
最 *Tsueʻ*, Most.
更 ˏ*Keng*, Change, more.
曲 *Chʻüʻ*, Crooked, injury, song.
曷 *Hoʻ*, Why not?
曳 *Yeʻ*, Drag.

## 74. 月

有 'Yiu, To have, to be.
宥 Yiu', Indulge, forgive.
月 Yue', Moon, month.
望 Wang', Look towards, hope, aspect, repute.
朝 ꜀Chau, ꜂chau, Morning, towards, palace, do homage.
勝 Sheng', Conquer, bear, surpass.
期 ꜀Ch'i, Period, expect.
服 Fu' (c) ꜀fu, Submit, hug.
朋 ꜀P'eng, Friend.
朔 So', North, first of a month.

## 75. 木

未 We', Not yet.
相 ꜂Siang, Mutual, together, help.
木 Mu', Wood, timber.
本 'Pen, Root, origin.
東 ꜂Tung, East.
樹 Shu', Tree, to plant.
果 'Kwo, Fruit, really.
榮 ꜀Yung, Glory.
樂 Lo', yo', Yo', Joy, music.
集 Chi', Collect.
極 Chi', Extreme, limit.
棄 Ch'i', Reject, leave, cast away.
業 Ye', Business, property, finally.
權 ꜀Ch'iuen, Authority, a steelyard weight, an exception.
末 Mo', Tree top, end, tip end, no more, worthless.
架 Chia', Frame.
條 T'iau, A rod, a classifier of long things, an article, a law.
束 Shu', Bind, control, encase.
槪 Kai', A stable.
機 ꜂Chi', Engine, opportunity.
植 Ch', Plant, fix.
根 ꜂Ken, Root.
橫 ꜀Heng, Perverse, crosswise.
棘 ꜀Chi, Thorns, brambles.
枝 ꜂Ch, A branch.
杯 ꜂Pe, A cup.
橄 'Kan, Chinese olive, it belongs to the terebinthaceae.
欖 'Lan, A kind of olive; the canarium.
板 'Pan, Plank, board.
柱 Chu', Pillar, prop.
樣 Yang', Sample, pattern.
樓 ꜀Leu, Loft, story.
枯 ꜂K'u, Withered.

核 *Ho*ʿ, Seed, kernel, compare, search.

格 *Ko*ʿ, Reform, come.

杖 *Chang*ʿ, Staff, cudgel, lean on.

某 ʾ*Meu*, Any, a certain one.

模 ˛*Mu*, Pattern, sample.

楷 ʾ*Ch'ia*, Model.

林 ˛*Lin*, Forest, grove.

榭 *Hie*ʿ, Terrace, arbor.

檻 ʾ*K'an*, Railing, cage.

楣 ˛*Me*, Door lintel.

構 *Keu*ʿ, Join, truss of a house.

材 ˛*Ts'ai*, Materials.

榻 *T'a*ʿ, A couch.

楮 ʾ*Ch'u*, Paper, mulberry.

楊 ˛*Yang*, Poplar, aspen.

柳 ʾ*Liu*, Willow.

梧 ˛*Wu*, } An ornamental tree
桐 ˛*T'ung*, } with large leaves.

桃 ˛*T'au*, Peach.

李 ʾ*Li*, Plum, *hing-li*, baggage.

松 ˏ*Sung*, Pine, fir.

栢 *Po*ʿ ʾ*Pai*, Cedar, cypress.

柵 *Cha*ʿ, Stockade, fence or pen of open work.

## 76. 欠

欠 *Chien*ʿ, Lack, owe, debt.

欲 *Ü*ʿ, Wish, desire, will.

次 *T's*ʿ, Order, next in order.

歟 ˛*Ü*, A final expressing admiration.

歡 ˏ*Hwan*, Joy, to like.

欣 ˏ*Hin*, Delight.

欺 ˏ*Ch'i*, Deceive, insult.

歌 ˏ*Ko*, A song.

歐 ˏ*En*, Sing, chant, recite.

## 77. 止

此 ʾ*Ts*ʿ, This.

歸 ˏ*Kwe*, Return, render, yield, belong.

止 ʾ*Chï*, Stop, cease, only.

歷 *Li*ʿ, Pass over, away, successive, experience.

正 *Cheng*ʿ, (c) ˏ*cheng*, Upright, correct, virtuous.

武 ʾ*Wu*, Military, used for *pu*, a step.

歲 *Sue*ʿ, A year, season.

步 *Pu*ʿ, Step.

歧 ˛*Ch'i*, Diverge, forked, *ch'i lu* a bye-way.

## 78. 歹

歹 ,Tai, Evil, bad.
死 'S, Death.
殊 ,Shu, Different, really.
殘 ,Ts'an, Cruel, barbarous.
殲 ,Chien, Kill, destroy, perish.
殆 Tai', Insecure, almost.
殤 Shang, Untimely death.
殂 'Tsu, Dissolution, death.

## 79. 殳

殳 ,Shu, A spear.
殺 Sha', (c) ,sha, To kill.
殿 Tien', Temple.
毀 'Hwe, Destroy.
殷 ,Yin, Great, flourishing.
般 ,Pan, A kind, the same.
殼 Ch'io', K'e, } Shell, husk.

## 80. 毋

毋 ,Wu, ,wu, Do not, a denial.
母 'Mu, Mother.
每 'Me, Each, every.
毒 Tu', (c) ,tu, Poison.
毓 Ü', Cherish, brood, nurture.

## 81. 比

比 'Pi, To compare.

## 82. 毛

毛 ,Mau, Hair, wool.
毫 ,Hau, Hair, down, a mote.

## 83. 氏

民 ,Min, People, a plebeian.
氏 Sh', Family, suffix to family name of a woman or other person.

## 84. 气

氣 Ch'i', Breath, any gaseous body, matter, anger.

## 85. 水

水 ,Shui, Water.
求 ,Ch'iu, Seek, desire, pray.
法 Fa', Law, mode, method.
溫 ,Wen, Tepid, warm, mild.
汝 'Ju, Thou.
沒 Mo', Sink, die, not, no.
深 ,Shen, Deep.
洗 ,Si, To wash.
河 ,Ho, River, canal.
治 Ch', Govern, manage.

沙 ,*Sha*, Sand.

洲 ,*Cheu*, Island, continent.

派 *P'ai'*, Divide, appoint.

海 '*Hai*, The sea.

污 ,*Wu*, Filthy.

滅 *Mie'*, Quench, destroy.

潔 ,*Chie*, Cleanse, purity.

波 ,*Po*, A wave.

活 *Hwo'* (c) ,*hwo*, Alive, mobile.

酒 '*Chiu*, Wine.

油 ,*Yiu*, Oil.

流 ,*Liu*, Flow, glide.

永 '*Yung*, Long, for ever.

濟 *Chi'*, Cross a ferry, to succor.

淫 ,*Yin*, Adulterous, profligate, excess.

泣 *Ch'i'*, To weep.

清 ,*Ch'ing*, Pure, clear.

洪 ,*Hung*, Great, vast.

沾 ,*Chan*, Moisten, tinge, infect.

濯 *Cho'*, Wash, wash the feet.

沐 *Mu'*, Bathe, bathe the head, receive favor.

漸 *Chien'*, Gradual.

泥 ,*Ni*, Mud.

澤 *Tse'*, A pool, favor.

灌 *Kwan'*, Pour, irrigate.

泉 *Ch'iuen*, Fountain, money.

江 ,*Kiang*, River.

洋 ,*Yang*, Ocean.

滿 '*Man*, Full.

源 ,*Yuen*, Source, fountain.

湖 ,*Hu*, Lake.

漢 *Han'*, Name of a river, of a dynasty, of the Chinese.

沉 ,*Ch'en*, To sink, perish.

淪 ,*Lun*, Eddy, gulf, sink, perish.

渴 '*K'o*, Thirst.

濱 ,*Pin*, Bank, brink.

溯 *So'*, Trace up, go against the current.

漏 *Leu'*, Leak, omit.

渡 *Tu'*, Ferry, to cross over.

消 ,*Siau*, Melt, waste away.

潦 '*Lau*, Flood, excess of rain.

浮 ,*Feu*, Float, swim, superficial.

渭 *Wei'*, Name of a turbid river.

津 ,*Chin*, A ford, ferry.

涉 *She'*, To wade, concern.

潮 *Ch'au*, Tide, damp.

潢 *,Hwang*, A lake, pool, *chwang hwang*, embellishment.

洛 *Lo'*, } Names of rivers.
泗 *Sï'*, }

淋 *,Lin*, Drip, trickle.

湍 *,Tw'an*, A torrent.

激 *Chi'*, Excite, impede.

濫 *Lan'*, A flood, excess, superfluous, intrusive, nominal.

測 *Ts'e'*, Estimate, measure.

泰 *T'ai'*, Vast, quiet, opulent.

渚 *'Chu*, An islet, sandbank.

淬 *Ts'ue'*, To dip, dye.

泅 *,Ch'iu*, To swim.

濕 *,Shï, (c) shï'*, Wet, damp, moist.

涕 *T'i'*, To weep.

淚 *Le'*, Tears.

浩 *Hau'*, Vast.

淵 *,Yuen*, Abyss.

滋 *,Ts*, To multiply.

## 86. 火

火 *'Hwo*, Fire.

無 *,Wu*, Not.

焉 *,Yen*, Euphonic.

爲 *,Wei*, Be, become, make, do.

然 *,Jan*, So, yet.

營 *,Ying*, Plan, plot, camp, legion.

焚 *,Fen*, Consume.

烈 *Lie'*, Fierce, brave.

烏 *,Wu*, A crow, black, what? where? how!

災 *,Tsai*, Calamity.

燔 *,Fan*, Burn.

烟 *,Yen*, Smoke, tobacco.

燬 *'Hwei*, Destroy by fire.

燃 *,Jan*, Kindle.

燈 *,Teng*, A lamp.

照 *Chau'*, Shine, enlighten.

熱 *Jo'*, Heat.

勳 *,Hiün*, Merit.

煩 *,Fan*, Vex, perplex, trouble.

燮 *Sie'*, Temper, mingle, blend.

燕 *Yen'*, *,yen*, A swallow, a feast.

熾 *Chï'*, Kindle.

燄 *Yen'*, Flame.

爍 *Sho'*, Flash, explode.

燦 *'Ts'an*, Brilliant.

爛 *Lan*ʿ, Bright, torn, rotten.
煇 ˏ*Hwei*, Splendor.
煌 ˎ*Hwang*, Lustre.
烹 ˏ*P'eng*, Bake, roast.
熙 ˏ*Hi*, Bright, glorious.
煮 '*Chu*, Boil, cook.

87. 爪

爭 ˏ*Cheng*, Contend, strive.
爰 ˎ*Yuen*, Therefore, at, in, next.
爵 *Tsio*ʿ, Rank, title, office.

88. 父

父 *Fu*ʿ, Father.
爺 ˎ*Ye*, Father, combined in various titles.

89. 爻

爾 '*Er*, Thou, a particle.

90. 爿

牀 ˎ*Ch'wang*, Bed, bedstead.

91. 片

片 *P'ien*ʿ, A strip, slip, leaf.
牖 *Yiu*ʿ, Door, window, to instruct.

92. 牙

牙 ˎ*Ya*, Teeth.

93. 牛

物 *Wu*ʿ, Thing, animal
牛 ˎ*Niu*, Cow, ox.
牡 '*Mu*, Male.
特 *T'e*ʿ, Special, intentional, an ox.
犢 *Tu*ʿ, A calf.
牧 *Mu*ʿ, Shepherd, herdsman.
牽 ˏ*Ch'ien*, Lead, draw.
牲 ˏ*Sheng*, Cattle, beasts for sacrifice.
牢 ˎ*Lau*, Firm, prison, a victim for sacrifice.

94. 犬

猶 ˎ*Yiu*, Yet, like.
獄 *Ü*ʿ, Prison, law-suit.
獸 *Sheu*ʿ, Wild beast.
獻 *Hien*ʿ, Present, offer.
犯 *Fan*ʿ, Violate, offend.
獲 *Hwo*ʿ, *hu*ʿ, Take, obtain.
獨 *Tu*ʿ, Alone, single, only.
狂 ˎ*Kw'ang*, Mad, foolish, sport.
犬 '*Ch'uin*, A dog.
獅 ˏ*Sh*, A lion.
狀 *Chwang*ʿ, Form, a lawyer's brief.

狹 *Hia'*, Narrow, stupid.
獵 *Lie'*, Catch, hunt.

## 95. 玄

率 *Shwai'*, Lead, imitate, all.
茲 *,Ts*, This, it.
玄 *,Hiuen*, Sombre, mysterious.

## 96. 玉

王 *,Wang*, King, prince.
理 *'Li*, A principle, to govern.
瑟 *She'*, A harp of many strings.
環 *,Hwan*, A ring, circle, around.
班 *,Pan*, Class, to distribute.
玉 *Ü'*, Gem, jade.
琴 *,Ch'in*, Harp, lute.
珍 *,Chen*, Pearl.
球 *,Ch'iu*, Globe.
璣 *,Chi*, An astronomical instrument.
玩 *Wan'*, Joy, amusement.
玷 *Tien'*, A flaw.
珥 *'Er*, Ear-ring, pendant.
珠 *,Chu*, Pearl, jewel.
璧 *Pi'*, A precious gem.
珩 *,Heng*, Emerald.

瑚 *,Hu*, Coral.
琳 *,Lin*, A kind of precious stone.
瑯 *,Lang*, Neck ornaments.
琥 *'Hu*, Amber.
玖 *'Kiu*, Ebony.
璀 *,Ts'ui*, Lustre of a gem.
璨 *'Ts'an*, Sparkling.
瑞 *Jui'*, Auspicious.

## 97. 瓜

瓜 *,Kwa*, A melon.

## 98. 瓦

瓦 *'Wa*, Title, earthen-ware.

## 99. 甘

甚 *Shen'*, (c) *,shen*, Intense, excessive, to the extent of.
甘 *,Kan*, Sweet, willing.

## 100. 生

生 *,Sheng*, Life, to impart life; produce.
產 *'Ch'an*, To give birth, an estate.
甦 *Su*, To revive.

## 101. 用

用 *Yung'*, Use.

## 102. 田

異 I', Different, strange.

當 ,Tang, Ought, proper, in, on.

由 ,Yiu, From, out of.

申 ,Shen, Extend, repeat.

田 ,T'ien, Field.

男 ,Nan, A male, a son.

界 Chie', Boundary.

畜 Hü', ch'u', Store up, cattle, to breed.

畢 Pi', Ended, finished.

留 ,Liu, Detain, delay.

甲 Chia', Mail, a cyclic character, the first.

畏 We, Fear, reverence.

畧 Lio', Brief, compendious, tactics.

疇 ,Ch'eu, A field.

番 ,Fan, Footstep, change, a time or times, barbarous, foreign.

畀 Pi', Give, bestow.

疆 ,Chiang, Bound, limit.

畫 Hwa', Painting, a pen stroke.

畝 'Mu, A mow, 7260 sq. ft.

## 103. 疋

疋 'P'i, A piece of cloth.

疑 ,I, Doubt, used also for 擬 to decide.

疏 ,Shu, Herbs, open, coarse.

楚 'Ch'u, Pain, grief.

## 104. 疒

病 Ping', Sickness.

疾 Chi', Malady.

痛 T'ung', ,t'eng, Pain.

痕 ,Hen, A scar, a blow.

## 105. 癶

登 ,Teng, Ascend.

發 Fa', ,fa, Raise, start, produce.

## 106. 白

百 Pe', 'Pai, } A hundred.

皆 ,Chie, All.

白 Po', ,pai, White.

皇 ,Hwang, Greatest, emperor.

的 Ti', Target, exact, a particle.

## 107. 皮

皮 ,P'i, Skin.

## 108. 皿

益 I', More, advantage.

盛 Sheng', Full, abundant. Ch'eng, Fill.

盈 ˓Ying, Full, overflowing.
盡 Chin', Exhaust, finish, altogether.
監 Chien', Note, survey.
盍 Ho', Why not?
皿 'Min, Vessel, instrument.
盜 Tau', Rob.
盟 ˓Meng, Alliance, pact.
盤 ˓P'an, Dish, board.
盪 Tang', A tub, large, enlarge.

## 109. 目

眞 ˏChen, True.
督 Tu', Supervise.
衆 Chung', Many.
目 Mu', Eye.
眷 Chiuen', A relative, to protect.
直 Ch', Straight.
置 Ch', Locate, dispose of.
省 'Sing, 'sheng, Examine, spare, province.
看 ˏK'an, Look, see.
眼 'Yen, Eyes.
瞽 'Ku, Blind.
瞶 Kw'e', Blind.
瞻 ˏChan, Look at.
矚 Chu, Observe intently.
眠 ˓Mien, Slumber.
睡 Shue', Sleep.
瞬 Shun', Wink of an eye.
盼 P'an', Look, hope.
睇 T'i', A glance.

## 110. 矛

矛 ˓Mau, Spear.
務 Wu', Business, earnestly.
矜 ˏChin, Boast, admire, pity.

## 111. 矢

知 ˏCh, Know.
矢 Sh', Arrow, an oath.
短 'Toan, Short.
矧 'Shen, How much more.

## 112. 石

石 Sh' (c) ˓shi, Stone.
破 P'o', Break, burst, open,
磐 ˓P'an, A broad rock.
磨 ˓Mo (c) ˏmo, A millstone.
硫 ˓Liu, Sulphur.
磬 Ch'ing', A stone bell or cymbal.
碼 Ma, Cornelian, a yard, numerical figures.

碯 *Nau*, Agate, cornelian.
碔 *'Wu*, A fine stone, but not a gem.
砆 *,Fu*, A stone, a false gem.
確 *Ch'io'*, Solid, real, reliable.

## 113. 示

神 *꜀Shen*, God, spirit.
祭 *Tsi'*, Sacrifice, offering.
福 *Fu'*, Happiness.
禮 *'Li*, Rites, politeness, propriety.
視 *Sh'*, To view, to treat.
禁 *Chin'*, Prohibit.
祝 *Chu'*, *꜀chu*, Bless, pray.
祈 *꜀Ch'i*, Pray, beg.
禱 *'Tau*, Supplicate, pray.
禍 *Hwo'*, Misery, calamity.
示 *Sh'*, Show, inform, a proclamation.
祖 *'Tsu*, Grandfather, ancestor.
祜 *'Hu*, Bliss, prosperity.
祀 *S'*, Sacrifice, offering.
禦 *'Ü*, Withstand, resist.
祥 *꜀Siang*, Prosperity, luck.

## 114. 禸

禽 *꜀Ch'in*, Fowls, birds.

## 115. 禾

禾 *꜀Ho*, Growing rice.
穌 *,Su*, Revive, *Yesu*, Jesus.
稱 *,Ch'eng*, Praise, address, weigh, fit.
穀 *Ku'*, Grain.
私 *,S*, Private, selfish.
種 *Chung'*, Plant, kind, sort.
稽 *,Chi*, Search, examine.
秉 *'Ping*, Hold fast, adhere, handful.
積 *Tsi'*, Collect, store up.
稅 *Shue'*, Taxes, duties.
穢 *Hwe'*, Filth.
移 *꜀I*, Move, change.
秘 *,Pi*, Secret.
程 *꜀Ch'eng*, Road, journey.
秋 *,Ch'iu*, Autumn.
廩 *'Lin*, Store-house.
穩 *'Wen*, Firm, secure.
秦 *꜀Ch'in*, Name of a dynasty.
秀 *Siu'*, Bloom, flourish, elegant.
穆 *Mu'*, Sublime, benign.

## 116. 穴

穴 *Hiue'*, Cave, tomb.

空 ,*K'ung*, Empty.

窘 '*Ch'ün*, Persecute.

窮 ,*Ch'iung*, Exhaust, poor.

竊 *Ch'ie'*, Steal, stealthy.

穹 ,*Ch'iung*, Lofty, canopy of heaven.

突 *T'u'*, Sudden, rush.

究 ,*Kiu*, Search out.

窓 ,*Chw'ang*, Window.

窺 ,*Kw'ei*, Pry, spy.

## 117. 立

立 *Li'*, Stand.

章 ,*Chang*, Chapter, display.

端 ,*Toan*, Correct, an item, commencement.

童 ,*T'ung*, Boy, maiden.

竭 *Chie'*, Exhaust, complete.

竟 *Ching'*, Finally.

竚 *Chu'*, Wait, expect.

競 *Ching'*, Strive, earnest.

## 118. 竹

第 *Ti'*, Number, mansion, only.

等 '*Teng*, Class, equal, &c.

節 *Chie'*, Joint, verse.

築 *Chu'*, Found, build.

答 *Ta'* \ ..

篇 ,*P'ien*, Essay, chapter, section.

笑 *Siau'*, Laugh, smile.

簡 '*Chien*, Brief, convenient.

筵 ,*Yen*, Feast, invite.

篤 '*Tu*, Real, sincere.

管 '*Kwan*, Govern.

算 *Soan'*, Estimate, calculate.

簪 ,*Tsen*, Hairpin.

筯 *Chu'*, Chopstick.

筆 '*Pi*, Pencil.

竹 *Chu'*, Bamboo.

簫 ,*Siau*, Flute, flageolet.

竽 ,*Ü*, Flute, piper.

## 119. 米

米 '*Mi*, Rice.

精 ,*Ching*, Essence, fine, accurate.

粗 ,*Ts'u*, Coarse.

糧 ,*Liang*, Provender.

粉 '*Fen*, Starch, flour.

## 120. 糸

約 *Yo'*, Agreement, narrow, sparing.

素 *Su‘*, Plain, unadorned, ordinary, hitherto.

細 *Si‘*, Fine, small.

緣 *ˏYuen*, Because, therefore, pre-established harmony.

終 ˏ*Chung*, End, final, not at all.

結 *Chie‘*, Tie, connect.

維 ˏ*We*, Connect, only, merely.

總 ˏ*Tsung*, Generally, altogether.

統 ’*T‘ung*, Entire, general.

絕 *Chiue‘*, Cut off, extinguish.

紀 *Chi‘*, Period of 12 years, a record.

經 ˏ*Ching*, Rule, classic, warp, longitude, experience.

編 ˏ*Pien*, To twine, compose verses or books.

納 *Na‘*, Pay, give, receive.

給 *Chi‘*, (c) ’*chi*, ’*kei*, Give.

綱 ˏ*Kang*, Main principles.

綿 ˏ*Mien*, { Floss, cottony silk,

緜 extended, connected.

縱 ˏ*Tsung*, Let loose, suppose, a direct line.

繼 *Chi‘*, To succeed, connect with.

繁 ˏ*Fan*, Numerous, abundant.

純 ˏ*Ch‘un*, Pure, sincere, perfect.

網 ’*Wang*, A net.

紅 ˏ*Hung*, Red.

綻 *Chan‘*, A rip, rent, hole.

索 ’*So*, A cord, to seek.

繫 *Hi‘*, Tie, bind.

系 *Hi‘*, Family line, connect.

緯 ’*We*, Transverse, woof, latitude.

緬 *Mien‘*, Fine threads, connected thought, ponder.

繚 ˏ*Liau* { Wind around, envi-

繞 ’*Jau*, ron, saunter.

縷 ’*Lü*, A filament, a nice distinction.

締 *T‘i‘*, Indissolubly joined, adapted.

綺 ’*Ch‘i*, Silk gauze.

絺 ˏ*Chï*, Grass cloth.

綌 ˏ*Hi*, Hemp cloth.

繡 *Siu‘*, Embroider, decorate.

絲 ˏ*S*, Silk thread, raw silk.

綠 *Lü‘*, Green.

累 ’*Le*, Often, entangle.

織 *Chï‘*, Weave.

組 *’Tsu*, Fringe, tape, badge of office.

紬 *‚Ch‘eu*, Draw threads for weaving, silk, pongee.

繹 *I‘*, Draw out, unravel.

緝 *Chi‘*, Twist, join, continue, compose ; pursue, seize.

## 121. 缶

缺 *Ch‘iue‘*, Deficit, few, gap, official post.

## 122. 网

罪 *Tsue‘*, Sin, guilt.

羅 *‚Lo*, A net, gauze.

罕 *’Han*, Rare, admire.

罰 *Fa‘*, Punish, fine.

罹 *‚Li, lo*, Encounter evil, grief.

署 *’Shu*, Yamên, office, manage, act pro tempore.

罔 *’Wang*, Without, privative.

## 123. 羊

羊 *‚Yang*, Sheep, goat.

羣 *‚Ch‘iün*, Herd.

義 *I‘*, Justice, righteousness, kindness, friendship, patriotism.

美 *’Me*, Beautiful.

羔 *‚Kau*, Lamb.

羞 *‚Siu*, Shame.

羨 *Sien‘*, Covet, long for.

羶 *‚Shan*, Fetid, rank odor.

## 124. 羽

翰 *Han‘*, A quill.

翼 *I‘*, Wing, aid.

習 *Si‘*, Repeat, imitate, learn.

翦 *’Chien*, Destroy.

翠 *Ts‘ue‘*, A green bird.

耀 *Yo‘*, *yau‘*, Splendor.

翕 *Hi‘*, Unite, combine.

翥 *’Chu*, To soar.

翔 *’Siang*, Gyrate.

翱 *‚Au*, Hover.

翹 *‚Ch‘iau*, High, raise the head.

## 125. 老

者 *’Che*, A relative ref. to persons and things.

老 *’Lau*, Old, aged.

耆 *‚Ch‘i*, Aged, an elder.

耇 *’Keu*, Superannuated, wrinkled.

## 126. 而

而 *‚Er*, And, but.

耑 ,*Chwen*, Solely, bent on.
耐 *Nai'*, Patience, perseverance.

## 127. 耒

耕 ,*Keng*, Plow.

## 128. 耳

耳 '*Er*, Ear, a euphonic.
聖 *Sheng'*, Sacred, sage, holy.
聽 ,*T'ing*, Hear, allow.
聞 ,*Wen*, Hear, perceive.
耶 ,*Ye*, Interrogative final, *Ye su*, Jesus.
聲 ,*Sheng*, Sound, report, fame.
聚 *Chü'*, Collect.
聰 ,*Ts'ung*, Wise, quick-eared.
職 *Ch'*, Office.
聾 ,*Lung*, Deaf.
聯 ,*Lien*, Unite, connect.

## 129. 聿

肇 *Chau'*, Commence, found.
肅 *Su'*, Solemn, serious.
肄 *I'*, Practice, labor.

## 130. 肉

能 ,*Neng*, Able, can.
肉 *Ju'*, *jeu'*, Flesh.
脫 *T'o'*, Extricate.
膏 ,*Kau*, Grease, anoint.
背 *Pei'*, Back, carry on the back, turn the back, recite.
胎 ,*T'ai*, The womb.
育 *Ü'*, Rear, nurture.
肯 '*K'en*, Willing.
腓 ,*Fe*, Leg bones.
肥 ,*Fei*, Fat.
膽 '*Tan*, Gall, courage.
腹 '*Fu*, Bosom, belly.
膚 ,*Fu*, Skin.
胞 ,*Pau*, Womb.
胚 '*P'i*, Conception, fœtus.
臚 ,*Lu*, Order, record.
脂 ,*Ch*, Fat, essence.
胡 ,*Hu*, Why? Northern barbarians.
腥 ,*Sing*, A fishy odor.
肴 ,*Yau*, Meats, viands.
臠 '*Loan*, Minced meat.
腐 '*Fu*, Decayed, rotten.
胥 ,*Hü*, Altogether, almost.

## 131. 臣

臣 ,*Ch'en*, Officer, liege.
臨 ,*Lin*, Arrive, confront.

臥 *Wo*ʿ, Lie down, sleep.

## 132. 自

自 *Tsʿ*, Self, of course, from.

臭 *Hiuʿ*, *ch'euʿ*, To smell, stench.

## 133. 至

至 *Chʿ*, Arrive at, most.

到 *Tauʿ*, To, at, arrive.

臺 ˛*T'ai*, Terrace, stage.

臻 ˏ*Chen*, Arrive at, most.

## 134. 臼

與 ʾ*Ü*, With, give, interrogative?

舊 *Chiuʿ*, Old, ancient.

興 ˏ*Hing*, Rise, raise, flourish.

舁 ˏ*Ü*, Bear aloft, sustain.

## 135. 舌

舍 *She*, Cottage, yield, give up.

## 137. 舟

舟 ˏ*Cheu*, Ship, vessel.

船 ˛*Chw'en*, Boat, ship.

## 138. 艮

良 ˛*Liang*, Good, virtuous, rather.

艱 ˏ*Chien*, Difficult.

## 139. 色

色 *Seʿ*, ʾ*shai*, Color, beauty, sensuality.

## 140. 艸

萬 *Wanʿ*, A myriad, all.

若 *Joʿ*, If, suppose, like, that, his, its.

蓋 *Kaiʿ*, Because, cover.

華 ˏ*Hwa*, Flower, glory.

蒙 ˛*Meng*, Simple, cover, receive favor.

苦 ʾ*K'u*, Bitter.

葬 *Tsangʿ*, Inter.

蓮 ˛*Lien*, Water lily.

蘭 ˛*Lan*, A flower, Aglaia odorata.

藏 ˛*Ts'ang*, Conceal, store.

荒 ˏ*Hwang*, Wild, waste, barren.

莫 *Moʿ*, No, not, must not

英 ˏ*Ying*, Bloom, brave, heroic.

花 ˏ*Hwa*, Flower.

藉 *Chieʿ*, Reliance, pretext, record.

葡 ˛*P'u* } Grape.
萄 ˛*T'au*, }

著 *Choʿ*, *chuʿ*, To send, publish, display. An affix expressive of completion.

落 Lo', lau', Fall.
苟 'Keu, If, doubtful, irregular.
蒼 ,Ts'ang, Azure.
薄 Po', ₍pau, Thin.
護 Hu', Protect.
荷 Ho', Lotus, to bear, receive favor.
蔽 Pi', Veil, to obscure.
藐 'Miau, Minute, slight.
藥 Yo', yau', Medicine.
蕪 ₍Wu, Weeds, rubbish.
薨 'Hung, Death of a noble.
菓 ,Kwo, Fruits.
葉 Ye', Leaves.
蘇 ,Su, or 穌, To revive.
草 'Ts'au, Grass.
苗 ₍Miau, Germ, aboriginal.
茂 Mau', Flourishing, abundant.
薦 Chien', Recommend.
葛 'Ko (c) ₍ko, Flax.
蔭 Yin', Shade, by privilege of birth.
苑 Yuen', Pasture, park.
芳 ,Fang, Fragrance.
藝 I', Plant, cultivate, craft, art.
蓄 Hü', Nourish, hoard.
菜 Ts'ai', Herbs.
薇 ,We, Pot herbs.
葵 ₍Kw'e, Malvaceous plants, the sunflower.
芥 Chie', Mustard.
芬 ,Fen, Perfume of flowers.
蕩 Tang', Vagrant, vast, wasteful.
蕃 Luxuriant.

## 141. 虍

處 'Ch'u, Ch'u', Place, dwell, to place.
虛 ,Hü, Empty, vain.
號 Hau', Sign, title, cry.
虔 ,Ch'ien, Earnest, devout.
虐 Nio', Oppress, injure.
虜 'Lo, Prisoner, ravage.

## 142. 虫

蛇 ₍She, Serpent.
蜜 Mi', Honey.
蟲 ₍Ch'ung, Insect, worm.
蠻 ₍Man, Savage.
螺 ₍Lo, A Small sea shell.

蝗 ˎHwang, Locust.
蝦 ˏHia, Shrimp, crawfish.
蛤 ʼKo, Oyster, muscle.
蠶 ˎTs'an, Silk-worm.
蛛 ˏChu, Spider.
蚓 ʼYin, Earth-worm.
蟬 ˎCh'an, A kind of locust.
蟻 Iʿ, Ants.
蠅 ˎYing, Flies.

## 143. 血

血 Blood.

## 144. 行

行 ˎHing, hang, Walk, act, hong.
街 ˏChie, Street.
衛 Weʿ, Protect, defend.
術 Shuʿ, Method.
衢 ˎCh'ü, Street, road.
衡 ˎHeng, Transverse.
衍 ʽYen, Inundate, amplify.
衒 ˎHiuen, Brag, boast, display, for 眩 to dazzle.

## 145. 衣

衣 ˏI, Clothes.
初 ˏCh'u, Beginning.
被 Peʿ, Receive, prefix to passive verbs.
裔 ˏI, Posterity, tribe.
哀 ˏAi, Grief, sorrow, melancholy.
襲 Siʿ, Lurk, take by surprise, hereditary.
衷 ˏChung, Heart, nature.
製 Chʿ, Manufacture.
衰 ˏShwai, Decay.
袍 ˎP'au, Mantle, robe.
囊 ˎNang, Bag, sack, yesterday.
補 ʼPu, Patch, mend.
表 ʼPiau, Outside, display, example.
裸 ʼLo, Naked.
裳 ˎCh'ang, Clothes, lower garments.
複 Fuʿ, Repeated, double.
裘 ˎCh'iu, Jacket, vest.
襟 ˏChin, Skirt.
袖 Siuʿ, Sleeve.
裝 ˏChwang, Adorn, repair, lade a ship.
裁 ˎTs'ai, Cut, trim, shear.
裂 Lieʿ, Rend, tear.

## 146. 襾

西 ,*Si*, West.

要 *Yau*ʿ, Wish, will, important.

覆 *Fu*ʿ, Reply, repeat, overturn.

覈 *Ho*ʿ, Investigate, search, verify, distinguish.

## 147. 見

見 *Chien*ʿ, *hien*ʿ, See, be seen, appear.

親 ,*Ch'in*, Kindred, intimacy, self, own.

現 *Hien*ʿ, At present, appear.

觀 ,*Kwan*, Behold, consider.

覺 *Chio*ʿ, *chiau*ʿ, Conscious, feel, awake.

覩 *Tu*ʿ, Look, see.

覲 *Chin*ʿ, Interview with a superior.

覿 *Ti*ʿ, See, face to face.

覓 *Mi*ʿ, Seek.

## 148. 角

角 *Chio*ʿ, '*chiau*, Horn, corner.

解 '*Chie*, Untie, explain.

觚 ꜀*Ku*, Square, law, plan, a square vessel, a wine cup.

## 149. 言

言 ꜀*Yen*, Words, speak.

謂 *We*ʿ, Say, call.

諸 ,*Chu*, Many, all, plural prefix, in, at.

訓 *Hiün*ʿ, Instruct.

詳 ꜀*Hiang*, Full, minute, in detail.

譬 *P'i*ʿ, Compare, parable.

試 *Sh*ʿ, Try, endeavor.

諭 *Ü*ʿ, Edict, command.

誡 *Chie*ʿ, Ordinance, commandment.

謀 ꜀*Mo*, Plan, plot.

該 ,*Kai*, Ought, altogether, the said.

謝 *Sie*ʿ, To thank, to decline.

許 '*Hü*, Promise, approve; much.

詛 '*Tsu*, Curse, imprecation.

請 '*Ch'ing*, Invite, request, inquire.

讚 *Tsan*ʿ, Praise.

記 *Chi*ʿ, Record, remember.

誠 ꜀*Ch'eng*, Sincere, honest.

證 *Cheng*ʿ, Evidence, witness.

語 '*Ü*, Words, discourse.

詣 *I*ʿ, Visit.

說 *Shwo*ʿ, Speak, narrative.

計 *Chi'*, Count, calculate.
誰 *ˏShue*, Who?
讓 *Jang'*, Yield, relinquish.
論 *Lun'*, *ˏlun*, Discourse, treatise.
誓 *Sh'*, Oath, swear.
識 *Sh'*, Know, remember.
議 *I'*, Discuss, negotiate.
變 *Pien'*, Turn, change.
訟 *Sung'*, Accuse, law-suit.
詞 *ˏTs'* Words, verses, statement.
託 *T'o'*, *(c) ˏt'o*, Entrust, pretend.
詔 *Chau'*, Edict, proclamation by the sovereign.
誘 *Yiu'*, Win, beguile, persuade.
誨 *Hwe'*, Instruct, admonish.
謳 *ˏEu*, Recite, sing.
誦 *Sung'*, Read, recite.
詩 *ˏSh*, Verses, poetry.
講 *'Chiang*, Speak, discourse.
誕 *Tan'*, Birth, advent of a great man, great, false.
譴 *'Ch'ien*, Rebuke, punish.
詭 *'Kwe*, Deceit.
謙 *'Ch'ien*, Modest.
讀 *Tu'*, *(c) ˏtu*, Read.
認 *Jen'*, Recognize, acknowledge.
誇 *ˏKw'a*, Boast.
詰 *Chie'*, Inquire.
謹 *'Chin*, Careful, respectful.
譽 *ˏÜ*, Praise.
謗 *Pang'*, Slander.
誤 *Wu'*, Mistake, error.
謬 *Miu'*, Error.
調 *ˏT'iau*, *tiau'*, Turn, temper, mix, musical air.
辯 *Pien'*, Eloquent, distinguish, vindicate.
訝 *Ya'*, Frightened, astonished.
諂 *'Ch'an*, Flattery.
譏 *ˏChi*, Ridicule.
評 *ˏP'ing*, Censure, criticism.
詠 *'Yung*, Sing.
諧 *ˏHie*, Harmony.
詎 *Chü'*, Who? How?
譜 *'Pu*, Record, catalogue.
諏 *ˏTseu*, Consult, inquire.
警 *'Ching*, Warn, caution, exhort, to respect.

## 150. 谷

谷 *Ku*ʿ, Valley.

## 151. 豆

豈 ʾ*Chʻi*, How ?

豐 ˏ*Feng*, Opulent.

豔 *Yen*ʿ, Beauty.

## 152. 豕

象 ˏ*Siang*, Elephant, ivory, figure, emblem.

豳 ˏ*Ping*, Name of a state.

豚 ˛*Tʻun*, A pig.

豪 ˛*Hau*, Rich, opulent.

豫 *Ü*ʿ, Beforehand, doubt, suspicion, luxury.

## 153. 豸

貌 *Mau*ʿ, Appearance, face.

貊 *Mo*ʿ, Barbarian.

## 154. 貝

賜 *Ts*ʿ, Bestow, confer.

贖 *Shu*ʿ, Redeem.

負 *Fu*ʿ, Bear on the back, turn the back; repudiate obligations.

責 *Che*ʿ (c) ˛*tse*, Rebuke, reprove.

財 ˛*Tsʻai*, Riches.

貴 *Kwei*ʿ, Honorable.

賽 *Sai*ʿ, Vie, display.

貧 *Pʻin*, Poor.

貨 *Hwo*ʿ, Goods.

賦 *Fu*ʿ, Conferred by heaven.

質 *Ch*ʿ, Talent, matter, pledge, hostage.

貪 ˏ*Tʻan*, Covet.

買 ʾ*Mai*, Buy.

賣 *Mai*ʿ, Sell.

貢 *Kung*ʿ, Tribute.

賢 ˛*Hien*, Worthy, wise, gifted.

賓 ˏ*Pin*, Guest, retainer.

賞 ʾ*Shang*, Reward.

賊 *Tse*ʿ (c) ˛*tsei*, Thief, steal, injure.

資 ˏ*Ts*, Means, supply, rely on.

貯 *Chu*ʿ, Hoard, store up.

賡 ˏ*Keng*, Repeat or continue a song.

## 155. 赤

赦 *She*ʿ, Forgive.

赤 *Cʻh*ʿ, Red, sincere, earnest.

赫 *Ho*ʿ, Awful, majestic.

## 156. 走

越 *Yue*ʿ, Pass, leap over.

起 ʾ*Chʻi*, Rise, raise.

走 ʾ*Tseu*, Walk, run, run away.

趨 ,*Ch'ü*, Run, run towards.
赴 *Fu'*, Go.
趁 *Ch'en'*, Avail of.

## 157. 足

路 *Lu'*, Road, way.
足 *Tsu' (c) ˛tsu*, Foot, enough.
踐 *Chien'*, Tread.
蹟 *Chi'*, Track.
跪 *Kwei'*, Kneel.
蹈 *'Tau*, Tread, stamp on.
躑 *Chi'*, Going back and forth.
躅 *Chu'*, To walk unsteadily.
躇 ˛*Chu*, Overleaping, hesitating.
躊 ˛*Ch'eu*, Undecided.
躋 *Chi'*, Cling, climb, rise.
跳 *T'iau'*, Leap.
躍 *Yo'*, Spring, dance.
跣 *'Sien*, Barefoot.
跽 *Kwei'*, Kneel.
踧 *Ts'u'*, } To walk reverently.
踖 *Si'*, }

## 158. 身

身 ,*Shen*, Body, person.
躬 ,*Kung*, Person, self.
軀 ,*Ch'ü*, Body, person.

## 159. 車

車 ,*Chü* ,*ch'e*, Wagon, chariot.
較 *Chiau'*, Compare.
軍 ,*Chiün*, Army.
轄 *Hia'*, Control.
載 *Tsai'*, Convey, a year.
輕 ,*Ch'ing*, Light.
輩 *Pei'*, Class, grade, generation.
輪 ˛*Lun*, Wheel.
輸 ,*Shu*, Rotate, pay out, lose, be beaten.
轉 ,*Chwen*, Turn.
輝 ,*Hwe*, Splendor, lustre.
輿 ˛*Ü*, Imperial domain.
輻 *'Fu*, Spokes of a wheel, with next to collect.
輳 ,*Ts'eu*, Hub of a wheel.
輔 *'Fu*, Aid.
轟 ,*Hung*, Booming, as of cannon.

## 160. 辛

幸 *Hing'*, Fortunate.
辜 ,*Ku*, Offence, guilt.
辭 ˛*T's*, Words, to decline.

速成漢語

辨 Pien', Distinguish.
辛 ,Sin, Bitter, acrid.

## 161. 辰

辱 Ju', Shame, disgrace.
農 ,Nung, Husbandman.
辰 ,Ch'en, Time, the 5th hour.

## 162. 辵

遂 ,Sue, Then, thereon, at once.
迦 ,Chia, A Buddhist name.
道 Tau', Way, method, truth, doctrine, reason.
過 Kwo', Pass, cross over, transgress.
逃 ,T'au, Escape, fly.
選 'Hiuen, Select, choose.
追 ,Chue, Pursue.
造 Tsau', Create, make.
遠 'Yuen, Far, long.
避 Pi', Avoid, escape.
迨 Tai', Until.
返 'Fan, Return.
適 Sh', Meet, suit, go.
遺 ,I, Omit, transmit, let fall, leave behind.
遵 ,Tsun, Observe, obey.
遣 'Ch'ien, Send.

違 ,We, Oppose, withdraw from.
逆 Ni', Contrary, resist.
遭 ,Tsau, Meet, encounter.
途 ,T'u, Path, road.
遍 Pien', Everywhere.
速 Su' (c) ,su, Hasten.
通 ,T'ung, Open, reasonable.
達 Ta', Open, intelligent, prosperous.
逐 Chu', Eject, persecute.
近 Chin', Near.
邀 ,Yau, Invite.
述 Shu', (c) ,shu, Narrate, relate.
進 Chin', Enter.
迫 P'o', Urge.
迷 ,Mi, Delude, astray.
遐 ,Hia, Remote.
邇 'Er, Near.
遄 ,Toan, Go and come, haste.
遊 ,Yiu, Roam, rove.
運 Yün', Revolve, circulate, transport.
還 ,Hwan, Return.
連 ,Lien, Connect, together.
迎 ,Ying, Meet, welcome.

遷 ,Ch'ien, Remove.
送 Sung, To give a present, escort away.
遁 Tun', Escape.
退 T'ue, Retire.
逾 ˛Ü, Leap over, surpass.
遜 Hiün', Yielding, modest.
迄 'Ch'ï, End, finish.
迹 Chi', Footstep.
迅 Hiün', Vivid, energetic.
逝 Sh', Passing, vanishing.
遽 Chü', Suddenly.
迢 ˛T'iau, Distant, remote.
遞 Ti', Transmit, distant.
遴 ˛Lin, Elect, choose.
迓 Ya', Meet, welcome, invite.
遑 ,Hwang, Leisure, vacant.
逸 I', Pleasure, escape.
遨 ˛Au, Roam, saunter.
邃 Sue, In the rear, far back, as a suite of rooms.
逢 ˛Feng, Meet.
邊 ,Pien, Side, border.

## 163. 邑

邑 I', City, district.

鄉 ,Hiang, Village, neighborhood, the country.
邦 ,Pang, Nation, state.
都 ,Tu, Capital city.
郊 ,Chiau, Suburban fields.
却 Ch'io', Reject, forsooth.
那 Na', 'na, That, how, where?
郇 ˛Hiün, Name of a place, Zion.
邪 ˛Sie, Oblique, perverse, corrupt.
部 Pu', Class, sort, bureau, board, volume.
鄰 ˛Lin, Neighbor.

## 164. 酉

醫 ,I, Heal.
醒 'Sing, Awake.
酬 ˛Ch'eu, Reciprocate, friendly intercourse.
釁 Hin', Fault, defect, quarrel.
酵 Kiau', Leaven, yeast.
配 P'ei', Unite, fit together.
釀 'Niang, Ferment.
酣 ,Han, Intoxicate.
酸 ,Soan, Sour.

## 165. 釆

釋 Sh', Loose, release, expound, Buddhist.

## 166. 里

里 ꜀*Li*, Neighborhood, Chinese mile, 1897½ Eng. ft. in geography, 1460½ ft., $\frac{1}{250}$ of a deg.

野 ʼ*Ye*, Pasture, wilderness.

重 *Chung*ʻ, ꜀*chʻung*, Heavy, double, again.

量 ꜀*Liang*, *liang*ʻ, Measure, capacity.

## 167. 金

金 ˏ*Chin*, Gold, metal.

錫 *Si*ʻ, Tin, bestow.

錄 *Lu*ʻ, Record, inscribe.

銀 ꜀*Yin*, Silver.

銅 ꜀*Tʻung*, Copper, brass.

鐵 ʼ*Tʻie*, Iron.

鑑 *Chien*ʻ, Mirror.

鑒 *Chien*ʻ, Inspect, oversee.

鑄 *Chu*ʻ, Cast, found.

錢 ꜀*Chʻien*, Cash, money.

釘 ꜀*Ting*, Nail.

鋒 ˏ*Feng*, Point, edge.

錯 *Tsʻo*ʻ, Mistake, scattered.

鑿 *Tso*ʻ, ꜀*tsau*, Bore, chisel.

鐲 *Cho*ʻ, Bracelet.

鐶 ꜀*Hwan*, Ring.

錦 ʼ*Chin*, Gilding, brocade.

鑲 ˏ*Siang*, Border, inlaid.

鐘 ˏ*Chung*, Bell, clock.

鑪 ꜀*Lu*, Furnace.

鏘 ˏ*Chʻiang*, } A jingling sound.

鏗 ˏ*Kʻeng*, }

鈴 ꜀*Ling*, A small bell.

鍾 ˏ*Chung*, To love, a measure, goblet.

鈞 ˏ*Chüün*, Equal, just, venerable, a weight of 30 catties.

## 168. 長

長 ʼ*Chang*, ꜀*Chʻang*, Long, elder, superior.

## 169. 門

門 ꜀*Men*, Gate, door.

闢 *Pʻi*ʻ, Open.

間 *Chien*ʻ, In, between.

開 ˏ*Kʻai*, Open.

閉 *Pi*ʻ, Shut.

閃 ʼ*Shan*, Dart.

闊 *Kʻo*ʻ, Wide.

閱 *Yue*ʻ, Look over, pass over.

閣 *Ko*ʻ, Gallery.

閑 ꜀*Hien*, Vacant, idle.

## 170. 阜

降 *Chiang*‘, ꜁*hiang*, Come down, send down, degrade, surrender.

隱 ’*Yin*, Hide, conceal.

陳 ꜁*Ch‘en*, Display, arrange, order of battle.

陷 *Hien*‘, Fall into, entrap.

隨 ꜁*Sue*, Follow, at option.

阿 ꜁*O*, Cringe, flatter, lean on, partial, diminutive, a prefix to names.

陰 ’*Yin*, The dark, or female principle.

除 ꜁*Chu*, Exclude, besides; in arithmetic, division.

隅 ꜁*Ü*, Corner.

際 *Chi*‘, Limit, border, junction.

阻 ’*Tsu*, Obstacle, hinder.

陸 *Lu*‘, Dry land, by land.

隙 *Hi*‘, A quarrel, cranny.

防 ꜁*Fang*, Guard against.

院 *Yuen*‘, Court, hall, office.

附 ’*Fu* (c) ꜀*fu*, Append.

險 ’*Hien*, Steep, perilous.

陟 *Ch*‘, Climb, promotion.

限 *Hien*‘, Limit.

## 172. 隹

雅 ’*Ya*, Refined, literary.

難 ꜁*Nan*, Hard, difficult.

離 ꜁*Li*, Leave.

雖 ꜁*Sue*, Though.

雜 *Tsa*‘, (c) ꜁*tsa*, Mixed, promiscuous.

雙 ꜀*Shwang*, Double, a pair.

雕 ꜀*Tiau*, Carve, adorn, tattoo.

雞 ꜀*Chi*, Chicken.

雀 *Ch‘io*‘, ’*ch‘iau*, Sparrow, bird.

雍 ꜀*Yung*, Harmony.

## 173. 雨

靈 ꜁*Ling*, Spirit, intelligent, effectual.

雨 ’*Ü*, Rain.

雲 ꜁*Yün*, Clouds.

震 *Chen*‘, Quake, convulse.

雪 ’*Hiue*, Snow.

露 *Lu*‘, Dew.

需 ꜀*Hü*, Need, must.

零 ꜁*Ling*, Scattering, remnant.

霄 ꜀*Siau*, A halo, fleecy clouds, heaven.

霞 ꜁*Hia*, Glow of sunset.

霓 ꜁*Ni*, Rainbow.

雷 ˛Lue, Thunder.
霜 ˏShwang, Frost.
霪 ˛Yin, Excessive rains.
霆 ˛T'ing, Sharp thunder.
電 Tien', Lightning.

## 174. 靑

靑 ˏCh'ing, Green.
靜 Ching', Still, silent.
眚 'Sheng, Fault, crime.

## 175. 非

非 ˏFe, Not, is not, wrong.
靡 ˛Mi, Profuse, not, without.

## 176. 面

面 Mien', Face.

## 177. 革

革 Ko', Leather, change, dismiss.
鞫 Chü', Judge, condemn.
韁 ˏChiang, Bridle.

## 178. 韋

韞 Yün', Guard, conceal.

## 180. 音

音 ˏYin, Voice, sound.
響 'Hiang, Echo.
韻 Yün', Rhyme.
韶 ˛Shau, Name of an air and instrument.

## 181. 頁

顯 'Hien, Reveal, display.
類 Le', Class, species.
頓 Tun', Bow the head, instantly, at once.
願 Yüen', Willing, desirous.
顧 Ku', Look, regard.
賴 Lai', Depend on.
順 Shun', Obey, yield, unimpeded.
預 Ü', Beforehand, prepare.
頌 Sung', Praise.
須 ˏHü, Must.
頒 ˏPan, Distribute.
頭 ˛T'eu, Head.
領 'Ling, Neck. Yin-ling, Stretch the neck.
頂 'Ting, Bear on the head, superlative.
顢 ˛Man, Large face.
頇 ˏHan, Bald; with the preceding, stupid.
頗 ˏP'o, Somewhat, rather, very.

題 ˓T'i, Theme, subject.
頃 ˏCh'ing, 100 mow, an instant.
頻 ˓P'in, Incessant, urgent.
顏 Yen', Color, countenance.
頑 ˓Wan, Stupid, perverse.

## 182. 風

風 ˏFeng, Wind, custom, influence.

## 184. 食

食 Sh', Eat, food.
餅 'Ping, Loaf, cake.
養 'Yang, Nourish.
飲 'Yin, Drink.
餘 ˓Ü, Overplus.
饑 ˏChi, Hunger, dearth.
飢 ˏChi, Hunger.
飾 Sh', Ornament.
饒 ˓Jau, Generous in fare, in treatment, forgive.
饔 ˏYung, Breakfast.
飧 ˏSun, Supper.
飽 'Pau, Full fed, satisfied.
飫 Ü', Sated, filled.
饌 'Choan, Meats, dressed food.
饈 ˓Siu, Viands, dainties.
餌 'Er, Pastry, bait, allurement.
飯 Fan', Boiled rice.

## 185. 首

首 'Sheu, Head, chief, beginning

## 186. 香

香 ˏHiang, Incense.
馨 ˏHing, Fragrance.

## 187. 馬

馬 'Ma, Horse.
驢 ˓Lü, An ass.
驅 ˏCh'ü, Drive, expel.
駭 ˏHai, Fright.
驕 ˏChiau, Pride.
駐 Chu', Reside.
驗 Yen', Test, bear a test.
駕 Chia', Equipage, the Emperor, thou.
驚 ˏChing, Take fright.
騎 ˓Ch'i, Ride, rider.
駝 ˓To, Camel.
驟 Cheu', Sudden, gallop.
駛 'Sh, Sail.
驥 Chi', A fine horse.

騰 ˏ*Teng*, Mount up, run swiftly.
驊 ˏ*Hwa*, An elegant horse.
騮 ˓*Liu*, A bay or sorrel.
馳 ˓*Ch'ï*, Run, gallop.
騁 ʾ*Ch'eng*, Run swiftly.

188. 骨

體 ʾ*T'i*, Body, substance, members, sympathy.
骨 ʾ*Ku* (c) ˓*ku*, Bone.

189. 高

高 ˏ*Kau*, High.

190. 髟

髮 *Fa'*, Hair.
髫 ˓*T'iau*, Loose ringlets, young, youthful.
髦 *Mau'*, Long locks.

191. 鬥

鬬 *Teu'*, Contend.
鬨 *Hung'*, A confused noise.

192. 鬯

鬱 *Ü'*, Fragrant, pent, vexed.

193. 鬲

鬻 *Ü'*, Buy, sell.
融 ˏ*Yung*, Bright, blend, harmonize.

194. 鬼

鬼 ʾ*Kwei*, Ghost, devil.
魔 ˓*Mo*, Devil, temptation.
魂 ˓*Hwun*, Soul.

195. 魚

魚 ˓*Ü*, Fish.
魯 ʾ*Lu*, Stupid, name of a kingdom.
鮮 ˏ*Sien*, Fresh, rare.
鱗 ˓*Lin*, Scales, fish.
鯤 ˏ*Kw'en*, Leviathan.
鰲 ˓*Au*, A monster said to sustain the earth.
鯨 ˏ*Ching*, Whale.
鱷 ˏ*Ngo'*, Alligator.

196. 鳥

鳥 ˏ*Niau*, Bird.
鴿 *Ko'*, (c) ˓*ko*, Dove, pigeon.
鳴 ˓*Ming*, Cry, sound.
鳳 *Feng'*, Phœnix.
鸞 ˓*Loan*, Bird of paradise.
鶴 *Ho'*, ˓*hau*, Stork, crane.
鴻 ˓*Hung*, Wild goose.
鵲 *Ch'io'*, Magpie, daw, jay.

197. 鹵

鹽 ˓*Yen*, Salt.

198. 鹿

麗 *Li*', Beautiful, splendid.
麟 *Lin, Ki-lin*, an animal which appears at the birth of a sage.
麈 '*Chu*, A deer with a bushy tail, a fly brush.
麤 *Ts'u*, Coarse. 粗, 觕.

199. 麥

麥 *Mo*', *mai*', Wheat.

200. 麻

麻 *Ma*, Hemp.
麽 *Mo*, *ma*, Minute, delicate, interrogative.

201. 黃

黃 *Hwang*, Yellow.

203. 黑

默 *Mo*', Silent.
黑 *Ho*', *he*, Black.
黨 '*Tang*, Clan, company.
黛 *Tai*', Dark green.

205. 黽

黽 *Min*', Strive, urge, a frog.

鼈 *Pie*', (c) *pie*, A turtle supposed to hear with its eyes.
黿 *Yuen*, Tortoise.
鼉 *T'o*, A large iguana.

206. 鼎

鼎 '*Ting*, A censer.

207. 鼓

鼓 '*Ku*, Drum, excite.

210. 齊

齊 *Ch'i*, Evenly, united, name of a state.
齋 *Chai*, Studio, penance.

211. 齒

齒 '*Ch*', Upper front teeth.
齡 *Ling*, Front teeth, sign of age.

212. 龍

龍 *Lung*, Dragon.

213. 龜

龜 *Kwei*, Tortoise.

214. 龠

籲 *Yo*', Supplicate.

# 語言自邇集

（*Yü Yen Tzŭ Êrh Chi: A Progressive Course Designed to Assist the Student of Colloquial Chinese as Spoken in the Capital and the Metropolitan Department*）

〔英〕威妥瑪（Thomas Francis Wade）編

《語言自邇集》，英國威妥瑪編。威妥瑪（Thomas Francis Wade，一八一八—一八九五），英國漢學家。生於英國倫敦，一八四二年來華，一八八八年任劍橋大學首任漢學教授。著有《漢字習寫法》、《文件自邇集》等。與英國翟理斯（Herbert Allen Giles）合創之北京官話拼音系統「威妥瑪-翟理斯式拼音」影響甚深。此書專供學習北京及直隸衙門通行之漢語口語，屬首次對十九世紀中期北京官話之語音、詞彙及語法系統進行深入研究，與威氏同時編撰之書面語教材《文件自邇集》互爲補充。書分兩卷，内容涵蓋發音、部首、練習、問答等。一八六七年初版四卷本，一八八六年再版三卷本，一九〇三年三版兩卷本。據一九〇三年上海版影印。

# 語言自邇集

(YÜ YEN TZŬ ÊRH CHI).

A

## PROGRESSIVE COURSE

DESIGNED TO ASSIST THE STUDENT OF

# COLLOQUIAL CHINESE

AS SPOKEN IN THE CAPITAL AND THE METROPOLITAN DEPARTMENT.

IN TWO VOLUMES.

THIRD EDITION. (ABRIDGED.)

PREPARED BY

THOMAS FRANCIS WADE,

*Sometime H.B.M.'s Minister in China,*

AND

WALTER CAINE HILLIER,

*Sometime Chinese Secretary to H.B.M.'s Legation, Peking.*

VOL. I.

SHANGHAI—HONGKONG—YOKOHAMA—SINGAPORE

KELLY AND WALSH, LIMITED.

1903

# PUBLISHERS' PREFACE TO THIRD (ABRIDGED) EDITION.

In producing the present reprint of Sir Thomas Wade's great work in an abridged form, the Publishers have acted upon advice which was approved by Sir Walter Hillier—the joint Author of the 2nd edition published in 1886—and also with the sanction of Sir Thomas Wade's executors.

Since 1886 so many new text-books on Colloquial Chinese have appeared, that much of the "Tzŭ Êrh Chi" has been superseded in the curriculum of studies prescribed for Student Interpreters in the British Legation. The "Hundred Lessons" and "Graduate's Wooing" have been abandoned for many years in favour of other works, and as the "Tzŭ Êrh Chi" was primarily intended for the use of Consular Students it was decided—for the time being at least—to reprint only those Parts which have continued to hold their own as a text-book.

The present reprint contains therefore only Parts I. to IV., that is to say, the introductory Parts on Pronunciation and the Radicals, followed by the Forty Exercises and Ten Dialogues. In the opinion of competent authorities the student of Colloquial Pekingese has in these four Parts an introduction to the language which will not fail to appear to him more and more valuable as he progresses. The collection of characters to which he is introduced has been so carefully made, that a sound knowledge of them will furnish a solid foundation upon which further studies of the language can securely rest.

So much has been said and written for and against Sir Thomas Wade's system of transliteration that we will here add no more to this perennial argument than a request to the tyro: and that is, to remember that it is the only system of romanisation which has so far attained any widespread and lasting success.

As was explained in the Preface to the original edition, the title "Yü Yen Tzŭ Êrh Chi" was suggested by a passage in the Confucian work known as "The Doctrine of the Mean," which implies that in the attainment of proficiency—as in the accomplishment of a journey—the start must be made from what is near. "*Tzŭ Êrh*" means "*from what is near*" while *Yü Yen . . . chi* means "expressions (or spoken words) . . . collection (or compilation). The whole is therefore fairly rendered in the English title as a "Progressive Course in Colloquial Chinese."

SHANGHAI,
*April* 1903

# PART I.

## PRONUNCIATION.

*ia.* With the vowels distinct; not *ya*, but as in the Italian *piazza, Maria.* In some syllables terminating in *ia, iang, iao,* the *ia* is in certain tones almost *éa* or *eyah.* This is oftener observable where the initial is *l, m,* or *n ;* but even with these the usage is capricious.

*iai.* The *iaj* in the Italian *vecchiaja.*

*iao.* The vowels as in *ia* and *ao,* with the terminal peculiarity of the latter. This sound is also modified by the *tone.*

*ie.* With the vowels distinct, as in the Italian *siesta, niente.* The *i* is modified, as in the case of *ia,* under similar circumstances; that is, in certain tones *ie* inclines to become *éé,* or *eyeh,* often making *lien, nien* almost *leyen, neyen.*

*io.* Shorter than the Italian *io;* more nearly the French *io* in *pioche.*

*iu.* As a final, nearly *eeyew* or *eeoo,* at all times longer than our *ew.* Thus *chiu* is not *chew,* but rather *chyew,* and the tone may make the vowel sounds even more distinct. In the syllables *liu, niu,* the *i* is affected as in *ia, ie;* they become almost *leyew, neyew.* In *chiung, hsiung* (the only syllables ending in consonants into which I have introduced *iu*), it must be admitted that in most instances, though not in all, the *iung* is rather *eeyōng* than *eeyoong,* the *ō* representing *o* in *roll.*

*o.* Something between the vowel-sound in *awe, paw,* and that in *roll, toll.* When single, it commences with a slight consonantal sound, part nasal and guttural, which the *'ng* inadequately expresses, and is inflected at the close as if an *a* or *ah* were appended to it. The tones seriously modify this syllable. As a final the power of the vowel remains the same, with the same terminal inflection, and not altogether divested of the guttural peculiarity which it is not within the compass of our alphabet to reproduce. Let the reader, as an experiment, try to pronounce *lo* as *law,* prolonging the *aw* in his throat.

*ou.* In reality *ĕō;* the vowel-sounds in *burrow* when all the consonants are withdrawn ; in English, nearest the *ou* in *round, loud.*

*ü.* When uttered alone, as it is at times for *yü,* or when a final, nearest the vowel-sound in the French *eût, tu.* In *ün* it is not so long as in the French *une;* but nearer the *ün* in the German *München.*

*üa.* Occurs only in the final *üan,* which in some tones is *üen ;* the *ü* as above, but the *a* much flatter than in the final *an;* nearer the *an* in *antic.*

*üe.* The *ü* as above, the *e* as in *eh;* the vowel-sounds in the French *tu es* represent this combination perfectly.

*üo.* A disputed sound, used, if at all, interchangeably with *io* in certain syllables.

*u.* When single (as at times instead of *wu*), and when a final, the *oo* in *too;* in *un* and *ung* it is shorter, as in the Italian *punto, lungo.* In the latter final it vacillates between *ung* and *ōng,* being nasalised at the close so as to produce a sound between the French *long* and *longue.*

*ua.* As we pronounce it in Juan ; nearly *ooa,* which in many instances contracts to *wa.* In the final *uan, uang* it is also sometimes *óa* or *oá,* as the tones may rule.

*uai.* As in the Italian *guai;* the above sound *ua,* with the *i* in *ai* appended to it; the *u* subject to the same changes as in *ua.*

*uei.* The *u* as in *ua*, *uai*, often in value *w;* the *ei* as in *ei* final; the vowel-sounds in the French *jouer* answer fairly to *uei.*

*uê.* The *u* as in *ua;* the *ê* as explained before. It is found only in the final *uên*, which sounds as if written *ú-ŭn*, frequently *wên* or *wun*. It is in many cases difficult to distinguish *uên* from *un;* for instance, *kun* from *kuên.*

*ui.* The *u* as above, followed enclitically by *i*, as if *oo-y;* the vowel-sounds in *screwy;* more enclitic than in the French *Louis* or the Italian *lui*. It is in some tones *uei.*

*uo.* The *u* as above, the *o* as in *lone;* the Italian *uo* in *fuori;* often *wo*, and, at times, nearly *ŏō.*

*ŭ.* Between the *i* in *bit* and the *u* in shut; only found with the initials *ss*, *tz*, *tz'*, which it follows from the throat, almost as if the speaker were guilty of a slight eructation. We have no vowel-sound that fairly represents it.

*Consonantal Sounds.*

*ch.* Before any of the above finals except *ih*, simply as in *chair*, *chip;* before *ih* it is softened to *dj;* *chih* being in many cases pronounced *djih.*

*ch'.* A strong breathing intervening between the initial *ch* and the vowel-sound, but without reduplicating the latter. Drop the first vowel in *cháhá*, or the italicised letters in *much-harm*, and the *ch-ha* remaining will give a fair idea of the syllable *ch'a*. This may also be obtained if we contrast the smooth syllable *cha* with *tcha*, the breathing becoming apparent in the greater effort needed to utter the latter syllable. The *ch'* does sometimes soften like the unaspirated *ch* before *ih*, but much more rarely.

*f.* As in *farm.*

*h.* As the *ch* in the Scotch *loch;* the *ch* of the Welch and Gaelic.

*hs.* A slight aspirate preceding and modifying the sibilant, which is, however, the stronger of the two consonants. To pronounce *hsing* let the reader try to drop the first *i* in *hissing*. He will exaggerate both the aspirate and the sibilant, but the experiment will give him a clear idea of the process. The aspiration is effected by closing the middle of the tongue upon the back of the palate before the tip of the tongue is raised for the sibilation. It differs from *sh*, although this difference is less observable before the diphthongs *ia*, *ie.*

*j.* Most nearly the French *j* in *jaune;* our *s* in *fusion*, or *z* in *brazier*, are the nearest imitation of which our alphabet admits. Some foreigners read *j* as *r*, but this I hold to be entirely wrong.

*k.* As *c* in *car*, *k* in *king;* but when following other sounds, often softened to *g* in *go*, *gate*. In the word *ko*, for instance, the Numerative proper to many nouns, when this is preceded by *na*, that, or *chê*, this, the *k* is softened, the two syllables being pronounced almost *nago*, *chêgo.*

*k'.* The aspirate as in *ch'*. Drop the italicised letters in *kick-hard* and you will have *k'a;* in *kick-her*, and you have *k'ê.*

*l.* As in English.

*m.* As in English.

*n.* As in English.

*ng.* A consonantal sound of partly nasal and partly guttural influence upon the vowels it precedes. To produce *nga*, take the italicised consonants in the French mo*n ga*lant; for *ngai*, in mo*n gai*llard; for *ngo*, in so*n go*sier. It is never so evident in a syllable pronounced by itself as when following another syllable that terminates in a vowel or in *n*.

*p.* As in English.

*p'.* The aspirate as in *ch'*, *k'*. Observe the manner in which an Irishman pronounces *p*arty, *p*arliament; or drop the italicised letters in *sla*p-*h*a*rd*, and you will retain *p'a*.

*s.* As in English.

*sh.* As in English.

*ss.* *ssŭ* is the only syllable in which this initial is found. The object of employing *ss* is to fix attention on the peculiar vowel sound *ŭ*, which, as stated above, it is so hard to reproduce.

*t.* As in English.

*t'.* As in *k'*, *p'*, etc. Observe an Irishman's pronunciation of *t* in *t*error, *t*orment; or drop the italics in *hi*t-*h*a*rd*, and you have *t'a*.

*ts.* As in *jetsam*, *catsup*; after another word, often softened to *ds* in *gladsome*.

*ts'.* The aspirate intervening as in *ch* and other initials. Let the reader drop the italicised letters in *be*ts-*h*a*rd*, and he will retain *ts'a*.

*tz.* Is employed to mark the peculiarity of the final *ŭ*, but is hardly of greater power than *ts*.

*tz'.* Like *ts'* above. This and the preceding initial are, like *ss*, only used before the *ŭ*.

*w.* As in English, but very faint before *u*, if indeed it exist at all.

*y.* As in English, but very faint before *i* or *ü*.

In the final *ao* I have followed the Manchu spelling, against Morrison and Williams, who write *aou*, *âu*. This, as I have admitted, is the approximate sound in certain tones.

The final *eh*, used only in *yeh*, may seem unnecessarily separated from *ieh*. In my opinion the consonant *y* is sufficiently plain to authorise it, and the tone-inflection is not less practicable in the syllable *yeh* than in *ieh*. So with the final *ên*.

In the final *ê* some confusion with *o* is unavoidable. I have endeavoured to guide myself by the Manchu, but find that although native teachers consign them to different finals, it is next to impossible in many words to say whether *ê* (or *ngê*), *chê*, *jê*, *kê*, *mê*, *tê*, or *o*, *cho*, *jo*, *ko*, *lo*, *mo*, *to*, be the correct orthography. The same is true with the aspirated *ch*, *k*, *t*; but I think that after the aspirate, in general, the *o* prevails, also that while none of these syllables, sometimes sounded as ending in *ê*, is exempt from the changes to *o*, there are many in *o* which never change to *ê*. It will be found that some natives incline more to the one and some more to the other.

The final *êi* is of doubtful existence even in *nêi*, which certainly ends in a sound somewhat different from the terminal of *lei*, *mei*. These have taken the place of *lui*, *mui*, the old orthography of the Mandarin as spoken in the South.

The finals *ên* and *êng* were originally substituted for *un* and *ung* in syllables beginning with *f*, *m*, *p*, after the latest native works published at Canton to teach the Cantonese to talk

Mandarin, and the modification has been found to be fully authorised by the Pekingese. The Manchu orthography of the 18th century was *fung, mung*, but always *fên, mên, pên.*

The *u* in *iung, ung*, and in *ua, uai* and other combinations, in which it figures both as *o* and *w*, has been retained nevertheless as the vowel most certainly to be recognised in the simplest form of the *sound*, and as the most convenient for exhibiting the variation of the *tone* without change of *syllable*, to which end, moreover, it was expedient to avoid using the initials *hw, kw.*

*Breathings.*

The aspirate which intervenes between the initials *ch, k, p, t, ts, tz*, and the vowels following them, is indicated, as will have been seen above, by an inverted comma, in preference to an *h*, lest the English reader, following his own laws of spelling, should be led to pronounce *ph* as in *triumph, th* as in *month*, and so on, which would be a serious error. The full recognition of the aspirate's value is of the last importance; the *tones* themselves are not of more. A speaker who says *kan* when he ought to say *khan* might as well speak of London for London.

**3. Tone.**—There is no subject on which it is more important to write, and none on which it is harder to avoid repeating what has been said by others.

The ideas of a Chinese are capable of expression in writing in some thousands of characters that may be used singly or in combination with each other. The sound of each of these is such that without much violence to fact we call it a monosyllable. The Chinese term this monosyllable *yin*. In no dialect known to us does the number of the *yin* exceed a few hundreds; hence great confusion to the ear, and distress to the memory when it would distinguish between sounds, characters, or ideas which it can only recall by an alphabetic denomination common to many. Under the *yin* or sound *i* in MORRISON'S Dictionary there are 1,165 characters, differing in form and meaning. Of this *yin* there are, however, subordinate divisions, the *shêng*, which we translate tones, keys in which the voice is pitched, and by which a variety of distinctions is effected, so delicate as to be retained only after long and anxious watching by the foreign ear, but so essential an acquisition that, until by practice his intonation be accurate, the foreign speaker is in hourly danger of making very laughable mistakes. A good deal that he says will no doubt be understood, but, whether he theorise or not on the matter, until his speech be *tonically* correct, no missionary or interpreter need imagine himself secure of being intelligible.

The term *tone* has been so long accepted as the equivalent of the Chinese *shêng* that it may be hardly worth while attempting to disturb the usage. It might be notwithstanding rendered with greater propriety *note*, in a musical sense, although no musical instrument to my knowledge is capable of exhibiting more than an approximation to the *shêng*. Dr. HAGER, in his folio on the Elementary Characters of the Chinese Language (1801), has tried to give an idea of the *shêng* as musical notes. The attempt has been repeated, I believe, more recently by the late Dr. DYER, the celebrated sinologue.

The number of the *shêng* differs in different dialects. Books recognise five. In the Peking dialect there are now four: 1st, the *shang-p'ing*, or upper-even tone; 2nd, the *hsia-p'ing*, or lower-even tone; 3rd, the *shang*, or ascending tone; 4th, the *ch'ü*, receding or departing tone.

In the 1st tone, the *upper-even*, it may be enough to observe, the vowel-sound, whether the word be pronounced quickly or slowly, proceeds without elevation or depression. One of our sinologues has not incorrectly styled it the *affirmative* tone.

In the 2nd tone, the *lower-even*, the voice is jerked, much as when in English we utter words expressive of doubt and astonishment.

In the 3rd tone, the *ascending*, the sound becomes nearly as abrupt, but more resembling what with us would indicate indignation and denial.

In the 4th tone, the *receding*, the vowel-sound is prolonged, as it were, regretfully.

The *ju*, or *entering*, an abrupt tone still recognised in studying the written language—that is to say, in committing Chinese books to memory—is now ignored in the practice of the spoken language of Peking; in this most of the words or characters ranged under it in the vocabularies having been transferred to the 2nd tone. But the *ju shêng* is not extinct in some other dialects.

It is simplest, as Mr. MEADOWS suggests, to distinguish the four tones of Pekingese by numbers. I write the *shêng* of the syllable *pa*, accordingly, as follows:—

$pa^1$, $pa^2$, $pa^3$, $pa^4$.

The sounds of the syllables repeated in the above order form a sort of a *chime*, which can only be learned by the ear, but which it is not difficult to learn. When he has caught it the student should never hear a new phrase without taking it to pieces and satisfying himself and his teacher, word by word, of the proper tone or note of each. So long as his teacher declines to pass his notation as correct, so long should he carefully repeat the word or words disputed.* When absent from the teacher he will be able to fortify his ear by recurrence to the Syllabary.

There is some danger of misleading a student who has *not* caught the chime, and once he has he will dispense with all illustration. We will hazard but one parallel, for better or for worse. Let A, B, C, D be four persons engaged in conversation, and a question be put by B regarding the fate of someone known to them all. In the four lines below I have supposed A to assert his death in the 1st tone; B to express his apprehension that he has

* To give an instance of the scrapes into which inaccuracy in the tones may betray the speaker, a gentleman who really speaks the language well was asking, in 1858, where $yen^1$, the salt for the supply of Peking, was obtained, and was told first, to his astonishment, that it was all imported by foreigners; objecting to this, and explaining that he meant fresh salt, or the salt consumed in daily food, he was yet more astonished to hear that it was $yen^2$, brought from the inland province of Honan; nor was it until after some minutes' cross-examination that the Chinese addressed, detecting his error and correctly intoning the syllable, replied, "from the salines of the province of course." The foreigner had been intoning $yen^2$, the sound for, amongst others, the word *salt*, as though it were $yen^1$, the sound for, amongst others, the word *smoke*; and the Chinese had believed the first question to refer to opium, commonly called smoke, and the second, in which some qualifications had been added, to refer to native tobacco.

been killed, in the 2nd ; C to scout this suspicion, in the 3rd ; and D to confirm it sorrowfully, in the 4th.

1. *shang-p'ing*, A. Dead.
2. *hsia-p'ing*, B. *Killed?*
3. *shang*, C. No!
4. *ch'ü*, D. Yes!

Now in this short dialogue, or tetralogue, English speakers would ordinarily so pitch the voice as to make the whole a tolerable approximation to the chime the student has to acquire; but the analogy would entirely mislead him were he not to qualify it by remembering that in the four words instanced the voice rises and falls according to the emotion of the speaker, whereas the pitch of *pa*³, *pa*⁴, or any other syllables, is independent of any such motive. The tone of the syllable has as little relation to its sense as the note allotted to any word in most of our songs has to its meaning. The distinction next to be observed is this, that while there is nothing to prevent the same word being allotted in different songs to any note in the scale, it is only by exception that in Chinese speech the place of a word in the tone-scale is ever exchanged for another. So *p'a*, to fear, is always *p'a*⁴; *chiao*, to teach, is at times *chiao*¹, at times *chiao*⁴; for with a new meaning a word will change its tone, sometimes even its sound.

As the student has been told above, however, the correct application of the tones will only come to him by the practice of the ear, and in order to discipline his ear a set of Tone Exercises has been prepared in another Part of this Colloquial Series. To these his attention is earnestly recommended.

**4. Rhythm.**—What tone is to the individual sound, rhythm is to the sentence. Like the tone, it can only be acquired from a native. The student must take careful note of the proper place of the emphasis. He must not be surprised to find the rhythm in apparent antagonism to the tone in some cases, especially when an adjective or adverb is formed by reduplication of a word, with the enclitic particle *ti* appended, as in *sung-sung-ti*, *hsieh-hsieh-ti*, where his teacher will refuse to recognise any difference between the tones of the two *hsieh*, although to our ear the accent of the second differs widely from that of the first, resting in some of these polysyllabic combinations on the one and in some on the other syllable.

5. And now for the sake of securing an accurate idea of the pronunciation of each syllable, let the student carefully follow a Pekingese through the Sound Table which occupies the next pages.

## SOUND TABLE,

*Or List of Syllables distinguished as belonging to the 1st, 2nd, 3rd, and 4th Tone Classes.*

NOTE.—The following sounds, *a, ai, an, ang, ao, ê, ên, êng, o, ou,* are as often pronounced *$^{ng}$a, $^{ng}$ai, $^{ng}$an,* and so on. *See* the remarks on the subject on page 6, under the initial *ng*.

| | | 1 | 2 | 3 | 4 |
|---|---|---|---|---|---|
| 1. | a, $^{ng}$a | 阿 | … | 阿 | 阿 |
| 2. | ai, $^{ng}$ai | 哀 | 埃 | 矮 | 愛 |
| 3. | an, $^{ng}$an | 安 | … | 俺 | 岸 |
| 4. | ang, $^{ng}$ang | 昂 | 昂 | … | … |
| 5. | ao, $^{ng}$ao | 熬 | 熬 | 襖 | 傲 |
| 6. | cha | 渣 | 劄 | 拃 | 乍 |
| 7. | ch'a | 叉 | 茶 | 扠 | 杈 |
| 8. | chai | 齋 | 宅 | 窄 | 債 |
| 9. | ch'ai | 拆 | 柴 | 冊 | … |
| 10. | chan | 沾 | … | 盞 | 站 |
| 11. | ch'an | 攙 | 饞 | 産 | 懺 |
| 12. | chang | 章 | … | 長 | 賬 |
| 13. | ch'ang | 娼 | 長 | 廠 | 唱 |
| 14. | chao | 招 | 著 | 找 | 兆 |
| 15. | ch'ao | 吵 | 巢 | 炒 | 鈔 |
| 16. | chê | 遮 | 摺 | 者 | 這 |
| 17. | ch'ê | 車 | … | 扯 | 撤 |
| 18. | chei | … | … | … | 這 |
| 19. | chên | 眞 | … | 枕 | 震 |
| 20. | ch'ên | 嗔 | 臣 | 磣 | 趁 |

| | | 1 | 2 | 3 | 4 |
|---|---|---|---|---|---|
| 21. | chêng | 正 | … | 整 | 正 |
| 22. | ch'êng | 稱 | 成 | 懲 | 秤 |
| 23. | chi | 雞 | 吉 | 己 | 記 |
| 24. | ch'i | 七 | 奇 | 起 | 氣 |
| 25. | chia | 家 | 夾 | 甲 | 價 |
| 26. | ch'ia | 掐 | … | 卡 | 恰 |
| 27. | ch'iai | … | … | 楷 | … |
| 28. | chiang | 江 | … | 講 | 匠 |
| 29. | ch'iang | 腔 | 牆 | 搶 | 戧 |
| 30. | chiao | 交 | 嚼 | 脚 | 叫 |
| 31. | ch'iao | 敲 | 橋 | 巧 | 俏 |
| 32. | chieh | 街 | 結 | 解 | 借 |
| 33. | ch'ieh | 切 | 茄 | 且 | 妾 |
| 34. | chien | 奸 | … | 減 | 見 |
| 35. | ch'ien | 千 | 錢 | 淺 | 欠 |
| 36. | chih | 知 | 值 | 指 | 志 |
| 37. | ch'ih | 赤 | 遲 | 尺 | 翅 |
| 38. | chin | 斤 | … | 錦 | 近 |
| 39. | ch'in | 親 | 勤 | 寢 | 唚 |
| 40. | ching | 睛 | … | 井 | 靜 |
| 41. | ch'ing | 輕 | 晴 | 請 | 慶 |
| 42. | chio | … | 角 | … | … |

語言自邇集



| | | 1 | 2 | 3 | 4 |
|---|---|---|---|---|---|
| 43. | ch‘io | … | … | … | 却 |
| 44. | chiu | 究 | … | 酒 | 救 |
| 45. | ch‘iu | 秋 | 求 | 糗 | … |
| 46. | chiung | … | … | 窘 | … |
| 47. | ch‘iung | … | 窮 | … | … |
| 48. | cho | 卓 | 濁 | … | … |
| 49. | ch‘o | 擉 | … | … | 綽 |
| 50. | chou | 週 | 軸 | 肘 | 晝 |
| 51. | ch‘ou | 抽 | 綢 | 醜 | 臭 |
| 52. | chü | 居 | 局 | 舉 | 句 |
| 53. | ch‘ü | 屈 | 渠 | 取 | 去 |
| 54. | chüan | 捐 | … | 捲 | 眷 |
| 55. | ch‘üan | 圈 | 全 | 犬 | 勸 |
| 56. | chüeh | 噘 | 絶 | 蹷 | 倔 |
| 57. | ch‘üeh | 缺 | 瘸 | … | 確 |
| 58. | chün | 君 | … | 菌 | 俊 |
| 59. | ch‘ün | … | 羣 | … | … |
| 60. | chüo | … | 爵 | … | … |
| 61. | ch‘üo | … | … | … | 却 |
| 62. | chu | 猪 | 竹 | 主 | 住 |
| 63. | ch‘u | 出 | 厨 | 處 | 處 |
| 64. | chua | 抓 | … | 爪 | … |
| 65. | ch‘ua | 欻 | … | … | … |
| 66. | chuai | 拽 | … | 跩 | 拽 |
| 67. | ch‘uai | 揣 | … | 揣 | 踹 |
| 68. | chuan | 專 | … | 轉 | 傳 |
| 69. | ch‘uan | 穿 | 船 | 喘 | 串 |
| 70. | chuang | 裝 | … | 奘 | 壯 |
| 71. | ch‘uang | 牕 | 牀 | 闖 | 創 |

| | | 1 | 2 | 3 | 4 |
|---|---|---|---|---|---|
| 72. | chui | 追 | … | … | 墜 |
| 73. | ch‘ui | 吹 | 垂 | … | … |
| 74. | chun | … | … | 准 | … |
| 75. | ch‘un | 春 | 純 | 蠢 | … |
| 76. | chung | 中 | … | 腫 | 重 |
| 77. | ch‘ung | 充 | 虫 | 寵 | 銃 |
| 78. | ch‘uo | 擉 | … | … | … |
| 79. | ê, $^{ng}$ê | 阿 | 額 | 我 | 惡 |
| 80. | ên, $^{ng}$ên | 恩 | … | … | 摁 |
| 81. | êng, $^{ng}$êng | 哼 | … | … | … |
| 82. | êrh | … | 兒 | 耳 | 二 |
| 83. | fa | 發 | 法 | 髮 | 法 |
| 84. | fan | 翻 | 煩 | 反 | 飯 |
| 85. | fang | 方 | 房 | 訪 | 放 |
| 86. | fei | 非 | 肥 | 匪 | 費 |
| 87. | fên | 分 | 墳 | 粉 | 分 |
| 88. | fêng | 風 | 縫 | … | 奉 |
| 89. | fo | … | 佛 | … | … |
| 90. | fou | … | 浮 | 否 | 埠 |
| 91. | fu | 夫 | 扶 | 斧 | 父 |
| 92. | ha | 哈 | 蝦 | 哈 | 哈 |
| 93. | hai | 咳 | 孩 | 海 | 害 |
| 94. | han | 頇 | 寒 | 喊 | 漢 |
| 95. | hang | 夯 | 行 | … | 項 |
| 96. | hao | 蒿 | 毫 | 好 | 好 |

| | | 1 | 2 | 3 | 4 |
|---|---|---|---|---|---|
| 97. | hê, hei | 黑 | ... | 黑 | ... |
| 98. | hên | ... | 痕 | 很 | 恨 |
| 99. | hêng | 哼 | 恆 | ... | 橫 |
| 100. | ho | 喝 | 河 | ... | 賀 |
| 101. | hou | 齁 | 候 | 吼 | 後 |
| 102. | hu | 忽 | 壺 | 虎 | 戶 |
| 103. | hua | 花 | 滑 | 話 | 話 |
| 104. | huai | ... | 懷 | ... | 壞 |
| 105. | huan | 歡 | 環 | 緩 | 換 |
| 106. | huang | 荒 | 黃 | 謊 | 晃 |
| 107. | huei, hui | 灰 | 回 | 悔 | 賄 |
| 108. | huên, hun | 昏 | 魂 | 渾 | 混 |
| 109. | hung | 烘 | 紅 | 哄 | 汞 |
| 110. | huo | 劐 | 活 | 火 | 貨 |
| 111. | hsi | 西 | 席 | 喜 | 細 |
| 112. | hsia | 瞎 | 霞 | ... | 夏 |
| 113. | hsiang | 香 | 詳 | 想 | 向 |
| 114. | hsiao | 消 | 學 | 小 | 笑 |
| 115. | hsieh | 些 | 鞵 | 血 | 謝 |
| 116. | hsien | 先 | 閒 | 險 | 限 |
| 117. | hsin | 心 | 尋 | ... | 信 |
| 118. | hsing | 星 | 行 | 醒 | 姓 |
| 119. | hsio | ... | 學 | ... | ... |
| 120. | hsiu | 修 | ... | 朽 | 袖 |
| 121. | hsiung | 兄 | 熊 | ... | ... |
| 122. | hsü | 須 | 徐 | 許 | 續 |
| 123. | hsüan, hsüen | 喧 | 懸 | 選 | 選 |
| 124. | hsüeh | 靴 | 穴 | 雪 | 穴 |
| 125. | hsün | 熏 | 巡 | ... | 汛 |

| | | 1 | 2 | 3 | 4 |
|---|---|---|---|---|---|
| 126. | hsüo | ... | 學 | ... | ... |
| 127. | i, yi | 衣 | 一 | 尾 | 易 |
| 128. | jan | ... | 然 | 染 | ... |
| 129. | jang | 嚷 | 瓤 | 嚷 | 讓 |
| 130. | jao | ... | 饒 | 繞 | 繞 |
| 131. | jê | ... | ... | ... | 熱 |
| 132. | jên | ... | 人 | 忍 | 任 |
| 133. | jêng | 扔 | ... | ... | ... |
| 134. | jih | ... | ... | ... | 日 |
| 135. | jo | ... | ... | ... | 若 |
| 136. | jou | 揉 | 柔 | ... | 肉 |
| 137. | ju | 如 | 如 | 入 | 入 |
| 138. | juan | ... | ... | 軟 | ... |
| 139. | jui | ... | ... | 蕋 | 瑞 |
| 140. | jun | ... | ... | ... | 潤 |
| 141. | jung | ... | 榮 | 氄 | ... |
| 142. | ka | 嘎 | 嘎 | 嘎 | 嘎 |
| 143. | k'a | 卡 | ... | 卡 | ... |
| 144. | kai | 該 | ... | 改 | 槩 |
| 145. | k'ai | 開 | ... | 慨 | ... |
| 146. | kan | 甘 | ... | 趕 | 幹 |
| 147. | k'an | 看 | ... | 砍 | 看 |
| 148. | kang | 剛 | ... | 堈 | 杠 |
| 149. | k'ang | 康 | 扛 | 抗 | 炕 |

| | | 1 | 2 | 3 | 4 |
|---|---|---|---|---|---|
| 150. | kao | 高 | … | 稿 | 告 |
| 151. | k'ao | 尻 | … | 考 | 靠 |
| | kê, k'ê; *see* ko, k'o. | | | | |
| 152. | kei | … | … | 給 | … |
| 153. | k'ei | 刻 | … | … | 刻 |
| 154. | kên | 根 | 哏 | … | 艮 |
| 155. | k'ên | … | … | 肯 | 掯 |
| 156. | kêng | 更 | … | 埂 | 更 |
| 157. | k'êng | 坑 | … | … | … |
| 158. | ko, kê | 哥 | 格 | 各 | 個 |
| 159. | k'o, k'ê | 可 | 可 | 渴 | 客 |
| 160. | kou | 溝 | 狗 | 狗 | 彀 |
| 161. | k'ou | 摳 | … | 口 | 叩 |
| 162. | ku | 估 | 骨 | 古 | 固 |
| 163. | k'u | 窟 | … | 苦 | 褲 |
| 164. | kua | 瓜 | … | 寡 | 掛 |
| 165. | k'ua | 誇 | … | 侉 | 跨 |
| 166. | kuai | 乖 | … | 拐 | 怪 |
| 167. | k'uai | … | … | 擓 | 快 |
| 168. | kuan | 官 | … | 管 | 慣 |
| 169. | k'uan | 寬 | … | 款 | … |
| 170. | kuang | 光 | … | 廣 | 逛 |
| 171. | k'uang | 誆 | 狂 | … | 況 |
| 172. | kuei | 規 | … | 詭 | 貴 |
| 173. | k'uei | 虧 | 揆 | 傀 | 愧 |
| 174. | kuên, kun | … | … | 滾 | 棍 |
| 175. | k'uên, k'un | 坤 | … | 閫 | 困 |
| 176. | kung | 工 | … | 礦 | 共 |
| 177. | k'ung | 空 | … | 孔 | 空 |

| | | 1 | 2 | 3 | 4 |
|---|---|---|---|---|---|
| 178. | kuo | 鍋 | 國 | 果 | 過 |
| 179. | k'uo | … | … | … | 闊 |
| 180. | la | 拉 | 邋 | 蝲 | 蠟 |
| 181. | lai | … | 來 | … | 賴 |
| 182. | lan | 藍 | 婪 | 懶 | 爛 |
| 183. | lang | 榔 | 狼 | 朗 | 浪 |
| 184. | lao | 撈 | 勞 | 老 | 澇 |
| 185. | lê | 勒 | … | … | 樂 |
| 186. | lêi, lei | 累 | 雷 | 累 | 類 |
| 187. | lêng | … | 稜 | 冷 | 愣 |
| 188. | li | 璃 | 離 | 禮 | 立 |
| 189. | lia | … | … | 倆 | … |
| 190. | liang | 量 | 凉 | 兩 | 諒 |
| 191. | liao | … | 聊 | 了 | 料 |
| 192. | lieh | 咧 | 咧 | 咧 | 列 |
| 193. | lien | 連 | 憐 | 臉 | 練 |
| 194. | lin | … | 林 | 檁 | 賃 |
| 195. | ling | … | 零 | 領 | 另 |
| 196. | lio | … | … | … | 略 |
| 197. | liu | 遛 | 留 | 柳 | 六 |
| 198. | lo | 撈 | 騾 | 裸 | 駱 |
| 199. | lou | 摟 | 樓 | 簍 | 陋 |
| 200. | lü | … | 驢 | 屢 | 律 |
| 201. | lüan | … | … | … | 戀 |
| 202. | lüeh | … | … | … | 略 |
| 203. | lün | 掄 | 倫 | 圇 | 論 |
| 204. | lüo | … | … | … | 略 |
| 205. | lu | 嚕 | 爐 | 櫓 | 路 |

| | | 1 | 2 | 3 | 4 |
|---|---|---|---|---|---|
| 206. | luan | … | … | … | 亂 |
| 207. | lun | … | 輪 | 圇 | 論 |
| 208. | lung | 窿 | 龍 | 隴 | 弄 |
| 209. | ma | 媽 | 麻 | 馬 | 罵 |
| 210. | mai | … | 埋 | 買 | 賣 |
| 211. | man | 顢 | 瞞 | 滿 | 慢 |
| 212. | mang | 茫 | 忙 | 莽 | … |
| 213. | mao | 貓 | 毛 | 卯 | 貌 |
| 214. | mei | … | 煤 | 美 | 昧 |
| 215. | mên | 捫 | 門 | … | 悶 |
| 216. | mêng | 懵 | 盟 | 猛 | 夢 |
| 217. | mi | 眯 | 迷 | 米 | 密 |
| 218. | miao | 喵 | 苗 | 藐 | 廟 |
| 219. | mieh | 咩 | … | … | 滅 |
| 220. | mien | … | 綿 | 勉 | 面 |
| 221. | min | … | 民 | 憫 | … |
| 222. | ming | … | 名 | … | 命 |
| 223. | miu | … | … | … | 謬 |
| 224. | mo | 摩 | 麽 | 抹 | 末 |
| 225. | mou | … | 謀 | 某 | … |
| 226. | mu | … | 模 | 母 | 木 |
| 227. | na | 那 | 拏 | 那 | 那 |
| 228. | nai | … | … | 奶 | 耐 |
| 229. | nan | 喃 | 男 | … | 難 |
| 230. | nang | 囔 | 囊 | 攮 | 齉 |
| 231. | nao | 撓 | 鐃 | 惱 | 鬧 |
| 232. | nei | … | … | … | 內 |
| 233. | nên | … | … | … | 嫩 |
| 234. | nêng | … | 能 | … | … |
| 235. | ni | … | 泥 | 擬 | 匿 |
| 236. | niang | … | 娘 | … | 釀 |
| 237. | niao | 嬲 | … | 鳥 | 尿 |
| 238. | nieh | 揑 | 呆 | … | 孽 |
| 239. | nien | 拈 | 年 | 捻 | 念 |
| 240. | nin | … | 您 | … | … |
| 241. | ning | … | 甯 | 擰 | 佞 |
| 242. | nio | … | … | … | 虐 |
| 243. | niu | 妞 | 牛 | 鈕 | 拗 |
| 244. | no | … | 挪 | … | 懦 |
| 245. | nou | … | … | … | 耨 |
| 246. | nü | … | … | 女 | … |
| 247. | nüeh | … | … | … | 虐 |
| 248. | nüo | … | … | … | 虐 |
| 249. | nu | … | 奴 | 努 | 怒 |
| 250. | nuan | … | … | 暖 | … |
| 251. | nun | … | … | … | 嫩 |
| 252. | nung | … | 濃 | … | 弄 |
| 253. | o, $^{ng}$o | 哦 | 訛 | … | 惡 |
| 254. | ou, $^{ng}$ou | 毆 | … | 偶 | 嘔 |
| 255. | pa | 八 | 拔 | 把 | 罷 |
| 256. | p‘a | 琶 | 扒 | … | 怕 |
| 257. | pai | 擗 | 白 | 百 | 拜 |

語言自邇集



| | | 1 | 2 | 3 | 4 |
|---|---|---|---|---|---|
| 258. | p'ai | 拍 | 牌 | [illegible] | 派 |
| 259. | pan | 班 | … | 板 | 半 |
| 260. | p'an | 攀 | 盤 | … | 盼 |
| 261. | pang | 幫 | … | 綁 | 謗 |
| 262. | p'ang | 胖 | 旁 | 膀 | 胖 |
| 263. | pao | 包 | 薄 | 保 | 抱 |
| 264. | p'ao | 抛 | 袍 | 跑 | 礮 |
| 265. | pei | 背 | … | 北 | 背 |
| 266. | p'ei | 披 | 陪 | … | 配 |
| 267. | pên | 奔 | … | 本 | 奔 |
| 268. | p'ên | 噴 | 盆 | … | 噴 |
| 269. | pêng | 繃 | … | … | 迸 |
| 270. | p'êng | 烹 | 朋 | 捧 | 碰 |
| 271. | pi | 逼 | 鼻 | 筆 | 必 |
| 272. | p'i | 批 | 皮 | 鄙 | 屁 |
| 273. | piao | 標 | … | 表 | 鰾 |
| 274. | p'iao | 漂 | 嫖 | 漂 | 票 |
| 275. | pieh | 憋 | 別 | 彆 | 彆 |
| 276. | p'ieh | 撆 | … | 撇 | … |
| 277. | pien | 邊 | … | 扁 | 便 |
| 278. | p'ien | 偏 | 便 | 諞 | 片 |
| 279. | pin | 賓 | … | … | 殯 |
| 280. | p'in | 拼 | 貧 | 品 | 牝 |
| 281. | ping | 兵 | … | 稟 | 病 |
| 282. | p'ing | 砰 | 憑 | … | 聘 |
| 283. | po | 波 | 駁 | 播 | 簸 |
| 284. | p'o | 坡 | 婆 | 笸 | 破 |
| 285. | pou * | 不 | … | … | … |
| 286. | p'ou | 掊 | … | 剖 | … |

| | | 1 | 2 | 3 | 4 |
|---|---|---|---|---|---|
| 287. | pu | 不 | 不 | 補 | 不 |
| 288. | p'u | 鋪 | 葡 | 普 | 鋪 |
| 289. | sa | 撒 | 瞰 | 洒 | 薩 |
| 290. | sai | 顋 | … | … | 賽 |
| 291. | san | 三 | … | 傘 | 散 |
| 292. | sang | 桑 | … | 嗓 | 喪 |
| 293. | sao | 騷 | … | 掃 | 掃 |
| 294. | sê | 嘶 | … | … | 嗇 |
| 295. | sên | 森 | … | … | … |
| 296. | sêng | 僧 | … | … | … |
| 297. | so | 唆 | … | 鎖 | 溯 |
| 298. | sou | 搜 | … | 叟 | 嗽 |
| 299. | su | 蘇 | 速 | … | 素 |
| 300. | suan | 酸 | … | … | 算 |
| 301. | sui | 雖 | 隨 | 髓 | 碎 |
| 302. | sun | 孫 | … | 損 | … |
| 303. | sung | 松 | .. | 竦 | 送 |
| 304. | sha | 殺 | … | 傻 | [illegible] |
| 305. | shai | 篩 | … | 色 | 曬 |
| 306. | shan | 山 | … | 閃 | 善 |
| 307. | shang | 商 | 晌 | 賞 | 上 |
| 308. | shao | 燒 | 杓 | 少 | 少 |
| 309. | shê | 賒 | 舌 | 捨 | 射 |
| 310. | shên | 身 | 神 | 審 | 愼 |
| 311. | shêng | 生 | 繩 | 省 | 賸 |
| 312. | shih | 失 | 十 | 使 | 事 |
| 313. | shou | 收 | 熟 | 手 | 獸 |

* Pronounced *pou* in poetry only.

| | | 1 | 2 | 3 | 4 |
|---|---|---|---|---|---|
| 314. | shu | 書 | 贖 | 數 | 數 |
| 315. | shua | 刷 | ... | 耍 | ... |
| 316. | shuai | 衰 | ... | 摔 | 率 |
| 317. | shuan | 拴 | ... | ... | 涮 |
| 318. | shuang | 雙 | ... | 爽 | 雙 |
| 319. | shui | ... | 誰 | 水 | 睡 |
| 320. | shun | ... | ... | ... | 順 |
| 321. | shuo | 說 | ... | ... | 朔 |
| 322. | ssŭ | 絲 | ... | 死 | 四 |
| 323. | ta | 答 | 搭 | 打 | 大 |
| 324. | t'a | 他 | ... | 塔 | 榻 |
| 325. | tai | 獃 | ... | 歹 | 代 |
| 326. | t'ai | 胎 | 擡 | ... | 太 |
| 327. | tan | 單 | ... | 膽 | 蛋 |
| 328. | t'an | 貪 | 談 | 坦 | 炭 |
| 329. | tang | 當 | ... | 擋 | 當 |
| 330. | t'ang | 湯 | 糖 | 躺 | 燙 |
| 331. | tao | 刀 | 擣 | 倒 | 道 |
| 332. | t'ao | 叨 | 逃 | 討 | 套 |
| 333. | tê | 叨 | 得 | ... | ... |
| 334. | t'ê | ... | ... | ... | 特 |
| 335. | tei | 鏑 | ... | 得 | ... |
| 336. | têng | 燈 | ... | 等 | 鐙 |
| 337. | t'êng | 鼟 | 疼 | ... | 櫈 |
| 338. | ti | 的 | 敵 | 底 | 地 |
| 339. | t'i | 梯 | 提 | 體 | 替 |
| 340. | tiao | 貂 | ... | ... | 弔 |
| 341. | t'iao | 挑 | 條 | 挑 | 跳 |
| 342. | tieh | 爹 | 疊 | ... | ... |
| 343. | t'ieh | 貼 | ... | 鐵 | 帖 |
| 344. | tien | 攧 | ... | 點 | 店 |
| 345. | t'ien | 天 | 田 | 餂 | 掭 |
| 346. | ting | 釘 | ... | 頂 | 定 |
| 347. | t'ing | 聽 | 停 | 梃 | 聽 |
| 348. | tiu | 丟 | ... | 唒 | ... |
| 349. | to | 多 | 奪 | 朶 | 惰 |
| 350. | t'o | 託 | 駝 | 妥 | 唾 |
| 351. | tou | 兜 | ... | 斗 | 豆 |
| 352. | t'ou | 偷 | 頭 | ... | 透 |
| 353. | tu | 督 | 毒 | 賭 | 妒 |
| 354. | t'u | 秃 | 塗 | 土 | 唾 |
| 355. | tuan | 端 | ... | 短 | 斷 |
| 356. | t'uan | ... | 團 | ... | ... |
| 357. | tui | 堆 | ... | ... | 對 |
| 358. | t'ui | 推 | ... | 腿 | 退 |
| 359. | tun | 敦 | ... | 盹 | 鈍 |
| 360. | t'un | 吞 | 屯 | ... | 褪 |
| 361. | tung | 冬 | ... | 懂 | 動 |
| 362. | t'ung | 通 | 同 | 統 | 痛 |
| 363. | tsa | 臢 | 雜 | 咱 | ... |
| 364. | ts'a | 擦 | ... | ... | ... |
| 365. | tsai | 栽 | ... | 宰 | 在 |
| 366. | ts'ai | 猜 | 才 | 彩 | 菜 |
| 367. | tsan | 簪 | 偺 | 攢 | 贊 |
| 368. | ts'an | 參 | 慚 | 慘 | 儳 |
| 369. | tsang | 贓 | 喒 | ... | 葬 |
| 370. | ts'ang | 倉 | 藏 | ... | ... |

| | | 1 | 2 | 3 | 4 |
|---|---|---|---|---|---|
| 371. | tsao | 遭 | 鑿 | 早 | 造 |
| 372. | ts'ao | 操 | 槽 | 草 | … |
| 373. | tsê | … | 則 | … | … |
| 374. | ts'ê | … | … | … | 策 |
| 375. | tsei | … | 賊 | … | … |
| 376. | tsên | … | … | 怎 | … |
| 377. | ts'ên | 參 | … | … | … |
| 378. | tsêng | 增 | … | 怎 | 增 |
| 379. | ts'êng | 蹭 | … | 層 | 蹭 |
| 380. | tso | 作 | 昨 | 左 | 作 |
| 381. | ts'o | 搓 | 矬 | … | 錯 |
| 382. | tsou | … | … | 走 | 奏 |
| 383. | ts'ou | … | … | … | 湊 |
| 384. | tsu | 租 | 足 | 祖 | … |
| 385. | ts'u | 粗 | … | … | 醋 |
| 386. | tsuan | 鑽 | … | 纂 | 揝 |
| 387. | ts'uan | 躥 | 攢 | … | 竄 |
| 388. | tsui | 堆 | … | 嘴 | 罪 |
| 389. | ts'ui | 催 | 隨 | … | 萃 |
| 390. | tsun | 尊 | … | 撙 | … |
| 391. | ts'un | 村 | 存 | 忖 | 寸 |
| 392. | tsung | 宗 | … | 總 | 縱 |
| 393. | ts'ung | 葱 | 從 | … | … |
| 394. | tzŭ | 資 | … | 子 | 字 |
| 395. | tz'ŭ | 齜 | 磁 | 此 | 次 |
| | us; *see* wu. | | | | |
| 396. | wa | 挖 | 娃 | 瓦 | 襪 |
| 397. | wai | 歪 | … | 舀 | 外 |
| 398. | wan | 灣 | 完 | 晚 | 萬 |
| 399. | wang | 汪 | 王 | 往 | 忘 |
| 400. | wei | 微 | 爲 | 委 | 位 |
| 401. | wên | 溫 | 文 | 穩 | 問 |
| 402. | wêng | 翁 | … | … | 甕 |
| 403. | wo | 窩 | … | 我 | 臥 |
| 404. | wu | 屋 | 無 | 武 | 物 |
| 405. | ya | 丫 | 牙 | 雅 | 壓 |
| 406. | yai | … | 涯 | … | … |
| 407. | yang | 央 | 羊 | 養 | 樣 |
| 408. | yao | 腰 | 遙 | 咬 | 要 |
| 409. | yeh | 噎 | 爺 | 野 | 夜 |
| 410. | yen | 煙 | 言 | 眼 | 沿 |
| 411. | yi | 揖 | 益 | … | 易 |
| 412. | yin | 音 | 銀 | 引 | 印 |
| 413. | ying | 應 | 迎 | 影 | 應 |
| 414. | yo | 約 | … | … | 樂 |
| 415. | yü | 愚 | 魚 | 雨 | 預 |
| 416. | yüan | 冤 | 原 | 遠 | 願 |
| 417. | yüeh | 曰 | 嶽 | … | 月 |
| 418. | yün | 暈 | 雲 | 允 | 運 |
| 419. | yu | 憂 | 油 | 有 | 右 |
| 420. | yung | 庸 | 容 | 永 | 用 |

# PART II.

## THE RADICALS.

# PART II.

## THE RADICALS.

6.—We now come to the written character, which the student must for the time be pleased to accept as made up of two parts, its Radical, and that part which is not its Radical. The latter part various sinologues have for fairly sufficient reasons agreed to term its Phonetic. In a large majority of words the phonetic indicates the sounds, that is to a certain extent. The radical, with a like limitation, indicates the category of the sense.

The radicals are 214 in number. Some of them are subject to modifications which entirely change their figure. The following General Table shows them arranged in 17 classes, according to the number of pencil strokes in each radical; that is, the radicals of one stroke in the first class, those of two in the second, and so on. Many radicals in the latter classes will be seen to be made up of radicals of fewer strokes, *e.g.*, 109, 180, 209.

Before each radical is a number marking its place in the general series, the name of the character so numbered, and its tone; after the character, its meaning, and then a number of characters, never exceeding three, which have been selected as illustrating the part that the radical after which they stand generally plays in the composition of characters, whether in its full or its modified form. The radicals that undergo modification are marked with an asterisk (*); and their modified forms are collected at the end of the General Table. This list of modified forms should be consulted as the radicals are being acquired.

The character, it has been said above, consists of its radical and its phonetic. Let the student turn to Radical 3 and he will see in the character given to illustrate its part in the composition that the radical *chu*, a point, stands on the top of it. The remainder, three horizontal strokes and a vertical one, are its phonetic. Let him turn to the 12th Radical, *pa*, eight, and he will see that it is placed under the phonetic in the characters given as examples. In the examples opposite the 64th Radical, *shou*, the hand, the radical stands in the first example, in full form, on the left of the phonetic; in the second, in modified form, also on the left; in the third, in full form, underneath the phonetic.

To look out a character in the dictionaries arranged according to radicals, it is essential, of course, in the first place to decide correctly under what radical it is classed. This point assured,—and the knowledge necessary to this end is sooner attained by practice than might be supposed,—the number of strokes in the phonetic must be accurately counted, because in the dictionaries in question the characters under each radical are subdivided into classes, according to the number of strokes in the phonetic. The counting of these, even where they are numerous, will not be found so formidable a task once the student becomes familiar with the radicals, for he will observe that the phonetic is either resolvable into other radical characters, or, in some instances, is simply a single radical character added to the radical;

and once he knows, as he soon will, the place of any radical in the General Table, he will recall the number of strokes composing it without the trouble of counting them.

Take the third example opposite the 85th Radical, *shui*, water. The radical itself is the abbreviated form of *shui:* the phonetic resolves itself into four radicals; the centre of the upper part is the 149th, of seven strokes; this is flanked on both sides by the 120th, of six strokes; and below is the 59th, of three strokes; making in all twenty-two strokes. In the second example of the 29th Radical, the phonetic is simply the 128th Radical; in the second example of the 75th Radical, the phonetic is that same radical repeated. The rule regarding the composition of the phonetic is not strictly universal, but by the beginner it may be accepted as very generally obtaining.

To assist the student in acquiring a working knowledge of the radicals, three test tables are subjoined.

The first contains all the characters chosen to illustrate the use of the radicals in the General Table, arranged in order of the number of their strokes collectively. When the student shall have examined the first 30, or 20, or even 10, of the radicals in the General Table, let him run down the right-hand column of the Test Table, and try to identify the radicals of the characters therein placed, turning to the General Table for assistance whenever his memory fails him. This will speedily acquaint him with the radicals and the part they most commonly play.

The second Test Table contains all the radicals redistributed in categories of subjects, according to the meaning of each. Some are in consequence repeated. At the top of the right-hand column, for instance, we have the 72nd, as the sun, followed by the 73rd, the moon; then the 72nd again, as day, followed by the 36th, as night. It is hoped that this will at the same time aid and exercise the memory; but it will not be of as great service to him as the following table, the third.

The third table exhibits the radicals in three classes, distinguished for brevity's sake as colloquial, classical, and obsolete. The colloquial are those which represent words used, many of them frequently, in conversation; the classical, those not met with in conversation but found in books and writing; the obsolete, those which, although the dictionaries allot them a signification, are no longer employed except as radical indices. The colloquial radicals are 142 in number, the classical 25, the obsolete 47.

The student is recommended, when he shall have examined the General Table sufficiently to have formed a definite idea of the nature and functions of the radical characters arranged in it, to betake himself to the Exercises in the Colloquial Radicals which immediately follow this third Test Table. In these he will find a number of short combinations of words, all of them, with the exception of one or two, which are separately explained, radical characters; arranged more or less in categories of subjects. If he will keep to these exercises till he really knows every character in them, he will be master of 138 of the 214 radicals, and he will have easy victory over the remaining 76.

The explanations set opposite the radicals in the General Table might often be expanded or modified, but will be found for the present sufficient.

---

## GENERAL TABLE.

### 1 Stroke.

| | | | | |
|---|---|---|---|---|
| 1. | *yi*$^{124}$ | 一 | one; unity. | 七 不 且 |
| 2. | *kun*$^{3}$ | 丨 | a stroke connecting the top with the bottom. | 中 |
| 3. | *chu*$^{3}$ | 丶 | a point; a period. | 主 |
| 4. | *p'ieh*$^{3}$ | 丿 | a line running obliquely to the left. | 久 乍 乏 |
| 5. | *yi*$^{14}$ | 乙 | a character in the time cycle of China; also used as *yi*, one. | 九 也 亂 |
| 6. | *chüeh*$^{2}$ | 亅 | a hooked end. | 了 事 |

### 2 Strokes.

| | | | | |
|---|---|---|---|---|
| 7. | *êrh*$^{4}$ | 二 | two. | 五 井 |
| 8. | *t'ou*$^{2}$ | 亠 | above. | 交 京 亮 |
| 9. | *jên*$^{2}$ | 人* | man. | 今 來 你 |
| 10. | *jên*$^{2}$ | 儿 | man. | 允 兆 兒 |
| 11. | *ju*$^{34}$ | 入 | in, into; to enter. | 內 全 兩 |
| 12. | *pa*$^{12}$ | 八 | eight. | 六 兵 典 |
| 13. | *chiung*$^{3}$ | 冂 | border waste-land. | 冒 冕 |
| 14. | *mi*$^{4}$ | 冖 | to cover over. | 冠 |
| 15. | *ping*$^{1}$ | 冫 | an icicle. | 冬 准 凑 |
| 16. | *chi*$^{13}$ | 几 | a stool. | 凡 凳 |
| 17. | *k'an*$^{3}$ | 凵 | able to contain. | 凸 凹 出 |
| 18. | *tao*$^{1}$ | 刀* | a knife; a sword. | 分 別 則 |
| 19. | *li*$^{4}$ | 力 | strength. | 助 勁 勸 |
| 20. | *pao*$^{1}$ | 勹 | to wrap round. | 勺 包 |
| 21. | *pi*$^{3}$ | 匕 | a spoon or scoop; a weapon | 北 匙 |
| 22. | *fang*$^{1}$ | 匚 | a chest. | 匠 匪 |
| 23. | *hsi*$^{3}$ | 匸 | able to contain or conceal. | 匹 |
| 24. | *shih*$^{2}$ | 十 | ten. | 千 半 南 |
| 25. | *pu*$^{3}$ | 卜 | to divine. | 占 卡 |
| 26. | *chieh*$^{2}$ | 卩* | a joint. | 危 却 |
| 27. | *han*$^{4}$ | 厂 | a ledge that shelters. | 底 厚 原 |

| | | | | |
|---|---|---|---|---|
| 28. | *ssŭ*$^{1}$; *mou*$^{3}$ | 厶 | private; selfish. | 去 參 |
| 29. | *yu*$^{4}$ | 又 | again. | 反 取 叠 |

3 Strokes.

| | | | | |
|---|---|---|---|---|
| 30. | *k'ou*$^{3}$ | 口 | the mouth. | 可 嗇 嚴 |
| 31. | *wei*$^{2}$ | 囗 | able to enclose. | 回 困 圖 |
| 32. | *t'u*$^{3}$ | 土 | earth. | 在 墓 壞 |
| 33. | *shih*$^{4}$ | 士 | a scholar. | 壯 壺 壽 |
| 34. | *chih*$^{3}$ | 夂 | to step onwards. | 夅 |
| 35. | *ts'ui*$^{1}$ | 夊 | to step slowly. | 夏 |
| 36. | *hsi*$^{1 2}$ | 夕 | evening. | 外 夜 夢 |
| 37. | *ta*$^{4}$ | 大 | great. | 太 天 奇 |
| 38. | *nü*$^{3}$ | 女 | a female. | 奶 好 姓 |
| 39. | *tzŭ*$^{3}$ | 子 | a son. | 孔 孫 學 |
| 40. | *mien*$^{2}$ | 宀 | roof of a cave. | 官 家 寒 |
| 41. | *ts'un*$^{4}$ | 寸 | an inch. | 專 尊 對 |
| 42. | *hsiao*$^{3}$ | 小 | little. | 少 尖 |
| 43. | *wang*$^{1}$ | 尢* | bent, as an ailing leg. | 就 |
| 44. | *shih*$^{1}$ | 尸 | a corpse. | 尺 屋 層 |
| 45. | *ch'ê*$^{4}$ | 屮 | sprouting; vegetation. | 屯 |
| 46. | *shan*$^{1}$ | 山 | a hill. | 峯 嶺 |
| 47. | *ch'uan*$^{1}$ | 巛* | streams. | 州 巡 |
| 48. | *kung*$^{1}$ | 工 | labour. | 左 巧 差 |
| 49. | *chi*$^{3}$ | 己 | self. | 巷 |
| 50. | *chin*$^{1}$ | 巾 | a napkin; head gear. | 布 帳 幫 |
| 51. | *kan*$^{1}$ | 干 | a shield; to concern. | 平 年 幹 |
| 52. | *yao*$^{1}$ | 幺 | small. | 幻 幾 |
| 53. | *yen*$^{3}$ | 广 | roof of a house. | 床 店 府 |
| 54. | *yin*$^{3}$ | 廴 | continued motion. | 廷 建 |
| 55. | *kung*$^{3}$ | 廾 | the hands folded, as in salutation. | 弄 |

| | | | | |
|---|---|---|---|---|
| 56. | *yi*$^{4}$ | 弋 | to shoot with the bow. | 式 |
| 57. | *kung*$^{1}$ | 弓 | a bow *(arcus).* | 弔 弟 張 |
| 58. | *ch'i*$^{4}$ | 彐* | pointed like a pig's head. | 彙 |
| 59. | *shan*$^{1}$ | 彡 | streaky, like hair. | 彩 |
| 60. | *ch'ih*$^{4}$ | 彳 | to step short. | 往 後 得 |

4 Strokes.

| | | | | |
|---|---|---|---|---|
| 61. | *hsin*$^{1}$ | 心 | heart; mind. | 必 愛 慢 |
| 62. | *ko*$^{1}$ | 戈 | a lance; a spear. | 成 我 或 |
| 63. | *hu*$^{4}$ | 戶 | a house door. | 房 扁 |
| 64. | *shou*$^{3}$ | 手* | the hand. | 拜 換 掌 |
| 65. | *chih*$^{1}$ | 支 | a prop; to issue money. | |
| 66. | *p'u*$^{1}$ | 攴* | to tap lightly. | 敀 散 敦 |
| 67. | *wên*$^{2}$ | 文 | stripes or streaks; ornament, as opposed to plainness; literature; unit of Chinese copper cash currency. | 斌 斑 |
| 68. | *tou*$^{3}$ | 斗 | Chinese measure=about 20 *chin*. *(See* 69.) | 料 斟 |
| 69. | *chin*$^{1}$ | 斤 | Chinese pound=about $1\frac{1}{3}$ lb. English; usually spoken of as a catty; *chin* also an axe. | 斧 斬 新 |
| 70. | *fang*$^{1}$ | 方 | square. | 旁 旗 |
| 71. | *wu*$^{2}$ | 无* | not. | 旣 |
| 72. | *jih*$^{4}$ | 日 | the sun; the day. | 昂 春 晝 |
| 73. | *yüeh*$^{14}$ | 曰 | to speak. | 更 書 替 |
| 74. | *yüeh*$^{4}$ | 月 | the moon. | 有 朋 朝 |
| 75. | *mu*$^{4}$ | 木 | wood; trees. | 本 林 柴 |
| 76. | *ch'ien*$^{4}$ | 欠 | to owe; to be deficient. | 次 欵 |
| 77. | *chih*$^{3}$ | 止 | to stop (*neuter*). | 正 步 武 |
| 78. | *tai*$^{3}$ | 歹* | decayed bones of a murdered man; bad. | 死 |
| 79. | *shu*$^{1}$ | 殳 | a quarter-staff. | 殺 |
| 80. | *wu*$^{24}$ | 毋 | *wu*, do not! | 每 |
| 81. | *pi*$^{3}$ | 比 | to compare; lay side by side. | |
| 82. | *mao*$^{2}$ | 毛 | hair, fur. | 毯 |
| 83. | *ch'i*$^{4}$ | 气 | vapour. | 氣 |

| | | | | |
|---|---|---|---|---|
| 84. | *shih*$^{4}$ | 氏 | family; one's house from past time till now. | 民 |
| 85. | *shui*$^{3}$ | 水* | water. | 永 河 灣 |
| 86. | *huo*$^{3}$ | 火* | fire. | 炕 炭 然 |
| 87. | *chao*$^{3}$ | 爪* | claws. | 爲 爵 |
| 88. | *fu*$^{4}$ | 父 | father. | 爺 |
| 89. | *yao*$^{2}$ | 爻 | crosswise. | 爽 |
| 90. | *ch'iang*$^{2}$ | 爿 | the Radical 91 reversed. | 牀 牆 |
| 91. | *p'ien*$^{4}$ | 片 | a slab of wood; a slice or piece. | 牕 |
| 92. | *ya*$^{2}$ | 牙 | the back teeth. | |
| 93. | *niu*$^{2}$ | 牛* | oxen; kine. | 牲 特 牽 |
| 94. | *ch'üan*$^{3}$ | 犬* | the dog. | 狗 獃 獸 |

5 Strokes.

| | | | | |
|---|---|---|---|---|
| 95. | *yüan*$^{2}$ | 玄 | black; originally *hsüan*$^{2}$, but not so read now. | 玆 率 |
| 96. | *yü*$^{4}$ | 玉* | precious stones. | 玻 瑞 璃 |
| 97. | *kua*$^{1}$ | 瓜 | the gourd. | 瓢 瓣 |
| 98. | *wa*$^{3}$ | 瓦 | tiles. | 瓶 |
| 99. | *kan*$^{1}$ | 甘 | sweet. | 甚 甜 |
| 100. | *shêng*$^{1}$ | 生 | to live; to produce. | 產 |
| 101. | *yung*$^{4}$ | 用 | to use. | 甬 |
| 102. | *t'ien*$^{2}$ | 田 | fields; arable land. | 男 留 略 |
| 103. | *p'i*$^{3}$ | 疋 | the bale or piece of cloth, silk, etc. | 疑 |
| 104. | *ni*$^{1\,4}$ | 疒 | disease. | 疼 病 |
| 105. | *po*$^{1\,4}$ | 癶 | back to back. | 發 |
| 106. | *pai*$^{2}$; *po*$^{1\,2}$ | 白 | white. | 百 的 皇 |
| 107. | *p'i*$^{2}$ | 皮 | skins; bark. | 皺 |
| 108. | *min*$^{3}$ | 皿 | covered dishes. | 盅 盆 盞 |
| 109. | *mu*$^{4}$ | 目 | the eye. | 看 盼 直 |
| 110 | *mou*$^{2}$; *mao*$^{2}$ | 矛 | a long lance. | 矜 |
| 111. | *shih*$^{3}$ | 矢 | arrows. | 知 矩 短 |

4

| | | | | |
|---|---|---|---|---|
| 112. | *shih*$^{2}$ | 石 | stone. | 破 硺 碎 |
| 113. | *ch'i*$^{2}$; *shih*$^{4}$ | 示 | spiritual power; revelation. | 祖 票 禁 |
| 114. | *jou*$^{3}$ | 禸 | the print of a fox's foot. | 禽 |
| 115. | *ho*$^{2}$ | 禾 | any kind of grain. | 秋 秦 |
| 116. | *hsüeh*$^{2\,4}$ | 穴 | a cave in the side of a hill. | 窖 窮 竄 |
| 117. | *li*$^{4}$ | 立 | to stand up or still. | 站 章 竪 |

**6 Strokes.**

| | | | | |
|---|---|---|---|---|
| 118. | *chu*$^{2}$ | 竹* | the bamboo. | 等 策 算 |
| 119. | *mi*$^{3}$ | 米 | rice uncooked. | 粗 粱 糞 |
| 120. | *mi*$^{4}$; *ssŭ*$^{1}$ | 糸 | raw silk as spun by the worm. | 紅 累 絲 |
| 121. | *fou*$^{3}$ | 缶 | earthenware. | 缺 罄 |
| 122. | *wang*$^{3}$ | 网* | a fishing net. | 罔 罕 罷 |
| 123. | *yang*$^{2}$ | 羊 | sheep. | 美 羞 羣 |
| 124. | *yü*$^{3}$ | 羽 | feathers. | 翁 翎 習 |
| 125. | *lao*$^{3}$ | 老 | old. | 考 者 |
| 126. | *êrh*$^{2}$ | 而 | and; but yet. | 耍 耐 |
| 127. | *lei*$^{3}$ | 耒 | the plough. | 耕 耨 |
| 128. | *êrh*$^{3}$ | 耳 | the ear. | 聞 聖 聽 |
| 129. | *yü*$^{4}$ | 聿 | a pencil. | 肅 |
| 130. | *jou*$^{4}$; *ju*$^{4}$ | 肉* | flesh; meat. | 服 肯 能 |
| 131. | *ch'ên*$^{2}$ | 臣 | minister; servant of the sovereign. | 臨 |
| 132. | *tzŭ*$^{4}$ | 自 | self; from. | 臭 |
| 133. | *chih*$^{4}$ | 至 | to come or to go; arrive at. | 臺 |
| 134. | *chiu*$^{4}$ | 臼 | a stone mortar. | 與 舉 舊 |
| 135. | *shê*$^{2}$ | 舌 | the tongue. | 舒 |
| 136. | *ch'uan*$^{3}$ | 舛 | at issue; in error. | 舞 |
| 137. | *chou*$^{1}$ | 舟 | ships; boats. | 船 |
| 138. | *kên*$^{4}$ | 艮 | limitation; also character in the time cycle. | 良 艱 |
| 139. | *sê*$^{4}$; *shai*$^{3}$ | 色 | colour. | 豔 |

| | | | | |
|---|---|---|---|---|
| 140. | *ts'ao*$^{3}$ | 艸* | plants ; herbs. | 花 草 葬 |
| 141. | *hu*$^{1}$ | 虍 | the tiger's streaks. | 虎 虐 號 |
| 142. | *ch'ung*$^{2}$; *hui*$^{4}$ | 虫 | reptiles having feet. | 虱 蜜 蝨 |
| 143. | *hsieh*$^{3}$; *hsüeh*$^{34}$ | 血 | blood. | 衆 |
| 144. | *hang*$^{2}$; *hsing*$^{2}$ | 行 | *hang*, a row, as of buildings ; *hsing*, to go, to do. | 街 衕 衚 |
| 145. | *yi*$^{1}$ | 衣 | clothes. | 衫 哀 表 |
| 146. | *ya*$^{4}$ | 襾* | to cover ; commonly mistaken for 西 (*hsi*$^{1}$), west, which is, strictly speaking, not a radical. | 要 |

**7 Strokes.**

| | | | | |
|---|---|---|---|---|
| 147. | *chien*$^{4}$ | 見 | to perceive, with the eye, nose, ear, or mind ; sometimes the sign of passive or reflective verbs. | 規 親 覺 |
| 148. | *chio*$^{23}$; *chiao*$^{3}$ | 角 | horns ; a corner. | 解 |
| 149. | *yen*$^{2}$ | 言 | words. | 訛 說 謬 |
| 150. | *ku*$^{13}$ | 谷 | a valley. | 欲 |
| 151. | *tou*$^{4}$ | 豆 | beans ; a sacrificial bowl of wood. | 豈 豐 |
| 152. | *shih*$^{3}$ | 豕 | the pig. | 象 |
| 153. | *chai*$^{4}$; *ti*$^{3}$ | 豸 | reptiles without feet. | 貌 |
| 154. | *pei*$^{4}$ | 貝 | the tortoise ; his shell ; hence, precious. | 貧 賊 賓 |
| 155. | *ch'ih*$^{34}$ | 赤 | flesh colour. | 赦 |
| 156. | *tsou*$^{3}$ | 走 | to walk or run. | 起 趕 |
| 157. | *tsu*$^{2}$ | 足 | the foot ; enough. | 跨 路 躄 |
| 158. | *shên*$^{1}$ | 身 | the body. | 躬 躲 |
| 159. | *ch'ê*$^{1}$; *chü*$^{1}$ | 車 | vehicles ; sedans. | 輩 載 輕 |
| 160. | *hsin*$^{1}$ | 辛 | bitter. | 辜 辭 辯 |
| 161. | *ch'ên*$^{2}$ | 辰 | the 5th horary period of the Chinese day, 7 to 9 A.M. ; also a character in the time cycle. | 辱 |
| 162. | *ch'o*$^{4}$ | 辵* | moving and pausing. | 迎 送 這 |
| 163. | *yi*$^{4}$ | 邑* | any centre of population. | 那 郡 郤 |
| 164. | *yu*$^{3}$ | 酉 | the 10th horary period, 5 to 7 P.M. ; also a character in the time cycle. | 酒 醫 醜 |
| 165. | *pien*$^{4}$ | 釆 | to part and distinguish ; not to be confused with 采 (*ts'ai*$^{3}$), colour. | 釋 |
| 166. | *li*$^{3}$ | 里 | a hamlet of 25 families ; the Chinese measure=about one-third of an English mile. | 重 野 量 |

### 8 Strokes.

| | | | | |
|---|---|---|---|---|
| 167. | *chin*$^1$ | 金 | the metals ; gold. | 針 錯 鑿 |
| 168. | *chang*$^3$; *ch'ang*$^2$ | 長* | to grow; long, length. | |
| 169. | *mên*$^2$ | 門 | a gate ; a door. | 開 間 關 |
| 170. | *fu*$^4$; *fou*$^4$ | 阜* | a mound of earth. | 阿 陋 陪 |
| 171. | *li*$^4$; *tai*$^4$ | 隶 | to reach to ; to arrive at. | 隸 |
| 172. | *chui*$^1$ | 隹 | short-tailed birds. | 隻 雙 雞 |
| 173. | *yü*$^3$ | 雨 | rain. | 雪 雲 |
| 174. | *ch'ing*$^1$ | 青 | sky-blue. | 靖 靜 |
| 175. | *fei*$^1$ | 非 | negative ; wrong. | 靠 |
| 176. | *mien*$^4$ | 面 | the face ; the outside. | |

### 9 Strokes.

| | | | | |
|---|---|---|---|---|
| 177. | *ke*$^2$; *ko*$^2$ | 革 | a hide stripped of hair; to strip the hide; to flay. | 靴 鞋 |
| 178. | *wei*$^2$ | 韋 | tanned hide. | 韓 |
| 179. | *chiu*$^3$ | 韭 | leeks. | 韮 |
| 180. | *yin*$^1$ | 音 | sound. | 韻 響 |
| 181. | *yeh*$^4$ | 頁 | the head ; leaf or page of a book. | 項 頭 類 |
| 182. | *fêng*$^1$ | 風 | wind. | 颳 飄 |
| 183. | *fei*$^1$ | 飛 | to fly, as birds. | |
| 184. | *shih*$^2$ | 食 | to eat. | 飲 餮 餓 |
| 185. | *shou*$^3$ | 首 | the head. | 馘 |
| 186. | *hsiang*$^1$ | 香 | fragrance. | 馨 馥 |

### 10 Strokes.

| | | | | |
|---|---|---|---|---|
| 187. | *ma*$^3$ | 馬 | the horse. | 騎 騾 驚 |
| 188. | *ku*$^3$ | 骨 | the bones. | 體 髓 |
| 189. | *kao*$^1$ | 高 | high. | |
| 190. | *piao*$^1$ | 髟 | shaggy. | 髮 鬍 鬚 |

語言自邇集



| | | | | |
|---|---|---|---|---|
| 191. | *tou*[4] | 鬥 | to fight; to emulate. | 鬧 鬬 |
| 192. | *ch'ang*[4] | 鬯 | a sacrificial bowl of porcelain; luxuriant vegetation; contentment. | 鬱 |
| 193. | *ko*[2]; *li*[4] | 鬲 | a sacrificial vase on crooked feet. | 融 鬻 |
| 194. | *kuei*[3] | 鬼 | spirits of the dead. | 魁 魂 魔 |

**11 Strokes.**

| | | | | |
|---|---|---|---|---|
| 195. | *yü*[2] | 魚 | fish. | 魯 鮮 鰲 |
| 196. | *niao*[3] | 鳥 | birds. | 鳳 鴨 鷹 |
| 197. | *lu*[3] | 鹵 | natural salts. | 鹹 鹽 |
| 198. | *lu*[4] | 鹿 | the deer species. | 麒 麗 麟 |
| 199. | *mai*[4]; *mo*[4] | 麥 | wheat. | 麪 |
| 200. | *ma*[2] | 麻 | hemp. | 麼 |

**12 Strokes.**

| | | | | |
|---|---|---|---|---|
| 201. | *huang*[2] | 黃 | yellow; clay colour. | 黈 [illegible] 黌 |
| 202. | *shu*[3] | 黍 | millet. | 黎 黏 |
| 203. | *hei*[1,3]; *hê*[4] | 黑 | black. | 點 黨 |
| 204. | *chih*[4] | 黹 | embroidery. | 黻 黼 |

**13 Strokes.**

| | | | | |
|---|---|---|---|---|
| 205. | *mêng*[3]; *min*[2] | 黽 | of the frog or toad kind; to exert oneself. | 黿 |
| 206. | *ting*[3] | 鼎 | a two-eared tripod used in sacrifice. | 鼐 |
| 207. | *ku*[3] | 鼓 | the drum, etc. | 鼕 鼗 |
| 208. | *shu*[3] | 鼠 | the rat kind. | |

**14 Strokes.**

| | | | | |
|---|---|---|---|---|
| 209. | *pi*[2] | 鼻 | the nose. | 齁 |
| 210. | *ch'i*[2] | 齊 | arranged in order. | 齋 齎 |

**15 Strokes.**

| | | | | |
|---|---|---|---|---|
| 211. | *ch'ih*[3] | 齒 | front teeth. | 齡 齧 |

### 16 Strokes.

| | | | | |
|---|---|---|---|---|
| 212. | *lung*[2] | 龍 | the dragon tribe. | 龔 龕 |
| 213. | *kuei*[1] | 龜 | the tortoise, turtle, etc. | 鼈 |

### 17 Strokes.

| | | | | |
|---|---|---|---|---|
| 214. | *yo*[4] | 龠 | flutes, pipes, etc. | 龢 |

The characters in the foregoing table marked with an asterisk (*) are, some generally, some always, modified when employed as radicals of other characters. In the following are given the modifications recognised in the great Chinese lexicon of K'ANG HSI. There are a few others allowed in manuscript, which will be acquired without great difficulty.

| | | | |
|---|---|---|---|
| 人 | 亻 | 爪 | 爫 |
| 刀 | 刂 | 牛 | 牜 |
| 卩 | 㔾 | 犬 | 犭 |
| 尢 | 尣 兀 | 玉 | 王 |
| 巛 | 川 | 竹 | ⺮ |
| 彐 | 彑 彐 | 网 | 罒 罓 |
| 心 | 忄 㣺 | 肉 | 月 |
| 手 | 扌 | 艸 | 艹 艹 |
| 攴 | 攵 | 襾 | 西 |
| 无 | 旡 | 辵 | 辶 |
| 歹 | 歺 | 邑 | 阝* |
| 水 | 氵 氺 | 長 | 镸 |
| 火 | 灬 | 阜 | 阝** |
| 艸 | 草 | | |

* This modified form of *i*[4] is written on the *right* of the phonetic, e.g., 郡.

* * This modified form of *fou*[3] is written on the *left* of the phonetic, e.g., 陳.

## RADICAL TEST TABLE I.

七九了久也凡勺千不中乏五井今六分匹反太天孔少尺屯弔且主乍允内
冬凸凹出包北半占卡去可外左巧布平幼必本正民永交兆全匠危回在争
奶好尖州年式成有次死每百考那你兵別助却底困壯巡床廷弄弟往我改
更步甬男罕良却阿事京來兒兩典卦取夜奇姓官店或房斧昂朋林武河炕
牀狗的直知罔者服肯花庞虱衫表迎陋亮冒冠則勁南屋巷建後扁拜春炭
牲玻甚皇盅盆看盼矜秋紅美要耐臭虐哀要郤重准匪厚原夏孫家峯差料
旁書柴殺氣特茲留疼病矩破祖秦窄站缺翁耕能草豈起赶躬辱酒針陪隻
送湊勒匙參專巢帳張彩得斬既晝爽率瓶甜產略票章粗累羞翎習船規訛
欲貧赦這野雪項冕壺寒尊就幾換掌散敦斌斑替朝欻毯然爲爺牽發短降
禽等策粱絲喬舒衆街衕輩辜量開問雲飲壘嗇幹廚橐愛斟新瑞蓋碎禁羣
墅葬號解象賊跨路載靖靴韮鳳亂澠圖墓尋夢對慢旗猷豎算聞臺與蜜說
貌賓槳輕融魁魂歷璃曆窗疑皺窮罷舞餓衞靠鞋颳養髮鬧黎學耨親錯隸
靜頭鴨糶嶺幫爵牆瓢糞聲舉艱韓緘鮮鼓黏點黻竈齋竄舊謬豐壁醫雙雞
馥騎婁壞獸臨關韻翳魯麒麗黼發軥類嚷辦覺辭釋響飄馨鹹麵贛篤齡蠶
辮騾魔鰲齋齧聽囂龔龕穌鶩體髓鬮麟豔鬚鷹灣[illegible][illegible]釁[illegible]鑿鬱

## RADICAL TEST TABLE II.

1 日月日夕
2 風雨气冫水
3 鬼示卜鬯豆鼎鬲
4 金鼓龠音
5 干支乙辛子酉辰艮爻
6 金木水火土
7 山川谷穴阜田冂
8 玉石鹵水
9 色青黄赤白黑玄
10 人儿氏自己父子女士臣
11 身心廾手足首頁而髟耳鼻面目見面
12 言曰口舌牙齒皮肉骨血气
13 力用工
14 尸首骨卩尢疒
15 入夂夊廴行走辵隶彳止立食
16 厶歹鬥攴
17 生長大小長幺
18 厂宀广襾口里門戶邑阜
19 衣巾黹
20 舟車皿几匕斗臼瓦缶
21 魚网牛耒糸皮革韋
22 刀匕干戈弋弓矢矛殳斤
23 凵勹匚匸
24 艸木竹瓜鬯屮禾米豆韭麥麻黍
25 辛甘香
26 牛羊犬豕馬鹿鼠
27 鳥隹虫豸龍魚龜黽角貝
28 羽飛爪内釆文彡虍髟
29 疋斗斤寸方長
30 一二八十
31 片比爿
32 无欠足齊
33 亠冖高彐聿
34 毋又癶舛非
35 丨丶丿亅

語言自邇集



## RADICAL TEST TABLE III.

### 1. Colloquial.

一二人入八刀力十卜又口土士大女子小寸尸山川工己巾干弓心戈戶
手支文斗斤方日月曰木欠止歹比毛氏水火爪父片牙牛犬玉瓜瓦甘生
用田疋白皮目矛矢石禾穴立竹米缶羊羽老而耳肉臣自至臼舌舛舟色
虫血行衣見覺言谷豆貝赤走足身車辛辰酉里金長門雨青非面革韭音
頁風飛食首香馬骨高鬥鬼魚鳥鹿麥麻黃黍黑鼎鼓鼠鼻齊齒龍

### 2. Classical.

乙几匕夕弋无殳毋爻玄皿耒聿艮豕豸邑阜韋鬯鬲鹵黹黽龜

### 3. Obsolete.

丨丶丿亅亠儿冂冖冫凵勹匚匸卩厂厶囗夂夊宀尢屮幺广廴廾彐彡彳
攴气爿疒癶示禸糸网艸虍襾辵釆隶隹髟龠

5

生牛肉、老[25]米、白[26]米、小[27]米子、老[28]玉米、黄[29]米、

9. 牛[1]羊、牛[2]馬、魚[3]虫、草[4]虫、牙[5]虫、虫[6]牙、毛[7]毛虫、羽[8]毛、羊[9]毛、皮[10]毛、毛[11]女、飛[12]鳥、高[13]飛、大[14]鹿、鹿[15]角、金[16]魚、魚[17]子、比[18]目魚、石[19]首魚、走[20]馬、老[21]馬、小[22]川馬、竹[23]馬、口[24]齒、靑[25]牛白馬、土[26]牛木馬、西[27]口馬、龍[28]爪、龍[29]門、門[30]龍舟、黄[31]羊子、小[32]山羊、羊[33]皮、香[34]牛皮、老[35]鼠、小[36]犬、犬[37]子、金[38]龜、龜[39]卜、長[40]虫、

10. 金[1]木水火土、田[2]土、大[3]田、瓜[4]田、一[5]田禾黍、山[6]水、山[7]川草木、西[8]山、山[9]谷、谷[10]口、西[11]方、大[12]風、西[13]風、風[14]水、風[15]言、羊[16]角風、香[17]風十里、土[18]音、水[19]音、山[20]音、水[21]色、一[22]色、大[23]雨、欠[24]雨、雨[25]水、十[26]日一雨、土[27]山子、黄[28]土、黑[29]土、鬼[30]火、金[31]鼓、金[32]瓜、木[33]瓜、木[34]耳、木[35]魚子、

11. 長[1]一寸、八[2]寸二、八[3]斗豆子、十[4]斤米、一[5]二疋、一[6]二頁、八[7]十二里、非[8]止一人、止[9]欠一文、八[10]口人、一[11]方、一[12]寸見方、斗[13]方、日[14]用斗金、

12. 日[1]日、月[2]月、一[3]日一見、山[4]高月小、月[5]色、月[6]夕、自[7]辰至酉、日[8]子、長[9]至日、

13. 靑[1]黄赤白黑、靑[2]白、黑[3]白、靑[4]黄赤[5]色、黄[6]而黑、香[7]色、月[8]白色、玉[9]色、女[10]色、

14. 火[1]石、山[2]子石、石[3]白子、石[4]門、石[5]人、石[6]馬、白[7]玉、金[8]口玉言、瓦[9]缶金玉、瓦[10]面、瓦[11]片。

## EXERCISES IN THE COLLOQUIAL RADICALS.

1\. 人[1]氏、門[2]氏、人[3]口、戶[4]口、自[5]己、子[6]女、女[7]子、女[8]人、父[9]子、老[10]子、貝[11]子、臣[12]子、大[13]臣、士[14]子、白[15]衣大士、文[16]士、文[17]人、鬼[18]子、

2\. 人[1]身、己[2]身、人[3]心、心[4]口、手[5]足、耳[6]目、方[7]面大耳、牙[8]齒、門[9]牙、口[10]舌、口[11]齒、口[12]音、目[13]力、骨[14]肉、尸[15]首、骨[16]血、血[17]心、黑[18]心、一[19]生心血、赤[20]心、二[21]人一心、鼻[22]子、骨[23]尸、手[24]心、手[25]面、面[26]目、見[27]面、面[28]見、一[29]面、面[30]子、面[31]生、

3\. 入[1]門、干[2]支、支[3]用、用[4]力、用[5]人、用[6]心、足[7]用、用[8]工、長[9]工、月[10]工、瓦[11]木工、土[12]木工、大[13]工、小[14]工、工[15]人、人[16]工火食、女[17]工、手[18]工、水[19]手、鼓[20]手、老[21]手、生[22]長、立[23]止、自[24]立、行[25]止、行[26]走、行[27]香、高[28]香、香[29]片、甘[30]心、鼎[31]力、人[32]力、一[33]齊、比[34]齊、食[35]言、比[36]方、小[37]心、齊[38]心、見[39]長、見[40]小、心[41]高、高[42]見、

4\. 大[1]小、子[2]比父高、父[3]老子小、老[4]小、心[5]歹、歹[6]人、小[7]人、高[8]大、身[9]高力大、又[10]高又大、人[11]老又曰二毛、

5\. 手[1]巾、雨[2]衣、皮[3]衣、女[4]衣、

6\. 舟[1]車、車[2]馬、二[3]馬車、車[4]門、水[5]車、小[6]車子、門[7]戶、大[8]門、小[9]門°二[10]門、門[11]口、門[12]面、土[13]門土戶、車[14]戶、走[15]馬大門、

7\. 刀[1]子、干[2]戈、矢[3]石、弓[4]矢、弓[5]刀石、一[6]力弓、十[7]力弓、牛[8]角弓、

8\. 西[1]瓜、黃[2]瓜、香[3]瓜、瓜[4]皮、瓜[5]子、禾[6]黍、黍[7]子、米[8]麥、麥[9]子、大[10]麥、小[11]麥、豆[12]角、黃[13]豆、黑[14]豆、小[15]麻子、竹[16]子、韭[17]黃、肉[18]片、用[19]刀片肉、牛[20]肉、羊[21]肉、鹿[22]肉、一[23]方肉、一[24]斤

# EXERCISES IN THE COLLOQUIAL RADICALS. KEY.

## 1.

1. *jên*$^2$ *shih*$^4$, a person from such or such a place; *e.g.*, What is he? He is a Canton *jên*$^2$ *shih*$^4$.
2. *mên*$^2$ *shih*$^4$, husband and wife's family name. The phrase is used to or of a married woman. Who are her husband's family (*mên*$^2$), and who her own (*shih*$^4$)?
3. *jên*$^2$ *k'ou*$^3$, men and women; males and females in a family.
4. *hu*$^4$ *k'ou*$^3$, families; *lit.*, doors and mouths; used in speaking of the population of a street, village, town.
5. *tzŭ*$^4$ *chi*$^3$, self, oneself.
6. *tzŭ*$^3$ *nü*$^3$, sons and daughters.
7. *nü*$^3$ *tzŭ*$^3$, a daughter.
8. *nü*$^3$ *jên*$^2$, a wife.
9. *fu*$^4$ *tzŭ*$^3$, father and son.
10. *lao*$^3$ *tzŭ*$^3$, a father. Proper name of an ancient philosopher.
11. *pei*$^4$ *tzŭ*$^3$, Chinese for *bei tsê*, a Manchu title of nobility.
12. *ch'ên*$^2$ *tzŭ*$^3$, public servants.
13. *ta*$^4$ *ch'ên*$^2$, minister of state; also the designation of certain particular officials of high rank.
14. *shih*$^4$ *tzŭ*$^3$, a hard student; a reading man.
15. *pai*$^2$ *i*$^1$ *ta*$^4$ *shih*$^4$, common designation of the goddess Kuan-yin.
16. *wên*$^2$ *shih*$^4$, a learned scholar.
17. *wên*$^2$ *jên*$^2$ (stronger than *shih*$^4$ *tzŭ*$^3$); scholar.
18. *kuei*$^3$ *tzŭ*$^3$, devil; only so used when applied to foreigners.

## 2.

1. *jên*$^2$ *shên*$^1$, a man's person.
2. *chi*$^3$ *shên*$^1$, one's own; as of affairs, property, etc.
3. *jên*$^2$ *hsin*$^1$, the heart or mind.
4. *hsin*$^1$ *k'ou*$^3$, the breast; *lit.*, heart's mouth.
5. *shou*$^3$ *tsu*$^2$, hand and foot (not literally, but figuratively); of the relationship of brothers.
6. *êrh*$^3$ *mu*$^4$, the sight and hearing, when spoken of as quick or not; *fig.*, a police detective; a spy, whether officially employed or otherwise.
7. *fang*$^1$ *mien*$^4$ *ta*$^4$ *êrh*$^3$, with square face and large ears; characteristics of manly beauty; at the same time, signs of a distinguished career.
8. *ya*$^2$ *ch'ih*$^3$, a tooth; the teeth.
9. *mên*$^2$ *ya*$^2$, the upper front teeth.
10. *k'ou*$^3$ *shê*$^2$, altercation; *lit.*, mouth and tongue.
11. *k'ou*$^3$ *ch'ih*$^3$, mouth and teeth; used specially with reference to the pronunciation, accurate or inaccurate, of the dental sounds. *See also* below, 9, 24.
12. *k'ou*$^3$ *yin*$^1$, mouth sounds, pronunciation.
13. *mu*$^4$ *li*$^4$, strength of sight.
14. *ku*$^3$ *jou*$^4$, bone and flesh (not literally, but figuratively); of intimate relationship.
15. *shih*$^1$ *shou*$^3$, a corpse; *lit.*, corpse and head.
16. *ku*$^3$ *hsüeh*$^3$, bone and blood; *fig.*, of intimate relationship.
17. *hsüeh*$^3$ *hsin*$^1$, blood, heart; the quality of a staunch friend, faithful, adherent.
18. *hei*$^1$ *hsin*$^1$, black heart; the opposite of *hsüeh*$^3$ *hsin*$^1$.
19. *yi*$^4$ *shêng*$^1$ *hsin*$^1$ *hsüeh*$^4$, whole life's heart blood; said of long-sustained application to a good purpose.

20. *ch'ih*$^4$ *hsin*$^1$, red heart; said of ministerial fidelity.
21. *êrh*$^4$ *jên*$^2$ *yi*$^1$ *hsin*$^1$, two persons of one mind; agreement; a union conducive to success.
22. *pi*$^2$ *tzŭ*$^3$, the nose.
23. *ku*$^3$ *shih*$^1$, a skeleton; *lit.*, bone and corpse.
24. *shou*$^3$ *hsin*$^1$, the palm of the hand; *lit.*, hand's heart.
25. *shou*$^3$ *mien*$^4$, inside of hand and fingers; applied figuratively to affairs that are easy to understand.
26. *mien*$^4$ *mu*$^4$, the face; *lit.*, face and eyes.
27. *chien*$^4$ *mien*$^4$, to see the face; to have a personal interview.
28. *mien*$^4$ *chien*$^4$, to see with one's own eyes; certainly a person; doubtfully a thing.
29. *yi*$^4$ *mien*$^4$, simultaneously; *lit.*, one and the same face; used of two acts done at the same time by the same agent.
30. *mien*$^4$ *tzŭ*$^3$, the outer face or outside, as opposed to the lining or inside, of clothes; applied also to the surface of affairs.
31. *mien*$^4$ *shêng*$^1$, a face such as one has not seen before; *lit.*, face raw or new; but used disapprovingly.

## 3.

1. *ju*$^4$ *mên*$^2$, to enter the doors; used figuratively of commencing a study. There is another phrase for entering a door literally. *
2. *kan*$^1$ *chih*$^1$, the stems and branches, *sc.* of the cyclic system by which time is reckoned in China.
3. *chih*$^1$ *yung*$^4$, expenditure; *lit.*, what is issued and used.
4. *yung*$^4$ *li*$^4$, to exert oneself; use strength.
5. *yung*$^4$ *jên*$^2$, to employ people with discrimination.
6. *yung*$^4$ *hsin*$^1$, to apply oneself; use the mind.
7. *tsu*$^2$ *yung*$^4$, enough to use; most commonly of revenue or income.
8. *yung*$^4$ *kung*$^1$, of application; to use labour.
9. *ch'ang*$^2$ *kung*$^1$, long labour; service on long engagement, as opposed to service described as *yüeh*$^4$ *kung*$^1$. (*See* 10.)
10. *yüeh*$^4$ *kung*$^1$, service by the month.
11. *wa*$^3$ *mu*$^4$ *kung*$^1$, the service employed on building, *lit.*, labour of tile and wood, *sc.* of tiler and carpenter.
12. *t'u*$^3$ *mu*$^4$ *kung*$^1$, labour employed on earth and wood, *sc.* in laying foundations.
13. *ta*$^4$ *kung*$^1$, in building; of the more skilled labour; employed.
14. *hsiao*$^3$ *kung*$^1$, of the less skilled labour, hodmen, etc.
15. *kung*$^1$ *jên*$^2$, house servants; also farm labourers.
16. *jên*$^2$ *kung*$^1$ *huo*$^3$ *shih*$^2$, expense of living; *lit.*, labour and subsistence.
17. *nü*$^3$ *kung*$^1$, needlework; *lit.*, women's work.
18. *shou*$^3$ *kung*$^1$, handiwork, specially that of tailors, joiners, carvers, etc.
19. *shui*$^3$ *shou*$^3$, sailor; boatman.
20. *ku*$^3$ *shou*$^3$, drummer.
21. *lao*$^3$ *shou*$^3$, old hand; experienced.
22. *shêng*$^1$ *chang*$^3$, bred and born; *lit.*, born and grown up.
23. *li*$^4$ *chih*$^3$, to come to a standstill.
24. *tzŭ*$^4$ *li*$^4$, able to stand alone; independent by reason of character or abilities.
25. *hsing*$^2$ *chih*$^3$, conduct, goings on (*q.d.* whether moving or still, out of doors or at home); used also of an affair: will it go on or not?
26. *hsing*$^3$ *tsou*$^3$, to move; be employed in a public office.

27. *hsing*² *hsiang*¹, the burning of incense in temples by officials. There is another term for the same sacrifice when performed by the people.
28. *kao*¹ *hsiang*¹, the tall sticks of incense.
29. *hsiang*¹ *p'ien*⁴, slices of fragrance; of scented tea.
30. *kan*¹ *hsin*¹, willing; *lit.*, with pleasant heart.
31. *ting*³ *li*⁴, strong, as a sacrificial tripod; complimentarily used to a person on whose superior influence the speaker relies.
32. *jên*² *li*⁴, produced by men's ability; *lit.*, strength, as opposed to spontaneous growth; artificial.
33. *yi*⁴ *ch'i*², all at the same time or together.
34. *pi*³ *ch'i*², to equalise the length or height of cords, poles, etc.: *pi*³, laying side by side; *ch'i*², to make even.
35. *shih*² *yen*², to eat words; break faith.
36. *pi*³ *fang*¹, for instance; by comparison; also used substantively as a parallel case.
37. *hsiao*³ *hsin*¹, careful; beware!
38. *ch'i*² *hsin*¹, unanimous.
39. *chien*⁴ *chang*³, to grow; *q.d.* to feel, or be the subject of growth; used of animals or vegetables; of man, morally or physically. *Chien*⁴ *ch'ang*², used of eminence of a particular quality or attainment; it is hardly colloquial.
40. *chien*⁴ *hsiao*³, view small; of a niggardly disposition.
41. *hsin*¹ *kao*¹, of lofty aims; noble ambition.
42. *kao*¹ *chien*⁴, far-seeing, as in politics, family affairs, etc. Complimentarily, another person's opinion; *lit.*, [your] lofty view or idea.

## 4.

1. *ta*⁴ *hsiao*³, large and small; hence, size.
2. *tzŭ*³ *pi*³ *fu*⁴ *kao*¹, the son taller than the father.
3. *fu*⁴ *lao*³ *tzŭ*³ *hsiao*³, the father old, the son young; used where the father is very old to have so young a son.
4. *lao*³ *hsiao*³, old and young.
5. *hsin*¹ *tai*³, of evil disposition.
6. *tai*³ *jên*², villains, such as thieves, murderers.
7. *hsiao*³ *jên*², the man morally small, as opposed to the *chün*¹ *tzŭ*³ (君子), the man morally and intellectually perfect.
8. *kao*¹ *ta*⁴, tall; lofty.
9. *shên*¹ *kao*¹ *li*⁴ *ta*⁴, tall of stature and of great strength.
10. *yu*⁴ *kao*¹ *yu*⁴ *ta*⁴, both tall (or high) and large.
11. *jên*² *lao*³ *yu*⁴ *yüeh*¹ *êrh*⁴ *mao*², when a man is old he is also said to be *êrh*⁴ *mao*², two-haired, *sc.* to have hair white and black.

*Obs.*—Colloquially, *yüeh*¹ is only used, as here, in proverbs, quotations, etc.

## 5.

1. *shou*³ *chin*¹, a handkerchief.
2. *yü*³ *i*¹, rain clothes; a waterproof dress.
3. *p'i*² *i*¹, clothes of fur, or lined with fur.
4. *nü*³ *i*¹, women's apparel.

## 6.

1. *chou*¹ *chü*¹, (politely) junk or cart, land or water carriage.
2. *ch'ê*¹, *ma*³, carts and horses.
3. *êrh*⁴ *ma*³ *ch'ê*¹, a cart with two horses; *êrh*⁴ *ma*³ *chü*¹, a name for the water tobacco pipe, more commonly spoken of as *shui*³ *yen*¹ *tai*⁴.
4. *ch'ê*¹ *mên*², the *porte cochère;* entrance by which carts, etc., are admitted.
5. *shui*³ *ch'ê*¹, water-cart.
6. *hsiao*³ *ch'ê*¹ *tzŭ*³, the small or single-wheeled cart or wheelbarrow.
7. *mên*² *hu*⁴, entrance gate or gates of a house.
8. *ta*⁴ *mên*², the greater gate; specially, an entrance gate.
9. *hsiao*³ *mên*², smaller entrance gate.
10. *êrh*⁴ *mên*², the gate you come to in Chinese premises after passing the *ta*⁴ *mên*², chief entrance gate.
11. *mên*² *k'ou*³, gateway, doorway.
12. *mên*² *mien*⁴, the front of a shop; *q.d.* its doorway face.
13. *t'u*³ *mên*² *t'u*³ *hu*⁴, mud buildings, as in villages, poor suburbs; *lit.*, doorways and window-spaces of earth.
14. *ch'ê*¹ *hu*⁴, carters in general; not used in Peking of one man.
15. *tsou*³ *ma*³ *ta*⁴ *mên*², any large gate of a house court through which there is room for horses to pass.

## 7.

1. *tao*¹ *tzŭ*³, a knife.
2. *kan*¹ *ko*¹, shield and spear; *fig.*, for war.
3. *shih*³ *shih*², the arrow and the stone; archery and slinging.
4. *kung*¹ *shih*³, bow and arrow; archery.
5. *kung*¹, *tao*¹, *shih*², bow, sword, and stone.

*Obs.*—Military graduates have to prove their strength by drawing the bow, exercise with the sword, and raising the stone.

6. *yi*¹ *li*⁴ *kung*¹, a bow that requires power equal to 1 catty weight to draw it; the bow easiest drawn.
7. *shih*² *li*⁴ *kung*¹, a bow of 10 catty power; really the stiffest bow an archer attempts to draw, though there are bows nominally of 16 catty power.
8. *niu*² *chiao*³ *kung*¹, cow-horn bow. All bows are stiffened with cow horn or iron, the latter, however, being for show.

## 8.

1. *hsi*¹ *kua*¹, water melon; *lit.*, Western melon.
2. *huang*² *kua*¹, cucumber; *lit.*, yellow melon.
3. *hsiang*¹ *kua*¹, the melon generally eaten as fruit; *lit.*, scented melon.
4. *kua*¹ *p'i*², rind of any gourd.
5. *kua*¹ *tzŭ*³, seeds of any gourd.
6. *ho*² *shu*³, rice and millet uncut.
7. *shu*³ *tzŭ*³, millet.
8. *mi*³ *mai*⁴, rice and wheat cut; as we say corn or grain.
9. *mai*⁴ *tzŭ*³, wheat.
10. *ta*⁴ *mai*⁴, barley.

11. *hsiao*³ *mai*⁴, wheat.
12. *tou*⁴ *chiao*³, a bean-pod ; *lit.*, bean-horn.
13. *huang*² *tou*⁴, the bean commonly eaten.
14. *hei*¹ *tou*⁴, black pulse.
15. *hsiao*³ *ma*² *tzŭ*³, cumin.
16. *chu*² *tzŭ*³, bamboo tree.
17. *chiu*³ *huang*², leeks ; *lit.*, leeks yellow.
18. *jou*⁴ *p'ien*⁴, slices of meat ; *p'ien*⁴ here a substantive.
19. *yung*⁴ *tao*¹ *p'ien*⁴ *jou*⁴, using knife slice meat ; to slice meat with a knife ; *p'ien*⁴ here a verb.
20. *niu*² *jou*⁴, beef.
21. *yang*² *jou*⁴, mutton.
22. *lu*⁴ *jou*⁴, venison.
23. *yi*⁴ *fang*¹ *jou*⁴, a lump or hunch (*lit.*, square) of meat.
24. *yi*⁴ *chin*¹ *shêng*¹ *niu*² *jou*⁴, 1 catty of fresh (or raw) beef.
25. *lao*³ *mi*³, old rice ; rice that has been some time in store.
26. *pai*² *mi*³, new (*lit.*, white) rice ; also rice of better quality than the *huang*² *mi*³. (*See* 29.)
27. *hsiao*³ *mi*³ *tzŭ*³, oats.
28. *lao*³ *yü*⁴ *mi*³, Indian corn of a certain age.
29. *huang*² *mi*³, a coarse rice ; not brought up to Peking.

## 9.

1. *niu*² *yang*², sheep and cattle.
2. *niu*² *ma*³, cattle and horses.
3. *yü*² *ch'ung*², insects that fish eat ; larvæ of gnats, etc.
4. *ts'ao*³ *ch'ung*², plants and insects, *q.d.* botany and entomology ; also any insects found in grass or plants.
5. *ya*² *ch'ung*², teeth insects. The Chinese believe toothache to be their work.
6. *ch'ung*² *ya*², a tooth, or teeth, suffering from insects ; aching.
7. *mao*² *mao*² *ch'ung*², hairy insect ; caterpillar.
8. *yü*³ *mao*², camlet ; also feathers and hair ; plumage of a bird.
9. *yang*² *mao*², wool.
10. *p'i*² *mao*², hair of fur ; also *fig.* of maladies not serious ; *q.d.* affecting the surface only.
11. *mao*² *nü*³, spinster ; a girl whose hair is still unparted on the forehead ; applied rather to young girls not of nubile years.
12. *fei*¹ *niao*³, birds ; *lit.*, flying birds.
13. *kao*¹ *fei*¹, flying high.
14. *ta*⁴ *lu*⁴, the red deer ; *lit.*, great deer.
15. *lu*⁴ *chio*², deer's horn.
16. *chin*¹ *yü*², gold fish.
17. *yü*² *tzŭ*³, fish eggs ; spawn.
18. *pi*³ *mu*⁴ *yü*², pair-fish, supposed to be inseparable ; *fig.*, of the married state.
19. *shih*² *shou*³ *yü*², a kind of sciæna ; commonly called the *huang*² *hua*¹ *yü*², yellow-flower fish, yellow marked or spotted fish.
20. *tsou*³ *ma*³, a horse that ambles along quietly ; such a horse as Chinese officials prefer to ride.
21. *lao*³ *ma*³, an old horse.
22. *hsiao*³ *ch'uan*¹ *ma*³, a Szechwan pony.
23. *chu*² *ma*³, horse made of bamboo.
24. *k'ou*³ *ch'ih*³, mouth's teeth ; *sc.* a horse's teeth, by which his age is known.
25. *ch'ing*¹ *niu*² *pai*² *ma*³, grey cow, white horse ; used literally ; but also figuratively, of marriages of which the conditions are astrologically objectionable.
26. *t'u*³ *niu*² *mu*⁴ *ma*³, ox of clay, horse of wood ; *fig.*, of stupid people.
27. *hsi*¹ *k'ou*³ *ma*³, a horse from the western frontier ; *lit.*, western mouths, *sc.* frontier passes.

28. *lung*$^{2}$ *chao*$^{3}$, dragon's claws ; as in embroidery, painting, etc.
29. *lung*$^{2}$ *mên*$^{2}$, the dragon's gate, through which candidates for degrees enter the examination hall.
30. *tou*$^{4}$ *lung*$^{2}$ *chou*$^{1}$, contending dragon boats ; the boats in which men race at the fête of the fifth moon.
31. *huang*$^{2}$ *yang*$^{2}$ *tzŭ*$^{3}$, a kind of antelope.
32. *hsiao*$^{3}$ *shan*$^{1}$ *yang*$^{2}$, a goat's kid.
33. *yang*$^{2}$ *p‘i*$^{2}$, a sheepskin.
34. *hsiang*$^{1}$ *niu*$^{2}$ *p‘i*$^{2}$, Russia leather, *sc.* scented cow-hide.
35. *lao*$^{3}$ *shu*$^{3}$, a rat, *sc.* an old rat.
36. *hsiao*$^{3}$ *ch‘üan*$^{3}$ (of one's own son), a little dog.
37. *ch‘üan*$^{3}$ *tzŭ*$^{3}$, dog, as in 36.
38. *chin*$^{1}$ *kuei*$^{1}$, a small kind of land tortoise.
39. *kuei*$^{1}$ *pu*$^{3}$, divination ; *lit.*, that practised with reference to the marks on a tortoise's back.
40. *ch‘ang*$^{2}$ *ch‘ung*$^{2}$, a serpent ; *lit.*, the long reptile.

## 10.

1. *chin*$^{1}$, *mu*$^{4}$, *shui*$^{3}$, *huo*$^{3}$, *t‘u*$^{3}$, metal, wood, water, fire, earth ; the five elements of the Chinese system.
2. *t‘ien*$^{2}$ *t‘u*$^{3}$, lands ; fields.
3. *ta*$^{4}$ *t‘ien*$^{2}$, the autumn crops, which are many and of large value as compared with those of spring.
4. *kua*$^{1}$ *t‘ien*$^{2}$, lands growing gourds, melons, etc.
5. *yi*$^{4}$ *t‘ien*$^{2}$ *ho*$^{2}$ *shu*$^{3}$, a field all rice or millet ; a well-filled field.
6. *shan*$^{1}$ *shui*$^{3}$, scenery ; *lit.*, hills and water ; also, the water on the hills ; torrents.
7. *shan*$^{1}$ *ch‘uan*$^{1}$, *ts‘ao*$^{3}$ *mu*$^{4}$, scenery ; landscape ; *lit.*, hills, streams, herbage (or plants), and trees. *Shan*$^{1}$ *ch‘uan*$^{1}$, the water system of a country.
8. *hsi*$^{1}$ *shan*$^{1}$, the hills to the west.
9. *shan*$^{1}$ *ku*$^{3}$, hill and valley ; valleys in the hills.
10. *ku*$^{3}$ *k‘ou*$^{3}$, a gorge, narrow pass ; *lit.*, valley's mouth.
11. *hsi*$^{1}$ *fang*$^{1}$, the western region ; western country ; often, specially, Thibet, the land of Buddha.
12. *ta*$^{4}$ *fêng*$^{1}$, high wind ; a gale.
13. *hsi*$^{1}$ *fêng*$^{1}$, west wind.
14. *fêng*$^{1}$ *shui*$^{3}$, air and water ; the influence superstitionsly attributed to certain aspects of buildings, localities, etc.
15. *fêng*$^{1}$ *yen*$^{2}$, words borne on the wind ; rumour.
16. *yang*$^{2}$ *chiao*$^{3}$ *fêng*$^{1}$, ram's horn wind ; a whirlwind ; name given to a child's convulsions.
17. *hsiang*$^{1}$ *fêng*$^{1}$ *shih*$^{2}$ *li*$^{3}$, fragrance blown 10 *li*.
18. *t‘u*$^{3}$ *yin*$^{1}$, sounds of the locality ; a local dialect.
19. *shui*$^{3}$ *yin*$^{1}$, water sounds ; *lit.*, the murmur of flowing water ; *fig.*, affection of one's proper accent caused by residence away from home, *q.d.* by drinking the water of the strange place.
20. *shan*$^{1}$ *yin*$^{1}$, sounds in hills ; an echo.
21. *shui*$^{3}$ *sê*$^{4}$, tint of water ; its pleasant tint, as in spring or autumn ; used also of the complexion of a handsome woman.
22. *yi*$^{4}$ *sê*$^{4}$, of uniform colour.
23. *ta*$^{4}$ *yü*$^{3}$, heavy rain.
24. *ch‘ien*$^{4}$ *yü*$^{3}$, there is a want of rain.
25. *yü*$^{3}$ *shui*$^{3}$, rain water ; also the name of one of the 24 periods into which the Chinese year is divided.
26. *shih*$^{2}$ *jih*$^{4}$ *yi*$^{4}$ *yü*$^{3}$, rain once in 10 days ; preceded by another sentence, wind once in five days ; weather to please farmers.

6

27. *t'u*$^{3}$ *shan*$^{1}$ *tzŭ*$^{3}$, an artificial mound in a garden, etc.; *t'u*$^{3}$ *shan*$^{1}$, a hill or mound of earth, as distinguished from one of rock.
28. *huang*$^{2}$ *t'u*$^{3}$, clay.
29. *hei*$^{1}$ *t'u*$^{3}$, black loam; specially of the dirty soil of Peking.
30. *kuei*$^{3}$ *huo*$^{3}$, devil fire, will-o'-the-wisp.
31. *chin*$^{1}$ *ku*$^{3}$, gong; *lit.*, metal and drum; *fig.*, sounds of war; the gong properly gives the signal to retire, the drum to advance.
32. *chin*$^{1}$ *kua*$^{1}$, a red gourd not eatable; one of the insignia borne on a pole at funerals and at certain state ceremonies.
33. *mu*$^{4}$ *kua*$^{1}$, papaya, BRIDGMAN (?). In the North a scented melon, not eaten, but used in medicine.
34. *mu*$^{4}$ *êrh*$^{3}$, a tree's ear; an edible lichen.
35. *mu*$^{4}$ *yü*$^{2}$ *tzŭ*$^{3}$, a hollow wooden vessel on which the Buddhist priest taps when chanting or begging.

## 11.

1. *ch'ang*$^{2}$ *yi*$^{2}$ *ts'un*$^{4}$, 1 inch long.
2. *pa*$^{2}$ *ts'un*$^{4}$ *êrh*$^{4}$, 8 inches 2 [tenths].
3. *pa*$^{1}$ *tou*$^{4}$ *tou*$^{4}$ *tzŭ*$^{3}$, 8 measures of pulse. The addition of *tzŭ*$^{3}$ to other nouns is common.
4. *shih*$^{2}$ *chin*$^{1}$ *mi*$^{3}$, 10 catties of rice.
5. *yi*$^{1}$ *êrh*$^{4}$ *p'i*$^{3}$, one or two bales of cloth, drapery, etc.
6. *yi*$^{1}$ *êrh*$^{4}$ *yeh*$^{4}$, one or two leaves of a book.
7. *pa*$^{1}$ *shih*$^{2}$ *êrh*$^{4}$ *li*$^{3}$, 82 *li*=some 27 miles.
8. *fei*$^{1}$ *chih*$^{3}$ *yi*$^{4}$ *jên*$^{2}$, not only one person.
9. *chih*$^{3}$ *ch'ien*$^{4}$ *yi*$^{1}$ *wên*$^{2}$, only one cash short.
10. *pa*$^{1}$ *k'ou*$^{3}$ *jên*$^{2}$, eight persons; *q.d.* such or such a family consisting of. The expression is no more to be taken literally than "half a dozen" with us.
11. *yi*$^{1}$ *fang*$^{1}$, a whole neighbourhood.
12. *yi*$^{2}$ *ts'un*$^{4}$ *chien*$^{4}$ *fang*$^{1}$, to be an inch square. The verb *chien*$^{4}$ is here reflective.
13. *tou*$^{3}$ *fang*$^{1}$, literally, bushel-square; the square or oblong space left often in the trelliswork of a Chinese window, to admit the light; said to derive its name from the size, not the form, of the space so reserved.
14. *jih*$^{4}$ *yung*$^{4}$ *tou*$^{3}$ *chin*$^{1}$, daily expend a measure of gold; expenditure of a wealthy man. Cf. our *pot* of money.

## 12.

1. *jih*$^{4}$ *jih*$^{4}$, every day.
2. *yüeh*$^{4}$ *yüeh*$^{4}$, every month.
3. *yi*$^{4}$ *jih*$^{4}$ *yi*$^{2}$ *chien*$^{4}$, to see or visit once every day.
4. *shan*$^{1}$ *kao*$^{1}$ *yüeh*$^{4}$ *hsiao*$^{3}$, mountains lofty, moon small; the moon rising behind lofty mountains; phrase used of the picturesque effect of such a scene.
5. *yüeh*$^{4}$ *sê*$^{4}$, moonlight; rather used of a moon old and bright.
6. *yüeh*$^{4}$ *hsi*$^{1}$, moonlit night; part of rather a high-flown phrase applied to the beauties of spring.
7. *tzŭ*$^{4}$ *ch'ên*$^{2}$ *chih*$^{4}$ *yu*$^{3}$, from about 8 A.M. to about 5 P.M. The Chinese day and night are divided into 12 two-hourly periods. The *ch'ên*$^{2}$ is the fourth before midnight; *yu*$^{3}$, the third from noon.
8. *jih*$^{4}$ *tzŭ*$^{3}$, a day.
9. *ch'ang*$^{2}$ *chih*$^{4}$ *jih*$^{4}$, of days lengthening after the winter solstice.

語言自邇集



## 13.

1. *ch'ing*$^1$, *huang*$^2$, *ch'ih*$^4$, *pê*$^2$, *hê*$^4$ (or, in Peking, *po*$^2$, *ho*$^4$); sky-blue or deep-green, yellow, blood-red, white, black.
2. *ch'ing*$^1$ *pai*$^2$, blue-white=pale blue.
3. *hei*$^1$ *pai*$^2$ (so pronounced in Peking colloquial), black and white, as of a chessboard's squares; also used when speaking of intense stupidity that cannot tell white from black.
4. *ch'ing*$^1$ *huang*$^2$, green and yellow. Unripe grain is said not to have reached the age when these colours mingle. The phrase is also applied to a sickly countenance.
5. *ch'ih*$^4$ *sê*$^4$, bright scarlet, such as is used on temples, etc.; also ruddy, as a person's complexion. In the latter sense it is pronounced in Peking *ch'ih*$^4$ *shai*$^3$.
6. *huang*$^2$ *êrh*$^2$ *hei*$^1$, yellow and yet black; said of the countenance in certain sickness.
7. *hsiang*$^1$ *sê*$^4$, the colour of *hsiang*$^1$, Chinese incense sticks, which we call joss-sticks; a pale yellow dye seen in silks, cloth, etc.
8. *yüeh*$^4$ *pai*$^2$ *sê*$^4$, moon-white (=pale blue) colour.
9. *yü*$^4$ *sê*$^4$, colour of jade; much the same as *yüeh*$^4$ *pai*$^2$ *sê*$^4$.
10. *nü*$^3$ *sê*$^4$, lust after women.

## 14.

1. *huo*$^3$ *shih*$^2$, a flint.
2. *shan*$^1$ *tzŭ*$^3$ *shih*$^2$, a rockery; the stones used to make one.
3. *shih*$^2$ *chiu*$^4$ *tzŭ*$^3$, a stone mortar.
4. *shih*$^2$ *mên*$^2$, a gate or doorway of stone; passage through a rockery; rock pass between hills.
5. *shih*$^2$ *jên*$^2$, human figure of stone.
6. *shih*$^2$ *ma*$^3$, stone horse.
7. *pai*$^2$ *yü*$^4$, white jade.
8. *chin*$^1$ *k'ou*$^3$ *yü*$^4$ *yen*$^2$, mouth of gold words of jade; such as the Emperor speaks; Imperial affirmations or predictions. Used with negatives in rejecting what is said to you by another, as *not* infallible. What you say, or he says, is *not* mouth of gold, etc.
9. *wa*$^3$, *fou*$^3$, *chin*$^1$, *yü*$^4$, tile, earthenware; gold, jade (or jewels). The first two are better to buy than the last; thrift is better than profusion.
10. *wa*$^3$ *mien*$^4$, tile face=the roof of a house.
11. *wa*$^3$ *p'ien*$^4$, a bit of tile.

# PART III.

## THE FORTY EXERCISES.

(CHINESE TEXT.)

## EXERCISE I.

1 十六。十九。二十。三十四。五十七。六十八。

2 第十七個。二三百。二三千。兩三千。三兩個。三五個。五六百個人。

3 第一。第二。十七。第一千八百六十五。

4 第一百萬零三百個。五十七萬零六百一十。七十萬零二十。

5 一百萬。三十五萬。五百萬零一。六萬零五百零七。十萬。

6 七萬零一百九十一。千萬。四十六萬一千。

7 五萬零八十八。九萬八千四百零二。一千零五。四千零七十二。八千三百六十七。一萬零六。一百零三。

8 一百一十八。二百五十四。九百九十九萬三千。

9 有幾個人來。有些個人。有好些個人。有多少人來。三萬多人。

10 數十個。幾十個。十幾個。兩個。幾個。不止十個。八九個。十來個。九個。十個。二百多。五千多。

11 長三寸四。一身一口。有幾口人。五斤牛肉。六斤羊肉。幾斤魚。

12 七斗麥子。九斗米。一斗黍子。

13 幾個牙。長幾萬里。至多四萬里。有山足高二百里。三百斤有零。

## EXERCISE I. KEY.

1

十二。十四。九十。七十三。四十五。一百九十九。

2

四萬零一百六十八。三百萬零一千二百二十四。八百二十九。二百九十二。

3

第二十一。第三百四十二。第八十。第六十七。有八九個人來。

4

第九百九十九。第七百萬零六千五百四十三。第三百萬零四千五百六十七。

5

五百萬零二百零一。三百萬零二十七。六千零四十。九十九萬九千九百九十九。

6

有好些個馬。有多少牛。牛馬有五十六。

7

有幾斤魚。有七斤零幾兩。六斗小米子。有十八斗米。十四斗豆子。

8

有十幾個人來。有五十多人來。有一百多個人來。一身一口。

9

有十來斤魚。十九斤牛肉。十七斤鹿肉。十四斗米。十八斗豆子。十斗小米子。

10

長多少里。長好些里。足一千七百里。足九百里。有山足高八里。

## EXERCISE II.

1 我們倆人。偺們倆。這麼大。那麼小。

2 甚麼人。甚麼東西。

3 那個人是誰。那個人是個好人。他是個買賣人。賣甚麼的。賣好些個東西。

4 我要好的有沒有。沒有了。這個很好。那個不好。這個人很好、那個人很不好。

5 他來了沒有。他沒來。有甚麼人來。沒有人來。有人來了。他是那‘兒的人。他不是這兒的人。

6 他們來了多少人。他們來了好些個人。有多少人在那兒。有十幾個人

7 這個是我們的。那個是他們的。這個是甚麼人的。這個東西是誰的。是我們的。這個東西你們有多少。有不多的。

8 我不要這個、他們要這個。他們的不大好。你們那兒有好的沒有。沒有好的。沒有狠好的、我們不要了。你們有這個東西沒有。我們不要這個東西。我買不了那麼些個。

9 這個了不得。那個了不了。

10 這個東西很好。這個東西好得很。

11 你要買馬、得‘買個好的。那馬買不得、毛長得不好。

12 那竹子長得很長。他來了你得‘走。

13 那個人比我的兒子高八寸多。你們是幾口人。我們是十來口人。

## EXERCISE II. KEY.

1 你的馬、我的羊。他的車。你們的米。我們的手巾。他們的刀子。

2 你們買、我們賣。他們要買東西。要買甚麼東西。要買好東西。我們這兒賣很好的東西。

3 這麼小、那麼大。這個山不是那麼高。

4 你有好馬沒有。我沒有。我們這兒賣好車、不賣馬。這個車不是好的。

5 這個馬是誰的。是我的。你有多少馬。我有三個馬。這兒有多少車。不狠多。

6 你是那‘兒的人。我是這兒的人。那個買賣人是那‘兒的人。他不是這兒的人。他賣的東西好不好。不很好。這兒的買賣人沒有很好的東西。我們倆買賣人賣好東西。

7 我要買東西、這兒有賣東西的沒有。不很多。有多少。有五個。我要買好些個東西、你賣不賣。你要甚麼東西。要好東西。

8 他有多少兒女。他有四個女兒、五個兒子。他五個兒子在這兒、他的女兒在那兒。我走了一百里。他是賣瓦的。我要買的是幾斗麥子。

9 你要得‘多少日子。我要得‘三個月。你用的是麥子是黍子。這是甚麼東西。這是黑豆。這兒魚不少。

10 那個東西是金的麼。不是金的、是黃土的。他鼻子很小。那鹿肉是很好。那黃羊子是這兒的麼。是這兒的。這兒的山水很好、

11 那個人長得很高。那長虫有三寸多長。他來了我得‘見他。

## EXERCISE III.

1 有人拿東西來了。有人來要拏那東西去。那東西很多、一個人拏不了去。

2 那人是拏不得、那人是拿不著的、那人是拿不了的。

3 屋裏。進屋裏來。這個屋子沒有人住。

4 住房子。這個房子比他那個房子好多了。

5 你們那兒有多少房子。有三十五間房子。你住的房子大小。我住的是三間小屋子。

6 他在家裏做甚麼。他沒在家。上那‘兒去了。上街去了。街上走着。街上的人很多。外頭土大。

7 你在那‘兒住。我在城裏頭住。是東城住着好、是西城住着好。他那人開的鋪子在那‘兒、是做甚麼買賣的。

8 他那鋪子東城有三個、西城有四個、我們這兒沒有那麼大的買賣。那個鋪子是我的。那鋪子裏買東西的人很多。

9 他來了沒有。他來了。他沒進來、過去往西去了。他上街買東西去了。他來過沒有。

10 這個道兒過得去麼。過不去。你上那‘兒去。我不上那‘兒去。你上那兒去過沒有。我沒去過。

11 你做甚麼來着。他沒起來。你這個人得‘起來了。那東西拿不起來。風起來了。起了大風。

12 要下雨。下過了大雨了。這麼大雨住不了。雨住了。這個東西拿得住拿不住。拿得住。你小心拿住了。

13 他那門開得開開不開。開不開。

## EXERCISE III. KEY.

1 你住在城裏頭。我在城外頭住。我住的房子有六間。你在那‘兒開鋪子、在那‘兒住家。

2 這個房子比那個房子大多了。這個房子有十間、那個房子有四間。大街上住房不很多、鋪子不少。

3 他住家在那‘兒。他在西城一個小小兒的房子裏住。他在那兒開鋪子是不是。他不是買賣人。

4 進屋裏來、街上有土。那屋門兒開了。他開着幾個鋪子。他開着三四個鋪子。開在那‘兒。開在東城。他的買賣大不大。不很大。

5 他在家裏做甚麼。他沒有甚麼做的、他出城去了、往那‘兒去了。往西去了。他要做甚麼。他要買車買馬。

6 我要買他的東西的。那個買賣人往那‘兒去了。我住的房子他知道不知道、他沒進過你的屋子、他是不知道。

7 他那個人的房子、比你我的房子好多了。他那房子有多少間。有八間、我的房子有六間、你的房子有四間。他那房子的口面大。

## EXERCISE IV.

1 有人說那個地方兒住不得。是誰說的。是我說的。你那‘兒知道。

2 這是誰家的房子。誰知道。我做不出來。他說不出來。他做過多少回。他做了一回。

3 外頭來了五六個人。是甚麼人。我不知道。

4 大人進來你們都得‘站起來。我在樓上坐著、他是在地下躺著。

5 你愛這個不愛。我不大愛。

6 你快些兒走、城門一關、你回不了家了。我身子乏、走不了。

7 把門開開。門開了。關上牕戶。把牕戶關上。牕戶關上了。

8 他在道兒上躺著、叫他起來。把門關上。

9 走著來的步下走著。他走了來的、我是坐車來的。他是步行來的。我在前頭走。他在後頭走。快走。我快走了。慢慢兒的走。

10 他那個人回來了沒有。他沒回來。他上那‘兒去了。上衙門去了。他去是坐轎子是坐車。坐頂小轎去的。他不大愛坐車。是他那頂轎子好。

11 是這兒的騾子好是那兒的騾子好。這兒騾子沒有那兒的好。這兒騾子比那兒的慢。那兒騾子驢都快。

12 他買的是馬麼。不是、買的是騾子驢。他買了多少。買了三頭騾子七個驢。

13 你是步行來的是騎馬來的。我是騎馬來的。我那匹馬跑得很快。

## EXERCISE IV. KEY.

1

他在樓上坐著、叫他快往這兒來。他不快來、來的很慢。我在頭裏坐車、他在後頭坐轎子。

2

叫他買兩輛車、四匹馬。他說這兒沒有馬。他說騾子比馬好。他買了騾子沒有。買了。他買了多少騾子。買了四頭。他買了驢沒有。他沒買、你沒叫他買驢。

3

他上衙門去是坐轎子是坐車。他是步行去的、他說是坐車坐轎子都不愛。他回來的不快。他在地下躺著、起不來。

4

那匹馬比這匹快。馬比騾子快、騾子比驢快。他到了沒到。沒到。他做甚麼。他慢慢兒的走著。叫他快來。

5

你有幾頂轎子。有兩頂。你的騾馬驢有多少。有四匹馬、三頭騾子、五個驢。你有車沒有。沒有、我的車都賣了。你站著做甚麼。不做甚麼。你愛坐著、我愛站著。

## EXERCISE V.

1 我要請先生教告你給我找了先生沒有。找著了、他不來、他說學生那麼多不肯來。先生請坐。請教，這是甚麼字。

2 叫人把那字典拿來。請先生找出那個字來要找甚麼字呢要找瞧字。

3 請問、這個字你認得不認得。這個字我還沒看見過呢。這個字你看見過沒有、那個字你還沒有看見過麼。真沒看見過。

4 你告訴我、他那個人的口音、有你的好沒有、我的口音不大甚麼好、他認得的字比我認得的多。

5 這個字你見過沒見過見過了。你告訴我是甚麼字。我不記得那個字了。還有不記得的字麼。那兒沒有呢、記得的少、不記得的多。

## EXERCISE V. KEY.

1 我請了先生來教我說話。你還要學寫字不要。請先生告訴我、我的口音正不正、不很正、你認得的字還不多。

2 那字典在那兒。在先生的屋裏、他那兒找字呢。他找的字、你請他給抄下來。先生不肯來。他告訴我、你的口音很不好、說話又不眞。

3 我的先生你見過沒有。我見他騎著馬、那馬跑的很快、他沒瞧見我。請拿字典找記字。我找著了。那個字你認得不認得。那個字我還沒瞧見過。

4 這幾個學生學甚麼。學寫字、學認字。他們的先生是誰。我不知道是誰。你見過沒有。見過。他在這兒教學生。那字你抄了沒有。還沒抄哪、要快抄。

5 你愛騎馬不愛。馬跑得快、我不愛騎他。這個馬好不好。不很好、他跑得慢。騎住了。

## EXERCISE VI.

1 他說的官話還可以、可是沒有你的好、他說的官話、還有土音。聽見說你得了幾本書、都看完了沒有。得是得了、看了不過一兩本。

2 我聽見說你學著官話呢、學得很好、那四聲你分得出分不出。都還可以分得開。

3 那一本書你看完了沒有。十分裏看了有七八分。明白不明白。有幾分不大明白、也有幾個字不認得。

4 你念了多少日子的書。我念了十個月的書。那書上的字都記得麼。記不了那麼多。忘了好些個了、還有記錯了的。

5 他那個人懂得官話不懂。我聽見人說他不懂得。他認得字不認得。字還認得、認過四五千字。你那兒知道呢。上月我們在一塊兒看書。我叫他抄寫、他行不行。沒有甚麼不行的。

6 你告訴我、他的話你聽得出來。聽不出來、

7 你念過的書、千萬不可忘了。不錯、你說得很是。

8 你會用我們這兒的字典麼。會用是會用、找字可得慢些兒。

## EXERCISE VI. KEY.

1 拿那一管筆給我。這個筆不好、還有好的沒有。好的沒有了、不好的還有兩三管。

2 拿一張紙、一塊墨、一管筆、寫字。你要我寫甚麼字。這書上不認得的字都寫。

3 我聽見說你學官話呢、你懂得不懂得。我不大懂、念的日子不多。

4 四聲你會分不會。都會分。肯字是那一聲。是上聲。不錯。你拿這張紙、寫那個字。你寫錯了。

5 那一本書你看完了沒有。看完了、也很明白。有不認得的字沒有。那兒沒有呢、不認得的多、認得的少。

6 我的話你懂不懂。你的口音這麼正、我很懂得。

7 你給我買一張紙、一管筆、可以不可以。可以。你還要墨不要。不要、要五張紙、兩管筆、明白不明白。都明白了。

## EXERCISE VII.

1 廚房。一把刀子。一把鍤子。一個炒勺。一個飯鍋。一個鍋蓋。一個茶碗。一個茶盅。一個酒杯。一個酒盅子。

2 他要上炕躺著。我在牀上躺著。你快把鋪蓋鋪上。那個人快上牀了。

3 那牀上有帳子沒有。他在牀上躺著、我在椅子上坐著。

4 這屋裏黑了、快拿燈來。桌子上的那蠟燈是誰拏了去了。是我給廚子拏過去了。廚房的火弄上還沒著呢。

5 飯鍋是煮飯的、鍋蓋就是飯鍋的蓋兒、茶碗茶盅也有有蓋兒的。

6 酒杯酒盅子這兩個東西不大很分、可也分得出來、本是酒杯比酒盅兒大。

7 那屋裏那些桌子椅子都壞了、說桌椅兩分、是兩張桌子八張椅子。

8 那個勺本大。勺子比勺小。匙子比勺子還小。說的是一把勺子一把匙子這都是京話這麼用。

9 你們屋裏有蓆子沒有。我們屋裏炕上都有蓆子。

10 你們那兒也用蠟燈麼。我們黑下也是用蠟燈。

11 你買了那麼些蠟是作甚麼用。都是家裏用。是廚房用麼。不是、都是黑下看書用的。

語言自邇集



## EXERCISE VII. KEY.

1 炕上的蓆子他給拏了去了。叫他給我拏來。這床上的鋪蓋在那兒。他也拏了去都賣了。

2 蠟燈在那兒在椅子上。把那蠟燈拏了去、拏個燈來。那燈你找著了沒有。這屋裏這麼黑、看不見燈在那兒。給我那蠟燈、我找去。

3 酒盅子比酒杯小。茶碗茶盅都可以說。蓋兒有大的有小的、飯鍋的蓋兒比茶碗的蓋兒大。

4 那屋裏帳子蓆子都壞了。你快去買帳子鋪蓋、把鋪蓋鋪好了。

5 給我一把刀子一把鍤子一把勺子。桌子上有刀子鍤子、沒有勺子。叫廚子給你一把勺子。

6 廚子煑飯用的飯鍋他那個人拏了去了、廚子說那飯他煑不了。我問那個人飯鍋是誰拏了去了、他說不知道是誰。

7 你那話說錯了。我沒說我看見他做的。我說的是你告訴我是他做的、你沒明白我的話。我明白不明白不用說、你找我的錯兒做甚麼。誰找你的錯兒、你做你的、我做我的。

8 我要分這塊紙給那五個人、給他的可得比那四個人的分兒大。你去請他把拏了去的我那兩本書還給我。

## EXERCISE VIII.

1 一條櫈子一個櫈子都說得。分的是長的多說條、方的多說個。話條子是學話用的。

2 花瓶。酒瓶。酒壺。茶壺。盤子。碟子。

3 點燈、吹燈。燒火。滅火。

4 倒水。你把這個水給倒了。他倒水去了。倒茶來。這東西站不住、倒下來了壞了。

5 空是沒有東西在裏頭、空手也說得。壺滿是把壺倒滿了。茶壺空了。酒壺滿了。那酒壺是空的是滿的。是空的。

6 那花瓶是甚麼人弄破了的。那是我弄破的、可沒有壞、收拾收拾還可以使得。那傢伙弄壞了、使不得。

7 那刀子鍤子勺子盤子碟子飯碗酒杯、這些個都是喫飯的傢伙

8 花瓶也算是傢伙麼。花瓶也可以算是傢伙。

9 爐子有大小不同。廚房裏做飯用的是爐子、炕裏燒的是爐子、屋裏燒的也是爐子。

10 叫人倒茶、是叫人把茶拿來倒在茶碗裏頭。你點了燈沒有。我點上了、他給吹滅了。

11 吹燈是人把燈吹滅了。燈滅了、火滅了、是燈火自己滅了。

12 那倆壺裏有水沒有。一個是空的、一個是滿的。你把那空的倒滿了水。

## EXERCISE VIII. KEY.

1 我眞不知道你要那麼些椅子做甚麼.

2 你還筭算、請了二十五個人來吃飯、你想、我們用的那幾張椅子、二十五個人還坐得下麼。

3 二十五個人坐不下、廚房裏的櫈子很使得。

4 有了櫈子可坐開了、請間櫈子在吃飯的屋子還好看不好看。還有碟子飯碗、得‘找幾個。可不知道往那‘兒去找去。

5 我們這兒有三十個飯碗。

6 那飯碗使不得、又有六個破的。

7 我不管破不破、叫人來收拾就得了。

8 我買了他一桌傢伙、還有廚房用的些個零碎東西、同燒火使的、他開的帳、你給筭一算錯不錯.

9 我不會筭帳。這是那‘兒的話、那先生還沒教給你認數目字麼。

10 那小寫的數目字我認得了、這都是大寫的我還不懂。

## EXERCISE IX.

1 前兒就是前天、昨兒昨天、今兒今天、明兒明天、後兒後天、都是那麼著。

2 天氣分得是天冷、天熱、天涼、天暖和、颳風、晴天、下雨、下雪、這些都在裏頭。

3 一點半鐘就是一點鐘兩刻。一下鐘就是一點鐘。

4 他那個人念過二十多年的書、不過做了五六個月的先生。這個人白日愛騎馬、黑下回家看書。

5 我今兒走、下月可以回來。你這個人今兒八下鐘還沒起來麽。

6 前年後年說得、前月後月不大很說。這兒天熱的時候兒下雨、天冷就下雪。

7 前四天颳北風、第二天天氣很冷。昨兒黑下下雨、夜裡住了、今兒天晴了。

8 今年天氣暖和得很、沒有去年那麼冷。今年的時令不正、這幾年誰見過四月裡還下雪呢。

9 我們倆到這兒好些年了。他是去年來的、我是上月到的、他們倆去年來過了。

## EXERCISE IX. KEY.

1 你那'一年到京裏來的.

2 我是今年到的。來的日子不多、不過有半年。

3 你的京話說的到很不錯。

4 那都是我在南方就學過的。

5 那就是了。你看這兒水土好不好。

6 這水土沒甚麼不好、時令很和平、熱到沒甚麼熱、我在這兒沒過過年、不知道冷怎麼樣。

7 在屋裏到很暖和、可是這麼說、要在外頭走幾天可了不得。

8 聽見說這兒的雪很大。

9 不是雪到少、一年不過下一二寸。我說的是颳風吹的冷。

10 你天天都做甚麼。

11 我天天七點半鐘起來、就喫點心、回頭請先生、念三點半鐘的書、就喫飯咯、回來騎馬出去。

12 那們今兒喫完了飯、你來和我騎馬去、行不行。

13 你瞧天氣涼了、要下雨、晴不了。

14 可不是麼、那們還是明兒個去好。明兒定甚麼時候兒去。

15 定一亮就走。涼到沒甚麼涼、快跑點兒就得了。

## EXERCISE X.

1 工夫。每年不是年年麼。每月就是月月、每天每日還是那麼樣。

2 他是早起起來、晌午上街、晚晌回家看書、到夜裏三更天就在炕上躺著天天都是這麼樣。

3 各自各兒、就是自己一個人。這個事情得你各自各兒去。那房子就是他各自各兒住著。

4 上半天下了雨、下半天晴了。前半夜還暖和、後半夜冷。三更天就是半夜。

5 夜裏那打更的打更、一夜有五更、頭一更就是定更。

6 天長做事的工夫多、天短沒有空兒、事情得擱著罷。

7 他多喒回來。他明兒回來罷。那茶壺擱在那兒了。擱在屋裏桌子上了。

8 天上的雲彩滿了就是陰天。今兒早起下的霧很大、那麼大的山都看不見了。

9 你在那兒站著做甚麼、快去罷。

10 那飯得了罷。還沒得、得一會子呢。那麼偺們還上街走一走罷。

## EXERCISE X. KEY.

1 昨兒晚上我聽見街上有好些個聲兒。你聽見是甚麼樣兒的聲兒。

2 就在門口兒有打木頭的聲兒。

3 那就是更夫打更的聲兒。每夜分作五更、頭一更是定更、第三更就是半夜。這打更的白日裏沒事、到夜裏就一點空兒也沒有。他就在那小房子裏各自各兒住著、也沒女人也沒兒子。不管晴天陰天都得出來、不能說今兒我擱著不管罷。一年到頭都是一樣。

4 今兒個滿天都是雲彩、陰的什麼都看不見了。

5 可不陰了麼。早起下大霧來著、到晌午可就晴了一會子。到黑上來、還不定晴不晴呢。

6 這時候一天比一天短了、偺們的夜書是打多早晚兒念起。

7 這會子不得工夫、先擱著罷。我打算過幾天再說。

## EXERCISE XI.

1 腌臢。乾淨。衣裳。靴子。鞋。襪子。把衣裳穿上。把靴子脫下來。一雙靴子。

2 那一雙靴子得補上一點兒皮子。他買了十雙襪子一條手巾。那也不算多。洗靴子溫和水使不得。

3 這盆水腌臢了、換乾淨的拏來我洗臉。那衣裳腌臢了、拏刷子給刷一刷。

4 這件衣裳破了、叫人來給補補罷。不用補罷、縫一縫也行了。一個臉盆。

5 你快起來罷、穿上衣裳。他脫了衣裳躺著。那一件衣裳他穿了好些日子沒換呢。

6 今兒個天冷、你得多穿一件衣裳。你見他的時候兒他是穿靴子是穿鞋呢。

7 這條手巾不乾淨、擱在臉盆裏洗一洗罷。你愛穿的是靴子是鞋。那都看我是做甚麼、在家裏沒事我就穿鞋、上衙門的時候兒可得穿靴子。

8 你那一雙皮鞋子這麼些日子老在那兒擱著、得刷一刷罷。不錯、你給刷罷。

9 你洗手是愛使涼水是愛使開水。兩樣兒都不好、涼水太涼開水太熱。最好的就是溫和水兒。

10 你快把這水倒在鍋裏溫一溫罷。那火要滅了。這水溫了半天老開不了。

## EXERCISE XI. KEY.

1 老太太告訴我說你今兒起的不大早。

2 不錯、昨兒晚上在外頭喫飯、回來晚了。道兒貧不好走、不用說靴子衣裳都弄髒了、就是臉也都髒的看不得。回家時就叫人拏溫和洗臉水兒來、把衣裳靴子都脫了、一看、襪子也破咯、得補咯。叫人拏雙鞋來、擱在炕爐子那兒、換了一身乾淨衣裳。哎呀、這靴子著了雨、不好脫、在我說還是穿鞋好。喫了碗茶、心裏就好點兒。可是夜裏的雨下的很可怕。你也出門來著嗎。

3 我是穿了一身好衣裳來著、不肯弄壞了、沒出門兒。

4 請喝茶。這話都不用說了。

5 這茶水開不開。

6 水在火上擱了半天、可不是開的嗎。

## EXERCISE XII.

1 女人們小的時候兒學針線、他們多一半不認得字。帽子是說一頂。裁縫裁衣裳縫衣裳都行。

2 你洗澡的時候兒不要把頭髮擱在水裏、頭髮一着水、老乾不了。

3 單衣裳是就有一面兒沒有裏兒的、夾衣裳是有裏兒有面兒的。棉衣裳是夾衣裳中間有棉花的。出汗。

4 砍肩兒是有前後沒有袖子的那一件衣裳。汗衫是儘裏頭穿的單衣裳。

5 褂子是儘外頭穿的衣裳、短的就叫馬褂子。這一條褲子是棉的是夾的。

6 帽子有小帽兒官帽兒兩様兒、官帽兒也分涼帽暖帽。

7 你會做針線不會。我不會。那麼着我就叫一個裁縫來把我那一件汗衫補了。

8 那一件砍肩兒裁了還沒縫呢。那一件破馬褂子得補了。拏撣子撣一撣衣裳上的土。

9 那一把木梳是誰梳頭的。洗澡是一身都洗。天天兒洗澡很好。

10 你老先生頭髮短得很、頂兒上也就沒有了。我有五十多了、是沒頭髮的時候兒了。

11 今年棉花多不多。少是不少、可沒有去年那麼多。

語言自邇集



## EXERCISE XII. KEY.

1 裁縫來了。

2 叫他進來。

3 您要做的都是什麼衣裳。

4 要褂子褲子砍肩兒、還要做穿在儘裏頭的那個甚麼。

5 您說的是小褂兒不是。

6 不錯、還要好幾件汗衫兒。

7 那個褂子您要棉的要夾的。

8 兩樣兒都不要、天氣太熱了。你做個單的就得咯。

9 袖子是做什麼樣兒的。

10 比我這個要長點兒。

11 你小心點兒這衣裳、都要比著身子裁、穿著就有樣兒了。我還告訴你、不要一穿就壞了。

12 您要是天天兒到晚上把衣裳攞乾淨了就老不壞了。

13 這衣裳得幾天就得了。

14 我很會做針線、不多日子就得了。

15 這個裁縫臟的看不得、他有點兒老不用胰子的樣兒、頭髮也不梳。

16 那是他沒有木梳罷。

## EXERCISE XIII.

1 賬目。花錢。花費。四吊錢的票子。不知道那個東西的輕重得拏秤稱一稱。

2 他欠人的賬目不少。他該的賬不下一千兩銀子。他還不了那麼些個罷。

3 我借錢是我把人家的錢拏來我使。我借給人錢是把我的錢拏給人使。

4 我們家裡天天兒的花費不很多。他愛花錢好花錢都說得。他那個人過於花錢、他的本錢快完了罷。

5 那個房子價錢不貴。這一件皮褂子價值很便宜。那個花瓶不值錢。今年的棉花很賤。他家裏一個大錢都沒有。

6 那當十的大錢裏頭、有七分是銅的有三分是鐵的。黃金比銀子重、鐵比銀子輕。

7 票子是一張紙上頭寫着錢數兒、買東西同銀子錢一個樣兒。那褂子他當了十吊錢的票子。

8 那花瓶兒他賣不賣。賣他是一定賣、你要可得花倆錢兒、他不是賤買的。

9 該當花錢的時候兒。誰怕花個一二兩、你這個人一開口、就是十兩八兩的話。

## EXERCISE XIII. KEY.

1 我打算上口外去、聽見說票子不好使、還是用銀子方便、還有那小銅錢兒、也得要點兒。

2 要是一定要、可是他們用的那個錢不是京裏使的那個錢罷。

3 不錯、京裏使的錢是一個當十個的大錢。這銀子到口外換著很費事。不用說銀子的價錢不同、就是平的大小也不一樣。

4 聽見說出了關、那兒的火食賤多了。

5 火食是賤、要是把這個車錢房錢算起來、花費可也不少呢。你回來的時候兒怕要該下好些賬。

6 要該賬是一定得還的。還不了、請你借給我點兒錢就是了。

7 你還打算借呢、先頭裏你短我好幾兩銀子老沒還我、還借這不太過於點兒嗎。

8 那就罷了。今兒銀子換多少錢。

9 今兒銀子換十七吊多錢。

10 那麼你給我平二十兩銀子罷。

11 平得了、拏了去罷。你這一道兒上太太平平的。

## EXERCISE XIV.

1 雞子兒。牛奶。燈油。香油。這菜弄得吃不得、快撤了去罷。燈油是豆子做的、香油是芝蔴做的、火油出在地裏。

2 我昨兒買了三百斤煤五十斤炭八十斤柴火四石米二百斤麪。天冷的時候兒煤炭用的多。

3 炕爐子是燒煤的多、火盆是用炭。火盆是屋裏用的、不是做飯做水的。

4 菜有生的有熟的、在火上做的都是熟菜、生菜在地下長出來就可以吃得。

5 你去給我買一個小雞子三四個雞子兒。還要牛奶不要。牛奶便宜、我就要幾斤。我們這兒買牛奶不論斤數兒、都是論碗論瓶。

6 買果子是論箇兒的多。你快弄飯去、飯得了就端上來。

7 你愛吃饅頭愛吃飯。兩樣兒都不愛、我愛喝湯。愛喝什麼湯呢。肉湯雞湯都好。

8 我明天要請人吃飯、給他們什麼菜好。不論甚麼菜都可以、他們都是偺們本家的人。

## EXERCISE XIV. KEY.

1 我今年的煤火錢花的不少.那煤的價兒一天比一天貴、柴火又出的不多、每月花的至少也得十三塊。

2 那是你燒那頂好的煤、都是口外來的。我燒的是炭、賤多着呢、廚房裏也好使。

3 聽見說你的廚子弄的菜倒不錯。

4 是、他做的湯和那奶油點心很好吃。你今兒在我這兒吃飯罷、好不好。來。把家伙端上來。告訴廚子做那個生菜小雞兒、用雞子兒香油和在一塊兒、教他使那個細鹽不使粗鹽。還要各樣兒的果子、叫他小心點兒買熟分的。

5 這個飯倒是不錯。我那個廚子不行、一點兒弄菜的本事都沒有。

6 那是他學的不好。請你喝點兒黃酒、我記得你不愛喝水。

7 今兒這個飯喫的很好。酒也喝得很足、這火也燒的頂暖和的、偺們倆還要甚麼咯。

## EXERCISE XV.

1 算計道路的遠近、直走近繞着走遠。東西南北。坐船。過河。那船上的客不少。

2 我們明天一早開船往南邊去。河裏的水淺、沒有海水深。他是南邊人。

3 你去年進京的時候兒在那兒住著呢。在客店裏住。我聽見說城外頭客店有不大好住的。那都看掌櫃的好不好、在我說人乏了那兒都好、到店裏不過歇着罷了。

4 你走路愛坐車愛坐船。那是看地方兒、南邊沒有車、走道兒的客人都是坐船。走河路都是小船兒、走海的船大。

5 你老前年坐海船不是受了累了麼。不錯、是颳大風。船在山東海邊兒上擱了淺、我們那些人辛苦的了不得。

6 船上吃飯是甚麼人管。也是船家管。船上的頭兒叫管船兒的、南邊就叫老大。

7 你算計是坐船貴是坐車貴。坐車比坐船花的錢多。沒有的話、那兒有車價比船價還貴呢。你不知道、北邊的車多是在車店裏擱着的、你要坐車那掌櫃的也要使幾個錢、還有天天兒住店的盤費沒算。

## EXERCISE XV. KEY.

1 刻下京城在北邊兒就叫北京。幾百年前南邊也有個京城、就是目下說的南京。

2 我和他進城去。我走的是直道兒很近、他繞着道兒走的、就很遠。

3 河有大小的不同。海比河大。河沒有海深。

4 河邊兒、海邊兒、那都是說河海邊兒上的地。邊兒上的水淺、中間的水可都很深。

5 人走水路得坐船。海面坐的船大、河裏走的都是小船兒。

6 坐船不用住店、坐車可得天天兒住店花的錢多。算計盤費還是坐船花的錢少、價值也比車價兒便宜。

7 掌櫃的是舖子裏管事的人。客店裏也有掌櫃的。

8 在我說、坐船坐車都好。坐船就是怕颳大風、坐車怕下大雨、那可都要受累。有一年我們坐車、道兒上下起雨來。一路連個賣吃兒的都沒有、很苦乏的了不得。後來到店裏、歇了一夜就好了。

## EXERCISE XVI.

1 那馱子太重、一個牲口馱不了。這些東西不好帶。這是甚麼話、裝在箱子裏就好帶了。

2 行李是走道兒的客人帶的東西。箱子有皮子做的、有木頭做的、甚麼都裝得。

3 包上包兒是把東西用甚麼包起來。他是拏毡子把那小箱子包起來了。

4 那口袋你帶了來做甚麼。是裝零碎東西的。道兒上到店裏就得餧牲口。

5 駱駝都是口外來的。你小心着行李、馱子都齊了就走。要不快點兒起身、怕趕不了城了。

6 跟班的是使喚的人。他叫跟班的把箱子裝在車上、車走了、他趕不上了。

7 牲口身上馱着的東西就叫馱子。驢馱子、騾馱子、都說得、馬馱子可不大說。

8 我出門去、他的跟班的在後頭追我、追了半天也沒趕上、我老遠的看見他跑、可不知道他是追我呢。

9 那個人在那兒呢。他出去了、你快跑可以趕得上他。他早走了、怕趕不上罷。無論趕得上趕不上、你快跑着追他就是了。

## EXERCISE XVI. KEY.

1 無論甚麼人出外、都得帶行李。

2 車快來了、你先打點行李箱子。衣包和口袋還得收拾收拾。

3 這屋裏的地毯有了土了、得拿出去打一打、桌子上鋪的布也很腌臟、得洗了。

4 叫馬夫把牲口餵上。一會兒我要出門、不用人跟着、告訴我跟班的、把我帶的東西給裝好了。

5 北邊地方帶東西都是用牲口、叫馱子。有驢馱子、騾馱子、駱駝馱的也叫馱子。駝轎是騾子駝的轎子。

6 你走的這樣快、我跟不上。

7 他出去工夫兒不大、你快追着告訴他、我還有東西給他帶呢。

8 我有點兒事使喚你、你到他那兒給借倆錢兒、無論他說是有無、一定得借點兒來。

9 他那個人好利害。

10 夏天熱的利害、冬天冷的利害、那都是很熱很冷的話頭兒。不冷不熱的時候兒就是春秋天兒。

## EXERCISE XVII.

1 人的頭裏頭有腦子、就叫腦袋。你這個辮子得梳了。人老了耳朶聽不眞、眼睛看不眞。

2 那個人鼻子眼睛長得很奇怪。我心疼這個馬、不肯叫他走乏了。

3 這個人很結實、那個人輭弱得很。本地的布結實。這個坐兒很輭和、

4 你的身子有病麼。沒有病、不過是身子輭弱。這一件事我實在管不了。我怎麼管得了那麼些個人。

5 這一匹馬很老實、你買他罷。看着是老實、你餧他幾天兒瞧罷、騎着怕拉不住。

6 偺們這五六年沒有見、你的鬍子都白了。是我這幾年病得利害、連家裏的人都不認得我。

7 道兒上躺着的那個人、兩腿都破了。腰上有病、直不起來。我的指頭疼。

8 你這麼慢走是身上有病麼。不是、是人老了、腰腿都輭了。這個事我實在做不來。

9 他的舌頭有病、連嘴唇子都破了。那女人的指甲那麼長、把他的胳臂抓破了。

10 你這麼拽着我、是有甚麼事麼、要沒事這麼拉拉拽拽是甚麼樣子呢。有話直說就是了。

## EXERCISE XVII. KEY.

1 這事叫人怎麼去和他說。你怎麼這麼軟弱。他那個人也不過是一個腦袋罷、你怕他做甚麼、

2 人到老來的時候兒、樣樣兒都不行、耳朶聽不明、眼睛也看不眞、說話連嘴唇子都不中用了。

3 春天的時候兒天氣太乾、我的嘴唇兒愛破。

4 這麼點兒頭髮就要打辮子、我看還沒有人的鬍子長呢。

5 你看他的鬍子多麼長。

6 你不要那麼拉拽着我、你的指甲長、弄壞你的指甲也不好、抓了我的胳臂也不好。

7 他腿上有病、走道兒拉着很疼。

8 我看他正在有力氣的時候兒、身子怎麼這麼軟弱。

9 這樣兒軟弱人、你連拉帶拽還怕不把他拉躺下。

10 今兒我看見一個人、面目長的很奇怪。

## EXERCISE XVIII.

1 年輕的人多愛刮臉、人到了四十多就有鬍子了。叫個剃頭的來、我要打辮子。女人們梳頭。

2 剃頭、剃的是那辮子以外的短頭髮。前些年不剃頭的那賊就叫長髮賊。

3 說人體面是說他是個好人、說他長得體面是說他長得好看。剃頭鋪。

4 他那屋子蓋得體面也說得。剃頭刮臉都是用剃頭刀。

5 我們本地人剃頭不使溫和水兒、也不用胰子。你乏了我背你罷。他肚子裏有學問。他上了吊了。

6 明天那地方官要斬幾個賊、聽見說斬賊的那一把刀不很快、不過重就是了。

7 你鼻梁兒上怎麼這麼黃。那是我咋兒叫人家打了一下兒。

8 四方的東西有四個楞兒、有四個角兒、刀楞兒可不說。

## EXERCISE XVIII. KEY.

1 李家那個小千金長得多麼好看、你瞧見沒有。

2 我瞧見了。重眉毛、大眼睛、高鼻梁兒、倆鬢角兒頭髮又黑又亮、顋頰的肉皮兒也很細、小下巴頦兒、長脖細腰兒、嗓子說話兒很眞、脚兒也不大、身體也不粗、果眞不錯。

3 他滿身骨頭疼、是身子有病麼。不是、是他老了、氣血不足了。

4 刮臉剃頭、都得找剃頭的。

5 人的胸前背後、也說前心後心、

6 口袋裝很重的東西、得背在脊梁背兒上、也可以擱在肩膀兒上。

7 你怎麼了、臉上氣色不好。在那兒躺着是肚子疼麼。

8 不是肚子疼、是我這隻脚的踝子骨叫個小人兒拿石頭打了一下兒。連波稜蓋兒都疼的了不得。

9 城門外頭吊着好些個人腦袋。有人告訴我說、都是斬下來的賊首級。

## EXERCISE XIX.

1 這一匹馬走的這麼慢、全是你沒餧足。

2 君上是百官萬民的主子。家生子兒是買的底下人生的兒女。

3 爵位尊、是說人做的官大、小官算不了有爵位。

4 管民的是文官、帶兵的是武官。

5 文武官的衣裳怎麼分。不大好分、不過是他們帶的補子不同。

6 各地方的官兵額數是有一定的、不過是不足的時候兒多、趕到月底要點名、就找些個人充數兒。

7 山東那塊兒出了個好缺、不知道是誰得.誰該着補就是誰。

8 拿銀錢買官、那就叫捐官。他那官是捐的麼。不是捐的、是出兵得的。

9 那帶兵的大官一點兒本事都沒有、前些日子、那賊都跑到山裏頭去、沒吃的了、他要當時追他們、很可以把他們殺退了。

10 貴姓。賤姓馬。

## EXERCISE XIX. KEY.

1 天下最大的就是君上、最多的就是民人。君上又叫主子、民人又說百姓。

2 我的一個同學的在西下做參贊、聽見說那樣兒官的爵位很尊貴。

3 他很懂得事、還用你給他參贊麽。

4 做武官是打當兵起來的多。

5 帶兵的官有定額。有缺就得補。有缺無人就是空缺。

6 額外的官是正額以外的官。

7 我打算找點兒事、沒找着、請你來給找個門路。

8 不管有錢沒錢、一定和人家要、是勒索。

9 我定東西的時候兒、說住了都要好的、怎麽你弄好些個不好的擱在裏頭充數兒。你要不給換好的、我全退回去。

10 叫你把桌子擱在屋子當中間兒、怎麽給擱在一邊兒了。底下我再告訴你話、可得記着能。

11 百家姓兒那一本書、是人的姓都有麽。

12 那兒能全有、不過是聽熟了的那些姓就是了。

13 你給我殺一隻小雞子。

## EXERCISE XX.

1 城門上的官兵是盤查出入人的。

2 國家定的律例是治理百姓的。

3 種地是小民的本分、夏天人人兒種地。

4 秋天種的麥子夏天收、就叫秋麥、春天種的麥子夏天收、就叫春麥。

5 那麼着、秋麥和春麥是一樣的麼。不能算一樣、秋麥總收的多。

6 近年天下大亂是官長治理的不好、普天下百姓都知道。

7 你那個兒子太不說理、告訴他甚麼話總不理會、不論甚麼事全愛說嘴

8 去年來了一羣賊、把那一片房子都燒了。那住着的人怎麼樣呢。他們早都跑了。

9 好些個人在一塊兒那叫一羣、馬牛羊數兒多了也說一羣。

10 你把我的名片拏到他那兒去、告訴他我晚半晌兒本人兒過去見他、有話說。

## EXERCISE XX. KEY.

1 普天下都有中國人。各國都有律例。律例是國家定出來治理百姓的。章程是各官立的。

2 昨兒有人把一羣羊趕到我地裏頭、把我種的麥子都給喫了。

3 看街的就是巡察各地面兒的官人。

4 我那些個書、不知是誰都給拉亂了、你給理一理罷。

5 那個人性子暴的利害、你理他做甚麽。

6 萬里長城是普天下七大奇裏的第一奇。聽見說是一位君上勒令百姓做的。

7 不錯。那君上無道之至、治理百姓過於刻苦、做完了城、沒有幾年天下就大亂了。

8 會生客之時、先得穿官衣。

## EXERCISE XXI.

1 你的主意怎麼樣、是去好、還是不去好呢。自然是去好。

2 把我那一個小棍兒拏來、我要出門。把我那一桿槍裝上、我要打鳥兒、可不定打的着打不着。

3 我昨兒把那桿槍拏起來、不知道是裝得了的、偶然放了一下兒。四面兒都有人、恰巧沒打着誰、要是打着了可了不得了。

4 背地裏拏東西不叫人知道、就是偷。把人家的東西硬拏了去、是奪。好些個賊、夜裏明火拏着槍刀到人家硬拏東西、就是搶。

5 說話沒有理、那算是混說。

6 我的洗澡水怎麼這麼混。打了不大的工夫兒、過一會兒就好了。

7 我那個學生過於懶惰、不愛用功。打他兩下兒看罷。

8 那一天有倆賊、一個拏着一條長槍、一個拏着一根大棍子、四下裏混打、恰巧來了一個人、拏著一桿槍。看見了那倆賊混打、趕着裝上槍就打。那賊呢。那拏槍的扔下槍就跑了。那拏棍子的叫槍子兒打著腿、跑不了咯。放槍的那個人是特意來的、還是偶然來的。怕是偶然來的、可也不定。

## EXERCISE XXI. KEY.

1 去年有十幾個賊、拏着槍刀進城來了、把我鋪子裏的東西搶的乾乾淨淨兒的了。一點鐘前、我那懶惰的底下人回家去了、他走的時候兒、沒把門關上。怕也是特意做的。

2 那些賊裏頭有一個把我砍了一下兒、我就請了個外國大夫給治好了。還有一個賊、拿着我裝好了的鳥槍、偶然給放了。

3 看街的聽見那槍的聲兒、就來瞧一瞧是甚麼事。他看見賊害了怕、一直的跑了。在道兒上看見個做官的、也不知同那個官、混說些甚麼話。

4 那做官的說、你不用說這些個、我就帶我的兵去拿那賊去。那些賊聽說快有兵來、都四散了。

5 這時候兒我那個底下人回來了、說他的事做完了。那做官的和他說、怕你和他們是一氣兒罷。他回的話都不真、就叫人拿棍子把他打了幾下兒。

6 你年輕的時候兒、要這麼懶惰、不愛念書、趕到長大了的時候、那兒還成得了人麼。不成人、就沒有過日子的路兒、沒路兒、自然得做賊找飯吃、昨兒個你把書扔下、同那客人們放槍去。他們散了以後你還不念書。

## EXERCISE XXII.

1 那人幹的事總不叫人知道。大約不是甚麼好事、不然他怎麼背人。可不是麼、人家常說、好話不背人、背人沒好話。

2 那一件事還沒辦妥當了.章程得'改、可不知道李大人准不准。大約沒甚麼更改的。

3 要幹甚麼事、先得'定規個准主意。

4 幹事的時候兒、心不擱在事上、那就叫失神。

5 定妥了辦事的法子總在他身上。

6 那個人有一件要事、得'趕着辦、他一點兒不忙、同人催他快着些兒、他不肯聽。

7 他在那兒拏倆胳臂混掄是幹什麼。怕是喝酒喝多了。

8 條約是各國和中國立定兩下裏往來的章程。

9 這樣兒菜是廚子專給你弄的、你倒不吃。

10 大凡帳目都是一條一條的那麼開。你這寫的全是參差不齊。

## EXERCISE XXII. KEY.

1 凡念書的時候兒、偶然有不懂得的話、若是用心揣摩、大約那意思就明白了。

2 昨兒我約他上西山去、他說先得‘回家去問一問准否。怕是不准他往遠處去。

3 寫信、寫文書、有寫錯了的地方兒、得‘拿一塊紙補在那錯字上、這就叫打補子。

4 你這麼失神、甚麼事都辦不妥當。

5 那花盆是我專心專意給你帶來的。你不要、這是瞧不起我罷。

6 這話說的眞胡鬧、我不要、是我不好意思白要你的東西。

7 這屋裏的傢伙都參差不齊、你給理一理罷。

8 你忙甚麼、客來還得‘一會子呢。

9 你幹甚麼去了。我一錯眼兒你就跑了。又得‘我拿棍子掄你幾下兒了。

10 他們向來定規的辦法、是不好更改的。

## EXERCISE XXIII.

1 城門口兒的地方兒窄、來往的車馬多。

2 外頭是甚麼人嚷。底下人和趕車的那兒吵呢。你出去告訴他們不要嚷嚷、看鬧出事來。

3 你看那兩個小人兒、一個很好看、一個長的眞醜。

4 那好看的笑話那長的醜的、那醜的生了氣、把茶碗摔碎了。有人說了他兩句、他害起怕來了、就說茶碗是掉下去的。

5 揝住他的辮子要拉了他去、他躺在地下把胳臂擱了。

6 晚飯吃多了、夜裏愛做夢。他叫馬摔了。

7 我告訴你一個笑話兒。昨兒我困的利害、在椅子上坐着就着了。同人把墨水兒倒在我嘴裏、我都不知道。

8 街道兒窄、那麼大的車拉不過去。

## EXERCISE XXIII. KEY.

1 昨兒個有兩個人在城上那個窄的地方兒吵嚷、一個長得好看、一個是很醜的。那好看的和那醜的說、沒二句話、這件事你倒底做不做。

2 那醜的說、我一則怕言語、二則乏的了不得。你自己去做罷、若是你不做、我怎麽能做呢。

3 那一個大笑起來了、就說、你這話說錯了、怎麽怕言語、怕是做不了罷。還不快去呢、這明明兒的是叫我把你摔下去。這話沒說完、那醜的就跑下去了。

4 你准是做夢罷、昨兒城上沒有人。

5 我前兒個、在前門大街那兒騎着馬、不知道甚麽人在後頭吵嚷、叫我那個馬開腿跑了去、不大會兒我就掉下去了、把踝子骨擱了一下兒。還好、擱的不大重、歇了一歇兒可就好了。那馬不知道跑到那兒去了、這會兒還沒找着呢。

6 我今兒走了一天、困極了。沒法子、最好是歇一夜、明兒就歇過乏兒來了。

## EXERCISE XXIV.

1 昨兒晚上那兒有人行兇。兇手拏住了、後來怕是要正法的。就地正法。

2 事情沒來之先、看見甚麼能知道日後的祥瑞、那就叫吉兆。

3 家裏日用的錢足了是寬綽。錢太少、過日子不足、就是貧窮。

4 過日子有准進的錢、那就叫產業。

5 那時候兒我甚麼都沒了、就找了一個朋友說、偺們這些年的相好、你幫我幾個錢、肯不肯。他說、沒有甚麼不肯、眞是不能。我們底根兒本有幾個錢、你是知道的、現在產業也沒了、連弄一個大錢都很費事。

6 你們這車、要是當天兒趕進城去、我多多兒的賞你們酒錢。

7 你多階起身、我要沒丢那銀子今兒就走、總在這三五天可就要動身。那麼着我們這就分手了。一路平安罷。

8 你們那鋪子怎麼不開了。我們去年就分手了。

9 八月十五、中秋節、正好賞月。

10 請你幫個忙兒、不然這件事今兒個完不了。

## EXERCISE XXIV. KEY.

1 他那個人的事情、眞不吉祥.

2 底根兒他有產業、過日子還很寬綽。有一年連月的不下雨、種的地全不收成、他家裏的事情就不順當了。本錢慢慢兒的都花完了、現在窮得很。他相好的朋友們、偶然還幫他幾個錢。

3 是他一個人兒丟了錢了、還是連累了人家了呢。

4 那些種地的人、多一半也丟了錢了、近來那個地方就很不安寗、我倒沒受甚麼累。怎麼是這麼着。在我說、事情不論吉凶都有個先兆兒。有一天我做了一個夢。夢見有一個人來、把我地裏的麥子都給燒了、這麼着、我就把麥子都生賣了。後來短了雨、我的錢倒是早已先得了。

5 請大人把這個瓶留下罷、我窮的很。朋友們不肯幫、把家裏的傢伙不是當就是賣、現在就有這一個了。

6 你不是姓張麼。怎麼窘成這個樣兒。前兩三年我記得你還有產業、日子還過得下去呢。

7 大人說的不錯、後來我丟了錢了、現在我就是個要飯兒的人了。

## EXERCISE XXV.

1 稱人您、是有點兒尊重人的意思。

2 家祖就是我父親的老子。旁人的父親就稱人家老翁。

3 令祖好阿、令尊好阿、是問人家的祖、人家父親的安。

4 向人說自己的弟兄、說的是家兄、舍弟。稱人家的弟兄、是說令兄、令弟。

5 奴才就是使喚的人、有是買的、有不是買的、還是說底下人的多。

6 今兒家祖回來、我得去迎接。後兒他們老翁下葬、我得去幫幫他們去。

7 生絲不是你們這兒的土貨麼。可不是麼、那絨可不是土貨、請您替我挑一點兒好的。

8 我兄弟給大人請安、他說他明兒怕不能來、找了個替工兒替他幾天。

9 我挑出來的那瓦盆總得挑着、擱在車上不行。

10 他把紙弄成團兒、往我臉上扔。

11 牲口駝的東西叫馱子、那是頭裏說過的、人肩膀兒上挑的東西叫挑子、人背上背的東西叫背子。

## EXERCISE XXV. KEY.

1 大前兒個我們家兄回家來了、帶着有二百多團絲、五十疋絨。我父親叫我接他去、就手兒幫着他、把貨拏進來。

2 那麽着令兄是個賣布的麽。

3 可不是麽。家父跟先祖、從前也是做那樣的買賣。您問這個話、有甚麽高見呢。

4 我們舍弟要買些個細絲、請您令兄給他挑點兒好的、行不行。

5 那有甚麽不行的、挑是一定給令弟挑、就是有一樣兒、價錢可怕長了、現在很貴呢。

6 您請罷、回來見。

7 昨兒個他們令祖下葬。我叫我的底下人去幫幫他們、這奴才們不肯聽我的話、到了兒沒去、旁人說那兒有鬼、他們害了怕了、說不去。後來我的孫子叫了他們一個來。他喳的一聲、慢慢兒的走過來、我那孫子就拏棍子、把他打了幾下兒。

8 您的底下人說的話有一點眞呢。那一天夜裏我打那兒過、看見一個鬼混跑。頭髮是紅的、臉是黃的、我一瞧見怕的我了不得。

9 這是那兒的話。准是你又喝多了。

## EXERCISE XXVI.

1 我們明兒上西山去罷。到那兒、就找個樹林子、在青草地裏坐着、又涼快、又沒土。你說好不好。

2 去倒沒有甚麼不能去的、我却想着還是在太陽地裏曬暖兒好、樹林子坐着時候兒還不對呢。

3 偺們倆人賽着跑罷。正對我的心、你的腿却比我的長、怕跑不過你。

4 他那倆兄弟利害得很、都是過於嗇刻、不肯花錢、他們的錢一天比一天增的多。

5 那葱這兩天貴、不分老嫩、都是二百錢一斤。

6 草木是花草樹木的總名。麥子出了苗兒了。火苗兒也說得。

7 苗子是四川東南的人、分生的熟的。

8 樹多叫樹林子。那桑樹林子綠森森的。

9 要把溼衣裳弄乾了、得鋪在日頭地裏曬一曬。曬乾了就疊起來。

10 聽見說、對過兒住的那個人疊次吞了人家好些個銀子。天有八下鐘了、小人兒們該睡覺了。

## EXERCISE XXVI. KEY.

1

那一天我們兩個人在樹林子裏𤞑着拉弓來着。天氣很好、日頭曬的還暖和、那一帶樹林子綠森森得好看。拉完了弓、我告訴他一個笑話兒。

2

我就說、從前有一個姓馬的、是個賣葱的。有一天他在桑樹林子裏頭就地兒睡、他起來的時候兒、看見有一個人在他跟前站着、大聲的笑。

3

他生了氣說、這兒有甚麼笑頭兒啊。那個人對他說、這個地方很溼、你瞧你的衣裳、都弄溼了、得鋪在太陽地裏曬一曬、而且你帶的貨也丟了。

4

那老頭兒瞧了一瞧、眞是口袋都空了。就說、不是你吃了我的嫩葱却是誰。他說、我沒白吃、給的價錢在那兒、說着就把幾個大錢扔在草裏。

5

那姓馬的想着眞是錢、向前拿去、一錯眼兒、那個人就沒了。錢也找不着了、這姓馬的知道不是人、却是個鬼。

6

那個人嗇刻的利害。他是打雲南那地方兒來的。我想他本是一個苗子、前幾年他做乾草的生意。他的銀錢、一個月比一個月增的多了、他疊次呑人家的錢、自己却不愛花。

## EXERCISE XXVII.

1 我們倆人起初很親熱、後來他待我傲慢、這麼着、我就和他絕了交了。

2 我昨兒到你那兒去拜會、怎麼不見。你這話有點兒不可憑罷、怕是你留下名片就走了。

3 你待我這麼傲慢、回來告訴你父親。憑你愛告訴誰就告訴誰、我都不怕。

4 某人告訴我說、你那一筆賬的銀子還沒交出來、你不慚愧麼。

5 那倆瓶、乍見的時候兒、好像是一對兒、細細兒的一瞧、尺寸就不一樣。

6 有人嫉妒我這個好兒、然而這也是件平常的事、而且也是我應當得的。

7 應當倆字的意思怎麼分別。沒有別的法子、總得看上下文就知道了.

8 會客的時候兒、主人在東邊兒坐、賓客在西邊兒坐、陪著的人在下邊兒坐、對不對、那總是看屋子的方向。

9 我素常不愛拜客。冬天得穿厚衣裳、夏天穿薄的。

10 寬厚是刻薄的對面兒。

## EXERCISE XXVII. KEY.

1 某人你們見過面麼。沒見過。我們也是今兒初次見。人很好、乍見就和他很熟。

2 聽見別人說、他原是厚道人、素日待人很好、行事也不刻薄。

3 要是和我認得的那個人比起來、我認得的那人可不是這麼樣。

4 憑他是誰、都待的傲慢。看見人有好的事、他就嫉妒。拿人的東西不懂得還、和他要、他也不慚愧。這樣兒的人、怎麼能不和他絕交呢。

5 我實在沒工夫兒辦、憑你辦去罷。

6 請客是請人吃飯。客應坐在上面、主人旁邊兒陪著。

7 你那個小鳥兒要他幹甚麼、交給我罷。得了、得了。你怎麼見人家的東西就要、

8 你一個人不肯去、我陪着你去、好不好。

## EXERCISE XXVIII.

1 那桌面兒不很光潤、把他擦一擦罷。

2 玻璃是外國來的東西不是。當初是外國貨、近來我們這兒也會做。料貨和玻璃有點兒分別。

3 那玻璃瓶子怎麼破了。不是碰破了的、是燒的時候兒就裂了。

4 牕戶紙裂了、叫裱糊匠來糊上。單張兒紙糊在什麼上頭是糊、雙張兒紙、糊在一塊兒是裱。

5 各行的手工人叫匠人的多、木匠、瓦匠、鐵匠、都說得。

6 布是棉花做的、紗是絲做的。

7 那一塊紗顏色兒淡了、必須染別的顏色兒。原舊的顏色兒是紅的、還可以染紅的、您要別的顏色兒、也可以染藍的。

8 你瞧那一疋紅紗顏色兒光潤不光潤。怎麼是光潤呢。那紗原來是好紗、又是新的、染的顏色又好看。這光潤不止於說紗、說別的也行。

9 我拿那個玻璃瓶來要擦一擦、碰在桌子上碰破了、收拾不收拾。不必收拾了。

10 他是甚麼行當兒。必是當廚子。你行幾。我們弟兄五個、我行二。

語言自邇集



## EXERCISE XXXVIII. KEY.

1 這屋裏糊的紙腌臟、叫個裱糊匠來給糊新的。

2 這一張畫兒你找個人給、裱一裱、裱的可別太厚了。

3 牕戶破了進風、拿張紙給糊上。

4 這紗你怎麼給染成這個顏色兒。我不是告訴你染藍的麼、你倒給染出紅的來了。顏色兒又淡、又不光潤。

5 我這褂子太舊了、穿不得了。

6 牕戶上的玻璃有了土了、必得拿布擦一擦、屋裏就不這麼黑了.

7 染東西的顏色在那'兒買。顏料鋪裏就賣.

8 你小心拿著那玻璃盃、別給碰了。

9 總沒下雨、天乾的利害。你瞧這桌面子都乾裂了.

10 買賣都分行。京城裏各行、最大的就是銀、酒、茶、布、四行.

14

## EXERCISE XXIX.

1 剛纔我們在這兒商量這件事情、再三的喊他過來、等了半天他不答應。我疑惑他沒聽見。

2 再三再四的請他把那個舊書套送給我、他總不答應、末末了兒、還是我買了個新的。

3 我們十個人從前定得湊錢做買賣。後來落下了兩個人、還有把本錢取回去的、我瞧這個、我也不肯再往裏入錢了。

4 我兄弟送我的那個箱子、叫你挪開點兒、怎麼挪那麼遠。

5 這米我量了不彀五石、一個單套兒車足拉的了。

6 在我說、這麼些個不止五石、不是二套車怕拉不了罷。

7 我是從南邊兒來的、向來沒坐過車、我們一到店裏、那趕車的就要錢。我疑惑著從來沒這個理、叫他等一等兒再來罷。

8 我永遠再不到他那兒去了。這是怎麼話說。你再斟酌斟酌罷、等一會兒沒了氣、就改了主意了。

9 那馬還不好好兒的拴上他。你看他把門碰壞了。那倒沒甚麼、叫個木匠來收拾收拾、就得了。

10 昨兒我叫他們買一百雞子兒送上山來。誰想他們道兒上、連丟帶碰、趕到了山上就沒甚麼了。

## EXERCISE XXIX. KEY.

1 我纔出門剛要走的時候兒、有人來找你。我說你不在家、叫他等一會兒再來。

2 借人家的傢伙、用完了不給送回去、還等著人家來取、使得麼.

3 從我到這兒來、總沒見東西落價兒。

4 這個錢鈌少的利害。我各處去湊、纔湊了這麼點兒。不彀我用的、給你罷。

5 他過日子、永遠是東挪西湊、老不彀花的。

6 把牲口拴上、一會兒就要套車。

7 我買了一套書。帶的錢不彀了、和你商量、要是身上有、借給我一點兒、行不行。

8 我疑惑他說的話不實、你到那兒給打聽打聽

9 你背著我做事不叫我知道、你可小心著。日後要是叫我打聽出來、我可不答應。

10 外頭有人喊、你答應一聲兒、出去看看是誰。

11 阿、原來又是他來了。從那天我說他以後他總沒有來。

12 他來了兩末兒、都趕上我在家、你說巧不巧。

13 我們辦這件事、想出兩個辦法來、請你給斟酌使那個好。

## EXERCISE XXX.

1 臺灣是中國東南海裏的地方兒、南北兩頭兒山嶺兒又多、又大、那山峯長得也很好看。

2 江河湖海、是天下大水的總名兒。

3 偺們這兒的小河兒很窄、有浮橋、就可以過去。那長江的江面有地方兒寬下裏和湖相同。

4 那長江之流打西到東、湖北來的船到江西去、一路都是順流。到了江西那兒的山水也可以。

5 那山峯的尖兒是個個不同。山峯是高而尖的、山嶺也高、就是沒有那尖的樣子。

6 尖兒那個字眼兒、甚麼刀尖兒筆尖兒都說得。

7 京城裏沒有甚麼河水、喝的都是井水。

8 京城的買賣大半在大街上開鋪子、衚衕小巷都是住家兒的多。

9 城外頭沒有甚麼人家兒的地方、就叫野地、連有墳墓的也算。

10 他是個鄉村兒的人、野的利害那墳地很大、必是闊人家兒的。

11 你會浮水麼。會是會、很遠了可不行。這道河浮的過去、浮不過去、河面兒太寬、浮不過去。

## EXERCISE XXX. KEY.

1 臺灣是中國的地方有二百多年了。南北下裏有峰嶺、裏頭有幾個頂高的山峰。地方不很寬闊、却有幾道小河兒、河邊兩面的田地、出產的東西很多。鄉村和城都有、裏頭住的人同民人一樣。我聽見說有幾個地方兒、住著野人、多一半兒是做賊過日子。他們都是散著住、不成鄉村。也有人說那些野人吃人。那兒做買賣的、大半和民人做、近來却有太西各國的船來往、外國人也有在那兒住著做買賣的。

2 中國有幾道江、也大也深、很可以走得大船。長水的時候兒、流得很快、往上走的船覺著很慢。往下流的水、在船上看着、覺得更快了。那小河兒又窄又灣、都是河船來往的、走道兒的人、可以打浮橋上過去。

3 那一國有幾個大湖、湖面很寬闊、大裏下和海一樣。湖裏頭也有山峰、大小船都可以走得。一有大風那浪眞利害。

4 有地方兒要做并很費事、那土太硬。

5 我有一位朋友、他住在一個小巷裏頭。那一天我去找他、我進錯了衚衕兒、沒找着他的家。

## EXERCISE XXXI.

1 我們倆人剛纔鬧著玩兒、他把棍子在我腦袋上打了一下兒。安靜點兒罷、別太粗了、總得想着你兄弟年幼、那麼重的手脚、他耐不得。

2 聽見說老爺欠安。沒有甚麼、不過身上有點兒不舒服。

3 我這件新褂子怕耐不得長。那可難說、要穿着常冒雨、自然壞的快。獃一獃兒。

4 他那羞辱人的樣子眞討人嫌。

5 男女、就是爺們娘兒們。賊把男女老少都殺了。

6 他一家子老幼都病了、是不分年高年輕的全不舒服。

7 和祖父一輩兒的是長輩、和兒孫一輩兒的是晚輩。

8 你怎麼這麼冒失碰着了我了、眞是討人嫌。我錯了、我錯了、實在是沒留神。

9 你過於笨的利害、爽快些兒辦罷。管我呢、你這麼獃頭獃腦的還要說人。

10 我們過日子眞艱難。耐着些兒罷、你這麼能耐人、難道一輩子不出頭麼。

## EXERCISE XXXI. KEY.

1 街上那兒有一個要玩意兒的。男女老幼好些個人在那兒看。你聽見說麼。

2 你還說呢。我纔剛上街的時候兒、看見好些個爺們娘兒們在那兒站着、我想着必是有甚麼玩意兒、不然那些人在那兒獃着臉兒看甚麼呢。我正要去看、恰巧有個人冒冒失失的問了我一句話、說、你不舒服、大好了。我一看、不是別人、是一家兒裏的一個平輩、長得又蠢又笨、也不知道說的都是那'兒的事。實在是討人嫌。

3 你說的不是某人麼。他父親我認得、人很安靜、說話行事也極爽快。前幾年他不大寬綽、近來看他那個樣兒倒很舒服。想是日子比原先好過一點兒咯、

4 你受人家的羞辱、就是耐着點兒也不難、爲甚麼生氣呢。

## EXERCISE XXXII.

1 他臨死的時候兒、他的兒孫們都爭起家產來咯.

2 良民是不犯國法的人。

3 大臣上朝的時候兒、不是進皇宮麼、不是進皇宮、皇宮是皇上住的地方兒、就是禁地、向例連大臣們都不准到的。

4 你把這幾件文書給號上、打儘頭裏的日子號起。

5 我們大人出了號令、禁止底下人要錢、要是犯了禁、必要治罪的。

6 幹這沒良心的事難免犯法。做良民比爲匪不强麼、反倒不要做、眞是怪事.

7 隨你們倆人鬪嘴兒、就是別打起來、要是打起來、那可不是玩意兒。

8 大赦天下.寬免犯人的罪名、總出於皇上的恩典。

9 你別在太陽地裏走、免得受熱。他那個病隨你怎麼治、早晚總是要死的。

10 朝廷隨地酌情建立地方官爲臨民的官。地方官治理的好、自然就能安靖了。

## EXERCISE XXXII. KEY.

1 好些年前、有一個人姓林、要做皇上。沒反以前、他先把他的死黨布散的各處都有、連皇宮禁地也有他的人。後來事情破了、他自己也叫人拿住了。他的死黨還在山東河南反了好幾個月。

2 百姓反了、皇上就令大臣平定那不安靖的地方兒。那大臣臨走的時候兒、得上朝去見皇上。

3 那文書是第幾號。還沒號上呢。

4 北京城建立的年分不遠。從前朝廷建立在南邊兒、皇上住的地方就說得是京、那城就叫南京。

5 鬬雞是良民不要的玩意兒。那是最不體面的事、也是應該例禁的。

6 我聽見說那姓李的犯了大罪、有人說他必是定死罪了、也是應該的、人要是明火、免不了死罪。那樣兒的人若不殺他、良民怎麼能彀過安靖日子呢。

7 這話是不錯的、然而那個姓李的、誰還想到他做賊呢。

8 你隨時來見我罷。我雖然不是有錢的、總能給你一碗飯吃、一杯茶喝。

9 那就是我的好朋友了、我最怕的是叫人家費事。你若是眞這麼樣兒叫我來見你、你瞧我還常來不常來呢。

15

## EXERCISE XXXIII.

1 那座廟門口兒牆上貼着告示、禁止娘兒們上廟燒香。

2 他們令祖死了、今兒個和尚去念經。和尚吃素。

3 俗語兒說、今日且吃今日飯、明天有事明天辦。剛剛兒和你的性情相對。

4 老爺廟是和尚廟麼。不錯、是和尚廟。關夫子、俗呌老爺。關夫子是文話、俗話就是老爺。

5 這文書得寫楷書、行書草字都不行。墨又得濃。

6 那山上廟裏頭的房子一層比一層高。

7 你抽空兒給我畫一張畫兒、行不行。早已過去的時候兒就是往古。

8 古來有位聖人姓孔、他的教後世呌做聖教。爲中國最尊重的。同時還有老子的教、呌做道教。佛教是西方僧家傳來的。尊佛爺出家的是僧家、俗說就呌和尚。尊老子出家的是道士。聖教又名儒教、儒教的人呌俗家。三教的總名就呌僧道儒。

9 京城的廟多、有的是和尚廟、有的是道士廟。在那兒念經的聲兒和人家唱曲兒一個樣。

10 我屋裏牆上掛的那張古畫兒、今兒拿新紙裱上一層。

## EXERCISE XXXIII. KEY.

1 古來、二千四百三十多年前的時候、中國有一位姓孔的、人人都稱他爲聖人。他平日說的話成了一本書、人看這個書就知道學好。好怎麼學呢、是這麼着。做官呢、替君上辦事總得用心、在家呢、還得尊重爺娘待弟兄該當疼愛、就是自己的女人、也要和和氣氣兒的、交朋友的心必須實在。能彀照著這麼行、就是儒教中的好人了。

2 寫字有眞字草字之分。眞字也叫楷書。寫楷書的時候、墨要濃纔好看。草字也叫草書。

3 怎麼叫草字。有人說是字寫出來和草一樣、就叫草字、這話可不知道對不對。

4 念書寫字都得專心、不可空念和唱曲兒一個樣。

5 佛是西方的聖人。傳他的教的書就叫佛經。佛經的道理、不過叫人靜心就是了。俗人不知、說是念了那個經、就能彀免罪、眞是胡說。

6 和尙是念佛經的人。他們的別名又說僧人。

7 前兒我見了一張告示在牆上貼着、上邊兒的字筆畫看不眞、下邊兒又有擦壞了的地方兒、也不知道是甚麼事。

## EXERCISE XXXIV.

1 這麼些日子纔回來、渴想渴想。彼此彼此、

2 打這塊兒往東一望、直到天邊兒上、都是水。

3 衆人都說皇上新近專派了一位大官察考倉庫裏頭銀米的數兒對不對。或銀或米若有短少、列位怕要得處分。依我說、他來不來碍不着偺們的事。

4 這一個打雜兒的有甚麼好處、你這麼戀戀不捨的。

5 你們年中進的錢甚麼是大宗兒。就是祖宗留下的產業阿。

6 老不下雨、鄉下人盼望的利害。昨兒剛長點兒雲彩、偏偏兒的又叫風颳散了、

7 另找一輛車罷、若是跨着轅兒必要弄一身土。

8 京城是五方雜處的地方兒。

## EXERCISE XXXIV. KEY.

1 中國各城裏頭都有倉有庫。倉是裝米的、庫是擱銀子的。這倉庫都有官人管理、銀子米若丟了、都爲官人是問。倉庫裡頭收着的銀子和米、年年總得'查一回。那一年我有一個朋友是管銀庫的、夜裡來了些個賊、打開庫門、把裏頭的銀子都搶了去了。那大官就叫我那朋友把丟了的銀子按原數兒補還、我那朋友那'兒有那麽些個現銀子呢、斟酌些日子、沒有法子、就跑了.

2 那有甚麽用處。就是跑到天邊兒上去、那官人還能拿不到麽、就是拿不到、也不能回家、就是回家、也不能常住阿。

3 依我看、還是等着聽處分、倒比滿地方兒跑强多了。

4 趕車的、你瞧阿、有個人坐在車後頭了、你還不往後抽麽。

5 去年我和你要那毛氊子你捨不得給我。如今你要送我、我偏不要咯。

## EXERCISE XXXV.

1 我那個時辰表給鐘表鋪裏送去、叫他們給修理修理。就手兒間他們我那個風雨表收什得了沒有。

2 他手裏捏着管筆、彷彿要寫甚麼。瓦盆兒是盆兒匠捏的。

3 那賊捏造告示、作爲官出的。

4 他帶的貨物捏報是行李、叫關上查出來、全都入了官了。

5 先灑水後掃地、不然那土就飛起來咯。

6 你那個小狗兒眞好看。毛兒也長、腿兒也短、耳朶也不小、就是嘴頭兒有點兒尖。

7 他們那兒打降、別就是要蓋房子罷。

8 若論圓扁的不同、西瓜是圓的、扁豆就是扁的、錢是又圓又扁的。

9 我沒犯法、人告我做賊、那不是我的冤、枉麼。

10 他近來的事情不好、那都是他的報應。我實在想不出甚麼法子來報答他待我的恩典。

## EXERCISE XXXV. KEY.

1 我看你那兒使喚的那個打雜兒的很好、做事很快、當屋子裏灑掃的很乾淨、我去了永遠見他拿着笤帚、在那兒掃地。我那個底下人野的利害、那麼大身量兒、走道兒老是前迸後跳的。成天家、不是打雞就是鬬狗、很彷彿小人兒的樣子。

2 還有一樣兒、沒開過眼。有一天、我的時辰表壞了、打算着要找人修理、擱在桌兒上了。他看見了、拿在手裏說、這是個甚麼呢、又圓又扁的。沒揑住、一失手掉的地下了。我問他表怎麼摔了、他揑報是狗跳在桌子上、往下一迸、碰下來的。還說要是訛他弄壞的。那可寃枉了他了。這樣兒的人我還怎麼用呢。

3 我看你用的那個人也不錯。本來是鄉下的人、粗率點兒也是有的、那樣兒人一定有力氣、往後要是砌牆、叫他幫著打碎做小工兒、倒也罷了。

## EXERCISE XXXVI.

1 這櫃子裏的抽屜拉不出來．你使勁一抽、就拉出來了。

2 那一件事就悞了是甚麼緣故．那緣故太多、不容易說。

3 您這位少爺今年多大歲數兒。小兒今年十八歲了、他的生日是六月初八、過年就要給他辦事咯。趕到您那兒辦喜事的日子我必要去道喜去。

4 你別打算欺哄我、我告訴你、那不是件容易事。我很是你的硬對兒、若論誆騙人、你可不是個兒。

5 可惜那個人過於糊塗、說不明白．就悞了我半天的工夫．

6 我們倆彼此很對勁。可惜他那個兒弟很會欺哄人、去年還誆騙了我幾兩銀子呢。

7 我最不喜歡他待有年紀兒人的那個樣子。我告訴你、那都是小的時候兒、老家兒不管他的緣故。

8 他是個安靜人、不論甚麼事都是從從容容兒的辦．

## EXERCISE XXXVI. KEY.

1 過了新年又長了一歲了。

2 你們老人家今年多大年紀。家父現在八十二歲了，這樣兒年紀也算得是有壽數兒的人了。

3 昨兒我等了你一天、你爲甚麼不找我去。有個緣故。我正要走、恰巧有個遠親來了、我沒法子、陪他坐着說話兒、就悞住了。過了半天他纔走了、天也不早了、我就沒找你去。

4 你們住的那地方兒上大街很近、買甚麼東西實在是便當。我們住的這小衚衕兒很不方便、買點兒甚麼眞不容易。

5 他那個人一點勁兒沒有、還想要學武、心裏有多麼糊塗。

6 你喜歡吃這菜不是、可惜沒了。

7 你別欺哄我、纔剛我看見了那抽屜裏頭還有好些個呢。

8 在鋪子裏買東西不欺哄人、街上買東西可得留神、多有賣不好的東西誆騙人銀錢的。

16

## EXERCISE XXXVII.

1 您公事忙不忙。也不算很忙、天天兒總有閒着的時候兒。

2 我有一件事情奉求。李老爺該我的那一筆賬我屢次上他那兒去要、他們的人總說沒空兒、不見我。您多偺閒着、託您替我要一要纔好。

3 昨兒我一個相好的、因爲孩子病、心裏煩悶、急要發信到鄉下問一問、託我替他雇一個人送信。我雇了一個人、打發他去了、到後半天他回來、說沒有找着。我知道他是撒謊、所以我不肯給他錢。

4 小價錢買來的、大價兒賣、那就是賺錢。貨是一兩銀子一斤買的、還是一兩銀子賣的、所以不能賺錢。

5 他帶着一車子私貨進城、門上的官人過來查問、他慌慌忙忙的說是行李。官人不信、把箱子打開一看、果然裝的都是私貨、所以全入了官了。

6 天上的星星雖多、掃帚星可不大常見。

7 我鄉下買了個所在、趕到夏天在那兒住着、小孩子們必是樂極了。

## EXERCISE XXXVII. KEY.

1 你平常做甚麼。怎麼我屢次的上你那兒去、你家裏的人、老答應說是你不在家、你想、我那'有工夫兒。不是公事、就是私事、家務又多。那'一樣兒不得'我辦、所以永遠沒閒空兒。

2 人若是悶得慌、到街上走一走最好。看見點兒可樂的事、心裏自然就不煩了。要是碰見下雨的日子、不能出去、可叫人急得慌。

3 有一件急事、得'煩個人給他送個信兒去。你閒着沒事、就奉求你給他個信兒。不行、我沒閒空兒、請另託別位罷。我想不論打發誰去都行。

4 那孩子愛撒謊我打發他雇車去、他回來告訴我街上沒車。我不信、打發別人去雇去了。不大的工夫兒就雇來了、我纔知道是那孩子要賺錢、趕車的不肯跟着他撒謊、所以沒雇成。

5 他的買賣很賺錢、所有各樣兒零碎貨物都賣、所以不能不賺錢。雖然是個雜貨鋪兒、買賣倒不錯。

## EXERCISE XXXVIII.

1 小兒得了在工部裏帖寫的差使、都是承您的情。

2 現任的官出了缺、上司就派員署理、趕到新派實任的來了、那署理的差使就完了。

3 六部的上司都稱堂官、堂官以下就是司官。新到衙門候補的司官、爲學習行走。

4 京城的衙門辦稿、不是司官就是書辦。供事是有頂戴的書辦、當的差使可就和書辦一樣。

5 文書發了之後、存起來的稿子就叫陳案。

6 他偷了我們墳上的樹、我寫了一個稟帖、上衙門去告他。那衙役們不給送進去、說先得給他們多少錢。你還不知道那衙門人的習氣麼、就是他老子去打官司、也是一樣兒的要錢。

7 新來的那位官員是做甚麼的。是上司派來的委員、問那明火案兒的口供。

## EXERCISE XXXVIII. KEY.

1 人要是辦錯了事、有了不是、得承當。這件事是甚麼人承辦。

2 無論差使大小、都得給國家出力。實任署任、都是一樣。

3 當官差就是當差使。辦私事不能說差使。

4 候補的官先得學習行走、那就是初到衙門的時候兒、學着當差。有缺就可以派着署。

5 最大的衙門是六部、部裡最大的官就是堂官、又說上司。一部分多少司、管各司的官兒叫司官、又說司員。稿子都是他們辦、也有交給書辦辦的。

6 書辦是書吏的俗名兒。事情辦妥了、稿子寫好了、給堂官看。那叫回堂畫稿。

7 凡各衙門有外差、得派委員去辦。

8 衙役、皂隸、是各衙門裡使喚作零碎事的官人。

9 供事是考來的、中了就有頂戴。比書辦尊貴些。

10 辦過了的官事文件、收存起來叫存稿。存稿裡有准過的、有不准的、可都是陳案。

## EXERCISE XXXIX.

1 他那一件事情成了、是他的命運好。在我說、不關運氣、都是他有志氣、肯用功的好處。

2 作善得福、作惡得禍、這都是天命所定自然之理。

3 他打直隸運來的米沒賺錢、連本兒都虧空了。

4 可惜那個人雖然聰明、到底脾氣不行。任憑待他怎麼好、總是抱怨。

5 天氣寒冷的時候兒、人得活動活動、身子纔不吃虧、不然、趕有了病、就後悔不來了。

6 你專在這不相干的事情上用功、有甚麼益處。你們老人家花了若干的銀子給你捐了官、你不正經當差使、這不是辜負老家兒的恩典麼。眞叫人家寒心阿。疼的要命。

7 這個學生極靈、又願意用功。其餘那些個孩子眞是不中用。

8 你臉上發了福了。舊年這個時候兒、看你那個樣兒就活不了。

9 把牕戶開開罷。那牕戶不是活的、開不開。

## EXERCISE XXXIX. KEY.

1 他的性情很好、一點兒脾氣都沒有、怎麼能得禍。況且長得也是很有福氣的樣兒。

2 人生來的命有好有歹、就是運氣、也不能一個樣兒。

3 無論做甚麼事、總得有志氣、自然成得了事。若一點兒志氣都沒有、一輩子也不用想有進益。

4 他那個人你別錯瞧了。說話行事倒很活動、一點兒也不死樣。人也極聰明、很有志氣。老在家裏、那兒也不願意去、最愛用功。

5 你借別人的錢、他怕你出利錢吃虧、替你還上。這是你的益處、你倒抱怨他多事。這不是辜負人家的好意麼、叫人寒心不寒心。日後他知道、和你要錢、准是要後悔的。

6 行善做惡那都在人。作惡的人悔改了、一樣也是善人。

7 這幾樣兒很好。給我留下。其餘的拿了去我不要。

8 這小狗兒很有靈性、我說甚麼他都懂得。

## EXERCISE XL.

1 你天天兒來不來都不要緊。若有緊急的事情、橫竪得叫你去。

2 可惜他蓋的那房子不像房子的式樣。好像馬棚似的、住着很不像樣兒。

3 那一所兒房子、通共有多少間。通共有一百多間、除了人住的、下賸還有四五十間。

4 我合算起來、有一萬兩銀子的外欠、除了還賬之外、下賸還有一二千兩銀子的盈餘。

5 我月月兒進的錢總不彀、沒有盈餘、反倒賸下些個賬目不能還。過這種樣兒的日子眞叫我傷心。

6 有人放槍、把他那小孩子打着了、傷的很重。

7 門旁邊兒的木頭是竪的、門上下的木頭是橫的。

8 在地下平擱的東西、說橫、說竪、那都是隨勢酌情的活動話、若是在面前直着的爲竪、在旁面的人就以爲是橫。

## EXERCISE XL. KEY.

1 我纔剛告訴你有件緊急的事、預先把馬備好了等着、到這時候兒你還沒預備呢。我不說你罷、你眞叫我着急、說你、你倒像我脾氣不好似的。

2 借們這賬得通長了算一算。我借過你幾次合在一塊兒、通共有多少錢。除去我還你的、下剩我算計着還有一點兒盈餘.

3 你借的錢多、還的錢少。那兒還有盈餘呢。

4 我瞧你外面倒像很明白、你怎麼連橫竪都不知道。叫你把畫兒掛上、竪的是在門兩旁掛的、橫的是在門上頭掛的。你都給掛錯了。

5 這件事、你交給我辦。橫竪我給你辦好了。

6 你不要說了。那一件事、你辦的好叫我傷心。上次我打算搭個天棚、託你給買蓆。誰想你一點準兒沒有。東西也沒買來、連你的面兒都見不着了。

請酒、大家先乾一杯。

15 請、請。

16 請茶。我可不布、都沒外人、自取罷。

17 那最好、大家讓起來、倒顯着拘泥、還是隨便的好。您瞧、剛說是不讓、怎麼又讓起來了。我們也得回敬纔是。

18 不是那麼着、這幾樣兒菜是我前兩天就打發人到櫃上告訴了、託他們鑪上用心給做一做、似乎比現弄的好點兒。我看諸公都不動筷兒、我不能不布一布。您何妨嚐一嚐。

19 諸位別住筷兒、總得吃飽呀。

20 我們都吃得飽了、酒也喝醉了、這樣兒的盛設叫您費心。

21 今兒沒甚麼可吃的、酒也不好、叫諸位屈量。

22 您那兒的話呢。今兒個也不說甚麼了、車來了、天也不早了、得回去了。過一天再到您府上道謝去。

23 豈敢、豈敢。您請便罷、我也不敢奉留了。

24 諸公還坐會兒、我先失陪。請了、請了、別送、別送、留步、留步、主人也不必送。請回去陪別位客罷。

25 我就到這兒候乘。

26 磕頭、磕頭。

27 再見、再見。

太早咯、不但別位客不能到齊、碰巧了連主人還未必能彀到呢。 5 我還要請教您、我若是領他這個情、似乎還得寫個回字兒罷。 6 那倒不用、您既是把帖子留下了、那就是您一準要去的憑據。 7 趕到要去的時候兒、還得繳還那個帖子不是。 8 不錯、這規矩是這麼着。您明兒去的時候兒、到了庄子的門口兒、先叫您的管家遞了您的名片。那門口兒伺候的人接過片子來、就頭裡帶着道兒、讓您進去、主人在那屋裡、就讓您到那屋裡。您見了主人、不用說、先作個揖、回來把那個請帖兒雙手遞給他、嘴裡說、我又來討擾、就抱愧的了不得、尊帖上下的字眼兒實在不敢當。主人一面接帖兒、一面也說兩句謙虛話。大家就坐下喝茶。等別的客都來齊了、那纔讓坐擺飯。 9 有時候兒客不能都到、若只短一半位、就不儘等着了。趕到來了、就讓在那空座兒上坐。爲甚麼呢、那座位都是主人早已算計定了的、到了入座的時候兒、雖然應該謙讓。主人萬不肯叫你們隨便坐。所以後來的有給他留下的空座兒、他來了也不用很讓、就坐下了。 10 哎呀、閣下來了、失迎的很、您恕我。 11 那兒的話、我來晚了罷、叫諸公受等。 12 不晚、不晚、也都剛到、咱們入席罷。 13 這個座兒實在有僭的很。 14 理當、理當。諸位

我倒有一個法子、今兒個忙些兒、沒空兒細說、請先生明兒過來、喒們再商量、行不行。 53 可以、沒有甚麼不行的、我就遵命了、明兒個幾點鐘兒。 54 明兒個喒們申初兒罷。 55 那們我失陪了。 56 您請。 57 請。

## 問答章之十

1 今兒早起有個朋友送了個帖兒來、是要請我在飯庄子上吃飯、我心裏有點兒猶豫、是爲甚麼呢、我想、貴國的一切見面兒應酬的禮節、我都不大很熟、倘若落了過節兒、倒教人家笑話。 2 您別那麼想阿、等我把那個俗套子告訴告訴您、您就明白了。您把那個帖兒給我瞧瞧。阿、原來是張大老爺請您在慶會堂吃飯阿、這個庄子好、地方又寬綽、屋子很涼快、我常去。他那個菜做的講究、樣樣兒都得味兒、誰家也沒有他那麼好、您去罷、樂得的大家談談、散散悶兒呢。 3 我聽說貴國請客、那帖子上定的時刻不能算準成、彷彿罷、寫的是午刻、必得未刻去纔好。 4 那看帖子是怎麼寫的、如果有個準字、就得到了那時候兒就去、張大老爺這帖子上沒有那準字、就寫的是四點鐘、您就是六點鐘去、也不晚、去的

實在有甚麽益處兒呢。29 三字經是三個字一句、爲的是小孩子容易念、那千
字文因爲沒有重字、小孩子念了、就可以認得一千字。30 念了這個之後、念甚
麽呢。31 常念的都是先念四書、後來念五經。32 您從念四書起、到念完了五
經、有幾年的工夫兒。33 兩頭兒算起來有六七年的工夫。34 阿、那五經念完
了、就是先生十四歲那一年。35 不錯、還沒到十四歲呢。36 先生從多大歲數
兒上開講。37 我從十二歲上纔開講。38 開講的時候兒、還是自己看註子、還
是聽先生的解說。39 我一開講的時候兒是聽先生的解說、講過一年多、就自
己看註子。後來作了二年多的詩合文章、纔進學。40 阿、十六歲中秀才、也就算
早阿、是先生的天分高。41 那兒的話呢。那也是徼倖。後來鄉試下了多少場、七
八年纔中了舉人。42 先生今年貴庚。43 我今年三十歲。44 先生中舉人之
後、這六年裡頭有甚麽公幹。45 沒有甚麽事情、前二年在家裡教書、後幾年在
外頭作幕、幫朋友。46 請問令友榮任是甚麽官。47 是山東的知縣、他去年不
在了、我纔回來的。48 先生作過幕那更好了。49 怎麽更好呢。50 好處是這
麽樣、我那朋友學話之後、還要學文書。51 可惜就是這個教話沒頭緒。52 那

## 問答章之九

1 有先生來要見老爺。 2 請進來。 3 進來了。 4 先生請坐。 5 請坐。
6 先生貴姓。 7 賤姓蘇。 8 先生到這兒來貴幹。 9 昨兒聽見一個相好的
說起閣下要請先生。 10 阿、必是那張先生說的。 11 不錯、是張先生說的。
12 張先生他告訴您是我要找先生、是我替別人找先生。 13 他沒告訴我詳細、
可不是閣下要請麽。 14 不是我要請、是一個相好的託我請。 15 令友還是貴
國的人麽。 16 是本國的人、到貴處日子不多。 17 既是新來的、我們的話恐怕
不懂罷。 18 不錯、漢話一句都不懂、漢字一個也不認得。 19 這麽着、我怎麽能
教給他書呢。 20 先生先得教他說話。話能說些兒、那看書再說。 21 他一字不
懂、我從那兒教起。 22 先生是老手了、在貴國教過多少門生、怎麽不能教他。
23 我們的教學那是另有一說。說話是不學而會的、至於念書、是從小兒背念熟
的、恐怕令友不能照着我們這兒的小孩子那麽費事罷。 24 那是自然的、也可
以商量一個法子。先生從多大念書。 25 我從七歲念起。 26 先生一念是先念
三字經、千字文麽。 27 不錯、先念的是那個。 28 貴國人都先念這兩個小書兒、

爺那些個鋪蓋甚麼的、可以僱一輛小車兒裝上、合老爺一塊兒走、其餘上船、打通州那們走。

72 按照那麼着、我就坐裝行李的那輛車麼。

73 老爺另僱一輛轎車兒坐、好罷。

74 那車是單套、是二套呢。

75 老爺要快、必得用二套的、現在雨水大、道兒不好走、三套的也不妨。

76 哎、道兒不好走、坐車不大對我的勁兒、在這兒雇馬、行不行。

77 騾子馬都可以雇、只怕我們的鞍子老爺騎着不合式。

78 我們那兒馬身上的傢伙我都帶着呢。

79 也怕不行、那馬鞍子我們的馬還可以備、那嚼帽子怕不肯戴。

80 嚼帽子是甚麼呢。

81 就是那馬腦袋上預備着安嚼子拴扯手的那傢伙。恐怕我們的馬戴不慣、要鬧性子。不如買匹外國馬、倒好。

82 外國馬在天津這兒那兒可以買。

83 行了、我們行裡有匹馬、是我們行中夥計的、他要賣、那馬很好、又老實又快、來往進京有三四回了。

84 那麼着、我就到行裡商量商量。還有那些個大箱子、運到通州的時候兒、雇甚麼人送進京去。

85 老爺就雇小的、好不好。

86 好、倒沒甚麼不好的、只怕這麼些日子你們行裡離不開你、不容你去。

87 行了、離得開、今兒打發我來不是聽老爺的吩咐來了麼。

合我要多少錢。 55 那倒難說、老爺會說我們的話、可以先合他商量、看他要的價兒若很多、不妨駁他、再還他個價兒。 56 那都行了。就是第二天進京、還得打那麼走。 57 早起離了河西務、還是往西北去、有二十多里是到安平、還有二十多里是馬頭、從馬頭還算有二十里地、到張家灣那個老城。 58 沒到張家灣、不是先有個小河兒麼。 59 不是、那城是南北下裡騎着河面兒的。老爺進了南門、順着大街過了河、就出北門。那北門外頭有兩股岔道兒、往北的是上通州去、往西偏着點兒的那就是進京的了。 60 接那兒到京還有多遠呢。 61 看老爺進那個門。若是城外店裡住、進沙窩門兒、還算有五十多里路、若是到城裡頭、走東便門、那是往北點兒、多個二三里地、也不算很遠。 62 上外國公館是進那個門好。 63 那外國公館都是在海岱門裡頭、御河橋一帶、在我說、是進東便門方便些兒。 64 很好、如今我明白了。還有一件事、我走的這麼快、我的行李怎麼樣呢。 65 老爺的行李有多少。 66 就是門外頭擱着的那些東西。 67 甚麼、那些大箱子也是老爺的麼。 68 原是啊。 69 老爺想兩天進京、恐怕不能都帶罷、不但用好些個大車費錢、還不能很快。 70 那麼、你說還有甚麼好法子。 71 依我說、老

18

好。河西務那兒還是那個店好。35 那兒有一個富興、一個順來、兩個都是大店。
一個在街南頭兒、一個在街北頭兒。36 這兩個是那個方便呢。37 若論房子
吃食都差不多兒、南頭兒方便、北頭兒方便、那是隨老爺的意。38 南的北的有
甚麼不同、相離的很遠麼。39 離的却不甚遠、河西務沒有這兒府城那麼大地
方、不過是個鎮店。一條長街、兩邊兒有些個鋪子甚麼的。40 這麼說起來、南的
北的有甚麼不一樣的。41 沒有甚麼不一樣的、是我向來給老爺們帶道、總是
一進街就住下的時候兒多。42 你說的、那是打天津去的、在南頭兒住、打京裡
來的、在北頭兒住、是不是。43 不錯、老爺明白。44 就是了。我到了店裡叫他們
弄甚麼菜好呢。45 老爺怕沒吃過我們的菜罷。46 沒吃過呢。47 阿、老爺還
沒吃過、不如從天津做一點兒好拿的菜帶着。48 甚麼、自己帶着、到了店裡不
吃他們的飯、他們願意麼。49 那倒沒甚麼、店裡還得他們的房錢。50 這房錢
有一定的價兒麼。51 我們人住店、差不多有一定的價兒、若是外國客人、怕那
掌櫃的他多要幾個錢。52 那掌櫃的就是店東麼。53 那都不定、有是店東做
掌櫃的、有是店東外請別人、替他照應買賣做掌櫃的。54 就是這個房錢大概

一道橋、到熱鬧街兒那兒、再打聽第二道橋、過了第二道橋、往西北就是進京的大道。 16 聽見說還有過河的地方兒、有沒有。 17 那是擺渡罷。擺渡是有。 18 擺渡是有、那車馬怎麼樣呢。 19 車馬沒甚麼、那都可以擺過去。 20 往後怎麼樣呢。 21 往後是這麼着、離了擺渡口兒還是順著大道走、到離天津三十多里的那個鎮店、叫浦口、就是頭段兒。 22 那兒呢、頭一段兒不是河西務麼。 23 河西務遠多了、那算是一天的道兒。過了浦口之後、先到楊村、後到南蔡村、挨晚兒的時候兒可以到河西務。這些地方兒相隔大約都是三十多里地。 24 按道兒說、這河西務離京還有多遠呢。 25 按道兒說、就算是中間兒了。在那兒住一夜、明兒個就進得了京咯。 26 住一夜是在那兒呢。 27 貴國的人向來有住店的有住廟的。 28 是店裡好、是廟裡好呢。 29 依我說、是店裡方便些兒。廟裡留客是格外的事情、一來、不定有房子沒有、二來、如果趕車的多、和尚不願意、再者、丟了東西、爲誰是問呢。 30 阿、店裡丟東西是店主人應管麼。 31 原是那麼着。還有一說、吃的喝的店裡都能預備、廟裡連廚房都沒有。 32 沒廚房、廟裡在那兒弄飯呢。 33 他們弄的都是素菜、葷的他們不能弄。 34 阿、那們不如店裡

來著、是不是。96可不是拏着呢、剛纔從我們那兒買的。97是小孫子跟他要來着麽。98不是、令孫哭了、他說、你別哭、我送給你點兒玩意兒。99就是這個畫兒算玩意兒、爲甚麽不送到小兒那兒去呢。100那張大爺的姪兒今兒早起到我們鋪子裡來、打聽令郎的住處。我們說知道您納、不知道他、他叫我們把畫兒送到府上就是了、過兩天他還要親自來呢。

## 問答章之八

1請老爺安。2好阿、你是甚麽人。3我是英順行打發來、給老爺帶路進京的。老爺定規多喒走。4明兒就要走。5老爺要走的是水路、是旱路呢。6是旱路好、是水路好。7水路呢、這兩天雨大、河水長了、上水的船拉着費事、再遇着北風、怕五六天到不了通州。8哎、這麽着那水路就不行。走旱路怎麽樣呢。9若是老爺明兒一早動身、趕着走、第二天晚上就可以到京、慢着點兒、第三天足行了。10這旱路你熟罷。11哎、這十幾年常來往、怎麽不熟呢。12我不用人帶道、你細細兒告訴我都是打那麽走、行不行。13可以、沒甚麽不行的。老爺出了城、東邊兒那個浮橋知道不知道。14那個知道。15您過了這

住麽。

65 他這會兒單搬出去了。

66 請問他住在甚麽地方兒。

67 他在交民巷、西頭兒路北，

68 他是在交民巷住麽。

69 眞的呵、你疑惑作甚麽。

70 我估摸是在城外頭住的。

71 離衙門那麽遠、不行、你怎麽估摸着是城外頭呢。

72 昨兒日頭落、碰見他的車、在琉璃廠。

73 那兒有這個話、他昨兒晚上在我這兒來着。

74 車是他的。他却沒在車上。

75 他沒在車上、你怎麽知道車是他的。

76 車上坐着個老婆子、他說是孟大爺的車。

77 老婆子抱着個孩子麽。

78 不錯、是個七八歲的小孩子。

79 必是我那小孫子、嗳、那早晚兒那兒去。

80 老爺放心、有點兒事情。

81 有點兒甚麽事情呢、車驚了麽。

82 不是、本來道兒不好走。

83 那麽、是車翻了麽。

84 也不然、是合對頭兒車碰了。

85 碰了、老沒說開麽、怎麽那早晚兒還在那兒呢。

86 倒不是沒說開。

87 是小孩子受了傷了麽。

88 却沒甚麽很利害、他從車上跳下來的時候兒把腿扭了一下兒。

89 可惡、知道那個車是誰的不知道。

90 就是那張爺、他姪兒的。

91 還是他呀、那麽送畫兒是作甚麽呢。

92 這畫兒是給您納令孫的。

93 特意買畫兒壓驚、是甚麽意思呢。

94 畫兒是先買的、並不是特意買的。

95 碰車的時候兒他手裡就拏着

30 那堂子衚衕住的張爺您納認識不認識。 31 張爺我認識就是他買的麼
32 還不是他。 33 不是他、提他作甚麼。 34 我提他有個原故。 35 有原故爲甚
麼不說呢。 36 您納太急、回來就明白了。 37 你這是要戲我的話、我不依。
38 那兒敢要戲您納。 39 有正經話爲甚麼不說。 40 提起來話兒長。 41 就是、
你不能說我進去了、你去罷。 42 噯、別忙、別忙、還有話說呢。 43 有話就快說、我
沒空兒。 44 那張爺您納說是認得。 45 那我先告訴你了。 46 他們令姪您納
認得不認得。 47 見過一次、不很熟。 48 叫送這個畫兒的就是他。 49 他叫送
來的。他多喒晚兒回來了。 50 甚麼回來呢、他出外來着麼。 51 他從前不是跟
官出去麼。 52 那個我不知道、是那年出去的。 53 我記得是前年往江西去了。
54 前年出去的、我從去年還見他在城裡頭呢。 55 那都不論、他給我送畫兒是
作甚麼。 56 本不是給您買的。 57 不是給我買的、你拏來作甚麼、我決不買這
個。 58 說甚麼買呀、錢是他給過了。 59 你這個來回話兒我始終不明白。
60 等我再告訴您幾句話。 61 就快說、別儘着躭悞工夫兒。 62 您納的少爺不
是在戶部有差使麼。 63 你這個人竟是打聽、小兒原是在戶部。 64 他不是單

是決不見他了。54 我是說着玩兒呢、來的是刻字匠、要錢來了。55 叫他月底再來罷。56 他先來過兩回了。57 不錯、是有的、我應許了還錢、是得給的。58 大人不必費事了、我替您開發了罷。

## 問答章之七

1 是你叫門麼。2 是我叫門。3 你是那兒的。4 我是城外頭來的。5 你找誰。6 找姓孟的。7 我就姓孟。8 阿、您納就是孟爺。9 不錯、我姓孟、找我作甚麼。10 廣文齋打發我來的。11 廣文齋不是書鋪麼。12 不錯、是書鋪。13 叫你送甚麼書來麼。14 不是送書來了。15 怎麼、手裡拏的不是書麼。16 不是書、竟是個書套。17 沒有書、竟送個空書套作甚麼。18 這書套不是空的。19 不是空的還裝着甚麼。20 裝着幾張畫兒。21 畫兒、怕不是送這兒來的罷。22 沒錯、是給這兒送來的。23 爲甚麼、我沒有買畫兒。24 我知道不是您納買的。25 那麼爲甚麼給我送了來。26 有別人給您納這兒買的。27 給我買畫是甚麼意思。28 買的意思您納倒不用打聽。29 到底是誰給買的。

33 體面有甚麼體面呢、那天穿的那褂子也不怎麼樣。 34 怎麼樣不怎麼樣、也算是値錢的、他騎的那騾子也是很好的。 35 我估摸他是坐車來的。 36 不是坐車、騎着騾子來的、那騾子十分的臕壯。 37 既然是這麼着、你既知道他這麼靠不住、又愛花錢、你還這麼護着他、是個甚麼道理。 38 人家從前很享福、如今沒有路兒了、我見了他、心裡怎麼能不憐恤。 39 噯、怎麼憐恤他是憑你、竟是有一句話、可不用託我給他找甚麼事情。 40 可惜了兒的、眼看着他這個人是要要飯的。 41 等他要飯的時候兒、給他頓飯吃到可以、叫我保他作甚麼我萬也不能。 42 按那天定的、約了他後兒來。 43 後兒他來了、你可以把我起先說的那話告訴他。 44 告訴他是大人一定不肯幫他麼。 45 不是那個話、是告訴他、我出了城了。 46 他若是問大人多喒回來。 47 你就說不知道多喒回來。 48 他若是天天兒來打聽呢。 49 憑他來多少回、總不許他進來。 50 我想、不如簡直的告訴他、若打算甚麼事、你轉託別人、不用倚靠大人咯、好不好。 51 那却不行、若是簡直的告訴他不肯相幫、必得把所以然的話細說明白了、那更不必了。 52 哼、院子裡說話不是徐丞的聲兒麼。 53 若是他、隨你用甚麼話推辭、我

私。16 怎麽、那個走私是叫官場中査着了。17 哎、您想一想、那官役勒索的錢多、官場中有不知道的理麽。18 勒索了不過三百兩銀子、也不算很多。19 你說是不多、這數兒也是應當合他們同事的均分的、那巡船上的人不但沒按着分兒分給同事的、他們自己留的也是彼此相爭。20 大家爲錢爭鬧、後來有個報了官的、是不是。21 就是了、官既知道這件事、便細究個水落石出、把老徐從重的罰了、連他的功名也革了。22 老徐像這麽丢臉、也難怪徐亦遮掩。23 遮掩、是該遮掩的、誰教他張揚來着、也不用編造他父親因朋友受累的這些假話呀。24 那可也過逾虛詐咯。25 他說這個話的時候兒我就有一半兒不信、我記得那李亦城合他父親很熟和、我心裡打着合他打聽打聽這個人。26 大概那姓李的說他沒有甚麽好話罷。27 一句好話也沒有。那徐亦他是很認得、徐亦頭裡求他給找一個事情、他心軟了、依了、沒考過就保舉了。28 是個甚麽差使。29 是個貼寫的事情、沒有一個月就不要他了。30 不要他、是因爲他行止不好。是因爲他沒本事呢。31 兩樣兒都不好、楷書所不能寫、怎麽能做貼寫呢、而且說的話一句也靠不住。32 那個人奇怪呀、沒有錢、穿的怎麽那麽體面呢。

19

78 那巡哨船早躲開了、徐丞他經過那樣兒的事、就長了一個見識、不照前次從豐、只給十兩銀子罷了。 79 他們依不依。 80 那'兒不依呢、他們都喝的半醉了、要摟他的船也不能了、他給的不論怎麼少都可以依得.

## 問答章之六

1 那旁岔話兒算結了。他那年辦洋葯是甚麼人託他的、他告訴了你沒有。

2 我不記得。 3 他不是說是他父親叫他去的麽。 4 那我實在是不記得咯。

5 不論你記得不記得、實在是他父親叫他買的、後來他父親關閉買賣的緣故、就是因爲這個。 6 那'兒呢、是他打算的不好麽。 7 打算的不好那一句話也有的、那'洋葯出口是往天津去的。 8 阿、在天津叫人摟出來了麽。 9 那船始終沒到天津、走到山東海面兒上叫海賊把船扣住了。 10 這麽着、老徐的資本全丟了罷。 11 不錯、不但丟了資本、連頂戴也丟了。 12 他原來有個功名麽、那我却不知道。 13 是、他就是頭年捐的。 14 是捐過阿。然而海賊那一案怎麽會干涉着他的功名呢、難道說他與海賊通了麽。 15 那却不因爲海賊、是因爲走

給一百兩銀子、是沒有的事、說是若不給三百兩是要全封了。57 這三百兩他給不給呢。58 他沒有這麼些個錢。59 沒有這麼些個錢、他還有甚麼法子辦呢。60 他寫了個字兒、叫他們跟上海洋行裡取錢。61 奇怪、他們也肯要這個字兒麼。噯、他出了這個虎口是個便宜。62 還有那、這不算所出了虎口。63 怎麼呢、那巡役們要了這個字兒又有甚麼反悔呢。64 不是那麼樣、他們大家沒商量妥的時候兒、柴船和巡船一塊兒往下走、撞了人家灣着的兩隻船。65 又是兩隻巡哨的船麼。66 不是關上的船、是欽差劉大人的船、一隻是預備他自己坐的、一隻是他下人坐的。67 可笑。還是半夜的時候兒麼。68 不到半夜、二更多天。69 二更多天、劉大人合底下人必都睡了罷。70 劉大人怕是在城裡頭公館裡、底下人們還在船上樂呀、唱阿的、鬧呢。71 就是那些個底下人們到底與海關上無干。72 原是呀、竟是徐沵那個柴船撞了他們的船先是一驚、後來心定了一定兒就合他要賠補的錢。73 要賠補甚麼呢。74 賠補他們受驚、賠補官船的損壞、隨便甚麼都算應賠補的。75 他甘心受他們這個、我不明白。76 一則是寡不敵衆、二則是他的膽虛。77 膽虛是應該膽虛。到了兒怎麼樣呢。

起來、辦洋藥的那一層、他還些微的有點兒難處。33 別是那洋藥短了罷。
34 短、是不短。價錢天天兒長、東西還足彀買的。35 賣的還是公然賣麼。36 也
不算公然、都是躉船棧房裡藏的。37 吃的時候兒還是在洋行裡麼。38 不是、
徐汆常去的是在窨衚衕兒裡頭、一個小鋪兒的後頭。39 阿、這徐汆也常上烟
館麼。眞是有甚麼老子有甚麼兒子。40 吃的也不大很利害。41 阿、自己不吃、
盡是替人家辦的罷。可是他那個難是甚麼呢。42 那時候兒烟禁沒開、他辦得
了要出洋、還躭悞了好些日子。43 底下怎麼出的口呢。44 有裝柴火的船、他
把烟下在裡頭偷着出口。45 我以爲上海的柴火都是進口的、出口是往那兒
去呢。46 去的地方兒大概不遠。那船裝的實在是柴火少洋藥多。47 所以鬧
出事來了。48 鬧出事來是這麼著、那柴火船順着水放下去、抽冷子有巡船來
抓住了。49 抓住了就把這貨封了麼。50 還沒有封、那些巡役們說你若不多
多兒給我們錢、可就要搜你的船了。51 巡役們跟他要多少錢呢。52 他們沒
說數兒、盡是叫他從豐。53 這徐汆他要給多少。54 他那人糊塗、說要給一百
兩。55 一百兩、那寔在從豐了、巡役們也不覺多麼。56 那兒不覺多、看柴火船

親賠本兒、不是眞的麼。
7 賠本兒、原是賠本兒、可不像他說的那麼賠本兒。
8 不是像他說的賠本兒、還是怎麼着呢。
9 他賠本兒全是他自己糊塗、自己拋費了、沒別的。
10 到底家裡養活的人口多。
11 他養活家口倒沒有那件事。不用提別的、那徐福慶早就不在了。
12 早去了世了麼、他那些個兒女却是誰養活呢。
13 他女兒在他沒去世之前就都死了、兒子單生了一個、就是這個撒謊的。
14 那怕大人是聽錯了罷。
15 一點兒也沒聽錯、我細細兒的考查過了、你不是說合徐家有親麼。
16 不錯、我說過。
17 這四五年來你都沒見過他們罷。
18 不止四五年、有九年十年的光景沒見了。
19 就是了。那老徐在布鋪作買賣、他的名聲怎麼樣。
20 那一時人就說他狂傲、沒有甚麼別的不好。
21 他不是很愛吃烟麼。
22 吃烟是有的、也有一點兒貪酒。
23 却原來。就是你在上海遇見那徐永他在那兒作甚麼。
24 他說是有人托他辦土貨出洋。
25 甚麼土貨呢、是茶葉、是湖絲。
26 有茶葉、有湖絲、有藥材。
27 這些土貨是要運到那兒去呢。
28 他說得是往北往南、我不記得、
29 他沒提辦洋貨麼。
30 他巧來提過、我不記得咯。
31 沒提過辦洋藥麼。
32 辦洋藥原有的、大人提到、我纔想

67 那倒是歲數還小呢、常愛病。 68 常愛病麽、是甚麽病。 69 打我母親死了他缺奶、後來不很足壯。 70 這實在可憐、還有你們弟兄們、量必可以幫着過日子。 71 我却很願意、可惜沒個道路。 72 你是長房的不是。 73 我排二。 74 可是、你大哥作甚麽呢。 75 他腿脚兒有殘疾、甚麽都不能幹。 76 噯、這個光景可了不得、還有你的兄弟可怎麽樣呢。 77 我父親收買賣的時候兒、他們還小呢、不能栽培他們念書、他們學的還算不深。 78 說來說去、你的意思是要託我給你找個事情、對不對。 79 大人肯這麽疼愛我、我感激的心一言難盡了。 80 就是、你今兒個來意實在是因爲這個不是。 81 不是大人先提起來、我實在是不敢開口。 82 也罷、等我給你打算打算、請你過了十天前後兒來、再說。 83 眞是承大人的提拔、我過幾天再來請安。 84 偺們過兩天見、請。 85 大人請坐。

## 問答章之五

1 龍田、那徐氶再來的時候兒你告訴他我出城去了。 2 噯、可惜、叫他白喜歡了、他怎麽得罪了大人了。 3 甚麽得罪呢、他那些個話通身都是假的。 4 怎麽呢、他不是徐福慶的兒子麽。 5 這徐福慶的兒子那却是恬。 6 他說他父

好了沒有。41 年紀這麼大、眼睛還算可以。42 那兒說到年紀、歲數兒合我差不多兒。43 家父今年六十九。44 我七十一、比他大兩歲。45 我父親要能彀像大人這麼硬朗、那是求之不得的了。46 怎麼不能呢、他沒有我受的累多。47 大人是爲國家當重任、辦事受的累多、我老子爲家業心裡也有他的辛苦。48 那是從前做買賣時候兒累的、如今是回家歇着了。49 回家、是回家、也是無可奈何。50 怎麼呢、買賣不好麼。51 也不盡是那麼様。52 怎麼呢、莫不是銀錢被了竊。53 比丟了還可惡、所掙的錢差不多兒叫人家都騙净了。54 可惜了兒的、是怎麼呢、欠主兒蹦了麼。55 大人、不是那麼様、我父親保的那個朋友跑了、56 可惡、令尊的精神就是因爲這個受傷、是不是。57 自然是、家裡人口多、沒力量養活、不免着急。58 你父親跟前你們幾個。59 我們弟兄四個、還有三個姐妹。60 這麼多呢、未必都在家裡罷。61 個個兒都在家裡。62 我想那姑娘都是出嫁的。63 本有兩個出了門子、給的都是武官、上回西路出兵都陣亡了。64 阿、他們倆孀婦就回家來麼。65 是、都回家來了、一個帶着兩個孩子、一個帶着六個孩子。66 噯、那人口眞纍的不少、還有一個姑娘沒出門子麼。

## 問答章之四

1 龍田。 2 大人叫我作甚麼。 3 院子裡那個人是誰。 4 那個人是姓徐的。 5 阿、是你認識的麼。 6 是我陳認識的。 7 你們倆是在那兒遇見的。 8 是在上海會過的。 9 是多喒呢。 10 好些年了。 11 你合他很有交情麼。 12 可以。我們本是個遠親。 13 你們是親戚麼。他作甚麼來了、你知道不知道。 14 不知道、大人要我問他麼。 15 問問他也好。 16 他說是來要見大人。 17 來見我作甚麼。 18 他說是他父親打發他來、給大人請安的。 19 他父親是作甚麼的呢。 20 從前是作買賣、現在閒着呢。 21 這人我所不記得、是個作甚麼買賣的。 22 西城那個大布鋪、大人那兒不記得。 23 阿、那徐福慶阿、他我還記得。來的是他兒子麼。 24 不錯、是他的兒子。 25 讓他進來。 26 大人讓你哪。 27 大人好。 28 請坐、請坐。 29 大人請坐。 30 請坐、請坐。來。 31 喳。 32 沏茶來。貴姓是徐麼。 33 賤姓徐。 34 徐福慶是你父親麼。 35 不錯、家父的名字是徐福慶。 36 前幾年我們就認識、他好阿。 37 托大人的福、打發我來給大人請安。 38 叫他惦記着、着實勞你的駕咯。 39 該當的。 40 我模模糊糊的記得他眼睛不大好、如今

那兒的人呢。104 是道兒上茶館兒裡的人。105 離城門有多遠兒。106 不遠兒、就在沙窩門兒外頭。107 是來順兒在那兒喝茶來著麽。108 不是喝茶、是喝酒、吃東西。109 你合他一塊兒吃麽。110 沒有、我出去拴鞭子去了。111 拴好了鞭子就回茶館兒了麽。112 趕我回來、他們先跑了。113 跑了、就是坑你的車錢麽。114 不但車錢、連茶館兒的飯錢都沒給。115 阿、他們跑了、茶館兒就是合你要這個錢麽。116 可不是麽、我不肯給、他們就打了我了。117 茶館兒打你這一層、我有甚麽法子。118 打不打沒甚麽要緊、請老爺找補我的車錢、我就走了。119 車錢還容易、把他的工錢折給你就是了。120 老爺可以這就賞罷、叫小的回去。121 車錢你放心罷、這個茶館兒裡的事情你合他沒話麽。122 沒話、沒話。請老爺給了錢、小的就回去。123 你實在是個忠厚人哪、肯擔待人家的不是、可是你回村兒裡、要告訴來順他老子、他兩個兒子沒有一個是材料兒的、這宗樣兒的人我決不要他們咯。

來順一個坐兒麽。72 還有他一個同伴兒。73 要快是那個的主意。74 來順僱車來的時候兒說若快、可以多加幾個錢。75 你們說明白了是多少錢。76 說定了的是五吊錢。77 連他要給加的錢都在裏頭麽。78 都說在一塊兒了、小的不訛人。79 車價還罷了、是因爲這個打架來着麽。80 總沒合他打架。81 怎麽了、你不是纔說挨了打了麽。82 小的說挨打、可不是他打的。83 不是他、是誰。84 有好些個人、小的不認得都是誰。85 都是來順帶了來的伴兒麽。86 不是、一個也不是來順帶來的。87 他們是搶東西的麽。88 也不然。嗳喲、說起來話長。89 就是話長你也得說了。90 請老爺補還我的錢、我就走了。91 別忙、別忙這件事我還得分晰明白。92 不値得就悞老爺的工夫。93 那你不用管、只要我問你甚麽你說甚麽。94 老爺還問甚麽呢。95 這個張來順是馬駒橋的人麽。96 他父親在村兒外頭種個菜園子。97 這麽著這來順兒必是你素來認得的。98 他小時候兒在街上玩兒、我常看見他。99 他小時候兒是老實阿、是琉璃呢。100 小的不肯說人的短處。101 不要你偏說短處、他有好處你不能彀說麽。102 請老爺補還我的車錢、我就走了。103 就是、毆打你的是

們是誰、要的是甚麼錢。 38 那天替老爺買的桌子、鋪子裡要錢。 39 那鋪子不是在西城麼。 40 不是、鋪子是在城外頭。 41 城外麼、離那個門近。 42 小的城外的道兒不大熟。 43 這鋪子在北邊兒在南邊兒、還不知道麼。 44 阿、小的想起來了、在安定門外。 45 這裡頭我有點兒不大明白的地方兒。 46 老爺不明白甚麼。 47 你這個人總得說實話。 48 小的不敢撒謊。 49 阿、院子裏甚麼人吵嚷呢。 50 小的出去看一看罷。 51 不用去。放窗戶罷。 52 唉、有個人闖進來、是甚麼事情。 53 你不是趕車的麼、闖進來幹甚麼。 54 噯哎、小的給老爺磕頭、求老爺作主。 55 作甚麼主呢。 56 噯哎、丟了錢、挨了打、求老爺伸冤。 57 你丟錢挨打、與我何干。 58 不關老爺的事、却關老爺的底下人。 59 我那個底下人、可是那個來順麼。 60 阿、不錯、就是他、我頭裏沒理會他。 61 他合你怎麼了。 62 我的車錢他那兒給了麼。 63 是北城來的那個車麼。 64 甚麼北城阿、我是馬駒橋店裏的。 65 咳、這個還得說詳細、你可小心細說罷。 66 小的若有一句謊、老爺要了我的腿都使得。 67 你們今兒是甚麼時候兒起的身。 68 雞叫的時候兒纔套車。 69 是單套、是二套。 70 是二套車、爲走的快。 71 車上就是這

## 問答章之三

1 來。2 隨進來問 老爺要甚麼。3 你是甚麼人。4 小的叫來福。5 你姓甚麼。6 小的姓張。7 你在這兒幹甚麼。8 小的是替哥哥來替工。9 你哥哥是誰。10 小的的哥哥叫來順。11 阿、就是給我看書房的那個來順兒麼。12 不錯、就是那個來順。13 他沒告假、怎麼走了呢。14 因爲老爺欠安、他不便告假。15 怎麼不等我好了呢。16 家裡有件很要緊的事。17 有甚麼要緊的事情呢。18 小的母親病的利害。19 既這麼着、怎麼他走了、你來了呢。20 他回去是小的的父親叫他、小的來是怕躭悞老爺這兒的工夫。21 阿、別的先勿論、底下人出門到底應當告假。22 請老爺饒他罷小的哥哥也快來了。23 你家裡離這兒遠近。24 不算很遠。25 怎麼不很遠。26 至多有四里地、還是在東城呢。27 是了、你這個人先回去罷。28 小的哥哥就得回來麼。29 到晚晌來也可以。30 阿、那不是來順來了麼。31 阿、叫他進來。你去罷。32 老爺沒有甚麼別的事使喚小的。33 沒事、你去罷。來順。34 小的糊塗、請老爺寬恕。35 你眞糊塗、出去爲甚麼不言語。36 老爺欠安、他們是急於合我要錢。37 他

成麼。

33 那是我們本家。

34 更好了、他新近不是放了巡撫了麼。

35 是阿、放的是河南巡撫。你納還有什麼高見。

36 我想你若還當着差使、那老大人必肯提拔你。

37 這是錯想了、你不知道、他向來不喜歡我。

38 你不過這麼想、甚麼是個對證兒。

39 他上次出外我求他帶我來着。

40 他怎麼囘答你的。

41 他說的就是天底下沒有人、我也不要你。

42 阿、他說的這麼言重、有甚麼緣故麼。

43 他恨我年輕的時候兒不勤儉。

44 唉、你放心罷。既往不咎。老大人那ʻ兒還那麼恨你。

45 你不知道、他還有別的話呢。

46 那ʻ兒有總不肯寬宥的話麼。

47 他說過、我無論到甚麼分兒上再不能照應你。

48 可惜、有這個好機會、你得不着益處兒。

49 沒法子、誰教我底根兒沒出息呢。

50 令尊留下的家產、專歸你一個人兒了、是還分給一家兒了呢。

51 還有我們家兄舍弟、一個人分了一分兒。

52 分的還是令兄的多呀。

53 不是、是三個人均分的。

54 留下的是銀錢哪、是產業呀。

55 有現銀子、也有房子、買賣。

56 身底下住房、你又不是長子、爲甚麼歸你。

57 從前先父在的時候兒、家兄就管買賣。

58 阿、就是你在家裡伺候令堂。

59 原是阿、因爲舍弟也是在外頭作幕。

## 問答章之二

1 您納騎的不是我們這兒的馬麽。2 不錯、是在貴處買的馬。3 是誰替你買的。4 店裡那些人替我挑的。5 他們合你要了多少錢。6 他們要了三十兩銀子。7 你給了沒給呢。8 我看着價錢多一點兒沒給。9 你到底給了多少銀子。10 我跟他們定規是二十二兩銀子。11 這匹馬從前是我的。12 阿、你爲甚麽賣了。13 因爲家裡沒錢纔賣了。14 不是因爲有甚麽毛病阿。15 一點兒毛病都沒有。16 你底跟兒多少錢買的。17 那時候兒有錢、買的貴。18 你那時候兒是有差使不是。19 我頭裡是當衙門、到先父去世的時候兒擱下了、回去料理家務。20 哎呀、令尊病的日子久麽。21 可不是麽、病了十來年呢。22 他納這些年的病誰照應家裡呢。23 我父親雖不能出門、還可以管家裡的事。24 令尊若是在世、你的差使還可以當麽。25 可以當不可以當、還不定。26 怎麽不定呢。27 差使的得項若是多些兒、我還願意當。28 你從前當着還得賠墊麽。29 倒沒那個、總得能多點兒纔寬綽。30 你別怪我說、你擱下的不當。31 那麽、依你納主意當時叫我怎麽辦呢。32 那王大人不是你們親

# 問答章之一

1 您貴處是那兒。 2 敝處是天津、沒領教。 3 我也是直隸人。 4 阿、原來是同鄉。 5 他那一位是那兒的人。 6 他是外國人。 7 到這兒來做甚麼、您知道不知道。 8 我不知道、您問他本人兒就知道了。 9 請問尊駕到我們這兒做甚麼。 10 我是個做買賣的。 11 您帶了來的都是甚麼貨。 12 都是東洋的油漆碎貨。 13 阿、您貴國是日本國麼。 14 不錯、是日本國。 15 怎麼呢、我聽見說過貴處出入很難。 16 頭裡却難、近來開了禁咯、就好些兒咯。 17 我們的商民也有上那兒去的沒有。 18 貴國的商民也有。 19 我們的人在那兒是那一省的人多. 20 他們多一半兒是打廣東福建去的。 21 他們的買賣大小呢。 22 只怕沒甚麼很大的罷。 23 爲甚麼呢、沒有本錢麼。 24 他們的本錢大概不很多。 25 沒錢往東洋去幹甚麼。 26 他們多一半兒是跟太西各國的人去的。 27 太西國的人帶他們去有甚麼益處兒。 28 是用他們管行作經手的。 29 他們合日本國的人對勁兒不對勁兒。 30 彼此怕都有點兒不相信罷。

# PART IV.

## THE TEN DIALOGUES.

(CHINESE TEXT.)

# 語言自邇集

(YÜ YEN TZŬ ÊRH CHI).

A

## PROGRESSIVE COURSE

DESIGNED TO ASSIST THE STUDENT OF

# COLLOQUIAL CHINESE

AS SPOKEN IN THE CAPITAL AND THE METROPOLITAN DEPARTMENT.

IN TWO VOLUMES.

THIRD EDITION. (ABRIDGED.)

PREPARED BY

THOMAS FRANCIS WADE,

*Sometime H.B.M.'s Minister in China,*

AND

WALTER CAINE HILLIER,

*Sometime Chinese Secretary to H.B.M.'s Legation, Peking.*

VOL. II.

SHANGHAI—HONGKONG—YOKOHAMA—SINGAPORE

KELLY AND WALSH, LIMITED.

1903

# PART III.

## THE FORTY EXERCISES.

**The Ordinal Numbers.**—Any cardinal number or group of cardinal numbers becomes Ordinal when *ti*4 is prefixed to it. Thus,

*liu*4, 6; *ti*4 *liu*4, 6th. *san*1 *pai*3 *ling*2 *êrh*4, 302; *ti*4 *san*1 *pai*3 *ling*2 *êrh*4, 302nd.

**7.** For purposes of numeration the following words will be constantly required:—

幾 *chi*3, some; how many?

數 *shu*4, number; several; some; but *shu*3, to count.

些 *hsieh*1, few; some.

多 *to*1, many; more.

少 *shao*3, few; less.

*to*1-*shao*3, how many? also, a good number.

When not interrogative more emphasis is laid on *to*1 than on *shao*3, but the tone is held to be the same.

**8.** In Exercise I, given below to illustrate the method of numeration, words are used which the student has already learned in the Radical Table. The following are new:—

有 *yu*3, to be; to have.

來 *lai*2, to come; adverbially, in numeration, to approach a total, but under, not in excess.

不 *pu*4, not; the tone varies before different characters.

好 *hao*3, good; adverbially, very; verbally, to recover.

個, 箇, *ko*4, one, or ones, of persons or things; the commonest numerative of a large number of nouns substantive; the second is the correct form of the character. The term numerative is explained below.

**The Numeratives.**—Chinese nouns substantive have commonly associated with them certain other nouns substantive, here styled Numeratives, between the meaning of which and their own there is an affinity. This may be generic, specific, formal, qualitative, and is sometimes so vaguely defined that nouns, being names of things in categories widely different, may have the same numerative. The latter, in virtue of this affinity, acts as the unit of the class, body, or other plurality that may be indicated by the noun on which it is dependent; and it should be borne in mind that a large number of numeratives are never used independently of those nouns to which they are related. We have in English nouns that do somewhat the same duty. We say so many *head* of oxen; so many *stand* of arms; a crew of so many *hands;* a fleet of so many *sail.* These are all plurals or collectives. If we were speaking of oxen, we might also say that there was not a *head* left; or if of arms, that every *stand* was destroyed. The Chinese numerative will be found to play both the parts here illustrated; but it also plays a part of its own. Where it comes between a number, one or more, and its substantive, it cannot be translated. For *yi*2 *ko*4 *jên*2, one man, *san*1 *ko*4 *jên*2, three men, the Cantonese, in the broken English which is the *lingua franca* of the open ports of China, would say, "one piece man," "three piece man." We have nothing analogous to this in our language.

There are many substantives which have no numerative, such in particular as are applied to the measure of time, space, quantity, etc.

As stated above, the numerative is itself a substantive, but in construction it will often represent our *one* or *ones,* the pronominal adjective indefinite.

*Obs.*—*Yi*1, one, changes its tone before *ko*4 and other numeratives.

## EXERCISE I.

1 十六. 十九. 二十. 三十四. 五十七. 六十八.

1. Sixteen. Nineteen. Twenty. Thirty-four. Fifty-seven. Sixty-eight.

2 第十七個. 二三百. 二三千. 兩三千. 兩三個. 三五個. 五六百個人.

2. The seventeenth person (or thing). Two or three hundred. Two or three thousand. Two or three thousand. Two or three persons or things. Three or five persons or things. Five or six hundred persons.

*Obs.*—The Chinese do also say three or four, four or five.

3 第一. 第二十七, 第一千八百六十五.

3. Number one; the first; also, figuratively, the best. Number twenty-seven; the twenty-seventh. Number one thousand eight hundred and sixty-five; or, the one thousand eight hundred and sixty-fifth.

4 第一百萬零三百個. 五十七萬零六百一十. 七十萬零二十.

4. The one million and three hundredth person (or thing). Five hundred and seventy thousand six hundred and ten. Seven hundred thousand and twenty.

*Obs.*—Six hundred and ten; the *yi*, one, before *shih* cannot be omitted. In reckoning myriads it is equally correct to use *yi* or to omit it. You may say *shih wan*, *shih pa wan*, or *yi shih wan*, *yi shih pa wan*.

5 一百萬. 三十五萬. 五百萬零一. 六萬零五百零七, 十萬.

5. A million. Three hundred and fifty thousand. Five million and one. Sixty thousand five hundred and seven. One hundred thousand.

6 七萬零一百九十一. 千萬. 四十六萬一千.

6. Seventy thousand one hundred and ninety-one. Ten millions; or, figuratively, any number; in any (or the utmost) degree; also, above all things. Four hundred and sixty-one thousand.

7 五萬零八十八。九萬八千四百零二。一千零五。四千零七十二。八千三百六十七。一萬零六。一百零三。

7. Fifty thousand and eighty-eight. Ninety-eight thousand four hundred and two. One thousand and five. Four thousand and seventy-two. Eight thousand three hundred and sixty-seven. Ten thousand and six. One hundred and three.

8 一百一十八。二百五十四。九百九十九萬三千。

8. One hundred and eighteen. Two hundred and fifty-four. Nine million nine hundred and ninety-three thousand.

9 有幾個人來。有些個人。有好些個人。有多少人來，三萬多人。

9. A number of people are come; or, How many people are come? There are some people. There are a good number of people. How many people are come? Upwards of thirty thousand.

10 數十個。幾十個，十幾個。兩個。幾個。不止十個。八九個。十來個。九個，十個。二百多。五千多。

10. Several score (*lit.*, tens); some score. Some score; or, How many score? Ten and more persons or things; or, How many over ten? Two persons or things. Some persons or things; or, How many? There are more than ten; *lit.*, [the number] does not stop at ten ones. Eight or nine. Near ten persons or things. Nine or ten persons or things. Two hundred and more. Five thousand and more.

*Obs.* 1.—Score: the Chinese have no word for score, but it is un-English to say some tens. Note that ten odd are supposed not to exceed fifteen.

*Obs.* 2.—Near ten, but below it: *lai* is only used with ten or a multiple of ten.

11 長三寸四，一身一口。有幾口人，五斤牛肉，六斤羊肉，幾斤魚，

11. Three inches four-tenths long. A single individual. There are some persons; or, How many persons are there? Five catties of beef. Six catties of mutton. Some catties of fish; or, How many catties of fish?

*Obs.* 1.—Four-tenths: understand the word *fên*, part (emphatically, tenth part), after *ssŭ*, four.

*Obs.* 2.—*K'ou* refers to individuals, male or female.

12 七斗麥子。九斗米，一斗黍子。

12. Seven measures of wheat. Nine measures of rice. One measure of millet.

13 幾個牙。長幾萬里，至多四萬里。有山足高二百里。三百斤有零。

13. Some teeth; or, How many teeth? Several myriads of *li* in length; some tens of thousands of miles long; or, How many myriads of miles long? At the most forty thousand *li*. There is a mountain (or there are mountains) full two hundred *li* high. Three hundred catties odd.

*Obs.*—Full: *see* Radical 157. The Chinese idea is rather to measure the heights of mountains by the length of the road by which they are ascended.

*Turn the following into Chinese.* (KEY, EXERCISE I.*)

1. Twelve. Fourteen. Ninety. Seventy-three. Forty-five. One hundred and ninety-nine.

2. Forty thousand one hundred and sixty-eight. Three million twelve hundred and twenty-four. Eight hundred and twenty-nine. Two hundred and ninety-two.

3. The twenty-first. The three hundred and forty-second. The eightieth. Number sixty-seven. Eight or nine men are coming.

4. The nine hundred and ninety-ninth. The seven million six thousand five hundred and forty-third. The three million four thousand five hundred and sixty-seventh.

5. Five million two hundred and one. Three million and twenty-seven. Six thousand and forty. Nine hundred and ninety-nine thousand nine hundred and ninety-nine.

6. There are a good many horses. How many oxen are there? There are fifty-six oxen and horses.

7. How many catties of fish are there? Seven catties and some ounces. Six measures of small millet. There are eighteen measures of rice. Fourteen measures of beans.

8. More than ten persons are coming. More than fifty persons are coming. A hundred odd persons are coming. A single individual.

9. There are about (but less than) ten catties of fish. Nineteen catties of beef. Seventeen catties of venison. Fourteen measures of rice. Eighteen measures of beans. Ten measures of small millet.

10. How many miles long? A good many. Full seventeen hundred *li*. Full nine hundred *li*. There are mountains fully eight *li* high.

**9. The Article.**—As will have been seen from Example 11 in the foregoing exercise, our Indefinite Article may be represented by *yi*[1], one, without any numerative. But if the substantive be one of those to which a numerative is assignable, that numerative will be commonly found between the *yi*[1] and the substantive. Sometimes the numerative will stand without the *yi*[1], as in *yu*[3] *ko*[4] *jên*[2] *lai*[2], for *yu*[3] *yi*[2] *ko*[4] *jên*[2] *lai*[2], there is a person come (or coming).

**10.** The Definite Article *the* is not uncommonly rendered by the demonstrative pronouns

這 *chê*[4], this; and 那 *na*[4], that;

* The Chinese text of this and all similar exercises will be found in vol. i.

but chiefly, if not always, when the thing or person indicated is for certain known to the hearer or has been recently referred to. But these are not the only equivalents.

**11. The Noun Substantive.**—One peculiarity of the Chinese Substantive has already been noticed—the employment, namely, of a large staff of words, themselves substantives, in close relation with other substantives, which from their most conspicuous function have been denominated Numeratives. By others they have also been styled Classifiers, as possessing in general a meaning in affinity with that of the nouns to which they are attached as adjuncts, or which, when detached from these, they represent.

Independently of these adjuncts, the Chinese substantive may be simple or compound.

Of the simple form, any substantive in the Radical Table is as good a specimen as another; such as *jên*², man; *shên*¹, body; *ma*³, horse; etc.

Of the compound form, there are instances of more kinds than one in the Exercises in the Colloquial Radicals (vol. i, p. 34); such as *shih*¹-*shou*³, a corpse (*lit.*, corpse-head); *k'ou*³-*shê*², altercation (*lit.*, mouth and tongue); *kan*¹-*ko*¹, war (*lit.*, shield and spear). These suffice to show that the words combined may be of like or of very different meaning. In the same Exercise will be found *ch'ên*²-*tzŭ*³, a minister of state; *shih*⁴-*tzŭ*³, a lettered man. The word *tzŭ*³, son, is largely added to other substantives.

兒 *êrh*², also meaning son, is used in the same way as frequently as *tzŭ*³; in Pekingese, more frequently. But neither of them can be appended *ad libitum*. Some substantives that take the one may at times take the other; and many do not take either.

*Obs.*—This *êrh* also sometimes plays a part in the formation of adverbs, especially of time and place.

Combinations of words, such as with us shipwright, horse-boy, landlord, etc., are common enough in Chinese; but, in view of the independent individuality of almost every Chinese word, it is in most instances safer to speak of the relation of the first word to the second as attributive, rather than as part of a compound substantive.

Some English substantives, it will soon be seen, require for the reproduction of their meaning a string of words. Thus *carter* is the driving-cart-one, or the one who drives the cart; neither of which combinations, however, would it be convenient to designate a compound substantive.

**12. Number.**—The plural of substantives may be effected by the reduplication of the simple word, but this not without limitation; or by the addition of a noun of multitude, sometimes preceding, sometimes following, the simple word; or, in certain cases, by the addition of the particle *mên*¹, explained below (13).

**13.** 們 *mên*¹, a word used colloquially to indicate the plural of personal substantives or pronouns, and apparently for no other purpose. Thus,

*ta*⁴ *jên*², your excellency, his excellency (*lit.*, great man).
*ta*⁴ *jên*² *mên*, your excellencies, their excellencies.

Experience will show that its use even with personal substantives is limited.

*Note.*—When the tone mark is omitted it must be understood that the character is so little emphasised as to carry no tone.

**14. The Noun Adjective.**—The Adjective, like the substantive, may be either a single word, such as *hao*$^3$, good, in Exercise I, or a combination of words of like or different significations.

**15. The Personal Pronoun.**—The Personal Pronouns singular are—

我 *wo*$^3$, the 1st person ; 你 *ni*$^3$, the 2nd ; 他 *t'a*$^1$, the 3rd.

**16.** Their plural is formed by the addition of the particle *mên*$^1$, just noticed (**13**). Thus,

*wo*$^3$*-mên*, we, us ; *ni*$^3$*-mên*, ye, you ; *t'a*$^1$*-mên*, they, them.

*Obs.*—*Ni*$^3$*-mên* is often used politely to a single individual.

**17.** 偺, 咱, *tsa*$^2$, properly *tsan*, is a pronoun of the first person peculiar to northern Chinese, but never used in the singular. In the plural, *tsa*$^2$*-mên* means you and I, or you and we, when the persons spoken of are present ; parties in the same undertaking or concern. The second form of *tsa*$^2$ is but an abbreviation of the first.

**18.** When animate beings are in question, any male or female, man or beast, may be indicated by *t'a*$^1$, he or she ; *t'a*$^1$*-mên*, they. But in speaking of inanimate things *t'a*$^1$ is used very sparingly.

In the constructions of the verb which we describe as impersonal, the pronoun *it* cannot be said to be visibly represented in Chinese.

**19.** 的 *ti*$^1$. This word, which is properly a substantive meaning a bright spot, the blot on a target, has come to perform various duties. Appended enclitically to substantives and pronouns, it forms, as we should say, the genitive or possessive case. Appended to adjectives or adjective constructions, it adverbialises them. It is sometimes a relative pronoun ; sometimes an indefinite pronoun, such as one, some, etc.

In all these cases it has presumably usurped the place of other words, notably that of the verb *tê*$^2$, noticed immediately below (**21**).

**20.** Attention is here directed to *ti*$^1$ as forming the **Possessive** of substantives or pronouns. Thus,

| | |
|---|---|
| *tzŭ*$^4$*-chi*$^3$*-ti*, of or belonging to oneself. | *ta*$^4$*-jên*$^2$*-ti*, his excellency's. |
| *wo*$^3$*-ti*, mine. | *wo*$^3$*-mên-ti*, ours. |
| *ni*$^3$*-ti*, thine. | *ni*$^3$*-mên-ti*, yours. |
| *t'a*$^1$*-ti*, his. | *t'a*$^1$*-mên-ti*, theirs. |

**21.** The following brief examples will help to confirm the student in his knowledge of the words just learned (**10–19**) :—

| | | | | | | | | |
|---|---|---|---|---|---|---|---|---|
| 己 *chi*$^3$ | 的 *ti* | 咱 *tsa*$^2$ | 人。*jên*$^2$ | 咱 *tsa*$^2$ | 的。*ti* | 你 *ni*$^3$ | 這 *chê*$^4$ | 這 *chê*$^4$ |
| 的 *ti* | 馬。*ma*$^3$ | 們 *mên* | 咱 *tsa*$^2$ | 們 *mên* | 他 *t'a*$^1$ | 我 *wo*$^3$ | 兒。*'rh* | 個。*ko*$^4$ |
| 馬。*ma*$^3$ | 我 *wo*$^3$ | 這 *chê*$^4$ | 們 *mên* | 兩 *liang*$^3$ | 們 *mên* | 他。*t'a*$^1$ | 那 *na*$^4$ | 那 *na*$^4$ |
| | 自 *tzŭ*$^4$ | 兒 *'rh* | 倆。*lia*$^3$ | 個 *ko*$^4$ | 的。*ti* | 你 *ni*$^3$ | 兒。*'rh* | 個。*ko*$^4$ |

This one. That one. This place here. That place there.

Thou, I, he ; we three. Thine. Theirs.

We two persons here. We two.

A horse (or horses) of our place here.

My own horse (*lit.*, myself's horse).

*Note.*—There is nothing to show whether *ma*, horse, in the 4th example, is singular or plural.

2

**22. The Relative Pronoun.**—It has just been observed (19) that *ti*¹ acts sometimes as a Relative Pronoun. In constructions such as The person who did, The thing which was done, *ti* may be allowed to be so characterised. But for caution's sake it should be borne in mind that the Chinese may not unfrequently be rendered by our participle, past or present, if not in other ways.

**23. The Interrogative Pronoun** *who, which, what,* which has been described by some grammarian as a relative in search of an antecedent, is in general rendered colloquially as below. There are other forms of higher style.

誰 *shui*², who, is never used but of persons.

甚 *shên*² 麽 *mo*¹, 嗎 *ma*¹. The combination *shên*²*-mo*¹, pronounced *shê*ⁿ²*-mo*¹, used alone, signifies *what,* but may stand before a personal noun, as in *shê*ⁿ²*-mo*¹ *jên*², what person? The character *shên* signifies extreme, but is then read *shên*⁴, and it may be surmised that it has come to be corruptly employed in this combination. Its adjunct *mo* is a negative interrogative particle; it is sometimes also used as a conjunction, as in *na*⁴ *mo*¹ *to*¹, as much as that; *chê*⁴ *mo*¹ *hsiao*³, as small as this. *Ma* is a strictly colloquial interrogative.

什 *shih*², a tithe, is sometimes written instead of *shên*², but the compound is none the less pronounced *shê*ⁿ²*-mo*, or *shê*²*-mo*.

那 *na*³, with *ko*⁴ or other numerative (*yi*¹, one, intervening or not), is interrogative, What person? What thing?

*Obs.*—It is *na*³, not *na*⁴, which we have met with above (10) as a demonstrative pronoun.

**24.** Thus, for Who? Whom? What person? we may have *shui*² or *she*ⁿ²*-mo jên*² or *na*³ *yi*² *ko*⁴ *jên*² or *na*³ *ko*⁴ *jên*².

For the interrogative *what, shê*ⁿ²*-mo* may stand alone; or the substantive representing the thing spoken of may be expressed, and without its numerative.

But *which,* if referring to one of many objects, animate or inanimate, will be rendered by *na*³, as above, followed by *yi*¹ and the numerative, or by the numerative without *yi*¹.

**25. The Verb.**—It will suffice for the moment to observe that in Chinese the Verb may be simple or compound—the compound verb being made up sometimes of the same verb reduplicated, sometimes of verbs of like or different meanings, sometimes of a verb and its object.

These remarks apply rather to verbs that we should designate Active or Neuter. The equivalent of our Passive formation is effected by prefixing to the verb concerned other verbs signifying to suffer, to receive, to perceive, etc., as the case may be.

Some verbs incontestably active are reinforced by other verbs, which, like the French *faire,* signify either to do or to cause to be done.

**26.** We have met above (8) two simple verbs: *yu*³, which means, as an active verb, to have, and as a verb substantive, to be; and *lai*², to come. The latter has something of this

sense even when used as an auxiliary, which it often is. The verb *yu*³ has also, though limitedly, auxiliary functions.

**27.** With these and the following verbs, although also possessing all of them independent powers, there may be effected, as auxiliaries, a fair proportion of the equivalents of our verbs' inflections.

**28.** 在 *tsai*⁴, to be; to be at; at; in the act of; in.

**29.** 是 *shih*⁴, to be; to be what ought to be, that is, right. Hence, in answer to a question, *shih*⁴ means *yes*, and *pu*² *shih*⁴, *no*; interrogatively, *shih*⁴ *pu*² *shih*⁴, is it so or not? is it right or not? The combination *pu*² *shih*⁴, not right, constantly occurs as a substantive meaning error, fault; or as an adjective or adverb, wrong, erroneously. It is well to remember, however, that the negative or affirmative in answer to a question is more frequently expressed in Chinese by the repetition, or partial repetition, of the question with the negative or affirmative prefixed than by the negative or affirmative alone. Thus,

*t'a*¹ *lai*² *pu*⁴ *lai*², is he coming? *t'a*¹ *pu*⁴ *lai*², he is not coming.
*shih*⁴ *t'a*¹ *pu*² *shih*⁴, it is he, is it not? *shih*⁴ *t'a*¹, it is he.

We could not say, without being guilty of a vulgarity, *pu*⁴ simply, in answer to the first question, and the simple affirmative *shih*⁴ would rarely be used in answer to the second. *See* Exercise III, 10 and note variations in tone of *pu*.

**30.** 得 *tê*², to get; to have; to possess; to accomplish. See *ti*¹, above (**19**). As an auxiliary, *tê*² follows the verb to which it is attached, indicating sometimes that the action of the first verb is completed, but oftener the possibility of its completion. It discharges, perhaps more than any other verb in Chinese, what we regard as the functions of our verb *can* and *cannot*. Of this more directly.

**31.** 了 *liao*³, 咯 *lo*¹, to end, or be ended, when following a verb, indicates the completion of an act, the occurrence of an event. It may often fairly be called a sign of the past tense. It is also freely used as a final expletive. *Lo* is much used as a colloquial termination.

When the negative *pu*⁴ (8) intervenes between the other verb and *liao*³, the construction is almost, if not quite, that represented by our potential auxiliaries.

Thus *lai*² *pu liao*³, it is not possible that [he] should come. This is said, however, when the speaker merely holds a strong opinion as to the impossibility. Were he to say *lai*² *pu tê**, he would affirm it more positively.

It should be remembered that, elsewhere as here, *tê*² and *liao*³, though both signify completion or achievement, are by no means identical in their functions as auxiliaries.

In the combinations *tê*² *liao*, it is finished or achieved, *liao*³ is the auxiliary of *tê*²; as we should say, it puts *tê* in the past tense.

**32.** 要 *yao*⁴, to want; to desire; to be about to. It is used, but by no means invariably, to indicate future time. The tense of the verb is as often as not shown by the context alone. But from its meaning of "to want," *yao*⁴ comes to represent our auxiliary *must*, both singly and in various combinations.

* *Note.*—The omission of tone marks sometimes, as in this case over the words *pu tê*, signifies that the rhythm of the sentence or the accent on one particular word render the unmarked words practically toneless.

With one of these the student of Pekingese cannot too soon become acquainted. Out of *tê*² and *yao*⁴, a corrupt monosyllable, *tei*³, has been formed, which is one of the most useful auxiliaries in the Peking colloquial. It is of course not recognised by native lexicographers, and has been represented in this course by the character *tê*², distinguished by a Chinese tone mark attached to it on the right side.

Another corrupt combination is *pieh*² 别, for *pu*² *yao*⁴, the imperative *do not*.

33. 沒 *mo*⁴ or *mu*⁴, not, is much less common than *pu*⁴, but is used in a few cases where *pu*⁴ is not used. While, for instance, *pu*⁴ is never used with *yu*³, to have or to be, *mo*⁴ or *mu*⁴ is never used with *shih*⁴, to be.

With *yu*³ it has formed the corrupt monosyllable *mei*², which will be found, however, before the verb *yu*³ itself, standing as a simple negative. Thus,

*mei*² *yu*³ *hao*³ *ti*, there are not any good ones.

When *mo*⁴ or *mei*² stands before another verb, that verb is generally in the past tense. Thus,

*t'a*¹ *lai*² *liao mei*² *yu*³, is he come or not?

*t'a*¹ *mei*² *lai*², he is not (has not) come.

If your question were, Is he coming or not? you would ask *t'a*¹ *lai*² *pu lai*², and the answer in the negative would be *t'a*¹ *pu*⁴ *lai*², he will not come (is not coming).

34. To recapitulate, the words just learned (21–33) are as follows:—

在 *tsai*⁴, to be; to be at; at.
是 *shih*⁴, to be; to be right.
得 *tê*², to possess; to obtain; to achieve.
要 *yao*⁴, to want; to will.
得' *tei*³ (*tê*² *yao*⁴), must.
了 *liao*³, to end; ended.
沒 *mo*⁴, *mu*⁴, not; *mei*² (=*mo*⁴ *yu*³), not to be.
誰 *shui*², who?
那 *na*³, what?
甚 *shên*⁴, extreme; but with *mo*¹, interrogative, and intoned *shên*².
什 *shih*², a tithe; but, like *shên*², used phonetically with the following *mo*¹, to express *what?* also *any*.
麼 *mo*¹, a negative interrogative particle.

35. Learn also the following:—

很, 狠 *hên*³, an intensive; as in *hên*³ *hao*³, very good. The second is a corrupt form.

東 *tung*¹, east; 西 *hsi*¹, west (*see* Radical 146). The combination *tung*¹-*hsi*¹ means a thing. Thus,

*hên*³ *hao*³ *ti tung*¹-*hsi*¹, very good thing (or things).

買 *mai*³, to buy; 賣 *mai*⁴, to sell. The combination *mai*³-*mai*⁴ means trade, business. Thus,

*ta*⁴ *mai*³-*mai*⁴, trade on a large scale.

---

## EXERCISE II.

1 我們倆人。偺們倆。這麽大。那麽小。

1. We two (men or women). You and I. As large as this. As small as that.

*Obs.*—In *chê-mo*, *na mo*, the *mo* has no interrogative power. The syllable is sometimes represented by *mên* (13), which, however, is then pronounced *mo*.

2 甚麽人。甚麽東西。

2. What man? What thing?

*Obs.*—Thing: *tung-hsi*, east and west; *q.d.*, everything between east and west.

3 那個人是誰。那個人是個好人。他是個買賣人。賣甚麽的。賣好些個東西。

3. Who is that man? That man is a good man. He is a trader. What does he sell? He sells a good many things.

*Obs.*—What does he sell? (*lit.*, he is a seller of what?) It would be equally correct to say *t'a mai ti shih shên mo*.

4 我要好的有沒有。沒有了。這個很好、那個不好。這個人很好、那個人很不好。

4. I want good ones; have [you] any? (or, are there any?) There are none; or, I have none left. This is very good; that is bad (or, this is a very good one; that one is bad). This man is very good; that man is very bad.

*Obs.*—I have none left: *liao* implies that there were some originally, but that they have gone.

5 他來了沒有。他沒來。有甚麽人來。沒有人來。有人來了。他是那兒的人。他不是這兒的人。

5. Is he come? He is not come. Who is it that is come? There is no one come. A person is come; or, there is someone come. What place is he from? He is not of this place.

*Obs.* 1.—In the last two examples *chê êrh*, *na êrh* are pronounced *chê 'rh*, *na 'rh*.

*Obs.* 2.—It is simplest to construe *ti* as the sign of the possessive case; *q.d.*, he is what place's man?

6 他們來了多少人。他們來了好些個人。有多少人在那兒。有十幾個人。

6. How many people is it that are come? A good number. How many people are there? Ten people and more.

*Obs.*—It would be equally correct in the answer to the first question to omit *t'a mên*.

7 這個是我們的。那個是他們的。這個是甚麼人的。這個東西是誰的。是我們的。這個東西你們有多少。有不多的。

7. This is ours. That is theirs. Whose is this thing? Whose is this thing? It is ours. How many have you of this article? Not many of them.

8 我不要這個。他們要這個。他們的不大好。你們那兒有好的沒有。沒有好的、有。很好的、我們不要了。你們有這個東西沒有。我們不要這個東西。我買不了那麼些個。

8. I do not want this one; they want it. Theirs is not very good. Have you got any good ones there? None good. Unless you have some very good ones, we do not want any. Have you got this thing? We do not want it. I cannot buy so many as that.

*Obs.* 1.—We do not want any: note the use of *liao* as a final expletive.
*Obs.* 2.—In the last example, *na-mo*, that, those; *hsieh ko*, indefinitely numerous ones.
*Obs.* 3.—I cannot buy, etc.: *liao*³, a potential auxiliary.

9 這個了不得。那個了不了。

9. This will never do; or this is a bad business. That is not to be done; or, that cannot be accomplished.

*Obs.*—The first *liao*, is the verb to finish, to accomplish; the second *liao*, though literally possessing the same meaning, does the duty of the verb *can*, or, with *pu*, cannot.

10 這個東西很好。這個東西好得很。

10. This thing is very good.

*Obs.*—*Hao tê hên* in the second example: there is no perceptible difference in the meaning of the two sentences.

11 你要買馬、得買好的。那個馬買不得、毛長得不好。

11. If you want to buy a horse you should (or, ought to) buy a good one. It won't do to buy that horse (*lit.*, that horse cannot be (=ought not to be) bought); he has a bad coat (*lit.*, the hair, *chang*³ *tê*², has grown, not good, or, not well).

*Obs.*—*Chang*³, to grow, not *ch'ang*², long (Radical 168); *see* next example. *Tê* is here an auxiliary completing the action of the verb *chang*³; *see* 20.

語言自邇集



12 那竹子長得很長. 他來了你得走.

12. Those bamboos have grown greatly. When he comes you must go; or, he is come and you must go.

*Obs.* 1.—*Chu* (Radical 118), the bamboo; *tzŭ* (Radical 39).
*Obs.* 2.—*chang*$^3$ *tê hên ch'ang*$^2$, have lengthened very long.

13 那個人比我的兒子高八寸多. 你們是幾口人. 我們是十來口人.

13. That man is upwards of eight inches taller than my son. How many in family are you? We are under ten.

*Obs.* 1.—*Lit.*, that man compared with my son [is] high eight inches [and] more.
*Obs.* 2.—See *k'ou* in the Colloquial Radicals; *lai* above in 8.

*Turn the following into Chinese.* (KEY, EXERCISE II.)

1. Thy horse. My sheep. His cart. Your rice. Our handkerchief. Their knife.

2. You buy, we sell. They want to buy things. What things do they want to buy? Good things. We here sell very good things.

3. As small as this; as large as that. This mountain is not as high as that (*q.d.*, as the height the other person declares it to be).

4. Have you any good horses? No. We sell good carts here; we do not sell horses. This cart is not a good one.

5. Whose is this horse? It is mine. How many horses have you? Three. How many carts are there here? Not very many.

6. What place are you from? I am of this place. What place is that trader from? He is not of this place. Does he sell good things? Not very good. The traders here have not very good things. We two traders sell good things.

*Obs.*—Trader: *lit.*, a buying selling man.

7. I want to buy things; are there any traders (sellers) here? Not very many. How many are there? Five. I want to buy a good many things; do you want to sell? (or, do you sell them?) What things do you want? Good things.

8. How many sons and daughters has he? Four daughters and five sons. His five sons are here; his daughters are there (in that place). I have walked a hundred *li*. He sells earthenware. What I want to buy is some bushels of wheat.

*Obs.*—Earthenware (Radical 98.)

9. How many days do you require? I want three months. Do you use wheat or millet? What are these things? They are black beans. There are many fish in this place (*lit.*, here the fish are not few).

10. Is that thing gold? No; it is clay. His nose is very small. Venison (deer flesh) is very good. Is the antelope (yellow sheep) found here? Yes. The scenery (Radical Exercises, 10, 6) here is very fine.

*Obs.*—Clay: *lit.*, yellow earth (*see* Radical 201.)

11. That man has grown very tall; or, he *is* very tall. That snake is more than three inches long. When he comes I must see him.

**36.** To return to verbs and verbal constructions. Note the following:—

拿 *na*$^2$, simply, to lay hold of a person or thing. Thus,

*na*$^2$ *jên*$^2$, to arrest a person. *na*$^2$ *chê*$^4$ *ko*$^4$ *tung*$^1$*-hsi*$^1$, lay hold of this thing.

**37.** 去 *ch'ü*$^4$, simply, to go, as opposed to *lai*$^2$, to come. Thus,

*wo*$^3$ *lai*$^2$, I come. *ni*$^3$ *ch'ü*$^4$, you go.

**38.** From combination of the above we get *na*$^2$ *lai*$^2$, to bring, and *na*$^2$ *ch'ü*$^4$, to take away—an object, of course, being expressed or understood. When expressed, the object, in the simpler phrases, is placed between *na*$^2$ and its adjunct *lai*$^2$ or *ch'ü*$^4$. Thus,

*na*$^2$ *shui*$^3$ *lai*$^2$, bring water here.

*na*$^2$ *chê*$^4$ *ko*$^4$ *tung*$^1$-*hsi*$^1$ *ch'ü*$^4$, take this thing away (*lit.*, laying hold of this thing go). There are exceptions to this rule of construction which will be noticed in their place.

**39.** Referring to Sections **30** and **31**, write out the following in Chinese :—

*na*$^2$ *tê*$^2$, can be laid hold of. *na*$^2$ *pu*$^4$ *tê*$^2$, cannot be, etc.

*na*$^2$ *tê*$^2$ *lai*$^2$, can be brought. *na*$^2$ *pu*$^4$ *lai*$^2$, cannot be, etc.

*na*$^2$ *tê*$^2$ *ch'ü*$^4$, can be taken away. *na*$^2$ *pu*$^4$ *ch'ü*$^4$, cannot be, etc.

Observe *na*$^2$ *tê*$^2$ *liao*$^3$, can be laid hold of; *na*$^2$ *pu*$^4$ *liao*$^3$, cannot be, etc. In these two the first differs nothing from *na*$^2$ *tê*$^2$; but *na*$^2$ *pu*$^4$ *liao*$^3$ will be found to have more force and scope than *na*$^2$ *pu*$^4$ *tê*$^2$.

**40.** With the following verbs, *lai*$^2$ and *ch'ü*$^4$ may discharge much the same function as when attached to *na*$^2$ :—

進 *chin*$^4$, to enter (as a door). 過 *kuo*$^4$, to pass over (as a river, hill, street).

出 *ch'u*$^1$, to go out of (as a door). 往 *wang*$^3$, to move towards, or in the direction of.

**41.** Thus, for instance :—

| | | | | | |
|---|---|---|---|---|---|
| 過 *kuo*$^4$ | 來。*lai*$^2$ | 往 *wang*$^3$ | 過 *kuo*$^4$ | 出 *ch'u*$^1$ | 進 *chin*$^4$ |
| 去。*ch'ü*$^4$ | 過 *kuo*$^4$ | 這 *chê*$^4$ | 山 *shan*$^1$ | 門 *mên*$^2$ | 門 *mên*$^2$ |
| | 來 *lai*$^2$ | 兒 *'rh* | 去，*ch'ü*$^4$ | 去。*ch'ü*$^4$ | 來。*lai*$^2$ |

To come in at the door. To go out of the door.
To go over (across) the hills.
To be coming in this direction (or, come here).
To pass backwards and forwards.

**42.** 過 *kuo*$^4$, to pass, is much used as an auxiliary in verbal constructions of past time.

**43.** 起 *ch'i*$^3$, to rise, followed by *lai*$^2$, may mean simply to rise from a lower position ; to get up. But the combination *ch'i*$^3$-*lai*$^2$, it will be seen, has a separate function.

It has been mentioned above (26) that *lai*$^2$ is frequently used as an auxiliary. This it is as indicating progressive action. The combination *ch'i*$^3$-*lai*$^2$, itself an auxiliary, must be rendered variously according to circumstances.

**44.** 到 *tao*$^4$, to arrive ; as *t'a*$^1$ *tao*$^4$ *liao*$^3$, he has arrived ; *t'a*$^1$ *mei*$^2$ *tao*$^4$, he has not arrived. It is used as an auxiliary with certain verbs implying movement, but with greater freedom in the southern than in the northern mandarin.

**45.** 著, 着, *cho*$^1$, also *chao*$^2$, written in the two forms here given. The first of these, however, is used in positions where the second would not be. Besides other parts, the word plays that of a most important auxiliary verb.

As *cho*$^1$, attached to several verbs it produces a participial inflection. Under other conditions, hereafter explained, *cho* is read *cho*$^2$. Thus,

*tsou*$^3$*-cho*, walking, going on foot.

But it must not be applied indiscriminately.

As *chao*$^2$, it resembles in power the verbs *tê*$^2$ and *liao*$^3$, and often means to meet with unexpectedly, or to catch, as a cold, etc. *See* Note at the end of Exercise XL.

We may say *na*$^2$ *pu*$^4$ *tê*$^2$, *na*$^2$ *pu*$^4$ *liao*$^3$, or *na*$^2$ *pu*$^4$ *chao*$^2$. But here again the selection of the auxiliary must depend on circumstances.

**46.** Learn the following substantives :—

房 *fang*$^2$, a house. 屋 *u*$^1$, or *wu*$^1$, a room. 舖 *p'u*$^4$, a shop.

These as often as not take *tzŭ*$^3$ after them. Thus, *fang*$^2$*-tzŭ*, *wu*$^1$*-tzŭ*, *p'u*$^4$*-tzŭ*.

**47.** 間 *chien*$^1$, a division or space ; the numerative of rooms and houses. (*See* Exercise XL, 3, Obs. 2.) Thus,

*yi*$^4$ *chien*$^1$ *fang*$^2$*-tzŭ*, a house. *liang*$^3$ *chien*$^1$ *wu*$^1$*-tzŭ*, two rooms.

*Obs.*—*Yi*$^4$, properly *yi*$^1$ ; *tzŭ*, properly *tzŭ*$^3$. The latter, when used thus encliticially, atonic.

But observe, *san*$^1$ *ko*$^4$ *p'u*$^4$*-tzŭ*, three shops.

間 *chien*$^1$ will also be found to act as a preposition of time or space ; in which case it follows its object.

**48.** Learn the following :—

家 *chia*$^1$, house, home ; also, family.
城 *ch'êng*$^2$, city wall ; city.
街 *chieh*$^1$, street.
道 *tao*$^4$, road, way ; also, to say (as will be seen later).
裏 *li*$^3$, inside of.
外 *wai*$^4$, outside of.
上 *shang*$^4$, above ; towards ; to ascend.
下 *hsia*$^4$, below ; to descend.
頭 *t'ou*$^2$, head ; end ; side.
住 *chu*$^4$, to stop oneself ; to stand firm ; to reside at.

**49.** The following are examples of some of the simplest uses of these words :—

| | | | | | | |
|---|---|---|---|---|---|---|
| 道 *tao*$^4$ | 家 *chia*$^1$ | 下 *hsia*$^4$ | 上。*shang*$^4$ | 外 *wai*$^4$ | 外。*wai*$^4$ | 家 *chia*$^1$ |
| 兒 *'rh* | 兒 *'rh* | 雨。*yü*$^3$ | 上 *shang*$^4$ | 頭。*t'ou*$^2$ | 裏 *li*$^3$ | 裏。*li*$^3$ |
| 上。*shang*$^4$ | 的。*ti* | 住 *chu*$^4$ | 街。*chieh*$^1$ | 街 *chieh*$^1$ | 頭。*t'ou*$^2$ | 城 *ch'êng*$^2$ |

In the house ; or, at home.

Outside the wall or city.

Inside. Outside.

Up (or, in) the street. To go up the street.

It rains (*lit.*, there descends rain).

Householders, as opposed to shopkeepers.

On the road.

Observe that *shang*$^4$, *li*$^3$, *wai*$^4$, used as prepositions, follow the object. So would *hsia*$^4$ as a preposition ; it is here used only as a verb.

**50.** Add these words :—

做 *tso*$^4$, to do ; as *tso*$^4$ *shih*$^4$ (252), to do business.

開 *k'ai*$^1$, to open ; hence, in composition, implying removal to greater or less distance. As *k'ai*$^1$ *mên*$^2$, to open the door.

3

## EXERCISE III.

1 有人拿了東西來。有人來要拏那東西去。那東西很多、一個人拏不了去。

1. There is a man here with things; or, a man is come with things; a man has brought things. A man is come to take away that thing (*i.e.*, with the wish or intention to take). Those things are too many for one man to take.

*Obs.* 1.—*Lit.*, there is a man [who] holding things is come.

*Obs.* 2.—If there were no *liao* at the end, it could mean that a man was come for the things; *q.d.*, *na*, to lay hands on, the thing.

*Obs.* 3.—That thing; *na* or *na ko*.

*Obs.* 4.—*Lit.*, those things [are] very many; one man cannot take [them] away.

*Obs.* 5.—Notice the *pu liao*, implying impossibility, between *na* and *ch'ü*. It might run, one man *na pu liao na tung-hsi ch'ü*.

2 那人是拏不得。那人是拿不著的。那人是拿不了的。

2. That man must not be seized (*e.g.*, because of his rank or other circumstance that makes it wrong to seize him). That man cannot be seized (there is no getting hold of him). That man is not to be seized, will never be seized (he is too powerful, too far off, etc.).

3 屋裏。進屋裏來。這個屋子沒有人住。

3. In a room. To come into the room. No one lives in this room.

4 住房子。這個房子比他那個房子好多了。

4. To live in a house. This house a great deal better than that one of his.

*Obs.* 1.—The *liao* at the end is merely expletive.

*Obs.* 2.—*T'a* = *t'a ti*, his that house.

5 你們那兒有多少房子。有三十五間房子。你住的房子大小。我住的是三間小屋子。

5. How many buildings have you over there? Thirty-five *chien*. Is the house you live in large or small? I live in a small room of three *chien*.

*Obs.* 1.—*Chien*: see Exercise XL, 3, Obs. 2.

*Obs.* 2.—Construe:—You reside(ing-*ti*) that house, [is it] large, [is it] small?

6 他在家裏做甚麼。他沒在家。上那'兒去了。上街去了。街上走着。街上的人很多。外頭土大。

6. What is he doing at home? He is not at home. Where is he gone? He is gone for a turn (*lit.*, up the street). Walking in the street. There is a great number of people in the street. There is a great deal of dust outside.

*Obs.*—*Shang*, verb and preposition.

7 你在那'兒住。我在城裏頭住。是東城住着好、是西城住着好。他那人開的舖子在那'兒、是做甚麼買賣的。

7. Where do you live? I live in the city. (or, in Peking, in the Tartar city). Is it better to live in the eastern or in the western division of the city? Where is that man's shop, and what business does he do?

*Obs.* 1.—If *hao* were omitted, this would continue the conversation, [Are you] *chu cho*, living, in the eastern city or in the western?

*Obs.* 2.—*Lit.*, that man's shop that he opens is where?

8 他那舖子東城有三個、西城有四個、我們這兒沒有那麼大的買賣。那個舖子是我的。那舖子裏買東西的人很多、

8. His shops are three in the east division of the city, and four in the west; we have no business so large here. That shop is mine. There is a large number of people buying things in that shop; or, the number of people, etc., is large.

*Obs.* 1.—His shops, *lit.*, his those shops.

*Obs.* 2.—We, *wo*[3]*-mên*, the person addressed being an outsider.

*Obs.* 3.—*Ti* has probably no more than a rhythmical function.

9 他來了沒有、他來了。他沒進來、過去往西去了。他上街買東西去了。他來過沒有。

9. Has he come? He has come. He did not come in; he went past, westwards. He is gone up the street to buy something. Has he ever been over here?

10 這個道兒過得去麼。過不去。你上那兒去。我不上那'兒去。你上那兒去過沒有。我沒去過。

10. Can you (or, one) get through by that way? You cannot get through (or, there is no thoroughfare). Where are you going? I am not going anywhere. Have you ever been there? No; I have never been there.

*Obs.*—The *na 'rh* in the first clause interrogative; in the second, indefinite—anywhere.

11 你做甚麼來着。他沒起來。你這個人得起來。那東西拿不起來。風起來了。起了大風。

11. What have you been doing? or, What were you doing (at the time)? He is not up (out of bed). *You* must get up. That thing cannot be lifted (it is too heavy). The wind has risen (is beginning, or has begun, to rise). It has come on to blow hard.

*Obs.* 1.—Observe the auxiliaries *lai* and *cho*, signifying past time.

*Obs.* 2.— You this man: *chê ko jên* may be added in anger or not; it merely emphasises the personal pronoun, first, second, or third. *Liao* has here no more than a rhythmical function.

12 要下雨。下過了大雨了。這麼大雨住不了。雨住了。這個東西拿得住拿不住。拿得住。你小心拿住了。

12. It is going to rain. It has rained heavily. Rain as heavy as this won't stop. The rain has stopped. Can [one] get a firm hold of this thing or not? [One] can get a firm hold of it. Be careful to keep a firm hold of it (to hold it fast).

*Obs.* 1.—In the construction of possibility or impossibility, the *tê* and *pu* come between the *na* and *chu*. But you say *na chu tung-hsi*; you must not say *na tung-hsi chu*.

*Obs.* 2.—Be careful: *lit.*, little heart, little being here used in the sense of fine, minute; *q.d.*, pay minute attention.

13 他那門開得開開不開。開不開。

13. Will his door open? (or, can that door of his be opened?) It won't open.

*Obs.*—*Lit.*, his that door open can open? open not [can] open? Open not [can] open. If the answer were *k'ai pu liao*, the impossibility would be more strongly affirmed than by *k'ai pu k'ai*.

*Turn the following into Chinese.* (KEY, EXERCISE III.)

1. You live inside the city. I live outside the city. I live in a house of six *chien*. Where do you keep a shop, and where do you live?

2. This house is much larger than that one. It has ten *chien;* that one has four. In the large streets there are not many dwelling-houses; [but] there are many shops there.

3. Where is his residence? He lives in a very small house in the west of the city. He keeps a shop there, does he not? He is not in trade.

*Obs.*—An intensive is often formed by the repetition of the adjective. Thus, *hsiao hsiao êrh ti*, very small.

4. Come into the room; it is dusty in the street. The door of that room is open. How many shops has he? Three or four. Where are they? They are in the east of the city. Does he do a large business? Not very large.

5. What is he doing at home? He has nothing to do; or, he does nothing (*lit.*, has not what to do). He has gone out of the city. Where has he gone? Towards the west. What does he want to do? He wants to buy horses and carts.

6. Where has that trader I wanted to buy things from gone? Does he know where I live? He does not know; he has not been into your room.

*Obs.* To know: 61.

7. That man's house is a much better one than mine or yours. How many *chi n'* has it got? Eight; mine has six, and yours has four. His house has a large frontage (*k'ou*$^{3}$ *mien*$^{4}$).

51. 知 *chih*$^{1}$, to know; commonly joined with *tao*$^{4}$, to say (48). Thus,

*wo*$^{3}$ *pu*$^{4}$ *chih*$^{1}$ *tao*$^{4}$, I cannot tell; *lit.*, I do not know to say.

52. 愛 *ai*$^{4}$ or *ngai*$^{4}$, to love or like. Thus,

*ni*$^{3}$ *pu*$^{2}$ *ai*$^{4}$ *t'a*$^{1}$ *mo*$^{1}$, do you not like him?

53. 話 *hua*$^{4}$, spoken language, what one says, as opposed to *wên*$^{2}$, language of books (Radical 67). Thus,

*t'a*$^{1}$ *ti*$^{1}$ *hua*$^{4}$ *hao*$^{3}$, his [style of] speaking is good.

54. 說 *shuo*$^{1}$, to say; as in *wo*$^{3}$ *shuo*$^{1}$, I say = this is my opinion. Also to speak; as *shuo*$^{1}$ *hua*$^{4}$, to speak language; or, the language spoken, as opposed to *wên*$^{2}$. But followed by a personal pronoun, *shuo*$^{1}$ means to blame: as *t'a*$^{1}$ *shuo*$^{1}$ *wo*$^{3}$, he blamed me.

55. Examples:—

| | | | | | | |
|---|---|---|---|---|---|---|
| 他 *t'a*$^{1}$ | 他 *t'a*$^{1}$ | 那 *na*$^{4}$ | 他。*t'a*$^{1}$ | 你 *ni*$^{3}$ | 道。*tao*$^{4}$ | 你 *ni*$^{3}$ |
| 說 *shuo*$^{1}$ | 說 *shuo*$^{1}$ | 人 *jên*$^{2}$ | 不 *pu*$^{2}$ | 愛 *ai*$^{4}$ | 我 *wo*$^{3}$ | 知 *chih*$^{1}$ |
| 的 *ti* | 的 *ti* | 說 *shuo*$^{1}$ | 大 *ta*$^{4}$ | 他 *t'a*$^{1}$ | 不 *pu*$^{4}$ | 道 *tao*$^{4}$ |
| 話 *hua*$^{4}$ | 很 *hên*$^{3}$ | 甚 *shên*$^{2}$ | 愛 *ai*$^{4}$ | 不 *pu*$^{2}$ | 知 *chih*$^{1}$ | 不 *pu*$^{4}$ |
| 好。*hao*$^{3}$ | 是。*shih*$^{4}$ | 麽。*mo*$^{1}$ | 他。*t'a*$^{1}$ | 愛 *ai*$^{4}$ | 道。*tao*$^{4}$ | 知 *chih*$^{1}$ |

Do you know? I do not.
Do you like him? Not much.
*Obs.—Ta*, great, used adverbially.
What is that man saying? What he says *hên*$^{3}$ *shih*$^{4}$, is quite (or, very) right (or, correct).
He speaks very well (good accent, form, sense).

56. 叫, 呌, *chiao*$^{4}$, to call; to bid. As *chiao*$^{4}$ *t'a*$^{1}$ *lai*$^{2}$, bid him come; call him here. The first is the form more commonly used. As will be seen later, it sometimes means to cause, and, as an auxiliary, can render an active verb passive.

57. 回 *hui*$^{2}$, to return; as *t'a*$^{1}$ *hui*$^{2}$ *lai*$^{2}$ *liao*, he is come back. Also, an occasion; as *liang*$^{3}$ *hui*$^{2}$, on two occasions.

58. 乏 *fa*$^{2}$, to be tired; as *wo*$^{3}$ *shên*$^{1}$-*tzŭ* *fa*$^{2}$ *liao*, I am (*lit.*, my person is) tired.

59. 站 *chan*$^{4}$, to stand upright, as distinguished from sitting, or lying down.

60. 躺 *t'ang*$^{3}$, to recline ; to lie down.

61. 坐 *tso*$^{4}$, to sit.

62. Examples :—

| | | | | | |
|---|---|---|---|---|---|
| 坐 *tso*$^{4}$ | 起 *ch'i*$^{3}$ | 乏 *fa*$^{2}$ | 來。*lai*$^{2}$ | 了。*liao* | 他 *t'a*$^{1}$ |
| 着。*cho* | 來。*lai*$^{2}$ | 了。*liao* | 走 *tsou*$^{3}$ | 叫 *chiao*$^{4}$ | 走 *tsou*$^{3}$ |
| 躺 *t'ang*$^{3}$ | 站 *chan*$^{4}$ | 你 *ni*$^{3}$ | 道 *tao*$^{4}$ | 他 *t'a*$^{1}$ | 回 *hui*$^{2}$ |
| 着。*cho* | 着。*cho* | 站 *chan*$^{4}$ | 兒 *'rh* | 回 *hui*$^{2}$ | 去 *ch'ü*$^{4}$ |

He is gone back on foot.

*Obs.—Tsou* here, on foot.

Call him back ; or, bid him return.

Tired with one's journey.

*Obs.—Tsou tao*, to go the road : probably, but not necessarily, on foot.

You stand up !

Standing up. Sitting. Lying down.

*Obs.—Cho* inflecting these verbs participially.

63. 關 *kuan*$^{1}$, to close, to shut ; as *kuan*$^{1}$ *mên*$^{2}$, shut the door. Also, a barrier or military frontier station ; also, an important point ; hence (as will be seen later), to bear upon, to concern.

64. 窗 *ch'uang*$^{1}$, a window ; colloquially, always followed by *hu*$^{4}$ (Radical 63). Thus,

*kuan*$^{1}$ *ch'uang*$^{1}$-*hu*$^{4}$, shut the window.

65. 樓 *lou*$^{2}$, an upper story ; also a storied building ; as *lou*$^{2}$ *shang*$^{4}$, upstairs.

*Obs.*—Its numerative in the latter case is not *chien*, but *tso*. *See* Part VIII.

66. 衙 *ya*$^{2}$, a bureau or official residence ; colloquially, not used alone, but with *mên*$^{2}$. Thus,

*shang*$^{4}$ *ya*$^{2}$-*mên*$^{2}$, to go to office.

67. 地 *ti*$^{4}$, the ground ; as *ti*$^{4}$ *hsia*$^{4}$, on the ground.

68. Examples :—

| | | | | | | |
|---|---|---|---|---|---|---|
| 在 *tsai*$^{4}$ | 人 *jên*$^{2}$ | 在 *tsai*$^{4}$ | 我 *wo*$^{3}$ | 有 *yu*$^{3}$ | 樓 *lou*$^{2}$ | 關 *kuan*$^{1}$ |
| 樓 *lou*$^{2}$ | 躺 *t'ang*$^{3}$ | 地 *ti*$^{4}$ | 要 *yao*$^{4}$ | 人 *jên*$^{2}$ | 上 *shang*$^{4}$ | 門 *mên*$^{2}$ |
| 上 *shang*$^{4}$ | 在 *tsai*$^{4}$ | 下 *hsia*$^{4}$ | 上 *shang*$^{4}$ | 上 *shang*$^{4}$ | 坐 *tso*$^{4}$ | 開 *k'ai*$^{1}$ |
| 坐 *tso*$^{4}$ | 地 *ti*$^{4}$ | 躺 *t'ang*$^{3}$ | 衙 *ya*$^{2}$ | 樓 *lou*$^{2}$ | 着 *cho* | 窗 *ch'uang*$^{1}$ |
| 着。*cho* | 下。*hsia*$^{4}$ | 着。*cho* | 門。*mên*$^{2}$ | 去。*ch'ü*$^{4}$ | 人。*jên*$^{2}$ | 戶。*hu*$^{4}$ |

Shut the door and open the window.

There is a person (or, persons) sitting upstairs.

*Obs.—Cho* marking present time.

Someone is gone upstairs (*lit.*, ascending the story is gone).

I want to go to office (to the *ya*$^2$-*mên*$^2$).

*Obs.*—*Shang*, going towards or to.

A person (or persons) stretched on the ground. (Two renderings.)

Sitting upstairs.

**69.** 步 *pu*$^4$, a pace. As *pu*$^4$ *hsia*$^4$ (**48**), on foot; *pu*$^4$ *hsia*$^4$ *tsou*$^3$, to go on foot. Also, with *hsing*$^2$ (Radical 144); as *pu*$^4$ *hsing*$^2$, to walk; *pu*$^4$ *hsing*$^2$ *tsou*$^3$, to go on foot.

**70.** 騎 *ch'i*$^2$, to bestride; as *ch'i*$^2$ *ma*$^3$, to ride on horseback.

**71.** 轎 *chiao*$^4$, a sedan-chair; as *tso*$^4$ *chiao*$^4$, to sit in a sedan-chair.

**72.** 頂 *ting*$^3$, the numerative of *chiao*$^4$, sedan-chair; as *san*$^1$ *ting*$^3$ *chiao*$^4$-*tzŭ*, three sedans. Also the numerative of caps. It means as well the crown of the head, as will be seen later.

**73.** 車 *ch'ê*$^1$ (Radical 159), cart or carriage; as *tso*$^4$ *ch'ê*$^1$, to sit in a cart.

**74.** 輛 *liang*$^4$, the numerative of *ch'ê*$^1$, cart; as *ssŭ*$^4$ *wu*$^3$ *liang*$^4$ *ch'ê*$^1$, four or five carts.

**75.** 馬 *ma*$^3$ (Radical 187), a horse.

**76.** 匹 *p'i*$^{1\,3}$, numerative of *ma*$^3$; as *pa*$^1$ *p'i*$^1$ *ma*$^3$, eight horses.

**77.** 騾 *lo*$^2$, a mule. Its numerative is *t'ou*$^2$ (**48**); as *san*$^1$ *t'ou*$^2$ *lo*$^2$-*tzŭ*, three mules. *Ko* (**8**) can also be used.

**78.** 驢 *lü*$^2$, a donkey. Its numerative is *t'ou*$^2$ (**48**); as *liang*$^3$ *t'ou*$^2$ *lü*$^2$, two donkeys. Mules and donkeys are spoken of collectively as *lo*$^2$-*tzŭ* *lü*$^2$. *Ko* (**8**) can also be used as the numerative of donkeys.

**79.** Examples:—

| | | | | | | |
|---|---|---|---|---|---|---|
| 買 *mai*$^3$ | 騎 *ch'i*$^2$ | 是 *shih*$^4$ | 他 *t'a*$^1$ | 我 *wo*$^3$ | 他 *t'a*$^1$ | 我 *wo*$^3$ |
| 了 *liao* | 騾 *lo*$^2$ | 騎 *ch'i*$^2$ | 賣 *mai*$^4$ | 要 *yao*$^4$ | 是 *shih*$^4$ | 是 *shih*$^4$ |
| 兩 *liang*$^3$ | 子 *tzŭ* | 馬 *ma*$^3$ | 騾 *lo*$^2$ | 買 *mai*$^3$ | 步 *pu*$^4$ | 坐 *tso*$^4$ |
| 輛 *liang*$^4$ | 來 *lai*$^2$ | 來 *lai*$^2$ | 子 *tzŭ* | 頂 *ting*$^3$ | 下 *hsia*$^4$ | 車 *ch'ê*$^1$ |
| 車。*ch'ê*$^1$ | 的。*ti* | 的 *ti* | 驢。*lü*$^2$ | 轎 *chiao*$^4$ | 走 *tsou*$^3$ | 來 *lai*$^2$ |
| | 我 *wo*$^3$ | 是 *shih*$^4$ | 他 *t'a*$^1$ | 子。*tzŭ* | 的。*ti* | 的。*ti* |

I came in a cart; *lit.*, I am seated in a cart come.

He goes (or, is or was going) on foot.

I want to buy a sedan chair.

*Obs.*—*Ting*=*yi ting*, one piece.

He sells (or, is selling) mules and donkeys.

Did he ride here on a horse or on a mule? *q.d.*, he, was he riding a horse hither, was he riding a mule hither?

I have bought two carts.

*Obs.*—Not *êrh liang*.

80. 快 *k'uai*$^4$, quick; as *na*$^4$ *p'i*$^2$ *ma*$^3$ *k'uai*$^4$, that horse [is] quick.

81. 慢 *man*$^4$, slow; as *na*$^4$ *lo*$^2$*-tzŭ* *man*$^4$, that mule [is] slow.

82. 前 *ch'ien*$^2$, before, in time or place.

83. 後 *hou*$^4$, behind, in time or place.

84. 都 *tou*$^1$ (properly *tu*$^1$), all, plurality; as *na*$^4$ *hsieh*$^1$ *jên*$^2$ *tou*$^1$ *hao*$^3$, those people are all good. Also, under some circumstances, both or either.

85. Examples:—

| | | | | | | |
|---|---|---|---|---|---|---|
| 頭 *t'ou*$^2$ | 不 *pu*$^2$ | 慢。*man*$^4$ | 走 *tsou*$^3$ | 騾 *lo*$^2$ | 頭 *t'ou*$^2$ | 我 *wo*$^3$ |
| 裏 *li*$^3$ | 是。*shih*$^4$ | 前 *ch'ien*$^2$ | 得 *tê*$^2$ | 子 *tzŭ* | 騾 *lo*$^2$ | 那 *na*$^4$ |
| 好。*hao*$^3$ | 他 *t'a*$^1$ | 頭 *t'ou*$^2$ | 快。*k'uai*$^4$ | 驢 *lü*$^2$ | 子 *tzŭ* | 匹 *p'i*$^2$ |
| | 後 *hou*$^4$ | 後 *hou*$^4$ | 他 *t'a*$^1$ | 都 *tou*$^1$ | 慢。*man*$^4$ | 馬 *ma*$^3$ |
| | 來 *lai*$^2$ | 頭 *t'ou*$^2$ | 走 *tsou*$^3$ | 好。*hao*$^3$ | 那 *na*$^4$ | 快。*k'uai*$^4$ |
| | 比 *pi*$^3$ | 都 *tou*$^1$ | 得 *tê*$^2$ | 我 *wo*$^3$ | 些 *hsieh*$^1$ | 那 *na*$^4$ |

That horse of mine is fast.

That mule is slow.

Those mules and donkeys are all good.

*Obs.*—Were the *hsieh* omitted, *lo* and *lü* would be singular, and *tou*=both.

I walk fast; *q.d.*, I walking achieve speed. He walks slow.

Front and rear both wrong; *lit.*, not what [the thing] should be, before or behind.

*Obs.*—*Tou pu*, all not, in such a context=neither.

He was better subsequently than he had been at first.

*Obs.* 1.—*Hou lai* may mean (as here) after a date already past, or hereafter. The combination *ch'ien lai* is not colloquial, nor is it analogous to *hou lai* in construction. In writing it means to proceed to or towards. It has also auxiliary power.

*Obs.* 2.—*T'ou li*: *q.d.*, within the beginning=at first. Also, in front; see Exercise IV, 1, English (p. 27). There are many other combinations signifying *before*, in some of which, as will be seen, *ch'ien* plays a part.

86. 把 *pa*$^3$, to hold; to take hold of. Frequently prefixed to what we call the object of the transitive verb. Thus,

*pa*$^3$ *na*$^4$ *mên*$^2$ *kuan*$^1$ *shang*$^4$, shut to that door.

As a substantive, *pa*$^3$ has various uses; amongst others, that of a numerative.

87. 給 *kei*$^3$ (properly *chi*$^3$), to give; as in *ni*$^3$ *kei*$^3$ *wo*$^3$ *yi*$^2$ *ko*$^4$, you give me one. Hence it often acts as *to* or *for*; as we should say, it forms the dative case. Thus,

*ni*$^3$ *kei*$^3$ *wo*$^3$ *na*$^2$ *yi*$^2$ *ko*$^4$ *lai*$^2$, bring one for me.

88. 跑 *p'ao*$^3$, to run, as a man; to gallop, as a horse. As *p'ao*$^3$ *ch'ü*$^4$ *liao*, ran off, or galloped away.

## EXERCISE IV

1 有人說那個地方兒住不得。是誰說的。是我說的。你那兒知道。

1. They say, or, some say (*lit.* there is a man, or there are men, who say), that that place is uninhabitable. Who is that says so? I (*lit.*, it is I that) say so. How do you know?

2 這是誰家的房子。誰知道。我做不出來。他說不出來。他做過多少回。他做了一回。

2. Whose house is this? (what family does it belong to?) Who knows? I can't do it. He can't tell. How many times has he done (or, made) it? He has done it once; *q.d.*, one turn.

*Obs.* 1.—*Ch'u-lai*, as an auxiliary completing the action of the verbs *tso* and *shuo*.

*Obs.* 2.—*Chi*[3] *hui*[2] would be equally correct.

3 外頭來了五六個人。是甚麼人。我不知道。

3. There are five or six people outside that have come. Who are they? I cannot say.

4 大人進來你們都得站起來。我在樓上坐著、他是在地下躺著。

4. When His Excellency comes in you must all stand up. I was (or am) sitting upstairs; he was or is lying on the ground.

*Obs.* 1.—Do not construe *ti*[4] *hsia*, below. We shall come presently to *ti*[3] *hsia*, below.

*Obs.* 2.—Were *liao*[3] placed after the first *lai*, the sentence would run, His Excellency has come in, etc.

N.B.—A *ta-jên* is not necessarily His Excellency, the title being applied to any official above a certain rank.

5 你愛這個不愛。我不大愛。

5. Do you like this? Not very much.

6 你快些兒走、城門一關、你回不了家了。我身子乏、走不了。

6. Walk a little faster; when once the city gate is shut you won't get home. I am too tired to walk any more.

*Obs.*—*Lit.*, my body is tired, walk [I] cannot.

7 把門開開。門開了。關上窗戶。把窗戶關上。窗戶關上了。

7. Open the door. The door is open. Shut the window. Shut the window. The window is shut.

*Obs.*—Shut; the *shang*[4] as an auxiliary completing the action of the verb *kuan*.

4

8 他在道兒上躺著、叫他起來、把門關上。

8. He is lying down in the road; tell him to get up. Shut the door.

*Obs.*—With verbs of motion *tao-'rh shang* means, on the way, on the road, while one is travelling.

9 走著來的。步下走著。他走了來的、我是坐車來的。他是步行來的。我在前頭走。他在後頭走。快走。我快走了。慢慢兒的走。

9. Walking here. Walking; or, to come or to go on foot; going on foot. He walked here; I came in a cart. He came on foot. I was walking in front; he was behind. Go fast; or, make haste and go (imperative). I am going shortly or soon. Go gently.

*Obs.* 1.—*Ti* at the end of the first clause is probably used corruptly for *tê*, as auxiliary completing the act of *tsou lai*.

*Obs.* 2.—In the second clause, if *ti* be not used for *tê*, a word signifying manner must be understood after *ti*, *q.d.*, my [manner of coming] *shih*, was, sit-in-cart-coming's manner.

*Obs.* 3.—There is a difference between *k'uai tsou* used imperatively and otherwise.

*Obs.* 4.—Note *liao* indicating future action.

10 他那個人回來了沒有。他沒回來。他上那'兒去了。上衙門去了。他去是坐轎子是坐車。坐小轎去的、他不大愛坐車。是他那頂轎子好。

10. Is that man come back or not? He is not back. Where did he go (is he gone to)? To the $ya^2$-$m\hat{e}n^2$ (office). Did he go in a chair or in a carriage? In a small chair; he does not much like being in a carriage. That chair of his is good; or, his is the better chair.

*Obs.*—*Yi*, one, colloquially omitted before *ting*, the numerative noun.

11 是這兒的騾子好、是那兒的騾子好。這兒騾子沒有那兒的好。這兒騾子比那兒的慢。那兒騾子驢都快。

11. Which are the better, the mules from this place or from that? The mules here are not so good as those there; *q.d.*, this place's mules are not (or, have not) that place's good. The mules here are slower than what you get there. Both the mules and donkeys from that place are fast.

12 他買的是馬麽。不是、買的是騾子驢。他買了多少。買了三頭騾子七個驢。

12. Is it horses that he is buying? No, he is buying (or, what he has bought are) mules and donkeys. How many has he bought? Three mules and seven donkeys. (*See* 78.)

13 你是步行來的是騎馬來的.我是騎馬來的.我那匹馬跑得很快.

13. Did you come on foot or on horseback? I rode here. That horse of mine gallops very fast.

*Turn the following into Chinese.* (KEY, EXERCISE IV.)

1. He is sitting upstairs; tell him to come here quickly. He won't come fast; he is coming very slowly. I went in front in a cart; he followed in a sedan-chair.

*Obs.*—In front, *t'ou*[2] *li*[3]. *See* 85, Obs. 2.

2. Tell him to buy two carts and four horses. He says there are no horses here. He says mules are better than horses. Has he bought mules? Yes. How many has he bought? Four. Has he bought any donkeys? No; you did not tell him to buy donkeys.

3. Has he gone to the *ya-mên* in a sedan-chair or in a cart? He has gone on foot; he says he does not like carts or sedans. He will not come back soon. He is lying on the ground; he can't get up.

4. That horse is faster than this one. Horses are faster than mules; mules are faster than donkeys. Has he arrived? No. What is he doing? He is walking slowly. Tell him to come quickly.

5. How many sedan-chairs have you? Two. How many mules, horses, and donkeys? Four horses, three mules, five donkeys. Have you any carts? No; I have sold all my carts. Why are you standing up? For no reason (*lit.*, I am not doing anything); you like sitting down; I like standing up.

*Obs.*—Why: *lit.*, to do what?

**89.** 請 *ch'ing*[3], to pray; to request. Hence, please; as in *ch'ing*[3] *tso*[4], please be seated.

**90.** 教 *chiao*[1], to teach; as *t'a*[1] *chiao*[1] *wo*[3] *shuo*[1] *hua*[4], he is teaching me to speak the language.

**91.** 看 *k'an*[4], to behold; to regard. As *wo*[3] *k'an*[4] *t'a*[1] *hao*[3], I think him good. *K'an*[1], to watch (*see* 526).

見 *chien*[4] (Radical 147), to see; to perceive. Often combined with *k'an*[4]; as *wo*[3] *mei*[2] *k'an*[4] *chien*[4], I have not seen him (or it).

**92.** 書 *shu*[1], a book; writings. As *k'an*[4] *shu*[1], to read or study.

**93.** 找 *chao*[3], to seek; to search for. As *chao*[3] *p'i*[1] *hao*[3] *ma*[3], to look out for a good horse.

**94.** 字 *tzŭ*[4], written words; Chinese characters.

**95.** 典 *tien*[3], a rule; a canon. With *tzŭ*[4] (94), a dictionary; *q.d.*, a word-canon. Thus, *na*[2] *tzŭ*[4] *tien*[3] *chao*[3] *tzŭ*[4], with (*lit.*, taking hold of) a dictionary to look out words.

*Obs.*—*Na* before the instrumental case.

96. 學 *hsiao*$^2$, also read *hsio*$^2$, *hsüeh*$^2$, *hsüo*$^2$, to learn. Also, to imitate; to follow, as an example. When combined with 生 *shêng*$^1$ (Radical 100), to be born, *hsio*$^2$-*shêng*$^1$ or *hsüeh*$^2$-*shêng*$^1$, a pupil.

97. 認 *jên*$^4$, to recognise. With *tzŭ* (94), to be able to read; as *t'a*$^1$ *pu*$^2$ *jên*$^4$ *tê* *tzŭ*$^4$, he cannot read (*lit.*, is not able to recognise characters).

98. Examples:—

| | | | | | | |
|---|---|---|---|---|---|---|
| 生 *shêng*$^1$ | 是 *shih*$^4$ | 找 *chao*$^3$ | 拏 *na*$^2$ | 我 *wo*$^3$ | 他 *t'a*$^1$ | 他 *t'a*$^1$ |
| 認 *jên*$^4$ | 學 *hsio*$^2$ | 找。*chao*$^3$ | 字 *tzŭ*$^4$ | 不 *pu*$^2$ | 看 *k'an*$^4$ | 要 *yao*$^4$ |
| 得 *tê*$^2$ | 字。*tzŭ*$^4$ | 這 *chê*$^4$ | 典 *tien*$^3$ | 認 *jên*$^4$ | 書。*shu*$^1$ | 請 *ch'ing*$^3$ |
| 字 *tzŭ*$^4$ | 那 *na*$^4$ | 個 *ko*$^4$ | 給 *kei*$^3$ | 得 *tê*$^2$ | 有 *yu*$^3$ | 人 *jên*$^2$ |
| 多。*to*$^1$ | 學 *hsio*$^2$ | 字 *tzŭ*$^4$ | 我 *wo*$^3$ | 請 *ch'ing*$^3$ | 字 *tzŭ*$^4$ | 教 *chiao*$^1$ |

He wants to engage (*lit.*, request) someone to read with him (*lit.*, to teach to read books).

There is a character (or, there are characters) which I do not know; please look [it] out in the dictionary for me.

*Obs.*—*Kei wo*, for me, *chao chao* (short for *chao yi chao*; *lit.*, seek a seek).

This character is the character *hsio*$^2$, to learn.

That pupil (or student) knows a number of characters.

99. 先 *hsien*$^1$, before (in time); as *hsien*$^1$-*shêng*$^1$ (Radical 100), a teacher; *lit.*, elder-born (Compare our senior, signor, sir). Thus,

*ch'ing*$^3$ *hsien*$^1$-*shêng*$^1$, to engage (*lit.*, request, or, to invite, send for) a teacher.

100. 抄 *ch'ao*$^1$, to copy; as *ch'ao*$^1$ *shu*$^1$, to copy writings or books. Often coupled with the following *hsieh*$^3$.

101. 寫 *hsieh*$^3$, to write; as *hsieh*$^3$ *tzŭ*$^4$, to write (*lit.*, write the character).

102. 眞 *chên*$^1$, true, truly; as *chê*$^4$ *shih*$^4$ *chên*$^1$ *hua*$^4$, this is true (*lit.*, true statement).

103. 正 *chêng*$^4$, upright, correct; as *k'ou*$^3$ *yin*$^1$ *chêng*$^4$, mouth sounds correct = accurate pronunciation.

104. 肯 *k'ên*$^3$, to wish, to choose to; as *t'a*$^1$ *pu*$^4$ *k'ên*$^3$ *lai*$^2$, he won't (does not choose to) come.

105. 還 properly *huan*$^2$, to return. Colloquially, *han*$^2$, *hai*$^2$, yet, still; as *wo*$^3$ *hai*$^2$ *yu*$^3$ *yi*$^2$ *ko*$^4$, I have still got one; I have got no more than one.

106. Examples:—

| | | | | | | |
|---|---|---|---|---|---|---|
| 肯 *k'ên*$^3$ | 還 *hai*$^2$ | 你 *ni*$^3$ | 說 *shuo*$^1$ | 他 *t'a*$^1$ | 先 *hsien*$^1$ | 請 *ch'ing*$^3$ |
| 不 *pu*$^4$ | 有 *yu*$^3$ | 口 *k'ou*$^3$ | 的 *ti*$^1$ | 不 *pu*$^4$ | 生 *shêng*$^1$ | 先 *hsien*$^1$ |
| 肯 *k'ên*$^3$ | 比 *pi*$^3$ | 音 *yin*$^1$ | 是 *shih*$^4$ | 肯 *k'ên*$^3$ | 還 *hai*$^2$ | 生 *shêng*$^1$ |
| 都 *tou*$^1$ | 他 *t'a*$^1$ | 不 *pu*$^2$ | 眞 *chên*$^1$ | 抄 *ch'ao*$^1$ | 沒 *mei*$^2$ | 進 *chin*$^4$ |
| 好。*hao*$^3$ | 好。*hao*$^3$ | 正。*chêng*$^4$ | 話。*hua*$^4$ | 寫。*hsieh*$^3$ | 來。*lai*$^2$ | 來。*lai*$^2$ |

Ask the teacher to come in.

*Obs.*—If the *ch'ing* were placed after *hsien-shêng*, this would mean, Please walk in, sir.

The teacher is not come yet.

He won't (does not want to) copy.

What is said is the truth.

Your pronunciation is incorrect ; you have a bad pronunciation.

There is another (or, there are others) better than he.

Whether [I, you, he] choose or not, it makes no difference (*q.d.*, assent or not assent), both are good. See *tou*$^{1}$ (**84**).

**107.** 瞧 *ch'iao*$^{2}$, to look at ; to see. As in *mei*$^{2}$ *ch'iao*$^{2}$ *kuo*$^{4}$, not to have seen [him, it]. Like *k'an*$^{4}$ (**91**), it is very commonly joined with *chien*$^{4}$ (Radical 147) ; as in *ch'iao*$^{2}$ *pu*$^{2}$ *chien*$^{4}$, unable to see. The forms *k'an*$^{4}$*-chien*$^{4}$ and *ch'iao*$^{2}$*-chien*$^{4}$ differ little in sense, but the latter seems to be used rather when the object is small enough to escape attention.

**108.** 告 *kao*$^{4}$, to announce; colloquially, most often coupled with *su*$^{4}$ (**109**). With *shih* (Radical 113), *kao*$^{4}$*-shih*$^{4}$, a proclamation.

**109.** 訴 *su*$^{4}$ or *sung*$^{4}$, to tell to ; to complain that. *Kao*$^{4}$*-su*$^{4}$, also pronounced *kao*$^{4}$*-sung*$^{4}$, to tell to ; as in *ni*$^{3}$ *kao*$^{4}$*-su*$^{4}$ *wo*$^{3}$, you tell me.

**110.** 問 *wên*$^{4}$, to ask ; to inquire. As in *wo*$^{3}$ *wên*$^{4}$ *t'a*$^{1}$ *ni*$^{3}$ *shih*$^{4}$ *shui*$^{2}$, I asked him, who are you ?

**111.** 記 *chi*$^{4}$, to record in writing ; but, colloquially, to remember. As *wo*$^{3}$ *pu*$^{2}$ *chi*$^{4}$ *tê*$^{2}$, I do not remember.

**112.** 呢 *ni*$^{1}$, a particle, generally, but not always, interrogative.

**113.** Examples :—

| | | | | | | |
|---|---|---|---|---|---|---|
| 那 *na*$^{3}$ | 甚 *shen*$^{2}$ | 大 *ta*$^{4}$ | 記 *chi*$^{4}$ | 瞧 *ch'iao*$^{2}$ | 還 *hai*$^{2}$ | 請 *ch'ing*$^{3}$ |
| 個 *ko*$^{4}$ | 麼 *mo*$^{1}$ | 很 *hên*$^{3}$ | 得 *tê*$^{2}$ | 瞧 *ch'iao*$^{2}$ | 沒 *mei*$^{2}$ | 你 *ni*$^{3}$ |
| 好 *hao*$^{3}$ | 話 *hua*$^{4}$ | 記 *chi*$^{4}$ | 不 *pu*$^{2}$ | 好 *hao*$^{3}$ | 看 *k'an*$^{4}$ | 告 *kao*$^{4}$ |
| 呢。*ni*$^{1}$ | 呢。*ni*$^{1}$ | 得。*tê*$^{2}$ | 記 *chi*$^{4}$ | 不 *pu*$^{4}$ | 見 *chien*$^{4}$ | 訴 *su*$^{4}$ |
| | 請 *ch'ing*$^{3}$ | 這 *chê*$^{4}$ | 得。*tê*$^{2}$ | 好。*hao*$^{3}$ | 過。*kuo*$^{4}$ | 他。*t'a*$^{1}$ |
| | 問 *wên*$^{4}$ | 是 *shih*$^{4}$ | 不 *pu*$^{2}$ | 你 *ni*$^{3}$ | 你 *ni*$^{3}$ | 我 *wo*$^{3}$ |

Please tell him.

I have not seen [him or it].

*Obs.—Hai :* merely intensive ; strictly, not yet seen, etc.

You look [at it and] see whether it is good or not.

Do you remember ?

[I] do not very well remember.

*Obs.*—Note the double intensive *ta*$^{4}$ *hên*$^{3}$.

What is this that you are saying ? (what is the meaning of such language ?)

I beg to ask [you] which is the better (or best) ?

*Obs.—Ch'ing*$^{3}$ preceding *wên*$^{4}$ : a respectful form of question ; sometimes also sarcastic.

## EXERCISE V.

1 我要請先生教書、你給我找了先生沒有。我找著了、他不來、他說學生那麼多他不肯來。先生請坐。請教、這是甚麼字。

1. I want to engage a teacher to teach me to read (*lit.*, books); have you found a teacher for me? [I] have found one, [but] he is not coming; he says that he won't come to so large a number of students. Teacher, please be seated. Be so good as to tell me what this character is.

*Obs.* 1.—*Lit.*, he says students being that many, he does not choose (refuses) to come.

*Obs.* 2.—Be so good: *ch'ing chiao* is a polite form of asking for information of an equal or superior on any subject.

2 叫人把那字典拿來。請先生找出那個字來。要找甚麼字呢。要找瞧字。

2. Tell someone to bring that dictionary here. Teacher, please look out that character. What character do you want looked out? The character *ch'iao*² (to see).

3 請問、這個字你認得不認得。這個字我還沒看見過呢。這個字你看見過沒有。那個字你還沒有看見過麼。眞沒看見過。

3. Do you know this character, sir? I have not met with (*lit.*, seen) this character. Have you met with this character? Have you never met with that character either? No, indeed; never.

*Obs.* 1.—Sir gives the force of the *ch'ing wên*, I beg to inquire.

*Obs.* 2.—The object *chê ko tzŭ* precedes the verb only for emphasis sake.

*Obs.* 3.—The two questions are different. In the first the speaker is in doubt; in the second he assumes a fact.

*Obs.* 4.—Either: *hai* or *han*, also, still.

*Obs.* 5.—Indeed: *chên*, truly, have [I] not seen [it or them].

4 你告訴我、他那個人的口音有你的好沒有。我的口音不大甚麼好、他認得的字比我認得的多。

4. Tell me is that man's pronunciation as good as yours? My pronunciation is not particularly good; he knows more characters than I.

*Obs.*—You might say equally well *mei shên mo hên hao.*

5 這個字你見過沒見過。見過了。你告訴我是甚麼字。我不記得那個字了。還有不記得的字麼。那'兒沒有呢。記得的少、不記得的多。

5. Have you [ever] met with (*lit.*, seen) this character? I have. Tell me what character it is. I do not remember the character. Are there any other characters that you do not remember? Of course there are; I remember but few compared with the number I forget.

*Obs.*—Of course there are: *lit.*, how, *na 'rh* [can it be that there should] not be, eh? This interrogative form of affirmation is very common.

*Turn the following into Chinese.* (KEY, EXERCISE V.)

1. I have asked a teacher to come and teach me to talk. Do you want to learn to write as well? Teacher, please tell me is my pronunciation correct? Not very correct; besides you do not know many characters.

*Obs.*—Besides: *lit.*, you recognised characters yet not many.

2. Where is that dictionary? It is in the teacher's room; he is looking out characters there. Ask him to copy them for me. The teacher does not wish to come. He tells me that your pronunciation is very far from good and that your diction is also incorrect.

*Obs.*—Also (Radical 29).

3. Have you seen my teacher? I saw him riding on horseback; the horse was galloping very fast, he did not see me. Please look out the character *chi* in the dictionary. I have found it. Do you recognise that character? I have never seen it.

4. What are these pupils learning? They are learning to write and to read. Who is their teacher? I do not know who he is. Have you ever seen him? Yes, he is here teaching the pupils. Have you copied those characters yet? Not yet, but I will copy them soon.

5. Do you like riding? If a horse gallops fast, I do not like to ride him. Is this horse a good one? Not very good; he does not gallop fast. Sit tight (on your horse).

*Obs.*—Sit tight: *lit.*, ride firm (48).

**114.** 紙 *chih*³, paper.

**115.** 張 *chang*¹, properly to open, to spread out; hence when used as the numerative of *chih*³, paper, a sheet. Also, the numerative of tables, chairs, etc.; also, a common surname.

**116.** 筆 *pi*³, a Chinese pencil; as *na*² *pi*³ *hsieh*³ *tzŭ*⁴, take a pen and write characters (*sc.*, to write *with* a pen).

**117.** 管 *kuan*³, a tube; the numerative of pencils. As *liang*³ *kuan*³ *pi*³, two pencils. Also, to superintend; to look after. *See* Exercise XV, 6, Obs. 2.

**118.** 墨 *mê*$^{4}$, *mo*$^{4}$, ink; as *pi*$^{3}$ *mo*$^{4}$, pen and ink (*fig.* for composition).

**119.** 塊 *k'uai*$^{4}$, a bit; a piece; the numerative of Chinese ink, which is in small cakes. As *san*$^{1}$ *k'uai*$^{4}$ *mo*$^{4}$, three cakes of ink.

**120.** 本 *pên*$^{3}$, the numerative of books; as *san*$^{1}$ *pên*$^{3}$ *shu*$^{1}$, three volumes, or, a three-volume book. Properly, *pên*$^{3}$ is the trunk of a tree, its root above ground; hence, primary, original; hence, under certain circumstances, the pronoun *this*, *self*.

**121.** Examples:—

| | | | | | |
|---|---|---|---|---|---|
| 筆 *pi*$^{3}$ | 抄 *ch'ao*$^{1}$ | 這 *ché*$^{4}$ | 筆 *pi*$^{3}$ | 張 *chang*$^{1}$ | 買 *mai*$^{3}$ |
| 都 *tou*$^{1}$ | 字 *tzŭ*$^{4}$ | 書 *shu*$^{1}$ | 兩 *liang*$^{3}$ | 白 *pai*$^{2}$ | 的 *ti* |
| 說 *shuo*$^{1}$ | 用 *yung*$^{4}$ | 多 *to*$^{1}$ | 塊 *k'uai*$^{4}$ | 紙 *chih*$^{3}$ | 是 *shih*$^{4}$ |
| 得。*tê*$^{2}$ | 筆 *pi*$^{3}$ | 少 *shao*$^{3}$ | 香 *hsiang*$^{1}$ | 十 *shih*$^{2}$ | 三 *san*$^{1}$ |
| | 拿 *na*$^{2}$ | 本。*pên*$^{3}$ | 墨。*mo*$^{4}$ | 管 *kuan*$^{3}$ | 十 *shih*$^{2}$ |

The purchase (that which is bought) is thirty sheets of white paper, ten pencils, and two pieces of scented ink.

*Obs.*—Scented: *hsiang*$^{1}$ (Radical 186).

How many volumes does this book consist of?

[When speaking of] copying [with a pencil], it is as correct to say *yung pi* (use the pencil) as *na pi* (take the pencil).

*Obs.* 1.—*Lit.*, [as to] copying characters, use pencil, take pencil, *tou*, all=both, may be said.

*Obs.* 2.—Use, *yung*$^{4}$ (Radical 101), here, like *na*$^{2}$, forms with its object our instrumental case; *sc.*, with a pencil.

**122.** 念 *nien*$^{4}$, to think of; to commit to memory; to repeat aloud; to study. Thus, *nien*$^{4}$ *shu*$^{1}$, to recite, as Chinese beginners do their books.

**123.** 完 *wan*$^{2}$, to end; hence sometimes used as an auxiliary to imply completion of an act, as *k'an*$^{4}$ *wan*$^{2}$, to have read [it] all (*lit.*, read ended).

**124.** 可 *k'o*$^{3}$, to be right; to be able. *K'o*$^{3}$ is also used idiomatically as an adverb or a disjunctive, in abatement of affirmation; and otherwise. Thus,

*k'o*$^{3}$ *pu*$^{2}$ *shih*$^{4}$, can it not be? (It certainly is; indeed it is.)

*k'o*$^{3}$ *shih*$^{4}$, it may be; but.

**125.** 以 *i*$^{3}$, properly, to use; hence employed as an instrumental preposition. With the preceding word *k'o*$^{3}$, it answers a question affirmatively, sometimes with reserve. sometimes not; or it may simply mean can, is able to, or, may possibly. With certain verbs it has an adverbial sense; as in *shih*$^{4}$ *i*$^{3}$ (34), therefore, accordingly.

126. Examples :—

| | | | | | | |
|---|---|---|---|---|---|---|
| 用 yung$^4$ | 話。hua$^4$ | 以。i$^3$ | 的 ti | 書 shu$^1$ | 月 yueh$^4$ | 他 t'a$^1$ |
| 我 wo$^3$ | 可 k'o$^3$ | 那 na$^4$ | 筆 pi$^3$ | 沒 mei$^2$ | 的 ti | 念 nien$^4$ |
| 不 pu$^4$ | 用 yung$^4$ | 可 k'o$^3$ | 墨 mo$^4$ | 看 k'an$^4$ | 書。shu$^1$ | 過 kuo$^4$ |
| 好 hao$^3$ | 不 pu$^4$ | 是 shih$^4$ | 還 hai$^2$ | 完。wan$^2$ | 那 na$^4$ | 三 san$^1$ |
| 說。shuo$^1$ | 可 k'o$^3$ | 眞 chên$^1$ | 可 k'o$^3$ | 他 t'a$^1$ | 本 pên$^3$ | 個 ko$^4$ |

He has been studying three months ; *lit.*, he has recited three months' books.

[I have] not read through that book ; *lit.*, have not completed reading it.

His composition is pretty fair.

*Obs.*—Note the power of *hai*, still, notwithstanding ; it modifies the abatement of *k'o i*.

*That* is the truth, no doubt.

*Obs.*—Without *k'o* the affirmation would be stronger.

Whether available or not, it is not for me to say.

*Obs.*—Construe thus :—[Whether man] *k'o yung*, can rightly, possibly, use [it or] not, I cannot well (or properly) say.

127. 官 *kuan*$^1$, an official. As an attributive, that which belongs to government ; as in *kuan*$^1$ *hua*$^4$, the government spoken language, commonly styled the mandarin dialect.

128. 民 *min*$^2$, the people ; as *kuan*$^1$ *min*$^2$, the government (or officials) and people.

129. 會 *hui*$^4$, as a verb, to meet, to come together ; also, to be competent to, to know how to, to understand. As *hui*$^4$ *shuo*$^1$, to be able to speak.

As a substantive, it means a conjuncture ; also a period of time. As *yi*$^4$ *hui*$^3$*-tzŭ* or *yi*$^4$ *hui*$^3$*-'rh*, a while. Note the change of tone. It is not to be confounded with *hui*$^2$ (57).

130. 分 *fên*$^1$, to divide ; a fraction ; specially, a tenth. As *shih*$^2$ *fên*$^1$, ten-tenths, a whole ; hence, adverbially, much, very ; as *shih*$^2$ *fên*$^1$ *hao*$^3$, very good. *Fên*$^4$, a set (*see* 153).

131. 聽 *t'ing*$^1$, to hear ; as *t'ing*$^1$ *hua*$^4$, to hear what is said=to obey. Also, to submit to, to comply with.

132. 明 *ming*$^2$, plain to the sight ; also, clear-seeing. As *ming*$^2$ *pai*$^2$ (*lit.*, clear white), intelligent ; intelligible.

133. Examples :—

| | | | | | | |
|---|---|---|---|---|---|---|
| 明 ming$^2$ | 不 pu$^4$ | 說 shuo$^1$ | 不 pu$^4$ | 房。fang$^2$ | 民 min$^2$ | 官 kuan$^1$ |
| 白。pai$^2$ | 出 ch'u$^1$ | 的 ti | 會 hui$^4$ | 那 na$^4$ | 人 jên$^2$ | 住 chu$^4$ |
| | 來。lai$^2$ | 官 kuan$^1$ | 說 shuo$^1$ | 人 jên$^2$ | 住 chu$^4$ | 的 ti |
| | 都 tou$^1$ | 話 hua$^4$ | 官 kuan$^1$ | 十 shih$^2$ | 的 ti | 是 shih$^4$ |
| | 說 shuo$^1$ | 我 wo$^3$ | 話。hua$^4$ | 分 fên$^1$ | 是 shih$^4$ | 衙 ya$^2$ |
| | 不 pu$^4$ | 聽 t'ing$^1$ | 他 t'a$^1$ | 好。hao$^3$ | 民 min$^2$ | 門。mên$^2$ |

[The building] that an official lives in is a *ya-mên*.

*Obs.*—This would be said in answer to the question, What is a yamên ? There are numbers of men in office who have no yamên.

5

What the people live in are *min*$^{2}$ *fang*$^{2}$ (houses of the people).

*Obs.*—In both these examples either *fang* or some similar word is understood after *chu ti*.

That is a very good man.

He cannot speak mandarin.

When he speaks mandarin (or, the mandarin that he speaks) I do not understand.

*Obs.* 1.—*Ch'u lai* is here more than auxiliary of time; it affects the meaning of *t'ing*$^{1}$.

*Obs.* 2.—Here also the speaker may be unintelligible on account of either the sound or the sense.

He cannot speak intelligibly at all.

*Obs.*—This might be because of lack of intelligence or of error in form.

134. 也 *yeh*$^{3}$, also; even. As *chê*$^{4}$ *ko*$^{4}$ *yeh*$^{3}$ *hao*$^{3}$, this one also is good; or, this one will do as well.

135. 懂 *tung*$^{3}$, to understand; as *tung*$^{3}$ *pu*$^{4}$ *tung*$^{3}$, do you understand or not?

136. 聲 *shêng*$^{1}$, sound; specially, the tones. As *ssŭ*$^{4}$ *shêng*$^{1}$, the four tones.

137. 平 *p'ing*$^{2}$, even; level; at peace; also (as will be seen later), ordinary, common.

138. 忘 *wang*$^{4}$, to forget. As *wang*$^{4}$ *pu*$^{4}$ *liao*$^{3}$, never can forget.

139. 錯 *ts'o*$^{4}$, to err; wrong. As *t'ing*$^{1}$ *ts'o*$^{4}$ *liao*, to mistake what is said; *lit.*, to hear wrong. When following active verbs in general, *ts'o*$^{4}$ affects them like our syllable *mis* prefixed; but generally, if not always, where the error is unintentional.

140. Examples:—

| | | | | | | |
|---|---|---|---|---|---|---|
| 眞 *chên*$^{1}$ | 這 *chê*$^{4}$ | 去 *ch'ü*$^{4}$ | 平 *p'ing*$^{2}$ | 那 *na*$^{4}$ | 土 *t'u*$^{3}$ | 那 *na*$^{4}$ |
| 是 *shih*$^{4}$ | 字 *tzŭ*$^{4}$ | 聲。*shêng*$^{1}$ | 下 *hsia*$^{4}$ | 四 *ssŭ*$^{4}$ | 話 *hua*$^{4}$ | 管 *kuan*$^{3}$ |
| 不 *pu*$^{2}$ | 我 *wo*$^{3}$ | 那 *na*$^{4}$ | 平 *p'ing*$^{2}$ | 聲 *shêng*$^{1}$ | 也 *yeh*$^{3}$ | 筆 *pi*$^{3}$ |
| 記 *chi*$^{4}$ | 忘 *wang*$^{4}$ | 不 *pu*$^{2}$ | 上 *shang*$^{3}$ | 是 *shih*$^{4}$ | 懂 *tung*$^{3}$ | 也 *yeh*$^{3}$ |
| 得。*tê* | 了 *liao*$^{3}$ | 錯。*ts'o*$^{4}$ | 聲 *shêng*$^{1}$ | 上 *shang*$^{4}$ | 得。*tê* | 好。*hao*$^{3}$ |

That pencil is also a good one (or, will do as well).

[He] also understands the local dialect.

*Obs.*—*T'u* (Radical 32): *see* Radical Exercises, 10, 18.

The four tones are the *shang-p'ing* (upper even), the *hsia-p'ing* (lower even), the *shang* (ascending), the *ch'ü* (departing).

*Obs.*—*Shang*$^{4}$ when applied to the third tone is *shang*$^{3}$.

That is quite right; *lit.*, that is not wrong.

*Obs.*—*Pu* changes its tones before *ts'o*, *shih*, and other words in the 4th tone.

This character I have forgotten; I really do not remember it.

## EXERCISE VI.

1 他說的官話還可以、可是沒有你的好。他說的官話還有土音。聽見說你得了幾本書、都看完了沒有。得是得了、看了不過一兩本。

1. His speaking [of] mandarin is passable, but not so good as yours. His mandarin has a certain local accent. I hear (or, one hears) that you have got some books; have you read them all through yet? I *have* got them, but I have not read more than one or two volumes.

*Obs.* 1.—In both sentences *hai* or *han* diminishes the force of the affirmation.
*Obs.* 2.—*K'o shih*, but.
*Obs.* 3.—Passable, *k'o i*; *lit.*, one can use, is tolerably available.
*Obs.* 4.—Local accent: *t'u yin*, sound of the locality or country. (*See* 140, Obs.)
*Obs.* 5.—*I have* got: *tê shih tê liao*, as to possessing, *shih*, it is a fact that [I] am in possession.

2 我聽見說你學著官話呢、學得很好、那四聲你分得出分不出。都還可以分得開。

2. I hear it said that you are learning mandarin, and getting on very well; can you distinguish the four tones? I can distinguish them all.

*Obs.*—I can distinguish: *lit.*, all still can [I] distinguish. Note the force of *han* or *hai*, still; *q.d.*, [obstacles or difficulties notwithstanding], still can I, etc.

3 那一本書你看完了沒有。十分裏看了有七八分。明白不明白。有幾分不大明白、也有幾個字不認得。

3. Have you done reading that book yet? (or, have you finished that book?) I have read about four-fifths of it; *lit.*, seven or eight-tenths. Do you understand it? There are portions of it that I do not well understand; there are also some characters [in it] that I do not know.

4 你念了多少日子的書。我念了十個月的書。那書上的字都記得麼。記不了那麼多。忘了好些個了、還有記錯了的。

4. How long have you been reading (studying)? I have been studying ten months. Do you remember all the characters in the book (or books) you have been studying? I cannot remember so many as that. I have forgotten a good number altogether, and there are some that I do not remember accurately (*lit.*, remember wrong).

5 他那個人懂得官話不懂。我聽見人說他不懂得。他認得字不認得。字還認得、認個四五千字。你那'兒知道呢。上月我們在一塊兒看書。我叫他抄寫、他行不行。沒有甚麼不行的。

5. Does he understand mandarin? I have heard people say that he does not. Does he know the written character? That he does; he has learned four or five thousand characters. How do you know? We read together last month. If I tell him to copy will he be able to? There is no reason why he should not.

*Obs.* 1.—Read together: *tsai yi k'uai-'rh*; *lit.*, in one piece (or, forming one piece).
*Obs.* 2.—Last month: *lit.*, the upper month. "Next month" is *hsia yüeh*, the lower month.
*Obs.* 3.—Will he be able to: *hsing pu hsing*, can he do or not? (*Hsing*, Radical 144.)

6 你告訴我、他的話你聽得出來聽不出來。

6. Tell me, do you understand him when he speaks?

7 你念過的書、千萬不可忘了。不錯、你說得很是。

7. You must on no account forget the books you read. Certainly not (you are quite right).

*Obs.*—On no account: *ch'ien wan* (thousand myriad), with a negative, *pu k'o* (must you not).

8 你會用我們這兒的字典麼。會用、會是會用、找字可得'慢些兒。

8. Can you use our dictionary? Yes, I can use it, but when I look out words I have to go slowly.

*Obs.* 1.—Our: *lit.*, our this place's.
*Obs.* 2.—*K'o* qualifies *tei*, must.

*Turn the following into Chinese.* (KEY, EXERCISE VI.)

1. Bring me that pencil. This pencil is not a good one; have you (*lit.*, is there) not another good one? Not a good one; I have two or three bad ones.

2. Take a sheet of paper, a cake of ink, and a pencil, and write some characters. What characters do you want me to write? All the characters you do not know in this book.

3. I hear that you are learning mandarin; do you understand it? Not very well; I have not been studying it long.

4. Can you distinguish the four tones? I can distinguish them all. What tone is *k'ên* in? The third. Right. Write that character on this sheet of paper. You have written it wrong.

*Obs.*—Can: *hui* (129).

語言自邇集



5. Have you finished that book yet? Yes, and I understand it perfectly. Are there any characters in it you do not recognise? Of course there are; the characters I know are few compared with those I do not know.

6. Do you understand me when I speak? Your pronunciation is so correct that I understand you very well.

7. Can you buy me a sheet of paper and a pencil? I can. Do you want ink too? No, I want five sheets of paper and two pencils; do you understand? Perfectly.

**141.** 炕 *k'ang*$^4$, the stove-bed, built of bricks.

**142.** 鋪 *p'u*$^1$, properly, to spread out, as a cloth. The numerative of *k'ang*$^4$, stove-bed; as *yi*$^4$ *p'u*$^1$ *k'ang*$^4$.

*Obs.*—Not to be confounded with the same character in a corrupt form (46), *p'u*$^4$, a shop.

**143.** 蓋 *kai*$^4$, to cover; a cover. With *p'u*$^1$ (142), as in *p'u*$^1$-*k'ai*$^4$, bedding; *q.d.*, that which is spread and that which covers. As a verb, in its sense of to cover, it is used as to build; as *kai*$^4$ *fang*$^2$-*tzŭ*, to build a house.

**144.** 蓆 *hsi*$^2$, a mat, such as is spread on a bed, on the floor, etc.; as *p'u*$^1$ *hsi*$^2$-*tzŭ*, to spread a mat (or mats).

**145.** 牀 *ch'uang*$^2$, a bedstead; one's bed. Its numerative is *chang*$^1$ (115) or may be *ko*$^4$; as *yi*$^1$ *chang*$^1$ *ch'uang*$^2$ or *yi*$^2$ *ko*$^4$ *ch'uang*$^2$.

**146.** 帳 *chang*$^4$, a curtain; as *chang*$^4$-*tzŭ*. Also an account, or accounts, as will be seen presently.

**147.** Examples:—

| | | | | | | |
|---|---|---|---|---|---|---|
| 下 *hsia*$^4$ | 兒 *'rh* | 帳 *chang*$^4$ | 上。*shang*$^4$ | 把 *pa*$^3$ | 鋪 *p'u*$^1$ | 那 *na*$^4$ |
| 鋪 *p'u*$^1$ | 蓋 *kai*$^4$ | 子。*tzŭ* | 牀 *ch'uang*$^2$ | 鋪 *p'u*$^1$ | 着 *cho* | 鋪 *p'u*$^1$ |
| 蓆 *hsi*$^2$ | 上。*shang*$^4$ | 把 *pa*$^3$ | 上 *shang*$^4$ | 蓋 *kai*$^4$ | 蓆 *hsi*$^2$ | 炕 *k'ang*$^4$ |
| 子。*tzŭ* | 地 *ti*$^4$ | 蓋 *kai*$^4$ | 沒 *mei*$^2$ | 鋪 *p'u*$^1$ | 子。*tzŭ* | 上 *shang*$^4$ |

There are mats spread on that stove-bed.
Spread the bedding; *q.d.*, on the *k'ang*.
There are no curtains to the bed.
Put on the cover; *lit.*, taking the cover, cover to; *shang* completing the action of the verb.
Spread mats (or, the mat) on the ground.

**148.** 桌, 卓 *cho*$^1$, *cho*$^2$, a table. Its numerative is *chang*$^1$ (115); as *san*$^1$ *chang*$^1$ *cho*$^1$-*tzŭ*, three tables. The character *cho*$^2$ is the ancient form.

**149.** 椅 *i*$^3$, a chair; its numerative is also *chang*$^1$.

**150.** 燈 *têng*$^1$, a lamp; a candlestick. Not a lantern unless joined with *lung*$^2$, of which more in its place.

**151.** 盞 *chan*$^3$, the numerative of *têng*$^1$, a lamp; as *liu*$^4$ *chan*$^3$ *têng*$^1$, six lamps.

**152.** 蠟 *la*$^4$, wax or tallow, animal or vegetable. The latter, made from the berry of the *Croton sebiferum*, is spoken of as *pai*$^2$ *la*$^4$, white wax; *huang*$^2$ *la*$^4$, beeswax.

153. Examples:—

| | | | | | | |
|---|---|---|---|---|---|---|
| 坐 *tso*$^{4}$ | 那 *na*$^{4}$ | 都 *tou*$^{1}$ | 上 *shang*$^{4}$ | 四 *ssŭ*$^{4}$ | 是 *shih*$^{4}$ | 那 *na*$^{4}$ |
| 的 *ti* | 張 *chang*$^{1}$ | 是 *shih*$^{4}$ | 那 *na*$^{4}$ | 張 *chang*$^{1}$ | 一 *yi*$^{4}$ | 一 *yi*$^{2}$ |
| 是 *shih*$^{4}$ | 椅 *i*$^{3}$ | 蠟 *la*$^{4}$ | 兩 *liang*$^{3}$ | 椅 *i*$^{3}$ | 張 *chang*$^{1}$ | 分 *fên*$^{4}$ |
| 誰。*shui*$^{2}$ | 子 *tzŭ* | 燈。*têng*$^{1}$ | 盞 *chan*$^{3}$ | 子。*tzŭ* | 桌 *cho*$^{1}$ | 桌 *cho*$^{1}$ |
| | 上 *shang*$^{4}$ | 在 *tsai*$^{4}$ | 燈, *têng*$^{1}$ | 桌 *cho*$^{1}$ | 子 *tzŭ* | 椅 *i*$^{3}$ |

That set consists of one table and four chairs.

*Obs.*—*Yi*$^{2}$ *fên*$^{4}$ one division. (*See* 130.)

The two *têng* on the table are *la têng* (candlesticks).

Who is it that is sitting on that chair?

154. 酒 *chiu*$^{3}$, Chinese wine; distilled spirit.

155. 盃 *pei*$^{1}$, a cup in which wine is drunk; as *chiu*$^{3}$ *pei*$^{1}$, a wine-cup.

156. 盅 *chung*$^{1}$, a cup, which may hold either tea or wine. Its numerative is *ko*$^{4}$. The word *chung*$^{1}$ is said to be less used in the South than in the North.

157. 茶 *ch'a*$^{2}$, tea.

158. 碗 *wan*$^{3}$, a bowl or cup, which may hold tea or rice; *ch'a*$^{2}$ *wan*$^{3}$, a tea-cup.

159. 飯 *fan*$^{4}$, properly cooked rice; generally, any cooked victuals; one's meals.

160. 喫 or 吃 *ch'ih*$^{1}$, to eat; *ch'ih*$^{1}$ *fan*$^{4}$, to eat a meal.

161. 喝 *ho*$^{1}$, to drink.

162. Examples:—

| | | | | | | |
|---|---|---|---|---|---|---|
| 好 *hao*$^{3}$ | 喝 *ho*$^{1}$ | 兩 *liang*$^{3}$ | 拿 *na*$^{2}$ | 喝 *ho*$^{1}$ | 喫 *ch'ih*$^{1}$ | 他 *t'a*$^{1}$ |
| 喫 *ch'ih*$^{1}$ | 過 *kuo*$^{4}$ | 個 *ko*$^{4}$ | 個 *ko*$^{4}$ | 過 *kuo*$^{4}$ | 過 *kuo*$^{4}$ | 喫 *ch'ih*$^{1}$ |
| 不 *pu*$^{4}$ | 三 *san*$^{1}$ | 酒 *chiu*$^{3}$ | 茶 *ch'a*$^{2}$ | 三 *san*$^{1}$ | 三 *san*$^{1}$ | 飯 *fan*$^{4}$ |
| 好 *hao*$^{3}$ | 盃 *pei*$^{1}$ | 盅 *chung*$^{1}$ | 碗 *wan*$^{3}$ | 碗 *wan*$^{3}$ | 碗 *wan*$^{3}$ | 去 *ch'ü*$^{4}$ |
| 喫。*ch'ih*$^{1}$ | 酒。*chiu*$^{3}$ | 兒。*'rh* | 來。*lai*$^{2}$ | 茶。*ch'a*$^{2}$ | 飯。*fan*$^{4}$ | 了。*liao*$^{3}$ |

He has gone to get his meal; *lit.*, to eat rice.

To have eaten three bowls of rice.

To have drunk three cups of tea.

Bring a tea-cup here.

Two wine-cups.

To have drunk three cups of wine.

[Is it] fit to eat (good for food)? (or, is it nice?)

163. 弄 *nung*$^{4}$, properly *lung*, to play tricks with. Colloquially used of numerous processes, moral or material; as with the following word *ts'ai*$^{4}$. It is often used also to represent the sound *lung*$^{2}$ in the Pekingese expression *lung*$^{2}$ *huo*$^{3}$, to light the fire; there is another *lung* (198) which appears equally admissible.

164. 菜 *ts'ai*$^{4}$, originally vegetable, but used generally of eatables; as *nung*$^{4}$ *ts'ai*$^{4}$, to prepare food.

165. 厨 *ch'u*$^{2}$, to cook; but, colloquially, oftenest found forming part of substantives. As *ch'u*$^{2}$-*fang*$^{2}$, the cook-house, *ch'u*$^{2}$-*tzŭ*, a cook.

166. 煎 *chien*$^{1}$, to fry; as *chien*$^{1}$ *yü*$^{2}$ (Radical 195), to fry fish.

167. 炒 *ch'ao*$^{3}$, to fry or broil; a drier process than *chien*$^{1}$. So, *ch'ao*$^{3}$ *jou*$^{4}$, to broil meat

168. 煑 *chu*$^3$, to boil, actively; as *chu*$^3$ *ts'ai*$^4$, to boil vegetables, or eatables generally.

169. 燒 *shao*$^1$, to burn; in cooking, to roast. As *shao*$^1$ *jou*$^4$, to roast meat, or meat roasted.

170. 壞 *huai*$^4$, to spoil, morally or materially; combined with various other verbs to indicative of ill result.

171. Examples:—

| | | | | | | |
|---|---|---|---|---|---|---|
| 飯 *fan*$^4$ | 飯 *fan*$^4$ | 子 *tzŭ* | 都 *tou*$^1$ | 分 *fên*$^1$ | 都 *tou*$^1$ | 那 *na*$^4$ |
| 都 *tou*$^1$ | 得 *tê*$^2$ | 很 *hên*$^3$ | 壞 *huai*$^4$ | 燒 *shao*$^1$ | 弄 *nung*$^4$ | 廚 *ch'u*$^2$ |
| 弄 *nung*$^1$ | 了 *liao* | 會 *hui*$^1$ | 了。*liao*$^3$ | 肉 *jou*$^4$ | 壞 *huai*$^4$ | 子 *tzŭ* |
| 好 *hao*$^3$ | 是 *shih*$^4$ | 煎 *chien*$^1$ | 這 *chê*$^4$ | 煑 *chu*$^3$ | 了、*liao* | 把 *pa*$^3$ |
| 了。*liao* | 菜 *ts'ai*$^4$ | 炒、*ch'ao*$^3$ | 廚 *ch'u*$^2$ | 肉 *jou*$^4$ | 不 *pu*$^4$ | 菜 *ts'ai*$^4$ |

The cook has spoiled all the dishes; roast meat and boiled are spoiled alike.

*Obs.* 1.—The cook *pa*, taking the *ts'ai*, eatables, *tou*, all, has he *nung*, in his treatment, preparation, *huai*, spoiled. The phrase *nung huai* may be applied to failure in the conduct of various operations.

*Obs.* 2.—Alike, *pu fên*, not distinguishing roast meat and boiled meat, all [has he] spoiled. The subject of *huai* is throughout *ch'u*$^2$-*tzŭ*, the cook.

This cook is very skilful (*lit.*, is very competent in frying); but *chien*$^1$ *ch'ao*$^3$ is here used of cooking in general.

[The expression] *fan*$^4$ *tê*$^2$ means that the meal is ready; *lit.*, that the victuals are cooked.

*Obs.* 1.—*Ts'ai*, the other eatables, and *fan*, the rice.

*Obs.* 2.—*Hao* here completes the action of *nung*; the food is *fully* prepared. But *nung pu hao*, said of anything, differs little from *nung huai* except in intensity. It may be applied to cooking, negotiation, building, a campaign, etc.

172. 鍋 *kuo*$^1$, the large pan in which things are cooked, notably rice; as *fan*$^4$-*kuo*$^1$, the rice-pan.

173. 刀 *tao*$^1$ (Radical 18), a knife; as *tao*$^1$-*tzŭ*.

174. 鍤 *ch'a*$^1$, a fork; as *ch'a*$^1$-*tzŭ*. The numerative of *tao* and *ch'a* is *pa*$^3$ (86).

175. 勺 *shao*$^2$, properly, a pan not so large as *kuo*$^1$ (172). As *shao*$^2$-*tzŭ*, a spoon; *fan*$^4$ *shao*$^2$-*'rh*, a spoon to ladle out rice with from the pan.

176. 匙 *ch'ih*$^2$, a smaller kind of spoon than *shao*$^2$. The difference is explained below in Exercise VII.

177. 傢 *chia*$^1$. The character is not found in the native dictionaries.

178. 伙 *huo*$^3$, nor is this character; combined, they include every variety of utensil. Familiarly, small arms may also be spoken of as *chia*$^1$-*huo*$^3$; spears, muskets, or any paraphernalia

179. Examples:—

| | | | | | |
|---|---|---|---|---|---|
| 勺 *shao*$^2$ | 一 *yi*$^4$ | 的 *ti* | 西 *hsi*$^1$ | 的。*ti* | 飯 *fan*$^4$ |
| 子 *tzŭ* | 把 *pa*$^3$ | 是 *shih*$^4$ | 都 *tou*$^1$ | 家 *chia*$^1$ | 鍋 *kuo*$^1$ |
| 兩 *liang*$^3$ | 鍤 *ch'a*$^1$ | 一 *yi*$^4$ | 是 *shih*$^4$ | 裏 *li*$^3$ | 是 *shih*$^4$ |
| 把 *pa*$^3$ | 子 *tzŭ* | 把 *pa*$^3$ | 傢 *chia*$^1$ | 用 *yung*$^4$ | 煑 *chu*$^3$ |
| 匙 *ch'ih*$^2$ | 三 *san*$^1$ | 刀 *tao*$^1$ | 伙。*huo*$^3$ | 的 *ti* | 飯 *fan*$^4$ |
| 子。*tzŭ* | 把 *pa*$^3$ | 子 *tzŭ* | 買 *mai*$^3$ | 東 *tung*$^1$ | 用 *yung*$^4$ |

The *fan*$^4$-*kuo*$^1$ (rice-pan) is used to boil rice

All things used in a house are *chia*$^1$-*huo*$^3$.

[The things] that have been bought are one knife, one fork, three large spoons, and two small spoons.

*Obs.* 1.—Note the numeratives.

*Obs.* 2.—In Tientsin spoons should be called *t'iao*$^2$-*kêng*$^1$ or *kêng*$^1$-*ch'ih*$^2$.

## EXERCISE VII.

1 廚房.一把刀子.一把鍤子.一個炒勺.一個飯鍋.一個鍋蓋.一個茶碗.一個茶盅.一個酒杯.一個酒盅子.

1. Kitchen. A knife. A fork. A frying-pan. A cooking-pan; a pan to cook rice. A cooking-pan lid. A tea-cup. A tea-cup. A wine-cup. A wine-cup. (*See* below, Example 6.)

2 他要上炕躺著.我在牀上躺著.你快把鋪蓋鋪上.那個人快上牀了.

2. He will (or, wants to) lie down on the stove-bed. I shall (or, am going to) lie (or, am lying) down on the bed. Be quick and make the bed; *lit.*, spread the bedding. That man will soon be laid out (is sick unto death).

*Obs.*—We may say *ch'uang shang* of lying down on the bed; but in *shang ch'uang* the *shang* is a verb, and has in this phrase only the special meaning assigned it in the translation. We may say *shang k'ang*, to ascend the stove-bed, of a person who is going to sleep upon one.

3 那牀上有帳子沒有.他在牀上躺著、我在椅子上坐著.

3. Are there curtains to that bed? He is (or was) lying on the bed; I am (or was) sitting on a chair.

4 這屋裏黑了、快拿燈來.桌子上的那蠟燈是誰拏了去了.是我給廚子拏過去了.廚房的火弄上了還沒著呢.

4. It is very dark in this room; bring a lamp here quick. Who took away the candlestick that was on the table? It was I that took it for the cook (or, took it over to give to the cook). The kitchen fire has been lighted, but is not well alight yet.

*Obs.* 1.—*Lung*$^4$: *see* 163.

*Obs.* 2.—The last word, read *chao*$^2$, is not here an auxiliary as in Exercise V, 1, but an independent verb signifying to throw out light.

5 飯鍋是煮飯的、鍋蓋,就是飯鍋的蓋兒.茶碗茶盅也有蓋兒的.

5. A rice-pan (*fan*$^4$-*kuo*$^1$) is a pan for boiling rice; the *kuo*$^1$-*kai*$^4$ is the cover of the rice-pan. Tea-cups, whether *ch'a*$^2$ *wan*$^3$ or *ch'a*$^2$ *chung*$^1$, [may] both have *kai*$^4$-*'rh*, covers.

*Obs.*—May both; *yeh yu*, also are there, *yu kai-'rh ti*, possessing cover ones—ones that have covers.

語言自邇集



6 酒杯酒盅子這兩個東西不大很分。可也分得出來、本是酒杯比酒盅兒大。

6. There is no great difference between a *chiu*³ *pei*¹ and a *chiu*³ *chung*¹-*tzŭ* (wine-cups of chinaware or metal), and yet they may be distinguished (they are distinguishable); the fact is that the *chiu pei* is larger than the *chiu chung*.

*Obs.* 1.—And yet: these two things [one can] not very much distinguish. [Although this be so] *k'o*, but, [one can] *yeh*, also, *fên, tê ch'u lai*, succeed in distinguishing; [for] *pên*, in reality, *shih*, it is a fact that, the *chiu pei* compared with the *chiu chung* is large.

*Obs.* 2.—The words *fên tê ch'u lai* may be rendered by the verb *distinguished* or the verbal adjective *distinguishable*; the mood and tense of the verb being entirely dependent on the context. In answer to the question, Can you (do) you distingnish or not? *fên tê ch'u lai*, I can (or do) distinguish, would be, as we say, in the present tense of the indicative mood.

*Obs.* 3.—*Pên*: see above (120). It forms part of various adverbial constructions in this sense.

7 那屋裏那些桌子椅子都壞了。說桌椅兩分、是兩張桌子八張椅子。

7. The chairs and tables in that room are all spoiled. [When one] speaks of two sets of chairs and tables, [what is meant] is two tables and eight chairs.

8 那個勺本大。勺子比勺小。匙子比勺子還小。說的是一把勺子、一把匙子、這都是京話這麼用。

8. The *shao*² is properly a large spoon. The *shao*²-*tzŭ* is smaller than the *shao*². The *ch'ih*²-*tzŭ* is still smaller than the *shao*²-*tzŭ*. One says *yi*⁴ *pa*³ *shao*²-*tzŭ* and *yi*⁴ *pa*³ *ch'ih*²-*tzŭ*; these are Pekingese idioms.

*Obs.*—*Lit.*, these all are in Peking spoken language thus used.

9 你們屋裏有蓆子沒有。我們屋裏炕上都有蓆子。

9. Have you mats in your apartment (or apartments)? There are mats on all the stove-beds in our apartments.

10 你們那兒也用蠟燈麼。我們黑下也是用蠟燈。

10. Do you also use candles in your part of the world? We also use candles at night in our part of the world.

*Obs.* 1.—*Lit.*, *la têng*, candlesticks; *ni mên na 'rh*, that place of yours.

*Obs.* 2.—At night, when darkness (blackness) has fallen: *hei* (Radical 203).

6

11 你買了那麼些蠟是作甚麼用. 都是家裏用. 是厨房用麼. 不是. 都是黑下看書用的.

11. What have you been buying such a quantity of wax for? For household use. Is it for kitchen use? No; it is for reading at night.

*Obs.* 1.—Construe the first question as two sentences, or with the first clause treated as the subject of the verb *shih*; *q.d.*, your purchase of that much wax is to make what use of? *Na mo*: *see* 23.

*Obs.* 2.—*Tso shên mo* is very common as Why? For what reason? Here with *yung* it is, For what purpose?

*Obs.* 3.—*Tou* in the last two replies is used rather for emphasis sake. We do not translate it necessarily in English.

*Obs.* 4.—In the last answer understand *la*, wax, after the *ti* at the close; *lit.*, it is all in the dark to read books use's [wax].

*Turn the following into Chinese.* (KEY, EXERCISE VII.)

1. He has taken away the mat that was on the stove-bed. Tell him to bring it to me. Where is the bedding belonging to this bed? He has taken it away too, and sold it all.

2. Where is the candlestick? On the chair. Take it away, and bring a lamp. Have you found the lamp? The room is so dark I cannot see where the lamp is. Give me the candlestick, and I will go and look for it.

3. A *chiu³ chung¹-tzŭ* (wine-cup) is smaller than a *chiu³ pei¹*. You may say either *ch'a² wan³* or *ch'a² chung¹* (tea-cup). *Kai⁴* (covers) are both large and small; the cover of a cooking-pan is larger than that of a tea-cup.

4. The curtains and mats in that room are all spoiled. Go at once and buy curtains and bedding, and make the bed.

5. Give me a knife and fork and spoon. There are knives and forks on the table, [but] no spoon. Tell the cook to give you a spoon.

6. That man has taken away the pan which the cook used for boiling rice; the cook says he can't boil the rice. I asked that man who had taken away the pan; he said he did not know who it was.

7. Your statement is not correct. I did not say I saw him do it; what I did say was that you told me he had done it. You didn't understand what I said. Whether I did or whether I didn't, why should you want to find fault with me? Who is finding fault with you? you do your [business] and I'll do mine.

*Obs.* 1—Whether, etc.: *lit.*, I did or did not [there's] no use saying.

*Obs.* 2.—Find fault with me: *lit.*, find (or, look for) my faults.

8. I want to divide this piece of paper amongst those five men, but I must give that one a larger piece than the other four. Go and ask him to return (105) those two books of mine that he took away.

*Obs.*—I want to divide, etc.: translate—I want to divide this piece of paper [and] give it to those five men; give[n] to him that one, however, must [be] compared with those four men's share, large.

**180.** 凳 *têng⁴*, a stool; a bench. Its numerative is the following substantive *t'iao²*; as *liang³ t'iao² têng⁴-tzŭ*, a couple of stools. You may equally well say *liang³ ko⁴ têng⁴-tzŭ*.

**181.** 條 *t'iao²*, a branch; a twig; the numerative of stools and many dissimilar things that are long and narrow, also of other articles.

語言自邇集



182. 倒 *tao*$^{4}$, to pour, actively; as *tao*$^{4}$ *ch'a*$^{2}$, to pour tea. (*See* below, Exercise VIII.) Also, on the reverse, or to reverse; as, *tao*$^{4}$ *pu*$^{2}$ *shih*$^{4}$, on the contrary, it is not so; *tao*$^{4}$ *kuo*$^{4}$ *lai*$^{2}$ to turn end for end. Read *tao*$^{3}$, to upset, or to be upset.

183. 壺 *hu*$^{2}$, a pot or kettle in which tea may be made, wine heated, etc.; as *ch'a*$^{2}$ *hu*$^{2}$, tea-pot. Its numerative is either *pa*$^{3}$ or *ko*$^{4}$.

184. 花 *hua*$^{1}$, flowers; also, to spend, to squander, or to dissipate, as will be seen later on.

185. 瓶 *p'ing*$^{2}$, a bottle or vase; as *hua*$^{1}$ *p'ing*$^{2}$, a flower-vase.

186. 破 *p'o*$^{4}$, to crack; to break. As *p'o*$^{4}$ *huai*$^{4}$, to ruin (or, be ruined) by breaking.

187. 收 *shou*$^{1}$, to receive; to recover; to put away. Both singly and in combination it has other meanings.

188. 拾 *shih*$^{2}$, to pick up; to put in order; with the preceding *shou*$^{1}$, to mend. The combination *shou*$^{1}$ *shih*$^{2}$ has various other uses.

189. Examples:—

| | | | | | | |
|---|---|---|---|---|---|---|
| 會 *hui*$^{4}$ | 都 *tou*$^{1}$ | 倒 *tao*$^{4}$ | 壺 *hu*$^{2}$ | 水 *shui*$^{3}$ | 花 *hua*$^{1}$ | 三 *san*$^{1}$ |
| 收 *shou*$^{1}$ | 破 *p'o*$^{4}$ | 了。*liao* | 裏 *li*$^{3}$ | 壺 *hu*$^{2}$ | 瓶 *p'ing*$^{2}$ | 條 *t'iao*$^{2}$ |
| 拾 *shih*$^{2}$ | 了 *liao* | 這 *chê*$^{4}$ | 的 *ti* | 拿 *na*$^{2}$ | 倒 *tao*$^{3}$ | 長 *ch'ang*$^{2}$ |
| 沒 *mei*$^{2}$ | 有 *yu*$^{3}$ | 傢 *chia*$^{1}$ | 水 *shui*$^{3}$ | 來。*lai*$^{2}$ | 了。*liao* | 櫈。*têng*$^{4}$ |
| 有。*yu*$^{3}$ | 人 *jên*$^{2}$ | 伙 *huo*$^{3}$ | 給 *kei*$^{3}$ | 把 *pa*$^{3}$ | 把 *pa*$^{3}$ | 那 *na*$^{4}$ |

Three long benches.
That flower-vase has been upset.
Bring the water-kettle here.
Pour the water out of that pot.
*Obs.*—The *liao*, pronounced *lo*, merely expletive. Note *kei*, for [me].
All these articles are (or, all this furniture is) broken; is there anyone that can repair them?

190. 盤 *p'an*$^{2}$, dishes. The numerative is *ko*$^{4}$; as *yi*$^{2}$ *ko*$^{4}$ *p'an*$^{2}$-*tzŭ*.

191. 碟 *tieh*$^{2}$, plates, saucers, smaller than *p'an*$^{2}$. The numerative is *ko*$^{4}$; as *ssŭ*$^{4}$ *ko*$^{4}$ *tieh*$^{2}$-*tzŭ*, four plates.

192. 點 *tien*$^{3}$, a point, a particle; to punctuate; to light, as a candle. Thus,

*tien*$^{3}$ *têng*$^{1}$, to light a lamp (or lamps).

As a particle, *yi*$^{4}$ *tien*$^{3}$-'*rh*, a minute point; used adverbially, a little, slightly.

193. 吹 *ch'ui*$^{1}$, to blow; as *ch'ui*$^{1}$ *têng*$^{1}$, to blow out a lamp or candle.

194. 滅 *mieh*$^{4}$, to extinguish, as a light, a fire; with the foregoing, *ch'ui*$^{1}$ *mieh*$^{4}$, to blow out.

195. 使 *shih*$^{3}$, to employ. As *shih*$^{3}$ *tê*$^{2}$, available, capable of being used; *shih*$^{3}$ *pu*$^{4}$ *tê*$^{2}$, cannot be used.

196. Examples :—

| | | | | | | |
|---|---|---|---|---|---|---|
| 些 *hsieh*$^1$ | 房 *fang*$^2$ | 誰 *shui*$^2$ | 點 *tien*$^3$ | 幾 *chi*$^3$ | 小。*hsiao*$^3$ | 盤 *p'an*$^2$ |
| 話 *hua*$^4$ | 火 *huo*$^3$ | 給 *kei*$^3$ | 燈。*têng*$^1$ | 個 *ko*$^4$ | 幾 *chi*$^3$ | 子 *tzŭ* |
| 都 *tou*$^1$ | 滅 *mieh*$^4$ | 滅 *mieh*$^4$ | 那 *na*$^4$ | 碟 *tieh*$^2$ | 個 *ko*$^4$ | 大 *ta*$^4$ |
| 使 *shih*$^3$ | 了。*liao* | 了。*liao* | 燈 *têng*$^1$ | 子。*tzŭ* | 盤 *p'an*$^2$ | 碟 *tieh*$^2$ |
| 得。*tê*$^2$ | 這 *chê*$^4$ | 厨 *ch'u*$^2$ | 是 *shih*$^4$ | 快 *k'uai*$^4$ | 子 *tzŭ* | 子 *tzŭ* |

*P'an*$^2$*-tzŭ* are larger than *tieh*$^2$*-tzŭ*.

Some *p'an*$^2$*-tzŭ* (dishes) and some *tieh*$^2$*-tzŭ* (plates or saucers).

Make haste and light the lamp.

Who put that lamp out?

The fire is gone out in the kitchen.

All these expressions may be employed.

197. 爐 *lu*$^2$, a stove. Its numerative is *ko*$^4$; as *yi*$^2$ *ko*$^4$ *lu*$^2$*-tzŭ*, a stove.

198. 籠 *lung*$^2$, properly, a cage; hence, joined with *têng*$^1$, a Chinese lantern; used verbally with *huo*$^3$, fire, as to light. *See* 163.

199. 空 *k'ung*$^1$, empty; hence, *k'ung*$^4$, leisure.

Observe the change of tone.

200. 滿 *man*$^3$, full.

201. 同 *t'ung*$^2$, same; with. As *chê*$^4$ *liang*$^3$ *ko*$^4$ *t'ung*$^2$ *pu*$^4$ *t'ung*$^2$, are these two the same or different? *t'a*$^1$ *t'ung*$^2$ *wo*$^3$ *ch'ü*$^4$, he is going (or, he went) with me.

202. 算 *suan*$^4$, to reckon, arithmetically; also, to consider as. Thus, *chê*$^4$ *suan*$^4$ *hao*$^3$, this one may regard as good.

203. 碎 *sui*$^4$, in fragments; in tatters. Hence, *ling*$^2$ *sui*$^4$ (5), fragmentary; odds and ends.

204. Examples :—

| | | | | | | |
|---|---|---|---|---|---|---|
| 碎 *sui*$^4$ | 算 *suan*$^4$ | 是 *shih*$^4$ | 的 *ti* | 爐 *lu*$^2$ | 的, *ti* | 爐 *lu*$^2$ |
| 東 *tung*$^1$ | 數 *shu*$^4$ | 同 *t'ung*$^2$ | 這 *chê*$^4$ | 子。*tzŭ* | 快 *k'uai*$^4$ | 子 *tzŭ* |
| 西。*hsi*$^1$ | 目。*mu*$^4$ | 我 *wo*$^3$ | 壺 *hu*$^2$ | 那 *na*$^4$ | 燒 *shao*$^1$ | 是 *shih*$^4$ |
| 沒 *mei*$^2$ | 那 *na*$^4$ | 來 *lai*$^2$ | 倒 *tao*$^4$ | 壺 *hu*$^2$ | 火。*huo*$^3$ | 燒 *shao*$^1$ |
| 空 *k'ung*$^4$ | 是 *shih*$^4$ | 的。*ti* | 滿, *man*$^3$ | 是 *shih*$^4$ | 快 *k'uai*$^4$ | 火 *huo*$^3$ |
| 兒。*'rh* | 零 *ling*$^2$ | 算 *suan*$^4$ | 他 *t'a*$^1$ | 空 *k'ung*$^1$ | 籠 *lung*$^2$ | 用 *yung*$^4$ |

A *lu*$^2$*-tzŭ* (stove or fireplace) is used for lighting a fire in.

Make haste and light a fire. Make haste and light the fire; *lit.*, the stove.

*Obs.—Shao huo* can only be used with reference to a furnace in which wood or millet stalks, etc., are used for fuel.

That pot is empty, but this one is full [this pot, on the other hand (182), is full].

He came with me.

To count up.

That is a thing (or, those are things) of small account.

I have no leisure; *q.d.*, to do what you ask me.

## EXERCISE VIII.

1 一條櫈子一個櫈子都說得分的是長的多說條、方的多說個、話條子是學話用的。

1. A stool or bench; you may also use $ko^4$ as the numerative of $t\hat{e}ng^4$. If a distinction is to be made, it is (or, the difference is) that $t'iao^2$ is oftener said of [benches that are] long, and $ko^1$ oftener of [stools that are] square. $Hua^4$ $t'iao^2$-$tz\breve{u}$ (*lit.*, slips of oral language) are what are used in learning a spoken language.

2 花瓶。酒瓶。酒壺。茶壺。盤子。碟子。

2. Flower-vase. Wine-bottle. Wine-kettle. Tea-pot. Dishes. Plates.

*Obs.*—The Chinese drink their wine warm.

3 點燈。吹燈。燒火。滅火。

3. Light the lamp. Blow out the lamp. Light the fire. Put out the fire.

4 倒水。你把這個水給倒了。他倒水去了。倒茶來。這東西站不住、倒下來了壞了。

4. To pour water. You pour out this water (=throw it away). He is gone to pour out (throw away) water. Pour tea here (=Serve tea). This thing would not stand up; it has overturned, and is spoiled.

*Obs.* 1.—*Lai*: *q.d.*, bring tea *in* and pour it out.

*Obs.* 2.—Overturned $tao^3$.

5 空是沒有東西在裏頭、空手也說得。壺滿了是把壺倒滿。茶壺空了。酒壺滿了。那酒壺是空的是滿的。是空的。

5. $K'ung^1$ means that there is nothing inside; you may also say $k'ung^1$ $shou^3$, empty-handed. [The words] $hu^2$ $man^3$ mean that something has been poured into the $hu^2$ (pot) until it was full. The tea-pot has been emptied. The wine-kettle has been filled. Has that wine-kettle anything in it? It is empty.

*Obs.* 1.—Construe:—*Hu man*, pot filled, is=means [that someone] taking the pot, *tao man*, has by pouring filled it.

*Obs.* 2.—Note the force of *liao*.

6 那花瓶是甚麼人弄破了的。那是我弄破的、可沒有壞、收拾收拾還可以使得。那傢伙弄壞了、使不得。

6. Who is it that has broken the (or that) flower-vase? I broke it, but it is not utterly spoiled; it can be mended, and (or, if it be mended) then some use can be made of it. That article is so badly injured that no use can be made of it.

*Obs.* 1.—Mend, mend, still can [one] use it. The reduplication of verbs and attributives is very colloquial. It has no special significance.

*Obs.* 2.—Construe:—That article [by some agency] breaking has been spoiled, or ruined; [one] cannot use it.

*Obs.* 3.—As a rule, even in what we consider passive or impersonal constructions, construe the verb as governed by a cause or personal agent.

7 那刀子鍤子勺子盤子碟子飯碗酒杯。這些個都是喫飯的傢伙。

7. Knives, forks, spoons, dishes, plates, bowls, and wine-cups, are all table utensils (*chia*[1] *huo*[3] for eating one's meals).

8 花瓶也算是傢伙麼。花瓶也可以算是傢伙。

8. Are flower-vases also considered *chia*[1] *huo*[3]? They may be so considered.

9 爐子有大小不同。廚房裏做飯用的是爐子、炕裏燒的是爐子、屋裏燒的也是爐子。

9. Stoves (*lu*[2]*-tzŭ*) are of different sizes, some larger, some smaller. The stove for cooking things in the kitchen is a *lu*[2]*-tzŭ*; so is the stove which is lit in the stove-bed; so also is the stove which is lit in one's room.

10 叫人倒茶、是叫人把茶拿來倒在茶碗裏頭。你點了燈沒有。我點上了、他給吹滅了。

10. When you tell a man to *tao*[4] *ch'a*[2] (pour tea), you mean, pour tea into the tea-cups. Have you lit the lamp? I lit it, but he blew it out.

*Obs.* 1.—The action of *tien* is completed by *shang*.

*Obs.* 2.—But he blew: *kei* (to give) before *ch'ui mieh* implies, idiomatically, that the act of the person in question was not to be expected. Were it omitted, the two acts would be simply distinguished: I lit it; he blew it out.

11 吹燈是人把燈吹滅了。燈滅了、火滅了。是燈火自己滅了。

11. *Ch'ui*[1] *têng*[1] (*lit.*, to blow lamp) means that someone is blowing it out (or, has done so). [The expressions] *têng*[1] *mieh*[4] *liao*, *huo*[3] *mieh*[4] *liao*, mean that the lamp (or fire) has gone out of itself.

12 那倆壺裏有水沒有。一個是空的、一個是滿的。你把那空的倒滿了水。

12. Is there water in those two kettles? One is empty, the other is full. Fill the empty one with water.

語言自邇集



*Turn the following into Chinese.* (KEY, EXERCISE VIII.)

1. I really don't know what you want so many chairs for.

2. Now just count, you have asked twenty-five people to dinner, and do you think that those few chairs of ours will seat five-and-twenty people?

3. If they won't seat twenty-five people, the benches in the kitchen will do very well.

4. With the benches we can seat them, [but] allow me to ask if benches would look well in the dining-room? Then there are the plates and rice-bowls; I must find some, but I don't know where to look for them.

*Obs.*—Seat them: *lit.*, [they] can sit open, *i.e.*, not too close.

5. We have thirty rice-bowls here.

6. They won't do; besides, six are broken.

7. I don't care whether they are broken or not, just send for someone to mend them.

8. I have bought a dinner set (*lit.*, table of utensils) of him, also some odds and ends for kitchen use, with some fire-irons (*lit.*, things used for lighting the fire); just add all this up for me and see if his account is correct.

*Obs.*—Just add up: *lit.*, he opened that account you for me reckon one reckon, wrong not wrong.

9. I can't do accounts; *lit.*, reckon bills. (*See* 146.) What do you mean by that; has not the teacher taught you the numerals (字目數)?

10. I know the numerals in their abbreviated form, but these are all written in the full (*lit.*, large) form, and I am not acquainted [with that] yet.

**205.** 今 *chin*¹, now; the present.

**206.** 年 *nien*², the year.

**207.** 時 *shih*², time.

**208.** 令 *ling*⁴, to command; a command; also, honourable. When combined with the foregoing, as *shih²-ling⁴*, the weather that prevails; the state of weather that the season demands.

**209.** 暖 *nuan*³, also *nan*³, warm.

**210.** 和 *ho*², *huo*², *hai*⁴, peace; together with; also, soft or gentle. Combined with *nuan*³ or *nan*³, warm; as the temperature in-doors or out-of-doors. Read *huo*⁴, to mix, as powder, flour, etc., with water.

**211.** 昨 *tso*², of yesterday.

**212.** 天 *t'ien*¹, heaven; a day.

**213.** Examples:—

| | | | | | | |
|---|---|---|---|---|---|---|
| 都 *tou*¹ | 日 *jih*⁴ | 天。*t'ien*¹ | 昨 *tso*² | 的 *ti* | 年。*nien*² | 今 *chin*¹ |
| 可 *k'o*³ | 子 *tzŭ* | 前 *ch'ien*² | 天。*t'ien*¹ | 時 *shih*² | 去 *ch'ü*⁴ | 年。*nien*² |
| 以 *i*³ | 多 *to*¹ | 兒。*'rh* | 昨 *tso*² | 令 *ling*⁴ | 年。*nien*² | 明 *ming*² |
| 說。*shuo*¹ | 少 *shao*³ | 多 *to*¹ | 兒。*'rh* | 暖 *nan*³ | 前 *ch'ien*² | 年。*nien*² |
| | 天 *t'ien*¹ | 少 *shao*³ | 前 *ch'ien*² | 和。*huo*² | 年 *nien*² | 後 *hou*⁴ |

This year. Next year. The year after next. Last year; *sc.*, the year that is gone.
The year before last the weather was warm.

*Obs.*—Note the special use of *ch'ien*, before, and *hou*, after, in these phrases.

Yesterday. Yesterday.

The day before yesterday. The day before yesterday.

[In how many days?] you may say *tó shaŏ jih-tzŭ* or *to shaŏ t'ién*.

214. 就 *chiu*$^4$, to follow as a consequence; consequently; then, in the time or argument.

215. 定 *ting*$^4$, to fix, make firm; hence, certain. As *yi*$^2$ *ting*$^4$, entirely certain.

216. 晝 *chou*$^4$, daytime.

217. 夜 *yeh*$^4$, night.

218. 晴 *ch'ing*$^2$, fine; clear.

219. 亮 *liang*$^4$, light as day.

220. Examples:—

| | | | | | | |
|---|---|---|---|---|---|---|
| 夜 *yeh*$^4$ | 天 *t'ien*$^1$ | 起 *ch'i*$^3$ | 道 *tao*$^4$ | 晝 *chou*$^4$ | 沒 *mei*$^2$ | 我 *wo*$^3$ |
| 裏 *li*$^3$ | 今 *chin*$^1$ | 來。*lai*$^2$ | 兒。*'rh* | 夜 *yeh*$^4$ | 有 *yü*$^3$ | 來 *lai*$^2$ |
| 可 *k'o*$^3$ | 兒 *'rh* | 昨 *tso*$^2$ | 天 *t'ien*$^1$ | 的 *ti* | 定 *ting*$^4$ | 他 *t'a*$^1$ |
| 以 *i*$^3$ | 下 *hsia*$^4$ | 兒 *'rh* | 亮 *liang*$^4$ | 都 *tou*$^1$ | 日 *jih*$^4$ | 就 *chiu*$^4$ |
| 到。*tao*$^4$ | 雨。*yü*$^3$ | 晴 *ch'ing*$^2$ | 就 *chiu*$^4$ | 走 *tsou*$^3$ | 子。*tzŭ* | 走。*tsou*$^3$ |

As soon as I come (or came) he goes (or went); *lit.*, then he goes.
There is no day fixed.
To travel both by day and night.
To rise at dawn; *lit.*, as soon as the heavens are bright, to rise.
It was fine yesterday; to-day it rains.
May arrive in the course of the night.

221. 鐘 *chung*$^1$, a bell; also, in modern Chinese, a clock.

222. 表 *piao*$^3$, the outside as opposed to the inside; hence, manifestation. In modern Chinese, a watch.

223. 刻 *k'ê*$^4$, to engrave; a short time; in modern Chinese, a quarter of an hour. Also, to oppress, as will be seen later.

224. 候 *hou*$^4$, to await; hence, when combined with *shih*$^2$, time, a time, the time.

225. Examples:—

| | | | | | | | |
|---|---|---|---|---|---|---|---|
| 刻。*k'ê*$^4$ | 說 *shuo*$^1$ | 鐘 *chung*$^1$ | 時 *shih*$^2$ | 辰 *ch'ên*$^2$ | 了。*liao* | 看 *k'an*$^4$ | 是 *shih*$^4$ |
| | 得。*tê*$^2$ | 三 *san*$^1$ | 辰 *ch'ên*$^2$ | 鐘。*chung*$^1$ | 這 *chê*$^4$ | 鐘 *chung*$^1$ | 甚 *shên*$^2$ |
| | 四 *ssŭ*$^4$ | 下 *hsia*$^4$ | 表。*piao*$^3$ | 那 *na*$^4$ | 鐘 *chung*$^1$ | 就 *chiu*$^4$ | 麼 *mo*$^2$ |
| | 點 *tien*$^3$ | 鐘 *chung*$^1$ | 三 *san*$^1$ | 表 *piao*$^3$ | 是 *shih*$^4$ | 知 *chih*$^1$ | 時 *shih*$^2$ |
| | 三 *san*$^1$ | 都 *tou*$^1$ | 點 *tien*$^3$ | 是 *shih*$^4$ | 時 *shih*$^2$ | 道 *tao*$^4$ | 候。*hou*$^4$ |

What o'clock is it?
Look at the clock and you will see (*lit.*, know).
This is a clock; *lit.*, a bell of *shih*$^2$ *ch'ên*$^2$ (Radical 162), hour periods.
That is a watch; *lit.*, an indicator of hour periods.
You may say [for three o'clock] *san tien chung* or *san hsia chung*, three points or three blows of the bell.

*Obs.*—*Hsia*, blows.

Three quarters past four.

226. 冷 *lêng*$^3$, cold; as in *chin*$^1$ *t'ien*$^1$ *lêng*$^3$, it is cold to-day.

227. 熱 *jê*$^{4}$, hot; as *pu*$^{4}$ *lêng*$^{3}$ *pu*$^{2}$ *jê*$^{4}$, neither hot nor cold.

228. 雪 *hsüeh*$^{3}$, snow; as *hsia*$^{4}$ *hsüeh*$^{3}$, it is snowing.

229. 涼 *liang*$^{2}$, cool; cold. As *liang*$^{2}$ *shui*$^{3}$, cold water. Often used with *k'uai*$^{4}$ (80), brisk or fresh; as *liang*$^{2}$ *k'uai*, cool (not cold).

230. 刮 *kua*$^{1}$, to rasp; to cut; to shave.

231. 颳 *kua*$^{1}$ (said to be a vulgar form of the above), to blow, as the wind.

232. 氣 *ch'i*$^{4}$, breath, air; the material influences of nature; morally, temper, anger; also (under certain circumstances, and in combination), aspect, appearance, taste, and smell. As *t'ien*$^{1}$ *ch'i*$^{4}$, weather; temperature.

233. Examples:—

| | | | | | | |
|---|---|---|---|---|---|---|
| 話。*hua*$^{4}$ | 我 *wo*$^{3}$ | 兒 *'rh* | 了 *liao* | 風 *fêng*$^{1}$ | 颳 *kua*$^{1}$ | 天 *t'ien*$^{1}$ |
| | 說 *shuo*$^{1}$ | 天 *t'ien*$^{1}$ | 半 *pan*$^{4}$ | 住 *chu*$^{4}$ | 起 *ch'i*$^{3}$ | 氣 *ch'i*$^{4}$ |
| | 了 *liao* | 涼 *liang*$^{2}$ | 夜 *yeh*$^{4}$ | 了 *liao* | 大 *ta*$^{4}$ | 冷。*lêng*$^{3}$ |
| | 半 *pan*$^{4}$ | 快。*k'uai*$^{4}$ | 的 *ti* | 下 *hsia*$^{4}$ | 風 *fêng*$^{1}$ | 天 *t'ien*$^{1}$ |
| | 天 *t'ien*$^{1}$ | 他 *t'a*$^{1}$ | 雪 *hsüeh*$^{3}$ | 雪。*hsüeh*$^{3}$ | 來 *lai*$^{2}$ | 氣 *ch'i*$^{4}$ |
| | 的 *ti* | 和 *hai*$^{4}$ | 今 *chin*$^{1}$ | 下 *hsia*$^{4}$ | 了。*liao* | 熱。*jê*$^{4}$ |

The weather is cold. The weather is hot.

A high wind has got up.

When the wind stopped, it snowed.

It snowed half the night. *Pan*$^{4}$: *see* 236.

To-day it is cool.

He had a long talk with me; *lit.*, half a day's talk.

234. 初 *ch'u*$^{1}$, the first; when first. As *ch'i*$^{3}$ *ch'u*$^{1}$, in the beginning. *Ch'i*$^{3}$, to rise: *see* 43.

235. 次 *tz'ŭ*$^{4}$, a time or turn; as *ch'u*$^{1}$ *tz'ŭ*$^{4}$, the first time. In a series, any place but the first.

236. 半 *pan*$^{4}$, half.

237. Examples:—

| | | | | | | |
|---|---|---|---|---|---|---|
| 二。*êrh*$^{4}$ | 月。*yüeh*$^{4}$ | 半 *pan*$^{4}$ | 上 *shang*$^{4}$ | 上 *shang*$^{4}$ | 他 *t'a*$^{1}$ | 兩 *liang*$^{3}$ |
| 兩 *liang*$^{3}$ | 正 *chêng*$^{1}$ | 個 *ko*$^{4}$ | 半 *pan*$^{4}$ | 月。*yüeh*$^{4}$ | 們 *mên*$^{2}$ | 個 *ko*$^{4}$ |
| 點 *tien*$^{3}$ | 月 *yüeh*$^{4}$ | 月。*yüeh*$^{4}$ | 月。*yüeh*$^{4}$ | 本 *pên*$^{3}$ | 初 *ch'u*$^{1}$ | 人 *jên*$^{2}$ |
| 半 *pan*$^{4}$ | 初 *ch'u*$^{1}$ | 一 *yi*$^{2}$ | 下 *hsia*$^{4}$ | 月。*yüeh*$^{4}$ | 次 *tz'ŭ*$^{4}$ | 初 *ch'u*$^{1}$ |
| 鐘。*chung*$^{1}$ | 一 *yi*$^{1}$ | 個 *ko*$^{4}$ | 半 *pan*$^{4}$ | 下 *hsia*$^{4}$ | 見 *chien*$^{4}$ | 見 *chien*$^{4}$ |
| | 初 *ch'u*$^{1}$ | 半 *pan*$^{4}$ | 月。*yüeh*$^{4}$ | 月。*yüeh*$^{4}$ | 面。*mien*$^{4}$ | 是 *shih*$^{4}$ |

When [it is said that] two people *ch'u*$^{1}$ *chien*$^{4}$, it means that they have seen each other for the first time.

Last moon. This moon. Next moon.

In the first half of the moon. In the last half of the moon.

A half moon. A month and a half.

The first and second days of the first moon.

*Obs.*—First moon: *chêng* (*see* 103); *q.d.*, the right or chief moon, to which all the rest are subordinate. Note the change of tone.

Half-past two o'clock.

## EXERCISE IX.

1 前兒就是前天、昨兒昨天、今兒今天、明兒明天、後兒後天、都是那麼著。

1. *Ch'ien-'rh*$^2$ is simply *ch'ien*$^2$ *t'ien*$^1$ (the day before yesterday); [and the combinations meaning] yesterday, to-day, to-morrow, and the day after to-morrow, all follow the same rule.

2 天氣分得是天冷、天熱、天涼、天暖和、颳風、晴天、下雨、下雪、這些都在裏頭。

2. The weather (*lit.*, air of the sky) is distinguished as cold, hot, cool, warm, windy, clear, rainy, snowy.

*Obs.*—The last clause is not translated; *chê hsieh*, these some, or many, all are inside, are all included.

3 一點半鐘就是一點鐘兩刻。一下鐘就是一點鐘。

3. An hour and a half is the same as an hour and two quarters. Both the following expressions, *yi*$^2$ *hsia*$^4$ *chung*$^1$ and *yi*$^4$ *tien*$^3$ *chung*$^1$, mean an hour.

4 他那個人念過二十多年的書、不過做了五六個月的先生。這個人白日愛騎馬、黑下回家看書。

4. That man there has studied upwards of twenty years; he has been a teacher only five or six months. It is this man's habit to ride in the day and to study in the evening when he comes home.

*Obs.* 1.—Habit: *ai* (52) to love = to be used to.
*Obs.* 2.—By day: *pai jih* precedes the verb.

5 我今兒走、下月可以回來。你這個人今兒八下鐘還沒起來麽。

5. I am going to-day, and may be back next moon. What! were you not up at eight o'clock to-day?

*Obs.*—You: *lit.*, you this man! reproachfully.

6 前年後年說得、前月後月不大很說。這兒天熱的時候兒下雨、天冷就下雪。

6. You may say both *ch'ien*$^2$ *nien*$^2$ for the year before last and *hou*$^4$ *nien*$^2$ for the year after next, but *ch'ien*$^2$ *yüeh*$^4$ and *hou*$^4$ *yüeh*$^4$ are not much used. At this place it rains in the hot weather and snows in the cold.

語言自邇集



7 前四天颳北風、第二天天氣很冷.昨兒黑下下雨、夜裡住了、今兒天晴了.

7. Four days ago it blew from the north, and the day following it was very cold. It rained last evening, but it stopped in the night, and it was fine this morning.

8 今年天氣暖和得很、沒有去年那麽冷.今年的時令不正、這幾年誰見過四月裡還下雪呢.

8. The weather is very mild this year; not so cold as it was last year. The weather is not seasonable this year; nobody has seen snow in the fourth moon for some years.

*Obs.*—Not seasonable: *pu chêng*, not correct.

9 我們倆到這兒好些年了.他是去年來的、我是上月到的、他們倆去年來過了.

9. We two have been here a good many years; or, it is many years since we came here. He came last year; I arrived last moon; they two came here last year.

*Obs.*—Not *tsa mên* (see 17) unless the person addressed is present.

*Turn the following into Chinese.* (KEY, EXERCISE IX.)

1. In what year did you arrive in Peking?

2. I came this year. I have not been here long; only half a year.

3. But you speak mandarin very correctly.

4. That is all owing to my having learned Chinese in the South (*lit.*, southern quarter). (Radical 70.)

5. That accounts for it. Do you find the climate here agree with you (good)?

*Obs.*—Climate: *lit.*, water and earth.

6. There is nothing the matter with it; the seasons are very equable, and the heat is nothing to speak of; but not having passed a winter here, I cannot say what the cold is like.

*Obs.* 1.—Equable: *ho² p'ing²* (210, 137).

*Obs.* 2.—Passed a winter: *lit.*, passed the [new] year.

7. It is warm enough in one's room, but it's pretty cold all the same if you go on a few days' trip.

*Obs.* 1.—All the same: *lit.*, but [though] it is thus said.

*Obs.* 2.—If: this is commonly expressed by the characters *yao⁴ shih⁴* (32, 29), the former being corruptly used for *jo*, of which more presently.

8. The snow, I am told, is very heavy here.

9. No, that is not the case; on the contrary, there is little snow,—only an inch or so falls during the year. What I referred to were the winds, which blow so cold.

*Obs.*—Only: *pu² kuo⁴*; *lit.*, not exceeding.

10. What do you do every day?

11. I rise every morning at 7.30 and have my breakfast, then I send for my teacher and read for three hours and a half, after which I dine and go out for a ride.

*Obs.* 1.—Breakfast, lunch, or any minor meal, is called in Peking "little heart," said to be short for four words (以點饑心) which, literally translated, mean "in order to satisfy slightly the hungry craving." Puddings are also called *tien hsin*.

*Obs.* 2.—"After which" or "afterwards" is often rendered by the words *hui*$^{2}$ *t'ou*$^{2}$, to turn the head; *hui lai*, to return, has the same force.

12. In that case come for a ride with me after your dinner to-day, will you?

13. Look at the weather; [it has turned] cold and is going to rain; I do not think it can possibly clear up.

14. So it is; in that case we had better go to-morrow. What time to-morrow shall we fix?

*Obs.* 1.—So it is: *see* 124.

*Obs.* 2.—Fix: 215.

15. Say daylight. The cold is nothing; after a short gallop we shall be all right.

**238.** 更 *ching*$^{1}$, properly *kêng*$^{1}$, to change; the watches of the night, of which there are five. When read *kêng*$^{4}$ it is an adjective of comparison; *na*$^{4}$ *kêng*$^{4}$ *hao*$^{3}$, that is better still.

**239.** 夫 *fu*$^{1}$, a man, especially a husband; commonly, any working man. As *chiao*$^{1}$-*fu*$^{1}$, a chair-bearer; *ma*$^{3}$-*fu*$^{1}$, a groom. Joined with *kung*$^{1}$ (Radical 48), work. *See* Exercise X, 1.

**240.** 每 *mei*$^{3}$, every; as in *mei*$^{3}$ *yi*$^{2}$ *ko*$^{4}$, every individual one.

**241.** 打 *ta*$^{3}$, to strike; as *t'a*$^{1}$ *ta*$^{3}$ *wo*$^{3}$, he is striking (or, has struck) me; also idiomatically combined with many verbs of action. It is also used as a preposition. Thus,

*ta*$^{3}$ *tso*$^{2}$ *t'ien*$^{1}$ *tao*$^{4}$ *chin*$^{1}$ *tien*$^{1}$, from yesterday until to-day.

*ta*$^{3}$ *na*$^{4}$ *'rh kuo*$^{4}$, to go by there.

**242.** 罷 *pa*$^{4}$, to end; to cause to cease. At the end of a sentence, "there's an end of it;" but sometimes used to imply doubt, like our Eh? or a command.

**243.** Examples:—

| | | | | | | |
|---|---|---|---|---|---|---|
| 你 *ni*$^{3}$ | 打。*ta*$^{3}$ | 甚 *shên*$^{2}$ | 回 *hui*$^{2}$ | 的。*ti* | 更 *ching*$^{1}$ | 夜 *yeh*$^{4}$ |
| 說 *shuo*$^{1}$ | 他 *t'a*$^{1}$ | 麼。*mo*$^{1}$ | 更。*ching*$^{1}$ | 每 *mei*$^{3}$ | 夫 *fu*$^{1}$ | 裏 *li*$^{3}$ |
| 他 *t'a*$^{1}$ | 有 *yu*$^{3}$ | 不 *pu*$^{4}$ | 打 *ta*$^{3}$ | 夜 *yeh*$^{4}$ | 是 *shih*$^{4}$ | 分 *fên*$^{1}$ |
| 罷 *pa*$^{4}$ | 不 *pu*$^{2}$ | 能 *nêng*$^{2}$ | 他 *t'a*$^{1}$ | 打 *ta*$^{3}$ | 打 *ta*$^{3}$ | 五 *wu*$^{3}$ |
| 了。*liao* | 是 *shih*$^{4}$ | 不 *pu*$^{4}$ | 做 *tso*$^{4}$ | 五 *wu*$^{3}$ | 更 *ching*$^{1}$ | 更。*ching*$^{1}$ |

The night is divided into five watches.
The *ching-fu* are the men who beat the watches (strike the changes).
A watch is struck five times every night.
What are you beating him for? I cannot do otherwise; or, he must be beaten.
If he has done wrong, reprove him and have done with it.

*Obs.*—Wrong: *pu shih*.

**244.** 早 *tsao*$^{3}$, early. As in *tsao*$^{3}$ *fan*$^{4}$, early rice; *sc.*, breakfast.

**245.** 晚 *wan*$^{3}$, late. As in *wan*$^{3}$ *fan*$^{4}$, the evening meal; dinner or supper.

246. 晌 *shang*$^{3}$, noon; coupled, colloquially, with the following *wu*$^{3}$, and often pronounced *shang*$^{2}$ *hu*$^{1}$. *Pan*$^{4}$ *shang*$^{3}$, half the day, or a long while; *wan*$^{3}$ *shang*$^{1}$, evening. Note the change of tone.

247. 午 *wu*$^{3}$, noon. See *ch'ên*$^{2}$, Radical Exercise XII, 7. The 24 hours of the day are divided by the Chinese into 12 *shih*$^{2}$-*ch'ên*$^{2}$. Of these, *wu*$^{3}$ represents the two hours from 11 A.M. to 1 P.M.

248. 咱 *tsan*$^{1}$, length of time; popular contraction of *tsao*$^{3}$ *wan*$^{3}$. As in *to*$^{1}$ *tsan*$^{1}$, the common phrase for When? *q.d.*, how soon, how early?

249. Examples:—

| | | | | | | |
|---|---|---|---|---|---|---|
| 你 *ni*$^{3}$ | 我 *wo*$^{3}$ | 不 *pu*$^{2}$ | 咱 *tsan*$^{1}$ | 沒 *mei*$^{2}$ | 午 *wu*$^{3}$ | 他 *t'a*$^{1}$ |
| 的 *ti* | 來 *lai*$^{2}$ | 定。*ting*$^{4}$ | 喫 *ch'ih*$^{1}$ | 回 *hui*$^{2}$ | 出 *ch'u*$^{1}$ | 早 *tsao*$^{3}$ |
| 罷。*pa*$^{4}$ | 的 *ti* | 他 *t'a*$^{1}$ | 的。*ti* | 家。*chia*$^{1}$ | 門 *mên*$^{2}$ | 起 *ch'i*$^{3}$ |
| | 晚。*wan*$^{3}$ | 來 *lai*$^{2}$ | 早 *tsao*$^{3}$ | 晚 *wan*$^{3}$ | 去 *ch'ü*$^{4}$ | 起 *ch'i*$^{3}$ |
| | 你 *ni*$^{3}$ | 的 *ti* | 晚 *wan*$^{3}$ | 飯 *fan*$^{4}$ | 下 *hsia*$^{4}$ | 來 *lai*$^{2}$ |
| | 走 *tsou*$^{3}$ | 早 *tsao*$^{3}$ | 都 *tou*$^{1}$ | 多 *to*$^{1}$ | 午 *wu*$^{3}$ | 晌 *shang*$^{3}$ |

He got up early, went out at noon, and had not returned in the afternoon.

*Obs.*—The afternoon is often spoken of as *hou pan t'ien*, the latter half of the day.

What is the dinner hour? It is uncertain.

*Obs.* 1.—Late (or evening) meal when can be eaten; *ti*=*tê*.

*Obs.* 2.—Early late both not fixed.

He came early; I came late (or, he came before me).

Go your own ways; or, mind your own business.

*Obs.*—Note *pa*, a command. *See* 242.

250. 件 *chien*$^{4}$, properly, to distinguish; a distinction; but best known as a numerative; amongst other substantives, numerative of *shih*$^{4}$, affairs (252).

251. 情 *ch'ing*$^{2}$, feelings; circumstances; very commonly combined with

252. 事 *shih*$^{4}$, affairs; a matter. *See* 257.

253. 擱 *ko*$^{1}$, a character of doubtful authority; primarily, to delay; but colloquially, to put; to place. As *ko*$^{1}$ *tsai*$^{4}$ *chê*$^{4}$ *'rh*, put it here.

254. 各 *ko*$^{4}$, each; every.

255. 樣 *yang*$^{4}$, kind; fashion. As *ko*$^{4}$ *yang*$^{4}$, every sort or kind.

256. 短 *tuan*$^{3}$, short. As *ch'ang*$^{2}$ *tuan*$^{3}$, long and short; hence, the length of.

257. Examples:—

| | | | | | | |
|---|---|---|---|---|---|---|
| 那 *na*$^{4}$ | 各 *ko*$^{4}$ | 各 *ko*$^{4}$ | 把 *pa*$^{3}$ | 那 *na*$^{4}$ | 那 *na*$^{4}$ | 這 *chê*$^{4}$ |
| 東 *tung*$^{1}$ | 樣 *yang*$^{4}$ | 樣 *yang*$^{4}$ | 那 *na*$^{4}$ | 椅 *i*$^{3}$ | 件 *chien*$^{4}$ | 件 *chien*$^{4}$ |
| 西 *hsi*$^{1}$ | 的 *ti* | 各 *ko*$^{4}$ | 桌 *cho*$^{1}$ | 子 *tzŭ* | 事 *shih*$^{4}$ | 事 *shih*$^{4}$ |
| 長 *ch'ang*$^{2}$ | 事 *shih*$^{4}$ | 樣 *yang*$^{4}$ | 子 *tzŭ* | 擱 *ko*$^{1}$ | 情 *ch'ing*$^{2}$ | 我 *wo*$^{3}$ |
| 短 *tuan*$^{3}$ | 都 *tou*$^{1}$ | 的 *ti* | 擱 *ko*$^{1}$ | 在 *tsai*$^{4}$ | 不 *pu*$^{4}$ | 不 *pu*$^{4}$ |
| 不 *pu*$^{4}$ | 懂 *tung*$^{3}$ | 都 *tou*$^{1}$ | 開 *k'ai*$^{1}$ | 那 *na*$^{3}$ | 好 *hao*$^{3}$ | 明 *ming*$^{2}$ |
| 同。*t'ung*$^{2}$ | 得。*te*$^{2}$ | 有。*yu*$^{3}$ | 些。*hsieh*$^{1}$ | 兒、*'rh* | 說。*shuo*$^{1}$ | 白。*pai*$^{2}$ |

I don't understand this thing (affair, matter).

That thing should not be spoken of. (It is not good to speak of that thing.)

Where shall that chair be put (or placed).

Move away (*lit.*, place apart) that table a little.

There are some of every kind.

[He] understands every kind of thing.

Those things are of different lengths.

258. 雲 *yün*$^{2}$, cloud; commonly coupled with *ts'ai*$^{3}$. As *yün*$^{2}$ *ts'ai*$^{3}$, clouds; *lit.*, cloud colour.

259. 彩 *ts'ai*$^{3}$, colours. As in *wu*$^{3}$ *ts'ai*$^{3}$, the five colours; *sc.*, blue, yellow, red, white, and black. It may also mean luck, as will be seen later.

260. 陰 *yin*$^{1}$, the female of the dual powers of nature; darkness; dark. *T'ai*$^{4}$ *yin*$^{1}$ (264), the moon, but not colloquially.

261. 陽 *yang*$^{2}$, the male power of nature; brightness; light. *T'ai*$^{4}$ *yang*$^{2}$ (264), the sun.

262. 霧 *wu*$^{4}$, mist. As in *hsia*$^{4}$ *wu*$^{4}$, a fog, or mist, has come on; *lit.*, there has descended a fog or mist.

263. 怕 *p'a*$^{4}$, to fear; hence, to doubt; hence used as perhaps.

264. 太 *t'ai*$^{4}$, properly the superlative of *ta*$^{4}$, great; used both as an adjective and an adverb.

265. Examples :—

| | | | | | |
|---|---|---|---|---|---|
| 大 *ta*$^{4}$ | 太 *t'ai*$^{4}$ | 陰 *yin*$^{1}$ | 的 *ti* | 颳 *kua*$^{1}$ | 滿 *man*$^{3}$ |
| 太 *t'ai*$^{4}$ | 陽。*yang*$^{2}$ | 天 *t'ien*$^{1}$ | 時 *shih*$^{2}$ | 風。*fêng*$^{1}$ | 天 *t'ien*$^{1}$ |
| 陽 *yang*$^{2}$ | 下 *hsia*$^{4}$ | 是 *shih*$^{4}$ | 候, *hou*$^{4}$ | 太 *t'ai*$^{4}$ | 的 *ti* |
| 看 *k'an*$^{4}$ | 的 *ti* | 看 *k'an*$^{4}$ | 白 *pai*$^{2}$ | 陽 *yang*$^{2}$ | 雲 *yün*$^{2}$ |
| 不 *pu*$^{4}$ | 霧 *wu*$^{4}$ | 不 *pu*$^{2}$ | 日 *jih*$^{4}$ | 平 *p'ing*$^{2}$ | 彩 *ts'ai*$^{3}$ |
| 出。*ch'u*$^{1}$ | 很 *hên*$^{3}$ | 見 *chien*$^{4}$ | 說 *shuo*$^{1}$ | 西 *hsi*$^{1}$ | 怕 *p'a*$^{4}$ |

With a sky so overcast, it will probably blow.

*Obs.* 1.—The first clause is pendent; [there being] a full heaven's clouds.

*Obs.* 2.—Probably : one fears that there will blow wind.

When the sun is nearly set.

*Obs.*—Nearly : *lit.*, is even with the west; but sunset is otherwise described.

When *yin t'ien* is used of the sky in the daytime, it means that the sun is not visible : *lit.*, the sun [one] cannot discern.

There is a very thick mist; the sun is not visible.

*Obs.*—There is : *hsia ti*, there has descended ; *ti*=*tê*.

語言自邇集



## EXERCISE X.

1 工夫.每年不是年年麼、每月就是月月、每天每日還是那麼樣.

1. Work. Every year (*mei*$^{3}$ *nien*$^{2}$) is the same as year after year (*nien*$^{2}$ *nien*$^{2}$), is it not? *Mei*$^{3}$ *yüeh*$^{4}$ is moon after moon (monthly); so with the phrases *mei*$^{3}$ *t'ien*$^{1}$ *mei*$^{3}$ *jih*$^{4}$ (daily).

*Obs.* 1.—Hence, time at man's disposal for work; hence, leisure; time taken up by anything. The *fu* in *kung-fu* cannot be explained.

*Obs.* 2.—Is it not? interrogative affirmative, common in Chinese.

*Obs.* 3.—So with: *lit.*, also is it so fashion.

2 他是早起起來、晌午上街、晚晌回家看書、到夜裏三更天就在炕上躺著.天天都是這麼樣.

2. He rises early, goes for a walk (*lit.*, up the street) at noon, comes home in the evening and reads, and in the third watch of the night he goes to bed. He does the same every day.

*Obs.*—Goes to bed: not *shang ch'uang*$^{2}$, which means to take to one's bed in mortal sickness. *See* Exercise VII, 2, Obs.

3 各自各兒、就是自己一個人.這個事情得‘你各自各兒去.那房子就是他各自各兒住著.

3. The expression *ko*$^{4}$ *tzŭ*$^{4}$ *ko*$^{3}$-*'rh* means simply one's individual self. In this matter it is essential that you should go yourself. He lives by himself in that house.

*Obs.* 1.—Essential: *tei* (*see* 30, 32).

*Obs.* 2.—By himself: either he is master or senior, or no outsiders live there.

*Obs.* 3.—Note the tone of the second *ko*.

4 上半天下了雨.下半天晴了.前半夜還暖和、後半夜冷.三更天就是半夜.

4. It rained in the forenoon, but the afternoon was fine. It was warm before midnight but cold after. The third watch is midnight.

*Obs.*—*Ch'ien pan t'ien* and *hou pan t'ien* would be equally correct.

5 夜裏那打更的打更.一夜有五更、頭一更就是定更.

5. As regards the watches which a watchman strikes during the night, the night is divided into five, the beginning of the first of which is the watch-setting.

6 天長做事的工夫多、天短沒有空兒、事情得'擱著罷。

6. When the days are long there is more time to do things; when they are short, one has not leisure for them, and they must just wait (be put aside).

*Obs.* 1.—Leisure: *k'ung⁴-'rh.* Note the change of tone. *See* 199.

*Obs.* 2.—Must just wait: *lit.*, affairs [one] *tei*, must, *ko cho*, put, or be putting [aside], *pa*, and that's all about it.

*Obs.* 3.—It is difficult to define the precise power of *cho* here. The Chinese seem to treat it as a mere expletive.

7 他多喒回來。他明兒回來罷。那茶壺擱在那'兒了。擱在屋裏桌子上了。

7. When will he be back? Probably to-morrow. Where is the tea-pot put? On the table in the room.

*Obs.*—Where put, etc. Construe:—That teapot [man has] put in what place?

8 天上的雲彩滿了就是陰天。今兒早起下的霧很大、那麼大的山都看不見了。

8. When the sky is overcast the day is said to be *yin¹* (dull, obscured). There was a thick mist this morning; even those big mountains were invisible.

*Obs.*—Overcast: *lit.*, the clouds in (*lit.*, on) the sky fill [the sky].

9 你在那兒站著做甚麼、快去罷。

9. What are you standing there for? be off at once.

10 那飯得了罷。還沒得、得'一會子呢。那麼偺們還上街走一走罷。

10. I suppose dinner is ready? No, it is not ready, and it will be some time yet before it is. In that case let us have another turn up the street.

*Obs.* 1.—I suppose: *pa* here = eh? *See* 243.

*Obs.* 2.—A time: *see* 129.

*Turn the following into Chinese.* (KEY, EXERCISE X.)

1. I heard a lot of noises in the street yesterday evening. What sort of noises did you hear?

2. [A sound like] someone striking wood outside the door.

*Obs.*—Outside the door: *mên k'ou-'rh*; *lit.*, the mouth of, or entrance to, the door.

3. That was the watchman striking the watches. The night is divided into five watches, the first of which is the watch-setting and the third is midnight. The watchman has nothing to do in the daytime, but he has not a moment's leisure at night. He lives quite by himself in that small house yonder, and has neither wife nor child. He has to be out in all weathers, wet or fine (*lit.*, not regarding fine days nor cloudy days); and he never can say, "I'll put aside my work to-day." From year's end to year's end (*lit.*, one year up to the head, *i.e.*, the end), it is always the same.

4. The sky has been completely overcast to-day, and so dull that one could see nothing at all.

5. Hasn't it been dull! There was a thick fog in the morning, but it lifted (*lit.*, cleared) for a while at noon. It may be fine towards dark, but that is uncertain.

*Obs.*—Towards dark: *lit.*, arriving at dark coming up.

6. The days are now getting shorter and shorter; whenever (*to*$^1$ *tsao*$^3$ *wan*$^3$, **248**) shall you and I commence our night studies? (*lit.*, our night book is from whenever reading commenced?)

7. We've no time at present; let it be for a bit. I propose to talk about that a day or two hence.

*Obs.*—Propose: *ta*$^3$ *suan*$^4$. *See* **241**.

**266.** 衣 *i*$^1$ (Radical 145), clothes; classically, upper garments.

**267.** 裳 *shang*$^1$, classically, a skirt; colloquially appended to *i*$^1$, clothes in general.

**268.** 骯 *a*$^1$, $^{ng}$*a*$^1$, *ang*$^1$, $^{ng}$*ang*$^1$, dirty; not used colloquially except in combination with the following.

**269.** 髒 *tsa*$^1$, *tsang*$^1$, dirty; used with the preceding *ang*$^1$ or *a*$^1$, but also without it. The combination is as often pronounced *a*$^1$-*tsa*$^1$ as *ang*$^1$-*tsang*$^1$.

**270.** 換 *huan*$^4$, to exchange.

**271.** 乾 *kan*$^1$, dry.

**272.** 淨 *ching*$^4$, clean. The compound *kan*$^1$-*ching*$^4$, however, means simply, clean; as dirty things are washed *kan*$^1$-*ching*$^4$, clean.

**273.** Examples:—

| | | | | | | |
|---|---|---|---|---|---|---|
| 把 *pa*$^3$ | 手 *shou*$^3$ | 我 *wo*$^3$ | 弄 *nung*$^4$ | 乾 *kan*$^1$ | 了 *liao*$^3$ | 你 *ni*$^3$ |
| 他 *t'a*$^1$ | 巾 *chin*$^1$ | 換 *huan*$^4$ | 飯 *fan*$^4$ | 淨 *ching*$^4$ | 不 *pu*$^4$ | 的 *ti* |
| 倒 *tao*$^4$ | 來。*lai*$^2$ | 一 *i*$^4$ | 弄 *nung*$^4$ | 的。*ti* | 得。*tê*$^2$ | 衣 *i*$^1$ |
| 出 *ch'u*$^1$ | 水 *shui*$^3$ | 條 *t'iao*$^2$ | 的 *ti* | 這 *chê*$^4$ | 你 *ni*$^3$ | 裳 *shang*$^1$ |
| 去 *ch'ü*$^4$ | 骯 *ang*$^1$ | 乾 *kan*$^1$ | 乾 *kan*$^1$ | 個 *ko*$^4$ | 快 *k'uai*$^4$ | 骯 *ang*$^1$ |
| 罷。*pa*$^4$ | 髒 *tsang*$^1$ | 淨 *ching*$^4$ | 淨。*ching*$^4$ | 廚 *ch'u*$^2$ | 去 *ch'ü*$^4$ | 髒 *tsang*$^1$ |
| | 了 *liao* | 的 *ti* | 給 *kei*$^3$ | 子 *tzŭ* | 換 *huan*$^4$ | 的 *ti* |

Your clothes are dreadfully dirty.

*Obs.*—*Liao pu tê*: *lit.*, in a manner that will never do. *See* Exercise II, 9.

Go and change them at once.

*Obs.*—*Lit.*, change clean [ones for them].

This cook cooks cleanly.

*Obs.*—*Lit.*, this cook, preparing rice, prepares it clean. Note *ti* for *tê*.

Bring me a clean handkerchief.

*Obs.*—Towels are also called *shou-chin*; but there is a special term for silk handkerchiefs.

The water is dirty; pour it away.

*Obs.*—Note the employment of *t'a* in referring to an inanimate object.

274. 刷 *shua*$^1$, to brush, as a hat or clothes. In brushing boots, shoes, furniture, etc., water is used.

275. 洗 *hsi*$^3$, to wash, as clothes, the hands, the face; coupled with the following *tsao*$^3$, to bathe.

276. 澡 *tsao*$^3$, with the foregoing, to bathe.

277. 臉 *lien*$^3$, the face.

278. 盆 *p'ên*$^2$, a basin; as *hsi*$^3$*-tsao*$^3$ *p'ên*$^2$, a bath tub.

279. 胰 *i*$^2$, soap made from hogs' lard; it always takes *tzŭ* after it. Coarse soap made from the bean is called *fei*$^2$*-tsao*$^4$, and a mixture of the two, *i*$^2$*-tsao*$^4$. The new characters will be met with later.

280. 最 *tsui*$^4$, much; very.

281. 温 *wên*$^1$, warm; often combined with *ho*$^2$ (210), but pronounced *huo*$^1$.

282. 梳 *shu*$^1$, a comb; to comb. When used as a noun it either takes *mu*$^4$, wood, before it, or is followed by *tzŭ*. Thus,

*mu*$^4$ *shu*$^1$ or *shu*$^1$*-tzŭ*, a comb.

*N.B.*—A woman's comb is called *lung*$^3$*-tzŭ*, with which she *shu*$^1$ *t'ou*$^2$, combs her hair (*lit.*, head).

283. 髮 *fa*$^3$, the hair; colloquially, it takes the prefix *t'ou*$^2$, the head, as *t'ou*$^2$ *fa*$^3$. Emphasis must be laid on the first character.

284. Examples :—

| | | | | | | |
|---|---|---|---|---|---|---|
| 澡 *tsao*$^3$ | 梳 *shu*$^1$ | 臉。*lien*$^3$ | 最 *tsui*$^4$ | 得 *tê*$^2$ | 洗 *hsi*$^3$ | 臉 *lien*$^3$ |
| 最 *tsui*$^4$ | 梳 *shu*$^1$ | 給 *kei*$^3$ | 熱 *jê*$^4$ | 乾 *kan*$^1$ | 手 *shou*$^3$ | 盆 *p'ên*$^2$ |
| 好。*hao*$^3$ | 頭 *t'ou*$^2$ | 我 *wo*$^3$ | 我 *wo*$^3$ | 淨 *ching*$^4$ | 用 *yung*$^4$ | 是 *shih*$^4$ |
| 刷 *shua*$^1$ | 髮。*fa*$^3$ | 一 *i*$^4$ | 洗 *hsi*$^3$ | 了。*liao* | 胰 *i*$^2$ | 洗 *hsi*$^3$ |
| 子。*tzŭ* | 早 *tsao*$^3$ | 把 *pa*$^3$ | 了 *liao* | 前 *ch'ien*$^2$ | 子 *tzŭ* | 臉 *lien*$^3$ |
| | 起 *ch'i*$^3$ | 木 *mu*$^4$ | 六 *liu*$^4$ | 兒 *'rh* | 就 *chiu*$^4$ | 用 *yung*$^4$ |
| | 洗 *hsi*$^3$ | 梳 *shu*$^1$ | 回 *hui*$^2$ | 個 *ko*$^4$ | 洗 *hsi*$^3$ | 的。*ti* |

A basin is used for washing the face.

In washing the hands, if you use soap you can wash them clean.

*Obs.*—Mark the force of *chiu*; *lit.*, washing the hands, using soap, you *then* washing obtain clean [ones].

The day before yesterday was the hottest [we have had]; I washed my face six times.

*Obs.*—The *ko* after *ch'ien-'rh* must be regarded as a simple colloquial expletive peculiar to Peking; the *êrh* is probably a corruption of *jih*, day.

Bring me a comb to comb my hair.

*Obs.*—Note the reduplication of the verb; *shu shu*, short for *shu i shu*, to comb a comb, or have a comb at.

It is best to bathe early.

A brush.

285. 針 *chên*$^1$, a needle.

語言自邇集



286. 線 *hsien*$^4$, thread; the numerative is *t'iao*$^2$. *Chên*$^1$*-hsien*$^4$ in combination means needlework.

287. 縫 *fêng*$^2$, to stitch together; read *fêng*$^4$, a seam or crack. *See* 737.

288. 補 *pu*$^3$, to patch; hence, to fill up a vacancy, make good a deficiency.

289. Examples:—

| | | | | | |
|---|---|---|---|---|---|
| 很 *hên*$^3$ | 的 *ti* | 都 *tou*$^1$ | 兒 *'rh* | 線。*hsien*$^4$ | 一 *i*$^2$ |
| 得 *tei*$^3$ | 衣 *i*$^1$ | 學 *hsio*$^2$ | 太 *t'ai*$^4$ | 這 *chê*$^4$ | 個 *ko*$^4$ |
| 縫 *fêng*$^2$ | 裳 *shang*$^1$ | 針 *chên*$^1$ | 小。*hsiao*$^3$ | 個 *ko*$^4$ | 針。*chên*$^1$ |
| 補 *pu*$^3$ | 破 *p'o*$^4$ | 線。*hsien*$^4$ | 女 *nü*$^3$ | 針 *chên*$^1$ | 一 *i*$^4$ |
| 了 *liao* | 得 *tê*$^2$ | 你 *ni*$^3$ | 人 *jên*$^2$ | 眼 *yen*$^3$ | 條 *t'iao*$^2$ |

A needle. A thread.

The eye of this needle is too small. *Chên*$^1$ *yen*$^3$*-'rh* is not used in Peking, but *chên*$^1$ *pi*$^2$*-'rh*.

*Obs.*—The eye of a needle is also called *chên pi*$^2$*-'rh*, the needle's nose; *chên yen*, without the *êrh*, means a stye in the eye, but *chên* must be emphasised.

Women all learn sewing.

Your clothes are very tattered; they must be mended.

*Obs.*—*Fêng pu*, to mend: *lit.*, stitch and patch.

290. 穿 *ch'uan*$^1$, to bore through; to put on clothes.

291. 鞋 *hsieh*$^2$, shoes.

292. 脫 *t'o*$^1$, to take off or away. Often used with *hsia*$^4$, below; as *t'o*$^1$ *hsia*$^4$, to take off.

293. 靴 *hsüeh*$^1$, boots; it takes *tzŭ* after it.

294. 雙 *shuang*$^1$, a pair.

295. 襪, 韈, *wa*$^4$, stockings; it takes *tzŭ* after it. The character is found under both radicals.

296. Examples:—

| | | | | | | |
|---|---|---|---|---|---|---|
| 雨 *yü*$^3$ | 穿 *ch'uan*$^1$ | 脫 *t'o*$^1$ | 不 *pu*$^4$ | 麼 *mo*$^1$ | 脫 *t'o*$^1$ | 一 *i*$^4$ |
| 就 *chiu*$^4$ | 雨 *yü*$^3$ | 一 *i*$^4$ | 了 *liao*$^3$ | 大 *ta*$^4$ | 靴 *hsüeh*$^1$ | 雙 *shuang*$^1$ |
| 不 *pu*$^2$ | 靴 *hsüeh*$^1$ | 身 *shên*$^1$ | 一 *i*$^4$ | 的 *ti* | 子。*tzŭ* | 襪 *wa*$^4$ |
| 怕 *p'a*$^4$ | 雨 *yü*$^3$ | 的 *ti* | 百 *pai*$^3$ | 靴 *hsüeh*$^1$ | 你 *ni*$^3$ | 子。*tzŭ* |
| 了。*liao* | 衣 *i*$^1$ | 衣 *i*$^1$ | 步 *pu*$^4$ | 子 *tzŭ* | 穿 *ch'uan*$^1$ | 穿 *ch'uan*$^1$ |
| | 下 *hsia*$^4$ | 裳、*shang*$^1$ | 了。*liao* | 走 *tsou*$^3$ | 那 *na*$^4$ | 鞋。*hsieh*$^2$ |

One pair of stockings.

To put on shoes.

To take off boots.

If you put on boots as big as that you won't be able to walk a hundred paces.

To take off all one's clothes.

With rain boots and rain clothes on, rain need not be dreaded.

*Obs.*—Rain boots are more commonly called *yü*$^3$ *hsüeh*, oil (or oiled) boots; the character for *yü* will be met with later.

## EXERCISE XI.

1 腌臢、乾淨。衣裳、靴子。鞋。襪子。把衣裳穿上。把靴子脫下來。一雙靴子。

1. Dirty. Clean. Clothes. Boots. Shoes. Stockings. Put on your clothes. Take off your boots. A pair of boots.

2 那一雙靴子得補上一點兒皮子。他買了十雙襪子、一條手巾。那也不算多。洗靴子溫和水使不得。

2. You must patch that pair of boots with a little leather. He has bought ten pairs of stockings and one handkerchief. That is not very many after all. Warm water will not do to wash boots in.

*Obs.*—After all: note the force of *yeh*; *lit.*, that also not reckoned many.

3 這盆水腌臢了、換乾淨的拏來我洗臉。那衣裳腌臢了、拏刷子給刷一刷。

3. The water in this basin is dirty; change it and bring me some clean water instead to wash my face. Those clothes are dirty; take a brush and brush them.

4 這件衣裳破了、叫人來給補補罷、不用補罷、縫一縫也行了。一個臉盆。

4. This garment is torn: call someone here to patch it. There is no occasion, I think, to patch it; it will do as well if it is sewn up. A wash-basin.

*Obs.*—The second *pa* implying doubt.

5 你快起來罷、穿上衣裳。他脫了衣裳躺著。那一件衣裳他穿了好些日子沒換呢。

5. Get up quickly and dress. He is (or was) lying down undressed (or, has taken off his clothes and is lying down). He has had that garment on for a number of days without changing it.

6 今兒個天冷、你得多穿一件衣裳。你見他的時候兒他是穿靴子是穿鞋呢。

6. It is cold to-day; you must put on something more. When you saw him had he got on boots or shoes?

*Obs.*—*Lit.*, when you saw him's time, he wore, etc. Note *ni*, the sign of the interrogative.

7 這條手巾不乾淨、擱在臉盆裏洗一洗罷。你愛穿的是靴子是鞋。那都看我是做甚麽在家裏沒事我就穿鞋、上衙門的時候兒可得穿靴子。

*Obs.*—That all depends: *lit.*, that [is] all to be seen.

7. This handkerchief is not clean; put it in the wash-hand basin and wash it. Do you prefer to wear boots or shoes? That all depends upon what I am doing; when I am at home with nothing to do I wear shoes, but when I go to the yamên I am obliged to wear boots.

8 你那一雙皮靴子這麽些日子老在那兒擱著、得刷一刷罷。不錯、你給刷罷。

8. Those leather boots of yours which have been lying by all this time, ought to be brushed, surely. You are quite right; suppose you brush them for me.

9 你洗手是愛使涼水是愛使開水。兩樣兒都不好、涼水太涼開水太熱。最好的就是溫和水兒。

9. Do you prefer cold water or boiling water to wash your hands in? Both are bad; cold water is too cold, boiling water is too hot. Warm water is the best.

10 你快把這水倒在鍋裏溫一溫罷。那火要滅了。這水溫了半天老開不了。

10. Be quick and pour this water into the pan and warm it. The fire is going out. The water has been on a long while and will not boil.

*Turn the following into Chinese.* (Key, Exercise XI.)

1. Your mother tells me you did not get up very early to-day.

*Obs.* 1.—Your mother, 老太太: *lit.*, the old lady or dame. *T'ai-t'ai* is a term of respect applied to the wives of officials and aged women; it is of comparatively modern origin, but nothing seems to be known about its derivation.

*Obs.* 2.—*Shuo*, to speak, generally follows *kao-su* when the latter is in the past tense.

2. Quite true; I was dining out yesterday evening, and came back late. The roads were really in a bad state, and, not to speak of my boots and clothes, which were all dirtied, my face even was not fit to be seen for grime. When I got home I called for warm water to wash it, and, taking off my clothes and boots, I saw at once that my stockings were in holes

and would have to be mended. I ordered the servants (men) to bring me a pair of shoes, and to put them on the stove of the *k'ang*, and had a change of clean clothes all over. *Ai ya!* when these boots of mine get wet with rain they are not easy to take off; in my opinion it is better to wear shoes. After I had taken a cup of tea I felt better (*lit.*, in the heart then good a little). But the way the rain came down in the night was enough to frighten one. Did you go out, too?

*Obs.* 1.—Get wet: *chao*$^{2}$ *yü*$^{3}$. *See* **45**.

*Obs.* 2.—In my opinion: *lit.*, in my saying. *See* **28**.

3. I had on a suit of good clothes which I did not want to get spoilt, [so] I did not cross (go out of) the door.

4. Please have some tea. Don't let us talk about this.

5. Is this water for the tea boiling?

6. The water has been on the fire for ever so long (half the day); of course it is boiling.

*Obs.*—Of course: *k'o pu shih*. *See* **124**.

**297.** 儘 *chin*$^{3}$, to the greatest extent; prefixed adverbially.

**298.** 摘 *chai*$^{1}$, to pluck off, as fruit, etc. (but not flowers).

**299.** 戴 *tai*$^{4}$, to wear on the head.

**300.** 撢 *tan*$^{3}$, to tap; to dust. With *tzŭ*, a duster.

**301.** 帽 *mao*$^{4}$, a cap; generally takes *tzŭ* after it.

**302.** 中 *chung*$^{1}$, middle; midst. Often used with *chien*$^{1}$, a division or space (**47**): as *chung*$^{1}$ *chien*$^{4}$-*'rh*, in the middle; or, the middle. Note the change of tone. It can also be used as a verb, to fulfil or accomplish, as will be seen later. Read *chung*$^{4}$, to pass an examination.

**303.** Examples:—

| | | | | | | |
|---|---|---|---|---|---|---|
| 了。*liao* | 帽 *mao*$^{4}$ | 帽 *mao*$^{4}$ | 土。*t'u*$^{3}$ | 帽 *mao*$^{4}$ | 中 *chung*$^{1}$ | 儘 *chin*$^{3}$ |
| | 子 *tzŭ* | 子 *tzŭ* | 你 *ni*$^{3}$ | 子。*tzŭ* | 間 *chien*$^{4}$ | 裏 *li*$^{3}$ |
| | 叫 *chiao*$^{4}$ | 摘 *chai*$^{1}$ | 一 *i*$^{2}$ | 拏 *na*$^{2}$ | 兒。*'rh* | 頭。*t'ou*$^{2}$ |
| | 風 *fêng*$^{1}$ | 下 *hsia*$^{4}$ | 進 *chin*$^{4}$ | 撢 *tan*$^{3}$ | 戴 *tai*$^{4}$ | 儘 *chin*$^{3}$ |
| | 颳 *kua*$^{1}$ | 來。*lai*$^{2}$ | 屋 *wu*$^{1}$ | 子 *tzŭ* | 帽 *mao*$^{4}$ | 前 *ch'ien*$^{2}$ |
| | 下 *hsia*$^{4}$ | 我 *wo*$^{3}$ | 裏 *li*$^{3}$ | 撢 *tan*$^{3}$ | 子。*tzŭ* | 頭。*t'ou*$^{2}$ |
| | 去 *ch'ü*$^{4}$ | 的 *ti* | 把 *pa*$^{3}$ | 撢 *tan*$^{3}$ | 摘 *chai*$^{1}$ | 正 *chêng*$^{4}$ |

At the very inside. At the very front. Right in the middle.
To wear a cap. To take off the cap.
Tap the dust off with a duster.
The moment you enter a room take your hat off.
My cap was blown off by the wind.

*Obs.*—Note the use of *chiao*, to call or cause, as an auxiliary, by means of which *kua*, to blow, becomes passive. There are other verbs which perform the same function, but of these more hereafter. *See* **56**.

**304.** 砍, 坎, *k'an*$^{3}$, to chop; to strike with a sword or like weapon (not with a stick, a spear, the hand, etc.). The second is the correct form, but the first is often used.

305. 肩 *chien*$^1$, shoulders; when linked with the foregoing, it means a waistcoat, *q.d.*, a garment that divides, or lies between, the shoulders.

306. 汗 *han*$^4$, sweat.

307. 衫 *shan*$^1$, a shirt; a shift. Generally used with the preceding.

308. 單 *tan*$^1$, single; a term applied to many kinds of documents. It also means only.

309. 夾 *chia*$^2$, double; read *chia*$^1$, to place between two objects. *See* Examples.

310. Examples:—

| | | | | | | |
|---|---|---|---|---|---|---|
| 裡。*li*$^3$ | 單 *tan*$^1$ | 收 *shou*$^1$ | 一 *i*$^4$ | 衣 *i*$^1$ | 汗 *han*$^4$ | 一 *i*$^2$ |
| | 子。*tzŭ* | 單 *tan*$^1$ | 天 *t'ien*$^1$ | 裳。*shang*$^1$ | 衫 *shan*$^1$ | 個 *ko*$^4$ |
| | 把 *pa*$^3$ | 給 *kei*$^3$ | 的 *ti* | 昨 *tso*$^2$ | 兒。*'rh* | 砍 *k'an*$^3$ |
| | 紙 *chih*$^3$ | 他。*t'a*$^1$ | 汗。*han*$^4$ | 天 *t'ien*$^1$ | 單 *tan*$^1$ | 肩 *chien*$^1$ |
| | 夾 *chia*$^1$ | 開 *k'ai*$^1$ | 寫 *hsieh*$^3$ | 我 *wo*$^3$ | 衣 *i*$^1$ | 兒。*'rh* |
| | 在 *tsai*$^4$ | 一 *i*$^2$ | 一 *i*$^2$ | 出 *ch'u*$^1$ | 裳，*shang*$^1$ | 一 *i*$^2$ |
| | 書 *shu*$^1$ | 個 *ko*$^4$ | 個 *ko*$^4$ | 了 *liao* | 夾 *chia*$^2$ | 件 *chien*$^4$ |

A waistcoat. A shirt.
Clothes without lining. Lined clothes.
I perspired all day yesterday.
Write a receipt and give it him.
Make a list.
Place the paper between [the leaves of] the book.

311. 棉 *mien*$^2$, the cotton plant; as *mien*$^2$ *hua*$^1$, raw cotton.

312. 褲 *k'u*$^4$, trousers, of which the numerative is *t'iao*$^2$ (181); it takes *tzŭ* after it.

313. 裁 *ts'ai*$^2$, to cut, as a tailor when shaping clothes; hence, *ts'ai*$^2$-*fêng*$^2$, a tailor, one who cuts and stitches.

*N.B.*—Emphasise *ts'ai*.

314. 褂 *kua*$^4$, an outer coat; as *ma*$^3$ *kua*$^4$-*tzŭ*, or *ma*$^3$ *kua*$^4$-*'rh*, a riding jacket, or short coat.

315. 袖 *hsiu*$^4$, a sleeve; it takes *tzŭ* after it.

316. Examples:—

| | | | | | |
|---|---|---|---|---|---|
| 衣 *i*$^1$ | 褂 *kua*$^4$ | 是 *shih*$^4$ | 褲 *k'u*$^4$ | 褲 *k'u*$^4$ | 棉 *mien*$^2$ |
| 裳。*shang*$^1$ | 子。*tzŭ*$^4$ | 夾 *chia*$^2$ | 子 *tzŭ* | 子。*tzu* | 衣 *i*$^1$ |
| 裁 *ts'ai*$^2$ | 袖 *hsiu*$^4$ | 的。*ti* | 是 *shih*$^4$ | 這 *chê*$^4$ | 裳。*shang*$^1$ |
| 縫。*fêng*$^2$ | 子。*tzŭ* | 一 *i*$^2$ | 單 *tan*$^1$ | 一 *i*$^4$ | 一 *i*$^4$ |
| | 裁 *ts'ai*$^2$ | 件 *chien*$^4$ | 的 *ti* | 條 *t'iao*$^2$ | 條 *t'iao*$^2$ |

Wadded clothes.
A pair of trousers. Is this pair of trousers single or lined?
A coat. Sleeves.
To cut out clothes. A tailor.

## EXERCISE XII.

1 女人們小的時候兒學針線、他們多一半不認得字。帽子是說一頂。裁縫裁衣裳縫衣裳都行。

1. Women in their childhood learn needlework; the majority of them cannot read. The numerative of caps is *ting*³. A tailor can both cut out and make up clothes.

*Obs.*—The majority: *lit.*, the excess half; *ta pan* would be equally correct.

2 你洗澡的時候兒不要把頭髮擱在水裏、頭髮一着水、老乾不了。

2. When you bathe, do not put your hair in the water; when once the hair gets wet, it takes a long time to dry.

*Obs.*—*Chao*², to come in contact with. *See* 45.

3 單衣裳是就有面兒沒有裏兒的、夾衣裳是有裏兒有面兒的。棉衣裳是夾衣裳中間有棉花的。出汗。

3. Clothes *tan*¹ (not lined), are such as have an outside with nothing inside it; clothes, *chia*² (lined), are such as have both a lining and an outside. Wadded garments are *chia*² (lined) with cotton in between. To perspire.

4 砍肩兒是有前後沒有袖子的那一件衣裳。汗衫是儘裏頭穿的單衣裳。

4. A *k'an*³*-chien*¹ is the article of dress which has a back and front and no sleeves. The *han*⁴*-shan*¹ is the garment without lining worn innermost of all.

5 褂子是儘外頭穿的衣裳、短的就叫馬褂子。這一條褲子是棉的是夾的。

5. The *kua*⁴*-tzŭ* is the garment worn outermost of all; when short it is called a *ma*³ *kua*⁴ (or riding jacket). Is this pair of trousers wadded or is it lined?

6 帽子有小帽兒官帽兒兩樣兒、官帽兒也分涼帽暖帽。

6. Caps are distinguished as small caps and official hats; while official hats are of two kinds, the cool (summer) cap and the warm (winter) cap.

語言自邇集



7 你會做針綫不會.我不會.那麼着我就叫一個裁縫來把我那一件汗ˋ衫補了.

7. Do you know how to sew? I do not. In that case I will call a tailor here to mend (patch) my shirt.

8 那一件砍肩兒裁了還沒縫呢.那一件破馬褂子得'補了.拏撣子撣一撣衣裳上的土.

8. The waistcoat is cut out but not put together yet. That torn riding coat should be mended. Tap the dust off the clothes with a duster.

9 那一把木梳是誰梳頭的.洗澡是一身都洗.天天兒洗澡很好.

9. Who is it that combs his hair with that (or the) wooden comb? The expression *hsi*[3]-*tsao*[3] means to bathe the whole body. It is a good thing to bathe every day.

*Obs.*—*Shu t'ou*, to comb the hair; *fa* can be omitted.

10 你老先生頭髮短得很、頂兒上也就沒有了.我有五十多了、是沒頭髮的時、候兒了.

10. Your hair, sir, is very short, and you have already become bald on the top of your head. I am more than fifty; it is time for one to lose one's hair.

*Obs.* 1.—Sir: *lit.*, old elder born; a polite term of address to an elderly person.

*Obs.* 2.—Note *ting*[3], the crown of the head; *t'ou* being understood. *See* 72.

*Obs.* 3.—More than fifty; it would be better to add the character *sui*[4] (952), but it has been omitted as it has not yet been introduced.

11 今年棉花多不多.少是不少、可沒有去年那麼多.

11. Is raw cotton plentiful this year? It is not, so to speak, scarce, but it is not so abundant as it was last year.

*Turn the following into Chinese.* (KEY, EXERCISE XII.)

1. The tailor has come.
2. Tell him to come in.
3. What clothes do you want made, sir?

*Obs.*—*Nin*[2] (您) is a polite form of the personal pronoun *ni*[3]. *See* 648.

4. Coats, trousers, and waistcoats; and, besides, I want you to make those what-do-you-call-'ems that one wears next the skin.

*Obs.*—What-do-you-call-'em: *lit.*, that what (with the possessive appended).

5. You mean under-shirts, don't you, sir?

*Obs.*—Under-shirts: *lit.*, little coats.

6. That's it; and I want a good many shirts too.

7. Do you want that coat wadded, sir, or lined?

8. I don't want it either way; the weather is too hot. If you make a single one that will do.

9. In what style are the sleeves to be made?

10. I want them a little longer than this [coat] of mine.

*Obs.*—Longer: *lit.*, compared with (Radical 81) this one, etc., long.

11. Be a little careful about these clothes; I want them all cut to [the shape of] my body, so that when worn they may have a style about them. And, I must tell you, I don't want them to wear out as soon as they are put on.

*Obs.* 1.—Cut to the shape of: *lit.*, comparing body cut.

*Obs.* 2.—Have a style: *lit.*, have kind or fashion (*yang*$^{4}$).

12. If you brush your clothes clean every evening, sir, they will not spoil for a long time.

13. In how many days will these clothes be ready?

14. I am very good at needlework; they will not be many days before they are ready.

15. This tailor is so dirty he isn't [fit] to be seen; he looks somewhat as if he had not used soap for a long time; his hair, too, is not combed.

*Obs.*—Dirty: *tsang* is often used without *ang*.

16. Possibly because he has not got a comb.

**317.** 金 *chin*$^{1}$ (Radical 167), metal, especially gold; gold is also termed *huang*$^{2}$ *chin*$^{1}$ (Radical 201), the yellow metal.

**318.** 銀 *yin*$^{2}$, silver.

**319.** 銅 *t'ung*$^{2}$, copper.

**320.** 鐵 *t'ieh*$^{3}$, iron.

**321.** 錢 *ch'ien*$^{2}$, coin, especially cash.

**322.** 吊 *tiao*$^{4}$, in Peking, a 500-cash note; elsewhere, a string of 1,000 copper cash. Also to hang or suspend.

**323.** 票 *p'iao*$^{4}$, a printed note or written order for money; also, a police warrant.

**324.** Examples:—

| | | | | | | |
|---|---|---|---|---|---|---|
| 是 *shih*$^{4}$ | 是 *shih*$^{4}$ | 我 *wo*$^{3}$ | 百 *pai*$^{3}$ | 銀 *yin*$^{2}$ | 子。*tzŭ* | 三 *san*$^{1}$ |
| 鐵 *t'ieh*$^{3}$ | 銅 *t'ung*$^{2}$ | 分 *fên*$^{1}$ | 個 *ko*$^{4}$ | 子 *tzŭ* | 三 *san*$^{1}$ | 十 *shih*$^{2}$ |
| 做 *tso*$^{4}$ | 做 *tso*$^{4}$ | 不 *pu*$^{4}$ | 錢 *ch'ien*$^{2}$ | 的 *ti* | 吊 *tiao*$^{4}$ | 兩 *liang*$^{3}$ |
| 的。*ti* | 的 *ti* | 出 *ch'u*$^{1}$ | 兒 *'rh* | 票。*p'iao*$^{4}$ | 錢。*ch'ien*$^{2}$ | 銀 *yin*$^{2}$ |
| | 那 *na*$^{3}$ | 那 *na*$^{3}$ | 裏 *li*$^{3}$ | 這 *chê*$^{4}$ | 三 *san*$^{1}$ | 子。*tzŭ* |
| | 個 *ko*$^{4}$ | 個 *ko*$^{4}$ | 頭 *t'ou*$^{2}$ | 一 *i*$^{4}$ | 兩 *liang*$^{3}$ | 金 *chin*$^{1}$ |

Thirty taels.

*Obs.*—*Liang*, two, is a measure of weight, commonly called a tael; 10 *liang* go to the *chin* or catty.

Gold.

Three *tiao* (elsewhere than in Peking, 3,000, or three strings of, cash).

A bank-note for three taels.

*Obs.*—In Peking, notes for silver are called *p'iao*, and notes for cash are called *p'iao-tzŭ*.

Amongst these hundred cash I cannot distinguish which are made of copper and which of iron.

325. 桿 *kan3*, properly, any straight pole or rod of wood; the numerative of spears, muskets, etc.

326. 秤 *ch'êng4*, a balance; a weighing beam. Scales are called 天平 *(t'ien1-p'ing2)*; a small steelyard has another name.

327. 稱 *ch'êng1*, to weigh; hence, to esteem. In certain combinations, to speak of; to designate; to speak. *Ch'êng1* is to weigh with a *ch'êng4*; *p'ing2 i p'ing2* is to weigh with a *t'ien1-p'ing2*. There is another term for weighing with a steelyard.

328. Examples:—

| | | | | | | |
|---|---|---|---|---|---|---|
| 麼 *mo* | 小、*hsiao3* | 這 *chê4* | 天 *t'ien1* | 麼、*mo* | 桿 *kan3* | 稱 *ch'êng1* |
| 多 *to1* | 稱 *ch'êng1* | 一 *i4* | 買 *mai3* | 稱 *ch'êng1* | 秤 *ch'êng4* | 東 *tung1* |
| 的 *ti* | 不 *pu4* | 桿 *kan3* | 來 *lai2* | 一 *i4* | 來。*lai2* | 西、*hsi1* |
| 米。*mi3* | 了 *liao3* | 秤 *ch'êng4* | 的 *ti* | 稱 *ch'êng1* | 做 *tso4* | 拏 *na2* |
| | 那 *na4* | 太 *t'ai4* | 米。*mi3* | 昨 *tso2* | 甚 *shên2* | 一 *i4* |

To weigh things.

*Obs.*—*Yao1 i yao1* (566) is also permissible and perhaps more popular.

Bring me a balance. What for? To weigh the rice we bought yesterday.

This balance is too small; it will not weigh so much rice as that.

329. 價 *chia4*, price; value.

330. 值 *chih2*, to be worth. As *chia4-chih2*, the price anything is worth or is valued at *chia4-ch'ien2* (321) is more common.

331. 貴 *kuei4*, dear; valuable; honourable; esteemed.

332. 賤 *chien4*, cheap.

333. 便 *p'ien2*, a popular pronunciation of *pien4*, convenient. Read *p'ien2* only when followed by *i2*; *see* below. *Fang1-pien4* (Radical 70), convenient; handy.

334. 宜 *i2*, to be befitting; morally, essential. As *p'ien2-i2*, cheap; advantageous; advantage.

335. 輕 *ch'ing1*, light.

336. 重 *chung4*, heavy. Read *ch'ung2*, to repeat; twice over (*see* Part IV, Dialogue IX, 29).

337. Examples:—

| | | | | | | |
|---|---|---|---|---|---|---|
| 不 *pu4* | 賤 *chien4* | 個 *ko4* | 木 *mu4* | 便 *p'ien2* | 兩 *liang3* | 這 *chê4* |
| 值 *chih2* | 得 *tê* | 銅 *t'ung2* | 頭 *t'ou2* | 宜。*i2* | 銀 *yin2* | 一 *i4* |
| 錢。*ch'ien2* | 很。*hên3* | 壺 *hu2* | 是 *shih4* | 鐵 *t'ieh3* | 子。*tzŭ* | 匹 *p'i1* |
| | 酒 *chiu3* | 的 *ti* | 輕 *ch'ing1* | 是 *shih4* | 不 *pu2* | 馬 *ma3* |
| | 瓶 *p'ing2* | 價 *chia4* | 的。*ti* | 重 *chung4* | 貴 *kuei4* | 值 *chih2* |
| | 子 *tzŭ* | 錢 *ch'ien2* | 那 *na4* | 的 *ti* | 很 *hên3* | 幾 *chi3* |

How many taels is this horse worth? It is not dear; it is very cheap.

Iron is heavy; wood is light.

That copper kettle is very cheap.

Wine bottles are valueless.

*Obs.*—*Pu chih ch'ien* may also mean to cost a trifle.

**338.** 借 *chieh*$^{4}$, to lend ; to borrow.

**339.** 賬 *chang*$^{4}$, a bill ; an account. This is a corrupt form of *chang*$^{4}$ (**146**) ; it is not recognised by the dictionaries, but is so universally used that it demands notice.

**340.** 該 *kai*$^{1}$, to owe anything ; morally, to owe duty ; ought. Often combined with *tang*$^{1}$ (**342**).

**341.** 費 *fei*$^{4}$, to expend money, pains, etc.

**342.** 當 *tang*$^{4}$, to represent ; to stand for. *Tang*$^{1}$, to act as ; suitable ; proper ; that which ought to be done. *Tang*$^{4}$, to pawn or pledge. *Tang*$^{1}$ or *tang*$^{4}$, an adverb of time.

**343.** 於 *yü*$^{2}$, in ; in the case or matter of ; proceeding out of. Used only in certain combinations.

**344.** 好 *hao*$^{4}$, to like much ; to be fond of. To be distinguished from *hao*$^{3}$, good.

**345.** Examples :—

| | | | | | | |
|---|---|---|---|---|---|---|
| 當 *tang*$^{4}$ | 做。*tso*$^{4}$ | 他 *t'a*$^{1}$ | 錢。*ch'ien*$^{2}$ | 他 *t'a*$^{1}$ | 這 *chê*$^{4}$ | 我 *wo*$^{3}$ |
| 天 *t'ien*$^{1}$ | 是 *shih*$^{4}$ | 好 *hao*$^{4}$ | 費 *fei*$^{4}$ | 該 *kai*$^{1}$ | 一 *i*$^{4}$ | 的 *ti* |
| 兒 *'rh* | 他 *t'a*$^{1}$ | 看 *k'an*$^{4}$ | 心 *hsin*$^{1}$ | 了 *liao* | 本 *pên*$^{3}$ | 錢 *ch'ien*$^{2}$ |
| 去 *ch'ü*$^{4}$ | 該 *kai*$^{1}$ | 書。*shu*$^{1}$ | 費 *fei*$^{4}$ | 好 *hao*$^{3}$ | 書 *shu*$^{1}$ | 都 *tou*$^{1}$ |
| 的。*ti* | 當 *tang*$^{1}$ | 這 *chê*$^{4}$ | 心。*hsin*$^{1}$ | 多 *to*$^{1}$ | 是 *shih*$^{4}$ | 借 *chieh*$^{4}$ |
| 他 *t'a*$^{1}$ | 做 *tso*$^{4}$ | 件 *chien*$^{4}$ | 當 *tang*$^{4}$ | 帳。*chang*$^{4}$ | 借 *chieh*$^{4}$ | 出 *ch'u*$^{1}$ |
| 當 *tang*$^{1}$ | 的。*ti* | 事 *shih*$^{4}$ | 鋪。*p'u*$^{4}$ | 過 *kuo*$^{4}$ | 了 *liao* | 去 *ch'ü*$^{4}$ |
| 廚 *ch'u*$^{2}$ | 我 *wo*$^{3}$ | 該 *kai*$^{1}$ | 當 *tang*$^{4}$ | 於 *yü*$^{2}$ | 來 *lai*$^{2}$ | 了。*liao* |
| 子。*tzŭ* | 是 *shih*$^{4}$ | 誰 *shui*$^{2}$ | 票。*p'iao*$^{4}$ | 費 *fei*$^{4}$ | 的。*ti* | 他 *t'a*$^{1}$ |

My money is all lent out.

This book of his is borrowed.

He owes a great many debts.

To spend too much money.

Much obliged to you.

*Obs.*—The expression is generally confined to thanks for favours which entail the exercise of mind rather than of body (*lit.*, I have spent your heart ; or, you have expended your mind or brain on me). The heart, according to the Chinese theory, is the seat of the intellect.

A pawnshop. A pawn-ticket.

He is very fond of reading.

Who ought to undertake this affair ? It is he that ought to do it.

I went on the same day (*q.d.*, the day on which it happened).

He acts as cook.

*Obs.*—*Tang* here implies either that his previous occupation was something different, or that cooking is only one of other crafts with which he is acquainted.

## EXERCISE XIII.

1 賬目。花錢。花費。四吊錢的票子。不知道那個東西的輕重、得拏秤稱一稱。

1. Accounts. To spend money (184). Expenses; expenditure. A four-*tiao* note. You must weigh it in the balance if you do not know its weight.

*Obs.*—The word *chang*⁴, as already explained, is not authorised by the native dictionaries; it is, however, a very common substitute for the correct form (146), and means, says a teacher, a memorandum of expenditure. *Mu*, the eye, combined with *chang* has something of the force of our word *heads*, in a discourse; sections, or other subdivisions.

2 他欠人的賬目不少。他該的賬、不下一千兩銀子。他還不了那麽些個罷。

2. He owes different people a great deal of money. He has bills outstanding to the extent of at least (not below) one thousand taels. I don't suppose he can pay that amount.

3 我借錢、是我把人家的錢拏來我使。我借給人錢、是把我的錢拏給人使。

3. The expression *wo*³ *chieh*⁴ *ch'ien*² means that I am getting money of people for my use. *Wo*³ *chieh*⁴ *kei*³ *jên*² *ch'ien*² means that I am letting another have my money for his use.

*Obs.* 1.—The expression: *lit.*, [the words] *wo chieh ch'ien* are=mean [that] I holding people's money bring it [to me] for my own use. *Chieh kei jên ch'ien* means [that I] holding my money take it [to people] for people's use.

*Obs.* 2.—People: *jên-chia*. The *chia* generalises *jên*, and has something of the force of our word *kind*, though *jên-chia* cannot bear so wide a meaning as mankind; *folks* would be a nearer rendering.

4 我們家裡天天兒的花費不很多。他愛花錢、好花錢、都說得。他那個人過於花錢。他的本錢快完了罷。

4. Our daily domestic expenditure is not large. It is equally correct to say *t'a ai*⁴ (he loves to spend) or *hao*⁴ (is fond of spending) money. That man spends too much; his capital must be nearly at an end.

*Obs.* 1.—Too much: *lit.*, is excessive, or exceeds, *yü*, in the matter of, spending money.

*Obs.* 2.—Capital or principal: *lit.*, root or stock of money.

5 那個房子價錢不貴。這一件皮掛子價值很便宜。那個花瓶不值錢。今年的棉花很賤。他家裏一個大錢都沒有。

5. That is not a dear house. The price asked (or paid) for this fur cloak is very small. That flower-vase is worth nothing. Cotton is very low this year. He has not got a cash to live on.

*Obs.*—Not a cash: *lit.*, he in his house one large cash even has not got. This might mean equally that his family were all in as great distress; but were it an object to isolate the individual, *shou*$^3$ *li*$^3$, in his hand, might be used instead of *chia li*.

6 那當十的大錢裏頭、有七分是銅的有三分是鐵的。黃金比銀子重、鐵比銀子輕。

6. Seven-tenths of those ten-cash pieces are copper, and three-tenths iron. Gold is heavier than silver; iron is lighter than silver.

*Obs.*—Ten-cash pieces: *lit.*, representing ten's large cash (342). The second *ti* is simplest construed as *ones*; *q.d.*, there are seven-tenths being copper ones, there are three-tenths being iron ones. Were it meant that each cash contained seven-tenths copper to three-tenths iron, the text might be variously modified: you might omit the *li-t'ou*, and then proceed, *tou shih ch'i fên t'ung san fên t'ieh*; or, retaining the *li-t'ou*, proceed, *yu ch'i fên t'ung san fên t'ieh*.

7 票子是一張紙上頭寫著錢數兒、買東西同銀子錢一個樣兒。那掛子他當了十吊錢的票子。

7. A *p'iao*$^4$*-tzŭ* is a paper note on which is written the number of cash it is worth; for buying things it is the same as coin. He has pawned that coat for notes to the value of ten *tiao* (or, for a ten-*tiao* note).

*Obs.*—A paper note: *lit.*, a *p'iao-tzŭ* is a strip of paper upon [which one] writes a number (or amount) of cash; [in] buying things [it is] with money [of] one and the same fashion. Instead of *i ko yang-'rh*, you may read *shih i ko yang*.

8 那花瓶兒他賣不賣。賣他是一定賣、你要、可得‘花倆錢兒、他不是賤買的。

8. Will he sell that flower-vase? He is sure to sell, but if you want it you will have to pay pretty well for it; he didn't buy it cheap.

*Obs.* 1.—*Hua lia chien-'rh*: *lit.*, spend a couple of cash; a Pekingese expression for putting one's hand in one's pocket.

*Obs.* 2.—*Ti* here stands for *tê*.

9 該當花錢的時候兒、誰怕花個一二兩、你這個人一開口、就是十兩八兩的話。

9. No one minds spending a tael or two when they have (or ought) to be spent, but it's nine or ten taels with you directly you open your mouth (you are too large in your ideas altogether).

*Obs.*—Ought: note the use of the two verbs with a similar meaning. *Kai* alone would be equally correct, but perhaps slightly less forcible; *tang* could also be used alone.

*Turn the following into Chinese.* (KEY, EXERCISE XIII.)

…s k'ou wai means … the Great Wall at … Kou or Cheng … (… kou) … the Great Wall … Shan hai kuan is … kuan … 4)

1. I am thinking of going beyond the frontier, [where] I hear that notes are not handy (*lit.*, not good to use)—silver being more convenient to use—and that one will want some small copper cash too.

*Obs.* 1.—Am thinking: where this is used in the sense of proposing to carry out a project, the word *suan*, to reckon, is commonly employed, preceded by the auxiliary *ta*³ (241).

*Obs.* 2.—The frontier: *k'ou* (Radical 30), a mouth or pass; *k'ou wai*, outside a pass or gateway on the Chinese frontier. In Peking, *k'ou wai* is understood to mean the region beyond the Great Wall.

2. You will certainly want some; but the cash they use [there] is not, I fancy, the cash used in the capital.

3. Quite right; the cash used in the capital are large cash, each representing ten [small ones]. When one gets beyond the frontier, changing silver gives a deal of trouble. Not only (*lit.*, there's no use saying) does the price of silver vary, but its amount when weighed varies too (*lit.*, the large and small of the *p'ing*, or scale, is also not the same).

4. I have heard that when one goes beyond the barrier living is much cheaper.

*Obs.* 1.—A barrier (63).

*Obs.* 2.—Living: *lit.*, fire and food (Radical 184).

5. Living is cheap, certainly; but if you reckon up the cart hire (*lit.*, money) and inn (*lit.*, house) money, expenses are by no means small. When you get back I fear you will owe many bills.

*Obs.*—If: *yao shih*, if it be that; *yao* (32) being corruptly used for another word, *jo*⁴ if, which will be met with later.

6. If I owe bills they must certainly be paid. If I cannot pay them I shall just ask you to lend me a little money.

*Obs.*—I shall just, etc.: *lit.*, [I will] request you to lend to me a little money, *chiu shih liao*, and that's all.

7. So you are thinking of borrowing again, eh? you owed me long ago a good many taels which you have not paid me back all this time; another loan would be a little too much, surely.

*Obs.* 1.—You owed: *lit.*, were short [to] me.

*Obs.* 2.—Too much: *t'ai kuo yü i tien'rh*, a little too excessive.

8. Well, well; let's say no more about it. What is the exchange for silver to-day?

*Obs.* 1.—Well, well, etc.: *lit.*, that then ended, *na chiu pa liao*.

*Obs.* 2.—Exchange: *lit.*, how many cash does silver (*i.e.*, the ounce of silver) change for?

9. To-day the tael changes for over seventeen *tiao*.

10. In that case weigh [out] for me twenty taels.

*Obs.*—Weigh: *p'ing* (327).

11. Here they are, weighed; take them. A prosperous journey to you.

*Obs.*—Prosperous journey: *lit.*, you on this road a great great, tranquility tranquility one. The reduplication is merely employed for the sake of euphony.

346. 煤 *mei*2, coal.

347. 炭 *t'an*4, charcoal.

348. 柴 *ch'ai*2, fuel; when used with *huo*3, fire, it means straw or reed fuel, shavings, etc.

349. 論 *lun*4, to discuss. As *pu*2 *lun*4, never mind; no matter.

350. 石 *tan*4, a corrupt form of *shih*2, stone (Radical 112); 100 catties are ordinarily called a *tan*4 or picul.

351. Examples :—

| | | | | | | |
|---|---|---|---|---|---|---|
| 少。*shao*3 | 賣 *mai*4 | 的。*ti* | 炭 *t'an*4 | 山 *shan*1 | 一 *i*2 | 煤 *mei*2 |
| 不 *pu*2 | 的。*ti* | 米 *mi*3 | 是 *shih*4 | 裡。*li*3 | 塊 *k'uai*4 | 炭 *t'an*4 |
| 論 *lun*4 | 不 *pu*2 | 是 *shih*4 | 過 *kuo*4 | 柴 *ch'ai*2 | 兒。*'rh* | 出 *ch'u*1 |
| 輕 *ch'ing*1 | 論 *lun*4 | 論 *lun*4 | 秤 *ch'êng*4 | 火。*huo*3 | 出 *ch'u*1 | 在 *tsai*4 |
| 重,*chung*4 | 多 *to*1 | 石 *tan*4 | 賣 *mai*4 | 煤 *mei*2 | 在 *tsai*4 | 那 *na*3 |

Where do coal and charcoal come from? From the hills.

*Obs.—Lit.*, coal, charcoal come out in what one piece, bit, or spot. *Na*3 *'rh* would be equally correct, but not perhaps so definite. Note *na i k'uai-'rh* pronounced *na*3 *k'uêrh*.

Fuel.

Coal and charcoal are sold by weight.

*Obs.—Lit.*, passing the beam sold.

Rice is sold by the picul.

*Obs.—Lit.*, reckoning the picul sold.

No matter whether many or few. No matter whether light or heavy.

352. 麪 *mien*4, flour.

353. 油 *yu*2, oil.

354. 芝 *chih*1, properly, the plant of immortality; used with *ma*2, the following character, it means sesame, and is pronounced *chih*1-*ma*2, the *chih*1 being emphasised.

355. 麻 *ma*2 (Radical 200), hemp.

356. 糖 *t'ang*2, sugar.

357. 鹽 *yen*2, salt.

358. 粗 *ts'u*1, coarse.

359. 細 *hsi*4, fine.

360. Examples :—

| | | | | | | |
|---|---|---|---|---|---|---|
| 細,*hsi*4 | 麻 *ma*2 | 糖 *t'ang*2 | 你 *ni*3 | 的 *ti* | 麪。*mien*4 | 菜 *ts'ai*4 |
| | 線 *hsien*4 | 是 *shih*4 | 們 *mên*1 | 鹽 *yen*2 | 我 *wo*3 | 油。*yu*2 |
| | 粗 *ts'u*1 | 好 *hao*3 | 的 *ti* | 粗,*ts'u*1 | 們 *mên*1 | 芝 *chih*1 |
| | 棉 *mien*2 | 吃 *ch'ih*1 | 細,*hsi*4 | 沒 *mei*2 | 這 *chê*4 | 麻。*ma* |
| | 線 *hsien*4 | 的,*ti* | 白 *pai*2 | 有 *yu*3 | 兒 *'rh* | 乾 *kan*1 |

Vegetable oil, made from the seeds of certain vegetables. It is also used to denote foreign salad oil.

Sesame. Flour.

*Obs.*—Note that *mien* used alone colloquially often means vermicelli.

Our salt here is coarse, not so fine as yours.

White sugar is nice to eat.

Twine is coarse; cotton thread is fine. *Ma*$^2$ *hsien*$^4$ is cobbler's thread. *Ma*$^2$ *shêng*$^2$-*'rh* is twine.

**361.** 湯 *t'ang*$^1$, broth.

**362.** 鷄 *chi*$^1$, chicken; as *chi*$^1$-*tzŭ*$^3$ *'rh*, fowls' eggs.

*N.B.*—Emphasise *tzŭ*.

**363.** 奶 *nai*$^3$, milk.

**364.** 果 *kuo*$^3$, fruit. Also, in certain combinations, a strong affirmative; certainly; if indeed.

**365.** 饅 *man*$^2$, a dumpling. Commonly used with *t'ou*$^2$, a head; as *man*$^2$-*t'ou*, Chinese bread, or steamed dumplings. Foreign bread is generally called *mien*$^4$-*pao*$^1$, flour balls, or rolls. The term *man*$^2$-*t'ou* has its origin in an incident in Chinese history, a certain general having caused paste effigies to be substituted for the human heads it was customary to offer as a propitiatory sacrifice when crossing a river in the country of the southern savages, in which he was operating.

**366.** 熟 *shu*$^2$, ripe; cooked. Hence, accustomed; familiar. Vulgarly, *shou*$^2$.

**367.** 端 *tuan*$^1$, in combination, morally upright; to place properly.

**368.** 撤 *ch'ê*$^4$, to remove.

**369.** Examples:—

| | | | | | | |
|---|---|---|---|---|---|---|
| 子。*tzŭ* | 個 *ko*$^4$ | 果 *kuo*$^3$ | 麼 *mo* | 也 *yeh*$^3$ | 了 *liao* | 鷄 *chi*$^1$ |
| 糖 *t'ang*$^2$ | 來。*lai*$^2$ | 子 *tzŭ* | 的 *ti* | 可 *k'o*$^3$ | 端 *tuan*$^1$ | 湯。*t'ang*$^1$ |
| 果 *kuo*$^3$ | 水 *shui*$^3$ | 熟 *shou*$^2$ | 都 *tou*$^1$ | 以 *i*$^3$ | 進 *chin*$^4$ | 山 *shan*$^1$ |
| 子。*tzŭ* | 果 *kuo*$^3$ | 了 *liao* | 撤 *ch'ê*$^4$ | 說。*shuo*$^1$ | 來。*lai*$^2$ | 羊 *yang*$^2$ |
| | 子。*tzŭ* | 摘 *chai*$^1$ | 下 *hsia*$^4$ | 這 *chê*$^4$ | 開 *k'ai*$^1$ | 奶。*nai*$^3$ |
| | 乾 *kan*$^1$ | 下 *hsia*$^4$ | 去。*ch'ü*$^4$ | 書 *shu*$^1$ | 飯 *fan*$^4$ | 飯 *fan*$^4$ |
| | 果 *kuo*$^3$ | 幾 *chi*$^3$ | 那 *na*$^4$ | 甚 *shên*$^2$ | 來 *lai*$^2$ | 好 *hao*$^3$ |

Chicken soup. Goat's milk.

When the food is ready, serve *(tuan)* it up. You can also say *k'ai* (serve it up).

*Obs.*—*Tuan fan* is, strictly speaking, to "serve up," and *k'ai fan* to "dish up." In the second sentence, *lai* implies the act of bringing to the table as well.

Take away these books and things.

*Obs.*—And things: *lit.*, and what ones.

That fruit is ripe; pluck some.

*Obs.*—*Chai*$^1$, to pluck (298).

Fresh fruit. Dry fruit. Jam.

*Obs.*—In Peking the term *shui kuo* is applied only to plums.

10

## EXERCISE XIV.

1 雞子兒.牛奶.燈油.香油.這菜弄得吃不得、快撤了去罷.燈油是豆子做的、香油是芝蔴做的.火油出在地裏.

1. Fowls' eggs. Cows' milk. Lamp oil. Sweet oil. The food is cooked [so badly] that it is uneatable; take it away at once. Lamp oil is made from the bean; sweet oil from sesame; mineral oils come out of the ground.

2 我昨兒買了三百斤煤,五十斤炭,八十斤柴火,四石米二百斤麪.天冷的時候兒煤炭用的多.

2. I bought yesterday three hundred catties of coal, fifty catties of charcoal, eighty catties of fuel, four piculs of rice, and two hundred catties of flour. When the weather is cold the consumption of coal and charcoal is larger.

3 炕爐子是燒煤的多、火盆是用炭.火盆是屋裏用的、不是做飯做水的。

3. Most stoves of stove-beds burn coal; in a chafing-dish one uses charcoal. A chafing-dish is for use in a room; it is not meant [for] cooking food or heating water with.

4 菜有生的有熟的、在火上做的都是熟菜、生菜在地下長出來就可以吃得.

4. Things to be eaten are either *shêng*[1] (raw) or *shou*[2] (cooked); all that are prepared over a fire are *shou*[2] (cooked); the *shêng*[1] *ts'ai*[4] are vegetables that may be eaten in their natural state.

*Obs.*—Natural state: *lit.*, the *shêng ts'ai* are [these; such as] growing out of the ground [man] thereon (or immediately) can eat. In Peking the term *shêng ts'ai* is confined to such vegetables as are never cooked.

5 你去給我買一個小雞子三四個雞子兒.還要牛奶不要.牛奶便宜、我就要幾斤.我們這兒買牛奶不論斤數兒、都是論碗論瓶.

5. You go and buy me a chicken and three or four eggs. Do you want any milk as well? I should like a few catties of milk if it is cheap. In this part of the world we do not buy milk by the catty, but by the cup or bottle.

*Obs.*—Milk by the catty: *lit.*, you do not consider (or reckon) the catties' number.

6 買果子是論箇兒的多。你快弄飯去、飯得了就端上來。

6. Fruit is generally bought by the piece. Go and get the food ready directly, and as soon as it is ready put it on the table.

*Obs.*—Food ready: *tê*, having achieved that which is in course of preparation. The expression *tê liao* is used of several other operations completed.

7 你愛吃饅頭愛吃飯。兩樣兒都不愛、我愛喝湯、愛喝什麼湯呢。肉湯雞湯都好、

7. Do you prefer bread or rice? Neither; I like broth. What kind of broth? Either meat soup or chicken broth suits me.

*Obs.*—Prefer: *ai* might also be rendered, what are you in the *habit* of eating?

8 我明天要請人吃飯、給他們什麼菜好。不論甚麼菜都可以、他們都是偺們本家的人。

8. I want to ask some people to dinner to-morrow; what had I better give them to eat? Anything will do for them; they are all our own immediate belongings (*lit.*, people of our own family stock).

*Obs.*—*Pên chia* is only used of blood relations.

*Turn the following into Chinese.* (KEY, EXERCISE XIV.)

1. This year I have spent no little money on coal and fuel. The price of coal keeps getting dearer every day, and, besides, there is not much "kindling" in the market (*lit.*, produced, *ch'u*[1]); my monthly expenditure must be at the very least thirteen dollars.

*Obs.* 1.—I have spent, etc.: *lit.*, my this year's coal fire money spent not little. *Hao*, short for *ch'ai hao*.

*Obs.* 2.—Note *yu* (Radical 29), also, besides.

*Obs.* 3.—At the very least: *chih*[4] *shao*[3] (Radical 133).

2. That is because you burn the best coal, which all comes from beyond the frontier. I burn charcoal, which is much cheaper; it can be used in the kitchen too.

*Obs.*—Much cheaper: *chien to cho ni*. It is difficult to explain the use of *cho* in this connexion; it appears to act as an intensive, and is said by the teachers to be a corruption of *cho shih*[2], in very truth, an expression that will be met with later. *See* Note on *cho* at the close of Exercise XL.

3. I hear your cook cooks by no means badly.

*Obs.*—By no means badly: *lit.*, on the reverse (*tao*[4], 182) not wrong. This use of *tao* is perhaps a colloquialism peculiar to Peking, but, like many idiomatic expressions of a similar nature, it is considered by northerners as indispensable to fluency of diction; it would not be incorrect to omit the *tao*, but the sentence would have an unfinished sound. It is the judicious use of these little auxiliaries that just makes the difference between a fluent and an awkward speaker.

4. Yes, he does; the soup and butter puddings he makes are very good indeed. Suppose you dine here at my place to-day. Here (*to the servant*)! Bring the [dinner] things. Tell the cook to make a chicken salad (*lit.*, raw vegetable chicken), with a mixture of eggs and sweet oil; tell him to use fine salt, not coarse. I want also every kind

of fruit, and tell him to be careful to buy them ripe.

*Obs.* 1.—Butter puddings: *lit.*, milk oil pudding (*tien*$^{3}$ *hsin*$^{1}$, Exercise IX, Eng., 11, Obs. 1; p. 52).

*Obs.* 2.—With a mixture: *lit.*, using eggs and sweet oil mix (*huo*$^{4}$, 210) together (*i k'uai-'rh*, in one place or piece).

*Obs.* 3.—Ripe: *shou*$^{2}$ *fên*$^{4}$; *lit.*, the ripe distinction one's. This is a localism.

5. This dinner I must say is excellent. Now my cook is no use; he has not the least bit of a turn for cooking.

*Obs.*—A turn for: *pên*$^{3}$ *shih*$^{4}$; *lit.*, root matter. This does not mean, as might be supposed from its formation, inborn qualities, but acquired ones.

6. This is because he learnt badly. Please take some wine; I remember that you don't like to drink water.

*Obs.*—Wine: *huang*$^{2}$ *chiu*$^{3}$, yellow wine, is the name given to a light wine that the Chinese commonly drink at their principal meal.

7. We have eaten a very good dinner to-day and drunk lots of wine; the fire, too, burns with plenty of warmth; what more can we two want?

*Obs.*—Lots: *lit.*, very enough (Radical 157).

370. 京 *ching*$^{1}$, the capital of a state, ancient or modern.

371. 遠 *yüan*$^{3}$, far.

372. 近 *chin*$^{4}$, near. *Yüan*$^{3}$-*chin*$^{4}$, in combination, means distance; *to*$^{1}$ *yüan*$^{3}$, how far.

373. 路 *lu*$^{4}$, a road; a way.

374. 直 *chih*$^{2}$, straight.

375. 繞 *jao*$^{4}$, winding.

376. Examples:—

| | | | | | | |
|---|---|---|---|---|---|---|
| 這 *chê*$^{4}$ | 來 *lai*$^{2}$ | 遠, *yüan*$^{3}$ | 京。*ching*$^{1}$ | 路, *lu*$^{4}$ | 兒。*'rh* | 到 *tao*$^{4}$ |
| 麽 *mo* | 告 *kao*$^{4}$ | 叫 *chiao*$^{4}$ | 近 *chin*$^{4}$ | 北 *pei*$^{3}$ | 有 *yu*$^{3}$ | 京 *ching*$^{1}$ |
| 繞 *jao*$^{4}$ | 訴 *su*$^{4}$ | 他 *t'a*$^{1}$ | 得 *tê*$^{2}$ | 京 *ching*$^{1}$ | 八 *pa*$^{1}$ | 城 *ch'êng*$^{2}$ |
| 着 *cho* | 我。*wo*$^{3}$ | 一 *i*$^{4}$ | 很。*hên*$^{3}$ | 南 *nan*$^{2}$ | 十 *shih*$^{2}$ | 有 *yu*$^{3}$ |
| 走 *tsou*$^{3}$ | 偺 *tsa*$^{2}$ | 直 *chih*$^{2}$ | 遠 *yüan*$^{3}$ | 京 *ching*$^{1}$ | 多 *to*$^{1}$ | 多 *to*$^{1}$ |
| 罷。*pa*$^{4}$ | 們 *mên*$^{2}$ | 進 *chin*$^{4}$ | 不 *pu*$^{2}$ | 東 *tung*$^{1}$ | 里 *li*$^{3}$ | 遠 *yüan*$^{3}$ |

How far is it to the capital?

*Obs.*—How far? *lit.*, [how] many far? When speaking of short distances, *yu*$^{3}$ *to*$^{1}$ *shao*$^{3}$ *lu*$^{4}$ is often used, or *chi*$^{3}$ *li*$^{3}$ *lu*$^{4}$, how many *li* of road, whether by land or water.

More than eighty *li*.

Peking, Nanking, Tokio.

Very near. Is it far?

Tell him to come straight in and tell me.

*Obs.* Had the sentence run, he *came* straight in and told me, *su* should be followed by *shuo*, to speak.

Suppose we take a roundabout in this direction.

*Obs.*—The *pa* at the close of this sentence has the force of "what do you think?" *i.e.*, expresses a doubt as to the willingness of the person addressed to comply with the suggestion.

377. 河 *ho*$^{2}$, a river.

378. 海 *hai*$^{3}$, the sea.

379. 邊 *pien*$^{1}$, side.

380. 深 *shên*$^{1}$, deep; morally, profound.

381. 淺 *ch'ien*$^{3}$, shallow. Morally, commonplace; not profound.

382. 隻 *chih*$^{1}$, numerative of ships, also of many other things, such as oxen, sheep, and chickens.

383. 船 *ch'uan*$^{2}$, a ship or boat.

384. Examples:—

| | | | | | | |
|---|---|---|---|---|---|---|
| 多 *to*$^{1}$ | 地 *ti*$^{4}$ | 的 *ti* | 那 *na*$^{4}$ | 兒 *'rh* | 隻 *chih*$^{1}$ | 海 *hai*$^{3}$ |
| 少 *shao*$^{3}$ | 方。*fang*$^{1}$ | 地 *ti*$^{4}$ | 一 *i*$^{4}$ | 上 *shang*$^{4}$ | 船。*ch'uan*$^{2}$ | 面 *mien*$^{4}$ |
| 樣 *yang*$^{4}$ | 海 *hai*$^{3}$ | 方 *fang*$^{1}$ | 條 *t'iao*$^{2}$ | 就 *chiu*$^{4}$ | 我 *wo*$^{3}$ | 兒 *'rh* |
| 兒 *'rh* | 裏 *li*$^{3}$ | 有 *yu*$^{3}$ | 河 *ho*$^{2}$ | 看 *k'an*$^{4}$ | 在 *tsai*$^{4}$ | 上 *shang*$^{4}$ |
| 的 *ti* | 頭 *t'ou*$^{2}$ | 深 *shên*$^{1}$ | 有 *yu*$^{3}$ | 見 *chien*$^{4}$ | 海 *hai*$^{3}$ | 有 *yu*$^{3}$ |
| 魚。*yü*$^{2}$ | 有 *yu*$^{3}$ | 的 *ti* | 淺 *ch'ien*$^{3}$ | 了。*liao* | 邊 *pien*$^{1}$ | 三 *san*$^{1}$ |

There are three ships on the sea.

*Obs.*—*Hai mien-'rh* implies distance.

I was on the shore and saw them; or, I saw them from the shore.

In that river there are shallow places and deep.

How many kinds of fish are there in the sea?

385. 客 *k'ê*$^{4}$, *k'o*$^{4}$, a stranger. Also, a guest; a passenger; a traveller. *Mai*$^{3}$ *k'o*, a customer.

386. 店 *tien*$^{4}$, a large shop; an inn.

387. 掌 *chang*$^{3}$, the palm of the hand; to superintend.

388. 櫃 *kuei*$^{4}$, the counter; a till; a cupboard; a wardrobe.

389. 計 *chi*$^{4}$, to reckon; to count.

390. Examples:—

| | | | | | |
|---|---|---|---|---|---|
| 算 *suan*$^{4}$ | 手 *shou*$^{3}$ | 櫃。*kuei*$^{4}$ | 店。*tien*$^{4}$ | 人。*jên*$^{2}$ | 來 *lai*$^{2}$ |
| 計 *chi*$^{4}$ | 掌。*chang*$^{3}$ | 掌 *chang*$^{3}$ | 衣 *i*$^{1}$ | 飯 *fan*$^{4}$ | 往 *wang*$^{3}$ |
| 帳 *chang*$^{4}$ | 手 *shou*$^{3}$ | 櫃 *kuei*$^{4}$ | 櫃。*kuei*$^{4}$ | 店。*tien*$^{4}$ | 的 *ti* |
| 目。*mu*$^{4}$ | 心。*hsin*$^{1}$ | 的。*ti* | 錢 *ch'ien*$^{2}$ | 茶 *ch'a*$^{2}$ | 客 *k'o*$^{4}$ |

Passing strangers.

A restaurant. A tea-shop.

*Obs.*—*Ch'a-tien* is not a "tea-house."

A wardrobe. A till.

An inn manager, or cashier of a shop; *q.d.*, the person who holds or superintends *(chang)* the till *(kuei)*.

The palm of the hand. The centre of the palm.

To do accounts.

*Obs.*—You can also say *suan chang*.

**391.** 能 *nêng²*, to be able.

**392.** 南 *nan²*, south.

**393.** 北 *pei³*, north.

**394.** 受 *shou⁴*, to receive; to suffer; hence used in many passive formations.

**395.** 累 *lei⁴*, entanglement; to entangle; to trouble.

**396.** 苦 *k'u³*, bitterness; bitter; grief; mental or physical suffering.

**397.** 歇 *hsieh¹*, to rest.

**398.** 連 *lien²*, to join; to connect; even. Often employed as the conjunction *and*.

**399.** Examples:—

| | | | | | | |
|---|---|---|---|---|---|---|
| 雨。*yü³* | 一 *i⁴* | 一 *i²* | 連 *lien²* | 辛 *hsing¹* | 累 *lei⁴* | 你 *ni³* |
| | 連 *lien²* | 個 *ko⁴* | 茶 *ch'a²* | 苦。*k'u³* | 了 *liao* | 去 *ch'ü⁴* |
| | 下 *hsia⁴* | 人 *jên²* | 也 *yeh³* | 歇 *hsieh¹* | 麼。*mo* | 年 *nien²* |
| | 了 *liao* | 也 *yeh³* | 不 *pu⁴* | 歇 *hsieh¹* | 一 *i²* | 走 *tsou³* |
| | 三 *san¹* | 看 *k'an⁴* | 能 *nêng²* | 乏 *fa²* | 路 *lu⁴* | 海 *hai³* |
| | 天 *t'ien¹* | 不 *pu* | 喝。*ho¹* | 兒 *'rh* | 眞 *chên¹* | 受 *shou⁴* |
| | 的 *ti* | 見。*chien⁴* | 連 *lien²* | 罷。*pa⁴* | 是 *shih⁴* | 了 *liao* |

When you went to sea last year did you suffer any hardship?

*Obs.*—Went to sea: *lit.*, walked or travelled the sea.

It was truly misery the whole voyage.

*Obs.*—*Hsin¹* or *hsing¹* (Radical 160).

Rest a bit.

*Obs.*—*Pa* is here an invitation; *hsieh hsieh* alone or *hsieh cho* is equally admissible.

I cannot even drink tea.

There was (or is) not even a single man to be seen.

Rain fell for three days consecutively.

*Obs.*—Consecutively: *lit.*, one connexion; *i.e.*, without a break.

## EXERCISE XV.

1 算計道路的遠近、直走近、繞着走遠。東西南北。坐船。過河。那船上的客不少。

1. A straight road is the shortest; a winding road is longer (or, as to distance, the straight road there is the shortest). North, south, east, and west. To be on board a ship. To cross a river. There are a good many passengers on board that ship (or boat).

*Obs.* 1.—A straight road, etc.: *lit.*, if you reckon *(suan-chi)* the distance *(yüan-chin)* of a road, it is nearer to walk straight than to go by a circuitous route.

*Obs.* 2.—Note the order in which the Chinese enumerate the points of the compass.

2 我們明天一早開船往南邊去。河裏的水淺、沒有海水深。他是南邊人。

2. We set sail the first thing to-morrow morning for the South. The water in the rivers is shallower than that of the sea. He is a southerner.

*Obs.* 1.—Set sail: *lit.*, open the boat; *q.d.*, let her loose from her moorings.

*Obs.* 2.—The first thing: *lit.*, the first early; the moment it is early.

3 你去年進京的時候兒在那兒住著呢。在客店裏住。我聽見說城外頭客店有不大好住的。那都看掌櫃的好不好、在我說人乏了那兒都好、到店裏不過歇着罷了。

3. When you went to Peking last year where did you live? I stopped at an inn. I have heard it said that the inns outside the city are some of them not very good to stay at. That is all according as the inn-keeper is a good or a bad one; in my opinion, when one is tired any place is good; all you go to an inn for is to rest yourself.

*Obs.*—All you go, etc.: *lit.*, [the object of]going to an inn [is] not more than to rest [or resting], and there an end.

4 你走路愛坐車、愛坐船。那是看地方兒。南邊沒有車、走道兒的客人都是坐船。走河路都是小船兒、走海的船大。

4. Do you prefer travelling by cart or in a boat? That depends upon the country I am in; there are no carts in the South, and travellers all go by water. The vessels used in river-travelling are small; sea-going vessels are larger.

5 你老前年坐海船不是受了累了麼。不錯、是颳大風、船在山東海邊兒上擱了淺、我們那些人辛苦的了不得。

5. In the voyage you made by sea, sir, the year before last, you had a hard time of it, hadn't you? I had; it blew hard, and the ship got ashore on the coast of Shantung; all of us who were on board suffered terribly.

*Obs.* 1.—Sir: *ni lao*, short for *ni lao hsien-shêng.* This abridged form is slightly less courteous than the longer address, but it is sometimes used. The student should bear in mind that the simple pronoun *ni*³ is only used when adressing inferiors, or persons with whom the speaker is on intimate terms; *nin* is more frequently used in Peking than *ni lao.*

*Obs.* 2.—Hard time: *lit.*, you *shou*, were the recipient of, suffered, trouble,

*Obs.* 3.—Got ashore: *lit.*, [the wind, or some accident] put the ship on a shoal [place].

*Obs.* 4.—Dreadfully: *lit.*, we, those persons=I and the others there, were troubled infinitely. The adjective *hsing k'u* is verbalised by *ti.*

6 船上吃飯是甚麼人管。也是船家管。船上的頭兒叫管船兒的、南邊就叫老大。

6. Who looks after the messing on board ship? The people of the ship look after it. The head man in a boat is called *kuan³-ch'uan²-'rh-ti;* in the South he is called *lao³-ta⁴* (*Anglicè*, lowdah).

*Obs.* 1.—The people of the ship: *ch'uan chia;* those who make *ch'uan*, the boat, *chia*, their home. *Yeh* implies that it is their business to look after the meals as well as other things.

*Obs.* 2.—Note *kuan³*, to look after (117).

7 你算計是坐船貴是坐車貴。坐車比坐船花的錢多。沒有的話。那兒有車價比船價還貴呢。你不知道、北邊的車多是在車店裏擱着的。你要坐車、那掌櫃的也要使幾個錢、還有天天兒住店的盤費沒算。

7. Which do you consider costs most, travelling by water or travelling in a cart? One spends more travelling in a cart. Nonsense; how can a cart be dearer than a boat? You don't understand; most of the carts in the North are put up in the cart inns, and if you want to employ carts the inn-keeper must also make his squeeze; then there are the daily inn expenses *en route* which you have not taken into account.

*Obs.* 1.—One spends: *hua ti*, though commonly so pronounced, should be written *hua tê*, the construction being, literally, sitting in a cart compared with sitting in a ship, [one] *hua tê*, succeeds in expending (comes to spend), more money.

*Obs.* 2.—Nonsense: *lit.*, not existing talk; you talk about what does not exist.

*Obs.* 3.—Squeeze: the word *shih*, property, to use, when placed as here means to use another's money, of course unfairly.

*Obs.* 4.—Travelling expenses: *p'an fei⁴*. *P'an* is, properly, a circular dish, bowl, or plate; it also means to travel backwards and forwards; to go to and fro, as when loading or unloading a vessel. *P'an fei* are therefore the expenses when travelling to and from a place; hence, travelling expenses generally.

*Turn the following into Chinese.* (KEY, EXERCISE XV.)

1. At the present moment the capital is in the North and is called Peking. Several hundred years ago there was also a capital in the South; it was the city now called Nanking.

*Obs.* 1.—Present moment: *k'ê*$^{4}$ *hsia*$^{4}$ (223)

*Obs.* 2.—Now: *lit.*, under the eye (Radical 109).

2. I went into the city with him. The road I went by was straight and very short; he went by a winding road, which was consequently very long.

*Obs.*—Consequently: *chiu*.

3. Rivers are of different sizes. The sea is bigger than a river. Rivers are not so deep as the sea.

4. *Ho*$^{2}$ *pie-'rh*$^{1}$ (the bank of a river), *hai*$^{3}$ *pie-'rh*$^{1}$ (the sea-shore), both refer to the ground at the side of a river or of the sea. The water at the side is shallow, but everywhere in the middle it is very deep.

5. People who journey by water must go by boat. The ships one goes by on the sea are large; the boats which sail on rivers are all small.

6. In a journey by boat there is no necessity for putting up at an inn, but going by cart one must put up at an inn every day, which costs a lot of money. Estimating the cost of the two, one spends less money travelling by boat; the price of a boat, too, is less than that of a cart.

7. The *chang*$^{3}$-*kuei*$^{4}$-*ti* is the manager of a shop. In an inn there is also a *chang*$^{3}$-*kuei*$^{4}$-*ti*.

*Obs.*—Manager: *lit.*, the man who superintends or controls matters.

8. In my opinion, to go by boat and by cart are both good [ways of travelling]. In a boat the one thing one has to fear is a high wind; in a cart, heavy rain; in either case one will have a bad time of it. One year we were travelling in a cart, and while we were on the road the rain began to fall. During the whole journey we did not fall in with (*lit.*, there was not) even one man selling food; we were very distressed and dreadfully fatigued. Eventually we came to an inn, where we rested a night and recovered.

*Obs.*—The one thing, etc.: *chiu shih pa*. Note this fresh use of *chiu*.

**400.** 李 *li*$^{3}$, plums; but in the phrase *hsing*$^{2}$-*li*$^{3}$, baggage, corruptly used for some other character.

**401.** 箱 *hsiang*$^{1}$, a trunk; a box. Alone, it takes *tzŭ* after it.

**402.** 包 *pao*$^{1}$, a bundle (*pao*$^{1}$-*'rh*). To make into a bundle, *pao*$^{1}$ *shang*$^{4}$ *pao*$^{1}$-*'rh*, *pao*$^{1}$ *shang*$^{4}$, or *pao*$^{1}$ *ch'i*$^{3}$ *lai*$^{2}$.

**403.** 袋 *tai*$^{4}$, a bag; a purse. Commonly used with *k'ou*$^{3}$, a mouth.

**404.** 氈, 毡, *chan*$^{1}$, felt or similar fabrics.

**405.** 毯 *t'an*$^{3}$ a carpet or rug; as *mao*$^{2}$ *t'an*$^{3}$-*tzŭ*, a woollen or hair carpet.

11

**406.** 布 *pu*$^{4}$, cotton fabrics. Also, as will be seen later, to spread out; to arrange: to distribute.

**407.** Examples :—

| | | | | | |
|---|---|---|---|---|---|
| 毯 *t'an*$^{3}$ | 口 *k'ou*$^{3}$ | 地 *ti*$^{4}$ | 來。*lai*$^{2}$ | 包 *pao*$^{1}$ | 李 *li*$^{3}$ |
| 子 *tzŭ* | 袋 *tai*$^{4}$ | 布 *pu*$^{4}$ | 氈 *chan*$^{1}$ | 起 *ch'i*$^{3}$ | 子。*tzŭ* |
| 鋪 *p'u*$^{1}$ | 小 *hsiao*$^{3}$ | 是 *shih*$^{4}$ | 帽 *mao*$^{4}$ | 這 *chê*$^{4}$ | 皮 *p'i*$^{2}$ |
| 在 *tsai*$^{4}$ | 米 *mi*$^{3}$ | 粗 *ts'u*$^{1}$ | 便 *p'ien*$^{2}$ | 個 *ko*$^{4}$ | 箱。*hsiang*$^{1}$ |
| 炕 *k'ang*$^{4}$ | 兒。*'rh* | 的。*ti* | 宜。*i*$^{2}$ | 衣 *i*$^{1}$ | 行 *hsing*$^{2}$ |
| 上。*shang*$^{4}$ | 把 *pa*$^{3}$ | 三 *san*$^{1}$ | 本 *pên*$^{3}$ | 裳 *shang*$^{1}$ | 李。*li*$^{3}$ |

Plums.
A leathern box (portmanteau). Baggage.
Wrap up these clothes.
*Obs.*—Note *chê ko* with a plural word.
Felt caps are cheap.
Native cotton fabrics are coarse.
*Obs.*—Native: *lit.*, original, proper, or indigenous to, the locality.
Three bags of millet.
Spread the carpet on the *k'ang*.

**408.** 餵 *wei*$^{4}$, to feed animals.

**409.** 駱 *lo*$^{4}$, described in native dictionaries as a white horse with a black mane; conversationally, only used with the following.

**410.** 駝 *t'o*$^{2}$, the camel with two humps, known to us as the Bactrian camel, and commonly called *lo*$^{4}$-*t'o*$^{2}$; to carry on the back, as a beast a burden.

*N.B.*—Emphasise *lo*$^{4}$.

**411.** 牲 *shêng*$^{1}$, cattle; beasts. Rarely used alone, and generally with *k'ou*, a mouth.

**412.** Examples :—

| | | | | | | |
|---|---|---|---|---|---|---|
| 一 *i*$^{4}$ | 他 *t'a*$^{1}$ | 得 *tei*$^{3}$ | 牲 *shêng*$^{1}$ | 着 *cho* | 那 *na*$^{4}$ | 叫 *chiao*$^{4}$ |
| 回 *hui*$^{2}$ | 駱 *lo*$^{4}$ | 好 *hao*$^{3}$ | 口 *k'ou* | 四 *ssŭ*$^{4}$ | 一 *i*$^{2}$ | 馬 *ma*$^{3}$ |
| 毛 *mao*$^{2}$ | 駝 *t'o* | 好 *hao*$^{1}$ | 是 *shih*$^{4}$ | 百 *pai*$^{3}$ | 個 *ko*$^{4}$ | 夫 *fu*$^{1}$ |
| 兒。*'rh* | 一 *i*$^{4}$ | 兒 *'rh* | 長 *ch'ang*$^{4}$ | 斤 *chin*$^{1}$ | 駱 *lo*$^{4}$ | 來 *lai*$^{2}$ |
| | 年 *nien*$^{2}$ | 的 *ti* | 騎 *ch'i*$^{2}$ | 煤。*mei*$^{2}$ | 駝 *t'o* | 餵 *wei*$^{4}$ |
| | 脫 *t'o*$^{1}$ | 餵 *wei*$^{4}$ | 的 *ti* | 這 *chê*$^{4}$ | 駝 *t'o*$^{2}$ | 馬。*ma*$^{3}$ |

Tell the *ma-fu* to come and feed the horse.
*Obs.*—*Ma-fu*: *lit.*, horse man (239).
That camel has a load of 400 catties of coal.
This beast is constantly ridden; he must be well fed.
Camels cast their coats once a year.
*Obs.*—*Lit*, camels one year put off one time wool.

語言自邇集



**413.** 跟 *kên*$^1$, the heel; hence, to follow, to accompany. It often takes the place of the preposition *with*; as *kên*$^1$ *wo*$^3$ *ch'ü*$^4$, go with me.

**414.** 班 *pan*$^1$, properly, any set of persons organised to act together, as a troop of players, a set of chair-bearers, a guard, etc. *Kên*$^1$*-pan*$^1$*-ti* or *kên*$^1$*-pa*$^1$*-'rh-ti*, the servant or servants of an official of rank; a general servant or valet is also called *hsia*$^4$ *jên*$^2$ (*lit.*, under man). By common usage, *kên*$^1$*-pa*$^1$*-'rh-ti* is the term applied to the servants of foreigners in Peking; there are other terms for domestics, which will be met with later.

**415.** 裝 *chuang*$^1$, to put into; to contain.

**416.** 帶 *tai*$^4$, a girdle (with *tzŭ*); to lead; to bring; also, as will be seen later, a stretch or strip of country, etc.

**417.** 馱 *to*$^4$, a beast's load.

**418.** Examples :—

| | | | | | | |
|---|---|---|---|---|---|---|
| 沒 *mei*$^2$ | 那 *na*$^4$ | 下 *hsia*$^4$ | 去。*ch'ü*$^4$ | 來。*lai*$^2$ | 外 *wai*$^4$ | 我 *wo*$^3$ |
| 有。*yu*$^3$ | 一 *i*$^4$ | 那 *ma*$^4$ | 這 *chê*$^4$ | 你 *ni*$^3$ | 帶 *tai*$^4$ | 的 *ti* |
| | 隻 *chih*$^1$ | 麼 *mo* | 個 *ko*$^4$ | 跟 *kên*$^1$ | 了 *liao* | 跟 *kên*$^1$ |
| | 船 *ch'uan*$^2$ | 多 *to*$^1$ | 箱 *hsiang*$^1$ | 我 *wo*$^3$ | 一 *i*$^4$ | 班 *pan*$^1$ |
| | 裝 *chuang*$^1$ | 的 *ti* | 子 *tzŭ* | 上 *shang*$^4$ | 匹 *p'i*$^1$ | 的 *ti* |
| | 好 *hao*$^3$ | 東 *tung*$^1$ | 裝 *chuang*$^1$ | 衙 *ya*$^2$ | 馬 *ma*$^3$ | 打 *ta*$^3$ |
| | 了 *liao* | 西。*hsi*$^1$ | 不 *pu*$^2$ | 門 *mên*$^2$ | 回 *hui*$^2$ | 口 *k'ou*$^3$ |

My servant has come back from beyond the frontier with a horse.

*Obs.—Ta*, here a preposition, from.

Go with me to the yamên.

This box won't hold all these things.

*Obs.*—Won't hold: *lit.*, put into not down.

Is that ship loaded yet? (Is the loading of it completed *(hao liao)*?)

**419.** 追 *chui*$^1$, to pursue; to follow up; to prosecute, as a claim or an inquiry. *Chui*$^1$ *shang*$^4$, to overtake.

**420.** 趕 *kan*$^3$, also to pursue. It appears to have much the same sense as the preceding, but also means to drive; as *kan*$^3$ *ch'ê*$^1$, to drive a cart; *kan*$^3$ *lü*$^2$, to drive a donkey.

**421.** 喚 *huan*$^4$, to call aloud; commonly combined with *chiao*$^4$, to call.

**422.** 無 *wu*$^2$, not to be; not to have. The opposite of *yu*$^3$, to be; to have.

**423.** 利 *li*$^{4}$, commonly, profit; advantage. Properly, sharp-edged; hence, with the following character, *hai*$^{4}$, terrible, terribly.

**424.** 害 *hai*$^{4}$, harm; hurt. Also, to receive or suffer injury, etc.; as *hai*$^{4}$ *ping*$^{4}$, to get ill, to catch an illness; *hai*$^{4}$ *p'a*$^{4}$, to be afraid.

**425.** Examples :—

| | | | | | | |
|---|---|---|---|---|---|---|
| 里 *li* | 錯 *ts'o*$^{4}$ | 熱 *jê*$^{4}$ | 在 *tsai*$^{4}$ | 們 *mên*$^{2}$ | 車 *ch'ê*$^{1}$ | 你 *ni*$^{3}$ |
| 無 *wu*$^{2}$ | 是 *shih*$^{4}$ | 得 *tê* | 那 *na*$^{4}$ | 趕 *kan*$^{3}$ | 的。*ti* | 快 *k'uai*$^{4}$ |
| 雲。*yün*$^{2}$ | 無 *wu*$^{2}$ | 利 *li*$^{4}$ | 兒 *'rh* | 快 *k'uai*$^{4}$ | 趕 *kan*$^{3}$ | 去 *ch'ü*$^{4}$ |
| | 心 *hsin*$^{1}$ | 害。*hai*$^{4}$ | 叫 *chiao*$^{4}$ | 些 *hsieh*$^{1}$ | 牛 *niu*$^{2}$ | 追 *chui*$^{1}$ |
| | 的。*ti*$^{1}$ | 他 *t'a*$^{1}$ | 喚。*huan*$^{4}$ | 兒。*'rh* | 的。*ti* | 他。*t'a*$^{1}$ |
| | 萬 *wan*$^{4}$ | 這 *chê*$^{4}$ | 天 *t'ien*$^{1}$ | 誰 *shui*$^{2}$ | 咱 *tsa*$^{2}$ | 趕 *kan*$^{3}$ |

Go after him quickly.
A carter. A herd-boy.
Let us get on quicker.
Who is calling (or crying) out there?
The day is terribly hot.
His error was unintentional.
Not a cloud all round.

**426.** Learn also the following :—

春 *ch'un*$^{1}$, spring. 秋 *ch'iu*$^{1}$, autumn.

夏 *hsia*$^{4}$, summer. 冬 *tung*$^{1}$, winter.

**427.** Examples :—

| | | | | | | |
|---|---|---|---|---|---|---|
| 明 *ming*$^{2}$ | 去 *ch'ü*$^{4}$ | 來。*lai*$^{2}$ | 颳 *kua*$^{1}$ | 天 *t'ien*$^{1}$ | 夏 *hsia*$^{4}$ | 春 *ch'un*$^{1}$ |
| 年 *nien*$^{2}$ | 年 *nien*$^{2}$ | 冬 *tung*$^{1}$ | 起 *ch'i*$^{3}$ | 的 *ti* | 天 *t'ien*$^{1}$ | 天 *t'ien*$^{1}$ |
| 冬 *tung*$^{1}$ | 夏 *hsia*$^{4}$ | 天 *t'ien*$^{1}$ | 涼 *liang*$^{2}$ | 時 *shih*$^{2}$ | 熱。*jê*$^{4}$ | 暖 *nuan*$^{3}$ |
| 天。*t'ien*$^{1}$ | 天。*t'ien*$^{1}$ | 冷。*lêng*$^{3}$ | 風 *fêng*$^{1}$ | 候 *hou*$^{4}$ | 秋 *ch'iu*$^{1}$ | 和。*huo* |

Spring is warm.
Summer is hot.
In autumn cool breezes begin to blow.
Winter is cold.
Last summer.
Next winter.

## EXERCISE XVI.

1 那駄子太重、一個牲口駝不了.這些東西不好帶.這是甚麼話、裝在箱子裏就好帶了.

1. That is too heavy a load; one animal cannot carry it. It will be difficult to carry all these things. What are you talking about? pack them in a box and you can carry them easily enough.

2 行李是走道兒的客人帶的東西.箱子有皮子做的、有木頭做的、甚麼都裝得.

2. The expression *hsing-li* comprises whatever a traveller carries with him. Trunks are made, some of leather, some of wood, and will hold all sorts of things.

3 包上包兒是把東西用甚麼包起來.他是拏毡子把那小箱子包起來了.

3. *Pao*[1] *shang pao*[1]*-'rh* (to make a bundle) is to wrap up things in anything. He has wrapped up that small box in a rug.

4 那口袋你帶了來做甚麼.是裝零碎東西的.道兒上到店裏就得餧牲口.

4. What have you brought that bag for? To put odds and ends into. On a journey the beasts have to be fed as soon as one arrives at an inn.

*Obs.*—Note the force of *chiu*, as soon as; *lit.*, arriving at an inn one must then and there *(chiu)* feed the animals.

5 駱駝都是口外來的.你小心着行李、駄子都齊了就走.要不快點兒起身、怕趕不了城了.

5. Camels all come from beyond the frontier. Take care of the baggage; when the packages are all there, we will start. If we don't get off quickly, I am afraid we sha'n't save the gates.

*Obs.* 1.—All there: *lit.*, if the baggage be all *ch'i*, complete (Radical 210).

*Obs.* 2.—Get off, start: *lit.*, raise the body; *q.d.*, to be on the move.

*Obs.* 3.—Save the gates: *lit.*, shall not catch up the city wall; *i.e.*, shall not reach the city in time to get in before the gates are shut.

6 跟班的是使喚的人。他叫跟班的把箱子裝在車上、車走了、他趕不上了。

6. The *kên¹-pan¹* are they who take orders (your servants). He ordered a servant to put his box (or boxes) into the cart (or carts), but the cart had started and he could not catch it up.

*Obs.* 1.—In southern "mandarin" an individual servant is spoken of as a *kên-pan*; in Peking as *kên-pan-ti*, or oftener, *kên-pa-'rh-ti*.

*Obs.* 2.—Take orders: *lit.*, are those whom [one] sends and calls.

7 牲口身上駝着的東西就叫馱子。驢馱子、騾馱子、都說得、馬馱子可不大說。

7. The things which a beast bears on its back are called a *to⁴-tzŭ*. One may speak of an ass or a mule *to⁴-tzŭ*, but seldom of a horse *to⁴-tzŭ*.

8 我出門去、他的跟班的在後頭追我、追了半天也沒趕上、我老遠的看見他跑、可不知道他是追我呢。

8. After I had gone out his servant came after me, but though he pursued me for a good while he did not overtake me; I did see him at a great distance running, but I did not know he was after me.

*Obs.* 1.—A good while: *lit.*, half the day.

*Obs.* 2.—A great distance: *lao*, old, is sometimes used as an adverb of intensity; you can say also *lao³ tsao³ ti*, very early.

9 那個人在那'兒呢。他出去了、你快跑可以趕得上他。他早走了、怕趕不上罷。無論趕得上趕不上、你快跑着追他就是了。

9. Where is that man? He has gone out; if you run fast [enough] you will be able to overtake him. He is gone some time (*lit.*, early); I fear it will not be possible to overtake him. Whether he is to be overtaken or not, you just run after him as hard as you can.

*Obs.* 1.—Fast enough: *lit.*, running quickly you will be able to achieve coming up with him.

*Obs.* 2.—As hard as you can: *lit.*, quick running pursue [him], then it will be right (or well).

*Turn the following into Chinese.* (KEY, EXERCISE XVI.)

1. Everyone, no matter who, when going on a journey must take baggage with him.

2. The cart will soon be here; get your luggage and boxes ready. The bundle of clothes and the bag have still to be made up.

*Obs.*—Get ready: *ta³ tien³* (*lit.*, beat and point); to arrange and check off. *Tien³*, short for *tien³ shu-'rh*, to count or check the number.

3. The carpet on the floor of this room is dusty, it must be taken out and beaten; the table-cloth is very dirty, too, and will have to be washed.

*Obs.*—Is dusty: *yu liao t'u liao.* Note the repetition of the particle *liao*, which does not here mark the past tense, but is simply a final expletive.

4. Tell the *ma-fu* to feed the animals. I am going out in a little while, and I don't want anybody with me; tell my boy to pack up the things I am taking with me.

*Obs.* 1.—Feed the beasts: *pa shêng-k'ou wei shang; shang* signifying the completion of the act. *Wei shêng-k'ou* would be equally correct.

*Obs.* 2.—With: *kên.*

5. For carrying things about with one, animals are always used in the North; these loads are called *to⁴-tzŭ*. There are donkey *to⁴-tzŭ* and mule *to⁴-tzŭ*; a camel's [load] may also be called a *to⁴-tzŭ*. *T'o²-chiao⁴* (a litter) is a *chiao⁴-tzŭ* (sedan-chair) carried by mules.

6. You walk so quickly I cannot keep up with you.

*Obs.* 1.—So: *lit.*, this kind or fashion.

*Obs.* 2.—Not keep up: *lit.*, follow not up.

7. He has not been gone out long; hurry after him and tell him I have some more things to give him to take.

*Obs.*—Long: not a great *kung-fu*, while.

8. I have a small matter I want to employ you on: go to him and borrow a little money for me; no matter whether he says he has or has not got any, you must positively get a small loan for me.

*Obs.* 1.—A little money: *lia ch'ien-'rh*; *lit.*, two cash.

*Obs.* 2.—For me: this is indicated here by the verb *lai*, to come.

9. He is a dreadful fellow.

*Obs.*—*Hao*, good, is often used as a substitute for *hên*, very.

10. Summer is dreadfully hot; winter is terribly cold; these are expressions for great heat and great cold. The seasons when it is neither hot nor cold are spring and autumn.

*Obs.*—Expression: *hua t'ou-'rh*; *lit.*, heads of talk.

**428.** 腦 *nao³*, the brains, when used with *tzŭ*; when followed by *tai⁴*, a bag, it means the head, but with the exception of the human head, the term *nao³ tai⁴* is only used for the heads of animals whose names are composed of more than one word, as *lao² hu³*, a tiger, etc.

**429.** 辮 *pien⁴*, the pigtail or queue worn by the Chinese.

**430.** 朶 *to³*, a bud; the lobe of the ear.

**431.** 眼 *yen³*, the eye; often used with the following; the numerative of wells.

**432.** 睛 *ching¹*, the pupil of the eye.

**433.** 嘴 *tsui³*, the mouth.

**434.** 唇 *ch'un²*, the lips.

**435.** 鬍 *hu²*, the beard or moustache.

**436.** Examples :—

| | | | | | | |
|---|---|---|---|---|---|---|
| 的 *ti* | 嘴 *tsui*$^3$ | 唇 *ch'un*$^2$ | 隻 *chih*$^1$ | 的 *ti* | 髮 *fa* | 大 *ta*$^4$ |
| 飯 *fan*$^4$ | 裡 *li*$^3$ | 上 *shang*$^4$ | 眼 *yen*$^3$ | 耳 *êrh*$^3$ | 打 *ta*$^3$ | 腦 *nao*$^3$ |
| 不 *pu*$^4$ | 說 *shuo*$^1$ | 的 *ti* | 睛。*ching*$^1$ | 朶 *to*$^3$ | 一 *i*$^4$ | 袋。*tai*$^4$ |
| 要 *yao*$^4$ | 好 *hao*$^3$ | 鬍 *hu*$^2$ | 打 *ta*$^3$ | 聽 *t'ing*$^1$ | 條 *t'iao*$^2$ | 梳 *shu*$^1$ |
| 說 *shuo*$^1$ | 話、*hua*$^4$ | 子 *tzŭ* | 辮 *pien*$^4$ | 不 *pu*$^4$ | 辮 *pien*$^4$ | 好 *hao*$^3$ |
| 話。*hua*$^4$ | 滿 *man*$^3$ | 短。*tuan*$^3$ | 子。*tzŭ* | 眞。*chên*$^1$ | 子。*tzŭ* | 了 *liao* |
| | 嘴 *tsui*$^3$ | 他 *t'a*$^1$ | 嘴 *tsui*$^3$ | 一 *i*$^4$ | 他 *t'a*$^1$ | 頭 *t'ou*$^2$ |

A big head.

When you have combed your hair well, do it into a pigtail. *See* **241.**

His ear is incorrect ; or, he does not hear distinctly.

One eye.

To plait the queue.

The hair on the lip is short.

He speaks fair.

Don't speak with your mouth full.

**437.** 胳 *ko*$^1$, *kê*$^1$, properly, the armpit ; not used alone.

**438.** 臂 *pei*$^4$, the arm in general.

**439.** 指 *chih*$^3$, the finger ; to point to ; to point out ; to point at. *Chih*$^2$*-t'ou*, the finger or toe. Note the change of tone.

**440.** 甲 *chia*$^3$, the nails. *Chih*$^1$*-chia*$^3$, the nails, whether of the hand or foot. Note the tone of *chih*, which must be emphasised.

**441.** 腰 *yao*$^1$, the loins ; the waist.

**442.** 腿 *t'ui*$^3$, the thigh ; the legs.

**443.** Examples :—

| | | | | | | |
|---|---|---|---|---|---|---|
| 短 *tuan*$^3$ | 乏 *fa*$^2$ | 有。*yu*$^3$ | 看。*k'an*$^4$ | 用 *yung*$^4$ | 粗。*ts'u*$^1$ | 那 *na*$^4$ |
| 拿 *na*$^2$ | 了。*liao* | 兩 *liang*$^3$ | 腰 *yao*$^1$ | 指 *chih*$^2$ | 你 *ni*$^3$ | 個 *ko*$^4$ |
| 不 *pu*$^4$ | 我 *wo*$^3$ | 條 *t'iao*$^2$ | 裡 *li*$^3$ | 頭 *t'ou*$^2$ | 的 *ti* | 人 *jên*$^2$ |
| 著 *chao*$^2$ | 的 *ti*$^1$ | 腿 *t'ui*$^3$ | 有 *yu*$^3$ | 指 *chih*$^3$ | 指 *chih*$^1$ | 的 *ti* |
| 他。*t'a*$^1$ | 胳 *ko*$^1$ | 都 *tou*$^1$ | 錢 *ch'ien*$^2$ | 給 *kei*$^3$ | 甲 *chia*$^3$ | 胳 *ko*$^1$ |
| | 臂 *pei*$^4$ | 走 *tsou*$^3$ | 沒 *mei*$^2$ | 我 *wo*$^3$ | 快。*k'uai*$^4$ | 臂 *pei*$^4$ |

That man's arm is thick.

Your nails are sharp.

Point it out to me with your finger.

Have you any money in your waistbelt?

*Obs.—Lit.*, in your waist ; a Chinaman's purse is attached to his girdle.

Both my legs are tired out with walking.

My arm is short ; I cannot get hold of him.

**444.** 結 *chieh*$^2$, to knot, bind, or collect together ; hence, to conclude, to finish. When used with the following as an adjective, it means substantial, strong, or vigorous, and is pronounced *chieh*$^1$*-shih*$^1$.

*N. B.*—The *chieh* must be emphasised.

445. 實 *shih*$^2$, true; sound; solid, as opposed to hollow. *Shih*$^2$ *tsai*$^4$, in reality; truly; really.

446. 軟 *juan*$^3$, soft.

447. 弱 *jo*$^4$, weak.

448. 抓 *chua*$^1$, to catch or claw hold of, as a man with his hand, or a bird with its talons; to clutch.

449. 拉 *la*$^1$, to pull; to drag.

450. 拽 *chuai*$^4$, to haul at. The dictionaries give a different sound to this character, but the colloquial pronunciation is as above.

451. Examples:—

| | | | | | | |
|---|---|---|---|---|---|---|
| 住 *chu*$^4$ | 拉 *la*$^1$ | 過 *kuo*$^4$ | 拽 *chuai*$^4$ | 結 *chieh*$^1$ | 弱 *jo*$^4$ | 我 *wo*$^3$ |
| 我 *wo*$^3$ | 破 *p'o*$^4$ | 來。*lai*$^2$ | 住 *chu*$^4$ | 實。*shih* | 沒 *mei*$^2$ | 的 *ti* |
| 的 *ti* | 了 *liao* | 不 *pu*$^2$ | 罷。*pa*$^4$ | 馬 *ma*$^3$ | 有 *yu*$^3$ | 身 *shên*$^1$ |
| 手 *shou*$^3$ | 衣 *i*$^1$ | 要 *yao*$^4$ | 把 *pa*$^3$ | 要 *yao*$^4$ | 去 *ch'ü*$^4$ | 子 *tzŭ* |
| 了。*liao* | 裳。*shang*$^1$ | 拉 *la*$^1$ | 桌 *cho*$^1$ | 跑 *p'ao*$^3$ | 年 *nien*$^2$ | 今 *chin*$^1$ |
| | 他 *t'a*$^1$ | 他 *t'a*$^1$ | 子 *tzŭ* | 把 *pa*$^3$ | 那 *na*$^4$ | 年 *nien*$^2$ |
| | 抓 *chua*$^1$ | 怕 *p'a*$^4$ | 拉 *la*$^1$ | 他 *t'a*$^1$ | 麼 *mo* | 軟 *juan*$^3$ |

I am weak this year, not so strong as I was last year.

The horse is going to bolt; hold on to him.

Haul that table over.

Don't drag him, or you may tear his clothes.

He grasped me by the hand.

452. 病 *ping*$^4$, illness; disease.

453. 疼 *t'êng*$^2$, pain, whether from wound or sickness; intensity of kindly feeling. *T'êng ai*$^4$, tender love, or to love tenderly.

454. 奇 *ch'i*$^2$, strange (in a good sense).

455. 怪 *kuai*$^4$, monstrous; strange (in a bad sense). Often used with the foregoing. *Kuai*$^4$ can also be used verbally; to take offence at; to be astonished at.

456. 怎 *tsên*$^3$, how? what? In Peking never met with colloquially except when followed by *mo*$^1$ (23), and then the final *n* is not heard, the dissyllable being pronounced *tsêm*$^3$-*mo*, with the emphasis on the first syllable.

457. Examples:—

| | | | | | |
|---|---|---|---|---|---|
| 這 *chê*$^4$ | 奇 *ch'i*$^2$ | 疼 *t'êng*$^2$ | 怪 *kuai*$^4$ | 疼 *t'êng*$^2$ | 我 *wo*$^3$ |
| 是 *shih*$^4$ | 怪 *kuai*$^4$ | 嘴 *tsui*$^3$ | 不 *pu*$^4$ | 的 *ti* | 病 *ping*$^4$ |
| 怎 *tsên*$^3$ | 不 *pu*$^4$ | 乾。*kan*$^1$ | 得 *tê*$^2$ | 了 *liao*$^3$ | 得 *tê* |
| 麼 *mo* | 奇 *ch'i*$^2$ | 你 *ni*$^3$ | 你 *ni*$^3$ | 不 *pu*$^4$ | 利 *li*$^4$ |
| 了。*liao* | 怪。*kuai*$^4$ | 說 *shuo*$^1$ | 頭 *t'ou*$^2$ | 得。*tê*$^2$ | 害。*hai*$^4$ |

I am terribly ill.

I am in awful pain.

No wonder your head is sore and your mouth dry.

*Obs.*—No wonder: *lit.*, [you] astonished not can [be] that, etc.

Don't you think it strange?

How is this? or, how did this come about?

## EXERCISE XVII.

1 人的頭裏頭有腦子、就叫腦袋。你這個辮子得梳了。人老了、耳朵聽不真、眼睛看不真。

1. A man's *t'ou*$^2$ has *nao*$^3$-*tzŭ* (brains) inside it, and is accordingly called *nao*$^3$-*tai*$^4$ (his brain bag). Your queue must be combed. When a man is old he can neither hear well (*lit.*, truly) with his ears nor see clearly (distinctly) with his eyes.

2 那個人鼻子眼睛長得很奇怪。我心疼這個馬、不肯叫他走乏了。

2. That man has a very odd-looking countenance. I am too fond of this horse to let him tire himself.

*Obs.*—Countenance: *lit.*, that man's nose and eyes = his face, growing has attained to singularity. In this and similar combinations, *chang*$^3$, to grow, must generally be construed *is*; much as we say is turning out, or, has turned out.

3 這個人很結實、那個人輭弱得很。本地的布結實。這個坐兒很輭和。

3. This man is very strong (sound); that man is very feeble. Native cloth is very strong. This seat is very soft (or comfortable).

*Obs.* 1.—Strong: note that *chieh*$^1$ must be strongly emphasised.
*Obs.* 2.—Note *tso*$^4$-*'rh*, a seat; there is another form of the character.
*Obs.* 3.—*Juan*$^3$-*huo*: *lit.*, soft and comfortable. Cf. *nuan*$^3$-*huo*, warm.

4 你的身子有病麽。沒有病、不過是身子輭弱。這一件事我實在管不了。我怎麽管得了那麽些個人。

4. Have you anything the matter with you? No, I am not ill; only weak. I really cannot manage (or, look after) this matter. How can I possibly look after (or control) so many men?

5 這一匹馬很老實、你買他罷。看着是老實、你餧他幾天兒瞧罷、騎着怕拉不住。

5. This horse is very quiet; won't you buy him? (or, you had better buy him). He looks quiet enough, but you feed him up for a few days, and then see; were you to ride him I doubt if you could hold him.

*Obs.*—Quiet: *lit.*, old and sound, sincere, or honest; the term is applied to men as well as animals.

6 偺們這五六年沒有見你的鬍子都白了.是我這幾年病得利害.連家裏的人都不認得我.

6. In these five or six years that you and I have not met your beard has turned quite white. That's because I have been sadly ailing for some years; even my own family don't recognise me.

7 道兒上躺着的那個人、兩腿都破了.腰上有病、直不起來.我的指頭疼.

7. That man who is lying on the road has both his legs injured (or ulcerated). To have something the matter with the back (loins) that makes it impossible to stand upright (or, straighten oneself). My finger is sore (or, pains me).

8 你這麼慢走是身上有病麼.不是、是人老了、腰腿都輭了.這個事我實在做不來.

8. Do you walk so slowly because you have something the matter with you? No, it is age which makes me weak both in the back and limbs. I really cannot do this.

9 他的舌頭有病、連嘴唇子都破了.那女人的指甲那麼長、把他的胳臂抓破了.

9. There is something the matter with his tongue, and both it and his lips have broken out. That woman's nails were so long that when she clutched hold of his arm they tore it.

10 你這麼拽着我、是有甚麼事麼、要沒事這麼拉拉拽拽是甚麼樣子呢.有話直說就是了.

10. Why do you drag at me like that? it is not seemly (*lit.*, what fashion is it?) to claw me so for no reason. [If] you have anything to say, just say it out straight.

*Obs.*—For no reason: *lit.*, if (*yao* for *jo*) you have no business, thus to drag drag, clutch clutch, is what fashion? There being talk straight speak, then it will do.

*Turn the following into Chinese.* (KEY, EXERCISE XVII.)

1. How can anyone go and speak to him about this matter? Why are you so weak? After all the man has only one head (*i.e.*, is much the same as anyone else), what are you afraid of him for?

*Obs.* 1.—How can, etc.: *lit.*, this matter cause men how go with him speak.

*Obs.* 2.—After all: *lit.*, also not more.

*Obs.* 3.—What for: *tso shên-mo.*

2. When a man comes to be old, he breaks down in every way; his ears do not hear distinctly, his eyes do not see true, and in speaking his lips even are of no use.

*Obs.*—Breaks down in every way: *yang yang-'rh tou pu hsing*; *lit.*, kind kind all not work, move, or act. Note the plurality obtained by repetition: *yang yang-'rh*, each or every kind; *jên jên-'rh*, each or every man. It must be remembered, however, that only certain substantives form the adjective pronoun *each* or *every* by duplication. We could not say, for instance, *cho cho*, every table; *i i*, every chair.

*Obs.* 2.—No use: *pu chung yung*, do not fulfil, or accomplish, use. See 303.

3. In spring the weather is too dry; my lips are liable to chap.

*Obs.* 1.—Weather: see 232.

*Obs.* 2.—Liable: this is frequently rendered by *ai*, to love, to be prone to.

4. With so little hair as this to make a pigtail! why! it appears to me it isn't so long as a man's beard.

5. Look what a long beard he has!

6. Don't pull me about like that, your nails are long; to spoil them would be a misfortune, and to scratch my arm would be equally so.

7. There is something the matter with his legs; in walking he drags them after him in great pain.

8. He appears to me to be just at the age when a man is strong; how is it that he is so weak?

*Obs.*—When a man is strong: *lit.*, the time when he has strength (*li*$^{4}$) and breath (*ch'i*$^{4}$).

9. Do you mean to say that if you haul and pull at a man in such a weak condition as this you can't pull him over on his back?

*Obs.*—*Lit.*, this kind of weak man; *lien*, together with, hauling, *tai*, and, clutching do you still fear not to pull him recumbent? Note the use of *lien* and *tai* as conjunctions.

10. I saw a man to-day with a very queer countenance.

*Obs.*—Countenance; *lit.*, face (*mien*) and eyes (*mu*).

458. 眉 *mei*$^{2}$, eyebrows.

459. 鬢 *pin*$^{4}$, the hair on the temples.

460. 腮 *sai*$^{1}$, the jaws; probably, inside the cheek. Generally combined with the following.

461. 頰 *chia*$^{4}$, *chieh*$^{4}$, the jaws; probably, the cheek on the outside.

462. 巴 *pa*$^{1}$, the name of a place; used corruptly as part of the combination *hsia*$^{4}$-*pa*$^{1}$, the chin.

463. 頦 *k'o*$^{1}$, the lower part of the face; colloquially, only used with the foregoing, with which it is identical.

464. Examples:—

| | | | | | | |
|---|---|---|---|---|---|---|
| 喝 *ho*$^{1}$ | 顋 *sai*$^{1}$ | 得 *tê* | 鬍 *hu*$^{2}$ | 巴 *pa*$^{1}$ | 顋 *sai*$^{1}$ | 眉 *mei*$^{2}$ |
| 了 *liao* | 就 *chiu*$^{4}$ | 很。*hên*$^{3}$ | 子。*tzŭ* | 頦 *k'o*$^{1}$ | 頰。*chieh*$^{4}$ | 毛。*mao*$^{2}$ |
| 酒 *chiu*$^{3}$ | 知 *chih*$^{1}$ | 看 *k'an*$^{4}$ | 眉 *mei*$^{2}$ | 兒。*'rh* | 下 *hsia*$^{4}$ | 鬢 *pin*$^{4}$ |
| 了。*liao* | 道 *tao*$^{4}$ | 他 *t'a*$^{1}$ | 毛 *mao*$^{2}$ | 連 *lien*$^{2}$ | 巴。*pa*$^{1}$ | 角 *chiao*$^{3}$ |
| | 他 *t'a*$^{1}$ | 兩 *liang*$^{3}$ | 長 *ch'ang*$^{2}$ | 鬢 *pin*$^{4}$ | 下 *hsia*$^{4}$ | 兒。*'rh* |

Eyebrows. The hair on the temples.

The cheeks. The chin. The chin. *Sai*$^1$ *chieh*$^4$ is the inside of the cheeks, the outside of which is called *lien*$^3$ *tan*$^4$*-tzŭ*; the gills of a fish are *sai*$^1$ *chieh*$^4$.

Whiskers. Very long eyebrows.

Look at his cheeks and you will see that he has been drinking.

465. 脖 *po*$^2$, the neck.

466. 嗓 *sang*$^3$, the throat, within and without.

467. 節 *chieh*$^2$, joints, of the bones, the bamboo, etc.

468. 剃 *t'i*$^4$, to shave; used only of shaving the head.

469. 刮 *kua*$^1$, to scrape with a knife; to scrape the hair off an animal's skin. *Kua*$^1$ *lien*$^3$, to shave the face.

470. Examples:—

| | | | | | | |
|---|---|---|---|---|---|---|
| 幾 *chi*$^3$ | 兒,*'rh* | 竹 *chu*$^2$ | 頭 *t'ou*$^2$ | 不 *pu*$^2$ | 子 *tzŭ* | 他 *t'a*$^1$ |
| 回 *hui*$^2$ | 你 *ni*$^3$ | 子 *tzŭ* | 節 *chieh*$^2$ | 要 *yao*$^4$ | 疼。*t'êng*$^2$ | 的 *ti* |
| 頭。*t'ou*$^2$ | 一 *i*$^2$ | 有 *yu*$^3$ | 兒,*'rh* | 這 *chê*$^4$ | 說 *shuo*$^1$ | 脖 *po*$^2$ |
| 刮 *kua*$^1$ | 個 *ko*$^4$ | 多 *to*$^1$ | 這 *chê*$^4$ | 麽 *mo* | 話 *hua*$^4$ | 子 *tzŭ* |
| 臉。*lien*$^3$ | 月 *yüeh*$^4$ | 少 *shao*$^3$ | 一 *i*$^4$ | 大。*ta*$^4$ | 嗓 *sang*$^3$ | 長。*ch'ang*$^2$ |
| | 剃 *t'i*$^4$ | 節 *chieh*$^2$ | 桿 *kan*$^3$ | 骨 *ku*$^2$ | 子 *tzŭ* | 嗓 *sang*$^3$ |

His neck is long.

My throat is sore.

Don't speak so loudly.

*Obs.—Pu yao chê mo ta sang-tzŭ shuo hua* would be equally correct.

Joints of the bones.

How many joints has this bamboo?

*Obs.—Chu* has another numerative, *kên*$^1$, which will be met with later.

How many times a month do you shave your head?

*Obs.*—Note that *t'i*$^4$ can only be used of shaving the head.

To shave the face.

471. 胸 *hsiung*$^1$, the breast; in Peking, commonly called *hsiung*$^1$ *p'u*$^2$*-tzŭ*. There is no recognised character for *p'u*, but the following is generally used, though its proper pronunciation is *fu*$^3$.

472. 脯 *fu*$^3$, *p'u*$^2$.

473. 背 *pei*$^4$, the back. *Pei*$^1$, to carry on the back.

474. 脊 *chi*$^3$, the spine.

475. 梁 *niang*$^2$, the spine; properly read *liang*$^2$, a horizontal beam. Note, *chi*$^2$*-niang*$^2$, the backbone, emphasising *chi*$^2$.

476. 膀 *pang*$^3$, the shoulders; seldom used alone.

477. 肚 *tu*$^4$, the belly. *Tu*$^3$, the entrails; used only of the entrails of animals.

**478.** Examples :—

| | | | | | | |
|---|---|---|---|---|---|---|
| 肚 tu$^4$ | 肩 chien$^1$ | 脊 chi$^2$ | 麽 mo | 你 ni$^3$ | 站 chan$^4$ | 胸 hsiung$^1$ |
| 子。tzŭ | 膀 pang$^3$ | 梁。niang$^2$ | 東 tung$^1$ | 背 pei$^4$ | 在 tsai$^4$ | 脯 p'u$^2$ |
| 指 chih$^2$ | 兒。'rh | 脊 chi$^2$ | 西。hsi$^1$ | 上 shang$^4$ | 我 wo$^3$ | 子 tzŭ |
| 頭 t'ou$^2$ | 肚 tu$^4$ | 梁 niang$^2$ | 椅 i$^3$ | 背 pei$^1$ | 的 ti | 疼。t'êng$^2$ |
| 肚 tu$^4$ | 子。tzŭ | 背 pei$^4$ | 背 pei$^4$ | 着 cho$^1$ | 背 pei$^4$ | 不 pu$^2$ |
| 兒。'rh | 腿 t'ui$^3$ | 兒。'rh | 兒。'rh | 甚 shên$^2$ | 後。hou$^4$ | 要 yao$^4$ |

My chest is sore.
Don't stand behind my back.
What are you carrying on your back?
The back of a chair.
The spine. The back between and below the shoulders.
The shoulders. The belly.
The calf of the leg. The fleshy tip of the finger.
*Obs.*—The thigh is ta$^4$-t'ui$^3$.

**479.** 波 po$^1$, waves. *Shui$^3$ po$^1$*, a ripple on the water.

**480.** 稜, 楞, lêng$^2$, an edge; both forms are admissible.

**481.** 脚, 腳, chiao$^3$, the feet; the first form is the commoner.

**482.** 踝 huai$^2$, the ankle; colloquially, used only in the combination *huai$^2$-tzŭ ku$^3$*, ankle-bone (or ankle).

**483.** 體 t'i$^3$, the body. With *mien$^4$*, the face (Radical 176), the combination means respectable; very commonly also, of persons and things, nice-looking.

**484.** 斬 chan$^3$, to behead.

**485.** 賊 tsei$^2$, robbers; rebels; any malefactors.

**486.** 級 chi$^2$, a step in gradation; the heads of criminals when cut off.

**487.** Examples :—

| | | | | | |
|---|---|---|---|---|---|
| 袋。tai$^4$ | 斬 chan$^3$ | 面 mien$^4$ | 了。liao | 骨。ku$^3$ | 波 po$^1$ |
| 長 ch'ang$^2$ | 下 hsia$^4$ | 的 ti | 他 t'a$^1$ | 兩 liang$^3$ | 稜 lêng$^2$ |
| 毛 mao$^2$ | 來 lai$^2$ | 人。jên$^2$ | 是 shih$^4$ | 脚 chiao$^3$ | 蓋 kai$^4$ |
| 賊。tsei$^2$ | 的 ti | 首 shou$^3$ | 個 ko$^4$ | 都 tou$^1$ | 兒。'rh |
| 老 lao$^3$ | 賊 tsei$^2$ | 級 chi$^2$ | 很 hên$^3$ | 走 tsou$^3$ | 踝 huai$^2$ |
| 賊。tsei$^2$ | 腦 nao$^3$ | 是 shih$^4$ | 體 t'i$^3$ | 疼 t'êng$^2$ | 子 tzŭ |

The knee-cap. The ankle-bone (or ankle).
I have walked till both my feet are sore.
He is a most respectable man.
*Shou$^3$-chi$^2$* is the head of a malefactor when cut off.
The long-haired rebels. An old thief.

## EXERCISE XVIII.

1 年輕的人多愛刮臉、人到了四十多就有鬍子了。叫個剃頭的來、我要打辮子。女人們梳頭。

1. Most young men are in the habit of shaving their faces; when men get to forty or upwards they have beards. Send for a barber; I want my hair dressed. Women comb (or dress) the hair.

*Obs.* 1.—Most: note that *to*[1] does not mean all, but the greater part.
*Obs.* 2.—*Shu t'ou* is only applied to the female *coiffure*.

2 剃頭、剃的是那辮子以外的短頭髮。前些年不剃頭的那賊就叫長髮賊。

2. In the [Chinese] tonsure, what is shaved off is the short hair growing outside the pigtail. Some years ago the outlaws who did not shave the head were called long-haired rebels.

*Obs.*—Outside: *i wai*. One of the senses of *i* is to follow, hence with words indicating place it means in the direction of; thus, *i tung*, to the east of; *i wai*, outside of. The sentence literally construed is, shaving the head, that which is shaved is the queue towards outside short hair.

3 說人體面是說他是個好人。說他長得體面是說他長得好看。剃頭鋪。

3. When you say a man is *t'i*[3]*-mien*[4] you mean that he is a person of good character; when you say that such a person is *chang*[3] *tê t'i*[3]*-mien*[4] you mean that he is good-looking. A barber's shop.

4 他那屋子蓋得體面也說得。剃頭刮臉都是用剃頭刀。

4. You can also say that that house of so-and-so's is *t'i*[3]*-mien*[4] (that it is erected, *kai*[4], in a respectable way). The *t'i*[4]*-t'ou*[2]*-tao*[1] (razor) is used both for shaving the head and the face.

5 我們本地人剃頭不使溫和水兒、也不用胰子。你乏了我背你罷。他肚子裏有學問。他上了吊了。

5. We natives use neither warm water nor soap in shaving the head. If you are tired I'll carry you on my back. He is a man of learning. He has hanged himself.

*Obs.* 1.—Note *hsio*[2]*-wên*[4], learning: the *hsio*[2] must be emphasised. The stomach is held by the Chinese to be the seat of intelligence.
*Obs.* 2.—*Shang tiao* (322) can only be used of suicide by hanging.

6 明天那地方官要斬幾個賊、聽見說斬賊的那一把刀不很快、不過重就是了.

6. The local authorities are going to behead several rebels (or malefactors) to-morrow; I am told that the sword with which criminals are beheaded is not very sharp, only heavy.

7 你鼻梁兒上怎麼這麼黃. 那是我昨兒叫人家打了一下兒.

7. How is it that the bridge of your nose is so yellow? Because someone hit me [there] yesterday.

*Obs.*—Hit: *lit.*, was hit by someone one blow. *Hsia*: *lit.*, a fall; *sc.*, a fall of the hand.

8 四方的東西有四個楞兒、有四個角兒、刀楞兒可不說.

8. Square things have four edges (*lêng*²) and four corners (*chiao*³); but [you can] not say *tao*¹ *lêng*²-*'rh* (the edge of a knife).

*Turn the following into Chinese.* (KEY, EXERCISE XVIII.)

1. How pretty that little girl belonging to the LI family has grown up to be; have you seen her?

*Obs.*—Girls are often called *ch'ien chin* (thousand [pieces of] gold), especially when speaking of them to their own parents.

2. Yes, I have seen her. She has heavy eyebrows, big eyes, and a high bridge to her nose; her hair on either temple is both black and bright; she has a fine skin, too, on her cheeks, a small chin, long neck, and slender waist, while she speaks out very distinctly; her feet also are not large, nor her figure clumsy; she is indeed [pretty], and no mistake.

*Obs.* 1.—Both: *yu* (Radical 29).

*Obs.* 2.—Figure: *lit.*, body and form, *shên*¹ *t'i*³.

*Obs.* 3.—Is indeed: *kuo*³ *chên*¹, in very truth.

3. Is it because he is ill that every bone in his body aches? No; it is because he is old and has not sufficient vitality.

*Obs.* 1.—Body: *man*³ *shên*; *lit.*, full body of *ku-t'ou*, bones, *t'êng*, that ache.

*Obs.* 2.—Vitality: *lit.*, breath and blood, *ch'i hsüeh*.

4. To get the head or the face shaved one must send for a barber.

5. For a man's *hsiung*¹-*ch'ien*² (breast) and *pei*⁴-*hou*⁴ (back) the expressions *ch'ien*²-*hsin*¹ and *hou*⁴-*hsin*¹ may be used.

6. The bag contains heavy articles and will have to be carried on the back, or it may be placed on the shoulders.

7. What is the matter with you? your face has a bad colour. Are you lying down there because you have a stomach-ache?

*Obs.* 1.—What is the matter: *lit.*, you how? *ni tsêm*³-*mo liao*.

*Obs.* 2.—Colour; *lit.*, aspect colour, *ch'i sê*⁴. *See* 232.

8. It is not my stomach that aches; it is the ankle-bone of this foot, which a boy hit with a stone. Both it and my knee are dreadfully painful.

*Obs.*—Boy: *lit.*, small man. There is another expression for a boy or child, which will be met with later.

9. There are a whole lot of men's heads hanging up outside the city gate. A man told me they were, every one of them, the heads of criminals who had been decapitated.

*Obs.*—Hanging: *tiao*⁴; *see* 322. There is another expression for to hang.

488. 君 *chün*$^1$, the Sovereign.

489. 民 *min*$^2$, the people, as distinguished from their governors.

490. 主 *chu*$^3$, a master. *Chün*$^1$ *chu*$^3$, the term adopted in the British Treaty to designate Her Majesty the Queen.

491. 爵 *chio*$^2$, *chüeh*$^2$, *chiao*$^2$, high rank, whether official or hereditary.

492. 位 *wei*$^4$, properly, the position of a person, the place where he stands or sits. Specially, high position; hence, the numerative of gentlemen, scholars, and officials, also of cannon.

493. 參 *ts'an*$^1$, to counsel. When combined with *jên*$^2$, a man, read *shên*$^1$; as *jên*$^2$-*shên*$^1$, ginseng. Also read *ts'ên*$^1$ (*see* 576).

494. 贊 *tsan*$^4$, to assist; as *ts'an*$^1$-*tsan*$^4$, to aid with counsel and advice. Also, an official title. *See* Examples.

495. 尊 *tsun*$^1$, honoured.

496. Examples:—

| | | | | | | |
|---|---|---|---|---|---|---|
| 這 *chê*$^4$ | 贊。*tsan*$^4$ | 是 *shih*$^4$ | 他 *t'a*$^1$ | 主 *chu*$^3$ | 民 *min*$^2$ | 君 *chün*$^1$ |
| 一 *i*$^2$ | 他 *t'a*$^1$ | 個 *ko*$^4$ | 的 *ti*$^1$ | 子。*tzŭ* | 人。*jên*$^2$ | 上。*shang*$^4$ |
| 位 *wei*$^4$ | 是 *shih*$^4$ | 甚 *shên*$^2$ | 爵 *chio*$^2$ | 家 *chia*$^1$ | 那 *na*$^4$ | 小 *hsiao*$^3$ |
| 是 *shih*$^4$ | 個 *ko*$^4$ | 麼 *mo* | 位 *wei*$^4$ | 主 *chu*$^3$ | 是 *shih*$^4$ | 民。*min*$^2$ |
| 誰。*shui*$^2$ | 尊 *tsun*$^1$ | 爵 *chio*$^2$ | 尊 *tsun*$^1$ | 兒。*'rh* | 個 *ko*$^4$ | 他 *t'a*$^1$ |
| | 重 *chung*$^4$ | 位。*wei*$^4$ | 貴。*kuei*$^4$ | 船 *ch'uan*$^2$ | 民 *min*$^2$ | 是 *shih*$^4$ |
| | 人。*jên*$^2$ | 參 *ts'an*$^1$ | 他 *t'a*$^1$ | 主。*chu*$^3$ | 房。*fang*$^2$ | 個 *ko*$^4$ |

The Sovereign. The people.

He is a man of the people.

*Obs.*—*Min jên* in general conversation is the designation applied to Chinese as distinguished from Tartars. In places in the provinces where there is no Tartar colony *min jên* may mean a private individual with no official rank or status; in Peking he is called *pai*$^2$ *jen*$^2$-*'rh*, *lit.*, a white man.

That is an ordinary dwelling-house.

*Obs.*—*Min fang*, in Peking, is a house which is the property of a private individual, as opposed to *kuan fang*, Government property.

The lord or master. The master of the house.

The captain of a ship.

His official position is honourable.

What rank has he?

*Obs.*—If *wei* were omitted the question would be understood of hereditary rank only.

The Assistant Resident in certain Chinese colonies. (Used by us as the term for diplomatic secretaries.)

He is an honourable man.

*Obs.*—*Lit.*, honourable and important.

Who is this gentleman?

13

497. 文 *wên*$^{2}$ (Radical 67), civilian, as opposed to the following.

498. 武 *wu*$^{3}$, military.

499. 兵 *ping*$^{1}$, soldier.

500. 缺 *ch'üeh*$^{1}$, to vacate; a vacancy; hence, in certain contexts, any official post. It also means short, or deficient.

501. 額 *ngê*$^{2}$, *ngo*$^{2}$, properly, the forehead; colloquially, as well as in writing, a fixed number.

502. 捐 *chüan*$^{1}$, to subscribe for a public purpose.

503. 充 *ch'ung*$^{1}$, to stand for; to stand in the place of; to act as; to play the part of. Often used with *tang*$^{1}$ (342). Also, to make up, as a number.

504. Examples:—

| | | | | | |
|---|---|---|---|---|---|
| 額 *ngo*$^{2}$ | 開 *k'ai*$^{1}$ | 過 *kuo*$^{4}$ | 出 *ch'u*$^{1}$ | 當 *tang*$^{1}$ | 文 *wên*$^{2}$ |
| 數。*shu*$^{4}$ | 缺。*ch'üeh*$^{1}$ | 兵 *ping*$^{1}$ | 兵。*ping*$^{1}$ | 兵。*ping*$^{1}$ | 官。*kuan*$^{1}$ |
| 捐 *chüan*$^{1}$ | 補 *pu*$^{3}$ | 沒 *mei*$^{2}$ | 你 *ni*$^{3}$ | 充 *ch'ung*$^{1}$ | 武 *wu*$^{3}$ |
| 官。*kuan*$^{1}$ | 缺。*ch'üeh*$^{1}$ | 有。*yu*$^{3}$ | 出 *ch'u*$^{1}$ | 兵。*ping*$^{1}$ | 官。*kuan*$^{1}$ |

Civil officials. Military officials.
To be a soldier. To be a soldier.
To go on a military expedition.
Have you been on active service?
To remove from office for sickness or misconduct; or, to vacate a post.
To fill, or succeed to, a vacancy.
A given number.
To purchase a grade of rank by subscribing to the State's necessities.

505. 殺 *sha*$^{1}$, to kill; also, adverbially, an intensive.

506. 退 *t'ui*$^{4}$, to retire; to drive back.

507. 勒 *lo*$^{4}$, to bind; to coerce. In combination read *lê*$^{2}$, as *lê*$^{2}$-*so*$^{3}$, to squeeze; to extort money. *Lei*$^{1}$, to hold in, as a horse; also, in combination, to strangle, as will be seen later.

508. 索 *so*$^{3}$, to demand; to extort.

509. Examples:—

| | | | | | | |
|---|---|---|---|---|---|---|
| 把 *pa*$^{3}$ | 捐 *chüan*$^{1}$ | 子。*tzŭ* | 人 *jên*$^{2}$ | 退 *t'ui*$^{4}$ | 人。*jên*$^{2}$ | 店 *tien*$^{4}$ |
| 馬 *ma*$^{3}$ | 出 *ch'u*$^{1}$ | 那 *na*$^{4}$ | 勒 *lê*$^{2}$ | 出 *ch'u*$^{1}$ | 賊 *tsei*$^{2}$ | 主 *chu*$^{3}$ |
| 勒 *lei*$^{1}$ | 銀 *yin*$^{2}$ | 個 *ko*$^{4}$ | 索 *so*$^{3}$ | 城 *ch'êng*$^{2}$ | 都 *tou*$^{1}$ | 兒 *'rh* |
| 著 *cho* | 子 *tzŭ* | 官 *kuan*$^{1}$ | 了 *liao* | 去。*ch'ü*$^{4}$ | 殺 *sha*$^{1}$ | 殺 *sha*$^{1}$ |
| 點 *tien*$^{3}$ | 來。*lai*$^{2}$ | 勒 *lê*$^{2}$ | 我 *wo*$^{3}$ | 那 *na*$^{4}$ | 退 *t'ui*$^{4}$ | 了 *liao* |
| 兒。*'rh* | 勒 *lei*$^{1}$ | 令 *ling*$^{4}$ | 五 *wu*$^{3}$ | 關 *kuan*$^{1}$ | 了。*liao* | 兩 *liang*$^{3}$ |
| | 住 *chu*$^{4}$ | 人 *jên*$^{2}$ | 兩 *liang*$^{3}$ | 上 *shang*$^{4}$ | 把 *pa*$^{3}$ | 個 *ko*$^{4}$ |
| | 馬。*ma*$^{3}$ | 家 *chia*$^{1}$ | 銀 *yin*$^{2}$ | 的 *ti* | 賊 *tsei*$^{2}$ | 客 *k'o*$^{4}$ |

The innkeeper killed two guests.

The rebels were repulsed with loss.

Drive the rebels out of the city.

*Obs.*—*T'ui* cannot be used promiscuously ; you could not, for instance, use it in speaking of driving a dog away.

The Custom House people squeezed me out of five taels.

That official compels people to subscribe money.

*Obs.*—*Chüan* is not generally used of subscriptions to a private object.

Pull the horse up.

*Obs.*—Up : *chu*, to a standstill.

Hold in your horse a bit.

510. 底 *ti*$^{3}$, the bottom ; below.

511. 全 *ch'üan*$^{2}$, all ; entire.

512. 姓 *hsing*$^{4}$, surname of family or tribe.

513. 名 *ming*$^{2}$, name, or cognomen, as distinguished from the surname.

514. Examples :—

| | | | | | | |
|---|---|---|---|---|---|---|
| 兒 *'rh* | 麽, *mo* | 不 *pu*$^{4}$ | 辛 *hsing*$^{1}$ | 石 *shih*$^{2}$ | 事 *shih*$^{4}$ | 樓 *lou*$^{2}$ |
| 地 *ti*$^{4}$ | 貴 *kuei*$^{4}$ | 好。*hao*$^{3}$ | 苦 *k'u*$^{3}$ | 頭。*t'ou*$^{2}$ | 的。*ti* | 底 *ti*$^{3}$ |
| 名 *ming*$^{2}$ | 姓。*hsing*$^{4}$ | 百 *po*$^{2}$ | 全 *ch'üan*$^{2}$ | 桌 *cho*$^{1}$ | 河 *ho*$^{2}$ | 下。*hsia*$^{4}$ |
| 叫 *chiao*$^{4}$ | 名 *ming*$^{2}$ | 姓。*hsing*$^{4}$ | 是 *shih*$^{4}$ | 子 *tzŭ* | 底 *ti*$^{3}$ | 底 *ti*$^{3}$ |
| 甚 *shê*$^{n2}$ | 子。*tzŭ* | 你 *ni*$^{3}$ | 用 *yung*$^{4}$ | 底 *ti*$^{3}$ | 下 *hsia*$^{4}$ | 下 *hsia*$^{4}$ |
| 麽, *mo* | 這 *chê*$^{4}$ | 姓 *hsing*$^{4}$ | 的 *ti*$^{1}$ | 下。*hsia*$^{4}$ | 全 *ch'üan*$^{2}$ | 人。*jên*$^{2}$ |
| | 塊 *k'uai*$^{4}$ | 甚 *shê*$^{n2}$ | 人 *jên*$^{2}$ | 他 *t'a*$^{1}$ | 是 *shih*$^{4}$ | 管 *kuan*$^{3}$ |

Downstairs.

Servants. A head servant or butler. *See* 414.

The bottom of the river is all stones.

Below the table ; or, underneath the table.

*Obs.*—This might also mean on the under face of the table ; but in that case it would be more accurate to say *cho*$^{1}$ *mien*$^{4}$*-'rh ti*$^{3}$ *hsia*$^{4}$.

His troubles are all owing to the inefficiency (worthlessness) of the people in his employ.

The people.

*Obs.*—*Lit.*, hundred surnames. Note the change in sound and tone of *pai*$^{3}$, a hundred.

What is your name (to inferiors) ?

What is your name (to equals and superiors)?

A name.

What is the name of this place ?

## EXERCISE XIX.

1 這一匹馬走的這麼慢，全是你沒餧足。

1. The reason this horse goes so slowly is all because you have not given him enough to eat.

2 君上是百官萬民的主子。家生子兒是買的底下人生的兒女。

2. The *chün*[1]*-shang*[4] (Sovereign) is lord over all his subjects, official and unofficial. *Chia*[1] *shêng*[1]*-tzŭ*[3]*-'rh* are the children born to bond-servants (while in a state of bondage).

*Obs.*—All subjects, etc.: *lit.*, lord over the hundred officials and myriad non-officials. *Wan* is often used to denote an infinite quantity or number. The Manchus more particularly speak of the Emperor as their *chu-tzŭ*, master.

3 爵位尊、是說人做的官大、小官算不了有爵位。

3. When you say that a man's position is honourable you mean that his office is considerable; a petty official is not considered to have "position."

4 管民的是文官、帶兵的是武官。

4. Officials who have charge of the people are *wên*[2] *kuan*[1] (civilians); those who command troops are *wu*[3] *kuan*[1] (military officers).

5 文武官的衣裳怎麼分。不大好分、不過是他們帶的補子不同。

5. What is the difference between the dress of civil and military officials? It is not very easy to distinguish between them; the only difference is that the *pu*[3]*-tzŭ* (or insignia) that they wear are not identical.

*Obs.*—*Pu*[3]*-tzŭ* is the name given to the square embroidered patch worn by officials on the breast and back of the court robe: on the civil "patch" birds are represented, each grade having a distinctive bird; on the military patch animals are depicted. The *pu-tzŭ* of princes and nobles of the highest grades are round.

6 各地方的官兵額數是有一定的不過是不足的時候兒多、趕到月底要點名、就找些個人充數兒。

6. The strength of the army in different places is fixed, but it is at most times under the proper complement; [so] when a muster is called at the end of the month some men are found to make up the number.

*Obs.* 1.—When: *lit.*, pursuing, arrive at, etc.; *i.e.*, when the end of the month is arrived at. Note *yüeh ti*, the end of the month.

*Obs.* 2.—Call the muster: *tien ming*; *lit.*, prick, or check, the names.

7 山東那塊兒出了個好缺、不知道是誰得。誰該着補就是誰。

7. A good vacancy has occurred over in Shantung; I don't know who will get it. The person whose turn it is will get it.

*Obs.*—Whose turn it is: *lit.*, who, owing to fill it, will then fill it. *Kai-cho* is frequently used in the above sense; were the *cho* omitted, *kai* would simply mean ought.

8 拿銀錢買官、那就叫捐官。他那官是捐的麼。不是捐的、是出兵得的。

8. When an office or rank is obtained by payment of money, that is called *chüan*$^{1}$ *kuan*$^{1}$ (to obtain an office by subscription). Was his office purchased? No; it was obtained by active military service.

9 那帶兵的大官一點兒本事都沒有、前些日子、那賊都跑到山裏頭去、沒吃的了、他要當時追他們、很可以把他們殺退了。

9. The high officer at the head of the troops has no ability whatever; some days ago the rebels escaped into the mountains, where they had nothing to eat; if he had pursued them at the time he could perfectly well have driven them back with loss.

*Obs.* 1.—*Ta kuan* might be either singular or plural.
*Obs.* 2.—Nothing to eat: *mei*, had not (*yu*, understood), *ch'ih ti*, eatables.

10 貴姓。賤姓馬。

10. May I ask your name? My name is Ma.

*Obs.*—*Lit.*, your honourable name? My common name, Ma.

*Turn the following into Chinese.* (Key, Exercise XIX.)

1. The greatest person in the Empire is the Sovereign; the most numerous body are the *min*$^{2}$-*jên*$^{2}$ (people). The Sovereign is also called the master, and the people, *po*$^{2}$ *hsing*$^{4}$ (the hundred surnames).

*Obs.* 1.—Empire: *t'ien*$^{1}$ *hsia*$^{4}$ (*lit.*, under Heaven); the idea being that the Emperor of China exercises sway over everything under Heaven.

2. A schoolfellow of mine is a *ts'an*$^{1}$-*tsan*$^{4}$ down West; I hear that the position of such officers is very honourable.

*Obs.* 1.—Schoolfellow: *t'ung*$^{2}$ *hsüo*$^{2}$; *lit.*, same learning. *Hsüo*$^{2}$, short for *hsüo*$^{2}$-*fang*$^{2}$, a school.

*Obs.* 2.—Down west: *hsi*$^{1}$ *hsia*$^{4}$; this is the general name given to Thibet and the portion of Chinese territory to the north-west of the Great Wall.

3. He thoroughly understands [the management of] affairs; is he likely to employ you to assist him?

*Obs.*—Employ: *ts'an-tsan* (494); emphasise *tsán*.

4. Most military officers rise from the ranks.

*Obs.*—Rise from the ranks: *lit.*, are from serving as soldiers risen (got up) most.

5. The number of officers in command of troops is fixed. Whenever there is a vacancy

it must be filled up. When there is a vacancy and nobody [to fill it up], it is a *k'ung*$^{1}$ (empty) vacancy.

6. Supernumerary officials are those in excess of the regular establishment.

*Obs.* 1.—Supernumerary: *ngo*$^{2}$ *wai*$^{4}$, outside the fixed number.

*Obs.* 2.—Regular: *chêng*$^{4}$ (103).

7. I have been casting about to find a bit of a job, but I have not been able to do so; so I have come to ask you to find some opening for me.

*Obs.* 1.—Have come, etc.: *ch'ing ni lai* may be read in two ways.

*Obs.* 2.—Opening: *mên*$^{2}$ *lu*$^{4}$; *lit.*, door and way; *i.e.*, a way of access to employment.

8. To insist on having money from a person whether he possesses it or not is to squeeze.

*Obs.*—To insist on having, etc.: *i*$^{2}$ *ting*$^{4}$ *han*$^{4}$ *jên*$^{2}$ *chia*$^{1}$ *yao*$^{4}$, positively from persons wanting.

9. When I fixed on the things, I insisted that I wanted all of them good; why have you put in a quantity of bad ones just to make up the number? If you don't exchange them for good ones, I shall throw the whole lot back on you.

*Obs.* 1.—Fixed on: *ting*$^{4}$.

*Obs.* 2.—Insisted: *shuo*$^{1}$ *chu*$^{4}$ *liao*, stood firm at the statement. *See* 48.

*Obs.* 3.—Throw back: *t'ui*$^{4}$ *hui*$^{2}$ *ch'ü*$^{4}$.

10. I told you to put the table in the middle of the room; why have you put it on one side? In future, when I tell you anything you must remember it.

*Obs.*—In future: *ti*$^{3}$ *hsia*$^{4}$, which can be applied to time as well as to material objects.

11. Are all the surnames of the people in the volume of the "*Po Chia Hsing?*"

12. How could they all be? [it] only [contains] those which one is familiar with, that's all.

*Obs.*—Familiar: *lit.*, have heard ripe.

13. Kill a fowl for me.

515. 國 *kuo*$^{2}$, a nation; a State; a Government.

516. 章 *chang*$^{1}$, a rule; a law. Often used with *ch'êng*$^{2}$ (519).

517. 律 *lü*$^{4}$, statutes.

518. 例 *li*$^{4}$, laws; amendments.

519. 程 *ch'êng*$^{2}$, a stage in a journey.

520. Examples:—

| | | | | | | |
|---|---|---|---|---|---|---|
| 例 *li*$^{4}$ | 程 *ch'êng*$^{2}$ | 中 *chung*$^{1}$ | 程 *ch'êng*$^{2}$ | 一 *i*$^{2}$ | 出 *ch'u*$^{1}$ | 那 *na*$^{4}$ |
| 不 *pu*$^{4}$ | 不 *pu*$^{4}$ | 國 *kuo*$^{2}$ | 你 *ni*$^{3}$ | 定 *ting*$^{4}$ | 來 *lai*$^{2}$ | 律 *lü*$^{4}$ |
| 同。*t'ung*$^{2}$ | 行。*hsing*$^{2}$ | 律 *lü*$^{4}$ | 知 *chih*$^{1}$ | 的 *ti* | 的。*ti* | 例 *li*$^{4}$ |
| | 各 *ko*$^{4}$ | 例。*li*$^{4}$ | 道 *tao*$^{4}$ | 章 *chang*$^{1}$ | 各 *ko*$^{4}$ | 是 *shih*$^{4}$ |
| | 國 *kuo*$^{2}$ | 這 *chê*$^{4}$ | 不 *pu*$^{4}$ | 程, *ch'êng* | 關 *kuan*$^{1}$ | 國 *kuo*$^{2}$ |
| | 的 *ti* | 些 *hsieh*$^{1}$ | 知 *chih*$^{1}$ | 這 *chê*$^{4}$ | 都 *tou*$^{1}$ | 家 *chia*$^{1}$ |
| | 律 *lü*$^{4}$ | 章 *chang*$^{1}$ | 道。*tao*$^{4}$ | 路 *lu*$^{4}$ | 有 *yu*$^{3}$ | 定 *ting*$^{4}$ |

Laws are made by the State.

*Obs.*—It would be equally correct, but perhaps more indefinite, to say simply *lü li shih kuo chia ting ti*. *Ch'u lai* in this connexion signifies completion of an act; made and promulgated.

Every Custom House has fixed regulations.

Do you know the road?

*Obs.*—*Lu ch'êng*: *lit.*, stages of a road. *Lu ch'êng* can only be applied to long distances divided into stages.

The penal code of China

These regulations won't do.

The laws of different countries are not identical.

語言自邇集



521. 巡 *hsün*2, to go the rounds.

522. 察 *ch'a*2, to inquire into.

523. 搜 *sou*1, to search, as the person, baggage, etc.

524. 動 *tung*4, to move ; and, less frequently, to be moved.

525. 種 *chung*4, to sow ; to cultivate. Read *chung*3 *'rh*, seeds. *Chung*3 (colloquially, *tsung*1), a kind or class.

526. Examples :—

| | | | | | | | |
|---|---|---|---|---|---|---|---|
| 東 *tung*1 | 不 *pu*2 | 的。*ti* | 幾 *chi*3 | 不 *pu*2 | 方 *fang*1 | 看 *k'an*1 |
| 西。*hsi*1 | 要 *yao*4 | 種 *chung*4 | 點 *tien*3 | 要 *yao*4 | 的 *ti* | 街 *chieh*1 |
| | 這 *chê*4 | 菜。*ts'ai*4 | 鐘 *chung*1 | 動 *tung*4 | 人。*jên*2 | 的 *ti* |
| | 種 *tsung*1 | 種 *chung*4 | 動 *tung*4 | 那 *na*4 | 搜 *sou*1 | 是 *shih*4 |
| | 樣 *yang*4 | 種 *chung*3 | 身。*shên*1 | 東 *tung*1 | 察 *ch'a*2 | 巡 *hsün*2 |
| | 兒 *'rh* | 兒。*'rh* | 種 *chung*4 | 西。*hsi*1 | 行 *hsing*2 | 察 *ch'a*2 |
| | 的 *ti* | 我 *wo*3 | 地 *ti*4 | 你 *ni*3 | 李。*li*3 | 地 *ti*4 |

The *k'an*1-*chieh*1-*ti* is the man who goes the round of the locality and sees (*q.d.*, that order is kept).

*Obs.*—Note that *k'an*1 means here to watch or keep guard over, and is in the first tone. *See* 91.

To search baggage.

Do not touch those things.

What time do you start ?

A farmer (or farm labourer).

To grow vegetables.

To sow seeds.

*Obs.*—Also called *tzŭ*3 *'rh*.

I don't want this kind of thing.

527. 治 *chih*4, to regulate ; to reform ; to restore order; good government as distinguished from disorder. Also, to treat medically ; *chih*4 *hao*3, to cure.

528. 理 *li*3, regulating principle or force. Also, to manage ; to regulate. Sometimes read *lü*3, to arrange ; to set in order. *Li*3 *hui*4 (129), to pay attention ; to observe ; to notice.

529. 暴 *pao*4, passionate; fierce. The opposite of *ho*2, soft ; gentle; accommodating (210).

530. 亂 *lan*4, *luan*4, disorder.

531. 急 *chi*2, quick in movement or temper.

532. 性 *hsing*4, nature ; natural disposition.

533. Examples :—

| | | | | | | |
|---|---|---|---|---|---|---|
| 急。*chi*2 | 那 *na*4 | 官 *kuan*1 | 道 *tao*4 | 治 *chih*4 | 方 *fang*1 | 百 *po*2 |
| 不 *pu*2 | 個 *ko*4 | 性 *hsing*4 | 理 *li*3 | 理。*li*3 | 官 *kuan*1 | 姓 *hsing*4 |
| 用 *yung*4 | 人 *jên*2 | 子 *tzŭ* | 不 *pu*2 | 治 *chih*4 | 一 *i*4 | 亂 *luan*4 |
| 著 *chao*2 | 說 *shuo*1 | 過 *kuo*4 | 錯。*ts'o*4 | 亂。*luan*4 | 點 *tien*3 | 得 *tê* |
| 急。*chi*2 | 話 *hua*4 | 於 *yü*2 | 這 *chê*4 | 這 *chê*4 | 兒 *'rh* | 很。*hên*3 |
| | 太 *t'ai*4 | 暴。*pao*4 | 個 *ko*4 | 個 *ko*4 | 不 *pu*2 | 地 *ti*4 |

The people are very disorderly (or turbulent); the local officials do not keep them in the slightest order.

Order and disorder ; or, to restore order.

This reasoning (or principle) is perfectly correct.

*Obs.*—*Tao*, morally, the right road ; *li*, the principle imparted to man, if he conform to which he will keep the right road. *Tao-li* is, hence, right principle ; next, any principle conformity to which produces the normal estate of men or things, the rationale or logical condition of anything. It is against *tao-li*, in the first sense, to steal ; but the *tao-li* of a thief is to steal, for he would not be a thief if he did not steal : a Chinese would say *mei chê ko tao-li*, it is not logical, there is no sense in such a proposition as that a man should be a thief and not steal. Lastly, the term *tao-li* is used as the principles collectively, the philosophic system, of any teacher. Confucianism is the *tao-li* of Confucius.

This official is too passionate.

That man talks too impetuously.

Do not get excited ; or, there is no occasion to excite yourself.

*Obs.*—Note the peculiar use of *chao*, which here means to put forth or give out; not as in the expression *chao*$^2$-*liang*$^3$, to catch, or meet with unexpectedly.

534. 普 *p'u*$^3$, universal.

535. 羣 *ch'ün*$^2$, a flock ; a drove ; a multitude.

536. 耕 *kêng*$^1$, to till ; also read *ching*$^1$, as *ching*$^1$ *ti*$^4$, to plough.

537. 總 *tsung*$^3$, to collect ; collectively. Hence, in any case ; never ; positively ; always.

538. 之 *chih*$^1$, used in books as the pronoun of the third person and the sign of the possessive ; also used in some instances in the spoken language.

539. Examples :—

| | | | | | | |
|---|---|---|---|---|---|---|
| 去、*ch'ü*$^4$ | 那 *na*$^4$ | 言 *yên*$^2$ | 國 *kuo*$^2$ | 地。*ti*$^4$ | 多。*to*$^1$ | 普 *p'u*$^3$ |
| 把 *pa*$^3$ | 一 *i*$^4$ | 之。*chih*$^1$ | 人。*jên*$^2$ | 我 *wo*$^3$ | 要 *yao*$^4$ | 天 *t'ien*$^1$ |
| 書 *shu*$^1$ | 羣 *ch'ün*$^2$ | 國 *kuo*$^2$ | 你 *ni*$^3$ | 總 *tsung*$^3$ | 種 *chung*$^4$ | 下 *hsia*$^4$ |
| 理 *lü*$^3$ | 羊 *yang*$^2$ | 家 *chia*$^1$ | 總 *tsung*$^3$ | 沒 *mei*$^2$ | 種 *chung*$^3$ | 的 *ti* |
| 一 *i*$^4$ | 趕 *kan*$^3$ | 之 *chih*$^1$ | 得 *tei*$^3$ | 看 *k'an*$^4$ | 兒 *'rh* | 人 *jên*$^2$ |
| 理。*lü*$^3$ | 到 *tao*$^4$ | 大 *ta*$^4$ | 去、*ch'ü*$^4$ | 見 *chien*$^4$ | 先 *hsien*$^1$ | 種 *chung*$^4$ |
| | 山 *shan*$^1$ | 官。*kuan*$^1$ | 總 *tsung*$^3$ | 過 *kuo*$^4$ | 得 *tei*$^3$ | 地 *ti*$^4$ |
| | 上 *shang*$^4$ | 把 *pa*$^3$ | 而 *êrh*$^2$ | 外 *wai*$^4$ | 耕 *ching*$^1$ | 的 *ti* |

The population of the world is mostly agricultural.

If you want to sow seeds you must first plough the land.

I have never seen a foreigner (or foreigners).

You will have to (must positively) go.

In a word ; speaking collectively.

*Obs.*—This is, strictly speaking, not colloquial, though the phrase is constantly used in conversation ; *chih* is here a final particle of no particular value.

The high officials of the State.

*Obs.*—*Ti* would here be more colloquial than *chih*, but the latter character is introduced to show its use in a possessive construction.

Drive that flock of sheep on to the hills.

Put the books in order.

## EXERCISE XX

1 城門上的官兵是盤査出入人的.

1. The guards on the city gates are [there] for [the purpose of] searching [the baggage of] persons entering and leaving the city.

2 國家定的律例是治理百姓的.

2. The laws passed by the State are for the administration of the people.

3 種地是小民的本分、夏天人人兒種地.

3. Farming is the proper business of the humbler classes; in the summer everyone is tilling the ground.

*Obs.*—Proper business: *pên*, that which is originally, *fên*⁴, the lot or share, *hsiao*³ *min*², of the humbler classes.

4 秋天種的麥子夏天收、就叫秋麥、春天種的麥子夏天收、就叫春麥.

4. Wheat sown in the autumn, which is gathered in the summer, is called *ch'iu*¹ *mai*⁴ (autumn wheat); wheat sown in the spring and gathered in the summer is called spring wheat.

5 那麼着、秋麥和春麥是一様的麼。不能算一様、秋麥總收的多。

5. In that case are autumn wheat and spring wheat identical? They cannot be considered so; the autumn wheat gives always a better yield.

6 近年天下大亂是官長治理的不好、普天下百姓都知道.

6. That the great disorder which has everywhere [prevailed] of late years is due to the maladministration of the authorities is a fact known to the people of the whole Empire.

*Obs.* 1.—Late: *chin*; *lit.*, near.

*Obs.* 2.—Authorities: *kuan ch'ang*³, the officials who *ch'ang*³, are superior; the expression is only used in speaking of the whole official class, in contradistinction to the *hsiao min*.

*Obs.* 3.—Maladministration: *chih-li*, in governing *ti*=*tê*, attained to, *pu hao*, badness.

*Obs.* 4.—Notice the construction of the whole sentence: [the fact that of] late years the Empire's great disorder is [the result of] the authorities' maladministration the entire Empire's people all know.

7 你那個兒子太不說理、告訴他甚麼話總不理會、不論甚麼事全愛說嘴。

7. That son of yours is altogether too unreasonable; he never pays attention to anything he is told, and has an opinion to offer on every subject going.

*Obs.* 1.—Unreasonable: *lit.*, does not speak reason.

*Obs.* 2.—Opinion to offer: *shuo tsui* often means boasting or self-glorification.

8 去年來了一羣賊、把那一片房子都燒了。那住着的人怎麼樣呢。他們早都跑了。

8. A horde of rebels came over there last year and burnt that whole lot of buildings. How about the occupants? They decamped long before the rebels came.

9 好些個人在一塊兒那叫一羣、馬牛羊數兒多了也說一羣。

9. A large number assembled together is said to be a *ch'ün*²; the same term may be applied to horses, oxen, and sheep in any number.

10 你把我的名片拏到他那兒去、告訴他我晚半晌兒本人兒過去見他、有話說。

10. Take my card to his place and tell him that I shall go over myself in the latter part of the afternoon to see him, as I have something to say to him.

*Obs.*—Note *ming-p'ien*, a visiting card (Radical 91). *See* 1,025.

*Turn the following into Chinese.* (KEY, EXERCISE XX.)

1. There are Chinamen all over the world. Every country has a penal code. The penal code was fixed by the State for the government of the people. Regulations are drawn up by the officials.

*Obs.*—Draw up: *li* (Radical 117).

2. A man yesterday drove a flock of sheep on to my ground, and they ate up all the wheat I had sown there.

3. The *k'an*¹*-chieh*¹*-ti* are official underlings who go the rounds and inspect every place.

4. Somebody, I don't know who, has been putting all my books into confusion; arrange them for me.

*Obs.*—Put into confusion: *la luan*; *lit.*, drag into confusion.

5. That man is dreadfully passionate; why do you pay any attention to him?

*Obs.*—Pay attention to: *li*³ (528).

6. The Great Wall (10,000 *li* long wall) is the first of the seven great wonders of the world. I have heard that it was a king who compelled his people to build it.

7. Quite right. That Sovereign was utterly without principle; he governed his people in an exceedingly oppressive way. Within a few years from the completion of the wall the whole Empire was in great disorder.

*Obs.* 1.—Utterly without, etc.: *lit.*, not principle to the utmost (Radical 133). This phrase is not strictly colloquial, though quite admissible in conversation. It has been introduced to show the use of the possessive *chih*.

*Obs.* 2.—Oppressive: *k'ê*⁴ *k'u*³. *See* 223.

8. It is necessary to put on the official dress when receiving a visitor who is a stranger.

*Obs.*—Stranger: *shêng k'o*; *lit.*, raw stranger (Radical 100).

540. 搶 *ch'iang*$^{3}$, to take by violence.

541. 奪 *to*$^{2}$, to snatch away.

542. 偷 *t'ou*$^{1}$, to steal ; to filch. Also, secretly ; stealthily.

543. 股 *ku*$^{3}$, classically, the leg or thigh. Colloquially, used of banditti, etc.; a gang or band.

544. 逃 *t'ao*$^{2}$, to fly, as a fugitive.

545. 竄 *ts'uan*$^{4}$, to escape or scuttle off, as rats or mice ; applied also to the escape of rebels or banditti.

546. 散 *san*$^{3, 4}$, to disperse. *San*$^{3}$, a medicinal powder.

547. 混 *hun*$^{3, 4}$, mingled in confusion, like the water of torrents. Read *hun*$^{2}$, stupid ; idiotic ; reckless. It also means muddy when applied to water, though, strictly speaking, another character of the same sound should be used.

548. Examples :—

他 *t'a*$^{1}$ 們 *mên* 把 *pa*$^{3}$ 行 *hsing*$^{2}$ 李 *li*$^{3}$ 搶 *ch'iang*$^{3}$ 了 *liao* 去 *ch'ü*$^{4}$ 了。*liao* 他 *t'a*$^{1}$

把 *pa*$^{3}$ 我 *wo*$^{3}$ 的 *ti* 筆 *pi*$^{3}$ 奪 *to*$^{2}$ 了 *liao* 去 *ch'ü*$^{4}$ 了。*liao* 偷 *t'ou*$^{1}$ 東 *tung*$^{1}$

西。*hsi*$^{1}$ 偷 *t'ou*$^{1}$ 偷 *t'ou*$^{1}$ 兒 *'rh* 的 *ti* 走。*tsou*$^{3}$ 他 *t'a*$^{1}$ 逃 *t'ao*$^{2}$ 走 *tsou*$^{3}$ 了。*liao*

四 *ssŭ*$^{4}$ 川 *ch'uan*$^{1}$ 那 *na*$^{4}$ 一 *i*$^{4}$ 股 *ku*$^{3}$ 賊 *tsei*$^{2}$ 散 *san*$^{4}$ 了 *liao* 一 *i*$^{2}$ 個 *ko*$^{4}$

個 *ko*$^{4}$ 兒 *'rh* 竄 *ts'uan*$^{4}$ 到 *tao*$^{4}$ 雲 *yün*$^{2}$ 南 *nan*$^{2}$ 去 *ch'ü*$^{4}$ 了。*liao* 混 *hun*$^{2}$ 水。*shui*$^{3}$

混 *hun*$^{4}$ 說。*shuo*$^{1}$ 混 *hun*$^{3}$ 和 *ho*$^{2}$ 在 *tsai*$^{4}$ 一 *i*$^{2}$ 塊 *k'uai*$^{4}$ 兒。*'rh* 他 *t'a*$^{1}$ 是 *shih*$^{4}$

個 *ko*$^{4}$ 混 *hun*$^{2}$ 小 *hsiao*$^{3}$ 子。*tzŭ*

They seized the baggage and went off with it.
He snatched my pen away from me.
To steal things.
To walk stealthily (*i.e.*, that no one shall know).
He has run away.
That band of robbers from Ssŭch'uan (Szechwan) has dispersed, and skulked off one by one into Yünnan.
Muddy water.
To talk wildly.
Jumbled together.
He is a reckless (or rowdy) youngster.

549. 懶 *lan*$^{3}$, idle ; commonly used with the following.

550. 惰 *to*$^{4}$. *Lan*$^{3}$-*to*$^{4}$, idle.

551. 棍 *kun*$^{4}$, a staff.

552. 扔 *jêng*$^{1}$, to cast ; to throw. Also read *jêng*$^{3}$.

553. 放 *fang*$^{4}$, to release ; to let go.

554. 槍 *ch'iang*$^1$, a spear; a musket. The numerative of the second is *kan*$^3$ (325) or *kên*$^1$; and of the first, *kan*$^3$, *kên*$^1$ (644), or *t'iao*$^2$.

555. Examples:—

| | | | | | | |
|---|---|---|---|---|---|---|
| 放 *fang*$^4$ | 邊 *pien*$^1$ | 用 *yung*$^4$ | 鳥 *niao*$^3$ | 槍 *ch'iang*$^1$ | 上 *shang*$^4$ | 那 *na*$^4$ |
| 他 *t'a*$^1$ | 兒 *'rh* | 不 *pu*$^4$ | 兒。*'rh* | 就 *chiu*$^4$ | 衙 *ya*$^2$ | 個 *ko*$^4$ |
| 麽。*mo* | 罷。*pa*$^4$ | 着 *chao*$^2$ | 那 *na*$^4$ | 打 *ta*$^3$ | 門, *mên*$^2$ | 人 *jên*$^2$ |
| 放 *fang*$^4$ | 放 *fang*$^4$ | 了 *liao* | 一 *i*$^4$ | 着 *chao*$^2$ | 他 *t'a*$^1$ | 懶 *lan*$^3$ |
| 他 *t'a*$^1$ | 了 *liao* | 扔 *jêng*$^1$ | 條 *t'iao*$^2$ | 了 *liao* | 放 *fang*$^4$ | 惰 *to*$^4$ |
| 罷, *pa*$^4$ | 他 *t'a*$^1$ | 在 *tsai*$^4$ | 棍 *kun*$^4$ | 一 *i*$^2$ | 了 *liao* | 不 *pu*$^2$ |
| | 罷。*pa*$^4$ | 一 *i*$^4$ | 子 *tzŭ* | 個 *ko*$^4$ | 一 *i*$^4$ | 愛 *ai*$^4$ |

That man is lazy; he does not like going to the yamên.

He fired a shot and hit a bird.

*Obs.*—Note *chao*; its special force will be seen later.

You have (or, will have) no use for that stick; you had better throw it aside.

*Obs.*—*Pa*, as before, may also be rendered imperatively.

Let him go.

*Obs.*—Note that *liao* is only an expletive, and might be omitted, though it has a certain force, as will be seen from the following sentences.

Let him go? Yes, let him go.

556. 恰 *ch'ia*$^4$, to coincide with exactly.

557. 巧 *ch'iao*$^3$, cunning; also, opportune, with or without the preceding.

558. 特 *t'ê*$^4$, special; particular.

559. 意 *i*$^4$, meaning; purpose.

560. 偶 *ou*$^3$, *ngou*$^3$, accidental.

561. 然 *jan*$^2$, thus by nature; as it were; positively. Affixed to many words and combinations with an adverbial force; as *jan*$^2$ *êrh*$^2$ (Radical 126), and yet; nevertheless.

562. Examples:—

| | | | | | | |
|---|---|---|---|---|---|---|
| 個 *ko*$^4$ | 那 *na*$^4$ | 不 *pu*$^2$ | 偶 *ou*$^3$ | 意 *i*$^4$ | 來 *lai*$^2$ | 他 *t'a*$^1$ |
| 人 *jên*$^2$ | 是 *shih*$^4$ | 是 *shih*$^4$ | 然 *jan*$^2$ | 的 *ti* | 的 *ti* | 恰 *ch'ia*$^4$ |
| 巧 *ch'iao*$^3$ | 自 *tzŭ*$^4$ | 特 *t'ê*$^4$ | 錯 *ts'o*$^4$ | 來 *lai*$^2$ | 很 *hên*$^3$ | 巧 *ch'iao*$^3$ |
| 得 *tê* | 然 *jan*$^2$ | 意 *i*$^4$ | 了 *liao* | 看 *k'an*$^4$ | 巧。*ch'iao*$^3$ | 來 *lai*$^2$ |
| 很。*hên*$^3$ | 的。*ti* | 做 *tso*$^4$ | 自 *tzŭ*$^4$ | 你。*ni*$^3$ | 我 *wo*$^3$ | 了。*liao* |
| | 這 *chê*$^4$ | 的。*ti* | 然 *jan*$^2$ | 我 *wo*$^3$ | 特 *t'ê*$^4$ | 你 *ni*$^3$ |

He came in the nick of time.

You have arrived most opportunely.

I came here purposely to see you.

*Obs.*—*T'ê i*, with special intent.

My mistake was accidental; of course it was not done intentionally.

*Obs.*—Of course: *tzŭ jan*, of itself thus.

That is a matter of course.

This man is very ingenious.

## EXERCISE XXI.

1 你的主意怎麼樣、是去好、還是不去好呢。自然是去好。

1. What is your opinion, should I go or not? Of course you had better go.

*Obs.*—Opinion: *lit.*, leading or dominant idea.

2 把我那一個小棍兒拏來、我要出門。把我那一桿槍裝上、我要打鳥兒、可不定打的着打不着。

2. Bring me that small cane (or stick) of mine; I am going out. Load my gun; I want to shoot some birds, though I am not certain that I shall hit any.

*Obs.*—Note *ta*, to fire or shoot at; *ta chao* or *ta liao*, to hit what is fired at. *Fang* (see next paragraph), to fire a gun.

3 我昨兒把那桿槍拏起來、不知道是裝得了的、偶然放了一下兒。四面兒都有人、恰巧沒打着誰、要是打着了可了不得了。

3. I picked up that gun yesterday without knowing it was loaded, and accidentally let it off. There were people all round me, but luckily I did not hit anyone; if I had, it would have been no end of a business.

*Obs.*—All round: *lit.*, on four sides.

4 背地裏拏東西不叫人知道、就是偷。把人家的東西硬拏了去、是奪。好些個賊、夜裏明火拏着槍刀到人家硬拏東西、就是搶。

4. When a person takes a thing unobserved without letting anyone know, that is *t'ou*[1] (to steal or pilfer). To take away anything from a person by force is *to*[2] (to snatch or seize violently). When a number of robbers armed with spears (or muskets) and swords go at night by the light of torches to a man's house and forcibly take his property, that is *ch'iang*[3] (robbery with violence).

*Obs.* 1.—Unobserved: *lit.*, in (or on) the ground behind the back; *i.e.*, where one cannot be seen.

*Obs.* 2.—Torchlight: *lit.*, the light or brightness of fire; burglary is often referred to as *ming-huo* simply, and the combined characters are never used in any other sense.

5 說話沒有理、那算是混說、

5. To talk without reference to reason (or, the right) is what is considered *hun*[4] *shuo*[1] (talking wildly).

6 我的洗澡水怎麼這麼混．打了不大的工夫兒．過一會兒就好了．

6. How is it that my bath water is so muddy? It hasn't been drawn very long; it will be all right after a little while.

7 我那個學生過於懶惰、不愛用功．打他兩下兒看罷．

7. That pupil of mine is too idle altogether; he won't study. Give him a thrashing, and then see how he does.

8 那一天有倆賊、一個拏着一條長槍、一個拏着一根大棍子、四下裏混打、恰巧來了一個人、拏著一桿槍．看見了那倆賊混打、趕着裝上槍就打．那賊呢．那拏槍的扔下槍就跑了、那拏棍子的叫槍子兒打著腿、跑不了咯．放槍的那個人是特意來的、還是偶然來的．怕是偶然來的、可也不定．

8. The other day two robbers, the one armed with a long spear, the other with a large staff, were assaulting people right and left, when it fortunately happened that someone with a musket came along. Seeing the robbers so engaged, he hurriedly loaded and fired. And what did the robbers do? The one with the spear threw it down and ran away; the one with the stick was struck by the bullet in the leg, so he couldn't run. Did the man who fired make his appearance designedly or by accident? Probably by accident, but I am not sure.

*Obs.* 1.—Note the numerative of *ch'iang*. Spears may be spoken of as *kan*, *kên*, or *t'iao*, but muskets are always *kan* or *kên* (644).

*Obs.* 2.—Right and left: *hsia li*, in the sense of direction. *Ssŭ hsia*, the four directions; properly, the four points of the compass. Cf. also *ssŭ mien-'rh* in paragraph 3.

*Obs.* 3.—Note *ch'iang-tzŭ*³, a bullet.

*Turn the following into Chinese.* (KEY, EXERCISE XXI.)

1. Last year over ten robbers armed with spears and knives came into the city and made a clean sweep of everything in my shop. An hour before this happened that lazy servant of mine had gone to his home, and when he went he did not shut the door. I am afraid this was done intentionally, too.

*Obs.* 1.—Clean sweep; *lit.*, took the things in my shop and robbed it clean; the word "clean" is repeated for euphony's sake, though it would be quite correct to say, simply, *kan-ching*.

*Obs.* 2.—Gone home: this may be rendered by *chia ch'ü liao*, *hui chia ch'ü liao*, or *shang chia ch'ü liao*.

2. One of the robbers gave me a cut, and I called in a foreign doctor, who cured me.

Another, seeing a fowling-piece of mine that was loaded, let it off by accident.

*Obs.* 1.—Cut (304).

*Obs.* 2.—Doctor: common called *tai-fu* (太夫), though there is a more literary term. Note *tai*$^{4}$, not *t'ai*$^{4}$.

*Obs.* 3.—Cure (527).

3. The *k'an*$^{1}$-*chieh*$^{1}$-*ti*, hearing the report of the gun, came to see what was the matter. On seeing the robbers he was frightened, and ran straight away. On the road he saw an official, and told him some confused story or other, I don't know what.

*Obs.* 1.—*K'an*$^{1}$-*chieh-ti*, the local constable. Note *k'an*$^{1}$, to watch (91).

*Obs.* 2.—Frightened: *hai liao p'a liao*. *See* 424.

*Obs.* 3.—Straight off: *lit.*, one straight ran. *See* 374.

4. The officer said, "That will do with that story. I will take my soldiers to the place forthwith, and arrest the robbers." When the robbers heard that the soldiers were coming directly, they all dispersed in different directions.

*Obs.*—That will do, etc.: *lit.*, you need not say all this.

5. By this time my servant had come back, saying that the business which had taken him out was finished. The official said to him, "I suspect you and they had an understanding." His rejoinder was so full of untruths that orders were given for him to get a few blows with a stick.

*Obs.* 1.—Understanding: *lit.*, I fear you with them were one breath; were in collusion.

*Obs.* 2.—Rejoinder: *lit.*, the talk he returned all not true.

6. If you are to be so idle when you are young, and dislike study, how will you succeed in life when you grow up? If you do not make a man of yourself, you will have no means of livelihood, and, without that, you will naturally have to seek your bread by thieving. Yesterday you threw away your book and went out shooting with the visitors. Even after they had gone you did not study.

*Obs.* 1.—Young: *lit.*, your years' light time.

*Obs.* 2.—Means of livelihood: *lit.*, a road of passing the days; a means of subsisting from one day to another.

**563.** 凡 *fan*$^{2}$, all whatsoever. Also, as will be seen later, vulgar; common.

**564.** 揣 *ch'uai*$^{3}$, to feel, or feel for, by thrusting in the hand; hence, in combination with the following word, to guess.

**565.** 摩 *mo*$^{1}$, to feel with the fingers.

**566.** 約 *yo*$^{1}$, *yüeh*$^{1}$, primarily, to bind; an agreement. *T'iao*$^{2}$ *yo*$^{1}$ (181) is the expression for treaty (*i.e.*, *yo*$^{1}$, an agreement; *t'iao*$^{2}$, in strips, sections, or clauses).

**567.** 准 *chun*$^{3}$, to authorise; true to a course.

**568.** 否 *fou*$^{3}$, if not; or, not. Rarely used colloquially.

**569.** Examples:—

| | | | | | | |
|---|---|---|---|---|---|---|
| 同 *t'ung*$^{2}$ | 不 *pu*$^{2}$ | 准 *chun*$^{3}$ | 不 *pu*$^{4}$ | 准 *chun*$^{3}$ | 揣 *ch'uai*$^{3}$ | 凡 *fan*$^{2}$ |
| 他 *t'a*$^{1}$ | 大 *ta*$^{4}$ | 不 *pu*$^{4}$ | 着。*chao*$^{2}$ | 不 *pu*$^{4}$ | 摩。*mo*$^{1}$ | 事 *shih*$^{4}$ |
| 去。*ch'ü*$^{4}$ | 長 *ch'ang*$^{2}$ | 准 *chun*$^{3}$ | 准 *chun*$^{3}$ | 准。*chun*$^{3}$ | 不 *pu*$^{4}$ | 總 *tsung*$^{3}$ |
| 大 *ta*$^{4}$ | 說。*shuo*$^{1}$ | 話 *hua*$^{4}$ | 否 *fou*$^{3}$ | 我 *wo*$^{3}$ | 知 *chih*$^{1}$ | 要 *yao*$^{4}$ |
| 約。*yo*$^{1}$ | 約 *yo*$^{1}$ | 裡 *li*$^{3}$ | 就 *chiu*$^{4}$ | 揣 *ch'uai*$^{3}$ | 道 *tao*$^{4}$ | 小 *hsiao*$^{3}$ |
| | 我 *wo*$^{3}$ | 可 *k'o*$^{3}$ | 是 *shih*$^{4}$ | 摩 *mo*$^{1}$ | 他 *t'a*$^{1}$ | 心。*hsin*$^{1}$ |

In all things great care should be taken.

To guess.

I do not know whether he will give his sanction or not.

I cannot guess.

*Chun*$^3$ *fou*$^3$ (to authorise or to negative) is the same as *chun*$^3$ *pu*$^4$ *chun*$^3$, but it is not often used in conversation.

He invited me to go with him.

Most probably.

570. 更 *kêng*$^1$, to change; but *kêng*$^4$, more, the sign of the comparative (*see* 238).

571. 改 *kai*$^3$, to change.

572. 妥 *t'o*$^3$, secure; satisfactory. Often used with *tang*$^1$ (342).

573. 專 *chuan*$^1$, single; special.

574. 失 *shih*$^1$, to lose; to miss.

575. 神 *shên*$^2$, spirits, divine or human; animal spirits.

576. 參 *ts'ên*$^1$, with the following *tz'ŭ*$^1$, irregular; uneven (*e.g.*, like foliage). Read also *ts'an*$^1$ and *shên*$^1$ (*see* 493).

577. 差 *tz'ŭ*$^1$, with *ts'ên*$^1$, irregular.

578. Examples:—

| | | | | | |
|---|---|---|---|---|---|
| 西 *hsi*$^1$ | 駱 *lo*$^4$ | 神 *shên*$^2$ | 念 *nien*$^4$ | 用 *yung*$^4$ | 這 *chê*$^4$ |
| 的、*ti* | 駝 *t'o* | 就 *chiu*$^4$ | 書、*shu*$^1$ | 更 *kêng*$^1$ | 章 *chang*$^1$ |
| 那 *na*$^4$ | 是 *shih*$^4$ | 有 *yu*$^3$ | 做 *tso*$^4$ | 改。*kai*$^3$ | 程 *ch'êng*$^2$ |
| 更 *kêng*$^4$ | 專 *chuan*$^1$ | 參 *ts'ên*$^1$ | 事 *shih*$^4$ | 他 *t'a*$^1$ | 妥 *t'o*$^3$ |
| 不 *pu*$^4$ | 駝 *t'o*$^2$ | 差 *tz'ŭ*$^1$ | 一 *i*$^4$ | 專 *chuan*$^1$ | 當 *tang*$^1$ |
| 行。*hsing*$^2$ | 東 *tung*$^1$ | 了。*liao* | 失 *shih*$^1$ | 心 *hsin*$^1$ | 不 *pu*$^2$ |

These regulations are satisfactory; they need not be amended.

He gives his whole attention to study.

In the transaction of business absent-mindedness at once leads to irregularity.

Camels are specially employed as beasts of burden.

That will answer still worse.

579. 忙 *mang*$^2$, to haste; busy.

580. 向 *hsiang*$^4$, to face towards; towards; direction.

581. 規 *kuei*$^1$, a rule; custom.

582. 幹 *kan*$^4$, to attend to business; business. It often takes the place of *tso*$^4$, to do.

583. 辦 *pan*$^4$, to administer; colloquially it has many meanings, as to purchase, to punish, etc. *Pan*$^4$-*tsui*$^3$ (433), to squabble.

584. 法 *fa*$^{2\,3}$, method; fashion. Read *fa*$^3$, law or laws. *Fa*$^4$ *kuo*$^2$, France; note the tone.

585. Examples :—

| | | | | | | |
|---|---|---|---|---|---|---|
| 會 *hui*$^4$ | 辦 *pan*$^4$ | 了。*liao* | 你 *ni*$^3$ | 明 *ming*$^2$ | 很 *hên*$^3$ | 我 *wo*$^3$ |
| 辦 *pan*$^4$ | 不 *pu*$^4$ | 這 *chê*$^1$ | 們 *mên* | 年 *nien*$^2$ | 忙。*mang*$^2$ | 們 *mên* |
| 事。*shih*$^4$ | 來 *lai*$^2$ | 個 *ko*$^4$ | 幹 *kan*$^4$ | 出 *ch'u*$^1$ | 我 *wo*$^3$ | 向 *hsiang*$^4$ |
| 忙 *mang*$^2$ | 的。*ti* | 法 *fa*$^2$ | 甚 *shên*$^2$ | 遠 *yüan*$^3$ | 定 *ting*$^4$ | 來 *lai*$^2$ |
| 甚 *shên*$^2$ | 他 *t'a*$^1$ | 子 *tzŭ* | 麼 *mo* | 門 *mên*$^2$ | 規 *kuei*$^1$ | 不 *pu*$^2$ |
| 麼。*mo* | 眞 *chên*$^1$ | 是 *shih*$^4$ | 來 *lai*$^2$ | 兒。*'rh* | 了 *liao* | 大 *ta*$^4$ |

Hitherto we have never been very busy.

*Obs.*—Hitherto: *lit.*, towards [the time that has now] come; *hsiang lai* with a negative can generally be rendered *never*.

I have decided to make a long journey next year.

*Obs.*—Decided: *lit.*, *ting*, have determined or laid down, *kuei*, as a definite line of action.

What have you come for?

This plan is impracticable.

He is really an able administrator.

What's your hurry?

586. 胡 *hu*$^2$, wildly; blindly.

587. 鬧 *nao*$^4$, to be in a rage; of events, to occur when they should not occur.

588. 掄 *lun*$^1$, *lün*$^1$, to whirl about, as a mace, etc.; to brandish, as the fist, etc.

589. 催 *ts'ui*$^1$, to urge.

590. Examples :—

| | | | | | | |
|---|---|---|---|---|---|---|
| 兒 *'rh* | 裡 *li*$^3$ | 忙 *mang*$^2$ | 槍 *ch'iang*$^1$ | 成 *ch'êng*$^2$ | 姓 *hsing*$^4$ | 不 *pu*$^2$ |
| 鬧 *nao*$^4$ | 鬧 *nao*$^4$ | 去 *ch'ü*$^4$ | 棍 *hun*$^4$ | 天 *t'ien*$^1$ | 鬧 *nao*$^4$ | 要 *yao*$^4$ |
| 了 *liao* | 嗓 *sang*$^3$ | 辦。*pan*$^4$ | 掄。*lun*$^1$ | 家 *chia*$^1$ | 了 *liao* | 胡 *hu*$^2$ |
| 個 *ko*$^4$ | 子 *tzŭ* | 他 *t'a*$^1$ | 催 *ts'ui*$^1$ | 拏 *na*$^2$ | 大 *ta*$^4$ | 鬧 *nao*$^4$ |
| 亂 *lan*$^4$ | 了。*liao* | 們 *mên* | 他 *t'a*$^1$ | 着 *cho* | 亂 *lan*$^4$ | 了。*liao* |
| 兒。*'rh* | 今 *chin*$^1$ | 家 *chia*$^1$ | 趕 *kan*$^3$ | 桿 *kan*$^3$ | 子。*tzŭ* | 百 *po*$^2$ |

Don't be disorderly.

There was a great outbreak of the people.

*Obs.*—Note that *lan*$^4$-*tzŭ* is a disturbance; *luan*$^4$, a state of disturbance. *Nao* can be used of the outbreak of an epidemic (see below).

To brandish a spear the whole day.

*Obs.*—The whole day: *lit.*, a complete day. The teachers can give no explanation of the use of *chia* in this connexion. We find the same sound in the expression *pu*$^1$ *chia*, it is not so; no.

Urge him to go and attend to it with all despatch.

Diphtheria has broken out in their house.

I have had a misfortune to-day.

## EXERCISE XXII.

1 那人幹的事總不叫人知道。大約不是甚麼好事、不然他怎麼背人。可不是麼。人家常說、好話不背人、背人沒好話。

1. That man never lets anyone know what he is about. Probably it is nothing very reputable, otherwise why should he be so secret about it? Yes, indeed; there is a common saying that "Good advice is not given in secret; secret advice is never good."

*Obs.* 1.—Otherwise: *pu*, were it not, *jan*, thus.

*Obs.* 2.—Secret: *pei⁴ jên*, behind people's backs. Cf. *pei ti li*.

2 那一件事還沒辦妥當了。章程得改、可不知道李大人准不准。大約沒甚麼更改的。

2. That matter is not satisfactorily disposed of yet. The regulations require alteration, but I do not know whether Li *ta-jên* will approve or not. Most probably no important alteration will take place.

*Obs.*—*Ta-jên*: this might be translated His Excellency, but it must be remembered that the title *ta-jên* is given to any officer of the third or higher grades of official rank.

3 要幹甚麼事、先得定規個准主意。

3. If one wants to engage in any affair one must first settle on a definite line of action.

4 幹事的時候兒、心不擱在事上、那就叫失神。

4. When one is engaged in any transaction and one's attention is not devoted to the matter [in hand], that is what is called *shih¹ shên²* (to be absent-minded).

*Obs.*—Attention devoted to: *lit.*, heart placed in or upon.

5 定妥了辦事的法子總在他身上。

5. The final determination of the way in which the thing is to be done rests entirely with him.

*Obs.*—Rests with him: *lit.*, is on his body; he bears the responsibility.

6 那個人有一件要事、得趕着辦、他一點兒不忙、同人催他快着些兒、他不肯聽。

6. That man had a matter of importance in hand which it was necessary he should dispose of promptly; but he would not hurry himself a bit, and when someone who was acting with him urged him to make a little more speed he would not listen.

*Obs.* 1.—Matter of importance: *yao*, short for *yao chin*³, a combination which will be met with later.
*Obs.* 2.—Acting with him: *t'ung jên*, short for *t'ung shih*⁴ *ti jên*.

7 他在那兒拏倆胳臂混掄是幹什麼。怕是喝酒喝多了。

7. What is he swinging his arms about there for? I suspect he has had too much to drink.

8 條約是各國和中國立定兩下裏往來的章程。

8. *T'iao*²-*yo*¹ (treaties) are the regulations for intercourse between their respective countries drawn up by different nations with China.

*Obs.*—*Lit.*, *t'iao-yo* are each nation's with China drawn up both sides going and coming regulations. *Wang lai*, going and coming; hence, interchange, whether of courtesies, correspondence, trade, or otherwise.

9 這樣兒菜是廚子專給你弄的、你倒不吃。

9. This dish was specially prepared for you by the cook, and yet you won't eat it.

10 大凡帳目都是一條一條的那麼開。你這寫的全是參差不齊。

10. Most accounts are drawn up item by item. These that you have written out are irregular and incomplete.

*Obs.* 1.—Most: *ta fan*; *lit.*, the great whole; hence, the majority.
*Obs.* 2.—Irregular: *ts'ên-tz'ŭ*; *lit.*, jaggedness. The irregularity here referred to is unevenness in the writing; *pu ch'i* may also mean uneven, though the context in this case rather indicates incompleteness than unevenness, which is already provided for by *ts'ên-tz'ŭ*. We can say that a certain number of persons *lai ch'i liao*, have all arrived, or that a hedge has been trimmed *pu ch'i*, unevenly.

*Turn the following into Chinese.* (KEY, EXERCISE XXII.)

1. Whenever you are studying and happen to meet an expression you do not understand, if you try diligently to get at it (*lit.*, guess) you will most probably understand its meaning.

2. Yesterday I invited him to go to the Western Hills; he said he must first go home to ask leave. I fear he will not be allowed to go any distance.

3. In writing letters and despatches, should there be any part written wrongly, a piece of paper must be put over the characters that are mis-written; this [operation] is called *ta*³ *pu*³-*tzŭ* (to put in a correction).

4. If you are absent-minded in this way, you will do nothing satisfactorily.

5. I brought that flower-pot purposely and specially for you. If you decline it, it shows (this is) you look down upon me.

*Obs.* 1.—Purposely and specially: *lit.*, with special heart and special intent.

*Obs.* 2.—Look down upon: *ch'iao pu ch'i*; *lit.*, you regard not elevated; *i.e.*, you don't look up to me. The reverse is *ch'iao tê ch'i*.

6. This is indeed nonsensical talk! I decline it because I do not feel at liberty to accept your things without having done anything to deserve them.

*Obs.* 1.—Nonsensical talk: *lit.*, this talk spoken is truly wild extravagance. I do not want is [because] I [could] not [with] good intent for nothing at all (*pai*[2]) want your things.

*Obs.* 2.—Note *pai*, white; hence, a synonym for nothing at all, in vain, etc. Cf. *pai, jên-'rh*, a private individual (p. 97).

7. The furniture of this room is all in disorder; put it to rights.

*Obs.* 1.—Disorder: *ts'ên-tz'ŭ pu ch'i*.

*Obs.* 2.—Put to rights: see 528.

8. What is your hurry? it will be a little time yet before the guests come.

9. What did you go away for? Directly I took my eyes off you, away you ran. I'll have to take a stick again and lay it about you a few times.

*Obs.* 1.—Took my eyes off: *lit.*, I, one erring (or straying) of the eyes (*i ts'o yên-'rh*), you then ran.

*Obs.* 2.—Lay it about you: *lun* (588).

10. The mode of action they have always (hitherto) laid down cannot well be altered or modified.

591. 語 *yü*[3], language; sayings.

592. 句 *chü*[4], a clause; a sentence.

593. 吵 *ch'ao*[1], *ch'ao*[3], to wrangle (of two or many).

594. 嚷 *jang*[3], to talk too loud. *Jang*[1], to chatter in a loud tone; also, to talk about matters that should be kept quiet; to let out a secret.

595. Examples:—

| | | | | | |
|---|---|---|---|---|---|
| 你 *ni*[3] | 起 *ch'i*[3] | 兩 *liang*[3] | 倆 *lia*[3] | 同。*t'ung*[2] | 各 *ko*[4] |
| 嚷 *jang*[3] | 來 *lai*[2] | 句 *chü*[4] | 不 *pu*[2] | 一 *i*[2] | 國 *kuo*[2] |
| 甚 *shê*[n2] | 了。*liao* | 話 *hua*[4] | 和 *ho*[2] | 句 *chü*[4] | 的 *ti* |
| 麽。*mo* | 少 *shao*[3] | 就 *chiu*[4] | 說 *shuo*[1] | 話。*hua*[4] | 言 *yen*[2] |
| 嚷 *jang*[1] | 嚷 *jang*[3] | 吵 *ch'ao*[3] | 不 *pu*[4] | 他 *t'a*[1] | 語 *yü*[3] |
| 嚷。*jang*[1] | 些。*hsieh*[1] | 鬧 *nao*[4] | 到 *tao*[4] | 們 *mên* | 不 *pu*[4] |

The languages spoken in different countries vary.

A sentence; also, once and for all.

Those two are not on good terms; before they have spoken two sentences they begin to quarrel.

*Obs.*—Note that *ch'ao nao* is verbal altercation (see also 583).

Make less noise.

What are you making such a noise about?

To chatter; also, to let out a secret; or, to talk about a matter which should be kept quiet.

596. 阿 *a*[1], an ejaculation; sometimes interrogative.

597. 訛 *ngê*$^2$, *ngo*$^2$, wrong; untrue. Colloquially, generally to defraud by false representation; to extort money under false pretences; to accuse wrongfully.

598. 笑 *hsiao*$^4$, to laugh; laughter.

599. Examples:—

| | | | | | |
|---|---|---|---|---|---|
| 就 *chiu*$^4$ | 不 *pu*$^4$ | 和 *han*$^4$ | 笑 *hsiao*$^4$ | 有 *yu*$^3$ | 你 *ni*$^3$ |
| 是 *shih*$^4$ | 該 *kai*$^1$ | 人 *jên*$^2$ | 的 *ti* | 甚 *shê*$^{n2}$ | 笑 *hsiao*$^4$ |
| 訛 *ngo*$^2$ | 的 *ti* | 家 *chia*$^1$ | 阿。*a*$^1$ | 麽 *mo* | 甚 *shê*$^{n2}$ |
| 人，*jên*$^2$ | 錢 *ch'ien*$^2$ | 要 *yao*$^4$ | 硬 *ying*$^4$ | 可，*k'o*$^3$ | 麽。*mo* |

What are you laughing at?
What is there to laugh at?
To insist upon payment of money that is not owed is extortion.

600. 衰 *shuai*$^1$, decayed; worn out.

601. 困 *k'un*$^4$, *k'uen*$^4$, surrounded; embarrassed; fatigued.

602. 極 *chi*$^2$, extreme; excess.

603. 夢 *mêng*$^4$, a dream.

604. Examples:—

| | | | | | | |
|---|---|---|---|---|---|---|
| 笑。*hsiao*$^4$ | 見 *chien*$^4$ | 話。*hua*$^4$ | 說 *shuo*$^1$ | 極 *chi*$^2$ | 夢。*mêng*$^4$ | 他 *t'a*$^1$ |
| 極 *chi*$^2$ | 一 *i*$^1$ | 熱 *jê*$^4$ | 了 *liao* | 了 *liao* | 他 *t'a*$^1$ | 氣 *ch'i*$^4$ |
| 好 *hao*$^3$ | 件 *chien*$^4$ | 極 *chi*$^2$ | 一 *i*$^2$ | 躺 *t'ang*$^3$ | 那 *na*$^4$ | 血 *hsüeh*$^3$ |
| 的 *ti* | 奇 *ch'i*$^2$ | 了。*liao* | 夜 *yeh*$^4$ | 在 *tsai*$^4$ | 個 *ko*$^4$ | 衰 *shuai*$^1$ |
| 事。*shih*$^4$ | 事。*shih*$^4$ | 我 *wo*$^3$ | 的 *ti* | 炕 *k'ang*$^4$ | 人 *jên*$^2$ | 了。*liao* |
| | 冷 *lêng*$^3$ | 夢 *mêng*$^4$ | 夢 *mêng*$^4$ | 上 *shang*$^4$ | 困 *k'un*$^4$ | 做 *tso*$^4$ |

His constitution is worn out.
To dream.
Being extremely tired (sleepy) he lay down on the *k'ang*$^4$, and talked in his sleep all through the night.
Extremely hot.
I dreamt a strange dream.
*Obs.*—Dreamt: *lit.*, saw in my dreams a strange thing.
A chuckle; or, ironical laugh.
A most excellent undertaking (or arrangement).

605. 貌 *mao*$^4$, personal appearance.

606. 相 *hsiang*$^4$, the physiognomy. This character will be met with later in a different tone.

607. 醜 *ch'ou*$^3$, ugly (morally or physically).

608. 摔 *shuai*$^1$, *shuai*$^3$, to throw; to dash down.

609. 掉 *tiao*$^4$, to hang (neuter); to fall down.

610. 撾 *ch'o*$^{1}$, *ch'uo*$^{1}$, to jar by a fall.

611. 揝 *tsuan*$^{4}$, to grasp in the hand.

612. Examples :—

| | | | | | | |
|---|---|---|---|---|---|---|
| 揝 *tsuan*$^{4}$ | 了。*liao* | 笑。*hsiao*$^{4}$ | 到 *tao*$^{4}$ | 下 *hsia*$^{4}$ | 得 *tê* | 相 *hsiang*$^{4}$ |
| 住 *chu*$^{4}$ | 把 *pa*$^{3}$ | 他 *t'a*$^{1}$ | 河 *ho*$^{2}$ | 來。*lai*$^{2}$ | 醜。*ch'ou*$^{3}$ | 貌 *mao*$^{4}$ |
| 我 *wo*$^{3}$ | 胳 *ko*$^{1}$ | 把 *pa*$^{3}$ | 裏 *li*$^{3}$ | 掉 *tiao*$^{4}$ | 一 *i*$^{2}$ | 長 *chang*$^{3}$ |
| 的 *ti* | 臂 *pei*$^{4}$ | 瓶 *p'ing*$^{2}$ | 去 *ch'ü*$^{4}$ | 下 *hsia*$^{4}$ | 件 *chien*$^{4}$ | 得 *tê* |
| 手 *shou*$^{3}$ | 撾 *ch'o*$^{1}$ | 子 *tzŭ* | 了 *liao* | 去。*ch'ü*$^{4}$ | 醜 *ch'ou*$^{3}$ | 好 *hao*$^{3}$ |
| 了。*liao* | 了。*liao* | 摔 *shuai*$^{1}$ | 很 *hên*$^{3}$ | 他 *t'a*$^{1}$ | 事。*shih*$^{4}$ | 看。*k'an*$^{4}$ |
| | 他 *t'a*$^{1}$ | 破 *p'o*$^{4}$ | 可 *k'o*$^{3}$ | 掉 *tiao*$^{4}$ | 掉 *tiao*$^{4}$ | 長 *chang*$^{3}$ |

Good-looking. Ugly.

*Obs.—Lit.*, appearance grown to, etc. *Hsiang mao* might equally well be placed before *ch'ou;* in either case *chang tê* is best not translated.

A disgraceful (or scandalous) business.

To fall down. To fall down.

*Obs.*—The use of *lai* and *ch'ü* will vary according to the position of the speaker with reference to the object fallen. Thus, were the speaker on foot he would say of a man on horseback, *t'a tiao hsia lai liao*, he has fallen off; if the speaker were on horseback too, he would say *t'a tiao hsia ch'ü liao.*

He fell into the river ; such a joke !

*Obs.*—We could say also *tiao tsai ho li.*

He dashed the bottle down and broke it.

To give a shock to one's arm.

He grasped me tightly by the hand.

613. 窄 *chai*$^{3}$, narrow.

614. 則 *tsê*$^{2}$, then ; in consequence.

615. 況 *k'uang*$^{4}$, besides.

616. 且 *ch'ieh*$^{3}$, also; in the next place. Also, under certain circumstances, temporarily.

617. Examples :—

| | | | | | | |
|---|---|---|---|---|---|---|
| 件 *chien*$^{4}$ | 地 *ti*$^{4}$ | 況 *k'uang*$^{4}$ | 兒 *'rh* | 不 *pu*$^{4}$ | 那 *na*$^{4}$ | 一 *i*$^{1}$ |
| 事 *shih*$^{4}$ | 方 *fang*$^{1}$ | 且 *ch'ich* | 窄 *chai*$^{3}$ | 穿 *ch'uan*$^{1}$ | 一 *i*$^{2}$ | 則。*tsê*$^{2}$ |
| 我 *wo*$^{3}$ | 兒 *'rh* | 又 *yu*$^{4}$ | 二 *êrh*$^{4}$ | 一 *i*$^{1}$ | 件 *chien*$^{4}$ | 二 *êrh*$^{4}$ |
| 且 *ch'ieh*$^{3}$ | 窄。*chai*$^{3}$ | 弄 *nung*$^{4}$ | 則 *tsê*$^{2}$ | 則 *tsê*$^{2}$ | 褂 *kua*$^{4}$ | 則。*tsê*$^{2}$ |
| 不 *pu*$^{2}$ | 那 *na*$^{4}$ | 髒 *tsang*$^{1}$ | 太 *t'ai*$^{4}$ | 袖 *hsiu*$^{4}$ | 子 *tzŭ* | 況 *k'uang*$^{4}$ |
| 問。*wên*$^{4}$ | 一 *i*$^{2}$ | 了。*liao* | 長 *ch'ang*$^{2}$ | 口 *k'ou*$^{3}$ | 我 *wo*$^{3}$ | 且。*ch'ieh*$^{3}$ |

In the first place. In the second place.

Moreover ; besides.

I won't put on that coat: in the first place, the sleeves are too narrow; in the second, it is too long ; and, moreover, it has been dirtied.

The place is narrow ; there is not much space.

I won't inquire into that matter for the moment (temporarily).

## EXERCISE XXIII.

1 城門口兒的地方兒窄、來往的車馬多。

1. There is but little space at the city gates for the number of carts and horses that are moving through them in opposite directions.

*Obs.—Lit.*, the city gates' mouth place narrow; coming and going carts and horses many.

2 外頭是甚麼人嚷、底下人和趕車的那兒吵呢。你出去告訴他們不要嚷嚷、看鬧出事來。

2. Who is it that is making such a noise outside? The servants and carters are wrangling about something. Go out and tell them not to make such a row, or they may get into trouble.

*Obs.* 1.—Note *jang*[1] *jang*[1], the noise of several people talking loudly; it cannot be used of the noise made by one person.

*Obs.* 2.—Get into trouble: *lit.*, *k'an*, [or they may] find trouble *(shih)* break out *(nao ch'u lai)*.

3 你看那兩個小人兒、一個很好看、一個長的真醜。

3. Look at those two little fellows; one of them is good-looking, the other very much the reverse.

4 那好看的笑話那長的醜的、那醜的生了氣、把茶碗摔碎了。有人說了他兩句、他害起怕來了、就說茶碗是掉下去的。

4. The good-looking one was making fun of the ugly one, and the latter, getting into a rage, smashed a tea-cup. Someone found fault with him for this, so he got frightened and said the tea-cup had fallen down.

*Obs.* 1.—Rage: *lit.*, begot, or generated, breath. *Ch'i*, air, breath: in Chinese physiology often untranslatable; it is best rendered matter; in this instance, wrath matter; the boy begot wrath matter; *i.e.*, got into a rage.

*Obs.* 2.—Found fault; *shuo*, to speak, followed by a personal noun or pronoun, means to blame; but when the same nouns or pronouns are so circumstanced as to be in what we call the dative case, *shuo* means to speak to.

5 揝住他的辮子要拉了他去、他躺在地下把胳臂擱了。

5. They took hold of his pigtail and were trying to drag him off, when he lay down and jarred his arm in doing so.

6 晚飯吃多了、夜裏愛做夢. 他叫馬摔了.

6. If you eat too heavy a late dinner you are liable to dream at night. He was thrown from his horse.

7 我告訴你一個笑話兒. 昨兒我困的利害、在椅子上坐着就着了. 同人把墨水兒倒在我嘴裏. 我都不知道.

7. I will tell you a comical story. Yesterday I was dreadfully tired, and went off to sleep as I sat in my chair. The people that were with me poured some liquid ink into my mouth without my knowing anything about it.

*Obs.*—Went off to sleep: *chao*² *liao*, short for *shui*⁴-*chao*² *liao*, to go off to sleep; this character will be met with later.

8 街道兒窄、那麼大的車拉不過去.

8. The street is too narrow for so large a cart to be taken through it.

*Turn the following into Chinese.* (KEY, EXERCISE XXIII.)

1. There were two men yesterday having an altercation in that narrow space on the top of the city wall, one a good-looking individual, the other very ugly. The good-looking one said to the ugly one, "There is only one of two answers, are you going to do this or are you not?"

*Obs.* 1.—One of two answers: *lit.*, there are not two sentences or two words about it.

*Obs.* 2.—Are you going to do this, etc., *lit.*, this matter you, *tao ti*, *au fond* (or eventually), do or not; *tao ti* is best not translated. Cf. also *tao liao*³ *'rh*.

2. The ugly one replied, "In the first place, I am afraid of what people will say; and in the second, I am terribly tired. Go and do it yourself; if you don't do it, how can I?"

*Obs.*—What people will say: *lit.*, I fear remarks (*yen-yü*). Note that *yen-yü* may mean to tell in the sense of to blab; also, to mention; *e.g.*, when you want me *yen-yü i shêng-'rh*, let me know.

3. The other burst out into a loud laugh and said, "You are wrong there; why are you afraid of what people will say? I expect you can't do it. If you don't go at once, it is very plain that I must pitch you down." The ugly fellow ran off before [the other] had finished what he was saying.

*Obs.* 1.—Very plain: *ming*² *ming*²-*'rh ti*.

*Obs.* 2.—Must pitch you down: *lit.*, this is evidently causing me (*chiao wo*) to take you and throw you down. Note *shuai*³ not *shuai*¹; *hsia ch'ü*, not *hsia lai*, the speaker being also on the wall.

4. You surely must have been dreaming; there was no one on the wall yesterday.

5. I was riding along the main street of the *ch'ien*² *mên*² the day before yesterday, when an altercation between some men behind me, I don't know who, sent my horse off at full speed. After a little I fell off, and gave a jar to my ankle. Luckily, the shock was not a

heavy one; I rested a bit and got all right. I don't know where the horse galloped to; he has not been found yet.

*Obs.* 1. Full speed: *lit.*, caused my horse to spread his legs (*k'ai t'ui*) and run off.

*Obs.* 2. Luckily: *hai hao*, it was yet good (or fortunate).

*Obs.* 3.—Yet: *lit.*, this while. *See* 129.

6. I have walked all day to-day and am extremely sleepy. There is no help for it; the best thing you can do is to rest for a night; you will have got over your fatigue by to-morrow.

*Obs.*—Got over your fatigue: *lit.*, rested over your fatigue (*hsieh kuo fa-'rh lai liao*).

618. 兆 *chao*$^4$, a presage; an omen.

619. 吉 *chi*$^2$, auspicious.

620. 凶 *hsiung*$^1$, inauspicious. Also, cruel; malevolent; hence applied to acts of violence or murder.

621. 祥 *hsiang*$^2$, good fortune; that which bodes good fortune.

622. 瑞 *jui*$^4$, the same as the foregoing *hsiang*$^2$.

623. Examples:—

| | | | | | | |
|---|---|---|---|---|---|---|
| 情 *ch'ing*$^2$ | 祥。*hsiang*$^2$ | 出 *ch'u*$^1$ | 吉 *chi*$^2$ | 出 *ch'u*$^1$ | 我 *wo*$^3$ | 吉 *chi*$^2$ |
| 凶 *hsiung*$^1$ | 祥 *hsiang*$^2$ | 兵 *ping*$^1$ | 兆。*chao*$^4$ | 了 *liao* | 們 *mên* | 兆。*chao*$^4$ |
| 暴。*pao*$^4$ | 瑞, *jui*$^4$ | 很 *hên*$^3$ | 去 *ch'ü*$^4$ | 一 *i*$^2$ | 家 *chia*$^1$ | 凶 *hsiung*$^1$ |
| | 性 *hsing*$^4$ | 吉 *chi*$^2$ | 年 *nien*$^2$ | 個 *ko*$^4$ | 裏 *li*$^3$ | 兆。*chao*$^4$ |

A good omen. An ill omen.

A good omen has occurred in our family.

Last year's campaign was most successful.

Prosperity.

*Obs.*—This phrase is seldom met with in conversation. The characters are constantly seen on shop signs.

A cruel and violent disposition.

624. 安 *ngan*$^1$, repose.

625. 寧, 甯 *ning*$^2$, tranquillity; the second form is now always used, the original character being tabooed, as it formed the *ming*$^2$, or personal designation, of the Emperor whose reign is styled Tao Kuang. When read *ning*$^4$, and followed by a negative, it becomes a term of comparison.

626. 順 *shun*$^4$, obedient; hence, following.

627. 寬 *k'uan*$^1$, broad; liberal.

628. 綽 *ch'o*$^4$, of exceeding extent (said of place, fortune, etc.); inseparable in the spoken language from *k'uan*$^1$.

16

629. Examples :—

| | | | | | | |
|---|---|---|---|---|---|---|
| 事 *shih*$^4$ | 綽。*ch'o*$^4$ | 他 *t'a*$^1$ | 順 *shun*$^4$ | 不 *pu*$^4$ | 亂 *luan*$^4$ | 安 *ngan*$^1$ |
| 都 *tou*$^1$ | 他 *t'a*$^1$ | 家 *chia*$^1$ | 水 *shui*$^3$ | 安 *ngan*$^1$ | 百 *po*$^2$ | 寧。*ning*$^2$ |
| 順 *shun*$^4$ | 們 *mên* | 裡 *li*$^3$ | 順 *shun*$^4$ | 寧 *ning*$^2$ | 姓 *hsing*$^4$ | 天 *t'ien*$^1$ |
| 當。*tang*$^1$ | 的 *ti* | 寬 *k'uan*$^1$ | 風。*fêng*$^1$ | 了。*liao* | 就 *chiu*$^4$ | 下 *hsia*$^4$ |

Peace and quietness (state of freedom from danger).
When the Empire is in disorder the people are not tranquil.
A fair wind and tide (or stream).
His family is in easy circumstances.
Everything goes smoothly with them.

630. 貧 *p'in*$^2$, poor.

631. 窮 *ch'iung*$^2$, extremity ; hence, poverty.

632. 窘 *chiung*$^3$, straitened (of space or fortune); not often used colloquially out of Peking.

633. 產 *ch'an*$^3$, to produce, as the earth its fruits ; productions ; property.

634. 業 *yeh*$^4$, a calling ; an occupation; hence, acquired property. It is also a sign of the past tense.

635. Examples :—

| | | | | | |
|---|---|---|---|---|---|
| 有 *yu*$^3$ | 也 *yeh*$^3$ | 一 *i*$^4$ | 家 *chia*$^1$ | 貧 *p'in*$^2$ | 他 *t'a*$^1$ |
| 甚 *shên*$^2$ | 沒 *mei*$^2$ | 點 *tien*$^3$ | 裏 *li*$^3$ | 窮 *ch'iung*$^2$ | 真 *chên*$^1$ |
| 麼 *mo* | 有。*yu*$^3$ | 兒 *'rh* | 很 *hên*$^3$ | 的 *ti* | 不 *pu*$^2$ |
| 出 *ch'u*$^1$ | 這 *chê*$^4$ | 產 *ch'an*$^3$ | 窘。*chiung*$^3$ | 人。*jên*$^2$ | 是 *shih*$^4$ |
| 產。*ch'an*$^3$ | 兒 *'rh* | 業 *yeh*$^4$ | 連 *lien*$^2$ | 他 *t'a*$^1$ | 個 *ko*$^4$ |

He is by no means a poor man.
His family is in very straitened circumstances.
They have absolutely no property.
What are the natural products of this place?

636. 朋 *p'êng*$^2$, a friend or companion; a person with whom one is in constant contact. Never used alone colloquially.

637. 友 *yu*$^3$, a friend; a person of kindred tastes or sentiments.

638. 賞 *shang*$^3$, to bestow on ; also, under certain circumstances, to take pleasure in, as a pretty sight.

639. 相 *hsiang*$^1$, mutual ; reciprocal ; but it also indicates the unreciprocated relation of one person or thing to another. *See* 606.

640. 幫 *pang*$^1$, to assist.

語言自邇集



**641.** Examples :—

| | | | | | |
|---|---|---|---|---|---|
| 多 *to*$^1$ | 幫 *pang*$^1$ | 姓 *hsing*$^4$ | 地 *ti*$^4$ | 一 *i*$^2$ | 這 *chê*$^4$ |
| 年 *nien*$^2$ | 着 *cho*$^1$ | 銀 *yin*$^2$ | 方 *fang*$^1$ | 個 *ko*$^4$ | 些 *hsieh*$^1$ |
| 的 *ti* | 我。*wo*$^3$ | 子。*tzŭ* | 官 *kuan*$^1$ | 朋 *p'êng*$^2$ | 花 *hua*$^1$ |
| 相 *hsiang*$^1$ | 我 *wo*$^3$ | 請 *ch'ing*$^3$ | 賞 *shang*$^3$ | 友 *yu*$^3$ | 盆 *p'ên*$^2$ |
| 好、*hao*$^3$ | 們 *mên* | 你 *ni*$^3$ | 給 *kei*$^3$ | 賞 *shang*$^3$ | 是 *shih*$^4$ |
| | 倆 *lia*$^3$ | 來 *lai*$^2$ | 百 *po*$^2$ | 的。*ti* | 我 *wo*$^3$ |

These flower-pots were presented to me by a friend.

The local officials rewarded the people.

*Obs.*—Note that in most instances *shang* is used of the gift of a superior to an inferior; in the preceding example it is used politely.

Please come and assist me.

We two have been good friends for many years.

— **642.** 留 *liu*$^2$, to keep; to detain.

**643.** 丢 *tiu*$^1$, to lose.

**644.** 根 *kên*$^1$, the root of a tree ; the numerative of sticks, spears, ropes, etc.

**645.** 現 *hsien*$^4$, now ; present time.

**646.** 別 *pieh*$^2$, do not ; a contraction of the words *pu*$^2$ *yao*$^4$. It will be met with presently in its proper signification.

**647.** Examples :—

| | | | | | | |
|---|---|---|---|---|---|---|
| 能 *nêng*$^2$ | 了。*liao* | 底 *ti*$^4$ | 根 *kên*$^1$ | 能。*nêng*$^2$ | 費 *fei*$^4$ | 留 *liu*$^2$ |
| 寫 *hsieh*$^3$ | 手 *shou*$^3$ | 根 *kên*$^1$ | 棍 *kun*$^4$ | 別 *pieh*$^2$ | 心 *hsin*$^1$ | 他 *t'a*$^1$ |
| 字。*tzŭ*$^4$ | 疼 *t'êng*$^2$ | 兒。*'rh* | 子。*tzŭ* | 給 *kei*$^3$ | 今 *chin*$^1$ | 吃 *ch'ih*$^1$ |
| | 現 *hsien*$^4$ | 到 *tao*$^4$ | 丢 *tiu*$^1$ | 丢 *tiu*$^1$ | 天 *t'ien*$^1$ | 飯。*fan*$^4$ |
| | 在 *tsai*$^4$ | 底 *ti*$^3$ | 不 *pu*$^4$ | 那 *na*$^4$ | 怕 *p'a*$^4$ | 費 *fei*$^4$ |
| | 不 *pu*$^4$ | 丢 *tiu*$^1$ | 了。*liao*$^3$ | 一 *i*$^4$ | 不 *pu*$^4$ | 心 *hsin*$^1$ |

Keep him to dinner.

Much obliged ; I am afraid I cannot to-day.

*Obs.*—Obliged : *lit.*, you have expended your thoughts ; one of many expressions of thanks.

Don't lose that stick.

*Obs.*—We might also say *pieh tiu na kên kun-tzŭ*, but in southern *kuan hua* this would mean don't throw it away.

It can't be lost.

At the root ; originally.

*Obs.*—Note *ti*$^4$, not *ti*$^3$.

Eventually (or, after all) it was lost.

My hand is sore ; I cannot write at present.

*Obs.*—At present : *lit.*, the now that is.

## EXERCISE XXIV.

1 昨兒晚上那兒有人行兇。兇手拏住了、後來怕是要正法的。就地正法。

1. A murder was committed there last night. The murderer has been seized, and will, I expect, eventually be executed. Execution at the scene of the crime.

*Obs.* 1.—Murder: *lit.*, a man there did a cruel action. Note that *hsing hsiung* may not mean to commit a murder, though it generally does.

*Obs.* 2.—Murderer: *hsiung shou*; *lit.*, murdering hand. *Shou*, the hand, is not unfrequently used in place of *jên*, the individual.

*Obs.* 3.—Executed: *chêng*, in legal phraseology, means to punish; *chêng fa*, to punish by the law, or as the law directs, is, however, limited to capital punishment.

2 事情沒來之先、看見甚麼能知道日後的祥瑞、那就叫吉兆。

2. When before a thing comes to pass there is something seen by which one can tell that there will be prosperity at some future date, that is called *chi² chao⁴* (an auspicious omen).

*Obs.*—When before: *lit.*, things not come's before; the word *chih* here, like *ti*, forming a number of words preceding it into a predicate of the word following it.

3 家裏日用的錢足了是寬綽。錢太少、過日子不足、就是貧窮。

3. When there is money enough in a house for daily use, that is called *k'uan¹-ch'o¹* (comfort). When there is not enough for daily need, that is *p'in²-ch'iung²* (poverty).

4 過日子有准進的錢、那就叫產業。

4. When there is a regular income to provide for daily subsistence, that is called *ch'an³-yeh⁴* (property producing a regular income).

*Obs.*—Regular income: *lit.*, certain incoming's money.

5 那時候兒我甚麼都沒了、就找了一個朋友說、偺們這些年的相好、你幫我幾個錢、肯不肯。他說、沒有甚麼不肯、真是不能。我們底根兒本有幾個錢、你是知道的、現在產業也沒了、連弄一個大錢都很費事。

5. I lost everything at that time, so I looked up a certain friend of mine and said to him, "We have been good friends all these years; will you help me with a little money?" He said, "It is not that I will not, but really that I cannot. We had a little money originally, as you know, but now our income has disappeared and we find very great difficulty in making a single cash."

6 你們這車、要趕當天兒趕進城去、我多多兒的賞你們酒錢。

6. If you can get your cart into the city in the one day I will give you a large *pourboire*.

7 你多喒起身。我要沒丟那銀子、今兒就走、總在這三五天可就要動身。那麼着我們這就分手了。一路平安罷、

7. When do you start? If I had not lost that silver I should have been off to-day, but I shall certainly start within the next three or four days. In that case we will say good-bye now. May you have a prosperous journey!

*Obs.*—Good-bye: *fên shou*; *lit.*, separate the hands. It is the custom amongst Chinese to shake hands, though not quite in the European fashion, when taking leave of each other for a long period; and the drawing away of the hands after such a leavetaking is *fên shou*.

8 你們那鋪子怎麼不開了。我們去年就分手了。

8. How is it that your shop is no longer open? We dissolved partnership last year.

*Obs.*—Note another meaning of *fên shou*.

9 八月十五、中秋節、正好賞月。

9. The 15th of the 8th moon, the Festival of Mid-autumn, is just the right time for viewing the moon.

*Obs.*—Festival: the Chinese year is divided into three principal periods or festivals (*chieh*; *lit.*, joints), exclusive of New Year's Day, to each of which a specific name is given; the first is on the 15th of the 1st moon (the Feast of Lanterns), the second on the 5th of the 5th moon, and the third as above.

10 請你幫個忙兒、不然這件事今兒個完不了。

10. Please come and lend me a hand, otherwise I sha'n't get through with this business to-day.

*Obs.*—Lend a hand: *lit.*, aid a haste; *q.d.*, a person who is in haste or busy.

*Turn the following into Chinese.* (KEY, EXERCISE XXIV.)

1. That man's affairs are certainly not prosperous.

2. Originally he had a regular income, and was in easy circumstances as regarded his daily needs. There came a year when there was no rain for months in succession, so he got no crops off his land, and his family affairs did not go smoothly. He spent all his capital by degrees, and now he is very poor. His intimate friends now and again (accidentally) help him along with a little money.

*Obs.*—Capital: *lit.*, root money.

3. Did he alone lose his money, or did he involve others in his misfortune?

*Obs.*—Involve: *lit.*, to connect *(lien)* in misfortune or trouble *(lei)*; in combination they form the verb to involve. The sentence, literally translated, runs: was it he one man lost money, yet was it [that he] involved other persons?

4. The greater part of the farmers thereabouts lost their money also, so the district has been far from quiet of late; I, however, did not suffer much inconvenience. [You ask me] why (*lit.*, how)? It was in this wise. In my opinion, things, whether good or evil, always give a presage of their advent. One day I dreamt a dream. I dreamt I saw a man come and burn all the wheat in my fields; so I sold the whole of it unripe [as it stood]. Afterwards we were short of rain, but I had got hold of my money long beforehand.

*Obs.* 1.—Of late: *lit.*, near coming *(chin lai)*.

*Obs.* 2.—However: *tao*. *See* 182.

*Obs.* 3.—Give a presage, etc.: *lit.*, all have a previous omen.

5. Please keep this jar, sir *(ta-jên)*; I am very poor. My friends won't assist me, so I have sold or pawned all my household furniture, and this one jar is all I've got [left].

*Obs.*—Note *p'ing*, a jar; *p'ing-tzŭ*, a bottle, or small jar.

6. Isn't your name CHANG? How have you become so poor as this? I remember two or three years back you had a regular income and could manage to live well enough.

*Obs.*—So poor: *lit.*, you how straitened *(chiung*$^{2}$*)* into *(ch'êng*$^{2}$*)* this kind?

7. What you say, sir, is quite true; I lost my money after that, and at present am a beggar.

*Obs.*—Beggar: *lit.*, wanting rice's man; the "man" may be omitted.

648. 您 *nin*$^{2}$, more commonly pronounced *ni-na*, which, again, is short for *ni lao jên chia*; politely, you my elder, you, sir, or madam.

649. 喳 *cha*$^{1}$ (rather *dja*$^{1}$), a sound taken from the Manchu; yes, sir, or madam.

650. 親 *ch'in*$^{1}$, intimate relationship.

651. 旁 *p'ang*$^{2}$, the sides.

652. 母 *mu*$^{3}$, a mother.

653. Examples :—

| | | | | | | |
|---|---|---|---|---|---|---|
| 的。*ti* | 走 *tsou*$^{3}$ | 車 *ch'ê*$^{1}$ | 大 *ta*$^{4}$ | 兒 *'rh* | 父 *fu*$^{4}$ | 來。*lai*$^{2}$ |
| 我 *wo*$^{3}$ | 人。*jên*$^{2}$ | 輛 *liang*$^{4}$ | 道 *tao*$^{4}$ | 的 *ti* | 親。*ch'in*$^{1}$ | 喳。*cha*$^{1}$ |
| 親 *ch'in*$^{1}$ | 我 *wo*$^{3}$ | 兩 *liang*$^{3}$ | 中 *chung*$^{1}$ | 人。*jên*$^{2}$ | 母 *mu*$^{3}$ | 您 *nin*$^{2}$ |
| 筆 *pi*$^{3}$ | 親 *ch'in*$^{1}$ | 旁 *p'ang*$^{2}$ | 間 *chien*$^{4}$ | 那 *na*$^{4}$ | 親。*ch'in*$^{1}$ | 要 *yao*$^{4}$ |
| 寫 *hsieh*$^{3}$ | 自 *tzŭ*$^{4}$ | 邊 *pien*$^{1}$ | 兒 *'rh* | 一 *i*$^{4}$ | 旁 *p'ang*$^{2}$ | 甚 *shên*$^{2}$ |
| 的。*ti* | 做 *tso*$^{4}$ | 兒 *'rh* | 走 *tsou*$^{3}$ | 條 *t'iao*$^{2}$ | 邊 *pien*$^{1}$ | 麽。*mo* |

Boy! Sir. What do you want, sir?

Father (Radical 88). Mother. Bystanders.

On that high road the middle is for carts and the two sides for people on foot.

*Obs.*—Note that *ch'ê* is generalised by the numerative following instead of preceding it.

I did it myself. I wrote it myself.

*Obs.*—We might also say *wo pên*$^{3}$ *jên-'rh*, my individual self.

654. 祖 *tsu*$^{3}$, ancestors.

語言自邇集



655. 翁 *wêng1*, an old man. Generally employed with the first character of a person's *hao4*, or literary appellation; thus, a man whose name was WANG, and his *hao4* YA3-T'ING2, could be spoken of or addressed as YA3 *wêng1*.

656. 兄 *hsiung1*, an elder brother.

657. 孫 *sun1*, a grandchild.

658. 舍 *shê4*, a cottage.

659. 弟 *ti4*, a younger brother.

660. Examples :—

| | | | | | | |
|---|---|---|---|---|---|---|
| 孫。*sun1* | 您 *nin2* | 兒 *êrh2* | 七 *ch'i2* | 老 *lao3* | 父 *fu4* | 我 *wo3* |
| 有 *yu3* | 跟 *kên1* | 子。*tzŭ* | 個。*ko4* | 翁。*wêng1* | 家 *chia1* | 的 *ti* |
| 五 *wu3* | 前 *ch'ien2* | 孫 *sun1* | 家 *chia1* | 我 *wo3* | 祖 *tsu3* | 祖 *tsu3* |
| 個 *ko4* | 幾 *chi3* | 子。*tzŭ* | 兄。*hsiung1* | 們 *mên* | 母。*mu3* | 上。*shang4* |
| 小 *hsiao3* | 位 *wei4* | 孫 *sun1* | 舍 *shê4* | 弟 *ti4* | 這 *chê4* | 家 *chia1* |
| 孫。*sun1* | 令 *ling4* | 女。*nü3* | 弟。*ti4* | 兄 *hsiung1* | 位 *wei4* | 祖 *tsu3* |

My ancestors. My grandfather. My grandmother.

*Obs.* 1.—My is implied by the use of *chia*, which is used only in referring to one's own relations.

*Obs.* 2.—We can also say *chia tsu*, my grandfather.

This old gentleman.

We are seven brothers.

*Obs.*—Note that *ti* precedes *hsiung* when the word is plural, but that *hsiung ti* means a younger brother.

My elder brother. My younger brother (*see* Exercise XXV, 4).

A son. A grandson. A granddaughter.

How many grandsons have you, sir?

*Obs.* 1.—Note *ling sun* when speaking of others; *hsiao sun* of one's own grandchildren. *See* 208.

*Obs.* 2—Have you: *kên ch'ien*; *lit.*, in your presence.

I have five grandsons.

661. 奴 *nu2*, a slave; but also used disparagingly of inferiors not slaves.

662. 才 *ts'ai2*, talent; but when coupled with *nu2*, the foregoing, it does not appear to affect its sense.

663. 迎 *ying2*, to go out to meet an equal or superior.

664. 接 *chieh1*, to receive a present; to greet a guest. Can be used with the foregoing.

665. Examples :—

| | | | | | | |
|---|---|---|---|---|---|---|
| 迎 *ying2* | 道 *tao4* | 才 *ts'ai2* | 那 *na4* | 得 *tei3* | 父。*fu1* | 奴 *nu2* |
| 接 *chieh1* | 兒 *'rh* | 們 *mên* | 壞 *huai4* | 去 *ch'ü4* | 快 *k'uai4* | 才。*ts'ai2* |
| 您。*nin2* | 趕 *kan3* | 走 *tsou3* | 必 *hsin1* | 迎 *ying2* | 回 *hui2* | 迎 *ying2* |
| | 不 *pu2* | 錯 *ts'o4* | 的 *ti* | 接。*chieh1* | 來 *lai2* | 接。*chieh1* |
| | 上 *shang4* | 了 *liao* | 奴 *nu2* | 我 *wo3* | 我 *wo3* | 家 *chia1* |

Slaves.

To receive; to go to meet, as a parent, visitor, etc.

My father will be back directly; I must go and receive him.

Those rascally servants of mine lost their way, and were not in time to receive you.

666. 葬, 塟, *tsang*$^4$, to bury; the first form appears to be more frequently used.

667. 絲 *ssu*$^1$, silk (spinning or winding) not yet made into a fabric.

668. 團 *t'uan*$^2$, a ball, a lump, as of silk, cotton, etc.

669. 絨 *jung*$^2$, woollen cloth; velvet; worsted; very coarse silk.

670. 尺 *ch'ih*$^3$, the Chinese foot, of 10 inches.

671. Examples:—

| | | | | | |
|---|---|---|---|---|---|
| 五。*wu*$^3$ | 長 *ch'ang*$^2$ | 是 *shih*$^4$ | 一 *i*$^4$ | 那 *na*$^4$ | 下 *hsia*$^4$ |
| 尺 *ch'ih*$^2$ | 三 *san*$^1$ | 論 *lun*$^4$ | 根 *kên*$^1$ | 絨 *jung*$^2$ | 塟, *tsang*$^4$ |
| 寸 *ts'un*$^4$ | 尺 *ch'ih*$^3$ | 尺 *ch'ih*$^3$ | 絲 *ssŭ*$^1$ | 三 *san*$^1$ | 一 *i*$^4$ |
| 過 *kuo*$^4$ | 二 *êrh*$^4$ | 賣 *mai*$^4$ | 線 *hsien*$^4$ | 尺 *ch'ih*$^3$ | 團 *t'uan*$^2$ |
| 長。*ch'ang*$^2$ | 寸 *ts'un*$^4$ | 的。*ti* | 絨 *jung*$^2$ | 寬。*k'uan*$^1$ | 絲。*ssŭ*$^1$ |

To bury.
A ball of silk.
That velvet is three feet wide.
A silken thread.
Velvet is sold by the foot.
Three feet two inches and a half in length.
Too long; *lit.*, feet and inches excessive length.
*Obs.*—Note *ch'ih*$^3$ *ts'un*$^4$ in combination, not *ch'ih*$^3$.

672. 貨 *huo*$^4$, goods; merchandise.

673. 昂 *ang*$^2$, rising; risen. Seldom used alone.

674. 替 *t'i*$^4$, to supply the place of; for; instead of.

675. 挑 *t'iao*$^1$, to carry on the shoulder; to select.

676. Examples:—

| | | | | | | |
|---|---|---|---|---|---|---|
| 菜 *ts'ai*$^4$ | 挑 *t'iao*$^1$ | 打 *ta*$^3$ | 長 *chang*$^3$ | 現 *hsien*$^4$ | 貴。*kuei*$^4$ | 買 *mai*$^3$ |
| 挑 *t'iao*$^1$ | 一 *i*$^2$ | 算 *suan*$^4$ | 了 *liao* | 在 *tsai*$^4$ | 絲 *ssŭ*$^1$ | 土 *t'u*$^3$ } |
| 了 *liao* | 個 *ko*$^4$ | 請 *ch'ing*$^3$ | 都 *tou*$^1$ | 昂 *ang*$^2$ | 貨 *huo*$^4$ | 貨 *huo*$^4$ } |
| 來, *lai*$^2$ | 好 *hao*$^3$ | 您 *nin*$^2$ | 說 *shuo*$^1$ | 貴 *kuei*$^4$ | 的 *ti* | 出 *ch'u*$^1$ |
| | 的。*ti* | 替 *t'i*$^4$ | 得, *tê* | 現 *hsien*$^4$ | 價 *chia*$^4$ | 口。*k'ou*$^3$ |
| | 把 *pa*$^3$ | 我 *wo*$^3$ | 我 *wo*$^3$ | 在 *tsai*$^4$ | 錢 *ch'ien*$^2$ | 昂 *ang*$^2$ |

To buy goods for export.
*Obs.*—Note *k'ou*, a port, sea or riverine; also, a pass, frontier or otherwise.
High price; rising in price.
The price of silk goods is *ang*$^2$-*kuei*$^4$ (high) just now, or *chang*$^3$ (has risen); you may say either.
I propose to ask you to choose me a good one.
Bring (carry with a pole) those vegetables here.

## EXERCISE XXV.

1 稱人您、是有點兒尊重人的意思。

1. To address a person as *nin*² (you, sir) conveys a certain idea of doing honour to the person addressed.

*Obs.—Lit.*, when one accosts anyone as *nin*, it is that there is a particle of honouring the person's intention,

2 家祖就是我父親的老子。旁人的父親就稱人家老翁。

2. *Chia*¹ *tsu*³ (my grandfather) is my father's father. The father of a third person is called his *lao*³ *wêng*¹.

*Obs.* 1.—Third person: *lit.*, side person. Though *lao wêng* is a term of respect, you do not use it when speaking to a man of his own father.

*Obs.* 2.—*Ch'êng*, here, to speak of; translated in Example 1 by *addressing*, because its object is there in the second person.

3 令祖好阿、令尊好阿、是問人家的祖、人家父親的安。

3. Is the honoured grandfather well? is the honoured worshipful one well? are inquiries after the well-being of the grandfather or father of the person addressed.

*Obs.*—Note the interrogative *a*.

4 向人說自己的弟兄、說的是家兄、舍弟。稱人家的弟兄、是說令兄、令弟。

4. In speaking to anyone of one's own brothers, the form used is *chia*¹ *hsiung*¹ (the elder brother of my family), *shê*⁴ *ti*⁴ (the younger brother of my cottage). In speaking to anyone else of his brother, the form is the honoured elder brother, or the honoured younger brother.

5 奴才就是使喚的人、有是買的、有不是買的、還是說底下人的多。

5. The term *nu*²-*ts'ai*² means, simply, servants, some are property (slaves). some are not; but the more common phrase is *ti*³ *hsia*⁴ *jên*² (inferiors).

*Obs.*—But the more common: *lit.*, [but] still is [it the fact that] saying *ti hsia jên's* [fashion is the] more frequent; or, the saying *ti hsia jên's* [people] predominate.

6 今兒家祖回ʻ來。我得ʻ去迎接。後兒他們老翁下葬、我得ʻ去。幫幫他們去。

6. My grandfather returns to-day, and I must go to meet him. Their father is to be buried the day after to-morrow, and I shall have to go and lend a hand at the funeral.

*Obs.* 1.—Buried, etc.: *lit.*, the day after to-morrow their father [they] bury; I must to help them go. *Hsia tsang* are two verbs compounded, not a verb and its object.

*Obs.* 2.—Here, as in many places, the object *(lao wêng)* preceding the verb may be made in our idiom the subject of a passive verb.

17

7 生絲不是你們這兒的土貨麼．可不是麼、那絨可不是土貨、請您替我挑一點兒好的．

7. Is not raw silk a product of your country here? To be sure it is; but velvet is not, and I shall be obliged to you to choose me some that is good.

*Obs.*—To be sure: *lit.*, can it not be?

8 我兄弟給大人請安、他說他明兒怕不能來、找了個替工兒替他幾天．

8. My younger brother presents his respects to you, sir; he says he is afraid he cannot come to-morrow, so he has found a substitute to act in his stead for a few days.

*Obs.* 1.—Note that *hsiung-ti*, in combination, means a younger brother or brothers, and *ti hsiung*, brothers, elder and younger.

*Obs.* 2.—Present respects: *ch'ing an*; *lit.*, request [to be informed of your] comfort or well-being.

*Obs.* 3.—Substitute; *lit.*, an instead-of workman.

9 我挑出來的那瓦盆總得'挑着、擱在車上不行．

9. You will have to carry those earthenware basins that I have chosen with a carrying pole; it won't do to put them in a cart.

*Obs.*—Note *t'iao*, to choose: *t'iao cho*, to carry with a pole.

10 他把紙弄成團兒、往我臉上扔．

10. He rolled some paper into a ball and threw it in my face.

*Obs.*—*Lit.*, he took paper, worked it [till it] formed a ball, towards my face threw it; *ch'êng* is often an auxiliary simply denoting completion of an action.

11 牲口駝的東西叫馱子、那是頭裏說過的、人肩髈兒上挑的東西叫挑子、人背上背的東西叫背子．

11. The load carried on the backs of animals is called a *to⁴-tzŭ*, as has been before explained; that carried by men with a pole over the shoulder is called a *t'iao¹-tzŭ*; and that carried by men on the back is called a *pei¹-tzŭ*.

*Obs.*—髈 and 膀 are identical.

*Turn the following into Chinese.* (KEY, EXERCISE XXV.)

1. Three days ago our elder brother returned home, bringing with him some 200 balls odd of silk and 50 bales of velvet. My father told me to go and meet him, and, while I was about it, to assist him in carrying in the goods.

*Obs.* 1.—Three days ago: *lit.*, the great day before yesterday.

*Obs.* 2.—While I was about it: *lit.*, following with the hand; *i.e.*, taking advantage of one job to do another (to take the opportunity).

2. Is your elder brother a draper, then?

3. To be sure. Father and an ancestor of his were also in that line of business. What object have you in asking?

*Obs.*—What object: *lit.*, you ask this talk have what lofty vision (or idea)?

4. My younger brother wants to buy some fine raw silk, [and I wish to] ask your brother to pick out a little good [stuff] for him; can it be done?

5. It can be done, of course; he will certainly select some silk for your brother; but there is one thing, I am afraid the price has gone up; it is very dear at present.

6. Good-bye, sir! *Au revoir!*

*Obs.* 1.—Good-bye: *lit.*, you please; *q.d.*, please do not remain on my account, or, please do not let me detain you.

*Obs.* 2.—*Au revoir*: *lit.*, returning see; we shall meet when you or I return, or by-and-by. These are two of the most common salutations in use; *nin ch'ing* may be also used for, that will do, thank you.

7. Their grandfather was buried yesterday. I told my servants to go and lend them a hand, but the rascals wouldn't listen to me, and never went at all. Some bystander had said there was a ghost over there, and they were so frightened that they refused to go. My grandson eventually called one of them to him. He gave a *cha* and came slowly across, whereupon my grandson gave him a few strokes with a stick.

*Obs.* 1.—Never: *tao liao$^3$-'rh*: *lit.*, to the finish.

*Obs.* 2.—A ghost: *kuei$^3$* (Radical 194).

8. What your servants say has some little truth in it. I passed the place the other night, and I saw a ghost running about in a wild sort of way. His hair was red, his face yellow, and the moment I saw him it frightened me terribly.

*Obs.* 1.—By: this is rendered by *ta$^3$* (241).

*Obs.* 2.—Frightened me terribly: *p'a ti wo liao pu tê*. Note *p'a* as an active verb.

9. What nonsense! You certainly must have had too much to drink again.

677. 想 *hsiang$^3$*, to think; to think of.

678. 却 *ch'io$^4$*, *ch'üeh$^4$*, properly, to reject a present; a strong disjunctive, to be rendered sometimes by *but*, sometimes by emphasis only.

679. 睡 *shui$^4$*, to sleep.

680. 覺 *chiao$^4$*, *chio$^2$*, *chüeh$^2$*. *Chiao$^4$* is properly to perceive, to feel, in which sense it is sometimes pronounced *chio$^2$* and *chüeh$^2$*; when joined with *shui$^4$*, to sleep (679), it is pronounced *chiao$^4$*; it does not seem to affect the sense of that word in any way.

681. Examples:—

| | | | | | | |
|---|---|---|---|---|---|---|
| 著 *chao$^2$* | 睡 *shui$^4$* | 說 *shuo$^1$* | 他 *t'a$^1$* | 你。*ni$^3$* | 到。*tao$^4$* | 我 *wo$^3$* |
| 身 *shên$^1$* | 覺 *chiao$^4$* | 我 *wo$^3$* | 昨 *tso$^2$* | 你 *ni$^3$* | 我 *wo$^3$* | 想 *hsiang$^3$* |
| 上 *shang$^4$* | 來 *lai$^2$* | 沒 *mei$^2$* | 兒 *'rh* | 想 *hsiang$^3$* | 常 *ch'ang$^2$* | 他 *t'a$^1$* |
| 覺 *chio$^2$* | 著。*cho* | 在 *tsai$^4$* | 來 *lai$^2$* | 他 *t'a$^1$* | 常 *ch'ang$^1$* | 明 *ming$^2$* |
| 著 *cho* | 我 *wo$^3$* | 家 *chia$^1$* | 過。*kuo$^4$* | 怎 *tsên$^3$* | 兒 *'rh* | 兒 *'rh* |
| 冷。*lêng$^3$* | 睡 *shui$^4$* | 我 *wo$^3$* | 他 *t'a$^1$* | 麽 *mo$^1$* | 的 *ti* | 可 *k'o$^3$* |
| | 不 *pu$^4$* | 却 *ch'io$^4$* | 們 *mên* | 樣。*yang$^4$* | 想 *hsiang$^3$* | 以 *i$^3$* |

I think he can arrive to-morrow.

I am continually thinking about you.

*Obs.*—For *ch'ang*, see 688.

What do you think of him?
He came yesterday, and they said I wasn't at home, but I was asleep.
*Obs.—Shui-chiao* does not necessarily imply sleep, but it does imply the attempt to sleep; *see* next example.
I cannot sleep; I feel cold.

682. 對 *tui*$^4$, opposite to; to agree with; a pair. It also sometimes takes the place of the preposition *to*, or marks the sign of the dative.

683. 賽 *sai*$^4$, to compete with.

684. 嗇 *sê*$^4$, niggardly; never used alone.

685. 吞 *t'un*$^1$, to swallow; to bolt down. Oftener used figuratively of peculation or avarice.

686. 疊 *tieh*$^2$, in folds or layers; to fold; repeatedly.

687. 增 *tsêng*$^1$, to add to.

688. 常 *ch'ang*$^2$, constant; continual.

689. Examples:—

| | | | | | | |
|---|---|---|---|---|---|---|
| 是 *shih*$^4$ | 裳 *shang*$^1$ | 吞 *t'un*$^1$ | 嗇 *sê*$^4$ | 馬, *ma*$^3$ | 面。*mien*$^4$ | 對 *tui*$^4$ |
| 平 *p'ing*$^2$ | 疊 *tieh*$^2$ | 人 *jên*$^2$ | 刻 *k'ê*$^4$ | 那 *na*$^4$ | 我 *wo*$^3$ | 面。*mien*$^4$ |
| 常 *ch'ang*$^2$ | 起 *ch'i*$^3$ | 家 *chia*$^1$ | 人 *jên*$^2$ | 青 *ch'ing*$^1$ | 們 *mên* | 輭 *juan*$^3$ |
| 的 *ti* | 來。*lai*$^2$ | 的 *ti* | 不 *pu*$^2$ | 馬 *ma*$^3$ | 賽 *sai*$^4$ | 是 *shih*$^4$ |
| 事。*shih*$^4$ | 增 *tsêng*$^1$ | 錢。*ch'ien*$^2$ | 好 *hao*$^4$ | 跑 *p'ao*$^3$ | 過 *kuo*$^4$ | 硬 *ying*$^4$ |
| | 多。*to*$^1$ | 把 *pa*$^3$ | 花 *hua*$^1$ | 得 *tê*$^2$ | 兩 *liang*$^3$ | 的 *ti* |
| | 却 *ch'io*$^4$ | 衣 *i*$^1$ | 錢。*ch'ien*$^2$ | 快。*k'uai*$^4$ | 回 *hui*$^2$ | 對 *tui*$^4$ |

The opposite; the reverse side; also, in front of.
Soft is the opposite of hard.
We tried the horses twice; the grey gallops the faster.
Niggardly men do not like to spend money.
*Obs.—Hao*$^4$.
To pocket (*lit.*, swallow) people's money.
Fold up the clothes.
*Obs.—Ch'i lai*, the auxiliary verb of *tieh*, does not necessarily imply movement upwards.
Many added.
It is nevertheless a matter of common occurrence.
*Obs.—P'ing-ch'ang* may also mean indifferent, as a person's reputation.

690. 葱 *ts'ung*$^1$, onions.

691. 苗 *miao*$^2$, sprouts; the first appearance of any vegetation above the ground belonging to the category of grasses.

692. 嫩 *nên*$^{4}$, *nun*$^{4}$, tender, fresh, or young, as opposed to tough, stale, or old.

693. 桑 *sang*$^{1}$, the mulberry tree.

694. 樹 *shu*$^{4}$, a tree.

695. 林 *lin*$^{2}$, a grove ; a wood ; a forest.

696. Examples :—

| | | | | | | |
|---|---|---|---|---|---|---|
| 兒 *'rh* | 我 *wo*$^{3}$ | 有 *yu*$^{3}$ | 桑 *sang*$^{1}$ | 來 *lai*$^{2}$ | 兒。*'rh* | 一 *i*$^{4}$ |
| 不 *pu*$^{2}$ | 要 *yao*$^{4}$ | 桑 *sang*$^{1}$ | 樹。*shu*$^{4}$ | 了。*liao* | 豆 *tou*$^{4}$ | 斤 *chin*$^{1}$ |
| 要 *yao*$^{4}$ | 嫩 *nên*$^{4}$ | 樹 *shu*$^{4}$ | 山 *shan*$^{1}$ | 樹 *shu*$^{4}$ | 苗 *miao*$^{2}$ | 葱。*ts'ung*$^{1}$ |
| 老 *lao*$^{3}$ | 雞 *chi*$^{1}$ | 林 *lin*$^{2}$ | 背 *pei*$^{4}$ | 林 *lin*$^{2}$ | 兒 *'rh* | 嫩 *nên*$^{4}$ |
| 的。*ti* | 子 *tzŭ*$^{3}$ | 子。*tzŭ* | 後 *hou*$^{4}$ | 子。*tzŭ* | 上 *shang*$^{4}$ | 苗 *miao*$^{2}$ |

A catty of onions.
Tender sprouts.
The beans have sprouted.
*Obs.*—Emphasise *shang :* not that *shang* verbalises *miao*.
A grove of trees ; or, a wood.
The mulberry tree.
At the back of the hill there is a mulberry grove.
I want soft-boiled eggs, not hard-boiled ones.

697. 森 *sên*$^{1}$, density, as of foliage.

698. 綠 *lü*$^{4}$, green ; the literary pronunciation is *lu*$^{4}$.

699. 草 *ts'ao*$^{3}$, grass ; plants not being trees.

700. 濕, 溼, *shih*$^{1}$, wet ; damp. The first form is the commoner.

701. 曬, 晒, *shai*$^{4}$, a verb describing the action of the sun's rays ; not necessarily to scorch. The second is a vulgar form.

702. Examples :—

| | | | | | | |
|---|---|---|---|---|---|---|
| 出 *ch'u*$^{1}$ | 裳 *shang*$^{1}$ | 我 *wo*$^{3}$ | 草 *ts'ao*$^{3}$ | 子 *tzŭ* | 的。*ti* | 葱 *ts'ung*$^{1}$ |
| 去 *ch'ü*$^{4}$ | 都 *tou*$^{1}$ | 一 *i*$^{4}$ | 鞋。*hsieh*$^{2}$ | 綠 *lü*$^{4}$ | 那 *na*$^{4}$ | 苗 *miao*$^{2}$ |
| 曬 *shai*$^{4}$ | 濕 *shih*$^{1}$ | 身 *shên*$^{1}$ | 草 *ts'ao*$^{3}$ | 森 *sên*$^{1}$ | 個 *ko* | 兒 *'rh* |
| 一 *i* | 了 *liao* | 的 *ti* | 帽 *mao*$^{4}$ | 森 *sên*$^{1}$ | 竹 *chu*$^{2}$ | 是 *shih*$^{4}$ |
| 晒。*shai*$^{4}$ | 拏 *na*$^{2}$ | 衣 *i*$^{1}$ | 兒。*'rh* | 的。*ti* | 林 *lin*$^{2}$ | 綠 *lü*$^{4}$ |

Onion sprouts are green.
How green that bamboo grove is !
Straw shoes. Straw hats.
All my clothes are wet ; take them out and dry them in the sun.

## EXERCISE XXVI.

1 我們明兒上西山去罷。到那兒、就找個樹林子、在青草地裏坐着、又涼快。又沒土。你說好不好。

1. Let's go to the Western Hills to-morrow. When we get there we will look for a grove of trees and sit down on the green grass, where we shall be both cool and free from dust. What do you say?

*Obs.*—Green grass: the word *ch'ing* applies to many other colours besides green; it may also mean glossy black, grey, or blue, and further qualifies the shades of certain primary colours.

2 去倒沒有甚麼不能去的、我却想着還是在太陽地裏曬暖兒好、樹林子坐着時候兒還不對呢。

2. There is nothing to prevent our going, but I think it would be better to bask in the sun; it is not the time of year to sit in the woods.

*Obs.*—*Lit.*, go there is not, on the contrary, any not being able to go's [reason]; I, however, think, still it is in the sun's place to warm better; in a wood sitting the time [is] not apposite.

3 偺們倆人賽着跑罷。正對我的心。你的腿却比我的長、怕跑不過你。

3. Let's have a race. It's just what I should like, but your legs are longer than mine, and I fear I can't beat you.

*Obs.*—Just what I should like: *lit.*, correctly agrees with my wishes (or feelings).

4 他那倆兒弟利害得很、都是過於嗇刻、不肯花錢、他們的錢一天比一天增的多。

4. Those two brothers of his are terrible fellows, they are both too niggardly; they won't spend anything, and their money increases every day.

5 那葱這兩天貴、不分老嫩、都是二百錢一斤。

5. Onions have been dear these last two days; old and young alike, they are all 200 cash the catty.

6 草木是花草樹木的總名。麥子出了苗兒了。火苗兒也說得。

6. The term *ts'ao*$^3$ *mu*$^4$ is generic of flowers, plants, and trees. The wheat has sprouted. You can also say *huo*$^3$ *miao*$^2$*-'rh* (the flame of a fire).

*Obs.*—Generic: *lit.*, all-including name.

7 苗子是四川東南的人、分生的熟的。

7. The Miaotzŭ are people to the south-east of Szechwan; they are divided into wild and reclaimed.

*Obs.*—Wild, etc.: *lit.*, unripe and ripe; reclaimed and unreclaimed.

8 樹多叫樹林子。那桑樹林子綠森森的。

8. A number of trees is called a *shu*$^4$ *lin*$^2$*-tzŭ*. How deep (or dense) the green of that mulberry grove is!

9 要把溼衣裳弄乾了、得鋪在日頭地裏曬一曬。曬乾了就疊起來。

9. If you want to dry damp clothes you should spread them out in a sunny place for the sun to shine upon them. When the sun has dried them they should be folded up.

*Obs.* 1.—To dry: *nung*, here, and often elsewhere, pronounced *nou*, verbalises the adjective *kan*, dry.
*Obs.* 2.—Sunny: *lit.*, you must spread them in a sun place; note *jih-t'ou*, the sun.

10 聽見說、對過兒住的那個人疊次吞了人家好些個銀子。天有八下鐘了、小人兒們該睡覺了。

10. I hear that the man who lives over the way has pocketed people's money over and over again. It's 8 o'clock; youngsters should be in bed.

*Obs.* 1.—Over the way: *lit.*, fronting over (or across).
*Obs.* 2.—Over and over: *lit.*, on repeated occasions.

*Turn the following into Chinese.* (KEY, EXERCISE XXVI.)

1. The other day we two were having an archery match in the grove. The weather was excellent, the sun's rays were warm, and that stretch of wood was of a lovely deep green. When we had finished our archery I told him a funny story.

*Obs.* 1.—Archery: *la kung* (Radical 57), to draw the bow.
*Obs.* 2.—A stretch: *i tai*. *See* 416.

2. I proceeded to say that once upon a time there was a man of the name of MA, who sold onions. He was sleeping one day on the ground in a mulberry grove, and when he got up he saw a man standing before him roaring with laughter.

*Obs.* 1.—Once upon a time: *lit.*, formerly.
*Obs.* 2.—Roaring with laughter: *lit.*, [with] great sound laugh[ing].

3. "What is there to laugh at here?" he asked in a rage. The man said to him, "The ground here is very damp; look at your clothes, they are all wet, and must be spread out in the sun to dry; besides, you have lost the merchandise you brought with you."

*Obs.* 1.—Asked in a rage: *lit.*, he begot rage, then said, here is what laughing head (or item)?

*Obs.* 2.—Said to him: *tui t'a shuo*; note *tui* as a preposition.

4. The old man gave a look, and, true enough, his bags were empty. "Then," said he, "if it isn't you who has eaten my young onions, who has?" "I've not eaten them for nothing," the other replied; "there's the money;" and as he spoke he threw some large cash into the grass.

*Obs.* 1.—Old man: *lit.*, old head; a common expression, but not often addressed to the individual.

*Obs.* 2.—There's the money: *lit.*, the price I have given is there; *kei ti* for *kei tê* (have given).

5. The man MA, thinking this really was money, went forward to get it, but the moment he took his eyes off the other, he was gone. The money, too, could not be found, so MA knew that it was not a man but a sprite.

6. That man is fearfully stingy. He comes from that place Yünnan. I think that by origin he is a Miaotzŭ, who, several years since, did a business in straw (dry grass). His money increases largely month by month; he has repeatedly pocketed other people's money, but he is not fond of spending it himself.

*Obs.*—Business: *shêng*$^1$ *i*$^4$; *lit.*, growing (or life) intention; a metaphorical synonym for trade, which a person engages in with, *i*, the intention, *shêng*, of growing (*q.d.*, rich), or of living. The metaphor was originally applied to the revival of vegetation in early spring.

703. 某 *mou*$^3$, certain; as, a certain man.

704. 乍 *cha*$^4$, suddenly; unexpectedly.

705. 和 *hai*$^4$, *ho*$^2$, together with; in relations with. *See also* 210.

706. 別 *pieh*$^2$, to distinguish; to separate; hence, another. *See also* 646.

707. 素 *su*$^4$, of uniform plainness; hence, uninterruptedly through past time; heretofore. Also, vegetable diet, as opposed to meat diet.

708. Examples:—

| | | | | | | |
|---|---|---|---|---|---|---|
| 來 *lai*$^2$ | 平 *p'ing*$^2$ | 我 *wo*$^3$ | 都 *tou*$^1$ | 別 *pieh*$^2$ | 開 *k'ai*$^1$ | 某 *mou*$^3$ |
| 的 *ti* | 素 *su*$^4$ | 分 *fên*$^1$ | 不 *pu*$^4$ | 告 *kao*$^4$ | 起 *ch'i*$^3$ | 人。*jên*$^2$ |
| 意 *i*$^4$ | 素 *su*$^4$ | 別 *pieh*$^2$ | 知 *chih*$^1$ | 訴 *su*$^4$ | 當 *tang*$^4$ | 我 *wo*$^3$ |
| 思，*ssŭ*$^1$ | 常 *ch'ang*$^2$ | 不 *pu*$^4$ | 道。*tao*$^4$ | 人。*jên*$^2$ | 鋪 *p'u*$^4$ | 和 *hai*$^4$ |
| | 是 *shih*$^4$ | 出 *ch'u*$^1$ | 乍 *cha*$^4$ | 別 *pieh*$^2$ | 來，*lai*$^2$ | 某 *mou*$^3$ |
| | 向 *hsiang*$^4$ | 來。*lai*$^2$ | 見 *chien*$^4$ | 人 *jên*$^2$ | 你 *ni*$^3$ | 人 *jên*$^2$ |

A certain person.
I have opened a pawnshop with So-and-so (or, a certain individual).
Don't tell anybody. Nobody else knows.
On suddenly seeing [them] I can't distinguish [which is which].
*P'ing*$^2$ *su*$^4$ and *su*$^4$ *ch'ang*$^2$ have the meaning of *hsiang*$^4$ *lai*$^2$ (heretofore, in all past time).

709. 原 *yüan*$^{2}$, origin ; beginning ; in fact.

710. 待 *tai*$^{4}$, towards ; to await ; to treat, or behave to.

711. 厚 *hou*$^{4}$, thick ; staunch ; liberal.

712. 薄 *pao*$^{2}$, *po*$^{2}$, thin.

713. Examples :—

| | | | | | | |
|---|---|---|---|---|---|---|
| 兒 *'rh* | 薄 *pao*$^{2}$ | 人。*jên*$^{2}$ | 他 *t'a*$^{1}$ | 毛 *mao*$^{2}$ | 熱。*jê*$^{4}$ | 我 *wo*$^{3}$ |
| 的。*ti* | 我 *wo*$^{3}$ | 這 *chê*$^{4}$ | 原 *yüan*$^{2}$ | 病。*ping*$^{4}$ | 那 *na*$^{4}$ | 們 *mên* |
| | 要 *yao*$^{4}$ | 一 *i*$^{4}$ | 是 *shih*$^{4}$ | 他 *t'a*$^{1}$ | 是 *shih*$^{4}$ | 倆 *lia*$^{3}$ |
| | 厚 *hou*$^{4}$ | 張 *chang*$^{1}$ | 個 *ko*$^{4}$ | 待 *tai*$^{4}$ | 原 *yüan*$^{2}$ | 原 *yüan*$^{2}$ |
| | 一 *i*$^{4}$ | 紙 *chih*$^{3}$ | 厚 *hou*$^{4}$ | 我 *wo*$^{3}$ | 來 *lai*$^{2}$ | 來 *lai*$^{2}$ |
| | 點 *tien*$^{3}$ | 太 *t'ai*$^{4}$ | 道 *tao*$^{4}$ | 好。*hao*$^{3}$ | 的 *ti* | 親 *ch'in*$^{1}$ |

We were warm friends at first.

*Obs.—Lit.*, intimate and hot.

That is an original flaw (or defect) ; one that has always been there.

*Obs.*—Note *mao-ping*, a flaw or defect : *mao*, a hair, hence a synonym for anything minute ; the term may be applied to moral, physical, or material blemishes.

He treats me well.

At bottom he is a staunch (liberal-minded) man.

*Obs.*—Staunch : *hou tao ; lit.*, of stout or staunch principles.

This sheet of paper is too thin ; I want a little thicker one.

714. 傲 *$^{ng}$ao*$^{4}$, proud.

715. 嫉 *chi*$^{4}$, not used in speaking without the following *tu*$^{4}$, with which it is identical in meaning.

716. 妒 *tu*$^{4}$, envious ; jealous.

717. 慚 *ts'an*$^{2}$, to be ashamed ; generally used with the following.

718. 愧 *k'uei*$^{4}$, to be ashamed ; shame.

719. Examples :—

| | | | | | |
|---|---|---|---|---|---|
| 心 *hsin*$^{1}$ | 真 *chên*$^{1}$ | 待 *tai*$^{4}$ | 地 *ti*$^{4}$ | 做 *tso*$^{4}$ | 他 *t'a*$^{1}$ |
| 裏 *li*$^{3}$ | 是 *shih*$^{4}$ | 人 *jên*$^{2}$ | 裏 *li*$^{3}$ | 了 *liao* | 嫉 *chi*$^{4}$ |
| 慚 *ts'an*$^{2}$ | 叫 *chiao*$^{4}$ | 傲 *$^{ng}$ao*$^{4}$ | 說 *shuo*$^{1}$ | 官。*kuan*$^{1}$ | 妒 *tu*$^{4}$ |
| 愧。*k'uei*$^{4}$ | 我 *wo*$^{3}$ | 慢。*man*$^{4}$ | 我 *wo*$^{3}$ | 背 *pei*$^{4}$ | 我 *wo*$^{3}$ |

He is jealous of my being an official.

*Obs.—Chi-tu* cannot be used of jealousy of the affections, the term for which is, literally, to eat vinegar (*ch'ih ts'u*$^{4}$).

Behind my back [he] says I treat people arrogantly.

*Obs.*—One of the primary meanings of *man*$^{4}$, slow, is indifferent or rude.

This really makes me feel ashamed.

18

720. 絕 *chüeh*$^{2}$, to cut off, to interrupt, as a stream, supplies, intercourse; to be so cut off.

721. 交 *chiao*$^{1}$, to interchange; intercourse; to hand over. *Chiao*$^{1}$-*ch'ing*$^{2}$, friendship.

722. 憑 *p'ing*$^{2}$, to lean upon; to depend on. Also, to let; to allow. It will be met with later in the sense of proof or evidence.

723. Examples :—

| | | | | | | |
|---|---|---|---|---|---|---|
| 交 *chiao*$^{1}$ | 交。*chiao*$^{1}$ | 交 *chiao*$^{1}$ | 們 *mên* | 話 *hua*$^{4}$ | 麽 *mo* | 憑 *p'ing*$^{2}$ |
| 給 *kei*$^{3}$ | 這 *chê*$^{4}$ | 情 *ch'ing*$^{2}$ | 是 *shih*$^{4}$ | 也 *yeh*$^{3}$ | 連 *lien*$^{2}$ | 他 *t'a*$^{1}$ |
| 我 *wo*$^{3}$ | 件 *chien*$^{4}$ | 總 *tsung*$^{3}$ | 多 *to*$^{1}$ | 沒 *mei*$^{2}$ | 一 *i*$^{2}$ | 們 *mên* |
| 辦 *pan*$^{4}$ | 事 *shih*$^{4}$ | 沒 *mei*$^{2}$ | 年 *nien*$^{2}$ | 有。*yu*$^{3}$ | 句 *chü*$^{4}$ | 說 *shuo*$^{1}$ |
| 罷。*pa* | 情 *ch'ing*$^{2}$ | 絕 *chüeh*$^{2}$ | 的 *ti* | 我 *wo*$^{3}$ | 實 *shih*$^{2}$ | 甚 *shên*$^{2}$ |

Let them say what they like (or, no matter what they say), there is not a word (*lit.*, sentence) of truth in it.

Ours is a friendship of long standing, which has never been interrupted.

***Obs.*—Friendship : *lit.*, interchange of feelings.**

You had better leave the settlement of this matter to me ; or, hand that matter over to me to deal with.

724. 賓 *pin*$^{1}$, guest, stranger, as opposed to *chu*$^{3}$, in the sense of host.

725. 拜 *pai*$^{4}$, to salute ; to visit ; to pay respects to.

726. 應 *ying*$^{1}$, to conform to what is right ; ought.

727. 陪 *p'ei*$^{2}$, to play second to, as a candidate in reserve ; to bear one's guest company.

728. Examples :—

| | | | | | | |
|---|---|---|---|---|---|---|
| 喝 *ho*$^{1}$ | 茶 *ch'a*$^{2}$ | 陪 *p'ei*$^{2}$ | 來 *lai*$^{2}$ | 應 *ying*$^{1}$ | 會。*hui*$^{4}$ | 有 *yu*$^{3}$ |
| 一 *i*$^{4}$ | 你 *ni*$^{3}$ | 客。*k'o*$^{4}$ | 得 *tê* | 該 *kai*$^{1}$ | 那 *na*$^{4}$ | 賓 *pin*$^{1}$ |
| 杯 *pei*$^{1}$ | 陪 *p'ei*$^{2}$ | 我 *wo*$^{3}$ | 巧 *ch'iao*$^{3}$ | 見 *chien*$^{4}$ | 麽 *mo* | 客 *k'o*$^{4}$ |
| 兒 *'rh* | 著 *cho* | 要 *yao*$^{4}$ | 請 *ch'ing*$^{3}$ | 他。*t'a*$^{1}$ | 著 *cho*$^{2}$ | 來 *lai*$^{2}$ |
| 罷。*pa*$^{4}$ | 我 *wo*$^{3}$ | 喝 *ho*$^{1}$ | 你 *ni*$^{3}$ | 你 *ni*$^{3}$ | 我 *wo*$^{3}$ | 拜 *pai*$^{4}$ |

A visitor has come to call. In that case I must see him.

***Obs.*—*Pai* is simply to leave a card ; *pai hui*, to call with the intention of seeing the host.**

You have come in the very nick of time ; please keep the guests company.

I am going to have a cup of tea ; will you join me ?

## EXERCISE XXVII.

1 我們倆人起初很親熱、後來他待我傲慢、這麽狂、我就和他絕了交了。

1. We were warm friends at first, but he afterwards behaved in an arrogant way, so I broke off relations with him.

2 我昨兒到你那兒去拜會、怎麽不見。你這話有點兒不可憑罷、怕是你留下名片就走了。

2. When I went to your place to call yesterday, how was it you wouldn't see me? I'm afraid your statement can't be altogether depended upon; I expect you just left your card and went away.

3 你待我這麽傲慢、回來告訴你父親。憑你愛告訴誰、就告訴誰、我都不怕。

3. If you treat me in this arrogant manner, I'll tell your father by-and-by. You may tell whom you please; I'm not afraid of anyone.

*Obs.*—You please: *lit.*, it depends on your liking to tell whom, then tell whom; I all not fear.

4 某人告訴我說、你那一筆賬的銀子還沒交出來、你不慚愧麽。

4. A certain person tells me that you have not yet handed over the money for that bill of yours; aren't you ashamed of yourself?

*Obs.*—Note *pi*, the numerative of bills or of items in a bill.

5 那倆瓶、乍見的時候兒、好相是一對兒、細細兒的一瞧、尺寸就不一樣。

5. When I first glanced at those two jars they appeared very like a pair, but directly I had a careful look at them, I found that their dimensions were not the same.

*Obs.*—Directly: note the force of *i*; *lit.*, minutely one look, feet and inches then not the same. *Ch'ih ts'un* may be used with reference to small articles as well as large.

6 有人嫉妒我這個好兒、然而這也是件平常的事、而且也是我應當得的。

6. Some people envy me this good fortune of mine, yet it is a matter of very ordinary occurrence, and, what is more, it was my turn to get it.

*Obs.*—Turn: note that *ying tang* might equally mean, deserve to get it. *See* Exercise XIX, 7, Obs.

7 應當倆字的意思怎麼分別。沒有別的法子、總得看上下文就知道了。

7. How can you distinguish the meaning of the two characters *ying tang?* The only way we can tell is too look at the context.

*Obs.*—Context: *lit.*, upper and lower text (literature, Radical 67). The sentence, literally translated, runs, there is no other way only (altogether) must look at upper and lower text (what goes before and after), then know.

8 會客的時候兒。主人在東邊兒坐、賓客在西邊兒坐、陪著的人在下邊兒坐、對不對。那總是看屋子的方向。

8. In entertaining (receiving) guests, the host sits on the eastern side and the guest on the western side, [while] those who help to entertain sit below; isn't that correct? That depends entirely upon the direction (*fang—lit.*, place) in which the room faces (*hsiang*).

*Obs.* 1.—Correct: does it agree or not (*q.d.*, with the facts)?
*Obs.* 2.—Note *fang hsiang*, the direction in which anything faces.

9 我素常不愛拜客。冬天得穿厚衣裳、夏天穿薄的。

9. As a general rule, I am not fond of paying visits. In winter thick clothes must be worn; in summer, thin.

10 寬厚是刻薄的對面兒。

10. *K'uan*[4]*-hou*[4] (generous, liberal-minded) is the opposite of *k'ê*[4]*-po*[2] (illiberal, unhandsome in conduct).

*Turn the following into Chinese.* (KEY, EXERCISE XXVII.)

1. Have you seen So-and-so before? No, we have not. We also have seen him to-day for the first time. He is a very good fellow, and I was very intimate with him from the first moment I met him.

*Obs.*—Seen: *chien kuo mien*, met face to face; it implies something more than seeing a person without being acquainted with him.

2. I have heard from other people that he is at bottom a staunch, liberal man; one who has all along treated people well, and who does his business without any meanness.

*Obs.*—Does his business, or business: *hsing shih.*

3. If I were to institute a comparison between him and the man I know, the latter

(the man I know) is by no means a fellow of this kind.

*Obs.*—By no means: this is implied by the word *k'o*[3].

4. He is arrogant to everybody, no matter who. Whenever anyone is in luck, he is envious. He takes people's things without understanding that they have to be returned; and when one asks him [for them], he feels no shame. How can one help breaking with a man of this kind?

*Obs.*—*Lit.*, how can [one] be able not with him to cut off relations?

5. I have really no time to do this; go and do it yourself if you like (or, manage it how you please).

6. To *ch'ing*[3] *k'o*[4] is to ask guests to a meal. Guests ought to be seated at the upper end, and the host should keep them company at the side.

7. What do you want that small bird of yours for? hand it over to me. There, there! Why do you want people's things whenever you see them?

*Obs.* 1.—Why? what for? *kan shên-mo.*

*Obs.* 2.—There (or, that will do)! *tê liao* (*lit.*, finished).

8. If you don't want to go by yourself, I will accompany you; what do you say?

729. 裱 *piao*[3], to paste two sheets of paper together; to mount a picture.

730. 糊 *hu*[2], to paste paper, cloth, etc., against another substance.

731. 匠 *chiang*[4], workman; artificer.

732. 染 *jan*[3], to dye.

733. 顏 *yen*[2], colours.

734. 紅 *hung*[2], red.

735. 藍 *lan*[2], blue.

736. 畫 *hua*[4], to draw or paint; a drawing or painting.

A dyer's shop.

Red colour. Blue colour.

*Obs.*—*Sê* (Radical 139): also read *shai*$^3$ or *shê*$^4$.

This piece of cloth won't take a red colour.

*Obs.*—We might also say *jan pu ch'u hung ti lai.*

738. 淡 *tan*$^4$, weak (as of tea); pale (as of colours).

739. 新 *hsin*$^1$, new.

740. 舊 *chiu*$^4$, old.

741. 紗 *sha*$^1$, crape.

742. Examples :—

| | | | | | |
|---|---|---|---|---|---|
| 淡 *tan*$^4$ | 毯 *t'an*$^3$ | 這 *chê*$^4$ | 是 *shih*$^4$ | 是 *shih*$^4$ | 這 *chê*$^4$ |
| 了。*liao* | 顏 *yen*$^2$ | 個 *ko*$^4$ | 舊 *chiu*$^4$ | 新 *hsin*$^1$ | 疋 *p'i*$^3$ |
| | 色 *sê*$^4$ | 地 *ti*$^4$ | 的。*ti* | 的 *ti* | 紗 *sha*$^1$ |

Is this piece of crape new or old?

The colour of this carpet is faded.

743. 必 *pi*$^4$, necessarily; must.

744. 須 *hsü*$^1$, must.

745. 光 *kuang*$^1$, brightness.

746. 潤 *jun*$^4$, moist; to moisten.

747. 玻 *po*$^1$ }
748. 璃 *li*$^2$ } (said to be derived from a Sanskrit word), glass of all kinds.

749. 料 *liao*$^4$, materials; often specially applied to vitreous ware. Also, to estimate; to measure. *See* Part V, Lesson III, Note 8; Part V, Lesson L, Note 4.

750. Examples :—

| | | | | | | |
|---|---|---|---|---|---|---|
| 好 *hao*$^3$ | 蓋 *kai*$^4$ | 摔 *shuai*$^3$ | 把 *pa*$^3$ | 兒。*'rh* | 潤 *jun*$^4$ | 這 *chê*$^4$ |
| 木 *mu*$^4$ | 房 *fang*$^2$ | 出 *ch'u*$^1$ | 玻 *po*$^1$ | 日 *jih*$^4$ | 必 *pi*$^4$ | 顏 *yen*$^2$ |
| 料。*liao*$^4$ | 子 *tzŭ* | 去 *ch'ü*$^4$ | 璃 *li*$^2$ | 光 *kuang*$^1$ | 須 *hsü*$^1$ | 色 *shê*$^4$ |
| 料 *liao*$^4$ | 必 *pi*$^4$ | 做 *tso*$^4$ | 瓶 *p'ing*$^2$ | 很 *hên*$^3$ | 染 *jan*$^3$ | 不 *pu*$^4$ |
| 貨。*huo*$^4$ | 得 *tei*$^3$ | 甚 *shên*$^2$ | 的 *ti* | 大。*ta*$^4$ | 深 *shên*$^1$ | 很 *hên*$^3$ |
| | 用 *yung*$^4$ | 麼。*mo* | 水 *shui*$^3$ | 你 *ni*$^3$ | 些 *hsieh*$^1$ | 光 *kuang*$^1$ |

The colour is not very glossy ; it will have to be dyed a little deeper colour.

*Obs.*—Note that *pi*, followed by *hsü* or *tei*, is more emphatic than either of the latter words used singly.

The sunlight is very strong.

*Obs.*—The sun's disc is called *jih kuang-'rh*, as are also the sun's rays.

Why do you throw away the water in the glass bottle ?

In building a house one must use good wood.

Vitreous ware (also a slang term for a person who is a fraud, spurious imitations of jade or agate being made of this vitreous ware).

751. 擦 *ts'a*$^1$, to rub with the hand or a cloth, etc.

752. 碰 *p'êng*$^4$, to run against ; to come violently in contact with.

753. 裂 *lieh*$^4$, to crack of itself, as wood or paper.

754. 行 *hang*$^2$, a vulgar modification of *hsing*$^2$ or *hang*$^2$ (Radical 144); a trade or calling ; a place of business ; a hong. Also, a column of characters.

755. Examples :—

| | | | | | |
|---|---|---|---|---|---|
| 不 *pu*$^2$ | 裡 *li*$^3$ | 一 *i*$^4$ | 紙 *chih*$^3$ | 碰 *p'êng*$^4$ | 擦 *ts'a*$^1$ |
| 在 *tsai*$^4$ | 幾 *chi*$^3$ | 行 *hang*$^2$ | 都 *tou*$^1$ | 人。*jên*$^2$ | 一 *i*$^4$ |
| 行 *hang*$^2$ | 位 *wei*$^4$ | 字。*tzŭ*$^4$ | 裂 *lieh*$^4$ | 那 *na*$^4$ | 擦。*ts'a*$^1$ |
| 問 *wên*$^4$ | 東 *tung*$^1$ | 你 *ni*$^3$ | 了。*liao* | 窗 *ch'uang*$^1$ | 小 *hsiao*$^3$ |
| 別 *pieh*$^2$ | 家。*chia*$^1$ | 們 *mên* | 開 *k'ai*$^1$ | 戶 *hu*$^4$ | 心 *hsin*$^1$ |
| 人。*jên*$^2$ | 我 *wo*$^3$ | 行 *hang*$^2$ | 行。*hang*$^2$ | 的 *ti* | 別 *pieh*$^2$ |

To give a thing a rub.

Take care ; don't bump against people.

The paper in that window is all cracked.

To carry on a wholesale (or mercantile) business ; or, to start a business.

A column (or row) of characters.

How many partners are there in your hong (or firm) ?

*Obs.*—Partners : *tung*, the east, is a synonym for a master or host, the east being by ancient custom the position occupied by the master of the house, and the west that by the guests ; hence, *tung-chia*, a master or proprietor, *chia* having much the same force as in *jên-chia*. It should be noticed that *tung-chia* is the term generally used by Chinese servants to denote their foreign masters, though native heads of households are seldom so spoken of. Cf. also *fang-tung*, the owner of a house.

I am not an expert ; ask someone else.

*Obs.*—Note *expert* : I am not in that line of business. It can be used with reference to any subject with which the speaker is unfamiliar.

## EXERCISE XXVIII.

1 那桌面兒不很光潤、把他擦一擦罷。

1. The top of that table is not very bright; give it a rub.

2 玻璃是外國來的東西不是。當初是外國貨、近來我們這兒也會做。料貨和玻璃有點兒分別。

2. Glass is a foreign article, isn't it? In the first instance it was a foreign product, but of late we have been able to make it here too. There is a slight difference between *liao*$^4$-*huo*$^4$ (vitreous ware) and *po*$^1$-*li*$^2$ (glass).

*Obs.*—In the first instance: *lit.*, at the time of (*tang*) commencement (*ch'u*).

3 那玻璃瓶子怎麼破了。不是碰破了的、是燒的時候兒就裂了。

3. How did that glass bottle get broken (or cracked)? It was not broken by a blow (collision); it cracked of its own accord in baking.

*Obs.*—Note the distinction: *p'o*, a break or crack from collision, etc.; *lieh*, spontaneous cracking. *Lieh* is never applied to glass except under the above conditions.

4 牕戶紙裂了、叫裱糊匠來糊上。單張兒紙糊在什麼上頭是糊、雙張兒紙、糊在一塊兒是裱。

4. The paper of the window is cracked; tell a paper-hanger to come and paste it up. To paste a single piece of paper upon anything is *hu*$^2$; two sheets of paper pasted together are *piao*$^3$.

*Obs.* 1.—Paper-hanger: *lit.*, pasting artisan.
*Obs.* 2.—Paste it up: *shang* indicates completion of the act, no upward movement.

5 各行的手工人叫匠人的多、木匠、瓦匠、鐵匠、都說得。

5. The term *chiang*$^4$ is applied to handicraftsmen in most trades; you may say *mu*$^4$ *chiang*$^4$ (a carpenter), *wa*$^3$-*chiang*$^4$ (a bricklayer), *t'ieh*$^3$-*chiang*$^4$ (a blacksmith).

*Obs.*—The character *hang* is not recognised by the dictionaries; from the original meaning of the character without the dot (namely, to move, the way or course of movement, the order of proceeding), it comes to mean class, calling, etc.

語言自邇集



6 布是棉花做的、紗是絲做的。

6. Shirtings are made of cotton; crape is made of silk.

7 那一塊紗顏色兒淡了、必須染別的顏色兒。原舊的顏色兒是紅的。還可以染紅的、您要別的顏色兒。也可以染藍的。

7. The colour of that piece of crape is faded; it must be dyed some other colour. The original colour was red, and it can be dyed red again; if you prefer some other colour, sir, it can be dyed blue.

*Obs.*—Original colour: *lit.*, original old colour.

8 你瞧那一疋紅紗顏色兒光潤不光潤。怎麼是光潤呢。那紗原來是好紗、又是新的、染的顏色又好看。這光潤不止於說紗、說別的也行。

8. Look at that piece of red crape and tell me if it is not *kuang*[1] *jun*[4]. What does *kuang*[1] *jun*[4] mean? That in the first place the crape is good crape; then that it is new; and, besides, that it is dyed a good colour. The expression *kuang*[1] *jun*[4] is not used only of crape; it is equally applicable to other things.

*Obs.* 1.—In the first place, etc.: *lit.*, that the crape in the first instance was good; again [that it] is new; the colour [men] dyeing it achieved = the colour that it is dyed, also is good to see.

*Obs.* 2.—Not used only: *lit.*, does not halt in (or at) the speaking of crapes; to speak of other things also it does.

9 我拿那個玻璃瓶來要擦一擦、碰在桌子上碰破了、收拾不收拾。不必收拾了。

9. I was bringing that glass bottle here to give it a rub, when I bumped it against the table and cracked it; shall it be mended? It need not be mended.

10 他是甚麼行當兒必是當廚子。你行幾、我們弟兄五個、我行二。

10. What is his craft (or, line of business)? He must be a cook. Where do you come in the family? We are five brothers, and I come second.

*Obs.* 1.—Craft: *lit.*, the trade or calling *(hang)* that he performs *(tang)*.

*Obs.* 2.—*Hang*, a list: hence, to be on a list; I am second in the list (or column) [of my generation]. Note the sisters do not count; *e.g.*, a man with two elder sisters and an elder brother would *hang êrh*; a girl, however, reckons her position in the family *quoad* her sisters in the same way.

19

*Turn the following into Chinese.* (KEY, EXERCISE XXVIII.)

1. The paper hung (pasted) in this room is dirty; call a paper-hanger to paper it afresh (*lit.*, paste new).

2. Find a man to mount this picture for me; but do not let the mounting be too thick.

3. The window is in holes (broken) and lets in the wind; get a sheet of paper and paste it up.

*Obs.*—Lets in: *chin*, to enter. Note that in this construction *chin* precedes its object.

4. Why have you dyed this piece of crape this colour? Didn't I tell you to dye it blue, and yet you have dyed it red? The colour is pale, too, and not glossy.

*Obs.*—Yet: *tao*, on the other hand.

5. This coat of mine is too old; it is unwearable.

6. There is dust on the glass in (on) the window; you must give it a rub with a piece of cloth, and the room will not be so dark.

7. Where can one buy the colours for dyeing things? They are sold in the colour (colour material) shops.

8. Take care how you carry that tumbler; don't bump it against anything.

9. There has been absolutely no rain; the weather has been terribly dry. Just look at this table top, it is all cracked with dryness.

10. Businesses are divided into hongs. Of the different hongs in the capital, the biggest are the silver (banks), wine, tea, and cloth hongs.

**756.** 剛 *kang*$^{1}$, properly, hard, which meaning in certain combinations it retains; with the following character it has an intensive force.

**757.** 纔 *ts'ai*$^{2}$, just now; but a moment ago. Also, only just; then; thereupon.

**758.** 再 *tsai*$^{4}$, again; the second time; then.

**759.** 等 *têng*$^{3}$, a class or grade; also, to wait.

**760.** Examples:—

| | | | | | | |
|---|---|---|---|---|---|---|
| 剛 *kang*$^{2}$ | 打 *ta*$^{3}$ | 等 *têng*$^{3}$ | 等。*têng*$^{3}$ | 再 *tsai*$^{4}$ | 了。*liao* | 他 *t'a*$^{1}$ |
| 兒 *'rh* | 我 *wo*$^{3}$ | 了。*liao* | 我 *wo*$^{3}$ | 說 *shuo*$^{1}$ | 等 *têng*$^{3}$ | 剛 *kang*$^{1}$ |
| 裝 *chuang*$^{1}$ | 來 *lai*$^{2}$ | 他 *t'a*$^{1}$ | 再 *tsai*$^{4}$ | 罷。*pa*$^{4}$ | 一 *i*$^{4}$ | 纔 *ts'ai*$^{2}$ |
| 得 *tê*$^{2}$ | 著。*cho* | 纔 *ts'ai*$^{2}$ | 不 *pu*$^{4}$ | 等 *têng*$^{3}$ | 會 *hui*$^{3}$ | 回 *hui*$^{2}$ |
| 下。*hsia*$^{4}$ | 剛 *kang*$^{1}$ | 剛 *kang*$^{1}$ | 能 *nêng*$^{2}$ | 一 *i*$^{4}$ | 兒 *'rh* | 來 *lai*$^{2}$ |

He came back a moment ago.

Wait a bit and we will see about it.

*Obs.*—*Tsai shuo* may also be translated literally.

Wait a bit. I can wait no longer.

He hit me just now.

*Obs.*—Note that *ts'ai-kang* and *kang-ts'ai* are interchangeable, but that the latter perhaps places the time in the more immediate present.

It will just (exactly) fit (pack in).

*Obs.*—Note the tone of the second *kang*.

761. 取 *ch'ü³*, to fetch; to bring; to take for oneself.

762. 送 *sung⁴*, to carry to; to present; to accompany.

763. 落 *la⁴*, *lao⁴*, *lo⁴*, down; to descend; to leave behind one; to leave out.

764. 永 *yung³*, eternal.

765. Examples:—

| | | | | | | |
|---|---|---|---|---|---|---|
| 回 *hui²* | 沒 *mei²* | 不 *pu⁴* | 落 *la⁴* | 去。*ch'ü⁴* | 一 *i⁴* | 順 *shun⁴* |
| 來。*lai²* | 落 *lao⁴* | 知 *chih¹* | 下。*hsia⁴* | 一 *i²* | 本 *pên³* | 便 *pien⁴* |
| 不 *pu²* | 兒 *'rh* | 道 *tao⁴* | 鳥 *niao³* | 個 *ko⁴* | 書 *shu¹* | 取 *ch'ü³* |
| 送 *sung⁴* | 了。*liao* | 他 *t'a¹* | 兒 *'rh* | 大 *ta⁴* | 我 *wo³* | 幾 *chi³* |
| 不 *pu²* | 他 *t'a¹* | 的 *ti* | 落 *lao⁴* | 錢 *ch'ien²* | 給 *kei³* | 吊 *tiao⁴* |
| 送。*sung⁴* | 永 *yung³* | 下 *hsia⁴* | 在 *tsai⁴* | 都 *tou¹* | 你 *ni³* | 錢 *ch'ien²* |
| | 遠 *yüan³* | 落。*lo⁴* | 樹 *shu⁴* | 沒 *mei²* | 送 *sung⁴* | 來。*lai²* |
| | 不 *pu⁴* | 他 *t'a¹* | 上。*shang⁴* | 有 *yu³* | 回 *hui²* | 這 *chê⁴* |

Fetch me a few strings of cash at the same time (while you are about it).

*Obs.*—At the same time: *shun pien*; *lit.*, following the convenience (*i.e.*, opportunity). Cf. *chiu shou-'rh* Exercise XXV, Eng., 1, Obs. 2; p. 130).

I will send this book back for you.

I have not omitted (left out) a single cash.

The bird has lighted on the tree.

I don't know his whereabouts (the place in which he has lighted).

He has no home (or, no person or place to whom or which he can go for help or shelter); to be thrown upon the world.

He will never come back.

*Obs.*—Never: *lit.*, in the infinite, or eternal, distance.

Don't [I pray] accompany me [to the door].

*Obs.*—This is a parting salutation in very common use, and it is polite so to address one's host when seeing one to the door. Another form is *liu² pu⁴*; *lit.*, detain your footsteps.

766. 湊 *ts'ou⁴*, to add to a body or number; to assemble, of men or things; active or neuter.

767. 挪 *no²*, to move a thing from one place to another.

768. 拴 *shuan¹*, to tie up animals or things.

769. 套 *t'ao⁴*, generally, a closely-fitting case or envelope. The numerative of *i-shang* clothes generally; as *i t'ao i-shang*, a suit of clothes.

770. Examples :—

| | | | | | | |
|---|---|---|---|---|---|---|
| 馬。*ma*$^3$ | 上。*shang*$^4$ | 一 *i*$^2$ | 書 *shu*$^1$ | 兒。*'rh* | 子。*tzŭ* | 我 *wo*$^3$ |
| 一 *i*$^2$ | 今 *chin*$^1$ | 個 *ko*$^4$ | 是 *shih*$^4$ | 把 *pa*$^3$ | 把 *pa*$^3$ | 們 *mên* |
| 套 *t'ao*$^4$ | 兒 *'rh* | 書 *shu*$^1$ | 四 *ssŭ*$^4$ | 馬 *ma*$^3$ | 牀 *ch'uang*$^2$ | 湊 *ts'ou*$^4$ |
| 套 *t'ao*$^4$ | 套 *t'ao*$^4$ | 套, *t'ao*$^4$ | 套。*t'ao*$^4$ | 拴 *shuan*$^1$ | 挪 *no*$^2$ | 了 *liao* |
| 杯。*pei*$^1$ | 騾 *lo*$^2$ | 把 *pa*$^3$ | 一 *i*$^2$ | 上。*shang*$^4$ | 在 *tsai*$^4$ | 五 *wu*$^3$ |
| | 子 *tzŭ* | 車 *ch'ê*$^4$ | 套 *t'ao*$^4$ | 這 *ché*$^4$ | 那 *na*$^4$ | 兩 *liang*$^3$ |
| | 套 *t'ao*$^4$ | 套 *t'ao*$^4$ | 書。*shu*$^1$ | 個 *ko*$^4$ | 邊 *pien*$^1$ | 銀 *yin*$^2$ |

We have got together (subscribed) five taels.
Remove the bed to that side.
Tie up the horses (or horse).
This book is in four covers.

*Obs.*—*T'ao* is the cover or wrapper in which the *pên* or volumes are encased.

A book within a cover. A book cover.
Get the cart ready.

*Obs.*—*Lit.*, harness the cart. The Chinese do not as a rule say *t'ao* of the horse or mule, but it would be correct to do so in the following sentence.

Will you harness the mule or the horse to-day?

*Obs.*—Note that there is another word for to saddle a horse, which will be come to in due course.

A set of cups that fit one within the other.

771. 商 *shang*$^1$, a trader ; to consult.

772. 量 *liang*$^2$, *liang*$^4$, to calculate ; to measure.

773. 殼, 够 *kou*$^4$, enough ; the second form is the correct one.

774. 斟 *chên*$^1$, properly, to pour out wine ; colloquially, it has not this sense, but is joined with *cho*$^2$ (*see* next word).

775. 酌 *cho*$^2$, combined with the foregoing *chên*$^1$, means to deliberate, whether with another or oneself ; it also means to pour out wine, but not colloquially.

776. Examples :—

| | | | | | | |
|---|---|---|---|---|---|---|
| 米。*mi*$^3$ | 罷。*pa*$^4$ | 你 *ni*$^3$ | 能 *nêng*$^2$ | 賽 *sai*$^4$ | 商 *shang*$^1$ | 那 *na*$^4$ |
| 分 *fên*$^4$ | 殼 *kou*$^4$ | 們 *mên* | 殼 *kou*$^4$ | 馬 *ma*$^3$ | 量 *liang*$^4$ | 一 *i*$^4$ |
| 量 *liang*$^4$ | 不 *pu*$^2$ | 去 *ch'ü*$^4$ | 去 *ch'ü*$^4$ | 去。*ch'ü*$^4$ | 著 *cho* | 天 *t'ien*$^1$ |
| 不 *pu*$^4$ | 殼。*kou*$^4$ | 斟 *chên*$^1$ | 不 *pu*$^4$ | 今 *chin*$^1$ | 出 *ch'u*$^1$ | 我 *wo*$^3$ |
| 輕。*ch'ing*$^1$ | 量 *liang*$^2$ | 酌 *cho*$^2$ | 能。*nêng*$^2$ | 兒 *'rh* | 城 *ch'êng*$^2$ | 們 *mên* |

The other day we were discussing the question of having races outside the city.
Can you go to-day or not?

*Obs.*—*Kou* here does not seem to affect the force of *nêng*.

Go and talk the matter over (or, consider it).

Is it enough? have you enough? enough?

To measure rice.

The weight is not light.

*Obs.*—*Fên*[4] *liang*[4]; *lit.*, the share or portion (*fên*[4]) contained in the *liang*[4], cubic capacity: note that *liang*[4] is a measure of capacity. We may say of a box that it has not *liang*[4]-*'rh*, capacity, to contain a certain quantity; also that a man's *chiu*[3] *liang*[4], capacity for wine, is great or small.

777. 疑 *i*[2], doubts; to doubt.

778. 惑 *huo*[4], to doubt; to bewilder. Not used alone in the spoken language.

779. 喊 *han*[3], to cry aloud; to halloo.

780. 答 *ta*[1], to reply.

781. 應 *ying*[4], echo; to echo; to respond to. Not to be confounded with *ying*[1] (726).

782. 從 *ts'ung*[2], proceeding from; forth from.

783. 末 *mo*[4], the end; *lit.*, the tip of anything that runs to a point. Read *mo-'rh*, a time or occasion; as *san*[1] *mo*[4]-*'rh*, three times.

784. Examples :—

| | | | | | | |
|---|---|---|---|---|---|---|
| 的。*ti* | 末 *mo*[4] | 前 *ch'ien*[2] | 答 *ta*[1]. | 天 *t'ien*[1] | 是 *shih*[4] | 你 *ni*[3] |
| | 了 *liao*[3] | 在 *tsai*[4] | 應 *ying*[4] | 他 *t'a*[1] | 眞 *chên*[1] | 這 *chê*[4] |
| | 兒 *'rh* | 外 *wai*[4] | 了 *liao* | 也 *yeh*[3] | 的。*ti* | 話 *hua*[4] |
| | 告 *kao*[4] | 頭 *t'ou* | 沒 *mei*[2] | 不 *pu*[4] | 我 *wo*[3] | 我 *wo*[3] |
| | 病 *ping*[4] | 做 *tso*[4] | 有。*yu*[3] | 答 *ta*[1] | 喊 *han*[3] | 疑 *i*[2] |
| | 回 *hui*[2] | 官 *kuan*[1] | 我 *wo*[3] | 應。*ying*[4] | 他 *t'a*[1] | 惑 *huo*[4] |
| | 來 *lai*[2] | 末 *mo*[4] | 從 *ts'ung*[2] | 你 *ni*[3] | 半 *pan*[4] | 不 *pu*[2] |

I have my doubts about the truth of what you say.

I hallooed for him ever so long, and yet he wouldn't answer (or, though I shouted to him, etc).

*Obs.* 1.—The *yeh* implies that the result was contrary to expectation or the natural order of things.

*Obs.* 2.—*Ta ying*: emphasise *ta*.

Did you agree (consent)?

*Obs.*—Agree: *lit.*, answer [in the affirmative].

I was formerly an official in the provinces, [but] I eventually (finally) reported myself as ailing (retired on the ground of ill-health), and came back.

*Obs.* 1.—Another expression for to retire from office is *kao t'ui* (506).

*Obs.* 2.—Note that *wai-t'ou*, as a general rule, when employed by a person in Peking, means anywhere in the Empire outside the capital.

*Obs.* 3.—Eventually; at the very last: *lit.*, at the tip of the finish. The reduplication of *mo* is perhaps slightly emphatic; we could also say *mo liao-'rh* or *mo hou*[4].

## EXERCISE XXIX.

1 剛纔我們在這兒商量這件事情、再三的喊他過來、等了半天他不答應、我疑惑他沒聽見。

1. We were discussing this affair here just now, and we called to him again and again to come; but after waiting ever so long he made no answer. I suspect he did not hear.

*Obs.*—Again and again: the *ti*, adverbial, standing for fashion; *q.d.*, three times' fashion.

2 再三再四的請他把那個舊書套送給我、他總不答應、末末了兒、還是我買了個新的。

2. I asked him again and again to make me a present of that old book cover, but he refused every time, and after all I had to buy a new one.

*Obs.*—After all: *lit.*, at the very end, still *(hai)* was it I bought a new one.

3 我們十個人從前定得湊錢做買賣。後來落下了兩個人、還有把本錢取回去的、我瞧這個、我也不肯再往裏入錢了。

3. Ten of us agreed some time ago to put some money into a business. Two afterwards withdrew, and others took out their capital; when I saw this I did not choose to put any more money in either.

*Obs.* 1.—Agreed: *ting tê*; most Pekingese would write and say *ti*.

*Obs.* 2.—To put money: *ts'ou*, properly written with Radical 159, means to converge, as the spokes to the nave of a wheel; here, *lit.*, to contribute money to do trade.

*Obs.* 3.—Withdrew: *lit.*, there dropped out two men.

*Obs.* 4.—And others, etc.: *lit.*, yet more there were laying-hand-on-capital took [it] back ones.

*Obs.* 5.—Did not choose: *pu k'ên* translates very well as decline or refuse, where there is evidence that a proposal has been made. Note *ju*, to enter, as an active verb.

4 我兄弟送我的那個箱子、叫你挪開點兒、怎麼挪那麼遠。

4. Because I told you to move the box away which my younger brother gave me, why should you have moved it so far?

*Obs.*—*Lit.*, [I] tell you to move apart my younger brother gave me's that box; [this being so] why move it thus far. *Ti* can often be translated which.

5 這米我量了、不彀五石、一個單套兒車足拉的了.

5. According to my measurement, this rice does not amount to five piculs, and a one-horse cart will draw it perfectly well.

*Obs.* 1.—One horse cart: *lit.*, single-harness cart.

*Obs.* 2. Perfectly well: *lit.*, enough dragging accomplish; note *liao*, here and below, to be able, *la tê liao*, *la pu liao*. The *tsu* is emphatic.

6 在我說、這麼些個不止五石、不是二套車怕拉不了從.

6. In my opinion this quantity is not so little as five piculs, and I don't think that less than two beasts will draw it.

*Obs.*—*Lit.*, quantity (*hsieh*) as this (*chê-mo*) does not stop at five piculs; if it is not a two-harness cart, [I] fear dragging not accomplish.

7 我是從南邊兒來的、向來沒坐過車、我們一到店裏、那趕車的就要錢、我疑惑著從來沒這個理、叫他等一等兒再來罷.

7. I come from the South; I have never travelled by cart before, and the moment we got to the inn the carter asked for his money. I suspected that this was not the rule, so I told him to wait a while and come again.

*Obs.* 1.—The moment: *lit.*, we once arrived in the inn, the carter thereon wanted money; *na*, that carter belonging to the cart just spoken of.

*Obs.* 2.—Not the rule: *lit.*, I suspected that hitherto there was not this *li*, a principle or rule that should obtain because it was just. The carter would plead that to pay at once was *li*, justice; the traveller suspects that this had never been the principle in accordance with which action ought to be taken.

8 我永遠再不到他那兒去了.這是怎麼話說、你再斟酌斟酌罷、等一會兒沒了氣、就改了主意了.

8. I will never go to his place again. What a remark to make! Think the matter over again; wait a while till your anger has gone, and you will have changed your mind (or decision).

*Obs.* 1.—What a remark! *lit.*, this is how talk to say! A vulgarism in frequent use in Peking; it is not necessarily a comment on a remark made, but is used under many conditions as an ejaculation of regret, surprise, or indignation; *e.g.*, the servant lets fall a glass and breaks it, upon which the master would ejaculate *chê shih tsêmmo hua shuo*.

*Obs.* 2.—Wait a while till; or, by-and-by when.

*Obs.* 3.—Note *mei liao ch'i liao*, not *mei liao ch'i-'rh liao*, which means dead; hence, care must be taken to omit the *êrh*.

9 那馬還不好好兒的拴上他.你看他把門碰壞了.那倒沒甚麼、叫個木匠來收拾收拾、就得了.

9. Why won't you tie that horse up properly? Look! he has bumped against the door and broken it. That doesn't signify; call a carpenter to mend it, and that matter will be settled.

*Obs.* 1.—Why won't you? *lit.*, you still (in spite of my orders or consequences) do not efficiently tie up that horse.

*Obs.* 2.—Doesn't signify: *lit.*, that, on the other hand, not what (= anything); call a carpenter to come and mend it, and there an end.

10 昨兒我叫他們買一百雞子兒送上山來.誰想他們道兒上、連丟帶碰、趕到了山上就沒甚麼了.

10. I told them yesterday to buy a hundred eggs and bring them to the Hills. Can you imagine it? what with what they broke and lost on the road, by the time they reached the Hills there were hardly any left.

*Obs.* 1.—Bring them: note that *lai* shows the speaker to be at the Hills himself.

*Obs.* 2.—Can you imagine, etc? *lit.*, who would have thought? in connexion with *(lien)* lost, together with *(tai)* bumping, coming up with arrival at the Hills [time] there was not anything [appreciable left]; *mei shêmmo* does not mean that there were none at all, but that the quantity was unappreciable. Note the conjunctions *lien* and *tai*; the Chinese seldom make use of the same conjunction twice running in the same sentence, whether conversationally or in writing.

*Turn the following into Chinese.* (KEY, EXERCISE XXIX.)

1. I had just got out of the door and was on the point of starting (walking) when a man came looking for you. I said you were not at home, and told him to come again by-and-by (later on).

2. To borrow people's furniture (or, utensils, tools, etc.), and not send it back when you have finished with it, but even wait till they come to fetch it, is that right?

*Obs.*—Is that right? *shih tê*, will [such conduct] do?

3. Since I came here, I have never seen the price of things fall.

4. This money is terribly short [of the amount]. I have been everywhere to [try and] get it together, and this trifle is all I have managed to raise *(ts'ou)*. It's not enough for my purpose; I'll give it to you, if you like.

*Obs.* 1.—Short: *ch'üeh shao* (*see* 500).

*Obs.* 2.—Is all: *ts'ai ts'ou liao chê-mo i tien-'rh*, I have only collected as little as this.

*Obs.* 3.—Not enough, etc.: *pu kou wo yung ti*, not enough my use's [purpose]; the use to which I want to put it.

5. With him it's a never-ending get-from-here and scrape-together-there for a livelihood; never enough for his expenses.

*Obs.*—*Lit.*, he, passing his days (getting his livelihood), eternally is east removing, west scraping together: ever *(lao)* not enough for spending's [purpose].

6. Tie up the beasts; I shall want to (or, am going to) put them in the cart shortly.

7. I have bought a book in a cover. I have not enough money with me, and I want

to ask you (*lit.*, consult with you) if you have any about you (*lit.*, on your body) to lend me a little ; can you?

*Obs.*—Can you? *hsing pu hsing.*

8. I doubt whether what he says is true ; inquire for me when you get there.

*Obs.* 1.—I doubt, etc.: *lit.*, I doubt (suspect) what he says is not true.

*Obs.* 2.—Inquire: *ta t'ing*, to beat about for information. *See* 241.

9. If you do things behind my back so that I shan't know, you just look out! If I find you out in future, I shall have some objections to make.

*Obs.*—*Lit.*, you, backing me, do things not causing me to know, you then (*k'o*, hypothetical particle) take care : a day hereafter if it is causing me to inquire out (*ch'u lai*, if the inquiry elicits the fact), then (*k'o*) I shall not agree. Note that the second *chiao* makes *ta t'ing* passive: if [your doings] are found out by me. *Ta ying* means here something stronger than mere objection, and implies that the matter will not be passed by with a mere protest.

10. There is a man calling out outside ; answer, and go out and see who it is.

*Obs.*—Answer: *lit.*, answer a sound.

11. Ah! and so it's he that has come again, is it? He has never been here since the day I gave him a blowing up.

*Obs.* 1.—And so: *yüan lai*, which cannot here be rendered by its ordinary meaning.

*Obs.* 2.—"Never" must not here be rendered by *yung yüan* and the negative, as this refers to the future.

12. He came twice, and on both occasions caught me at home ; unlucky, wasn't it?

*Obs.* 1.—Twice: *liang mo'rh*; though *hui*$^2$ would do as well.

*Obs.* 2.—Caught me at home: *kan shang wo tsai chia*, caught me up at home.

*Obs.* 3.—Unlucky: *ch'iao*$^3$, which can be used in a bad as well as a good sense.

13. We have thought out two plans for managing this affair, and would ask you to consider which we had better employ.

785. 臺 *t'ai*$^2$, a terrace.

786. 灣 *wan*$^1$, curving ; to curve ; a bay or indentation.

787. 江 *chiang*$^1$, a river ; see *ho*$^2$ (377). *Chiang*$^1$ is never used of a small stream, though *ho*$^2$ may be applied to large ones.

788. 湖 *hu*$^2$, a lake.

789. 流 *liu*$^2$, to flow ; not to be confounded with *liu*$^4$, a current.

790. 浪 *lang*$^4$, waves, larger than *po*$^1$ (479).

791. 闊、濶, *k'uo*$^4$, spacious ; hence, wealthy. Both forms are admissible.

792. Examples :—

| | | | | | | |
|---|---|---|---|---|---|---|
| 得 *ti* | 沒 *mei*$^2$ | 浪 *lang*$^4$ | 濶。*k'uo*$^4$ | 兒 *'rh* | 一 *i*$^4$ | 臺 *t'ai*$^2$ |
| 快。*k'uai*$^4$ | 有 *yu*$^3$ | 就 *chiu*$^4$ | 風 *fêng*$^1$ | 就 *chiu*$^4$ | 灣，*wan*$^1$ | 灣。*wan*$^1$ |
| 順 *shun*$^4$ | 甚 *shên*$^2$ | 起 *ch'i*$^3$ | 大 *ta*$^4$ | 到 *tao*$^4$ | 再 *tsai*$^4$ | 一 *i*$^2$ |
| 流。*liu*$^2$ | 麽 *mo*$^1$ | 來。*lai*$^2$ | 海 *hai*$^3$ | 了。*liao* | 繞 *jao*$^4$ | 個 *ko*$^4$ |
| 頂 *ting*$^3$ | 波 *po*$^1$ | 太 *t'ai*$^4$ | 裡 *li*$^3$ | 大 *ta*$^4$ | 一 *i*$^2$ | 灣 *wan*$^1$ |
| 流。*liu*$^2$ | 浪。*lang*$^4$ | 湖 *hu*$^2$ | 的 *ti* | 江 *chiang*$^1$ | 個 *ko*$^4$ | 子。*tzŭ* |
| | 流 *liu*$^2$ | 裡 *li*$^3$ | 波 *po*$^1$ | 寬 *k'uan*$^1$ | 灣 *wan*$^1$ | 灣 *wan*$^1$ |

Formosa.
A curve ; a bay.
To bend, as a bow, one's back in bowing, etc.
Round one turn more, and there we are.
Large rivers are wide.
When the wind is high the waves in the sea rise.
There are no great waves on the T'ai-hu (lake).
It flows quickly ; glides quickly.
To float with the current.
Against the current.

*Obs.*—*Shun*$^{4}$ *liu*, with the emphasis on *shun*, means smooth, as the hair of a dog or cat brushed the right way. It should be borne in mind that *shun liu* does not mean going with the stream when propelling power is used, nor does it mean a fair or favourable current ; the character for this is *liu*$^{4}$, which will be met with later. *Cf.* also *shun fêng*, *ting fêng* (*see* 72).

793. 浮 *fou*$^{2}$, *fu*$^{2}$, floating ; movable. *Fu*$^{4}$ *shui*$^{3}$, to swim.

794. 橋 *ch'iao*$^{2}$, a bridge.

795. 井 *ching*$^{3}$, a well.

796. 坑 *k'êng*$^{1}$, a pit, natural or artificial ; also, to cheat or swindle (*see* Part IV, Dialogue III, 113).

797. 衚 *hu*$^{2}$ }
798. 衕 *t'ung*$^{2}$ } a small street; an alley. Generally pronounced *hu*$^{2}$-*t'ung*$^{4}$-*'rh*.

799. 巷 *hsiang*$^{4}$, a small street; an alley. Not so common as the above.

800. Examples :—

| | | | | | |
|---|---|---|---|---|---|
| 颳 *kua*$^{1}$ | 裡 *li*$^{3}$ | 那 *na*$^{4}$ | 頭 *t'ou*$^{2}$ | 那 *na*$^{4}$ | 水 *shui*$^{3}$ |
| 風 *fêng*$^{1}$ | 頭 *t'ou*$^{2}$ | 一 *i*$^{4}$ | 橋。*ch'iao*$^{2}$ | 邊 *pien*$^{1}$ | 面 *mien*$^{4}$ |
| 走 *tsou*$^{3}$ | 有 *yu*$^{3}$ | 條 *t'iao*$^{2}$ | 井 *ching*$^{3}$ | 兒 *'rh* | 兒 *'rh* |
| 小 *hsiao*$^{3}$ | 個 *ko*$^{4}$ | 衚 *hu*$^{2}$ | 水 *shui*$^{3}$ | 有 *yu*$^{3}$ | 上 *shang*$^{4}$ |
| 巷 *hsiang*$^{4}$ | 深 *shên*$^{1}$ | 衕 *t'ung*$^{4}$ | 好 *hao*$^{3}$ | 個 *ko*$^{4}$ | 浮 *fou*$^{2}$ |
| 好。*hao*$^{3}$ | 坑。*k'êng*$^{1}$ | 兒 *'rh* | 喝。*ho*$^{1}$ | 石 *shih*$^{2}$ | 著。*cho* |

Floating on the water.
There's a stone bridge there.
Well water is good to drink.
In that lane there is a deep hole.
When the wind blows it is best to walk along the small alleys.

語言自邇集



801. 野 *yeh*$^3$, properly, uninhabited ground, but often country as opposed to town. Hence, wild ; savage.

802. 鄉 *hsiang*$^1$, a village ; a region. Often used with the following.

803. 村 *ts'un*$^1$, a village ; a hamlet. Smaller than *hsiang*$^1$.

804. 墳 *fên*$^2$, a grave ; a tomb ; the mound or monument above a grave, but not a head-stone or tablet.

805. 墓 *mu*$^4$, a grave ; a tomb. Rarely used without the preceding word *fên*$^2$.

806. 峯 *fêng*$^1$, the peak of a hill.

807. 嶺 *ling*$^3$, a height not peaked.

808. 尖 *chien*$^1$, a projecting point, of a knife, hill, etc.

809. Examples :—

| | | | | | | |
|---|---|---|---|---|---|---|
| 的。*ti* | 鄉 *hsiang*$^1$ | 兒 *'rh* | 嶺 *ling*$^3$ | 野 *yeh*$^3$ | 墓。*mu*$^4$ | 那 *na*$^4$ |
| 那 *na*$^4$ | 下 *hsia*$^4$ | 的 *ti* | 冬 *tung*$^1$ | 草。*ts'ao*$^3$ | 這 *chê*$^4$ | 一 *i*$^2$ |
| 是 *shih*$^4$ | 人 *jên*$^2$ | 山 *shan*$^1$ | 天 *t'ien*$^1$ | 鄉 *hsiang*$^1$ | 兒 *'rh* | 片 *p'ien*$^4$ |
| 個 *ko*$^4$ | 從 *ts'ung*$^2$ | 峯 *fêng*$^1$ | 過 *kuo*$^4$ | 村 *ts'un*$^1$ | 沒 *mei*$^2$ | 野 *yeh*$^3$ |
| 墳 *fên*$^2$ | 門 *mên*$^2$ | 很 *hên*$^3$ | 不 *pu*$^2$ | 兒。*'rh* | 野 *yeh*$^3$ | 地 *ti*$^4$ |
| 地。*ti*$^4$ | 頭 *t'ou*$^2$ | 尖。*chien*$^1$ | 去。*ch'ü*$^4$ | 這 *chê*$^4$ | 雞。*chi*$^1$ | 全 *ch'üan*$^2$ |
| | 村 *ts'un*$^1$ | 他 *t'a*$^1$ | 前 *ch'ien*$^2$ | 個 *ko*$^4$ | 野 *yeh*$^3$ | 是 *shih*$^4$ |
| | 來 *lai*$^2$ | 是 *shih*$^4$ | 邊 *pien*$^1$ | 山 *shan*$^1$ | 花。*hua*$^1$ | 墳 *fên*$^2$ |

The whole of that waste ground is occupied by graves.

*Obs.* 1.—*P'ien*, the numerative of spaces of ground, generally large ; the word "whole" is rendered by *i*.

*Obs.* 2.—Waste : *yeh* can only be properly applied to places at a distance from human habitations.

There are no pheasants here.

Wild flowers. Wild grasses.

A village.

*Obs.*—The term can be applied to any collection of houses, large or small, where there is no resident official.

This mountain pass is impassable in winter.

The peak ahead of us is very sharp pointed.

He is a countryman, and comes from Mên-t'ou Ts'un.

*Obs.*—Mên-t'ou Ts'un, the village of Mên-t'ou.

That is a cemetery.

## EXERCISE XXX.

1 臺灣是中國東南海裏的地方兒、南北兩頭兒山嶺兒又多、又大、那山峯長得也很好看。

1. T'aiwan (Formosa) is a place in the sea, south-east of China, the northern and southern extremities of which are very mountainous, the heights being of considerable elevation; the mountain scenery is at the same time very picturesque.

*Obs.*—Very mountainous: the mountain heights are both numerous and large. Were they not lofty as well as extensive, their *tao-'rh*, or extent (48), would be *ch'ang*, long, or *k'uan*, broad; but not *ta*, great.

2 江河湖海、是天下大水的總名兒。

2. The phrase *chiang*[1] *ho*[2] *hu*[2] *hai*[3] (rivers, streams, lakes, and seas) designates in general terms the greater waters of the Empire.

3 偺們這兒的小河兒很窄、有浮橋兒就可以過去。那長江的江面有地方兒寬下裏和湖相同。

3. Our small rivers here are so narrow that they can be crossed by movable bridges. The Great River (the Yangtze) is as broad as a lake in many places.

*Obs.* 1.—The Great River: the *chiang mien*, surface, of the Great (*lit.*, long) River in its breadth with a lake [is] mutually (639) the same.

*Obs.* 2.—Breadth: *hsia li*, in the direction of, *k'uan*, its breadth. Cf. *ssŭ hsia li*, in every direction. We may also invert the expression, as *ch'ang li hsia*, *k'uan li hsia*, but the meaning is precisely the same.

4 那長江之流打西到東、湖北來的船到江西去、一路都是順流。到了江西那兒的山水也可以。

4. The course of the Great River is from west to east; vessels from Hupeh to Kiangsi go with the stream the whole way. The scenery when you get to Kiangsi is rather fine.

*Obs.*—Rather fine: *lit.*, will do; is tolerably good.

5 那山峯的尖兒是個個不同。山峯是高而尖的、山嶺也高、就是沒有那尖的樣子。

5. The mountain peaks in a *shan*[1]-*fêng*[1] are no two alike. A *shan-fêng* is lofty and pointed; a *shan*[1]-*ling*[3] is also a height, but not of peaked form.

*Obs.*—Also a height: the construction is somewhat elliptical; *q.d.*, a *shan-ling* is also high [like a *shan-fêng*, but when it is a *shan-ling*] *chiu* then, there is not that pointed form.

6 尖兒那個字眼兒、甚麼刀尖兒筆尖兒都說得。

6. The term *chien¹-'rh* may be equally applied to the point of a knife, a pencil, or the like.

*Obs.* 1.—Term: *lit.*, character eye. It is extremely difficult to analyse this expression with any success, but its force can be seen at once by illustration; thus, of *hung*, red, one would say that the *tzŭ*, character, was *hung*, and that it was a *tzŭ yen-'rh*, term, for a particular *yen-shê*, colour.

*Obs.* 2.—The like: understand *chê tsung* (525) *yang-tzŭ ti*, this kind of ones, after *pi chien*. Were *tao chien* and *pi chien* omitted, the sentence would run—can be applied to anything. Note *shên-mo*, any, anything.

7 京城裏沒有甚麼河水、喝的都是井水。

7. There is no river water to speak of in the capital; what is drunk is well water.

8 京城的買賣大半在大街上開鋪子、衚衕小巷都是住家兒的多。

8. Trade in the capital is for the most part conducted in shops on the great streets; the houses in the lanes and small streets are principally dwelling-houses.

9 城外頭沒有甚麼人家兒的地方、就叫野地、連有墳墓的也算。

9. The country outside the city walls where there are comparatively few habitations is called *yeh³ ti⁴*; even when there are graves in it it is so regarded.

*Obs.* 1.—Where: *lit.*, outside the walls a not-having-men's-houses' place [men] consequently (*chiu*) call *yeh ti*.

*Obs.* 2.—Regarded: *lit.*, together with having grave's [place men] also reckon *yeh ti*.

10 他是個鄉村兒的人、野的利害。那墳地很大、必是闊人家兒的。

10. He is a yokel (villager), and dreadfully raw. That cemetery is very large, and must belong to a wealthy family.

11 你會浮水麼。會是會、很遠了可不行。這道河浮的過去、浮不過去。河面兒太寬、浮不過去。

11. Can you swim? I can swim, but I can't swim very far. Could you swim across this river? It is too wide for me to swim across.

*Obs.*—It is contended by purists that *fu⁴*, to swim, should be written 鳧.

*Turn the following into Chinese.* (KEY, EXERCISE XXX.)

1. Formosa has been Chinese territory for more than two hundred years. There are mountain ranges in the north and south in which are several very lofty peaks. The country (place) is not very extensive, but [in it] there are some small rivers, the fields on the banks of which produce many things. It contains both villages and towns, the inhabitants of which are of the same type as the Chinese (*min² jên²*, common people). I am told that there are several places inhabited by savages, most of whom make their living by thieving. They are (live) scattered about, and do not form village [communities]. Some people, too, say that these savages are cannibals. The people who do business there deal (do it) for the most part with Chinese; of late, however (*ch'io*), ships from the various European countries have frequented the place, and there are foreigners who have taken up their residence there in order to carry on business.

*Obs.* 1.—Has been: *lit.*, Formosa *is* Chinese territory *there are* two hundred years.

*Obs.* 2.—In the north and south; cf. Exercise XXX, 3, Obs. 2.

*Obs.* 3.—Fields: *t'ien ti* (Radical 102).

*Obs.* 4.—Produce: *ch'u ch'an* (*see* 635), with the possessive; the produced things many.

*Obs.* 5.—Same type as: *t'ung min jên* (Chinese subjects) *i ko yang*.

*Obs.* 6.—Savages: *yeh jên*, men of the wilds.

*Obs.* 7.—They live scattered about: *t'a mên san³ cho chu*, they scattered live, and do not form *(ch'êng)* villages.

*Obs.* 8.—Frequented: *lit.*, of late, however, there are (have been) extreme-west *(tai hsi)* various-nation's vessels [that] come [and] go. *T'ai hsi kuo* is a common term for foreign countries in general.

2. China has several rivers, both large and deep, which are perfectly navigable for large vessels. When the water rises (grows), [the current] flows very rapidly, and upward-bound junks find it very slow [work]. The downward current, as seen from a boat [proceeding against the stream], appears to flow with even greater rapidity [than it does]. The small rivers are narrow and winding, and are navigated only by river boats; travellers by road may cross them by floating bridges.

*Obs.* 1.—Perfectly navigable: *lit.*, very much can walking accomplish large vessels.

*Obs.* 2.—Downward current: *lit.*, the water that flows downwards.

3. That country possesses *(yu)* several large lakes, which (the surfaces of which) are very extensive and resemble the sea in size. In the lakes, too, there are mountain peaks; they are navigable for both large and small vessels. The moment there is a high wind the waves are really terrible.

*Obs.*—Size: *ta li hsia*. *See* Exercise XXX, 3, Obs. 2.

4. There are some places where the making of wells is a matter of great labour; the ground is too hard.

*Obs.*—Labour: *hên fei shih*; *lit.*, much expends effort (matter).

5. I have a friend who lives in a small street. I went to look him up the other day, but I got into the wrong lane and did not find his house.

**810.** 男 *nan²*, male.

**811.** 爺 *yeh²*, properly, a father; but forming part of certain appellations of honour, also of other words.

**812.** 娘 *niang²*, properly, a mother; but in certain combinations, any woman.

**813.** 幼 *yu⁴*, of tender years.

**814.** 輩 *pei*$^{4}$, a class; an order; a generation.

**815.** Examples :—

| | | | | | | |
|---|---|---|---|---|---|---|
| 比 *pi*$^{3}$ | 子。*tzŭ* | 老 *lao*$^{3}$ | 們。*mên* | 你 *ni*$^{3}$ | 我 *wo*$^{3}$ | 男 *nan*$^{2}$ |
| 他 *t'a*$^{1}$ | 比 *pi*$^{3}$ | 幼。*yu*$^{4}$ | 娘 *niang*$^{2}$ | 們 *mên* | 的 *ti* | 女。*nü*$^{3}$ |
| 長 *chang*$^{3}$ | 我 *wo*$^{3}$ | 老 *lao*$^{3}$ | 兒 *'rh* | 少 *shao*$^{4}$ | 男 *nan*$^{2}$ | 女 *nü*$^{3}$ |
| 一 *i*$^{2}$ | 晚 *wan*$^{3}$ | 少。*shao*$^{4}$ | 們。*mên* | 爺 *yeh*$^{2}$ | 人。*jên*$^{2}$ | 人。*jên*$^{2}$ |
| 輩。*pei*$^{4}$ | 一 *i*$^{2}$ | 一 *i*$^{2}$ | 娘 *niang*$^{2}$ | 好。*hao*$^{3}$ | 老 *lao*$^{3}$ | 那 *na*$^{4}$ |
| | 輩。*pei*$^{4}$ | 輩 *pei*$^{4}$ | 家。*chia*$^{1}$ | 爺 *yeh*$^{2}$ | 爺。*yeh*$^{2}$ | 是 *shih*$^{4}$ |

Man and woman.

One's wife; a woman.

*Obs.*—*Nü jên* could only be used of the speaker's own wife.

That is my husband.

Your worship; or, a gentleman; the title Mr.

*Obs.*—*Lao-yeh* was originally the title given to *chü jên*, or graduates of the second grade, but it is now universally applied to any officials below the rank of District Magistrate, or indeed any person of education and social standing; it answers very much to our Esquire.

Is your son well?

*Obs.*—*Shao*$^{4}$, not *shao*$^{3}$. Note that the polite language *ni mên* is either singular or plural.

Men. Women.

*Obs.*—Pronounce *nia*$^{2}$-*'rh mên*.

A wife's family.

Old and young. Old and young.

*Obs.*—Note *shao*$^{4}$.

A generation.

Of a generation later than I.

Of a generation earlier than he.

**816.** 玩 *wan*$^{2}$, to trifle; to play.

**817.** 耍 *shua*$^{3}$, to flourish, as a weapon in fencing; to play.

**818.** 蠢 *ch'un*$^{3}$, loutish in form or mind, or both.

**819.** 笨 *pên*$^{4}$, of things, unwieldy; of persons, stupid.

**820.** 獃 *tai*$^{1}$, silly; idiotic; abstracted; abstractedly.

**821.** Examples :—

| | | | | | | |
|---|---|---|---|---|---|---|
| 耍 *shua*$^{3}$ | 的。*ti* | 這 *chê*$^{4}$ | 笨 *pên*$^{4}$ | 法 *fa*$^{2}$ | 他 *t'a*$^{1}$ | 年 *nien*$^{2}$ |
| 錢。*ch'ien*$^{2}$ | 他 *t'a*$^{1}$ | 事 *shih*$^{4}$ | 人 *jên*$^{2}$ | 子 *tzŭ* | 鬧 *nao*$^{4}$ | 輕 *ch'ing*$^{1}$ |
| 別 *pieh*$^{2}$ | 是 *shih*$^{4}$ | 情 *ch'ing*$^{2}$ | 獃 *tai*$^{1}$ | 笨。*pên*$^{4}$ | 著 *cho* | 的 *ti* |
| 耍 *shua*$^{3}$ | 個 *ko*$^{4}$ | 不 *pu*$^{2}$ | 頭 *t'ou*$^{2}$ | 他 *t'a*$^{1}$ | 玩 *wan*$^{2}$ | 人 *jên*$^{2}$ |
| 笑 *hsiao*$^{4}$ | 書 *shu*$^{1}$ | 是 *shih*$^{4}$ | 獃 *tai*$^{1}$ | 是 *shih*$^{4}$ | 兒。*'rh* | 好 *hao*$^{4}$ |
| 我。*wo*$^{3}$ | 獃 *tai*$^{1}$ | 玩 *wan*$^{2}$ | 腦 *nao*$^{3}$ | 個 *ko* | 這 *chê*$^{4}$ | 玩 *wan*$^{2}$ |
| | 子。*tzŭ* | 兒 *'rh* | 的。*ti* | 蠢 *ch'un*$^{3}$ | 個 *ko*$^{4}$ | 耍。*shua*$^{3}$ |

Young people are fond of play (or, practical joking).
He is playing (or joking).
This method is rude, clumsy.
He is a loutish fellow.
A silly creature.
This business (or matter) is no joke (or, child's play).
He is dazed with study; a bookworm absorbed in his books.
To gamble.
Don't [try and] fool me.

822. 冒 *mao4*, properly, a covering for the head; a word descriptive of obtrusiveness, of doing that which one ought to let alone, of things that happen inopportunely; out of place.

823. 爽 *shuang3*, of weather, bright, cheery; of persons, lively, free from care. Also, to break, as a promise; or to fail in, as an engagement. It also means to be in error.

824. 靜 *ching4*, at rest, as opposed to unquiet.

825. 舒 *shu1*, properly, open; unrolled. Often combined with the following.

826. 服 *fu2*, complying; obedient. It has many meanings besides.

827. 艱 *chien1*, very difficult; but used in combination with the following *nan2* without intensifying its meaning.

828. 難 *nan2*, difficult. *Nan4*, difficulties or misfortunes.

829. 哈 *ha1*, the sound of loud laughter.

830. Examples :—

| | | | | | | |
|---|---|---|---|---|---|---|
| 大 *ta4* | 舒 *shu1* | 兒 *'rh* | 舒 *shu1* | 爽 *shuang3* | 身 *shên1* | 冒 *mao1* |
| 笑。*hsiao4* | 服。*fu* | 都 *tou1* | 服。*fu* | 快 *k'uai4* | 子 *tzŭ* | 著 *cho2* |
| 你 *ni3* | 他 *t'a1* | 是 *shih4* | 你 *ni3* | 人。*jên2* | 爽 *shuang3* | 雨 *yü3* |
| 別 *pieh2* | 爽 *shuang3* | 艱 *chien1* | 這 *chê4* | 安 *an1* | 快。*k'uai4* | 兒 *'rh* |
| 打 *ta3* | 了 *liao* | 難 *nan* | 話 *hua4* | 靜 *ching4* | 天 *t'ien1* | 走。*tsou3* |
| 哈 *ha1* | 約 *yo1* | 的。*ti* | 我 *wo3* | 人。*jên2* | 氣 *ch'i4* | 他 *t'a1* |
| 哈。*ha1* | 了。*liao* | 難 *nan2* | 不 *pu4* | 這 *chê4* | 爽 *shuang3* | 是 *shih4* |
| | 他 *t'a1* | 道 *tao4* | 服。*fu2* | 房 *fang2* | 快。*k'uai4* | 個 *ko4* |
| | 哈 *ha1* | 說 *shuo1* | 連 *lien2* | 子 *tzŭ* | 他 *t'a1* | 冒 *mao4* |
| | 哈 *ha1* | 你 *ni3* | 走 *tsou3* | 住 *chu4* | 是 *shih4* | 失 *shih4* |
| | 的 *ti* | 不 *pu4* | 道 *tao4* | 著 *cho* | 個 *ko4* | 鬼, *kuei3* |

To walk in the rain.
He is a blundering fool (a person who says and does the wrong thing at the wrong time).
In brisk health.
Bracing, cheerful weather.
He is a smart, energetic fellow; also, a man who speaks to the point and acts with promptitude.

A quiet, steady man.

This is a comfortable house to live in.

*Obs.*—It would not be incorrect to say *chê shih ko shu fu fang tzŭ*, but the first rendering is preferable, as there are many cases in which *shu fu* cannot be used as a simple qualifying adjective; thus, we could not say *shu fu ma*, a comfortable horse, or *shu fu i tzŭ*, a comfortable chair, but would have to insert the verbs to ride and to sit on respectively, as in the example above.

I am not satisfied with this statement of yours; or, I object to or protest against what you say.

[He] finds difficulty even in walking.

You don't mean to say (*lit.*, it is hard to say, you cannot say with truth) that you are not comfortable.

*Obs.*—*Tao*, to say (*see* 48). *Shuo* may be omitted.

He has broken his compact.

He roared with laughter.

Don't humbug me; or, don't "stuff me up."

**831.** 耐 *nai*$^4$, to endure, either in the sense of to put up with or to last.

**832.** 羞 *hsiu*$^1$, shame; to be ashamed.

**833.** 辱 *ju*$^4$, *ju*$^3$, to insult.

**834.** 討 *t'ao*$^3$, to exact; to demand; to provoke.

**835.** 嫌 *hsien*$^2$, to dislike.

**836.** Examples:—

| | | | | | | |
|---|---|---|---|---|---|---|
| 飯 *fan*$^4$ | 賬 *chang*$^4$ | 他 *t'a*$^1$ | 懶 *lan*$^3$ | 也 *yeh*$^3$ | 這 *chê*$^4$ | 耐 *nai*$^4$ |
| 的。*ti* | 的。*ti* | 不 *pu*$^4$ | 做 *tso*$^4$ | 沒 *mei*$^2$ | 個 *ko*$^4$ | 過 *kuo* |
| 他 *t'a*$^1$ | 你 *ni*$^3$ | 乾 *kan*$^1$ | 的 *ti* | 羞 *hsiu*$^1$ | 不 *pu*$^2$ | 這 *chê*$^4$ |
| 嫌 *hsien*$^2$ | 不 *pu*$^2$ | 淨。*ching*$^4$ | 討 *t'ao*$^3$ | 辱 *ju*$^4$ | 耐 *nai*$^4$ | 兩 *liang*$^3$ |
| 少 *shao*$^3$ | 害 *hai*$^4$ | 他 *t'a*$^1$ | 人 *jên*$^2$ | 他 *t'a*$^1$ | 長。*ch'ang*$^2$ | 天 *t'ien*$^1$ |
| 了。*liao* | 羞 *hsiu*$^1$ | 是 *shih*$^4$ | 嫌。*hsien*$^2$ | 們。*mên* | 那 *na*$^4$ | 就 *chiu*$^4$ |
| | 麼。*mo* | 來 *lai*$^2$ | 我 *wo*$^3$ | 好 *hao*$^4$ | 個 *ko*$^4$ | 好 *hao*$^3$ |
| | 討 *t'ao*$^3$ | 討 *t'ao*$^3$ | 嫌 *hsien*$^2$ | 吃 *ch'ih*$^1$ | 人 *jên*$^2$ | 了。*liao* |

Get over the next two days (or, few days) and you will be all right.

This won't last long (or, wear well).

And yet that man did not insult them.

[Men who are] fond of eating and lazy at work (people who like to live at another person's expense) provoke people's dislike.

I object to his want of cleanliness.

He has come for payment of his bill (or, to dun for debts).

Are you not ashamed? Have you no shame?

*Obs.*—*See* 424.

A beggar.

He objects that it is not enough; he is not satisfied with what he has got.

## EXERCISE XXXI.

1 我們倆人剛纔鬧著玩兒、他把棍子在我腦袋上打了一下兒。安靜點兒罷、別太粗了、總得想着你兄弟年幼、那麼重的手脚、他耐不得。

1. We two were skylarking together just now, and he hit me over the head with a stick. Be a little more quiet; don't be too rough: you must remember that your brother is of tender years and cannot stand such rough treatment.

*Obs.*—Rough treatment: *lit.*, cannot endure such rough hands and feet [as you lay upon him].

2 聽見說老爺欠安、沒有甚麼、不過身上有點兒不舒服。

2. I hear, sir, that you are a little indisposed. It's nothing at all to speak of; I am only a little out of sorts.

*Obs.* 1.—Indisposed: *lit.*, deficient in repose (624); this is a polite form of address reserved for equals or superiors.

*Obs.* 2.—Out of sorts: *lit.*, on (or in) my body not comfortable.

3 我這件新褂子怕耐不得長。那可難說、要穿着常冒雨、自然壞的快。歇一歇兒。

3. This new coat of mine won't last long, I am afraid. It's difficult to say; if you wear it continually in the rain of course it will soon be spoilt. To take a spell.

*Obs.*—Spell: *tai*, to abstract oneself; *q.d.*, from work that is engaging one's attention.

4 他那羞辱人的樣子眞討人嫌。

4. That insulting manner of his is really most annoying.

5 男女、就是爺們娘兒們。賊把男女老少都殺了。

5. The words *nan*², *nü*³ mean simply men and women. The rebels slew all, without distinction of age or sex.

6 他一家子老幼都病了、是不分年高年輕的全不舒服。

6. Were you to say his whole family, *lao*³ and *yu*⁴, were sick alike, you would mean that both those who were of respectable age and those who were of tender years were all indisposed without distinction.

*Obs.*—Respectable age: *lit.*, years high; *q.d.*, piled up, as opposed to the lesser burden of years, which is *ch'ing*, light.

7 和祖父一輩兒的是長輩、和兒孫一輩兒的是晚輩。

7. The generation which is the contemporary of your father and your grandfather is the *chang*³ *pei*⁴ (senior generation); that which is the contemporary of your son and grandson is the *wan*³ *pei*⁴ [junior (or later) generation].

*Obs.* 1.—Contemporary: *lit.*, the with [a man's] grandfather and father one and the same generation's ones are the senior generation, etc.

*Obs.* 2.—Grandfather: *see* 660, where *tsu fu* combined make one word; they are here separate.

8 你怎麽這麽冒失、碰着了我了、眞是討人嫌。我錯了、我錯了、實在是沒留神。

8. Why are you so careless? You have bumped up against me; it is really most annoying. I beg your pardon.

*Obs.*—I beg your pardon: *lit.*, I am wrong, I am wrong; I really did not pay attention. There are other forms of apology, such as *yu tsui* (852), etc.

9 你過於笨的利害、爽快些兒辦罷。管我呢、你這麽獃頭獃腦的還要說人。

9. You are too dreadfully awkward; be a little more smart. Mind your own business; an idiot like yourself to attempt (want) to find fault with other people!

*Obs.*—Mind your own business (or, what is that to you?): *lit.*, do you take charge of (or mind) me? Great emphasis must be laid on *kuan*, which, preceding a character in the third tone, is of course in the second. The expression must be used with discretion, as it is not very polite. Emphasise the final *jên*.

10 我們過日子眞艱難。耐着些兒罷、你這麽能耐人、難道一輩子不出頭麽。

10. It is indeed a hard task for us to live from day to day. Be a little patient; such an able man as you will surely not remain in obscurity all his life.

*Obs.* 1.—Able: *nêng nai*, ability; *lit.*, the ability that is acquired by patient application. The term, however, is not confined to skill acquired by practice. Cf. also *nêng kan*, capable, able, or capability (582).

*Obs.* 2.—Obscurity: *lit.*, not put out the head; come to the front; make oneself prominent; also, to take the lead.

*Turn the following into Chinese.* (KEY, EXERCISE XXXI.)

1. In the street yonder there is a fellow going through some performance. A whole lot of people, men and women, old and young, are looking at him. Have you heard of it?

*Obs.*—Performing: *shua wan i êrh; lit.*, brandishing playthings. The term is used of any performance, such as juggling, performing with a dancing bear, etc.

2. You've just found that out, have you? When I was out in the street a little while ago I saw a lot of men and women standing there; I thought there must be some performance or other going on, otherwise what would a lot of people be gaping at? I was just going to have a look, when, at the very moment, a man in a blundering manner put a question to me; said he, "You haven't been very well, have you quite recovered?" I gave one glance, and saw it was no other than a certain member of our family of the same generation as myself; he had grown loutish and awkward, and I have no idea what his conversation was all about. He is certainly a disagreeable creature.

*Obs.* 1.—You've just found that out: *ni hai shuo ni*, you still (or just) speak of it, is an idiomatic colloquialism something equivalent to "that's stale news; other people knew all about it long ago, and talked the matter out, but you are still talking about it."

*Obs.* 2.—Otherwise: *pu jan*, were it not thus.

*Obs.* 3.—Gaping at: *tai-cho lien-'rh k'an*, looking with abstracted faces. Note the participial force of *cho*.

3. Isn't the man you speak of So-and-so? I know his father; a very steady man, exceedingly brisk, both in action and speech. Several years ago he was not very well off, but I judge from his appearance of late that he is now very comfortable. Times, I imagine, are somewhat easier with him than they used to be in the early days.

*Obs.* 1.—In action: *hsing shih*, in the putting through (causing to progress) of business.

*Obs.* 2.—Judge from: *lit.*, of late looking at his that fashion (appearance), on the other hand *(tao)* very comfortable.

*Obs.* 3.—Times are somewhat easier, etc.: *lit.*, [I] think it is days compared with original (*yüan*) before (*hsien*) good to pass a little.

4. If you are insulted by people it is not very hard to bear with them a little; why get into a rage?

837. 皇 *huang*$^2$, august; imperial.

838. 宮 *kung*$^1$, an imperial palace.

839. 朝 *ch'ao*$^2$, properly, to see the Emperor, as at Court; any dynasty of China. Read *chao*$^1$, the morning; not used colloquially.

840. 廷 *t'ing*$^2$, properly, a hall of assembly; specially, the Emperor's Court.

841. Examples:—

| | | | | | |
|---|---|---|---|---|---|
| 朝 *ch'ao*$^2$ | 朝 *ch'ao*$^2$ | 時 *shih*$^2$ | 皇 *huang*$^2$ | 方 *fang*$^1$ | 皇 *huang*$^2$ |
| 衣 *i*$^1$ | 去 *ch'ü*$^4$ | 候。*hou*$^4$ | 城。*ch'êng*$^2$ | 就 *chiu*$^4$ | 上 *shang*$^4$ |
| 戴 *tai*$^4$ | 應 *ying*$^1$ | 朝 *ch'ao*$^2$ | 明 *ming*$^2$ | 是 *shih*$^4$ | 住 *chu*$^4$ |
| 朝 *ch'ao*$^2$ | 該 *kai*$^1$ | 廷。*t'ing*$^2$ | 朝 *ch'ao*$^2$ | 皇 *huang*$^2$ | 的 *ti* |
| 帽。*mao*$^4$ | 穿 *ch'uan*$^1$ | 上 *shang*$^4$ | 的 *ti* | 宮。*kung*$^1$ | 地 *ti*$^4$ |

The place where the Emperor lives is the Imperial Palace.

*Obs.*—The Emperor: *lit.*, the august [one] above.

The Imperial city.

In the time of the Ming dynasty.
The Court.
When one goes to Court one ought to put on a Court dress and hat.

842. 建 *chien*$^{4}$, to set up ; to establish.

843. 臨 *lin*$^{2}$, to descend ; to approach to. Colloquially, rarely, except in time.

844. 強 *ch'iang*$^{2}$, energetic. Often, over-energetic ; violent ; also, superior to. *Ch'iang*$^{3}$, to insist on against a person's will or inclination. *Chiang*$^{4}$, obstinate ; self-willed.

845. 良 *liang*$^{2}$, virtuous ; good.

846. 禁 *chin*$^{4}$, to prohibit.

847. Examples :—

| | | | | | | |
|---|---|---|---|---|---|---|
| 良 *liang*$^{2}$ | 嘴。*tsui*$^{3}$ | 利 *li*$^{4}$ | 比 *pi*$^{3}$ | 候 *hou*$^{4}$ | 立 *li*$^{4}$ | 各 *ko*$^{4}$ |
| 民。*min*$^{2}$ | 耍 *shua*$^{3}$ | 害。*hai*$^{4}$ | 別 *pieh*$^{2}$ | 強 *ch'iang*$^{3}$ | 的。*ti* | 衙 *ya*$^{2}$ |
| 臨 *lin*$^{2}$ | 錢 *ch'ien*$^{2}$ | 沒 *mei*$^{2}$ | 人 *jên*$^{2}$ | 要 *yao*$^{4}$ | 他 *t'a*$^{1}$ | 門 *mên*$^{2}$ |
| 民 *min*$^{2}$ | 是 *shih*$^{4}$ | 有 *yu*$^{3}$ | 強。*ch'iang*$^{2}$ | 我 *wo*$^{3}$ | 臨 *lin*$^{2}$ | 是 *shih*$^{4}$ |
| 的 *ti* | 禁 *chin*$^{4}$ | 良 *liang*$^{2}$ | 強 *ch'iang*$^{2}$ | 的 *ti* | 走 *tsou*$^{3}$ | 朝 *ch'ao*$^{2}$ |
| 官。*kuan*$^{1}$ | 止 *chih*$^{3}$ | 心。*hsin*$^{1}$ | 暴 *pao*$^{4}$ | 錢。*ch'ien*$^{2}$ | 的 *ti* | 廷 *t'ing*$^{2}$ |
| | 的。*ti* | 強 *chiang*$^{4}$ | 的 *ti* | 他 *t'a*$^{1}$ | 時 *shih*$^{2}$ | 建 *chien*$^{4}$ |

Yamêns are established by the Court.
When he was on the point of starting he insisted on having my money.
He is superior to other people.
He is terribly violent.
Devoid of moral sense (or conscience).

*Obs.—Liang hsin, lit.*, virtuous heart, is the innate goodness of man, who, according to Chinese ethics, is born virtuous.

To answer (argue with) a superior.
Gambling is prohibited.
Honest (law-abiding) subjects.
The official in direct relations with the people (the Chih-hsien, commonly called the District Magistrate).

848. 為 *wei*$^{2}$, to do ; to be.

849. 匪 *fei*$^{3}$, wrongdoing, in a grave sense ; wrongdoer.

850. 反 *fan*$^{3}$, to turn upside down ; on the contrary ; hence, to rebel.

851. 犯 *fan*$^{4}$, to stumble against ; to offend ; to incur a penalty.

852. 罪 *tsui*$^{4}$, properly, punishment ; also, offences, great or small. *See* Exercise XXXI, 8, Obs.

853. 死 *ssŭ*$^{3}$, to die.

854. 黨 *tang*$^{3}$, a gang ; a band ; a political party ; a class.

855. Examples :—

| | | | | | | |
|---|---|---|---|---|---|---|
| 他 t'a$^1$ | 麼 mo | 是 shih$^4$ | 死 ssŭ$^3$ | 法 fa$^3$ | 了。liao | 那 na$^4$ |
| 叫 chiao$^4$ | 罪 tsui$^4$ | 一 i$^1$ | 了。liao | 的 ti | 難 nan$^2$ | 地 ti$^4$ |
| 人 jên$^2$ | 名。ming$^2$ | 黨 tang$^3$ | 這 chê$^4$ | 人 jên$^2$ | 爲 wei$^2$ | 方 fang$^1$ |
| 勒 lei$^1$ | 應 ying$^1$ | 的。ti | 些 hsieh$^1$ | 總 tsung$^3$ | 你 ni$^3$ | 的 ti |
| 死 ssŭ$^3$ | 該 kai$^1$ | 應 ying$^1$ | 賊 tsei$^2$ | 得 tei$^3$ | 們 mên | 土 t'u$^3$ |
| 了。liao | 死 ssŭ$^3$ | 該 kai$^1$ | 匪 fei$^3$ | 治 chih$^1$ | 了。liao | 匪 fei$^3$ |
| | 罪。tsui$^4$ | 甚 shên$^2$ | 都 tou$^1$ | 罪。tsui$^4$ | 犯 fan$^4$ | 反 fan$^3$ |

The bad characters of that place have rebelled.

*Obs.*—*T'u fei* must be natives of the locality. *Fei* can be applied to any individual who is guilty of grave misdemeanours, but it is generally understood to refer to banditti or rebels.

Sorry to have troubled you; much obliged.

*Obs.*—*Nan wei* is constantly used courteously, "May I trouble you to," "Much obliged," both as a request for a favour and as an acknowledgment of one. Distinguish *wei$^2$ nan$^2$*, to be in difficulties, difficult.

It is essential that those who break the laws be punished.

*Obs.*—*Chih tsui*, to treat an offence; *q.d.*, with punishment. *Chih ping*, to treat a complaint; *q.d.*, with medicine.

Dead.

*Obs.*—Of persons it is common to use the euphemism *kuo ch'ü liao*, he has passed away; or *pu tsai liao*, he is no more.

These bandits are all of one gang.

*Obs.*—*Tsei fei* must be bandits or rebels.

What penalty ought they to receive?

*Obs.*—*Tsui ming*: what is the name of the punishment (what particular penalty) [they] ought [to receive].

It should be death.

He was strangled. *See* 507.

*Obs.*—Note that there is another term for the punishment of death by strangulation.

856. 爭 *chêng$^1$*, to emulate; to wrangle; to fight with.

857. 鬪 *tou$^4$*, to fight, with or without arms; but not used of war.

858. 號 *hao$^4$*, a signal, visible, as a flag; audible, as a bugle call; a verbal order; a sign, style, or number. Also, to call, or the name by which a person is called by his friends, in contradistinction to his *ming$^2$*, or cognomen by which he is known to his family.

859. 靖 *ching$^4$*, quiet, as a country free from disorder.

860. Examples :—

| | | | | | |
|---|---|---|---|---|---|
| 頭 t'ou$^2$ | 靖。ching$^4$ | 字 tzŭ$^4$ | 了。liao | 下 hsia$^4$ | 土 t'u$^3$ |
| 兒。'rh | 年 nien$^2$ | 號。hao$^4$ | 貴 kuei$^4$ | 裡 li$^3$ | 匪 fei$^3$ |
| 口 k'ou$^3$ | 號。hao$^4$ | 地 ti$^4$ | 行 hang$^2$ | 爭 chêng$^1$ | 同 t'ung$^2$ |
| 號。hao$^4$ | 甚 shên$^2$ | 方 fang$^1$ | 是 shih$^4$ | 鬪 tou$^4$ | 百 po$^2$ |
| 號 hao$^4$ | 麼 mo | 不 pu$^4$ | 甚 shên$^2$ | 起 ch'i$^3$ | 姓 hsing$^4$ |
| 衣。i$^1$ | 號 hao$^4$ | 安 an$^1$ | 麼 mo | 來 lai$^2$ | 兩 liang$^3$ |

The local rowdies and the people began (or, have begun) to fight with each other.

What is the style of your hong?

The country is disturbed.

The style of a reign, *i.e.*, that by which its years are called; thus, TAO KUANG *wu nien*, the fifth year of TAO KUANG.

What is the number (*sc.*, of a despatch, house in a street, etc.).

*Obs.—Hao t'ou-'rh; lit.*, the number of distinguishing mark on the head, front, or top.

A password.

A soldier's uniform.

*Obs.*—So called from the *hao*, the distinctive number or name of regiment, marked on the circular patch which is sewn on the breast and back of most soldiers' jackets.

861. 恩 *ngên*¹ grace; goodness shown to an inferior.

862. 赦 *shê*⁴, pardon; amnesty. Used only of Imperial pardons.

863. 免 *mien*³, to avoid; to cause to avoid; to dispense with; to forego. Hence also, under certain circumstances, to let off; to pardon.

864. 隨 *sui*², following after; according to.

865. Examples :—

| | | | | | | |
|---|---|---|---|---|---|---|
| 隨 *sui*² | 錢。*ch'ien*² | 口 *k'ou*³ | 下 *hsia*⁴ | 回 *hui*² | 是 *shih*⁴ | 皇 *huang*² |
| 事。*shih*⁴ | 隨 *sui*² | 亂 *luan*⁴ | 免 *mien*³ | 來 *lai*² | 打 *ta*³ | 上 *shang*⁴ |
| 隨 *sui*² | 時 *shih*² | 說。*shuo*¹ | 得 *tê* | 的。*ti* | 黑 *hei*¹ | 的 *ti* |
| 你 *ni*³ | 來。*lai*² | 難 *nan*² | 費 *fei*⁴ | 隨 *sui*² | 龍 *lung*² | 恩 *ngên*¹ |
| 的 *ti* | 隨 *sui*² | 免 *mien*³ | 事。*shih*⁴ | 便 *pien*⁴ | 江 *chiang*¹ | 典。*tien*³ |
| 便。*pien*⁴ | 時 *shih*² | 費 *fei*⁴ | 隨 *sui*² | 坐 *tso*⁴ | 赦 *shê*⁴ | 他 *t'a*¹ |

The Emperor's bounty or goodness.

*Obs.—ngên tien : tien*, the standard, canon, or law of bounty or favour. The term, though now universally applied to acts of kindness shown by superiors to inferiors, was originally confined to Imperial acts of grace, which were a *tien*, canon, standard, or law for others to follow.

He came back pardoned from the Black Dragon River (the Amoor).

*Obs.*—The Amoor region is a common place of banishment for officials and soldiers guilty of crimes.

Sit down as you like, to save bother.

To talk recklessly; to let one's tongue run away with one.

Expenditure of money is hardly avoidable.

*Obs.—Nan* has here almost the sense of a negative; unavoidable. It is often thus used courteously.

Come from time to time.

To be guided by circumstances.

*Obs.—Lit.*, according to time following after (or up) matters; to deal with a matter as [the conditions of] the moment require.

As you please; or, at your convenience.

*Obs.*—This may be used either courteously or otherwise.

## EXERCISE XXXII.

1 他臨死的時候兒、他的兒孫們都爭起家產、來咯。

1. As his end approached his sons and grandsons began to wrangle about the property.

2 良民是不犯國法的人。

2. *Liang*² *min*² (good subjects; or, virtuous people) are those who do not offend against the laws.

3 大臣上朝的時候兒、不是進皇宮麼、不是進皇宮、皇宮是皇上住的地方兒、就是禁地、向例連大臣們都不准到的。

3. When high officers go to Court, do they not enter the *huang*² *kung*¹? No; the *huang*² *kung*¹ is the place in which the Emperor lives, and is forbidden ground, which even high officials have never been allowed to visit.

*Obs.*—Never: *lit.*, [by] heretofore [existing] law are not permitted to go to.

4 你把這幾件文書給號上、打儘頭裏的日子號起。

4. Number these despatches for me, commencing the numbers with the earliest date.

*Obs.*—Commencing, etc.: *lit.*, from the very front days numbering commence.

5 我們大人出了號令、禁止底下人耍錢、要是犯了禁、必要治罪的。

5. Our chief (or master) has issued an order forbidding the servants to gamble; if the prohibition is disregarded, [the offender] will certainly be punished.

*Obs.*—*Ti*: *lit.*, the *fan chin*, disregard of the prohibition, certainly will be (*yao*) a punished one.

6 幹這沒良心的事、難免犯法、做良民比爲匪不強麼、反倒不愛做、真是怪事。

6. You will hardly escape a breach of the laws if you pursue this unprincipled business. Would it not be better to behave as an honest citizen than to act in an illegal manner? and yet you won't behave like one; it is really most strange.

*Obs.*—Note that *wei fei* may mean to play the robber, or become a rebel, though the title can be earned by the commission of any act of an intentionally illegal nature; thus, smuggling, brawling, gambling, etc., come within the category of *wei fei*.

7 隨你們倆人鬭嘴兒、就是別打起來、要是打起來、那可不是玩意兒。

7. You two may squabble as much as you please, only don't come to blows, for that would be beyond a joke.

*Obs.*—As much as you please: *sui*, short for *sui pien*, according to your convenience or inclination.

8 大赦天下。寬免犯人的罪名、總出於皇上的恩典。

8. A general amnesty. The pardon of criminals always proceeds from the Emperor's bounty.

*Obs.* 1.—Note that *shê* can only be applied to Imperial pardons or the diminution of sentences by Imperial command. An offence against a private individual can be *k'uan mien*, condoned (*lit.*, liberal remission; *q.d.*, of penalties remitted); a more common expression is *jao*[4].

*Obs.* 2.—Criminal: *fan jên*, a man who offends; *q.d.*, against the laws.

9 你別在太陽地裏走、免得受熱。他那個病隨你怎麼治、早晚總是要死的。

9. Don't walk in the sun, and you won't get sunstroke. It doesn't matter how you treat his complaint, he must die sooner or later.

*Obs.* 1.—Sunstroke: *shou jê* can be used of any complaint caused by the action of the sun, whether directly or indirectly.

*Obs.* 2.—Doesn't matter: *lit.*, you may treat his complaint according to how [you please].

10 朝廷隨地酌情建立地方官、為臨民的官。地方官治理的好、自然就能安靖了、

10. The Sovereign is guided by places and circumstances in his establishment of local authorities to be in near relations with the people. If the local authorities govern wisely (well), quiet naturally prevails.

*Obs.*—Is guided: *lit.*, following (acting according to) place, considering circumstances establishes officers [for the government of] the locality. *Ti-fang kuan* does not include exclusively judicial, fiscal, or educational authorities, nor, in the capital, the departments of the central government, unless these be executive. *Ching* (859) must not be confounded with *ching* (824); the former applies to conditions of place, and the latter to the character or state of the individual.

*Turn the following into Chinese.* (KEY, EXERCISE XXXII.)

1. A great many years ago there was a man called LIN who wanted to be Emperor. Before he rebelled he distributed his sworn confederates here and there [till] they were [posted] everywhere: his men were even [to be found] in the forbidden ground of the Imperial Palace. His arrangements (the affair) subsequently got known (*lit.*, was broken), and he himself was arrested. His sworn followers continued in rebellion for very many months in Shantung and Honan.

*Obs.* 1.—Sworn confederates: *ssŭ*[3] *tang*[3], confederates to the death.

*Obs.* 2.—Distributed: *pu san* (406), arranged and distributed.

2. When the people rebel, the Emperor sends (orders) a high official to pacify the disturbed country. When the high official is about to start he has to go to Court to see the Emperor.

*Obs.*—Pacify: *p'ing ting; lit.*, to level and fix.

3. What is the number of that despatch? It has not yet been numbered.

4. The date of the establishment of the northern capital (the city of Peking) is not far back (*yüan*$^3$). The court was formerly established in the South; the place where the Emperor resides is called *ching*$^1$ (the capital), and so that city was called *Nan-ching* (the "southern capital").

*Obs.*—Date: *nien fên; lit.*, year distribution, the place it occupies in the cyclical distribution of time.

5. Cockfighting is a pastime in which virtuous people do not indulge. It is a most disreputable amusement (matter), and ought to be prohibited by law.

6. I hear that that fellow Li has committed a grave crime; some people say that he is certain to be sentenced to death. He deserves it, for when men become burglars they cannot escape capital punishment. If men of that stamp are not put to death, how can honest people gain a quiet livelihood?

*Obs.*—Burglars: *see* Exercise XXI, 4, Obs. 2.

7. What you say is quite correct; still, who would have thought that the man Li would have become a robber?

8. Come and see me from time to time. Although I am not a rich man, I am always able to give you a bowl of rice to eat and a cup of tea to drink.

9. Then you will be my true friend, for what I particularly dread is giving people trouble. If you will really let me come to see you in this way, you will see whether I shall come often or not.

*Obs.* 1.—True friend: *lit.*, good friend.

*Obs.* 2.—Let me, etc.: *chiao wo.*

866. 古 *ku*$^3$, ancient.

867. 世 *shih*$^4$, an age; a generation.

868. 孔 *k'ung*$^3$, properly, a hole; the surname of Confucius.

869. 聖 *shêng*$^4$, virtuous as heaven; sainted; canonised.

870. 儒 *ju*$^2$, generally, a scholar; specially, a Confucianist, as opposed to the Taoist and Buddhist.

871. Examples:—

| | | | | | |
|---|---|---|---|---|---|
| 夫 *fu*$^1$ | 儒 *ju*$^2$ | 稱 *ch'êng*$^1$ | 稱 *ch'êng*$^1$ | 是 *shih*$^4$ | 從 *ts'ung*$^2$ |
| 子。*tzŭ*$^3$ | 教。*chiao*$^1$ | 他 *t'a*$^1$ | 他 *t'a*$^1$ | 尊 *tsun*$^1$ | 古 *ku*$^3$ |
| 古 *ku*$^3$ | 後 *hou*$^4$ | 的 *ti* | 爲 *wei*$^2$ | 重 *chung*$^4$ | 至 *chih*$^4$ |
| 玩 *wan*$^2$ | 世。*shih*$^4$ | 教 *chiao*$^4$ | 聖 *shêng*$^4$ | 孔 *k'ung*$^3$ | 今 *chin*$^1$ |
| 鋪。*p'u*$^4$ | 孔 *k'ung*$^3$ | 爲 *wei*$^2$ | 人 *jên*$^2$ | 子 *tzŭ*$^3$ | 都 *tou*$^1$ |

In all ages Confucius has been honoured and styled the Sacred Man, and his doctrine has been styled Confucianism.

*Obs.*—*Lit.*, from of old till now all have (are) honoured Confucius.

語言自邇集



Future generations; posterity.

K'ung Fu-tzŭ (Confucius).

*Obs.* The great master Confucius: *fu-tzŭ*, a sage, a master, a distinguished man. Emphasise ...

A "curio" shop.

*Obs.—Ku wan: lit.*, ancient gems; applied to any objects of *vertu* that are not absolutely new.

872. 佛 *fo*², Buddha.

873. 廟 *miao*⁴, a temple.

874. 座 *tso*⁴, properly, a seat or throne; also, the numerative of cities, temples, etc.

875. 僧 *sêng*¹, a Buddhist priest.

876. 俗 *su*², properly, common; in vulgar use; but under certain conditions, a layman. Also, with *chia*¹, Confucian.

877. 尙 *shang*⁴, properly, eminent; but most commonly a conjunction, not in frequent use colloquially. When linked to *ho*² (210), it is merely phonetic; as *ho*²-*shang*⁴, a Buddhist priest.

*N.B.*—Emphasise *ho*².

878. Examples:—

| | | | | | | |
|---|---|---|---|---|---|---|
| 古。*ku*³ | 有 *yu*³ | 方 *fang*¹ | 人 *jên*² | 位 *wei*⁴ | 這 *chê*⁴ | 拜 *pai*⁴ |
| 尙 *shang*⁴ | 文 *wên*² | 的 *ti* | 一 *i*² | 和 *ho*² | 一 *i*² | 佛 *fo*² |
| 且。*ch'ieh*³ | 廟。*miao*⁴ | 風 *fêng*¹ | 個 *ko*⁴ | 尙。*shang*⁴ | 座 *tso*⁴ | 爺。*yeh* |
| 回 *hui*² | 俗 *su*² | 俗。*su*² | 老 *lao*³ | 三 *san*¹ | 廟 *miao*⁴ | 和 *ho*² |
| 敎。*chiao*⁴ | 家。*chia*¹ | 各 *ko*⁴ | 道。*tao*⁴ | 個 *ko*⁴ | 有 *yu*³ | 尙 *shang*⁴ |
| | 上 *shang*⁴ | 城 *ch'êng*² | 地 *ti*⁴ | 僧 *sêng*¹ | 幾 *chi*³ | 廟。*miao*⁴ |

To worship Buddha.

A Buddhist temple.

How many priests are there in this temple?

Three priests and a servant (or, temple coolie).

*Obs.*—A temple servant is *lao*³-*tao*⁴, but the character of the latter sound is merely phonetic: indeed, both may be. Note that Taoist priests are also styled *lao-tao*.

The customs, or morality, of a district (or locality).

*Obs.*—In addition to its original meaning, wind, *fêng*, also means manner, deportment, or style; as *fêng su*, the manner that is common or in vulgar use.

Every city has a Confucian temple (or temples).

*Obs.*—*Wên miao: lit.*, temples of literature, as opposed to *wu miao, lit.*, military temples, temples to *Kuan Ti*, or *Lao-yeh*, the God of War.

A layman, as opposed to *ho*²-*shang*⁴, a priest.

*Obs.*—When priests renounce their vows and become laymen they are said to *huan su* (105), return to laymen.

Early antiquity.

Besides; moreover.

The Mahomedan faith.

*Obs.*—A Mussulman is called a *hui hui* or *hui-tzŭ*, though the latter is slightly opprobrious. The term *hui-hui* is said to be a reproduction of Turkish sounds.

879. 傳 *ch'uan*$^{2}$, to communicate by tradition; to propagate by preaching; to convey a message; to be a medium of communication. *Chuan*$^{4}$, a record or chronicle.

880. 經 *ching*$^{1}$, a canonical book or Buddhist *sutra;* also, to pass through or by. In composition, a sign of the past tense.

881. 楷 *ch'iai*$^{3}$, *k'ai*$^{3}$, properly, the stalk of grain; applied to a clerkly kind of Chinese writing somewhat corresponding to our round text.

882. 率 *shuai*$^{4}$, to follow one's nature; properly, in a good sense, but in the example given below, careless.

883. 更 *kêng*$^{4}$, before adjectives, more. Distinguish *kêng*$^{1}$, to change (570).

884. 濃 *nung*$^{2}$, thick, of fluids.

885. Examples:—

| | | | | | | |
|---|---|---|---|---|---|---|
| 淡 *tan*$^{4}$ | 兒 *'rh* | 楷 {*ch'iai*$^{3}$ / *k'ai*$^{3}$} | 好 *hao*$^{3}$ | 話。*hua*$^{4}$ | 時 *shih*$^{2}$ | 傳 *ch'uan*$^{2}$ |
| 的 *ti* | 更 *kêng*$^{4}$ | 書 *shu*$^{1}$ | 些 *hsieh*$^{1}$ | 名 *ming*$^{2}$ | 傳 *ch'uan*$^{2}$ | 教 *chiao*$^{4}$ |
| 對 *tui*$^{4}$ | 不 *pu*$^{4}$ | 寫 *hsieh*$^{3}$ | 難。*nan*$^{4}$ | 臣 *ch'ên*$^{2}$ | 流 *liu*$^{2}$ | 的。*ti* |
| 面 *mien*$^{4}$ | 好 *hao*$^{3}$ | 得 *tê* | 他 *t'a*$^{1}$ | 傳，*chuan*$^{4}$ | 下 *hsia*$^{4}$ | 五 *wu*$^{3}$ |
| 兒。*'rh* | 了。*liao* | 草 *ts'ao*$^{3}$ | 昨 *tso*$^{2}$ | 他 *t'a*$^{1}$ | 來 *lai*$^{2}$ | 經 *ching*$^{1}$ |
| | 濃 *nung*$^{2}$ | 率 *shuai*$^{4}$ | 兒 *'rh* | 經 *ching*$^{1}$ | 的。*ti* | 是 *shih*$^{4}$ |
| | 是 *shih*$^{4}$ | 今 *chin*$^{1}$ | 寫 *hsieh*$^{3}$ | 過 *kuo*$^{4}$ | 傳 *ch'uan*$^{2}$ | 古 *ku*$^{3}$ |

Missionaries.

The Five Classics (or Canons) have been handed down by tradition from ancient times.

*Obs.*—*Lit.*, ancient times transmitted flowing down come.

To convey a message.

A biography (or record) of illustrious officials.

*Obs.*—Illustrious: *ming*, short for *ch'u ming*, to make a name.

He has been through a deal of trouble.

He wrote his round text yesterday carelessly, and to-day even worse.

*Obs.*—*Ts'ao*, grass, amongst other meanings, has that of "hasty;" hence its combination with *shuai*.

*Nung*$^{2}$ (thick, glutinous) is the opposite of *tan*$^{4}$ (733) (weak, watery).

886. 貼 *t'ieh*$^{1}$, to stick; to be sticking to, as a placard on a wall.

887. 牆 *ch'iang*$^{2}$, a wall.

888. 層 *ts'êng*2, layers or sections of various things, from front to rear, side to side, top to bottom.

889. 掛 *kua*4, to hang up; to be hung up.

890. 示 *shih*4 (Radical 113), to proclaim; a proclamation.

891. Examples :—

| | | | | | |
|---|---|---|---|---|---|
| 一 *i*4 | 兩 *liang*3 | 上。*shang*4 | 個 *ko*4 | 有 *yu*3 | 各 *ko*4 |
| 層 *ts'êng*2 | 層 *ts'êng*2 | 這 *chê*4 | 套 *t'ao*4 | 告 *kao*4 | 城 *ch'êng*2 |
| 的 *ti* | 道 *tao*4 | 事 *shih*4 | 兒 *'rh* | 示 *shih*4 | 的 *ti* |
| 擱 *ko*1 | 理。*li*3 | 裡 *li*3 | 掛 *kua*4 | 貼 *t'ieh*1 | 門 *mên*2 |
| 起 *ch'i*3 | 一 *i*4 | 頭 *t'ou*2 | 在 *tsai*4 | 着。*cho* | 口 *k'ou*3 |
| 來。*lai*2 | 層 *ts'êng*2 | 有 *yu*3 | 牆 *ch'iang*2 | 弄 *nung*4 | 兒 *'rh* |

At the gates of every city there are proclamations posted.

*Obs.*—Proclamations : *lit.*, informing proclamations. *Shih* is not used alone colloquially.

Make a loop and hang it up on the wall.

In this matter there is a two-fold principle.

Place it (or them) in layers, one above the other.

*Obs.*—One above the other : this is indicated by *ch'i lai*.

892. 唱 *ch'ang*4, to sing.

893. 曲 *ch'ü*3, one kind of songs. Also, crooked; tortuous.

894. 抽 *ch'ou*1, to draw one out of many, as a stick from a faggot.

895. Examples :—

| | | | | | | |
|---|---|---|---|---|---|---|
| 灣 *wan*1 | 抽 *ch'ou*1 | 他 *t'a*1 | 把 *pa*3 | 唱 *ch'ang*4 | 唱 *ch'ang*4 | 他 *t'a*1 |
| 的 *ti* | 身。*shên*1 | 有 *yu*3 | 線 *hsien*4 | 罷 *pa*4 | 曲 *ch'ü*3 | 唱 *ch'ang*4 |
| 往 *wang*3 | 曲 *ch'ü*1 | 事 *shih*4 | 抽 *ch'ou*1 | 我 *wo*3 | 兒。*'rh* | 得 *tê* |
| 東 *tung*1 | 曲 *ch'ü*1 | 不 *pu*4 | 出 *ch'u*1 | 們 *mên* | 唱 *ch'ang*4 | 好 *hao*3 |
| 流。*liu*2 | 灣 *wan*1 | 能 *nêng*2 | 來。*lai*2 | 聽。*t'ing*1 | 一 *i*2 | 聽。*t'ing*1 |

He sings pleasantly.

To sing ballads.

Give us a song; let's hear you.

Draw out the thread.

He is occupied and cannot get away (*lit.*, draw himself out; *q.d.*, from his work).

[The river] takes a winding course to the east.

*Obs.*—We can also say *wan*1 *wan*1 *ch'ü*3 *ch'ü*3. *N.B.*—*Wan wan ch'ü*3 *ch'ü*3, but *ch'ü*1 *ch'ü*1 *wan wan*.

## EXERCISE XXXIII.

1 那座廟門口兒牆上貼着告示、禁止娘兒們上廟燒香。

1. There is a proclamation posted (pasted) on the wall at the gate of that temple prohibiting women from going there to burn incense.

2 他們令祖死了、今兒個和尚去念經、和尚吃素。

2. Their grandfather is dead, and to-day the Buddhist priests are going there to hold a service (recite canons). Priests eat maigre (or, are vegetarians). (*See* 707.)

3 俗語兒說、今日且吃今日飯、明天有事明天辦。剛剛兒和你的性情相對。

3. The proverb says, "Just eat the rice you've got to-day; deal to-morrow with what comes to-morrow (don't look ahead; live for the moment)." This exactly corresponds with your disposition.

*Obs.* 1.—Just: *ch'ieh*; *lit.*, temporarily (616).
*Obs.* 2.—Exactly: *kang-kang*³*-'rh*. *See* 760.

4 老爺廟是和尚廟麼。不錯、是和尚廟。關夫子、俗叫老爺。關夫子是文話、俗話就是老爺。

4. Are *Lao*³*-yeh miao*⁴ (temples to *Lao-yeh*, the God of War) Buddhist temples? Yes. *Kuan*¹ *Fu*¹*-tzŭ*³ is commonly called *Lao-yeh*. *Kuan Fu-tzŭ* is *wên*² *hua*⁴ (the literary style); in colloquial parlance he is *Lao-yeh*.

5 這文書得寫楷書、行書草字都不行、墨又得濃。

5. This *wên*²*-shu*¹ (despatch) must be written in round (clerkly) characters; neither running hand nor "grass characters" (the much abbreviated form) will do. The ink, too, must be thick.

6 那山上廟裏頭的房子一層比一層高。

6. Each tier of buildings in that temple on the hill is higher than the other (the one below it).

7 你抽空兒給我畫一張畫兒、行不行。早已過去的時候兒就是往古。

7. Can you find time to draw me a picture? *Wang*³ *ku*³ (past antiquity) is time long gone by.

*Obs.*—Find time: *lit.*, pull out [a portion of] leisure.

8 古來有位聖人姓孔。他的教後世叫做、聖教。為中國最尊重的。同時還有老子的教、叫做道教。佛教是西方僧家傳來的。尊佛爺出家的是僧家。俗說就叫和尚。尊老子出家的是道士。聖教又名儒教。儒教的人叫俗家。三教的總名就叫僧道儒。

8. In ancient times there was a sainted man called (whose surname was) K'UNG. His doctrine was entitled by subsequent generations the *shêng*[4] *chiao*[4] (the doctrine of the Sainted Man). It is that most honoured in China. There was also contemporaneous with this the doctrine of *Lao*[3]-*tzŭ*, which is called the doctrine of *tao*[4] (reason or right). The doctrine of Buddha was propagated (or preached) by the *sêng*[1]-*chia*[1] (priests) from the West. Those who leave their homes for the honour of Buddha are *sêng-chia;* in common parlance they are called *ho*[2]-*shang*[4]. Those who leave their homes for the honour of *Lao*[3]-*tzŭ* are *tao*[4]-*shih*[4] (priests of *tao*). The *shêng*[4] *chiao*[4] (doctrine of Confucius) is also called *ju*[2] *chiao*[4]. Persons belonging to the *ju*[2] *chiao*[4] are called *su*[2]-*chia*[1] (members of the ordinary persuasion). The three sects (or persuasions) are spoken of collectively as *sêng*[1] *tao*[4] *ju*[2] (Buddhism, Taoism, and Confucianism).

*Obs.* 1.—Most honoured: *ti* representing *chiao;* it is the China most honours one.

*Obs.* 2.—Also called: *lit.*, other name.

*Obs.* 3.—Collectively: *lit.*, the three doctrines all-including term is *sêng tao ju*. Notice the *chiu* after the subject *tsung ming;* it emphasises, but is untranslatable in English.

9 京城的廟多、有的是和尚廟。有的是道士廟。在那兒念經的聲兒和人家唱曲兒一個樣。

9. There are many temples in the capital; some are temples of Buddhist priests, some are temples of Taoist priests. The recital of the books in these sounds as if people were singing songs.

*Obs.*—Sounds as if: *lit.*, the in that place reciting book's sound is with men singing songs one (or, the same) fashion. *Nien*, to recite: *see* 122.

10 我屋裏牆上掛的那張古畫兒。今兒拿新紙裱上一層。

10. I pasted a fresh piece of paper to-day under (or, at the back of) that old picture that hangs on the wall of my room.

*Obs.* 1.—*Hua*, a picture, may also mean a scroll with characters written on it.

*Obs.* 2.—Under: *lit.*, on, but it must have been under, or at the back of, the picture.

*Turn the following into Chinese.* (KEY, EXERCISE XXXIII.)

1. In ancient days, more than 2,430 years ago, there lived (was) in China a man named K'UNG, who is styled by everybody the Sacred Man. A book has been compiled (made up) from his everyday conversations, by reading which men [can] know how to follow after the right. How it is followed after is in this wise. As an official, in conducting affairs as the agent (on behalf) of one's Sovereign, one must be circumspect (use attention); at home, one must also honour one's father and mother, be tenderly affectionate towards one's brothers, and even *(chin shih)* one's wife should be treated with amiability, while one's friendships must be genuine. If [you] can act in this manner [you] are a good Confucianist (*lit.*, a good man in the middle of the Confucian sect).

*Obs.* 1.—Everyday conversation: *lit.*, of his ordinary (*p'ing*, 137) days spoken talk [men] have formed (*ch'êng liao*) a book.

*Obs.* 2.—Follow after: *lit.*, imitate, *hsiao*$^4$ (96).

*Obs.* 3.—In this wise, etc.: the sentence is interrogative; how is the right imitated? it is thus.

*Obs.* 4.—Amiable, amiability: *ho ch'i*; *lit.*, harmonious breath. It is here reduplicated for the sake of euphony.

*Obs.* 5.—Genuine friendship: *lit.*, the interchange (*chiao*, 721) [of relations with] friends must positively [be] *shih tsai*, true; *pi hsü*, there must, *shih*, truth, *tsai*, be present.

2. Written characters are distinguished as *chên*$^1$ (the proper character) and *ts'ao*$^3$ ("grass," or running, character). The proper (or round) text is also called *ch'iai*$^3$ (or *k'ai*$^3$) *shu*$^1$. When one is writing the ordinary character the ink must be thick for it to look well. The "grass character" is also called *ts'ao*$^3$ *shu*$^1$.

*Obs.*—Written characters: *lit.*, [in] writing characters there is the *chên tzŭ* and *ts'ao tzŭ's* (*chih*) distinction (*fên*).

3. Why are they called "grass characters"? Some people say they are so called [because] when written the characters are just like grass, but I don't know whether this statement is correct or not.

*Obs.*—They are so called: *lit.*, there are men say it is the character written out with grass one and the same, then (therefore) called *ts'ao tzŭ*. The origin of the term is more generally supposed to be derived from *ts'ao*, in its meaning of careless, hasty.

4. Recitation and writing require undivided (special) attention; one ought not to recite without thinking (*lit.*, empty, or emptily, recite), as if one were singing a ballad.

5. Buddha is the Sacred Man of the West. The books which propagate his faith are called the Buddhistic books (or *sutras*). The principle of the Buddhistic canon is simply to give men tranquillity of mind, that is all. [This] the common people do not know, [for] they talk of being able to escape retribution for their sins by reciting these canonical books, which is really nonsense.

*Obs.* 1.—Simply to give, etc.: *lit.*, not exceeding (*pu kuo*) cause (*chiao*) men to tranquillise [their] hearts, and there an end.

*Obs.* 2.—Escape retribution for sins: *mien tsui*. *Mien tsui*, forgiveness of sins in a religious sense.

6. *Ho*$^2$-*shang*$^4$ are the men who recite the books of Buddha. Another name for them is *sêng*$^1$ *jên*$^2$.

7. The day before yesterday I saw a proclamation posted on the wall, the writing on the upper portion of which I could not see distinctly, while the lower portion was rubbed and torn in places, so I don't know what it was about.

*Obs.*—The writing on the upper portion: *lit.*, the upper side's characters pen strokes [I] saw not distinctly (true).

語言自邇集



896. 倉 *ts'ang*$^{1}$, a granary.

897. 庫 *k'u*$^{4}$, a store-room.

898. 宗 *tsung*$^{1}$, a sort; also used as a collective, pluralising the noun that precedes it

899. 考 *k'ao*$^{3}$, to compare; to examine competitively.

900. Examples:—

| | | | | | | |
|---|---|---|---|---|---|---|
| 回 *hui*$^{2}$ | 是 *shih*$^{4}$ | 我 *wo*$^{3}$ | 不 *pu*$^{4}$ | 宗 *tsung*$^{1}$ | 沒 *mei*$^{2}$ | 管 *kuan*$^{3}$ |
| 的。*ti* | 一 *i*$^{4}$ | 們 *mên* | 能 *nêng*$^{2}$ | 事 *shih*$^{4}$ | 有 *yu*$^{3}$ | 倉 *ts'ang*$^{1}$ |
| | 年 *nien*$^{2}$ | 的 *ti* | 做。*tso*$^{4}$ | 情 *ch'ing*$^{2}$ | 銀 *yin*$^{2}$ | 的。*ti* |
| | 考 *k'ao*$^{3}$ | 學 *hsio*$^{2}$ | 祖 *tsu*$^{3}$ | 我 *wo*$^{3}$ | 子。*tzŭ* | 庫 *k'u* |
| | 三 *san*$^{1}$ | 生 *shêng*$^{1}$ | 宗。*tsung*$^{1}$ | 萬 *wan*$^{4}$ | 這 *chê*$^{4}$ | 裡 *li*$^{3}$ |

The custodian of a granary.
There is no silver in the treasury.
I cannot on any account do things of this kind.
Ancestors.
Our pupils are examined three times a year.

901. 如 *ju*$^{2}$, if; as.

902. 若 *jo*$^{4}$, if.

903. 雜 *tsa*$^{2}$, miscellaneous; not uniform.

904. 另 *ling*$^{4}$, additional.

905. 派 *p'ai*$^{4}$, properly, the branches or ramifications of a stream. Hence, to distribute; to allot; to send on a mission.

906. Examples:—

| | | | | | | |
|---|---|---|---|---|---|---|
| 如 *ju*$^{2}$ | 另 *ling*$^{4}$ | 雜 *tsa*$^{2}$ | 倒 *tao*$^{4}$ | 了。*liao* | 派 *p'ai*$^{4}$ | 這 *chê*$^{4}$ |
| 同。*t'ung*$^{2}$ | 外 *wai*$^{4}$ | 貨 *huo*$^{4}$ | 有 *yu*$^{3}$ | 若 *jo*$^{4}$ | 人 *jên*$^{2}$ | 件 *chien*$^{4}$ |
| 如 *ju*$^{2}$ | 的。*ti* | 鋪。*p'u*$^{4}$ | 一 *i*$^{4}$ | 是 *shih*$^{4}$ | 辦 *pan*$^{4}$ | 事 *shih*$^{4}$ |
| 今。*chin*$^{1}$ | 另 *ling*$^{4}$ | 那 *na*$^{4}$ | 點 *tien*$^{3}$ | 另 *ling*$^{4}$ | 理 *li*$^{3}$ | 情 *ch'ing*$^{2}$ |
| | 外 *wai*$^{4}$ | 飯 *fan*$^{4}$ | 兒 *'rh* | 派 *p'ai*$^{4}$ | 就 *chiu*$^{4}$ | 如 *ju*$^{2}$ |
| | 還 *hai*$^{2}$ | 錢 *ch'ien*$^{2}$ | 邊 *pien*$^{1}$ | 人 *jên*$^{2}$ | 雜 *tsa*$^{2}$ | 果 *kuo*$^{3}$ |
| | 有。*yu*$^{3}$ | 是 *shih*$^{4}$ | 兒。*'rh* | 我 *wo*$^{3}$ | 亂 *luan*$^{4}$ | 不 *pu*$^{4}$ |

If someone is not sent to attend to it, this affair will all be in a mess.
*Obs.—Ju kuo: lit.*, if indeed (see 364). *Ju jo* would not be incorrect.
If somebody else is sent instead, I shall then have a slight chance.
*Obs.* 1.—*Jo shih*, commonly pronounced *yao shih*, and often so written.
*Obs.* 2.—Chance: *lit.*, margin or verge; *q.d.*, of hope.
A grocer's shop. (Not much used in Peking.)
The allowance (money) for food is not included.
Besides that there are.
Like; similar to.
Now.
*Obs.—Lit.*, as now. The origin of this expression is obscure.

907. 盼 p'an$^4$, to look for anxiously.

908. 望 wang$^4$, to expect; to hope; to look towards; towards.

909. 列 lieh$^4$, separated in due order.

910. 衆 chung$^4$, a number of persons; all; everyone.

911. 渴 k'o$^3$, thirsty; to thirst for.

912. Examples:—

他 t'a$^1$ 們 mên 列 lieh$^4$ 位 wei$^4$ 正 chêng$^4$ 盼 p'an$^4$ 望 wang$^4$
着 cho 你 ni$^3$ 來 lai$^2$ 可 k'o$^3$ 巧 ch'iao$^3$ 你 ni$^3$ 就 chiu$^4$
來 lai$^2$ 了。liao 衆 chung$^4$ 位 wei$^4$ 老 lao$^3$ 爺 yeh$^2$ 們 mên
好。hao$^3$ 沒 mei$^2$ 有 yu$^3$ 指 chih$^3$ 望 wang$^4$ 了。liao 明 ming$^2$
兒 'rh 去 ch'ü$^4$ 望 wang$^4$ 看 k'an$^4$ 你。ni$^3$ 渴 k'o$^3$ 了 liao
別 pieh$^2$ 喝 ho$^1$ 涼 liang$^2$ 水。shui$^3$ 一 i$^2$ 個 ko$^4$ 打 ta$^3$
雜 tsa$^2$ 兒 'rh 的。ti

These gentlemen were just hoping you would come, and, most opportunely, here you are.

Are your honours all well?

There is no hope.

*Obs.—Lit.*, there is no indication, nothing to point to (nothing on which to base) hope.

I'll look you up to-morrow.

*Obs.—Wang k'an* is more familiar than *pai*, or *pai hui*, and can only be reciprocally used by equals on intimate terms, or by superiors to inferiors.

When you are thirsty don't drink cold water.

A coolie.

*Obs.—Lit.*, one who does (*ta*, verb of action) *tsa*, miscellaneous [jobs]. The word "coolie" (? k'u$^3$ li$^4$, hard labour) is not known in Peking except as an Anglo-Chinese term.

913. 依 i$^1$, to lean against; closely following. Hence, according to; to accede to; to comply with. Hence, pu$^4$ i$^1$, to object; I won't stand it. *See* Part IV, Dialogue VII, 37.

914. 戀 lien$^4$, lüan$^4$, to be warmly attached to a person or place.

915. 跨 k'ua$^4$, to bestride; to be seated with one leg hanging.

916. 轅 yüan$^2$, the shaft of a cart; the side gates leading into the outer court of a yamên.

917. 捨 shê$^3$, to let go; to part with; not to detain.

918. 礙, 碍 ngai$^4$, to obstruct; to interfere with. The second character is only an abbreviation of the first. In Peking the ng is hardly sounded, if at all.

919. Examples:—

人 jên$^2$ 出 ch'u$^1$ 遠 yüan$^2$ 門 mên$^2$ 難 nan$^2$ 免 mien$^3$
依 i$^1$ 戀 lien$^4$ 父 fu$^4$ 母。mu$^3$ 跨 k'ua$^4$ 車 ch'ê$^1$
轅 yüan$^2$ 兒。'rh 轅 yüan$^2$ 門。mên$^2$ 他 t'a$^1$ 是 shih$^4$
捨 shê$^3$ 不 pu$^4$ 得 tê$^2$ 銀 yin$^2$ 子。tzŭ 別 pieh$^2$
怕 p'a$^4$ 不 pu$^2$ 礙 ai$^4$ 不 pu$^2$ 礙。ai$^4$ 你 ni$^3$
去 ch'ü$^4$ 罷 pa$^4$ 碍 ai$^4$ 手 shou$^3$ 碍 ai$^4$ 脚 chiao$^3$
兒 'rh 的。ti 依 i$^1$ 我 wo$^3$ 說。shuo$^1$

When a man goes on a long journey he can hardly help feeling unwilling to leave his father and mother.

*Obs.*—*I lien* is generally used in connexion with love for parents or elders, not of love for children, which is *lien* alone, or *shê pu tê*. *Lien* can also be used of addiction to a vice; *e.g.*, a man *lien*, clings to, his opium pipe.

To sit on the shafts of a cart.

*Obs.*—Note *yê-'rh*$^{2}$, not *yüa-'rh*$^{2}$.

The outer gates of a yamên.

He cannot part with (is loth to part with) his money.

Don't be afraid; its nothing (or, there is no harm done; there is no harm in it; it doesn't matter).

Be off with you! you're in my way.

I should say (*lit.*, according to my statement).

920. **彼** *pi*$^{3}$, that, as opposed to this.

921. **此** *tz'ŭ*$^{3}$, this.

922. **處** *ch'u*$^{4}$, a place; but *ch'u*$^{3}$, in composition, to live in a place. Also, to manage; to punish. Hence, *ch'u*$^{3}$ *fên*$^{4}$, official penalties (see *infra*).

923. **偏** *p'ien*$^{1}$, to lean towards. Hence, partial; specially; particularly.

924. **或** *huo*$^{4}$, expressive of uncertainty; if; perhaps; either; or.

925. Examples:—

| | | | | | | |
|---|---|---|---|---|---|---|
| 我 *wo*$^{3}$ | 甚 *shên*$^{2}$ | 兄 *hsiung*$^{1}$ | 這 *chê*$^{4}$ | 相 *hsiang*$^{1}$ | 分 *fên*$^{1}$ | 彼 *pi*$^{3}$ |
| 偏 *p'ien*$^{1}$ | 麽 *mo* | 弟 *ti*$^{4}$ | 有 *yu*$^{3}$ | 待。*tai*$^{4}$ | 彼 *pi*$^{3}$ | 此 *tz'ŭ*$^{3}$ |
| 不 *pu*$^{2}$ | 偏 *p'ien*$^{1}$ | 或 *huo*$^{4}$ | 甚 *shên*$^{2}$ | 各 *ko*$^{4}$ | 此 *tz'ŭ*$^{3}$ | 總 *tsung*$^{3}$ |
| 去。*ch'ü*$^{4}$ | 向 *hsiang*$^{4}$ | 待 *tai*$^{4}$ | 麽 *mo* | 處。*ch'u*$^{4}$ | 總 *tsung*$^{3}$ | 要 *yao*$^{4}$ |
| 處 *ch'u*$^{3}$ | 的 *ti* | 朋 *p'êng*$^{2}$ | 好 *hao*$^{3}$ | 處 *ch'u*$^{4}$ | 是 *shih*$^{4}$ | 商 *shang*$^{1}$ |
| 分。*fên*$^{4}$ | 地 *ti*$^{4}$ | 友 *yu*$^{3}$ | 處。*ch'u*$^{4}$ | 處。*ch'u*$^{4}$ | 一 *i*$^{2}$ | 量。*liang*$^{4}$ |
| | 方 *fang*$^{1}$ | 他 *t'a*$^{1}$ | 或 *huo*$^{4}$ | 到 *tao*$^{4}$ | 樣 *yang*$^{4}$ | 他 *t'a*$^{1}$ |
| | 兒。*'rh* | 沒 *mei*$^{2}$ | 待 *tai*$^{4}$ | 處。*ch'u*$^{4}$ | 兒 *'rh* | 不 *pu*$^{4}$ |

We must each consult the other; or, both parties will have to consult each other.

He treats all alike without distinction.

*Obs.*—*Lit.*, he, not distinguishing this one or that, collectively is one fashion treating [people].

Everywhere. Everywhere. Everywhere.

What advantage is there in this? or, what advantage (or, good points) has this?

Neither to his brothers nor to his friends does he show any marks of partiality.

I just won't go.

*Obs.*—It is difficult to give the exact force of *p'ien* in this combination; I should do so and so (or, you want me to), but I will *p'ien*, diverging from the proper path, do something quite the contrary.

Official penalties (the penalties, heavy or light, imposed upon officials for dereliction of duty).

## EXERCISE XXXIV.

1 這麼些日子纔回來、渴想渴想。彼此彼此。

1. What a time you have been away! I have been longing to see you. The feeling is mutual.

*Obs.*—*Lit.*, these many days only then return! [I have] thirstily thought [of you]. We two, we two (in the relation of reciprocity). *K'o hsiang* is a common salutation amongst friends meeting after a separation.

2 打這塊兒往東一望、直到天邊兒上、都是水。

2. Looking from this spot in an easterly direction one can see nothing but water right up to the horizon.

*Obs.*—*Lit.*, from this spot towards the east, one look [in] one [unbroken] straightness as far as the edge of heaven, all is water.

3 衆人都說皇上新近專派了一位大官察考倉庫裏頭銀米的數兒對不對。或銀或米若有短少、列位怕要得處分。依我說、他來不來碍不着偺們的事。

3. Everybody says that the Emperor has recently specially deputed a high official to examine the amounts of silver and rice in the treasury and granary [and see if] they are correct. If either the rice or silver are short [of the proper amount], all you gentlemen will receive (get) penalties I expect. I should say that it can't matter to us whether he comes or not.

*Obs.* 1.—Recently: *hsin chin*; *lit.*, in the new (fresh) proximity, *q.d.*, of time.

*Obs.* 2.—Correct: *tui pu tui*; if it agrees [with the registered amount] or not.

*Obs.* 3.—It won't matter to us: *ai pu chao*; *lit.*, interfering not succeed in our matter, *chao* being a particle indicating successful completion of an action (*see* 45; also Note at the close of Exercise XL).

4 這一個打雜兒的有甚麼好處、你這麼戀戀不捨的。

4. What good points (or qualities) does this coolie possess that you should be so loth to part with him?

5 你們年中進的錢甚麼是大宗兒。就是祖宗留下的產業阿。

5. In what does the chief portion of your yearly income consist? In the property left us by our ancestors.

6 老不下雨、鄉下人盼望的利害。昨兒剛長點兒雲彩、偏偏兒的又叫風兒颳散了。

6. There has been no rain for ever so long, and the country-folk are longing (hoping dreadfully) for it to come. Yesterday, just as a few clouds had made their appearance (grown), the wind most provokingly again blew them all away.

*Obs.*—Most provokingly: *p'ien p'ien* could here be fairly rendered "I'll be hanged if the wind," etc.

7 另找一輛車、若是跨着轅兒、必要弄一身土。

7. You had better get (find) another cart; if you sit on the shafts [of this one] you are sure to get covered with dust.

*Obs.*—Get covered with dust: *lit.*, make (163) one body's dust (*ti*, understood).

8 京城是五方雜處的地方兒。

8. The capital is a place with a miscellaneous population.

*Obs.*—*Lit.*, the capital is a five-quarters-miscellaneous-residing's place. Note *ch'u³*, not *ch'u⁴*. The fifth quarter is the centre.

*Turn the following into Chinese.* (KEY, EXERCISE XXXIV.)

1. In every city of China there are granaries and treasuries. Granaries are for holding (containing) rice; treasuries for putting silver into. These granaries and treasuries all have official underlings in charge of them, and when rice or money is lost, these official underlings are in all cases responsible. The money and rice contained in the treasuries and granaries have to be inspected once every year. Some years ago (that year) I had a friend who was in charge of a treasury; some robbers came in the night, broke (beat) open the door, and carried off the whole of the treasure. The high officials thereupon called upon my friend to make good the silver stolen; but of course he had no such sum in ready money, and after deliberating for some days, [he could think of] no plan, so he ran away.

*Obs.* 1.—Note *kuan jên*, official underlings; *kuan*, officials.

*Obs.* 2.—Are responsible: *lit.*, *wei*, it is, *kuan jên*, the official underlings, *shih*, that are, *wên*, asked.

*Obs.* 3.—To make good: *lit.*, according to the original quantity patching return.

*Obs.* 4.—Of course, etc.: *lit.*, my friend, where had [he] so much now (=ready) money as that?

2. What was the use of that? Even if he had run to the ends of the earth (the horizon) couldn't the police have got hold of him? and even if they could not manage to arrest him, he would be unable to return to his home; supposing he did return, he could not live there permanently.

*Obs.*—The police, etc.: *lit.*, the official underlings yet able seizing not arrive [at success]?

3. As I regard it, it would have been far better for him to have waited and submitted to his penalty than to have run all over the country.

*Obs.*—Waited and submitted to, etc.: *lit.*, *têng cho*, waiting, *t'ing*, to have accepted or submitted to (131), his *ch'u fên*; *tao*, on the contrary, compared with the whole (full) place running superior (*ch'iang*) much.

4. Carter! look, there's a man sitting behind the cart! why don't you whip behind?

*Obs.*—Whip behind: *wang hou ch'ou* (894): a Pekingese idiom.

5. You wouldn't part with that woollen carpet when I asked you for it last year; if you were to make me a present of it now I just wouldn't take it (want it).

926. 揑 *nieh*$^1$, to hold between the fingers, as a flower; to work up, as clay.

927. 灑, 洒 *sa*$^3$, to sprinkle water; the second character being an abbreviation of the first.

928. 掃 *sao*$^3$, to sweep: when combined with the following it is pronounced *sao*$^4$, and means a large broom.

929. 帚 *chou*$^3$, a broom.

930. 砌 *ch'i*$^4$, to raise in courses or layers, as a wall.

931. 硂, 夯 *hang*$^1$, to beat the ground for building, before bricks or stones are laid. This character, according to some authorities, should be written in the second form.

932. Examples :—

| | | | | | | |
|---|---|---|---|---|---|---|
| 再 *tsai*$^4$ | 房 *fang*$^2$ | 出 *ch'u*$^1$ | 拏 *na*$^2$ | 灑 *sa*$^3$ | 小 *hsiao*$^3$ | 揑 *nieh*$^1$ |
| 砌 *ch'i*$^4$ | 子 *tzŭ* | 個 *ko*$^4$ | 個 *ko*$^4$ | 了 *liao* | 牛 *niu*$^2$ | 着 *cho*$^2$ |
| 牆。*ch'iang*$^2$ | 先 *hsien*$^1$ | 道 *tao*$^4$ | 掃 *sao*$^4$ | 滿 *man*$^3$ | 兒 *'rh* | 筆。*pi*$^3$ |
| | 得 *tei*$^3$ | 兒 *'rh* | 帚 *chou*$^3$ | 地 *ti*$^4$ | 當 *tang*$^4$ | 揑 *nieh*$^1$ |
| | 打 *ta*$^3$ | 來。*lai*$^2$ | 掃 *sao*$^3$ | 下 *hsia*$^4$ | 玩 *wan*$^2$ | 了 *liao* |
| | 硂 *hang*$^1$ | 要 *yao*$^4$ | 雪 *hsüeh*$^3$ | 的 *ti* | 意 *i*$^4$ | 一 *i*$^2$ |
| | 後 *hou*$^4$ | 蓋 *kai*$^4$ | 掃 *sao*$^3$ | 水。*shui*$^3$ | 兒。*'rh* | 個 *ko*$^4$ |

Holding a pencil in the fingers.

He moulded a small cow (out of clay) for a plaything.

He sprinkled the whole ground (or, the whole floor) with water; or, he spilt the water all over the floor.

Sweep the snow away with a broom and make a path.

In building a house the ground has to be prepared first, and the walls then raised.

語言自邇集



933. 狗 *kou*$^{3}$, a dog.

934. 修 *hsiu*$^{1}$, to put or keep in order; to repair; to revise.

935. 圓 *yüan*$^{2}$, round.

936. 扁 *pien*$^{3}$, flat and thin; also, a tablet hung over the door of a room or house. Note that *p'ing* (137) is used of a flat surface without reference to thickness.

937. 幌 *huang*$^{3}$, a shop sign, whether of wood or any design indicating the nature of the goods sold or business done.

938. 表 *piao*$^{3}$, properly, the outside. Hence, to manifest; hence, a watch.

939. Examples:—

| | | | | | |
|---|---|---|---|---|---|
| 幌 *huang*$^{3}$ | 扁 *pien*$^{3}$ | 有 *yu*$^{3}$ | 兒 *'rh* | 表。*piao*$^{3}$ | 一 *i*$^{4}$ |
| 子 *tzŭ* | 了。*liao* | 扁 *pien*$^{3}$ | 的 *ti* | 修 *hsiu*$^{1}$ | 條 *t'iao*$^{2}$ |
| 是 *shih*$^{4}$ | 酒 *chiu*$^{3}$ | 的。*ti* | 尺 *ch'ih*$^{3}$ | 房 *fang*$^{2}$ | 狗，*kou*$^{3}$ |
| 布 *pu*$^{4}$ | 舖 *p'u*$^{4}$ | 大 *tai*$^{4}$ | 有 *yu*$^{3}$ | 子。*tzŭ* | 修 *hsiu*$^{1}$ |
| 做 *tso*$^{4}$ | 子 *tzŭ* | 夫 *fu*$^{1}$ | 圓 *yüan*$^{2}$ | 畫 *hua*$^{4}$ | 理 *li*$^{3}$ |
| 的。*ti* | 的 *ti* | 掛 *kua*$^{4}$ | 的 *ti* | 道 *tao*$^{4}$ | 鐘 *chung*$^{1}$ |

A dog.

*Obs.*—Note the numerative.

To mend clocks and watches.

*Obs.*—*Lit*, to mend and regulate.

To repair a house.

Rulers are round or flat.

*Obs.*—Rulers: *lit.*, drawing lines's feet. *Ch'ih* is also a foot measure or rule.

The doctor has started in practice.

*Obs.*—*Lit.*, has hung up his signboard. Note that a *pien* can only be placed over the door, or horizontally; there are exceptions to this rule, but in such cases the *pien* is called *li pien* (Radical 117), an upright tablet.

Wine-shop signs are made of cotton cloth.

940. 冤 *yüan*$^{1}$, to be aggrieved.

941. 枉 *wang*$^{3}$, properly, not straight; hence, injustice.

942. 迸 *pêng*$^{4}$, to jump off the ground with both legs; to bound. This rendering is not recognised by the dictionaries.

943. 跳 *t'iao*$^4$, to jump off the ground; generally, with one leg.

944. 嚇 *hsia*$^4$, to frighten; to scare. In composition, read *ho*$^4$.

945. Examples :—

| | | | | | |
|---|---|---|---|---|---|
| 了 *liao* | 非 *ching*$^3$ | 有 *yu*$^3$ | 迸 *pêng*$^4$ | 枉 *wang*$^3$ | 那 *na*$^4$ |
| 我 *wo*$^3$ | 去 *ch'ü*$^4$ | 人 *jên*$^2$ | 上 *shang*$^4$ | 他 *t'a*$^1$ | 不 *pu*$^2$ |
| 一 *i*$^2$ | 了。*liao* | 跳 *t'iao*$^4$ | 牆 *ch'iang*$^2$ | 麼。*mo* | 是 *shih*$^4$ |
| 跳。*t'iao*$^4$ | 嚇 *hsia*$^4$ | 下 *hsia*$^4$ | 去。*ch'ü*$^4$ | 你 *ni*$^3$ | 冤 *yüan*$^1$ |

Is not that doing him an injustice (or, accusing him wrongfully)?

Jump up on the wall.

A man has jumped into the well.

Gave me a fright; or, made me jump.

*Obs.—Lit.*, frightened me a jump; *t'iao*, however, refers to the action of the heart, not of the body.

946. 造 *tsao*$^4$, to make.

947. 報 *pao*$^4$, to announce; to give notice of. Hence, a newspaper; a gazette; to recompense.

948. 彷 *fang*$^3$, to resemble.

949. 彿 *fu*$^2$, only used with the foregoing *fang*$^3$. As *fang*$^3$-*fu*$^2$, to resemble; to seem; seemingly.

950. 笤 *t'iao*$^2$, with *chou*$^3$ (929), a small broom.

951. Examples :—

| | | | | | | |
|---|---|---|---|---|---|---|
| 樣 *yang*$^4$ | 彿 *fu* | 著 *cho* | 票。*p'iao*$^4$ | 造 *tsao*$^4$ | 得 *tei*$^3$ | 要 *yao*$^4$ |
| 子。*tzŭ* | 要 *yao*$^4$ | 把 *pa*$^3$ | 有 *yu*$^3$ | 了 *liao* | 報 *pao*$^4$ | 造 *tsao*$^4$ |
| 京 *ching*$^1$ | 掃 *sao*$^3$ | 笤 *t'iao*$^2$ | 個 *ko*$^4$ | 一 *i*$^4$ | 官。*kuan*$^1$ | 房 *fang*$^2$ |
| 報。*pao*$^4$ | 地 *ti*$^4$ | 帚 *chou*$^3$ | 人 *jên*$^2$ | 張 *chang*$^1$ | 他 *t'a*$^1$ | 子 *tzŭ* |
| | 的 *ti* | 彷 *fang*$^3$ | 拏 *na*$^2$ | 銀 *yin*$^2$ | 揑 *nieh*$^1$ | 先 *hsien*$^1$ |

Before building a house you must give notice to the authorities.

*Obs.—Tsao* is not the common word for building a house, which is *kai*$^4$.

He forged a cheque (or, bank note).

A man is holding a broom as if he were going to sweep the ground.

*Obs.—Lit.*, there is a man holding a broom [with a] seemingly wanting-to-sweep-the-ground's appearance.

The "Peking Gazette."

## EXERCISE XXXV.

1 我那個時辰表給鐘表鋪裏送去、叫他們給修理修理。就手兒問他們我那個風雨表收什得了沒有。

1. Send that watch of mine to the watch-makers' and tell them to repair it for me. You can take the opportunity to ask them whether the repairs to my barometer are finished.

*Obs.* 1.—Watch: *lit.*, an indicator of *shih ch'ên*, time, or periods of time; there are 12 *shih ch'ên* in the 24 hours. A watch can also be called *piao³* simply, but special care must be taken not to append the common affix *tzŭ*.

*Obs.* 2. Barometer: *lit.*, wind and rain indicator; the term is naturally a modern one. Cf. also *han² shu³ piao*, an indicator of cold and heat; *q.d.*, a thermometer.

2 他手裏捏着管筆、彷彿要寫甚麼。瓦盆兒是瓦盆兒匠捏的。

2. He has hold of a pencil in his fingers, as if he wanted to write something. Earthenware bowls are made by the hand of the potter.

3 那賊捏造告示作爲官出的。

3. The rebels forged a proclamation which was to pass as one issued by the authorities.

*Obs.* 1.—To pass as: *tso wei*, both verbs, and both here meaning to play a part, to act as.

*Obs.* 2.—Issued: *ch'u*, to issue, here an active verb, of which *kuan*, officer, or the government, is the subject; *lit.*, to act as an authorities-issue-one = one that is issued by the authorities.

4 他帶的貨物捎報是行李。叫關上查出來、全都入了官了。

4. He returned the merchandise he had with him as baggage, which being detected at the Customs station, the whole was confiscated.

*Obs.* 1.—Being detected: *chiao*, *lit.*, to cause; *q.d.*, [some agent or incident] caused [the inspector] at (*shang*) the Customs station to find out [the truth] = [the truth] was discovered by the Customs. There is not in Chinese any verb properly passive, but the passive construction is effected by a verb like *shou*, to receive, *pei*, to suffer, or by statement of the action that caused what was received or suffered; the action being indicated by one active verb, the subject of which, whether agent or incident, is understood.

*Obs.* 2.—Confiscated: *lit.*, all entered into the official [custody].

5 先灑水後掃地、不然、那土就飛起來咯。

5. Sprinkle water before you sweep the floor, otherwise the dust will fly about.

6 你那個小狗兒眞好看。毛兒也長、腿兒也短、耳朵也不小、就是嘴頭兒有點兒尖。

6. That is certainly a very nice-looking little dog of yours. His coat is long, his legs are short, and his ears are not small; only his muzzle is a little [too] pointed.

24

7 他們那兒打[illegible]、别就是要蓋房子罷.

7. They must be going to build a house there that they are preparing the ground.

*Obs.*—They must be, etc.: *pieh chiu shih*; *lit.*, it is not then other than [to] build a house, I expect. *Pieh*, to distingush, has here the force of deciding between two alternatives; [it can't be] other than to build. The *chiu* may be dispensed with.

8 若論圓扁的不同、西瓜是圓的、扁豆就是扁的、錢是又圓又扁的。

8. As regards the difference between *yüan*² (round) and *pien*³ (flat), a water melon is round and a broad bean is flat; a cash is both the one and the other.

*Obs.*—As regards, etc: *lit.*, if [one would] discuss *yüan* and *pien's* unsameness.

9 我沒犯法、人告我做賊、那不是我的寃枉麽。

9. If I have not broken the law and I am accused of being a thief, that is an injustice to me, is it not?

*Obs.*—Note *tso tsei*, to be a thief.

10 他近來的事情不好、那都是他的報應。我實在想不出甚麽法子來報答他待我的恩典。

10. That his affairs of late have not gone well is entirely the reward of his own misdeeds. I really can't think of any way of repaying his goodness to me.

*Obs.*—Reward of misdeeds: *pao ying*, answering recompense, can only be applied to the reward of evil-doing.

---

*Turn the following into Chinese.* (KEY, EXERCISE XXXV.)

1. I notice that the coolie you have there is a very good one: he does things very promptly, and keeps the rooms extremely clean; whenever I go [to your house] I always see him there with a broom sweeping up. That servant of mine is a terrible boor; with that tall figure of his, when he walks he is constantly jumping about in one direction or another. The whole day long, if he is not driving (beating) the fowls he is worrying (*tou*) the dogs, for all the world like a youngster.

*Obs.* 1.—Promptly; *k'uai*⁴ *tang*¹ (342), *lit.*, quickly and properly; but *tang*, it is maintained, has no force at all in this connexion. Cf. *shun tang* (626), favourable, free from obstruction; *pien tang* (333), convenient.

*Obs.* 2. Keeps clean, etc.: *lit.*, in the room sprinkles and sweeps (*ti* for *tê*) very clean.

*Obs.* 3.—Tall figure, etc.: *lit.*, as great body measurement (*shên liang*, stature) as that. *Shên liang* refers to height only, not girth.

*Obs.* 4.—Jumping about, etc.: *lit.*, a forward jumping (*pêng*) backward bounding (*t'iao*) one.

2. Another thing [about him is that he] is quite inexperienced. One day, my watch being out of order (spoilt), I had put it on

the table intending to look for a man to mend it. He saw it, and, taking it in his hand, said, "What sort of a thing is this? it's both round and flat." He was not holding it tightly, so it slipped from his hand and fell to the ground. I asked him why he threw my watch down, and he concocted a story (falsely reported) that the dog had jumped on the table, and in jumping off had knocked the watch down. He went on to say that if I falsely asserted (597) that he had damaged the watch, he would be the victim of an injustice. How can I employ a man of this kind?

*Obs.* 1.—Inexperienced: *lit.*, has not opened his eyes; has never seen anything.

*Obs.* 2.—Hold tightly: he had not *nieh chu*, pinched it to.

*Obs.* 3.—Slipped from his hand, etc.: *lit.*, one l[illegible]ing of the hand (*shih shou*, 574), it fell to the ground.

3. It seems to me that your servant is good enough (*lit.*, also not wrong). He is a rustic by origin, and, though a little rough and careless, that kind of man is sure to be strong (muscular), and if you should be building a wall by-and-by, you can get him to help in beating the ground (pile-driving), or in helping the masons; for that he will do well enough.

*Obs.* 1.—And though, etc.: *lit.*, rough and careless a little, also there is (*shih yu*) of it (*ti*).

*Obs.* 2.—Helping the masons: *tso hsiao kung-'rh*, *lit.*, to do little jobs, refers especially to the work done by a bricklayer's assistant, who is called *hsiao kung-tzŭ*; the bricklayer, or master mason, being a *ta kung-tzŭ*.

**952.** 歲, 歳 *sui*[4], the year; but used more limitedly than *nien*[2]. The second is the correct form.

**953.** 紀 *chi*[4], anciently, a period of twelve years; hence, any period of years. Verbally, to reckon a period.

**954.** 壽 *shou*[4], old age.

**955.** Examples:—

| | | | | | | |
|---|---|---|---|---|---|---|
| 壽。*shou*[4] | 人。*jên*[2] | 年 *nien*[2] | 紀。*chi*[4] | 多 *to*[2] | 萬 *wan*[4] | 歲 *sui*[4] |
| | 您 *nin*[2] | 紀 *chi*[4] | 有 *yu*[3] | 大 *ta*[4] | 歲 *sui*[4] | 數 *shu*[4] |
| | 高 *kao*[1] | 的 *ti* | 了 *liao* | 年 *nien*[2] | 爺。*yeh*[2] | 兒。*'rh* |

One's age.

The Emperor; *lit.*, the lord of 10,000 years.

How old are you?

*Obs.*—This is not a very polite form, the ordinary one being *kuei*[4] *kêng*[1], which will be met with later.

A man of mature years; well advanced in life. Not applied to persons under sixty.

What is your age, sir?

*Obs.*—This form is only used to men over forty years of age, the limit being generally indicated by the moustache, which is seldom allowed to grow before that age, unless in the case of officials of a certain rank.

**956.** 因 *yin*[1], a cause; because of.

**957.** 爲 *wei*[4], because of. Not to be confounded with *wei*[2] (848).

**958.** 緣 *yüan*[2], origin; clue; cause.

**959.** 故 *ku*[4], ancient; a cause of.

**960.** 耽, 躭 *tan*[1], to loiter; to delay. The second is the commoner form.

961. Examples :—

| | | | | | |
|---|---|---|---|---|---|
| 那 *na*$^{4}$ | 爲 *wei*$^{4}$ | 會 *hui*$^{4}$ | 你 *ni*$^{3}$ | 有 *yu*$^{3}$ | 爲 *wei*$^{4}$ |
| 緣 *yüan*$^{2}$ | 甚 *shên*$^{2}$ | 兒 *'rh* | 躭 *tan*$^{1}$ | 病 *ping*$^{4}$ | 甚 *shên*$^{2}$ |
| 故 *ku*$^{4}$ | 麽 *mo*$^{1}$ | 纔 *ts'ai*$^{2}$ | 擱 *ko*$^{1}$ | 不 *pu*$^{4}$ | 麽。*mo* |
| 難 *nan*$^{2}$ | 緣 *yüan*$^{2}$ | 來 *lai*$^{2}$ | 到 *tao*$^{4}$ | 能 *nêng*$^{2}$ | 因 *yin*$^{1}$ |
| 說。*shuo*$^{1}$ | 故 *ku*$^{4}$ | 因 *yin*$^{1}$ | 這 *chê*$^{4}$ | 去。*ch'ü*$^{4}$ | 爲 *wei*$^{4}$ |

Why?

I cannot go because I am unwell.

What is the reason for delaying your arrival until now?

*Obs.*—*Lit.*, you delay put [on one side] until this while, only then come is because of what cause? *Tan* is never used alone colloquially, being generally combined with *ko*, as above, or with *wu* (962).

The reasons are hard to give (or, difficult to explain).

962. 悞, 誤 *wu*$^{4}$, to leave undone; to fail in doing; to be in error; to hinder. Both forms are used.

963. 容 *jung*$^{2}$, *yung*$^{2}$, alone, to receive; to contain; to tolerate; to allow; also, the countenance. But with the following *i*$^{4}$, easy.

964. 易 *yi*$^{4}$, *i*$^{4}$, alone, to change; but with *jung*$^{2}$, easy.

965. Examples :—

| | | | | | | |
|---|---|---|---|---|---|---|
| 從 *ts'ung*$^{1}$ | 討 *t'ao*$^{3}$ | 屋 *wu*$^{1}$ | 辦。*pan*$^{4}$ | 躭 *tan*$^{1}$ | 悞 *wu*$^{4}$ | 怎 *tsên*$^{3}$ |
| 從 *ts'ung*$^{1}$ | 人 *jên*$^{2}$ | 裡 *li*$^{3}$ | 這 *chê*$^{4}$ | 悞 *wu*$^{4}$ | 會 *hui*$^{4}$ | 麽 *mo* |
| 容 *jung*$^{1}$ | 嫌 *hsien*$^{2}$ | 容 *jung*$^{2}$ | 桌 *cho*$^{1}$ | 工 *kung*$^{1}$ | 他 *t'a*$^{1}$ | 躭 *tan*$^{1}$ |
| 容 *jung*$^{1}$ | 沒 *mei*$^{2}$ | 不 *pu*$^{2}$ | 子 *tzŭ* | 夫 *fu*$^{1}$ | 的 *ti* | 悞 *wu*$^{4}$ |
| 兒 *'rh* | 人 *jên*$^{2}$ | 下。*hsia*$^{4}$ | 尺 *ch'ih*$^{2}$ | 那 *na*$^{4}$ | 意 *i*$^{4}$ | 了 *liao* |
| 的。*ti* | 能 *nêng*$^{2}$ | 他 *t'a*$^{1}$ | 寸 *ts'un*$^{4}$ | 不 *pu*$^{4}$ | 思 *ssŭ*$^{1}$ | 半 *pan*$^{4}$ |
| | 容 *jung*$^{2}$ | 過 *kuo*$^{4}$ | 太 *t'ai*$^{4}$ | 容 *jung*$^{2}$ | 了。*liao* | 天。*t'ien*$^{1}$ |
| | 他。*t'a*$^{1}$ | 於 *yü*$^{2}$ | 大 *ta*$^{4}$ | 易 *i*$^{4}$ | 別 *pieh*$^{2}$ | 我 *wo*$^{3}$ |

How is it you have delayed so long?

I have mistaken his meaning (or intention).

*Obs.*—*Lit.*, I have mistakenly understood. *See* 129.

Don't delay.

It is not easy to manage (or, deal with).

This table is (the dimensions of this table are) too large; there is not space for it in the room.

He is too aggravating; no one can tolerate him.

In a leisurely (or deliberate) manner.

966. 勁 *chin*$^{4}$, muscular strength; also, in combination, inclination.

967. 塗 *t'u*$^{2}$, *tu*$^{4}$, properly, mud; but in *hu*$^{2}$-*tu*$^{4}$, stupid, read *tu*$^{4}$.

968. 喜 *hsi*$^{3}$, joy; to be pleased; to like.

969. 歡 *huan*¹, to rejoice; to show pleasure.

970. 惜 *hsi*¹, to pity; to feel for; to like; to spare; to save (economically).

971. Examples :—

| | | | | | | |
|---|---|---|---|---|---|---|
| 們 *mên* | 可 *k'o*³ | 你 *ni*³ | 喜 *hsi*³ | 途 *tu*⁴ | 勁 *chin*⁴ | 這 *chê*⁴ |
| 倆 *lia*³ | 惜 *hsi*¹ | 道 *tao*⁴ | 歡 *huan*¹ | 極 *chi*² | 兒, *'rh* | 兩 *liang*³ |
| 很 *hên*³ | 得 *tê* | 喜。*hsi*³ | 他, *t'a*¹ | 了 *liao* | 他 *t'a*¹ | 天 *t'ien*¹ |
| 對 *tui*⁴ | 很。*hên*³ | 他 *t'a*¹ | 喜 *hsi*³ | 我 *wo*³ | 那 *na*⁴ | 身 *shên*¹ |
| 勁 *chin*⁴ | 愛 *ai*⁴ | 的 *ti* | 事。*shih*⁴ | 實 *shih*² | 個 *ko*⁴ | 上 *shang*⁴ |
| 兒 *'rh* | 惜 *hsi*¹ | 少 *shao*⁴ | 我 *wo*³ | 在 *tsai*⁴ | 人 *jên*² | 沒 *mei*² |
| | 他 *t'a*¹ | 爺 *yeh*² | 給 *kei*³ | 不 *pu*⁴ | 糊 *hu*² | 有 *yu*³ |

These two days past I have had no strength in my body (I have felt limp).
That man is utterly stupid; I certainly do not like him.
A wedding (generally); a birth, etc.; any event which is the subject of congratulation.
I congratulate you.
His son is much to be pitied.
*Obs.—Lit.*, his son is a [men] ought to (may) pity one (*tê=ti*) very.
To be fond of.
Those two hit it off (get on together, suit each other) very well.
*Obs.—Lit.*, their muscle corresponds. The origin of this expression is said to be found in the explanation that as their muscular strength corresponds, is equal, each would be careful not to come to blows with the other.

972. 欺 *ch'i*¹, to deceive.

973. 哄 *hung*³, to beguile.

974. 誆, 誑 *k'uang*¹, to attempt to gain one's end by lies, false promises, etc.

975. 騙 *p'ien*⁴, to defraud one of.

976. 屜 *t'i*⁴, a drawer; a tray.

977. Examples :—

| | | | | | | |
|---|---|---|---|---|---|---|
| 把 *pa*³ | 個 *ko*⁴ | 誆 *k'uang*¹ | 他 *t'a*¹ | 方 *fang*¹ | 有 *yu*³ | 那 *na*⁴ |
| 那 *na*⁴ | 抽 *ch'ou*¹ | 騙 *p'ien*⁴ | 把 *pa*³ | 兒。*'rh* | 欺 *ch'i*¹ | 個 *ko*⁴ |
| 個 *ko*⁴ | 屜 *t'i*⁴ | 了 *liao* | 人 *jên*² | 你 *ni*³ | 哄 *hung*³ | 人 *jên*² |
| 關 *kuan*¹ | 抽 *ch'ou*¹ | 去, *ch'ü*⁴ | 家 *chia*¹ | 別 *pieh*² | 人 *jên*² | 老 *lao*³ |
| 上 *shang*⁴ | 出 *ch'u*¹ | 把 *pa*³ | 的 *ti* | 哄 *hung*³ | 的 *ti* | 實 *shih*² |
| 罷。*pa*⁴ | 來 *lai*² | 這 *chê*⁴ | 表 *piao*³ | 我。*wo*³ | 地 *ti*⁴ | 沒 *mei*² |

That man is honest, and does not cheat in any way.
*Obs.—Lit.*, has not cheating men's places.
Don't deceive me.
He did a man out of his watch.
Pull this drawer out and shut that one to.

## EXERCISE XXXVI.

1 這櫃子裏的抽屜拉不出來。你使勁一抽、就拉出來了。

1. The drawer in this wardrobe (or, chest of drawers) won't come (pull) out. Give it a good hard pull and you will get it out.

*Obs.*—Good hard pull, etc. : *lit.*, you use muscle one pull out, and you will drag it out.

2 那一件事就悞了是甚麼緣故、那緣故太多、不容易說。

2. What is the reason why that affair has not succeeded (or, has lagged)? There are a great many reasons; too many to make it easy to tell them.

3 您這位少爺今年多大歲數兒。小兒今年十八歲了、他的生日是六月初八、過年就要給他辦事咯。趕到您那兒辦喜事的日子我必要去道喜去。

3. What is the age of this son of yours, sir? My son is eighteen; his birthday is on the 8th of the 6th moon; next year we are going to marry him. When the wedding day comes I shall be sure to go and offer my congratulations.

*Obs.*—Marry : *lit.*, we want to arrange matters for him ; *yao* being a sign of the future tense. Note that the father speaks of his son's marriage as *pan shih* simply, not *hsi shih*.

4 你別打算欺哄我、我告訴你、那不是件容易事。我很是你的硬對兒、若論詎騙人、你可不是個兒。

4. Don't try and deceive me, for [allow] me to tell you, it is not an easy matter. I am quite a match for you, and if you come to (discuss) cheating, you are not up to my form.

*Obs.*—Up to my form ; *pu shih ko-'rh* : *lit.*, are not a piece, *q.d.*, of a piece with me. The expression is a slang one.

5 可惜那個人過於糊塗、說不明白。就悞了我半天的工夫。

5. What a pity it is that that man is so exceedingly stupid that he cannot make himself intelligible. He has taken up ever so much of my time.

*Obs.*—Exceedingly : exceeds in the matter of stupidity. *See* 343.

6 我們倆彼此很對勁、可惜他那個兄弟很會欺哄人、去年還誆騙了我幾兩銀子呢。

6. He and I suit each other very well. Unfortunately, his brother is a great cheat; he did me out of some taels last year.

*Obs.*—Great cheat: is very competent (well knows how) to cheat people.

7 我最不喜歡他待有年紀兒人的那個樣子。我告訴你、那都是小的時候兒、老家兒不管他的緣故。

7. I particularly object to his manner towards elderly people. I'll tell you the reason [of his behaviour]; it's all because his elders did not keep him in order in his childhood.

*Obs* 1.—I'll tell you the reason, etc.; *lit.*, I tell you that all is in childhood elders not control him's cause. It would not be incorrect were *yüan ku* to precede the cause, as in the translation.

*Obs.* 2.—Elders: *lao chia-'rh*, the elders of his family, inclusive of relations, such as uncles, aunts, etc.

8 他是個安靜人、不論甚麼事都是從從容容兒的辦。

8. He is a steady fellow, and does everything, no matter what, in a quiet, methodical way.

*Turn the following into Chinese.* (KEY, EXERCISE XXXVI.)

1. After the new year you will be a year older.

*Obs.*—The Chinese reckon age by the year, commencing with the 1st of the 1st moon, the fraction of the year counting in favour of the child; thus, a child born in the 10th moon would be two years old on the 1st of the following 1st moon.

2. How old is your father? My father is now eighty-two. A person of his years may be considered an aged man.

*Obs.*—A person of his years, etc.: *lit.*, [with] this kind of age he also can be considered to be a possessing longevity number's man.

3. Yesterday I waited the whole day for you; why did you not go and look me up? There was a reason for it. I was just going to start, when at the moment, as luck would have it, a distant relation turned up (came); there was nothing for it but to sit down and talk with him, and there I was kept. He only left after a long time, and as it was then getting late, I did not go and look you up.

*Obs.* 1.— I sat with him, etc.; *lit.*, there being no plan I accompanied (entertained, *p'ei*) him sitting down [and] talked, being delayed to the spot (*tan wu chu liao*); the *chu* indicating the impossibility of getting away.

*Obs.* 2.—He only left, etc.: *lit.*, after half a day had passed he only then (*ts'ai*) left.

4. It is quite near for you to get into the main street where you live, which is very convenient indeed for buying anything [one wants]. The little lane in which we live is most inconvenient; it is by no means easy to buy anything, however small.

*Obs.*—By no means easy: *lit.*, to buy a little of anything truly not easy.

5. That man has not an atom of muscle about him, and yet he thinks of learning

military [exercises] (studying for the army). How foolish he is !

*Obs.*—How foolish : *lit.*, in his heart there is how much stupidity !

6. You like this vegetable, don't you? Unfortunately (it's a pity), there isn't any more.

7. Don't deceive me; just now I saw there was a whole lot in that drawer.

8. You are not cheated when you buy things in shops, but when you buy them in the street you have to look out; they mostly sell you bad things and cheat you out of your money.

*Obs.* 1.—You are not cheated : *lit.*, in the shops buy things [they] do not cheat people.

*Obs.* 2.—Mostly : *to* (7).

978. 屢 *lü*$^3$, frequent.

979. 公 *kung*$^1$, public; just disinterested. Also, as will be seen later, a gentleman.

980. 私 *ssŭ*$^1$, private; illicit; interested.

981. 務 *wu*$^4$, business; the verb *must*.

982. Examples :—

| | | | | | | |
|---|---|---|---|---|---|---|
| 道 *tao*$^4$ | 私。*ssŭ*$^1$ | 賣 *mai*$^4$ | 私 *ssŭ*$^1$ | 事 *shih*$^4$ | 的 *ti* | 屢 *lü*$^3$ |
| 人。*jên*$^2$ | 他 *t'a*$^1$ | 人 *jên*$^2$ | 事。*shih*$^4$ | 務 *wu*$^4$ | 說 *shuo*$^1$ | 次。*tz'ŭ*$^4$ |
| 私 *ssŭ*$^1$ | 是 *shih*$^4$ | 不 *pu*$^4$ | 家 *chia*$^1$ | 必 *pi*$^{2\,4}$ | 他。*t'a*$^1$ | 我 *wo*$^3$ |
| 情。*ch'ing*$^2$ | 個 *ko*$^4$ | 准 *chun*$^3$ | 務。*wu*$^4$ | 用 *yung*$^4$ | 辦 *pan*$^4$ | 屢 *lü*$^3$ |
| | 公 *kung*$^1$ | 走 *tsou*$^3$ | 買 *mai*$^3$ | 心。*hsin*$^1$ | 公 *kung*$^1$ | 次 *tz'ŭ*$^4$ |

Many times.

I have reprimanded him time after time.

In transacting public business there must positively be attention (attention is essential).

*Obs.*—Note that *wu pi* is stronger than either *pi* or *wu* alone. We can either say *wu pi*$^2$ or *wu pi*$^4$.

Private affairs.

Household affairs.

Merchants are not authorised (forbidden) to smuggle.

*Obs.*—Smuggle : *lit.*, walk secretly.

He is a just man (a man of just principles).

A private understanding; or, private relations, in a good or a bad sense. Where one of the parties is a woman, always in a bad sense.

983. 閒 *hsien*$^2$, empty; without occupation; leisure.

984. 悶 *mên*$^4$, sad; in low spirits.

985. 慌 *huang*$^1$, an intensive of adjectives describing disagreeable sensations. Also, scared; agitated.

986. 樂 *lê*$^4$, *lo*$^4$, joy in the heart; gladness in the countenance. Also, to laugh.

987. 煩 *fan*$^2$, to put, or be put to, trouble.

988. 急 *chi²*, quick in movement or temper; rushing of water. With *chao²* (45), anxious; eager; impatient. ← See 5-31

989. Examples:—

| | | | | | | |
|---|---|---|---|---|---|---|
| 他 *t'a¹* | 的。*ti* | 帶 *tai⁴* | 散 *san⁴* | 要 *yao⁴* | 的 *ti* | 我 *wo³* |
| 那 *na⁴* | 別 *pieh²* | 了 *liao* | 悶。*mên⁴* | 請 *ch'ing³* | 慌。*huang¹* | 沒 *mei²* |
| 話 *hua⁴* | 着 *chao²* | 去。*ch'ü⁴* | 這 *chê⁴* | 客 *k'o⁴* | 我 *wo³* | 有 *yu³* |
| 他 *t'a¹* | 急。*chi²* | 慌 *huang¹* | 包 *pao¹* | 樂 *lo⁴* | 悶 *mên⁴* | 閒 *hsien²* |
| 樂 *lo⁴* | 我 *wo³* | 慌 *huang¹* | 兒 *'rh* | 一 *i¹* | 死 *ssŭ³* | 空 *k'ung⁴* |
| 了。*liao* | 告 *kao⁴* | 忙 *mang²* | 煩 *fan²* | 樂 *lo⁴* | 了。*liao* | 兒。*'rh* |
| | 訴 *su⁴* | 忙 *mang²* | 你 *ni³* | 散 *san⁴* | 我 *wo³* | 悶 *mên⁴* |

I have no leisure. *See* 199.

Much bored; intensely dull.

I am bored to death.

I want to ask some guests to have a good time, and dispel my melancholy (cheer me up a bit).

May I trouble you to take this parcel with you?

Flurried; flustered.

Don't be anxious (get excited; or, be impatient).

When I told him that (or, gave him that message), he laughed.

990. 奉 *fêng⁴*, properly, to raise the hands, as when presenting anything; to receive, as orders, an appointment, etc.

991. 求 *ch'iu²*, to request; to crave; to seek.

992. 託 *t'o¹*, to commission; to request one to act as agent.

993. 發 *fa¹*, to issue forth; to cause to issue; to send.

994. 信 *hsin⁴*, good faith; to believe; a letter. Also, to follow, as one's inclination.

995. Examples:—

| | | | | | |
|---|---|---|---|---|---|
| 不 *pu⁴* | 的 *ti* | 個 *ko⁴* | 託 *t'o¹* | 您。*nin²* | 我 *wo³* |
| 得 *tê²* | 話 *hua⁴* | 人 *jên²* | 您 *nin²* | 求 *ch'iu²* | 有 *yu³* |
| 的。*ti* | 我 *wo³* | 送 *sung⁴* | 替 *t'i⁴* | 老 *lao³* | 件 *chien⁴* |
| 信 *hsin⁴* | 不 *pu²* | 信 *hsin⁴* | 我 *wo³* | 爺 *yeh²* | 事 *shih⁴* |
| 口 *k'ou³* | 信。*hsin⁴* | 去。*ch'ü⁴* | 打 *ta³* | 的 *ti* | 奉 *fêng⁴* |
| 說。*shuo¹* | 信 *hsin⁴* | 你 *ni³* | 發 *fa¹* | 恩。*ngên¹* | 求 *ch'iu²* |

I have a favour to ask of you.

I crave Your Honour's clemency (or favour). Would you (I would commission you to) send a man for me with a letter (or, to take a letter)?

*Obs.*—Note *sung hsin*, to send a letter; *sung hsin-'rh*, to send a message.

I do not believe what you say.

It is incredible.

To be free with one's tongue; to say what comes into one's head.

*Obs.*—Note *hsin* in the sense of to follow one's inclination.

**996.** 雇 *ku*$^4$, to hire, as a servant, horse, conveyance; not said of a house, furniture, etc.

**997.** 孩 *hai*$^2$, a child.

**998.** 撒 *sa*$^1$, to scatter from the hand, as seed, etc.

**999.** 謊 *huang*$^3$, falsehood.

**1000.** 賺 *chuan*$^4$, to gain, as money.

**1001.** 星 *hsing*$^1$, a star.

**1002.** 所 *so*$^3$, properly, a place; the relative pronoun *that which*. With the verb *yu*$^3$, to be, it means all. With *i*$^3$ (125), it means therefore, consequently (*see* 125).

**1003.** Examples:—

雇 *ku*$^4$ 一 *i*$^2$ 個 *ko*$^4$ 小 *hsiao*$^3$ 孩 *hai*$^2$ 子 *tzŭ* 送 *sung*$^4$ 信。*hsin*$^4$
雇 *ku*$^4$. 船。*ch'uan*$^2$ 好 *hao*$^3$ 孩 *hai*$^2$ 子 *tzŭ* 去 *ch'ü*$^4$ 玩 *wan*$^2$ 兒 *'rh*
去 *ch'ü*$^4$ 罷。*pa*$^4$ 他 *t'a*$^1$ 常 *ch'ang*$^2$ 撒 *sa*$^1$ 謊 *huang*$^3$ 所 *so*$^3$ 以 *i*$^3$
沒 *mei*$^2$ 人 *jên*$^2$ 信 *hsin*$^4$ 他。*t'a*$^1$ 說 *shuo*$^1$ 謊 *huang*$^3$ 話。*hua*$^4$ 掃 *sao*$^4$
帚 *chou*$^3$ 星。*hsing*$^1$ 流 *liu*$^2$ 星。*hsing*$^1$ 雖 *sui*$^1$ 然 *jan*$^2$ 他 *t'a*$^1$ 的 *ti*
本 *pên*$^3$ 事 *shih*$^4$ 大 *ta*$^4$ 也 *yeh*$^3$ 不 *pu*$^4$ 能 *nêng*$^2$ 賺 *chuan*$^4$ 錢。*ch'ien*$^2$
所 *so*$^3$ 有 *yu*$^3$ 的 *ti* 書 *shu*$^1$ 全 *ch'üan*$^2$ 好。*hao*$^3$

To hire a small boy to carry a letter.

*Obs.*—Note that *hai-tzŭ* may mean a boy or a girl.

To hire (or charter) a boat or ship.

Go and play, that's a good child.

He constantly tells lies, so nobody believes him.

To say what is not the truth; to tell a falsehood.

A comet. A meteor.

Although his ability is great, he cannot make money.

*Obs.*—It would be equally correct to say *t'a ti pên shih sui jan ta.*

All the books that there are are good.

*Obs.*—All that there are: *lit.*, that which there are of (*ti*) books are all good. Note that *so yu* must be followed by some word signifying all, such as *tou* or *ch'üan*, the *so yu* being only intensive.

## EXERCISE XXXVII.

1 您公事忙不忙。也不算很忙、天天兒總有閒着的時候兒。

1. Do your public duties keep you busy, sir? I cannot be considered to be very busy, as I always have some leisure time during each day.

2 我有一件事情奉求。李老爺該我的那一筆賬、我屢次上他那兒去要、他們的人總說沒空兒。不見我。您多偺閒着、託您替我要一要纔好。

2. I have a favour to ask of you. I have been time after time to Li *lao-yeh's* place to ask for payment of that account which he owes me, but his people always say that he is not at leisure, and he won't see me. Would you, when you have nothing to do, ask him for payment on my behalf?

*Obs.*—The final *ts'ai hao*, then it will be all right, is omitted in the translation, as it seems unnecessary to the completion of the sentence.

3 昨兒我一個相好的、因爲孩子病、心裏煩悶、急要發信到鄉下問一問、託我替他雇一個人送信。我雇了一個人、打發他去了、到了後半天他回來、說沒有找着。我知道他是撒謊、所以我不肯給他錢。

3. Yesterday a friend of mine who was in great distress about a child of his in the country that is ill, wanted to send a note off at once to inquire how he was, and asked me to hire someone to take it. I did hire a man, and sent him off, but he came back in the afternoon and said that he had not been able to find the place. I knew he was not telling the truth, so I would not give him any money.

*Obs.* 1.—In the afternoon: *tao*, when the time came to be afternoon.
*Obs.* 2.—Find the place: *see* Note on *chao* at the end of Exercise XL.

4 小價錢買來的。大價兒賣、那就是賺錢。貨是一兩銀子一斤買的、還是一兩銀子賣的、所以不能賺錢。

4. To buy cheap and sell dear is *chuan*[4] *ch'ien*[2] (to make money). The goods cost a tael a catty and were sold at a tael a catty; there is consequently nothing made on the transaction.

*Obs.*—To buy: *ti* representing the goods, or any like word; *lit.*, [when men] at a great price sell [they] at a small price bought *ti*, goods, articles = the goods bought by them, *na chiu*, that then = such a transaction, is making money.

5 他帶着一車子私貨進城、門上的官人過來查問、他慌慌忙忙的說是行李、官人不信、把箱子打開一看、果然裝的都是私貨、所以全入了官了。

5. He brought a barrow-load of smuggled goods into the city, [and when] the official underlings at the gate came forward to ask what they were (*lit.*, to search and inquire), he said in a flurried sort of way that it was personal baggage. They didn't believe him, and when they opened the boxes they saw at once that, sure enough, the boxes contained nothing but contraband articles, which were consequently all confiscated.

*Obs.* 1.—Note *ch'ê-tzŭ*, or *hsiao ch'ê-tzŭ*, a barrow.

*Obs.* 2.—Sure enough: *kuo jan*; *lit.*, indeed, in very truth, thus, they were, etc.

6 天上的星星雖多、掃帚星可不大常見。

6. Although there are plenty of stars in the sky, comets are not often seen.

7 我鄉下買了個所在、趕到夏天在那兒住着、小孩子們必是樂極了。

7. I have bought a place in the country and when we come to live there in the summer the children are sure to be as happy as possible (happy in the extreme).

*Obs.*—Place: *so tsai*; *lit.*, where [one] is. It is difficult to account for the use of *tsai* in this connexion, though colloquially *so* is seldom used without it in its meaning of place.

*Turn the following into Chinese.* (KEY, EXERCISE XXXVII.)

1. What do you generally occupy yourself with? How is it that on the repeated occasions that I have been to your place your servants always answer me that you are not at home. Just think! what spare time have I got? If it is not public business [that occupies me], it is private, and my household affairs, too, are numerous. Nothing of any kind can be done without me, so I have never any leisure time.

*Obs.* 1.—Spare time: *kung fu*, short for *hsien*[2] *kung fu*.

*Obs.* 2.—Nothing of any kind, etc.: *lit.*, what one kind not must I manage?

*Obs.* 3.—So: *see* 1002.

2. If a man is out of spirits, the best thing he can do is to take a walk in the streets. When he sees some trifle that amuses him (in which he can find pleasure), his mind of course is no longer troubled. If one chances on a rainy day, so that one cannot go out, it makes one very impatient.

*Obs.*—Chances on: *lit.*, runs against.

3. I have a pressing matter [in hand], and must trouble somebody to take a message to him. You are at leisure and have nothing to do, so I beg you to take him the message. I cannot (it won't do), I have no time to spare; please ask somebody else. In my

語言自邇集



opinion it will be all the same (all will do) no matter whom you send.

4. That child is given to lying. I sent him to hire a cart, and he came back and told me there were no carts on the street. I didn't believe him, and sent another person to hire one. It came in a short time, [so] I knew that the boy wanted to make a squeeze (make money), and that the bargain was not concluded because the carter wouldn't follow suit in the lie (*lit.*, follow him in lying).

*Obs.* 1.—It came in a short time: *lit.*, in not a great while, then it hired came.

*Obs.* 2.—The bargain, etc.: *lit.*, therefore the hiring was not completed.

5. His business pays well; he sells miscellaneous articles of every kind, so he cannot but make money. Although it's a grocer's shop, the business is a first rate one.

**1004.** 承 *ch'êng*$^{2}$, to receive or undertake on commission; to be the recipient of, as favours.

**1005.** 差 *ch'ai*$^{1}$, to send, whether as an envoy or, on ordinary occasions, as an official messenger. Read *ch'a*$^{1}$, different; to differ: *ch'a*$^{4}$, to be out; wrong.

**1006.** 任 *jên*$^{4}$, to hold an office; the office so held. Also, a trust or burden; to allow, in the sense of *p'ing*$^{2}$ (722).

**1007.** 署 *shu*$^{3}$, an official bureau. *Shu*$^{4}$, provisional tenure of office.

**1008.** 習 *hsi*$^{2}$, to practise when learning.

**1009.** Examples:—

| | | | | | | |
|---|---|---|---|---|---|---|
| 不 *pu*$^{4}$ | 署 *shu*$^{4}$ | 不 *pu*$^{2}$ | 使。*shih*$^{3}$ | 差。*ch'ai*$^{1}$ | 承 *ch'êng*$^{2}$ | 這 *chê*$^{4}$ |
| 多。*to*$^{1}$ | 理。*li*$^{3}$ | 是 *shih*$^{4}$ | 三 *san*$^{1}$ | 差 *ch'ai*$^{1}$ | 了。*liao* | 事 *shih*$^{4}$ |
| 不 *pu*$^{4}$ | 學 *hsio*$^{2}$ | 實 *shih*$^{2}$ | 年 *nien*$^{2}$ | 人。*jên*$^{2}$ | 承 *ch'êng*$^{2}$ | 情 *ch'ing*$^{2}$ |
| 差 *ch'a*$^{1}$ | 習 *hsi*$^{2}$ | 任 *jên*$^{4}$ | 任 *jên*$^{4}$ | 都 *tou*$^{1}$ | 情。*ch'ing*$^{2}$ | 沒 *mei*$^{2}$ |
| 甚 *shên*$^{2}$ | 一 *i*$^{4}$ | 不 *pu*$^{2}$ | 滿 *man*$^{3}$ | 說 *shuo*$^{1}$ | 承 *ch'êng*$^{2}$ | 有 *yu*$^{3}$ |
| 麽。*mo* | 年。*nien*$^{2}$ | 過 *kuo*$^{4}$ | 了。*liao* | 有 *yu*$^{3}$ | 問。*wên*$^{4}$ | 人 *jên*$^{2}$ |
| | 差 *ch'a*$^{1}$ | 是 *shih*$^{4}$ | 他 *t'a*$^{1}$ | 差 *ch'ai*$^{1}$ | 聽 *t'ing*$^{1}$ | 應 *ying*$^{1}$ |

Nobody has undertaken this business (*lit.*, consented to undertake).

*Obs.*—*Ying*$^{1}$, although in the 1st tone, has the force of *ying*$^{4}$ (781), not of *ying*$^{1}$ (726).

To be the recipient of favours or good offices; I am obliged to you for your good offices.

Thanks for your kind inquiries.

An office servant or messenger (*lit.*, one who waits to be sent on an errand).

A yamên "runner"; or, to send a person, *q.d.*, on an errand.

They all say they have official business.

*Obs.*—*Ch'ai shih*: *lit.*, official sending employment; employment in an official capacity.

The time for which the post is held expires in three years.

His is not the substantive (actual) appointment; he is only acting.

To learn for a year; a year's novitiate.

Almost; very nearly the same.

Little difference.

*Obs.*—This and the foregoing phrase, which are in constant use, may be varied to *ch'a pu yüan*$^{3}$ *liao* (371), *ch'a pu liao to shao*, etc.

1010. 部 *pu*$^4$, any great category; a tribunal or board; the numerative of books.

1011. 堂 *t'ang*$^2$, a large hall; in certain departments of State, collective of the chiefs ot the establishment.

1012. 司 *ssŭ*$^1$, to manage; to direct; to manage one of the departments in a great office; the department so managed.

1013. 委 *wei*$^3$, to depute, as a higher officer a lower.

1014. 員 *yüan*$^2$, any officer of civil or military service.

1015. 吏 *li*$^4$, properly, to exercise authority over others, is used with reference to the civil service in various ways; also, to mean clerks.

1016. 役 *i*$^4$, *yi*$^4$, properly, any employé; but especially such people as constables, etc.

1017. 皂 *tsao*$^4$, properly, black; the *tsao* of *fei-tsao*, soap (*see* 279).

1018. 隸 *li*$^4$, properly, one under the authority of another.

1019. Examples:—

| | | | | | | |
|---|---|---|---|---|---|---|
| 幾 *chi*$^3$. | 麼, *mo* | 書 *shu*$^1$ | 極 *chi*$^2$ | 那 *na*$^4$ | 上. *shang*$^4$ | 六 *liu*$^4$ |
| 位 *wei*$^4$ | 一 *i*$^4$ | 辦 *pan*$^1$ | 了。*liao* | 些 *hsieh*$^1$ | 司 *ssŭ*$^1$ | 部 *pu*$^4$ |
| 官 *kuan*$^1$ | 班 *pan*$^1$ | 不 *pu*$^4$ | 書 *shu*$^1$ | 衙 *ya*$^2$ | 派 *p'ai*$^4$. | 的 *ti* |
| 員。*yüan*$^2$ | 皂 *tsao*$^4$ | 差 *ch'a*$^1$ | 吏 *li*$^4$ | 役 *yi*$^4$ | 委 *wei*$^3$ | 堂 *t'ang*$^2$ |
| | 隸。*li*$^4$ | 甚 *shên*$^2$ | 同 *t'ung*$^2$ | 壞 *huai*$^4$ | 員。*yüan*$^2$ | 官。*kuan*$^1$ |

The chiefs of the Six Boards in the capital.

*Obs.*—Both Presidents and Vice-Presidents of Boards are so called, as also chiefs of other departments.

The high authorities (or, chief of the department) are sending a weiyuan (or deputy).

*Obs.*—The word *wei-yüan* has become anglicised in China.

Those yamên runners are utterly corrupt (or depraved).

*Shu li* are almost the same as *shu pan* (yamên clerks) (there is no appreciable difference).

*Obs.*—*Shu li* are clerks in a provincial yamên; *shu pan* are clerks in a metropolitan Board. Note the tone.

A body of runners (or lictors).

*Obs.*—They are probably so called from the colour of the dress they wear; in Peking the black coat is not insisted on. For *pan*, *see* 414.

Several officials (or, how many?).

1020. 供 *kung*$^1$, properly, to supply for use. *Kung*$^4$, to accuse; evidence.

1021. 稟 *ping*$^3$, to represent to a superior; the petition or document in which the representation is made. The original form took the 115th Radical, under which it will be found in the dictionary.

1022. 帖 *t'ieh*$^3$, a slip of silk or paper with writing on it; also, under certain circumstances, read *t'ieh*$^4$.

**1023.** 存 *ts'un*$^{2}$, to preserve; to retain.

**1024.** 稿 *kao*$^{3}$, the rough draft of a document.

**1025.** Examples :—

| | | | | | |
|---|---|---|---|---|---|
| 屜 *t'i*$^{4}$ | 把 *pa*$^{3}$ | 地 *ti*$^{4}$ | 說 *shuo*$^{1}$ | 帖 *t'ieh*$^{3}$ | 我 *wo*$^{3}$ |
| 裡。*li*$^{3}$ | 稿 *kao*$^{3}$ | 方 *fang*$^{1}$ | 得。*tê* | 告 *kao*$^{4}$ | 寫 *hsieh*$^{3}$ |
| 上 *shang*$^{4}$ | 子 *tzŭ* | 官、*kuan*$^{1}$ | 口 *k'ou*$^{3}$ | 他。*t'a*$^{1}$ | 了 *liao* |
| 供。*kung*$^{1}$ | 存 *ts'un*$^{2}$ | 起 *ch'i*$^{3}$ | 供、*kung*$^{1}$ | 供 *kung*$^{1}$ | 一 *i*$^{2}$ |
| 名 *ming*$^{2}$ | 在 *tsai*$^{4}$ | 稿 *kao*$^{3}$ | 稟 *ping*$^{3}$ | 他 *t'a*$^{1}$ | 個 *ko*$^{4}$ |
| 帖 *t'ieh*$^{3}$ | 抽 *ch'ou*$^{1}$ | 子。*tzŭ* | 報 *pao*$^{4}$ | 也 *yeh*$^{3}$ | 稟 *ping*$^{3}$ |

I have written a petition accusing him (I have brought an action against him).
One can also say *kung* (implicating him).
Oral evidence.
To petition (report to) the local authorities.
To draw out (to prepare) a draft.
Keep the draft in the drawer.
To make offerings to an idol (or, before the tablets of ancestors).
A visiting card.

*Obs.*—Also called *ming-p'ien* (see Exercise XX, 10, Obs.). The difference is technical; any teacher will explain it.

**1026.** 陳 *ch'ên*$^{2}$, to spread out; hence, to state. Here, and very commonly, stale; used.

**1027.** 案 *$^{ng}$an*$^{4}$, in legal or official language, a case or question. Also, the correspondence regarding a case; hence, records.

**1028.** 照 *chao*$^{4}$, properly, to reflect light; hence, according to.

**1029.** 式 *shih*$^{4}$, a fashion; the fashion.

**1030.** Examples :—

| | | | | | | |
|---|---|---|---|---|---|---|
| 沒 *mei*$^{3}$ | 式 *shih*$^{4}$ | 辦。*pan*$^{4}$ | 陳 *ch'ên*$^{2}$ | 辦 *pan*$^{4}$ | 都 *tou*$^{1}$ | 不 *pu*$^{2}$ |
| 了 *liao*$^{3}$ | 樣。*yang*$^{4}$ | 照 *chao*$^{4}$ | 米。*mi*$^{3}$ | 的。*ti* | 是 *shih*$^{4}$ | 論 *lun*$^{4}$ |
| 咯。*lo* | 這 *chê*$^{4}$ | 着 *cho* | 按 *$^{ng}$an*$^{4}$ | 我 *wo*$^{3}$ | 照 *chao*$^{4}$ | 誰 *shui*$^{2}$ |
| 照 *chao*$^{4}$ | 一 *i*$^{2}$ | 現 *hsien*$^{4}$ | 照 *chao*$^{4}$ | 喜 *hsi*$^{3}$ | 着 *cho* | 起 *ch'i*$^{3}$ |
| 會。*hui*$^{4}$ | 案 *$^{ng}$an*$^{4}$ | 在 *tsai*$^{4}$ | 公 *kung*$^{1}$ | 歡 *huan*$^{1}$ | 陳 *ch'ên*$^{2}$ | 稿 *kao*$^{3}$ |
| | 還 *hai*$^{2}$ | 的 *ti* | 道 *tao*$^{4}$ | 吃 *ch'ih*$^{1}$ | 案 *$^{ng}$an*$^{4}$ | 子 *tzŭ* |

No matter who prepares the draft, it is always done according to the precedents on record.

*Obs.*—Precedents: *lit.*, old cases.

I like to eat old rice.
To act (or, deal with a matter) in accordance with justice.
According to the present style (or fashion).
This case is not yet finished (or closed).
An official communication; or, to write officially.

*Obs.*—The term is almost exclusively confined to correspondence between foreign and Chinese officials.

## EXERCISE XXXVIII.

1 小兒得了在工部裏帖寫的差使、都是承您的情。

1. I am entirely indebted to your good offices for my son's [success in] obtaining the post of copyist in the Board of Works.

*Obs.*—The post of copyist: *lit.*, slip-writing employment. Note *t'ieh*⁴, not *t'ieh*³; *t'ieh*⁴ (886) can also be used, but the tone is as above.

2 現任的官出了缺、上司就派員署理、趕到新派實任的來了、那署理的差使就完了。

2. The present incumbent of the post is dead, and the chief has sent an officer to act; when the newly appointed substantive incumbent arrives, the acting man's duties will be at an end.

*Obs.*—Dead: *lit.*, has created a vacancy; the term used in official reports for announcing the decease of an official in active employment.

3 六部的上司都稱堂官、堂官以下就是司官。新到衙門候補的司官、爲學習行走。

3. The superior officers of the Six Boards are called the *t'ang*² *kuan*¹; those under them are the *ssŭ*¹ *kuan*¹ (sub-chiefs, or chiefs of departments). An expectant *ssŭ kuan* newly come to any yamên serves a novitiate.

*Obs.* 1.—Expectant; *lit.*, waiting to fill; *hou* being here the verb to wait.

*Obs.* 2.—Novitiate: *lit.*, is, or acts as, [one who] to learn by practice moves [therein].

4 京城的衙門辦稿、不是司官就是書辦。供事是有頂戴的書辦、當的差使可就和書辦一樣。

4. The drafts of public documents in the yamêns in the capital, when not prepared by sub-chiefs of departments, are prepared by the *shu*¹ *pan*¹ (clerks). *Kung*⁴ *shih*⁴ are clerks with an official button; their duties are, however, of the same nature as those of the *shu*¹ *pan*¹.

5 文書發了之後、存起來的稿子就叫陳案。

5. When a despatch has been sent off, the draft that is placed in the archives is called a *ch'ên*² *ngan*⁴ (a case or correspondence of the past no longer in hand).

6 他偷了我們墳上的樹、我寫了一個墳帖、上衙門去告他。那衙役們不給送進去、說先得給他們多少錢。你還不知道那衙門人的習氣麼、就是他老子去打官司、也是一樣兒的要錢。

6. He stole some trees from our cemetery, so I wrote a petition and went to the yamên to bring an action against him. The *ya yi* would not send it in for me, however, and said I must first give them so much money. Don't you yet know the ways of those yamên people? even if the father of one of them were to go to law, they would want money just the same.

*Obs.* 1.—Ways: *hsi-ch'i*, habit or manner; *ch'i*, the aspect, air, or temper, *hsi*, acquired by practice. Used only in a bad sense.

*Obs.* 2.—Go to law: *ta*, verb of motion, to undertake, *kuan ssŭ*, an action at law. The derivation of the term is obscure.

7 新來的那位官員是做甚麼的。是上司派來的委員、問那明火案兒的口供。

7. What has the official that is newly arrived come to do? He is a *wei-yüan* sent by the chief to take evidence in that burglary case.

*Turn the following into Chinese.* (KEY, EXERCISE XXXVIII.)

1. If a man makes a mistake in anything he does (*lit.*, manages a matter wrongly), and is in fault, he must *ch'êng² tang¹* (abide the consequences; *lit.*, accept what he ought to get). Who undertakes this business?

2. In official business, whether great or small, one ought in all cases to serve one's country with zeal; and it is all one whether the appointment be substantive or acting.

*Obs.*—Serve with zeal: *lit.*, for (*kei*) the State put forth strength.

3. *Tang¹ kuan¹ ch'ai¹* is the same as *tang¹ ch'ai¹ shih³* (to have official duties). The management of private affairs cannot be termed *ch'ai¹ shih³*.

4. Expectant officials must first serve a novitiate, that is, learn their official duties when they first come to a public office. When a vacancy occurs they may be sent to act.

5. The largest public offices are the Six Boards, and the highest officials in these are the *t'ang² kuan¹* (chiefs); they are also called *shang⁴ ssŭ¹*. A Board is divided into so many *ssŭ¹* (departments), and the officials in charge of the departments are called *ssŭ¹ kuan¹* (chiefs of departments) or *ssŭ¹ yüan²*. The drafts are prepared by them, but there are some handed over to the *shu¹ pan¹* (clerks) to do.

6. *Shu¹ pan¹* is the common name for *shu¹ li⁴*. When a matter is duly transacted and the draft finished, it is given to the chiefs of the Board to read. That is called *hui² t'ang² hua⁴ kao³* (to lay before; *lit.*, to report) to the chiefs for signature.

7. When any public office has outside business, an official must be deputed to transact it.

8. *Ya*$^2$ *yi*$^4$ and *tsao*$^4$ *li*$^4$ are the underlings employed in every yamên to perform miscellaneous duties.

9. *Kung*$^4$ *shih*$^4$ get their appointments by examination; when they pass they get a button. It is a more honourable appointment than that of *shu*$^1$ *pan*$^1$ (*lit.*, they are more honourable, etc.).

*Obs.*—To pass an examination: *chung*$^4$ (302).

10. The correspondence in official matters that are concluded is stowed away and called *ts'un*$^2$ *kao*$^3$ (archived drafts). Of the archived drafts some have been sanctioned and others not, but they are all archives.

**1031.** 脾 *p'i*$^2$, the part of the stomach that produces digestion.

**1032.** 禍 *huo*$^4$, adversity; calamity.

**1033.** 福 *fu*$^2$, prosperity.

**1034.** 命 *ming*$^4$, decree, of fate or of a superior; with *hsing*$^4$ (532), and sometimes without, existence.

**1035.** 運 *yün*$^4$, to convey; to bring to pass.

**1036.** Examples:—

| | | | | | |
|---|---|---|---|---|---|
| 氣 *ch'i*$^4$ | 禍 *huo*$^4$ | 氣。*ch'i*$^4$ | 急。*chi*$^2$ | 太 *t'ai*$^4$ | 脾 *p'i*$^2$ |
| 好。*hao*$^3$ | 麼。*mo* | 這 *chê*$^4$ | 他 *t'a*$^1$ | 暴。*pao*$^4$ | 氣。*ch'i*$^4$ |
| 運 *yün*$^4$ | 天 *t'ien*$^1$ | 不 *pu*$^2$ | 很 *hên*$^3$ | 性 *hsing*$^4$ | 他 *t'a*$^1$ |
| 貨。*huo*$^4$ | 命，*ming*$^4$ | 是 *shih*$^4$ | 有 *yu*$^3$ | 兒 *'rh* | 脾 *p'i*$^2$ |
| | 運 *yün*$^4$ | 大 *ta*$^4$ | 福 *fu*$^2$ | 又 *yu*$^4$ | 氣 *ch'i*$^4$ |

Temper; also, eccentricity of character.

*Obs.*—For *ch'i*, see Exercise XXXVIII, 6, Obs. 1.

His temper is too passionate.

He is also of a quick (or impatient) temperament.

He has a very prosperous air; or, he is a prosperous (or happy) man.

Is not this a great calamity?

The decrees of Heaven.

Good fortune.

*Obs.*—*Lit.*, the *ch'i* [that the revolutions of fate bring] round.

To convey merchandise.

**1037.** 志 *chih*$^4$, resolution.

**1038.** 益 *yi*$^2$, *yi*$^4$, addition; advantage. Colloquially, far oftener *yi*$^2$ than *yi*$^4$.

**1039.** 活 *huo*$^2$, alive; living.

**1040.** 聰 *ts'ung*$^1$, quick to apprehend what one hears.

**1041.** 願 *yüan*$^4$, to wish; to be willing.

**1042.** 功 *kung*$^1$, exertion in a good cause.

**1043.** Examples :—

| | | | | | |
|---|---|---|---|---|---|
| 用 *yung*$^4$ | 聰 *ts'ung*$^1$ | 看 *k'an*$^4$ | 在 *tsai*$^4$ | 志 *chih*$^4$ | 他 *t'a*$^1$ |
| 功。*kung*$^1$ | 明。*ming*$^2$ | 他 *t'a*$^1$ | 沒 *mei*$^2$ | 空 *k'ung*$^1$ | 很 *hên*$^3$ |
| 怕 *p'a*$^4$ | 他 *t'a*$^1$ | 外 *wai*$^4$ | 有 *yu*$^3$ | 活 *huo*$^2$ | 有 *yu*$^3$ |
| 活 *huo*$^2$ | 不 *pu*$^2$ | 面 *mien*$^4$ | 益 *yi*$^2$ | 百 *pai*$^3$ | 志 *chih*$^4$ |
| 不 *pu*$^4$ | 願 *yüan*$^4$ | 兒 *'rh* | 處。*ch'u*$^4$ | 歲。*sui*$^4$ | 氣。*ch'i*$^4$ |
| 了。*liao*$^3$ | 意 *i*$^4$ | 很 *hên*$^3$ | 我 *wo*$^3$ | 實 *shih*$^2$ | 無 *wu*$^2$ |

He is a man of great resolution.

"Without resolution one may live a hundred years in vain."

Really there is no advantage.

*Obs.—Yi ch'u: lit.*, places of advantage

His appearance, to my eye, is that of a very intelligent man.

He is unwilling to exert himself.

I fear he can't live.

**1044.** 虧 *k'uei*$^1$, to be deficient.

**1045.** 辜 *ku*$^1$, properly, fault: specially, ingratitude; to be ungrateful for.

**1046.** 負 *fu*$^4$, to turn the back on; to bear on the back.

**1047.** 抱 *pao*$^4$, to hold in the bosom or the arms; hence, to cherish.

**1048.** 怨 *yüan*$^4$, resentment.

**1049.** Examples :—

| | | | | | | |
|---|---|---|---|---|---|---|
| 把 *pa*$^3$ | 負 *fu*$^4$ | 願 *yüan*$^4$ | 要 *yao*$^4$ | 辦 *pan*$^4$ | 虧。*k'uei*$^1$ | 他 *t'a*$^1$ |
| 孩 *hai*$^2$ | 了 *liao* | 意 *i*$^4$ | 叫 *chiao*$^4$ | 結 *chieh*$^2$ | 這 *chê*$^4$ | 本 *pên*$^3$ |
| 子 *tzŭ* | 我 *wo*$^3$ | 抱 *pao*$^4$ | 他 *t'a*$^1$ | 了。*liao* | 件 *chien*$^4$ | 錢 *ch'ien*$^2$ |
| 抱 *pao*$^4$ | 的 *ti* | 怨 *yüan*$^4$ | 念 *nien*$^4$ | 從 *ts'ung*$^2$ | 事 *shih*$^4$ | 虧 *k'uei*$^1$ |
| 進 *chin*$^4$ | 好 *hao*$^3$ | 着 *cho* | 誓 *shu*$^1$ | 前 *ch'ien*$^2$ | 多 *to*$^1$ | 空 *k'ung*$^1$ |
| 來。*lai*$^2$ | 心 *hsin*$^1$ | 我 *wo*$^3$ | 他 *t'a*$^1$ | 我 *wo*$^3$ | 虧 *k'uei*$^1$ | 了。*liao* |
| | 了。*liao* | 辜 *ku*$^1$ | 不 *pu*$^2$ | 很 *hên*$^3$ | 你 *ni*$^3$ | 吃 *ch'ih*$^1$ |

His capital was encroached upon; he lost some of his capital.

To suffer loss; to get the worst of an encounter; to have a bad time.

*Obs.—Lit.*, to eat (=suffer) loss.

It is almost entirely owing to you that this matter has been settled.

*Obs.*—Owing to you: *lit.*, this matter, for the most part, if you had not been there (if your aid had been wanting), would [not] have been settled. *Chieh*, completed; *lit.*, to knot (see 444). *To k'uei* may be freely rendered, I am greatly indebted to you.

Formerly I wanted him very much to study; he was unwilling, and felt resentment against me, being ungrateful to me for my good intentions.

*Obs.*—Ungrateful: *k'uei* (1044) *fu* is as often used in Peking as *ku fu*.

Bring the child in.

**1050.** 寒 *han*$^2$, cold.

**1051.** 悔 *hui*$^3$, to repent, of good or evil.

**1052.** 善 *shan*$^4$, virtuous.

**1053.** 惡 *$^{ng}$o*$^4$, *$^{ng}$ê*, vicious.

**1054.** Examples :—

| | | | | | |
|---|---|---|---|---|---|
| 不 *pu*$^4$ | 不 *pu*$^4$ | 了。*liao* | 了 *liao* | 了。*liao* | 他 *t'a*$^1$ |
| 能 *nêng*$^2$ | 能 *nêng*$^2$ | 善 *shan*$^4$ | 錢 *ch'ien*$^2$ | 我 *wo*$^3$ | 們 *mên* |
| 都 *tou*$^1$ | 都 *tou*$^1$ | 人 *jên*$^2$ | 如 *ju*$^2$ | 當 *tang*$^1$ | 如 *ju*$^2$ |
| 算 *suan*$^4$ | 算 *suan*$^4$ | 惡 *$^{ng}$o*$^4$ | 今 *chin*$^1$ | 初 *ch'u*$^1$ | 今 *chin*$^1$ |
| 是 *shih*$^4$ | 善 *shan*$^4$ | 人。*jên*$^2$ | 後 *hou*$^4$ | 多 *to*$^1$ | 寒 *han*$^2$ |
| 惡。*$^{ng}$o*$^4$ | 也 *yeh*$^3$ | 人 *jên*$^2$ | 悔 *hui*$^3$ | 花 *hua*$^1$ | 苦 *k'u*$^3$ |

They are now in bitter poverty.

I spent too much to begin with (at first), and now I regret it.

*Obs.*—Regret: *lit.*, after regrets. When verbalised, to repent or regret.

Good men and bad men.

Men cannot all be accounted good, and yet they cannot all be accounted bad.

**1055.** 其 *ch'i*$^2$, used in particular locutions as the definite article: *the* person or thing.

**1056.** 餘 *yü*$^2$, surplus; remainder.

**1057.** 靈 *ling*$^2$, spiritual; intelligent.

**1058.** Examples :—

| | | | | | |
|---|---|---|---|---|---|
| 得 *tê* | 玩 *wan*$^2$ | 很 *hên*$^3$ | 上 *shang*$^4$ | 其 *ch'i*$^2$ | 那 *na*$^4$ |
| 起 *ch'i*$^3$ | 意 *i*$^4$ | 靈 *ling*$^2$ | 他。*t'a*$^1$ | 餘 *yü*$^2$ | 孩 *hai*$^2$ |
| 來。*lai*$^2$ | 兒 *'rh* | 便 *pien*$^4$ | 他 *t'a*$^1$ | 的 *ti* | 子 *tzŭ* |
| | 都 *tou*$^1$ | 甚 *shên*$^2$ | 心 *hsin*$^1$ | 比 *pi*$^3$ | 很 *hên*$^3$ |
| | 拏 *na*$^2$ | 麼 *mo* | 裡 *li*$^3$ | 不 *pu* | 靈 *ling*$^2$ |

That child is very intelligent; the others cannot be compared with him.

*Obs.*—Others: *lit.*, the (*ch'i*) remaining ones all compare not up to (or above) him.

He is very quick, and is good at any accomplishment.

*Obs.*—Note *wan-i-'rh*, accomplishments, such as music, archery, etc.

語言自邇集



## EXERCISE XXXIX.

1 他那一件事情成了、是他的命運好.在我說、不關運氣、都是他有志氣、肯用功的好處.

1. That success of his is due to his luck. I do not attribute it to his luck; I think it was all due to his own merits, his determination and industry.

*Obs.* 1.—Not attribute: *lit.*, in my saying=opinion, it is not connected with luck. See *kuan* (63), to concern

*Obs.* 2.—All due: *lit.*, wholly is it that he has resolution-and-willingness-to-use-exertion's good points, or advantage.

2 作善得福、作惡得禍、這都是天命所定自然之理.

2. That good deeds bring happiness and evil deeds misfortune is a natural principle ordained by the laws of Heaven.

3 他打直隸運來的米沒賺錢、連本兒都虧空了.

3. He has not made anything on the consignment of rice that he brought from Chihli, and has even lost some of his capital.

*Obs.* 1.—Consignment: *lit.*, the from Chihli conveyed coming (*ti*) rice.

*Obs.* 2.—Note that *tou* does not here mean all, but both: both the profits were absorbed, and some of the capital as well.

4 可惜那個人雖然聰明、到底脾氣不行.任憑待他怎麽好、總是抱怨.

4. What a pity it is that although that man is intelligent, he has an impossible temper. No matter how well one treats him, he is sure to grumble (*lit.*, feel resentment).

*Obs.* 1.—No matter how: *jên p'ing*, you may as you please treat him well, etc.

*Obs.* 2.—His temper: note that one can speak of a man's *p'i-ch'i* being good, or of his having no *p'i-ch'i*, eccentricities of character or temper, at all.

5 天氣寒冷的時候兒、人得活動活動.身子纔不吃虧、不然趕有了病、就後悔不來了.

5. When the weather is cold, people must move about, and then their bodily health will not suffer; otherwise, when they get ill, they will repent in vain.

*Obs.* 1.—Note *kan*³, when, short for *kan tao*, when they arrive at.

*Obs.* 2.—Repent in vain: *hou hui pu lai*; *lit.*, repentance won't come, there will be no result from repentance. *Lai* must here be treated as *hsing*, to succeed, to have good results, or some similar word.

6 你專在這不相干的事情上用功。有甚麼益處。你們老人家花了若干的銀子給你捐了官、你不正經當差使。這不是辜負老家兒的恩典麼。眞叫人家寒心阿。疼的要命。

6. What do you gain by devoting your energies to these undertakings which do not concern you? Your father spent all that money in buying you an official post, and yet you won't carry out your official duties as you should. Isn't this ingratitude for the goodness of your parents to you? You really estrange people [by your conduct]. The pain is unendurable (*lit.*, killing).

*Obs.* 1.—All that money: *jo kan*; *lit.*, as these ones. *Kan* (Radical 51) is explained in the native dictionaries to be equivalent in this combination to *ko*, one or ones; and by a process of amplification which it is not necessary here to go through, the two characters can be shown to mean as many as these or this. The expression is in common use colloquially, and may be positive as well as comparative, as *jo kan jên*, a whole lot of people.

*Obs.* 2.—As you should, properly: *chêng ching*; *lit.*, the straight length. Hence, the proper or direct route; morally, properly, respectably. *Cf. chêng ching jên*, a respectable person.

*Obs.* 3.—To estrange: *lit.*, cause people's hearts to be cold. *Han hsin*, a cold heart, refers to the coldness engendered by ingratitude.

7 這個學生極靈。又願意用功。其餘那些個孩子眞是不中用。

7. This student is most intelligent, and, besides, is willing to exert himself. The rest of the children are really no good at all. (*See* 302).

8 你臉上發了福了。舊年這個時候兒、看你那個樣兒就活不了。

8. You are quite fat in the face. This time last year, to judge from your appearance, you could not live.

*Obs.* 1.—Fat in the face: *lit.*, your face has put forth happiness.

*Obs.* 2.—Last year: *lit.*, the old year; *chiu* often taking the place of *ch'ü*.

9 把牕戶開開罷。那牕戶不是活的、開不開。

9. Open that window. The window is a fixture; it won't open.

*Obs.*—Fixture: *huo* can be used of anything that can be moved or taken to pieces; as, for instance, the stock of a gun, which is *huo ti*, can be taken off. The converse is *ssŭ ti*; *lit.*, dead, a fixture, or a dummy.

*Turn the following into Chinese.* (KEY, EXERCISE XXXIX.)

1. He has a very good disposition, and has not a grain of temper; how can any calamity befall him? Besides, he looks a prosperous man.

*Obs.*—He looks prosperous: *lit.*, growing has attained a very-much-possessing-prosperity's manner.

2. The *ming*[4] (fortune) of a man at his birth may be good or evil; and even *yün*[4] *ch'i*[4] (luck) is not all of one kind.

3. No matter what one does, one must have resolution, and then success is a matter of course. If a man has not the slightest

語言自邇集



resolution, he need not think to make any way all his life.

*Obs.* Way, progress: *chin yi*$^{4}$; *lit.*, advancement [on the path of] gain, advantage. Note the tone.

4. Don't you make any mistake about that man. In speech and action he has plenty of "go," and is not in the least a "stick." He is exceedingly intelligent withal, and has lots of resolution. He is always at home, and won't go anywhere, being so very fond of work.

*Obs.* 1.—Don't make a mistake: *lit.*, him that man do not you wrongly regard (*ch'iao*).

*Obs.* 2.—"Go:" *huo tung*, lively movement; the converse of which is *ssŭ yang*, inanimate, *lit.*, dead fashion.

5. You borrow other people's money, and he, fearing the payment of interest may cause you loss, pays it back for you. This is an advantage to you, and yet you resent his interference. Isn't this ingratitude for a well-intentioned [act] on his part, and won't it disgust people with you (estrange them)? If he finds it out (knows) by-and-by, and duns you for the money, you will certainly repent it.

*Obs.* 1.—Interference: *to shih*; *lit.*, many matters, a term applied to a busybody or a person who interferes in matters with which he has no concern.

*Obs.* 2. Certainly repent: *chun chih hou hui ti*, it is assuredly a to-be-a-hereafter repented of *ti*, action, or some similar word; hereafter being rendered by *yao*, the sign of the future.

6. The doing of good or the doing of evil depends entirely on a man himself. An evil-doer who repents and reforms (*hui*$^{3}$ *kai*$^{3}$) is equally a good man.

*Obs.*—Depends on: *tsai*, is in, or rests with.

7. These different sorts are all good. Leave them. You can take the rest away; I don't want them.

8. This little dog is very quick; whatever I say he understands.

*Obs.*—Very quick: *hên yu ling hsing*; *lit.*, very much has an intelligent disposition or nature.

**1059.** 緊 *chin*$^{3}$, tight; pressing. Also, extreme; hence, when used with *yao*$^{4}$, to want, which may precede or follow it, important.

**1060.** 預 *yü*$^{4}$, beforehand. When so used it is generally coupled with *hsien*$^{1}$, before; it is also found in combination with the next character.

**1061.** 備 *pei*$^{4}$, to prepare; ready.

**1062.** 通 *t'ung*$^{1}$, passing from one point to another without hindrance; to understand.

**1063.** 共 *kung*$^{4}$, collectively; together with.

**1064.** 合 *ho*$^{2}$, united; agreeing with.

**1065.** Examples:—

| | | | | | | |
|---|---|---|---|---|---|---|
| 很 *hên*$^{3}$ | 不 *pu*$^{4}$ | 個 *ko*$^{4}$ | 備 *pei*$^{4}$ | 沒 *mei*$^{2}$ | 去。*ch'ü*$^{4}$ | 不 *pu*$^{2}$ |
| 合 *ho*$^{2}$ | 通，*t'ung*$^{1}$ | 道 *tao*$^{4}$ | 馬。*ma*$^{3}$ | 有，*yu*$^{3}$ | 屋 *wu*$^{1}$ | 要 *yao*$^{4}$ |
| 意。*i*$^{4}$ | 通 *t'ung*$^{1}$ | 兒 *'rh* | 預 *yü*$^{4}$ | 預 *yü*$^{4}$ | 子 *tzŭ* | 緊。*chin*$^{3}$ |
| 正 *chêng*$^{4}$ | 共 *kung*$^{4}$ | 通 *t'ung*$^{1}$ | 備 *pei*$^{4}$ | 先 *hsien*$^{1}$ | 預 *yü*$^{4}$ | 趕 *kan*$^{3}$ |
| 合 *ho*$^{2}$ | 三 *san*$^{1}$ | 不 *pu*$^{4}$ | 下 *hsia* | 告 *kao*$^{4}$ | 備 *pei*$^{4}$ | 緊 *chin*$^{3}$ |
| 式，*shih*$^{4}$ | 十 *shih*$^{2}$ | 通。*t'ung*$^{1}$ | 馬，*ma*$^{3}$ | 訴 *su*$^{4}$ | 好 *hao*$^{3}$ | 送 *sung*$^{4}$ |
| | 個。*ko*$^{4}$ | 路 *lu*$^{4}$ | 這 *chê*$^{4}$ | 我，*wo*$^{3}$ | 了 *liao* | 信 *hsin*$^{4}$ |

It does not matter; it is not important.

Send the letter as quickly as possible.

Is the room prepared?

Tell me beforehand.

Get the horse ready; saddle the horse (not harness him, for which *see* 770).

Have the horse ready.

*Obs.*—Note the difference; *hsia* has here the force of to be in waiting.

Can one get through by this road?

No thoroughfare.

Altogether thirty.

Very much to my liking.

*Obs.*—We can say also *ho wo ti i.*

It just suits.

*Obs.*—*Lit.*, exactly agrees with the pattern.

1066. 除 *ch'u*$^2$, to take away; to subtract from. With *fei*$^1$ (Radical 175), except.

1067. 剩, 賸 *shêng*$^4$, to remain, as the balance of a sum. The second is the correct character, though the first form is generally used.

1068. 盈 *ying*$^2$, excess; overplus.

1069. 像 *hsiang*$^4$, properly, a figure resembling; to resemble; to seem like.

1070. 似 *ssŭ*$^4$, *shih*$^4$ (differently pronounced under different circumstances), resembling.

1071. Examples:—

| | | | | | | |
|---|---|---|---|---|---|---|
| 非 *fei*$^1$ | 的 *ti* | 子 *tzŭ* | 流 *liu*$^2$ | 盈 *ying*$^2$ | 一 *i*$^4$ | 除 *ch'u*$^2$ |
| 他 *t'a*$^1$ | 老 *lao*$^3$ | 長 *chang*$^3$ | 水 *shui*$^3$ | 餘, *yü*$^2$ | 千 *ch'ien*$^1$ | 了 *liao* |
| 去 *ch'ü*$^4$ | 子。*tzŭ* | 得 *tê* | 似 *shih*$^4$ | 花 *hua*$^1$ | 銀 *yin*$^2$ | 花 *hua*$^1$ |
| 不 *pu*$^4$ | 照 *chao*$^4$ | 很 *hên*$^3$ | 的。*ti* | 錢 *ch'ien*$^2$ | 子。*tzŭ* | 費 *fei*$^4$ |
| 行。*hsing*$^2$ | 像。*hsiang*$^4$ | 像 *hsiang*$^4$ | 這 *chê*$^4$ | 好 *hao*$^3$ | 沒 *mei*$^2$ | 下 *hsia*$^4$ |
| | 除 *ch'u*$^2$ | 他 *t'a*$^1$ | 孩 *hai*$^2$ | 像 *hsiang*$^4$ | 有 *yu*$^3$ | 剩 *shêng*$^4$ |

After deducting the expenditure there remains a balance of *Tls.* 1,000.

There is no surplus (nothing over).

To spend money as fast as water flows; money goes as water flows.

*Obs.*—Note that *ssŭ* is always pronounced *shih* when followed by *ti*.

This child is very like his father.

To photograph.

Except he goes, it won't do.

1072. 橫 *hêng*$^2$, horizontal, as opposed to perpendicular.

語言自邇集



**1073.** 竪, 豎 *shu*$^4$, perpendicular, as opposed to horizontal.

**1074.** 傷 *shang*$^1$, of a man's person or feelings, to wound; to injure. Also of many things beside, animate and inanimate.

**1075.** 棚 *p'êng*$^2$, a mat-shed; a pent-house; an awning.

**1076.** 搭 *ta*$^1$, to place on; to pile up; to put up. Also, to join, as a party of people; to add.

**1077.** Examples:—

| | | | | | | |
|---|---|---|---|---|---|---|
| 個 *ko* | 傷 *shang*$^1$ | 的 *ti* | 去。*ch'ü*$^4$ | 兒 *'rh* | 豎 *shu*$^4$ | 把 *pa*$^3$ |
| 涼 *liang*$^2$ | 心。*hsin*$^1$ | 牛。*niu*$^2$ | 我 *wo*$^3$ | 上 *shang*$^4$ | 起 *ch'i*$^3$ | 這 *chê*$^4$ |
| 棚 *p'êng*$^2$ | 夏 *hsia*$^4$ | 受 *shou*$^4$ | 打 *ta*$^3$ | 人 *jên*$^2$ | 來 *lai*$^2$ | 一 *i*$^4$ |
| 好。*hao*$^3$ | 天 *t'ien*$^1$ | 傷。*shang*$^1$ | 傷 *shang*$^1$ | 家 *chia*$^1$ | 橫 *hêng*$^2$ | 根 *kên*$^1$ |
| 搭 *ta*$^1$ | 搭 *ta*$^1$ | 我 *wo*$^3$ | 了 *liao* | 過 *kuo*$^4$ | 在 *tsai*$^4$ | 木 *mu*$^4$ |
| 船。*ch'uan*$^2$ | 一 *i*$^2$ | 很 *hên*$^3$ | 他 *t'a*$^1$ | 不 *pu*$^2$ | 道 *tao*$^4$ | 頭 *t'ou*$^2$ |

Set that log of wood upright; people can't pass when it is lying across the road.
I have wounded his cow.
To suffer injury (of persons or things).
I am very distressed in mind.
In summer it is a good thing to put up an awning.
To take passage on board a ship.

**1078.** 準 *chun*$^3$, to adjust; to equalise. Hence, a rule; accurate; accuracy; certain; sure. The character is interchangeable with *chun*$^3$ (567), but the latter is the form in more common use.

**1079.** 勢 *shih*$^4$, property; power; authority; hence, power to change. Also, appearance of power; aspect; condition.

**1080.** Examples:—

| | | | | | |
|---|---|---|---|---|---|
| 派 *p'ai*$^4$ | 一 *i*$^2$ | 二 *êrh*$^4$ | 兩 *liang*$^3$ | 有 *yu*$^3$ | 他 *t'a*$^1$ |
| 兒 *'rh* | 座 *tso*$^4$ | 分。*fên*$^1$ | 銀 *yin*$^2$ | 我 *wo*$^3$ | 的 *ti* |
| 不 *pu*$^4$ | 廟 *miao*$^4$ | 隨 *sui*$^2$ | 子 *tzŭ* | 的 *ti* | 天 *t'ien*$^1$ |
| 小 *hsiao*$^3$ | 的 *ti* | 勢。*shih*$^4$ | 總 *tsung*$^3$ | 準 *chun*$^3$ | 平 *p'ing*$^2$ |
| 呢。*ni* | 勢 *shih*$^4$ | 這 *chê*$^4$ | 差 *ch'a*$^4$ | 一 *i*$^4$ | 沒 *mei*$^2$ |

His balance is not so true as mine; it is invariably two candareens out on every tael.

*Obs.*—*T'ien-p'ing*, a balance for weighing silver (*see* **326**). Note *ch'a*$^4$ (*see* **1005**).

According to circumstances.

This is an imposing looking temple.

*Obs.*—*Lit.*, this temple's *shih p'ai-'rh*, distributed appearance (=the way in which it is laid out), is not small. The term can be applied to persons, also to any pageant or procession, such as a funeral *cortége*, a wedding, etc.

27

## EXERCISE XL.

1 你天天兒來不來都不要緊。若有緊急的事情、橫竪得叫你去。

1. Whether you come every day or not is of no consequence. If there be anything of pressing importance you will have to be sent for in any case.

*Obs.* 1.—In any case: *hêng shu* (here read *hêng*[4] *shih*); *lit.*, horizontally or perpendicularly, whichever way you take it.

*Obs.* 2.—Note the force of *lai* and *ch'ü*, showing that the person addressed is at the moment at the place to which he will have to come when sent for. Emphasise *chiao*.

2 可惜他蓋的那房子不像房子的式樣。好像馬棚似的、住着很不像樣兒。

2. It is a pity that he has built that house so unlike what a house ought to be. It looks just like a stable, and is by no means a seemly place for him to live in.

*Obs.* 1.—Looks just like: *hao=hên*. Note the object resembled between *hsiang* and *shih*, the two words which combine to produce our verb resemble; the latter had better be translated as a noun, *q.d.*, much like a horse-shed's likeness.

*Obs.* 2.—A stable is commonly called *ma hao* (858), *ma p'êng* being, strictly speaking, a lean-to without doors or windows.

*Obs.* 3.—Seemly or suitable: not like the appearance, *q.d.*, that a house in which he lives should have.

3 那一所兒房子、通共有多少間。通共有一百多間、除了人住的。下賸還有四五十間。

3. How many *chien*[1] are there in that house (or, block of buildings)? There are altogether more than a hundred; some forty or fifty over and above what people are living in.

*Obs.* 1.—House: note that *i so fang-tzŭ* means the whole of the rooms or separate buildings forming one block, courtyard, or set of courtyards comprising one establishment; *i tso fang-tzŭ* would be one building, as, for instance, that on one side of a courtyard, but the expression is not common.

*Obs.* 2.—*Chien* is not, strictly speaking, the numerative of rooms or houses, but is a noun indicating a certain space measurement. Chinese houses are not spoken of as containing so many rooms, but so many *chien*, the *chien* being the space between any four of the pillars that support the roof; thus, if we spoke of a *ssŭ chien wu-tzŭ* or *ssŭ chien fang-tzŭ*, we should mean that there were four such spaces in the room or house, or, in other words, that the roof was supported by ten pillars, five on a side; a house of 100 *chien* would be a house that contained 100 such spaces, irrespective of the number of rooms. The student is requested to modify the rendering given of *chien* in 47 in accordance with the above explanation: *yi chien fang-tzŭ* is not a house irrespective of the number of *chien* it contains (which is *yi tso fang-tzŭ*), but a house of one *chien*.

*Obs.* 3.—Over and above: *lit.*, having excluded the persons inhabiting ones, below remaining still are there 40 or 50 *chien*.

4 我合算起來、有一萬兩銀子的外欠、除了還賬之外、下賸還有一二千兩銀子的盈餘.

4. I put the total of what is due to me at ten thousand taels, and after paying my own debts I shall have a credit balance of one or two thousand taels.

*Obs.* 1.—What is due to me: *wai ch'ien*; *lit.*, outside owings, the converse of which is *ch'ien wai*.

*Obs.* 2.—After paying: read *huan*⁴, not *han* or *hai*.

5 我月月兒進的錢總不彀、沒有盈餘、反倒賸下些個賬目不能還、過這種樣兒的日子眞叫我傷心.

5. My monthly income is never sufficient, I have nothing left from it; on the contrary, I have some debts remaining that I cannot pay. I am sorely distressed at having to live in this way.

6 有人放槍、把他那小孩子打着了、傷的很重.

6. A man let a gun off and hit his little child, which he hurt very badly.

7 門旁邊兒的木頭是豎的、門上下的木頭是橫的.

7. The doorposts of a door are perpendicular; the [beams of] wood above and below the door are horizontal.

8 在地下平擱的東西、說橫、說豎、那都是隨勢酌情的活動話、若是在面前直着的爲豎、在旁面的人就以爲是橫.

8. The direction of things laid flat will be said to be perpendicular or horizontal conditionally; if [the direction of] a thing lying end on to a person be held to be perpendicular, it will be regarded as horizontal by anyone whose face is turned at right angles to that of the first person.

*Obs.* 1.—Conditionally: *lit.*, on the ground laid flat of a thing the saying *hêng* and the saying *shu* are all 'according-to-the-case-and-considering-the-circumstances' *huo tung hua*, movable expressions.

*Obs.* 2.—End on: *lit.*, if that before [one's] face *chih*, in a right line, confronting, be *shu*, [whoever] *tsai*, may be, a side-facing man, then will regard it as *hêng*.

*Obs.* 3.—Held to be: *wei*², to make of, as in *tso wei*.

*Obs.* 4.—Regarded: the same verb *wei* preceded by *i*, to use, here acting as the sign of the objective case of a noun, the object of *wei*, understood; *q.d.*, of the direction specified, the side-facing man makes horizontal = he regards it as horizontal. Treat *i wei* as the verb to regard, remembering that the object may either precede the combination or come between its two parts. It is equally correct to say *chê ko i wei shih hêng* and *i chê ko wei hêng*.

*Turn the following into Chinese.* (KEY, EXERCISE XL.)

1. I told you just now I had a very important matter to attend to, and that you were to get the horse ready saddled in waiting for me; and even at this hour you have not got it ready. If I don't scold you, you will put me in a temper, and if I do, it will look as if my temper was bad.

2. Our accounts must be gone into from end to end. Putting together what I have borrowed from you at different times, what does the total amount to? After deducting what I have repaid you, I estimate that I have a small sum over to the good.

*Obs.*—From end to end: *t'ung ch'ang*, the complete length (1062).

3. You have borrowed more than you have repaid. How can you have any balance to the good?

4. From your appearance I should say you were a very intelligent man, and yet (how) you don't know horizontal from perpendicular. I told you to hang up the drawings; the perpendicular ones to be hung at the two sides of the door, and the horizontal one over the top. You have hung them all wrong.

5. You hand this matter over to me to deal with. In any case I will manage it all right for you.

6. Say nothing about it. You managed that other affair in a way that distressed me very much. The last time I thought of putting up an awning (sky awning) I asked you to buy mats for me. To my surprise (who would think?), you were not in the least to be depended on (had not a grain of accuracy). You did not buy the articles, and I couldn't even catch a sight of your face.

NOTE.—*Cho*$^{2}$ or *chao*$^{2}$ is written in the two different forms given in **45**, but the second is that more commonly employed, except when *cho* signifies to command. It is especially used in this latter sense in Imperial Decrees, to express the "We will" of the Emperor. When preceding adjectives or adverbs, it is read both *cho* and *chao*. We have, for instance, *cho shih*, of that which is real and true, *bonâ fide*; *cho lo*, of the settlement of a doubt, claim, inquiry, etc.; but *chao chi*, anxious, duly eager, or over-eager, and from the latter, impatient. After verbs, when nothing intervenes, it is most commonly, almost universally, *cho*, as in *tsou cho*, going, *p'ao cho*, running; but if the auxiliary *tê*, or *pu* representing *pu tê*, come between it and the verb, it is invariably *chao*, as in *chao tê chao*, has found or can find, *chao pu chao*, cannot find. In either case, whether *chao* or *cho*, after a verb its meaning is almost identical with that of *tê*, which, again, as has been before observed, is often corruptly supplanted by *ti*. The probability is that the *ti* used now to produce what we call the inflection of the possessive case was originally *tê*, and it is reducible to an equivalent of *tê* in almost every construction in which we find it, except perhaps those which we should term adverbial; those, that is, where *ti* may be rendered by our terminations *like* as in *sailorlike*, or wise in *crosswise*. Even in these *tê* would do their duty, but as the parallel constructions in classical written Chinese are formed by *jan*, thus, and there is between the primitive meaning of *jan* and that of *ti* a certain affinity, it may be safer to infer that in these *ti* figures in its earlier and uncorrupted sense. This was brightness, manifestness, like the white part of a target; hence, that which is evident. The word *jan*, originally the flashing of fire, came to mean *thus* by apparently a similar process.

# CHINESE WEIGHTS AND MEASURES.*

LENGTH.—As in England we commence with barleycorns, so in China have the natives started with a certain number of kernels of grain; whether disposed lengthwise or crosswise is disputed. One grain is held to make a *fên*$^{1}$ (分); 10 *fên* a *ts'un*$^{4}$ (寸), the Chinese inch; 10 *ts'un* a *ch'ih*$^{3}$ (尺), the Chinese cubit, covid, or foot; and 10 *ch'ih* a *chang*$^{4}$ (丈). The *ch'ih*, says the Chrestomathy, fixed by the Mathematical Board at Peking is 13.125 English inches, that used by tradesmen in Canton varies from 14.625 inches to 14.81 inches, and that employed by the engineers of public works is 12.7 inches, while that by which distance is usually measured is 12.1 inches nearly. The *li*$^{3}$ (里), or mile, is 1,897$\frac{1}{2}$ English feet; and 192$\frac{1}{2}$ *li* used to be reckoned for a degree of latitude or longitude. But the European mathematicians at the capital, deviating from their predecessors, divided the degree into 250 *li*, reducing it to 1,826 English feet, or the tenth part of a French league; and this, at present, is the established measure. Accordingly, the *li* is a little *more* than one-third of an English mile.

The *fên* may be taken as equivalent to a line in rough calculations; it is (calling the *ch'ih* 14.625 inches) exactly 1.015625 of the twelfth of an inch. The *ts'un* in Canton is equal to 1.21875 of an inch, or one inch and one-fifth. The *chang* is frequently used by carpenters and other artizans in measuring their work; its length of course depends on that of the *ch'ih* employed, but it is usually about 14.35 feet.

*N.B.*—The *chang* of the Foreign Trade Tariff of 1858 is 141 English inches; the *ch'ih*, 14.1 English inches.

LAND MEASURE.—Five *ch'ih*, Chinese feet, make one *pu*$^{4}$ (步), pace; 240 *pu*$^{4}$ one *mou*$^{3}$ (畝) or *mu*$^{3}$ = about one-sixth of an English acre; and 100 *mou* one *ch'ing*$^{3}$ (頃).

WEIGHT.—It must be borne in mind that, except copper cash, the Chinese have no current coin, and that, except where foreign coin is employed, all payments in silver are calculated with reference to weight. The maximum money weight is the *liang*$^{3}$ (兩), say ounce, commonly known as the *tael*, the subordinate divisions of which are the *ch'ien*$^{2}$ (錢) or mace, *fên*$^{1}$ (分), candarin, *li*$^{2}$ (釐), cash; the three last-named denominations respectively equalling the one-tenth, one-hundredth, and one-thousandth of the *liang*. The cash of the copper currency, which should properly be worth a tael a thousand, are spoken of as *t'ung*$^{2}$ (銅) *ch'ien*$^{2}$ or *ch'ien*, the latter term being moreover generic of money, like our word cash.

In what we should call avoirdupois, the weights to be remembered, in addition to the above, are the *chin*$^{1}$ (斤 or 觔) catty, or Chinese pound of 16 *liang* or ounces, the ounce being subdivided, as in money weight. The *chin* is equal to about 1$\frac{1}{3}$ lb. English, and 100 *chin* make the *tan*$^{4}$ (擔) or *shih*$^{2}$ (石), known by us as the picul = 133$\frac{1}{3}$ lb. English. The characters *tan* and *shih* are used interchangeably at Peking, but the latter is never used with its proper sound, being called *tan*$^{4}$, and almost invariably written 石.

* Condensed from the "Chinese Chrestomathy," the highly valuable work compiled by the late Dr. BRIDGMAN.

# PART IV.

## THE TEN DIALOGUES.

# PART IV.

## THE TEN DIALOGUES.

### DIALOGUE I.

1. What part of the country are you from, sir?

2. I am a T'ien-ching (Tientsin) man; may I ask your country?

3. I am a Chihli man too.

4. Ah! we are fellow-provincials, then.

5. Who is that gentleman?

6. He is a foreigner.

7. Do you know what brings him here?

8. I do not; you had better ask him himself.

9. May I ask what brings you to our country, sir?

10. I am in business.

11. What have you brought with you, sir?

12. Small things in the Japanese lacquer-ware way.

13. Oh! you are from Japan, sir?

14. Yes; I am a Japanese.

15. Indeed! I had been told that no one could get into Japan or out of it.

16. That difficulty did exist once, but of late the restrictions have been removed, and intercourse is an easier matter than it used to be.

17. Have any of our merchants gone over there yet?

18. There are some Chinese merchants and subjects there.

19. From what province of China do the majority of them go?

20. The greater part are from the provinces of Kwangtung and Fukien.

21. Do they do a large business?

22. Not very large, I should imagine.

2. 敝 *pi*$^4$ 2. 津 *chin*$^1$, *ching*$^1$ 2. 領 *ling*$^3$ 9. 駕 *chia*$^4$ 12. 洋 *yang*$^2$ 12. 漆 *ch'i*$^1$, *ch'ü*$^4$ 19. 省 *shêng*$^3$ 20. 廣 *kuang*$^3$ 22. 只 *chih*$^3$

1. *Obs.*—What part: *kuei*, honourable, for the possessive pronoun of the second person.

2. *Obs.* 1.—I am: *pi*, vile, in ill condition, for the possessive of the first pronoun; my humble place is T'ien-chin or T'ien-ching. *Obs.* 2.—May I ask: *lit.*, I have not *ling*, received your instruction; you have not said whence you come.

4. *Obs.*—Fellow-provincials: *hsiang*, properly, village; both the speakers are men of the province of Chihli.

8. *Obs.*—Himself: *lit.*, him, the individual man.

9. *Obs.*—Sir: *tsun chia*; *lit.*, honoured chariot.

12. *Obs.* 1.—Japanese: *tung yang*; *lit.*, the eastern sea; the sea or ocean; hence, foreign. *Obs.* 2.—Lacquer-ware: *ch'i*, the gum with which lacquerware is covered.

15. *Obs.*—No one: *nan*, difficult, is as often as not used for impossible.

16. *Obs.* 1.—Did exist: *t'ou li*, in the beginning, formerly, *ch'io*, notwithstanding, [however easy now, it was] nevertheless difficult. *Obs.* 2.—Removed: *k'ai*, to open, *chin*, the prohibitions; hence, the state of things is *hao hsieh-'rh*, somewhat better.

19. *Obs.*—Province: *shêng*, of which there are 18 in China.

20. *Obs.*—Kwangtung: *kuang*, broad.

22. *Obs.*—I should imagine: *chih p'a*; *lit.*, I only fear.

23. Why not? haven't they money?

24. Well, I should say not much.

25. Why do they go to Japan, then, if they haven't money?

26. Most of them have accompanied Europeans.

27. What do Europeans carry them with them for?

28. It is to take charge of their hongs and to act as brokers for them.

29. Do they get on well with the Japanese?

30. Neither has much confidence in the other, I imagine.

28. 作 *tso*[4] 30. 異 *i*[4]

28. *Obs.* 1.—Act as: *tso* is but another form of *tso* (*see* Part III, 50). *Obs.* 2.—Brokers: *ching*, in the sense of to pass through, *shou*, the hand.

30. *Obs.*—Confidence: *hsiang hsin*, reciprocal trust, faith, or belief in each other (*pi tz'ŭ*).

---

## DIALOGUE II.

1. Is not the horse you are riding, sir, a horse of our country here?

2. Yes; it was bought in your country.

3. Who bought it for you?

4. The people in the horse-yard chose it for me.

5. How much did they ask you for him?

6. They asked thirty taels.

7. Did you give it?

8. I did not; I thought they asked too much.

9. And how much did you give?

10. I closed with them for twenty-two taels.

11. The horse was mine once.

12. Was he really? why did you sell him?

13. I sold him because I wanted money.

14. It was not on account of any defect was it?

15. Not at all; he had no defect whatever.

16. What did you pay for him in the first instance?

17. A good deal; I had money then.

18. Ah! you had something in the public service, had you not?

19. I was in a public office until my father died; I gave up my employment then, and returned home to look after my family affairs.

20. Dear me! was your father long ill?

21. Oh yes; pretty near ten years.

22. And during his illness who took charge of his family?

1. 納 *na*[4] 20. 哎 *ai*[1] 20. 呀 *ya*[1] 20. 久 *chiu*[3]

1. *Obs.*—Sir: *ni-na*. See *nin*, above (Part III, 648).

9. *Obs.*—And how much: [though you did not give what they asked] *tao ti*, in the end, etc.

19. *Obs.* 1.—Father died: *hsien fu*, my late father, *ch'ü*, departed from, *shih*, the world. *Obs.* 2.—Gave up: *ko hsia*, laid down, the appointment. *Obs.* 3.—Look after: *liao li*; the first word signifying here the calculation, the second the administration, required in *chia wu*, household business.

20. *Obs.* 1.—Dear me! *ai ya*. *Obs.* 2.—Your father: *ling tsun*; both words signifying honourable. *Obs.* 3.—Long: *jih-tzŭ chiu*, days long enduring.

22. *Obs.* 1.—His illness: *t'a-na*, like *ni-na*, a respectful form; pronounced *t'an-na*. *Obs.* 2.—Took charge: *chao ying*, looked to everything, and met every requirement.

23. He was able to attend to his affairs in-doors, though he could not go out.

24. Should you have remained in office had you not lost your father?

25. I might have remained or I might not; I am not sure.

26. How not sure?

27. I would have staid in the place if there had been more to be made out of it.

28. Did your salary in it not cover your expenses?

29. Well, it did; still a little addition was required to make one comfortable.

30. Don't think it odd if I say that you were wrong to give up your place?

31. Why, what do you think I ought to have done?

32. Is not His Excellency WANG your connexion by marriage?

33. More; he is my blood relation.

34. Better still; was not he made Governor of a province the other day?

35. He was; Governor of Honan. But what do you imply by your question, sir?

36. My idea is that were you still in public employ His Excellency WANG would beyond doubt be willing to give you a lift.

37. You are wrong; he never liked me.

38. That's all imagination; what evidence have you that he did not?

39. The last time he left home I asked him to take me with him.

40. And what answer did he make?

41. He said, "If there were not another man in the world, I wouldn't have you."

| | | | | |
|---|---|---|---|---|
| 27. 項 *hsiang*4 | 28. 墊 *tien*4 | 32. 王 *wang*2 | 34. 撫 *fu*3 | 36. 拔 *pa*2 |
| 28. 賠 *p'ei*2 | 31. 依 *i*1 | 32. 戚 *ch'i*4 | 36. 提 *t'i*2 | 38. 證 *cheng*4 |

23. *Obs.*—He: note that a son cannot speak of his father as *t'a*.

24. *Obs.*—Remained in office: *tang*1, here to perform.

25. *Obs.*—*To-shao ch'ien:* in Peking as often pronounced *to-'rh ch'ien.*

27. *Obs.*—More to be made: *hsiang*, properly, the neck; items; subdivisions. *Tê hsiang*, the items, sums, obtained; specially used of the profits or pickings of an office.

28. *Obs.*—Cover expenses: *p'ei*, to make up a deficiency, but, popularly, to lose money; *tien*, to advance money. *P'ei tien*, to lose the advances made.

29. *Obs.*—Well: [though I could have wished more] *tao*, yet, I had not to *p'ei tien*.

30. *Obs.* 1.—Think it odd: *kuai*, to be angry with. *Obs.* 2.—Were wrong: in laying down your office you were *pu tang*1, not right.

31. *Obs.*—You think: *i*, to follow, to lean against, according to; *lit.*, in that case, according to your idea, [you would have] *chiao*, caused me to do what?

32. *Obs.* 1.—His Excellency: WANG *ta-jên*; the two last words make an honourable appellative proper to a large number of officials whom, however, we should not style Excellency. *Obs.* 2.—Connexion: *ch'in ch'i*, related by marriage. Emphasise *ch'in*.

34. *Obs.*—Made governor: *fang*, to let go (in the higher grades of office, to appoint), *hsün fu*, the former character signifying to go rounds, as a watch; the latter, to soothe, to conciliate. Under the present dynasty, the chie, authority over a single province, with a few exceptions.

35. *Obs.*—Imply by your question: *lit.*, what is your lofty view, the view of your superior intelligence?

36. *Obs.*—Give you a lift: *t'i*, to lift or pick up, *pa*, to pluck or pull up; *t'i* also means to mention or allude to (*see* Dialogue IV, 81). *T'i pa*, to help on anyone in preference to others; to show preference to.

37. *Obs.*—Never liked: he heretofore has not *hsi huan*, rejoiced in, me.

38. *Obs.*—Evidence: *lit.*, what is a *tui chêng?* the latter word *(chêng)* signifying witness, that *tui*, accords with what you advance.

39. *Obs.* 1.—Last time: *shang tz'ŭ*, the time, or turn, last above the present. *Obs.* 2.—Left home: *lit.*, wen outside; said of anyone going to some distance to trade, on duty, etc.

42. Dear me! was there any reason for such sternness?

43. He can't bear me because I was idle and extravagant when I was young.

44. Oh! be easy about that. Bygones are bygones. His Excellency surely doesn't continue to bear you such illwill now.

45. You don't know; he said more than what I have told you.

46. But not that he would never forgive you?

47. He said that no matter what luck he might have, he would never show me any favour again.

48. What a pity that with such an opportunity as this you shouldn't be able to avail yourself of it.

49. There is no help for it; it's no one's fault but my own that I did not make better use of my time long ago.

50. Did your father's property all come to you, or was it divided?

51. Not all to me; my two brothers, elder and younger, have each a share.

52. Has your elder brother a larger share than the rest?

53. No; it is equally divided amongst the three of us.

54. What sort of property was it, money?

55. There was some ready money and some house property, and business as well.

56. How came the house to you when you were not the eldest son?

57. While my father was alive my eldest brother always looked after the shop.

58. Oh! and you live in the house to take care of your mother?

59. Exactly, my younger brother being also away from home; he has got a private secretary's place somewhere or other.

| | | | | |
|---|---|---|---|---|
| 43. 恨 *hên*⁴ | 44. 唉 *ai*¹ | 46. 宥 *yu*⁴ | 50. 歸 *kuei*¹ | 58. 伺 *tz'ŭ*¹ |
| 43. 勤 *ch'in*² | 44. 旣 *chi*⁴ | 48. 機 *chi*¹ | 53. 均 *chün*¹ | 59. 幕 *mu*⁴ |
| 43. 儉 *chien*³ | 44. 咎 *chiu*¹ ⁴ | 49. 息 *hsi*¹ ² | 54. 哪 *na*¹ | |

43. *Obs.* 1.—Can't bear: *hên*, to hate, to be wrath with. *Obs.* 2.—Idle: was not *ch'in*, diligent, and *chien*, economical.

44. *Obs.* 1.—Oh! *ai*, an interjection. *Obs.* 2.—Bygones: *chi*, of time that is past; since. *Chi wang*, as to what is past, or, since the thing is past, *pu chiu*¹, there is no fault [imputed].

46. *Obs.*—Forgive: *yu*, to forgive; *k'uan yu*, to have the liberality to forgive.

47. *Obs.*—Luck: *lit.*, no matter what share of promotion, wealth, etc., he might reach.

48. *Obs.*—Opportunity: *chi*, motive power, *hui*, to meet, to come across; the meeting with the motive power that will accomplish a certain object in view.

49. *Obs.*—Better use: *hsi*, properly, rest; the profit, interest, accruing on money put out. *Ch'u hsi*, to make profit, or the profit made; colloquially, seldom used except in a moral sense. Emphasise *ch'u*.

50. *Obs.*—All come: *chuan*, exclusively, *kuei*, to revert to.

53. *Obs.*—Equally; *chün*, in even shares.

54. *Obs.* 1.—Was it: *na*, an interrogative particle. *Obs.* 2.—Property: *ch'an yeh* may mean land, house, or business.

56. *Obs.* 1.—The house: *lit.*, the dwelling-house below your person. *Obs.* 2.—Eldest: *chang*³; cf. *chang pei*, an elder generation.

57. *Obs.*—Alive: *tsai*, existing.

58. *Obs.* 1.—Take care of: *tz'ŭ hou*, to wait on; both words meaning to wait, to wait for. *Obs.* 2.—Your mother: *ling t'ang*; the latter word, properly a hall, being elliptically used for *hsüan t'ang*, a poetical term for mother.

59. *Obs.*—Private secretary: *mu*, properly, a curtain or screen, behind which the secretary would sit, his employer being in court. The term has a classical origin.

## DIALOGUE III.

1. Come here, somebody!

2. Here, sir! what did you want, sir?

3. Who are you?

4. My name is LAI-FU.

5. What is your surname?

6. My surname is CHANG.

7. What do you do here?

8. I came to do my elder brother's work.

9. Who is your elder brother?

10. My brother's name is LAI-SHUN.

11. What, the LAI-SHUN who looks after the library?

12. Yes; the same.

13. How came he to go away without asking leave?

14. He thought he oughtn't to trouble you about leave, sir, when you were unwell.

15. Why couldn't he wait till I was well again?

16. He was wanted at home on very particular business.

17. What particular business?

18. His mother was very ill.

19. If so, why should you and he have changed places?

20. He went because father desired it, and I came for fear your work might not be done, sir.

21. Well, be all that as it may, servants should never leave the house without asking leave.

22. Don't be hard on my brother, sir, pray; he will be back soon.

23. Is your house far from this?

24. I should not call it very far.

25. What do you mean by not very far?

26. It's not more than four *li* at the most; it's in the Eastern Division too.

27. Well, in the meanwhile you can go home.

28. Must my brother come back directly?

29. It will do if he is here by to-night.

30. Oh, here is LAI-SHUN himself!

31. Ah! tell him to come here. You can go.

32. You have no further orders for me, sir?

33. None whatever; you go. Here, LAI-SHUN!

34. I have made a sad mistake, sir, but I hope you will forgive me.

8. 哥 *ko*$^{1}$ 21. 勿 *wu*$^{34}$ 23. 離 *li*$^{2}$
13. 假 *chia*$^{4}$ 22. 饒 *jao*$^{2}$ 34. 恕 *shu*$^{4}$

4. *Obs.*—My name: *hsiao ti*, the little one; servants so style themselves to their masters; in a court, prisoners and witnesses do the same. Differently used farther on, in Part V, Lesson LXXXVII.

8. *Obs.*—Elder brother: *ko-ko*; borrowed from the Manchu language. Notice *t'i* first as the preposition instead of, and then as the verb to replace, or to do instead of.

13. *Obs.*—Ask leave: *chia*, to rest, to take a holiday; not to be confounded with *chia*$^{3}$, false. *Kao chia*, to give notice of leave.

14. *Obs.*—He oughtn't: *pu pien*, it was not expedient, convenient, befitting, that he should.

19. *Obs.*—If so: since it is *chê-mo-cho*, thus.

21. *Obs.*—Be all that: *wu*$^{4}$, a negative imperative particle; *lit.*, of other matters, before [I speak of this most essential matter] do not speak. Colloquially, *wu*$^{3}$.

22. *Obs.*—Don't be hard: *jao*, to forbear, to pardon, to excuse. *See* Part III, Exercise XXXII, 8, Obs. I.

23. *Obs.*—Far from: *li*, to separate; hence, from; is your house from this far or near?

27. *Obs.*—In the meanwhile: *hsien*, before your brother comes.

28. *Obs.*—Directly: *chiu*, now.

34. *Obs.*—Forgive me: *k'uan shu*. *Shu*, properly, to forbear doing to others what one does not wish done to oneself; hence, to show mercy.

35. It was a mistake indeed ; why did you go out without saying a word to me?

36. You were not well, sir, and they were pressing me for the money.

37. Who were *they*, and what was *the* money?

38. The shop, sir, where I bought the table for you the other day wanted to be paid for it.

39. Isn't that shop in the Western Division?

40. No, sir ; outside the walls.

41. Outside the walls! near which gate?

42. I don't know much about the town outside the walls, sir.

43. But you know whether the shop was north or south of this, don't you?

44. Oh! I remember ; it's outside the Anting Gate.

45. There's something I don't quite understand in all this.

46. What is it you don't understand, sir?

47. You have got to speak the truth, mind.

48. I shouldn't venture to tell you a lie, sir.

49. Halloo! who is it that's making such a noise in the court?

50. Shall I go out and see, sir?

51. No, you needn't go. Shut (let down) the window.

52. Dear me! what can the matter be? there's someone coming rushing into the house.

53. Why, you are a waggoner, are you not? what do you mean by rushing in in this way?

54. Oh, sir! my humble service to you ; I want you to stand my friend, sir.

55. What do you mean?

56. Oh, sir! justice, if you please ; I've been thrashed and I've lost my money.

57. And what have I to do with your thrashing or your losses?

58. If you have nothing to do with it, sir, your servant has, at any rate.

59. Which servant? what, LAI-SHUN here, perhaps?

60. Ah! yes, indeed ; that is the man ; I didn't notice him before.

61. What has he had to do with you?

62. He hasn't paid me my fare.

63. Your fare from the Northern Division?

64. Northern Division? I belong to an inn at Foal's Bridge.

65. Dear, dear! this really requires explanation ; take care what you say.

| | | | |
|---|---|---|---|
| 48. 敢 *kan*$^{3}$ | 54. 噯 *ai*$^{1}$ | 56. 伸 *shên*$^{1}$ | 64. 駒 *chü*$^{1}$ |
| 49. 院 *yüan*$^{4}$ | 54. 磕 *k'o*$^{1}$ | 57. 與 *yü*$^{3}$ | 65. 咳 *hai*$^{1}$ |
| 52. 闖 *ch'uang*$^{3,4}$ | 56. 挨 *ai*$^{2}$, *ngai*$^{2}$ | 57. 何 *ho*$^{2}$ | 65. 詳 *hsiang*$^{2}$ |

36. *Obs.*—Pressing: *lit.*, they were impatient in the matter of *(yü)* from me wanting money.

48. *Obs.*—Venture: *kan*, to dare.

49. *Obs.*—Court: *yüan*, an enclosure surrounded by walls ; the open spaces between the buildings in a Chinese house are so called.

52. *Obs.* 1.—Dear me! *ai*$^{2}$, here an interjection indicative of surprise or regret. *Obs.* 2.—Rushing in : *ch'uang*$^{3}$, to burst a way into ; said of man or beast. In Peking, *ch'uang*$^{4}$.

54. *Obs.* 1.—Oh, sir! *ai*, a mere exclamation. *Obs.* 2.—Humble service: *k'o*, to knock, *t'ou*, the head ; perform a kotow. *Obs.* 3.—Stand my friend: *lit.*, I pray you, sir, to *tso chu*, to play the master, to manage my business for me.

56. *Obs.* 1.—Have been thrashed: *ngai*; originally, to beat ; more commonly, side by side with. In northern mandarin, to suffer, to be the recipient of ; hence, when with other verbs, what we should call a sign of the passive. *Obs.* 2.—Justice : *lit.*, I pray you, sir, *shên*, stretch out so as to straighten, *yüan*, my wrong.

57. *Obs.*—To do with: *yü*, with ; your loss of money, etc., has with me, ho kan, what connexion or concern?

64. *Obs.*—Foal's Bridge: *chü*, a horse, an ass, or a mule, not full grown. Ma-chü Ch'iao is a village a few miles east of Peking.

65. *Obs.* 1.—Dear, dear! *hai*, an interjection. *Obs.* 2.—Explanation: *lit.*, this *hai*, still, requires *hsiang hsi*, explicit and minute explanation.

66. You may take my leg off, sir, if I say a word that's not true.

67. What time did you start this morning?

68. The cart was put to at cock-crow.

69. Had you one beast or two?

70. A pair; we were to go quick.

71. Had you no passenger but LAI-SHUN here?

72. There was a companion of his as well.

73. And which of the two was it that proposed to go so fast?

74. LAI-SHUN hired the cart, and when he came to hire it he said that if I made haste he would pay me something extra.

75. What did you and he agree should be the fare?

76. It was settled that I was to have five *tiao*.

77. Including the extra charge for speed?

78. Yes, the extra fare included; I never take in anybody.

79. Oh! the fare is fair enough; was it about this you came to blows?

80. We didn't come to blows at all.

81. What! didn't you say just now that you had a thrashing?

82. Yes; but it was not LAI-SHUN that thrashed me.

83. Who then?

84. A number of people; I don't know any one of them.

85. What, a lot of people headed by LAI-SHUN?

86. No, no; LAI-SHUN did not bring anyone.

87. They were thieves then?

88. No, not thieves either. Oh dear! it's a long story to tell.

89. Well, but you have got to tell it, whether it be long or short.

90. Oh, sir! please pay me the fare that's due to me and I'll go about my business.

91. Not so fast; I want to clear up this business.

92. It's not worth taking up your time, sir.

93. Don't you trouble yourself about that; all you've got to do is to answer my questions.

94. Well, sir, what do you want me to tell you?

95. Is CHANG LAI-SHUN here a Foal's Bridge man?

96. His father is a market-gardener outside the village.

97. Oh! then of course LAI-SHUN is an old acquaintance of yours?

98. I used to see him when he was quite a little fellow playing about the streets.

| | | |
|---|---|---|
| 72. 伴 *pan*⁴ | 79. 架 *chia*⁴ | 91. 晰 *hsi*¹ |
| 74. 加 *chia*¹ | 88. 喲 *yo*¹ | 96. 園 *yüan*² |

70. *Obs.*—*Wei*⁴, for, going quickly.

72. *Obs.*—Companion: *pan*, a partner, an associate.

74. *Obs.*—Extra: *chia*, to add to; *lit.*, he said if I made haste he could add some cash.

78. *Obs.*—Take in: *ngo* (*see* Part III, 597).

79. *Obs.*—Came to blows: *chia*, properly, a frame; to ward off blows; with *ta*, to fight, with arms or without.

88. *Obs.*—Oh dear; *ai yo*, an interjection.

91. *Obs.*—To understand: *hsi*, bright, clear; I must *fên hsi*, distinguish one part from another, *ming-pai*, clearly.

93. *Obs.*—All you have to do; *chih*, only; I only require that when I ask you something you say that something.

96. *Obs.*—Gardener; *yüan*, a garden; his father keeps (*lit.*, opens) a *ts'ai yüan*, vegetable garden, as distinct from *hua yüan*, a flower garden, *kuo mu yüan*, an orchard.

99. Was he honest as a boy, or the reverse?

100. Sir, I had rather not tell tales of anybody.

101. But I don't want you specially to tell tales; you can tell me any good you know of him, can't you?

102. Sir! please pay me my fare and let me go about my business.

103. Well, tell me; where did the people come from who fell upon you?

104. They belonged to a tea-house on the road.

105. How far from the city?

106. Not far; just outside the Sha-wo Gate.

107. And LAI-SHUN had some tea there?

108. No, no tea; some spirits and something to eat besides.

109. Did you breakfast with him?

110. No; I was away getting my whip mended.

111. Well, and when it was mended you came back to the house?

112. Yes, I came back; and when I got back I found that they were off.

113. Off! having done you out of your fare?

114. Yes, and not only me but the tea-house as well.

115. Oh! that was it; and the tea-shop wanted you to pay your passengers' bill?

116. That *was* it; and when I wouldn't pay they set upon me.

117. Well, so far as the beating you got at the tea-house goes, I don't see that I can do anything for you, eh?

118. Oh! the beating doesn't signify; but please, sir, pay me my fare, and let me go about my business.

119. There is no difficulty about the fare; I shall stop it out of LAI-SHUN's wages for you.

120. Could you give it me at once, sir, if you please, and let me go home?

121. Don't disturb yourself about the fare; but have you nothing to say to him about what took place at the tea-shop?

| | | | |
|---|---|---|---|
| 103. 毆 *ou*[1] | 106. 沙 *sha*[1] | 110. 鞭 *pien*[1] | 119. 折 *chê*[2] |
| 104. 館 *kuan*[3] | 106. 窩 *wo*[1] | 114. 但 *tan*[4] | |

99. *Obs.*—Reverse: *liu li*, slippery, evasive, dishonest, not to be depended upon. *Liu li* is, *lit.*, glassware (*see* Dialogue VII, 72); hence, metaphorical for a slippery customer, commonly called *liu li ch'iu*[2]-*'rh* "a glass marble."

100. *Obs.*—Tell tales: to tell people's *tuan ch'u*, short places, demerits; *ch'ang ch'u* is a man's special merit.

103 *Obs.*—Fell upon: *ngou*, to beat, with or without a weapon.

104. *Obs.*—Tea-house: *kuan*, a term to be differently translated according to circumstances; a school, an hotel the temporary residence of an official travelling on duty, etc.

106. *Obs.*—Gate: *Sha-wo*, popularly pronounced *Sha-hou*; *lit.*, dust, or sand, nest. *Wo* is the nest or lair of bird or beast.

110. *Obs.*—Whip: *pien*; mended, *shuan*, as before, to tie to, or round.

112. *Obs.* 1.—When: *kan*, as before, to overtake, to come up to. *Obs.* 2.—They were off: they had, before the time so described, run away.

113. *Obs.*—Done you out of: *k'êng* (*see* Part III, 796).

114. *Obs.*—Not only: *tan*, only; not only the waggon fare, *lien*, also, etc.

117. *Obs.*—So far as: *ts'êng*; *lit.*, a layer; hence, a stage in proceedings, an incident.

119 *Obs.*—Stop it: *chê*, properly, to snap off; here, as elsewhere, to deduct from one account in favour of another. Also read *shê*[2] (*see* Part V, Lesson XXVII, 13).

海上絲綢之路文獻集成 科技與文化編

122. No, no; nothing whatever. Please pay me my fare, sir, and let me go home.

123. Well, you are a right good fellow to put up with your neighbour's wrongdoing in this way; but when you get back to your village, you may tell LAI-SHUN's father that neither of his sons is any good, and that I will have nothing whatever to do with such servants.

123. 忠 *chung*$^{1}$ 123. 擔 *tan*$^{1}$ 123. 材 *ts'ai*$^{2}$ 123. 決 *chüeh*$^{2}$

123. *Obs.* 1.—Right good: *chung*, honest, loyal; *hou*, thick (morally, sound, liberal, the opposite of mean). *Obs.* 2.—Put up with: *tan*$^{1}$, to bear on the shoulder, but read *tan*$^{4}$ when used materially; *tan tai* to behave towards men as one bearing their *pu shih*, faults, on one's own shoulder. *Obs.* 3.—But when: *ching*, a strong disjunctive. *Obs.* 4.—Any good: *ts'ai liao*, *lit.*, materials; neither of them is of the material that makes a good, useful, or honest man. *Obs.* 5.—Nothing whatever: *chüeh*; *lit.*, to cut; positively, decidedly.

---

## DIALOGUE IV.

1. LUNG-T'IEN!
2. Sir!
3. Who is that in the court?
4. His name is HSÜ.
5. Oh! a man you know, is it?
6. Yes, sir; an old acquaintance.
7. Where did you meet?
8. We met at Shanghai.
9. When was that?
10. Many years ago.
11. Were you intimate?
12. Pretty well, sir; we are distantly connected.
13. Oh, you're connected? Do you know what he has come for?
14. No, sir, but I can ask him; shall I?
15. Do; I have no objection.
16. He says he is come to see Your Excellency.
17. Come to see me! what about?
18. His father has sent him to pay his respects, he says.
19. His father! what is his father?
20. He was in business once; at present he has no occupation.
21. I don't remember the man at all; what line of business was he in?
22. Surely you remember the large draper's shop in the Western Division, sir?
23. Oh! HSÜ FU-CH'ING; I do remember him. It's *his* son, is it?
24. His son, sir.

4. 徐 *hsü*$^{2}$ 6. 識 *shih*$^{2\,4}$ 7. 遇 *yü*$^{4}$ 23. 慶 *ch'ing*$^{4}$

1. *Obs.*—LUNG-T'IEN! the name of the person addressed, not the surname; this, in familiar intercourse, especially with a junior, is omitted. Were the surname expressed, it would precede the name as above in Dialogue III, 95.

4. *Obs.*—HSÜ: a surname. There are in all China but some 540 single-syllabled surnames, with perhaps 30 of two syllables.

5. *Obs.*—Know: *shih*, to know, to recognise.

6. *Obs.*—Old acquaintances: *ch'ên*, old, of things long in use; also, stale (*see* Part III, 1028).

7. *Obs.*—Meet: *yü*, to meet by accident.

18. *Obs.*—Respects: sent to *ch'ing*, for *ch'ing wên*, to beg to be allowed to inquire after your *an*, health, comfort.

21. *Obs.*—The man: *q.d.*, this man is one *so*, whom, I do not remember; the addition of the *so* is held to emphasise the affirmation.

23. *Obs.*—HSÜ FU-CH'ING: *ch'ing*, prosperity, congratulations upon prosperity; here, part of a man's name.

語言自邇集



25. Ask him to step in.

26. His Excellency begs you will walk in.

27. I hope Your Excellency is well.

28. Take a seat! take a seat!

29. When Your Excellency is seated.

30. Take a seat! take a seat! Here, somebody!

31. *Dja!*

32. Some tea! Your name is Hsü, sir?

33. Hsü, at your service, sir.

34. The son of Hsü Fu-ch'ing?

35. Hsü Fu-ch'ing is my father.

36. I used to know him years ago; I hope he is well.

37. Very well, thank you, sir; he sent me to inquire after Your Excellency's health.

38. It was very good of him to think of me, I am sure, and very good of you to take so much trouble.

39. Oh, sir, it was no more than my simple duty.

40. Your father used to suffer from his eyes, if I remember rightly; are they any better now?

41. His eyesight is pretty good, thank you, considering his age.

42. Age! why, he is much the same age as I am!

43. He is sixty-nine, sir.

44. Then I beat him by two years, for I am seventy-one.

45. I should be well satisfied if he looked as hearty as Your Excellency.

46. Well, I don't understand why he should not; he has not gone through what I have.

47. As a public man Your Excellency has had great cares no doubt; but my poor father has had his domestic financial anxieties.

48. But they are over now that he has retired from business.

49. Yes, sir, he *has* retired, but that was because he could not help himself.

| | | | |
|---|---|---|---|
| 25. 讓 *jang*⁴ | 37. 托 *t'o*¹ | 38. 勞 *lao*² | 45. 朖 *lang*² ⁴ |
| 32. 沏 *ch'i*¹ | 38. 惦 *tien*⁴ | 40. 摸 *mo*¹ | 49. 奈 *nai*⁴ |

25. *Obs.*—Ask him: *jang*, properly, to concede to; hence, to offer to, to invite to benefit by. Very commonly used of invitations to eat, to drink, to smoke, etc.

32. *Obs.*—Some tea: *ch'i*, to pour boiling water on tea.

33. *Obs.*—Your service: *chien*, cheap, lowly; like *pi* (*see* Dialogue I, 2), for the pronoun of the first person.

37. *Obs.*—Thank you: *t'o*, the same as *t'o* (*see* Part III, 992), to be beholden to, *fu*, the prosperity, of the person addressed; *q.d.*, goodness, which Heaven rewards by making him prosper, has a beneficial influence on the speaker.

38. *Obs.* 1.—Good of him: *chiao*, to cause, as elsewhere, puts the verb in the passive; *tien*, to be anxious about persons or things; not recognised by the dictionaries. *Obs.* 2.—I am sure: *chao shih*, in very truth. *Obs.* 3.—Take trouble: *lao*, trouble, to trouble. *Lao chia*, to trouble the chariot, politely for to trouble you; it is also frequently used in the sense of "thank you."

40. *Obs.*—If I remember: *mo*, a word not used separately from *hu*; the combination implying dimness of sight or sense; dimly remember. The character *mo* is not recognised by the native dictionaries, and is probably a corruption of *mo*, to feel, or the same phonetic with the 72nd or 109th Radical.

42. *Obs.*—Much the same: *ch'a*¹, properly, diverging; not to be confounded with the same character read *ch'ai*¹ (*see* Part III, 1005), or *tz'ŭ*¹ (*see* Part III, 577). *Ch'a pu to*, differing not much, nearly the same as.

45. *Obs.* 1.—As hearty: *ying*, hard; *lang*⁴, properly *lang*², tall. There is, strictly speaking, no character to represent this latter sound. *Obs.* 2.—Well satisfied: *lit.*, if my father could be like Your Excellency that hearty, that [would be a thing that though] one asked for it, one could not obtain it; too good a thing to be got.

49. *Obs.*—Not help: *nai*, properly, a certain fruit, but as used in this phrase, untranslatable. *Wu nai ho* and *wu k'o nai ho* both mean that the case is without any remedy; there is no help for it.

29

50. Oh, indeed! he was unfortunate in business?

51. Not exactly, sir.

52. No? then was he robbed?

53. Far worse, sir; he was cheated out of almost all the money he had made.

54. Dear me! I'm sorry to hear that; how was it? did someone who owed him money make off with it?

55. No, sir, a friend he went security for—

56. Absconded! how abominable! and the loss has told on your father's health, has it?

57. Naturally, sir; he has a large family and nothing to give them.

58. How many are there of you?

59. Four sons and three daughters.

60. But not all at home?

61. Every one at home, sir.

62. I thought your father's daughters were all married?

63. Two of them were married to officers of the army, but their husbands were killed in that last campaign in the West.

64. And their widows are come home again?

65. Yes, sir; one with her two children, and the other with six.

66. That is a large family to keep, indeed; and there is another lady unmarried?

67. She is quite a young thing, and always ailing.

68. Ah! what does she suffer from?

69. My mother died while she was a baby at the breast, and she never throve afterwards.

| | | | | |
|---|---|---|---|---|
| 51. 竟 *ching*$^{4}$ | 53. 惡 *wu*$^{4}$ | 56. 精 *ching*$^{1}$ | 60. 未 *wei*$^{4}$ | 63. 亡 *wang*$^{2}$ |
| 52. 莫 *mo*$^{4}$ | 53. 掙 *chêng*$^{4}$ | 57. 養 *yang*$^{3}$ | 62. 姑 *ku*$^{1}$ | 64. 孀 *shuang*$^{1, 4}$ |
| 52. 被 *pei*$^{4}$ | 54. 繃 *pêng*$^{1}$ | 59. 姐 *chieh*$^{3}$ | 62. 嫁 *chia*$^{4}$ | 64. 婦 *fu*$^{4}$ |
| 52. 竊 *ch'ieh*$^{4}$ | 55. 保 *pao*$^{3}$ | 59. 妹 *mei*$^{4}$ | 63. 陣 *chên*$^{4}$ | |

51. *Obs.*—*Ching*, a strong disjunctive; then, but then, only, nothing but; when followed by a negative, never.

52. *Obs.* 1.—No? *mo*, generally, negative imperative; *mo pu*, if it were not; was it not then that he was robbed? *Obs.* 2.—Robbed: *pei*, to cover (hence, to suffer; hence, sign of the passive); *ch'ieh*, to steal, to pilfer.

53. *Obs.* 1.—Worse: *wu*, to hate; *k'o wu*, deserving hate, detestable, abominable. *Obs.* 2.—Made: *chêng*, to make an effort, as when trying to extricate oneself from bonds; *chêng ch'ien*, to make money by exertion.

54. *Obs.*—Make off with: did the *ch'ien chu*, debtor, *pêng*, flick it, the money, away? *Pêng*, which is not a recognised character, is used of the action of a bowstring, or of a piece of wood so set as to propel anything, upon the missile propelled.

55. *Obs.*—Security: *pao*, to secure, to ensure, in any sense.

56. *Obs.*—Health: *ching*, properly, minute, subtle; *ching*, the spirit within one, as distinguished from *shên*, its external manifestation; *ching shên*, animal spirits, health.

57. *Obs.*—Nothing to give: *lit.*, he has not *li liang*, resources wherewith to, *yang huo*, to keep them alive: *yang*, to feed, to rear, man or beast.

59. *Obs.*—Daughters; *chieh*, elder sisters of the speaker; *mei*, his younger sisters.

60. *Obs.*—But not: *wei*, not, not yet; *wei pi*, it does not necessarily follow.

61. *Obs.*—All: *ko ho-'rh*, every individual.

62. *Obs.* 1.—Daughters: *kù-niang*, a spinster. *Obs.* 2.—Married: *chia*, of the woman married, to leave home.

63. *Obs.* 1.—Married: those they were given to were military officers. *Obs.* 2.—Killed: *chên*, a rank, the ranks of a force; *wang*, to die; *chên wang*, died in battle; were killed the last time that in the West, *lit.*, on the western road (beyond the frontier) there was a *ch'u ping*, going forth to war.

64. *Obs.*—Widows: *shuang*$^{1}$, widowed (in Peking, *shuang*$^{4}$); *fu*, a wife. *Fu-jên* is used of any woman.

67. *Obs.*—Always ailing: *ai*, to love; here and often, in the sense of "to be used to."

69. *Obs.* 1.—While: *ta*, proceeding from; hence, at the time when. *Obs.* 2.—At the breast: *ch'üeh nai*, she wanted, was deficient in, milk. *Obs.* 3.—Throve: *tsu chuang*, sufficiently vigorous.

70. This is very sad, really; but you and your brothers are doing something for the family, I suppose.

71. I should be very glad to do anything, but unfortunately I can get nothing to do.

72. Are you the eldest son?

73. The eldest but one, sir.

74. Well, but what is your eldest brother about?

75. He is a cripple and quite unfit for anything.

76. Well, this is a terrible case; and your younger brothers?

77. They were quite children when my father gave up business, and as he couldn't pay for their schooling they have been very imperfectly educated.

78. Well, I suppose the long and the short of it is that you want me to find you a place, eh!

79. Oh, Your Excellency, I should be inexpressibly grateful if you would take so much interest in me.

80. And that was the real object of your visit to-day, wasn't it?

81. Indeed, I shouldn't have presumed to mention the subject, sir, if you had not alluded to it.

82. Well, I'll see what I can do for you; be so good as to call again about ten days hence.

83. I am greatly indebted to you for the preference you are showing me, sir; I will wait on Your Excellency again in a few days.

84. Good-bye, then, for the present.

85. Good-bye to Your Excellency.

| | | | | |
|---|---|---|---|---|
| 70. 憐 *lien*$^{2}$ | 75. 殘 *ts'an*$^{2}$ | 76. 景 *ching*$^{3}$ | 77. 培 *p'ei*$^{2}$ | 79. 激 *chi*$^{1}$ |
| 73. 排 *p'ai*$^{2}$ | 75. 疾 *chi*$^{2}$ | 77. 栽 *tsai*$^{1}$ | 79. 感 *kan*$^{3}$ | 79. 盡 *chin*$^{4}$ |

70. *Obs.*—Very sad: *lien*, to compassionate; *k'o lien*, that rightly may be, deserves to be, pitied; but it is used simply as to pity. *Obs.* 2.—For *liang*, *see* Part III, 772.

71. *Obs.*—But: *lit*, I, *ch'üeh*, for all that may be argued to the contrary, am very willing; *k'o hsi*, lamentably, there is no *tao-lu*, road.

72. *Obs.*—Eldest son: *chang*$^{3}$ *fang*; *lit.*, the chamber first in order. The sons, while children, are all in one apartment: as each one marries, he has a room to himself; the eldest will be first married.

73. *Obs.*—Eldest but one: *p'ai*, to arrange in order. *P'ai êrh*, I stand second among the sons; a daughter might say it of her place among her sisters. Cf. also *hang*, Part III, Exercise XXVIII, 10.

75. *Obs.*—Cripple: *ts'an chi*, dreadfully ailing in the legs and feet. *Ts'an*, to destroy, to seriously injure (hence, cruel); *chi*, ailments in general

76. *Obs.* 1.—Terrible case: *kuang ching*, circumstance; the latter word, alone, being more strictly applicable to scenery, features of a landscape. *Obs.* 2.—*K'o*, is properly, may properly be said to be, *liao pu tê*, infinite, &c., in its badness.

77. *Obs.* 1.—Gave up: *shou*, here in the sense of to pack up, as a huckster his wares. *Obs.* 2—Pay for schooling: *tsai p'ei*, properly, of trees; *tsai*, to plant; *p'ei*, to pile earth round the roots; could not take care of them [so as to enable them] to read. *Obs.* 3.—Imperfectly: *lit.*, their learning [though they have some] *hai*, or *han*, for all that, cannot either be considered deep.

79. *Obs.* 1.—Interest: *t'êng ai*, to tenderly love. *Obs.* 2.—Grateful: *kan chi*; the character *kan* meaning to move the heart, or to have the heart moved; *chi*, the outbursting of the heart moved. *Obs.* 3.—Inexpressibly: *chin*, to exhaust, words will hardly exhaust.

81. *Obs.*—Allude to: *t'i*, properly, to pick up (*see* Dialogue II, 36).

83. *Obs.*—Preference: *t'i pa*; the first word as in 81; the second means, to draw one out of a bundle. *T'i pa*, to help on anyone in preference to others (*see* Dialogue II, 36).

## DIALOGUE V.

1. LUNG-T'IEN! when HSÜ YUNG calls again, you tell him I've left town.

2. Poor fellow! he'll be sadly disappointed; what has he done to offend Your Excellency?

3. Offend! his whole story was a tissue of falsehoods from beginning to end.

4. Why, isn't he the son of HSÜ FU-CH'ING?

5. Oh, yes; he's HSÜ FU-CHING's son.

6. And didn't his father fail as he said?

7. He did fail; but not as he said.

8. How did he fail then?

9. It was his own extravagance and folly that broke him; nothing else.

10. Still he has an immense family to support.

11. Nothing of the sort. In the first place, HSÜ FU-CH'ING himself has been dead some years.

12. Dead some years! and who maintains all those sons and daughters of his?

13. His daughters all died before him, and he never had any son but this impostor.

14. Sir, I think Your Excellency must be misinformed on that point.

15. Not in the least; I've been making very careful inquiries. Didn't you say that you were connected with these people by marriage?

16. I did.

17. But you have seen nothing of them for four or five years?

18. Oh, more than that; nine or ten years.

19. Just so. Now, when old Hsü kept the draper's shop, what was his character?

20. They used to say he was a very proud man; I never heard anything else against him.

21. Wasn't he very much given to smoking opium?

22. He did smoke, certainly; and he was a little fond of his glass too.

23. Exactly. Now, when you met his son at Shanghai, what was he doing there?

24. He said he had been commissioned to buy produce for exportation.

25. What produce, tea or silk?

| | | |
|---|---|---|
| 9. 拋 p'ao[1] | 20. 狂 k'uang[2] | 22. 貪 t'an[1] |
| 15. 查 ch'a[2] | 21. 烟 yen[1] | 25. 葉 yeh[4] |

1. *Obs.*—HSÜ YUNG: *yung*, eternal; here the name of the man surnamed Hsü.

2. *Obs.* 1.—Disappointed: *pai hsi huan*, *lit.*, to rejoice in vain; the literary equivalent is *shih wang* (失望). *Obs.* 2.—Offend: *tê tsui*, to get blame of you; before *ta-jên* understand *yü* (see Part III, 343), in the sense of "from" or "of."

3. *Obs.*—Beginning to end: *t'ung shên*, entire body.

9. *Obs.*—Extravagance: *p'ao*, to let go suddenly of what is held in the hand; *p'ao fei*, to spend without restraint.

15. *Obs.*—Careful inquiries: *kao ch'a*, the latter character being indentical in the colloquial language with *ch'a* (*see* Part III, 522).

20. *Obs.*—Proud: *k'uang*, of unbridled temper or passions; *k'uang ao*, ungovernably proud, contemptuous.

21. *Obs.*—Smoking: *yen*, smoke of any kind. *Ch'ih yen*, to eat smoke, to smoke; nowadays more particularly used of opium-smoking, at least in conversation with foreigners. Opium is often particularised as *ta yen*.

22. *Obs.*—Fond of his glass: *t'an*, to covet, to desire immoderately.

24. *Obs.*—Produce: *t'u huo*, merchandise of the place or country.

25. *Obs.*—Tea: *yeh*, a leaf; *ch'a yeh*, tea leaves, tea in the market.

26. Tea and silk and medicines.

27. And where were they to have been carried?

28. I forget whether he said north or south.

29. And did he say nothing about purchasing imports?

30. He may possibly have done so, but I don't remember.

31. Nothing about opium?

32. Yes, yes; now you mention it, I recollect that he had some little difficulty about his opium.

33. There wasn't as much as he wanted in the market, I suppose.

34. Oh yes. The price of the drug was rising every day, but there was plenty of it to be bought.

35. What publicly?

36. Not exactly; it was stowed away in the receiving ships or in warehouses.

37. And had it to be smoked on foreign premises?

38. No; the divan HSÜ YUNG used to frequent was in the back of a small house up a narrow street.

39. Oh, he used to frequent a divan, did he? Like father, like son.

40. Well, he didn't smoke so much after all.

41. Only purchased it for others, eh? And what was the difficulty he got into about it?

42. The prohibitions against the trade were still in force, and after he had purchased what he wanted, he couldn't get it away for a long time.

43. And how did he succeed at last?

44. He shipped it in a boat freighted with firewood, and smuggled it out of port.

45. I thought firewood all came *to* Shanghai; where could it be going to *from* the port?

46. Probably to some place in the neighbourhood. The junk, you may be sure, had more opium than firewood on board.

47. And so he got into a scrape?

48. Yes; his junk was dropping down the tide when a revenue cruiser pounced upon her.

26. 湖 *hu*$^{2}$ 26. 材 *ts'ai*$^{2}$ 36. 躉 *tun*$^{3}$ 36. 藏 *ts'ang*$^{2}$

26. 藥 *yao*$^{4}$ 32. 微 *wei*$^{1}$ 36. 棧 *chan*$^{4}$

26. *Obs.* 1.—Silk: *Hu ssŭ*, properly, silk of Hu-chou Fu, in the province of Chê-chiang (Chêkiang), but used generically of the finer silk. *Obs.* 2.—Medicines: *yao*, drug; *ts'ai*, materials; the latter word used particularly of timber.

27. *Obs.*—Carried: *yün*, to convey (*see* Part III, 1035).

29. *Obs.*—Imports: *yang huo*, foreign commodities (*see* Dialogue I, 12).

30. *Obs.*—May possibly have: *ch'iao lai*, *lit.*, coming by chance; *ch'iao* is short for *p'êng ch'iao* (*see* Part III, 752), casually, by chance.

31. *Obs.* 1.—Nothing about: *lit.*, did he not mention that he was *pan*, managing, engaged in, an operation of (that is, as it is very commonly used, buying). *Obs.* 2.—Opium: *yang yao*, foreign drug, drug from the seas; hence, abroad.

32. *Obs.*—Some little: *wei*, minute; *hsieh wei i tien*, a very common diminutive.

35. *Obs.*—Publicly: *kung jan*; the latter word as in Part III, 561.

36. *Obs.* 1.—Receiving ships: *tun ch'uan*; the first character meaning to buy wholesale. *Obs.* 2—Warehouses: *chan fang*. *Obs.* 3.—Stored: *ts'ang*, to conceal, to put out of sight.

44. *Obs.*—Smuggled it out: *t'ou*, to steal; *t'ou-cho*, stealthily, went out of port.

48. *Obs.*—Pounced: *ch'ou lêng-tzu*, an expression indicating unlooked-for occurrences; on a sudden *chua chu*, clapped the paw, or claw, upon, and held or stopped the boat. The word *lêng*, cold, may refer to the shock of any occurreuce unlooked for, but *ch'ou*, to draw, is scarcely explicable.

49. And put the cargo under seal?

50. No; but the tidewaiters threatened to search her if Hsü Yung didn't behave liberally.

51. How much did they ask?

52. They named no sum: they only said he must be liberal.

53. And what did he offer?

54. Well, like a fool, he offered a hundred taels.

55. That was pretty liberal; didn't the Custom House people think so?

56. They thought it much too liberal for a boat loaded with fuel, and they said that unless he paid down three hundred taels they would seize the whole cargo.

57. And did he pay three hundred taels?

58. He hadn't got it to pay.

59. Then how did he manage?

60. He gave them an order on a foreign house in Shanghai.

61. I wonder they took it. He was in great luck to get away at all.

62. But he didn't get away immediately, that was the best of it.

63. What, did the Customs people repent of their bargain after they had got the order for the money?

64. No; but while all this negotiation had been going on the Customs boat and the junk had been dropping down the tide side by side, and they ran foul of two other boats that were lying at anchor.

65. What, two other cruisers?

66. No, not cruisers; two boats belonging to the Imperial Commissioner Liu; one for himself and the other for his suite.

67. Capital! Was it very late at night?

68. Not very late; about nine o'clock.

69. Still, the Commissioner and his people were all asleep, I suppose?

70. The Commissioner, I should think, was at his rooms in the city; but his people were laughing and singing and keeping it up on board.

71. But his people had no concern with a Customs question?

49. 封 *fêng*[1]　61. 虎 *hu*[3]　65. 哨 *shao*[4]　66. 劉 *liu*[2]

52. 豐 *fêng*[1]　64. 撞 *chuang*[4]　66. 欽 *ch'in*[1]

49. *Obs.*—Under seal: *fêng*, properly, to stop up an orifice; here, to close by pasting certain official papers over a door, hatch, etc.

50. *Obs.*—Tidewaiter: there is another term for the tidewaiters in the employ of the Foreign Customs.

52. *Obs.*—Handsome: *fêng*, abounding, plenteous; *ts'ung fêng*, in an abounding manner, in the most abounding manner.

60. *Obs.* 1.—An order: *lit.*, he wrote *ko tzŭ-'rh*, a [paper of] characters; applicable to any note, memorandum, etc. *Obs.* 2.—On a house: *kên*, commonly, following, in the presence of; here, of or from; of the foreign house *ch'ü ch'ien*, to take the money.

61. *Obs.*—Get away: *hu*, the tiger; that he got out of the tiger's mouth was his *p'ien i*, advantage.

62. *Obs.*—But he didn't, etc.: *lit.*, but there was more [to come]; this wasn't yet to be considered entirely *(so)* getting out of the tiger's mouth.

64. *Obs.* 1.—Ran foul: *chuang*, to run up against; collision of persons or things. *Obs.* 2.—At anchor: *wan* (*see* Part III, 786); there, a bay; but here and often, to be at anchor.

65. *Obs.*—Cruisers: *shao*, properly, to whistle, or to make the like sound; hence, to make it as a signal; *hsün shao ch'uan*, circulating signal-making vessels.

66. *Obs.* 1.—Not cruisers: *kuan*, here short for *hai kuan*, Maritime Customs establishment. *Obs.* 2.—Commissioner: *ch'in*, imperial; *ch'ai*, envoy. *Obs.* 3.—Liu, a surname.

72. True, but when his boat ran bump up against them, it frightened them, and then, when they had recovered from their alarm, they came down on him for compensation.

73. Compensation for what?

74. For the fright, and damage done to the Imperial Commissioner's boats, and anything else you please.

75. I wonder HSÜ YUNG didn't show fight.

76. They were too many for him, and, besides, he had a guilty conscience.

77. As well he might have. But how did it all end?

78. The Customs boat had hauled off, but his experience in her case had taught him not to be too liberal this time, so he offered the Commissioner's people ten taels only.

79. And they were satisfied?

80. Oh yes; they would have taken anything; they were much too far gone to overhaul his junk.

72. 驚 *ching*[1] 76. 寡 *kua*[3] 76. 膽 *tan*[3] 78. 躲 *to*[3]
74. 損 *sun*[3] 76. 敵 *ti*[2] 76. 虛 *hsü*[1] 80. 醉 *tsui*[4]

72. *Obs.*—Frightened: *ching*, a word indicating surprise, but also terror.

74. *Obs.*—Damage: *sun*, to injure; *sun huai*, to injure seriously.

76. *Obs.* 1.—Too many: *kua*, the few, could not *ti*, stand before, as equal to, *chung*, the many. *Obs.* 2.—Guilty conscience: *tan*, the liver, was *hsü*, the opposite of *shih*, true, sound, solid. With the Chinese the liver is the seat of courage. Compare our term white-livered.

78. *Obs.* 1.—Had hauled off: *tsao*, early, some time before; *to*, to withdraw; *to k'ai*, to get out of the way. *Obs.* 2.—Experience: he *ching kuo*, having passed through that [other affair], *chang*, had added a piece of *chien shih*, ..ing and knowing.

80. *Obs.* 1.—Oh yes: *lit.*, how should they not consent? *Obs.* 2.—Too far gone: they had all drunk to a state *pan tsui*, semi-intoxication.

---

## DIALOGUE VI.

1. Well, to return to his fabrications. Did he tell you whom he was buying opium for?

2. I forget.

3. He didn't tell you it was for his father?

4. I don't remember, really.

5. It *was* for his father, however, and his father's bankruptcy was due to this very transaction.

6. It was a bad speculation?

7. In one sense, yes; the opium was shipped for Tientsin.

8. What, and seized there?

9. It never arrived; the junk it was on board of was taken by pirates off the Shantung coast.

10. And old HSÜ lost all the money he had invested in it?

1. 岔 *ch'a*[4] 9. 始 *shih*[3] 9. 終 *chung*[1] 9. 扣 *k'ou*[4] 10. 資 *tzu*[1]

1. *Obs.*—To return: *lit.*, that digression let us consider ended; *ch'a*, a forked road; *p'ang-ch'a*, branching off from one side; *chieh*,[2] to tie a knot, to close an affair or a conversation.

5. *Obs.*—Bankruptcy: *kuan pi*, *lit.*, to close (a business), is used only of failure; for to retire from business, *see* Dialogue IV, 77.

9. *Obs.* 1.—Never: *shih*,[3] beginning, *chung*,[1] end; *shih chung*, from first to last. *Obs.* 2.—Taken by pirates: *lit.* was by sea robbers *k'ou*[4] *chu*, kept fast; *k'ou* is properly to strike, as one knocking at a door.

10. *Obs.*—Invested: *tzŭ*,[1] properly, goods; here, money; *tzŭ pên*, capital.

11. Yes, and not only that, but his button to boot.

12. But I didn't know that he had any rank.

13. He had purchased a grade the year before.

14. Purchased a grade! But how could the piracy affect his rank? it is not alleged that he was in relations with the pirates, surely?

15. The piracy did not affect it, but the smuggling did.

16. What, did the smuggling come to the knowledge of the authorities?

17. Do you suppose large sums are ever extorted without the knowledge of the authorities?

18. Three hundred taels was not so very large a sum.

19. Quite large enough to be divided; and the cruiser's people not only kept more than their share, but fought about what they kept.

20. And then one told on the rest?

21. Precisely; and once the authorities got wind of it, the whole operation was traced to its source, and old HSÜ had to pay the heaviest fine that could be inflicted, and was stripped of his rank as well.

22. Well, one can't wonder at HSÜ YUNG's desire to keep his father's disgrace quiet.

23. Certainly not, he wasn't obliged to publish such a thing; but that is no reason why he should come here with a long invention about his father being the victim of misplaced confidence.

24. That was too bad, I admit.

| | | | | |
|---|---|---|---|---|
| 14. 涉 *shê*[4] | 21. 究 *chiu*[1] | 22. 遮 *chê*[1] | 23. 揚 *yang*[2] | 24. 逾 *yü*[4] |
| 16. 場 *ch'ang*[3] | 21. 罰 *fa*[2] | 22. 掩 *yen*[3] | 23. 編 *pien*[1] | 24. 詐 *cha*[4] |

11. *Obs.*—Button: *ting tai; lit.*, that which is borne on the crown of the head; but it means, generally, the insignia of office.

12. *Obs.*—Rank: *kung ming*, elliptically, for the credit one has gained, the name one is leaving; commonly used for official rank, whether obtained by merit or purchase.

14. *Obs.* 1.—But: *jan êrh*, often pronounced *jan 'rh*; the case being *jan*, thus, *êrh*, yet,——. *Obs.* 2.—Could affect: *shê*, properly, to ford; *kan shê*, to be affected by prejudicially; *q.d.*, the thing *kan*, strikes me, I am *shê*, implicated in it; as a man fording a stream is wet by the water. *Obs.* 3.—Not alleged: *nan tao* (*see* Part III, 830). *Obs.* 4.—In relations: *t'ung*, to penetrate; here, to be in communication with, to be in league with.

15. *Obs.*—Smuggling: *tsou ssŭ*; the *ssŭ* is applied to any act unauthorised by law; a Chinese here understands *huo*, goods, after it, and treats *tsou*, to go, as an active verb. Compare our phrase to *run* goods.

16. *Obs.*—Authorities: *ch'ang*, an arena; *kuan ch'ang chung*, in the official arena, amongst the authorities.

19. *Obs.*—Divided: with their *t'ung shih*, fellows in the business, *chün fên*, in equal parts shared; *t'ung shih* is equally applicable to associates in a lawful undertaking, those one acts with.

21. *Obs.* 1.—Traced: *chiu*, to investigate; they carefully investigated [in such wise that there was] a water-descending stone-appearing, a discovery of the truth. *Obs.* 2.—Heaviest: *ts'ung chung* (see *ts'ung fêng*, Dialogue V, 52). *Obs.* 3.—Fine: *fa*, properly, to punish; but, colloquially, to fine. *Obs.* 4.—Stripped: *kê* (Radical 177); *lit.*, to skin.

22. *Obs.* 1.—Father's disgrace: *tiu lien*, to lose, to throw away, face. *Obs.* 2.—To keep quiet: *chê*, to screen wholly, *yen*, to half-screen; *chê yen* may be used literally, but is oftener figurative.

23 *Obs.* 1.—Publish: *chang yang*; the first word meaning to spread wide, the second, to raise high. *Obs.* 2.—Invention: *pien*, to weave; *pien tsao*, to fabricate a story.

24. *Obs.*—Too bad: *yü*, to overpass, to exceed, *cha*, falsehood; *kuo yü*, to exceed in, *hsü cha*, what is empty and false.

25. I half mistrusted him at the time, and I resolved to ask Li Yung-ch'êng about him; I knew that he used to be very intimate with his father.

26. And his account of him was not satisfactory, I suppose?

27. Not at all. He knows Hsü Yung very well; he was weak enough to recommend him for a place once without examining him.

28. As what?

29. As an office copyist; but he didn't keep the place a month.

30. Why not? was he ill-conducted or incompetent?

31. Both; he could not write round hand at all, so he was of no use as a copyist; and they never could believe a word that he said.

32. I wonder how he contrives to dress as well as he does, with nothing to live on.

33. The coat he had on the other day was no great things, I am sure.

34. Great things or not, it was a coat that must have cost something; and so must that mule he was on.

35. I thought he came in a cart.

36. No, he rode here; on a stout mule in very good case.

37. And yet, with all you know of his dishonesty and extravagance, you seem inclined to take his part.

38. I can't help pitying people that have known better days, when I see them in extremity.

39. Pity him as much as you will; but don't ask me to get him employment, for I won't do it.

40. He'll be on the streets before long, poor fellow.

| | | | | |
|---|---|---|---|---|
| 26. 概 *kai*$^{4}$ | 31. 靠 *k'ao*$^{4}$ | 35. 摸 *mo*$^{1}$ | 36. 壯 *chuang*$^{4}$ | 38. 享 *hsiang*$^{3}$ |
| 27. 舉 *chü*$^{3}$ | 35. 估 *ku*$^{1,3}$ | 36. 驃 *piao*$^{1}$ | 37. 護 *hu*$^{4}$ | 38. 恤 *hsü*$^{1}$ |

25. *Obs.* 1.—Intimate: *shou ho*; *ho*, short for *ho p'ing*. *Obs.* 2.—Resolved: *ta-cho*. *Obs.* 3.—To ask: *ta t'ing*, to inquire.

26. *Obs.* 1.—I suppose: *ta kai*, in all probability. *Obs.* 2.—Account: *shuo*, not here to blame, but to talk of.

27. *Obs.*—Recommend: *chü*, classically, to raise; *pao chü*, to recommend, to guarantee the goodness of, a person. That man formerly besought him *kei chao*, for him to seek, something; he being in heart *juan*, soft, consented; not having examined him, *chiu*, yet proceeded, to recommend him.

29. *Obs.*—Office copyist: *t'ieh hsieh*; *lit.*, to write memoranda that are *t'ieh*, appended, to the document. *See* Part III, Exercise XXXVIII, 1, Obs., for another form of the same character.

30. *Obs.*—Ill-conducted: *hsing chih*, moving and being stationary (=conduct under all conditions), not good.

31. *Obs.* 1.—Not write round hand at all: *lit.*, as to *ch'iai shu*, round hand, *so*, it was what, he could not write; the *so*, as before observed, is sometimes regarded by a Chinese, however, as intensive or emphasising, not as a relative pronoun. *Obs.* 2.—Believe: *k'ao*, to lean against, to rely upon; *k'ao pu chu*, not to be relied on.

32. *Obs.*—Wonder: *lit.*, that man is strange: being without money, how is it that what he wears is so respectable.

33. *Obs.*—No great things: also not anything.

35. *Obs.*—I thought: *ku*$^{1}$ *mo*, from *ku* (in Peking, *ku*$^{3}$), to estimate, as number or value; *mo*, to feel with the fingers.

36. *Obs.*—Good case: *piao chuang*, sleek and stout; *piao* not used except of beasts.

37. *Obs.*—Take his part: *hu*, to protect.

38. *Obs.* 1.—Better days: having formerly *hsiang*, enjoyed, *fu*, happiness. *Obs.* 2.—Pitying: *lien*, to pity (*see* Dialogue IV, 70); *hsü* means the same as *lien*.

40. *Obs.* 1.—Poor fellow: *k'o-hsi-liao-'rh-ti*, one deserving of pity. *Obs.* 2.—Pitying: *yen k'an-cho*, while the eye is beholding. *Obs.* 3.—On the streets: he will, or is about to, want rice.

41. Well, when he comes to want a meal I'll give it him; but recommend him for any place I will not.

42. He was to be here the day after to-morrow.

43. Then tell him what I told you.

44. That you will have nothing to say to him, sir?

45. No; that I am gone out of town.

46. And if he asks when you are likely to be back?

47. You can't say; you don't know how long I shall be away.

48. But if he should be calling every day to find out?

49. Let him call as often as he likes, he is not to be admitted.

50. Wouldn't it be better to tell him plainly that he mustn't count on Your Excellency's support?

51. No, no; that will involve explanations into which I am still less inclined to enter with him.

52. If I don't mistake, I hear his voice in the yard.

53. Then you may just put him off in the best way you can, for see him I won't.

54. I was only joking; it's the block-cutter come for his money.

55. Let him come at the end of the month.

56. The man has been here twice already, sir.

57. So he has, and I promised to pay him; so he must be paid.

58. I'll pay him, sir; don't trouble yourself.

| | | | |
|---|---|---|---|
| 41. 頓 *tun*$^4$ | 50. 簡 *chien*$^3$ | 50. 倚 *i*$^3$ | 53. 推 *t'ui*$^1$ |
| 49. 許 *hsü*$^3$ | 50. 轉 *chuan*$^3$ | 52. 哼 *hêng*$^1$ | 53. 辭 *tz'ŭ*$^2$ |

41. *Obs.* 1.—A meal: *tun*, originally, to bow the head a time or turn: hence, one time of eating. *Obs.* 2.—Recommend: *pao*, to guarantee (*see* above, 27, *pao chü*).

42. *Obs.*—Was to be here: according to what was that day agreed to, you *yo*, engaged, him to come the day after to-morrow.

43. *Obs.*—What I told you: *ch'i hsien*, at the beginning.

49. *Obs.*—He is not to be: *hsü*, to permit; I do not permit him to come in.

50. *Obs.* 1.—Better: *pu ju*, nothing so good as; interrogatively, would it not be best? *Obs.* 2.—Plainly: *chien chih*, from *chien*, concise, summary, and *chih*, straight. *Obs.* 3.—Mustn't count: *lit.*, if you are *ta suan*, speculating on anything, do you *chuan*, turning round, commission someone else; *chuan*, as here, constantly used as a disjunctive; *q.d.*, so far from commissioning you, *chuan*, on the contrary, commission someone else. *Obs.* 4.—Your Excellency's support: it is of no use *i k'ao*, to lean against Your Excellency; *i* and *k'ao* are nearly identical in meaning.

51. *Obs.* 1.—No, no: note the force of *ch'io* as above. *Obs.* 2.—Explanations: *lit.*, it will be necessary to tell him minutely and plainly *so i jan ti hua*, words stating the *so i jan*, wherefore thus; the reason why.

52. *Obs.*—If I don't mistake: *hêng*, here, an interrogative word, ah? what? also, an ejaculation or grunt.

53. *Obs.* 1.—Put him off: *t'ui tz'ŭ*, to push or put forward excuses; the latter word meaning originally language. *Kao tz'ŭ*, to make one's excuses, is to take leave. As a verb, *tz'ŭ* means to decline; also, to dismiss from one's employ. *Obs.* 2.—See him I won't: *chüeh*, positively, decidedly; a strong affirmative.

54. *Obs.*—Block-cutter: *k'o*$^1$, to engrave; not to be confounded with the same character read *k'o*$^4$ (*see* Part III, 223); *k'o-tzŭ chiang*, a type-cutter.

57. *Obs.*—Promised: *ying hsü*; both words in the sense of responding favourably to what is proposed, promising to perform.

58. *Obs.*—I'll pay him: *lit.*, I for you, sir, will *k'ai fa*, distributingly issue; *k'ai fa* in strictness applying to the settlement of a number of accounts.

# DIALOGUE VII.

1. Was it you who were knocking at the door?

2. It was I.

3. Where are you from?

4. I am from outside the city.

5. Who are you looking for?

6. A person named MÊNG.

7. Well, that's my name.

8. Oh! you are Mr. MÊNG?

9. Yes, I am MÊNG; what do you want of me?

10. I was sent from the Kuang Wên Chai.

11. Is not the Kuang Wên Chai a bookseller's?

12. Yes, a bookseller's.

13. What book is it you were told to bring?

14. I have not brought any book.

15. What, isn't that a book you have in your hand?

16. No; it's a book cover, not a book.

17. If you have no books, why bring an empty book cover?

18. The book cover is not empty.

19. If it isn't, what has it got inside?

20. A few drawings.

21. Drawings! you've come to the wrong house, I suspect.

22. No, it's all right; I was to bring them here.

23. How so? I've bought no drawings.

24. No; I know that it was not you who bought them.

25. Well, then, why bring them to me?

26. Someone bought them for your house.

27. What could anyone have meant by buying drawings for me?

28. Oh, sir, you needn't ask what his motive was.

29. Well, but who was it that bought them for me?

30. Do you know Mr. CHANG who lives in the T'ang-tzŭ Hu-t'ung?

31. I do know him; and it was he, was it?

32. No, it was not he.

33. Not he! then why mention him?

34. I have a reason for mentioning him.

35. If you have, why don't you state it?

36. You're in a great hurry, sir; you will understand more about it presently.

37. Come, I won't stand this; you're quizzing me.

38. Quizzing! I shouldn't think of such a thing.

39. But why not speak, if you have got anything serious to say?

6. 孟 *mêng*[4]　　10. 齋 *chai*[1]　　37. 戲 *hsi*[4]

1. *Obs.*—Knocking: *lit.*, calling, *sc.*, someone to come out.

6. *Obs.*—MÊNG: a family name; the surname of the philosopher known to us as Mencius.

10. *Obs.*—Kuang Wên Chai: *chai*, properly, a swallow's nest; a pavilion in which to repose; elegantly used of certain shops (*see* below, Part V, Lesson LXXX, 2).

16. *Obs.*—Book cover: *t'ao* (*see* Part III, 769); here, the cover of pasteboard and cloth in which Chinese volumes are wrapped.

30. *Obs.*—T'ang-tzŭ Hu-t'ung: *see* Part III, 797; *t'ang*, properly, a hall; *t'ang-tzŭ* may also mean a bathing establishment, but is specially the name of the chapel in which the Emperor sacrifices to his ancestors.

36. *Obs.*—Presently: *hui lai*, in a turn of time; not, when you return.

37. *Obs.*—Quizzing: *hsi*, to play, dramatically or otherwise; this is *shua hsi*, joking language; I *pu i*, will not submit to it (*see* Part III, 913).

39. *Obs.*—Serious: *chêng ching*, *lit.*, upright and straight; often used as we vulgarly use the word regular; here, the opposite of *shua hsi*, fun.

40. It's a long story to tell.

41. Well, if you can't tell it me, I'll go in; be off with you!

42. Stop, stop! don't be in such a hurry; I've got something more to say.

43. Be quick about it then; I've no time to waste.

44. You say you know Mr. CHANG, sir?

45. Yes, I told you so before.

46. Do you know his nephew, sir?

47. Not well; I've seen him once.

48. Well, it is he that ordered these drawings to be sent to you.

49. He ordered them? When did he return?

50. Return? has he been absent?

51. Wasn't he away with some officer?

52. I don't know; what year was it?

53. I recollect his going to Kiangsi the year before last.

54. Indeed! I've seen him in Peking ever since last year.

55. Never mind; what did he send me the drawings for?

56. It was not for you that he bought them.

57. Then what have you brought them here for? I am not going to buy them, I can assure you.

58. Buy them! no; he has paid for them.

59. Well, I do not understand one word of all these contradictions.

60. But you will if you let me say a few words more.

61. Quick, then; don't keep me here all day.

62. Isn't your son employed in the Board of Revenue?

63. You do nothing but ask questions; my son *is* under the Board of Revenue.

64. He doesn't live with you, does he?

65. He has a separate establishment at present.

66. May I ask where his house is?

67. He lives at the west end of Chiao Min Hsiang, on the north side of the way.

68. Lives in Chiao Min Hsiang?

69. To be sure he does; what makes you doubt it?

70. I thought he lived in the Chinese town.

71. What, all that way from the Board's office? that would never do; what made you think he lived in the Chinese town?

72. I met his cart yesterday at sunset in the Liu-li Ch'ang.

73. How could that be? he was here with me last night.

74. The cart was his, but he wasn't in it.

75. How did you know, then, that the cart was his?

76. An old woman in the cart said that it was Mr. MÊNG's cart.

46. 姪 *chih*$^{2}$ 65. 搬 *pan*$^{1}$ 72. 琉 *liu*$^{2}$ 72. 廠 *ch'ang*$^{3}$ 76. 婆 *p'o*$^{2}$

46. *Obs.*—Nephew: *chih*, the son of a brother, not of a sister.

61. *Obs.*—All day: *chin-cho*, completely, utterly.

62. *Obs.* 1.—Your son: see *shao*, Part III, **815**; his junior worship. *Obs.* 2.—Board of Revenue: Hu Pu; *lit.*, the Department of the Population = of the Census.

64. *Obs.*—Does not live with you: *tan chu*, to live alone, apart from parents or brothers.

65. *Obs.*—Separate establishment: *pan*, to remove from one place to another; not used of small things; specially used of a change of residence; he at this time has in singleness removed [his establishment] out, *sc.*, of his father's house.

72. *Obs.* 1.—Sunset: *jih-t'ou lao*. *Obs.* 2.—Liu-li Ch'ang: *lit.*, glassware manufactory; the name of a street in the outer, or Chinese, city. *Liu*, glassware; *li*, as in *po-li*; *ch'ang*, properly, a large booth.

76. *Obs.*—Old woman: *p'o*, any married woman.

77. An old woman with a child in her arms?

78. Exactly; a child some seven or eight years old.

79. Dear me! it must have been my grandson; where could he have been going so late?

80. Don't be alarmed, sir; they had met with a little accident.

81. What was it, pray? had the mule taken fright?

82. No; the fact is that the roads were in a bad state.

83. Oh! and the cart had been upset?

84. No, not that either; it and another cart had run against each other.

85. Well, and were they still discussing the collision at that hour?

86. It wasn't that any discussion they might have had wasn't over.

87. Then the little boy was hurt?

88. Not severely; he jumped out of the cart, and in jumping out he sprained his leg.

89. Confound that other cart! do you know whose it was?

90. It belonged to Mr. CHANG's nephew.

91. Mr. CHANG's nephew! and the drawings that he has sent——?

92. Are for your grandson, sir.

93. But why should he buy drawings, of all things in the world, to pacify the child?

94. He had bought the drawings; he didn't buy them on purpose for the child.

95. And he had them with him in his hand, I suppose, when the carts came into collision?

96. Yes, he had; he had just bought them at our shop.

97. And did the child ask him for them?

98. No; your grandson cried, and he said, "Don't cry, and I'll send you something to play with."

99. Oh! and these drawings are for him to play with; but why didn't you take them to my son's house instead of bringing them here?

100. Mr. CHANG's nephew came to our shop this morning to find out where your son lived, sir. We said we couldn't say, but that we knew your house; and then he told us to bring the drawings here; he'll call himself in a day or two.

| | | | |
|---|---|---|---|
| 83. 翻 *fan*$^{1}$ | 93. 壓 *ya*$^{1}$ | 98. 哭 *k'u*$^{1}$ | 100. 府 *fu*$^{3}$ |
| 88. 扭 *niu*$^{3}$ | 94. 並 *ping*$^{4}$ | 100. 郎 *lang*$^{2}$ | |

79. *Obs.*—So late: *na tsao wan* = such a time of day.

83. *Obs.*—Upset: *fan*; originally, flight or other movement backwards and forwards.

84. *Obs.*—Run against each other: the cart had with a *tui-t'ou-'rh ch'ê*, an opposing cart, made collision.

85. *Obs.*—Still discussing: *lit.*, the collision having taken place, had they *lao*, in so long a time, not *shuo k'ai*, talked it out, thoroughly explained it.

88. *Obs.*—Sprained: *niu*, to twist; here, twisted, or sprained, the leg.

93. *Obs.*—To pacify: *ya*, properly, to press down, to suppress; *ching*, fright.

94. *Obs.*—*Ping* is a copulative particle meaning with; also; moreover; when followed by a negative it intensifies the negation.

98. *Obs.*—Cried: *k'u*, to cry, as a human being.

100. *Obs.* 1.—Your son: *lang*, properly, a male, a man: *ling lang*, your son's, *chu ch'u*, abiding place. *Obs.* 2.—The word *sir* is introduced here in the translation to give the force of *ling*, honoured. *Obs.* 3.—Here: *fu*, properly, a treasury, a palace; politely, *fu shang*, your residence; the *shang* also indicating the superiority of the person addressed. *Obs.* 4.—Himself: *ch'in tzŭ*, his own self.

## DIALOGUE VIII.

1. Your servant, sir.

2. How do you do? Who are you?

3. I have been sent by the Ying Shun Hong to show you the way to Peking, sir. When do you propose going, sir?

4. I want to be off to-morrow.

5. Do you intend to go by land or by water, sir?

6. Which is the better way?

7. I should say by land; the river will be so high with the heavy rains we have had these last few days that it will be hard work tracking the boat up stream, and if you were to come in for a northerly wind, I don't think you could fetch T'ung Chou in five or six days.

8. Dear me! it won't do to go by water, then. How about going by land?

9. If you were off to-morrow morning, sir, and pushed on, you ought to be at Peking by the following evening; if you took your time, you would be well able to reach it on the third day.

10. Do you know the land road well?

11. Know it well? I should think I did; I've been travelling it back and forward for these ten years and more.

12. Then can you tell me enough about it to enable me to dispense with a guide, supposing I don't take one?

13. Yes; there is no difficulty about that. Do you know the floating bridge to the east as you leave this city, sir?

14. Yes, I know the bridge.

15. When you are on the other side of it, sir, you will be in a street where there is a good deal going on; you must inquire there for another bridge, and when you are across the second bridge, you will be in a road going north-west, which is the high road to Peking.

16. I have heard that one has to cross a river somewhere; is there one?

17. You mean the ferry, I suppose. There *is* a ferry.

18. There is a ferry! and how do the carts and horses manage?

19. There is no trouble with them; they can be ferried over.

20. Well, and after the ferry, what then?

21. When you leave the ferry station, you keep along the high road for thirty odd *li* from Tientsin, when you come to a market town called P'u-k'ou; that is the first stage.

3. 英 *ying*$^1$ 9. 州 *chou*$^1$ 17. 渡 *tu*$^4$ 12. 段 *tuan*$^4$

5. 旱 *han*$^4$ 17. 擺 *pai*$^3$ 21. 浦 *p'u*$^3$

3. *Obs.*—Ying Shun Hong: *ying*, properly, bursting into flower; hence, gallant, heroic; *shun*, obedient, that flows without check. *Ying shun* might translate as the Prosperous; the hong, mercantile firm, whose sign is Prosperity. *Ying* is the character employed to denote England, commonly called *ying kuo*.

5. *Obs.*—By land: *han*, dry.

7. *Obs.*—T'ung Chou: *chou*, one of the minor jurisdictions into which a *fu*, prefecture, is ordinarily divided. See *hsien*, Dialogue IX, 47.

9. *Obs.*—Were off: *tung shên*, to move the person; specially, to start on a journey.

13. *Obs.*—Floating bridge: *fou ch'iao* or *fu ch'iao*.

15. *Obs.*—Good deal going on: *jê nao chich-'rh*, a bustling street.

17. *Obs.*—Ferry: *pai-tu*; from *pai*, to shake, as the ferryman must the boat, and *tu*, to cross water.

21. *Obs.* 1.—Ferry station: *k'ou*, the mouth; on the sea-coast, a port; here, specially, of the hollow in the banks where they are touched by the ferry boat going and returning. *Obs.* 2.—P'u-k'ou: *p'u*$^3$, a bend in the bank of a river; here read *p'u*$^3$. *Obs.* 3.—Stage: *tuan*; properly, a piece, a section.

22. What, isn't the first stage Ho-si Wu?

23. No, sir; Ho-si Wu is a long way on; it's the end of the first day's journey. When you have passed through P'u-k'ou, you come next to Yang Ts'un, and after that to Nan-ts'ai Ts'un, and you may then reach Ho-si Wu towards nightfall. These places are all something over thirty *li* from each other.

24. And how much of the road to Peking are you supposed to have done when you get to Ho-si Wu?

25. It's about half way. You spend the night there, and you may be in Peking next day.

26. And where does one pass the night?

27. Some of your countrymen stop at the inns, sir; some in the temples.

28. Which are the better, the inns or the temples?

29. I think the inns more convenient myself. At the temples strangers are taken in only now and then, and it is not certain, in the first place, whether there is accommodation to be had in them or not; then, if there is a large number of carters, the priests do not like it; and, besides, if anything is missing there is no one to make responsible.

30. Ah! then the innkeeper has to look to it if things are lost at an inn, has he?

31. Yes, sir; that's the way of it. And there is another consideration, the inns can get you what you want to eat or drink; in the temples there is not even a kitchen.

32. No kitchen! then where do the people cook?

33. The people in the temples cook nothing but maigre; they may not cook meat.

34. Humph! one will be best off in an inn then. Which is the best inn in Ho-si Wu?

35. There is the Fu Hsing and the Shun Lai, both of them large inns; one stands at the south end of the street, and the other at the north.

36. And which will it suit me best to go to?

37. It must be for you to decide, sir, whether it suits you best to stop at a south end inn or an inn at the north end; the fare and accommodation are pretty much the same at both.

38. What does it signify whether I stop at the inns north or the inns south? are they a great way apart?

39. No great way apart; Ho-si Wu is not a large place like our city here; it is only a market town, one long street with some shops and so forth on either side of it.

| | | | |
|---|---|---|---|
| 23. 楊 *yang*² | 23. 隔 *ko*² | 33. 葷 *hun*¹ | 35. 興 *hsing*¹ |
| 23. 蔡 *ts'ai*⁴ | 29. 格 *ko*² | 35. 富 *fu*⁴ | 39. 鎮 *chên*⁴ |

23. *Obs.* 1.—Yang Ts'un: *lit.*, the village of the family of Yang. *Obs.* 2.—Nan Ts'ai Ts'un: the southern village of the family of Ts'ai. *Obs.* 3.—From each other: *hsiang kê*, or *ko*, mutually separated.

24. *Obs.*—Much of the road: *lit.*, speaking according to, with reference to, the length of the road.

25. *Obs.*—About half way: *lit.*, it may be reckoned to be *chung chien*, in the middle.

29. *Obs.*—Now and then: *kê*, or *ko*, from various other meanings comes to signify a bound or rule; *ko wai*, beyond rule; in the temples *liu k'o*, the keeping strangers, is an extraordinary thing, a thing not usual.

33. *Obs.*—Maigre: *su* (*see* Part III, 707), but here used of food which is not meat; *hun*, properly, that which has a relish, but simply meat or fish when opposed to *su*, maigre.

35. *Obs.* 1.—Fu Hsing: *fu*, rich; *fu hsing*, wealth and prosperity; say, the sign of the Well-to-do. *Obs*, 2.—Shun Lai: the inn to which guests come *shun*, in an uninterrupted stream; say, the Ever-going.

37. *Obs.*—Fare: *ch'ih shih*.

39. *Obs.* 1.—Market town: *chên*, properly, to control; amongst other meanings it has that of a town, less in importance than a district city. *Obs.* 2.—Some shops: *p'u-tzŭ*, shops, *shên-mo ti*, and anything you like.

40. Very well; then what difference is there between the north end and the south?

41. There is no difference; but the gentlemen I have shown the road to have in most instances put up at the inn nearest at hand after they had got into the town.

42. You mean, put up at the south end if they were going from Tientsin, and at the north coming from Peking, don't you?

43. Exactly so, sir.

44. All right. Now, when I get to my inn, what had I best tell them to get ready for me?

45. I don't suppose you have tried our Chinese fare, have you, sir?

46. No, I have not.

47. Well, if you have not, sir, you had best have something that will carry got ready at Tientsin, and take it with you.

48. Take it with me! but if I don't feed at the inn, they won't like it, will they?

49. It doesn't signify; the inn people will charge you for your accommodation.

50. Is there any fixed sum that one pays for one's lodging?

51. *We* pay much the same under any circumstances, but the man in charge will probably make a foreign traveller pay a little more than we do.

52. Is the man in charge the proprietor of the inn?

53. There is no rule; in some cases the proprietor takes charge himself, sometimes he engages a man in charge to look after the business for him.

54. I understand. And how much is it likely that I shall be asked to pay for my lodging?

55. I can hardly tell, but you speak Chinese, sir, and so you can have a talk with them about that before you take your rooms; if their charge is too high, there's no harm in objecting to it and offering something less.

56. Yes, that will do very well. Now, to get to Peking next day, which way am I to go?

57. After leaving Ho-si Wu in the morning, you still keep north-west, and, at twenty odd *li* on, you come to An-p'ing, and at some twenty *li* more, to Ma-t'ou; and then, twenty *li* from Ma-t'ou, you come to the old walled town of Chang-chia Wan.

58. Isn't there a small stream somewhere before you reach Chang-chia Wan?

59. No, sir; the town is on the river, part north of it, and part south. You will go in at the south gate, up the main street, across the river, and out by the north gate. Outside the gate there is a forked road; the road north takes you to T'ung Chou; the other, which bears west, takes you to Peking.

60. How far is it from that to Peking?

61. That depends on the gate you go in by, sir. If you stop at an inn in the Chinese city, you will go in by the Sha-wo Gate, and that is some fifty *li* from Chang-chia Wan; if you are going into the city by the East Wicket, you must keep north two or three *li*; no great distance farther.

55. 妨 *fang*[1]　　　55. 駁 *po*[2]

41. *Obs.*—Nearest at hand: *i chin chieh*, once they entered the street.

47. *Obs.*—With you: *pu ju*, there is nothing so good as that, *ts'ung*, at, Tientsin [the place *from* which you are moving], you should *tso*, having prepared, a little good-to-carry victuals, *tai-cho*, carry them with you.

55. *Obs.* 1.—No harm: *pu fang*, no hurt, no objection. *Obs.* 2.—Objecting: *po*, properly, to turn sharp round; to contradict.

59. *Obs.* 1.—On the river: *ch'i-cho*, bestriding the river face. *Obs.* 2. Forked road: two *ku*, *lit.*, limbs, of a diverging road. *Obs.* 3. Bears west: *p'ein*, swerving from a right line, leaning off the perpendicular, which in this case is north.

60. *Obs.*—From that: *chieh* is here used in the same sense as *ta*, from.

62. Which gate should one go in by to get to the Foreign Legations?

63. They are all inside the Ha-ta Gate, in the neighbourhood of the Imperial Canal Bridge; I should say the best way would be by the East Wicket.

64. Very good; I understand perfectly. There is another question I want to ask, if I am to go so fast, what am I to do with my baggage?

65. How much baggage have you, sir?

66. Those things lying outside the door.

67. What, are all those large cases yours too, sir?

68. To be sure they are.

69. If you intend to be in Peking in two days, I am afraid you must leave some of the baggage behind, sir; you would have to pay a good deal for the hire of so many large carts, and, not only that, it would be impossible for you to go any pace.

70. Well, then, what do you recommend me to do?

71. I think, sir, you might hire a small cart to carry your bedding and all that sort of thing with you, and ship the rest of the baggage by T'ung Chou.

72. In that case do I ride in the cart with the baggage I take with me?

73. Better hire another small cart to ride in, sir; don't you think so?

74. Will they be carts with one beast or two?

75. If you want to get on, sir, you must have two beasts; indeed, you might well have three, for there will be a good deal of water on the roads after the rain, and they will be heavy.

76. Ah! but if the roads are so heavy I don't much fancy riding in a cart; can I hire a horse here?

77. Yes, sir, or a mule; but I am afraid our saddles will not do for you.

78. I've got English saddlery and all that sort of thing with me.

79. I don't think that will do all the same; the saddle might be put on one of our horses, but I don't think he would stand the *chiao²-mao⁴-tzŭ*.

80. What is the *chiao-mao-tzŭ* (head-piece)?

81. It is the gear on a horse's head for attaching the bit and reins to. What I am afraid of is that as the horse is not used to carrying the like he might be restive. I should say you would do better to buy a foreign horse.

| | | | |
|---|---|---|---|
| 63. 岱 *tai⁴* | 69. 恐 *k'ung³* | 79. 嚼 *chiao²* | 81. 慣 *kuan⁴* |
| 63. 御 *yü⁴* | 77. 鞍 *an¹* | 81. 扯 *ch'ê³* | |

63. *Obs.* 1.—Ha-ta Gate: properly, Hai Tai; the name given the gate by the late dynasty; *tai*, classically, a hill. *Obs.* 2.—Imperial Canal Bridge: *yü*, properly, to drive a chariot; when prefixed to certain words, imperial.

69. *Obs.*—Afraid: *k'ung*, the same in meaning as *p'a*, with which it is joined.

73. *Obs.*—Small cart: *chiao ch'ê-'rh*, or *chiao ch'ê-tzŭ*, a passenger cart; with a top, as opposed to *ta ch'ê*, or *ch'ang³ ch'ê*, a large or open cart (*see* Dialogue VII, 72); *hsiao ch'ê*, also a passenger cart; *hsiao ch'ê-tzŭ*, a wheel-barrow.

77. *Obs.* 1.—Afraid: *chih p'a*, I only fear. *Obs.* 2.—Saddles: *an*.

79. *Obs.* 1.—Be put on: *lit.*, our horses *hai*, after all, can *pei*, take on the back. *Obs.* 2.—*Chiao*: properly, to bite, whether of man or beast; here, short for *chiao-tzŭ*, a bit (*see* 81).

81. *Obs.* 1.—Reins: *ch'ê*, to draw; *ch'ê³ shou*, the bridle used by a rider. *Obs.* 2.—Not used: *kuan*, accustomed to. *Obs.* 3.—Restive: *nao hsing-tzŭ*, to let his temper break out, to give way to temper.

31

82. But how am I to buy a foreign horse here at Tientsin?

83. There's a horse in our hong that one of the gentlemen wants to sell; he is a very good horse, quiet and fast, and he has been to Peking and back three or four times.

84. Good; I'll go to the hong and have a talk about it. And now, when these boxes go up to T'ung Chou, whom can I hire to go with them to Peking?

85. Would it do to hire me, sir?

86. It would do very well, but I doubt whether the house will let you go; I don't think they could spare you for so many days.

87. They can spare me, sir; what did they send me here to-day for but to take your orders?

83. 夥 *huo*$^{3}$  87. 吩 *fên*$^{1}$  87. 咐 *fu*$^{4}$

83 *Obs.* 1.—Gentlemen: *huo*, originally, a number of persons or things; thence, the same with, associated with; *huo chi*, one who is associated with one in a place, sometimes as a partner, but more generally as a paid *employé*. *Obs.* 2.—Quiet: *lao-shih*, honest; hence, simple; when applied to animals, inoffensive.

86. *Obs.*—Let you go: *jung*$^{2}$, the same character as that read *yung* in Part III, 963, but here meaning to allow, to tolerate; I fear [the people] in your hong *li pu k'ai*, unable to separate from you, will not let you go.

87. *Obs.*—Orders: *fên fu*, to give orders to; the combination is not well explained by the dictionaries. By some teachers the two words are said to mean no more than they would without the Radical *k'ou*, namely, to allot to different persons their several functions.

---

## DIALOGUE IX.

1. [*Servant.*] There's a teacher who wishes to see you, sir.

2. [*Master.*] Ask him to walk in.

3. The teacher, sir.

4. [*Master, to the Teacher.*] Take a seat, please.

5. [*Teacher.*] Thank you, sir; pray be seated.

6. May I ask your name, sir?

7. My name is Su.

8. And your business with me is——?

9. I heard that you wanted to engage a teacher, sir; a friend of mine mentioned it yesterday.

10. Ah! it must have been CHANG *hsien-shêng* who was speaking of it.

11. It was CHANG *hsien-shêng*.

12. Did he tell you that I was looking out for a teacher for myself or for someone else?

13. He did not specify whether it was for yourself or not, sir; is it not for yourself?

14. It is not; I do not want a teacher myself, but a friend of mine has commissioned me to engage one for him.

15. Is your friend a countryman of your own, sir?

16. He is; he has not been in China long.

7. 蘇 *su*$^{1}$  9. 閣 *ko*$^{2}$

7. *Obs.*—Su: *su*, properly, reviving; here, a surname.

9. *Obs.*—Sir: *ko*, properly, an upper story; *ko-hsia* in ancient times applied only to certain ministers; now, as used in the text, sir.

13. *Obs.*—Specify: he did not tell me *hsiang hsi*, explicitly.

17. Then he does not understand Chinese, I suppose?

18. He does not speak a word of Chinese, nor does he know a character.

19. How am I to read with him then?

20. You will have to teach him to talk first. When he begins to speak, we shall see what can be done in the written language.

21. But how am I to begin if he doesn't know a character?

22. Oh, sir, a teacher of your experience, who has had so many pupils among your own countrymen, will not find it impossible to teach him, surely?

23. Teaching as we are taught is another affair. We become able to speak Chinese without learning it, and we acquire the written language by learning books off by heart when we are very young; but I don't think it likely that your friend will put himself to the trouble of keeping to the same order of proceeding as our Chinese boys.

24. That of course not; still we may hit upon something. How old were you when you began to read, may I ask?

25. I began at seven.

26. Did you begin with the Three-character Classic and the Poem in a Thousand Characters?

27. Yes; they were my first studies.

28. The Chinese all begin with those little books; what is the real advantage of their so doing?

29. The Three-character Classic is in sentences of three characters each, and this makes it easy for little children to commit it to memory; the Poem in a Thousand Characters has no character twice repeated, and therefore, when they have learned this, they know a thousand characters.

30. And what do they learn after these?

31. As a rule, the Four Books, and, after these, the Five Canons.

32. How many years did it take you, sir, to learn them all, from the time you began the Four Books until you knew the Five Canons?

33. Some six or seven years from the beginning of the course to the end of it.

34. Ah! then by the time you had learned the Five Canons you were fourteen?

35. Yes, in my fourteenth year.

36. And how old were you when you began to have them explained to you?

37. I was twelve years of age.

38. Did you study the commentary, or did you have the text explained to you orally by your teacher?

18. 漢 *han*4 36. 講 *chiang*3 38. 註 *chu*4

18. *Obs.*—Chinese: *han*, the name of the dynasty which commenced about B.C. 200; now applied generally to all men and things Chinese.

19. *Obs.*—Read with: *chiao kei*; the *kei* being untranslatable in English; grammatically, we should say that it puts *t'a* in the dative case.

22. *Obs.* 1.—Experience: *lao shou*, an old hand. *Obs.* 2.—Pupils: *mên-shêng*; the word *shêng* being construed as man; those who come to the *mên*, gate or door, of the *hsien-shêng*, teacher.

23. *Obs.* 1.—Without learning: *êrh*, and yet; we do not learn, and yet we are able. *Obs.* 2.—Learn by heart *pei nien*, *lit.*, backing recite; *pei*, short for *pei-cho shu*, with one's back to the book, *i.e.*, without looking at it.

29. *Obs.*—Twice repeated: *ch'ung*2 (*see* Part III, 336).

31. *Obs.*—Five Canons: *ching* (*see* Part III, 885); here specially of the five great classical books of China.

36. *Obs.*—Explained: *chiang*, properly, to tell; specially, to explain the meaning of a character or a text; *k'ai chiang*, to begin explaining.

38. *Obs.*—Commentary: *chu*, properly, to make a note of; thence, to annotate.

39. At first, by my teacher; but after listening to his explanations a year or so, I began to read the commentary myself. Then I worked at prose and verse composition some two years or more, and then I graduated.

40. At sixteen! that was early; you must be a first-rate man.

41. Nothing of the kind, indeed; it was all luck. I had to stand several examinations for my licentiate's degree, and I didn't get it for seven or eight years after.

42. May I ask your age?

43. I am thirty.

44. And what has been your occupation in the six years since you took your licentiate's degree?

45. I have been doing nothing to speak of; I took pupils at home for the first two years, and for some time after that I acted as private secretary to a friend.

46. What office did your friend hold?

47. He was magistrate of a district in Shantung; he died last year, and I came home again.

48. Your having acted as a private secretary is an additional recommendation.

49. How an additional recommendation?

50. In this respect: my friend, who wishes to engage you, will want to study official correspondence when he has learned the spoken language.

51. It's a pity that one can't see one's way to beginning the spoken language.

52. I have a plan, but I am too busy to-day to explain it; could you come and see me to-morrow and talk it over with me?

53. By all means; I'll wait on you to-morrow as you desire, sir; at what o'clock?

54. Shall we say between three and four?

55. Very good, sir; then I take my leave.

56. Good-day.

57. Good-day.

| | | | |
|---|---|---|---|
| 39. 詩 *shih*$^1$ | 41. 徼 *chiao*$^3$ | 42. 庚 *kêng*$^1$ | 51. 緒 *hsü*$^4$ |
| 40. 中 *chung*$^4$ | 41. 倖 *hsing*$^4$ | 46. 榮 *jung*$^2$ | 53. 遵 *tsun*$^1$ |
| 40. 秀 *hsiu*$^4$ | 41. 試 *shih*$^4$ | 47. 縣 *hsien*$^4$ | 54. 申 *shên*$^1$ |

39. *Obs.* 1.—Prose composition: *wên chang; lit.*, forms of literature, literature which conforms to the rules of composition; *shih*, poetry, is not included in the term. *Obs.* 2.—Graduated: *chin hsio*, to enter *hsio*, the colleges, or literary establishments, of which the graduates who have taken the first degree are members.

40. *Obs.* 1.—Early: what, at sixteen, *chung*$^4$ (not to be confounded with the same character read *chung*$^1$), you obtained the degree of *hsiu ts'ai*, fine talent, your B.A. *Obs.* 2.—*Chung*$^4$: properly, to hit a mark; *hsiu*, fair, elegant. *Obs.* 3.—First-rate man: your *t'ien jên*, share of ability assigned you by Heaven, is *kao*, of high degree.

41. *Obs.* 1.—All luck: *chiao*, amongst many meanings, has that of a byway; *hsing*, properly, fortunate; *chiao hsing*, generally, of success beyond merit. *Obs.* 2.—Licentiate: *hsiang shih, lit.*, village trial; an allusion to ancient competitive examination in one's native district, but now technically signifying the examination for the second degree held in the capital of the province.

42. *Obs.*—Your age: *kêng*, one of the characters used in the Chinese time cycle; colloquially, as here, the years of one's age.

46. *Obs.*—What office: *jung*, properly, of vegetation, flourishing; used as here, complimentarily; *jung jên*, your post.

47. *Obs.*—District: *hsien*, one of the minor jurisdictions into which a prefecture is divided; somewhat less important than a *chou*; the magistrate governing it is called a *chih-hsien*, as in the *chou*, a *chih-chou*.

50. *Obs.*—Correspondence: *wên-shu*, generic of all official documents.

51. *Obs.*—See one's way: *hsü*, a skein of silk; *t'ou hsü*, the clue to unravel a skein.

53. *Obs.*—As you desire: *tsun*, to obey; I will just obey your commands.

54. *Obs.*—Three and four: *shên*, the ninth of the 12 two-hour periods into which the 24 hours are divided; it extends from 3 to 5 P.M.; *shên ch'u*, the first part of the period *shên*.

55. *Obs.*—Take leave: *shih* (*see* Part III, 574), to lose, to deprive oneself of [the pleasure of] *p'ei*, bearing you company.

## DIALOGUE X.

1. This morning a friend of mine sent me an invitation to dinner at a restaurant; I am in two minds about going, because it seems to me that as I am not very well up in any of your forms of social etiquette, I should raise a laugh at my expense if I were to omit any of the usual formalities.

2. Don't imagine that; when I have told you what the ordinary formalities are, you will understand what to do. Let me have a look at your invitation. Oh! I see; its CHANG *ta lao-yeh*, who asks you to dine at the Ch'ing Hui T'ang; that's a capital restaurant; it is roomy, and the apartments are very cool; I often go there myself. They are very particular there about the cooking, and everything is palatable; there is no establishment that comes up to it; you'd better go; you'll be glad to have a chat with them all, and wake yourself up a bit.

3. I have heard that the time stated on Chinese invitations cannot be considered absolute; for instance, when noon is the hour given, one should go at about 2 P.M. to be in order.

4. That depends on how the invitation is worded; if the character *chun*³ (precisely) occurs, one must go at the hour named. The character *chun* does not occur in CHANG *ta lao-yeh's* invitation, which names four o'clock simply, so if you go at six you won't be late. If you go too early, not only will the other guests not have all assembled, but it may chance even that your host has not arrived.

| | | | | | |
|---|---|---|---|---|---|
| 虛 | 1. 莊 *chuang*¹ | 1. 豫 *yü*⁴ | 1. 禮 *li*³ | 2. 究 *chiu*¹ | 3. 未 *wei*⁴ |
| | 1. 猶 *yu*² | 1. 酬 *ch'ou*² | 1. 倘 *t'ang*³ | 2. 味 *wei*⁴ | |

1. *Obs.* 1.—Invitation: *t'ie-'rh*, a slip of paper in the form of a memorandum; anything extending over one sheet is not generally included in the term (*see* Part III, 1022). Cf. *shuo t'ie-'rh*, a memorandum generally; *ch'ing t'ie-'rh*, an invitation. *Obs.* 2.—Restaurant: *chuang*, *lit.*, a large place of business, also a village, is only applied in this connexion to a restaurant which does not supply lodging accommodation. *Obs.* 3.—In two minds: *yu yü*, or *yu yi*⁴, indecision; *yu*, *lit.*, a monkey; *yü*, an elephant; both supposed to be suspicious animals, and hence typical of doubt or indecision. *Obs.* 4.—Etiquette: *ying ch'ou ti li chieh*, *lit.*, the items *(chieh)* of *li*, observances (ritual or ceremonial), belonging to *(ti) ying ch'ou*, social requirements; *ying* and *ch'ou*, both mean to return, as a compliment, though the latter in certain combinations means also to recompense. *Ying ch'ou* is applied only to the amenities of society; we can say *t'a ti ying ch'ou ta*, or *to*, his social duties are numerous, or he has a large circle of friends. *Obs.* 5.—If: *t'ang*; seldom used without *jo* in conversation. *Obs.* 6.—Omit: *la* (see Part III, 763). *Obs.* 7.—Formalities, observances: *kuo chieh*; *chieh* (short for *li chieh*, as above), the formalities, *kuo*, that pass.

2. *Obs.* 1.—Ordinary formalities: *su t'ao-tzŭ*, *lit.*, common casing, suit, or set; *t'ao*, an envelope or casing (*see* Part III, 769), is here, as in the phrase *i t'ao i-shang*, a suit of clothes, a numerative of some such word as ceremony, form, etc., understood, of which it takes the place; hence, the affix *tzŭ*. *See* observations on the numeratives, Part III, 8. *Obs.* 2.—Ch'ing Hui T'ang: this might be rendered the Hall of Happy Meetings; for *ch'ing*, *see* Dialogue IV, 23. *Obs.* 3.—Particular: *chiang chiu*, *lit.*, in the dishes they prepare they very much explain and inquire; they give particular directions [as to how the food should be cooked], and inform themselves [as to the manner in which these directions are carried out]; *chiu*, to inquire into, to examine; it will be found later in another combination. *Obs.* 4.—[illegible] *wei-'rh* (pronounce [illegible]), a flavour [illegible] *wei*, taste, flavour, [illegible] *wei-'rh* [illegible] *Obs.* [illegible]—Glad [illegible] *t'ê* (emphasise *tê*), *lit.*, gladly obtain; [illegible] Part III, 989.

[illegible] *Obs.* 1.—[illegible] *ch'êng* has here no special force [illegible] being the important word, and therefore [illegible] *Obs.* 2.—Noon: *wu k'ê*, one of the eight *k'ê*, or divisions, in the *shih ch'en*, or hour period, *wu* (*see* Part III, 225), which [illegible] from 11 A.M. [illegible]; *wu k'ê* is indefinite and [illegible] mean any quarter between 11 and 1. To make it precise [illegible] character would be required; thus, *wu ch'u* (*see* Dialogue IX, 51) *êrh k'ê* would be the second division in the [illegible], or commencing [illegible] of the *wu* period; in other words, [illegible] the next period [illegible].

5. There is another point upon which I want the benefit of your advice: if I accept his hospitality, it seems to me that I ought to send him an answer.

6. There is no occasion; your retention of the invitation is a proof of your positive intention to go.

7. When I go I shall have to give up the invitation, sha'n't I?

8. Yes; the custom is this. When you go, you should, on arrival at the door of the restaurant, tell your servant to hand in your card. The people in attendance at the door will take your card, and, showing you the way in, will invite you to enter whatever room the host may be in. When you see your host, I need not remind you that you should in the first place salute him, after which you should take the letter of invitation and present it to him with both hands, saying as you do so, "Here I am bothering you again; I am as ashamed of myself as I can be; I am not worthy of the terms you have applied to me in your invitation." The host, as he takes the invitation from you, will also make some depreciatory remark about himself, and everybody will then sit down and take tea. When all the guests have arrived, you will be invited to take your places, and dinner will be put on the table.

9. It sometimes happens that all the guests cannot come; and if only one is wanting, you do not keep on waiting for him. When he does turn up, he is invited to take the vacant seat. The seats that the different guests shall take have all been determined beforehand by the host, so when you come to table, although you are bound to protest, he is certain not to allow you to sit as you please. A vacant seat is thus reserved for a guest who comes late, and when he does arrive he can sit down without much formality.

*[The guest is now supposed to have met his host, and made his bow and speech.]*

10. [*Host.*] Here you are, sir! I have been remiss in not going to meet you; pray forgive me.

5. 領 *ling*³ 6. 據 *chü*⁴ 8. 矩 *chü*³ ⁴ 8. 揖 *i*¹ 8. 謙 *ch'ien*¹
5. 乎 *hu*¹ 7. 繳 *chiao*³ 8. 遞 *ti*⁴ 8. 擾 *jao*³

5. *Obs.* 1.—Accept his hospitality: *ling*, here, to receive, to accept; if I receive his *ch'ing*, politenesses (tokens of friendly sentiment). *Ling* can also be applied to the drawing of pay, etc.; it further means the neck; hence, *ling-tzŭ*, a collar. *See also* Dialogue I, 2. *Obs.* 2.—It seems to me: *hu* is here a particle implying doubt; for *ssŭ*, see Part III, 1070.

6. *Obs.*—Proof: *p'ing*, to lean upon (*see* Part III, 722); *chü*, to lay hold of, the something reliable that one lay's hold of; hence, proof, evidence.

7. *Obs.*—*Chiao*, to deliver up, to surrender.

8. *Obs.* 1.—Custom: *kuei* (*see* Part III, 581), *lit.*, a pair of compasses, a rule, custom; *chü*⁴, a carpenter's square; hence also, a rule or custom; the two are never used apart in the above sense. *Obs.* 2.—When you go: *ming-'rh* is often used indefinitely of some future date not very far remote. *Obs.* 3.—*Ti*, to hand in or over to; for *jang*, to invite, *see* Dialogue IV, 25. *Obs.* 4.—Salute: *tso i*, to make the Chinese bow with the hands folded. *Obs.* 5.—Bothering: *jao*, to bother, to give trouble to, to incommode; for *t'ao*, see Part III, 834 and 836. *Obs.* 6.—Ashamed: *pao k'uei*, *lit.*, carry shame in my bosom; *see* Part III, 718. *Obs.* 7.—Not worthy: *lit.*, I dare not act as (represent myself to be) the person you treat me as (*see* Part III, 342, *tang*⁴); I cannot play the part you assign to me; a very common depreciatory expression applicable to almost any compliment or civility. There are of course many other forms of saluting a host than the one here given. *Obs.* 8.—Depreciatory: *ch'ien*, humble, modest; *hsü*, empty, in the sense of deficiency (*see* Dialogue V, 76). *Obs.* 9.—One: note *i pan wei*; this is a pure colloquialism. The *pan* must not be emphasised.

9. *Obs.*—Formality: *jang*, to invite; in the present instance, in the sense of to yield, to give way to others in which sense it is frequently used.

10. *Obs.*—Remiss, etc.: *shih ying*, failed to meet you.

11. [*Guest.*] Not at all; I'm late, I'm afraid, and have kept all you gentlemen waiting.

12. [*Host.*] No, no; they've only just arrived; let's get to dinner.

13. [*Guest.*] I'm guilty of great assumption in taking this place.

14. [*Host.*] It's yours by right. Pray take wine all of you: we'll begin with a bumper.

15. [*To host.*] Your health.

16. [*Host.*] Please begin. I won't help you; we're all intimates here, and each one must help himself.

17. [*Guest.*] That's the best way; if we all begin to press each other to eat, it will look too formal; we'd much better go as we please. There you are! we've just agreed to dispense with formalities, and you are commencing them. We shall have to return the compliment to make it right.

18. [*Host.*] No, I am not. I sent a man a day or two ago to the manager's office to tell him to beg them in the kitchen to pay particular attention to the cooking of the dishes, and they seem to me rather better than those not made to order. I notice you gentlemen won't get your chopsticks to work, so I am obliged to help you. You might taste them.

* * * * *

19. [*Host.*] Don't put your chopsticks down; you must all make a good meal.

20. [*Guest.*] We've all had as much as we can eat, and more wine than we can carry, and are very much obliged to you for your excellent dinner.

21. [*Host.*] There has been nothing fit for you to eat to-day, and the wine is so bad that you have not done justice to your drinking powers.

22. [*Guest.*] What are you talking about? I'll say no more to-day, as my cart has come, and it's no longer early, so I must be getting home. I shall call shortly at your house to offer my thanks.

| | | | | |
|---|---|---|---|---|
| 11. 諸 *chu*¹ | 17. 顯 *hsien*³ | 17. 敬 *ching*⁴ | 18. 嚐 *ch'ang*² | 21. 屈 *ch'ü*¹ |
| 12. 席 *hsi*² | 17. 拘 *chü*¹ | 18. 竈 *tsao*⁴ | 19. 飽 *pao*³ | 22. 謝 *hsieh*⁴ |
| 13. 僭 *chien*⁴ | 17. 泥 *ni*⁴ ² | 18. 筷 *k'uai*⁴ | 20. 盛 *shêng*⁴ | |

11. *Obs.* 1.—All you gentlemen: *chu*, all; for *kung*, *see* Part III. 979. *Obs.* 2.—Kept you waiting: *lit.*, caused you *shou*, to endure [the trouble of], *têng*, waiting.

12. *Obs.*—Get to dinner: *hsi*, a repast or banquet; let's enter upon our repast.

13. *Obs.*—Assumption: *chien*, to usurp, to assume what does not belong to one; [in taking] this seat I am indeed guilty of much assumption.

14. *Obs.*—A bumper: *lit.*, let us all drain a cup.

16. *Obs.*—Help you: *pu*, to distribute (*see* Part III. 406).

17. *Obs.* 1.—Look: *hsien*, manifest, apparent; *hsien cho*, apparently; hence, to appear to be, to look as. *Obs.* 2.—Formal, conventional: *chü*, to grasp, to adhere to; *ni*⁴, bigoted, opinionated; *chü ni*, a grasping at what one conceives to be the proper thing; *ni*², mud. *Obs.* 3.—Return the compliment: *ching*, to honour, to show respect to.

18. *Obs.* 1.—Manager's office: *kuei shang*; *lit.*, in, or at, the counter. *Obs.* 2.—Kitchen: *tsao*, a furnace, or cooking range, of a large establishment; *shang*, as above. *Obs.* 3.—*K'uai*, a chopstick; also called *k'uai-tzŭ*. *Obs.* 4.—*Ch'ang*, to taste: properly written without the radical "mouth."

19. *Obs.*—Make a good dinner: *ch'ih pao*, eat till you are full, or satisfied.

20. *Obs.*—Excellent dinner: *shêng*, superlative, excellent, fine, etc.; *shê*, to spread, to lay out, to arrange; hence, what is so laid out, *q.d.*, a dinner. Cf. our slang word "spread."

21. *Obs.*—Not done justice, etc.: *ch'ü*, *lit.*, crooked, or bent awry; also, a wrong or grievance, to do wrong to; *liang*, capacity (*see* Part III, 776, Obs.); here, capacity for drink.

22. *Obs.*—Offer my thanks: *tao*, to say, to give expression to, *hsieh*, thanks; *hsieh hsieh nin*, thank you, sir.

23. [*Host.*] I couldn't think of such a thing. Please yourself about going, I beg; I won't venture to detain you.

24. [*Guest.*] Are you gentlemen going to sit a while? in that case I must take my leave before you? Good-bye, good-bye; don't see me to the door, pray; stop where you are; there's no occasion for our host either to see me out; now, please, return and see to your other guests.

25. [*Host.*] I'll come no further; I'll see you into your cart.

26. [*Guest.*] Thanks, many thanks.

27. [*Host.*] *Au revoir.*

23. 豈 *ch'i*[3] 25. 乘 *ch'êng*[2]

23. *Obs.* 1.—Couldn't think of: *lit.*, how could I venture (to trouble you, or some such phrase, understood); *ch'i* is the interrogative particle how or what, but only used in certain set phrases. The above is one of the commonest of polite phrases, and is used with as much frequency as *pu kan tang* (*see* above 8, Obs. 7). *Obs.* 2.—Detain: *fêng liu.* It is difficult to give the exact force of *fêng* in this phrase; it means, properly, to raise the hands when presenting anything (*see* Part III, 990); to do an act of homage or respect; hence, the respect that such an act implies.

24. *Obs.*—Stop where you are: *liu pu*, *lit.*, detain your footsteps; only used politely.

25. *Obs.*—Get into your cart: *ch'êng shang*, to mount, as a horse or a chariot; not used colloquially except in polite conversation.

26. *Obs.*—Many thanks: *k'o t'ou* is a common expression for thanks, but not to an inferior.

国家出版基金项目
NATIONAL PUBLICATION FOUNDATION

# 海上絲綢之路文獻集成

總主編　陳支平　陳春聲

## 科技與文化編 95

主編　王揚宗　葉　農

海峽出版發行集團
THE STRAITS PUBLISHING & DISTRIBUTING GROUP
福建人民出版社

# 本册目次

# 榕腔初學撮要

（*A Manual of the Foochow Dialect*）

〔美〕摩嘉立（Caleb Cook Baldwin）編譯

# 榕腔初學撮要　解題

《榕腔初學撮要》，美國摩嘉立編譯。摩嘉立（Caleb Cook Baldwin，一八二〇—一九一一），美國公理會傳教士。生於美國新澤西州，一八四八年來華，居福州近半世紀，一八九五年返美。此書係福州方言學習教材，正文含語法，短語，商業，宗教、文學、政府，雜集，短語短句所用字詞及其英語簡釋，英漢詞彙等内容。據一八七一年福州版影印。

同治十年

# 榕腔初學撮要

摩嘉立編譯

福州美華書局印

A

# MANUAL

OF THE

# FOOCHOW DIALECT.

BY

REV. C. C. BALDWIN,

*Of the American Board Mission.*

---

FOOCHOW:

METHODIST EPISCOPAL MISSION PRESS.

1871.

# PPEFACE.

This Manual is designed to facilitate the study of the Foochow Dialect in its construction, idioms, and some of its common terms and phrases. The aim has been to present the elementary rules and principles of the dialect in such simple forms and connections as to aid the student in the beginning of his task. Familiar examples and brief explanations are introduced under the various subjects treated in the work.

The plan and scope of the volume appear in the Index. Its extent and practical availability as a Manual are seen from the number of Chinese words and expressions introduced in various forms as single or compound names and terms, as examples, as set phrases, and as Chinese equivalents of English words. The number of such words and expressions is estimated to be in Part 1st, 800, Part 2d, 1130, Part 3d, 720, Part 4th, 730, Part 5th, 1220, Part 6th, 1150, Part 7th, 2850, giving an aggregate of 8600. Making a reduction of $\frac{1}{4}$ to $\frac{1}{3}$ from this aggregate on account of repetitions of the same word or expression, there will remain about 6000 different words, terms, and phrases. These may be memorized and employed as models by the learner in the prosecution of his studies.

The first sixteen pages of the Manual, comprising orthography and explanations, is taken—with slight modifications and additions—from the Introduction of the Alphabetic Dictionary in the Foochow Dialect. The orthography being the same, the Romanized Chinese words of the Manual, with rare exceptions as in case of a few commercial and other technical terms, may be readily found in the Dictionary, where discriminations in meaning are more fully developed. The two works may therefore be used together with advantage.

It should be observed, however, that some of the Romanized words have no Chinese characters to represent them in the Dictionary, also that the characters—when employed—are not always the same in the two works. For some statements on this subject of representing colloquial words by Chinese characters, the student is referred to the second page in the Introduction to the Dictionary, also to page 47 of the Manual.

Parts 2d and 6th and most of Part 5th were prepared by Mrs. C. C. Baldwin. The phrases of Part 2d may be thoroughly analyzed and studied by referring to the Vocabulary in Part 6th for the meanings of single words and compound terms. The Tables of Relationship in Part 5th—as regards arrangement and extent— are a new feature in works of this kind. By means of the Index on pages 182 & 183, reference may be made to the table or tables, in which any given term occurs, in order to ascertain its meaning.

The multiplicity of tonic marks and diacritical points and accents has made it difficult—not to say impossible—to secure entire accuracy in printing. The whole work has been reviewed and a list of the more important corrections inserted. The context and the student's knowledge of the orthography will usually suffice to correct any trivial errors that may still remain.

The cordial thanks of the author are due to Rev. R. S. Maclay, D. D. for his contribution of Part 3d on Commercial Terms, as well as for valuable suggestions on various points during the progress of the work and for aid in correcting proof-sheets : also to the Methodist Episcopal Mission of Foochow for generously undertaking the expense and labor of printing and publication.

With these brief introductory remarks, the volume is sent forth in the earnest desire that it may be of service to any who wish to investigate this dialect, and especially to missionaries preparing to labor for the evangelization of the Chinese people.

C, C. B.

FOOCHOW, March 15th, 1871.

# INDEX.

# CORRECTIONS.

| Page | Line | Correction |
|---|---|---|
| *Page* 11. | *Line* 33. | —*wi*(last word on page) read *wí*. |
| 15. | 17. | —p. 595 and p. 610 refer to the Aphabetic Dictionary in the Foochow Dialect. |
| 25. | 22. | —*twaí*$^{2}$ read *twai*$^{2}$. |
| 31. | 6. | —*nióh*$_{2}$ read *nioh*$_{2}$. |
| 34. | 25. | —*mwóí*$^{2}$ read *mwoí*$^{2}$. |
| 35. | 2. | —*mwóí*$^{2}$ read *mwoí*$^{2}$. |
| 43. | 4. | —꜀*ui* read ꜀*ui*. |
| 57. | 15. | —꜀*Kwong* read ꜀*Kwong*. |
| 61. | 8. | —꜀*í* read ꜀*i*. |
| 61. | 35. | —erase (or ꜀*seu*). |
| 71. | 9. | —꜀*chiéng* read ꜀*chiêng*. |
| 71. | 11. | —*nioh*, read *nioh*$_{2}$. |
| 75. | 33. | —*yiok*, read *yok*,. |
| 78. | 6. | —I am under obligation to you, read I owe my company, *i. e.*, excuse my leaving you. |
| 82. | 7. | —꜀*mó* read ꜀*mó*. |
| 87. | 14. | —after dinner read after noon. |
| 99. | 30. | —*hó*$^{2}$ read *ho*$^{2}$. |
| 105. | 26. | —*ngwoi*$^{2}$ read *ngwoí*$^{2}$. |
| 105. | 28. | —*ngwoi*$^{2}$ read *ngwoî*$^{2}$. |
| 108. | 26. | —ʿ*Kwang* ʿ*k*ʿ*au*, read ꜀*Kwang* ʿ*k*ʿ*au*. |
| 109. | 23 | —*K*ʿ*ié*$^{2}$ read *Kiĕ*$^{2}$. |
| 110. | 32. | —꜀ *Ching* read ꜀ *Ching*. |
| 123. | 13. | —二百 read 百二. |
| 152. | 27. | —*Sioh*, read *Sioh*$_{2}$. |
| 160. | 22. | —for *p*ʿ*ek*, classifier of *horses*, use 匹 instead of 疋. |
| 178. | 15. | —P. read M. |
| 184. | 17. | —ʿ*siéu* read ʿ*sieu*. |
| 186. | 15. | —꜀*ié* read ꜀*ié*. |
| 188. | 13. | —꜀*Su* read ꜀*Su*. |
| 208. | 4. | —*mók*, read *mok*,. |
| 232. | 16. | —*ngiah*$_{2}$ read *ngiăh*$_{2}$. |
| 232. | 20. | —*swoi*$^{2}$ read *swoî*$^{2}$. |

# MANUAL

## OF THE

# FOOCHOW DIALECT.

## PART I. GRAMMAR.

In the following pages, under the general term of GRAMMAR, the prominent rules and principles of the science, as they exist in the Foochow Dialect, are expressed in simple definitions and statements. These are generally illustrated by short examples in Chinese characters and their Romanized equivalents, with translations into English. The proper construction and idioms of the dialect, thus brought to view, will prepare the student for the study of PHRASES.

### ORTHOGRAPHY.

The system of orthography adopted in this Manual is essentially that known as the system of Sir William Jones. It was used in Romanizing the languages of India and the Pacific Islands, and the dialects of the North American Indians.

VOWELS.

| | | | |
|---|---|---|---|
| 1. *a*, | as | in | *far*, *father*. |
| 2. *á*, | ,, | ,, | *care*, *fair*, or as *e* in *there*. |
| 3. *ă*, | ,, | ,, | *hat*, *sat*, *fathom*. |
| 4. *e*, | ,, | ,, | *they*, *prey*, or as *a* in *name*. |
| 5. *é*, | ,, | ,, | *met*, *seven*, *error*. |
| 6. *ë*, | ,, | ,, | *her*, or as *i* in *bird*. |
| 7. *i*, | ,, | ,, | *machine*. |
| 8. *í*, | ,, | ,, | *pin*, or as the second *i* in *infinite*. |
| 9. *o*, | ,, | ,, | *no*, *note*, *report*. |
| 10. *ó*, | ,, | ,, | *for*, *lord*, or as *a* in *fall*. |
| 11. *u*, | ,, | ,, | *bull*, but oftener as *o* in *move*, or *oo* in school. |
| 12. *ü*, | ,, | ,, | the French *l'une*, *jeune*. |

DIPHTHONGS in the first tone.

1. *ai*, as in *aisle*, *aye*, *while*.
2. *au*, ,, *ow* in *now*, *howl*.
3. *eu*, } have the sounds of the component vowels.
4. *iă*, }
5. *ié*, }
6. *io*, }
7. *iu*, as *ew* in *pew*, *chew*.
8. *oi*, has the sound of the component vowels.

TRIPHTHONG in the first tone.

1. *ieu*, has the sound of the component vowels.

CONSONANTS.

1. *ch*, as in church.
2. *ch'*, the aspirate *ch*, or the same as *ch* with an additional *h*, which is always represented by the Greek *spiritus asper*, or mark of rough breathing.
3. *h*, as in *hand* at the beginning of words, while at the end it is not fully enunciated, but marks an abrupt closing of the vocal organs.
4. *k*, as in *king* at the beginning of words, while at the end it is a suppressed *k* sound, and (like the *h*) marks an abrupt closing of the vocal organs.
5. *k'*, the aspirate *k*.
6. *l*, as in *lay*.
7. *m*, ,, ,, *may*.
8. *n*, ,, ,, *nay*.
9. *ng*, ,, ,, *singing*, both at the beginning and end of words.
10. *p*, ,, ,, *pay*.
11. *p'*, the aspirate *p*.
12. *s*, as in *say*.
13. *t*, ,, ,, *tame*.
14. *t'*, the aspirate *t*.
15. *w*, as in *want*, *wing*, *swan*, in the beginning and middle of words.
16. *y*, as in *yore*.

*The native standard of pronunciation* is a work called 戚林八音合訂 *Ch'ek Ling Paik Ing Hak Teng*, or more simply the *Paik Ing*, or Eight Tone Book. As seen from the full title it is a compilation of the works of two authors, *Ch'ek* and *Ling*. The page is divided by a horizontal line. The lower section is by *Ling*, and the characters are arranged by a system of 20 initials and 35 finals. As a dictionary, it is somewhat more comprehensive than the upper part, but it is not used as a standard of pronunciation. The upper section is ascribed originally to *Ch'ek* (a military chieftain of the Ming dynasty, known familiarly as 戚叅將 *Ch'ek ch'ang chiong)*, and is the only standard of pronunciation for the Foochow dialect. It is a dictionary in which all the characters are systematically arranged according to their sounds. Each simple word has three elements, an initial sound, a final sound, and a tone. The initials are termed *che t'au*, word-heads. The finals are termed *che mó*, word-mothers, or fundamental generic sounds. To represent the former, 15 characters, having the 15 different initial sounds, are used. To represent the latter, 33 characters are in like manner employed.

The original number of finals was 36, but three of these became obsolete on account of identity in sound with other three in the list. They are divided metrically into 3s, 7s, and 5s, by native teachers, and are regarded as yielding a good poetic sense in the order in which they stand. The sign †(placed after) marks the three obsolete finals.

春花香 *Ch'ung Hwa Hiong*, The spring flowers (are) fragrant,
秋山開 *Ch'iu Sang K'ai;* The autumnal hills unfold;
嘉賓歡歌須金†杯 *Ka Ping Hwang Kó Sü King Pwí*,
The worthy guests, joyous in song, must (take) the golden bowls,
孤燈光輝燒銀缸 *Ku Teng Kwong Hwi Sieu Ngũng Kong.*
(While) the single lamp brilliantly burns in its silver cup.
之東郊 *Chi Tĕng Kau*, Go forth to the eastern wild,
過西橋 *Kwo Sá Kio;* And cross the western bridge;
鷄聲催初天 *Kié Siăng Ch'oi Ch'ĕ T'iéng*,
The voice of the cock hastens the opening dawn,
奇梅†歪遮†溝 *K'iă Mwí Wai Chiă Keu.*
The rare almond, drooping, veils the water-course.

The system of initials, finals, and tones constitutes the alphabet of the language. All the characters of the *Paik Ing* are arranged under the 33 finals, as the leading element or symbol, with the subdivision into 15 classes under each final according to the initial sounds of the characters, and the farther subdivision into 7 classes under each initial according to their tones. In practice, however, it will be found that for a considerable number of possible combinations of the initials and finals with their tonic inflections, there are neither written characters nor colloquial words in this dialect. The above arrangement of characters with their definitions constitutes a Chinese Alphabetic Dictionary.

By referring to the Tables below, the student will observe that an *initial* sound is a single consonant or two consonants combined, and that no vowel is ever used as an initial. (Words under the *eng* initial, however, may be regarded as beginning with the vowel of the final sound or with *w* or *y*). It is also seen that a *final* sound consists of a vowel or vowels, sometimes preceded by *w* or *y*, and sometimes followed by *h*, *k*, or *ng*.

### Tones.

The tonic marks belong properly to the Romanized orthography of the language, as the tone is always an essential part of the word. In theory and as commonly spoken of, there are eight tones in this dialect, but practically only seven, as the second and sixth are identical, and the characters and spoken words having this peculiarity of sound are invariably referred to the second tone. The tonic marks are the same as those used in Williams' Tonic Dictionary. They consist of semicircles and semicircles combined with horizontal strokes. Their position at the corners of characters and words indicates the tone, as seen in the following diagram:—

| 1. | 2. | 3. | 4. | 5. | 6. | 7. | 8. |
|---|---|---|---|---|---|---|---|
| ꜀丹 | ꜂胆 | 旦꜄ | 答꜆ | ꜁談 | ꜂胆 | 淡꜅ | 達꜇ |
| ꜀Tang. | ꜂Tang. | Tang꜄. | Tak꜆. | ꜁Tang. | ꜂Tang. | Tang꜅. | Tak꜇. |

The poetical division of the tones is into 平聲 *꜁ping ꜀siăng*, the even tones, and 仄聲 *chah꜆ ꜀siăng*, the deflected or oblique tones. The *first* and *fifth* tones belong to the former, and all the others to the latter class.

The tones are now commonly distinguished into two orders or grades, 上聲 *siong*$^2$ ꜀*siăng*, the *upper* or primary tones, and 下聲 *ha*$^2$ ꜀*siăng*, the *lower* or secondary tones. They are as follows:—

1. 上平 *siong*$^2$ ꜀*ping*, the upper even tone.
2. 上上 *siong*$^2$ ꜂*siong*, or *siong*$^2$ *siong*$^2$, the upper rising tone.
3. 上去 *siong*$^2$ *k‘ëü*꜄, the upper departing or diminishing tone.
4. 上入 *siong*$^2$ *ik*$_2$ ,, ,, entering or abrupt tone.
5. 下平 *ha*$^2$ ꜀*ping*, the lower even tone.
6. 下上 *ha*$^2$ ꜂*siong*, or *hă*$^2$ *siong*$^2$ the lower rising tone.
7. 下去 *ha*$^2$ *k‘ëü*꜄ the lower departing or diminishing tone.
8. 下入 *ha*$^2$ *ik*$_2$ ,, ,, entering or abrupt tone.

DESCRIPTION OF THE TONES. The names given to the tones above are merely translations of the Chinese terms and furnish a very imperfect idea of their nature. The following very concise, lucid, and scientific description, with diagrams of the tones, is from the pen of Rev. Charles Hartwell of the American Board Mission.

"The tones have five elements, which are pitch, quality of voice, inflection, stress, and time.

The *first* tone has the pitch of a third, is the *head tone* in quality of voice, and is without inflection, without stress, and long in time.

The *second* tone is a minor third below the first, and has the pitch of sharp one. It is near the *orotund* in quality of voice, is without inflection, has the thorough stress, and is long in time.

The *third* tone begins on the pitch of a fifth below—as in diagram No. 1—and gradually rises to the key note. Or, with a consonant initial, begins on the key note of the voice—as in diagram No. 2—drops to a fifth below, and returns to the key note. It is long in time.

The *fourth* tone is like the third in pitch and inflection, but ends abruptly with a strong vanishing stress. It is pronounced more quickly than the third, but is properly long in time, as is shown by its changing to the first and second tones in combination, which are both long tones.

The *fifth* tone, beginning on the fifth of the voice in pitch with a strong radical stress, descends rapidly and is short in time. Sometimes, with consonant initials, it seems to take the form indicated in Diagram No. 2, the stress commencing with the vowel sound.

The *sixth* tone is the same as the second.

The *seventh* tone begins on the key-note of the voice, rises to the pitch of a second with strong emphasis, and descends with thorough stress to about a fifth below. It is lóng in time.

The *eighth*. tone has the pitch of a third, is without inflection, and is short in time. It ends very abruptly, though with less stress than the fourth tone.

## DIAGRAMS OF THE FOOCHOW TONES

*IN THEIR FULL FORM.*

No. 1. *Upper series.*

*Lower series.*

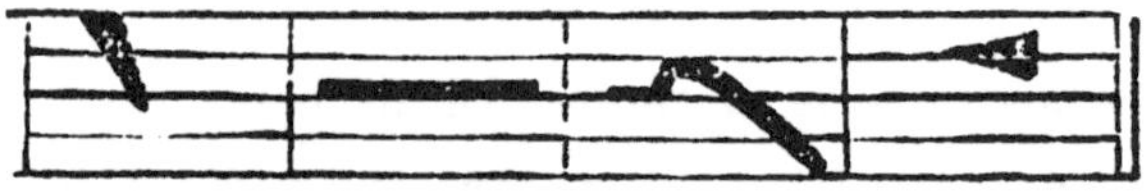

No. 2. Or, *Upper series thus.*

*Lower series thus.*

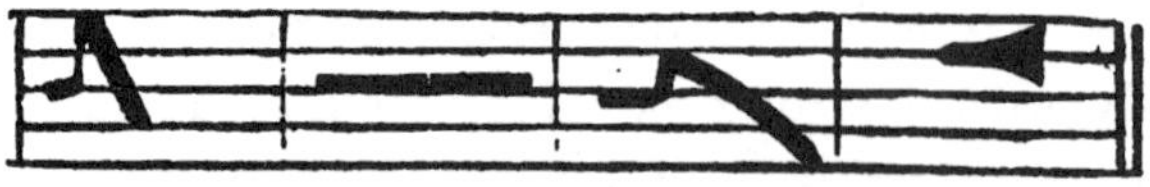

In the above diagrams the middle line is designed to represent the key-note of the speaker's voice".

The Rev. M. C. White, M. D., formerly a member of the Methodist Episcopal Mission, Foochow, now a Professor in Yale College, U. S. A., after careful study of the dialect, published the results of his investigations in the Methodist Quarterly Review. We quote his graphic delineation of the tones.—"The *first*, or *primary smooth tone*, called *siong*$^2$ ꜀*ping*, is a uniform even sound, enunciated a little above the ordinary speaking key, but neither elevated nor depressed, from the commencement to the close of the word. It is, in this respect, like the enunciation of a note in music; it may, therefore, be called the singing tone, or the musical monotone.

The *second*, or *primary high tone*, called *siong*$^2$ ꜂*siong*, is enunciated in the ordinary speaking key, and the voice usually falls a note at the close, as at the end of a sentence in unimpassioned discourse. In connected discourse, however, the second tone is sustained, and turns upward, like the vanishing stress of unaccented words in common conversation. In attempting to pronounce the letters *a-e*, we notice that *e* is pronounced either a note higher, or lower, than *a*. So, also, if we take the pains to listen attentively when *a* alone is pronounced, we shall notice that it has its ending or vanishing movement, turned upward one note; or, if spoken like the close of a sentence, where the voice falls in the usual way, we shall perceive that the vanishing movement of *a* turns downward one note. This is exactly the variety of enunciation, distinguished by the *second*, or *siong*$^2$ ꜂*siong*, tone in this dialect.

The *third*, or *primary diminishing tone*, called *siong*$^2$ *k'ëü*꜄, is what elocutionists call the *rising third*, and is heard in English on the emphatic word in a direct question, as, Does it *rain?*" where the voice turns upward, through the interval of two notes of the octave.

The *fourth*, or *primary abrupt tone*, call *siong*$^2$ *ik*$_2$ turns the voice upward through the same interval as the *third tone;* but it terminates abruptly, as though the voice was suddenly interrupted in an effort to pronounce a final *h*. In words which, in other tones, end in *ng*, the abrupt close of the fourth tone sounds somewhat like a suppressed or half-uttered *k*, but the clicking sound of the *k* is not heard. If a person should attempt to ask the question, "Can you open the *lock?*" and be suddenly stopped before enunciating the final clicking sound of the *k*, he would give to the last word the *primary abrupt tone*.

The *fifth*, or *secondary smooth tone*, called *ha*$^2$ *꜀ping*, is a quick forcible enunciation, commencing about two notes above the ordinary key, and suddenly dropping down, at the close, to the key note. It is what is called by elocutionists the *falling third*, and, when emphatic, the *falling fifth*. It is sometimes called the scolding tone. It is heard in a petulant enunciation of the emphatic words in the sentence, " *No!* I'll do no such *thing*".

The *sixth tone* is identical with the *second*, and no words are arranged under it; that is, no *secondary high*, or *rising tone*, has yet been invented in this dialect.

The *seventh* or *secondary diminishing tone*, called *ha*$^2$ *k'ü'*, is a guttural downward circumflex. It is, in English, expressive of peculiar emphasis, frequently indicating rebuke, scorn, or contempt, as,

" *Whence*, and what art thou, *execrable shape?*
. . . *Back* to thy *punishment*,
*False fugitive*."

"You wrong me every way; you *wrong* me, Brutus."

The words *very many*, if spoken with forcible emphasis, would also exhibit the tone under consideration.

This is probably the most difficult tone in the language to enunciate correctly, under all circumstances.

The *eighth*, or *secondary abrupt tone*, called *ha*$^2$ $ik_2$ closes abruptly, like the *fourth tone*, but differs from it by being enunciated on a uniform pitch, a little above the ordinary key. The eighth tone is an abrupt termination of the first tone, in the same manner as the fourth tone is an abrupt termination of the third."

### The tones in Combination.

When words are enunciated singly, the tones appear in their full form and are marked in their elements and distinctive peculiarities. But in compound terms or names, and in phrases whose component words are in regimen, or close construction, they assume striking peculiarities, which in some cases involve a radical change. *These peculiarities relate to the first or leading word of the term or phrase.* The only exception that we have noticed is when the following word is a mere suffix or unimportant word, in which case the leading word usually retains its ordinary character as to tone.

The *first* tone (leading) is usually spoken with a very strongly marked accent as in ꜀*sing* ꜀*sang* (teacher), ꜀*ki* ꜂*chi* (a foundation).

The *second* tone (leading) has the peculiar inflection noticed above in the description of tones. It sometimes imparts to the voice a slightly sarcastic accent, especially when the following word is in the 3d or 7th tone, as in ꜂*siong sëü*꜄ (reward), ꜂*ka mó*꜆ (to feign).

The *third* and *seventh* tones (leading) cannot be distinguished from the *first* (leading). They have the same strongly marked accent. This is easily tested in colloquial terms which have no generally accepted character to represent the leading word. Native teachers, in *borrowing* a character for it, often disagree. One, perhaps, will use a first tone, another a third tone, and another a seventh tone, character.

The *fourth* tone (leading), when ending in *h*, has the quality of the *first* tone (leading); when ending in *k*, that of the *second* tone (leading). The following are familiar examples:—*tiăh*꜇ ꜀*hwa* (to pluck flowers), *k'ah*꜇ ꜀*t'iăng* (a parlor), *tóh*꜇ ꜂*kiăng* (a small table), spoken as ꜀*tó* ꜂*kiăng* (a small knife), *paik*꜇ ꜀*ing* (the eight tones), *ch'ek*꜇ *ngwok*꜇ (the seventh month), *t'iék*꜇ *liĕng*꜆ (an iron chain).

The *fifth* tone (leading) is spoken in a low or depressed tone of the voice without marked emphasis. The inexperienced student in his effort to speak words of this tone *in regimen*, according to the rules laid down for the tones *in their full form*, misses the sound entirely, and enunciates it like the *first* tone in regimen, saying ꜀*niĕng pwang*꜄ instead of ꜁*niĕng pwang*꜄ (a year and a half), ꜀*pu sak*꜇ instead of ꜁*pu sak*꜇ (a Budhist idol). The distinction is very apparent in the comparative pronunciation of such phrases as ꜀*ki* ꜂*chi* (a foundation), and ꜁*ki* ꜂*chi* (chess-men).

The *sixth* tone is obsolete, or the same as the *second.*

The *seventh* tone (leading) is the same as the *third* tone (leading), q. v.

The *eighth* tone (leading) has no marked distinction—as that prevailing in the *fourth* tone—between words ending in *h* and *k*. In the city of Foochow it is enunciated in a depressed tone of voice like the *fifth* tone (leading), while in the suburbs, and probably in the country, it is often heard with a strongly marked accent like the *first* tone (leading). This may be regarded as a kind of country brogue. In phrases having the *second* word in the *fifth* tone, this peculiar brogue is less evident, which is due to the strong radical stress or emphasis pertaining to that tone. Examples,—*pah*꜈ ꜂*ma* (a white horse),

MAN. 2.

*sioh*₂ *ˌpi* (a stone tablet), *siăh*₂ *ˌta* (to drink tea), *pah*₂ *t'ak*ˎ (the white pagoda), *hok*₂ *ˌseng*, (a pupil), *hak*₂ *e*ˀ (agreeable), *nik*₂ *ˌt'au* (the sun).

### Importance of the tones.

The nature and peculiarities of the tones are noticed above. But it is very important to learn and apply them correctly in practice. "In English, various tones or inflections of the voice are used to give force and animation to language; but in Chinese, the tone is an essential part of the word in all circumstances; while rhetorical effect is given to discourse by accentuation, rapidity or slowness of utterance, and peculiarities of manner, as well as varieties of pitch of the voice, and gesticulation". To a novice the Chinese tones may seem of no more importance than the accents or inflections of his own language, which never alter the meaning of single words, though they may affect the force and meaning of a sentence as a whole. Careful study and observation soon correct the misapprehension. He discovers that in the *spoken* language, words of the same spelling and tone constantly occur, whose meaning is determined by the connection and circumstances of discourse, as *ˌsang* which may mean *hill*, *coat*, *beget*, or *three:* but that words of the same spelling and *different* tone are also very numerous, as *ˌsang*, hill, *'sang*, sparing, *sang*' scatter, *ˌsang*, clear, as weather, and *sang*² silent; and *ˌkau*, hook, *'kau*, nine, *kau*' doctrine, *ˌkau*, a monkey, and *kau*² thick. In these instances, the connection of the discourse will not always serve to convey one's meaning. Inadvertence or an effort to give a word a peculiar force or inflection in a *foreign style* of speaking may fail to inform the listener correctly; or produce very incongruous expressions, as saying the sky is *ˌsang*, hill, instead of *ˌsang*, fair or clear, or calling the number *'kau*, nine, by the name *ˌkau*, a monkey. A servant brings his master a *bundle of wood* instead of a *fork* for the table, the mistake being due to the master's saying *ˌch'a* (wood) instead of *ˌch'a* (fork). The incident furnishes an apt, practical illustration of the importance of the tones of Chinese words.

### Tables.

The following Tables exhibit the system of Romanized Orthography, as used in writing the words or vocables of this dialect. An approximate representation of the sounds is all that can be hoped for in this department. Some students prefer *i* and *u* to *y* and *w* where these occur in the system. Good arguments may be adduced for either set of letters. But it should be observed that such arguments are partial in their application and do not affect the system as a whole, when the tones and their combinations, as well as the vowel and consonant sounds, are considered. It is hoped that the system adopted in this work will be readily acquired and prove serviceable to the student.

# TABLE I. The initials and the finals, with the characters used in the Paik Ing to represent them, and their alphabetic value in Roman letters.

NOTE. The 11th initial (eng) denotes simply the absence of any initial consonant, hence the blank on the right in the column of alphabetic values.

| FIFTEEN INITIALS. | | | | THIRTY-THREE FINALS. | | | | | | | |
|---|---|---|---|---|---|---|---|---|---|---|---|
| 1 | Liu | 柳 | L | 1 | Ch'ung | 春 | ung | 17 | Sieu (d) | 燒 | ieu |
| 2 | Piéng | 邊 | P | 2 | Hwa | 花 | wa | 18 | Ngüng | 銀 | üng |
| 3 | Kiu | 求 | K | 3 | Hiong | 香 | iong | 19 | Kong | 缸 | ong |
| 4 | K'e | 氣 | K' | 4 | Ch'iu (d) | 秋 | iu | 20 | Chi | 之 | i |
| 5 | Tá | 低 | T | 5 | Sang | 山 | ang | 21 | Tĕng | 東 | ĕng |
| 6 | P'ó | 波 | P' | 6 | K'ai | 開 | ai | 22 | Kau | 郊 | au |
| 7 | T'a | 他 | T' | 7 | Ka | 嘉 | a | 23 | Kwo (b) | 過 | wo |
| 8 | Cheng | 曾 | Ch | 8 | Ping | 賓 | ing | 24 | Sá | 西 | á |
| 9 | Nik | 日 | N | 9 | Hwang | 歡 | wang | 25 | Kio (c) | 橋 | io |
| 10 | Si | 時 | S | 10 | Kó | 歌 | ó | 26 | Kié | 雞 | ié |
| 11 | Eng | 鶯 | | 11 | Sü | 須 | ü | 27 | Siăng | 聲 | iăng |
| 12 | Mung | 蒙 | M | 12 | Pwí (a) | 杯 | wí | 28 | Ch'oi | 催 | oi |
| 13 | Ngü | 語 | Ng | 13 | Ku | 孤 | u | 29 | Ch'ë | 初 | ë |
| 14 | Ch'ok | 出 | Ch' | 14 | Teng | 燈 | eng | 30 | T'iéng | 天 | iéng |
| 15 | Hi | 喜 | H | 15 | Kwong | 光 | wong | 31 | K'iă | 奇 | iă |
| | | | | 16 | Hwi | 輝 | wi | 32 | Wai | 歪 | wai |
| | | | | | | | | 33 | Keu | 溝 | eu |

NOTE. Much difficulty is experienced in Romanizing some of the final sounds.

(a) Some would write the *pwí* final *pwe;* others prefer the form *pwoi.*

(b) Some give to the *kwo* final an additional slight *a* or *ë* sound, writing it *kwoa* or *kwoë.*

(c) Some would write the *kio* final *küo;* others prefer the form *kioa* or *kioë.*

Perhaps none of these forms fully represent the required sounds, which are accurately learned only by imitating the native mode of pronunciation.

(d) The vowel sounds of the *ch'iu* and *sieu* finals are often confounded—by teachers as well as others—especially in the suburbs and country. The same remark holds in reference to the *pwí* and *hwi* finals, the tendency being to use *wi* instead of *wí*.

## TABLE II. Primary syllables or words, formed

*Note.* Words, composed of the *eng* initial and either of the

| | | Liu 柳 | Piéng 邊 | Kiu 求 | K‘e 氣 | Tá 低 | P‘ó 波 |
|---|---|---|---|---|---|---|---|
| Ch‘ung | 春 | lung | pung | kung | k‘ung | tung | p‘ung |
| Hwa | 花 | lwa | pwa | kwa | k‘wa | twa | p‘wa |
| Hiong | 香 | liong | piong | kiong | k‘iong | tiong | p‘iong |
| Ch‘iu | 秋 | liu | piu | kiu | k‘iu | tiu | p‘iu |
| Sang | 山 | lang | pang | kang | k‘ang | tang | p‘ang |
| K‘ai | 開 | lai | pai | kai | k‘ai | tai | p‘ai |
| Ka | 嘉 | la | pa | ka | k‘a | ta | p‘a |
| Ping | 賓 | ling | ping | king | k‘ing | ting | p‘ing |
| Hwang | 歡 | lwang | pwang | kwang | k‘wang | twang | p‘wang |
| Kó | 歌 | ló | pó | kó | k‘ó | tó | p‘ó |
| Sü | 須 | lü | pü | kü | k‘ü | tü | p‘ü |
| Pwí | 杯 | lwí | pwí | kwí | k‘wí | twí | p‘wí |
| Ku | 孤 | lu | pu | ku | k‘u | tu | p‘u |
| Teng | 燈 | leng | peng | keng | k‘eng | teng | p‘eng |
| Kwong | 光 | lwong | pwong | kwong | k‘wong | twong | p‘wong |
| Hwi | 輝 | lwi | pwi | kwi | k‘wi | twi | p‘wi |
| Sieu | 燒 | lieu | pieu | kieu | k‘ieu | tieu | p‘ieu |
| Ngüng | 銀 | lüng | püng | küng | k‘üng | tüng | p‘üng |
| Kong | 釭 | long | pong | kong | k‘ong | tong | p‘ong |
| Chi | 之 | li | pi | ki | k‘i | ti | p‘i |
| Tëng | 東 | lëng | pëng | këng | k‘ëng | tëng | p‘ëng |
| Kau | 郊 | lau | pau | kau | k‘au | tau | p‘au |
| Kwo | 過 | lwo | pwo | kwo | k‘wo | two | p‘wo |
| Sá | 西 | lá | pá | ká | k‘á | tá | p‘á |
| Kio | 橋 | lio | pio | kio | k‘io | tio | p‘io |
| Kié | 雞 | lié | pié | kié | k‘ié | tié | p‘ié |
| Siăng | 聲 | liăng | piăng | kiăng | k‘iăng | tiăng | p‘iăng |
| Ch‘oi | 催 | loi | poi | koi | k‘oi | toi | p‘oi |
| Ch‘ë | 初 | lë | pë | kë | k‘ë | të | p‘ë |
| T‘iéng | 天 | liéng | piéng | kiéng | k‘iéng | tiéng | p‘iéng |
| K‘iă | 奇 | liă | piă | kiă | k‘iă | tiă | p‘iă |
| Wai | 歪 | lwai | pwai | kwai | k‘wai | twai | p‘wai |
| Keu | 溝 | leu | peu | keu | k‘eu | teu | p‘eu |

**by combining each initial with each final.**

finals *hiong*, *sieu*, *kio*, *siăng*, *t‘iéng*, and *k‘iă*, begin with *y*.

| T‘a 他 | Cheng 曾 | Nik 日 | Si 時 | Eng 鶯 | Mung 蒙 | Ngü 語 | Ch‘ok 出 | Hi 非 |
|---|---|---|---|---|---|---|---|---|
| t‘ung | chung | nung | sung | ung | mung | ngung | ch‘ung | hung |
| t‘wa | chwa | nwa | swa | wa | mwa | ngwa | ch‘wa | hwa |
| t‘iong | chiong | niong | siong | yong | miong | ngiong | ch‘iong | hiong |
| t‘iu | chiu | niu | siu | iu | miu | ngiu | ch‘iu | hiu |
| t‘ang | chang | nang | sang | ang | mang | ngang | ch‘ang | hang |
| t‘ai | chai | nai | sai | ai | mai | ngai | ch‘ai | hai |
| t‘a | cha | na | sa | a | ma | nga | ch‘a | ha |
| t‘ing | ching | ning | sing | ing | ming | nging | ch‘ing | hing |
| t‘wang | chwang | nwang | swang | wang | mwang | ngwang | ch‘wang | hwang |
| t‘ó | chó | nó | só | ó | mó | ngó | ch‘ó | hó |
| t‘ü | chü | nü | sü | ü | mü | ngü | ch‘ü | hü |
| t‘wí | chwí | nwí | swí | wí | mwí | ngwí | ch‘wí | hwí |
| t‘u | chu | nu | su | u | mu | ngu | ch‘u | hu |
| t‘eng | cheng | neng | seng | eng | meng | ngeng | ch‘eng | heng |
| t‘wong | chwong | nwong | swong | wong | mwong | ngwong | ch‘wong | hwong |
| t‘wi | chwi | nwi | swi | wi | mwi | ngwi | ch‘wi | hwi |
| t‘ieu | chieu | nieu | sieu | yeu | mieu | ngieu | ch‘ieu | hieu |
| t‘üng | chüng | nüng | süng | üng | müng | ngüng | ch‘üng | hüng |
| t‘ong | chong | nong | song | ong | mong | ngong | ch‘ong | hong |
| t‘i | chi | ni | si | i | mi | ngi | ch‘i | hi |
| t‘ëng | chëng | nëng | sëng | ëng | mëng | ngëng | ch‘ëng | hëng |
| t‘au | chau | nau | sau | au | mau | ngau | ch‘au | hau |
| t‘wo | chwo | nwo | swo | wo | mwo | ngwo | ch‘wo | hwo |
| t‘á | chá | ná | sá | á | má | ngá | ch‘á | há |
| t‘io | chio | nio | sio | yo | mio | ngio | ch‘io | hio |
| t‘ié | chié | nié | sié | ié | mié | ngié | ch‘ié | hié |
| t‘iăng | chiăng | niăng | siăng | yăng | miăng | ngiăng | ch‘iăng | hiăng |
| t‘oi | choi | noi | soi | oi | moi | ngoi | ch‘oi | hoi |
| t‘ë | chë | në | së | ë | më | ngë | ch‘ë | hë |
| t‘iéng | chiéng | niéng | siéng | yéng | miéng | ngiéng | ch‘iéng | hiéng |
| t‘iă | chiă | niă | siă | yă | miă | ngiă | ch‘iă | hiă |
| t‘wai | chwai | nwai | swai | wai | mwai | ngwai | ch‘wai | hwai |
| t‘eu | cheu | neu | seu | eu | meu | ngeu | ch‘eu | heu |

## TABLE III. FINALS, AS MODIFIED BY TONES.

*Note.* The *eng* initial is placed at the head of this table, as it denotes the absence of any initial consonant, and therefore gives the simplest form of all the finals through each tone. Hence all words spoken without an initial consonant, or beginning with *w* or *y*, are classed under this initial. See *Note* on preceding page.

| Eng | 鶯 | 上平 | 上上 | 上去 | 上入 | 下平 | 下上 | 下去 | 下入 |
|---|---|---|---|---|---|---|---|---|---|
| Ch'ung | 春 | ung | ung | ong | ok | ung | ung | ong | uk |
| Hwa | 花 | wa | wa | wa | wah | wa | wa | wa | wah |
| Hiong | 香 | iong | iong | iong | iok | iong | iong | iong | iok |
| Ch'iu | 秋 | iu | iu | eu | euh | iu | iu | eu | iuh |
| Sang | 山 | ang | ang | ang | ak | ang | ang | ang | ak |
| K'ai | 開 | ai | ai | ai | aih | ai | ai | ai | aih |
| Ka | 嘉 | a | a | a | ah | a | a | a | ah |
| Ping | 賓 | ing | ing | eng | ek | ing | ing | eng | ik |
| Hwang | 歡 | wang | wang | wang | wak | wang | wang | wang | wak |
| Kó | 歌 | ó | ó | ó | óh | ó | ó | ó | óh |
| Sü | 須 | ü | ü | ëü | ëüh | ü | ü | ëü | üh |
| Pwí | 杯 | wí | wí | woí | woíh | uí | wí | woí | wíh |
| Ku | 孤 | u | u | o | oh | u | u | o | uh |
| Teng | 燈 | eng | eng | aing | aik | eng | eng | aing | ek |
| Kwong | 光 | wong | wong | wong | wok | wong | wong | wong | wok |
| Hwi | 輝 | wi | wi | oi | oih | ui | wi | oi | wih |
| Sieu | 燒 | ieu | ieu | ieu | ieuh | ieu | ieu | ieu | ieuh |
| Ngüng | 銀 | üng | üng | ëüng | ëük | üng | üng | ëüng | ük |
| Kong | 缸 | ong | ong | aung | auk | ong | ong | aung | ok |
| Chi | 之 | i | i | e | eh | i | i | e | ih |
| Tëng | 東 | ëng | ëng | aëng | aëk | ëng | ëng | aëng | ëk |
| Kau | 郊 | au | au | au | auh | au | au | au | auh |
| Kwo | 過 | wo | wo | wo | woh | wo | wo | wo | woh |
| Sá | 西 | á | á | á | áh | á | á | á | áh |
| Kio | 橋 | io | io | io | ioh | io | io | io | ioh |
| Kié | 雞 | ié | ié | ié | iéh | ié | ié | ié | iéh |
| Siăng | 聲 | iăng | iăng | iăng | iăk | iăng | iăng | iăng | iăk |
| Ch'oi | 催 | oi | oi | ói | óih | oi | oi | ói | oih |
| Ch'ë | 初 | ë | ë | aë | aëh | ë | ë | aë | ëh |
| T'iéng | 天 | iéng | iéng | iéng | iék | iéng | iéng | iéng | iék |
| K'iă | 奇 | iă | iă | iă | iăh | iă | iă | iă | iăh |
| Wai | 歪 | wai | wai | wai | waih | wai | wai | wai | waih |
| Keu | 溝 | eu | eu | aiu | aiuh | eu | eu | aiu | euh |

It appears, from Table III and its note of explanation, that there are 90 final syllables, which (as belonging to the *eng* initial) are also independent words or vocables. They may be arranged alphabetically as follows:—

*a, á, aë, aëh, aëk, aëng, ah, áh, ai, aih, aik, aing, aiu, aiuh, ak, ang, au, auh, auk, aung, e, ë, eh, ëh, ek, ëk, eng, ëng, eu, ëü, euh, ëüh, ëük, ëüng, i, iă (yă), iăh (yăh), iăk (yăk), iăng (yăng), ié, iéh, iék (yék), iéng (yéng), ieu (yeu), ieuh (yeuh), ih, ik, ing, io (yo), ioh (yoh), iok (yok), iong (yong), iu, iuh, o, ó, oh, óh, oi, ói, oih, óih, ok, ong, u, ü, uh, üh, ui, uí, uk, ük, ung, üng, wa, wah, wai, waih, wak, wang, wi, wí, wih, wíh, wo, woh, woí, woíh, wok, wong.*

The tables II and III also furnish the data for ascertaining the number of vocables produced by the combination of initials with finals and the modification by tones. The whole number is (15X33X 7) 3465. Besides these, there are two words not strictly referable to the table of initial and final sounds, viz., the semi-vocal nasal *ng*ʾ (no, not) on p. 595, and the word ˛*ngiau*, on p. 610, composed of the initial *ng*ˋand a final compounded of *i* and *au*, — making the whole number of vocables 3467. But probably less than half of these are in actual use. This paucity of vocables or monosyllabic words is largely compensated by the very frequent union of two or more words, virtually forming polysyllables, to express simple ideas. Thus the number of words is in effect increased to several thousands, which give to this dialect "a richness and variety of expression but little inferior to that of many alphabetic languages."

PRACTICAL SUGGESTIONS. These relate principally to the acquisition of the spoken language.

1. Study thoroughly the Orthography, comprising the rudiments of the language with the elements of initial, final, and tone in single words, as given in the Tables.

2. Practice on the rudiments and tables *with the native teacher*, learning to enunciate as he does. No extent or thoroughness of independent study can ever compensate for deficiency in such practice.

3. Notice the important changes which occur in combination of tones, as given on pages 8 and 9.

4. Also observe how the final consonants *h*, *k*, and *g*, and some of the initials, are often half-suppressed or seem wholly to disappear in the easy, native mode of speaking. Very close attention should be given to these idiomatic changes, so soon as thoroughness is attained in enunciating words singly. This is essential to ease and accuracy in public address and common conversation.

5. It will be found useful to practice writing out, in the Romanized form, simple phrases heard in conversation. This will serve to fix them in the memory, and to draw the attention to many important words or particles, which otherwise might not be thoroughly learned for years.

6. The student should by no means confine himself to his books and teacher, but should mingle with common people and observe carefully their modes of speaking. The union of study and observation will help to form a style, alike removed from coarseness and excessive refinement, while exclusive study with a teacher will tend to the formation of a book-colloquial style, not fully or readily understood by the people at large.

### Parts of Speech.

In reference to their uses and meanings, Chinese characters are often classed as 活字 $wak_2$ $che^2$, living words, 實字 $sik_2$ $che^2$, real words, and 虛字 ꜀*hū* $che^2$ empty words. A verb is a $wak_2$ $che^2$, a noun is a $sik_2$ $che^2$, and a preposition is a ꜀*hū* $che^2$. But of course the native nomenclature is designed to embrace all Chinese words. We adopt the English terms for the different *parts of speech*, as the one most likely to prove satisfactory to the student, and as a convenient mode of exhibiting the nature of Chinese words and their relative position in a sentence. The *parts of speech* are numbered and treated of in their order, after which other words, not properly classible under them, are noticed under distinct headings. This arrangement gives the student an insight into this dialect, as contrasted with his own language, and may help him to avoid using foreign idioms in his early attempts to speak a strange tongue.

# 1. ARTICLE.

There is properly no *article* in this dialect, and nouns are often used without any adjunct corresponding to it.

伊是好侬 *꜀i se*$^2$ *꜂hó ꜁nĕng*, he is (a) good man.
厝野高 *ch'io꜄ ꜂yă ꜁keng*, (the) house (is) very high.

The nearest equivalent for the *indefinite article, a* or *an*, is the numeral *sioh*$_2$ one, or the same numeral with a classifier.

一日 *sioh*$_2$ *nik*$_2$ one day or *a* day.
一點鐘 *sioh*$_2$ *꜂teng ꜀chŭng*, one hour or *an* hour.
一隻侬 *sioh*$_2$ *chiăh꜆ ꜁nĕng*, one man or *a* man.

The coll. word *꜂la*—probably a corruption of *꜂chiă*—also stands for the article *a*, 務喇侬 *o*$^2$ *꜂la ꜁nĕng*, there was *a* man, or a certain man.

The nearest equivalent for the *definite article, the*, is the pronominal adjective or demonstrative pronoun *꜂chiă*, this, that.

啫馬 *꜂chiă ꜂ma*, this horse or *the* horse.
啫筆 *꜂chiă pek꜆* this pencil or *the* pencil.

It is apparent, from the examples given above, that the Chinese equivalents for the English articles *a, an, the*, correspond in meaning to the Saxon *ane* and *thät* from which the latter are derived.

# 2. NOUN.

*Proper nouns or names.* There is no mode of *capitalizing* these, as in western languages. The names of persons, however, are sometimes marked—as in christian books—by a perpendicular line on the right, and the names of places by two such marks or by four inclosing lines. When, in writing, the Chinese wish to mention a person with honor, his name is made to begin a new column, or is raised a space or two above, or has a blank left before it. These honorary distinctions may serve to indicate names of persons to the English student, when the perpendicular stroke is not used.

*Patronymics or surnames.* These invariably precede the proper or given name, as 林發祥 *꜁Ling hwak꜆ ꜁sióng*, instead of 發祥林 *Hwak꜆ ꜁siong ꜁ling.* In the name of a married woman, the full, written form includes both her husband's and her father's surnames.

MAN. 3.

as 陳林氏 ˛*Ting* ˛*Ling se*² or 陳門林氏 ˛*Ting* ˛*mwong* ˛*ling se*² designates a woman whose husband's surname is ˛*Ting*, and father's ˛*Ling*. The terms ˛*mwong* and *se*² in this and like examples simply mean "family". In English the name may be rendered Mrs. Ting-Ling.

*Common nouns or names*, as in other languages, comprise a numerous class of words. Their position in the sentence and other accidents are noticed below under *properties of nouns*.

*Collective nouns* are common nouns which denote a number of persons or things considered collectively or in one body, as 軍 ˛*kung*, an army, 羣 ˛*kung*, a flock, 家 ˛*ka*, a family, 會 *hwoi*² an assembly.

*Compound nouns* consist of two or more words, united to describe a single object. They occur very frequently in this dialect, and compensate for the paucity of simple nouns or names. They are formed in three ways—by prefixing or affixing nouns to the principal word, or by prefixing such verbs as 拍 *p'ah*˒ to beat, 做 *chó*˒ to do, to make, to be.

(1) With noun-prefixes.

司傅 ˛*sa ho*² a master, skilled workman, instructor.
土司傅 ˛*t'u* ˛*sa ho*², a mason.
海邊 ˋ*hai* ˛*piéng*, the sea-side.
嘴舌 *ch'oi*˒ *siék*˒ the tongue.

(2) With noun-suffixes.

刀仔 ˛*tó* ˋ*kiăng*, a small knife.
仈仔 ˛*nĕng* ˋ*kiăng*, a small human image or toy.

In these instances the word ˋ*kiăng* is a diminutive, indicating a child or small specimen of the object named.

(3) With verb-prefixes.

做廚 *chó*˒ ˛*tio*, to-be-cook—a cook.
做先生 *chó*˒ ˛*sing* ˛*sang*, to-be-a-physician—a physician.
做生理 *chó*˒ ˛*seng* ˋ*li*, to-do-trade—a trader, a merchant.
拍鐵 *p'ah*˒ *t'iék*˒ to-beat-iron—a blacksmith.
坐齋 *sói*² ˛*chá*, to-sit-in-school—a schoolmaster.

Sometimes the words 其𠆧 ꜁*ki* ꜁*nĕng* (its man or the man of) are added to such forms, as 做生意其𠆧 *chó*꜄ ꜀*seng e*꜄ ꜁*ki* ꜁*nĕng*, to-do-trade-its-man, or the-man-of-doing-trade, i. e., a trader. In this and like instances we have a verb of being or action, a noun of art, profession, material, or other object, and a noun denoting the actor, preceded by the sign of the genitive, all combined as the equivalent of a single English word.

### Properties of nouns.

The Chinese noun has no inflection. Its properties are determined by its position in the sentence or by the use of additional words.

**Person.** The persons of proper nouns, especially the *first* and *second* persons, are sometimes distinguished, as in English, by prefixing the pronouns 我, 汝, 伊, ꜂*ngwai*, ꜂*nü*, ꜀*i* (I, thou, he) to the proper names. This usage, however, is not common in the spoken language, where the following rules may be observed.

(1) For the *first* person the pronoun alone, or a humble, self-depreciating term, with or without the pronoun prefixed, is commonly used.

(2) The *second* person is likewise indicated by the pronoun alone, or by some term of respect or title of rank belonging to the individual, with or without the pronoun prefixed.

(3) The *third* person is indicated in ordinary discourse in the usual way. After pointing out the individual by name, it is common to speak of him in subsequent discourse by the pronoun 伊 ꜀*i*, he, or 啫𠆧, ꜂*chiă* ꜁*nĕng*, that person, or by his name or peculiar title, as 王 ꜁*wong*, the king, 老爹 ꜂*ló* ꜀*tiă*, His Honor, the officer, 先生 ꜀*sing* ꜀*sang*, the teacher.

**Gender.** The most prominent terms to designate the sexes are 男 ꜁*nang*, male, and 女 ꜂*nü*, female. These are restricted in usage to the human species.

The more common colloquial terms are 唐晡 ꜁*tong* ꜀*pwo*, a male, and 諸娘 ꜀*chü* ꜁*niong*, a female, or 唐晡𠆧 ꜁*tong* ꜀*pwo* ꜁*nĕng*, a man, and 諸娘𠆧 ꜀*chü* ꜁*niong* ꜁*nĕng*, a woman. The term 唐晡仔 ꜁*tong* ꜀*pwo* ꜂*kiăng*, is used for boy, and 仔 ꜂*kiăng* alone for son. The word 弟 *tié*꜅ (little brother) is a familiar appellation for boy or lad. The term 諸仈仔 ꜀*chü* ꜁*nëng* ꜂*kiăng* is used for girl or daughter. The word 妹 *mwoi*꜄ (little sister) is a familiar appellation for a girl. The term 男女仔 ꜁*nang* ꜂*nü* ꜂*kiăng* is a comprehensive one for boys and girls, or sons and daughters.

To distinguish the gender of the lower animals, the word 雄 *kaëk*꜆ is placed after, and 牯 ꜂*këng* either before or after, the name to designate the male, and the word 𤛇 ꜂*mó* after the name to designate the female, as 牛牯 ꜁*ngu* ꜂*këng*, a bull, 牯猪 ꜂*këng* ꜀*tü* or 猪雄 ꜀*tü kaëk*꜆ a boar, 雞雄 ꜀*kié kaëk*꜆ a cock, 雞𤛇 ꜀*kié* ꜂*mó*, a hen.

There seems to be some distinction in usage between ꜂*këng* and *kaëk*, the terms for male. The work ꜂*këng* is restricted to quadrupeds, while *kaëk*꜆ is a more general term, applied to quadrupeds, birds, &c.

Nouns of the *common* gender are such as 鳥 ꜂*cheu*, birds, 雞 ꜀*kié*, fowls, 獸 *seu*꜄ wild beasts, 頭牲 ꜁*t'au* ꜀*sang*, animals.

Nouns not included in the above classes are *neuter*. But it may be observed in conclusion that the Chinese cosmogonal system supposes dual principles in nature, termed 陰陽 ꜀*ing* ꜁*yong*. The ꜁*yong* is the superior or *male* principle, comprising such objects as heaven, sun, day, while the ꜀*ing* is the inferior and recipient or *female* principle, comprising such as earth, moon, water, night. This system, logically carried out, would make all nouns masculine or feminine.

**Number.** As Chinese nouns do not admit of inflection, the property of number is determined, (1) by the context, (2) more commonly—to form the plural—by duplicating the noun, or (3) by certain words prefixed or affixed, or (4) by the use of a numeral and classifier.

The usual suffix—mostly employed in the written language—is 等 ꜂*teng*, a class or collection of individuals.

In the spoken language, the following and like forms occur:—

仈仈 ꜁*nëng* ꜁*nëng*, all men, all persons.
各仈 *kauk*꜆ ꜁*nëng*, each one, everybody.
衆仈 *chëüng*꜅ ꜁*nëng*, the whole concourse, the multitude.

諸位 *꜀chü oi*$^2$ all the places, seats, or guests.
大家伙 *tai*$^2$ *꜀ka ꜁nëng*, great-family-persons, i. e., all here present.

**Case.** The *nominative* before and after the verb, or the subject and predicate forms, occur as in English, as 啫伙是賊 *꜂chiă ꜁nëng se*$^2$ *ch'ek꜇* that man is a thief.

The *possessive* or *genitive* is formed by the insertion of *꜁ki* (often contracted into *꜁i*) between possessor and thing possessed. It means literally his, hers, its, or theirs, and is analogous to the sign *of*, or to the apostrophe and letter *s*, as in 椆其門 *꜁tiu ꜁ki ꜁mwong*, closet-its-door, the door of the closet, or the closet's door.

Sometimes the sign *꜁ki* is omitted, when the first noun may be parsed as an adjective qualifying the second, or as forming with it a compound noun, as 伙厝 *꜁nëng ch'io꜄* men's houses or human abodes, 國號 *kwok꜆ hó*$^2$ nation's title, dynasty's name, or national title, dynastic name.

The *objective* or *accusative* is distinguished by its position.

(1) It follows the governing verb.

寫字 *꜂siă che*$^2$ to write characters or words.
煮飯 *꜂chü pwong*$^2$ to boil rice.

(2) It precedes the verb and has the word *t'á꜄* or *k'á꜄* as its sign.

替伊拍 *k'á꜄ ꜀i p'ah꜆* for-him-beat—to beat him.

(3) It precedes verbs in the imperative, and its classifier is often separated and placed after the verb.

書掏來讀 *꜀chü ꜁tó ꜁li t'ëk꜇* book-take-come-read—bring the book and read.

肉去買二觔 *nük꜇ k'ó꜄ ꜂má lang*$^2$ *꜀kŭng*, pork-go-buy-two-pounds—go and buy two pounds of pork.

(4) It follows the governing preposition, expressed or understood.

共伙 *kaëng*$^2$ *꜁nëng*, with persons, 至尾 *kau꜄ ꜂mwi*, unto the end.

去鼓山 *k'ó꜄ ꜂ku ꜀sang*, to go (to) Kushan.

The *independent* or *vocative* is denoted by the word 阿 ꜀*ó*, following the noun. But this rather belongs to the written language. In the colloquial the particles 吓 ꜀*a* and 𠯿 ꜀*á* are used, the latter being often enunciated with considerable emphasis or stress.

主吓 ꜂*chio* ꜀*a*, Lord! O Lord!

先生吓 ꜀*sing* ꜀*sang* ꜀*a*, or ꜀*sing* ꜀*sang* ꜀*á*, Ho, Teacher!

The *dative* and *ablative* often have no distinguishing mark. When preceded by a preposition they may be parsed as objectives or accusatives in like regimen.

### Classifiers or Numeratives.

These form a very peculiar and important class of nouns in regimen with other nouns. Some are collectives or nouns of multitude. In their literal sense they indicate a common accident or quality, pertaining to the members of the class of objects made the subject of discourse, as state, condition, shape, size, use, material, etc. They occur very frequently in the spoken language, and in common or diffuse composition, but are seldom required in the higher, classic styles.

The Chinese noun, as already observed, has no inflection. Most common nouns seem to be regarded as names of things in the abstract, or as mere ideal quantities. They require a numeral and a classifying word to individualize and define them. Hence the Chinese, in their crude attempts to speak English, think it necessary generally to use such adjuncts; for instance, saying "two-piece-men" instead of "two men".

The classifiers are such words as 個 ꜂*ka* (or ꜂*a*), 其 ꜀*ki*, 隻 *chiăh*꜆, an individual (person or thing), 枳 ꜂*chi*, skein, small bunch, 合 *hak*꜇ pair, 結 *kaik*꜆ bunch, 對 *tói*꜄ piece, 丸 ꜀*wong*, lump or ball (as seen in List of Classifiers in a subsequent part of the volume). They are termed *classifiers* by some because they relate to individuals as pertaining to a class, and *numeratives* by others, because used in combination with numeral adjectives to indicate the number of individuals made the subject of discourse.

The following rules should be observed.

(1) Usually several nouns have the same classifier, as 架 *ka꜃*, the classifier of bedsteads, closets, clocks, ladders, etc., 粒 *lak꜅* the classifier of stars, beads, buttons, scars, grains, fruits, etc.

(2) When the same vocal sound is used as the name of different objects, their different classifiers distinguish them to the ear of the listener, as 椆一架 *꜀tiu sioh꜅ ka꜃*, one closet, 綢一疋 *꜀tiu sioh꜅ p'ek꜁* one piece of silk-goods. The same terms, *written in Chinese characters*, are of course plainly distinguished by the different characters for *closet* and *silk-goods*.

(3) The numeral and classifier are placed—

Sometimes before the noun.

二把轎 *lang꜄ ꜂pa kieu꜄* two sedans.

Sometimes after the noun.

轎二把 *kieu꜄ lang꜄ ꜂pa*, sedans-two, i. e., two sedans.

And usually after a verb in the imperative mood.

剪刀仔去買三把 *꜀ka ꜀tó ꜂kiăng k'ó꜃ ꜂mā ꜀sang ꜂pa*, scissors-go-buy-three-pairs, i. e., go and buy three pairs of scissors.

(4) The general rule is that *every noun, preceded by a numeral, has its appropriate classifier or numerative.*

To this there are some exceptions, as

(a) In some collective nouns, which are also used as classifiers.

一羣 *sioh꜅ ꜀kung*, one flock.

二主 *lang꜄ ꜂chio*, two families.

(b) In some nouns designating fixed sets or numbers.

八營 *paik꜁ ꜀yăng*, the eight camps.

八卦 *paik꜁ kwa꜃* the eight diagrams.

三國 *꜀sang kwok꜁* The Three States.

(c) In nouns referring to some division of time.

三日 *꜀sang nik꜅* three days.

八年 *paik꜁ ꜀niĕng*, eight years.

二工 *lang꜄ ꜀kĕng*, two (days') work.

(d) In the following and similar instances. These, however, are only *partial* exceptions to the general rule, as the classifier may be optionally omitted or retained.

In answering such questions as, "How many have shares?" the reply may be 三仈 *꜀sang ꜁nëng*, or 三個仈 *꜀sang ꜂a ꜁nëng*, three persons.

In some nouns preceded by the numerals from *twenty* upward, as 二十六仈 *ne$^2$ sek$_2$ lëk$_2$ ꜁nëng*, or 仈二十六隻 *꜁nëng ne$^2$ sek$_2$ lëk$_2$ chiăh꜆* twenty six men, 百二仈 *pah꜆ ne$^2$ ꜁nëng*, or 仈百二隻 *꜁nëng pah꜆ ne$^2$ chiăh꜆* one hundred and twenty men.

The *importance of a discriminating use* of the clasisfiers is readily tested. The term 三杯 *꜀sang ꜀pwi*, properly means *three cupfuls*, while 杯三隻 *꜀pwi ꜀sang chiăh꜆* means simply *three cups*. So the use of *wrong* classifiers would produce incongruous expressions, like a *drove* of sedans, a *kernel* of rope, a *sheet* of grain in English.

## 3. PRONOUNS.

In respect to properties of *number* and *case* the pronouns are subject to the same rules as nouns.

In common conversation, when the relation of the three persons or parties, and the nature of the subject spoken of, are well understood, the personal pronouns are more frequently omitted than in English.

*The personal pronoun of the first person.*

SINGULAR.

| | | | | |
|---|---|---|---|---|
| Nom. | 我 *꜂Ngwai,* | 儂家 *꜁Nëng ꜀ka,* | 奴 *꜁Nu.* | I. |
| Poss. | 我其 *꜂Ngwai ꜁ki,* | &c. | &c. | My or Mine. |
| Obj. | 我 *꜂Ngwai,* | 儂家 *꜁Nëng ꜀ka,* | 奴 *꜁Nu.* | Me. |
| Ind. | ,, | ,, | ,, | Me or I. |

PLURAL.

| | | | | |
|---|---|---|---|---|
| Nom. | 我仈 *꜂Ngwai ꜁nëng,* or | 我各仈 *꜂Ngwai kauk꜆ ꜁nëng,* | &c. | We. |
| Poss. | 我仈其 *꜂Ngwai ꜁nëng ꜁ki.* | &c. | &c. | Our or Ours. |
| Obj. | 我仈 *꜂Ngwai ꜁nëng,* or | 我各仈 *꜂Ngwai kauk꜆ ꜁nëng,* | &c. | Us. |
| Ind. | ,, ,, | ,, ,, | ,, | We. |

The pronoun *꜂Ngwai* is used in addressing inferiors, also informally and rather impolitely in speaking to equals. The pronoun *꜁Nëng ꜀ka* is a term commonly used in addressing equals. The pronoun

꜀*Nu* (lit. slave, servant) is used in addressing superiors. It is also very generally used as a term of real or affected humility and self-depreciation, when the speaker wishes to honor or flatter the one whom he addresses.

Other terms, conveying the idea of inferiority or domesticity, often occupy the place of the possessive, *my*, *mine*. They are practical illustrations of the custom of speaking in humble or depreciatory terms of what belongs to one's self.

The following are familiar instances of such usage:—

家父 ꜀*ka ho*$^2$, domestic-father—my father.
內人 *nói*$^2$ ꜀*ing*, inner or secluded person—my wife.
賤內 *chiéng*$^2$ *nói*$^2$ ignoble-secluded-one—my wife.
賤恙 *chiéng*$^2$ *yong*꜃ mean-sickness—my sickness.
舍侄 *siă*꜃ *tik*꜁ cottage-nephew—my nephew.
敝友 *pe*$^2$ ꜂*iu*, abject-friend—my friend.
敝店 *pe*$^2$ *taing*꜃ wretched-shop—my shop.
小仈 ꜂*sieu* ꜀*nĕng*, small-man—my humble self.

*The personal pronoun of the second person*, 汝 ꜂*nü*, Thou, may be tabulated like that of the *first* person.

Instead of ꜂*nü*, the name or appropriate title of the person addressed is very often used, as 先生 ꜀*sing* ꜀*sang*, teacher, 大仈 *twai*$^2$ ꜀*nĕng*, great man, 老爺 ꜂*ló* ꜀*ié*, venerable sire.

Other terms, the counterparts of those in the *first* person, are used for the possessive, *thy*, *thine*. They exhibit the Chinese mode of honoring others by speaking respectfully of what belongs to them.

The following are instances:—

令正 *leng*$^2$ *cheng*꜃, excellent-correct—your wife.
令尊 *leng*$^2$ ꜀*chong*, excellent-honored—your father.
尊君 ꜀*chong* ꜀*kung*, honored-chief—your father.
尊齒 ꜀*chong* ꜂*ch'i*, honored-teeth—your age?
高壽 ꜀*kó seu*$^2$ exalted-age or life—your age?
高見 ꜀*kó kiéng*꜃, exalted- opinion—your opinion.
貴國 *koi*꜃ *kwok*꜁ your honorable country.
貴姓 *koi*꜃ *seng*꜃, ,, ,, surname.
貴東 *koi*꜃ ꜀*tung*, ,, ,, employer.

*The personal pronoun of the third person*, 伊 ꜀*i*, He, She, It, may be tabulated like those of the *first* and *second*.

Instead of 伊 ꜀*i*, the terms 啫 仈 ‘*chiă* ꜀*nĕng*, this or that person, and 啫 乇 ‘*chiă nóh*꜆ this or that thing, &c., are often used.

*Compound Personal Pronouns*. The terms for *self*, *selves*, are 自 家 *che*$^{2}$ ꜀*ka*, or *chĕü*$^{2}$ ꜀*ka*, and 本 身 ‘*pwong* ꜀*sing*, the latter meaning *lit.*, own body. The single words *che*$^{2}$ and *chĕü*$^{2}$ are also used, as 自 做 *che*$^{2}$ *chó*ʾ to do one's self, 自 稱 *che*$^{2}$ ꜀*ch‘ing* or *chĕü*$^{2}$ ꜀*ch‘ing*, to style or praise one's self, 自 瞞 自 *che*$^{2}$ ꜀*mwang* *che*$^{2}$ self-deceive-self—to deceive one's self.

The terms *che*$^{2}$ ꜀*ka* and ‘*pwong* ꜀*sing* are both used for either of the three persons, the connection showing which one is intended. But, for definiteness, the simple pronouns are prefixed, as 我 自 家 ‘*ngwai che*$^{2}$ ꜀*ka*, I, myself, 汝 自 家 ‘*nü che*$^{2}$ ꜀*ka*, You, yourself, 伊 自 家 ꜀*i che*$^{2}$ ꜀*ka*, He, himself, 我 本 身 ‘*ngwai* ‘*pwong* ꜀*sing*, I, myself, &c.

The term 伊 自 家 ꜀*i che*$^{2}$ ꜀*ka*, and 伊 本 身 ꜀*i* ‘*pwong* ꜀*sing* are used for *itself*, as applied to lower animals. The former is also applied to inanimate objects.

*The Interrogative Pronouns* are formed by prefixing the words 世 *sié*ʾ 乜 *miéh*꜆ and 俤 *tié*$^{2}$ to other words.

(1) 世 *sié*ʾ is always followed by *nóh*꜆ (thing), making a compound interrogative, as 世 乇 *sié*ʾ *nóh*꜆ what? 世 乇 乇 *sié*ʾ *nóh*꜆ *nóh*꜆ what thing? 世 乇 仈 *sié*ʾ *nóh*꜆ ꜀*nĕng*, what person? 世 乇 名 *sié*ʾ *nóh*꜆ ꜀*miăng*, what name? what's the matter?

(2) 乜 *miéh*꜆ is sometimes used *independently* for the interrogative *what?* And sometimes, like *sié*ʾ, is followed by 乇 *nóh*꜆ (thing), as 乜 時 候 *miéh*꜆ ꜀*si haiu*$^{2}$ what time? 乜 乇 *miéh*꜆ *nóh*꜆ what? 乜 乇 乇 *miéh*꜆ *nóh*꜆ *nóh*꜆ what thing?

(3) 俤 *tié*$^{2}$ is always followed by a noun, or by a classifier, with or without a numeral prefixed, as 俤 仈 *tié*$^{2}$ ꜀*nĕng*, what person? who? 俤 仈 裡 *tié*$^{2}$ ꜀*nĕng*, ‘*tié*, at whose house? 俤 隻 *tié*$^{2}$ *chiăh*꜆ or 俤 一 隻 *tié*$^{2}$ *sioh*$_{2}$ *chiăh*꜆ which one? The term 苛 俤 代 ꜀*k‘ó tié*$^{2}$ *tai*$^{2}$

榕腔初學撮要

( elliptically ꜀k'ó tié² ) wherefore? why so? is more properly classed as an interrogative adverbial phrase.

The *Relative Pronouns* have no proper equivalent. Their place is supplied by ꜁ki or ꜁ki ꜂chiă, placed before the noun which indicates the subject, as 一暝來其伙講 *sioh꜆ ꜁mang ꜁li ꜁ki ꜁nĕng ꜂kong*, or 一暝來其啫伙講 *sioh꜆ ꜁mang ꜁li ꜁ki, ꜂chiă ꜁nĕng ꜂kong*, the person, who came yesterday, said—

The *Compound Relative, what* (that which), is expressed by 所 ꜂*su*, as 伊所做其代 ꜀*i* ꜂*su chó*꜄ ꜁*ki tai*² that-which-he-did-its-business—the business which he did. But the common terms used in speaking for this pronoun, and for the compounds, *whoever, whichever, whatever, whosoever*, &c., are the interrogative pronouns. The connection always determines the usage.

賣曉的講世乇 *má² ꜂hieu tek꜆ ꜂kong sié꜄ nóh꜆* did not know what (he) said.

俤伙欲做大 *tié² ꜁nĕng ói꜄ chó꜄ twai²* whoever wishes to be great—

在汝做世乇 *chai² ꜂nü chó꜄ sié꜄ nóh꜆*, as-you-please-do-what—whatever you may please to do.

The terms 凡 ꜁*hwang* and 大凡 *tai² ꜁hwang* (all, in general) are also frequently used, but properly belong to the written language, as 凡欲來其伙 ꜁*hwang ói꜄ ꜁li ꜁ki ꜁nĕng*, all-wish-come-its-persons—whosoever wishes to come.

The *Demonstrative Pronouns* are 只 ꜂*chi*, 啫 ꜂*chiă*, 許 ꜂*hü* or ꜂*hi*, 那 ꜂*hiă*, 𠲥 ꜁*chui*, 回 ꜁*hui*.

(1) Used *adjectively*, 只 ꜂*chi*, 啫 ꜂*chiă*, 許 ꜂*hü* or ꜂*hi*, and 那 ꜂*hiă*.

(a) ꜂*Chi* (this) as a pronominal adjective, qualifies some nouns, as 只隻 ꜂*chi chiăh*꜆ this one, 只邊 ꜂*chi* ꜀*peng*, this side, 只面 ꜂*chi meng*꜄ this face or surface, 只帮 ꜂*chi* ꜀*pong*, this time. It also qualifies classifiers with their numeral or adjective prefixes, as

只一隻 ꜂*chi sioh꜆ chiăh꜆* this one.
只二條 ꜂*chi lang²* ꜁*teu*, these two threads or strips.
只幾樣 ꜂*chi* ꜂*kwi yong²* these few sorts.

(b) ʿ*Chiă*, this, is also used in the sense of *that* as a pronominal adjective, as 啫仈 ʿ*chiă* ꜀*nĕng*, this or that person, 啫乇 ʿ*chiă nóh*꜆ this or that thing.

(c) ʿ*hü* or ʿ*hi*, and ʿ*hiă*, that, are the correlatives of ʿ*chi* and ʿ*chiă*, this, as 許隻 ʿ*hü chiăh*꜆ or ʿ*hi chiăh*꜆ that one, 許二樣 ʿ*hü lang*² *yong*² or ʿ*hi lang*² *yong*² those two kinds, 那𣍐 ʿ*hiă* ʿ*k*ʿ*wang*, that form or manner.

(2) Used *independently*. The demonstratives 只 ʿ*chi* and 許 ʿ*hü* are sometimes so used, as 毛只毛許 ꜀*mó* ʿ*chi* ꜀*mó* ʿ*hü*, neither this nor that, i. e., no cause whatever.

The correlatives 嘰 ꜀*chuí* and ꜀*huí* are used only as *independent* demonstratives, as they never qualify nouns.

嘰是好 ꜀*chuí se*² ʿ*hó*, this is good.

嘰好囘呆 ꜀*chuí* ʿ*hó* ꜀*huí* ꜀*ngai*, this good and that bad, i. e., this is the better.

囘伓比嘰 ꜀*huí ng*² ʿ*pi* ꜀*chuí*, that not comparable to this.

The same words also form compound terms with their correlates ʿ*chiă* and ʿ*hiă*.

啫嘰 ʿ*chiă* ꜀*chuí*, this ! this thing ! this here !

那囘 ʿ*hiă* ꜀*huí*, that ! that thing ! that there !

(3) Used *adverbially*. The demonstratives 只 ʿ*chi*, 許 ʿ*hü* or ʿ*hi*, are frequently so used.

只高 ʿ*chi* ꜀*keng*, so high, 只滿好 ʿ*chi* ʿ*mwang* ʿ*hó*, so very good, 只裡 ʿ*chi* ʿ*tié* (this-within) in here, and 只塊 ʿ*chi wai*ʾ, used for ꜀*chu wai*ʾ here, 許大 ʿ*hü twai*² or ʿ*hi twai*² so large, 許久 ʿ*hü* ꜀*ong*, or ʿ*hi* ꜀*ong*, so long a time, 許裡 ʿ*hü* ʿ*tié* or ʿ*hi* ʿ*tié* (that-within) in there, and ʿ*hü wai*ʾ or ʿ*hi wai*ʾ, used for ꜀*hu wai*ʾ there.

## 4. ADJECTIVES.

The Chinese *adjective* has no declension of gender, number and case.

Adjectives precede the nouns which they qualify, as 好仈 ʿ*hó* ꜀*nĕng*, a good man. But sometimes the sign of the possessive or genitive is interposed, in which case the adjective becomes the name of the thing possessed, as 好其仈 ʿ*hó* ꜀*ki* ꜀*nĕng*, a man of goodness, i. e., a good man.

When an adjective follows a noun, it becomes a predicate, the substantive verb being often understood, as 乇好 *nóh*͵ ʿ*hó*, the thing (is) good, 厝高 *ch'io*ʾ ꜀*keng*, the house (is) high.

THE POSITIVE degree denotes absolute or simple quality, and is expressed by a single word as in other languages.

THE COMPARATIVE degree is formed—

(1) By prefixing 故 *ko*ʾ still, still more, to the *positive*, as 故好 *ko*ʾ ʿ*hó*, better. The word 更 *kaing*ʾ is also used, but often with the force of *the*, or *all the*, as 更呆 *kaing*ʾ ꜀*ngai*, the worse, all the worse.

(2) By the addition of 去 *k'ó*ʾ, (go) or 過 *kwo*ʾ (pass), to the positive, with or without the sign *ko*ʾ, when a formal comparison is instituted between two subjects.

只隻大去許隻 ʿ*chi chiăh*͵ *twai*² *k'ó*ʾ ʿ*hŭ chiăh*͵ this one (is) larger than that one.

故高過山 *ko*ʾ ꜀*keng kwo*ʾ ꜀*sang*, higher than the mountains.

(3) By interposing 比 ʿ*pi* (to compare) between the objects compared, and placing the comparative adjective after them.

汝比伊故呆 ʿ*nŭ* ʿ*pi* ꜀*i ko*ʾ ꜀*ngai*, you are worse than he.

(4) An adverbial comparative is formed by the use of 莾 ʿ*mwong*, or 越 *wok*₂.

莾久莾好 ʿ*mwong* ꜀*ong* ʿ*mwong* ʿ*hó*, the longer (time) the better.

越遲越呆 *wok*₂ ꜀*ti wok*₂ ꜀*ngai*, the later the worse.

THE SUPERLATIVE degree is formed—

(1) By prefixing to the positive such words as 盡 *cheng*² 頂 ʿ*ting*, 野 ʿ*yă*, 極 *kik*₂ 上 *siong*², as 盡好 *cheng*² ʿ*hó*, (exhaustive-good) wholly good, 頂好 ʿ*ting* ʿ*hó*, (top-good) the best, 野好 ʿ*yă* ʿ*hó*, very good, 極好 *kik*₂ ʿ*hó*, extremely good, 上好 *siong*² ʿ*hó*, superiorly good, first rate.

(2) By prefixing other words, which give completeness, emphasis, or intensity to the idea, and may be classed as superlative forms, as 真 ꜀*ching*, truly, 太 *k'ak*͵ too, very, remarkably, 秃 *t'uk*₂ blunt, the very end or extreme, 𫝥 *nioh*₂ how, how very, i. e., very, extremely, 十分 *sek*₂ ꜀*hung*, (ten-candareens) wholly, entirely, 十全 *sek*₂ ꜀*chiong* (ten-complete) completely, perfectly.

(3) By reduplicating the adjective and sometimes following it with 着 *tioh*$_2$ which indicates fullness or completeness of the quality, as 明明 ꜀*ming* ꜀*ming*, very clear or plain, 細細着 *sá*ʾ *sá*ʾ *tioh*$_2$ very small, 高高 ꜀*keng* ꜀*keng*, or 高高着 ꜀*keng* ꜀*keng tioh*$_2$ very high.

(4) By such suffixes as 的極 *tek*꜆ *kik*$_2$ 之至 ꜀*chi che*ʾ.

大的極 *twai*$^2$ *tek*꜆ *kik*$_2$ extremely great.

毛理之至 ꜀*mó* ʿ*li*· ꜀*chi che*ʾ exceedingly unreasonable.

The *signs* of the comparative and superlative are sometimes *wholly omitted*, when the connection or attendant circumstances clearly determine which of the two degrees is intended.

嚌好 ꜀*chui* ʿ*hó*, this (is) the better, or the best.

長一尺 ꜀*tong sioh*$_2$ *ch'ioh*꜆ one foot the longer, or the longest.

*Defference in quality*, or other accidents, is expressed—

(1) *Definitely*, by prefixing the ordinals.

第一好 *tá*$^2$ *ek*꜆ ʿ*hó*, the-first-good—the first quality, the best.

第二好 *tá*$^2$ *ne*$^2$ ʿ*hó*, the-second-good—the second quality.

(2) *Indefinitely*, by the use of such words as, 贏 ꜀*yăng* (win) and 輸 ꜀*sio* (lose), or the full, idiomatic forms 贏去 ꜀*yăng k'ó*ʾ and 輸去 ꜀*sio k'ó*ʾ, with or without the comparative sign 故 *ko*ʾ.

嚌故贏去囘 ꜀*chui ko*ʾ ꜀*yăng k'ó*ʾ ꜀*hui*, this excels (is better than) that.

汝輸去伊 ʿ*nü* ꜀*sio k'ó*ʾ ꜀*i*, you are inferior to him.

Also by the use of the term 故毛拿 *ko*ʾ ꜀*mó niăh*$_2$ or 故不如 *ko*ʾ *pok*꜆ ꜀*ü*, often followed by 樣 *yong*$^2$ (form, fashion) at the close of the sentence. 故毛拿伊樣 *ko*ʾ ꜀*mó niăh*$_2$ ꜀*i yong*$^2$ still-not-equal-to-him-style—not comparable to his, or to what he has made or done.

The idea of *great difference* in quality, &c., is expressed by such adjuncts as 的佤 *tek*꜆ *sá*$^2$, 野佤 ʿ*yă sá*$^2$, 的遠 *tek*꜆ *hwong*$^2$.

好的佤 ʿ*hó tek*꜆ *sá*$^2$ very much better,

高野佤 ꜀*keng* ʿ*yă sá*$^2$, very much higher.

差的遠 ꜀*ch'a tek*꜆ *hwong*$^2$ differs far, very different from.

The idea of *slight difference* in quality, &c., is expressed by such adjuncts as 些微 ꜀*niă nói*ʾ, 一滴仔 *sioh*$_2$ *tek*꜆ ʿ*kiăng*, 一知知 *ek*꜆ ꜀*ti* ꜀*ti*, with or without the comparative sign 故 *ko*ʾ.

故好些微 *ko' 'hó ꜀niă nói'* a little better.
大一滴仔 *twai² sioh꜅ tek꜀ 'kiăng,* a little larger.
差一知知 *꜀ch'a ek꜀ ꜀ti ꜀ti,* differs or lacks a trifle.

The idea of *inferior* quality, &c., in the *positive* degree is expressed by such prefixes as 毛世乇 *꜁mó sié' nóh꜀* or 毛乜乇 *꜁mó miéh꜀ nóh꜀* 毛箬 *꜁mó nióh꜅* 賣樣 *má² yong²* 毛野 *꜁mó 'yă.*
毛世乇好 *꜁mó sié' nóh꜀ 'hó,* not very good.
毛箬高 *꜁mó nioh꜅ ꜁keng,* not very high.
賣樣熱 *má² yong² yék꜅* not very hot, only a little warm.
毛野遠 *꜁mó 'yă hwong²* not very far, quite near.

The idea of *ordinary* or *passable* quality, &c., is expressed by the prefix 也務 *yă² o²* (also has or is).
也務好 *yă² o² 'hó,* pretty good, tolerably fair.

Numeral Adjectives consist of single words from *one* to *ten,* as 一 *sioh꜅* or *ek꜀* one, 二 *lang²* or *ne²* two, 三 *꜀sang,* three, 四 *se'* four, 五 *ngo²* five, 六 *lëk꜅* six, 七 *ch'ek꜀* seven, 八 *paik꜀* eight, 九 *'kau,* nine, 十 *sek꜅* or 一十 *ek꜀ sek꜅* ten; and of two or more words from *eleven* onward, as 十一 *sek꜅ ek꜀ eleven,* 十二 *sek꜅ ne²* twelve, 二十 *ne² sek꜅* twenty, 二十一 *ne² sek꜅ ek꜀* twenty one, 二十二 *ne² sek꜅ ne²* twenty two, 三十 *꜀sang sek꜅* thirty, 一百 *sioh꜅ pah꜀* one hundred, 一千 *sioh꜅ ꜀ch'iéng,* one thousand, 一萬 *sioh꜅ wang²* ten thousand.

In using the duplicate forms for *one* and *two,* the student must discriminate very carefully. Thus 10 is *sek꜅* or *ek꜀ sek꜅* not *sioh꜅ sek꜅* 20 is *ne² sek꜅* not *lang² sek꜅* 11 is *sek꜅ ek꜀* not *sek꜅ sioh꜅* 21 is *ne² sek꜅ ek꜀* not *ne² sek꜅ sioh꜅.*

Ordinal Numbers are formed by prefixing the serial word 第 *tá²* to numeral adjectives, as 第一 *tá² ek꜀* the first, 第二 *tá² ne²* the second, 第三 *tá² ꜀sang,* the third. The word 頭 *꜁t'au* (head) is also used for the *first,* as 頭節 *꜁t'au chiék꜀* the first verse.

In the *spoken* language, the word 第 *tá²* is used up to the *tenth,* and sometimes to the *nineteenth,* after which the numerals alone are used as ordinals.

In speaking *informally* on common subjects, the word 第 *te*$^2$ is often omitted entirely, as 一 二 三 *ek*꜄ *ne*$^2$ ꜀*sang*, and 四 五 六 *se*ᵓ *ngo*$^2$ *lëk*$_2$ may mean *first, second, third*, and *fourth, fifth, sixth*, as well as one, two, three, and four, five, six.

The *months of the year* have no ordinal prefix, as 正月 ꜀*chiăng ngwok*$_2$ the first month, 二月 *ne*$^2$ *ngwok*$_2$ the second month, 三月 ꜀*sang ngwok*$_2$ the third month. To express a given number of months, a distinctive form is used, as 三 個 月 日 ꜀*sang* ᶜ*a ngwok*$_2$ *nik*$_2$ three months' days, i. e., three months.

The ordinal for *days of a month* is the word 初 ꜀*ch'ë*, used up to the *tenth* day, after which the numerals alone are used, as 初 一 ꜀*ch'ë ek*꜄ the first (day of the month), 初 二 ꜀*ch'ë ne*$^2$ the second, 初 十 ꜀*ch'ë sek*$_2$ the tenth, 十 一 *sek*$_2$ *ek*꜄ the eleventh, 三 十 ꜀*sang sek*$_2$ the thirtieth. It is common in speaking of the current day of the month to prefix the word "to-day" as 今 旦 初 九 ꜀*king tang*ᵓ ꜀*ch'ë* ᶜ*kau*, to-day (is) the ninth.

## 5. VERBS.

As Chinese verbs are not conjugated, they are the same through all the *moods* and *tenses*. These properties are determined by the sense or connection, or by the use of auxiliaries.

### Moods.

The Indicative, as 我 拍 ᶜ*ngwai p'ah*꜄ I strike, 汝 坐 ᶜ*nü sói*$^2$ You sit, 伊 去 ꜀*i k'ó*ᵓ He goes. But these and other verbs in different connections and without distinctive signs might be in other moods.

The Subjunctive. Its most common sign in the colloquial is 哪 *na*$^2$ (lit., only), as 伊哪務來我就 ꜀*i na*$^2$ *o*$^2$ ꜀*li* ᶜ*ngwai cheu*$^2$, if he comes, then I—.Other common signs are the verbs 驚 ꜀*kiăng* (to fear) and 恐 怕 ᶜ*k'üng p'a*ᵓ or ᶜ*hung p'a*ᵓ (to fear lest) used as auxiliaries, as 驚 伊 䠡 跋 ꜀*kiăng* ꜀*i dá*$^2$ *pwak*$_2$ I fear he will fall, lest he falls or will fall, 恐 怕 盪 雨 ᶜ*hung p'a*ᵓ *taung*$^2$ ᶜ*ü*, lest it should rain. These two expressions may also be rendered in the *potential* mood.

The following are used as auxiliary terms in writing, and in more formal styles of conversation:—若使 *yok*$_2$ *ʿsü*, 若凡 *yok*$_2$ *꜀hwang*, 假使 *ʿka ʿsü*, 設使 *siek*$_2$ *ʿsü*, if, supposing that; 可比 *ʿk'ó ʿpi*, 比喻 *ʿpi ëü*$^2$ 比論 *ʿpi laung*$^2$, 比方 *ʿpi ꜀hwong*, to illustrate, for the sake of comparison, if for instance; and 雖然 *꜀ch'wi ꜀yong*, though, although.

The Potential is indicated by such auxiliary signs as 𠊎 *á*$^2$ 着 *tioh*$_2$ 通 *꜀t'ëng*, 欲 *ói*ʾ 該 *꜀kai*, 該當 *꜀kai ꜀tong*, 應當 *꜀ing ꜀tong*, 應該 *꜀ing ꜀kai*, 應該着 *꜀ing ꜀kai tioh*$_2$ as 𠊎拍 *á*$^2$ *p'ah*ʾ can or may strike, 着講 *tioh*$_2$ *ʿkong*, must say, 通做 *꜀t'ëng chó*ʾ must or ought to do, 該來 *꜀kai ꜀li* or 應該來 *꜀ing ꜀kai ꜀li*, ought to come.

The Imperative is simply the verb with or without the pronoun, as 來 *꜀li* or 汝來 *ʿnü ꜀li*, come or come thou. Sometimes the interjection 吓 *꜀a*, is added, as 汝來吓 *ʿnü ꜀li ꜀a*, come thou!

The *imperative* is also indicated by such words as 莽 *ʿmwong*, merely, just, 來 *꜀li*, to come, 去 *k'ó*ʾ to go, as 莽坐 *ʿmwong sói*$^2$ just sit! 來食 *꜀li siăh*$_2$ come eat, 去講 *k'ó*ʾ *ʿkong*, go say. The last two and similar phrases are really double imperatives, though often the words *꜀li* and *k'ó*ʾ seem merely to denote the beginning of the action of the following verb.

The Infinitive has no distinctive sign. It follows a noun, pronoun, adjective, or verb.

駛伙去 *ʿsai ꜀nëng k'ó*ʾ cause a person to go, send some one.
叫我做 *kieu*ʾ *ʿngwai chó*ʾ call me to do.
好做 *ʿhó chó*ʾ good (easy) to do.
毛敢講 *꜀mó ʿkang ʿkong*, not dare to say.

Participial Mood or Participle. The particle 禮 *ʿlá*, equivatent to *is*, or *is in the act of*, may be regarded as the sign of the *present* participle. It forms, with the following verb, a participial verb, as 禮寫 *ʿlá ʿsiă*, is writing, 禮講 *ʿlá ʿkong*, is saying.

The sign of the *past* or *perfect* participle is 旣然 *ke*ʾ *꜀yong* (since, already), as 旣然來 *ke*ʾ *꜀yong ꜀li*, having come.

The suffixes 了 *ʿlau*, 完 *꜀wong*, 完了 *꜀wong ʿlau*, also form the *past* participle, as 寫了 *ʿsiă ʿlau*, or 寫禮了 *ʿsiă ʿlá ʿlau*, written, 做完 *chó*ʾ *꜀wong*, done, made, 啫話講完了 *ʿchiă wa*² *ʿkong ꜀wong ʿlau*, these words having been said, having finished saying these words.

## Tenses.

The Present Tense is distinguished—

(1) By the sense or connection, 我欲 *ʿngwai ói*ʾ I wish, 汝甘願呶 *ʿnü ꜀kang ngwong*² *꜀pá*, are you willing? 伊是好仈 *꜀i se*² *ʿhó ꜀nĕng*, he is a good man, 伊賣曉的 *꜀i má*² *ʿhieu tek*ͽ he does not know.

(2) By the use of the particle 禮 *ʿlá*, which makes participial verbs in this tense, as 伊禮做 *꜀i ʿlá chó*ʾ, he is doing.

(3) By prefixing an adverb of present time, as 伶 *꜀tang*, 現在 *hiêng*² *chai*² now, at present, as in 伶做 *꜀tang chó*ʾ now do or does, 現在去 *hiêng*² *chai*² *k'ó*ʾ now go or goes.

But in these and many like phrases, the *time* is ambiguous. Often it is properly *the immediate future*, and the two phrases above may be rendered "now about to do", "now about to go". Except when the connection clearly indicates the element of time, the insertion of 禮 *ʿlá* is needed to form the *present*, as 伊伶禮做 *꜀i ꜀tang ʿlá chó*ʾ he is now doing.

The Past Tense is formed—

(1) By the auxiliaries 務 *o*² 仈曾 *paik*ͽ *꜀cheng*, and by 曾 *꜀cheng* alone, when it is preceded by the negative 昧 *mwói*² (not yet), as 務看 *o*² *k'ang*ʾ has seen, 仈曾講 *paik*ͽ *꜀cheng ʿkong*, has said, have already said, 昧曾做將換 *mwói*² *꜀cheng chó*ʾ *꜀chiong wang*² not yet have done so, never have done so.

(2) By the suffixes 了 *ʿlau*, 完了 *꜀wong ʿlau*, as 我寫了 *ʿngwai ʿsiă ʿlau*, I have written, 我做完了 *ʿngwai chó*ʾ *꜀wong ʿlau*, I have done or finished (it).

(3) By the use both of auxiliaries and suffixes, as 我務看了 *ʿngwai o*² *k'ang*ʾ *ʿlau*, I have seen.

(4) By the auxiliaries 已 *ʿi* and 已今 *ʿi ꜀king*, which are also signs of the past tense, but properly belong to the written language, or to more formal discourse.

(5) By the use of adverbs or other words, involving the idea of past time, as 伊昧來 ꜀*i mwói*$^2$ ꜁*li*, he has not yet come, 當時伊教百姓 ꜀*tong* ꜁*si* (or ꜀*tong* ʻ*chiă* ꜁*si haiu*$^2$) ꜀*i ka*ʾ *pah*꜆ *sang*ʾ at that time he taught the people.

The Pluperfect follows the rules of the *imperfect* or *first past*. It is readily distinguished in such forms as 昧死已前伊務講 *mwoi*$^2$ ʻ*si* ʻ*i* ꜁*seng* ꜀*i o*$^2$ ʻ*kong*, not-yet-died-before, he-had-said—before he died he said or had said. In this and like instances, the *pluperfect* resolves itself into the *imperfect*.

The Future Tense is formed—

(1) By the auxiliaries 剝 *pwoh*꜆ 將剝 ꜀*chiong pwoh*꜆ 就剝 *cheu*$^2$ *pwoh*꜆ 僻 *á*$^2$, 就僻 *cheu*$^2$ *á*$^2$, as 剝做 *pwoh*꜆ *chó*ʾ will do, about to do, 僻拍 *á*$^2$ *pʻah*꜆ will strike, 將剝去 ꜀*chiong pwoh*꜆ *kʻó*ʾ or 就剝去 *cheu*$^2$ *pwoh*꜆ *kʻó*ʾ about to go, or forthwith about to go.

In the last and like instances, the words ꜀*chiong* and *cheu*$^2$ convey the idea of *immediate future* in time.

(2) By the use of adverbs and other words, involving the idea of future time, as 後 *haiu*$^2$ and 後來 *haiu*$^2$ ꜁*lai*, afterwards, 將來 ꜀*chiong* ꜁*lai*, hereafter, 毛箬久 ꜁*mó nioh*꜇ ꜁*ong*, in not a very long time, 回頭 ꜁*huí* ꜁*tʻau*, turn-the-head—in a little while, and ꜁*ha* ʻ*tiăng*, soon, shortly.

These are sometimes followed by 就 *cheu*$^2$ (then, forthwith) as a sort of sign of the future, as 毛箬久就起身 ꜁*mó nioh*꜇ ꜁*ong* *cheu*$^2$ ʻ*kʻi* ꜀*sing*, not-very-long-then-rise-body—will start shortly.

The *substantive verb* 是 *se*$^2$ (to be) is often wholly omitted in simple sentences. In such cases *time* or *tense* is determined by the meaning of the other words, or by the general sense, connection, or circumstances, as 人洒 ꜁*nëng sá*$^2$ the persons (are or were) many, 時候便 ꜁*si haiu*$^2$ *piéng*$^2$ the time (was, is, or will be) convenient, 伶好囉 ꜀*tang* ʻ*hó* ꜁*ló*, now (it is) well!

## Passive Voice.

The words used as signs of the *passive* are 乞 *kʻëük*꜆ (to give), 受 *seu*$^2$ (to receive or suffer), 見 *kiéng*ʾ (to see or experience).

(1) When *k'ëük*ↄ is used, it is always followed by the word denoting the agent or actor.

乞佽講 *k'ëük*ↄ *꜀nëng ꜂kong*, gave-persons-to-say—to be talked about by people.

乞老爹拍 *k'ëük*ↄ *꜂ló ꜀tiă p'ah*ↄ give-officers-to-beat—to be beaten by the officers.

(2) When *seu*² is used, the actor may or may not be mentioned, as 受拍 *seu*² *p'ah*ↄ to receive a beating, 受伊拍 *seu*² *꜀i p'ah*ↄ receive-his-beating—to be beaten by him.

In such instances *seu*² becomes the principal verb, while *p'ah*ↄ and *꜀i p'ah*ↄ many be parsed as *verbal nouns*, or phrases in the accusative.

(3) When 見 *kiëng*ↄ is used, it is followed immediately by the principal verb; and the word denoting the agent or actor, if mentioned, precedes the sign.

見怪 *kiëng*ↄ *kwai*ↄ to be offended at, to take offence.
莫見怪 *móh*₂ *kiëng*ↄ *kwai*ↄ don't be offended.
乞汝見笑 *k'ëük*ↄ *꜂nü kiëng*ↄ *ch'ieu*ↄ give-you-to-be-laughed-at—to be laughed at by you.

In the last instance, *k'ëük*ↄ is the principal sign, and the phrase may be rendered "receive or suffer your laughing". The more common form is simply 乞汝笑 *k'ëük*ↄ *꜂nü ch'ieu*ↄ, laughed at by you.

## Reduplicated Verbs.

The verb is frequently repeated in Chinese to emphasize the idea or to denote prolonging of the action or suffering. Sometimes, however, such repetition sems to be a mere euphonism, adding nothing to the essential idea of the verb. The following are familiar instances:—扼扼 *aik*ↄ *aik*ↄ to press with the hand, 看看 *k'ang*ↄ *k'ang*ↄ to see, to examine or consider, 念念 *naing*² *naing*² to repeat, to recite, 行行 *꜀kiăng ꜀kiăng*, to walk onward, 沃沃 *woh*ↄ *woh*ↄ to water, to irrigate.

# 6. ADVERBS.

(1) Some adverbs may be compared like adjectives, as 慢 *maing²* slowly, 故慢 *ko' maing²* more slowly, 盡慢 *cheng² maing²* very slowly.

(2) They also become intensive or superlative by reduplication, as 快快 *k'â' k'â'* very quickly, 好好 *'hó 'hó*, very well.

(3) Many adjectives are used adverbially, as always seen by the context. The following are instances:—好 *'hó* (good) well, 呆 *ˏngai* (bad) badly, 少 *'chieu* (few) seldom, 私 *ˏsü*, (private) privately, 眞 *ˏching* (true) truly, 正 *chiăng'* (correct) correctly.

(4) Adverbs and adverbial phrases may be classed as in other languages, as follows:—

(a) *Of place.* 只塊 *ˏchu wai'* here, 許塊 *ˏhu wai'* there, 冬那 *ˏtëng 'në*, where, 裡 *'tié* or 裡勢 *'tié tié'* inside, 處處 *ch'ëü' ch'ëü'* everywhere, 別位 *pekˎ oi²* elsewhere, 上勢 *siong² sié'* or *ˏkú 'teng*, above, 下底 *a² 'tú*, below, 前斗 *ˏseng 'tau*, before, 後斗 *a² 'tau*, behind.

(b) *Of time.* 伶 *ˏtang* and 現在 *hiéng² chai²* now, 今旦 *ˏking tang'* to-day, 從來 *ˏchüng ˏlai*, and 向來 *hiong' ˏlai*, heretofore, 將來 *ˏchiong ˏlai*, hereafter, 只古 *'chi 'u*, just now, 早先 *'cha ˏleng*, a while ago, 就 *cheu²* then, forthwith, 卽刻 *chekˎ k'aikˎ* and 直頭 *tikˎ ˏt'au*, at once, directly, 昧 *mwoi²* not yet, 面候 *miéng² au²* when, 有時 *'iu ˏsi*, sometimes, 許久 *'hü ˏong*, so long a time, 常常 *ˏsiong ˏsiong*, and 時常 *ˏsi ˏsiong*, and 時刻 *ˏsi k'aikˎ* constantly, *ˏseu* or *ˏseu ˏseu*, frequently, 少 *'chieu* or 少的 *'chieu tekˎ* seldom, 仅 *po²* moreover, 再 *chai'* or *kai'* again, 一回 *siohˎ ˏhúi*, once, *ˏha 'tiăng*, soon, presently.

(c) *Of order.* 就 *cheu²* then, next, 然後 *ˏyong haiu²* afterwards, 竟然 *keng' ˏyong*, and 畢竟 *pekˎ keng'* after all, at last, finally.

(d) *Of negation or prohibition.* 伓 *ng²* not, 毛 *ˏmó*, no, not, 莫 *móhˎ* (including the auxiliary, *do*), do not, don't.

(e) *Of contingence.* 或且 *hĕk꜇ ꜂ch'iă*, perhaps, peradventure, 毛該再 *꜁mó ꜀kai chai꜄*, a final adverbial term, contracted into *꜁ma chai꜄* or *꜂ma tai꜄*, perhaps, probably, 倠是 *ă² se²* may be, possibly, perhaps.

(f) *Of interrogation.* 將樣 *꜀chiòng yong²* how? 將其 *꜀chiong ꜁ki*, why? 將樣其 *꜀chiong yong² ꜁ki*, why? how? 苛俤 *꜀k'ó tiĕ²* or 苛俤代 *꜀k'ó tiĕ² tai²* wherefore? why thus? 冬那 *꜀tĕng ꜂nĕ*, where, how? as in 冬那是將換 *꜀tĕng ꜂nĕ se² ꜀chiong wang²* how is it thus—it is not at all so, 箬 *nioh꜇* how, as in 箬壞 *nioh꜇ wai²*, how many? 箬洒 *nioh꜇ să²* how much or many?

(g) *Of defect, exclusion, likeness, etc.* 差不多 *꜀ch'a pok꜆ ꜀tó*, nearly, almost, 少的 *꜂chieu tek꜆* seldom, 險些 *꜂hiĕng ꜀sié*, almost, within a little, 獨獨 *tuk꜇ tuk꜇* only, 將換 *꜀chiong wang²* thus, so, 漸漸 *chiĕng² chiĕng²*, or *꜁si ꜀niă nói꜄*, by degrees, gradually, by little and little.

## 7. PREPOSITIONS.

Prepositions are not so numerous as in some other languages; and often the sentence assumes in this respect an elliptical form, even when the language furnishes the proper prepositional word or phrase.

There are two classes of prepositions, (1) those consisting of a single word, some of which are verbals, (2) compounds or prepositional phrases. In reference to *position* they may be arranged in two classes, as follows :—

(1) *Preceding* the noun or pronoun. 在 *chai²*, in, at, into, upon, 落 *lóh꜇* in, at, 自 *chëü²* and 從 *꜁chüng*, from, commencing from or at, 由 *꜁iu*, from, by, through, out of, 照 *chieu꜄* and 憑 *꜁ping*, according to, as, 駛 *꜂sai* and 用 *ëüng²* by means of, as a cause, instrument, material, etc., 共 *kaëng²* with, along with, for, 對 *tói꜄* opposite, to, towards, face to face with, 因 *꜀ing* or 因爲 *꜀ing oi²* for, on account of, in behalf of, 替 *t'á꜄* or *k'á꜄* for, instead of, 近 *këüng²* and 傍 *paung²* by, near, next to, close to, 至 *kau꜄* to, unto, till, 向 *hiong꜄* towards, 透 *t'au꜄* through, 趁 *t'eng꜄* or *t'ai꜄* by, through, as a road, an opportunity.

(2) *Following* the noun or pronoun. 下 *hu²* or *a²* below, 後 *au²* behind, 前 *꜀seng*, before, in front of, 面前 *meng꜄ ꜀seng*, in front of, in presence of, 上 *siong²* or 面上 *meng꜄ siong²* upon, on the top of, 頂 *꜂ting* or *꜀kà ꜂teng*, on the summit or top of, 中 *꜀tong*, 大中 *tai² ꜀tong*, 中 *꜀tüng*, and 中間 *꜀tüng ꜀kang*, in the middle of, amidst, among, 對面 *tói꜄ meng꜄* opposite to, 裡 *꜂tié* or 裡勢 *꜂tié tié꜄* in, within, 外 *ngié²* or 外斗 *ngié² ꜂tau*, without, outside of.

## 8. CONJUNCTIONS.

㑚 *po²* 也 *yă²* and, also, 也毛 *yă² ꜀mó*, 也伓 *yă² ng²* neither, nor, 共 *kaĕng²* together with, and, 零 *꜀ling*, and, as a surplus, 連 *꜀liéng*, in connection with, and, 兼 *꜀kiéng*, 㑚兼 *po² ꜀kiéng*, in addition to, 因 *꜀ing*, 因爲 *꜀ing oi²* for, because, 㑚 *na²* only, if, 㑚毛 *na² ꜀mó*, 㑚伓 *na² ng²* unless, 惟獨 *꜀mi tuk꜆* but, only, 總 *꜂chung*, 故 *ko꜄* but, yet, still, 或 *hĕk꜆* either, or, 吓 *꜂a*, or, 何況 *꜀hó hwong꜄* how much more, 若使 *yok꜆ ꜂sü*, 若凡 *yok꜆ ꜀hwang*, 假使 *꜂ka ꜂sü*, 設使 *siék꜆ ꜂sü*, if, supposing that, 驚 *꜀kiăng*, 恐怕 *꜂k'ŭng p'a꜄* or *꜂hung p'a꜄*, lest, 到底 *tó꜄ ꜂tí*, at the last, on the contrary, or, 故此 *ko꜄ ꜂ch'ü*, 因此 *꜀ing ꜂ch'ü*, therefore, hence, 所以 *꜂su ꜂i*, 所以然 *꜂su ꜂i ꜀yong*, for what reason, wherefore, whence, 就 *cheu²* 學將換 *óh꜆ ꜀chiong wung²* then, thereupon, 雖然 *꜀ch'wi ꜀yong*, although.

## 9. INTERJECTIONS.

(1) The particles 吓 *꜀a* and 嘩 *꜀á* are used after the noun, as signs of the independent or vocative case. The latter is used in familiar or informal address, and is often spoken with considerable stress of voice.

主吓 *꜂chio ꜀a*, Lord! O Lord!

先生吓 *꜀sing ꜀sang ꜀a*, or *꜀sing ꜀sang ꜀á*, Ho, Teacher!

Instead of 吓 *꜀a*, the word 阿 *꜀ó* is sometimes used in books, as a sign of the vocative.

(2) The following is a list of interjections used *independently*, or as mere *exclamations;* asterisks being used in the places where there are no Chinese characters for the word or words.

* * * *aë*$^2$ a familiar call, ho ! halloo ! you there !

唉吓 *꜀ai ꜁a* or *꜀ai a*$^2$ a tone of surprise, or admiration, ah !

唉 *꜁ai* or *ai*$^2$ a tone of surprise, also of prohibition, stop !

哀哉 *꜀ai ꜀chai*, ah ! alas !

喏 *꜁chiă*, there ! there 'tis ! so, you have it !

嘘 *꜁ch'ü*, hoot ! shoo! also a term of contempt, uttered with the middle finger thrust out.

哯 *꜁ë* or *꜁ë ꜁ë*, ho ! halloo !

* * * *eh꜆* or *eh꜆ eh꜆* a tone of refusal, spoken pettishly, will ! won't ! according to circumstances.

* * * *ha꜄*, an answer to a call—well, what is it?

* * * *꜀há*, an assent to a statement, yes, it's so !

* * * *꜁há háh꜇* a mocking, irritating term, as said to a crying child.

* * * *haë*$^2$ *haë*$^2$ shame ! shame ! uttered while drawing the fore-finger over the cheek.

咳 *꜁hai*, a tone of surprise or pity, ah ! alas ! also used by coolies in bearing burdens.

喊 *hai*$^2$ ah ! oh ! stop !

那囘 *꜂hiă ꜁huí*, that ! that there ! used in trying to recall a thought or subject.

好 *꜂hó*, good ! well !

* * * *hó꜄* an answer to a call, similar to *ha꜄*.

唉阿 *꜀hoi ꜁ó*, a term of regret or surprise, oh ! ah !

* * * *꜁hoi*, halloo! you there !

怪的是 *kwai꜄ tek꜆ se*$^2$ or *꜁hwa tek꜆ se*$^2$ why, it's just so ! that must be it !

嘮嚕 *꜁lio lio*$^2$ / *꜀lu ꜀lu* } are sounds used in calling dogs.

啊啊 *ó*$^2$ *ó*$^2$ yes, that's it !—said on apprehending a meaning or when another understands and does a thing properly.

唉阿 *꜀oi ꜁ó*, a term of regret or surprise, oh ! ah !

* * * *꜁oi*, halloo ! you there !

* * * *ói*$^2$ an answer to a call, ay !

慘 *꜂siăng* (also 儺慘 *á*$^2$ *꜂siăng* and 該慘 *꜀kai ꜂siăng*). ah ! alas ! what a pity !

慘隻慘 ‘*siăng chiăh*₎ ‘*siăng*, how very lamentable !

* * * ₅*tē*, there ! there it is !

很 ‘*t‘eng*, or 艥很 *á*² ‘*t‘eng*, ah ! what a pity !

哇哇 *to*˒ *to*˒ or ₅*tu to*˒ sounds used in calling fowls.

* * * ₍*wai* ₅*a*, (or ₅*ó* or *a*²) tones of wonder or astonishment.

* * * *wai*˒ ₅*a* (or ₅*ó* or *a*²) ah, most wonderful !

* * * ₍*wi* (rarely used) an exclamation of surprise, uttered with the hands thrown out in an excited manner.

## Supplement.

Some of the words, treated and construed as *parts of speech*, often occur in peculiar connections in a sentence. These, with various other words used as prefixes or suffixes, may be termed *enclitics*, though not always corresponding fully to the authorized definition of that term. They require a distinct notice, and are embraced under the following divisions.

### I. Final Particles or Enclitic Words.

These are of different kinds and their force is usually apparent from the context.

(1) Those that are interjectional, emphatic, or euphonic.

(a) 吓 ‘*a*, as in 是吓 *se*² ‘*a*, it is so !

(b) 吓 ₅*a* and 艥 ₅*á* (also signs of the vocative, q. v.).

是吓 *se*² ₅*a*, it is so indeed !

伊講吓 ₍*i* ‘*kong* ₅*a*, he said—

來食飯艥 ₅*li siăh*₂ *pwong*² ₅*á*, come and eat the rice (i. e., your meal).

(c) 伊唉 ₍*i* ₅*ai* (or ‘*nü* ₅*ngai*) is an enclitic phrase.

毛拿伊唉 ₅*mó niăh*₂ ₍*i* ₅*ai* (or ‘*nü* ₅*ngai*), no (way of) managing him or it !

毛法拿伊唉 ₅*mó hwak*₎ *niăh*₂ ₍*i* ₅*ai*, no possible way of managing it !

(d) 囉 ₍*ló* or ‘*ló*, a euphonic equivalent of commas and period in a vocal enumeration of articles or subjects.

椅囉棹囉書囉 ‘*ié* ₍*ló*, *tóh*₎ ₍*ló*, ₍*chü* ₍*ló*, chairs, tables, books.

Man. 6.

(e) 囉 ʿló, a particle following such verbs as 叫 kieuʾ and 稱 ˓ch'ing, as in 名叫囉世乇 ˓miăng kieuʾ ʿló siéʾ nóh˒, name called what, i. e., by what name is he or it called?

(f) 囉 ˓ló, as in 來囉 ˓li ˓ló, has come!
好囉 ʿhó ˓ló, good! well done!
伮佬囉 po² lau² ˓ló, (they) moreover were aged.
是囉 se² ˓ló, it is indeed so!
剁死囉 pwoh˒ ʿsi ˓ló, about to die! nearly dead!

(g) 阿 ˓ó or 呵 ˓ó, an interjectional particle, mostly used in books and about the same as ˓a in the spoken language.
伊務福呵 ˓i o² hok˒ ˓ó, he is blessed!
儺救自家阿 á² keuʾ che² ˓ka ˓ó, can save himself!
伓是死是困着阿 ng² se² ʿsi, se² k'aungʾ tioh₂ ˓ó, is not dead, is asleep!

(h) 嗒 ˓pu or ˓mu, as in 都乇一隻嗒 ˓tu ˓mó sioh₂ chiăh˒ ˓pu, wholly not one even, i. e., there's not even a single one!

(2) Those that usually follow an important word in a sentence, and indicate fullness or completion of the sense. Some, however, as the particles 禮 ʿlá and 兜 ˓tau, seem to have a prepositional or adverbial force; and the former, placed between verbs, is conjunctive or merely euphonic.

The following is a list of some of the words of this class, with examples of their separate and combined uses:—

走 ʿchau, 啫 ˓chiă, 出 ch'ok˒, 見 kiéngʾ, 過 kwoʾ, 起 ʿk'i, 去 k'óʾ, 禮 ʿlá (also a sign of the present participle, q. v.), 來 ˓li, 落 lóh₂ 死 ʿsi, 兜 ˓tau, 的 tek˒ 着 tioh₂ 轉 ʿtiong, 倒 ʿtó.

跑走 ˓p'au ʿchau, or 臂走 piéʾ ʿchau, to run away.
行啫過 ˓kiăng ˓chiă kwoʾ to walk by or past.
賣看的出 má² k'angʾ tek˒ ch'ok˒ can't-see-it-out—can't discern or find out clearly.
儺看的見 á² k'angʾ tek˒ kiéngʾ, can see it.
行過 ˓kiăng kwoʾ, to walk by.
趟起 kok˒ ʿk'i, or 趟起來 kok˒ ʿk'i ˓li, to rise up.
落去 lóh₂ k'óʾ, to go down, to descend.

榕腔初學撮要

走去 *꜂chau k‘ó꜄*, to run away.

病好去 *pang꜅ ꜂hó k‘ó꜄*, the sickness well, i. e., healed.

記禮務講 *ke꜄ ꜂lá o꜅ ꜂kong*, it has been written, saying—

圍禮尅 *꜀ui ꜂lá k‘aik꜆* to environ and crowd.

遏落溝禮去 *taung꜅ lóh꜇ ꜀kau ꜂lá k‘ó꜄* fell down into the ditch.

上來 *siong꜅ ꜁li*, to come up, to ascend.

上去 *siong꜅ k‘ó꜄* to go up, to ascend.

叫起來 *kieu꜄ ꜂k‘i ꜁li*, to call or cry out.

刣死 *꜁t‘ai ꜂si*, to kill-dead—to put to death.

地垰 *te꜅ ꜀tau* or *tié꜅ ꜀tau*, on the ground.

南門垰 *꜁nang ꜁mwong ꜀tau*, at or near the South Gate.

曉的 *꜂hieu tek꜆* to know, to understand.

做的巧 *chó꜄ tek꜆ ꜂k‘ieu*, to do or make ingeniously.

賣奪的去 *má꜅ tok꜇ tek꜆ k‘ó꜄*, cannot be taken away by violence.

毛的入 *꜁mó tek꜆ ꜂tié*, cannot enter into.

討的着 *꜂t‘ó tek꜆ tioh꜇* sought out, found.

去着 *k‘ó꜄ tioh꜇* or 去着了 *k‘ó꜄ tioh꜇ ꜂lau*, have been (to that place).

討的轉 *꜂t‘ó tek꜆ ꜂tiong*, to require (and get it) back.

跌倒 *pwak꜇ ꜂tó*, to fall down, as a person does.

拍倒 *p‘ah꜆ ꜂tó*, to knock down; fallen, knocked over.

### 2. Interrogative Particles and Forms.

(1) 吓 *꜂a*, used in the spoken language, and 阿 *꜂ó*, in books, are equivalent to the disjunctive *or*, and are followed by the negative *꜁mó*, no, not.

務吓毛 *o꜅ ꜂a ꜁mó*, is this so or not? have (you) or not?

務將換阿毛 *o꜅ ꜀chiong wang꜅ ꜂ó ꜁mó*, is it so or not? have (you done) so or not?

(2) 囉 *꜁ló*, *꜀ló*, or *꜂ló*—the sound being somewhat fugacious or indefinite—is also equivalent to *or*, and is followed by the negative *not yet*.

食飯囉昧 *siăh꜇ pwong꜅ ꜁ló mwoi꜅*, have you eaten rice (your meal) or not yet?

(3) 囉叭 ꜁*ló* ꜀*pá*, is an interrogative term, meaning "or not", or analogous to the term ꜁*ló mwoi*$^2$ (or not yet).

伊去囉叭 ꜀*i k'ó*ʾ ꜁*ló* ꜀*pá*, has he gone or not, i. e., has he yet gone?

(4) 呢 ꜀*ni* and 哩 ꜀*li* (or ꜁*ni* and ꜁*li*, as both the tone and initial are sometimes indefinite) are interrogatives, following more or less closely in the sentence such terms as, 將 ꜀*chiong* or 將樣 ꜀*chiong yong*$^2$ how? 將其 ꜀*chiong* ꜁*ki*, why? 世毛 *sié*ʾ *nóh*꜇ what? 俤伙 *tié*$^2$ ꜁*nëng*, who? 冬那 ꜀*tëng* ʿ*në*, where? how? 代駛 *tai*$^2$ ʿ*sai*, what need? why? 苛俤 ꜀*k'ó tié*$^2$ or 苛俤代 ꜀*k'ó tié*$^2$ *tai*$^2$ why? wherefore?

伶將做呢 ꜀*tang* ꜀*chiong chó*ʾ ꜀*ni*, now how (shall we) do?
將樣講哩 ꜀*chiong yong*$^2$ ʿ*kong* ꜀*li*, how say? how does (he) say?

伊講啫話將其呢 ꜀*i* ʿ*kong* ʿ*chiă wa*$^2$ ꜀*chiong* ꜁*ki* ꜀*ni*, he says these words, why? why does he say so?

俤伙𠈀赦罪呢 *tié*$^2$ ꜁*nëng á*$^2$ *siă*ʾ *chói*$^2$ ꜀*ni*, who can forgive sin?

(5) 麼 ꜁*mó*, often used in books and analogous to 叭 ꜀*pá* or ꜁*pá*.

(6) 叭 ꜀*pá* or ꜁*pá*—the sound being somewhat indefinite—is a final interrogative, about equivalent to "*or not*" or "*or not yet*" in a full translation of the sentence.

伶去叭 ꜀*tang k'ó*ʾ ꜀*pá*, now shall we go?
𠈀是叭 *á*$^2$ *se*$^2$ ꜀*pá*, is it perhaps or probably so?
好叭 ʿ*hó* ꜀*pá*, is it well (so)? will it do (so)?

(7) A sentence is also made to assume an interrogative form—

(a) By repeating a verb or an adjective with a negative interposed.

做伓做 *chó*ʾ *ng*$^2$ *chó*ʾ will (you) do it or not?
好伓好 ʿ*hó ng*$^2$ ʿ*hó*, good (so) or not?

(b) By interposing a verb or an adjective between positives and negatives, or placing the same after them.

𠈀曉的賣 *á*$^2$ ʿ*hieu tek*꜇ *má*$^2$ do (you) understand or not?
𠈀賣來 *á*$^2$ *má*$^2$ ꜁*li*, will (he) come or not?
𠈀賣俊 *á*$^2$ *má*$^2$ *chong*ʾ is it excellent or not? is it not fine?

### 3. Colloquial Prefixes.

These seem to be imperfect reduplications of a following noun, verb, or participial noun. They are mostly in the *fifth*, or *eighth*, tone, and have the same initial as the principal word.

The following are familiar examples:—

叉 叉 *꜀ch'a ꜀ch'a*, forks; 角 角 *kĕk꜆ kaĕk꜆* a corner; 扛 扛 *꜀kwang kwang²* a bail, handle; 礐 礐 *k'ok꜆ k'auk꜆* a cavity, a plash; 匡 匡 *꜀k'wong ꜀k'wong*, frames, marked spaces; *꜀kĕ kaĕh꜆* a choking sound, a half-suppressed cackling; *꜀k'ĕng ꜂k'ĕng sau꜄* a dry, hacking cough; *꜀nü nĕük꜆* or *nük꜆ nĕük꜆* rumpled, as a sleeve shoved up, *met.*, to squat and skulk out of sight.

### 4. Colloquial Euphonic Prefixes.

These comprise a peculiar class of words, prefixed to certain verbs in this dialect. So far as has been noticed, they occur only under the 賓 *꜀ping* and 之 *꜀chi* finals. They always have the same *initial* and *tone* as the following, principal word. If there are exceptions to this rule, the variation will probably be due to a change in the initial sound of the latter in easy, flowing speech. As heard in various connections and applications, these prefixes often seem to convey the idea of a continuance of the action to completion. But some native teachers have described them as initial, auxiliary, or euphonic sounds, merely serving to effect an easy utterance of the principal word.

The following are selected, as samples, from over 160 instances of this class of words, as found in the Alphabetic Dictionary of the Foochow Dialect. As the prefixes are mere colloquialisms, the Chinese character for the principal word only is inserted.

詛 *chė꜄ cho꜄*, to curse, 畫 *e² wa²* to sketch, 化 *he꜄ hwa꜄* to burn, as idol-paper, 舞 *꜂i ꜂u*, to brandish, 安 *꜀ing ꜀eng*, to place, 刮 *kek꜆ kauk꜆* to scrape, 擒 *꜁k'ing ꜁k'iéng*, to clutch, 開 *꜀k'i ꜀k'wi*, to open, 犂 *꜁li ꜁lá*, to plow, 賣 *me² má²* to sell off, 拈 *꜀ning ꜀niéng*, to take, 迎 *꜁nging ꜁ngiăng*, to parade or carry in procession, 簸 *pe꜄ pwai꜄* to winnow, 拍 *p'eh꜆ p'ah꜆* to beat, 鑲 *꜀sing ꜀siong*, to insert or inlay, 糴 *tih꜆ tiăh꜆* to buy, as rice, 吐 *t'e꜄ t'o꜄* to vomit, 重 *꜁t'ing ꜁t'ŭng*, to pile up.

## The Same Words used as Different Parts of Speech.

The following are familiar instances of such use:—

下 *a*$^{2}$, v. to descend: *a*$^{2}$, prep. (after the noun) under, below.
就 *cheu*$^{2}$, adv. forthwith, at once : *cheu*$^{2}$, conj. then, in that case.
少 ‘*chieu*, adj. few, not many : ‘*chieu*, adv. sparingly, seldom.
照 *chieu*’, v. to shine upon, to illumine : *chieu*’, prep. according to.
眞 ꜀*ching*, adj. true, genuine : ꜀*ching*, adv. truly, really ; very, extremely.
深 ꜀*ch‘ing*, adj. deep ; abstruse, profound : ꜀*ch‘ing*, adv. fully, implicitly, profoundly.
春 ꜀*ch‘ung*, n. spring : ꜀*ch‘ung*, adj. vernal.
用 *ëüng*$^{2}$, v. to use, to employ ; *ëüng*$^{2}$, prep. by, with, by means of.
好 ‘*hó*, adj. good, excellent ; ‘*hó*, adv. well, suitably ; easily ; extremely.
囘 ꜁*huí*, v. to return : ꜁*huí*, n. a time, a turn.
因 ꜀*ing*, and ꜀*ing oi*$^{2}$, prep. for, because of : ꜀*ing*, and ꜀*ing oi*$^{2}$, conj. for, since, because.
共 *kaëng*$^{2}$, prep. with ; for, in behalf of : *kaëng*$^{2}$, conj. and, also ; as, like to.
至 *kau*’, v. to reach, to arrive at : *kau*’, prep. till, until.
驚 ꜀*kiăng*, v. to fear, to dread : ꜀*kiăng*, conj. for fear that, lest.
故 *ko*’, a sign of the comparative, more : *ko*’, adv. or conj. still, yet.
落 *lóh*꜇ v. to descend, to fall : *lóh*꜇ prep. in, at.
侬 ꜁*nëng*, n. a man, person : ꜁*nëng*, adj. human.
伩 *po*$^{2}$, adv. again, once more : *po*$^{2}$, conj. and, also.
駛 ‘*sai*, v. to use, to employ, to cause : ‘*sai*, prep. by, with, by means of.
上 *siong*$^{2}$ v. to go up, to ascend ; *siong*$^{2}$ prep. (after the noun) on, upon.
天 ꜀*t‘iéng*, n. heaven, sky, weather : ꜀*t‘iéng*, adj. celestial, aerial.
文 ꜁*ung*, n. letters, literature : ꜁*ung*, adj. literary, civil, not military.
畫 *wa*$^{2}$ n. a drawing, painting, picture : *wa*$^{2}$ v. to draw, to paint.
約 *yok*꜇ n. an agreement, a contract : *yok*꜇ v. to agree, to contract.

# PART II. PHRASES.

It may be observed that a large proportion of the Phrases are in constant use among the people ; in regard to such there is a degree of satisfaction not experienced in reference to those which pertain exclusively to foreign matters and modes of operation. These are rather translations from English into Chinese than otherwise ; or, the phraseology, if already in use, is confined to certain classes, and might appear *foreign* to the people at large. The most of these are found under headings 13 and 28.

Many brief expressions, suitable for beginners will be found scattered throughout the various sections of this Part of the Manual. These may be conveniently marked and studied first by the student.

It will readily be perceived from a glance at Literal Translations that strict renderings from Chinese into English would be far removed from an easy style. It has seemed preferable to give free translations, and to refer the student to the Chinese and English Vocabulary, contained in this volume, for the meaning of single words *as they appear in the phrases.*

It is recommended that, so far as is practicable, the phrases should be used as models by which to construct other sentences. For instance, in the expression *kieu'* *₍i ˋk'ó'* 𠯈伊去 call-him-go —tell him to go, by substituting for *k'ó'* 去 (to go) the verbs *chó'* 做 (to do, to make), *sói*² 坐 (to sit), etc., we have at once a large number of phrases which are universally known and used.

It will be found that, in accordance with native usage, characters have been borrowed, and sometimes *coined,* to represent colloquial sounds. The borrowed characters, as defined in the dictionaries, may be found to differ widely in meaning from the sense intended in the particular places where they occur in the phrases.

It will also be seen that characters are employed which do not represent the sounds. In such cases they have been selected with reference to the meaning.

The Romanized Chinese words in parentheses are alternate forms of the word or words immediately preceding.

## 1. DISCRIMINATION IN THE USES OF WORDS.

Mistakes sometimes originate from attaching to a Chinese word *all* the significations belonging to its *more comprehensive* English equivalent, and thus applying it too extensively. *Lau*$^2$ 佬 means *old*, but its use is far more restricted than the word *old* in English; it is applied only to animate objects, some say only to man, while *ko*$^2$ 舊 (old) is applied mostly, if not always, to inanimate objects. If we use *lau*$^2$ 佬 instead of *ko*$^2$ 舊 in the phrase *ko*$^2$ *꜀ki sau*ᵓ *ᶜch'iu ꜀tó ꜀li*, 舊其掃箒掏來 (bring the old broom), we make the sense ludicrous, by saying, "Bring the *aged*, or *venerable*, broom." A person is not *ᶜtoi* 短 (short) but *ᶜá*, 矮 (short, low). We *kié*ᵓ 寄 (send) *things*, not *men*. We *keu*ᵓ 救 (save) *men*, not *things*. The direction to *keu*ᵓ 救 (save) a leg of mutton till to-morrow would bewilder the servant, as *keu*ᵓ 救 means *to save* only in the sense of *to rescue, to deliver*. *Clothing* may be too *naung*$^2$ 嫩 (small) but not too *sá*ᵓ 細 (small); a *child* may be either *naung*$^2$ or *sá*ᵓ. We *tai*ᵓ 戴 (put on) a *hat*, but *sëüng*$^2$ 穿 (put on) *clothing*, and *shoes* and *stockings*. *Ch'eng*ᵓ 凊 and *taĕng*ᵓ 凍 both mean *cold*, but we never say the *weather* is *taĕng*ᵓ and only in a few instances that *things* are *ch'eng*ᵓ. We *꜀ka* 剪 with scissors, and *sioh*꜂ 削 or *kak*꜂ 割 with a knife, but *ch'ói*ᵓ 剉 or *ᶜk'ang* 砍 or *p'wai*ᵓ 破 with an ax or like instrument. *꜀K'ing* 傾 means to pour from a spout, but *piăng*ᵓ 併 to pour, as from a bowl, or to empty, as refuse from a dust-pan. *Tó*ᵓ 倒 is much like *piăng*ᵓ. Cloth is *꜀pany chiăng*ᵓ 平正 (poor, inferior). A man is *꜀küng* 窮 poor (in purse), and *꜀soi* 衰 poor (in flesh).

Some of the examples given below illustrate still farther the introductory remark in regard to the origin of a certain class of mistakes, and also show that a single word in Chinese sometimes expresses an idea which requires circumlocution in English. Also that the same English word with its qualifying phrases may be represented by several different Chinese equivalents.

Bring the book over here, 書掏過來 *꜀Chü ꜀tó kwo*ᵓ *꜀li*.
Bring the child over here, 伲仔抱過來 *Nié*$^2$ *ᶜkiăng pó*$^2$ *kwo*ᵓ *꜀li*.

Bring the chair over here, 椅掇過來 ʻ*Ié tauk*˃ *kwo*ʾ ˳*li.*
Bring the (empty) sedan over here, 轎拍過來 *Kieu*² *p'ah*˃ *kwo*ʾ ˳*li.*
Bring the tea over here (in both hands), 茶捧過來 ˳*Ta* ˳*p'ung kwo*ʾ ˳*li.*
Bring the basket (by the bail, etc.) over here, 簗扛過來 ˳*Lai kwang*² *kwo*ʾ ˳*li.*
Bring the child over here (on the back), 伲仔邁過來 *Nié*² ʻ*kiăng mai*² *kwo*ʾ ˳*li.*
Bring the flour over here (as in bags across the shoulder), 麪粉扛過來 *Miéng*² ʻ*hung* ˳*k'ong kwo*ʾ ˳*li.*
Bring the water over here (in buckets on a cooly-stick), 水擔過來 ʻ*Chwi* ˳*tang kwo*ʾ ˳*li.*
Bring the box over here (as carried by two), 箱扛過來 ˳*Siong* ˳*kong kwo*ʾ ˳*li.*
Bring the salt over here (by boat), 鹽下過來 ˳*Siéng ha*² *kwo*ʾ ˳*li.*

## 2. LITERAL TRANSLATIONS.

What is this? 嚽是世乇 ˳*Chuí se*² *sié*ʾ *nóh*˃*?* (This is what?)
This is a pencil, 嚽是筆 ˳*Chuí se*² *pek*˃ (This is pencil.)
What is this made of? 嚽是世乇做其 ˳*Chuí se*² *sié*ʾ *nóh*˃ *chó*ʾ ˳*ki?* (This is what made of?)
This is made of wood, 嚽是柴做其 ˳*Chuí se*² ˳*ch'a chó*ʾ ˳*ki.* (This is wood made of.)
Where did this come from? 嚽是冬那來 ˳*Chuí se*² ˳*tëng* ʻ*në* ˳*li?* (This is whence came?)
This came from the sea, 嚽是海禮來 ˳*Chuí se*² ʻ*hai* ʻ*lá* ˳*li.* (This is sea from came.)
This came from a foreign country, 嚽是外國禮來 ˳*Chuí se*² *ngwoi*² *kwok*˃ ʻ*lá* ˳*li.* (This is foreign country from came).
Who made this? 嚽是俤侬做其 ˳*Chuí se*² *tié*² ˳*nëng chó*ʾ ˳*ki?* (This is what person made thing?)
I made this myself, 嚽是我自家做其 ˳*Chuí se*² ʻ*ngwai che*² ˳*ka chó*ʾ ˳*ki.* (This is myself made thing.)
Whose is this? 嚽是俤侬其 ˳*Chuí se*² *tié*² ˳*nëng* ˳*ki?* (This is what person's?)
This is mine, 嚽是奴其 ˳*Chuí se*² ˳*nu* ˳*ki.* (This is mine.)

### 3. THE NOUN *TAI*$^2$ OR *TAI*$^2$ *KIÉ*꜃, BUSINESS.

To have business, to have trouble, 務代計 *O*$^2$ *tai*$^2$ *ié*꜃ *(kié*꜃ *).*
What business? What is the matter? 世毛代計 *Sié*꜃ *nóh*꜁ *tai*$^2$ *ié*꜃*?*
To attend to a matter of business, 幹代計 *Kang*꜃ *tai*$^2$ *ié*꜃.
The business is urgent, 代計急 *Tai*$^2$ *ié*꜃ *kek*꜁.
Now what work shall (I) do first? 佮先做世毛代計 ꜀*Tang* ꜀*seng chó*꜃ *sié*꜃ *nóh*꜁ *tai*$^2$ *ié*꜃*?*
To do the work thus—will it answer or not? 代計將換做𠅬駛的賣 *Tai*$^2$ *ié*꜃ ꜀*chiong wang*$^2$ *chó*꜃ *á*$^2$ ꜂*sai tek*꜁ *má*$^2$ *?*
There will not be time enough to do the work, 代計做伓付 *Tai*$^2$ *ié*꜃ *chó*꜃ *ng*$^2$ *ho*꜃.
The matter is settled, 代計定着了 *Tai*$^2$ *ié*꜃ *tiăng*$^2$ *tioh*$_2$ ꜂*lau.*
Can the matter be effected? 啫代𠅬成賣 ꜂*Chiă tai*$^2$ *á*$^2$ ꜀*siăng má*$^2$ *?*
(You) must assist him about the work, 代計着帮伊齊做 *Tai*$^2$ *ié*꜃ *tioh*$_2$ ꜀*pong* ꜀*i* ꜀*chi chó*꜃.
A trifling affair, 毛𨋢𠊎其代 ꜀*Mó kak*$_2$ *siăh*$_2$ ꜀*ki tai*$^2$. 小可其代 ꜂*Sieu* ꜂*hó* (꜂*k'ó)* ꜀*ki tai*$^2$.

### 4. THE NOUNS ꜂*HWÍ*, FIRE, AND ꜀*CH'A*, WOOD.

Kindle a fire, 起火 ꜂*K'i* ꜂*hwí.* 火起一隻 ꜂*Hwí* ꜂*k'i sioh*$_2$ *chiăh*꜁ (spoken fast ꜂*hwí* ꜂*k'i liăh*꜁.)
Blow the fire, 嗙火 ꜀*Pung* ꜂*hwí.* 火嗙灼 ꜂*Hwí* ꜀*pung tioh*$_2$.
Kindle (a fire) in the stove, 起火爐 ꜂*K'i* ꜂*hwí* ꜀*lu.*
The fire will not kindle, or burn, 火賣灼 ꜂*Hwí má*$^2$ *tioh*$_2$.
The fire is too hot, 火太猛 ꜂*Hwí k'ak*꜁ ꜂*mang.*
There is too little fire, 火太微 ꜂*Hwí k'ak*꜁ ꜀*mi.*
Withdraw (the fuel so as to extinguish) the fire, 火退 ꜂*Hwí t'ói*꜃.
Light a lamp-lighter, 具火 *Këü*$^2$ ꜂*hwí.*
Light a lamp, 點火 ꜂*Tiéng* ꜂*hwí,* (or *tok*꜁ ꜂*hwí*) or 火點一隻 ꜂*Hwí* ꜂*tiéng sioh*$_2$ *chiăh*꜁.
Extinguish the lamp, 火嗙過 ꜂*Hwí* ꜀*pung kwo*꜃.
Light a match, 自來火掏來劃 *Chëü*$^2$ ꜀*lai* ꜂*hwí* ꜀*tó* ꜀*li* ꜀*wa.*
Bring two (or a few) bundles of wood, 柴扛二把來 ꜀*Ch'a kwang*$^2$ *lang*$^2$ ꜂*pa* ꜀*li.*

Take a stick of wood and split it up, 柴掏一塊破 *꜀Ch'a ꜀tó sioh꜆ tói꜄ p'wai꜄.*

Put two (or a few) sticks of wood in the stove, 柴掏二塊凸火爐禮 *꜀Ch'a ꜀tó lang² tói꜄ ꜂t'u ꜂hwi ꜀lu ꜂lá.*

The weather is very cold and a large quantity of wood is consumed, 睹天盡凊柴燒的大 *꜂Chiă ꜀t'iéng cheng² ch'eng꜄ ꜀ch'a ꜀sieu tek꜀ twai².*

## 5. THE ADJECTIVE ꜂HÓ, GOOD.

Not good, 伓好 *Ng² ꜂hó.* 毛好 *꜀Mó ꜂hó.*
Very good, 頂好 *꜂Ting ꜂hó.* 盡好 *Cheng² ꜂hó.*
The first good—the best, 第一好 *Tá² ek꜀ ꜂hó.*
Beautiful, 生的好 *꜀Sang tek꜀ ꜂hó.*
So very good, 只滿好 *꜂Chi ꜂mang ꜂hó.*
Tolerably good—does pretty well, 野務好 *꜂Yă o² ꜂hó.*
Just right—just the thing, 正正好 *Chiăng꜄ chiăng꜄ ꜂hó.*
Quite inferior, 毛世毛好 *꜀Mó sié꜄ nóh꜀ ꜂hó.*
Very pleasant to hear, 野好聽 *꜂Yă ꜂hó ꜀t'iăng.*
Not easy to read—difficult to read, 伓好讀 *Ng² ꜂hó t'ëk꜆.*
Very laughable, 盡去好笑 *Cheng² k'ó꜄ ꜂hó ch'ieu꜄.*
Good-looking. Good weight, over weight, 好看 *꜂Hó k'ang꜄.*
Select good ones, 揀好其 *꜂Keng ꜂hó ꜀ki.*
Cannot recover—is not yet well, 病賣好 *Pang² má² ꜂hó.*
A good (benevolent) heart will have a good reward, 好心務好報 *꜂Hó ꜀sing o² ꜂hó pó꜄.*
He is very good, kind, polite, etc., 伊做仈野好 *꜀I chó꜄ ꜀nëng ꜂yă ꜂hó.*
Extremely good, 好的很 *꜂Hó tek꜀ ꜂heng (or ꜂t'eng).*

## 6. THE NEGATIVE *NG²*, NOT, PRECEDING CERTAIN ADJECTIVES.

The word *ng²* 伓 a negative particle, which often precedes verbs, is also used before a few simple and verbal adjectives, as *ng² ꜂hó,* 伓好 not good, *ng² tioh꜆* 伓着 not right, *ng² tëüng꜄* 伓中 not fit, and some others.

The adjectives in the following phrases, if used *alone* (not antithetically), would not be preceded by *ng²* 伓 but by *má²* 賣 or in some cases by *꜀mó* 毛 to express negation. A general definition of these phrases would be—*just the thing, just right, medium*.

Neither large nor small, 伓大伓細 *Ng² twai² ng² sá꜄*.

Neither salt nor fresh, 伓鹹伓䀹 *Ng² ꜀keng ng² ꜂chiăng*.

Neither long nor short, 伓長伓短 *Ng² ꜀tong ng² ꜂toi*.

Neither tall nor low, 伓高伓矮 *Ng² ꜀keng ng² ꜂á*.

Neither hot nor cold (as weather), 伓熱伓凊 *Ng² yék꜆ ng² ch'eng꜄*.

Neither strong nor weak (as tea, etc.), 伓濃伓淡 *Ng² ꜀nüng ng² tang²*.

Neither narrow nor wide, 伓窄伓闊 *Ng² chah꜆ ng² k'wak꜆*.

## 7. THE VERB *K'Ó꜄*, TO GO, TO DEPART.

As Chinese verbs have no inflection, the tense is determined by other words in regimen, as *꜀king tang꜄ k'ó꜄* 今旦去 to go to-day; *sioh꜆ ꜀mang k'ó꜄* 一暝去 went yesterday. *꜂Lá*, 禮 the present participial prefix of the verb, is not used in connection with *k'ó꜄* 去 (to go) nor with *꜀li* 來 (to come); but we have, instead, *꜂lá ꜀kiăng*, 禮行 (is walking), i. e., is in the act of going or coming.

Tell, or request, him to go, 叫伊去 *Kieu꜄ ꜀i k'ó꜄*.

He need not go, 伊伓駛去 *꜀I ng² ꜂sai k'ó꜄*.

Will not let him go, 伓乞伊去 *Ng² k'ëük꜆ ꜀i k'ó꜄*.

Defer to go a little, 慢塊去 *Maing² nói꜄ (nai꜄) k'ó꜄*.

Let us go! Go! 去吓 *K'ó꜄ ꜀a!*

He is the one to go, 是伊去 *Se² ꜀i k'ó꜄*.

Let us go now! Go now! 伶去 *꜀Tang k'ó꜄!*

Does he wish to go or not? 伊欲去伓欲去 *꜀I ói꜄ k'ó꜄ ng² ói꜄ k'ó꜄?*

He does not dare to go, 伊毛敢去 *꜀I ꜂mang (꜀mó ꜂kang) k'ó꜄*.

He is not willing to go, He will not go, 伊伓肯去 *꜀I ng² ꜂k'ing k'ó꜄*.

He has gone, 伊去了 *꜀I k'ó꜄ ꜂lau*.

Has he gone yet? 伊去囉昧 *꜀I k'ó꜄ ꜀ló mwoi²?*

He has not gone yet, 伊昧去 *꜀I mwoi² k'ó꜄*.

Where has he gone? 伊去冬那 ꜀I k'ó꜄ ꜁tëng ꜂në?

He has gone to the city, 伊去城裏 ꜀I k'ó꜄ ꜁siăng ꜂tié.

Why has he gone? 伊將其去 ꜀I ꜀chiong ꜁ki k'ó꜄?

He has gone and will return soon, 伊去就來 ꜀I k'ó꜄ cheu$^2$ ꜁li.

He has been gone but a short time, 伊去毛箬久 ꜀I k'ó꜄ ꜁mó nioh$_2$ ꜁ong.

He has been gone a long time already, 伊去野久了 ꜀I k'ó꜄ ꜂yă ꜁ong ꜂lau.

He has never yet gone (been) there, 伊昧去着 ꜀I mwoi$^2$ k'ó꜄ tioh$_2$.

He has already gone (been) there, 伊去着了 ꜀I k'ó꜄ tioh$_2$ ꜂lau.

He has just gone, 伊隻隻去 ꜀I chiăh꜆ chiăh꜆ (or ꜂chi ꜂u, or ꜂chi ꜁tong) k'ó꜄.

He has gone above (up stairs), 伊去崎頂 ꜀I k'ó꜄ ꜁ká ꜂teng.

He has gone below stairs, 伊去下底 ꜀I k'ó꜄ a$^2$ ꜂tá.

He has seldom gone (been) there, 伊少的去 ꜀I ꜂chieu tek꜆ k'ó꜄.

He has very frequently gone (been) there, 伊去野純 ꜀I k'ó꜄ ꜂yă ꜁seu.

Will he go or not? Does he wish to go or not? 伊去伓去 ꜀I k'ó꜄ ng$^2$ k'ó꜄?

He will not go, He does not wish to go, 伊伓去 ꜀I ng$^2$ k'ó꜄.

He *will* go (is bent on going), He is about to go, 伊剝去 ꜀I pwoh꜆ k'ó꜄.

(I think) he will not go (implying his unwillingness to go), 伊伓成去 ꜀I ng$^2$ ꜁siăng k'ó꜄.

He may (will probably) go next year, 伊明年𫢗去 ꜀I ꜁mang ꜁niéng á$^2$ k'ó꜄.

Is there any one going to *Ch'ong seng* to day? 今旦倉前務其去吓毛 ꜀King tang꜄ ꜀Ch'ong ꜁seng o$^2$ ꜁i (꜁ki) k'ó꜄ ꜂a ꜁mó?

He cannot go, 伊毛擔當去 ꜀I ꜁mó ꜀tang ꜀tong k'ó꜄.

He cannot go (as from illness), 伊賣去 ꜀I má$^2$ k'ó꜄.

He cannot go (as from want of leisure), 伊毛的去 ꜀I ꜁mó tek꜆ k'ó꜄, 伊賣去的 ꜀I má$^2$ k'ó꜄ tek꜆.

He must go, 伊着去 ꜀I tioh$_2$ k'ó꜄.

He must not go, 伊伓通去 ꜀I ng$^2$ ꜀t'ëng k'ó꜄.

He must go again. He must go to still another place, 伊故着去 *꜀I ko꜄ tioh$_2$ k'ó꜄*.

If he should go, 伊𠍽務去 *꜀I na$^2$ o$^2$ k'ó꜄*.

One hundred cash gone (spent), 錢去一百 *꜁Chiéng k'ó꜄ sioh$_2$ pah꜆*.

The verb *K'ó꜄* 去 is frequently used as an enclitic or adjunct of a verb, or adjective, and signifies the completion of an act, or process; also in making comparisons, when it is about equivalent to *than*. In pronunciation the consonant is often wholly lost and the vowel sound seems only a catch of the breath. The word *k'ó꜄* 去 as a termination is sometimes pronounced *꜀ó*, as in *꜁mwong ꜀kwong ꜀ó*, shut the door; here the sense is plainly *k'ó꜄* as it denotes completion of action in the preceding verb. It should be observed that, in this as in many other instances, there is danger of giving too much emphasis to final particles.

To become bad or spoiled (as things), 呆去 *꜁Ngai k'ó꜄*.

Is dead, 死去 *꜂Si k'ó꜄*.

Sin forgiven, 罪赦去 *Chói$^2$ siă꜄ k'ó꜄*.

Cannot be escaped. Cannot be forgiven, 賣免的去 *Má$^2$ ꜂miéng tek꜆ k'ó꜄*.

Have forgotten, 賣記的去 *Má$^2$ ke꜄ tek꜆ k'ó꜄*.

What a pity! 可惜的去 *꜂K'ó sek꜆ tek꜆ k'ó꜄*.

This is *very* good, 𡅏盡去好 *꜁Chuí cheng$^2$ k'ó꜄ ꜂hó*.

This is better than that, 𡅏故好去囘 *꜁Chuí ko꜄ ꜂hó k'ó꜄ ꜁huí*.

## 8. THE VERB *SIĂH$_2$* TO EAT, TO SMOKE.

To eat breakfast, 食早 *Siăh$_2$ ꜂cha*.

To eat a lunch, or dessert, 食點心 *Siăh$_2$ ꜂tiéng ꜀sing*.

To eat rice—take a meal, 食飯 *Siăh$_2$ pwong$^2$*.

To take medicine, 食藥 *Siăh$_2$ yoh$_2$*.

To drink liquor to intoxication, 食酒醉 *Siăh$_2$ ꜂chiu choi꜄*.

Have (you) eaten yet? 食囉味 *Siăh$_2$ ꜁ló mwoi$^2$?*

Have (you) finished eating yet? 食完囉味 *Siăh$_2$ ꜁wong ꜁ló mwoi$^2$?*

(I) have finished eating, 食完了 *Siăh$_2$ ꜁wong ꜂lau*.

(I) have not finished eating yet, 食味完 *Siăh$_2$ mwoi$^2$ ꜁wong*.

Am only half through eating, 食半闌城 *Siăh₂ pwang' ꜀lang ꜀ch'iăng.*

It was all eaten up by him, 都乞伊食完去 *꜀Tu k'ëük, ꜀i siăh₂ ꜀wong k'ó'.*

Have eaten to the full—have eaten enough, 食飽了 *Siăh₂ ʻpa ʻlau.*

Nothing to eat, 毛乇食 *꜀Mó nóh, siăh₂.*

It is not eatable, 賣食的 *Má² siăh₂ tek,.*

It is eatable, 𫾫食的 *Á² siăh₂ tek,.*

Can (he) eat or not?—is he well enough to eat? 𫾫食賣食 *Á² siăh₂ má² siăh₂?*

Cannot eat it down, 賣食的入 *Má² siăh₂ tek, ʻtié.*

If eaten, it will poison people to death, 𫾫食死伙 *Á² siăh₂ ʻsi ꜀nëng.*

To go to a feast, *lit.*, go to drink wine, 去食酒 *K'ó' siăh₂ ʻchiu.*

To "eat his," i. e., he (the employer) furnishing the food, 食伊其 *Siăh₂ ꜀i ꜀ki.*

To find one's own food, as an employé does, 自家食 *Che² ꜀ka siăh₂.*

To smoke tobacco, 食烟 *Siăh₂ ꜀hong.*

Can (you) smoke tobacco? 𫾫食烟賣 *Á² siăh₂ ꜀hong má²?*

To smoke opium, 食烟 *Siăh₂ ꜀hong,* or 食鴉片 *Siăh₂ ꜀a p'iéng'.*

## 9. THE VERB *CHÓ'*, TO DO, TO MAKE, TO BE.

To do work, 做代計 *Chó' tai² ié'.*

This is done well. Has done it well, 做的好 *Chó' tek, ʻhó.*

This is poorly done. Has done it poorly, 做的呆 *Chó' tek, ꜀ngai.*

There will not be time enough to do it, 做伓付 *Chó' ng² ho'.*

To do a thing wrong, 做錯 *Chó' tang².*

To do reversely or in the wrong order, 單倒做 *꜀Tang tó' chó'.*

Has done it faultlessly, 做都毛錯 *Chó' ꜀tu ꜀mó tang².*

This is not the way to do it, 伓是將換做 *Ng² se² ꜀chiong wang² chó'.*

Difficult to do, 啊做 *꜀Ó chó'.*

To contract for doing or making, 定做 *Tiăng² chó'*.
He acts in his own peculiar way, 伊做伊 *꜀I chó' ꜀i*.
To be an officer, 做老爹 *Chó' ꜂ló ꜀tiă*.
To be a doctor, 做先生 *Chó' ꜀sing ꜀sang*.
One engaged in trade—a trader, 做生意其 *Chó' ꜀seng e' ꜁ki*.
One who works in mud—a mason, 做土其 *Chó' ꜁t'u ꜁ki*.

## 10. THE VERBS ꜁KIĂNG, TO WALK, AND KWO' TO PASS OVER.

Walk in! (as said by one within), 行入來 *꜁Kiăng ꜂tié ꜁li*.
Walk in! (said when both persons are without), 行入 *꜁Kiăng ꜂tié*.
Step aside a little, 行邊些微 *꜁Kiăng ꜀piéng ꜀niă nói'*.
To go wrong, 行錯 *꜁Kiăng lang²*.
Have walked till I pant excessively, 行盡惑 *꜁Kiăng cheng² hĕk꜇*.
(And so) avoid walking such a distance, 免的行許遠 *꜂Miéng tek꜆ ꜁kiăng ꜂hü hwong²*.
Have walked till my feet ache very much, 胶行盡瘦 *꜀K'a ꜁kiăng cheng² ꜀sŏng*.
It is very slippery walking, 行盡滑 *꜁Kiăng cheng² kŏk꜇*.
The clock don't go, 自鳴鐘賣行 *Chĕü² ꜁ming ꜀chüng mă² ꜁kiăng*.
The bread is not risen (enough to bake), 包行昧高 *꜀Pau ꜁kiăng mwoi² ꜁keng*.
Has gone out—away from home, 過位 *Kwo' oi²*, or 過塊 *Kwo' tói'*.
Has gone over the bridge, 去過橋 *K'ó' kwo' ꜁kio*.
Has not come over yet, 昧過來 *Mwoi² kwo' ꜁li*.
Pass a little beyond (a certain place), 再行過些微 *Chai' ꜁kiăng kwo' ꜀niă nói'*.
Creep over here! 扒過來 *꜁Pa kwo' ꜁li*.
Come over here! 行過來 *꜁Kiăng kwo' ꜁li*.
Can't leave to go away, 賣行的過位 *Mă² ꜁kiăng tek꜆ kwo' oi²*.
This disease is contagious, 啫病傑過 *꜂Chiă pang² ă² kwo'*.

榕腔初學撮要

## 11. THE VERBS TO OPEN AND TO SHUT OR CLOSE.

To open the eyes, 目睭擘開 *Mek$_2$ ꜀chiu pah꜅ ꜀k'wi.*

To open the eyes wide, 目睭擘大 *Mek$_2$ ꜀chiu pah꜅ twai$^2$.*

To open the mouth, 嘴擘起 *Ch'oi꜃ pah꜅ ꜂k'i.*

To open the door, 門開起 *꜁Mwong ꜀k'wi ꜂k'i.*

Close the book! 書合去啵 *꜀Chü hak$_2$ k'ó ꜁pó!* (a phrase implying haste.)

Close the fan, 扇合去 *Siéng꜃ hak$_2$ k'ó.*

Close (your) mouth, 嘴合去 *Ch'oi꜃ hak$_2$ k'ó*, 嘴咖禮 *Ch'oi꜃ ꜂mau ꜂lá.*

Shut (your) hand, 手合去 *꜂Ch'iu hak$_2$ k'ó.*

Shut (your) hand tight, 手擵緊 *꜂Ch'iu ꜀ma ꜂king.*

Close (your) eyes, 目睭尅去 *Mek$_2$ ꜀chiu k'aik꜅ k'ó.*

Shut the door, 門關去 *꜁Mwong ꜀kwong ꜀ó*, 關門 *꜁Kwong ꜁mwong*, 門掩去 *꜁Mwong ꜂ang ꜀ó.*

## 12. LOSING, SEEKING, FINDING, BORROWING, LENDING.

I have lost my pencil, 筆柏湯去 *Pek꜅ p'ah꜅ taung$^2$ k'ó.*

My pencil is gone, 筆毛去 *Pek꜅ ꜁mó k'ó.*

Have you seen it? 務看見吓毛 *O$^2$ k'ang꜃ kiéng꜃ ꜂a ꜁mó?*

I have not seen it, 毛看見 *꜁Mó k'ang꜃ kiéng꜃.*

Where did you put it? 汝放着冬那 *꜂Nü pong꜃ tioh$_2$ ꜀tëng ꜂në?*

This morning I put in on the table and now it is gone, 早起按棹禮佮毛去 *꜂Cha ꜂k'i ꜀eng tóh꜅ ꜂lá ꜀tang ꜁mó k'ó.*

This is very stange! 嚽希倖 *꜁Chuí ꜀hi haing꜃!*

Go quick and look for it! 快去討 *K'á꜃ k'ó꜃ ꜂t'ó!*

You must look all around for it, 滿塊都着討 *꜂Mwang tói꜃ ꜀tu tioh$_2$ ꜂t'ó.*

Things cannot be stolen by persons in the house, 只裡乇賣毛 *꜂Chi ꜂tié nóh꜅ má$^2$ ꜁mó.*

That, of course! 回自然 *꜁Huí chëü$^2$ ꜁yong!*

I only fear that strangers may have been in and taken it, 哪驚生混仈入來掏阿 *Na$^2$ ꜀kiăng ꜀sang hong$^2$ ꜁nëng ꜂tié ꜁li ꜁tó ꜀ó* (or *tai꜃ ꜂ch'iu ꜀ó.*)

Look for it slowly (carefully), 慢慢討 *maing$^2$ maing$^2$ ꜂t‘ó.*

I have found the pencil, 筆討着了 *Pek꜆ ꜂t‘ó tioh꜇ ꜂lau.*

Where did you find it? 冬那討着 *꜀Tĕng ꜂nĕ ꜂t‘ó tioh꜇?*

It fell on the floor, 湯落地下 *Taung$^2$ lóh꜇ te$^2$ a$^2$.*

It was hidden by the chair, 乞椅遞禮 *K‘ëük꜆ ꜂ié tá$^2$ ꜂lá.*

If there was no one to take it, certainly it could not be gone, 毛伙掏總賣毛 *꜀Mó ꜀nĕng ꜀tó ꜂chung má$^2$ ꜀mó.*

I have just been to buy cloth, 只長去攏布 *꜂Chi ꜀tong k‘ó꜄ ꜂tong pwo꜄.*

I put my umbrella in his shop and forgot to take it, 傘放伊店禮賣記的掏 *꜂Sang pong꜄ ꜀i taing꜄ ꜂lá má$^2$ ke꜄ tek꜆ ꜀tó.*

You must go and look for it, 汝着去討 *꜂Nü tioh꜇ k‘ó꜄ ꜂t‘ó.*

I have looked for it and can't find it, 討了毛塊討 *꜂T‘ó ꜂lau ꜀mó tói꜄ (nói꜄) ꜂t‘ó.*

It has been picked up by some one, 乞伙拾去 *K‘ëük꜆ ꜀nĕng k‘ak꜆ k‘ó꜄.*

It is because you were not careful, 是汝毛小心 *Se$^2$ ꜂nü ꜀mó ꜂sieu ꜀sing.*

What a pity! 可惜的 *꜂K‘ó sek꜆ tek꜆!*

It takes money to buy one! 去買都着錢 *K‘ó꜄ ꜂má ꜀tu tioh꜇ ꜀chiéng.*

Treat it as of no worth! let it go! 看破毛値伊 *K‘ang꜄ p‘ó꜄! ꜀mó tih꜇ ꜀i!*

Next time be careful, 下二回着細二 *A$^2$ ne$^2$ ꜀huí tioh꜇ sá꜄ ne$^2$.*

I wish to get some good Shantung pears, 剝値好其山東梨 *Pwoh꜆ tih꜇ ꜂hó ꜀ki ꜀Sang ꜀Tĕng ꜀li.*

The junks have not yet arrived, 現在船昧至 *Hiéng$^2$ chai$^2$ ꜀sung mwoi$^2$ kau꜄.*

There are none in the shops, 店禮都毛 *Taing꜄ ꜂lá ꜀tu ꜀mó.*

There are none to be found, 毛塊尋 *꜀Mó tói꜄ (nói꜄) ꜀sing.*

If there is a good place in some *Hong*, please get me the situation, 行禮郇務好其地方替奴尋一隻 *꜀Ong ꜂lá na$^2$ o$^2$ ꜂hó ꜀ki te$^2$ ꜀hwong t‘á꜄ ꜀nu ꜀sing sioh꜇ chiăh꜆.*

At present the vacancies are all filled up—none can be found, 只前到缺都滿去毛塊尋 *ʻChi ꜀seng nóʼ k'wok꜀ ꜀tu ʻmwang k'ŏ—꜀mó tóiʼ (nóiʼ) ꜀sing.*

Some one inquires for the teacher to speak (with him), 仈討先生講話 *꜀Nĕng ʻt'ó ꜀sing ꜀sang ʻkong wa².*

To lend a borrowed article, 轉借 *ʻTiong chioh꜀.*

This is a very good fan, lend it to me a while, 啫扇野好借奴一下 *ʻChiă siéngʼ ʻyă ʻhó, chioh꜀ ꜀nu sioh꜀ a².*

Don't be offended—it is one I borrowed myself, 莫怪奴自家也是借其 *Móh꜀ kwaiʼ—꜀nu che² ꜀ka yă² se² chioh꜀ ꜀ki.*

Of whom did you borrow it? 是共帝仈借其 *Se² kaĕng² tié² ꜀nĕng chioh꜀ ꜀ki?*

It was borrowed from my older brother, 是奴兄禮借其 *Se² ꜀nu ꜀hiăng ʻlá chioh꜀ ꜀ki.*

I'll trouble you to borrow it for me a little while, 豈動汝轉借一下 *ʻK'i taĕng² ʻnü ʻtiong chioh꜀ sioh꜀ a².*

I think your brother will certainly be willing (to lend it to me), 諒必令兄能肯 *Liong² pek꜀ leng² ꜀hing á² ʻk'ing.*

There is no such thing as his lending you and not lending me, 毛喇借汝伓借奴 *꜀Mó ʻla chioh꜀ ʻnü ng² chioh꜀ ꜀nu.*

Fear he will not be willing to lend it, 驚伊伓肯借 *꜀Kiăng ꜀i ng² ʻk'ing chioh꜀.*

I'll (only) borrow it to-day and will return it to you to-morrow, 今旦借明旦就還汝 *꜀King tangʼ chioh꜀ ꜀ming tangʼ cheu² ꜀teng ʻnü.*

## 13. DOMESTIC MATTERS.

### THE TABLE.

Set the table, 排棹 *꜀Pá tóh꜀.*

Spread the cloth straight, 棹單舒正正 *Tóh꜀ tauʼ ꜀ch'ü chiăngʼ chiăngʼ.*

Put on a clean table-cloth, 棹單換潔其 *Tóh꜀ tauʼ wang² t'ah꜀ ꜀ki.*

At each place set one plate, two forks, two knives, one soup spoon, one salt cellar, one tumbler, and one napkin, 一位着排一吓盤义二把刀二把湯瓢一把鹽碟一隻玻璃杯一隻手巾一條. *Sioh$_2$ oi$^2$ tioh$_2$ ꜁pá sioh$_2$ ʿa ꜁pwang, ꜀chʻa lang$^2$ ʿpa, ꜀tó lang$^2$ ʿpa, ꜀tʻong ꜁pʻieu sioh$_2$ ʿpa, ꜁siéng tiĕk$_2$ sioh$_2$ chiăh꜆, ꜀pó ꜁lá ꜀pwí sioh$_2$ chiăh꜆, ʿchʻiu ꜀küng sioh$_2$ ꜁teu.*

On the waiter place the tea pot, hot water pot, sugar bowl, cream jug, and spoon-holder, 茶盤禮按茶婆囉湯鑵囉糖甕囉牛乳鑵囉貯茶瓢其杯都按許裡 *꜁Ta ꜁pwang ʿlá ꜀eng ꜁ta ꜁pó ꜀ló, ꜀tʻong kwangʾ ꜀ló, ꜁tʻong aĕngʾ ꜀ló, ꜁ngu ꜁neng kwangʾ ꜀ló, ʿtio ꜁ta ꜁pʻieu ꜁ki ꜀pwí ꜀tu ꜀eng ʿhü ʿtié.*

Place the caster in the center of the table, 椒料架按桌大中 *꜀Chieu laiu$^2$ kaʾ ꜀eng tóh꜆ tai$^2$ ꜀tong.*

We have invited guests for to-day, 今旦請仈客 *꜀King tangʾ ʿchʻiăng ꜁nĕng kʻah꜆.*

Set three extra places, 着多排三位 *Tioh$_2$ ꜀tó ꜁pá ꜀sang oi$^2$.*

Gather up the dishes—clear off the table, 收碗 *꜀Siu ʿwang.*

THE KITCHEN.

Go and boil water to make tea, 去炮茶 *Kʻóʾ pʻauʾ ꜁ta.*

Make the tea with boiling water, 冲茶湯着滾 *꜀Chʻüng ꜁ta ꜀tʻong tioh$_2$ ʿkung.*

The tea-leaves have no strength—add more, 茶葉都毛料故着添 *꜁Ta nioh$_2$ ꜀tu ꜁mó laiu$^2$—koʾ tioh$_2$ ꜀tʻiéng.*

The tea is too weak, 茶太淡 *꜁Ta kʻak꜆ tang$^2$.*

Do not make the tea too strong, 茶伓通太濃 *꜁Ta ng$^2$ ꜀tʻĕng kʻak꜆ ꜁nüng* (or *tengʾ*.)

Use only a small quantity of tea-leaves, 茶葉摕少一滴仔 *꜁Ta nioh$_2$ ꜀ma ʿchieu sioh$_2$ tek꜆ ʿkiăng* (or *ʿchieu nek꜆ ʿkiăng*).

Add boiling water, 滾湯掏來提 *ʿKung ꜀tʻong ꜁tó ꜁li ꜁tiăng.*

Add still more hot water, 湯故着提 *꜀Tʻong koʾ tioh$_2$ ꜁tiăng.*

Do you wish more tea? 茶故値伓値 *꜁Ta koʾ tih$_2$ ng$^2$ tih$_2$?*

Boil rice, 煮飯 *ʿchü pwong$^2$.*

To cook rice, as in a bowl set in water, 炖飯 *Tong$^2$ pwong$^2$.*

Boil a bowl of congee, 粥煮一碗 *Chĕük*ʾ *ᶜchü sioh*$_2$ *ᶜwang.*

When you put the rice over to boil, put in salt, 米一落鼎鹽就着下 *ᶜMi sioh*$_2$ *lóh*$_2$ *ᶜtiăng* *꜁siĕng cheu*$^2$ *tioh*$_2$ *ha*$^2$.

Boil the milk, 牛乳掏去滚一下 *꜁Ngu* *꜁neng* *꜁tó k'ó*ʾ *ᶜkung sioh*$_2$ *a*$^2$.

Take the milk off as soon as it boils, 牛乳一滚就着掏起 *꜁Ngu* *꜁neng sioh*$_2$ *ᶜkung cheu*$^2$ *tioh*$_2$ *꜁tó ᶜk'i.*

Fear it will have a scorched taste, 驚伊能臭燋阿 *꜀Kiăng* *꜀i á*$^2$ *ch'au*ʾ *꜁niăng* *꜀ó.*

Skim the milk, 撇牛乳油 *P'iĕk*ʾ *꜁ngu* *꜁neng* *꜁iu.*

Make butter, 拍牛乳油 *P'ah*ʾ *꜁ngu* *꜁neng* *꜁iu.*

Boil ten eggs, 雞蛋煞十其 *꜀Kiĕ laung*$^2$ *sak*$_2$ *sek*$_2$ *꜁ki.*

Boil the eggs rather soft, 雞蛋煞淺些微 *꜀Kiĕ laung*$^2$ *sak*$_2$ *ᶜchi'ĕng* (*ᶜch'ing*) *꜀niă nói*ʾ.

Boil them thoroughly (hard), 煞透 *Sak*$_2$ *t'au*ʾ.

Bake the beef, 牛肉掏來鏉 *꜁Ngu nük*$_2$ *꜁tó* *꜁li ngó*$^2$.

Roast the beef, 牛肉掏來燒 *꜁Ngu nük*$_2$ *꜁tó* *꜁li* *꜀sieu.*

Cut the beef into slices and broil it, 牛肉削一片一片掏來烘 *꜁Ngu nük*$_2$ *sioh*ʾ *sioh*$_2$ *p'iĕng*ʾ *sioh*$_2$ *p'iĕng*ʾ *꜁tó* *꜁li* *꜀hĕng.*

Fry the pork, 肉掏來煎 *Nük*$_2$ *꜁tó* *꜁li* *꜀chiĕng.*

Fricassee the fowl, 雞掏來炡 *꜀Kiĕ* *꜁tó* *꜁li* *꜁kong.*

Bake the fowl and baste it frequently with the gravy—do not let it get dry, 雞掏去鏉汁着許久許久沃沃賭伓通乞伊乾 *꜀Kiĕ* *꜁tó k'ó*ʾ *ngó*$^2$ *chaik*ʾ *tioh*$_2$ *ᶜhü* *꜁ong* *ᶜhü꜁ong woh*ʾ *woh*ʾ *꜁chiă* (or *p'wak*ʾ *p'wak*ʾ *꜁chiă*, or *ho*ʾ *ho*ʾ *꜁chiă*) *ng*$^2$ *꜀t'ĕng k'ĕük*ʾ *꜀i* *꜀ta.*

Boil the fowl and put Shantung vermicelli in the soup, 雞放鼎禮煞山東粉就放賭雞湯禮煮 *꜀Kiĕ pong*ʾ *ᶜtiăng* *ᶜlá sak*$_2$ *꜀Sang* *꜀Tĕng* *ᶜhung cheu*$^2$ *pong*ʾ *ᶜchiă* *꜀kiĕ* *꜀t'ong* *ᶜlá* *ᶜchü.*

Sprinkle salt on the beef, 鹽着穢牛肉禮 *꜁Siĕng tioh*$_2$ *iĕ*$^2$ *꜁ngu nük*$_2$ *ᶜlá.*

Make bread to day, 今旦做包 *꜀King tang*ʾ *chó*ʾ *꜀pau.*

Knead the bread thoroughly, 包劑着挼很很着 *꜀Pau chá*$^2$ *tioh*$_2$ *꜁nui* (or *꜀seu*) *ᶜheng* *ᶜheng tioh*$_2$.

Do not let the bread stand too long lest it sour, 包劑伓通按太久驚伊儺酸 *꜀Pau chá$^{2}$ ng$^{2}$ ꜀t‘ĕng ꜀eng k‘ak꜆ ꜁ong ꜀kiăng ꜀i á$^{2}$ ꜀song.*

Do not make the fire too hot lest the bread burn, 火伓通太猛包驚伊儺焦 *꜂Hwí ng$^{2}$ ꜀t‘ĕng k‘ak꜆ ꜂mang ꜀pau ꜀kiăng ꜀i á$^{2}$ ꜀chieu.*

Make sponge cake, 做雞蛋糕 *Chó꜄ ꜀kiĕ laung$^{2}$ ꜀kó.*

Beat the whites and yolks separately, 雞蛋二下柏黃做黃柏精做精柏 *꜀Kiĕ laung$^{2}$ lang$^{2}$ a$^{2}$ p‘ah꜆, ꜁wong chó꜄ ꜁wong p‘ah꜆, ꜀ching chó꜄ ꜀ching p‘ah꜆.*

Put the beans to soak, 豆掏來浸 *Tau$^{2}$ ꜁tó ꜁li cheng꜄.*

Skin the pomelo, 枹掏去刣 *꜀P‘au ꜁tó k‘ó꜄ ꜁t‘ai.*

Skin the orange, 桔掏去擘 *Kek꜆ ꜁tó k‘ó꜄ pah꜆.*

This pork is watered, 睹肉是灌水其 *꜂Chiă nük꜇ se$^{2}$ kwang꜄ ꜂chwi ꜁ki.*

This goat's meat is inflated with air, 睹羊肉是唪其 *꜂Chiă ꜁yong nük꜇ se$^{2}$ ꜁pung ꜁ki.*

What do you wish for breakfast,? 今旦食早食世乇 *꜀King tang꜄ siăh꜇ ꜂cha siăh꜇ siĕ꜄ nóh꜆?*

The knife will rust, 刀儺生鉎 *꜀Tó á$^{2}$ ꜀sang ꜀sing.*

The bucket leaks, 水桶漏 *꜂Chwi ꜂t‘ĕng lau$^{2}$.*

Draw a bucket of water, 水潒一桶 *꜂Chwi ch‘iong$^{2}$ sioh꜇ ꜂t‘ĕng.*

Bring a load of water, 水擔一担 *꜂Chwi ꜀tang sioh꜇ tang꜄.*

The water is roiled—put it to settle, 水渾着澄清 *꜂Chwi ꜁hung—tioh꜇ ꜁ting ꜀ch‘ing.*

Scour the forks and knives, 叉刀掏去磨 *꜀Ch‘a ꜀tó ꜁tó k‘ó꜄ ꜁mwai.*

THE BEDROOM.

Make the bed, 舒被鋪 *꜀Ch‘ü p‘woi$^{2}$ ꜀p‘wo.*

Air the bedclothes daily, 被鋪日日着涼 *P‘woi$^{2}$ ꜀p‘wo nik꜇ nik꜇ tioh꜇ ꜁liăng.*

Loop up the bed-curtain and tie it, 帳縛起 *Tiong꜄ pwoh꜇ ꜂k‘i.*

Brush out the mosquitoes, 摔蚊虫 *Saĕk꜆ (or pwang$^{2}$) ꜁hung ꜁mwong.*

Sweep the bedroom daily, 房裡日日着掃 ꜁Pung ʻtiě nik$_2$ nik$_2$ tioh$_2$ sauʼ.

After sweeping dust everything, 掃了滿塊都着拂 Sauʼ ʻlau ʻmwang tŏiʼ ꜀tu tioh$_2$ hok꜆.

Wash the wash-bowl daily, 面桶日日着洗 Mengʼ ʻt'ěng nik$_2$ nik$_2$ tioh$_2$ ʻsá.

Wash the wash-stand daily, 面架日日駛水撖 Mengʼ kaʼ nik$_2$ nik$_2$ ʻsai ʻchwi ʻkang.

Arrange the table—putting the things in their places, 收拾棹乇着排好 ꜀Siu sik$_2$ tóh꜆—nóh꜆ tioh$_2$ ꜁pá ʻhó.

Pile up the books nicely, 書着疊好 ꜀Chü tioh$_2$ t'ak$_2$ ʻhó.

Wash the floor, 洗板棚 ʻSá ʻpeng ꜁pang.

Wash the matting, wringing the cloth out dry, it should not be too wet, 蓆着撖布捧乾伓通太濫 Ch'ioh$_2$ tioh$_2$ ʻkang, pwoʼ ch'ong$^2$ ꜀ta, ng$^2$ ꜀t'ěng k'ak꜆ lang$^2$.

### LAMPS.

Trim the lamps daily, 燈馬日日着收拾 ꜀Ting ʻma nik$_2$ nik$_2$ tioh$_2$ ʻk'a lak꜆.

Fill up the lamps daily, 油日日着添溢 ꜁Iu nik$_2$ nik$_2$ tioh$_2$ ꜀t'iěng tiěng$^2$.

Add a little more oil, 油再添些微 ꜁Iu kaiʼ ꜀t'iěng ꜀niă nóiʼ.

This oil is not good—it gives poor light, 啫油平正賣光 ʻChiă ꜁iu ꜁pang chiăngʼ—má$^2$ ꜀kwong.

The lamp is dim, 燈馬賣光 ꜀Ting ʻma má$^2$ ꜀kwong.

Cut the wick even, 燈芯着剪平 ꜀Tiěng ꜀sing tioh$_2$ ʻcheng ꜁pang.

Wash the lamp-chimney daily, 玻璃管日日着洗 ꜀Pó ꜁lá ʻkwong nik$_2$ nik$_2$ tioh$_2$ ʻsá.

Cannot scour (this spot) off, 鐳賣去 Laĕʼ má$^2$ k'óʼ.

It was so originally, and I cannot wash it off, 生成啫款洗賣去 ꜀Seng ꜁siăng ʻchiă ʻk'wang, ʻsá má$^2$ k'óʼ.

### WASHING AND IRONING.

Take the clothes and wash them, 衣裳擲去洗 ꜀I ꜁siong ꜁tó k'óʼ ʻsá.

Must not spill the water all over the house, 水伓通泎一厝 *ʻChwi ng$^2$ ꜀tʻĕng chiăkꜝ꜁sioh$_2$ chʻioʼ.*

Take the table-cloth and wash the stained place, 棹單掏去沾 *Tŏhꜝ tauʼ ꜁tó kʻóʼ ꜀chiéng.*

In washing be careful not to break the buttons, 洗衣裳着細膩鈕伓通洗破去 *ʻSá ꜀i ꜁siong tioh$_2$ sáʼ ne$^2$ kʻaiuʼ ng$^2$ ꜀tʻĕng ʻsá pʻwaiʼ kʻóʼ.*

In washing the clothes use the wash-board, 洗衣裳駛衣裳板鑢 *ʻSá ꜀i ꜁siong ʻsai ꜀i ꜁siong ʻpeng laëʼ.*

Wash with soap, 獲胰皂洗 *Kʻek$_2$ ꜁i chó$^2$ ʻsá.*

In washing rub this very lightly with your hands lest it be torn, 𡁻那好輕輕汔驚伊𠱓破 *꜁Chúá na$^2$ ʻhó ꜀kʻing ꜀kʻing chʻiăkꜝ ꜀kiăng ꜀i á$^2$ pʻwaiʼ.*

Wash them twice over, 着洗二過 *Tioh$_2$ ʻsá lang$^2$ kwoʼ.*

Spread the clothes on the grass to bleach, 衣裳鋪草菲禮曝 *꜀I ꜁siong ꜀pʻwo ʻchʻau ʻpʻi ʻlá pʻwoh$_2$.*

Sprinkle them frequently with water, 許久許久着駛水涺涺啫 *ʻHü ꜁ong ʻhü ꜁ong tioh$_2$ ʻsai ʻchwi hoʼ hoʼ ꜁chiă.*

Starch the clothes — do not starch them too stiff, 衣裳着漿伓通漿太𤞣 *꜀I ꜁siong tioh$_2$ ꜀chiong—ng$^2$ ꜀tʻĕng ꜀chiong kʻakꜝ kʻeuʼ.*

Iron the clothes to-morrow, 明旦着熨衣裳 *꜁ming tangʼ tioh$_2$ okꜝ ꜀i ꜁siong.*

Iron them smooth, 着熨光 *Tioh$_2$ okꜝ ꜀kwong.*

Sprinkle the clothes before ironing, 熨衣裳着駛水涺 *Okꜝ ꜀i ꜁siong, tioh$_2$ ʻsai ʻchwi hoʼ.*

### SEWING.

Go call the tailor to come here to-morrow, 去叫衣裳司傅明旦來 *Kʻóʼ kieuʼ ꜀i ꜁siong ꜀sa ho$^2$ ꜁ming tangʼ ꜁li.*

When did he say he would come? 伊講面候𠱓來 *꜀I ʻkong miéng$^2$ au$^2$ á$^2$ ꜁li.*

He said his work was pressing and he could not come to-morrow, 伊講工夫急明旦毛的來 *꜀I ʻkong ꜀kĕng ꜀hu kekꜝ ꜀ming tangʼ ꜀mó tekꜝ ꜀li.*

Must wait a few days and then he will have leisure, 着等幾日過隻務閒 *Tioh$_2$ ‘ting ‘kwi nik$_2$ kwo’ chiăh꜆ o$^2$ ꜀eng.*

The tailor has come! 衣裳司傅來囉 *꜀I ꜀siong ꜀sa ho$^2$ ꜀li ꜀ló!*

I wish this garment to be made and finished to day—will there be time enough? 啫衣裳今旦欲完付吓伓付 *‘Chiă ꜀i ꜀siong ꜀king tang’ ói’ ꜀wong—ho’ ‘a ng$^2$ ho’?*

Do not (take the stitches) through on the right side, 伓通透面 *Ng$^2$ ꜀t‘ĕng t‘au’ meng’.*

Take small stitches, 針着幼 *꜀Cheng tioh$_2$ eu’.*

Sew it rather coarsely, 紩粗些微 *T‘iĕng’ ꜀ch‘u ꜀niă nói’.*

Sew it the width of a seam smaller, 紩入一縫 *T‘iĕng’ ‘tiĕ sioh$_2$ p‘ong’.*

Do not pucker (the seam)—sew it even, 伓通晌紩平直 *Ng$^2$ ꜀t‘ĕng nĕŭk꜆—t‘iĕng’ ꜀pang tik$_2$.*

In quilting make the stitches small both inside and outside, 㧖裡面針討幼哩 *꜀Hong ‘li meng’ ꜀cheng ‘t‘ó eu’ ꜀li.*

In hemming make the stitches small on the outside, 繳面針着幼 *꜀Ch‘ieu meng’ ꜀cheng tioh$_2$ eu’.*

Baste straight, 搭直直着 *Tak꜆ tik$_2$ tik$_2$ tioh$_2$.*

At the beginning and end backstitch firmly, 頭尾着交有 *꜀T‘au ‘mwi tioh$_2$ ꜀kau taing$^2$.*

Don't draw the thread too tight, 線伓通太雄 *Siăng’ ng$^2$ ꜀t‘ĕng k‘ak꜆ ꜀hŭng.*

Make the stitches even, i. e., of the same length, or in the same line, 針胶着純 *꜀Cheng ꜀k‘a tioh$_2$ ꜀seu.*

Turn it down even (as a hem)—don't get it irregular, 撇純莫大細賭 *Piĕk꜆ ꜀seu—móh$_2$ twai$^2$ sá’ ‘tu.*

In stitching take each stitch into the preceding, 釘針胶肘針胶 *Teng’ ꜀cheng ꜀k‘a ‘tiu ꜀cheng ꜀k‘a.*

In backstitching make the seam straight, 交針着純直直着 *꜀Kau ꜀cheng tioh$_2$ ꜀seu tik$_2$ tik$_2$ tioh$_2$.*

Do not take the stitches irregularly, i. e., long and short, or up and down, 莫高下針 *Móh$_2$ ꜀keng kiă$^2$ ꜀cheng.*

MAN. 9.

In sewing on the edging, hold it tightly with the left hand so that it may be scant, 𦇐花後手着夾有 *˓Long ˓hwa au$^2$ ʿch'iu tioh˒ kek˒ taing$^2$.*

Full the edging, a little, 花着放緩些微 *˓Hwa tioh˒ pongʾ nëüng$^2$ ˓niă nóiʾ.*

In making the button-holes pull the thread tight, 紩鈕門穿線扱緊哩 *T'iéngʾ k'aiuʾ ˓mwong ˓ch'iong siăngʾ ch'iăk˒ ʿking ˓li.*

Hold the button-hole straight and make the stitches regular—not in and out, 鈕門着拈直針胶着達平 *K'aiuʾ ˓mwong tioh˒ ˓niéng tik˒ ˓cheng ˓k'a tioh˒ tak˒ ˓pang.*

Sew the buttons on strong, 紩鈕着紩有有着 *T'iéngʾ k'aiuʾ tioh˒ t'iéngʾ taing$^2$ taing$^2$ tioh˒.*

Make the binding of the neck even, 綑頟着純純闊 *ʿK'ung ʿliăng tioh˒ ˓seu ˓seu k'wak˒.*

Have sewed it too near the edge, 紩太墘 *T'iéngʾ k'ak˒ ˓kiéng.*

Put a piece of cloth under (as to patch), 布套裡勢 *Pwoʾ t'óʾ ʿtié tiéʾ.*

This thread is much tangled, 啫線野亂 *ʿChiă siăngʾ ʿyă naungʾ.*

*Different sizes of sewing silk beginning with the coarsest.*

中鎖 *˓Tüng ʿsó*, as that used in queues.
鎖線 *ʿSó siăngʾ*, as for shoe-tassels.
二扣 *Ne$^2$ k'aiuʾ*, a very coarse kind.
三扣 *˓Sang k'aiuʾ*, } sizes between the preceding and the next.
粗衣 *˓Ch'u ˓i*, }
純衣 *˓Seu ˓i*, a medium size.
大衣 *Tai$^2$ ˓i*, }
葛衣 *Mok˒ ˓i*, } finest varieties.
蘇衣 *˓Su ˓i*, }

## 14. ILLNESS, AILMENTS.

Sick, ill, 破病 *P'waiʾ pang$^2$.*

Indisposed, 身體𠍴抖托 *˓Sing ʿlá ng$^2$ ʿt'au lóh˒ (t'óh˒).*

The whole body (in distress) and can't bear it, 一身體賣制的 *Sioh˒ ˓sing ʿlá má$^2$ chiéʾ tek˒.*

To ache all over, 一身痛 *Sioh$_2$ ꜀sing t‘iăng꜃*.

Aches dreadfully! 隻叫囉痛 *Chiă꜁ kieu꜃ ꜂ló t‘iăng꜃!* 那痛二痛 *꜂Hiă t‘iăng꜃ ne$^2$ t‘iăng꜃!*

The whole body—can't drag it up! 一身賣拖的起 *Sioh$_2$ ꜀sing mă$^2$ ꜀t‘wa tek꜁ ꜂k‘i!*

The feet and hands relaxed and aching, 胶手𪘊𪘊瘦 *꜀K‘a ꜂ch‘iu lŭk$_2$ luĕk꜁ ꜀song.*

The mouth all coated and food tasteless, 嘴厚食毛味 *Ch‘oi꜃ kau$^2$ siăh$_2$ ꜀mó e$^2$.*

All chilled and numbed, 生寒凊𤄯 *꜀Ch‘ang ꜀kang ch‘eng꜃ pe꜃.*

The pulse slow and weak, 脈沉 *Mah$_2$ ꜀t‘eng.*

The pulse full and quick (feverish), 脈大 *Mah$_2$ twai$^2$.*

Fear (you) have taken a heavy cold, 驚是風寒受的深 *꜀Kiăng se$^2$ ꜀hung ꜀hang seu$^2$ tek꜁ ꜀ch‘ing.*

Now (you) must bring it out (by medicine), 伶着表 *꜀Tang tioh$_2$ ꜂pieu* ( or *t‘óh꜁*).

Now must take a sweat, 伶着發汗 *꜀Tang tioh$_2$ hwak꜁ kang$^2$.*

The sweating must (be made to) extend to the feet, then it will do well, 汗着透胶隻好 *Kang$^2$ tioh$_2$ t‘au꜃ ꜀k‘a chiăh꜁ ꜂hó.*

Just now (the fever, has subsided, 只長隻退和 *꜂Chi ꜀tong chiăh꜁ t‘ói꜃ ꜀hwo.*

Now must not expose (yourself) to the wind, 伶伓通引風 *꜀Tang ng$^2$ ꜀t‘ĕng ꜂yăng ꜀hung.*

Don't know what this eruption is, 賣曉的生世毛 *mă$^2$ ꜂hieu tek꜁ ꜀sang sié꜃ nóh꜁.*

At first it was only a small pimple, 起先𨑨一粒仔 *꜂K‘i ꜀seng na$^2$ sioh$_2$ lak$_2$ ꜂kiăng.*

Has now become as large as a cup, 伶變務甌大 *꜀Tang piĕng꜃ e$^2$ ꜀eu twai$^2$.*

Now it is suppurating and aches very badly, 伶禮灌膿盡痛 *꜀Tang ꜂lá kwang꜃ (chó꜃) ꜀nĕng cheng$^2$ t‘iăng꜃.*

As for sleeping, I can't get asleep, 困賣困的着 *K‘aung꜃ mă$^2$ k‘aung꜃ tek꜁ tioh$_2$.*

Now have a chill and then hot or feverish, 也柏寒柏熱 *Yă$^2$ p‘ah꜁ ꜀kang p‘ah꜁ yék$_2$.*

The boil has not yet come to a head, 膿頭故昧現 ꜀Nĕng ꜀tʻau koʼ mwoi$^2$ hiĕng$^2$.

It will take a few days more, then it will burst, 故着務幾日隻䚡剝膿 Koʼ tioh꜇ o$^2$ ʻkwi nik꜇ chiăh꜇ á$^2$ pauk꜇ ꜀nĕng.

To have a boil, 生瘀 ꜀Sang hwong ʼ.

To have a whitlow, 生蛇頭 ꜀Sang ꜀sié ꜀tʻau.

To catch a fall and sprain the hand, 跌一倒手跌撳去 Pwak꜇ sioh꜇ ʻtó ʻchʻiu pwak꜇ ꜀chʻŭng ꜀ó.

To wrench the foot, 胶撇 ꜀kʻa piek꜇.

A little better, 差些微 ꜀Chʻa ꜀niă nóiʼ.

No perceptible change for the better, 賣見差 má$^2$ kiĕngʼ ꜀chʻa.

Now am entirely recovered! 伶都脫體囉 ꜀Tang ꜀tu tʻauk꜇ ʻtʻá ꜀ló!

## 15. QUANTITY.

Is there any? 務吓毛 O$^2$ ʻa ꜀mó?

There is, 務吓 O$^2$ ꜀a.

Probably there is some, 䚡務吓 Á$^2$ o$^2$ ꜀a.

Probably there is none, 䚡毛吓 Á$^2$ ꜀mó ꜀a.

Do not know whether there is any or not, 賣曉的務吓毛 Má$^2$ ʻhieu tek꜇ o$^2$ ʻa ꜀mó.

How much is there left? 剩箬壞呢 Tiong$^2$ nioh꜇ wai$^2$ ꜀ni?

There is not much left, 剩毛箬壞 Tiong$^2$ ꜀mó nioh꜇ wai$^2$.

There is only a little left, 儕剩一滴仔 Na$^2$ tiong$^2$ sioh꜇ tek꜇ ʻkiăng. 剩伓際事 Tiong$^2$ ng$^2$ chié$^2$ sëü$^2$.

There is a large quantity left, 剩野晒吓 Tiong$^2$ ʻyă sá$^2$ ꜀a. 剩堆山 Tiong$^2$ ꜀toi ꜀sang.

There is not one left, 都毛剩一隻嗒 ꜀Tu ꜀mó tiong$^2$ sioh꜇ chiăh꜇ ꜀pu.

Too small a quantity, too few, 太少嗒 Kʻak꜇ ʻchieu ꜀pu.

Too large a quantity, 太晒吓 Kʻak꜇ sá$^2$ ꜀a.

What quantity must be used? 着駛箬壞呢 Tioh꜇ ʻsai nioh꜇ wai$^2$ ꜀ni?

The smaller part (lit., the small half), 細半 Sáʼ pwangʼ.

The larger part (lit., the large half), 大半 Twai$^2$ pwangʼ.

A cupful, 一杯 Sioh꜇ ꜀pwi.

A cup *full*, 一杯溢 *Sioh$_2$ ꜀pwí tiéng$^2$.*

Half a cup, 半杯 *Pwang’ ꜀pwí.*

A little more than half a cup, 大半杯 *Twai$^2$ pwang’ ꜀pwí.*

A little less than a cup, 一杯少些微 *Sioh$_2$ ꜀pwí ‘chieu ꜀niă nói’.*

A little more than a cup, 一杯好些微 *Sioh$_2$ ꜀pwí ‘hó ꜀niă nói’.*

About a cupful, 約略一杯 *Yokˏ liok$_2$ sioh$_2$ ꜀pwí.*

A cup and a half, 杯半 *꜀Pwí pwang’.*

Two cups and a half, 二杯半 *Lang$^2$ ꜀pwí pwang’.*

Running over! 浡 *P‘ak$_2$!*

Full and running over, 澎澎溢 *꜀P‘ang ꜀p‘ang tiéng$^2$.*

Make double the quantity (mentioned in the recipe), 做二料 *Chó’ lang$^2$ laiu$^2$.*

A half-side of anything, 半爿 *Pwang’ ꜀peng.*

The larger half-side, 大半爿 *Twai$^2$ pwang’ ꜀peng.*

The smaller half-side, 細半爿 *Sá’ pwang’ ꜀peng.*

A half length, 半長 *Pwang’ ꜀tong.*

The longer half-length, 大半長 *Twai$^2$ pwang’ ꜀tong.*

The shorter half-length, 細半長 *Sá’ pwang’ ꜀tong.*

To cut into two equal sections, 削對稜 *Siohˏ tói’ leng’.*

To cut (with scissors) into two equal lengths, 剪對段 *‘Ka tói’ ꜀tong.* 剪半段 *‘Ka pwang’ ꜀tong.* 剪二橛 *‘Ka lang$^2$ kwok$_2$.*

To cut with scissors into two equal parts lengthwise, 剪半爿 *‘Ka pwang’ ꜀peng.* 剪對爿 *‘Ka tói’ ꜀peng.*

Half the road, i. e., half the distance, 半路中 *Pwang’ tio$^2$ ꜀tong.*

The whole piece, 軀躿塊 *꜀Kó ꜀long tói’.*

The whole piece (of goods), 軀躿疋 *꜀Kó ꜀long p‘ekˏ.*

## 16. ACCOUNTS.

Will it be necessary to buy? shall I buy? 駛伓駛買 *‘Sai ng$^2$ ‘sai ‘má?* (*‘sang ‘sai ‘má?*).

Must buy, 着買 *Tioh$_2$ ‘má.*

He has gone to buy things—make purchases, 伊去買乇 *꜀I k‘ó’ ‘má nóhˏ.*

How much shall (I) buy? 着買箬壞 *Tioh$_2$ ʻmá nioh$_2$ wai$^2$?*

There is none in the market (lit., no place to buy), 毛塊買 *꜀Mó tói꜂ (nói꜂) ʻmá.*

How much money do you offer? 汝價錢還箬壞 *ʻNü ka꜂ ꜀chiéng ꜀teng nioh$_2$ wai$^2$?*

This is not worth so much, 啫毛伓値只塊錢 *ʻChiă nóh꜁ ng$^2$ tek$_2$ ꜀chu wai꜂ ꜀chiéng.*

(You) dislike the price as too dear, 嫌貴 *꜀Hiéng koi꜂.*

Everything is expensive, 諸毛都貴 *꜀Chü nóh꜁ ꜀tu koi꜂.*

It is too dear, can't make a bargain, 太貴賣成花 *K'ak꜁ koi꜂ má$^2$ ꜀siăng ꜀hwa.*

It is neither cheap nor dear, 也毛便宜也毛多長 *Yă$^2$ ꜀mó ꜀peng ꜀ngié yă$^2$ ꜀mó ꜀tó ꜀tong.*

Can't afford to buy it, 買賣起 *ʻMi má$^2$ ʻk'i.*

Add (give) a few more (cash), 再添幾隻 *Kai꜂ ꜀t'iéng ʻkwi chiăh꜁.*

How much did you give for this? 𡅏箬壞錢買其 *꜀Chuí nioh$_2$ wai$^2$ ꜀chiéng ʻmá ꜀ki?*

What is the price of this? 𡅏箬壞錢 *꜀Chuí nioh$_2$ wai$^2$ ꜀chiéng?*

Two hundred cash, 二百錢 *Lang$^2$ pah꜁ ꜀chiéng.*

Let it go at 150, 百五就是 *Pah꜁ ngo$^2$ cheu$^2$ se$^2$.*

150 is very cheap, 百五野便宜 *Pah꜁ ngo$^2$ ʻyă ꜀peng ꜀ngié.*

Shall lose money (on it), 鞋折本 *Á$^2$ siék$_2$ ʻpwong.*

Sold by the pound, 論觔賣 *Laung$^2$ ꜀kŭng mă$^2$.*

What is the price *per* pound? 一觔箬壞 *Sioh$_2$ ꜀kŭng nioh$_2$ wai$^2$?*

Not enough to meet the cost, 伓彀本 *Ng$^2$ kau꜂ ʻpwong.*

Very cheap, 野賤 *ʻYă siăng$^2$.*

Buy the worth of this money, 盡只塊錢買 *Cheng$^2$ ꜀chu wai꜂ ꜀chiéng ʻmá.*

To reckon accounts, 算數 *Saung꜂ so꜂.*

To write down an account, 記數 *Ke꜂ so꜂.*

To settle up an account, 還數 *꜀Teng so꜂.*

In all how much cash? 都着箬壞錢 *꜀Tu tioh$_2$ nioh$_2$ wai$^2$ ꜀chiéng?*

In purchasing how much did you overrun the amount in hand? 長駛箬壞錢 ꜁Tong ʻsai nioh꜇ wai꜅ ꜁chiêng?

How much money still remains? 錢存箬壞 ꜁Chiêng ꜁chong nioh꜇ wai꜅? 故剩箬壞錢 Koʼ tiong꜅ nioh꜇ wai꜅ ꜁chiêng?

Monthly pay (of employés), 月資 Ngwok꜇ ꜀chü.

How much are the wages? 工錢箬壞 ꜀Kĕng ꜁chiêng nioh꜇ wai꜅?

A teacher's stipend, 束脩 Sok꜆ ꜀siu.

To take pay in advance, 錢先支 ꜀Chiêng ꜀seng ꜀chiê.

How much can you earn (or gain) a day? 一日儩聽的箬壞錢 Sioh꜇ nik꜇ á꜅ tʻengʼ tek꜆ nioh꜆ wai꜅ ꜁chiêng?

Can't earn (or gain) much, 賣聽的箬壞 Má꜅ tʻengʼ tek꜆ nioh꜇ wai꜅.

To owe people money, 欠伙錢 Kʻiêngʼ ꜁nĕng ꜁chiêng (or chai꜅.)

To make out a bill, or list of prices, 開單 ꜀Kʻwi ꜀tang.

## 17. BARGAINING WITH A CABINET-MAKER.

I wish to have a closet made of ꜁Nang muk꜇ wood, 我欲做楠木裯一隻 ʻNgwai óiʼ chóʼ ꜁nang muk꜇ ꜁tiu sioh꜇ chiăh꜆.

Width four feet, height six feet five inches, 闊四尺高六尺五 Kʻwak꜆ seʼ chʻioh꜆ ꜀keng lĕk꜇ chʻioh꜆ ngo꜅.

Inside five stories (i. e., of shelves and drawers), 裏勢五層 ʻTiê tiêʼ ngo꜅ ꜁cheng.

The middle story (is to have) two drawers, 大中層二個揩 Tai꜅ ꜀tong ꜁cheng lang꜅ ʻa tʻáʼ.

On the outside, long, paneled, doors, 外斗廣東堵其門直透 Ngiê꜅ ʻtau ʻkwong ꜀tĕng ʻtu ꜁ki ꜁mwong tik꜇ tʻauʼ.

Use thick brass hinges, 駛粗厚銅具台蝉釘 ʻSai ꜀chʻu kau꜅ ꜁tĕng ꜁ki hiăk꜇ ꜁siêng tengʼ.

Use the money-safe (kind) of lock, 駛夾幔鎖 ʻSai kak꜆ mang꜅ ʻsó.

Two coats of varnish, 明漆雙過 ꜁Ming chʻek꜆ ꜀sĕng kwoʼ.

The materials must all be good, 柴料都著好 ꜁Chʻa laiu꜅ ꜀tu tioh꜇ ʻhó.



榕腔初學撮要

In your opinion, workman, what will the price be? 乞司傅看着務碆壞錢 *K'ëük, ,sa ho² k'ang' tioh, o² nioh, wai² ,chiêng?*

How many days will it take to make it? 幾日𠏹做便 *'Kwi nik, á² chó' piêng²?*

Teacher, at present wood-material is all dear, 先生只帮柴料都貴 *,Sing ,sang 'chi ,pong ,ch'a liiu² ,tu koi'.*

Can't be compared with former times, 伓比前倒將換 *Ng² 'pi ,seng tó' (,ó') ,chiong wang².*

Simply *making* it would require twenty days' work, 郁做胚着做二十工 *Na² chó' ,p'wi tioh, chó' ne² sek, ,kêng.*

Besides this it must be varnished twice and brass (fittings) nailed on, 故着漆雙過連釘銅 *Ko' tioh, ch'ek, ,sëng kwo' ,liêng teng' ,têng.*

It will certainly require a month and a half to make and finish it, 總着月半日隻𠏹便 *'Chung tioh, ngwok, pwang' nik, chiă', á² piêng².*

The price will be 10 dollars, 價錢十塊 *Ka' ,chiêng sek, tói'.*

If the teacher will use different sorts of hard wood, 比喻先生郁肯駛雜有 *'Pi ëü² ,sing ,sang na² 'k'ing 'sai chak, taing²,*

Then it will not require so much money, 就伓駛只塊錢 *Cheu² ng² 'sai ,chu wai' ,chiêng,*

And I'll reckon it at 8 dollars—about that figure, 科的八塊做賍 *,K'wo tek, paik, tói' chó' ,chong,*

(But if you) wish to use that kind of wood, (the ,Nang muk,) I must have thus much cash, 剝駛喏柴着務只㗂 *Pwoh, 'sai 'chiă ,ch'a tioh, o² 'chi sá²,*

Teacher, is it not that you dislike my price? 是伓是汝先生嫌奴貫 *Se² ng² se² 'nü ,sing ,sang ,hiêng ,nu koi'.*

## 18. EXCURSIONS, TRAVELING.

Where are you going to-day? 今旦去冬那 *,King tang' k'ó' ,têng 'në?*

Are you going to the city to-day? 今旦務入城吓毛 *,King tang' o² 'tié ,siăng 'a ,mó?*

Have business to-day and cannot go, 今旦務代計毛的去 ꜀*King tang*꜄ *o*$^2$ *tai*$^2$ *iė*꜄ ꜁*mó tek*꜆ *kʻó*꜄.

I shall go after a few days, 二日儺去 *Lang*$^2$ *nik*$_2$ *á*$^2$ *kʻó*꜄.

Shall walk to day, shall not take a chair, 今旦那行伓坐轎 ꜀*Kïng tang*꜄ *na*$^2$ ꜁*kiăng* (or *pwo*$^2$ ꜁*heng*) *ng*$^2$ *sói*$^2$ *kieu*$^2$.

Call two chair-bearers, 吼扛轎其二隻 ꜂*Hau* ꜀*kong kieu*$^2$ ꜁*ki lang*$^2$ *chiăh*꜆.

Are we to go one way only, or to go and return? 單倒吓來囘 ꜀*Tang tó*꜄ ꜂*a* ꜁*lai* ꜁*huí?*

How much will the fare be for the round trip? 來囘箬壞錢 ꜁*Lai* ꜁*huí nioh*$_2$ *wai*$^2$ ꜁*chiéng?*

The fare there and back will be 200 cash, 來囘二百錢 ꜁*Lai* ꜁*hui lang*$^2$ *pah*꜆ ꜁*chiéng.*

What is the fare for only one way? 單倒箬壞錢 ꜀*Tang tó*꜄ *nioh*$_2$ *wai*$^2$ ꜁*chiêng?*

The fare one way is 120 cash, 單倒百二 ꜀*Tang tó*꜄ *pah*꜆ *ne*$^2$.

Raise (the poles, so that the person can enter), 升起 ꜀*Sing* ꜂*kʻi.*

Carry the sedan carefully, must not knock against things, 轎扛細膩伓通撞 *Kieu*$^2$ ꜀*kong sá*꜄ *ne*$^2$, *ng*$^2$ ꜀*tʻĕng pʻaung*$^2$.

Keep step! 骹步着討好 ꜀*Kʻa pwo*$^2$ *tioh*$_2$ ꜂*tʻó* ꜂*hó* (or ꜁*seu*, or ꜁*chá*).

Look above! Look below! Look *straight* on both sides!—so as to avoid collision, stumbling, etc. 看上 *Kʻang*꜄ *siong*$^2$*!* 看底 *Kʻang*꜄ ꜂*tá!* 看正 *Kʻang*꜄ *chiăng*꜄*!*

Slippery, and will fall! 滑溜 *Kok*$_2$ *leu*꜄*!*

Sit straight! (not to one side), 坐正 *Sói*$^2$ *chiăng*꜄*!*

Sit still! 坐定 *Sói*$^2$ *tiăng*$^2$*!*

Do you know the road? 路仈伓仈 *Tio*$^2$ *paik*꜆ *ng*$^2$ *paik*꜆ (꜂*peng paik*꜆).

We have been over this road before, 啫路行着了 ꜂*Chiă tio*$^2$ ꜁*kiăng tioh*$_2$ ꜂*lau.*

We have not been over this road before, 啫路昧行着 ꜂*Chiă tio*$^2$ *mwoí*$^2$ ꜁*kiăng tioh*$_2$.

Have gone wrong and must turn back, 行錯着囘頭 ꜁*Kiăng tang*$^2$ *tioh*$_2$ ꜁*huí* ꜁*tʻau* (or ꜁*huí* ꜂*tiong* ꜁*tʻau*).

Man. 10.

Here (we) must turn off, 是只塊轉灣 *Se² ꜀chu wai˃ ˓tiong ꜀wang.*

If (you) do not know the road, (you) must inquire, 伓八路着借們 *Ng² paik˃ tio² tioh₂ chioh˃ mwong˃.*

Allow me to inquire the way to ꜀Ming Kaing² ꜀Sang within the city, 乞奴借們啫去城裏閩縣山着趁冬那行 *K'ëük˃ ꜀nu chioh˃ mwong˃ ꜀chiă, k'ó˃ ꜀siăng ˓tié ꜀Ming Kaing² ꜀Sang tioh₂ t'eng˃ tëng ˓në ꜀kiăng?*

Turn off at the right hand, 轉灣掏筯手 *˓Tiong ꜀wang ꜀tó tëü² ˓ch'iu.*

Turn off at the left hand, 轉灣掏碗手 *˓Tiong ꜀wang ꜀tó ˓wang ˓ch'iu.*

Walk straight forward, 一直行 *Ek˃ tik₂ ꜀kiăng.*

How much farther are we to go? 故務箬壞路 *Ko˃ o² nioh₂ wai² tio²?*

Still one ˓li and over, 故務里把路 *Ko˃ o² ˓li ˓pa tio².*

Put down the sedan! 囘 ꜀*Huí!* or 囘手 ꜀*Huí ˓ch'iu!*

What time shall we come to bring you back? 幾點鐘來接轎 *˓Kwi ˓teng ꜀chüng ꜀li chiék˃ kieu²?*

Wait here, I shall return soon, 汝倻落只塊等就轉去 *˓Nü na² lóh₂ ꜀chu wai˃ ˓ting, cheu² ˓tiong k'ó˃.*

I am going to Kushan to-morrow, 明旦剝去鼓山 ꜀*Ming tang˃ pwoh˃ k'ó˃ ˓Ku ꜀Sang.*

Will you go by road or by boat? 趁路去吓趁船去呢 *T'eng˃ tio² k'ó˃ ˓a t'eng˃ ꜀sung k'ó˃ ꜀ni?*

Shall go by boat, 趁船禮去 *T'eng˃ ꜀sung ˓lá k'ó˃.*

Carry the sedan to the landing (where the boat is to stop), 轎拍去許邊道頭等 *Kieu² p'ah˃ k'ó˃ ˓hü ꜀peng tó² ꜀t'au ˓ting.*

At what hour will you start? 幾點去 *˓Kwi ˓teng k'ó˃.*

What will be the state of the tide to-morrow? 明旦世毛水市 ꜀*Ming tang˃ sié˃ nóh˃ ˓chwi ch'e²?*

The tide will not be favorable early to-morrow morning, 明旦早水市討賣着 ꜀*Ming tang˃ ˓cha ˓chwi ch'e² ˓t'ó má² tioh₂.*

It will be better to go somewhat late, 遲一滴仔去故好 ꜀*Ti sioh₂ tek˃ ˓kiăng (or ꜀ti nek˃ ˓kiăng) k'ó˃ ko˃ ˓hó.*

榕腔初學撮要



The tide will be full to-morrow at 9 o'clock, 明旦九點鐘水漲溢 ˏ*Ming tang*’ ‘*kau* ‘*teng* ꜀*chüng* ‘*chwi* ‘*tong tiéng*$^2$.

We will start at the ebb of the tide, 水汐隻開頭 ‘*Chwi p‘wong*’ *chiăh*꜁ ꜀*k‘wi* ˏ*t‘au*.

Ten o'clock will be just the right time to go, 十點去正正好 *Sek*$_2$ ‘*teng k‘ó*’ *chiăng*’ *chiăng*’ ‘*hó*.

What luggage will you take? 帶世毛去 *Tai*’ *sié*’ *nóh*꜁ *k‘ó*’?

Bedding, a trunk and provision basket, 鋪蓋皮箱一隻伙食籃一隻 ꜀*P‘wo kai*’ ˏ*p‘ui* ꜀*siong sioh*$_2$ *chiăh*꜁ ‘*hwi sik*$_2$ ˏ*lang sioh*$_2$ *chiăh*꜁.

Will it be necessary to call coolies? 駛伓駛叫擔担呢 ‘*Sai ng*$^2$ ‘*sai* (or ‘*sang* ‘*sai*) *kieu*’ ꜀*tang tang*’ ꜀*ni*?

Just go and call two, 莽去叫二隻 ‘*Mwong k‘ó*’ *kieu*’ *lang*$^2$ *chiăh*꜁.

How many chair-bearers shall I call? 轎夫叫幾隻 *Kieu*$^2$ ꜀*hu kieu*’ ‘*kwi chiăh*꜁?

There will be two chairs—each will have three men, 二頂轎都是三其擺 *Lang*$^2$ ‘*ting kieu*$^2$ ꜀*tu se*$^2$ ꜀*sang* ˏ*ki* ‘*pai*.

In all call six, 攏總叫六其 ‘*Lung* ‘*chung kieu*’ *lĕk*$_2$ ˏ*ki*.

Going up the mountain is hard work—get men who are accustomed to it, 上嶺吃虧吓着務行慣其 *Siong*$^2$ ‘*liăng k‘ek*꜁ ꜀*k‘wi* ˏ*a* — *tioh*$_2$ *o*$^2$ ˏ*kiăng kwang*’ ˏ*ki*.

How far is it from here to the city? 只塊去城裡路務若遠 ꜀*Chu wai*’ *k‘ó*’ ˏ*siăng* ‘*tié tio*$^2$ *o*$^2$ *nioh*$_2$ *hwong*$^2$.

Only 3 or 4 ‘*li*, 那務三四里 *Na*$^2$ *o*$^2$ ꜀*sang se*’ ‘*li*.

How great is the distance from here to Amoy? 去厦門若壞路 *K‘ó*’ *A*$^2$ ˏ*Mwong nioh*$_2$ *wai*$^2$ *tio*$^2$?

A few days' travel, 務幾日路 *O*$^2$ ‘*kwi nik*$_2$ *tio*$^2$.

Is it far from here to America? 去花旂國路偌遠吓賣 *K‘ó*’ ꜀*Hwa* ˏ*Ki Kwok*꜁ *tio*$^2$ *á*$^2$ *hwong*$^2$ ‘*a má*$^2$.

The distance is great, 野遠 ‘*Yă hwong*$^2$.

The distance by sea and land is about 40 or 50 days (travel), 船連路約畧着務四五十日 ˏ*Sung* ꜀*liéng tio*$^2$ *yiok*꜁ *liok*$_2$ *tioh*$_2$ *o*$^2$ *se*’ *ngo*$^2$ *sek*$_2$ *nik*$_2$.

## 19. LANGUAGE, TALKING.

Can you speak the colloquial? 儺講平話吓賣 Á$^{2}$ ᶜkong ꜀pang wa$^{2}$ ᶜa má$^{2}$?

I can understand what is said but cannot speak, 儺曉的聽賣曉的講 Á$^{2}$ ᶜhieu tek꜆ ꜀t‘iăng má$^{2}$ ᶜhieu tek꜆ ᶜkong.

He speaks remarkably well, 伊講野平 ꜀I ᶜkong ᶜyă ꜀pang.

He speaks pretty well, 伊講野務平 ꜀I ᶜkong ᶜyă o$^{2}$ ꜀pang.

He talks a jargon, 伊話講野咬 ꜀I wa$^{2}$ ᶜkong ᶜyă ngauᵓ.

He speaks with a brogue, 伊講話務腔 ꜀I ᶜkong wa$^{2}$ o$^{2}$ ꜀k‘iong.

His brogue is very heavy, 腔野重 ꜀K‘iong ᶜyă taĕng$^{2}$.

He does not speak clearly (as to sense), 伊講話賣了離 ꜀I ᶜkong wa$^{2}$ má$^{2}$ ᶜlieu lié$^{2}$.

He stammers in speaking, 伊講話急舌 ꜀I ᶜkong wa$^{2}$ kek꜆ siék$_{2}$.

What he says is very good to hear, 伊講話盡好聽 ꜀I ᶜkong wa$^{2}$ cheng$^{2}$ ᶜhó ꜀t‘iăng.

One can never fully learn this language, 啫話學賣盡 ᶜChiă wa$^{2}$ óh$_{2}$ má$^{2}$ cheng$^{2}$.

This language is difficult to learn, 啫話阿學 ᶜChiă wa$^{2}$ ꜀ó óh$_{2}$.

Cannot learn so as to imitate perfectly, 學賣像 Óh$_{2}$ má$^{2}$ ch‘iong$^{2}$.

Don't speak! 莫講話 Móh$_{2}$ ᶜkong wa$^{2}$.

Don't speak, Don't tell about it, 莫做聲 Móh$_{2}$ chóᵓ ꜀siăng.

Talk a little lower, 細聲些微 Sáᵓ ꜀siăng ꜀niă nóiᵓ.

Don't make such a clamor of voices, 莫昂昂叫 Móh$_{2}$ ꜀ngong ꜀ngong kieuᵓ.

(You) talk too loud, 聲音太大 ꜀Siăng ꜀ing k‘ak꜆ twai$^{2}$.

Be still! Don't talk! 默默着 Sang$^{2}$ sang$^{2}$ tioh$_{2}$!

It shall be as you say. No matter what was said (it did no good), 在汝將樣講 Chai$^{2}$ ᶜnü ꜀chiong yong$^{2}$ ᶜkong.

Must not say that, 嘴伓通講 ꜀Chuí ng$^{2}$ ꜀t‘ĕng ᶜkong.

Of course it's so—does not need farther talking about, 伓是仅講 Ng$^{2}$ se$^{2}$ po$^{2}$ ᶜkong.

Have said it again and again, 講囉仅講 ᶜKong ᶜló po$^{2}$ ᶜkong.

He calls and you won't answer, 伊叫汝伓應 ꜀I kieu꜄, ꜂nü ng$^2$ eng꜄.

He is calling, 伊禮叫 ꜀I ꜂lá kieu꜄.

Have given directions already, 吩咐了 ꜀Hung ho꜄ (no꜄) ꜂lau.

Go and tell him, 去共伊講 K'ó꜄ kaĕng$^2$ ꜀i ꜂kong.

Have told him, 共伊講了 Kaĕng$^2$ ꜀i ꜂kong ꜂lau.

Is talked about by people (as bad), 乞仈講 K'ëük꜆ ꜁nĕng ꜂kong.

Is slandered by people, 乞仈讒譖 K'ëük꜆ ꜁nëng ꜁chang chaing꜄.

Sit down and chat, 坐坐冇講 Sói$^2$ sói$^2$ p'ang꜄ ꜂kong.

Very lively times! 盡鬧熱 Cheng$^2$ nau$^2$ yék$_2$!

He is making a great ado with me (about it), 伊共奴禮鬧 ꜀I kaĕng$^2$ ꜁nu ꜂lá nau$^2$.

What did he say? 伊講世乇 ꜀I ꜂kong sié꜄ nóh꜆? 伊將講 ꜀I ꜀chiong (or ꜀chiong yong$^2$) ꜂kong?

Can't exhaust the subject, 賣講的盡 Má$^2$ ꜂kong tek꜆ cheng$^2$.

## 20. VISITING, POLITE AND FAMILIAR TERMS.

Please come in and sit down, 請入坐 ꜂Ch'iăng ꜂tié sói$^2$.

Don't be ceremonious—let us both sit (said by visitor), 莫拘齊坐 Móh$_2$ ꜀kü—꜁chá sói$^2$.

Have you taken breakfast yet? 食早囉昧 Siăh$_2$ ꜂cha ꜁ló mwoi$^2$.

Have you eaten dinner yet? 食晝昧 Siăh$_2$ tau꜄ mwoi$^2$?

I have eaten, 食了 Siăh$_2$ ꜂lau, 偏囉 ꜀P'iêng ꜁ló, (this last not used by common people).

I have not eaten yet, 昧食 Mwoi$^2$ siăh$_2$.

Where is your mansion? 府上着冬那 ꜂Hu siong$^2$ tioh$_2$ ꜀tëng ꜂në?

Where is your house? 厝着冬那 Ch'io꜄ tioh$_2$ ꜀tëng ꜂në?

What is your honorable surname? 貴姓 Koi꜄ seng꜄?

What is your surname? 姓乜 Sang꜄ miéh꜆? or 姓乜乇 Sang꜄ miéh꜆ nóh꜆?

This year what is your exalted age? (to an old person), 今年高壽 ꜀King ꜁niêng ꜀kó seu$^2$?

How old are you this year? 今年明箬壞歲 ꜀King ꜁niêng ꜁mang nioh$_2$ wai$^2$ hwoi꜄?

Please (take) some tea, 請茶 ꜂Ch'iăng ꜁ta.

Please (take) some refreshments, 請點心 ʿ*Chʻiăng* ʿ*tiéng* ꜀*sing.*

Don't be ceremonious, 莫細膩 *Móh*$_{2}$ *sáʾ ne*$^{2}$.

Thanks for tea, 多謝茶 ꜀*Tó siă*$^{2}$ ꜀*ta.*

Sit longer, 莽再坐 ʿ*Mwong chaiʾ sói*$^{2}$.

I have troubled you! 吵嘈 ʿ*Chʻau* ꜀*á!* or 打擾 ʿ*Ta* ʿ*yeu!*

I am under obligation to you, 欠陪 *Kʻiéngʾ* ꜀*puí.*

How dare I presume to! 豈敢 ʿ*Kʻi* ʿ*kang* (or ʿ*kʻi* ʿ*kiăng*).

At a future day when at leisure call again and sit, 下日務閒再入來坐 *A*$^{2}$ *nik*$_{2}$ *o*$^{2}$ ꜀*eng chaiʾ* ʿ*tié* ꜀*li sói*$^{2}$.

I have failed in politeness, but do not be offended (said to the visitor), 失禮莫見怪 *Sek*ʾ ʿ*lá, móh*$_{2}$ *kiéngʾ kwaiʾ*.

Walk carefully (so as not to fall — said mostly to women), 行好 ꜀*Kiăng* ʿ*hó.*

Walk slowly (a parting salutation), 慢慢行 *Maing*$^{2}$ *maing*$^{2}$ ꜀*kiăng.*

Please (return and) enter (your house—as said by the visitor), 請入 ʿ*Chʻiăng* ʿ*tié.*

It was by mistake! i. e., excuse me! 悞做 *Ngwo*$^{2}$ *chóʾ!*

I have offended (somewhat like the polite phrase "I beg pardon"), 得罪 *Tuik*ʾ *chói*$^{2}$.

I congratulate you! 拱喜 ʿ*Küng* ʿ*hi!* and 且喜 ʿ*Chʻiă* ʿ*hi!* the latter used only by women—the former by both sexes.

Thanks! (for a gift or for a great favor done), 多謝 ꜀*Tŏ siă*$^{2}$*!* 謝謝 *Siă*$^{2}$ *siă*$^{2}$*!*

Thanks! (for a trifling favor done), 豈動 ʿ*Kʻi taëng*$^{2}$*!* 多勞 ꜀*Tŏ* ꜀*ló.*

Thanks for the loan! 謝借 *Siă*$^{2}$ *chioh*ʾ*!*

May I trouble you? 勞動 ꜀*Ló tong*$^{2}$*?*

I have alarmed (disturbed) you, 驚動 ꜀*King tong*$^{2}$.

Am blessed with your favor! 叨福 ꜀*Tʻó hok*ʾ*!*

May you prosper pecuniarily! (a New Year's salutation), 發財 *Hwak*ʾ ꜀*chai!*

May we both prosper! (said in reply to the preceding), 齊發 ꜀*Chá hwak*ʾ*!*

A happy New Year! 拜年, 拜年 *Paiʾ* ꜀*niéng! Paiʾ* ꜀*niéng!*

How old are you (to a middle-aged person)? 尊齒 ꜀*Chong* ꜂*ch'i?*

How old are you (to a young person)? 尊庚 ꜀*Chong* ꜀*keng?*

How old are you (to a child)? 幾歲 ꜂*Kwi hwoí*꜄*?*

How many months old (is the infant)? 幾個月日 ꜂*Kwi* ꜂*a ngwok*$_2$ *nik*$_2$*?*

Not a year old yet, 昧晬 *Mwoi*$^2$ *chói*꜄.

13 months old, 晬一 *Chói*꜄ *ek*꜅.

### 21. TALK WITH A TEACHER.

I am a foreigner just come to Foochow, 奴是外國僥來福州 ꜁*Nu se*$^2$ *ngwoí*$^2$ *kwok*꜅ *chiăh*꜅ ꜁*li Hok*꜅ ꜀*Chiu,*

And do not know how to speak this dialect, 賣曉的講只塊話 *Má*$^2$ ꜂*hieu tek*꜅ ꜂*kong* ꜀*chu wai*꜄ *wa*$^2$.

And now I invite the Teacher 伶請先生 ꜀*Tang* ꜂*ch'iăng* ꜀*sing* ꜀*sang*

To teach me to speak the language and read books, 教奴講話連讀書 *Ka*꜄ ꜁*nu* ꜂*kong wa*$^2$ ꜁*liéng t'ĕk*$_2$ ꜀*chü.*

According to the Teacher's opinion, now that I am just beginning, 乞先生看奴伶僥起手 *K'ĕük*꜅ ꜀*sing* ꜀*sang k'ang*꜄ ꜁*nu* ꜀*tang chiăh*꜅ ꜂*k'i* ꜂*ch'iu,*

What would it be best for me to learn first? 着先學世毛好 *Tioh*$_2$ ꜀*seng óh*$_2$ *sié*꜄ *nóh*꜅ ꜂*hó?*

It is important first to repeat over the eight tones, 要緊着先呼八音 *Yeu*꜄ ꜂*king tioh*$_2$ ꜀*seng* ꜀*k'u paik*꜅ ꜀*ing,*

And to read the initials and finals intelligibly, 字頭字母着讀分明 *Che*$^2$ ꜁*t'au che*$^2$ ꜂*mó tioh*$_2$ *t'ĕk*$_2$ ꜀*hung* ꜁*ming,*

Must not do it confusedly (so as to confound them with each other), 伓通含糊 *Ng*$^2$ ꜀*t'ĕng* ꜁*hang* ꜁*hu.*

Must certainly study these a year or half a year, 的着讀至一年半載 *Tek*꜅ *tioh*$_2$ *t'ĕk*$_2$ *kau*꜄ *sioh*$_2$ ꜁*niéng pwang*꜄ ꜂*chai,*

And know how to combine initials with finals, 字頭字母𫧃曉的敠 *Che*$^2$ ꜁*t'au che*$^2$ ꜂*mó á*$^2$ ꜂*hieu tek*꜅ *ch'ëüng*꜄.

Only then will it do, i. e., will you have studied these enough, 僥𫧃駛的 *Chiăh*꜅ *á*$^2$ ꜂*sai tek*꜅.

The Eight Tone (book) has how many initials and finals? 八音箬壞字頭共字母 *Paik꜆ ꜀Ing nioh$_2$ wai$^2$ che$^2$ ꜁t'au kaëng$^2$ che$^2$ ꜂mó?*

There are 36 finals (only 33 in use) and 15 initials, 三十六字母十五字頭 *꜀Sang sek$_2$ lĕk$_2$ che$^2$ ꜂mó sek$_2$ ngo$^2$ che$^2$ ꜁t'au.*

Being able to repeat these perfectly, 𠲎呼熟熟着 *Á$^2$ ꜀k'u sŭk$_2$ sŭk$_2$ tioh$_2$,*

Then of course in speaking and reading you will not miss the tone, 自然講話讀書賣走音 *Chëü$^2$ ꜁yong ꜂kong wa$^2$ t'ĕk$_2$ ꜀chü má$^2$ ꜂chau ꜀ing.*

As to the *꜀piéng* initial and the *꜀p'ó* initial, 學啫邊字頭共波字頭 *Óh$_2$ ꜂chiă ꜀piéng che$^2$ ꜁t'au kaëng$^2$ ꜀p'ó che$^2$ ꜁t'au,*

The *꜁kiu* initial and the *k'e꜄* initial, 求字頭共氣字頭 *꜁Kiu che$^2$ ꜁t'au kaëng$^2$ k'e꜄ che$^2$ ꜁t'au,*

The *꜀cheng* initial and the *ch'ok꜆* initial, 曾字頭共出字頭 *꜀Cheng che$^2$ ꜁t'au kaëng$^2$ ch'ok꜆ che$^2$ ꜁t'au,*

The *꜀tá* initial and the *꜀t'a* initial, 低字頭共他字頭 *꜀Tá che$^2$ ꜁t'au kaëng$^2$ ꜀t'a che$^2$ ꜁t'au,*

(These) are generally confounded with each other (by foreigners), 多的多𠲎混 *꜀Tó tek꜆ ꜀tó á$^2$ hong$^2$,*

(And you) must know how to distinguish (between these), 着𠲎曉的分別 *Tioh$_2$ á$^2$ ꜂hieu tek꜆ ꜀hung piék꜆.*

I truly do not know (about these things), 奴其實賣曉的 *꜁Nu ꜁ki sik$_2$ má$^2$ ꜂hieu tek꜆,*

And depend upon the Teacher to instruct me, 藉汝先生教奴 *Chiă$^2$ ꜂nü ꜀sing ꜀sang ka꜄ ꜁nu.*

We will now read the 5th chapter of Matt. commencing at the 10th verse, 伶讀馬太第五章十節起 *꜀Tang t'ĕk$_2$ ꜂Ma T'ai꜄ tá$^2$ ngo$^2$ ꜀chiong sek$_2$ chiék꜆ ꜂k'i,*

And ending with the 27th verse, 至二十七節止 *Kau꜄ ne$^2$ sek$_2$ ch'ek꜆ chiék꜆ ꜂chi.*

Read the 6th chapter of Daniel, 讀但以理第六章 *T'ĕk$_2$ Tang꜄ ꜂I ꜂Li tá$^2$ lĕk$_2$ ꜀chiong,*

Read it in the character and render it into colloquial, 連讀連說 *꜁Liéng t'ĕk$_2$ ꜁liéng siok꜆.*

If you, Teacher, hear me make mistakes, you must tell me, 汝先生聽奴郍務錯就着講 *‘Nü ꜀sing ꜀sang ꜀t‘iăng ꜁nu na$^2$ o$^2$ tang$^2$ cheu$^2$ tioh$_2$ ‘kong.*

## 22. READING AND WRITING.

Can (you) read? 字仈伓仈 *Che$^2$ paik꜇ ng$^2$ paik꜇* (or *‘peng paik꜇*)?

Only know one or two (i. e., a few) characters, 郍仈一二字 *Na$^2$ paik꜇ sioh$_2$ lang$^2$ che$^2$.*

Can you write? 㑐寫字賣 *Á$^2$ ‘siă che$^2$ má$^2$?*

Do not know how to write, 賣曉的寫 *Má$^2$ ‘hieu tek꜇ ‘siă.*

He is writing a letter, 伊禮寫批 *꜀I ‘lá ‘siă ꜀p‘ié.*

Must seal the letter, 批着封啫 *꜀P‘ié tioh$_2$ ꜀hung ꜁chiă.*

Take this writing (or chit) across the way, 啫字掏去許邊 *‘Chiă che$^2$ ꜁tó k‘ó’ ‘hü ꜀peng.*

Take this letter to the city to Mr. Ling's, 批掏去城裏林先生 *꜀P‘ié ꜁tó k‘ó’ ꜁siăng ‘tié ꜁Ling ꜀sing ꜀sang.*

Will (they) return an answer (by me)? 務囘批吓毛 *O$^2$ ꜁huí ꜀p‘ié ‘a ꜁mó?*

Shall (I) wait for an answer? 駛伓駛等囘批 *‘Sai ng$^2$ ‘sai* (or *‘sang ‘sai*) *‘ting ꜁huí ꜀p‘ié?*

To read aloud, to study, 讀書 *T‘ëk$_2$ ꜀chü.*

How many years have you studied? 書讀幾年 *꜀Chü t‘ëk$_2$ ‘kwi ꜁niéng?*

To read a book silently, to peruse, 看書 *K‘ang’ ꜀chü.*

To recite a lesson by reading it (as Chinese children do), 定書 *Teng$^2$ ꜀chü.*

To recite memoriter with the back to the teacher, 背書 *Pwoi$^2$ ꜀chü.*

Have not learned it perfectly—cannot recite it, 讀昧熟賣背 *T‘ëk$_2$ mwoi$^2$ sük$_2$—má$^2$ pwoi$^2$.*

Have studied this book through, 只一本讀過了 *‘Chi sioh$_2$ ‘pwong t‘ëk$_2$ kwo’ ‘lau.*

To miss (skip) a line in reading, 讀過行 *T‘ëk$_2$ kwo’ ꜁hong.*

To read only one leaf, 郍讀一頁 *Na$^2$ t‘ëk$_2$ sioh$_2$ hiék$_2$.*

## 23. EMOTIONS AND CHARACTERISTICS.

Very much pleased, 頂歡喜 ꜂*Ting* ꜀*hwang* ꜂*hi.*

Very much displeased, 盡去伓歡喜 *Cheng*$^2$ *k'ó*꜃ *ng*$^2$ ꜀*hwang* ꜂*hi.*

Nothing to be displeased about, 毛毛伓歡喜 ꜀*Mó nóh*꜁ *ng*$^2$ ꜀*hwang* ꜂*hi.*

Not at all well pleased, 毛乜毛歡喜 ꜀*Mó miéh*꜁ *nóh*꜁ ꜀*hwang* ꜂*hi.*

Not suited, 伓中意 *Ng*$^2$ *tëüng*꜃ *e*꜃.

Sorrowful at heart, 苦吓心禮 ꜂*K'u* ꜂*a* ꜀*sing* ꜂*lá.*

Very sorrowful at heart, 心禮盡苦 ꜀*Sing* ꜂*lá cheng*$^2$ ꜂*k'u.*

Am anxious about him day and night, 日暝禮思量伊 *Nik*꜁ ꜀*mang* ꜂*lá* ꜀*sü* ꜀*liong* ꜀*i.*

Angry at heart, 氣吓心禮 *K'e*꜃ ꜂*a* ꜀*sing* ꜂*lá.*

Angry the whole day, 一日受氣至暗 *Sioh*꜁ *nik*꜁ *seu*$^2$ *k'e*꜃ *kau*꜃ *wang*꜃.

Very amiable, 盡好愛 *Cheng*$^2$ ꜂*hó t'iăng*꜃.

Not amiable, 伓好愛 *Ng*$^2$ ꜂*hó t'iăng*꜃.

Very reserved, very sullen, 野嚛 ꜂*Yă heng*$^2$.

Very restless, very mischievous, 盡賤 *Cheng*$^2$ *chiéng*$^2$.

Don't be so restless! Don't be so mischievous! 莫賤 *Móh*꜁ *chiéng*$^2$!

To act so as to cause others to hate one, 討伙嫌 ꜂*T'ó* ꜀*nëng* ꜀*hiéng.*

To act so as to make people scold, 討伙罵 ꜂*T'ó* ꜀*nëng ma*꜃.

Is hated by people, 乞伙嫌 *K'ëük*꜁ ꜀*nëng* ꜀*hiéng.*

This man is very honest, 啫伙野老實 ꜂*Chiă* ꜀*nëng* ꜂*yă* ꜂*ló sik*꜁.

This man is very trustworthy, 啫伙野妥當 ꜂*Chiă* ꜀*nëng* ꜂*yă* ꜂*t'io taung*꜃.

Very faithful or reliable, 野忠厚 ꜂*Yă* ꜀*tüng haiu*$^2$.

Very assiduous (makes himself generally useful), 野力落 ꜂*Yă lik*꜁ *lóh*꜁.

Works diligently, 做代計野勤緊 *Chó*꜃ *tai*$^2$ *ié*꜃ ꜂*yă* ꜀*k'üng* ꜂*king.*

Memory poor, 記才平正 *Keʾ ꜁chai ꜁pang chiăngʾ.*
Patient in disposition, 性耐 *Sangʾ nai$^2$* or 耐心 *Nai$^2$ ꜀sing.*
Hasty in temper, 性急 *Sangʾ kekˏ* or 急氣 *Kekˏ k'eʾ.*

## 24. TIMES AND SEASONS.

The current year, 本年 *ʻPwong ꜁niĕng.*
Last year, 去年 *K'ŏʾ ꜁niĕng* or 去年明 *K'ŏʾ ꜁niĕng ꜁mang.*
Year before last, 昨年 *Sóh$_2$ ꜁niĕng.*
Year previous to year before last, 乇昨年 *Nóhˏ sóh$_2$ ꜁niĕng.*
Next year, 明年 *꜁Mang ꜁niĕng* or 來年 *꜁Lai ꜁niĕng.*
Year after next, 後年 *Au$^2$ ꜁niĕng.*
Year after year-after-next, 乇後年 *Nóhˏ au$^2$ ꜁niĕng.*
What year of the Emperor T'ungti is this? 今年同治幾年 *꜀King ꜁niĕng ꜁Tung Te$^2$ ʻkwi ꜁niĕng?*
What month is this? 啫月是幾月 *ʻChiă ngwok$_2$ se$^2$ ʻkwi ngwok$_2$?*
It is the tenth month, 是十月 *Se$^2$ sek$_2$ ngwok$_2$.*
What day of the month is it? 今旦砮壞 *꜀King tangʾ nioh$_2$ wai$^2$?* 今旦乜乇日子 *꜀King tangʾ miĕhˏ nóhˏ* (or *siĕʾ nóhˏ*) *nik$_2$ ʻchi?* 今旦是幾 *꜀King tangʾ se$^2$ ʻkwi?* 今旦面候 *꜀King tangʾ miĕng$^2$ au$^2$?*
To-day is which of the first ten days of the month? 今旦初幾 *꜀King tangʾ ꜀ch'ĕ ʻkwi?* 今旦幾吓 *꜀King tangʾ ʻkwi꜁a?*
What day of the month is it from the 11th to the 19th? 今旦十幾 *꜀King tangʾ sek$_2$ ʻkwi?*
What day of the month is it, from the 20th to the 30th? 今旦廿幾 *꜀King tangʾ nik$_2$ ʻkwi?*
The 1st, 10th, 11th, 20th, 21st, 初一初十十一二十廿一 *꜀Ch'ĕ ekˏ, ꜀ch'ĕ sek$_2$, sek$_2$ ekˏ, ne$^2$ sek$_2$, nik$_2$ ekˏ.*
Which is the intercalary month of this year? 今年閏幾月 *꜀King ꜁niĕng nong$^2$ ʻkwi ngwok$_2$?*
The 5th is the intercalary month, 閏五 *Nong$^2$ ngo$^2$.*
We on the other side (of the world) intercalate one day every four years, 儂家許邊四年隻閏一日 *꜁Nĕng ꜀ka ʻhü ꜀peng seʾ ꜁niĕng chiăhˏ nong$^2$ sioh$_2$ nik$_2$.*

In China how many months are reckoned in a year? 中國一年應幾個月日 ꜀Tüng Kwok꜅ sioh$_2$ ꜁niéng eng’ ‘kwi ‘a ngwok$_2$ nik$_2$?

Twelve months, 十二個月日 Sek$_2$ ne$^2$ ‘a ngwok$_2$ nik$_2$.

The long months have 30 days, 月大三十日 Ngwok$_2$ twai$^2$ ꜀sang sek$_2$ nik$_2$.

The short months have only 29 days, 月小郁廿九日 Ngwok$_2$ ‘sieu na$^2$ niék꜅ ‘kau nik$_2$.

A year has about 5 or 6 long months, 一年約略五六個月日大 Sioh$_2$ ꜁niéng yok꜅ liok$_2$ ngo$^2$ lëk$_2$ ‘a ngwok$_2$ nik$_2$ twai$^2$.

There are four seasons in a year—Spring, Summer, Autumn, and Winter, 一年應四季春夏秋冬 Sioh$_2$ ꜁niéng eng’ se’ kié’—꜀Ch‘ung, Ha$^2$, ꜀Ch‘iu, ꜀Tëng.

The 1st, 2nd, and 3d months are the Spring Season, 正二三三個月日是春季 ꜀Chiăng ne$^2$ ꜀sang, ꜀sang ‘a ngwok$_2$ nik$_2$ se$^2$ ꜀Ch‘ung kié’.

How many days are there in a week? 一禮拜應幾日 Sioh$_2$ ‘lá pai’ eng’ ‘kwi nik$_2$?

There are seven days in a week, 七日一禮拜 Ch‘ek꜅ nik$_2$ sioh$_2$ ‘lá pai’.

A week hence, 下一禮拜 A$^2$ sioh$_2$ ‘lá pai’.

A week ago, 先一禮拜 ꜀Seng sioh$_2$ ‘lá pai’.

What day is it to-day? 今旦拜幾 ꜀King tang’ pai’ ‘kwi?

To-day is Saturday, 今旦拜六 ꜀King tang’ pai’ lëk$_2$.

To-morrow will be Sunday, 明旦禮拜日 ꜁Ming tang’ ‘lá pai’ nik$_2$.

Day after to-morrow will be Monday, 後日是拜一 Au$^2$ nik$_2$ se$^2$ pai’ ek꜅.

We must not work on Sunday, 禮拜日伓通做代 ‘Lá pai’ nik$_2$ ng$^2$ ꜀t‘ëng chó’ tai$^2$.

In Winter the days are short and the nights long, 冬天日短暝長 ꜀Tëng ꜀t‘iëng nik$_2$ ‘toi ꜁mang ꜁tong.

There are 12 ꜁si ꜁sing (Chinese hours) in a day, 一日應十二時辰 Sioh$_2$ nik$_2$ eng’ sek$_2$ ne$^2$ ꜁si ꜁sing.

The ˛*Si* ˛*Sing* are as follows,—

| | | | | |
|---|---|---|---|---|
| 子 ʻ*Chü*, | 11 P. M.—1 A. M. | | 午 ʻ*Ngu*, | 11 A. M.—1 P. M. |
| 丑 ʻ*T'iu*, | 1 A. M.—3 ,, | | 未 *E*$^2$, | 1 P. M.—3 ,, |
| 寅 ˛*Ing*, | 3 ,, —5 ,, | | 申 ˓*Sing*, | 3 ,, —5 ,, |
| 卯 ʻ*Mau*, | 5 ,, —7 ,, | | 酉 ʻ*Iu*, | 5 ,, —7 ,, |
| 辰 ˛*Sing*, | 7 ,, —9 ,, | | 戌 *Sok*ˎ, | 7 ,, —9 ,, |
| 巳 *Sëü*$^2$, | 9 ,, –11 ,, | | 亥 *Hai*$^2$, | 9 ,, –11 ,, |

There are two hours in a ˛*si* ˛*sing*, 一時辰應二點鐘 *Sioh*$_2$ ˛*si* ˛*sing engʾ lang*$^2$ ʻ*teng* ˓*chüng*.

What time is it now? 只長幾點 ʻ*Chi* ˛*tong* ʻ*kwi* ʻ*teng?* 只長幾下 ʻ*Chi* ˛*tong* ʻ*kwi a*$^2$ *?*

Four o'clock, 四點 *Seʾ* ʻ*teng*.

It is 15 minutes to 4 o'clock, 四點差一刻 *Seʾ* ʻ*teng* ˓*ch'a sioh*$_2$ *k'aik*ˎ.

It is 10 minutes past 4 o'clock, 四點過十分 *Seʾ* ʻ*teng kwoʾ sek*$_2$ ˓*hung*.

Half past four, 四點半 *Seʾ* ʻ*teng pwangʾ*.

Has the clock struck four yet? 四點鐘響昧 *Seʾ* ʻ*teng* ˓*chüng* ʻ*hiong mwoi*$^2$ *?*

The clock has struck, 鐘響了 ˓*Chüng* ʻ*hiong* ʻ*lau*.

The clock has just struck, 鐘隻隻響 ˓*Chüng chiăh*ˎ *chiăh*ˎ ʻ*hiong*.

The clock struck a long time since, 鐘響野久 ˓*Chüng* ʻ*hiong* ʻ*yă* ˛*ong*.

Do not know whether the clock has struck or not—have not heard it. 鐘賣曉的響囉昧昧聽見 ˓*Chüng má*$^2$ ʻ*hieu tek*ˎ ʻ*hiong* ˛*ló mwoí*$^2$*—mwoí*$^2$ ˓*t'iăng kiĕngʾ*.

The clock has stopped and don't go, 自鳴鐘停去賣行 *Chëü*$^2$ ˛*ming* ˓*chüng* ˛*ting k'óʾ—má*$^2$ ˛*kiăng*.

Wind the clock, 自鳴鐘着開 *Chëü*$^2$ ˛*ming* ˓*chüng tioh*$_2$ ˓*k'wi*.

The days pass away very swiftly, 一日過一日盡快 *Sioh*$_2$ *nik*$_2$ *kwoʾ sioh*$_2$ *nik*$_2$ *cheng*$^2$ *k'áʾ* or 日子快過 *Nik*$_2$ ʻ*chi* ˓*kié kwoʾ*.

Is it daybreak yet? 天光囉昧 ꜀*T‘iĕng ꜀kwong ꜁ló mwoi$^2$?*

It is not daybreak yet, 天故昧光 ꜀*T‘iĕng ko*ꜗ *mwoi$^2$ ꜀kwong.*

The day has just dawned, 天寢寢光 ꜀*T‘iĕng ‘ch‘ing ‘ch‘ing* (or *chiăh*ꜗ *chiăh*ꜗ, or *‘p‘u ‘p‘u*) ꜀*kwong.*

It is not broad daylight yet, 天昧大光 ꜀*T‘iĕng mwoi$^2$ twai$^2$ ꜀kwong.*

The day has fully dawned, 天大光 ꜀*T‘iĕng twai$^2$ ꜀kwong.*

It is midday, 日頭中午 *Nik$_2$ ꜁t‘au ꜀tong ‘ngu.* 日頭罩 *Nik$_2$ ꜁t‘au tau*ꜗ.

It is almost sundown, 日頭剝落山 *Nik$_2$ ꜁t‘au pwoh*ꜗ *lóh$_2$ ꜀sang.*

It is nearly dark (almost night), 今剝暗囉 ꜀*Tang pwoh*ꜗ *ang*ꜗ ꜁*ló.*

How many watches are there in a night? 一晡務幾更 *Sioh$_2$ ꜀pwo o$^2$ ‘kwi ꜀kang?*

There are five watches, 務五更 *O$^2$ ngo$^2$ ꜀kang.*

The first watch, the 2nd watch, the 3d watch, the 4th watch, the 5th watch, 定更二更三更四更五更 *Tiăng$^2$ ꜀kang, ne$^2$ ꜀kang, ꜀sang ꜀kang, se*ꜗ *꜀kang, ngo$^2$ ꜀kang.*

Have come late, 來的遲 ꜁*Li tek*ꜗ ꜁*ti.*

Have come too early, 太早來 *K‘ak*ꜗ *‘cha ꜁li.*

Have (you) leisure to-day? 今旦務閒吓毛 ꜀*King tang*ꜗ *o$^2$ ꜁eng ‘a ꜁mó?*

Have no leisure to do it to-day, 今旦毛閒做 ꜀*King tang*ꜗ ꜁*mó ꜁eng chó*ꜗ.

Saw (him) a little while ago, 早先隻看見 *‘Cha ꜀seng (꜀leng) chiăh*ꜗ *k‘ang*ꜗ *kiĕng*ꜗ.

Has just this moment gone out, 只長隻出去 *‘Chi ꜁tong chiăh*ꜗ *ch‘ok*ꜗ *k‘ó*ꜗ.

Has just this moment come, 只古隻隻來 *‘Chi ‘u chiăh*ꜗ *chiăh*ꜗ ꜁*li.*

Wait a little, 頂一下 *‘Ting sioh$_2$ a$^2$* or 頂一刻古 *‘Ting sioh$_2$ k‘aik*ꜗ *(siăk*ꜗ*) ‘ku.*

He sat only a short time, 伊坐毛箬久 ꜀*I sói$^2$ ꜁mó nioh$_2$ ꜁ong.*

Wait till after a little while, 等噶偵囉慢 *‘Ting ꜁ha ‘tiăng ꜁ló maing$^2$.*

It will be done in a short time, 些微久儺完 *꜀Niă nói꜄ ꜁ong á² ꜁wong.*

It will only ache a moment (as in extracting a tooth), 鄉痛一久 *Na² t'iăng꜄ sioh꜅ ꜁ong.*

To work at a thing half a day, i. e., to be long in doing it, 做半日 *Chó꜄ pwang꜄ nik꜅* or 做半晒日 *Chó꜄ pwang꜄ sá² (꜀seng) nik꜅.*

Saw (it) on a former occasion, 前帮看見 *꜁Seng ꜀pong,* (or *꜁seng ꜂hŭ ꜀pong) k'ang꜄ kiĕng꜄.*

At that time was not aware of it, 許一久賣曉的 *꜂Hŭ sioh꜅ ꜁ong má² ꜂hieu tek꜆.*

(He) came on a former occasion, 許前到務來 *꜂Hŭ ꜁seng tó꜄ (nó꜄) o² ꜁li.*

Will go after dinner, 過晝就去 *Kwo꜄ tau꜄ cheu² k'ó꜄.*

To take dinner at noon, 日頭晝食飯 *Nik꜅ ꜁t'au tau꜄ siăh꜅ pwong².*

The season has passed (as for fruits), 過時 *Kwo꜄ ꜁si.*

## 25. THE WEATHER.

The sun shines very brightly to-day, 今旦日頭野大 *꜀King tang꜄ nik꜅ ꜁t'au ꜂yă twai².*

The weather is fair to-day, 今旦天晴 *꜀King tang꜄ ꜀t'iĕng ꜁sang.*

It is not so warm to-day as it was yesterday, 今旦故毛一暝許熱 *꜀King tang꜄ ko꜄ ꜁mó sioh꜅ ꜁mang ꜂hŭ yék꜅.*

It is warmer to-day than yesterday, 今旦故熱去一暝 *꜀King tang꜄ ko꜄ yék꜅ k'ó꜄ sioh꜅ ꜁mang.*

It is very warm in here—must go out and take the breeze, 只裡盡熱着出去涼風 *꜂Chi ꜂tié cheng² yék꜅ tioh꜅ c'hok꜆ k'ó꜄ ꜁liong ꜀hung.*

To-day there is a south wind and the weather is mild, 今旦南風天暖 *꜀King tang꜄ ꜁nang ꜀hung ꜀t'iĕng ꜂nong.*

The weather is fine for washing clothes, 赌天好洗衣裳 *꜂Chiă ꜀t'iĕng ꜂hó ꜂sá ꜀i ꜁siong.*

There is a drought, no rain falls, 天做旱毛湯雨 *꜀T'iĕng chó꜄ ang² ꜁mó taung² ꜂ü.*

The fields and gardens are all dried up, 田園都㪚去 *꜁Ch'eng ꜁hwong ꜀tu ꜀ta k'óʾ.*

There is no sun to-day, 今旦毛日頭 *꜀King tangʾ ꜁mó nik꜇ ꜁t'au.*

To-day the weather is dull and cloudy, 今旦陰烏天 *꜀King tangʾ ꜀eng ꜀u ꜀t'iéng.*

To-day it is sometimes sunny and sometimes cloudy, 今旦高低日 *꜀King tangʾ ꜀keng kiă$^2$ nik꜇.*

The sky is very dark—it is going to rain, 天野烏剢盪雨 *꜀T'iéng ʿyă ꜀u—pwoh꜆ taung$^2$ ʿü.*

Rainy weather, 盪雨天 *Taung$^2$ ʿü ꜀t'iéng.*

It rained yesterday and day before yesterday, 一暝昨日下雨 *Sioh꜇ ꜁mang sóh꜇ nik꜇ ha$^2$* (or *taung$^2$*) *ʿü.*

A silent rain, 病啞雨 *Pang$^2$ ʿa ʿü.*

A fine rain (more than mist), 雨仔 *ʿÜ ʿkiăng.*

The fog (or haze) is dense to-day, 今旦霿厚 *꜀King tangʾ ꜁mwo kau$^2$.*

The dew falls, 落露 *Lóh꜇ loʾ.*

There is a heavy dew, 露厚 *Loʾ kau$^2$* or 露大 *Loʾ twai$^2$.*

The weather is very cool to-day, 今旦野凉 *꜀King tangʾ ʿyă ꜁liong.*

The afternoons are cool, 下罩時𠏹凉 *A$^2$ tauʾ ꜁si á$^2$ ꜁liong.*

The weather is very cold to-day—it will snow, 今旦盡凊𠏹盪雪 *꜀King tangʾ cheng$^2$ ch'engʾ—á$^2$ taung$^2$ siok꜆.*

Frost fell last night, 一暝晡落霜 *Sioh꜇ ꜁mang ꜀pwo lóh꜇ ꜀song.*

There is no wind at all, 一滴風都毛 *Sioh꜇ tek꜆ ꜀hung ꜀tu ꜁mó.*

The breeze has just sprung up, 只長起風 *ʿChi ꜁tong ʿk'i ꜀hung.*

The wind blows hard, 風透 *꜀Hung t'auʾ.*

Do not go into the wind, 伓通吹風 *Ng$^2$ ꜀t'ĕng ꜀ch'wi ꜀hung.*

Do not sit in the wind, 伓通落風頭坐 *Ng$^2$ ꜀t'ĕng lóh꜇ ꜀hung ꜁t'au sói$^2$.*

The wind blows so hard, (you) must put on (more) clothing, 風只透着穿衣裳 *꜀Hung ʿchi t'auʾ tioh꜇ sëüng$^2$ ꜀i ꜁siong.*

There is going to be a typhoon, 剢做風颱 *Pwoh꜆ chóʾ ꜀hung ꜀t'ai.*

## 26. A CONFLAGRATION.

There was a fire last night, 一暝晡火燒厝 Sioh$_2$ ꜁mang ꜀pwo ꜂hwi ꜀sieu ch'io꜃.

The fire was very large, 燒盡大吓 ꜀Sieu cheng$^2$ twai$^2$ ꜁a.

Had you heard of it? 伓長囉昧 Paik꜅ ꜁tiong ꜁ló mwoi$^2$?

I had heard of it, 伓長了 Paik꜅ ꜁tiong ꜂lau.

I had not heard of it, 昧伓長 Mwoi$^2$ paik꜅ ꜁tiong.

How many buildings were burnt? 燒若壞間吓 ꜀Sieu nioh$_2$ wai$^2$ ꜀kang ꜁a?

I have heard it said some five or six hundred, 聽伊講務五六百間 ꜀T'iăng ꜀i ꜂kong o$^2$ ngo$^2$ lëk$_2$ pah꜅ ꜀kang.

Four or five persons were burnt to death, 伙燒死四五隻 ꜁Nëng ꜀sieu ꜂si se꜃ ngo$^2$ chiăh꜅.

This is very lamentable! 儕盡去凄慘吓 ꜁Chuí cheng$^2$ k'ó꜃ ꜀ch'á ꜂ch'ang ꜁a!

At whose place did the fire commence? 俤伙裡起火 Tié$^2$ ꜁nëng ꜂tié ꜂k'i ꜂hwi?

I have heard it said the fire commenced at a dye-shop, 聽伊講是染店禮起火 ꜀T'iăng ꜀i ꜂kong se$^2$ ꜂niéng taing꜃ ꜂lá ꜂k'i ꜂hwi.

Some say it was done by an incendiary, 也務講是伙放火 Yă$^2$ o$^2$ ꜂kong se$^2$ ꜁nëng pong꜃ ꜂hwi.

At what time did it commence burning? 乜毛時候燒起 Miéh꜅ nóh꜅ ꜁si haiu$^2$ ꜀sieu ꜂k'i?

It was the 2d watch when it commenced burning, 務二更燒起 O$^2$ ne$^2$ ꜀kang ꜀sieu ꜂k'i.

At daylight it was still burning, 天光故禮燒 ꜀T'iéng ꜀kwong ko꜃ ꜂lá ꜀sieu.

Has the fire diminished now? 只長火緩去囉叭 ꜂Chi ꜁tong ꜂hwi nëüng$^2$ k'ó꜃ ꜁ló ꜀pá?

The fire has gone down now, 只長火落地了 ꜂Chi ꜁tong ꜂hwi lóh$_2$ te$^2$ ꜂lau.

Now the fire is out, 只長火煞去 ꜂Chi ꜁tong ꜂hwi sak꜅ k'ó꜃.

MAN. 12.

## 27. PROMISCUOUS PHRASES.

Supposed (he) was not in, 漢的毛着禮 *Hang' tek, ˏmó tioh₂ ˋlá.*

Take this and paste it on the wall, 嚽掏去貼墙禮 *ˏChuí ˏtó k'ó' t'aik, ˏch'iong ˋlá.*

What are (you) laughing at? 笑世毛 *Ch'ieu' sié' nóh,?*

The longer (time) the better, 越久越好 *Wok₂ ˏong wok₂ ˋhó.*

The opposite shop, 對面店 *Tói' meng' taing'.*

Opposite the shop, 店對面 *Taing' tói' meng'.*

Struck by thunder, 乞雷公拍 *K'ëük, ˏlai ˏkung p'ah,* or 乞雷拍 *K'ëük, ˏloi p'ah,.*

Went out just now, 只長出門 *ˋChi ˏtong ch'ok, ˏmwong.*

Cannot overtake him, 賣逐的着 *Má² tük₂ tek, tioh₂* or 逐賣着 *Tük₂ má² tioh₂.*

Won't listen, 伓肯聽 *Ng². ˋk'ing ˏt'iăng,* or 伓聽 *Ng² ˏt'iăng.*

Did not hear, Can not hear, 伓聽見 *Ng² ˏt'iăng kiéng'.*

Will it answer? 僫駛的賣 *Á² ˋsai tek, má²?* 僫賣駛的 *Á² má² ˋsai tek,?*

Either (or any) way will do, 都駛的 *ˏTu ˋsai tek,.*

This is what may indeed be called fine! 嚽隻叫囉俊 *ˏChuí chiăh, kieu' ˋló chong'!*

Truly beautiful, 真作佳 *ˏChing chauk, ˏka.*

Fortunately saw it, 做化看見 *Chó' hwa' k'ang' kiéng'.*

*Such* a way! 啫欵勢 *ˋChiă ˋk'wang sié'!*

Will do it presently, 回頭做 *ˏHuí ˏt'au chó'.*

Why did he do so? (How should I) know! 伊將其將換做曉的 *ˏI ˏchiong ˏki ˏchiong wang² chó'? ˋHieu tek,!*

Is not in, Is not here (or there), 毛着禮 *ˏMó tioh₂ ˋlá.*

Have not seen it for a very long time, 斷真久毛看見 *Taung² ˏching ˏong ˏmó k'ang' kiéng'.*

To tie in a hard knot, 拍結纇 *P'ah, kiék, ˏloi.*

To stand aside, Stand aside! 僻邊 P'iăh꜆ ꜀piĕng.

Go and inform him, 去通知伊 K'ó꜄ ꜀t'ung ꜀ti ꜀i.

Have you met this man before? 喏伙務會着昧 ꜂Chiă ꜁nĕng o$^2$ hwoi$^2$ tioh$_2$ mwoi$^2$?

Have met him before, 會着了 Hwoi$^2$ tioh$_2$ ꜂lau.

Are the things ready? 乇便囉昧 Nóh꜆ piĕng$^2$ ꜁lô mwoi$^2$?

Improper, inconvenient, 伓便 Ng$^2$ piĕng$^2$.

Inconvenient, unhandy, 伓便急 Ng$^2$ piĕng$^2$ kek꜆.

Very uncertain, 大乇定着 Twai$^2$ ꜁mô tiăng$^2$ tioh$_2$.

There is an odd one (in number), 奇一隻 ꜀K'iă sioh$_2$ chiăh꜆.

To beat in two separate portions (as whites and yolks of eggs), 二下拍 Lang$^2$ a$^2$ p'ah꜆.

To beat two (i. e. a few) strokes, 拍二下 P'ah꜆ lang$^2$ a$^2$.

One to each person, 一伙一隻 Sioh$_2$ ꜁nĕng sioh$_2$ chiăh꜆.

Every body has something to say (about it), 一伙一句 Sioh$_2$ ꜁nĕng sioh$_2$ kwo꜄.

Each locality has its own customs or usages, 一位一位例 Sioh$_2$ oi$^2$ sioh$_2$ oi$^2$ liê$^2$.

Language unlike and dress different, 話語不同穿戴各樣 Wa$^2$ ꜂ngü pok꜆ ꜁tung sëüng$^2$ tai꜄ kauk꜆ yong$^2$.

Has not the power to control or decide it, 賣主的意 má$^2$ ꜂chio tek꜆ e꜄.

No alternative—no other way, 乇法的 ꜁Mó hwak꜆ tek꜆.

Take this letter to Ch'ong Seng and call at Kwang Ing Chang as you return, 批掏去倉前轉來躋觀音井 ꜀P'iĕ ꜁tó k'ó꜄ ꜀Ch'ong ꜁Seng, ꜂tiong ꜁li ꜂wa ꜀Kwang ꜀Ing ꜂Chang.

Go first to Twai Liăng and then to Ch'ong Seng, 先去大嶺後去倉前 ꜀Seng k'ó꜄ Twai$^2$ ꜂Liăng haiu$^2$ k'ó꜄ ꜀Ch'ong ꜁Seng.

Both ends, 兩頭尾 ꜂Liong ꜁t'au ꜂mwi.

To turn end for end, 拍轉頭 P'ah꜆ ꜂tiong ꜁t'au, 俥轉頭 ꜀Ch'iă ꜂tiong ꜁t'au.

To turn the other side up or about, 板轉爿 ꜂Peng ꜂tiong ꜁peng.

To turn the inside out, 板轉裏 ꜂Peng ꜂tiong ꜂li.

Done! finished! 完囉 ꜁Wong ꜁ló!

## 28. FORMS OF PRAYER.

The prayers introduced here, though in a connected form, will be found, when analyzed, to consist of many set phrases in common use among the native christians. Their semi-classical character is unavoidable owing to the poverty of the colloquial as regards religious terms. It should be considered that christian literature is of comparatively recent growth in Foochow, and that forms of expression which are now used only among certain classes must in time become universal. Other *moral and religious terms* may be found *as definitions* in the English and Chinese vocabulary at the close of the Manual.

### THE LORD'S PRAYER.

Our Heavenly Father in heaven, 奴各伙其天父着天禮
*꜁Nu kauk꜇ ꜁nëng ꜁ki ꜀T'iëng Ho$^2$ tioh$_2$ ꜀t'iëng ʿlá,*

We desire Thy name to be hallowed, 願汝其名成聖 *Ngwong$^2$ ʿnü ꜁ki ꜁miăng ꜁siăng sengʾ.*

We desire Thy kingdom immediately to flourish, 願汝其國就徦興旺 *Ngwong$^2$ ʿnü ꜁ki kwok꜇ cheu$^2$ á$^2$ ꜀hing wong$^2$.*

We desire Thy will to prevail universally 願汝其旨意通行
*Ngwong$^2$ ʿnü ꜁ki ʿchi eʾ ꜀t'ung ꜁heng*

Upon earth the same as in heaven, 著地共著天禮一樣
*Tioh$_2$ te$^2$ kaëng$^2$ tioh$_2$ ꜀t'iëng ʿlá sioh$_2$ yong$^2$.*

Our daily food we pray Thee to grant us to-day, 日用其糧草求汝今旦賜伙家 *Nik$_2$ ëüng$^2$ ꜁ki ꜁liong ʿch'ó ꜁kiu ʿnü ꜀king tangʾ sëüʾ ꜁nëng ꜀ka.*

We forgive others who sin against us, 伙家赦得罪伙家其伙 *꜁Nëng ꜀ka siăʾ taik꜇ chói$^2$ ꜁nëng ꜀ka ꜁ki ꜁nëng,*

We pray Thee also to forgive our sins, 求汝也赦伙家其罪 *꜁Kiu ʿnü yă$^2$ siăʾ ꜁nëng ꜀ka ꜁ki chói$^2$.*

Do not cause us to meet with temptation, 莫駛伙家遇著誘惑 *Móh$_2$ ʿsai ꜁nëng ꜀ka ngëü$^2$ tioh$_2$ ʿiu hëk$_2$,*

But deliver us that we may escape from evil, 著救伙家脫離兇惡 *Tioh$_2$ keuʾ ꜁nëng ꜀ka t'wak꜇ lié$^2$ ꜀hüng auk꜇:*

For the kingdom, power, and glory, 因國共權柄榮耀
*꜀Ing kwok꜇, kaëng$^2$ ꜁kwong pangʾ, ꜁ing yeu$^2$,*

All belong to Thee, 都屬著汝 *꜀Tu sük$_2$ tioh$_2$ ʿnü.*

Unto myriads of ages, 至萬萬世 *Kauʾ wang$^2$ wang$^2$ sieʾ*.

This is what our hearts truly desire, 實心所願 *Sik$_2$ ˛sing ʿsu ngwong$^2$*.

The following prayers *in their Chinese form* were originally furnished by a native preacher; they appear here with a few slight alterations.

### Prayer for the Sabbath.

O Lord God of the Sabbath! 安息日其主上帝吓 *˛Ang sekʾ nik$_2$ ˛ki ʿChio Siong$^2$ Táʾ ˛a!*

I, a sinner, bow before thy throne, 罪亻人跪汝臺前 *Chói$^2$ ˛nĕng koi$^2$ ʿnü ˛tai ˛seng.*

I render thanks to God for preserving me in health and prosperity 感謝上帝保護奴平安 *ʿKang siă$^2$ Siong$^2$ Táʾ ˛pó ho$^2$ ˛nu ˛ping ˛ang*

Through another week, 伋過一禮拜 *Po$^2$ kwoʾ sioh$_2$ ʿlá paiʾ*.

On this day I can again observe the Sabbath, 至今旦䚋再守啫安息日 *Kauʾ ˛king tangʾ á$^2$ chaiʾ ʿsiu ʿchiă ˛ang sekʾ nik$_2$*,

And remember God's 記念上帝 *Keʾ niéng$^2$ Siong$^2$ Táʾ*

Great work of creation and great grace of salvation and redemption, 造化大功連救世贖罪大恩 *Chó$^2$ hwaʾ twai$^2$ ˛kung ˛liéng keuʾ sieʾ sük$_2$ chói$^2$ twai$^2$ ˛ong.*

I have been dull and ignorant heretofore, 奴亻人一向蒙昧 *˛Nu ˛nĕng ekʾ hiongʾ ˛mang mwoi$^2$*,

And have not known God nor obeyed the heavenly doctrine, 伓八上帝毛憑天道 *Ng$^2$ paikʾ Siong$^2$ Táʾ ˛mó ˛ping ˛t'iéng tó$^2$*.

And not only have I violated the sabbath, 不止郁犯啫安息日 *Pokʾ ʿchi na$^2$ hwang$^2$ ʿchiă ˛ang sekʾ nik$_2$*

This particular command, 只一條其誡 *ʿChi sioh$_2$ ˛teu ˛ki kaiʾ*,

But my sins of every kind are numberless, 件件其罪講也賣盡 *Yong$^2$ yong$^2$ ˛ki chói$^2$ ʿkong yă$^2$ má$^2$ cheng$^2$*.

And now I pray God, 伶求上帝 *˛Tang ˛kiu Siong$^2$ Táʾ*.

To regard the Savior's merits, 念救主其功勞 *Niéng$^2$ Keuʾ ʿChio ˛ki ˛kung ˛ló,*

Forgive all my sins, 赦奴諸般其罪 *Siă꜄ ꜀nu ꜀chü ꜀pwang ꜀ki chói꜅,*

And help me on this day, 助奴落只一日 *Chaë꜅ ꜀nu lóh꜇ ꜂chi sioh꜇ nik꜇,*

Not only to rest from outward labor, 不止那外面工夫停止 *Pok꜆ ꜂chi na꜅ ngwoi꜅ miéng꜅ ꜀këng ꜀hu ꜀ting ꜂chi,*

But also cause that my heart 也駛奴心裏 *Yă꜅ ꜂sai ꜀nu ꜀sing ꜂tié*

May be troubled by no worldly anxieties, 都毛俗慮吵擾 *꜀Tu ꜀mó sük꜇ lëü꜅ ꜂ch'au ꜂yeu;*

That so I may with my whole heart and will serve God, 㑚盡心盡意奉事上帝 *Á꜅ cheng꜅ ꜀sing cheng꜅ e꜄ hong꜅ sëü꜅ Siong꜅ Tá꜄,*

Diligently study the heavenly doctrine, 勤緊學啫天道 *꜀K'üng ꜂king óh꜇ ꜂chiă ꜀t'iëng tó꜅,*

And examine my feelings, 連查察心緒 *꜀Liéng ꜀cha ch'ak꜆ ꜀sing sëü꜅;*

Pray with a devout heart, 虔心祈禱 *꜀Kiëng ꜀sing ꜀ki ꜂tó,*

And not profitlessly pass this holy day, 毛空過啫聖日 *꜀Mó ꜀k'ëng kwo꜄ ꜂chiă seng꜄ nik꜇.*

Also grant that the doctrine which I hear 仅賜奴所聽其道理 *Po꜅ sëü꜄ ꜀nu ꜂su ꜀t'iăng ꜀ki tó꜅ ꜂li*

I may understand more clearly (than heretofore), 㑚更明白會悟 *Á꜅ kaing꜄ ꜀ming pek꜇ hwoi꜅ ngwo꜅,*

And treasure it in my heart 存落心裏禮 *꜀Chong lóh꜇ ꜀sing ꜂tié ꜂lá*

To be food for my soul, 做養靈魂其糧草 *Chó꜄ ꜂yong ꜀ling ꜀hung ꜀ki ꜀liong ꜂ch'ó;*

And that I may know how to serve God, 㑚曉的服事上帝 *Á꜅ ꜂hieu tek꜆ huk꜇ sëü꜅ Siong꜅ Tá꜄,*

Believe in and submit to Jesus, 信服耶穌 *Seng꜄ huk꜇ ꜀Yă ꜀Su,*

And obtain inexhaustible happiness, 得無窮盡其福 *Taik꜆ ꜀u ꜀küng cheng꜅ ꜀ki hok꜆.*

Moreover, I pray God on this day 仅求上帝落只一日 *Po꜅ ꜀kiu Siong꜅ Tá꜄ lóh꜇ ꜂chi sioh꜇ nik꜇*

Also to bestow grace on preachers of the word, 也施恩落傳道其𠊎 *Yă꜅ ꜀sié ꜀ong lóh꜇ ꜀tiong tó꜅ ꜀ki ꜀nëng.*

Wherever they may be, 毛論着冬那 ꜁*Mó laung*$^2$ *tioh*꜇ ꜀*tĕng* ꜂*nē;*

That they may all have the Holy Spirit's assistance, 都得聖神幇助 ꜀*Tu taik*꜆ *Seng*꜄ ꜁*Sing* ꜀*pong chaē*$^2$,

So that they may explain the truth, 𣍐解說眞理 *Á*$^2$ ꜂*ká siok*꜆ ꜀*ching* ꜂*li*,

Reform people by their exhortations, and thus cause the doctrines they preach 勸化世人駛所傳其道 *K'wong*꜄ *hwa*꜄ *sié*꜄ ꜁*ing*, ꜂*sai* ꜂*su* ꜁*tiong* ꜁*ki tó*$^2$

To be like good seed sown in fertile ground, 就像好種落肥地 *Cheu*$^2$ *ch'iong*$^2$ ꜂*hó* ꜂*chŭng lóh*꜇ ꜁*pui te*$^2$,

All bringing forth fruit, 都𣍐結實 ꜀*Tu á*$^2$ *kiék*꜆ *sik*꜇.

Also bestow thy grace on believers, 也施恩乞信道其伙 *Yă*$^2$ ꜀*sié* ꜀*ong k'ĕŭk*꜆ *seng*꜄ *tó*$^2$ ꜁*ki* ꜁*nĕng*,

That on this day 落只一日 *Lóh*꜇ ꜂*chi sioh*꜇ *nik*꜇

They may obtain thy blessing more (than ever before), 更得汝其祝福 *Kaing*꜄ *taik*꜆ ꜂*nü* ꜁*ki chĕük*꜆ *hok*꜆,

So that their conduct may be more perfect, 德行更好 *Taik*꜆ *haing*$^2$ *kaing*꜄ ꜂*hó*,

And they be the light of the world, 𣍐做世間伙其光 *Á*$^2$ *chó*꜄ *sié*꜄ ꜀*kang* ꜁*nĕng* ꜁*ki* ꜀*kwong*,

And glorify God, 榮耀上帝 ꜁*Ing yeu*$^2$ *Siong*$^2$ *Tá*꜄.

Also may God bestow mercy upon the Chinese, 㑚求上帝施恩落中國伙 *Po*$^2$ ꜁*kiu Siong*$^2$ *Tá*꜄ ꜀*sié* ꜀*ong lóh*꜇ ꜀*Tŭng Kwok*꜆ ꜁*nĕng*,

Whether old or young, high or low, 毛論老幼高低 ꜁*Mó laung*$^2$ ꜂*ló eu*꜄, ꜀*kó* ꜀*tá*,

That they may soon together obey 早早𣍐齊憑 ꜂*Cha* ꜂*cha á*$^2$ ꜁*chá* ꜁*ping*

God's will, 上帝其旨意 *Siong*$^2$ *Tá*꜄ ꜁*ki* ꜂*chi e*꜄,

And together obey the command to keep the Sabbath, 齊守安息日其誡命 ꜁*Chá* ꜂*siu* ꜀*ang sek*꜆ *nik*꜇ ꜁*ki kai*꜄ *meng*$^2$,

Believe in and follow Jesus, 信從耶穌 *Seng*꜄ ꜁*chŭng* ꜁*Yă* ꜀*Su*,

And after death together enjoy the happiness of Heaven, 死後齊享天堂其福氣 ꜂*Si hau*$^2$ ꜁*chá* ꜂*hiong* ꜀*t'iĕng* ꜁*tong* ꜁*ki hok*꜆ *k'e*꜄.

I, a sinner, am originally very vile, 奴罪仈本來是極賤 *꜁Nu chói$^2$ ꜁nëng ʻpwong ꜁lai se$^2$ kik$_2$ chiéng$^2$,*

And now, resting wholly on the Savior's merit, 伶全靠救主其功勞 *꜀Tang ꜁chiong k'óʾ Keuʾ ʻChio ꜁ki ꜀kung ꜁ló,*

I earnestly pray (unto Thee) O God, 懇求上帝 *ʻK'ong ꜁kiu Siong$^2$ Táʾ,*

Hoping that Thou wilt hear my prayer, 望汝聽奴祈禱 *Wong$^2$ ʻnü ꜀t'iăng ꜁nu ꜁ki ʻtó.*

This is what my heart truly desires, 實心所願 *Sik$_2$ ꜀sing ʻsu ngwong$^2$.*

## MORNING PRAYER.

Jehovah God, 耶和華上帝 *꜁Yă ꜁Hwo ꜁Hwa Siong$^2$ Táʾ,*

Most exalted, most holy Lord, 是至尊至聖其主宰 *Se$^2$ cheʾ ꜀chong, cheʾ sengʾ ꜁ki ʻChio ʻChai,*

I, a sinner, have received Thy care 罪仈蒙汝照顧 *Chói$^2$ ꜁nëng ꜁mung ʻnü chieuʾ koʾ*

During another night, 仅過一晡 *Po$^2$ kwoʾ sioh$_2$ ꜀pwo,*

And have prosperity both in body and soul, 身心都得平安 *꜀Sing ꜀sing ꜀tu taik$_2$ ꜁ping ꜀ang.*

I now bow before God's throne, 伶跪落上帝臺前 *꜀Tang koi$^2$ lóh$_2$ Siong$^2$ Táʾ ꜁tai ꜁seng,*

And thank Thee for Thy favor, 感謝汝其恩惠 *ʻKang siă$^2$ ʻnü ꜁ki ꜀ong hié$^2$.*

I also pray Thee to grant that through this day 仅求汝賜奴今旦一日 *Po$^2$ ꜁kiu ʻnü sëüʾ ꜁nu ꜀king tangʾ sioh$_2$ nik$_2$*

What I think, do, and say, 所想所做所講 *ʻSu ʻsiong, ʻsu chóʾ, ʻsu ʻkong,*

May all accord with thy truth, 都合汝其眞理 *꜀Tu hak$_2$ ʻnü ꜁ki ꜀ching ʻli;*

And that I may not meet with temptation and evil, 毛遇着誘惑呆惡其代 *꜁Mó p'aung$^2$ tioh$_2$ ʻiu hëk$_2$ ꜁ngai aukʾ ꜁ki tai$^2$.*

My former sins are exceedingly many, 奴從前罪惡儷的佷 *꜁Nu ꜁chüng ꜁chieng chói$^2$ aukʾ sá$^2$ tekʾ ʻheng,*

And I pray God 求上帝 *꜁Kiu Siong$^2$ Táʾ*

To have regard to the Savior's merits and forgive me, 念救主其功勞赦奴 *Niéng² Keu' ʻChio ꜀ki ꜀kung ꜀ló siă' ꜀nu.*

The food that is needful for me to-day 奴今旦所駛用其糧草 *꜀Nu ꜀king tang' ʻsu ʻsai ëüng² ꜀ki ꜀liong ʻch'ó*

I also pray Thee to grant me, 也求汝賜奴 *Yă² ꜀kiu ʻnü sëü' ꜀nu.*

Moreover, I pray God to send down the Holy Spirit 伋求上帝降聖神 *Po² ꜀kiu Siong² Tá' kaung' Seng' ꜀Sing*

To renew my heart, 感化奴心 *ʻKang hwa' ꜀nu ꜀sing,*

To banish wicked thoughts, 除去呆惡其念頭 *꜀Tü k'ó' ꜀ngai auk꜀ ꜀ki niéng² ꜀t'au,*

And cause a good heart to spring up, 駛啫善心發起 *ʻSai ʻchiă siéng² ꜀sing hwak꜀ ʻk'i,*

So that I may bear the fruits of the Spirit, 倸結聖神其菓子 *Á² kiék꜀ Seng' ꜀Sing ꜀ki ʻkwí ʻchi,*

And glorify God, 歸榮耀上帝 *꜀Kwi ꜀ing yeu² Siong² Tá'.*

Also take care of my parents, brothers, sisters, 連照顧奴罷奶兄弟姊妹 *꜀Liéng chieu' ko' ꜀nu pa² ʻná, ꜀hiăng tié², ʻchiă mwoi',*

Relatives and friends, 共親朋戚友 *Kaëng² ꜀ch'ing ꜀peng ch'ek꜀ ʻiu,*

That they may soon reject the wrong and return to the right, 早早棄邪歸正 *ʻCha ʻcha k'e' ꜀siă ꜀kwi chiăng',*

And believe and obey the gospel, 信從福音 *Seng' ꜀chüng hok꜀ ꜀ing,*

So that during this life we may together have prosperity, 生前齊得平安 *꜀Seng ꜀chiéng ꜀chá taik꜀ ꜀ping ꜀ang,*

And after death together enjoy eternal happiness, 死後齊享永福 *ʻSi haiu² ꜀chá ʻhiong ʻing hok꜀.*

I also pray God 伋求上帝 *Po² ꜀kiu Siong² Tá'*

To bestow grace upon churches everywhere, 施恩落各處其教會 *꜀Sié ꜀ong lóh꜀ kauk꜀ ch'ëü' ꜀ki kau' hwoi²,*

And grant that the conduct of all may be perfect, 賜仈仈德行純全 *Sëü' ꜀nëng ꜀nëng taik꜀ haing² ꜀sung ꜀chiong,*

That they may affectionately regard and love each other 相親相愛 *꜀Song ꜀ch'ing ꜀song t'iăng'*

Like members of the same household, 像做一厝其伙一樣
*Ch'iong꜅ chó꜃ sioh꜇ ch'io꜃ ꜁ki ꜁nĕng sioh꜇ yong꜅.*

Thus praying, 將換祈禱 *꜀Chiong wang꜅ ꜁ki ꜂tó,*

I trust in the Savior's merits, 是託救主其功勞 *Se꜅ t'auk꜆ Keu꜃ ꜂Chio ꜁ki ꜀kung ꜁ló.*

This is what my heart truly desires, 實心所願 *Sik꜇ ꜀sing ꜂su ngwong꜅.*

Evening prayer.

Thanks be to the All-wise, All-powerful, Heavenly Father 感謝全智全能其天父 *꜂Kang siă꜅ ꜁chiong te꜃, ꜁chiong ꜁neng ꜁ki ꜀T'iéng Ho꜅*

That he has again preserved me through another day, 伋保護奴再過一日 *Po꜅ ꜀pó ho꜅ ꜁nu chai꜃ kwo꜃ sioh꜇ nik꜇,*

And that I have had clothing, food, and prosperity, 得啫衣食平安 *Taik꜆ ꜂chiă ꜀i sik꜇ ꜁ping ꜀ang,*

And have not met with calamity, or sickness and pain, 毛遇着災害病痛 *꜁Mó p'aung꜅ tioh꜇ ꜀chai hai꜅ pang꜅ t'iăng꜃.*

God's favor is very great, 上帝其恩大的極 *Siong꜅ Tá꜃ ꜁ki ꜀ong twai꜅ tek꜆ kik꜇;*

Truly it is higher than the heavens, 眞眞比天故高 *꜀Ching ꜀ching ꜂pi ꜀t'iéng ko꜃ ꜀keng,*

And deeper than the sea, 比海故深 *꜂Pi ꜂hai ko꜃ ꜀ch'ing.*

I, a sinful man, receive this deep (great) favor, 罪伙受啫深恩 *Chói꜅ ꜁nĕng seu꜅ ꜂chiă ꜀ch'ing ꜀ong,*

And have nothing to give in return, 毛乇報答 *꜁Mó nóh꜆ pó꜃ tak꜆.*

But I earnestly pray the Heavenly Father 惟獨切切求天父 *꜁Mi tuk꜇ ch'iék꜆ ch'iék꜆ ꜁kiu ꜀T'iéng Ho꜅*

To help me through my whole life with a warm heart to do good, 助奴一生熱心行善 *Chaē꜅ ꜁nu ek꜆ ꜀seng yék꜇ ꜀sing ꜁heng siéng꜅,*

And thus glorify my Heavenly Father, God, 歸榮耀天父上帝 *꜀Kwi ꜁ing yeu꜅ ꜀T'iéng Ho꜅ Siong꜅ Tá꜃.*

Examining, for the day, my heart, 奴今旦中間查察心裏 *꜁Nu ꜀king tang꜃ ꜀tüng ꜀kang ꜀cha ch'ak꜆ ꜀sing ꜂tié,*

Together with my words and actions, 共所講所做其代
Kaëng$^2$ ʻsu ʻkong ʻsu chóʼ ꜁ki tai$^2$,

I have many errors 務俩差錯 O$^2$ sá$^2$ ꜀chʻa chʻauk꜆.

In my service of God and treatment of men 奉事上帝看待衆𠆧 Hong$^2$ sëü$^2$ Siong$^2$ Táʼ kʻangʼ tai$^2$ chëüngʼ ꜁nëng

There have been many deficiencies, 務俩欠缺 O$^2$ sá$^2$ kʻiëngʼ kʻwok꜆.

I pray Thee to regard Jesus' merits, 求汝着念耶穌其功勞 ꜁Kiu ʻnü tioh$_2$ niëng$^2$ ꜁Yă ꜀Su ꜁ki ꜀kung ꜁ló,

And pardon my sins, 赦奴罪愆 Siăʼ ꜁nu chói$^2$ ꜀kʻiëng.

If it please Thee grant me this night 合汝旨意賜奴今晡 Hak$_2$ ʻnü ʻchi eʼ sëüʼ ꜁nu ꜀king ꜀pwo

Again to have peaceful sleep, 再得平安好困 Chaiʼ taik꜆ ꜁ping ꜀ang ʻhó kʻaungʼ,

And let me not fall into temptation and sin, 毛遇着誘惑罪惡其代 ꜁Mó pʻaung$^2$ tioh$_2$ ʻiu hëk$_2$ chói$^2$ auk꜆ ꜁ki tai$^2$.

Strengthen me in mind and body so that to-morrow when I rise 補奴心力至明旦𧼮起 ʻPwo ꜁nu ꜀sing lik$_2$ kauʼ ꜁ming tangʼ kok꜆ ʻkʻi

I may the better with my whole heart serve God, 更解盡心服事上帝 Kaingʼ á$^2$ cheng$^2$ ꜀sing huk$_2$ sëü$^2$ Siong$^2$ Táʼ,

And keep Thy commands, 守汝誡命 ʻSiu ʻnü kaiʼ meng$^2$.

If I should suddenly die, 那務伓存意過世 Na$^2$ o$^2$ ng$^2$ ꜁chong eʼ kwoʼ siéʼ,

I pray Thee to consider the Savior's merits, 求汝念救主其功勞 ꜁Kiu ʻnü niëng$^2$ Keuʼ ʻChio ꜁ki ꜀kung ꜁ló,

Pardon my sins, and save my soul, 赦奴其罪救奴其靈魂 Siăʼ ꜁nu ꜁ki chói$^2$, keuʼ ꜁nu ꜁ki ꜁ling ꜁hung.

Moreover I pray God 伋求上帝 Po$^2$ ꜁kiu Siong$^2$ Táʼ

Also to protect those composing the church, 也保護會中其𠆧 Yă$^2$ ꜀pó hó$^2$ hwoi$^2$ ꜀tüng ꜁ki ꜁nëng,

Whether pastors, ministers, or private members, 毛論牧師教士會友 ꜁Mó laung$^2$ muk$_2$ ꜀sü, kauʼ sëü$^2$ hwoi$^2$ ʻiu,

And grant that they and their households 賜伊連一厝𠆧 Sëüʼ ꜀i ꜁liéng sioh$_2$ chʻioʼ ꜁nëng

May also all have prosperity, 也都得平安 Yă$^2$ ꜀tu taik꜆ ꜁ping ꜀ang.

I, a sinful man, 奴罪仈 ꜀Nu chói$^2$ ꜀nĕng

Originally (of my self) dare not approach Thee and pray, 本來毛敢近前祈禱 ‘Pwong ꜀lai ꜀mó ‘kang kĕüng$^2$ ꜀seng ꜀ki ‘tó;

And now I wholly rest on the Savior's merits, 伶全藉救主其功勞 ꜀Tang ꜀chiong chiă$^2$ Keu’ ‘Chio ꜀ki ꜀kung ꜀ló,

Desiring the Heavenly Father graciously to grant (my requests), 望天父恩准 Wong$^2$ ꜀T‘iĕng Ho$^2$ ꜀ong ‘chung.

This is what my heart truly desires, 寔心所願 Sik꜁ ꜀sing ‘su ngwong$^2$.

GRACE AT MEALS.

Thanks to (Thee), Heavenly Father, for granting so many things 感謝天父賜只俩毛 ‘Kang siă$^2$ ꜀T‘iĕng Ho$^2$ sëü’ ‘chi sá$^2$ nóh꜁

To nourish my body, 養奴肉體 ‘Yong ꜀nu nŭk꜁ ‘t‘á.

I, a sinful man, receive this great favor, 罪仈受啫鴻恩 Chói$^2$ ꜀nĕng seu$^2$ ‘chiă ꜀hung ꜀ong,

And have nothing to give in return, 毛毛報答 ꜀Mó nóh꜁ pó’ tak꜁,

But only at each meal with a true heart I return thanks, 惟有頓頓都務寔心感謝 ꜀Mi ‘iu taung’ taung’ ꜀tu o$^2$ sik꜁ ꜀sing ‘kang siă$^2$.

Now I moreover pray the Heavenly Father to grant that the truth 伶再求天父賜眞理 ꜀Tang chai’ ꜀kiu ꜀T‘iĕng Ho$^2$ sëü’ ꜀ching ‘li

May nourish my soul, 養奴靈魂 ‘Yong ꜀nu ꜀ling ꜀hung,

And (wilt Thou) cause me day and night to ponder it 駛奴日暝思慕 ‘Sai ꜀nu nik꜁ ꜀mang ꜀sü mwo$^2$

As one who is hungry and thirsty, 就像飢渴一樣 Cheu$^2$ ch‘iong$^2$ ꜀ki k‘ak꜁ sioh꜁ yong$^2$.

Thus thanking Thee for favors 將換謝恩 ꜀Chiong wang$^2$ siă$^2$ ꜀ong

I trust in the merits of the Savior, 是託救主其功勞 Se$^2$ t‘auk꜁ Keu’ ‘Chio ꜀ki ꜀kung ꜀ló.

This is what my heart truly desires, 實心所願 Sik꜁ ꜀sing ‘su ngwong$^2$.

# PART. III.
# COMMERCIAL TERMS.

The following sections contain a large portion of the terms and phrases used in commerce. An effort has been made to approximate a uniform Commercial nomenclature; and to effect this we have adopted, as far as practicable, the terms and phrases used with reference to this subject at the other Treaty Ports of China. The English sentences given on the following pages are nearly the same as those used by the Rev. J. Macgowan in his excellent Manual of the Amoy Colloquial; and, as far as it was possible for us to do so, we have used the characters he has employed to represent the phrases in Chinese. In the Romanized translation of the Chinese sentences, we have not always aimed at a literal translation, but in many cases have given the colloquial equivalents which are in general use among the people of Foochow.

## 1. Merchandize.

| | | |
|---|---|---|
| Cotton (raw), | *꜁Miĕng ꜀hwa,* | 綿花 |
| Cotton yarn, | *꜁Miĕng ꜀sa,* | 綿紗 |
| Shirtings, | *꜁Yong pwo꜄,* | 洋布 |
| White shirtings, | *P'ieu꜄ pah꜇ ꜁yong pwo꜄,* | 漂白洋布 |
| Gray shirtings, | *꜂Pwong saik꜆ ꜁yong pwo꜄,* | 本色洋布 |
| Red shirtings, | *꜁Ĕng ꜁yong pwo꜄,* | 紅洋布 |
| Yellow shirtings, | *꜁Wong ꜁yong pwo꜄,* | 黃洋布 |
| Blue shirtings, | *꜁Lang ꜁yong pwo꜄,* | 藍洋布 |
| Colored shirtings, | *꜂Ngu saik꜆ ꜁yong pwo꜄,* | 五色洋布 |
| Dyed shirtings, | *꜂Niĕng saik꜆ ꜁yong pwo꜄,* | 染色洋布 |
| Twilled cloths, | *꜁Siă ꜁ung ꜁yong pwo꜄,* | 斜紋洋布 |
| Prints, | *Eng꜄ ꜀hwa pwo꜄,* | 印花布 |
| Do. large flowers, | *Twai꜅ ꜀hwa pwo꜄,* | 大花布 |
| Do. small flowers, | *Sá꜄ ꜀hwa pwo꜄,* | 小花布 |
| Gingham, | *꜂Liu ꜁teu pwo꜄,* | 柳條布 |
| Chintz, | *꜁Yong ꜀hwa, ꜀Hwa pwo꜄,* | 洋花 花布 |
| Woolen cloths, | *꜁Ni,* | 呢 |
| Broadcloth, | *Twai꜅ ꜁ni,* | 大呢 |

| | | | |
|---|---|---|---|
| Long ells, | *P'ek*ꜗ ꜀*chié*, | 嗶吱 | |
| Camlets, | ʿ*Ü* ꜀*sa*, ʿ*Ü taung*², | 羽紗 | 羽緞 |
| Spanish stripes, | ꜁*Ni*, | 呢 | |
| Cassimere, | ʿ*Sieu* ꜁*ni*, | 小呢 | |
| Bombazettes, | ʿ*Ü* ꜁*mó pwo*ʾ, | 羽毛布 | |
| Damask, | ʿ*Ü* ꜁*ling*, | 羽綾 | |
| Raw silk, | ꜀*Si*, | 絲 | |
| Silk thread, | ꜀*Si siăng*ʾ, | 絲線 | |
| Silk stuffs, | ꜁*Tiu*, | 綢 | |
| Silks and satins, | ꜁*Tiu taung*², | 綢緞 | |
| Plain lusters, | ʿ*Ü* ꜁*tiu*, | 羽綢 | |
| Brocaded lusters, | ꜀*Hwa* ʿ*ü* ꜁*tiu*, | 花羽綢 | |
| Blankets, or rugs, | ꜀*Chiéng*, | 氈 | |
| Fustians, | ꜁*Huí* ꜁*üng*, | 回絨 | |
| Velvet, | ꜁*Üng*, | 絨 | |
| Gauze, | ꜁*Ló*, | 羅 | |
| Do. silk, | ꜀*Sa*, | 紗 | |
| Silk Camlet, | *Siăng*ʾ *chaiu*ʾ, | 線縐 | |
| Satin, | *Kong*ʾ *taung*², | 貢緞 | |
| Do. figured, | ꜀*Hwa kong*ʾ, | 花貢 | |
| Crape, | *Chaiu*ʾ ꜀*sa*, | 縐紗 | |
| Grass-cloth, | *Ha*² *pwo*ʾ, *Chá*ʾ *pwo*ʾ, | 夏布 | 紵布 |
| Thread, | *Siăng*ʾ, | 線 | |
| Opium, | ꜀*A p'iéng*ʾ ꜁*t'u*, | 鴉片土 | |
| Do. Patna, | ꜀*Kung*, *La*ʾ, | 公喇 | |
| Do. Malwa, | *Pah*ꜗ ꜁*p'uí*, *Pah*ꜗ ꜁*ná*, | 白皮 | 白坭 |
| Do. Benares, | ꜀*Chié*, ꜀*Kó* | 膏 | |
| Do. Turkey, | ꜀*King* ꜀*hwa*, | 金花 | |
| Mockquee, | *Muk*ꜗ ʿ*ngi*, | 木耳 | |
| Tobacco leaf, | ꜀*Hong nioh*ꜗ | 煙葉 | |
| Camphor, | ꜀*Chiong* ʿ*nó*, | 樟腦 | |
| Sulphur, | ꜁*Liu* ꜁*hwong*, | 硫磺 | |
| Saltpetre, | ꜀*Sieu*, | 硝 | |
| Brass wire, | ꜁*Tĕng* ꜀*si*, ꜁*Tĕng siăng*ʾ, | 銅絲 | 銅線 |
| Copper sheets, | ꜁*Ĕng* ꜁*tĕng p'iéng*ʾ, | 紅銅片 | |
| Copperas, | ꜀*Ch'ang* ꜁*hwang*, | 生礬 | |

| | | |
|---|---|---|
| Sandalwood, | *꜁T'ang ꜀hiong,* | 檀香 |
| Sapanwood, | *꜀Su mëk₂,* | 蘇木 |
| Bark-mangrove, | *Kau꜃ ꜀ting ꜁p'ui,* | 校杒皮 |
| Ebony, | *꜀U muk₂* | 烏木 |
| Cloves, | *꜀Ting ꜀hiong,* | 丁香 |
| Dried shrimps, | *꜁Ha ꜂mi,* | 蝦米 |
| Birds-nests, | *Yéng꜃ ꜀wo,* | 燕窩 |
| Coral, | *꜀Tang ꜁hu,* | 珊瑚 |
| Isinglass, | *꜁Ngü ꜀ka,* | 魚膠 |
| Beche-de-mer, | *꜂Hai ꜀seng,* | 海參 |
| Beef-sinews, | *꜁Ngu ꜀küng,* | 牛筋 |
| Shell-fish, | *꜁Loi,* | 螺 |
| Sharks-fins, | *꜁Ngü ch'ié꜃,* | 魚翅 |
| Dried fish, | *꜁Ngü ꜂siong,* | 魚鯗 |
| Do. beef, | *꜁Ngu nük₂ ꜀pa,* | 牛肉羓 |
| Pepper, | *꜁Hu ꜀chieu,* | 楜椒 |
| Rice, | *꜂Mi,* | 米 |
| Beans and peas, | *Tau²,* | 荳 |
| Bean-cake, or pomace | *Tau² ꜀k'u,* | 荳坵 |
| Bean-relish, | *Tau² sié²,* | 荳豉 |
| Wheat, | *Mah₂,* | 麥 |
| Rock-candy, Sugar-candy, | *꜀Ping ꜁t'ong, ꜀Chiong ꜀ping, ꜁T'ong ꜀song,* or *꜁T'ong ꜀t'ong,* | 冰糖 糖霜 |
| White loaf-sugar, | *꜁Pwong kiék꜅ ꜁t'ong,* | 盆結糖 |
| Rattan, | *꜁Ting,* | 籐 |
| Umbrellas, | *꜂Ü ꜂sang,* | 雨傘 |
| Crockery, | *꜁Chü k'e꜃,* | 磁器 |
| Pearls, | *꜀Ting ꜀chio,* | 珍珠 |
| Mother-of-pearl, | *P'aung² k'aëk꜅,* | 蚌殼 |
| Tortoise-shell, | *Tai² ngwoi²,* | 玳瑁 |
| Iron, | *T'iék꜅,* | 鐵 |
| ,, cast, | *Chio꜃ t'iék꜅,* | 鑄鐵 |
| ,, pig, | *꜀Ch'ang t'iék꜅,* | 生鐵 |
| ,, bars, | *T'iék꜅ ꜁teu,* | 鐵條 |
| Lead, | *꜁Yong,* | 鉛 |

| | | |
|---|---|---|
| Whiting, | *꜁Iu ꜂hung,* | 油粉 |
| White-lead, | *꜁Yong ꜂hung,* | 鉛粉 |
| Red ,, | *꜀King ꜀tang,* | 金丹 |
| Spelter, zinc, | *Pah꜇ ꜁yong,* | 白鉛 |
| Tin, or pewter, | *Sek꜆,* | 錫 |
| Sheet-tin, | *꜁Yong t'iék꜆ p'iéng꜄,* <br> *꜂Mà ꜀ang t'iék꜆,* | 洋鐵片 <br> 馬鞍鐵 |
| Brass, | *꜁Tĕng,* | 銅 |
| Copper, | *꜁Ĕng ꜁tĕng,* | 紅銅 |
| ,, white, | *Pah꜇ ꜁tĕng,* | 白銅 |
| Steel, | *Kaung꜄,* | 鋼 |
| Flints, | *꜂Hwí sioh꜇,* | 火石 |
| Fans, | *Siéng꜄,* | 扇 |
| Cow's horns, | *꜁Ngu kaĕk꜆,* | 牛角 |
| Hides, | *꜁Ngu ꜁p'uí,* | 牛皮 |
| Shoes, | *꜁Á,* | 鞋 |
| Agar-agar, | *꜂Hai ch'ai꜄,* | 海菜 |
| Betel-nut, | *꜀Ping ꜁long ꜂chi,* | 梹榔子 |
| Oil, | *꜁Iu,* | 油 |
| Watches, | *꜂Pieu, ꜁Si ꜁sing ꜂pieu,* | 錶 時辰表 |
| Clocks, | *꜁Si ꜀chŭng, Chĕü꜅ ꜁ming ꜀chŭng,* | 時鐘 自鳴鐘 |
| Telescopes, | *꜀Ch'iéng ꜂li kiăng꜄,* | 千里鏡 |
| Tea, | *꜁Ta,* | 茶 |
| Bohea, | *꜂U ꜁i,* | 武彝 |
| Congou, | *꜀Kĕng ꜀hu,* | 工夫 |
| Hyson, | *꜂Hi ꜀ch'ung,* | 喜春 |
| Imperial, | *꜁Yéng ꜀chio,* | 圓珠 |
| Souchong, | *꜂Sieu ꜂chŭng,* | 小種 |
| Oolong, | *꜀U ꜁lŭng,* | 烏龍 |
| Pekoe, | *Seu꜅ ꜁mi,* | 壽眉 |
| ,, flowery, | *Pah꜇ ꜁hó,* | 白毫 |
| ,, orange, | *꜀Hwa ꜀hiong,* | 花香 |
| Twankey, | *꜁Sŭng ꜀k'á,* | 松溪 |
| Young Hyson, | *꜂Ŭ ꜁chiéng,* | 雨前 |
| Gunpowder, | *꜀Chio ꜀chié,* | 珠芝 |

榕腔初學撮要



## 2. Words and Phrases.

| | | |
|---|---|---|
| Account, an, | *Soʼ mĕk$_2$, Soʼ haung$^2$,* | 數目　　數項 |
| ,, book, | *Soʼ pʻwo$^2$,* | 數簿 |
| ,, adjust, | *Hwoi$^2$ soʼ,* | 會數 |
| ,, balance, | *˓Chong soʼ,* | 存數 |
| ,, charge, to, | *Siong$^2$ soʼ,* | 上數 |
| ,, ,, to my, | *Siong$^2$ ʻngwai ˓ki soʼ,* | 上我之數 |
| ,, to close, | *˓Kʻwang soʼ,* | 環數 |
| ,, collect an, | *ʻTʻó soʼ,* | 討數 |
| ,, pay an, | *˓Chʻing soʼ,* | 清數 |
| ,, make out an, | *˓Kʻwi ˓tang,* | 開單 |
| ,, receipt, | *˓Siu ˓tang.* | 收單 |
| Ad valorem, | *ʻKu kaʼ,* | 估價 |
| Advance money, | *˓Seng chʻok˒ ˓chiéng,* | 先出錢 |
| Advantageous, | *ʻHó taik˒ leʼ,* | 好得利 |
| Advertise, to, | *Chʻok˒ kóʼ pah$_2$* | 出告白 |
| Agree on price, | *Kaʼ ˓chiéng ʻkong tiăng$^2$ tioh$_2$,* | 價錢講定着 |
| Agreement, an, | *Yok˒,* | 約 |
| ,, make an, | *Kaĕng$^2$ ˓i yok˒, Lik$_2$yok˒,* | 與伊約　立約 |
| Amount, | *Kĕüng$^2$ kiéʼ,* | 共計 |
| Arbitrate, to, | *˓Tieu ʻchʻü,* | 調處 |
| Arbitrator, an, | *˓Kung ˓chʻing,* | 公親 |
| Assistant, an, | *ʻHwo keʼ,* | 夥計 |
| Assort, to, | *˓Hung ˓kwi loi$^2$,* | 分歸類 |
| Balance of account due, | *Tóiʼ ˓tü ngwoi$^2$ koʼ kʻiéngʼ,* | 對除外尙欠 |
| Balance of account on hand, | *Tóiʼ ˓tü ngwoi$^2$ koʼ ˓chong,* | 對除外尙存 |
| Bale, a, | *ʻKʻung,* | 綑 |
| Bank, a (government) | *˓Chiéng kwoh$_2$,* | 錢局 |
| ,, (private), | *˓Chiéng taingʼ,* | 錢庄 |
| Bank bill, cash, | *˓Chiéng pʻieuʼ,* | 錢票 |
| ,, ,, silver, | *˓Ngüng ˓tang,* | 銀單 |
| Bankrupt, | *˓Ong ʻtó, Taingʼ ʻtó,* | 行倒　　店倒 |

MAN. 14.

| | | |
|---|---|---|
| Bargain, (make a), | ‘Kong tiăng$^2$ tioh$_2$, | 講定着 |
| Barter, to, | Hwo’ wang$^2$ hwo’, | 貨換貨 |
| Basket, a, | ꜁Lëng, ꜁Lang, ꜀K‘wong, ꜁Lai, | 籠 籃 筐 箂 |
| Beacon, a, | Ke’ hô$^2$ ꜁ki t‘ak꜆, | 記號之塔 |
| Bill, a, | ꜁Ngüng ꜀tang, | 銀單 |
| ,, protest a, | Ng$^2$ ꜀chié, | 不支 |
| ,, accept a, | ‘Chung ꜀chié, | 准支 |
| ,, of exchange, | Tói$^2$ ꜀tang, | 兌單 |
| ,, of lading, | Chai’ hwo’ ꜀tang, | 載貨單 |
| Bond, a, | Yok꜆ che$^2$, | 約字 |
| Book-keeper, a, | ‘Kwang so’, ‘Chiong so’, ‘Chiong ꜁pwong, | 管數 掌數 掌權 |
| Borrow, to, | Chioh꜆ ꜁li, | 借來 |
| Bottomry bond, to make a, | ꜀Chiong ꜁sung chó’ taung’, | 將船爲當 |
| Bottomry bond, to close a, | ꜀Chiong ꜁sung ‘ku k‘ëük꜆ ꜀i, | 將船估與伊 |
| Box, a, | ꜀Siong, | 箱 |
| Breach of faith, | Sek꜆ seng’, Sek꜆ yok꜆, | 失信 失約 |
| Bribe, to, | ‘Wí lo$^2$, | 賄賂 |
| Broker, a, | ꜀King ‘ki ꜁nëng, ꜁Nga ꜁nëng, | 經紀人 牙人 |
| Brokerage, | ꜀T‘iu ꜁t‘au, ꜀T‘iu hong$^2$, ꜁Nga ëüng$^2$, | 抽頭 抽分 牙用 |
| Buoy, a, | ꜁P‘eu ꜀hu, ꜁P‘u t‘aëng’, | 浮桴 浮艬 |
| Buy, to, | ‘Má, | 買 |
| Buyer, a, | ‘Má k‘ah꜆, | 買客 |
| Calculate, | Saung’ so’, | 筭數 |
| Cancel, to, | ꜀Keu ꜀sieu, | 鈎消 |
| Capital, | ‘Pwong, ‘Pwong ꜁chiéng, | 本 本錢 |
| Captain, | ‘Hwi ‘tiong, Twai$^2$ ꜀kung, | 夥長 舵公 |
| Cargo, | Chai’, Sai$^2$ | 儎 |
| ,, boat, | Pauk꜆ ꜁sung, | 艊船 |
| ,, discharge, | ‘K‘i hwo’, Siong$^2$ ‘chwi, | 起貨 上水 |

| | | |
|---|---|---|
| Cargo, take in, | *Ch‘ok꜁ ‘chwi, Te’, Te’ hwo’,* | 出水 置 置貨 |
| ,, owner of, | *Hwo’ ‘chio,* | 貨主 |
| Cash, (money) | *꜀Chiéng, ꜀Ngṻng, ꜀Hwang,* | 錢 銀 番 |
| ,, on hand, | *‘Su ꜀chong ꜀ki ꜀ngṻng,* | 所存之銀 |
| Cask, a, | *꜀K‘wong,* | 桯 |
| Catalogue, a, | *Chak꜁ hwo’ ꜀tang,* | 什貨單 |
| Catty, a, | *꜀Kṻng,* | 斤 |
| Certificate, a, | *꜀Ping ꜀tang,* | 憑單 |
| ,, drawback, | *꜀Chong p‘ieu’,* | 存票 |
| ,, exemption (foreign produce), | *‘Miéng ꜀tṻng ꜀ching ꜀tang,* | 免重徵單 |
| Certificate, export (native produce), | *꜀Siu swoi’ ꜀tang,* | 收稅單 |
| Certificate, re-export (native produce), | *‘I ꜀wong chiăng’ swoi’ ꜀ping ꜀tang,* | 已完正稅憑單 |
| Change, to, | *Wang², Tói²,* | 換 兌 |
| ,, money, | *Wang² ꜀ngṻng ꜀chiéng,* | 換銀錢 |
| Charter a ship, | *Póh꜁ ꜀sung,* | 贌船 |
| Charterer (individual) | *Póh꜁ ꜀sung ꜀ki ꜀nĕng,* | 贌船之人 |
| ,, (a firm) | *Póh꜁ ꜀sung ꜀ki ꜀ong,* | 贌船之行 |
| Charter bond, | *Póh꜁ ꜀sung ꜀ki che²,* | 贌船之字 |
| Chop, a, a mark, | *Che² hó²,* | 字號 |
| Coast trade, duty receipt, | *Pwang’ swoi’ hó² ꜀siu,* | 半稅號收 |
| Coast trade, deposit duty memo., | *Chang² ꜀chong pwang’ swoi’ ngiéng² ꜀tang,* | 暫存半稅驗單 |
| Coast trade, deposit duty receipt, | *Chang² ꜀chong ꜀ki ꜀chong p‘ieu’,* | 暫存之存票 |
| Commerce, | *꜀Seng ‘li,* | 生理 |
| Commission, | *꜀T‘iu ꜀hung,* | 抽分 |
| ,, Agent, | *꜀Sing ꜀heng, ꜀Nga ꜀nĕng,* | 承行 牙人 |
| Commodity, | *Hwo’,* | 貨 |
| Compensate, | *꜀Puí,* | 賠 |
| Comprador, Ship, | *‘Má paing²,* | 買辦 |

| | | |
|---|---|---|
| Comprador, a shroff, | *ʿChiong koi$^2$,* | 掌櫃 |
| Confiscate, | *˓Chʿüng ˓kwang, Muk˒ ˓kwang,* | 充官　沒官 |
| Consign a vessel, | *˓Sung kiéʾ ˓ong,* | 船寄行 |
| ,, goods, | *Kiéʾ hwoʾ,* | 寄貨 |
| Consignee, | *˓Ong ˓ka,* | 行家 |
| Consul, a, | *ʿLiăng sëü$^2$ ˓kwang,* | 領事官 |
| Contents, | *ʿSu ˓chong ˓ki nóh˒,* | 所裝之物 |
| Contraband, | *Hwang$^2$ kengʾ,* | 犯禁 |
| Contract, | *Lik˒ yok˒,* | 立約 |
| Convey, to, | *Chaiʾ nóh˒ kʿóʾ,* | 載物去 |
| Coolie, | *˓Tang ˓këng,* | 擔工 |
| Copartner, | *Hak˒ ʿhwo keʾ, Kak˒ ʿhwo,* | 合夥計　合夥 |
| Copy, to, | *˓Chʿau,* | 抄 |
| Correspondence, | *Kiéʾ sengʾ ˓lai ʿwong,* | 寄信來往 |
| Correspondent, | *Kiéʾ sengʾ ˓ki ˓nëng,* | 寄信之人 |
| Cost, | *Kaʾ ˓chiéng,* | 價錢 |
| Costly, | *Koiʾ, Kaʾ koiʾ,* | 貴　價貴 |
| Count, to, | *Soʾ, Saungʾ, Saungʾ soʾ,* | 數　算　算數 |
| Counting house, | *Soʾ ˓pung,* | 數房 |
| Courier, a, | *˓Chʿiéng ʿli ʿma, ˓Pʿau ˓mwong ˓chü,* | 千里馬　跑文書 |
| Credit, give, | *˓Siă, ˓Siă soʾ,* | 賒　賒數 |
| Creditor, | *˓Chai ʿchio,* | 財主 |
| Custom, a, | *˓Hung sük˒, Sük˒ lié$^2$,* | 風俗　俗例 |
| Custom-house, | *Swoíʾ ˓kwang, ʿKwang ʿkʿau, Swoíʾ ʿkwang,* | 稅關　關口　稅館 |
| Customs, | *Swoíʾ ˓ngüng,* | 稅銀 |
| ,, levy, | *˓Siu swoíʾ,* | 收稅 |
| ,, pay, | *Póʾ swoíʾ, ˓Tau swoíʾ, Nak˒ swoíʾ,* | 報稅　投稅　納稅 |
| ,, defraud, | *Lauʾ swoíʾ, ʿChau swoíʾ,* | 漏稅　走稅 |
| ,, Commissioner of, | *Swoíʾ o$^2$ ˓si,* | 稅務司 |
| Customs, clerk in, | *Hiék˒ paing$^2$,* | 協辦 |
| ,, Interpreter in, | *˓Hwang ik˒ ˓kwang,* | 繙譯官 |

| | | |
|---|---|---|
| Customs, Linguist in, | *꜀T'ung sëü*$^2$, | 通事 |
| Customs banker, | *꜀Kwang ꜁ngũng hó*$^2$, | 官銀號 |
| ,, tariff, | *Chaik꜆ lié*$^2$, | 則例 |
| ,, godown, | *Ngiéng*$^2$ *hwo꜄ chang*$^2$ *꜁pung*, | 驗貨棧房 |
| ,, shed, jetty, | *Ngiéng*$^2$ *hwo꜄ ꜂ma ꜁t'au*, | 驗貨碼頭 |
| Customer, | *꜂Má k'ah꜆*, | 買客 |
| Damaged goods (by water), | *Sek꜆ ꜂chwi hwo꜄*, *Sëük꜆ ꜂chwi hwo꜄*, | 濕水貨 |
| Date, | *꜁Niéng ngwok*$_2$ *nik*$_2$ *꜂chi*, | 年月日子 |
| Day book, | *꜁Liu ꜂chwi p'wo*$^2$, | 流水簿 |
| Dear, | *Koi꜄*, | 貴 |
| Debt, | *Chai꜄*, | 債 |
| Debt, in, | *K'iéng꜄ chai꜄*, | 欠債 |
| Debtor, | *K'iéng꜄ chai꜄ ꜀ki ꜁nëng*, *K'iéng꜄ ho*$^2$, | 欠債之人 欠戶 |
| Deduct, | *K'aiu꜄ ꜁tü*, | 扣除 |
| Defraud, | *꜀K'i p'iéng꜄*, | 欺騙 |
| Defray, | *Ch'ok꜆ ꜂sai hié꜄*, | 出使費 |
| Demand, | *Tói꜄ ꜀i ꜂t'ó*, | 對伊討 |
| Demurrage, | *T'aik꜆ kwo꜄ aing*$^2$ *꜀ki ꜁ngũng*, | 貼過限之銀 |
| Deposit, to, | *K'ié꜄ chai*$^2$ *tek꜆*, *Kié꜄ tong꜄*, | 寄在的 寄頓 |
| Desk, writing, | *꜂Siă che*$^2$ *tóh꜆*, | 寫字棹 |
| Discharge (servant), | *꜁Sü*, | 辭 |
| ,, cargo, | *꜂K'i hwo꜄*, *Sìong*$^2$ *꜂chwi*, | 起貨 上水 |
| Discount, to, | *K'aiu꜄ ꜂tá*, *K'aiu꜄ chiék꜆*, | 扣底 扣折 |
| Dissolve partnership, | *꜀Siu ꜁pwang*, | 收盤 |
| Dollar, a, | *꜀Hwang sioh*$_2$ *tói꜄*, | 番一員 |
| Draft, a, | *꜁Ngũng ꜀tang*, *Tói*$^2$ *꜀tang*, | 銀單 兌單 |
| ,, to give, | *꜂Siă tói*$^2$ *꜀tang*, | 寫兌單 |
| Drawback certificate, | *꜁Chong p'ieu꜄*, | 存票 |
| Dun, to, | *P'aik꜆ so꜄*, | 迫數 |
| Duplicate, | *Ho꜄*, | 副 |
| Duty (Customs), | *Swoi꜄ ꜁ngũng*, | 稅銀 |

| | | |
|---|---|---|
| Duty, pay, | *Nak˒ swoi’*, | 納稅 |
| ,, export, | *Ch‘ok˒ ‘k‘au swoi’*, | 出口稅 |
| ,, import, | *‘Tiĕ ‘k‘au swoi’*, | 入口稅 |
| Dyed goods, | *‘Niĕng ˓ki pwo’*, | 染之布 |
| Earnest money, | *Tiăng$^{2}$ ˓ngüng, Tiăng$^{2}$ ˓chiĕng*, | 定銀　定錢 |
| Embark, to, | *Lóh˒ ˓sung*, | 落船 |
| Employ, persons, | *Ch‘iăng’*, | 倩 |
| ,, things, | *Ëüng$^{2}$, ‘Sai*, | 用　使 |
| Employment, | *˓King ‘ki, Sëü$^{2}$ ngiĕk˒* | 經紀　事業 |
| Endorse, | *˓Ch‘iĕng ˓miăng*, | 簽名 |
| Envelope, an, | *˓P‘iĕ tói$^{2}$, ˓P‘iĕ ˓p‘uí*, | 信囊　信皮 |
| Erase, to, | *˓Tu k‘ó’, ˓Tu mwak˒*, | 塗去　塗抹 |
| Estate, (lands and houses), | *Ngiĕk˒ ‘sang*, | 業產 |
| Estate, (property of all kinds), | *˓Ka ngiĕk˒*, | 家業 |
| Estimate, to, | *‘Ku ka’*, | 估價 |
| Examine, to, | *˓Cha, ‘Sing ch‘ak˒*, | 查　省察 |
| Exemption certificate (foreign produce), | *‘Miĕng ˓tüng ˓ching ˓tang*, | 免重徵單 |
| Exhibit, to, (goods), | *˓Pá*, | 排 |
| Exorbitant price, | *˓Hung ngwoi$^{2}$ koi’*, | 分外貴 |
| Expend, to, | *Ëüng$^{2}$ ˓chiĕng*, | 用錢 |
| Expenditure, | *‘Sai hiĕ’*, | 使費 |
| Exports, | *Ch‘ok˒ ‘k‘au hwo’*, | 出口貨 |
| Export certificate, | *˓Siu swoi’ ˓tang*, | 收稅單 |
| ,, duty receipt, | *Ch‘ok˒ ‘k‘au hó$^{2}$ ˓siu*, | 出口號收 |
| ,, manifest, | *Ch‘ok˒ ‘k‘au ˓ch‘ong ‘k‘au ˓tang*, | 出口艙口單 |
| ,, duty memo., | *Ch‘ok˒ ‘k‘au nói$^{2}$ te$^{2}$ hwo’ swoi’ ngiĕng$^{2}$ ˓tang*, | 出口內地貨稅驗單 |
| ,, duty, | *Ch‘ok˒ ‘k‘au swoi’*, | 出口稅 |
| Fine, | *Eu’, ˓Ching*, | 幼　精 |
| Fine, to, | *Hwak˒ ˓ngüng, Hwak˒ ˓chiĕng*, | 罰銀　罰錢 |

| | | |
|---|---|---|
| Forged writing, | *ʻKa pek˒ chek˒*, | 假筆跡 |
| Forgery of another's name, | *ʻKa che$^2$ hó$^2$*, | 假字號 |
| Fraud, a, | *˓Pau pe$^2$*, | 包弊 |
| Freight a ship, | *˓Pau chaiʾ hwoʾ*, | 包儎貨 |
| Freight, cargo, | *Chaiʾ, Sai$^2$*, | 儎 |
| Freights, | *Chaiʾ ˓ngüng*, | 儎銀 |
| Fulfill, | *˓Ü yok˒, ˓Ping yok˒, Chieuʾ yok˒*, | 如約 憑約 照約 |
| Godown, a, | *Chang$^2$ ˓pung*, | 棧房 |
| Gold, | *˓King*, | 金 |
| ,, dust, | *˓King ˓sa, ˓King ˓sai*, | 金沙 |
| Goods, | *Hwoʾ*, | 貨 |
| Gross weight, | *Mwoi$^2$ chiăng$^2$ taĕng$^2$, Mwoi$^2$ ˓tü tʻah˒*, | 未淨重 未除淨 |
| Guarantee, to, | *ʻPó neng$^2$, ʻPó ʻliăng*, | 保認 保領 |
| Guarantor, | *ʻPó neng$^2$ ˓ki ˓nĕng*, | 保認之人 |
| Handwriting, | *Pek˒ chek˒*, | 筆跡 |
| Harbor, inner, | *˓Sung póh˒ te$^2$ ˓hwong*, | 船泊地方 |
| ,, outer, | *ʻKʻau ngwoi$^2$*, | 口外 |
| ,, master, | *ʻLi ˓sung ˓tʻiăng*, | 理船廳 |
| High price, | *˓Kó kaʾ*, | 高價 |
| Hong, a, | *˓Ong*, | 行 |
| House, a, | *Chʻioʾ*, | 厝 |
| ,, owner of, | *Chʻioʾ ʻchio*, | 厝主 |
| House-rent, | *Chʻioʾ ˓chu*, | 厝租 |
| Imports, | *ʻTié ʻkʻau hwoʾ*, | 入口貨 |
| Import duty, | *ʻTié ʻkʻau swoiʾ*, | 入口稅 |
| ,, ,, memo., | *Ngiéng$^2$ ˓tang*, | 驗單 |
| ,, ,, receipt, | *ʻTié ʻkʻau hó$^2$ ˓siu*, | 進口號收 |
| ,, ,, receipt* | *˓Yong ˓sung swoiʾ ˓tang, ˓Ĕng ˓tang*, | 洋船稅單 紅單 |
| ,, manifest, | *ʻTié ʻkʻau ˓chʻong ʻkʻau ˓tang*, | 進口艙口單 |

* Kept by the merchant, and enabling him to sell the produce at the port of entry or send it into the country.

| | | |
|---|---|---|
| Inadequate, | ꜀Mó kau’ ngiăh$_2$, | 無至額 |
| Incorrect, | Ng$^2$ se$^2$, O$^2$ tang$^2$, | 不是 有錯 |
| Indemnify, to, | ꜀Puí, | 賠 |
| Ingot of silver, | ꜀Ngwong ‘pó, | 元寶 |
| Ink, | Mĕk$_2$, | 墨 |
| Inkstand, | Mĕk$_2$ kwang’, Mĕk$_2$ ꜀hu, | 墨罐 墨壺 |
| Insecure, | Ng$^2$ ‘ung, | 不穩 |
| Insolvent, | ꜀Ong ‘tó, | 行倒 |
| Installments, pay by, | ꜀T‘ang ꜀teng, | 攤還 |
| Insure, | ‘Pó ꜀ka, | 保家 |
| Insurance policy, | ‘Pó ꜀ka p‘ieu’, | 保家票 |
| Interest, | Le’ ꜀chiéng, Le’ ꜀ngŭng, | 利錢 利銀 |
| Invoice of goods, | Chai’ hwo’ ꜀tang, | 載貨單 |
| Jetty, | Tó$^2$ ꜀t‘au, | 道頭 |
| Landlord, | Ch‘io’ ‘chio, Ngiék$_2$ ‘chio, | 厝主 業主 |
| Lawful, | Hak$_2$ hwak꜆, | 合法 |
| Lease, a, | Tiéng$^2$ ꜀p‘ié, ꜀Chu ‘pong, | 佃批 租榜 |
| Ledger, a, | ‘Chung p‘wo$^2$, | 總簿 |
| Lend, to, | Chioh꜆ ꜀nĕng, | 借人 |
| Letter, a, | ꜀Chŭ seng’, ꜀P‘ié seng’, | 書信 |
| ,, book, | ꜀Ch‘au seng’ p‘wo$^2$, | 抄信簿 |
| License, a, | Chek꜆ chieu’, | 執照 |
| Lighthouse, | Wong$^2$ ꜀lau, | 望樓 |
| Lightship, | ꜀Ting ꜀sung, | 燈船 |
| Lose, to, | Sek꜆ lóh$_2$, P‘ah꜆ ꜀mó, | 失落 打無 |
| Loss, | Siék$_2$ ‘pwong, | 折本 |
| Lot, the whole, | Chó’ sioh$_2$ chiăh꜆, ‘Lung ‘chung, | 作一個 攏總 |
| Mace, a, | Sioh$_2$ ꜀chiéng ꜀ngŭng, | 一錢銀 |
| Mail bag, | ꜀Siu seng’ tói$^2$, | 收信袋 |
| ,, carrier, | ꜀Ch‘iéng ‘li ‘ma, | 千里馬 |
| Manage, to, | Paing$^2$ sëü$^2$, Paing$^2$ ‘li, | 辦事 辦理 |
| Manifest, ship's, | Pó’ swoi’ ꜀tang, | 報稅單 |
| ,, Export, | Ch‘ok꜆ ‘k‘au ꜀ch‘ong ‘k‘au ꜀tang, | 出口 艙口單 |

| | | |
|---|---|---|
| Manifest, Import, | ‘Tié ‘k‘au ꜀ch‘ong ‘k‘au ꜀tang, | 進口艙口單 |
| Market, (street), | ꜀Ká ch‘e[2], | 街市 |
| ,, price, | Ch‘e[2] ka’, | 市價 |
| Memorandum book, | ꜁Chong ke’ p‘wo[2], | 存記簿 |
| Merchandise, | Hwo’, | 貨 |
| Merchant, | ꜀Seng ‘li ꜁ki ꜁nĕng, ꜀Siong ꜁ing, | 生理之人 商人 |
| Miscellaneous. | ꜁Ling ꜀sing, ꜁Ling ch‘ói’ | 零星 零碎 |
| Mistake, | Ch‘auk꜆, Tang[2], | 錯 |
| Money, | ꜁Ngũng ꜁chiéng, ꜁Chiéng, | 銀錢 錢 |
| ,, changer, | ꜁Chiéng taing’ ꜁ki ꜁nĕng, | 錢店之人 |
| ,, lender, | Pong’ chai’ ꜁ki ꜁nĕng, | 放債之人 |
| Monopoly, | ꜀Pau ‘má ꜀pau má[2], ꜀Tang ꜁mwong tuk꜆ ch‘e[2], | 包買包賣 單門獨市 |
| Monthly, | Ngwok꜆ ngwok꜆, | 月月 |
| Mortgage, a, | ‘Teng k‘ié’, | 典契 |
| ,, to, | ‘Teng, | 典 |
| Mortgagee, | ‘Teng ‘chio, ꜁Chai ‘chio, | 典主 財主 |
| Mortgager, | ꜁Ngwong ‘chio, ‘Teng ak꜆ ꜁ki ꜁nĕng, | 原主 典押之人 |
| Muster, a, | Hwo’ yong[2], | 貨樣 |
| Net-weight, | Chiăng[2] taĕng[2], ꜁Tü t‘ah꜆ | 淨重 除淨 |
| Non-payment (at time specified), | Kwo’ aing[2], | 過限 |
| Note-book, | ꜁Chong ke’ p‘wo[2], | 存記簿 |
| Notify, to, | ꜀T‘ung ꜀ti, Pó’, | 通知 報 |
| Number, to, | Ke’ so’, | 記數 |
| Offer, to make an, | Ch‘ok꜆ ka’, | 出價 |
| Opportunity, | ꜀Ki hwoi[2], | 機會 |
| ,, embrace an, | T‘eng’ ꜀ki hwoi[2], ꜁Chüng ꜀ki hwoi[2], | 趁機會 從機會 |
| Order for money, | ꜁Ngũng ꜀tang, | 銀單 |
| Oversee, to, | ‘Kwang ‘li, | 管理 |
| Owe, to, | K‘iéng’, | 欠 |
| Particulars, | ꜁Teu yong[2], | 條件 |

MAN. 15.

| | | |
|---|---|---|
| **Partner, a,** | *꜂Hwo ke꜄,* | 夥計 |
| **Pass custom-house inspection,** | *Kwo꜄ ngiéng²,* | 過驗 |
| **Passport, a,** | *꜁Sui ꜁heng chek꜆ chieu꜄,* | 隨行執照 |
| **Pay ready money,** | *Hiéng² ꜁ngũng,* | 現銀 |
| **Picul, a,** | *Sioh꜇ tang꜄,* | 一担 |
| **Percentage, a,** | *꜀T'iu ꜀hung,* | 抽分 |
| **Permit, to land,** | *꜂K'i hwo꜄ pó꜄ ꜀tang,* | 起貨報單 |
| **,, to ship (duty being paid),** | *Ch'ok꜆ hwo꜄ pó꜄ ꜀tang,* | 出貨報單 |
| **Permit, to re-export,** | *Po² ch'ok꜆ ꜂k'au pó꜄ ꜀tang,* | 復出口報單 |
| **,, to tranship,** | *꜁Pwang ꜁sung pó꜄ ꜀tang,* | 搬船報單 |
| **,, to open hatches,** | *꜀K'wi ꜀ch'ong che²,* | 開艙字 |
| **Piece, (of cloth)** | *Sioh꜇ p'ek꜆,* | 一疋 |
| **Piece-goods,** | *Pwo꜄ p'ek꜆,* | 布疋 |
| **Pilot, a,** | *Pong꜄ ꜂kĕng, ꜂Ing ꜂chwi,* | 放港 引水 |
| **,, fees,** | *Pong꜄ ꜂kĕng ꜁ki ꜀kĕng ꜁chiéng,* | 放港之工錢 |
| **Port clearance,** | *꜁Ĕng ꜁pá,* | 紅牌 |
| **Post-office,** | *꜁Mwong ꜀chü ꜂kwang,* | 文書館 |
| **Postage,** | *꜂Chiu ꜀chü,* | 酒資 |
| **Premium, on sycee,** | *꜁Ung ꜁ngũng ꜁ki t'aik꜆ ꜂chwi,* | 紋銀之貼水 |
| **,, ,, dollars,** | *꜁Ngũng ꜂chwi,* | 銀水 |
| **Price,** | *Ka꜄,* | 價 |
| **,, current,** | *꜁Si ka꜄, ꜁Ong ꜁ching,* | 時價 行情 |
| **,, fair,** | *꜀Kung tó² ka꜄,* | 公道價 |
| **,, fall in,** | *Lóh꜇ ka꜄,* | 落價 |
| **,, rise in,** | *꜂K'i ka꜄,* | 起價 |
| **Prime cost,** | *꜁Ngwong ka꜄,* | 原價 |
| **Profit,** | *Taik꜆ le꜄ ꜁chiéng, Taik꜆ le꜄,* | 得利錢 得利 |
| **Profitable,** | *Á² taik꜆, O² ꜁chiéng t'eng꜄* | 能得 有錢聽 |

| | | |
|---|---|---|
| Promise, | *Eng’ ꜀sing, Eng’ ‘hü, ‘Hü,* | 應承　應許　許 |
| Promise, break a, | *Sek꜁ seng’, Sek꜁ yok꜁,* | 失信　失約 |
| Punctual in payment, | *꜀Mó ꜀t‘wa k‘iĕng’,* | 無拖欠 |
| Purchase, to, | *‘Má,* | 買 |
| Receipt, | *꜀Siu ꜀tang,* | 收單 |
| ,, export duty, | *Ch‘ok꜁ ‘k‘au swoi’ ꜀siu ꜀tang,* | 出口稅收單 |
| ,, import duty, | *‘Tiĕ ‘k‘au swoi’ ꜀siu ꜀tang* | 入口稅收單 |
| Receipts and expenses, | *Ch‘ok꜁ ik꜁ ꜀ki ꜀ngüng,* | 出入之銀 |
| Receiver of stolen goods, | *꜀Wo ꜀ko,* | 窩家 |
| Reckon, to, | *Saung’ so’,* | 算數 |
| Rectify a mistake, | *‘Kai* or *‘kwi,* | 改 |
| Refund, to, | *꜀Heng* or *꜀teng,* | 還 |
| Register, ship's, | *꜀Sung ꜀pá,* | 船牌 |
| Remit money, | *Kiĕ’ ꜀ngüng,* | 寄銀 |
| Rent, | *꜀Chu,* | 租 |
| Retail, to, | *꜀Ling ch‘ói’ má$^2$, Ch‘ói’ má$^2$,* | 零碎賣　碎賣 |
| Revenue, | *Hiong’ ꜀ngüng, ‘T‘ong haung$^2$,* | 餉銀　帑項 |
| Rough draft, | *‘Ch‘ó ‘kó,* | 草稿 |
| Safe, | *‘Ung taung’, ‘T‘io taung’,* | 穩當　妥當 |
| ,, House, | *‘Küng ko’ ꜀ki ꜀ong,* | 鞏固之行 |
| ,, business, | *‘Ung taung’ ꜀ki ꜀seng ‘li,* | 穩當之生理 |
| ,, investment, | *Ha$^2$ ‘pwong se$^2$ ‘ung taung’,* | 下本是穩當 |
| Sale, | *꜀Sieu ꜀t‘au, O$^2$ ‘chio che$^2$* | 消頭　有主字 |
| ,, for, | *Hwak꜁ má$^2$,* | 發賣 |
| ,, no, | *Má$^2$ ꜀sieu ꜀t‘au, ꜀Mó ‘chio che$^2$,* | 無消頭　無主字 |
| Same as pattern, | *꜀Ping yong$^2$, Chieu’ yong$^2$,* | 憑樣　照樣 |

海上絲綢之路文獻集成 科技與文化編

| | | |
|---|---|---|
| Same as before, | *꜀I keu$^2$*, | 依舊 |
| Sample, | *Hwoʾ yong$^2$*, | 貨樣 |
| Sample, to sell by, | *Chieuʾ yong$^2$ má$^2$*, | 照樣賣 |
| ,, to buy by, | *Chieuʾ yong$^2$ ‘má*, | 照樣買 |
| Scales, | *꜀T‘iĕng ꜀pang ꜀tó*, | 天平駝 |
| Seal, a, | *Engʾ*, | 印 |
| ,, to, | *Engʾ, Kaiʾ engʾ*, | 印 蓋印 |
| ,, a letter, | *꜀Hung sengʾ*, | 封信 |
| Sealing wax, | *‘Hwí ch‘ek꜁*, | 火漆 |
| Security, a (person), | *‘Pó neng$^2$ ꜀nĕng*, | 保認人 |
| ,, a (pledge), | *Taungʾ*, | 當 |
| Sell, to, | *Má$^2$*, | 賣 |
| ,, by package sample, | *꜀Ping yong$^2$ ꜀pau ꜀li má$^2$* | 憑樣包來賣 |
| Sell, at prime cost, | *꜀Ping ‘pwong má$^2$*, | 憑本賣 |
| Send a letter, | *Kiéʾ sengʾ*, | 寄信 |
| ,, a remittance, | *Kiéʾ ꜀ngŭng*, | 寄銀 |
| Settle an account, | *꜀Ch‘ing soʾ*, | 清數 |
| Share, a, | *Sioh$_2$ ‘ku*, | 一股 |
| Ship, a, | *꜀Sung*, | 船 |
| Shipwreck, | *꜀Sung p‘ah꜁ p‘waiʾ*, | 船打破 |
| Ship's papers, | *꜀Sung ꜀pá*, | 船牌 |
| Shipping order (to land or ship cargo), | *꜀Pau ha$^2$ che$^2$*, | 包載字 |
| Shroff, a, | *‘Chiong koi$^2$*, | 掌櫃 |
| Shop, a, | *Taingʾ*, | 店 |
| Sign, to, | *꜀Ch‘iĕng ꜀miăng, Wa$^2$ hó$^2$*, | 簽名、畫號 |
| Signature, a, | *꜀Hwa ak꜁*, | 花押 |
| Silver, | *꜀Ngŭng*, | 銀 |
| ,, pure, | *꜀Ung ꜀ngŭng*, | 紋銀 |
| Smuggle, to, | *Lauʾ swoíʾ*, | 漏稅 |
| Speculate, to, | *P‘aung$^2$ chóʾ hwaʾ*, | 遇造化 |
| String of cash, | *Sioh$_2$ tieuʾ ꜀chiéng*, | 一吊錢 |
| Sufficient, | *Kauʾ ngiăh$_2$*, | 至額 |
| Suit, to (please), | *Hak$_2$ eʾ*, | 合意 |

榕腔初學撮要

| | | |
|---|---|---|
| Suitable, (proper), | *Hak$_2$ ꜀ngi,* | 合宜 |
| Supercargo, | *Ch'ok꜁ ꜂hai,* | 出海 |
| Survey of the hatches, | *Ngiéng$^2$ ꜀sung che$^2$,* | 驗船字 |
| Sycee, | *꜀Ngwong ꜂pó,* | 元寶 |
| Tael, a, | *Sioh$_2$ ꜂liong,* | 一兩 |
| Take an inventory, | *꜂Teng hwo꜃,* | 點貨 |
| Tariff, | *Chaik꜁ lié$^2$,* | 則例 |
| Tea-boy, | *꜀Ta ꜀pung, ꜀Ta k'o꜃,* | 茶房 茶庫 |
| Teaman, | *꜀Ta k'ah꜁,* | 茶客 |
| Tidewaiter, | *Sau꜃ ꜀ping,* | 哨兵 |
| Tonnage dues memo., | *꜀Sung ch'a꜃ ngiéng$^2$ ꜀tang,* | 船鈔驗單 |
| ,, ,, receipt, | *꜀Sung ch'a꜃ hó$^2$ ꜀siu ꜀tang,* | 船鈔號收單 |
| Total, | *Këüng$^2$ kié꜃,* | 共計 |
| Trade, (a craft), | *꜀Këng ngié$^2$,* | 工藝 |
| Trade, (commerce), | *꜀Seng ꜂li, ꜀Seng e꜃,* | 生理 生意 |
| Trader, a, | *Chó꜃ ꜀seng ꜂li ꜀ki ꜀nëng,* | 做生理之人 |
| Transfer an account, | *꜀Ch'au so꜃, ꜀Pwang so꜃,* | 抄數 盤數 |
| Transit duty memo., | *Chai꜃ ong$^2$ ꜂tié nói$^2$ te$^2$ ꜀ki ꜂k'au swoi꜃ ngiéng$^2$ ꜀tang,* | 再運入內地之口稅驗單 |
| ,, pass, | *Chai꜃ ong$^2$ ꜂tié nói$^2$ te$^2$ ꜀ki swoi꜃ ꜀tang,* | 再運入內地之稅單 |
| Transmit, to, | *Kié꜃,* | 寄 |
| Transport, to, | *Ong$^2$ hwo꜃ k'ó꜃,* | 運貨去 |
| Treasure, | *꜀Ngüng haung$^2$,* | 銀項 |
| Treaty, a, | *꜀Hwo yok꜁,* | 和約 |
| Undersell, to, | *Kaung꜃ ka꜃ ꜀li hwang꜃, ꜂Chieu ꜂ch'ü ꜀tó ꜀lai,* | 降價來喚 少取多來 |
| Unjust, | *꜀Mó ꜀kung tó$^2$,* | 無公道 |
| Unlawful, | *꜀Mó hak$_2$ hwak꜁,* | 無合法 |
| Unprofitable, | *꜀Nang taik꜁ le꜃,* | 難得利 |
| Unrecoverable debt, | *꜀Mó tói꜃ ꜀siu so꜃,* | 無處收數 |
| Unsafe, | *꜀Mó ꜂t'io taung꜃,* | 無妥當 |
| Unsold, | *Ko꜃ mwoi$^2$ má$^2$,* | 尙未賣 |
| Usage, custom, | *꜀Hung sük$_2$, Sük$_2$ lié$^2$,* | 風俗 俗例 |

| | | |
|---|---|---|
| Usury, | *Taëng² le’*, | 重利 |
| Value, to (goods), | *‘Ku*, | 估 |
| Valuable, | *‘Pó pwoí’*, *Tek˒ ˓chiéng*, | 寶貝 値錢 |
| War-tax, | *˓Lié ˓king*, | 厘金 |
| Warrant, to, | *‘Pó ‘liăng*, | 保領 |
| Weigh, to, | *˓Ch‘ing taëng²*, | 稱重 |
| Wharfage, | *Tó² ˓t‘au swoí’*, | 道頭稅 |
| Wholesale, buy, | *˓Mó ch‘ói’ ‘má*, | 無碎買 |
| „ sell, | *˓Mó ch‘ói’ má²*, | 無碎賣 |
| Worth, to be, | *Tek˒*, | 値 |
| Write, to, | *‘Siă*, | 寫 |
| Yard, one, | *Sioh˒ ‘ma*, | 一碼 |

## 3. Buying and Selling.

| | | |
|---|---|---|
| Goods of the first quality, | *Siong² ‘hó ˓ki hwo’*, | 上好之貨 |
| Goods of the worst quality, | *Kik˒ ˓ngai ˓ki hwo’*, | 極歹之貨 |
| What is the current price of these goods now? | *‘Chiă hwo’ hiéng² ˓si sié’ nóh˒ ˓ong ˓ching*, | 此貨現時甚麽行情 |
| Examine the goods carefully, | *Hwo’ tioh˒ sá’ ne² k‘ang’*, | 貨着詳細看 |
| What is the price of this? | *˓Chuí sié’ nóh˒ ka’*, | 此甚麽價 |
| I am afraid it is too dear, | *˓Kiăng k‘ak˒ koi’*, | 恐太貴 |
| Fair price, | *‘Ló sik˒ ka’*, *˓Kung ˓pang ka’*, | 老實價 公平價 |
| Reduce the price a little, | *Ka’ tioh˒ ‘keng ˓niă nói’*, | 價着減少許 |
| Cannot reduce much, | *Má² ‘keng tek˒ ‘yă sá²*, | 不減得太多 |
| What will you sell them for? | *‘Nü pwoh˒ má² nioh˒ wai² ˓chiéng*, | 爾要賣若干錢 |
| $ 3.75, at the least, | *Kik˒ ‘chieu ˓sang tói’ ch‘ek˒ kaëk˒ pwang’*, | 極少三員七角半 |

| | | |
|---|---|---|
| How many yards in a piece? | *Sioh$_2$ p‘ek꜅ o$^2$ ‛kwi ‛ma,* | 一疋有幾碼 |
| This is what I paid for it, | *꜀Chuí se$^2$ ‛ngwai chieuʼ ‛pwong ꜀chiéng ꜀ki kaʼ,* | 此是我照本之價 |
| I am selling for what I gave, | *‛Ngwai se$^2$ ꜀ping ‛pwong má$^2$,* | 我是照本賣 |
| Let us split the difference, | *꜀Chá niong$^2$ sioh$_2$ pwangʼ,* | 齊讓一半 |
| I want ready money, | *‛Ngwai pwoh꜅ tih$_2$ hiéng$^2$ ꜀ngüng,* | 我要現銀 |
| That will never do, | *꜀Chuí t‘auʼ ‛tá má$^2$ ‛sai tek꜅,* | 此終是不使的 |
| Send me the bill in due time, | *Kauʼ ꜀si tioh$_2$ ꜀k‘wi ꜀tang k‘ëük꜅ ‛ngwai,* | 到時着開單來與我 |
| Pay me in Mexicans, | *‛Ngwai pwoh꜅ tih$_2$ ‛nü ‛cheu ꜀hwang,* | 我要爾鳥番 |
| You must give me at least a month's credit, | *Kik$_2$ ‛chieu yă$^2$ tioh$_2$ ꜀siă ‛ngwai sioh$_2$ ‛ka ngwok$_2$ nik$_2$,* | 極少亦着賒我到一個月 |
| I lose too much by the discount, | *‛Ngwai siék$_2$ k‘ak꜅ sá$^2$ ꜀ngüng ‛chwi,* | 我折太多銀水 |
| Bring a muster and let me see, | *Hwoʼ yong$^2$ ꜀tó ꜀li k‘angʼ,* | 貨樣拿來看 |
| Does that include the duty? | *Swoíʼ ꜀ngüng o$^2$ chai$^2$ nói$^2$ ꜀mó,* | 稅銀有在內無 |
| These piece-goods are too coarse, | *P‘ek꜅ ꜀t‘au k‘ak꜅ ꜀ch‘u,* | 疋頭太粗 |
| The goods are all of the same quality, | *Hwoʼ ꜀tu se$^2$ sioh$_2$ yong$^2$,* | 貨皆是一樣 |
| I want to charter a ship, | *‛Ngwai óiʼ póh$_2$ ꜀sung,* | 我欲𨂿船 |
| When do you expect the ship's arrival? | *‛Nü p‘ah꜅ saungʼ ꜀sung miéng$^2$ au$^2$ kauʼ,* | 爾打算船何時到 |
| I cannot tell you now, | *‛Chiă ꜀si haiu$^2$ má$^2$ ‛hieu tek꜅,* | 此時候未知 |

| | | |
|---|---|---|
| I will give you $20.00 a bale, | Sioh$_2$ ꜀pau ꜂ngwai k‘ëük꜆ ꜂nü ne$^2$ sek$_2$ tói꜄, | 一包我與爾二十員 |
| No, I cannot afford to do so, | Má$^2$ ꜂sai tek꜆ ꜂ngwai siék$_2$ ꜂pwong k‘ak꜆ sá$^2$, | 不使得我折本太多 |
| How many pieces have you? | ꜂Nü o$^2$ ꜂kwi p‘ek꜆, | 爾有幾疋 |
| I don't know, I have not counted them yet, | ꜂Ngwai má$^2$ ꜂hieu tek꜆ ꜀tu mwoi$^2$ saung꜄, | 我不知尙未筭 |
| What is the price of six catties grey shirting, | Lĕk$_2$ ꜀küng ꜂pwong saik꜆ ꜁yong sié꜄ nóh꜆ ka꜄, | 六斤本色洋何價 |
| One tael six mace five, | Sioh$_2$ ꜂liong lĕk$_2$ ꜁chiéng pwang꜄, | 一兩六錢半 |
| How many pieces are there in a bale? | Sioh$_2$ ꜂k‘ung ꜂kwi p‘ek꜆, | 一綑幾疋 |
| You must give me a receipt, | ꜂Nü tioh$_2$ ꜂siă sioh$_2$ ꜀t‘iong ꜀siu ꜀tang k‘ëük꜆ ꜂ngwai, | 爾着寫一張收單與我 |

## 4. On Teas.

| | | |
|---|---|---|
| How much tea is there in the market? | ꜀Ká siong$^2$ o$^2$ nioh$_2$ wai$^2$ ꜁ta, | 街上有若干茶 |
| You have to pay the duty, | Swoí꜄ ꜁ngüng se$^2$ ꜂nü ch‘ok꜆, | 稅銀是爾出 |
| Who pays the commission? | Se$^2$ tié$^2$ ꜁nĕng ch‘ok꜆ ꜀t‘iu ꜀hung, | 是誰出抽分 |
| The buyer pays it, | ꜂Má ꜂chio tioh$_2$ ch‘ok꜆, | 買的着出 |
| These goods are troublesome to sell, | ꜂Chiă hwo꜄ ꜁nang ꜀sieu, | 此貨難消 |
| When will you come and take the goods away? | ꜂Nü miéng$^2$ au$^2$ ꜁li ꜀pwang hwo꜄, | 爾何時來搬貨 |
| I'll buy the whole from you, | ꜂Ngwai ꜂lung ꜂chung kaĕng$^2$ ꜂nü ꜂má, | 我要一齊與汝買 |

| | | |
|---|---|---|
| I don't want to sell by retail, | ʻNgwai ˛mó ˛ling chʻóiʼ má$^2$, | 我不零碎賣 |
| Call again next week, | A$^2$ ʻlá paiʼ kaiʼ ˛li, | 後禮拜再來 |
| Do these goods suit you? | ʻChiă hwoʼ á$^2$ hak$_2$ ʻnŭ eʼ ˛pá, | 此貨能合爾意麼 |
| Make an offer, | ʻNŭ tioh$_2$ chʻok˒ kaʼ, | 爾着出價 |
| You always sell worthless goods, | ʻNŭ ˛tu se$^2$ má$^2$ ˛ngai hwoʼ, | 爾都是賣歹貨 |
| No one wants these goods, | ʻChiă hwoʼ ˛mó ˛nĕng tih$_2$, | 此貨無人要 |
| Try and sell them for me, | ʻNŭ tʻáʼ ʻngwai chʻeʼ má$^2$ kʻangʼ, | 爾代我試賣看 |
| The market is very dull now, | Hiéng$^2$ chai$^2$ ˛ká chʻe$^2$ má$^2$ ˛sieu ˛tʻau, | 現時街上無消頭 |
| The market is very brisk now, | ʻChiă ˛si haiu$^2$ ˛ká chʻe$^2$ twai$^2$ ˛sieu ˛tʻau, | 此時街上大消頭 |
| Don't you know the price has come down? | ʻNŭ má$^2$ ʻhieu tek˒ ˛ong ˛ching o$^2$ lóh$_2$ ˛pá, | 爾不知行情有落麼 |
| There is not much tea in the country, | ˛Sang ʻtié ˛mó siéʼ nóh˒ ˛ta, | 山內無甚麼茶 |
| It is too common, | ˛Chuí se$^2$ kʻak˒ ˛chʻu, | 此是太粗 |
| This is the first crop, | ˛Chuí se$^2$ ˛tʻau ˛chʻung ˛ki ˛ta, | 此是頭春之茶 |
| This belongs to a tea-man, | ʻChiă ˛ta se$^2$ ˛ta kʻah˒ ˛ki ˛ta, | 此茶是茶客之茶 |
| What is the name of this chop? | ʻChiă ˛ta kieuʼ siéʼ nóh˒ che$^2$ hó$^2$, | 此茶叫甚麼字號 |
| Bring me a muster chest, | ʻNŭ ˛tó sioh$_2$ ˛siong ˛li chóʼ yong$^2$, | 爾取一箱茶來做樣 |
| What is the gross weight? | Mwoi$^2$ tʻiăh˒(˛siong, ˛lai, etc.) nioh$_2$ wai$^2$, | 未拆淨若干 |
| What is the net weight? | ˛Tŭ tʻiăh˒ nioh$_2$ wai$^2$, | 除拆若干 |
| I shall weigh in the afternoon, | ʻNgwai a$^2$ tauʼ pwoh˒ kwoʼ chʻengʼ, | 我下午要過秤 |

MAN. 16.

| | | |
|---|---|---|
| How many piculs do you make it? | *ʿNü saungʾ nioh꜂ wai$^{2}$ tangʾ,* | 爾算若干担 |
| It needs firing, | *Tioh꜂ kwoʾ pwoi$^{2}$,* | 着過焙 |
| You must let me have the same as sample, | *ʿNü tioh꜂ chieuʾ yong$^{2}$ ꜀tó k'ëük꜂ ʿngwai,* | 爾着照樣拿與我 |
| Show me the Green tea musters, | *Lioh꜂ ꜀ta yong$^{2}$ ꜀tó k'ëük꜂ ʿngwai k'angʾ,* | 綠茶樣拿與我看 |
| Your teas are rather dusty, | *ʿNü ꜀ta k'ak꜂ ch'óiʾ,* | 爾之茶較碎 |
| Your offer is too low, | *ʿNü kaʾ ꜀teng k'ak꜂ kiă$^{2}$,* | 爾價還太低 |
| I will give you 25 taels for ½ chest, | *Pwangʾ ꜀siong ʿngwai k'ëük꜂ ʿnü ne$^{2}$ sek꜂ ngo$^{2}$ ʿliong,* | 半箱我與爾廿五兩 |
| I think the price will stand, | *ʿNgwai k'angʾ ʿchiă kaʾ ꜀mó ʿk'i ꜀mó lóh꜂,* | 我看此價無起無落 |
| Ask the tea-boy, | *Tioh꜂ mwongʾ ꜀ta ꜀pung,* | 着問茶房 |

## 5. The Shroff.

| | | |
|---|---|---|
| Put these dollars in boxes, | *꜀Ngüng tioh꜂ ëüng$^{2}$ ꜀siong ꜀li ꜀chong,* | 銀着用箱來裝 |
| 4,000 dollars in each box, | *Kauk꜂ ꜀siong seʾ ꜀ch'ieng tóiʾ,* | 各箱四千員 |
| Seal them with the house-seal, | *Ëüng$^{2}$ ʿpwong ꜀ong ꜀ki ꜀hung ꜀teu ꜀li ꜀hung,* | 用本行之封條來封 |
| Stamp them with the house-mark, | *Mengʾ siong$^{2}$ ʿsiă ʿpwong ꜀ong ꜀ki che$^{2}$ hó$^{2}$,* | 面上寫本行之字號 |
| Get this dollar tested, | *꜀Tó ʿchi sioh꜂ tóiʾ ꜀ngüng k'óʾ k'angʾ,* | 拿此銀一員去看 |
| It has a cracked sound | *꜀Ngüng ꜀siăng ʿa ʿa,* | 銀聲啞啞 |
| Weigh these dollars, | *ʿChiă ꜀ngüng tioh꜂ kwoʾ ch'engʾ,* | 此銀着過秤 |
| What is the rate of exchange to-day? | *꜀King tangʾ ꜀ngüng ʿchwi se$^{2}$ nioh꜂ wai$^{2}$,* | 今日銀水是若何 |
| Sycee 4 % premium, | *꜀Ngwong ʿpó sioh꜂ pah꜂ ʿliong tioh꜂ ꜀ka seʾ ʿliong ꜀ngüng ʿchwi,* | 元寶每百兩着加四兩銀水 |

## 6. Godown Man.

| | | |
|---|---|---|
| Godown man, | ꜂*Kwang chang*$^2$, | 管棧 |
| Hire two cargo boats, | *Tioh*$_2$ *ch‘iăng*꜃ *lang*$^2$ ꜀*teu pauk*꜁ ꜀*sung*, | 着倩二條艀船 |
| Go alongside the ship, | *Tioh*$_2$ ꜂*lĕng* ꜀*sung* ꜀*piéng*, | 着倚船邊 |
| Give this order to the chief mate, | ꜂*Chiă* ꜀*tang tioh*$_2$ ꜀*kau k‘ĕük*꜁ ꜀*sung* ꜀*ki twai*$^2$ ꜂*hwo*, | 此單着交與船中大夥 |
| Where does the ship lie? | ꜀*Sung póh*$_2$ ꜀*tĕng* ꜂*nĕ*, | 船拋何處 |
| 100 bales of cotton, | *Sioh*$_2$ *pah*꜁ ꜀*pau* ꜀*miéng* ꜀*hwa*, | 一百包綿花 |
| 3,000 piculs of rice, | ꜂*Mi* ꜀*sang* ꜀*ch‘iéng tang*꜃, | 米三千担 |
| Take care and don't get the cotton wet, | *Sá*꜃ *ne*$^2$ ꜀*miéng* ꜀*hwa ng*$^2$ ꜀*t‘ĕng p‘ah*꜁ *lang*$^2$, | 謹慎綿花不可打濕 |
| Have you weighed the rice? | ꜂*Mi o*$^2$ *kwo*꜃ ꜀*liong* ꜀*mó*, | 米有過量無 |
| One bag 120 catties, | *Sioh*$_2$ *tói*$^2$ *pah*꜁ *ne*$^2$ ꜀*kŭng*, | 一袋二百斤 |
| Is that net quantity? | *O*$^2$ ꜀*tü t‘ah*꜁ *mwoi*$^2$, | 有除净未 |
| No, it includes the bag, | ꜀*Mó*, ꜀*liéng tói*$^2$ *saung*꜃, | 無連袋筭 |
| Deliver 300 bundles to him, | *Tioh*$_2$ ꜀*kau k‘ĕük*꜁ ꜀*i* ꜀*sang pah*꜁ ꜀*pau*, | 着交與他三百包 |
| When you deliver the goods count the tallies, | ꜂*Nü* ꜀*kau hwo*꜃ *tioh*$_2$ *saung*꜃ ꜀*t‘iu*, | 你交貨着筭籌 |
| Get twenty men to pack, | *Kieu*꜃ *ne*$^2$ *sek*$_2$ ꜀*nĕng* ꜀*li* ꜀*chong*, | 叫二十人來裝 |
| Tell the comprador to pay them, | *Kieu*꜃ ꜂*chiong koi*$^2$ *saung*꜃ ꜀*chiéng k‘ĕük*꜁ ꜀*i*, | 叫掌櫃筭錢與他 |
| You must keep your eyes on those coolies, | ꜂*Nü tioh*$_2$ *ch‘ëü*꜃ ꜂*chiă chó*꜃ ꜀*kĕng* ꜀*ki* ꜀*nĕng*, | 你着督此做工之人 |
| Mark all the bags of tea, | ꜀*Ta tói*$^2$ ꜀*tu tioh*$_2$ *eng*꜃ ꜂*la che*$^2$ *hó*$^2$, | 茶袋俱着印個字號 |

# PART IV. RELIGION, LITERATURE, GOVERNMENT.

## 1. SECTS.

*꜀Ü kau꜄*, 儒教 the sect of the Learned, Confucianism—the term *꜀ü* (Ju) was first adopted A. D. 1150, as an appellation for those who followed Chuhi in his speculations about the Great Extreme.

*Tô$^2$ kau꜄*, 道教 the sect of Rationalists, Tauism, founded by Lautsz', who was born B. C. 604.

*Sek꜇ kau꜄* 釋教 Budhism, introduced into China about A. D. 66.

*꜀Ü tô$^2$ sek꜇ ꜁sang kau꜄* 儒道釋三教 the three sects, Confucianism, Tauism, Budhism.

*꜀U ꜀ui kau꜄* 無爲教 the non-action sect or esoteric Budhism, a sect of mystic Budhists (Edkins' Religious Condition of the Chinese People, pp. 260—267).

*꜀Wong kau꜄* 黃教 the Yellow sect, Shamanism, prevailing in Mongolia and Tibet.

*Wak$_2$ huk$_2$* 活佛 the Living Budha, the Delai Lama, or Grand Lama.

*꜁T'iu ꜁küng kau꜄* 抽筋教 the sect of those that pluck out the sinew, a designation of the Jews in *꜁K'ai ꜁hung* (Kaifung) 開封 the capital of Honan—the Jews probably entered China, B. C. 205 or 258.

*꜀Hui ꜀hui kau꜄* 回回教 Mohammedism or Islamism—its adherents entered China during the T'ang dynasty (A. D. 620—907) within a century after the hegira.

*꜂King kau꜄* 景教 the Illustrious Doctrine, a term for the religion of the Nestorians, who probably entered China as early as A. D. 505. The Nestorian tablet, *꜂King kau꜄ ꜁pi* 景教碑 commemorating "the diffusion of the illustrious religion of *Tai$^2$*

*꜀ching* 大秦 (Ta-tsin) Judea", was erected A. D. 781 at *꜀Sá ꜀ang* (Singan) 西安 the capital of Shensi, and discovered A. D. 1625 by some workmen.

*꜀T'iéng ꜂chio kau꜄* 天主教 Religion of the Lord of Heaven, Roman Catholicism, introduced into China, A. D. 1292.

*꜀Yă ꜀su kau꜄* 耶穌教 Religion of Jesus, Protestant Christianity, introduced into China, A. D. 1807.

The following terms occur in metaphysical disquisitions on cosmogony by Tauist and other writers—

*T'ai꜄ kik꜇* 太極 the Great Extreme, the primordial principle or cause, which produced the dual powers, or which, through these powers, evolved the universe.

*꜀Ing ꜀yong*, 陰陽 the dual principles, or powers, *yin* and *yang*, the inferior and superior, or female and male, principles in nature, which by their mutual action formed the outlines of all existences.

*꜀Pwang ꜂ku*, 盤古 Pwanku, the first man, described as produced from chaos by the dual powers and then as chiseling it into shape.

## 2. WORSHIPED OBJECTS, GODS, GODDESSES.

The following classification is adopted for the sake of convenience. As regards the first two of its three divisions, it is somewhat artificial. Gods that "have hair and are not vegetarians, and whose names are used in regular and lay Tauist chants or prayers" are popularly classed as Tauist deities. Hence some of those in the first division might be referred to the second, or Tauist, class.

An asterisk * denotes that the object is a state god, or is worshiped by officers of government. The letters (s. a.) indicate that offerings and sacrifices are presented in the 2d and 8th months, in *spring and autumn*. Placed before a date, the letter (b.) indicates the *birthday* of a god; the letter (i.) with the figures (1 & 15), the burning of *incense* on the 1st and 15th of each month; the letter (w.) the time of more formal *worship*.

NATIONAL AND ANCESTRAL OBJECTS OF WORSHIP.

꜀*T'iéng*, 天 Heaven (i. 1 & 15), ꜁*Hwong* ꜀*T'iéng*, 皇天 Imperial Heaven ; ꜀*T'iéng Te²* 天地 * Heaven and Earth (s. a.).

*Haiu²* ꜂*T'u*, 后土 Imperial Land or Earth, gods of the Land, as worshiped on the left of the grave.

꜁*Sing* ꜁*Ki*, 神祇 * Celestial and terrestrial gods, Saturn and Cybele (s. a.).

*Siä² chek*꜄ 社稷 * gods of land and grain, the Chinese Ceres (s. a).

*Nik₂ Ngwok₂* 日月 * Sun and Moon, ꜀*Hung* ꜁*Hung*, ꜁*Loi* ꜂*Ü*, 風雲雷雨 * Winds, Clouds, Thunder, and Rain (s. a.).

꜁*Nang* ꜂*Teu*, 南斗 South Peck (Pole) — rules life ; *Paĕk*꜄ ꜂*Teu* (꜂*Tau*) 北斗 North Peck (Pole or Dipper) — rules death (i. 1 & 15).

꜂*Teu* ꜂*Mu*, 斗母 Peck-mother, a guardian of children (i. 1 & 15, w. 8 m. 15 d.).

*Sĕü*꜄ ꜂*hai*, 四海 the Four Seas ; *Sĕü*꜄ *tuk₂* 四瀆 the Four Rivers; ꜂*Ngu ngok₂* 五嶽 the Five Mountains.

*Siong² tá*꜄ 上帝 the Supreme Ruler — the Supreme Intelligence, Governing Power or Providence, as worshiped by ancient monarchs and mentioned in the Shoo-king and Odes.

꜁*Hiéng Tá*꜄ 玄帝 * or ꜁*Hiéng* ꜀*T'iéng Siong² Tá*꜄ 玄天上帝 Somber Ruler or Supreme Ruler of the somber heavens, also styled North Ruler and Governor of Water to prevent conflagrations (b. 3m. 3d.).

꜀*Sang* ꜁*Hwong*, 三皇 the Three Emperors, *viz.*, *Huk₂* ꜀*hi*, 伏羲 Fuh-hi or Fohi, inventor of the eight diagrams; ꜁*Sing* ꜁*nung*, 神農 the divine husbandman, who first practiced agriculture and studied about herbs ; ꜁*Wong Tá*꜄ 黃帝 Yellow Emperor, inventor of letters and implements, and discoverer of the silk-worm (i. 1 & 15).

꜂*Kwi* ꜁*sing*, 鬼神 spirits or *manes*, gods; ꜁*Sing* ꜁*ming* 神明 spiritual intelligences, the immortal gods.

꜁*Sing* ꜂*chü* ꜁*pá*, 神主牌 or ꜁*pá t'ó*꜄ 牌套 the ancestral tablet, abode of the *manes* (daily incense).

*ʿChu ꜀chung,* 祖宗 ancestors, and *꜀Kung ꜁pó,* 公婆 one's ancestors of the four past generations, as worshiped in the tablet (daily incense).

*Wang² swoí ꜄ ꜁pá,* 萬歲牌 * the imperial tablet (w. winter solstice, 1m. 1d., and on birthday). *T'ai꜄ Mieu²* 太廟 the Great Temple (of the tablets of deceased monarchs at the capital) (i. 1 & 15, s. a.).

*A² kai꜄* 下界 (the spirits of) the lower world, miserable orbate ghosts, to whom offerings are made mostly in the 7th moon.

*Seng꜄ ꜁wong,* 聖王 the Sage Kings (of remote antiquity), as Yau and Shun.

*Seng꜄ ꜁ing,* 聖人 * sages, the sage (Confucius) (i. 1 & 15, s. a.), *Seng꜄ ꜁hiéng,* 聖賢 or *Seng꜄ ꜁hiéng ꜁ing,* 聖賢人 sages and philosophers.

*꜁Ung ꜀ch'iong tá꜄ ꜀kung,* 文昌帝君 * the god of literature, said to be the *ʿChié ꜁mi ꜀sing,* 紫微星 or North Star (b. 2m. 3d., i. 1 & 15, s. a.).

*꜀K'wi ꜀sing,* 魁星 * also a god of literature, the *꜀Kié* 奎 star (god) in Andromeda or Pisces, pictured as standing before *꜁Ung ꜀ch'iong tá꜄ ꜀kung,* and "kicking the Dipper" (*꜀k'wi ꜀sing t'ek꜀ ʿtau*), (b. 8m. 15d., i. 1 & 15).

### Tauist Deities.

*꜀Sang ꜀ch'ing,* 三清 the Three Pure Ones, *viz., T'ai꜄ Siong² ʿLó ꜀Kung* 太上老公 also called *ʿLó ʿChü* 老子 or Lautsz', founder of Rationalism, *꜁Ngwong ʿSü ꜀T'iéng ꜀chong,* 元始天尊 and *꜀T'ung ꜀T'iéng Kau꜄ ʿChio* 通天教主.

*Ngŭk꜀ ꜁Hwong,* 玉皇 (sometimes styled *Siong² Tá꜄* or Supreme Ruler), the Pearly Emperor, chief god of the Tauist pantheon (b. 1m. 9d.).

*꜁Wong ꜀t'iéng ꜀kung,* 王天君 King, heavenly prince, represented by a huge image with three eyes, in temples of the Pearly Emperor (b. 6m. 16d.).

*ʿHwi ꜁sing,* 火神 styled *ʿHwi Tá꜄* 火帝 * the god of fire (b. 6m. 13d., i. 1 & 15, s. a.).

꜀*Kwang Tá*꜄ * 關帝 (also styled ꜀*Kwang* ꜂*ló* ꜁*ié*, 關老爺 ꜀*Kwang* ꜀*hu* ꜂*chü*, 關夫子 and ꜂*U seng*꜄ 武聖) the Chinese Mars, god of war (b. 5m. 13d., i. 1 & 15, s. a.)

꜂*Ngu Tá*꜄ 五帝 the Five Rulers, who expel pestilential influences and demons, borne in processions in the 5—7 months: their names are ꜀*Tiong*, 張 ꜀*Chüng*, 鍾 ꜁*Lau*, 劉 ꜂*Sü*, 史 *Tieu*² 趙 (b. 5m. 1—5d): they are variously supposed to represent the Five Directions, or the Five Elements, or the Five Colors: their two classes of attendants or police are called respectively ꜁*Tong* ꜀*pang* ꜂*kwi*, 長班鬼 tall demons, or *Ch'ek*꜆ ꜁*ié*, 七爺 seventh sirs, and ꜂*Á paik*꜆ ꜂*kwi*, 矮八鬼 short demons, or *Paik*꜆ ꜁*ié*, 八爺 eighth sirs.

꜁*Ngiéng* ꜁*ló* ꜁*wong*, 閻羅王 (also styled ꜁*Ngiéng* ꜁*ló* ꜀*t'iéng* ꜂*chü*, 閻羅天子), the Emperor or king of *hades*, judge of spirits, specifically the judge in the 5th of the 10 halls.

*T'ai*꜄ ꜀*sang*, 泰山 * Great Mountain, also styled ꜁*Ing seng*꜄ *tá*꜄ 仁聖帝 Benevolent, sage emperor—said to be a grandson of ꜁*Hiéng tá*꜄, the Somber Ruler (b. 3m. 28d, i. 1 & 15, s. a.).

꜁*Siǎng* ꜁*hwong*, 城隍 * Municipal Guardian, or Lord of the Province, the Provincial Governor (b. 2m. 22d, i. 1 & 15, s. a.).

*Tai*² ꜁*wong*, 大王 Great King, the Constable of a precinct or ward (i. 1 & 15).

*Wok*꜇ ꜁*wong*, 越王 * or ꜁*Ming wok*꜇ ꜁*wong*, 閩越王 King of the Min country, who reigned in the Han dynasty—his temple is on Great Temple Hill, Foochow, and he is worshiped in times of drought (s. a.).

꜁*Ngwong sói*꜄ 元帥 the god of musicians, actors, pugilists and players in general, said to be the third son of the Pearly Emperor (b. 8m. 23d.)—his attendants are *Tang*² *ne*² *pah*꜆ 鄭二伯 *Tang*² *ne*² ꜂*mu*, 鄭二姆 ꜀*U* ꜀*kó*, 烏哥 *Pah*꜇ *tié*², 白俤 ꜁*Ling* ꜂*keu*, 靈狗.

꜂*Ngu* ꜂*hiéng*, 五顯 a god, said to have been a thief and sometimes called "god of thieves", but now very generally reverenced (b. 4m. 8d.).

*Pah*꜇ ꜁*mieu pwang*꜄ ꜀*t'iéng* ꜂*ngu* ꜂*hiéng* ꜀*kung*, 澤苗半天五顯公 the Mid-heaven Duke, Ngu-hiéng, of Pah-mieu (village

榕腔初學撮要

where the worship originated—is worshiped without any image under the open sky (b. 8m. 17d.).

*ʻKau saiʾ* 九使 (also styled *ʻkau saiʾ ꜀ié*, 九使爺 and *ʻkau saiʾ ꜀wong*, 九使王) the god of courtesans.

*꜀Tŭ ek꜁ saiʾ* 猪一使 the god of swine.

*ʻLu ꜀pang*, 魯班 the patron god of carpenters and those who use the chisel and the saw.

*Hoʾ yok꜆* 傅說 the patron god of masons and plasterers.

*ʻNü ꜀wo*, 女媧 Pandora, who "melted stones to repair the heavens," patron goddess of stone-cutters.

*ʻKwi kok꜁ ʻchü*, 鬼谷子 the god of diviners and fortune-tellers.

*Yoh꜆ ꜀wong ʻchu ꜀sü*, 藥王祖師 (? also styled *꜀Song ꜀ching ꜀ing*, 孫眞人) the god of medicine, apothecaries, and doctors (b. 3m. 3d.).

*꜀I ꜀kwang tai² ꜀wong*, 醫官大王 the god of surgery or the healing art, as worshiped by friends of the sick.

*꜀Chai ꜀sing*, 財神 gods of wealth (b. 2m. 2d.).

*ʻT'u te² ꜀kung*, 土地公* "Lord of the land", a god of wealth, worshiped in shops, banks, custom-houses and yamêns, (b. 2m. 12d.).

*ʻNgu kok꜁ ꜀sing*, 五穀神 * spirits of the grains (s. a.).

*Chauʾ ꜀kung Chauʾ ʻma*, 灶君灶媽* gods of the kitchen (b. 8m. 3d, daily incense, w. 12m. 23d & 24d.).

*P'auʾ ꜀sing*, 炮神 * spirits of cannons; *꜀Ki*, 旗 or *꜀Ki tuk꜆* 旗纛 * flags, banners.

*꜀Mwong ꜀sing*, 門神 spirits of the doors.

*Oiʾ ꜀ti ꜀küng*, 尉遲恭 * and *꜀Ching sëük꜁ ʻpó*, 秦叔寶 * names of two divinities pictured on yamên-doors.

*꜀Sing ꜀tu*, 神荼 and *Ok꜁ ʻlwi*, 鬱壘 the names of two divinities, written on doors as charms to keep out evil spirits.

*꜀Hu sëüʾ*, 符使 also called *꜀Kung ꜀chó*, 功曹 Messengers, Mercurii, as pictured on bits of paper and "sent on their errand" by burning them.

*ʻMa ʻchu*, 媽祖 * or *ʻMa ʻchu ꜀pó*, 媽祖婆 Goddess of sailors, also styled *꜀T'iéng haiu²* Queen of heaven, *꜀T'iéng haiu² ꜀niong ꜀niong*, 天后娘娘 Her Ladyship Queen of heaven, and

˛T'iéng siong² seng˒ ˓mu, 天上聖母 Holy Mother in the heavens above (b. 3m. 23d., i. 1 & 15, s. a.)—her two chief attendants are ˛Ch'iéng ˓li ˓ngang, 千里眼 the Thousand-mile-eye, and Song² ˛hung ˓ngi, 順風耳 the Favoring-wind-ear.

˛Ling ˓chwi ˓ná, 臨水奶* (also styled ˛Niong ˓ná, 娘奶 Mother), a native of the southern suburbs of Foochow in the T'ang dynasty, goddess of midwifery and of children under 16 years of age (b. 1m. 15d., s. a.).

˛Pó ˛kwang ˛Pó ˓ná, 婆官婆奶 the assistants, of "Mother", who constitute two classes of 36 and 72 respectively.

˓Hu ˛pó ˓ná, 虎婆奶* Tiger-dame-mother, a goddess on the back of a tiger (styled ˓hu ˛ié, Sir Tiger), guardian of sick children (s. a.).

Pah₂ ˛kié ˓sieu ˓chiă, 白雞小姐* the White-Cock Officer's Daughter, a goddess, named Paik˒ ˛hi, 栢姬 with an image of (her faithful) white cock by her side (b. 7m. 7d.)—her temple is near the governor's yamên.

˛Chio ˓ma, 珠媽* goddess of small-pox (s. a.); ˓Mëng ˓ma, 疹媽* goddess of measles (s. a.).

˛Siéng ˛kiéng ˓ná, 簷前奶 or Ch'ek˒ ˛sing ˓ná, 七星奶 Mother of Eaves, or the Seven Stars, a guardian of children (b. 7m. 7d, daily incense).

˛Tiong ˛siéng (coll. ˛Tiong ˛seng), 張仙 a certain genius, shooting ˛T'iéng ˓keu, 天狗 the sky-dog, or dog in the sky—a picture hung in bedrooms and worshiped by married women to "keep children from being devoured by the dog" (daily incense).

˓Ch'iong ˛chiéng ˓hu, 搶錢虎 Snatch-cash-tiger (styled ˓hu ˛ié, Sir Tiger), god of gamblers or blacklegs (daily incense, w. 2 & 16 of mo.).

˛Kau seng˒ ˛wong, 猴聖王 Monkey-Sage-King, worshiped with offerings of fruits under banians, &c., to propitiate his favor "so that he may not trouble children"—his attendants are Haik˒ ˛kau, 黑猴 Black Monkey, and Pah₂ t'o˒, 白兎 White Rabbit.

˛Hu ˛li, 狐狸, or ˛Hu ˛li ˛ma, 狐狸猫 the fox, or fox-elfin, styled ˛Hu ˛siéng, 狐仙* Fox-genius, ˛Siéng ˛ié, 仙爺 Sir

Genius, and ꜀Hu ꜀siéng ꜁ié, 狐仙爺 Sir Fox-genius—worshiped as "Keeper of the Seals" (without image or picture) by the Viceroy and other high mandarins (i. 1 & 15); also with offerings of fruits, etc., by the friends of "those possessed with the fox-elf".

꜁Lüng ꜁sing, 龍神 * the Dragon, worshiped as Bestower of rain in times of drought (i. 1 & 15. s. a.).

꜁Ngu ꜁t'au, 牛頭 the Ox-headed, ꜂Ma miéng² 馬面 the Horse-faced, ꜀Kié ꜁t'au, 雞頭 the Cock-headed, and Ak꜆ chiong꜄, 鴨將 the Duck-generals—are attendants of the Five Rulers, the King of hades, the Great Mountain, and the Lord of the Province.

BUDHIST DEITIES.

꜁Pu sak꜆ 菩薩 Budhist gods or idols.

Huk₂ Budh; ꜀Sang ꜂pó huk₂ 三寶佛 the Three Precious Budhs (꜀Kiă siék꜆ 迦葉 Sek꜆ ꜀kiă, 釋迦 and ꜁Meu ꜁ná, 牟尼), the past, present, and future Budhs; ꜁Ü ꜁lai, 如來 is a common term applied to them.

Sek꜆ ꜀kiă ꜁meu ꜁ná, 釋迦牟尼 Shakya-muni; ꜀Ó ꜁mi ꜁t'ó huk₂ 阿彌陀佛 Amida-Budha.

꜁Mi lek₂ 彌勒 or ꜁Mi ꜁ná huk₂ 彌尼佛 a fat, laughing Budh (in the front hall of monasteries), the future (some say the *past*) Budha.

꜀Kwang ꜀ing, 觀音 * or ꜀Kwang ꜀ing huk₂ 觀音佛 or ꜀Kwang sié꜄ ꜀ing, 觀世音 the Goddess of Mercy, sometimes represented as a man—worshiped as the *giver of children* by married women (b. 2m. 19d, i. 1 & 15, w. 9, 19, 29, of mo.).

Pek₂ ꜀i tai² sëü² 白衣大士 the white-robed-great-personage—a title of Kwanyin.

꜁Kiă ꜁lang, 伽藍 certain Budhs who record human actions.

Kang꜄ ꜀chá, 監齋 styled ꜀Kiéng ꜁t'ó ꜁ló ꜁wong, 堅陀羅王 god of the Budhist kitchen—the name also applied to the god of the refectory.

꜁Ui ꜁tó (or ꜁ui ꜁nó) 韋馱 the wand-bearer (back of the fat Budh in the front hall or temple).

꜂Chung ꜁t'i, 準提 the name of a many-handed Budh.

ʻP'wo ˛ang, 普庵 a Budha, as represented on paper-charms.

Sëü' ˛chiu huk˛ 泗洲佛 a Budh worshiped in shrines at street-corners (b. 6m. 1d, i. 1 & 15).

Ne² sek˛ se' oi² ˛chü ˛t'iéng, 二十四位諸天 the Twenty-four Personages of the Heavens (b. 4m. 24d, w. by female vegetarians in the 4th month, also on the 4th, 14th, and 24th, of each month).

Sëü' tai² ˛king ˛kong, 四大金剛 the four gigantic sentinels in the front hall, subduers of demons.

˛Heng ˛Ha ne² chiong', 哼哈二將 the Vociferating Generals, Heng and Ha.

Sek˛ paik˛ ˛ló hang' 十八羅漢 the 18 disciples, as arranged on the left and right in the main hall.

Te² chaung² ˛wong, 地藏王 named Muk˛ ˛liéng, 目連 a deified Budhist who "delivers spirits from limbo" (b. 7m. 29d.).

## 3. SAGES AND PHILOSOPHERS.

ʻK'ung ʻchü, 孔子 or ʻK'ung ˛hu ʻchü, 孔夫子 Confucius, named ˛K'iu, 丘 and styled Tëüng² ˛ná, 仲尼 born B. C. 549 or 553, 8m. 27d. ?—his tablet occupies the central place in Confucian temples.

Sëü' p'woi' 四配 the Four Associates or Assessors, viz., ˛Ngang ʻchü, 顏子 or ˛Ngang ˛huí, 顏回 a favorite and chief disciple of Confucius; ˛Cheng ʻchü, 曾子 or ˛Cheng ˛seng, 曾參 a voluminous writer and the author or compiler of the Classic on Filial Piety; ʻChü ˛sü, 子思 or ʻK'ung ngek˛ 孔伋 grandson of Confucius; Maing² ʻchü, 孟子 Mencius—their tablets are in niches on the left and right, or east and west, below that of Confucius.

Sek˛ tiék˛ 十哲 the Ten Wise Ones, viz., ʻMing ʻchü, 閔子 (ʻMing ʻsong, 閔損 ʻMing ʻchü ˛k'iéng, 閔子騫); Tëüng² ˛üng, 仲雍 (ʻYéng ʻchü, 冉子); ʻChü kong' 子貢 (˛Twang muk˛ ʻchü, 端木子 ˛Twang muk˛ sëü' 端木賜); ʻChü lo² 子路 (Tëüng² ʻchü, 仲子 Tëüng² ˛iu, 仲由); ʻChü ha² 子夏 (Pok˛ ʻchü, 卜子 Pok˛ ʻchü ha² 卜子夏); ʻYéng paik˛ ˛ngiu, 冉伯牛 (ʻYéng ʻchü, 冉子 ʻYéng ˛keng, 冉耕); ʻYéng ˛kiu, 冉求 (Yéng ʻchü, 冉子); ʻChai

*꜂ngó,* 宰我 (*꜂Chai ꜂chü,* 宰子 *꜂Chai ꜁ü,* 宰予); *꜂Chü ꜁iu,* 子游 (*꜁Ngiong ꜂chü,* 言子 *꜁Ngiong ꜂yéng,* 言偃); *꜂Chü ꜀tiong,* 子張 (*꜀Chiong ꜀song ꜀sü,* 顓孫須 *꜀Chiong ꜀song ꜂chü,* 顓孫子)—their tablets are on the east and west, below those of the Four Associates.

*Ch'ek꜆ sek꜇ ne[2] ꜁hiéng ꜁ing,* 七十二賢人 the 72 worthies or philosophers, disciples of the Sage—their tablets are on the east and west, in the outer court.

*꜀Sang ꜀ch'iéng ꜁tu tá[2] ꜂chü,* 三千徒弟子 the 3000 disciples, including the 72 worthies.

## 4. AUTHORS.

*꜁Ung ꜁wong,* 文王 the Literary Prince, about B. C. 1150, author of the Book of Changes.

*꜀Chiu ꜀kung,* 周公 Lord Chow or Duke of Chow, about B. C. 1112, author of the Chow Ritual.

*꜂Ló ꜂chü,* 老子 or *꜂Ló ꜀kung,* 老君 Lautsz', born B. C. 604 in the (now) province of Hupeh, author of Classic on Reason and Virtue.

*꜀Sü ꜂ma ꜀ch'iéng,* 司馬遷 the Herodotus of China, or earliest Chinese historian, about B. C. 104 in the Han dynasty, author of the Historical Records.

*꜀Sü ꜂ma ꜀kwong,* 司馬光 a historian of the Sung (*Saëng꜄*) dynasty in the 11th century, author of General Mirror to Use in Governing.

*K'ok꜆ ꜁Ngwong,* 屈原 a noted minister of the feudal state *꜂Ch'u,* 楚 B. C. 300—225, in the Chow dynasty, the most ancient of Chinese poets, author of the Dissipation of Sorrows.

*꜂Li pek꜇* 李白 or *꜂Li t'ai꜄ pek꜇* 李太白 of the T'ang, and *꜀Su ꜀tung ꜀p'ó,* 蘇東坡 of the Sung, dynasty, the two most celebrated of Chinese poets.

*꜀Pang ꜀chieu,* 班昭 or *꜁Chó tai[2] ꜀ka* (or *꜀ku,*) 曹大家 a celebrated authoress, about A. D. 80, who wrote the Instructions (*hong꜄*) on Female Duties—the mother of the emperor Shangti of the Eastern Han was her pupil.

*Ting seu²* 陳壽 a court-historian of the Eastern Chin, about A. D. 350, author of History of the Three States.

*Chio hi,* 朱熹 styled *Chio chü,* 朱子 or *Chio hu chü,* 朱夫子 Chuhi, the celebrated philosopher and commentator of the 12th century.

*T'iăng chü,* 程子 Chêngtzu, a disciple of Chuhi, who wrote comments on the Great Learning.

*Ma twang ling,* 馬端齡 of Loping, Kiangsi, often called Matwanling of Poyang, author of Antiquarian Researches, in the Sung (*Saëng*) dynasty, about A. D. 1275.

*Wong paik, haiu²,* 王伯厚 author of the Trimetrical Classic in the Sung (*Saëng*) dynasty.

*Chiu sëü² hing,* 周嗣典 author of the Millenary Classic in the Liang dynasty, about A. D. 550.

*Li si chiéng,* 李時沾 author of the Herbal in the Ming dynasty.

*Ch'ek, ch'ang chiong* 戚叅將 a military chief of the Ming dynasty, author of chief part of the Foochow Eight Tone Book.

*K'ong hi,* 康熙 and *Üng cheng* 雍正 the emperors Kanghi and Yungching, A. D. 1662—1735, authors of the Sacred Edict and explanations.

*Sü kié ü,* 徐繼畬 a governor of Fookien in the reign of Taokwang, author of a Geography.

## 5. BOOKS.

*Sëü k'o chiong chü chung muk,* 四庫全書總目 General Catalogue of all the Books in the Four Libraries, the Imperial Catalogue.

### The Classics.

*Ngu king,* 五經 the Five Classics, or Canonical works, mostly emended and compiled by Confucius—

*Ik, king,* 易經 Book of Changes, by Wênwang, the Literary Prince, about B. C. 1150.

*Chü king,* 書經 Shooking, or Book of Historical Documents, containing a brief history of China from the emperor Yao, B. C. 2357 to P'ing Wang of the Chow dynasty, B. C. 770.

*꜀Si ꜀king,* 詩經 Book of Odes, arranged under four heads, *Kwok꜁ ꜀hung,* 國風 National Airs, *꜂Sieu ꜂nga,* 小雅 Lesser Eulogies, *Tai$^{2}$ ꜂nga,* 大雅 Greater Eulogies, and *Söüng$^{2}$* 頌 Praises (used at imperial sacrifices).

*꜂Lá ke꜃,* 禮記 Record of Rites or Ceremonies (embracing additions made after Confucius' time), partly written by Lord Chow, with comments by two brothers, named *Tai꜃ taik꜁* 戴德 and *Tai꜃ seng꜃* 戴信 (familiarly called *Tai$^{2}$ tai꜃* 大戴 and *꜂Sieu tai꜃* 小戴 elder and younger *Tai꜃*.

*꜀Ch'ung ꜀Ch'iu,* 春秋 Spring and Autumn, chronicles of events from the era of P'ing Wang to the times of Confucius, B. C. 721–480, about 242 years, as reckoned by some—the only one of the five classics that can be properly called Confucius' own work.

*Söü꜃ ꜀chü,* 四書 the Four Books, Books of the Four Philosophers—

*Tai$^{2}$ hok꜁* 大學 the Great Learning, commonly ascribed to *꜀Cheng ꜀seng,* 曾參 i. e. *꜀Cheng ꜂chü,* 曾子 a disciple of Confucius, though an ancient tradition assigns the authorship to his grandson, *꜂Chü ꜀sü,* 子思.

*꜀Tüng ꜁üng,* 中庸 the Doctrine of the Mean, ascribed to *꜂Chü ꜀sü.*

*Laung$^{2}$ ꜂Ngü,* 論語 the Digested Conversations, or Confucian Analects, comprising the sayings of Confucius—in two parts, *Siong$^{2}$ laung$^{2}$* 上論 or *Hok꜁ ꜁i,* 學而 and *Ha$^{2}$ laung$^{2}$* 下論 or *꜀Siéng cheng꜃* 先進.

*Maing$^{2}$* 孟 the works of Mencius—in three parts, *Siong$^{2}$ maing$^{2}$* 上孟 or *꜁Liong hié$^{2}$ ꜁wong,* 梁惠王 *꜀Tüng maing$^{2}$* 中孟 or *꜁Lié ꜁leu,* 離婁 and *Ha$^{2}$ maing$^{2}$* 下孟 or *Kó꜃ ꜂chü,* 告子.

*Hau꜃ ꜀king,* 孝經 a Classic on Filial Piety, in 18 short sections, commonly ascribed to *꜀Cheng ꜂chü*—it contains Confucian apothegms on that subject.

*Sek꜁ ꜀sang ꜀king,* 十三經 the 13 classics, a compilation by order of T'ai-tsung, the second emperor of the T'ang dynasty—it comprises *Ik꜁ ꜀king,* 易經 Book of Changes, *꜀Si ꜀king,* 詩經 Book of Odes, *꜀Chü ꜀king,* 書經 Book of Historical Documents, *꜂Chó tiong$^{2}$* 左傳 *꜀Kung ꜁yong tiong$^{2}$* 公羊傳 and *Kok꜁ ꜁liong tiong$^{2}$* 穀粮傳 three editions of Spring and Autumn, ꜂Li ke꜄ 禮記 or K‘ëük꜆ ꜂lá, 曲禮 Record of Rites, ꜀Chiu ꜂lá, 周禮 Rites of Chow, ꜁Ngi ꜂lá, 儀禮 Forms of Etiquette, Laung꜅ ꜂ngü, 論語 the Confucian Analects, ꜂I ꜂nga, 爾雅 a kind of ancient dictionary, Hau꜄ ꜀king, 孝經 the classic on Filial Piety, Maing꜅ 孟 the works of Mencius.

Chio꜄ 註 comments, commentaries, Chio꜄ saë꜄ 註疏 annotations, annotated classics.

### Other Common School-Books.

꜂Sieu hok꜇ 小學 the Lesser Learning, or Juvenile Instructor, in two volumes, compiled by Chuhi and designed as a counterpart of the Tai꜅ hok꜇ Great Learning.

꜀Sang che꜅ ꜀king, 三字經 the Trimetrical Classic, containing 1068 characters in 178 double lines, compiled by Wang Paihou of the Sung (Saëng꜄) dynasty.

꜀Ch‘iéng che꜅ ꜁ung, 千字文 the Thousand Character Book, or Millenary Classic, containing one thousand different characters, by Chou Ssu-hsing of the Liang dynasty, about A. D. 550.

Pah꜆ ꜀ka sang꜄, 百家姓 the Hundred Family Surnames, or list of Chinese surnames, in reality containing over 450, of which 30 are double.

꜀Sing luk꜇ ꜂k‘ié ꜁mung, 聲律啟蒙 Youth's Instructor in Sounds, Rules and Examples of Antithetical Words from one to over ten.

꜀Ch‘iéng ꜀ka ꜀si, 千家詩 Odes (or Poetical Selections) from Many Authors, as "repeated by Siă꜅ ꜀hwong taik꜆ 謝枋德 i. e. Tiék꜇ ꜀sang, 叠山 at the close of the Yuen and beginning of the Ming".

꜁Tong ꜀si, 唐詩 Songs of the T‘ang dynasty, three hundred in number, in pentameters or heptameters, also called ꜀Si hwak꜆ ik꜇ ꜁mwong, 詩法入門 Rules for Learning to make poetry.

꜀Ch‘ing ꜁hung chik꜇ 青雲集 the Azure Ladder Collection, a simple poetizing instructor or manual.

Sek꜇ swoi꜄ ꜁neng ꜁ung, 十歲能文 Ten-years-old-can-essay, i. e. can write essays at the age of ten—the name of a Volume of Progressive Lessons on the art of composing.

*꜀Ch'u hok꜆ chik꜆* 初學集 Young Student's Collection, or selected model essays of authors, at the close of the Ming, and beginning of the Ta-ch'ing, dynasties.

*꜂Ku ꜁ung*, 古文 Ancient Literature, excerpts from old authors on various subjects, from the era of the ancient monarchs down to the Ming dynasty.

MISCELLANEOUS WORKS.

*꜀Lië ꜀só*, 離騷 the Dissipation of Sorrows, by the poet Ch'ü Yüan.

*Tó² taik꜇ ꜀king*, 道德經 Classic on Reason and Virtue, a philosophical work by Lautsz', the founder of Tauism.

*꜂Sü ke꜄* 史記 Historical Records, in 130 chapters, by Ssu Mach'ien, about B. C. 104—the model for subsequent histories.

*꜀Chü te² ꜀t'ung kang꜄* 資治通鑑 General Mirror to Use in Governing, in 294 chapters, by Ssu Makwang of the Sung (*Saëng꜄*) dynasty.

*꜀T'ung kang꜄ ꜀kong muk꜆* 通鑑綱目 General Mirror and Synopses or Summaries, or a general mirror of history by Chuhi, the foundation of the work being the T'ung-chien of Ssu Makwang.

*꜀Kong kang꜄ e² ꜀ti lioh꜆* 綱鑑易知錄 History made Easy, a compiled abridgment of the preceding work.

*꜁Ung kiëng꜄ ꜀t'ung ꜂k'ó*, 聞見通考 the Complete Antiquarian Researches, by Ma Twanling, about A. D. 1275.

*꜀Keng chek꜇ ꜁tu ꜀si*, 耕織圖詩 Plates and Odes on Tilling and Weaving, written in the Sung (*Saëng꜄*) dynasty—is widely circulated to teach and encourage the people.

*Seng꜄ ëü²* 聖諭 or *Seng꜄ ëü² ꜂kwong hong꜄* 聖諭廣訓 the Sacred Edict or Injunctions, a politico-moral treatise, in 16 maxims or apothegms, written by Kanghi and amplified by his successor Yungching.

*꜂Pwong ꜂ch'ó*, 本草 an Herbal, in 52 chapters, comprising subjects pertaining to the vegetable, mineral and animal kingdoms, by Li Shihchan in the Ming dynasty.

*Tai² ꜂tiëng*, 大典 Great Classic, in 22,877 chapters, of the Emperor Yungloh of the Ming dynasty, A. D. 1403.

ˏSang ˏchai ˏtu, 三才圖 Plates (illustrating) the Three Powers (heaven, earth, man, i. e. the whole universe), in 130 volumes.

ˏIng ˏk'wang che' liok₂ 瀛寰志略 Universal Geography, by Governor Hsü Chiyü, in the 28th year of Taokwang, A. D. 1848—the materials for the work were collected at Amoy "by examining foreign maps, etc., and by personal interviews with the American scholar, 'Nga pe² 'li, 雅禆理 (Abeel) and others".

ˏKa 'pó ˏchiong chik₂ 家寶全集 or ˏTiong ˏka 'pó, 傳家寶 Complete Collection of Family Jewels, comprising minute specifications of duties and 100 rules for students, by Sik₂ ˏsing ˏking ˏt'iéng ˏki (Shihchêngchin T'ienchi) 石成金天基 of Yangchou, Kiangsu.

ˏK'wo ˏtiong ˏteu lié² 科場條例 the Regulations about Literary Examinations.

Cheng' ˏsing, 搢紳 or Cheng' ˏsing ˏchiong ˏchü, 搢紳全書 Complete lists of Official Grades and Appointments, the Chinese Red Book.

ˏSeu ˏsing ke' 搜神記 Records of researches about the Gods.

ˏSing ˏsiéng ˏt'ung kang' 神仙通鑑 General Mirror of Gods and Genii, containing brief notices of their names and origin.

### Dictionaries.

Siok, ˏung 'kai che² 說文解字 Treatise on the Meanings of Characters, published A. D. 150.

Pwoi² ˏung ong² 'hu, 佩文韻府 Thesaurus or Cyclopedia of Collated Characters and Sounds, in 130 volumes, by 76 learned doctors, who labored 8 years at the work under Kanghi's personal superintendence, published in the 50th year of his reign, A. D. 1711.

ˏK'ong ˏhi che² 'tiéng, 康熙字典 Kanghi's Dictionary—an abridgment of the Thesaurus and a standard authority on the readings and definitions of characters.

Ch'ek, ˏling paik, ˏing hak₂ teng' 戚林八音合訂 or simply Paik' ˏIng, 八音 the Eight Tone Book, a compilation of the works of two authors, Ch'ek and Ling, the standard of pronunciation in the Foochow Dialect.

### NOVELS.

‹*Sieu siok*› 小說 novels, novelettes ; ‹*Yă* ‹*sü*, 野史 tales, stories.

‹*Sang kwok*› *che*› 三國誌 History of the Three (contending) States (*Sük*₂ 蜀 *Ngoi*² 魏 ‹*Ngu*, 吳) including the period A. D. 170—317, a historical novel by ‹*Ting seu*² 陳壽 about A. D. 350.

‹*Lieu* ‹*chá*, 聊齋 or ‹*Lieu* ‹*chá che*› *e*² 聊齋誌異 the Easy Study's Record of Strange Things, or Pastimes of the Study, in 16 vols., remarkable for purity, force, and copiousness of style, about A. D. 1679.

‹*Hung* ‹*leu mong*› 紅樓夢 Dreams of the Red Chamber.

‹*Chwi* ‹*hu* (or ‹*hü*), 水滸 Water's Bank, or Robber's Retreat, a story of the pirate or robber, *Saĕng*› ‹*kong*, 宋江 styled *Kik*₂ ‹*si* ‹*ü*, 及時雨 Timely Rain, who "lived at the close of the Sung dynasty and became a loyal officer".

‹*Sá* ‹*iu ke*› 西遊記 Record of Western Rambles—story of the conflicts of the Ape (‹*kau seng*› ‹*wong*) with the Pearly Emperor.

### 6. SCHOOLS, COLLEGES, HALLS.

‹*Chá*, 齋 a primary school ; ‹*Chü* ‹*chá*, 書齋 or *Hok*₂ ‹*tong*, 學堂 a school-room, a seminary.

*Ngiê*² *óh*₂ 義學 a free school, in which there is no charge for tuition.

‹*Chü yéng*² 書院 a college ; *Wok*₂ ‹*sang*, 越山 *Hong*² ‹*tié*, 鳳池 ‹*Ngó* ‹*hung*, 鰲峰 and *Cheng*› *ngiê*² 正誼 the names of four colleges in Foochow.

‹*K'ó* ‹*pang*, 考棚 an examination-hall, place of examinations for the first degree at the Literary Chancellor's.

*Kong*› *yéng*² 貢院 the provincial examination-hall, place of examination for the second degree, also for the third degree at Peking.

‹*King* ‹*lwang taing*² 金鑾殿 the Imperial Palace—where the Hanlin examination is held.

‹*Hang* ‹*ling yéng*² 翰林院 or ‹*Hang* ‹*ling* ‹*kwang*, 翰林館 the Imperial College at Peking.

## 7. TEACHERS AND EXAMINERS.

*꜀Sing ꜀sang,* 先生 or *Ka' ꜀chá ꜀sing ꜀sang,* 教齋先生 or *Sói*$^2$ *꜀chá ꜀sing ꜀sang,* 坐齋先生 a school-teacher.

*꜀Sang ʿtiong,* 山長 or *꜀Chü yéng*$^2$ *꜀sang ʿtiong,* 書院山長 a college instructor or professor.

*Hok*$_2$ *yéng*$^2$ 學院 or *hok*$_2$ *꜁tai,* 學臺 a Literary Chancellor, who examines under-graduates for the first degree.

*ʿChio ʿk'ó,* 主考 and *ho' ʿk'ó,* 副考 or *ʿChio ho' ʿk'ó,* 主副考 the First and Second Examiners, who examine candidates for the second degree.

*ʿChung ꜁choi,* 總裁 or *Twai*$^2$ *ʿchung ꜁choi,* 大總裁 the Examiners of candidates for the third degree.

*꜁Hwong tá'* 皇帝 the Emperor, by or before whom candidates for the fourth degree are examined.

## 8. REVIEWS AND EXAMINATIONS.

*꜀Ung ꜀chü,* 温書 to review lessons at school.

*Sioh*$_2$ *꜀ung,* 一温 a review of three days' lessons; *Sioh*$_2$ *sik*$_2$ 一習 a review of six days' lessons; *Sioh*$_2$ *꜁sung,* 一旬 a review of 9 days' lessons on the 10th day.

*Ngwok*$_2$ *k'wo'* 月課 monthly trials in composing; *Chó' k'wo'* 做課 to write trial-essays, as in school or college.

*ʿK'ó ꜀chü yéng*$^2$ 考書院 a college-examination.

*ʿK'ó se',* 考試 or *ʿSieu se',* 小試 the examinations for the first or Siutsai degree.

*Swoi' ʿk'ó,* 歲考 and *꜀K'wo ʿk'ó,* 科考 the two examinations in the 3 years' term of a Literary Chancellor.

*ʿK'ó ꜁mi ꜁chai,* 考遺才 a trial-examination of the Siutsai from the 11th name in the 3d grade to the end of the class, held about a month previous to examinations for the 2d degree.

*꜀K'wo ꜁tiong,* 科場 also called *꜀hiong ꜀k'wo,* 鄉科 or *꜀hiong se',* 鄉試 the provincial examinations for the second or Küjin degree.

*Hwoi*$^2$ *꜀k'wo,* 會科 also called *hwoi*$^2$ *se',* or *hwoi*$^2$ *sëü'* 會試 the examinations at the capital for the third or Chinshih (chinsz') degree.

*Taing$^2$ se*꜄ 殿試 or ꜁*tieu* ꜂*k'ó*, 朝考 the examinations at the palace for the fourth or Hanlin degree.

## 9. PUPILS, GRADUATES, DEGREES.

*Hok$_2$* ꜀*seng*, 學生 a scholar, a pupil.

꜁*Tung* ꜀*seng*, 童生 an under - graduate, a candidate for the first degree.

*Seu*꜄ ꜁*choi*, 秀才 THE FIRST DEGREE, A. B., a Siutsai graduate.

*K'ó*꜄ ꜂*k'ó se*꜄, 去考試 ꜂*tié* ꜂*sieu* ꜁*tiong*, 入小場 to enter for the first degree.

*Cheng*꜄ *óh$_2$* 進學 or *cheng*꜄ *seu*꜄ ꜁*choi*, 進秀才 to obtain the Siutsai degree.

*P'wang*꜄ ꜁*ngwong*, 泮元 the first of the Siutsai graduates.

*Ik$_2$* ꜀*seng*, 佾生 or *pe$^2$* ꜂*ch'ü*, 備取 under (Siutsai) graduates, the reserved class of promising candidates for the next Siutsai examination.

꜀*Cheng* ꜀*seng*, 增生 the "additional" class or advanced grade, as attained by examination before a new Chancellor after the stipendiary list is filled.

꜂*Ling* ꜀*seng*, 廩生 a stipendiary Siutsai; ꜂*Pwo* ꜂*Ling*, 補廩 enrolled on the list of stipendiaries; ꜂*Ling* ꜀*á* ꜂*pó*, 廩挨保 the two stipendiaries who act as sureties for the under-graduates.

*Kong*꜄ ꜀*seng*, 貢生 the *kong* or breveted Siutsai, graduates who attain such grade by imperial favor, or merit, or certain rules in a given number of years, or a good character and special examinations previous to the triennial examinations for the 2d degree; or by payment of certain fees entitling them, though not regular Siutsai, to compete for that degree.

꜂*Ling kong*꜄ 廩貢 or *swoi*꜄ *kong*꜄ 歲貢 an advanced grade from the ꜂*ling* ꜀*seng* after from 9 to 12 years.

꜀*Iu kong*꜄ 優貢 the excelling or good-character grade, given at a special examination before the Chancellor and Governor.

*Pak$_2$ kong*꜄ 拔貢 a selected Siutsai, as breveted by the Governor—a selection of one only from each Hsien or district, once in 12 years.

*Kang*’ ꜀*seng*, 監 生 a purchased grade, entitling one, though not a regular Siutsai, to compete for the Küjin degree; ꜀*Kiong kang*’ 捐 監 to purchase the Siutsai degree or standing.

‘*Kü* ꜁*ing*, 舉 人 THE SECOND DEGREE, A. M., a Küjin graduate.

*K‘ó*’ ꜀*k‘wo* ꜁*tiong*, 去 科 場 or ‘*tié twai*$^{2}$ ꜁*tiong*, 入 大 場 to enter for the second degree.

*Tëüng*’ ‘*kü*, 中 舉 or *tëüng*’ ‘*kü* ꜁*ing*, 中 舉 人 to obtain the Küjin degree.

*Kä*’ ꜁*ngwong*, 解 元 the first of the Küjin graduates.

꜀*King* ꜀*k‘wi*, 經 魁 the 2d to the 5th, inclusive; ‘*A* ꜀*k‘wi*, 亞 魁 the 6th to the 12th, inclusive; ꜁*Ung* ꜀*k‘wi*, 文 魁 from the 13th to the end of the graduating class.

*Ho*’ ‘*pong*, 副 榜 the secondary list or class, the under (Küjin) graduates.

*Cheng*’ *sëü*$^{2}$ 進 士 THE THIRD DEGREE, L. L. D., a Chinshih( Chinsz’) graduate.

*Siong*$^{2}$ ꜀*king*, 上 京 or ‘*tié* ꜀*king*, 進 京 to "go to the capital" (to enter for the third degree).

*Tëüng*’ *cheng*’ *sëü*$^{2}$, 中 進 士 to obtain the Chinshih degree.

*Hwoi*$^{2}$ ꜁*ngwong*, 會 元 the first of the Chinshih graduates.

*Hwoi*$^{2}$ ꜀*k‘wi*, 會 魁 the 2d to the 18th of these graduates.

꜁*Hang* ꜁*ling*, 翰 林 THE FOURTH DEGREE, or Imperial Collegiate grade, which may be termed an *office* rather than a *degree*.

‘*Teng* ꜁*hang* ꜁*ling*, 點 翰 林 to class or enroll as imperial collegians.

*Chaung*$^{2}$ ꜁*ngwong* (coll. ꜀*chó* ꜁*ngwong*), 狀 元 ‘*Pong* ‘*ngang*, 榜 眼 ꜀*T‘ang* ꜀*hwa*, 探 花 and ꜁*Tiong* ꜁*lu*, 傳 臚 the first four of the Hanlin.

*Ek*꜁ *kak*꜁ 一 甲 the first class or grade, those who enter the Imperial College.

*Ne*$^{2}$ *kak*꜁ 二 甲 the second class, those who enter the Boards, as *Pwo*$^{2}$ ꜁*wong*, 部 員 petty Board-officers.

꜀*Sang kak*꜁ 三 甲 the third class, those who are appointed to District Magistracies.

꜁*Pang* ꜁*t‘au cheng*’ *sëü*$^{2}$ 平 頭 進 士 level-head-chinshih—those failing to attain to either of the three classes.

## 10. THE EMPIRE, THE CENTRAL GOVERNMENT.

꜀*T'iéng a*$^{2}$ 天下 the world, the empire.

*Kwok*꜆ 國 a state, country, kingdom, empire.

*Kwok*꜆ ꜀*ka*, 國家 the state; *Kwok*꜆ *hwak*꜆ 國法 the laws; *Pah*꜆ *sang*꜄ 百姓 the people.

*Kwok*꜆ *cheng*꜄ 國政 or *cheng*꜄ *sëü*$^{2}$ 政事 national government; *Te*$^{2}$ *kwok*꜆ 治國 to rule the country or empire.

꜀*Tüng kwok*꜆ 中國 or ꜀*tüng* ꜁*hwa*, 中華 the Middle Kingdom, China.

*Tai*$^{2}$ ꜀*ch'ing kwok*꜆ 大清國 the Great Pure, or Manchu, empire, A. D. 1644.

*Kwok*꜆ ꜁*tieu*, 國朝 a dynasty; ꜁*Tieu tói*$^{2}$ 朝代 a dynasty, dynasties; *Kwok*꜆ *hó*$^{2}$ 國號 the name or style of a dynasty; ꜁*Niéng hó*$^{2}$ 年號 name of a reign.

꜀*King* ꜁*siăng*, 京城 the capital; *Paëk*꜆ ꜀*king*, 北京 Peking; ꜀*King pó*꜄ 京報 the Peking Gazette.

꜁*Hwong tá*꜄ 皇帝 the emperor, styled ꜀*t'iéng* ꜂*chü*, 天子 Son of Heaven.

*T'ai*꜄ ꜂*chü*, 太子 the crown-prince; in general the emperor's sons, usually styled *ak*꜇ ꜀*kó*, *ne*$^{2}$ ꜀*kó*, ꜀*sang* ꜀*kó*, 阿哥, 二哥, 三哥, first brother, second brother, third brother, &c.

꜁*Hwong t'ai*꜄ ꜂*chü*, 皇太子 the crown-prince, heir-apparent; ꜀*Kung* ꜂*chio*, 公主 the emperor's daughters.

꜁*Hwong haiu*$^{2}$ 皇后 the empress; ꜁*Hwong* ꜀*hi*, 皇妃 imperial concubines.

꜁*Hwong t'ai*꜄ *siong*$^{2}$ 皇太上 or *t'ai*꜄ *siong*$^{2}$ ꜁*hwong*, 太上皇 the father of the emperor; ꜁*Hwong t'ai*꜄ *haiu*$^{2}$ 皇太后 the empress dowager.

꜁*Hwong* ꜀*ch'ing kwok*꜆ *ch'ek*꜆ 皇親國戚 the imperial kindred.

꜀*King* ꜁*lwang taing*$^{2}$ 金鑾殿 the imperial palace; ꜀*Küng* ꜂*wong*, 宮苑 or ꜀*küng* ꜂*wong* ꜂*tié*, 宮苑裡 the imperial harem, seraglio.

꜀*Küng* ꜂*nü*, 宮女 or ꜀*küng* ꜁*ngó*, 宮娥 maids of honor; *T'ai*꜄ *kang*꜄ 太監 eunuchs.

*Chiok*˃ 爵 a degree or rank of nobility, as the 5 following—
*˛Kung ˛heu paik*˃ *˓chü ˛nang*, 公侯伯子男 duke, marquis, earl, viscount, baron.

*˓P'ing*, 品 or *˓p'ing ngek*˃ 品級 an official rank or grade—there are nine such ranks, each of which is farther distinguished into *chiăng*˃, 正 principal or chief, and *chëüng*² 從 secondary or subordinate.

*Ek*˃ *˓p'ing*, 一品 the first (highest) of the 9 ranks; *˓Kau ˓p'ing*, 九品 the ninth (lowest) rank; *Chiăng*˃ *ek*˃ *˓p'ing*, 正一品 the chief-first rank; *Chëüng*² *˓kau ˓p'ing*, 從九品 the subordinate-ninth rank.

*˓Ting*, 頂 the official ball or button — worn on the top of the cap; *˓Ting tai*˃ 頂帶 to wear an official button.

*Chiăng*˃ *˛tu*, 正途 the correct or straight road—offices gained by the regular, competitive examinations; *˛K'wo kak*˃ *ch'ok*˃ *˛sing*, 科甲出身 to gain office by literary success.

*˛P'iéng ˛tu*, 偏途 the partial or oblique road—offices gained by irregular or exceptional modes, as *˛Kung ˛kung*, 軍功 by military merit, *˓Pó ˓kü*, 保舉 by responsible recommendation, *Ngié*² *sëü*² 議敘 by official conference, *Lié*² *˛kiong*, 例捐 by customary contribution or payment of fees.

*˛Sing ˓chü*, 臣子 a minister, an officer, officers.

*Ngëü*² *˛ling ˛kung*, 御林軍 and *Se*² *woi*² 侍衛 Imperial Guards.

*T'ai*˃ *˓chü t'ai*˃ *˛sü*, 太子太師 *T'ai*˃ *˓chü t'ai*˃ *ho*˃ 太子太傅 *Tai*˃ *˓chü t'ai*˃ *˓pó*, 太子太保 the tutors of the emperor's sons—of the chief 1st rank.

*˓Sü ˛kwang*, 史官 an annalist, a historiographer; *˓Chó ˓sü*, 左史 and *Eu*² *˓sü*, 右史 the two court-historians.

*Ngëü*² *˓sü*, 御史 a censor, censors—of the subordinate 1st rank.

*˛K'ing ˛ch'á*, 欽差 an imperial envoy or commissioner.

*˛Hung ˛wong*, 封王 to invest with kingly rank, as by an imperial rescript.

*Chiăng*˃ *sai*˃ 正使 and *Ho*˃ *sai*˃ 副使 imperial legates or envoys, bearers of a rescript or decree—of the chief 1st rank.

*Nói*² *kóh*˃ 內閣 the Inner Council, the Cabinet; *˛Kung ˛ki tai*² *˛sing*, 軍機大臣 the General Council of State.

*Tai*$^2$ *hok*$_2$ *sëü*$^2$ **大學士** chief doctors or chancellors—of the chief 1st rank; *Hiék*$_2$ *paing*$^2$ *tai*$^2$ *hok*$_2$ *sëü*$^2$ **協辦大學士** assistant chancellors.

꜂*Chai siong*꜃ **宰相** a premier; ꜂*Chó eu*$^2$ *siong*꜃ **左右相** the two chief ministers or premiers—of the chief 1st rank.

*Lëk*$_2$ *pwo*$^2$ **六部** the Six Boards—*Le*$^2$ *pwo*$^2$ **吏部** B. of Civil Office, *Ho*$^2$ *pwo*$^2$ **戶部** B. of Population and Revenue, ꜂*Lá pwo*$^2$ **禮部** B. of Rites, ꜀*Ping pwo*$^2$ **兵部** B. of War, ꜀*Hing pwo*$^2$ **刑部** B. of Punishments, ꜀*Këng pwo*$^2$ **工部** B. of Works.

*Siong*$^2$ ꜀*sü*, **尙書** President of a Board—of the subordinate 1st rank; *Se*$^2$ ꜀*long*, **侍郎** Vice-president of a Board—of the chief 2nd rank.

꜀*Long* ꜀*tüng*, **郎中** directors, assistants of a vice-president—of the chief 5th rank; ꜀*Wong ngwoi*$^2$ **員外** under-secretaries, clerks; ꜂*Chio sëü*$^2$ **主事** managers.

꜂*Li* ꜀*hwang yéng*$^2$ **理藩院** Court for the Government of Foreigners, the Colonial Office.

꜀*Tu ch'ak*꜁ *yéng*$^2$ **都察院** the All-Examining Court or Censorate.

꜀*T'ung cheng*꜃ ꜀*si*, **通政司** the Court of Memorial or Representation, and Appeal.

*Tai*$^2$ ꜂*li se*$^2$ **大理寺** the Court of Judicature.

꜀*Hang* ꜀*ling yéng*$^2$ **翰林院** the Imperial College; ꜂*Chiong yéng*$^2$ *hok*$_2$ *sëü*$^2$ **掌院學士** the two presidents or senior members of the college.

*Kwok*꜁ ꜂*chü kang*꜃ **國子監** the National College—for teaching graduates of the lower degrees.

꜀*K'ing* ꜀*t'iéng kang*꜃ **欽天監** the Imperial Astronomical College.

*T'ai*꜃ ꜀*siong se*$^2$ **太常寺** the Sacrificial Court.

*T'ai*꜃ *puk*$_2$ *se*$^2$ **太僕寺** superintendents or overseers of H. I. M's Stud.

꜀*Kwong lük*$_2$ *se*$^2$ **光祿寺** the Banqueting House, subordinate to the Board of Rites.

꜀*Hung* ꜀*lu se*$^2$ **鴻臚寺** the Ceremonial Court.

*T'ai*꜃ ꜀*i yéng*$^2$ **太醫院** the Supreme Medical Hall.

꜀*Chung* ꜀*ing* ꜂*hu*, **宗人府** Board of the Imperial Kindred—is entirely under the Emperor's management.

## 11、PROVINCIAL GOVERNMENT.

ʿ*Seng*, 省 a province; *Hok*ˎ *kiong*ˀ ʿ*seng*, 福建省 the Fookien province.

ʿ*Seng* ˛*siăng*, 省城 the provincial capital.

ʿ*Hu*, 府 the chief divisions of a province, a department, a prefecture.

˛*Chiu*, 州 an inferior department, one that is less than a prefecture.

*Kaing*² 縣 the sub-divisions of a prefecture, a district.

˛*Tu*, 都 or ʿ*Li*, 里 the sections of a district, a township.

˛*Hiong*, 鄉 or ˛*hiong* ˛*ch'ong*, 鄉村 or ˛*hiong* ˛*kang*, 鄉間 a village, a hamlet.

*P'wo*ˀ 舖 the wards or districts of a city or town.

*Siă*² 社 or ʿ*king siă*² 境社 a neighborhood or hamlet, a collection of houses with a local temple.

˛*Ung* ˛*kwang*, 文官 civil officers; ʿ*U* ˛*kwang*, 武官 military officers; ˛*ung* ʿ*u paik*ˎ ˛*kwang*, 文武百官 all the mandarins, civil and military.

ʿ*Iu* ˛*si*, 有司 judges, magistrates; ʿ*Ló* ˛*tiă*, 老爹 His Honor, an officer.

˛*Hiong* ˛*sing*, 鄉紳 "those wearing sashes", the gentry; ˛*Sing* ˛*ki*, 紳耆 the gentry and the elders.

### Civil Officers.

˛*Cheng* ˛*kong* ˛*si*, 僧綱司 the Budhist superintendent in a department—is of the subordinate 9th rank.

˛*Cheng hwoi*² ˛*si*, 僧會司 Budhist superintendent in a district.

*Tó*² ʿ*ki* ˛*si*, 道紀司 and ˛*Ing* ˛*yong óh*ˎ 陰陽學 Tauist superintendents or overseers.

ʿ*Tiĕng le*² 典吏 and *Le*² ˛*wong*, 吏員 two petty ranks, promotions from the clerkship.

ʿ*Tiĕng* ʿ*sü*, 典史 a grade above the last, rank of a ʿ*Chwi le*ˀ 水利 or *Pwo*² ˛*nga*, 捕衙.

*Pwo*² ˛*nga*, 捕衙 or *pwo*² ˛*t'iăng*, 捕廳 the general superintendent of a prison, a district magistrate's assistant.

*꜀Sung ꜂kiĕng,* 巡檢 the supervisor of a township, a sheriff—of the subordinate 9th rank.

*Kaing² ꜁sing,* 縣丞 or *꜀hung kaing²* 分縣 a deputy district magistrate—of the chief 8th rank.

*꜀Ti kaing²* 知縣 a district magistrate—of the chief 7th rank.

*꜀Chiu ꜁tung,* 州同 the deputy of a *chiu* magistrate—of the subordinate 6th rank.

*꜀Ti ꜀chiu,* 知州 the magistrate of a *chiu,* or inferior department—of the subordinate 5th rank.

*꜁Tung ꜀ti,* 同知 or *꜀hung ꜂hu,* 分府 a deputy prefect—of the chief 5th rank.

*꜂Hai ꜁hwong (꜁wong),* 海防 a marine inspector—of the *tung-ti* rank.

*꜀Ti ꜂hu,* 知府 a prefect—of the subordinate 4th rank.

*Tó² ꜁tai,* 道臺 an intendant of circuit—of the chief 4th rank; *꜀Si tó²* 司道 commissioners and intendants.

*꜁Liong tó²* 糧道 commissioner of the land-tax; *꜁Siéng tó²* 鹽道 the salt commissioner.

*Ang꜄ ꜀si,* 按司 or *ang꜄ ch'ak꜄ ꜀si,* 按察司 or *ngiék꜅ ꜁tai,* 臬臺 the criminal judge—of the chief 3d rank.

*Pwo꜄ ꜀si,* 布司 or *pwo꜄ cheng꜄ ꜀si,* 布政司 or *꜀hwang ꜁tai,* 藩臺 a provincial treasurer—of the subordinate 2d rank.

*꜂U yéng²* 撫院 or *꜂u ꜁tai,* 撫臺 a provincial governor, lieutenant-governor—of the subordinate or chief 2d rank.

*꜂Chung tok꜄* 總督 or *chié꜄ ꜁tai,* 制臺 a viceroy, governor-general—of the chief 2d or subordinate 1st rank; *Tok꜄ ꜂u,* 督撫 Viceroy and Provincial Governor.

*Óh꜅ ꜀kwang,* 學官 or *kau꜄ ꜀kwang,* 教官 styled *óh꜅ ꜂ló ꜀sü,* 學老師 a superintendent of education—of the chief 8th rank; *Kau꜄ seu²* 教授 and *Kau꜄ ëü²* 教諭 the superintendents of education in a *hu* (prefecture) and a *kaing* (district).

*Hok꜅ yéng²* 學院 or *hok꜅ ꜁tai,* 學臺 a Literary Chancellor.

### The Army.

*꜀Ping,* 兵 or *꜀ping ꜀ting,* 兵丁 or *꜀ping sëü²* 兵士 a soldier.

*꜀Kung ꜀yăng,* 軍營 an army; *꜁Yăng ꜁pwang,* 營盤 a camp.

*Paik*ˎ ˏ*ki*, 八旗 the eight banners, the Tartar troops.

*Paik*ˎ ˏ*yăng*, 八營 the eight camps or grand military divisions, the Chinese troops.

MILITARY OFFICERS.

*Sek*ˎ ˏ*sang* ˏ*sing kau*ˀ ˋ*chung* ˏ*ping*, 十三陞至總兵 thirteen promotions, or grades, to the generalship—ˋ*Sieu hiong*ˀ 小餉 the small rations or pay, *Twai*² *hiong*ˀ 大餉 the large pay, ˋ*Ma* ˏ*ping*, 馬兵 a cavalry man, *Ngwoi*² ˋ*wi*, 外委 a petty rank, one promoted from the cavalry, a corporal or sergeant, ˏ*King chié*ˀ 經制 a lieutenant, ˋ*Pa* ˋ*chung*, 把總 a centurion, a captain, ˏ*Ch'iêng* ˋ*chung*, 千總 a chiliarch, ˋ*Siu pe*² 守備 a major, ˏ*Tu* ˏ*si*, 都司 a military officer of the 5th grade or rank, ˏ*Iu kek*ˎ 遊擊 a lieutenant-colonel, ˏ*Ch'ang chiong*ˀ 叅將 a colonel, *Ho*ˀ *chiong*ˀ 副將 a brigadier, ˋ*Chung* ˏ*ping*, 總兵 a general, a commander.

ˏ*T'i tok*ˎ 提督 a commander-in-chief, *Lük*ˎ *tio*² ˏ*t'i tok*ˎ 陸路提督 chief of the land forces, a major-general; ˋ*Chwi* ˏ*sü* ˏ*t'i tok*ˎ 水師提督 an admiral.

*Chiong*ˀ ˏ*kung*, 將軍 a general, commander of the Manchu garrison in a city; ˏ*Tu* ˋ*t'ung*, 都統 a major-general of Tartars.

ˏ*Ngwong sói*ˀ 元帥 a generalissimo; *Tok*ˎ ˏ*ping twai*² ˏ*ngwong sói*ˀ 督兵大元帥 one specially appointed as commander-in-chief of the troops.

MANDARIN'S OFFICE OR YAMEN.

ˏ*Nga* ˏ*mwong*, 衙門 a yamên, a mandarin's residence and office.

*Lĕk*ˎ ˏ*pung*, 六房 the six departments of a yamên, corresponding to the Six Boards at the capital.

*Tô*² ˋ*tiong*, 道長 the head-clerk of a department (of the ˋ*Tiêng le*² grade); also the chief of a company of police.

ˏ*Sü* ˏ*ié*, 師爺 an officer's private secretary and adviser; ˏ*Chü paing*² 書辦 official clerks or writers.

*Twai*² ˏ*ié*, 大爺 the great sirs or sires, official attendants and managers.

榕腔初學撮要

꜁*Mwong siong*$^2$ 門上 or ꜁*mwong* ꜁*t'au,* 門頭 an official door-keeper, a major-domo.

꜁*Tiong wa*$^2$ 傳話 an interpreter; *Tik*$_2$ ꜁*tong,* 值堂 those serving by turns, as scribes or interpreters.

꜀*Ch'á yăh*$_2$ 差役 or ꜁*ngwong* ꜀*ch'á,* 原差 police, messengers, bailiffs; *Ché*$^2$ *lá*$^2$ 皂隸 lictors, runners.

꜂*Ma k'wai*꜃ 馬快 a thief-catcher, as at the district magistrate's; *Ang*꜃ *chek*꜇ 案緝 a thief-catcher at a military office.

*Nik*$_2$ *pó*꜃ 日報 a daily gazette or circular—prepared for officials and gentry.

꜁*Ching* ꜂*ü pó*꜃ 晴雨報 a weather-circular, as prepared for the higher officers by the district magistrate.

*Kó*꜃ *se*$^2$ (spoken *kó*꜃ *che*$^2$) 告示 an official proclamation.

### Punishments and Tortures.

*Kwok*꜇ *hwak*꜇ 國法 the laws; *Hwang*$^2$ *hwak*꜇ 犯法 or *hwang*$^2$ *kwok*꜇ *hwak*꜇ 犯國法 to transgress the laws.

꜁*Ch'iu hwang*$^2$ 囚犯 a culprit, a criminal; ꜁*Ch'iu* ꜁*lĕng,* 囚籠 a cage in which a criminal is carried.

꜀*Ch'au* ꜀*ka,* 抄家 to sequestrate one's property.

*Muk*$_2$ ꜀*kwang,* 沒官 or ꜀*kwi* ꜀*kwang,* 歸官 to confiscate to the government.

*Kaung*꜃ *ngek*꜇ 降級 to degrade; *kaung*꜃ ꜀*sang ngek*꜇ 降三級 degraded three ranks or degrees.

*Kaik*꜇ *chek*꜇ ꜁*liu eng*$^2$ 革職留任 deprived of insignia of rank but retaining office.

꜀*Ch'ang,* 參 to depose; a deposition, an impeachment; ꜀*ch'ang* ꜁*wong,* 參員 a degraded or deposed officer.

꜂*Piéng,* 貶 to censure, to degrade; ꜂*piéng k'ó*꜃ 貶去 degraded and sent away or exiled.

*Pa*$^2$ *chek*꜇ ꜁*ui* ꜁*ming,* 罷職爲民 to be dismissed from office and become a citizen.

꜁*Hing,* 刑 punishment, torture; ꜁*Hing këü*$^2$ 刑具 instruments of torture.

ʿ*Ngu* ꜀*hing*, 五 刑 the five (inferior or light) punishments, *viz.*, ꜀*Kiă*, 枷 canguing, *P'ah*꜆ 拍 beating, ʿ*Chang*, 椶 squeezing (the fingers), *Kek*꜇ 夾 squeezing (the ankles), ꜀*Kwong*, 關 imprisonment.

꜀*Kiă*, 枷 a cangue, to cangue; *P'ah*꜆ ꜀*kiă*, 拍 枷 to beat and cangue.

*P'ah*꜆ *ch'oi*ʾ ʿ*p'á*, 拍 嘴 巴 to beat the cheeks—with a leathern flap or thong, called ꜀*p'ui* ʿ*chiong*, 皮 掌.

*Twai*² ʿ*peng*, 大 板 and ʿ*Sieu* ʿ*peng*, 小 板 the large and small bamboos for beating culprits; *P'ah*꜆ *se*ʾ *sek*꜇ ʿ*peng*, 拍 四 十 板 to inflict 40 blows—the legal limit with the large bamboo.

ʿ*Chang* ʿ*chi*, 椶 指 an instrument made of sticks and strings for squeezing the fingers; *Siong*² ʿ*chang* ʿ*chi*, 上椶指 to be tortured with a *chang-chi*.

*Kek*꜇ *kong*ʾ 夾 棍 an instrument for squeezing the ankles; *Siong*² *kek*꜇ *kong*ʾ 上 夾 棍 to be tortured with a *kek-kong*.

꜀*Kang*, 監 or ꜀*kang* ꜀*ló*, 監 牢 or ꜀*ló ngwoh*꜇ 牢 獄 a prison; ꜀*Kang hwang*² 監 犯 or ꜀*kang* ꜀*ch'iu*, 監 囚 a prisoner.

꜀*Kwong* ꜀*kang*, 關 監 to shut up in prison, to imprison.

*Keng*ʾ ʿ*chi*, 禁 子 or *keng*ʾ ʿ*chi pah*꜆ 禁 子 伯 a jailer, a turnkey; ʿ*Nü keng*ʾ ʿ*chi*, 女禁子 or *keng*ʾ ʿ*chi* ʿ*ma*, 禁 子 媽 a female jailer.

꜀*K'a k'ó*ʾ 胶 靠 and ʿ*Ch'iu k'ó*ʾ 手 靠 or ꜀*K'a* ʿ*ch'iu k'ó*ʾ 胶 手 靠 fetters and manacles.

The five *superior or heavy* punishments are—

ʿ*Chang*, ʿ*Kieu*, ꜀*Kung*, ꜀*Liu*, ꜀*Tu*, 斬 絞 軍 流 徒 Beheading, Strangling, Banishment to the Garrisons, Banishment 3000 *li* from home, and Banishment 1000 *li* or to another province.

꜀*T'ai* ꜀*t'au*, 刣 頭 to behead; *Sá*ʾ *kak*꜆ 細 割 to execute by "cutting into small pieces"; ꜀*ling* ꜀*ti sá*ʾ *kak*꜆ 淩 遲 細 割 to cut to pieces ignominiously and slowly.

ʿ*Kieu* ʿ*si*, (coll. ʿ*ka* ʿ*si*), 絞 死 to execute by strangling.

*Mwong*ʾ *chói*² 僴 罪 to exile for crime.

*Mwong*ʾ ꜀*ch'üng* ꜀*kung*, 罔充軍 or *mwong*ʾ ʿ*k'iéng*, 罔遣 to banish (beyond the frontiers) to the garrisons.

*Mwong*ʾ ꜁*liu*, 罔流 to banish 3000 *li* from one's home.

*Mwong*ʾ ꜁*tu*, 罔徒 to banish 1000 *li* or to another province.

### Extrajudicial Punishments.

꜀*Sü* ꜁*hing*, 私刑 private torture, that which is unauthorized, or "not written in the laws of the Great Pure Dynasty".

꜀*K'wi* ꜀*sing taiu*ʾ 魁星吊 to be suspended (by a leg and an arm, so as to resemble the posture of) ꜀*k'wi* ꜀*sing*, a god of literature.

*Siong*² ꜀*hwa* ꜁*mi ka*ʾ 上畫眉架 to be fastened to "the thrush or hopping-bird's frame", i. e., a frame consisting of a post and two cross-pieces.

꜁*Kau pó*² ꜁*t'ó*, 猴抱桃 a monkey grasping a peach—a torture so called from the prisoner's fancied resemblance to that object, when suspended by one arm over a pole with his hands tied together under one or both legs.

*Koi*² *liéng*² 跪鍊 to kneel on chains—often accompanied with a severe flogging.

*Siong*² ꜀*t'ong* ꜁*sié*, 上湯蛇 to be tortured with hot-water snakes, i. e., hollow coils of pewter or other metal about the arms, into which boiling water is poured.

*Söüng*² *t'iék*ʾ *siăng*ʾ ʿ*long*, 穿鐵線襉 to wear a shirt of iron-wire—the shirt is made to press the body closely by pulling an attached cord, and the protruding skin and flesh is rasped or cut off.

*Lóh*₂ ꜀*hwi tói*² 落灰袋 (to be smothered to death by having the head) put into a bag of lime.

ʿ*Tiéng chioh*ʾ 點燭 to be lighted (like) a candle—the culprit is wound in cotton yarn, which is thoroughly saturated with oil and set on fire.

*K'ié*² ꜁*lëng*, 跬籠 to stand in a (wooden) cage—till death ensues from exhaustion and starvation.

*Wak*₂ ꜁*mai*, 活埋 to be buried alive.

# PART V. MISCELLANY.

## 1. NUMERALS.

| | Full forms. | Abbreviations. | |
|---|---|---|---|
| 1 | 一 壹 | 〡〇 | *Sioh$_2$, Suoh$_2$, Ek꜁.* |
| 2 | 二 貳 弍 | 〢〇 | *Lang$^2$, Ne$^2$.* |
| 3 | 三 叁 | 〣〇 | *꜀Sang.* |
| 4 | 四 肆 | 〤〇 | *Se꜃.* |
| 5 | 五 伍 | 〥〇 | *Ngo$^2$.* |
| 6 | 六 陸 | 〦〇 | *Lĕk$_2$.* |
| 7 | 七 柒 | 〧〇 | *Ch'ek꜁.* |
| 8 | 八 捌 | 〨〇 | *Paik꜁.* |
| 9 | 九 玖 | 〩〇 | *꜂Kau.* |
| 10 | 十 拾 | 〸 | *Sek$_2$.* |
| 11 | 十一 拾壹 | 〸〡 | *Sek$_2$ ek꜁.* |
| 12 | 十二 | 〸〢 | *Sek$_2$ ne$^2$.* |
| 13 | 十三 | 〸〣 | *Sek$_2$ ꜀sang.* |
| 20 | 二十 廿 | 〹 | *Ne$^2$ sek$_2$, Niék꜁.* |
| 21 | 二十一 廿一 | 〹〡 | *Niék꜁ ek꜁.* |
| 22 | 二十二 廿二 | 〹〢 | *Niék꜁ ne$^2$.* |
| 40 | 四十 | 〤〸 | *Se꜃ sek$_2$, Siék꜁.* |
| 41 | 四十一 | 〤〸〡 | *Siék꜁ ek꜁.* |
| 42 | 四十二 | 〤〸〢 | *Siék꜁ ne$^2$.* |
| 100 | 一百 | 〡百 | *Sioh$_2$ pah꜁.* |
| 101 | 一百〇一 | 〡百〇〡 | *Sioh$_2$ pah꜁ ꜀ling sioh$_2$.* |
| 102 | 一百〇二 | 〡百〇〢 | *Sioh$_2$ pah꜁ ꜀ling lang$^2$.* |
| 110 | 百一 | 百〡 | *Pah꜁ ek꜁.* |
| 111 | 一百一十一 | 百〡〡 | *Sioh꜁ pah꜁ ek꜁ sek$_2$ ek꜁,*<br>*Pah꜁ ek꜁ ek꜁ (or sioh$_2$).* |
| 115 | 一百一十五 | 百〡〥 | *Sioh$_2$ pah꜁ ek꜁ sek$_2$ ngo$^2$.*<br>*Pah꜁ ek꜁ ngo$^2$,* |
| 120 | 百二 | 百〢 | *Pah꜁ ne$^2$.* |
| 121 | 一百二十一 | 百〢〡 | *Pah꜁ ne$^2$ sioh$_2$.* |

| | | | |
|---|---|---|---|
| 122 | 一百二十二 | [illegible] | *Pah› ne$^{2}$ lang$^{2}$.* |
| 125 | 一百二十五 | [illegible] | *Pah› ne$^{2}$ ngo$^{2}$.* |
| 200 | 二百 | [illegible] | *Lang$^{2}$ pah›.* |
| 210 | 二百一十 | [illegible] | *Ne$^{2}$ pah› ek›.* |
| | | | *Lang$^{2}$ pah› ek› sek$_{2}$ ek›.* |
| 211 | 二百一十一 | [illegible] | *Ne$^{2}$ pah› ek› ek›.* |
| | | | *Ne$^{2}$ pah› ek› sioh$_{2}$.* |
| 215 | 二百一十五 | [illegible] | *Lang$^{2}$ pah› ek› sek$_{2}$ ngo$^{2}$.* |
| 220 | 二百二十 | [illegible] | *Ne$^{2}$ pah› ne$^{2}$.* |
| 221 | 二百二十一 | [illegible] | *Lang$^{2}$ pah› niék› ek›.* |
| 1000 | 一千 | [illegible] | *Sioh$_{2}$ ꜀ch'iéng.* |
| 1001 | 一千零一 | [illegible] | *Sioh$_{2}$ ꜀ch'iéng ꜁ling sioh$_{2}$* |
| 1010 | 一千零一十 | [illegible] | *Sioh$_{2}$ ꜀ch'iéng ꜁ling sek$_{2}$ ꜁ki.* |
| 1100 | 一千一百 | [illegible] | *꜀Ch'iéng ek›.* |
| 1202 | 一千二百零二 | [illegible] | *꜀Ch'iéng ne$^{2}$ ꜁ling lang$^{2}$.* |
| 1220 | 一千二百二十 | [illegible] | *꜀Ch'iéng ne$^{2}$ lang$^{2}$.* |
| 1221 | 一千二百二十一 | [illegible] | *꜀Ch'iéng ne$^{2}$ niék› ek›.* |
| 10,000 | 一萬 | [illegible] | *Sioh$_{2}$ wang$^{2}$.* |
| 14,000 | 一萬四千 | [illegible] | *Wang$^{2}$ se›.* |
| 100,000 | 一億 | | *Sioh$_{2}$ e›.* |
| 1,000,000 | 一兆 | | *Sioh$_{2}$ tieu$^{2}$.* |

*E› tieu$^{2}$* 億兆 Myriads, an innumerable multitude.

*Sioh$_{2}$ lang$^{2}$ chiăh›* 一二隻 One or two.

*Lang$^{2}$ ꜀sang pah›* 二三百 *꜀Sang lang$^{2}$ pah›* 三二百 Two or three hundred.

*ʻKwi chiăh›* 幾隻 A few units, a few of, several.

*Sek$_{2}$ ʻkwi,* 十幾 10 and a few units.

*Pah› ʻkwi,* 百幾 100 and a few tens.

*꜀Ch'iéng ʻkwi,* 千幾 1000 and a few hundreds.

*Sek$_{2}$ ꜁tü chiăh›* 十餘隻 Ten and a few more.

*Sek$_{2}$ siong$^{2}$* 十上 Over 10. *Niék› siong$^{2}$* 廿上 Over 20.

*Pah› ʻpa,* 百把 or *Pah› siong$^{2}$* 百上 Over 100.

*Pah› ʻpa lang$^{2}$* 百把二 100 and over to 200.

*꜀Ch'iéng ʻpa,* 千把 or *꜀Ch'iéng siong$^{2}$* 千上 Over 1000.

*Sioh$_{2}$ tieu›* 一吊 1000 (cash).

## 2. ORDINALS.

Ordinals are formed by prefixing the word *tâ*$^2$ 第 to numerals. This particle is used through 10 and sometimes as far as through 19, but in ordinary conversation it is generally omitted, and the simple numerals are employed. For further explanation see pages 31 and 32.

## 3. ARITHMETICAL TABLES.

In these tables the terms *eng*ˀ, *saung*ˀ, and *se*$^2$ used for "make", might in some cases be employed interchangeably.

### Troy Weight.

Used in weighing gold and silver; the higher denominations *hung*, *chiéng*, *liong*, also used in weighing thread and medicines. The *liong* or tael is equal to 583⅓ grs. Troy.

| | |
|---|---|
| 10 millionths make 1 *si*.<br>*Sek*$_2$ *hwok*ˎ *eng*ˀ *sioh*$_2$ ꜀*si*. | 十忽應一絲 |
| 10 *si* make 1 *hó*.<br>*Sek*$_2$ ꜀*si eng*ˀ *sioh*$_2$ ꜁*hó*. | 十絲應一毫 |
| 10 *hó* make 1 *lié*.<br>*Sek*$_2$ ꜁*hó eng*ˀ *sioh*$_2$ ꜁*lié*. | 十毫應一厘 |
| 10 *lié* make 1 candareen.<br>*Sek*$_2$ ꜁*lié eng*ˀ *sioh*$_2$ ꜀*hung*. | 十厘應一分 |
| 10 candareen make 1 mace.<br>*Sek*$_2$ ꜀*hung eng*ˀ *sioh*$_2$ ꜁*chiéng*. | 十分應一錢 |
| 10 mace make 1 ounce.<br>*Sek*$_2$ ꜁*chiéng eng*ˀ *sioh*$_2$ ꜂*liong*. | 十錢應一兩 |

### Avoirdupois Weight.

The *küng* or Chinese pound varies from 12 to 21oz. The standard is 16 oz. and about equal to the English pound. The catty of 16 taels is 1⅓lb. avoirdupois. A picul is 133⅓ English pounds.

| | |
|---|---|
| 10 mace make 1 ounce.<br>*Sek*$_2$ ꜁*chiéng eng*ˀ *sioh*$_2$ ꜂*liong*. | 十錢應一兩 |
| 16 ounces make 1 pound.<br>*Sek*$_2$ *lĕk*$_2$ ꜂*liong eng*ˀ *sioh*$_2$ ꜀*küng*. | 十六兩應一觔 |
| 100 pounds or catties make 1 load or picul.<br>*Sioh*$_2$ *pah*ˎ ꜀*küng eng*ˀ *sioh*$_2$ *tang*ˀ. | 一百觔應一担 |

### Linear Measure.

The *Ch'ioh꜃* or Chinese foot varies in length and is distinguished by different names, as common foot, domestic foot, tailor's foot, Peking foot. The common foot (*꜀pang ch'ioh꜃*) is about ¼ of an Eng. inch shorter than the Eng. foot. The *li* or Chinese mile is 360 paces and is computed by some to be 1897½ Eng. feet.

10 *tenths* make 1 inch. 十分筭一寸
*Sek$_2$ ꜀hung saung꜂ sioh$_2$ ch'aung꜂.*

10 inches make 1 foot. 十寸筭一尺
*Sek$_2$ ch'aung꜂ saung꜂ sioh$_2$ ch'ioh꜃.*

5 feet make 1 pace or stride. 五尺筭一步
*Ngo$^2$ ch'ioh꜃ saung꜂ sioh$_2$ pwo$^2$.*

10 feet make 1 rod or pole. 十尺筭一丈
*Sek$_2$ ch'ioh꜃ saung꜂ sioh$_2$ taung$^2$.*

3 feet make 1 yard. 三尺筭一碼
*꜀Sang ch'ioh꜃ saung꜂ sioh$_2$ ꜁ma.*

10 miles make 1 league. 十里筭一舖
*Sek$_2$ ꜁li saung꜂ sioh$_2$ p'wo꜂.*

*Sioh$_2$ ꜀na,* 一挪 the space between the ends of the thumb and middle finger when extended, span of about 7 Chinese inches.

*Sioh$_2$ ꜀ch'iéng,* 一揃 the space between the extremities of the extended arms, fathom of 5 or 6 feet.

*Pwang꜂ ꜀ch'iéng,* 半揃 (also called *sioh$_2$ pek$_2$* 一拔 or *sioh$_2$ pié꜂ ꜁ch'iu,* 一臂手) a half *ch'iéng* or fathom.

### Square Measure.

(See Gibson's Chin. Arith.)

The *mu* or Chinese acre is estimated, 6. 61 *mu* equal to an English acre.

100 inches make 1 foot. 一百寸筭一尺
*Sioh$_2$ pah꜃ ch'aung꜂ saung꜂ sioh$_2$ ch'ioh꜃.*

25 feet make 1 pace. 二十五尺筭一步
*Ne$^2$ sek$_2$ ngo$^2$ ch'ioh꜃ saung꜂ sioh$_2$ pwo$^2$.*

4 paces make 1 rod or pole. 四步筭一丈
*Se꜂ pwo$^2$ saung꜂ sioh$_2$ taung$^2$.*

6 poles make 1 rood. 六丈算一分

*Lĕk*$_2$ *taung*$^2$ *saung*’ *sioh*$_2$ ꜀*hung*.

10 roods make 1 acre. 十分算一畝

*Sek*$_2$ ꜀*hung saung*’ *sioh*$_2$ ‘*mu*.

100 acres make 1 *k‘ing*. 一百畝算一頃

*Sioh*$_2$ *pah*$_{ɔ}$ ‘*mu saung*’ *sioh*$_2$ ‘*k‘ing*.

### Wine Measures.

*Pwong*’ *kau*’ 半斠 one half of a *kau*, about a gill, the smallest wine-measure.

*Sioh*$_2$ *kau*’ 一斠 one *kau*, 2 gills or half a pint.

*Kau*’ *pwong*’ 斠半 one and a half *kau*, 3 gills.

*Lang*$^2$ *kau*’, 二斠 two *kau*, 4 gills or 1 pint.

*Se*’ *kau*’, 四斠 four *kau*, 2 pints or 1 quart.

The earthen jar or ꜀*ting*, 埕 used for containing wine, holds from 180 to 220 gills.

### Dry Measure.

The *ching* or Chinese pint varies in capacity. The government measure is somewhat larger than that of the shops. The latter or common *ching* contains nearly an Eng. quart.

3 tubes or cups make 1 pint. 三管應一升

꜀*Sang* ‘*kwong eng*’ *sioh*$_2$ ꜀*ching*.

10 gills make 1 pint. 十合應一升

*Sek*$_2$ *kak*$_{ɔ}$ *eng*’ *sioh*$_2$ ꜀*ching*.

10 pints make 1 peck. 十升應一斗

*Sek*$_2$ ꜀*ching eng*’ *sioh*$_2$ ‘*tau*.

10 pecks make 1 load. 十斗應一担

*Sek*$_2$ ‘*tau eng*’ *sioh*$_2$ *tang*’.

### Measure of Time.

The *si sing* or Chinese hour is equal to two hours of clock-time.

60 seconds make 1 minute.
*Lĕk$_2$ sek$_2$ ʿmieu se$^2$ sioh$_2$ ꜀hung.*
六十秒是一分

60 minutes make 1 hour.
*Lĕk$_2$ sek$_2$ ꜀hung se$^2$ sioh$_2$ ʿteng.*
六十分是一點

15 minutes make 1 quarter.
*Sek$_2$ ngo$^2$ ꜀hung se$^2$ sioh$_2$ k'aik꜁.*
十五分是一刻

4 quarters make 1 hour.
*Seʾ k'aik꜁ se$^2$ sioh$_2$ ʿteng.*
四刻是一點

24 hours (or 12 ꜂si ꜂sing) make 1 day.
*Ne$^2$ sek$_2$ seʾ ʿteng ꜀chŭng se$^2$ sioh$_2$ nik$_2$.*
二十四點鐘是一日

7 days make 1 week.
*Ch'ek꜁ nik$_2$ se$^2$ sioh$_2$ ʿlá paiʾ.*
七日是一禮拜

12 months make 1 year.
*Sek$_2$ ne$^2$ ʿa ngwok$_2$ nik$_2$ se$^2$ sioh$_2$ ꜂niéng.*
十二個月日是一年

The "intercalar year" (has) 13 months.
*Nong$^2$ ꜂niéng sek$_2$ ꜀sang ʿa ngwok$_2$ nik$_2$.*
閏年十三個月日

The long months have 30 days.
*Ngwok$_2$ twai$^2$ ꜀sang sek$_2$ nik$_2$.*
月大三十日

The short months have 29 days.
*Ngwok$_2$ ʿsieu ne$^2$ sek$_2$ ʿkau nik$_2$.*
月小二十九日

One year has 360 days (as commonly reckoned).
*Sioh$_2$ ꜂niéng engʾ ꜀sang pah꜁ lĕk$_2$ sek$_2$ nik$_2$.*
一年應三百六十日

60 years make one cycle.
*Lĕk$_2$ sek$_2$ ꜂niéng se$^2$ sioh$_2$ ꜂lung kak꜁ ʿchü.*
六十年是一輪甲子

### Circular and Angular Measure.

60 seconds make 1 minute.
*Lĕk$_2$ sek$_2$ ʿmieu se$^2$ sioh$_2$ ꜀hung.*
六十秒是一分

60 minutes make 1 degree.
*Lĕk$_2$ sek$_2$ ꜀hung se$^2$ sioh$_2$ to$^2$.*
六十分是一度

360 degrees make 1 circumference or circle.
*꜀Sang pah꜁ lĕk$_2$ sek$_2$ to$^2$ se$^2$ sioh$_2$ ꜂yéng ꜂k'wang.*
三百六十度是一圓環

## 4. CLASSIFIERS OR NUMERATIVES,

ALPHABETICALLY ARRANGED.

(See pages 22, 23, and 24).

| Classifiers. | | Names of things under their respective classifiers. |
|---|---|---|
| *꜂A,* | 個 | Persons, cash, feet, hands, months, etc. |
| *A*$^{2}$ | 吓 | Times, repetitions, etc. |
| *Chaik꜁* | 節 | Joints, as of fingers, bamboo, sugar-cane. |
| *Chak꜁* | 匝 | Showers of rain. |
| *꜂Chang,* | 盞 | Lanterns. |
| *Chau꜃* | 灶 | Families. |
| *꜀Cheng,* | 層 | Stories, as of pagodas, baskets; steps of stairs, rounds of ladders, etc. |
| *꜂Chi,* | 只 | Skeins, small bunches of fresh flowers, incense-sticks, coiffure-cord, etc. |
| *Chiăh꜁* | 隻 | Persons and things generally. |
| *꜂Chio,* | 主 | Owners, householders, families. |
| *Chó*$^{2}$ | 座 | Cities, towers, churches, mountains, volcanoes. |
| *꜀Chong,* | 賍 | Businesses, affairs. |
| *Ch‘iéng꜃* | 槧 | Stalks or boughs of flowers. |
| *꜀Ch‘iéng,* | 揃 | A measure—from tip to tip of the hands extended. |
| *Ch‘iong꜃* | 串 | Strings of beads, cash, etc. |
| *Ch‘oi꜃* | 嘴 | Persons composing a household, also mouthfuls. |
| *꜀Ch‘ong,* | 床 | Blankets, counterpanes, sheets, mattresses, bed-curtains. |
| *Hak*$_{2}$ | 合 | Pairs of certain things, as closets, bottles, lanterns, also married couples. |
| *Hek*$_{2}$ | 畫 | Strokes of characters. |
| *Hiék*$_{2}$ | 頁 | Lobes of livers and lungs. |
| *Ho꜃* | 付 | Sets, as of 10 bowls, 10 pairs of chopsticks, 5 buttons, pairs of ear-rings. |
| *Hok꜁* | 幅 | Breadths of cloth. |
| *꜀Hong,* | 行 | Lines, columns of characters, scratches, long marks, etc. |

| | | |
|---|---|---|
| *Hong*$^2$ | 分 | Shares, portions. |
| ꜀*Huí*, | 佪 | Times, repetitions. |
| *Huk*$_2$ | 服 | Packages or doses of medicine, to be taken, or used externally. |
| ꜂*Ka*, | 個 | Persons, cash, months. |
| *Ka*꜄ | 架 | Bedsteads, closets, clocks, ladders, etc. |
| *Kaik*꜆ | 結 | Bunches of vermicelli. |
| ꜀*Kang*, | 橺 | Houses, shops, bedrooms. |
| ꜀*Ki*, | 其 | Persons, cash, inkstones, tea-kettles, etc. |
| *Kwa*꜄ | 掛 | Strings or bunches, as of beads, keys, fire-crackers. |
| *Kwo*꜄ | 句 | Sentences (written or spoken), times, repetitions. |
| *Kwok*꜆ | 笏 | Blocks of ink. |
| *Kwok*$_2$ | 橛 | Pieces, bits, as of thread or cord ; also transverse sections, as of potatoes, timber. |
| ꜂*Kwong*, | 捲 | Rolls of things, spools or reels of cotton. |
| *Kwong*꜄ | 卷 | Scrolls, manuscripts, books. |
| ꜀*K'a*, | 胶 | One of a pair, as of shoes, stockings, ear-rings, bracelets, legs of pork and mutton. |
| ꜂*K'eu*, | 口 | Frying-pans, fills of a pipe, ponds, betel-nut in leaves, also persons as requiring food. |
| ꜀*K'iă*, | 奇 | Single ones of pairs, as shoes, stockings. |
| ꜀*K'u*, | 鍦 | Sections of a fish, as cut transversely. |
| ꜂*K'ung*, | 綑 | Rolls, as of paper, cloth, bedding; also coils of rope. |
| ꜀*K'ŭng*, | 囷 | Piles, heaps, stacks, as of clothes, straw, stones, wood. |
| *K'wong*$^2$ | 匡 | Rectangular or ruled spaces. |
| *Laiu*$^2$ | 料 | Lots of ingredients, as in medicinal or culinary recipes. |
| *Lak*$_2$ | 粒 | Stars, beads, grains of rice, buttons, peanuts, fruit, scars, particles of dust, etc. |
| ꜀*Lau*, | 流 | Times, repetitions. |
| *Leng*꜄ | 瓣 | Lobes, carpels, triangular sections of fruit. |
| *Leu*$^2$ | 綹 | Locks of hair. |
| ꜂*Liăng*, | 領 | Pieces of matting or carpet. |
| ꜂*Liu*, | 綹 | False beards or cues, periwigs. |

| | | |
|---|---|---|
| *Lóh*꜇ | 落 | Houses. |
| ꜀*Loi*, | 縲 | Pimples, bites. |
| *Loi*꜅ | 類 | Sorts, as of men, goods, etc. |
| ꜁*Long*, | 鄉 | Lengths of grass-cloth-nettle thread, each consistting of 4 or 5 separate threads. |
| ꜁*Miăng*, | 名 | Persons enrolled; police, chair-bearers, coolies, etc. |
| *Miéng*꜅ | 面 | Drums, gongs, mirrors. |
| ꜁*Mwong*, | 門 | Guns, cannon, fire-crackers, reports of crackers and firearms ; officers. |
| *Ngá*꜅ | 枝 | Branches, as of trees. |
| ꜂*Pa*, | 把 | Things with handles, as knives, forks, spoons, shovels, tongs, fans ; also needles, sedans, bundles of wood, handfuls. |
| ꜁*Pá*, | 排 | Rows, sets of things arranged or spread out, companies of soldiers, etc. |
| *Paing*꜅ | 瓣 | Petals ; sections or divisions, as of melons, pumpkins. |
| ꜀*Pau*, | 包 | Packages of needles, cake, sugar, clothes, etc. |
| ꜂*Peng*, | 板 | Lots or sets, as of bean-curd cakes, ladies' dress-trimmings ; also beats in music. |
| ꜀*Pi* (or ꜁*pi* ꜀*ti*), | 蕐 | Clusters, as of grapes ; bunches, as of keys. |
| ꜀*Pié* or ꜁*p'ié*, | 披 | Leaves of greens. |
| ꜀*Pwang*, | 班 | Orders, ranks, classes, companies, as of actors, police, officers. |
| ꜁*Pwo*, | 朶 | Flowers. |
| *Pwoh*꜇ | 縛 | Bunches of things tied up, as paper, fruit, etc. |
| ꜂*Pwong*, | 本 | Volumes of books, pens, theatrical exhibitions. |
| *P'á*꜄ | 瓣 | Carpels, lobes, sections, as of oranges, pomelos. |
| *P'á*꜄ | 拜 | Kneelings, acts of homage. |
| *P'ek*꜆ | 疋 | Horses, pieces of goods. |
| *P'iéng*꜄ | 片 | Thin things, slips, strips; clouds. |
| ꜂*P'ung*, | 捧 | Double-handfuls. |
| *P'wo*꜅ | 部 | Treatises, chronicles. |
| *Sai*꜅ | 載 | Boat-loads of goods. |
| ꜀*Sëng*, | 雙 | Pairs, as of shoes, stockings, chopsticks. |

| | | |
|---|---|---|
| *꜀Siăng,* | 聲 | Reports, as of guns, fire-crackers, etc. |
| *Siéng꜄* | 墻 | Doors, windows, bents of houses, lengths of side-walls. |
| *꜀Sing,* | 身 | Small images of persons, idols, idol-gods. |
| *꜂Siu,* | 首 | Hymns, stanzas. |
| *Sok꜆* | 束 | Same as *pwoh꜇* q. v. |
| *Swoi꜅* | 稅 | Furrows of a field, seams in sewing, etc. |
| *꜁Tá,* | 題 | Themes, subjects, essays. |
| *Tang꜄* | 担 | Cooly-loads. |
| *꜀Tau,* | 株 | Trees, timber, plants. |
| *Taung꜄* | 頓 | Meals. |
| *꜁Teu,* | 條 | Long things, as ropes, threads, roads, collars; boats, ships. |
| *Tiăng꜅* | 錠 | Ingots of gold and silver. |
| *꜂Ting,* | 頂 | Hats, caps, sedans. |
| *To꜅* | 杜 | Bunches, as of peanuts, beans (exposed for sale). |
| *꜀Toi,* | 堆 | Heaps, as of refuse, lime. |
| *Tói꜄* | 塊 | Pieces or fragments of things. |
| *꜀Tong,* | 墩 | Villages, hamlets. |
| *꜂Tong,* | 黨 | Bunches, packages, as of paper, or idol-paper. |
| *꜂Tu,* | 堵 | Rooms, apartments, lengths or spaces of plastering. |
| *T'aik꜆* | 貼 | Plasters, parcels or doses of medicine. |
| *꜁T'au,* | 頭 | Animals, birds, fish, reptiles, also burdens on the ends of a carrying-stick. |
| *꜂T'iăng,* | 領 | Beds in a garden. |
| *꜀T'iong,* | 張 | Sheets of paper, charms, cards of invitation, gaming-cards; tables, chairs, etc. |
| *T'iong꜅* | 杖 | Stalks of sugar-cane. |
| *꜀T'ó,* | 刀 | Parcels of paper. |
| *T'ó꜄* | 套 | Suits of clothes, sets of furniture, etc. |
| *꜁T'ŭng,* | 重 | Folds or thicknesses. |
| *꜀T'wa,* | 拖 | Girdles, sets of silk-thread for queues, strings of fish. |
| *Wah꜇* | 畫 | Strokes of characters. |
| *꜁Wong,* | 丸 | Lumps or balls, as of earth, dough. |
| *Yék꜇.* | 葉 | Petals, sheets of gold or silver foil. |
| *Yong꜅* | 件 | Articles, commodities, garments, subjects, affairs. |

## 5. ASIA AND ITS COUNTRIES.

—:o:—

| | | | |
|---|---|---|---|
| ASIA | Yashiya | 亞西亞 | ꜂A ꜀sá ꜂a |
| SIBERIA | Olossŭ-shu kuo | 俄羅斯屬國 | ꜁Ngó ꜁ló ꜀sŭ sŭk꜇ |
| TOORKISTAN | Hsiyü | 西域 | ꜀Sá mik꜇ [kwok꜆ |
| TURKEY | T'uerhch'i | 土耳其 | ꜂T'u ꜂ngi ꜁ki |
| JUDEA | Yut'aikuo | 猶太國 | ꜁Iu t'ai꜄ kwok꜆ |
| ARABIA | Yalapai | 亞喇伯 | ꜂A lak꜇ paik꜆ |
| PERSIA | Possŭ | 波斯 | ꜀P'ó ꜀sŭ |
| BELOOCHISTAN | Peiluchih | 俾路芝 | ꜀Pi lo꜅ ꜀chie |
| AFGHANISTAN | Ofuhan | 阿富汗 | ꜀Ó ho꜄ hang꜅ |
| INDIA | T'ienchukuo | 天竺國 | ꜀T'iéng tĕŭk꜆ kwok꜆ |
| | Yintu | 印度 | Eng꜄ to꜅ |
| BURMAH | Mientien | 緬甸 | ꜂Miéng tiéng꜅ |
| SIAM | Hsienloo | 暹羅 | ꜁Siéng ꜁ló |
| ANNAM | Annan | 安南 | ꜀Ang ꜁nang |
| | Kuangnan | 廣南 | ꜂Kwong ꜁nang |
| LEWCHEW | Liuch'iu | 琉球 | ꜁Liu ꜁k'iu (꜁kiu) |
| JAPAN | Jihpên | 日本 | Nik꜇ ꜂pwong. |
| CHINA | Chungkuo | 中國 | ꜀Tŭng kwok꜆ |
| | Chunghua | 中華 | ꜀Tŭng ꜁hwa |
| | Tach'ingkuo | 大清國 | Tai꜅ ꜀ch'ing kwok꜆ |
| MANCHURIA | Manchou | 滿州 | ꜂Mwang ꜀chiu |
| MONGOLIA | Mêngku | 蒙古 | ꜁Mung ꜂ku |
| ILI | Yili | 伊犂 | ꜀I ꜁lá |
| TIBET | Hsit'sang | 西藏 | ꜀Sá chaung꜅ |
| COREA | Kaoli | 高麗 | ꜀Kó ꜁lá |
| | Chaohsien | 朝鮮 | ꜁Tieu ꜀siéng |
| FORMOSA | T'aiwan | 臺灣 | ꜁Tai꜀wang(꜀wang) |

In the following sections, numbered 6, 7, 8, 9, 10, most of the names in the first columns, as also in the 2d column of section 7, are taken from Williams' Map of China.

## 6. THE PROVINCES OF CHINA

### AND THEIR SUB-DIVISIONS.

The Eighteen ꜂*Seng*, 省 or Provinces are divided into *fu*, 府 *t'ing*, 廳 *chou*, 州 and *hsien*, 縣 termed in the Foochow dialect ꜂*hu* ꜀*t'iăng*, ꜀*chiu*, and *kaing*$^2$. A *fu* is a large portion of a province, and is usually called a department or prefecture. A *t'ing* is smaller than a *fu*, and is either like it governed by an officer directly subject to the heads of the provincial government (and hence called *tik*$_2$ *lá*$^2$ 直隸), or else forms a subordinate part of a *fu*. A *chou* is a division similar to a *t'ing*, and like it either independent of other divisions, or forming part of a *fu*. The difference between the two consists in the government of a *t'ing* resembling that of the *fu* more nearly than that of a *chou* does. In accordance with the above explanation, they may be termed *independent* or *subordinate* departments. A *hsien* is a small division or subordinate part of a *fu*, or of an independent *t'ing* or *chou*, and is usually styled a district. As the division called *t'ing* is rarely met with, it is often omitted from the classification by European writers (See Chinese Repository, VOL. IV., pp. 54 & 55.

In the following table, the figures indicating the number of the chief and subordinate divisions in each province are taken from an article by Walter T. Lay, Esqr., in the Chinese Recorder, July, 1870.

| PROVINCES | Mand'n Sound | Character | Foochow Sound | Fu | T'ing | Chou | Hsien |
|---|---|---|---|---|---|---|---|
| Chihli | Chihli | 直隸 | *Tik*$_2$ *lá*$^2$ | 11 | | 23 | 123 |
| Shantung | Shantung | 山東 | ꜀*Sang* ꜀*tĕng* | 10 | | 11 | 96 |
| Shansi | Shanhsi | 山西 | ꜀*Sang* ꜀*sá* | 9 | | 16 | 85 |
| Honan | Honan | 河南 | ꜁*Ó* ꜁*nang* | 9 | 1 | 10 | 96 |
| Kiangsu | Chiangsu | 江蘇 | ꜀*Kong* ꜀*su* | 8 | 3 | 6 | 62 |
| Nganhwui | Anhui | 安徽 | ꜀*Ang* ꜀*hwi* | 8 | | 9 | 50 |
| Kiangsi | Chianghsi | 江西 | ꜀*Kong* ꜀*sá* | 13 | 2 | 2 | 75 |
| Chehkiang | Chêchiang | 浙江 | *Chiék*꜆ ꜀*kong* | 11 | 3 | 1 | 75 |
| Fuhkien | Fuchien | 福建 | *Hok*꜆ *kiong*꜄ | 10 | | 2 | 62 |
| Hupeh | Hupei | 湖北 | ꜁*Hu paĕk*꜆ | 10 | | 8 | 60 |
| Hunan | Hunan | 湖南 | ꜁*Hu* ꜁*nang* | 9 | 4 | 7 | 64 |
| Shensi | Shanhsi | 陝西 | ꜂*Siéng* ꜀*sá* | 7 | 7 | 10 | 73 |
| Kansuh | Kansu | 甘肅 | ꜀*Kang sĕŭk*꜆ | 8 | 2 | 13 | 49 |
| Sz'chuen | Ssuch'uan | 四川 | *Sĕŭ*꜄ ꜀*ch'iong* | 12 | 9 | 19 | 112 |
| Kwangtung | Kuangtung | 廣東 | ꜂*Kwong* ꜀*tĕng* | 9 | 2 | 11 | 78 |
| Kwangsi | Kuanghsi | 廣西 | ꜂*Kwong* ꜀*sá* | 11 | | 18 | 47 |
| Kweichau | Kueichou | 貴州 | *Koi*꜄ ꜀*chiu* | 12 | 5 | 14 | 33 |
| Yunnan | Yünnan | 雲南 | ꜁*Hung* ꜁*nang* | 14 | 5 | 29 | 39 |

## 7. THE PROVINCES OF CHINA

### AND THEIR CAPITALS.

| PROVINCES | Capitals | Mand'n Sound | Character | Foochow Sound |
|---|---|---|---|---|
| Chihli | Pauting | Paoting-fu | 保定府 | ‘Pó teng$^2$ ‘hu |
| Shantung | Tsinan | Chinan-fu | 濟南府 | Chá’ ˛nang ,, |
| Shansi | Taiyuen | T‘aiyüan-fu | 太原府 | T‘ai’ ˛ngwong ,, |
| Honan | Kaifung | K‘aifêng-fu | 開封府 | ˛K‘ai ˛hung ,, |
| Kiangsu | Kiangning | Kiangning-fu | 江寗府 | ˛Kong ˛ning ,, |
| Nganhwui | Nganking | Anch‘ing-fu | 安慶府 | ˛Ang k‘eng’ ,, |
| Kiangsi | Nanchang | Nanch‘ang-fu | 南昌府 | ˛Nang ˛ch‘iong ,, |
| Chehkiang | Hangchau | Hangchou-fu | 杭州府 | ˛Hong ˛chiu ,, |
| Fuhkien | Foochow | Fuchou-fu | 福州府 | Hok˒ ˛chiu ,, |
| Hupeh | Wuchang | Wuch‘ang-fu | 武昌府 | ‘U ˛ch‘iong ,, |
| Hunan | Changsha | Ch‘angsha-fu | 長沙府 | ˛T iong ˛sa ,, |
| Shensi | Singan | Hsian-fu | 西安府 | ˛Sá ˛ang ,, |
| Kansuh | Lanchau | Lanchou-fu | 蘭州府 | ˛Lang ˛chiu ,, |
| Sz'chuen | Chingtu | Ch‘êngtu-fu | 成都府 | ˛Sing ˛tu ,, |
| Kwangtung | Canton | Kuangchou-fu | 廣州府 | ‘Kwong ˛chiu ,, |
| Kwangsi | Kweilin | Kueilin-fu | 桂林府 | Kiè’ ˛ling ,, |
| Kweichau | Kweiyang | Kueiyang | 貴陽府 | Koi’ ˛yong ,, |
| Yunnan | Yunnan | Yünnan | 雲南府 | ˛Hung ˛nang ,, |

## 8. PREFECTURES OF FOOKIEN PROVINCE.

| | | | |
|---|---|---|---|
| Fuhchau | Fuchou-fu | 福州府 | Hok˒ ˛chiu ‘hu |
| Hinghwa | Hsinghua-fu | 興化府 | ˛Hing hwa’ ‘hu |
| Tsiuenchau | Ch‘uanchou-fu | 泉州府 | ˛Chiong ˛chiu ‘hu |
| Changchau | Changchou-fu | 漳州府 | ˛Chiong ˛chiu ‘hu |
| Fuhning | Funing-fu | 福寗府 | Hok˒ ˛ning ‘hu |
| Yenping | Yenp‘ing-fu | 延平府 | ˛Yong ˛ping ‘hu |
| Kienning | Chienning-fu | 建寗府 | Kiong’ ˛ning ‘hu |
| Shauwu | Shaowu-fu | 邵武府 | Sieu$^2$ ‘u ‘hu |
| Tingchau | T‘ingchou | 汀州府 | ˛T‘ing ˛chiu ‘hu |
| Lungngan | Lungyen-chou | 龍巖州 | ˛Lũng ˛ngang ˛chiu |
| Yungchun | Yungch‘un-chou | 永春州 | ‘Ing ˛ch‘ung ˛chiu |
| Taiwan | T‘aiwan-fu | 臺灣府 | ˛Tai ˛wang ‘hu |

## 9. DISTRICTS OF FOOCHOW PREFECTURE.

| | | | |
|---|---|---|---|
| Min | Min-hsien | 閩縣 | ꜁Ming kaing$^2$ |
| Haukwan | Houkuan-hsien | 侯官縣 | Au$^2$ ꜀kwang kaing$^2$ |
| Changloh | Changlo-hsien | 長樂縣 | ꜁Tiong lóh꜇ kaing$^2$ |
| Fuhtsing | Fuch'ing-hsien | 福清縣 | Hok꜆ ꜀ch'iăng kaing$^2$ |
| Lienkiang | Lienchiang-hsien | 連江縣 | ꜁Lièng (꜁leng) ꜀kong kaing$^2$ |
| Loyuen | Loyüan-hsien | 羅源縣 | ꜁Ló ꜁ngwong kaing$^2$ |
| Mintsing | Minch'ing-hsien | 閩清縣 | ꜁Ming ꜀ch'iăng kaing$^2$ |
| Yungfuh | Yungfu-hsien | 永福縣 | ꜂Ing hok꜆ kaing$^2$ |
| Kutien | Kut'ien-hsien | 古田縣 | ꜀K'u ꜁ch'eng kaing$^2$ |
| Pingnan | P'ingnan-hsien | 屏南縣 | ꜁Ping ꜁nang kaing$^2$ |

## 10. TREATY PORTS, ETC.

| | | | |
|---|---|---|---|
| Kiungchau | Ch'iungchou | 瓊州 | ꜁King ꜀chiu |
| Macao | Aomên | 澳門 | Ó꜄ ꜁mwong |
| Hongkong | Hsiangchiang | 香港 | ꜀Hiong ꜂kĕng |
| Canton | Kuangtung | 廣東 | ꜂Kwong ꜀tĕng |
| Whampoa | Huangpu | 黃埔 | ꜁Wong pwo$^2$ (꜀p'wo) |
| Swatow | Shant'ou | 汕頭 | Sang꜄ ꜁t'au |
| Amoy | Hsiamên | 廈門 | A$^2$ ꜁mwong |
| Kulangsu | Kulanghsü | 鼓浪嶼 | ꜂Ku laung$^2$ sëü$^2$ |
| Foochow | Fuchou | 福州 | Hok꜆ ꜀chiu |
| Pagoda Anchorage | Lohsingt'a | 羅星塔 | ꜁Ló ꜀sing t'ak꜆ |
| Takao | Takow | 打狗 | ꜂Ta ꜂keu |
| Taiwan | T'aiwan | 臺灣 | ꜁Tai ꜁wang |
| Tamsui | Tanchui | 淡水 | Tang$^2$ ꜂chwi |
| Kilung | Chilung | 雞籠 | ꜀Kiĕ ꜁lĕng |
| Wanchau | Wênchou | 溫州 | ꜀Ung ꜀chiu |
| Ningpo | Ningpo | 甯波 | ꜁Ning ꜀p'ó |
| Chinhai | Chênhai | 鎮海 | Teng꜄ ꜂hai |
| Chusan | Tinghai | 定海 | Teng$^2$ ꜂hai |
| Puto | P'ut'o | 普陀巖 | ꜂P'wo ꜁tó ꜁ngang |
| Shanghai | Shanghai | 上海 | Siong$^2$ ꜂hai |
| Woosung | Wusung | 吳淞 | ꜁Ngu ꜁sŭng |

| | | | |
|---|---|---|---|
| Chinkiang | Chênchiang | 鎮江 | *Teng˒ ˓kong* |
| Nanking | Nanching | 南京 | *˓Nang ˓king* |
| Kiukiang | Chiuchiang | 九江 | *ʿKiu ˓kong* |
| Hankow | Hankʻou | 漢口 | *Hang˒ ʿkʻau* |
| Yentai | Yentʻai | 煙臺 | *˓Yĕng ˓tai* |
| Chefoo | Chihfou | 芝罘 | *˓Chiĕ ˓pʻeu* |
| Tientsin | Tʻienchin | 天津 | *˓Tʻiĕng ˓ching* |
| Taku | Taku | 大沽 | *Tai² ˓ku* |
| Peking | Peiching | 北京 | *Paĕk˒ ˓king* |
| Niuchwang | Niuchuang | 牛莊 | *˓Ngiu ˓chong* |
| Yingtsz' | Yingtzu | 營子 | *˓Ing ʿchŭ* |
| Kalgan | Changchiakʻou | 張家口 | *˓Tiong ˓ka ʿkʻau* |
| Kiachta | Chʻiakʻotʻu | 恰克圖 | *Kʻak˒ kʻaik˒ ˓tu* |
| | Maimaichʻêng | 買賣城 | *ʿMá mai² ˓siăng* |

## 11. CHINESE CHRONOLOGY

### AND DYNASTIES.

According to Chinese mythology, Pwanku, the first man, was succeeded by three rulers, called the Celestial, Terrestrial, and Human sovereigns, after whom flourished the two monarchs, Yu-chʻao (Having-nests) and Suijên (Match-man or Prometheus). This mythological history ends with the appearance of Fuhhi, and their chronology should not be charged with the long periods antecedent, varying from foty-five to five hundred thousand years . . . . . The accession of Fuhhi is placed in the Chinese annals, B. C. 2852, or eight years after the death of Enos, 1152 years after the creation, and 508 before the deluge, according to the commonly received chronology of Usher . . . . . . But reckoning according to Hales' chronology, we bring the commencement of ancient Chinese history, 303 years subsequent to the deluge, 47 before the death of Noah, and about three centuries before the confusion of tongues (See Middle Kingdom, VOL. II, pages 198 and 199).

The Chinese compute time by a cycle of 60 years, which was formed in the 61st year of 皇帝 *˓Wong ti˒*, the Yellow Emperor, by his minister 大撓 *Tai² ʿNau* (*˓nau*). The 10 characters, called *sek˒ ˓kang*, the ten stems, or *˓Tʻiĕng ˓kang*, 天干 celestial stems, were combined with the 12 horary characters, called *sek꜁ ne$^2$ ꜀chié,* 十二支 the twelve branches, or *Te$^2$ ꜀chié,* 地支 terrestrial branches, so as to form couplets, which were employed as the names of successive years. Six repetitions of the "stems" (6X10) with five repetitions of the "branches" (5X12) formed the cycle.

## The 10 stems are

甲 乙 丙 丁 戊 已 庚 辛 壬 癸

*Kak꜁ Ek꜁ ‘Ping ꜀Ting Mwo$^2$ ‘Ki ꜀Keng ꜀Sing ꜀Ing Koi꜄*

## The 12 branches are

子 丑 寅 卯 辰 巳 午 未 申 酉 戌 亥

*‘Chü ‘T‘iu ꜀Ing ‘Mau ꜀Sing Sëü$^2$ ‘Ngu E$^2$ ꜀Sing ‘Iu Sok꜁ Hai$^2$*

The 61st year of Hwangti being the first year of the first cycle, 74 cycles were completed A. D. 1803. The following table shows with sufficient minuteness the computation for the present century.

| | | | | | |
|---|---|---|---|---|---|
| 1801 | 辛酉 | *꜀Sing ‘iu,* | .... | .... .... | .... .... .... |
| 1802 | 壬戌 | *꜀Ing sok꜁* | 1834 | 甲午 | *Kak꜁ ‘ngu,* |
| 1803 | 癸亥 | *Koi꜄ hai$^2$* | .... | .... .... | .... .... .... |
| 1804 | 甲子 | *Kak꜁ ‘chü,* | 1844 | 甲辰 | *Kak꜁ ꜀sing,* |
| 1805 | 乙丑 | *Ek꜁ ‘t‘iu,* | .... | .... .... | .... .... .... |
| 1806 | 丙寅 | *‘Ping ꜀ing,* | 1854 | 甲寅 | *Kak꜁ ꜀ing,* |
| 1807 | 丁卯 | *꜀Ting ‘mau,* | .... | .... .... | .... .... .... |
| 1808 | 戊辰 | *Mwo$^2$ ꜀sing,* | 1864 | 甲子 | *Kak꜁ ‘chü,* |
| 1809 | 已巳 | *‘Ki sëü$^2$* | .... | .... .... | .... .... .... |
| 1810 | 庚午 | *꜀Keng ‘ngu,* | 1870 | 庚午 | *꜀Keng ‘ngu,* |
| 1811 | 辛未 | *꜀Sing e$^2$* | 1871 | 辛未 | *꜀Sing e$^2$* |
| 1812 | 壬申 | *꜀Ing ꜀sing,* | 1872 | 壬申 | *꜀Ing ꜀sing,* |
| 1813 | 癸酉 | *Koi꜄ ‘iu,* | .... | .... .... | .... .... .... |
| 1814 | 甲戌 | *Kak꜁ sok꜁* | 1880 | 庚辰 | *꜀Keng ꜀sing,* |
| 1815 | 乙亥 | *Ek꜁ hai$^2$* | .... | .... .... | .... .... .... |
| 1816 | 丙子 | *‘Ping ‘chü,* | 1890 | 庚寅 | *꜀Keng ꜀ing,* |
| .... | .... .... | .... .... .... | .... | .... .... | .... .... .... |
| 1824 | 甲申 | *Kak꜁ ꜀sing,* | 1900 | 庚子 | *꜀Keng ‘chü,* |

Besides the cyclic mode of computation, the Chinese reckon from the beginning of each emperor's reign. This is the ordinary way of indicating the dates of current events. Thus the 6th day of June, 1870, according to the Chinese calendar, is written 同治九年五月初八日 ꜀*Tung te*$^2$ ꜂*kau* ꜀*niĕng ngo*$^2$ *ngwok*꜅ ꜀*ch'ĕ paik*꜄ *nik*꜅ T'ungchih, 9th year, 5th month, 8th day.

In Morrison's View of China, published in the year 1817, the dynasties and individual reigns are given from the reigning emperor, 嘉慶 ꜀*Ka k'eng*꜄ A. D. 1816, up through the Three Sovereigns, 三皇 ꜀*Sang* ꜀*hwong*, B. C. 2622–3369, and through the *three lines* of sovereigns of the fabulous period, *viz.*, 人皇氏 ꜀*Ing* ꜀*hwong se*$^2$, 9 brothers, 18000 years, 地皇氏 *Te*$^2$ ꜀*hwong se*$^2$, 11 brothers, 18000 years, and 天皇氏 ꜀*T'iĕng* ꜀*hwong se*$^2$, 12 brothers, 45000 years. Before these was 盤古 ꜀*Pwang* ꜂*ku*, the first man, or the "first who appeared after the heavens and earth were separated".

Chronological lists by subsequent writers, having greater facilities for correctness as to arrangement and dates, differ considerably from that work. They also differ somewhat from each other, but the chief discrepancies are confined to the periods preceding A. D. 24.

The lists of dynasties and sovereigns, found in the Chinese Repository, Vol. 10, p. 123, *et seq.*, are based on the native works, ꜀*Kong kaṅg*꜄ *e*$^2$ ꜀*ti lioh*꜅ 綱鑑易知錄 and ꜀*Sang* ꜀*ngwong kak*꜄ ꜂*chŭ*, 三元甲子. The following 8 periods are arranged from data furnished by those lists. A comparison of these with the corresponding periods in the two Tables immediately succeeding them, will show discrepancies of the kind referred to above.

| | | | |
|---|---|---|---|
| 1. The Three August Sov'ns | 三皇 | ꜀*Sang* ꜀*hwong* | Mythological Period |
| 2. ,, Five Sovereigns | 五帝 | ꜂*Ngu tá*꜄ | B.C. 2852—2206 |
| 3. ,, Hea Dynasty | 夏朝 | *Ha*$^2$ ꜀*tieu* | ,, 2205—1767 |
| 4. ,, Shang Dynasty | 商朝 | ꜀*Siong* ꜀*tieu* | ,, 1766—1123 |
| 5. ,, Chow Dynasty | 周朝 | ꜀*Chiu* ꜀*tieu* | ,, 1122—250 |
| 6. ,, Tsin Dynasty | 秦朝 | ꜀*Ching* ꜀*tieu* | ,, 249—247 |
| 7. ,, After Tsin Dynasty | 後秦 | *Haiu*$^2$ ꜀*ching* | ,, 246—203 |
| 8. ,, Han Dynasty | 漢朝 | *Hang*꜄ ꜀*tieu* | ,, 202—A.D.24 |

# Synoptical Table of Chinese Dynasties.

**Arranged from Chronological Tables by Wm. Fredk. Mayers, Esq., as published in the Journal of the North - China Branch of the Royal Asiatic Society, December, 1867—with the corresponding Foochow names of the dynasties.**

| Names of the Dynasties | | | Duration | |
|---|---|---|---|---|
| The Three Sovereigns | 三皇 | *꜀Sang ꜀hwong* | ... ... ... | Fabulous |
| ,, Five Rulers | 五帝 | *꜂Ngu tá꜃* | B.C. 2852–2206 | period. |
| ,, Hia Dynasty | 夏朝 | *Ha² ꜀tieu* | ,, 2205–1767 | Legendary |
| ,, Shang ,, (also called Yin 殷) | 商朝 | *꜀Siong ꜀tieu* | ,, 1766–1123 | period. |
| ,, Chow ,, | 周朝 | *꜀Chiu ꜀tieu* | ,, 1122–250 | Semi-historical |
| ,, Ts'in ,, | 秦朝 | *꜀Ching ꜀tieu* | ,, 249–247 | |
| ,, After T'sin ,, | 後秦 | *Haiu² ꜀ching* | ,, 246–203 | |
| ,, Han ,, | 漢朝 | *Hang꜃ ꜀tieu* | ,, 202–A.D.24 | |
| ,, Eastern Han ,, | 東漢 | *꜀Tëng hang꜃* | A. D. 25–220 | |
| ,, After Han ,, | 後漢 | *Haiu² hang꜃* | ,, 221–264 | |
| ,, Tsin ,, | 晉朝 | *Cheng꜃ ꜀tieu* | ,, 265–419 | |
| ,, North'rn Sung ,, | 北宋 | *Paëk꜅ saëng꜃* | ,, 420–478 | and |
| ,, Ts'i ,, | 齊朝 | *꜀Chá ꜀tieu* | ,, 479–501 | |
| ,, Liang ,, | 梁朝 | *꜀Liong ꜀tieu* | ,, 502–556 | |
| ,, Ch'èn ,, | 陳朝 | *꜀Ting ꜀tieu* | ,, 557–588 | |
| ,, Sui ,, | 隋朝 | *꜀Sui ꜀tieu* | ,, 589–617 | |
| ,, T'ang ,, | 唐朝 | *꜀Tong ꜀tieu* | ,, 618–906 | |
| ,, After Liang ,, | 後梁 | *Haiu² ꜀liong* | ,, 907–922 | |
| ,, ,, T'ang ,, | 後唐 | ,, *꜀tong* | ,, 923–935 | |
| ,, ,, Tsin ,, | 後晉 | ,, *cheng꜃* | ,, 936–946 | |
| ,, ,, Han ,, | 後漢 | ,, *hang꜃* | ,, 947–950 | historical |
| ,, ,, Chow ,, | 後周 | ,, *꜀chiu* | ,, 951–959 | |
| ,, Sung ,, | 宋朝 | *Saëng꜃ ꜀tieu* | ,, 960–1126 | |
| ,, South'rn Sung ,, | 南宋 | *꜀Nang saëng꜃* | ,, 1127–1279 | |
| ,, Yüan ,, | 元朝 | *꜀Ngwong ꜀tieu* | ,, 1280–1367 | |
| ,, Ming ,, | 明朝 | *꜀Ming ꜀tieu* | ,, 1368–1643 | period |
| ,, Ts'ing ,, | 清朝 | *꜀Ch'ing ꜀tieu* | ,, 1644–1862* | |

* Year of accession of the reigning Emperor 同治 T'ungchih.

MAN. 22.

# Synoptical Table of Chinese Dynasties.

(By Walter T. Lay, Esqr., in Chinese Recorder, August, 1870.)

The number of sovereigns here given—239—is exclusive of those who reigned during the period styled the Three Emperors. That period is one of much obscurity, and consequently no reliable data are at hand on which to base a calculation.

| Name of Dynasty | | Duration of Dynasty | Years | No. of Sovereigns |
|---|---|---|---|---|
| The Three Emperors | 三皇 | B.C. 3314—2570 | 745 | .. |
| ,, Five do | 五帝 | ,, 2569—2179 | 391 | 5 |
| ,, Sia | 夏朝 | ,, 2178—1767 | 412 | 17 |
| ,, { Shang | 商朝 | ,, 1766—1374 | 393 | 17 |
| ,, { Yin | 殷朝 | ,, 1373—1123 | 251 | 11 |
| ,, Chow | 周朝 | ,, 1122—771 | 352 | 12 |
| ,, Eastern Chow | 東周朝 | ,, 770—249 | 522 | 23 |
| | | Interregnum | 27 | |
| ,, Ch'in | 秦朝 | ,, 221—207 | 15 | 2 |
| ,, Han | 漢朝 | ,, 206—A.D.24 | 230 | 14 |
| ,, Eastern Han | 東漢朝 | A.D. 25—220 | 196 | 12 |
| ,, Second Han | 後漢朝 | ,, 221—264 | 44 | 2 |
| ,, Western Chin | 西晉朝 | ,, 265—316 | 52 | 4 |
| ,, Eastern Chin | 東晉朝 | ,, 317—419 | 103 | 11 |
| ,, Sung | 宋朝 | ,, 420—478 | 59 | 8 |
| ,, Ch'i | 齊朝 | ,, 479—501 | 23 | 5 |
| ,, Liang | 梁朝 | ,, 502—556 | 55 | 4 |
| ,, Ch'ên | 陳朝 | ,, 557—588 | 32 | 5 |
| ,, Sui | 隋朝 | ,, 589—617 | 29 | 3 |
| ,, T'ang | 唐朝 | ,, 618—906 | 289 | 20 |
| ,, Five Dynasties. { How Liang | 後梁朝 | ,, 907—922 | 16 | 2 |
| ,, Five Dynasties. { ,, T'ang | 後唐朝 | ,, 923—935 | 13 | 4 |
| ,, Five Dynasties. { ,, Chin | 後晉朝 | ,, 936—946 | 11 | 2 |
| ,, Five Dynasties. { ,, Han | 後漢朝 | ,, 947—950 | 4 | 2 |
| ,, Five Dynasties. { ,, Chow | 後周朝 | ,, 951—959 | 9 | 3 |
| ,, Sung | 宋朝 | ,, 960—1126 | 167 | 8 |
| ,, Southern Sung | 南宋朝 | ,, 1127—1279 | 153 | 10 |
| ,, Yuan | 元朝 | ,, 1280—1367 | 88 | 9 |
| ,, Ming | 明朝 | ,, 1368—1643 | 276 | 17 |
| ,, Ch'ing | 清朝 | ,, 1644—1861 | 218 | 7* |
| Total number of Sovereigns, | | | | 239 |

*Still reigning.

## 12. FAMILY RELATIONSHIPS.

The Chinese trace relationships to a very minute extent. It is hoped the terms, as here arranged in the form of Tables, may be convenient for reference.

General Remarks. *Pah*꜁ 伯 used alone, or as a terminating title of relationship, denotes that the person bearing it is older, and *chëük*꜁ 叔 in like manner denotes that he is younger, than one's father. The practice of the wife and her relatives in calling her husband's brothers *pah*꜁ 伯 and *chëük*꜁ 叔 is complimentary, or in imitation of her children.

All great-grandchildren of one's four great-grandfathers and belonging, of course, to the same generation as one's self, are divided into two classes. 1. Those of the same surname as one's self, called ꜀*hiĭng tiê*² 兄弟 and ʻ*chiă mwoi*ʼ 姐妹 (brothers and sisters): these embrace the children of one's father (also called ꜀*pau* ꜀*hing tá*² 胞兄弟 and ꜀*pau* ʻ*chiă mwoi*ʼ 胞姐妹), the children of one's paternal uncle, and the grandchildren, by male line, of one's paternal grandfather's brother. 2. Those of different surname from one's self: these are called ʻ*pieu* ꜀*hing tá*² 表兄弟 and ʻ*pieu* ʻ*chiă mwoi*ʼ 表姐妹 (i. e., *pieu* brothers and sisters) and are divided into three classes, *viz.*, *Keu*² ʻ*pieu*, 舅表 ꜀*Ku* ʻ*pieu*, 姑表 and ꜀*I* ʻ*pieu*, 姨表 according to the line of descent.

When terms of relationship, as commonly used, are indefinite, more minute distinctions are made by the use of additional terms, as ꜀*pau* ꜀*hing tá*² 胞兄弟 own brothers, i. e. sons of the same father, *chëük*꜁ *pah*꜁ ꜀*hing tá*² 叔伯兄弟 paternal-uncle-brothers, i. e., sons of paternal uncle.

The Romanized words are the colloquial equivalents of the Chinese characters.

A heavy horizontal line indicates the termination of a line of relationship so far as here represented.

## Introductory Terms.

Ancestors, 祖宗 ʻ*Chu* ꜀*chung*. Descendants, 仔孫 ʻ*kiăng* ꜀*song*. Husband, 唐晡 ꜀*Tong* ꜀*pwo*. Wife, 老媽 *Lau*² ʻ*ma*. Husband and wife, 夫妻 ꜀*Hu* ꜀*ch'á*, or 夫婦 ꜀*Hu ho*² or 老公媽 *Lau*² ꜀*kung* ʻ*ma*. Parents, 郎奶 *Pa*² ʻ*ná*. Children, 仔伲 ʻ*Kiăng* ꜀*nié*.

## Tables.

### No. 1.

PATERNAL ANCESTORS (BY MALE LINE), AND DESCENDANTS.

| | | |
|---|---|---|
| P. grandf's p. grandfather, | 高 祖 | ‘Lô twai$^2$ ꜀kung. |
| P. grandf's p. grandmother, | 高祖妣 | ‘Lô twai$^2$ ‘ma. |
| P. grandfather's father, | 曾 祖 | Twai$^2$ ꜀kung. |
| P. grandfather's mother. | 曾祖妣 | Twai$^2$ ‘ma. |
| P. grandfather, | 祖 | ꜀Kung. |
| P. grandmother, | 妣 | ‘Ma. |
| Father, | 父 | ꜁Nong ma$^2$. |
| Mother, | 母 | ꜁Nong ‘nâ. |
| Self, | 己 | ‘Pwong ꜀sing. |

| | | | |
|---|---|---|---|
| Son, 子 | ‘Kiăng. | Daughter, 女 | ꜀Chü ꜁nëng ‘kiăng. |
| Son's wife, 媳 | ꜀Sing mo$^2$. | Her husband, 壻 | ꜁Nié sai᾽. |

| | | | |
|---|---|---|---|
| Son's son, | Son's daughter, | Daughter's son, | Daughter's dau. |
| 孫 | 孫女 | 外孫 | 外孫女 |
| ꜀Song. | ꜀Chü ꜁nong ꜀song. | Ngiê$^2$ ꜀seng ꜀song.* | Ngiê$^2$ ꜀seng ꜀song ‘nü.† |
| His wife, | Her husband, | His wife, | Her husband, |
| 孫婦 | 孫壻 | 外孫婦 | 外孫女壻 |
| ꜀Song ꜀sing mo$^2$. | ꜀Song sai᾽. | Ngiê$^2$ ꜀seng ꜀sing mo$^2$. | Ngiê$^2$ ꜀seng ꜀song sai᾽. |

| | | |
|---|---|---|
| Son's son's son, | Son's son's dau. | *Also called Ngiê$^2$ ꜀seng. |
| 曾孫 | 曾孫女 | †Also called Ngiê$^2$ ꜀seng ꜀chü ꜁nong ꜀song, and Ngiê$^2$ ꜀seng ‘nü. |
| ꜀Cheng ꜀song. | ꜀Cheng ꜀song ‘nü. | |
| His wife, | Her husband, | |
| 曾孫婦 | 曾孫女壻 | |
| ꜀Song ꜀sing mo$^2$. ꜀Cheng ꜀song ꜀sing mo$^2$. | ꜀Song sai᾽. ꜀Cheng ꜀song ‘nü sâ᾽. | |

Great-great-grandson (by male line), 元孫 ꜁Ngwong ꜀song. Great-great-great-grandson (by male line), 來孫 ꜁Lai ꜀song.

## No. 2.

### Great Uncle.

| P. grandfather's elder brother. | P. grandf's younger brother, |
|---|---|
| 伯祖<br>*Pah꜆ ꜀kung.*<br>His wife, 伯妣 *꜂Mu ꜁pó.* | 叔祖<br>*Chëük꜆ ꜀kung.*<br>His wife, 叔妣 *꜂Sing ꜁pó.* |

| P. grandf's bro's elder son, | P. grandf's bro's younger son, | P. grandf's bro's daughter, |
|---|---|---|
| 堂伯<br>*Pah꜆* or<br>*꜁Tong pah꜆.*<br>His wife,<br>堂姆<br>*꜂Mu.* | 堂叔<br>*Chëük꜆*, or<br>*꜁Tong chëük꜆.*<br>His wife,<br>堂嬸<br>*꜂Sing.* | 堂姑<br>*꜀Ku*, or<br>*꜁Tong ꜀ku.*<br>Her husband,<br>堂姑夫<br>*꜀Ku ꜀hu.* |

| Their children, | Her children, |
|---|---|
| 從堂兄弟 從堂姐妹<br>*꜀Hiăng tiĕ²*, *꜂Chiă mwoi꜄.* | 表兄弟 表姐妹<br>*꜂Pieu ꜀hing tá²*, *꜂Pieu ꜂chiă mwoi꜄.* |

| | | | |
|---|---|---|---|
| Wife of *꜂pieu ꜀hing* | 表兄 | is *꜂pieu ꜂só*, | 表嫂 |
| Wife of *꜂pieu tá²* | 表弟 | is *꜂pieu tá² ho²*, | 表弟婦 |
| Husband of *꜂pieu ꜂chiă* | 表姐 | is *꜂pieu ꜂chiă ꜀hu*, | 表姐夫 |
| Husband of *꜂pieu mwoi꜄* | 表妹 | is *꜂pieu mwoi꜄ ꜀hu*, | 表妹夫 |

## No 3.

### Great Aunt.

| | | |
|---|---|---|
| P. grandf's sister, | 姑妣 | *꜀Ku ꜁pó.* |
| Her husband, | 姑祖 | *꜀Ku ꜀kung.* |

| P. grandf 's sister's elder son, | P. grandf 's sister's younger son, | P. grandf's sister's daughter, |
|---|---|---|
| 表伯<br>*꜂Pieu pah꜆.*<br>His wife,<br>表姆<br>*꜂Pieu ꜂mu.* | 表叔<br>*꜂Pieu chëük꜆.*<br>His wife,<br>表嬸<br>*꜂Pieu ꜂sing.* | 表姑<br>*꜂Pieu ꜀ku.*<br>Her husband,<br>表姑夫<br>*꜂Pieu ꜀ku ꜀hu.* |

| Their children, |
|---|
| 表兄弟 表姐妹<br>*꜂Pieu ꜀hing tá²*, *꜂Pieu ꜂chiă mwoi꜄.* |

## No. 4.
### Great Uncle.

| | | |
|---|---|---|
| P. grandm's brother, | 舅 祖 | *Keu² ꜀kung.* |
| His wife, | 舅祖妣 | *Keng² ‘ma.* |

| P. grandm's bro's elder son, | P. grandm's bro's younger son, | P. grandm's bro's daughter, |
|---|---|---|
| 表伯 | 表叔 | 表姑 |
| *‘Pieu pah꜆.* | *‘Pieu chĕŭk꜆.* | *‘Pieu ꜀ku.* |
| His wife, | His wife, | Her husband, |
| 表姆 | 表嬸 | 表姑夫 |
| *‘Pieu ‘mu.* | *‘Pieu ‘sing.* | *‘Pieu ꜀ku ꜀hu.* |

Their children,
表兄弟 *‘Pieu ꜀hing tá²,* 表姐妹 *‘Pieu ‘chiă mwoiʾ.*

## No. 5.
### Great Aunt.

| | | |
|---|---|---|
| P. grandm's sister, | 姨 妣 | *꜀I ‘ma.* |
| Her husband, | 姨 祖 | *꜀I ꜀kung.* |

| P. grandm's sister's elder son, | P. grandm's sister's younger son, | P. grandm's sister's daughter, |
|---|---|---|
| 表伯 | 表叔 | 表姑 |
| *‘Pieu pah꜆.* | *‘Pieu chĕŭk꜆.* | *‘Pieu ꜀ku.* |
| His wife, | His wife, | Her husband, |
| 表姆 | 表嬸 | 表姑夫 |
| *‘Pieu ‘mu.* | *‘Pieu ‘sing.* | *‘Pieu ꜀ku ꜀hu.* |

Their children,
表兄弟 *‘Pieu ꜀hing tá²,* 表姐妹 *‘Pieu ‘chiă mwoiʾ.*

## No. 6.
### Paternal Uncle.

| Father's elder bro., | Father's young. bro., |
|---|---|
| 伯 | 叔 |
| *Pah꜆.* | *Chĕŭk꜆* or *꜀Ka.* |
| His wife, | His wife, |
| 姆 | 嬸 |
| *‘Mu.* | *꜀Ka ‘sing.* |

P. uncle's children,
親堂兄弟 *꜀Hiăng tiĕ²,* 親堂姐妹 *‘Chiă mwoiʾ.*

## No. 7.
### Paternal Aunt.

| Father's sister, |
|---|
| 娘姑 |
| *꜀Niong ꜀ku.* |
| Her husband, |
| 姑夫 |
| *꜀Ku ꜀hu.* |

P. aunt's children,
表兄弟 *‘Pieu ꜀hing tá²,* 表姐妹 *‘Pieu ‘chiă mwoiʾ.*

# No. 8.

## Brother.

| | |
|---|---|
| Elder brother, 兄 ꜀Hiăng. His wife, 兄嫂 ꜀Hiăng ʻsó. | Younger brother, 弟 Tiĕ$^{2}$. His wife, 弟婦 Tiĕ$^{2}$ ꜀sing mo$^{2}$. Tiĕ$^{2}$ ꜀ing. |
| Brother's son, 侄 ꜀Song. His wife, 侄婦 ꜀Song ꜀sing mo$^{2}$. | Brother's daughter, 侄女 ꜀Chü ꜀nong ꜀song. Her husband, 侄壻 ꜀Song saiꜗ. |

| | | | |
|---|---|---|---|
| Bro's son's son, 侄孫 ꜀Song ʻkiăng.* His wife, 侄孫婦 ꜀Song ꜀sing mo$^{2}$. | Bro's son's dau., 侄孫女 ꜀Chü ꜀nong ꜀song Her husband, 侄孫壻 ꜀Song saiꜗ. | Bro's dau's son, 外甥 Ngiĕ$^{2}$ ꜀seng. His wife, 外甥媳婦 Ngiĕ$^{2}$ ꜀seng ꜀sing mo$^{2}$. | Bro's dau's dau., 外甥女 Ngiĕ$^{2}$ ꜀seng ʻnü. Her husband, 外甥女壻 Ngiĕ$^{2}$ ꜀seng ꜀song saiꜗ. |
| Bro's son's son's son, 曾侄孫 ꜀Song ʻkiăng. | Bro's son's son's dau., 曾侄孫女 ꜀Song ʻkiăng. | Bro's dau's son's son, 外甥孫 Ngiĕ$^{2}$ ꜀seng ꜀song. | Bro's dau's son's dau., 外甥孫女 Ngiĕ$^{2}$ ꜀seng ꜀song ʻnü. |

* The term ꜀song ʻkiăng is indefinite, having a wider application than represented in this table.

## No. 9.

### Sister.

| Elder sister, | Younger sister, |
|---|---|
| 姐 | 妹 |
| *‘Chiă.* | *Mwoi’.* |
| Her husband, | Her husband, |
| 姐夫 | 妹夫 |
| *‘Chiă ꜀hu.* | *Mwoi’ ꜀hu.* |

| Sister's son, | Sister's daughter, |
|---|---|
| 外甥 | 外甥女 |
| *Ngié$^{2}$ ꜀seng.* | *Ngié$^{2}$ ꜀seng ‘nü.* |
| His wife, | Her husband, |
| 外甥媳婦 | 外甥女壻 |
| *Ngié$^{2}$ ꜀seng ꜀sing mo$^{2}$.* | *Ngié$^{2}$ ꜀seng ꜀song sai’.* |

| Sister's son's son, | Sister's son's dau., |
|---|---|
| 外甥孫 | 外甥孫女 |
| *Ngié$^{2}$ ꜀seng ꜀song.* | *Ngié$^{2}$ ꜀seng ꜀song ‘nü.* |
| His wife, | Her husband, |
| 外甥孫媳婦 | 外甥孫女壻 |
| *Ngié$^{2}$ ꜀seng ꜀song ꜀sing mo$^{2}$.* | *Ngié$^{2}$ ꜀seng ꜀song sai’.* |

## No. 10.

### Maternal Ancestors.

| | | |
|---|---|---|
| M. grandf's father, | 外曾祖 | *Ngié$^{2}$ twai$^{2}$ ꜀kung.* |
| M. grandf's mother, | 外曾祖妣 | *Ngié$^{2}$ twai$^{2}$ ‘ma.* |
| M. grandfather, | 外祖 | *Ngié$^{2}$ ꜀kung.* |
| M. grandmother, | 外祖妣 | *Ngié$^{2}$ ‘ma.* |

## No. 11.

### Great Uncle.

| | |
|---|---|
| M. grandf's elder bro., | M. grandf's younger bro., |
| 外伯祖 | 外叔祖 |
| *Pah꜁ ꜀kung.* | *Chĕük꜁ ꜀kung.* |
| His wife, | His wife, |
| 外伯妣 | 外叔妣 |
| *꜂Mu ˛pó.* | *꜂Sing ˛pó.* |
| M. grandf's brother's son, | M. grandf's bro's daughter, |
| 堂舅 | 堂姨 |
| *˛Nìong keu[2].* | *˛Nìong ˛i.* |
| His wife. | Her husband, |
| 堂妗 | 堂姨夫 |
| *˛Nìong keng[2].* | *˛I ꜀hu.* |

Their children,

| | |
|---|---|
| 表兄弟 | 表姐妹 |
| *꜂Pieu ꜀hing tá[2],* | *꜂Pieu ꜂chiă mwoí꜃.* |

## No. 12.

### Great Aunt.

| | | |
|---|---|---|
| M. grandf's sister, | 姑妣 | *꜀Ku ˛pó.* |
| Her husband, | 姑祖 | *꜀Ku ꜀kung.* |

| | |
|---|---|
| M. grandf's sister's son, | M. grandf's sister's daughter, |
| 表舅 | 表姨 |
| *꜂Pieu keu[2].* | *꜂Pieu ˛i.* |
| His wife. | Her husband, |
| 表妗 | 表姨夫 |
| *꜂Pieu keng[2].* | *꜂Pieu ˛i ꜀hu.* |

Their children,

| | |
|---|---|
| 表兄弟 | 表姐妹 |
| *꜂Pieu ꜀hing tá[2],* | *꜂Pieu ꜂chiă mwoí꜃.* |

## No. 13.

### Great Uncle.

| | | |
|---|---|---|
| M. grandmother's brother, | 舅祖 | *Keu$^{2}$ ꜀kung.* |
| His wife, | 舅妣 | *Keng$^{2}$ ‘ma.* |

| M. grandm's bro's son, | M. grandm's bro's daughter, |
|---|---|
| 表舅 | 表姨 |
| *‘Pieu keu$^{2}$.* | *‘Pieu ꜁i.* |
| His wife, | Her husband, |
| 表妗 | 表姨夫 |
| *‘Pieu keng$^{2}$.* | *‘Pieu ꜁i ꜀hu.* |

Their children,

表兄弟 *‘Pieu ꜀hing tâ$^{2}$,* 表姐妹 *‘Pieu ‘chiă mwoi’.*

## No. 14.

### Great Aunt.

| | | |
|---|---|---|
| P. grandm's sister, | 姨妣 | *꜁I ‘ma.* |
| Her husband, | 姨祖 | *꜁I ꜀kung.* |

| M. grandm's sister's son, | M. grandm's sister's daughter, |
|---|---|
| 表舅 | 表姨 |
| *‘Pieu keu$^{2}$.* | *‘Pieu ꜁i.* |
| His wife, | Her husband, |
| 表妗 | 表姨夫 |
| *‘Pieu keng$^{2}$.* | *‘Pieu ꜁i ꜀hu.* |

Their children,

表兄弟 *‘Pieu ꜀hing tâ$^{2}$,* 表姐妹 *‘Pieu ‘chiă mwoi’.*

| No. 15. Maternal Uncle. | No. 16. Maternal Aunt. |
|---|---|
| Mother's brother, | Mother's sister, |
| 母舅 *꜁Niong keu$^{2}$.* | 母姨 *꜁Niong ꜁i.* |
| His wife, | Her husband, |
| 母妗 *꜁Niong keng$^{2}$.* | 母姨夫 *꜁I ꜀hu.* |

Their children,

表兄弟 *‘Pieu ꜀hing tâ$^{2}$,* 表姐妹 *‘Pieu ‘chiă mwoi’.*

## No. 17.
## Adopted Relatives.

| | | |
|---|---|---|
| Adopted Father, | 誼父 | *K'ié꜃ ꜀nong ma².* |
| ,, Mother, | 誼母 | ,, *꜂ná.* |
| ,, Son (retaining own surname), | 誼子 | ,, *꜂kiăng.* |
| Adopted Daughter (retaining own surname), | 誼女子 | ,, *꜀chü ꜀nĕng꜂kiăng.* |
| Adopted Dau's husband, | 誼女壻 | ,, *꜀nié sai꜃.* |
| ,, Brothers, | 誼兄弟 | *Ngié² ꜀hiăng tié².* |
| ,, Sisters, | 誼姊妹 | ,, *꜂chiă mwoi꜃.* |
| Son of one's adopted son, or the adopted son himself as related to the adopted paternal grandfather, | 誼孫 | *Ngié² ꜀song.*<br>*K'ié꜃ ꜀song.* |
| Wife's adopted Father, | 誼丈人 | *Ngié² ꜀tiong ꜀nĕng.*<br>*K'ié꜃ ꜀tiong ꜀nĕng.* |
| ,, ,, Mother, | 誼岳母 | *Ngié² ꜂tiong꜂ná.*<br>*K'ié꜃ ꜂tiong꜂ná.* |

## No. 18.
## Husband's Relatives.

| | | |
|---|---|---|
| Husband's paternal grandfather, | 夫祖父 | *Twai² ꜀kung.* |
| His wife, | 夫祖母 | ,, *꜂ma.* |
| Husband's paternal uncle older than his (i.e., husband's) father, | 夫伯 | *Pah꜄ ꜀kung.* |
| His wife, | 夫伯姆 | *꜂Mu ꜀pó.* |
| Husband's paternal uncle younger than his (i. e., husband's) father, | 夫叔 | *Chëük꜄ ꜀kung.* |
| His wife, | 夫叔嬸 | *꜂Sing ꜀pó.* |
| Husband's paternal aunt, | 夫姑 | *꜀Ku ꜀pó.* |

| | | |
|---|---|---|
| Her husband, | 夫姑丈 | ꜀Ku꜀kung. |
| Husband's father, | 夫父 | Lau$^2$ ꜀kwang. |
| ,, mother, | 夫母 | ꜁Tai꜀ka. |
| ,, brothers, | 夫兄弟 | Twai$^2$ pah꜆. Sá꜄chëŭk꜆. |
| Their wives, | 夫嫂夫弟婦 | Pah꜆꜂hang. Sá꜄꜂sing. |
| Husband's brother's son, | 夫姪 | ꜀Song. |
| ,, sisters, | 夫姊妹 | Twai$^2$ ꜀ku. Sá꜄ ꜀ku. |
| Their husbands, | 夫姊妹丈 | ꜀Ku꜀hu. |
| Husband's sister's son, | 夫甥 | Ngié$^2$ ꜀seng. |

## No. 19.

## Wife's Relatives.

| | | |
|---|---|---|
| Wife's paternal grandfather, | 岳祖父 | Ngié$^2$ ꜀ka twai$^2$ ꜀kung. |
| His wife, | 岳祖母 | ,, ,, twai$^2$ ꜂ma. |
| Wife's paternal uncle older than her (i. e., wife's) father, | 岳伯 | ,, ,, pah꜆ ꜀kung. |
| His wife, | 岳伯姆 | ,, ,, ꜂mu꜁pó. |
| Wife's paternal uncle younger than her (i. e., wife's) father, | 岳叔 | ,, ,, chëŭk꜆ ꜀kung. |
| His wife, | 岳叔嬸 | ,, ,, ꜂sing꜁pó. |
| Wife's paternal aunt, | 岳姑 | ,, ,, ꜀ku꜁pó. |
| Her husband, | 岳姑丈 | ,, ,, ꜀ku꜀kung. |
| Wife's father, | 岳父 | ꜁Tiong꜁nëng. |
| ,, mother, | 岳母 | ꜂Tiong꜂ná. |
| ,, brothers, | 舅兄弟 | Twai$^2$ sá꜄ keu$^2$. |
| Their wives, | 舅嫂舅弟婦 | Twai$^2$ sá꜄ keng$^2$. |
| Wife's brother's son, | 內侄 | Ngié$^2$ ꜀ka꜀song. |
| Wife's sisters, | 大細姨 | Twai$^2$ sá꜄ ꜁i. |
| ,, sister's husband, | 襟兄弟 | ꜁Tëng꜁mwong. |
| ,, sister's son, | 襟侄 | ꜁Tëng ꜁mwong ꜁ki ꜂kiăng. |

# No. 20.

## Terms Pertaining

## To Families Related By Marriage.

**These terms are used by others as well as by members of such families. A *꜀ch'ing ꜀ka twai$^2$ ꜀kung* is the paternal grandfather of the relative acquired by marriage.**

| | | |
|---|---|---|
| Paternal grandfather, | 姻太祖 | *꜀Ch'ing ꜀ka twai$^2$ ꜀kung.* |
| ,, grandmother, | 姻太祖妣 | ,, ,, *twai$^2$ ꜂ma.* |
| Father, | 姻翁 | *꜀Ch'ing ꜀ka.* |
| Mother, | 姻母 | ,, *꜂mu.* |
| Paternal uncle, | 姻伯祖 | ,, *꜀ka pah꜆ ꜀kung.* |
| His wife, | 姻伯妣 | ,, ,, *꜂mu ꜁pó.* |
| Paternal uncle, | 姻叔祖 | ,, ,, *chëük꜆ ꜀kung.* |
| His wife, | 姻叔妣 | ,, ,, *꜂sing ꜁pó.* |
| Paternal aunt, | 姻姑妣 | ,, ,, *꜀ku ꜁pó.* |
| Her husband, | 姻姑祖 | ,, ,, *꜀ku ꜀kung.* |
| Brothers (of the husband), | 姻伯 | ,, ,, *pah꜆.* |
| | 姻叔 | ,, ,, *chëük꜆.* |
| Their wives, | 姻姆 | ,, ,, *꜂mu.* |
| | 姻嬸 | ,, ,, *꜂sing.* |
| Sister (of the husband), | 姻姑 | ,, ,, *꜀ku.* |
| Her husband, | 姻姑丈 | ,, ,, *꜀ku ꜀hu.* |
| Brother (of the wife), | 姻舅 | ,, ,, *keu$^2$.* |
| His wife, | 姻妗 | ,, ,, *keng$^2$.* |
| Sister (of the wife), | 姻姨 | ,, ,, *꜁i.* |
| Her husband, | 姻姨丈 | ,, ,, *꜁i ꜀hu.* |

# Index to Preceding Tables.

The figures from 1 to 20 refer to No. of Table. The principal terms in common use may be found by reference to the first or leading word in the Index, but sometimes by a following word, e. g., ꜁*i*, aunt, though not appearing alone, is found under ꜁*niong*.

## 13. TITLES OF ADDRESS, ETC.

### Pertaining to Relatives.

꜀*I,* 阿 a common prefix of terms of relationship, as in the three following—

꜀*I* ꜀*ka,* 阿家 ꜀*i* ꜀*tiă,* 阿爹 ꜀*i* ꜁*ié,* 阿爺 ꜀*i* ꜀*kwang,* 阿官 ꜀*i ma*$^2$ 阿罷 a father, as his children call him.

꜀*I* ꜂*ná,* 阿奶 ꜀*i* ꜀*ma,* 阿嬤 also ꜀*i* ꜂*mu,* 阿姆 ꜀*i* ꜂*sing,* 阿孀 and ꜀*i* ꜂*só,* 阿嫂 a mother, as her children call her.

꜀*I* ꜀*kó,* 阿哥 elder brother.

꜁*Tong* ꜀*pwo* ꜁*nëng,* 唐晡伙 one's husband, the term used by a wife in speaking of her husband; she also calls him "the father" of their eldest child, or uses some term by which others address or speak of him, as 姑爺 ꜀*ku* ꜁*ié,* 先生 ꜀*sing* ꜀*sang,* 相公 *siong*꜄ ꜀*këng,* 阿家 ꜀*i* ꜀*ka.*

꜀*Hu* ꜀*ka,* 夫家 your husband.

꜀*Siéng* ꜀*hu,* 先夫 or ꜀*siéng* ꜁*ing,* 先人 my deceased husband.

꜂*Ló* ꜂*siéu,* 老小 a wife, his wife, your wife.

*Chiéng*$^2$ *nói*$^2$ 賤內 or *nói*$^2$ ꜁*ing,* 內人 my wife; *ch'io*꜄ ꜂*tié,* 厝裡 my wife, his wife, your wife; a husband also calls his wife "the mother" of their eldest child.

꜀*Siéng sek*꜆ 先室 my deceased wife.

꜀*Chong* ꜀*hu* ꜁*ing,* 尊夫人 or *leng*$^2$ *cheng*꜄ 令正 also ꜂*nü* ꜂*ló* ꜂*sieu,* 汝老小 or ꜂*nü* ꜀*i* ꜂*só,* 汝阿嫂 your wife.

꜁*I* ꜂*chiă,* 姨姐 or ꜁*i* ꜁*niong,* 姨娘 term for a father's concubine, as used by his children and other relatives.

꜀*Siéng ho*$^2$ 先父 my late father; ꜀*siéng* ꜂*mu,* 先母 my late mother.

*Sëü*$^2$ *ho*$^2$ 嗣父 and *sëü*$^2$ ꜂*mu,* 嗣母 adopted parents, as one (adopted as a son by relatives of the same surname) calls them.

### Among Acquaintances or Strangers.

꜀*I pah*꜆ 阿伯 or *pah*꜆ *pah*꜆ 伯伯 ꜀*I chëük*꜆ or 阿叔 or *chük*꜆ *chëük*꜆ 叔叔 uncle! a compellation of middle-aged men.

*Ek*꜆ *chëük*꜆ 一叔 first uncle! *Ne*$^2$ *chëük*꜆ 二叔 second uncle!—terms in addressing persons younger than one's father.

*Pah*꜆ ꜀*kung,* 伯公 and *chëük*꜆ ꜀*kung,* 叔公 great uncles—terms in addressing aged men.

꜀Chièng pwoi꜄ 前輩 senior! venerable sir!

Lau² ꜀nĕng, 佬仈 aged man or woman.

꜀Kó, 哥 elder brother—a term of respect, used as a suffix of the given name, as in Cheng꜄ ꜀ngwong ꜀kó, 正元哥 Brother Cheng Ngwong.

Twai² ꜀kó, 大哥 great brother! a respectful compellation of an elder acquaintance or stranger. Ne² ꜀kó, 二哥 second brother! a compellation for a younger acquaintance or stranger.

Sá꜄ ꜀kó, 細哥 little brother! a respectful compellation for another's sons up to 7 or 8 years of age.

꜀Tiė tiė² 俤俤 my boy! my lad!

꜀I ꜂mu, 阿姆 and ꜀I ꜂sing, 阿嬸 brother's wife! a compellation of middle-aged women.

꜂Mu ꜀pó, 姆婆 and ꜂Sing ꜀pó, 嬸婆 great aunts—terms in addressing aged women.

꜀I ꜀pó, 阿婆 or ꜀Pó ꜀pó, 婆婆 old lady! madam! dame!

꜀I ꜂só, 阿嫂 or ꜂Pieu ꜂só, 表嫂 sister-in-law—madam, Mrs., a compellation of young married women.

꜀Hiong a² ꜂só, 鄉下嫂 a country-woman, a field-woman; ꜀Hiong a² mwoi꜄ 鄉下妹 a country lass.

꜀Ku ꜀niong, 姑娘 or ꜂Sieu ꜂chiă, 小姐 daughters of the gentry, etc., young ladies, unmarried girls.

Mwoi꜄ ꜀kó, 妹哥 or Mwoi꜄ ꜀kwang, 妹官 his or your daughter, young miss.

꜀Mui mwoi꜄ 妹妹 a pet name for a little girl, sis!

꜀I ꜂ná, 阿奶 mother! nurse!

꜂Ná ꜀ma, 奶嫲 a nurse, a female servant, as in wealthy families.

Ch'io꜄ (house) 厝 a suffix in names of married women, as ꜀Ting ch'io꜄ 丁厝 a wife or widow of "the house" or surname of ꜀Ting—a compellation used in familiar address and in calling those of lower rank.

### Official Compellations, Etc.

Twai² ꜀nĕng, 大人 great man—compellation of high officers.

꜂Ló ꜀tiă, 老爹 an officer, His Honor, the Officer.

꜂Ló ꜀ié, 老爺 a compellation of subordinate civil officers;

*Twai*² *ʿló ˏié*, 大老爺 term for a district magistrate, marine inspector, etc.

*Twai*² *ʿló*, 大老 a compellation of military officers, as brigadiers, colonels.

*ʿChung ˏié*, 總爺 a compellation of lower officers, as majors, chiliarchs, centurions or captains.

*Tʻaiˀ ʿló*, 太老 and *ʿló tʻaiˀ ˏié*, 老太爺 compellations of an officer's father.

*Tʻaiˀ ʿná*, 太奶 *ʿló tʻaiˀ*, 老太 and *ʿló ˏtʻai tʻaiˀ* 老太太 compellations of an officer's mother.

*Lau*² *tʻaiˀ ʿló*, 佬太老 and *lau*² *tʻaiˀ ʿná*, 佬太奶 compellations for an officer's grandfather and grandmother.

*ˏTʻai tʻaiˀ* 太太 Her Ladyship, an officer's wife.

*ˏI tʻaiˀ* 姨太 term for an officer's concubine.

*Sieuˀ ˏié*, 少爺 young gentleman, an officer's son; *Sieuˀ ˏié ˏniong*, 少爺娘 or *sieuˀ ˏná ʿná*, 少奶奶 an officer's son's wife.

*Siongˀ ˏkëng*, 相公 Sir! Respected Sir! *Siongˀ ˏkëng ˏniong*, 相公娘 Madam! Mistress!

*Twai*² *siongˀ ˏkëng*, 大相公 and *Ne*² *siongˀ ˏkëng*, 二相公 compellations for first and second brothers.

*ˏSing ˏsang*, 先生 Teacher! *ˏSing ˏsang ʿmu*, 先生母 or *ˏsing ˏsang ˏniong*, 先生娘 Teacher's wife, Madam.

*ʿLó ˏsü*, 老師 venerable master, a compellation for an instructor, professor, superintendent of education, geomancer, etc.

*ˏSü ʿmu*, 師母 instructor's wife; *ˏSü ˏku*, 師姑 instructor's sister.

*ˏSa ho*² 師傅 skilled workman, one practiced in a trade, art, or profession; *ˏSa ho*² *ˏniong*, 師傅娘 workman's or master's wife.

*Twai*² *ˏié*, 大爺 and *Ne*² *ˏié*, 二爺 great sires and second sires, official attendants and managers.

*ˏSü ˏié*, 師爺 an officer's private secretary and adviser.

*ʿPó ʿtiong ˏkung*, 保長公 the common appellation for a constable.

*ʿLó chiongˀ* 老將 term for a soldier.

*ʿLó ʿpeng*, 老板 the master of a shop, boss!

## 14. SHOP CARDS.

復　利

凡遇關津自行納稅[12]

本行自運呢羽嗶吱[1]
洋廣各色什貨住福[2][3]
省南臺倉前橋頭觀
音井坐南朝北開張[4][5]
概憑大價發售無不[6][7]
小心揀選以圖永遠
馳名貨真價一童叟[8][9]
無欺凡士商賜顧者[10]
請認本行招牌爲記
庶不致悞[11]　○

剪斷摺皺概不退換[13]

HOK꜆ LE꜄ RENEW PROFIT.

1. ꜂*Pwong* ꜁*ong chëü*$^{2}$ *ong*$^{2}$ ꜁*ni* ꜂*ü p‘ek*꜆ ꜀*chié*, Our establishment itself imports woolens camlets serges, 2. ꜁*Yong* ꜂*Kwong kauk*꜆ *saik*꜆ *sik*꜆ *hwo*꜄, And all kinds of miscellaneous goods from foreign parts and Canton, 3. *Chëü*$^{2}$ *Hok*꜆ ꜂*seng* ꜁*Nang* ꜁*tai* ꜀*Ch‘ong* ꜁*chiéng* ꜁*kio* ꜁*t‘eu* ꜀*Kwang* ꜀*ing* ꜂*ching*, Located in Foochow Nantai at the head of Ch‘ong-seng bridge Kwang-ing-chang, 4. *Chó*$^{2}$ ꜁*nang* ꜁*tieu paëk*꜆ Situated with the back to the South and fronting the North, 5. ꜀*K‘ai* ꜀*Tiong*, (Here) we open (shop), 6. *K‘ai*꜄ ꜁*ping tai*$^{2}$ *ka*꜄ *hwak*꜆ ꜁*siu*, Wholly follow wholesale prices in offering for sale, 7. ꜁*U pok*꜆ ꜂*sieu* ꜀*sing* ꜂*keng* ꜂*song* ꜂*i* ꜁*tu* ꜂*ing* ꜂*wong* ꜁*ti* ꜁*ming*, Not without careful minds (i. e. very carefully) select (our goods) planning for a lasting and wide reputation, 8. *Hwo*꜄ ꜀*ching ka*꜄ *ek*꜆ Goods genuine price one, 9. ꜁*Tung* ꜂*seu* ꜁*u* ꜀*k‘i*, The young and the old we do not cheat, 10. ꜁*Hwang sëü*$^{2}$ ꜀*siong sëü*꜄ *ko*꜄ ꜂*chiă* ꜂*ch‘ing neng*$^{2}$ ꜂*pwong* ꜁*ong* ꜀*chieu* ꜁*pá* ꜁*ui ke*꜄, All gentlemen and merchants (i. e., all persons) who patronize us will please to recognize our establishment's sign as a mark or reminder, 11. *Sëü*꜄ *pok*꜆ *te*꜄ *ngwo*$^{2}$, Then probably (doubtless) they will not fall into mistakes.

12. ꜁*Hwang ngëü*$^{2}$ ꜀*kwang* ꜀*ching chëü*$^{2}$ ꜁*heng nak*꜆ *swoi*꜄, All falling in with excise stations (custom-houses) must themselves pay in the duties, 13. ꜂*Cheng twang*$^{2}$ *chiék*꜆ *chaiu*꜄ *k‘ai*꜄ *pok*꜆ *t‘ói*꜄ *wang*$^{2}$, After cutting off folding rumpling (purchasers) cannot at all bring back and exchange (the goods).

信來號布庄

本[1]號創立有年開[2]在
閩省南臺中亭半街
坐[3]東向西採[4]辦蘇松
梭布自[5]設染坊精染
大紅眞青各色布疋
無[6]不小心揀選貨[7]眞
價實[8]四方共信遠邇
馳名近[9]因無恥之徒
專備低貨假冒本庄
同音字號混[10]人耳目
以期圖利特[11]此佈知
凡[12]客商 賜顧者請
認本庄招牌爲記庶[13]
不致悞 ○

*SENGʾ ꜁LAI HÓ$^2$ PWOʾ ꜀CHONG.*

1. *ʿPwong hó$^2$ chʿaungʾ lik꜃ ʿiu ꜁niĕng*, 2. *꜀Kʿai chai$^2$ ꜁Ming ʿSeng ꜁Nang ꜁tai ꜀Tüng ꜁ting pwangʾ ꜀ká*, 3. *Chó$^2$ ꜀tu̇ng hiongʾ ꜀sá*, 4. *ʿÇhʿai paing$^2$ ꜁Su ꜁Süng ꜀só pwoʾ*, 5. *Chëü$^2$ siék꜂ ʿniéng ꜀hwong ꜀ching ʿniéng tai$^2$ ꜁hung ꜀ching ꜀chʿing kauk꜂ saik꜂ pwoʾ pʿek꜂*, 6. *꜁Upok꜂ ʿsieu ꜀sing ʿkeng ʿsong*, 7. *Hwoʾ ꜀ching kaʾ sik꜃* 8. *Sëüʾ ꜀hwong këüng$^2$ sengʾ ʿwong ʿi ꜁ti ꜁ming*, 9. *Këüng$^2$ ꜀ing ꜁u ʿtʿi ꜀chi ꜁tu ꜀chiong pe$^2$ ꜀tá hwoʾ ʿka mó$^2$ ʿpwong ꜀chong ꜁tung ꜀ing che$^2$ hó$^2$*, 10. *Hong$^2$ ꜁ing ʿngi muk꜃ ʿi ꜀ki ꜁tu le$^2$*, 11. *Tek꜃ ʿchʿü pwoʾ ꜀ti*, 12. *꜁Hwang kʿaik꜂ ꜀siong sëüʾ koʾ ʿchiă ʿchʿing neng$^2$ ʿpwong ꜀chong ꜀chieu ꜁pá ꜁ui keʾ*, 13. *Sëüʾ pok꜂ teʾ ngwo$^2$.*

**Believe-come Sign Cotton-cloth Shop.**

**1. Our style established for years, 2. Opened in Min provincial city Nantai midway of Tongting street, 3. Seated to the East fronting the West, 4. Select and prepare Su (chow) and Süng (konghu) woven cotton cloth, 5. Self establish a dye-shop finely dye deep red genuine black all colors cotton-piece-goods, 6. Not without careful mind select, 7. Goods genuine price true, 8. Four quarters all trust far near wide reputation, 9. Just now because shameless fellows are wholly bent prepare inferior goods counterfeit our shop same sound style, 10. Confuse men's ears eyes to plan for gain, 11. We specially publish this to inform, 12. All customers traders bestowing patronage please recognize our shop's sign as mark or reminder, 13. Probably (doubtless) not fall into mistakes.**

## 15. WEDDING CARDS.

**Invitations to a feast at the bride's house on the day preceding marriage.**

### To a gentleman.

1. *꜀Ch'u ch'ek꜆ nik꜇ oi꜅ ꜁pau tik꜇ ꜂tiong ꜂nü Paik꜆ Hok꜆ ꜀ü ꜀kwi*, 2. *꜀Ch'u lĕk꜇ nik꜇ kiék꜆ ꜀siong ꜀p'ang ka꜄ ꜀kwang ꜁ü*, 3. *Sĕü꜄ sok꜆*

4. *꜁Ling ꜂Iu ꜁Ing ꜂ling tik꜇ ꜀Sing ꜀Hiong chai꜄ pai꜄*.

1. I have selected the 7th day for my nephew's eldest daughter, Paik Hok, to be married. 2. On the 6th day, the wine cups having been cleansed, may we drag you here, Sir, to view the chariot. 3. Excuse me from sending again to hasten you.

4. Ling Iu Ing and his nephew, Sing Hiong, repeatedly pay their respects.

[1] 初七日爲胞侄長女百福于歸[2]初六日

潔觴攀

駕觀輿

[3] 恕速

[4] 林友仁領姪心香再拜

### To a lady.

1. *꜀Ch'u lĕk꜇ nik꜇ oi꜅ ꜀hu tik꜇ ꜂tiong ꜂nü Paik꜆ Hok꜆ pai꜄ keng꜄*, 2. *Kiék꜆ ꜀siong keng꜄ nga꜅ ꜁ngü ꜀hiong ꜂lá hwoí꜄* 3. *Se꜅ haiu꜅ ꜂chó ꜀chié*.

4. *꜁Ling ꜁mwong ꜁Ting se꜅ ꜂ling ꜀hu tik꜇ ho꜅ ꜂Hü se꜅ cheng꜄ ꜁üng pai꜄*.

1. I have selected the 6th day for my husband's nephew's eldest daughter, Paik Hok, to make the trial toilet. 2. Have cleansed the wine cups and will respectfully welcome you in the fish (ornamented) chariot to teach us the ceremonies. 3. I await the early oiling (of your chariot wheels), i. e., your early arrival.

4. Mrs. Ling, formerly Miss Ting, with the wife of her husband's nephew, formerly Miss Hü, properly attired will pay their respects to you.

[1] 初六日爲夫侄長女百福拜鏡潔[2]觴

敬迓

魚軒禮誨

[3] 氏候

早脂

[4] 林門陳氏領夫姪婦

許氏正容拜

| INVITATIONS to the marriage feast at the bridegroom's house. | |
|---|---|
| To a gentleman. | |
| 1. *꜀Cheu ꜀ch'u ch'ek꜇ nik꜉ oi$^2$ ch'ëü꜊ ꜂nang Kwok꜇ ꜂Ing seu$^2$ sek꜇ ꜁hi ꜂yong*, 2. *꜀P'ang ka꜊ sëü꜊ ꜀kwong*, 3. *Sëü꜊ ꜀p'eng*.<br>4. *꜂Lau ꜂Tieu ꜂Sing chai꜊ pai꜊*.<br>5. *Chëü$^2$ ꜂Yong ꜀tong ꜂ting*.<br><br>1. I have selected the 7th day for our second son Kwong Ing's marriage-feast. (May I) drag you, Sir, to bestow light. 3. Excuse me from sending again to hasten you.<br>4. Lau Tieu Sing repeatedly pays his respects.<br>5. We reside at Yong Tong Ting. | 諏[1]初七日爲次男國英受室喜筵攀[2]<br>駕賜光<br>恕[3]伻<br>劉[4]朝成再拜<br>住[5]洋墩亭 |
| To a lady. | |
| 1. *꜀Chiéng ꜀ch'u ch'ek꜇ nik꜉ ꜁ing ch'ëü꜊ ꜂nang ho$^2$ ꜂Ling se$^2$ mieu$^2$ hiéng$^2$*, 2. *꜁Hi ꜂yong keng꜊ nga$^2$ ꜀hiong ꜀kü ꜁ld hwoi꜊*, 3. *Se$^2$ haiu$^2$ ꜁chó ꜀chié*.<br>4. *꜂Lau ꜂mwong ꜂Ting se$^2$ cheng꜊ sëük꜇ pai꜊*.<br><br>1. I have selected the 7th day to lead forth (or introduce) my second son's bride, Miss Ling, to pay respects to the ancestors. 2. Have prepared a joyous feast and will respectfully welcome you in your fragrant chariot to teach us the ceremonies. 3. I await the early oiling.<br>4. Mrs. Lau, formerly Miss Ting, correctly and respectfully presents compliments. | 詹[1]初七日引次男婦林氏廟見喜[2]筵<br>敬迓<br>香車禮誨<br>[3]氏候早脂<br>劉[4]門陳氏正肅拜 |

## 16. FUNERAL CARD.

訃[1]

不孝[2]朝瑞侍奉無狀禍[3]延

顯妣

皇[4]清例授孺人晉贈安人陳[5]太安人前月得病痛[6]此

本月初四日丑時終於內寢距[7]生於乾隆庚戌

年十月三十日戌時享[8]壽七十有九哀[9]此訃

聞

謹[10]以初十日凶服告成

十[11]一、十二日領帖

孤[12]哀子林朝瑞泣血

出[13]繼男朝安泣稽顙

期[14]服孫邦元稽顙

降[15]服孫邦大力昌拭淚

功[16]服曾孫成平喜稽首

住[17]銀湘浦

1. Card announcing decease. 2. The unfilial *Tieu Soi* in serving has been destitute of good conduct (i. e. very worthless). 3. And caused (this) calamity to befall his illustrious mother. 4. Who by the Imperial Pure (dynasty's) customary bestowal (of honorary degree) is *U Ing*, with the additional conferment of *Ang Ing*. 5. Mrs. Ting T'ai Ang Ing was taken ill the previous month. 6. And, alas! in the present month, the 4th day, at the *T'iu* hour, expired in the inner chamber. 7. Born in the *Keng sok* year of *Kieng Lung*, the 10th month, 30th day, *Sok* hour. 8. And was 79 years of age. 9. We mournfully communicate the information of this (sad event). 10. We have carefully selected the 10th day when the mourning apparel will be announced complete (i. e., when we will begin to wear mourning). 11. On the 11th and 12th days we will receive (your) cards (i. e. visits of condolence).

12. The orphan *Ling Tieu Soi* weeps tears of blood. 13. The given-away-son, *Tieu Ang*, weeps and performs the *kotau*. 14. The one-year-mourning grandson, (son of *Tieu soi*) *Pang Ngwong*, performs the *kotau*. 15. The nine-months'-mourning grandsons (sons of *Tieu Ang*) *Pang Lik*, *Pang Tai*, and *Pang Ch'iong*, wipe their tears. 16. The five-months'-mourning great-grandsons (sons of *Pang Ngwong*) *Sing Ping* and *Sing Hi* perform the *kotau*. 17. We reside at Ngung Siong P'wo.

## 17. EXERCISES ON COMBINATION OF TONES.

( See Explanations on pages 8 & 9. )

| | | |
|---|---|---|
| **1st & 1st.** | **1st & 5th.** | **2d & 2d.** |
| 東家 ꜀*Tung* ꜀*ka* | 功勞 ꜀*Kung* ꜁*ló* | 攏總 ꜂*Lung* ꜂*chung* |
| 花香 ꜀*Hwa* ꜀*hiong* | 聰明 ꜀*Ch'ung* ꜁*ming* | 孔子 ꜂*K'ung* ꜂*chü* |
| 挑唆 ꜀*T'ieu* ꜀*só* | 風寒 ꜀*Hung* ꜁*hang* | 米粉 ꜂*Mi* ꜂*hung* |
| 陰間 ꜀*Ing* ꜀*kang* | 温和 ꜀*Ung* ꜁*hwo* | 長子 ꜂*Tiong* ꜂*chü* |
| 中秋 ꜀*Tüng* ꜀*ch'iu* | 花盆 ꜀*Hwa* ꜁*pwong* | 保守 ꜂*Pó* ꜂*siu* |
| 先生 ꜀*Sing* ꜀*sang* | 相量 ꜀*Song* ꜁*liong* | 手指 ꜂*Ch'iu* ꜂*chai* |
| 高陞 ꜀*Kó* ꜀*sing* | 珊瑚 ꜀*Tang* ꜁*hu* | 豈敢 ꜂*K'i* ꜂*kang* |
| **1st & 2d.** | **1st & 7th.** | **2d & 3d.** |
| 君子 ꜀*Kung* ꜂*chü* | 憂悶 ꜀*Iu mong*꜅ | 穩當 ꜂*Ung taung*꜄ |
| 瘋軟 ꜀*Hung* ꜂*niong* | 相讓 ꜀*Song niong*꜅ | 轉唇 ꜂*Tiong ch'io*꜄ |
| 誇口 ꜀*K'wa* ꜂*k'eu* | 災難 ꜀*Chai nang*꜅ | 賞賜 ꜂*Siong sëü*꜄ |
| 穿手 ꜀*Ch'iong* ꜂*ch'iu* | 安靜 ꜀*Ang cheng*꜅ | 手臂 ꜂*Ch'iu pié*꜄ |
| 空想 ꜀*K'ëng* ꜂*siong* | 公道 ꜀*Kung tó*꜅ | 顯應 ꜂*Hiëng eng*꜄ |
| 山頂 ꜀*Sang* ꜂*ting* | 高傲 ꜀*Kó ngó*꜅ | 倚靠 ꜂*Ai k'ó*꜄ |
| 雞母 ꜀*Kié* ꜂*mó* | 加倍 ꜀*Ka pwoi*꜅ | 改變 ꜂*Kai piéng*꜄ |
| **1st & 3d.** | **1st & 8th.** | **2d & 4th.** |
| 春菜 ꜀*Ch'ung ch'ai*꜄ | 孤獨 ꜀*Ku tuk*꜇ | 總督 ꜂*Chung tok*꜆ |
| 張罩 ꜀*Tiong tau*꜄ | 煙盒 ꜀*Hong ak*꜇ | 軟法 ꜂*Niong hwak*꜆ |
| 乾燥 ꜀*Kang só*꜄ | 葱白 ꜀*Ch'ëng pah*꜇ | 享福 ꜂*Hiong hok*꜆ |
| 今旦 ꜀*King tang*꜄ | 翻譯 ꜀*Hwang ik*꜇ | 感激 ꜂*Kang kek*꜆ |
| 擔担 ꜀*Tang tang*꜄ | 生活 ꜀*Seng wak*꜇ | 猛答 ꜂*Mang tak*꜆ |
| 安慰 ꜀*Ang oi*꜄ | 金箔 ꜀*King póh*꜇ | 彩色 ꜂*Ch'ai saik*꜆ |
| 開印 ꜀*K'wi eng*꜄ | 風俗 ꜀*Hung sük*꜇ | 緊急 ꜂*King kek*꜆ |
| **1st & 4th.** | **2nd & 1st.** | **2d & 5th.** |
| 兵卒 ꜀*Ping chok*꜆ | 滾湯 ꜂*Kung* ꜀*t'ong* | 總裁 ꜂*Chung* ꜁*choi* |
| 公爵 ꜀*Kung chiok*꜆ | 寡居 ꜂*Kwa* ꜀*kü* | 有時 ꜂*Iu* ꜁*si* |
| 三百 ꜀*Sang pah*꜆ | 酒盃 ꜂*Chiu* ꜀*pwi* | 採蓮 ꜂*Ch'ai* ꜁*leng* |
| 加一 ꜀*Ka ek*꜆ | 小心 ꜂*Sieu* ꜀*sing* | 早年 ꜂*Cha* ꜁*niéng* |
| 家法 ꜀*Ka hwak*꜆ | 點心 ꜂*Tiéng* ꜀*sing* | 左營 ꜂*Chó* ꜁*yăng* |
| 棕索 ꜀*Chëng sóh*꜆ | 海參 ꜂*Hai* ꜀*seng* | 鎖匙 ꜂*Só* ꜁*sié* |
| 中國 ꜀*Tüng kwok*꜆ | 管家 ꜂*Kwang* ꜀*ka* | 舉人 ꜂*Kü* ꜁*ing* |

| 2d & 7th. | |
|---|---|
| 仰望 | ‘Ngiong wong$^2$ |
| 手段 | ‘Ch‘iu taung$^2$ |
| 懶惰 | ‘Lang tó$^2$ |
| 改換 | ‘Kai wang$^2$ |
| 吵鬧 | ‘Ch‘au nau$^2$ |
| 品貌 | ‘P‘ing mau$^2$ |
| 引導 | ‘Ing tó$^2$ |
| 五臟 | ‘Ngu chaung$^2$ |

| 2d & 8th. | |
|---|---|
| 手鐲 | ‘Ch‘iu sóh$_2$ |
| 搶奪 | ‘Ch‘iong tok$_2$ |
| 打獵 | ‘Ta lak$_2$ |
| 扁盒 | ‘Piéng ak$_2$ |
| 手脈 | ‘Ch‘iu mah$_2$ |
| 小麥 | ‘Sieu mah$_2$ |
| 抵敵 | ‘Tá tik$_2$ |
| 本日 | ‘Pwong nik$_2$ |

| 3d & 1st. | |
|---|---|
| 送親 | Saëng’ ˏch‘ing |
| 唱歌 | Ch‘iong’ ˏkó |
| 相公 | Siong’ ˏkëng |
| 救兵 | Keu’ ˏping |
| 繡花 | Seu’ ˏhwa |
| 楱根 | Ch‘eu’ ˏküng |
| 散班 | Sang’ ˏpwang |
| 按司 | Ang’ ˏsi |

| 3d & 2d. | |
|---|---|
| 貢棗 | Kong’ ‘chó |
| 救火 | Keu’ ‘hwí |
| 繡補 | Seu’ ‘pwo |
| 送禮 | Saëng’ ‘lá |
| 讚美 | Chang’ ‘mi |
| 太子 | T‘ai’ ‘chü |
| 禁止 | Keng’ ‘chi |
| 面桶 | Meng’ ‘t‘ëng |

| 3d & 3d. | |
|---|---|
| 進貢 | Cheng’ kong’ |
| 糞倒 | Pong’ tó’ |
| 貴恙 | Koi’ yong’ |
| 獻祭 | Hiong’ chié’ |
| 報稅 | Pó’ swoi’ |
| 看戲 | K‘ang’ hié’ |
| 嘆氣 | T‘ang’ k‘e’ |
| 告假 | Kó’ ka’ |

| 3d & 4th. | |
|---|---|
| 唱曲 | Ch‘iong’ k‘woh, |
| 四隻 | Se’ chiăh, |
| 面色 | Meng’ saik, |
| 報答 | Pó’ tak, |
| 刺客 | Ch‘ëü’ k‘aik, |
| 鑄鐵 | Chio’ t‘iék, |
| 降級 | Kaung’ ngek, |
| 利息 | Le’ sek, |

| 3d & 5th. | |
|---|---|
| 秀才 | Seu’ ςchoi |
| 幼童 | Eu’ ςtung |
| 向來 | Hiong’ ςlai |
| 素常 | So’ ςsiong |
| 楱排 | Ch‘eu’ ςpá |
| 太平 | T‘ai’ ςping |
| 價錢 | Ka’ ςchiéng |
| 應承 | Eng’ ςsing |

| 3d & 7th. | |
|---|---|
| 相貌 | Siong’ mau$^2$ |
| 秀茂 | Seu’ maiu$^2$ |
| 燦爛 | Ch‘ang’ lang$^2$ |
| 告狀 | Kó’ chaung$^2$ |
| 聽候 | T‘eng’ haiu$^2$ |
| 面上 | Meng’ siong$^2$ |
| 篡位 | Ch‘wa’ oi$^2$ |
| 妒忌 | To’ ke$^2$ |

| 3d & 8th. | |
|---|---|
| 楱木 | Ch‘eu’ muk$_2$ |
| 數目 | So’ mĕk$_2$ |
| 穢濁 | Woi’ chok$_2$ |
| 布帛 | Pwo’ pek$_2$ |
| 半截 | Pwang’ chek$_2$ |
| 看脈 | K‘ang’ mah$_2$ |
| 漂白 | P‘ieu’ pah$_2$ |
| 四十 | Se’ sek$_2$ |

| 4th & 1st. | |
|---|---|
| 伯公 | Pah, ˏkung |
| 客廳 | K‘ah, ˏt‘iăng |
| 壁邊 | Piăh, ˏpiéng |
| 摘花 | Tiăh, ˏhwa |
| 束修 | Sok, ˏsiu |
| 歇工 | Hiok, ˏkëng |
| 喫虧 | K‘ek, ˏk‘wi |
| 敕封 | T‘ek, ˏhung |

| 4th & 2d. | |
|---|---|
| 百九 | Pah, ‘kau |
| 拍打 | P‘ah, ‘ta |
| 桌頂 | Tóh, ‘ting |
| 燭斗 | Chioh, ‘tau |
| 不止 | Pok, ‘chi |
| 熨斗 | Ok, ‘tau |
| 出疹 | Ch‘ok, ‘mëng |
| 闥板 | T‘ak, ‘peng |

| 4th & 3d. | |
|---|---|
| 拍破 | P‘ah, p‘wai’ |
| 桌罩 | Tóh, tau’ |
| 剝去 | Pwoh, k‘ó’ |
| 借問 | Chioh, mwong’ |
| 不孝 | Pok, hau’ |
| 決斷 | Kiok, twang’ |
| 答應 | Tak, eng’ |
| 急性 | Kek, sang’ |

**4th & 4th.**

曲尺 Kʻwoh꜇ chʻioh꜇
尺七 Chʻioh꜇ chʻek꜇
脚色 Kioh꜇ saik꜇
乜毛 Miéh꜇ nóh꜇
歇息 Hiok꜇ sek꜇
插燭 Chʻak꜇ chioh꜇
蟋蟀 Sek꜇ sauk꜇
一叔 Ek꜇ chëük꜇

**4th & 5th.**

隔暝 Kah꜇ ꜁mang
客房 Kʻah꜇ ꜁pung
拍呆 Pʻah꜇ ꜁ngai
借錢 Chioh꜇ ꜁chiéng
出門 Chʻok꜇ ꜁mwong
設辭 Siék꜇ ꜁sü
搭船 Tak꜇ ꜁sung
橘皮 Kek꜇ ꜁pʻuí

**4th & 7th.**

百二 Pah꜇ ne$^2$
借貸 Chioh꜇ tai$^2$
尺五 Chʻioh꜇ ngo$^2$
僻靜 Pʻiăh꜇ cheng$^2$
出痘 Chʻok꜇ tau$^2$
雪洞 Siok꜇ taëng$^2$
鴨蛋 Ak꜇ laung$^2$
執事 Chek꜇ sëü$^2$

**4th & 8th.**

拍折 Pʻah꜇ siék$_2$
益目 Yăh꜇ mëk$_2$
剝値 Pwoh꜇ tih$_2$
百六 Pah꜇ lëk$_2$
約畧 Yok꜇ liok$_2$
夾合 Kak꜇ hak$_2$
瞎目 Hak꜇ mëk$_2$
急舌 Kek꜇ siék$_2$

**5th & 1st.**

崇安 ꜁Chung ꜀ang
同鄉 ꜁Tĕng ꜀hiong
逢三 ꜁Hung ꜀sang
文章 ꜁Ung ꜀chiong
紅花 ꜁Ĕng ꜀hwa
全家 ꜁Chiong ꜀ka
緣因 ꜁Yong ꜀ing
琉光 ꜁Liu ꜀kwong

**5th & 2d.**

房裡 ꜁Pung ʿtié
船主 ꜁Sung ʿchio
紅紙 ꜁Ĕng ʿchai
華表 ꜁Hwa ʿpieu
糧草 ꜁Liong ʿchʻó
娘奶 ꜁Nong ʿná
言語 ꜁Ngiong ʿngü
求懇 ꜁Kiu ʿkʻong

**5th & 3d.**

裙鏡 ꜁Kung kiăngʾ
蒙蔽 ꜁Mung peʾ
全副 ꜁Chiong hoʾ
詳細 ꜁Siong sáʾ
年半 ꜁Niéng pwangʾ
平秤 ꜁Pang chʻengʾ
埋葬 ꜁Mai chaungʾ
蠻笑 ꜁Mang chʻieuʾ

**5th & 4th.**

魂魄 ꜁Hung pʻaĕk꜇
强惡 ꜁Kiong auk꜇
油漆 ꜁Iu chʻek꜇
顔色 ꜁Ngang saik꜇
臺閣 ꜁Tai kóh꜇
迎接 ꜁Nging chiék꜇
提督 ꜁Tʻi tok꜇
挪毛 ꜁Nó nóh꜇

**5th & 5th.**

裁縫 ꜁Choi ꜁pʻung
拳頭 ꜁Kung ꜁tʻau
榮華 ꜁Ing ꜁hwa
龍船 ꜁Liong ꜁sung
時常 ꜁Si ꜁siong
題緣 ꜁Tá ꜁yong

**5th & 7th.**

華麗 ꜁Hwa lá$^2$
傳道 ꜁Tiong tó$^2$
郎罷 ꜁Nong ma$^2$
償命 ꜁Siong miăng$^2$
酬謝 ꜁Siu siă$^2$
綢緞 ꜁Tiu taung$^2$

**5th & 8th.**

羊肉 ꜁Yong nük$_2$
來歷 ꜁Lai lik$_2$
茶葉 ꜁Ta nioh$_2$
凌辱 ꜁Ling ük$_2$
刑罰 ꜁Hing hwak$_2$
長樂 ꜁Tiong lóh$_2$

**7th & 1st.**

順風 Song$^2$ ꜀hung
柱珠 Tʻeu$^2$ ꜀chio
岸邊 Ngiăng$^2$ ꜀piéng
大家 Tai$^2$ ꜀ka
令尊 Leng$^2$ ꜀chong
念經 Naing$^2$ ꜀king

**7th & 2d.**

順理 Song$^2$ ʿli
話語 Wa$^2$ ʿngü
瓦頂 Ngwa$^2$ ʿting
上好 Siong$^2$ ʿhó
妗媽 Keng$^2$ ʿma
賀喜 Hó$^2$ ʿhi
濾水 Lëü$^2$ ʿchwi

7th & 3d.

奉教 Hong$^2$ kau꜄
壽數 Seu$^2$ so꜄
病痛 Pang$^2$ t'iăng꜄
怒氣 No$^2$ k'e꜄
令箭 Leng$^2$ chiéng꜄
斷契 Twang$^2$ k'ié꜄
餓頓 Ngó$^2$ taung꜄
被面 P'woi$^2$ meng꜄

7th & 4th.

樣式 Yong$^2$ sek꜆
五隻 Ngo$^2$ chiăh꜆
第一 Tá$^2$ ek꜆
會伯 Hwoi$^2$ pah꜆
蛋殼 Laung$^2$ k'aĕk꜆
治國 Te$^2$ kwok꜆
硬法 Ngaing$^2$ hwak꜆
辨別 Piéng$^2$ piék꜆

7th & 5th.

諒來 Liong$^2$ ꜁lai
暫時 Chang$^2$ ꜁si
大伙 Twai$^2$ ꜁nĕng
下南 A$^2$ ꜁nang
令堂 Leng$^2$ ꜁tong
道人 Tó$^2$ ꜁ing
舊年 Keu$^2$ ꜁niéng
就來 Cheu$^2$ ꜁li

7th & 7th.

定動 Teng$^2$ taĕng$^2$
順便 Song$^2$ piéng$^2$
奉命 Hong$^2$ meng$^2$
玳瑁 Tai$^2$ ngwoi$^2$
另外 Leng$^2$ ngwoi$^2$
命令 Meng$^2$ leng$^2$
犯病 Hwang$^2$ pang$^2$
皂隸 Chó$^2$ lá$^2$

7th & 8th.

閏月 Nong$^2$ ngwok$_2$
上截 Siong$^2$ chek$_2$
受納 Seu$^2$ nak$_2$
定着 Tiăng$^2$ tioh$_2$
五十 Ngo$^2$ sek$_2$
二十 Ne$^2$ sek$_2$
鬧熱 Nau$^2$ yék$_2$
後日 Au$^2$ nik$^2$

8th & 1st.

白丁 Pah$_2$ ꜀ting
落霜 Lóh$_2$ ꜀song
學官 Óh$_2$ ꜀kwang
綠丹 Lioh$_2$ ꜀tang
目睭 Mek$_2$ ꜀chiu
佛龕 Huk$_2$ ꜀k'ang
學生 Hok$_2$ ꜀seng
牧師 Muk$_2$ ꜀sü

8th & 2d.

白棗 Pah$_2$ ꜂chó
鐲仔 Sóh$_2$ ꜂kiăng
藥粉 Yoh$_2$ ꜂hung
食酒 Siăh$_2$ ꜂chiu
踏斗 Tak$_2$ ꜂tau
族譜 Chuk$_2$ ꜂p'wo
秫米 Suk$_2$ ꜂mi
若使 Yok$_2$ ꜂sü

8th & 3d.

白菜 Pah$_2$ ch'ai꜄
莫笑 Móh$_2$ ch'ieu꜄
局騙 Kwoh$_2$ p'iéng꜄
射箭 Sioh$_2$ chiéng꜄
禿蒂 T'uk$_2$ te꜄
雜貨 Chak$_2$ hwo꜄
納稅 Nak$_2$ swoi꜄
力氣 Lik$_2$ k'e꜄

8th & 4th.

縛束 Pwoh$_2$ sok꜆
一貼 Sioh$_2$ t'aik꜆
石塔 Sioh$_2$ t'ak꜆
糶粟 Tiăh$_2$ ch'ioh꜆
律法 Luk$_2$ hwak꜆
獨一 Tuk$_2$ ek꜆
蠟燭 Lak$_2$ chioh꜆
勒迫 Lek$_2$ p'aik꜆

8th & 5th.

白糖 Pah$_2$ ꜁t'ong
麥芽 Mah$_2$ ꜁nga
石頭 Sioh$_2$ ꜁t'au
玉牌 Ngwoh$_2$ ꜁pá
掘土 Kuk$_2$ ꜁t'u
茯苓 Huk$_2$ ꜁ling
合床 Hak$_2$ ꜁ch'ong
日頭 Nik$_2$ ꜁t'au

8th & 7th.

綠豆 Lioh$_2$ tau$^2$
箬[illegible] Nioh$_2$ sá$^2$
石臼 Sioh$_2$ k'o$^2$
食飯 Siăh$_2$ pwong$^2$
律例 Luk$_2$ lié$^2$
絶嗣 Chiok$_2$ sëü$^2$
合倍 Hak$_2$ pwoi$^2$
極妙 Kik$_2$ mieu$^2$

8th & 8th.

擇日 Tah$_2$ nik$_2$
白食 Pah$_2$ siăh$_2$
玉鐲 Ngwoh$_2$ sóh$_2$
拿賊 Niăh$_2$ ch'ek$_2$
毒藥 Tuk$_2$ yoh$_2$
韎額 Mwak$_2$ ngiăh$_2$
直截 Tik$_2$ chek$_2$
寂寞 Chik$_2$ mok$_2$

# PART VI.

## VOCABULARY OF WORDS AND TERMS IN PART SECOND.

This Vocabulary is prepared with special reference to the study of Part II, and the words are generally defined only in the senses there employed. Compound terms are often treated as single words, no definitions being given of their component parts. Such terms may usually be found under the first word, but sometimes under a following word as being more important in idea.

——:o:——

꜀*A*, 鴉 as in ꜀*a p'iêng'* 鴉片 opium.

ʿ*A*, 吓 The disjunctive *or;* a classifier; a connective or euphonic particle.

ʿ*A*, 啞 Mute, dumb, silent.

꜁*A*, 吓 An interjectional, emphatic, and euphonic particle.

*A²* 下 Below, down; next, future; a time, a while; a portion.

*A²* 厦 as in *A²* ꜁*Mwong*, 厦門 Amoy.

ʿ*Á*, 矮 Short, low in stature.

*Á²* 艓 Can, will; do, does; is; probably.

*Aëng'* 甕 A jar, vase, pitcher, etc.

꜀*Ang*, 安 Still, settled, safe, calm, peaceful; rest.

ʿ*Ang*, 闇 To shut the door.

*Ang'* 暗 Dark, as night.

*Ang²* 旱 Drought.

*Au²* 後 After in time or place, behind: *au²* ʿ*ch'iu*, 後手 the left hand; *au² nik*꜆ 後日 day after to-morrow; *au²* ꜁*niêng*, 後年 year after next.

*Auk*꜆ 惡 Wicked.

꜀*Cha*, 查 To examine.

ʿ*Cha*, 早 Early, soon; formerly; breakfast: ʿ*cha* ꜀*seng*, 早先 just now, a short time since; ʿ*cha* ʿ*k'i*, 早起 morning.

꜁*Chá*, 齊 Together; at the same time.

*Chá²* 劑 Dough.

*Chaë²* 助 To assist.

*Chah*꜆ 窄 Narrow.

꜀*Chai*, 災 Natural calamities; divine judgments, misfortunes.

ʿ*Chai*, 載 A year.

*Chai'* 再 Again; then, further, continued.

*Chai'* 債 A debt.

꜁*Chai*, 才 Ability, talents.

꜁*Chai*, 財 Wealth, goods.

*Chai²* 在 To be in; as, according to.

*Chaik͵* 汁 Gravy.

*Chak₂* 雜 Various, mixed.

꜀*Chang*, 讒 as in ꜀*chang chaing*꜄ 讒譖 to slander.

꜂*Chau*, 走 To escape; to vary from.

*Chauk͵* 作 as in *chauk͵* ꜀*ka*, 作佳 handsome, beautiful.

*Che*꜄ 至 To arrive at, to come; the summit, the end; very, most.

*Che*² 字 A character, a letter; an epistle, a chit: *che*² ꜀*t'au*, 字頭 initials; *che*² ꜂*mó*, 字母 finals.

*Che*² 自 or *che*² ꜀*ka*, 自家 Self, one's self.

꜀*Cheng*, 針 A needle, a pin; a stitch: ꜀*cheng* ꜀*k'a*, 針胶 a stitch.

꜀*Cheng*, 曾 One of the 15 initials.

꜂*Cheng*, 剪 To cut with scissors, to clip even.

*Cheng*꜄ 浸 To soak.

꜀*Cheng*, 層 A story of a building; a shelf, a layer; a degree above.

*Cheng*² 盡 To exhaust; exhausted, finished; very, extremely, to the utmost degree.

*Cheu*² 就 Then, immediately, soon; that is, just so: *cheu*² *se*² 就是 that is, to wit, viz.

*Chëü*² 自 Self: *chëü*² ꜀*yong*, 自然 self-existent, of course; *chëü*² ꜀*ming* ꜀*chüng*, 自鳴鐘 a clock.

*Chëük͵* 祝 as in *chëük͵* *hok͵* 祝福 to bless, to bestow favors.

*Chëük͵* 粥 Congee.

*Chëüng*꜄ 衆 A multitude, a concourse of at least three persons.

꜂*Chi*, 只 Only, merely; so much, thus much; here; this, this one: ꜂*chi* ꜀*tong*, 只長 just now, a moment ago.

꜂*Chi*, 旨 Intention; will, purpose.

꜂*Chi*, 止 To stop, to rest.

꜂*Chiă*, 姐 An older sister.

꜂*Chiă*, 啫 This, that, these, those.

꜀*Chiă*, 啫 A euphonic and emphatic particle.

*Chiă*² 藉 To trust in, to rely or depend on.

*Chiăh͵* 僅 One, single; just, just now, then, just then.

*Chiăk͵* 泎 To spill.

꜀*Chiăng*, 正 as in ꜀*chiăng* *ngwok₂* 正月 the first month of the year.

꜂*Chiăng*, 䱹 Fresh, not salt; insipid.

*Chiăng*꜄ 正 Correct, straight, not awry; exactly; in the center; right.

꜀*Chié*, 支 To draw, as wages.

*Chié*꜄ 際 as in *ng*² *chié*꜄ *sëü*² 伓際事 a trifling amount.

*Chié*꜄ 制 To control, to endure, to bear up under.

*Chiék͵* 接 To receive, to go to

bring back, as a sedan.

*Chiék*͵ 節 A verse.

͵*Chiéng*, 煎 To fry, as pork.

͵*Chiéng*, 沾 To wash out, as a spot.

͵*Chiéng*, 前 Before in time or place.

͵*Chiéng*, 錢 Cash, money.

*Chiéng*² 賤 Base, vile, low; mischievous, restless, as children.

͵*Chieu*, 焦 Burnt, scorched.

͵*Chieu*, 椒 as in ͵*chieu laiu*² 椒料 spices.

ʿ*Chieu*, 少 Little, few, less; seldom.

*Chieu*ʾ 照 To shine on; to care for: *chieu*ʾ *ko*ʾ 照顧 to take care of.

͵*Ching*, 眞 True, sincere.

͵*Ching*, 精 The white of an egg.

ʿ*Chio*, 主 Lord; the chief, the head: ʿ*chio* ʿ*chai*, 主宰 a ruler; ʿ*chio e*ʾ 主意 to control, to decide.

*Chioh*͵ 借 To borrow; to lend; to beg of.

͵*Chiong*, 章 A chapter, a section.

͵*Chiong*, 將 How, in what way? ͵*chiong wang*² 將換 so, thus; ͵*chiong* ͵*ki*, 將其 why?

͵*Chiong*, 漿 Starch; to starch.

͵*Chiong*, 全 All, complete, the whole.

͵*Chiu*, 州 A department less than a prefecture.

͵*Chiu*, 睭 as in *mek*͵ ͵*chiu*, 目睭 the eye.

ʿ*Chiu*, 酒 Wine.

*Chó*ʾ 做 To do, to act; to make; to build; to be: *chó*ʾ *hwa*ʾ 做化 fortunately.

*Chó*² 造 as in *chó*² *hwa*ʾ 造化 to create.

*Chó*² 皂 as in ͵*i chó*² 胰皂 soap.

*Chói*ʾ 晬 A full year of age—used in reference to children.

*Chói*² 罪 Sin; breach of etiquette.

͵*Chong*, 賍 as in *chó*ʾ ͵*chong*, 做賍 thereabouts, about that amount.

͵*Chong*, 尊 Honorable, exalted, respected: ͵*chong* ʿ*chʿi*, 尊齒 and ͵*chong* ͵*keng*, 尊庚 (what is) your age?

*Chong*ʾ 俊 Fine, excellent.

͵*Chong*, 存 To remain, still on hand; also as in *ng*² ͵*chong e*ʾ 伓存意 unexpectedly, suddenly.

͵*Chu*, 只 as in ͵*chu wai*ʾ 只塊 here; this many.

͵*Chü*, 書 A book.

͵*Chü*, 諸 as in ͵*chü nóh*͵ 諸乇 all, every thing.

͵*Chü*, 資 Pay, wages, as in *ngwok*͵ ͵*chü*, 月資 monthly wages.

ʿ*Chü*, 子 11 P. M.—1. A. M.

ʿ*Chü*, 煮 To boil in water.

͵*Chui*, 嚌 This.

ʿ*Chung*, 准 To grant.

ʿ*Chung*, 總 All; certainly.

꜀Chüng, 鍾 A bell, a clock.
꜂Chüng, 種 Seed.
꜁Chüng, 從 To follow, to comply with; from: ꜁chüng ꜁chiéng, 從前 formerly.
꜂Chwi, 水 Water: ꜂chwi ch'e² 水市 the tide, time or state of the tide.
꜀Ch'a, 差 A mistake, an error, a fault; to differ; a little better, as from illness.
꜀Ch'a, 叉 A fork.
꜁Ch'a, 柴 Wood.
꜀Ch'á, 悽 as in ꜀ch'á ꜂ch'ang, 悽慘 lamentable, pitiable.
Ch'ak꜀ 察 To examine, to scrutinize.
꜀Ch'ang, 生 A superlative, very, completely, all over.
꜂Ch'au, 吵 To annoy, to disturb, to trouble.
꜂Ch'au, 草 or ꜂ch'au ꜂p'i, 草菲 grass.
Ch'au꜄ 臭 Offensive to the smell.
Ch'auk꜀ 錯 To err, to do wrong.
꜀Ch'ë, 初 The beginning—used before the ordinals for the first 10 days of the month.
Ch'ek꜀ 漆 Varnish; to varnish.
Ch'ek꜀ 七 Seven; the seventh.
Ch'eng꜄ 凊 Cold, as the weather or the person.
꜁Ch'eng, 田 A field.
Ch'ëü꜄ 處 as in kauk꜀ ch'ëü꜄ 各處 every place, every-where.
Ch'ëüng꜄ 敠 To unite: ch'ëüng꜄ che² 敠字 to spell.
꜂Ch'i, 齒 The teeth; age, years.
꜀Ch'iă, 俥 To turn round.
꜂Ch'iă, 且 as in ꜂ch'iă ꜂hi, 且喜 joy to you!
Ch'iăk꜀ 汒 To rub, as in washing clothes between the hands.
Ch'iăk꜀ 伮 To twitch, to pull at.
꜂Ch'iăng, 請 To request, to invite; to beg; please, as in please sit.
꜁Ch'iăng, 俶 To finish, to complete, as a job partly done.
Ch'iék꜀ 切 Earnest, eager.
꜂Ch'iéng, 淺 Superficially, in a slight degree.
꜀Ch'ieu, 鍬 To hem, to fell.
Ch'ieu꜄ 笑 To laugh.
꜀Ch'ing, 清 Pure, clear.
꜀Ch'ing, 深 Deep; heavy, as a cold.
꜀Ch'ing, 親 To love; intimate, near, as kindred: ꜀ch'ing ch'ek꜀ ꜁peng ꜂iu, 親戚朋友 or ꜀ch'ing ꜁peng ch'ek꜀ ꜂iu, 親朋戚友 relatives and acquaintances.
꜂Ch'ing, the same as ꜂ch'iéng, 淺 slightly.
꜂Ch'ing, 寢 Just now, just.
Ch'io꜄ 厝 A house.
Ch'ioh꜀ 尺 A foot (in measure).
Ch'ioh꜅ 蓆 Matting.
꜀Ch'iong, 穿 A hole, an opening; to bore through.
꜁Ch'iong, 墻 A thick, solid wall.

*Ch'iong²* 像 Like, similar.
*Ch'iong²* 潒 To draw (water).
꜀*Ch'iu*, 秋 Autumn.
꜂*Ch'iu*, 手 The hand.
*Ch'oi*꜄ 嘴 The mouth.
*Ch'ói*꜄ 砍 To cut down, to lop off.
*Ch'ok*꜆ To go out; one of the 15 initials.
꜀*Ch'ong*, 倉 A storehouse for rice or salt: ꜀*Ch'ong* ꜁*Seng*, 倉前 a locality on the S. side of the Min, Foochow.
*Ch'ong²* 搶 To wring out.
꜀*Ch'u*, 粗 Coarse, coarsely; stout, heavy: ꜀*ch'u* ꜀*i*, 粗衣 a certain size of sewing silk, as on p. 66.
꜀*Ch'ü*, 舒 To spread out.
꜀*Ch'ung*, 春 The spring of the year.
꜀*Ch'üng*, 冲 To pour on boiling water in order to steep.
꜁*Ch'üng*, 摐 To sprain.
꜀*Ch'wi*, 吹 To blow, as the wind; to be exposed to the wind.
*E*꜄ 意 Will, purpose, wish.
*E²* 未 1—3. P. M.
*E²* 味 Taste, flavor.
*Ek*꜆ 一 One, the first; the whole, throughout.
꜀*Eng*, 安 To place, to lay down, to let stand, as dough.
꜀*Eng*, 陰 as in ꜀*eng* ꜀*u*, 陰烏 dark, muggy, as the atmosphere.
*Eng*꜄ 應 To answer; to amount to.
꜁*Eng*, 閒 Leisure.
꜀*Eu*, 甌 A cup.
*Eu*꜄ 幼 Fine, small, young.
*Ëüng²* 用 To use, to expend.
꜁*Ha*, as in ꜁*ha* ꜂*tiăng*, 嚄等 soon, after a little while.
*Ha²* 下 To fall, as rain; to sprinkle in.
*Ha²* 夏 Summer.
*Ha²* 下 To transport, as by boat.
꜂*Hai*, 海 The sea.
*Hai²* 害 To injure; calamity.
*Hai²* 亥 9—11. P. M.
*Haing²* 行 Actions, conduct.
*Haiu²* 後 After in time, late, behind.
*Hak*₂ 合 Accordant to; to close, to shut.
*Hang*꜄ 漢 To suppose; to give notice.
꜁*Hang*, 含 Confused; shabbily: ꜁*hang* ꜁*hu*, 含糊 careless, slovenly.
꜁*Hang*, 寒 as in ꜀*hung* ꜁*hang*, 風寒 a cold.
꜂*Hau*, 哮 To call.
꜂*Heng*, 很 Very, exceedingly.
꜁*Heng*, 行 To do, to perform.
*Heng²* 噤 Reserved, sullen, silent, mum.
*Hĕk*₂ 惑 To pant, to puff.
꜀*Hĕng*, 烘 To toast, to broil.
꜀*Hi*, 希 as in ꜀*hi* *haing*꜄ 希倖 unaccountable.
꜂*Hiă*, 那 Very, exceedingly.
*Hiăk*₂ 合 as in *hiăk*₂ ꜁*siéng*, 合蟬 hinges.

꜀*Hiăng*, 兄 An older brother.
*Hiĕk*꜇ 頁 A classifier.
꜁*Hiĕng*, 嫌 To dislike, to hate.
*Hiĕng*꜅ 現 To appear; plain, open: *hiĕng*꜅ *chai*꜅ 現在 now, the present.
꜂*Hieu*, 曉 To know.
꜀*Hing*, 兄 An older brother.
꜀*Hing*, 興 To flourish.
꜂*Hiong*, 响 To strike, as a clock.
꜂*Hiong*, 享 To enjoy.
*Hiong*꜄ as in *ek*꜆ *hiong*꜄ 一向 heretofore.
*Ho*꜄ 付 Time enough.
*Ho*꜄ 洱 To sprinkle with the hand or water-pot; to baste, as meat.
*Ho*꜅ 父 A father.
꜂*Hó*, 好 Good, right, well, properly; more, very; well, as from sickness.
*Hok*꜆ 福 Happiness, good fortune; happy: *hok*꜆ *k'e*꜄ 福氣 happiness; *Hok*꜆ ꜀*Chiu*, 福州 Foochow; *Hok*꜆ ꜀*Ing*, 福音 the gospel.
*Hok*꜆ 拂 To brush, to dust.
꜀*Hong*, 煙 Tobacco; opium.
꜁*Hong*, 行 A row, a line.
꜁*Hong*, 杭 To quilt.
*Hong*꜅ 奉 To obey, to follow.
*Hong*꜅ 混 Confused, indistinct: ꜀*sang hong*꜅ 生混 strange, unknown.
꜀*Hu*, 夫 as in ꜀*kĕng* ꜀*hu*, 工夫 work.



꜀*Hu*, 夫 A porter, a workman.
꜂*Hu*, as in ꜂*hu siong*꜅ 府上 your house.
꜂*Hŭ*, 許 That, the other; so, thus: ꜂*hŭ* ꜂*tié*, 許裡 in there; ꜂*hŭ* ꜁*ong* ꜂*hŭ* ꜁*ong*, 許久許久 occasionally, frequently.
꜁*Huí*, 回 To turn round; to return back; to put down, as a sedan; a time: ꜁*huí* ꜂*ch'iu*, 回手 to set down, as a load; ꜁*huí* ꜀*t'au*, 回頭 to turn in order to retrace one's steps; a little while.
꜁*Huí*, 佪 That—the correlate of this.
*Huk*꜇ 服 To serve.
꜀*Hung*, 封 To seal up.
꜀*Hung*, as in ꜀*hung ho*꜄ (or *no*꜄) 吩咐 to direct, to give orders to.
꜀*Hung*, 風 Wind, air: ꜀*hung* ꜀*t'ai*, 風颱 a typhoon; ꜀*hung* ꜁*t'au*, 風頭 in the wind or draught.
꜀*Hung*, 分 A minute; to separate, to divide: ꜀*hung* ꜁*ming*, 分明 clearly; ꜀*hung piĕk*꜆ 分別 to discriminate.
꜀*Hung*, 蚊 as in ꜀*hung* ꜁*mwong*, 蚊門 a mosquito.
꜂*Hung*, 粉 Flour, powder; also as in ꜀*Sang* ꜀*Tĕng* ꜂*hung*, 山東粉 Shantung vermicelli.
꜁*Hung*, 魂 The soul.
꜁*Hung*, 渾 Roiled.
꜁*Hung*, 洪 Great, vast.

꜀*Hüng*, 兇 Malevolent, cruel: ꜀*hüng auk*꜆ 兇惡 wicked.

꜁*Hüng*,雄 Tight, taut, stretched.

꜀*Hwa*, 花 Flowers; edging: ꜀*Hwa* ꜁*ki kwok*꜆ (Flowery-flag-country) 花旗國 the United States.

*Hwa*꜄ 化 To change, to transform.

*Hwak*꜆ 法 A rule, law: ꜁*mó hwak*꜆ *tek*꜆ 毛法的 no alternative.

*Hwak*꜆ 發 To manifest, to spring up; to bring out, as perspiration: *hwak*꜆ ꜁*chai*, 發財 to become rich.

꜀*Hwang*, 歡 as in ꜀*hwang* ꜂*hi*, 歡喜 to rejoice, to be pleased.

*Hwang*² 犯 To violate, as a law.

꜂*Hwí*, 火 Fire.

꜂*Hwí*, as in ꜂*hwí sik*꜇ 伙食 food, provisions.

꜁*Hwo*,和 Harmony; genial, mild.

*Hwoi*꜄ 歲 A year of one's age.

*Hwoi*² 會 To meet, to visit; to understand, to know: *kau*꜄ *hwoi*² 教會 a church (of members); *hwoi*² ꜂*iu*, 會友 a church member.

*Hwong*꜄ 瘋 A boil.

꜁*Hwong*, 園 A garden.

*Hwong*² 遠 Far, distant.

꜀*I*, 衣 or ꜀*i* ꜁*siong*, 衣裳 clothes; ꜀*i sik*꜇ 衣食 clothing and food.

꜀*I*, 伊 He, him, she, her, it.

꜁*I*, used for ꜁*ki*, 其 one, any one.

꜁*I*, as in ꜁*i chó*² 胰皂 soap.

꜂*Ié*, 椅 A chair.

*Ié*² 積 To sprinkle, as powder.

꜀*Ing*, 因 For, because.

꜀*Ing*, 音 Sound, voice, tone.

꜂*Ing*, 永 Eternal.

꜁*Ing*, as in ꜁*ing yeu*² 榮耀 glory; to glorify.

꜁*Ing*, 人 A man, a human being.

꜁*Ing*, 寅 3--5 A. M.

꜂*Iu*, as in ꜂*iu hëk*꜇ 誘惑 to tempt, to mislead.

꜂*Iu*, 酉 5--7 P. M.

꜁*Iu*, 油 Oil.

꜀*Ka*, 剪 To cut with scissors.

*Ka*꜄ 價 Price, value of a thing.

*Ka*꜄ 教 To teach.

*Ka*꜄ 架 An open frame, etc., a stand.

꜂*Ká*, 解 To loosen; to explain.

*Kaëng*² 共 With, of, in behalf of; as, like to.

*Kai*꜄ 蓋 To cover, a cover.

*Kai*꜄ 再 Again.

*Kai*꜄ 誡 Rule of conduct.

*Kaing*꜄ 更 The better, the more.

*Kaing*² 縣 A district.

*Kak*꜆ 夾 as in *kak*꜆ *mang*² 夾幔 a money-safe.

*Kak*꜆ 割 To cut, as with a knife.

*Kak*꜇ 鉀 as in ꜁*mó kak*꜇ *siăh*꜇ 毛鉀食 unimportant.

꜀*Kang*, 更 A watch of the night.

꜀*Kang*, 間 In the midst of: *sié*꜄ ꜀*kang*, 世間 this world.

꜀*Kang*, 櫚 A classifier.

꜂*Kang*, 敢 To dare.

꜂*Kang*, 感 To move the feelings;

榕腔初學撮要

ʻkang siâ² 感謝 to thank; ʻkang hwa' 感化 to improve, to convert.

ʻKang, 㧡 To wipe with a cloth.

Kang' 幹 To attend to, as business.

˛Kang, 寒 Affected by the cold, chilled.

Kang² 汗 Perspiration.

˛Kau, 交 or ˛kau ˛cheng, 交針 to backstitch.

ʻKau, 九 Nine, the ninth.

Kau' 教 Doctrines, a religious sect.

Kau' 㲃 Enough, sufficient.

Kau' 至 To arrive at, to, unto.

Kau² 厚 Thick, not thin, dense; very superior; furred, as the tongue.

Kauk, 各 Each, every: kauk, yong² 各樣 strange, odd.

Kaung' 降 To descend; to send down, to confer.

Ke' 記 To remember; to write down, as an account: ke' ˛chai, 記才 the memory.

Kek, 桔 The mandarin orange.

Kek, 急 Hasty, impatient; urgent: kek, siek₂ 急舌 a stammering tongue.

Kek₂ 夾 To hold tightly.

ʻKeng, 揀 To select.

˛Keng, 高 High, tall; up: ˛keng kiă² 高下 high and low, uneven, fluctuating, as prices.

˛Keng, 鹹 Salt, not fresh.

˛Kĕng, 工 Work; a day's work.

Keu' 救 To save from evil: Keu' ʻChio, 救主 the Savior.

Kĕü² 具 as in kĕü² ʻhwi, 具火 to strike a light.

Kĕüng² 近 Near, to come near.

˛Ki, 飢 Hungry.

˛Ki, 其 One, any one; a numerative; a sign of the possessive.

˛Ki, 旗 A flag.

˛Ki, 祈 or ˛ki ʻtó, 祈禱 to pray.

Kiă² 下 Low, not elevated.

˛Kiăng, 驚 Afraid.

ʻKiăng, 仔 A son, a child; a diminutive of persons, animals, and things.

ʻKiăng, used for ʻkang, 敢 as in ʻk'i ʻkiăng, 豈敢 how dare!

˛Kiăng, 行 To walk, to go.

˛Kie, 雞 The barnyard fowl.

˛Kie, 快 Quickly, rapidly.

Kie' 季 Seasons of the year.

Kie' 寄 To send, as things.

Kiek, as in kiek, ˛loi, 結纇 a hard knot; kiek, sik₂ 結實 to bear fruit.

Kieng' 見 To see, to perceive; sign of the passive.

˛Kieng, 墘 The edge, the border; near the edge.

˛Kieng, 虔 Correct, devout.

Kieu' 叫 To call, to command; to term.

Kieu² 轎 A sedan.

Kik₂ 極 Extremely.

˛King, as in ˛king tong² 驚動

to alarm, to disturb.
˛King, 今 Now, this, to, as in ˛king tang˒ 今日 to-day; ˛king ˛niéng ˛mang, 今年暝 this year.
ʻKing, 緊 Tightly.
˛Kio, 橋 A bridge.
˛Kiu, 求 To beg, to ask, to supplicate; one of the 15 initials.
Ko˒ 顧 To care for.
Ko˒ 故 More; still, still more, still again.
Ko² 舊 Old, as things.
˛Kó, 糕 a cake.
˛Kó, 高 High, exalted.
˛Kó, as in ˛kó ˛long, 䡤軇 the whole.
Koi˒ 貴 Dear, expensive; honorable.
Koi² 跪 To kneel.
Kok˒ 趜 To rise up, as a person.
Kok₂ 滑 Slippery; to slip.
˛Kong, 扛 To carry between two, to bear burdens on a pole between two.
ʻKong, 講 To talk, to speak, to say.
˛Kong, 炡 To boil soft, as meat, to fricassee.
ʻKu, as in ʻchi ʻku (ʻu) 只古 just now, a moment ago.
ʻKu, 鼓 A drum: ʻKu ˛Sang, 鼓山 Drum Mountain—on the N. side of the Min near Foochow.
˛Kü, 拘 To stand on ceremony.
˛Kung, 公 Just, fair, equitable.
˛Kung, 功 A good service, work, or affair; merit.
ʻKung, 滾 To boil—an intransitive verb.
˛Küng, 觔 A pound.
˛Küng, as in ʻchʻiu ˛küng, 手巾 a napkin.
ʻKüng, as in ʻküng ʻhi, 拱喜 joy to you! I congratulate you!
˛Küng, 窮 Poor, indigent; to exhaust.
Kwai˒ 怪 Offended.
˛Kwang, as in ˛Kwang ˛Ing ʻChang, 觀音井 a locality on the south side of the Min, Foochow.
Kwang˒ 慣 Accustomed to, practiced in.
Kwang˒ 灌 To water, as meat; to suppurate.
Kwang˒ 鑵 An earthen pitcher, etc.
Kwang² 扤 To carry by the bail, or as a bundle by the string.
˛Kwi, 歸 To revert to.
ʻKwi, 幾 A few; an interrogative of quantity, how many? what?
ʻKwi, as in ʻkwi ʻchi, 果子 fruit.
Kwo˒ 過 To pass over, to go beyond; to do over; to be contagious, as a disease; times: kwo˒ sié˒ 過世 to die.
Kwo˒ 句 A sentence, a phrase.
Kwok˒ 國 A country, a kingdom.
Kwok₂ 楲 A classifier.
˛Kwong, 關 To shut.
˛Kwong, 光 Light, not dark; smooth.

ʻKwong, 管 A tube: ˓pó ˓lá ʻkwong, 玻璃管 a lamp-chimney.

ʻKwong, as in ʻKwong ˓Tĕng, 廣東 Canton.

˓Kwong, 權 or ˓kwong pangʼ 權柄 power, authority.

˓Kʻa, 骹 The foot.

ʻKʻa, as in ʻkʻa lak˒ 收拾 to mend, to put to rights; to adjust.

Kʻáʼ 快 Quickly, speedily.

Kʻah˒ 客 A guest.

Kʻaik˒ 尅 To close (the eyes).

Kʻaik˒ 刻 15 minutes; a little while.

Kʻaiuʼ as in ne² kʻaiuʼ 二扣 a particular size of sewing-silk; see p. 66.

Kʻaiuʼ 鈕 A button: kʻaiuʼ ˓mwong, 鈕門 or kʻaiuʼ ˓mwong ˓chʻiong, 鈕門穿 a button-hole.

Kʻak˒ 渴 Thirsty.

Kʻak˒ 太 A superlative, in excess, too much.

Kʻak˒ 拾 To pick up.

ʻKʻang, 砍 To chop, to fell, to cut down.

Kʻangʼ 看 To see, to look; to treat, to regard; to read silently.

Kʻaungʼ 困 To sleep: kʻaungʼ tioh₂ 困着 asleep.

Kʻeʼ 棄 To reject.

Kʻeʼ 氣 To be angry, temper, spirit; one of the 15 initials.

Kʻek˒ as in kʻek˒ ˓kʻwi, 吃虧 pain, suffering; distressed.

Kʻek₂ 獲 To use, to employ, with, by.

˓Kʻĕng, 空 In vain, to no purpose.

Kʻeuʼ 殏 Stiff, as clothes.

Kʻĕük˒ 乞 To give, to let; a sign of the passive.

ʻKʻi, 起 To lift up; up; to build, to kindle; beginning; after verbs denotes completion of action; an enclitic: ʻkʻi ˓seng, 起先 at first; ʻkʻi ʻchʻiu, 起手 to commence.

ʻKʻi, 豈 as in ʻkʻi ʻkang, 豈敢 how dare! ʻkʻi taĕng² 豈動 (or 起動) thanks for your trouble!

˓Kʻiă, 奇 One, a single one; the odd numbers.

˓Kʻiéng, 愆 A fault, error, sin.

Kʻiéngʼ 欠 To owe, deficient in.

˓Kʻing, 輕 Light, not heavy; lightly.

ʻKʻing, 肯 To be willing, to consent.

˓Kʻing, 傾 To pour from a spout.

˓Kʻiong, 腔 Brogue, foreign accent.

ʻKʻó, as in ʻkʻó sek˒ 可惜 what a pity!

Kʻóʼ 靠 To rest or depend on.

Kʻóʼ 去 To go, to depart, gone, past; spent, as money; than; denotes completion of sense of the preceding word: kʻóʼ ˓niéng ˓mang, 去年暝 last year.

ʻK'*ong*, 悃 Urgently.

꜀K'*ong*, 扛 To carry, as across the shoulder.

꜀K'*u*, 呼 To recite, to repeat.

ʻK'*u*, 苦 Sorrowful.

ʻK'*ung*, 綑 To bind, as an edge with cloth.

꜀K'*üng*, 勤 or ꜀*k'üng* ʻ*king*, 勤緊 diligent, sedulous.

K'*wak*꜆ 闊 Wide.

ʻK'*wang*, 欵 Style, manner, way.

꜀K'*wi*, 開 To open, to begin; to make out, as a bill; to wind, as a clock.

꜀K'*wo*, 科 To reckon, to estimate, as prices.

K'*wok*꜆ 缺 A deficiency; vacancy.

K'*wong*ʾ 勸 To exhort.

ʻ*La*, 喇 A, that, such a thing as.

ʻ*Lá*, 禮 Worship; etiquette, politeness; forms the present participle; a prepositional or adverbial particle.

*Laë*ʾ 攎 To scour, to rub.

*Laëk*꜆ 籠 Loosened, relaxed.

꜁*Lai*, 來 To come: ꜁*lai* ꜁*huí*, 來回 to and fro; ꜁*lai* ꜁*niéng*, 來年 next year.

꜁*Lai*, 筙 A basket.

꜁*Lai*, as in ꜁*lai* ꜀*kung*, 雷公 thunder.

*Laiu*² 料 Materials of which things are made; strength, as of tea, etc.; sets of materials, as in a recipe.

*Lak*꜇ 粒 A classifier.

꜁*Lang*, 籃 A basket.

*Lang*² 濫 Wet.

*Lang*² 二 Two, a few.

ʻ*Lau*, 了 Sign of the past tense, have, has; already.

*Lau*² 佬 Old, aged, as persons.

*Lau*² 漏 To leak.

*Laung*² 論 According to; in reference to: ꜁*mó laung*² 毛論 irrespective of.

*Laung*² 蛋 An egg.

*Lëk*꜇ 六 Six, the sixth.

*Lëk*꜇ 籠 A colloquial prefix.

꜀*Leng*, the same as ꜀*seng* in ʻ*cha* ꜀*seng*, 早先 a short time ago.

*Leng*ʾ 稜 A classifier.

*Leng*² 令 A law; excellent, worthy, your.

*Leu*ʾ 溜 To slide, to slip down.

*Lëü*² 慮 To think upon anxiously.

ʻ*Li*, 理 Doctrine.

ʻ*Li*, 裏 The inner surface, the lining.

ʻ*Li*. 里 The Chinese mile—according to some, equal to 1897½ Eng. feet.

꜁*Li*, 來 To come.

꜁*Li*, 梨 A pear.

꜁*Li*, 哩 A euphonic particle.

*Liăh*꜆ the same as *chiăh*꜆ 隻 or *sioh*꜇ *chiăh*꜆ 一隻 one.

ʻ*Liăng*, 嶺 A mountain ridge, a road over a peak: *Twai*² ʻ*Liăng*, 大嶺 a locality on the south side of the Min, Foochow.

*ʿLiăng*, 領 A collar, the neck, as of a dress.

*˛Liăng*, 涼 To air.

*Lié*$^2$ 離 Removed from, separate: *tʿwak*˒ *lié*$^2$ 脫離 to escape, to get rid of.

*Lié*$^2$ 例 Customs, rules, regulations.

*˛Liéng*, 連 And, in addition to.

*ʿLieu*, 了 as in *ʿlieu lié*$^2$ 了離 clear, as to sense.

*Lik*$_2$ 力 Strength: *lik*$_2$ *lóh*$_2$ 力落 active and ready, as to do extra work.

*˛Ling*, 林 A surname.

*˛Ling*, 靈 as in *˛ling ˛hung*, 靈魂 the soul.

*ʿLiong*, 兩 Two, a couple.

*˛Liong*, 涼 Cool, fresh: *˛liong ˛hung*, 涼風 to take the air.

*˛Liong*, as in *˛liong ʿchʿó*, 糧草 food, provisions.

*Liong*$^2$ 諒 To think, to suppose.

*Lo*˒ 露 Dew.

*˛Ló*, 囉 A euphonic particle, equivalent to commas and periods in a vocal enumeration of things.

*ʿLó*, 囉 A euphonic particle after certain verbs.

*ʿLó*, 老 Old, a term of respect: *ʿló sik*$_2$ 老實 honest.

*˛Ló*, 囉 A disjunctive, or; an emphatic and euphonic particle.

*˛Ló*, 勞 To labor; to trouble one: *˛ló tong*$^2$ 勞動 to trouble one (for a favor); also as in *˛kung ˛ló*, 功勞 merit.

*Lóh*$_2$ 落 To place, to put in; to stay in a place; in, upon, down.

*˛Loi*, 雷 Thunder.

*˛Long*; 𦃀 To sew over and over, to overhand.

*˛Lu*, 爐 A furnace, a stove.

*ʿLung*, as in *ʿlung ʿchung*, 攏總 all.

*˛Ma*, 𢭃 To take with the hand, to grasp; to shut the hand tightly.

*ʿMa*, 馬 as in *ʿma tʿai*˒ 馬太 Matthew.

*Ma*˒ 罵 To scold.

*ʿMá*, 買 To buy.

*Má*$^2$ 賣 To sell; cannot, will not, is not.

*Mah*$_2$ 脈 The pulse.

*Mai*$^2$ 邁 To carry on the back.

*Maing*$^2$ 慢 Slow, slowly; to delay, to defer, as one's going.

*ʿMang*, 猛 Hot, glowing, as fire.

*ʿMang*, a corruption of *˛mó ʿkang*, 毛敢 not dare.

*ʿMang*, a corruption of *ʿmwang*, 滿 (full) very.

*˛Mang*, 暝 Night.

*˛Mang*, 明 as in *˛mang ˛niéng ˛mang*, 明年暝 next year.

*˛Mang*, 蒙 Dull of apprehension; ignorant, simple.

*ʿMau*, 𠲎 To close the mouth.

*ʿMau*, 卯 5—7 A. M.

*Mek*₂ as in *mek*₂ *꜀chiu*, 目睭 the eye.

*Meng*꜄ 面 The face; the surface, outside.

*Meng*² 命 To command; a decree.

꜂*Mi*, 米 Uncooked rice.

꜁*Mi*, as in ꜁*mi tuk*₂ 惟獨 but, only; ꜁*mi* ꜂*iu*, 惟有 only have or is.

꜁*Mi*, 微 Small, trifling, mean.

꜁*Miăng*, 名 A name; fame, honor.

*Miéh*꜆ 乜 What? also as in *miéh*꜆ *nóh*꜆ 乜毛 what? any to speak of.

꜂*Miéng*, 免 To avoid, to escape; to forgive.

*Miéng*² 面 The surface; that which is anterior: *miéng*² *au*² 面候 (perhaps a corruption of *miéh*꜆ ꜁*seng au*² 乜前候) when? what time or day of the month?

*Miéng*² as in *miéng*² ꜂*hung*, 麪粉 wheat flour.

꜁*Ming*, 明 Clear: ꜁*ming tang*꜄ 明旦 to-morrow; ꜁*ming pek*₂ 明白 to understand clearly; ꜁*ming ch'ek*꜆ 明漆 a kind of varnish.

꜁*Ming*, 閩 as in ꜁*Ming kaing*² ꜁*sang*, 閩縣山 Name of a hill in the S. E. quarter of Foochow.

꜁*Mó*, 無 No, none, not, cannot; to be gone, missing, stolen: ꜁*mó tói*꜄ 無塊 nowhere; ꜁*mó hwak*꜆ 無法 no alternative.

*Móh*₂ 莫 A negative of prohibition, do not!

*Mok*꜆ as in *mók*꜆ ꜀*i*, 莫衣 a particular size of sewing silk; see p. 66.

*Muk*₂ 木 Wood.

꜁*Mung*, 蒙 To receive, or be grateful for, as favors.

꜂*Mwang*, 滿 Full, entire, all.

꜁*Mwai*, 磨 To sharpen, or scour, as knives.

꜂*Mwí*, 尾 The end.

꜁*Mwo*, 霧 Haze, fog.

*Mwo*² 慕 To think fondly of.

*Mwoi*꜄ 妹 A younger sister.

*Mwoi*² 昧 Blind, ignorant; not yet.

꜂*Mwong*, 莾 Just, only just, merely.

*Mwong*꜄ 憫 To ask, to inquire about.

꜁*Mwong*, 門 A door.

*Na*² 郍 Only, simply; if, when.

꜂*Ná*, 奶 A mother.

*Nai*꜄ the same as *nói*꜄ 塊 a little.

*Nai*² 耐 Patient.

꜁*Nang*, as in ꜁*nang muk*₂ 楠木 a hard, yellowish wood, suitable for furniture.

꜁*Nang*, 南 South.

*Nau*² 鬧 To make a great ado about: *nau*² *yék*₂ 鬧熱 a bustle, a great stir.

*Naung*꜄ 亂 Tangled.

*Naung*² 嫩 Small.

*Ne*$^2$ 二 Two, the second; a superlative, very.

*Nek*꜄ 啀 as in *nek*꜄ *nek*꜄ 啀啀 a little.

꜀*Neng*, as in ꜀*chiong* ꜀*neng*, 全能 powerful.

꜀*Neng*, 乳 Milk.

꜀*Nĕng*, as in ꜀*nĕng* ꜁*ka*, 儂家 I, we, us.

꜀*Nĕng*, 膿 Pus, matter: ꜀*nĕng* ꜀*t'au*, 膿頭 the head, or core of a boil.

꜀*Nĕng*, 人 A man, a person.

*Nĕŭk*꜄ 朒 To draw, as a seam, to pucker.

*Nĕŭng*$^2$ 緩 Slack, as a rope; diminished, as a conflagration.

꜁*Ni*, 呢 An interrogative particle.

꜁*Niă*, as in ꜁*niă* *nói*꜄ 些微 a little.

꜀*Niăng*, 燋 Scorched, burnt.

*Nié*$^2$ as in *nié*$^2$ ꜂*kiăng*, 伲仔 children.

*Niĕk*꜄ 廿 A contraction of *ne*$^2$ *sek*$_2$ 二十 twenty.

꜁*Niéng*, 拈 To hold or take in the hand.

꜂*Niéng*, 染 To dye.

꜀*Niéng*, 年 A year.

*Niéng*$^2$ 念 To think, to consider: *niéng*$^2$ ꜀*t'au*, 念頭 thoughts.

*Nik*$_2$ 日 A day: *nik*$_2$ ꜀*t'au*, 日頭 the sun; *nik*$_2$ *nik*$_2$ 日日 daily; *nik*$_2$ ꜂*chi*. 日子 days, time.

*Nik*$_2$ 廿 A corruption of *ne*$^2$ *sek*$_2$ 二十 twenty.

MAN. 27.

*Nioh*$_2$ 箬 How (much)? a superlative, very: *nioh*$_2$ *wai*$^2$ 箬壞 how much or many?

*Nioh*$_2$ 葉 A leaf.

*No*꜄ the same as *ho*꜄ 咐 q. v.

*Nó*꜄ the same as *tó*꜄ 倒 q. v.

*Nóh*꜄ 乇 A thing, the third before or after in years, as on page 83; similarily used in reference to days.

*Nói*꜄ used for *tói*꜄ 塊 a place: ꜂*mwang* *nói*꜄ 滿塊 every place, every-where.

꜂*Nong*, 暖 Mild, as the weather.

*Nong*$^2$ 閏 An intercalary month, to intercalate.

꜀*Nu*, 奴 I, me--used in polite phrase and by inferiors.

꜂*Nü*, 汝 You: ꜂*nü* ꜀*ki*, 汝其 yours.

꜀*Nui*, 挼 To knead.

*Nŭk*$_2$ 肉 Flesh, meat; pork: *nŭk*$_2$ ꜂*t'á*, 肉體 the body.

꜀*Nŭng*, 濃 Rich, as liquids; deep, as color.

*Ng*$^2$ 伓 Not, neither; will not, not wish.

꜀*Ngai*, 呆 Bad, evil, wicked; spoiled; poorly.

*Ngau*꜄ 咬 Confused, jumbled; jargon, brogue.

*Ngĕü*$^2$ 遇 To meet with.

*Ngié*$^2$ 外 or *ngié*$^2$ ꜂*tau*, 外斗 outside.

*Ngo*$^2$ 五 Five, the fifth.

*Ngó*$^2$ 燉 To bake.

꜀*Ngong*, 昻 as in ꜀*ngong* ꜀*ngong kieu*꜄ 昻昻叫 a din, a clamor of voices.

꜂*Ngu*, 午 11 A. M.—1 P. M.

꜀*Ngu*, 牛 A cow, an ox.

꜂*Ngwai*, 我 I, me.

*Ngwo*² 誤 To err, to mistake; accidentally.

*Ngwo*² as in *hwoi*² *ngwo*² 會悟 to arouse one's self so as to perceive clearly, noticing, discerning.

*Ngwoi*² 外 Outside, outward.

*Ngwok*₂ 月 A lunar month.

*Ngwong*² 願 To desire.

*O*² 務 To be, is, it is; do, did; have, has.

꜁*Ó*, 阿 A final particle.

꜁*Ó*, used for *k'ó*꜄ 去 to denote completion of action.

꜁*Ó*, 婀 Hard, difficult.

*Óh*₂ 學 To learn: as, as to, according to.

*Oi*² 位 A place, a seat.

*Ói*꜄ 欲 To wish, to desire.

*Ok*꜄ 熨 To iron.

꜁*Ong*, 恩 or ꜁*ong hiê*² 恩惠 favor, grace, benefits.

꜀*Ong*, 行 A hong.

꜀*Ong*, 久 A long time, a period of time.

꜂*Pa*, 飽 Full, satisfied; over, excess.

꜂*Pa*, 把 A classifier.

꜀*Pa*, 扒 To climb, to clamber, to creep.

*Pa*² as in *pa*² ꜂*ná*, 罷奶 parents.

꜁*Pá*, 叭 An interrogative particle.

꜀*Pá*, 排 To arrange in order.

*Pah*꜄ 百 A hundred: *pah*꜄ *ngo*² 百五 one hundred and five tens, i. e., 150; *pah*꜄ *ne*² 百二 120.

*Pah*꜄ 擘 To break apart, to open; to skin, as an orange.

꜂*Pai*, 擺 A sort of term for sedan-men (when more than two—so as to take turns).

*Pai*꜄ 拜 To bow to, to show honor to, to salute; it precedes the ordinal numbers for the days of the week after the Sabbath: *pai*꜄ ꜂*kwi*? 拜幾 what day of the week is it? *sioh*₂ ꜂*lá pai*꜄ 一禮拜 one week.

*Paik*꜄ 八 Eight; the eighth: *Paik*꜄ ꜁*Ing*, 八音 the eight tones; the Eight Tone Book.

*Paik*꜄ 仈 To be acquainted with.

꜀*Pang*, 平 Level, even, uniform; colloquial: ꜀*pang tik*₂ 平直 straight; ꜀*pang chiăng*꜄ 平正 poor, inferior.

꜀*Pang*, as in ꜂*peng* ꜀*pang*, 板棚 a board floor.

*Pang*² 病 Ill; sickness: *pang*² ꜂*a*, 病啞 dumb, silent.

꜁*Pau*, 包 Bread.

*Pauk*꜄ 剝 To burst, to break, as a boil.

*Pe*² 痺 Numbed.

*Pek*꜄ 必 Certainly.

*Pek*⌋ 筆 A pen, a pencil.

⌊*Peng*, 邊 Side, way, direction.

‘*Peng*, as in ‘*peng paik*⌋ a corruption of *paik*⌋ *ng*² *paik*⌋ 𠆧伓𠆧 acquainted with or not?

‘*Peng*, 板 A board; to invert, to turn over.

⌊*Peng*, 爿 A side, a part.

⌊*Peng*, as in ⌊*peng* ‘*iu*, 朋友 a friend, an acquaintance.

⌊*Peng*, as in ⌊*peng* ⌊*ngié*, 便宜 cheap.

‘*Pi*, 比 to compare: ‘*pi ëü*² 比喻 for instance, to illustrate.

*Piăng*’ 倂 To pour, to empty out.

*Piék*⌋ 撇 To turn down, as a hem.

*Piék*⌋ 蹩 Lame, bent, wrenched.

⌊*Piéng*, 邊 The side, the border; one of the 15 initials.

*Piéng*’ 變 To change, to alter.

*Piéng*² 便 Convenient, proper; ready, done, finished: *piéng*² *kek*⌋ 便急 convenient, handy.

‘*Pieu*, 表 To show, to manifest; to bring out, as an ailment, etc.

⌊*Ping*, 平 Tranquil, peaceful: ⌊*ping* ⌊*ang*, 平安 well and happy, free from trouble, prosperous.

⌊*Ping*, 憑 To obey, to follow.

*Po*² 仅 Again.

⌊*Pó*, as in ⌊*pó* ⌊*lá*, 玻璃 glass.

⌊*Pó*, 保 or ⌊*pó ho*² 保護 to preserve, to protect.

*Pó*’ 報 or *pó*’ *tak*⌋ 報答 to recompense; a recompense.

⌊*Pó*, as in ⌊*tá* ⌊*pó*, 茶婆 a metal teapot.

⌊*Pó*, 嚗 A final emphatic sound.

*Pó*² 抱 To carry in the arms, to embrace.

*Pok*⌋ 不 Not.

⌊*Pong*, 帮 To assist; a period of time.

*Pong*’ 放 To put down, to place; to loosen, to hold loosely: *pong*’ ‘*hwi*, 放火 to set fire to, incendiarism.

⌊*Pu*, 嗒 An interjectional particle.

⌊*Pui*, 肥 Fat; fertile.

⌊*Puí*, 陪 To keep one company, as in sitting, laughing, or talking with him.

⌊*Pung*, 房 A room, a chamber.

⌊*Pung*, 㖸 To blow with the mouth, to inflate with air: ⌊*pung kwo*’ 㖸過 to blow out (a lamp).

*Pwak*² 跋 To fall, as a person.

⌊*Pwang*, 般 A sort, manner, kind.

*Pwang*’ 半 A half: *pwang*’ ⌊*lang* ⌊*ch‘iăng*, 半闌𢦶 half-done.

⌊*Pwang*, 盤 A plate, a tray.

*Pwang*² 拌 To brush away, to strike with limber things.

⌊*Pwí*, 杯 A cup.

⌊*Pwo*, 晡 or ⌊*mang* ⌊*pwo*, 暝晡 night: *sioh*² ⌊*mang* ⌊*pwo*, 一暝晡 last night.

‘*Pwo*, 補 To mend, to repair, to recruit, as the body.

*Pwo*’ 布 Cotton cloth.

*Pwo*2 步 A step: *pwo*2 ꜀*heng*, 步行 to walk.

*Pwoh*, 剁 Will, shall, about to; bent on.

*Pwoh*2 縛 To tie up.

*Pwoi*2 背 To recite with the back to the teacher.

‘*Pwong*, 本 Origin, source; this, the present; capital in trade; a classifier: ‘*pwong* ꜀*lai*, 本來 originally.

*Pwong*2 飰 Boiled or steamed rice.

*P‘ah*, 拍 To beat, to strike; to do, to effect—a verb of varied signification according to context.

*P‘ak*2 浡 Running over.

*P‘ang*’ 冇 Empty, loose: *p‘ang*’ ‘*kong*, 冇講 to chat.

꜀*P‘ang*, 澎 Full, up to the brim, overflowing.

꜀*P‘au*, 枹 A pomelo.

*P‘au*’ 炮 To boil water for tea.

*P‘aung*2 橦 To collide, to knock against.

*P‘aung*2 遇 To meet with, as temptation.

*P‘ek*, 疋 A classifier.

*P‘iăh*, 僻 To step to one side; to get out of another's way.

꜀*P‘ié*, 批 A letter, an epistle.

*P‘iék*, 撇 To skim off.

꜀*P‘iéng*, as in ꜀*p‘iéng* ꜀*ló*, 偏囉 have eaten—phrase borrowed from the Court dialect.

*P‘iéng*’ 片 A slice.

꜀*P‘ieu*, 瓢 A spoon.

꜀*P‘ó*, 波 One of the 15 initials.

*P‘ó*’ 破 Worthless.

*P‘ong*’ 縫 A seam's width.

‘*P‘u*, the same as the particle ‘*ch‘ing*, 寢 just, just now.

꜀*P‘uí*, 皮 Leather.

꜀*P‘ung*, 捧 To carry in both hands.

*P‘wai*’ 破 To break, to tear, to split, as with an ax: *p‘wai*’ *pang*2 破病 sick, ill.

*P‘wak*, 潑 To sprinkle, to baste, as meat.

꜀*P‘wí*, 胚 In the rough, unfinished.

꜀*P‘wo*, 鋪 To spread: *p‘woi*2 ꜀*p‘wo*, 被鋪 or ꜀*p‘wo kai*’ 鋪蓋 bedding.

*P‘woh*2 曝 To sun.

*P‘woi*2 被 A coverlet, a comfortable.

*P‘wong*’ 汳 To ebb, to flow out, as the tide.

꜀*Sa*, as in ꜀*sa ho*2 司傅 a skilled workman.

‘*Sá*, 洗 To wash.

*Sá*’ 細 Minute, small: *sá*’ *ne*2 細膩 careful, ceremonious.

*Sá*2 侕 Many, much.

*Saëk*, 捽 To thresh, to brush out.

‘*Sai*, 駛 Need, use; necessary; answering the purpose; to use, to cause.

*Sak*˒ 煞 To stop, to cease.

*Sak*$_2$ 煞 To boil in water.

˓*Sang*, 生 To bear, to produce, to bring forth; to grow: ˓*sing* ˓*sang*, 先生 a teacher, a physician; ˓*sang hong*$^2$ 生混 strange, unknown.

˓*Sang*, 山 A mountain, a hill: ˓*Sang* ˓*Tĕng*, 山東 Shantung.

˓*Sang*, 三 Three, the third.

‘*Sang*, 傘 An umbrella.

‘*Sang*, as in ‘*sang* ‘*sai*, a corruption of ‘*sai ng*$^2$ ‘*sai*, 駛伓駛 is it necessary or not?

*Sang*˒ 性 The natural disposition, temper, spirit.

*Sang*˒ 姓 The surname.

˓*Sang*, 晴 Fair, as the weather.

*Sang*$^2$ 默 To be silent, not to speak.

*Sau*˒ 掃 To sweep: *sau*˒ ‘*ch‘iu*, 掃箒 a broom.

*Saung*˒ 筭 To reckon, to cipher.

*Se*˒ 四 Four, the fourth.

*Se*$^2$ 是 Is, am, are, it is.

*Sek*˒ as in ˓*ang sek*˒ 安息 to stop, to rest, to repose.

*Sek*˒ as in ‘*k‘ó sek*˒ 可惜 what a pity! alas!

*Sek*˒ 失 To lose, to drop; a failure.

*Sek*$_2$ 十 Ten, the tenth.

˓*Seng*, 生 Life; to bear, to produce: ˓*seng* ˓*chiĕng*, 生前 the present life; ˓*seng e*˒ 生意 trade; ˓*seng* ˓*siăng*, 生成 originally.

˓*Seng*, 先 First, before, early, formerly.

˓*Seng*, perhaps a corruption of *sá*$^2$ 佤 much.

*Seng*˒ 聖 Sage, perfect; holy.

*Seng*˒ 信 To believe.

*Seng*˒ 性 A surname.

˓*Seng*, 前 In front of; formerly: ˓*seng tó*˒ 前到 time, occasion.

˓*Sĕng*, 雙 Double, twofold.

˓*Seu*, 純 Uniform; regularly; constantly, frequently: ˓*seu* ˓*i*, 純衣 a particular size of sewing-silk, see p. 66.

*Seu*$^2$ 壽 Age, longevity.

*Seu*$^2$ 受 To receive, to take, as a cold: *seu*$^2$ *k‘e*˒ 受氣 to be angry.

*Sëü*˒ 賜 To give, to bestow, as a superior does.

*Sëü*$^2$ 祀 To serve, to obey.

*Sëü*$^2$ 士 A learned man: *kau*˒ *sëü*$^2$ 教士 a christian minister.

*Sëü*$^2$ 巳 9—11 A. M.

*Sëüng*$^2$ 穿 To put on clothing, to dress: *sëüng*$^2$ *tai*˒ 穿戴 what is worn, dress and cap, etc.

‘*Si*, 死 To die, dead.

海上絲綢之路文獻集成 科技與文化編

꜀*Si*, 時 Time; season, as for fruit: ꜀*si* ꜀*sing*, 時辰 a Chinese hour —equaling two hours Eng.; ꜀*si haiu*$^2$ 時候 time.

‘*Siă*, 寫 To write.

*Siă*’ 赦 To forgive.

꜀*Siă*, 邪 Wrong; depraved.

*Siă*$^2$ 謝 To thank; thanks.

*Siăh*$_2$ 食 To eat, to drink, to smoke: ꜀*mó kak*$_2$ *siăh*$_2$ 毛𠰸食 unimportant.

*Siăk*꜇ as in *sioh*$_2$ *siăk*꜇ ‘*ku*, same as *sioh*$_2$ *k‘aik*꜇ ‘*ku*, 一刻古 a little while.

꜁*Siăng*, 聲 A voice, a tone in speaking or music; a noise, a sound.

*Siăng*’ 線 Thread, sewing silk.

꜀*Siăng*, 城 A walled city.

꜀*Siăng*, 成 To complete: ꜀*siăng* ꜁*hwa*, 成花 to complete the flower, i. e., bargain.

*Siăng*$^2$ 賤 Cheap.

꜁*Sié*, 施 To bestow, to grant.

*Sié*’ 世 The world, an age: *kwo*’ *sié*’ 過世 to die; *sié*’ *nóh*꜇ 世乇 what? any, some, particularly.

*Sié*’ 勢 Way, manner, fashion.

꜀*Sié*, as in ꜀*sié* ꜀*t‘au*, 蛇頭 a whitlow.

*Siék*$_2$ as in *siék*$_2$ ‘*pwong*, 折本 to lose in trade.

*Siék*$_2$ 舌 The tongue.

*Siéng*’ 扇 A fan.

꜀*Siéng*, 塩 Salt, table-salt.

*Siéng*$^2$ 善 Good, excellent.

꜁*Sieu*, 燒 To burn, to roast.

‘*Sieu*, as in ‘*sieu* ‘*hó* (or ‘*k‘ó*) 小可 small, petty; ‘*sieu* ꜁*sing*, 小心 careful.

*Sik*$_2$ as in ꜁*siu sik*$_2$ 收拾 to put in order.

*Sik*$_2$ 實 Real, true, sincere, honest: ꜀*ki sik*$_2$ 其實 truly.

꜁*Sing*, as in ꜁*tiéng* ꜁*sing*, 燈芯 a wick.

꜁*Sing*, 身 The body.

꜁*Sing*, 鋥 Rust.

꜁*Sing*, 申 3—5. P. M.

꜁*Sing*, 陞 To raise, as sedan-poles.

꜁*Sing*, 心 The mind, the understanding, the heart: ꜁*sing sëü*$^2$ 心緒 the feelings of the heart.

꜀*Sing*, 辰 7—9. A. M.

꜀*Sing*, 尋 To seek for.

꜀*Sing*, 神 A spirit: *seng*’ ꜀*sing*, 聖神 the Holy Spirit.

*Sioh*꜇ 削 To cut, as with a knife.

*Sioh*$_2$ 一 One, the whole; each, every; throughout; as soon as: *sioh*$_2$ ꜀*mang*, 一暝 yesterday.

*Siok*꜇ 雪 Snow.

*Siok*꜇ 說 To explain, to render from classical into colloquial.

꜁*Siong*, 箱 A box, a trunk.

‘*Siong*, 想 To think, to consider.

*Siong*$^2$ 上 To rise, to ascend; above; exalted, supreme:

榕腔初學撮要



*Siong*$^2$ *Táʾ* 上帝 Supreme Ruler, God.

꜀*Siu*, 收 To gather, to collect.

ʻ*Siu*, 守 To observe, to keep, as the sabbath.

*Soʾ* 數 An account, to count.

ʻ*Só*, 鎖 A lock.

*Sóh*$_2$ as in *sóh*$_2$ *nik*$_2$ 昨日 day before yesterday; *sóh*$_2$ ꜁*niéng*, 昨年 year before last.

꜀*Soi*, 衰 Poor, lean in flesh.

*Sói*$^2$ 坐 To sit.

*Sok*꜆ as in *sok*꜆ ꜀*siu*, 束脩 a teacher's stipend.

*Sok*꜆ 戌 7—9, P. M.

꜀*Song*, 痠 Aching, as from fatigue.

꜀*Song*, 酸 Sour.

꜀*Song*, 相 Mutually.

꜀*Song*, 霜 Frost.

꜀*Su*, as in ꜀*su* ꜀*i*, 蘇衣 a fine size of sewing-silk, see p. 66.

ʻ*Su*, 所 That which.

꜀*Sü*, 師 A leader, a teacher: *muk*$_2$ ꜀*sü*, 牧師 a pastor, a christian minister.

꜀*Sü*, 思 To think: ꜀*sü* ꜁*liong*, 思量 to think anxiously about.

*Sük*$_2$ 熟 Ripe; perfectly.

*Sük*$_2$ 屬 To belong to.

*Sük*$_2$ 俗 Common, ordinary.

*Sük*$_2$ 贖 To atone for; to redeem.

꜁*Sung*, 船 A boat, a junk, a ship.

꜁*Sung*, 純 Perfect.

꜀*Ta*, 乾 Dry.

ʻ*Ta*, as in ʻ*ta* ʻ*yeu*, 打擾 I have troubled you—a polite phrase.

꜁*Ta*, 茶 Tea.

꜀*Tá*, 低 Low, humble; one of the 15 initials.

ʻ*Tá*, 底 The base, the bottom: *a*$^2$ ʻ*tá*, 下底 below, beneath.

*Táʾ* 帝 An emperor.

*Tá*$^2$ 第 A series; forms the ordinal numbers.

*Tá*$^2$ 遮 To cover, to screen.

*Taëngʾ* 凍 Cold, as things.

*Taëng*$^2$ 重 Heavy; strong, as brogue.

*Taiʾ* 戴 To put or wear on the head, as cap or flowers; to wear, as ear-rings, finger-rings, bracelets.

*Taiʾ* 帶 To carry along with one.

꜁*Tai*, 臺 A platform, stage, throne.

*Tai*$^2$ 代 or *tai*$^2$ *kiéʾ* (or *iéʾ*) 代計 business, work; a matter.

*Tai*$^2$ as in *tai*$^2$ ꜀*tong*, 大中 in the center; the midst: *tai*$^2$ ꜀*i*, 大衣 a particular size of sewing-silk, see p. 66.

*Taik*꜆ 得 To obtain, to have.

*Taik*꜆ 德 Virtue, moral excellence.

*Taingʾ* 店 A shop.

*Taing*$^2$ 有 Hard, not soft; firm, tightly.

*Tak*꜆ 搭 To baste (in sewing).

*Tak*$_2$ 達 or 踏 To take uniform stitches—not in and out, not long and short.

꜀*Tang*, 伶 Now.

꜀*Tang*, 單 A bill, a receipt; single, one: ꜀*tang tó*ʾ 單到 one way; in a wrong or reverse order.

꜀*Tang*, 擔 To carry on the ends of a cooly-stick across the shoulder.

*Tang*ʾ as in *Tang*ʾ ʿ*I* ʿ*Li*, 但以理 Daniel.

*Tang*ʾ 担 A cooly-load, a burden carried on the ends of the stick across the shoulder.

*Tang*² 錯 A mistake, an error.

*Tang*² 淡 Poor, weak, as liquids; light, as a shade or color.

*Tau*ʾ 罩 A cover; midday, noon, dinner: *tóh*꜆ *tau*ʾ 棹罩 a table-cloth; *a*² *tau*ʾ 下罩 afternoon.

*Tau*² 豆 Beans.

*Tauk*꜆ 掭 To take or carry in the hands, as a chair.

*Taung*ʾ 頓 A meal.

*Taung*² 盪 To fall.

*Taung*² 斷 Interrupted, discontinued.

*Te*ʾ 智 Wise: ꜀*chiong te*ʾ 全智 all-wise.

*Te*² 地 The earth, the globe; the ground: *te*² ꜀*hwong*, 地方 a place, situation, employment; *te*² *a*² 地下 the floor, the ground.

*Tek*꜆ 滴 A drop; *met.*, a very little.

*Tek*꜆ 的 A euphonic particle; denotes completion of sense; after ʿ*chieu* 少 (a little) and ꜀*tó* 多 (much, many), it makes an adverbial sense; certainly; see pages 42 & 43.

*Tek*꜇ 値 To be worth in price.

ʿ*Teng*, 點 The stroke of a clock, an hour: ʿ*teng* ꜀*chüng*, 點鍾 o'clock.

ʿ*Teng*, as in ꜁*ká* ʿ*teng*, 崎頂 above.

*Teng*ʾ 濃 Strong, as liquids.

*Teng*ʾ 釘 To nail; to stitch.

꜁*Teng*, 還 To return (a thing), to repay; to offer a price: ꜁*teng so*ʾ 還數 to pay up an account.

*Teng*² 定 To recite by reading, as Chinese children do.

꜀*Tëng*, 東 East: ꜀*tëng* ʿ*në*, 東那 where? how?

꜀*Tëng*, 冬 Winter.

꜁*Tëng*, 銅 Brass.

꜁*Teu*, 條 A classifier.

*Tëü*² 筯 Chopsticks.

*Tëüng*ʾ 中 Suitable, fit: *tëüng*ʾ *e*ʾ 中意 pleased with.

꜀*Ti*, 知 To know: ꜀*t'ung* ꜀*ti*, 通知 to inform one.

꜁*Ti*, 遲 Late.

꜀*Tiă*, 爹 A father: ʿ*ló* ꜀*tiă*, 老爹 an officer.

ʿ*Tiăng*, 鼎 A frying-pan.

꜁*Tiăng*, 埕 To add or pour in (more water).

*Tiăng²* 定 Steady, fixed, certain: *tiăng²* ꜀*kang*, 定更 the first watch of the night.

ʿ*Tiĕ*, 入 To enter.

ʿ*Tiĕ*, 裡 In, within, inside: ʿ*tiĕ tiĕ*ʾ (*siĕ*ʾ) 裡勢 within.

*Tiĕ²* 俤 An interrogative pronoun, preceding a noun or classifier, which? what?

*Tiĕ²* 弟 A younger brother.

*Tiĕk*₂ 碟 A saucer, a small plate.

꜀*Tiĕng*, as in ꜀*tiĕng* ꜀*sing*, 燈芯 a wick.

ʿ*Tiĕng*, 點 To light, as lamps.

ʿ*Tiĕng*, as in ʿ*tiĕng* ꜀*sing*, 點心 tiffin, lunch.

*Tiĕng²* 滝 Full.

*Tih*₂ 値 To wish: ꜁*mó tih*₂ 毛値 not wish, to reject.

*Tik*₂ 直 Straight: *ek*ʾ *tik*₂ 一直 straight ahead; *tik*₂ *t'au*ʾ 直透 straight through.

꜀*Ting*, as in ꜀*ting* ʿ*ma*, 燈馮 a lamp.

ʿ*Ting*, 頂 Very; a classifier; to wait, to delay.

꜁*Ting*, 澄 To settle, to become clear, as water.

꜁*Ting*, 停 To rest, to stop.

ʿ*Tio*, 貯 To contain, to hold.

*Tio²* 路 A road, a path.

*Tioh*₂ 灼 To kindle, kindled.

*Tioh*₂ 着 To be at or in, to be present; ought, must; marks completion of action, as also attainment of a certain state or condition: *ng² tioh*₂ 怀着 not right.

ʿ*Tiong*, 轉 To turn, to return home; to do by proxy, to pass over to another.

*Tiong*ʾ 帳 A bed-curtain.

꜁*Tiong*, 傳 To proclaim; to be reported or noised abroad.

*Tiong²* 剩 To be over, residual, there remains.

ʿ*Tiu*, 肘 To place by, up to.

꜁*Tiu*, 棡 A closet, a cupboard.

꜀*Tó*, 刀 A knife.

꜀*Tó*, 多 Much, many, more, mostly: ꜀*tó* ꜁*tong*, 多長 dear, expensive, extravagant.

ʿ*Tó*, 倒 To fall, a fall; to lie down.

*Tó*ʾ 倒 To pour, to empty out.

*Tó*ʾ as in ꜁*seng tó*ʾ (or *nó*ʾ) 前到 time, occasion.

꜁*Tó*, 掏 To take, to carry.

*Tó²* 道 A path, road; doctrine: *tó²* ꜁*t'au*, 道頭 a wharf, landing.

*Tóh*ʾ 桌 A table.

꜀*Toi*, 堆 A multitude, mass: ꜀*toi* ꜀*sang*, 堆山 a large quantity.

ʿ*Toi*, 短 Short (in length).

*Tói*ʾ 塊 A piece; a place; a dollar; a classifier.

*Tói*ʾ 對 To pair, to match: *tói*ʾ *meng*ʾ 對面 the opposite side, opposite to.

*Tok*ʾ 篤 To light, as a lamp.

꜀*Tong*, as in ꜁*mó* ꜀*tang* ꜀*tong*, 毛擋當 cannot.

꜀*Tong*, 中 In the midst of.

ʻ*Tong*, 漲 To rise, as the tide.

ʻ*Tong*, 党 To buy, as piece-goods.

꜀*Tong*, 長 Long in time or measure; more, exceeding: *pwang*ʼ ꜀*tong*, 半長 a half-length.

꜀*Tong*, 堂 A temple; a mansion.

*Tong*$^{2}$ 動 To move, to excite: ʻ*kang tong*$^{2}$ 感動 to move, to influence (the mind), as the Holy Spirit does.

*Tong*$^{2}$ 炖 To cook or heat in an inner tube or vessel.

꜀*Tu*, 都 All, altogether, wholly.

ʻ*Tu*, 堵 A section, a panel.

꜀*Tü*, 除 To destroy, to banish.

*Tük*$_{2}$ 逐 To pursue: *tük*$_{2}$ *mä*$^{2}$ *tioh*$_{2}$ 逐賣着 cannot overtake (him).

꜀*Tung*, 同 Together, alike: ꜀*Tung te*$^{2}$ 同治 the present Emperor of China (1871).

꜀*Tüng*, 中 The middle, the center, in the middle of; medium: ꜀*Tüng Kwok*꜁ 中國 China; ꜀*tüng* ʻ*só*, 中鎖 a certain size of sewing silk, see p. 66.

꜀*Tüng*, as in ꜀*tüng haiu*$^{2}$ 忠厚 honest, unselfish, faithful.

*Twai*$^{2}$ 大 Large, great; much; full and quick, as the pulse.

꜀*T'a*, 他 One of the 15 initials.

ʻ*T'á*, 體 The body.

*T'á*ʼ 替 To substitute, for, instead of, in behalf of.

*T'á*ʼ 櫃 A drawer.

*T'ah*꜁ 潔 Clean, pure.

꜀*T'ai*, 刣 To kill; to skin, as a pomelo.

*T'aik*꜁ 貼 To paste up or on.

*T'ak*$_{2}$ 疊 To pile up.

ʻ*T'au*, as in ʻ*t'au tóh*꜁ (*t'óh*꜁) 抖托 well, free from illness.

*T'au*ʼ 透 To pass through, throughout, extending to; to blow strong or fresh.

꜀*T'au*, 頭 The head, the first, the beginning.

*T'auk*꜁ 託 To intrust to, to rely on.

*T'auk*꜁ as in *t'auk*꜁ ʻ*t'á*, 脫體 to recover from sickness.

*T'ëk*$_{2}$ 讀 To read aloud, to study.

ʻ*T'eng*, perhaps a corruption of ʻ*heng*, 很 very, exceedingly.

*T'eng*ʼ 趁 By, through.

*T'eng*ʼ 賺 To gain, to earn.

꜀*T'eng*, 沉 Sunk, low, weak.

꜀*T'ëng*, 通 Ought, must.

ʻ*T'ëng*, 桶 A pail, bucket, tub.

꜀*T'iäng*, 聽 To hear, to listen; to obey, to understand.

*T'iäng*ʼ 痛 To ache, to be in pain.

*T'iäng*ʼ 愛 To love.

꜀*T'iéng*, 天 Heaven, heavenly; the sky, the weather; a season of the year: ꜀*t'iéng* ꜀*tong*, 天堂 heaven.

꜀*T'iéng*, 添 To add to.

*T'iéng*ʼ 紩 To sew.

ʻ*T'io*, as in ʻ*t'io taung*ʼ 妥當 trusty.

ʻ*T'iu*, 丑 1—3 A.M.

꜀*T'ó*, 叨 To feel deeply grateful, as in ꜀*t'ó hok*꜆ 叨福 very thankful for the benefit, blessed with your favor!

꜂*T'ó*, 討 To seek, to ask for; to aim to effect; to induce, to bring on one's self, as punishment, etc.

*T'ó*꜄ 套 To put under, as a piece in patching.

*T'óh*꜆ the same as ꜂*pieu* 表 to bring out (a disease).

*T'ói*꜄ 退 To withdraw, to subside; to extinguish (fire) by removing (the wood).

꜀*T'ong*, 湯 Hot water; soup, broth.

꜁*T'ong*, 糖 Sugar.

꜂*T'u*, 凸 To thrust in, to put in.

꜁*T'u*, 土 Earth, mud.

꜀*T'ung*, 通 To go through: ꜀*t'ung* ꜀*ti*, 通知 to inform; ꜀*t'ung* ꜁*heng*, 通行 current, as coin or doctrine.

꜀*T'wa*, 拖 To drag.

꜀*U*, 烏 Black, dark.

꜂*U*, a contraction of ꜂*ku*, 古 q.v.

꜁*U*, 無 No, not, none.

꜂*Ü*, 雨 Rain.

꜀*Wa*, 劃 To scratch, to rub, as a match.

꜂*Wa*, 躠 To turn aside, to call at on one's way.

*Wa*² 話 Words, language: *wa*² ꜂*ngü*, 話語 language, speech.

꜀*Wang*, 彎 To bend, to curve; to turn.

꜂*Wang*, 碗 A bowl, dishes.

*Wang*꜄ probably a corruption of *ang*꜄ 暗 dark.

*Wang*² 換 To exchange, to change.

*Wang*² 萬 A myriad; 10,000.

*Woh*꜆ 沃 To water; to baste, as meat.

*Wok*꜇ 越 a sign of the comparative, the more, increasingly.

꜁*Wong*, 完 To finish, finished; wholly, entirely, perfectly.

꜁*Wong*, 黃 The yolks of eggs.

*Wong*² 望 To hope, to expect, to desire.

*Wong*² 旺 To flourish.

꜂*Yă*, 野 Extremely, very: ꜂*yă o*² 野務 somewhat, tolerably.

꜁*Yă*, 耶 as in ꜁*Yă* ꜀*Su*, 耶穌 Jesus; ꜁*Yă* ꜁*Hwo* ꜁*Hwa*, 耶和華 Jehovah.

*Yă*² 也 Also, moreover.

꜂*Yăng*, 引 To receive, to get, to contract by exposure.

*Yĕk*꜇ 熱 Warm, hot.

*Yeu*꜄ as in *yeu*꜄ ꜂*king*, 要緊 important.

*Yoh*꜇ 藥 Medicine.

*Yok*꜆ as in *yok*꜆ *liok*꜇ 約略 about so much, about that.

꜂*Yong*, 養 To nourish; to improve, as one's heart.

꜁*Yong*, 羊 A goat.

*Yong*² 樣 Manner.

*Yong*² 件 A classifier of wide application: *yong*² *yong*² 件件 all, everything.

# PART VII.

## ENGLISH AND CHINESE VOCABULARY.

This Vocabulary comprises merely a selection from the more common English words, and usually but one or two simple colloquial equivalents for each word. The list, however, is partially supplemented by the numerous words occurring in the preceding part of the Manual, which may be found by headings of subjects.

The general plan and design of the volume also preclude a very minute discrimination in usages of words. The student should be particularly guarded on this point, the importance of which is noticed on pages 48 & 49. For fuller renderings and distinctions in meaning, reference may be readily made by the Romanized words to the Alphabetic Dictionary of the Foochow Dialect.

———:o:———

### A

A, an, 一 *sioh*$_2$ or *ek*$_)$.
Abacus, 算盤 *saungʼ ꜁pwang.*
Ability, 本事 *ʻpwong sëü*$^2$.
Able, 𠊎 *á*$^2$, 能 *꜁neng.*
Abominable, 可惡 *ʻk'ó oʼ.*
Above, 崎頂 *꜁ká ʻteng,* 上 *siong*$^2$.
Absent, 毛着禮 *꜁mó tioh*$_2$ *ʻlá.*
Accompany, 齊去 *꜁chá k'óʼ.*
According to, 憑 *꜁ping,* 照 *chieuʼ.*
Account, n. 數 *soʼ.*
Accuse, 告 *kóʼ.*
Accustomed, 慣 *kaingʼ,* 熟 *sük*$_2$.
Ache, 痛 *t'iăngʼ*; 疼 *꜀song.*
Acid, 酸 *꜀song.*
Acknowledge, 認 *neng*$^2$.
Acrid, 辣 *lak*$_2$.
Across, 横 *꜁hwang.*
Actions, 行 *haing*$^2$.
Active, 活 *wak*$_2$ 活動 *wak*$_2$ *tong*$^2$.
Add, 加 *꜀ka,* 添 *꜀t'iéng.*
Adieu, (walk slowly!) 慢行 *maing*$^2$ *꜁kiăng.*
Adopted, 誼 *ngié*$^2$, 契 *k'iéʼ.*
Adultery, 姦淫 *꜀kang ꜁ing.*
Advance, v. 行前 *꜁kiăng ꜁seng.*
Advent, as of Christ, 降世 *kaungʼ siéʼ.*
Advise, 勸 *k'wongʼ.*
Affair, 代 *tai*$^2$, 事 *sëü*$^2$.
Afflictions, 患難 *hwang*$^2$ *nang*$^2$.
Afraid, 驚 *꜀kiăng.*
Africa, 亞非利加 *ʻA ꜀hi le*$^2$ *꜀ka.*
After, 後 *haiu*$^2$ or *au*$^2$.
Afternoon, 下晝 *a*$^2$ *tauʼ.*
Again, 再 *kaiʼ,* 佊 *po*$^2$.
Agate, 瑪瑙 *ʻma ʻnó.*
Age, (one's) 年歲 *꜁niéng hwoiʼ.*

Agriculture, 耕種 ꜀keng chëüng꜄.
Ague, 柏腹寒 p'ah꜆ pok꜆ ꜁kang.
Air, n. 氣 k'e꜄, 風 ꜀hung.
Alive, 活 wak꜇.
All, 都 ꜀tu, 攏總 ꜂lung ꜂chung.
Allow, 容 ꜁üng, 准 ꜂chung.
Almanac, 王曆 ꜁wong lik꜇ 通書 ꜀t'ung ꜀chü.
Almond, 杏仁 haing꜅ ꜁ing.
Almost, 差不多 ꜀ch'a pok꜆ ꜀tó.
Alms, (to give) 施濟 sië꜄ chá꜄.
Aloes, 蘆薈 ꜁lu kwoi꜄.
Alone, 獨獨 tuk꜇ tuk꜇.
Also, 也 yă꜅.
Altar, 壇 ꜁tang.
Although, 雖然 ꜀c'hwi ꜁yong.
Alum, 礬 ꜁hwang.
Always, 時常 ꜁si ꜁siong.
Amber, 琥珀 ꜂hu p'aëk꜆.
America, 亞美利駕 ꜂A ꜂mi le꜅ ka꜄.
Amiable, 好愛 ꜂hó t'iăng꜄.
Among, 中間 ꜀tüng ꜀kang.
Amount to, 應管 eng꜄ ꜂kwang.
Ancestor, 祖宗 ꜂chu ꜀chung.
Anchor, n. 矴 teng꜄.
Ancient, 古早 ꜂ku ꜂cha.
And, 連 ꜁liéng, 零 ꜁ling.
Angel, 天使 ꜀t'iéng sëü꜄.
Angle, n. 角 kaëk꜆.
Angry, 受氣 seu꜅ k'e꜄, 使性 ꜂sai sang꜄.
Ankle, 骹牛目 ꜀k'a ꜁ngu mĕk꜇.
Annoy, 吵 ꜂ch'au, 吵擾 ꜂ch'au ꜂yeu.
Another, 別隻 pek꜇ chiăh꜆.
Answer, 應 eng꜄.
Ant, 螻蟻 ꜀ëng ngië꜅.
Antecedents, 來歷 ꜁lai lik꜇.
Anvil, 鐵砧 t'iëk꜆ ꜂tong.
Anxious, 慮 lëü꜅.
Ape, n. 猴 ꜁kau.
Appear, 出現 ch'ok꜆ hiéng꜅.
Appoint, 立 lik꜇ 封 ꜀hung.
Apprentice, 徒弟 ꜁tu tá꜅.
Apricot, 青仔 ꜀ch'ang ꜂kiăng.
Apron, 圍身裙 ꜁ui ꜀sing ꜁kung.
Arithmetic, 算學 saung꜄ hok꜇.
Arm, n. 手臂 ꜂ch'iu pié꜄.
Army, 軍營 ꜀kung ꜁yăng.
Arouse, 撥醒 pwak꜆ ꜂ch'ang.
Arrange, 排 ꜁pá.
Arrive, 至 kau꜄.
Arrow, 箭矢 chiéng꜄ ꜂ch'i.
Arsenic, 信 seng꜄, 人言 ꜁ing ꜁ngiong.
Ascend, 上 siong꜅.
Ashamed, 羞禮 ꜂sieu ꜂lá.
Ashes, 火灰 ꜂hwi ꜀hu.
Asia, 亞細亞 ꜂A sá꜄ ꜂a.
Ask, 問 mwong꜄.
Ass, 驢 ꜁lë.
Assembly, 會 hwoi꜅.
Assort, 類 loi꜅.
Asthma, 痚疾 ꜀heu chik꜇.
Astonished, 錯愕 ch'auk꜆ ngauk꜆.
Astronomy, 天文 ꜀t'iéng ꜁ung.
Asylum, (foundling) 養育堂 ꜂yong ük꜇ ꜁tong.
Authority, 權柄 ꜁kwong pang꜄.

Autumn, 秋天 ꜀ch'iu ꜀t'iéng.
Avoid, 避 pié$^{2}$, 免 ‘miéng.
Awake, 清醒 ꜀ch'ing ‘ch'ang.
Awl, 鉾 chaung’.
Ax, 斧頭 ‘p'wo ꜁t'au.

**B.**

Back, n. 背 ꜀p'iăng or pwoi’.
Bad, 呆 ꜁ngai, 惡 auk꜆.
Bag, 袋 tói$^{2}$, 囊 ꜁nong.
Baggage, 行李 ꜁heng ‘li.
Bail, (as of bucket) 扣 kwang$^{2}$.
Bait, 餌 ne’.
Bake, 熬 ngó$^{2}$.
Ball, n. 球 ꜁kiu, 丸 ꜁wong, (cannon-) 鉛子 ꜁yong ‘chi.
Balustrade, 欄檮 ꜁lang ꜁tó.
Bamboo, 竹 tëük꜆.
Banian, 榕槕 ꜁süng ch'eu’.
Banish, 們非 mwong’ chói$^{2}$.
Bank, (river) 岸 ngiăng$^{2}$, (for money) 錢店 ꜁chiéng taing’.
Baptism, 洗禮 ‘sá ‘lá.
Bark, n. 皮 ꜁p'uí.
Bark, v. (as dogs) 吠 poi$^{2}$.
Barley, 大麥 twai$^{2}$ mah꜆ (pearl-) 薏苡 e’ ‘mi.
Barometer, 風雨針 ꜀hung ‘ü ꜀cheng.
Barrel, (cask) 楻 ꜁k'wong.
Basin, (earthen) 砵 pwak꜆.
Basket, 籃 ꜁lang, 筙 ꜁lai.
Bat, 枇杷豈蒸 ꜁pi ꜁pa tau$^{2}$ kiék꜆ 蝙蝠 ‘piéng hok꜆.
Be, 是 se$^{2}$.
Bead, 珠 ꜀chio.
Bean, 荳 tau$^{2}$.
Beard, 鬚 ꜀sü.
Bearer, (sedan-) 轎夫 kieu$^{2}$ ꜀hu.
Beast, 獸 seu’, 頭牲 ꜁t'au ꜀sang.
Beautiful, 好看 ‘hó k'ang’ 生的好 ꜀sang tek꜆ ‘hó.
Because, 因 ꜀ing, 因爲 ꜀ing oi$^{2}$.
Beche-de-mer, 海参 ‘hai ꜀seng.
Bedding, 鋪蓋 ꜀p'wo kai’.
Bedstead, 眠床 ꜁ming ꜁ch'ong.
Bee, 蜂 ꜀p'ung.
Beef, 牛肉 ꜁ngu nük꜇.
Before, (in time) 先 ꜀seng.
Beg, 求 ꜁kiu.
Beget, 生 ꜀sang, 養 ‘yong.
Beggar, 乞食 k'ëük꜆ siăh꜇.
Begin, 起手 ‘k'i ‘ch'iu.
Beginning, 起頭 ‘k'i ꜁t'au.
Behead, 刣頭 ꜁t'ai ꜁t'au.
Behind, (in place) 後斗 a$^{2}$ ‘tau.
Believe, 信 seng’.
Bell, 鍾 ꜀chüng, (small hand-) 鈴鈴 ꜀ling ꜀ling.
Belly, 腹老 pok꜆ ‘ló, 腹 pok꜆.
Below, 下 a$^{2}$ 下底 a$^{2}$ ‘tá.
Bench, 椅條 ‘ié ꜁teu.
Bend, v. 拗彎 ‘a ꜀wang.
Benevolence, 恩德 ꜀ong taik꜆.
Bent, 彎 ꜀wang, 曲 k'woh꜆.
Betelnut, 梹榔 ꜀ping ꜁long.
Betroth, 做親 chó’ ꜀ch'ing.
Between, 大中 tai$^{2}$ ꜀tong, 中間 ꜀tüng ꜀kang.
Beyond, 外 ngié$^{2}$ or ngwoi$^{2}$.
Bible, 聖經 seng’ ꜀king.
Bile, 膽 ‘tang.
Bird, 鳥 ‘cheu.

Birthday, 生日 ꜀sang nik$_2$.
Bite, 咬 ka$^2$.
Bitter, 苦 ꜂k‘u.
Black, 烏 ꜀u, 大青 twai$^2$ ꜀ch‘ang.
Blame, v. 責 chaik꜆.
Blaspheme, 褻瀆 siĕk꜆ tuk$_2$.
Bleach, 漂白 p‘ieu꜄ pah$_2$.
Bleat, 咩 máh꜆.
Blind, 青盲 ꜀ch‘ang ꜁mang.
Blinds, 簾 ꜁liéng, (venetians) 鱟頁門 hau꜄ hiăk$_2$ ꜁mwong.
Blood, 血 haik꜆.
Blow, (as the wind) 吹 ꜀ch‘wi, (with the mouth) 嗙 ꜁pung.
Blue, 藍 ꜁lang.
Board, n. 板 ꜂peng.
Boast, 誇 ꜀k‘wa.
Boat, 船 ꜁sung.
Body, 身 ꜀sing, 肉身 nŭk$_2$ ꜀sing.
Boil, v. 滾 ꜂kung, 煮 ꜂chü, 煞 sak$_2$.
Boils, hwong꜄ 瘡 ꜀ch‘ong.
Bolt, n. 閂 ch‘aung꜄.
Bone, 骨 kauk꜆.
Book, 書 ꜀chü.
Boot, 靴 ꜀k‘wo.
Bore, 鋑 lói꜄ 銇 lói$^2$.
Borrow, 借 chioh꜆.
Bottle, 瓶 ꜁ping.
Bottom, 底 ꜂tá.
Bow, (mil. weapon) 弓 ꜀kŭng.
Bow the head, 俓頭 k‘iăng꜄ ꜁t‘au.
Bowl, 碗 ꜂wang.
Box, n. 箱 ꜀siong, (small) 盒 ak$_2$.
Boy, 唐哺仔 ꜁tong ꜀pwo ꜂kiăng.
Bracelet, 手鐲 ꜂ch‘iu sóh$_2$.
Braid, n. 辮線 piéng$^2$ siăng꜄.
Brain, 頭腦 ꜁t‘au ꜂nó.
Branch, 枝 ngá$^2$ ⿰木臭枝 ch‘eu꜄ ngá$^2$.
Brass, 銅 ꜁tëng.
Bread, 包 ꜀pau.
Break, 拍破 p‘ah꜆ p‘wai꜄.
Breath, 氣 k‘e꜄.
Breed, n. 種 ꜂chŭng.
Bribe, 買囑 ꜂má chëŭk꜆ 賄賂 ꜂wí lo$^2$.
Brick, 磚 ꜀chiong.
Bride, 新人 ꜀sing ꜁ing.
Bridegroom, 新郎 ꜀sing ꜁long.
Bridge, 橋 ꜁kio.
Briers, 莿草 ch‘ié꜄ ꜂ch‘au.
Bright, 光 ꜀kwong, 明 ꜁ming.
Brimstone, 硫磺 ꜁liu ꜁hwong.
Bring, 掏來 ꜁tó ꜁li.
Brittle, 脆 ch‘wói꜄.
Broad, 闊 k‘wak꜆.
Brood, 菢 po$^2$.
Broom, 掃箒 sau꜄ ꜂ch‘iu.
Brother, 兄弟 ꜀hiăng tié$^2$.
Brown, 紫 ꜂chié.
Brush, 刷 sauk꜆, 拂 hok꜆.
Bucket, 桶 ꜂t‘ëng.
Bud, v. 發芽 pwok꜆ ꜁nga.
Budh, 佛 huk$_2$.
Build, 起 ꜂k‘i.
Bundle, 包 ꜀pau, 把 ꜂pa, 包袱 ꜀pau huk$_2$.
Burden, 担 tang꜄.
Burn, 燒 ꜀sieu and ꜁hang.
Burst, 剝 pauk꜆.
Bury, 埋 ꜁mai, 葬 chaung꜄.

Business, 代計 tai$^{2}$ ié꜄ 事 sëü$^{2}$.
Bustle, 鬧熱 nau$^{2}$ yék$_{2}$.
Butt, v. 觝 taëk꜆.
Butter, 牛乳油 ꜁ngu ꜁neng ꜁iu.
Butterfly, 蚨蝶 ꜁hu tiék$_{2}$.
Button, 鈕 k‘aiu꜄, (of a cap) 帽頂 mó$^{2}$ ꜂ting.
Buy, 買 ꜂má.

## C

Cabbage, 白菜 pah$_{2}$ ch‘ai꜄.
Cage, 籠 ꜁lëng.
Cake, 餅 ꜂piăng, 糕 ꜀kó, (steamed) 粿 ꜂kwi.
Calamity, 災 ꜀chai, 禍 hwo$^{2}$.
Calico, (figured) 花布 ꜀hwa pwo꜄.
Call, v. 叫 kieu꜄ and ꜂hau.
Camel, 駱駝 lok$_{2}$ ꜁tó.
Camellia, 茶花 ꜁ta ꜀hwa.
Camlet, 羽毛 ꜂ü ꜁mó.
Camphor, (gum) 樟腦 ꜀chiong ꜂nó.
Can, 儺 á$^{2}$ 務擔當 o$^{2}$ ꜀tang ꜀tong.
Canal, 河 ꜁ó.
Candle, 燭 chioh꜆.
Cangue, n. & v. 枷 ꜁kiă.
Canister, 罌 ꜀ing.
Cannon, 炮 p‘au꜄ 銃 ch‘ëüng꜄.
Cannot, 賣 má$^{2}$, 毛擔當 ꜁mó ꜀tang ꜀tong.
Cap, 帽 mó$^{2}$.
Cardinal points, 四方 sëü꜄ ꜀hwong.
Careful, 細膩 sá꜄ ne$^{2}$, 小心 ꜂sieu ꜀sing, 細心 sá꜄ ꜀sing.
Carpenter, 木司傅 muk$_{2}$ ꜀sa ho$^{2}$.

Carpet, 地毡 te$^{2}$ ꜀chiéng, 毯 ꜂t‘ang.
Carry, 掏 ꜁tó, 抱 pó$^{2}$, (on ends of a stick) 擔 ꜀tang, (between two) 扛 ꜀kong, (on the back) 邁 mai$^{2}$.
Carve, 雕 ꜀teu, 刻 k‘aik꜆.
Cash, 錢 ꜁chiéng.
Casket, 盒 ak$_{2}$ 寶盒 ꜂pó ak$_{2}$.
Cassia, 桂 kié꜄.
Cast, (mold or found) 鑄 chio꜄.
Castor-oil, 蓖蔴油 ꜀pi ꜁mwai ꜁iu.
Cat, 貓 ꜁ma, 貓仔 ꜁ma ꜂kiăng.
Cataract, (surg.) 上翳 siong$^{2}$ ié꜄.
Catty, 觔 ꜀kŭng.
Cauliflower, 芥藍花 kai꜄ ꜁lang ꜀hwa.
Cause, v. 使 ꜂sai.
Cauterize, 灸 ko꜄.
Ceiling, 倒仰 tó꜄ ꜂ngiong.
Centipede, 蜈蚣 ꜁ëng ꜁ëng.
Certain, 定着 tiăng$^{2}$ tioh$_{2}$.
Chaff, 粗糠 ꜀ch‘u ꜀k‘ong.
Chain, 鍊 liéng$^{2}$.
Chair, 椅 ꜂ié.
Chamber, 房裏 ꜁pung ꜂tié.
Change, v. 換 wăng$^{2}$ 變 piéng꜄.
Chapter, 章 ꜀chiong.
Character, (word) 字 che$^{2}$.
Charcoal, 炭 t‘ang꜄.
Charms, (written) 符 ꜁hu.
Chaste, 貞節 ꜀ting chiék꜆.
Chat, v. 冇講 p‘ang꜄ ꜂kong.
Cheap, 便宜 ꜁peng ꜁ngié, 賤 siăng$^{2}$.

Cheek, 面頰 *meng꜄ ꜂p‘á.*
Chess, 象棋 *ch‘iong² ꜁ki.*
Chestnut, 栗子 *lik꜇ ꜂chi.*
Chicken-pox, 水珠 *꜂chwi ꜀chio.*
Child, 伲仔 *niē² ꜂kiăng.*
Chimney, 烟筒 *꜀yéng ꜁tĕng.*
Chin, 下頦 *a² ꜁pa* or *a² ꜁hai.*
China-aster, 菊花 *kĕük꜆ ꜀hwa.*
China-root, 茯苓 *huk꜇ ꜁ling.*
Chips, 柴配 *꜁ch‘a p‘woi꜄.*
Chisel, 鑿 *ch‘ĕk꜇.*
Choke, 骾 *꜂kang.*
Cholera, 病吐瀉 *pang² t‘o꜄ siă꜄.*
Choose, 揀 *꜂keng.*
Chopsticks, 筯 *tĕü².*
Christ, 基督 *꜀Ki Tok꜆.*
Christianity, 耶穌教 *꜁Yă ꜀su kau꜄.*
Church, 教會 *kau꜄ hwoi²* 聖會 *seng꜄ hwoi²* (building) 禮拜堂 *꜂lá pai꜄ ꜁tong.*
Cinnamon, 桂皮 *kiē꜄ ꜁p‘uí.*
Circle, 環 *꜁k‘wang.*
City, 城 *꜁siăng.*
Clamor, 囉嘈 *꜁ló ꜁chó.*
Clamp, 鉗 *꜁k‘i.*
Class, n. 類 *loi²* 等 *꜂teng,* 班 *꜀pang.*
Classic, 經 *꜀king.*
Classify, 類 *loi².*
Clean, *t‘ah꜆* 他格 *t‘ah꜆ kaik꜆.*
Clear, 清 *꜀ch‘ing,* 明 *꜁ming.*
Clever, 聰明 *꜀ch‘ung ꜁ming,* 伶俐 *꜁ling le².*
Climate, 水土 *꜂chwi ꜂t‘u.*
Climb, 扒上 *꜁pa siong².*

Clock, 鐘 *꜀chŭng,* 自鳴鐘 *chĕü² ꜁ming ꜀chŭng.*
Cloth, 布 *pwo꜄,* (woolen) 呢 *꜁ni.*
Clothes, 衣裳 *꜀i ꜁siong.*
Cloud, 雲 *꜁hung.*
Clove, 丁香 *꜀ting ꜀hiong.*
Club, (stick) 棍 *kong꜄.*
Coagulate, 凝 *ngik꜇.*
Coal, (fossil) 煤炭 *꜁muí t‘ang꜄.*
Coarse, 粗 *꜀ch‘u.*
Cockroach, 咬蜈 *ka² sak꜇ (lak꜇),* (large) 蜈蝴 *sak꜇ ꜂mó.*
Cocoon, 蠶繭絲 *꜁ch‘eng ꜂keng ꜀si.*
Coffin, 棺材 *꜀kwang ꜁ch‘ai.*
Cold, (med.) 風寒 *꜀hung ꜁hang.*
Cold, a. 凊 *ch‘eng꜄,* 凍 *taĕng꜄.*
Colic, 痧 *꜀sa,* 着痧 *tioh꜇ ꜀sa.*
Collar, 領 *꜂liăng.*
Colloquial, 平話 *꜁pang wa².*
Color, 色 *saik꜆* 顏色 *꜁ngang saik꜆.*
Comb, n. 頭梳 *꜁t‘au ꜀sĕ,* (fine) 篦梳 *pe² ꜀sĕ.*
Come, 來 *꜁li.*
Comfort, 安慰 *꜀ang oi꜄.*
Commandment, 誡 *kai꜄,* 命令 *meng² leng².*
Common, 平常 *꜁pang ꜁siong.*
Communion, 心交 *꜀sing ꜀kau.*
Company, 陣 *teng².*
Compare, 比併 *꜂pi p‘iăng².*
Compel, 干 *꜀kang* or *꜀ang.*
Complete, a. 全 *꜁chiong,* 十分 *sek꜇ ꜀hung.*

MAN. 29.



榕腔初學撮要

Compliments, 請安 ʻch'iăng ꜀ang.
Comprador, 買辦 ʻmá paing².
Concave, 凹裏 nah꜆ (náh꜆) ʻtié.
Concern, concernment, 干過 ꜀kang kwo꜄, 干涉 ꜀kang siék꜇.
Concubine, 細婆 sá꜄ ꜁pó.
Condemn, 定罪 tiăng² chói².
Confer, (bestow) 賜 sëü꜄.
Confess, 認 neng².
Confiscate, 沒官 muk꜇ ꜀kwang.
Congee, 粥 chëük꜆ (thin) 泔 ʻang.
Congratulate, 拱喜 ʻküng ʻhi.
Conquer, 贏 ꜁yăng.
Conscience, 良心 ꜁liong ꜀sing.
Consequences, 關係 ꜀kwang hié².
Constipation, 積宿 chek꜆ sëük꜆.
Consul, 領事 ʻliăng sëü².
Consult, 商量 ꜀song ꜁liong.
Consumption, 跌痨 t'iék꜇ ꜁ló.
Contagious, 傳染 ꜁tiong ʻniéng, 倠過 á² kwo꜄.
Contain, 包 ꜀pau, 貯 ʻtio.
Contract, 約 yok꜆ (shorten) 縮短 t'ëük꜆ ʻtoi.
Contribute, (money) 捐 ꜀kiong.
Convenient, 便 piéng².
Convert, 感化 ʻkang hwa꜄, 變化 piéng꜄ hwa꜄.
Convex, 窩窩 ꜀wo ꜀wo.
Cool, a. 凉 ꜁liong.
Cool, v. 凉凍 ꜁liăng taëng꜄.
Coolie, 擔扁擔索 ꜀tó ꜀peng ꜀tang sóh꜆.
Copper, 銅 ꜁tëng.
Copperas, 生礬 ꜀ch'ang ꜁hwang.
Copy, n. 稿 ʻkó.
Copy, v. 抄 ꜀ch'au, 盤 ꜁pwang.
Coral, 珊瑚 ꜀tang ꜁hu.
Cord, 索 sóh꜆ (small) 線 siăng꜄.
Cork, (stopple) 塞 sek꜆.
Corner, 角 kaëk꜆.
Corpse, 身屍 ꜀sing ꜀si.
Cotton, 棉花 ꜁miéng ꜀hwa.
Cough, 嗽 sau꜄.
Count, 數 so꜄ 點 ʻteng.
Country, 國 kwok꜆ (the) 鄉下 ꜀hiong a².
Court, (law) 官堂頂 ꜀kwang ꜁tong ʻting.
Cover, v. k'aing꜄ 遮 ꜀chiă.
Covet, 貪 ꜀t'ang.
Cow, 牛㸬 ꜁ngu ʻmó.
Cowardly, 膽小 ʻtang ʻsieu.
Coxcomb, 雞髻 ꜀kié kwoi꜄.
Crab, 蟹 há² 蟳 ꜁sing, 蠘 ch'iék꜇ (small land-) 蟛蜞 ꜁p'ang ꜁k'i.
Crack, n. & v. i. 𡽶 pek꜆.
Crane, 鶴 hok꜇.
Crape, 縐紗 chaiu꜄ ꜀sa.
Create, 創造 ch'aung꜄ chó² 造化 chó² hwa꜄.
Creator, 造化其主 chó² hwa꜄ ꜁ki ʻchio.
Creek, 浦 ʻp'wo.
Creep, 扒 ꜁pa.
Crevice, 隙 p'ong꜄ or ꜁p'ung p'ong꜄.
Cricket, 蟋蟀 sek꜆ sauk꜆.
Crisp, 酥 ꜀su, 脆 ch'woi꜄.
Crockery, 硋器 ꜁hai k'e꜄.

榕腔初學撮要

**Crooked**, 彎 ꜀wang, 曲 k'woh꜄.
**Crop**, (of fowls, birds) 腒 ꜀kai.
**Cross**, n. 十字架 sek$_2$ che$^2$ ka꜃.
**Crosswise**, 橫 ꜁hwang, or ꜂ta ꜀lang ꜁hwang.
**Crouch**, 蹲 ꜁ch'iong, or ꜁ku ꜀tung ꜁ch'iong.
**Crow**, (ornith.) 老鴉 ꜂lô ꜀wa.
**Crowd**, v. 尅 k'aik꜄.
**Cruet-stand**, 椒料架 ꜀chieu laiu$^2$ ka꜃.
**Crust**, 皮 ꜁p'ui, 殼 k'aĕk꜄.
**Cry**, v. 啼 ꜁t'ié, 啼嘛 ꜁t'ié ꜁ma.
**Crystal**, 水晶 ꜂chwi ꜀ching.
**Cucumber**, 菜瓜 ch'ai꜃ ꜀kwa.
**Cue**, 頭髮辮 ꜁t'au hwok꜄ piéng$^2$.
**Cuff**, n. 袖頭 ꜂wong ꜁t'au.
**Cup**, 杯 ꜀pwi, 甌 ꜀eu.
**Curd**, (bean-) 荳腐 tau$^2$ hô$^2$.
**Curiosities**, 古董 ꜂ku ꜂tung.
**Current**, a. 通行 ꜀t'ung ꜁heng.
**Curse**, v. 詛 cho꜃.
**Curtain**, 簾 ꜁liéng, (bed-) 帳 tiong꜃.
**Cushion**, 褥 ük$_2$ 墊 taing$^2$.
**Custom**, 風俗 ꜀hung sük$_2$ (tribute) 稅 swoi꜃.
**Cut**, 割 kak꜄ 削 sioh꜄ 裁 ꜁choi, (with shears) ꜀ka, 剪 ꜂cheng.
**Cymbals**, 鈸 pwak$_2$.

# D

**Daily**, 日日 nik$_2$ nik$_2$.
**Damp**, 濕 nong꜃.
**Dangerous**, 危 ꜁ngui.
**Dare**, v. i. 敢 ꜂kang.
**Dark**, (as night) 暗 ang꜃.
**Darn**, 繡 seu꜃, 繡補 seu꜃ ꜂pwo.
**Date**, (fruit) 棗 ꜂chó.
**Daughter**, 諸娘仔 ꜀chü ꜁nëng ꜂kiăng.
**Day**, 日 nik$_2$ 日子 nik$_2$ ꜂chi.
**Daylight**, 天光 ꜀t'iéng ꜀kwong.
**Dead**, 死了 ꜂si ꜂lau, 殂 ꜁chu or ꜁të.
**Deaf**, 耳聾 nge$^2$ ꜁lëng.
**Dear**, (in price) 貴 koi꜃.
**Debt**, 欠項 k'iéng꜃ haung$^2$.
**Deceive**, 騙 p'iéng꜃.
**Decide**, 決意 kiok꜄ e꜃, 決斷 kiok꜄ twang꜃.
**Declivity**, 崎 k'ié꜃.
**Deduct**, 扣 k'aiu꜃, 除 ꜁tü.
**Deed**, (bond) 契 k'ié꜃.
**Deep**, 深 ꜀ch'ing.
**Deer**, 鹿 lëk$_2$.
**Defeated**, 敗 pai$^2$, 輸 ꜀sio.
**Deficiency**, 缺 k'wok꜄.
**Deformed**, 殘疾 ꜁chang chik$_2$.
**Degrade**, (in rank) 革 kaik꜄ 降級 kaung꜃ ngek꜄.
**Delay**, v. 挨 ꜀á, 挨延 ꜀á ꜁yong.
**Delicate**, 幼 eu꜃ 細嫩 sá꜃ naung$^2$.
**Delirious**, 發狂 hwak꜄ ꜁kwong.
**Demon**, 鬼 ꜂kwi.
**Denomination**, 號 hó$^2$.
**Depraved**, 邪 ꜁siă.
**Depute**, 委 ꜂wi.
**Descend**, 下 a$^2$, 落 lóh$_2$ 降 kaung꜃.
**Descendants**, 仔孫 ꜂kiăng ꜀song.
**Deserve**, 該當 ꜀kai ꜀tong.

Despair, 絶望 chiok꜇ wong꜅.
Despise, 看輕 k‘ang꜄ ꜀k‘ing.
Destiny, 命 miăng꜅ 數 so꜄.
Destroy, 毀 ꜂hwi, 除 ꜁tü, 滅 miék꜇.
Devil, 魔鬼 ꜁mó ꜂kwi.
Devout, 虔心 ꜁kiéng ꜀sing.
Dew, 露 lo꜄.
Diagonal, 斜 ch‘iă꜅ or ch‘ié꜅.
Diagrams, (the eight) 八卦 paik꜆ kwa꜄.
Dialect, 土話 ꜂t‘u wa꜅ 本地話 ꜂pwong te꜅ wa꜅.
Diamond, 金剛石 ꜀king ꜀kong sioh꜇ 金剛鑽 ꜀king ꜀kong ꜂chong.
Diarrhea, 病瀉 pang꜅ siă꜄.
Dice, 骰子 ꜁tau ꜂chi.
Dictionary, 字典 che꜅ ꜂tiéng.
Die, 死 ꜂si, 過世 kwo꜄ sié꜄.
Differ, 差 ꜀ch‘a.
Difficult, 艱難 ꜀kang ꜁nang.
Dig, 掘 kuk꜇ (a well) 開井 ꜀k‘wi ꜂chang.
Digest, 消化 ꜀sieu hwa꜄.
Dilemma, 兩難 ꜂liong ꜁nang.
Diligent, 勤緊 ꜁k‘üng ꜂king.
Dim, 暮 mwo꜅.
Diminish, 減少 ꜂keng ꜂chieu.
Dinner, 晝 tau꜄.
Dip, (up or out) 舀 ꜂yeu, (as a sop) 揾 ong꜄.
Dirt, 土 ꜁t‘u.
Dirty, 齷齪 auk꜆ ch‘auk꜆ or ꜀la ꜀cha.
Disappear, 變毛 piéng꜄ ꜁mó.
Disciple, 門生 ꜁mwong ꜀seng, 門徒 ꜁mwong ꜁tu.
Disclosed, 露出 lo꜄ ch‘ok꜆.
Discount, n. 銀水 ꜁ngüng ꜂chwi, 扣頭 k‘aiu꜄ ꜁t‘au.
Discourse, v. 論 laung꜅.
Discriminate, 辨別 piéng꜅ piék꜆ 分別 ꜀hung piék꜆.
Disease, 症 cheng꜄, 疾 chik꜇.
Disgrace, v. 壓落 tah꜆ lóh꜇ 凌辱 ꜁ling ük꜇.
Disheveled, 亂 naung꜄.
Disinclined, 毛心 ꜁mó ꜀sing.
Disjointed bone, 骨榾 kauk꜆ chwah꜇.
Dismiss, 辭 ꜁sü, 放 pong꜄.
Dispensary, 醫館 ꜀i ꜂kwang.
Disposition, (of mind) 性 sang꜄, 心性 ꜀sing sang꜄ 癖性 p‘ek꜆ seng꜄.
Dispute, 毆 pauk꜆.
Distribute, 分 ꜀pwong, 分發 ꜀hung hwak꜆.
Disturb, 吵 ꜂ch‘a or ꜂ch‘au, 吵擾 ꜂ch‘au ꜂yeu, (by noise) ꜁cha.
Diuretic, 利水 le꜄ ꜂chwi.
Dive, 謎水 me꜅ ꜂chwi.
Divide, 分 ꜀pwong 匀 ꜁üng.
Divination, 卜卦 pauk꜆ kwa꜄.
Dizzy, 眩 ꜁hing.
Do, 做 chó꜄ 行 ꜁heng, 爲 ꜁ui, (don't!) 莫 móh꜇.
Doctrine, 教 kau꜄ 道 tó꜅.
Dog, 犬 ꜂k‘eng, 犬仔 ꜂k‘eng ꜂kiăng.
Dollar, 番 ꜀hwang, (Mexican) 鳥番 ꜂cheu ꜀hwang.

Dominoes, 骨牌 *kauk꜆ ꜁pá.*
Door, 門 *꜁mwong.*
Double, a. 雙倍 *꜀sëng pwoi$^2$.*
Doubt, v. 可疑 *꜂k'ó ꜁ngi.*
Dough, 劑 *chá$^2$.*
Dove, 白鴿 *pah$_2$ tak꜆.*
Down, (to go) 下 *a$^2$* 落 *lóh$_2$.*
Drag, 拖 *꜀t'wa.*
Dragon, 龍 *꜁lüng.*
Dragon-fly, 蟆蚨 *꜁ma ꜁hu.*
Draw, (pictures) 畫 *wa$^2$*, (water) 潒 *ch'iong$^2$*, (a sword) 拔 *pek$_2$.*
Drawer, 匵 *t'á꜄.*
Dream, n. 夢 *maëng꜄.*
Dregs, 渣粕 *꜀cha p'óh꜆* 糟粕 *꜀chau p'óh꜆.*
Drink, 食 *siăh$_2$* 啜 *ch'iok꜆* 飲 *꜂ing.*
Drop, n. & v. (as liquids) 滴 *tek꜆.*
Drop, (let fall) 拍蕩 *p'ah꜆ taung$^2$.*
Drought, 做旱 *chó꜄ ang$^2$.*
Drown, 浸死 *cheng꜄ ꜂si.*
Drum, n. 鼓 *꜂ku.*
Dry, a. *꜀ta,* 乾 *꜀kang.*
Dry, v. (in the sun) 曝 *p'woh$_2$* (at the fire) 烘 *꜀hëng.*
Duck, 鴨 *ak꜆.*
Dull, 鈍 *꜀tong*, (in mind) 蒙昧 *꜁mang mwoi$^2$* or *꜁mung mwoi$^2$.*
Dumb, 病啞 *pang$^2$ ꜂a.*
Dun, v. 討數 *꜂t'ó so꜄.*
Dung, n. 屎 *꜂sai,* 糞 *pong꜄.*
Dusk, 含暗晡 *꜁hang ang꜄ ꜀pwo.*
Dust, n. 塕塵 *꜀ung ꜁ting.*

Duty, 本分 *꜂pwong hong$^2$.*
Dye, 染 *꜂niéng.*
Dysentery, 病痢 *pang$^2$ le$^2$* 血痢 *haik꜆ le$^2$.*

## E

Each, 各 *kauk꜆* 每 *꜂mwi.*
Ear, 耳 *nge$^2$* 耳仔 *nge$^2$ ꜂kiăng.*
Ears, (of grain) 穗 *soi꜄.*
Early, 早 *꜂cha.*
Earn, 賺 *t'eng꜄.*
Earnest, 迫切 *p'aik꜆ ch'iék꜆* 熱心 *yék$_2$ ꜀sing.*
Earth, 地 *te$^2$*, (soil) 土 *꜁t'u.*
Earthenware, 硋器 *꜁hai k'e꜄.*
Earthquake, 地定動 *te$^2$ teng$^2$ taëng$^2$.*
East, 東 *꜀tëng* or *꜀tung.*
Easy, 容易 *꜁üng e$^2$.*
Eat, 食 *siăh$_2$.*
Ebb, 水汐 *꜂chwi p'wong꜄.*
Echo, 倒埕聲 *tó꜄ ꜁tiăng ꜀siăng.*
Eclipse, 蝕 *sek꜆.*
Economical, 省 *꜂sang,* 儉省 *kiéng$^2$ ꜂sang.*
Edge, 邊 *꜀piéng,* 墘 *꜁kiéng.*
Egg, 蛋 *laung$^2$.*
Egg-plant, 紫菜 *꜂chié ch'ai꜄.*
Either, 或 *hĕk$_2$.*
Elastic, 韌 *nong$^2$.*
Elbow, 手單 *꜂ch'iu ꜀tang.*
Electricity, 電氣 *tiéng$^2$ k'e꜄.*
Elegant, 雅 *꜂nga,* 雅緻 *꜂nga te꜄.*
Elements, (five) 五行 *꜂ngu ꜁heng.*
Elephant, 象 *ch'iong$^2$.*
Eloquence, 口才 *꜂k'eu ꜁chai.*

**Emaciated**, 衰 ₍soi.
**Embankment**, 墻 pa’ or ang$^2$.
**Embrace**, v. 抱 pó$^2$, (include) 包 ₍pau.
**Embroider**, 繡花 seu’ ₍hwa.
**Emetic**, 吐藥 t‘o’ yoh₎.
**Emperor**, 皇帝 ₍hwong tá’.
**Employer**, 東家 ₍tung ₍ka.
**Empty**, 空 ₍k‘ĕng.
**Emulate**, 賽贏 swoí’ ₍yăng.
**Enclose**, 圍 ₍mi.
**End**, 尾 ‘mwi, 煞尾 sak₎ ‘mwi.
**Enemy**, 仇人 ₍siu ₍ing, 仇敵 ₍siu tik₎.
**England**, 大英國 tai$^2$ ₍ing kwok₎.
**Engrave**, 雕刻 ₍teu k‘aik₎.
**Enjoy**, 享 ‘hiong.
**Enough**, 務彀 o$^2$ kau’.
**Enter**, 入 ‘tiĕ.
**Entice**, 誘惑 ‘iu hĕk₎.
**Envelope**, (letter-) 批袋 ₍p‘ié tói$^2$.
**Envy**, 妒忌 to’ ke$^2$.
**Epidemic**, 時症 ₍si cheng’.
**Epilepsy**, 癇瘋 kang’ ₍hung.
**Epistle**, 批 ₍p‘ié, 信 seng’.
**Epsom salts**, 朴硝 p‘auk₎ ₍sieu.
**Equator**, 赤道 ch‘ek₎ tó$^2$.
**Escape**, 走 ‘chau.
**Essay**, (lit.) 文章 ₍ung ₍chiong.
**Establish**, 立 lik₎ 設立 siék₎ lik₎.
**Eternal**, 永遠 ‘ing ‘wong.
**Etiquette**, 禮 ‘lá, 禮數 ‘lá so’.
**Europe**, 歐羅巴 ₍Eu ₍ló ₍pa.
**Evening**, 半晡 pwang’ ₍pwo.
**Every**, 各 kauk₎.
**Exact**, a. 正正 chiăng’ chiăng’.
**Examine**, 查 ₍cha, (judic.) 審 ‘sing.
**Example**, 樣 yong$^2$, 模樣 ₍mwo yong$^2$.
**Excel**, 贏 ₍yăng.
**Excessive**, 太過 t‘ai’ kwo’, 過分 kwo’ hong$^2$.
**Exchange**, 換 wang$^2$, 駁 pauk₎.
**Excite**, 撩 ₍lieu, 激 kek₎ 惹 ‘niă.
**Executioner**, 劊子手 kwoi’ ‘chü ‘ch‘iu.
**Exhaust**, 盡 cheng$^2$.
**Exhort**, 勸 k‘wong’.
**Exist**, 着 tioh₎ 務 o$^2$ 存 ₍chong.
**Expel**, 逐出 tŭk₎ ch‘ok₎.
**Expiate**, 贖 sŭk₎.
**Explain**, 解說 ‘ká siok₎.
**Extend**, (as the hand) 穿 ₍ch‘iong, 凸 ‘t‘u.
**Extort**, 勒索 lek₎ sauk₎.
**Extract**, (teeth) 取齒 ‘ch‘ü ‘ngai.
**Extremely**, 極 kik₎ 盡 cheng$^2$.
**Eye**, n. 目 mĕk₎ 目睭 mek₎ ₍chiu.
**Eyebrow**, 眉毛 ₍mi ₍mó.

## F

**Face**, n. 面 meng’.
**Fact**, 實事 sik₎ sëü$^2$.
**Faction**, 黨 ‘tong.
**Fade**, 退色 t‘ói’ saik₎.
**Faint**, 失去 sek₎ k‘ó’.
**Faith**, 信德 seng’ taik₎.
**Fall**, as a person, 跌 pwak₎.
**False**, 假 ‘ka.
**Fame**, 名聲 ₍miăng ₍siăng.

Family, 家 ꜀ka, 家法 ꜀ka hwak꜁.
Famine, 飢荒 ꜀ki ꜀hwong.
Fan, n. 扇 siéngʾ.
Fan, v. 搧扇 yăk꜆ siéngʾ.
Fanning-mill, 風扇 ꜀hung ꜀siéng.
Far, 遠 hwong².
Fare, (boat-) 船債 ςsung chaiʾ.
Fat, a. 肥 ςpui, 肥水 ςpui ‘chwi.
Fate, 天數 ꜀t‘iéng soʾ.
Father, 郎罷 ςnong ma².
Fatigued, 辛苦 ꜀sing ‘k‘u, 弱毛力 yok꜁ ςmó lik꜆.
Favor, 恩 ꜀ong.
Fear, v. 驚 ꜀kiăng.
Feast, n. 酒 ‘chiu, 酒席 ‘chiu sik꜆.
Feather, 毛 ςmó.
Fee, 禮 ‘li, 花綵 ꜀hwa ‘ch‘ai.
Feeling, 情 ςching.
Feign, 假冒 ‘ka mó².
Feignedly, 醡醡勢 taʾ taʾ siéʾ.
Felt, n. 毡 ꜀chiéng.
Female, a. 女 ‘nü, 㹻 ‘mó.
Fertile, 肥 ςpui.
Fervent, 熱心 yék꜆ ꜀sing.
Festival, 節 chaik꜁.
Fever, 熱病 yék꜆ pang².
Few, 少 ‘chieu.
Fickle, 浮 ςp‘eu, 浮燥 ςp‘eu sóʾ.
Field, 田 ςch‘eng.
Fierce, 惡 auk꜁, 兇惡 ꜀hŭng auk꜁.
Fig, 無花果 ςu ꜀hwa ‘kwo.
Fight, v. 相拍 ꜀song p‘ah꜁.
File, n. & v. 鑢 laëʾ.
Filial, 孝順 hauʾ song².
Fill, 填滿 ςteng ‘mwang, (with liquid) 傾溢 ςk‘ing tiéng².
Filter. v. 濾 lëü² 澤 tek꜆.
Fins, 翅 ch‘iéʾ.
Find, (found) 討着 ‘t‘ó tioh꜆.
Fine, a. 幼 euʾ.
Fine, v. 罰錢 hwak꜆ ςchiéng.
Finger, n. 手指 ‘ch‘iu ‘chai.
Finish, v. 做完 chóʾ ςwong.
Fir, 杉 ꜀sang, 松 ςsüng.
Fire, n. 火 ‘hwi.
Fire-engine, 水龍 ‘chwi ςlüng.
Fish, n. 魚 ςngü.
Fish, v. 討魚 ‘t‘ó ςngü.
Fist, n. 拳頭 ςkung ςt‘au.
Fit, a. 合 hak꜆ 合宜 hak꜆ ςngi.
Flag, 旗 ςki.
Flame, n. 火熖 ‘hwi yéng².
Flat, (level) 平 ςpang, (low) 扁 ‘piéng.
Flatter, ꜀hë me² 諂媚 ‘t‘iéng me² 奉承 hong² ςsing.
Flay, 剝皮 pwoh꜁ ςp‘uí.
Flea, 咬蚤 ‘ka ‘chau.
Flesh, 肉 nük꜆.
Flexible, 軟 ‘niong.
Flint, 火石 ‘hwi sioh꜆.
Float, v. 浮 ςp‘u.
Flock, 羣 ςkung.
Floor, 板棚 ‘peng ςpang.
Flour, (wheat) 麪粉 miéng² ‘hung, (rice) 糗 ch‘áʾ.
Flow, v. 流 ςlau.
Flower, n. 花 ꜀hwa.
Fly, n. 苔蠅 ꜀pu ςsing.
Fly, v. 飛 ꜀pwi.

Foam, n. 水浡 ʿ*chwi p‘wok*꜂.
Fog, 雺霧 ꜁*mwo o²*.
Fold, n.(one-) 一倍 *sioh*꜂ *pwoi²*.
Fold, v. 摺 *chiĕk*˒.
Follow, 跟 ꜀*kŭng*.
Food, 伙食 ʿ*hwi sik*꜂ 粮草 ꜁*liong* ʿ*ch‘ó*.
Foolish, 戇 *ngaung²*, 獃 ꜀*tai*.
Foot, 骹 ꜀*k‘a*, (measure) 尺 *ch‘ioh*˒.
For, 因 ꜀*ing*, 爲因 ꜀*ing oi²*, (in behalf of) 替 *k‘á*ʾ or *t‘á*ʾ, 共 *kaëng²*.
Forbid, 禁 *keng*ʾ.
Ford, v. 涉水 *lak*꜂ ʿ*chwi*.
Forehead, 額頭 *ngiah*꜂ ꜁*t‘au*.
Foreign, 番 ꜀*hwang*, 洋 ꜁*yong*.
Forenoon, 上罩 *siong² tau*ʾ.
Forever, 拍長 *p‘ah*˒ ꜁*tong*, 透底 *t‘au*ʾ ʿ*tá*.
Forget, 賣記的 *má² ke*ʾ *tek*˒.
Forgive, 赦 *siă*ʾ 免 ʿ*miéng*.
Fork, n. 叉 ꜀*ch‘a*.
Formerly, 起先 ʿ*k‘i* ꜀*seng*, 從前 ꜁*chŭng* ꜁*chiéng*.
Fortunate, 吉 *kek*˒.
Fortunately, 做化 *chó*ʾ *hwa*ʾ.
Foundation, 基 ꜀*ki*.
Foursquare, 四角 *se*ʾ *kaëk*˒.
Fowl, 雞 ꜀*kié*, (birds) 鳥 ʿ*cheu*.
Fowling-piece, 鳥銃 ʿ*neu* ꜀*ch‘iong*.
Fox, 狐狸 ꜁*hu* ꜁*li*.
Fragrant, 香 ꜀*hiong*.
Frame, n. 架 *ka*ʾ.
France, 佛蘭西 *Huk*꜂ ꜁*lang* ꜀*sá*.
Freeze, 凝冰 *ngik*꜂ ꜀*ping*.
Freight, 船債 ꜁*sung chai*ʾ.
Fresh, 新鮮 ꜀*sing* ꜀*siéng*, 鮮 ꜀*ch‘iéng*.
Friend, 朋友 ꜁*peng* ʿ*iu*.
Fringe, n. 繸 *soi*ʾ 纓 ꜀*ing*.
Frog, 水雞 ʿ*chwi* ꜀*kié*.
From, 由 ꜁*iu*, 自 *chëŭ²* 從 ꜁*chŭng*.
Front, (in) 前斗 ꜁*seng* ʿ*tau*, 面前 *meng*ʾ ꜁*seng*.
Frost, 霜 ꜀*song*.
Froth, n. 浡 *p‘wok*꜂.
Fruit, 果子 ʿ*kwi* ʿ*chi*.
Fry, 煎 ꜀*chiéng*, 煎炒 ꜀*chiéng* ʿ*ch‘a*.
Full, 滿 ʿ*mwang*, 溢 *tiéng²*.
Funeral, 送葬 *saëng*ʾ *chaung*ʾ.
Furs, 皮貨 ꜁*p‘ui hwo*ʾ.
Furnace, 灶 *chau*ʾ, 爐 ꜁*lu*.
Furrow, n. 稅 *swoi²*.
Fussy, 浮燥 ꜁*p‘eu só*ʾ.
Future, 將來 ꜀*chiong* ꜁*lai*.

## G

Gain, n. 利 *le*ʾ, 利息 *le*ʾ *sek*˒.
Gain, v. 賺 *t‘eng*ʾ or *chwang*ʾ.
Gall, n. 膽 ʿ*tang*.
Gamble, 賭錢 ʿ*tu* ꜁*chiéng*.
Game, (wild) 野味 ʿ*yă e²*.
Gap, 谷谷 *k‘iăk*꜂ *k‘iăk*˒.
Gape, 擘嘴 *pah*˒ *ch‘oi*ʾ.
Garden, 園 ꜁*hwong*.
Garlic, 蒜 *saung*ʾ.
Garter, 襪帶 *wak*꜂ *tai*ʾ.
Gate, 門 ꜁*mwong*.
Gather, 收 ꜀*siu*, 收拾 ꜀*siu sik*꜂.
Gauze, 紗 ꜀*sa*, 紗羅 ꜀*sa* ꜁*ló*.

Gay-colored, 綵色 ꜂ch'ai saik꜆.
Gazette, (Peking-) 京報 ꜀king pó꜄.
Gem, 玉 ngwoh꜇ 寶石 ꜂pó sioh꜇.
Genealogy, 族譜 chuk꜇ ꜂p'wo.
Generation, 代 tói$^2$.
Genii, 仙 ꜀siĕng, 神仙 ꜁sing ꜀siĕng.
Gentry, 鄉紳 ꜀hiong ꜀sing.
Genuine, 真 ꜀ching, 正 chiăng꜄.
Geography, 地理 te$^2$ ꜂li.
Geomancy, 地理 te$^2$ ꜂li, 風水 ꜀hung ꜂chwi.
Get, 得來 taik꜆ ꜁li.
Giggle, 嬉嬉笑 ꜀hi ꜀hi ch'ieu꜄.
Gild, 貼金 t'aik꜆ ꜀king, 鍍金 to$^2$ ꜀king.
Gills, 魚翅 ꜁ngü ꜀ch'i.
Gimlet, 手鑚 ꜂ch'iu chaung꜄.
Ginger, 薑母 ꜀kiong ꜂mó.
Ginseng, 人參 ꜁ing ꜀seng.
Girdle, n. 帶 tai꜄.
Girl, 諸娘仔 ꜀chü ꜁nĕng ꜂kiăng.
Give, 乞 k'ëük꜆.
Gizzard, 肣 keng$^2$.
Glad, 歡喜 ꜀hwang ꜂hi.
Glass, 玻璃 ꜀pó ꜁lá.
Glazing, n. 釉 eu$^2$.
Globe, 球 ꜁kiu.
Glory, 榮耀 ꜁ing yeu$^2$.
Gloves, 手絡 ꜂ch'iu lóh꜆.
Glue, 膠 ꜀ka, 水膠 ꜂chwi ꜀ka.
Gnat, 蠓仔 ꜂mëng ꜂kiăng.
Gnaw, 咬 ka$^2$, (a bone) 齰骨 ꜀k'á kauk꜆.
Go, 去 k'ó꜄, 往 ꜂wong.

Goat, 山羊 ꜀sang ꜁yong.
Go-between, 成行 ꜁sing ꜁heng.
God, 上帝 Siong$^2$ tá꜄, (gods) 神明 ꜁sing ꜁ming.
Gold, 金 ꜀king.
Gong, 鑼 ꜁ló.
Good, 好 ꜂hó, 善 siĕng$^2$.
Goods, 貨 hwo꜄.
Goose, 鵝 ꜁ngié.
Gospel, 福音 Hok꜆ ꜀ing.
Gourd, 瓠 ꜁pu.
Govern, 管 ꜂kwang, 治 te$^2$.
Grace, 恩 ꜀ong, 恩典 ꜀ong ꜂tiĕng.
Graft, v. 接模 chiĕk꜆ ch'eu꜄.
Grain, 五穀 ꜂ngu kok꜆.
Granary, 倉 ꜀ch'ong.
Grapes, 葡萄 ꜁pwo ꜁tó.
Grasp, v. 擒 ꜁k'iéng, or ꜀ma.
Grass, 草 ꜂ch'au.
Grasscloth, 綀布 chá꜄ pwo꜄ 夏布 ha$^2$ pwo꜄.
Grasshopper, 草蜢 ꜂ch'au ꜂mang.
Grate, n. 爐承 ꜁lu ꜁sing.
Grate, v. 鑢 laë꜄, (as potatoes) 切 ch'iăk꜆.
Gratis, 白 pah꜇ or pah꜇ pah꜇.
Grave, n. 墓 mwo꜄.
Gravy, 汁 chaik꜆.
Grease, 油 ꜁iu.
Green, 綠 lioh꜇ (color of plants) 青 ꜀ch'ang.
Gridiron, 鐵箅 t'iĕk꜆ pe꜄.
Grief, 苦 ꜂k'u, 苦楚 ꜂k'u ꜂ch'u.
Grind, (in a mill) 磨 mó$^2$ (by rubbing) 磨 ꜁mwai.

Groan, 嘆氣 *t‘ang꜃ k‘e꜃*.
Ground, n. 地 *te$^{2}$* 土 *꜀t‘u*.
Grow, 長大 *꜂tiong twai$^{2}$*.
Gruff, 伏獨 *huk꜁ tuk꜁*.
Guava, 番石榴 *꜀hwang sioh꜁ ꜀liu*.
Guest, 人客 *꜀nëng k‘ah꜁*.
Guild, 行友 *꜀ong ꜂iu*.
Guitar, 琵琶 *꜀pi ꜀pa*.
Gun, 銃 *ch‘ëüng꜃* 炮 *p‘au꜃*.
Gunpowder, 火藥 *꜂hwi yoh꜁*.
Gust, 拍風做颶 *p‘ah꜁ ꜀hung chó꜃ pó꜃*.
Gutter, 水溝 *꜂chwi ꜀kau*.
Gypsum, 石膏 *sioh꜁ ꜀kó*.

## H

Hail, n. 雹 *p‘ëk꜁*.
Hair, 毛 *꜀mó*, (of the head) 頭髮 *꜀t‘au hwok꜁*.
Half, 半 *pwang꜃*.
Hall, 堂 *꜀tong*, 廳 *꜀t‘iăng*.
Halo, 暈 *wong$^{2}$*.
Ham, (cured) 火腿 *꜂hwi ꜂t‘oi*.
Hammer, n. 鉄鎚 *t‘iék꜁ ꜀t‘ui*.
Hand, n. 手 *꜂ch‘iu*.
Handkerchief, 手巾 *꜂ch‘iu ꜀küng*.
Handle, n. 柄 *pang꜃*.
Happen on, 遇着 *p‘aung$^{2}$ tioh꜁*.
Happiness, 福 *hok꜁*.
Hard, 有 *taing$^{2}$* 硬 *ngaing$^{2}$*.
Harelip, 缺嘴 *k‘iék꜁ ch‘oi꜃*.
Harmony, 和氣 *꜀hwo k‘e꜃*.
Harrow, n. 耞耙 *꜀kiă (꜀kié) pa$^{2}$*.
Harvest, 收成 *꜀siu ꜀sing*.
Hasp, 門搭 *꜀mwong tak꜁*.

Hatch, v. 菢蛋 *po$^{2}$ laung$^{2}$*.
Hate, v. 嫌 *꜀hiéng*.
Have, 務 *o$^{2}$*, 有 *꜂iu*.
Hawk, 鷂 *yeu$^{2}$* and *lau$^{2}$ yoh꜁*.
He, 伊 *꜀i*.
Head, 頭 *꜀t‘au*.
Heal, 醫 *mwok꜁* or *꜀i*.
Heap, n. & v. 堆 *꜀toi*.
Hear, 聽見 *꜀t‘iăng kiéng꜃*.
Heart, 心 *꜀sing*.
Heat, n. 熱氣 *yék꜁ k‘e꜃*.
Heaven, 天 *꜀t‘iéng*.
Heavy, 重 *taëng$^{2}$*.
Heel, 跤單 *꜀k‘a ꜀tang*.
Hell, 地獄 *te$^{2}$ ngwoh꜁*.
Helm, 舵 *twai$^{2}$*.
Help, 帮 *꜀pong*, 助 *chaë$^{2}$*.
Hem, v. 鍬 *꜀ch‘ieu*.
Hemp, 蔴 *꜀mwai*.
Herb, 草 *꜂ch‘au* or *꜂ch‘ó*.
Herd, n. 羣 *꜀kung*.
Here, 只塊 *꜀chu wai꜃*.
Heresy, 異端 *e$^{2}$ ꜀twang*, 邪教 *꜀siă kau꜃*.
Heron, (white) 白鷺 *pah꜁ lo$^{2}$*.
Hiccough, 拍呃 *p‘ah꜁ aëh꜁*.
Hide, n. 皮 *꜀p‘ui*.
Hide, v. (one's self) 屈 *k‘ok꜁*.
High, 高 *꜀keng* or *꜀kó*.
Hill, 山 *꜀sang*.
Hinge, 合蟬 *hak꜁ (hiăk꜁) ꜀siéng*.
Hire, v. (as workmen) 倩工 *ch‘iăng꜃ ꜀këng*, (things) 租 *꜀chu*, (a boat) 討船 *꜂t‘ó ꜀sung*.
Hoarse, 聲音啞 *꜀siăng ꜀ing ꜂a*.
Hoe, n. 鋤頭 *꜀t‘ü ꜀t‘au*.

**Hold**, v. 拈手 ꜀niéng ꜂ch‘iu, (contain) 貯 ꜂tio.
**Hole**, 空 ꜀k‘ĕng, 空籠 ꜀k‘ĕng ꜀lĕng.
**Hollow**, a. 空冇 ꜀k‘ĕng p‘ang꜃.
**Holy**, 聖 seng꜃.
**Honest**, 老實 ꜂ló sik$_2$.
**Honey**, 蜜 mik$_2$.
**Hong**, 行 ꜁ong.
**Honorable**, 尊貴 ꜀chong koi꜃.
**Hood**, 風帽 ꜀hung mó$^2$.
**Hoof**, 蹄 ꜁tá.
**Hook**, n. 鉤 ꜀kau, 籠臂鉤 ꜁lĕng pié꜃ ꜀kau.
**Hoop**, n. & v. 箍 ꜀k‘u.
**Hop**, v. 跔跤 ꜁k‘wo ꜀k‘a.
**Hope**, 望 wong$^2$, 倚望 ꜂ai wong$^2$.
**Horizon**, 天邊 ꜀t‘iéng ꜀piéng.
**Horn**, 角 kaĕk꜄.
**Horse**, 馬 ꜂ma.
**Hospital**, 醫館 ꜀i ꜂kwang.
**Hot**, 熱 yék$_2$.
**Hound**, n. 獵犬 lak$_2$ ꜂k‘eng.
**Hour**, 點鐘 ꜂teng ꜀chŭng, (Chinese) 時辰 ꜁si ꜁sing.
**House**, 厝 ch‘io꜃.
**How**, 將 ꜀chiong, 將樣 ꜀chiong yong$^2$.
**Humble**, 謙虛 ꜀k‘iéng ꜀kü.
**Hungry**, 腹老饑 pok꜄ ꜂ló ꜀kwi (or ꜀eu).
**Hunt**, v. (as game) 打獵 ꜂ta lak$_2$.
**Hurt**, 傷 ꜀siong, 害 hai$^2$.
**Husband**, 唐脯 ꜁tong ꜀pwo.
**Hymn**, 詩 ꜀si, 神詩 ꜁sing ꜀si.

# I

**I**, 我 ꜂ngwai, 奴 ꜁nu, 儂家 ꜁nĕng ꜀ka.
**Ice**, 冰 ꜀ping.
**Idea**, 意 e꜃ 意思 e꜃ sëü꜃.
**Idol**, 菩薩 ꜁pu sak꜄ 神像 ꜁sing ch‘iong$^2$.
**If**, 倻 na$^2$, 假使 ꜂ka ꜂sü.
**Imitate**, 憑 ꜁ping, 學樣 óh$_2$ yong$^2$.
**Immerse**, 浸 cheng꜃ 搵 ong꜃.
**Immortality**, 長長活 ꜁tong ꜁tong wak$_2$ 永生 ꜂ing ꜀seng.
**Implicate**, 帶累 tai꜃ loi$^2$.
**Important**, 要緊 yeu꜃ ꜂king.
**Impose upon**, 欺負 ꜀k‘i ho$^2$.
**Imprison**, 關監 ꜀kwong ꜀kang.
**Incarnation**, 降生 kaung꜃ ꜀seng.
**Incense**, n. 香 ꜀hiong.
**Inch**, 寸 ch‘aung꜃.
**Include**, 包 ꜀pau.
**Incomparable**, 無雙 ꜁u ꜀sëng.
**Increase**, 加 ꜀ka, 加增 ꜀ka ꜀cheng.
**Index**, 目錄 muk$_2$ lioh$_2$.
**Indian-corn**, 腰邊橐 ꜀yeu ꜀piéng p‘au꜃.
**Indigo**, 靛 taing$^2$.
**Individual**, 位 oi$^2$, (thing) 隻 chiăh꜄ 其 ꜁ki.
**Indulgent**, 寬容 ꜀k‘wang ꜁ŭng.
**Infant**, 細仔 sá꜃ ꜂kiăng.
**Infectious**, 儺過 á$^2$ kwo꜃, 傳染 ꜁tiong ꜂niéng.
**Inferior**, kiă$^2$, 下 a$^2$.
**Inform**, 通知 ꜀t‘ung ꜀ti, 漢 hang꜃.

Ingenious, 巧 ꜂*k'ieu.*

Ingot, 錠 *tiăng$^2$*, 元 寶 錠 ꜀*ngwong* ꜂*pó tiăng$^2$.*

Inheritance, 家 業 ꜀*ka ngiék*꜁.

Injure, 害 *hai$^2$*, 傷 ꜀*siong.*

Ink, 墨 *mĕk*꜁.

Inkstone, 硯 *ngiéng*꜃.

Inn, 客 店 *k'ah*꜃ *taing*꜃.

Innocent, 毛 罪 ꜀*mó chói$^2$.*

Inquest, 驗 屍 *ngiéng$^2$* ꜀*si.*

Insane, 癲 ꜀*tiéng*, 癲 狂 ꜀*tiéng* ꜀*kwong.*

Insect, 虫 ꜀*t'ĕng.*

Insert, *ch'ĕüng*꜃ 插 *ch'ak*꜃.

Inside, (within) 裡 勢 ꜂*tié tié*꜃.

Insipid, 味 饕 *e$^2$* ꜂*chiăng.*

Instant, n.—刻古 *sioh*꜁ *k'aik*꜃ ꜂*ku.*

Instead of, 替 *t'á*꜃ or *k'á*꜃.

Instigate, 挑 剔 ꜀*t'ieu* *t'aĕk*꜃ 挑 唆 ꜀*t'ieu* ꜀*só*, 撩 ꜀*lieu.*

Instrument, 家 私 ꜀*ka* ꜀*si.*

Intelligent, 聰 明 ꜀*ch'ung* ꜀*ming.*

Intend, 存 意 ꜀*chong e*꜃.

Intercalary, 閏 *nong$^2$.*

Intercede, 替 求 *t'á*꜃ ꜀*kiu.*

Interest, n. (profit) 利 *le*꜃.

Interfere, (meddle) 察 *ch'ak*꜃.

Interpreter, 傳 話 ꜀*tiong wa$^2$*, 通 事 ꜀*t'ung sĕü$^2$.*

Interval, 衕꜃ *laĕng*꜃, 衕꜃空꜃ *laĕng*꜃ *k'aĕng*꜃.

Intestines, 腹 腸 *pok*꜃ ꜀*tong.*

Intoxicated, 酒 醉 ꜂*chiu choi*꜃.

Inundation, 大 水 *twai$^2$* ꜂*chwi.*

Invent, 創 製 *ch'aung*꜃ *chié*꜃.

Invigorate, 補 力 ꜂*pwo lik*꜁.

Invite, 請 ꜂*ch'iăng.*

Iron, n. 鐵 *t'iék*꜃.

Iron, v. (as clothes) 熨 *ok*꜃.

Irrigate, 沃 *woh*꜃.

Is, 是 *se$^2$* 務 *o$^2$.*

It, 伊 ꜀*i*, 啫 乇 ꜂*chiă nóh*꜃.

Itch, n. 瘍 疙 ꜀*kó ló$^2$.*

Itch, v. 雞 癢 *á$^2$ siong$^2$.*

Ivory, 牙 ꜀*nga.*

## J

Jackass, 驢 牯 ꜀*lĕ* ꜂*kĕng.*

Jacket, 短 衫 ꜂*toi* ꜀*sang*, 褂 *kwa*꜃.

Jars, (various sorts of) 罌 ꜀*ing*, 甕 *aĕng*꜃, 瓶 ꜀*ping*, 缸 ꜀*kong*, 埕 ꜀*ting.*

Jaundice, 黃 癉 ꜀*wong* ꜂*tang.*

Jaw, 牙 槽 ꜀*nga* ꜀*só.*

Jerusalem, 耶路撒冷 ꜀*Yă lo$^2$ sak*꜃ ꜂*leng.*

Jessamine, 茉 莉 花 *mĕk*꜁ (or *mek*꜁) *le$^2$* ꜀*hwa.*

Jest, 蠻 笑 ꜀*mang ch'ieu*꜃.

Jetty, (landing) 道 頭 *tó$^2$* ꜀*t'au.*

Join, 合 *hak*꜁ 接 *chiék*꜃.

Joint, 節 *chaik*꜃.

Journal, 日 記 *nik*꜁ *ke*꜃.

Judge, v. 審 ꜂*sing*, 審 判 ꜂*sing p'wang*꜃.

Jug, 瓶 ꜀*ping.*

Juice, 汁 *chaik*꜃ 漿 ꜀*chiong.*

Jump, 跳 *t'ieu*꜃, (as insects) *p'ih*꜁.

Just, a. 公 平 ꜀*kung* ꜀*pang.*

Justify, 稱 義 ꜀*ch'ing ngié$^2$.*

Jut out, 凸 出 ꜂*t'u ch'ok*꜃.

## K

Kaleidoscope, 百花筒 *pah, ꜀hwa ꜁tëng.*
Kernel, 核 *hok₂* 枳 *ʿchi.*
Key, 鎖匙 *ʿsó ꜁sié.*
Kick, 踢 *t'ek,.*
Kidnap, 拐 *ʿkwai.*
Kidneys, 內腎 *nói² seng².*
Kill, 刣 *꜁t'ai.*
Kiln, 窰 *꜁yeu.*
Kind, n. 樣 *yong²* 類 *loi².*
Kindle, 起火 *ʿk'i ʿhwi.*
King, 王 *꜁wong.*
Kingdom, 國 *kwok,.*
Kiss, 烝嘴 *꜀ching ch'oi'.*
Kitchen, 灶前 *chau' ꜁seng.*
Kite, (paper-) 紙鷂 *ʿchai yeu².*
Knee, 胶屈頭 *꜀k'a pok, ꜁t'au.*
Kneel, 跪 *koi².*
Knife, 刀 *꜀tó.*
Knit, 織 *chek,.*
Knot, n. 纇 *꜀loi,* (in wood) 櫑 *꜀loi.*
Know, 曉的 *ʿhieu tek,* 仈 *paik,.*

## L

Label, 標條 *꜀pieu ꜁teu,* 僉 *꜀ch'iêng.*
Lacking, 少 *ʿchieu,* 缺 *k'wok,.*
Lacquer, 漆 *ch'ek,.*
Ladder, 梯 *꜀t'ai,* 樓梯 *꜁lau ꜀t'ai.*
Lady, 娘 *꜁niong.*
Lake, 湖 *꜁hu* or *꜁u.*
Lamb, 羊仔 *꜁yong ʿkiăng.*
Lame, 跛胶 *ʿp'iăng ꜀k'a.*
Lamp, 燈馬 *꜀ting ʿma.*
Land, n. 地 *te².*
Landlord, 厝主 *ch'io' ʿchio,* 地主 *te² ʿchio.*
Language, 話 *wa².*
Lantern, 燈籠 *꜀ting ꜁lëng.*
Lard, 猪油 *꜀tü ꜁iu.*
Large, 大 *twai².*
Last, a. 尾 *ʿmwi.*
Late, 遲 *꜁ti.*
Lathe, 俥架 *꜀ch'iă ka'.*
Laugh, 笑 *ch'ieu'.*
Law, 律法 *luk₂ hwak,.*
Lazy, 懶 *ʿlang,* 懶惰 *ʿlang tó².*
Lead, n. 鉛 *꜁yong.*
Lead, v. 邀 *꜀yeu,* 帶 *tai'.*
Leaf, 箬 *nioh₂* (of a book) 頁 *hiék₂.*
Leak, 漏 *lau².*
Lean, a. 衰 *꜀soi,* 瘦 *saiu'.*
Learn, 學 *óh₂.*
Lease, n. 租榜 *꜀chu ʿpong.*
Leather, 皮 *꜁p'ui.*
Leaven, v. 發酵 *hwak, ꜁pui.*
Leech, 螞蜞 *ʿma ꜁k'i.*
Left, (side) 左邊 *ʿchó ꜀peng.*
Leisure, 閒 *꜁eng.*
Lend, 借 *chioh,.*
Leper, 孤老 *꜀ku ʿló.*
Leprosy, 癩 *lai²,* 上癩 *siong² lai²,* 病腿 *pang² ʿt'oi.*
Lesson, 課 *k'wo'.*
Level, 平 *꜁pang,* or *꜁pang ʿtiăng.*
Liberal, 厚 *haiu².*
Licentious, *hwah,* 放肆 *hwong' sëü'.*
Lick, 舐 *liăk,.*
Licorice, 甘艸 *꜀kang ʿch'ó.*

Lie, (down) 倒 ᶜtó, (speak falsely) 野講 ᶜyă ᶜkong, 莽講 ᶜmwong ᶜkong.
Life, 活命 wak$_2$ miăng$^2$.
Light, n. & a. 光 ꜀kwong, (not heavy) 輕 ꜀k'ing, (in color) 淡 tang$^2$, 淺 ᶜch'iĕng.
Light, v. 點 ᶜtiĕng and tok꜆.
Lightning, 閃電 ᶜniăng niăngᵓ.
Lily, 百合花 paik꜆ hak$_2$ ꜀hwa.
Lime, 灰 ꜀hwi.
Line, 線 siăngᵓ, (mark) 行 ꜀hong.
Lining, 裏 ᶜli.
Lion, 獅 ꜀sai.
Lip, 嘴皮 ch'oiᵓ ꜀p'ui.
Literati, 讀書仈 t'ĕk$_2$ ꜀chü ꜀nĕng.
Little, n. 一滴仔 sioh$_2$ tek꜆ ᶜkiăng.
Live, 活 wak$_2$.
Liver, 肝 ꜀kang.
Lizard, 蝘 ᶜchiĕng.
Load, n. 担 tangᵓ, (boat-) 儎 $^2$ sai$^2$.
Loadstone, 熁石 hiĕk꜆ sioh$_2$.
Loathe, 厭 yĕngᵓ 厭棄 yĕngᵓ k'eᵓ.
Lock, n. & v. 鎖 ᶜsó.
Lodge, v. (over night) 隔暝 kah꜆ ꜀mang.
Loins, 腰 ꜀yeu.
London, 倫敦 ꜀Lung ꜀tung.
Long, 長 ꜀tong, (in time) ꜀ong.
Longevity, 長命 ꜀tong miăng$^2$, 壽 seu$^2$.
Look, 看 k'angᵓ, 覷 ch'ëüᵓ.
Loose, a. 鬆 ꜀sĕng, 寬 ꜀k'wang.
Loosen, 解 ᶜkă.
Loquat, 枇杷 ꜀pi ꜀pa.
Lord, 主 ᶜchio.
Lost, 拍毛 p'ah꜆ ꜀mó.
Lottery, 花會 ꜀hwa hwoi$^2$.
Louse, 虱蝨 saik꜆ ᶜmó.
Love, 愛 t'iăngᵓ.
Low, a. 下 kiă$^2$, (in hight or stature) 矮 ᶜá, (in price) 賤 siăng$^2$, 低 ꜀tá.
Lump, 對 tóiᵓ.
Lungs, 肺 hiéᵓ.
Lust, 私慾 ꜀sü ük$_2$.
Lye, 鹼水 ꜀kiĕng ᶜchwi.

## M

Machine, 家私 ꜀ka ꜀si, 機 ꜀ki.
Mackerel, 馬胶 ᶜma ꜀k'a.
Mad, 發狂 hwak꜆ ꜀kwong.
Magic, 法術 hwak꜆ suk$_2$.
Magpie, 胶鵲 ꜀k'a ch'ioh꜆.
Majestic, 威風 ꜀wi ꜀hung.
Make, 做 chóᵓ, 作 chauk꜆.
Male, 男 ꜀nang, (of animals) 雄 kaĕk꜆ 牯 ᶜkĕng.
Man, 仈 ꜀nĕng, 人 ꜀ing.
Manage, 料理 ꜀lieu ᶜli, 辦 paing$^2$.
Mandarin, 官府 ꜀kwang ᶜhu.
Manilla, 小呂宋 ᶜSieu ᶜlü songᵓ.
Manis, ꜀la ᶜli, 穿山甲 ꜀ch'iong ꜀sang kak꜆.
Manner, 樣 yong$^2$.
Manure, v. 潑料 p'wak꜆ laiu$^2$.
Many, 佴 sá$^2$, 多 ꜀tó.
Map, 地理圖 te$^2$ ᶜli ꜀tu.
Mark, v. 畫 wah$_2$.

榕腔初學撮要

Marrow, 骨髓 *kauk꜁ ‘ch‘oi.*

Marry, (a wife) 討親 *‘t‘ó ꜀ch‘ing,* (a husband) 嫁使 *ka’ sai’,* 出嫁 *ch‘ok꜁ ka’,* 出閣 *ch‘ok꜁ kóh꜁* 做客 *chó’ ah꜁.*

Mason, 土司傅 *꜀t‘u ꜀sa ho$^{2}$.*

Mat, 蓆 *ch‘ioh꜁$_{2}$.*

Match, n. (paper-) 紙煤 *‘chai ꜀muí* or *‘chai ꜀hĕng,* (lucifer-) 自來火 *chëü$^{2}$ ꜀lai ‘hwi.*

Match, v. 合 *hak꜁$_{2}$* 對 *tói’.*

Materials, 料 *laiu$^{2}$.*

Mattress, 褥 *ük꜁$_{2}$* (straw-) 草苫 *‘ch‘au chaing’.*

Meal, (one) 一頓 *sioh꜁$_{2}$ taung’.*

Mean, (base) 賤 *chiéng$^{2}$.*

Measles, 疹 *‘mĕng.*

Measure, v. 量 *꜀liong.*

Meat, 肉 *nük꜁$_{2}$.*

Mediator, 中保 *꜀tüng ‘pó.*

Medicine, 藥 *yoh꜁$_{2}$.*

Melon, 瓜 *꜀kwa.*

Melt, 鎔 *꜀yong,* 化 *hwa’.*

Mend, *‘k‘a lak꜁* 補 *‘pwo.*

Menses, 月經 *ngwok꜁$_{2}$ ꜀king.*

Mercury, 水銀 *‘chwi ꜀ngüng.*

Mercy, 慈悲 *꜀chü ꜀p‘i.*

Merit, 功勞 *꜀kung ꜀ló.*

Method, 方法 *꜀hwong hwak꜁.*

Microscope, 顯微鏡 *‘hiéng ꜀mi kiăng’.*

Middle, 大中 *tai$^{2}$ ꜀tong,* 中 *꜀tüng.*

Mildew, 斑 *꜀peng.*

Military, 武 *‘u.*

Milk, n. 乳 *꜀neng.*

Mill, 磨 *mó$^{2}$.*

Millet, 黍 *‘së* and *꜀taï.*

Mind, n. 心 *꜀sing,* 心裡 *꜀sing ‘tié.*

Miracle, 神跡 *꜀sing chek꜁* 異跡 *e$^{2}$ chek꜁.*

Mirror, 鏡 *kiăng’.*

Mischievous, 賤作 *chiéng$^{2}$ chauk꜁.*

Misery, 苦楚 *‘k‘u ‘ch‘u.*

Miss, v. 賣着 *mă$^{2}$ tioh꜁$_{2}$* 失誤 *sek꜁ ngwo$^{2}$.*

Mistake, n. 錯 *tang$^{2}$.*

Mix, 攪 *꜀k‘au,* 調 *꜀teu* and *꜀seu.*

Moist, 濕 *nong’.*

Molasses, 糖水 *꜀t‘ong ‘chwi.*

Moldy, 生醭 *꜀sang ‘p‘u.*

Monastery, (Tau.) 觀 *kwang’,* (Bud.) 寺 *se$^{2}$.*

Money, 錢 *꜀chiéng.*

Monkey, 猴 *꜀kau.*

Month, moon, 月 *ngwok꜁$_{2}$.*

More, 故俪 *ko’ sá$^{2}$.*

Moreover, 仅 *po$^{2}$,* 故連 *ko’ ꜀liéng.*

Morning, 早起頭 *‘cha ‘k‘i ꜀t‘au.*

Mortgage, n. 典契 *‘teng k‘ié’.*

Mosquito, 蚊門 *꜀hung ꜀mwong.*

Moss, 青苔 *꜀ch‘ang ꜀t‘i.*

Mostly, 多的 *꜀tó tek꜁* 居多 *꜀kü ꜀tó.*

Moth, (candle-) 火蛾 *‘hwi ꜀ngó,* (in clothes, etc.) 蠹魚 *‘tu ꜀ngü.*

Mother, 娘奶 *꜀nong ‘ná.*

Mountain, 山 *꜀sang.*

Mourning, (to wear) 帶孝 *tai꜃ ha꜃*.
Mouth, 嘴 *ch'oi꜃*, 口 *꜂k'eu*.
Move, 動 *taëng$^2$* or *tong$^2$*.
Moxa, 艾 *ngié꜃*.
Much, 侕 *sá$^2$*, 多 *꜀tó*.
Mud, 土 *꜁t'u*.
Mulberry-tree, 桑榠 *꜀song ch'eu꜃*.
Mule, 騾 *꜁ló*.
Multiply, (arith.) 乘 *꜁sing*.
Murderer, 兇手 *꜀hüng ꜂ch'iu*.
Muscle, 筋 *꜀küng*.
Mushroom, 菰 *꜀ku*, 香菰 *꜀hiong ꜀ku*.
Musical instruments, 樂器 *ngok꜇ k'e꜃*.
Musk, 麝香 *siă$^2$ ꜀hiong*.
Must, 着 *tioh꜇* 的着 *tek꜆ tioh꜇*.
Mustaches, 嘴鬚 *ch'oi꜃ ꜀ch'iu*.
Mustard, 芥辣 *kai꜃ lak꜇*.
Mutton, 羊肉 *꜁yong nük꜇*.
Mutual, 相 *꜀song* or *꜀siong*.
My, mine, 我其 *꜂ngwai ꜁ki*.
Myriad, 萬 *wang$^2$*.
Myrrh, 沒藥 *muk꜇ yoh꜇*.

## N

Nail, n. 釘 *꜀ting*.
Nail, v. 釘 ꜃ *teng꜃*.
Naked, 赤身 *ch'iăh꜆ ꜀sing*.
Name, 名 *꜁miăng* or *꜁ming*.
Napkin, 手巾 *꜂ch'iu ꜀küng*.
Narrow, 窄 *chah꜆*.
Native, 本地 *꜂pwong te$^2$*, 土 *꜂t'u*.
Natural, 生成 *꜀seng ꜁siăng*.
Nature, 性 *seng꜃*.
Navel, 腹臍 *pok꜆ ꜁sai*.
Near, 近 *köüng$^2$*.
Near-sighted, 近覷 *köüng$^2$ ch'ëü꜃* or *köüng$^2$ ne꜃*.
Neck, 脰骨 *tau$^2$ kauk꜆*.
Needle, 針 *꜀cheng*.
Neighboring, 隔壁 *꜀kang piăh꜆*.
Nephew, 姪 *tik꜇*.
Nest, *seu꜃*, 窩 *꜀wo*, 巢 *꜁chau*.
Net, (fishing-) 縊 *maëng$^2$*.
New, 新 *꜀sing*.
News, 新聞 *꜀sing ꜁ung*.
Newspaper, 新聞紙 *꜀sing ꜁ung ꜂chai*.
New York, 紐約 *꜂Niu yok꜆*.
Nickname, 花名 *꜀hwa ꜁miăng*.
Niece, 姪女 *tik꜇ ꜂nü*.
Night, 暝晡 *꜁mang ꜀pwo*, 夜 *yă$^2$*.
Nightmare, 乞魅壓 *k'ëük꜆ ꜂mai tah꜆*.
Nip, v. 扭 ꜃ *neu꜃*, 攝 *niék꜆*.
No, 伓是 *ng$^2$ se$^2$*, 毛 *꜁mó*.
Noble, 尊貴 *꜀chong koi꜃*.
Noise, (clamor) 囉嘈 *꜁ló ꜁chó*.
Noon, 日晝 *nik꜇ tau꜃*, 正午 *chiăng꜃ ꜂ngu*.
North, 北 *paëk꜆* (-east) 東北 *꜀tëng paëk꜆*.
Nose, 鼻 *p'e꜃*.
Not, 伓 *ng$^2$*, 毛 *꜁mó*.
Notch, n. 缺 *k'iék꜆*.
Nothing, 毛毛 *꜁mó nóh꜆*.
Notice, v. 顧 *ko꜃*.
Noun, 實字 *sik꜇ che$^2$*.

Novel, n. 小說 ꜂sieu siok꜆ 野史 ꜂yă ꜂sü.

Now, 伶 ꜀tang, 現在 hiêng$^2$ chai$^2$.

Numb, 痺 pe꜄, 痳 ꜁ma.

Number, n. 數目 so꜄ mĕk$_2$ (No.) 第 tă$^2$.

Numerals, 數目字 so꜄ mĕk$_2$ che$^2$.

Nun, 尼姑 ꜁ná ꜀ku.

Nunnery, 庵 ꜀ang.

Nurse, v. (suckle) 喚乳 hwang꜄ ꜁neng.

Nutmeg, 荳蔻 taiu$^2$ k‘aiu꜄.

## O

O! 唉吓 ꜀ai ꜁a or ꜀ai a$^2$.

Oar, 槳 ꜂chiong.

Obey, 聽嘴 ꜀t‘iăng ch‘oi꜄.

Oblique, 歪 ꜀wai, 斜 ꜁siă.

Obstacle, 關絆 ꜀kwang pwang꜄.

Obstinate, 拗 au꜄.

Ocean, 洋 ꜁yong.

Odd, 奇 ꜀k‘iă, 單 ꜀tang, (strange) 奇特 ꜁ki tek$_2$.

Odor, (fragrant) 香 ꜀hiong, (offensive) 臭味 ch‘au꜄ e$^2$.

Of course, 自然 chëü$^2$ ꜁yong.

Offended at, 怪 kwai꜄.

Offer, v. (as to the gods) 獻 hiong꜄, 供 këüng꜄.

Office, 職 chek꜆ 任 eng$^2$.

Officer, 老爹 ꜂ló ꜀tiă.

Often, ꜁seu, 屢次 lëü꜄ ch‘ëü꜄.

Oil, 油 ꜁iu.

Old, 佬 lau$^2$, (as things) 舊 ko$^2$.

Oleander, 夾竹桃 kak꜆ tëük꜆ ꜁t‘ó.

Olive, 橄欖 ꜂ka (꜂kang) ꜂lang.

One, 一 sioh$_2$ or ek꜆.

Onion, 葱 ꜀ch‘ëng.

Only, 㑚 na$^2$, 獨獨 tuk$_2$ tuk$_2$.

Open, v. 開 ꜀k‘wi.

Ophthalmia, 眼症 ꜂ngang cheng꜄.

Opinion, 意見 e꜄ kiêng꜄.

Opium, 鴉片 ꜀a p‘iêng꜄.

Opportunity, 機會 ꜀ki hwoi$^2$.

Oppose, 抵敵 ꜂tá tik$_2$.

Opposite, 對面 tói꜄ meng꜄.

Or, 或 hĕk$_2$.

Orange, (coolie-) 柑 ꜀kang, (mandarin-) 橘 kek꜆.

Order, n. 次序 ch‘ëü꜄ sëü$^2$.

Originally, 本體 ꜂pwong ꜂tá (꜂t‘á), 本來 ꜂pwong ꜁lai.

Other, 別隻 pek$_2$ chiăh꜆.

Ought, 該當 ꜀kai ꜀tong.

Ounce, 兩 ꜂liong.

Outside, 外 ngiê$^2$, 外斗 ngiê$^2$ ꜂tau.

Oven, 鐓爐 ngó$^2$ ꜁lu.

Owe, 欠 k‘iêng꜄.

Owl, 貓王鳥 ꜁ma ꜁hung ꜂cheu (꜁ma ꜁wong ꜂cheu).

Owner, 主伙 ꜂chio ꜁nëng.

Ox, 牛 ꜁ngu.

Oyster, 蠣 tié$^2$.

## P

Pace, 步 pwo$^2$.

Paddles, 扒楫 ꜁pa siék꜆ (or tiék꜆).

Paddy, 粟 ch‘ioh꜆.

Page, (of a book) 板 ꜂peng.

Pagoda, 塔 t‘ak꜆.

Pain, 痛 *t‘iăng’*.
Paint, v. 油 *꜁iu*, or *sok$_2$*.
Pair, 雙 *꜀sĕng*, 合 *hak$_2$*.
Palate, 舌仔 *siĕk$_2$ ‘kiăng*.
Palm, (gomuti-) 棕榥 *꜀chĕng ch‘eu’*.
Palm, (of hand) 手掌 *‘ch‘iu ‘chiong*, 巴掌 *꜀pa ‘chiong*.
Palsy, 瘋軟 *꜀hung ‘niong*.
Pan, (cooking-) 鼎 *‘tiăng*.
Panel, 堵 *‘tu*.
Pant, *hĕk$_2$* 喘 *‘ch‘wang*.
Panther, 豹 *pau’*.
Pantry, 伙食房 *‘hwi sik$_2$ ꜁pung*.
Paper, n. 紙 *‘chai*.
Parable, 比喻 *‘pi ĕü$^2$*.
Parade-ground, 較場 *ka’ ꜁tiong*.
Parasol, 日照 *nik$_2$ chieu’*.
Pardon, 赦 *siă’*, 免 *‘miéng*.
Pare, 刡 *꜀p‘ié* and *꜁miéng*.
Parents, 罷奶 *pa$^2$ ‘ná*.
Parlor, 客廳 *k‘ah꜆ ꜀t‘iăng*.
Parrot, 鸚哥 *꜀eng ꜀kó*.
Partial, 偏爿 *꜀p‘iéng ꜁peng*.
Partition, v. 截 *chek$_2$*.
Partner, 夥計 *‘hwi e’ (ke’)*.
Pass, v. 行過 *꜁kiăng kwo’*.
Paste, n. & v. 糊 *꜁ku*.
Pasteboard, 紙坯 *‘chai ꜀p‘wi*.
Pastor, 牧師 *muk$_2$ ꜀sü*.
Patch, v. 臺補 *꜁tai ‘pwo*.
Patient, 忍耐 *‘ üng nai$^2$*.
Pattern, n. 樣 *yong$^2$*.
Pave, 鋪 *꜀p‘wo*.
Pawn, v. 當 *taung’* 押 *ak꜆*.
Pay, 還 *꜁heng* or *꜁teng*.

Peace, 安 *꜀ang*, 平安 *꜁ping ꜀ang*, (general) 太平 *t‘ai’ ꜁ping*, (fraternal or international) 和 *꜁hwo*.
Peach, 桃 *꜁t‘ó*.
Peacock, 孔雀 *‘k‘ung ch‘iok꜆*.
Peacock's feather, 翎 *꜁ling*.
Peanut, 花生 *꜀hwa ꜀seng*.
Pear, 梨 *꜁li*.
Pease, 金豆 *꜀king tau$^2$*.
Peck, n. (10 *꜀ching*) 斗 *‘tau*.
Peck, v. 啄 *tauk꜆*.
Pecul, (133⅓ lbs.) 担 *tang’*.
Pen, pencil, 筆 *pek꜆*.
Pendulum, 擺 *‘pai*.
Peony, 牡丹 *‘mu ꜀tang*.
People, 百姓 *pah꜆ sang’*.
Pepper, 胡椒 *꜁hu ꜀chieu*.
Peppermint, 薄荷 *pok$_2$ ꜁hó*.
Perceive, 見覺 *kiéng’ kaĕk꜆*.
Percentage, 分 *꜀hung*, (what) 幾分 *‘kwi ꜀hung?*
Perch, v. 泊 *póh$_2$*.
Perfect, a. 全 *꜁chiong*.
Perfume, 香 *꜀hiong*.
Perhaps, 或且 *hĕk$_2$ ‘ch‘iă*.
Persimmon, 柿 *k‘e$^2$*.
Person, 位 *oi$^2$*, 伙 *꜁nĕng*.
Perspiration, 汗 *kang$^2$*.
Pervious, 通 *꜀t‘ĕng*, 透 *t‘au’*.
Pestle, 槌 *꜁t‘ui*.
Petal, 花瓣 *꜀hwa paing$^2$*.
Petition, 稟 *‘ping*.
Pewter, 錫 *sek꜆*.
Pheasant, 雉雞 *te$^2$ ꜀kié*.
Phenix, 鳳 *hong$^2$*.

海上絲綢之路文獻集成 科技與文化編

Phlegm, 痰 ˛t'ang, 痰渤 ˛t'ang p'wok˛.
Physician, 郎中 ˛long ˛tüng, 醫生 ˛i ˛seng, 先生 ˛sing ˛sang.
Pick up, 拾起 k'ak˃ ʻk'i.
Picul, (133⅓ lbs.) 担 tang˃.
Piece, 塊 tói˃, (of cloth) 疋 p'ek˃.
Pigeon, 白鴿 pah˛ tak˃.
Pigment, 顏料 ˛ngang laiu².
Pile up, 疊 t'ak˛.
Pill, 藥丸 yoh˛ ˛wong.
Pillow, 枕頭 ʻchiéng ˛t'au.
Pin, n. 毛鼻針 ˛mó p'e˃ ˛cheng, 揿針 piék˃ ˛cheng.
Pin, v. 掬 këük˃.
Pinafore, 灠遮 ʻlang ˛chiă.
Pincers, 鑷鑷 kiék˃ niék˃.
Pinch, n. (pugil) 一撮 sioh˛ ch'auk˃.
Pinch, v. 扭˃ neu˃.
Pine, n. 杉柴 ˛sang ˛ch'a.
Pine-apple, 黃梨 ˛wong ˛li.
Pistol, 手銃 ʻch'iu ch'ëüng˃.
Pit, 坑 ˛k'ang.
Pitch, v. 丟 ˛liu and hiéng˃.
Pitcher, 水瓶 ʻchwi ˛ping.
Pitiable, 受愛 seu² wai˃, 凄凉 ˛ch'á ˛liong.
Pity, v. 可憐 ʻk'ó ˛leng.
Placard, n. 告白 kó˃ pah˛.
Place, n. 位處 oi² ch'ëü˃.
Plain, a. 明白 ˛ming pek˛ (unadorned) 樸實 p'auk˃ sik˛.

Plaintiff, 原告 ˛ngwong kó˃.
Plait, v. 拾裥 k'ak˃ ʻkiéng.
Plan, n. 計 kié˃, 計策 kié˃ ch'aik˃.
Plan, v. 拍算 p'ah˃ saung˃.
Plane, n. 推刀 ˛t'oi ˛tó.
Plane, v. 推 ˛t'oi.
Plant, v. 栽 ˛chai, 種 chëüng˃.
Plantain, 芭蕉果 ˛pa ˛chieu ʻkwo.
Plaster, n. 灰 ˛hwi, (med.) 膏藥 ˛kó yoh˛.
Plaster, v. 塗 ˛tu.
Plat, v. (braid) 辮 piéng².
Plate, n. 盤 ˛pwang, (small) 碟 tiék˛.
Plays, (theatrical) 戲 hié˃.
Play, v. 客遊 k'ah˃ ˛lieu.
Pleased, 歡喜 ˛hwang ʻhi, 悅意 yok˛ e˃.
Pledge, n. 做當 chó˃ taung˃.
Plot, v. 謀 ˛meu.
Plow, n. & v. 犂 ˛lá.
Pluck, v. (as fruit) 摘 tiăh˃.
Plug, n. & v. 塞 sek˃ or saik˃.
Plum, 李 ʻli.
Pocket, 袋 tói².
Pock-marked, 痳 ˛ma.
Poem, 詩 ˛si.
Point, n. 尖頭 ˛chiéng ˛t'au.
Poison, n. 毒 tuk˛ or tëk˛.
Poison, v. t'au˃, (to death) t'au˃ ʻsi, 毒死 tuk˛ ʻsi.
Poke, 搠 taëk˃.
Pole, (bamboo-) 竹筦 tëük˃ aung², (north) 北極 paëk˃ kik˛.

Police, 差役 ꜀ch‘á yăh꜁.
Politeness, 禮數 ꜂lá so꜃.
Pomegranate, 石榴 sioh꜁ ꜀liu.
Pomelo, 枹 ꜀p‘au.
Pond, 池 ꜀tié.
Poor, 窮 ꜀küng.
Poppy, 鶯粟 ꜀eng sëük꜁.
Porcelain, 磁器 ꜀chü k‘e꜃.
Pork, 猪肉 ꜀tü nük꜁ 肉 nük꜁.
Port the helm, 挨柁 ꜀á twai$^2$.
Post, (pillar) 柱 t‘eu$^2$.
Potash, 鹻 ꜀kiéng.
Potato, 蕃薯 ꜀hwang ꜀sü.
Pottery, 硋器 ꜀hai k‘e꜃.
Pound, n. 觔 ꜀küng.
Pound, v. mó꜃, 擂 lói$^2$.
Pour, (from a spout) 傾 ꜀k‘ing, (out or away) 倂 piăng꜃.
Powder, n. (medicinal) 藥散 yoh꜁ ꜂sang.
Practiced, 熟 sük꜁.
Praise, 褒美 ꜀pó ꜂pi, 稱讚 ꜀ch‘ing chang꜃.
Pray, 祈禱 ꜀ki ꜂tó.
Preach, 講書 ꜂kong ꜀chü, 傳道 ꜀tiong tó$^2$.
Precious, 寶貝 ꜂pó pwoi꜃.
Preface, 序頭 sëü$^2$ ꜀t‘au.
Pregnant, 帶娠 tai꜃ ꜀sing.
Prepare, 辦 paing$^2$, 預備 ëü$^2$ pe$^2$.
Prescription, (med.) 藥方 yoh꜁ ꜀hwong.
Present, n. 禮物 ꜂lá uk꜁.
Present, v. 送 saëng꜃.
Press, v. 壓 tak꜁ (with the hand) 扼 aik꜁.
Price, n. 價 ka꜃, 價錢 ka꜃ ꜀chiéng.
Prick, v. tóh꜁ and ꜀teng.
Prickly-heat, 疿 poi꜃.
Priest, 祭司 chié꜃ ꜀si, (Bud.) 和尙 ꜀hwo siong$^2$, (Tau.) 道人 tó$^2$ ꜀ing, (lay Tau.) 道大 ꜀tó tai$^2$, 道士 tó$^2$ sëü$^2$.
Print, 印 eng꜃.
Prison, 監 ꜀kang.
Private, 私家 ꜀sai ꜀ka, 私 ꜀sü.
Procession, (to carry in) 迎 ꜀ngiăng.
Proclaim, 傳 ꜀tiong.
Proclamation, (gov.) 告示 kó꜃ che$^2$.
Prodigal, n. 浪子 laung$^2$ ꜂chü.
Profit, n. & v. 益 yăh꜁.
Profound, 深奥 ꜀ch‘ing ó꜃.
Prohibit, 禁 keng꜃.
Promise, v. 應承 eng꜃ ꜀sing, 應許 eng꜃ ꜂hü.
Proof, 憑據 ꜀ping këü꜃.
Prop, n. & v. 肘 ꜂tiu.
Prophet, 先知 ꜀siéng ꜀ti.
Propitious, (as gods) 靈應 ꜀ling eng꜃, 偕聖 á$^2$ siăng꜃, (as time, etc.) 吉 kek꜁.
Prostitute, n. 白面 pah꜁ meng꜃, 妓女 ke$^2$ ꜂nü.
Protect, 保護 ꜂pó ho$^2$ or ꜀pó ho$^2$, 庇蔭 ꜂pi eng꜃.
Proud, 驕傲 ꜀kieu ngó$^2$.
Proverb, 俗語話 sük꜁ ꜂ngü wa$^2$.
Providence, 天 ꜀t‘iéng.

榕腔初學撮要



Provoke, 激 kek꜁ 惹 ‘niă.
Prunes, 梅 ςmui.
Prussia, 普魯士 ‘P‘wo ꜀lu sëü$^2$.
Prussian blue, 洋藍 ςyong ςlang.
Public, 公 ꜀kung.
Pull, 拔 pek$_2$ or ꜀pi.
Pulley, 綷餅 luk$_2$ ‘piăng.
Pulp, 蘢 ςnong, 漿 ꜀chiong.
Pump, n. 水挑 ‘chwi ꜀t‘ieu.
Pump, v. 挑水 ꜀t‘ieu ‘chwi.
Pumpkin, 金瓜 ꜀king ꜀kwa.
Punish, 罰 hwak$_2$ (whip) 拍 p‘ah꜁.
Punishment, (official) 刑 ςhing.
Punka, 風扇 ꜀hung siéngʾ.
Pupil, 學生 hok$_2$ ꜀seng, (of the eye) 烏仁 ꜀u ςning.
Purgative, 瀉藥 siăʾ yoh$_2$.
Purple, 紫 ‘chié.
Pursue, 逐 tük$_2$ 追 ꜀twi.
Pus, 膿 ςnëng.
Push, 擲 ‘t‘iăng.
Putty, 油灰 ςiu ꜀hwi.

## Q

Quadruped, 獸 seuʾ.
Quality, 等 ‘teng, 色 saik꜁.
Quarrel, 相爭 ꜀song ꜀chang.
Queen, 王后 ςwong haiu$^2$.
Quench, 滅 miék$_2$ (thirst) 止渴 ‘chi k‘ak꜁.
Question, 問 mwongʾ.
Quick, 快 k‘áʾ, 趕緊 ‘kang ‘king.
Quiet, 靜 cheng$^2$.
Quill, (barrel of a) 毛管 ςmó ‘kwong.
Quilt, n. 棉被 ςmiéng p‘woi$^2$.
Quilt, v. 杭 ςhong.
Quince, 木瓜 muk$_2$ ꜀kwa.
Quinine, 咖哪 ꜀kiă ‘na.
Quinsy, 喉蛾 ςheu ςngó.
Quire, 刀 ꜀t‘ó.
Quota, 份頭 hong$^2$ ςt‘au, 股 ‘ku.
Quote, 引 ‘ing.

## R

Rabbit, 兎 t‘oʾ.
Radicals, 字部 che$^2$ pwo$^2$.
Rag, 破布 p‘waiʾ pwoʾ.
Rain, n. 雨 ‘ü.
Rainbow, 虹 k‘ëüng$^2$.
Raise, 起 ‘k‘i, 掏起 ςtó ‘k‘i.
Raisins, 葡萄乾 ςpu ςtó ꜀kang.
Rake, 鈀搭 ςpa tak꜁ (bamboo-) 鈀濟 ςpa cháʾ.
Rancid, 臊 ꜀ch‘ó.
Rank, n. 等 ‘teng, (official) 品 ‘p‘ing.
Rapids, 瀨 laiʾ.
Rare, 罕 ‘hang, 少 ‘chieu.
Rat, 老鼠 ‘ló ‘ch‘ü.
Rattan, 籐 ςting.
Raw, 生 ꜀ch‘ang.
Razor, 剃刀 t‘iéʾ ꜀tó.
Read, 讀 t‘ëk$_2$.
Ready, 便 piéng$^2$.
Real, 實 sik$_2$ 眞 ꜀ching.
Reap, 割 kak꜁.
Reason, n. 道 to$^2$, 理 ‘li, (cause) 緣故 ςyong koʾ.
Rebel, v. 做反 chóʾ ‘hwang.
Receive, 受 seu$^2$, 接 chiék꜁.

Recite, 背書 *pwoi$^2$ ꜀chü.*
Reckon, 筭 *saungᵓ.*
Recognize, 認 *neng$^2$.*
Recommend, 保薦 *ᶜpó chiéngᵓ.*
Recompense, n. & v. 報 *póᵓ.*
Record, v. 記 *keᵓ*, 載 *chaiᵓ.*
Rectum, 臟頭 *chaung$^2$ ꜀t‘au.*
Red, 紅 *꜀ĕng.*
Redeem, 贖 *sŭk꜆.*
Reform, v. i. 改過 *ᶜkai kwoᵓ*, 棄邪歸正 *k‘eᵓ ꜀siă ꜀kwi chengᵓ.*
Refuse, n. 糞倒 *pongᵓ tóᵓ.*
Register, n. 册 *ch‘ah꜆*, 錄 *lioh꜆.*
Regret, 退悔 *t‘óiᵓ hwoiᵓ.*
Regulate, 料理 *꜀lieu ᶜli.*
Reign, v. 坐位 *sói$^2$ oi$^2$.*
Reject, 棄 *k‘eᵓ.*
Rejoice, 歡喜 *꜀hwang ᶜhi.*
Relations, (the five) 五倫 *ᶜngu ꜀lung.*
Relatives, 親戚 *꜀ch‘ing ch‘ek꜆.*
Release, 放 *pongᵓ*, 解 *ᶜká.*
Religion, (doctrine) 教 *kauᵓ.*
Rely, 藉 *chiă$^2$*, 靠 *k‘óᵓ.*
Remainder, 剩其 *tiong$^2$ ꜀ki*, 其餘 *꜀ki ꜀ü.*
Remember, 記 *keᵓ.*
Rent, w. 租 *꜀chu*, 出租 *ch‘ok꜆ ꜀chu.*
Repent, 悔改 *hwoiᵓ ᶜkai.*
Repine, 怨 *wongᵓ.*
Report, v. 報 *póᵓ.*
Reprove, 責備 *chaik꜆ pe$^2$.*
Reputation, 名聲 *꜀miăng ꜀siăng.*
Reside, 住 *teu$^2$.*

Resin, 柏膠 *pak꜆ ꜀kau.*
Responsibility, (to bear) 當 *꜀tong.*
Rest, 歇 *hiok꜆*, 安歇 *꜀ang hiok꜆.*
Resurrection, 復活 *po$^2$ wak꜆.*
Retain, 留 *꜀lau.*
Retract, 翻聲 *꜀hwang ꜀siăng.*
Return, v. i. 轉 *ᶜtiong*, 回 *꜀huí.*
Revenge, 報仇 *póᵓ ꜀siu.*
Revere, 敬 *kengᵓ.*
Reverse, (turn end for end) 拍轉頭 *p‘ah꜆ ᶜtiong ꜀t‘au.*
Revise, 改 *ᶜkwi.*
Revolve, 俥俥轉 *꜀ch‘iă ꜀ch‘iă ᶜtiong.*
Reward, 賞 *ᶜsiong.*
Rheumatism, 瘋 *꜀hung.*
Rhubarb, 大黃 *tai$^2$ ꜀wong.*
Ribs, 肋條骨 *lĕk꜆ ꜀teu kauk꜆.*
Rice, 米 *ᶜmi*, (paddy) 粟 *ch‘ioh꜆*, (boiled) 飯 *pwong$^2$*, (in the ear) 稻 *teu$^2$.*
Rich, 富 *poᵓ.*
Ride, 騎 *꜀k‘ié.*
Ridicule, v. 恥笑 *ᶜt‘i ch‘ieuᵓ.*
Right, 正 *chiăngᵓ*, 是 *se$^2$*, (side) 右邊 *eu$^2$ ꜀peng.*
Righteousness, 義理 *ngié$^2$ ᶜli.*
Ring, n. 環 *꜀k‘wang.*
Ringworm, 癬 *ᶜch‘iăng.*
Rinse, 滈盪 *꜀kó laung$^2$.*
Ripe, 熟 *sŭk꜆.*
Rise up, 趉起 *kok꜆ ᶜk‘i.*
River, 江 *꜀kĕng*, 河 *꜀ó.*
Road, 路 *tio$^2$.*
Roast, 燒 *꜀sieu.*
Rob, 奪 *tok꜆* 搶奪 *ᶜch‘iong tok꜆.*

榕腔初學撮要

Robe, 袍 ꜀pó.
Rocket, 九頭龍 ꜂kau ꜀t'au ꜀lŭng.
Rocking-chair, 險'椅 hiăng' ꜂ié.
Rogue, 仙家 ꜀siéng ꜀ka.
Roll, 捷' liéng' and ꜀ka ꜀lau, (up) 捲 ꜂kwong.
Rolling-pin, 研棍 ꜂ngiéng kong'.
Rome, 羅馬 ꜀Ló ꜂ma.
Roof, 厝瓦頂 ch'io' ngwa² ꜂ting.
Room, 房 ꜀pung, 廳 ꜀t'iăng.
Roost, 泊 póh₂.
Root, n. 根 ꜀kŭng.
Rope, 索 sóh₎.
Rose, 長春花 ꜀tiong ꜀ch'ung ꜀hwa.
Rot, 腐 po² or ꜂ang po², 腐爛 po² lang².
Rough, 粗 ꜀ch'u, 莿莿 ch'ié' ch'ié'.
Round, 圓 ꜀yéng.
Row, n. (line, rank) 行 ꜀hong.
Row, v. 盪槳 t'aung' ꜂chiong.
Rub, 擦' ch'aĕ', 磨 ꜀mwai.
Rudder, 舵 twai².
Rude, 粗俚 ꜀ch'u ꜀la.
Rug, 毡條 ꜀chiéng ꜀teu.
Ruin, 敗 pai², 壞 hwai².
Rule, v. 管 ꜂kwang.
Ruminate, 轉磨 ꜂tiong mó².
Rumple, 衤+芻 chaiu' or naiu'.
Run, pié' 跑 ꜀p'au.
Russia, 俄羅斯 ꜀Ngó ꜀ló ꜀sŭ.
Rust, v. 生鉎 ꜀sang ꜀sing.

## S

Sabbath, 安息日 ꜀ang sek₎ nik₂.
Sable, (fur) 貂皮 ꜀tieu ꜀p'uí.
Sacrifice, v. 祭 chié'.
Saddle, 馬鞍 ꜂ma ꜀ang.
Safe, a. 安穩 ꜀ang ꜂ung.
Sage, (man) n. 聖人 seng' ꜀ing.
Sail, n. 風篷 ꜀hung ꜀p'ung.
Salary; 俸身 hong' ꜀sing.
Salt, n. 鹽 ꜀siéng.
Salt, a. 鹹 ꜀keng.
Salt, v. 醃 siéng'.
Saltpetre, 硝 ꜀sieu.
Salute, 請安 ꜂ch'iăng ꜀ang.
Same, 同 ꜀tĕng, 一樣 sioh₂ yong².
Sample, 樣 yong².
Sand, 沙 ꜀sai.
Sandal-wood, 檀 ꜀t'ang.
Sap, 汁 chaik₎.
Satin, 緞 taung².
Satisfied, 足意 chëük₎ e'.
Saucer, 碟 tiék₂ 碟仔 tiék₂ ꜂kiăng.
Save, 救 keu', (things) 藏 ꜀chong, 留 ꜀lau.
Savior, 救主 keu' ꜂chio.
Saw, n. & v. 鋸 këü'.
Say, 講 ꜂kong.
Scab, 痞 ꜂p'i.
Scald, 炡 ꜀kong, 炕 t'auk₎.
Scales, (fish-) 魚鱗 ꜀ngü ꜀ling.
Scar, 疤 ꜀pa, 痕 ꜀hong, 跡 chiăh₎.
Scarce, 少 ꜂chieu.
Scatter, 散 sang'.

Scheme, n. 計 *kiéʾ*.
School, 齋 *꜀chá*.
Scissors, 剪刀仔 *꜀ka ꜀tó ‘kiăng*.
Scold, 駡 *maʾ*.
Scoop, n. 鏟箕 *‘ch‘iăng ꜀ki*.
Scorched, 燋着 *꜀chieu tioh$_2$* and *꜁niăng*.
Scour, 鑢 *laëʾ*.
Scrape, 刮 *kauk꜆*.
Scratch, 挖 *wak꜆* 爬 *꜁pa*.
Screen, n. 屏風 *꜁ping ꜀hung*, (of cloth or bamboo-splints) 簾 *꜁liéng*.
Screw, n. 螺絲 *꜁loi ꜀si*.
Scrofula, 瀝 *lek$_2$*.
Scrotum, 腎脬 *leng$^2$ ꜀p‘a*.
Scull, n. 櫓 *‘lu*.
Scurf, 垢 *‘kau*.
Sea, 海 *‘hai*.
Seal, 印 *engʾ*, (up) 封 *꜀hung*.
Seam, 線稅 *siăngʾ swoi$^2$*.
Search, 搜 *꜀seu*, 搜尋 *꜀seu ꜁sing*.
Seasons, (four) 四季 *seʾ kiéʾ*.
Seat, n. 位 *oi$^2$*.
Secretions, 精液 *꜀ching ik$_2$*.
Sect, 教門 *kauʾ ꜁mwong*.
Security, (to be) 做保 *chóʾ ‘pó*.
Sedan, 轎 *kieu$^2$*.
See, 看 *k‘angʾ*, 看見 *k‘angʾ kiéngʾ*.
Seed, 種 *‘chŭng*, (of fruits) 核子 *hok$_2$ ‘chi*.
Seek, 尋 *꜁sing*, 討 *‘t‘ó*.
Seize, 拿 *niăh$_2$* 擒 *꜁k‘iéng*.
Seldom, 少的 *‘chieu tek꜆* 罕的 *‘hang tek꜆*.

Self, 自家 *che$^2$ ꜀ka*.
Selfish, 私心 *꜀sü ꜀sing*.
Sell, 賣 *má$^2$*.
Semen, 精 *꜀ching*.
Send, 差遣 *꜀ch‘á ‘k‘iéng*, 駛去 *‘sai [꜀i] k‘óʾ*, (things) 寄 *kiéʾ*.
Senses, (five) 五官 *‘ngu ꜀kwang*.
Sentence, (of words) 句 *kwoʾ*.
Servant, 駛嘴 *‘sai ch‘oiʾ*.
Sesame, 油蔴 *꜁iu ꜁mwai*.
Set, n. 副 *hoʾ*.
Settle, (accounts) 算清 *saungʾ ꜀ch‘ing*.
Severe, 嚴 *꜁ngiéng*, 重 *taëng$^2$*.
Sew, 紩 *t‘iéngʾ*.
Sewer, 暗溝 *angʾ ꜀kau*.
Shaddock, 橙 *꜁cheng*.
Shadow, 影 *‘ong*.
Shake, v. t. 搖 *꜁yeu*, (v. i.) 定動 *teng$^2$ taëng$^2$*.
Shall, 將欲 *꜀chiong pwoh꜆*.
Shallow, 淺 *‘ch‘iéng*.
Shape, 樣式 *yong$^2$ sek꜆*, 形 *꜁hing*.
Share, n. 份 *hong$^2$* 股 *‘ku*.
Shark, 鯊魚 *꜀sai ꜁ngü*.
Sharp, 利 *le$^2$*.
Shave, (with a razor) 剃 *t‘iéʾ*.
Shavings, 柴配 *꜁ch‘a p‘woiʾ*.
Shears, *꜀ka ꜀tó*, 虎爪 *‘hu ‘chau*.
Sheath, 鞘 *sieuʾ*.
Shed, n. 廠 *‘ch‘iong*.
Shed, v. (skin) 脫殼 *t‘aungʾ k‘aëk꜆* (feathers) 脫毛 *t‘aungʾ ꜁mó*.
Sheep, 棉羊 *꜁miéng ꜁yong*.
Sheet, (of paper) 張 *꜀t‘iong*.

Shelf, 架層 ka꜄ ꜁cheng.
Shell, 殼 k'aëk꜆.
Shin, 骹臁 ꜀k'a ꜁liéng.
Shine, 照 chieu꜄.
Ship, 洋船 ꜁yong ꜁sung.
Shirk work, 躲工 lio$^2$ ꜀këng.
Shirt, 襉 ꜂long.
Shoe, 鞋 ꜁á.
Shoot, (a gun) 放銃 pong꜄ ch'ëüng꜄, (an arrow) 射箭 sioh꜇ chiéng꜄, (birds) 拍鳥 p'ah꜆ ꜂cheu.
Shop, 店 taing꜄, 舖 p'wo꜄.
Shore, n. 岸 ngiàng$^2$.
Short, 短 ꜂toi.
Shot, 鉛子 ꜁yong ꜂chi.
Shoulder, 肩頭 ꜀kiéng ꜁t'au.
Shout, v. 呼꜄ kaë꜄, 喝 hak꜆.
Shovel, (fire-) 火鈀 ꜂hwi ꜁pa.
Show, (point out) 指 ꜂pi.
Shrimp, 蝦 ꜁ha.
Shrine, 龕 ꜀k'ang.
Shut, (a door) 關 ꜀kwong, (a fan) 合 hak꜇ (the eyes) 尅 k'aik꜆.
Shuttle, 梭 ꜀só.
Sick, 破病 p'wai꜄ pang$^2$.
Sickle, 鐮鍥 ꜁liéng kaik꜆.
Side, 傍邊 ꜁pong ꜀piéng.
Sift, 篩 ꜀t'ai.
Sigh, v. 嘆氣 t'ang꜄ k'e꜄.
Sign-board, 招牌 ꜀chieu ꜁pá.
Silk, 絲 ꜀si, 綢 ꜁tiu.
Silk-worm, 蠶繭 ꜁ch'eng ꜂keng.
Silver, 銀 ꜁ngüng.
Similar, 相像 ꜀song ch'iong$^2$.
Sin, n. 罪 chói$^2$.

Sin, v. 犯罪 hwang$^2$ chói$^2$; (against) 得罪 taik꜆ choi$^2$.
Sinew, 筋 ꜀kŭng.
Sing, 唱 ch'iong꜄.
Single, 單 ꜀tang, 隻 chiăh꜆.
Sink, 沉 ꜁t'eng.
Sister, (elder) 姐 ꜂chiă, (younger) 妹 mwoi꜄.
Sit, 坐 sói$^2$.
Skein, 枳 ꜂chi.
Sketch, 畫 wa$^2$.
Skill, 手段 ꜂ch'iu taung$^2$.
Skim, 撇 p'iék꜆.
Skin, n. 皮 ꜁p'uí.
Skull, 頭骯骨 ꜁t'au ꜂wang kauk꜆.
Sky, 天 ꜀t'iéng.
Slack, 鬆 ꜀sëng and nëüng$^2$.
Slander, 誹謗 ꜁pai (꜁pá) paung꜄, 毀謗 ꜂hwi paung꜄.
Slave, (male) 奴才 ꜁nu ꜁ch'ai, (female) 丫頭 ꜀a ꜁t'au.
Sleep, 困 k'aung꜄.
Sleepy, 睶 ꜂ch'ung, 欲困 ói꜄ k'aung꜄.
Sleeve, 手袖 ꜂ch'iu ꜂wong.
Slice, n. 片 p'iéng꜄.
Slice, v. 削 sioh꜆.
Slip, v. 滑 kok꜇.
Slow, 慢 maing$^2$.
Small, 細 sá꜄, 嫩 naung$^2$.
Small-pox, 出痘 ch'ok꜆ tau$^2$.
Smart, v. 痠 ꜀song, 痠澀 ꜀song saik꜆.
Smell, v. 嚊 pe$^2$.
Smoke, 烟 ꜀ing, 火烟 ꜂hwi ꜀ing.

Man. 32.

Smooth, 光 ꜀*kwong*.
Snail, 田螺 ꜁*ch'eng* ꜁*loi*.
Snake, 佬蛇 *lau*$^2$ ꜁*sié*.
Snare, v. 當 ꜀*tong*.
Sneeze, 喝嚏 *hak*꜆ *ch'e*$^2$.
Snore, 鼾 ꜁*hang*.
Snow, n. 雪 *siok*꜆.
Soak, 浸 *cheng*꜄.
Soap, 胰皂 ꜁*i chó*$^2$, 油垢 ꜁*iu* ꜀*k'u*.
Sofa, 匟牀 *k'aung*꜄ ꜁*ch'ong*.
Soft, 腝 *naëng*꜄.
Solder, 銲 *ang*$^2$.
Soldier, 兵 ꜀*ping*.
Solid, 實 *sik*$_2$.
Son, 仔 ꜂*kiăng*, 子 ꜂*chü*.
Song, 曲 *k'woh*꜆ 歌 ꜀*kó*.
Soon, 就 *cheu*$^2$.
Soot, 烏烟 ꜀*u* ꜀*yéng*.
Soul, 靈魂 ꜁*ling* ꜁*hung*.
Sound, n. 聲音 ꜀*siăng* ꜀*ing*.
Soup, 湯 ꜀*t'ong*.
Sour, 酸 ꜀*song*.
South, 南 ꜁*nang*.
Sow seed, 欜種 *ié*$^2$ ꜂*chüng*.
Soy, 豉油 *sié*$^2$ ꜁*iu*.
Spade, 鏵 ꜁*hwa*.
Speak, 講話 ꜂*kong wa*$^2$.
Spear, 鎗 ꜀*ch'iong*.
Species, 種 ꜂*chüng*, 類 *loi*$^2$.
Spectacles, 眼鏡 ꜂*ngiăng ngiăng*꜄.
Spend, 駛 ꜂*sai*, 用 *üng*$^2$, 費 *hié*꜄.
Spice, 椒料 ꜀*chieu laiu*$^2$.
Spider, 蜘蛛 ꜀*t'i* ꜀*t'ü*, and ꜂*ma* ꜀*lai* ꜁*ié*.
Spill, 泎 *chiăk*꜆.
Spirit, n. 神 ꜁*sing*, 靈 ꜁*ling*.
Spit, v. 呸瀧 *p'oi*꜄ ꜂*lang*.
Splendid, 華麗 ꜁*hwa li*$^2$.
Split, v. 破 *p'wai*꜄.
Sponge, 海絨 ꜂*hai* ꜁*üng*.
Spoon, 瓢 ꜁*p'ieu*.
Spout, n. 嘴 *ch'oi*꜄.
Spread, 鋪 ꜀*p'wo*, 舒 ꜀*ch'ü*.
Spring, n. (season) 春天 ꜀*ch'ung* ꜀*t'iéng*, (of water) 泉 ꜁*chiong*.
Sprinkle, *ho*꜄ 潑 *p'wak*꜆.
Sprout, v. 發芽 *pwok*꜆ ꜁*nga*.
Spurt, v. t. (water) 噴水 *p'ong*꜄ ꜂*chwi*.
Square, a. 四角 *se*꜄ *kaëk*꜆.
Squeeze, 挾 *kek*$_2$ 硌 *k'iăk*꜆.
Squirrel, 胡鼠 ꜁*hu* ꜂*ch'ü*.
Stab, 劄 *t'aek*꜆ and *keh*꜆ or *kih*$_2$.
Staff, 杖 *t'iong*$^2$.
Stain, n. 暈 *wong*$^2$, 跡 *chiăh*꜆.
Stairs, 踏斗 *tak*$_2$ ꜂*tau*.
Stammer, *tăh*$_2$ and *tih*$_2$ or *chih*$_2$.
Stamp, n. 戳 *chek*$_2$ 戳記 *chek*$_2$ *ke*꜄.
Stand, v. 跬 *k'ié*$^2$.
Staple, (of iron or brass) 碢鎢目 ꜁*ku* ꜀*chwi mĕk*$_2$.
Star, 星 ꜀*sing*.
Starch, n. & v. 漿 ꜀*chiong*.
Starve, 餓 *ngó*$^2$.
Steal, 偷 ꜀*t'au*. 偷拘 ꜀*t'au* ꜁*tö*.
Steam, n. 湯氣 ꜀*t'ong k'e*꜄.
Steam, v. 炊 ꜀*ch'wi*.
Steel, 鋼 *kaung*꜄.
Steelyard, 秤 *ch'eng*꜄.
Steep, a. 崎 *k'ié*꜄.

Step, 腳潑 ꜀k‘a p‘wak꜇ (in stairs) 層 ꜀cheng.
Stick, v. (adhere) 鉀 kak꜇.
Stiff, 硬 ngaing꜅.
Still, a. 靜 cheng꜅, (silent) sang꜅.
Stir, v. 動 taëng꜅ or tong꜅.
Stockings, 襪 wak꜇.
Stomach, 胃 oi꜅, 脾胃 ꜀pi oi꜅.
Stone, n. 石 sioh꜇.
Stoop, v. 覆 p‘ok꜆ or p‘ok꜆ kiă꜅.
Stop, 歇 hiok꜆, 止 ‘chi, 停 ꜀ling.
Stove, 鐵爐 t‘iék꜆ ꜀lu.
Straight, 直 tik꜇.
Strain, (to filter) 濾 lëü꜅.
Strangle, 絞’死 saung’ ‘si.
Straw, 稿 ‘kó.
Streaks, 紋 ꜀ung.
Street, 街 ꜀ká, 街中 ꜀ká ꜀tong.
Strength, 力 lik꜇ 力量 lik꜇ liong꜅.
Strict, 嚴 ꜀ngiéng, 緊 ‘king.
Strike, 拍 p‘ah꜆ 打 ‘ta.
String, v. 串 ch‘iong’.
Stroke, (of pencil) 畫 wah꜇ or hek꜇.
Stubborn, 拗 au’, 心硬 ꜀sing ngaing꜅.
Study, v. 讀書 t‘ëk꜇ ꜀chü.
Stuff, n. 料 laiu꜅.
Stuffing, (as of cakes) 餡 ang꜅.
Stumble, 着踢 tioh꜇ t‘ek꜆.
Stupid, 戇 ngaung꜅, 獃 ꜀tai.
Submit, 降伏 ꜀hong huk꜇.
Subscribe money, 題錢 ꜀tá ꜀chiéng.
Subtract, 扣 k‘aiu’.
Successive, 陸續 lük꜇ sük꜇.
Suck, 欶 sóh꜆.
Suckle, 喚乳 hwang’ ꜀neng.
Sudorific, 出汗藥 ch‘ok꜆ kang꜅ yoh꜇.
Suet, 油板 ꜀iu ‘peng.
Sugar, 糖 ꜀t‘ong.
Sugar-cane, 樜 chiă’.
Suitable, 中駛 tëüng’ ‘sai.
Sulphur, 硫磺 ꜀liu ꜀hwong.
Sum, 共計 këüng꜅ kié’.
Summer, 夏天 ha꜅ ꜀t‘iéng.
Sun, 日 nik꜇ 日頭 nik꜇ ꜀t‘au.
Sunday, 禮拜日 ‘lá pai’ nik꜇.
Sunflower, 向日葵 hiong’ nik꜇ ꜀ki.
Supper, 暝 ꜀mang.
Support, v. 扶 ho꜅.
Surface, 面 meng’.
Surgery, 外科 ngwoi꜅ ꜀k‘wo.
Surname, 姓 sang’.
Suspend, 掛 kwa’, 吊 taiu’.
Swallow, n. (ornith.) 燕 yéng’.
Swallow, v. 吞 ꜀t‘ong.
Swear, 詛嘴 cho’ ch‘oi’.
Sweat, n. 汗 kang꜅.
Sweep, v. 掃 sau’.
Sweet, 甜 ꜀tiéng, 甘 ꜀kang.
Swell, 腫 ‘chüng.
Swim, 泅水 ꜀siu ‘chwi.
Swine, 猪 ꜀tü.
Swing, v. 輪 ꜀lung.
Sword, 刀 ꜀tó, 劍 kiéng’.
Sycee, 元寶銀 ꜀ngwong ‘pó ꜀ngüng, 紋銀 ꜀ung ꜀ngüng.
Syphon, 掬 këük꜆.

# T

Table, 桌 tóh꜀.
Tablet, 牌 ꜁pá, (stone-) 碑 ꜀pi.
Tael, 兩 ꜂liong.
Tail, 尾 ꜂mwi.
Take, 掏 ꜁tó, 拈 ꜀niéng.
Talk, v. 講話 ꜂kong wa².
Tall, 漢馬高 hang꜄ ꜂ma ꜁keng.
Tallow-tree, 桕模 k'ëüng² ch'eu꜄.
Tally, n. 籌 ꜁t'iu.
Tame, a. 熟 sük₂ 老實 ꜂ló sik₂.
Tan, v. 礬皮 ꜁hwang ꜁p'ui.
Tape, 帶仔 tai꜄ ꜂kiăng.
Tares, 稗 p'á꜄.
Target, 靶 ꜂pa.
Taro, 芋 wo².
Tartar, (Manchu) 滿州 ꜂mwang ꜀chiu, (Mongol) 蒙古 ꜁mung ꜂ku.
Tassel, 縒 soi꜄.
Taste, n. 味 e².
Tea, 茶 ꜁ta, (-leaf) 茶葉 ꜁ta nioh₂.
Tea-taster, 茶師 ꜁ta ꜀sü.
Teach, 教 ka꜄, 教導 ka꜄ tó꜄.
Teacher, 先生 ꜀sing ꜀sang.
Tear, v. ꜂t'ié, 破 p'wai꜄, 擘 pah꜀.
Tears, 目滓 mek₂ ꜂chai.
Telescope, 千里鏡 ꜀ch'iéng ꜂li kiăng꜄.
Tell, 通知 ꜀t'ung ꜀ti, 漢 hang꜄.
Temple, 廟 mieu², 殿 taing².
Tempt, 謠惑 ꜁yeu hëk₂.
Tendon, 筋 ꜀küng.
Terrace, 臺 ꜁tai.
Testimony, 口供 ꜂k'eu ꜀küng.
Thank, 多謝 ꜀tó siă².

The, 啫 ꜂chiă, (ordinal) 第 tá².
Theatricals, 做戲 chó꜄ hié꜄.
There, 許塊 ꜀hu wai꜄.
Therefore, 故此 ko꜄ ꜂ch'ü.
Thermometer, 寒暑針 ꜁hang ꜂sü ꜀cheng.
Thick, 厚 kau², (as paste) kük₂.
Thief, 賊 ch'ek₂.
Thigh, 腿 ꜂t'oi.
Thimble, 頂針 ꜂t'ing ꜀cheng.
Thin, 薄 póh₂ (as paste) 清 ꜀ch'ing.
Thing, 乇 nóh꜀ 物 uk₂.
Think, 想 ꜂siong, 思想 ꜀sü ꜂siong.
Thirst, 嘴渴 ch'oi꜄ k'ak꜀.
This, 啫 ꜂chiă, (indep. pron.) 儕 ꜁chuí.
Thread, 線 siăng꜄.
Threaten, 嚇 hiăh꜀.
Thresh, 摔 saëk꜀.
Threshold, 門限 ꜁mwong taing².
Throat, 喉嚨 ꜁hë (꜁hó) ꜁lëng.
Through, 通透 ꜀t'ëng t'au꜄.
Throw, 丟 ꜀liu, (down) chóh₂.
Thunder, n. 雷公 ꜁lai (꜁loi) ꜀kung.
Thus, 將換 ꜀chiong wang².
Ticket, 標條 ꜀pieu ꜁teu.
Tickle, v. t. ꜁ki teh꜀ (tih₂), v. i. 僟癢 á² ꜁siong.
Tide, (ebb) 水汐 ꜂chwi p'wong꜄, (flood) 水漲 ꜂chwi ꜂tong.
Tie, v. 縛 pwoh₂ (a knot) 結纇 kaik꜀ ꜁loi.
Tiffin, 點心 ꜂tiéng ꜀sing.

榕腔初學撮要

Tiger, 佬虎 *la² ʻhu (lau² ʻhu).*
Tight, 緊 *ʻking*, (taut) 雄 *꜀hŭng.*
Tile, 瓦 *ngwa².*
Till, v. 耕種 *꜀keng chëŭng꜄.*
Time, 時候 *꜀si haiu².*
Tin, 錫 *sek꜆.*
Tinder, 火艾 *ʻhwi ngié꜄.*
Tinfoil, 錫箔 *sek꜆ póh꜇.*
Toad, 蝦蟆 *꜀ha ꜀ma.*
Toast, v. 烘 *꜀hĕng.*
Tobacco, 煙 *꜀hong.*
Toe, 胶指 *꜀k'a ʻchai.*
Together, 齊 *꜀chá*, or *꜀chá ꜀chá.*
Toil, 勞苦 *꜀ló ʻk'u.*
Tomato, 蛇蛋 *꜀sié laung².*
Tone, 音 *꜀ing*, 聲 *꜀siăng.*
Tongs, 火鉗 *ʻhwi ꜀k'ing.*
Tongue, 嘴舌 *ch'oi꜄ siék꜇.*
Too, 太 *k'ak꜆.*
Tool, 家私 *꜀ka ꜀si.*
Tooth, 齒 *ʻngai*, and *ʻk'i* or *ʻch'i.*
Top, 頂 *ʻting.*
Torch, 火把 *ʻhwi ʻpa.*
Tortoise, 龜 *꜀kwi.*
Toss, 險 *hiéng꜄.*
Touch, ʻ按 *ʻeng*, 摸 *꜀mwo.*
Tough, 韌 *nong².*
Towards, 向 *hiong꜄*, 朝 *꜀tieu.*
Toys, 客遊乇 *k'ah꜆ ꜀lieu nóh꜆.*
Trade, n. 生意 *꜀seng e꜄.*
Trample on, 躇 *ch'iăk꜇* or *ch'ŭk꜇.*
Transgress, 犯 *hwang².*
Translate, 翻譯 *꜀hwang ik꜇.*
Transparent, 通瓏 *꜀t'ëng ꜀lëng.*
Transport, v. 運 *ong².*
Trap, (rat-) 老鼠杏 *ʻló ʻch'ü k'iăk꜆.*
Travel, v. 行路 *꜀kiăng tio².*
Tray, 盤 *꜀pwang.*
Tread, v. 胶踏 *꜀k'a tak꜇.*
Treasury, 庫 *k'o꜄.*
Treat, 看待 *k'ang꜄ tai².*
Treaty, 和約 *꜀hwo yok꜆.*
Tree, 樹 *ch'eu꜄.*
Tremble, 斗斗戰 *ʻteu ʻteu chiéng꜄.*
Tribute, 貢 *kong꜄.*
Trough, 槽 *꜀só.*
Trousers, 褲 *k'o꜄.*
True, 真 *꜀ching*, 實 *sik꜇.*
Try, (make trial) 試 *ch'e꜄.*
Tub, 桶 *ʻt'ëng*, 胶桶 *꜀k'a ʻt'ëng.*
Tube, 筒 *꜀tëng*, 管 *ʻkwong.*
Tumor, 瘤 *꜀liu*, 瘋瘤 *꜀hung ꜀liu.*
Tune, 調 *tieu².*
Turbid, 渾 *꜀hung*, 濁 *chok꜇.*
Turkey, (ornith.) 火雞 *ʻhwi ꜀kié.*
Turn, v. 轉彎 *ʻtiong ꜀wang*, (as a screw or in a lathe) 俥 *꜀ch'iă.*
Turnip, 菜頭 *ch'ai꜄ ꜀t'au.*
Turtle, 鱉 *piék꜆.*
Twilled, 斜紋 *꜀siă ꜀ung.*
Twins, 雙生 *꜀sëng ꜀sang.*
Twist, v. 搓 *꜀ch'ó*, 攮 *꜀nong.*
Type, (metallic) 鉛字 *꜀yong che².*
Typhoon, 風颱 *꜀hung ꜀t'ai.*

## U

Ugly, 生的呆 *꜀sang tek꜆ ꜀ngai.*
Ulcer, 瘡 *꜀ch'ong.*
Umbrella, 傘 *ʻsang.*
Unbind, 解 *ʻká.*

Uncle, 伯 *pah꜅* 叔 *chĕük꜅* (maternal) 娘舅 *꜀niong keu$^2$*.
Under, 下 *a$^2$*, 下底 *a$^2$ ꜂tá*.
Understand, 曉的 *꜂hieu tek꜅*.
Unicorn, 麒麟 *꜀ki ꜀ling*.
Uniform, a. *꜀seu*, 純 *꜀sung*.
Unite, 合 *hak$_2$* 連 *꜀liêng*.
United States of America, 合衆國 *Hak$_2$ chĕüng꜄ kwok꜅* 大美國 *Tai$^2$ ꜂mi kwok꜅*.
Universal, 普遍 *꜂p'wo p'iêng꜄*.
Unnecessary, 伓駛 *ng$^2$ ꜂sai*.
Unrighteous, 不義 *pok꜅ ngiê$^2$*.
Upon, 面上 *meng꜄ siong$^2$*, *꜀*崎頂 *꜀ká ꜂teng*.
Upset, 拍倒 *p'ah꜅ ꜂tó*.
Upstairs, 樓頂 *꜀lau ꜂ting*.
Urge, 勉勵 *꜂miêng lá$^2$*.
Urinate, *꜀na nieu$^2$* 小便 *꜂sieu ꜀piêng*.
Urine, 尿 *nieu$^2$*.
Use, v. 駛 *꜂sai*, 用 *ëüng$^2$*.
Useful, 中駛 *tëüng꜄ ꜂sai*.
Usurp, 佔 *chiêng꜄*.
Utmost, 極 *kik$_2$* 盡 *cheng$^2$*.

## V

Vacant, 空 *꜁k'ëng*, 虛 *꜁hü*.
Vacation, (to give a) 放假 *pong꜄ ka꜄*.
Vaccinate, 種痘 *chĕüng꜄ tau$^2$*.
Vagabond, n. 歹仔 *꜂p'ai ꜂kiăng*.
Vainly, 空喬 *꜁k'ĕng ꜀ngieu*.
Varnish, 漆 *ch'ek꜅*.
Vase, 瓶 *꜀ping*.
Vegetable, 菜 *ch'ai꜄*.
Veil, n. 帕 *p'a꜄*.
Vein, 血筋 *haik꜅ ꜁küng*.
Velvet, 絨 *꜀üng*.
Ventilate, 通風 *꜁t'ëng ꜁hung*.
Veranda, 走馬樓 *꜂chau ꜂ma ꜀lau*.
Verb, 活字 *wak$_2$ che$^2$*.
Verdigris, 銅綠 *꜀tëng lioh$_2$*.
Vermicelli, 麪 *miêng$^2$*.
Vermilion, 銀硃 *꜀ngüng ꜁chio*.
Verse, 節 *chiêk꜅*.
Very, 盡 *cheng$^2$*, 頂 *꜂ting*, 極 *kik$_2$* 野 *꜂yă*.
Vessel, 器 *k'e꜄*, (boat) 船 *꜀sung*.
Vest, (waistcoat) 甲仔 *kak꜅ ꜂kiăng*.
Vial, 瓶 *꜀ping*.
Vibrate, *꜁*輪 *꜁lung*, 擺 *꜂pai*.
Viceroy, 總督 *꜂chung tok꜅*.
Village, 鄉村 *꜁hiong ꜁ch'ong*.
Vinegar, 醋 *ch'o꜄*.
Violent, 強 *꜀kiong*, 惡 *auk꜅*.
Virtue, 德 *taik꜅*.
Visiting-card, 片單 *p'iêng꜄ ꜁tang*, 名片 *꜀miăng p'iêng꜄*.
Vitriol, (blue) 膽礬 *꜂tang ꜀hwang*.
Viviparous, 胎生 *꜁t'ai ꜁seng*.
Voice, 聲音 *꜁siăng ꜁ing*.
Volume, 本 *꜂pwong*, 部 *p'wo$^2$*.
Vomit, 吐 *t'o꜄*, 嘔 *꜂au*.
Vow, 許愿 *꜂hü ngwong$^2$*.

## W

Wade, 涉水 *lak$_2$ ꜂chwi*.
Wager, v. 賭輸 *꜂tu ꜀sio*.
Wages, 工錢 *꜁këng ꜀chiêng*.
Waist, 腰 *꜁yeu*.
Wait, 等 *꜂ting*.

Walk, 行 ꜁kiàng.
Wall, 墻 ꜁ch'iong, (of laths and plaster) 土壁 ꜂t'u piăh꜆.
Walnut, 核桃 hok꜇ ꜁t'ó.
War, 動刀兵 tong꜅ ꜀tó ꜀ping.
Ward, (of a town) 鋪 p'wo꜄, 鄉 ꜀hiong.
Warlike, 武 ꜂u.
Warm, 熱 yék꜇.
Warn, 警戒 ꜂king kai꜄.
Warped, 翹 ꜁ngau, 蹺 k'ieu꜄.
Warrant, n. 票 p'ieu꜄.
Warrant, v. 包 ꜀pau, 保 ꜂pó.
Wash, 洗 ꜂sá.
Washington, 華盛頓 ꜁Hwa seng꜅ tong꜄.
Waste, v. 花費 ꜀hwa hié꜄.
Watch, n. (of the night) 更 ꜀kang, (a time-piece) 錶 ꜂pieu.
Watch, v. aung꜄.
Water, 水 ꜂chwi.
Water-melon, 西瓜 ꜀sá ꜀kwa.
Waves, n. 風浪 ꜀hung laung꜅.
Wave, v. 舞 ꜂u.
Wax, 蠟 lak꜇.
Weak, 弱 yok꜇.
Wealth, 錢財 ꜁chiéng ꜁chai.
Wean, 斷乳 taung꜅ ꜁neng.
Wear, (as clothes) 穿꜅ sëüng꜅, (as a cap, flowers, etc.) 戴 tai꜄.
Weary, 倦力 siăh꜇ lik꜇, 弱 yok꜆.
Weather, 天 ꜀t'iéng.
Weave, 織 chek꜆.
Wedge, n. & v. 尖 ꜀chiéng.
Weed, v. 薅草 ꜀hau ꜂ch'au.
Week, 一禮拜 sioh꜇ ꜂lá pai꜄.
Weigh, 稱 ꜀ch'ing.
Well, n. 井 ꜂chang.
Well, a. 好 ꜂hó.
West, 西 ꜀sá.
Wet, 濫 lang꜅.
Wet-nurse, ꜁neng hwang꜄, 朧奶 ꜁neng ꜂ná.
Wharf, 道頭 tó꜅ ꜁t'au.
What, 世乇 sié꜄ nóh꜆, (that which) 所 ꜂su.
Wheat, 小麥 ꜂sieu mah꜇.
Wheel, 車輪 ꜀ch'iă ꜁lung.
When, 面候 miéng꜅ au꜅, 箸古 nioh꜇ ꜂u.
Where, 冬那 ꜀tëng ꜂në.
Whetstone, 刀石 ꜀tó sioh꜇.
Whip, n. 鞭 ꜀piéng, (switch) 箠 ꜁ch'uí.
Whirlwind, 捲螺風 ꜂kwong ꜁loi ꜀hung.
Whiskers, 鬚 ꜀sü, 胡鬚 ꜁hu ꜀sü.
White, 白 pah꜇.
Who, 俤仈 tié꜅ ꜁nëng.
Whole, ꜁kó ꜁long, 全 ꜁chiong.
Why, 將其 ꜀chiong ꜁ki.
Wick, 燈芯 ꜀tiéng ꜀sing.
Wide, 闊 k'wak꜆.
Wife, 佬媽 lau꜅ ꜂ma.
Wild, 野 ꜂yă.
Will, n. (mental) 志氣 che꜄ k'e꜄.
Will, (auxil.) 刹 pwoh꜆, 將刹 ꜀chiong pwoh꜆.
Willing, 肯 ꜂k'ing, 願 ngwong꜅.
Willow, 柳 ꜂liu.
Win, 贏 ꜁yăng.
Wind, n. 風 ꜀hung.

Window, 檻門 ʿk'ang ꜀mwong.
Wine, 酒 ʿchiu.
Wing, 翼 sik꜆.
Wink, 目睭睛睛 mek꜆ ꜀chiu t'iăk꜄ t'iăk꜄.
Winnow, 簸 pwai꜄, 扇 ꜀siĕng.
Winter, 冬天 ꜀lĕng ꜀t'iĕng.
Wipe, 拭 ch'ek꜄ (with wet cloth) ʿkang.
Wire, 線 siăng꜄.
Wise, 智꜄ óh꜄.
Wish, 欲 ói꜄, 值 tih꜆.
With, 共 kaĕng꜆.
Within, 裡勢 ʿtié tié꜄, 內 nŏi꜆.
Without, 外斗 ngié꜆ ʿtau, 外 ngwoi꜆.
Woe, 禍 hwo꜆, 災禍 ꜀chai hwo꜆.
Wolf, 豺狼 ꜀ch'ai ꜀long.
Woman, 諸娘伙 ꜀chü ꜀niong ꜀nĕng.
Womb, 胎 ꜀t'ai.
Wonder, 奇特 ꜀ki tek꜆.
Wood, 木 muk꜆ 柴 ꜀ch'a.
Wool, 羊毛 ꜀yong ꜀mó.
Woolens, 呢 ꜀ni, 毡 ꜀chiéng.
Word, (written) 字 che꜆, (spoken) 話 wa꜆.
Work, 工 ꜀kĕng, 工夫 ꜀kĕng ꜀hu.
World, 世間 sié꜄ ꜀kang.
Worms, 蟲 ꜀t'ĕng.
Wormwood, 茵蔯 ꜀ing ꜀ting.
Worship, 拜 pai꜄, 禮拜 ʿlá pai꜄.
Worth, a. 值錢 tek꜆ ꜀chiéng.
Worthy, a. 倠中 á꜆ tĕüng꜄.

Wound, n. 傷 ꜀siong.
Wound, v. 拍傷 p'ah꜄ ꜀siong.
Wrap, 包 ꜀pau, 拍包 p'ah꜄ ꜀pau.
Wring, ch'ong꜆.
Wrinkle, 縐 chaiu꜄, 皺 naiu꜄.
Wrist, 手管 ʿch'iu ʿkwang.
Write, 寫 ʿsiă.
Wrong, 錯 tang꜆ 伓着 ng꜆ tioh꜆.
Wry, 歪 ꜀wai.

## Y

Yam, 薯 ꜀sü.
Yard, 一碼 sioh꜆ ʿma.
Yarn, (cotton-) 棉紗線 ꜀miĕng ꜀sa siăng꜄.
Year, 年 ꜀niĕng, (of age) 歲 hwoi꜄.
Yeast, 酵 ꜀pui, 包酵 ꜀pau ꜀pui.
Yellow, 黃 ꜀wong.
Yes, 是 se꜆, 正是 chiăng꜄ se꜆.
Yesterday, 一暝 sioh꜆ ꜀mang.
Yet, (still) 故 ko꜄, (not yet) 昧 mwoi꜆.
Yield, (give place to) 讓 niong꜆.
Yoke, n. 牛軛 ꜀ngu kah꜄.
Yolk, 蛋黃 laung꜆ ꜀wong.
You, 汝 ʿnü, (plu.) 汝各伙 ʿnü kauk꜄ ꜀nĕng.
Young, 後生 hau꜆ ꜀sang.

## Z

Zealous, 熱心 yék꜆ ꜀sing.
Zebra, 虎斑馬 ʿhu ꜀peng ʿma.
Zenith, 天中中 ꜀t'iĕng ꜀tong ꜀tong.
Zodiac, 黃道 ꜀wong tó꜆.
Zone, 道 tó꜆.

—:o:—

# 汕頭方言初階

（*First Lessons in the Swatow Dialect*）

〔美〕斐姑娘（Adele Marion Fielde）编

《汕頭方言初階》，美國斐姑娘編。斐姑娘（Adele Marion Fielde，一八三九—一九一六），全名阿黛爾・瑪麗安・菲爾德，美北浸信會女傳教士。生於美國紐約，一八六五年至曼谷，頗用心於潮州方言之學習，一八七三至一八八九年至汕頭。此書係潮汕方言學習教材，設二百課，每課設十二單字、雙音詞或片語，先注羅馬字音，後釋以英文，末附汕頭方言羅馬字音索引。是書排版，每課内容皆置於雙數頁，單數頁悉爲空白，僅分左右兩欄。此次收録，將單數頁删去，僅留一頁以示其式樣。據一八七八年汕頭版影印。

汕頭方言初階

# FIRST LESSONS

IN THE

# SWATOW DIALECT.

BY

A. M. FIELDE.

FESTINA LENTE.

SWATOW:
PRINTED BY THE "SWATOW PRINTING OFFICE COMPANY."
1878

# DIRECTIONS FOR USING THIS BOOK.

1st.

Learn perfectly, from a native teacher, the eight tones as given in the exercise on page 3.

2nd.

Learn from pages 5 and 6 the Chinese sounds represented by the letters used in Romanizing them.

3rd.

Learn how to pronounce correctly words with and without the aspirate, and with and without the nasal, using the exercises on page 7.

4th.

Learn to count accurately from pages 9 and 10.

5th.

Learn the lessons in their order, completely mastering each before beginning the next one. Be able to write the Chinese characters from memory, to translate the English into Chinese, and the Chinese into English, and look for fuller definitions of the same words in Williams' Dictionary.

6th.

Exercise the ear more than the eye in learning the language.

A. M. F.

Swatow, 1877.

## TONES.

Every Chinese word has a tone, inseparable from its pronunciation. In the Tîe Ciu dialect there are eight tones, which can be acquired only from a living teacher. Many Chinese teachers know no names for the tones; and different teachers place them in different orders. The following order is perhaps most usual.

| *Chinese Name.* | | | |
|---|---|---|---|
| 上平 | cīe$^n$ phê$^n$, | upper even. | |
| 上上 | cīe$^n$ sǐang, | upper high. | |
| 上去 | cīe$^n$ khà, | upper going. | |
| 上入 | cīe$^n$ jîp, | upper entering. | |
| 下平 | ĕ phê$^n$, | lower even. | |
| 下上 | ĕ siăng, | lower high. | |
| 下去 | ĕ khà, | lower going. | |
| 下入 | ĕ jîp, | lower entering. | |

*Tonal Marks.*

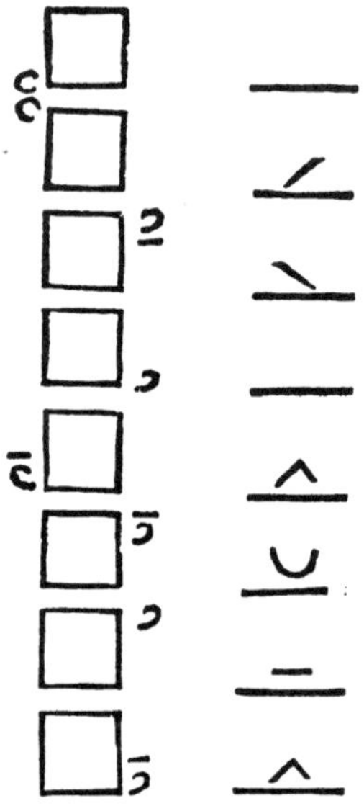

These names do not express the relative sounds of the tones, but appear to be purely arbitrary. Words in the entering tones always end in the sound of h, k, p, or t. In speaking, the tone of a word is greatly modified by its relation to other words in the sentence, and all are obscure except that of the most emphatic word, which has its tone fully enunciated. The same syllable is seldom found in all the eight tones.

汕頭方言初階



## EXERCISES IN THE TONES.

| | | | | | | | | | |
|---|---|---|---|---|---|---|---|---|---|
| 司 | si | 低 | ti | 刀 | to | 紛 | hun | 邦 | pang |
| 死 | sí | 抵 | tí | 短 | tó | 粉 | hún | 榜 | páng |
| 四 | sì | 帝 | tì | 戴 | tò | 奮 | hùn | 放 | pàng |
| 薛 | sih | 滴 | tih | 卓 | toh | 弗 | hut | 北 | pak |
| 時 | sî | 池 | tî | 逃 | tô | 魂 | hûn | 房 | pâng |
| 是 | sĭ | 弟 | tĭ | 在 | tŏ | 混 | hŭn | 謗 | păng |
| 示 | sī | 地 | tī | 袋 | tō | 份 | hūn | 方 | pāng |
| 蝕 | sîh | 碟 | tîh | 擇 | tôh | 佛 | hût | 縛 | pâk |

| | | | | | | | | | |
|---|---|---|---|---|---|---|---|---|---|
| 烘 | hang | 溫 | un | 心 | sim | 貞 | ceng | | sia |
| 罕 | háng | 蘊 | ún | 審 | sím | 腫 | céng | 寫 | sía |
| 漢 | hàng | 搵 | ùn | 沁 | sìm | 政 | cèng | 赦 | sìa |
| 謁 | hak | 鬱 | ut | 濕 | sip | 則 | cek | 錫 | siah |
| 韓 | hâng | 紜 | ûn | 忱 | sîm | 嘗 | cêng | 斜 | sîa |
| 限 | hăng | 慍 | ŭn | 甚 | sĭm | 靖 | cĕng | 社 | sĭa |
| 巷 | hāng | 運 | ūn | | sīm | | cēng | 射 | sīa |
| 學 | hâk | 睡 | ût | 習 | sîp | 澤 | cêk | 席 | sîah |

## ROMAN LETTERS.

The sounds of Chinese words cannot be exactly represented by Roman letters, used as in English. In this book the Roman letter whose sound in English approximates the Chinese sound, is taken as the symbol of that sound, and the exact pronunciation must be acquired from the Chinese themselves.

The vowels when followed by consonants are much shortened, especially when followed by h, k, t and p.

The aspirate does not coalesce with a consonant preceding it, but is sounded independently.

The sounds of p, k and t when not followed by the aspirate are so repressed as to resemble those of b, g and d.

Of the consonants all occur as initials, but only h, k, m, n, ng, p and t as finals.

ⁿ at the end of a word indicates that the vowels of the word are sounded nasally.

In all cases the pronunciation of the Chinese word should be learned through the ear and from a native teacher, and the Romanized words should be relied upon only as a help to the memory in learning.

The pronunciation of the same word varies greatly in the different districts. That followed in these lessons is that of the Departmental City.

# SOUNDS OF THE LETTERS.

*Vowels.*

| | | | | | | | | |
|---|---|---|---|---|---|---|---|---|
| a | as | in | far, | in | 鴉 | a, | 匣 | âp. |
| e | ,, | ,, | they, | ,, | 啞 | é, | 掖 | êk. |
| i | ,, | ,, | machine, | ,, | 衣 | i, | 邑 | ip. |
| o | ,, | ,, | no, | ,, | 烏 | o, | 屋 | ok. |
| ɵ | ,, | | aw in fawn, | ,, | 蠔 | ɵ̂, | 桌 | tɵh. |
| u | ,, | | oo ,, tool, | ,, | 有 | ŭ, | 搵 | ùn. |
| ʉ | ,, | | French u, | ,, | 餘 | ʉ̂, | 恩 | ʉn. |
| w | ,, | | o in one | ,, | 完 | ŵn, | 萬 | bw̄n. |

*Consonants.*

| | | | | | | | | |
|---|---|---|---|---|---|---|---|---|
| b | as | in | bar, | in | 馬 | bé, | 麥 | bêh. |
| g | ,, | ,, | gay, | ,, | 牙 | gê, | 鵝 | gɵ̂. |
| h | ,, | ,, | hot, | ,, | 魚 | hʉ̂, | 貪 | tham. |
| j | ,, | ,, | jam, | ,, | 字 | jī, | 絨 | jông. |
| k | ,, | ,, | kick, | ,, | 膠 | ka, | 角 | kak. |
| l | ,, | ,, | lad, | ,, | 路 | lō, | 拉 | la. |
| m | ,, | ,, | mat, | ,, | 夜 | mê, | 迷 | mî. |
| n | ,, | ,, | not, | ,, | 籃 | nâ, | 艱 | kan. |

| | | | | | | | | |
|---|---|---|---|---|---|---|---|---|
| p | as | in | pop, | in | 巴 | pa, | 立 | lîp. |
| s | ,, | ,, | so, | ,, | 順 | sŭn, | 實 | sît. |
| t | ,, | ,, | tilt, | ,, | 茶 | tê, | 得 | tit. |
| ng | ,, | ,, | sing, | ,, | 籠 | lâng, | 言 | ngn̂. |
| c | ,, | ,, | chair | ,, | 止 | cí, | 船 | cûn. |

*This last is a sound between ch in chair, and ts in fits.*

*The vowels found in combination are*

| | | | | | | | | |
|---|---|---|---|---|---|---|---|---|
| ai | as | in | 來 | lâi, | 勿 | mài, | 哀 | ai. |
| au | ,, | ,, | 後 | ău, | 老 | láu, | 頭 | thâu. |
| ia | ,, | ,, | 亦 | ĭa, | 益 | iah, | 養 | iáng. |
| ie | ,, | ,, | 窰 | îe, | 藥 | îeh, | 廟 | bīe. |
| io | ,, | ,, | 妖 | io, | 永 | ióng, | 慾 | îok. |
| iu | ,, | ,, | 油 | îu, | 硫 | lîu, | 守 | síu. |
| oa | ,, | ,, | 大 | tōa, | 帶 | tòa, | 舵 | tŏa. |
| oi | ,, | ,, | 鞋 | oî, | 代 | thòi, | 狹 | oîh. |
| ua | ,, | ,, | 活 | ûah, | 我 | úa, | 滿 | múa. |
| ue | ,, | ,, | 說 | sueh, | 額 | thue, | 話 | ūe. |
| ui | ,, | ,, | 醫 | ui, | 碓 | tùi, | 瑞 | sŭi. |

## EXERCISES IN THE ASPIRATES.

| *Not Aspirated.* | | *Aspirated.* | | *Not Aspirated.* | | *Aspirated.* | |
|---|---|---|---|---|---|---|---|
| 角 | kak. | 壳 | khak. | 毒 | tâk. | 讀 | thâk. |
| 江 | kang. | 匡 | khang. | 躭 | tam. | 貪 | tham. |
| 九 | káu. | 口 | kháu. | 卒 | cut. | 出 | chut. |
| 旗 | kî. | 其 | khî. | 層 | cân. | 田 | chân. |
| 鑑 | kàm. | 勘 | khàm. | 牌 | pâi. | 徘 | phâi. |
| 競 | kĕng. | 虹 | khĕng. | 榜 | páng. | 紡 | pháng. |
| 圭 | kui. | 虧 | khui. | 備 | pì. | 譬 | phì. |

## EXCERCISE IN THE NASALS.

| *Not Nasal.* | | *Nasal.* | | *Not Nasal.* | | *Nasal.* | |
|---|---|---|---|---|---|---|---|
| 趙 | tĭe. | 丈 | tĭe$^{n}$. | 沙 | sua. | 山 | sua$^{n}$. |
| 婢 | pĭ. | 辮 | pĭ$^{n}$. | 哇 | ua. | 鞍 | ua$^{n}$. |
| 碑 | pi. | 邊 | pi$^{n}$. | 家 | ke. | 耕 | ke$^{n}$. |
| 播 | pùa. | 半 | puà$^{n}$. | 嫁 | kè. | 徑 | kè$^{n}$. |
| 砂 | sa. | 衫 | sa$^{n}$. | 招 | cie. | 章 | cie$^{n}$. |

## NASAL AND ASPIRATED.

| | | | | | | | |
|---|---|---|---|---|---|---|---|
| 坑 | khe$^{n}$. | 醒 | ché$^{n}$. | 腔 | khie$^{n}$. | 潘 | phûa$^{n}$. |
| 墻 | chîe$^{n}$. | 星 | che$^{n}$. | 平 | phê$^{n}$. | 痛 | thìa$^{n}$. |
| 鮮 | chi$^{n}$. | 閂 | chùa$^{n}$. | 聘 | phìa$^{n}$. | 炭 | thòa$^{n}$. |

## CHINESE LETTERS.

As the spoken and written languages are unlike, a colloquial sentence written in the characters which would represent its sounds, would not to a Chinese scholar correctly express its meaning. Many colloquial words have no written character. In such case a character of similar signification, with a star following it, has been used in this book.

汕頭方言初階



## FIGURES.

| | | | | |
|---|---|---|---|---|
| 1 | cêk. | 19 | câp káu. | 2,076 |
| 2 | nŏ. | 20 | jī câp. | 3,506 |
| 3 | sa$^{n}$. | 23 | jīh sa$^{n}$. | 4,728 |
| 4 | sì. | 35 | sâp ngŏ. | 5,206 |
| 5 | ngŏ. | 44 | sîp sì. | 5,782 |
| 6 | lâk. | 56 | ngôp lâk. | 6,008 |
| 7 | chit. | 69 | lâk káu. | 6,703 |
| 8 | poih. | 78 | chit poih. | 7,543 |
| 9 | káu. | 94 | kâup sì. | 7,600 |
| 10 | câp. | 100 | cêk peh. | 7,030 |
| 11 | câp it. | 105 | peh lân ngŏ. | 8,000 |
| 12 | câp jī. | 150 | peh ngŏ. | 8,764 |
| 13 | câp sa$^{n}$. | 382 | sa$^{n}$ peh poih jī. | 9,706 |
| 14 | câp sì. | 570 | ngŏ peh chit. | 9,900 |
| 15 | câp ngŏ. | 853 | poih peh ngŏ câp sa$^{n}$. | 9,830 |
| 16 | câp lâk. | 900 | káu peh. | 17,846 |
| 17 | câp chit. | 1,000 | cêk choi$^{n}$. | 40,700 |
| 18 | câp poih. | 10,000 | cêk bw̄n. | 97,015 |

## NUMERALS.

| | | | | | |
|---|---|---|---|---|---|
| 1 | 一 | cêk. | One, | 壹 | cêk. |
| 2 | 二 | nŏ. | Two, | 弍 | nŏ. |
| 3 | 三 | sa$^{n}$. | Three, | 叄 | sa$^{n}$. |
| 4 | 四 | sì. | Four, | 肆 | sì. |
| 5 | 五 | ngŏ. | Five, | 伍 | ngŏ. |
| 6 | 六 | lâk. | Six, | 陸 | lâk. |
| 7 | 七 | chit. | Seven, | 柒 | chit. |
| 8 | 八 | poih. | Eight, | 捌 | poih. |
| 9 | 九 | káu. | Nine, | 玖 | káu. |
| 10 | 十 | câp. | Ten, | 拾 | câp. |
| 50 | 五十 | ngŏ câp. | Eleven, | 拾壹 | câp-it. |
| 100 | 百 | peh. | Twenty two, | 念弍 | jīh-jī. |
| 1000 | 千 | choi$^{n}$. | Thirty four, | 卅肆 | sâp-sì. |
| 1st | 第一 | tŏi$^{n}$ it. | Hundred, | 陌 | peh. |
| 2d | 第二 | tŏi$^{n}$ jī. | Thousand, | 阡 | choi$^{n}$. |
| 5th | 第五 | tŏi$^{n}$ ngŏ. | Ten thousand, | 萬 | bw̄n. |
| 10th | 第十 | tŏi$^{n}$ câp. | Hundred thousand, | 億 | êk. |
| 200dth | 第二百 | tŏi$^{n}$ nŏ peh. | Million. | 兆 | tiŏ. |

## TIMES.

| | | |
|---|---|---|
| 子時 | cú sî, | 11 to 1 A.M. |
| 丑時 | thíu sî, | 1 „ 3 „ |
| 寅時 | în sî, | 3 „ 5 „ |
| 卯時 | báu sî, | 5 „ 7 „ |
| 辰時 | sîn sî, | 7 „ 9 „ |
| 巳時 | cĭ sî, | 9 „ 11 „ |
| 午時 | ngŏ sî, | 11 „ 1 P.M. |
| 未時 | bĭ sî, | 1 „ 3 „ |
| 申時 | sin sî, | 3 „ 5 „ |
| 酉時 | íu sî, | 5 „ 7 „ |
| 戌時 | sut sî, | 7 „ 9 „ |
| 亥時 | hăi sî, | 9 „ 11 „ |
| 定更 | an ke$^n$, | first watch. |
| 二更 | jĭ ke$^n$, | second „ |
| 三更 | sa$^n$ ke$^n$, | third „ |
| 四更 | sì ke$^n$, | fourth „ |
| 五更 | ngŏ ke$^n$, | fifth „ |
| 永遠 | íong íen, | eternally. |

| | | |
|---|---|---|
| 清晨 | * mn̄g khí, | morning. |
| 上午 | * cĭe$^n$ kùa, | forenoon. |
| 中午 | * jît tàu, | noonday. |
| 下午 | * ĕ kùa, | afternoon. |
| 黃昏 | * mê hng, | evening. |
| 半夜 | pùa$^n$ mê, | midnight. |
| 日間 | * jît kùa, | daytime. |
| 夜間 | * mê kùa, | night-time. |
| 明天 | * mùa khí, | to-morrow. |
| 明日 | * mùa jît, | to-morrow. |
| 昨天 | * ca jît, | yesterday. |
| 前天 | côi$^n$ jît, | day before yesterday. |
| 明年 | * mê nî, | next year. |
| 初旬 | chiu sûn, | the first ten days of the month. |
| 中旬 | * jîh sûn, | the middle ten days. |
| 月尾 | guêh búe, | the last ten days of the month. |
| 拜一 | pài it, | Monday. |
| 禮拜日 | lói pài jît, | Sunday. |

## LESSON I.

| | | | |
|---|---|---|---|
| 我 | úa; I, me. | 去 | khṳ̀; go. |
| 爾 | lṳ́; you, singular. | 欲 | ài$^{n}$; wish, will. |
| 伊 | i; he, she, it, they. | 不 | put, m̄, m̆; no, not. |
| 我等 | * ún, ẃn; we, excluding the hearer. | 也 | īa, a; or, whether. |
| 們俺 | * nán; we, including the hearer. | 呢 | * nē; interrogative, expressing doubt. |
| 們汝 | * nín; you, plural. | 嗎 | * mē; interrogative particle. |

| | |
|---|---|
| 1 úa khṳ̀: úa m̄ khṳ̀. | 1 I go: I go not. |
| 2 úa ài$^{n}$ khṳ̀: úa m̆ khṳ̀. | 2 I will go: I won't go. |
| 3 úa m̄ ài$^{n}$ khṳ̀. | 3 I do not wish to go. |
| 4 lṳ́ ài$^{n}$ a m̄ ài$^{n}$? | 4 Do you want it or not? |
| 5 i ài$^{n}$, nán ài$^{n}$. | 5 They want it and we want it. |
| 6 nín ài$^{n}$, ẃn m̄ ài$^{n}$. | 6 You want it, we don't. |
| 7 nín khṳ̀, ún m̄ khṳ̀. | 7 You go, we are not going. |
| 8 úa ài$^{n}$ khṳ̀, i m̄. | 8 I shall go, he will not. |
| 9 lṳ́ ài$^{n}$ khṳ̀ a m̆? | 9 Do you wish to go or not? |
| 10 khṳ̀ a m̄ khṳ̀, úa ài$^{n}$. | 10 Whether I go or not I want it. |
| 11 nín khṳ̀ a m̄ khṳ̀, ún ài$^{n}$ khṳ̀. | 11 Whether you go or not, we are going. |
| 12 i ài$^{n}$, úa m̆. | 12 He wants it, and I won't give it to him. |
| 13 úa m̆ ài$^{n}$ khṳ̀. | 13 I have decided not to go. |
| 14 lṳ́ ài$^{n}$, mē? | 14 Do you want it? |
| 15 khṳ̀ a m̄ khṳ̀, nē? | 15 Are you going or not? |
| 16 lṳ́ úa m̆ khṳ̀. | 16 You and I won't go. |
| 17 nín ài$^{n}$ a m̄? | 17 Do you want it or not? |
| 18 nín ài$^{n}$, mē? | 18 Do you want it? |
| 19 i ài$^{n}$ khṳ̀, mē? | 19 Is she going to go? |
| 20 ài$^{n}$ a m̄ ài$^{n}$, nē? | 20 Do they want it? |
| 21 ẃn ài$^{n}$ m̆ khṳ̀. | 21 We are going to decide not to go. |
| 22 ài$^{n}$ khṳ̀ a m̄? | 22 Are you going or not? |
| 23 ài$^{n}$ khṳ̀ a m̆? | 23 Do you wish to go or not? |
| 24 m̄ khṳ̀: m̆ khṳ̀. | 24 Am not going: won't go. |

13

## LESSON II.

| | | | |
|---|---|---|---|
| 是 | sĭ; be, is, are. | 勿 | mài; do not. |
| 有 | ŭ; has, have. | 無 | bô; no, not. |
| 來 | lâi; come. | 未 | būe; not yet. |
| 知 | cai; know. | 甚 | sĭm; superlative. |
| 叫 | kìe; call. | 什 | * sih; interrogative. |
| 好 | hó; well, good. | 麼 | * mih; interrogative. |

| | |
|---|---|
| 1 sĭ lú a m̄ sí, nē? | 1 It is you is it not? |
| 2 sĭ, a m̄ sĭ? | 2 Is it so or not? |
| 3 sĭ, mē? hó, mē? | 3 Is it so? Is it well? |
| 4 sĭ hó a m̄ hó? | 4 Is it good or bad? |
| 5 úa ŭ; lú būe ŭ. | 5 I have; you have not yet. |
| 6 lâi, hó lâi khù. | 6 Come, let's go. |
| 7 m̄ cai i ŭ a bô. | 7 I do not know whether he has any or not. |
| 8 ài$^{n}$ ŭ: ài$^{n}$ bô. | 8 Will be: about not to be. |
| 9 bô mih ài$^{n}$: bô mih cai. | 9 Do not much wish it: do not very well know. |
| 10 i būe cai lú ài$^{n}$ lâi. īa sĭ. | 10 He does not yet know you are coming. If. |
| 11 lú hó khù kìe i lâi. | 11 You go and call him. |
| 12 bô kìe, i bô lâi. | 12 If you do not call him he will not come. |
| 13 i īa sĭ lâi. | 13 Should he come. |
| 14 úa m̄ cai kìe i. | 14 I did not think to call him. |
| 15 ài$^{n}$ kìe i a būe? lú īa sĭ bô lâi. | 15 Do you want to call him yet? Should you not come. |
| 16 i ài$^{n}$ lâi a būe? | 16 Is he coming yet? |
| 17 lâi ŭ, m̄ cai hó a m̄ hó. | 17 Some have come, I do not know whether they are good or not. |
| 18 sĭm hó: sĭm m̄ hó. | 18 The best: the very worst. |
| 19 bó sĭm mih hó. | 19 Not very good. |
| 20 lâi lâi, khù khù. | 20 Going to and fro. |

## LESSON III.

人 nâng, jîn; man, person.
物 mûeh; things.
屋 * chù; house.
在 tŏ; be, dwell.
個 kâi; one, a classifier.
的 * kâi; possessive.

別 pi̍et, pa̍t; other.
毋 bô; prohibitory particle.
此 chṳ́, cí; this, here.
彼 pí, hṳ́; that, there.
這 cé, cí; this, here.
那 ná, hṳ́; that, there.

| | |
|---|---|
| 1 nâng nâng: bô nâng. | 1 Everybody: nobody. |
| 2 cí kâi nâng sĭ hó nâng. | 2 This is a good man. |
| 3 ĭa sĭ ŭ nâng lâi. | 3 Should anybody come. |
| 4 bô pa̍t nâng tŏ. | 4 There is no one else here. |
| 5 hṳ́ kâi mûeh sĭ m̄ hó. | 5 That thing is bad. |
| 6 lṳ́ ài<sup>n</sup> khṳ̀ chṳ̀ a būe? | 6 Are you going home yet? |
| 7 cí cêk kâi m̄ hó. | 7 This one is not good. |
| 8 ài<sup>n</sup> hṳ́ cêk kâi. | 8 I want that one. |
| 9 tŏ hṳ́ bô nâng tŏ. | 9 There is no one there. |
| 10 kâi kâi sĭ hó. | 10 Every one of them is good. |
| 11 lâi, kâi nâng, kâi nâng. | 11 Come one by one. |
| 12 tŏ lṳ́: tŏ i. | 12 As you like: it is his affair. |
| 13 bô nâng cai. | 13 Nobody knows. |
| 14 nâng nâng ài<sup>n</sup>. | 14 Everybody wants it. |
| 15 bô pa̍t nâng lâi. | 15 No one else came. |
| 16 cí kâi bô mih hó. | 16 This is not very good. |
| 17 bô lṳ́ khṳ̀. | 17 You shall not go. |
| 18 bô lṳ́ lâi. nâng mûeh. úa kâi. | 18 You will not be allowed to come. People. Mine. |
| 19 nín kâi chù: ṳ́n kâi mûeh. | 19 Your house: our things. |
| 20 bô pi̍et pí chṳ́. | 20 Not distinguishing between this and that. |
| 21 pa̍t nâng: pa̍t mûeh. | 21 Other people: other things. |
| 22 hṳ́ kâi nâng sim hó. | 22 That man is excellent. |
| 23 i tŏ úa kâi chṳ̀. | 23 It is at my house. |
| 24 hṳ́ kâi chù bô nâng tŏ. | 24 There is no one at that house. |
| 25 cí kâi mûeh sĭ lṳ́ kâi a m̄ sĭ? pa̍t mûeh. | 25 This thing is yours is it not? Something else. |

## LESSON IV.

| | |
|---|---|
| 鍾 ceng; a cup. | 挈 * khîeh; take in one hand. |
| 房 pâng; a room. | 做 cò, coh; make, do. |
| 門 mn̂g; door. | 睡 * ût, gût; sleep, lie. |
| 牆 chîe$^{n}$; wall. | 醒 ché$^{n}$; waken. |
| 放 pàng; put, let. | 到 kàu; arrive at. |
| 給 * khṳt; let, give. | 了 lío; already. |

| | |
|---|---|
| 1 hó khṳt i cai. | 1 Let him know. |
| 2 mài khṳt nâng cai. | 2 Do not let any body know. |
| 3 bô khṳt lṳ́ khîeh. | 3 Shall not let you take it. |
| 4 bô ceng hó khṳt i. | 4 There is no cup to give him. |
| 5 pât nâng ài$^{n}$ ût lío. | 5 Other people want to sleep. |
| 6 lṳ́ cai i kàu chù a būe? | 6 Do you know whether he has gotten home yet? |
| 7 i gût khṳ̀ lío. | 7 He has gone to sleep. |
| 8 cò lâi sĭ m̄ hó. | 8 It is not well done. |
| 9 cí kâi, úa m̄ ài$^{n}$, khṳ̀ khîeh pât kâi lâi. | 9 I do not want this one, go and bring another. |
| 10 i kàu, úa ài$^{n}$ lâi khṳ̀. m̄ sĭ i kâi. | 10 When he comes, I am going to go. Is not his. |
| 11 cò kàu ài$^{n}$ hó lío. | 11 It is nearly done. |
| 12 ài$^{n}$ kàu a būe? | 12 Are we nearly there? |
| 13 i ût ché$^{n}$ lío. | 13 She has woke up. |
| 14 hṳ́ kâi mn̂g sĭ nán kâi. | 14 That door is ours. |
| 15 bô pât mûeh hó khîeh. mài khṳt i cò. | 15 There was nothing else to take. Do not let him do it. |
| 16 cí kâi kìe cò mih kâi? | 16 What do you call this? |
| 17 pàng i khṳ̀. m̄ cai. | 17 Let him go. Unaware. |
| 18 ài$^{n}$ khṳ̀ gût a būe? | 18 Are you going to bed yet? |
| 19 khîeh kâi ceng khṳt i. | 19 Get a cup and give him. |
| 20 lṳ́ tŏ cò mih kâi? | 20 What are you making? |
| 21 hṳ́ kâi sĭ sih mih nâng? | 21 What man is that? |
| 22 lṳ́ ài$^{n}$ cò sih mih kâi? | 22 What are you going to make? |
| 23 cí kâi sĭ sih mih chîe$^{n}$? | 23 What wall is this? |
| 24 pâng mn̂g. | 24 Door of a room. |
| 25 cò lṳ́ khṳ̀: i cò i khṳ̀. | 25 Go you along: he went his way. |

# LESSON V.

| | | | |
|---|---|---|---|
| 看 | thói$^{n}$; look. | 內 | lăi; in, inside. |
| 見 | kìen, kì$^{n}$; perceive. | 外 | gūa; out, outer. |
| 聽 | thia$^{n}$; hear, heed. | 速 | mé; sok; quick. |
| 摸 | mông; feel, with hands. | 快 | * khùe; speedily. |
| 摺 | * thăng; touch. | 緩 | mān; slow. |
| 事 | sṳ; business. | 㲌 | kàu; sufficient. |

| | |
|---|---|
| 1 úa thói$^{n}$ kì$^{n}$. gūa nâng. | 1 I see. Outsiders. |
| 2 úa thói$^{n}$ m̄ kì$^{n}$. | 2 I do not see. |
| 3 thia$^{n}$ kì$^{n}$: thia$^{n}$ m̄ kì$^{n}$. | 3 Hear: do not hear. |
| 4 ài$^{n}$ thói$^{n}$ hó thói$^{n}$, mài thăng. | 4 Look if you want to, but do not touch it. |
| 5 ŭ sih mih sṳ? | 5 What is the matter? |
| 6 lṳ́ tŏ hṳ́ bô sṳ. | 6 You have no business there. |
| 7 lṳ́ lâi thói$^{n}$ mih kâi? | 7 What did you come to see? |
| 8 m̄ hó kì$^{n}$ nâng. | 8 Not fit to be seen. |
| 9 mài khṳ̀ thia$^{n}$ i. | 9 Do not heed him. |
| 10 tŏ cí lăi ŭ sa$^{n}$ nâng. | 10 There are three people in here. |
| 11 i tŏ chù lăi. | 11 He is in the house. |
| 12 hṳ́ gūa bô nâng tŏ. | 12 There is no one out there. |
| 13 pàng tŏ pâng lăi. | 13 Put it in the room. |
| 14 pàng tŏ chîe$^{n}$ gūa. | 14 Put it outside the wall. |
| 15 úa ùt m̄ kàu. | 15 I did not sleep enough. |
| 16 bô sìm mih pât sṳ. | 16 Nothing else is the matter. |
| 17 khìeh kàu líο. | 17 Have already got enough. |
| 18 mé mé lâi, mān mān khṳ̀. | 18 Come quickly, go slowly. |
| 19 i mān mān ài$^{n}$ lâi. | 19 He is coming after awhile. |
| 20 lṳ́ hó khùe khùe cò. | 20 Do it quickly. |
| 21 i mông lâi, mông khṳ̀. | 21 He felt all around. |
| 22 bô sìm mih ài$^{n}$. | 22 Does not much want it. |
| 23 úa ŭ sa$^{n}$ càp gūa. | 23 I have over thirty. |
| 24 i khìeh ŭ sì peh gūa. | 24 He took over four hundred. |
| 25 i ŭ sṳ. sok sok nē! | 25 He has an affair on hand. Be quick! |
| 26 lăi gūa bô mûeh. | 26 There was nothing inside nor outside. |

## LESSON VI.

水 cúi; water, fluid.
汲 * pûah; to draw water.
走 cáu; run.
行 kîaⁿ; walk.
何 hô̤: tī; what?
處 chù: kò̤; place.

多 tɵ; ke; cōi; many, much.
少 cíe; sío; few, little.
早 cá; early.
晏 ùaⁿ; late.
遲 chî; late, slow.
太 * khah; too.

1 lṳ́ àiⁿ khṳ̀ tī kò̤?
2 àiⁿ khṳ̀ pûah cúi.
3 cáu mé mé kìe i.
4 cáu lâi cí kò̤. cáu khṳ̀.
5 mài khṳ̀ hṳ́ kò̤.
6 hó̤ mān mān kîaⁿ.
7 cí kâi sĭ tī nâng kâi? hô̤ chù? ŭ tɵ sío.
8 i ŭ cōi cōi kâi.
9 i bô̤ tŏ̤ hṳ́ kò̤.
10 i tŏ̤ tī kò̤? úa m̄ cai.
11 pàng tŏ̤ cí kò̤.
12 pàng tŏ̤ tī kò̤?
13 i àiⁿ tī cêk kâi?
14 àiⁿ kìe tī cêk nâng?
15 m̄ hó̤ sĭ cōi, hó̤ sĭ cíe. kîaⁿ m̄ kàu.
16 nâng mûeh cōi.
17 i khîeh tī kâi?
18 lṳ́ khah ùaⁿ lâi.
19 cá cá lâi, mài ùaⁿ.
20 mài khîeh khah cōi.
21 cúi khah cíe.
22 ŭ ke ke nâng lâi.
23 lṳ́ kîaⁿ khah mé.
24 lṳ́ lâi khah chî líʊ.
25 lṳ́ mài chî mān lâi.
26 úa àiⁿ ke ke.

1 Where are you going?
2 I am going to draw water.
3 Run quickly and call him.
4 Run here. Run away.
5 Do not go there.
6 Walk slowly.
7 To which person does this belong? Where? Have more or less.
8 He has a great many.
9 He is not there.
10 Where is he? I don't know.
11 Put it here.
12 Where did you put it?
13 Which one does he want?
14 Which do you wish to call?
15 The good are many, the bad few. Cannot walk there.
16 A great crowd.
17 Which did he take?
18 You come too late.
19 Come early, don't be late.
20 Do not take too many.
21 There is too little water.
22 Many people came.
23 You walk too fast.
24 You have come too late.
25 Do not be late in coming.
26 I want much.

## LESSON VII.

出 chut; go out.
入 jîp; enter.
買 bói; buy.
賣 bōi; sell.
能 lêng, ŏi; can, able.
不能 * bŏi; cannot.

識 sek; pat; acquainted with.
曾 cêng; sign of the past.
得 tit; attain, can.
得 * tò; may, able.
着 tîeh; must, right, hit.
過 kùe; pass, surpass.

| | | |
|---|---|---|
| 1 | àiⁿ, kâi àiⁿ, bŏi tit tîeh. | As for wanting it, I want it, but can't get it. |
| 2 | úa m̄ pat i. | I do not know him. |
| 3 | i ŏi kîaⁿ, ŏi cáu. | He can walk and run. |
| 4 | ŏi cò tit: m̄ cò tit. | That will do: that won't do. |
| 5 | cò tit lâi: cò m̄ lâi. | It can be done: cannot be done. |
| 6 | m̄ cai tîeh a m̄ tîeh. | Do not know whether it hit. |
| 7 | ŏi tit jîp a bŏi? | Can we go in? |
| 8 | ŏi tit jîp, bŏi tit chut. | You can go in but can't come out. |
| 9 | m̄ cai i ŏi a bŏi. | I do not know whether he can. |
| 10 | kìe i chut lâi. | Tell him to come out. |
| 11 | mài jîp khù. . kìen sek. | Do not go in. Knowledge. |
| 12 | mài i jîp lâi. | Do not let him come in. |
| 13 | cí kâi tîeh a m̄ tîeh? | Is this right or wrong? |
| 14 | úa àiⁿ chut mn̂g. | I am going out. |
| 15 | i chut mn̂g khù. | She has gone out. |
| 16 | i chut mn̂g a būe? | Is she married yet? |
| 17 | úa pat thóiⁿ kìⁿ. | I have seen it before. |
| 18 | úa m̄ pat thóiⁿ kìⁿ. | I never saw it before. |
| 19 | úa pat tò cò. | I know how to do it. |
| 20 | úa thiaⁿ m̄ pat tò khù, | I do not understand. |
| 21 | cí kâi hó kùe há kâi. | This is better than that. |
| 22 | úa pat thiaⁿ kùe. | I have heard it before. |
| 23 | úa m̄ cêng thiaⁿ kìⁿ. | I have not heard. |
| 24 | put lêng cò tit. | That will not do. |
| 25 | i tŏ bói bōi. | He is buying and selling. |
| 26 | àiⁿ bōi, bōi m̄ tîeh. | I wished to sell but could not. |
| 27 | úa m̄ pat tò cò. | I do not know how to do it. |

## LESSON VIII.

覔 chūe; seek.
碍 gāi; hinder.
叉 che; fork.
刀 to; knife.
匙 sî; spoon.
箸 tū; chopsticks.

盤 pûa$^n$; plate.
鹽 îam; salt.
塊 kə̀; piece, lump.
枝 ki; branch, a classifier.
把 pé; bunch, handful.
定 tīa$^n$; certain, secure.

| | |
|---|---|
| 1 chūe lâi, chūe khù, chūe m̄ tîeh. | 1 Looked all about but could not find it. |
| 2 ŏi chūe tîeh a bŏi? | 2 Can you find it? |
| 3 īa sĭ m̄ kì$^n$ khù, hó khù chūe. | 3 If it is lost go and look for it. |
| 4 ŏi cə̀ nâng: bŏi cə̀ nâng. | 4 Can be somebody: be nobody. |
| 5 lú tîeh cə̀ hó nâng. | 5 You must be a good boy. |
| 6 bô nâng pàng i chut. | 6 Nobody let him out. |
| 7 lú ŭ kìe úa, mē? | 7 Have you called me? |
| 8 sì ki che m̄ kì$^n$ khù. | 8 Four forks are missing. |
| 9 hú ki to, khîeh lâi. | 9 Bring that knife. |
| 10 lâk ki sî pàng tŏ cí kə̀. | 10 Put the six spoons here. |
| 11 bói ŭ cêk pé tū. | 11 Bought a bundle of chopsticks. |
| 12 cêk pé tū jī câp ki. gāi tîeh. | 12 There are twenty chopsticks in one bundle. Impede. |
| 13 chit ki che pàng tŏ pûa$^n$. | 13 Put the seven forks on a tray. |
| 14 chūe cêk pé îam. | 14 Seek a handful of salt. |
| 15 bói ŭ cêk kə̀ îam. | 15 Bought a lump of salt. |
| 16 pàng cêk kə̀, cêk kə̀. | 16 Put it piece by piece. |
| 17 tîeh ŭ ngŏ ki che. | 17 There must be five forks. |
| 18 pí chú mài gāi. | 18 Do not let this and that clash. |
| 19 lú mài gāi tîeh úa kâi sū. | 19 Do not you interfere with my business. |
| 20 úa m̄ gāi lú. | 20 I won't hinder you. |
| 21 sū tīa$^n$ tîeh líο. | 21 The matter is settled. |
| 22 tīa$^n$ ài$^n$ chūe kàu i tîeh. | 22 I will certainly seek till I find him. |
| 23 cə̀ tīa$^n$: bô tīa$^n$ tîeh. | 23 Give security: not exactly. |

# LESSON IX.

| | | | |
|---|---|---|---|
| 坐 | cŏ; sit. | 隻 | ciah; a classifier. |
| 住 | cŭ, tĭu; reside. | 椅 | ĭ$^n$; a chair. |
| 食 | cîah; eat, drink. | 索 | seh; rope, cords. |
| 將 | cang; make use of. | 飽 | pá; full, satisfied. |
| 將 | ciang; sign of the future. | 幾 | * kúi; how many? |
| 條 | tîo; a strip, a classifier. | 耳 | * tĭa$^n$; intensifying particle. |

| | |
|---|---|
| 1 jîp: cŏ. | 1 Come in: sit down. |
| 2 ài$^n$ cŏ pàng tĭ kò? | 2 Where are you going to sit? |
| 3 lâi cŏ pàng cí kò. | 3 Come and sit here. |
| 4 lṳ́ tĭu tŏ tĭ kò? | 4 Where do you live? |
| 5 lṳ́ sĭ cŭ tŏ hṳ́ kò, a m̄ sĭ? | 5 You reside there, do you not? |
| * cang seh. | Use ropes. |
| 6 cîah a būe? būe. | 6 Have you eaten yet? Not yet. |
| 7 ciang lâi, úa ài$^n$ khṳ̀. | 7 I am going some time. |
| 8 i ciang kàu líou. | 8 He has about reached here. |
| 9 i ciang ài$^n$ khṳ̀. | 9 He is about to go. |
| 10 ciang lâi, bŏi tit khṳ̀ | 10 In the future he cannot go. |
| 11 cang ciah ĭ$^n$ lâi cŏ. | 11 Take a chair and sit down. |
| 12 lṳ́ tŏ cîah mih kâi? | 12 What are you eating? |
| 13 i cîah pá líou. | 13 He has finished eating. |
| 14 cîah kàu ài$^n$ pá. | 14 Nearly through the meal. |
| 15 tŏ cîah būe pá. | 15 Not yet through the meal. |
| 16 cîah kàu pá pá. | 16 Eat quite enough. |
| 17 i m̄ kàu cîah. | 17 He has not enough to eat. |
| 18 mài cîah khah cōi. | 18 Do not eat too much. |
| 19 i cîah khah pá. | 19 He has eaten too much. |
| 20 seh ŭ kúi tîo? | 20 How many ropes are there? |
| 21 lṳ́ ŭ kúi ciah ĭ$^n$? | 21 How many chairs have you? |
| 22 úa jîp khṳ̀, i tŏ cŏ. | 22 When I entered he was sitting. |
| 23 put kùe cîah pá tĭa$^n$. | 23 Ate no more than enough. |
| 24 ŭ kâi pûa$^n$ tĭa$^n$ tĭa$^n$. | 24 Have only a plate. |
| 25 ĭ$^n$, ŭ kúi ciah? | 25 How many chairs have you? |
| 26 put kùe sa$^n$ ciah tĭa$^n$. | 26 Not more than three. |
| 27 ŭ cêk ciah tĭa$^n$ tĭa$^n$. | 27 I have only one. |

## LESSON X.

| | | | |
|---|---|---|---|
| 頭 | thâu; head. | 加 | kia, ke; add, increase. |
| 面 | mīn; face. | 零 | lân; a few. |
| 手 | chíu; hands. | 困 | khùn; exhausted. |
| 脚 | kha; feet. | 倦 | kw̆n; fatigued. |
| 肚 | tó; belly. | 疲 | phî; lassitude. |
| 洗 | sói; wash. | 乏 | hêk; weary. |

| | |
|---|---|
| 1 cang cúi sói mīn. khṳ̀ kì$^n$ i mīn. | 1 Get some water for washing your face. Go and and see him. |
| 2 i tó khùn, ài$^n$ cîah. | 2 He is hungry. |
| 3 i kâi nâng khùn hêk. | 3 He is tired out. |
| 4 i kha chíu cōi. | 4 He is always in motion. |
| 5 ŭ lân nâng lâi. | 5 A few people came. |
| 6 úa kîa$^n$ kàu hêk lío. | 6 I have walked till I am tired. |
| 7 ŭ ke lân kâi. | 7 There are a few more. |
| 8 i bô kha, bô chíu. | 8 He has neither hands nor feet. |
| 9 i ŭ nŏ ciah chíu. | 9 He has two hands. |
| 10 ài$^n$ cò lâk ciah kha kâi. | 10 I want to have it made with six legs. |
| 11 cò sa$^n$ ciah î$^n$ thâu. | 11 Make three high stools. |
| 12 pàng tŏ chîe$^n$ kha. | 12 Put it by the wall. |
| 13 i cŏ tŏ mn̂g kha. | 13 He sat by the door. |
| 14 ŭ ke cêk kâi tīa$^n$. | 14 There is only one more. |
| 15 bô lân kâi. | 15 There are scarcely any. |
| 16 chíu pûa$^n$: kha pûa$^n$. | 16 Back of the hand: instep. |
| 17 úa m̄ ài$^n$ ke. | 17 I do not want any more. |
| 18 nâng sĭm sĭ phî kw̆n. | 18 I am exceedingly weary. |
| 19 lṳ́ tīa$^n$ a m̄ tīa$^n$? | 19 Are you certain about it? |
| 20 nâng khùn kw̆n bŏi cò sĭm mih sṳ̄. | 20 I am languid and can do nothing. |
| 21 cí kâi nâng sĭm sĭ phî. | 21 This person is very indolent. |
| 22 nâng phî, lâi khṳ̀ ût, hó. | 22 If you are tired, you better lie down. |
| 23 gūa mīn: lăi mīn. | 23 The exterior: the inner surface. |
| 24 thia$^n$ tŏ tó lăi. | 24 Take it into your mind. |
| 25 bô ke kâi tó lâi cîah. | 25 No more appetite. |

# LESSON XI.

| | | | |
|---|---|---|---|
| 家 | ke; family. | 粒 | lîap; a classifier of small, round objects. |
| 柑 | kaⁿ; orange. | 回 | hûe; return, revert to. |
| 皮 | phûe; skin, bark. | 丢 | tiu; to throw. |
| 碗 | úaⁿ; a bowl. | 抛 | * sek; to fling. |
| 盃 | pue; a cup. | 棄 | * tīo; relinquish. |
| 件 | kĭaⁿ; items. | 咸 | * hăm; all, jointly. |

| | | |
|---|---|---|
| 1 | thâu ke bô tŏ. | The master is not in. |
| 2 | úa àiⁿ hûe ke. | I am going home. |
| 3 | khù sói pûaⁿ úaⁿ. | Go wash the dishes. |
| 4 | pue ceng hăm kâi khîeh khù. | Take all the cups. |
| 5 | ceng pûaⁿ khîeh káu kâi. | Take nine saucers. |
| 6 | cí kâi mûeh kĭaⁿ úa m̄ àiⁿ. | I do not want these things. |
| 7 | cí kâi mûeh, kĭaⁿ, kĭaⁿ hó. | These things are each good. |
| 8 | i cêk ke nâng. | That whole family. |
| 9 | bói câp lîap kaⁿ. | Buy ten oranges. |
| 10 | kaⁿ bói ŭ kúi lîap? i m̄ cai nâng. | How many oranges did you buy? He became unconscious. |
| 11 | m̄ àiⁿ, hó khù bōi tīo. | If you don't want it, sell it. |
| 12 | i nâng hăm kâi m̄ àiⁿ. | None of them want it. |
| 13 | mài tiu tīo i. | Do not throw it away. |
| 14 | hó kâi mûeh kĭaⁿ, m̄ hó sek tīo. | You should not cast away good things. |
| 15 | lú hó khùe khùe sek tīo. | Cast it away quickly. |
| 16 | kaⁿ phûe hó tiu tīo. | Throw away the orange peel. |
| 17 | hăm ke nâng kâi kâi hó. | Every one of the family is good. |
| 18 | cí lîap kaⁿ hó cîah. | This is a good orange. |
| 19 | pûaⁿ úaⁿ mûeh kĭaⁿ. | Table furniture. |
| 20 | cêk pue, cêk pue, cîah sĭm cōi. | Cup by cup he drank a great quantity. |
| 21 | cí kâi úaⁿ tū khù sói. | Wash these bowls and chopsticks. |
| 22 | cí hûe tŏ ke lăi chut lâi. | Came this time from home. |
| 23 | cí kĭaⁿ phûe sĭ hó phûe. | This leather is good leather. |
| 24 | cí lîap kaⁿ khîeh pàng úaⁿ lăi. | Take this orange and put it in the bowl. |

## LESSON XII.

| | |
|---|---|
| 床 chn̂g; a table. | 間 koi$^{n}$; classifier of rooms. |
| 桌 toh; a table. | 座 cō; classifier of houses. |
| 櫃 kūi$^{n}$; chest of drawers. | 眠 mîn; sleep. |
| 心 sim; heart. | 輔 hŭ; assist. |
| 大 tăi, tōa; great. | 予 * pun; give. |
| 細 sòi; ìu$^{n}$; fine; small. | 數 * kúi; several. |

| | |
|---|---|
| 1 mîn chn̂g: mîn í$^{n}$. | 1 Bedstead: sofa. |
| 2 toh kūi$^{n}$; chn̂g kūi$^{n}$: | 2 Sideboard: side table. |
| 3 cí ciah toh khah sòi. | 3 This table is too small. |
| 4 i kâi gūa mīn sĭ hó, sim lăi sĭ m̄ hó. | 4 His appearance is good, but he has a bad heart. |
| 5 tŏ bói chn̂g í$^{n}$ mûeh kĭa$^{n}$. | 5 Buying furniture. |
| 6 hṳ́ cêk cō chù ŭ ngŏ koi$^{n}$ pâng. | 6 That house has five rooms. |
| 7 hṳ́ kâi toh kūi$^{n}$ ŭ sì ciah kha. | 7 That side table has four legs. |
| 8 i sĭ hó sim kâi nâng. | 8 He is a good hearted man. |
| 9 lṳ́ sòi sim khṳ̀ cò. | 9 Go and do it carefully. |
| 10 cí kâi tōa kùe hṳ́ kâi. | 10 This is larger than that. |
| 11 i ŏi tōa a bŏi? | 11 Will it grow larger? |
| 12 cí cō chù tōa sòi ŭ kúi koi$^{n}$ pâng. | 12 This house has several rooms, large and small. |
| 13 i bŏi tōa. | 13 It will not grow larger. |
| 14 lṳ́ kâi sim tăi hó, úa hŭ lṳ́. | 14 Your intentions are very good: I will help you. |
| 15 cí kâi tăi jîn cò sṳ̄ sĭm sòi sim. | 15 This great man transacts business very carefully. |
| 16 lṳ́ hó pàng sim. | 16 Be of easy mind. |
| 17 cí kúi kĭa$^{n}$ mûeh, khîeh khṳ̀ pun i. | 17 Take these several things and give them to him. |
| 18 tōa sòi ŭ sa$^{n}$ câp. | 18 There were thirty, great and small. |
| 19 cí kâi khah sòi; ŭ pât kâi a bô? ìu$^{n}$ ìu$^{n}$. | 19 This is too small; are there any other ones? Very minute. |
| 20 nín kúi nâng khṳ̀ hŭ i cò. | 20 You all go and help him do it. |

## LESSON XIII.

| | |
|---|---|
| 嘴 chùi; mouth. | 痛 thìa$^n$; painful. |
| 舌 cíh; tongue. | 上 sĭang; superior. |
| 齒 khí; teeth. | 盡 cĭn; uttermost. |
| 唇 tûn; lips. | 甚 * căi; very. |
| 火 húe; fire. | 還 hŵn; still, yet. |
| 顧 kù; regard. | 共 kāng; kah; with, and. |

| | |
|---|---|
| 1 i chùi ŏi. | 1 He is an able speaker. |
| 2 i kâi chùi cíh m̄ hó. | 2 He is a gossiping person. |
| 3 i kâi khí thìa$^n$. | 3 She has toothache. |
| 4 cí kâi sĭang hó. | 4 This is excellent. |
| 5 cí kâi hó căi. | 5 This is very good. |
| 6 cí kâi cĭn hó. | 6 This is the best. |
| 7 i hŵn ŭ. | 7 He still has some. |
| 8 úa thói$^n$ ŭ húe cíh chut lâi. | 8 I saw flames coming out. |
| 9 hŵn lío m̄ kàu. | 9 There is not yet enough. |
| 10 m̄ cai i hŵn ŭ a bô. | 10 I do not know whether he has any more or not. |
| 11 thìa$^n$ căi. | 11 Very painful. |
| 12 ŏi thìa$^n$ a bŏi? | 12 Does it hurt you? |
| 13 i sĭang ài$^n$. | 13 He wants it exceedingly. |
| 14 pàng húe. | 14 To set on fire. |
| 15 lú ài$^n$ ke sĭm mih kâi? | 15 What more do you want? |
| 16 hŵn ŭ ke, mē? | 16 Have you more? |
| 17 lú kù úa, úa kù lú. | 17 Regard me, and I shall you. |
| 18 lú hŵn thìa$^n$, mē? | 18 Are you still in pain? |
| 19 lú kāng i thói$^n$ kù. | 19 Be considerate of him. |
| 20 khìeh kâi pue, kah kâi úa$^n$. | 20 Take a cup and a bowl. |
| 21 lú kah úa hó khù. | 21 You and I should go. |
| 22 tōa kah sòi cĭn hó. | 22 The large and the small are both extremely good. |
| 23 sĭang hó kâi cĭn khìeh. | 23 Bring all the best ones. |
| 24 cí kâi khí gāi tìeh chùi tûn. | 24 This tooth interferes with the lip. |
| 25 i chùi tûn thìa$^n$. | 25 Her lip is sore. |

# LESSON XIV.

芒 * mê; spark, flash.
前 côi$^{n}$; in front of.
先 soi$^{n}$; before.
後 ău; after.
撮 cheh; a quantity.
所 só; that which.
論 lŭn; discuss.
現 hīn; plainly.
今 kìa$^{n}$, kim, ta$^{n}$; now.
在 căi; now.
就 cĭu; cū; then, thereupon.
幾 * jìeh; how.

| | | |
|---|---|---|
| 1 | i tŏ chù côi$^{n}$. | He is in front of the house. |
| 2 | bô lŭn côi$^{n}$ ău. | Whether before or behind. |
| 3 | i kìa$^{n}$ thâu mīn côi$^{n}$. | He walks ahead. |
| 4 | hīn kim kâi nâng, lâi lŭn soi$^{n}$ kâi nâng. | Those of present time talk of those of former times. |
| 5 | lṳ́ côi$^{n}$ ău khṳ̀ chŭe thói$^{n}$ tŏ m̄e; m̄ tŏ, cĭu m̄ ài$^{n}$. | You go and look around and see if it is there; if it is not I don't want it. |
| 6 | pàng i kâi mīn côi$^{n}$. | Put it before him. |
| 7 | lṳ́ soi$^{n}$ kìa$^{n}$. hīn căi khṳ̀. | You go first. Go now. |
| 8 | úa soi$^{n}$ khṳ̀, ău lṳ́ lâi. | I will go first, you come after. |
| 9 | khìeh cheh cúi lâi pun úa cìah. húe mê. | Bring me a drink of water. A spark. |
| 10 | hṳ́ cêk cheh îam pàng tŏ úa$^{n}$. | Put that salt in the bowl. |
| 11 | i bô só put tŏ. | He is omnipresent. |
| 12 | i bô só put cai. | He is omniscient. |
| 13 | i bô só put lêng. | He is almighty. |
| 14 | ŏi thói$^{n}$ kì$^{n}$ hīn hīn. | Can see it plainly. |
| 15 | i hīn kim ài$^{n}$ khṳ̀. | He is going to go now. |
| 16 | úa ta$^{n}$ lâi khṳ̀. | I am going to go now. |
| 17 | lṳ́ ŭ jìeh cōi? | How much have you? |
| 18 | ŭ jìeh hó kâi? | How good ones have you? |
| 19 | put lŭn sih mih nâng. | Whatever person. |
| 20 | lṳ́ só cò kâi sṳ̄. | What you did. |
| 21 | úa hīn căi ài$^{n}$ khṳ̀. | I shall go now. |
| 22 | cí cheh mûeh hăm kâi ài$^{n}$ bōi. | I want to sell all this lot of things. |

## LESSON XV.

| | | | |
|---|---|---|---|
| 歲 | * hùe; a year. | 阿 | a; a prefix to names. |
| 年 | nî; a year. | 老 | lău, láu; aged. |
| 子 | cṳ́, kía$^{n}$; child; little. | 幼 | iù$^{n}$; small, young. |
| 孩 | * nô$^{n}$; child; infant. | 新 | sin; new. |
| 顯 | híen; manifest. | 舊 | kū; old. |
| 生 | se$^{n}$; life; produce. | 久 | kú; a long time. |

| | | |
|---|---|---|
| 1 | lṳ́ ŭ jîeh cōi hùe? | How old are you? |
| 2 | úa sa$^{n}$ câp gūa hùe. | I am over thirty. |
| 3 | i nî hùe cōi. | He is advanced in years. |
| 4 | sin nî ài$^{n}$ kàu. | The new year is near. |
| 5 | kim nî úa ài$^{n}$ khṳ̀. | I shall go this year. |
| 6 | kū nî i m̄ pat lâi. | Last year he did not come. |
| 7 | hṳ́ cêk nî i jîh gūa hùe. | That year he was over twenty. |
| 8 | ău nî: ău nî. | Year after next: in after years. |
| 9 | i ŭ sa$^{n}$ kâi kía$^{n}$. | She has three children. |
| 10 | cêk ciah í$^{n}$ kía$^{n}$. | A little chair. |
| 11 | cêk ki to kía$^{n}$. | A little knife. |
| 12 | i híen hīn khut nâng thói$^{n}$. | He appeared so that people could see him. |
| 13 | lău iù$^{n}$, hăm kâi lâi. | Old and young, all came. |
| 14 | nín kâi lău tōa ài$^{n}$ lâi mē? | Are your old people coming? |
| 15 | lău nâng ke. | Venerable head of the family. |
| 16 | i kâi nâng lău tōa. | He is aged. |
| 17 | i khṳ̀ kú líó. | He went a long time ago. |
| 18 | lṳ́ kú m̄ pat lâi. cṳ́ sòi. | You have not been here for a long time. Be careful. |
| 19 | i kú kú tŏ. | It is always there. |
| 20 | úa hīn căi lâi khṳ̀. | I am going to go now. |
| 21 | lṳ́ lâi ŭ jîeh kú? | How long since you came? |
| 22 | bói kàu ta$^{n}$ ŭ jîeh kú? | How long since you bought it? |
| 23 | nâng nâng sṳ́ ài$^{n}$. | What everyone wants. |
| 24 | i se$^{n}$ a nô$^{n}$ líó. | She already has a child. |
| 25 | cí kâi a nô$^{n}$ kía$^{n}$ se$^{n}$ kàu ta$^{n}$ ŭ jîeh kú? | How long since this child was born? |

## LESSON XVI.

| | | | |
|---|---|---|---|
| 爹 | tia; father. | 姊 | cí, cé; elder sister. |
| 爸 | pa; papa. | 妹 | mūe; younger sister. |
| 父 | pĕ; father. | 客 | kheh; guest. |
| 母 | bó, âi, ne; mother. | 位 | ūi; seat, place, person. |
| 兄 | hiaⁿ; elder brother. | 性 | sèⁿ; temper, disposition. |
| 弟 | tĭ; younger brother. | 詢 | sûn; inquire after. |

| | | | |
|---|---|---|---|
| 1 | úa kâi a tia bô tŏ. | 1 | My father is not in. |
| 2 | i bô pĕ, bô bó. | 2 | He has neither father nor mother. |
| 3 | i ǹiⁿ cò hiaⁿ tĭ. | 3 | They are going to be brethren. |
| 4 | i bô kíaⁿ tĭ. | 4 | She has no male children. |
| 5 | i a nôⁿ kíaⁿ cōi. | 5 | She has many children. |
| 6 | a nôⁿ, lâi cí kò. | 6 | My child, come here. |
| 7 | ŭ nâng kheh lâi. | 7 | Visitors have come. |
| 8 | i sĭ gūa chù nâng. | 8 | He is a foreigner. |
| 9 | ǹiⁿ khì cò nâng kheh. | 9 | I am going out visiting. |
| 10 | pàng tŏ nâng kheh pâng. | 10 | Put it in the guest room. |
| 11 | i ǹiⁿ cŏ tōa ūi. | 11 | He will sit in the chief seat. |
| 12 | hú cêk ūi lău nâng sĭ lú kâi a pĕ a m̄ sĭ? | 12 | That old man is your father, is he not? |
| 13 | i m̄ cêng ŭ kíaⁿ. | 13 | She has had no children. |
| 14 | i būe cêng ŭ. | 14 | She has not yet had. |
| 15 | i cí mūe sì nâng. | 15 | The four sisters. |
| 16 | i hiaⁿ tĭ nŏ nâng. | 16 | The two brothers. |
| 17 | lú hiaⁿ tĭ jĭeh cōi nâng? ún hiaⁿ tĭ lâk nâng. | 17 | How many brothers are there of you? Six. |
| 18 | lú ŭ kúi kâi hiaⁿ tĭ? | 18 | How many brothers have you? |
| 19 | úa sĭ a hiaⁿ, ŭ saⁿ kâi a tĭ. | 19 | I am the eldest, and have three brothers. |
| 20 | úa tōa i saⁿ hùe. ŏi tōa cí kâi a bŏi? | 20 | I am three years older than he. Is it bigger than this? |
| 21 | úa kâi âi ǹiⁿ lâi sûn nín. | 21 | My mother is coming to inquire after you. |
| 22 | lú kâi húe sèⁿ tōa căi. | 22 | Your irascibility is extreme. |
| 23 | i kâi sim sèⁿ sĭm hó. | 23 | His temper is excellent. |

## LESSON XVII.

男 lâm; ta-po; human male.
女 nńg; ca-bó; female.
夫 hu; ang; man; husband.
婦 hŭ; bó; woman; wife.
姿 cṳ; graceful.
娘 nîe; lady; mother.

飯 pn̄g; boiled rice.
姓 sè$^{n}$; surname; clan.
請 chía$^{n}$; invite.
用 ēng; use; employ.
裝 * chɵ̄; hold; contain.
裝 cuang; tie$^{n}$; ,affect; dress.

| | | |
|---|---|---|
| 1 | ŭ ēng: bɵ̂ ēng. | Useful: useless. |
| 2 | cí kâi ŭ sih mih ēng? | Of what use is this? |
| 3 | thâu ke nîe tɵ̆ mē? | Is your mistress in? |
| 4 | cí kâi pue chɵ̄ mih kâi? | What is in this cup? |
| 5 | cang kâi pn̄g úa$^{n}$ khṳ̀ chɵ̄. | Take a rice bowl to hold it. |
| 6 | chɵ̄ pàng pn̄g úa$^{n}$. | Put it in a rice bowl. |
| 7 | ài$^{n}$ chía$^{n}$ nâng kheh. | Going to invite company. |
| 8 | cí cêk ūi cṳ nîe kía$^{n}$. | This young lady. |
| 9 | i se$^{n}$ kâi cṳ nîe kía$^{n}$. | She has given birth to a daughter. |
| 10 | i se$^{n}$ kâi ta-po kía$^{n}$. | She has given birth to a son. |
| 11 | i sɵ́ se$^{n}$ kâi kía$^{n}$, sĭ ta-po, a sĭ cṳ nîe? | Is the child she has borne male or female? |
| 12 | i hu hŭ nɵ̆ nâng lâi. | Husband and wife both came. |
| 13 | ài$^{n}$ ēng cɵ̀ sĭm mih kâi? | What are you going to make of it? |
| 14 | hŭ jîn nâng m̄ hɵ́ khṳ̀. | Women should not go. |
| 15 | lâm nńg hăm kâi khṳ̀. | Male and female, all went. |
| 16 | i bɵ̂ bó, bɵ̂ kía$^{n}$. | He has no wife nor children. |
| 17 | i soi$^{n}$ ŭ kâi ang. | She formerly had a husband. |
| 18 | hṳ́ kâi a nô$^{n}$ sĭ ta-po a sĭ ca-bó? tie$^{n}$ cɵ̀. | Is that child a boy or a girl. Affect to be. |
| 19 | i ŭ kâi ke ău. | He has a wife. |
| 20 | úa cêk se$^{n}$ m̄ pat thói$^{n}$. | I never in all my life saw—. |
| 21 | lṳ́ sih mih sè$^{n}$? | What is your surname? |
| 22 | nín cêk sè$^{n}$, lâm nńg jîeh cōi nâng? | Male and female, how many are there in your clan? |
| 23 | chía$^{n}$ kâi cṳ nîe nâng kheh. | Invite a lady guest. |
| 24 | chía$^{n}$ i kâi ang lâi cîah pn̄g. tie$^{n}$. | Invite her husband to come and eat. To decant liquors. |
| 25 | nńg cɵ̀ lâm cuang. | A woman in men's clothes. |

## LESSON XVIII.

| | |
|---|---|
| 惜 sieh; compassionate. | 妻 chi, cía, bó; wife. |
| 愛 ài; love, kindness. | 相 siang, sie; mutual. |
| 擺 pái; spread out. | 干 kan; concerning; result. |
| 自 cṳ̆; from; self. | 與 ṳ́, kāi, kio; for, with, to. |
| 自 * ka; self. | 可 khó, hó; may. |
| 己 kí, kĭ; self. | 以 í$^{n}$; by that means. |

| | |
|---|---|
| 1 cí kĭa$^{n}$ sṳ̄ ṳ́ úa bô kan. | 1 This affair is nothing to me. |
| 2 cí kâi sṳ̄ ka kĭ khó í$^{n}$ cò tit. | 2 This business I can myself get along with. |
| 3 ka kĭ ài sieh ka kĭ. | 3 Take care of yourself. |
| 4 nín ang cía sĭm sĭ siang ài. | 4 You are very fond of each other. |
| 5 lṳ́ hó khùe khùe kio úa pái toh. só í$^{n}$. | 5 Set the table quickly for me. Therefore. |
| 6 úa kāng i sie pat. | 6 I am acquainted with him. |
| 7 cṳ̆ cá: cṳ̆ soi$^{n}$. | 7 Aforetime: formerly. |
| 8 hó cîah. | 8 The meal is ready. |
| 9 bô mûeh hó cîah. | 9 There is nothing edible. |
| 10 kan lṳ́ bô sṳ̄. | 10 It is nothing to you. |
| 11 úa ṳ́ lṳ́ bô kan. | 11 I have nothing to do with you. |
| 12 bô siang kan. | 12 It is of no consequence. |
| 13 khó í$^{n}$. cṳ̆ kí. | 13 It will do. One's self. |
| 14 i nŏ nâng sie sieh. | 14 The two love each other. |
| 15 khó sieh căi. | 15 It is a great pity. |
| 16 i cṳ nîe nâng hó sieh. | 16 Those women are lovable. |
| 17 lṳ́ m̄ sieh úa. | 17 You are not kind to me. |
| 18 úa sĭm sĭ sieh lṳ́. | 18 I love you much. |
| 19 lṳ́ būe ŭ pái toh. | 19 You have not yet set the table. |
| 20 i bô kùe: i ŭ kùe. | 20 He is not at fault: is at fault. |
| 21 úa ka kĭ bô. | 21 I myself have none. |
| 22 lṳ́ kio úa bói nŏ kâi. | 22 Buy two for me. |
| 23 lṳ́ kāi úa cò. | 23 You do it for me. |
| 24 í$^{n}$ chṳ̀, khṳ̀ cò. | 24 Thereby went and did it. |
| 25 úa lâi ŭ sa$^{n}$ nî kú. | 25 I came three years ago. |
| 26 i lâi ŭ lâk nî. | 26 He has been here six years. |

## LESSON XIX.

| | |
|---|---|
| 金 kim; gold. | 還 hâiⁿ; hôiⁿ; give back. |
| 銀 n̂gn; silver. | 借 cieh; borrow, lend. |
| 錢 cîⁿ; cash. | 使 sái; send, spend, cause. |
| 席 sîah; a feast. | 使 sài; messenger. |
| 算 sǹg; reckon. | 欠 khìam; lack, owe. |
| 數 sìo; count. | 頗 phó; heh; somewhat, rather. |

| | |
|---|---|
| 1 úa cieh kùe i ngŏ kâi n̂gn. | 1 I borrowed five dollars from him. |
| 2 úa ngŏ kâi n̂gn cieh i. | 2 I lent him five dollars. |
| 3 i chut sài gūa chù. | 3 He sent an ambassador abroad. |
| 4 cí kâi n̂gn tîeh hâiⁿ i. | 4 You must repay him this money. |
| 5 úa khìam lú sîah n̂gn jîeh cōi, úa sǹg hâiⁿ lú. | 5 I will repay you what I owe you for the repast. |
| 6 cí kâi sĭ kim cò. | 6 This is made of gold. |
| 7 lú só cieh kâi n̂gn tîeh hâiⁿ i. | 7 You must pay him the money you borrowed. |
| 8 i cîⁿ n̂gn cōi. | 8 He has much money. |
| 9 i bô cîⁿ, bô n̂gn. | 9 He has neither cash nor dollars. |
| 10 lú khìam i jîeh cōi? | 10 How much do you owe him? |
| 11 i khìam úa lân kâi cîⁿ tīaⁿ. phó cai. phó cōi. | 11 He owes me only a few cash. Know somewhat. Rather many. |
| 12 taⁿ àiⁿ sǹg sìo. | 12 Will now settle accounts. |
| 13 lú sìo, thóiⁿ ŭ jîeh cōi kâi. | 13 You count, and see how many there are. |
| 14 hŵn ŭ heh cōi. | 14 There are still a good many. |
| 15 i sái heh cōi cîⁿ. | 15 He spends a good deal. |
| 16 sái i khù khîeh. | 16 Send him for it. |
| 17 i sĭ heh tōa kâi. | 17 It is a rather large one. |
| 18 àiⁿ cang kim cò, a sĭ àiⁿ cang n̂gn cò? sǹg sìo. | 18 Do you want it made of gold or of silver? Reckon up. |
| 19 lú sǹg m̄ tîeh. | 19 You have reckoned wrongly. |
| 20 soiⁿ sǹg kàu tīaⁿ tîeh. | 20 First reckon exactly. |
| 21 àiⁿ khù kùe nî. | 21 Going to spend New Year. |
| 22 i ŭ cōi kùe úa. | 22 He has more than I. |
| 23 i kâi a pĕ kùe khù. | 23 His father has passed away. |

## LESSON XX.

| | |
|---|---|
| 牛 gû; ox, cattle. | 車 chia; car, cart. |
| 馬 bé; horses. | 飼 chī; feed; rear. |
| 猪 tṳ; swine. | 講 káng; tàⁿ; say. |
| 膋 lâ; fat, tallow. | 話 ūe; speech. |
| 肉 nêk; flesh, meat. | 彳 chit; to step. |
| 油 îu; oil. | 亍 chok; to walk. |

| | | |
|---|---|---|
| 1 | lṳ́ kîaⁿ lâi chit chok kìe. | You came noisily. |
| 2 | gû bé chit chok kìe kîaⁿ khṳ̀. nâng bé. | The cows and horses went clattering away. Troops. |
| 3 | úa thiaⁿ kìⁿ lṳ́ kîaⁿ khṳ̀ chit chok kìe. | I heard the patter of your feet as you went. |
| 4 | nín hiaⁿ tī kíaⁿ chit chit chok chok tī kò lâi? | From where do you boys come scampering? |
| 5 | àiⁿ bói cêk kò gû nêk. | Will buy a piece of beef. |
| 6 | i cîah tṳ nêk cōi. | He eats much pork. |
| 7 | cí kâi îu, tī kò lâi? | Where did this oil come from? |
| 8 | cang cêk kò gû lâ. | Use a piece of suet. |
| 9 | mài khah cōi tṳ lâ. | Do not put in too much lard. |
| 10 | lṳ́ só tàⁿ kâi ūe, úa thiaⁿ m̄ kìⁿ. | I did not hear what you said. |
| 11 | úa m̄ pat thiaⁿ i tàⁿ. | I have not heard him say. |
| 12 | cí kâi sī sih mih ūe? | What sort of talk is this? |
| 13 | i ṳ̄ cêk ciah bé chia. | He has a wagon. |
| 14 | i ŏi tàⁿ ūe a bŏi? | Can he talk? |
| 15 | àiⁿ chī kàu i tōa. | I will keep him till he is grown. |
| 16 | chī kaù tōa lío cīu m̄ àiⁿ i. | After she had brought him up, she did not want him. |
| 17 | tṳ bó seⁿ ṳ̆ lâk ciah tṳ kíaⁿ. thiaⁿ káng. | The sow has given birth to six pigs. Hear discourses. |
| 18 | gû bó seⁿ gû kíaⁿ. | Cows produce calves. |
| 19 | úa thiaⁿ lṳ́ tàⁿ cīu sī. | I will do as you say. |
| 20 | i tàⁿ ūe m̄ hó thiaⁿ. | He spoke indecently. |
| 21 | i tŏ bé thâu. | He is at the pier. |
| 22 | mài kio nâng tàⁿ. | Do not tell anybody. |

## LESSON XXI.

- 樹 tû; a cupboard.
- 樓 lâu; an upper story.
- 路 lō; road, path.
- 巷 hāng; lane, street.
- 塗 thô; earth, soil.
- 擔 tà$^n$; burden, a picul.

- 起 khí; rise, build, begin.
- 擔 ta$^n$; carry on a pole over the shoulder.
- 曝 phâk; to sun.
- 濕 sip; tâm; wet.
- 乾 * ta; dry.
- 重 têng; layers.

| | | |
|---|---|---|
| 1 | lí khù kāng i tà$^n$. | You go and tell him. |
| 2 | úa ài$^n$ kio i tà$^n$. | I shall tell him. |
| 3 | i chī tu, chī gû. | He rears hogs and cows. |
| 4 | cîah tû: tû kía$^n$. | A food safe: little cupboard. |
| 5 | cí tîo hāng hó khù tī kò? | Where does this road lead to? |
| 6 | cí kâi tâm tâm kâi lō khí thâu phâk ta lío. | This muddy road is beginning to get dry. |
| 7 | cí tà$^n$ mûeh hó ta$^n$ pàng sa$^n$ têng lâu kò. | Carry this carry of things and put them in the third story. |
| 8 | phâk ta ŭ kúi têng lío. | Several layers have dried. |
| 9 | i khí thâu tà$^n$ ūe. | He began to speak. |
| 10 | bô lō hó kîa$^n$. | There is no road to walk in. |
| 11 | kìe kâi nâng lâi ta$^n$ thô. | Call a man to carry earth. |
| 12 | phâk kàu ta ta. | Sun it till it is dry. |
| 13 | ta$^n$ jîh gūa tà$^n$ thô. sip sip. | Carried over twenty loads of earth. Dank. |
| 14 | úa ta$^n$ ŭ sâp gūa tà$^n$. | I have carried over thirty loads. |
| 15 | lí ta$^n$ ŭ kúi tà$^n$? | How many loads did you carry? |
| 16 | i tǒ cáu bé lâu kîa$^n$ lâi, kîa$^n$ khù. | He is walking back and forth on the verandah. |
| 17 | cí cêk cō chù khí kàu ta$^n$ ŭ jîeh kú lío? | How long since this house was built? |
| 18 | i ài$^n$ khí kâi cáu bé lâu. | He will build a verandah. |
| 19 | m̄ sī hí cêk tîo lō. | It is not that road. |
| 20 | lō tâm tâm m̄ hó kîa$^n$. | The road is very wet, so that one cannot well walk. |
| 21 | ta$^n$ khí kîa$^n$ cuang. | Carry the luggage. |
| 22 | cuang kúi tà$^n$ îu khù bōi. | Decant several piculs of oil for selling. |

## LESSON XXII.

天 thi$^{n}$; thien; the firmament.
地 tǐ; the earth.
山 sua$^{n}$; hills, mountain.
海 hái; sea.
溪 khoi; river, stream.
河 hô; large river.

邊 pi$^{n}$; pôi$^{n}$; pien; margin.
旁 phâng; phîa$^{n}$; side.
墘 kî$^{n}$; shore; brink; brim.
隔 kêh; divide, partition.
格 keh; limit, pattern, reach.
次 chù; the next; secondary.

| | |
|---|---|
| 1 úa ài$^{n}$ kùe khoi. | 1 I wish to cross the river. |
| 2 bw̄n mûeh sǐ thi$^{n}$ sǐang tōa. | 2 Of all things heaven is greatest. |
| 3 i lâi kàu hái kî$^{n}$ lío. | 3 He has already reached the beach. |
| 4 i cǒ tǒ lō phâng. | 4 He sits by the roadside. |
| 5 pàng tǒ tû kha pi$^{n}$. | 5 Put it by the wardrobe. |
| 6 pàng tǒ chîe$^{n}$ kha pi$^{n}$. | 6 Put it by the wall. |
| 7 hīn cǎi khoi bô cúi, só ī$^{n}$ bǒi tit khù. | 7 There is now no water in the river, therefore we cannot go. |
| 8 i cîah khoi cúi. | 8 He drinks river water. |
| 9 i keh hái. | 9 It is across the sea. |
| 10 i kâi chù tǒ sua$^{n}$ kha. | 10 His house is at the foot of the hill. |
| 11 lō pi$^{n}$: lō phâng. | 11 Beside the road. |
| 12 lō kî$^{n}$; lō phîa$^{n}$. | 12 Beside the road. |
| 13 hái pi$^{n}$: hái pien. | 13 By the sea side. |
| 14 pàng hú cêk pôi$^{n}$. | 14 Put it on that side. |
| 15 ài$^{n}$ cò jîeh cōi keh? | 15 How many partitions will you have made? |
| 16 hú cêk tîo khoi hô kâi cúi hó cîah. | 16 The water of that river is good to drink. |
| 17 i sǐ chù pi$^{n}$ nâng. | 17 He is a neighbour. |
| 18 cí aū ài$^{n}$ cò chù pi$^{n}$. | 18 Hereafter they are going to be neighbours. |
| 19 i sǐ sua$^{n}$ lăi nâng. | 19 He is a countryman. |
| 20 i cǒ tǒ sua$^{n}$ phîa$^{n}$. | 20 He sat on the hill side. |
| 21 ài$^{n}$ pàng tǐ kâi ūi chù? | 21 Where will you put it? |
| 22 thi$^{n}$ tǐ lăi, sua$^{n}$ cōi, a sǐ khoi hô cōi? | 22 Are there more mountains or more rivers in the world? |
| 23 ài$^{n}$ kêh cò nǒ keh. | 23 Will make two pigeonholes. |

# LESSON XXIII.

目 mâk; the eye.
睛 * ciu; the eyeball.
眉 bâi; brow; crescent.

毛 mô; hair; feathers.
草 cháu; grass; weeds.
茅 * me; rank grass.

日 jı̂t; sun; day.
月 gûeh; moon; month.
本 pún; pn̂g; classifier of books; own; origin.

分 hun; a tenth; to divide.
分 hūn; a part or share.
分 pun; distribute.

---

1 câp hun: poih hun.
2 saⁿ hun: ngŏ hun.
3 lṳ́ ŭ kúi pn̂g?
4 gûeh bâi: mâk bâi.
5 i mâk ciu thìaⁿ.
6 i seⁿ lâi mâk ciu sòi.
7 i sĭ pn̂g tṳ̆ nâng.
8 cí kâi sĭ i kâi pn̂g hu.
9 cí kò sĭ i kâi pn̂g tṳ̆.
10 i pun cò nŏ ki.
11 jı̂t thâu: gûeh nîe.
12 jı̂t jı̂t: kíaⁿ jı̂t.
13 poih gûeh, câp sì. kùe hūn.
14 ău jı̂t: ău jı̂t.
15 i bô thâu mô.
16 jı̂t chut: jı̂t jı̂p.
17 khṳ̀ chūe cháu me.
18 i ke kúi jı̂t àiⁿ lâi.
19 keh ke saⁿ jı̂t.
20 keh ke cêk jı̂t.
21 úa bô pún sṳ.
22 sĭ lṳ́ kâi pn̂g hūn.
23 nín kâi ke, pun a būe?
24 lṳ́ hūn lăi pun ŭ jîeh cōi?
25 cí kĭaⁿ mûeh kàu kúi hun hó?
26 cí kâi gûeh hūn, sĭ úa cò. úa hūn lăi kâi sṳ.

1 The whole: eight tenths.
2 Thirty per cent: one half.
3 How many volumes have you?
4 The new moon: eyebrow.
5 He has sore eyes.
6 He has naturally small eyes.
7 He is a native.
8 This is her own husband.
9 This is his own country.
10 It separated into two branches.
11 The sun: the moon.
12 Every day: to-day.
13 The fourteenth of the eighth month. Exceed one's sphere.
14 Hereafter: day after to-morrow.
15 He has no hair.
16 Sunrise: sunset.
17 Go and seek ferns.
18 He will come in a few days.
19 Three days afterward.
20 In one day more.
21 I have not the wherewith.
22 It is your duty.
23 Is your estate divided yet?
24 How much was there in your share?
25 What proportion of this is good?
26 This portion of the month I do it. That within my sphere.

## LESSON XXIV.

| | | | |
|---|---|---|---|
| 合 | hâh; accord. | 衆 | cèng, cùa$^{n}$; all. |
| 合 | hâp; united; join. | 全 | chŵn, cn̂g; all; whole. |
| 爲 | ûi; do; effect. | 從 | chông; since, from. |
| 爲 | ūi; ŭi; because; for; help. | 從 | chông; tùe; follow. |
| 亂 | lŭan; confused. | 從 | cŭang; clan; subordinate. |
| 妄 | buáng; thèng; disorderly. | 由 | îu; through, by. |

1 siang hâh; m̄ siang hâh.
2 i hâp ke ài$^{n}$ lâi.
3 hâh mâk, m̄ hâh mâk.
4 lṳ́ chông tī kò̤ lâi?
5 cí kâi chŵn m̄ hó̤.
6 ūi tîeh cí kâi sṳ̄.
7 ūi tîeh i kâi pē bó̤.
8 cèng nâng ài$^{n}$.
9 cn̂g kâi khîeh lâi.
10 chông côi$^{n}$ m̄ pat thói$^{n}$ kì$^{n}$.
11 chông soi$^{n}$ bô̤ cí kâi sṳ̄.
12 i sĭ cŭang hia$^{n}$ tī.
13 úa bô̤ lêng ûi.
14 úa tà$^{n}$, nín tăi ke thia$^{n}$.
15 tăi ke, lâi thói$^{n}$.
16 ài$^{n}$ cò̤, tîeh cò̤ kàu chŵn.
17 úa tùe lṳ́ lâi khṳ̀.
18 chông lâi: chông kim í$^{n}$ ău.
19 hṳ́ ciah gû kía$^{n}$ tùe tě̤ chia ău.
chŵn lêng.
20 sim m̄ hó̤ lŭan.
21 mài buáng cò̤: mài thèng cò̤.
22 mài lŭan tà$^{n}$.
23 îu nín cùa$^{n}$ nâng cò̤.
24 îu ka kī hâh mâk, m̄ îu cèng nâng ài$^{n}$.
25 tîeh chông i kâi ṳ̄e.

1 Agreeing; disagreeing.
2 The entire family is coming.
3 Suiting or not suiting the taste.
4 Where did you come from?
5 This is altogether bad.
6 Because of this affair.
7 On account of his parents.
8 All men want it.
9 Bring the whole of it.
10 I never before saw it.
11 Formerly there was no such thing.
12 They are cousins.
13 I have not the ability.
14 While I speak, you all listen.
15 All come and look.
16 If you are going to do it, you must finish it.
17 I will go along with you.
18 Heretofore: henceforth.
19 That calf is following the wagon.
Almighty.
20 Do not be agitated.
21 Do not do it carelessly.
22 Do not speak incoherently.
23 Do it through you all.
24 Because it suits me, not because of people's wishes.
25 Must comply with his directions.

# LESSON XXV.

| | |
|---|---|
| 鼻 phī$^{n}$; nose. | 竿 ko̤; reed; staff. |
| 嗅 * phī$^{n}$; smell. | 香 * phang; fragrant. |
| 竹 tek; bamboo. | 臭 * chàu; stinking. |
| 另 * lêng; besides. | 易 kōi; easy. |
| 換 ūa$^{n}$; exchange. | 難 lân, o̤h; difficult. |
| 輩 pùe, hùe; class, sort. | 各 kak; each. |

| | |
|---|---|
| 1 i sĭang kōi cîah húe. | 1 It is very easy to burn. |
| 2 kak nâng kak nâng kâi sṳ̄. | 2 Each persons affairs are his own. |
| 3 kak nâng kak nâng kâi. | 3 Each one's things are his own. |
| 4 lâm cṳ́ hùe tŏ̤ cí gūa, nńg cṳ́ hùe tŏ̤ hṳ́ lăi. | 4 The menkind are to be out here, and the women in there. |
| 5 i ŭ phī$^{n}$, i kâi phī$^{n}$ bŏi phī$^{n}$ phang chàu. | 5 He has a nose, but he cannot smell. |
| 6 khṳ̀ chūe ki tek ko̤ lâi. | 6 Go and find a bamboo pole. |
| 7 mài lêng ūa$^{n}$ lâi. | 7 Do not come again. |
| 8 m̄ cai i lêng gūa ŭ a bê̤. | 8 Do not know whether he has any besides. |
| 9 i a nô$^{n}$ kía$^{n}$ hùe m̄ cai. | 9 The children do not know. |
| 10 hŭ jîn hùe m̄ hó̤ khṳ̀. | 10 Women should not go. |
| 11 i cṳ nîe hùe bê̤ lâi. | 11 The ladies did not come. |
| 12 kàu sǹg sìo kâi jît. | 12 At the day of reckoning. |
| 13 hṳ́ kâi mûeh o̤h chūe. | 13 That thing is hard to find. |
| 14 sĭ kōi, sĭ o̤h, tîeh cò̤ kàu chŵn. | 14 Hard or easy, it must be completed. |
| 15 ŏi phang a bŏi? | 15 Is it fragrant? |
| 16 i kâi chùi chàu. | 16 His breath is offensive. |
| 17 cí kâi ài$^{n}$ ūa$^{n}$ cò̤ hṳ́ kâi. cí kĭa$^{n}$ mûeh lân cò̤. | 17 I want to exchange this for that. This is difficult to make. |
| 18 kōi cò̤: o̤h cò̤. | 18 Easily done: hard to do. |
| 19 sĭ tek cò̤ kâi. | 19 It is made of bamboo. |
| 20 ke sì jît ài$^{n}$ lêng ūa$^{n}$ khṳ̀. | 20 Going again in three days. |
| 21 lṳ́ tōa pùe, a i tōa pùe? | 21 Are you or he the older? |
| 22 cí kâi ūe lân tà$^{n}$. | 22 This language is hard to speak. |
| 23 cai lân, put lân. | 23 Knowing the difficulty overcomes it. |

# LESSON XXVI.

認 jīn; recognize; confess.
讀 thâk; read aloud.
寫 sía; write.
說 sueh; discourse.
聲 sia$^{n}$; sound.
書 cṳ; book.

册 cheh; book, schedule.
畫 ûeh; line, mark.
紙 cúa; paper.
信 sìn; epistle; trust.
攏 lóng; act with; all together.
總 cóng; all.

| | |
|---|---|
| 1 úa pat tō̤ jīn. | 1 I recognize him. |
| 2 lṳ́ pn̂g cṳ cheh khìeh lâi. | 2 Bring your book. |
| 3 i tŏ̤ thâk cṳ. | 3 He is reading (aloud). |
| 4 i tŏ̤ thói$^{n}$ cṳ. | 4 He is reading (silently). |
| 5 úa thia$^{n}$ i kâi sia$^{n}$ sueh. | 5 I heard his voice. |
| 6 thâk kàu tōa sia$^{n}$. | 6 Read loud. |
| 7 lṳ́ thâk khah sòi sia$^{n}$. | 7 You read too low. |
| 8 hó̤ chut sia$^{n}$. | 8 Let out your voice. |
| 9 ŏi thâk, hṳ̂n lío bŏi sueh. | 9 Can read but not explain. |
| 10 lṳ́ ŏi thâk cṳ a bŏi? | 10 Can you read? |
| 11 ài$^{n}$ sía pàng cí pn̂g cheh kò̤. káng sueh. | 11 I will write it in this book. Discourse about. |
| 12 i tŏ̤ sía sìn. | 12 He is writing a letter. |
| 13 úa bô̤ cúa hó̤ sía. | 13 I have no paper to write on. |
| 14 lṳ́ ŭ kúi pn̂g cheh? | 14 How many books have you? |
| 15 úa ŭ chit pn̂g. | 15 I have seven. |
| 16 chíu mâk: kha mâk. | 16 The wrist bone: the ankle bone. |
| 17 lṳ́ tà$^{n}$ lâi m̄ tîeh. | 17 What you just said was wrong. |
| 18 úa pun ŭ peh gūa pn̂g cṳ cheh. | 18 I distributed over a hundred books. |
| 19 lṳ́ tī jît ài$^{n}$ lâi? | 19 What day are you coming? |
| 20 hṳ́ cêk jît i bô̤ tŏ̤. | 20 That day he was not there. |
| 21 cṳ lóng cóng thâk chṳ̂n. | 21 Finish reading all the books. |
| 22 thói$^{n}$ cṳ cheh tîeh jīn ûeh. lṳ́ m̄ hó̤ sìn. | 22 In reading you must know the strokes. Don't believe it. |
| 23 mài sía ke cíe ûeh. i m̄ jīn. | 23 Do not write more or less strokes. He won't confess. |
| 24 cṳ cheh lóng cóng khìeh lâi. | 24 Bring all the books. |

# LESSON XXVII.

字 jī; letters.
音 im; sound.
語 gṳ́; speech, language.
筆 pit; pen, pencil.
墨 bâk; ink.
寄 kìa; send by another.

抄 chau; to copy.
描 bîe; trace through paper.
竭 kîet; exhaust.
力 lât; strength.
句 kù; word, sentence.
讀 tāu; a clause.

1 tîeh thâk ŭ kù ŭ tāu.
2 ài$^{n}$ kāi lṳ́ tà$^{n}$ kù ūe.
3 cṳ kâi kù tāu tîeh jīn.
4 kak chù kak chù kâi im gṳ́.
sua$^{n}$ kîet, hái kîet.
5 cêng thâk lŭn gṳ́ a būe?
6 lṳ́ pat jī mē?
7 ŭ hûe jī a bô?
8 thâk kàu ŏi jīn jī.
9 cí kâi jī sĭ chau kâi a sĭ bîe kâi?
10 ŏi thia$^{n}$ kì$^{n}$ i kâi sia$^{n}$ im.
11 i bô sĭm mih kîet lât.
12 tà$^{n}$ só í$^{n}$, khṳt úa cai.
13 ŭ sì kâi, cĭu hó. ēng put kîet.
14 lṳ́ tà$^{n}$ lâi kâi ūe sĭ tîeh.
15 lṳ́ hó tà$^{n}$ tīa$^{n}$ tîeh.
16 i m̄ cai hun pîet jī im.
17 tîeh hun pîet tī kâi hó tī kâi m̄ hó.
18 ca jît i cai cí kâi sṳ̄, i cĭu m̄ khṳ̀.
19 úa pat thâk kùe.
20 sĭ, hó tà$^{n}$ sĭ, m̄ sĭ hó tà$^{n}$ m̄ sĭ.
21 lṳ́ m̄ chut lât.

1 Read with regard to the stops.
2 I want to speak a word with you.
3 You must discern the clauses.
4 Each place has its own dialect.
Land and sea used up.
5 Have you read the Discourses yet?
6 Can you read?
7 Is there an answer?
8 Read till you know the letters.
9 Are these characters copied or traced?
10 Can hear the sound of it.
11 He is not very diligent.
12 Tell me the reasons for it.
13 If I had four, it would do. Inexhaustible.
14 What you just said is right.
15 Say precisely what you will do.
16 He does not distinguish between the sounds of the letters.
17 You must discriminate between the good and the bad.
18 Had he known this yesterday, he would not have gone.
19 I have read it before.
20 If it is so, say it is so, if not so, say it is not so.
21 You do not exert yourself.

## LESSON XXVIII.

喊 hàm; call aloud.
離 lî; leave.
開 khui, khai; open, unfold.
閉 * kueⁿ; to shut.
待 thăi; wait for.
欵 khṳ́n; to wait on; sort.
等 thĕng; tán; wait, expect.
候 hāu; time; wait.
時 sî; time; season.
上 cĭeⁿ; ascend:
上 cīeⁿ; upper; upon.
落 lô̤h; descend; let down.

| | | |
|---|---|---|
| 1 | bô̤ nâng pat cĭeⁿ thiⁿ. | No one has ascended to heaven. |
| 2 | cĭeⁿ cĭeⁿ, lôh lôh. | Ascending and descending. |
| 3 | bô̤ sî hāu hó̤ cò̤. | I have no time to do it. |
| 4 | i tī kâi sî hāu àiⁿ lâi? | When is he coming? |
| 5 | hīn căi sih mih sî hāu? | What time is it now? |
| 6 | bô̤ sĭm mih hun pîet. | There is not much distinction. |
| 7 | kàu cí lâi m̄ pat thóiⁿ. | Until now I never saw it. |
| 8 | khui mn̂g: kueⁿ mn̂g. | Open the door: shut the door. |
| 9 | khṳ́n thăi i hó̤. | Treat him well. |
| 10 | i bô̤ mih khṳ́n thăi úa. pun khui. | He did not show me much courtesy. Apportion. |
| 11 | khṳ́n thăi nâng kheh. | Entertain a guest. |
| 12 | hàm i lî khui. | Tell him to withdraw. |
| 13 | lî khui. khai hâh. | To depart from. Folding. |
| 14 | cèng nâng tŏ̤ tán lṳ́. | All the people expect you. |
| 15 | thăi úa; tán úa; thĕng úa. | Wait for me. |
| 16 | ŏi jîeh tōa? ŏi jîeh hó̤? | How large is it? How good is it? |
| 17 | i tàⁿ pât mih ūe. | He speaks another language. |
| 18 | lâi kâi gūa gûeh. | Came over a month ago. |
| 19 | ngŏ hūn lô̤h cêk hūn. | Put in one fifth of it. |
| 20 | cò̤ saⁿ hūn lô̤h cêk hūn. | Put in one third of it. |
| 21 | cĭn sim thâk, cĭu mé mé pat. | If you give your whole mind to reading you will soon know how. |
| 22 | jīn m̄ chut: hṳ̂n m̄ jīn. | Do not recognize: do not yet recognize. |
| 23 | cīeⁿ kúi jît. cí khṳ́n. | A few days ago. This kind. |
| 24 | i cĭeⁿ suaⁿ cīeⁿ. | He went up on the mountain. |
| 25 | hṳ́ cêk sî. hṳ́ cêk khṳ́n. | At that time. That sort. |

# LESSON XXIX.

| | |
|---|---|
| 按 àn; press; according to. | 樣 īe$^n$; se$^n$; mode; pattern. |
| 肖 sĭo; jîen; similar. | 怎 cè; căi; why; how; what. |
| 如 jû; as; like. | 屢 lú; ē; reiterated. |
| 似 sŭ; chĭe$^n$; similar. | 呢 nî; interrogative. |
| 挪 * cìe$^n$; thus; hither. | 好 * chin; very. |
| 這 * hìe$^n$; thus; thither. | 像 sìe$^n$; chĭe$^n$; likeness. |

| | |
|---|---|
| 1 lâm cú hùe cŏ tŏ cìe$^n$ pôi$^n$, hŭ jîn, nńg cú hùe cŏ tŏ hìe$^n$ pôi$^n$. | 1 The men sit on this side, and the women sit on that side. |
| 2 jû cìe$^n$ se$^n$ cè. lú lú. | 2 Do thus. Again and again. |
| 3 īa sĭ hìe$^n$ se$^n$ cè. | 3 Should you do like that—. |
| 4 cè lâi cìe$^n$ se$^n$ sĭ m̄ hó. | 4 It is badly done thus. |
| 5 căi se$^n$ īe$^n$? | 5 What sort of thing is it? |
| 6 sĭ cìe$^n$ se$^n$. | 6 That is the way it is. |
| 7 chin chĭe$^n$: m̄ chin chĭe$^n$. | 7 Much alike: not much alike. |
| 8 chíu àn sim cè. | 8 Did it heart and hand. |
| 9 àn cìe$^n$ se$^n$ cè. īe$^n$ sìe$^n$. | 9 Do like this. Effigy. |
| 10 àn hìe$^n$ se$^n$ cè. | 10 Act in that way. |
| 11 úa cè ŏi? úa căi tit cai? | 11 How can I? How do I know? |
| 12 i cè nî m̄ lâi? | 12 Why does he not come? |
| 13 i se$^n$ lâi chin chĭe$^n$ i kâi a bó cêk īe$^n$. ē ē. | 13 She looks just like her mother. Time after time. |
| 14 cè chin chĭe$^n$ cìe$^n$ se$^n$. | 14 Make it about like this. |
| 15 i sĭo i a pĕ. | 15 He resembles his father. |
| 16 i jîen i a hia$^n$. | 16 He resembles his brother. |
| 17 se$^n$ lâi jîen jîen. | 17 They are (born) just alike. |
| 18 cè lâi jîen jîen. | 18 They are made just alike. |
| 19 nŏ nâng kâi mīn siang sŭ. | 19 The faces of the two resemble each other. |
| 20 cí kâi kio hú kâi siang sŭ. tie$^n$ īe$^n$. | 20 This and that are similar. Affect a style. |
| 21 ài$^n$ cè căi se$^n$ īe$^n$? | 21 How do you want it to be made? |
| 22 se$^n$ lâi căi se$^n$ īe$^n$ cĭu sĭ chin chĭe$^n$. | 22 The sort of thing produced is very similiar. |
| 23 i kâi sìe$^n$ sĭo a m̄ sĭo? | 23 Is the likeness a good one? |

# LESSON XXX.

| | | | |
|---|---|---|---|
| 鳥 | cío; a bird. | 咬 | kă; bite. |
| 雞 | koi; a fowl. | 打 | phah; strike. |
| 鴨 | ah; a duck. | 比 | pí; compare. |
| 翼 | * sit; wings. | 問 | mn̄g; inquire. |
| 狗 | káu; a dog. | 同 | tâng; agreeing. |
| 飛 | pue; fly. | 豈 | khá; how should it. |

| | |
|---|---|
| 1 m̄ sī cie$^n$ se$^n$. | 1 It is not so. |
| 2 lú cò nī ŏi hie$^n$ mé lâi? | 2 How is it that you are come so soon? |
| 3 i sī tà$^n$ cie$^n$ se$^n$ a m̄ sī? | 3 He said so did he not? |
| 4 cò àn úa cie$^n$ se$^n$ cò. | 4 Do as I am doing. |
| 5 àn cío pue hie$^n$ mé. | 5 As fast as a bird flies. |
| 6 nŏ kâi m̄ sie tâng. | 6 The two are not alike. |
| 7 ŏi sie tâng a bŏi? | 7 Are they alike? |
| 8 hái káu: cúi ah: sua$^n$ koi. | 8 A seal: teal: pheasant. |
| 9 hái koi bó: ah cíh. | 9 A sea gull: duck's bill. |
| 10 mài sía hie$^n$ mé. | 10 Do not write so fast. |
| 11 koi ang: koi bó: koi kia$^n$. | 11 Cock: hen: chicken. |
| 12 i lâi mn̄g hāu lú. | 12 He has come to pay his respects to you. |
| 13 se$^n$ lâi sie tâng sie tâng. | 13 They are exactly alike. |
| 14 se$^n$ lâi m̄ siang tâng. | 14 They are not alike. |
| 15 cie$^n$ se$^n$ kâi nâng. | 15 That sort of people. |
| 16 cèng nâng tâng sim. | 16 They are all of one mind. |
| 17 cèng nâng tà$^n$ ūe m̄ tâng sim. | 17 They all spoke different minds. |
| 18 hó cang sih mih kâi khó pí i? | 18 What can be taken to compare with it? |
| 19 bô khó pí: bô hó pí. | 19 Incomparable. |
| 20 m̄ tâng īe$^n$. | 20 Not agreeing in kind. |
| 21 khó pí ŭ cêk ciah cío. | 21 It is as if there were a bird—. |
| 22 cie$^n$ se$^n$ cò, khá ŏi a bŏi? | 22 Could it thus be done? |
| 23 ciang lâi sī ŭ cò nī? | 23 How will it be in the future? |
| 24 ah pí cío ia ŭ sit, khá ŏi tâng cío pue, mē? | 24 Ducks like birds have wings, but can they fly as do birds? |
| 25 i sie phah, sie kă. | 25 They strike and bite each other. |

## LESSON XXXI.

想 sie$^{n}$; to think.
里 lí; one tenth of a league.
塘 * phò; about 3½ miles.
寸 chùn; inch.
尺 chieh; a foot.
丈 tn̆g; ten feet.
長 tn̂g; long.
短 tó; short.
高 kau; kûi$^{n}$; high.
低 ti; kĕ; low.
下 ĕ; below; following.
下 ē; a time; once.

| | |
|---|---|
| 1 úa sie$^{n}$ m̄ chut. | 1 I cannot think of it. |
| 2 ŏi sie$^{n}$ kì$^{n}$ a bŏi? | 2 Can you think it out? |
| 3 úa kâi sim sie$^{n}$. côi$^{n}$ nî. | 3 My thoughts. Year before last. |
| 4 câp lí cò cêk phò. | 4 Ten lí make a league. |
| 5 cêk lí lō jîeh cōi tn̆g tn̂g? ău, nŏ nî. | 5 How many tn̆g in one lí of length? Two years after. |
| 6 câp hun cò cêk chùn. | 6 Ten tenths make an inch. |
| 7 câp chùn cò cêk chieh. | 7 Ten inches make a foot. |
| 8 câp chieh cò cêk tn̆g. | 8 Ten feet make a tn̆g. |
| 9 sie$^{n}$ tn̂g, sie$^{n}$ tó. | 9 Think it all over. |
| 10 kau í$^{n}$ ài$^{n}$ cò kúi chieh kûi$^{n}$? | 10 How many feet high will you make the dining chairs? |
| 11 nín nŏ nâng bô mih kûi$^{n}$ kĕ. | 11 You two are not very different in height. |
| 12 lú úa lâi kì$^{n}$ kâi kau ti. | 12 Let us see which is ablest. |
| 13 lú kâi nâng kûi$^{n}$ kùe i kâi nâng. ŏi tó cí kâi a bŏi? | 13 You are taller than he. Is it any shorter than this? |
| 14 ĕ hûe mài lâi. | 14 Another time do not come. |
| 15 hâh cò cêk ē khà. | 15 Take them all at once. |
| 16 chíu ĕ. kàu kì$^{n}$. | 16 Dependents. Opinion. |
| 17 lú ŭ sih mih kau kì$^{n}$? | 17 What is your opinion? |
| 18 pàng tŏ chn̂g ĕ. | 18 Put it under the table. |
| 19 ĕ jît: ĕ chù. | 19 Another day: next time. |
| 20 ĕ gûeh; ĕ mīn. | 20 The following month: under surface. |
| 21 tn̂g tó cò cêk ē sǹg. | 21 Reckon them all together, the long ones, and the short ones. |
| 22 cêk ē cêk ē thia$^{n}$ kì$^{n}$. | 22 Hear it stroke after stroke. |
| 23 thi$^{n}$ ĕ nâng mûeh. | 23 All under heaven. |
| 24 cò kàu chit chieh tn̂g. | 24 Make it seven feet long. |

## LESSON XXXII.

市 chĭ; market.
街 koi; street.
船 cûn; boat.
帆 phâng; sail.
方 hng; region.
頂 téng; top.

底 tói; bottom.
搭 tah; go on board.
較 * ío; comparative, more.
代 thòi; instead of.
方 pang, pāng; side, extent.
方 huang; cìaⁿ; thereupon.

| | | |
|---|---|---|
| 1 | i tó lăi bô̤ mûeh. | There is nothing in the fellow. |
| 2 | lṳ́ àiⁿ kìⁿ úa mih sṳ? | On what account do you wish to see me? |
| 3 | jît ŏi jîeh ùaⁿ? | How late in the day is it? |
| 4 | thăi i tōa. | Wait till he is grown. |
| 5 | i kâi kîaⁿ m̄ tîeh; i kâi cò̤ sṳ. phâng cûn. | His misdemeanor; his behaviour. Sail boats. |
| 6 | téng tûn: ĕ tûn. | Upper lip: under lip. |
| 7 | chíu tói: kha tói. | Palm: sole of the foot. |
| 8 | lṳ́ ŏi sái cûn a bŏi? | Can you manage a boat? |
| 9 | tah m̄ tîeh cûn. | Did not reach the boat. |
| 10 | ío tōa: ío hó̤: ío tó̤. | Larger: better: shorter. |
| 11 | úa thòi lṳ́ cò̤. | I will do it in your stead. |
| 12 | cang cí kâi thòi hṳ́ kâi. | Take this instead of that. |
| 13 | úa àiⁿ tah lṳ́ khṳ̀. | I wish to take passage with you. |
| 14 | pàng lôh chṳ̂ng téng. | Set it on the top of the table. |
| 15 | ŭ ngṳ̂, bô̤ mûeh kĭaⁿ hó̤ bói. | I have money, but there is nothing to buy. |
| 16 | bô̤ tī hng hó̤ pàng. | There is no room for it. |
| 17 | cò̤ sì pang sì pang. | Make it perfectly square. |
| 18 | huang kim. tōa pāng. | Now a days. On a large scale. |
| 19 | bw̄n pang; bw̄n mûeh. | Everywhere; everything. |
| 20 | úa hàm lṳ́, lṳ́ huang hó̤ lâi. cò̤ hó̤ cìaⁿ hó̤ lâi. | When I call you, you then come. Do it and then come. |
| 21 | cí hûe úa huang thóiⁿ kìⁿ. | I just now saw it. |
| 22 | úa tŏ̤ koi chĭ huang lâi. | I just came from market. |
| 23 | cûn cí hûe hó̤ sái phâng. | The sail can now be raised. |
| 24 | gūa hng nâng. koi chĭ. | Foreigners. Market. |

## LESSON XXXIII.

布 pò; cloth; spread down.
寒 kûa$^{n}$; ngân; hâng; cold.
冷 chìn; né; cold.
熱 jîet; jûah; hot.
闊 khùa$^{n}$; khuah; wide.
寬 khwn; khua$^{n}$; broad; gentle.

狹 oîh; narrow.
深 chim; deep.
淺 chíen; shallow.
偕 * cò-pû; together.
通 thong; permeate; everywhere
亦 īa; also; moreover.

| | |
|---|---|
| 1 cí cêk tîo lō oîh oîh. | 1 This road is very narrow. |
| 2 thi$^{n}$ sî m̄ hó. | 2 The weather is bad. |
| 3 thi$^{n}$ sî hó căi. | 3 The weather is very fine. |
| 4 thong koi chī, bô nâng pat. | 4 Through all the market, there is no one who knows. |
| 5 lṳ́ tī sî ài$^{n}$ lôh cûn? | 5 When are you going on board? |
| 6 chim kùe hái. | 6 Deeper than the sea. |
| 7 i kâi chùi khuah khuah. | 7 His mouth is very wide. |
| 8 sî hāu ài$^{n}$ kàu. | 8 The time is at hand. |
| 9 chn̂g pò: mīn pò. ìu$^{n}$ pò. | 9 Table-cloth: towel. Fine cloth. |
| 10 pât kâi tī hng īa ŭ. | 10 Other countries also have. |
| 11 úa īa ŭ lân kâi. | 11 I also have a few. |
| 12 cí kĭa$^{n}$ pò sĭm khwn khuah, īa kûa$^{n}$ jûah hó ēng; hó cò-pû lâi khṳ̀ bói. | 12 This kind of cloth is very wide, and is good for both cold and warm weather; come with me and buy some. |
| 13 cí kâi oîh khah jûah; cò-pû lâi khṳ̀ khwn khuah. hái tói. | 13 This narrow space is too hot; come with me to spacious quarters. Bottom of the sea. |
| 14 hó khua$^{n}$ khua$^{n}$ kîa$^{n}$. | 14 Walk leisurely. |
| 15 khua$^{n}$ khua$^{n}$ cò. | 15 Do it comfortably. |
| 16 chim sĭe$^{n}$. jîet căi. | 16 Deep thinking. Bustling. |
| 17 thi$^{n}$ sî ngân chìn. | 17 The weather is very cold. |
| 18 phah né úa kâi sim. | 18 Chills my affections. |
| 19 thong thi$^{n}$ ĕ. se$^{n}$ kûa$^{n}$. | 19 The whole earth. Ague. |
| 20 mài lŭn chim chíen. | 20 Whether deep or shallow. |
| 21 mài lŭn khuah oîh. | 21 Whether wide or narrow. |
| 22 ài$^{n}$ kûa$^{n}$ jûah thong ēng. | 22 What can be used for both hot and cold weather. |

# LESSON XXXIV.

衫 saⁿ; clothes.
褲 khò; trowsers.
異 ī, keh; strange.
平 phêng; peace; adjust.
平 phêⁿ, pêⁿ; level, even.
差 cha, tāⁿ; err; differ.

曉 híο; comprehend.
返 tn̂g; return.
反 hŵn; póiⁿ; turn.
掀 hien; lift, jerk, whisk.
翻 hwn; flutter; turn over.
轉 cŵn; tn̂g; revolve.

1 saⁿ khò tû. ŏi ngân a bŏi?
2 cha m̄ to; cha put to.
3 lứ kāng úa cə̀-pû khù.
4 nán cə̀-pû lâi khù.
5 khîeh tn̂g khù hâiⁿ i.
6 ún ka kī kâi saⁿ khò khîeh m̄ tîeh. kûaⁿ jîet.
7 nŏ kâi pêⁿ pêⁿ cêk īeⁿ.
8 phêⁿ īeⁿ: pheⁿ pheⁿ īeⁿ.
9 hŵn kùe lâi: póiⁿ kùe lâi.
10 hien kùe lâi.
11 i hwn lâi hwn khù.
12 hwn cu.
13 ēng n̂gn ūaⁿ cə̀ mûeh kìe cə̀ bói.
14 bói líο bŏ ēng.
15 m̄ sī ēng cîⁿ n̂gn hŏ bói.
16 lứ tàⁿ tāⁿ.
17 cêk híο cīu bŏi tāⁿ.
18 tîeh lêng ūaⁿ cŵn cə̀.
19 hwn tn̂g kùe lâi, úa thóiⁿ.
20 lêng ūaⁿ tn̂g chùi tàⁿ.
21 lứ hŏ pàng pêⁿ.
22 lứ phêng jît cə̀ mih sū?
23 phêng sim lâi lūn.
24 i seⁿ lâi keh īeⁿ.
25 ī nâng: ī sū.
26 lứ cêk cŵn sīeⁿ, sim cīu phêng.

1 A clothes-press. Are you cold?
2 Not much difference.
3 You go with me.
4 We will go together.
5 Go back and return it to him.
6 We did not get even our own clothes. Chills and fever.
7 The two are just alike.
8 Alike: just alike.
9 Turn it over sidewise.
10 Lift it up and invert it.
11 He rolled back and forth.
12 Turn the leaves of a book.
13 To exchange money for things is called buying.
14 Of no use after being bought.
15 Not to be bought with money.
16 You mistook in speaking.
17 Comprehend it and you won't err.
18 Must do it all over again.
19 Turn it over that I may see it.
20 Say it over again.
21 Put it down level.
22 What did you heretofore do?
23 Discuss candidly.
24 He is naturally different.
25 Strangers: strange affair.
26 You think it over, and you will be reconciled to it.

# LESSON XXXV.

| | |
|---|---|
| 夜 | mê; night. |
| 歇 | hiah; cease; stop. |
| 響 | híang; emit sound. |
| 晴 | cê$^{n}$; clear sky. |
| 昏 | hun, hng; obscure. |
| 光 | kuang, kng; light. |
| 明 | mêng; bright; clear. |
| 暗 | àm; dark; secret. |
| 間 | kan; space; between. |
| 霎 | siap; short time. |
| 隨 | sûi; accord; forthwith. |
| 鍾 | ceng; a bell. |

| | | |
|---|---|---|
| 1 | lú ŭ sî ceng a bô? | Have you a clock? |
| 2 | úa sûi sî ài$^{n}$ khù. | I am going immediately. |
| 3 | sûi chíu cai kue$^{n}$ mûg. | Close the door after you. |
| 4 | câp im ceng. | A music box. |
| 5 | úa mêng mêng kāng lú tà$^{n}$. | I tell you plainly. |
| 6 | siap sî kan jĭt àm lío, mê hng tĭeh cí kò hiah. | It will very soon be dark, you must stop here to-night. |
| 7 | lú kâi mâk hun àm. | Your eyes are dim. |
| 8 | thi$^{n}$ kng lío, ceng cò nî būe híang? | It is daylight, why has not the bell rung yet? |
| 9 | thi$^{n}$ kng cá ài$^{n}$ khù. | Will go at daylight. |
| 10 | thi$^{n}$ sî cê$^{n}$ mêng lío. | The weather is fair now. |
| 11 | thi$^{n}$ ài$^{n}$ cê$^{n}$ lío. | The sky is clearing. |
| 12 | thi$^{n}$ būe kng cíu khù. | Went before daylight. |
| 13 | mê sî, nâng tŏ ût. siap sî kan. | In the night when people were asleep. A little while. |
| 14 | mêng nâng m̄ cò àm sū. bô nâng cai cí kâi sū. | Intelligent people do not do dark deeds. No one knows this. |
| 15 | sî ceng hiah kîa$^{n}$. | The clock has stopped. |
| 16 | kàu thói$^{n}$ kì$^{n}$ sū sĭ cìe$^{n}$ se$^{n}$, úa sûi sî cíu hiah. | When I saw it was so, I at once stopped. |
| 17 | mê hng kía$^{n}$. jĭt àm. | Early evening. At dark. |
| 18 | ceng híang ŭ siap sî. | The bell rung a little while ago. |
| 19 | jĭt ài$^{n}$ àm lío. | It is almost dark. |
| 20 | jĭt būe àm. cêk siap sî. | About dark. A moment. |
| 21 | sî ceng ŏi híang a bŏi? | Does this clock strike? |
| 22 | thi$^{n}$ kng cá hó lâi. | Come at daylight. |
| 23 | ŏi kng, ŏi àm. | Can produce light or darkness. |

## LESSON XXXVI.

紅 âng; red.
青 che<sup>n</sup>; green; blue.
烏 o; black.
白 pêh; white; clear.
藍 lâm; chí<sup>n</sup>; indigo; blue.
綠 lêk; bright green.

赤 chiah; a light brown.
黃 n̂g; yellow.
染 ní; jíam; dye.
色 sek; color.
跟 kun; the heel.
竟 * io; ío; but.

1 chim âng: chíen âng.
2 it lâm: jī lâm: sa<sup>n</sup> lâm.
3 tûn âng, khí pêh.
4 âng sū: pêh sū.
5 âng mô nâng.
6 lêk lêk. âng thâu cûn.
7 pàng âng. kun sûi.
8 ŏi mêng pêh a bŏi?
9 lú ài<sup>n</sup> tī cêk sek?
10 i kâi mīn âng âng.
11 ài<sup>n</sup> jíam cò lâm sek.
12 i kâi mīn che<sup>n</sup> che<sup>n</sup>.
13 i kâi nâng mêng pêh.
14 cò nî ŏi hìe<sup>n</sup> mêng pêh?
15 úa ài<sup>n</sup> ní n̂g sek, lú io ní cò chiah sek. chiah kha.
16 cí cêk ciah cío kâi sek sī cù se<sup>n</sup> kâi a sī nâng ní kâi? jît mê cò.
17 cí kâi sī i kâi pn̂g sek.
18 chūe thien che<sup>n</sup> sek kâi.
19 i mâk ciu o o.
20 úa sim sìe<sup>n</sup> sī úa kâi, io sī lú kâi. jît jîet.
21 i chông côi<sup>n</sup> cêng kun kùe úa.
22 i kun sûi úa lâi.
23 i kun sûi úa nŏ nî lío.

1 Dark red: light red.
2 Navy blue: dark blue: pale blue.
3 Red lips and white teeth.
4 Happy affair: sad affair.
5 Red haired people; foreigners.
6 Pea green. A junk.
7 Have dysentery. Tag after.
8 Do you comprehend?
9 Which colour do you want?
10 His face was very red.
11 Will dye it blue.
12 He is very pale.
13 He is intelligent.
14 How can he be so well informed?
15 I wanted it coloured yellow, but you have dyed it brown. Natural footed.
16 Is the colour of this bird natural or is it artificial? Worked day and night.
17 This is its natural colour.
18 Seek an azure one.
19 His eyes are black.
20 I thought it was mine, but it is yours. The sun is hot.
21 He formerly attended upon me.
22 He followed me here.
23 He has served me two years.

# LESSON XXXVII.

| | | | |
|---|---|---|---|
| 風 | huang; wind. | 轟 | * tâng; roar; crash. |
| 風 | hong; fame; usage. | 澆 | * ak; èng; sprinkle. |
| 雨 | hŏ; rain. | 吹 | chue; to blow as wind. |
| 雷 | lûi; thunder. | 飄 | * thâu; to blow; swirl. |
| 電 | tĭen; lightning. | 暫 | cĭam; briefly. |
| 颶 | * thai; cyclone. | 罕 | hán; seldom. |

| | |
|---|---|
| 1 huang cúi. tōa huang. | 1 Geomancy. A gale. |
| 2 huang thai. hong sia$^{n}$. | 2 Typhoon. Rumour. |
| 3 mâi khut huang chue tĭeh. | 3 Do not let the wind blow on it. |
| 4 mâi i phâk jĭt. | 4 Do not let the sun shine on it. |
| 5 lûi tâng, huang thâu, âi$^{n}$ lôh hŏ líο. hŏ lâi. | 5 It thunders, and the wind whistles, it is going to rain. It rains. |
| 6 thi$^{n}$ o âm, âi$^{n}$ lôh hŏ. lú thói$^{n}$ âi$^{n}$ cò huang thai mē? | 6 The sky is dark, it is going to rain. Do you think there will be a typhoon? |
| 7 kì$^{n}$ tĭeh hŏ cĭu bô ēng. | 7 If it is exposed to the rain it will be of no use. |
| 8 tĭen kuang ău, lûi cĭu ai$^{n}$ tâng. | 8 After it has lightened, it will thunder. |
| 9 mâi i kì$^{n}$ huang. | 9 Do not expose it to wind. |
| 10 cí kúi sî hán lôh hŏ; cháu tĭeh cai ak cúi. | 10 It seldom rains of late; the grass must be watered. |
| 11 i hán tit lâi kì$^{n}$ úa. | 11 He seldom comes to see me. |
| 12 huang thai thâu lâi sĭm tōa; tĭeh ŭ lûi tâng, huang ŏi hiah. hán tit ŭ cí kĭa$^{n}$ sū. | 12 A great typhoon is blowing; should it thunder the wind would cease. This seldom happens. |
| 13 khut hŏ ak tĭeh. | 13 Wet by the rain. |
| 14 khut hái cúi ak tĭeh. | 14 Wet by sea water. |
| 15 cai khù èng cúi. | 15 Think to sprinkle it. |
| 16 úa put kùe cĭam lâi. | 16 I have only just come. |
| 17 lú cĭam cŭ kúi jĭt. | 17 You stay but a few days. |
| 18 cí kĭa$^{n}$ sū sĭ nâng hong sia$^{n}$ kâi. peh sè$^{n}$. | 18 This is a report. The people generally. |
| 19 huang thâu, hŏ lôh. | 19 The wind blows, and it rains. |

## LESSON XXXVIII.

| | | | |
|---|---|---|---|
| 雪 | seh; snow. | 叢 | câng; classifier of trees. |
| 名 | mîa; name. | 摘 | tiah; to pluck. |
| 花 | hue; flower. | 拔 | pôih; to pull out. |
| 樹 | chhīu; tree. | 留 | lîu; lâu; lay up; detain. |
| 葉 | hìeh; leaf. | 發 | hwt; to shoot forth. |
| 根 | kun; root. | 拔 | * máng; to pull up. |

| | | |
|---|---|---|
| 1 | i kâi mîa sia$^n$ hó. | His reputation is good. |
| 2 | thi$^n$ hwt o àm ài$^n$ lóh hŏ. | The sky darkens, it will rain. |
| 3 | i mák ciu hue hue. | His sight is dim. |
| 4 | cí kâi chháu hó máng tīo. | Pull up these weeds. |
| 5 | lu ciang lâi kâi mîa sí phang. | Your future name will be fragrant. |
| 6 | i sih mih mîa jī? | What is his name? |
| 7 | lí kìe cò sih mih mîa? | What is your name? |
| 8 | hue koi. chhīu hìeh. | A turkey. Leaf of a tree. |
| 9 | cí câng chhīu, chhīu ki, chhīu kun, chhīu phûe, lóng cóng mài lâu i. | Do not leave any of this tree, branches, roots, or bark. |
| 10 | chhīu thâu. | Largest part of the trunk. |
| 11 | i kâi mīn seh seh pêh. | Her face is of snowy whiteness. |
| 12 | cí kúi câng hue, máng tīo. | Pull up these plants. |
| 13 | cí câng hue hwt lâi hó thói$^n$; tiah kúi ki lâi. | These flowers have sprung up very prettily; pick a few. |
| 14 | cí câng hue khui lâi seh seh pêh. mîa sek. | This flower has blossomed snowy white. Reputation. |
| 15 | thi$^n$ ài$^n$ lóh seh. | It is going to snow. |
| 16 | kun mài pôih tīo, i hŵn ŏi hwt. | Do not pull out the root, and it will sprout again. |
| 17 | lâu pàng ĕ jīt cìah. | Leave it to eat another day. |
| 18 | lâu i mài khù. | Detain him from going. |
| 19 | cí cêk câng chhīu būe ŭ khui hue, soi$^n$ hwt hìeh. | Before this tree blossoms it puts out leaves. |
| 20 | lí kâi úa lîu sim cò. | Do it carefully for me. |
| 21 | mê nî ŏi hwt hue. | Next year it will bear flowers. |

## LESSON XXXIX.

| | | | |
|---|---|---|---|
| 田 | chân; a rice field. | 子 | cí; seed; offspring. |
| 園 | hn̂g; unwatered fields. | 種 | céng; seed. |
| 雲 | hûn; clouds. | 種 | cèng; to plant. |
| 工 | khang; kang; kong; work. | 徙 | súa; remove. |
| 夫 | hu; khùe; work. | 僱 | kò; hire. |
| 菓 | kúe; kúai$^{n}$; fruit. | 匠 | chīe$^{n}$; artizan. |

| | |
|---|---|
| 1 cɵ̀ chân khang khùe. | 1 Work in the fields. |
| 2 ceh chân hn̂g nâng. | 2 A tiller of the soil. |
| 3 cí kɵ̀ hn̂g, hó kò cɵ̀ khang khùe hùe lâi cèng kúe cí. chân hn̂g. | 3 Hire labourers to plant seed in this garden. Plantation. |
| 4 cí câng kúe cí hó kò nâng súa kùe hìe$^{n}$ pôi$^{n}$ hn̂g kɵ̀ cèng. | 4 Hire men to remove these seedlings and plant them in the further garden. |
| 5 ŭ hó céng cí, tîeh ŭ hó chân hn̂g lâi cèng cĭu hó. | 5 If having good seed, you have good ground to plant it in, it is well. |
| 6 kò kâi hue chīe$^{n}$ lâi cèng hue. | 6 Hire a gardener to come and plant flowers. |
| 7 hn̂g lăi kâi kúe cí hó cîah lío. | 7 The fruit of the garden is already fit to eat. |
| 8 ēng sim, kang hu cèng. | 8 Plant it nicely with care. |
| 9 che$^{n}$ kúai$^{n}$ hó tiah khṳ̀ bōi. | 9 Pick the fruit and sell it. |
| 10 kò cûn khṳ̀ bói kúi īe$^{n}$ hó che$^{n}$ kúai$^{n}$ lâi. | 10 Hire a boat and go and buy various fresh fruits. |
| 11 céng cí cèng lôh chân hn̂g; būe hó súa. | 11 Plant the seed in the field; do not transplant it yet. |
| 12 cí câng chīu súa pàng pât kɵ̀. ēng sim. | 12 Remove this tree to another place. Put your mind on it. |
| 13 ŏi ceh chân hn̂g, īa ŏi cɵ̀ khang khùe. | 13 He can work in the fields, and can work at a trade. |
| 14 cɵ̀ kang hu, kang hu. | 14 Do it in a workmanlike manner. |
| 15 thong thi$^{n}$ lóng cóng sĭ pêh hûn. pò chân. | 15 The sky is covered with white clouds. Plant rice. |

## LESSON XL.

| | | | |
|---|---|---|---|
| 燈 | teng; a lamp. | 燒 | sie; warmth; heat. |
| 籠 | lâng; a cage. | 灰 | hue; lime. |
| 爐 | lô; stove; grate. | 燒 | * hîa$^{n}$; put on fuel. |
| 柴 | châ; wood. | 灶 | càu; fireplace. |
| 炭 | thòa$^{n}$; coal. | 滾 | kún; to boil. |
| 點 | tíam; dot. | 住 | * nā; stay. |

| | |
|---|---|
| 1 húe thòa$^{n}$ lôh ke cêk cheh. | 1 Put on some more coal. |
| 2 khí húe pàng húe lô. | 2 Build a fire in the grate. |
| 3 khù chūe mûeh hîa$^{n}$. | 3 Going to gather fuel. |
| 4 ŭ kúi tíam ceng? | 4 What o'clock is it? |
| 5 ta$^{n}$ hó tíam teng. | 5 Light the lamps now. |
| 6 i ŏi cò hue kang. | 6 He can do mason's work. |
| 7 sĭ hue thô cò kâi. | 7 It is made of mortar. |
| 8 teng lâng bô tŏ. | 8 The lantern is not here. |
| 9 ŭ sì tíam gūa ceng líO. | 9 It is past four o'clock. |
| 10 hîa$^{n}$ kún çúi. | 10 Boil some water. |
| 11 bô châ hó hîa$^{n}$ càu. sie hue. | 11 There is no wood to heat the range. To burn lime. |
| 12 cío lâng bô khù. | 12 The bird-cage is gone. |
| 13 hiah kha, tíam kía$^{n}$. | 13 Stop a minute. |
| 14 tíam teng kâi sî hāu. | 14 Time for lighting the lamps. |
| 15 hiah ŭ cêk tíam ceng kú. | 15 Stopped an hour ago. |
| 16 khîeh cheh châ khù càu ĕ hîa$^{n}$ sie cúi. | 16 Take some wood to the kitchen and heat some water. |
| 17 cêk lō àm, tîeh tíam teng lâng. nā pàng cí kò. | 17 The road is dark, you must light the lantern. Stay here. |
| 18 tíam ki teng khù khí húe lô. | 18 Light a lamp and go and build a fire in the grate. |
| 19 mê hng kúi nâng ài$^{n}$ nā tŏ cí kò, tîeh khîeh ke cheh châ thòa$^{n}$ pàng càu ĕ ēng. | 19 To-night several people will stay here; get some more wood and coal and put in the kitchen to use. |
| 20 cúi kún a būe? | 20 Does the water boil yet? |
| 21 lâu i nā kò sie hue. | 21 Have him stay to burn lime. |

# LESSON XLI.

| | | | |
|---|---|---|---|
| 鐵 | thih; iron. | 重 | tăng; tŏng; weighty. |
| 銅 | tâng; copper. | 輕 | khin; light; trivial. |
| 鉛 | în; lead. | 磨 | bûa; to rub; grind. |
| 錫 | siah; pewter. | 磨 | bō; millstones. |
| 晶 | cia$^n$; crystal. | 滑 | kût; smooth. |
| 缶 | hûi; earthen. | 吹 | * pûn; blow, as with the mouth. |

| | | |
|---|---|---|
| 1 | pêh tâng: âng tâng: n̂g tâng. | White copper: red copper: brass. |
| 2 | pêh thih: cúi cia$^n$. | Tin: crystal. |
| 3 | ŭ jîeh tăng? | How heavy is it? |
| 4 | ŏi jîeh kût? | How smooth is it? |
| 5 | mài tà$^n$ khah tăng. | Do not speak too forcibly. |
| 6 | tăng sṳ: khin sṳ. | Important affair: trivial matter. |
| 7 | cò sṳ̄ khin khin, mài khah tăng. | Do things quietly, do not be too emphatic. |
| 8 | thih soh. în pit. | Iron chain. Lead pencil. |
| 9 | húe châ: châ pé. | Matches: wood in bundles. |
| 10 | tîeh thói$^n$ tŏng i. | You must esteem it. |
| 11 | lú thói$^n$ tâng thih tăng, a în siah tăng? | Do you consider brass and iron, or lead and pewter the heavier? |
| 12 | tîeh khin khin pûn, m̄ hó pûn khah tăng. | You must blow it lightly, do not blow it too strongly. |
| 13 | cí ki teng hó pûn tīo. | Blow out this lamp. |
| 14 | cí kò cúi cia$^n$ kio úa bûa kût kût. | Rub this piece of crystal very smooth for me. |
| 15 | tâng, thih, în, siah, hûi, cí ngŏ īe$^n$, tī īe$^n$ ēng ío cōi? tà$^n$ ūe khin khin. | Which is most used, copper, iron, lead, pewter or earthen? Speak gently. |
| 16 | cí kâi bō tăng kùe cí kò thih. | This millstone is heavier than this lump of iron. |
| 17 | cí kò lō kût. tîeh khin khin kîa$^n$. | This road is slippery. We must walk softly. |
| 18 | cí kò tâng khîeh khù bûa kng kng, bûa kàu hó thói$^n$ kì$^n$ nâng. cṳ̆ lâi húe. | Take this copper and rub it bright, so you can see your face in it. Matches. |

## LESSON XLII.

藥 îeh; medicine.
身 sin; the body.
病 pēⁿ; sick.
症 cèng; disease.
醫 ui; heal; cure.
痊 chŵn; convalescent.

致 tì; tend to.
缺 khih; khueh; deficient.
欠 * cûah; lack; diminish.
愈 jú; well; more; exceed.
烘 hang; cieh; dry by a fire.
凡 hŭam; hûam; all.

| | |
|---|---|
| 1 khùe khùe cáu khí. | 1 Get up quickly. |
| 2 i būe cáu khí. tì kàu. | 2 He is not yet up. So that. |
| 3 cá cá cáu khí. i ŭ pēⁿ. | 3 Get up early. He is sick. |
| 4 lṳ́ tī cêk jît khí sin? | 4 What day did you start? |
| 5 i tì ŭ sih mih pēⁿ cèng? | 5 What disease has he? |
| 6 lṳ́ tîeh cîah îeh. | 6 You must take medicine. |
| 7 ŏi ui a bŏi? huang lô. | 7 Can it be cured? Furnace. |
| 8 i hŵn khueh khìam cōi. | 8 He still lacks much. |
| 9 úa m̄ cai chéⁿ khí lâi. | 9 I did not think to wake up. |
| 10 cŏ pàng úa cí sin piⁿ. | 10 Sit here beside me. |
| 11 i pēⁿ ío hó, būe chŵn jú. | 11 He is better, but not well yet. |
| 12 cí īeⁿ pēⁿ oh ui. jú mé jú hó. | 12 This sort of disease is hard to cure. The quicker the better. |
| 13 chīu sin. khih chùi. | 13 Trunk of a tree. Hare-lip. |
| 14 i sĭm ŏi ui pēⁿ cèng; cêk cîah i kâi îeh, pēⁿ cĭu chŵn jú. | 14 He is very able in the cure of diseases; when you have once taken his medicine you are well. |
| 15 hŭam pēⁿ cèng tîeh cîah îeh huang ŏi chŵn jú. | 15 For all diseases medicine must be taken in order to get well. |
| 16 hŭam seⁿ cò nâng. | 16 All born men. |
| 17 hŭam nâng tì ŭ khih chùi kâi pēⁿ, tîeh cai soiⁿ ui. | 17 Any one who has a hare-lip must have it cured at first. |
| 18 i tŏ cieh sie. | 18 He is warming himself. |
| 19 lṳ́ cêk khueh îeh, cĭu tì kàu pēⁿ bŏi chŵn jú. | 19 You at first lacked medicine, thereupon the ailment became incurable. |
| 20 mài cûah îeh, pēⁿ cĭu khùe chŵn jú. | 20 If there be no lack of medicine, the ailment will quickly be cured. |
| 21 saⁿ tâm, khṳ̀ hang ta. | 21 Your jacket is wet; go and dry it. |

# LESSON XLIII.

茶 tê; tea.
米 bí; uncooked rice.
菜 chài; vegetables.
舖 phò; shop.
餅 pía$^{n}$; biscuit.
沖 chong; infuse.

配 phùe; accompany.
煎 cien; to stew dry.
已 ĭ$^{n}$; sign of the past.
經 keng; passed by or through.
𠖃 tau; retain; keep.
瓜 kue; the melon species.

| | |
|---|---|
| 1 ceh chân nâng. bí phò. | 1 A farmer. A rice shop. |
| 2 bô sĭm mih kang hu. | 2 Not nicely put together. |
| 3 pue jîp thi$^{n}$ hûn. | 3 Fly to the clouds. |
| 4 i būe lâi cò lá kâi khang khùe, i m̄ pat cò. | 4 He never made one till he came to work for you. |
| 5 i ài$^{n}$ cien cò lâ. | 5 He is going to make it into lard. |
| 6 put tit ĭ$^{n}$: put tit put ĭ$^{n}$. | 6 Inevitable: cannot do otherwise. |
| 7 cîah pía$^{n}$ phùe tê. | 7 Eat biscuit with tea. |
| 8 cí cêk ūi cu nîe kía$^{n}$ phùe khut nâng a būe ŭ? tau lâu. | 8 Is this young lady betrothed yet? Detain. |
| 9 ĭ$^{n}$ keng cò lío. | 9 The betrothal is accomplished. |
| 10 pêh chài thâu: âng chài thâu. | 10 Turnips: beets. |
| 11 ài$^{n}$ bói mûeh phùe. n̂g thâu kía$^{n}$. | 11 Will buy the accompaniments of rice. Carrots. |
| 12 lâ ĭ$^{n}$ keng cien hó lío. | 12 The lard is already tried out. |
| 13 tê bí: tê pûa$^{n}$: tê ceng. | 13 Tea leaves: saucer: tea-cup. |
| 14 khù tê phò, bói tê bí, lâi chong tê; ún ĭ$^{n}$ keng bói ŭ pía$^{n}$ hó phùe. | 14 Go to the tea shop, buy some tea, and steep it; we have bought the tea biscuits already. |
| 15 khù pía$^{n}$ phò thói$^{n}$ bōi ŭ kue cí a bô. | 15 Go to the grocery and see whether they sell fruit or not. |
| 16 ŭ hó bí, tîeh ŭ hó chài lâi phùe jú hó. | 16 Having good rice, it is better to have good vegetables with it. |
| 17 úa ĭ$^{n}$ keng ú i khù, mài tau lâu i. | 17 I have already let him go, do not detain him. |
| 18 úa tau lâu lá lâi cí chong tê cîah. | 18 I will detain you to come here and make some tea. |

# LESSON XLIV.

| | | | |
|---|---|---|---|
| 角 | kak; horn; corner. | 對 | tùi; pair, opposite, by. |
| 靂 | leh, lêh; a clap. | 肥 | pûi; fat, rich. |
| 敢 | ká$^{n}$; dare. | 瘦 | sán; sò; thin, lean. |
| 貯 | tíu; khǹg; chō; put away. | 殼 | khak; shell; hollow. |
| 孔 | khang; khóng; a hole. | 偕 | kāi, kŭa; jointly. |
| 空 | khong; khang; empty | 灰 | hu; embers, dust. |

| | |
|---|---|
| 1 i tùi sua$^{n}$ kha keng kùe. | 1 He came by the foot of the hill. |
| 2 i sie kāng cîah. | 2 They eat together. |
| 3 cí koi$^{n}$ chù sĭ i kŭa úa sie kāng kâi. ūa$^{n}$ sa$^{n}$. | 3 This house is his and mine together. Change clothes. |
| 4 lâ lêh khah pûi. | 4 There is too much fat in it. |
| 5 sa$^{n}$ kak: ngŏ kak. | 5 Triangular: pentangular. |
| 6 i kâi phī$^{n}$ khang sòi. | 6 His nostril is small. |
| 7 khǹg khah kú cĭu ài$^{n}$ chàu. | 7 If kept too long it will smell. |
| 8 i kŭa úa tâng cò. | 8 He acts conjointly with me. |
| 9 i kâi thâu khak thìa$^{n}$. | 9 His head aches. |
| 10 úa cò ká$^{n}$? khang khak. | 10 How dare I? Hollow. |
| 11 úa tīa$^{n}$ tīeh m̄ ká$^{n}$. | 11 I surely dare not. |
| 12 lú ká$^{n}$, sĭ, bô ài$^{n}$ kāng úa tà$^{n}$! thâu khak úa$^{n}$. | 12 You dare, dare you, not to tell me! A skull. |
| 13 lú khǹg tŏ tó lăi, mài kio nâng tà$^{n}$. | 13 Lay it up in your mind, and do not tell anybody. |
| 14 lú kio úa khǹg pàng kò. | 14 You keep it for me. |
| 15 khong cú: mêng cú. | 15 Confucius: Mencius. |
| 16 kŭa lú tùi mīn cŏ. | 16 Your vis-a-vis. |
| 17 gû kak sĭ khang khak kâi, a m̄ sĭ? sĭ. | 17 A cow's horn is hollow, is it not? It is. |
| 18 sie cò húe hu. | 18 Burn it to ashes. |
| 19 pûa$^{n}$ úa$^{n}$ mài leh leh kìe. | 19 Do not clatter the dishes. |
| 20 lú kâi mīn cò nî ŏi hìe$^{n}$ sán sò? tùi mīn. | 20 Why is your face so thin? Opposite. |
| 21 tùi cí kâi khang jîp khì. | 21 Go in through this hole. |
| 22 chō pàng khak tói. | 22 Put it away in the shell. |
| 23 úa kāi lú cò tùi thâu. | 23 I am your rival. |

## LESSON XLV.

| | | | |
|---|---|---|---|
| 耳 | hī$^{n}$; ear; handle. | 立 | līp; establish. |
| 尾 | búe; tail; end. | 嫁 | kè; marry a husband. |
| 聘 | phìa$^{n}$; phèng; betrothal. | 小 | síe; sío; small. |
| 古 | kó; anciently. | 並 | pēng; together with. |
| 娶 | chūa; take a wife. | 兼 | kiam; additionally. |
| 設 | siet; to institute; if. | 及 | kīp; concerning; till. |

| | |
|---|---|
| 1 kang cī$^{n}$: gūeh kang. | 1 Wages: work by the month. |
| 2 lūn kīp mih sṳ̄? | 2 What does it relate to? |
| 3 kīp sî. kīp chṳ́. | 3 Seasonable. Concerning this. |
| 4 cí kâi kio hṳ́ kâi put siang kīp. sío sṳ̄; síe khó sṳ̄. | 4 This and that do not relate to each other. Trivial matter. |
| 5 kīp kàu úa lâi kâi sî hāu. | 5 Until the time when I come. |
| 6 lṳ́ hó phèng i lâi. | 6 You engage her to come. |
| 7 kè chūa kâi sṳ̄ sī kó nâng siet līp kâi. cêk mê. | 7 Marrying and giving in marriage was established of old. The whole night. |
| 8 lṳ́ kâi cáu kía$^{n}$ kè tī kò? | 8 Where is your daughter married? |
| 9 lṳ́ kâi tau kía$^{n}$ chūa tī kò? | 9 From where did your son take his wife? |
| 10 siet sái lṳ́ ōi kiam i kâi sṳ̄, cīu khut lṳ́ cò. | 10 Supposing that you can take his business in addition, I will let you. |
| 11 sío jîn nâng siet līp to sī m̄ hó sṳ̄. pēng kiam. | 11 What ignorant people establish is much of it bad. Furthermore. |
| 12 pēng bô phìa$^{n}$ n̂gn cò lêng chūa bó? | 12 Without betrothal money how can one take a wife? |
| 13 līp sim àì$^{n}$ kè. | 13 Made up her mind to marry. |
| 14 chông thâu kàu búe. | 14 From beginning to end. |
| 15 cṳ̀ kó kīp kim pēng bô koh īe$^{n}$. sío jîn. | 15 From ancient times till now there is no difference. Rude. |
| 16 lṳ́ kâi hī$^{n}$ síe sim thia$^{n}$. | 16 Give careful hearing. |
| 17 chông kó kàu kim. | 17 From olden times till now. |
| 18 chūa jīp kè chut. | 18 Marry in and marry out. |
| 19 kiam kīp pât nâng. | 19 Refer it to so one else. |
| 20 cò sṳ̄ bô thâu bô búe. | 20 There is neither head nor tail to it. |
| 21 cò sṳ̄ ū thâu ū búe. | 21 Systematically done. |
| 22 cío búe: gû búe. | 22 Bird's tail: ox tail. |

# LESSON XLVI.

| | | | |
|---|---|---|---|
| 譬 | phì; illustrate. | 假 | ké; false. |
| 喻 | jŭ; compare; enforce. | 死 | sí; die; dead. |
| 成 | sêng; cîa$^n$; consummation. | 活 | ûah; alive; moving. |
| 理 | lí; regulate; doctrine. | 世 | sì; the world. |
| 雙 | sang; pair; couple. | 昨 | ca; cá; recently. |
| 眞 | cin; true. | 昔 | cá; formerly. |

| | |
|---|---|
| 1 tŏ kó cá ŭ. | 1 In ancient times there were. |
| 2 lṳ́ tà$^n$ ìu$^n$ sia$^n$, úa kâi hĭ$^n$ thia$^n$ m̄ kì$^n$. ké cuang. | 2 You speak low, I do not hear you. Disguise. |
| 3 úa chông kó kàu kim m̄ pat thia$^n$ kì$^n$. cêk sì. | 3 From old time till now, I never heard this. A generation. |
| 4 búe kía$^n$. mn̂g hĭ$^n$. | 4 Youngest child. Door-knocker. |
| 5 soi$^n$ kîa$^n$ phìa$^n$, ău chūa bó. | 5 First effect the betrothal, afterward bring home the wife. |
| 6 lâm chūa bó, nn̂g kè ang. | 6 Men take wives, women marry husbands. |
| 7 kó kim cêk ĭe$^n$. | 7 In the past and the present it is the same. |
| 8 ca mê ŭ nâng kûa$^n$ sí. | 8 Last night people froze to death. |
| 9 cang thói$^n$ kì$^n$ kâi lâi phì jŭ thói$^n$ m̄ kì$^n$ kâi. | 9 Make use of the visible to illustrate the invisible. |
| 10 cí kâi mûeh sĭ se$^n$ sêng ŭ, a sĭ nâng cò kâi? | 10 Is this thing natural or artificial? |
| 11 sĭ cin a sĭ ké? | 11 Is it true or false? |
| 12 lṳ́ chut sì tŏ tĭ kò? | 12 Where were you born? |
| 13 cêk sin khut i phah kàu ài$^n$ sí. | 13 He was beaten almost to death by them. |
| 14 lṳ́ ciang lâi m̄ cai cò nî sí. | 14 You do not know what sort of death you will die. |
| 15 sì sṳ sĭ cìe$^n$ se$^n$ kîa$^n$. | 15 That is the way of the world. |
| 16 lṳ́ hṳ̂n m̄ cai sí ûah! | 16 You are still unaware of the consequences! |
| 17 phì jŭ tit hó, cí kâi lí cĭu mêng pêh. | 17 If the parable be complete, the doctrine will be made clear. |
| 18 sêng sang: sêng tùi. | 18 Complete pair: perfect couple. |
| 19 sì cīe$^n$ kâi sṳ ài$^n$ cò, tîeh cò tit cîa$^n$. | 19 In transacting wordly business, you must carry it to a consummation. |
| 20 sí kâi: ûah kâi. | 20 Immovable one: movable ones. |

# LESSON XLVII.

保 pó; protect; benefit.
仗 cĭang; weapons; rely on.
意 ì; ideas; desires.

思 sù; ideas; thoughts.
塡 thîen; supply a deficiency.
佑 ĭu; aid; help.

俗 sôk; common.
教 kà; teach; instruction.
被 pĭ; pun; sign of the passive voice.
受 sĭu; receive.
拿 * lîah; catch, seize.
基 ki; foundation.

| | | |
|---|---|---|
| 1 | ŭ cêk kù sôk gú cìe$^{n}$ se$^{n}$ tà$^{n}$. lú cò nî sĭe$^{n}$? | There is a proverb which says so. What do you think? |
| 2 | lú hó sĭu i kà. | Receive his instructions. |
| 3 | būe ŭ khí chù tîeh soi$^{n}$ thîen tī kha. | Before you build a house you must lay a foundation. |
| 4 | pó chŵn tī hng. | Protect the whole country. |
| 5 | úa cí kĭa$^{n}$ sū chŵn chŵn cĭang lú kio úa lí. | I wholly rely on you to adjust this matter for me. |
| 6 | m̄ cai i kâi ì. | I do not know what his idea is. |
| 7 | tŏ tī kò khut i lîah tîeh? | Where was he when caught by him? |
| 8 | tà$^{n}$ tăi ì. pó ĭu. | Tell the sense of it. Protect. |
| 9 | ŭ sih mih ì sù? | What is the meaning of it? |
| 10 | bô ì sù. sí nâng cío. | Senseless. A vulture. |
| 11 | m̄ hâh i kâi ì. | Not according with his idea. |
| 12 | sì sôk nâng tà$^{n}$. | Common people say. |
| 13 | hú īe$^{n}$ khah sôk. | That kind is too common. |
| 14 | jû lú ì. ké ì. | As you wish. Pretend. |
| 15 | pàng húe kâi nâng khut i lîah tîeh a būe? | Has the incendiary been caught by him yet? |
| 16 | ki tī thîen hó a būe? | Are the foundations laid yet? |
| 17 | sih mih ì sù? pĭ úa thói$^{n}$ kì$^{n}$. | What does it mean? Seen by me. |
| 18 | pó ĭu i cêk ke nâng. | Protect the whole family. |
| 19 | lú kâi ì sù pun úa thói$^{n}$ chut. | Your intentions have been discovered by me. |
| 20 | úa pun i lîah tîeh. | I was caught by him. |
| 21 | pĭ úa kà sa$^{n}$ nî, hong sôk cĭu tńg cò hó lío. i cò nî tà$^{n}$? | If taught by me for three years, their habits would become good. What does he say? |
| 22 | kim jît ŭ phah cĭang, mē? | Was there fighting to-day? |

## LESSON XLVIII.

| | | | |
|---|---|---|---|
| 考 | kháu; deceased male ancestors. | 伯 | peh; husband's or father's elder brother. |
| 妣 | pí; deceased female ancestors. | 叔 | cek; husband's or father's younger brother. |
| 公 | kong; public; grandfather. | 始 | sí; origin; commencement. |
| 媽 | má; grandmother. | 終 | cong; termination. |
| 祖 | có; ancestor. | 太 | thài; great. |
| 哥 | ko̤; elder brother. | 閏 | jūn; intercalary. |

1 khui ki có. — 1 The founder of the family.

2 sí có kháu pí. — 2 Remote ancestors.

3 có pĕ; lăi kong. — 3 Paternal grandfather.

4 có bó̤; lăi má. — 4 Paternal grandmother.

5 gūa có pĕ; gūa kong. — 5 Maternal grandfather.

6 gūa có bó̤; gūa má. — 6 Maternal grandmother.

7 cêng có pĕ bó̤. — 7 Great grand parents.

8 lău có pĕ bó̤. — 8 Great grand parents.

9 kau có pé bó̤. — 9 Great great grandparents.

10 thài kau có pĕ bó̤. — 10 Great great great grandparents.

11 tōa peh, jī peh. tăi jîn. — 11 Eldest and next to the eldest uncle. Great man.

12 peh pĕ, cek pĕ. có ke. — 12 Father's elder and younger brother. Ancestral home.

13 i khṳ̀ lí kong sṳ̄. — 13 He is gone on public business.

14 tâng a kong má sĭ cek peh hiaⁿ tĭ. — 14 Those having the same grand parents are cousins.

15 i bô̤ sí, bô̤ cong. — 15 It has no beginning nor end.

16 saⁿ nî kâi jūn gûeh. — 16 There is an intercalary month once in three years.

17 cieh mn̄g cí ūi a peh nín thài kong tŏ̤ ke mē? kong tī. — 17 Inquire of this elderly man, if your great grandfather is at home. A common.

18 a ko̤, nán a cek khṳ̀ tī kò̤? — 18 Brother, where is uncle?

19 a peh, nán a má àiⁿ hàm a ko̤ khṳ̀ tàⁿ ūe. — 19 Uncle, grandmother wishes to speak with brother.

20 a cek kong. — 20 Grandfather's younger brother.

21 lṳ sí cong tîeh ṳ̆i i. cong kú. — 21 From first to last you must help him. Always.

# LESSON XLIX.

舅 kŭ; mother's or wife's brothers.
姑 ko; father's or husband's sisters.
姨 î; mother's or wife's sisters.
丈 tĭe$^n$; husband of a ko, or a î.
嫂 sɵ́; elder brother's wife.
姆 ḿ; wife of a peh.
嬸 sím; wife of a cek.
妗 kĭm; wife of a kŭ.
舅 * ta-kua$^n$; husband's father.
姑 * ta-ke; husband's mother.
岳父 * tĭe$^n$-nâng; wife's father.
岳母 * tĭe$^n$-ḿ; wife's mother.

1 nín a tĭe$^n$-nâng, tĭe$^n$-ḿ tɵ̆ tī kɵ̀ tīu? — 1 Where do your wife's father and mother live?

2 a sɵ́, nín ta-kua$^n$ tɵ̆ cɵ̀ sih mih sṳ̄? — 2 Sister-in-law, what is your husband's father doing?

3 nín ta-ke kim nî ŭ jîeh cōi hùe? — 3 How old is your husband's mother?

4 lău ḿ, ún a ko chía$^n$ lṳ́ kŭa a sím lâi cîah pn̄g. — 4 Auntie, my aunt invites you and the younger aunt to come and eat rice.

5 bɵ́ kŭ: chi kŭ. — 5 Mother's brother: wife's brother.

6 tōa bɵ́ kŭ. — 6 Mother's eldest brother.

7 sòi chi kŭ. — 7 Wife's younger brother.

8 tōa síe ḿ. — 8 Eldest sister-in-law.

9 tōa ko: sòi ko. lău ḿ. — 9 Father's elder sister: father's younger sister. Aunt.

10 tōa bɵ́ î. — 10 Mother's elder sister.

11 úa tɵ̆ có ke tah cûn, lâi kàu cí kɵ̀, chit kâi gûeh cúi lō. — 11 In coming by ship from my own country here, I was seven months on the way.

12 lṳ́ tī sî ài$^n$ khṳ̀ có ke? — 12 When are you going to your native land?

13 úa phah sǹg ke kúi nî ài$^n$ khṳ̀. — 13 I have calculated upon going in a few years more.

14 chía$^n$ nín kâi a sím hùe, lâi thia$^n$. — 14 Invite your women folks to come and hear.

15 úa kâi a sɵ́ lâi mn̄g hāu lṳ́. — 15 My sister-in-law has come to inquire after you.

16 khá m̄ sĭ lṳ́ kâi a ko? — 16 Is it not your aunt?

17 ko ciang. húe mê ko. — 17 Indulgent: easy with. Firefly.

## LESSON L.

媳婦 * sim-pŭ; son's wife.
兒 jî; child.
郎 n̂g; sister's or daughter's husband.
壻 sài; daughter's or younger sister's husband.
甥 seng; sister's children.
孫 sun; grandchildren.
思 sṳ; reflect, consider.
表 píe; exterior.
堂 thâng; household; venerable.
堂 tn̂g; hall; chapel; house.
親 chin; near relations.
族 côk; tribe; kindred.

| | | |
|---|---|---|
| 1 | lṳ́ hó̤ sṳ sĭe$^{n}$. | Reflect upon it. |
| 2 | sin n̂g; sin nîe. | Bridegroom; bride. |
| 3 | î píe cí mūe. | Female maternal cousins. |
| 4 | thâng hia$^{n}$ tĭ: cŭang hia$^{n}$ tĭ. | Cousins: second cousins. |
| 5 | î píe hia$^{n}$ tĭ. | Male maternal cousins. |
| 6 | chin hia$^{n}$ tĭ. côk hia$^{n}$ tĭ. | Own brothers. Male relatives. |
| 7 | ko píe. | Father's sister's child. |
| 8 | i bô̤ kía$^{n}$, bô̤ jî. | She is childless. |
| 9 | cáu sun; ca-bó sun. | Granddaughter or niece. |
| 10 | tau sun; ta-po sun. | Grandson or nephew. |
| 11 | chūa sim-pŭ. | Bring home a daughter-in-law. |
| 12 | i ài$^{n}$ cò̤ chin. | They are going to marry. |
| 13 | gūa seng. chin chùi. | Sister's child. Kiss. |
| 14 | i būe ŭ chut mn̂g. | She is not yet married. |
| 15 | jî sài. mūe sài. | Husband. Younger sister's husband. |
| 16 | lṳ́ kâi gūa seng cêng chūa sim-pŭ a būe? | Has your nephew yet brought home a daughter-in-law? |
| 17 | nín chin, thâng, cŭang, jîeh cōi nâng? | How many are there of you, brothers, cousins, and second cousins? |
| 18 | n̂g kŭ kâi kía$^{n}$ cĭu sĭ píe hia$^{n}$ tĭ; cáu kía$^{n}$ cĭu sĭ píe cí mūe. | The sons and daughters of the men connected with us by our female relatives are cousins. |
| 19 | tâng tn̂g kâi hia$^{n}$ tĭ cí mūe pí côk lăi kâi hia$^{n}$ tĭ cí mūe ío chin. | Brothers and sisters of the same household are more near than those of the same clan. |
| 20 | ŭ jîeh cōi kía$^{n}$ sun? | How many descendants? |
| 21 | cí kâi sĭ úa kâi kía$^{n}$ sài. | This is my daughter's husband. |
| 22 | lău nâng sṳ tîeh sun hùe. | The old man considers the young ones. |

## LESSON LI.

姪 tîet; brother's child.
岳 ngâk; wife's parents.
繼 kì; successive.
嫡 tek; the true wife.
庶 sù; many; nearly.
乳 jú; nǐ; ni; breast; milk.
妾 chiap; concubine.
養 íang; nourish; adopt
胞 pau; uterine.
胎 tho; the womb.
足 cok; full; the foot.
者 cía; particle arresting attention.

| | | |
|---|---|---|
| 1 | i sǐ sang se$^n$ kâi. | They are twins. |
| 2 | cí kâi kía$^n$ sǐ i íang kâi. | This child is adopted by her. |
| 3 | i sǐ tek bɵ́ se$^n$ kâi. | He is the true wife's child. |
| 4 | ngâk bɵ́. kì bɵ́. | Wife's mother. Step-mother. |
| 5 | sù bɵ́ kâi kía$^n$. | Inferior wife's child. |
| 6 | bɵ́ chin. jú bɵ́. | Own mother. Foster mother. |
| 7 | ni bɵ́. gû nǐ. | Wet nurse. Cow's milk. |
| 8 | se$^n$ cía, íang cía, pê$^n$ pê$^n$ âi sieh. | Those begotten, and those adopted are alike loved. |
| 9 | i kâi ngâk bɵ́ sǐ sù kâi, m̄ sǐ tek kâi. | His wife's mother is the inferior, not the superior wife. |
| 10 | pě chiap ŭ kía$^n$ cía cǐu sǐ sù bɵ́. | A father's concubine, having children, is a sù bɵ́. |
| 11 | khẃn thăi kì bɵ́ kāng chin bɵ́ cêk īe$^n$. | Treat a step-mother the same as an own mother. |
| 12 | lṳ́ kâi tîet, tîeh kò kâi ni bɵ́ lâi chī nǐ. | You must hire a wet nurse to nurse your nephew. |
| 13 | chiap, kìe cɵ̀ jī nang, sa$^n$ nâng, chiah kha. | Concubines are called second, or third, or large footed persons. |
| 14 | íang kía$^n$ thăi lău. | Rear a child for one's old age. |
| 15 | thâu the se$^n$ kâi kía$^n$. | The first begotten son. |
| 16 | pau hia$^n$ tǐ phì jŭ cɵ̀ chíu cok. | Own brothers are as the hand and the foot. |
| 17 | kàu cok. câp cok. | Enough. The full measure. |
| 18 | ŭ pē$^n$ cía, tîeh cai ui sin hūn. cîah ni. | The sick must heal their bodies. To nurse. |
| 19 | tâng pau cí mūe. | Sisters, having the same mother. |
| 20 | i kì i a pě kâi sṳ̄. côi$^n$ nâng; ǎu bó. | He succeeds to his father's business. His first, and second wife. |

## LESSON LII.

| | | | |
|---|---|---|---|
| 聖 | sìa$^{n}$; holy, pure. | 尖 | ciam; pointed. |
| 鹹 | kîam; salted. | 慘 | chám; distressing. |
| 淡 | cía$^{n}$; fresh, not salt. | 悽 | chi; suffering. |
| 稚 | cí$^{n}$; fresh, tender. | 涼 | lîang; cool. |
| 酥 | so; crisp, flaky. | 乘 | * lā; take advantage of. |
| 圓 | î$^{n}$; round. | 脂 | * nî; juice, gum. |

| | | |
|---|---|---|
| 1 | cai cok. soi$^{n}$ cai nâng. | Contented. A seer. |
| 2 | gû nĭ îu. gû nĭ pía$^{n}$. | Butter. Cheese. |
| 3 | cí kâi a nô$^{n}$ kêh ni a būe? chi chám. | Is this child weaned yet? Excruciating. |
| 4 | hâh sìa$^{n}$ cu só tà$^{n}$. | As the holy book says. |
| 5 | huang chue kùe hâi mīn cĭu ŏi lîang. | The wind having blown over the sea is cool. |
| 6 | tâng kâi a pĕ, tâng kâi a bó. | The same father and the same mother. |
| 7 | huang chue lâi kàu lîang. | The wind blows cool. |
| 8 | kong chin. kîam chhài. | A mediator. Salt vegetable. |
| 9 | chīu nî. | The gum of a tree. |
| 10 | kîam kâi hó kùe cía$^{n}$ kâi. | The salt is better than the fresh. |
| 11 | cúi cía$^{n}$, hó pûah lâi cîah; īa sĭ kîam cĭu m̄ ài$^{n}$. | If the water is fresh, draw some to drink; if salt I don't want it. |
| 12 | úa thói$^{n}$ lú cí$^{n}$ cí$^{n}$. | To me you look youthful. |
| 13 | cŏ pàng mûg kha lā lîang. | Sat by the door enjoying the coolness. |
| 14 | cí$^{n}$ kâi nî ío ke. | This is more juicy. |
| 15 | àn lîap ka$^{n}$ hìe$^{n}$ î$^{n}$. | As round as an orange. |
| 16 | thâu ciam, sin î$^{n}$. | Pointed head and round body. |
| 17 | khó sieh i chi chám. | Pity his distress. |
| 18 | i chi chám căi; lú tîeh thói$^{n}$ kù i. | He suffers greatly; you must take care of him. |
| 19 | lêh îam khah cíe; m̄ kàu kîam. | Too little salt was put in; it is not salt enough. |
| 20 | khùa bói kúi kà î$^{n}$ kâi so pía$^{n}$. îeh î$^{n}$. | Go and buy a few round crisp-cakes. Pills. |
| 21 | cí kâi a nîe kía$^{n}$, kha ciam, chíu ìu$^{n}$. | This little lady has pointed feet and small hands. |

# LESSON LIII.

| | | | |
|---|---|---|---|
| 利 | * lāi; sharp. | 彎 | wn; bending, curved. |
| 鈍 | tun; dull, blunt. | 曲 | khek; crooked. |
| 朋 | * jūn; tough. | 惡 | ak; wicked, evil. |
| 脆 | * chə̀; tender. | 善 | sĭen; righteous. |
| 黏 | lîam; liam; sticky. | 足 | * lă; enough. |
| 直 | tît; straight. | 連 | lîen; connect; even. |

1 sim tîeh tît, m̄ hó wn khek. — 1 The mind must be upright, not tortuous.

2 i thâu mô khek khek. — 2 Her hair is curly.

3 sìo bâk tît a būe? — 3 Is the account balanced yet?

4 i lāi kùe te. — 4 It is sharper than a knife.

5 te tun, hó khîeh khù bûa lāi. — 5 The knife is dull, take it and go and sharpen it.

6 nêk khah jūn, te khah tun. — 6 The meat is too tough, the knife too dull.

7 cí cêk kə̀ gû nêk chə̀ chə̀, hó cîah. — 7 This piece of beef is very tender and good to eat.

8 cí tîo lō wn wn khek khek. — 8 This road is very crooked.

9 sĭen kâi nâng sim tît, ak kâi nâng sim wn. — 9 The righteous have an upright mind, the wicked a perverted one.

10 cêk lîen chit wn, poih khek, huang kàu hú kə̀. — 10 A series of seven bends and eight crooks in arriving there.

11 cî$^{n}$ n̂gn ēng kàu lú lă. — 11 Use as much money as you need.

12 chíu lîam lîam, hó khù sói. — 12 Your hands are sticky, wash them.

13 wn lâi wn khù. — 13 To curve back and forth.

14 ak nâng sĭe$^{n}$ ak sù. — 14 The wicked devise wickedness.

15 sĭen cía ciang lâi ŏi cĭe$^{n}$ thien tn̂g. lă lío. — 15 The righteous will by-and-bye go to heaven. That is enough.

16 i kâi ūe tà$^{n}$ lâi lāi căi. — 16 He spoke very sharply.

17 pĕng m̄ sí cìe$^{n}$ se$^{n}$. — 17 It is not at all so.

18 lîen jît thâu huang. — 18 For successive days the wind has blown.

19 lîen kîp pât nâng. — 19 It involves other people.

20 lú kía$^{n}$ jît chía$^{n}$ nâng kheh cə̀ kúi ciah sîah, sîah cêk ciah cə̀ jîeh cōi cî$^{n}$? liam tŏ hú búe. — 20 How many guests did you invite to day, and how much did each repast cost you? Paste it on at the end.

# LESSON LIV.

| | | | | |
|---|---|---|---|---|
| 吊 | tìo; hang, suspend. | 隨便 | * | jŭan; either; as you like. |
| 代 | tŏ; a generation. | 便宜 | * | phi$^n$; cheap. |
| 遠 | íen; hn̆g; far. | 便 | | pĭen; convenient. |
| 近 | kŭn; near. | 便 | * | pīn; ready. |
| 陋 | lŏ; ugly. | 貴 | | kùi; costly; noble. |
| 粗 | cho; coarse. | 苦 | | khó; bitter; difficult. |

| | |
|---|---|
| 1 kŭn lâi kâi hong sôk m̄ hó. | 1 Recent customs are bad. |
| 2 i se$^n$ lâi cho lŏ. cho pò. | 2 He is ugly. Coarse cloth. |
| 3 tìo khui tŏ hú kò. | 3 Hang it up there. |
| 4 mài khó i cò. | 4 Do not trouble him to do it. |
| 5 hn̆g kŭn cêk ie$^n$ phi$^n$ kùi. | 5 Far and near the price is the same. |
| 6 i hn̆g hn̆g kò lâi. | 6 It comes from a great distance. |
| 7 kîa$^n$ khah hn̆g cĭu ŏi phî kŭn. íen kŭn. | 7 If you walk too far you will be weary. Far and near. |
| 8 kŭn kò kùi, hn̆g kò cĭu phi$^n$. hûam jîn. | 8 Near by it is dear, far off it is cheap. Common people. |
| 9 hn̆g tō kâi có. | 9 Remote ancestors. |
| 10 hŭam se$^n$ tŏ sì kan. | 10 All born into the world. |
| 11 pīn a būe? būe ŭ pīn. | 11 Ready yet? Not yet ready. |
| 12 sûi pĭen ài$^n$ khù. | 12 Shall go when it is convenient. |
| 13 chông úa kâi pĭen. | 13 Suiting my convenience. |
| 14 cìe$^n$ se$^n$ m̄ pĭen. | 14 That is inconvenient. |
| 15 káu tíam, pĭen hó lâi. | 15 It will be convenient for you to come at nine o'clock. |
| 16 cí kâi pĭen sĭ. cho phûe. | 16 This is just it. Coarse skin. |
| 17 sûi pĭen hó; jŭan. | 17 Whichever you please. |
| 18 lú thói$^n$ sĭ phi$^n$ a sĭ kùi? | 18 Do you consider it cheap or dear? |
| 19 úa chin mâk thói$^n$ kì$^n$. | 19 I saw it with my own eyes. |
| 20 úa chin hĭ$^n$ thia$^n$ kì$^n$. | 20 I heard it with my own ears. |
| 21 khó thâu, mài khó búe. | 21 Endure hardness at the beginning and not have it at the end. |
| 22 lú hó kùi tŏng i. | 22 You should value it. |
| 23 hú kâi kùi tŏng kùe cí kâi. hn̆g hn̆g. | 23 That is more valuable than this. Very far. |

## LESSON LV.

酸 sng; sour.
甜 tîam; sweet.
硬 ngĕ; hard.
軟 nńg; soft.
辛 * hiam; pungent.
美 múi; ngía; handsome.

厚 kău; thick; strong.
薄 pôh; thin; weak.
嗇 siap; harsh; astringent.
偷 thau; pilfer; stealthily.
賊 chât; rob; thief.
涉 * ĕ; wade; ford.

| | | |
|---|---|---|
| 1 | mûeh kìa$^n$ î$^n$ keng bói pīn pīn lío. | The things have already been bought, and are ready. |
| 2 | cha tît hn̆g. | Vastly different. |
| 3 | pńg tī bói bô, tîeh khù pât kò bói. | If there are none to be bought here, go elsewhere and buy. |
| 4 | ŏi jîeh ngĕ? ŭ jîeh kău? se$^n$ ngĕ. | How hard is it? How thick is it? Surely. |
| 5 | sng ka$^n$ kía$^n$. khut nâng phah. | Limes. Beaten by some one. |
| 6 | bô lú jîp cí lăi. | Won't let you come in here. |
| 7 | só kùe khù kâi nî kìe cò cá nî. | Years that are past are called former years. |
| 8 | sng tîam căi, chŵn bŏi siap. | An acidulated sweet, not in the least acrid. |
| 9 | úa thói$^n$ kì$^n$ kâi chât ĕ kùe khoi thau khîeh mûeh. | I saw a thief wade across the river to steal things. |
| 10 | i kâi sè$^n$ ngĕ căi. | He is of obdurate disposition. |
| 11 | lú âi$^n$ bói kău kâi, a pôh kâi? | Do you wish to buy a thick one or a thin one? |
| 12 | tê chong kău kău, mài pôh. | Make the tea very strong. |
| 13 | cí ie$^n$ tê khah siap. | This sort of tea is too bitter. |
| 14 | mài lôh khah hiam. | Do not make it too peppery. |
| 15 | sĭ. sĭ mē? sĭ cìe$^n$ se$^n$. | It is so. Is it so? It is thus. |
| 16 | cí kâi se$^n$ lâi ngía kùe hú kâi. tê pôh. | This is more beautiful than that. The tea is weak. |
| 17 | i sĭ tŏi$^n$ it ngía. | It is very handsome. |
| 18 | m̄ hó cò chât. mó. | Do not be a thief. Do not. |
| 19 | i lâi thau thói$^n$. | He came to slyly see. |
| 20 | cí kâi sĭ i kâi múi ì. | This is his fine idea. |

## LESSON LVI.

- 獅 sai; lion.
- 熊 hîm; bear.
- 貓 ngio; cat.
- 驢 lṳ̂; mule.
- 騾 lɵ̂; ass.
- 鵝 gɵ̂; goose.

- 鷹 eng; eagle kind.
- 些 * cē; has the effect of er on an adjective.
- 些 se; little; somewhat.
- 須 su; ought; servicable.
- 會 hŭe; society; convene.
- 會 * ŏi; likely; will be; apt.

| | | |
|---|---|---|
| 1 | cĭu ŏi lɵ̂h hŏ. su ēng. | It will then rain. Needful. |
| 2 | mé cē. mān cē. cíe cē. | Quicker. Slower. Fewer. |
| 3 | ke cē. cá cē. ùa<sup>n</sup> cē. | More. Earlier. Later. |
| 4 | chim cē. chíen cē. tōa cē. | Deeper. Shallower. Larger. |
| 5 | hn̆g se su. tōa se su. | A little further. Rather larger. |
| 6 | chut se su. lɵ̂h se su. | Go out a little. Lower somewhat. |
| 7 | ŏi sng a bŏi? ŏi tîam. | Is it sour? It is sweet. |
| 8 | sai sĭ hán thói<sup>n</sup> kì<sup>n</sup> kâi. | A lion is seldom seen. |
| 9 | cí ciah hîm sĭ nâng hîm m̄ sĭ káu hîm. | This bear is the brown bear, not the white-necked bear. |
| 10 | ngio ài<sup>n</sup> khṳ̀ thau cîah gɵ̂ nêk. | The cat is going to slyly eat the goose meat. |
| 11 | lṳ̂ ŏi kîa<sup>n</sup> hn̆g lō a sĭ lɵ̂ ŏi kîa<sup>n</sup> hn̆g lō? | Which can travel farthest the mule or the ass? |
| 12 | eng hiah tɵ̆ chīu kɵ̀. | The eagle perches in trees. |
| 13 | sìa<sup>n</sup> hŭe. kong hŭe. | The church. Public assembly. |
| 14 | hŭe tn̂g. hŭe kùe mīn. | A church. Have met before. |
| 15 | m̄-cai ŏi cê<sup>n</sup> a bŏi. | Do not know whether it will clear. |
| 16 | cí ciah gɵ̂ khah sán. | This goose is too lean. |
| 17 | chông úa kâi ì sṳ̀. | According to my ideas. |
| 18 | cìe<sup>n</sup> se<sup>n</sup> huang sêng cɵ̀ nâng. | Thus you may become somebody. |
| 19 | cúi tōa. thi<sup>n</sup> o àm. | The tide is rising. The sky is dark. |
| 20 | nâng hɵ́. tɵ̆ cí. | The man is good. It is here. |
| 21 | tɵ̆ lṳ́ mīn côi<sup>n</sup>. | It is before your face. |
| 22 | úa thói<sup>n</sup> cɵ̀ hɵ́. | I regard it as being good. |
| 23 | i ài<sup>n</sup> cɵ̀ tōa. | He wishes to be greatest. |
| 24 | cɵ̀ sì sôk nâng tà<sup>n</sup>. | According to the saying of the common people. |

## LESSON LVII.

| | | | |
|---|---|---|---|
| 麟 | lîn; a fabulous animal. | 虎 | hóⁿ; tiger. |
| 龍 | lêng; a dragon. | 龜 | ku; tortoise. |
| 蛇 | cûa; serpent. | 象 | chïeⁿ; elephant. |
| 魚 | hû; fish. | 虫 | thâng; worm; insect. |
| 蠍 | hiet; scorpion. | 蝦 | hê; prawns. |
| 蟻 | hïa; ant. | 蟹 | hŏi; crabs. |

| | |
|---|---|
| 1 lêng hê. hái gô. cêk búe hû. | 1 Lobster. Pelican. One fish. |
| 2 lău hóⁿ. cháu thâng. | 2 A fierce tiger. Insects. |
| 3 pêh hóⁿ kă lú! | 3 The white tiger devour you! |
| 4 pêh hïa, o hïa, âng hïa. | 4 White ants, black ants, red ants. |
| 5 phì jŭ cò hû. | 5 Likened unto a fish. |
| 6 lú lâi cò úa kâi kíaⁿ. | 6 You come and be my child. |
| 7 lîah hû kâi nâng. | 7 A fisherman. |
| 8 sói saⁿ nâng. i seⁿ pēⁿ. | 8 Washerman. He is sick. |
| 9 lâi phah sí cêk tîo cûa. | 9 Come and kill a snake. |
| 10 ngio thâu cío. hóⁿ hŏi. | 10 Owl. Spotted crab. |
| 11 mûeh kïaⁿ bōi m̄ khù. | 11 Could not sell the things. |
| 12 bōi m̄ kàu pn̂g cîⁿ. | 12 Did not sell for first cost. |
| 13 taⁿ àiⁿ bōi. bōi tīo lío. | 13 Now wish to sell. Already sold. |
| 14 sì kha cûa. ŭ pēⁿ cía. | 14 Lizard. The sick. |
| 15 lîn hán hán khut nâng thóiⁿ kìⁿ. káu bó cûa. | 15 The lîn is very seldom seen by people. Lizard. |
| 16 lîn m̄ cîah ûah mûeh. | 16 The lîn does not eat living things. |
| 17 lêng kâi mûeh ŏi tōa, ŏi sòi, ŏi tn̂g, ŏi tó; bô tïaⁿ tîeh kâi. | 17 Dragons are large and small, long and short; they are not of any certain size. |
| 18 mài khut hiet kíaⁿ kă tîeh. | 18 Do not get bitten by a scorpion. |
| 19 hê hó cîah, a sī hŏi hó cîah? | 19 Which is the best for eating, prawns or crabs? |
| 20 ku khak. lêng cûn. | 20 Tortoise shell. Dragon boat. |
| 21 cûa kâi phûe hó cò îeh, mē? | 21 Is the skin of a snake good for medicine? |
| 22 chïeⁿ kâi nêk hó cîah. | 22 The elephant's flesh is edible. |
| 23 cûa bô kha ŏi kïaⁿ. | 23 Serpents walk without legs. |

## LESSON LVIII.

豹 pà; leopard.
鱟 hāu; the king crab.
蚶 ham; scallop.
蠔 ê; oyster.
鼈 pih; turtle.
犀 sai; rhinoceros.

甲 kah; naily substance.
鱗 lân; scales.
爪 jíu; claws.
牙 gê; tusks.
蹄 tôi; hoof.
鰓 chi; gills.

1 ah tôi kha. hāu peh cheh.
2 hāu peh cheh ài$^{n}$ cè sí kâi, a sĭ ài$^{n}$ cè ûah kâi?
3 hó$^{n}$ se$^{n}$ pà jî.
4 cí kâi hāu jîeh tăng?
5 cí cheh ham ŭ jîeh cōi lîap?
6 ê khah sòi lîap.
7 pih kah ŏi jîeh kùi; ài$^{n}$ bói cè îeh.
8 bói cheh sai gû phûe khù cîah cĭu hó.
9 hê kâi lân cōi, a lêng kâi lân cōi?
10 chĭe$^{n}$ gê hó cè tū.
11 ngŏ jío lêng.
12 lîn kâi búe chin chĭe$^{n}$ gû búe; tôi chin chĭe$^{n}$ bé tôi.
13 nâng tà$^{n}$ hó$^{n}$ khui jío cĭu m̄ khui gê, khui gê cĭu m̄ khui jío; sĭ mē?
14 pât ĭe$^{n}$ hê cĭn sĭ nŏ kâi chi; ŭ cêk ĭe$^{n}$ hê, cĭu sĭ sì kâi chi.
15 chíu kah, kha kah.

1 Web-footed. Venitians.
2 Do you want the slats of the shutters fixed or movable?
3 The tiger gives birth to the leopard.
4 How heavy is this king-crab?
5 How many scallops are there in this lot?
6 The oysters are too small.
7 How dear is turtle shell? I want to buy some for medicine.
8 You better buy some rhinoceros skin and take it.
9 Which has the most scales, the fish or the dragon?
10 Elephant tusks are good for making chop-sticks.
11 The five clawed dragon.
12 The tail of the lîn is like that of an ox; its hoofs are like a horse's.
13 People say that if a tiger has claws it has no tusks; if it has tusks it has no claws; is it so?
14 Other species of fish have but two gills; there is one species having four gills.
15 Finger-nails, toe-nails.

# LESSON LIX.

| | | | |
|---|---|---|---|
| 都 | to; altogether; general; probably; fine. | 惟 | jûi; but; precisely; consist in; and. |
| 搔 | * pê; scratch. | 爬 | pê; peh; clamber; climb. |
| 匍 | * pê; creep. | 虱 | sat; lice. |
| 癢 | * cĭe$^n$; to itch. | 蚊 | bun; gnats. |
| 拋 | * pha; fling out. | 虻 | máng; mosquito. |
| 梳 | siu; comb; brush. | 網 | măng; net; sew coarsely. |

| | |
|---|---|
| 1 to sĭ cĭe$^n$ se$^n$. | 1 It is probably so. |
| 2 cĭe$^n$ **kò m̄** pê, **khù** pê thìa$^n$ **kò**. | 2 Not scratching where it itches but where it aches. |
| 3 chit **cŏ**, poih pê, káu hwt gê. | 3 Sit up at seven months, creep at eight, teeth at nine. |
| 4 kâi a nô$^n$ kía$^n$ **tŏ** pê. | 4 A child creeps. |
| 5 i peh cĭe$^n$ chù téng. | 5 He climbs up on the roof. |
| 6 **lú** kâi mīn khut máng kă kàu cêk tíam cêk tíam âng âng. | 6 Your face has been bitten by mosquitoes till it is all little red dots. |
| 7 bun kă nâng pí máng kă, jú cĭe$^n$, jú thìa$^n$. | 7 The bites of gnats itch and ache more than mosquito bites. |
| 8 cá cē khí lâi, siu thâu. | 8 Rise earlier and comb your hair. |
| 9 châ siu; în siu; kak siu. | 9 Wooden comb; lead comb; horn comb. |
| 10 pha cêk ē măng, pha tīeh câp búe **hû**. | 10 At one cast of the net caught ten fish. |
| 11 thâu sat, sin sat. | 11 Head lice, body lice. |
| 12 tu, gû, ngio, káu, lóng cóng ŏi se$^n$ sat. | 12 Swine, oxen, cats and dogs, all have lice. |
| 13 nín a tia khīeh măng **khù** khoi kî$^n$ pha **hû**. | 13 Your father took the net to the river side to fish. |
| 14 i pê kùe sua$^n$. | 14 He clambered over the mountain. |
| 15 jûi sĭ **lú** tà$^n$, úa huang siang sìn. | 15 Since you say so, I thereupon believe it. |
| 16 lu **m̄ hó** siang sìn i. | 16 You should not trust him. |
| 17 úa siang sìn **lú** cĭu sĭ. | 17 I believe you then. |
| 18 úa to **m̄**, jûi sĭ **lú** âi$^n$. | 18 I did not altogether wish to, but you wanted to. |

## LESSON LX.

| | | | |
|---|---|---|---|
| 站 | khĭa; stand up; stage. | 枯 | ko; withered; sere. |
| 寓 | ngŏ; khĭa; sojourn; lodge. | 眩 | hîn; dizzy. |
| 豎 | * khĭa; perpendicular. | 有 | tōi$^{n}$; solid; durable. |
| 橫 | hûe$^{n}$; horizontal. | 冇 | phà$^{n}$; porous. |
| 斜 | sîa; aslant; sloping. | 穩 | ún; stable; safe. |
| 崎 | khi; kĭa; steep; rough. | 啞 | é; dumb. |

| | | |
|---|---|---|
| 1 | i cêk pôi$^{n}$ chíu ko ta. | One of his arms is withered. |
| 2 | i kâi thâu khak hîn. | Her head is dizzy. |
| 3 | ōi hîn cûn a bōi? | Are you sea-sick? |
| 4 | i kâi sin hūn tōi$^{n}$, úa kâi sin hūn phà$^{n}$. | His flesh is solid, mine is flabby. |
| 5 | khĭa tŏ sang pôi$^{n}$. | Stand on the two sides. |
| 6 | khĭa khí lâi. i cè nî tà$^{n}$? | Stand up. What does he say? |
| 7 | lú khĭa khí tŏ tī kò? | Where do you live? |
| 8 | lú ngŏ tŏ tī kò? | Where do you live? |
| 9 | úa khĭa tŏ îeh phò lăi. | I live at a drug shop. |
| 10 | sim sū nâng nâng ŭ, tōi$^{n}$ phà$^{n}$ m̄ sie tâng. | All men have motives, but not of like strength. |
| 11 | hûe$^{n}$ tît pê$^{n}$ pê$^{n}$ tōa. | The same breadth and length. |
| 12 | cí kâi nâng é, bōi tà$^{n}$ ūe. | This man is dumb. |
| 13 | thâu hîn, mâk àm. | Dizzy and blind. |
| 14 | cí tîo lō khah kĭa. | This road is too steep. |
| 15 | hue hîeh ko ta khù; cai ak cúi. | The leaves of the plants are dried up; think to water them. |
| 16 | ài$^{n}$ pàng khĭa, a ài$^{n}$ pàng tît? | Do you want to place it upright or horizontally? |
| 17 | jît sîa heh hn̆g lío. | The sun is almost down. |
| 18 | cìe$^{n}$ se$^{n}$ pàng m̄ ún, tîeh lêng pàng ún cē. | It is not firmly placed: you must render it steadier. |
| 19 | tōi$^{n}$ thòa$^{n}$ pí phà$^{n}$ thòa$^{n}$ ío ke cî$^{n}$. | Solid coal compared with porous coal, is the more costly. |
| 20 | é kâi nâng kì$^{n}$ tîeh nâng cĭu ài$^{n}$ tà$^{n}$ ūe. | A dumb man, seeing other people, wishes to speak. |
| 21 | hàm i khĭa khui cē. | Tell him to stand off a little. |

# LESSON LXI.

| | | | |
|---|---|---|---|
| 迫 | pek; urgent. | 滿 | múa; complete; entire. |
| 切 | chiet; pressing. | 滿 | * tĭ$^{n}$; full; replete. |
| 要 | ìo; important. | 緊 | kín; pressing. |
| 亂 | * jṳ̂; tangled; disorderly. | 錯 | chò; mistaken. |
| 整 | cía$^{n}$; amend; adjust. | 滴 | tih; drop; drip. |
| 𪇒 | * jû; neat; orderly. | 堤 | toi; a dike. |

| | |
|---|---|
| 1 i kâi thâu mê jṳ̂ jṳ̂. | 1 His hair is unkempt. |
| 2 bô cêk tíam cha chò. | 2 Not in the least wrong. |
| 3 i múa tī kò khṳ̀. | 3 He went everywhere. |
| 4 chiet ìo; m̄ hó cò chò. | 4 It is important; do not make a mistake. |
| 5 i ŭ chò jîp, to bô chò chut. | 5 He makes mistakes on the credit, but not on the debit side. |
| 6 mâk chiet ìo mài chò thói$^{n}$, sim chiet ìo mài chò sĭe$^{n}$. | 6 Important that the eyes make no error in seeing, and the mind no error in thinking. |
| 7 múa lō koh ĭe$^{n}$ phang. | 7 The entire way a variety of odors. |
| 8 sṳ̄ kín kín. | 8 The business is pressing. |
| 9 sṳ̄ ŏi kín a bŏi? | 9 Is the matter urgent? |
| 10 sî jît khah kín pek. | 10 The time is too pressing. |
| 11 lṳ́ pek kàu úa cìe$^{n}$ kín cò nî? kín pek. | 11 Why do you urge me so pressingly? Urgent. |
| 12 ŭ sih mih chiet ìo a bô? | 12 Is there anything specially important? |
| 13 cí kĭa$^{n}$ mûeh khîeh khṳ̀ cía$^{n}$ lí hó. | 13 Take this and go and get it repaired. |
| 14 chù lăi kâi mûeh pái kàu jû jû. | 14 Arrange the household stuff in fine order. |
| 15 chō mài khah tĭ$^{n}$. | 15 Do not fill it too full. |
| 16 lôh kàu i tĭ$^{n}$ tĭ$^{n}$. | 16 Put in till it is quite full. |
| 17 hŏ cúi tih múa sin. | 17 The rain dripped all over me. |
| 18 cêk tíam cêk tih bô cha chò. | 18 Not the least bit in error. |
| 19 toi téng, toi lăi, toi gūa, to hó kîa$^{n}$. | 19 The top, the inside and the outside of the dike may be traversed. |
| 20 cúi cêk tih cêk tih, tih lôh lâi. | 20 The water drops, drop by drop. |

## LESSON LXII.

| | |
|---|---|
| 歹 táⁱi; pháⁱi; vicious. | 荒 * hng; famine. |
| 伙 húe; goods; comrade. | 拗 áu; obstinate. |
| 極 kêk; extreme. | 蠻 mân; fierce; savage. |
| 必 pit; surely. | 壯 càng; robust. |
| 餓 gō̤; starve. | 强 kîang; strong. |
| 飢 ki; dearth; scarcity. | 番 hwn; foreign. |

| | | |
|---|---|---|
| 1 | lṳ́ tîeh cai hó̤ tái. | You must know good and evil. |
| 2 | m̄ cai hó̤ phái. | Not discern good and evil. |
| 3 | a tie$^{n}$ bŏi áu mân, a ko ia bô̤ tái ì, ang cía nō̤ nâng sim siang ài. | Uncle is not perverse, and aunt is not vicious, so the husband and wife are fond of each other. |
| 4 | ke húe cía$^{n}$ lí hó̤, khang khùe cò̤ chut lâi huang hó̤. | Have the tools in good order and the work done with them will then be good. |
| 5 | hṳ́ kâi ti hng tōa ki hng, bí kùi căi. | There is a great famine in that region and rice is very dear. |
| 6 | cí kĭa$^{n}$ mûeh kêk hó̤ cîah. | This is exceedingly delicious. |
| 7 | i kâi nâng kêk hó̤, pit bô̤ cò̤ áu mân kâi sṳ̄. | He is extremely good, and certainly does no malicious thing. |
| 8 | i khṳ̀ hwn pôi$^{n}$ kàu ta$^{n}$ ŭ sa$^{n}$ câp nî kú. | He went to foreign parts thirty years ago. |
| 9 | cí kâi nâng kêk khîang càng. | This man is exceedingly strong. |
| 10 | cí kĭa$^{n}$ sṳ̄ kêk áu mân. | This is a most atrocious business. |
| 11 | kîa$^{n}$ kàu cí kò̤ tó lăi ki gō̤. | In walking here I became famished. |
| 12 | cṳ̆ sí. gō̤ sí. húe thâu. | Suicide. Starve to death. A cook. |
| 13 | hàm húe thâu lâi cía$^{n}$ lí cîah. | Call the cook to come and get dinner. |
| 14 | lṳ́ cí kĭa$^{n}$ sṳ̄ áu lí căi; lṳ́ mài khah mân. | Your are very perverse about this; do not be too vehement. |
| 15 | i kâi nâng khîang khîang càng càng cò̤ ŏi sí? | When he is so robust, how is it that he will die? |
| 16 | hwn nâng. pit pit ài$^{n}$. | Foreigners. Surely will. |
| 17 | hwn pôi$^{n}$ lâi kâi. | An importation. |

# LESSON LXIII.

取 chú; assume; get.
儉 khĭam; frugal.
澀 * siap; stingy.
漸 cĭam; gradual.
利 lĭ; shrewd; profitable.
害 hāi; injurious.

防 hûang; screen; ward off.
險 hĭam; danger; abyss.
危 ngûi; huang; imminent.
懶 lán; languid.
惰 tŏa$^{n}$; lazy.
憨 ngà; stupid; foolish.

| | |
|---|---|
| 1 ngà sìe$^{n}$. tà$^{n}$ ngà ūe. | 1 Foolishly thought. Stupid speech. |
| 2 cí kâi nâng thói$^{n}$ tīeh gūa mīn ngà, i kâi sim lăi sīm sī lĭ hāi. | 2 This person's appearance would be considered foolish, but his mind is very subtle. |
| 3 híam híam khut lú tà$^{n}$ kàu úa ài$^{n}$. | 3 Almost persuaded by you to wish for it myself. |
| 4 i lán tŏa$^{n}$ căi. | 4 He is very indolent. |
| 5 cĭam cĭam bô khù. | 5 Gradually disappeared. |
| 6 i kâi nâng cò sū khah khĭam siap. | 6 He transacts business too economically. |
| 7 ca mê kâi huang cĭam cĭam thàu, cĭam cĭam lĭ hāi. | 7 The wind last night gradually became more violent and destructive. |
| 8 lú hó cai hûang i. | 8 You better beware of him. |
| 9 i pē$^{n}$ huang híam căi; tīeh cai hûang ău sū. | 9 He is dangerously ill; you must guard against consequences. |
| 10 lú tŏ i cûn lí sū, sī cìah i, a sī cìah ka kī. | 10 In managing affairs on his boat, does he furnish your food, or do you yourself? |
| 11 úa cìah ka kī. | 11 I supply my own food. |
| 12 tek ke phah cúi, hû thâu thìa$^{n}$. | 12 When you beat the water with a bamboo, the fishes' heads ache. |
| 13 cí kâi nâng sīm hó chú. | 13 This person is very suitable. |
| 14 cí kīa$^{n}$ sū sīm khó chú. | 14 This thing is very appropriate. |
| 15 cí kâi sū cīu úa thói$^{n}$ kī$^{n}$ lâi, cêk bô khó chú. | 15 This affair, as I understand it, is wholly inappropriate. |
| 16 cí kâi sî hāu sī ngûi kâi sî hāu. huang híam sí. | 16 This season is a dangerous time. Very nearly died. |
| 17 lú só phah sn̄g sī ngà căi. | 17 Your conclusion is a foolish one. |

# LESSON LXIV.

奶 nái; madam; lady.
跛 * kúai; lame; limp.
愚 ngû; uninstructed.
泥 * lok; slush; mire.
耽 tam; obstruct; prevent.
誤 gō; thwart; hamper.

益 iah; benefit; use.
間 * làn; omit; space between.
嫌 hìam; reproach.
驕 kio; haughty; confident.
傲 ngău; arrogant.
添 thiam; thi$^n$; add; extra.

---

1 tōa nái, jī nái, sa$^n$ nái.
2 lú mài tam gō úa.
3 kúai kha kâi nâng cíe.
4 lú m̄ hó kio ngău.
5 bô sím mih lī iah.
6 lú mài hāi i.
7 phah kàu i kúai kha.
8 lú mài gō tīeh sū.
9 hāi kàu i kúai kha.
10 phah kàu i cêk sin thìa$^n$ cài.
kúai kha cía.
11 hìam i kio ngău.
12 ngû kâi nâng m̄ thong lí.
13 hō lôh kàu lō lok lok.
14 sa$^n$ mīn ngō mâk, ē jīt mài tà$^n$ tn̂g té kha ūe.
15 lú mài chūe ūe.
16 mài tam gō i kâi sî hāu.
17 làn cêk keh, cêk keh sía.
18 thi$^n$ ke lâu kâi.
19 ū nâng kheh lâi, thiam ke kúi ie$^n$ chài.
20 úa cí hûe tam sim cài.
21 bói ū, bói bô, mài tam gō.
22 mài cò bô iah kâi sū, khù hāi ū iah kâi su.
23 lú mài tam tà$^n$ úa.

1 Eldest, second, and third, wives.
2 Do not you hinder me.
3 There were but few lame people.
4 Do not be proud.
5 No special benefit.
6 Do not you harm him.
7 Beat him till he was lamed.
8 Do not you thwart the thing.
9 Occasioned his being lame.
10 Beat him till he ached all over.
The lame.
11 Reprove his arrogance.
12 Rude people do not comprehend correct principles.
13 Rained till the road is miry.
14 As there were but five eyes to the three faces, do not hereafter say her feet were large or small.
15 Do not make excuses.
16 Do not waste his time.
17 Write in the alternate spaces.
18 Put in a few more.
19 A guest has come, add a few more kinds of vegetables.
20 I am this time much disappointed.
21 Whether you buy or not, don't delay.
22 Do not let that which is useless, injure what is beneficial.
23 Do not disappoint me.

## LESSON LXV.

淨 cĕng; limpid; only.
清 cheng; clean; clear.
潔 kiet; khih; pure.
混 hŭn; turbid; confuse.
敗 * ien; tainted.
裏 * tói; interior; inside.

生 * cheⁿ; raw; unripe.
熟 sêk; ripe; cooked.
消 sio; digest; dissolve.
消 * sie; transpire; news.
息 sit; message; respire.
神 sîn; gods; spirit.

| | | |
|---|---|---|
| 1 | sin ke cheng pêh. | Elegible to office. |
| 2 | sói cheng khih cheng khih. | Wash very clean. |
| 3 | tói mīn kâi ien, gūa mīn bŏi ien. | The inside is tainted but the outside is not. |
| 4 | cheⁿ kâi kōi ien, sêk kâi mān ien. | The raw easily spoils, the cooked will keep longer. |
| 5 | ŭ sih mih hó sie sit? | What is the news? |
| 6 | i ŭ kìa sie sit a bô? | Did he send any message? |
| 7 | kàu sì nî kú bô sie sit. | No tidings for four years. |
| 8 | lí mài hŭn úa. | Do not you disturb me. |
| 9 | sîn sài. mn̄g sîn. | Angels. Consult the gods. |
| 10 | sîn, ŭ kâi cin, ŭ kâi ké. | Of gods there are false and true. |
| 11 | cí kâi nâng sèⁿ lâi ŭ sieh sîn. | This person has a guardian angel. |
| 12 | cí kâi nâng thóiⁿ tìeh bô sîn. | This person appears spiritless. |
| 13 | sêk kâi mûeh kōi sio. | Cooked things digest easily. |
| 14 | cìeⁿ sì tó lăi m̄ sio cìah. | Did not digest the last meal. |
| 15 | cìeⁿ kúi jît ŭ sie sit. | There was tidings a few days ago. |
| 16 | cí kúi jît ío sêk líо. | Lately they are riper. |
| 17 | kiet cĕng tī hng. | Clean the country. |
| 18 | cheⁿ sêk mài sie hŭn. | D'ont mingle the green and ripe. |
| 19 | mài hŭn úa sǹg sìo. | Do not disturb my calculation. |
| 20 | tī tói ŭ sih mih tŏ? | What is inside the earth? |
| 21 | khoi tói kâi cúi cheng khih. | The water in the river is clean. |
| 22 | o hûn pun huang chue sio. | The wind has dispersed the clouds. |
| 23 | cêk jît sio ŭ jîeh cōi bí? | How much rice is consumed in a day? |
| 24 | tī íeⁿ mûeh sio ío cōi? | Of which thing is the most used? |
| 25 | tī kò sio ío ke? | Where is the greatest consumption? |

## LESSON LXVI.

富 pù; rich; affluent.
峰 hong; a high peak.
貧 khio; phîn; poor; penniless.
窮 khîong; poor; exhausted.
嚴 ngîam; stern; strict.
密 * cât; thick; close together.

密 mît; bât; mi; close; tight.
朽 * àu; rotten; decayed.
爛 nūa; rotten; corrupt.
糜 mî; rotten; pulpy.
皺 jìo; wrinkled.
嶇 khu; uneven.

| | |
|---|---|
| 1 phîn kâi cōi, pù kâi cíe. | 1 The poor are many, the rich few. |
| 2 cí kâi nâng hŵn sĭ hó. | 2 Here is yet another good man. |
| 3 cí câng hue hŵn sĭ ngía. | 3 Here is one more handsome flower. |
| 4 cò bât bât, mài làn khang. | 4 Make it tight, do not leave holes. |
| 5 lăi pâng. bât mn̂g. | 5 Private room. Panneled door. |
| 6 chùi hâp mi mi. | 6 Shut the mouth tight. |
| 7 hâp mi. mi bât. | 7 Close tight. Close and tight. |
| 8 lú hó ngîam ngîam kà i. | 8 Teach him strictly. |
| 9 mài khah ngîam. | 9 Do not be too severe. |
| 10 cí kĭa$^{n}$ sū mît mît khù cò. | 10 Go and do this privately. |
| 11 i thâu mô cât cât. | 11 His hair is very thick. |
| 12 cí câng chīu hwt khí lăi hîeh cât cât. | 12 This tree has come up with thick foliage. |
| 13 i ŭ mît sìn kìa úa cai. i nâng khio căi. | 13 He sent a private letter to inform me. They are very poor. |
| 14 cí câng chīu àu khù lío. | 14 This tree has rotted. |
| 15 i cêk sin kâi nêk mî nūa. | 15 All his flesh is rotten |
| 16 i mīn phûe jìo. | 16 His face is winkled. |
| 17 lú mài jìo bâi. | 17 Do not frown. |
| 18 sua$^{n}$ lō khi khu. | 18 The path is rough. |
| 19 lō kût kût khi khu khi khu. | 19 The road is slippery and rough. |
| 20 mî nūa kâi pē$^{n}$ m̄ hó thèng cîah mûeh. | 20 With this putrid disease, you must not eat carelessly. |
| 21 cí lîap kúe cí khah sêk; ài$^{n}$ mî líο. khio khîong. | 21 This fruit is too ripe; it is about to rot. Poor. |
| 22 cí kâi nâng nūa căi. | 22 This man is very corrupt. |
| 23 i sĭ phîn khîong nâng. | 23 He is a poor man. |
| 24 cêk nî bô sie bô sit. | 24 For a year there has been no tidings from him. |

## LESSON LXVII.

好 hàu$^{n}$; fond of; addicted to.
奇 khî; rare; unexpected.
怪 kùai; strange; weird.
濁 * lô; turbid; roiled.
閃 * sih; glisten.
爍 * iap; sparkle.

皆 kai; all; altogether.
腐 hu; hū; rotten; carius.
弱 jîak; weak; frail.
賢 hîen; gâu; wise.
正 cia$^{n}$; cìa$^{n}$; correct; right.
歪 chúa; awry.

| | | |
|---|---|---|
| 1 | cia$^{n}$ gûeh, jîh it. | The 21st of the first month. |
| 2 | lú kŭn jît cìa$^{n}$ khù, ta$^{n}$ hŵn ài$^{n}$ khù! | You went recently and now you want to go again! |
| 3 | iap cêk sih cĭu bô khù. | Flashed once then disappeared. |
| 4 | úa tà$^{n}$ lâi cìa$^{n}$ a m̄ cìa$^{n}$? | Was what I just said correct? |
| 5 | lú tà$^{n}$ lâi cìa$^{n}$ cìa$^{n}$. | You just spoke correctly. |
| 6 | tán ēng bô, cìa$^{n}$ hó bói. | Wait till it is all used up, then buy some. |
| 7 | chau kâi cṳ; sía cìa$^{n}$ cìa$^{n}$. | Make the copy correct. |
| 8 | i kâi chùi sĭm bât. | He is close-mouthed. |
| 9 | i sĭang hàu$^{n}$ tà$^{n}$ ūe. | She is very loquacious. |
| 10 | nâng se$^{n}$ phîn khîong pù kùi kai îu thi$^{n}$. | Poverty and wealth are alike from heaven. |
| 11 | i bô khí, mûeh tîeh mî mî cìa$^{n}$ cîah tit lôh. | He is toothless, and the things must be pulpy so that he can eat them. |
| 12 | i cò sṳ̄ khî khî kùai kùai. | He does marvelously. |
| 13 | chut khî kâi sṳ̄. | An extraordinary event. |
| 14 | cí kâi nâng khî hó. | This is an uncommonly good man. |
| 15 | i sin cĭe$^{n}$ khùn jîak, mài kùai i. hîen jîn. | He is feeble, do not startle him. Sages. |
| 16 | cúi lô, m̄ hó cîah, ēng cheng kâi. | The water is dirty, do not drink it, use clean. |
| 17 | thói$^{n}$ tîeh iap iap sih. | Saw it glitter. |
| 18 | mûeh pit soi$^{n}$ hu, ău cĭu ŏi se$^{n}$ thâng. | Things must be rotten before they breed worms. |
| 19 | cò cìa$^{n}$, mài cò chúa. | Make it exact, not awry. |
| 20 | i ài$^{n}$ cò gâu. | He wants to be a wiseacre. |

## LESSON LXVIII.

帽 lō; a hat.
閾 * tŏi$^{n}$; threshold.
梯 thui; stairs; ladder.
扣 khà; knock; beat.
掃 sàu; sweep; brush.
扭 * cŭn; wring; grasp.

破 phùa; broken; ragged.
眨 * nih; wink the eye.
傷 sie$^{n}$; siang; wound; hurt.
實 sı̂t; real; true.
失 * ka; let drop down.
落 * lâuh; fall; drop.

| | |
|---|---|
| 1 nêk hu nūa. nih mâk. | 1 Putrid meat. To wink. |
| 2 i ka kī cŭ sìa$^{n}$ cŭ hîen. | 2 He is holy and wise of himself! |
| 3 hó kio gâu nâng tâng sí, mài kio ngô nâng tâng se$^{n}$. | 3 Better to die with the wise than to live with the foolish. |
| 4 cí kâi nâng phī$^{n}$ chúa chùi chúa. phah phùa. | 4 This man's nose and mouth are crooked. To break. |
| 5 khî ī. khî cu. | 5 Astonishing. Rare books. |
| 6 ta$^{n}$ ŭ kúi tíam ceng? | 6 What o'clock is it now? |
| 7 lôh ke tíam kía$^{n}$. | 7 Put in a little more. |
| 8 thi$^{n}$ kong nih mâk. | 8 It lightens. |
| 9 cí kò pò lâu pàng kò sói pûa$^{n}$ úa$^{n}$ tia$^{n}$ tīa$^{n}$. | 9 Keep this cloth and wash only the dishes with it. |
| 10 mài i ka lâuh. | 10 Do not let it drop. |
| 11 cŭn kàu i ta ta. | 11 Wring it dry. |
| 12 sói mn̂g tŏi$^{n}$ kha. | 12 Wash the threshold. |
| 13 sàu lâu thui. | 13 Sweep the stairs. |
| 14 kâi tê ceng kah kâi tê pûa$^{n}$ khîeh lâi. | 14 Bring a tea-cup and saucer. |
| 15 i tŏ lâu thui kha. | 15 He is at the foot of the stairs. |
| 16 lú ŭ tà$^{n}$ sı̂t ūe a bô? | 16 Did you speak the truth? |
| 17 tîeh, ài$^{n}$ tà$^{n}$ sı̂t. | 17 Certainly, you speak truly. |
| 18 cá sòi, mài khà phùa. | 18 Be careful, do not break it. |
| 19 lú jı̂p lâi, tîeh khà mn̂g. | 19 You must knock when you enter. |
| 20 i téng bō ka lâuh. | 20 His hat dropped off. |
| 21 mn̂g tŏi$^{n}$ m̄ hó khĭa. | 21 Do not stand in the door. |
| 22 cí kâi pue khut lú khà phùa. | 22 You have broken this cup. |
| 23 phah kàu tăng sie$^{n}$. | 23 Beaten till badly hurt. |
| 24 tà$^{n}$ ūe mài thèng sie$^{n}$ nâng. | 24 Do not so speak as to wound people. |

# LESSON LXIX.

| | | | |
|---|---|---|---|
| 廳 | thia$^n$; the main room. | 貼 | tah; paste on. |
| 鍋 | * tía$^n$; an iron pan. | 引 | ín; lead; conduct. |
| 帚 | síu; cíu; broom. | 帶 | * chūa; guide. |
| 板 | * pang; a board. | 閂 | chùa$^n$; bar; bolt. |
| 口 | kháu; mouth; outside. | 結 | kat; kit; knit; bolt; end. |
| 膏 | kɵ; hard grease. | 又 | īu; moreover; also. |

| | | |
|---|---|---|
| 1 | bɵ̂ siang. úa khɵ́ siang i. | No harm done. I grieve for him. |
| 2 | lăi siang pē$^n$. siang sim. | Internal disease. Grieved at heart. |
| 3 | khin sie$^n$, tăng sie$^n$. | Slight wound, deep wound. |
| 4 | sît căi, sĭ sie$^n$ kúi kɵ̀. | In truth, was wounded in a few spots. |
| 5 | ka lâuh thô, tī kɵ̀ sie$^n$ tîeh? | Where was it injured in falling? |
| 6 | ka lâuh khù, īa bŏi phùa, īa bŏi sie$^n$. | Was not broken nor injured in falling. |
| 7 | cí kɵ̀ jī tah pàng thia$^n$ tang. | Stick this letter up in the parlour. |
| 8 | cí câng chīu kat sît líο. | This tree has borne fruit. |
| 9 | ài$^n$ ût tîeh cai chùa$^n$ mn̂g. | Before retiring, bar the door. |
| 10 | bɵ̂ kɵ îeh hɵ́ tah sie$^n$ kháu. | No ointment to put on the bruise. |
| 11 | īu ín chūa ke cêk nâng lâi kit cɵ̀ cé mūe. | Induced still another person to join the sisterhood. |
| 12 | i kâi chùi tûn hâp mi mi. | His lips were tightly closed. |
| 13 | cí cêk kháu tía$^n$ ín chūa i khîeh khṳ̀ thia$^n$ ău khǹg. | Induce her to take this pan and put it away behind the parlour. |
| 14 | ín chūa nâng kheh jîp nâng kheh thia$^n$. | Lead the guest into the reception room. |
| 15 | khîeh sàu síu lâi sàu lâu pâng. sì kɵ̀ pang. | Bring a broom and sweep the floor. Four boards. |
| 16 | úa lâi khṳ̀ gūa kháu. | I am going out. |
| 17 | i tɵ̆ gūa kháu. | He is out of doors. |
| 18 | mn̂g kit. kit mn̂g. | A bolt. Bolt the door. |
| 19 | gû lâ kit cɵ̀ cêk kɵ̀. | The suet has set in a lump. |
| 20 | kɵ îeh tah líο kit kín. | The salve hardened after putting on. |
| 21 | thia$^n$ mn̂g kâi mn̂g chùa$^n$ chùa$^n$ hɵ́. | Put up the bar of the door of the main room. |
| 22 | ka lâuh tɵ̆ lâu pang kɵ̀. | It dropped on the floor. |

## LESSON LXX.

| | | | |
|---|---|---|---|
| 筅 | chói$^{n}$; a small broom. | 鎔 | îe$^{n}$; fuse metals; melt. |
| 埃 | ai; eng; dust. | 拭 | chit; wipe with a dry cloth. |
| 塵 | tîn; têng; dust. | 㮣 | * jâ; wipe with a wet cloth. |
| 副 | hù; a set; aid. | 摺 | cih; fold up. |
| 桶 | tháng; tub; bucket. | 單 | toa$^{n}$; alone; single. |
| 擦 | chìu; scrub; scour. | 獨 | tôk; sole; only. |

| | | |
|---|---|---|
| 1 | chit tīo eng têng. | Wipe off the dust. |
| 2 | tê 'sî chŵn hù chit kàu kim kim. n̂gn toa$^{n}$. | Rub all the tea-spoons very bright. Money order. |
| 3 | cang cí kâi pêh thih tháng sói pûa$^{n}$ úa$^{n}$. | Use this tin pan for washing the dishes. |
| 4 | sa$^{n}$ khò cih hó pàng tû lăi. | Fold up the clothes and put them in the press. |
| 5 | cí cheh bí bói jîeh cōi cî$^{n}$? | What did you pay for this rice? |
| 6 | i toa$^{n}$ se$^{n}$ cí kâi kía$^{n}$. | She has had only this child. |
| 7 | toa$^{n}$ toa$^{n}$ ŭ cí cêk kâi. | There is only this one. |
| 8 | lú hŵn lío jâ būe kàu. | You have not yet rubbed it enough. |
| 9 | khí ŭ chìu îeh a bê? | Do you use tooth powder? |
| 10 | tôk it kâi cin sîn. | The sole true God. |
| 11 | toa$^{n}$ tôi. sang tôi. | Undivided hoof. Divided hoof. |
| 12 | ēng koi mê chói$^{n}$ lâi sàu tīo tîn ai. | Take a feather brush and brush off the cobwebs. |
| 13 | tek chói$^{n}$. hī$^{n}$ chói$^{n}$. | Bamboo brush. Ear broom. |
| 14 | cí kha tháng chō ŭ kúi hù pûa$^{n}$ úa$^{n}$? | How many sets of dishes does this tub hold? |
| 15 | kha tháng. mīn tháng. cúi tháng. tìo tháng. pûah tháng. nŏ hī$^{n}$ tháng. | Wash tub. Wash basin. Water bucket. Bailed pail. Drawing pail. Two eared kettle. |
| 16 | sie kàu jîet ŏi îe$^{n}$ a bŏi? | If heated will it melt? |
| 17 | kim, n̂gn, tâng oh îe$^{n}$; toa$^{n}$ toa$^{n}$ în siah kōi îe$^{n}$. | Gold, silver and brass are hard to melt; lead and pewter only melt easily. |
| 18 | thong sin chìu sói. | Scrub the whole person. |
| 19 | cìa$^{n}$ hù. hù sài. | Principal and vice. Assistant. |

## LESSON LXXI.

| | |
|---|---|
| 應 | eng; ought; proper. |
| 應 | èng: a lot; correspond. |
| 應 | ìn; answer; respond. |
| 當 | tng; adequate; suitable. |
| 當 | tǹg; pawn; pledge. |
| 當 | tàng; serve a purpose. |
| 孝 | hàu; filial; dutiful. |
| 該 | kai; ought; deserve. |
| 宜 | ngî; proper; fit. |
| 需 | su; need; forced. |
| 鬚 | chiu; beard; tassel. |
| 誰 | * tîang; person. |

| | | |
|---|---|---|
| 1 | cò̤ lâi m̄ hâh mâk. | They do not please me. |
| 2 | tôk kía<sup>n</sup> bô̤ hàu. | An only son is undutiful. |
| 3 | pit su kîa<sup>n</sup> hàu pĕ bó̤. | Must obey parents. |
| 4 | i sĭ put hàu kâi kía<sup>n</sup>. | He is an unfilial son. |
| 5 | i jîeh cōi kâi hàu cá̤ hàu hŭ. | How many sons and daughters-in-law is she? |
| 6 | i ṳ̆ hàu sim. | He has a filial heart. |
| 7 | eng hūn tit jîeh cōi? | What was your portion? |
| 8 | lṳ́ eng kai cìe<sup>n</sup> se<sup>n</sup> tà<sup>n</sup>. | You should say so. |
| 9 | sĭ lṳ́ tng eng kai cò̤ kâi. | It is what you ought to do. |
| 10 | lṳ́ pit su tîeh khṳ̀ cò̤. | You must certainly do it. |
| 11 | úa mn̄g i, i m̄ ìn. | I asked him and he did not answer. |
| 12 | lṳ́ î<sup>n</sup> keng ìn úa hó̤ cíu eng kai tîeh cìe<sup>n</sup> se<sup>n</sup> kîa<sup>n</sup>. | What you have said you would do, you should do. |
| 13 | cêk èng bói jîeh cōi cî<sup>n</sup>; sǹg úa thia<sup>n</sup>. | How much did you pay for the lot; reckon it up. |
| 14 | ṳ̆ kìe ṳ̆ ìn. | The demand brings the supply. |
| 15 | kìe kàu i ìn. | Call till he answers. |
| 16 | cîe ĕ siang èng. | The former and latter correspond. |
| 17 | tùi tùi èng úa kâi ūe. | Exactly fulfills my words. |
| 18 | m̄ kai cìe<sup>n</sup> se<sup>n</sup>. | It should not be so. |
| 19 | kai jîeh cōi n̂gn? | How much should he pay? |
| 20 | lṳ́ kai sí. tî tîang? | You deserve to die! Who's there? |
| 21 | tng sî i ío sòi. | When he was small. |
| 22 | i kâi phò tǹg khṳt úa. | He has pawned his shop to me. |
| 23 | cêk nâng tng câp nâng. | One man equal to ten men. |
| 24 | i nŏ̤ nâng nî hùe siang tng. | The age of the two is equal. |
| 25 | m̄ ká<sup>n</sup> tng. m̄ hâh ngî. | I dare not presume. Improper. |

## LESSON LXXII.

| | |
|---|---|
| 主 cú; owner; lord. | 擔 tam; bear; sustain. |
| 拜 pài; reverence; kneel to. | 救 kìu; rescue; save. |
| 鴉 a; a crow. | 安 an; uaⁿ; peaceful. |
| 羊 îeⁿ; sheep kind. | 慰 ùe; comfort; soothe. |
| 綿 mî; floculent; refuse silk. | 貌 mău; appearance. |
| 禮 lói; rites; decorum. | 莿 chì; spines; prickles. |

| | |
|---|---|
| 1 i sîang úa kâi tàng. | 1 He is caught by my stratagem. |
| 2 mài sîang nâng kâi tàng. | 2 Do not be taken in by people. |
| 3 lú pài sih mih sîn? | 3 What gods do you worship? |
| 4 hûe pài. pài kìⁿ. | 4 Return a visit. Pay respects to. |
| 5 i pat lói sìo. | 5 He knows the rules of society. |
| 6 i kâi lói mău hó. | 6 He has good manners. |
| 7 chit jît cêk kâi lói pài. | 7 Sunday once in seven days. |
| 8 lói pài tn̂g. lói mûeh. | 8 A church. Formal presents. |
| 9 lói sìo. sío jîn nâng. | 9 Etiquette. A rude person. |
| 10 thiⁿ sìo. kìu sì cú. | 10 Destiny. The Saviour. |
| 11 lú uaⁿ sim khù cò. | 11 Do it with a restful mind. |
| 12 phêng an! mn̄g uaⁿ. | 12 Peace! Inquire after. |
| 13 chíaⁿ lú uaⁿ. uaⁿ sîn. | 13 I salute you. Set up a god. |
| 14 uaⁿ ùe i kâi sim. o a. | 14 Comfort him. A crow. |
| 15 mīn mău. bô lói. | 15 Countenance. Unceremonious. |
| 16 úa tam tng i. | 16 I take his responsibility. |
| 17 cí tîo lō seⁿ chì. | 17 This road is thorny. |
| 18 kìu! bô kìu. | 18 Help! No salvation. |
| 19 i seⁿ lâi bô îeⁿ bô sìeⁿ. | 19 He has no form nor likeness. |
| 20 uaⁿ hiah. uaⁿ cō. | 20 Stop and rest. Sit at ease. |
| 21 ãiⁿ bîe i kâi îeⁿ sìeⁿ. | 21 Will sketch his likeness. |
| 22 lú khù kìu èng i. | 22 You go to his relief. |
| 23 cí kâi lói úa tng m̄ khí. | 23 I am not up to these formalities. |
| 24 i bŏi tit tîeh kìu. | 24 He cannot be saved. |
| 25 i m̄ sī toaⁿ toaⁿ úa kâi kìu cú. tam tng. | 25 He is not my Saviour alone. Become responsible for. |
| 26 mî îeⁿ, suaⁿ îeⁿ ŭ hun pîet. | 26 There is a difference between sheep and goats. |

## LESSON LXXIII.

餐 chan; a meal.
頓 * tǹg; meal; spell; turn.
柚 ìu; pummelo.
梨 lâi; the pear kind.
李 lí; the plum kind.
梅 bûe; prunes.

奈 năi; a yellow plum.
桃 thô; peaches.
檨 * sūai$^n$; mango.
蔗 cìa; sugar-cane.
橘 kit; limes.
薯 cṳ̂; potatoes.

| | | |
|---|---|---|
| 1 | ŭ. ŭ mē? būe ŭ. | I have. Have you? Have not yet. |
| 2 | ŭ ēng. i ŭ sṳ̄. | Useful. He has business. |
| 3 | i ŭ lí. tîeh ŭ. | He is in the right. Must be. |
| 4 | pit tîeh ŭ. ŭ jîeh cōi? | Certainly. How many are there? |
| 5 | lṳ́ hó khṳ̀ ua$^n$ ùe i. | You go and console her. |
| 6 | ke cú; ke cú nîe. | Master; mistress. |
| 7 | lṳ́ ka kī cú ì. | Decide for yourself. |
| 8 | i bŏi cú ì. | She cannot choose for herself. |
| 9 | hó$^n$ ài$^n$ cîah îe$^n$. | Tigers eat sheep. |
| 10 | hâh ngî a m̄ hâh ngî? | Is it proper or not? |
| 11 | chù cú tŏ tī kò? | Where is the owner of the house? |
| 12 | cí kâi sṳ̄ cò m̄ hâh ngî. | This affair is unjustifiable. |
| 13 | cêk jît sam chan. | Three meals a day. |
| 14 | ŭ nâng cîah sa$^n$ tǹg, ŭ nâng cîah nŏ tǹg. | Some people eat three meals, and some eat two. |
| 15 | mīn jû thô hue. | Face like a peach blossom. |
| 16 | cîah tǹg, gō tǹg ŭ sio kâi. | Eat a meal and fast a meal and some will digest. |
| 17 | tăi chan. cá tǹg. | Dinner. Breakfast. |
| 18 | mê hng tǹg. cêk tǹg pn̄g. | Supper. A meal. |
| 19 | tǹg tǹg cîah nêk. | Eat meat every meal. |
| 20 | ŭ sî ŭ, ŭ sî bô. | Sometimes has, sometimes has not. |
| 21 | ŭ kâi m̄ pīen. | Some are not expedient. |
| 22 | hŭam só ŭ. cêk lîap năi. | Whatever there is. A plum. |
| 23 | i sĭ tī hng cú. | He is the owner of the place. |
| 24 | lâi phûe. lâi sim. | Pear rind. Core of a pear. |
| 25 | tiah kúi liap kit ka$^n$. | Pick a few sour oranges. |
| 26 | hwn lâi. hwn cṳ̂. | Pine apples. Irish potatoes. |

# LESSON LXXIV.

形 lêng; form; shape.
規 kui; eustom; rule.
矩 kṳ́; usage; regulation.
包 pau; wrap; bundle.
衣 i; garments; dress.
服 hôk; clothes.

符 hṳ̂; agree, as an impression with a seal.
雜 câp; heterogenous.
奴 nô; servant; slave.
婢 pĭ; slave.
體 thói; body; substance.
個 * tiang; classifier.

| | | |
|---|---|---|
| 1 | ài$^{n}$ khṳ̀ pun tī tîang? | To whom will you give it? |
| 2 | cí kâi sĭ tī tîang kâi? | Whose is this? |
| 3 | m̄ cai sĭ tī tîang. | Do not know who it is. |
| 4 | i lâi tiang sî, úa tŏ cîah. | When he came, I was eating. |
| 5 | cá tiang sî ŭ. | Aforetime there was. |
| 6 | hṳ́ tiang sî ŭ. | At that time there was. |
| 7 | i tī tiang sî ài$^{n}$ kàu? | When will he arrive? |
| 8 | ŭ tiang sî i lâi. | He sometimes comes. |
| 9 | lṳ́ tiang sî ài$^{n}$ khṳ̀? | When are you going? |
| 10 | tīa$^{n}$ kui. nńg pĭ. | Settle a rate. Female slave. |
| 11 | kak hâng kak hâng kâi kui. | Each guild has its own rules. |
| 12 | kui cìa$^{n}$. pau khí lâi. | Admonitions. Bundle it up. |
| 13 | kui kṳ́ sĭ nâng nâng tîeh ŭ. | All must practise propriety. |
| 14 | i bô̤ kui bô̤ kṳ́. | He is lawless. |
| 15 | lṳ́ úa siang kui cìa$^{n}$. | We admonish each other. |
| 16 | pau kín. cêk pau. | Wrap up tight. A package. |
| 17 | m̄ siang hṳ̂. | The parts do not match. |
| 18 | i kâi sim câp. | His mind is distracted. |
| 19 | câp sek. sin thói. | Variegated. The body. |
| 20 | cò̤ câp kang. | Do all sorts of work. |
| 21 | ēng i cò̤ phah câp. | Take him as man of all work. |
| 22 | hêng mău se$^{n}$ lâi mih īe$^{n}$? | What is his appearance? |
| 23 | cí pau i hôk jîeh cōi kĭa$^{n}$? hṳ̂ hâh. | How many garments in this bundle? Matching. |
| 24 | ke cú sĭ ke cú kâi i hôk, nô pĭ sĭ nô pĭ kâi i hôk; ŭ hun pîet. | The master's dress and the servant's dress are different. |
| 25 | i sin thói nńg jîak. | He is weak in body. |

## LESSON LXXV.

體 * thi; thí; respectable.
貼 thiap; supply; adjacent.
磚 cng; bricks.
箱 sie$^{n}$; chest; box.
鞋 ôi; shoes.
圍 ûi; enclosure.

蕊 lúi; classifier of flowers.
張 tie$^{n}$; classifier of things in sheets.
領 nía; classifier of upper garments; collar.
被 phŭe; a blanket.
綑 khún; roll; bind.
疋 phit; a whole piece.

1 ŭ thí mīn.
2 hêng thói. sìa$^{n}$ thói.
3 kâi pûa$^{n}$, ki pit, kò cng.
4 kha sie$^{n}$, ciah cûn.
5 tîo seh, tie$^{n}$ cúa.
6 nía phŭe, pé tṳ̄.
7 pn̂g cheh, pau îeh.
8 lîap ka$^{n}$, lúi hue, câng chīu.
9 cō chù, ûi chân, koi$^{n}$ pâng.
10 búe hṳ̂, khún pò.
11 téng bō, phit pò.
12 sang ôi, tùi koi.
13 cêk tîo cûa pue lôh lâi.
14 cêk ūi tăi jîn.
15 sa$^{n}$ sói ŭ kúi nía?
16 úa hán tit ŭ. chía$^{n}$ būe.
17 i ŭ lói; ŭ kui kṳ́.
18 lăi tói ŭ.
19 thiap sin kâi i hôk.
20 thiap sin kâi nô pĭ.
21 úa thói thiap lṳ́.
22 ǹi$^{n}$ ní cò thô hue sek.
23 i kâi i sa$^{n}$ âng âng.
24 i m̄ hàu$^{n}$ thia$^{n}$.
25 i m̄ hàu$^{n}$ tà$^{n}$.
26 phŭe khún hó, khǹg pàng sie$^{n}$ tói.
27 câp gūa phit pò khún cò cêk ē.

1 Honored and dignified.
2 Bodily frame. Emperor's person.
3 A tray, a pen, a brick.
4 A box, a boat.
5 A rope, a sheet of paper.
6 A blanket, a bunch of chop-sticks.
7 A book, a packet of medicine.
8 An orange, a flower, a tree.
9 A house, a field, a room.
10 A fish, a roll of cloth.
11 A hat, a piece of cloth.
12 A pair of shoes, a pair of fowls.
13 A snake glided by.
14 A great man.
15 How many jackets did you wash?
16 I seldom have. Wait a moment.
17 He is well bred.
18 There are some inside.
19 Garments next the body.
20 Body servants.
21 I accommodate you.
22 Will dye it pink.
23 His garments were red.
24 He is not willing to obey.
25 He would not say.
26 When you have rolled up the blanket, put it in the chest.
27 Over ten pieces of cloth rolled up together.

## LESSON LXXVI.

| | | | |
|---|---|---|---|
| 生 | seng; means of living; doctor. | 更 | keⁿ; a watch of the night. |
| 免 | míen; dispense with; evade. | 上 | * tèng; on; in; near. |
| 賺 | thàn; earn; profit. | 慈 | chṳ̂; mercy; kindness. |
| 妥 | thó; secure; prepared. | 諸 | cu; all; implying doubt. |
| 補 | pó; repair; recruit. | 倘 | tháng; if; supposing. |
| 睡 | sŭi; to sleep. | 若 | jîak; if; same as; then. |

| | |
|---|---|
| 1 mn̂g seng. ui seng. cṳ seng. | 1 Disciple. Physician. Scholar. |
| 2 cìaⁿ seng, síe seng. | 2 Great and inferior actors. |
| 3 míen kǐⁿ. seng lí. | 3 He need not come in. Business. |
| 4 míen lâi. cu hûam. | 4 He need not come. Totally. |
| 5 míen. cu ūi. | 5 It is unnecessary. You, sirs. |
| 6 cu cṳ́ peh ke. | 6 All classes of authors. |
| 7 cu jû ŭ cí kâi ieⁿ, hó bói. | 7 If there is this kind, buy some. |
| 8 cu jû ŭ cí kâi sṳ̄, cò nî? | 8 If this happens, then what? |
| 9 kâi gûeh thàn jîeh cōi cîⁿ? | 9 How much do you earn per month? |
| 10 tháng jîak thàn ŭ cîⁿ, tîeh cai cîah pó îeh. | 10 If you earn money, you must take a tonic. |
| 11 cí kĭaⁿ sṳ̄ tîeh lí thó thiap. | 11 This business must be thoroughly done. |
| 12 cí kâi nâng thó tàng. | 12 This man is reliable. |
| 13 cí kù ūe tàⁿ lâi m̄ thó. | 13 That was not well said. |
| 14 i tŏ pó ôi. chṳ̂ bó. | 14 He mends shoes. Loving mother. |
| 15 pó îeh. pó saⁿ. | 15 A restorative. Mend clothes. |
| 16 pó n̂gn cúi. jû jîak. | 16 Make up the deficiency of weight in money. It seems—. |
| 17 saⁿ phùa, sĭ àiⁿ kit a sĭ àiⁿ pó? | 17 Do you want the hole in the garment darned or patched? |
| 18 chíaⁿ kâi lói seng lâi kìaⁿ lói. | 18 Invite a master of ceremonies to perform the rites. |
| 19 jĭt bô pá chan cêk tǹg, mê bô ún sŭi saⁿ keⁿ. | 19 Without one full meal in the day, there will not be three watches of sound sleep in the night. |
| 20 chíu tèng. sin tèng. | 20 In the hand. On the body. |
| 21 chṳ̂ sim. chṳ̂ ài. | 21 Tender heart. Affection. |
| 22 tháng jîak. jîak sĭ. | 22 Premising. If it be so. |
| 23 jîak sĭ bô hŏ. | 23 If there be no rain. |

## LESSON LXXVII.

沙 sua; sand.
石 cîeh; stone.
鋼 kǹg; steel.
木 bâk; timber.
鉎 se$^{n}$; cast iron.
礬 hṳ̂n; alum.
榕 * sêng; banyan.
硫 lîu; sulphur.
靛 tōi$^{n}$; indigo.
膠 ka; glue.
漆 chak; varnish.
璇 sūan; gems.

| | | |
|---|---|---|
| 1 | phah i. ŏi tit phah i. | Beat him. Can beat him. |
| 2 | úa jîak īa sĭ phah i. | If I should beat him. |
| 3 | úa ciang ài$^{n}$ phah i. | I am about to beat him. |
| 4 | tîeh phah i. phah! | Must beat him. Strike! |
| 5 | hàm i phah i. | Tell him to beat him. |
| 6 | tŏ phah i. sêng chîu. | Is beating him. Banyan. |
| 7 | úa í$^{n}$ keng phah i líao. | I have already beaten him. |
| 8 | i būe jīn, úa í$^{n}$ keng phah hŏ́ líao. | Before he confessed, I had already beaten him. |
| 9 | pĕ būe kàu, úa ciang ài$^{n}$ phah hŏ́ líao. | Before his father comes, I shall have beaten him. |
| 10 | úa pĭ i phah. | I am beaten by him. |
| 11 | úa ŏi khṳt nâng phah. | I can be beaten. |
| 12 | úa īa sĭ khṳt nâng phah. | If I am beaten by anybody. |
| 13 | ciang lâi úa ài$^{n}$ sĭu i phah. | Sometime I shall take a beating from him. |
| 14 | tîeh sĭu i phah. | Must take his beating. |
| 15 | hàm i sĭu phah. | Tell him to take the beating. |
| 16 | tŏ sĭu i phah. | Getting a beating from him. |
| 17 | úa í$^{n}$ keng khṳt i phah hŏ́ líao. | I have already been beaten by him. |
| 18 | i būe cêng khṳt i lîah, úa soi$^{n}$ sĭu phah. | Before he was caught, I had been beaten. |
| 19 | lṳ́ būe cêng ŏi tà$^{n}$ chut pit ài$^{n}$ sĭu i phah. | Before you can say anything you will surely be beaten. |
| 20 | pêh hṳ̂n. che$^{n}$ hṳ̂n. | Alum. Copperas. |
| 21 | bâk sat. pó thiap. | Bed bugs. Make up a loss. |
| 22 | lîu n̂g. míen kúi sî. | Brimstone. It won't be long. |

## LESSON LXXVIII.

| | | | |
|---|---|---|---|
| 赴 | hù; arrive; repair to. | 或 | hôk; uncertain; either. |
| 順 | sŭn; yield to; obey. | 堆 | tun; pile; pile up. |
| 及 | * hù; to effect; avail. | 嚇 | heh; scare; intimidate. |
| 蓆 | chîeh; matting. | 喝 | toah; shout at; reprimand. |
| 預 | ṳ̆; ready; provided. | 癬 | síen; ringworm. |
| 備 | pĭ; prepare; provide. | 鏽 | sang; rust. |

| | | |
|---|---|---|
| 1 | úa ài<sup>n</sup> khṳ̀ hù sîah. | I am going to repair to supper. |
| 2 | hù m̄ tîeh cûn. | Did not catch the boat. |
| 3 | hù hŭe. hù sṳ̄. | Attend a meeting. Attend to business. |
| 4 | cûn ài<sup>n</sup> khui, kîa<sup>n</sup> khùe cē cìa<sup>n</sup> hù. | The boat is about to start, walk faster so as to get it. |
| 5 | jît khah ùa<sup>n</sup>; kîa<sup>n</sup> kàu hṳ́ kò m̄ hù. | It is too late in the day; to go there is impraticable. |
| 6 | sṳ̄ lí kàu hó cĭu m̄ hù. | To settle the matter is unavailing. |
| 7 | chîeh pau. cháu chîeh. | A matting bag. Straw mat. |
| 8 | soi<sup>n</sup> ṳ̆ pĭ hó. | Get ready beforehand. |
| 9 | úa m̄ cêng ṳ̆ cí kâi sṳ̄. | I am not yet prepared for this. |
| 10 | ṳ̆ pĭ phah bô pĭ. | Forewarned is forearmed. |
| 11 | í<sup>n</sup> keng ṳ̆ pĭ pīn lío. | Already quite prepared. |
| 12 | í<sup>n</sup> keng pĭ cok líο. | Already fully provided. |
| 13 | hôk cía i ài<sup>n</sup> lâi. | Perhaps he will come. |
| 14 | thô tun pàng hue hn̂g. | Pile the earth in the garden. |
| 15 | tun cò cêk tun. | Pile it up in a pile. |
| 16 | i sĭ heh lṳ́ kâi. | He is browbeating you. |
| 17 | mài heh toah i. | Do not threaten him. |
| 18 | mùa tĭ kò thèng heh nâng. pĭ pīn a būe? | Frightening people everywhere. Are they made ready yet? |
| 19 | lṳ́ heh i, toah i. | You bully and scold her. |
| 20 | lṳ́ toah i cò mé cē. | You shout out at him to hurry. |
| 21 | se<sup>n</sup> síen. se<sup>n</sup> sang. | Have tetter. Get rusty. |
| 22 | heh sí nâng. | Scare people to death. |
| 23 | cí kĭa<sup>n</sup> sṳ̄ kio úa lí thó thiap thó thiap. | Regulate this business throughly for me. |
| 24 | i pó thiap úa. | He made it up to me. |

## LESSON LXXIX.

| | | | |
|---|---|---|---|
| 糕 | ke; cakes; pastry. | 參 | siam; ginseng. |
| 粿 | kúe; loaf; cake. | 卵 | n̆g; eggs. |
| 粥 | mûe; congee. | 糖 | thn̂g; sugar. |
| 飯湯 | * ám; porridge. | 粉 | hún; flour. |
| 湯 | thng; soup. | 㬲 | kà$^n$; yeast. |
| 酒 | cíu; wine. | 麵 | mī; wheaten. |

| | |
|---|---|
| 1 jĭak i lâi lṳ́ kāng i tà$^n$. | 1 If he comes, you tell him. |
| 2 cu jû ŭ n̂gn cĭu hó̤ bói. | 2 If there is money then buy. |
| 3 jĭak īa sĭ i m̄ hàu$^n$ cĭu hiah. | 3 If he don't want to, then stop. |
| 4 siet jĭak hó̤ cò̤ cĭu cò̤. | 4 If it is well to do it then do it. |
| 5 siet sái i tà$^n$ cí kâi ūe—. | 5 Suppose that he says this—. |
| 6 hôk cía i thia$^n$ lṳ́ tà$^n$. | 6 Perchance he may listen to you. |
| 7 īa sĭ m̄ tŏ̤, lṳ́ tńg lâi. | 7 If he is not there, come back. |
| 8 thi$^n$ sĭ hó̤ cĭu ài$^n$ cò̤. koi n̆g ke. | 8 (If) the weather is good I will work. Sponge-cakes. |
| 9 ŭ hó̤ huang cĭu ài$^n$ khṳ̀. | 9 (If) the wind is fair I will go. |
| 10 ŭ kang cĭu ŭ n̂gn. | 10 If work, then pay. |
| 11 ŭ pn̄g cĭu ài$^n$ cĭah. | 11 If there is any rice I will eat. |
| 12 ŭ cûn cĭu ài$^n$ tah cûn; bô̤ cûn cĭu ài$^n$ kĭa$^n$ lō. kà$^n$ bó̤. | 12 If there is a boat I will go by boat; if there is no boat then I will walk. Yeast. |
| 13 ŭ nâng jĭp lâi lṳ́ cĭu lâi hàm. | 13 If any one comes in, then come and call me. |
| 14 i lâi khĭeh cĭu pun i khĭeh. thng sĭ. | 14 If he comes to get it, then let him have it. Spoon. |
| 15 ŭ cĭu hó̤; bô̤, cĭu bô̤ siang kan. | 15 If there is, then well; if not, then no matter. |
| 16 ŭ nâng khṳ̀, úa ài$^n$ cò̤-pû khṳ̀. | 16 If anybody goes, then I want to go along. |
| 17 cá jĭt soi$^n$ ŭ pĭ, kim jĭt ŏi tit tĭeh hù cûn. pn̄g ám. mī hún. | 17 If you had yesterday made ready, to-day you might have embarked. Rice water. Flour. |
| 18 bô̤ kìu sì cú ui i, tī tĭang ŏi tit ui i? | 18. If the Saviour had not healed him, who could have healed him? |

## LESSON LXXX.

茄 kîe; egg-plant.
笋 sún; sprouts.
芽 gê; buds; shoots.
薑 kieⁿ; ginger.
巾 kun; napkin.
粟 chek; unhusked rice.

罇 cun; bottle; flask.
煲 * ue; earthen pot.
甌 au; a covered cup.
鑵 kẁn; jar; cruse.
碟 tîh; little plates.
釭 kang; kng; jar.

1 bô eí nŏ nâng bô ēng.
2 i tàⁿ, bô sŭn Mosai kâi kui kú cĭu bŏi tit kìu. o thn̂g.
3 lú m̄ hàuⁿ cĭu hiah.
4 mài lău ui seng khù lío, kim jît cĭu sĭ àiⁿ bói îeh.
5 ŭ cîⁿ thàn, úa cĭu lâi. pêh thn̂g.
6 úa tah cûn kâi sî hāu, lú īa sĭ thóiⁿ kìⁿ úa—.
7 pó thiap saⁿ hun cúi. cúi kng.
8 mài hiah tŏ hú kò, kim jît cĭu kàu.
9 pó thiap i kâi kang cîⁿ.
10 lâk jît thàn, cêk jît hiah.
11 míen thĕng hāu kú.
12 míen ēng cò.
13 jîak īa sĭ bói sêng, hó lâi kāi úa tàⁿ.
14 i kâi sim ngĕ kùe thih.
15 úa sŭn lú cĭu sĭ.
16 cò bâk kang kâi, lâi lío.
17 i saⁿ khò būe ŭ pīn.
18 húe cîeh. thàn cîah.

1 If you do not have these two men, all is useless.
2 They said, if you do not observe the law of Moses you cannot be saved. Brown sugar.
3 If you don't want to, then stop.
4 If the venerable physician had not gone, to-day we should have bought medicine.
5 If there is money to made, I will come. White sugar.
6 If you see me when I am embarking—.
7 Add three tenths to make up the deficiency. Water jar.
8 If we had not stopped there we should have arrived to-day.
9 Supply the deficiency in his wages.
10 Work six days and stop one.
11 Unnecessary to wait long.
12 There is no need to do it.
13 If you succeed in buying it, come and tell me.
14 His heart is harder than iron.
15 I will obey you.
16 The carpenter has already come.
17 His clothes are not ready.
18 Flint. Earn a living.

## LESSON LXXXI.

筒 tâng; tube; cylinder; a gill.

糴 tı̂ah; buy (rice.)

噴 pûn; spurt; snort.

拈 liam; pinch up.

扛 kng; carry on a pole between two.

携 * kŭa$^n$; carry at the side by a handle.

背 * pì; carry in a cloth on the back.

負 * iă; carry on the back.

抱 phŏ; clasp in the arms.

夾 kôih; carry under the arm.

戴 tì; carry on the head.

從 * tāng; during; from.

---

1 kie$^n$ n̂g. tek sún.
2 kúi kâi kîe pàng ue tói.
3 cí kâi sua$^n$ se$^n$ lâi kio sún cêk ıe$^n$. phŏ a nô$^n$.
4 cí lîap hue cí hwt gê lío.
5 lôh hŏ thi$^n$, hue bâk cĭu kōi chut gê.
6 che$^n$ kie$^n$ ŏi sio cîah.
7 chíu kun. thâu kun.
8 sua ue. tê kẁn. hue kang.
9 hue kng. tōi$^n$ kng. húe hu sek.
10 cúi kng. tê au.
11 au úa$^n$ pûa$^n$ tîh. húe hu.
12 i kâi thâu tì kim bō.
13 tāng chut sì kàu ta$^n$.
14 tāng cá, úa pat sói.
15 cŭ tāng úa lâi cĭu bŏi.
16 tāng soi$^n$ ŭ kâi.
17 tāng cá jı̂t ă pí pīn lío.
18 i pì a nô$^n$ khù tîah bí.
19 bō, sí tì tŏ thâu tèng kâi mûeh.
20 kāng cîeh pê$^n$ tōi$^n$.
21 pûn cêk chùi cúi.
22 pûn tâng. bí tâng.
23 cí ıe$^n$ pía$^n$ cêk tâng jîeh cōi cî$^n$? kŭa$^n$ cúi.
24 chíu liam cêk lúi hue lâi phı̄$^n$ phang. khut i kôih khù.

1 Tumeric. Bamboo sprouts.
2 Put the egg-plants in the pot.
3 This mountain is shaped like a cone. Carry the baby.
4 This flower-seed has sprouted.
5 In rainy weather plants readily germinate.
6 Fresh ginger aids digestion.
7 Handkerchief. Head-cloth.
8 An eared pot. Tea-pot. Vase.
9 Flower-pot. Blue dye pot. Gray.
10 Water-jar. Covered tea-cup.
11 The dishes. Ashes.
12 He wore a crown.
13 From his birth till now.
14 I washed it a little while ago.
15 From the time I came it has not.
16 There used to be some.
17 It has been ready since yesterday.
18 She went, carrying the baby, to buy rice.
19 A hat is worn on the head.
20 As solid as a stone.
21 Spurt out a mouthful of water.
22 Chinese flute. Rice measure.
23 How much are these cakes per roll? Carry water.
24 Picked a flower to smell. Carried off under his arm.

## LESSON LXXXII.

胡 hû; hô; Tartar.
玉 gêk; jade; precious stone.
典 tíen; canon; ritual.
辣 lûah; biting; hot.
醋 chò; vinegar.
椒 cie; pepper.

葱 chang; onions.
芋 ō; taro.
芥 kài; mustard.
豆 tāu; beans; pulse.
葛 kuah; creepers.
蒜 sàg; garlic.

| | |
|---|---|
| 1 hû cie. pêh hû cie. | 1 Black pepper. White pepper. |
| 2 hû jîn. âng cie. | 2 Tartars. Cayenne pepper. |
| 3 hiam cie. hue cie. | 3 Chillies. Red peppers. |
| 4 kài lûah. chùi chàu. | 4 Ground mustard. Bad breath. |
| 5 i kâi nâng ŭ hiam lûat. | 5 He is a fiery fellow. |
| 6 lûah kie$^{n}$. tāu hū. | 6 Pungent ginger. Bean-curd. |
| 7 lí būe pat cîah tîeh lûah kie$^{n}$. hŭ jîn. | 7 You do not know what it is to suffer. Women. |
| 8 hwn kuah. jī tíen. | 8 Sweet potatoes. Dictionary. |
| 9 cúi ō. lêk tāu. ng tāu. | 9 Water taro. Green peas. Dry peas. |
| 10 o mâk tāu tùi pêh mâk tāu. | 10 Disagreement between equals. |
| 11 bói kúi lîap chang thâu. | 11 Buy a few onions. |
| 12 cîah sàg thâu cîah lío chùi ŏi chàu. | 12 If you eat garlic your breath will be bad. |
| 13 àng cêk lîap kài cí hìe$^{n}$ tōa. | 13 As large as a mustard seed. |
| 14 cí kâi sĭ gêk a sĭ cîeh? | 14 Is this jade or stone? |
| 15 bê sĭm mih hun pîet. | 15 Not much distinction. |
| 16 ta$^{n}$ ài$^{n}$ chau sìo. | 16 Will now transfer the account. |
| 17 cang cí kâi jī tíen kâi jī kāi úa chau kùe lâi. | 17 Copy the characters in this dictionary for me. |
| 18 cí cheh chò sng căi. | 18 This vinegar is very sour. |
| 19 cí īe$^{n}$ hê tîeh ŭ kie$^{n}$ chò, cìa$^{n}$ hó cîah. | 19 This sort of fish needs ginger vinegar to make it edible. |
| 20 kó tíen. tíen sît. | 20 Ancient records. Document. |
| 21 tíen kù. tíen tŏng. | 21 Ordinances. Consider valuable. |
| 22 kài chài. tī tāu. | 22 Mustard greens. Pea-nuts. |
| 23 ō thâu. khah hiam lûah. | 23 Yams. Too peppery. |
| 24 sàg thâu, sàg hieh. | 24 Garlic roots and tops. |

# LESSON LXXXIII.

| | | | |
|---|---|---|---|
| 典 | tói<sup></sup>ⁿ; to mortgage. | 孝 | * hà; mourning. |
| 掛 | kùa; khùa; suspend; anxious. | 裙 | kûn; petticoat. |
| 慮 | lṳ̆; anxious; care for. | 袖 | * ńg; sleeve. |
| 帶 | tòa; girdle; draw on. | 頸 | * ăm; neck. |
| 拖 | thoa; to drag. | 頦 | hâi; chin. |
| 束 | sok; pâk; hâ; to gird. | 腰 | ie; waist. |

| | | |
|---|---|---|
| 1 | ku ie. phŭe toa ⁿ. | Hump-back. Quilt cover. |
| 2 | i sî sî hâ kûn. | She always wears a petticoat. |
| 3 | ài ⁿ sói cêk tùi ńg kháu kah kâi ăm nía. sok tòa. | Going to wash a pair of cuffs and a collar. Fasten a belt. |
| 4 | hâ i kâi ăm. | Put it around his neck. |
| 5 | i cang phûe tòa hâ ie. pâk ie. | He girded himself with a leathern girdle. Gird. |
| 6 | i ĕ hâi ciam ciam. | His chin is sharp. |
| 7 | i khṳ̀ tìo ám sí. | He went and hung himself. |
| 8 | thói ⁿ kàu ăm tn̂g tn̂g. | Looking with outstretched neck. |
| 9 | tìo ăm cṳ̆ cĭn. | Suicide by hanging. |
| 10 | tìo ăm seh. | Hangman's rope. |
| 11 | chù sĭ kio nâng tói ⁿ kâi. | The house is a mortgaged one. |
| 12 | i kâi phò ài ⁿ tói ⁿ khṳ̄t nâng. | His shop is to be mortgaged. |
| 13 | cí koi ⁿ chù chut tói ⁿ. | This house is to mortgage. |
| 14 | ŭ tói ⁿ, bê bōi. | To be mortgaged, not sold. |
| 15 | i tòa hà sa ⁿ nî. | He wears mourning three years. |
| 16 | lṳ́ mien ēng kùa lṳ̆ úa. | You need not be anxious about me. |
| 17 | ie tèng kùa ki te. | A knife hung at the waist. |
| 18 | tòa hâ kûi ⁿ cē, cìa ⁿ bŏi thoa tîeh thô ĕ. | Gird it up a little higher so it will not drag on the ground. |
| 19 | sa ⁿ ńg mài cò khah khuah. | Do not make the sleeves too wide. |
| 20 | i ēng jîeh cōi kûn sa ⁿ kè cáu kía ⁿ. | How many suits for her daughter's wedding outfit? |
| 21 | lṳ̆ kàu ău lâi kâi sṳ̄. | Take thought for the future. |
| 22 | i lṳ́ sṳ̄ ío tn̂g. | He makes precautionary plans. |
| 23 | úa sĭm khùa sim. | I am very anxious. |
| 24 | sî ceng kùa tŏ thia ⁿ tèng. | Hang the clock in the main room. |

## LESSON LXXXIV.

糊 hû; foolish; confused.
煮 cṳ́; cook; boil; steep.
煲 pû; sâh; cook with water.
椿 ceng; pound with pounder.
蒸 * chue; cook with steam.
醃 * lŏ; to pickle.

糊 * kô; paste.
斬 cám; to chop.
砍 * tok; split.
削 siak; hew.
批 phoi; pare.
刮 * kueh; scrape; abrade.

---

1 cṳ́ cîah. cṳ́ pn̄g.
2 cṳ́ sêk. hû sueh.
3 hû lŭan. hû hŭn.
4 pû cúi cò̤ kô.
5 bí ceng pêh pêh.
6 pn̄g mài cṳ́ khah mî.
7 cám chîu lîah cío.
8 lŏ kàu jît cìaⁿ hó̤ cîah.
9 seⁿ hó̤, cṳ́ pn̄g pêh.
10 cí kâi a sim nâng mîa ke chue kúe.
11 cí tieⁿ jī cang kô tah pàng lō tèng khṳt nâng thóiⁿ.
12 phoi tīo i kâi phûe.
13 siak kàu ciam ciam.
14 cí kâi siah tê kṳ̀n ēng kueh te, kueh i kng.
15 tī tîang siet lîp khí thâu pû mûeh cṳ́ mûeh ?
16 koi nn̆g hó̤ sâh sêk.
17 i kíaⁿ jît khí thâu lâi.
18 thâu cêk kâi cīu sī.
19 khĭa khui cē, mài i tok tîeh.
20 cám kúi ki châ lâi pû pn̄g. cám tīo.
21 mô̤ kueh cheng khih, cìaⁿ hó̤ chue.

1 Cooking food. Boil rice.
2 Cook through. Nonsensical.
3 Incoherent. Not perspicuous.
4 Heat water for making paste.
5 Pound the rice very white.
6 Do not cook the rice too soft.
7 Cut down the tree to catch the bird.
8 Pickle it enough and it is good.
9 The handsome are good cooks.
10 This woman is a skillful cake-maker.
11 Get paste and stick this placard up by the road to be seen.
12 Pare off its rind.
13 Whittle it to a point.
14 Use a scraper and scrape this pewter tea-pot bright.
15 Who first invented cooking?
16 Boil the eggs hard.
17 He began to come to-day.
18 It is the one at the top.
19 Stand off a little, so he won't hit you (in splitting.)
20 Chop a few sticks of wood to boil the rice. Chop off.
21 Scrape the hair off clean, then steam it.

## LESSON LXXXV.

器 khì; vessel; utensil.
具 kŭ; implement.
裂 lìh; lì; split; tear; rip.
剝 pak; peh; peal; flay.
攪 ká; beat; stir.
攪 * lă; stir around.
抹 buah; rub on; smear.
割 kuah; cut; divide.
攙 cham; mingle; mix.
勻 * câu; even; equal.
腫 céng; swell; enlarge.
核 hût; kernel; stone.

| | | |
|---|---|---|
| 1 | khì kŭ. kim n̂gn khì. | Utensils. Gold and silver vessels. |
| 2 | m̄ sêng khì kâi nâng. | A man unfit for the place. |
| 3 | cí kâi nâng sĭm sĭ síe khì. | This man is very small minded. |
| 4 | gêk khì. hŏ kŭ. | Jade vessel. Umbrella and clogs. |
| 5 | cêk hù tê kŭ. | A set of dishes for making tea. |
| 6 | thia$^n$ kì$^n$ cí kâi ūe, i cĭu lìh tĭo i kâi sa$^n$. | When he heard this, he at once rent his garments. |
| 7 | i ka kĭ lìh khui. lì tĭo. | It split open itself. Tear. |
| 8 | i kâi i hôk phùa lìh. | His garments were tattered. |
| 9 | pun huang chue lìh. | Torn by the wind. |
| 10 | lìh cò chit poih kò. | Ripped into seven or eight pieces. |
| 11 | lìh mâk. phah lìh. | Fissured eye. To rive. |
| 12 | i kâi phûe pak kàu cheng khih. | Peal its skin off clean. |
| 13 | peh tĭo phûe cìa$^n$ hó cìah. | Peal off the skin then eat it. |
| 14 | koi n̆g ká câu câu. | Beat the eggs thoroughly. |
| 15 | koi n̆g ke tîeh lă câu. | Stir the cake thoroughly. |
| 16 | a nô$^n$ kía$^n$ hùe lă lă ká. | Children are always stirring. |
| 17 | buah khui, cĭu hó kùe. | Brush it aside so we can pass. |
| 18 | buah tĭo lêng ūa$^n$ sía. | Rub out and write again. |
| 19 | peh tĭo phûe, khà tĭo hût, ău sâh thn̂g, sâh mî mî, kìe cò ke. | Take off the skin, take out the stones, stew in sugar to a pulp, and call it jam. |
| 20 | buah îeh. buah ke îeh. | Rub on medicine. Smear with salve. |
| 21 | cang cí kâi îeh buah kúi jĭt, ău cìa$^n$ bŏi céng. | Smear on this medicine for a few days then it will not swell. |
| 22 | kuah tĭ. cham câu câu. | Cede territory. Mix evenly. |
| 23 | tĭ kha pun cúi kuah kàu kĭa kĭa. | The foundation has been cut off sharp by the water. |

## LESSON LXXXVI.

| | | | |
|---|---|---|---|
| 東 | tang; east. | 秋 | chiu; autumn. |
| 西 | sai; west. | 冬 | tang; winter. |
| 南 | lâm; south. | 季 | khùi; season; crop. |
| 北 | pak; north. | 逢 | hông; meet unexpectedly. |
| 春 | chun; spring. | 再 | cài; again; likewise. |
| 夏 | hē; summer. | 旬 | * cûn; moment. |

| | | | |
|---|---|---|---|
| 1 | lú kâi sìo kuah pàng úa. | 1 | Turn your account over to me. |
| 2 | kuah cò nǒ pôi$^{n}$. | 2 | Cut it into two portions. |
| 3 | sa$^{n}$ sì ie$^{n}$ cham cò cêk ē. | 3 | Three or four kinds mingled. |
| 4 | cham ke cêk choh lôh khù. | 4 | Mix in a little more. |
| 5 | mài cham tîeh m̄ hó kâi. | 5 | Do not mix in the bad ones. |
| 6 | mài sie cham. | 6 | Do not mingle them. |
| 7 | cí īe$^{n}$ mûeh cham tîeh hú ie$^{n}$ bô ēng khù. | 7 | This sort is so mixed with that as to be rendered useless. |
| 8 | buah m̄ câu. | 8 | Not rubbed on evenly. |
| 9 | tăi ke pun câu câu. | 9 | All share alike. |
| 10 | sai pak. tang lâm. | 10 | Northwest. Southeast. |
| 11 | tang pak. sai lâm. | 11 | Southwest. Northeast. |
| 12 | lú kâi chun chiu jîeh cōi? | 12 | How advanced in years are you? |
| 13 | chun khùi kâi i hôk. | 13 | Autumn garments. |
| 14 | ko bâk hông chun cài hwt gê. | 14 | Sere trees bud again in spring-time. |
| 15 | chun hun, chiu hun, jît mê pê$^{n}$ pun. | 15 | At the vernal and autumnal equinox, the days and nights are equal. |
| 16 | sî sî hông tîeh i. | 16 | Always coming across him. |
| 17 | hē húe thi$^{n}$. | 17 | The hot season. |
| 18 | ôih lō sie hông. | 18 | Met in a narrow path. |
| 19 | tang jît khó ài. | 19 | The winter sun is desirable. |
| 20 | cêk nî sì khùi. | 20 | One year has four seasons. |
| 21 | cīe$^{n}$ khùi, ĕ khui. | 21 | Early and late crop. |
| 22 | úa cí cûn kàu, | 22 | I this instant arrived. |
| 23 | cí cûn mûeh tîeh khù. | 23 | Must go this instant. |
| 24 | lú cí cûn tà$^{n}$ kâi. | 24 | What you just now say. |
| 25 | hú cêk cûn ŭ. | 25 | At that moment there was. |

## LESSON LXXXVII.

擘 peh; sunder; break in two.
半 pùa$^{n}$; half; part of.
半 * ùe; a piece of; half.
答 tap; reply.
插 chah; insert.
鑿 châk; chisel.

祈 khî; pray.
禱 táu; suplicate.
跪 kūi; kneel.
緣 îen; cause.
故 kù; reason.
因 in; because.

---

1 lú cài tà$^{n}$ mêng pêh.
2 i sī pak pôi$^{n}$ lâi kâi.
3 i hē thi$^{n}$ sī khù pak thâu.
4 tang thi$^{n}$ sī ngân.
5 lú tāng soi$^{n}$ ía sī mài hiah, cí cūn cíu kàu.
6 tang thi$^{n}$ sī cháu bâk lóng cóng ko ta. kù chú.
7 lú m̄ hó cài cìe$^{n}$ se$^{n}$.
8 úa cài sa$^{n}$ kio i tà$^{n}$.
9 úa cài m̄ lâi líu.
10 che$^{n}$ chun put lâi.
11 peh m̄ khui.
12 cêk tōa pùa$^{n}$. kù ì.
13 pùa$^{n}$ mê. pùa$^{n}$ jît.
14 pùa$^{n}$ sì. pùa$^{n}$ cú.
15 cêk nâng, pùa$^{n}$ nâng.
16 bô pùa$^{n}$ nâng tō.
17 pùa$^{n}$ lō. bô îen bô kù.
18 pùa$^{n}$ ū, pùa$^{n}$ bô.
19 lâu cêk ùe pun úa.
20 cham cêk síe ùe cíu hó.
21 i ìn tap m̄ lâi.
22 chah bōi tit jîp.
23 cí kâi khang chak tōa cē. in ūi tîeh.
24 ū sih mih îen kù?
25 kūi lôh khù, khî táu.

1 Please repeat it clearly.
2 They come fom the north.
3 They go north in summer.
4 In winter it is cold.
5 If you had not before stopped, you would now have arrived.
6 In winter, vegetation is all dried up. Therefore.
7 Do not again do so.
8 I told him again and again.
9 I'll never come again.
10 Youthful days never return.
11 Did not succeed in sundering.
12 The larger portion. Obstinate.
13 Midnight. Half a day.
14 Middle aged. Son-in-law.
15 Scarcely any body.
16 Nobody at all there.
17 Halfway. No reason for it.
18 Now it appears, then it is gone.
19 Keep a half for me.
20 Mix in less than half.
21 He could not answer.
22 Not succeed in inserting it.
23 Chisel this hole out a little larger. Because.
24 What is the cause of it?
26 Kneel down and pray.

## LESSON LXXXVIII.

| | |
|---|---|
| 猴 kâu; monkey. | 倒 tó; fall over. |
| 鼠 chú; rat species. | 顛 tin; tien; apex; upset. |
| 兎 thò; hare. | 倒 tò; táu; invert; pour out. |
| 獺 thoah; beaver. | 縛 pâk; fasten; bind. |
| 甕 àng; a jar. | 果 kúa$^n$; really; truly. |
| 末 bûah; leavings; powder. | 然 jîen; truly; however. |

| | |
|---|---|
| 1 cí cêk ûe pun pât nâng. | 1 Give this piece to some one else. |
| 2 kuah cêk pùa$^n$. | 2 Cut off half of it. |
| 3 lú cêk ûe, úa cêk ûe. | 3 You half and I half. |
| 4 in ūi tīeh cí kìa$^n$ sū. | 4 Because of this affair. |
| 5 mài tin tò cò. | 5 Do not make it upside down. |
| 6 úa hàm lú cìe$^n$ se$^n$, lú tin tò hìe$^n$ se$^n$. | 6 I tell you this way, and you do the other way. |
| 7 mài tien tien táu táu. | 7 Do not turn things upside down. |
| 8 i pùa$^n$ mê kàu. | 8 He arrived at midnight. |
| 9 lâi ū pùa$^n$ kâi gûeh. | 9 Came a fortnight ago. |
| 10 ûn in i kâi a hia$^n$ bô lâi. | 10 Because his brother did not come. |
| 11 hāi i tó lôh khì. | 11 Made it tumble down. |
| 12 i kìa$^n$ kàu pùa$^n$ mê. | 12 He walked till midnight. |
| 13 kâi, pùa$^n$ kâi, ū. | 13 There is scarcely one. |
| 14 kìa$^n$ kàu pùa$^n$ lō cìu hiah. | 14 Went half way, then stopped. |
| 15 gûeh pùa$^n$ kha àì$^n$ khì. | 15 Will go the middle of the month. |
| 16 pùa$^n$ pêh, pùa$^n$ o. | 16 Mottled black and white. |
| 17 ûn in sī cò nī? | 17 Why is all this? |
| 18 cío pue pùa$^n$ thi$^n$. | 18 Bird flying in mid heaven. |
| 19 pùa$^n$ thi$^n$ lûi. | 19 A species of noisy beetle. |
| 20 i lâi pài hāu lú. | 20 He comes to pay his respects to you. |
| 21 a mú nâng sô chah kâi ûgn hue. tò tìo. | 21 Women's head ornaments. Pour it out. |
| 22 kúa$^n$ jîen sī. | 22 It is certainly so. |
| 23 nō kâi se$^n$ lâi jîen jîen. | 23 The two are precisely alike. |
| 24 îeh bûah. pêh îeh bûah. | 24 Powdered medicine. Quinine. |
| 25 pâk kàu kín kín. | 25 Fasten it tight. |
| 26 tò pàng úa$^n$ kò. | 26 Pour it into a bowl. |
| 27 tie$^n$ cò kúi àng. | 27 Decant it into several jars. |

## LESSON LXXXIX.

| | | | |
|---|---|---|---|
| 切 | * côih; to slice; mince. | 圈 | kho; a circle. |
| 截 | coĭh; intercept; cut off. | 靜 | cĕⁿ; quiet; still. |
| 午 | * kùa; period of six hours. | 默 | * tīam; still; silent. |
| 槽 | cô; a trough. | 井 | céⁿ; a well. |
| 溝 | kau; a ditch. | 號 | hō; a sign; mark. |
| 袋 | tō; a pocket; bag. | 而 | jû; yet; but; still. |

| | |
|---|---|
| 1 kó cá ŭ, hīn kim bô. | 1 Anciently there was, but there are none now-a-days. |
| 2 jīak jîen sī. | 2 If it is really so. |
| 3 kīam chài àng. | 3 The hollow above the collar bone. |
| 4 ka kī cŭ seⁿ jîen. | 4 It is itself naturally so. |
| 5 cúi àng. hûi àng. | 5 Water jar. Earthen jar. |
| 6 tāu gê àng. cīeh àng. | 6 Bean-sprout jar. Stone jar. |
| 7 tò tê lâi cīah. | 7 Pour out some tea to drink. |
| 8 phah tó. phah m̄ tó. kho tīo. | 8 Knock down. Did not succeed in knocking down. Blot out. |
| 9 tó tŏ tī. pò tō. | 9 Fell on the ground. Bag. |
| 10 côih cêk kò mī pau. | 10 Cut a piece of bread. |
| 11 tŏ pùaⁿ lō khut i côih cŭ. côih cŭ. | 11 Was stopped by him midway. Intercept. |
| 12 côih cò sì côih. | 12 Cut it into four slices. |
| 13 jû kúaⁿ sī cīeⁿ seⁿ. | 13 If it be really so. |
| 14 cŭ jîen, jû jîen. | 14 Underived, self-existent. |
| 15 só íⁿ jîen. tháng kho kha. | 15 These reasons. Bandy legged. |
| 16 tng jîen kâi lí. | 16 Its natural properties. |
| 17 cīeⁿ kùa; ĕ kùa. | 17 Forenoon; afternoon. |
| 18 mê kùa; jīt kùa. | 18 Night time; daytime. |
| 19 jû kim, jû ău. | 19 Now and henceforth. |
| 20 ngŏ nâng jû íⁿ. | 20 Five men in all. |
| 21 cí kâi jû íⁿ. | 21 Only this and nothing more. |
| 22 tīam cĕⁿ kâi tī hng. | 22 A quiet spot. |
| 23 lú hó tīam tīam. | 23 You keep still. |
| 24 bé cô. cúi kau. tháng kho. | 24 Manger. Drain. Hoops. |
| 25 n̂gn tō. céⁿ kho. | 25 Purse. Well rounds. |

# LESSON XC.

失 sit; lose; slip; err.
祠 sû; sacrifice to ancestors.
拗 áu; twist off; break.
拗 * á; snap; break.
折 cìh; snap in two.
折 * cih; compensate.

稱 cheng; denominate.
稱 chèng; fit; corresponding.
呼 hu; breath out; call.
碎 chùi; fragments.
醉 cùi; drunken.
哩 lī; adverbial particle denoting excessively.

| | | |
|---|---|---|
| 1 | i kâi sa$^{n}$ ŭ kâi àm tē. | Her dress had a secret pocket. |
| 2 | úa kho cè hē. | I will make a circle for a mark. |
| 3 | lú kâi phò hē, cè mih hē? | What is the sign of your shop? |
| 4 | i cè kâi àm hē. | He made a secret sign. |
| 5 | i àm cĕ$^{n}$ cè kâi sū, ta$^{n}$ híen hīn chut lâi líɑ. | What he did secretly, is now come to light. |
| 6 | ngio chú. ngio chú kía$^{n}$. | Rat. Mouse. |
| 7 | i cŏ tŏ cé$^{n}$ kî$^{n}$. | He sat beside the well. |
| 8 | ua$^{n}$ cĕ$^{n}$. àm cĕ$^{n}$. | Quietly. Privately. |
| 9 | buah o cè hē. | Blacken it for a mark. |
| 10 | lō li hn̆g, tó li khùn. | The road long, the belly empty. |
| 11 | cí tîo cúi kau khah ôih īa khah chíen. cíu cùi. | This ditch is too narrow and too shallow. Drunk. |
| 12 | thi$^{n}$ li lêh hŏ. pùa$^{n}$ kâi n̂gn. | It rains so. Half-dollar. |
| 13 | úa li m̄ tán lú. | I shan't wait for you. |
| 14 | àm cĕ$^{n}$ cîah cî$^{n}$. | Take a bribe. |
| 15 | sit ì; sit sim. | Miss his purpose; lose heart. |
| 16 | àm cĕ$^{n}$ thàn. àm cĕ$^{n}$ thói$^{n}$. | Secret gain. Secretly saw. |
| 17 | àm coh cĕ$^{n}$. sit lói. | Prowling about. Disrespectful. |
| 18 | sit chíu; sit kha. | Lose hold; slip up. |
| 19 | sit húe. sit cúi. | Catch fire. Slip into the water. |
| 20 | bw̄n bê cêk sit. | Not the least mistake in it. |
| 21 | sit sîn. sit sé. | Absent minded. Driven homeless. |
| 22 | sû tn̂g. se$^{n}$ sû. | Ancestral hall. Image of one living. |
| 23 | cih cè jîeh cōi cî$^{n}$? | How much in compensation? |
| 24 | áu cìh; á cìh. | Bend to breaking; snap short off. |
| 25 | cih cîah. cheng hu. | Pay for rations. Designate. |
| 26 | chèng ì. pò chùi. | Suit the taste. Rags. |

## LESSON XCI.

成 sîa$^{n}$; a tenth; full.
漿 cie$^{n}$; a thick fluid.
扇 sì$^{n}$; a fan.
銼 chò; file.
斧 pó; hatchet; to hack.
鋤 tâ; hoe; mattock.

汁 cap; juice; sap.
弄 * mûeh; meddle with.
漏 lāu; leak; filter.
挖 * líu; to dig out.
掘 kût; dig; delve.
斷 tn̂g; break off.

1 cîa$^{n}$ jît. cêk sîa$^{n}$ sìo.
2 cih cò chit sîa$^{n}$ sn̂g.
3 i ài$^{n}$ poih sîa$^{n}$.
4 bô sîa$^{n}$ sìo.
5 bí cie$^{n}$. mī cie$^{n}$. cúi cie$^{n}$.
6 ài$^{n}$ líu tī kha.
7 cúi lāu. ŏi lāu a bŏi?
8 ah mô sì$^{n}$. chù téng ŏi lāu.
9 pó thâu. tâ thâu. ki chò.
10 ēng tâ thâu kio úa kût tn̂g.
11 cí tîo soh ài$^{n}$ tn̂g.
12 khat i mûeh tīo.
13 pó thâu pàng tŏ chīu kha.
14 lá kâi tâ thâu mài líu tn̂g cí câng chīu kan.
15 hâ cap lāu chut kwn gūa. kût pó.
16 lá mài mûeh tīo cí ki chò.
17 cí tîo thih, ēng chò lâi chò tn̂g.
18 mài kût khah chim.
19 cap lāu tīo sa$^{n}$ sîa$^{n}$ khà.
20 cí īe$^{n}$ kúe cí ío ŭ cap.
21 cang pó thâu tok chùi chùi. líu kâi khang.
22 lá mài mûeh tîeh úa.
23 líu cé$^{n}$. gô mô sì$^{n}$.
24 cí lîap ka$^{n}$ bô mih cap.

1 The entire day. A tenth of them.
2 A dividend of seven tenths.
3 He wants eighty per cent.
4 Not the full number.
5 Congee. Starch. Broth.
6 Will dig the foundation.
7 A filter. Does it leak?
8 Duck's feather fan. The roof leaks.
9 An axe. A hoe. A file.
10 Chop it off for me with the hoe.
11 This rope is going to break.
12 Destroyed by him.
13 Put the axe by the tree.
14 Do not, in digging, cut off this root with the hoe.
15 The fish gravy has leaked out of the pot. A pick.
16 Do not handle and spoil this file.
17 File this bar of iron in two with a file.
18 Do not dig too deep.
19 Three tenths of the sap has run out.
20 This sort of fruit is more juicy.
21 Take an axe and cut it up fine. Dig a hole.
22 Do not meddle with me.
23 Dig a well. Goose feather fan.
24 This orange is not very juicy.

## LESSON XCII.

| | | | |
|---|---|---|---|
| 螺 | lô; spiral; a conch. | 香 | hiang; hie$^{n}$; fragrant. |
| 螄 | si; spiral shells. | 氣 | khì; breath; vital force. |
| 熏 | hun; fumigate; smoke. | 腿 | thúi; the thigh. |
| 烟 | in; smoke; vapour. | 指 | * cói$^{n}$; cńg; toes; fingers. |
| 霧 | bū; mist; vapour. | 指 | cí; kí; to point; refer. |
| 濛 | mông; fog; small rain. | 遮 | cia; screen; cover. |

| | | | |
|---|---|---|---|
| 1 | lô khak. lô si. | 1 | Sea shells. Corkscrew. |
| 2 | hun nêk. hun ta. | 2 | Smoked meat. Dry at a fire. |
| 3 | cúi hun. hun tîng. | 3 | Smoking tobacco. Tobacco pipe. |
| 4 | pue chú. in tâng. | 4 | Flying squirrel. Chimney. |
| 5 | pàng in húe. cîah hun. | 5 | Let off fireworks. To smoke. |
| 6 | hie$^{n}$ in. o in. | 6 | Smoke of pastilles. Lamp-black. |
| 7 | cúi in. húe hun cûn. | 7 | Steam. Steam boat. |
| 8 | húe chia. thi$^{n}$ hwt bū. | 8 | Steam-car. It is misty. |
| 9 | pùa$^{n}$ sua$^{n}$ ìn bū. | 9 | Low thick vapour. |
| 10 | sòi hŏ mông mông. | 10 | Drizzling mist. |
| 11 | thi$^{n}$ sî hwt mông. | 11 | The weather is foggy. |
| 12 | sie hie$^{n}$. kîa$^{n}$ hie$^{n}$. | 12 | Burn incense. Worship. |
| 13 | hie$^{n}$ hu. hie$^{n}$ lô. | 13 | Ashes of incense. Incense pot. |
| 14 | tíam kúi kí hie$^{n}$. | 14 | Light a few incense sticks. |
| 15 | hie$^{n}$ châ. hie$^{n}$ bûah. | 15 | Sandal-wood. Incense powder. |
| 16 | i khui hie$^{n}$ phò. | 16 | He has an incense shop. |
| 17 | hiang khì. tê hiang. | 17 | Fragrance. Aroma of tea. |
| 18 | sîn khì. bô sîn khì. | 18 | Vitality. No vigor. |
| 19 | lú cîe$^{n}$ sî kâi khì sek hó. | 19 | Your countenance is healthy. |
| 20 | huang khì pē$^{n}$. se$^{n}$ khì. | 20 | Miasmatic disease. Get angry. |
| 21 | hong khì. khì sí nâng. | 21 | Climate. Exasperate one. |
| 22 | lîah i lâi chut khì. | 22 | Bring him to vent spite on. |
| 23 | chiu thi$^{n}$ hó thi$^{n}$ khì. | 23 | Fine autumn weather. |
| 24 | hē thi$^{n}$ kâi thi$^{n}$ khì jûah. | 24 | Summer weather is hot. |
| 25 | mài phī$^{n}$ tîeh thô khì. | 25 | Don't breath the malaria. |
| 26 | thi$^{n}$ khì. khì lât. | 26 | Temperature. Energy. |
| 27 | hŏ cia. cia jît. | 27 | Umbrella. Screen from the sun. |
| 28 | lú kí úa thói$^{n}$. | 28 | You point it out to me. |

汕頭方言初階



## LESSON XCIII.

| | | | |
|---|---|---|---|
| 氣 | * khùi; nervous matter. | 劍 | kìam; straight sword. |
| 避 | pī; avoid; escape. | 鞍 | uaⁿ; saddle. |
| 閃 | síam; evade; spun. | 步 | pō; step; pace. |
| 壁 | piah; partition; wall. | 傘 | sùaⁿ; umbrella; shelter. |
| 影 | íaⁿ; shadow; image. | 表 | * pie; a watch. |
| 帓 | * mua; shawl; wrap. | 糞 | pùn; ordure. |

| | |
|---|---|
| 1 i ŭ khùi ŭ lât. | 1 He has stamina. |
| 2 i bŏ kò chut khùi. | 2 No way to vent his feelings. |
| 3 i sim khùi thìaⁿ. | 3 His nerves are disordered. |
| 4 lŏh kha khùi. | 4 Lose strength in the legs. |
| 5 pī sì. jìt íaⁿ. | 5 Seclude one's self. A shadow. |
| 6 pī cêk pôiⁿ, khut i kùe. | 6 Dodge one side to let him pass. |
| 7 keh piah. kìa piah. | 7 Partition wall. Precipice. |
| 8 cìeh piah. chíeⁿ piah. | 8 A cliff. Dividing wall. |
| 9 keh piah kâi. cêk nía mua. | 9 Next door neighbours. A shawl. |
| 10 mīn piah. gûeh íaⁿ. | 10 Opposite wall. Night shadow. |
| 11 nâng íaⁿ. hue íaⁿ. | 11 Person's shadow. Shadow of plants. |
| 12 ŭ íaⁿ. bŏ íaⁿ. | 12 Evident. Without evidence. |
| 13 tŏ íaⁿ. tîo mua. | 13 Cast a reflection. A long shawl. |
| 14 mua cêk nía mua. | 14 Wrap up in a shawl. |
| 15 mua tŏ sin tèng. | 15 Wrapped around the person. |
| 16 kìam nêk, kìam khak. | 16 Sword and scabbard. |
| 17 i kâi cìh lāi căi, kio kìam cêk ieⁿ. cí mih sŭ? | 17 He is very sarcastic. What does it refer to? |
| 18 i kâi ie kùa ki kìam. | 18 He wore a dirk. |
| 19 phīⁿ uaⁿ. bé uaⁿ. | 19 Bridge of the nose. A saddle. |
| 20 cŏ tŏ bé uaⁿ téng. | 20 Sit on a saddle. |
| 21 bé tîeh ŭ uaⁿ cŏ khù cìaⁿ ún. | 21 There must be a saddle on the horse in order to sit steadily. |
| 22 pō kìaⁿ. cêk pō cêk pō. | 22 Go on foot. Step by step. |
| 23 cò sŭ tîeh lâu tī pō. | 23 Leave some room for grace. |
| 24 lêng kìaⁿ, hóⁿ pō. | 24 A proud bearing. |
| 25 gŏ kìaⁿ, ah pō. | 25 A mediocre appearance. |
| 26 hŏ sùaⁿ. sì pie. pûi pùn. | 26 Umbrella. A watch. Manure. |

## LESSON XCIV.

| | |
|---|---|
| 表 pío; make known. | 撐 the$^n$; to pole a boat. |
| 陰 im; obscure; dark. | 辮 pi$^n$; the queu. |
| 陽 îang; brilliant; male. | 辮 pī$^n$; to braid. |
| 雹 phâk; hail. | 犁 lôi; plough. |
| 槳 cíe$^n$; an oar. | 照 cìe; enlighten; like. |
| 棹 * kò; to row. | 刷 sueh; brush; brush on. |

| | | |
|---|---|---|
| 1 | kio úa pío mêng pêh. | Represent it plainly to me. |
| 2 | pío chut i kâi khî ī. | Disclose its wonders. |
| 3 | píe chin. | Relatives of a different surname. |
| 4 | im kan. îang kan. | Hades. The land of the living. |
| 5 | im lîang. thi$^n$ sī im im. | Cool and shady. Dull weather. |
| 6 | kuang im. im îang. | Duration. The dual powers. |
| 7 | cí lăi khah im. | It is too dark in here. |
| 8 | sieh chùn im. | Improve the moments. |
| 9 | thài îang, thài im. | The sun and moon. |
| 10 | lôh phâk. cìe piah. | To hail. Illuminated wall. |
| 11 | cìe kì$^n$ thong sin. | Illuminate the body. |
| 12 | gûeh cìe jīp pâng lăi. | The moon shines into the room. |
| 13 | jīt cìe. sueh pêh. | The sun shines. To whitewash. |
| 14 | cìe kì$^n$ nâng ía$^n$. | Reflect one's image. |
| 15 | cìe lú tà$^n$. hŵn cìe. | As you say. Reflected light. |
| 16 | cìe koi chī kâi ïe$^n$. | According to the market. |
| 17 | cìe cí kâi ïe$^n$ khì cò. | Make according to this pattern. |
| 18 | tìo kúi ki teng lâng cìe kàu lō kng kng. | Hang up some lanterns to light the road. |
| 19 | cêk ki sueh kía$^n$. | A white-wash brush. |
| 20 | poih cíe$^n$ cûn. | An eight oared boat. |
| 21 | sī ài$^n$ the$^n$ a sī ài$^n$ kò? | Shall we pole or row? |
| 22 | pi$^n$ kio úa pī$^n$ hó. | Braid my queu for me. |
| 23 | chân ēng gû khì lôi. | Take the ox to plough the field. |
| 24 | cieh kâi lôi lâi lôi chân. | Borrow a plough for ploughing. |
| 25 | khîeh sa$^n$ ki cíe$^n$ lôh cûn. | Take three oars to the boat. |
| 26 | pì ki kìam tŏ sin tèng. | Carry a rapier on the person. |
| 27 | bô kha pō, bô nâng ía$^n$. | No signs of it. |

汕頭方言初階



# LESSON XCV.

命 mīa; life; lot; fate.
命 mĕng; command; charge.
蜂 phang; bee; wasp.
蜜 bı̂t; honey; sweet.
嶼 sṳ̆; an island.
鎖 sɵ́; lock.
蓮 nôi; lily; lotus.
麻 mûa; hemp.
穀 * kak; grains; corn.
菽 * sek; soy; pulse.
麥 bêh; wheat.
蠟 lâh; wax.

1 cáu khṳ̀ síam hŏ.
2 síam mn̂g. cṳ kı̀am.
3 tɵ kı̀am. hɵ́ mīa.
4 khó mīa. thien mĕng.
5 sèⁿ mīa. sǹg mīa.
6 ŏi cîah tn̂g mīa.
7 tɵ́ mīa. uaⁿ mīa.
8 it it jû mĕng.
9 sŭn i kâi mĕng.
10 úa mĕng i cɵ̀ cìeⁿ seⁿ.
11 mīa pɵ̂h. seⁿ mīa.
12 bı̂t phang. n̂g phang.
13 úa khó mīa nâng.
14 phang bı̂t. tı̂am kùe bı̂t.
15 sɵ́ sı̂. sɵ́ thâu.
16 sɵ́ mn̂g. nôi hue.
17 bı̂t lâh. ngŏ kak.
18 bɵ̂ suaⁿ bɵ̂ sṳ̆.
19 nôi khui hue lío.
20 mûa tāu sek bêh.
21 bɵ̂ hŏ, bí bŏi hwt khí lâi, nâng gɵ̄ sí.
22 hái sṳ̆. mı̄ bêh.
23 cí kâi sṳ̆ kìe cɵ̀ mih mîa?
24 pak bêh cɵ̀ mı̄ ío hɵ́ cîah. bêh chân.
25 nôi hue khui kâi sı̂ hāu kìe cɵ̀ hē thiⁿ.

1 Run under shelter from rain.
2 Screen doors. Students' rapier.
3 Weapons. Happy lot.
4 Luckless. Fate.
5 Existence. Calculate fortunes.
6 Have a long life.
7 Short-lived. Easy life.
8 Everything done as required.
9 Obey his commands.
10 I ordered him to do so.
11 Luck is bad. Horoscope.
12 Honey bee. Hornet.
13 I am an ill-fated one.
14 Honey. Sweeter than honey.
15 Key. A lock.
16 Lock the door. Lotus flower.
17 Beeswax. All kinds of grains.
18 The open sea.
19 The lotus has blossomed.
20 All sorts of crops.
21 If there be no rain the rice does not come up, and people starve.
22 Islands. Wheat.
23 What is this island called?
24 The northern wheat makes better flour. Wheat-field.
25 The time when lilies blossom is called summer.

## LESSON XCVI.

雀 chiak; ciah; sparrow.
露 lō; dew.
霜 sng; frost.
冰 pia$^n$; ice.
旗 kî; a flag.
收 siu; receive; gather in.

執 * khîa; to hold; carry.
執 cip; retain; engage in.
鑽 cǹg; auger.
銃 chèng; gun.
鑼 lô; gongs.
鼓 kó; drums.

| | |
|---|---|
| 1 mûa ciah cío. nôi cí. | 1 The house sparrow. Lotus seeds. |
| 2 n̂g chiak. phah chèng. | 2 Goldfinch. Fire a gun. |
| 3 khîa hŏ sùa$^n$. cǹg kía$^n$. | 3 Carry an umbrella. Gimlet. |
| 4 khîa pit ǹi$^n$ cìa$^n$. | 4 Should hold the pen upright. |
| 5 lṳ́ thói$^n$ i kâi chíu tèng khîa ki mih mûeh? | 5 What do you think that is which he holds in his hand? |
| 6 chíu khîa ki sì$^n$. | 6 Held a fan in his hand. |
| 7 kak cip cêk ì. | 7 Each retains his own notions. |
| 8 kak cip cêk sueh. cip ì. | 8 Each holds to his own explanation. Obstinate. |
| 9 kak cip cêk lí. | 9 Each maintains his own doctrine. |
| 10 lṳ́ īa sĭ cip ka kī kâi ì, sṳ̄ cĭu m̄ tît. | 10 If you persist in your own idea the matter will not be settled. |
| 11 kâi nâng cip cêk kĭa$^n$ sṳ̄. | 11 Each man attends to one sort of business. |
| 12 cip sṳ̄ jîeh cōi nâng? | 12 How many managers are there? |
| 13 hue lō cúi. lō cúi tăng. | 13 Perfumery. Heavy dew. |
| 14 mé jît, tăng lō. | 14 Hot sun makes heavy dew. |
| 15 thi$^n$ sî tăi chìn, lôh sng lôh seh. hue kî. | 15 Very cold weather with frost and snow. U. S. flag. |
| 16 sng sĭ thi$^n$ téng lôh kâi; pia$^n$ sĭ cúi kat kâi. | 16 Frost falls from the sky; ice is congealed water. |
| 17 khîa kî cò hō. | 17 Hold up a flag as a signal. |
| 18 ngŏ kak tōa siu sêng. | 18 The harvest home. |
| 19 chèng îeh, chèng cí. | 19 Powder and shot. |
| 20 siu kuah. siu khí. | 20 Reap the harvest. Gather up. |
| 21 siu phò. phah kó. | 21 Shut up shop. Beating drums. |
| 22 siu bói. phah lô. | 22 Buyer. Sound gongs. |

## LESSON XCVII.

| | |
|---|---|
| 搥 tûi; to beat; pommel. | 猜 chai; ieh; guess; doubt. |
| 鎚 thûi; hammer; mallet. | 血 hueh; blood. |
| 槌 thûi; beetle; club. | 燭 cek; candle. |
| 舀 ío; íe; to bale out; dip. | 臺 thâi; tâi; stand; platform. |
| 搖 îo; îe; to wag; rock. | 送 sàng; present; wait on. |
| 殺 suah; thâi; to kill. | 鹿 têk; a deer. |

| | | |
|---|---|---|
| 1 | saⁿ kak bêh. tûi phah. | Buckwheat. To thump. |
| 2 | tûi saⁿ cîeh. | Stone to pound clothes on. |
| 3 | tûi îeh. tûi lô kó. | Pound up drugs. Strike gongs. |
| 4 | jú tûi ke ē, jú hó. | The more you pound it the better. |
| 5 | ēng thih thûi khà tûi, m̄ hó ēng châ thûi. | Use a hammer to pound it, do not use a beetle. |
| 6 | phah thih thûi. phah kó thûi. | A sledge hammer. Drumstick. |
| 7 | tâng lô thûi. tâng thûi. | Gong hammer. A mace. |
| 8 | íe cêk tōa úaⁿ. | Bale out a big bowl full. |
| 9 | íe m̄ ta. | You can't bale it dry. |
| 10 | íe mài khah tīⁿ. | Do not dip it too full. |
| 11 | îe thâu, îe chíu. | Shake the head, and the hand. |
| 12 | îe lâi îe khù. | Rock back and forth. |
| 13 | îe i câu. | Shake it up thoroughly. |
| 14 | mài suah seⁿ mīa. | Do no murder. |
| 15 | thâi nâng, pàng húe. | Murder and arson. |
| 16 | thâi thâu. suah sí. | Decapitate. Put to death. |
| 17 | suah seⁿ. thâi sí nâng. | Butcher animals. Murder. |
| 18 | lú ieh thóiⁿ sī sih mûeh. | You guess what it is. |
| 19 | lú kâi sim mài thèng chai. | Do not be curious. |
| 20 | ieh m̄ tîeh. lú chai thói. | Can't guess. Guess at it. |
| 21 | ciang lâi jîak àiⁿ thâi i. tûi ie. | If in future you wish to kill it—Thump the loins. |
| 22 | suah hueh. cek tâi. | Shed its blood. Candlestick. |
| 23 | têng tâi. lâu thâi. | A trellis. A platform. |
| 24 | sàng lói mûeh. | Make formal presents. |
| 25 | sàng kîaⁿ. têk kak. | Accompany. Antlers. |
| 26 | lâh cek. têk nêk. | Wax taper. Venison. |

# LESSON XCVIII.

棺 kuaⁿ; kwn; coffin.
跨 * hûah; to straddle.
籐 tîn; rattan.
織 cit; keⁿ; weave.
嘑 * hā; roar; hum.
吐 thò; to vomit.
踏 tâh; to tread on.
舉 kṳ́; elevate.
動 tŏng; tāng; shake.
轎 kīe; sedan chair.
湧 éng; waves.
罪 cŭe; sin; offense.

| | | |
|---|---|---|
| 1 | sŭn huang siang sàng. | May you have a fair wind. |
| 2 | sàng khut lṳ́. | I give this to you. |
| 3 | sie sàng. tîn íⁿ. | Reciprocate gifts. Rattan chair. |
| 4 | kìu seⁿ mīa. sàng i khṳ̀. | Save life. Accompany him. |
| 5 | sàng sŭn huang. kīe hu. | Favorable wind. Chair bearers. |
| 6 | lṳ́ sàng i kàu tī kò? | How far did you go with him? |
| 7 | i sàng lṳ́ kúi kīaⁿ mûeh. | He presents you several things. |
| 8 | cí kâi sī nâng sàng kâi. | This was a present. |
| 9 | kuaⁿ bâk. hā hā kìe. | A coffin.. Gurgle. |
| 10 | siu kwn. kúi tîo tîn. | To encoffin. Several rattans. |
| 11 | i būe ŭ siu kwn. | He is not yet encoffined. |
| 12 | hûah m̄ kùe. hûah kùe. kha tâh. | Can't straddle across. Straddled across. Foot-stool. |
| 13 | ío tŏng nâng sim. | Agitate the feelings. |
| 14 | cit pò: keⁿ pò. cŏ kīe. | Weave cloth. Go in a sedan. |
| 15 | cit cháu chîeh; cit chíu kun. | Weave matting; weave napkins. |
| 16 | cit chut ŭ hue jī. | Weave in figures. |
| 17 | mài hā hā kìe. | Do not vociferate. |
| 18 | chīu, khut huang chue tîeh, hā hā kìe. | The trees, blown by the wind, reverberate. |
| 19 | nâng bé hā hā kìe tùi cí kò kùe. kng kīe. | A crowd went clamoring past here. Bear a sedan. |
| 20 | kha tâh íⁿ. kha mài tâh. | Foot-stool. Don't tread on it. |
| 21 | lṳ́ mài tâh tîeh úa. | Do not you step on me. |
| 22 | kṳ́ chíu. kong kṳ́ kâi nâng. | Raise the hand. Candidate put forth by the public. |
| 23 | kṳ́ tŏng tōa pāng. | A good deportment. |
| 24 | kṳ́ mâk bô chin. | A stranger in a strange land. |

## LESSON XCIX.

| | | | |
|---|---|---|---|
| 脫 | thut; escape; relinquish. | 價 | kè; price. |
| 脫 | * thǹg; pak; strip; take off. | 貨 | hùe; wares. |
| 穿 | * chēng; put on garments. | 界 | kài; boundary. |
| 穿 | * chng; perforate; bore. | 髓 | chúe; marrow. |
| 篩 | thai; sieve; sift. | 骨 | kut; bone. |
| 値 | * tâk; worth; value. | 橋 | kîe; bridge. |

| | |
|---|---|
| 1 úa bô̤ pńg cîⁿ, phò lăi bô̤ hùe. | 1 I have no capital, so my shop has no stock. |
| 2 bói sih mih kè cîⁿ, lṳ́ hó̤ tàⁿ mêng. | 2 Tell plainly what price you bought it for. |
| 3 cí sang ôi sih mih kè cîⁿ? tâk cîⁿ. | 3 What is the price of this pair of shoes? Costly. |
| 4 pak chiah kha. pak tīo bō̤. | 4 Bare-footed. Take off a hat. |
| 5 bé uaⁿ kîe. chēng saⁿ. | 5 An arched bridge. Wear clothes. |
| 6 thut phûe. chng cîⁿ. | 6 Cast the skin. String cash. |
| 7 thâu khak kng kng; bô̤ tì bō̤. | 7 Bare-headed; no hat on. |
| 8 khó̤ íⁿ thut sin. | 8 Managed to escape. |
| 9 cí kâi nâng sĭm sì thut sôk. | 9 This person is very refined. |
| 10 bô̤ kò̤ hó̤ chut thut. | 10 No way of egress. |
| 11 thǹg tīo saⁿ. thǹg tīo ôi. | 11 Undress. Take off your shoes. |
| 12 chēng tn̂g saⁿ. kut thâu. | 12 Wear a long gown. The bones. |
| 13 thut tīo i kâi chin. | 13 Break off a betrothal. |
| 14 chng hīⁿ. chēng khò. | 14 Perforate the ears. Put on trowsers. |
| 15 i kâi i hôk chēng chut lâi sĭm hó̤ thóiⁿ. tī kài. | 15 She was very prettily dressed. A boundary. |
| 16 chng hó̤, tìo pàng chīu tèng. | 16 Bore a hole through it and hang it up in a tree. |
| 17 sî kè. chĭ kè. | 17 Current rate. Market price. |
| 18 kè cîⁿ kùi căi. | 18 The price is exorbitant. |
| 19 bô̤ kè. bô̤ tàⁿ kè. | 19 Priceless. No false price. |
| 20 sît kè. bô̤ nŏ̤ kè. | 20 The real price. No two prices. |
| 21 hùe mûeh. pêh kut. | 21 Stock in trade. Dry bones. |
| 22 kak īeⁿ hùe se, m̄ tân. | 22 All descriptions of goods. |
| 23 kut nêk. hṳ̂ thâu chúe. | 23 Blood relations. Fish brains. |

## LESSON C.

| | |
|---|---|
| 趕 | kúa$^{n}$; pursue; hasten. |
| 逐 | tôk; jīo; drive; press. |
| 嚷 | jíang; clamor; bawl. |
| 捧 | * put; take with both hands. |
| 滅 | mît; exterminate. |
| 原 | ngŵn; origin; innate. |
| 流 | lâu; flow; circulate. |
| 唾 | * nŭa; saliva; spittle. |
| 唾 | * phùi; to spit out. |
| 容 | îong; bear with; style. |
| 准 | cún; permit; grant. |
| 求 | khîu; beseech; beg. |

| | | |
|---|---|---|
| 1 | lṳ́ kâi cŭe sí tăng. | Your offense is great. |
| 2 | huang éng tōa cǎi. | It is very rough. |
| 3 | éng hìe$^{n}$ tōa úa m̄ ká$^{n}$ khṳ̀. | The waves are so high, I dare not go. |
| 4 | mài jíang. pek chiet khîu. | Do not yell. Beg urgently. |
| 5 | úa tit cŭe lṳ́. | I have offended you. |
| 6 | kúa$^{n}$ khùe cē. kúa$^{n}$ lō. | Hurry up. Go faster. |
| 7 | kúa$^{n}$ chut. jīo m̄ tîeh lío. | Drive out. Couldn't overtake. |
| 8 | lṳ́ tîeh kúa$^{n}$ kín cò. | Do it as quick as you can. |
| 9 | lṳ́ jīo úa m̄ tîeh. | You can't catch up with me. |
| 10 | kúa$^{n}$ cí hûe sŭn cúi, hó khui cûn. | Let us start now and avail ourselves of the tide. |
| 11 | lṳ́ hó khṳ̀ jīo i mé cē. | You go and hurry him up. |
| 12 | jīo kàu bô mn̂g bô lō. | Driven to extremities. |
| 13 | kúa$^{n}$ tôk. jīo tío. tôk chut. | Expel. Drive away. Exorcise. |
| 14 | jīo i chut khṳ̀. îong i. | Drive him out. Bear with him. |
| 15 | lṳ́ hó khut úa khîu. | Grant my petition. |
| 16 | khîu khṳ̀, cún a m̄ cún? | Was the petition granted? |
| 17 | gūa mīn tŏ jíang khá sĭ lṳ́ a m̄ sĭ? | It was you halooing out there, was it not? |
| 18 | lṳ́ jíang mih sṳ̄? | What are you clamoring about? |
| 19 | i jíang tó khùn. | He bawls because he is hungry. |
| 20 | îong úa tà$^{n}$ cêk kù ūe. | Let me speak a word. |
| 21 | phī$^{n}$ kì$^{n}$ bûe, nŭa cúi cĭu lâu. kúa$^{n}$ lâu. | Smelling plums makes the mouth water. Follow the tide. |
| 22 | cìe ngŵn ìe$^{n}$. | The same as before. |
| 23 | phùi nŭa. ngŵn lâi. | To expectorate. Previously. |
| 24 | mît tīo khṳ̀. mît côk. | Exterminated. Extinct clan. |
| 25 | mît mn̂g. ngŵn nâng. | Extinct family. First owner. |

## LESSON CI.

| | | | |
|---|---|---|---|
| 流 | lîu; class; fluid; vagrant. | 罷 | pă; desist; quash. |
| 下 | hĭa; lower; below. | 遇 | ngŏ; to meet; happen. |
| 稷 | cek; glutinous millet. | 貪 | tham; covet; bent on. |
| 黍 | sú; millet. | 耍 | * chá$^n$; loiter; play. |
| 跡 | ciah; foot-mark; trace. | 耍 | * sńg; frolic; sport. |
| 約 | ieh; contract; treaty. | 裘 | hîu$^n$; wadded jacket. |

| | | |
|---|---|---|
| 1 | pńg ngŵn. ngŵn ì. | Primarily. First intention. |
| 2 | ngŵn lâi sĭ cìe$^n$ se$^n$. | It was originally so. |
| 3 | ngŵn m̄ kai cìe$^n$ se$^n$. | By rights it should not be so. |
| 4 | lâu cúi tōa. lâu hueh. | The tide is rising. To bleed. |
| 5 | lâu mâk cap. lâu tĭ$^n$. | Shed tears. The tide is full. |
| 6 | nńg lîu. lîu lôh. | Womankind. Squatters. |
| 7 | hĭa lîu. huang lîu. | Lower classes. A hearsay. |
| 8 | tn̂g lâu cúi. lîu lî sit só. | Everflowing water. Vagabonds. |
| 9 | îong mău. m̄ îong i. | Style and looks. Not endure him. |
| 10 | lân îong. pau îong. | Inexcusable. Long enduring. |
| 11 | chông îong. cún úa khîu. | Forbear. Grant my request. |
| 12 | khá sĭ îong kōi? | Is it so easy? |
| 13 | úa m̄ cún lú cìe$^n$ se$^n$ cò. | I will not allow you to do so. |
| 14 | khîu mîa. | Strive for a reputation. |
| 15 | lú ài$^n$ thâk cṳ, pĭen sĭ thâk cṳ, m̄ hó chá$^n$. | If you are going to read, read, and not loiter. |
| 16 | bô ía$^n$, bô ciah. | There is no evidence of it. |
| 17 | úa cai ía$^n$ ciah. | I know its marks. |
| 18 | ŏi kîa$^n$ sîn só cò kâi sṳ̄ ciah. m̄ hó sńg. | Can work miracles. Do not play. |
| 19 | mît ieh. tham sim. | Private understanding. Covetous. |
| 20 | lú bói mûeh hó, cĭu lâi, mài khṳ̀ tī kò chá$^n$. | When you have bought the things then come back; do not go loitering about. |
| 21 | lú thia$^n$ úa pĭen thia$^n$, m̄ thia$^n$, pĭen pă. | If you listen to me, well and good; if not that ends it. |
| 22 | pă chĭ. pă kang. | Closed market. Strike for wages. |
| 23 | ngŏ tîeh. sie ngŏ. | It happened. Meet each other. |

## LESSON CII.

| | | | |
|---|---|---|---|
| 管 | kŵn; rule; sway. | 蠶 | chôiⁿ; silkworm. |
| 管 | * kńg; a duct; tube. | 蠹 | cù; weevil. |
| 脊 | cit; ciah; spine; ridge. | 蟀 | sut; cricket. |
| 鰭 | * nîa; dorsal fin. | 鱷 | ngâk; crocodile. |
| 翅 | sît; chì; side fins. | 魦 | sua; shark. |
| 冠 | * kùe; comb of birds. | 鮔 | * gô; porpoise. |

| | |
|---|---|
| 1 lṳ́ kúaⁿ úa m̄ tîeh. | 1 You cannot keep up with me. |
| 2 úa kâi cûn mé, kúaⁿ i kâi cûn tit tîeh. | 2 My boat is a fast one, and can overtake his boat. |
| 3 kúaⁿ cí ciah hóⁿ, kúaⁿ kàu jîeh hn̆g? | 3 How far did you pursue the tiger? |
| 4 kúaⁿ cí kâi lâu, ío mé kàu. | 4 If we follow this tide we shall arrive sooner. |
| 5 lṳ́ tŏ có ke tī tiang sî khí sin lâi cí kò? | 5 When did you start from your country to come here? |
| 6 khí sin a būe? | 6 Have they started yet? |
| 7 poih gûeh àiⁿ khí sin. | 7 Will start in the eighth month. |
| 8 cí ciah káu ŏi kă nâng a bŏi? | 8 Is this dog apt to bite? |
| 9 i thóiⁿ cò khî hùe. | 9 He considered it a rare article. |
| 10 lôh hùe. khí hùe. | 10 Ship off goods. Land goods. |
| 11 chut hùe. hùe kha. | 11 Take delivery of goods. Garblings. |
| 12 bô ie ciah kut. mô kńg. | 12 No backbone. Hair duct. |
| 13 á chíu cóiⁿ kut. | 13 Crack the finger joints. |
| 14 jī sía lâi ŭ kut lât. kùi kut. | 14 The characters are vigorously written. A fine figure. |
| 15 kut piⁿ nêk. kut thâu hu. | 15 Meat next the bone. Bone dust. |
| 16 cîeh kài. sì kài. | 16 A boundary stone. This world. |
| 17 pun tī kài. bí thai. | 17 Settle the boundaries. Rice sieve. |
| 18 thai bí. pă chíu. koi mô kńg. | 18 Sift rice. Stop work. Quill. |
| 19 tâk jîeh cōiⁿ cîⁿ? | 19 How much is it worth? |
| 20 sì tâk cîⁿ kâi mûeh. | 20 It is very valuable. |
| 21 m̄ tâk cêk kâi cîⁿ. | 21 Not worth a single cash. |
| 22 àiⁿ pă put lêng. | 22 Could not cease from it. |
| 23 kŵn lí. siu kŵn. | 23 Govern. Take control. |

汕頭方言初階



## LESSON CIII.

| | | | |
|---|---|---|---|
| 漢 | hàn; relating to China. | 呢 | nî; broad cloth. |
| 晚 | mńg; evening; late. | 棉 | mî; cotton plant. |
| 線 | sùaⁿ; thread; cord. | 羅 | lê̤; open worked. |
| 髮 | hwt; hair; moss. | 紗 | se; gauze; cotton. |
| 絲 | si; silk; fiber. | 縐 | jìo; crape. |
| 羽 | ú; bunting; plumes. | 絨 | jông; woolen cloth. |

| | | |
|---|---|---|
| 1 | ngŏ̤ kìⁿ. ngŏ̤ hâh. | See unexpectedly. Occurrences. |
| 2 | i kâi ngŏ̤ hâh sĭm hó̤. | He had first rate luck. |
| 3 | nâng seⁿ chiet ìo sī ngŏ̤ hâh. gê̤ mê̤ kńg. | Luck is the important thing in life. A goose-quill. |
| 4 | i ngŏ̤ tîeh sih mih sṳ? | What happened to him? |
| 5 | úa m̄ pat ngŏ̤ tîeh i. | I never happened to meet him. |
| 6 | ngŏ̤ tîeh lê̤h hŏ. | It happened to rain. |
| 7 | ngŏ̤ ŭ sih mih sṳ? | What happened? |
| 8 | bê̤ hêng ciah. Ĭ ciah. | No clue of him. Miracles. |
| 9 | kha ciah. sim ciah. | Foot-print. Sentiments. |
| 10 | mît ciah. mî hue. | Destroy the traces. Raw cotton. |
| 11 | mài mûeh seⁿ ciah. | Do not disfigure it. |
| 12 | lîp hâp ieh. tham cîah. | Make a treaty. Gluttonous. |
| 13 | ŭ àm ieh. cóng kẃn. | A secret agreement. Overseer. |
| 14 | ieh úa cè̤-pû khṳ̀. | Agreed that I should go with him. |
| 15 | sía ieh sìo. chù cit. | Write the bargain. Ridge of roof. |
| 16 | se sùaⁿ. lê̤ se. ú mê̤. | Spool-cotton. Gauze. Plumes. |
| 17 | m̄ jû ieh. | Not according to contract. |
| 18 | tham ût. tham cîⁿ. | Sleep inordinately. Avaricious. |
| 19 | câp hùe phò. kẃn sìo. | Fancy store. Book-keeper. |
| 20 | kẃn i m̄ cŭ. kẃn sṳ. | He is beyond control. Boss. |
| 21 | kẃn ke. kẃn hn̂g. ú se. | Steward. Janitor. Camlet. |
| 22 | lṳ́ kẃn ĕ jîeh cōiⁿ nâng? | How many do you oversee? |
| 23 | bâk mî. mî hue tō̤. | Cotton plant. Cotton bale. |
| 24 | lê̤ măng. lê̤ pò. hó̤ hàn. | A net. Lace. Lusty. |
| 25 | tōa hàn. thiⁿ hàn, hûn hàn. | Tall and stout. Milky way. |
| 26 | hàn jîn. múa jîn. | Chinamen. Manchus. |
| 27 | lê̤ hàn. lê̤ pûaⁿ. | Budhist worthies. Compass. |

## LESSON CIV.

| | | | |
|---|---|---|---|
| 苧 | tĭu; species of hemp. | 願 | ngw̆n; wish; desire. |
| 渡 | tō; ferry; ford. | 甘 | kam; agreeable; willing. |
| 闢 | phek; open up. | 肯 | khéng; hàu$^{n}$; willing; assenting. |
| 闢 | * pit; crack; disclose. | 堪 | kham; worthy; sustain. |
| 縫 | * phāng; a chink; crack. | 牽 | khan; lead; pull. |
| 鳳 | hŏng; phenix. | 完 | ŵn; finish; conclude. |

| | | |
|---|---|---|
| 1 | si sùa$^{n}$. si pò. | Sewing silk. Silk cloth. |
| 2 | si hwt. tĭu sùa$^{n}$. | Unspun silk. Linen thread. |
| 3 | bâk sùa$^{n}$. tĭu pò. | A line made with ink. Linen. |
| 4 | tâng sùa$^{n}$; thih sùa$^{n}$. | Brass wire; iron wire. |
| 5 | khîang hàn. hó hàn nâng. | Robust. Chieftains. |
| 6 | mî se. khan gû. | Cotton yarn. Take care of cows. |
| 7 | cí kâi pò, sĭ chôi$^{n}$ si ke$^{n}$ kâi, a sĭ mî se ke$^{n}$ kâi? | Is this cloth made of silk or of cotton? |
| 8 | lú cêk tîo pò âi$^{n}$ lì cò nŏ ûe, lú cêk ûe úa cêk ûe. lú hó khan i khù. | Tear that strip of cloth into two parts, one for you and one for me. You lead him. |
| 9 | tah tō cûn khù. khui phek. | Go by ferry boat. Develop. |
| 10 | kùe tō. kam sim. | Cross the ferry. Submissive. |
| 11 | úa cò kam? | How can I be willing? |
| 12 | lú kāng úa bói cêk peh cî$^{n}$ si sùa$^{n}$. | You buy a hundred cash worth of sewing silk for me. |
| 13 | úa kam ngw̆n. | I am willing and desirous. |
| 14 | lú khéng khù, mē? | Are you willing to go? |
| 15 | khéng a m̄ khéng? | Are you willing, or not? |
| 16 | kham kai tit phah. | Deserving of a whipping. |
| 17 | se$^{n}$ phāng: pit phāng. | To crack open. |
| 18 | tah thi$^{n}$ kng cá kâi tō cûn, kùe khoi. tō thâu. | Take the early ferry-boat across the river. The ferry. |
| 19 | cá tō: ùa$^{n}$ tō. | Early boat: late boat. |
| 20 | chûg pit phāng líо. | The table has cracked. |
| 21 | sin ceng kâi chîe$^{n}$ kōi pit phāng. m̄ hàu$^{n}$. | Newly pounded walls easily crack. Unwilling. |
| 22 | cò kàu ŵn chŵn. | Finish it completely. |

# LESSON CV.

| | |
|---|---|
| 招 | cie; make known; induce. |
| 招 | * îah; beckon. |
| 招 | cio; assume; confess. |
| 醬 | cìe$^{n}$; condiments. |
| 擂 | lûi; to triturate. |
| 哭 | khàu; to cry; weep. |
| 笑 | chìe; smile; laugh. |
| 戲 | hì$^{n}$; theatre; play. |
| 熬 | ngâu; simmer; seethe. |
| 燉 | tŭn; boil by putting the dish into water. |
| 湖 | hû; ô; a lake. |
| 星 | che$^{n}$; a star. |

| | | |
|---|---|---|
| 1 | úa sim sṓ ngw̆n. | What my heart desires. |
| 2 | ŵn líο sim ngw̆n. | Gratified the heart's desire. |
| 3 | cṳ̆ ngw̆n. m̄ ngw̆n. | Own free will. Averse. |
| 4 | ēng ŵn líο. ŵn chŵn. | All used up. All concluded. |
| 5 | ŵn kang. ŵn pĭ. | Finish the job. All made ready. |
| 6 | ŵn líο. tà$^{n}$ ŵn líο. | Got through. Through speaking. |
| 7 | m̄ kham. kham ēng. | Unworthy. Fit to use. |
| 8 | sĭu khó lân kham? | How can I bear this suffering? |
| 9 | kam kit. kam hō. | A willing bond. Timely rain. |
| 10 | cṳ̆ kam. kam kam kâi. | Voluntary. Luscious ones. |
| 11 | kam cháu. khan lîen. | Liquorice. Implicate. |
| 12 | khan si. khan kùa. | Stretch silk. Held in suspense. |
| 13 | cí kâi tī hng sĭm khai phek. | This place has a wide view. |
| 14 | khai phek: khui phek. | Having a fine prospect. |
| 15 | mài làn phāng. | Do not leave chinks. |
| 16 | cṳ̆ cio. cio hu. | Bring upon one's self. Wait upon. |
| 17 | chut cie thiap. cie thiap. | Issue a handbill. A poster. |
| 18 | cie ua$^{n}$. mài khàu. | Proclaim amnesty. Don't cry. |
| 19 | cie nâng lâi cə̀ kang. | Advertise for laborers. |
| 20 | cie ang. | To take a son-in-law. |
| 21 | i cṳ̆ cio jīn. | He owns to the charge. |
| 22 | sĭ i cie ín lâi kâi. | The one introduced by him. |
| 23 | îah i lâi. cie i lâi bói. cie i lâi. | Beckon to him. Lead him to buy. Induce him to come. |
| 24 | tāu cìe$^{n}$. lûi thûi. | Bean-sauce. A pestle. |
| 25 | hì$^{n}$ chìe. khṳ̀ thói$^{n}$ hì$^{n}$. | Ridicule. Go to the theatre. |
| 26 | hì$^{n}$ kía$^{n}$. hì$^{n}$ sńg. | Actors. To frolic; tease. |
| 27 | cə̀ hì$^{n}$. che$^{n}$ kuang. | Perform a play. Starlight. |

## LESSON CVI.

| | | | |
|---|---|---|---|
| 珠 | cu; a pearl; bead. | 串 | chẁn; pak; to string on. |
| 珍 | tien; precious; rare. | 乾 | * kua$^{n}$; cured by drying. |
| 寶 | pó; valuable; noble. | 乾 | kang; clean; entirely. |
| 貝 | pùe; rich; precious. | 廚 | tô; sît; kitchen. |
| 砲 | phàu; cannon; fireworks. | 怱 | chong; hurried. |
| 臼 | khŭ; a mortar. | 捷 | * tīam; continuously. |

| | | |
|---|---|---|
| 1 | ké cu; cin cu. | False pearls; real pearls. |
| 2 | cu pó. cêk pak cu. | Jewelry. A string of beads. |
| 3 | kùa phī$^{n}$ phang kâi hie$^{n}$ cu. | Wear a scent bag. |
| 4 | hâ mâk hŭn cu. | Mixing fish-eyes and pearls. |
| 5 | mê mêng cu. khî tien. | A brilliant gem. Exquisite. |
| 6 | tien tŏng. tien pó. | To prize. Precious things. |
| 7 | lê kè pó. âng pó cîeh. | Invaluable. A ruby. |
| 8 | lú pat pó. | You are a judge of the value. |
| 9 | lâm pó cîeh. pó sua hún. | A sapphire. Emery. |
| 10 | pó tŏng. pó pùe. | To esteem. Valuable. |
| 11 | ūe tà$^{n}$ lâi m̄ cêk chẁn. | That just said is irrelevant. |
| 12 | chùn kùe khù. | To string through. |
| 13 | i kio i chẁn tâng. | They were banded together. |
| 14 | àm cĕ$^{n}$ kio i sie chẁn. | Secretly leagued with them. |
| 15 | chẁn hâh. chẁn thong. chẁn phàu. | Banded together. Intercommunicate. String of fire crackers. |
| 16 | hō phàu. cêk mn̂g phàu. | Signal gun. A cannon. |
| 17 | phàu thâi. phàu chia. | A fort. Gun-carriage. |
| 18 | cí cêk mn̂g phàu hó phùe ŭ jîeh cōi húe îeh, jîeh tăng kâi phàu cí? | How much powder, and how heavy a cannon ball, are required to load this cannon? |
| 19 | mn̂g kha khŭ. bí khŭ. | Socket for door-pivot. Rice mortar. |
| 20 | kang cĕng. bōi kang cĕng. | Limpid. All sold out. |
| 21 | phâk cè kua$^{n}$. | Dry it in the sun. |
| 22 | cêk nâng kang cêk pue. | Each person drained a glass. |
| 23 | tô pâng. húe sît. | Kitchen. Cook-room. |
| 24 | úa cêk sî chong chong. | I was in a desperate hurry. |
| 25 | lú hó tīam tīam kia$^{n}$. | You walk right along. |

# LESSON CVII.

弓 keng; a bow; a measure.
箭 cì$^{n}$; arrow; bowshot.
拉 la; pull; tug; drag.
射 sīa; shoot; spurt.
獵 lâh; hunt; the chase.
農 lông; agriculture.

鬼 kúi; ghost; a spirit.
魔 mô; demon.
屐 kîah; clogs.
桅 ûi; mast.
舵 tōa; tăi; rudder,
猶 îu; even; so; rather.

1 i chong chong cĭu khù. — 1 He went hurriedly off.

2 bô lói. lông hu; lông jîn. — 2 Uncivil. A farmer.

3 i cè i tīam tīam khù. — 3 He went right along.

4 i tīam tīam tà$^{n}$ cêk jît. — 4 He talked on the whole day.

5 i cè i tīam tīam tà$^{n}$, m̄ kù pât nâng. — 5 He talked right on without regard to any one else.

6 úa pàng i tīam tīam tà$^{n}$ kàu ŵn. lâh káu. — 6 I let him talk right on till he had done. Hunting dog.

7 thi$^{n}$ tīam tīam lôh hŏ. — 7 It rains incessantly.

8 la múa keng. la cŭ. — 8 Draw a bow. Hold fast.

9 khui ngĕ keng. hó cì$^{n}$. — 9 Draw a stiff bow. Good shot.

10 jîeh cōi keng pō. — 10 How many bowshots is it?

11 híang keng híang cì$^{n}$. — 11 A whizzing bow and arrow.

12 khui keng m̄ pàng cì$^{n}$. — 12 Empty threats.

13 cí ki keng khah tăng, la m̄ khui. húe cì$^{n}$. — 13 This bow is too heavy, I can't draw it. A rocket.

14 pùa$^{n}$ nâng, pùa$^{n}$ kúi. — 14 Half man, half devil.

15 á wn cí kâi keng. — 15 Bend this bow.

16 lông ke. lah jîn. — 16 Agriculturalists. Sportsman.

17 bé cì$^{n}$. phah lâh. — 17 Mounted bowmen. To hunt.

18 pō cì$^{n}$. mô kúi. — 18 Unmounted bowmen. Evil spirit.

19 pàng né cì$^{n}$. tăi kong. — 19 Shoot at a venture. Helmsman.

20 cêk cì$^{n}$ kâi tī. sīa cì$^{n}$. — 20 A bowshot. Shoot arrows.

21 kuang im sŭ cì$^{n}$. — 21 Time flies like an arrow.

22 àm cì$^{n}$ sie$^{n}$ nâng. — 22 To secretly injure.

23 jît ía$^{n}$ sīa jîp lâi. — 23 The sunshine streamed in.

24 sīa tîeh cêk ciah cío. — 24 Shot a bird.

25 phâng cûn. ûi búe. — 25 Sailing vessels. The mast head.

## LESSON CVIII.

| | | | |
|---|---|---|---|
| 腦 | náu; brains; head. | 腮 | sai; jaws; jowl. |
| 袋 | * tài; case; cover. | 肝 | kua$^{n}$; liver. |
| 伸 | sin; vindicate; redress. | 脛 | * kăn; gizzard; tripe. |
| 伸 | * chun; stretch out. | 膽 | tá$^{n}$; the gall; courage. |
| 冤 | wn; ill usage; vex. | 肺 | hùi; the lungs. |
| 迷 | mî; bewitch; delude. | 嗎 | * hē$^{n}$; interrogative assent. |

| | | |
|---|---|---|
| 1 | lú thói$^{n}$ kì$^{n}$ kúi, hē$^{n}$. | What are you afraid of? |
| 2 | lú tà$^{n}$ kúi ūe. | You speak empty words. |
| 3 | kúi sîn. īu hó. | Supernatural beings. Better. |
| 4 | kúi thâu kúi náu. | To eaves drop, and peep about. |
| 5 | i khut kúi mî tîeh. | He is possessed by a devil. |
| 6 | lú hó sin i kâi wn. | You should redress his wrong. |
| 7 | wn kúi. tōa ûi. | Unavenged spirit. Mainmast. |
| 8 | kúi húe. sa$^{n}$ ki ûi. | Will-o'-wisp. Three-masted. |
| 9 | kúi lîah kúi. | A rogue catching a rogue. |
| 10 | lĭ hāi kùe kúi. | Hatefuler than a devil. |
| 11 | tŏa búe. lîah tŏa. cûn tăi. | The part of the rudder in the water. Steer. Rudder. |
| 12 | bô thâu náu. | No head for the matter. |
| 13 | náu ău kì$^{n}$ sai. náu tài. | See the jaws from behind the head. Pericranium. |
| 14 | chun chíu, chun kha. | Stretch out the arm and leg. |
| 15 | chun tît kha. | Stretched out, as dead. |
| 16 | chun tn̂g chut lâi. | Stretch it forth. |
| 17 | sin wn. īu tōa. | Obtain redress. Even larger. |
| 18 | wn ke cè kú cîa$^{n}$ chin ke, chin ke cè kú cîa$^{n}$ wn ke. | The estranged at length wed, and the wedded become estranged. |
| 19 | hàm wn; kìe wn. hē$^{n}$. | Declare a grievance. Yes. |
| 20 | hun mî m̄ cai nâng. | Stupefied or dazed. |
| 21 | mî sit lō thâu. | To lose the road. |
| 22 | cip mî. sim kua$^{n}$ thâu. | Wilfully dull. The chest. |
| 23 | ài$^{n}$ ní tu kua$^{n}$ sek. | Color it dark brown. |
| 24 | kua$^{n}$ húe. tá$^{n}$ cap. | Temper. The bile. |
| 25 | tá$^{n}$ tōa. bô tá$^{n}$. | Courageous. Cowardly. |

## LESSON CIX.

| | |
|---|---|
| 純 sûn; unmixed. | 商 siang; su; kàu; trade. |
| 釘 tèng; to nail. | 兩 níe; an ounce. |
| 釘 teng; a nail. | 斤 kun; pound or catty. |
| 量 lĭang; capacity. | 升 seng; a pint. |
| 量 lîang; take counsel. | 斗 táu; a peck. |
| 量 nîe; measure. | 畝 bó; Chinese acre. |

| | |
|---|---|
| 1 se$^{n}$ kua$^{n}$ húe. kua$^{n}$ húe tōa. | 1 Get angry. High-tempered. |
| 2 i sim kua$^{n}$ m̄ hó. | 2 His disposition is bad. |
| 3 úa tōa tá$^{n}$ lâi tà$^{n}$. | 3 I venture to come and tell. |
| 4 hùi húe. sûn cĕng. | 4 Fever. All uniform. |
| 5 sûn pêh. sûn che$^{n}$. | 5 Pure white. Unmixed green. |
| 6 sûn o. sûn chŵn. | 6 Plain black. Sincere. |
| 7 sûn si. tèng thih teng. | 7 Pure silk. Drive a nail. |
| 8 cang teng khù tèng mûeh. | 8 Take a nail and nail a thing. |
| 9 tèng kín. thí lĭang i. | 9 Nail fast. Respect him. |
| 10 khut bít phang tèng tīeh. | 10 Stung by a honey bee. |
| 11 i ŏi tèng nâng. | 11 It is apt to sting people. |
| 12 hái lĭang. lát lĭang. | 12 Capacity. Powers. |
| 13 cò sū tīeh lĭang lát. | 13 Do things with ability. |
| 14 cū lĭang. hó lĭang. | 14 Self-esteem. Fine abilities. |
| 15 siang lĭang. khì lĭang. | 15 Good feeling. Calibre. |
| 16 nîe thói$^{n}$ jīeh tn̂g. | 16 Measure and find its length. |
| 17 nîe bí, nîe pò. | 17 Measure rice, measure cloth. |
| 18 seng lí. sì hái thong siang. | 18 Business of a merchant. Commerce. |
| 19 siang lîang; kàu nîe. | 19 Consult about; talk it over. |
| 20 su nîe. siang kheh. | 20 To bargain. A trader. |
| 21 îam siang. cêk seng bí. | 21 Salt-merchant. Pint of rice. |
| 22 câp lâk níe ûi cêk kun. | 22 Sixteen ounces are a pound. |
| 23 câp cî$^{n}$ ûi cêk níe. | 23 Ten mace make a tael. |
| 24 câp hun ûi cêk cî$^{n}$. | 24 Ten candareen make a mace. |
| 25 jīeh cōi kun níe? | 25 What is the weight of it? |
| 26 bô kun táu. cêk bó chân. | 26 Somersault. Acre of rice-field. |
| 27 nō tâng cò cêk seng. | 27 Two gills make a pint. |
| 28 câp seng cò cêk táu. | 28 Ten pints make a peck. |

# LESSON CX.

| | |
|---|---|
| 頃 khŵ́n; 100 acres. | 煎 * luah; to fry in oil. |
| 手 * síu; person; handy. | 煏 pek; to toast. |
| 眷 kŵ̀n; kindred; regard. | 仙 sien; an immortal. |
| 周 ciu; environ; circulate. | 筋 kun; sinews; tendon. |
| 週 ciu; a year; revolve. | 眼 ngán; the eye. |
| 炒 chá; to fry dry. | 焙 pūe; dry over a fire. |

| | | |
|---|---|---|
| 1 | câp hun ûi cêk bó. | Ten tenths make an acre. |
| 2 | cêk bó chân siu jîeh cōi chek? ke kŵ̀n. | How much paddy from an acre of ground? The family. |
| 3 | chue síu. keng cì$^n$ síu. phàu síu. suah síu. cu síu. cúi síu. phah síu. | Players on wind instruments. Archers. Gunners. Executioner. Copyist. Waterman. Pugilist. |
| 4 | láu chíu. mîa chíu. kùe chíu. sêk chíu. | An old hand. A skilled hand. To transfer. An expert. |
| 5 | hó cò chíu. chíu ĕ. | Work of art. Subordinates. |
| 6 | cīe$^n$ chíu; ĕ chíu. | On the left; on the right. |
| 7 | ĕ chíu; cīe$^n$ chíu. | Another time; the other time. |
| 8 | cīe$^n$ chíu kang; ĕ chíu kang. pêh chíu cò. | Master workman; apprentices. Do a thing off hand. |
| 9 | cīe$^n$ chíu sĭ úa cò; ĕ chíu sĭ i lâi cò. | The other time I did it; next time he does it. |
| 10 | pêh chíu sêng ke. | A self-made man. |
| 11 | khang chíu. che$^n$ chíu. | Empty-handed. A raw hand. |
| 12 | sa$^n$ ciah chíu. sŭn chíu. | Light-fingered. By the way. |
| 13 | cŭ kŵ̀n. kŵ̀n kù. | Household. Regard kindly. |
| 14 | ciu bât. ciu chŵ̂n. | Well defined. Bring about. |
| 15 | ciu cai. sì ciu ûi. | General knowledge. All around. |
| 16 | ciu nî, ciu pûeh, ciu jît. | Complete year, month or day. |
| 17 | sîn sien; sien nâng. | Invisible beings; fairies. |
| 18 | cúi sien hue. thien sien. | The narcissus. Angels. |
| 19 | tī sien. kìam sien. | A human immortal. Fencer. |
| 20 | sien kut. poih sien. | Fairy-like. The eight genii. |
| 21 | che$^n$ kun. tōa kun. | Veins. Tendons of the body. |
| 22 | hueh kun. mī kun. | Blood vessels. Tough dough. |

## LESSON CXI.

泡 phàu; to soak soft.
額 hîah; forehead; fixed.
顖 sìn; sìn; the sinciput.
鬢 pìn; hair on the temple.
頰 * kih; side of face; cheeks.
仁 jîn; humanity; kernel.
腎 sĭen; kidneys.
齦 n̂gn; the gums.
齦 * ngoih; to crunch.
喉 âu; throat; windpipe.
嚨 lêng; aesophagus.
起 khí; sort; class.

| | | |
|---|---|---|
| 1 | ŭ ngán bô cu. âu lêng. | Undiscriminating. Throat. |
| 2 | ngán côiⁿ ŭ sū, mē? | Have you immediate business? |
| 3 | hŏng ngán. pìn piⁿ. | Long, narrow eye. The temple. |
| 4 | hó ngán lât. hîah sìo. | Quick perceptions. Legal number. |
| 5 | thóiⁿ m̄ cĭeⁿ ngán. | Look upon with contempt. |
| 6 | ngán sîn. âu lêng kíaⁿ. | Expression of the eye. Palate. |
| 7 | hîah mīn sìn. hîah kak. | The forehead. Above the temple. |
| 8 | îeh tah pìn piⁿ. | Stick medicine on the temple. |
| 9 | sien nâng thâu. | The image in the eye. |
| 10 | mâk ciu jîn. pêh jîn. | The eyeball. White of the eye. |
| 11 | mâk chì mô. hîah kĕ. | The eyelashes. Forehead low. |
| 12 | sìn mn̂g; hîah sìn. | The fontanel in a babe. |
| 13 | ŭ hîah a bô hîah? | Is there a fixed rate? |
| 14 | kih kau. o jîn. | The cheeks. The iris. |
| 15 | jîn ài. thô jîn, tāu jîn. | Benevolence. Meat of peach-stone, and pea-nut. |
| 16 | sĭen cí ĭeⁿ. sim sĭen. | Oval. The heart and reins. |
| 17 | khí n̂gn. ngoih khí. | The gums. Grate the teeth. |
| 18 | âu lêng thìaⁿ. âu ta. | Throat sore. Thirsty. |
| 19 | âu seⁿ gô. koi nn̆g jîn. | Quinsy. Yolk of an egg. |
| 20 | ngĕ âu. nn̂g ân. | Windpipe. Aesophagus. |
| 21 | lá kâi âu bô siaⁿ sĭ ŵn in lá pek chiet kāng nâng sie jíang. | You are hoarse because you have been so vehemently scolding. |
| 22 | hŭam àiⁿ cîah kâi mûeh pit àiⁿ kùe âu lêng. | Whatever is eaten must pass down the throat. |
| 23 | tàⁿ ūe tŏ âu lêng tói. | Talk in a whisper. |
| 24 | cí khí, hú khí, m̄ tâng ĭeⁿ. | The two sorts are unlike. |

## LESSON CXII.

帶 lih; tih; rootlets; stems.
腭 ngâk; roof of the mouth.
肩 koi$^{n}$; the shoulder.
胸 heng; the thorax.
坪 phîa$^{n}$; beach; flats.
嶺 nía; a ridge; range.
臂 pì; forearm.
節 coih; festival; term.
節 cak; joint; restrain.
肘 * thn̆g; elbow.
膝 chek; the knee.
脇 hîap; side of the body.

| | | |
|---|---|---|
| 1 | jíang kàu âu bɵ̂ sia$^{n}$. | Scream till hoarse. |
| 2 | lú ìn tap m̄ kong. úa kāi i cɵ̀ tong pɵ́. | Your answer is not to the point. I will be bail for him. |
| 3 | tong kì$^{n}$. | An intermediate agent. |
| 4 | ŭ nɵ̆ khí, cêk khí sĭ tîam, cêk khí si kîam. | There are two kinds, one is sweet and one is salt. |
| 5 | mâk kha phûe. heng côi$^{n}$. | Eyelids. The breast. |
| 6 | âu lêng kńg. âu lêng lih. | The tonsils. The palate. |
| 7 | heng côi$^{n}$ kut. kun lih. | The breast bone. Rootlets. |
| 8 | pn̄g sî kut; koi$^{n}$ kah. | Shoulder blade. |
| 9 | kue sêk, lih lɵ̂h. heng kua$^{n}$ côi$^{n}$. | The melon being ripe the stem falls off. The breast. |
| 10 | tiah tīo lih. | Pick off the stems. |
| 11 | cīe$^{n}$ ngâk. koi$^{n}$ thâu. | Roof of the mouth. Shoulder. |
| 12 | khui heng sa$^{n}$. | Jacket opening in front. |
| 13 | koi heng; ku heng. | A projecting breast bone. |
| 14 | tûi heng. sim heng. | Beat the breast. Disposition. |
| 15 | sim heng khuah. chek ĕ. | Magnanimous. One's children. |
| 16 | i kâi sim heng lêng ūa$^{n}$ kio nâng m̄ tâng. | His disposition is different from other people's. |
| 17 | hái phîa. khoi phîa. | Flats by a sea or river. |
| 18 | sua$^{n}$ nía. nía thâu. kùe nía. nía lō. nía kha. kîa$^{n}$ kàu pùa$^{n}$ nía hiah hêk. nía téng. | Mountain range. High peaks. To pass. The pass. Foot of the pass. Went half up the steep and stopped to rest. Highest point. |
| 19 | chíu pì. sî coih. | The arm. Stated times. |
| 20 | chíu thn̆g. cńg kah. | Elbow. Thumb-nail. |
| 21 | phah chek kŭi. | Bend the knees. |

## LESSON CXIII.

膕 * wt; hinge joint.
腕 ŵn; the wrist.
籬 lî; fence or wattle.
臁 lîam; calf of the leg.
踉 * te$^{n}$; heel of the foot.
胃 ūi; the stomach.
盂 u; a porringer.
脉 mêh; the pulse.
痰 thâm; phlegm.
汗 kūa$^{n}$; perspiration.
腸 tn̂g; intestines.
腋 * keh; arm-pit.

| | | |
|---|---|---|
| 1 | cí kâi nía kûi$^{n}$ căi; lîen cío ài$^{n}$ pue kùe khù hŵ̂n sĭ eh. | This is a lofty ridge; it would be difficult for even a bird to fly over it. |
| 2 | kùe cí kâi nía hìa$^{n}$ pôi$^{n}$ m̄ cai sih mih tī kài. | It is unknown what country is beyond this range. |
| 3 | hŭ úa cêk pì kâi lât. | Lend us a hand. |
| 4 | cồ coih. kùe coih. | Keep holiday. Spend holiday. |
| 5 | cak ēng. cak khĭam. | Economize. Be frugal. |
| 6 | cńg thâu kong; kha cńg thâu kong; kha cńg kía$^{n}$; cói$^{n}$ kah; kha cńg kah. | The thumb; the big toe; small toes; finger nails; toe nails. |
| 7 | chíu cói$^{n}$, kha cói$^{n}$. | The fingers and toes. |
| 8 | chíu cńg thâu, kha cńg thâu. | All the fingers and toes. |
| 9 | chíu cak. | A finger ring, finger joint. |
| 10 | hiap ĕ. thâu khak chúe. | The side. The brains. |
| 11 | ka kī kâi hueh mêh. | One's own kith and kin. |
| 12 | kha tn̂g tó. thâm kŵ̀n. | Calf of the leg. Spittoon. |
| 13 | sío jîn khì. kha ău te$^{n}$. | Ill-bred. The heel of the foot. |
| 14 | i bô̂ sih mih khì lât. | He has not much energy. |
| 15 | lâi cŏ̤ úa kha thâu u. | Come sit on my knee. |
| 16 | lâu kūa$^{n}$. sim heng ôih. | Perspire. Illiberal. |
| 17 | àn mêh. chíu ŵn. | Feel the julse. The wrist. |
| 18 | ŵn lât. phîa$^{n}$ lî kut. | Strength of wrist. The ribs. |
| 19 | tek lî. tău lî. | Bamboo fence. Trellis for peas. |
| 20 | kha lîam kut. sim tn̂g. | Shin bone. Bowels. |
| 21 | hó̤ sim tn̂g. cêk mêh. | Kindly disposed. Of one blood. |
| 22 | mêh lí. | Philosophy of the pulse. |
| 23 | hwt kūa$^{n}$ îeh. pío kūa$^{n}$. | A sudorific. Produce sweat. |

## LESSON CXIV.

| | |
|---|---|
| 島 táu; island; rock. | 野 ía; desert; wild. |
| 谷 kok; ravine; gulch. | 壩 pà; low banks. |
| 洞 tāng; cave; gorge. | 埠 po; mart; port. |
| 穴 hŵt; den; cavern. | 禦 gṳ̆; cause to desist. |
| 巢 châu; tàu; nest. | 鳴 mêng; to cry out; buzz. |
| 曠 khùang; vacant. | 温 un; tepid; genial. |

| | | |
|---|---|---|
| 1 | keh tháng ĕ. un cúi. | The arm-pit. Tepid water. |
| 2 | cúi ūi kháu. hái táu. | Pit of the stomach. Islet. |
| 3 | ūi kháu khui. un sêk. | Have an appetite. Familiarize. |
| 4 | khù ūi húe. un pó. | Cleanse the blood. Tonics. |
| 5 | khui ūi. kha lîam phīⁿ. | Excite an appetite. Shin. |
| 6 | m̄ khui ūi. suaⁿ kok. | Not appetizing. Valleys. |
| 7 | hâng ūi. hŵn ūi. | Indigestion. Turn the stomach. |
| 8 | ūi ngâu. un ūi. | Weak stomach. Warm the stomach. |
| 9 | un cu. un pá. | Review studies. Warm and fed. |
| 10 | suaⁿ mêng kok èng. | The vales echo the hills. |
| 11 | khong kok. kok kháu. | A gorge. Bed of a torrent. |
| 12 | mêng wn. ía sèⁿ. | Cry out for redress. Restive. |
| 13 | cío mêng, bé mêng, têk mêng. mêng kó. | The cry of a bird, a horse a deer. Sound a drum. |
| 14 | sien tāng. tāng hŵt. | Fairy grotto. Cavern. |
| 15 | tāng pâng hue cek. | The nuptial chamber. |
| 16 | hīa hŵt. cío tàu. | Ant-hole. Bird's nest. |
| 17 | tît tît khù phah chât kâi châu hŵt. | Straightway go and destroy the robber's den. |
| 18 | put jîp hóⁿ hŵt uaⁿ tit hóⁿ cú. bô châu hŵt. | You do not enter a tiger's den and quietly take the cubs. Houseless. |
| 19 | khùang ía. pêh hwt. | Wilderness. Self-sown. |
| 20 | cháu ía. chân ía. | Desert. A common. |
| 21 | ía jîn. suaⁿ pà. | A rustic. Low banks. |
| 22 | po thâu. îam po. | A port. A salt depot. |
| 23 | tōa po thâu. keh ĕ. | A great mast. Arm-pit. |
| 24 | bô nâng gṳ̆ i tit cŭ. | Nobody can withstand him. |

## LESSON CXV.

城 sîa$^{n}$; city; citadel.
邑 ip; city; fief.
鄉 hie$^{n}$; village; country.
里 lí; neighborhood.
寨 cē; a hold; stockade.
村 chng; hamlet.

池 tî; pool; pond.
江 kang; river; canal.
掘 khut; hole; cave.
喪 sàng; lose; bereft.
室 sit; abiding place.
浴 êk; to bathe.

| | | |
|---|---|---|
| 1 | âu lêng gṳ̆. sói êk. | Adam's apple. To bathe. |
| 2 | tī tîang ká$^{n}$ khṳ̀ gṳ̆ i. | Who ventures to withstand him? |
| 3 | kha wt; chíu wt. | Knee joint; elbow joint. |
| 4 | úa pat kàu i ke. | I have been to his house. |
| 5 | lăi sit. sit ke. | Inner room. Household. |
| 6 | sàng sim. sàng sè$^{n}$ mīa. | Discouraged. Lost his life. |
| 7 | phah êk. jṳ̂ êk. | Take a bath. Sponge bath. |
| 8 | hṳ́ kâi hie$^{n}$ lí se$^{n}$ tɵ̆ tī kɵ̀? | Where does that village stand? |
| 9 | cûn í$^{n}$ keng jîp kang kháu. | The boat has entered the river. |
| 10 | sîa$^{n}$ chîe$^{n}$: sîa$^{n}$ mn̂g. | City wall: gate of the city. |
| 11 | sái i khṳ̀ sîa$^{n}$ lăi. | Send him into the city. |
| 12 | ip jîn. sîa$^{n}$ lái hùe. | Towns-folk. City people. |
| 13 | sîa$^{n}$ chĭ nâng. tûng hie$^{n}$. | City-people. Towns-man. |
| 14 | hie$^{n}$ ĕ. ĭ hie$^{n}$. | The country. Strange country. |
| 15 | hṳ̂ tî; nói tî. | Fish pond; lotus pond. |
| 16 | sói êk koi$^{n}$. se$^{n}$ tî khut. | Bath house. Full of hollows. |
| 17 | cúi khut. hie$^{n}$ lí kía$^{n}$. | A tank. A little village. |
| 18 | cí kâi hie$^{n}$ chng ciu ûi lóng cóng sĭ tî khut. | All around this village there are pools and caves. |
| 19 | hie$^{n}$ chng kâi nâng cōi nâng ká$^{n}$ khṳ̀ tî sói êk. | Of the villagers there are many who dare bathe in the pools. |
| 20 | chut sîa$^{n}$ mn̂g gūa cĭu sĭ kang cúi. hie$^{n}$ lí gūa. | Outside the city gate is the river. Outside the village. |
| 21 | tāng cí sîa$^{n}$ kàu nín cē lăi ŭ jîeh cōi lí lō? | How far is it from this city to your village? |
| 22 | kîa$^{n}$ kàu tî kî$^{n}$ khut kî$^{n}$ kɵ̀, tîeh cai thói$^{n}$ lō. | Having arrived at the pools look to your steps. |
| 23 | cí kang pi$^{n}$ ŭ jîeh cōi hie$^{n}$ chng? | How many villages are there by this river? |

# LESSON CXVI.

| | | |
|---|---|---|
| 坑 | khe$^n$; pit; trench. | |
| 坎 | khàm; precipice. | |
| 坎 | khám; pit. | |
| 坷 | khó; uneven. | |
| 崩 | pang; fall in ruins. | |
| 涸 | khó; dry up; ebb. | |
| 陷 | hām; pitch down. | |
| 泉 | cûa$^n$; a spring. | |
| 源 | ngŵn; source. | |
| 皇 | hûang; sovereign. | |
| 帝 | tì; potentate. | |
| 少 | sìo; juvenile. | |

| | | |
|---|---|---|
| 1 | sua$^n$ khe$^n$. kĭa khàm. | A ravine. Precipice. |
| 2 | khe$^n$ cúi tùi cí kò lâu lêh lâi. lâu khó. | The water of the ravine runs down here. The tide ebbs. |
| 3 | cêk pôi$^n$ sĭ kĭa sua$^n$, cêk pôi$^n$ sĭ chim khe$^n$. | One side is a steep mountain, the other a deep ravine. |
| 4 | khe$^n$ khàm. káu cûa$^n$. | A gorge. The other world. |
| 5 | cí tĭo khe$^n$ kâi ngŵn thâu tŏ sua$^n$ téng, ŏi chut cûa$^n$ ciu nî bŏi khó. | The source of this stream is a mountain spring which flows all the year round. |
| 6 | khàm kha. cé$^n$ cûa$^n$. | Foot of the cliff. Wellspring. |
| 7 | sim khám. khám khó. | Pit of the stomach. Irksome. |
| 8 | hām hāi. hām khe$^n$. | Unjustly implicate. Pitfall. |
| 9 | khe$^n$ hām. sîa$^n$ hām. | Entrap. The city has fallen. |
| 10 | sua$^n$ pang, tī hām. | A landslide; state in ruin. |
| 11 | chîe$^n$ pang tĭo khà. | The wall has fallen down. |
| 12 | cúi kháu pang khà. | The spout is demolished. |
| 13 | hŏ lêh kàu sua$^n$ thô pang cêk lō. cúi khí thâu khó. | Rained till the soil slid on to the whole path. Tide begins to ebb. |
| 14 | cúi cûa$^n$; pue cûa$^n$. | A fountain; a cascade. |
| 15 | n̂g cûa$^n$ bê láu sìo. | In the grave there are no years. |
| 16 | cúi ngŵn thâu. sìo nî. | Headwaters. Youthful. |
| 17 | cîah cúi tîeh su tîeh ngŵn thâu. láu sìo. | In drinking think of the fountain. Young and old. |
| 18 | hûang tì. hûang tì ūi. | Emperor. The throne. |
| 19 | sam hûang ngŏ tì. | The famed eight-rulers. |
| 20 | gêk hûang sĭang tì. | The highest of the gods. |
| 21 | tì hûang tì bē. pang hām. | Wear a crown. Fall, as a cliff. |
| 22 | ngŵn cûa$^n$ kún kún. | A boiling spring. |

# LESSON CXVII.

| | | | |
|---|---|---|---|
| 王 | ûang; king; royal. | 縣 | kūi$^{n}$; a district. |
| 君 | kun; ruler. | 京 | kia$^{n}$; capital. |
| 國 | kok; kingdom. | 官 | kua$^{n}$; official. |
| 省 | sé$^{n}$; province; save. | 軍 | kun; troops. |
| 府 | hú; prefecture; gentlemen. | 衙 | gê; tribunal. |
| 州 | ciu; a political division. | 塔 | thah; pagoda. |

| | | |
|---|---|---|
| 1 | kun ûang. kok kun. | Princes. The sovereign. |
| 2 | hú kun. kok ûang. | The deceased. The king. |
| 3 | kok ke. ûang ke. | Reigning family. The king. |
| 4 | gūa kok. sé$^{n}$ cî$^{n}$. | Foreign lands. Save money. |
| 5 | kok ke kâi sū. ûang bō. | National affairs. A crown. |
| 6 | sé$^{n}$ kang. kua$^{n}$ hú. | Save labor. Magistrates. |
| 7 | cò kua$^{n}$. lâk kua$^{n}$. | In office. The Six Boards. |
| 8 | kua$^{n}$ lō. gê mn̂g. pak kia$^{n}$. | Highway. Yamun. Peking. |
| 9 | lō tèng. sìa chan. | By the road. The sacrament. |
| 10 | cí kìa$^{n}$ sū ōi cò tit sêng cìu sĭ tŏ hú sîa$^{n}$. | If this thing can be accomplished, it will be at Hu city. |
| 11 | kua$^{n}$ hú í$^{n}$ keng chut gê mn̂g. gūa kok nâng. | The magistrates had left the court. Foreigners. |
| 12 | nín cêk sé$^{n}$ ŭ jîeh cōi hú ciu thia$^{n}$ kūi$^{n}$. | How many political divisions has your province? |
| 13 | tong kok kāng ŭ câp poih sé$^{n}$. ûang ke mûeh. | China has eighteen provinces. Appurtenances of kings. |
| 14 | úa kìa sìn lâi khà hue kì kok khut úa kâi chin nâng. hú sîa$^{n}$. | I am sending a letter to my relatives in America. The prefectural city. |
| 15 | tong kok kâi hûang tì cŏ ūi kàu ta$^{n}$ ŭ jîeh cōi nî; lú kāng úa tà$^{n}$. | How long since the Emperor of China ascended the throne; you tell me. |
| 16 | kia$^{n}$ kua$^{n}$ pí kak sé$^{n}$ kâi kua$^{n}$ ío tōa. | The officers of the capital are greater than those of the provinces. |
| 17 | cŭ cá ŭ cêk ki kua$^{n}$ kun tùi thah kha keng kùe. | A while ago a staff of officers went past the pagoda. |
| 18 | kun bé. sam kun. | A regiment. The army. |

## LESSON CXVIII.

| | | | |
|---|---|---|---|
| 爺 | îa; sire; noblemen. | 邦 | pang; region. |
| 權 | khŵn; authority. | 赦 | sìa; pardon. |
| 督 | tok; order; oversee. | 往 | úang; pass. |
| 法 | huap; law; rules. | 初 | chiu; first-ten days of the moon. |
| 度 | tō; measure; limit. | 初 | che; beginning. |
| 犯 | hŭam; transgress. | 常 | sîe$^{n}$; frequent. |

| | |
|---|---|
| 1 tōa lău îa. sìo îa. | 1 Your honor. Young squire. |
| 2 thài îa. úang sî. | 2 Your worship. In the past. |
| 3 jī îa, sam îa. îa mn̂g. | 3 Official attendant and his servant. Clerks in yamun. |
| 4 sîe$^{n}$ sî. phêng sîe$^{n}$ nâng. | 4 Constantly. Common people. |
| 5 sîe$^{n}$ sîe$^{n}$ ŭ. ĭ sîe$^{n}$. | 5 Always have. Unusual. |
| 6 jû sîe$^{n}$. sîe$^{n}$ sîe$^{n}$. | 6 As customary. Frequently. |
| 7 tán chut chiu. | 7 Wait till the first of the month. |
| 8 chiu it, chiu sì. | 8 First and fourth of the month. |
| 9 che thâu ē. che se$^{n}$. | 9 From the beginning. First born. |
| 10 a che ke. che lâi. | 10 A raw hand. Newly come. |
| 11 che sî. tng che. | 11 In the beginning. At first. |
| 12 che che kâi sî hāu. | 12 At the very first. |
| 13 che chut. che chù. | 13 First of the season. First-time. |
| 14 lṳ́ tāng chiu kúi lâi? | 14 What day did you come? |
| 15 kía$^{n}$ jît m̄ cai chiu kúi. | 15 Do not know what day it is. |
| 16 kim jît sĭ jîh kúi? | 16 What day of the month is it? |
| 17 che khui thi$^{n}$ tī. | 17 At the creation. |
| 18 bô lâi úang. ŭ lâi úang. | 18 No intercourse. Intercourse. |
| 19 úang sîe$^{n}$. úang jît. úang hẃn ēng jîeh kú. | 19 Heretofore. How long does it take to go and come? |
| 20 í$^{n}$ úang. úang lâi ciu bûk. | 20 Gone. Current account. |
| 21 i úang úang cìe$^{n}$ se$^{n}$. | 21 It often happens so. |
| 22 sìa cŭe. tăi sìa thi$^{n}$ ĕ. | 22 Pardon offences. General amnesty. |
| 23 sìa kùe lṳ́ cêk chù lío. | 23 I have once forgiven you. |
| 24 huap bô khó sìa. | 24 The law does not pardon. |
| 25 sìa míen. khŵn lât tōa. | 25 Forgive. Great power. |
| 26 cóng tok. hŭam huap tō. | 26 Governor. Violate the rules. |

# LESSON CXIX.

| | | | |
|---|---|---|---|
| 感 | kám; excite; act upon. | 怒 | náu; nō; anger. |
| 化 | hùe; change; alter. | 解 | kói; loosen; explain. |
| 謝 | sīa; acknowledge; decline. | 改 | kói; amend; change. |
| 恨 | hŭn; resentment. | 廨 | kòi; deliver over. |
| 怨 | ẁn; abhor; dislike. | 律 | lût; statute; usage. |
| 惡 | * ló; ù; hate; scorn. | 累 | lūi; lŭi; bind; involve. |

| | |
|---|---|
| 1 ŭ khŵn; bê khŵn; chông khŵn; khŵn lí; ló hŭn; khó hŭn; ẁn hŭn. | 1 Authoritative; without authority; yield to expediency; control; hate; odious; bear a grudge. |
| 2 tok kang. tok lí. | 2 Oversee work. To direct. |
| 3 kà tok. kok huap. | 3 Instruct. Laws of a country. |
| 4 lói huap. tăi huap kok. | 4 Code of politeness. France. |
| 5 siet huap; lîp huap. | 5 Establish rules. |
| 6 hû huap. cìa$^{n}$ huap. | 6 Lay a spell. Correct laws. |
| 7 bê huap. huap tō. | 7 No expedient. Regulations. |
| 8 ēng sih mih huap? | 8 What plan can be resorted to? |
| 9 tō se$^{n}$ kùe jît. | 9 For the time being. |
| 10 tō sìo. tō jît. | 10 Periods. Spend the day. |
| 11 bê tō. ēng khù kùe tō. | 11 Limitless. Spend extravagantly. |
| 12 tō lĭang. lĭang tō. | 12 Moderate. Good natured. |
| 13 tōa tō; sòi tō; tn̂g tō; tó tō; huap lût. | 13 Generous; contracted; wide latitude; limited; law. |
| 14 chíu cńg thau chun chut lâi io ŭ tn̂g tó. | 14 All the fingers cannot be of the same length. |
| 15 sîn sien phah kó ŭ sî tā$^{n}$. | 15 Even angels sometimes beat the drum out of time. |
| 16 hŭam jîn. hŭam cŭe. | 16 A criminal. Commit a crime. |
| 17 hŭam huap. che hŭam. | 17 Transgress law. First offence. |
| 18 cài hŭam. hŭam tîeh. | 18 Repeated offences. Encounter. |
| 19 kám sīa. kám èng. | 19 Thank you. Recompense. |
| 20 kám hùe. kói tīo. | 20 Lead to repentance. Unloose. |
| 21 nâng ŭ cŭe cè nî lêng tit kói thut? lŭi lá. | 21 How can a sinner be set free? Obliged to you. |
| 22 khat i thoa lūi tîeh. | 22 Was implicated by him. |

## LESSON CXX.

| | | | |
|---|---|---|---|
| 常 | chîang; customary. | 兵 | piaⁿ; soldier; troops. |
| 羣 | khûn; flock. | 卒 | cut; retainess. |
| 椰 | ia; gê; cocoa. | 武 | bú; military. |
| 戰 | cìen; battle. | 擊 | * kâk; beat, as with stones. |
| 將 | cìang; leader. | 丟 | * hâm; phiaⁿ; kâk; to throw away. |
| 后 | hŏ; a sovereign. | 丁 | teng; adult. |

| | |
|---|---|
| 1 lé sieⁿ eng kai kám sia i a mien? tàⁿ m̄ pat tó khà. | 1 What do you think as to its being necessary to thank him? Not know what to say. |
| 2 phêng chîang. úang chîang. | 2 Commonplace. Heretofore. |
| 3 chîang chîang. bé íⁿ. | 3 Habitual. Carpenter's bench. |
| 4 piaⁿ bé. ûang bé. | 4 Dragoons. Imperial horse. |
| 5 châ bé. cêk khûn îeⁿ. | 5 Saw-horse. Flock of sheep. |
| 6 bú cìang. cìen kah. | 6 A general. Armour. |
| 7 cìen kŭ. cìen cìang. | 7 Weapons. Warriors. |
| 8 cìen tī. cìen cûn. | 8 Battle-ground. Ship of war. |
| 9 sio hùe. m̄ hùe. | 9 Digestion. Indigestible. |
| 10 kà hùe. sie hùe. | 10 Improve by teaching. Burn charms. |
| 11 hùe seⁿ. ûang hùe. | 11 Metamorphoses. Civilization. |
| 12 hùe cîⁿ. hùe sin. | 12 Burn mock money. Transform. |
| 13 cōi sīa. sīa thiap. | 13 Many thanks. Card of thanks. |
| 14 sīa cíu. sīa kheh. | 14 After dinner call. Decline a visit. |
| 15 sīa sì. kit ŵn. | 15 Die. Harbour animosity. |
| 16 mài ŵn thiⁿ, ŵn tī, ŵn pât nâng; tîeh ŵn ka kī. | 16 Be not dissatisfied with heaven, earth, and men, but with yourself. |
| 17 hwt nō. kói ûaⁿ. kói cìaⁿ. | 17 Get angry. Exchange. Revise. |
| 18 kói kùe. kói jît. | 18 Amend. Change the day. |
| 19 kói mêng pêh. kói sueh. | 19 Explain clearly. Make clear. |
| 20 kòi hŭam. | 20 Deliver up the prisoner. |
| 21 îa cí. gê cí khak. | 21 Cocoa-nut. Cocoa-nut shells. |
| 22 piaⁿ cìang. láu cìang. | 22 Military leader. A general. |
| 23 ûang hŏ. thài hŏ. | 23 Empress. Empress dowager. |
| 24 bé piaⁿ. pō piaⁿ. | 24 Cavalry. Infantry. |
| 25 sío cut. nâng teng. | 25 Camp-followers. People. |

## LESSON CXXI.

| | | | |
|---|---|---|---|
| 瓢 | * hia; a calabash. | 印 | ìn; stamp; seal. |
| 柄 | pè$^{n}$; handle; haft. | 驗 | ngīam; verify. |
| 令 | lĕng; order; occasion. | 塞 | sat; stop up; abstruct. |
| 封 | hong; invest with. | 屍 | si; carcase. |
| 封 | huang; seal up. | 葬 | cǹg; bury; entomb. |
| 契 | khòi; covenant. | 鉋 | * thiu; a plane; to plane. |

| | | | |
|---|---|---|---|
| 1 | pia$^{n}$ teng. hō̤ lĕng. | 1 | Soldiers. A written order. |
| 2 | lĕng nâng se$^{n}$ khì. | 2 | Make one vexed. |
| 3 | léng nâng ài sieh. | 3 | Cause people to love. |
| 4 | sî lĕng. khṳ̂n pè$^{n}$. | 4 | Times and seasons. Power. |
| 5 | bô̤ ūe pè$^{n}$. châ hia. | 5 | Nothing plausible. A dipper. |
| 6 | hŏ sùa$^{n}$ pè$^{n}$, sì$^{n}$ pè$^{n}$, to̤ pè$^{n}$, pó thâu pè$^{n}$. | 6 | Handle of an umbrella, fan, knife, and axe. |
| 7 | cêk huang sìn; cêk huang n̂gn; huang m̂g. | 7 | A letter; a money packet; a sealed door. |
| 8 | huang ìn. huang tâng. | 8 | Close the seals. An envelope. |
| 9 | huang cûn. hong sîn. | 9 | Impress a boat. Deify. |
| 10 | hong kua$^{n}$. sí si. | 10 | Appoint to office. A corpse. |
| 11 | hong pĕ bó̤. | 11 | Invest parents with a title. |
| 12 | pêh khòi; âng khòi; khòi kía$^{n}$; khòi pĕ; khòi cò̤ hia$^{n}$ tĭ. | 12 | Unstamped deed; stamped deed; devoted child; a god-father; covenant brothers. |
| 13 | chù khòi. ieh khòi. | 13 | Deed of a house. Contract. |
| 14 | sat phī$^{n}$. sat chùi. | 14 | Cold in the head. Silenced. |
| 15 | cúi cô̤ sat khṳ̀, cúi bŏi kîa$^{n}$. | 15 | The trough is obstructed so the water does not flow. |
| 16 | sin si; si sin. si chin. | 16 | A dead body. The mourners. |
| 17 | ngīam toa$^{n}$. ngīam si. | 17 | A permit. Hold an inquest. |
| 18 | ngīam thói$^{n}$. èng ngīam. | 18 | Examine into. Verified. |
| 19 | ngīam sie$^{n}$; ngīam kùe líο. | 19 | Inspect the injuries. Proven. |
| 20 | chía$^{n}$ ngīam. hâp cǹg. | 20 | Invite examination. Bury together. |
| 21 | cǹg sua$^{n}$; cǹg huang cúi. | 21 | The burial ground. |
| 22 | sàng cǹg. cǹg kim. | 22 | Carry to the grave. Inurn. |
| 23 | cǹg kua$^{n}$. thiu pê$^{n}$ pê$^{n}$. | 23 | Encoffin. Plane it even. |

## LESSON CXXII.

蓋 kài; overtop; screen.
蓋 kùa; a cover.
蓋 khap; set; imprint.
蓋 khàm; cover with a cover.
蓋 kah; wrap up.
蓋 kám; a cover; cover up.

傢 ke; tools; gear.
伙 húe; furniture.
夥 húe; comrade.
計 kì; comrade.
計 kòi; scheme; compute.
繡 sìu; embroider.

| | |
|---|---|
| 1 thiu cìh. cêk ki thiu. | 1 Blade of a plane. A plane. |
| 2 thiu kût kût. cia kài. | 2 Plane it smooth. To screen. |
| 3 kài in. kài thâu, kài mīn. | 3 Because that. Screen head and face. |
| 4 kài au. kài mi mi. | 4 Covered tea-cup. Cover up closely. |
| 5 kài sì. khap cè hō. | 5 World-wide. Set a mark. |
| 6 khìeh kài au kùa khàm kài au. khap ìn. | 6 Take the cover and cover the covered cup. To print. |
| 7 kah phūe, kah hīuⁿ, kah saⁿ. | 7 Wrap up in a coverlet, wadded jacket, and tunic. |
| 8 kài úaⁿ kùa pit khà. | 8 The cover of the bowl is broken. |
| 9 khàm pò phâng, khàm kàu àm àm. | 9 Cover with an awning so it will be very shady. |
| 10 mûeh kīaⁿ khàm kín kín, mài ngio chú thau cìah. | 10 Cover the things closely so they will not be eaten by rats. |
| 11 tê kŵn kùa. sieⁿ kùa. | 11 Tea-pot lid. Trunk lid. |
| 12 khàm au kùa. háh húe. | 12 Covered basin cover. A pall. |
| 13 kah tó, kah koiⁿ thâu. | 13 Wrap the belly and shoulders. |
| 14 kah khah mi khah jûah. | 14 Bundled up too warm. |
| 15 kùa khah sòi, khàm m̄ lôh. | 15 The cover is too small to fit. |
| 16 khàm koiⁿ cháu chù, tŏ suaⁿ kha kè tīu. | 16 Has set up a straw shed, and lives at the foot of the hill. |
| 17 cí kè ŭ khàm phâng, ío lîang. khap lâi m̄ hīn. | 17 The awning here makes it cooler. Not printed clearly. |
| 18 lí tìeh khap sì cìaⁿ sì cìaⁿ, khap khí lâi cìaⁿ hó thóiⁿ. mĕng lĕng. | 18 You must set it squarely down and then the imprint will look well. Mandate. |
| 19 tíaⁿ kám. kám mi mi. | 19 Spider cover. Cover tightly. |
| 20 ke húe. húe kì. sìu hue. | 20 Tools. Partner. Embroider. |

## LESSON CXXIII.

| | | | |
|---|---|---|---|
| 營 | îa$^n$; camp; military. | 學 | hâk; ôh; learn. |
| 營 | îong; plan; cast about. | 習 | sîp; practice: used to. |
| 機 | ki; secret; moving power. | 示 | sī; make known. |
| 機 | kui; machine; loom. | 髯 | jíam; lîam; moustache. |
| 洩 | sîap; ooze; divulge. | 尼 | nî; a nun. |
| 債 | cè; debt; freight. | 婆 | phûa; an old wife. |

| | |
|---|---|
| 1 kòi khui mêng pêh. | 1 Compute it exactly. |
| 2 ēng kòi hām hāi nâng. | 2 Use a malicious stratagem. |
| 3 kāng kòi jîeh cōi? | 3 How much altogether? |
| 4 àm kòi. îa$^n$ pûa$^n$. | 4 A dark plot. A camp. |
| 5 kòi sn̂g hó, cìa$^n$ lâi. | 5 Decide upon it, then come. |
| 6 îa$^n$ pâng. jîp îa$^n$ tng pia$^n$. | 6 Barracks. Enlist as a soldier. |
| 7 thau îa$^n$. keng îong. | 7 Surprise a camp. Shrewd. |
| 8 îong se$^n$. îong ûi. | 8 Get a living. Attend to business. |
| 9 mîa ke keng îong. | 9 Fertile in ways and means. |
| 10 kun ki. chia kui thâu. | 10 Army tactics. A chain pump. |
| 11 ki hŭe. ki khì. | 11 Opportunities. Machine. |
| 12 ki bât. thien ki. chia kui. | 12 Occult. Destiny. Lathe. |
| 13 kì$^n$ ki. ki pêh pò. | 13 Improve the chance. Long cloth. |
| 14 ēng cĭn sim ki. | 14 Use every device to attain it. |
| 15 cit pò kui. cêk kui pò. | 15 A loom. A web of cloth. |
| 16 sū ki sîap lāu. | 16 The plan has leaked out. |
| 17 sîap tîeh khì. cè cú. | 17 Lost its savour. Creditor. |
| 18 thien ki m̄ hó sîap lāu. cè kía$^n$. | 18 Should not divulge the designs of heaven. Debtor. |
| 19 khìam cè su hâi$^n$ cè. | 19 Debts must be paid. |
| 20 pàng cè. cíu cè. | 20 Shave notes. Tavern score. |
| 21 cī$^n$ cè sòi kù. | 21 The debt is of little consequence. |
| 22 hâk sîp. khui ôh. | 22 Learn. Begin to study. |
| 23 ôh bú; ôh tn̂g; ôh kua$^n$; lé ôh tit pat, mē? | 23 Practice military exercises; school-room; superintendent of schools; can you learn? |
| 24 kà sī. nî ko. tau lâu. | 24 Educate. A nun. Detain. |
| 25 lău phûa. lău a phûa. | 25 The wife. My good woman. |

## LESSON CXXIV.

| | | | |
|---|---|---|---|
| 剪 | ka; shear; clip. | 虹 | khĕng; rainbow. |
| 鉸 | ka; pivot; hasp. | 篾 | bīh; splints; slats. |
| 哀 | ai; sorrow; woful. | 業 | ngîap; patrimony; trade. |
| 料 | līo; estimate; strass; stuff. | 士 | sṳ̄; scholar; statesman. |
| 朝 | chîo; dynasty; facing. | 他 | tha; that; other. |
| 朝 | cio; early. | 威 | ui; majesty; awful. |

| | |
|---|---|
| 1 cai cōe. jīn cūe. | 1 Aware of his sin. Confess sin. |
| 2 ka to. ka pò. ka saⁿ khò. | 2 Scissors. Cut cloth. Cut out clothes. |
| 3 i ŏi ka ŏi cò. cêk cio. | 3 She can cut and fit. In a trice. |
| 4 lāi to kuah cúi m̄ tn̄g. | 4 No knife will divide water. |
| 5 bûa ka to phah só sì. | 5 Preparing to do mischief. |
| 6 hûi khì cn̂g kâi pit khù. | 6 The crockery is all cracked. |
| 7 i ōh chùi ōh cīh. | 7 He mimics them. |
| 8 lú mài ōh ieⁿ ōh sieⁿ. | 8 Don't you imitate him. |
| 9 àiⁿ ōh sía jī pit soiⁿ tīeh ōh bīe. | 9 If you would learn to write, you must first learn tracing. |
| 10 bói cêk peh ki thih teng. | 10 Buy a hundred nails. |
| 11 ai khàu. ai ŭn kâi siaⁿ. | 11 Weeping. A piteous wailing. |
| 12 thâu khàu, thâu khîu. | 12 Crying while she besought. |
| 13 ai cú. ai ai pĕ bó. | 13 Motherless bairn. Alas, my parents. |
| 14 ai khîu. cìo līo. | 14 Supplicate. To oversee. |
| 15 lio lí. lio sṳ̄ jû kìⁿ. | 15 Manage. You will find it so. |
| 16 put chut úa só līo. | 16 It is no more than I expected. |
| 17 bé lio. put lio. cṳ̄ lio. | 17 Provender. Unforeseen. I think. |
| 18 kiaⁿ lio. lio khì. | 18 Best sort of strass. Imitation stone. |
| 19 chân lio. îeh lio. sek lio. | 19 Fertilizers. Drugs. Coloring stuff. |
| 20 lio mûeh. lân lio. | 20 Materials. It is hard to say. |
| 21 cṳ̄ lio cò m̄ lâi. | 21 I think it cannot be done. |
| 22 cá chîo. cŏ chîo. | 22 Ancient dynasties. Hold court. |
| 23 chîo kìⁿ. pn̄g chîo. | 23 Go to court. Our dynasty. |
| 24 chîo pâng. chîo hôk. | 24 Audience room. Court dress. |
| 25 cŏ tang chîo sai. | 25 Sit on the east facing west. |
| 26 nŏ nâng cŏ sie chîo. | 26 The two sit facing each other. |
| 27 sṳ̄ ngîap; ke ngîap. | 27 Employment; estate. |

# LESSON CXXV.

靈 lêng; disembodied agency.
竅 khìo; aperture; pore.
懇 khṳ́n; importunate.
囘 * khùn; a moment.
停 thêng; stop; arrange.
止 cí; halt; desist.

其 khî; whatever; wherever.
餘 ṳ̂; overplus; remnants.
抵 tú; abut; mulct.
抵 tí; bear the consequences.
報 pò̤; requite; inform.
賞 síeⁿ; reward.

1 sṳ̆ cut; kun sṳ̆. hâk sṳ̆.
2 sṳ̆, lông, kong, siang. tha nâng. tha hng. îu tha khṳ̀.
3 ui hong; hóⁿ ui; ṳ̆ ui; hwt ui; ui ngîam; ui bú; kuaⁿ ui. bô̤ ui khì; ui lêng.
4 lêng ki. bw̄n bw̄n seⁿ lêng.
5 im lêng. lêng ī. lêng èng.
6 m̄ khui khìo. lêng khìo.
7 káu khìo. chit khìo.
8 sim khìo. khṳ́n khîu.
9 tán cêk khùn kíaⁿ.
10 ke cêk khùn kíaⁿ.
11 thêng kang; thêng chíu; thêng cí; thêng tṳ̀g.
12 saⁿ thêng lō íⁿ keng kîaⁿ líu nō̤ thêng.
13 m̄ cí saⁿ kâi. cí hueh.
14 cí i m̄ cṳ̆. khî ṳ̂.
15 bô̤ tīaⁿ cí. cí âu.
16 cai khî it, m̄ cai khî jī.
17 khî tang. khî chṳ̀. sie tú.
18 ṳ̂ tī. ṳ̆ ṳ̂.
19 bô̤ ṳ̂. ṳ̂ lât.
20 tú tit cṳ̆. tāi tí.
21 tí cṳ̆e. tú sìo, tí sìo.

1 Warriors. Cabinet minister.
2 Scholars, farmers, mechanics, and merchants. That man. Other places. Let it go.
3 Awful; terrible; dignified; threatening; solemnity; martial; august. Undignified; efficacy.
4 Effective contrivance. The living.
5 Ghosts. Supernatural. Effective.
6 Uncomprehending. Accumen.
7 Passages of the body. The senses.
8 The intellect. Beg earnestly.
9 Wait a minute.
10 Presently.
11 Stop work; stay your hand; cease; well arranged.
12 Of the three stages we have already walked two.
13 Not merely three. Staunch blood.
14 It can't be stopped. What is over.
15 No definite object. Quench thirst.
16 Know one but not the other.
17 Therein. The next. Abut on.
18 Unused space. More than enough.
19 None to spare. Extra force.
20 It will not give way. In general.
21 Bear the blame. Pay a mulct.

## LESSON CXXVI.

| | | | |
|---|---|---|---|
| 媒 | bûe; a go-between. | 汛 | sìn; guard house. |
| 朋 | phêng; friend; consort. | 塘 | tn̂g; post-station. |
| 友 | íu; companion. | 杆 | kua$^n$; staff; post. |
| 僕 | pôk; vassal; menial. | 眙 | * hoi; blinking. |
| 裔 | ĭ; posterity. | 聾 | lâng; deaf. |
| 禁 | kìn; restrict; forbid. | 非 | hui; negative. |

| | | |
|---|---|---|
| 1 | tí mĭa. tú i. | Compensate for a life. Mulct him. |
| 2 | tú nâng mĭa. | Make atonement for a life. |
| 3 | pò èng. pò tap. pò ak. | Requite. Reward. Revenge. |
| 4 | mài cang ak pò ak. pò kía$^n$. | Requite not evil. Courier. |
| 5 | pò i cai. tit tîeh síe$^n$. | Inform him. Get a reward. |
| 6 | tîeh ŭ cêk kâi nâng khùa kāng i tà$^n$ ūe; kāng i tà$^n$ ūe kâi nâng kìe cò bûe. phêng íu. | There must be some person to go and do the talking; the one who does the talking is called a go-between. Friend. |
| 7 | bûe phûa. | An old woman who settles matches. |
| 8 | sĭa bûe nâng. | Remunerate the go-between. |
| 9 | kua$^n$ bûe; sĭ kua$^n$ siet kâi tĭ hng, hŭam hŭ jîn, hŭam tăng cŭe kâi, kua$^n$ cĭu kìm i tŏ hú kò; jû eng kai lêng ūa$^n$ kè kâi, cĭu sûi kua$^n$ bûe cú ì hwt kè. | An official go-between: the magistrate appoints a place where undutiful wives may be shut up; and from there they are again married off according to the will of the go-between. |
| 10 | chin phêng. sa$^n$ phêng sì íu. | A relative. A coterie of friends. |
| 11 | hó phêng. lău phêng íu. | Good friend. Old friend. |
| 12 | íu ài. iah íu. | Fraternal. Helpful friend. |
| 13 | nô pôk. pĭ pôk. | Man servant. Servants. |
| 14 | ău ĭ. ĭ sun. îa$^n$ sìn. | Posterity. Descendants. Guard-house. |
| 15 | pôk pôk. sìn tĭ kua$^n$. | Drudge. Station-master. |
| 16 | câp lí cĭu ŭ kâi tn̂g. | The stations are a league apart. |
| 17 | îa$^n$, tn̂g, sìn, sa$^n$ kĭa$^n$. | Three sorts of halting places. |
| 18 | ûi kua$^n$; kî kua$^n$. | A mast; a flag-staff. |
| 19 | ké cò hĭ$^n$ lâng. | Pretended to be deaf. |
| 20 | mài kio nâng sĭ hui. | Do not contradict people. |

# LESSON CXXVII.

| | | | |
|---|---|---|---|
| 㾕 | * heⁿ; asthmatic. | 疥 | kòi; the itch; a scratch. |
| 瀉 | sìa; purge; flow off. | 瘡 | chng; an eruption. |
| 痘 | cu; tāu; small-pox. | 痂 | phí; scab of a sore. |
| 斑 | pang; poiⁿ; blotched; mottled. | 疱 | phă; a blister. |
| 癩 | * thûe; a boil; ulcer. | 瘤 | lîu; tumor; wen. |
| 膿 | lâng; pus; slough off. | 痸 | * chái; spasms; fits. |

| | | |
|---|---|---|
| 1 | khùn kíaⁿ i àiⁿ lâi. | He is coming presently. |
| 2 | chíaⁿ thêng cŭ khùn kíaⁿ. | Stop a little while. |
| 3 | hó hiah hêk cêk khùn kíaⁿ. | Rest a little while. |
| 4 | hó thêng kha cêk khùn kíaⁿ. | Stay your steps a little. |
| 5 | cĭam chíaⁿ thêng chíu cêk sî. | Just stay your hand a moment. |
| 6 | chíaⁿ thêng kang câp jît. | Let us stop work for ten days. |
| 7 | ngŏ lói pài, thêng bói bōi cêk jît. kìm cí. | When Sunday occurs, traffic stops for a day. Prohibit. |
| 8 | lú seⁿ kòi, tîeh cîah lîu n̂g bûah. | You have itch, and must take sulphur. |
| 9 | úa cá mê gût bô cêk khùn kíaⁿ. hó khì hueh. | I slept scarcely any last night. Fresh and plump. |
| 10 | cí pńg cheh cĭam pàng tŏ cí kò, khùn kíaⁿ úa lâi khîeh tńg. kìm tī. | I will leave this book here, and in a little while come and get it. Forbidden ground. |
| 11 | úa pat ngŏ tîeh i. | I have met him before. |
| 12 | kìm cut. kìm sîaⁿ. | Turnkey. The closed citadel. |
| 13 | mâk hoi hoi. sîa cío mâk. | Squint-eyed. Cross-eyed. |
| 14 | heⁿ pēⁿ. sìa îeh. sìa tó. | Asthma. A purgative. Purging. |
| 15 | nêk lîu. húe sìa; jûah sìa. | Fleshy tumor. Fever with purging. |
| 16 | sìa nŏ chù. sìa cúi. | Purged twice. Open a sluice. |
| 17 | chut cu. cieⁿ cúi. tāu cieⁿ. | Have small-pox. Pustules. Virus. |
| 18 | cèng cu; cèng tāu. mīn poiⁿ. | Vaccinate. Pock-marked. |
| 19 | poiⁿ kùe hóⁿ hŏi. | More spotted than a tiger-crab. |
| 20 | pàng lâng. lâng hueh. | Let out the pus. Bloody sloughing. |
| 21 | phí būe hó peh tīo. | Do not pick off the scab yet. |
| 22 | kit phí. hueh lîu. | Form a scab. Vascular tumor. |
| 23 | tîeh îeⁿ chái. tu bó chái. | Have fits. Convulsions. |
| 24 | seⁿ chng. kha seⁿ phă. | Have a humor. Foot is blistered. |

# LESSON CXXVIII.

瘰 lêk; king's evil.
抽 thiu; lift; draw; levy.
* 痘 tāu; chicken-pox.
* 疹 mûe; measles.
痠 sng; aching.
腹 pak; the caul.
* 咳 ka; hack; cough.
嗽 sàu; clear the throat.
狂 khûang; sío; insane.
癲 tien; crazed; silly.
且 chía$^{n}$; moreover; still.
土 thó; earth; territory.

| | |
|---|---|
| 1 i sǐ úa kâi sim pak kâi phêng íu, m̄ pí sǐ cíu nêk kâi phêng íu. | 1 He is my bosom friend and it is not as if he were merely a boon companion. |
| 2 i kio úa sǐ chin, hui pí tha nâng. | 2 He is my own near relative, and it is not as if he were another. |
| 3 hàu$^{n}$ sueh sǐ hui ūe pǐen sǐ sǐ hui nâng. | 3 He who is fond of gossip, is a gossip. |
| 4 bô hui ká$^{n}$ sǐ lé? hui lói. | 4 Is it really you? Indecent. |
| 5 sǐ sǐ a sǐ hui? | 5 Is it a fact or is it not? |
| 6 hui jîen. cá mńg. | 6 Really not so. Early and late. |
| 7 pit hui bô kù. | 7 It is certainly not without a cause. |
| 8 khá hui kù ì! | 8 How can it be unintentional! |
| 9 ka sàu hó lío. thiu kan. | 9 His cough is cured. Cramp. |
| 10 thiu khí lâi. cúi thó hó. | 10 Draw it up. The soil is good. |
| 11 ke it thiu. thiu tīo tói. | 11 Add a tithe. Take out the bottom. |
| 12 thiu sin cò i khù. | 12 He took himself off. |
| 13 cîah tāu, cîah mûe. | 13 Have chicken-pox and measles. |
| 14 sng thìa$^{n}$. kut sng. | 14 Aching. Rheumatic pains. |
| 15 kha sng, chíu nńg. | 15 Weak and weary. |
| 16 tó pak tōa. i sǐ sío. | 16 A big paunch. He is crazy. |
| 17 kháu bît, pak kìam. | 17 Honey tongued and false hearted. |
| 18 kháu sǐ, sim hui. | 18 Specious and insincere. |
| 19 cí pak ûi hun. | 19 Betrothed before birth. |
| 20 ka sàu. khûang pē$^{n}$. | 20 Cough. Insanity. |
| 21 hwt khûang. sío káu. | 21 Out of his head. Mad dog. |
| 22 khûang huang, mé hŏ. | 22 Furious gusts and driving rain. |
| 23 tien khûang. hwt tien. | 23 Raving mad. Become delirious. |
| 24 cu tien. úa chía$^{n}$ mn̄g lé. | 24 Pedantic. Let me now ask you. |

## LESSON CXXIX.

| | | | |
|---|---|---|---|
| 文 | bûn; literary; elegant. | 榻 | thap; pen-case. |
| 經 | kia$^{n}$; keng; classics. | 行 | * cūe; line; column; seam. |
| 詩 | si; poems; odes. | 章 | cie$^{n}$; chapter; essay. |
| 易 | îah; diagrams. | 念 | līam; learn by heart. |
| 硯 | ɪ$^{n}$; ink-stone. | 講 | * ôh; narrate; recite. |
| 遍 | pìn; pìen; circuit; whole. | 記 | kì; record; remember. |

| | |
|---|---|
| 1 ɪ$^{n}$ pûa$^{n}$. pit tâng. | 1 Writing tray. Pen holder. |
| 2 sueh bûn. pêh bûn. | 2 Discuss letters. Plain text. |
| 3 ôh kó. lâi līam úa thia$^{n}$. | 3 Tell stories. Recite it to me. |
| 4 chía$^{n}$ kîa$^{n}$ chía$^{n}$ khàu. | 4 Crying as he walked along. |
| 5 bun lí; sî bûn; kó bûn; bûn cie$^{n}$; bûn huap; bûn ôh. | 5 Style; current literature; ancient literature; fine writing; grammar; scholar. |
| 6 ngŏ kia$^{n}$; kia$^{n}$ cu; îah kia$^{n}$; cu kia$^{n}$; si kia$^{n}$; sîn si. | 6 Five classics; the classics; the diagrams; history; poetry; hymns. |
| 7 hwn sa$^{n}$ pìen. līam keng. kó si. ôh si kù. tăi hâk. | 7 Review three times. Chant passages. Ancient poetry. Recite rhymes. Great Science. |
| 8 sît jī; ûah jī; hu jī. | 8 Nouns; verbs; particles. |
| 9 pit bâk ɪ$^{n}$ khîeh lâi. | 9 Bring writing implements. |
| 10 kì tit. m̄ kì tit khù. | 10 Remember. Quite forgotten. |
| 11 làn cêk cūe. pío cie$^{n}$. | 11 Omit a column. A memorial. |
| 12 pìn tī n̂g kim. | 12 All the earth is golden. |
| 13 thâk ke kúi pìen. | 13 Read it a few times more. |
| 14 pìen koi$^{n}$ pâng. kì hō. | 14 The whole room. A mark. |
| 15 thâk sêk líao hó hwn. | 15 Read it perfectly then review. |
| 16 kua$^{n}$ ūe; pêh ūe; thó ūe. | 16 Court dialect; common language; unlearned speech. |
| 17 bûn bú. bûn jîn. bûn kua$^{n}$, bú kua$^{n}$. | 17 Civil and military. Literary men. Civil and military officers. |
| 18 lú thâk ŭ kúi cie$^{n}$? | 18 How many chapters have you read? |
| 19 thâk cêk pìen úa thia$^{n}$. | 19 Read it over to me once. |
| 20 bô cūe. pit cūe. se$^{n}$ cūe. | 20 Seamless. To crack. Cracked. |

## LESSON CXXX.

| | |
|---|---|
| 寮 lîo; hut; shed. | 廟 bīe; fane; temple. |
| 庫 khò; treasury; magazine. | 棚 pê$^n$; staging; shed. |
| 監 kam; prison; oversee. | 倉 chng; granary; bin. |
| 獄 gêk; prison; jail. | 行 hâng; warehouse; guild. |
| 庵 am; religious house. | 勞 lâu; labor; toil. |
| 宮 keng; temple; palace. | 釣 tìe$^n$; to hook; bait. |

| | | |
|---|---|---|
| 1 | bûn ngía; sĭ cí tĭeh nâng kâi īe$^n$ sìe$^n$. | Intellectual; refers to the appearance of persons. |
| 2 | lá hó ôh úa thia$^n$. ôh kó. bé pâng. gêk cut. | Relate it to me. Narrate stories. Stable. Jailor. |
| 3 | cí nō kù ūe sĭ cí tī cêk kīa$^n$ sū tà$^n$? ŭ lâu lá. | What do these two sentences refer to? Have troubled you. |
| 4 | lá kí cêk kīa$^n$ sū lâi phì jŭ úa thia$^n$. chhâ lîo. | Point out something which will illustrate it. Wooden shed. |
| 5 | n̂gn khò; chng khò; tī gêk. | Treasury; storehouses; hell. |
| 6 | kìm kam, siu kam. cŏ kam. | Put in jail. Be in prison. |
| 7 | cáu kam hŭam. kam tok. | Escaped prisoner. To boss. |
| 8 | am tn̂g. jîp am. | Budhist temple. Enter a nunnery. |
| 9 | nî ko am. lâm am. | A nunnery. A monastery. |
| 10 | ûang keng. keng bīe. | Royal palace. Temple. |
| 11 | ôh keng. tŏ né keng; phah lôh né keng. | College. Sent to the residence for discarded concubines. |
| 12 | ke bīe; có bīe. sîn bīe. | Ancestral temple. Idol temple. |
| 13 | hì$^n$ pê$^n$; tah pê$^n$; lō thâu pê$^n$; ke$^n$ pê$^n$; cháu lîo. | Theatrical stage; put up a staging; shed by the road; watchman's shed; hut. |
| 14 | chek chng. khui chng. hùe chng. hâng phò. | Granary. Dispense grain. Depot. Place of business. |
| 15 | hâng ke. tâng hâng. | Head manager. Same firm. |
| 16 | cai hâng, m̄ cai hâng. | Versed or not versed in this business. |
| 17 | hâng hùe. lâu sîn. | Wares. Careworn. |
| 18 | i sĭ sih mih hâng tàng kâi nâng? tìe$^n$ hê. pâng lîo. | What is his craft? Catch fish. Shanty. |
| 19 | lâu lât. lâu sim. tìe$^n$ ko. | To labor. Be anxious. Fish-pole. |

## LESSON CXXXI.

| | | | |
|---|---|---|---|
| 殿 | tōi$^{n}$; palace; temple. | 鋪 | pho; spread; bedding. |
| 關 | kwn; bar; belong to. | 楹 | ê$^{n}$; beams. |
| 館 | kw̃n; hall; caravansary. | 桷 | kak; rafters; lath. |
| 層 | cân; tier; degrees. | 堵 | tú; a brace; impede. |
| 窗 | theng; window. | 蕉 | cie; plantains. |
| 瓦 | hĭa; tiles; flags. | 巧 | khá; dextrous; apt. |

| | | |
|---|---|---|
| 1 | lâu lú kio úa cò. | Trouble you to do it for me. |
| 2 | lâu tŏng. m̄ ká$^{n}$ lâu tŏng lú. | To trouble. Dare not bother you. |
| 3 | chù kak. kwn sim. | Roof slats. Attentive. |
| 4 | keng tōi$^{n}$. tōi$^{n}$ ĕ. | Palace. Crown prince. |
| 5 | kim tōi$^{n}$. khui kwn. | Golden halls. Unbar. |
| 6 | nín kùi hú tŏ tĭ kò? | Where are your gentlemen? |
| 7 | pàng kwn. kwn kháu. | Let pass. Place for passing. |
| 8 | m̄ kwn úa sū. | It is none of my business. |
| 9 | lú bô kwn sim thói$^{n}$. | You did not pay attention. |
| 10 | se$^{n}$ sí kâi kwn thâu. | A matter of life and death. |
| 11 | ui kw̃n; cíu kw̃n; kong kw̃n; cu kw̃n; hŭe kw̃n; kau lâu kw̃n; kw̃n tĭ; khui kw̃n, kói kw̃n. | Hospital; tavern; public hall; library; club-house; restaurant; a post; open and close a session. |
| 12 | sa$^{n}$ cân lâu. theng mn̂g. ŭ kúi cân? thi$^{n}$ theng. cân chut put khîong. ŭ cân chù. hâng theng. tâng theng phêng íu. | Three story building. Window. How many steps up? Skylight. Endless series. Has gradations. Poor student. Fellow students and classmates. |
| 13 | pho hĭa; pho cháu chîeh; pho siet; phah pho; tâng pho; pho pang. | Lay tiles; spread matting; set in order; make up a bed; bed-fellow; bed boards. |
| 14 | tú sat. tú chùi. tú cŭ. khîeh ki mûeh khù tú, tú kín kín. | Wall up. Gag the mouth. Obstruct. Take something and brace it very firmly. |
| 15 | keng cie. khî khá. | Bananas. Ingenious. |
| 16 | khá chie$^{n}$; khá ie$^{n}$; khá kang; sòi khá. | Cunning hand; curious pattern; skilled work; complex. |

# LESSON CXXXII.

| | | | |
|---|---|---|---|
| 排 | pâi; place properly. | 耞 | * ké<sup></sup>ⁿ; flail. |
| 列 | lîet; range; state. | 鍫 | * chîang; shovel. |
| 鐶 | hŵn; ring; link. | 紛 | hun; confused. |
| 鋸 | kṳ̀; saw; toothed. | 難 | lān; difficulty. |
| 鐮 | lîam; sickle. | 災 | cai; calamity. |
| 鈎 | kau; hook; barb. | 患 | hŭam; tribulation. |

| | |
|---|---|
| 1 lṳ́ pâi hâng tōiⁿ kúi? | 1 Which are you, among the sons? |
| 2 kúi nâng cŏ̤ cò̤ cêk pâi. | 2 All sit down in a row. |
| 3 îeⁿ pâi kut. tu pâi kut. | 3 Mutton chops. Ribs of pork. |
| 4 ūaⁿ pâi. pâi tît tît. | 4 Rearrange. Set straight. |
| 5 pâi lîet nŏ̤ pôiⁿ. | 5 Ranged on two sides. |
| 6 khui lîet mêng pêh. | 6 State the case clearly. |
| 7 pâi cò̤ cêk lîet. | 7 Place them in file. |
| 8 cêk lîet jîeh cōi câng chīu? | 8 How many trees in each row? |
| 9 chíu hŵn; kha hŵn; hīⁿ hŵn; mn̂g hŵn; tâng hŵn. | 9 A bracelet; anklet; ear-ring; door-knocker; brass ring. |
| 10 kṳ̀ khí; kṳ̀ tio. | 10 Teeth of a saw; saw it off. |
| 11 kau lîam; lîam to̤. | 11 Pruning-hook; sickle. |
| 12 tìeⁿ kau; kau chut lâi; hīⁿ kau; kau lîen. | 12 Fish-hook; hook it out; ear-drop; coadjutors. |
| 13 khîa ki kéⁿ khṳ̀ phah chek. | 13 Take a flail and thresh rice. |
| 14 phûe chîang. sòi kṳ̀. | 14 A crow-bar. Small saw. |
| 15 chîang kúi kâi khang. | 15 Shovel out some holes. |
| 16 nâng mûeh hun hun. | 16 Everybody in confusion. |
| 17 hun lŭan; sim hun hun. | 17 Bustling; perplexed. |
| 18 pâi lān, kói hun. | 18 Explain a misunderstanding. |
| 19 cai lān; cúi cai, húe cai; thien cai; cai hāi. | 19 Adversity; flood and fire; calamity; afflictive. |
| 20 hŭam lān; bô̤ ău hŭam. | 20 Affliction; no sad results. |
| 21 put hŭam bô̤ nâng, cí hŭam bô̤ cîⁿ. | 21 Not distressed for lack of men but for lack of money. |
| 22 kṳ̀ tek, kâi kṳ̀, khí ío bât. | 22 Thinned out bamboos grow better. |
| 23 cí ki êⁿ m̄ hó̤ kṳ̀ khah tó̤. pâi cò̤ cêk tît. | 23 Do not saw this beam off too short. Set them in a row. |

## LESSON CXXXIII.

耙 pê; a harrow.
押 ah; compel; escort.
押 ap; pawn; keep.
架 kè; frame; rack.
枕 cím; pillow; contiguous.
帳 tà; tìe$^{n}$; curtain; tent.

寢 chím; sleep; rest.
鏡 kìa$^{n}$; a reflecting surface.
視 sì; see; behold.
歸 kui; return; revert.
簾 lîam; splint screen.
勺 * sîeh; a ladle.

| | | |
|---|---|---|
| 1 | ah khù kìm, ak khù thâi. | Take to prison, to execution. |
| 2 | kam ah jîeh kú? | How long was he under arrest? |
| 3 | ah hûe khù. ah hāu. | Escort back. Compel to wait. |
| 4 | úa ah i m̄ cŭ. | I could not arrest him. |
| 5 | ah hùe. síe ap. | Convoy goods. Pawn-shop. |
| 6 | ah sàng nâng. | The guard of a prisoner. |
| 7 | ēng kúi nâng khù ah i? | How many must go to his arrest? |
| 8 | ap sìo. lôh kâi hue ap. | Leave security. Put on a mark. |
| 9 | ap tît lío. câp jī kè. | Settled by pledges. A cross. |
| 10 | sa$^{n}$ kè; bō kè. | Clothes-horse; hat rack. |
| 11 | kè mûeh. cio kè. | Support a thing. Head off. |
| 12 | kè khí. cím thâu. ău cím. | Prop up. Pillow. Occiput. |
| 13 | hī$^{n}$ cím. cím tîeh. sie cím. | Hollow pillow. Touching. Adjoin. |
| 14 | cím kùe khù cē. | Overlap them a little. |
| 15 | cím pi$^{n}$ ūe. tâng cím. | Private talk. Using one pillow. |
| 16 | máng tìe$^{n}$. siet tìe$^{n}$. | Mosquito bar. Fix a curtain. |
| 17 | pho tìe$^{n}$. tâng chím. | Canopy. Bed-fellow. |
| 18 | chím cîah put ua$^{n}$. | No leisure to eat or sleep. |
| 19 | kìa$^{n}$ thâi. chíu kìa$^{n}$. | Mirror. Hand mirror. |
| 20 | cìe sin kìa$^{n}$. choi$^{n}$ lí kìa$^{n}$. | A pier-glass. A telescope. |
| 21 | peh hue kìa$^{n}$. mêng kìa$^{n}$. | A kaleidoscope. A reflector. |
| 22 | mâk kìa$^{n}$. mâk kŭn sì. | Spectacles. Near-sighted. |
| 23 | kìa$^{n}$ hue cúi gûeh. | Reflected flowers and moon. |
| 24 | sì sū. sîa sì. | Examine a case. Side glance. |
| 25 | sì nâng jû kí. | View others as yourself. |
| 26 | tît sì. mn̂g lîam. | Direct observation. Door screen. |
| 27 | sì sí jû kui. | Look upon death as going home. |
| 28 | tń̂g kui pń̂g kok. | Return to native land. |

## LESSON CXXXIV.

| | | | |
|---|---|---|---|
| 除 | tû; subtrnct; besides. | 微 | mûi; trifling; minute. |
| 傳 | thûn; promulgate. | 隱 | ún; obscured; retired. |
| 拾 | sîp; collect; arrange. | 藏 | chûng; conceal. |
| 伴 | phūa$^n$; associate. | 壺 | hû; a tankard. |
| 半 | * khùeh; a piece. | 林 | lîm; forest; grove. |
| 鉢 | puah; earthen basin. | 之 | cu; in regard to. |

| | | |
|---|---|---|
| 1 | kui hâi$^n$ lú. lîam lâi. | Give back to you. Secluded. |
| 2 | hieh lôh kui kun. | The leaves revert to the roots. |
| 3 | cí kâi nâng kui kun tīa$^n$ tîeh hó. káu kui. | This man's antecedents are good. Arithmetical processes. |
| 4 | nâng sí kui thó. | Men die and return to dust. |
| 5 | pun kui pn̂g hâng. | Analyze the constituents. |
| 6 | kui cūe pàng i kò. | The sin reverts upon him. |
| 7 | kui tû. tû tīo hà hôk. | Division. Lay aside mourning. |
| 8 | tû pē$^n$. tû hāi. | Remove disease. Suppress evil. |
| 9 | tû hui sĭ lú—. | Premising that it be you—. |
| 10 | tû chú cu gūa cīu bô. | Besides this, there are none. |
| 11 | tû siu ău, hûn khìam jîeh cōi? | Besides what has been received, how much is due? |
| 12 | cám cháu, tû kun. | Completely eradicate it. |
| 13 | tû sí nâng! | Enough to kill any body! |
| 14 | híen mûi kìa$^n$. mûi sòi. | Microscope. Atomic. |
| 15 | thói$^n$ tîeh mûi mûi. | See the least specks. |
| 16 | mûi mûeh; mûi chìe. | A trifle; a passing smile. |
| 17 | ún mûi; ún chûng; ún ún. | Abstruse; hidden; occult. |
| 18 | ún sŭ; ún mîa, ún sè$^n$. | Retired scholar; retired life. |
| 19 | cŭ ún sua$^n$ lîm. | Hid away in the country. |
| 20 | chîu lîm; têk lîm. | Forest; bamboo copse. |
| 21 | chûng kàu mi mi. | Very closely concealed. |
| 22 | cíu hû. thûn kà. | Wine-jug. Propagate doctrines. |
| 23 | thûn sueh; thûn lĕng; thûn ūe; có thûn; thûn sì. | Legend; promulge orders; transmit information; tradition; make known. |
| 24 | siu sîp. phūa$^n$ lêng. | Gather up. Watch by the dead. |

## LESSON CXXXV.

| | | | |
|---|---|---|---|
| 蛆 | chu; maggots; larva. | 俯 | hú; phak; stoop down. |
| 談 | thâm; phûeh; converse. | 伏 | hôk; lie prostrate. |
| 修 | siu: adjust; renovate. | 務 | bŭ; business; make effort. |
| 難 | lâng; harass; vex. | 奏 | càu; celebrate; perform. |
| 爆 | * pòng; pop; burst. | 樂 | gâuh; music. |
| 畫 | ūe; draw; paint. | 每 | múe; every; each. |

| | | |
|---|---|---|
| 1 | bô hó kâi tâng phŭa$^{n}$ put jû tôk kîa$^{n}$. | If you have not good company it is best to walk alone. |
| 2 | kìe úa sie phŭa$^{n}$. | Called me to go with him. |
| 3 | phûeh kàu pùa$^{n}$ mê. | Chatted until midnight. |
| 4 | ieh tīa$^{n}$ jı̍t cí. im gâuh. | Fix a certain day. The octave. |
| 5 | cí pńg cu cheh sĭ sía kâi a sĭ ìn kâi? put jû. | Is this book written or printed? Nothing like. |
| 6 | thâm lŭn; thó thâm. | Discuss. Local pronunciation. |
| 7 | chìe thâm. thâm pia$^{n}$. | Repartee. Discuss the war. |
| 8 | mài khù kāng i phûeh ūe. | Do not go and talk with him. |
| 9 | thâm kó lŭn kim. | Talking of things old and new. |
| 10 | i bô mih sîn khì, mài kio i phûeh khah kú. | He has not much vitality, do not talk too long with him. |
| 11 | cîh se$^{n}$ chu. cúi se$^{n}$ chu. | Festers on the tongue. Wigglers. |
| 12 | phak lôh khù. phak ké. hú hôk. hôk pia$^{n}$. | To stoop down. Bend over. Bow down. Troops in ambush. |
| 13 | múe sî; múe jı̍t; múe nî; múe nâng; múe sū; múe múe jû chú. | Every time; every day; every year; each person; every affair; always like that. |
| 14 | siu lí; siu pó; siu sin; siu sim; lâng ûi. | Regulate; repair; act well; cultivate the mind; harass. |
| 15 | sū bŭ. bŭ pit. | Business. Indispensable. |
| 16 | kong bŭ; ke bŭ; gūa bŭ; bŭ gūa. | Public affairs; private affairs; outside affairs; strive for something else. |
| 17 | pòng phùa khù. pòng lìh. | Burst assunder. Cracked open. |
| 18 | kha tháng pòng kho. | The tub has burst its hoop. |
| 19 | càu gâuh. gâuh khì. | Make merry. Musical instruments. |
| 20 | gâuh sia$^{n}$. ūe sua$^{n}$ cúi. | Musical. Draw landscapes. |

## LESSON CXXXVI.

爆 * phòng; explode.
譭 hûi$^n$; defame; slander.
謗 păng; vilify; malign.
和 hûa; concord; union.
尊 cun; venerate; honor.
敬 kèng; revere; respect.

搶 chíe$^n$; clutch; engross.
僻 phiah; phìa$^n$; partial; base.
站 căm; a stage of a journey.
提 thî; bring forward.
浮 phû; lift up; rise; float.
暈 * kông; fuddled; dull.

| | | |
|---|---|---|
| 1 | lṳ́ m̄ hó lâng ûi pât nâng. | You should not harass others. |
| 2 | hûi$^n$ păng. hûa phêng. | Slander. At peace. |
| 3 | hûa khì. káng hûa. | Complaisant. Treat of peace. |
| 4 | hûa ieh. hûa sŭn, hûa hó. | Treaty of amity. Accordant. |
| 5 | sim hûa khì phêng. | Reconciliation after strife. |
| 6 | cun kùi. cun kèng. | Venerate. Reverence. |
| 7 | hâu kèng. kèng tŏng. | Revere. Hold in esteem. |
| 8 | chíe$^n$ pêh. chíe$^n$ soi$^n$. chíe$^n$ khùe chíu. chíe$^n$ cì$^n$ hó$^n$. chíe$^n$ tit khà. | Make a clean sweep. Thrust one's self forward. Snatch out of the hand. Robber. Take by force. |
| 9 | cip phiah, sè$^n$ phìa$^n$. put jû. | Prejudiced. It is the best way. |
| 10 | cêk căm lō. thî kîp. | One stage. In regard to. |
| 11 | kúa$^n$ kâu jît àm cia$^n$ kâu căm. phû khí lâi. | Followed till dark before reaching the stopping place. Float up. |
| 12 | thî khí. thî hûang. | Suggest. To warn against. |
| 13 | thî ché$^n$ i kâi sim. | Intimate it to him. |
| 14 | thî phû. thâu kông kông. | To bring to notice. Heavy headed. |
| 15 | pât nâng bô kâi sṳ̄, lṳ́ m̄ hó hûi$^n$ păng. | When other people have done nothing, you should not malign them. |
| 16 | nín hia$^n$ tī tîeh siang kèng siang àì. | You boys must be respectful and kind to each other. |
| 17 | lî mîn chíe$^n$. phû phà$^n$. | Secretly appropriate. Become light. |
| 18 | kúi ie$^n$ hûa cò cêk ē. | Several sorts united in one. |
| 19 | thî khí i kâi mîa úa cíu se$^n$ khì. ŏi phòng. | If you introduce his name I shall be angry. Explosive. |
| 20 | lṳ́ tîeh cun i cò tŏa. | You must defer to him. |
| 21 | i kèng lṳ́, lṳ́ cò nî tin tò hûi$^n$ păng i? | He honors you, why do you turn about and slander him? |

## LESSON CXXXVII.

| | | |
|---|---|---|
| 磕 | khâp; to hit against. | |
| 瞌 | * tak; to nod. | |
| 叩 | khàu; tap; knock the head. | |
| 考 | kháu; question; examine. | |
| 抖 | * hì$^{n}$; shake; quiver. | |
| 交 | kau; blend; hand over. | |
| 盞 | cúa$^{n}$; cup; wine saucer. | |
| 疑 | gî; doubt; suspect. | |
| 瞞 | mûa; deceive; hide. | |
| 饒 | jîo; fertile; affluent. | |
| 聞 | bŭn; to hear. | |
| 梭 | so; shuttle. | |

| | | |
|---|---|---|
| 1 | khâp thâu, khâp hîah. | To run against each other. |
| 2 | sie tak thâu. i tŏ tak. | Nod to each other. He is nodding. |
| 3 | tak mâk gût. chai gî. | Asleep and nodding. Suspicion. |
| 4 | khâp thâu; khàu thâu. | Kneel and knock the head. |
| 5 | sa$^{n}$ kŭi, káu khàu. | Three kneelings and nine knockings. |
| 6 | khàu kì$^{n}$. kháu mn̄g. | Visit a superior. Examine. |
| 7 | kháu m̄ tîeh. kháu tit tîeh. kháu jîeh kûi$^{n}$? kháu tîeh it téng. | Not pass examination. Pass the examination. How high did he stand? In the first grade. |
| 8 | hì$^{n}$ tīo eng têng. sin bŭn cúa. | Shake the dust off. Newspaper. |
| 9 | kau chíu. kau í$^{n}$. kau pue, ūa$^{n}$ cúa$^{n}$. | To hand to one, to swap. Armchair. Wedding cups. |
| 10 | teng cúa$^{n}$. kau sa$^{n}$ tíam. | Lamp cup. Just three o'clock. |
| 11 | sim gî se$^{n}$ àm kúi. | The imagination creates ghosts. |
| 12 | kŭi lôh khṳ̀ khâp thâu. | Kneel and hit the forehead. |
| 13 | i mih sṳ̄ to cai. | He is well informed. |
| 14 | khîeh ṳ̂n sái ṳ̂n. | Spends all he gets. |
| 15 | ēng cía mài gî; gî cía mài ēng. | Do not distrust what you use nor use what you distrust. |
| 16 | gî pē$^{n}$. ṳ́n mûa. kau hâi$^{n}$. | Irresolute. Secret. Deliver over. |
| 17 | sît put siang mûa. | I will hide nothing from you. |
| 18 | pù jîo. jîo sêk. so kía$^{n}$. | Fertile. Abundant. Shuttle. |
| 19 | câp poih so cûn. | Eighteen shuttle-shaped boats. |
| 20 | pûi jîo kâi tī hng. | Fertile tract of land. |
| 21 | hṳ́ kò kâi nâng khio. | The people there are poor. |
| 22 | lṳ́ mûa úa m̄ tit. | You cannot deceive me. |
| 23 | cî$^{n}$ n̂gn lŭn kau chíu. | Money passes from hand to hand. |
| 24 | lṳ́ cêng mûa i, i sĕ í$^{n}$ ài$^{n}$ gî lṳ́. | You have deceived him, therefore he will distrust you. |

## LESSON CXXXVIII.

可 * thang; the wherewith.
針 cam; needel; pin.
暑 sú; summer heat.
縷 * nn̂g; to hem; overstitch.
縷 nîap; to darn; fell.
縫 * thī$^{n}$; sew; baste.

渴 kuah; thirsty; dry.
吞 thun; swallow; gulp.
嚼 * pō; chew; ruminate.
剃 thì; shave.
臨 lîm; lîam; while; come to.
織 * chiah; crochet; knit.

| | |
|---|---|
| 1 pùa$^{n}$ sìn, pùa$^{n}$ gî. | 1 Half believing, half doubting. |
| 2 úa bô thang hó hâi$^{n}$. | 2 I have not the wherewith to pay. |
| 3 bô thang ēng, tîeh lâi bói. | 3 If you have not what you need use, you must buy some. |
| 4 bô thang hó chēng. | 4 Not wherewith to be clothed. |
| 5 bô thang hó cò. | 5 Nothing to do it with. |
| 6 ŭ thang cîah, ŭ thang ēng. | 6 Something to eat and to use. |
| 7 cam khang, cam búe. | 7 Eye and point of a needle. |
| 8 sî pie cam, sî ceng cam. | 8 Hand of a watch and clock. |
| 9 cam pō khah tn̂g; mài chiah hìe$^{n}$ tn̂g. | 9 The stitches are too long; do not take them so long. |
| 10 phang chì. huang hŏ cam. hâng sú cam. cam tùi. | 10 Sting of a bee. Barometer. Thermometer. Identical. |
| 11 cí kúi kù cṳ sĭ cam tùi kua$^{n}$ hú sueh. kau cam. | 11 These sentences are indicative of the official words. Backstitch. |
| 12 cí cie$^{n}$ cṳ kâi ì kio tŏi$^{n}$ it cie$^{n}$ kâi ì cam tùi. | 12 The meaning of this chapter elucidates that of the first. |
| 13 cam phī$^{n}$. chng cam. | 13 Eye of needle. Thread a needle. |
| 14 hâng lâi sú úang. | 14 Heat and cold alternate. |
| 15 sĭu sú. sie$^{n}$ sú. | 15 Sun-stroke. Injured by the heat. |
| 16 sú khì. khṳ̀ sú. | 16 Sultry heat. Cooling. |
| 17 âu ta; âu kuah. thì thâu. | 17 Thirsty. Shave the head. |
| 18 cí kuah; kói kuah. pō mî. | 18 Quench thirst. Chew fine. |
| 19 kîam cúi âu ta nâng cîah. | 19 The thirsty will drink any water. |
| 20 thun lôh khṳ̀. thun m̄ lôh. | 20 Swallow it. Could not swallow. |
| 21 thun lîap îeh î$^{n}$. thì to. | 21 Swallow a pill. Razor. |
| 22 lîam kuah khṳ̀ kût cé$^{n}$. | 22 Wait till thirsty, then dig a well. |
| 23 chiah lâi ngía căi. | 23 It is very neatly stitched. |

# LESSON CXXXIX.

| | | | |
|---|---|---|---|
| 陞 | seng; ascend; rise. | 全 | * kàu; whole one. |
| 降 | kàng; descend; degrade. | 宿 | suah; sojourn; halt. |
| 降 | * hâng; reduce to terms. | 舐 | cĭ; lick; lap. |
| 投 | tâu; have recourse to. | 齧 | ngiet; gnaw; craunch. |
| 罵 | mē; revile; abuse. | 拍 | tah; phah; pat. |
| 蝕 | sih; incroach on; lose. | 抄 | so; rub with the hand. |

| | | |
|---|---|---|
| 1 | seng kuaⁿ. seng thiⁿ. | Promoted in rank. Go to heaven. |
| 2 | ŭ seng, ŭ kàng. | Some were promoted, some degraded. |
| 3 | cí jît kàu seng! | May you soon be promoted! |
| 4 | seng kî. seng tñg. | Raise a flag. Sit on the bench. |
| 5 | kàng lîm. kàng sì. kàng lôh. kàng seⁿ. | Come from the sky. Descend into the world. Decended. Be born. |
| 6 | hâng piaⁿ. tâu hâng. kui hâng. tâu hiah. tâu mêng. tâu bûn cu. ūe m̄ tâu ki, pùaⁿ kù te. | Quelled troops. Surrendered. Return to allegiance. Seek a lodging. Make known to. Hand in dispatches. Of unwelcome words, half a sentence is too much. |
| 7 | jît sìh; gueh sìh. | Eclipse of the sun and moon. |
| 8 | bōi sìh pñg cêk ûe. | Sold for half its cost. |
| 9 | suaⁿ ngîap pĭ a pĕ sô bōi tīo. khí thâu kàu suah búe. cìah m̄ tìeh cúi thó. | The estate which was sold by his father. From beginning to end. The climate disagrees with him. |
| 10 | sio sìh; ēng sìh. | Waste away; wear away. |
| 11 | kàu lîap; kàu kâi; kàu phit; kàu tàⁿ; kàu koiⁿ chù; kàu ciah cûn. | A whole pill; a whole one; the whole piece; whole picul; the whole house; the whole of the boat. |
| 12 | ŏi khí thâu bŏi suah búe. | Can begin but cannot end. |
| 13 | lṳ́ cá mê tŏ tī kò hiah suah? suah hiah. | Where did you stop last night? Take lodging. |
| 14 | gû bó cĭ gû kíaⁿ. | The cow licks her calf. |
| 15 | káu tŏ ngiet tṳ kut. | The dog gnaws a bone. |
| 16 | tah i kâi kôiⁿ thâu. | Pat him on the shoulder. |
| 17 | so i kâi thâu khak. | Stroke his head. |
| 18 | i hàuⁿ sñg, lṳ́ tìeh mē i. | He is fond of play; you must scold him. |

## LESSON CXL.

| | | | |
|---|---|---|---|
| 輪 | lûn; wheel; rotate. | 遭 | cūa; time; occasion. |
| 輦 | lín; barrow; transport. | 遭 | cau; encounter; endure. |
| 圈 | khwn; khuang; encircle. | 趺 | * pûah; fall; slip down. |
| 摧 | * léng; push; thrust. | 背 | pùe; pŭe; back; behind. |
| 啼 | thî; crow; coo; wail. | 襪 | bûeh; stockings. |
| 囘 | * hăn; times; turns. | 吮 | cuh; to suck. |

| | | |
|---|---|---|
| 1 | chiah ìu$^{n}$ ìu$^{n}$. cam kang. | Stitch it neatly. Needle work. |
| 2 | thì$^{n}$ bât bât. thì$^{n}$ kau cam. | Sew it closely. Backstitch it. |
| 3 | thì$^{n}$ khah cho. thì$^{n}$ ìu$^{n}$ ìu$^{n}$. | Sewed too coarsely. Sew finely. |
| 4 | sĭ ke$^{n}$ a sĭ chiah? | Is it woven or knitted? |
| 5 | lûn tîeh i. sie lûn. | It is his turn. Take turns. |
| 6 | lûn cẃn. chia lûn. | Revolve. Cart wheel. |
| 7 | lûn cûn. hĭ$^{n}$ lûn. | Wheeled boat. Rim of the ear. |
| 8 | lûn hŵn. lûn lîu. | Turning wheel. In rotation. |
| 9 | lín chia. lín kùe lâi. | A wheel-barrow. Roll it over. |
| 10 | lín tōa phàu. mn̂g khwn. | Gun-carriage. Door-casing. |
| 11 | mâk kìa$^{n}$ khuang. kìa$^{n}$ khuang. cío khuang. | Rim of spectacles. Frame of a picture. Bird ring. |
| 12 | kîa$^{n}$ m̄ chut khuang. | Not go outside the ring. |
| 13 | ûi cò cêk khwn. | Form a circle around it. |
| 14 | kîa$^{n}$ cêk tōa khwn. | Went on a wide circuit. |
| 15 | mài léng i pûah. | Do not push him down. |
| 16 | léng tó. léng khui. | Push over. Push open. |
| 17 | thî thî khàu khàu. | Moaning and weeping. |
| 18 | koi thî sa$^{n}$ lôh. | The cock crew the third time. |
| 19 | o a tŏ kìe. khù kúi hûe; khù kúi tńg; khù kúi hăn; khù kúi chù. khù cêk cau; khù cêk cūa. khù sì cūa lío. | The crows are cawing. Went several times. Went once. I have been there four times already. |
| 20 | cūa cūa ngŏ lú m̄ tîeh; cí cūa ngŏ tîeh lío. | Time after time I missed you; this time I have met you. |
| 21 | cau huang; cau cúi cai; cau lān; cau chât. | Meet with storms; encounter floods; endure hardship; fall among thieves. |
| 22 | siang pŭe. pùe ău. | Back to back. Behind it. |

## LESSON CXLI.

| | |
|---|---|
| 牌 pâi; tablet; buckler. | 壓 * teh; crush; repress. |
| 旨 cí; scope; decree; will. | 抑 * jih; press down. |
| 簿 phŏ; register; record. | 鑄 cù; cast in a mould. |
| 揾 ùn; dip; immerse. | 領 nía; receive; manage. |
| 浸 cìm; soak; immerse. | 式 sek; sample; a dime. |
| 積 cek; hoard; increase. | 鏟 * lĭu; shovel; spade. |

| | |
|---|---|
| 1 cieh pâi. húe pâi. chía" pâi. tîn pâi. cêk hù cúa pâi. hī" pâi. síe" n̂gn pâi. hó" thâu pâi. phah pâi. | 1 Stone tablet. Express. A permit. Rattan shield. A pack of cards. Flat ear-rings. A medal. Yamun tablets. Gamble. |
| 2 cuh nĭ. cuh hueh. cuh cap. cuh kàu ta. | 2 To nurse. Suck the blood. Suck the juice. Suck dry. |
| 3 cie" cí. cí ì. kam cí. | 3 Synopsis. Purpose. Delicious. |
| 4 sìo phŏ. cìe" phŏ. jît kì phŏ. hâh sek. | 4 Account book. Enter in account. Diary. Like the sample. |
| 5 ùn cúi. ùn tâm. | 5 Dip in the water. Wet, by dipping. |
| 6 cìm sí. cìm thn̂g. | 6 Drowned. Merge in sugar. |
| 7 cek ak, cek sĭen. | 7 Accumulate guilt or merit. |
| 8 cek cî" n̂gn. cek nî. | 8 Amass wealth. Added years. |
| 9 cek cò cêk ē. | 9 Pile it up together. |
| 10 teh sí. teh cŭ. | 10 Crush to death. Repress. |
| 11 jih lôh khù. jih jîp. | 11 Pressed down. Press it in. |
| 12 cù cî". cù phàu. cù ûang pó. teh m̄ cŭ. | 12 Coin money. Cast cannon. Coin sycee. Cannot suppress. |
| 13 ûang pó cêk kò ngŏ câp níe tăng; sĭ n̂gn. | 13 A sycee is fifty ounces in weight, and is of silver. |
| 14 nía cî". nía sū hú. | 14 Receive money. A consul. |
| 15 úa m̄ ká" kāng i pau nía. | 15 I dare not be bail for him. |
| 16 úa bô pún nía. | 16 I have not the ability. |
| 17 chau kùe phŏ. | 17 Transfer the account. |
| 18 nía toa"; siu toa"; hùe toa"; n̂gn toa". | 18 Order; receipt; bill of lading; draft. |
| 19 kak sek. lâk sek. | 19 All sorts. Six dimes. |
| 20 lú hāi i pûah lôh khù. | 20 You made him fall down. |

## LESSON CXLII.

| | |
|---|---|
| 桑 * sûi; the mulberry tree. | 敗 pāi; subvert; ruin. |
| 柿 săi; persimmon. | 廢 hùi; degenerated. |
| 店 tìam; stand; inn. | 壞 hŭai; spoiled; destroyed. |
| 埕 tîa$^n$; arena; an area. | 德 tek; virtue; goodness. |
| 場 tîe$^n$; floor for drying grain; arena. | 瞌 * siap; sleepy; dull. |
| 載 cài; convey; load; lade. | 道 tău; tŏ; path; principle. |

| | |
|---|---|
| 1 sng sûi. âng săi. | 1 Mulberries. Persimmons. |
| 2 thŵn tău lí. tău lō. | 2 Promulge doctrines. The way. |
| 3 sìn tek. pāi hŭai. hùi hŭai. | 3 Faith. Spoiled. Ruined. |
| 4 cí ciah cûn ōi cài kúi nâng? | 4 How many will this boat carry? |
| 5 mâk siap. âng săi kîe. | 5 Sleepy. Tomatoes. |
| 6 âng săi kîe cìe$^n$. săi pía$^n$. | 6 Catsup. Dried persimmons. |
| 7 lú sĭ cìe$^n$ se$^n$ ìeh úa. | 7 That is what you promised me. |
| 8 thia$^n$ tŏ lí kâi sî hāu m̄ hó mâk siap. | 8 At the time of preaching, you should not get sleepy. |
| 9 săi pía$^n$ khîeh khù gūa tîa$^n$ phâk. im tek. | 9 Put the dried persimmons to sun in the area. Goodness. |
| 10 mài pāi hŭai tîeh i kâi tek. cek tek. | 10 Do not destroy his worth. Increase in virtue. |
| 11 tìam lăi kâi mûeh kĭa$^n$ lóng cóng hùi hŭai khù. | 11 All the things in the stall were spoiled. |
| 12 khùe khùe cài sng sûi hîeh lâi chĭ chôi$^n$. | 12 Speedily carry mulberry leaves to feed the silk-worms. |
| 13 ìam tîe$^n$. pāi tîe$^n$. | 13 Salt pans. Spoiled market stuff. |
| 14 bí tîe$^n$. hâ tîe$^n$. | 14 Rice stall. Fish stall. |
| 15 bûn tîe$^n$ kháu líò, cìu kháu bú tîe$^n$. | 15 The literary candidates will be examined, then the military. |
| 16 cìa$^n$ tău. tăi tău. | 16 Correct doctrine. The great doctrine. |
| 17 lú kâi cûn cài mih kâi? | 17 What does your boat carry? |
| 18 lō tău phêng. pāi hŭai. | 18 The road is safe. Subvert. |
| 19 tŏ cí koi$^n$ tìam suah hiah. | 19 Lodge at this inn. |
| 20 tìam ke. tìam phò. mê tìam. hiah kheh. | 20 Taverns. Eating stand. Lodgings. Lodgers. |
| 21 kheh thâu phò. phò cú. | 21 Hotel. The proprietor of an inn. |

# LESSON CXLIII.

盆 phûn; a basin.
閒 ôi$^{n}$; leisure; unoccupied.
游 îu; idle; rove and enjoy.
稅 sùe; rent; duties on goods.
租 co; rent; income.
緄 kún; trim; bind; cord.

選 sẃn; choose; select.
擇 tê̤h; pick out; prefer.
振 cín; stimulate; rouse.
振 * tin; joggle; stir.
復 hôk; again; return.
圖 tô; map; plan.

| | | |
|---|---|---|
| 1 | mīn phûn. îu hì$^{n}$. | A wash basin. Frequent theatres. |
| 2 | ôi$^{n}$ tī; ôi$^{n}$ mûeh; ôi$^{n}$ ūe; ôi$^{n}$ sṳ̄; ôi$^{n}$ nâng; ŭ ôi$^{n}$. | Vacant ground; unused thing; idle talk; trifling; idler; at leisure. |
| 3 | îu chíu hàu$^{n}$ ôi$^{n}$. | The idler loves to loaf about. |
| 4 | úa m̄ kw̄n nâng kâi ôi$^{n}$ sṳ̄. úa m̄ ôi$^{n}$. | I have nothing to do with their foolishness. I am busy. |
| 5 | ôi$^{n}$ sĭ ôi$^{n}$ hui. | It is idle gossip. |
| 6 | sùe phò. sùe kẃn. | Rent a shop. Custom-house. |
| 7 | siu tī sùe. cí īe$^{n}$ mûeh ài$^{n}$ kùe sùe ēng jîeh cōi cî$^{n}$? | Collect ground rent. How much is the duty on this article? |
| 8 | cí koi$^{n}$ chù sĭ ka kī kâi a sĭ sùe kâi? tī tô. | Is this house your own or is it hired? An atlas. |
| 9 | siu hâng co. lṳ́ ŭ jîeh cōi koi$^{n}$ hâng phò co nâng? | Collect store-rent. How many shops have you rented to people? |
| 10 | i cêk nî toa$^{n}$ toa$^{n}$ siu co n̂gn cĭu ŭ câp bw̄n. | In a year he receives a hundred thousand dollars of rents alone. |
| 11 | ài$^{n}$ kún o. kún tîo. kún pĭ$^{n}$, kún kim pĭ$^{n}$. | Will bind it with black. Trimming. Braid for trimming. Trim with gold braid. |
| 12 | sẃn tê̤h kâi ngía kâi. | Pick out a pretty one. |
| 13 | che$^{n}$ cî$^{n}$ bw̄n sẃn. | One good cash in ten thousand. |
| 14 | tê̤h cheng khih cheng khih. | Pick it over till it is clean. |
| 15 | lṳ́ tê̤h tī cêk kâi? | Which do you prefer? |
| 16 | cûn co. hôk se$^{n}$, hôk ûah. | Boat-hire. Return to life. |
| 17 | ui cín sì hái. tăi cín ke sia$^{n}$. | He is one who can arouse the whole country. His energy has made his family famous. |
| 18 | mài tin tăng. hûe hôk. | Don't stir. Return an answer. |
| 19 | chíu bōi tin tăng. | Cannot move his hands. |

## LESSON CXLIV.

圖 thû; reckon on; scheme.
退 thè; withdraw; decline.
夢 māng; dream.
究 kìu; search out; examine.
追 tui; follow; pursue.
徒 thû; follower; futile.

含 * kâm; hold in the mouth.
含 hâm; tolerate; full.
毬 kîu; a ball; globe.
功 kong; meritorious.
功 * kang; strength; efficacy.
播 * ìa; scatter; sow.

| | |
|---|---|
| 1 tham thû. thû mîa thû lĭ. lú thói$^{n}$ cí kĭa$^{n}$ sū ŭ thû a bô thû? | 1 Calculate upon. Scheme how to become powerful. Do you think there is likelihood of this? |
| 2 cí kâi kía$^{n}$ tĭ bô thû. | 2 This boy is of no account. |
| 3 cí kĭa$^{n}$ sū oh thû. | 3 This is hard to calculate on. |
| 4 tô hêng. hêng tô. | 4 A sketch. The outline. |
| 5 to tô. tè thè. | 5 Map of the country. Shirk. |
| 6 thè chin. thè cî$^{n}$. | 6 Break a betrothal. Abate the price. |
| 7 thè hùe phò. thè sek. | 7 Warehouse. Faded out. |
| 8 thè pō. thè ău. thè sū. thè pia$^{n}$. | 8 Step backward. Draw back. Withdraw from the business. Retreat. |
| 9 cìen pāi, thè cáu. | 9 When defeated, beat a retreat. |
| 10 māng kì$^{n}$. cêk tîe$^{n}$ tōa māng. | 10 Dreamed. One long dream. |
| 11 māng m̄ kàu kâi sū. | 11 Dream did not come to pass. |
| 12 káng kìu. kháu kìu. | 12 Elucidate. Find out by questions. |
| 13 tui kìu. chim kìu. ngîam kìu. tui kúa$^{n}$. | 13 Pursue the investigation. Search into. Examine strictly. To chase. |
| 14 lú tùe úa kâi chùi búe tà$^{n}$. | 14 You say it after me. |
| 15 tui m̄ tîeh. kín kín tui. | 15 Did not overtake. A close chase. |
| 16 tui hong i kâi pĕ bó. | 16 Get posthumous honors for parents. |
| 17 tui su. tui pia$^{n}$. | 17 Reflect upon. Soldiers in pursuit. |
| 18 thû tĭ. mn̂g thû. hâm chìe. | 18 Pupil. Disciple. Smile. |
| 19 bô lói cu thû. | 19 An uncivil rascal. |
| 20 thû lâu bô iah. | 20 Trouble without advantage. |
| 21 thû lâu bô kong. | 21 Effort without achievment. |
| 22 hue hâm hâm, būe khui. | 22 Flower just ready to open. |
| 23 pau hâm. hái hâm. | 23 Inclosed in. Lenient. |
| 24 lú kâi chùi tèng kâm sih mûeh? | 24 What have you in your mouth? |

# LESSON CXLV.

| | | | |
|---|---|---|---|
| 念 | lĭam; reflect upon. | 集 | cîp; convene; compile. |
| 作 | cak; do; act. | 戒 | kài; inhibit; caution. |
| 專 | cwn; single; sole. | 刑 | hêng; legal punishment. |
| 變 | pìen; pì$^{n}$; change. | 刑 | * hîa$^{n}$; jurisprudence. |
| 騙 | phìen; delude; cheat. | 罰 | hŵt; offense; penalty. |
| 聚 | cŭ; assemble. | 部 | pŏ; tribunal; total. |

| | |
|---|---|
| 1 kang lât. ēng kang. | 1 Efficacy. Work hard. |
| 2 kong lâu. sêng kong. | 2 Merit. Finished work. |
| 3 ŭ kong. kong tek. | 3 Meritorious. Virtue. |
| 4 kong mîa. mīn phûn kè. | 4 Honor. A wash-stand. |
| 5 ciang kong pó cŭe. | 5 Make merit offset sin. |
| 6 cîah ua$^{n}$ ôi$^{n}$ kâi pn̄g. | 6 Eat the bread of idleness. |
| 7 tán úa ôi$^{n}$, úa kio lú cè-pû chut koi. | 7 Wait till I am at leisure and I will go out with you. |
| 8 sói ŏi thè sek. | 8 If washed it will fade. |
| 9 i cè mn̂g thû. kì lĭam. | 9 He is a disciple. Recollect. |
| 10 úa kì lĭam i. | 10 I bear her in mind. |
| 11 cín cak. cwn mn̂g. | 11 To encourage. A specialty. |
| 12 cwn kò ciah cûn. | 12 To charter a boat. |
| 13 cwn sim cwn ì. | 13 With all the heart and mind. |
| 14 cwn mn̂g ui mâk. | 14 The specialty of an oculist. |
| 15 cwn khŵn. cwn it. | 15 Having sole power. Particularly. |
| 16 cŭ cwn. cwn cwn. | 16 Take on one's self. Especially. |
| 17 cak ûi. pē$^{n}$ hwt cak. | 17 Doings. The ailment has returned. |
| 18 i ŏi pìen cè nâng. | 18 It will change into a man. |
| 19 máng sĭ îu chu pìen hùe kâi; chu sĭ îu chàu cúi sé se$^{n}$ kâi. | 19 Mosquitoes are generated from larvae; larvae are produced in stagnant water. |
| 20 kói pì$^{n}$. pìen thong. pìen sim. pì$^{n}$ mīn. | 20 Reform. Adapt to. Change the mind. Change countenance. |
| 21 cè chât kâi nâng bŏi tit phìen chù pi$^{n}$; thâu cîah kâi nâng bŏi tit phìen ngĕ âu. | 21 The thief cannot deceive his neighbour; one who steals food does not deceive his throat. |
| 22 cŭ cîp. hêng hŵt. | 22 Assemble. Punishment. |
| 23 hîa$^{n}$ pŏ. | 23 Board of Punishments. |

## LESSON CXLVI.

| | | | |
|---|---|---|---|
| 向 | hìang; towards; from. | 忍 | lún; jím; bear; suffer. |
| 誡 | kài; injunction. | 守 | cíe<sup></sup>ⁿ; síu; keep; guard. |
| 召 | tīo; summon; cite. | 吏 | lī; officer; deputy. |
| 差 | che; envoy; send. | 戶 | hŏ; an inner door. |
| 承 | sêng; accept; succeed. | 耐 | nāi; endure; forbear. |
| 賜 | sṳ̀; confer; bestow. | 括 | kwt; inclose; include. |

| | |
|---|---|
| 1 hŵn hŵn hôk hôk. | 1 Repeatedly; to reiterate. |
| 2 hôk mĕng. | 2 Report on a commission. |
| 3 ôi tói hṳ̂ lún kàu chùi chúa. pau kwt. síe sṳ̀. | 3 The sole enduring till its mouth is awry. Contain. To reward. |
| 4 ku chìe pih bṳ̂ mṳ̂. | 4 Pot calls kettle black. |
| 5 cíe$^n$ pn̄g bŏi nūa; cíe$^n$ bó bŏi tōa. kài khúu. | 5 A watched pot never boils. Live sparingly. |
| 6 hŭam sṳ̄ khí thâu lân. | 6 Everything begins with difficulty. |
| 7 sêk lêng se$^n$ khá. | 7 Familiarity produces skill. |
| 8 ūe hó$^n$ ūe phûe, lân ūe kut; cai nâng cai mīn, put cai sim. | 8 You paint the tiger's skin, not his bones; you know men's faces, not their hearts. |
| 9 bṳ̂ î$^n$ cap īa lâi. | 9 Half a loaf better than no bread. |
| 10 hîa$^n$ pâng. kîa$^n$ hêng. | 10 Criminal bureau. To punish. |
| 11 lâk pŏ; tī pŏ; lói pŏ; hŏ pŏ; pia$^n$ pŏ; hîa$^n$ pŏ; kang pŏ. lún m̄ khṳ̀; nāi m̄ khṳ̀; jím m̄ khṳ̀. | 11 The six Boards; the Board of Civil Office; of Rites; of Revenue; of War; of Punishments; of Works. Cannot endure it. |
| 12 jím khì thun sia$^n$. | 12 Restrain anger by silence. |
| 13 nāi tit khṳ̀. m̄ nāi. | 13 Can stand it. Not durable. |
| 14 jím m̄ cŭ. cíe$^n$ chù. | 14 I cannot bear it. Watch the house. |
| 15 síu pńg hūn. | 15 Keep to your own business. |
| 16 mn̂g hŏ. cûn hŏ. | 16 Household. Boat people. |
| 17 hŏ kháu. hìang tī cêk pôi$^n$? | 17 Population. Which way does it face? |
| 18 mn̂g hŏ siang tùi. | 18 The families are of equal rank. |
| 19 ke ke hŏ hŏ cīe$^n$ se$^n$. | 19 Every family does thus. |
| 20 hìang lâi. cêk hìang. | 20 Hitherto. For a while. |
| 21 hìang côi$^n$ khṳ̀. tam sêng. | 21 Go ahead. Guarantee. |

## LESSON CXLVII.

| | |
|---|---|
| 痕 hûn; scar; mark; trace. | 許 hú; allow; acquiesce. |
| 付 hù; enjoin on; give to. | 近 * bûa; approach. |
| 託 thôh; intrust to. | 接 ciap; cih; meet; connect. |
| 牧 môk; have oversight. | 黠 * sek; knowing; wily. |
| 師 su; sai; master. | 奈 năi; resource. |
| 進 cìn; advance; progress. | 棧 càng; a loft; go-down. |

| | | |
|---|---|---|
| 1 | hìang i cieh ñgn. | Borrow money from him. |
| 2 | hìang úa tàⁿ. | Attend to what I say. |
| 3 | hìang pak. jī cap sì hìang. | Facing north. Points of compass. |
| 4 | sim hìang hìang àiⁿ khù sñg. | His mind is on his play. |
| 5 | sêng jīn. sêng sīu. sai pĕ. sêng tng. sêng ciap. | Confessed. Accepted. Boss. Undertaken. Take in charge. |
| 6 | m̄ cai ŏi tit sêng ciap i kâi ūi a bŏi. | Do not know whether he can supersede him. |
| 7 | cí cêk kù ūe pau kwt lóng cóng. èng hú. hú phùe. | This sentence includes it all. Grant. Betroth to. |
| 8 | ŭ cêk hō bun kíaⁿ kìe cŏ o bun. mâk cap hûn. | There is a species of gnat called black gnat. Traces of tears. |
| 9 | mài ûeh seⁿ hûn. | Do not get it scratched. |
| 10 | cñg kah hûn. hù thoh. | Mark of thumb nail. To commission. |
| 11 | kau hù. hù lâi. | Transfer. Receive from. |
| 12 | sĭ lú hú úa kâi. | It is what you permitted me. |
| 13 | ē jît m̄ hú lú cieⁿ seⁿ. | I shall not allow it again. |
| 14 | hù thoh lú. môk su. | Commit it to you. Pastor. |
| 15 | thoh lú. môk îeⁿ. | Commission you. Tend sheep. |
| 16 | kìa chi, thoh cú. | Commit to wife and children. |
| 17 | láu su. sai hiaⁿ tī. su îa. cúi su. kà su. kun su. pâng su; cō su. | Learned man. Chums. Secretary. Marines. Teacher. Strategist. Examiners. |
| 18 | sie ciap. cìn kŭn; kìaⁿ bûa. | To splice. To approach. |
| 19 | cìn côiⁿ. bûa lâi. | Make progress. Draw near. |
| 20 | cham che lō thâu. | Place where roads meet. |
| 21 | jû hô? hô pit jû chú? | What way? What need of this? |
| 22 | bô khó năi hô; bô năi hô. | There is no help for it. |

## LESSON CXLVIII.

屬 sôk; belong to.
睬 chái; notice; greet.
捨 sía; relinquish.
怕 phà$^n$; dread; fear.
財 châi; wealth; profits.
械 hăi; gyves; device.

哰 lô; gabbling.
咩 meh; bleating.
咯 kok; clucking.
啾 cok; sputtering.
喔 ok; twittering.
呀 ă; final particle.

| | |
|---|---|
| 1 cò chúa chùi. càng pâng. | 1 Making faces. Go-down. |
| 2 sù pun ẃn. càng co. | 2 Bestow it upon us. Storage. |
| 3 lú kì$^n$ cóng tok căi tit ká$^n$? sok ĕ. | 3 As for seeing the governor, how dare you? Subordinates. |
| 4 eng kai cò mih sū cìa$^n$ ŏi tit phêng an? | 4 What should be done in order to be at peace? |
| 5 lú cīe$^n$ jît só cò kâi sū sĭ būe cêng kāi úa tà$^n$. | 5 What you did the other day you have not yet told me. |
| 6 lú phah sùg ài$^n$ chía$^n$ tī kâi ui seng lâi? thien châi. | 6 Which doctor have you decided to call? A windfall. |
| 7 lú cài tit cai cí kâi sū? | 7 How could you know this? |
| 8 lú cai mêng, ă? | 8 You comprehend, do you? |
| 9 i m̄ chái nán. | 9 They pay no attention to us. |
| 10 lú sĭ ài$^n$ sàng sè$^n$ mīa ă? | 10 You want to lose your life, do you? |
| 11 lú ká$^n$, sĭ, ài$^n$ sía tīo lú kâi se$^n$ mīa, ă? | 11 You dare be willing to lay down your life, dare you? |
| 12 lú ài$^n$ chŵn sía tīo ke ngîap ă? | 12 Your would wholly sacrifice your property, would you? |
| 13 thiap jîeh cōi cìa$^n$ kàu cok? | 13 How much will suffice? |
| 14 hó cò nî siu sîp? | 14 How can it be regulated? |
| 15 ciap i sia$^n$ búe tà$^n$. | 15 Say it after him. |
| 16 tāng cá kak úa sĭ lú ă? cí kâi sĭ sôk tī tîang? | 16 The one that hit me a while ago was you, was it? Whose is this? |
| 17 mài chái i. hwt châi. | 17 Don't notice him. Get rich. |
| 18 tham se$^n$ phà$^n$ sí. | 18 Covet life and dread death. |
| 19 châi cú. khì hăi. kun hăi. | 19 Rich man. A contrivance. Weapons. |
| 20 lô lô kìe. meh meh kìe. kok kok kìe. cok cok kìe. | 20 Gabble. Bleat. Clucking. Sputtering. |

## LESSON CXLIX.

| | | | |
|---|---|---|---|
| 淪 | lûn; whirl; engulf. | 兆 | tĭo; omen; prognostic. |
| 亡 | bûang; destroyed; lost. | 板 | pán; tune; a plank. |
| 福 | hok; happiness. | 板 | póiⁿ; slab; a register. |
| 局 | kêk; a game; affair. | 彩 | chái; variegated; lucky. |
| 吉 | kit; fortunate. | 雕 | tio; engrave; carve. |
| 凶 | hiong; unfortunate. | 刻 | khek; sculpture; carve. |

| | | |
|---|---|---|
| 1 | sim ǹiⁿ cîah, bô nāi cîah m̄ lôh. kêk gūa. | I would like to eat, but I am full. A neutral. |
| 2 | nâng ūi chái sí; cío ūi cîah bûang. | Men die for sake of wealth; birds perish for sake of food. |
| 3 | úa jíang kàu âu bô siaⁿ, i hṳ̂n lío m̄ chái úa. | I halooed till I was hoarse, but he paid no attention to me. |
| 4 | kĭaⁿ kĭaⁿ sĭ úa sô sôk. | Every one of them belongs to me. |
| 5 | úa sôk tŏ thiⁿ, lú sok tŏ tĭ. | I am of heaven, you of earth. |
| 6 | sí bûang. bûang jîn. | Exterminated. Fugitive. |
| 7 | lûn hûe. lûn bûang. | Chaotic. Lost in perdition. |
| 8 | ŭ hok khì. bŏi tit lío kêk. | Blessed. You can't bring it about. |
| 9 | tng kêk cía, mî. m̄ sêng kêk. | The dullest are those who play the game. A flash in the pan. |
| 10 | îeh kêk; cîⁿ kêk; ui kêk. | Dispensary; mint; hospital. |
| 11 | kêk phìen. jîp nâng kâi kêk. | Play a trick. Fell into the trap. |
| 12 | kêk gūa kâi nâng. kong kêk. cie siang kêk. cṳ kêk. cóng kêk. hun kêk. lŭn tăi kêk. | A looker-on. A council. Steamboat office. Printing office. A depot. An association. Considering the best interests of. |
| 13 | kit tĭo. hiong tĭo. | Auspicious sign. Bad omen. |
| 14 | kit jît, kit sṳ, kit jîn. | Lucky day, affair, fellow. |
| 15 | tăi kit lĭ chĭ. | Good chance for a speculation. |
| 16 | hiong cheⁿ; hiong nî. | Baleful star; unpromising year. |
| 17 | pò hiong, pò kit. | Convey bad or good tidings. |
| 18 | m̄ pat pán. cêk kò póiⁿ. | Not know the tune. A slab. |
| 19 | kó pán kâi nâng. | An old-fashioned person. |
| 20 | tùi pán. sam pán. | Follow the tune. A row-boat. |
| 21 | pán thâu. kuang chái. | The une. Brilliant. |

# LESSON CL.

芒 mâng; sword-grass.
緞 tn̄g; satin; glazed cloth.
秧 ng; young rice; sprouts.
棋 kî; a game, like chess.
簡 kán; terse; condense.
遺 jṳ̆i; entail; bequeath.

咥 hí; snicker; titter.
呵 ho̤; giggle; expel the breath.
啞 a; caw; babble.
繞 * în; to wind up.
解 * tháu; unwind.
黑 hek; black; dark; dull.

| | | |
|---|---|---|
| 1 | hí hí kìe. ho̤ ho̤ kìe. a a kìe. kî kêk. | Tittering. Giggling. Cawing. Game of chess. |
| 2 | hue tn̄g. o tn̄g. | Brocade. Black satin. |
| 3 | chĭe$^n$ kî. kî pûa$^n$. kî cí. | Chess. Chess-board. Chess-men. |
| 4 | bô̤ chái. hó̤ chái. chái thâu. | No chance. Good chance. A chance. |
| 5 | ngŏ chái, che$^n$, n̂g, chiah, pêh, hek. jṳ̆i mĕng. | The five colors, green, yellow brown, white, black. Dying orders. |
| 6 | ûi kî. jṳ̆i hĭa. | A game like chess. Bequeath. |
| 7 | jṳ̆i cṳ. jṳ̆i lô̤h lâi kâi. | A will. Inherited. |
| 8 | jṳ̆i pak kâi kía$^n$. àm hek. | A posthumous son. Benighted. |
| 9 | jṳ̆i pun kía$^n$ sun. | Left to his descendants. |
| 10 | hek pêh lân hun. | Good and bad indistinguishable. |
| 11 | hek àm. tà$^n$ kán. kán kán. | Dusky. Be brief. Laconic. |
| 12 | kán lîak. cak lîak. | A synopsis. Summary. |
| 13 | cí tîo sùa$^n$ hó̤ tháu tīo. | Unwind this thread. |
| 14 | în bûa cí tîo so̤h. | Wind up this rope. |
| 15 | m̄ cai cí kĭa$^n$ mûeh khá hù lṳ́ ēng mē? | I do not know whether this will suit your use. |
| 16 | lṳ́ būe sĭ hàm úa lî khṳ̂i ka kī kâi tī hng, ă! | You call one to leave my own land, do you! |
| 17 | bô̤ pât hō̤ sṳ̄ ŏi tit tô̤ pī cí kâi sí. în bûa. | There is no other way to escape this death. Wind it up. |
| 18 | lṳ́ khá kì tît lṳ́ hṳ́ tng sî só̤ tà$^n$, mē? | Do you remember what you then said? |
| 19 | ŏi tit pí ciang lâi kâi hok khì a bŏi? | Can it compare with the bliss of the future? |
| 20 | hô̤ í$^n$ cai? | How should I know? |
| 21 | kha m̄ eng tng tîeh cìe$^n$ se$^n$? | Ought it not to be so? |

## LESSON CLI.

| | | | | | |
|---|---|---|---|---|---|
| 播 | p̀ua; strew; promulgate. | | 徹 | thiet; pervious. |
| 辨 | pĭen; discriminate. | | 透 | thàu; throughout. |
| 駁 | poh; dispute; argue. | | 勉 | míen; constrain. |
| 辯 | pĭen; dispute; wrangle. | | 弜 | kíang; compel; force. |
| 叅 | cham; concerned with. | | 篦 | pìn; a fine tooth comb. |
| 莫 | môk; a negative, | | 甚 | nĕ; intensifying particle. |

| | |
|---|---|
| 1 ki cháu tíam lō. | 1 Every blade of grass gets its own drop of dew. |
| 2 cò̤ nî hó̤ cò̤ kâi huap; lṳ́ khá pat a m̄ pat? | 2 How would it do to make it a rule; do you know? |
| 3 ìn tap lâi m̄ tùi pán. | 3 The answer is not to the point. |
| 4 ĕ jît sĭ ká$^{n}$ lâi hîam pĕ bó̤, mē? cham pài. | 4 Hereafter dare he reproach his parents for it? Obeisance. |
| 5 khá m̄ sĭ eng kai lâu mâk cap? hun pĭen. thong thiet. | 5 Is it not a thing to weep for? Discriminate. Perspicacity. |
| 6 khá m̄ sĭ tng eng kai cìe$^{n}$ se$^{n}$? m̄ pĭen cin ké. | 6 Ought it not to be so? Not discriminating between true and false. |
| 7 cò̤ kàu nĕ tùi tùi. | 7 Made just exactly the same. |
| 8 lṳ́ kâi ūe mài kîp tîeh úa. | 8 Do not put your sayings upon me. |
| 9 sêng cîe$^{n}$ khí ĕ. | 9 The first involves the second. |
| 10 cêk kù cêk kù pĭen tit mêng pêh. pĭen pîet. | 10 Explain it sentence by sentence. Distinguish between. |
| 11 pĭen m̄ chut. thiet tói. | 11 Did not discriminate. Penetrate. |
| 12 pĭen poh. pĭen lŭn. | 12 Contradict. Debate. |
| 13 míen lât. míen kíang. | 13 Strenuous. Do by constraint. |
| 14 i míen kíang khṳ̀ cò̤. | 14 He forced himself to do it. |
| 15 míen kíang i khṳ̀ cò̤. | 15 Compel him to go and do it. |
| 16 kíang khîu. kíang kàu i hàu$^{n}$. | 16 Prevail on. Urge him to consent. |
| 17 pù kùi môk kíang khûi. | 17 Rank should not prevail. |
| 18 kíang kì. míen kíang kîa$^{n}$. | 18 Try to recall. Do by compulsion. |
| 19 môk hui sĭ lṳ́! môk hui sĭ. | 19 You don't say it is you! Can't but be. |
| 20 môk sueh—. môk tăi. | 20 Wonder not if—. None greater. |
| 21 môk tăi kâi kong lâu. | 21 No greater merit than this. |
| 22 sueh tit thiet. thàu thiet. | 22 Explain clearly. Thoroughly. |

## LESSON CLII.

| | |
|---|---|
| 透 | * thàng; pass through. |
| 亮 | lïang; clear; sonorous. |
| 縮 | kiu; sok; shrink. |
| 言 | ngân; a word; speech. |
| 觀 | kwn; observe; display. |
| 黨 | táng; faction; sort. |
| 拆 | thiah; break open. |
| 挽 | máng; túi; pull. |
| 更 | kèng; still; more. |
| 更 | keng; change; amend. |
| 詳 | sîang; examine into. |
| 行 | hĕng; actions. |

| | | |
|---|---|---|
| 1 | chìm kàu thàu thàu. | Soak it thoroughly. |
| 2 | thàng kùe hìe$^{n}$ pôi$^{n}$. thàng kàu hǘ tói tói. | Pass it through to the other side. Pass it down to the bottom. |
| 3 | tŏ lí thàng căi. | The doctrine is very comprehensive. |
| 4 | thàng sim. sêk thàng. | Throughout the heart. Quite ripe. |
| 5 | úa thói$^{n}$ thàng i kâi sü. | I see through his affairs. |
| 6 | hío m̄ thàu. mêng lïang. | Not understand. Transparent. |
| 7 | híang lïang. lïang se. | Musical. Lustrous gauze. |
| 8 | cheng lïang. sok tó. | Neat and clean. Shrunk up. |
| 9 | sói, i ŏi kiu bŭa. | If washed it will shrink. |
| 10 | thè sok. ngân gǘ. siet ngân. | Retreat. Words. Hypothesis. |
| 11 | hue ngân. khá gǘ. | Exaggeration. Eloquence. |
| 12 | kháu chut tōa ngân. | Bragging, talking big. |
| 13 | sit ngân. khui ngân. ngân gūa kâi ì. | Slip of the tongue. Begin to speak. An implied meaning. |
| 14 | ôi$^{n}$ kwn. tăi kwn. | Sight-seeing. Great performance. |
| 15 | kwn thien bûn. tâng táng. | Astrology. Same faction. |
| 16 | chât táng. kat táng. | Band of robbers. Form cabals. |
| 17 | hie$^{n}$ táng. thiah sìn. | Village junto. Open a letter. |
| 18 | thiah pi$^{n}$. thiah huang. | Unbraid the queu. Open a packet. |
| 19 | jú kèng tōa. jû kèng hó. | Still larger. Still better. |
| 20 | keng ūa$^{n}$; keng pìen; keng kói; keng i; keng lûn. | Substitute; change; alter; change the dress; alternate. |
| 21 | cham sîang. sîang mn̄g. | Take counsel about. Ask the facts. |
| 22 | sîang sòi. sîang bûn. | The details. Official report. |
| 23 | m̄ sîang. hūe sîang. | Not particularly. Joint inquiry. |
| 24 | tek hĕng. ngân hĕng. | Virtues. Words and actions. |
| 25 | hó sim hó hĕng. | If the heart be good, the conduct will be good. |

## LESSON CLIII.

| | |
|---|---|
| 艱 kan; hardships. | 踼 thak; kick. |
| 淹 * im; inundate. | 觸 * tak; butt; gore. |
| 接 * sùa; follow in connection. | 觸 chok; excite; stirred. |
| 損 sún; diminish; lose. | 纔 châi; lím; thereupon. |
| 跳 thìo; leap; jump. | 喈 ki; chirping. |
| 舞 bú; posture making. | 嘻 hi; snickering. |

| | |
|---|---|
| 1 cí cêk pé tū thiah khui. | 1 Undo this bundle of chop-sticks. |
| 2 cí cêk ngân. sueh khuah. | 2 This specific word. Unfold clearly. |
| 3 lú hó sueh sòi sîang. | 3 Explain it minutely. |
| 4 bw̄n sì tà$^{n}$ bŏi ŵn. | 4 Myriads that cannot be counted. |
| 5 lú kwn thói$^{n}$ ka kī kâi sū. | 5 Attend to your own business. |
| 6 cip kín cí kâi toa$^{n}$. | 6 Hold fast to this check. |
| 7 jú mé jú hó. | 7 The quicker the better. |
| 8 i jú kèng se$^{n}$ khì. | 8 He was all the more angry. |
| 9 jú cōi jú hó. | 9 The more the better. |
| 10 cí kâi pí hú kâi jú kèng sòi. kan lân. | 10 This compared with that is still smaller. Hardships. |
| 11 i jú kèng chut sia$^{n}$. | 11 He made a still louder noise. |
| 12 jú chut lât jú m̄ kîa$^{n}$. jú hâh úa sim; jú hâh cin lí. ak táng. | 12 The more strength he put out the less it moved. More in accordance with my feelings; with true principles. The wicked. |
| 13 lâi thia$^{n}$ lú kâi kim ngân. | 13 Came to hear your discourses. |
| 14 lú m̄ cai jîeh kan khó! | 14 You do not know how hard it is! |
| 15 i khù thìo khoi sí. | 15 He went and drowned himself. |
| 16 bŏi tì kàu ŭ sih mih sū. | 16 Cannot lead to any thing. |
| 17 tì kàu i ŏi hâi$^{n}$ úa. | 17 So that he can repay me. |
| 18 cí kâi ūe lím lím líu, úa cìu jîp lâi sùa tà$^{n}$—. | 18 This being said, I went in and continued saying—. |
| 19 bŏi sún tîeh cêk tîo thâu mô. | 19 Not lose one hair of your head. |
| 20 kan khó. thìo lôh lâi. | 20 Difficult. Jump down. |
| 21 thìo bú. thìo kùe lâi. | 21 Dance, leap. Jump over it. |
| 22 cêk thak kha. bé thak nâng. | 22 At one kick. Horses kick people. |
| 23 thak tîeh kha. úa lím lím lâi. | 23 Stubbed his toe. I just came. |

## LESSON CLIV.

纏 tî$^n$; to bandage; bother.
了 a; a crotch; fork.
了 hai; a tine.
議 ngí; to deliberate.
任 jĭm; sustain; trust.
任 jīm; an office; post.

職 ceh; duty; office.
望 mō̤; gaze; look.
望 bŭang; full moon.
哈 hah; chuckling.
喁 ngông; agape.
哇 ua; screaming.

| | | |
|---|---|---|
| 1 | khṳt gû tak tîeh. | Gored by a bull. |
| 2 | kha thak tîeh cîeh. | Stumbled over a stone. |
| 3 | mài thak tîeh kha. | Do not stumble. |
| 4 | nŏ̤ ciah gû sie tak. | Two cows butting each other. |
| 5 | tak tîeh úa kâi mâk. | Came within my sight. |
| 6 | chok tîeh i cĭu se$^n$ khì. | Excited his wrath. |
| 7 | chok hŭam tîeh i. | Make one's self obnoxious to him. |
| 8 | chòk khí úa kâi sim. | Stirred up my feelings. |
| 9 | cìe$^n$ se$^n$ châi sĭ tŏ̤ lí. | That is just the principle. |
| 10 | úa huang châi lâi. | I have but just come. |
| 11 | cìe$^n$ se$^n$ châi sĭ. | That is just the thing. |
| 12 | lṳ́ chía$^n$ úa, úa huang châi lâi. ua ua kìe. | If you invite me then I shall come. Screaming. |
| 13 | lṳ́ ô̤h hó̤ hó̤, úa châi khṳt lṳ́. | When you have learned it, then I will give it you. |
| 14 | úa lím lím ài$^n$ khṳ̀ lṳ́ kò̤ cŏ̤, lṳ́ cĭu lâi. | Just as I was going to sit with you, you came. |
| 15 | tî$^n$ kha. tî$^n$ thâu pò. | Bind the feet. A turban. |
| 16 | lṳ́ mài tî$^n$ kha tî$^n$ chíu. | Don't you hang around me. |
| 17 | cí kĭa$^n$ sṳ̄ i tāng mêng khí lâi tî$^n$ kàu jĭt tàu. | He was bothering about here from morning till noon. |
| 18 | a che. khui a, pun a. | A crotch. To fork off. |
| 19 | hia thâu. ngí lŭn. | Young slave girl. To discuss. |
| 20 | kong ngí. ngí sṳ̄. | Public debate. Criticise. |
| 21 | jĭm ēng. jĭm ì. ceh jĭm. sìn jĭm. | Employ. Get your wish. Responsibility. Confide in. |
| 22 | cĭe$^n$ jīm. cīe$^n$ jīm. lâu jīm. cih jīm. | Enter on an office. Former incumbent. Retain a post. Take office. |
| 23 | ngông ngông. hah hah kìe. | Agape. Laughing aloud. |

## LESSON CLV.

| | | | |
|---|---|---|---|
| 紐 | níu; button; knob. | 喜 | hí; joy; delight. |
| 絆 | * phàng; loop. | 謬 | nĭu; fallacious. |
| 素 | sù; formerly. | 辭 | sî; decline; leave; resign. |
| 素 | * sò; plain; simple. | 辭 | sû; words; argument. |
| 告 | kò; indict; accuse. | 菩 | phû; phô; idol; god. |
| 告 | kàu; inform; announce. | 薩 | sat; third class of saints. |

| | | |
|---|---|---|
| 1 | hīn jīm. ceh síu. | Present incumbent. Manage. |
| 2 | sì ceh. kú mō. | Hereditary title. Long expected. |
| 3 | hí chut mō gūa. | Beyond all expectation. |
| 4 | bô só mō. sit mō. | Nothing to hope for. Lose hope. |
| 5 | mō m̄ kì$^n$. mō kàu ta$^n$. | Cannot see. Expected till now. |
| 6 | thong pò. sa$^n$ níu, níu phàng. | Public notice. Button and loop. |
| 7 | níu hó. phêng sù. | Button it up. Heretofore. |
| 8 | sù sè$^n$. phêng jît. | Uniform character. Formerly. |
| 9 | sù m̄ sie pat. | Have not known each other. |
| 10 | sù lâi m̄ ua$^n$ hūn. | Does not mind his own business. |
| 11 | sò cuang. sò i hôk. | Plainly dressed. Plain dress. |
| 12 | chēng khù sò sò thói$^n$ tìeh kèng hó. tǒ mō. | If plainly dressed she would look better. Gazing. |
| 13 | ngŵn kò. pí kò. | Plaintiff. Defendant. |
| 14 | kò sī. chut kò sī. | Proclamation. Issue an edict. |
| 15 | phǒ kò. ài$^n$ khù kò i. | Pleader. Going to impeach him. |
| 16 | kàu sî. kàu pêh. kàu thò. tăi nĭu. pŭe nĭu. cha nĭu. nĭu thŵn. | I take leave. Notification. Renounce. A great mistake. Blunder. Error. Misleading. |
| 17 | úa kāi lú sie sî. sueh sû. sî pìet. sî kìa$^n$ thiap. m̄ sî lâu khó. pò pi$^n$. | I take leave of you. Plea. Take leave. A p. p. c. card. Does not avoid toil. Selvedge. |
| 18 | gú sû; ngân sû. sû kù hó. | A rejoinder. An apt remark. |
| 19 | kak cip cêk sû. | Each held to his own notion. |
| 20 | phô sat. pài phû sat. | Idols. Worship idols. |
| 21 | phêng sù i sĭ cò ui seng. | He was formerly a doctor. |
| 22 | í$^n$ keng chut ŭ cí kâi kò sī. níu khang. | When this proclamation had been issued. Button hole. |

## LESSON CLVI.

| | |
|---|---|
| 撞 cŭang; bump; collide. | 逆 ngêk; resist; oppose. |
| 邪 sîa; depraved; bad. | 挑 thie; pick; select. |
| 誦 sŏng; chant; hum. | 爭 ce$^{n}$; wrangle; strive. |
| 齋 ce; abstain; study. | 快 khùai; khùa$^{n}$; glad. |
| 責 ceh; reprove; reproach. | 歡 * hua$^{n}$; gratified; pleased. |
| 屑 * chua$^{n}$; a sliver. | 樂 lâk; pleasure; joy. |

| | | |
|---|---|---|
| 1 | hí lâk. hí khì; hí ìong. hí hua$^{n}$; hua$^{n}$ hí. sang hí. pò hí. | Happy. Happy look. Delighted. Two happy events come together. Foretokens luck. |
| 2 | úa kăi lú hua$^{n}$ hí. | I congratulate you. |
| 3 | sie cŭang. cŭang tīeh. cŭang thâu cŭang hīah. cûn thâu sie cŭang. | Run against each other. Bump. Thumped foreheads. The two boats collided. |
| 4 | pêh cŭang. cŭang pán. cŭang mn̂g. cŭang phùa. | Go in on pretense. Make a discord. Thump the door. Break against. |
| 5 | sîa tău. sîa huap. sîa sîn. sîa sim. kói sîa kui cìa$^{n}$. sîa khì. sĭu sîa. | Heretical doctrine. Unlawful rules. False gods. Corrupt heart. Forsake the wrong and return to the right. Mad. Contaminated. |
| 6 | sŏng sìn si. sŏng keng. | Sing hymns. Chant liturgies. |
| 7 | ce kài. cîah ce. cu ce. ài$^{n}$ khì jîp cu ce. | Abstinence. Fast. Student's room. Going to school. |
| 8 | cŭ ceh. ceh hŵt. ceh mn̄g. kùe ceh. ceh pĭ. | Self-reproach. Punish. Question. Punish. Reprimand. |
| 9 | khut chua$^{n}$ chah ìip cńg kah tói. châ chua$^{n}$. tok ceh. | Got a sliver under my nail. A splinter. Expel. |
| 10 | i ài$^{n}$ tui ceh lú. | He will chastise you. |
| 11 | ngêk lâu, ngêk huang. | Against wind and tide. |
| 12 | ngêk cú. mài ngêk i kâi ì. hŵn ngêk. ngêk táng. | Froward child. Do not oppose his wishes. Rebel. Rebels. |
| 13 | thie teng. thie khui. thie sŵn. thie sìu. | Raise the wick. Pick open. Pick out. Select for a hareem. |
| 14 | sie ce$^{n}$ sie jíang. ce$^{n}$ soi$^{n}$. khùa$^{n}$ ûah. khùai lâk. | Quarreling together. Strive to excel. Comfortable. Happy. |

## LESSON CLVII.

杉 sam; deal; pine.
恐 khíong; apprehensive.
畏 ùi; fear; dread.
默 mît; somber; secret.
拓 thak; to poke.
膜 môh; a film; filmy.

首 síu; head; chief.
勸 khǹg; exhort.
樟 cie$^{n}$; camphor.
償 sîe$^{n}$; indemnify.
賠 pûe; make up a loss.
叛 pw̆n; revolt; rebel.

1 thie phùa thûe. mài mō ău.
2 i cŭang tîeh thâu.
3 àì$^{n}$ sêng cí kâi ki hŭe.
4 sam kía$^{n}$. sam cə̀ kâi.
5 khíong phà$^{n}$. khíong ùi.
6 ùi síu ùi búe.
7 sĭang ùi. síu kūi$^{n}$.
8 hŭe síu. kîa$^{n}$ kàu mn̂g síu.
9 síu búe siang kù. mît lĭam.
10 ûi síu. chut síu. hú síu; khàu síu; hôk síu.
11 mît mît khù cə̀. mît sī. mît sía. mît ĭu.
12 khí thak. thak i khui.
13 thăng phùa mô̤h. tī tāu jîn mô̤h.
14 cêk têng nĕ mô̤h mô̤h.
15 khǹg kòi. khǹg míen. khǹg sì bûn. khǹg hûa. siang khǹg.
16 ce$^{n}$ pĭen. cie$^{n}$ chīu.
17 sîe$^{n}$ nâng mīa. pûe sîe$^{n}$. sîe$^{n}$ hâi$^{n}$. sîe$^{n}$ îeh kè$^{n}$.
18 pûe lói. cìe pûe. pûe hâi$^{n}$. pûe put sĭ.
19 hw̆n ngêk. hẃn pw̆n. pŭe pw̆n. lî pw̆n. pw̆n chât. m̄ ùi.

1 Open a boil. Don't look behind.
2 He bumped his head.
3 Will take advantage of this chance.
4 A young pine. Made of deal.
5 Fearful. Afraid of.
6 I want nothing to do with it.
7 Much afraid. The leading district.
8 The leader. Reached the street door.
9 Look after both ends. Meditate.
10 Acts as leader. Turn state's evidence. Bend the head down.
11 Did it secretly. A vision. Write from memory. Secret help.
12 Tooth-pick. Poke it open.
13 Break the film. The thin skin on kernels of pea-nuts.
14 A very filmy layer.
15 Exhort. Incite. Moral tracts. Exhort to peace. Admonish each other.
16 Bicker. Camphor-tree.
17 Indemnify for a life. Indemnify. Restore. Repay for the medecine.
18 Return a call. Pay the value. Repay. I own I am wrong.
19 To revolt. Insurrection. Conspire against. Throw off allegiance. A rebel. No fear.

## LESSON CLVIII.

訟 sŏng; litigation.
訴 sù; to state; expose.
舉 * tiè$^{n}$; raise; lift.
脹 tiè$^{n}$; puffy; swollen.
杖 cĭang; staff; cudgel.
拐 kúai; staff; crutch.

驚 kia$^{n}$; alarm; scare.
贖 sôk; redeem; ransom.
掩 * a$^{n}$; to cover up.
覆 * à$^{n}$; to snuggle.
匿 nêk; clandestine.
匿 * tìam; elude search.

| | |
|---|---|
| 1 kia$^{n}$ ùi. kàu sù. | 1 Afraid. Accusation and defense. |
| 2 lú ŭ kò, úa li ŭ sù. | 2 You may accuse, I can refute. |
| 3 hàu$^{n}$ sŏng. sŏng sû. | 3 Fond of litigation. An indictment. |
| 4 kia$^{n}$ sí nâng. kia$^{n}$ ĭ. | 4 Scare anybody to death. Frightful. |
| 5 chah sŏng. mâk tìe$^{n}$ phû. | 5 Enter into a case. Lift the eyes. |
| 6 úa tìe$^{n}$ khí mâk khù thói$^{n}$. | 6 I raised my eyes, and looked. |
| 7 chíu tìe$^{n}$ tît, kha tìe$^{n}$ tît. | 7 Lift your hand and foot. |
| 8 kha khîeh phû. chíu khîeh khí. | 8 Raise your foot. Lift your hand. |
| 9 céng tìe$^{n}$. tìe$^{n}$ lâng. cúi tìe$^{n}$. khì tìe$^{n}$. tó tìe$^{n}$. pá tìe$^{n}$. sio tìe$^{n}$. | 9 Swollen. Puffed up with pus. Dropsical. Flatulent. Belly swollen. Repletion. Relieve swelling. |
| 10 kúai cĭang. cip cĭang. | 10 Old man's staff. Chief mourners. |
| 11 cĭang ceh poih câp. | 11 Gave him eighty blows. |
| 12 phah jîeh cōi tek pói$^{n}$? | 12 How many blows did he get? |
| 13 cĭang cêk peh. | 13 Inflict a hundred blows. |
| 14 sôk tńg lâi; sôk cŭe; sok cŭe kìu nâng; sôk hûe. | 14 Ransom; commute a punishment; redeem; take out of pawn. |
| 15 cang pò a$^{n}$ mi i kâi mâk. | 15 Blindfold him. |
| 16 a$^{n}$ sat cúi khang. | 16 Stop up the leak. |
| 17 koi bó à$^{n}$ koi kía$^{n}$ tŏ i sît ĕ. à$^{n}$ a nô$^{n}$. | 17 The hen hovers the chickens under her wings. Snuggle a baby. |
| 18 à$^{n}$ bûa sin pi$^{n}$. a$^{n}$ phī$^{n}$. | 18 Snuggle it up. Hold the nose. |
| 19 cŭ sòi à$^{n}$ kàu tōa. | 19 Brought it up from a baby. |
| 20 a$^{n}$ mīn. a$^{n}$ m̄ cŭ. | 20 Cover the face. It won't stay shut. |
| 21 a$^{n}$ cêk pôi$^{n}$. lîah hû. | 21 Cover half. Blind man's buff. |
| 22 a$^{n}$ mi. a$^{n}$ sí. a$^{n}$ kín. | 22 Cover close. Smother. Stop tight. |
| 23 a$^{n}$ mâk cáu tìam. chân nêk. | 23 Hide and seek. Abscond. |
| 24 tìam tŏ hú lăi. nêk mîa. | 24 Hidden away there. Anonymous. |

# LESSON CLIX.

佔 * âⁿ; usurp; take by force.
與 ṳ́; consort with; in.
誑 * kuang; delude; mislead.
讐 chîu; enemy; abhor.
敵 têk; foe; rival.
枉 úang; oppress; needless.
屈 khut; crouch; to wrong.
居 kṳ; dwell; dwellings.
脯 pó; dried meat.
倡 chìang; leader; starter.
暢 thìang; joyous.
臣 chîn; vassal; statesman.

| | | |
|---|---|---|
| 1 | aⁿ lâi, aⁿ khṳ̀, aⁿ m̄ kàu hâiⁿ i. | All I can rake and scrape there is not enough to pay him. |
| 2 | nêk thiap. ôiⁿ kṳ. | Anonymous placard. Live at ease. |
| 3 | âⁿ úa kâi chù. kuang phìen. | Seized my house. To deceive. |
| 4 | âⁿ nâng kâi chi nńg. | Take other people's wives. |
| 5 | chân tī pun i âⁿ khṳ̀. | Took possession of my fields. |
| 6 | tī hng cí kúi nî pun i cĭam cĭam âⁿ khṳ̀. | He has been for several years gradually usurping the land. |
| 7 | àiⁿ âⁿ, cĭu sī. | He wants to usurp it, that's it. |
| 8 | lṳ́ thóiⁿ âⁿ tit khṳ̀ mē! | You see whether he can grab it! |
| 9 | sŏ âⁿ kâi. mài kuang úa. | What he seized. Do not mizzle me. |
| 10 | úa bô ṳ́ sṳ̄. | I am not concerned in it. |
| 11 | kuang lṳ́ kâi cîⁿ a sī kuang lṳ́ kâi ńgn? | Have I fooled you about about your cash, or your dollars? |
| 12 | úa kâi ūe sī bô siang kuang kâi. chìang síu. chìang khí thâu. | My words are not misleading. The inventor. The leader: guide. |
| 13 | úa kio lṳ́ bô wn bô chîu. | I have no disagreement with you. |
| 14 | pò chîu. chîu têk. chîu hṳ̀n. | Got revenge. Enemy. Detest. |
| 15 | tùi têk. têk chíu. kṳ cŭ. | Inimical. Competitor. Reside. |
| 16 | têk tit cŭ, têk m̄ cŭ. | Could or could not master him. |
| 17 | têk kok, têk piaⁿ. | Enemy's country and troops. |
| 18 | úang khut. tōa wn úang. | Oppress. A great wrong |
| 19 | úang hùi sim sîn. | You have lost all your pains. |
| 20 | úang kṳ nâng sì. | You are of no use in the world. |
| 21 | put úang lṳ́ ēng hìeⁿ cōi kang. | You need not take so much pains. |
| 22 | lêng khut lêng sin. | He can stoop or stand. |
| 23 | khut suah hó nâng. | Kill an innocent man. |
| 24 | kṳ sim. tê kṳ. thìang khùai. | Heart set upon. Tea shop. Joyous. |

# LESSON CLX.

| | |
|---|---|
| 情 chêng; human passions. | 賒 chia; on credit. |
| 才 châi; capacity; talents. | 花 * hua; waste; spend. |
| 納 nâp; receive; take in. | 張 tie$^{n}$; appoint; adjust. |
| 搲 * sa; claw; catch up; grab. | 張 ciang; display; publish. |
| 迎 ngêng; go out and receive. | 揚 îang; spread abroad. |
| 鄰 lîn; contiguous; near. | 乖 kuai; sulky; crafty. |

| | |
|---|---|
| 1 cham lâi cham khù. | 1 Intermingling. |
| 2 bōi tit pĭen poh. | 2 No chance for argument. |
| 3 sō̤ mn̄g hui sō̤ tap. | 3 What was asked was not answered. |
| 4 lú sō̤ ìn tap hui úa sō̤ mn̄g. | 4 Your answer is not to my question. |
| 5 lú kói sueh i thia$^{n}$. | 5 You explain it to him. |
| 6 khìo thâu mé. khìo thâu mān. | 6 Ready ability. Slow perceptions. |
| 7 ău lâi lú cĭu kì$^{n}$ i kâi kat búe. kîam ah pó. tie$^{n}$ īe$^{n}$. | 7 You will see the upshot of it all. Dried salt duck. Strut. |
| 8 thói$^{n}$ cí kâi nâng cè̤ nî kat kêk. | 8 See what end he comes to. |
| 9 káng kìu kàu kat búe. | 9 Explain the consequences. |
| 10 kun chîn. khûn chîn. tāi chîn. bûn chîn. | 10 Prince and ministers. Courtiers. High officials. Civil officers. |
| 11 cêk cūe hûn. kháu châi. | 11 A crease. Fluency of speech. |
| 12 ŭ nâng chêng, bô̤ nâng chêng. | 12 Have or have not a kind heart. |
| 13 bô̤ chêng; pô̤h chêng. tō̤ chêng. ēng chêng. bô̤ châi chêng. sît chêng. chêng lí. | 13 Ungrateful. Grateful. Cordial. Stolid. The real circumstances. Common sense. |
| 14 ciap nâp. ngêng cih. | 14 Welcome. Meet and welcome. |
| 15 lăi châi; gūa châi. | 15 Education; endowments. |
| 16 chìe nâp. nâp lîang. | 16 Smilingly take. Get a cool breeze. |
| 17 lú nâp a m̄ nâp? | 17 Do you take it in or not? |
| 18 sa lâi sa khù m̄ kàu ēng. sa tîeh i kâi sa$^{n}$. sa ki tûi khù jīo i. sa tîeh. | 18 All I could rake and scrape was not sufficient. Caught up his jacket. Catch up a club and drive him away. Clawed. |
| 19 sit ngêng. ngêng huang. | 19 Not meet at the door. Face the wind. |
| 20 lîn kŭn. lîn kok. | 20 Neighboring. Conterminous states. |
| 21 sì lîm. chia bói. | 21 Neighbors. Buy on credit. |
| 22 ciang îang. kuai ciang. | 22 Bruit abroad. Cross-grained. |

## LESSON CLXI.

享 híang; enjoy.
義 ngī; righteousness.
悟 ngŏ̤; arouse; aware.
充 chong; fill; fulfill.
壇 tûa$^n$; an altar; terrace.
閞 * aih$^n$; uai$^n$; ûaih$^n$; creak.

誇 khua; boast.
波 pe; ripple; wave.
卽 ciet; soon; then; that is.
甚 * ŭa; very; much.
至 cì; reach to; very.
最 cùe; exceedingly.

| | |
|---|---|
| 1 sṳ̄ būe líe kat. | 1 The affair is not terminated. |
| 2 sat pìn. chia sìo. | 2 Fine tooth comb. Credit account. |
| 3 cí kâi ūe tà$^n$ kàu thong thiet. | 3 Tell all the consequences. |
| 4 im tīo i kâi tī hng. | 4 Inundated his grounds. |
| 5 ta$^n$ lím lím cìa$^n$ lâi. | 5 Have only just now come. |
| 6 i lím lím khṳ̀ lío. | 6 He has just now gone. |
| 7 huang pīen. huang khó̤. | 7 All ready. Quite suitable. |
| 8 cèng kua$^n$ ài$^n$ siang ngí. | 8 The nobles will consult. |
| 9 nín cèng nâng chông úa cía cĭu se$^n$, m̄ chông úa cía cĭu sí. sì cì. bô̤ só̤ put cì. | 9 Those who follow me will live, those who do not follow me will die. All around. Universal. |
| 10 ì mō̤ ciang lâi ŏi tit cò̤ tōa kua$^n$. cì hó̤. cùe sòi. | 10 Hopes hereafter to be a great mandarin. The best. Very small. |
| 11 lṳ́ kio úa thòi chia. | 11 Have it charged to you for me. |
| 12 lṳ́ kāi úa chia lâi. | 12 You charge it to me. |
| 13 hua tīo i kâi ke ngīap. | 13 Spent his property. |
| 14 cêk nâng cú tie$^n$ m̄ jû nŏ̤ nâng kàu nīe. | 14 The lordship of one is not so good as the council of two. |
| 15 khai ciang. khua ciang. ciang kùa. îang pe. | 15 Open out. Self-laudatory. Festoon. Dash up in waves. |
| 16 kuai khá. khah kuai. cúi pe. | 16 Wily. Too cunning. Ripples. |
| 17 pe phêng. khua kháu. | 17 Smooth water. Boastful. |
| 18 híang hok. ngī cé$^n$. ngī pia$^n$. jîn ngī. ngī chng. ngī pě. ngī khì. ngī pôk. | 18 Enjoy happiness. Public well. Patriot volunteers. Righteous. Public granary. Adopted father. Honorable. Faithful servant. |
| 19 cṳ̌ ngŏ̤. ché$^n$ ngŏ̤. | 19 Bethink one's self. Arouse. |
| 20 chong múa; chong cok. cì chṳ́. | 20 Fill full. On this account. |

## LESSON CLXII.

| | |
|---|---|
| 贏 | * îa$^{n}$; beat; excel; win. |
| 輸 | su; beaten; lose; submit. |
| 强 | * kîe$^{n}$; kĭang; superior to. |
| 辯 | * ǹ; argue; dispute. |
| 擲 | tă$^{n}$; toss down; pitch. |
| 骰 | tâu; dice. |
| 片 | phìen; flake; slip; thin. |
| 寧 | lêng; rather. |
| 可 | * kŏ; rather; better. |
| 味 | bī; taste; flavor. |
| 道 | * sò; savor; taste. |
| 喋 | * sap; chattering. |

| | | |
|---|---|---|
| 1 | jĭm tŭi m̄ tñg. | Endure beating without breaking. |
| 2 | nâng kèng tŏng lŭ́. | People respect you. |
| 3 | nâng kŭi tōng kùe îe$^{n}$. | Men are more worthy than sheep. |
| 4 | ǹi$^{n}$ pun cŏ kúi a. | Will separate into several branches. |
| 5 | thiap pi$^{n}$. mîa phìen. | A facing. A visiting card. |
| 6 | pŭi thiap; lói thiap. | Visiting card of several folds. |
| 7 | úa kâi ūe khut lŭ́ tin tŏ cŏ khŭ̀. i m̄ ùi nâng. | My words were perverted by you. He is afraid of nobody. |
| 8 | khut lŭ́ khñg kàu úa kâi sim cêk pùa$^{n}$ ài$^{n}$ khŭ̀. cih sìn. | Was advised by you till I half wished to go. Receive a letter. |
| 9 | jī ke. jī ke hua$^{n}$ hí. | Both parties. Both are pleased. |
| 10 | îang mîa îang sia$^{n}$. | Spread his name and fame. |
| 11 | îang îang tit ì. | Every one to his liking. |
| 12 | îang chíu. chong tng. | Flourish the hands. Fill a station. |
| 13 | i cong kú m̄ ngŏ. | He never fully understands. |
| 14 | chong kong. îa$^{n}$ cî$^{n}$. | Revert to the state. Win money. |
| 15 | cì chêng cì lí kâi ūe. | Language of the utmost truth. |
| 16 | à îa$^{n}$. phah îa$^{n}$. cáu îa$^{n}$. | Out argue. Beat. Outrun. |
| 17 | su kio îa$^{n}$ tùi mīn. | Losing is the opposite of winning. |
| 18 | cáu su kâi nâng. sie à. | The loser in running. Dispute. |
| 19 | cí choh kîe$^{n}$ kùe hŭ́ choh. | This is superior to that. |
| 20 | tă$^{n}$ tâu. tă$^{n}$ tîeh. | Throw dice. Cast and hit it. |
| 21 | phìen sî. côih phìen. hĭa phìen. | Little while. Shave thin. Potsherds. |
| 22 | lêng kŏ m̄ ài$^{n}$. lêng kŏ sí. | Rather not. Rather die. |
| 23 | lêng kŏ pun lŭ́. | Rather give it to you. |
| 24 | bī sò. hŏ bī. sit bī. hâh bī. khì bī. kam bī. | Flavour. Luscious. Lose savour. Palatable. Odor. Delicious. |
| 25 | bô bī bô sò. sap sap kìe. | Insipid. Loquacious. |

## LESSON CLXIII.

| | | | | |
|---|---|---|---|---|
| 懼 | kŭ; fear; awe. | | 溺 | nêk; doating; excessive. |
| 與 | * chap; consort with. | | 毀 | húiⁿ; break down; raze. |
| 渣 | ca; pheh; settlings; dregs. | | 顫 | cìen; to shiver. |
| 鍊 | lïen; discipline; wrought. | | 顫 | * khìu; toǹg; trembling. |
| 試 | chì; try; test. | | 某 | móng; that one. |
| 賤 | cūaⁿ; mean; ignoble. | | 綾 | lîn; damask. |

1 ài chêng. nêk ài. kèng ài. ài sieh ke ke. jī ke ài sieh. tit i ài sieh.
2 khah ài sieh tì sêng ẁn.
3 khá ŭ nâng ài sieh a bô?
4 pī sïa lêng ín chūa.
5 lú mài kiaⁿ chéⁿ i.
6 pī chîu têk chìe.
7 i sïu nâng úang khut.
8 khut i kuang phìen.
9 ŭ cìeⁿ seⁿ kì. ciet sī.
10 lîn kŭn kâi sïaⁿ khut i húiⁿ tïo. ngŏ bī kè.
11 kùi cūaⁿ. lïen kâi khì kŭ.
12 à i m̄ kùe.
13 à lâi à khù. hïa cūaⁿ.
14 bô lí à kàu ŭ lí. i tōa kiaⁿ kŭ.
15 à m̄ khù.
16 thâi ïaⁿ kâi nâng.
17 cáu su kâi nâng.
18 lú kâi sū ciet úa kâi sū.
19 ciet sī. ciet jĭt. lú ciet khù.
20 kiaⁿ kàu khìu; kiaⁿ kàu toǹg.
21 sim kiaⁿ nêk cìen.
22 hwt cìen. thong sin hwt cìen.
23 chì thóiⁿ. chì i lïen i.
24 móng kò ŭ kâi bïe. kau chap.

1 The affections. Foolish fondness. Reverential love. Love much. Reciprocal love. Gain his love.
2 Inordinate love engenders hate.
3 Would anyone love such?
4 Lead by the Holy Spirit.
5 Do not wake him up.
6 Laughed at by his enemy.
7 He was oppressed.
8 Was deluded by him.
9 It is thus recorded. That is it.
10 The neighboring city was destroyed by him. Cruet-stand.
11 High and low. A tried weapon.
12 Cannot out argue him.
13 To bandy words. Base born.
14 Make the worse appear the better reason. He greatly fears.
15 Cannot carry the point.
16 The victor, in fighting.
17 The defeated, in running.
18 Your business is mine.
19 At once. Soon. Go at once.
20 Trembling from fright.
21 So terrified that the flesh creeps.
22 To shiver. He shook all over.
23 Try it and see. Discipline him.
24 In a certain place was a temple. To associate.

## LESSON CLXIV.

戚 chek; cîa$^n$; kin.
餉 hìang; taxes; duties.
納 * lâp; to pay stated sums.
粮 nîe; rations; taxes in kind.
閉 * hip; cover tight; smother.
卑 pui; plebeian; mean.

凍 tòng; freeze; congeal; icy.
鑷 niap; forceps; nip.
激 kek; worry; vex; beat upon.
辦 pōi$^n$; phōi$^n$; manage; do.
瓣 * hah; petals of a flower.
匣 âp; casket; little box.

1 m̄ cai ùn cúi i cìu aîh$^n$ aîh$^n$ kìe. tok pōi$^n$.
2 i kâi sè$^n$ chêng hó.
3 būe ū cih tîeh lú kâi sìn.
4 chut khù ngêng cih i.
5 būe cêng cih cîang, soi$^n$ khí ai.
6 hŵn sin, mîn chn̂g cìu aîh$^n$ aîh$^n$ kìe. pui cūa$^n$.
7 cí tîeh sih mih sū?
8 bô nâng ciap nâp i.
9 bô ūa hn̄g. cûah m̄ ūa.
10 i sī cì jîn tek kâi hū jîn.
11 híang hok cì kêk.
12 cúi tòng. hô tòng. tòng soh. tòng sí. tòng cúi.
13 mài kau chap i.
14 chin chek: chin cîa$^n$.
15 kok chek. gūa chek.
16 hìang kŵn. hìang n̂gn. hìang toa$^n$. kùe hìang. pia$^n$ hìang. lâp hìang.
17 lâp jîeh cōi co n̂gn?
18 lâp ûang nîe. bí nîe. kháu nîe.
19 lú cêng ŵn nîe a būe?
20 cî$^n$ nîe. kang nîe.
21 hwt nîe. nîe cháu. lâp nîe.
22 niap kía. pōi$^n$ i kâi sū.

1 If you do not think to dip it in water it will creak. Oversee.
2 His disposition is good.
3 Not yet received your letter.
4 Go out and greet him.
5 Before he had received the mourning staff, he began to mourn.
6 When he turns over, the couch creaks. Low and mean.
7 What does this refer to?
8 No one received him.
9 Not far. Does not lack much.
10 She is a most faithful woman.
11 Obtain the highest bliss.
12 Water freezes. River frozen. Icy. Freeze to death. Ice water.
13 Do not associate with him.
14 Relatives, of another surname.
15 Emperor's kin. Distant kin.
16 Custom house. Revenue. Receipt for duties. Pass the custom-house. Rations. Pay duty.
17 How much rent does he pay?
18 Pay taxes. Eatables. Victuals.
19 Have you paid your taxes yet?
20 Salary. Provisions for a journey.
21 Pay wages. Fodder. Pay rations.
22 Tweezers. Manage his business.

# LESSON CLXV.

| | |
|---|---|
| 整 * sṳ̆; set in order. | 縋 tūi; let down by a rope. |
| 窰 îe; a kiln; furnace. | 蠕 * so̤; squirm; wriggle. |
| 誓 sī; cūa; oath. | 矮 ói; low of stature. |
| 幹 kàn; capable. | 贅 cùe; wen; tautology. |
| 掌 cíeⁿ; palm of the hand. | 贅 cŭi; appendage. |
| 收 * khieh; collect; gather. | 呀 * ō̤; ā; ōi; vocative. |

| | |
|---|---|
| 1 i cì chiet àiⁿ khṳ̀. | 1 It is of the utmost importance that he should go. |
| 2 sṳ̆ lí hó̤ lío, khah mān. | 2 When ready, it was too late. |
| 3 cì tōa. cì sìa. cì khiet. | 3 Greatest. Holiest. Purest. |
| 4 sĭang kûiⁿ. sĭang jîet. sĭang mān. | 4 Tallest. Hottest. Slowest. |
| 5 sĭm mé. sĭm kú. sĭm ngía. | 5 Quickest. Longest. Handsomest. |
| 6 cùe hn̆g. cùe sĭen, cùe ngĭ. | 6 Farthest. Most righteous. |
| 7 câp hun hó̤. câp hun huaⁿ hí. | 7 Perfectly good. Wholly pleased. |
| 8 cûah ho̤h cōi. phōiⁿ cŭe. | 8 Much diminished. To punish. |
| 9 pí lṳ́ ío gâu. pĭ phōiⁿ. | 9 Wiser than you. Make ready. |
| 10 pí cí ío khin. sṳ̆ lí. | 10 Lighter than this. Regulate. |
| 11 jú kèng chéⁿ ngŏ̤. hĭa îe. | 11 More watchful. Kiln for tiles. |
| 12 pí lṳ́ ío ŭ lât. pí lṳ́ kèng hó̤. | 12 Compared with you, is the stronger. Better than you. |
| 13 pōiⁿ tit hó̤. hûi îe. îe mn̂g. sie îe. | 13 Well managed. Pottery kiln. Mouth of a furnace. Pit. |
| 14 hwt sī. tng thiⁿ mêng sī. | 14 Take oath. Swear before Heaven. |
| 15 lêng kàn. châi kàn. kàn sih mih sṳ̄? kàn tăi sṳ̄. hip sí. hip sie. | 15 Power. Talent. What is he able to do? Capable of great things. Suffocated. Warm up. |
| 16 hue îe. thòaⁿ îe. | 16 Lime kiln. Charcoal kiln. |
| 17 i so̤ khṳ̀. chíu cíeⁿ. | 17 He wriggled off. Palm of the hand. |
| 18 i tŏ̤ khieh hìang. | 18 He is employed in the Customs. |
| 19 khieh mûeh hîaⁿ. khieh cîⁿ. khieh sîp. khieh cò̤ cêk ē. | 19 Collect fuel. Collect money. Store up. Gather it together. |
| 20 a pĕ, ōi! a cé ā! chù piⁿ ō̤! | 20 Father! Sister! Neighbor! |
| 21 ói cṳ́. hṳ̂ lân cùe. cŭi sài. | 21 A dwarf. A wart. Daughter's husband, living in the house. |

## LESSON CLXVI.

志 cì; will; purpose.
憑 pêng; what can be proven.
據 kṳ̀; testimony; evidence.
證 cèng; proof; testify.
服 hôk; serve; what serves.
事 sṳ̄; serve; obey.

獻 hìen; offer in worship.
祭 cì; bring oblation.
題 * chìn; lift up.
提 * tìe; adhere; stick.
啄 toh; to peck; pick.
啜 chueh; sip; suck.

1 cí kìa$^n$ ío ìa$^n$; hṳ́ kìa$^n$ ío su. chì cē.
2 bōi su kùe hṳ́ kâi.
3 úa ŏi cáu ìa$^n$ i.
4 lêng kò sí, m̄ khṳ̀.
5 kìe$^n$ kùe hia$^n$ tī.
6 kìe$^n$ kùe pât kok.
7 ìa$^n$ kùe hṳ́ kìa$^n$.
8 su kùe cí cêk kìa$^n$.
9 mài tà$^n$ khah cùe.
10 jîp cūi; cie cūi.
11 ŭ cí khì. lîp cì. tāi cì. bô cí khì kâi nâng. sim cì ngē; sim cì ńng.
12 ŭ pêng. pêng tong.
13 bô pêng kṳ̀. pêng lṳ́ tà$^n$.
14 kháu sueh bô pêng.
15 pêng toa$^n$. kṳ̀ síu. ŭ hó cò cèng kṳ̀.
16 bô cèng bô kṳ̀. cò cèng kì$^n$. cèng sìt. ŭ hó ûi cèng.
17 hôk sṳ̄. hìen cì. cì bûn.
18 chìn m̄ phû. chìn phû.
19 tah m̄ tìe. cío toh cìah.
20 chueh tê. toh m̄ phùa.
21 bô năi i hô.
22 năi hô, năi hô?
23 kùe năi hô kìe.

1 This sort is superior; that sort is inferior. Try it.
2 Is not inferior to that one.
3 I can outrun him.
4 I rather die than go.
5 Superior to his brethren.
6 Excelling other kingdoms.
7 Surpassing that sort.
8 Inferior to this kind.
9 Do not reiterate too much.
10 Go to live with a wife's father.
11 Resolute. Fix the resolve. Great purpose. A shiftless fellow. Strong resolves; weak resolution.
12 There is proof. A broker.
13 Unfounded. It is as you say.
14 Words do not serve for proof.
15 Receipt. Guard vigilantly. There is proof of it to be had.
16 There is no proof of it. Be a witness. Proof. There is proof.
17 Serve. Make offerings. Elegy.
18 Lift without raising. Lift and raise.
19 It does not stick. Birds eating.
20 Sip tea. Could not peck it open.
21 There is no help for it.
22 What can be done now?
23 Cross the Budhist Styx.

# LESSON CLXVII.

奉 hŏng; offer or take respectfully.
稱 * téng; weigh; adjust.
秤 chìn; steelyard.
存 chûn; retain; left over.
毒 tâk; poison; noxious.
靠 kŏ; khàu; depend on.

倚 í$^{n}$; úa; rely on; lean on.
依 i; conform to; trust to.
賴 nāi; n̄g; depend on; trust.
賴 * lūa; falsely accuse.
胝 * lang; callous: corns.
遵 cun; comply; obey.

| | |
|---|---|
| 1 ke húe lien kú. cun síu. | 1 A long tried weapon. Obey. |
| 2 móng kâi lău m. | 2 A certain old woman. |
| 3 móng nâng; móng jı̂t; móng sî. | 3 That man; that day; at the time. |
| 4 tŏ móng kə̀ cə̀ móng sṳ̄. móng mûeh. | 4 In a certain place, doing a certain thing. That thing. |
| 5 cí hō nâng. hṳ́ hō mûeh. cí hō chù. | 5 This sort of person. That stamp of thing. This kind of house. |
| 6 mài khṳ̀ chap i kâi sṳ̄. chap jı̂p i kâi táng. | 6 Have nothing to do with his affairs. Entered that cabal. |
| 7 nêk cúi. nêk ńng. | 7 Submerged. Infanticide. |
| 8 hŏng sṳ̆. hŏng mĕng. thû lūa. | 8 Serve. Get orders. False accuser. |
| 9 téng thói$^{n}$ ŭ jîeh cōi kṳn. khîeh ki chìn khṳ̀ téng. | 9 Weigh it, and see how many catties. Take steelyards and weigh. |
| 10 cîah chûn kâi. bō chûn. chûn sim. chûn lâu. pó chûn. ēng chûn. siu chûn. | 10 The food left. Nothing left. Settled purpose. Keep back. Conserve. Remnants. Store up. |
| 11 ŭ kâi tâk ŭ kâi bŏi. | 11 Some are poison, some are not. |
| 12 tâk sim. tâk îeh. tâk chíu. tâk hāi. tâk khì. tâk sí nâng. hôk tâk. lîu tâk. | 12 Malicious. A poison. Villain. Malevolent. Malaria. Poison people. Poisoned. General bane. |
| 13 í$^{n}$ kŏ. bô i bô kŏ. khàu m̄ cŭ. khàu sua$^{n}$ cîah sua$^{n}$, khàu cúi cîah cúi. | 13 Lean against. Nothing to depend upon. Unreliable. Landsmen depend on land, watermen on water. |
| 14 m̄ i lṳ́. i lṳ́ kâi ūe. i jîen; i kū. cun i. | 14 I cannot agree with you. As you say. As usual. Compliant. |
| 15 úa tŏ chîe$^{n}$. úa tŏ í$^{n}$. bô nāi cṳ thû. bô hó n̄g. mài lūa nâng. | 15 Lean against the wall. Recline in a chair. Loafer. No dependence. Don't falsely accuse. |

## LESSON CLXVIII.

| | | | |
|---|---|---|---|
| 蹲 | * chn̂g; squat; crouch. | 强 | * chìo; powerful; strong. |
| 伏 | * pū; to brood; hover. | 弱 | * phûh; feeble; weak. |
| 唆 | sɵ; set at variance. | 巴 | pa; clap; slap. |
| 創 | chàng; create; found. | 枷 | kê; the cangue. |
| 造 | cău; construct; make. | 綢 | tîu; pongee. |
| 刮 | * kíam; khau; scrape out. | 痣 | kì; a mole; a spot. |

| | | |
|---|---|---|
| 1 | hâh cíeⁿ. tùe kín kín. | Join the palms. Adhere tightly. |
| 2 | kōi jû hŵn cíeⁿ. | As easy as turning the hand. |
| 3 | phah i cêk ē pa cíeⁿ. | Give him a slap. |
| 4 | hôk tâk thû lūa. | A self poisoned accuser. |
| 5 | hìen cì sîn. chàng sì kài. | Offer to gods. Create the world. |
| 6 | úa chìn i m̄ phû. | I cannot raise it up. |
| 7 | lʉ́ ciang lâi ŭ hɵ́ cʉ jît. | You will have a prosperous life. |
| 8 | kàⁿ bɵ́ m̄ kàu, i m̄ phû. | With too little yeast it will not rise. |
| 9 | m̄ cai cɵ̀ nî mûeh sí. i khŵn thăi lʉ́ jîeh hɵ́? | I do not know how he was killed. How did he treat you? |
| 10 | lʉ́ mài khʉ̀ hôk sʉ̆ i. | Do not go and serve them. |
| 11 | lʉ́ tîeh jím năi. | You must have patience. |
| 12 | hêng lí. hêng lí cōi. | Luggage. Much baggage. |
| 13 | úa àiⁿ khʉ̀ koi chī; tùi tī kɵ̀ khʉ̀? ak tâk. | I wish to go to the market; which is the way? Virulent. |
| 14 | i bɵ̂ ang bɵ̂ kíaⁿ hɵ́ khʉt i n̂g. | She has no husband nor children to depend on. |
| 15 | koi ciang cháu, cɵ̀ tàu, seⁿ n̆ng, chn̂g lɵ̂h khʉ̀ pū kíaⁿ. | A hen takes grass, makes a nest, lays eggs, broods on them, and hatches chickens. |
| 16 | sɵ sŏng. kà sɵ; sɵ kà. | Stir up litigation. Stir up strife. |
| 17 | chàng cău. chàng sʉ̄ ngîap. khai chàng. chàng sí. chàng hŭe tn̂g. sin chàng. | Create. Found an estate. Originate. To make first. Found a church. Newly founded. |
| 18 | cău hùe. chɵ cău. khí cău. khá cău. cău ngûn. | Form out of. Invent. Begin. Skillful work. A fabrication. |
| 19 | i li chìo, ún li phûh. | They are strong and we are weak. |
| 20 | kì chiu. kíam cheng khih. | Hair on a mole. Scrape it clean. |

# LESSON CLXIX.

| | | | |
|---|---|---|---|
| 螫 | * tìng; sting. | 訣 | kwt; occult doctrines. |
| 禍 | hŭa; woe; misery. | 散 | sùaⁿ; scatter; disperse. |
| 稀 | hi; sleazy; sparse. | 捡 | lìam; to pinch up. |
| 疏 | se; open; distant; coarse. | 鬮 | khau; lot; ballot. |
| 卜 | pok; phok; divine; guess. | 煤 | bûe; fossil coal; soot. |
| 卦 | khùe; cast future events. | 阻 | cé; impede; stop. |

| | |
|---|---|
| 1 ciang cîeh kâk sí. | 1 Stone him to death. |
| 2 ciang phì jŭ kà i. | 2 Teach him by parables. |
| 3 ciang hó ūe khǹg i. | 3 Entreat him with good words. |
| 4 cang pò cia mi mi. | 4 Screen closely with a cloth. |
| 5 khut n̂g phang tàng; ŭ phang tâk tŏ nêk tói, tì kàu i céng thìaⁿ. | 5 Was stung by a bee; there is bee venom in the flesh, so that it is swollen and aches. |
| 6 hiet tàng tîeh i. pok khùe. | 6 Scorpions sting him. Wizzard. |
| 7 cun úa kâi ì. | 7 Comply with my wishes. |
| 8 khut hŏ ak thàu thàu. | 8 Wet through by the rain. |
| 9 būe ŭ thiⁿ tī, būe ŭ nâng mûeh, būe cêng chàng cău bw̄n mûeh cu côiⁿ, ŭ cí cêk ūi sîn. hŭa hŭam. | 9 Before there were heavens or earth, before there were people, before all things were created, there was this God. Calamities. |
| 10 hi hi. thiⁿ téng kâi cheⁿ hi hi. pò hi. hi se. | 10 Sparse. The stars are far apart. Cloth sleazy. Sleazy. |
| 11 mûe pû hi cē. | 11 Make the porridge thinner. |
| 12 se thong. se châi. se sit. | 12 Clear out. Enlarge. Mislaid. |
| 13 bê chin se kău pêh. chīu lîm hi se. húe bûe. | 13 No difference on account of kinship. Sparse trees. Soot. |
| 14 i ké cuang cò pok khùe. pìen khùe. | 14 He disguised himself as a fortune teller. Luck has changed. |
| 15 phok thóiⁿ hó a m̄ hó. | 15 Divine whether good or ill. |
| 16 kháu kwt. sùaⁿ khui. sùaⁿ lío. | 16 Gibberish. Dispersed. Scattered. |
| 17 liam khau. bûe thòaⁿ. | 17 Draw lots. Mineral coal. |
| 18 có cí. có keh. có gāi. có lān. có huang. | 18 Make to stop. Impede. Retard. Hardships. Head wind. |
| 19 cúa bûe; cúa ín. | 19 Paper match, which holds fire. |

## LESSON CLXX.

| | | | |
|---|---|---|---|
| 勢 | sì; influence; power. | 合 | * kap; unite; mix. |
| 散 | * súa$^{n}$; medical powders. | 挖 | uai; to scoop out. |
| 找 | táu; exchange; barter. | 評 | phêng; discuss; revise. |
| 梁 | nîe; girder; bridge. | 批 | phoi; criticise; lease. |
| 鞭 | pi$^{n}$; a whip; lash. | 費 | * tî; hùi; expend; trouble. |
| 靴 | hia; boots. | 況 | khùang; moreover. |

| | | |
|---|---|---|
| 1 | hú khẁn nâng. bī sò. | That sort of people. Relish. |
| 2 | sng, kam, khó, hiam, kîam, kìe cè ngō bī. | Sour, sweet, bitter, spicy and salt, are the five tastes. |
| 3 | sua$^{n}$ tien hái bī. kùe bī. | All sorts of dainties. Past its prime. |
| 4 | í$^{n}$ keng chong hó lío, bī sò khut nâng ēng khù, só chûn kâi phoh kìe cè ca. | When it is steeped, and the relishable part has been used what is left is called dregs. |
| 5 | í$^{n}$ cí kĭa$^{n}$ sū tō se$^{n}$. | By this means he lives. |
| 6 | í$^{n}$ cí kù ūe ŏi tit jîp. | By this saying can enter in. |
| 7 | í$^{n}$ cúi kek sí. mīn kì. | Drowned by the waters. Freckles. |
| 8 | í$^{n}$ to thâi sí. phah cíe$^{n}$. | Slain by a knife. Clap the hands. |
| 9 | í$^{n}$ lú ūe tīa$^{n}$ lú cūe. | Condemn you by your words. |
| 10 | thói$^{n}$ chíu cíe$^{n}$ hûn. | Scrutinize the lines in the hand. |
| 11 | bûa to cîeh. îang pi$^{n}$. | Whetstone. Flourish a whip. |
| 12 | cèng kŭ. tíam sim. | Testimony. Stay the stomach. |
| 13 | sì lât. khẁn sì. hêng sì. | Influence. Authority. Aspect. |
| 14 | îeh súa$^{n}$. kap cè súa$^{n}$. | Mixed drugs. Make up powders. |
| 15 | táu ngn, táu cî$^{n}$. táu ūa$^{n}$. | Change money. Exchange. |
| 16 | hó sì thâu. sì lĭ kâi nâng. | Good omen. Sycophant. |
| 17 | sì só pit jîen. hùi sū. | I am compelled to do so. Fussy. |
| 18 | sêng sì. lâi sì sĭm hiong. | Improve the occasion. Savage looking. |
| 19 | kap îeh. kap pâng. kap hue sua. kap sek lĭo. kap kín. | Mix drugs. Room together. Mix mortar. Mix dye stuffs. Unite. |
| 20 | phī$^{n}$ nîe. tháng nîe. | Bridge of the nose. Bucket handle. |
| 21 | hia àng. bûeh àng. | Leg of boot. Leg of stocking. |
| 22 | khùang chía$^{n}$. hô khùang! | Still further. How much more! |
| 23 | phêng lŭn. phoi phêng. | Discuss the merits. Revise. |
| 24 | phoi toa$^{n}$. phoi hûe. | A lease. Official reply. |

## LESSON CLXXI.

| | | | |
|---|---|---|---|
| 掩 | * hŏiⁿ; closed; shut. | 梘 | kán; soap. |
| 右 | ĭu; cìaⁿ; on the right. | 吟 | ngîm; intone; hum. |
| 左 | có; tò; on the left. | 唱 | chìang; sing; carol. |
| 懷 | hûai; to harbour; cherish. | 泳 | * bī; to dive under water. |
| 希 | hi; expect; rare. | 泅 | sîu; swim; float. |
| 硃 | cu; vermilion. | 乃 | nái; may be; then; but. |

1 phok khà sĭ kit a sĭ hiong? mn̂g pok. khí bûe.

2 phoi mêng. phâng phoi. phoi poh. nía phōiⁿ.

3 hùi sim. hùi tīo. hùi tīo i kâi ke ngîap.

4 úa kâi mn̂g hŏiⁿ tŏ kà m̄ cêng chùaⁿ. sîu kùe khoi.

5 măng saⁿ; chiah sêng kâi saⁿ.

6 lâi liam khau khìeh thóiⁿ tī nâng kâi. bī cúi.

7 cí kìaⁿ sṳ̄ kàu tói sĭ cò nî; lí káng kìu úa thiaⁿ.

8 cìah chûn kâi, lâu pàng mùa khí. kap bûa.

9 sèng kùe i. sèng pāi nái piaⁿ ke sieⁿ sṳ̄.

10 cieⁿ seⁿ nái sĭ. nái hàm lí khà. ĭu chíu, có chíu.

11 cìaⁿ chíu, tò chíu kèng cōi nâng tàⁿ.

12 ĭu pôiⁿ, có pôiⁿ.

13 có ĭu. có tău.

14 có sṳ ĭu sieⁿ. kúai kha. ôh i kúai kha kìaⁿ.

15 hi hán. hûai hŭn. hûai phŏ. hûai m̄ hó ì.

16 n̂gn cu. cu pit.

17 hi mō. hi khî.

1 Was the divination lucky or unlucky? Guess fates. Embers.

2 Comment on. Side notes. Reverse the decision. Take a lease.

3 I' ve put you to trouble. Use up. Spent his property.

4 My door is closed but not yet bolted. Swim across the river.

5 A seamless garment.

6 Draw lots to see whose it shall be. Dive into the water.

7 What is the gist of this matter; you explain it to me.

8 What is left after eating, put aside till to-morrow. To double.

9 Overcome him. Victory or defeat is wounds for soldiers.

10 Thus it is. But I may call you. Right and left hand.

11 Right and left hand is the more common way of speaking.

12 On the right and left sides.

13 Near by. Erroneous doctrines.

14 Thinking of this way and that way. Lame. Imitate his limping.

15 Seldom. Cherish ill-will. To hug. Harbour evil thoughts.

16 Vermilion. Red pencil.

17 Hope. Rare.

## LESSON CLXXII.

䉲 nâ; a bailed basket.
筐 kheng; basket without a bail.
籮 lûa; deep open basket.
笠 lôih; a splint hat.
葫 ô; a low; round basket.
箕 ki; two-eared basket.

假 * hĕ; vacation.
使 * só; spend; use.
囊 láng; lâng; sack; bag.
勝 sèng; superior; excel.
勝 seng; adequate; bear.
景 kéng; prospect; aspect.

1 bûe thòa$^n$ sĭ îu sua$^n$ tói kâi thô só se$^n$ chut lâi kâi; húe thòa$^n$ sĭ îu nâng cám chû pàng tŏ îe tói sie kâi.
2 ŏi khí húe pun nâng cieh sie.
3 mài khà cò kîe$^n$ kùe khà cò. chĭ nâ.
4 tng jĭt í$^n$ kèng sa nîe kùe.
5 ài$^n$ sim lĭam tĭa$^n$ tīa$^n$.
6 ńng siu hó se$^n$; lâm siu hó sí.
7 cí kâi mûeh kĭa$^n$ cò cêk hûe lóng cóng tà$^n$ khù. só hùi.
8 ŭ jîeh cōi pûa$^n$ tî?
9 hô khùang cí kĭa$^n$ kèng kan khó! pùn ki.
10 hô khùang cí kâi kèng kùi tŏng! só hùi. hwn kán.
11 khùang chía$^n$ sĭ úa lâi.
12 úa míen ēng só hùi tîeh pûa$^n$ tî. chĭ nâ hĭ$^n$.
13 lú só hùi i jîeh cōi pûa$^n$ tî?
14 lôih kùa. tek lôih.
15 sèng kéng. kuang kéng. pái kéng. múi kéng. sŭn kéng. chok kéng se$^n$ chêng.
16 m̄ seng jĭm. put seng ngân. pàng hĕ.

1 Fossil coal comes from the mountains; charcoal comes from men's cutting down trees and charring them in a kiln.
2 Build a fire and warm one's self.
3 Not to do it is better than to do it. A market basket.
4 The day when the bargain was made.
5 Wish only remembrance of it.
6 For women an easy child-birth; for men an honorable death.
7 Take all these things away at one time. Expenditure.
8 How much is the fare?
9 How much more difficult then is this! A carrying basket.
10 How much more valuable then is this! Expenses. Soap.
11 Furthermore, I am come.
12 I need not expend any thing for fare. Bail of a basket.
13 How much was your passage?
14 A conical cover. Bamboo hat.
15 Picturesque. Prospect. To display. Fine site. Well situated. Cautious and discreet.
16 Inadequate to the post. Beyond description. Give a vacation.

## LESSON CLXXIII.

齊 côi; even; complete; at once.
濟 chì; tranquilize; classify.
治 tī; rule well; remedy.
滂 * pŏng; pōng; splash; bang.
陟 thek; to mount; go up.
類 lūi; species; class.
褥 jôk; mattress; cushion.
班 pan; grade; series.
民 mîn; the people.
譯 êk; interpret; translate.
等 téng; class; order; rank.
寡 kúaⁿ; few; solitary.

| | | |
|---|---|---|
| 1 | bói cêk kò̤ thúi sim nêk. | Buy a piece of lean meat. |
| 2 | kéng khùang hó̤ mē? | Are the prospects favorable? |
| 3 | lṳ́ mài có̤ cí i. nâng téng. | Do not prevent him. People. |
| 4 | i tn̂g kùe i a pĕ cêk pôiⁿ chíu. tī pēⁿ. sí káng kíaⁿ. | He is his father's right-hand. Practise medicine. A cast away. |
| 5 | chíaⁿ cèng hiaⁿ tī lâi cí pài tn̂g hŭe côi úa ŭ ūe àiⁿ kāng i tàⁿ. put téng. | Invite the brethren to meet here at the chapel; I have something I wish to say to them. Unlike. |
| 6 | siu sîp côi cíaⁿ. | Arrange them methodically. |
| 7 | cêk côi lâi. nĕ côi côi. | Come all at once. Very uniform. |
| 8 | ke húe m̄ côi cò̤ hó̤ cò̤ khang khùe? tī gêk. | The tools not being complete how can we work? Try causes. |
| 9 | chì pĭ. bw̄n mûeh chì pĭ, cí khìam tang huang. | All ready. All things are ready, and merely lack east wind. |
| 10 | put lêng chì ke uaⁿ lêng tī kok? | If you cannot govern a family how can you rule a kingdom? |
| 11 | chì chŵ̂n; côi cn̂g. | Complete throughout. |
| 12 | côi sim. m̄ côi. | Of one mind. Not uniform. |
| 13 | phah pŏng sîu. pōng pōng kìe. | Splashing about. Banging. |
| 14 | mn̂g pōng pōng kìe. | The door is slamming. |
| 15 | thek sí káng kíaⁿ lâu. | To float on the tide. |
| 16 | thek suaⁿ. thek cĭeⁿ thui téng. thek khí khṳ̀. thek m̄ khí. | Ascend a hill. Mount a ladder. Mount up. Cannot get up. |
| 17 | i sĭ thâng lūi. cío lūi. sĭen lūi. ak lūi. tâng lūi. ĭ lūi. | It is of the insect order. Bird kind. Righteous. Wicked. Same species. Strange kind. |
| 18 | hun cò̤ jîeh cōi téng? | Divided into how many classes? |
| 19 | lûn pan. cêk pan nâng. | Take turns. A class of men. |
| 20 | síu kúaⁿ hŭ jîn. êk ūe. | A widow. Translate. |

## LESSON CLXXIV.

乞 khut; beg; ask alms.
童 thông; young; lad.
扶 hû; uphold; help.
洪 âng; a flood.
洪 hông; vast; immense.
賭 tó; pûah; gamble; risk.
勒 lêk; bridle; restrain.
司 si; preside over; control.
浪 lăng; billows; surges.
梏 * gô; manacles.
鐐 lîo; fetters.
鏈 lîen; lock and chain.

1 khó sīeⁿ. khó ló hŭn. khó ceh pĭ. bô khó hîam.
1 Thinkable. Fit to hate. Blamable. Irreproachable.

2 cêk jît năi tit khù.
2 Can stand it for one day.

3 lí ŭ cîah hun mē?
3 Do you smoke?

4 ñg hun; sêk hun; o hun; cúi hun; cheⁿ hun; phīⁿ hun.
4 Tobacco; dry; dark; smoked through water; green; snuff.

5 îe nâ. hue lûa. phang hieⁿ âp. hieⁿ lâng.
5 Cradle. Lime basket. A perfume box. Incense bag.

6 bō âp. gêk âp. âp kíaⁿ. to âp. kìam âp.
6 Hat-box. Alabaster box. Tiny box. Sheath of a knife. Scabbard.

7 bói cêk tùi pùn ki.
7 Buy a couple of eared baskets.

8 tîeh cò pàng âp, i kâi hiang khì cìaⁿ bŏi cáu.
8 You must put it in a box, so the scent will not be lost.

9 cí kâi to kìam tîeh ŭ âp; bô kâi âp khíong ùi gō tîeh ka kī sieⁿ tîeh sin.
9 This sword must have a scabbard; without a scabbard I fear accidentally wounding myself.

10 bîh nâ. bîh lôih.
10 Splint basket. A reed hat.

11 sĭang téng; hĭa téng.
11 First-rate; second-rate.

12 kúaⁿ put têk cèng.
12 I am no match for so many.

13 khut cîah. khîu khut.
13 Beggar. Supplicate.

14 thông lâm. thông ñg. thông nî. sîn thông.
14 A youth. A virgin. Youthful. A bright lad.

15 hû i khí lâi. hû chíu.
15 Help him up. Support.

16 âng cúi. hông hok.
16 The deluge. Vast happiness.

17 phah kuaⁿ si. pûah cìⁿ.
17 Institute a law-suit. Gamble.

18 tó khì. cŭ tó. tó thâu. tó tîeⁿ. kìm tó. huang lăng.
18 Disgusted at. Get gamblers together. A stake. Gaming hall. Prohibit gaming. Billows.

## LESSON CLXXV.

雌 chṳ̂; bó; nùa; female.
雄 hîong; kang: kak; male.
牝 phín; bó; lán; female.
牡 móng; kó; kang; male.
騎 khîa; to ride.
一 * cē; once; one time.
糠 khng; chaff; husks.
糟 cau; sediment; dregs.
忘 bûang; forget; neglect.
墳 phûn; grave; mound.
墓 mô; tomb; sepulcher.
碑 pi; tablets; pillars.

| | | |
|---|---|---|
| 1 | sieⁿ láng bô i hôk. | No clothes in his bag. |
| 2 | kŭn lâi kâi kéng khùang hó mē? thóiⁿ múi kéng. | How go the times with you? See the fine view. |
| 3 | cí kâi kéng sek hó căi. | The aspect is fine. |
| 4 | kŭn lâi kâi kéng khùang m̄ hó. khîa koiⁿ bé. | The immediate prospect is bad. Ride on the shoulder. |
| 5 | lṳ́ chíaⁿ thĕng cêk thĕng. | Please wait a little while. |
| 6 | só si hô sṳ̄? | What does he preside over? |
| 7 | pûah su, pûah îaⁿ. | Lose or win in gaming. |
| 8 | êk cò pn̄g tī ūe. | Translate into the vernacular. |
| 9 | lêk seh. khîa sīa. | A bridle. Mounted archers. |
| 10 | lṳ́ cò lṳ́ khṳ̀, úa cò úa khṳ̀. khîa bé. | You go your way and I will go mine. Ride a horse. |
| 11 | àiⁿ khui kâi cṳ ce. | Going to open a school. |
| 12 | cí kâi hieⁿ lí ŭ cṳ ce. | This village has a school. |
| 13 | cōi cōi nâng sie hŭ à. | Many joined in the clamor. |
| 14 | koi ang; koi bó; ah bó; ah hêng; cío bó; cío kak; gû bó; gû kó; be bó; be kó; ciah bó; ciah kang; sai bó; sai kang; koi nùa; tṳ bó; tṳ lán. | Cock; hen; duck; drake; female bird; male bird; cow; bull; mare; horse; female sparrow; male sparrow; lioness; lion; pullet; sow; female pig. |
| 15 | khîa hóⁿ lân hĭa. | He who rides a tiger finds it difficult to dismount. |
| 16 | bêh khng. cho khng. | Wheat bran. Paddy chaff. |
| 17 | phîn cūaⁿ cṳ kau put khó bûang; cau khng cṳ chi put hĭa thâng. | Mean connections cannot be ignored; nor can a wife from the dregs of the people suit a mansion. |

# LESSON CLXXVI.

撚 * jûe; rub between the hands.
斂 líam; repress; gather in.
搓 so̤; roll under the hand.
氈 ci$^n$; felt; drugget.
兩 líang; both; dual.
少 * síam; wanting; short.

打 tá; thám; do; act on.
扮 pàn; apparel; rig out.
聽 thèng; hearken and decide.
廊 lâng; porch; corridor.
互 hû; dovetail; mutual.
鶴 hô̤h; a crane.

1 cíu cau.
2 cau nêk; cau hṳ̂.
3 phûn mŏ̤. mŏ̤ pi. cîeh pi. pi kì.
4 bûang kì. bûang pún.
5 hùi chím bûang cîah.
6 bô̤ nâng siu kŵn.
7 mīn mău cho lŏ. pêh hô̤h.
8 put tīo thô pùn.
9 tī tîang cò̤ thong sṳ̄? hûe ūe kâi nâng. kau hû.
10 khua$^n$ khua$^n$ líam sòi.
11 i cáu khṳ̀ tìam.
12 i tìam tŏ̤ tī kò̤?
13 thám khak. jîp líam.
14 bâk cîh; kat cîh. siu líam.
15 bī sng kâi sè$^n$ to̤ líam.
16 so̤ sùa$^n$. so̤ hie$^n$. so̤ cò̤ cêk kò̤. so̤ cúa tîo. so̤ chíu.
17 ci$^n$ bō̤. jû cŏ̤ cam ci$^n$. líang pôi$^n$ sie thâi.
18 líang sim siang hâh. líang phâng. m̄ tá kín.
19 tá thèng. tá pàn. tá chiu huang. síam chìn.
20 n̄g pàn lâm cuang.
21 nîe síam táu; síam chieh.

1 Dregs left after distilling spirits.
2 Corned meat; corned fish.
3 A grave. A grave-stone. Stone tablet. Inscription.
4 Forget. Forget a benefactor.
5 Lose sleep and forget to eat.
6 There is no one to take charge.
7 He is very ugly. White crane.
8 Clear away the rubbish.
9 Who acts as interpreter? The interpreter. Blended.
10 Gradually diminish.
11 He ran and hid.
12 Where is he hidden?
13 Tie a knot. Enshroud.
14 Tongue-tied. Neutralize.
15 Acids are neutralizing.
16 Twist thread. Roll incense sticks. Roll it into a lump. Make allumettes. Rub the hands.
17 Felt hat. Uneasy as if sitting on needles. Civil war.
18 Congenial minds. Both sides. Not important.
19 Inform yourself. Costume. Raise the wind. Short weight.
20 Women in men's clothes.
21 Short measure in pecks; in feet.

## LESSON CLXXVII.

紡 pháng; spin; reel.
績 ceh; splice threads.
撈 lîo; skim or rake out.
濾 * tè; strain through a cloth.
咽 * kṳ̆; swallow; gulp.
哽 kéⁿ; choke; stick.

回 * ût; turn; revolve.
敷 * chu; lay; spread out.
敷 hu; apply; arrange.
露 lò; divulge; expose.
涿 tâp; tok; trickle; drop.
撐 thèⁿ; prop; support.

| | |
|---|---|
| 1 thèng i lâi. pháng se. | 1 Come as he likes. Spin yarn. |
| 2 thèng khî cṳ̆ jîen. | 2 Let it be as it may. |
| 3 thèng thiⁿ îu mīa. | 3 As Heaven decrees. |
| 4 hû siang kau hâh. kṳ̆ lôh. | 4 To dovetail together. Swallow. |
| 5 hû siang lâi úang. | 5 Constant intercourse. |
| 6 i tŏ pháng ceh. ceh mûa. | 6 She is spinning. Twist hemp. |
| 7 phah soh; ká soh. lîo khí. | 7 Make ropes. Haul up. |
| 8 hái tói mông cam. | 8 Dredge in the sea for a needle. |
| 9 lîo ô khak. | 9 Dredge for oyster shells. |
| 10 kṳ̆ m̄ lôh. | 10 Could not swallow it. |
| 11 cò cêk chùi kṳ̆ lôh khṳ̀. | 11 Swallow at one mouthful. |
| 12 kṳ̆ líо mài kéⁿ tîeh. | 12 Do not choke in swallowing it. |
| 13 kéⁿ tîeh hṳ̂ kut. | 13 Choked with a fish-bone. |
| 14 âu lêng kéⁿ tîeh. | 14 Stuck in his throat. |
| 15 ût tn̂g thâu; hûe tn̂g thâu. | 15 Turn the head around. |
| 16 mài ût chúa. hû siang. | 16 Do not twist about. Responsive. |
| 17 chu cháu chîeh. tâp tâp tih. | 17 Lay down matting. Patter. |
| 18 hu îeh. put hu ēng. | 18 Put on medicine. Insufficient. |
| 19 lṳ́ hṳ́ kò īa sĭ put hu, li lâi úa cí kò khîeh. | 19 If you have not enough there, come here and get some. |
| 20 chiah sin lò thói. | 20 Stark naked. |
| 21 lò hêng. lò kut. | 21 Show the shape. Emaciated. |
| 22 mâk khah lò. khah lò kut. | 22 Hollow-eyed. Bones prominent. |
| 23 tâp tâp kìe. tok tok kìe. | 23 Pattering. Trickling. |
| 24 khui mn̂g thèⁿ theng. | 24 Open the doors and windows. |
| 25 i àiⁿ ka lâuh, khîeh ki mûeh khṳ̀ thèⁿ. | 25 It is going to fall, get something and prop it up. |
| 26 tè tīo phoh. | 26 Strain out the dregs. |

## LESSON CLXXVIII.

| | |
|---|---|
| 案 | ùa$^{n}$; case in law. |
| 審 | sím; investigate; judge. |
| 判 | phẁn; decide; verdict. |
| 駭 | hái; startled; scared. |
| 槍 | chie$^{n}$; a spear; pike. |
| 沉 | tîm; sink; lost. |
| 沫 | * phûeh; froth; foam. |
| 漬 | cù; to drench; tint. |
| 漬 | * sə̀; to sop up; wipe up. |
| 急 | kip; hasty; urgent. |
| 急 | * ân; tight; straightened. |
| 鯨 | khêng; ang; whale. |

| | |
|---|---|
| 1 ùa$^{n}$ kìa$^{n}$; ùa$^{n}$ chn̂g; kong ùa$^{n}$; kat ùa$^{n}$; ùa$^{n}$ bûn; ùa$^{n}$ îu; ùa$^{n}$ chêng; tōa ùa$^{n}$, sìo ùa$^{n}$; mīa ùa$^{n}$; ôi$^{n}$ ùa$^{n}$; tìo ùa$^{n}$; tīa$^{n}$ ùa$^{n}$; chûn ùa$^{n}$; hẃn ùa$^{n}$; hwn ùa$^{n}$. | 1 A case in court; the Bench; an action; close the case; official records; merits of the case; circumstances of the case; important and unimportant cases; murder case; a case that may be postponed; order a case up; give decision; copy on file; revise the case; rehear the case. |
| 2 ùa$^{n}$ cōi$^{n}$; kū ùa$^{n}$; sím ùa$^{n}$; tō ùa$^{n}$; mn̄g ùa$^{n}$; bô thâu kong ùa$^{n}$. | 2 At the bar; an old case; judge a case; in court; try a case; no cause for action. |
| 3 sím phẁn. sím mn̄g. tùi sím. sím sît. ngîam sím. | 3 To judge. Judicial inquiry. Confront witnesses. Final judgment. Severe inquiry. |
| 4 hăi phà$^{n}$. hăi ī. kia$^{n}$ hăi. hái ang. kín kip. | 4 Scared. Astonishing. Startle. A whale. Urgent. |
| 5 khùi kip. sū kip. kàu kip. kip cèng. | 5 Out of breath. No time to lose. Report danger. Virulent disease. |
| 6 lú kâi sim mài kip. | 6 Do not be in such a hurry. |
| 7 kip kip jû lût lĕng. | 7 As hasty as Mercury. |
| 8 túi ân ân. phûe ân ân. | 8 Draw it tight. Skin drawn tight. |
| 9 cù kàu thàng thàng. | 9 Thoroughly drenched. |
| 10 sə̀ kàu ta ta. | 10 Wipe it up dry. |
| 11 tîm lûn. tîm mît. tîm nêk. tîm tói. | 11 Irretrievably lost. Ruined. Drowned. Sunk to the bottom. |
| 12 gû nī phûeh. lâu phûeh. | 12 Cream. Froth at the mouth. |

# LESSON CLXXIX.

伏 * bih; secretly; ambushed.
捲 * kauh; kn̄g; to roll up.
窺 íam; kui; to peek; peep.
伺 sĭ; reconnoitre; spy.
伺 sū; to wait upon.
探 thàm; spy; explore.
偵 bîe; ceng; to spy out.
恩. un; grace; favor.
搬 pua"; remove; move.
焚 ûn; to scorch; burn.
脫 * lut; to shed.
菰 * ko; mould; mushrooms.

| | | |
|---|---|---|
| 1 | ì kìen. jîn ài. kong ngĭ. pún nía. kong phêng. se$^{n}$ ko. kong tău. sū hāu. | Opinion. Charity. Just. Ability. Welfare. Mouldy. Justice. To wait upon. |
| 2 | phùa nūa. peh sè$^{n}$. | Sloughing ulcers. The people. |
| 3 | bih thói$^{n}$ i tà$^{n}$ mih ūe. | Secretly find out what he says. |
| 4 | lí cē$^{n}$ cē$^{n}$ bih thói$^{n}$ i cò mih sū. pua$^{n}$ chù, pua$^{n}$ ke. | You quietly spy out what he is doing. Change one's residence. |
| 5 | úa bih cêk kùa thia$^{n}$ i nŏ nâng tŏ tà$^{n}$ àm cē$^{n}$ ūe. | I kept hidden a long while and heard the two in secret conclave. |
| 6 | lîam kauh khí. thàm kía$^{n}$. | Roll up the curtain. A spy. |
| 7 | cháu chîeh kn̄g hó, khîeh khí. sū hāu kâi nâng. | When you have rolled up the mat, put it away. Attendants. |
| 8 | mài khù thau íam i. | Do not go and peek at him. |
| 9 | nâng ài$^{n}$ kui sĭ i. | Some are going to reconnoitre it. |
| 10 | tá thàm. thàm mn̄g. thàm thói$^{n}$. thàm thia$^{n}$. | To sound one. To inquire into. Explore. Try to hear about. |
| 11 | ceng thàm. bîe thói$^{n}$. | Explorer; scout. To spy out. |
| 12 | khai un. un chêng. | Show favor to. Kindness. |
| 13 | un chiang chîu pò. | Requite evil for good. |
| 14 | i pua$^{n}$ khù pât kò. | He has moved to another place. |
| 15 | ûn hie$^{n}$. ûn sie. ûn hùe. ûn kàu thàng thàng. | Burn incense. Burn. Burn up. Burn it all up clean. |
| 16 | tŏ ún có ke, chiu thi$^{n}$ sî chīu bâk kâi hîeh cĭu khí thâu lut; kàu tang thi$^{n}$ sî cĭu lóng cóng lut ŵn khù. | In our country, in the autum the trees begin to shed their leaves, and in winter they have shed them all. |
| 17 | ài$^{n}$ ūe kâi chù kêk khut lí thói$^{n}$. kám un. | I will draw a plan of the house, for you to see. Grateful. |

# LESSON CLXXX.

概 khài; summing up.
騌 cang; mane.
鬃 cang; coiffure.
鬃 cáng; wig; peruke.
拳 khûn; the fist.
題 tôi; subscribe; compose.

題 thî; to bring to notice.
染 * ǹe; spot; infect.
魂 hûn; the wits; the manes.
魄 phek; the animal spirit.
熨 ù; ut; to iron; rub.
痺 * ngûi; numb.

| | |
|---|---|
| 1 khì khài. cêk khài. | 1 Resumé. Altogether. |
| 2 i kâi khì khài hó cǎi. | 2 His general appearance is fine. |
| 3 tǎi khài. khûn thâu. | 3 On the whole. The fist. |
| 4 bé cang mô. tu cang mô. | 4 Horse's mane. Hog's bristles. |
| 5 siu cang; tá cang. thâu cang. ké cáng. | 5 Arrange the coiffure. The head-dress. False hair. |
| 6 khûn thâu sai pě. phah khûn. thî khí. | 6 A teacher of boxing. Boxing. To prompt. |
| 7 tôi cîⁿ. tôi si. | 7 Subscribe money. Compose verses. |
| 8 lú soiⁿ thî thâu. | 8 You first broach the matter. |
| 9 sòi tôi tōa cò. | 9 Make to much of a small matter. |
| 10 mài khut i ǹe tîeh. | 10 Do not let him daub you. |
| 11 cí ieⁿ pēⁿ ŏi ǹe nâng. | 11 This disease is contagious. |
| 12 ǹe tîeh saⁿ sì nâng. | 12 Infected three or four people. |
| 13 lêng hûn. hûn phêk. sam hûn chit phek. | 13 Soul. The departed soul. Three souls and seven spirits. |
| 14 kiaⁿ kàu bô hûn. | 14 Frightened out of his wits. |
| 15 bô sim bô hûn. sit hûn. | 15 Abstracted. Lose the wits. |
| 16 lú káⁿ sǐ hûn m̄ tǒ sin. | 16 You have n't your wits about you. |
| 17 hûn pue phek sùaⁿ. | 17 The soul departs, the life ceases. |
| 18 kha chíu nĕ ngûi ngûi. | 18 My hands and feet are very numb. |
| 19 ut táu. ut saⁿ khò. | 19 A flat-iron. Iron clothes. |
| 20 cêk khài ŭ jîeh cōi? | 20 How much in one lot? |
| 21 chíu máng i bé cang mô. | 21 Holding on to the mane. |
| 22 kíaⁿ jît kâi cang siu khù ngía cǎi. sai kíaⁿ. | 22 Your coiffure is very prettily arranged to-day. Apprentice. |
| 23 lú kâi cang ŭ ciap cáng a bô? úa kong tǎu hâiⁿ lú. | 23 Do you wear false hair? I will give you fair pay. |

## LESSON CLXXXI.

吝 lĭen; sordid; stingy.
柔 jîu; flexible; meek.
睦 môk; affable.
索 sok; demand; bind.
惑 hôk; delude; lead astray.
憤 hún; ardor; zeal.

悲 pui; commiserate.
誘 íu; entice; lure.
訓 hùn; instruct; teach.
泣 khip; grieve; lament.
忽 hut; disregard; abruptly.
品 pín; rank; conduct.

| | | |
|---|---|---|
| 1 | tham lĭen. hûa môk. lêk sok. kau kṳ́. chṳ̂ pui. kà hùn. | Covetousness. Harmony. Extortion. Elevation. Compassion. Education. |
| 2 | thèng cò̤. kat khó. khin hut. hwt hún. jîn ngĭ. hùe kói. | Careless. Perseverance. Contempt. Zeal. Benevolence. Repentance. |
| 3 | ṳn tíen. lĭen sieh. pún hĕng. hêng ûi. íu hôk. gî hôk. | Favour. Close-fisted. Character. Behaviour. Temptation. Suspicion. |
| 4 | ai khip. m̄ lĭen. | Vexation. Open-handed. |
| 5 | sok mīa. hùn sī. hut jîen. pín mău. un jîu. | Involve one's life. Instructions. Abruptly. Countenance. Meek. |
| 6 | hut mêng hut àm. sĭang pín. | It appeared and disappeared suddenly. The best sort. |
| 7 | bô̤ pín. kêk pín. pín phêng. ín íu. íu phìen. mî hôk. hôk sì. | Abandoned. Highest rank. Classify. Entice. Befool. Inveigle. Delude mankind. |
| 8 | thî thî khàu khàu. hún nō̤. khàu khip. sîap hún. | Sobbing and crying. Angry. Lament. Vent his feelings. |
| 9 | jîu jîak. nn̂g jîu. sèⁿ chêng jîu. hut ngŏ̤. | Gentle. Pliant. Meek disposition. It happened. |
| 10 | sẃn nn̂g jîu kâi. | Pick out a limp one. |
| 11 | lṳ́ tôi jîeh cōi cîⁿ? | How much did you subscribe? |
| 12 | lṳ́ mài khah lĭen. | Do not be too stingy. |
| 13 | un jîu hieⁿ. môk côk. | An humble village. United clan. |
| 14 | hún khì. kṳ̆ sí. | Ardor. Choked to death. |
| 15 | íu i khṳ̀ cò̤ m̄ hó̤ sṳ̄. | Tempt him to wickedness. |
| 16 | hut khîang hut jîak. | Regardless of strength or weakness. |

## LESSON CLXXXII.

慧 hŭi; clever; intelligent.
智 tì; sagacious; prudent.
畜 thek; thiok; cattle; animals.
歷 lêh; to pass by or to.
良 lîang; benignant.
兇 hiong; malevolent.

術 sût; tricks; arts.
黴 bûe; mouldy; grimed.
曆 * lâh; heavenly bodies.
搖 * ît; to zigzag; wave.
虐 ngîak; harsh; cruel.
暴 pău; cruel; fierce.

| | |
|---|---|
| 1 un hŭi. tì hŭi. thek se$^{n}$. sîa sût. kwt sût. châi hù. bâk kang sai pĕ. | 1 Kindness. Wisdom. Brute. The black art. Superstitions. Clerk. Master carpenter. |
| 2 lûi kong ît húe. | 2 It thunders and lightens. |
| 3 ît chíu mài tà$^{n}$. | 3 Motion to him not to tell. |
| 4 chie$^{n}$ cêk ē ît, nâng cĭu kîa$^{n}$. sa$^{n}$ khò khîeh khùa ŭ huang kə̀; cêk ē ît cĭu kōi ta. hiong chíu. | 4 When the spear is waved they go on. Put the clothes in a windy place; if they flap they will easily dry. Murderer. |
| 5 hiong khûn phah put tit nâng chìe mīn. | 5 Even the hand of violence cannot strike a smiling face. |
| 6 hiong ak. hiong pău. kîa$^{n}$ hiong. pău pē$^{n}$. | 6 Wickedly cruel. Fierce and cruel. Act cruelly. Violent illness. |
| 7 khîang hiong pău ak. | 7 Unscrupulous and violent. |
| 8 ai sia$^{n}$. lâi lêh. lêh lâi. | 8 A moaning. Annals. Continuously. |
| 9 kau lâu. láu sît. mn̂g seng. kun cṳ́. | 9 Restaurant. Innocent. Disciples. Modest; cultured. |
| 10 ceng se$^{n}$, lâk thiok. | 10 All sorts of animals. |
| 11 chât sûi sío jîn, ŭ sî tì sèng kun cṳ́. | 11 The thief though uneducated is somtimes sharper than the cultured. |
| 12 lêh nî. lêh kú. lêh chîo. lêh lêh khṳ́ sìo. lâh jît. | 12 For a series of years. Long since. Successive dynasties. I can count all to this time. Almanac. |
| 13 lîang sim. lîang sĭen. lîang jîn. bô lîang sim. lîang ke hŭ ńng. huap sût. | 13 Conscientious. Virtuous. My goodman. Hard hearted. Gentelwomen. Magical rules. |
| 14 lîang bé. lîang cai. lîang lêng. pău ngîak. | 14 Gentle horse. Genius. Natural skill. Cruel. |

## LESSON CLXXXIII.

| | |
|---|---|
| 僞 ngŭi; counterfeit; false. | 禽 khîm; feathered creatures. |
| 奸 kang; traitorous; corrupt. | 獸 sìu; wild animals. |
| 偶 ngó; image; abruptly. | 畧 lîak; somewhat. |
| 人 * ang; effigy; image. | 帮 pang; classifier; succor. |
| 頑 ngŵn; passive; mulish. | 助 cŏ; assist; succor. |
| 欺 khi; cheat; abuse. | 誠 sêng; real; sincere. |

| | |
|---|---|
| 1 cà ngŭi. sim sût. ngŭi sim. bô phìen bô ngŭi. | 1 Hypocritical. Designs. False hearted. Guileless. |
| 2 kang cà. kang chîn. láu kang. kang hîong. kang chât. kang táng. | 2 Fraudulent. Traitorous. Traitor. Inordinate. Villain. Traitorous cabal. |
| 3 khîm sìu. peh sìu. | 3 Wild beasts. All kinds of beasts. |
| 4 nâng mīn sìu sim. | 4 Man's face and beast's heart. |
| 5 pue khîm cáu sìu. | 5 Birds and beasts. |
| 6 ngó sìeⁿ. bâk ngó. ngó ngŏ. pài ngó sìang. ngó jîen. | 6 Images. Effigy. Happened. Worship idols. Unforeseen. |
| 7 ang kíaⁿ. ang thâu. | 7 A doll. A mask. |
| 8 ngŵn ngĕ. khìam iak. | 8 Obdurate. Frugality. |
| 9 pang cŏ. pang pó. | 9 To aid. To eke out. |
| 10 sêng sît. cìah m̄ kam bī. | 10 Sincere. Not relish food. |
| 11 ngŵn cìeh. ngŵn mîn. phî ngŵn. tăi lîak. | 11 Inert stone. Unlettered people. Stupid. On an average. |
| 12 khi nâng. khi sim. | 12 Rascal. Deceive one's self. |
| 13 lŕ mài khi i sòi. | 13 Do not abuse the little ones. |
| 14 lîak lîak hío. | 14 I comprehend it slightly. |
| 15 pang chùi. cêk pang cûn. | 15 Speak for another. A fleet. |
| 16 thâu pang tê. | 16 First gathering of tea. |
| 17 ah pang. pang thiap. pang chíu. pang tòa kuaⁿ. | 17 The escort. To eke out. Help. Lieutenant-colonel. |
| 18 hŭ cŏ. sêng sim. | 18 Assist. True-hearted. |
| 19 cŏ lŕ cêk pì cu lât. | 19 I will lend you a helping hand. |
| 20 sêng kèng. sêng ì. cì sêng. nâng sŏ íⁿ ī khîm sìu cía tŏ tī kò? | 20 Real reverence. Truthful. Perfect sincerity. Wherein is the difference between men and beasts? |

海上絲綢之路文獻集成 科技與文化編

## LESSON CLXXXIV.

| | | | |
|---|---|---|---|
| 息 | sek; rest; savings. | 殃 | iang; misfortune. |
| 謀 | mông; stratagem. | 謙 | khiam; unobtrusive. |
| 虛 | hu; vacant; untrue. | 遜 | sùn; humble; docile. |
| 疾 | cît; sickness; touchy. | 憂 | iu; mournful. |
| 凌 | lêng; treat vilely. | 悶 | būn; sad; unhappy. |
| 辱 | jôk; insult; shame. | 恭 | kiong; venerate; polite. |

| | |
|---|---|
| 1 an sek. kòi mông. cît pēⁿ. lêng jôk. cai iang. khiam sùn. | 1 Sabbath. Stratagem. Disease. Insults. Misfortunes. Humility. |
| 2 iu būn. cúi po hûn. jìo hûn. bô hûn ciah. | 2 Grief. Ripples on water. Puckered. No trace of it. |
| 3 jím jôk. sīu jôk. khut i jôk tîeh. jôk kok. bōi jôk tîeh i. lêng ngîak. | 3 Endure insults. Receive insults. Insulted by him. To disgrace the country. Does not dishonor him. Maltreat. |
| 4 khi lêng. hiah sek. chut sek. cú sek. seⁿ sek. sek nō. | 4 Abuse. To rest. Perquisites. Posterity. Bear interest. Pacify. |
| 5 mông hāi. mông seⁿ. mông sū tō nâng, sêng sū tō thiⁿ. mông châi kù suah. cú mông. | 5 Plot against. Devise means of living. Man proposes but heaven disposes. To murder for money. Contriver of plots. |
| 6 jíum cît. kip cît. cît sì. | 6 Infected. Urgent. Iritably. |
| 7 khiam hu. kùe khiam. khiam kiong. put sùn. | 7 Lowly. Too retiring. Unobtrusive. Disrespectful. |
| 8 kiong hí! khang hu. kiong kiong kèng kèng. | 8 Happy New Year! Unoccupied. Reverently and in awe. |
| 9 kiong kèng put jû chông mēng. hu ngân. | 9 Obedience is better than subserviency. Idle prating. |
| 10 hu sim. sim hu. hu jī. hu tō kuang im. hu thûn. hu jîak. hu phû. | 10 Unprejudiced. Apprehensive. Adverbs. Waste the time. Idle tales. Decrepid. Nonsensical. |
| 11 cè chût nâng sim hu. | 11 The thief ever fears danger. |
| 12 hu mîa, hu lí. | 12 Vain is fame, empty are riches. |
| 13 chêng hu ùi cūe. | 13 Conscious that he merits punishment. |

## LESSON CLXXXV.

| | | | |
|---|---|---|---|
| 榮 | îong; splendor; glory. | 誣 | bû; false; lie. |
| 耀 | ĭo; lustrous; bright. | 贖 | * chíu; ransom. |
| 咒 | ìu; curse; imprecate. | 聰 | chong; astute. |
| 詛 | * cu; curse; swear. | 違 | ûi; oppose; disregard. |
| 吠 | pūi; to bark; howl. | 癭 | eng; goitre; a wen. |
| 狺 | * ngā; snarling. | 猇 | * hău$^{n}$: yelping. |

| | |
|---|---|
| 1 îong ĭo. cìu cu. iak kûi tō. kuang ĭo. | 1 Glory. Malediction. To average. Magnificent. |
| 2 ĭo mâk. iông jôk. | 2 Dazzle the eyes. Glory and shame. |
| 3 kuang có ĭo cong. | 3 Illustrious ancestors. |
| 4 hu bû. bû sueh. bû hām. bû kò. bû lŭa. ûi ngêk. ûi pŭe. bû sì hôk mîn. | 4 Visionary. Falsehood. Involve unjustly. Falsely accuse. Falsely charge. Oppose. Disobey. Misleading and deluding mankind. |
| 5 chíu nâng, chíu mûeh. | 5 Ransom people, or things. |
| 6 cìu mē. kú ûi lío. | 6 To curse. Long since I saw you. |
| 7 pêh lôh. chong mêng. | 7 Tell more than the facts. Astute. |
| 8 chong mêng tì hŭi. | 8 Very quick witted. |
| 9 ûi mĕng. ûi kà. bô ûi. | 9 Disregard orders. Disobey instructions. Let none disregard. |
| 10 îang hŏng im ûi. | 10 Agree to his face, and oppose behind his back. |
| 11 se$^{n}$ eng. put khe sa$^{n}$ jît. | 11 Has a wen. Only three days. |
| 12 nŏ ciah káu sie ce$^{n}$ cîah. | 12 Two dogs fighting over food. |
| 13 i phû tŏ cúi mīn lâu. | 13 It floats on the water. |
| 14 pŭe ău ngí lŭn nâng. tng mīn kāng i tà$^{n}$. | 14 Talk about people behind their back. Say it to his face. |
| 15 cí kĭa$^{n}$ sū úa cai sĭ bû i kâi. chíu tńg lâi. | 15 I know this is calumnious about him. To ransom. |
| 16 káu ngā ngā kìe, sĭ sie ce$^{n}$ sih mûeh? tău hĕng. | 16 What is the dog snarling at? Cleverness. |
| 17 jíang kàu koi thî káu pūi. pūi kàu jîeh kú. | 17 Scolded till the cocks crew and the dogs barked. Bark long. |
| 18 tī tîang phah kàu ŭn kâi káu hău$^{n}$ hău$^{n}$ kìe. | 18 Somebody beat our dog till it yelped. |

## LESSON CLXXXVI.

| | |
|---|---|
| 壓 iap; press down; repress. | 喘 chẃn; pant. |
| 負 hŭ; bear on the back. | 鼾 * hûa$^{n}$; to snore. |
| 忠 tong; loyal; honest. | 皻 * thîo; a pimple. |
| 元 ngŵn; first; primary. | 痱 pùi; prickly heat. |
| 摩 mo; rub; feel. | 吼 háu; roaring of beasts. |
| 猥 * hĭn; howling. | 嘷 * hm̄; growling. |

| | |
|---|---|
| 1 khi iap. khi kun. khi hŭ. pŭe hŭ. | 1 Oppress. Deceive the ruler. Impose upon. Carry on the back. |
| 2 hŭ un. hŭ khut. hŭ sim. hŭ ieh. | 2 Forget favors. Suffer a wrong. Unappreciative. Break a treaty. |
| 3 hûang thi$^{n}$ put hŭ khó sim nâng. iap kia$^{n}$. | 3 Heaven never ignores the sorrowful. Calm one's fears. |
| 4 iap tó. tong kău. | 4 Overthrow. Honest hearted. |
| 5 i sĭ ciang sì lât iap i. | 5 He conquered him by his strength. |
| 6 mo so. khùi chẃn. | 6 To stroke. Shortness of breath. |
| 7 i gût kàu tŏ hûa$^{n}$. | 7 He is asleep and snoring. |
| 8 tong ngĭ. tong sim. sai háu. | 8 Faithful. Sincere. Lions roar. |
| 9 thûe ciah. kuah tîeh kâi hûn. sie$^{n}$ hûn. huang háu. | 9 Scar of a boil. Scar of a cut. Scar of a wound. Wind roars. |
| 10 ngŵn nî; ngŵn jît. ngŵn khì put cok. ngŵn sí. ngŵn mê. | 10 The first year; first day. His constitution is not sound. In the beginning. First night. |
| 11 cáu kàu chẃn. | 11 Ran till out of breath. |
| 12 cêk mīn se$^{n}$ kàu cĭn sĭ pùi. hó$^{n}$ hm̄ hm̄ kìe. | 12 Her face is a covered with prickly heat. Tigers growl. |
| 13 mīn cìe$^{n}$ se$^{n}$ hoh cōi thîo. | 13 His face is all pimply. |
| 14 cêk mê hûa$^{n}$ kàu thi$^{n}$ kng. | 14 Snored until daylight. |
| 15 n̂gn cêk peh ngŵn. | 15 A hundred dollars. |
| 16 cia$^{n}$ gûeh chiu it kìe cò ngŵn jît. | 16 The first day of the first month is called the first day. |
| 17 káu cêk ē thăng tîeh, i cĭu hm̄ hm̄ kìe. | 17 If you touch the dog he growls. |
| 18 káu hĭn hĭn kìe sĭ thói$^{n}$ kì$^{n}$ sih mûeh? | 18 What does the dog see, that he is howling so? |
| 19 úa cē thói$^{n}$ cĭu cai. | 19 If I see it once I shall know. |

汕頭方言初階



## LESSON CLXXXVII.

| | | | |
|---|---|---|---|
| 抛 | * tīo; to toss up. | 韻 | ūn; rhymes. |
| 搖 | * hit; vibrate. | 例 | lī; classify; rules. |
| 攬 | * lám; hug; clasp. | 潑 | cuah; phuah; spatter. |
| 柱 | thĭo; pillar; column. | 躍 | iak; skip; leap. |
| 嘗 | sîeⁿ; to taste. | 裏 | lí; lining; inside. |
| 派 | phài; branch; ramify. | 僚 | lîo; colleague. |

| | | |
|---|---|---|
| 1 | nâng ciu sin hɵh cōi chù tŏng mêh. | In the whole body there are many throbbing pulses. |
| 2 | mài kiaⁿ tŏng i. | Do not startle him. |
| 3 | lâu tŏng lṳ́ kâi kùi pō. | I have disturbed you. |
| 4 | cí iēⁿ m̄ tŏng úa kâi sim. | This does not stir my heart. |
| 5 | hâh lī. sêng lī. ûi lī. | According to usage. Become a custom. Transgress the rules. |
| 6 | bô͘ lī put khó͘ khí; ŭ lī put khó͘ cí. | Without rules one cannot begin; with rules one may not stop. |
| 7 | cuah cêk lâu téng. | Spattered all over the floor. |
| 8 | cúi mài cuah tîeh chîeⁿ. | Do not bespatter the wall. |
| 9 | phuah kàu cêk sin lok lok. | Spattered all over him. |
| 10 | khut éng phuah tîeh. | Bespattered by the waves. |
| 11 | lṳ́ kâi cíeⁿ kò͘ lío kâi cúi mài phuah tîeh cûn lăi. iak iak. | Row so that the water from your oar will not spatter into the boat. Frisk about. |
| 12 | cí īeⁿ pò hó͘ cò͘ saⁿ lí. | This cloth is good for linings. |
| 13 | ēng lîn cò͘ lí. | Use damask for the lining. |
| 14 | tâng lîo. peh lîo. kuaⁿ lîo. lîo sôk. | Compeers. The Magistracy. Fellow officers. Colleague. |
| 15 | khò thúi. cheng khih sìeⁿ. | Legging. Clean appearance. |
| 16 | sie lám koiⁿ. lám kín kín. | Embrace. Hug tight. |
| 17 | tng mīn. pŭe ău. cîeh thĭo. sam thĭo. | To one's face. Behind one's back. Stone pillar. A post. |
| 18 | lṳ́ sîeⁿ thóiⁿ hó͘ mē. sîeⁿ sin bī. chì sîeⁿ. sîeⁿ cē. sîeⁿ cêk chùi. | Taste and see if it is good. Taste the first fruits. Taste it. Taste a little of this. Taste some. |
| 19 | phài thâu. cìaⁿ phài. | Precedence. Upright. |

## LESSON CLXXXVIII.

吵 chau; clamor.
鬧 nău; tumult.
撜 tia"; phòng; khâp; thump.
遇 * tn̄g; to meet.
掲 kiah; lṳ̂; thn̄g; poke.
簸 pùa; winnow.
脾 phî; the spleen.
氏 sĭ; family; a woman.
導 tău; lead; conduct.
謎 mĭ; riddle; puzzle.
瓶 pâng; a gurglet.
私 sai; underhand.

| | |
|---|---|
| 1 tăi chau cék tîe". si ūn. chau chau nău nău. | 1 A great hubbub. Rhymes. In violent altercation. |
| 2 ang cía chau nău. | 2 Man and wife quarreling. |
| 3 ŭ nău sṳ̄. tăi nău. nău cíu. náu phî" khì. tăi nău cêk tîe". nău i hôk. | 3 There is a tumult. A riot. A drunken rout. Berate whims. Great tumult. Trouble about clothes. |
| 4 phî khì. im ūn. | 4 Whimsies; temper. To rhyme. |
| 5 sih mih sĭ? hô hng nâng sĭ? tī kò nâng sĭ? | 5 What clan? What family is it? What gens are they? |
| 6 ín tău. hùn tău. khai tău, khui tău. | 6 Lead rightly. District instructor. To show the right way. |
| 7 phah mĭ. chai mĭ. mĭ gṳ́. é mĭ. ṳ́n gṳ́. | 7 Make riddles. Guess puzzles. Conundrum. Enigma. Riddle. |
| 8 cáu sai. sai sim. sai hùe. soi" kong, ău sai. sai ĕ. sai chêng. | 8 Smuggle. Partial. Smuggled goods. Public before private interests. Secretly. Selfish. |
| 9 cîh búe. kiah i khui. lṳ̂ khṳ̀ cē. thn̄g jîp. | 9 Tip of the tongue. Poke it aside. Poke it away. Poke it in. |
| 10 jîp mî. | 10 Stuff it with cotton. |
| 11 pùa ki. pùa ki kah. pùa bí. cûn tŏ pùa. | 11 Winnowing fan. A cobra. Winnow rice. The boat pitches. |
| 12 tŏ koi chĭ tn̄g tîeh i. | 12 I met him in the street. |
| 13 mài tia" tîeh. phòng tîeh. phòng tîeh thâu. | 13 Do not touch it. Bumped against. Bumped his head. |
| 14 khap tîeh i cĭu hó. | 14 If you come across him, all right. |
| 15 kia" khui cē cìa" bōi tia" tîeh. ŭ tia" tîeh úa. | 15 Walk off a little so it won't thump you. It hit me. |
| 16 i kâi phî khì m̄ hó. | 16 His temper is bad. |

# LESSON CLXXXIX.

| | | | |
|---|---|---|---|
| 謙讓 | * the khiam; unassuming. | 嫉妒 | cît kò; jealousy. |
| 虛假 | * pêh cía$^n$; to tell lies. | 失落 | * sua îa; to spill. |
| 詛誓 | * cìu cūa; imprecate. | 踞躅 | kek chok; hobble. |
| 衰颯 | sue sap; declining. | 鷺鷥 | lĭo si; the heron. |
| 旋渦 | * ká cn̄g; whirlpool. | 棕蓑 | cang sui; coir cloak. |
| 戲法 | * pa hì$^n$; jugglery. | 急速 | * kek chok; hurried. |

| | |
|---|---|
| 1 cò pa hì$^n$ kâi nâng. | 1 A juggler. |
| 2 huang lô theng, sŭ kó cì$^n$ khang; ue kía$^n$ chùi, jû lĭo si pâng; cie$^n$ mīn hîa$^n$ húe, ĕ mīn kún; câp kún poih kún cong kú ngân. cúi hun tâng. | 2 A draught like the holes in ancient cash; a spout like a heron shaped pitcher; on the upper surface build a fire and the under surface boils; it boils and boils but is always cold. Water pipe. |
| 3 î$^n$ cie$^n$ sĭ nâng cêk kâi mĭ gú, kŭa mĭ tói. | 3 The above is one of our riddles, and its answer. |
| 4 lú mài the khiam. | 4 Do not pretend you can't. |
| 5 cìe$^n$ se$^n$ tà$^n$ sĭ kùe the khiam lío. i kò ŏi kâi nâng cōi, lú hŭam sŭ tîeh the khiam, m̄ hó cŭ sĭ ŏi. | 5 In so saying you are much too modest. There there are many skillful people; you must be modest, and not laud yourself. |
| 6 lú mài tà$^n$ pêh cía$^n$. | 6 You must not tell lies. |
| 7 lú ká$^n$ kăng úa cìu cūa, mē? | 7 Dare you swear to it? |
| 8 cìe$^n$ se$^n$ cò sŭ khah sue sap. | 8 To act thus is too shabby. |
| 9 lú cìu cūa bô ēng. | 9 To make oath to it is useless. |
| 10 cí kâi nâng cí ău sue sap căi. | 10 This man has lately grown very old. |
| 11 lú mài thói$^n$ i kâi nâng ie$^n$ sĭ sue sap; i sĭ kâi phî khì cìe$^n$ se$^n$. thói$^n$ nâng cò pa hì$^n$. | 11 Do not consider his debilitated appearance; it is his habit to look so. See the jugglery. |
| 12 cúi tĕ cí kò ká cn̄g. | 12 The water here eddies. |
| 13 khîeh hó hó, mài sua îa. | 13 Take it carefully, don't spill it. |
| 14 cí kĭa$^n$ sŭ cò kàu kek kek chok chok. hāi úa cí kĭa$^n$ sŭ cò lâi khah kek chok. | 14 This thing is done all amiss. Made me do this thing all higgledy piggledy. |

## LESSON CXC.

| | |
|---|---|
| 玻璃 po lî; glass. | 螟蛉 mêng lêng; the sphex. |
| 緝繭 niap kói$^n$; plaits. | 和尚 * hûe sīe$^n$; priest. |
| 作揖 * ip că; salutations. | 慌張 huang ciang; flurried. |
| 戲弄 * pa lói; tease. | 生疏 * che$^n$ hūn; bashful. |
| 趣味 chù bī; amusing. | 放肆 hùang sù; impudent. |
| 裁縫 châi hông; tailor. | 了哥 lío ko; parrot. |

| | |
|---|---|
| 1 i kâi tău hēng chim. | 1 He is very clever. |
| 2 khak kek chok; cò m̄ kîp. sî hāu m̄ hó khah kek chok. kâi po lî theng. | 2 Too soon; I cannot make it in time. The time should not be too pressing. A window. |
| 3 po lî pue. chù bī căi. | 3 Goblet. Very interesting. |
| 4 ài$^n$ niap kúi kâi kói$^n$. | 4 Will lay several plaits. |
| 5 cí kâi îeh tah lío ĕ jĭt bŏi niap kói$^n$. | 5 Put on this medicine and afterward the skin won't pucker. |
| 6 i kâi mīn tèng niap kâi kói$^n$. | 6 He has the scar on his face. |
| 7 i kâi kûn niap cōi cōi kói$^n$. | 7 Her petticoat has many tucks. |
| 8 kio i ip că. i ia ip kâi că. kîa$^n$ ip că kâi lói. | 8 Salute him. He also bowed. Make formal bows. |
| 9 cha m̄ to phêng téng. | 9 About the same rank. |
| 10 mài pa lói i. | 10 Do not meddle with him. |
| 11 cí kîa$^n$ mûeh bô chù bī. | 11 This is uninteresting. |
| 12 hàm châi hông lâi cò. | 12 Call a tailor to do it. |
| 13 mêng lêng kâi kía$^n$. | 13 An adopted child. |
| 14 hûe sīe$^n$ pài koi. hue sīe$^n$ ài$^n$ tôi nâng kâi cî$^n$, cīu chut lâi múa koi múa hāng, lîam keng pài kŭi, cīu kìe cò hûe sīe$^n$ pài koi. | 14 Priests kneeling in the street. When the priests take the peoples contributions, they come out in all the streets and lanes, chanting and kneeling, and it is called worshipping the street. |
| 15 lú huang huang ciang ciang ài$^n$ khù tī kò? | 15 Where are you going in such trepidation? |
| 16 cí kâi nâng hùang sù căi. | 19 This fellow is very disorderly. |
| 17 i chĭ ciah lío ko ŏi tà$^n$ ūe. lú mài huang ciang. | 17 He has a parrot that can talk. Don't be in a flurry. |

## LESSON CXCI.

| | | | |
|---|---|---|---|
| 先生 | sin seⁿ; teacher. | 稱讚 | * e lṓ; praise. |
| 恐怕 | * pa lak; perhaps. | 羞恥 | * sío lí; ashamed. |
| 中間 | * tìn tang; centre. | 廉恥 | lîam chí; decency. |
| 大概 | * chìn chái; not exact. | 滿團 | phû thŵn; a hassock. |
| 躒𨅝 | * lí dí; to get on. | 多少 | * lân lṓ; a little. |
| 魯鈍 | lú tūn; dull, stupid. | 侍者 | * sì cái; butler. |

| | |
|---|---|
| 1 láu sin seⁿ mài khṳ̀ lío, kim jı̍t cı́u àiⁿ cìah sìa chan. i tŏ cŏ seng lí. | 1 If the old teacher had not gone, we should to-day have taken the communion. He trades. |
| 2 i pa lak bŏ lâi. | 2 Perhaps he will not come. |
| 3 thiaⁿ tìn tang tìo ki teng. cêk nâng cŏ tŏ tìn tang; nŏ nâng cŏ tŏ líang pôiⁿ. lân lṓ ìam. | 3 In the center of the parlour hung a lamp. One sits in the center, and two sit on the two sides. A little salt. |
| 4 chìn chái cŏ cìu hṓ. lṳ́ hṓ chìn chái i. lṳ́ tìeh sòi sim lí; mài chìn chìn chái chái. | 4 To do it slightly will answer. Do not be exact with him. You must carefully direct it; do not be inexact about it. |
| 5 i cŏ i lí dí khṳ̀. lṳ́ kâi mâk tìeh cai thóiⁿ, mài lí dí kìaⁿ. | 5 He went right along. You must use your eyes, and not just get you along. |
| 6 i cŏ seng lí kíaⁿ. | 6 He sells small wares. |
| 7 lṳ́ mài thèng e lṓ. | 7 Do not thoughtlessly laud. |
| 8 mài sái i síο lí. | 8 Do not make him ashamed. |
| 9 nâng tìeh ŭ lîam chí. bŏ lîam chí. cai lîam chí. | 9 People must be decent. Indecent. Regard decency. |
| 10 bói kúi kâi phû thŵn. | 10 Buy a few hassocks. |
| 11 lân lṓ mûeh kìaⁿ chìn chái bōi. mài e lṓ úa. | 11 Sell these few things as best you can. Don't praise me. |
| 12 ēng i cŏ sì cái. | 12 Employ him as butler. |
| 13 kŏ hṳ̂ thâu kah kŏ hṳ̂ búe. | 13 The two are equally insipid. |
| 14 cêk tn̂g kûiⁿ káu chieh bŏ ēng. i kâi nâng lú tūn. | 14 For reaching ten feet, a nine foot pole won't do. He is stupid. |
| 15 pa lak ŭ hŏ. | 15 Perhaps it will rain. |

## LESSON CXCII.

蒼蠅 * hô sîn; a fly.
狗蚤 * ka cáu; a flea.
蟯螂 * ka cŭah; cockroach.
蜈蚣 gê kang; centipede.
守宫 * cîⁿ lêng; lizzard.
蜻蜓 * sua me; dragon fly.
草蜢 cháu mé; grasshopper.
蜘蛛 ti tu; a spider.
水蛭 * hô khî; a leech.
蝙蝠 * pît pô; a bat.
蚯蚓 kău ún; earth worm.
蝦蟆 * kap pô; toad.

1 ti tu măng. ti tu si.
2 būe cêng sêng măng kìe cò ti tu si.
3 kap pô ŏi cîah hô sîn.
4 cêk mûeh hăh cêk ìeh; ka cáu bô nŭa lîah m̄ tîeh.
5 gê kang ŏi jīo ka cŭah.
6 cîⁿ lêng kă nâng lĭ hăi kùe gê kang.
7 sua me sĭ sih mih pìⁿ kâi? i ŏi sua me kîaⁿ.
8 lîah cheh cháu mé khìa chī cío. lîah m̄ tîeh.
9 ti tu ŏi cuh nâng kâi tâk; hô khî ŏi cuh nâng kâi hueh. pît pô hîⁿ.
10 kap pô pak phûe ka kī cîah.
11 tī kò kâi kău ún kìe kàu hìeⁿ tōa siaⁿ?
12 tī tîang lîah ŭ cêk ciah pît pô jîp lâi.
13 ti tu chùi. hô sîn kău. cháu mé kha thúi. ka cŭah chiu.
14 cìm cúi hô khî.
15 gê kang kă, koi bô ù; cîⁿ lêng kă. khí tōa chù.

1 Spider's web. Spiders film.
2 Before it is made into a web, it is called spider's silk.
3 Toads eat flies.
4 Each thing to its use; without spittle fleas couldn't be caught.
5 Centipedes drive away roaches.
6 The bite of a lizzard is more hurtful than that of a centipede.
7 What is a dragon fly evolved from? He walks on his hands.
8 Catch some grasshoppers to feed the birds. Couldn't catch.
9 Spiders suck poison from people; leeches suck their blood. Big round ears.
10 The toad takes off his skin and eats it himself.
11 Where is it that the angle worms squeak so loud?
12 Somebody caught a bat and brought it in.
13 Spider shaped spout. Flies are thick. Spindle legs. Beard like a cat's whiskers.
14 Leaches kept in soak.
15 If a centipede bites you rub it with a chicken; if a lizzard bites you, prepare your coffin.

# LESSON CXCIII.

| | | | |
|---|---|---|---|
| 欠伸 | * huah hì; yawn; gape. | 內瞕 | lăi ciang; stone blind. |
| 噴嚏 | * ka thì; sneeze. | 嘆氣 | * tháu khùi; sigh. |
| 打呃 | phah eh; hiccough. | 鼻涕 | * chek cúi; a cold. |
| 呃逆 | eh ngêk; belch. | 瘟疫 | un mût; pestilence. |
| 嗟嘆 | ca thàng; groan. | 癩瘋 | * thái ke; leprosy. |
| 瞎眼 | * che$^{n}$ mê; blind. | 滯氣 | thì khì; constipation. |

| | |
|---|---|
| 1 hē cì lûi, kuah tîu, mua cang sui. lṳ́ huah hì sĭ mâk siap a m̄ sĭ? | 1 When it lightens in summer, cut hemp and drape your raincloak. Do you yawn from sleepiness? |
| 2 phah ka thì. khat i kûa$^{n}$ kàu phah ka thì. | 2 To sneeze. You let him be chilly till he is sneezing. |
| 3 che$^{n}$ mê ŭ mâk ciu kng hùe khan. | 3 The blind have those who can see to lead them. |
| 4 phù nâng cí$^{n}$ n̂gn, thái ke sè$^{n}$ mīa. | 4 To the rich their money; to the leprous, their life. |
| 5 cí ie$^{n}$ ìeh hó kìu un mût. | 5 This medicine cures the plague. |
| 6 chek cúi sĭ síe khó kâi pē$^{n}$; thì khì sĭ ío tăng kâi pē$^{n}$; ài$^{n}$ ui, tîeh cíu thì khì ui. | 6 A cold is a slight ailment; the bilious habit is a more serious one which must first be cured. |
| 7 cíah kàu phah eh. | 7 Drank until he hiccoughed. |
| 8 eh ngêk kâi pē$^{n}$, khin kâi tîeh cíah sŭn khì ìeh; tăng kâi tîeh cíah pó ìeh. | 8 For belching, if it is slight take a sedative; if serious you must take a tonic. |
| 9 thái ke à kàu mì; thâm húe à kàu sí. | 9 The leper denies it till he is carius; the consumptive till he is dead. |
| 10 lṳ́ tháu khùi mih sṳ̄? | 10 What are you sighing about? |
| 11 pûah cí$^{n}$ bŏi su, tŏi$^{n}$ it kang hu; cò chât bŏi sí, tŏi$^{n}$ it seng lí. | 11 If you gamble and do not lose, it is the neatest work; if you steal and are not killed, it is the best business. |
| 12 lṳ́ míen êng ca thàng; pât nâng kâi mâk che$^{n}$ mê pí lṳ́ lăi ciang kâi mâk kèng m̄ hó thói$^{n}$. te pùa$^{n}$. | 12 You need not groan; other people's blind eyes, compared with your bright and whole blind eyes, are worse to look at. Now and then. |
| 13 lṳ́ tăng tī tiang sĭ che$^{n}$ mê? | 13 How long have you been blind? |

## LESSON CXCV.

葡萄 phû thɵ̂; grapes.
鵪鶉 an chun; quails.
駱駝 lɵ̂h thɵ̂h; camel.
斑鳩 * kŭ ku; pigeon.
鷓鴣 ciah ko; partridge.
蛺蝶 îap tîap; butterfly.

白鴿 * hún cío; a dove.
狐狸 hô lâi; a fox.
橄欖 ka$^{n}$ ná; olives.
檳榔 pin lɵ̂; betel.
柘榴 sîeh lîu; pomegranate.
孔雀 khóng chieh; peacock.

1 phû thɵ̂ che$^{n}$ sek.
2 phû thɵ̂ cíu. an chun tɵ̄.
3 lɵ̂h thɵ̂h kut. cí kâi sĭ phì jŭ kâi ūe. m̄ pat hùe cang phêng sîe$^{n}$ kâi mûeh kĭa$^{n}$, thói$^{n}$ cɵ̀ khî ĭ, pat kùe thói$^{n}$ tîeh sĭ bɵ̂ ēng kâi, cí kâi mûeh phì jŭ cɵ̀ lɵ̂h thɵ̂h kut.
4 kŭ ku thâu. cíah ko lō. îap tîap phâng. hún cío n̆ng. hô lâi phûe. pin nɵ̂ cí. ka$^{n}$ ná cap. sîeh lîu khí. khóng chieh ngán.
5 phîn khîong nâng tie$^{n}$ īe$^{n}$, tie$^{n}$ cɵ̀ pù nâng, nâng ài$^{n}$ hì$^{n}$ chìe i cĭu tà$^{n}$ cí nɵ̆ kù ūe; chíu lîah an chun bɵ́; cùi kâm chàu pin lɵ̂. pn̆g pn̆g lîah an chun sĭ an chun kak, sĭ tâk cî$^{n}$ kâi. an chun bɵ́ sĭ m̄ tâk cî$^{n}$; pin nɵ̂ īa tɵ pùa$^{n}$ sĭ ŭ cî$^{n}$ nâng cîah. kâm lîap ka$^{n}$ ná.
6 ún cí kɵ̀ kâi nâng tɵ pùa$^{n}$ sĭ cìe$^{n}$ se$^{n}$ tá pàn.

1 A purple color.
2 Wine. A bag to hold quails.
3 A camel's bone. This is figurative language. When the ignorant take a commonplace thing and consider it a prize, the knowing see that it is a useless article, and they figuratively call the a thing camel's bone.
4 The trigger. A natural path. Side sails. Doves' eggs. Foxes' pelts. The betel nut. Olive vinegar. The seeds of the pomegranate. Peacock feather.
5 When a poor man dresses up and pretends to be rich, if people wish to laugh at him they say these two lines; "the holds a quail in his hand, and betel nut in his mouth". If one is to carry around a quail it should be the male bird, which is costly. The female bird is inexpensive; and wealthy men occasionally chew betel. Holding an olive in his mouth.
6 We people here occasionally dress in that way.

## LESSON CXCIV.

約畧 iak lîak; for the most part.
大畧 * chŏ lîak; slightly.
約諒 iak lĭang; thereabouts.
遭塌 * tak n̄ng; to waste.
度數 * pang bŏ; distances; periods.
交代 kau tài; deliver over to.

好多 * ku ūa; ever so many.
無法 * bô pō; irremediable.
約度 * iak pān; average.
鬧熱 lāu jîet; busy.
排塲 phâi chîang; elegant.
妥貼 * iap thiap; neat.

1 tī gû ūa^n koi^n.
2 iak lîak sĭ sa^n tíam ceng.
3 úa chŏ lîak cai.
4 úa put kùe chŏ lîak ŏi.
5 iak lĭang ŭ kio i kau tài.
6 mài tak n̄ng tīo mûeh.
7 ku ūa jît sĭ jîeh cōi jît kâi pang bŏ?
8 lú chēng kàu hìe^n phâi chîang sĭ ài^n khù tī kò thói^n nâng lāu jîet, m̄ sĭ?
9 i chēng khù sui sĭ bô mih phâi chîang; siu sîp khù sĭm sĭ côi cía^n iap thiap.
10 sa^n phò lō kâi pang bŏ.
11 iak lĭang câp jît kâi pang bŏ. cìe^n se^n bô pō.
12 cía cĭu bô pō lío; lú tán kàu ku ūa jît cìa^n lâi.
13 ku ūa nâng, ku ūa nî.
14 i se^n lâi phâi chîang căi.
15 cêk nî cêk nî kâi kìen sek.
16 bô kìen sek kâi nâng; m̄ hŏ ēng i. bô pō.
17 úa kau tài kàu thŏ thiap thŏ thiap; lú cò nî cêk ē lāu jîet cĭu m̄ kì tit khù? lāu jîet căi.

1 An earthquake.
2 It was about three o' clock.
3 I know a little about it.
4 I am only mediocre.
5 Has about delivered it to him.
6 Do not waste things.
7 Ever so many days is about how many days?
8 You are dressed so finely because you are going somewhere where there s a crowd, are you?
9 Although not very handsomly dressed, her attire is very neat and orderly.
10 Three leagues distant.
11 A period of about ten days. There is thus no recourse.
12 There is no help for it; wait some days and then come.
13 Ever so many people and years.
14 He is very fine looking.
15 Each year has its own experience.
16 A man without experience; do not employ him. No way.
17 I delivered it intact; how is it that in the bustle you have forgotten all about it? A great deal going on.

## LESSON CXCVI.

遊玩 * thit thô; recreation.
後生 * hău seⁿ; youthful.
逼挾 pek hīap; over awe.
支派 ciⁿ phài; a tribe.
松柏 sêng peh; the pine tree.
公正 * kuaⁿ ciaⁿ; rectitude.

慌遽 * chîh chôh; flustered.
慌忙 huang mâng; flurried.
垢穢 * nah sap; dirty.
濫妄 * lăm sám; careless.
腌臢 * chi gî; disgusting.
潮濕 * ip cîp; dark and damp.

| | |
|---|---|
| 1 i kâi nâng kuaⁿ ciaⁿ. | 1 He is an upright man. |
| 2 lú tîeh kuaⁿ ciaⁿ tàⁿ. | 2 You must speak the truth. |
| 3 i kâi mîa sek m̄ hó. | 3 His reputation is bad. |
| 4 nín cí cêk ciⁿ phài ŭ jîeh cōi nâng? | 4 In your tribe here how many people are there? |
| 5 hău seⁿ nâng hàuⁿ thit thô. | 5 Young people are fond of pleasure. |
| 6 khan i khù thit thô. | 6 Lead him out for a walk. |
| 7 pĭ i pek hīap. | 7 Intimidated by him. |
| 8 cò sū m̄ hó chîh chôh. | 8 Do not be in a fluster. |
| 9 i huang mâng khí sin. | 9 He started in a hurry. |
| 10 sim lăi kâi nah sap pí sin gūa kâi nah sap jú kèng tîeh cai lí cheng khih. | 10 It is more important to remove the impurity of the heart than the uncleanness of the body. |
| 11 i tàⁿ ūe lăm sám. | 11 He speaks recklessly. |
| 12 lú m̄ hó lăm sám thî phû i kâi mîa. | 12 You should not heedlessly introduce his name. |
| 13 cí tieⁿ chîg chi gî căi. | 13 This table is filthily dirty. |
| 14 cí lăi khah ip cîp. | 14 It is too dank in here. |
| 15 kín pháng bô hó se. | 15 Urgent spinning makes bad yarn. |
| 16 nah sap nâng cò nah sap sū. kuaⁿ ciaⁿ hó thit thô. | 16 Dirty people do dirty things. Proper recreation. |
| 17 i kâi nâng bōi lám sám, só íⁿ i kâi mîa sek hó. | 17 This person is not negligent, therefore his reputation is good. |
| 18 i kâi sim tīaⁿ, só íⁿ i cò sū bōi huang mâng. | 18 His mind is made up, so he acts without precipitation. |
| 19 sim lăi cêk ē huang mâng só íⁿ cò sū ciu chîh chôh. | 19 His mind is agitated so he does things in a fluster. |

# LESSON CXCVII.

| | |
|---|---|
| 蝴蝶 * bói îah; butterfly. | 軟脚 * ńg nî; palsy. |
| 痢疾 lĭ cit; dysentery. | 欄杆 lân kan; balusters. |
| 瀉肚 * làu sái; diarrhea. | 妬忌 kò kĭ; envy. |
| 疳積 kam cek; worms. | 條繩 * gê lan; picture cord. |
| 黄疸 * n̂g sua; jaundice. | 廢疾 * phùa sieⁿ; maimed. |
| 癱瘓 * kŵn pien; paralysis. | 茂盛 mŏng sĕng; luxuriant. |

| | |
|---|---|
| 1 sĭ eng kai, m̄ sĭ thau ôiⁿ. ńg nî pēⁿ. | 1 It is proper, and not stolen leisure. The palsy. |
| 2 kuaⁿ ciaⁿ, mîn bē sū. | 2 Officials being upright, the people rest. |
| 3 bói îah thâu kâi ôi. | 3 An ornamented shoe. |
| 4 tieⁿ, bŏi sí, lĭ cit; gō, bŏi sí, sieⁿ huang. | 4 If you can eat, having dysentery you won't die; if you fast, having rheumatism, you won't die. |
| 5 tieh cai kŵn kù. | 5 Must be well attended to. |
| 6 n̂g sua pēⁿ sĭ to in sip jiet tì kâi. | 6 Jaundice generally arises from being in damp hot places. |
| 7 i kâi sim lăi kò kĭ. | 7 He is at heart envious. |
| 8 lŕ mài tam tāⁿ úa. | 8 Do not disappoint me. |
| 9 ēng kòi mông lîah i. | 9 Caught him by a stratagem. |
| 10 khut i ceh pĭ bē ūe hó ìn tap. | 10 When reprimanded by him had nothing to answer. |
| 11 khut i lêng jôk, cêk kù ūe m̄ káⁿ ìn. | 11 When insulted by him dare not answer by a single word. |
| 12 pí pât nâng ío láu sit. | 12 More harmless than others. |
| 13 lân kan àiⁿ cò cieh kâi, a sĭ àiⁿ cò châ kâi? | 13 Do you want the balusters made of stone or of wood? |
| 14 siu lâi iap iap thiap thiap. | 14 Very neatly arranged. |
| 15 cí kò kâi hue bâk mŏng sĕng căi. thông seng. | 15 The shrubbery here is very luxuriant. Pupil. |
| 16 bói tìo gê lan soh lâi pâk. | 16 Buy some cord and fasten it. |
| 17 thong sin kún lân kan pìⁿ. | 17 The whole suit trimmed with gimp. |
| 18 lŕ ĭu m̄ sĭ kŵn pien, ĭu m̄ sĭ ńg nî, cò nî ciu jit gût; m̄ pat thóiⁿ kìⁿ lŕ khí lâi kiaⁿ. | 18 You are not paralyzed nor palsied, why do you lie all day; I never saw you get up and walk. |

## LESSON CXCVIII.

| | |
|---|---|
| 諂媚 thíam mĭ; cajole. | 譏誚 ki chío; ridicule. |
| 興旺 heng ŭang; prosper. | 譏笑 * phì sìe; deride. |
| 姦淫 kang îm; adultery. | 砰硼 pīn pōng; boisterous. |
| 淫慾 îm îok; passions. | 懇求 * koh lô; expostulate. |
| 憐憫 lîen míen; merciful. | 寂寞 sok môk; desolate. |
| 倉皇 chang hûang; flurried. | 鬱結 * ut cût: melancholy. |

| | |
|---|---|
| 1 i cìe$^{n}$ se$^{n}$ **cò** sĭ thíam mĭ i. | 1 He does that to cajole him. |
| 2 thíam mí kâi nâng sĭ cōi. | 2 Flatterers are many. |
| 3 cí kúi nî heng ŭang căi. | 3 These few years it has prospered. |
| 4 kang îm kâi **sū m̄ hó cò**. | 4 You must not commit adultery. |
| 5 îm îok tîeh cai kìm cí. | 5 The passions must be controled. |
| 6 cí kâi nâng **hó**; úa sĭm sĭ lîen míen i. | 6 This man is good; I am very compassionate toward him. |
| 7 **lú** mài chang hûang; úa kio **lú** sie hŭ. | 7 Do not be agitated; I will help you. |
| 8 **lú m̄ hó** chut chùi cíu ki chío nâng. | 8 Do not open your mouth to ridicule people. |
| 9 ka kī **m̄** cai jîeh **hó**, kì$^{n}$ mīn cĭu ài$^{n}$ phì sìe nâng. | 9 Without knowing how good they are, whenever he sees people he derides them. |
| 10 lâu téng **cò** nî pīn pōng kìe sĭ sih mih **sū**? | 10 What is that racket going on up stairs? |
| 11 **lú** tîeh **koh lô** kàu i hàu$^{n}$. | 11 You must urge till he is willing. |
| 12 cí kúi jìt **bô** nâng lāi **cŏ** phûeh sĭ sok môk căi. | 12 These few days no one has come to chat and it is lonesome. |
| 13 **lù** ka kī kkĭa khí ōi sok môk mē? chang hûang. | 13 Are you lonely, living all by yourself? Fearful. |
| 14 sim lăi sĭe tîeh sok sok môk môk sĭm sí **m̄ hó**. | 14 Thinking that extreme solitude was very bad. |
| 15 **lú** sim lăi ut cût sih mih **sū**? | 15 What are you melancholy about? |
| 16 i kâi sim heng ôih sòi, cêk kĭa$^{n}$ **sū** cū ut ut cût cût. | 16 He is small minded, and is made sullen by any sort of thing. |
| 17 kîa$^{n}$ lō mài pīn pōng kìe. | 17 In walking do not make a racket. |
| 18 thói$^{n}$ kì$^{n}$ nâng kan khó, cĭu lîen míen i. | 18 Seeing any person in trouble he has compassion on him. |

# LESSON CXCIX.

| | | | |
|---|---|---|---|
| 秀才 | sìu châi; first literary degree. | 巫術 | bû sût; sorcerer. |
| 舉人 | **kṳ́** jîn; second degree. | 妖精 | io cia; fairies. |
| 進士 | cìn **sṳ̆**; third degree. | 琥珀 | hó<sup>n</sup> phek; amber. |
| 翰林 | hâng lîm; fourth degree. | 奢侈 | chia chí; luxurious. |
| 霹靂 | phek lêk; violent; clap. | 奥妙 | àu mīo; mysterious. |
| 煩惱 | hŵn **ló**; sorrowful. | 褻瀆 | siet tôk; blaspheme. |

| | |
|---|---|
| 1 úa thói<sup>n</sup> nín a nîe kâi ì **sṳ̀** sĭ ut cût; **lṳ́** **hó** **khṳ̀** koh **lô** i mài. | 1 I see that your mother's idea is that she is aggrieved; go and expostulate with her. |
| 2 lîp sìu châi ău cĭu **khṳ̀** sé<sup>n</sup> sîa<sup>n</sup> kháu **kṳ́** jîn; tèng **kṳ̀** jîn ău cĭu **khṳ̀** kia<sup>n</sup> sîa<sup>n</sup> kháu cìn **sṳ̆**; tèng cìn **sṳ̆** ău cĭu **khṳ̀** tōi<sup>n</sup> chì, tōi<sup>n</sup> chì ău īu **khṳ̀** chîo kháu, cĭu tíam hâng lîm. | 2 After taking the first degree one goes to the provincial city and is examined for the second degree; then to Peking, for the third; then to the palace, and afterwrd before the Court for examination for the fourth and highest. |
| 3 thông seng sa<sup>n</sup> nî **nŏ** **chṳ̀** **khṳ̀** hú sîa<sup>n</sup> kháu sìu châi. | 3 Students go twice in three years to the Hu city examinations. |
| 4 kháu **kṳ́** jîn, kháu cìn **sṳ̆** kháu hâng lîm sĭ sa<sup>n</sup> nî cêk **chṳ̀**. | 4 Examinations for the second third and fourth degrees are held once in three years. |
| 5 úa thói<sup>n</sup> cí kĭa<sup>n</sup> **sṳ̄** i sĭ kù ì **cô** kâi. lûi sia<sup>n</sup> phek lêk. | 5 I consider him very obstinate about this thing. Clap of thunder. |
| 6 **lṳ́** míen ēng hŵn **ló**. | 6 You need not be sad. |
| 7 i sĭ bû sût kâi nâng. | 7 He is a wizard. |
| 8 i sĭ îang mīn **khṳ̀** **cô**. | 8 He did it openly. |
| 9 tâng sin; tâng ki; thói<sup>n</sup> sìa<sup>n</sup> phûa; **lôh** sîn phûa. | 9 A person supposed to be possesed by a god. |
| 10 hŭam ŏi ûah kâi mûeh cêk ē kú nî cĭu **to** ŏi sêng io cia. | 10 All living things when they once become aged, may become fairies; or many of them may. |
| 11 ēng mûeh **m̄** **hó** khah chia chí. | 11 You should not be too lavish. |
| 12 cí kâi **tău** lí sĭm sĭ àu mīo. | 12 This doctrine is very deep. |
| 13 mài thèng siet tôk i. | 13 Do not thoughtlessly desecrate it. |

## LESSON CC.

甚是多 * tōa bó mûeh; a great deal.

忽然間 * hûh cē kìe; suddenly.

發寒顫 * phah chùn lūn; shudder.

顫料料 * noi noi sih; quiver.

慄慄戰 * tâp tâp tùn; shiver.

半斜掩 * hăm a hŏi; ajar.

點子呢 * sut kía<sup></sup>ⁿ nih; a little bit.

荊棘中 * chì nâ phè; brambles.

約其畧 * iak bó lĭang; thereabout.

頗大畧 * chó lí lîak; somewhat.

聽造化 thèng cău hùe; incidentally.

耶華華 * īa-hûa-hûa; Jehovah.

| | |
|---|---|
| 1 úa cí kò tōa bó mûeh. | 1 I have ever so much here. |
| 2 úa tōa bó mûeh sū būe cêng lí. | 2 I have a great number of matters not yet arranged. |
| 3 tōa bó mûeh nâng ài" lâi. | 3 Ever so many are coming. |
| 4 hûh cē kìe cíu ŭ tōa bó mûeh. | 4 Suddenly there was a great deal. |
| 5 hûh cē kìe bô khù. | 5 Suddenly disappeared. |
| 6 úa thói" tîeh cĭu phah chùn lùn. kia" kàu phah chùn lūn. | 6 When I saw it I shuddered. So frightened that he trembled. |
| 7 khì kàu noi noi sih. | 7 So angry that he quivered. |
| 8 ùi kàu tâp tâp tùn. | 8 So scared that he shook. |
| 9 úa mn̂g hăm a hŏi. | 9 My door is ajar |
| 10 úa chûn tíam kía" nih tīa". | 10 I have only a little bit left. |
| 11 chûn bô cêk sut kía" nih. | 11 Scarcely a bit left. |
| 12 sua îa cêk sut kía". | 12 Spilled a little bit. |
| 13 iak bó lĭang ài" hó lío. | 13 Just about done. |
| 14 cí kâi sī chó lí lîak hó. ĕ jît cò kang hu cē kèng hó. | 14 This is tolerably good. Another time make it nicer. |
| 15 i tìam tŏ chì nâ phè tói. | 15 He hid in the underbrush. |
| 16 i thèng cău hùe ài" lâi. | 16 He will come now and then. |
| 17 cí kĭa" sū thèng lá kâi cău hùe. | 17 Let this matter be at any time when you like. |
| 18 i chó lí lîak cò sī îa" kùe lá kâi. | 18 What he does without pains is superior to yours. |
| 19 mn̂g pàng hăm a hŏi. | 19 Set the door ajar. |
| 20 i thèng cău hùe mûeh. | 20 He now and then does some. |
| 21 cêk kĭa" mûeh noi noi sih. | 21 Something quivers. |
| 22 īa-hûa-hûa cu gūa bô ŭ pât kâi sîn. | 22 Beside Jehovah there is no God. |

C LESSON.

汕頭方言初階



C LESSON.

C. LESSON.



E.



G.



H.

汕頭方言初階



H. LESSON.

汕頭方言初階

K. LESSON.

K. LESSON

K. LESSON.



L.

M. LESSON.

汕頭方言初階

S. LESSON.

T. LESSON.

汕頭方言初階



T. LESSON.



U.



W.

国家出版基金项目
NATIONAL PUBLICATION FOUNDATION

# 海上絲綢之路文獻集成

總主編 陳支平 陳春聲

## 科技與文化編 96

主編 王揚宗 葉農

海峽出版發行集團
THE STRAITS PUBLISHING & DISTRIBUTING GROUP
福建人民出版社

# 本册目次

# 廣東方言讀本

（*A Chinese Chrestomathy in the Canton Dialect*）

〔美〕裨治文（Elijah Coleman Bridgman）編

《廣東方言讀本》，美國裨治文編。裨治文（Elijah Coleman Bridgman，一八〇一—一八六一），又名高理文、貝滿，美國基督教新教傳教士。一八三〇年自波士頓至廣州，向馬禮遜學習漢語，編輯《中國叢報》。此書係美國人編纂之首部漢語教材，或名《廣東語模範文章注釋》、《廣東語句選》、《廣東土話文選》等。正文凡十七章，每章分若干部分，每部分含若干條目，詞、短語或句子等條目以英文、漢字及廣東話羅馬字拼音相對照，再對較難條目出注。據一八四一年澳門版影印。

A

# CHINESE CHRESTOMATHY

IN THE

# CANTON DIALECT.

BY E. C. BRIDGMAN.

MACAO.

S. WELLS WILLIAMS.

M DCCC XLI.

# PREFACE.

WITH much solicitude this Chrestomathy is now presented to the friends and patrons of Chinese literature in general, and in particular to the members of the "Society for the Diffusion of Useful Knowledge in China," under whose auspices it was commenced.

Reference to the table of contents, with a glance at the body of the work, will afford an idea of what is comprised in the volume.

The books and native assistants employed in preparing the work — and always availed of as much as possible — need not be here specified; it would, however, be unjust to pass without grateful acknowledgment — the aid afforded by Mr. J. R. Morrison in reading and revising large portions of the manuscript — by Mr. Robert Thom in preparing the fifth and sixth sections on commercial affairs — and by Mr. S. Wells Williams in preparing the chapters on Natural History, with some other minor portions, and the whole of the Index. By the kind assistance of these gentlemen the value of the work has been very much enhanced.

For the errors which the critical reader cannot fail to observe, some explanation is due. A few words have different meanings, which must be indicated by different orthography, or tones, or both; all these are to be carefully distinguished from those words that have no such diversity of usage. Many of the errors in the orthography of Chinese words, and in their tones and aspirates, are attributable to the withdrawal of native assistants engaged to aid in compiling the work. This withdrawal was occasioned by the shutting up of foreigners in Canton, and the disturbed state of political affairs which ensued. The inconveniences, hindrances, and losses arising from this source have been many. The want of a well-established standard (there being no translation of any dictionary printed in this dialect) has been an additional cause of embarrassment.

The information respecting China and its productions, the people and their customs, the government and its laws, &c., &c., contained in the volume, will render it of value to the general scholar, while it will form a convenient manual in particular for the student of the language.

If the Chrestomathy, by serving these purposes, shall aid in bringing about a better state of relations between foreigners and the Chinese, and in facilitating a more friendly intercourse, desirable and useful alike to all, the object of its publication will be fully gained.

E. C. B.

*Macao, June 10th,* 1841.

廣東方言讀本

# CONTENTS.

## INTRODUCTION.



*CHAPTER I.*

## STUDY OF CHINESE.



*CHAPTER II.*

## THE HUMAN BODY.



*CHAPTER III.*

## THE KINDRED RELATIONS.

CHAPTER IV.

## CLASSES OF MEN.



CHAPTER V.

## DOMESTIC AFFAIRS.



CHAPTER VI.

## COMMERCIAL AFFAIRS.



CHAPTER VII.

## MECHANICAL AFFAIRS.

CONTENTS.

## CHAPTER VIII.

## ARCHITECTURE.



## CHAPTER IX.

## AGRICULTURE.



## CHAPTER X.

## THE LIBERAL ARTS.



## CHAPTER XI.

## MATHEMATICS.



## CHAPTER XII.

## GEOGRAPHY.

*CHAPTER XIII.*

## MINERALOGY.



*CHAPTER XIV.*

## BOTANY.



*CHAPTER XV.*

## ZOOLOGY.



*CHAPTER XVI.*

## MEDICINE.



*CHAPTER XVII.*

## GOVERNMENTAL AFFAIRS.

# INTRODUCTION.

## I. OBJECT OF THE CHRESTOMATHY.

THE Chrestomathy is designed to furnish a series of easy lessons comprising, as its title indicates, *simple instruction*, or that which is plain and useful. Its object is threefold: to aid foreigners in learning the Chinese, to assist native youth in acquiring the English tongue, and to show how far this language can be expressed and acquired through the medium of the Roman letters. Throughout the work, the English, the Chinese characters, and their sounds, occupy three parallel columns on each page. The Chinese, in the middle column, is written in the local dialect, only excepting the extracts from the classics and other standard works, law phrases, with forms of edicts, &c. The English, in the column on the left, is a translation of the Chinese; and the sounds, or the Romanized Chinese, fill the column on the right. A few notes and explanations, designed to illustrate the text, are supplied at the bottom of each page.

Used from time immemorial,—often by clans having but little intercourse with each other, perhaps in some instances by tribes once distinct from the Chinese,—this language has gradually branched into dialects, some more and some less removed from the original tongue. These dialects differ from each other, like the cognate languages of Europe; and the principal ones, like the Italian and its kindred branches, require separate elementary treatises to facilitate their acquisition. Of such works the Chinese have a few; these few, however, are of little value, and none of them have yet been translated. For acquiring a knowledge of the *Chinese Language*, appropriately so styled—or that form of it generally used by the literati and by the officers of government, and hence sometimes, perhaps erroneously, called the mandarin or court dialect—the works of Prémare, Marshman, Morrison, and Rémusat, are well known and highly approved. For studying one of the principal dialects of Fukien, Mr. Medhurst's Dictionary is a valuable help. But, excepting a small Vocabulary published by Dr. Morrison in 1829, no work of any note has yet been provided for the student in this dialect—a dialect spoken by all the inhabitants of this metropolis, and by great numbers in adjacent cities and villages. Such neglect of this dialect, after more than two centuries of intercourse with the people of Canton, ought not to be continued; and it is hoped that the Chrestomathy, appearing under circumstances, and in a time like the present, will be received with approbation, and be found useful to those for whom it is designed.

## II. CHARACTER OF THIS DIALECT.

Diversities in the modes of speech, and deviations from the most approved usages, exist in every tongue; and it is often difficult to determine which of several usages should be regarded as the standard. That now most prevalent in Peking, among the people about the court, differs considerably from that once dominant, and still extensively used, known as the Nanking dialect, or the language of the southern court. In their present position, foreigners are unable to ascertain even the number of dialects spoken within the empire. They cannot be few. How-

D

ever, with reference to such as are known, some particulars may be here noticed. In the first place, the differences, between the colloquial style and that generally used in books, *seem* to be greater in the Chinese than they are in most other languages. These differences are not everywhere the same. For example, in that dialect given in Mr. Medhurst's Dictionary, the differences between the colloquial and the written idioms are far greater than they are in the dialect of Canton. In the second place, standard works, which form the great body of national literature, are read and understood with nearly equal ease by people in every part of the empire, however much their local dialects may differ from the style of those works. In the third place, the system of intonation, except in a few instances, appears to be one and the same in all the dialects. But it is not true, (as some have supposed,) that Chinese books can be understood by people of the neighboring states—Lewchew, Japan, &c.,—unless, like all other foreigners and like the Chinese themselves, they have by dint of study acquired a knowledge of the language. And, in the fourth place, the characters preserve an unvarying form in all parts of the empire: a partial exception to this, however, is occasioned by the use of well-known characters, slightly changed to express new local phrases; in all such cases, regard is had only to the *sound* of the characters; while the addition, usually that of *hau* 口 (a mouth) to the left side, indicates that the character is changed. For instance, the three characters 喊嗙唥 used to express the sound of the word *hampaláng* (all), have no meaning in themselves when used in this collocation, their united sound being alone attended to and recognized. So with names of persons, countries, &c. When the word is well known, the *hau* is usually omitted, as 美士 *mí sz'* for Mr.; 先士 *sín sz'* for cents, &c.

The characteristics of the Canton dialect are limited to the pronunciation, choice, and collocation of words. In these three particulars, the deviations from the standard language are less than in many of the other dialects; still they are too numerous to be here specified. A reference to Morrison's Dictionary will show the principal differences in pronunciation. And a careful comparison, throughout the following pages, of the extracts from standard works with the sections written in the local dialect will in a measure illustrate its peculiarities in the choice and collocation of words. The books written in this dialect are but few, and they are sometimes accompanied with glossaries, containing explanations of the dialectical words and phrases.

## III. ORTHOGRAPHY ADOPTED.

The system of orthography proposed by sir William Jones, afterwards recommended by Mr. Pickering, and now adopted, with some variations, throughout almost all India, in the islands of the Pacific, and among the native tribes of North America, seems better fitted than any other to express the sounds of the Chinese language. And with few exceptions and alterations, it has been followed in this work. The system is too well-known to need here any explanations, and too generally approved to need any defense. The changes made in it are such as the peculiarities of the Chinese language necessarily require. In defining the letters, no attempt has been made to distinguish the double vowels from the true diphthongs, nor to separate the consonants into different classes.

### Vowels and Diphthongs.

1. *a* pronounced as in *quota*, *America*, *agreeable*, and like short *u* in *tun*, *pun*.
2. *á* pronounced as in *calm*, *balm*, *father*.
3. *é* pronounced as *a* in *may*, *lay*, and as *ei* in *neigh*.

4. { *i* pronounced short as in *pin, sin, sing.*
{ *í* pronounced long as in *machine, marine, police.*

5. *ó* pronounced as in *lord,* as *aw* in *awful,* and as *a* in *all, tall.*

6. *ò* pronounced as in *no, so;* or as *ow* in *snow, flow, glow.*

7. { *u* pronounced as in *bull, pull;* or as *oo* in *foot, book.*
{ *ú* pronounced as in *rule;* or *oo* in *school, fool.*

8. *ü* pronounced as in *l'une*; the French sound.

9. { *ai* pronounced as in *aisle;* as *ie* in *tie;* or as *i* in *life,* but closer.
{ *ái* pronounced nearly like the word *aye.*

10. { *au* pronounced as *ou* in *plough, our;* or as *ow* in *cow, brow,* but closer.
{ *áu* pronounced like the preceding, with the *a* long.

11. *éu* pronounced with both letters distinct, resembling the colloquial contraction *say' em.*

12. *íú* pronounced as *ew* in *pew,* but more open or lengthened.

13. *oi* pronounced as in *oil;* or *oy* in *joy, alloy.*

14. *ui* pronounced nearly as in *fluid, ruined,* but more open.

15. *úi* pronounced like the preceding, with *u* long.

CONSONANTS.

16. *ch* pronounced as in *chair, cheap.*

17. *f* pronounced as in *fine, fair, face.*

18. *h* pronounced as in *he, home, house.*

19. *k* pronounced as in *kite, key, king.*

20. *kw* pronounced as *qu* in *quite, quash.*

21. *l* pronounced as in *lane, lay, low, long.*

22. *m* pronounced as in *may, man, much.*

23. *n* pronounced as in *nay, new, no.*

24. *ng* pronounced as in *singing*; as an initial sound it may be represented by sounding the word *hanging,* omitting the first two letters.

25. *p* pronounced as in *pay, pomp, pound.*

26. *s* pronounced as in *son, sea, say.*

27. *sh* pronounced as in *shall, she, show.*

28. *sz'* pronounced with a strong emission of breath, as if followed by *i* half suppressed.

29. *t* pronounced as in *time, tune, tent.*

30. *ts* pronounced as in *wits, bits.*

31. *tsz'* pronounced like *sz',* with only the addition of a *t.*

32. *w* pronounced as in *wind, woe, will.*

33. *y* pronounced as in *young, your, youth.*

## IV. DIACRITICAL MARKS.

The spiritus lenis (') is used to denote the omission of an imperfect vowel, as in the case of *sz'* and *tsz',* above. The spiritus asper (ʽ) indicates a rough breathing, or the omission of the *h.* Semicircular marks, (ʿ) like the sign for a degree cut in two, and placed at one of the four corners of a word as is done by the Chinese, indicate and distinguish the four upper tones; similar marks, with a line underneath, (ʿ) placed in the same manner, indicate the lower series of tones.

## V. EXPLANATION OF THE TONES.

The authority for the intonations, as marked in the Chrestomathy, is a small Chinese Tonic Dictionary (see page 4), in which more than seven thousand of the most common characters are arranged into classes and orders, according to their tones. Systematic and close attention to these is especially important when commencing the study of the language. Analysis of them has the same relation to speaking, that tuning an instrument has to music. The musician's first business is to tune his instruments; until he does this, there is no music. So, without proper intonation, there is no speaking Chinese correctly. Definitions and rules can serve only as auxiliaries; and perhaps the examples adduced in English, on account of the diversities of pronunciation among foreigners, may lead some into error. Whenever practicable, therefore, recourse should be had to the *voice of the best native speakers*, as the ultimate standard of appeal. The student of music could never learn to sing correctly by the use of notes alone; but on this account he surely would not discard their use. Frequent practice with a master, with careful attention to the rudiments of the science, would be his best course. So the only way to learn to pronounce Chinese correctly, is constant practice with natives, carefully discriminating and noting the tones.

The eight tones marked in the Chrestomathy are formed into two series, four in each. Uniting these two we have a fourfold division, resembling what rhetoricians call the absolute modifications of the voice, or cardinal sounds, capable of subdivision. These are thus described by Chinese grammarians in a stanza taken from the *Hónghí Tsz' Tín*, or Imperial Dictionary of Kanghe.

平 聲 平 道 莫 低 昂 ꜁P'ing ꜀shing, ꜁p'ing tò² mók₂ ꜁tai ꜁ngóng;
上 聲 高 呼 猛 烈 強 ꜂Shéung ꜀shing, ꜀kò ꜀f'ú ꜂mang lít₂ ꜁kéung;
去 聲 分 明 哀 遠 道 H'ü' ꜀shing, ꜀fan ꜁ming ꜀oi ꜂ün tò²;
入 聲 短 促 急 收 藏 Yap₂ ꜀shing, ꜂tün tsuk꜆ kap꜆ ꜀shau ꜁ch'óng.

These four tones are usually illustrated, in Chinese lexicons, by a diagram representing a man's hand, in the following manner.

2. *Shéung shing*, or Rising tone.

3. *H'ü shing*, or Receding tone.

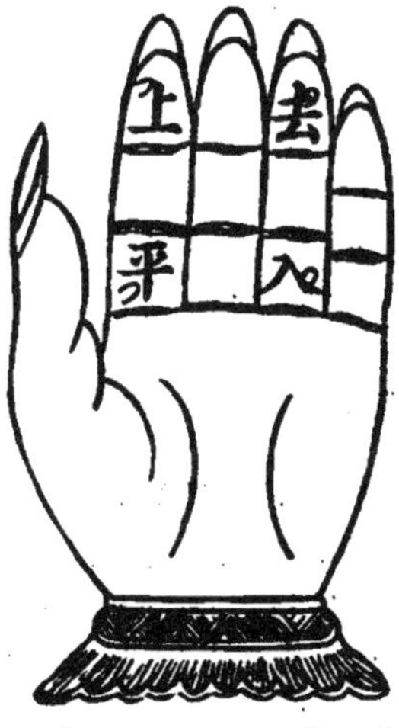


1. *P'ing shing*, or Even tone.

4. *Yap shing*, or Entering tone.

1. *P'ing shing*, or the monotone, is an even sound, and is fairly represented by a horizontal line. It is characterized by an entire absence of all inflection of voice. It may be quick or

slow, harsh or soft, on a high or low key; but it always continues in regard to elevation, precisely where it commenced. The following lines afford instances resembling it in English verse.

High on a throne of royal state, which far
Outshone the wealth of Ormuz or of Inde,
Or whēre the gōrgeous Eāst, with richest hānd,
Shōw'rs on her kings barbāric, pearls and gold,
Satan exalted sat.

2. *Shéung shing*, ascending tone, or rising inflection, turns the voice upwards, ending higher than it began. In English, it is heard invariably in the direct question. In the following lines, which afford instances of this tone, the acute accent (´) indicates the shéung shing.

My mother! when I learn'd that thou wast déad,
Say, wast thou conscious of the tears I shéd?
Hover'd thy spirit o'er thy sorrowing són,
Wretch even thén, life's journey just begún?

3. *H'ü shing*, the receding tone, is a distinct prolongation of the voice, diminishing, while it is prolonged; in English, it is used in the indirect question, and also in the language of scorn, surprise, authority, and alarm. In the two following examples, it is indicated by the grave (`) accent.

Hènce! hòme, you idle creatures, get you hòme,
You blòcks, you stònes, you wòrse than senseless things!

4. *Yap shing*, the entering tone, is an abrupt, short sound. In English, it occurs in words like *hit*, *hop*, &c.

A repetition of the description of these four tones, by varying the phraseology and presenting them in a different point of view, will perhaps throw on them additional light.

The *p'ing shing* is precisely the musical monotone, well represented by two parallel lines, indicating that it admits, neither of inflection in the tone, nor of variation in the volume, of voice, the *evenness* of the tone, alluded to in the term *p'ing*, precluding both. The *shéung shing* is that rising inflection, which is heard in our own language in every question that indicates some degree of surprise, and in the common expressions *ah! indeed!* The *h'ü shing*, a monotone like the p'ing shing, has this distinctive difference, that it is a *diminuendo*, or an inverted swell, and therefore may be pictured to the eye by the common musical mark of that expression. The Chinese call it the 'departing tone,' because it dies away upon the ear like the tones of receding music. The *yap shing* may be regarded as an abrupt monotone, in this dialect always preceding *p*, *t*, or *k*, hence deriving its characteristic ending. If one will pronounce the English word *lock*, only omitting the final consonants, he will give the true *yap shing*.

Each of these four tones, being subdivided, form the two series, noticed above, one of which may be considered primary, and the other secondary, the two being parallel to each other. The four tones, forming the first series, may be regarded as the fundamental modifications of the voice; and the four forming the second series, considered as counterpart or parallel to the first series, may be described in precisely the same terms as the first four tones, since they are distinguished from them only by being uttered on a lower key. Following out this arrangement, a well-defined system is formed, presenting in a narrow space all the tones, and all the vowel and diphthongal sounds, which occur in this dialect, in a tabular form, as exhibited on the two following pages.

E

Ords. **FIRST SERIES. Comprising the Upper Tones.**

| No. | 1 | 2 | 3 | 4 | P'ing shing. | Shéung shing. | H'ü shing | Yap shing | Meaning of the words, the heads of the orders and classes. |
|---|---|---|---|---|---|---|---|---|---|
| 1 | 先 | 鮮 | 線 | 屑 | ‹sín | ‘sín | sín’ | sít› | Before, moss, thread, bits. |
| 2 | 威 | 偉 | 畏 | | ‹wai | ‘wai | wai’ | | Dignity, great, awe. |
| 3 | 幾 | 紀 | 記 | | ‹kí | ‘kí | kí’ | | Several, to record, to remember. |
| 4 | 諸 | 主 | 著 | | ‹chü | ‘chü | chü’ | | All, master, to publish. |
| 5 | 修 | 叟 | 秀 | | ‹sau | ‘sau | sau’ | | Adorn, venerable man, elegant. |
| 6 | 東 | 董 | 凍 | 篤 | ‹tung | ‘tung | tung’ | tuk› | East, to rule, cold, real. |
| 7 | 英 | 影 | 應 | 益 | ‹ying | ‘ying | ying’ | yik› | Excellent, shadow, answer, beneficial. |
| 8 | 賓 | 稟 | 嬪 | 畢 | ‹pan | ‘pan | pan’ | pat› | Guest, petition, court lady, ended. |
| 9 | 張 | 掌 | 帳 | 着 | ‹chéung | ‘chéung | chéung’ | chéuk› | To draw out, to rule, curtain, to order. |
| 10 | 剛 | 講 | 降 | 角 | ‹kóng | ‘kóng | kóng’ | kók› | Strong, to speak, to descend, horn. |
| 11 | 朝 | 沼 | 照 | | ‹chíú | ‘chíú | chíú’ | | Morning, pool, to illumine. |
| 12 | 孤 | 古 | 故 | | ‹kú | ‘kú | kú’ | | Alone, ancient, old. |
| 13 | 鴛 | 婉 | 怨 | 乙 | ‹ün | ‘ün | ün’ | üt› | Drake, yielding, animosity, curved. |
| 14 | 皆 | 解 | 介 | | ‹kái | ‘kái | kái’ | | All, to open, firm or uncorrupted. |
| 15 | 登 | 等 | 凳 | 德 | ‹tang | ‘tang | tang’ | tak› | Ascend, sort, stool, virtue. |
| 16 | 師 | 史 | 四 | | ‹sz’ | ‘sz’ | sz’’ | | Master, history, four. |
| 17 | 金 | 錦 | 禁 | 急 | ‹kam | ‘kam | kam’ | kap› | Metal, embroidery, prohibit, hasty. |
| 18 | 交 | 絞 | 教 | | ‹káu | ‘káu | káu’ | | Intercourse, to strangle, to teach. |
| 19 | 栽 | 宰 | 載 | | ‹tsoi | ‘tsoi | tsoi’ | | To plant, to rule, to contain. |
| 20 | 兼 | 檢 | 劍 | 刦 | ‹kím | ‘kím | kím’ | kíp› | Joined, to examine, sword, to rob. |
| 21 | 津 | 贐 | 進 | 卒 | ‹tsun | ‘tsun | tsun’ | tsut› | A ford, presents, to enter, soldiers. |
| 22 | 雖 | 髓 | 歲 | | ‹sui | ‘sui | sui’ | | Although, marrow, year. |
| 23 | 科 | 火 | 貨 | | ‹fó | ‘fó | fó’ | | Order or sort, fire, cargo. |
| 24 | 緘 | 減 | 鑒 | 甲 | ‹kám | ‘kám | kám’ | káp› | To bind, to diminish, mirror, armor. |
| 25 | 翻 | 反 | 泛 | 發 | ‹fán | ‘fán | fán’ | fát› | To fly, to rebel, to float, to issue. |
| 26 | 家 | 賈 | 嫁 | | ‹ká | ‘ká | ká’ | | House, price, to marry (a husband). |
| 27 | 官 | 管 | 貫 | 括 | ‹kún | ‘kún | kún’ | kút› | Officer, tube, to connect, to inclose. |
| 28 | 魁 | 賄 | 誨 | | ‹fúi | ‘fúi | fúi’ | | Headmost, a bribe, to teach. |
| 29 | 遮 | 者 | 蔗 | | ‹ché | ‘ché | ché’ | | Screen, this, sugar cane. |
| 30 | 干 | 趕 | 幹 | 割 | ‹kón | ‘kón | kón’ | kót› | A shield, to pursue, business, to cut. |
| 31 | 甘 | 敢 | 紺 | 蛤 | ‹k‘óm | ‘k‘óm | k‘óm’ | k‘óp› | Sweet, daring, purple, a clam. |
| 32 | N. B. *In these two orders, no words occur in this series.* | | | | | | | | |
| 33 | | | | | | | | | |

| Ords. SECOND SERIES, Comprising the Lower Tones. | | | | | | | | | |
|---|---|---|---|---|---|---|---|---|---|
| No | 1 | 2 | 3 | 4 | Pʻing shing. | Shéung shing. | Hü shing | Yap shing | Meaning of the words, the heads of the orders and classes. |
| 1 | 連 | 璉 | 鍊 | 列 | ꜁lín | ꜃lín | lín꜅ | lít꜇ | To unite, gem, chain, to separate. |
| 2 | 迷 | 米 | 袂 | | ꜁mai | ꜃mai | mai꜅ | | To deceive, rice, cuff of the sleeve. |
| 3 | 宜 | 議 | 貳 | | ꜁í | ꜃í | í꜅ | | Right, deliberate, the second. |
| 4 | 除 | 佇 | 住 | | ꜁chü | ꜃chü | chü꜅ | | To exclude, to stand, to dwell. |
| 5 | 留 | 柳 | 陋 | | ꜁lau | ꜃lau | lau꜅ | | To detain, willow, base or mean. |
| 6 | 容 | 勇 | 用 | 欲 | ꜁yung | ꜃yung | yung꜅ | yuk꜇ | Manner, brave, use, to wish. |
| 7 | 靈 | 領 | 令 | 力 | ꜁ling | ꜃ling | ling꜅ | lik꜇ | Spiritual, the neck, to order, strength. |
| 8 | 文 | 敏 | 問 | 勿 | ꜁man | ꜃man | man꜅ | mat꜇ | Letters, celerity, to ask, do not. |
| 9 | 陽 | 仰 | 樣 | 藥 | ꜁yéung | ꜃yéung | yéung꜅ | yéuk꜇ | Light, to look up, pattern, physic. |
| 10 | 王 | 往 | 旺 | 鑊 | ꜁wóng | ꜃wóng | wóng꜅ | wók꜇ | King, to go, abundance, a pan. |
| 11 | 寮 | 了 | 料 | | ꜁líú | ꜃líú | líú꜅ | | A window, finished, to estimate. |
| 12 | 無 | 母 | 務 | | ꜁mú | ꜃mú | mú꜅ | | Without, mother, business. |
| 13 | 元 | 軟 | 願 | 月 | ꜁ün | ꜃ün | ün꜅ | üt꜇ | Origin, flexible, desire, moon. |
| 14 | 鞋 | 蟹 | 懈 | | ꜁hái | ꜃hái | hái꜅ | | Shoes, crab, lazy. |
| 15 | 盟 | 猛 | 孟 | 墨 | ꜁mang | ꜃mang | mang꜅ | mak꜇ | To swear, fierce, first, ink. |
| 16 | 詞 | 似 | 自 | | ꜁tsz' | ꜃tsz' | tsz'꜅ | | Sentence, like, self. |
| 17 | 吟 | 衽 | 任 | 入 | ꜁yam | ꜃yam | yam꜅ | yap꜇ | To chant, lappet, to sustain, to enter. |
| 18 | 茅 | 卯 | 貌 | | ꜁máu | ꜃máu | máu꜅ | | Rushes, luxuriant, countenance. |
| 19 | 臺 | 殆 | 代 | | ꜁tʻoi | ꜃tʻoi | tʻoi꜅ | | Terrace, dangerous, instead of. |
| 20 | 嚴 | 染 | 驗 | 業 | ꜁ím | ꜃ím | ím꜅ | íp꜇ | Severe, to dye, to examine, occupation. |
| 21 | 倫 | 卵 | 論 | 律 | ꜁lun | ꜃lun | lun꜅ | lut꜇ | Relation, egg, discourse, law. |
| 22 | 雷 | 累 | 類 | | ꜁lui | ꜃lui | lui꜅ | | Thunder, to involve, species. |
| 23 | 鵝 | 我 | 臥 | | ꜁ngó | ꜃ngó | ngó꜅ | | Goose, I or we, to sleep. |
| 24 | 藍 | 覽 | 纜 | 蠟 | ꜁lám | ꜃lám | lám꜅ | láp꜇ | Blue, to look, rope, wax. |
| 25 | 闌 | 懶 | 爛 | 辣 | ꜁lán | ꜃lán | lán꜅ | lát꜇ | Fading, lazy, broken, pungent. |
| 26 | 牙 | 雅 | 迓 | | ꜁ngá | ꜃ngá | ngá꜅ | | Teeth, elegant, to receive. |
| 27 | 門 | 滿 | 悶 | 末 | ꜁mún | ꜃mún | mún꜅ | mút꜇ | Door, full, grief, the end. |
| 28 | 梅 | 每 | 昧 | | ꜁múi | ꜃múi | múi꜅ | | Plum, each, obscure. |
| 29 | 蛇 | 社 | 射 | | ꜁shé | ꜃shé | shé꜅ | | Snake, local deities, to shoot. |
| 30 | 寒 | 旱 | 翰 | 褐 | ꜁hón | ꜃hón | hón꜅ | hót꜇ | Cold, drought, pencil, hempen cloth. |
| 31 | 含 | 頷 | 憾 | 合 | ꜁hóm | ꜃hóm | hóm꜅ | hóp꜇ | To endure, jaws, indignation, to unite. |
| 32 | 彭 | 棒 | 硬 | 額 | ꜁pʻáng | ꜃pʻáng | ngáng꜅ | ngák꜇ | Abundant, a mace, stiff, forehead. |
| 33 | 吾 | 五 | 悟 | | ꜁'ng | ꜃'ng | 'ng꜅ | | My or our, five, to perceive. |

Each of these thirty-three orders is characterized by its termination. All words ending with *ín* and *ít*, for example, belong to the first order; all ending with *óng* and *ók* belong to the tenth; those with *ím* and *íp*, to the twentieth; and those in *ón* and *ót*, to the thirtieth. So of all others; the order to which any word belongs is ascertained by its termination—that always being, or else including, a vowel or diphthongal sound. Further, each of these orders is distributed into eight—or, when the *yap shing* is wanting, into six—classes, according to the tones, as explained above. Thus the arrangement of all the characters in this dialect and their pronunciation depend on these two particulars: first, on the vowel or diphthongal sound; and secondly, on the tone. By the vowel or diphthongal sound and the consonants following them, the order is ascertained, and by the tone the class. In the second series, the initial sounds of the words do not always correspond to those in the first series; this results from the fact, that there are not in every order, a double series of words having the same initials. For example, in the first order, *꜀sín, ꜂sín, sín꜄, sít꜆*, form the first series, and *꜁lín, ꜃lín, lín꜅, lít꜇*, the second series; *lín* and *lít* being substituted for *sín* and *sít*.

ORDER I. *Sín, sít.* There are few or no deviations under this order, the vowel being the long and easy sound of the Italian *i*, like *ee* in meet, feet, &c.

ORDER II. *Wai.* Here there is no deviation from the sound of *ai*, as defined above, though the sound of *ai* in some words in this order is occasionally heard lengthened to *ái* as in the 14th order. It will be seen that in the fourth and eighth classes of this order the *yap shing* is wanting, as they are also in all the other orders where the words do not end with a consonant.

ORDER III. *Kí.* This is the same vowel as in the 1st order, and there seem to be only a few exceptions to, or slight deviations, from it in some words where the long *í* sound approximates nearly to the *é* of the 29th order, pronounced like *ay* in *may, pay, say*, &c.

ORDER IV. *Chü.* Here the sound of the vowel remains throughout the same; there are a few instances, however, in which it closely resembles *ui*, in the 22d order; the two are liable to be confounded, and should be carefully distinguished.

ORDERS V and VI. *Sau. Tung, tuk.* In these, the sounds of the terminations *au* in the 5th, and *ung* in the 6th are preserved without change. Yet there is the same tendency to lengthen the sound of *au* to that of *áu* in order 18th perceptible in some words under the first of these orders that has just been noticed under the 2d order.

ORDER VII. *Ying, yik.* Not unfrequently this vowel approximates to, and sometimes actually becomes a short *e*; thus *hing* and *ping* are changed to *heng* and *peng*; *kik* and *shik* to *kek* and *shek*; and so of some others under this order. However, even in those cases where *e* has become the common sound, the words will be readily understood if they are pronounced with *i*, according to the standard. A much more frequent change of words under this termination is that of the *i* into *a*; as for *sing, ming, ting*, to say *sang, mang, tang*, but still the change is of such a nature that an educated native easily distinguishes all these words from those of the 15th order.

ORDER VIII. *Pan, pat.* In a few words, especially those ending in the *yap shing*, the *a* in *abundant* comes very near to the long *á* of the 25th order; in which cases they are liable to be confounded with words of that order.

ORDER IX. *Chéung, chéuk.* The variations in the pronunciation of *éung* and *éuk* are few; in some instances the *u* approximates to the sound of *a*, in *quota*.

ORDERS X and XI. *Kóng, kók. Chíú.* There are no essential deviations under either of these orders.

ORDER XII. *Ká*. Probably in more than one half of the words forming this order, the *ú* is exchanged for *ò*; and many seem to range somewhere between the two, giving the sound of *o* in *so*, *no*, &c., so that it is difficult to determine which of the letters *ú* or *ò* should be used. In some cases, the sound of the vowel will be heard approximating to the *ú* by one ear, while by other persons the same word will be sounded as if it terminated in *ò*; most of the words, however, are uniformly pronounced by all persons ending either in *ò* or *ú*.

ORDER XIII. *Ün*, *üt*. In all words under this order, the French sound of the vowel is uniformly retained, being always followed by *n* or *t*.

ORDER XIV. *Kái*. In all these, there is uniformly the long sound of *ái*; but there is at times a little difficulty in distinguishing them from words of the 2d order where those run into this.

ORDER XV. *Tang*, *tak*. Here, as in *pan* and *pat*, and in other orders having short vowels, there is a tendency to change the short into the long vowel; some words placed here in the Tonic Dictionary are usually heard sounded long.

ORDER XVI. *Sz'*. There seems to be no word in the English language which has the sound given to those under this order; it will be nearly attained if pronounced according to the directions above, on page iii.

ORDER XVII. *Kam*, *kap*. Here likewise the vowel sometimes shows a disposition, though rather less than in some of the other orders having short vowels, to claim affinity with the *á* in *calm*, and thus to run into the 24th order.

ORDER XVIII. *Káu*. Here the full broad sound of *á* is invariably retained, distinguishing the words under this from those in the 5th order.

ORDERS XIX and XX. *Tsoi*. *Kím*, *kíp*. The *oi* of order 19, in a very few cases approaches the *ái* of the 14th. The terminations *ím* and *íp* are throughout uniform.

ORDER XXI. *Tsun*, *tsut*. The sound of *u*, as defined on page iii, is preserved in all the words in this order. By disregarding the vowel, the Chinese sometimes confound these words with those of the 8th order, under *pan* and *pat*, and it will require close attention to discriminate between the two.

ORDER XXII. *Sui*. In some words, the *ui* is a little more open and prolonged than in others; care should be taken not to confound these words with those of the 4th or 28th orders.

ORDER XXIII. *Fó*. The long *ó* of this order is in a very few cases shortened, so that it resembles that in *no*, *so*.

ORDERS XXIV, XXV, and XXVI. *Kám*, *káp*. *Fán*, *fát*. *Ká*. The variations under these three orders are few or none, each one being easily distinguished from all others, and uniform within itself.

ORDER XXVII. *Kún*, *kút*. The full broad sound of the *ú*, as *oo* in *school*, followed by *n* and *t*, characterizes this order, and easily distinguishes it from all the others.

ORDER XXVIII. *Fúi*. There is a distinct relationship between the sound of *úi* in this, and the *ui* in the 22d order, but the words under this order are uniform; care is, however, requisite to distinguish the two.

ORDER XXIX. *Ché*. The words under this head are uniform, and easily distinguished from all the others, except it may be a few in the 3d order, when the *i* approaches to the sound of *é* as here given.

ORDER XXX. *Kón*, *kót*. The vowel here, as in the 23d order, is usually full and broad, nor will any word comprised in it be easily confounded with those of any other order.

ORDER XXXI. *K'óm*, *k'óp*. Not only are *m* and *p* here used instead of *n* and *t*, in the preceding order, but the vowel *ó* is slightly changed, by abruptly closing the mouth when

F

the sound is but half uttered;—the former is like the sound *brawn, lawn,* this more like *comb, roam,* the change in the sound of *ó* being occasioned by the different terminating consonant.

ORDER XXXII. *P'áng, ngáng, ngák.* The words under this order are few, though several which are placed in the 15th order are sounded as if belonging to this. The vowel *á* is uniformly sounded long.

ORDER XXXIII. *'Ng.* By dropping the vowel in *ing*, and retaining the full sound of the *ng*, the scholar will give the true nasal here required.

It may be observed concerning these variations, that they are for the most part caused by an endeavor to multiply and extend the number of different sounds in conversation. There being no sound to Chinese characters, derivable from their component strokes, as the sounds of English words are derivable from the letters of which they are composed, the true sound of any character can only be learned by rote; and this too is the great source of the dialectical variations in pronunciation. These variations need give the student no trouble, as they will be easily learned by the ear. Besides these variations in the final vowel sound, there are a few occurring in the initial consonant, which are heard at Macao and other places near the coast. For instance, the initial *sh* is usually heard as *s;* as for *shui* (water) to say *sui; sáng sing* for *sháng shing*, provincial city, &c.; the sounds *tsz'* and *sz'* are sounded like a hard hissing *tchí* and *chí* differing from the common *chí* by its forced enunciation as if attempting to say *tsz':* in both these deviations, an approach to the Fukien dialect is observed. A few words, which, at Canton, are spoken without any initial vowel, are in Macao heard beginning with *ng*; as *ngí* (two) for *í; ngín* or *ngün* (words) for *ín; ngít* (hot) for *ít; ín* (worthy) is pronounced *hín*. These variations, together with that of sounding almost all the words comprised under the 7th order ending in *ing* and *ik*, as if they were written *ang* and *ak*, constitute the principal discrepancies in the dialect as is it spoken in the two cities, and the intermediate neighboring places. These are, however, not very important, and the word or phrase will be understood sounded either way.

## VI. THE GENERAL LANGUAGE.

That form of the Chinese most prevalent among the literati and at court, constituting the general language of the country, ought not to be overlooked by those who commence with any one of the dialects. Without going into lengthened details, a few observations here respecting it will help to exhibit more clearly the character and value of this dialect.

The language should be viewed as a whole. The dialectical diversities are chiefly in speaking, not in writing. There are local phrases, for some of which written characters exist, while for others there are none. These diversities, however numerous they may be, do not very materially affect the language of the country, properly so called. The great body of Chinese writings, like that of England, or of France, or of Germany, constitutes one uniform language, and is everywhere equally well understood. By the Chinese themselves their writings are always thus regarded. Their literature is one; and they have but one language. This every child, on learning to read, studies; for therein, with scarcely an exception, all books and all papers written for publication appear. The scholar therefore who learns to read only in a provincial dialect, may be as thoroughly versed in the literature of his country, and may become as familiar with its idioms, as the one who employs only that pronunciation prevalent among the literati, officers of government, and traveled gentlemen. Ability to use this pronunciation, in the conversational style current in all the high circles of the empire, is regarded by the Chi-

nese as so essential, that an education is hardly considered finished if this part be wanting. In like manner, the foreign student, who commences with any one of the dialects, should early direct his attention to the general language, and be careful not to neglect too long that pronunciation and conversational style which only can enable him to hold free converse with gentlemen and travelers wherever he may go. For this pronunciation, recourse must be had to native masters. For the language itself, as it appears in books, portions of the Chrestomathy afford very good examples, quoted from standard authors. All parts of the volume, however, even those sections which follow most closely the Canton local dialect, will probably be intelligible to every educated Chinese who reads them in any part of the country.

Fragments, like the inscription on the bath of Táng, first emperor of the Sháng dynasty, whose reign commenced 1766, B. C., prove that this language was early reduced to writing. Portions of the Book of Odes and Book of Records are confessedly of a very ancient date, and show too that many words in early use were homophonous. The number of syllables given in Morrison's Dictionary is 411; these by the use of tones and aspirates are increased to more than fifteen hundred. The number specified in the Tonic Dictionary is 1582; under each of these are arranged several homophonous words, varying from three or four to twenty, thirty, and more. Thus under *tsing*, following the Tonic Dictionary, occur these six, viz., 精睛菁旌蜻晶 each written differently, with a signification different from the others; yet the six are all pronounced precisely alike. This characteristic of the language may be exemplified by the words *rite, right, write,* and *wright,* in English; when spoken they are alike in sound, as these six Chinese words when spoken, or when their sounds are denoted by Roman letters, are all alike; yet when written as the Chinese write them, they are as unlike as *rite, right, write, wright.* But while these homophonous words are few in English, in Chinese they are exceedingly numerous, and constitute one of the greatest difficulties in learning the language.

A complete history of the Chinese literature is a great desideratum. It would settle some difficult questions, and throw light on this 'hard speech.' Valuable sketches have been given by several writers. The introductory papers to the dictionaries of Morrison and Medhurst, and an article in the Chinese Repository, vol. III. pp. 14—37, are probably among the best.

An alphabetical list of the syllables, similar to that in Morrison's Dictionary, is introduced here, the sounds of the characters being represented by the same system of orthography that has been employed in the body of the Chrestomathy. The list is intended to exhibit all the syllables in the general language, excepting only the varieties occasioned by the tones and aspirates; and it will enable the student, without referring to any other work, to form an opinion of the general language, and to mark the principal differences in pronunciation between it and this dialect. To aid him in marking these differences between the two, the sound of the characters is given in both, and in separate columns. Besides the vowels and diphthongs used in the Chrestomathy, the following additional ones are required in the general language; viz., *e* as in *where*, or like *ai* in *chair*; and *ei*, which is pronounced open nearly like *ey* in the words *bey* and *dey*.

*Note.*—In this list of syllables, commencing on the next page, the sounds as used in the court dialect are given in the first column after the Chinese characters, and the sounds of the local dialect in the second. In a few instances, two words occur in the first column having the same sound, as *'án* and *'án, chá* and *chá, che* and *che*; in each of these cases, the vowel in the second of the two words, if it be a final one as in *chá* and *che*, must be pronounced somewhat short and abrupt. So in all cases of the *yap shing*, where in the provincial dialect the vowel is followed by *p, t,* or *k*, it is pronounced short and abrupt: such are *chí, chó, chue, fá, hiá, &c.* It will be seen also, that analogy does not hold in all cases: thus *hiáng* becomes *héung* in one case, while *kiáng* becomes *kóng* in another; so *che* becomes *chip* in one, and *chít* in another instance.

| | | | | | | | | | | | |
|---|---|---|---|---|---|---|---|---|---|---|---|
| 亞 | á | á | 春 | chun | chun | 協 | hie | híp | 惹 | jé | yé |
| 額 | a | ngák | 中 | chung | chung | 陷 | hien | hám | 熱 | je *or* jue | ít |
| 艾 | 'ai | ngai | 撾 | chwá | chá | 忻 | hin | yan | 然 | jen | ín |
| 安 | 'án | ón | 嘬 | chwái | chái | 行 | hing | hang | 日 | ji | yat |
| 岸 | 'án | ngón | 壯 | chwáng | chóng | 學 | hió | hók | 入 | jin | yan |
| 恩 | 'an | yan | 乏 | fá | fát | 頊 | hiu | huk | 仍 | jing | ying |
| 卬 | áng | ngóng | 凡 | fán | fán | 休 | hiú | yau | 若 | jó | yéuk |
| 澳 | 'áu | ò | 分 | fan | fan | 穴 | hiue | yüt | 汝 | jü | yü |
| 區 | 'au | au | 方 | fáng | fóng | 玄 | hiuen | hün | 辱 | ju | yuk |
| 查 | chá | chá | 否 | fau | fau | 熏 | hiun | fan | 軟 | juen | yün |
| 閘 | chá | cháp | 非 | fei | fí | 凶 | hiung | hung | 蕋 | juì | yui |
| 差 | chái | chái | 縛 | fŏ | fŏk | 火 | hò | fò | 閏 | jun | yun |
| 斬 | chán | chám | 父 | fú | fú | 合 | hó | hóp | 戎 | jung | yung |
| 章 | cháng | chéung | 弗 | fu | fat | 乎 | hú | ú | 改 | kái | koi |
| 召 | cháu | chíú | 風 | fung | fung | 吁 | hü | hü | 干 | kán | kón |
| 紬 | chau | chau | 赫 | ha | hak | 紅 | hung | hung | 跟 | kan | kan |
| 者 | ché | ché | 害 | hái | hoi | 化 | hwá | fá | 抗 | káng | kóng |
| 折 | che | chít | 旱 | hán | hón | 滑 | hwá | wát | 更 | kang | kang |
| 摺 | che | chíp | 恨 | han | han | 淮 | hwái | wai | 告 | káu | kò |
| 占 | chen | chím | 杭 | háng | hóng | 喚 | hwán | fún | 忌 | kí | kí |
| 知 | chí | chí | 亨 | hang | hang | 昏 | hwan | fan | 及 | ki | káp |
| 尺 | chi | chik | 浩 | háu | hò | 黃 | hwáng | wóng | 加 | kiá | ká |
| 參 | chin | chan | 後 | hau | hau | 橫 | hwang | wáng | 甲 | kiá | káp |
| 正 | ching | ching | 希 | hí | hí | 活 | hwó | út | 介 | kiái | kái |
| 卓 | chó | chéuk | 檄 | hi | hat | 忽 | hwu | fat | 江 | kiáng | kóng |
| 主 | chú *or* chü | chü | 下 | hiá | há | 徊 | hwui | úi | 叫 | kiáu | kíú |
| 竹 | chu | chuk | 狹 | hiá | háp | 衣 | í | í | 茄 | kié | ké |
| 啜 | chue | chüt | 駭 | hiái | hoi | 讓 | jáng | yéung | 劫 | kie | kíp |
| 川 | chuen | chün | 向 | hiáng | héung | 饒 | jáu | íú | 劍 | kien | kím |
| 追 | chúi | chui | 孝 | hiáu | háu | 肉 | jau | yuk | 角 | kió | kók |

| | | | | | | | | | | | |
|---|---|---|---|---|---|---|---|---|---|---|---|
| 客 | ka | hák | 濫 | lán | lám | 貊 | ma | mak | 耨 | nau | náu |
| 口 | kau | hau | 浪 | láng | lóng | 買 | mái | mái | 囊 | náng | nóng |
| 巾 | kin | kan | 冷 | lang | lang | 曼 | mán | mán | 哽 | ngang | ngáng |
| 京 | king | king | 老 | láu | lò | 忙 | máng | móng | 訛 | ngó | ngó |
| 菊 | kiu | kuk | 里 | lí | lí | 孟 | mang | mang | 尼 | ní | ní |
| 決 | kiue | küt | 兩 | liáng | léung | 冒 | máu | mò | 娘 | niáng | néung |
| 犬 | kiuen | hün | 了 | liáu | líú | 牟 | mau | mau | 鳥 | niáu | níú |
| 均 | kiun | kwan | 列 | lie | lít | 乜 | mé | mat | 攝 | nie | níp |
| 窮 | kiung | kung | 連 | lien | lín | 米 | mí | mai | 年 | nien | nín |
| 九 | kiú | kau | 力 | li | lik | 妙 | miáu | míú | 匿 | ni | nik |
| 個 | kò | kó | 畧 | lió | léuk | 烕 | mie | mít | 虐 | nió | yéuk |
| 各 | kó | kók | 呂 | lü | lü | 面 | mien | mín | 牛 | niú | ngau |
| 古 | kú | kú | 劣 | liue | lüt | 妹 | mei | múi | 紉 | nin | yan |
| 去 | kü | hü | 戀 | liuen | lün | 密 | mi | mat | 寧 | ning | ning |
| 谷 | ku | kuk | 律 | liu | lut | 繆 | miú | mau | 挪 | nò | nó |
| 工 | kung | kung | 流 | liû | lau | 民 | min | man | 諾 | nó | nók |
| 瓜 | kwá | kwá | 勒 | la | lak | 名 | ming | ming | 奴 | nú | nú |
| 刮 | kwa | kwát | 林 | lin | lam | 摩 | mò | mó | 嫩 | nun | nün |
| 快 | kwái | fái | 令 | ling | ling | 末 | mó | mút | 女 | nü | nü |
| 官 | kwán | kún | 羅 | lò | ló | 母 | mú | mò | 恧 | nu | nuk |
| 困 | kwan | kwan | 洛 | ló | lók | 木 | mu | muk | 農 | nung | nung |
| 光 | kwáng | kwóng | 路 | lú | lò | 門 | mun | mún | 內 | nui | noi |
| 肱 | kwang | kwang | 樓 | lau | lau | 蒙 | mung | mung | 暖 | nuán | nün |
| 圭 | kwei | kwai | 陸 | lu | luk | 滿 | muán | mún | 痾 | ò | ó |
| 果 | kwò | kwó | 倫 | lun | lun | 那 | ná | nó | 惡 | ó | ók |
| 國 | kwó | kwók | 弄 | lung | lung | 納 | na | náp | 巴 | pá | pá |
| 圣 | kwu | kwat | 雷 | lui | lui | 乃 | nái | nái | 八 | pá | pát |
| 拉 | lá | láp | 卵 | luán | lün | 南 | nán | nám | 俳 | pái | pái |
| 喇 | lá | lát | 馬 | má | má | 能 | nang | nang | 扮 | pán | pán |
| 來 | lái | loi | 帓 | má | mút | 鬧 | náu | náu | 旁 | páng | póng |

| | | | | | | | | | | | |
|---|---|---|---|---|---|---|---|---|---|---|---|
| 朋 | pang | pang | 小 | siáu | síú | 順 | shun | shun | 跌 | tie | tít |
| 本 | pan | pún | 些 | sié | sé | 耍 | shwá | shá | 天 | tien | tín |
| 剖 | pau | pau | 屑 | sie | sít | 刷 | shwá | shát | 的 | ti | tik |
| 包 | páu | páu | 先 | sien | sín | 衰 | shwái | shui | 丟 | tiú | tíú |
| 比 | pí | pí | 夕 | si | sik | 爽 | shwáng | shóng | 丁 | ting | ting |
| 表 | piáu | píú | 削 | sió | séuk | 說 | shwó | shüt | 佗 | tò | tó |
| 别 | pie | pít | 序 | sü | tsü | 水 | shui | shui | 奪 | tó | tüt |
| 片 | pien | pín | 雪 | siue | süt | 心 | sin | sam | 土 | tú | tò |
| 丕 | pei | pí | 宣 | sieun | sün | 姓 | sing | sing | 斗 | tau | tau |
| 匹 | pi | pat | 戌 | siú | sut | 所 | sò | shó | 則 | tsa | tsak |
| 彪 | piú | píú | 旬 | siun | tsun | 索 | só | sók | 匝 | tsá | tsáp |
| 白 | pa | pák | 脩 | siú | sau | 素 | sú | sú | 才 | tsái | tsoi |
| 品 | pin | pan | 沙 | shá | shá | 叟 | sau | sau | 残 | tsán | tsán |
| 丙 | ping | ping | 殺 | shá | shát | 夙 | su | suk | 倉 | tsáng | tsóng |
| 波 | pò | pó | 晒 | shái | shái | 損 | sun | sün | 曾 | tsang | tsang |
| 泊 | pó | pók | 山 | shán | shán | 宋 | sung | sung | 早 | tsáu | tsò |
| 布 | pú | pò | 上 | sháng | shéung | 綏 | sui | shui | 妻 | tsí | tsai |
| 卜 | pu | puk | 少 | sháu | shíú | 算 | suán | sün | 將 | tsiáng | tséung |
| 笨 | pung | pún | 佘 | shé | shé | 士 | sz' | sz' | 俏 | tsiáu | tsíú |
| 半 | puán | pung | 舌 | she | shít | 得 | ta | tak | 且 | tsié | ché |
| 色 | sa | shik | 善 | shen | shín | 大 | tá | tái | 妾 | tsie | tsíp |
| 撒 | sá | sát | 尸 | shí | shí | 塔 | tá | táp | 千 | tsien | tsín |
| 腮 | sái | soi | 十 | shi | shap | 太 | tái | tái | 七 | tsi | tsat |
| 三 | sán | sám | 申 | shin | shan | 丹 | tán | tán | 雀 | tsió | tséuk |
| 森 | sán | sham | 升 | shing | shing | 當 | táng | tóng | 取 | tsü | tsü |
| 桑 | sáng | sóng | 爍 | shó | shéuk | 等 | tang | tang | 絶 | tsiue | tsüt |
| 生 | sang | shang | 殳 | shü | shü | 刀 | táu | tò | 全 | tsiuen | tsün |
| 掃 | sáu | sò | 書 | shú | shü | 地 | tí | tí | 夋 | tsiun | tsun |
| 西 | sí | sai | 手 | shau | shau | 刁 | tiáu | tíú | 酒 | tsiú | tsau |
| 相 | siáng | séung | 朮 | shu | shut | 爹 | tié | té | 侵 | tsin | tsam |

| | | | | | | | | | | | |
|---|---|---|---|---|---|---|---|---|---|---|---|
| 請 | tsing | tsing | 冬 | tung | tung | 爲 | wei | mí | 又 | yú | yau |
| 左 | tsò | tsó | 兌 | túi | túi | 未 | wí | wai | 一 | yi | yat |
| 作 | tsó | tsók | 段 | tuán | tün | 我 | wò | ngó | 吟 | yin | yam |
| 祖 | tsú | tsò | 兀 | 'u | ngat | 嚄 | wó | wók | 應 | ying | ying |
| 走 | tsau | tsau | 五 | ú | 'ng | 勿 | wu | mat | 約 | yó | yéuk |
| 足 | tsu | tsuk | 翁 | 'ung | yung | 丫 | yá | á | 于 | yü | yü |
| 攢 | tsuán | tsün | 而 | 'rh | í | 押 | yá | áp | 曰 | yue | üt |
| 寸 | tsun | tsün | 瓦 | wá | ngá | 隘 | yái | ái | 元 | yuen | ün |
| 宗 | tsung | tsung | 穵 | wá | wát | 仰 | yáng | yéung | 玉 | yu | yuk |
| 罪 | tsui | tsui | 外 | wái | ngoi | 夭 | yáu | íú | 云 | yun | wan |
| 子 | tsz' | tsz' | 丸 | wán | ün | 也 | yé | yá | 用 | yung | yung |
| 督 | tu | tuk | 文 | wan | man | 葉 | ye | íp | | | |
| 屯 | tun | tun | 王 | wáng | wóng | 言 | yen | ín | | | |

## VII. CHINESE GRAMMAR.

Regarding the grammar of this language no very small amount of matériel has been collected by Prémare, in his Notitia Linguæ Sinicæ. The E'lémens de la Grammaire Chinoise by Rémusat is however a much more methodical and useful work. By analyzing the language, and by marking attentively the modes of expression, the student will soon perceive—as well expressed in the résumé of Rémusat—that generally:

In every Chinese sentence, in which nothing is understood, the elements of which it is composed are arranged in the following order; the subject, the verb, the complement direct, and the complement indirect.

Modifying expressions precede those to which they belong: thus, the adjective is placed before the substantive, subject or complement; the substantive governed before the noun that governs it; the adverb before the verb; the proposition incidental, circumstantial, or hypothetical, before the principal proposition, to which it attaches itself by a conjunctive adjective, or by a conjunction expressed or understood.

The relative position of words and phrases thus determined, supplies the place often of every other mark intended to denote their mutual dependence, their character whether adjective or adverbial, positive, conditional, or circumstantial.

If the subject is understood, it is because it is a personal pronoun, or that it has been expressed above, and that the same substantive that is omitted is found in the preceding sentence, and in the same quality of subject, and not in any other.

If the verb is wanting, it is because it is the substantive verb, or some other easily supplied, or one which has already found a place in the preceding sentences, with a subject or complement not the same.

If several substantives follow each other, either they are in construction with each other, or they form an enumeration, or they are synonymes which explain and determine each other.

If several verbs succeed each other, which are not synonymous, and are not employed as auxiliaries, the first ones should be taken as adverbs, or as verbal nouns, the subjects of those which follow, or these latter as verbal nouns the complements of those which precede.

Here ends the summary of Rémusat. The student will find that Chinese sentences are generally short, and simple in their construction, the parts of each proposition being arranged in their natural order. And if he turns to the Chinese 文法 *man fát*, or 'laws of language,' he will find all words arranged into two great divisions. Those in the first are called 實字 *shat tsz'*, essential words, which are subdivided into 死字 *sz' tsz'*, dead or inactive words, i. e. nouns; and into 活字 *út tsz'*, living or active words, i. e. verbs. Those in the second are called 虛字 *hü tsz'*, or particles, which comprise, 起語辭 *hí yü tsz'*, initials; 接語辭 *tsip yü tsz'*, conjunctions; 歎語辭 *tán yü tsz'*, exclamations; 歇語辭 *hít yü tsz'*, finals; 轉語辭 *chün yü tsz'*, words denoting transition, &c. He will further perceive that these 'laws of language,' which constitute the grammar of the Chinese, have reference mainly to the construction of phrases and sentences. Practice in analyzing sentences—so as to be able in each case easily to distinguish the subject, the attribute, and the verb—or the subject and predicate—will show him that the character and uses of words are determined, not from their forms, but from the *position* they occupy. Chinese words have no variations in form, such as are made by the conjugation and declension of Latin or Greek verbs and nouns; but by position, their character and uses are greatly varied.

Those Chinese who best understand the use of their own language, give great weight to the *hü tsz'*,—these 'wings of Mercury,'—considering their right employment as the most important and the most difficult part of grammar.

## VIII. CHINESE LITERATURE.

The writings of the Chinese are exceedingly numerous, and great is the variety of style. From the days of Confucius down to our own times, during a period of more than twenty-three hundred years, there has been one uninterrupted series of authors. The Five Classics and Four Books taken collectively are somewhat less copious than the Old and New Testaments, with which however they are not to be compared, either in diversity and beauty of composition, or in purity and elevation of sentiment. Still the precepts given, the duties inculcated, and the prohibitions made, are remarkable, and have elicited an inquiry whether we should not look on these writings, as given by God, for the moral government of this people? Poetry and prose here have not assumed precisely the same forms as they did among the Greeks and Romans; but before passing judgment on the relative value of eastern and western authors, the student should examine and weigh well the merits of each. He may easily estimate the value of Grecian and Roman literature, for the whole ground on which the estimate is to be made, has been repeatedly surveyed, and every great problem worked out ready for use; but with regard to eastern literature, the case is different. Before one can be able to pass an accurate judgment on the whole body of Chinese lore, he must have enjoyed a much longer and a far more intimate acquaintance with this people and their writings, than any foreigner now living can boast of. The naturalist need not examine every individual in either of the kingdoms of nature, in order to determine the character and qualities of all its species. Nor is it necessary to read all Chinese books before you venture to form an opinion respecting the literature of this nation. It is requisite, however, to know what works exist, and also to know something of the circumstances under which they were written, before sentence be pronounced on their respective merits.

China is full of books, and schools, and colleges. New authors are continually springing up, though comparatively few of them gain much celebrity. The press is active, and the traffic in books is a lucrative and most honorable branch of trade. Individuals have their libraries, and government its collections. Of these there are catalogues, some of which contain simply the titles of books with the names of their authors; but others, in addition to the titles and names, give brief notices of their contents, intimating in few words what each work contains. Of the imperial library at Peking, there are catalogues in both these forms. A selection of authors from one of them, while it may serve as a guide for the student in collecting a library, will at the same time afford valuable data for forming an opinion regarding the merits, variety, and extent of Chinese literature.

## IX. STUDENT'S LIBRARY.

THAT catalogue of books in the imperial library—noticed in the third Annual Report of the Society for the Diffusion of Useful Knowledge in China—is probably one of the best ever published. It is called Yam ting, Sz' Fú tsün Shü Tsung Muk, 欽定四庫全書總目 General Catalogue of all the Books in the Four Libraries, [published] by Imperial Authority. This catalogue is in itself a very valuable work, comprised in one hundred and twelve duodecimo volumes of 140 or 150 pages each. As indicated by its title, the works enumerated in the catalogue are arranged into four great departments, which are subdivided into sections. From the many works comprised in each section, the names of only a few can here be enumerated. Such is the character of the titles of Chinese books that it is hardly practicable in all cases to translate them, and therefore in the following list the titles have sometimes been literally translated, in other instances, an equivalent has been substituted.

### First Division.

### KING PÒ, 經部 CLASSICAL WRITINGS.

| §1. BOOK OF CHANGES. | 易類 | *Yik Lui.* |
|---|---|---|
| 1. Tsz'hiá's Memoir on the Book of Changes, in eleven chapters. By Pu Tsz'hiá. | 子夏易傳十一卷卜子夏撰 | Tsz' há Yik Chün, shap yat kün. Puk Tsz' há chán. |
| 2. Commentary on Chau's Book of Changes, in ten chapters. By Wáng Pei of Wei (i. e. of the dynasty Wei). | 周易註十卷魏王弼撰 | Chau Yik Chü, shap kün. Ngai Wóng Pak chán. |
| 3. The original meaning of Chau's Book of Changes, in twelve chapters. By the philosopher Chü of Sung. | 周易本義十二卷宋朱子撰 | Chau Yik pún í, shap í kün. Sung Chü tsz' chán. |

§1. The Yi King is the oldest and most admired literary work extant among the Chinese. The number of treatises on it of various kinds, such as memoirs, commentaries, &c., enumerated in the imperial catalogue, is about 1450. The Yi King treats of general philosophy as supposed to have been taught by Fuhí. By some European writers it has been called a "book of riddles."—The word *kün*, here rendered *chapter*, is usually an arbitrary division, and varies in length from 20 to 100 and more pages, and may be translated chapter, book, part, or section, according to its relative length, and the character of the work in hand.

H

| | | |
|---|---|---|
| 4. Treatise on the Diagrams in the Book of Changes, in three chapters. By Wú Jinkie of Sung. | 易圖說三卷宋吳仁傑撰 | Yik Tò Shüt, sám kün. Sung 'Ng Yan kít chán. |
| §2. Book of Records. | 書類 | *Shü Lui.* |
| 5. Complete Exposition of the Ancient Records, in forty chapters. By Lin Chíkí of Sung. | 尙書全解四十卷宋林之奇撰 | Shéung Shü tsün kái, sz' shap kün. Sung Lam Chí kí chán. |
| 6. Treatise on the Book of Records, in thirty-five chapters. By Lü Tsúhien of Sung. | 書說三十五卷宋呂祖謙撰 | Shü shüt, sám shap 'ng kün. Sung Lü Tsò hím chán. |
| 7. Geographical Researches in the nine ancient provinces, in three chapters. By Sun Chingtsi of the reigning dynasty. | 九州山水考三卷國朝孫承澤撰 | Kau Chau shán shui Háu, sám kün. Kwók chíú Sün Shing chák chán. |
| 8. The Meanings of the Book of Records compared, in six chapters. By Kiáng Cháusi of the reigning dynasty. | 書經參義六卷國朝姜兆錫撰 | Shü King tsám Í, luk kün. Kwók chíú Kéung Chíú sik chán. |
| §3. Book of Odes. | 詩類 | *Shí Lui.* |
| 9. The true Meaning of Máu's Book of Odes, in forty chapters. By Máu Hang of Hán. | 毛詩正義四十卷漢毛亨撰 | Mò Shí ching í, sz' shap kün. Hón Mò Hang chán. |
| 10. Miscellaneous Memoirs on the Book of Odes, in twenty chapters. By Sú Chi of Sung. | 詩集傳二十卷宋蘇轍撰 | Shí tsap Chün, í shap kün. Sung Sú Chít chán. |
| 11. Geographical Researches on the Book of Odes, in six chapters. By Hwáng Yinglun of Sung. | 詩地理考六卷宋黃應麟撰 | Shí Tí lí Háu, luk kün. Sung Wóng Ying lun chán. |
| 12. Researches respecting the birds, beasts, plants, and trees mentioned in Máu's Book of Odes, in twenty chapters. By Wú Yü of Ming. | 毛詩鳥獸艸木考二十卷明吳雨撰 | Mò Shí níú, shau, tsò, muk, Háu, í shap kün. Míng 'Ng Yü chán. |
| §4. Book of Rites. | 禮類 | *Lai Lui.* |
| 13. Critical Exposition of Chau's Ritual, in forty chapters. By Wáng Cháuyü of Sung. | 周禮詳解四十卷宋王昭禹撰 | Chau Lai tséung kái, sz' shap kün. Sung Wóng Chíú yü chán. |

§2. To the foreign student the Shü King is much more interesting than the Yi King. Its moral sentiments are the purest and best in the language.

§3. These writings, in point of excellence, are second only to the Shü King. They are short, sententious, and often very hard to understand.

§4. The writings on ceremonial observances are exceedingly voluminous, and though much studied by the Chinese, are but little valued by foreign students. They exercise great influence in forming the manners of the people.

| | | |
|---|---|---|
| 14. Miscellaneous observations on Rites and Ceremonies, in seventeen chapters. By lord Ngau Kí of Yuen. | 儀禮集說十七<br>卷元敖繼公撰 | Í Lai tsap shüt, shap tsat kün. Yün Ngò Kai kung chán. |
| 15. Miscellaneous Remarks on the Ceremonial Records, in one hundred and sixty chapters. By Wei Tei of Sung. | 禮記集說一百<br>六十卷宋衛湜<br>撰 | Lai Kí tsap shüt, yat pák luk shap kün. Sung Wai Tai chán. |
| 16. General Researches respecting the Five Ceremonies, in two hundred and sixty-two chapters. By Tsin Hwuitien of the reigning dynasty. | 五禮通考二百<br>六十二卷國朝<br>秦蕙田撰 | 'Ng Lai Tung Háu, í pák luk shap í kün. Kwók chíú Tsun Wai tín chán. |
| §5. SPRING AND AUTUMN ANNALS. | 春秋類 | *Chun Tsau Lui.* |
| 17. The correct meaning of Tsò's Memoir on the Spring and Autumn Annals, in sixty chapters. | 春秋左傳正義<br>六十卷 | Chun Tsau Tsó Chüm ching í, luk shap kün. |
| 18. Commentary upon Kungyáng's Memoir on the Spring and Autumn Annals, in twenty-eight chapters. | 春秋公羊傳注<br>疏二十八卷 | Chun Tsau Kung yéung Chün chü shó, í shap pát kün. |
| 19. Commentary upon Kuliáng's Memoir on the Spring and Autumn Annals, in twelve chapters. | 春秋穀梁傳注<br>疏二十卷 | Chun Tsau Kuk léung Chün chü shó, í shap kün. |
| §6. FILIAL DUTY. | 孝經類 | *Háu King Lui.* |
| 20. The Correct Meaning of the classic Filial Duty, in three chapters, with Comments by Yuentsung the illustrious emperor of Táng. | 孝經正義三卷<br>唐元宗明皇帝<br>御註 | Háu King Ching Í, sám kün, Tóng Yün tsung ming wóng tai yü chü. |
| 21. A clear Exposition of the ancient text of the classic Filial Duty, in one chapter. By an anonymous writer. | 古文孝經指解<br>一卷不著編輯<br>者名氏 | Kú man Háu King chí kái, yat kün. Pat chü pín tsap ché ming shí. |
| §7. GENERAL OBSERVATIONS ON THE FIVE CLASSICS. | 五經總義類 | *'Ng King tsung í Lui.* |
| 22. Writings Explanatory of the classical and canonical Books, in thirty chapters. By Lu Yuenláng of Táng. | 經典釋文三十<br>卷唐陸元朗撰 | King Tín shik man, sám shap kün. Tóng Luk Yün lóng chán. |

§5. These annals were compiled by Confucius. Brief notices of them, and of other sacred writings of the Chinese, are to be found in chapter I., section 3, of the Chrestomathy: see pages 13, 14, and 15.

§6. The Hiáu King is comprised in a very few pages; it is however highly valued, and much read. Its object is indicated by its title.

§7. Under this head, the Five Classics are treated of as a whole, the several works being considered collectively, in the same manner as the Four Books are usually regarded as one work.

| | | |
|---|---|---|
| 23. The Plates of the Six Classics, in six books. By Yáng Kiá of the Sung dynasty. | 六經圖六卷宋楊甲撰 | Luk King Tò, luk kün. Sung Yéung Káp chán. |
| §8. The Four Books. | 四書類 | *Sz' Shü Lui.* |
| 24. Various Inquiries on the Four Books, in thirty-nine chapters. By the philosopher Chü of Sung. | 四書或問三十九卷宋朱子撰 | Sz' Shü wák Man, sám shap kau kün. Sung Chü tsz' chán. |
| 25. Researches respecting the persons and things mentioned in the Four Books, in forty chapters, with a supplement in eight chapters. By Sie Yingkí. | 四書人物考四十卷補考八卷明薛應旂撰 | Sz' Shü yan mat Háu, sz' shap kün; Pò Háu pát kün. Ming Sít Ying kí chán. |
| 26. Exposition of the Four Books, made easy for young students, in ten chapters. By Cháu Sz'yáu of the reigning dynasty. | 四書初學易知解十卷國朝鄒嗣堯撰 | Sz' Shü Ch'ó Hók í chí kái, shap kün. Kwók chíú Chíú Sz' yíú chán. |
| 27. The Meaning of the Four Books explained by clauses and sentences, in nineteen chapters. By Fán Yingting of the reigning dynasty. | 四書句讀釋義十九卷國朝范凝鼎撰 | Sz' Shü Kü Tau shik í, shap kau kün. Kwók chíú Fán Ying ting chán. |
| §9. Musical Works. | 樂類 | *Ngók Lui.* |
| 28. Writings on Music, in two hundred chapters. By Chin Yáng of Sung. | 樂書二百卷宋陳暘撰 | Ngók shü, í pák kün. Sung Chan Yéung chán. |
| 29. Musical Pieces for the scholar's lute, in three chapters. By Wáng Háujen of Ming. | 琴譜三卷明汪浩然撰 | Kam Pò, sám kün. Ming Wóng Hò ín chán. |
| 30. Musical canons, in thirty-six chapters. By Hwáng Tsó of Ming. | 樂典三十六卷明黃佐撰 | Ngók Tín, sám shap luk kün. Ming Wóng Tsó chán. |
| 31. Treatise on Dancing, in twelve chapters. By Cháng Mí of Ming. | 舞志十二卷明張敉撰 | Mò Chí, shap í kün. Ming Chéung Mí chán. |
| §10. Normal Education. | 小學類 | *Síú Hók Lui.* |
| 32. A Commentary on the Book of Elegances, in eleven chapters, commented upon by Kwó Pó of Tsin. | 爾雅註疏十一卷晉郭璞註 | Í Ngá Chü shó, shap yat kün. Tsun Kwók Puk chü. |

§9. In chapter X., sec. 2, the subject of music is treated of at considerable length, and the *mò*, or dancing of the Chinese, is also there spoken of; see page 356.

§10. The *'Rh Yé* is a work which now commonly appears in three volumes, quarto, embellished with engravings, and is apparently an abridgment of that by Kwó Pó. It is highly valued by the Chinese: 'it is a kind of dictionary.'

| | | |
|---|---|---|
| 33. Explanation of the Names of Things, in eight chapters. By Liú Hí of Hán. | 釋名八卷漢劉熙撰 | Shik ming, pát kün. Hon Lau Hí chán. |
| 34. Treatise on the Meaning of Words, in thirty-three chapters. By Hü Shin of Hán. | 說文解字三十卷漢許愼撰 | Shüt Man Kái tsz', sám shap kün. Hón Hü Shan chán. |
| 35. Classification of Words, in forty-five chapters. The original work written by Sz'má Kwáng. | 類篇四十五卷舊本題司馬光撰 | Lui Pín, sz' shap 'ng kün. Kau pún tai Sz' má Kwóng chán. |
| 36. The six Sources for Derivation of Words, in thirty-three chapters. By Tái Tung of Yuen. | 六書故三十三卷元戴侗撰 | Luk Shü Kú, sám shap sám kün. Yün Tái Tung chán. |
| 37. A Dictionary, in five chapters. By Lí Wanchung of Yuen. | 字鑑五卷元李文仲撰 | Tsz' Kám, 'ng kün. Yün Lí Man chung chán. |
| 38. Kánghí's Dictionary, in forty-two chapters. | 康熙字典四十二卷 | Hóng hí Tsz' tín, sz' shap í kün. |
| 39. Treatise on the Literature of Western Scholars. By Kin Nikó of the Ming dynasty. | 西儒耳目資明金尼閣撰 | Sai Yü í muk Tsz'. Ming Kam Ní kók chán. |

## Second Division.

### SZ' PÒ, 史部 HISTORICAL WRITINGS.

| §1. NATIONAL HISTORIES. | 正史類 | *Ching sz' Lui.* |
|---|---|---|
| 40. Historical Records, in one hundred and thirty chapters. By Sz'má Tsien of the Hán dynasty. | 史記一百三十卷漢司馬遷撰 | Sz' Kí, yat pák sám shap kün. Hón Sz' má Tsín chán. |
| 41. The Obscurities of the Historical Records investigated, in thirty chapters. By Sz'má Ching of Táng. | 史記索隱三十卷唐司馬貞撰 | Sz' Kí Sòk Yan, sám shap kün. Tóng Sz' má Ching chán. |

The works arranged under the head of *Siú Hók Lui* are rudimental, having reference to explanations of things, and the words or names by which they are denoted. The *Shwó Wan* and *Lú Shü* are very often quoted in the Dictionary of Kánghí: the object of the first is to explain the orthography of words by an exhibition of their component parts: the object of the second is to show whence words are derived, and refers them all to six general principles of derivation. Kánghí's Dictionary is in general use throughout the empire, and is a very valuable work.

§1. The historical writings of the Chinese are very prolix, often extending through many minute and uninteresting details. Sometimes however they are concise, animated, and graphic, in an admirable degree.

I

| | | |
|---|---|---|
| 42. History of the Hán dynasty, in one hundred and twenty chapters. By Pán Kò of Hán. | 漢書一百二十卷漢班固撰 | Hón Shü, yat pák í shap kün. Hón Pán Kú chán. |
| 43. History of the Three Kingdoms, in sixty-five chapters. By Chin Shau of Tsin. | 三國志六十五卷晉陳壽撰 | Sám Kwok Chí, luk shap 'ng kün. Tsun Chan Shau chán. |
| §2. ANNALS. | 編年類 | *Pín nín Lui.* |
| 44. General Mirror to aid in Government; two hundred and ninety-four chapters. By Sz'má Kwáng of Sung. | 資治通鑑二百九十四卷宋司馬光撰 | Tsz' Chí Tung Kám, í pák kau shap sz' kün. Sung Sz' má Kwóng chán. |
| 45. An extended Supplement to the General Mirror for aiding Government, in five hundred and twenty chapters. By Lí Shau of Sung. | 續資治通鑑長編五百二十卷宋李燾撰 | Tsuk Tsz' Chí Tung Kám chéung Pín, 'ng pák í shap kün. Sung Lí Shau chán. |
| §3. COMPLETE RECORDS. | 紀事本末類 | *Kí sz' pún mút Lui.* |
| 46. Narrative of the Subjugation of the Two Golden streams [in the reign of Kienlung], in one hundred and fifty-two chapters; by imperial authority. | 欽定平定兩金川方略一百五十二卷 | Yam ting Ping ting Léung Kam chün fóng Léuk, yat pák 'ng shap í kün. |
| 47. Narratives respecting Formosa, in seventy chapters; published by imperial authority. | 欽定臺灣紀略七十卷 | Yam ting Toi wán Kí Léuk, tsat shap kün. |
| 48. History Unraveled, in one hundred and sixty chapters. By Má Siú of the reigning dynasty. | 繹史一百六十卷國朝馬驌撰 | Yik Shí, yat pák luk shap kün. Kwok chíú Má Sau chán. |
| §4. SEPARATE RECORDS. | 別史類 | *Pit sz' Lui.* |
| 49. Ancient Records, in sixty chapters. By Sú Chi of Sung. | 古史六十卷宋蘇轍撰 | Kú Sz', luk shap kün. Sung Sú Chít chán. |
| 50. A Universal History, in two hundred chapters. By Ching Tsiáu of Sung. | 通志二百卷宋鄭樵撰 | Tung Chí, í pák kün. Sung Ching Tsíú chán. |

42, 43. There are distinct histories of every dynasty, usually compiled from the records of the government, and which have, of course, the best claim to authenticity. The History of the Three Kingdoms is very much admired by the Chinese, chiefly for its *style*, for in its narrative it is admitted that the writer has not restricted himself to simple facts.

§2. These annals are for the most part the production of private individuals, drawn from the general histories. Sz'má Kwáng's annals form a highly finished and one of the best digested histories that Chinese scholars have produced.

§3. Under this head are narratives of distinct events, traced from their beginning to their end. The History Unraveled is a work of great labor and highly valued.

| | | |
|---|---|---|
| 51. A Supplement to the Universal History, by imperial authority, in five hundred and twenty-seven chapters. | 欽定續通志五百二十七卷 | Yam ting, Tsuk Tung Chí 'ng pák í shap tsat kün. |
| § 5. MIXED HISTORIES. | 雜史類 | *Tsap Sz' Lui.* |
| 52. National Sayings, in two hundred and eleven chapters. By Wei Cháu of Wú. | 國語二十一卷吳韋昭注 | Kwók Yü, í shap yat kün. 'Ng Wai Chíú chü. |
| 53. Miscellanies of the Shady-Hill Establishment in one hundred chapters. By Wáng Shíching of the Ming dynasty. | 弇山堂別集一百卷明王世貞撰 | Ím Shán Tóng pít tsap, yat pák kün. Ming Wóng Shai ching chán. |
| 54. Historical accounts of Corea, in one volume. By I' Hien of Ming. | 朝鮮紀事一卷明倪謙撰 | Chíú sín Kí sz', yat kün. Ming Ngai Hím chán. |
| 55. History of the Country of Tsú, in sixty chapters. By Liú Táunán of Ming. | 楚紀六十卷明廖道南撰 | Tsò Kí, luk shap kün. Ming Líú Tò nam chán. |
| §6. OFFICIAL PAPERS. | 詔令奏議類 | *Chíú ling tsau í Lui.* |
| 56. Imperial proclamations and orders of Táng, in one hundred and thirty chapters. | 唐大詔令集一百三十卷 | Tóng tái chíú ling tsap, yat pák sám shap kün. |
| 57. Memorials to the Throne from high ministers of state, in one hundred and fifty chapters. | 諸臣奏議一百五十卷 | Chü shan tsau í, yat pák 'ng shap kün. |
| 58. Memorials of celebrated ministers of state during successive dynasties, in three hundred and fifty chapters. | 歷代名臣奏議三百五十卷 | Lik toi ming shan tsau í, sám pák 'ng shap kün. |
| §7. MEMOIRS. | 傳記類 | *Chün Ki Lui.* |
| 59. Memoirs of Confucius, in five chapters. The original work by Hú Shunchi of the Sung dynasty. | 孔子編年五卷舊本題宋胡舜陟撰 | Hung tsz' pín nín, 'ng kün. Kau pún tai Sung U' Shun chik chán. |
| 60. Memoirs of Distinguished Ladies in ancient times, in seven chapters; with a Supplement to the same in one chapter. By Liú Hiáng of the Hán dynasty. | 古列女傳七卷續列女傳一卷漢劉向撰 | Kú lít Nü Chün, tsat kün; tsuk lít Nü Chün, yat kün. Hón Lau Héung chán. |

§6. These official papers comprise a large variety of subjects, and are perhaps among the most authentic portions of the historical writings of the Chinese.

§7. There are extant separate memoirs, or biographical narratives, of almost all distinguished persons of every age; they afford one of the best sources for studying the national character of the Chinese. The lives of queens, empresses, and other females, have been ably written.

| | | |
|---|---|---|
| 61. Narrative of a Western Embassy, in one volume. By Liú Yu of the Yuen dynasty. | 西使記一卷元劉郁撰 | Sai Sz' Kí, yat kün. Yün Lau Yuk chán. |
| §8. Historical Excerpta. | 史鈔類 | *Sz' Sháu Lui.* |
| 62. The Seventeen Histories in complete and distinct parts, comprised in two hundred and seventy-three chapters. By Lü Tsúkien of the Sung dynasty. | 十七史詳節二百七十三卷宋呂祖謙撰 | Shap tsat Sz' Tséung Tsit, í pák tsat shap sám kün. Sung Lui Tsò hím chán. |
| 63. Conversations on Ancient and Modern affairs, in twelve chapters. By Wáng Yingkiáu of Ming. | 古今彝語十二卷明汪應蛟撰 | Kú Kam í Yü, shap i kun. Ming Wóng Ying káu chán. |
| 64. Historical Woof, in three hundred and thirty chapters. By Chin Yunsi of the reigning dynasty. | 史緯三百三十卷國朝陳允錫撰 | Sz' Wai, sám pák sám shap kün. Kwok chíú Chan Wan sik chán. |
| §9. Records of neighboring States. | 載記類 | *Tsoi Ki Lui.* |
| 65. Account of Foreign States, in ten chapters. By Fán Chó of the Táng dynasty. | 蠻書十卷唐樊綽撰 | Mán Shü, shap kün. Tong Fán Chéuk chán. |
| 66. Account of the Uncultivated parts of Kiángnán, in ten chapters. By Lung Kwan of Sung. | 江南野史十卷宋龍袞撰 | Kóng nám Yé Sz', shap kün. Sung Lung Kwan chán. |
| 67. An Historical Narrative of Corea, in six chapters. | 朝鮮史略六卷 | Chíú sín Sz' Léuk, luk kün. |
| §10. Of Times and Seasons. | 時令類 | *Shí Ling Lui.* |
| 68. An Extensive Record of the seasons of the Year, in four chapters. By Chin Yuentsing of Sung. | 歲時廣記四卷宋陳元靚撰 | Sui shí Kwóng Kí, sz' kün. Sung Chan Yün tsing chán. |
| 69. Miscellaneous Explanations of the four seasons, in four chapters. By Lí Tái of Ming. | 四時氣候集解四卷明李泰撰 | Sz' Shí Hí Hau tsap kái, sz' kün. Ming Lí Tái chán. |
| §11. Geographical Treatises. | 地理類 | *Tí Li Lui.* |
| 70. Description of the whole Universe when at peace, in one hundred and ninety-three chapters. By Ngó Sz' of the Sung dynasty. | 太平寰宇記一百九十三卷宋樂史撰 | Tái ping wán Yü Kí, yat pák kau shap sám kün. Sung Ngok Sz' chán. |

§8. There is extant another work, or a continuation of the seventeen historians, which is called the *twenty-one histories*. It is often referred to and much valued.

§9. These refer to states and tribes which are in part or entirely dependent on the Chinese and extend of course only to those who are on, or within, their borders. The mountain tribes on the northwest of Kwángtung come under this head.

| | | |
|---|---|---|
| 71. A Complete Statistical account of the Empire under the reigning dynasty, in five hundred chapters. | 大清一統志五百卷 | Tái Tsing yat Tung Chí, 'ng pák kün. |
| 72. A full Statistical Account of the province of Canton, in sixty-four chapters. By Hó Julun and others of the reigning dynasty. | 廣東通志六十四卷國朝郝玉麟等撰 | Kwóng tung Tung Chí, luk shap sz' kün. Kwók chíú Kók Yuk lun tang chán. |
| 73. Memorials and other papers on the Management of Canals, in four chapters. By Kin Pú of the reigning dynasty. | 治河奏績書四卷國朝靳輔撰 | Chí Hó tsau chik Shü, sz' kün. Kwók chíú Kan Pò chán. |
| 74. Researches respecting the origin of the Mántchous, in twenty chapters, by imperial authority. | 欽定滿洲源流考二十卷 | Yam ting Mún chau iin lau Háu, í shap kün. |
| 75. A Geographical Account of the *Lòfau* hills, in twelve chapters. By Táu Kingyi of the reigning dynrsty. | 羅浮山志十二卷國朝陶敬益撰 | Ló fau Shán Chí, shap í kün. Kwók chíú Tau King yik chán. |
| §12. On the Magistracy. | 官職類 | *Kún Chik Lui.* |
| 76. The six Canons of Táng, in thirty chapters. By Yuentsung the illustrious emperor of the Táng dynasty. | 唐六典三十卷唐元宗明皇帝御撰 | Tóng luk Tín, sám shap kün. Tóng Yün tsung ming wong tai yü chán. |
| 77. Drafts of documents of the Board of Rites, in one hundred and ten chapters. | 禮部志稾一百十卷 | Lai Pò Chí Kò, yat pák shap kün. |
| 78. A Description of the Magistracy in every age and of every rank, in sixty-three chapters; by imperial authority. | 欽定歷代職官表六十三卷 | Yam ting lik toi chik kún píú, luk shap sám kün. |
| 79. A Golden Mirror for the magistracy, in twelve chapters. By Niú Tiensu of the reigning dynasty. | 百僚金鑑十二卷國朝牛天宿撰 | Pák líú. Kam. Kám, shap í kün. Kwók chíú Ngau Tín suk chán. |
| §13. On the Constitution. | 政書類 | *Ching shü Lui.* |
| 80. A complete Governmental Directory, in two hundred chapters. By Tò Yiú of Táng. | 通典二百卷唐杜佑撰 | Tung Tín, í pák kün. Tóng Tò Yau chán. |

§11. Number 71 is the best statistical work extant on the Chinese empire; and No. 72 is one of the best for the province of Canton. There are similar works for all the provinces, departments, and districts of the empire, the whole forming a body of works on statistics unequaled for its extent and minuteness in any country. No. 75 is a popular work: the Lòfau hills are in this province, about a hundred miles northwest from the city of Canton.

J

| | | |
|---|---|---|
| 81. Complete Antiquarian Researches, in three hundred and forty-eight chapters. By Má Tuánlin of Yuen. | 文獻通考三百四十八卷元馬端臨撰 | Man Hín Tung Háu, sám pák sz' shap pát kün. Yün Má Tün lam chán. |
| 82. Supplement to the Complete Antiquarian Researches, in two hundred and fifty-two chapters. By imperial authority. | 欽定續文獻通考二百五十二卷 | Yam ting Tsuk Man Hín Tung Háu, í pák 'ng shap í kün. |
| 83. Collected Statutes of the Great Pure dynasty, in one hundred chapters. By imperial authority. | 欽定大清會典一百卷 | Yam ting Tá Tsing Úi Tín, yat pák kün. |
| 84. Complete Statistical Account of the eight Banners first collection, in two hundred and fifty chapters. | 八旗通志初集二百五十卷 | Pát Kí Tung Chí chó tsap, í pák 'ng shap kün. |
| 85. Laws and Statutes of the Great Pure dynasty, in forty-seven chapters. | 大清律例四十七卷 | Tái Tsing Lut Lai, sz' shap tsat kün. |
| § 14. Books of Reference. | 目錄類 | *Muk Luk Lui.* |
| 86. Chícháí's Catalogue of Books, with explanations of their contents, in twenty-two chapters. By Chin Chinsun of Sung. | 直齋書錄解題二十二卷宋陳振孫撰 | Chik chái Shü luk Kái tai, í shap í kün. Sung Chan Chan sün chán. |
| 87. Catalogue of Books belonging to the house of *Tsienking*, in thirty-two chapters. By Hwáng Yütsi of the reigning dynasty. | 千頃堂書目三十二卷國朝黃虞稷撰 | *Tsín king* tóng Shü Muk, sám shap í kün. Kwók chíú Wóng Yü tsik chán. |
| § 15. Criticisms on History. | 史評類 | *Sz' Ping Lui.* |
| 88. Miscellaneous Remarks on the Three Kingdoms, in two volumes. By Táng King of Sung. | 三國雜事二卷宋唐庚撰 | Sám Kwók tsap sz', í kün. Sung Tóng King chán. |
| 89. Observations on Men and Things, in thirty-four volumes. By Ching Hien of Ming. | 人物論三十四卷明鄭賢撰 | Yan Mat Lun, sám shap sz' kün. Ming Ching Ín chán. |
| 90. Táisz' Observations on the Laws, in one hundred chapters. By Cháng Chísiáng of Ming. | 太史史例一百卷明張之象撰 | Tái sz' Sz' Lai, yat pák kün. Ming Chéung Chí tséung chán. |

§ 13. The works arranged under this head exhibit and explain all the forms and duties of the government in all its numerous branches. For an account of No. 83, and extracts from it, see page 564 and sequel; for No. 85, see page 533, &c.

§ 14. These are apparently similar to the catalogue of the imperial library, from which this selection is made.

## Third Division.

### TSZ' PÒ, 子部 PROFESSIONAL WRITINGS.

| § 1. Philosophical Works. | 儒家類 | *Yü Ká Lui.* |
|---|---|---|
| 91. Domestic Sayings of Confucius, in ten chapters, with comments by Wáng Su of Wei. | 孔子家語十卷<br>魏王肅註 | Hung tsz' Ká Yü, shap kün. Ngai Wòng Suk chü. |
| 92. Learning, of Emperors, in eight chapters. By Fán Tsúyü of Sung. | 帝學八卷宋范<br>祖禹撰 | Tai Hók, pát kün. Sung Fán Tsò yü chán. |
| 93. A Miscellaneous Commentary on the Primary Lessons, by the philosopher Chü of Sung. | 小學集註六卷<br>宋朱子撰 | Síú Hók tsap chü, luk kün. Sung Chü tsz' chán. |
| 94. Conversations of the philosopher Chü, in one hundred and forty chapters. | 朱子語類一百<br>四十卷 | Chü tsz' Yü lui, yat pák sz' shap sz' kün. |
| 95. Notes on Reading, in sixty-one chapters. By Chin Tsiú of the Sung dynasty. | 讀書記六十一<br>卷宋眞德秀撰 | Tuk shü Kí, luk shap yat kün. Sung Chan Tak sau chán. |
| 96. Treatise on the Mind, in one volume. By Chin Tsiú of Sung. | 心經一卷宋眞<br>德秀撰 | Sam King, yat kün. Sung Chan Tak sau chán. |
| 97. Rules for Reading, by the philosopher Chü, in four chapters. Compiled by Cháng Hung and Tsí Hí of Sung. | 朱子讀書法四<br>卷宋張洪齊熙<br>同編 | Chü tsz' Tuk shü Fát, sz' kün. Sung Chéung Hung Tsai Hí tung pín. |
| 98. A full and complete Treatise on the Passions, in seventeen chapters. | 性理大全書十<br>七卷 | Sing Lí tái tsün shü, shap tsat kün. |
| 99. Treatise on Filial Duty for women, in one volume. By lady Ching of Táng. | 女孝經一卷唐<br>鄭氏撰 | Nü Háu King, yat kün. Tóng Ching shí chán. |
| 100. Plates and Remarks explanatory of the Great Extreme, in fourteen chapters. By Wáng Tsz'hwái of the reigning dynasty. | 太極圖說論十<br>四卷國朝王嗣<br>槐撰 | Tái Kik Tò Shüt Lun, shap sz' kün. Kwók Chíú Wóng Tsz' wái chán. |

§ 1. The *yü ká* is the school of the literati, comprising all the wise and the learned men of the nation, who follow the principles of Confucius, their great master. Their writings are numerous; and in point of excellence are second only to the ancient classics. The writings of some of the followers of the sage are such as would probably be preferred to those of Confucius by all and any but Chinese.

| | | |
|---|---|---|
| 101. Education of females, in six chapters. By Lán Tingyuen (or Luchow) of the reigning dynasty. | 女學六卷國朝藍鼎元編 | Nü Hók, luk kün. Kwók chíú Lám Ting yün pín. |
| §2. MILITARY AUTHORS. | 兵家類 | *Ping Ká Lui.* |
| 102. Writings on Defences of Cities, in four chapters. | 守城錄四卷 | Shau shing Luk, sz' kün. |
| 103. Military Records, in four chapters. By Hó Liáng-chin of Ming. | 陣紀四卷明何良臣撰 | Chan Kí, sz' kün. Ming Ho Léung shan chán. |
| 104. Memoirs of a hundred Generals, in one hundred chapters. By Cháng Yü of Sung. | 百將傳一百卷宋張預撰 | Pák Tséung Chün, yat pák kün. Sung Chéung Yü chán. |
| 105. Soldier's Mirror, in eleven chapters. By Tang Tinglò of the reigning dynasty. | 兵鏡十一卷國朝鄧廷羅撰 | Ping King, shap yat kün. Kwok chíú Tang Ting lò chán. |
| §3. WRITERS ON LAW. | 法家類 | *Fát Ká Lui.* |
| 106. The original works of the philosopher Kwán, in twenty-four chapters. By Kwán Chung. | 管子二十四卷舊本題管仲撰 | Kún tsz', í shap sz' kün. Kau pún tai Kún Chung chán. |
| 107. Requisites for the proper execution of punishment. By Páng Tiensi of Yuen. | 政刑類要一卷元彭天錫撰 | Ching Ying lui íú, yat kün. Yün Páng Tín sik chán. |
| §4. WRITERS ON HUSBANDRY. | 農家類 | *Nung Ká Lui.* |
| 108. The chief Essentials regarding Husbandry, Silk, Clothes, and Food, in two chapters. By Lú Mingshen of the Yuen dynasty. | 農桑衣食撮要二卷元魯明善撰 | Nung Song, í shik tsüt íú, í kün. Yün Lú Ming shín chán. |
| 109. A complete Work on Agricultural Operations, in sixty chapters. By Shü Kwángkí of Ming. | 農政全書六十卷明徐光啟撰 | Nung Ching tsün shü, luk shap kün. Ming Chü Kwóng kai chán. |
| 110. Plates and Odes on Tillage and Weaving. By Lú Chau of the Sung dynasty. | 耕織圖詩宋樓璹撰 | King Chik Tò Shí. Sung Lau Chau chán. |
| §5. MEDICAL WRITERS. | 醫家類 | *Í Ká Lui.* |
| 111. The Plain Questions of Hwángtí, in twenty-four chapters, commented on by Wáng Ping of Táng. | 黃帝素問二十四卷唐王冰註 | Wóng tai sú Man, í shap sz' kün. Tong Wóng Ping chü. |

§2. The military school, or *ping ká*, is respectable only for its numbers. The writings of its professors are worthless.

§3. The number of writers on law is not large; their works are occupied with the history of the laws and with the principles involved in them.

§4. For the views of the Chinese on agriculture, see chap. IX, *passim*.

| | | |
|---|---|---|
| 112. Treatise on Difficult Cases, in two chapters. By Tsin Yuejin of Chau. | 難經二卷周秦越人撰 | Nán King, í kün. Chau Tsun Yüt yan chán. |
| 113. Rules to aid in General Practice, in four hundred and twenty-six chapters. By Chau Ting and Wáng Su of Ming. | 普濟方四百二十六卷明周定王橚撰 | Pò Tsai Fóng, sz' pák í shap luk kün. Ming Chau Ting, Wóng Suk chán. |
| 114. Treatise on the Buffalo, in three chapters. By Tsáu Fú of Táng. | 水牛經三卷唐造父撰 | Shui Ngau King, sám kün. Tóng Tsò Fú chán. |
| 115. Veterinary Miscellany, in four chapters; with a supplementary work in one chapter. By Yü Jin and Yü Ki of Ming. | 療馬集四卷附錄一卷明喻仁喻傑同撰 | Líú Má tsap, sz' kün, fú luk yat kün. Ming Yü Yan, Yü Kít tung chán. |
| §6. Astronomical and Mathematical Writers. | 天文算法類 | *Tín Man Sün Fát Lui.* |
| 116. New Treatise on the laws of Celestial Phenomena, in three chapters. By Sú Sung of Sung. | 新儀象法要三卷宋蘇頌撰 | San Í Tséung Fát íú, sám kün. Sung Sú Tsung chán. |
| 117. A new work on Mathematics, in one hundred chapters. By Sü Kwángkí and the European Lunghwámin and others under the Ming dynasty. | 新法算書一百卷明徐光啟及西洋人龍華民等撰 | San Fát Sün shü, yat pák kün. Ming Tsü Kwóng kai kap Sai yéung yan *Lung-wá-man* tang chán. |
| §7. Magical Calculations. | 術數類 | *Shut Shò Lui.* |
| 118. Treatise on the Great Original, in ten chapters. By Yáng Hiung of Hán. | 太元經十卷漢揚雄撰 | Tái Yün King, shap kün. Hón Yéung Hung chán. |
| 119. On the Site for a House, two chapters: according to the original memoir called the House of Hwángtí. | 宅經二卷舊本題日黃帝宅經 | Chák King, í kün. Kau pún tai üt Wóng tai Chák King. |
| 120. A Minute Inquiry into the Laws of Divination, in four chapters. By Hú Hü of the reigning dynasty. | 卜法詳考四卷國朝胡煦撰 | Puk Fát Tséung Háu, sz' kün. Kwok chíú Ü Kü chán. |

§5. The works on medicine are numerous and copious, but they have not been much read by foreigners. For a brief account of the practice and science of medicine among the Chinese, see chapter XVI., page 497.

§6. In this section are found several works which have been prepared by the aid of foreigners, chiefly the Jesuits connected with the Astronomical Board. The native works are not of much value.

§7. The works on magical calculations appear not to have been investigated by any foreigner, and it is not probable they ever will be. Some works under this head are published by imperial authority.

K

| | | |
|---|---|---|
| **§ 8. Fine Arts.** | **藝術類** | *Ngai Shut Lui.* |
| 121. Records of Distinguished Painters of successive ages. By Cháng Yenyuen of Táng. | 歷代名畫記十卷唐張彥遠撰 | Lik toi Ming Wá Kí, shap kün. Tóng Chéung Í'n yün chan. |
| 122. Siuenhó's Works on Writing, in twenty chapters. | 宣和書譜二十卷 | Sün wó shü Pò, í shap kün. |
| 123. A Collection of Seals, in eight chapters. By Chü Siánghien of the reigning dynasty. | 印典八卷國朝朱象賢撰 | Yan Tín, pát kün. Kwok chíú Chü Tséung ín chán. |
| 124. Extensive and Complete collection of Musical Pieces, in ten chapters. By Yáng Piáuching of Ming. | 琴譜大全十卷明楊表正撰 | Kam Pò Tái Tsün, shap kun. Ming Yéung Píú ching chán. |
| 125. Works on Archery, in four chapters. By Kú Yu of the Ming dynasty. | 射書四卷明顧煜撰 | Shé Shü, sz' kün. Ming Kú Yuk chán. |
| **§ 9. Collections.** | **譜錄類** | *Pò luk Lui.* |
| 126. The Student's Apparatus, in five chapters. By Sú Yikien of Sung. | 文房四譜五卷宋蘇易簡撰 | Man Fóng Sz' Pò, 'ng kun. Sung Sú Yik kán chán. |
| 127. Memoir on Tea, in three chapters. By Lu Yü of Táng. | 茶經三卷唐陸羽撰 | Chá King, sám kün. Tong Luk Yü chán. |
| 128. Memoir on the Wines of the northern hills. By Chü Yichung of the Sung dynasty. | 北山酒經三卷宋朱翼中撰 | Pak shán Tsau King, sám kün. Sung Chü Yik Chung chán. |
| 129. The most Important Things to be known in diet, in eight chapters. By Kú Ming of Yuen. | 飲食須知八卷元賈銘撰 | Yam Shik sü chí, pat kun. Yün Kú Ming chán. |
| 130. An Account of Insects, in ten chapters. By Shin Hungching of Ming. | 蟲天志十卷明沈宏正撰 | Chung Tín Chí, shap kun. Ming Sham Wing ching chán. |
| **§ 10. Miscellaneous Authors.** | **雜家類** | *Tsáp Ká Lui.* |
| 131. Notices of Men and Things, in three chapters. By Liú Sháu of Wei. | 人物志三卷魏劉邵撰 | Yan mat che, sán kün. Ngai Líú Shíú chán. |

§ 8. Chapter X, on the Liberal Arts, contains a summary view of the Chinese ideas on the fine arts. See page 353.

§ 9. The collections are divided into two parts, collections of manufactured things, and of natural productions: in the first are comprised coins, ink, &c.; in the second are included several branches of natural history. One of the best works on Natural History, however, is arranged under § 5, with the Medical Writers. It is the *Pún Ts'ò* by Lí Shíchan; an account of it is inserted on pages 436, and 508.

| | | |
|---|---|---|
| 132. General Observations on Manners and Customs, in ten chapters; with a supplement in one chapter. By Ying Sháu of Hán. | 風俗通義十卷<br>附錄一卷漢應<br>邵撰 | Fung Tsuk tung Í, shap kün, fú luk yat kün. Hon Ying Shíú chán. |
| 133. Stories about the Eastern deserts of Tsí, in twenty chapters. By Chau Mie of Sung. | 齊東野語二十<br>卷宋周密撰 | Tsai Tung Yé Yü, í shap kün. Sung Chau Mat chán. |
| 134. Ancient and modern Accounts of the Seas, in one hundred and forty-two chapters. By Lu Tsie of the Ming dynasty. | 古今說海一百<br>四十二卷明陸<br>楫編 | Kú Kam Shüt Hoi, yat pák sz' shap í kün. Ming Luk Yap pín. |
| 135. Verity and reasonableness of Christianity, in two chapters. By Matthew Ricci under the Ming dynasty. | 天主實義二卷<br>明利瑪竇撰 | Tín Chü Shat Í, í kün. Ming Lí Má tau chán. |
| §11. Encyclopædias. | 類書類 | *Lui Shü Lui.* |
| 136. Cursory Researches at the Mountain Hall, in two hundred and twenty-eight chapters, with twelve supplementary chapters. By Páng Táiyi of the Ming dynasty. | 山堂肆考二百<br>二十八卷補遺<br>十二卷明彭大<br>翼撰 | Shán Tóng sz' Háu, í pák í shap pát kün; pò wai shap í kün. Ming Páng Tái yik chán. |
| 137. The Remembrancer and Tonic Treasury, in four hundred and forty-four chapters. By imperial authority. | 御定佩文韻府<br>四百四十四卷 | Yü Ting Púi Man Wan Fú, sz' pák sz' shap sz' kün. |
| 138. The Great Classical Work of Yungló in twenty-two thousand eight hundred and seventy-seven chapters. | 永樂大典二萬<br>二千八百七十<br>七卷 | Wing lók Tái Tín, í mán í tsín pát pák tsat shap tsat kün. |
| 139. Collection of Plates Illustrative of all Things, in 106 chapters. By Wáng Chí of Ming. | 三才圖會一百<br>六卷明王圻撰 | Sám Tsoi Tò Úi, yat pák luk kún. Ming Wóng Chít chán. |
| §12. Light Literature. | 小說類 | *Síú Shüt Lui.* |
| 140. Court and Country completely Described, in six chapters, according to the original of Cháng Tsu of the Táng dynasty. | 朝野僉載六卷<br>舊本題唐張鷟<br>撰 | Chíú Yé Kím Tsoi, luk kün, kau pún tai Tóng Chéung Tsuk chán. |

135. There are some other works by Ricci in the imperial library.

138. Yungló was the third emperor of the Ming dynasty, whose reign commenced A. D. 1403, and was a great patron of learning.

139. The *sám tsoi* are heaven, earth, and man, and the phrase is intended to denote all things in the whole universe, including whatsoever appertains to heavenly, earthly, and human affairs.

| | | |
|---|---|---|
| 141. Amusing Tale dreamed at the North River, in 20 chapters. By Sun Kwánghien of Sung. | 北夢瑣言二十卷宋孫光憲撰 | Pak mung shó ín, í shap kün. Sung Sün Kwóng hín chán. |
| 142. Comments on the (monsters of the) Mountains and Seas, in eighteen chapters. By Wú Jinchin of the reigning dynasty. | 山海經廣註十八卷國朝吳任臣撰 | Shán Hoi King kwóng Chü, shap pát kün. Kwók chíú 'Ng Yam shan chán. |
| 143. Records of Researches concerning the Gods, in twenty chapters; according to the original of Hán Páu of Tsin. | 搜神記二十卷舊本題晉干寶撰 | Sau Shan Kí, í shap kün, kau pún tai Tsun Kón Pò chán. |
| §13. Budhistic Writings. | 釋家類 | *Shik ká Lui.* |
| 144. Concerning the origin of Budhism, in twenty chapters. Written by the Budhist Chíshing of the Táng dynasty. | 開元釋教錄二十卷唐釋智昇撰 | Hoi Yün Shik káu luk, í shap kün. Tóng Shik Chí shing chán. |
| 145. Memoirs of the high Budhistic priests of Sung, in 30 chapters. By the Budhist Tsánning of Sung. | 宋高僧傳三十卷宋釋贊寧撰 | Sung Kò Tsang chün, sám shap kün. Sung Shik Tsán ning chán. |
| 146. Complete Records of the Budhistic Fathers, in fifty-four chapters, by the Budhist Chímò of the Sung dynasty. | 佛祖統紀五十四卷宋僧志磐撰 | Fat tsò Tung Kí, 'ng shap sz' kün. Sung Tsang Chí mó chán. |
| §14. Writings of the Rationalists. | 道家類 | *Tò Ká Lui.* |
| 147. An Exposition of the Canonical Work on True Virtue, in two chapters. By Sú Chi of Sung. | 道德經解二卷宋蘇轍撰 | Tò Tak King Kái, í kün. Sung Sú Chít chán. |
| 148. Memoirs of Demigods, in two chapters. By Liú Hiáng of Hán. | 列仙傳二卷漢劉向撰 | Lít Sín chün, í kün. Hón Laú Héung chán. |
| 149. Memoirs of Gods and Demigods, in ten chapters. By Kó Hung of Tsin. | 神仙傳十卷晉葛洪撰 | Shan Sín Chün, shap kün. Tsun Kót Hung chán. |
| 150. Expositions of the philosopher Chwáng, in three chapters. By Wú Shísháng of the present dynasty. | 莊子解三卷國朝吳世尚撰 | Chóng tsz' Kái, Sám kún. Kwók chíú 'Ng Shai shéung chán. |

§13. Budhism, though sometimes patronized by the emperors of China and supported by large and numerous monasteries, is nevertheless but little esteemed by men of letters.

§14. The writings of this sect rank no higher, and are perhaps less valued, than those of the Budhists. The work on Virtue has been translated into Latin by one of the French sinologues. The "three religions" of the Chinese are much blended one with the other.

# Fourth Division.

## TSAP PÒ, 集部 MISCELLANIES.

| | | |
|---|---|---|
| §1. Poetry of Tsu. | 楚辭類 | *Tsò Tsz' Lui.* |
| 151. The Poetry of Tsú in paragraphs and sentences; seventeen chapters. By Wáng Yi of Hán. | 楚辭章句十七卷漢王逸撰 | Tsò Tsz' Chéung kü, shap tsat kün. Hón Wóng Yat chán. |
| 152. Poetical Beauties illustrated with plates, in two volumes. Published by imperial authority. | 欽定補繪離騷全圖二卷 | Yam ting Pò úi Lí Sò tsün tò, í kün. |
| 153. Commentary on the Dissipation of Sorrows, in one volume. By Kú Shingtien of the reigning dynasty. | 離騷解一卷國朝顧成天撰 | Lí Sò Kái, yat kün. Kwók chíú Kú Shing tín chán. |
| §2. Individual Collections. | 別集類 | *Pít Tsap Lui.* |
| 154. Lí Táipa's Collection (of odes), in thirty chapters. By Lí Táipa of Táng. | 李太白集三十卷唐李太白撰 | Lí Tái pak Tsap, sám shap kün. Tóng Lí Tái pák chán. |
| 155. Collection for Domestic Entertainment, in eighty chapters. By Sz'má Kwáng of Sung. | 傳家集八十卷宋司馬光撰 | Chün Ká Tsap, pát shap kün. Sung Sz' má Kwóng chán. |
| 156. Tungpò's Complete Collection, in one hundred and fifteen chapters, by Sú Shi of Sung. | 東坡全集一百十五卷宋蘇軾撰 | Tung pó Tsün Tsap, yat pák shap 'ng kün. Sung Sú Shik chán. |
| §3. General Collections. | 總集類 | *Tsung Tsap Lui.* |
| 157. The complete Poems of Táng, in nine hundred chapters; by imperial authority. | 御定全唐詩九百卷 | Yü ting Tsün Tóng Shí, kau pák kün. |
| 158. Poetry by ladies, in fourten chapters. Compiled by Tien Fhang of the Ming dynasty. | 詩女史十四卷明田藝蘅編 | Shí nü Sz', shap sz' kün. Ming Tín Ngai hang pín. |
| §4. On the art of Poetry. | 詩文評類 | *Shí man Píng Lui.* |
| 159. Treatise on Poetical Composition, in one volume. By Chin Yitsang of Yuen. | 文說一卷元陳繹曾撰 | Man Shüt, yat kün. Yün Chan Yik tsang chán. |

This fourth division comprises a large variety of works which might be appropriately classed under the head of polite literature or belles-lettres. Nearly one third of the catalogue is occupied with the names of these works.

§2. Epistles, essays, inscriptions, with a large variety of poetical pieces form this collection. The first author is highly esteemed among the Chinese.

L

| | | |
|---|---|---|
| 160. Poetical Sayings of successive ages, in eighty chapters. By Wú Kinghiu of the reigning dynasty. | 歷代詩話八十卷國朝吳景旭撰 | Lik toi Shí Wá, pát shap kün. Kwók chíú 'Ng King huk chán. |
| 161. History of the Poetry of the Sung dynasty, in one hundred chapters. By Lí Ngó of this dynasty. | 宋詩紀事一百卷國朝厲鶚撰 | Sung Shí Kí sz', yat pák kün. Kwók chíú Lai Ngok chán. |
| §5. Odes and Songs. | 詞曲類 | *Tsz' Huk Lui.* |
| 162. Odes on Wine, in two chapters. By Tsz' Hwui of the Sung dynasty. | 酒邊詞二卷宋子諲撰 | Tsau pín Tsz', í kün. Sung Tsz' Wai chán. |
| 163. Odes on the White Clouds of the Mountains, in eight chapters. By Cháng Yen of Sung. | 山中白雲詞八卷宋張炎撰 | Shán chung Pák Wan Tsz', pát kün. Sung Chéung I'm chán. |
| 164. Fragmentary Odes of successive ages, in one hundred and twenty chapters; published by imperial authority. | 御定歷代詩餘一百二十卷 | Yü ting, Lik toi Shí ü, yat pák í shap kün. |
| 165. Records of the odes of Táng, in sixteen chapters. By Tung Fungyuen of the Ming dynasty. | 唐詞紀十六卷明董逢元撰 | Tóng Tsz' Kí, shap luk kün. Ming Tung Fung ün chán. |

From the preceeding list an idea may be formed of the general scope and characters of Chinese literature. The subject will be better exhibited by recapitulation, in a tabular form.

*I. Classical Writings.*

§ 1. Book of Changes.
§ 2. Book of Records.
§ 3. Book of Odes.
§ 4. Book of Rites.
§ 5. Spring and Autmn Annals.
§ 6. Filial Duty.
§ 7. General Observations on the Five Classics.
§ 8. The Four Books.
§ 9. Musical Works.
§ 10. Normal Education.

*II. Historical Writings.*

§ 1. National Histories.
§ 2. Annals.
§ 3. Complete Records.
§ 4. Separate Records.
§ 5. Mixed Histories.
§ 6. Official papers.
§ 7. Memoirs.
§ 8. Historical Excerpta.
§ 9. Records of neighboring states.
§ 10. Of Times and Seasons.
§ 11. Geographical treatises.
§ 12. On the Magistracy.
§ 13. On the Contitution.
§ 14. Books of Reference.
§ 15. Criticisms on History.

*III. Professional Writings.*

§ 1. Philosophical Works.
§ 2. Military Authors.
§ 3. Writers on Law.
§ 4. Writers on Husbandry.
§ 5. Medical Writers.
§ 6. Astronomical and Mathematical Writers.
§ 7. Magical Calculations.
§ 8. Fine Arts.
§ 9. Collections.
§ 10. Miscellaneous Authors.
§ 11. Encyclopedias.
§ 12. Light Literature.
§ 13. Budhistic Writings.
§ 14. Writings of the Rationalitss.

*IV. Micellanies.*

§ 1. Poetry of Tsú.
§ 2. Individual Collections.
§ 3. General Collections.
§ 4. On the Art of Poetry.
§ 5. Odes and Songs.

## X. METHOD OF STUDY.

The questions, how shall I begin, and how shall I proceed with the study of the Chinese language, have been so often asked by those who were commencing with it, that some suggestions

relative thereto will not be out of place here. At first view the difficulties seem to be very many and great. The student finds the characters entirely different in form from those of alphabetic languages; changes, such as are occasioned by conjugation and declensions, are wanting; while homophonous words, synonymous terms, and peculiar phrases, are superabundant. All these things, however, need not discourage him; for, with all its difficulties, native children easily acquire ability to speak, and read, and write it. The foreigner should learn the Chinese language as these children do; he should talk, talk, talk; read, read, read; write, write, write; and while thus talking, and reading, and writing, he should bring to his assistance whatever aid can be derived from books and teachers.

Special care should always be taken not to overstrain the mind. By attempting to compass too much at once, the memory is weakened, the intellectual faculties are fatigued, debility and disgust ensue, and study, becoming irksome, is either abandoned or dragged on without success. No one should read many books, until the general principles of the language, with a few select lessons, comprising say eight or ten hundred characters, have been made perfectly familiar. Some students justly complain of having gone over too much ground, rambling from book to book: no course can be worse than this. It will not often be necessary to dwell long at once on a single word, or phrase, or sentence; but the exact and full force of each word should be sought for and acquired. In order to proceed with pleasure and success all the efforts should be natural and easy. *With the mind undisturbed and free, the learner should daily and hourly speak and read; repeat again and again the same; hear others read and speak; write and rewrite what he hears and reads; peruse and reperuse it:* and he should assiduously persevere in these exercises, until the language becomes as familiar as his own. (See Jahn on the study of oriental languages.)

In using the Chrestomathy as a text-book — after first perusing the Introduction so as to become familiar both with the system of orthography and with that of the tones — the exercises in conversation, Sections first and second, may be commenced with. While these are being acquired, the two series of tones, given on pages VI and VII, should be so fixed in the memory, that any word in the dialect, when heard by the student, may be referred to its proper order. The two series of tones and Sections first and second being rendered familiar, the learner may pass on to the third Section and commit it to memory *à la Chinoise*, as recommended by Prémare. He need not stop at line eighty-eight, but go on and acquire the whole of the Trimetrical Classic, at the same time repeating the preceding lessons and studying Section fourth.—The Thousand Character Classic and the Odes for Children, noticed on page 8th, may be read in the some manner as the Trimetrical Classic, after this latter is completed.

Thus far the attention of the student will have been confined to talking and reading, under the tuition of the best native masters he can procure. It will now be time to take up the pencil, to the doing of which and to the system of writing, Sections fifth and sixth will afford an easy introduction. Henceforth talking and reading and writing will be carried on simultaneously, yet so varied as to afford that change which is rest.

At this stage, having thoroughly acquired the first chapter of the Chrestomathy "with the three (little) volumes in large characters," the student will have gained a stock of fifteen or eighteen hundred characters. These he should repeatedly examine and analyze, mark their component parts, and see to which of the 214 classes of characters, as given in Kánghí's dictionary, each one belongs. For this purpose, he should keep by his side a copy of that work, with a copy of Morrison's also,—in which latter the radicals, or heads of the 214 classes, are fully explained. With this system of classification, he should thoroughly acquaint himself, which he can easily do with the aid of a teacher and Kánghí's dictionary, if Morrison's be not at hand.

On no account should the student be anxious to hurry on from these preliminary exercises: The ground already gone over, he should review and rereview so as to know all the characters, and be able to recognize them at once wherever they may occur. It should be a rule, in the early part of his course, not to leave behind many characters or phrases of which he has not gained perfect mastery. Continual repetition, without any very laborious efforts, will fix the language fast in the memory.

*Gutta cavat lapidem, non vi, sed sæpe cadendo.*

Children and unlettered men learn languages rapidly by such frequent repetition: with these persons it is the only way they can learn; and with the scholar, though it be not the only, it is the surest and the most easy method for successful study.

*Legendum potius multum quam multa.*

The reading of Chinese books,—such as tracts, essays, &c.,—composed by foreignes, is a very questionable course. When the style is purely Chinese, all the phrases having been selected or formed by native masters, as in the case of Esop's Fables, it cannot be objected to. Thoghrout the Chrestomathy, care has been taken not to introduce any phrases or sentences except those either composed by Chinese or selected from their books. The only exceptions to this remark are to be found in those terms, which are (or were supposed to be) new to the Chinese. It is a true remark, that "the only way to impress upon the mind of a pupil the genius of a foreign tongue, is to impress upon it the phraseology of *native* speakers or writers. The habit of conception in conformity whith the models thus furnished will follow of itself. The pratice of expressing English conceptions in the words of a foreign language, for the purpose of learning it, *is not only useless but positively injurious.*" The practice of committing to memory select phrases and sentences should be continned, in order to funish good supplies of these models. To his list of selections, it will be well for the studant occasionly to add paragraphs and short pieces taken from the best native authors.

When a few chapters of the Chrestomathy have been made familiar, with the Sacred Edict and the three little works above named, the History of the Three Kingdoms and the Four Books may be taken up. These two works thoroughly mastered, and the Chrestomathy studied to the end, the student will be able to lay his own course, selecting from among the thousands of Chinese authors such works as may best suit his own taste and purposes.

# CHINESE CHRESTOMATHY.

## CHAPTER I.

## STUDY OF CHINESE.

## 習唐話篇一

Tsáp, ˏT'óng wá'; ˏp'ín yat,.

### Section First.

### EXERCISES IN CONVERSATION.

### 習言第一章

Tsáp, ˏín; tui' yat, ˏchéung.

| | | |
|---|---|---|
| 1. Teacher! (says the learner; to whom the former replies,) | 先生 | ˏSín ˏshang! |
| You compliment me. | 好話 | ʻHò wá'! |
| 2. I think of learning the Chinese language. | 我想學唐話噃 | ʻNgó ʻséung hók, ˏT'óng wá' pó'. |
| Do you indeed? | 你要學唐話呀 | ʻNí íú' hók, ˏT'óng wá' ˏmé? |

### *Notes and Explanations.*

TSAP is composed of *two wings*, placed over *white*, which are supposed to indicate repetition, like the motion of a bird's wings when flying; hence it comes to mean exercise, practice. *T'óng*, the name of one of the most celebrated dynasties, is an appellative of the Chinese: *wá*, formed of *words* placed on the left of *tongue*, signifies speech, language, or to speak; *T'óng wá*, then, is the language of the Chinese. *P'ín* is one of the terms used to denote a chapter; *yat* means one or first; *p'ín yat* is chapter first. *I'n* is the common term for word, to utter words; *tsáp ín*, denotes practice in words, or exercises in conversation. *Tai yat* is an ordinal; *tai*, formed of two parts, *bamboo* placed above *steps*, signifies number; *yat* is one; the two mean number one, or first. *Chéung*, formed of *sound* written above *ten*, indicates something perfect, a complete piece, as of music, or a section of a book.

1. *Sínshang* is a phrase compounded of *sín*, before, and *shang*, born; hence it means a senior, a superior, a teacher. *Hò wá*, literally, well spoken, is a complimental phrase, equivalent to saying, I am unworthy of the excellent title you give me: *hò*, formed of *son* placed on the right of *daughter*, signifies good, excellent.

2. *Ngó* is the personal pronoun I, commonly used in conversation: *ní* is its correlative, used in like manner for the second person singular. *Séung*, having a *tree* for its

| | | |
|---|---|---|
| 3. Yes; is it well to do so or not? | 係好唔好呢 | Hai'; ‘hò ˏ’m ‘hò ˓ní? |
| It is well. | 好吖 | ‘Hò ˓á! |
| 4. How shall I begin? | 起首點樣學呢 | ‘Hí ‘shau ‘tím yéung' hók, ˓ní? |
| First learn to speak in conversation. | 先學講說話咯 | ˓Sín hók, ‘kóng shüt, wá' lók,. |
| 5. Do you suppose I am able to learn? | 你估我學得唔學得呢 | ‘Ní ‘kú ‘ngó hók, tak, ˏ’m hók, tak, ˓ní? |
| Most certainly you are able. | 過頭唎 | Kwó' ˏt‘au ˓lé. |
| 6. I fear I am not. | 我怕唔學得啩 | ‘Ngó p‘á' ˏ’m hók, tak, kwá'. |
| You need not fear, for you have good vocal organs. | 唔怕你好鉗口 | ˏ’M p‘á', ‘ní ‘hò ˏk‘ím ‘hau. |

upper left hand part, and for the right an *eye*—an eye looking among trees, or something connected, attached to,—with *heart* close beneath, means the heart attached to, thinking of, reflecting on, or to contemplate: *íú*, directly below *séung*, means to seek, to desire; it is formed by writing *nü*, a *daughter*, a female, beneath a *canopy* or covering. *Hók*, to learn, is compounded of four parts; viz. *to imitate*, placed on a *mortar*, the two forming the top of the character, standing on a *cover*, the middle horizontal line, suspended over a *child*, which makes the lower part and completes the word. *Pó* and *mé* are particles, the first a dubitative, the second an interrogative:—You desire learn Chinese language, eh?

3. *Hai* is a direct affirmative: *ní* is an interrogative particle: *'m* is a negative one, formed of *five*, with two *mouths*, one on the left and one beneath; it is not found in native lexicons: Yes; good not good? that is, I do desire to learn the Chinese; do you think it well for me to undertake the task? *Hò á*, is the direct, unqualified, affirmative answer.

4. *Híshau* is a compound phrase: *hí* is formed of *already* placed close on the right of *to walk*, thus indicating, already on foot, raised up, beginning; *shau* represents the *human head*, and the *hair* upon it; hence its meaning, head foremost, beginning; *híshau*, therefore, is equivalent to raising up, or making a beginning. *Tím yéung* is a simple phrase: *tím*, being formed of the radical *black* or black spots and *divination*, literally means to point, to dot, to mark with dots; in this dialect it has the interrogative meaning of how, what; *yéung* is mode, fashion, manner; *tím yéung* is what manner, or simply how: begin how learn? that is, how shall I commence the study of the Chinese? *Sín*, as above, means before, first, or in the first place: *kóng*, *shüt*, and *wá*, each having *ín* or *words* on the left, usually, when standing alone, mean to speak; here, *shütwá* may be regarded as a compound phrase, signifying conversation. *Lók* is a particle used in answering a question.

5. *Kú* is to conjecture, to form an opinion: Is it your opinion that I can succeed in learning the language according to my wishes?—*tak* having the sense of obtaining that for which one seeks;—or, do you deem it impracticable? Or, as the Chinese phrase it, You think I learn can, not learn can, eh? Pass over the head, is the literal reply; *kwó-t‘au* is a compound phrase, denoting that you have more than the needful ability; *kwó* is to pass over; *t‘au* is, in many instances, synonymous with *shau*, from the form of which it differs only in having the two strokes at the top removed to the bottom, with a *leguminous plant* placed on its left side. *Lé* is an affirmative particle.

6. *P‘á* is formed of *heart* and *white:* the Chinese suppose that the heart, like the face, turns pale under the excitement of fear: it should be observed, that in *p‘á*, both the form and position of the *heart* are different from what they are in *séung* (above in No. 2.); in the latter, it is at the bottom in four strokes, in the other it has but three strokes, and is placed on the left side of the character. *Kwá* is a dubitative particle: *hau* is the

| | | |
|---|---|---|
| 7. It is really very difficult. | 實守難呀 | Shat₂ ‘shau ˏnán á’. |
| Not so. | 唔難 | ˏ’M ˏnán. |
| 8. The tones are difficult. | 聲音係難咯 | ‹Shing ‹yam hai² ˏnán lók›. |
| You must carefully listen. | 你用心聽啊 | ‘Ní yung² ‹sam ‹t‘ing ‹ó. |
| 9. It is difficult to distinguish these tones. | 難分個的聲㗎 | ˏNán ‹fan kó’ tik› ‹shing ‹é. |
| There are merely eight of them. | 不過都係八聲啫 | Pat› kwó’ ‹tò hai² pát› ‹shing ‹ché. |
| 10. How are the eight tones uttered? | 八聲點樣講呢 | Pát› ‹shing ‘tím yéung² ‘kóng ‹ní? |
| Four of them high, and four low. | 四個上四個下 | Sz” kó’ shéung² sz” kó’ há². |
| 11. What do you mean by high and low? | 上下係乜野呀 | Shéung² há² hai² mat› ‘yé á’? |
| By and by you will understand. | 慢慢就曉得咯 | Mán² mán² tsau² ‘híú tak› lók›. |
| 12. Where shall I commence? | 向邊處埋手呢 | Héung’ ‹pín ch‘ü’ ˏmai ‘shau ‹ní? |
| Commence with the four high tones. | 向上四聲先埋手咯 | Héung’ shéung² sz” ‹shing ‹sín ˏmai ‘shau lók›. |

common word for mouth: *k‘ím*, formed of *sweet* placed on the right of *metal*, usually means forceps; but joined with *hau* it denotes the faculties of speech, the vocal organs.

7. *Shatshau* is a phrase: *shat*, formed of *pearls* strung together beneath a *covering*, means affluent, full, solid, real; *shau* here resembles *shat* in its meaning, though it usually signifies to guard, to maintain; I maintain that it is really difficult. *Nán*, difficult, has eleven strokes on the left, and eight on the right; the latter are supposed to resemble *short tailed birds*. *A’* is an intensitive particle.

8. *Shing* and *yam* are synonyms, denoting sounds generally, but here refer to the tones of voice: *yam*, though commonly regarded as a simple character, is composed of *to erect* and *sun; shing* has an *ear* placed beneath eleven strokes: *yung* signifies to use, to employ. *Sam* is the heart, or mind. *T‘ing* has *ten*, *four*, and *one*, above *heart* on the right of an *ear* above a *king*, and means to hear, to listen, to discriminate sounds. *O’* is an admonitive particle.

9. *Fan*, having *eight* above a *knife*, signifies to divide. *Kótik* is a definitive, and *é* is an affirmative, particle. *Pat kwó*, literally, not exceeding, is equivalent to merely. *Tò* commonly signifies an imperial residence; here it implies all, the whole. *Ché* is a restrictive particle. Literally, the sentence runs thus: not exceeding all are eight tones only.

10. *Kó* is a numerical particle. *Shéung* is high, *há*, low: four of the tones are uttered on a high key, and four on a low one.

11. *Mat* is an interrogative particle: *yé*, formed of *mile* placed on the left of the pronoun *I* or *me*, usually means wild, wilderness; but in the phrase *mat yé*, it signifies thing: what things are the tones? *Mán mán* is leisurely, or by and by. *Tsau*, then, is formed by placing *more* on the right of *metropolis*. *Híú* has *sun* on the left of twelve strokes, meaning high, i. e. the sun high up; hence it signifies to enlighten, and joined with *tak*, to get light, to understand.

12. *Héung*, having a *mouth* within a *cave*, means toward, at, or upon: *pín ch‘ü* is where, what place or part. *Mai* means to bury, but in this dialect it is used for approaching; when followed by hand, it signifies joining, taking in hand, or making a beginning.

| | | |
|---|---|---|
| 13. How are they uttered? | 點樣講呢 | ʻTím yéung$^{2}$ ʻkóng ‹ní? |
| The four high tones are elevated and also shrill, acute, and clear. | 上四聲高而且響又輕又清 | Shéung$^{2}$ sz" ‹shíng ‹kò, ‹í ʻch'é ʻhéung, yau$^{2}$ ‹hing, yau$^{2}$ ‹ts'ing. |
| 14. And the four low tones, how are they uttered? | 下四聲呢 | Há$^{2}$ sz" ‹shing ‹ní? |
| With a depressed voice, grum, grave, and thick. | 下四聲沉而且啞又重又濁 | Há$^{2}$ sz" ‹shing ‹ch'am, ‹í ʻch'é ʻá, yau$^{2}$ chung$^{2}$, yau$^{2}$ chuk$_{2}$. |
| 15. How can a knowledge of these be acquired? | 點樣至曉得呢 | ʻTím yéung$^{2}$ chí' ʻhíú tak$_{2}$ ‹ní? |
| By examination of the Tonic Dictionary. | 睇分韻就曉得咧 | ʻT'ai ‹Fan Wan$^{2}$ tsau$^{2}$ ʻhíú tak$_{2}$ ‹lé. |
| 16. What is the Tonic Dictionary? | 分韻係乜野呀 | ʻFan Wan$^{2}$ hai$^{2}$ mat$_{2}$ ʻyé á'? |
| It is the name of a book. | 分韻係書名 | ‹Fan Wan$^{2}$ hai$^{2}$ ‹shü ‹ming. |
| 17. But I fear I am unable to read Chinese books. | 我怕唔曉得讀唐書唻 | ʻNgó p'á' ‹'m ʻhíú' tak$_{2}$ tuk$_{2}$ ‹T'óng ‹shü ‹é. |
| Then I will teach you to read. | 我教你讀唉 | ʻNgó káu' ʻní tuk$_{2}$ ‹é. |
| 18. This is unnecessary, for I wish first to learn to speak. | 唔使我愛先學講 | ‹'M ʻshai, ʻngó oi' ‹sín hok$_{2}$ ʻkóng. |

13, 14. *Kò* and *ch'am*, elevated and depressed, *héung* and *á*, shrill and grum, *hing* and *chung*, acute and grave, *ts'ing* and *chuk*, clear and dull, are opposites: the sounds of these eight words, in some degree, indicate their respective meanings, and to a practiced Chinese eye, the same is true also with respect to their forms. *I, ch'é*, and *yau*, are connective particles, meaning and, also, further: the last one in the present case is not required in the English, yet it cannot be omitted in the Chinese.

15. *Chí* means to attain, to arrive at the highest degree; here the sense is, How can I arrive at, or acquire, a good knowledge of the tones? *T'ai*, having an *eye* on the left, signifies to look, to examine. *Fan Wan*, literally divided tones, is a small book, bound sometimes in one or two, but oftener in four thin volumes: it consists of two small works, both of which commence on the first page and run through the whole book: one is a collection of letters, &c., occupying the upper half of each page, and the other is the work here named, in which all the words commonly used in this dialect are arranged according to their tones.

16. *Shü* is formed of *pencil* and *to speak;* hence its meaning, to write or what is written, a book. *Ming*, formed of *evening* and *mouth*, signifies name, or to name.

17. *Tuk*, formed by placing *words* on the left of *to sell*, means to read or to study. *Káu*, a law, rule, precept, or system of ethics, here means to teach: it is composed of *to imitate*, *child*, and *letters;* or, according to another derivation, of *to imitate*, *child*, and *to beat*—this being considered by the Chinese as an essential part of education—knowledge must be beaten into the young and simple.

18. *Shai* means to use, to employ, to be of use, needful, necessary. *Oi*, with a *heart* in the centre, is to love, to think on with affection; here it is equivalent to *tú:* see No. 2. *Kóm wá*, so eh, i. e. Do you say so! *Kóm* is a local word used for *kóm*

廣東方言讀本

| | | |
|---|---|---|
| If so, then you must imitate the sounds of my voice. | 咁話你跟住我個口講嚹 | ‘Kóm wá$^2$, ‘ní ‹kan chü’ ‘ngó kó’ ‘hau ‘kóng lá’. |
| 19. I fear I cannot do this. | 怕唔學得你噉咋 | P‘á’ ‚’m hók$_2$ tak› ‘ní ‘kóm chá’. |
| Try, try. | 試一試吔 | Shí’ yat› shí’ ‹é. |
| 20. I cannot utter the sounds correctly. | 唔講得正嘅 | ‚’M ‘kóng tak› ching’ ké’. |
| If so, then try again, repeating the experiment, | 唔正番轉頭再講 | ‚’M ching’, ‹fán ‘chün ‚t‘au tsoi’ ‘kóng. |
| 21. How long before I shall be able to speak correctly? | 幾耐至學得會呢 | ‘Kí noi$^2$ chí’ hók$_2$ tak› ‘úi ‹ní? |
| Do not trouble yourself on that point. | 唔使問幾耐 | ‚’M ‘shai man$^2$ ‘kí noi$^2$. |
| 22. But I wish quickly to be able to speak. | 我想快的會 | ‘Ngó ‘séung fái’ tik› ‘úi. |
| Then study assiduously, often repeating what you learn. | 勤力學多幾回囉 | ‚K‘an lik$_2$ hók$_2$, ‹tó ‘kí ‚úi ‹ló. |
| 23. [Besides often repeating,] is there any other way to facilitate the study? | 有乜捷徑有冇呢 | ‘Yau mat› tsít$_2$ king’ yau$^2$ ‘mò ‹ní? |
| Yes; it can be done by first clearly distinguishing the labials, linguals, gutturals, dentals, and nasals. | 有先分清唇舌喉牙鼻等音囉 | ‘Yau; ‹sín ‹fan ‹tsing ‘shan, shít$_2$, ‚hau, ‚ngá, pí$^2$, ‘tang ‹yam ‹ló, |

to dare, or to presume. ***Kanchü***, to follow, to imitate, derives its meaning from ***foot***, which forms the left part of ***kan***: ***chü*** means to dwell, and is here used instead of ***tsui***, to follow. ***Kó*** joined to ***ngó*** indicates the possessive case. ***Lá*** is a particle.

19. ***Chá*** is a particle implying doubt. ***Shí yat shí***, try one try, make one effort; if you fear you cannot learn, yet you can make the attempt, can begin, can try: ***shí*** is formed of ***words*** placed on the left of a ***rule*** or pattern.

20. ***Ching*** is right, straight, or a correct manner; I cannot speak correct as you do; if you cannot, then back turn head again speak, meaning, you must repeat the trial: ***fán chün t‘au*** is a phrase nearly equivalent to ***tsoi***, again.

21. ***Kínoi***, a compound phrase, is formed of ***kí*** a distributive particle, and ***noi***, duration, length of time: in what length of time, ***chí*** can I arrive at or acquire, ***hók tak*** by learning, ***úi*** the ability — of speaking the dialect correctly?

22. ***Fáitik*** is quickly: ***fái*** is compounded of ***heart*** and ***flowing***. ***Lik*** is nerve, strength, and forms a part of ***kan***, which itself means diligent: ***tó*** much, many, often, ***kí*** several, ***úi*** repetitions; that is, many several repetitions.

23. ***Tsít king*** is a phrase, meaning a short way; Is there any short way? The sentence is elliptical;—besides the oft repetitions which you have recommended, is there any other short way to acquire the language? ***Yau mò*** are opposites, have not have; in form ***mò*** differs from ***yau*** only in having the two strokes removed from the middle of the character. ***Shan*** the lips, ***shít*** the tongue, ***hau*** the thorax, ***ngá*** the teeth, and ***pí*** the nose,

CHI. CHR. 2

| | | |
|---|---|---|
| 24. How can you distinguish so many? | 咁多點樣分呢 | Kóm' ‹tó, 'tím yéung$^2$ ‹fan ‹ní? |
| By careful attention, this can be easily done. | 細心就分得啫 | Sai' ‹sam, tsau$^2$ ‹fan tak› ‹ché. |
| 25. It is also necessary to hear them spoken. | 都要聽過至做得 | ‹Tò íú' ‹t'ing kwó' chí' tsò$^2$ ‹tak›. |
| Come then, listen while I repeat them. | 咁話你聽我講嚟 | 'Kóm wá$^2$, 'ní ‹t'ing 'ngó 'kóng lá'. |
| 26. Please proceed. | 請講 | 'Ts'ing 'kóng. |
| They are as follows: i. Pan, P'áng, Fán, are labials. | 如賓彭翻就係唇音嘅 | ‹Ü: ‹pan, ‹p'áng, ‹fán, tsau$^2$ hai$^2$ ‹shan ‹yam ‹lá. |
| ii. Tung, Tang, Tsoi, are linguals. | 東登栽就係舌音嘅 | ‹Tung, ‹tang, ‹tsoi, tsau$^2$ hai$^2$ shít$_2$ ‹yam ‹lá. |
| iii. Kóm, Káu, Kám, are gutturals. | 甘交鍼就係喉音嘅 | ‹Kóm, ‹káu, ‹kám, tsau$^2$ hai$^2$ ‹hau ‹yam ‹lá. |
| iv. Sín, Sau, Sz', are dentals. | 先修師就係牙音嘅 | ‹Sín, ‹sau, ‹sz', tsau$^2$ hai$^2$ 'ngá ‹yam ‹lá. |
| v. 'Ng, Ngáng, Ngák, are nasals. | 吾硬額就係鼻音嘅 | ‹'Ng, Ngáng$^2$, Ngák$_2$, tsau$^2$ hai$^2$ pí$^2$ ‹yam ‹lá. |
| 27. Such then being the proper way to learn, what course shall I now pursue? | 咁話而家學乜野好呢 | 'Kóm wá$^2$, ‹í ‹ká hók$_2$ mat› 'yé 'hò ‹ní? |
| Whatever you find most convenient. | 隨便學咯 | ‹Ts'ui pín$^2$ hók$_2$ lók›. |

followed by *tang yam* classes of sounds, denote the labials, linguals, &c., or the classes of sounds formed by the lips, tongue, &c.: these five characters are thought to resemble the vocal organs which they severally specify.

24. *Kóm tó* so many! or being so many, how can they be distinguished? *Sai sam*, literally small heart, is equivalent to *yung sam;* be careful, then you can distinguish them.

25. *Tò* here has the sense of also—it is also necessary, *t'ing kwó* to have heard them pronounced, *chí* in order to arrive at, *tsò tak* the doing successfully—of the business in question. *Kóm wá* so speak, if such is your view of the case and such your wishes, then come on, listen while I repeat the five classes of sounds; or literally *ní t'ing* you hear, *ngó kóng* I speak.

26. *Ts'ing kóng*, I beg you will repeat to me examples of the five classes which you have specified: *ü*, literally, so or thus, is equivalent to the phrase, they are the following, viz., the labials, &c. N. B. These five are merely the leading or fundamental sounds of this description, which are modified and blended in almost every possible variety.

27. *Kóm wá*, used as a phrase, varies in its meaning according to the subject. The meaning of the whole sentence is, I regard what you have recommended as the *tsít king*, or best method of acquiring the language, and I wish now to know what course

| | | |
|---|---|---|
| 28. I wish to learn the dialect of Canton. | 我要學廣東省城俗話 | ʻNgó fú' hók, ʻKwóng ˌtung ʻsháng ˏshing tsuk, wá'. |
| If so, then it is requisite to take up one topic after another and proceed in order. | 咁樣就要逐一逐二學嚹 | ʻKóm yéung', tsau' fú' chuk, yat, chuk, í' hók, lá'. |
| 29. Very well; I thank you very much; please wait a few days, when I shall be obliged if you will come again and teach me. | 呀好多得多得等遲幾日再請先生番嚟教 | A'' ʻhò; ˌtó tuk, ˌtó tak, ʻtang ˏch'í ʻkí yat, tsoi' ʻts'ing ˌsín ˌshang ˌfán ˏlai káu'. |
| Good bye. | 請呀 | ʻTs'ing á'. |
| 30. Good bye. | 請呀 | ʻTs'ing á'. |

to pursue; how and where I shall commence: *íká* is a compound phrase, meaning now, a signification differing entirely from the original and common meaning, which is *í* and or also, *ka* family. *Tsui* to follow, *pín* convenient, agreeable; that is, in your study you may follow the course most agreeable and convenient to yourself.

28. *Kwóngtung*, (pronounced *Kwángtung* in the court dialect,) wide east, is the proper name of the province of which the city Canton is the metropolis: *sháng* province, *shing* city, are used for the provincial city, the capital of the province, the metropolis; *tsuk wá* is the common dialect. *Kóm yéung* such being your wishes, *tsau fú* then it is requisite, *chuk yat* to hasten one, *chuk í* to hasten two; that is, to take up one subject after another, and proceed methodically in your study.

29. *A' hò* yes good, this is what I like. *Tó tak* repeated is a common phrase for expressing gratitude; much I have received, much I have received by your kindness, and therefore thank you much. *Tang* wait, or please wait, *ch'í* delaying for, *kí yat* a few days, *tsoi* again or when again, *ts'ing* I will thank, *sínshang* you, *fán lai* back come, *káu* teach: i. e. please wait for a few days when I shall feel much obliged (and of course thank you,) if you will come again and give me further instruction. The teacher signifies his consent by saying *ts'ing á*, good bye.

## Section Second.

## EXERCISES IN CONVERSATION.

### 習言第二章
Tsáp, ˏín; tai' í' ˌchéung.

| | | |
|---|---|---|
| 1. Please sit down, (says the learner; and to whom the teacher replies,) | 請坐 | ʻTs'ing tsó'. |
| Very well! | 呀好 | A'' ʻhò. |

### *Notes and Explanations.*

1. *Ts'ing*, in polite intercourse is used, when taking leave, when meeting, and in the midst of discourse; it is composed of *words* and *pure*, and means to ask, to beg, to announce to, which are varied according to the subject and the occasion.

| | | |
|---|---|---|
| 2. I now think of learning to read, with what book shall I begin? | 而家想學讀書喺乜野書起呢 | ꜁Í ꜀ká ꜂séung hók꜊ tuk꜊ ꜀shü, ꜂hai mat꜄ ꜂yé ꜀shü ꜂hí ꜀ní? |
| With the three volumes in the large character. | 三簿大字書起咯 | ꜀Sám pò꜊ tai꜊ tsz'꜊ ꜀shü ꜂hí lók꜄. |
| 3. Where are those volumes to be obtained? | 邊處有個的書呢 | ꜀Pín ch'u꜄ ꜂yau kó꜄ tik꜄ ꜀shü ꜀ní? |
| At the bookseller's shop. | 書舖就有唎 | ꜀Shü p'ó꜄ tsau꜊ ꜂yau ꜀lé. |
| 4. I beg you will buy a copy of them for me. | 請你同我買一套 | ꜂Ts'ing ꜂ní ꜁t'ung ꜂ngó ꜂mai yat꜄ t'ò꜄. |
| I will do so. | 做得 | Tsò꜊ tak꜄. |
| 5. Are you able to rehearse those volumes? | 你念得過個簿書唔念得呢 | ꜂Ní ním꜊ tak꜄ kwó꜄ kó꜄ pò꜊ ꜀shü, ꜁'m ním꜊ tak꜄ ꜀ní? |
| Perhaps I can. | 或者做得 | Wák꜊ ꜂ché tsò꜊ tak꜄. |
| 6. Are you able to write them? | 寫得出唔寫得呢 | ꜂Sé tak꜄ ch'ut꜄ ꜁'m ꜂sé tak꜄ ꜀ní? |
| Some parts of them I can write. | 寫得的 | ꜂Sé tak꜄ tik꜄. |
| 7. Please write a few lines. | 請你寫幾行 | ꜂Ts'ing ꜂ní ꜂sé ꜂kí ꜁hóng. |
| Very well. | 呀好 | A'꜊ ꜂hò. |

2. *Hai*, differing from *hai*, (sec. i: 3.,) only in having a *mouth* added on the left, means with, and is used only in conversation. The three volumes in large characters are the Trimetrical Classic, the Hundred Family Names, and the Thousand Character Classic. The first derives its name from the arrangement of the work, having three characters in a line; these lines, however, are doubled, and the volume contains one hundred and seventy-eight double lines. The Hundred Family Names, arranged in a similar manner, with four characters in each single line, contains between four and five hundred names of families, worked into rhyme: being an unreadable book, its place in the school-room is supplied by another little volume, styled *Yau Hók Shí*, or Odes for Children. The Thousand Character Classic is so named, because it is composed of a thousand characters, no one of which is repeated in the volume. This work is said to have been composed in a single night, and so great was the mental exertion of its author, that all the hair of his head turned gray.

4. *T'ung ngó* is with me, or for me,—I beg you to purchase for me, *yat tò* one set or a copy of the three volumes. *Tsò tak*, do can, or can do,—what you request can be done; I will buy the books for you.

5. *Ním*, composed of *now* and *heart*, means to ponder, to read; in this dialect it means to recite a lesson without a book; *wákché* is a compound phrase, implying doubt; perhaps, or it may be, that I can rehearse those volumes.

6. Write can [come] out, not write can eh? is the literal reading of this question: to which the answer is, write can a little;—a little is a local signification of the word *tik* differing from its use in books, where it is employed to denote the genitive or possessive case.

## Section Third.

# EXERCISES IN READING.

## 習讀第三章

Tsáp$_2$ tuk$_2$; tai$^2$ ‹sám ‹chéung.

| | | |
|---|---|---|
| 1. Men at their birth: are in nature pure; | 人之初 性本善 | ‚Yan ‹chí ‹ch‘ó: sing’ ‘pún shín$^2$; |
| 2. In this all are alike: but they differ in practice. | 性相近 習相遠 | Sing’ ‹séung kan$^2$: tsáp$_2$ ‹séung ‘ün. |
| 3. If left uneducated: nature deteriorates. | 苟不教 性乃遷 | ‘Kau pat› káu’: sing’ ‘nái ‹ts‘ín. |
| 4. In the path of education: foremost is application. | 教之道 貴以專 | Káu’ ‹chí tò$^2$: kwai’ ‘í ‹chün. |
| 5. Anciently, Mang's mother: selected a residence; | 昔孟母 擇鄰處 | Sik› Mang$^2$ ‘mò: chák$_2$ ‚lun ‘ch‘ü; |
| 6. And as her son did not learn: she cut out her web. | 子不學 斷機杼 | ‘Tsz’ pat› hók$_2$: tün$^2$ ‹kí ‘ch‘ü. |

### *Notes and Explanations.*

1. These lines are taken from the Trimetrical Classic, or Sám Tsz’ King. *Yan* is the generic term for man; *ch‘ó*, beginning or man's beginning, is formed of *knife* placed on the right of *clothes;* in composition, the character *í* clothes or to clothe should be carefully distinguished from *shí* to manifest; *shí* has but one dot on the right side, while the other has two, as in *ch‘ó*. *Sing*, composed of *heart* and *to be born*, signifies nature; *pún* is root or origin; man's original nature, *shín* is good. N. B. The colon is used in the two columns of English merely to make them correspond to the division in the column of Chinese.

2. *Séung* has the sense of mutually, universally; men are universally, *kan* alike or kindred in their nature, but *ün* unlike, differing from one another, in their practice; *kan* and *ün* are opposites. This is a saying of Confucius.

3. *Kau* is a suppositive particle; if, or supposing that children are not educated—*pat* being a negative particle,—under such circumstances, their nature, *nái ts‘ín* is removed from what it was originally.

4. *Tò* means the way or course of education; *káu chí tò* education's way, *kwai* is made high in value, of prime importance, *í* by, *chün* close attention—of both teacher and pupil.

5. Mang, or Mangtsz’, is the original of what has been latinized into Mencius. The character of this distinguished philosopher was formed by his mother before he was born. So careful was she in all that she did and said, that at his birth he was superior to other mortals. Thrice she removed her residence solely for his benefit. First, she lived in the vicinity of tombs; there her boy learned to weep and wail. Next, she lived near a slaughter-house; there he learned to imitate the butcher. From thence she removed, and *chák* selected, *lun* a neighborhood, in which *chü* to reside: this was close by a school, where the boy had constant opportunity to witness good deportment. ‘Here,’ said the mother, ‘is the place for my son to reside.’ One day, the boy becoming tired of his book while at school, and returning home, his mother seized a knife, and cut from her loom a piece of cloth when it was yet unfinished. Alarmed at her conduct he fell on his knees before her, begging to know what she meant. ‘This web,’ said she, ‘is like my boy's learning: an accumulation of threads form inches; of inches feet are formed, and of feet yards; but if the web be cut asunder, it will never be completed. So it is with your studies.’ By this illustration the lad was roused to diligence; and his subsequent life showed how much could be effected by a mother's attention.

6. *Kí* the loom, and *ch‘ü* a shuttle are, by metonymy, used to denote the cloth woven in the loom.

| | | |
|---|---|---|
| 7. Tau of I'nshán: had good regulations; | 竇燕山 有義方 | Tau' ˌI'n ˌshán: ʻyau í' ˌfóng; |
| 8. And educated his five sons: who all became renowned. | 教五子 名俱揚 | Káu' ʻʻng ʻtsz': ˌming ˌk'ü ˌyéung. |
| 9. To nurture without educating: is the father's fault; | 養不教 父之過 | ʻYéung patˌ káu': fú' ˌchí kwó'; |
| 10. To teach without rigor: shows the master's indolence. | 教不嚴 師之惰 | Káu' patˌ ˌím: ˌsz' ˌchí tó'. |
| 11. That a child should not learn: is an improper thing; | 子不學 非所宜 | ʻTsz' patˌ hókˌ: ˌfí ʻshó ˌí; |
| 12. For if he do not learn: then what can he do when old? | 幼不學 老何爲 | Yau' patˌ hókˌ: ʻlò ˌhó ˌwai? |
| 13. A gem unwrought: is a useless thing; | 玉不琢 不成器 | Yukˌ patˌ téukˌ: patˌ ˌshing hí'; |
| 14. So a man unlearned: is a senseless being. | 人不學 不知義 | ˌYan patˌ hokˌ: patˌ ˌchí í'. |
| 15. Those who are children: at that tender age, | 爲人子 方少時 | ˌWai ˌyan ʻtsz': ˌfóng shíú' ˌshí, |
| 16. With teacher and friends: ought to learn politeness. | 親師友 習禮儀 | ʻTs'an ˌsz' ʻyau: tsápˌ ʻlai ˌí. |
| 17. Héung, when nine years old: warmed his father's bed; | 香九齡 能溫席 | ˌHéung ʻkau ˌling: ˌnang ˌwan tsikˌ; |
| 18. Duty to parents: ought carefully to be observed. | 孝於親 所當執 | Háu' ˌü ˌts'an: ʻshó ˌtóng chapˌ. |
| 19. Yung, when four years old: gave up his pears; | 融四歲 能讓梨 | ˌYung sz' sui': ˌnang yéung' ˌlí; |

7. Tau, the most celebrated master of his age, was a native of I'n (Yen), one of the ancient states of China; he gained his high reputation by the rigid discipline he maintained in his school: his five sons all became distinguished statesmen, and generation after generation, they preserved their father's good regulations, and maintained the honor and reputation of the family. "Such is the advantage of sustaining a rigid course of paternal instruction."

8. *K'ü* all, the names of all the five sons, or the reports of what they were and of what they did, *yéung* were spread abroad.

9. *Yéung*, formed of *sheep* placed above *eating*, signifies to nourish, to bring up: this neglect of providing for the instruction of children, *fú chí kwó* is the fault of the father—for which he is to be blamed.

10. *I'm* is that grave magisterial deportment which the Chinese deem indispensable for a school-master, and which is neglected, if neglected at all, only because he is lazy.

11. Children not learn, not thing proper—children ought to learn: *shó*, a place, a thing, here refers to children's neglecting to learn, which conduct is, *fí í* improper.

12. *Yau*, composed of *small* and *strength*, is the opposite of *lò*, or persons advanced to old age; *hó wai*, used as an interrogative, is equivalent to the direct negative,—they are useless, or those who grow up uneducated can do nothing.

13, 14. In these two lines, which are quoted from the Book of Rites, education is compared to the work of the lapidary: *yuk* refers to the gem in its unwrought state, and *hí* to the ornaments into which it is formed by the artist; *pat shing* means unfinished articles, which are useless; *pat chí*, not to know, is equivalent to being destitute of, *í* correct principles of conduct—it is being without any sense of propriety, or becoming like a brute.

15, 16. *Wai yan tsz'*, being men's sons, or while you are children, *fóng* then, *shíú* young in years, *shí* time, or while you are yet young, *ts'an* be near to, or follow and imitate a teacher, associate with and copy after good friends, in order, *tsáp* to practice, and become a proficient in, *lai í* good manners.

17, 18. *Háu* is the duty which children owe, *ü* to, *ts'an* their parents; *shó* this thing, or duty, *tóng* ought, *chap* to be carefully held or observed. The precept is adduced here in order to add force to the example of the illustrious Héung, who when only nine years old used to drive the musketoes from, and cool, his father's bed in summer, and warm it in winter.

| | | |
|---|---|---|
| 20. Duty to seniors: ought early to be understood. | 弟於長 宜先知 | Tai$^{2}$ ‹ü ‘chéung: ˏí ‹sín ‹chí. |
| 21. First practice filial and fraternal duties: next see and hear. | 首孝弟 次見聞 | ‘Shau háu’ tai$^{2}$: ts‘z’’ kín’ ˏman. |
| 22. Understand classification: investigate first principles. | 知某數 識某文 | ‹Chí ‘mau shò’: shik› ‘mau ˏmau. |
| 23. Units advance to tens: tens ascend to hundreds; | 一而十 十而百 | Yat› ˏí shap$_{2}$: shap$_{2}$ ˏí pák›; |
| 24. Hundreds to thousands: and thousands to myriads. | 百而千 千而萬 | Pák› ˏí ‹ts‘ín: ‹ts‘ín ˏí mán$^{2}$. |
| 25. The three powers: are heaven, earth, and man. | 三才者 天地人 | ‹Sám ˏts‘oi ‘ché: ‹t‘ín tí$^{2}$ ˏyan. |
| 26. The three lights: are the sun, moon, and stars. | 三光者 日月星 | ‹Sám ‹kwóng ‘ché: yat$_{2}$ üt$_{2}$ ‹sing. |
| 27. There are three ties: that of prince and minister, justice; | 三綱者 君臣義 | ‹Sám ‹kóng ‘ché: ‹kwan ˏshan í$^{2}$; |
| 28. Of father and son, affection: of husband and wife, kindness. | 父子親 夫婦順 | Fú$^{2}$ ‘tsz’ ‹ts‘an: ‹fú ‘fú shun$^{2}$. |
| 29. Spring and summer: autumn and winter, | 曰春夏 曰秋冬 | Üt$_{2}$ ‹ch‘un há$^{2}$: üt$_{2}$ ‹ts‘au ‹tung, |
| 30. These four seasons: revolve unceasingly. | 此四時 運不窮 | ‘Ts‘z’ sz’’ ˏshí: wan$^{2}$ pat› ˏk‘ung. |
| 31. North and south: east and west, | 曰南北 曰西東 | Üt$_{2}$ ˏnám pak›: üt$_{2}$ ‹sai ‹tung, |
| 32. These four points: converge to the centre. | 此四方 應乎中 | ‘Ts‘z’ sz’’ ‹fóng: ying’ ˏú ‹chung. |

19, 20. *Yung* was the youngest of several sons; being presented one day with a box of pears, they all strove for the largest and best except Yung, who selected the smallest; a bystander observing this, asked why he did so; "I am the youngest, and ought to take the least," was his sage reply. *Tai* means a younger brother, and also to act the part of such an one, a duty which he owes, *ü chéung* to superiors or seniors, and which, *í sín chí*, ought early to be understood and observed: *nang*, in the phrases *nang wan* and *nang yéung*, means literally able, or to be able, and implies the actual doing of what is expressed in the word which follows it; as he did warm the bed, he did give up the pears; or simply, he warmed the bed, he gave up the pears.

21, 22. *Shau* first of all, *hau tai*, we must do all our duty to our parents, and discharge all our obligations as younger brothers; *ts‘z’* next, *kín man* see and hear, i. e. acquire general knowledge. *Chí mau shò*, literally know certain numbers, and *shik mau man* understand certain principles;—in acquiring general knowledge, classify it, and investigate the principles.

23. The classification commences with this line and is continued on to the 53d. *Yat í shap*, is literally one and ten; the simple numbers commence with one and rise to ten; thence, by a common multiple ten, they may be increased indefinitely.

25. According to the cosmogony of the Chinese, man is placed on an equality with heaven and earth; and together they form a kind of triad, and hence are called the three powers.

27, 28. *Kóng* is a strong band, or regulator: of these there are three, justice, affection, and kindness, which are the ties of the social and civil compact. "The upright prince in his palace is the regulator of his ministers; the upright father at home is the regulator of his children; and the upright husband is the regulator of his wife: these three being upright, then the prince will be immaculate, the minister good, the father compassionate, the son dutiful, the husband kind, the wife submissive, the empire quiet, and nations at peace."

29. This phraseology is peculiar: *üt*, to speak, is used here to fill up the measure, and may be translated thus: *üt ch‘un há*, what we call (or to wit,) spring and summer. It answers nearly to the latin word videlicet, as often used in English composition.

31, 32. *Sz’ fóng* are the four cardinal points of the compass; and, considering the earth as one vast plain, are supposed to converge to a common centre.

| | | |
|---|---|---|
| 33. Water and fire: wood, metal, and earth, | 曰水火　木金土 | Üt, 'shui 'fó: muk, ˛kam 't'ò, |
| 34. These five elements: are the original of material forms. | 此五行　本乎數 | 'Ts'z' 'ng ˏhang: 'pún ˏú shò'. |
| 35. Benevolence and justice: propriety, wisdom, and truth; | 曰仁義　禮智信 | Ut, ˏyan í': 'lai chí' sun', |
| 36. These five virtues: are not to be confounded. | 此五常　不容紊 | 'Ts'z' 'ng ˏshéung: pat, ˏyung lun'. |
| 37. Rice, millet, and pulse: wheat, panicum, and rye, | 稻梁菽　麥黍稷 | Tò' ˏléung shuk,: mak, 'shü tsik, |
| 38. Are the six kinds of grain: on which men subsist. | 此六穀　人所食 | 'Ts'z' luk, kuk,: ˏyan 'shó shik,. |
| 39. Horses, oxen, and sheep: poultry, dogs, and swine, | 馬牛羊　鷄犬豕 | 'Má ˏngau ˏyéung: ˛kai 'hün 'ch'í, |
| 40. Are six kinds of animals: which men rear. | 此六畜　人所飼 | 'Ts'z' luk, ch'uk,: ˏyan 'shó tsz''. |
| 41. Joy and anger: sorrow and fear, | 曰喜怒　曰哀懼 | Üt, 'hí nò': üt, ˛oi kü', |
| 42. Love, hatred, and desire: are the seven passions. | 愛惡欲　乃七情 | Oi' ú' yuk,: 'nái ts'at, ˏts'ing. |
| 43. Gourd, earth, and skin: wood, stone and metal, | 匏土革　木石金 | ˏP'áu 't'ò kák,: muk, shek, ˛kam, |
| 44. Silk and bamboo: form eight musical instruments. | 絲與竹　乃八音 | ˛Sz' 'ü chuk,: 'nái pát, ˛yam. |
| 45. Gt.-grandsire's sire, gt.-gdsire, grandsire: sire, and self; | 高曾祖　父而身 | ˛Kò ˛tsang 'tsò: fú' ˏí ˛shan; |
| 46. One's own son: with one's grandson, | 身而子　子而孫 | ˛Shan ˏí 'tsz': 'tsz' ˏí ˛sün, |
| 47. Great-grandson: and great-grandson's son, | 自子孫　至元曾 | Tsz'' 'tsz' ˛sün: chí' ˏün ˛tsang, |

33, 34. These five elements are supposed, by a constant succession of changes, mutually to destroy and reproduce each other; and in this way they constitute the *pún* or basis, *ú* in or of which, *shò* numbers or things numbered consist; i. e. they are the original elements of all things.

35, 36. *Yan*, genuine philanthropy, pure benevolence; *í*, justice, moral rectitude, good intention, guilelessness; *lai*, decorum, politeness, exact propriety; *chí*, discretion, knowledge, understanding, wisdom; *sun*, unsuspicious confidence, truth, a *man* of his *word;* these five are, *shéung* the great cardinal virtues, which, *pat yung* will not endure or allow of, *lun* disorder or derangement.

37, 38. *Tò* is the general name for rice, of which there are many varieties; *léung* is the spiked Barbadoes millet; *shuk* is the common name for pulse; *shü* is the panicled millet; *tsik* also may perhaps be a species of millet; *yan shó shik*, men things-which eat; i. e. the vegetables which they eat.

39, 40. *Má* includes horses, asses, and several kinds of mules; *ngau* designates the whole bovine race; *kai* is used here as a general term for all kinds of poultry; *hün* is also a general term for the many varieties of dogs; *ch'uk* is limited to domesticated animals; *tsz'* means to feed, to give food to; *yan shó tsz'*, men things-which feed, i. e. the animals which men rear.

41, 42. These seven passions are regarded as natural feelings, common to all men; when rightly governed they render their possessor good; but if left uncontroled, they lead to evil: for the sake of euphony, *nái* is dropped in some editions, and another word is added to the end of the line to rhyme with *kü* above in the preceding line.

43, 44. *Nái pát yam* are eight sounds; the several objects specified here are the materials used in making the eight kinds of musical instruments for giving the eight sounds.

45—48. A modern author says: "my own generation forms one class, my father's one, my grandfather's one, my great-grandfather's one, my great-great-grandfather's one; thus above me are four classes: my son's is one, my grandson's one, my great-grandson's one, my great-

| | | |
|---|---|---|
| **48.** Are nine degrees of kindred: constituting the human relations. | 乃九族 人之倫 | ʿNái ʿkau tsuk$_2$: ˏyan ˓chí ˏlun. |
| **49.** Affection of father and son: agreement of husband and wife; | 父子恩 夫婦從 | Fú$^2$ ʿtsz' ˓yan: ˓fú ʿfú ˏts'ung; |
| **50.** The elder brother's love: the younger one's respect; | 兄則友 弟則恭 | ˓Hing tsak˒ ʿyau: tai$^2$ tsak˒ ˓kung; |
| **51.** Precedence observed: in the intercourse of friends; | 長幼序 友與朋 | ʿChéung yau' tsü$^2$: ʿyau ʿú ˏp'ang; |
| **52.** Honor from the prince: fidelity from his ministers: | 君則敬 臣則忠 | ˓Kwan tsak˒ king': ˏshan tsak˒ ˓chung: |
| **53.** These are the ten duties: on all alike binding. | 此十義 人所同 | ʿTs'z' shap˒ í$^2$: ˏyan ʿshó ˏt'ung. |
| **54.** Every teacher of youth: should clearly elucidate; | 凡訓蒙 須講究 | ˏFán fan' ˏmung: ˓su ʿkóng kau'; |
| **55.** Adduce proofs and illustrations: plainly marking the periods. | 詳訓詁 明句讀 | ˏTs'éung fan' ʿkú: ˏming kü' tau$^2$. |
| **56.** He who is a scholar: must have a beginning. | 爲學者 必有初 | ˏWai hók$_2$ ʿché: pít˒ ʿyau ˓ch'ó. |
| **57.** The Primary Lessons finished: he comes to the Four Books. | 小學終 至四書 | ʿSíú Hók$_2$ ˓chung: chí' Sz'' ˓Shü. |
| **58.** Confucius' Conversations: are in twenty chapters. | 論語者 二十篇 | Lun$^2$ ʿYü ʿché: í$^2$ shap$_2$ ˓p'ín. |

great-grandson's one; thus there are four classes below me: these, including myself, are the nine classes or degrees of kindred. The following is a literal translation: great-great-grandfather, great-grandfather, grandfather, father, and self, self and son, son and grandson, from son and grandson to great-grandson and great-grandson's son, are nine classes, men's relations. *Tsuk* means the successive generations of those who are united by blood.

49—53. The *yan chí lun* are here indicated, being those which subsist between father and son, husband and wife, elder and younger brothers, friends and associates, prince and ministers: these ten parties have their respective obligations: *fú tsz' yan* father and son's affection; *yan* kindness, when predicated of the father, is tender regard; but when referred to the son, it signifies filial duty, and such is the twofold meaning of the word here; *ts'ung* in like manner here means both the kindness of the husband, and the gentleness of the wife: *hing tsak yau* elder brother then love, i. e. they must love their younger brothers, and these must respect elder brothers; *chéung yau tsü*, senior and junior's order, or the order of precedence must be observed, *yau ú p'ang* in the intercourse of friends: *kwan tsak king*, prince then honor, the prince must give due honor or consideration to his ministers, while they must be faithful to him: these are, *shap í* the ten obligations, *yan shó t'ung* men things which agree—which all men, in their respective stations, ought carefully to discharge. The import of the whole is, that every son must dutifully serve his parents, every minister must be faithful to his prince; and so of the others.

54. With this line commences the second division of knowledge, that of the scientific investigation, specified in the 22d line above.

55. *Tau* is in form the same as *tuk* to read, but differing from it in tone, it receives a new signification; words of this kind frequently occur.

56. *Wai* to act, to be, *hók ché* a scholar; i. e. the scholar, or every scholar, *pít yau* must have, *ch'ó* a beginning—a suitable beginning of his studies.

57. The Primary Lessons were compiled about seven hundred years ago by Chü fútsz', and form six distinct parts, treating on education and the common duties of life; these lessons, *chung* being finished, the student next, *chí* enters on the study of the *Sz' Shü*, Four Books. These are; 1. the Superior Lessons; 2. the True Medium; 3. Conversations of Confucius; 4. Writings of Mencius. The Four Books were brought together into their present shape by Ching fútsz', who flourished about eight hundred years ago.

58, 59. The *Lun Yü* are the Conversations of Confucius, divided into twenty chapters, in which, *kwan tai tsz'* the collective body of his disciples, *kí* recorded his words, actions, &c. This work has been, not inaptly, compared to Boswell's Life of Johnson.

| | | |
|---|---|---|
| 59. His disciples have [therein]: recorded his good sayings. | 羣弟子 記善言 | ꜀Kw'an tai' 'tsz': kí' shín' ꜀ín. |
| 60. The works of Mencius: are in seven chapters; | 孟子者 七篇止 | Mang' 'tsz' 'ché: ts'át꜃ ꜀p'ín 'chí; |
| 61. He discourses on reason and virtue: benevolence and justice. | 講道德 說仁義 | 'Kóng tò' tak꜃: shüt꜃ ꜁yan í'. |
| 62. The author of the True Medium: was Tsz'sz'. | 作中庸 子思筆 | Tsók꜃ ꜀Chung ꜁Yung: 'Tsz' ꜀sz' pat꜃. |
| 63. 'True' is unperverted: 'medium' is unchangeableness. | 中不偏 庸不易 | ꜀Chung pat꜃ ꜀p'ín: ꜁yung pat꜃ yik꜄. |
| 64. The author of the Superior Lessons: was Tsang; | 作大學 乃曾子 | Tsók꜃ Tái' Hók꜄: 'nái ꜀Tsang 'tsz'; |
| 65. From personal and domestic: he goes to national, rule. | 自修齊 至平治 | Tsz'' ꜀sau ꜁ts'ai: chí' ꜁p'ing chí'. |
| 66. When Filial Duty: and the Four Books are understood, | 孝經通 四書熟 | Háu' ꜀King ꜀t'ung: Sz'' ꜀Shü shuk꜄, |
| 67. Then the six classics: may be commenced. | 如六經 始可讀 | ꜁U luk꜄ ꜀king: 'ch'í 'kó tuk꜄. |
| 68. The Odes, Records, Changes: Ritual, Spring and Autumn, | 詩書易 禮春秋 | ꜀Shí ꜀Shü Yik꜄: 'Lai ꜀Ch'un ꜀Ts'au, |
| 69. Called the six classics: ought to be well studied. | 號六經 當講求 | Hò' luk꜄ ꜀king: ꜀tóng 'kóng ꜁k'au. |
| 70. The systems of changes: by Fukhí and Shannung, with | 有連山 有歸藏 | 'Yau ꜁Lín ꜀Shán: 'yau ꜀Kwai ꜁Ch'óng, |
| 71. That of the Chau dynasty: were three complete works. | 有周易 三易詳 | 'Yau ꜀Chau Yik꜄: ꜀sám yik꜄ ꜁ts'éung. |

60, 61. Mang tsz', the name of the man, is here used to designate his works, just as we say Johnson or Milton when we refer to the works of those writers. *Tsz'* and *fútsz'* are terms of respect, nearly equivalent to philosopher: *kóng* and *shüt* are synonyms, and the latter serves as a connective, at the same time it fills the measure of the verse.

62, 63. *Tsók* means to make, or the maker, *pat* is the Chinese pencil; the pencil of Tsz'-sz' was the maker of the Chung Yung, i. e. this work was written by his hand; he was a grandson of Confucius, and the work consists chiefly of the ethical sayings of the sage, and originally formed a part of the Book of Rites.

64. *Tái Hók*, magna scientia, is explained to mean that learning which is suitable for persons who are advanced in years. This work was also originally a chapter of the Book of Rites; but is now one of the Four Books, and forms a counterpart to the *Síú Hók* or Primary Lessons.

65. *Tsz'* means from; *sau* is self-government; *tsai* is the government of a family; *chí* means to rule well a state, province, or kingdom; and *ping* is to keep in order an empire: these are the leading topics of the essay, which was reduced to writing by *Tsang*, one of the disciples of Confucius.

66, 77. *Háu King* is, as the name signifies, a treatise on filial duty, consisting of conversations between Confucius and Tsang; it is divided into eighteen short sections, and is commonly published with the Primary Lessons: *tung* and *shuk* are synonyms, each meaning thoroughly studied, well understood; *ü* as, such as, or works such as, *luk king* the six classics, *ch'í* begin, *kó* can, *tuk* to read; i. e. the treatise on Filial Duty and the Four Books being well understood, the student may commence the study of the higher classics.

68, 69. Spring and Autumn is a single work; but the Ritual originally formed two separate treatises, and these several works, collectively, *hò* were styled, *luk king* the six classics, *tóng* deserving, *kóng* explanation, and *kau* investigation.

70, 71. *Yau* there was, *Lín Shán* 'connected hills,' a so named treatise on the changes, written by *Fukhí; yau* there was, *Kwai Ch'óng* another work of the same kind written by the emperor Shannung; *yau* there was, *Chau Yik* the Changes of Chau, written by king Wan (or Wan wáng); *sám yik* three systems of changes, *ts'éung* complete and entire. These are unitedly called the *Yik King*, or the Book of Changes.

| | | |
|---|---|---|
| 72. The royal and ministerial canons: the instructions and injunctions, | 有典謨 有訓誥 | 'Yau 'tín ,mò: 'yau fan' kò', |
| 73. The vows and commands: are included in the Records. | 有誓命 書之奧 | 'Yau shai$^{2}$ ming$^{2}$: ‹shü ‹chí ò'. |
| 74. My lord Chau: was the author of the Chau Ritual. | 我周公 作周禮 | 'Ngó ‹Chau ‹kung: tsók› ‹Chau 'Lai. |
| 75. He instituted six Boards: for the general government. | 著六官 存治體 | Chü' luk$_{2}$ ‹Kún: ,ts'ün chí$^{2}$ 'tai. |
| 76. The elder and younger Tai: commented on the Ritual; | 大小戴 註禮記 | Tái$^{2}$ 'síú Tái': chü' 'Lai Kí'; |
| 77. Transmited the sage's words: & completed the ritual and music. | 述聖言 禮樂備 | Shut$_{2}$ shing' ,ín: 'lái ngók$_{2}$ pí$^{2}$. |
| 78. The National Airs: the two Eulogies, and the Songs, | 曰國風 曰雅頌 | Üt$_{2}$ Kwók› ‹Fung: üt$_{2}$ 'Ngá Tsung$^{2}$, |
| 79. Styled the Four Odes: are worthy to be rehearsed. | 號四詩 當諷詠 | Hò$^{2}$ Sz" ‹Shí: ‹tóng fung' wing$^{2}$. |
| 80. The odes having ceased: Spring and Autumn was made; | 詩既亡 春秋作 | ‹Shí kí' ,móng: ‹Ch'un ‹Ts'au tsók›; |
| 81. Which by praise and blame: separate the good and bad. | 寓褒貶 別善惡 | Yü$^{2}$ ‹pò 'pín: pít$_{2}$ shín$^{2}$ ók›. |

72, 73. *Shü*, the Book of Records, contains six different kinds of state papers, referring to times before Confucius: 1. *tín* were the imperial ordinances, which were regarded as unalterable; 2. *mò* included drafts or plans, drawn up by ministers as laws of action for their sovereigns; 3. *fan* denotes those instructions which the chief ministers prepared for their sovereign, opening and delineating the path in which he should walk; 4. *kò* were imperial proclamations, given for the instruction and admonition of the whole empire; 5. *shai* were vows taken by the emperors; for example, when an army was going out to battle, the monarch, worshiping towards heaven, vowed in the presence of his leaders, that he would reward the faithful and punish the unfaithful among his troops; 6. *ming* were the emperor's mandates, given to his great ministers.

74. *Kung* is an honorary title nearly equivalent to lord; *ngó Chau*, our Chau dynasty, i. e. my lord of the Chau (Chow) dynasty, *tsók* made, *Chau Lai* the Chau Ritual; he was the son of king Wan, mentioned above, and younger brother of the martial king (Wú wáng), the first monarch of the Chau dynasty, which arose B. C. 1122. The family name of this line of monarchs, which are very renowned in Cuinese history, was *Kí*, and in some editions it is written *ngó Kí kung*.

75. *Chü* is to institute, lord Kí instituted six Boards, the prototypes, probably, of the modern ones; *tsün* to maintain, *chí* governmental, *tai* operations, i. e. to preserve and govern the body politic.

76, 77. These two brothers, *chü* wrote commentaries on the *Lai*, and their work was styled *Lai Kí*, the Book of Rites; it was divided into forty-nine *p'ín* or chapters, two of which, the True Medium and the Superior Lessons, have been taken to form parts of the Four Books: the other chapters constitute the Book of Rites, one of the Five Classics: *shut* is to narrate, or add by way of comment; they narrated the sayings of the sage, and in this way, *lai ngók pí* both the ritual and musical services were rendered complete.

78, 79. *Hò Sz' Shí* named Four Odes, *üt* viz., *Kwók Fung* National Airs, which were annually collected and presented to the emperor, and by him submitted to his ministers, to enable them to know the character of those whom they had to govern; *Ngá* Eulogies, forming two parts,—*Síú* the Lesser, and *Tái* the Greater;—these were employed on state occasions, at imperial audiences and banquets; *Tsung* were Songs of praises, used at the imperial sacrifices; *tóng* worthy, *fung wing* to be rehearsed and sung.

80, 81. The odes, *kí móng* having been discontinued, Confucius, in order to supply their place, commenced his Annals, which cover a period of 242 years; they were compiled from the records of his native state, the modern Shántung: *yü* in them are found recorded, *pò pín* commendations and censures, *pít* distinguishing, *shín* the good, *ók* from the bad. From this

| | | |
|---|---|---|
| 82. [On the Annals] are three commentaries: by Kungyéung, | 三傳者 有公羊 | ˛Sám Chün$^{2}$ ˊché: ˊyau ˛Kung ˛yéung, |
| 83. The family of Tsó: and by Kukléung. | 有左氏 有穀梁 | ˊYau ˊTsó shí$^{2}$: ˊyau Kuk$_{3}$ ˛léung. |
| 84. The classics understood: read the philosophical writers; | 經既明 方讀子 | ˛King kí$^{3}$ ˛ming: ˛fóng tuk$_{2}$ ˊtsz'; |
| 85. Select important parts: and commit them to memory. | 撮其要 記其事 | Ts'üt$_{3}$ ˛k'í iú$^{3}$: kí$^{3}$ ˛k'í sz$^{2}$. |
| 86. Of these there are five: by Sun and by Yéung, | 五子者 有荀揚 | ˊ'Ng ˊtsz' ˊché: ˊyau ˛Sun ˛Yéung, |
| 87. By Manchung: and by Lò and Chóng. | 文中子 及老莊 | ˛Man ˛chung ˊtsz': kap$_{2}$ ˊLò ˛Chóng. |
| 88. The classics and philosophers understood: read next general history. | 經子通 讀諸史 | ˛King ˊtsz' ˛t'ung: tuk$_{2}$ ˛chü ˊsz'. |

characteristic, the work received its name; the commendations are life-giving like spring; the censures are life-withering like autumn; hence Spring and Autumn Annals.

82, 83. These three, in their respective commentaries, endeavored to complete and render more lucid the annals, which had been commenced by their master.

84—87. *Tsz'* is here used to denote the philosophical writers; of these, *tsüt* select, *kí iú* the most eminent, or parts from the writings of the most eminent, and, *kí k'í sz'* commit them to memory: *'ng tsz'* are five of *shap tsz'*, or ten authors, often referred to by the Chinese, and whose writings form a body of literature, second only to their classics.

88. *Chü sz'*, literally all histories, i. e. general history, which however refers only to their own country. From this line, the Sám Tsz' King proceeds with a brief summary of the history of the Chinese empire, and closes with examples and exhortations, intended to encourage the young student.

## Section Fourth.

## EXERCISES IN CONVERSATION.

### 習言第四章

Tsap$_{2}$ ˛ín; tai$^{2}$ sz$^{2}$ ˛chéung.

| | | |
|---|---|---|
| 1. Stop, stop! I wish to understand the meaning of what you have written. | 莫自莫自我要曉得點解至做得 | ˊMó tsz$^{2}$, ˊmó tsz$^{2}$! ˊngó iú$^{3}$ ˊhiú tak$_{3}$ ˊtím ˊkái, chí$^{3}$ tsò$^{2}$ tak$_{3}$. |
| It is easily understood, I will explain it to you. | 易曉我講你知呵 | I$^{2}$ ˊhiú, ˊngó ˊkóng ˊní ˛chí ˛ó. |

### *Notes and Explanations.*

1. *Mók* is the common pronunciation of *mó;* with this latter tone and sound it is frequently used in conversation. I wish now to understand, *tím kái* how explain, or what is the meaning of what you have written, *chí* then arrive at, *tsò* do, *tak* obtain; i. e. I shall then have obtained what I wish, when you have explained to me those lines, which you have copied from the Sám Tsz' King. N. B. The learner is supposed to interrupt his teacher, when he

廣東方言讀本



| | | |
|---|---|---|
| 2. What is the meaning of this character? (pointing to the first in the 3d section.) | 呢個字點解呢 | ‹Ní kó' tsz'² 'tím 'kái ‹ní? |
| It is called *yan*, and denotes *man*. | 呢個人字指凡人 | ‹Ní kó' ˏ*yan* tsz'², 'chí ˏfán ˏyan. |
| 3. (Pointing to the second he asks again,) And this? | 呢個呢 | ‹Ní kó' ‹ní? |
| This is *chí*, a particle. | 呢個之字係虛字 | ‹Ní kó' ‹*chí* tsz'² hai² ‹hü tsz'². |
| 4. I know it is a particle, but what is its meaning? | 我知係虛字⿰口知點解呢 | 'Ngó ‹chí hai² ‹hü tsz'², ‹chí 'tím 'kái ‹ní? |
| It means man's beginning, the time when he is born. | 只係人於初生個陣時咁咯 | Chat› hai² ˏyan ‹ü ‹ch'ó ‹shang, kó' chan' ˏshí, 'kóm lók›. |
| 5. And this, (pointing to the third,) what is its meaning? | 呢個又點呢 | ‹Ní kó', yau² 'tím ‹ní? |
| This is *ch'ó*, and it signifies *beginning*. | 呢個初字就係始初咁解 | ‹Ní kó' ‹*ch'ó* tsz'² tsau² hai² ‹ch'í ‹ch'ó, 'kóm 'kái. |
| 6. What is the meaning of the three when joined together? | 三個合埋點呢 | ˏSám kó' hóp› ˏmái 'tím ‹ní? |
| They mean man at his birth, when first separated from his mother's womb. | 人於初生離母胎時咁解咯 | ˏYan ‹ü ‹ch'ó ‹shang ˏli 'mò ‹t'oi ˏshí, 'kóm 'kái lók›. |
| 7. What is the meaning of the next three? | 下頭三個又點呢 | Há² ˏt'au ‹sám kó' yau² 'tím ‹ní? |
| They mean, that the nature of all men, when first born is good. | 凡人初生之性本來係善咁咯 | ˏFán ˏyan ‹ch'ó ‹shang ‹chí sing' 'pún ˏloi hai² shín², 'kóm lók›. |

has written eighty-eight lines, by calling for an explanation of what has been written; the conversation commences with the line '*yan chí ch'ó, sing pún shín*,' and may be extended at the pleasure of the learner.

2. *Níkó* means this; *chí*, the finger, here signifies to point with the finger, *níkó yan tsz'* this man character points to all men; i. e. it denotes the species, or man generally.

3. *Níkó chí tsz'* this character *chí*, *hai* is, *hü tsz'* an empty character, or a particle. By this vague term the Chinese intend to express connective or euphonic particles, in distinction from the *shat tsz'*, or solid words, such as nouns, verbs, &c.

4. In the phrase *chí tím kái ní?* the particle *chí* has the sense of but or yet: *chat* merely, *hai* is, *yan* man, *ü* at, *ch'ó* beginning, *shang* born, *kó* that, *chan* moment, *shí* time, *kóm* so, *lók* indeed; that is, the particle merely denotes the point of time, at which man is born. The phrase *yan chí ch'ó* may be rendered in various ways, thus; man's beginning, man at his birth, man at the time of his birth; &c.

6. Here the same idea is repeated, literally thus; man at beginning born separated mother's womb time, so explain indeed. The sentiment is explicitly expressed, that the child when first born possesses a good nature.

7. *Há t'au* below head, *sám kó* the three, also how? All men beginning born 's nature

CHI. CHR. 5

| | | |
|---|---|---|
| 8. Is there really such a doctrine! Where did it originate? | 眞有個的道理<br>喺邊處黎呢 | ‹Chan ‘yau kó’ tik› tò$^{2}$ ‘lí! ‘Hai ‹pín ch‘ü’ ‹lai ‹ní? |
| It was the general sentiment expressed by the ancient sages and wise men. | 歷古聖賢都係<br>咁講嘅嚹 | Lik$_{2}$ ‘kú shing’ ‹ín ‹tò hai$^{2}$ ‘kóm ‘kóng ké’ lá’. |
| 9. Were there any who doubted its correctness? | 有人思疑有冇<br>呢 | ‘Yau ‹yan ‹sz’ ‹í, ‘yau ‘mò ‹ní? |
| In the second book of Mencius, the philosopher Kungtò called it in question. | 下孟裏頭公都<br>子思疑 | Há$^{2}$ Mang$^{2}$ lüi$^{2}$ ‹t‘au ‹Kung ‹tò ‘tsz’ ‹sz’ ‹í. |
| 10. How was this? | 點思疑呢 | ‘Tím ‹sz’ ‹í ‹ní? |
| Having first quoted several cases, bearing on the question, he said (to Mencius), Now, you say, nature is good, are then all these false? | 佢先引幾說黎<br>講故此話今曰<br>性善然則彼皆<br>非與咁 | ‘K‘ui ‹sín ‘yan ‘kí shüt› ‹lai ‘kóng, kú’ ‘ts‘z’ wá$^{2}$, ‹kam üt$_{2}$ sing’ shín$^{2}$, ‹ín tsak› ‘pí ‹kái ‹fí ‹yü, ‘kóm. |
| 11. What was the answer of Mencius? | 孟夫子點答呢 | Mang$^{2}$ ‹fú ‘tsz’ ‘tím táp› ‹ní? |
| He waved the question, by introducing the subject of the passions. | 孟夫子擰情黎<br>推度話佢知 | Mang$^{2}$ ‹fú ‘tsz’ ‹ning ‹ts‘ing ‹lai ‹ch‘ui tók$_{2}$ wá$^{2}$ ‘k‘ui ‹chí. |
| 12. Well, you have explained enough for the present; to-morrow I will thank you to come again. | 做得嚹聽日請<br>先生番嚟 | Tsò$^{2}$ tak› lá’; ‹t‘ing yat$_{2}$ ‘ts‘ing ‹sín ‹shang ‹fán ‹lai. |

original come is good, so indeed! i. e. the meaning of the three next characters is, that the nature of all men is good at the time when they are first born.

8. Truly have that doctrine! In what place come eh? *Tò lí* means what is reasonable, or right, a just sentiment, a true doctrine, or simply a doctrine, or sentiment: *hai pín ch‘ü lai* may be correctly rendered, either, From what place did it originate? or, With whom did it originate? *lik* pass, *kú* ancient, *shing* sages, *ín* worthies, *tò* all, *hai* were, *kóm* so, *kóng* speaking, *ké lá* even so! that is, this was the sentiment, which the sages and worthies generally held through the successive ages of antiquity.

9. *Yau yan* have men, *sz’ í* doubting, *yau mò ní* have not have eh? i. e. were there any who doubted the correctness of the sentiment? Below Mang inside head, referring to the second book of Mencius, *Kungtò tsz’* the philosopher Kungtò (who is there introduced), *sz’ í* doubted, i. e. called in question the correctness of the sentiment.

10. *K‘ui* refers to Kungtò, who having first, *yan* adduced, *kí shüt* several sayings, *lai kóng* come speak, *kú ts‘z’* with reference to these sayings, (which were in opposition to what Mencius had advanced,) *wá* said or asked, Now you say the nature of man is good, *ín* are, *tsak* then, *pí* the sayings which I have adduced, *kái* all, *fí* false or erroneous? *yü* is an interrogative particle: *kóm* thus, or in this manner, Kungtò expressed his doubts of the correctness of the sentiment in question. See *Mang tsz’*, *kün luk*, *tai luk chéung*.

11. *Táp* is to answer, to give an answer: *ning* is to bring, or to take up as a topic of conversation; *ts‘ing* denotes man's natural disposition, or the passions, (sec. iii: 42.,) Mencius

| | | |
|---|---|---|
| Very good. | 好 | 'Hò. |
| 13. Good morning. | 請咧請咧 | 'Ts'ing lé'! 'ts'ing lé'! |
| Good bye. | 請呀請呀 | 'Ts'ing á'! 'ts'ing á'! |

taking up the subject of the passions, *lai* brought it, *ch'ui* to push, *tók* to measure, i. e. he made it take the place of the other, and in this way he waved the point at issue; *wá k'ui chí* speak him know, i. e. in his conversation with Kungtò.

12. *Tsò tak lá*, these words mean, you have explained as far as I desire you to do at this time; *ting yat* but to-morrow, please come again and renew your explanations. The teacher answers *hò* good, or I will do so, the reply being usually attended with a deferential bow, and then he takes his leave.

## Section Fifth.

## EXERCISES IN WRITING.

### 習寫第五章

Tsap$_{2}$ 'sé; tai$^{2}$ ''ng ‹cheung.

| | | |
|---|---|---|
| 1. How, Sir, do the Chinese commence learning to write? | 先生唐人點樣初學寫字呢 | ‹Sín ‹shang, ‹T'òng ‹yan 'tím yéung$^{2}$ ‹ch'ó hók$_{2}$ 'sé tsz'$^{2}$ ‹ní? |
| The teacher is requested at first to guide the child's hand, holding the pencil, to write copies in red ink. | 請先生把手執筆寫紅硃字先咯 | 'Tsing ‹sín ‹shang 'pá 'shau chap› pat› 'sé ‹hung ‹chü tsz'$^{2}$ ‹sín lók›. |
| 2. Are there any rules for writing? | 寫字有乜方法有冇呢 | 'Sé tsz'$^{2}$ 'yau mat› ‹fóng fát›, 'yau 'mò ‹ní? |
| Yes; there are rules for holding the pencil, for making the separate strokes, and for combining them into characters. | 有嗾有執筆法使筆法裝字法 | 'Yau ‹é; 'yau chap› pat› fát›, 'shai pat› fát›, ‹chóng tsz'$^{2}$ fát›. |

### *Notes and Explanations.*

1. *Sínshang* is often used in the sense of Sir and Mr., and in many instances, as in the present, may be well translated by Sir: *pá shau* is to grasp the hand; the teacher, standing up, grasps the child's hand and guides both it and the pencil: *chá pat* is to hold the pencil: *sé* is to write, *hung chü tsz'* red characters, *sín* in the first place; i. e. at first, when the child begins learning to write, he is furnished with copies written in red ink, and a pencil which he takes in his hand; then at the child's request, the teacher, grasping his hand, guides the pencil slowly and carefully over each of the characters in the copy.

2. *Fóng fát* is a common phrase for rules, such as rules, or instructions, for studying, writing, painting, and other similar arts; the two words are synonymous, and are often used separately in the same sense which they have here.

| | | |
|---|---|---|
| 3. How is the pencil to be held? | 點樣執呢 | 'Tím yéung² chap˒ ˓ní? |
| As Wóng Yaukwan held it. | 學王右軍執囉 | Hók˔ ˏWóng Yau² ˓kwan chap˒ ˓ló. |
| 4. How can I know how he held it? | 點知佢點樣執呢 | 'Tím ˓chí ˁk'ui 'tím yéung² chap˒ ˓ní? |
| By inspecting his copy-book. | 睇佢個筆陣圖囉 | 'T'ai ˁk'ui kó' pat˒ chan² ˏt'ò ˓ló. |
| 5. I have done so, and yet I do not at all understand how it is to be held. | 睇都唔曉得晒嘅 | 'T'ai, ˓tò ˏ'm 'híú tak˒ sái' ké'. |
| Then I will teach you: let the thumb be placed with the back towards the body, facing outwards; let the fore and middle fingers, with the back turned outwards, be brought near it, facing the body; thus holding fast the pencil: let the fourth and little fingers, placed close together, be brought part way in [beyond the pencil] pointing towards you, so holding the pencil, with the fist half open and hollow within, and with the fingers close together: this is the best way to hold the pencil. | 我教你呵頭指挨身向外二指中指挨外向身咁樣揸住個枝筆使無名指尾指疊埋伸一半入裏頭指住自巳咁樣執住好似半開嘅拳一樣總要拳空指密爲好 | ʻNgó káu' ʻní ˓ó: ˏt'au 'chí ˓ái ˓shan héung' ngoi²; í² 'chí, chung' 'chí, ˓ái ngoi² héung' ˓shan; 'kóm yéung² ˓chá chü² kó' ˓chí pat˒: 'shai ˏmò ˏming 'chí, ʻmí 'chí, típ˔ ˏmái, ˓shan yat˒ pún' yap˔ ʻlü ˏt'au, 'chí chü² tsz'² 'kí, 'kóm yéung² chap˒ chü², 'hò 'tsz' pún' ˓hoi ké' ˏk'ün yat˒ yéung², 'chung íú' ˏk'ün ˓hung 'chí mat˔; ˏwai 'hò. |

3. *Wóng Yaukwan* is the author of a system of writing, answering in many respects to those which are common in the west; the work contains twelve plates illustrating the several ways of holding the pencil, together with full explanations, to which are appended examples of all the different strokes used in writing Chinese, and characters showing the mode of their use. The one on the opposite page is intended to represent a Chinese master sitting at his table, engaged in writing.

4. *Pat chan t'ò* pencil order plates, i. e. plates illustrating the order, or manner, of holding the pencil.

5. *T'ai* I have looked, *tò* and yet, do not understand it, *sái ké* altogether, or entirely, i. e. I have examined the plates, and yet do not at all understand the subject.

6. *T'au chí* the thumb is also called *tái chí* the great finger: *í chí* the forefinger is also called *shik chí* the eating finger, from the part it often takes with the Chinese in supplying the mouth with food: *shai* is to use or let,—let *mò ming chí* the nameless or the fourth, and *mí chí* the last or little finger, *típ mái* placed one on the other, *shan* be brought, *yat pún* one half, *yap* entering, *lüt'au* within [side of the pencil], *chí chü* pointing towards, *tsz' kí* yourself, *hò tsz'* just as, *pún* half, *hoi* opened, *ké* being (being opened), *k'ün* the fist, *yat yéung* in one and the same manner; *chung* moreover, *íú* it is required, *k'ün* that the fist, *hung* be hollow, *chí mat* with the fingers close together; *wai hò* to be good, i. e. this is the good, or the best way to hold the pencil.

6. Though [I am able] to hold the pencil, yet I do not know which part of the character should be written first.

執住個枝筆每
個字唔知寫邊
的先呢

Chap› chü² kó' ‹chí pat›, ʽmúi kó' tsz'² ‚'m ‹chí ʻsé ‹pín tik› ‹sín ‹ní?

Distinguishing between the upper and the lower, the right and left parts, proceed from the upper to the lower, writing the left side first and then the right; if you doubt this, you may examine the eight rules in the character Wing.

以上下左右分
由上至下先左
後右唔信你睇
永字八法呵

ʽI' shéung² há² ʻtsó yau² ‹fan, ‚yau shéung² chí' há², ‹sín ʻtsó hau² yau²; ‚'m sun', ʽní ʻt'ai ʽWing tsz'² pát› fát› ‹ó.

7. Eternal. — ʽWing.

i. A dot, slanting. — Tím, tsik› chak›.

ii. A horizontal line, curbed. — ‹Wáng, tsik› lak‚.

iii. A perpendicular line, erect. — ʽNò, tsik› shü².

iv. A hook, quick leaping. — Yéuk›, tsik› ‹k'au.

v. A spike, pointed upwards. — Ch'ák›, tsik› t'íú'.

vi. A sweep, rapidly brushing outwards. — Léuk‚, tsik› p'ít›.

vii. A stroke, bill shaped, quickly sweeping. — Téuk›, tsik› fat›.

viii. A dash, slowly moving outwards. — Chák›, tsik› nát‚.

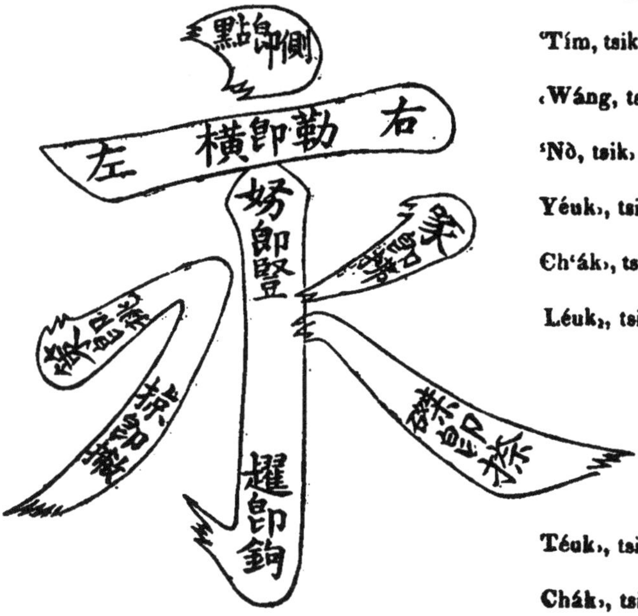


6. Hold fast the pencil, every character not know to write, [which] side of first eh? Although you have told me how to hold the pencil, yet I know not which part of even a single character should be written first,—which part is to be written first? *Ní* gives this interrogative form to the sentence, which otherwise would be declarative: the learner says that he does not know where to begin to write a single character; *í* using, *shéung há* upper and lower, *tsó yau* left and right, *fan* divisions, proceed in writing, *yau shéung* from the upper parts, *chí há* to the lower; also, *sín tsó* first write the left part, *hau yau* afterwards the right; *'m sun* not believing this, *ní t'ai* you may examine for confirmation, *Wing tsz' pát fát* the eight rules which are based on the eight parts of the character *Wing*. The Wing Tsz' Pát Fát is also used as the name of a little work on writing, from which the directions given above are chiefly selected.

7. This character is regarded as containing all the simple strokes required in writing Chinese; and both their names and the modes of writing them are briefly expressed in the respective parts, as here numbered.

8. A dot. (i.)

側 丶

This is made by a slant of the pencil, which moving [first] towards the right, is then turned round towards the left. It has 18 forms. Avoid the ox-head shape.

側筆而成向右轉左生一十八法忌牛頭

Chak꜄.

Chak꜄ pat꜄ ꜁í ꜁shing, héung꜄ yau꜄ ꜂chan ꜂tsó. ꜀Shang yat꜄ shap꜅ pát꜄ fát꜄. Kí꜄ ꜁ngau ꜁t'au.

9. A horizontal line. (ii.)

勒 一

This is made by a leap of the pencil, which stopping short on a point is drawn off to the left. It has 6 forms. Avoid making it with drooping shoulders.

趯筆而成駐鋒廻左生六法忌垂肩

Lak꜅.

Yéuk꜅ pat꜄ ꜁í ꜁shing, chü꜄ ꜀fung ꜁úi ꜂tsó. ꜀Shang luk꜅ fát꜄. Kí꜄ ꜁shui ꜀kín.

10. A perpendicular line. (iii.)

努 丨

Here the pencil must not be held perfectly erect, for then the stroke will lack body. It has 12 forms. Avoid the wasp-like waist.

筆不可直直則無力生一十二法忌蜂腰

꜂Nò.

Pat꜄ pat꜄ ꜂hó chik꜅, chik꜅ tsak꜄ ꜁mò lik꜅. ꜀Shang yat꜄ shap꜅ í꜄ fát꜄. Kí꜄ ꜀fung ꜀íú.

11. A hook. (iv.)

趯 亅

The pencil brought down is made to diverge a little, and raised upwards with a jerk. It has 14 forms. Avoid a resemblance to a crane's knees.

殺筆斜行借勢而起生一十四法忌鶴膝

Yéuk꜅.

Shát꜄ pat꜄ ꜁ts'é ꜁hang, tsé꜄ shai꜄ ꜁í ꜂hí. ꜀Shang yat꜄ shap꜄ sz꜄ fát꜄. Kí꜄ hók꜅ sat꜄.

---

8. This *chak*, slant, is commonly called *tím*, a dot. It has, either simple or compound, eighteen different forms, which, from some real or imaginary resemblance to certain objects, are called by their names; thus, pearl drop; plum seed; almond seed; goat's horns; cock's crest. These names, often very fanciful, are given to assist the memory. They are found in most of the Chinese copy-books, and ought to be carefully examined by every one who desires to write the character correctly with ease and elegance.

9. This *lak*, bit or curb, is commonly called *wáng*, a horizontal line; the pencil, being placed down carefully on the left, is carried rapidly off to the right, where, *chü fung* it is brought to a dead halt, *úi* thence recoiling, *tsó* towards the left. The ends of the line are compared to a man's shoulders, and ought, for the sake of beauty, to be erect and square, and not bent down or drooping.

10. *Nò*, a strong line, is usually called *shü* or *chik*, both meaning a perpendicular line: among the twelve forms assumed by this line, there are two or three which exhibit a crooked or deflected shape, one is called a crooked rule, and another a golden city.

11. *Yéuk*, a quick leap, is commonly called *k'au*, a hook. In most of the forms, the hook is turned to the left; in a few instances it takes the opposite direction; the shaft also takes a variety of forms: new moon, flying goose, swimming goose, dragon's tail, &c., are some of the names of these forms.

| | | |
|---|---|---|
| **12. A spike. (v.)** | 策  | **Ch'ák,.** |
| This resembles a part of a broken line, with the point thrown upwards. It has 6 forms. Avoid the shape of a nail's head. | 卽折異畫仰鋒<br>上搨生六法忌<br>釘頭 | Tsik, chít, í² wák₂, 'yéung ‹fung shéung' kít,. ‹Shang luk, fát,. Kí² ‹ting ‹t'au. |
| **13. A sweep. (vi.)** | 掠  | **Léuk₂.** |
| The best form of this is made by turning the pencil's point off to the left, with a heavy stroke. It has 8 forms. Avoid the shape of a rat's tail. | 筆鋒左出肥舒<br>爲貴生八法忌<br>鼠尾 | Pat, ‹fung 'tsó ch'ut,, ‹fí ‹shü ‹wai kwai'. ‹Shang pát₂ fát₂. Kí² 'shü 'mí. |
| **14. A stroke. (vii.)** | 啄  | **Téuk,.** |
| This is made by a sudden jerk of the pencil, and should be short and slender. It has 12 forms. Avoid the shape of a broken splinter. | 臥筆疾掩畧帶<br>瘦意生一十二<br>法忌斷柴 | Ngó² pat, tsat₂ 'ím, léuk₂ tái' sau' í'. ‹Shang yat, shap₂ í² fát,. Kí² tün² ‹shái. |
| **15. A dash. (viii.)** | 磔  | **Chák₂.** |
| Here the pencil delicately rises, and then spreads off with a full stroke. It has 6 forms. Avoid the shape of a broom. | 筆微仰而徐開<br>其勢生六法忌<br>撒帚 | Pat, ‹mí 'yéung ‹í, ‹ch'ü ‹hoi ‹k'í shai'. ‹Shang luk₂ fát,. Kí² sát, 'chau. |
| 16. Are there also rules for forming the characters? Come and examine the copy-plates of professor Shiú Ying. | 重有裝字嘅呢<br>你嚟睇邵瑛先<br>生寫個法帖啊 | Chung² 'yau ‹chóng tsz'² ké' ní? 'Ní ‹lai 't'ai Shiú² ‹Ying ‹sín ‹shang 'sé ‹ní kó' fát, t'íp, ‹ó. |

12. *Ch'ák*, a spike, is also called *t'íú*, pointing upwards, to prick or stir up; in one form it resembles the hook.

13. *Léuk*, a sweep, means to plunder; it is also called *p'ít* which has nearly the same sense; the allusion is derived from the *sweeping* course of those who plunder.

14. *Téuk*, a stroke, means also to strike with the bill, as a bird does in feeding; it is likewise called *fat*, which means to strike, to brush, to wave.

15. *Chák* is to pull in pieces, and is commonly called *nát;* golden knife, crying duck, frightened snake, roaming fish, playing fish, and double eyes, are the names of its forms.

16. The work of *Shíú Ying* contains a series of copies, ninety-two in number, each of which is accompanied by a short rule, for guidance of the learner. The work is in octavo; printed on thick stiff paper like pasteboard; the characters are white upon a black ground. The paper is all in one piece, folded between two boards, like a fan.

## Section Sixth.

## EXERCISES IN WRITING.

習寫第六章
Tsáp$_{2}$ ʿsé; tai$^{2}$ luk$_{2}$ ˏchéung.

| | | |
|---|---|---|
| 1. Universe. Fixed. Repose. | 宙定寧 | Chau$^{2}$. Ting$^{2}$. ˏNing. |
| In characters of this form, the upper part should cover all the lines below it. | 天覆者凡畫皆冒於其下 | ˏT'ín fau$^{2}$ ʿché, ˏfán wák$_{2}$ ˏkái mò$^{2}$ ˏü ˏk'í há$^{2}$. |
| 2. Extreme. Sacred. A cover. | 至聖蓋 | Chíʾ. Shingʾ. K'oiʾ. |
| In characters of this form, the lower part should support all the lines above it. | 地載者有畫皆托於其上 | Tí$^{2}$ tsoiʾ ʿché, ʿyau wák$_{2}$ ˏkái tók› ˏü ˏk'í shéung$^{2}$. |
| 3. A class. Youth. Immediately. | 部幼即 | Pò$^{2}$. Yauʾ. Tsik›. |
| In these prominence is given to the left part, it being elevated, while the right is depressed. | 讓左者左昂右低 | Yéung$^{2}$ ʿtsó ʿché, ʿtsó ˏngóng, yau$^{2}$ ˏtai. |
| 4. Read. Rainbow. Meritorious deeds. | 讀蝀績 | Tuk$_{2}$. Tungʾ. Tsik$^{2}$. |
| In these prominence is given to the right, it being extended, while the left is contracted. | 讓右者右伸左縮 | Yéung$^{2}$ yau$^{2}$ ʿché, yau$^{2}$ ˏshan, ʿtsó shuk›. |

### *Notes and Explanations.*

1. These are the copies of Shíú Ying. The large characters are selected only with reference to their form, and stand entirely independent of each other; their literal meaning is given, that it may be fixed in the memory during the exercise of writing. *T'ín fau ché*, the celestial canopy, denotes the upper part of the character; and in this dialect is called *ˏlam ˏp'ung ˏt'au:* the literal translation of the rule is,—celestial covering the, every line all covered in it below: *wák*, like *lak* (sec. v: 9.), means a horizontal line, or to draw such a line.

2. *Tí tsoi ché*, terrestrial support, denotes the lower line; *yau* there being, *wák* lines, *kái* all, *tók* [should be] supported, *ü* on, *k'í* it, *shéung* above: *yau wák* here is nearly equivalent to *fán wák;* the latter means every line, the former signifies whatever lines there are;—each phrase thus denoting all the lines.

3, 4. The student will not fail to notice a correspondence—sometimes antithetical, some-

| | | |
|---|---|---|
| 5. Glad. I or me. Rest. | 喜吾安 | ‘Hí. ˏ’Ng. ˏÓn. |
| In these, the transverse line through the middle should be well extended. | 橫擔者中畫宜長 | ˏWáng ˏtám ‘ché, ˏchung wák, ˏí ˏch‘éung. |
| 6. Armor. Even. Spear. | 甲平干 | Káp,. ˏP‘ing. ˏKón. |
| In these, the perpendicular line should be drawn perfectly straight through the middle. | 直卓者中豎宜正 | Chik, ch‘éuk, ‘ché, ˏchung shü’ ˏí ching’. |
| 7. Grapes. A caterpillar. A bean. | 葡蜀葛 | ˏP‘ò. Chuk, Kót,. |
| In characters of this form, the body of the hook should not be either too crooked or too short. | 勾拏法其身不宜曲短 | ˏKau ˏná fát,, ˏk‘í ˏshan pat, ˏí h‘uk, ‘tün. |
| 8. A sentence. A broad spoon. Do not. | 句勺勿 | Kui’. Ch‘éuk,. Mat,. |
| In characters of this form, the shape of the hook should not be too straight or too long. | 勾衄法其勢不可直長 | ˏKau nuk, fát,, ˏk‘í shai’ pat, ‘hó chik, ˏch‘éung. |
| 9. Left. In. Particolored. | 左在尨 | ‘Tsó. Tsoi’. P‘óng. |
| In these, the horizontal line should be short, and the sweep long. | 畫短撇長 | Wák, ‘tün, p‘it, ˏch‘éung. |

times correlative—in many of the following rules; there is likewise a similar correspondence between the terms used in the same rules; *ngóng* and *tai*, *shan* and *shuk*, are examples of this usage.

5, 6. The long horizontal line in the one, and the long perpendicular line in the other, of these are to be noted: the former should be well extended both ways; it has been by the Chinese compared to the two ends of a pole, on which a burden is suspended to be carried on the shoulders of two men.

7, 8. In both of these the long crooked line should be noted; from the shape into which it is bent, it is called *kau* a hook; *ná* means to seize or catch; *nuk* is a sabre, or the nose made bloody by the sabre: *kau ná fát* the hook catching form, *k‘í shan* its body, *pat* not, *í* should be, *h‘uk* crooked, *tün* short, i. e. it ought not to be too crooked or too short, but should be open nearly like the two sides of a square: in the *kau nuk fát*, the hook should be more short and contracted, “ because it has not so much to contain,” as may be seen by inspection. N. B. The hook in these examples, and the celestial canopy (sec. vi: 1.), are both among the six forms specified sec. v: 9.

| | | |
|---|---|---|
| 10. Right. Being. Ashes. | 右有灰 | Yau$^{2}$. $^{s}$Yau. ꜀Fúi. |
| In these, the horizontal line should be long, and the sweep short. | 畫長撇短 | Wák$_{2}$ $_{s}$ch‘éung, p‘ít$_{›}$ ‘tün. |
| 11. Wood. The origin. Vermilion. | 木本朱 | Muk$_{2}$ ‘Pún. ꜀Chü. |
| Here the horizontal line should be short, the perpendicular long, the sweep and dash well extended. | 畫短直長撇捺宜伸 | Wák$_{2}$ ‘tün, chik$_{2}$ $_{s}$ch‘éung, p‘ít$_{›}$ nát$_{2}$ $_{s}$í ꜀shan. |
| 12. Joy. A wood. To build mud walls. | 樂棐築 | Lók$_{›}$. ‘Fí. Chuk$_{›}$. |
| Here the horizontal line should be long, the perpendicular short, the sweep and dash contracted. | 畫長直短撇捺宜縮 | Wák$_{2}$ $_{s}$ch‘éung, chik$_{2}$ ‘tün, p‘ít$_{›}$ nát$_{2}$ $_{s}$í shuk$_{›}$. |
| 13. Ten. Above. Below. | 十上下 | Shap$_{2}$. Shéung$^{2}$. Há$^{2}$. |
| In these, the transverse line should be long, and the perpendicular short. | 橫長直短 | $_{s}$Wáng $_{s}$ch‘éung, chik$_{2}$ ‘tün. |
| 14. Talent. A dry measure. A well. | 才斗井 | $_{s}$Ts‘oi. ‘Tau. ‘Tsing. |
| In these the transverse should be short, and the perpendicular long. | 橫短直長 | $_{s}$Wáng ‘tün, chik$_{2}$ $_{s}$ch‘éung. |
| 15. Great. Second. Also or with. | 丕亞並 | ꜀P‘í. A‘$^{2}$. Ping$^{2}$. |
| When there are horizontal lines at the top and bottom, the former must be short, the latter long. | 上下有畫須上短而下長 | Shéung$^{2}$ há$^{2}$ ‘yau wák$_{2}$, ꜀sü shéung$^{2}$ ‘tün $_{s}$í há$^{2}$ $_{s}$ch‘éung. |
| 16. Eye. Self. Because. | 目自因 | Muk$_{2}$. Tsz‘$^{2}$. ꜀Yan. |
| When there are perpendicular lines on the right and left, that on the left must be limited, and the right prolonged. | 左右有直宜左收而右展 | ‘Tsó yau$^{2}$ ‘yau chik$_{2}$, $_{s}$í ‘tsó ꜀shau, $_{s}$í yau$^{2}$ ‘chín. |

**10, 11.** In these and similar examples, the learner will easily ascertain the parts which are the object of the rules, and need not, therefore, be detained with any notes or explanations.

| | | |
|---|---|---|
| **17. A dry measure. Streams. A country.** | 升 川 邦 | ‹Shing. ‹Ch‘ün. ‹Póng. |
| When there is a sweep on the left, and a perpendicular line on the right, the former should be contracted, and the latter extended downwards. | 左撇右直須左縮而右垂 | ‘Tsó p‘ít›, yau$^2$ chik$_2$, ‹sü ‘tsó shuk›, ‹í yau$^2$ ‹shui. |
| **18. Him. Disgrace. Large.** | 伊 僇 侈 | ‹I′. Luk$_2$. ‹Ch‘í. |
| When there are perpendicular lines on the left, and sweeps on the right, the former should be collected and contracted, and the latter open and extended. | 左直右撇宜左斂而右放 | ‘Tsó chik$_2$, yau$^2$ p‘ít›, ‹i ‘tso ‘lím, ‹í yau$^2$ fóng’. |
| **19. Also. Truly. None.** | 亦 然 無 | Yik$_2$. ‹I′n. ‹Mò. |
| When there are dots on the two lower corners, one reclining on the right and the other on the left with its point elevated, their tops ought to converge towards the middle of the character, so as to give it a diversified appearance. | 點複者宜偃仰向背以求變 | ‘Tím fuk› ‘ché, ‹í ‘ín ‘yéung héung’ púi’, ‘í ‹k‘au pín’. |
| **20. Three. Imperial order. Pencil.** | 三 冊 聿 | ‹Sám. Chák›. Lut$_2$. |
| When there are several horizontal lines, they ought to be diversified like scales and feathers, to prevent stiffness of appearance. | 畫重者宜鱗羽参差以化板 | Wák$_2$ ‹ch‘ung ‘ché, ‹í ‹lun ‘ü ‹ts‘ám ‹ts‘z’, ‘í fá’ ‘pán. |
| **21. Although. Look back. A body.** | 雖 顧 體 | ‹Sui. Kú’. ‘T‘ai. |

19. *Fuk ché* means double, or a double garment: the allusion is to a short coat or frock, worn by the Chinese, which, being open on the two sides, has four corners at the bottom: figures or flowers are embroidered on the corners, and there are stripes up and down on the back, or as in some cases the garment is merely figured along the bottom; this description of characters is thought to resemble the back of such a dress; *ín*, to sleep, or lie inclined in a sleeping posture, denotes the position of the dot on the right, and *yéung* to look upwards, denotes the dot on the opposite corner; the two dots, *í* ought, *héung* to correspond to each other, facing in towards, *púi* the back, which is formed by the two middle lines or dots, as the case may happen to be, *í k‘au pín* to seek change, i. e. to give diversity.

20. In this the reference is to, *ts‘ám ts‘z’* the uneven and variegated appearance of, *lun* fish scales, and *ü* bird's feathers: the several horizontal lines should be drawn in this manner, *í fá pán*, to metamorphose the board, i. e. to remove the appearance of stiffness.

廣東方言讀本

| | | |
|---|---|---|
| When both sides are alike, the right and the left should be equal. | 兩平者左右宜均 | ‘Léung ˏp‘ing ‘ché, ‘tsó yauʼ ˏí ˎkwan. |
| 22. Thanks. Charioteer. Tree. | 謝御樹 | Tséʼ. Yüʼ. Shüʼ. |
| When three are united [side by side], the middle one should be made perfectly regular. | 三合者中間務正 | ˎSám hópˏ ‘ché, ˎchung ˎkán mòʼ chingʼ. |
| 23. Imperial car. Sound. Detention. | 鑾嚮留 | ˏLün. ‘Héung. ˏLau. |
| When the character is in two parts, the upper and lower being equally divided, the [lines in the] middle may be a little increased or diminished, as the case requires. | 二段者上下平分中微加饒減 | Iʼ tünʼ ‘ché, shéungʼ háʼ ˏp‘ing ˎfan, ˎchung ˏmí ˎká ˏíú ‘kám. |
| 24. Essay. Ideas. To implicate. | 章意累 | ˎChéung. Iʼ. Luiʼ. |
| In these examples, three parts being united one above the other, the upper and the lower, though extended or contracted, must be evenly arranged. | 三聯者頭尾伸縮間仍要勻停 | ˎSám ˏlün ‘ché, ˏt‘au ‘mi ˎshan shukˏ ˎkán, ˏying íúʼ ˏwan ˏt‘ing. |
| 25. Inhale. To call. Peak. | 吸呼峰 | Hapˏ. ˏFú. ˎFung. |
| When the left side is small, make its top even with the other. | 左傍小者齊其上 | ‘Tsó ˏpóng ‘siú ‘ché, ˏts‘ai ˏk‘í shéungʼ. |
| 26. To know. Lady's headdress. Small. | 知鈿細 | ˎChí. ˏTín. Saiʼ. |
| When the right side is small, make its bottom even with the other. | 右邊少者齊其下 | Yauʼ ˎpín ‘shíú ‘ché, ˏts‘ai ˏk‘í háʼ. |
| 27. To vociferate. Barbarous. Utensil. | 囂嚚器 | ˎHíú. ˏNgau. Híʼ. |

24. *Kán* here denotes amid; amid the extensions or contractions of the top and bottom, *ying* still, there must be a due proportion and compactness maintained; the meaning of the word here and in 22 differs somewhat, though in the main they are alike.

| | | |
|---|---|---|
| When a part occurs four times on the outside of a character, the positions must be such as to give the whole a square form. | 外四叠者體格必整方 | Ngoi' sz' típ, 'ché, 't'ai kák, pít, 'ching ,fóng. |
| 28. Incisor teeth. You. A succession. | 齒 爾 繼 | 'Ch'í. 'I'. Kai'. |
| When a part is repeated four times within a character, the repetitions ought to be arranged close together in uniform order. | 內四叠者布置宜勻密 | Noi' sz' típ, 'ché, pò' chí' ,í ,wan mat,. |
| 29. Seven. Also. What? | 七 也 乜 | Ts'at,. 'Yá. Mat,. |
| In characters of this form, the horizontal line should not be level, for then it would destroy all beauty of shape. | 斜勒者不宜平平則失勢 | ,Ts'é lak, 'ché, pat, ,í ,p'ing, ,p'ing tsak, shat, shai'. |
| 30. Say. Go away. Moreover. | 云 去 且 | ,Wan. Hü'. 'Ch'é. |
| In characters of this form, the horizontal line should not be inclined, for then it would be inelegant. | 平勒者不宜倚倚則無儀 | ,P'ing lak, 'ché, pat, ,í 'í, 'í tsak, ,mò ,í. |
| 31. Ten cubits. A cubit. And. | 丈 尺 又 | Chéung'. Ch'ek,. Yau'. |
| When the dash is freely extended, it is very necessary to contract the head and shorten the sweep. | 縱捺之字必要攢頭收尾 | Tsung' nát, ,chí tsz', pít, íú' tsün' ,t'au ,shau 'mí. |
| 32. Martial. Complete. Several. | 武 成 幾 | 'Mò. ,Shing. ,Kí. |
| In giving free extension to the hooked line, care should be taken to prevent its being too slender or too much bent. | 縱戈之法最忌力弱身彎 | Tsung' ,kwó ,chí fát,, tsui' kí' lik, yéuk, ,shan ,wán. |

27, 28. *Típ* is to repeat, or reiterate; and *típ ché* are the repetitions: *t'ai kák*, the body marks, denote the limits of the character; which, *pít* must be, *ching* arranged, *fóng* in a square. Again, the several repetitions of the part on the inside ought to be, *wan* uniform, and, *mat* close together.

32. In these examples the hook is called *fí ngán* the flying goose; it is one of the fourteen forms of the hook mentioned in sec. v: 11. When extended as in 34, the name of floating or swimming goose is applied to it.

| | | |
|---|---|---|
| 33. Desist. Must. The will. | 息必志 | Sik,. Pít,. Chí'. |
| When the hooked line is horizontal, there is no danger of its being too much bent. | 横戈不厭曲 | ₛWáng ꜀kwó pat, ím' h'uk,. |
| 34. Chief. Throw. Diligence. | 魁拋勉 | ꜀Fuí. ꜀P'au. ˤMín. |
| In these where the hook is extended, it should compass the part on its side. | 伸勾貴抱持 | ꜀Shan ꜀kau kwai' ˤp'ò ₛchi. |
| 35. Heaven. Father. Letters. | 天父文 | ꜀T'ín. Fú². ₛMan. |
| In such characters as have the sweep and dash placed across each other, and attached to a part above, they must be exactly in the middle. | 承上之乂正中<br>為貴 | ₛShing shéung² ꜀chí ꜀chá ching² ꜀chung ₛwai kwai'. |
| 36. Horse. Rest. Being or doing. | 馬焉為 | ˤMá. ₛI'n. ₛWai. |
| In characters of this form—resembling horse's teeth, the point of the hook should shoot up towards the middle of the four dots. | 馬齒法其拏勾<br>之鋒宜注射四<br>點之半 | ˤMá ˤch'í fát,, ₛk'í ₛná ꜀kau ꜀chí ꜀fung, ₛí chü' shé² sz' ˤtím ꜀chí pún'. |
| 37. To adjust. Conversation. Millet. | 燮談黍 | Sít,. ₛT'ám. ˤShü. |
| When the dash is repeated, it should vary, being now contracted, and now extended. | 重捺者須有縮<br>有伸 | ₛCh'ung nát, ˤché, ꜀sü ˤyau shuk, ˤyau ꜀shan. |
| 38. Clear. Already. Wilderness. | 明既野 | ꜀Ming. Kí'. ˤYé. |
| Characters, having a level top, should have their upper parts even. | 上平之字宜齊<br>首 | Shéung² ₛp'ing ꜀chí tsz'², ₛí ₛts'ai ˤshau. |
| 39. Morning. Time. After. | 朝辰後 | ꜀Chíú. ₛShan. Hau². |

33. In these examples the hook is called a 'horizontal spear,' from its resemblance to a spear, thrown down in a horizontal position.

| | | |
|---|---|---|
| Characters of this form should be even at the foot. | 下平之字宜齊足 | Há² ‹p'ing ‹chí tsz'², ‹í ‹ts'ai tsuk›. |
| 40. Prohibition. A grove. A forest. | 禁林森 | Kam'. ‹Lam. ‹Sham. |
| When the hook is repeated, sometimes it should retain the full form, at others it should be suppressed. | 疊趯者當或挑或駐 | Típ› yéuk› 'ché, ‹tóng wák› ‹t'íú wák› chü², |
| 41. Dates. Small. Elder brother. | 棗戔哥 | 'Tsò. ‹Tsín. ‹Kó. |
| When there is a hook above and one below, the latter should be more prominent than the other. | 上下勾趯者下勾明而上勾暗 | Shéung² há² ‹kau yéuk› 'ché, há² ‹kau ‹ming, ‹í shéung² ‹kau óm'. |
| 42. Cap of manhood. A crown. To dwell. | 冠冕宅 | ‹Kún. 'Mín. Chák›. |
| When one hook hangs downwards, and the other turns upwards, the former should be contracted, and the latter extended. | 俯仰勾挑者俯勾縮而仰勾伸 | 'Fú 'yéung ‹kau ‹t'íú 'ché, 'fú ‹kau shuk›, ‹í 'yéung ‹kau ‹shan. |
| 43. Mandarin duck. Pigeon. Brightness. | 鴛鳩輝 | ‹Ŭn. ‹Kau. ‹Fai. |
| The bended hook in these examples ought to be turned back and contracted. | 屈勾之勢退縮斯宜 | Wat› ‹kau ‹chí shai' t'ui' shuk› ‹sz' ‹í. |
| 44. Equal. Everywhere. All. | 齊普皆 | ‹Ts'ai. 'P'ò. ‹Kái. |
| If the upper part of a character requires much space, give it an open appearance. | 上占地步者聽其上寬 | Shéung² chím' tí² pò² 'ché, t'ing' ‹k'í shéung² ‹fún. |

43. The *wat kau*, or bended hook, is the small one in the left part of the character, and is one of the six forms of the spike, or stroke pointing upwards, described in sec. v: 12; the technical name given to it is *shuk kau*, the hewn hook, and it also occurs in the lower part of *i* clothes, *chéung* long, &c.

44, 45. *Chím* means to usurp: *tí pò* denotes a pace or measure of ground, much room: *t'ing*, differing both in its meaning and tone from the same form of the character in sec. i: 8, is here synonymous with *yam*, which means to allow or permit: this, however, is a metaphorical sense of the word, it denotes a magisterial *hearing* of a representation and the subsequent *sanctioning* of it. *Fún* and *fút* are nearly synonymous; the former refers to an open displayed mode of writing, the latter implies breadth simply.

廣東方言讀本



| | | |
|---|---|---|
| **45.** The whole. Ten thousand. Solitary. | 衆萬禹 | Chung'. Mán$^{2}$. ˢYü. |
| If the lower part of a character requires much space, let it be broad. | 下占地步者任其下濶 | Há$^{2}$ chím' tí$^{2}$ pò$^{2}$ 'ché, yam$^{2}$ ˛k'í há$^{2}$ fút˒. |
| **46.** Ascend. Yield. Tranquil. | 騰讓靖 | ˛T'ang. Yéung$^{2}$. Tsing$^{2}$. |
| If the right side requires much space, it may be extended without fear. | 右占者右不妨於獨豐 | Yau$^{2}$ chím' 'ché, yau$^{2}$ pat˒ ˛fóng ˛ü tuk˛ ˛fung. |
| **47.** Respect. Offer. Arrange. | 敬獻劉 | King'. Hín'. ˛Lau. |
| If the left side requires much space there is no fear of its being too great. | 左占者左無嫌於偏大 | 'Tsó chím' 'ché, 'tsó ˛mò ˛ím ˛ü ˛p'ín tái$^{2}$. |
| **48.** Assistant. Distinguish. Spreading. | 弼辨衍 | Pat˛. Pín$^{2}$. 'Ín. |
| If both the right and left sides require much space, the middle should yield to them. | 左右占者中宜遜 | 'Tsó yau$^{2}$ chím' 'ché, ˛chung ˛í sun'. |
| **49.** Much. Pencil. To excite. | 蕃筆衝 | ˛Fán. Pat˒. ˛Ch'ung. |
| If the middle requires much space, let it be enlarged. | 中間占者中獨雄 | ˛Chung ˛kán chím' 'ché, ˛chung tuk˛ ˛hung. |
| **50.** A thrush. Fear. To fumigate. | 鶯驚釁 | ˛Ang. ˛King. Yau$^{2}$. |
| If the upper and lower parts require much space, then the middle must be small. | 上下占者中小 | Shéung$^{2}$ há$^{2}$ chím' 'ché, ˛chung 'síú. |
| **51.** A phœnix. Fly. Breath. | 鳳飛氣 | Fung$^{2}$. ˛Fí. Hí'. |

46, 47. *Pat fóng* no fear, *ü* in, *tuk* it alone, *fung* being expanded or extended: *mò ím* no dread, *ü* in, *p'ín* a one-sided, *tái* greatness or largeness; in these cases, the two sides are not required to balance each other.

| | | |
|---|---|---|
| The long hooked line in characters of this form ought to be bent and strong. | 縱腕宜曲勁 | Tsung' 'ún, ꜁í h'uk꜆ king². |
| 52. See. Original. Hair. | 見元毛 | Kín'. ꜁Yün. ꜁Mò. |
| If the hooked line is in a horizontal position, it should be well rounded and extended. | 横腕貴圓雋 | ꜁Wáng 'ún, kwai' ꜁ün tsun'. |
| 53. Hall. To rule. Bottom. | 庭尹底 | ꜁Ting. ꜃Wan. ꜂Tai. |
| In giving freedom to the sweep, avoid making it like a rat's tail. | 縱撇惡鼠尾 | Tsung' p'ít꜆, ú' 'shü ꜃mí. |
| 54. Friend. Turn back. Skin. | 友反皮 | ꜃Yau. 'Fán. ꜁P'í. |
| When there are successive sweeps, they must not be made parallel like a set of teeth. | 聯撇忌排牙 | ꜁Lün p'ít꜆, kí² ꜁pái ꜁ngá. |
| 55. To practice. Necessity. Figure. | 修須形 | ꜀Sau. ꜀Sü. ꜁Ying. |
| When there are three sweeps in succession, the head of the lower one must point to the middle of the one immediately above it. | 三撇法以下撇首頂上撇之腹 | ꜀Sám p'ít꜆ fát꜆, ꜃í há² p'ít꜆ 'shau, 'ting shéung² p'ít꜆ ꜀chí fuk꜆. |
| 56. To rule. Flow. Sea. | 治流海 | Chí². ꜁Lau. 'Hoi. |
| Where three dots are placed on the side, the point of the lower one must be directed upwards near the end of the top one, with which it corresponds. | 三點法以下點𡚒鋒與上點駐筆相應 | ꜀Sám 'tím fát꜆, ꜃í há² 'tím ꜁t'ai ꜀fung ꜃ü shéung² 'tím chü' pat꜆ ꜀séung ying'. |
| 57. Is. To run. To loiter. | 是走辵 | Shí². 'Tsau. Ch'éuk. |
| Here the character *puk*, 'divination,' must be straight, not deflected, extending from the middle of the upper part, in a rectangular position. | 卜字直無偏與上截中縫正對 | *Puk*꜆ tsz'² chik꜇ ꜁mò ꜀p'ín, ꜃ü shéung² tsít꜇ ꜀chung ꜁fung ching' tui'. |

53. In this place, *ú* is used as a verb, and means nearly the same as *kí* (sec. v: 13); in the Sám Tsz' King (sec. iii: 42), it has the same sound but is there used as a noun.

| | | |
|---|---|---|
| 58. A sexagenarian. Old. Examine. | 耆老考 | ꜁K‘í. ꜃Lò. ꜂Háu. |
| Here the character *t‘ò*, ‘earth,’ must be straight, not deflected, the perpendicular line corresponding with the left one in the part beneath. | 土字直無偏與下截左豎正對 | ꜂*T‘ò* tsz꜅ chik꜇ ꜁mò ꜀p‘ín, ꜃ü há꜅ tsít꜇ ꜂tsó shü꜅ ching꜄ tui꜄. |
| 59. Perfume. Abundant. Bind. | 馨繁繫 | ꜀Hing. ꜁Fán. Hai꜅. |
| When many parts are brought together, they must receive, yield to, and blend with, each other in such a manner, as prevent confusion. | 錯綜者貫迎讓穿揷而惡紛紜 | Ts‘ók꜆ ꜀tsung ꜂ché, kwai꜄ ꜁ying yéung꜅ ꜀ch‘ün ch‘áp꜆ ꜁á ú꜄ ꜀fan ꜁wan. |
| 60. Succession. To bind. A girdle. | 繼纏屬 | Kai꜄. ꜁Ch‘ín. Chuk꜆. |
| If the parts are very close together, they must be well arranged, without being at all blended. | 縝密者宜布置安排而嫌擠雜 | Shan꜅ mat꜇ ꜂ché, ꜁í pò꜄ chí꜄ ꜀ón ꜁pái, ꜁í ꜁ím ꜀tsai tsáp꜇. |
| 61. Carriage. Middle. Handkerchief. | 車中巾 | ꜀Kü. ꜀Chung. ꜀Kan. |
| Here the perpendicular line should be tapering like a needle, otherwise the beauty is lost. | 應懸針者而垂露焉則無韻 | ꜀Ying ꜁ün ꜀cham ꜂ché, ꜁í ꜁shui lò꜅ ꜁ín, tsak꜆ ꜁mò wan꜅. |
| 62. Eminent. Single. Ended. | 卓單畢 | Ch‘éuk꜆. ꜀Tán. Pat꜆. |
| Here the lower point of the perpendicular line should be blunt, otherwise it will want firmness. | 當垂露者而懸針焉則無力 | ꜀Tóng ꜁shui lò꜅ ꜂ché, ꜁í ꜁ün ꜀cham ꜁ín, tsak꜆ ꜁mò lik꜇. |
| 63. Regular. Lord. King. | 正主王 | Ching꜄. ꜂Chü. ꜁Wóng. |
| In characters of a regular form, the lines must be large. | 形本自正而骨力必堅 | ꜁Ying ꜂pún tsz꜅ ching꜄, ꜁í kwat꜆ lik꜇ pít꜆ ꜀kín. |
| 64. Change. But. Strength. | 易乃力 | Yik꜇. ꜃Nái. Lik꜇. |

| | | |
|---|---|---|
| Though the body of these ought to be slightly aslant, yet they must be regular in the centre. | 體雖宜斜而字心必正 | 'T'ai ‹sui ˏí ˏts'é, ˏí tsz'ˎ ‹sam pít› ching'. |
| 65. The body. Ear. Precious. | 身 耳 貝 | ‹Shan. 'I'. Púi'. |
| When the character is slender, its form must not be too short. | 字本瘦者其形勿短 | Tsz'ˎ 'pún shau' 'ché, ˏk'í ˏying matˎ 'tün. |
| 66. White. Work. To say. | 白 工 曰 | Pákˎ. ‹Kung. Ŭtˎ. |
| When the body of the character is short, the strokes of the pencil must be full, | 身本矮者用筆宜肥 | ‹Shan 'pún 'ai 'ché, yungˎ pat› ˏí ˏfí. |
| 67. To unite. To assemble. Decree. | 合 會 命 | Hópˎ. Úiˎ. Ming›. |
| In a covering over the lower part of the character, as in these examples, the sweep and dash should be equal. | 蓋下之法撇捺宜均 | K'oi' háˎ ‹chí fát›, p'ít› nátˎ ˏí ‹kwan. |
| 68. A guitar. Each. Valley, | 琴 各 谷 | ˏK'am. Kók›. Kuk›. |
| In characters embracing a part beneath, the right and left sides should correspond to each other. | 趲下之勢左右相稱 | Ch'an' háˎ ‹chí shai', 'tsó yauˎ ‹séung ch'ing›. |
| 69. To stop. Hill. Male. | 止 山 公 | 'Chí. ‹Shán. ‹Kung. |
| Although the lines ought to be full in these, yet they must not be too heavy. | 雖宜肥而勿腫 | ‹Sui ˏí ˏfí, ˏí matˎ 'chung. |
| 70. To complete. Inch. Divination. | 了 寸 卜 | 'Líú. Ts'ün'. Puk›. |
| Although the lines ought to be slender in these, yet they must not be made too much so. | 雖宜瘦而勿癯 | ‹Sui ˏí shau', ˏí matˎ ˏk'ü. |

64. The meaning of the rule given for characters of this form seems to be that, though the body leans a little out of the perpendicular, it must not lose the centre of gravity. It is literally *tsz' sam pít ching*, the heart of the character must be kept right—which may be understood either verbally or tropically.

| | | |
|---|---|---|
| 71. Above. Below. Thousand. | 上下千 | Shéung$^{2}$. Há$^{2}$. ꜀Ts‘ín. |
| When the lines are few and open, give them breadth. | 踈者豐之 | ꜀Shó ‘ché, ꜀fung ꜀chí. |
| 72. Mule. Tortoise. Crocodile. | 驘龜鼉 | ꜀Ló. ꜀Kwai. ꜁T‘ó. |
| When the lines are numerous and close together, they should be evenly arranged. | 密者匀之 | Mat$_{2}$ ‘ché, ꜁wan ꜀chí. |
| 73. Bright. Accumulated rocks. Rumbling. | 晶磊轟 | ꜀Tsing. ꜂Lui. ꜀Kwang. |
| When a character is formed by several repetitions of another, they should be orderly arranged. | 堆疊者消納之 | ꜁Tui típ$_{2}$ ‘ché, ꜀síú nap$_{2}$ ꜀chí. |
| 74. A furnace. Spirit. Anxious. | 爨靈鬱 | ‘Ts‘un. ꜁Ling. Wat$_{,}$. |
| When the lines are accumulated, they must be distinctly written. | 積累者清晰之 | Tsik$_{,}$ lui$^{2}$ ‘ché, ꜀ts‘ing ts‘ik$_{,}$ ꜀chí. |
| 75. The mouth. A field. From. | 口田由 | ‘Hau. ꜁T‘ín. ꜁Yau. |
| The lower horizontal line here should be a little prolonged, so as to support the end of the perpendicular one [on the right]. | 下畫宜微長以承右竪之末 | Há$^{2}$ wak$_{2}$ ꜁í ꜁mí ꜁ch‘éung, ꜂í ꜁shing yau$^{2}$ shü$^{2}$ ꜀chí mút$_{2}$. |
| 76. A man. Stem. A portico. | 丁芋亭 | ꜀Ting. ꜀Ting. ꜁T‘ing. |
| In these the end of the hook ought to be a little bent down, as if intended to hook up something from beneath. | 末勾宜微拖似有帶下之勢 | Mút$_{2}$ ꜀kau ꜁í ꜁mí ꜀t‘ó, ‘tsz$^{2}$ ‘yau tai$^{2}$ há$^{2}$ ꜀chí shai$^{2}$. |
| 77. Distant. To repay. To reach to. | 遠還逮 | ꜂Ün, ꜁W án. Tai$^{2}$. |

73, 74. *Tui típ* means to pile stones or other things on top of each other in a regular manner, and *tsik lui* implies that the things are heaped one upon another in the best manner they will admit of; *síú* disperse, *nap* receive, *chí* them, meaning, that the strokes must give and accommodate to each other in an orderly manner: again, *ts‘ing* distinctly, *ts‘ik* clearly,

| | | |
|---|---|---|
| The part in the middle, when surrounded in this manner, ought to have its top rather larger than its bottom. | 之遶中字宜於<br>上畧大而下小 | ‹Chí ʻíú ‹chung tsz'², ‹í ‹ü shéung² léuk₂ tai² ‹í há² ʻsíú. |
| 78. Do not. A particle. A dart. | 莫矣矢 | Mók₂. ʻÍ. ʻCh'í. |
| When the horizontal line is long, and the sweep short, the dash on the right must not be used, (but a dot should be placed in its stead.) | 畫長撇短者右<br>不宜用捺 | Wák₂ ‹ch'éung p'ít› ʻtün ʻché, yau² pat› ‹í yung² nát₂. |
| 79. Make. Look up. To walk. | 作仰行 | Tsók›. ʻYéung. ‹Hang. |
| Here the left perpendicular line may be short, and the right long. | 左竪不嫌短右<br>竪不嫌長 | ʻTsò shü² pat› ‹ím ʻtün, yau² shü² pat› ‹ím ‹ch'éung. |
| 80. Minister. Great. Beautiful. | 臣巨佳 | ‹Shan. Kü². ‹Kái. |
| Here the left may be long, and the right short. | 左竪不嫌長右<br>竪不嫌短 | ʻTsó shü² pat› ‹ím ‹ch'éung, yau² shü² pat› ‹ím ʻtün. |
| 81. Palace. Empty. Indulgence. | 宮空宥 | ‹Kún. ‹Hung. Yau². |
| Here the hook in the covering, when made to resemble a bird looking at its breast, is elegant. | 寶蓋之勾宛如<br>鳥之覗胷乃妙 | ʻPò k'oi² ‹chí ‹kau ʻün ‹ü ʻníú ‹chí shí² ‹hung ʻnái míú. |
| 82. Partridge. Luminous. Congee. | 鷓赫鬻 | Ché². Hak›. Chuk›. |
| When horizontal lines are arranged close together, it is necessary that they resemble the carved work of the artist, in order to produce a beautiful character. | 排攢之畫必如<br>工之鏤物乃佳 | ‹P'ái ʻtsün ‹chí wák₂ pít› ‹ü ‹kung ‹chí lau² mat₂ ʻnái ‹kái. |
| 83. A seal. To knock head. Compassionate. | 印叩卹 | Yan². Kau². Sut›. |

*chí* them, implying that the strokes should be regularly and distinctly written, preserving to each a due proportion in forming the whole.

82. *P'ái tsün* gives the idea of regularly arranged articles, as if for presentation to a superior, or as if arranging the materials of a book for publication, *chí wák* such strokes must be

| | | |
|---|---|---|
| Characters in which *tsít*, 'a seal,' occurs, must conform to these examples. | 從卩之字准此 | ꜂Ts'ung *tsít*꜃ ꜀chí tsz'꜄ 'chun 'ts'z'. |
| 84. Wilderness. A surname. Neighbor. | 郊鄭鄰 | ꜀Káu. Ching'. ꜁Lun. |
| Characters in which *yap*, 'a city,' occurs, must conform to these. | 從邑之字准此 | ꜂Ts'ung *yap*꜃ ꜀chí tsz'꜄ 'chun 'ts'z'. |
| 85. Islet. Barracks. Step. | 陼隖陔 | 'Chü. 'Ú. ꜁Hoi. |
| Characters in which *fau*, 'a mound,' occurs, must conform to these. | 從阜之字准此 | ꜂Ts'ung *fau*' ꜀chí tsz'꜄ 'chun 'ts'z'. |
| 86. Ascend. Protruding. Horary character. | 登發癸 | ꜀Tang. Fát꜀. Kwai'. |
| Characters in which *pút*, 'a mound,' occurs, must conform to these. | 從癶之字准此 | ꜂Ts'ung *pút*꜃ ꜀chí tsz'꜄ 'chun 'ts'z'. |
| 87. Sacrifice. A surname. To examine. | 祭蔡察 | Tsai'. Tsoi'. Chát꜀. |
| Characters in which this nameless part occurs, must conform to these. | 從夗之字准此 | ꜂Ts'ung * * * ꜀chí tsz'꜄ 'chun 'ts'z'. |
| 88. Many voices. Whole. To collect. | 臮衆聚 | K'í'. Chung'. Tsui'. |
| Characters in which *sám yan*, 'three men,' occurs, must conform to these. | 從三从之字准此 | ꜂Ts'ung ꜀*sám* ꜁*yan* ꜀chí tsz'꜄ 'chun 'ts'z'. |
| 89. A family. Elephant. Heroic. | 家象豪 | ꜀Ká. Tséung'. ꜁Hò. |
| Characters in which *ch'í*, 'a pig,' occurs, must conform to these. | 從豕之字准此 | ꜂Ts'ung '*ch'í* ꜀chí tsz'꜄ 'chun 'ts'z'. |

---

like the artist's, *lau mat* engraved thing or work, *nái* is, *kái* beautiful; *míú* in the preceding number implies beauty from grace, *kái* beauty from regularity.

84, 85. The two characters *yap* and *fau* are radicals, and in composition are, with a few exceptions, always contracted as in these examples; the only difference is in their position with respect to the other part of the character, the former being placed on the right, and the latter on the left side.

| | | |
|---|---|---|
| **90. To look down. Benevolence. Cease.** | 俯仁休 | **'Fú. ˏYan. ˏYau.** |
| When the character *yan*, 'man,' is placed on the side, it must be in this manner. | 單人傍字准此 | ˏTán ˏ*yan* ˏp'óng tsz'$^{2}$ 'chun 'ts'z'. |
| **91. Slowly. Compliance. Afterwards.** | 徐循後 | **ˏTs'ü. ˏTs'un. Hau$^{2}$.** |
| When the character man is doubled on the side, it must be in this manner. | 雙人傍字准此 | ˏShéung ˏ*yan* ˏp'óng tsz'$^{2}$ 'chun 'ts'z'. |
| **92. Milk. Rebellion. To wrap.** | 乳亂包 | **'Yü. Lün$^{2}$. ˏPáu.** |
| The character *üt*, an inverted hook, must be placed as in these examples. | 從乙之字准此 | ˏTs'ung *üt*$_{2}$ ˏchí tsz'$^{2}$ 'chun 'ts'z'. |

92. In learning to write these lessons, a little patience on the part of the student and considerable care will be requisite at starting, but the habit of holding the pencil in the erect position will soon become easy to the hand, and well proportioned characters will be the result. The Chinese mode, of laying a piece of thin paper over the copy, and writing the character repeatedly, is a good one in order to learn to write well, while it also acquaints the learner with the form and structure of the character. After some freedom with the pencil is thus acquired, a painted board, called *fan pái*, is procured, on which the characters are written again and again in an open, bold manner with a pencil dipped in blackened water, which just leaves a trace; by this means a free hand is acquired, and the form of characters indelibly impressed upon the memory. The Chinese are great admirers of calligraphy, and take unwearied pains to write their numerous characters in a uniform, proportionate, and elegant manner. Of the two points to be regarded, correctness and elegance, the former only is absolutely required of candidates at the literary examinations; but it adds greatly to the consideration in which they are held, if to this quality they add neatness and freedom. A stiffly written character, however correct may be the proportion of its parts, is little less displeasing to the eye of a Chinese than one written carelessly and out of proportion. In these copies, repeated writing is attended with the more advantage, inasmuch as the student has both the sound and signification of the characters before him with which he can associate their shape; and although there are some advantages in acquiring the meaning of characters when combined in sentences, yet it is of prime importance to have a single leading meaning in the mind for each character.

宇宙定寧至聖孟蓋勅部幼即讀蝀議續喜吾妻安
甲平干午葡萄蜀葛句勻匀勿左在尤尨右有厷灰
木本朱東樂桀簗梟十上下士才斗丰井丕正亞並
目自因固川升邪邦伊侈傪修亦赤然無三冊冉聿
雖顧顧體御謝樹術鑾響需留章意素累吸呼峰峻
和知鈿細囂囂器器齒爾爽鹽此七也乜云去且旦
丈尺史又武成或幾恩息必志勉旭魁拋天父外文
鷁鳩輝頻鳥馬焉為師明既野朝故辰後燓談茶黍
禁林森懋隶叜哥柔冠冕冦宅雲普皆齊衆表萬禹
施騰讓靖敬獻歛劉弼辨衍仰蕃肇衝擲鸞鶯驚釁

風鳳飛氣先見元毛庭居尹底友及反皮參修須形
治洪流海是足走尨者耆老考簪聲緐繁繼纖纓纚
車申中巾卓犖單畢易乃毋力正主本王身目耳貝
白工曰四會合金命琴吝各谷土止山公了寸卜才
上下千小贏齋龜鼉晶磊轟森爨鬱靈糜口日田由
丁芓寧亭遠邉遂逮莫奚矢契作仰冲行叵巨於佳
宫空宥宰鷊赫鬭鬻卭印叩卹郄郊鄭鄰陼隖陔阪
登癹發癸祭蔡察登氺泉衆聚家象豪豕仁儀俯休
從徐循後乳亂色包

書有六體曰篆曰隸曰楷曰行曰艸曰宋

書有六體曰篆曰隸曰楷曰行曰艸曰宋

書有六體曰篆曰隸曰楷曰行曰草曰宋

書有六體曰篆曰隸曰楷曰行曰草曰宋

書有六體曰篆曰隸曰楷曰行曰草曰宋

書有六體曰篆曰隸曰楷曰行曰草曰宋

廣東方言讀本

### EXPLANATION OF THE PLATES.

The copies of Shíú Ying are repeated in the first of these two sheets, printed in the common manner and size of type of Chinese books, and being presented on one sheet will afford the scholar a good exercise in writing. It will be observed, that in the plate there are four characters given under each rule, instead of three as in the preceding copies; this is according to the original book, but the space in the column did not admit the whole. An attentive examination of the sheet and comparison with the characters already given, and also a comparison of the characters with each other, will enable the learner to ascertain some of the modifications the same parts are susceptible of when placed differently.

The second plate contains specimens of the six different styles of writing employed by the Chinese. The same characters are given in each column, and read perpendicularly, thus:

*‹Shü ʿyau luk› ʿt'ai; üt› sün², üt› lai², üt› ʿk'ái, üt› ‹hang, üt› ʿt'sò, üt› Sung'.*

Of writing, there are six forms, viz., the *sün* or seal character, the *lai* or style of official persons, the *k'ái* or pattern style, the *hang* or running hand, the *t'sò* or abbreviated running hand, and the *Sung* or style of the Sung dynasty. A short account of these various styles is here added.

1. The *Sün shü*. This, from its present most common use, has been called by Europeans the seal character. Next to the original hieroglyphics, it is the most ancient style of writing, and includes many varieties, either fanciful inventions or modifications of various ages; its chief distinctions are however two, the greater and the inferior *sün*. The former belongs more exclusively to seals and stamps, and is often seen on the goods and wares of the Chinese, resembling an interminable labyrinth of rectangular lines; the latter is frequently used for ornamental inscriptions and prefaces to books, as well as for seals; a specimen of it is given in the first column of the plate on the right hand.

2. The *Lai shü*, style of official attendants. This was introduced during the Tsun dynasty, near the commencement of the Christian era. It was formed for the use of writers in the public offices, and has derived its name from this circumstance. It is now chiefly used for inscriptions and prefaces of works. See a specimen in the second column.

3. The *K'ái shü*, pattern style. This has been formed by the gradual improvements of good writing, and from it all the modern forms have originated. A Chinese can have no claim to literary merit among his countrymen who cannot write neatly as well as correctly in this style. The third column is an example of this kind, as are also the writing copies on the preceding pages.

4. The *Hang shü*. This may be literally translated the running hand, and to a certain extent it is so; but it does not admit of entire freedom. The pencil may be carried from stroke to stroke, without being raised from the paper; but no forms of abbreviation unauthorized by the dictionaries may be introduced, nor may any of the component parts of a character be thrown out. It is the common business hand of a neat writer, and is also frequently used in prefaces of books. Individuals often adopt unsanctioned abbreviations to a greater or less extent, according as custom has authorized or education habituated them, which in a measure serves to characterize their handwriting.

5. The *T'sò tsz'*, or 'plant character,' is the name given to a freer description of running hand than the preceding. It is full of abbreviations, which render it very difficult even to a well-educated native. Not only are abbreviated forms adopted, but even from them many lines are thrown out, and the pencil may be carried from one character to another almost *ad libitum*. This style is partially employed in the ordinary writing of the man of business, but to understand it fully, requires a particular study. Its chief use therefore is in inscriptions, and sometimes also in prefaces, particularly those of aged writers.

6. The *Sung t'ai*, style of the Sung dynasty, was introduced as a more elegant form of printing than any of the others, under the dynasty whose name it bears. Printing in China, by means of carved wooden plates, was invented in the early part of the tenth century. The Sung family obtained the supremacy about forty years after; and this style was gradually formed during the period that it retained the throne. Since that time, it is not known that any material alteration has taken place in its form; an example of it is given in the sixth column.

# CHAPTER II.

# THE HUMAN BODY.

# 身體篇二

‚Shan ‛t‘ai; ‚p‘ín í².

## Section First.

## SHAPE AND MOTIONS OF THE HEAD.

### 頭類第一章

‚T‘au lui²; tai² yat, ‚cheung.

| | | |
|---|---|---|
| 1. Man's head. | 人頭 | ‚Yan ‚t‘au. |
| 2. The skull, or head. | 頭壳 | ‚T‘au hók,. |
| 3. A great head. | 大頭 | Tái² ‚t‘au. |
| 4. A small head. | 細頭 | Sai² ‚t‘au. |
| 5. A long head. | 長頭 | ‚Ch‘éung ‚t‘au. |
| 6. A round head. | 圓頭 | ‚Ün ‚t‘au. |
| 7. A flat head. | 扁頭 | ‛Pín ‚t‘au. |

### *Notes and Explanations.*

Shant‘ai denotes the human body, not that of animals. The original form of *shan* is said to resemble the human body; but, when standing by itself, it may signify the body of an animal or of any object; body is also the leading signification of *t‘ai*, which is formed of *bones* and a *vessel filled:* the two united form an appropriate term, denoting the human body, and that only. The Chinese language abounds with terms of this description. *T‘au lui* denotes a collection of phrases relating to the head; in another place, it might stand as the title of a chapter on heads.

1, 2. For uses of *t‘au* see chap. I. sec. i: 5, 20, &c. *Yan t‘au* means, either a human head, or human heads, there being nothing in the phrase to define the number, which may be one or a thousand. *Hók* literally means a covering; joined with *t‘au* it denotes the skull, and in common phraseology simply the head: the common form of the character, which is here used, is an abridged one.

3—7. These terms denote the shape of the head; there are many other expressions, borrowed from objects of nature or art, for the same ideas; but they are often vulgar, and need not be enumerated.

廣東方言讀本

| | | |
|---|---|---|
| 8. The forehead. | 額頭 | Ngák꜇ ꜁t'au. |
| 9. Droop the head. | 垂頭 | ꜁Shui ꜁t'au. |
| 10. Hang down the head. | 低頭 | ꜀Tai ꜁t'au. |
| 11. Lift up the head. | 舉頭 | ꜂Kü ꜁t'au. |
| 12. Elevate the head. | 擔頭 | ꜀Tám ꜁t'au. |
| 13. Raise the head. | 擡頭 | ꜁T'oi ꜁t'au. |
| 14. Nod the head; or give assent. | 點頭 | ꜂Tím ꜁t'au. |
| 15. Nod the head; or give permission. | 噏頭 | Ngap꜇ ꜁t'au. |
| 16. Shake the head; or give a refusal. | 擰頭 | Ning꜅ ꜁t'au. |
| 17. Shake the head; or refuse assent. | 搖頭 | ꜁Íú ꜁t'au. |
| 18. Move the head. | 喐頭 | Yuk꜆ ꜁t'au. |
| 19. Incline the head. | 側頭 | Chak꜆ ꜁t'au. |
| 20. Turn round the head. | 回頭 | ꜁Úi ꜁t'au. |
| 21. Turn back the head. | 轉頭 | ꜂Chün ꜁t'au. |
| 22. Bow down the head to the ground. | 嗑亅 | ꜀K'ó ꜁t'au. |

8. *Ngák* is the space which extends from the hair on the top of the head to the eyebrows; it is followed by *t'au* partly for the sake of euphony, and partly in order to render the expression more definite. The temples are called *ngák꜇ kók꜆*, horns or corners of the forehead.

9, 10. The movements of the head described here and in the following sentences, down to the twenty-third, are made by one's self—they are one's own actions. It may be I, you, he, or they: as, he lifts up his head; lift up your head, &c. The person, whether first, second, or third; and the number, mode, &c. may be easily ascertained from the circumstances of the case, and the context of the sentence. *Shui* and *tai* are synonyms; and whether used separately, or joined as in *shui tai t'au*, they denote that drooping or bending down of the head, which is witnessed in sorrow, dejection, submission, meditation, &c.

11—13. These have a signification nearly the opposite of the preceding, and the three are so nearly alike that they are used interchangeably.

14, 15. These both denote the nod of the head, that natural and easy expression of assent or permission, which is everywhere so readily understood that none can mistake it. *Ngap* is a colloquial term.

16, 17. *Ning* never occurs except in conversational style; it denotes a shorter and quicker motion than is expressed by *íú*, which is the slow movement of the head from side to side.

18. *Yuk* simply denotes motion, without any reference to its direction, or object; *yuk t'au* may be in the imperative mode, meaning, move your head; or, if referring to a third person, it may signify he moves his head.

19. *Chak t'au* is to incline the head in order to listen, or the turning of it upon one shoulder in a listless attitude.

20, 21. These are used literally for turning round the head, and figuratively for returning, or sending anything back.

22, 23. *K'ó t'au* and *k'au t'au* signify one and the same act—a ceremony which originated in early times, and is perpetuated in the homage which children do to their parents, and the

| | | |
|---|---|---|
| 23. Knock the head upon the ground. | 叩頭 | K'au' ˏt'au. |
| 24. Wash the head. | 洗 丨 | 'Sai ˏt'au. |
| 25. Comb the head. | 梳 丨 | ˏShó ˏt'au. |
| 26. Shave the head. | 剃 丨 | T'ai' ˏt'au. |
| 27. Bind the head with a turban. | 包 丨 | ˏPáu ˏt'au. |
| 28. Bind the head with a bandage. | 勒 丨 | Lakˎ ˏt'au. |
| 29. Lean the head on the hand. | 托 丨 | T'ókˎ ˏt'au. |
| 30. Rest the head on a pillow. | 枕 丨 | 'Cham ˏt'au. |
| 31. Oil the head. | 油 丨 | ˏYau ˏt'au. |
| 32. To decapitate. | 斬 丨 | 'Chám ˏt'au. |
| 33. Cut off the head. | 斷 丨 | Tün' ˏt'au. |
| 34. Beat the head. | 打 丨 | 'Tá ˏt'au. |
| 35. A headach. | 頭痛 | ˏT'au t'ung'. |
| 36. Pain in the head. | 頭疾 | ˏT'au ts'ekˎ. |
| 37. Giddiness; or vertigo. | 頭昏 | ˏT'au ˏwan. |
| 38. Heaviness of the head. | 頭重 | ˏT'au chung'. |
| 39. Cut off men's heads. | 殺人頭 | Shátˎ ˏyan ˏt'au. |

people to their sovereign and their deities. The *modus operandi* has varied under different dynasties: the present formula is three kneelings and nine knockings of the head—*sám kwai kau k'au!*

24. In this and the following sentences, down to the thirty-fourth, the action is *upon* the head, and may be performed by one's self, or by a second or third person. The perpendicular mark which is used here instead of *t'au* denotes a repetition of the character immediately above it, and is the same mark that is employed for that purpose in Chinese books and dictionaries.

26. *T'ai t'au* is the shaving of the head now practiced throughout China, a custom which was introduced by the reigning family, and required of every male subject as a token of submission to the Mantchou conquerers.

27, 28. In some parts of the empire the people occasionally dress their heads with a turban, which is denoted by *páu t'au: lak t'au* refers to the dressing of the head with bandages, or binding it fast with cords or thongs.

32, 33. *Tün* is the term used in the Penal Code to denote decapitation; *chám*, etymologically, means the *chariot cut*, and is the common word for the same idea. The head is severed from the body by a sword, and usually at a single stroke.

35—38. By these phrases action *in* the head is denoted; *t'ung* is severe pain; *ts'ek*, compounded of *sickness* and *arrow* or dart, is used to express that thrilling pain sometimes felt in the temples, and other parts of the head.

39. The remaining part of this section consists of miscellaneous phrases; and in some of them there is a repetition of the ideas expressed in preceding sentences in fewer characters;

| | | |
|---|---|---|
| 40. The head has pain. | 頭有痛 | ˏT'au ʿyau t'ung'. |
| 41. The head is heavy. | 頭係重 | ˏT'au hai$^{2}$ chung$^{2}$. |
| 42. Did not nod the head; or give assent. | 唔揖頭 | ˏ'M ngap$_{2}$ ˏt'au. |
| 43. Did not lift up the head. | 不舉頭 | Pat˒ ʿkü ˏt'au. |
| 44. Certainly will shake the head; or give a refusal. | 必擰頭 | Pít˒ ning$^{2}$ ˏt'au. |
| 45. Certainly will cut off the head. | 必斬丨 | Pít˒ ʿchám ˏt'au. |
| 46. Wash the head clean. | 洗淨丨 | ʿSai tsing$^{2}$ ˏt'au. |
| 47. Comb the head smooth. | 梳光丨 | ˎShó ˎkwóng ˏt'au. |
| 48. Shave the head smooth. | 剃滑丨 | T'ai' wát$_{2}$ ˏt'au. |
| 49. Gray hairs come imperceptibly. | 不覺白頭 | Pat˒ kók˒ pák$_{2}$ ˏt'au. |
| 50. Excessive headache. | 頭疾到極 | ˏT'au tsek˒ tò' kik$_{2}$. |
| 51. Being dejected, drooping the head. | 喪氣垂頭 | Sóng' hí' ˏshui ˏt'au. |
| 52. So sick as not to be able to raise the head. | 病不起頭 | Peng$^{2}$ pat˒ ʿhí ˏt'au. |
| 53. Unwilling to bend down the head; or will not assent. | 不肯低頭 | Pat˒ ʿhang ˎtai ˏt'au. |
| 54. Private conversation. | 交頭接耳 | ˎKáu ˏt'au tsíp˒ ʿí. |
| 55. A lady. | 粉面油頭 | ʿFan mín$^{2}$ ˏyau ˏt'au. |
| 56. Went away and never returned. | 一去不回頭 | Yat˒ hü' pat˒ ˏúi ˏt'au. |
| 57. Meeting without bowing to each other. | 相逢不點頭 | ˎSéung ˏfung pat˒ ʿtím ˏt'au. |
| 58. Refusing to bow on seeing each other. | 撞見唔揖頭 | Chóng$^{2}$ kín' ˏ'm ngap$_{2}$ ˏt'au. |

---

thus *shát yan t'au* is used for *shát t'au:* and *t'au yau t'ung*, for *t'au t'ung*—different phrases for the same idea.

49. *Pat kók* is unconsciously, imperceptibly; gray hairs come upon one before he is aware of it; old age gains upon a man imperceptibly.

50. *Kik* is the extreme point, the highest degree, implying that the throbbing pain in the head, *tò kik* has reached an excessive degree.

51. *Sóng hí* is to lose the breath, the courage, or to become dejected; in which case the head droops; here the agent is to be supplied, he, she, or they according to the case in hand.

52. This elliptical mode of expression is very common in Chinese: *peng* sick, i. e. sick to such a degree as to be unable to raise the head; it is like the phrase in English, 'sick abed.'

54. Literally, this means, 'joining heads, receiving ears;' putting heads together, and whispering in each other's ears, so that the by-standers may not hear what is said.

55. Here and elsewhere it will be seen, that common phraseology may go far to illustrate manners, customs, and character: from the common practice of ladies using rouge and oil on the face and head, the terms *fan mín yau t'au* have come to denote the person using them.

57, 58. Both these phrases express one and the same idea, namely, the refusal of old acquaintances to recognize and bow to each other when accidentally brought together.

59, 60. Here too, in both phrases the same idea is expressed; the first phrase is often

| | | |
|---|---|---|
| 59. Most assuredly it is wrong to assent. | 是必唔好噏頭 | Shí' pít, ,'m 'hò ngap, ,t'au. |
| 60. On no account is it right to assent. | 千祈唔好噏頭 | ,Ts'ín ,k'í ,'m 'hò ngap, ,t'au. |
| 61. The head is man's glory. | 頭乃人之元首 | ,T'au 'nái ,yan ,chí ,ün 'shau. |
| 62. I would rather be decapitated than do it. | 情願割頭亦唔做 | ,Ts'ing ün' kót, ,t'au yik, ,'m tsò'. |
| 63. Go and never return. | 絶跡唔使回頭 | Tsüt, tsik, ,'m 'shai ,úi ,t'au. |
| 64. I will go and never return here again. | 呢處絶跡我唔回頭 | ,Ní ch'ü' tsüt, tsik, 'ngó ,'m ,úi ,t'au. |
| 65. I beg to ask how this character *t'au* is used? | 請問呢個頭字點使呢 | 'Ts'ing man' ,ní kó' *,t'au* tsz'' 'tím 'shai ,ní. |
| It is used in a great variety of ways. | 有好多使處 | 'Yau 'hò ,tó 'shai ch'ü'. |
| 66. (Thus for example,) What price, Sir, do you want for this? | 事頭公個的貨要乜價錢呢 | Sz'' ,t'au ,kung, kó' tik, fó' íú' mat, ká' ,ts'ín ,ní? |
| 67. This shop has certainly good wares and honest prices. | 呢間舖頭果然係貨眞價實喇 | ,Ní ,kán p'ò' ,t'au 'kwó ,ín hai' fó' ,chan ká' shat, ,lé. |
| 68. That sort is of a good mark and of the best quality. | 個樣係頭號最好的野 | Kó' yéung' hai' ,t'au hò' tsui' 'hò tik, 'yé. |
| 69. In doing an affair, he begins but never finishes. | 做事有頭無尾 | Tsò' sz'' 'yau ,t'au ,mò 'mí. |
| 70. All affairs are intrusted to me to manage. | 乜事都係要我頭當 | Mat, sz'' ,tò hai' fú' 'ngó ,tóng ,t'au. |

employed by superiors in giving instructions to inferiors, charging them not to give any information on this or that topic about which they may chance to be interrogated: the other expression is rather the language of request;—a thousand times I pray you, or I intreat you on all accounts, not to give him the least information.

61. The phrase *ün shau* means the chief, that which guides and governs, or which has the preëminence; hence the crown or the glory.

62. *Ts'ing ün* is one's own wish or choice; if my head should be cut off in case I would not do a specified action, *yik 'm tsò* even then I would not do it, I would prefer decapitation.

63, 64. The first of these two phrases refers to the expulsion of a servant or any other inmate of an establishment; the second relates to the voluntary abandonment of a house in disgust or anger; *tsüt tsik*, to obliterate footsteps, here means never, and implies the final departure, so that the prints of the feet—the footsteps—will never be retraced.

66—70. In these examples, the general meaning of *t'au* is that of chief, first. *Kung* is a term of respect added to *sz't'au*, 'head of affairs,' and is equivalent to Mr.; it is the respectful address in common use for a shopman, or indeed the director of almost any work or business. 'Doing affairs has head but no tail,' is an expression for those shiftless, thriftless persons who never accomplish what they undertake.

## Section Second.

# PARTS AND MOTIONS OF THE EYE.

## 眼類第二章

ʿNgán lui$^{2}$; tai$^{2}$ í$^{2}$ ˏchéung.

| | | |
|---|---|---|
| 1. Large eyes. | 大眼 | Tái$^{2}$ ʿngán. |
| 2. Small eyes. | 細丨 | Sai$^{3}$ ʿngán. |
| 3. Prominent eyes. | 突丨 | Tat$_{2}$ ʿngán. |
| 4. Sunken eyes. | 深丨 | ˏSham ʿngán. |
| 5. Bleareyed; lippitudo. | 爛丨 | Lán$^{2}$ ʿngán. |
| 6. Good eyes; or healthy eyes. | 好丨 | ʿHò ʿngán. |
| 7. Weeping eyes; epiphora. | 淚丨 | Lui$^{2}$ ʿngán. |
| 8. Moist eyes. | 濕丨 | Shap$_{3}$ ʿngán. |
| 9. Bright eyes; or keen-eyed. | 慧丨 | Wai$^{2}$ ʿngán. |
| 10. Blindness; amaurosis. | 盲丨 | ˏMáng ʿngán. |
| 11. Blindness; or closed eyes. | 密丨 | Mat$_{2}$ ʿngán. |
| 12. Dim-eyed. | 朦丨 | ˏMung ʿngán. |
| 13. Both eyes. | 雙丨 | ˏShéung ʿngán. |
| 14. One eye. | 單丨 | ˏTán ʿngán. |

### *Notes and Explanations.*

Muk is the radical word for the organ of vision, which it somewhat resembles; and it forms a part of nearly all the terms which refer to optics. *Ngán*, which has *muk* placed on the left of *kan*, is the character most in use to denote the eyes.

1, 2. The fondness of the Chinese for opposite terms, which appear in almost all they write and say, often assists in defining their most common words. Here we have three sets of them: To say, 'the sunken eye is the eye which is not prominent, and the prominent eye is that which is not sunken,' is their common mode of defining terms.

7, 8. *Lui* and *shap* are often used interchangeably; the former denotes the greatest profusion of humors.

9. This is the really good eye, characterised as the brilliant, the piercing, the intelligent eye,—'an eye which is not dull or stupid.'

10, 11. In common discourse the only distinction made between these two terms is this,—the first is used when speaking of a person, the second when speaking to a person who is blind. This distinction results, perhaps, from the etymology of the two characters: *máng* is the dead eye, the evacuated eye, or that in which the parts are ruined: *mat* signifies what is small, close, or hidden; and literally therefore, *mat ngán* is the eye which is closed up.

| | | |
|---|---|---|
| 15. Vacant eyes; haggard looks. | 虛眼 | ‹H'ü ʻngán. |
| 16. Acute ophthalmia. | 熱眼 | Ít, ʻngán. |
| 17. Inflamed eyes. | 赤眼 | Ch'ik› ʻngán. |
| 18. Red eyes. | 紅眼 | ‹Hung ʻngán. |
| 19. Cross-eyed or squinting; strabismus. | 斜眼 | ‹Ts'é ʻngán. |
| 20. Open the eyes. | 開眼 | ‹Hoi ʻngán. |
| 21. Shut the eyes. | 閉眼 | Pai' ʻngán. |
| 22. Close the eyes. | 合眼 | Hóp, ʻngán. |
| 23. Internal angle of the eye. | 眼頭 | ʻNgán ‹t'au. |
| 24. External angle of the eye. | 眼尾 | ʻNgán ʻmí. |
| 25. The corners of the eye. | 眼角 | ʻNgán kók›. |
| 26. The eyelids; palpebræ. | 眼盖 | ʻNgán koi'. |
| 27. The eyebrows; supercilia. | 眼眉 | ʻNgán ‹mí. |
| 28. The eyeball. | 眼睛 | ʻNgán ‹tsing. |
| 29. The crystaline lens of the eye. | 眼珠 | ʻNgán ‹chü. |
| 30. The pupil of the eye. | 瞳人 | ‹T'ung ‹yan. |
| 31. The pupil of the eye. | 眸子 | ‹Mau ʻtsz'. |
| 32. The white of the eye. | 眼白睛 | ʻNgán pák, ‹tsing. |
| 33. The iris of the eye. | 眼黑睛 | ʻNgán hak› ‹tsing. |
| 34. The eyelashes; cilia. | 眼揖毛 | ʻNgán yap› ‹mò. |

15. The *h'ü ngán* is that of the debauchee or idiot—the haggard or vacant stare of one whose mental powers are distracted, or in ruins, or both.

17, 18. These two terms are synonymous, and denote redness or inflammation of the eyes, whether occasioned by anger, by disease, or by excessive drinking.

19. *Ts'é ngán* may be used for any distortion of the eyes, or for looking askance, as well as for the strabismus.

28. This and all the other terms in this section are translated in the common and popular sense, in which they are used by the Chinese. Hence perfect accuracy is not, in all cases, to be expected.

29. This is literally the 'pearl of the eye;' and, though sometimes referred to the orb of the eye, seems admirably fitted to designate the crystalline lens. This use of it is supported by a reference to the eye of the fish.

30, 31. Both these, like the word pupil, seem to refer not less to the miniature image of any object which is formed on the eye, than to the perforation through which the rays of light pass into it: their literal meaning is, the child of the eye.

32, 33. *Pák* and *hak*, white and black, refer to the external appearance of the eye, to that which appears white, and to that which appears discolored.

| | | |
|---|---|---|
| 35. Do not cut my eyes. | 勿割親眼 | Mat$_2$ kót› ‹ts'an 'ngán. |
| 36. Invisible; or what the eye has never seen. | 目所不見 | Muk$_2$ 'shó pat› kín'. |
| 37. Lawless; or regardless of the laws. | 目無法紀 | Muk$_2$ ‚mò fát› 'kí. |
| 38. Fixed attention; or the eyes riveted. | 目不轉睛 | Muk$_2$ pat› 'chün ‹tsing. |
| 39. In the twinkling of an eye. | 一瞬之間 | Yat› 'shun ‹chí ‹kán. |
| 40. Vanished in the twinkling of an eye. | 轉眼成空 | 'Chün 'ngán ‚shing ‹hung. |
| 41. Open both eyes. | 擘開雙眼 | Mák› ‹hoi ‹shéung 'ngán. |
| 42. You must not open your eyes. | 唔好掙開眼 | ‚'M 'hò ‹chang ‹hoi 'ngán. |
| 43. This eye is ruined. | 呢隻眼壞了 | ‚Ní chek› 'ngán wái$^2$ 'líú. |
| 44. Unacquainted with the world. | 有眼不識人 | 'Yau 'ngán pat› shik› ‚yan. |
| 45. The eyes are blurred, and cannot see distinctly. | 眼花看不眞 | 'Ngán ‹fá hón' pat› ‹chan. |
| 46. Though my eyes are tired, I am indisposed to sleep. | 倦眼尙未思眠 | Kün$^2$ 'ngán shéung$^2$ mí$^2$ ‹sz' ‚mín. |
| 47. The eye closed, and all sensation lost. | 瞑目無所知覺 | ‚Ming muk$_2$ ‚mò 'shó ‹chi kók›. |
| 48. What is the disease in that man's eye? | 個個人個隻眼係乜野症 | Kó' kó' ‚yan kó' chek› 'ngán hai$^2$ mat› 'yé ching'? |

35. *Ts'an* here means at, or into; the phrase is used to admonish the careless barber not to injure his employer's eyes; for, after the tonsure, these organs are usually subjected to a probing with a pointed instrument almost as sharp as the razor itself.

36. Eye thing which not see—what the eye has never seen, is said with reference to things or beings invisible to mortal eyes.

37. Eye without law rules—void of respect to the laws, denotes a lawless person, who acts regardless of all the laws of the land, and who deserves to be treated as an outlaw.

38. *Chün tsing*, the turning or rolling of the eyes, preceded by *muk pat*, gives the idea of fixed attention.

39, 40. Both these phrases denote the shortest period of time: the first is, literally, one turn of the eyes' duration; the second is elliptical, and is used when speaking of the destruction of property by fire or flood, and of all those pleasures which, *chün ngán* in the twinkling of an eye, *shing* become, *hung* vacant or empty, i. e. cease to exist.

41, 42. *Mák* and *chang* express that exertion which is necessary to open the eyes, when one is afraid or unwilling to have them inspected, or when the lids have become attached to each other, or confined by disease; they are also often used with *hoi* merely for the sake of euphony, without adding anything to the force of the latter.

43. *Wái* expresses the act of destruction; and *líú*, joined to it, denotes that the act is already complete, and the object—the eye in this case—past recovery.

44. Having eyes, not understanding men—denotes one who is unable to appreciate character, and is said in scorn of an opponent.

46. Weary eyes, still not yet desiring sleep—refers not to that restlessness which disqualifies for sleep, but to a desire or necessity of engaging in some business requiring immediate attention.

47. *Ming muk* refers to that extreme point of sickness or stupefaction, when the subject is entirely senseless, so that he can neither see, hear, nor feel.

| | | |
|---|---|---|
| It is the cataract. | 係綠水灌瞳神 | Hai[2] luk[2] 'shui kún' ˏt'ung ˏshan. |
| 49. The following is an elegant saying: Words may act a deceitful part, but the eye cannot play the rogue. | 成語云言猶可以僞爲眸子則有不容僞者 | ˏShing 'yü ˏwan: ˏín ˏyau 'hó 'í ngai[2] ˏwai ˏmau 'tsz' tsak, 'yau pat, ˏyung ngai[2] 'ché. |
| 50. The eye is the best index of a man's character. | 存乎人者莫良於眸子 | ˏTs'ün ˏú ˏyan 'ché, mók[2] ˏléung ˏü ˏmau 'tsz'. |

48. *Ching* is disorder or disease: the name for the cataract—green water poured [into the] pupil—is descriptive of the disease, as it is viewed by those who are ignorant of the eye's structure: *t'ung shan* is here used for the pupil instead of *t'ung yan;* but the phrase *luk shui kún t'ung yan* is more frequently heard from the lips of the common people, than the former phrase, *luk shui kún t'ung shan.*

49. *Shing* means to complete, to finish; *shing yü* is a finished, or elegant saying: *wan*, to say, is equivalent to the English phrase, 'as follows;' and, when the structure of a sentence requires, as in *shing yü wan*, it may be translated thus, there is an elegant saying, namely; words perhaps may serve deceitful action, eye pupil then has what not permits deception, i. e. a man may deceive another by words, but he cannot do this by his eye, for that cannot be made to play the hypocrite; *tsak yau*, then has, refers to the time when the eye is brought into question,—do you speak of the eye, *then* I must say of it, that it will never deceive.

50. Possessed by man things, none good as the eye, freely construed means, that, Of all the parts of the human body, no one is so sure an index of character as the eye.

## Section Third.

## FORM AND FUNCTIONS OF THE NOSE.

鼻 類 第 三 章
Pí[2] lui[2]; tai[2] ˏsám ˏchéung.

| | | |
|---|---|---|
| 1. The nose. | 鼻哥 | Pí[2] ˏkó. |
| 2. A false nose. | 鑲鼻 | ˏSéung pí[2]. |
| 3. A flat nose. | 扁鼻 | 'Pín pí[2]. |
| 4. A high nose. | 高鼻 | ˏKò pí[2]. |

### *Notes and Explanations.*

Pí is one of the radical characters of the language, and is the common term for the organ of smelling: *kó* added to it in the first phrase, *pí kó*, is merely euphonic.

2. The false nose is an artificial one, sometimes made to supply the place of the natural organ, when by any misfortune it has been removed: *séung* means to inlay; and *séung pí*, is, literally, an inlaid nose.

3—5. *Pín pí* is the common flat nose, characteristic of the people of the southern provinces of this empire; *kò pí* is the high Roman nose; and *kau pí* is a prominent and hooked nose.

| | | |
|---|---|---|
| 5. A hooked nose. | 勾鼻 | ‹Kau pí$^2$. |
| 6. A great nose. | 大丨 | Táí$^2$ pí$^2$. |
| 7. A small nose. | 細丨 | Sai' pí$^2$. |
| 8. To bore the nose. | 穿丨 | ‹Ch'ün pí$^2$. |
| 9. To pinch the nose. | 捻丨 | Níp$_2$ pí$^2$. |
| 10. Cover the nose. | 掩丨 | 'Ím pí$^2$. |
| 11. To snort, or blow through the nose. | 噴丨 | P'an' pí$^2$. |
| 12. To sneeze. | 噴嚏 | P'an' t'ai'. |
| 13. The nose free and open. | 鼻通 | Pí$^2$ ‹t'ung. |
| 14. Stoppage of the nose. | 鼻塞 | Pí$^2$ sak›. |
| 15. Obstruction of the nose. | 丨萌 | Pí$^2$ ‚mang. |
| 16. Pain of the nose. | 丨痛 | Pí$^2$ t'ung'. |
| 17. Polypus of the nose. | 丨蛇 | Pí$^2$ ‚shé. |
| 18. Bridge of the nose. | 丨梁 | Pí$^2$ ‚léung. |
| 19. Sides of the nose. | 丨子 | Pí$^2$ 'tsz'. |
| 20. Cartilage of the nose. | 丨柱 | Pí$^2$ 'ch'ü. |
| 21. End of the nose. | 丨準 | Pí$^2$ 'chun. |
| 22. The nostrils. | 丨吼 | Pí$^2$ ‹lung. |
| 23. The nose regaled with flowers. | 花撲鼻 | ‹Fá p'ok› pí$^2$. |
| 24. White nose; or a crafty fellow. | 白鼻哥 | Pák$_2$ pí$^2$ ‹kó. |
| 25. Red nose. | 紅鼻哥 | ‚Hung pí$^2$ ‹kó. |
| 26. The nose affected by [the use of] wine. | 酒攻鼻 | 'Tsau ‹kung pí$^2$. |

11, 12. *P'an* expresses a forcible emission of breath from the mouth or nose, implying usually contempt or disgust. The colloquial phrase for sneezing is *'tá hat› ‹chí*, the sound of the two last words being an attempt to imitate the noise made in the act of sneezing.

13—15. *T'ung* denotes the organ in a perfectly healthy state; *sak* is an entire stoppage; *mang* a partial one.

22. A striking instance is here afforded of the vulgar misapplication of characters which occurs now and then in the provincial dialects. In this dialect, the nostril is called *pí lung*, but in books it is *pí kung*, the same characters as are here used, except the second has no *hau* or mouth on the side. Now in writing the colloquial phrase, they wish to approach as near as may be to the written character, and therefore take this same *kung*, adding a mouth on the side, but still calling it *lung*. Its proper sound, however, is *hau*, and it means to low, to bellow, to vociferate.

| | | |
|---|---|---|
| 27. A blotched nose. | 酒渣鼻 | ꜂Tsau ꜀chá pí꜄. |
| 28. Water flowing from the nose. | 流鼻涕 | ꜁Lau pí꜄ t'ai꜄. |
| 29. Nose bleeding; or hemorrhage of the nose. | 流鼻血 | ꜁Lau pí꜄ hüt꜅. |
| 30. An aquiline nose. | 鸚哥鼻 | ꜀Ang ꜀kó pí꜄. |
| 31. A snort of defiance. | 鬭鼻氣 | Tau꜄ pí꜄ hí꜄. |
| 32. Bringing the nose near in order to smell. | 以鼻就嗅 | ꜂Í pí꜄ tsau꜄ ch'au꜄. |
| 33. To inhale the effluvia. | 以鼻取氣 | ꜂Í pí꜄ ꜂ts'ü hí꜄. |
| 34. To judge of odors by the smell. | 以鼻審氣 | ꜂Í pí꜄ ꜂sham hí꜄. |
| 35. To distinguish odors by the smell. | 以鼻辨氣 | ꜂Í pí꜄ pín꜄ hí꜄. |
| 36. What makes your nose bleed? | 你爲乜事流鼻血 | ꜂Ní wai꜄ mat꜅ sz꜄ ꜁lau pí꜄ hüt꜅. |
| It is caused by present excitement. | 因爲呢排熱氣 | ꜀Yan wai꜄ ꜀ní ꜁p'ái ít꜅ hí꜄. |
| 37. What is that growing in that man's nose? | 個個人個鼻生乜野 | Kó꜄ kó꜄ ꜁yan kó꜄ pí꜄ ꜀shang mat꜅ ꜂yé. |
| It is a polypus. | 生鼻蛇 | ꜀Shang pí꜄ ꜁shé. |
| 38. What is a polypus? | 鼻蛇係乜野 | Pí꜄ ꜁shé hai꜄ mat꜅ ꜂yé? |
| It is a small fleshy excrescence growing in the nostril and stopping it up. | 係鼻窿生一条肉塞住個鼻窿 | Hai꜄ pí꜄ ꜀lung ꜀shang yat꜅ ꜁t'íú yuk꜅, sak꜅ chü꜄ kó꜄ pí꜄ ꜀lung. |

27. *Tsau chá pí*, wine dregs' nose, is that which is infected with pimples caused by excessive use of wine, or by an unhealthy state of the blood.

30. The shape denoted by *ang kó pí* or parrot nose is the same as that by *kau pí;* this form of the nose is seldom seen among the natives of the southern provinces, though more frequently observed among the Tartars and northern Chinese.

32. With nose approach smell, specifies the act of bringing the nose near to an object of smell: *tsau* means to approach near, and *ch'au* is the odor of anything, whether fragrant or the contrary.

33, 34. With nose to take effluvia: the precise meaning of *hí* must be determined by the context, or circumstances of the case in which it occurs; it may be the simple atmospheric air, or the same surcharged with any gas or odor: *sham* means to judge, test, or determine the qualities of; *pín* has here a sense analagous to *sham*, referring to the act of discriminating: *í pí* is with the nóse, or by means of the nose—it being used as the organ or instrument by which we judge of whatever comes in contact with the olfactory nerves.

36. *Wai* is here distinguished both in its tone and in its signification from the same form of the character in No. 49 of the last section: there it means to act, here it signifies for; *wai mat sz'* for what reason? to which the answer is, *yan wai* for this reason, or because of. *ní p'ái* present, *ít hí* inflamed breath, i. e. excitement, resulting from intemperate eating, drinking, or exercise.

## Section Fourth.

# FORM AND FUNCTIONS OF THE MOUTH.

## 口類第四章
ʻHau lui$^{2}$; tai$^{2}$ sz$^{3}$ ꜀cheung.

| | | |
|---|---|---|
| 1. A great mouth. | 大口 | Tái$^{2}$ ʻhau. |
| 2. A small mouth. | 細丨 | Sai$^{3}$ ʻhau. |
| 3. A distorted mouth. | 歪丨 | ꜀Wái ʻhau. |
| 4. Close the mouth. | 緘丨 | ꜀Kám ʻhau. |
| 5. Open the mouth. | 開丨 | ꜀Hoi ʻhau. |
| 6. Keep silence. | 合丨 | Hóp$_{2}$ ʻhau. |
| 7. Stop the mouth; or to gag. | 塞丨 | Sak$_{3}$ ʻhau. |
| 8. To procure a livelihood. | 糊丨 | ꜁Ú ʻhau. |
| 9. Bitterness in the mouth. | 口苦 | ʻHau ʻfú. |
| 10. Dryness of the mouth. | 丨乾 | ʻHau ꜀kón. |
| 11. The mouth eats. | 丨食 | ʻHau shik$_{2}$. |
| 12. The mouth drinks. | 丨飲 | ʻHau ʻyam. |
| 13. To hold fluid in the mouth. | 丨含 | ʻHau ꜁hóm. |
| 14. To chew food; or to masticate. | 丨嚼 | ʻHau tséuk$_{2}$. |
| 15. To gnaw with the teeth. | 丨齧 | ʻHau ngát$_{2}$. |

## *Notes and Explanations.*

HAU, 'the mouth,' say the Chinese, 'denotes that with which people eat and speak: its form is represented by the character.' It stands in Hónghí's imperial dictionary as the thirtieth radical, and forms a part of most of those words which refer to eating and speaking.

3, 4. *Wái* is compounded of *not* and *regular;* hence its meaning, irregular, distorted: *kám* means to bind with cords, to envelop, to close up; here it denotes one's voluntary act of closing the mouth, and in that way keeping silence, or, as we often say, holding the tongue.

7. The phrase *sak hau* is used in both a literal and figurative sense: a band of robbers, when they have seized on a person and are afraid that his cries will alarm the neighborhood, take care to stop his mouth; and if it happen that their nefarious acts have come to the ears of a local officer, or to any one else who may be willing to bring them to justice, again they take care to stop his mouth, which is usually done by bribing him or 'buying his mouth.'

8. The phrase *ú hau*, is, literally, to paste the mouth, or to stop it with boiled rice, and is in common use to denote the idea of procuring personal support, or that which is merely sufficient to supply daily wants—it is the 'living from hand to mouth.'

| | | |
|---|---|---|
| 16. The lips. | 口唇 | ‘Hau ˏshun. |
| 17. Polite. | 好口 | ‘Hò ‘hau. |
| 18. Veracious. | 直丨 | Chikˎ ‘hau. |
| 19. Loquacious. | 多丨 | ˓Tó ‘hau. |
| 20. Obscene. | 粗丨 | ˓Tsò ‘hau. |
| 21. A harelip. | 崩丨 | ˓Pang ‘hau. |
| 22. Stammering. | 漏丨 | Lau’ ‘hau. |
| 23. Open the mouth. | 擘開口 | Mákˎ ˓hoi ‘hau. |
| 24. Close the mouth. | 閉埋丨 | Pai’ ‘mái ‘hau. |
| 25. Embarrassed. | 難開丨 | ˏNán ˓hoi ‘hau. |
| 26. Indisposed to speak. | 冇口講 | ‘Mò ‘hau ‘kóng. |
| 27. True to his word. | 有口齒 | ‘Yau ‘hau ‘ch‘í. |
| 28. Regardless of the truth. | 冇口齒 | ‘Mò ‘hau ‘ch‘í. |
| 29. Very slow of speech. | 咁口訥 | Kóm’ ‘hau nutˎ. |
| 30. Fluency of speech. | 好口角 | ‘Hò ‘hau kókˎ. |
| 31. Eloquent. | 有口才 | ‘Yau ‘hau ˏts‘oi. |
| 32. Strife of words. | 爭口氣 | ˓Chang ‘hau hi’. |
| 33. Written testimony is necessary. | 口話無凴 | ‘Hau wá’ ˏmò ˏp‘ang. |

25. *Nán hoi hau*, difficult to open the mouth, denotes that embarrassment which one feels in presenting a second demand on the kindness of a friend: he feels embarrassed, and finds it difficult to broach the subject, or to *hoi hau*.

26—28. Literally these phrases read thus: no mouth to speak, meaning that one is indisposed to speak; having mouth and teeth, denoting one who is true to his word; and without mouth and teeth, or one who is regardless of the truth.

29. *Kóm* in a high degree, *hau* the mouth, *nut* slow to speak: *nut* does not imply any lack of knowledge, but simply backwardness in giving utterance to thoughts: in the Conversations of Confucius it is said of the good man, *yukˎ nutˎ ˓ü ˏin, ˏí ‘man ˓ü hang’*, ‘he is slow to speak, and prompt to act.’

30, 31. Good mouth corners, and having mouth power, both express nearly the same idea, and are applied to those who are able to speak well.

32. *Hau hi*, the breath of the mouth, here denotes mere words: *chang* is to contend: hence the meaning of the phrase, war of words, or logomachy, a mode of settling quarrels much practiced by the Chinese, to which is often added a lusty tug at the cue, and many demonstrations of a hostile dispostion, but bloody noses or broken heads are seldom a consequence of these wordy battles.

33. Mouth words no proof, is a phrase used to express the necessity of having written testimony, because the circumstances of a given case are such, that, *hau wá* words of the mouth, *mò p‘ang* afford no proof, i. e. no sufficient evidence of the truth or fact in question.

廣東方言讀本

| | | |
|---|---|---|
| 34. Charming eloquence. | 口角春風 | ʻHau kók› ‹ch'un ‹fung. |
| 35. It is useless to say more. | 不用費唇舌 | Pat› yung[2] fai[3] ‚shun shít‚. |
| 36. Talebearing is a fruitful source of mischief. | 口舌是非多 | ʻHau shít‚ shí[2] ‹fí ‹tó. |
| 37. A sweet mouth and a slippery tongue. | 口甜舌滑 | ʻHau ‚tím shít‚ wát‚. |
| 38. Words come from the mouth in perfect sentences. | 出口成文 | Ch'ut› ʻhau ‚shing ‚man. |
| 39. He must be true to his word. | 須用口齒 | ‹Sü yung[3] ʻhau ʻch'í. |
| 40. Unable to procure a livelihood. | 唔究糊口 | ‚'M kau[3] ‚ú ʻhau. |
| 41. I cannot endure such venomous words. | 不堪毒口 | Pat› ‹hóm tuk‚ ʻhau. |
| 42. Bitter words are good medicine. | 苦口涼藥 | ʻFú ʻhau ‚léung yéuk‚. |
| 43. Disease enters by the mouth. | 病從口入 | Peng[2] ‚ts'ung ʻhau yap‚. |
| 44. Mischief proceeds from the mouth. | 禍從口出 | Wó[2] ‚ts'ung ʻhau ch'ut›. |
| 45. Yes in the mouth, and no in the heart. | 口是心非 | ʻHau shí[2] ‹sam ‹fí. |
| 46. The mouth specious and the heart perverse. | 亻乖心歪 | ʻHau ‹kwái ‹sam ‹wái. |
| 47. From the mouth come peace and war. Peace is mild, but war is destructive: from the words of the mouth, then, are these two diverse effects. How greatly ought such springs of evil and of good to be feared! | 惟口出好興戎<br>好善也戎兵也<br>言發於口則有<br>二者之分利害<br>之幾可畏如此 | ‚Wai ʻhau ch'ut› ʻhò ‹hing ‚yung. ʻHò, shín[2] ʻyá: ‚yung, ‹ping ʻyá; ‚ín fát› ‹ü ʻhau, tsak› ʻyau í[2] ʻché ‹chí ‹fan. Lí[2] hoi[2] ‹chí ‹kí ʻhò wai[3] ‚ü ʻt'sz'. |

34. *Ch'un fung*, the vernal breezes, are used figuratively for what is mild, gentle, pleasing: hence the phrase denotes an utterance that is charming, like the zephyrs of spring.

35. *Fai shun shít*, an expenditure of the lips and tongue, refers to a case where words are unavailing, or *pat yung* without use.

36. Mouth and tongue [much, then there will be] right and wrong much, is a counterpart to one of the proverbs of an ancient king, 'Where there is no talebearer, strife ceaseth.'

38. This refers to that natural conversation, which, in accuracy and elegance, is comparable to the finished style of written composition.

43, 44. Disease enters through the mouth, because of intemperance in eating and drinking: mischief proceeds from the mouth, because of unguarded words.

47. These words, *wai hau ch'ut hò hing yung*, are from the closing part of an address of the ancient chieftain Shun to his successor U, found in the Shü King, or Book of Records, and must have been uttered more than 4000 years ago. They remind us of the inspired penman's words, "out of the same mouth proceedeth blessing and cursing." Literally translated, they run thus, the mouth promotes good, and excites weapons of war. The twenty-four words which follow are exegetical, and of a later date.

## Section Fifth.

# PARTS AND FUNCTIONS OF THE EAR.

### 耳類第五章
ʻÍ luiʼ; taiʼ ʻʼng ˓chéung.

| | | |
|---|---|---|
| 1. The ear. | 耳朶 | ʻÍ ʻtó. |
| 2. Cavity of the ear. | 耳窿 | ʻÍ ˓lung. |
| 3. Deafness of the ears. | 耳聾 | ʻÍ ˛lung. |
| 4. Acute ears. | 耳聰 | ʻÍ ˓tsʻung. |
| 5. Ringing in the ears. | 丨鳴 | ʻÍ ˓ming. |
| 6. Stoppage of the ear. | 丨塞 | ʻÍ sak˒. |
| 7. Dull ears. | 唔好耳 | ˛ʼM ʻhò ʻí, |
| 8. To feign deafness. | 詐耳聾 | Cháʼ ʻí ˛lung, |
| 9. Regardless of admonition. | 冇耳性 | ʻMò ʻí singʼ. |
| 10. No ear to hear. | 冇耳聽 | ʻMò ʻí ˓tʻing. |
| 11. No ear to receive what is said. | 冇耳裝 | ʻMò ʻí ˓chóng. |
| 12. Incline the ear to hear. | 側耳聽 | Chak˒ ʻí tʻingʼ. |
| 13. Give ear to hear. | 附耳聽 | Fúʼ ʻí tʻingʼ. |

## *Notes and Explanations.*

THE organ of hearing is thought to be represented by the character *í*, the common term to denote the ear; the present form differs from its original, which presents an outline of the external ear; *tó*, in the phrase *í tó*, is merely a euphonic particle, used in speaking of certain classes of objects which are pendulous or globular.

3, 4. The words *lung* and *tsʻung* are opposite in their signification: the first denotes the sense of hearing when it is lost or has become extremely dull; the latter is used when the organ is quick to perceive and discriminate.

5. Ringing in the ears is that sensation of sound which one sometimes perceives, and for which he can assign no cause, though for the moment it seems as distinct and real as the ringing of a bell. The same idea is expressed in No. 32, below.

9. No ear nature—denotes one who is regardless of whatever is said to him, as though the natural functions of his ears had ceased to perform the duties of their office.

10, 11. The meaning of *tʻing* and *chóng* in these two phrases is nearly the same: the latter often means to put into, to store up, which shade of thought is here retained.

12, 13. *Chak í tʻing* is the turning of the ear in any direction which will facilitate hearing; *fú* denotes the act of bringing it near for this purpose. *Tʻing*, in these two examples, it will be perceived, has a different intonation from the preceding number; it has the same use as in chap. I., sect. 6: 44.

| | | |
|---|---|---|
| 14. A deaf ear. | 耳無聞 | ꜂Í ꜁mò ꜁man. |
| 15. The ears pierced with flags. | 插耳旗 | Ch'áp꜅ ꜂í ꜁kí. |
| 16. To bore the lobes of the ears. | 錐丨珠 | ꜀Chui ꜂í ꜀chü. |
| 17. An acute ear. | 好丨鬼 | ʻHò ꜂í ʻkwai. |
| 18. Both ears very long. | 兩丨垂肩 | ꜂Léung ꜂í ꜁shui ꜀kín. |
| 19. He has many eyes and ears [in his employ]. | 佢丨目多 | ʻK'ui ꜂í muk꜇ ꜀tó. |
| 20. When I have washed my ears, I will listen to you. | 洗丨聆音 | ʻSai ꜂í ꜁ling ꜀yam. |
| 21. Having heard you thro' I will now wash my ears. | 聽過洗耳 | ꜀T'ing kwó꜄ ʻsai ꜂í. |
| 22. His words are still sounding in my ears. | 言猶在丨 | ꜁Ín ꜁yau tsoi² ꜂í. |
| 23. Stop both ears. | 塞埋兩丨 | Sak꜅ ꜁mái ꜂léung ꜂í. |
| 24. Can cleanse the ear by candle-light. | 燈前取丨 | ꜀Tang ꜁tsín ʻts'ü ꜂í. |
| 25. The ear ought not to hear lewd sounds. | 耳不聽淫聲 | ꜂Í pat꜅ t'ing꜄ ꜁yam ꜀shing. |
| 26. Those who have long ears, will enjoy long life. | 丨長命必長 | ꜂Í ꜁ch'éung, ming² pít꜅ ꜁ch'éung. |
| 27. Very charming sounds. | 好撩丨既聲 | ʻHò ꜁líú ꜂í ké꜄ ꜀shing. |
| 28. Close both ears. | 揜埋兩隻丨 | ʻAm ꜁mái ꜂léung chek꜅ ꜂í. |

14. An ear without hearing is the listless ear, and denotes one who, having ears, yet hears not, either in a natural or moral sense.

15. This is part of a punishment often inflicted on persons in Canton, for petty thefts and other similar misdemeanors: two little *kí* or flags are prepared, having shafts about a foot long, which are, *ch'áp í* thrust into or pierced through the ears, one on each side of the head; in this condition, with his hands chained behind him, the evildoer is led through the streets, one soldier going on before him beating a gong, and another following him with a rattan, which is smartly applied to the poor man's naked back.

18. Both ears depending to the shoulders denotes one who has very long ears; among the common people, however, this physiognomy is sometimes regarded as a presage of sitting down on the dragon's seat, or the throne.

19. This expression, and another one similar, 'He has many hands and feet,' are applied to officers of government who keep in pay a number of spies secretly to ascertain the actions of the people, or to other persons, who watch their enemies closely.

20, 21. Washed ears listen [to] sounds—is a respectful expression, implying that the person may have been hearing what was vile or rude, and when the impression of the sounds is washed away, he will be attentive. The other phrase has a reference to an ancient statesman in the time of the emperor *Yú*, named Hüyau, who, whenever he heard anything vile or mendacious, would wash his ears after it, as if to remove the impression of the words.

22. This was spoken by an ancient sage, and refers to the instructions of his father; the whole sentence is, *꜁Ín ꜁yau tsoi² ꜂í, ꜁í kí꜄ ꜀chí yéuk꜇ ꜁hó?* his words are still sounding in my ears, and how can I discard them?

24. Another line usually accompanies this, and both may be seen hanging up at the barber's door; literally they read thus: 'lamp before receive ears, moon beneath shave heads'—intending to set forth the man's skill, which is so great that he can perform all the manipulations of tonsure and toilet as well by night as by day.

| | | |
|---|---|---|
| 29. Cut the ear to make a remembrancer. | 切耳做記號 | Ts'ít꜀ ꜂í tsò² kí' hò². |
| 30. When her ears are bored she will become a lady. | 錐丨變姑娘 | ꜀Chui ꜂í pín' ꜀kú ꜁néung. |
| 31. Cut off your ears and make you a branded debtor. | 割丨變債墪 | Kot꜀ ꜂í pín' chái' 'tan. |
| 32. Draw an ear upon the wall to hear [your idle tales]. | 畫丨上牆聽 | Wák₂ ꜂í ꜂shéung ꜁ts'éung ꜀t'ing. |
| 33. An ear may be behind the adjoining wall, take care! | 隔牆防有耳 | Kák꜀ ꜁ts'éung ꜁fóng ꜂yau ꜂í. |
| 34. Passes in at one ear and out at the other. | 左丨入右丨出 | 'Tsó ꜂í yap₂ yau² ꜂í ch'ut꜀. |
| 35. If he does not obey, then pull his ears. | 唔聽話扭丨仔 | ꜁'M ꜀t'ing wá² 'nau ꜂í 'tsai. |
| 36. A credulous ear receives everything that is said. | 丨朶軟信人講 | ꜂Í 'tò ꜂yün sun² ꜁yan 'kóng. |
| 37. Sound ringing in both ears. | 兩隻丨嚶嚶聲 | ꜂Léung chek꜀ ꜂í ꜀ying ꜀ying ꜀shing. |
| 38. A sudden clap of thunder, giving no time to close the ears. | 迅雷不及掩丨 | Sun' ꜁lúi pat꜀ k'ap₂ 'ím ꜂í. |
| 39. When the mind is absent, the ear does not hear. | 心唔在丨就唔聽見 | ꜀Sam ꜁'m tsoi² ꜂í tsau² ꜁'m ꜀t'ing kín'. |
| 40. Take him by the ear and lead him back. | 扭住丨朶拉佢番嚟 | 'Nau chü' ꜂í 'tó ꜀lái 'k'ui ꜀fán ꜁lai. |
| 41. You do not at all give ear to what I say. | 你都唔俾耳聽我講 | ꜂Ní ꜀tò ꜁'m 'pí ꜂í ꜀t'ing ꜂ngó 'kóng. |
| 42. My ears are a little dull of hearing. | 我對耳有的咁多撞聾 | ꜂Ngó túi' ꜂í ꜂yau tí꜀ kóm' ꜀tó chóng² ꜁lung. |

29. Cut ears make memory mark—is said to one who is troubled with a treacherous memory; therefore he is admonished, 'Cut your ears to make a mark which will assist your memory.'

30. This is said of the little girl, while yet she is called 'child', and has nothing in her dress to indicate that she is a girl; but when her ears are decked with jewels, the question of her ladyship will no longer be doubtful.

31. *Chái tan* is used to denote one who is deeply involved in debt, but the origin of the term is doubtful: *chái* is a debtor, and *tan* is a signal chimney, built of brick or stone on eminences, in which fires are lighted as a signal of alarm: *tan* has other significations; and the phrase *chái tan* is written sometimes in forms different from that above.

32. This is the language of angry reproach: if you must give utterance to such language as you now use, draw an ear upon the wall to listen to your idle vociferations, for my ears, which are accustomed to the truth, are not to be attacked in this rude manner.

33. *Kák ts'éung* the adjoining wall, *fóng* fear, *yau* have, *í* an ear; you must be careful what you say, for behind the adjoining wall there may be some one who will hear you speak.

36. *Yün* is applied to what is weak, flexible, yielding, both physically and morally: here it is applied to those who readily believe whatever is said, regardless of the matter told them, or of the source from whence it comes.

42. *Túi í*, a pair of ears, is the same as *léung chek í*, two piece [of] ears, i. e. both ears; the phrase is idiomatic, and preceded by *ngó* simply means my ears: *tí-kóm-tó*, a jot-so-

| | | |
|---|---|---|
| 43. The words you speak are not worthy of being heard. | 你講的唔入耳<br>旣說話 | ‘Ní ‘kóng tik› ˏ’m yapˎ ˏí ké’ shüt› wá[2]. |
| 44. He closed his ears as if he heard nothing. | 塞埋兩耳當作<br>唔聽見 | Sak› ˏmái ˋléung ˋí, tóng’ tsók› ˏ’m ‹t‘ing kín’. |
| 45. In shaving your head this morning, you omitted to clean out your ears. | 今日剃頭未取<br>乾淨耳 | ‹Kam yat› t‘ai’ ˏt‘au, mí[2] ‘ts‘ü ‹kón tsing[2] ˋí. |
| 46. Mencius said, the desire of the mouth towards flavors, of the eye towards colors, of the ear towards sounds, of the nose towards scents, and of the four members towards ease, is natural; yet, these desires being imparted by heaven, the superior man does not speak of them merely as natural inclinations. | 孟子曰口之於<br>味也目之於色<br>也耳之於聲也<br>鼻之於臭也四<br>肢之於安佚也<br>性也有命焉君<br>子不謂性也 | Mang[2] ‘tsz’ ütˎ, ‘hau ‹chí ‹ü mí[2] ˋyá, mukˎ ‹chí ‹ü shik› ˋyá, ˋí ‹chí ‹ü ‹shing ˋyá, pí[2] ‘chí ‹ü ch‘au’ ˋyá, sz” ‹chí ‹chí ‹ü ‹ón yatˎ ˋyá; sing’ ˋyá; ˋyau ming[2] ˏín, ‹kwan ‘tsz’ pat› wai[2] sing’ ˋyá. |

much, is a common local phrase, denoting 'a little,' in degree, or in quantity; *tí* is the same as *tik*, the change in pronounciation is made merely for the sake of euphony; in most cases the *k* in *tik* is sounded very slightly: *chóng lung* is a sudden stroke of deafness, not that which is habitual: the whole sentence, as used in conversation, is equivalent to our common phrase, 'I beg your pardon,'—meaning, I did not distinctly hear what you said, please repeat it.

43. *Ní kóng tik* you speak that, or, that which you speak; *ké* is of, or belongs to, *shüt wá* words, or that class of words, '*m* which is unfit, *yap í* to enter the ear.

44. The words '*m t'ing kín*, not hear see, mean not to perceive by the sense of hearing, or to be deaf; *tóng tsók* to make as if, i. e. to feign: he closed his ears and acted as if he did not hear; he pretended to be deaf.

45. This is uttered in reproof for not hearing; were your ears open, or were you attentive as you ought to be, there would be no difficulty in hearing what is said to you.

46. This beautiful sentence is selected from the closing chapter of the conversations of Mencius. The sentence which succeeds it is antithetical to it, as follows; "the exercise of love between parents and children, of equity between princes and ministers, of propriety between hosts and guests, of wisdom among the virtuous, and of accordance on the sage's part with celestial principles, is ordained of heaven; yet such exercises being subjects of natural effort, the superior man does not speak of them wholly as heavenly gifts." The purpose of the sage, in these remarks was to restrain men from the unreserved obedience of what is called natural inclinations, and to urge on them the importance of exerting themselves to seek after gifts, considered as heavenly, and therefore supposed to be unattainable by ordinary men. The superior man, he here tells us, does not regard our inclinations purely as *sing*, natural and beyond the the power of restraint, but as being also *ming*, heavenly endowments, which are to be rightly employed for good.

## Section Sixth.

# FORM AND EXPRESSION OF THE FACE.

## 面類第六章
Mín² lui²; tai² luk₂ ₑcheung.

| | | |
|---|---|---|
| 1. The human face. | 人面 | ₛYan mín². |
| 2. A smiling face. | 笑面 | Síú' mín². |
| 3. A square face. | 方面 | ₑFóng mín². |
| 4. A round face. | 圓面 | ₛÜn mín². |
| 5. A broad face. | 濶面 | Fút₃ mín². |
| 6. A lean face. | 瘦面 | Shau' mín². |
| 7. The visage; or the human countenance. | 面容 | Mín² ₛyung. |
| 8. The complexion. | 面色 | Mín² shik₃. |
| 9. A flushed countenance. | 面赤 | Mín² ch'ik₃. |
| 10. A pallid countenance. | 面青 | Mín² ₑts'ing. |
| 11. A dark countenance. | 面黑 | Mín² hak₃. |
| 12. To meet together. | 會面 | Úi² mín². |
| 13. A personal interview. | 見面 | Kín' mín². |
| 14. To turn the back upon a person. | 背面 | Púi' mín². |
| 15. Being face to face. | 對面 | Túi' mín². |
| 16. Being in the presence of a person. | 當面 | ₑTóng mín². |
| 17. Being of little reputation. | 薄面 | Pók₂ mín². |

## *Notes and Explanations.*

MÍN was originally intended as a picture of the human face: it now denotes the face, the countenance, the front, the surface; also to front, to face, to see; and it often enters into the composition of those characters which, in any way, relate to the face. As an index of what man is, the face has come to signify character, reputation, &c.

12. This denotes coming into the presence of a person, and may be spoken of few or many: *úi* means to come together, to associate; an association, a society, a band.

14—16. *Púi mín*, literally back face, signifies the act of one person turning his back upon another in scorn or disgust; the phrase may also mean the back: *túi mín* is face to face, one being over against another: *tóng mín* is simply being in the presence of, without regard to the position of the parties.

| | | |
|---|---|---|
| 18. Having a good reputation. | 有面 | ʻYau mín$^2$. |
| 19. Having lost reputation. | 失丨 | Shat꜀ mín$^2$. |
| 20. Having preserved reputation. | 留丨 | ꜁Lau mín$^2$. |
| 21. Reputation; or a good name. | 體丨 | ʻT'ai mín$^2$. |
| 22. Mutually turning their backs on each other. | 相背面 | ꜀Séung púi' mín$^2$. |
| 23. A smiling face. | 面帶笑 | Mín$^2$ tái' síú'. |
| 24. A very lank face. | 丨太瘦 | Mín$^2$ t'ái' shau'. |
| 25. A benignant countenance. | 丨寬容 | Mín$^2$ ꜀fún ꜁yung. |
| 26. A fair complexion. | 好面色 | ʻHò mín$^2$ shik꜀. |
| 27. I did not see him. | 不會面 | Pat꜀ úi$^2$ mín$^2$. |
| 28. I did not obtain an interview. | 不見丨 | Pat꜀ kín' mín$^2$. |
| 29. To choose in the presence of others. | 當面揀 | ꜀Tóng mín$^2$ ʻkán. |
| 30. A good reputation. | 好體面 | ʻHò ʻt'ai mín$^2$. |
| 31. Without reputation. | 冇體丨 | ʻMò ʻt'ai mín$^2$. |
| 32. To destroy one's reputation. | 丟了丨 | ꜀Tíú ʻlíú mín$^2$. |
| 33. Personal esteem. | 有情丨 | ʻYau ꜁ts'ing mín$^2$. |
| 34. Seeking reputation. | 想討丨 | ʻSéung ʻt'ò mín$^2$. |
| 35. Ashamed to be seen. | 無體丨 | ꜁Mò ꜁t'ai mín$^2$. |
| 36. It is difficult to get a sight of him. | 難逢一面 | ꜁Nán ꜁fung yat꜀ mín$^2$. |

17—21. Thin face, having face, lost face, retained face, substantial face, all have reference to reputation, or a good name: *pók mín* is a modest term used when speaking of one's own character; *t'ai* is often used in connection with *mín*, thus, *k'ui yau t'ai mín*, he has a substance and face, is respectable, or has a good reputation.

24. *T'ái* written in this form, with an aspirate, denotes what is very great, or what exists in an eminent degree.

26. A good face color is applied to those whose countenances indicate health and good spirits, and not to personal beauty; a slight tinge of red on the cheeks, clear eyes, &c., are the well known indications.

27, 28. These refer to cases in which one goes to the house of another: *pat úi mín*, cannot meet the face, because the person sought does not choose to appear; *pat kín mín*, did not see he face, because the person sought was absent from home.

29. This is said of selecting goods, or anything else, where the choice is made in the presence of interested parties.

32. The reputation is here supposed to be destroyed by improper conduct; the phrase, therefore, is true to the letter, *tíú* casting away the reputation.

36. This is said when one, in pursuit of another, repeatedly fails to find him in the place where he is ordinarily to be seen.

| | | |
|---|---|---|
| 37. It is a long time since we met. | 許久一面 | ‘Hü ‘kau yat› mín$^{2}$. |
| 38. A single conversation. | 一面之詞 | Yat› mín$^{2}$ ‹chí ‹ts‘z’. |
| 39. A single interview. | 一丨之交 | Yat› mín$^{2}$ ‹chí ‹káu. |
| 40. Praising to the face, and slandering to the back. | 面舉背毀 | Mín$^{2}$ ‘kü púi’ ‘wai. |
| 41. Excessive insolence. | 過面相欺 | Kwó’ mín$^{2}$ ‹séung ‹hí. |
| 42. An open mistake. | 當丨錯過 | ‹Tóng mín$^{2}$ ts‘ó’ kwó’. |
| 43. I have spoken with him. | 覿丨講過 | Tik› mín$^{2}$ ‘kóng kwó’. |
| 44. Gazing at each other in amazement. | 面丨相窺 | Mín$^{2}$ mín$^{2}$ ‹séung ‹kw‘ai. |
| 45. By a personal interview friendship is restored. | 見丨着情 | Kín’ mín$^{2}$ chéuk$_{2}$ ‹ts‘ing. |
| 46. There is joy upon his countenance. | 面上有喜色 | Mín$^{2}$ shéung$^{2}$ ‘yau ‘hi shik›. |
| 47. Its virtues will presently appear. | 當面就見功 | ‹Tóng mín$^{2}$ ts‘au$^{2}$ kín’ ‹kung. |
| 48. He turned away his face, without noticing me. | 反面不識人 | ‘Fán mín$^{2}$ pat› shik› ‹yan. |
| 49. Leave me a little reputation. | 留遠的薄面 | ‹Lau ‹wán tik› pók$_{2}$ mín$^{2}$. |
| 50. If so, all reputation is lost. | 咁樣冇體丨 | ‘Kóm yéung$^{2}$, ‘mò ‘t‘ai mín$^{2}$. |
| 51. Repeatedly failed in seeing him. | 幾次不見丨 | ‘Kí tsz’’ pat› kín’ mín$^{2}$. |
| 52. It is difficult to break from personal esteem. | 情靣上難過 | ‹Ts‘ing mín$^{2}$ shéung$^{2}$ ‹nán kwó’. |
| 53. Ashamed to go and see him. | 無靣去見人 | ‹Mò mín$^{2}$ hü’ kín’ ‹yan. |
| 54. It is absolutely necessary to report in person. | 必須面稟方可 | Pít› ‹sü mín$^{2}$ ‘pan ‹fóng ‘hó. |
| 55. Diligence will secure a reputation. | 勤力方討得面 | ‹K‘an lik$_{2}$ ‹fóng ‘t‘ò tak› mín$^{2}$. |

41. Pass face give insult, is susceptible of two meanings: insulting beyond endurance; or insulting one who passes before you as a mere stranger.

42. *Ts‘ó kwó* is an error of any kind, which has been committed in the presence of others; and this fact, on detection of the error, is given in extenuation.

43. See face speak pass—I have seen and spoken with him—is a mode of saying that one has enjoyed an interview for consultation, &c.

45. Seeing the face creates kind feeling, a phrase derived from the usual experience of mankind, that when differences have arisen between absent parties, either by slanderous imputations or personal enmity existing between them, kind feeling and friendship is restored by a personal interview.

47. Now presence immediately see virtue—is said by the druggist, and others, in commendation of their commodities.

52. *Ts‘ing mín* denotes that feeling which springs from personal acquaintance, or it is that personal regard which constrains one to befriend another under all circumstances. The character *mín*, partially contracted as in this example, often occurs in manuscripts and cheap publications.

54. Must necessarily in person report to my superior, then it will be well: the case is such that it cannot be stated in writing, nor intrusted to a second person.

| | | |
|---|---|---|
| 56. There is no color in his face. | 面上冇的血色 | Mín² shéung² ʿmò tik› hüt› shik›. |
| 57. His countenance is not as good as it was last year. | 面色唔似舊年 | Mín² shik› ꜀'m ʿtsz' kau² ꜀nín. |
| 58. The debtor must frequently pay respects to the creditor. | 欠債不離常見面 | Hím' chái' pat› ꜀lí ‹shéung kín' mín². |
| 59. Under the mask he may appear in public. | 帶笑面致見得人 | Tái' siú' mín² chí' kín' tak› ꜀yan. |
| 60. The man who has a bold face will get rich. | 滿面春光必發財 | ʿMún mín² ‹ch'un ‹kwóng pít› fát› ꜀ts'oi. |
| 61. Men's minds differ like their faces. | 人心不一如其面然 | ꜀Yan ‹sam pat› yat› ꜀ü ꜀k'í mín² ꜀ín. |

60. The whole face spring bright must produce wealth, i. e. a bold prompt person of this description is supposed to be fitted for the acquisition of wealth. The phrase *ch'un kwóng* refers to the vivacity and freshness which is observed in nature, and especially birds, on the approach of spring.

## Section Seventh.

## THE FOUR LIMBS.

### 四肢類第七章

Sz'' ‹chí lui²; tai² ts'át› ‹chéung.

| | | |
|---|---|---|
| 1. The palm of the hand. | 手掌 | ʿShau ʿchéung. |
| 2. The finger nails. | 手甲 | ʿShau káp›. |
| 3. The elbow. | 手踭 | ʿShau ‹cháng. |
| 4. The arm. | 手臂 | ʿShau pí'. |

### *Notes and Explanations.*

CHÍ, formed of *flesh* placed on the left of *branches*, denotes branches of flesh, the extremities of the human body: *sz' chí*, the four extremities, are the hands and feet. Both parts of *chí* are found among the radicals; and, in composition, generally give to the words into which they enter something of their original signification.

1, 2. *Shau* is the common word for the hand; it is one of the radicals, and enters into the composition of a very large class of words, where, in a great many instances, in indicates some act performed by the hand, or to which it is related.

| | | |
|---|---|---|
| 5. The wrist. | 手腕 | ʻShau ʻún. |
| 6. A paralytic hand. | 跛手 | ˏPai ʻshau. |
| 7. The fist. | 拳頭 | ˏK'ün ˏt'au. |
| 8. A finger. | 手指 | ʻShau ʻchí. |
| 9. The thumb. | 公指 | ˏKung ʻchí. |
| 10. The forefinger. | 食指 | Shikˎ ʻchí. |
| 11. The middle finger. | 中指 | ˏChung ʻchí. |
| 12. Little finger. | 小指 | ʻSíú ʻchí. |
| 13. Knuckles. | 手節 | ʻShau tsitˎ. |
| 14. Striæ on the skin at the ends of the fingers. | 指模 | ʻChí ˏmò. |
| 15. Ring finger. | 無名指 | ˏMò ˏming ʻchí. |
| 16. Both hands. | 一對手 | Yatˎ túiʾ ʻshau. |
| 17. One hand. | 一隻手 | Yatˎ chekˎ ʻshau. |
| 18. A thievish hand. | 三隻手 | ˏSám chekˎ ʻshau. |
| 19. Right and left hands. | 左右手 | ʻTsó yauʾ ʻshau. |
| 20. Stretch out the hand. | 伸開手 | ˏShan ˏhoi ʻshau. |
| 21. Draw back the hand. | 縮埋手 | Shukˎ ˏmái ʻshau. |
| 22. Walking hand in hand. | 拖拉手 | ˏT'ó ˏlái ʻshau. |
| 23. Handcuffed. | 鎖住手 | ʻSó chüʾ ʻshau. |
| 24. Burning the hand. | 燒親手 | ˏShíú ˏts'an ʻshau. |

6. *Pai*, formed of *skin* on the right of *feet*, means lameness in the feet; it is also used in reference to other parts of the body: *pai shau* is the hand deprived of the power of muscular motion.

7. *K'ün*, considered etymologically, signifies the hand rolled up, i. e. the fist: *t'au* is an idiomatic addition, serving to make the phrase more definite and euphonic.

18. *Sám chek shau*, three hands, denotes an expert thief, who employs one hand more than is done by honest people.

21. This is used not only for drawing the hand back from any object or pursuit, but it also designates the hand that is drawn back and is remaining idle.

22. *T'ó lái shau*, take and lead by the hand, is said of two persons walking hand in hand, as children often do when playfully passing along in the street.

23. *Só* means a lock or to lock; *chü* denotes that the action is being effected, and that the hands are already bound fast; the whole phrase, therefore, denotes being handcuffed.

24. *Ts'an*, like *chü* in the preceding phrase, denotes that the action has already taken effect,—that the hand is in contact with the fire: *ts'an shau* is also used for one's own hand, and sometimes it implies the whole arm, as *shau* alone frequently does.

| | | |
|---|---|---|
| 25. Good workmanship. | 好手勢 | ‘Hò ‘shau shai’. |
| 26. To beat the palm of the hand. | 打扌板 | ‘Tá ‘shau ‘pán. |
| 27. To mark with the finger. | 打指模 | ‘Tá ‹chí ‹mò. |
| 28. A beginner; or one just entering upon a science. | 初學手 | ‹Ch‘ó hók› ‘shau. |
| 29. Not yet commenced. | 未開扌 | Mí’ ‹hoi ‘shau. |
| 30. Crooked fingers. | 手指攣 | ‘Shau ‘chí ‹lüü. |
| 31. Under the instep of the foot. | 脚板堂 | Kéuk› ‘pán ‹t‘óng. |
| 32. The little toe. | 脚指尾 | Kéuk› ‘chí ‘mí. |
| 33. The heel. | 脚睜頭 | Kéuk› ‹cháng ‹t‘au. |
| 34. Wound the feet. | 打跛脚 | ‘Tá ‹pai kéuk›. |
| 35. Pain in the knees. | 膝頭痛 | Sat› ‹t‘au t‘ung’. |
| 36. To shake hands with mutual joy. | 握手相歡 | Ak› ‘shau ‹séung ‹fún. |
| 37. To raise high with the hand. | 一扌擎起 | Yat› ‘shau ‹king ‘hí. |
| 38. The extremities as cold as ice. | 四肢冰冷 | Sz” ‹chí ‹ping ‘láng. |
| 39. Restore to the original possessor. | 交還原手 | ‹Káu ‹wán ‹ün ‘shau. |
| 40. Walking hand in hand. | 携手同行 | ‹Kw‘ai ‘shau ‹t‘ung ‹hang. |
| 41. To use much gesticulation. | 手舞足蹈 | ‘Shau ‘mú tsuk› tò’. |
| 42. Bear it in both hands. | 兩手捧住 | ‘Léung ‘shau ‘fung chü’. |

25. This is said of any kind of work which is well executed by the hand: *shai*, power, skill, beauty, here denotes the effect which is produced by the power of the hand.

27. To strike the finger's lines refers to a custom among the Chinese of daubing the tip of the forefinger in ink, and making an impression of it upon the paper in connexion with the signature of the writer, for the sake of greater security; this practice is observed only in important documents, especially those relating to the purchase and sale of human beings. If the striæ on the finger tips are in divergent lines, they are called *ts‘ám*, a corn fan; if they are convergent, and somewhat oval, around the little protuberance at the end of the finger, they are called *ló*, a spiral univalve. When a careless servant drops a vessel, the indignant mistress cries out, *‘shau ‘chí ‘mò ‹ló?* have your fingers no shells? meaning that where the striæ are in ovals, a safer hold is supposed to be had of the article, because there are some of them which turn up towards the tip of the finger.

31. *Kéuk* is the common word for feet used in conversation; in books and in elevated style, *tsuk* is often used in its stead: *pán* is a flat board, *t‘óng* is a hall; the two words denote that part of the foot which is immediately under the instep: *kéuk chéung*, or *kéuk pán*, are names for the bottom of the foot.

32. For the toes, as among us, there are no individual names, except for the great toe which is called *kéuk› ‘chí ‹kung*, and for the little one, named as above.

34. *Pai* is used here in a modified sense, denoting a severe bruising, but not sufficient to destroy the feet or render them useless.

| | | |
|---|---|---|
| 43. He is a very active person. | 快手快脚 | Fái' 'shau fái' kéuk,. |
| 44. With depending hands he must stand and wait. | 垂亻侍立 | ,Shui 'shau shí' lap,. |
| 45. Procure the assistance of another person. | 假亻於人 | 'Ká 'shau ‹ü ,yan. |
| 46. He folds his hands and waits for death. | 斂亻待斃 | 'Lím 'shau toi' pai'. |
| 47. Being hand-bound he has no way to act. | 束亻無策 | Ch'uk, 'shau ,mò ch'ák,. |
| 48. He is indifferent to those who are in distress. | 袖亻傍觀 | Tsau' 'shau ,p'óng ,kún. |
| 49. Two partners in trade. | 對亻夥計 | Túi' 'shau 'fó kí'. |
| 50. To make a display of one's skill. | 演吓手勢 | 'Ín 'há 'shau shai'. |
| 51. Succeeding according to one's wishes. | 得心應手 | Tak, ‹sam ying' 'shau. |
| 52. He avails himself of an experienced hand. | 以資熟亻 | 'Í ‹tsz' shuk, 'shau. |
| 53. Counting by one's fingers. | 屈指計算 | Wat, 'chí kai' süin'. |
| 54. Very beautiful fingers. | 十指纖纖 | Shap, 'chí ‹ts'ím ‹ts'ím. |
| 55. Fingers like the vernal shoots of bamboo. | 指如春笋 | 'Chí ,ü ‹ch'un 'sun. |
| 56. The beginning of an enterprise is difficult. | 唔好入手 | ,'M 'hò yap, 'shau. |

43. Quick hands and quick feet, denotes one who is very active in the execution of whatever he undertakes.

44. This is said of the servant, child, or pupil, in attendance on his superior; his hands must hang down straight, and in an erect attitude, he must stand near his superior, so that he may readily hear and attend to his commands.

45. To borrow a hand from another, is to procure the assistance of others in the performance of business.

46. This is said of one who, being in danger, ought to exert himself; but instead of so doing, he merely folds his hands and waits for the calamity to overtake him.

47. His hands are bound and he is without ways and means for action; he is in circumstances where he can do nothing, however well disposed.

48. When one is in distress, or in any imminent danger, the person who happens to be present at the moment, *tsau shau* sleeves his hands, or folds them up in his broad sleeves, and looks on the sufferer without making any effort to succor him.

49. *Fókí* is a partner in business, a companion or comrade in the common pursuits of life, excepting only those of a literary character: *kí*, in other phrases, is pronounced *kai*.

52. The capitalist, for instance, in establishing a commercial house, will endeavor, *í tsz'* to avail himself of the services, or will intrust the management of the new house to, *shuk shau* a ripe hand, one who has had experience in such business.

53. Bending down the fingers to count is common among the Chinese; as the person counts one, he bends down the thumb, and thus proceeds till he reaches five, when all the fingers are bent down; he then, proceeding on from six to ten, reverses the order, throwing open one finger after another: if the number is above ten, the same process is repeated.

54, 55. *Shap chí*, ten fingers, is an idiomatic expression for *the* fingers; *ts'ím ts'ím*, small small, denote what is fine and delicate, and are here descriptive of tapering and beautiful fingers: *ch'un sun* expresses the same idea.

56. *Yap shau*, entering the hand, is the beginning of an undertaking; *'m hò* denotes that it is not easy, i. e. that it is beset with difficulties.

| | | |
|---|---|---|
| 57. As easy as turning over the hand. | 易如反掌 | Í² ꜀ü ʻfán ʻchéung. |
| 58. More than can be numbered by the fingers. | 指不勝屈 | ʻChí pat꜆ ꜀shing wat꜆. |
| 59. He acts in great confusion. | 手忙脚亂 | ʻShau ꜁móng kéuk꜆ lün². |
| 60. He stands a tiptoe in expectation. | 兀高脚望 | Ngat꜇ ꜀kò kéuk꜆ móng². |
| 61. He is very swift on foot. | 兩脚如飛 | ꜂Léung kéuk꜆ ꜁ü ꜀fí. |
| 62. Limbs and body are very languid. | 肢體怠倦 | ꜀Chí ʻt'ai ꜂t'oi kün². |
| 63. The hands and feet are mutually dependent. | 手足相依 | ʻShau tsuk꜆ ꜀séung ꜀í. |
| 64. Dear to each other as the hands and feet. | 亅足至親 | ʻShau tsuk꜆ chí꜄ ꜀ts'an. |
| 65. His feet are fettered, and he is unable to advance. | 裹足不前 | ʻKwó tsuk꜆ pat꜆ ꜁ts'ín. |
| 66. He embraced her feet and wept. | 抱足而哭 | ꜂P'ò tsuk꜆ ꜁í huk꜆. |
| 67. The inferior must not tread on his superior's shadow. | 足不履影 | Tsuk꜆ pat꜆ ꜂lí ʻying. |
| 68. As intimate as the hands and feet. | 情同手足 | ꜁Ts'ing ꜁t'ung ʻshau tsuk꜆. |
| 69. I reside in the little cottage. | 小廬寄亅 | ʻSíú ꜁lò kí꜄ tsuk꜆. |
| 70. He resides in the vallies of the mountain. | 深山托亅 | ꜀Sham ꜀shán t'ók꜆ tsuk꜆. |
| 71. He comes to the river to wash his feet. | 臨流濯亅 | ꜁Lam ꜁lau chók꜇ tsuk꜆. |
| 72. Languor spread over all the limbs. | 四肢困懈 | Sz" ꜀chí kw'an꜄ hái². |
| 73. To feel with the hand. | 以手探之 | ꜂Í ʻshau t'ám꜄ ꜀chí. |
| 74. To cover the face with the hand. | 以亅掩面 | ꜂Í ʻshau ʻim mín². |
| 75. He impedes my progress. | 拖丨帶脚 | ꜀T'ó ʻshau tái꜄ kéuk꜆. |

58. Fingers not sufficient to bend down, denotes a number so large that it cannot be counted by the fingers, in the manner stated above.

59. This is said of one who comes to his business in such a state of perturbation, that all the motions of his hands and feet are made in confusion and disorder.

63, 64. Both of these phrases are intended to exhibit the relation of brothers: they are as dependent on, and as dear to, each other, as the hands and feet.

65. *Kwó* means to wrap up, to bandage; *kwó tsuk* denotes impediment of any kind which prevents one from advancing rapidly: *꜁ch'ín kéuk꜆* is the phrase used to express the act of dressing the little foot of the females.

66. This is said of the little child, or of any one else, who in great distress throws himself down and clings about the feet of another, weeping and begging for pardon or assistance.

67. It is deemed disrespectful for an inferior person of any grade, to tread on the shadow of a superior.

68. The affection expressed here is nearly the same as that in No. 64, but the reference is, not to brothers, but to friends.

69, 70. The first of these is said of one's self; into the little cottage I place my feet: the second is said of a scholar or statesman who seeks retirement in the deep places among hills: into the recesses of the mountains he throws his feet.

| | | |
|---|---|---|
| 76. Embracing with both arms. | 雙手攬住 | ‹Shéung ‘shau ‘lám chü$^{2}$. |
| 77. Transmitted from one to another. | 上交下手 | Shéung$^{2}$ ‹káu há$^{2}$ ‘shau. |
| 78. An unskillful workman. | 冇的手段 | ‘Mò tí› ‘shau tün$^{2}$. |
| 79. Surely he cannot reside here. | 斷難駐足 | Tün$^{2}$ ꜀nán chü$^{2}$ tsuk›. |
| 80. Detained by the moonlight. | 明月留足 | ꜀Ming üt$_{2}$ ꜀lau tsuk›. |
| 81. Their feet are bound with scarlet bands. | 赤繩繫足 | Ch‘ik› ꜀shing hai$^{2}$ tsuk›. |
| 82. Lend a helping hand. | 助一臂之力 | Chó$^{2}$ yat› pí’ ‹chí lik$_{2}$. |
| 83. Brothers are like hands and feet. | 兄弟如手足 | ‹Hing tai$^{2}$ ꜀ü ‘shau tsuk›. |
| 84. The palm of one hand laid on the back of the other. | 手板踏扌背 | ‘Shau ‘pán táp$_{2}$ ‘shau púi’. |
| 85. Sitting down with the hands holding the knees. | 扌抱膝頭坐 | ‘Shau ‘p‘ò sat› ꜀t‘au tsó$^{2}$. |
| 86. His hands and feet have no place to rest. | 扌足無所措 | ‘Shau tsuk› ꜀mò ‘shó ts‘ó’. |
| 87. He strikes as soon as he speaks. | 口起手就起 | ‘Hau ‘hí ‘shau tsau$^{2}$ ‘hí. |
| 88. You may look at it, but must not touch it. | 眼看扌勿動 | ‘Ngán hón’ ‘shau mat$_{2}$ tung$^{2}$. |
| 89. Do not refuse to me the thing I desire. | 莫個失手勢 | Mók$_{2}$ kó’ shat› ‘shau shai’. |
| 90. He has not yet commenced. | 唔曾開扌做 | ꜀’M ꜀ts‘ang ‹hoi ‘shau tsò$^{2}$. |

75. He draws back my hands and my feet, is said by one who is hindered by a person from making rapid advances.

76. *Shau* is here used for the arms: *chü*, as in No. 23, denotes action being performed: the phrase is used to express the conduct of the affectionate child, in spreading out both hands and throwing them around the neck of its beloved parent.

77. This may be used in various cases, where the idea is that of handing or transmitting anything from a superior to an inferior, or from a predecessor to his successor.

78. *Shau tün* is nearly synonymous with *shau shai* in No. 25; *mò tí* without a bit—of skill, an artificer who exhibits not the slightest degree of skill,

79. It is very hard to stop the feet, denotes the great difficulty one experiences in maintaining even a temporary residence in any given place: it is a place in which he cannot reside.

80. The bright moon detains the feet, is said of one who, being abroad in the moonlight with agreeable companions, is unwilling to return home.

81. *Ch‘ik shing* is equivalent to hymeneal bands: like the phrase, "matches are made in heaven," the words refer to the destiny which is supposed to bind certain parties so indissolubly to each other, that in due time, come what may, they will be husband and wife. This form of *tsuk* is an abbreviated one which frequently occurs.

84. This is descriptive of the idle manner of Budha, who is represented in images sitting on the ground, with his hands before him, having the palm of the one on the back of the other.

86. He has so much to do and is in such confusion, that he seems not to know what to do with himself, i. e. he has no place to rest his hands and feet.

87. A word and a blow, and the blow comes first, is said by a servant of his passionate master, who strikes even while he is telling him his faults.

89. *Shau shai* here denotes things or objects which one desires, and which he needs; he therefore begs they may not be refused to him.

| | | |
|---|---|---|
| 91. The golden lilies are seen beneath the screen. | 簾下露金蓮 | ˏLím há$^{2}$ lò$^{2}$ ˎkam ˏlín. |
| 92. He holds my wrist, [and prevents my action.] | 佢拗我手頸 | ˓K'ui 'áu ˓ngó 'shau 'keng. |
| 93. He cannot move hand or foot. | 四肢不能舉 | Sz" ˎchí patˀ ˏnang 'kü. |
| 94. In the palm of the hand to form strings of cash. | 手板做錢串 | 'Shau 'pán tsò$^{2}$ ˏtsín ch'ün'. |
| 95. Passed from one hand to another. | 左手交右手 | "Tsó 'shau ˎkáu yau$^{2}$ 'shau. |
| 96. Both the palm and the back of the hand are alike. | 手板肉手背肉 | 'Shau 'pán yuk$_{2}$, 'shau púi' yuk$_{2}$. |
| 97. He lives from hand to mouth. | 左手嚟右手去 | "Tsó 'shau ˏlai yau$^{2}$ 'shau h'ü'. |
| 98. Make motions with your hands to let me know. | 打手面話我聽 | "T'á 'shau mín$^{2}$ wá$^{2}$ ˓ngó ˎting. |
| 99. No one can tell when we shall meet again. | 未審何時握手 | Mí$^{2}$ 'sham ˏhó ˏshí akˀ 'shau. |
| 100. Never act without some motive. | 手足不可妄動 | 'Shau tsukˀ patˀ 'kó móng$^{2}$ tung$^{2}$. |
| 101. Both hands and feet are asleep. | 手又痺脚又痺 | 'Shau yau$^{2}$ pí' kéukˀ yau$^{2}$ pí'. |
| 102. Always busily employed at work. | 手不停脚不住 | 'Shau patˀ ˏt'ing kéukˀ patˀ chü$^{2}$. |
| 103. He has lost an intimate friend. | 失一手足朋友 | Shatˀ yatˀ 'shau tsukˀ ˏp'ang ˓yau. |
| 104. With the palm of his hand he is able to destroy men. | 俾手板就殺人 | 'Pí 'shau 'pán tsau$^{2}$ shátˀ ˏyan. |
| 105. For transacting business an experienced hand is the best. | 辦事不如老手 | Pán$^{2}$ sz"$^{2}$ patˀ ˏü ˓lò 'shau. |
| 106. When the heart is afraid, the hands and the feet tremble. | 心驚手脚就振 | ˎSam ˎking 'shau kéukˀ tsau$^{2}$ chan'. |

91. Screen beneath appear the golden lilies: doors in China are usually defended by screens suspended from the lintel, and hanging down nearly to the threshold; from behind these screens the female inmates often seek to get a glimpse at those who are passing in the streets, but in doing this they are liable to expose their "little feet," which are called golden lilies.

94. This is the complaint of a man that he has no capital to commence business with; what profit will there be in opening a shop, if I must string nothing but cash all day long?

95. This phrase is used in exchanging articles in barter or for money: when I deliver to you the goods in one hand, I must receive their equivalent at the same time in the other.

96. To say, that the palm and the back of the hand are both fleshy, is to prevent the exhibition of partiality in dispensing favors; both persons are alike worthy.

97. By the left hand it comes, by the right hand it goes: everything is expended and no surplus remains from day to day.

99. No one can determine at what time we shall again grasp each other's hands: this is said by friends when they are taking leave of each other.

100. The hands and feet should never move without some good design, for whenever in motion, they are liable to do harm.

104. A faithless man, who never abides by his word, *pí shau pán*, using the palm of his hand for a sword, i. e. without any weapon, is able to kill men.

## Section Eighth.

## THE COLLECTIVE PARTS OF THE BODY.

### 百體類第八章
Pák, ʻt'ai lui²; tai² pát, ˏchéung.

| | | |
|---|---|---|
| 1. A very long neck. | 好長頸 | ʻHò ˏchéung ʻkeng. |
| 2. A broad back. | 背脊濶 | Púi² tsek, fút,. |
| 3. Bones as naked as billets of wood. | 骨瘦如柴 | Kwat, shau² ˏü ˏch'ái. |
| 4. Mucus and tears mingle and flow down together. | 涕淚交流 | ʻTai lui² ˏkáu ˏlau. |
| 5. Bowels in disorder. | 肚腹不好 | ʻTò fuk, pat, ʻhò. |
| 6. Bind up the hair and take the book. | 束髮受書 | Ch'uk, fát, shau² ˏshü. |
| 7. The hair is as white as silver. | 髮白如銀 | Fát, pák, ˏü ˏngan. |
| 8. To beat the breast and stamp the feet. | 捶胸頓足 | ˏCh'ui ˏhung tun² tsuk,. |
| 9. The hairs of the head have become white. | 頭毛轉白 | ˏT'au ˏmò ʻchün pák,. |
| 10. The sinews and joints are not yet come to maturity. | 筋節未足 | ˏKan tsít, mí² tsuk,. |
| 11. Engraved on my bones, and inscribed on my heart. | 刻骨銘心 | Hák, kwat, ʻming ˏsam. |

### *Notes and Explanations.*

PA'K T'AI, the hundred [parts of the] body, are used to denote all the parts, external and internal, considered collectively. In Hónghí's Imperial Dictionary, *t'ai* is called a mansion, having twelve departments, which are explained to be the bones, the flesh, the hairs, the blood, &c., all arranged in order. The decimal numbers, ten, hundred, thousand, and myriad, are in frequent use among the Chinese to denote a certain set of things, or an indefinite number collectively considered, or, as in some cases, to express the completeness of a thing or action.

3, 4. These two phrases are descriptive of persons who have become emaciated, and are suffering from intemperance.

5. This phrase often occurs in the provincial Court Circular, where it appears as the reason given by an officer for asking leave of absence from his post of duty: *tò* and *fuk* are nearly synonymous terms for the belly.

6. This is said of the boy who has arrived at the age when he must, *ch'uk fát* have his hair tied up in two little tufts on the top of his head, and, *shau shü* take in hand his books, i. e. it is time for him to commence going to school.

8. Under the pressure of extreme grief it is common among the Chinese, especially females, to beat their breasts and stamp their feet.

10. *Kan tsít* are here used to denote the whole framework of the child's body, at an age when the bones and muscles, &c., of the limbs have not become firm enough to enable it to walk; it is still a tender infant.

11. The man who has received a favor from another, feeling unable to requite it, says he will engrave it on his bones, and inscribe it on his heart.

| | | |
|---|---|---|
| 12. A firm and inflexible disposition. | 鐵石心腸 | T'ít꜆ shek꜆ ꜀sam ꜁ch'éung. |
| 13. He is very honest and faithful. | 鐵膽銅肝 | T'ít꜆ ꜂tám ꜁t'ung ꜀kón. |
| 14. Violent anger will injure the liver. | 怒氣傷肝 | Nò꜅ hí꜄ ꜀shéung ꜀kón. |
| 15. Bold and heaven-daring. | 膽大包天 | ꜂Tám tái꜅ ꜀páu ꜁t'ín. |
| 16. The lungs are affected with disease. | 肺家受病 | Fai꜄ ꜀ká shau꜅ peng꜅. |
| 17. The brains are run out. | 腦漿迸出 | ꜃Nò ꜀tséung ping꜄ ch'ut꜅. |
| 18. The contents of the chest and of the abdomen. | 五腑六臟 | ꜃'Ng ꜂fú luk꜇ chóng꜅. |
| 19. Gray headed. | 頭髮間花白 | ꜁T'au fát꜆ kán꜄ ꜀fá pák꜇. |
| 20. Do you not fear he will pull out the roots of your tongue? | 唔怕勾利根 | ꜁'M p'á꜄ ꜀kau lí꜅ ꜀kan. |
| 21. The Adam's apple is remarkably prominent. | 喉欖高過頭 | ꜁Hau ꜂lám ꜀kò kwó꜄ ꜁t'au. |
| 22. The tears trickle down upon his breast. | 珠淚滴胸膛 | ꜀Chü lui꜅ tik꜆ ꜀hung ꜁t'óng. |
| 23. The heart beats continually. | 心口不歇跳 | ꜀Sam ꜂hau pat꜆ hít꜆ t'íú꜄. |
| 24. Holding fast under the arm. | 咖嚹底挾住 | Ká꜆ lák꜆ ꜂tai kíp꜇ chü꜅. |
| 25. Do not fear breaking your ribs. | 唔怕折骿骨 | ꜁'M p'á꜄ chít꜆ ꜀p'eng kwat꜆. |
| 26. The shoulders are higher than the ears. | 膊頭高過耳 | Pók꜆ ꜁t'au ꜀kò kwó꜄ ꜃í. |
| 27. The tears flow down in streams. | 眼水淋淋漓 | ꜃Ngán ꜂shui ꜁lam ꜁lam ꜁lí. |
| 28. The hair of the head is all in confusion. | 頭髮粒粒亂 | ꜁T'au fát꜆ lap꜇ lap꜇ lün꜄. |

12, 13. These have nearly the same sense, each being applied to persons of high integrity and great firmness: they denote a character like that of the Indian chief, described in the following couplet:

> "Like monumental bronze, firm and unmov'd his look,
> A heart that pity touch'd, but never shook."

15. Gall so large as to encircle the heavens, is a common phrase used to designate a person of great boldness.

18. *'Ng fú* and *luk chóng* are very often used to denote the whole of the internal parts of the body, all that is contained both in the chest and abdomen.

20. There is allusion here to the supposed king of hades, and the question is put to one who speaks without any regard to the truth: talking so, are you not afraid of sinking to hades, and having your tongue hooked out by its king? *Lí kan* are the roots of the tongue; *lí* is the colloquial term in use to denote the tongue, and this character is used to express the sound.

22. *Hung* is the usual term for the breast; *t'óng* added to it renders the phrase more definite.

23. *Sam hau* the heart, *pat* does not, *hít* cease, *t'íú* to leap; it beats incessantly—said of a person under the excitement of fear.

24. *Ká lák tai* is the hollow place under the shoulder, the armpit; *kíp chü* holding fast under the arm; the term by which the armpit is here designated is a vulgar one, and is written with other characters as well as these.

25. This is said by way of reproof and admonition to one who seems reluctant to work, as if he were afraid of breaking his ribs.

| | | |
|---|---|---|
| 29. The malady has penetrated even into the marrow of his bones. | 壞到入骨髓 | Wái' tò' yap, kwat, 'sui. |
| 30. His back is very stiff. | 背脊實係硬 | Púi' tsek, shat, hai' ngáng'. |
| 31. His heels are bruised by excessive walking. | 行爛脚睜皮 | ,Háng lán' kéuk, ,cháng ,p'í. |
| 32. By three blows of the bamboo to break the skin. | 三板打開皮 | ,Sám 'pán 'tá ,hoi ,p'í. |
| 33. Peel off your skin and make a drum of it to beat upon. | 剝皮捫鼓打 | Mók, ,p'í ,mún 'kú 'tá. |
| 34. The skin is extremely rough. | 皮膚粗到極 | ,P'í ,fú ,ts'ò tò' kik,. |
| 35. Do not insult a gray-headed man. | 莫欺白髮人 | Mók, ,hí pák, fát, ,yan. |
| 36. To shave the head in order to remove vexatious cares. | 削髮除煩惱 | Séuk, fát, ,chü ,fán 'nò. |
| 37. His breast is devoid of all solid learning. | 胸中無實學 | ,Hung ,chung ,mò shat, hók,. |
| 38. There is no fixed purpose in his breast. | 胸中無定見 | ,Hung ,chung ,mò ting' kín'. |
| 39. Not lost a single hair. | 唔失一條毛 | ,'M shat, yat, ,t'íú ,mò. |
| 40. Both cheek bones are very high. | 兩拳骨太高 | 'Léung ,k'ün kwat, t'ái' ,kò. |
| 41. Aged men's bones are weak. | 年老筋骨衰 | ,Nín 'lò ,kan kwat, ,shui. |
| 42. In young persons the bones are strong. | 年少好骨力 | ,Nín shíú' 'hò kwat, lik,. |
| 43. Singleness and sincerity of heart. | 一副熱心腸 | Yat, fú' ít, ,sam ,ch'éung. |
| 44. One who is very bold can kill robbers. | 大膽殺得賊 | Tái' 'tám shát, tak, ts'ák,. |
| 45. The heart is in the middle of the body. | 心在身之中 | ,Sam tsoi' ,shan ,chí ,chung. |
| 46. Green is related to wood, and affects the liver. | 青屬木入肝 | ,Ts'ing shuk, muk, yap, ,kón. |

29. This is said of one who has become exceedingly debased, the evil having entered into the very marrow of his bones.

32. *Pán* a board, refers to the long and heavy bamboo, which is used in beating criminals: it is not unusual for the person appointed to inflict this punishment, to receive money in order to secure a light use of the bamboo; otherwise it is expected that, *sám pán* by three blows of it, the skin of the criminal will be beaten off.

33. I will peel off your skin and stretch it on a drum head, to beat upon—as if it were a cow's hide: this is said in anger, and to intimidate.

36. By shaving off the hair of the head, as persons often do in China, when they wish to enter the monasteries, they imagine that they will be enabled, *chü* to remove, *fán nò* their vexatious cares,

38. *Kín* is frequently used in the sense of purpose, and *ting kín* is a fixed purpose: *mò* there is none, *hung chung* in the breast: the man has no decision of character.

43. *Yat fú* denotes several parts combined so as to form one whole; *ít*, fervid, ardent, in a secondary sense signifies sincerity; *sam ch'éung* the mind: the mind single and sincere.

46—50. The *'ng shik*, the *'ng hang*, and the *'ng fú* are here combined in a manner which may assist the memory; but it is not easy to understand how the five colors are related to the five elements [Chap. I. Sec. iii: 34.], or in what manner they affect the five viscera.

| | | |
|---|---|---|
| **47.** Red is related to fire, and affects the heart. | 赤屬火入心 | Ch‘ik› shuk$_2$ ‘fó yap$_2$ ‹sam. |
| **48.** Yellow is related to earth, and affects the spleen. | 黃屬土入脾 | ‚Wóng shuk$_2$ ‘t‘ò yap$_2$ ‚p‘í. |
| **49.** White is related to metal, and affects the lungs. | 白屬金入肺 | Pák$_2$ shuk$_2$ ‹kam yap$_2$ fai’. |
| **50.** Black is related to water, and affects the kidneys. | 黑屬水入腎 | Hak› shuk$_2$ ‘shui yap$_2$ shan’. |
| **51.** His personal appearance is extremely fine. | 佢容貌極好 | ‘K‘ui ‚yung máu$^2$ kik$_2$ ‘hò. |
| **52.** He is fond of quietude, and averse to moving about. | 好靜不好動 | Hò’ tsing$^2$ pat› hò’ tung$^2$. |
| **53.** A most beautiful countenance. | 了不得清秀 | ‘Líú pat› tak› ‹ts‘ing sau’. |
| **54.** It is difficult to find a person so dignified. | 難得咁莊重 | ‚Nán tak› kóm’ ‹chóng chung$^2$. |
| **55.** In his demeanor he is more graceful than other men. | 形容勝過人 | ‚Ying ‚yung shing’ kwó’ ‚yan. |
| **56.** In excellence and elegance perfectly complete. | 眞盡善盡美 | ‹Chan tsun$^2$ shín$^2$ tsun$^2$ ‘mí. |
| **57.** Neither a very fat nor a very lean man. | 不肥不瘦人 | Pat› ‚fí pat› shau’ ‚yan. |
| **58.** His face begins to be furrowed with age. | 面皮起皺咯 | Mín$^2$ ‚p‘í ‘hí tsau’ lók›. |
| **59.** A homely face will insure a good fortune. | 醜樣必好命 | ‘Ch‘au yéung$^2$ pít› ‘hò ming$^2$. |
| **60.** The pockmarks are marks of beauty. | 痘皮痘得俏 | Tau$^2$ ‚p‘í tau$^2$ tak› ts‘íú’. |
| **61.** The whole face is covered with black spots. | 一面都係蔴麥 | Yat› mín$^2$ ‹tò hai$^2$ ‚má mak$_2$. |
| **62.** No traces of him are left behind. | 佢踪跡唔留的 | ‘K‘ui ‹tsung tsik› ‚’m ‚lau tik›. |
| **63.** To subdue men by strength is the rule of force. | 以力服人者霸 | ‘Í lik$_2$ fuk$_2$ ‚yan ‘ché pá’. |
| **64.** Its shadow even I have not yet seen. | 影都未曾見過 | ‘Ying ‹tò mí$^2$ ‚ts‘ang kín’ kwó’. |
| **65.** He walks as haughtily as if he would tread men under his feet. | 推倒人咁豪氣 | ‹T‘úi ‘tò ‚yan kóm’ ‚hò hí’. |

52. *Tsing* and *tung*, rest and motion, are opposites: *hò*, good, by a change of intonation becomes a verb, and means to esteem good, to be fond of, or to love.

53. *Líúpattak* is nearly equivalent to *shatshau*, Chap. I. Sec. i: 7; *ts‘ing* clear, *sau* blooming; superlatively clear and beautiful.

55. *Ying*, form, shape; *yung*, manner, carriage; the two united denote conduct, demeanor; his form and manner rise above and overpass other men.

56. Truly consummately excellent and consummately good, may be said of either men or things, which are of superior excellence.

59, 60. *Yéung*, fashion or manner, here denotes the face; the phrase is used to console one who has a homely bride: the second phrase is similar, implying that the esteem for a person is so great and sincere, that his deformities, in the estimation of his friend, become marks of real beauty.

63. *Fuk yan* is to subdue men, or to keep them in a subdued state: the Chinese have two modes of doing this; one is the rule of reason, about which they vaunt themselves so highly, the other is that described above.

64. *Ying* may refer to person or persons as well as to things: I have not only not seen the thing or person, but even so much as the shadow thereof, not yet has been seen—by me.

| | | |
|---|---|---|
| 66. Every enterprise depends on human energy. | 全凴個點精神 | ˏTs'unˏ p'ang kó' 'tím ‹tsing ˏshan. |
| 67. When a man ceases to breathe, then he dies. | 呼吸停則氣斷 | ‹Fú hap› ˏt'ing tsak› hí' tün'. |
| 68. A man gapes because he is sleepy. | 打喊嚕係眼瞓 | 'Tá hám' lò$^2$ hai$^2$ 'ngán fan'. |
| 69. His tears flow up over his forehead. | 流淚流上額頭 | ˏLau lui$^2$ ˏlau 'shéung ngák$_2$ ˏt'au. |
| 70. One sneezes because he has taken cold. | 打乞痴係冷着 | 'Tá hat› ‹ch'í hai$^2$ 'láng chéuk$_2$. |
| 71. Do not laugh at those who are poor. | 切勿笑人貧窮 | Ts'ít› mat$_2$ síú' ˏyan ˏp'an ˏk'ung. |
| 72. The calls of the rich are quickly answered. | 發財呼喚就靈 | Fát› ˏts'oi ‹fú fún' tsau$^2$ ˏling. |
| 73. Long whiskers render a person hateful. | 胡連鬚令人厭 | ˏÚ ˏlín ‹sü ling$^2$ ˏyan ím'. |
| 74. Able to recognize persons by their tones of voice. | 聽聲就認得人 | T'ing' ‹shing tsau$^2$ yan$^2$ tak› ˏyan. |
| 75. Nothing is more feared than empty purses. | 最怕腰頭無錢 | Tsui' p'á' ‹iú ˏt'au ˏmò ˏts'ín. |
| 76. You must brace up your chin when you talk. | 托住下耙至講 | T'ók› chü$^2$ há$^2$ ˏp'á chí' 'kóng. |
| 77. The heart is the residence of divine intelligence. | 心爲神明之舍 | ‹Sam ˏwai ˏshan ˏming ‹chí shé'. |
| 78. Why regret a hair's expense. | 何惜一毛之費 | ˏHó sik› yat› ˏmò ‹chí fai'. |
| 79. A single hair even was not left. | 一条毛都有剩 | Yat› ˏt'iú ˏmò ‹tò 'mò shing$^2$. |
| 80. Do not bequeath [to him] a single hair. | 勿遺下一條毛 | Mat$_2$ ˏwai há$^2$ yat› ˏt'iú ˏmò. |
| 81. The mouth has honey, the belly has a sword. | 口有蜜腹有劍 | 'Hau 'yau mít› fuk› 'yau kím'. |
| 82. A shameful affair is called a sweaty countenance. | 事可愧曰汗顏 | Sz'$^2$ 'hó, kwai' üt$_2$ hón$^2$ ˏngán. |
| 83. I do not fear pulling out a single hair. | 拔一毛何畏焉 | Pát$_2$ yat› ˏmò ˏhó wai' ˏín. |
| 84. To be so pressed as to burn the eyebrows. | 以應燃眉之急 | 'Í ying' ˏín ˏmí ‹chí kap›. |

69. This is said of the truant boy, who, on being reproved, gives feigned tokens of sorrow; he sheds "dry tears."

73. *Ling yan ím*, cause men to dislike—those who have them; i. e. those who have long whiskers, cause themselves to be disliked; this expression is very applicable to this people, in whom the whiskers become, if allowed to grow, merely a patch of course, straggling hairs, worthy of being disliked.

74. This is said appropriately of blind persons, who are remarkable for recognizing people from the tones of their voice.

75. *I'ú* is the waist or loins, and *t'au* is added merely for euphony: around their loins the Chinese wear a girdle, having a small pouch or wallet suspended from it in front, which serves them for purses: the sentence is literally, most feared loins head no money.

76. This admonition is addressed to the willful or malicious liar; he must have recourse to this precautionary measure, else he will be in danger of losing his chin.

80. To a lazy spendthrift, nothing ought to be bequeathed, for it will be worse than useless.

83. A man who is rich and well established in business does not mind the trifling losses which may happen to him; he is able to sustain exactions and mishaps.

84. This phrase is used by a man who is in great need of money, and is obliged to apply for a loan; he wants the assistance as much as he requires a pair of eyebrows.

| | | |
|---|---|---|
| **85.** As if they had seen his inmost thoughts. | 如見其肺肝然 | ꜁Ü kín' ꜁k'í fai' ꜀kón ꜁ún. |
| **86.** The eyebrows will not retain a [grain of] sand. | 眼眉唔藏得沙 | ꜂Ngán ꜁mí ꜁'m ꜁chóng tak꜇ ꜀shá. |
| **87.** All things occur according to a fixed allotment. | 萬事聽從命跌 | Mán$^2$ sz'$^2$ ꜀t'ing ꜁tsung ming$^2$ tít꜇. |
| **88.** The secretions ceasing, the measure of life terminates. | 津液竭命數終 | ꜀Tsun yat꜈ kít꜈ ming$^2$ shò' ꜀chung. |
| **89.** The animal spirits are the gift of heaven; the bones and joints are from the earth. | 精神者天之分<br>骨骸者地之分 | ꜀Tsing ꜁shan ꜂ché ꜀t'ín ꜀chí ꜀fan; kwat꜇ ꜁hoi ꜂ché tí$^2$ ꜀chí ꜀fan. |
| **90.** A beautiful person has her cheeks red as the almond flower, mouth like the peach's bloom, waist slender as the willow leaf, eyes bright as autumnal ripples, and footsteps like the flowers of the water lily. | 美人稱紅杏臉<br>櫻桃口楊柳腰<br>秋波眼蓮花步 | ꜂Mí ꜁yan ꜀ch'ing ꜁hung hing' ꜂lím, ꜀ying ꜁t'ò ꜂hau, ꜁yéung ꜂lau ꜀iú, ꜀ts'au ꜀p'ó ꜂ngán, ꜁lín ꜀fá pò$^2$. |
| **91.** I beg to ask why the human body is called a microcosm. | 請問人身何以<br>稱爲小天地 | ꜂Ts'ing man$^2$ ꜁yan ꜀shan ꜁hò ꜂í ꜀ch'ing ꜁wai ꜂síú ꜀t'ín tí$^2$. |
| In reply it may be stated: the circuit of the heavens has three hundred and sixty divisions (or degrees); the human frame has also three hundred and sixty divisions: in the heavens are stars and constellations, with the sun and moon; in man also are the heart, liver, spleen, and lungs: hence he is called little heaven and earth, &c. &c. | 答曰週天三百<br>六十度人身骨<br>節亦三百六十<br>度天有星辰日<br>月於其中人亦<br>有心肝脾肺於<br>其內故名之曰<br>小天地云云 | Táp꜇ üt꜈: ꜀chau ꜀t'ín ꜀sám pák꜇ luk꜈ shap꜈ tò$^2$; ꜁yan ꜀shan kwat꜇ tsít꜇ yik꜈ ꜀sám pák꜇ luk꜈ shap꜈ tò$^2$; ꜀t'ín ꜂yau ꜀sing ꜁shan yat꜈ üt꜈ ꜀ü ꜁k'í ꜀chung; ꜁yan yik꜈ ꜂yau ꜀sam, ꜀kón, ꜁p'í, fai', ꜀ü ꜁k'í noi$^2$; kú' ꜁ming ꜀chí üt꜇ ꜀síú ꜀t'ín tí$^2$, ꜁wan, ꜁wan. |

**85.** Here there had been, it is supposed, an opportunity for the person in question to show out without restraint his whole character; hence those around him knew him as well as if they had seen his inmost parts.

**90.** These are a few of the metaphors used by the Chinese to describe beauty; the figure of autumnal ripples alludes to the dancing reflection of the sun upon a ruffled lake; the impression of the small foot of a Chinese lady in the path is supposed to resemble the flowers of the water lily.

**91.** This is one of several reasons, which the Chinese give for comparing man to the universe. *Wan, wan*, saying, saying, at the close, is equivalent to &c., &c.

# CHAPTER III.

# THE KINDRED RELATIONS.

# 親誼篇三

‹Ts‘an í$^{2}$; ‹p‘ín ‹sám.

---

## Section First.

## OF PARENTS.

### 雙親類第一章

‹Shéung ‹ts‘an lui$^{2}$; tai$^{2}$ yat› ‹chéung.

---

| | | |
|---|---|---|
| 1. Pray sit down; (says the host, to whom his friend responds,) | 請坐 | ‘Ts‘ing tsó$^{2}$. |
| Pray sit down. | 請坐 | ‘Ts‘ing tsó$^{2}$. |
| 2. What is your honorable surname? (asks the guest.) | 尊姓呀 | ‹Tsün sing’ á’? |
| My humble surname is Lau; (replies the host.) | 小姓劉 | ‘Síú sing’ ‹Lau. |
| 3. Is your honored father well? | 尊大人納福唉 | ‹Tsün tai$^{2}$ ‹yan náp$_{2}$ fuk› ‹é? |
| My father is very well, I thank you. | 家父藉福 | ‹Ká fú$^{2}$ tsik$_{2}$ fuk›. |
| 4. Is your honored father at home? | 令尊在家唔在 | Ling$^{2}$ ‹tsün tsoi$^{2}$ ‹ká ‹’m tsoi$^{2}$? |

## *Notes and Explanations.*

TS‘AN Í, used as a phrase, comprehends all the relations which are constituted by blood, marriage, adoption, &c. *T's'an* near or akin; *í* what is suitable for man, order, friendship; the two terms include all who are near and dear—the kindred relations.

1. This conversation may be supposed to occur between the master of a house and a visitor. The latter happens to call at the residence of the former, in company with a friend. After the ceremonies of introduction are finished, the master of the house requests his new friend to sit down, which he does, at the same time requesting his host to sit down also. Both being seated,

2. The visitor, leading the conversation, asks, honorable surname eh? The host replies, Mean surname is Lau. *Sing* refers to the name of the family: my surname, or the name of my family, is Lau. With the Chinese it is deemed polite for strangers, on meeting, to inquire for each other's names and surnames: inquiry for the latter is always made first.

3. Does the honorable great man enjoy happiness? The family's father, *tsik* has borrowed, *fuk* happiness; i. e. he derives health and happiness from your favor, for which I have to thank you.

| | | |
|---|---|---|
| He has gone abroad and has not yet returned. | 家父出外未回 | ‹Ká fú$^2$ ch'ut› ngoi$^2$ mí$^2$ ˏúi. |
| 5. What is the age of your honored and aged father? | 尊翁今年貴庚 | ‹'Tsün ‹yung ‹kam ˏnín kwai$^3$ ‹kang? |
| He has vainly passed eighty years. | 家父虛度八十 | ‹Ká fú$^2$ ‹h'ü tò$^2$ pát› shap$_2$. |
| 6. So old, and yet gone abroad! | 咁尊誠重出外 | Kóm$^3$ ‹tsün ˏshing, chung$^2$ ch'ut› ngoi$^2$! |
| He is compelled to do so in order to gain a livelihood. | 爲口奔馳呀 | Wai$^2$ 'hau ‹pan ˏch'í á$^3$. |
| 7. Oh, you speak in too humble terms, for your honored father is very affluent indeed! | 好話你令尊優優有餘嘅咯 | 'Hò wá$^2$; 'ní ling$^2$ ‹tsün ‹yau ‹yau 'yau ˏü ké$^3$ lòk›! |
| He affluent! were he like you, sir, then truly he would be well off. | 邊得如尊駕咁就好吱 | ‹Pín tak›! ˏü ‹tsün ká$^3$ 'kóm tsau$^2$ 'hò ‹chí. |
| 8. You speak in too humble terms, for your aged father is very strong and robust. | 好話你老人家就究壯健咯噃 | 'Hò wá$^2$; 'ní 'lò ˏyan ‹ká tsau$^2$ kau$^3$ chóng$^3$ kín$^2$ lók› pó$^3$. |
| Of late he has been rather feeble and infirm. | 近日都帶踭咯 | Kan$^2$ yat$_2$ ‹tò tái$^3$ ‹chang lók›. |
| 9. When you see your mother, I will thank you to present to her my compliments. | 令壽堂處代我話聲請安 | Ling$^2$ shau$^2$ ˏt'óng ch'ü$^3$ toi$^2$ 'ngó wá$^2$ ‹shing 'ts'ing ‹ón. |
| She is unworthy to receive [such honor]. | 唔敢當 | ˏ'M 'kóm ‹tóng. |
| 10. I must now beg to take my leave and return home. | 我告辭番去咯 | 'Ngó kò$^3$ ˏts'z$^3$ ‹fán hü$^3$ lok›. |
| Good bye. | 請呀 | 'Ts'ing á$^3$. |

4. **Excellency's honorable in the house, not in?** *Ling* is here applied to the person addressed, and *tsün* is used for his father: is your father at home?

5. The honorable aged this year [has what] rich age? Family's father, *h'ü* in vanity, has passed eighty years.

6. So old, yet gone abroad! *Tsün* has here the sense of venerated; *shing* is honest, and hence aged: so venerable and so aged! considering the two terms as combined, they convey the single idea of aged. *Wai hau* for the mouth, *pan ch'í* running hither and thither.

7. The guest tells his host that he is too modest; by abasing yourself and your father, you reflect too much honor on me; for your honored father, *yau yau*, *yau ü* is rich rich, having an overplus. *Pín tak*, literally, where get it? *tsün ká* is applied by the host as a term of respect to his friend and visitor.

8. *Kau* means to investigate, to carry to the utmost extreme; hence, the sense in which it is here used, very—very strong and robust: *chang* (often pronounced *cháng*,) denotes the heels; the phrase, *tò tái chang*, only can drag the heels, is descriptive of the infirm person who is scarcely able to lift his feet from the floor; and as he walks, therefore, can merely drag one foot along after the other.

9. Excellent longevity hall place, for me speak sound wish repose: ladies in China are seldom present at the interviews of friends; any reference to them must be made through their husbands, brothers, fathers, or sons: the son, answering for his mother, says, *'m kóm tóng*, cannot presume to receive—such unmerited honor.

10. I announce departure return go away; in this connection, *kò* has the sense of to beg, in the language of courtesy.

| | | |
|---|---|---|
| Good bye. | 請呀 | ʻTs'ing á'. |
| 11. My father commands. | 家嚴吩咐 | ‹Ká ‚ím ‹fan fú'. |
| 12. My father does not believe. | 父親唔信 | Fú² ‹ts'an ‚'m sun'. |
| 13. The orders of my mother. | 家慈之命 | ‹Ká ‚ts'z' ‹chí ming². |
| 14. Orders received from my repected mother. | 承嚴慈命 | ‚Shing ‚ím ‚ts'z' ming². |
| 15. Is you papa well? | 你阿爸好呀 | ʻNí á' ‹pá ʻhò ‹á? |
| 16. Your father is willing. | 老太爺情願 | ʻLò ta'i² ‚yé ‚ts'ing üin². |
| 17. My father's eyes are dim. | 老人家眼盹 | ʻLò ‚yan ‹ká ʻngán tun². |
| 18. No one knows a son so well as his father. | 知子莫若父 | ‹Chí ʻtsz' mók₂ yéuk₂ fú². |
| 19. Indulgent mothers spoil most of their children. | 慈母多敗兒 | ‚Ts'z' ʻmò ‹tó pái² ‚í. |
| 20. Papa, do not listen to his deceitful words. | 爹爹勿聽讒言 | ‹Té ‹té mat₂ t'ing' ‚ts'ám ‚ín. |
| 21. Your deceased father's good name still remains. | 先君威名尚在 | ‹Sín ‹kwan ‹wai ‚ming shéung² tsoi². |
| 22. The grave of a father [whose surname was] Wóng. | 黃公府君之墓 | ‚Wóng ‹kung ʻfú ‹kwan ‹chí mò². |
| 23. Filial respect and obedience are due to papa. | 阿爹本應孝順 | A' ‹ché ʻpún ‹ying háu' shun². |
| 24. The years of papa complete a full cycle. | 阿爺年登花甲 | A' ‚yé ‚nín ‹tang ‹fá káp›. |
| 25. His father is very affectionate. | 佢老子實守慈 | ʻK'ui ʻlò ʻtsz' shat› ʻshau ‚ts'z'. |
| 26. When will papa alter his place of residence? | 阿爹幾時遷居 | A' ‹té ʻkí ‚shí ‹ts'ín ‹kü? |
| 27. Your honored father's handwriting. | 令尊大人筆跡 | Ling² ‹tsün tái² ‚yan pat› tsik›. |
| 28. Your father gives his consent. | 老太君肯嘅咯 | ʻLò t'ái² ‹kwan ʻhang ké' lók›. |

11, 12. *Ká ím* family's majesty; *ím* denotes what is stern and majestic; the phrase denotes my father, and is equivalent to *fú ts'an;* the former is deemed the most elegant, but the latter is the most common.

13, 14. *Ká ts'z'* family's loving-one, i. e. the mother of the family, my mother; the word *ts'z'* means that affection and carefulness which a mother is supposed always to feel towards her offspring, and in this sense it is also applied to the care which animals take of their young. The other sentence, received respected loving-one's orders, is a more formal phrase, where *ím* indicates the respect which is due to one's mother.

17. *Lò yan ká* may be applied to one's own father, or to the father of a second or third person; the former use is the most frequent.

19. Indulgent mothers, *tò* in a great majority of instances,—say eight in ten, more or less,—spoil their children.

21. The former prince's awe-bearing name still remains: *sín kwan* is used to denote the deceased father of one to whom you are speaking; the phrase may also be used in reference to the deceased father of a third person, and it is employed by a son when writing or speaking of his deceased parent.

28. *Lò t'ái kwan*, and *lò t'ái yé* (No. 16,) are applied to the father of the person addressed; they may also be applied to a third person's father.

| | | |
|---|---|---|
| 29. My father's illness is not yet overcome. | 家嚴病體未愈 | ‹Ká ˏím ping$^2$ ʿt'ai mí$^2$ ü$^2$. |
| 30. My father has been gone a long time. | 家君去了好耐 | ‹Ká ‹kwan hü' ʿliú ʿhò noi$^2$. |
| 31. Your father has already promised. | 你老頭應承嘅 | ʿNí ʿlò ˏt'au ‹ying ˏshing ké'. |
| 32. My father has not been out for a long time. | 老父冇出好耐 | ʿLò fú' ʿmò ch'ut› ʿhò noi$^2$. |
| 33. Your mother wishes it to be in this manner. | 令壽堂愛咁樣 | Ling$^2$ shau$^2$ ˏt'óng oi' ʿkóm yeung$^2$. |
| 34. How long since your mother's decease? | 老太安過幾耐 | ʿLò t'ái' ‹ón kwó' ʿkí noi$^2$? |
| 35. My mother's strength is gradually decreasing. | 母親年力漸衰 | ʿMò ˏts'an ˏnín lik$_2$ tsím' ‹shui. |
| 36. My mother's sorrows are great beyond measure. | 家母憂思過度 | ‹Ká ʿmò ‹yau ‹sz' kwó' tò$^2$. |
| 37. I beg my honored mother will excuse me. | 母親大人寬宥 | ʿMò ‹ts'an tái$^2$ ˏyan ‹fún yau$^2$. |
| 38. It was done by your deceased father before he died. | 令考先時做過 | Ling$^2$ ʿhau ‹sín ˏshí tsò' kwó'. |
| 39. It was never seen by your deceased mother. | 令妣未曾見過 | Ling$^2$ ʿpí mí$^2$ ˏtsang kín' kwó'. |
| 49. Congratulating your mother on the anniversary of her birthday. | 老安人處祝壽 | ʿLò ‹ón ˏyan ch'ü' chuk› shau$^2$. |
| 41. Her ladyship is enjoying very excellent health. | 老太太好壯健 | ʿLò t'ái' t'ái' ʿhò chóng' kín$^2$. |
| 42. (a) Among the Sacred Commands is this, 'Be zealously filial and fraternal, and so give due weight to man's relations.' | 聖諭云敦孝弟以重人倫 | Shing' Yü$^2$ ˏwan, ‹Tun háu' tai$^2$, ʿí chung$^2$ ˏyan ˏlun. |
| (b) Our sacred predecessor, the august emperor Pious, during a reign of sixty-one years, imitated his ancestors and honored his parents, with unbounded dutifulness. He published, under imperial authority, a work enti- | 我聖祖仁皇帝臨御六十一年法祖尊親孝思不匱欽定孝經 | ʿNgó shing' ʿtsò, ˏyan ˏwóng tai', ˏlam yü$^2$ luk$_2$ shap$_2$ yat›, ˏnín, fát› ʿtsò ‹tsün ˏts'an, háu' ‹sz' pat› kwai$^2$. ‹Yam |

30. *Ká kwan*, like *ká fú*, is for the most part used to designate one's own father; the family's prince, i. e. my father.

31. *Lò t'au* old head, and *lò ts'z'* old child (No. 25), are both used to denote father; whether it be my father, your father, or his father, may usually be determined by the connection in which the terms occur.

34. *Lò t'ái ón* differs from *ling shau t'óng* only in this, that the former is used in reference to the person both while living and when dead.

42. *Shing Yü* is the title of a book, usually published in two small volumes, octavo. It contains sixteen injunctions or commands, written by Hónghí, each containing seven characters, arranged as in the one here given.

(*a*) *Tun* zealously perform, *háu tai* the filial and fraternal duties, *í* in that way or thereby, *chung* give weight to, *yan lun* men's relative duties. (Chap. I. Sec. iii: 48.)

(*b*) *Yungching*, the son and successor of Hónghí, in order to give more weight to his father's commands, wrote short explanatory treatises on each of them, enforcing the duties inculcated; the number of characters in each is given at the end of it; the first contains six hundred and thirty-two, of which about one third are here introduced.

tled, 'An Exposition of the Treatise on Filial Duty,' wherein the text of this classical work is fully explained, and its doctrinal principles are distinctly unfolded. His simple design was to govern the empire by the influence of filial piety. Hence, of the sixteen commands of his sacred majesty, the first relates to the filial and fraternal duties, as the source of all those principles which he would inculcate.

衍義一書衍釋
經文義理詳貫
無非孝治天下
之意故聖諭十
六條首以孝弟
開其端

ting, Háu' King 'Yn Í, yat shü; 'ín shik king man í' 'lí ts'éung kún'. Mò fí háu' chí t'ín há chí í'. Kú', shing' yü shap luk t'íu, 'shau 'í háu' tai, hoi k'í tün.

(c) We, having received the high imperial trust, and reflecting on the admonitions of times past, will fully explain the meaning of his instructions, by unfolding in the first place the doctrines of filial and fraternal duties. These we promulgate, soldiers and people, for your improvement.

朕丕承鴻業追
維徃訓推廣立
教之思先申孝
弟之義用是與
爾兵民人等宣
示之

Cham, 'p'í shing hung íp, chui 'wai 'wóng fan', t'ui 'kwóng lap káu' chí sz', sín shan háu' tai chí í. Yung shí 'ü 'í ping man yan 'tang, sün shí chí.

(d) Now filial duty is a fixed law of heaven, a universal principle of earth, and a duty obligatory on all people.

夫孝者天之經
地之義民之行
也

Fú háu' 'ché, t'ín chí kíng tí chí í, man chí hang 'yá.

(e) Do those, who are undutiful, never consider the heartfelt love of their parents

人不知孝父母
獨不思父母愛

Yan pat chí háu' fú 'mò, tuk pat sz' fú 'mò, oi'

---

*Ngó* is used like our, in such phrases as our ancestors, or rulers. *Shing tsò yan wóng tai* is an honorary title, which was given to Hónghí after his demise by his imperial son; it is called the *míú hò*, the temple designation, because it is recorded in the temple of ancestors. *Lam* is to superintend, to look down upon, or to come down to in order to govern; *yü* connected with it, has a similar meaning: the two joined are equivalent to holding the reigns of supreme government, directing the helm of state.

*Yam* denotes that the business, whatever it may be with which it is connected, is done by imperial authority: *ting* has here more than its primary sense to fix; it means to make, to publish. For *Háu King*, see Chap. I, Sec. iii: 66, *ín í*, unfolding the meaning, is used as a part of the title of the book, denoting commentary or exposition; *yat shü* one volume: *king man* is the text, as distinguished from comments.

*Mò fí* in no other way than, *háu* by the influence of filial duty, *chí* to govern, *t'ín há* the empire, *chí í* this intention, i. e. his intention was nothing more nor less than that of governing the whole empire through the influence of filial duty.

(c) *Cham* is the imperial We, the word which denotes the emperor, and is applied to no other person; it occurs only in documents where the emperor speaks of himself, and corresponds to the use of the plural number by western potentates. *Yung shí* using these [instructions of Hónghí], *ü* to, *í ping man yan tang* you soldiers and people, *sün shí chí* we promulgate them for your improvement.

towards them as children? At that time when they were yet in their mother's arms, unable to feed themselves if hungry, or to put on clothes if cold, it was their parents, who judged for them by their tones of voice and the expressions of their countenances;—who were rejoiced by their smiles, and grieved by their cries;—and who, when their children began to walk, followed them every step; and when sick, took neither sleep nor food: thus nourishing and educating them. When arrived at manhood, then also, to provide them wives and to secure them a livelihood, they carefully considered a hundred expedients, exhausting for them all their thoughts and strength. The goodness of parents is, indeed, unbounded as the high heavens!

子之心乎方其未離懷抱饑不能自哺寒不能自衣爲父母者審音聲察形色笑則爲之喜啼則爲之憂行動則跬步不離疾痛則寢食俱廢以養以教至於成人復爲授家室謀生理百計經營心力俱捽父母之德實同昊天罔極

'tsz' ‹chí ‹sam ‚ú? ‹Fóng ‚k'í mí$^{2}$ ‚lí ‚wái 'p'ò, ‹kí pat› ‚nang tsz'$^{2}$ ‹pò, ‚hón pát› ‚nang tsz'$^{2}$ í', ‚wai fú$^{2}$ 'mò 'ché 'sham ‹yam ‹shing ch'át› ‚ying shik›; siú' tsak› ‚wai ‹chí 'hí; ‚t'ai tsak› ‚wai ‹chí ‹yau; ‚hang tung$^{2}$ tsak› ‹wá pò$^{2}$ pat› ‚lí; tsat› t'ung' tsak› 'ts'am shik$_{2}$ ‹k'ü fai'; 'í 'yéung 'í káu'. Chí' 'ü ‚shing ‚yan, fuk$_{2}$ ‚wai shau$^{2}$ ‹ká shat›, ‚mau ‹shang 'lí, pák› kai' ‹king ‚ying, ‹sam lik$_{2}$ ‹k'ü sui'. Fú$^{2}$ 'mò ‹chí tak›, shat$_{2}$ ‚t'ung hò$^{2}$ ‹t'in 'móng kik$_{2}$!

(e) *Tuk pat sz'* only not consider; while they regard everything else, how is it that they neglect only this one? that is, father and mother loving son's heart. The particle *ú* marks the interrogation.

## Section Second.

## OF ANCESTORS.

### 高曾祖類第二章

‹Kò ‹tsang 'tsò lui$^{2}$; tai$^{2}$ í$^{2}$ ‹chéung.

1. What is your lofty surname, Sir?

高姓呀

‹Kò sing' á'?

My poor surname is Wóng...... And your's, Sir?

賤姓黃駕上呢

Tsín$^{2}$ sing' ‚Wóng ... Ká' shéung$^{2}$ ‹ní?

### *Notes and Explanations.*

*Kò*, *tsang*, and *tsò*, denote the three generations in a direct line, immediately above one's own father, as will appear in the sequel, and as already stated in Chap. I, Sec. iii: 45.

1. This conversation may be supposed to occur between two strangers. One, on entering

| | | |
|---|---|---|
| 2. Léung .... And how, Sir, is your great-great-grandfather ? | 梁呀尊駕令高<br>祖呢 | ˏLéung á'! ‹Tsün ká' ling$^{2}$ ‹kò 'tsò ‹ní. |
| He is deceased. | 高祖過身咯 | ‹Kò 'tsò kwó' ‹shan lók›. |
| 3. Where is your great-grandfather ? | 曾祖呢 | ‹Tsang 'tsò ‹ní ? |
| He has returned home with my grandfather. | 曾祖共祖鄉旋 | ‹Tsang 'tsò kung$^{2}$ 'tsò ‹héung ˏsün. |
| 4. Are they both well ? | 佢二位好呀 | ˢK'ui í$^{2}$ wai$^{2}$ 'hò ‹á ? |
| Very well, I thank you. | 托賴 | T'ók› lái$^{2}$. |
| 5. What honorable pursuits now engage their attention at home ? | 令公祖鄉旋有<br>乜貴幹呀 | Ling$^{2}$ ‹kung 'tsò ‹héung ˏsün, 'yau mat› kwai' kón' á' ? |
| They are living in quiet retirement. | 閒居啫 | ˏHán ‹kü ‹ché. |
| 6. Ah truly, it is delightful to dwell in calm retirement! How old are they ? | 好咧享清福哩<br>嘷今年幾大嚹 | 'Hò lé', 'héung ‹ts'ing fuk› ‹lé pé$^{2}$! ‹Kam ˏnín 'kí tái' lá' ? |
| My great-grandfather is eighty-eight, and my grandfather is nearly seventy. | 曾祖兩個八祖<br>亦七十將來 | ‹Tsang 'tsò ˢléung kó' pát›, 'tsò yik$_{2}$ ts'át› shap$_{2}$ ‹tséung ˏloi. |

---

the residence of the other, inquires, Lofty surname eh? The other replies, Poor surname [is] Wong; and then inquires for the surname in these terms, *ká shéung ní?* This phrase is derived from the equestrian period in the north of China, when every gentleman had his carriage: *ká shéung* denotes riding in a chariot, and is here used for the person that rides, or is worthy to do so; it is elliptical, for the whole phrase would be, and you, Sir, on the chariot, [what is your surname?]

2. He answers, [my surname is] Léung; and then proceeds to inquire for the ancestors of the family. *Tsünká* is here united, and conveys the simple idea of Sir; *ling* is you, and *kò tsò* denotes high ancestor, i. e. Sir, your high ancestor? The object of the question is to ascertain if his great-great-grandfather is yet alive; and hence the answer, the lofty ancestor, *kwó* has passed [from], *shan* the body—he is dead.

3. *Tsang tsò ní?* Your great-grandfather? This question comes in the same elliptical form, but without the least obscurity. In like manner *kò*, in the phrases *kò tsang tsò*, *kò sing*, and *kò tsò*,—and *tsò*, whether used separately or in the phrases *kò tsang tsò*, *kò tsò*, and *tsang tsò*,—have in each instance a precise and definite meaning, which will be ascertained by a careful examination of the several phrases in which the two terms occur: *héung* is used to denote a village, a town, and also the country, in contradistinction to a residence in a city or metropolis; *sün* is to return; they have returned to their home in the country.

4. They two gentlemen well eh? *Wai*, formed of *man* and *erect*, denotes a person of consideration; and both in its derivation and common usage corresponds well with the word gentleman. *T'ók lái* depending on you, i. e. by favor derived from you, they are well.

5. Your great-grandfather and grandfather to the country returning, have what rich business eh? *Kung* is used here as a substitute for *tsang*, great-grandfather: *hán* in leisure, *kü* they dwell.

6. *Hò lé!* it is very good to do so, *héung* enjoying, *ts'ing fuk* pure happiness: *kam nín* this year, *kí tái lá* how great in years—are they? Two eights is eighty and eight. In China, where marriages take place when the parties are young, the difference of twenty between the ages of father and son, is not unusual.

| | | |
|---|---|---|
| 7. Indeed! It is by no means strange then, that they should seek retirement. | 嘜呀唔怪得佢<br>歸隱咯 | ‹Ai ‹yá! ‚'m kwai' tak› ‘k‘ui ‹kwai ‘yan lók›. |
| You speak in too flattering terms! for it is only a slight degree of bodily indisposition that induces them to go into retirement. | 好話亦係因身<br>體有的唔爽故<br>此番去嘅 | ‘Hò wá²! yik₂ hai² ‹yan ‹shan ‘t‘ai ‘yau tí› ‚'m ‘shóng, kú' ‘ts‘z' ‹fán hü' ké'. |
| 8. Truly a sufficient reason; for the condition of aged people is like that of a lamp before the wind. Therefore, when decrepitude overtakes them, they ought to go to their homes in the country. Are they well at present? | 係咯老人家事<br>如風前燭有乜<br>依郁就要鄉旋<br>爲是近日好呀 | Hai² lók›; ‘lò ‚yan ‹ká sz'² ‚ü ‹fung ‚ts‘in chuk›. ‘Yau mat› ‹í yuk›, tsau² iú² ‹héung ‚sün ‚wai shí². Kan² yat₂ ‘hò ‹á? |
| I have of late heard that they are not very well. | 近日聽見都唔<br>係實守好呀 | Kan² yat₂ ‹t‘ing kín' ‹tò ‚'m hai² shat₂ ‘shau ‘hò á'. |
| 9. If you are sending home any letter, I beg you will add a line for me, and present to them my compliments and best wishes for their happiness. | 有乜書信回鄉<br>代我寫多句在<br>令太祖公前叱<br>名請吓安 | ‘Yau mat› ‹shü sun' ‚úi ‹héung, toi² ‘ngó ‘sé ‹tó kü', tsoi² ling² t‘ái' ‘tsò ‹kung ‚ts‘ín, ch‘ik› ‚ming ‘ts‘ing ‘há ‹ón. |
| Truly they are unworthy of your honors. | 豈敢豈敢 | ‘Hí ‘kóm! ‘Hí ‘kóm! |
| 10. Having a little trifling business requiring attention I will on another day therefore do myself the pleasure of waiting on you. | 我因有些賤事<br>改日再來聽教 | ‘Ngó ‹yan ‘yau ‹sé tsín' sz'², ‘koi yat₂ tsoi' ‚loi ‹t‘ing káu'. |
| I am unworthy, I am unworthy of such attention. | 不敢不敢 | Pat› ‘kóm! pat› ‘kóm! |

7. *Ai yá* is an exclamation of surprise, uttered on hearing that they were so old: *'m kwai tak* it is not suprising—that they being so advanced in years, *kwai* should return, *yan* to private life—retirement; *hò wá* you flatter, for it is not simply to enjoy private life that they have gone to their home in the country, *yik* but also, *hai* it is, *yan* because, *shan t'ai* their bodies, *yau* have, *ti* a little, *'m shóng* indisposition; therefore, *kú ts'z'* because of this they have gone home, &c.

8. The similitude of a lamp before the wind expresses the great danger there is from any slight mishaps which will hazard the life of an aged person, as a gentle puff of wind will extinguish a lamp. *Yau mat í yuk* having some feebleness and trembling: the phrase is local.

9. Having any letter returning home, for me write additional sentence, in your great-grandfather and grandfather's presence, repeat [my] name, beg [for them] repose. To this message, in behalf of his great-grandfather and grandfather, the other replies *how dare! how dare!* How dare they receive the honors you give them, i. e. they are unworthy of the attention with which you honor them.

10. *T'ing káu*, to listen to instructions, is here used as a complimentary phrase. *Pat kóm, pat kóm*, which is equivalent to *hí kóm hí kóm*, and *pat kóm tóng*, is uttered in behalf of the speaker, in reply to the compliment just received.

| | | |
|---|---|---|
| 11. Please return! please return! | 請回請回 | 'Ts'ing ˏúi! 'ts'ing ˏúi! |
| Only a step or two! only a step or two! | 行吓啫行吓啫 | ˏHang 'há ˏché! ˏhang 'há ˏché! |
| 12. Good bye! | 請呀 | 'Ts'ing á'! |
| Good bye! | 請呀 | 'Ts'ing á'! |
| 13. Great-great-grandfather departed this life long ago. | 高祖去世已久 | ˏKò 'tsò h'ü' shai' 'í 'kau. |
| 14. Great-grandfather is about seventy [years old]. | 曾祖上下七十 | ˏTsang 'tsò shéung$^{2}$ há$^{2}$ ts'át, shap$_2$. |
| 15. From ancestors it has come down to the present time. | 太公留到而家 | T'ái' ˏkung ˏlau tò' ˏí ˏká. |
| 16. Possessions bequeathed by ancestors. | 祖公遺下產業 | 'Tsò ˏkung ˏwai há$^{2}$ 'ch'án íp$_2$. |
| 17. My grandfather while living commanded it. | 阿公在生吩咐 | A' ˏkung tsoi$^{2}$ ˏshang ˏfan fú$^{2}$. |
| 18. My grandfather's picture is as natural as life. | 阿爺音容宛在 | A' ˏyé ˏyam ˏyung 'ún tsoi$^{2}$. |
| 19. When did your grandfather commence his fairy ramblings? | 令祖幾時仙遊 | Ling$^{2}$ 'tsò 'kí ˏshí ˏsín ˏyau? |
| 20. My father two months ago rejected this life. | 家祖前月棄世 | ˏKá 'tsò ˏts'ín üt$_2$ hí' shai'. |
| 21. He was interred by the side of my deceased grandmother. | 同先祖妣合葬 | ˏT'ung ˏsín 'tsò 'pí hóp$_2$ tsóng'. |
| 22. This was previously determined by my deceased grandfather. | 先祖考預定嘅 | ˏSín 'tsò 'háu ü$^{2}$ ting$^{2}$ ké'. |
| 23. (*a*) Among the Sacred Commands is this, 'Cherish warm attachment to kindred, and so display union and concord.' | 聖諭云篤宗族以昭雍睦 | Shing' Yü' ˏwan, Tuk, ˏtsung tsuk$_2$, 'í ˏch'íú ˏyung muk$_2$. |

11. The strangers, so regarded on first meeting, by their conversation become friends: the guest, having intimated that he must leave, on retiring from the house is followed by the host, to whom he says, *ts'ing úi, ts'ing úi!* I beg you to return, I beg you to return! meaning, do not put yourself to so much trouble. The host, who does not wish to be exceeded in politeness, says I will, *hang há ché, hang há ché!* walk a little, walk a little!

18. *Yam* and *yung*, sound and countenance, are used for portrait, *ún* as if, *tsoi* in being; the portrait of my grandfather is as natural as life; the terms *á kung* and *á yé* here used for grandfather are the most frequently employed in common intercourse in this region; in the neighboring province of Fukkín, he is sometimes called *tái fú* great father, a term which corresponds to the English word.

19. *Sín yau*, fairy ramblings, are used for death: the sense of the question is, when did your father die? But to avoid the unwelcome term they use *sín yau*,—a phrase which gives the Chinese the same train of ideas that was awakened in a Greek or Roman by "walking the Elysian fields."

20. *Hí shai*, cast off life, is equivalent to *h'ü shai*, depart this life, both being used to denote death.

23. This is the second of the sixteen injunctions of Hónghí: like the first, given in the preceding section, it is comprised in seven characters: what follows is the amplification of his son Yungching.

(b) In the Book of Records it is said, "He thereby promoted attachment among all his kindred, who being at concord...." Thus the emperor Yiú commenced the promulgation of his instructions by promoting concord among his kindred.

書曰以親九族九族既睦是帝堯首以睦族示教也

ˏShü üt꜀, ˋí ꜀ts'an ˋkau tsuk꜁ ˋkau tsuk꜀ kí' muk꜀. Shí' tai' ꜀Yiú ˋshau ˋí muk꜀ tsuk꜁ shí' káu' ˋyá.

(c) In the Book of Rites it is said, "If remote ancestors are honored, then immediate progenitors will be respected." If immediate progenitors are respected, then kindred will be united.

禮曰尊祖故敬宗敬宗故收族

ˋLai üt꜀, ꜀tsün ˋtsò kú' king' ꜀tsung. King' ꜀tsung kú' ꜀shau tsuk꜀.

(d) He who understands the duties of man will certainly attach great weight to concord among kindred.

明人道必以睦族爲重也

꜀Ming ꜀yan tò' pít꜁ ˋí muk꜁ tsuk꜀ ꜀wai chung' ˋyá.

(e) The degrees of kindred in a family are like the streamlets of a fountain, or the branches of a tree: although the streams differ in being more or less remote, and the branches in being more or less close, yet there is but one trunk and one fountain-head.

夫家之有宗族猶水之有分派木之有分枝雖遠近異勢踈密異形要其本源則一

꜀Fú ꜀ká ꜀chí ˋyau ꜀tsung tsuk꜀, ꜀yau ˋshui ꜀chí ˋyau ꜀fan p'ái', muk꜀ ꜀chí ˋyau ꜀fan ꜀chí; ꜀sui ˋün kan' í' shai', ꜀shò mat꜀ í' ꜀ying, iú' ꜀k'í ˋpún ꜀ün tsak꜁ yat꜁.

(f) Therefore a man's conduct towards his kindred should be like [what is witnessed in] the body: the four limbs and the collective members of which require a free passage for the blood through every part, while all are mutually affected by the pain and irritation of each.

故人之待其宗族也必如身之有四肢百體務使血脈相通而痾癢相關

Kú' ꜀yan ꜀chí toi' ꜀k'í ꜀tsung tsuk꜀ ˋyá, pít꜁ ꜀ü ꜀shan ꜀chí, ˋyau sz' ꜀chí pak꜁ ˋt'ai, mò' ˋsz' hüt꜁ mak꜀ ꜀séung ꜀t'ung, ꜀í ꜀hó ˋyéung ꜀séung ꜀kwán.

(g) In the Ritual of Chau this same idea is maintained, where, for the instruction of the people, six virtues are enumerated: after filial duty, and fraternal affection, the

周禮本此意以教民著爲六行日孝日友而繼

꜀Chau ˋLai ˋpún ˋts'z' í', ˋí káu' ꜀man chü' ꜀wai lok꜀ hang', üt꜀ háu', üt꜀ ˋyau, ꜀í

(b) The quotation from the Book of Records is broken, the writer extracting only enough to cover the point in question. The Book of Records, the Book of Rites, and the Ritual of Chau are names of portions of the Chinese classical works.

(e) The imperial author seems to have erred in a part of his illustrations, conforming rather to the popular notions than to the reality; he conceives a fountain sending forth its streams, which as they flow on branch off into a multitude of other rivulets, quite forgetting that the reverse was the truth; had he described an artificial fountain, throwing its jets in all directions, the figure would have been more appropriate, but this seems not to have been the

| | | |
|---|---|---|
| next is concord. This is, indeed, a constant duty, invariably enjoined in every age. | 曰睦誠古今不易之常道也 | kai' üt, muk,. ,Shing 'kú ,kam pat, yik, ,chí ,shéung tò' 'yá! |

idea in his mind; however, a popular idea will often afford a good comparison, even if it does not tally with rigid philosophy. The allusion to the root, trunk, branches and leaves of a tree to illustrate the progressive increase of a family is more suitable.

## Section Third.

## OF SONS AND GRANDSONS.

## 子孫類第三章

'Tsz' ,sün lui'; tai' ,sám ,chéung.

| | | |
|---|---|---|
| 1. The emperor's son. | 元子 | ,Yün 'tsz'. |
| 2. The heir apparent. | 太子 | T'ái' 'tsz'. |
| 3. The eldest son. | 長子 | 'Chéung 'tsz'. |
| 4. The eldest son by the wife. | 冢子 | 'Ch'ung 'tsz'. |
| 5. A prodigal son. | 浪子 | Lóng' 'tsz'. |
| 6. A son; or heir. | 子嗣 | 'Tsz' tsz''. |
| 7. The second son. | 次子 | Ts'z' 'tsz'. |
| 8. My own son. | 親生仔 | ,Ts'an ,shang 'tsai. |
| 9. An adopted son. | 承繼仔 | ,Shing kai' 'tsai. |
| 10. An adopted son of a different surname. | 螟蛉子 | ,Ming ,ling 'tsz'. |

### *Notes and Explanations.*

1, 2. YÜN is the first, the principal—the principal sons in the empire; it is sometimes used like *t'ái tsz*, for the heir apparent, though usually applied to all the sons of the emperor.

6. This phrase is used for both son and heir, but it is most frequently limited to the former; and in this use, that of son, the second term is very often dropped.

8. *Ts'an* here denotes one's own: *tsai* is in constant use not only for son, a human being, but it is also applied to the young of animals and birds, and often added to the specific name of little things in general, and in many of its uses corresponds to the diminutive termination *ulus* in Latin; in this instance it is equivalent to *tsz'*, a son, or *ts'z' tsz'* in the preceding example.

9, 10. *Shing kai tsai*, to receive in the line of succession a son, when one has no son of his own: this is usually done with few, and sometimes with no, formalities; as a general rule the adopted son is taken from the nearest branch, and in case no son is found among those who

廣東方言讀本



| | | |
|---|---|---|
| 11. A posthumous son. | 懷腹子 | ˬWái fukˀ ʻtsz'. |
| 12. A prodigal son. | 敗家仔 | Pái² ˬká ʻtsai. |
| 13. Devising means for the support of sons and grandsons. | 爲子孫計 | Wai² ʻtsz' ˬsün kai'. |
| 14. The son of a sister adopted as one's own. | 姑子歸宗 | ˬKú ʻtsz' ˬkwai ˬtsung. |
| 15. Daily increasing family, [or population.] | 生齒日繁 | ˬShang ʻch'í yat₂ ˬfán. |
| 16. One taken and brought up as a foster-child. | 攞嚟養嘅 | ʻLó ˬlai ʻyéung ké'. |
| 17. The sons and daughters of others. | 人仔人女 | ˬYan ʻtsai ˬyan ʻnü. |
| 18. Sons and grandsons inheriting honors. | 子孫襲蔭 | ʻTsz' ˬsün tsáp₂ yam'. |
| 19. Supported by labors of sons and grandsons. | 子亻代勞 | ʻTsz' ˬsün toi² ˬlò. |
| 20. A numerous and prosperous posterity. | 子亻發達 | ʻTsz' ˬsün fátˀ tát₂. |
| 21. A numerous and thriving posterity. | 子亻昌盛 | ʻTsz' ˬsün ˬch'éung shing². |
| 22. Descendants few and impoverished. | 子亻衰微 | ʻTsz' ˬsün ˬshui ˬmí. |
| 23. An infant child fondled at the breast. | 孩提之童 | ˬHoi ˬt'ai ˬchí ˬt'ung. |
| 24. [Children] playing about the parent's knees. | 依稀膝下 | ˬÍ ˬhí satˀ há². |
| 25. Without sons and grandsons. | 冇仔冇孫 | ʻMò ʻtsai ʻmò ˬsün. |
| 26. A grandson born of the wife of the eldest son. | 長子嫡亻 | ʻChéung ʻtsz' tikˀ ˬsün. |
| 27. A dutiful son and a worthy grandson. | 孝子賢亻 | Háu' ʻtsz' ˬhín ˬsün. |
| 28. Being dependent on sons and grandsons. | 倚賴子亻 | ʻÍ lái² ʻtsz' ˬsün. |
| 29. May you have a hundred sons and a thousand grandsons. | 百子千亻 | Pákˀ ʻtsz' ˬts'ín ˬsün. |

bear the same family name, then one is taken of a different surname, and is styled *ming ling tsz'*, a name derived from an insect, a sort of ichneumon fly, which is by the Chinese supposed to be barren, there being no sexes. This insect (so the Chinese say,) seizes on a young grub of some other species, and buries it up in a little clayey cell; then after flying around it with a loud buzzing noise for a few days, the covering of the little cell breaks open, and a perfect insect of its own species comes out.

15. Begetting teeth daily more numerous, i. e. a daily or constantly increasing number of eaters.

17. This is said in apology for harsh treatment; they are not my own children, and consequently I need not treat them kindly.

18. *Tsáp yam* is to inherit honors; there are in China certain honors conferred with the express condition that they shall pass down to sons and grandsons, &c.

19. Sons and grandsons for [their parents and grandparents] laboring; this is said with reference to those who are supported by their children and grandchildren, and who of course have nothing to do for themselves.

30—34. These phrases are applied to those who, having attained to manhood, give themselves up to feel, judge, and act, like children; the phrase *p'í hí* skin spirits, the external ap-

| | | |
|---|---|---|
| 30. A childish disposition. | 小兒皮氣 | ʻSíú ˏí ˏp'í hí'. |
| 31. A childish judgment. | 小兒度量 | ʻSíú ˏí tò² léung². |
| 32. Childish pursuits. | 小兒事業 | ʻSíú ˏí sz'² íp₂. |
| 33. Childish conduct. | 小兒所爲 | ʻSíú ˏí ʻshó ˏwai. |
| 34. Childlike sports. | 小兒好反斗 | ʻSíú ˏí hò' ʻfán ʻtau. |
| 35. They are not my own children. | 唔係親生嘅 | ˏ'M hai² ˏts'an ˏshang ké'. |
| 36. Sons and grandsons innumerable. | 子孫不勝數 | ʻTsz' ˏsün pat˒ ˏshing ʻshò. |
| 37. Involved by the conduct of one's sons and grandsons. | 爲子孫所累 | Wai² ʻtsz' ˏsün ʻshó lui². |
| 38. Children becoming great, rescue their parents from poverty. | 仔大救爺貧 | ʻTsai tái² kau' ˏyé ˏp'an. |
| 39. A foster-child can never become dear as one's own. | 養子唔得貼肉 | ʻYéung ʻtsz' ˏ'm tak˒ t'íp˒ yuk₂. |
| 40. An adopted child certainly will not prove true. | 契仔斷有真心 | K'ai' ʻtsai tün' ʻmò ˏchan ˏsam. |
| 41. Little children are very fond of play. | 小兒實守鷦鷯 | ʻSíú ˏí shat₂ ʻshau ˏtsíú ˏlíú. |
| 42. My son has grown up to manhood. | 小兒年已長大 | ʻSíú ˏí ˏnín ʻí ʻchéung tái². |
| 43. The boy is at school studying his books. | 幼兒學裏攻書 | Yau' ˏí hók₂ ʻlui ˏkung ˏshü. |
| 44. Clever children and grandchildren will be loved. | 子孫乖令人愛 | ʻTsz' ˏsün ˏkwái ling² ˏyan oi'. |
| 45. A son's son mourns a year for his father's parents. | 內丨係一年服 | Noi² ˏsün hai² yat˒ ˏnín fuk₂. |
| 46. A daughter's children mourn nine months for their mother's parents. | 外丨九個月服 | Ngoi² ˏsün ʻkau kó' üt₂ fuk₂. |
| 47. A great grandson is a distant relation. | 曾丨已經疎的 | ˏTsang ˏsün ʻí ˏking ˏshó tik˒. |
| 48. A great-great-grandson is of course still more distant. | 玄丨自然更疎 | ˏÜn ˏsün tsz'² ˏín kang' ˏshó. |

pearance of the person and the internal feelings of the mind, expresses the disposition, carriage, and bearing of an individual.

39. *T'íp yuk*, join flesh, conveys the idea of relation by blood: a foster-child, not being related by blood, can never be as tenderly loved as one who is of the same blood.

41. Small children extremely [like] wrens: the gambols and playfulness of children are not inaptly compared to the ceaseless motions and domestic habits of this universal favorite.

42. *Síú í*, my little son, is used in polite circles when speaking of one's own son, and means simply my son.

43. *Hók* is here used to denote the place where scholars assemble—the school-room; *kung shü*, to attack books, is a common phrase for expressing the idea of studying.

47—49. *Tsang sün* is an added grandson; *chung sün* a redoubled grandson: *tsang* means to add to, as in adding one story to another in building; *chung* means to lay one blow on after another, or to arrange one layer or stratum upon another.

海上絲綢之路文獻集成 科技與文化編

| | | |
|---|---|---|
| 49. A second grandson and a great-grandson are the same. | 重孫曾孫一樣 | Chung² ꜀sün ꜀tsang ꜀sün yat꜂ yéung². |
| 50. Nephew's sons are somewhat remote relations. | 姪丨疎皮隔節 | Chat₂ ꜀sün ꜀shó ˏp'í kák꜂ tsít꜂. |
| 51. Children and grandchildren succeed to their parents' estates. | 子丨承祖父業 | ʻTsz' ꜀sün ˏshing ʻtsò fú² íp₂. |
| 52. A line of descendants as long as the vines of the melon. | 子丨瓜瓞綿長 | ʻTsz' ꜀sün ꜀kwá tít₂ ˏmín ˏch'éung. |
| 53. Children and grandchildren laboring for the emperor. | 子丨出力皇家 | ʻTsz' ꜀sün ch'ut꜂ lik₂ ˏwóng ꜀ká. |
| 54. Unsuccessful and unhappy posterity. | 子丨唔承得福 | ʻTsz' ꜀sün ˏ'm ˏshing tak꜂ fuk꜂. |
| 55. To have ugly children is equal to being childless. | 子丨醜如無有 | ʻTsz' ꜀sün ʻch'au ˏü ˏmò ʻyau. |
| 56. Those born of the wife are the principal children. | 正出就係嫡子 | Ching' ch'ut꜂ tsau² hai² tik꜂ ʻtsz'. |
| 57. Those born of concubines are the common children. | 庶出便是庶子 | Shü' ch'ut꜂ pín² shí² shü' ʻtsz'. |
| 58. Your son confesses his own guilt. | 孩兒自知有罪 | ˏHoi ˏí tsz'² ꜀chí ʻyau tsúi². |
| 59. The child ought to comply with the parent's wishes. | 兒子當體親心 | ˏÍ ʻtsz' ꜀tóng ʻt'ai ꜀ts'an ꜀sam. |
| 60. An adopted son treated as one's own child. | 義子當作親生 | Í² ʻtsz' tóng' tsok꜂ ꜀ts'an ꜀shang. |
| 61. My daughter is not yet betrothed. | 小女尚未成人 | ʻSíú ʻnü shéung² mí² ˏshing ˏyan. |
| 62. My daughter has tasted the nuptial presents. | 小女食人茶禮 | ʻSíú ʻnü shik₂ ˏyan ˏch'á ʻlai. |
| 63. My daughter has no nuptial presents of value. | 小女冇乜粧奩 | ʻSíú ʻnü ʻmò mat꜂ ꜀chóng ˏlím. |
| 64. My daughter has not yet exchanged her final nuptial presents. | 小女未過大禮 | ʻSíú ʻnü mí² kwò' tái² ʻlai. |
| 65. My daughter has not commenced her nuptial lamentations. | 小女未開嘆情 | ʻSíú ʻnü mí² ꜀hoi t'án' ˏts'ing. |
| 66. My niece carefully observes the domestic rites. | 姪女謹守閨門 | Chat₂ ʻnü ʻkan ʻshau ꜀kwai ˏmún. |
| 67. Laboring as a slave for one's posterity. | 做子孫嘅奴才 | Tsò² ʻtsz' ꜀sün ké' ˏnò ˏts'oi. |
| 68. Good examples transmitted to posterity. | 留規謨與子孫 | ˏLau ꜀kwai ˏmò ʻü ʻtsz' ꜀sün. |

50. Nephew grandson separated a skin, sundered a joint; there is one skin between the parties, they are separated by a joint, which alludes to the successive joints of the bamboo, as if one was passed, or there were two folds of skin: the two phrases are similar, though they are usually joined in this connection.

52. *Kwá tít* is the vine of the melon: *mín ch'éung*, cotton extended, or spun out: the phrase denotes a long line of descendants.

55. *Ch'au* is ugly in person and manner, every way bad, base, vile; a child that is a curse and not a blessing to its parents.

| | | |
|---|---|---|
| 69. When will the marriage of your son be consummated? | 令郎幾時榮娶 | Ling² ꜀lóng ʿkí ꜀shí ꜀wing ts'ü' ? |
| 70. Your son has changed his heart and purpose. | 令郎回心轉意 | Ling² ꜀lóng ꜀úi ꜀sam ʿchün í'. |
| 71. Your son does not yet give his consent. | 令公郎未允肯 | Ling² ꜀kung ꜀lóng mí² ʿwan ʿhang. |
| 72. According to what your son declared. | 據你令郎講嘅 | Kü' ʿní ling² ꜀lóng ʿkóng ké'. |
| 73. The dutiful and obedient child will be blessed with dutiful and obedient children. | 孝順還生孝順子 | Háu' shun² ꜀wán ꜀shang háu' shun² ʿtsz'. |
| 74. Those who have been perverse and obstinate will be recompensed in having children with like tempers. | 忤逆還生忤逆兒 | ʿ'Ng yik₂ ꜀wán ꜀shang ʿ'ng yik₂ ꜀í. |
| 75. Children and grandchildren will doubtless enjoy the happiness of having sons and grandsons. | 兒孫自有兒孫福 | ꜀Í ꜀sün tsz'² ʿyau ꜀í ꜀sün fuk₁. |
| 76. The hawk breeds the hawk, and the dove bears the dove. | 鷹生鷹子鶻生鶻兒 | ꜀Ying ꜀shang ꜀ying ʿtsz', wat₂ ꜀shang wat₂ ꜀í. |
| 77. Dwellers on the mountains will have provisions enough, and have only to fear that their children will be clownish. | 山居柴米足只怕子孫愚 | ꜀Shán ꜀kü ꜀chái ʿmai tsuk₁, chat₁ p'á' ʿtsz' ꜀sün ꜀ü. |
| 78. If you would have children enjoy good health, let them always experience a little hunger and cold. | 若要小兒安常帶三分饑與寒 | Yéuk₂ iú' ʿsíú ꜀í ꜀ón, ꜀shéung tái' ꜀sám ꜀fan ꜀kí ʿü ꜀hòn. |
| 79. (*a*) The meaning of his imperial majesty may be thus explained: | 萬歲爺意思說 | Mán² sui' ꜀yé í' sz'² shüt₁: |
| (*b*) All men who are born into the world, have nine ranks of relations; how are these denominated? | 人生在世都有個九族怎麼叫做九族呢 | ꜀Yan ꜀shang tsoi² shai' ꜀tò ʿyau kó' ʿkau tsuk₂. ʿTsam ꜀mó kíú' tsò² ʿkau tsuk₂ ꜀ní? |
| (*c*) My own generation is one grade: my father's is one; my grandfather's is one; that of my grandfather's father is one; and that of my grandfather's grandfather is | 我自己是一輩我的父親一輩我的爺一輩我 | ʿNgó tsz'² ʿkí shí² yat₁ púi'; ʿngó tik₁ fú² ꜀ts'an yat₁ púi'; ʿngó tik₁ ꜀yé yat₁ púi'; ʿngó |

76. Like father, like son, "a chip of the old block," denoting that children naturally partake of the characteristics of their parents.

79. (*a*) *Mán sui yé*, ten thousand year's gentleman, is an epithet applied to the reigning emperor: it is here applied to Yungching, by an officer of the government who wrote copious commentaries on the explanatory treatises of that emperor (see Chap. III. Sec. i: 42, *b*). This extract is from the second commentary, written on the first part of that which was given in the last section.

one; thus above me are four grades: my son's generation is one grade; my grandson's is one; that of my grandson's son is one; and that of my grandson's grandson is one; thus below me are four grades of relations: including myself in the estimate, there are in all nine grades. These are brethren, and though each grade belongs to a different house or family, yet they are all my relations. And these are called the nine grades of relations.

輩一共兒孫重玄是四算這兄的人九
一又頭的的的的輩有已輩弟戶族做
親爺上我我我我一也自九的各的叫
父的我輩丨丨丨是邊我是兒門我個
的爺是四一一一又下連共輩各是這
爺我輩有子子孫丨我輩着九們便了族

,yé tik, fú2 ,ts'an yat, púi'; 'ngó ,yé tik, ,yé yau2 yat, púi'; shí2 'ngó shéung2 ,t'au kung2 'yau sz" púi'; 'ngó tik, ,í 'tsz' yat, púi'; 'ngó tik, ,sün 'tsz' yat, púi'; 'ngó tik, chung2 ,sün yat, púi'; 'ngó tik, ,ün ,sün yau2 shí2 yat, púi'; shí2 'ngó há2 ,pín 'yá 'yau sz" púi': ,lín 'ngó tsz'2 'kí sün' chéuk,, kung2 shí2 'kau púi'. Ché' 'kau púi' ,í tik, tai2 ,hing ,mún, kók, ,mún kók, ú2 tik, pín2 shí2 'ngó tik, tsuk, ,yan 'líú. Ché' kó' kíú' tsò2 'kau tsuk,.

(d) All men also have their remote ancestors and their immediate progenitors. How are these denominated? Those who are the farthest above me are remote ancestors; but those who are nearer are called immediate progenitors.

宗宗是些
祖祖頭近
有做上親宗
都叫最再做
人麽我祖叫
人怎呢老就

,Yan ,yan ,tò 'yau 'tsò ,tsung. 'Tsam ,mó kíú' tsò2 'tsò ,tsung ,ní? 'Ngó tsui' shéung2 ,t'au shí2 'lò 'tsò; tsoi' ,ts'an kan2 ,sé tsau2 kíú' tsò2 ,tsung.

(e). Now who is there of you who is not the descendant of remote ancestors and immediate progenitors? And who is there who has not the nine ranks of relations?

那傳沒
人宗個呢
些祖那族
這是的九
們不來個
你個下有

'Ní ,mún ché' ,sé ,yan, 'ná kó' pat, shí2 'tsò ,tsung ,ch'ün há2 ,loi tik,, 'ná kó' mút, 'yau kó' 'kau tsuk, ,ní?

(c) *Púi* denotes class, order, or grade; the context here shows its exact meaning; there are two slightly different forms of this character occurring in the first and third lines. This passage, with slight variations in the phraseology, was given, Chap. I. Sec. iii: 45, in a note.

## Section Fourth.

## OF HUSBAND AND WIFE.

### 夫婦類第四章
‹Fú ʻfú lui'; tai' ‹sz' ‹chéung.

| | | |
|---|---|---|
| 1. Originally coupled husband and wife. | 原配夫妻 | ‚Yün p'úi' ‹fú ‹ts'ai. |
| 2. Husband and wife affianced by their parents. | 結髮夫妻 | Kít› fát› ‹fú ‹ts'ai. |
| 3. Mildness and gentleness between husband and wife. | 和順夫婦 | ‚Wó shun' ‹fú ʻfú. |
| 4. Husband and wife mild and gentle. | 夫婦和順 | ‹Fú ʻfú ‚wó shun'. |
| 5. The husband mild and the wife gentle. | 夫和婦順 | ‹Fú ‚wó ʻfú shun'. |
| 6. Kindness and love between husband and wife. | 恩愛夫妻 | ‹Yan oi' ‹fú ‹ts'ai. |
| 7. Husband and wife both living to a good old age. | 夫婦偕老 | ‹Fú ʻfú ‹kái ʻló. |
| 8. Husband and wife living in peace and harmony. | 夫婦和諧 | ‹Fú ʻfú ‚wó ‚hái. |
| 9. Husband and wife assist and protect each other. | 夫妻保守 | ‹Fú ‹ts'ui ʻpò ʻshau. |
| 10. Husband and wife turning their eyes from each other in dislike. | 夫妻反目 | ‹Fú ‹ts'ai ʻfán muk›. |
| 11. The husband sings, and the wife follows in unison. | 夫唱婦隨 | ‹Fú ch'éung' ʻfú ‚ts'ui. |
| 12. The husband is the regulator of the wife. | 夫爲妻綱 | ‹Fú ‚wai ‹ts'ai ‹kóng. |

### *Notes and Explanations.*

*Fú* denotes one that may be depended on, or who is able to sustain important trusts or bear heavy burdens: *fú*, composed of *woman* and *broom*, referring to the domestic duties of a wife, means also to submit to, one whose duty it is to submit; both the explanations denote a married woman.

1, 2. These two phrases express nearly the same idea, designating a couple, neither of whom has ever before been married or betrothed; *p'úi* is a consort, to consort, or those who are consorted: *kít fát*, to tie the hair in a knot, denotes the intimate relation which subsists between the husband and wife, in that case where the parties were affianced by their parents: *ts'ai* is the wife, properly so called.

3—5. In each of these three sentences the same terms occur, and in each conveying essentially the same idea.

10. This is done in times of calamity, when misfortune overtakes them, or when perplexities and disappointments arise; the expression is also used for the jars and disagreements which sometimes cause man and wife to look askance at each other.

11. This phrase is intended to indicate perfect harmony between the husband and wife in all their pursuits and feelings.

12. *Kóng* is explained and illustrated in Chap. I, Sec. iii: 28; the husband is the controler of the wife.

| | | |
|---|---|---|
| 13. Cherishing his wife, and supporting his children. | 養妻活兒 | 'Yéung ‹ts'ai út› ˏí. |
| 14. A chaste widow, nourishing orphan children. | 節婦撫孤 | Tsít› 'fú 'fú ‹kú. |
| 15. My husband has gone out of the house. | 丈夫去出門 | Chéung' ‹fú h'ü' ch'ut› ˏmún. |
| 16. My husband is not at home. | 男人唔喺企 | ˏNám ˏyan ˏ'm 'hai 'k'i. |
| 17. The old man has not yet returned. | 老公未番嚟 | 'Lò ‹kung mí' ‹fán ˏlai. |
| 18. I do not see that the goodman has returned. | 良人未見回 | ˏLéung ˏyan mí' kín' ˏúi. |
| 19. My wife has no children. | 正妻冇所出 | Ching' ‹ts'ai 'mò 'shó ch'ut›. |
| 20. How many children has your concubine? | 妾侍生幾個 | Ts'íp› shí' ‹shang 'kí kó'? |
| 21. My wife's conduct is in the highest degree correct. | 正室極正大 | Ching' shat› kik› ching' tái'. |
| 22. The old woman has been dead a long time. | 老婆死好耐 | 'Lò ˏp'ó 'sz' 'hò noi'. |
| 23. Husband and wife are like garments. | 夫妻如衣服 | ‹Fú ‹ts'ai ˏü ‹í fuk›. |
| 24. The husband and wife are like a ferry-boat. | 夫妻渡客船 | ‹Fú ‹ts'ai tò' hák› ˏshün. |
| 25. The husband is brave, and the wife gentle. | 夫剛而婦柔 | ‹Fú ‹kóng ˏí 'fu ˏyau. |
| 26. If the husband is virtuous, the wife will also be virtuous. | 夫賢婦亦賢 | ˏFú ˏín 'fu yik› ˏín. |
| 27. The widow must not put on gay attire. | 寡婦切勿粉飾 | 'Kwá 'fú ts'ít› mat› 'fan shik›. |
| 28. The eldest son's wife ought to govern the family. | 冢亻理應掌家 | 'Ch'ung 'fú 'lí ‹ying 'chéung ‹ká. |
| 29. The widow ought to be chaste in her conduct. | 孀亻須要貞節 | ‹Séung 'fú ‹sui íú' ‹ching tsít›. |
| 30. The master has gone abroad to sell his goods. | 官人負販在外 | ‹Kún ˏyan fú' fán' tsoi' ngoi'. |
| 31. The husband and wife happy as fish in the water. | 夫妻如魚得水 | ‹Fú ‹ts'ai ˏü ˏü tak› 'shui. |
| 32. Husband and wife both equally advanced in age. | 夫妻白髮齊眉 | ‹Fú 'fú pák› fát› ˏts'ai ˏmí. |

15—18. *Chéungfú*, *námyan*, and *lòkung*, are all in common use when speaking of one's own husband; *léungyan*, the goodman, or my husband, occurs in writing, but is seldom used in conversation.

19—21. *Ching ts'ai* is used in opposition to *ts'íp shí*, the wife and the concubine; the latter term denotes one who is inferior to the wife: no person can lawfully have but one *ts'ai*, though the number of concubines is unlimited: *ching shat* is the same as *ching ts'ai*.

23. If one dies the other can marry again, just as one can procure a new garment when an old one is worn out.

24. When the boat reaches the shore the passengers quit it, and on reaching another river seek for another boat: so when one of a couple dies, the other wanders alone till another consort is found.

31. The fish in its element is supposed to be perfectly peaceful and happy, and in that condition becomes a fit emblem of what those ought to be who are joined in wedlock.

32. Husband and wife white hairs equal eyebrows; this is often written in congratulatory letters, expressive of the wish that both parties may live to the same good old age.

| | | |
|---|---|---|
| 33. Husband and wife unwilling to part from each other | 夫妻不忍分手 | ‹Fú ‹ts'ai pat› 'yan ‹fan 'shau. |
| 34. Husband and wife remaining constant to old age. | 夫妻白頭相守 | ‹Fú ‹ts'ai pák$_2$ ‹t'au ‹séung 'shau. |
| 35. Husband and wife being on a perfect level. | 夫妻檯面咁平 | ‹Fú ‹ts'ai ‹toi mín$^2$ kom' ‹p'ing. |
| 36. Husband and wife living in peace even to old age. | 夫婦同諧到老 | ‹Fú 'fú ‹t'ung ‹hái tò' 'lò. |
| 37. The husband and wife honor each other as guests. | 丨丨相敬如賓 | ‹Fú ‹ts'ai ‹séung king' ‹ü ‹pan. |
| 38. The husband and wife must not sit on the same mat. | 丨丨不同席坐 | ‹Fú 'fú pat› ‹t'ung ts'ik$_2$ tsó$^2$. |
| 39. Decorum binds husband and wife to their own spheres. | 丨丨以別爲禮 | ‹Fú 'fú 'i pít$_2$ ‹wai 'lai. |
| 40. Husband and wife eat of the fruit cultivated by their own hands. | 丨丨灌園食力 | ‹Fú 'fú kún' ‹ün shik$_2$ lik$_2$. |
| 41. Politeness between husband and wife must not be neglected. | 丨丨體不可失 | ‹Fú 'fú 'lai pat› 'hó shat›. |
| 42. Husband and wife living in peace, indicates a good principled family. | 丨丨和家道正 | ‹Fú 'fú ‹wó ‹ká tò$^2$ ching'. |
| 43. Husband and wife must not live in contention. | 丨丨勿作仇人 | ‹Fú 'fú mat$_2$ tsók› ‹ch'au ‹yan. |
| 44. Husband and wife like wayside acquaintances. | 丨丨如陌路人 | ‹Fú 'fú ‹ü mak$_2$ lò$^2$ ‹yan. |
| 45. On the third morning the bride visits her home. | 新婦三朝回門 | ‹San 'fu ‹sám ‹chíu ‹úi ‹mún. |
| 46. The bride does obeisance in the hall in this way. | 新抱拜堂咁樣 | ‹San 'p'ò pái' ‹t'óng 'kóm yéung$^2$. |
| 47. My wife died several years ago. | 賤內過身幾年 | Tsín$^2$ noi$^2$ kwó' ‹shan 'ki ‹nín. |
| 48. Have you yet contracted for a second marriage? | 繼室成番唔曾 | Kai' shat› ‹shing ‹fán ‹'m ‹ts'ang? |
| 49. Of what place is your betrothed wife? | 配室成邊處呀 | P'úi' shat› ‹shing ‹pín ch'ü' á'? |
| 50. My wife has no energy for managing her affairs. | 渾家爲人軟弱 | Wan$^2$ ‹ká ‹wai ‹yan 'un yéuk$_2$. |
| 51. A spouse whose partner is dead, is said to have spilled the tea. | 失婚係打瀉茶 | Shat› ‹fan hai' 'tá sé' ‹ch'á. |

39. Husband and wife by separation act according to the rules of propriety, i. e. by duly maintaining the line of separation between each other, and each performing the alloted duties, they act as they are bound to do by the rules of propriety.

40. Water the garden, eat strength, i. e. living by the sweat of the brow; this is said of those who, in retirement, prefer labor to leisure.

44. *Mak lò* is a narrow pathway in the fields, traveled only by persons on foot, who pass by each other without stopping to bow or for any other civilities: when the feelings of husband and wife are alienated, they treat each other in the same cold and indifferent manner.

45, 46. New wife third morning returns to the door—of her own father and mother, to take final leave of them: new bride worships the hall this manner, i. e. in the hall, at a specified time, and in a prescribed manner, she does obeisance to her new relatives.

47. The mean one of the inner apartment has passed away from the body several years since, i. e. she died a long time ago.

| | | |
|---|---|---|
| 52. My second betrothed is yet but a green girl! | 填房係青頭女 | ꜁T'ín ꜁fóng hai$^{2}$ ꜀ts'ing ꜁t'au ꜂nü. |
| 53. The equal wife is not a concubine. | 平妻唔係妾侍 | ꜁P'ing ꜀ts'ai ꜁'m hai$^{2}$ ts'íp꜅ shí$^{2}$. |
| 54. My wife has a slight knowledge of letters. | 拙荊頗識吓字 | Chüt꜅ ꜀king ꜂p'ó shik꜅ ꜂há tsz'$^{2}$. |
| 55. A wife succeeding the first is the same as the first. | 續絃妻如正室 | Tsuk$_{2}$ ꜁ín ꜀ts'ai ꜁ü ching' shat꜅. |
| 56. Sir, has your honorable lady joy? | 尊夫人有喜未 | ꜀Tsün ꜀fú ꜁yan ꜂yau ꜂hí mí$^{2}$? |
| 57. So worthy a lady surely ought to be loved. | 如夫人應寵愛 | ꜁Ü ꜀fú ꜁yau ꜀ying ꜂ch'ung oi'. |
| 58. Married again she will prove a hard stepmother. | 番頭婆使秤砣 | ꜀Fán ꜁t'au ꜁p'ó ꜂shai ch'ing' ꜁t'ó. |
| 59. Has your worthy lady yet tasted of the ginger and wine? | 令寵有薑酒飲未 | Ling$^{2}$ ꜂ch'ung ꜂yau ꜀kéung ꜂tsau ꜂yam mí$^{2}$? |
| 60. The marriage of husband and wife in this life, results from causes that existed in a preceding one. | 前世有緣今世結 | ꜁Ts'ín shai' ꜂yau ꜁ün, ꜀kam shai' kít꜅. |
| 61. When the husband has great riches the wife will be honored. | 夫婿有錢妻就貴 | ꜀Fú ꜂sai ꜂yau ꜁ts'ín, ꜀ts'ai tsau$^{2}$ kwai'. |
| 62. The wife is not to be regarded as criminal; if she do wrong the husband must answer for the same. | 婦人無罪罪在夫男 | ꜂Fú ꜁yan ꜁mò tsúi$^{2}$, tsúi$^{2}$ tsoi$^{2}$ ꜀fú ꜁nám. |
| 63. (a) Memoirs of several ladies of antiquity. | 典故列女傳 | ꜂Tín kú' lít$_{2}$ ꜂Nü Chün$^{2}$. |
| (b) Part first; Book first. | 卷之一上 | ꜂Kün ꜀chí yat꜅; Shéung$^{2}$. |

51. After a couple are affianced, if one dies before the nuptials are celebrated, the survivor is said to have spilled the tea, because the nuptial presents, of which tea is a part, have been exchanged in vain.

52. *T'ín fóng*, to fill the house, denotes the person who is to occupy the place in the family vacated by the decease of the first wife.

53. A concubine is sometimes unwilling to be known under her proper designation, and requires her attendants to call her *p'íng ts'ai*, and to say to visitors that *'m hai ts'íp shí*, which is in fact an imposition.

54. *Chüt* is illiterate; *king* is one whose head is adorned with flowers, etc.; the two words are used by the literary gentleman as a humble designation of his wife.

55. *Ín* is the string of a musical instrument, *tsuk* is to splice; the wife who succeeds the first after her decease, is every way her equal.

56, 57. *Fú yan* is a term of respect applied to wives of official people, and by courtesy to those of private gentlemen: *yau hí* having joy refers to the joy of being a father—the joy of joys with the Chinese, especially in case of the first son and heir: *ü fú yan* is a complimental appellation of a concubine.

58. *Fán t'au p'ó* is a woman who has married a second time, and such an one it is supposed, *shai* will use, *ch'ing t'ó* the weight of the steelyards—to throw at her children-in-law.

59. The idea is the same as in No. 56; *kéung* and *tsau*, ginger and wine, are said to be used plentifully immediately before parturition, under the impression that they will give strength to both mother and child.

62. It is the bounden duty of the husband, as the regulator of his wife, to see that she always keeps in her place and does her duty; hence his liability to be punished in her stead.

(c) In the education of females, the first object of attention is their virtue; the second is their language; the third is their deportment; and the fourth, their appropriate work.

女子之學一曰婦德二曰婦言三曰婦容四曰婦工

‘Nü ‘tsz’ ‚chí hók,, yat, üt, ‘fú tak,; í² üt, ‘fú ‚ín; ‚sám üt, ‘fú ‚yung; sz” üt, ‘fú ‚kung.

(d) Confucius said, Let the woman be in subjection to the man.

孔子曰婦人伏於人也

‘Hung ‘tsz’ üt,, ‘Fú ‚yan fuk, ‚ü ‚yan ‘yá.

(e) Therefore, she has no part in the direction of affairs; but there are three whom she must obey;—while under her paternal roof she must obey her father; after marriage she must obey her husband; and when he is dead she must obey her [eldest] son; in no case may she presume to follow her own will.

是故無專制之義有三從之道在家從父適人從夫夫死從子無所敢自遂也

Shí² kú’, ‚mò ‚chün chai’ ‚chí í²; ‘yau ‚sám ‚ts‘ung ‚chí tò²; tsoi² ‚ká ‚ts‘ung fú²; shik, ‚yan ‚ts‘ung ‚fú; ‚fú ‘sz’ ‚ts‘ung ‘tsz’; ‚mò ‘shó ‘kòm tsz’² sui² ‘yá.

(f) There are seven causes for putting away a wife; namely, disobedience to her parents, barrenness, wantonness, jealousy, incurable disease, loquacity, and thievishness.

婦有七去不順父母去無子去淫去妬去有惡疾去多言去竊盜去

‘Fú ‘yau ts‘át, h‘ü’; pat, shun² fú² ‘mò h‘ü’; ‚mò ‘tsz’ h‘ü’; ‚yam h‘ü’; tò’ h‘ü’; ‘yau ók, tsat, h‘ü’; ‚tó ‚ín h‘ü’; sít, tò² h‘ü’.

(g) There are five things which prevent a woman from being taken as a wife; if she belong to a vicious family, a rebellious family, to one whose members have suffered capitally, to one afflicted with incurable disease, or if she be the eldest child and has no brother,—in these several circumstances, she is not to be taken.

女有五不取逆家子不取亂家子不取世有刑人不取世有惡疾不取喪父長子不取

‘Nü ‘yau ‘’ng pat, ‘ts‘ü; yik, ‚ká ‘tsz’ pat, ‘ts‘ü; lün² ‚ká ‘tsz’ pat, ‘ts‘ü; shai’ ‘yau ‚ying ‚yan pat, ‘ts‘ü; shai’ ‘yau ók, tsat, pat, ‘ts‘ü; sóng’ fú² ‚chéung ‘tsz’ pat, ‘ts‘ü.

63. (a) This is the title of a small work in two volumes: *tin kú* refers to the persons—those of classical and ancient times: *chün* biographical memoirs.

(b) *Kün* is equivalent to book or chapter, used very commonly in Chinese works, to mark the large divisions into which they are arranged: the first volume is divided into three parts, the first is termed *shéung*, the second *chung*, and the third *há*.

(c) *Yat üt*, &c. are terms used in specifying particulars, as, in the first place, in the second place, &c; or to denote order, as, the first, the second: this, and paragraphs *(d) (e) (f)*, are selected from the first page of the first volume.

(g) This and the following paragraph are from the *Siú Hók*, or Primary Lessons; see *Kün í*, or Part second, in the last section of chapter 3d, which treats of the line of separation between husband and wife.

| | | |
|---|---|---|
| (*h*) There are three cases in which she is not to be divorced; if the family whence she was taken does not exist for her to return to, if she has been in mourning three years, or if her husband once poor has become rich;—in these several circumstances, she must not be put away. | 有三不去有所取無所歸不去與更三年喪不去前貧賤後冨貴不去 | ʻYau ‹sám pat› h'ü'; ʻyau ʻshó ʻts'ü ‚mò ʻshó ‹kwai pat› h'ü'; ʻü ‹kang ‹sám ‚nín ‹sóng pat› h'ü'; ‚ts'ín ‚p'an tsín² hau² fú' kwai' pat› h'ü'. |

(*h*) If she has been in mourning three years for her husband's parents, the period fixed by law. By comparing the various reasons here given for divorcing, refusing, or retaining a woman as a wife, it is very apparent that Chinese moralists never thought of elevating females above the ignorant and degraded state in which they found them.

## Section Fifth.

# OF BROTHERS.

## 兄弟類第五章
‹Hing tai² lui²; tai² ʻ'ng ‹cheung.

| | | |
|---|---|---|
| 1. Brothers having the same parents. | 同胞兄弟 | ‚T'ung ‹páu ‹hing tai². |
| 2. Cousins having the same grandfather. | 嫡堂〃〃 | Tik› ‚t'óng ‹hing tai². |
| 3. Cousins having the same great-grandfather. | 疎堂〃〃 | ‹Shó ‚t'óng ‹hing tai². |
| 4. Cousins who have the same uncles. | 叔伯〃〃 | Shuk› pák› ‹hing tai². |
| 5. Cousins having the same great-great-grandfather. | 同房〃〃 | ‚T'ung ‚fóng ‹hing tai². |
| 6. Cousins belonging to the same family. | 族中〃〃 | Tsuk‚ ‹chung ‹hing tai². |

### *Notes and Explanations.*

HING, formed of *mouth* and *man*, denotes the elder brother, who has a right to speak and to direct: *tai* is a successor, a younger brother: this compound term is used with much latitude, being applied to kinsmen of almost every degree of relationship, and to persons who are engaged in the same profession and pursuit.

1. *Páu*, formed of *flesh* and an *envelop*, (perhaps that which surrounds the fetus,) denotes children born of the same parents, or uterine brothers.

2, 3. *Tóng*, temple or hall, is used for those who dwell in the same hall; *tik*, formed of *woman* and *equal*, denotes those who have one and the same grandfather, and are cousins by blood: *shó t'óng hing tai*, extended hall brothers, are the sons of the *tik tóng*.

4. Younger and older uncles, older and younger brothers, are the same as No. 2; they are paternal cousins.

5. *T'ung fóng*, same room brothers, are those who spring from one and the same branch, or progenitor.

6. *Tsuk chung* is used in a more comprehensive sense than the preceding, and includes those who have the same family name: they are fellow-clansmen.

| | | |
|---|---|---|
| 7. He is my brother by adoption. | 過繼兄弟 | Kwó꜄ kai꜄ ꜀hing tai$^{2}$. |
| 8. Brothers who have different surnames. | 異姓丨丨 | Í$^{2}$ sing꜄ ꜀hing tai$^{2}$. |
| 9. Brothers who are closely bound to each other. | 結義丨丨 | Kít꜆ í$^{2}$ ꜀hing tai$^{2}$. |
| 10. Brothers who have passed through trials together. | 過江丨丨 | Kwó꜄ ꜀kóng ꜀hing tai$^{2}$. |
| 11. Brothers in trials and afflictions. | 患難丨丨 | Wán$^{2}$ nán$^{2}$ ꜀hing tai$^{2}$. |
| 12. Brothers who are living on terms of intimacy. | 換帖丨丨 | Ún$^{2}$ t'íp꜆ ꜀hing tai$^{2}$. |
| 13. Brothers who are pledged for each other's support. | 拜會丨丨 | Pái꜄ úi$^{2}$ ꜀hing tai$^{2}$. |
| 14. Brothers without sincere affection for each other. | 酒肉丨丨 | ꜂Tsau yuk꜇ ꜀hing tai$^{2}$. |
| 15. Love one another as brothers. | 友于丨丨 | ꜃Yau ꜁yü ꜀hing tai$^{2}$. |
| 16. Friends through successive generations. | 世兄世丨 | Shai꜄ ꜀hing shai꜄ tai$^{2}$. |
| 17. Elder and younger brothers by adoption. | 蘭丨蘭丨 | ꜁Lán ꜀hing ꜁lán tai$^{2}$. |
| 18. Good and affectionate brothers. | 宜丨宜丨 | ꜁Í ꜀hing ꜁í tai$^{2}$. |
| 19. The same to each other as brothers. | 如丨如丨 | ꜁Ü ꜀hing ꜁ü tai$^{2}$. |
| 20. The eldest brother acts in the father's stead. | 長丨當父 | ꜂Chéung ꜀hing tóng꜄ fú$^{2}$. |
| 21. The elder brother walks foremost. | 阿哥先行 | Á꜄ ꜀kó ꜀sín ꜁hang. |
| 22. The younger brother follows after him. | 細佬跟尾 | Sai꜄ ꜃ló ꜀kan ꜃mí. |
| 23. The lesser portion belongs to the youngest brothers. | 細佬少的 | Sai꜄ ꜃ló ꜂shíú tik꜆. |
| 24. The larger portion belongs to the eldest brother. | 大佬多的 | Tái$^{2}$ ꜃ló ꜀tó tik꜆. |

7. My adopted brother is used by the legitimate son when speaking of one who has been adopted by his parents.

8. This is applied, not only to those who are brothers by blood, born of the same mother by different fathers, but to members of a society, and also to intimate friends.

9. *Kít í*, bound in righteousness, is applied to friends who are pledged to defend each other: this pledge is often given before an altar.

10, 11. *Kwó kóng*, across the rivers, i. e. in all circumstances, and in all places, and in all seasons, however calamitous, remaining true to each other: *wán nán*, trials and afflictions, convey the same idea.

12. Exchanged card brothers, i. e. friends who have exchanged cards, and who by their frequent intercourse are living on terms of intimacy.

13. Worshiped associate brothers, i. e. friends who have associated, and worshiped before an altar in token of their attachment to one another.

17. These are so called by the legitimate sons of the father who has adopted them; the son calls those older than himself *lán hing*, and the younger *lán tai*: here *lán*, the name of a fragrant and beautiful flower, the *Aglaia odorata*, has been substituted for *kai*, because the latter, in this connection, has become infamous.

20. This is done only after the decease of the father: in like manner, after the decease of the mother, the eldest daughter succeeds to her place in the management of domestic affairs.

| | | |
|---|---|---|
| 25. Brothers separated from each other. | 手足分離 | ʿShau tsuk› ‹fan ˏlí. |
| 26. Senior brothers take precedence of the junior. | 兄先弟後 | ‹Hing ‹sín tai$^{2}$ hau$^{2}$. |
| 27. Elder brothers should be kind, and the younger ones respectful. | 丨友丨恭 | ‹Hing ʿyau tai$^{2}$ ‹kung. |
| 28. Brothers disagreeing among themselves. | 丨弟唔和 | ‹Hing tai$^{2}$ ˏ'm ˏwó. |
| 29. Calling each other brothers. | 丨丨相稱 | ‹Hing tai$^{2}$ ‹séung ‹ch'ing. |
| 30. Brothers living in perfect harmony. | 丨丨怡怡 | ‹Hing tai$^{2}$ ˏí ˏí. |
| 31. Brothers living together without contention. | 丨丨無故 | ‹Hing tai$^{2}$ ˏmò kú'. |
| 32. Patrimony divided among brothers. | 丨丨分家 | ‹Hing tai$^{2}$ ‹fan ‹ká. |
| 33. Brothers obtaining honors at the same examination. | 丨丨同科 | ‹Hing tai$^{2}$ ˏt'ung ‹fó. |
| 34. Brothers ought to live in harmony and concord. | 丨丨要和睦 | ‹Hing tai$^{2}$ íú' ˏwó muk$_{2}$. |
| 35. Brothers help and support each other. | 丨丨相扶持 | ‹Hing tai$^{2}$ ‹séung ˏfú ˏch'í. |
| 36. The brothers are several in number. | 丨丨有幾人 | ‹Hing tai$^{2}$ ʿyau ʿkí ˏyan. |
| 37. Brothers having different countenances. | 丨丨不同貌 | ‹Hing tai$^{2}$ pat› ˏt'ung máu$^{2}$. |
| 38. The hearts of brothers are all different. | 丨丨心各向 | ‹Hing tai$^{2}$ ˏsam kók› héung›. |
| 39. Brothers, the members of one family. | 丨丨一家親 | ‹Hing tai$^{2}$ yat› ‹ká ‹ts'an. |
| 40. The older brother cannot take care of the younger. | 丨不能顧弟 | ‹Hing pat› ˏnang kú' tai$^{2}$. |
| 41. They are like truly affectionate brothers. | 如果好兄丨 | ˏÜ ʿkwó ʿhò ‹hing tai$^{2}$. |
| 42. Cousins within the fifth generation. | 五服內丨丨 | ʿ'Ng fuk$_{2}$ noi$^{2}$ ‹hing tai$^{2}$. |
| 43. Brothers with the same father but different mothers. | 同父各母兄弟 | ˏT'ung fú$^{2}$ kók› ʿmò ‹hing tai$^{2}$. |
| 44. Cousins belonging to the same generation. | 同班輩嘅丨丨 | ˏT'ung ‹pán púi' ké' ‹hing tai$^{2}$. |
| 45. An only son, without any brothers. | 孤獨仔冇丨丨 | ‹Kú tuk$_{2}$ ʿtsai ʿmò ‹hing tai$^{2}$. |
| 46. No elder brother above, no younger brother below me. | 上無丨下無丨 | Shéung$^{2}$ ˏmò ‹hing, há$^{2}$ ˏmò tai$^{2}$. |
| 47. Think on the affection which subsists among brothers. | 念在丨弟之情 | Ním$^{2}$ tsoi$^{2}$ ‹hing tai$^{2}$ ‹chí ˏts'ing. |

24. This is not so determined by the laws of the empire; the phrase merely intimates that it is natural and right to give precedence to the oldest, not only in matters of ceremony, but in the common intercourse of life.

25. The hands and feet are used by metonymy to denote brothers, who are often compared to them. See Chap. II, Sec. vii: 83.

42. *Fuk* here has a secondary meaning derived from the custom of wearing badges of mourning for each other, which is done by those within five generations.

44. This includes those who stand in one and the same generation, having descended from one and the same ancestor.

| | | |
|---|---|---|
| 48. His brothers contend for the patrimony. | 佢丨弟爭家產 | ʻK'ui ˏhing tai$^{2}$ ˏchang ˏká ʻch'án. |
| 49. Brothers with the same heart and united strength. | 兄弟同心協力 | ˏHing tai$^{2}$ ˏt'ung ˏsam híp lik. |
| 50. All men have brothers, but I alone have none. | 人皆有丨丨我<br>獨無 | ˏYan ˏkái ʻyau ˏhing tai$^{2}$ ʻngó tuk ˏmò. |
| 51. All who dwell within the four seas are brothers. | 四海之內皆兄<br>弟也 | Sz$^{2}$ ʻhoi ˏchí noi$^{2}$ ˏkái ˏhing tai$^{2}$ ʻyá. |
| 52. The elder brother not acting the part of an elder brother, and the younger not acting the part of a younger. | 丨唔似丨弟唔<br>似弟 | ˏHing ˏ'm ʻtsz' ˏhing, tai$^{2}$ ˏ'm ʻtsz' tai$^{2}$. |
| 53. To dwell with a friend is easy, to dwell with a brother is difficult. | 處朋友易處丨<br>弟難 | ʻCh'ü ˏp'ang ʻyau í$^{2}$, ʻch'ü ˏhing tai$^{2}$ ˏnán. |
| 54. If the elder brother loves the younger, the latter will honor the former. | 兄愛其弟弟必<br>敬其兄 | ˏHing oi$^{2}$ ˏk'í tai$^{2}$, tai$^{2}$ pít king$^{2}$ ˏk'í ˏhing. |
| 55. While you have plenty of good living, there will be no lack of friends; but when calamities come, where will there be one to help you? | 有酒有肉多丨<br>弟患難何曾見<br>一人 | ʻYau ʻtsau ʻyau yuk ˏtó ˏhing tai$^{2}$; wán$^{2}$ nán$^{2}$ ˏhó ˏts'ang kin$^{2}$ yat ˏyan? |
| 56. (*a*) In early times there lived in the department of Pingyéung, in Shánsai, a wise personage, called the monarch Yíú. This monarch most ardently loved his kindred. | 當初山西平陽<br>府有個聖人叫<br>做堯帝這個堯<br>帝最是疼愛他<br>族人的 | ˏTóng ˏch'ó ˏShán ˏsai ˏPing ˏyéung ʻfú, ʻyau kó$^{2}$ shing$^{2}$ ˏyan, kíú$^{2}$ tsò$^{2}$ ˏYíú tai$^{2}$. Ché$^{2}$ kó$^{2}$ ˏYíú tai$^{2}$ tsui$^{2}$ shí$^{2}$ t'ung$^{2}$ oi$^{2}$ ˏt'á tsuk$^{2}$ ˏyan tik. |
| (*b*) In an ancient book it is well said, If people truly honor and respect their ancestors, then there will be no | 古書上說的好<br>人若果然尊敬 | ʻKú ˏshü shéung$^{2}$ shüt tik ʻhò; ˏyan yéuk ʻkwó ˏín |

50, 51. The first of these phrases was uttered by one of the disciples of Confucius; the second was given by the sage in reply, intending to cheer his desponding mind; this expression, 'within the four seas,' is a descriptive term for the empire, which in ancient times was supposed to be thus surrounded.

(*a*) This extract forms a continuation of that which is given at the end of the third section of this chapter: *Shánsai*, one of the most ancient provinces, is situated westward from the capital Pakking; *Pingyéung fú* is a few miles east of the Yellow river, near the centre of the province. The place is noticeable as being the residence of the progenitors of the nation from very ancient times.

(*b*) *Tsò* remote ancestors, and *tsung* immediate progenitors, sometimes denote the collective body of ancestors, or the great progenitor, of a family; the context and the sequel of this extract require such a rendering of the two terms.

one who does not ardently love his kindred.

祖宗再没有一個不疼愛族人的

‹tsün king' ʻtsò ‹tsung, tsoi' mút› ʻyau yat› kó' pat› t'ung' oi' tsuk› ‹yan tik›.

(*c*) Why am I ardently to love my kindred? Because these kindred, although some of them are more nearly and others are more remotely related to me, are all found, on examination, to be the descendants from my own great progenitor. Allowing you that we are several tens in number, or even several hundreds, we are yet all one.

爲甚麽族人我要疼愛他呢這些族人雖然有親門兒的有遠門兒的究竟都是我一個祖宗傳留下來凴你幾十丁幾百丁却總是一個人

Wai² sham² ‹mó tsuk› ‹yan ʻngó fú' t'ung' oi' ‹t'á ‹ní? Ché' ‹sé tsuk› ‹yan, ‹sui ‹in ʻyau ‹ts'an ‹mún ‹í tik›, ʻyau ʻün ‹mún ‹í tik›, kau' ʻking ‹tò shí² ʻngó yat› kó' ʻtsò ‹tsung ‹ch'ün ‹lau há² ‹loi. ‹P'ang ʻní ʻkí shap› ‹ting, ʻkí pák› ‹ting, kéuk› ʻtsung shí² yat› kó' ‹yan.

(*d*) We are just like water which is divided into streams. Look at a fountain; as it flows onward, it divides into several streams, or into several tens of streams. On examination, however, these are found to come from one single fountain, and not from two different sources.

就如水有分派的一般你看一股泉流將下去分作幾條分作幾十條究竟都是這一股兒泉的水并不曾有兩股水

Tsau² ‹ü ʻshui ʻyau ‹fan p'ái' tik› yat› ‹pún. ʻNí hón' yat› ʻkú ‹ts'ün ‹lau ‹tséung há² h'ü² ‹fan tsók› ʻkí ‹t'iú, ‹fan tsók› ʻkí shap› ‹t'iú. Kau' ʻking ‹tò shí² ché' yat› ʻkú ‹í ‹ts'ün tik› ʻshui, ping² pat› ‹ts'ang ʻyau ʻléung ʻkú ʻshui.

(*e*) In like manner we resemble a tree, with its leaves and branches. Look at a tree; as it grows and rises upwards, it has a thousand branches and ten thousand leaves. Yet on examination all these are found to have sprung forth from one single trunk,

又如樹木有枝葉的一般你看一顆樹長將起來千枝萬葉究竟都是一個根兒上發出來的

Yau² ‹ü shü² muk›, ʻyau ‹chí íp› tik› yat› ‹pún. ʻNí hón' yat› ʻfó shü², ʻchéung ‹tséung ʻhí ‹loi, ‹ts'ín ‹chí mán² íp›. Kau' ʻking ‹tò shí² yat› kó' ‹kan ‹í shéung² fát› ch'ut› ‹loi tik›.

(*f*) So likewise it is with these kindred; they are all (offspring of) my one great

既然這些族人都是我祖宗一

Kí' ‹in ché' ‹sé tsuk› ‹yan ‹tò shí² ʻngó ʻtsò ‹tsung yat› kó'

(*d*) *Kú* a division is here used as the distinctive epithet of a fountain; *yat kú ts'ün* is simply, a fountain.

progenitor. This one progenitor is the body; I, with these kindred, are its two hands and two feet, the ten fingers on the hands, and the ten toes on the feet, with the ears, eyes, lips, and nose.

個人祖宗就是一個身子我和這些族人就是兩手兩脚手上的十個指頭脚上的十個指頭頭上的耳朶眼睛嘴鼻子的一般了

ˏyan. ʽTsò ‹tsung tsau' shí' yat› kó' ‹shan ʽtsz'; ʽngó ˏwó ché' ‹sé tsuk, ˏyan, tsau' shí' ʽléung ʽshau ʽléung kéuk›, ʽshau shéung' tik› shap, kó' ʽchí ˏt'au, kéuk› shéung' tik› shap, kó' ʽchí ˏt'au, ˏt'au shéung' tik› ʽí ʽtó, ʽngán ‹tsíng, ʽtsui, pí' ʽtsz' tik› yat› ‹pún ʽlíú.

(*g*) Reflect on this a little. Suppose, for illustration, that an ulcer breaks out on some one part of my body; or suppose I wrench my hand, or sprain my leg; would it not be hard to say that the whole body will be unaffected?

你們想一想假如我身上有一處兒生個瘡或者閃了手跌了腿渾身上難道受用麼

ʽNí ˏmún ʽséung yat› ʽséung. ʽKá ˏü; ʽngó ‹shan shéung' ʽyau yat› ch'ü' ˏí ‹shang kó' ‹ch'óng, wák, ʽché ʽshím ʽlíú ʽshau, tít› ʽlíú ʽt'úi, wan' ‹shan shéung' ˏnán tò' shau' yung' ‹mó?

(*h*) So it is among your kindred; if you openly involve them in difficulties, cozen them, and cause them to suffer, would it not be hard to say that you will be free from suffering?

你們若是在族人跟前陷害他鑾騙他叫他不得受用難道你就得受用麼

ʽNí ˏmún yéuk, shí' tsoi' tsuk, ˏyan ‹kan ˏts'ín hám' hoi' ‹t'á, ‹ò p'in' ‹t'á, kíú' ‹t'á pat› tak› shau' yung', ˏnán tò' ʽní tsau' tak› shau' yung' ‹mó?

(*i*) Therefore men ought most ardently to love their kindred. (For it is with them,) just as it is with one's body; if one part is pained, then every part is pained; and if one part is irritated, then the whole is irritated. Such is harmony and concord among kindred.

所以人要着實疼愛族人就如我一個身子一處疼便處處都疼有一處癢便處處都癢這纔是和睦宗族呢

ʽShó ʽí ˏyan íú' chéuk› shat, t'ung' oi' tsuk, ˏyan. Tsau' ˏü ʽngó yat› kó' ‹shan ʽtsz', ʽyau yat› ch'ü' t'ung', pín' ch'ü' ch'ü' ‹tò t'ung', ʽyau yat› ch'ü' ʽyéung pín' ch'ü' ch'ü' ‹tò ʽyéung. Ché' ˏts'oi shí' ˏwó muk, ‹tsung tsuk, ‹ní.

(*g*) *Ká ü* to borrow a comparison, or suppose a case for the sake of illustration: *nán tò*, hard to say, is used here, as often elsewhere, as an interrogative form of speech, to mark a strong negation.

## Section Sixth.

# OF NEAR AND DISTANT RELATIONS.

## 內外親類第六章
Noi$^2$ ngoi$^2$ ‹ts'an lui$^2$; tai$^2$ luk͵ ‹chéung.

| | | |
|---|---|---|
| 1. Great-great-grandfather. | 高祖 | ‹Kò ʻtsò. |
| 2. Great-great-grandmother. | 高祖母 | ‹Kò ʻtsò ʻmò. |
| 3. Great grandfather. | 曾祖 | ‹Tsang ʻtsò. |
| 4. Great-grandmother. | 曾祖母 | ‹Tsang ʻtsò ʻmò. |
| 5. Great-grandfather. | 太公 | T'ái' ‹kung. |
| 6. Great-grandmother. | 太婆 | T'ái' ͺp'ó. |
| 7. Grandfather. | 祖父 | ʻTsò fú$^2$. |
| 8. Grandfather. | 阿公 | Á' ‹kung. |
| 9. Grandmother. | 祖母 | ʻTsò ʻmò. |
| 10. Grandmother. | 阿婆 | Á' ͺp'ó. |
| 11. Father. | 父親 | Fú$^2$ ‹ts'an. |
| 12. Mother. | 母親 | ʻMò ‹ts'an. |
| 13. Father's concubine. | 庶母 | Shü' ʻmò. |
| 14. Father's concubine. | 阿姐 | Á' ʻtsé. |
| 15. Sons. | 兒子 | ͺÍ ʻtsz'. |
| 16. Daughter-in-law. | 媳婦 | Sik͵ ʻfú. |
| 17. Daughters. | 女兒 | ʻNü ͺí. |
| 18. My daughter. | 小女 | ʻSíú ʻnü. |
| 19. Son-in-law. | 女婿 | ʻNü sai'. |

### *Notes and Explanations.*

***Noi ngoi ts'an***, inner and outer relations, might embrace the kindred relations of every degree, both near and remote; all the kith and kin of an individual. This section includes most of the terms in common use, omitting, however, a part of those synonyms which have been already given.

13, 14. These two terms are used by children when speaking to or of their father's concubine: the latter is the most frequently used when speaking to her.

| | | |
|---|---|---|
| 20. Grandson's wife. | 孫媳婦 | ‹Sün sik› ‘fú. |
| 21. Granddaughter. | 孫女 | ‹Sün ‘nü. |
| 22. Granddaughter's husband. | 孫婿 | ‹Sün sai’. |
| 23. Great-grandson. | 曾孫 | ‹Tsang ‹sün. |
| 24. Great-grandson's wife. | 曾孫媳婦 | ‹Tsang ‹sün sik› ‘fú. |
| 25. Great-great-grandson. | 玄孫 | ‚Ün ‹sün. |
| 26. Great-great-grandson's wife. | 玄孫媳婦 | ‚Ün ‹sün sik› ‘fú. |
| 27. Elder brother. | 大哥 | Tái$^{2}$ ‹kó. |
| 28. Elder brother. | 大佬 | Tái$^{2}$ ‘lò. |
| 29. Elder brother's wife. | 大嫂 | Tái$^{2}$ ‘sò. |
| 30. Elder brother's wife. | 阿嫂 | Á’ ‘sò. |
| 31. Younger brother. | 細佬 | Sai’ ‘lò. |
| 32. Younger brother's wife. | 弟婦 | Tai$^{2}$ ‘fú. |
| 33. Younger brother's wife. | 細嬸 | Sai’ ‘sham. |
| 34. Elder sister. | 姊 | ‘Tsz’. |
| 35. Elder sister's husband. | 姊丈 | ‘Tsz’ chéung$^{2}$. |
| 36. Elder sister's husband. | 姊夫 | ‘Tsz’ ‹fú. |
| 37. Elder sister's husband. | 姊婿 | ‘Tsz’ sai’. |
| 38. Elder sister's husband. | 外兄 | Ngoi$^{2}$ ‹hing. |
| 39. Younger sister. | 妹 | Múi$^{2}$. |
| 40. Younger sister's husband. | 妹夫 | Múi$^{2}$ ‹fú. |
| 41. Younger sister's husband. | 妹丈 | Múi$^{2}$ chéung$^{2}$. |
| 42. Younger sister's husband. | 妹婿 | Múi$^{2}$ sai’. |
| 43. Father's elder brother. | 伯父 | Pák› fú$^{2}$. |
| 44. Father's elder brother's wife. | 伯母 | Pák› ‘mò. |
| 45. Father's younger brother. | 叔父 | Shuk› fú$^{2}$. |
| 46. Father's younger brother's wife. | 阿嬸 | Á’ ‘sham. |

34. This is sometimes read *tsé*, but the form of the character remains unchanged; and *tsz’* is deemed the correct pronunciation.

| | | |
|---|---|---|
| 47. Father's elder sister. | 姑母 | ꜀Kú ꜂mò. |
| 48. Father's younger sister. | 姑姊 | ꜀Kú ꜂tsz'. |
| 49. Father's sister's husband. | 丨丈 | ꜀Kú chéung꜃. |
| 50. Nephew; or brother's son. | 姪 | Chat꜆. |
| 51. Nephew's wife. | 姪婦 | Chat꜆ ꜂fú. |
| 52. Niece; or brother's daughter. | 姪女 | Chat꜆ ꜂nü. |
| 53. Niece's husband. | 丨婿 | Chat꜆ sai꜃. |
| 54. Nephew's son. | 丨孫 | Chat꜆ ꜀sün. |
| 55. Nephew's son's wife. | 丨孫婦 | Chat꜆ ꜀sün ꜂fú. |
| 56. Nephew's daughter. | 丨孫女 | Chat꜆ ꜀sün ꜂nü. |
| 57. Nephew's daughter's husband. | 丨孫婿 | Chat꜆ ꜀sün sai꜃. |
| 58. Father's paternal elder uncle. | 伯公 | Pák꜆ ꜀kung. |
| 59. Father's paternal elder uncle's wife. | 伯婆 | Pák꜆ ꜁p'ó. |
| 60. Father's paternal younger uncle. | 叔公 | Shuk꜆ ꜀kung. |
| 61. Father's paternal younger uncle's wife. | 丨婆 | Shuk꜆ ꜁p'ó. |
| 62. Maternal grandfather. | 外祖 | Ngoi꜃ ꜂tsò. |
| 63. Maternal grandfather. | 外公 | Ngoi꜃ ꜀kung. |
| 64. Maternal grandmother. | 外祖母 | Ngoi꜃ ꜂tsò ꜂mò. |
| 65. Maternal grandmother. | 外婆 | Ngoi꜃ ꜁p'ó. |
| 66. Maternal grandfather's elder brother. | 外伯公 | Ngoi꜃ pák꜆ ꜀kung. |
| 67. Maternal uncles. | 母舅 | ꜂Mò ꜂k'au. |
| 68. Maternal uncles. | 舅父 | ꜂K'au fú꜃. |
| 69. Maternal uncle's wife. | 妗母 | ꜂K'am ꜂mò. |
| 70. Maternal uncle's wife. | 舅母 | ꜂K'au ꜂mò. |
| 71. Mother's elder sister. | 姨母 | ꜁I ꜂mò. |
| 72. Mother's younger sister. | 丨姐 | ꜁Í ꜂tsé. |
| 73. Mother's sister's husband. | 丨丈 | ꜁Í chéung꜃. |
| 74. Maternal grandmother's sister. | 丨婆 | ꜁Í ꜁p'ó. |
| 75. Maternal grandmother's sister's husband. | 姨公 | ꜁Í ꜀kung. |

| | | |
|---|---|---|
| 76. Paternal grandfather's sister's husband. | 丈公 | Chéung' ‹kung. |
| 77. Paternal grandfather's sister's husband. | 姑公 | ‹Kú ‹kung. |
| 78. Paternal grandfather's sister. | 姑婆 | ‹Kú ˏp'ó. |
| 79. Wife's father. | 岳丈 | Ngók, chéung'. |
| 80. Wife's father. | 外父 | Ngoi' fú'. |
| 81. Wife's mother. | 岳母 | Ngók, ʿmó. |
| 82. Wife's mother. | 外母 | Ngoi' ʿmò. |
| 83. Wife's elder brother. | 大舅 | Tái' ʿk'au. |
| 84. Wife's elder brother. | 內兄 | Noi' ‹hing. |
| 85. Wife's younger brother. | 細舅 | Sai' ʿk'au. |
| 86. Wife's younger brother. | 內弟 | Noi' tai'. |
| 87. Wife's brother's wife. | 妗娘 | ʿK'am ˏnéung. |
| 88. Wife's elder sister. | 大姨娘 | Tái' ˏí ˏnéung. |
| 89. Wife's elder sister's husband. | 襟兄 | ‹K'ám ‹hing. |
| 90. Wife's younger sister. | 細姨娘 | Sai' ˏí ˏnéung. |
| 91. Wife's younger sister's husband. | 襟弟 | ‹K'am tai'. |
| 92. Wife's nephew. | 內姪 | Noi' chat,. |
| 93. Wife's nephew's wife. | 內丨婦 | Noi' chat, ʿfú. |
| 94. Wife's niece. | 內丨女 | Noi' chat, ʿnü. |
| 95. Wife's niece's husband. | 內丨婿 | Noi' chat, sai'. |
| 96. Elder male cousins of different surname. | 表兄 | ʿPíú ‹hing. |
| 97. Wives of these elder cousins. | 表嫂 | ʿPíú ʿsò. |
| 98. Younger male cousins of different surname. | 表弟 | ʿPíú tai'. |
| 99. Wives of these younger cousins. | 表弟婦 | ʿPíú tai' ʿfú. |
| 100. Elder female cousins of different surname. | 表姊 | ʿPíú ʿtsz'. |
| 101. Husbands of these cousins. | 表姊夫 | ʿPíú ʿtsz' ‹fú. |

96—98. This includes, (1.) *kú píú hing*, my father's sisters' sons older than myself; (2.) *í píú hing*, my mother's sisters' sons older than myself; and (3.) *k'au píú hing*, my mother's brother's sons older than myself; *píú tai* includes the sons of the same families who are younger than myself.

| | | |
|---|---|---|
| 102. Younger female cousins of different surname. | 表妹 | ʻPíú múiʼ. |
| 103. Husbands of these cousins. | 表妹夫 | ʻPíú múiʼ ˏfú. |
| 104. Father's elder male cousins of different surname. | 表伯 | ʻPíú pákˎ. |
| 105. The wives of these cousins. | 表伯母 | ʻPíú pákˎ ʻmò. |
| 106. Father's younger male cousins of different surname. | 表叔 | ʻPíú shukˎ. |
| 107. Their wives. | 表丨母 | ʻPíú shukˎ ʻmò. |
| 108. Their wives. | 表嬸 | ʻPíú ʻsham. |
| 109. Father's elder female cousins of different surname. | 表姑母 | ʻPíú ˏkú ʻmò. |
| 110. Father's younger female cousins of different surname. | 丨姑姐 | ʻPíú ˏkú ʻtsé. |
| 111. Their husbands. | 丨丨丈 | ʻPíú ˏkú chéungʼ. |
| 112. Grandfather's elder male cousins of different surname. | 丨伯公 | ʻPíú pákˎ ˏkung. |
| 113. Their wives. | 丨伯婆 | ʻPíú pákˎ ˏp'ò. |
| 114. Grandfather's younger male cousins of different surname. | 丨叔公 | ʻPíú shukˎ ˏkung. |
| 115. Their wives. | 丨丨婆 | ʻPíú shukˎ ˏp'ò. |
| 116. Grandfather's female cousins of different surname. | 丨姑婆 | ʻPíú ˏkú ˏp'ò. |
| 117. Their respective husbands. | 丨丈公 | ʻPíú chéungʼ ˏkung. |
| 118. Cousin's son. | 丨姪 | ʻPíú chatˎ. |
| 119. Cousin's son's wife. | 丨丨婦 | ʻPíú chatˎ ʻfú. |
| 120. Cousin's daughter. | 丨丨女 | ʻPíú chatˎ ʻnü. |
| 121. Cousin's daughter's husband. | 丨丨壻 | ʻPíú chatˎ saiʼ. |
| 122. Cousin's grandson. | 丨丨孫 | ʻPíú chatˎ ˏsün. |
| 123. Cousin's grandson's wife. | 丨丨孫婦 | ʻPíú chatˎ ˏsün ʻfú. |
| 124. Cousin's granddaughter. | 丨丨孫女 | ʻPíú chatˎ ˏsün ʻnü. |
| 125. Cousin's granddaughter's husband. | 表丨孫壻 | ʻPíú chatˎ ˏsün saiʼ. |
| 126. Sister's son. | 外甥 | Ngoiʼ ˏshang. |
| 127. Sister's son's wife. | 外甥婦 | Ngoiʼ ˏshang ʻfú. |
| 128. Sister's daughter. | 外甥女 | Ngoiʼ ˏshang ʻnü. |

118—125. The descendants here mentioned are all on the mother's side, who, when she marries, merges her own surname in that of her husband.

| | | |
|---|---|---|
| 129. Sister's daughter's husband. | 外甥婿 | Ngoi² ‹shang saiʼ. |
| 130. Sister's grandson. | 外甥孫 | Ngoi² ‹shang ‹sün. |
| 131. Sister's grandson's wife. | 外丨丨婦 | Ngoi² ‹shang ‹sün ʻfú. |
| 132. Father's maternal uncle. | 舅公 | ʻK‘au ‹kung. |
| 133. Father's maternal uncle's wife. | 妗婆 | ʻK‘am ˏp‘ó. |
| 134. Father's maternal grandfather. | 外太公 | Ngoi² t‘áiʼ ‹kung. |
| 135. Father's maternal grandmother. | 外太婆 | Ngoi² t‘áiʼ ˏp‘ó. |
| 136. Son's wife's father. | 親家 | ‹Ts‘an ‹ká. |
| 137. Son's wife's mother. | 親家母 | ‹Ts‘an ‹ká ʻmó. |
| 138. Son's wife's mother. | 親家奶 | ‹Ts‘an ‹ká ˏnái. |
| 139. Son's wife's grandfather. | 太親家 | T‘áiʼ ‹ts‘an ‹ká. |
| 140. Son's wife's grandfather. | 老姻翁 | ʻLò ˏyan ‹yung. |
| 141. Son's wife's grandmother. | 太姻母 | T‘áiʼ ‹yan ʻmò. |
| 142. Husband's elder brother. | 大伯 | Tái² pák›. |
| 143. Husband's elder brother. | 伯爺 | Pák› ˏyé. |
| 144. Husband's elder brother's wife. | 大伯母 | Tái² pák› ʻmò. |
| 145. Husband's younger brother. | 細叔 | Saiʼ shuk›. |
| 146. Husband's younger brother. | 叔爺 | Shuk› ˏyé. |
| 147. Husband's younger brother's wife. | 細嬸 | Saiʼ ʻsham. |
| 148. Husband's sister. | 姑娘 | ‹Kú ˏnéung. |
| 149. Husband's sister's husband. | 姑爺 | ‹Kú ˏyé. |

# CHAPTER IV.

# CLASSES OF MEN.

# 人品篇四

ˏYan ˋpan; ˏpʻín sz˝.

## Section First.

## OF SAGES.

## 聖人類第一章

Shingˋ ˏyan lui²; tai² yatˎ ˏchéung.

| | | |
|---|---|---|
| 1. Confucius is the chief of sages. | 至聖孔子 | Chíˋ shingˋ ˋHung ˋtsz. |
| 2. The maxims of the sages are wide-spreading as the ocean. | 聖謨洋洋 | Shingˋ ˏmò ˏyéung ˏyéung. |
| 3. The doctrines of the sages are profound as the abyss. | 丨道淵源 | Shingˋ tò² ˏün ˏyün. |
| 4. The virtue of the sages is lofty and sublime. | 丨德巍巍 | Shingˋ takˎ ˏngai ˏngai. |
| 5. The sages teach mankind. | 丨人教人 | Shingˋ ˏyan káuˋ ˏyan. |
| 6. [Confucius] is the teacher and pattern of ten thousand generations. | 爲萬世師表 | ˏWai mán² shaiˋ ˏsz ˋpiú. |
| 7. How great are the doctrines of the sages! | 大哉聖人之道 | Tái² ˏtsoi shingˋ ˏyan ˏchí tò²! |
| 8. The three sovereigns are called ancient sages. | 三皇號爲故聖 | ˏSám ˏwóng hò² ˏwai kúˋ shingˋ. |
| 9. The five monarchs are styled royal kings. | 五帝皆曰聖王 | ˋNg taiˋ ˏkái ütˎ shingˋ ˏwóng. |

### *Notes and Explanations.*

The classification here adopted is of the most general kind—several minor ones being disregarded: for example, all persons holding office in the national government are divided into nine *pan*, classes or ranks, which are subdivided into principal and secondary; another division ranges the whole community into four classes, namely, scholars, husbandmen, mechanics, and merchants.

1. The meaning of *shing* will be better understood by a careful inspection of the phrases in which it occurs, than from any formal definition; as an appellative it is used to denote a class of persons of the very highest order.

2—4. These are not consecutive extracts, but independent phrases; and require, therefore, to be considered separately.

| | | |
|---|---|---|
| 10. The early sages were Yíú, Shun, U, and T'óng. | 先聖堯舜禹湯 | ‹Sín shing' ‚Yíú, Shun$^2$, ʻÜ, ‹T'óng. |
| 11. The later sages were Man, Mò, and the prince of Chau. | 後丨文武周公 | Hau$^2$ shing' ‚Man, ʻMò, ‹Chau ‹kung. |
| 12. An age without sages and worthies is unstable. | 世無聖賢不立 | Shai' ‚mò shing' ‚ín pat› lap$_2$. |
| 13. The sages never yet were faultless. | 聖人未嘗無過 | Shing' ‚yan mí' ‚shéung ‚mò kwó'. |
| 14. The sages established rules for man's instruction. | 丨人立法教人 | Shing' ‚yan lap$_2$ fát› káu' ‚yan. |
| 15. Sages even are but men. | 丨人亦猶人矣 | Shing' ‚yan yik$_2$ ‚yau ‚yan ʻí. |
| 16. The government of sages is an unofficial rule. | 丨人之政不莅而治 | Shing' ‚yan ‹chí ching' pat› lí$^2$, ‚í chí$^2$. |
| 17. To the virtue of the sages nothing can be added. | 聖人之德無以加矣 | Shing' ‚yan ‹chí tak› ‚mò ʻí ‹ká ʻí. |
| 18. How vast are the doctrines of the sages! unchangeable through the lapse of ages. | 聖德悠悠百世不改 | Shing' tak› ‚yau ‚yau pák› shai' pat› ʻkoi! |
| 19. The sages are the messengers of heaven and earth. | 聖人者天地之使也 | Shing' ‚yan ʻché ‹t'ín tí$^2$ ‹chí ʻsz' ʻyá. |
| 20. The great and renovating:—this is called sage. | 大而化之之謂聖 | Tái$^2$ ‚í fá' ‹chí, ‹chi wai' shing'. |
| 21. The love of the sages towards mankind is seen in their virtuous conduct. | 丨人之愛人以德 | Shing' ‚yan ‹chí oi' ‚yan ʻi tak›. |
| 22. The sages at their birth are possessed of knowledge. | 聖人則生而知之 | Shing' ‚yan tsak› ‹shang ‚í ‹chí ‹chí. |
| 23. He, who looking upward comprehends the celestial phenomena, and downward perceives the terrestrial operations, is a sage. | 仰識天文俯明地理者聖也 | ʻYéung shik› ‹t'ín ‚man, ʻfú ‚ming tí' ʻlí ʻché, shing' ʻyá. |
| 24. The moral maxims of the early and the later sages are the same. | 先聖後丨其揆一也 | ‹Sín shing' hau$^2$ shing' ‚k'í ʻkw'ai yat› ʻyá. |
| 25. Confucius said, The people of the west have sages. | 孔子曰西方之人有聖者 | ʻHung ʻtsz' üt$_2$, ‹Sai ‹fóng ‹chí ‚yan ʻyau shing' ʻché. |

25. This phrase is found in Hónghi's dictionary, under the word *Fat* (Budha), where the correctness of applying it to Budha is denied. The quotation presents a topic of interesting

廣東方言讀本



| | | |
|---|---|---|
| 26. The doctrines of the sages are deep and abstruse, beyond the reach of common men. | 聖道奧妙非凡<br>人所能及 | Shing' tò² ò' míú², ‹fí ‹fán ‹yan 'shó ‹nang kap₂. |
| 27. Without the institutes of sages, how can future generations be stable? | 無聖人之法後<br>世何以能立 | ‹Mò shing' ‹yan ‹chí fát₂, hau² shai' ‹hó 'í ‹nang lap₂? |
| 28. Those who in ancient times were called wise men, are now esteemed fools! | 古之所謂聖今<br>之所謂愚也 | 'Kú ‹chí 'shó wai² shing', ‹kam ‹chí 'shó wai² ‹yü 'yá! |
| 29. Sacrificial Ritual for the Temple of Sages; with plates. | 聖廟祀典圖考 | Shing' míú² tsz'' 'tín; ‹t'ò 'háu. |
| 30. Confucius! Confucius! How great is Confucius! | 孔子孔子大哉<br>亅子 | 'Hung 'tsz'! 'Hung 'tsz'! Tái² ‹tsoi 'Hung 'tsz'! |
| Before Confucius, there never was a Confucius! | 孔子之<br>前從無亅子 | 'Hung 'tsz' ‹chí ‹ts'ín, ‹Ts'ung ‹mò 'Hung 'tsz'! |
| Since Confucius, there never has been a Confucius! | 孔子之後更無<br>亅子 | 'Hung 'tsz' ‹chí hau², Kang' ‹mò 'Hung 'tsz'! |
| Confucius! Confucius! How great is Confucius! | 孔子孔<br>子大哉亅子 | 'Hung 'tsz'! 'Hung 'tsz'! Tái² ‹tsoi 'Hung 'tsz'! |

inquiry. To what region the words refer, and whether they point to one or more persons, are points which remain to be ascertained: the sentence is literally, Western region's people have sage, or sages.

29, 30. This is an interesting book, comprised in twelve, (sometimes in thirteen) volumes, containing portraits and brief accounts of Confucius, and of 144 other distinguished persons. In a few instances the portraits are wanting. The extract here given is taken from the eleventh volume of the work, which contains a series of seventy plates, illustrative of Confucius' life.

## Section Second.

## OF WORTHIES.

### 賢人類第二章
‹Ín ‹yan lui²; tai² í² ‹chéung.

| | | |
|---|---|---|
| 1. Worthy, having many talents. | 賢多才也 | ‹Ín ‹tó ‹ts'oi 'yá. |
| 2. Worthy, synonymous with good. | 賢猶善也 | ‹Ín ‹yau shín² 'yá. |

### *Notes and Explanations.*

WORTHIES hold the next rank after the sages, as will be seen in the following phrases. The *ín yan* is the man of genius, endowed with superior intellectual faculties.

1, 2. In the dictionary of Hónghí these two phrases are given to define the word *ín*; it de-

| | | |
|---|---|---|
| 3. In retirement he left no worthy man. | 野無遺賢 | ʻYé ˏmò ˏwai ˏín. |
| 4. The worthies retire from the world. | 賢者辟世 | ˏĬn ʻché pí$^2$ shaiʼ. |
| 5. A kingdom without able men is unstable. | 國無賢不立 | Kwókˎ ˏmò ˏín patˎ lap$_2$. |
| 6. Having the capacities of a worthy man. | 有賢人之才 | ʻYau ˏín ˏyan ˓chí ˏtsʻoi. |
| 7. Great worthies are second only to the sages. | 大丨幾亞聖 | Tái$^2$ ˏín ˓kí áʼ shingʼ. |
| 8. When you see a worthy man, try to equal him. | 見丨思齊焉 | Kinʼ ˏín ˓szʼ ˏtsʻai ˏín. |
| 9. Without able men, how can the world be governed? | 無丨何以治世 | ˏMò ˏín ˏhó ʻí chí$^2$ shaiʼ? |
| 10. In the school of Confucius were seventy-two worthies | 孔門七十二賢 | ʻHung ˏmún tsátˎ shapˎ í$^2$ ˏín. |
| 11. The worthy man never does aught that is mean or contracted. | 刻薄之事非賢者所爲 | Hakˎ pók$_2$ ˓chí sz"$^2$ ˓fí ˏin ʻché ʻshó ˏwai. |
| 12. From being an able, one may become a wise, man. | 由賢而後能至聖 | ˏYau ˏín ˏí hau$^2$ ˏnang chíʼ shingʼ. |
| 13. The perfect man does honor to those of superior worth, and is indulgent to all. | 君子尊賢而容衆 | ˓Kwan ʻtszʼ ˓tsün ˏín ˏí ˏyung chungʼ. |
| 14. The inmost thoughts of the worthy abide constantly in the paths of sages. | 賢者之深心存於聖道 | ˏĬn ʻché ˓chí ˓sham ˓sam ˏtsʻün ˓ü shingʼ tò$^2$. |
| 15. The words and actions of worthies may be made the patterns for succeeding ages. | 賢人之言行可爲後世法 | ˏĬn yan ˓chí ˏín hang$^2$ ʻhó ˏwai hau$^2$ shaiʼ fátˎ. |
| 16. When men have attained the rank of worthies they can be admitted to the sacrifices in the temple of sages. | 賢者而後能入祀於聖祠 | ˏĬn ʻché ˏí hau$^2$ ˓nang yap$_2$ tsz"$^2$ ˏü shingʼ ˏtsʻzʼ. |
| 17. Do men of worth enjoy such pleasures as these? | 賢者有此樂乎 | ˏĬn ʻché ʻyau ʻtsʻzʼ lók$_2$ ˏú? |
| 18. They enjoy it only after they become men of worth. | 賢者而後樂此 | ˏI'n ʻché ˏí hau$^2$ lók$_2$ ʻtsʻzʼ. |

notes the possession of many talents or great genius; and in respect to moral quality its meaning is equivalent to the word good, or virtuous. Hence the truly worthy man is both good and great.

3. This is said of an ancient sovereign who brought into his service every man of genius and virtue, unwilling that any such should remain in obscurity.

7. Mencius is called *á shing*, a sage of the second order; but the phrase here contains the general proposition, that eminent worthies are second only to the sages.

16. This privilege is granted only by the emperor to those, who, during their lifetime, were distinguished for their virtues and talents. In 1837, it was granted to Wan Yükú, late of Shuntak, who was once the tutor of his present majesty.

17, 18. This question was put to Mencius, when in the pleasure ground of his king, to whom he replied as above.

## Section Third.

## OF EXCELLENT MEN.

### 君子類第三章

꜀Kwan ꜂tsz' lui꜅; tai꜅ ꜀sám ꜀chéung.

| | | |
|---|---|---|
| 1. Worthy of praise and joy is the perfect man! | 嘉樂君子 | ꜀Ká lók꜇ ꜀kwan ꜂tsz'! |
| 2. The excellent man labors on fundamentals. | 君子務本 | ꜀Kwan ꜂tsz' mò꜅ ꜂pún. |
| 3. The excellent man is not a mere tool. | 丨子不器 | ꜀Kwan ꜂tsz' pat꜆ hí꜄. |
| 4. The excellent man rises in knowledge. | 丨子上達 | ꜀Kwan ꜂tsz' shéung꜅ tát꜇. |
| 5. The excellent man is humble and lowly. | 謙謙君子 | ꜀Hím ꜀hím ꜀kwan ꜂tsz'. |
| 6. The perfect man keeps in the path of rectitude. | 君子中庸 | ꜀Kwan ꜂tsz' ꜀chung ꜁yung. |
| 7. An eminent man of learning. | 爲學之君子 | ꜁Wai hók꜇ ꜀chí ꜀kwan ꜂tsz'. |
| 8. An eminently sincere and faithful man. | 誠實之丨子 | ꜁Shing shat꜇ ꜀chí ꜀kwan ꜂tsz'. |
| 9. An eminently kind and virtuous man. | 良善之丨子 | ꜁Léung shín꜅ ꜀chí ꜀kwan ꜂tsz'. |
| 10. The excellent man examines himself. | 君子求諸己 | ꜀Kwan ꜂tsz' ꜁k'au ꜀chü ꜂kí. |
| 11. The excellent man is never contentious. | 丨子無所爭 | ꜀Kwan ꜂tsz' ꜁mò ꜂shó ꜀chang. |
| 12. The excellent man is deeply versed in justice. | 丨子喻於義 | ꜀Kwan ꜂tsz' ü꜅ ꜀ü í꜅. |
| 13. The perfect man is always in the right. | 丨子而時中 | ꜀Kwan ꜂tsz' ꜁í ꜁shí ꜀chung. |
| 14. Be thou a scholar of eminent virtue! | 女爲君子儒 | ꜂Yü ꜁wai ꜀kwan ꜂tsz' ꜁ü! |
| 15. The eminent man's influence is like the wind. | 丨子之德風 | ꜀Kwan ꜂tsz' ꜀chí tak꜆ ꜀fung. |
| 16. The excellent man is ardently attached to his kindred. | 君子篤於親 | ꜀Kwan ꜂tsz' tuk꜆ ꜀ü ꜀ts'an. |

### *Notes and Explanations.*

KWANTSZ' is one eminently distinguished for what is amiable and laudable; he is the excellent, the eminent, or the perfect, man. The term is applicable both to sages and to worthies.

2. *Pún* here denotes the cardinal duties of life; and it is to these that the excellent man directs his undivided attention.

4. This is antithetical to what the base man does, who, *há tát* descends in knowledge—sinks down in ignorance and vice.

11. He searches into his own conduct in order to learn his errors, and turn from them. An admirable practice!

14. This was said by Confucius to one of his disciples, admonishing and encouraging him to rise to the rank of an eminent scholar, and not sink down to that of a poor and worthless one.

15. The person here spoken of is elevated to office; in which station his mild sway will

| | | |
|---|---|---|
| 17. The perfect man does not repine at heaven. | 君子不怨天 | ‹Kwan ‘tsz’ pat› ün’ ‹t‘ín. |
| 18. The excellent man's will abides by justice. | 丨子志存乎義 | ‹Kwan ‘tsz’ chí’ ‹ts‘ün ˏú í$^2$. |
| 19. The excellent man's first care is virtue. | 丨子先慎乎德 | ‹Kwan ‘tsz’ ‹sín shan$^2$ ˏú tak›. |
| 20. He conforms to reason in all his conduct. | 丨子遵道而行 | ‹Kwan ‘tsz’ ‹tsun tò$^2$ ˏí ˏhang. |
| 21. He never takes food to excess. | 丨子食無求飽 | ‹Kwan ‘tsz’ shik$_2$ ˏmò ˏk‘au ‘páu. |
| 22. He encourages others in good works. | 丨子成人之美 | ‹Kwan ‘tsz’ ˏshing ˏyan ‹chí ‘mí. |
| 23. He is one who has read extensively. | 丨子博學於文 | ‹Kwan ‘tsz’ pók› hók$_2$ ‹ü ˏman. |
| 24. He neither grieves nor mourns to excess. | 丨子不憂不懼 | ‹Kwan ‘tsz’ pat› ‹yau pat› kü›. |
| 25. He is a man of perfect virtue. | 丨子成德之名 | ‹Kwan ‘tsz’ ˏshing tak› ‹chí ˏming. |

move the people to good, as easily as the wind waves and bends down the grass in the meadows, or moves the leaves on the trees.

25. *Kwantsz’* is the name or designation of one possessing perfect virtue. This is the definition given by Hónghí to the term when it is used to denote the moral character of men. It is in frequent use for the head of a nation, family, &c.

## Section Fourth.

## OF JUST MEN.

## 義士類第四章

Í$^2$ sz’$^2$ lui$^2$; tai$^2$ sz’ ‹chéung.

| | | |
|---|---|---|
| 1. The just man is unmindful of himself. | 義士忘身 | Í$^2$ sz’$^2$ ˏmóng ‹shan. |
| 2. The charitable man succors the poor. | 義士濟貧 | Í$^2$ sz’$^2$ tsai’ ˏp‘an. |
| 3. The just man never utters empty words. | 義士無虛言 | Í$^2$ sz’$^2$ ˏmò ‹h‘ü ˏín. |
| 4. The honorable man does not disgrace himself. | 義士不辱身 | Í$^2$ sz’$^2$ pat› yuk$_2$ ‹shan. |
| 5. The just man vindicates the oppressed. | 義士打報不平 | Í$^2$ sz’$^2$ ‘tá pò’ pat› ‹p‘ing. |
| 6. The just man seeing one in danger rescues him. | 義士見危必拯 | Í$^2$ sz’$^2$ kín’ ˏngai pít› ‘ch‘ing. |

### *Notes and Explanations.*

THE class of persons here noticed is characterized by a high degree of rectitude, honor, and generosity; and may be styled the just, the honorable, the charitable. Justice is their most prominent feature.

1. He is unmindful of his own person in scenes of danger; and in the defense of the rights of a friend is regardless of any consequences that may befall himself.

5. This is of similar import, but exhibits more generosity: *pat p‘ing*, the one who is uneven, i. e. for the wronged party, *tá pò* he pays back what is due from him to his adversary.

| | | |
|---|---|---|
| 7. The word of the just man is sure. | 義士一言爲定 | Í2 sz'2 yat› ꜀ín ꜀wai ting2. |
| 8. The just man does not fear in the prospect of death. | 義士見死不怕 | Í2 sz'2 kín' ʽsz' pat› p'á'. |
| 9. It is difficult to change a just man's determination. | 義士志操難易 | Í2 sz'2 chí' ‹ts'ò ꜀nán yik2. |
| 10. The just man utterly disregards poverty and riches. | 義士竟忘貧富 | Í2 sz'2 ʽking ꜀móng ‹p'an fú'. |
| 11. In his intercourse with friends, he forgets himself. | 義士處友忘身 | Í2 sz'2 ʽchü ʽyau ꜀móng ‹shan. |
| 12. His words are precious as gold and gems. | 義士言如金石 | Í2 sz'2 ꜀ín ꜀ü ‹kam shek2. |
| 13. His word is worth a thousand pieces of gold. | 義士千金一諾 | Í2 sz'2 ‹ts'ín ‹kam yat› nók2. |
| 14. The just man will die for his country. | 義士爲國亡身 | Í2 sz'2 ꜀wai kwók› ꜀móng ‹shan. |
| 15. He will sooner die than disgrace his trust. | 義士死不辱命 | Í2 sz'2 ʽsz' pat› yuk2 ming2. |
| 16. The honorable man is not offended by things of no importance. | 義士不以小事介懷 | Í2 sz'2 pat› ʽí ʽsíú sz'2 kái' ꜀wái. |
| 17. In whatsoever the just man does, he neither seeks for fame nor gain. | 義士所爲不計名利 | Í2 sz'2 ʽshó ꜀wai pat› kai' ꜀ming lí2. |
| 18. It is difficult to find a just man among those who are rich. | 義俠之士富中難求 | Í2 háp2 ‹chí sz'2 fú' ‹chung ꜀nán ꜀k'au. |
| 19. The just man will sooner die than swerve from his integrity. | 義士之節寧死不屈 | Í2 sz'2 ‹chí tsít› ꜀ning ʽsz' pat› wat›. |
| 20. To spoil those who are rich for the relief of the poor, is worthy of a just man. | 刦富濟貧者亦義士也 | Kíp› fú' tsai' ꜀p'an ʽché yik2 í2 sz'2 ʽyá. |
| 21. The just man's heart cannot be swayed by riches or honors. | 義士之心富貴不能動 | Í2 sz'2 ‹chí ‹sam fú' kwai' pat› ꜀nang tung'. |
| 22. In the prosecution of duty, the just man is not influenced by personal considerations. | 義士操守不問己之有無 | Í2 sz'2 ‹ts'ò ʽshau pat› man2 ʽkí ‹chí ʽyau ꜀mò. |

13. Just man thousand gold one not, i. e. the slightest promise of the just man is a sufficient guaranty; even where thousands of gold are at stake, his word is better than any bonds or deeds—for these may be destroyed, that cannot.

15. *Ming* is a trust or commission of any kind with which one is charged, and which the just man will not disgrace, even though his life should be sacrificed. It must be confessed that the Chinese moralists have described many of the characteristics of virtue and integrity in their writings, however widely the people may have strayed from them in their practice: they have not been left without reprovers.

20. It is the miserly and heartless who are here denoted by the rich; such persons in times of famine and distress refuse to help the poor out of their calamities.

## Section Fifth.

## OF PHILANTHROPISTS.

## 仁人類第五章

ˏYan ˏyan lui²; tai² ‘’ng ꜀chéung.

| | | |
|---|---|---|
| 1. Philanthropy is humanity. | 仁者人也 | ˏYan ‘ché ˏyan ‘yá. |
| 2. The philanthropist loves mankind. | 亻者愛人 | ˏYan ‘ché oi’ ˏyan. |
| 3. He finds his delight in benevolence. | 亻者安仁 | ˏYan ‘ché ꜀ón ˏyan. |
| 4. He does not grieve to excess. | 亻者不憂 | ˏYan ‘ché pat꜃ ꜀yau. |
| 5. The benevolent man has no equal. | 亻者無敵 | ˏYan ‘ché ˏmò tik₂. |
| 6. The benevolent man is fearless. | 亻者有勇 | ˏYan ‘ché ‘yau ‘yung. |
| 7. Philanthropy is love to man. | 愛仁者爲仁 | Oi’ ˏyan ‘ché ˏwai ˏyan. |
| 8. Possessing the air of a philanthropist. | 有亻者之風 | ‘Yau ˏyan ‘ché ꜀chí ꜀fung. |
| 9. The benevolent man bears others on his heart. | 仁者以人爲心 | ˏYan ‘ché ‘í ˏyan ˏwai ꜀sam. |
| 10. He is known by his munificence. | 亻者以財發身 | ˏYan ‘ché ‘i ˏts‘oi fát꜃ ꜀shan. |
| 11. He is guarded in his words. | 亻者其言也訒 | ˏYan ‘ché ˏk‘í ˏín ‘yá yan². |
| 12. The philanthropist only can love mankind. | 惟仁者能好人 | ˏWai ˏyan ‘ché ˏnang hò’ ˏyan. |
| 13. Philanthropic thoughts are cherished in his heart. | 心存仁人之念 | ꜀Sam ˏts‘ün ˏyan ˏyan ꜀chí ním². |
| 14. When I truly desire to be benevolent, then I am benevolent. | 我欲亻斯仁至矣 | ‘Ngó yuk₂ ˏyan ꜀sz’ ˏyan chí’ ‘í. |

### *Notes and Explanations.*

YAN YAN is one who possesses love towards mankind; a philanthropist; a benevolent, or a kindhearted, man.

1. *Yan ché* may, according to the context, mean either the philanthropist, or philanthropy: in the abstract it has been defined by Chinese philosophers, *sam chí tak* virtue of the heart, and *oi chí lí* the principle of love,

5. No one can surpass him: *tik* has the sense of wrangler; a senior wrangler would be *mò tik*, without an equal.

6. His consciousness of rectitude not only relieves him from fear, but makes him bold and courageous.

10. By the use of his property and possessions, he makes himself conspicuous, whilst one of an opposite character degrades himself for the sake of gain.

11. 'Put a knife to thy throat if thou be a man given to appetite,' is a good proverb; this is of similar import, and was intended to check the loquacity of one of the sage's disciples: *yan* is composed of *words* and a sharp pointed *weapon*, and denotes speech that is well-guarded.

| | | |
|---|---|---|
| 15. But the benevolent man banishes him. | 惟仁人放流之 | ˏWai ˏyan ˏyan fóng' ˏlau ‹chí. |
| 16. To subdue self, and return to rectitude is philanthropy. | 克己復禮爲仁 | Hak› ʻkí fuk› ˁlai ˏwai ˏyan. |
| 17. Love all men, and endear yourself to the benevolent. | 汎愛衆而親仁 | Fán' oi' chung', ˏí ‹ts'an ˏyan. |
| 18. The philanthropist never does aught that is cruel. | 殘忍非仁者之所爲 | ˏTs'án ˁyan ‹fí ˏyan ʻché ‹chí ʻshó ˏwai. |
| 19. The philanthropist, in loving his fellow-men, commences at home and reaches those who are remote. | 仁者愛人由親及疏 | ˏYan ʻché oi' ˏyan ˏyau ‹ts'an kap› ‹shó. |
| 20. The philanthropist always has mercy and kindness in his thoughts. | 仁者常以恤憐爲念 | ˏYan ʻché ˏshéung ˁí sut› ˏlín ˏwai ním'. |
| 21. The misanthropist cannot long endure extreme poverty. | 不仁者不可以久處約 | Pat› ˏyan ʻché pat› ʻhó ˁí ʻkau ʻch'ü yéuk›. |
| 22. Every truly benevolent man will measure others by himself. | 凡仁人必推己以度人 | ˏFán ˏyan ˏyan pít› ‹t'úi ʻkí ˁí tók› ˏyan. |
| 23. Those who do not love mankind cannot be regarded as philanthropists. | 不愛人者不可以爲仁人 | Pat› oi' ˏyan ʻché pat› ʻhó ˁí ˏwai ˏyan ˏyan. |
| 24. What man is void of benevolence? But there are those who do not practice it. | 人孰無仁惟人不行仁矣 | ˏYan shuk› ˏmò ˏyan? ˏWai ˏyan pat› ˏhang ˏyan ˁí. |
| 25. The philanthropic mind never suspects a man will do what is unkind. | 仁人之念不疑人作不仁 | ˏYan ˏyan ‹chí ním' pat› ˏí ˏyan tsók› pat› ˏyan. |

15. *Chí* refers to a traitorous man, with whom it was dangerous to come in contact; it was therefore necessary to keep such an one at a distance.

21. His disposition being bad, he will have recourse to theft and robbery, breaking through every restraint, rather than suffer in his own person the evils of poverty.

24. 'Man who without benevolence? Yet man not practice benevolence truly,' is the literal rendering of this sentence; the substantive verb is embodied in the final particle *í*. The last sentence might also be rendered, But [there is to be found] the man who does not practice it.

## Section Sixth.

## OF GOOD MEN.

### 善人類第六章

**Shín$^{2}$ ꜁yan lui$^{2}$; tai$^{2}$ luk$_{2}$ ꜀chéung.**

| | | |
|---|---|---|
| 1. A lover of virtue. | 樂善之人 | Lók$_{2}$ shín$^{2}$ ꜀chí ꜁yan. |
| 2. Delights in doing good, and loves to communicate. | 好丨樂施 | Hò’ shín$^{2}$, lók$_{2}$ ꜀shí. |
| 3. The excellent man loves virtue. | 樂丨君子 | Lók$_{2}$ shín$^{2}$ ꜀kwan ‘tsz’. |
| 4. Advancing in virtue, and forsaking evil. | 遷丨改過 | ꜀Ts‘ín shín$^{2}$, ‘koi kwó’. |
| 5. Goodness only is precious. | 惟丨爲寶 | ꜁Wai shín$^{2}$ ꜁wai ‘pò. |
| 6. A man of pure goodness. | 純丨之人 | ꜁Shun shín$^{2}$ ꜀chí ꜁yan. |
| 7. The good men became rich. | 善人是富 | Shín$^{2}$ ꜁yan shí$^{2}$ fú’. |
| 8. Equally associated with good men. | 與善人爲偶 | ‘Ü shín$^{2}$ ꜁yan ꜁wai ‘ngau. |
| 9. The good man does virtuous deeds. | 善人行善事 | Shín$^{2}$ ꜁yan ꜁hang shín$^{2}$ sz’$^{2}$. |
| 10. The good man's heart is perfectly upright. | 善人心端正 | Shín$^{2}$ ꜁yan ꜀sam ꜀tün ching’. |
| 11. The good man will understand reason. | 丨人必明道 | Shín$^{2}$ ꜁yan pít꜄ ꜁ming tò$^{2}$. |
| 12. Loving virtue, he is unmindful of power. | 好善而忘勢 | ꜀Hò’ shín$^{2}$ ꜁í ꜁móng shai’. |
| 13. Seeing a good man, fear lest you be not his equal. | 見善如不及 | Kín’ shín$^{2}$ ꜁ü pat꜄ k‘ap$_{2}$. |
| 14. When U heard good words he bowed. | 禹聞善言則拜 | ‘Ü ꜁man shín$^{2}$ ꜁ín tsak꜄ pái’. |
| 15. The good man's heart abides in virtue. | 善人心恒存善 | Shín$^{2}$ ꜁yan ꜀sam ꜁hang ꜁ts‘ün shín$^{2}$. |
| 16. The good man desires others to become good. | 丨人欲人爲善 | Shín$^{2}$ ꜁yan yuk$_{2}$ ꜁yan ꜁wai shín$^{2}$. |

### *Notes and Explanations.*

GOOD, according to some Chinese authors, is a natural endowment of man; his nature, they say, is free from evil. Others maintain, that the sages only are immaculate—purely good, that the common people become so by education, while the lower classes will remain base in spite of education. *Shín* denotes what is good, virtuous, or goodness, virtue, moral worth.

1, 2. These give the prominent traits of the good man; he is a lover of virtue; he delights in doing good; and loves to communicate good to others.

7. This is said of one of the ancient dynasties; its gratuities to those who were good, who had done good service to the state, were great, and in this way they were enriched.

12. The good man who takes delight in virtue, finds no occasion for the exercise of brute force: he is powerful in goodness.

13. See good, seeming not to reach; i. e. whenever you see a good man, look on yourself as not having attained to his rank in virtue.

| | | |
|---|---|---|
| 17. Those who have good hearts do good deeds. | 有善心行善事 | ꜂Yau shín꜄ ꜀sam ꜁hang shín꜄ sz꜅. |
| 18. If there be good men, then keep near them. | 善人則親近之 | Shín꜄ ꜁yan tsak꜆ ꜀ts‘an kan꜄ ꜀chí. |
| 19. The doing of good can remove evil. | 爲善可以消災 | ꜁Wai shín꜄ ꜂hó ꜃í ꜀síú ꜀tsoi. |
| 20. The doing of good will induce great happiness. | 爲善則招百福 | ꜁Wai shín꜄ tsak꜆ ꜀chíú pák꜆ fuk꜆. |
| 21. The good man is worthy to be a guide. | 善人可以爲師 | Shín꜄ ꜁yan ꜂hó ꜃í ꜁wai ꜀sz꜄. |
| 22. He led on all the people to do good. | 取諸人以爲善 | ꜂Tsü ꜀chü ꜁yan ꜃í ꜁wai shín꜄. |
| 23. Select (for imitation) those who are good, and follow them. | 擇其善者而從之 | Chák꜇ ꜁k‘í shín꜄ ꜂ché ꜁í ꜁ts‘ung ꜀chí. |
| 24. It is only the good man who can protect himself from miseries. | 惟善人可以保身 | ꜁Wai shín꜄ ꜁yan ꜂hó ꜃í ꜂pò ꜀shan. |
| 25. Those who are able to do virtuously may be styled good men. | 人能行善則曰善人 | ꜁Yan ꜁nang ꜁hang shín꜄ tsak꜆ üt꜇ shín꜄ ꜁yan. |
| 26. The virtuous man does not do deeds of wickedness. | 行惡之事善人弗爲 | ꜁Hang ók꜆ ꜀chí sz꜅ shín꜄ ꜁yan fat꜆ ꜁wai. |
| 27. The good man's heart is pure, and free from evil. | 善人之心純一而無惡 | Shín꜄ ꜁yan ꜀chí ꜀sam ꜁shun yat꜆ ꜁í ꜁mò ók꜆. |

22. This was the ancient monarch Ü, who himself taking great delight in virtue, encouraged and led on all his people in the same good paths.

## Section Eleventh.

## OF HEROES.

### 英雄類第七章
꜀Ying ꜁hung lui꜄; tai꜄ ts‘át꜆ ꜀chéung.

| | | |
|---|---|---|
| 1. A youthful hero. | 年少英雄 | ꜁Nín shíú꜄ ꜀ying ꜁hung. |
| 2. Convene the heroes. | 招集英〡 | ꜀Chíú tsap꜇ ꜀ying ꜁hung. |
| 3. The hero of the age. | 當世英〡 | ꜀Tóng shai꜄ ꜀ying ꜁hung. |

### *Notes and Explanations.*

YINGHUNG denotes an illustrious person, one who is distinguished for valor and intrepidity; and corresponds to the word hero or heroine.

| | | |
|---|---|---|
| 4. Acquaint yourself with heroes. | 結識英雄 | Kít, shik, ‹ying ˏhung. |
| 5. The spirit of a hero. | 英雄氣概 | ‹Ying ˏhung hí' koi'. |
| 6. A hero buried in obscurity. | 英丨埋沒 | ‹Ying ˏhung ˏmái mút,. |
| 7. The heroes assemble together. | 英丨聚會 | ‹Ying ˏhung tsü² úi'. |
| 8. The hero does not ask if there be evil omens. | 英丨不問咎 | ‹Ying ˏhung pat, man² kau'. |
| 9. Two heroes cannot dwell in the same place. | 英丨不並立 | ‹Ying ˏhung pat, ping² lap,. |
| 10. Never inquire whence the hero's origin. | 英丨莫問出處 | ‹Ying ˏhung mók, man² ch'ut, ch'ü'. |
| 11. Of a hero's actions it is difficult to judge. | 英丨作事難測 | ‹Ying ˏhung tsók, sz" ˏnán chak,. |
| 12. Long have I heard of the hero's name. | 久聞英雄之名 | 'Kau ˏman ‹ying ˏhung ‹chí ˏming. |
| 13. Where now are the heroes of the past age! | 一世英丨安在 | Yat, shai' ‹ying ˏhung ‹on tsoi'! |
| 14. All around seek for the heroes of the land. | 遍訪天下英雄 | P'ín' 'fóng ‹t'ín há² ‹ying ˏhung. |
| 15. The hero views death like going home. | 英雄視死如歸 | ‹Ying ˏhung shí² 'sz' ˏü ‹kwai. |
| 16. A hero without opportunity to display his prowess. | 英丨無用武之地 | ‹Ying ˏhung ˏmò yung' 'mò ‹chí tí². |
| 17. The hero seeks death, and is not solicitous about his life. | 英丨問死不問生 | ‹Ying ˏhung man² 'sz' pat, man² ‹shang. |
| 18. The hero's name penetrates the ear like the voice of thunder. | 英丨之名如雷貫耳 | ‹Ying ˏhung ‹chí ˏming ˏü ˏlúi kún' 'í. |
| 19. In the mountain forests the heroes lie concealed. | 山林內英雄歸隱 | ‹Shán ˏlam noi² ‹ying ˏhung ‹kwai 'yan. |
| 20. Do not make the heroes of the world ridicule you. | 勿使天下英雄貽笑 | Mat, 'sz' ‹t'ín há² ‹ying ˏhung ˏí síú². |
| 21. When the purse is drained of gold the hero becomes dispirited. | 床頭金盡英丨失志 | ˏChóng ˏt'au ‹kam tsun² ‹ying ˏhung shat, chí'. |
| 22. The spirit of a hero cannot be swayed by music, by beauty, or by gain. | 英雄志氣非聲色貨利所能移 | ‹Ying ˏhung chí' hí' ‹fí ‹shing shik, fó' lí' 'shó ˏnang ˏí. |

4. Tie acquaintance with heroes, i. e. seek their acquaintance, and become intimately attached to them.

10. If he acts well the part of a hero it is enough, and it is of little consequence whether he came from a rich or a poor family.

## Section Eighth.

## OF BARDS.

### 騷人類第八章

‹Sò ‚yan lui²; tai² pát› ‹chéung.

| | | |
|---|---|---|
| 1. The bard is a retired scholar. | 騷人逸士 | ‹Sò ‚yan yat₂ sz'². |
| 2. The intoxicated bard sings boisterously. | 丨人醉酒狂吟 | ‹Sò ‚yan tsui' 'tsau ‚kw'ong ‚yam. |
| 3. He will put off his vests of fur to exchange them for wine. | 丨人解裘換酒 | ‹Sò ‚yan 'kái ‚k'au ún² 'tsau. |
| 4. He seeks the wine-shop to sooth his passions. | 丨人覔肆怡情 | ‹Sò ‚yan mik› sz'' ‚í ‚ts'ing. |
| 5. The bard finds his delight in poetry and wine. | 丨人詩酒自娛 | ‹Sò ‚yan ‹shí 'tsau tsz'² ‚yü. |
| 6. He uses a gem-goblet to purchase the spring wines. | 丨人玉壺買春 | ‹Sò ‚yan yuk₂ ‚ú ʿmái ‹ch'un. |
| 7. The bard will pawn his clothes to pay his bills for wine. | 丨人典衣以償酒債 | ‹Sò ‚yan 'tín ‹í ʿí ‚ch'éung 'tsau chái'. |
| 8. The bard always satisfies his poetical cravings with wine. | 丨人常以酒充詩饑 | ‹Sò ‚yan ‚shéung ʿí 'tsau ‹ch'ung ‹shí ‹kí. |
| 9. The bard is a debtor for wine wherever he may reside. | 丨人酒債恒處不無 | ‹Sò ‚yan 'tsau chái' ‚hang ch'ü' pat› ‚mò. |
| 10. In purchasing wine the bard does not heed an empty purse. | 丨人沽酒不計囊空 | ‹Sò ‚yan ‹kú 'tsau pat› kai' ‚nóng ‚hung. |
| 11. The bard prides himself on his poetical and drinking powers. | 丨人以詩酒傲性情 | ‹Sò ‚yan ʿí ‹shí 'tsau ngò² sing' ‚ts'ing. |

## *Notes and Explanations.*

Sò YAN is a popular term for those who devote themselves to the writing of poetry, deriving its origin from a composition written by *Wat Yün*, a talented minister of state under the Chau dynasty; the poem was called *Lí Sò*, or the Dissipation of Sorrows. *Wat Yün* committed suicide by drowning, and in memory of him the annual festival of the dragon boats is celebrated.

2. *Tsau* is a generic term used by the Chinese for all kinds of wines and spirits, as well those which are fermented as distilled: their liquors are generally manufactured by distillation more or less strong.

4. *Sz'* denotes a shop, and is often used as an appropriate term for those houses where wines and other liquors are sold and drank: they are the gin-palaces and the bar-rooms of the Chinese.

6. Spring is here used by metonymy for wine, which in ancient times was stored up in cel-

| | | |
|---|---|---|
| 12. Great fondness for wine, and wild enthusiasm in poetry, are characteristics of the bard. | 酒僻詩狂騷人態度 | ʻTsau pʻik› ‹shí ˏkwʻong ‹sò ˏyan tʻái’ tò[2]. |
| 13. The bard regards his sojourn in the world as a long journey. | 騷人以處世爲大夢 | ‹Sò ˏyan ʻí ʻchʻü shai’ ˏwai tái[2] mung[2]. |
| 14. The poet esteems riches and honors light as the dust of the earth. | 騷人輕富貴如塵土 | ‹Sò ˏyan ‹hing fú’ kwai’ ˏü ˏchʻan ʻtò. |
| 15. The genius of the poet never goes beyond the bounds of what is pure and elevated. | 騷人志氣不外清高 | ‹Sò ˏyan chí’ hí’ pat› ngoi’ ‹tsʻing ‹kò. |
| 16. Those who are charmed with poetry and wine are called bards. | 躭於詩酒謂之騷人 | ‹Tám ‹ü ‹shí ʻtsau wai[2] ‹chí ‹sò ˏyan. |
| 17. The bard in purchasing wine does not grudge the money on the head of his staff. | 亻人沽酒不計杖頭錢 | ‹Sò ˏyan ʻkú ʻtsau pat› kai’ chéung[2] ˏtʻau ˏtsʻín. |
| 18. 'Catch the moon in the midst of the sea,' was the incoherent language of an intoxicated bard. | 海中撈月騷人酒後狂言 | ʻHoi ‹chung ‹láu üt[2], ‹sò ˏyan ʻtsau hau[2] ˏkwʻong ˏín. |
| 19. The poet, though he encounters dangers, never grieves thereat. | 騷人卽遭危困未見其憂 | ‹Sò ˏyan tsik› ‹tsò ˏngai kwʻan’ mí[2] kín’ ˏkʻí ‹yau. |
| 20. The poet accomplishes what other men have not the power to effect. | 騷人作事爲人所不能爲 | ‹Sò ˏyan tsók› sz[2] ˏwai ˏyan ʻshó pat› ˏnang ˏwai. |
| 21. In his songs the bard celebrates his wine, and he takes his wine to give spirit to his songs. | 騷人以詩言酒意以酒道詩情 | ‹Sò ˏyan ʻí ‹shí ˏín ʻtsau í’, ʻí ʻtsau tò[2] ‹shí ˏtsʻing. |
| 22. Who is it, except the bard, that daily returns home full of wine from the booths on the banks of the river? | 每日江頭盡醉歸者非騷人而何哉 | ʻMúi yat[2] ‹kóng ˏtʻau tsun[2] tsui’ ‹kwai ʻché ‹fí ‹sò ˏyan ˏí ˏhó ‹tsoi? |

lars, and opened usually only in spring; and hence the spring purchase became a current phrase for filling the domestic goblets.

17. It is said that, in ancient times, aged men when going abroad with staff in hand, bind a few pieces of money around the staff's head, for cases of special emergency: even these the bard would willingly give for his wine.

18. This is said of the celebrated *Lí Táipák*, who, in consequence of some designs which he supposed were formed against his life, committed suicide by plunging into the sea, to catch the moon!

22. Wine-houses were erected in pleasant retreats, on elevated ground near the banks of rivers. From these it was usual for bards to return home thoroughly intoxicated.

## Section Ninth.

# OF THE MIDDLING CLASSES.

## 中品類第九章

‹Chung ‘pan lui’; tai’ ‘kau ‹chéung.

| | | |
|---|---|---|
| 1. Men of the highest order are good without instruction; men of the middling class are so after instruction; whilst those of the lowest are bad in spite of instruction. | 上品之人不教而善中品之人教而後善下品之人教而不善 | Shéung’ ‘pan ‹chí ˏyan pat› káu’ ˏí shín’; ‹chung ‘pan ‹chí ˏyan káu’ ˏí hau’ shín’; há’ ‘pan ‹chí ˏyan káu’ ˏí pat› shín’. |
| 2. Those of the highest order are sages, worthies, the excellent, the philanthropic, the good, the just, the upright, the dutiful, the constant, heroes, poets, lovers of knowledge, men of genius, and of wisdom. | 聖賢君仁善義忠孝烈英騷儒才智謂之上品 | Shing’, ˏin, ‹kwan, ˏyan shín’, í’, ‹chung, hau’, lít›, ‹ying, ‹sò, ˏyü, ˏts‘oi, chí’, wai’ ‹chí shéung’ ‘pan. |
| 3. Husbandmen, mechanics, physicians, diviners, astrologers, soldiers, woodcutters, fishermen, hunters, musicians, and watchmen, are of the middling class. | 農工醫卜星兵樵漁獵樂更保謂之中品 | ˏNung, ‹kung, ‹í, puk›, ‹sing, ‹ping, ˏts‘íú, ˏü, líp›, ngók›, ‹kang ‘pò, wai’ ‹chí ‹chung ‘pan. |
| 4. Players, servants, jugglers, vagabonds, robbers, thieves, pettifoggers, gamblers, swindlers, and cheats, are of the lowest class. | 戲奴術爛盜賊訟賭光詭惡牙謂之下品 | Hí’, ˏnò, shut›, lán’, tò’, ts‘ak›, tsung’, ‘tò, ‹kwóng, ‘kwai, ók› ˏngá, wai’ ‹chí há’ ‘pan. |
| 5. Those who till and reap the fields are called *husbandmen.* | 耕耘田畝謂之農夫 | ‹Kang ˏwan ˏt‘ín ‘mau wai’ ‹chí ˏnung ‹fú. |
| 6. Those who traffic in goods, going and coming from place to place, are called *merchants.* | 往來販貨則謂商人 | ‘Wóng ˏloi fán’ fó’ tsak› wai’ ‹shéung ˏyan. |

### *Notes and Explanations.*

THESE divisions afford a tolerably correct estimate, in a moral and intellectual light, of the principal classes of society among the Chinese.

2. Several of these words have been already explained: *chung* denotes upright and faithful, and is usually applied to good ministers of state; *hau* is applied to those who fulfill all their duties as sons; *lít* is applied to those who are constant and faithful and steadfast in what is good; *yü* are the literati, once the pure lovers of learning.

6, 7. *Shéung* is often used indiscriminately for merchants and traders of all kinds, whether conducting business on a large or small scale.

| | | |
|---|---|---|
| 7. Those who reside in shops and factories, with their goods, are called *tradesmen.* | 店行坐貨是之謂賈 | Tím' ‹hóng tsó² fó' shí² ‹chí wai² 'kú. |
| 8. Those who by the cure of diseases succor mankind, are called *physicians.* | 療疾濟世便稱醫生 | ˏLíú tsat₂ tsai' shai' pín² ‹ch'ing ‹í ‹shang. |
| 9. Those who drop the screen and sell divinations, are called *diviners*, or masters of divination. | 垂簾賣卜號曰占卦先生 | ˏShui ˏlím mái² puk₎ hò² üt₂ ‹chím kwá' ‹sín ‹shang. |
| 10. Those who examine the stars and calculate destinies are called *astrologers*, or the calculators of fates. | 推星度理稱爲擇日先生 | ‹T'úi ‹sing tók₂ 'lí ‹ch'ing ˏwai chák₂ yat₂ ‹sín ‹shang. |
| 11. Those who defend and protect forts, garrisons, and guardhouses are called *soldiers.* | 防護砲臺營汛號曰兵丁 | ˏFóng ú² p'áu' ˏt'oi ˏying sun' hò² üt₂ ‹ping ‹ting. |
| 12. Those who go to the hills and gather faggots are named *woodcutters.* | 入山採薪名爲樵子 | Yap₂ ‹shán 'ts'oi ‹san ˏming ˏwai ˏts'íú 'tsz'. |
| 13. Those whose occupation is in fishing are called *fishermen.* | 捕魚爲業謂之漁翁 | Pò² ˏü ˏwai íp₂ wai² ‹chí ˏü ‹yung. |
| 14. Those who play on the eight kinds of musical instruments are called *musicians.* | 掌奏八音謂之樂生 | 'Chéung tsau' pát₎ ‹yam wai² ‹chí ngók₂ ‹shang. |
| 15. Those who report the hour [of the night] in the streets are called *watchmen.* | 閭閻報漏號曰更夫 | ˏLíu ˏím pò' lau² hò² üt₂ ‹kang ‹fú. |
| 16. Those who abandon their families and shave clean their heads are called *Budhists.* | 出家削髮名曰禪僧 | Ch'ut₎ ‹ká séuk₎ fát₎ ˏming üt₂ ˏshím ‹sang. |
| 17. Those who gather their hair into a tuft and pin it in a knob are called *rationalists.* | 束髮叅冠則爲道士 | Ch'uk₎ fát₎ ‹ts'ám ‹kún tsak₂ ˏwai tò² sz'². |

9. These divines usually take up their quarters by the wayside, where they hang up a screen, made of cloth or bamboo, on which is written their advertisements, giving notice of what they can do, &c.

10. Besides divination and astrology, there are among the Chinese many other branches of the occult sciences practiced, as geomancy, chiromancy, fortune-telling, &c., by persons who exercise great influence over their credulous countrymen.

## Section Tenth.

# OF THE LOWER CLASSES.

## 下品類第十章

‹Há$^{2}$ ʻpan lui$^{2}$; tai$^{2}$ shap$_{2}$ ‹chéung.

| | | |
|---|---|---|
| 1. Those who do not engage in any occupation are called *drones.* | 不執一藝曰冇用人 | Pat› chap› yat› ngai$^{2}$ üt$_{2}$ ʻmò yung$^{2}$ ˏyan. |
| 2. Those who decapitate thieves and robbers are called *executioners.* | 誅斬賊盜呼爲殺手 | ‹Chü ʻchám ts'ak$_{2}$ tò$^{2}$ ‹fú ˏwai shát› ʻshau. |
| 3. Those who take care of prisons and prisoners are named *jailers.* | 收管監犯名曰禁卒 | ‹Shau ʻkún ‹kám fán$^{2}$ ˏming üt$_{2}$ kam' tsut›. |
| 4. Those who personate the ancients, and exhibit themselves as actors are called *players.* | 倣古演劇謂之戲子 | ʻFóng ʻkú ʻín k'ek$_{2}$ wai$^{2}$ ‹chí hí' ʻtsz'. |
| 5. Those whose persons have been sold to others are called *slaves.* | 賣身與人名爲奴僕 | Mái$^{2}$ ‹shan ʻü ˏyan ˏming ˏwai ˏnò puk$_{2}$. |
| 6. Those who perambulate the streets, begging their bread, are called *beggars.* | 沿途丐食謂之乞兒 | ˏÜn ˏt'ò k'oi' shik$_{2}$ wai$^{2}$ ‹chí hat› ˏí. |
| 7. Those who are expert and dexterous in playing tricks are called *jugglers.* | 演弄巧法謂之術士 | ʻÍn lung$^{2}$ ʻháu fát› wai$^{2}$ ‹chí shut$_{2}$ sz'$^{2}$. |
| 8. Abandoned fellows who wander about regardless of life are called *vagabonds.* | 亡命之徒呼爲爛仔 | ˏMóng ming$^{2}$ ‹chí ˏt'ò ‹fú ˏwai lán$^{2}$ ʻtsai. |
| 9. Those who plunder in large bands are called *robbers.* | 大夥打劫名爲強盜 | Tái$^{2}$ ʻfo ʻtá kíp› ˏming ˏwai ˏk'éung tò$^{2}$. |
| 10. Those who procure a livelihood by stealing and secreting goods are called *thieves.* | 偷竊爲生號爲賊仔 | ˏT'au sít› ˏwai ‹shang hò$^{2}$ ˏwai ts'ak$_{2}$ ʻtsai. |

### *Notes and Explanations.*

THE terms given in the fourth paragraph of the preceding section, with a few others of the like character, are explained in the following phrases.

10. This class of persons, when they commit their depredations on the rivers and coasts, or high seas, are called *hoi ts'ak*, sea thieves, i. e. pirates.

| | | |
|---|---|---|
| 11. Those who excite and support unfounded litigations are called *pettifoggers.* | 包攬詞訟謂之訟棍 | ˓Páu ˋlám ˏtsz' tsung² wai² ˓chí tsung² kwan'. |
| 12. Those who make themselves adepts in all kinds of gambling are called *gamblers.* | 精通賭具名爲賭棍 | ˓Tsing ˓t'ung 'tò kü² ˏming ˏwai 'tò kwan'. |
| 13. Those who deceive their intimate friends are called *swindlers.* | 欺騙親朋謂之光棍 | ˓Hí p'ín' ˓ts'an ˏp'ang wai² ˓chí ˓kwóng kwan'. |
| 14. Those who practice deception the world calls *cheats.* | 圖詐僞世號詭譎人 | ˏTò chá' ngai² shai' hò² 'kwai kwat˒ ˏyan. |
| 15. Those who never do well, whether moving or at rest, are called *wicked men.* | 動靜不善謂之惡人 | Tung² tsing² pat˒ shín² wai² ˓chí ók˒ ˏyan. |
| 16. Women who act as talebearers are called *tattlers.* | 女爲說客名曰牙婆 | ˋNü ˏwai shui' hák ˏming üt² ˏngá ˏp'ó. |

11—13. *Tsung kwan* a contentious stick, *tò kwan* a gambling stick, and *kwóng kwan* a bare stick, are phrases in which the word *kwan* a pole or stick expresses an unfeeling, selfish person, from whom no relenting or favor can be expected. The latter term sometimes denotes those who make it their inhuman delight and gain to stir up collisions and broils among their fellow-men for their own purposes.

16. Literally this sentence runs thus: 'women act talking visitors by name are called teeth dames,' i. e. tattlers. The character here called *shui* is also usually known as *shüt*, with nearly the same meaning.

# CHAPTER V.

# DOMESTIC AFFAIRS.

# 日用篇五

Yat, yung²; ‹p'ín ‘'ng.

## Section First.

## OF RENTING HOUSES.

## 租賃房屋第一章

‹Tsò yam² ‹fong uk›; tai² yat› ‹chéung.

| | | |
|---|---|---|
| 1. To whom do the houses in the city of Canton really belong? | 廣東省城之屋<br>究屬何人 | ‘Kwóng ‹tung ‘shàng ‹shing ‹chí uk› kau’ shuk› ‹shó ‹yan? |
| Every house has its own landlord. | 各業各主 | Kók› íp› kók› ‘chü. |
| 2. If [as it is commonly said,] there is not a foot of ground that does not belong to the sovereign, by what tenure do the people hold the ground as their own? | 尺地莫非王土<br>何得自專爲己<br>所有 | Ch‘ik› tí² mók› ‹fi ‹wóng ‘t‘ò ‹hó tak› tsz’² ‹chün ‹wai ‘kí ‘shó ‘yau? |
| They receive the right of occupancy thereof, for building, from the magistracy, with a stamped deed, which they retain in testimony of their right; after this they may sell the houses [built thereon]. | 與官承地蓋造<br>領紅契收執爲<br>憑後方能轉賣<br>其屋 | ‘Ü ‹kún ‹shing tí² k‘oi’ tsò², ‘ling ‹hung k‘ai’ ‹shau chap› ‹wai ‹p‘ang; hau² ‹fong ‹nang ‘chün mái² ‹k‘í uk›. |

### Notes and Explanations.

Yat yung, literally, ‘daily use,’ are terms used to designate whatsoever appertains to domestic concerns, such as furniture, food, clothing, &c. The chapter seems to require some remarks respecting the tenure of houses, and the names of their various apartments, to afford which this and the second section are intended; some of the topics here incidentally touched upon will be more fully treated in subsequent chapters.

1. Wide eastern provincial city's houses, de facto, belong to what man? i. e., To whom do the houses of the city of the province Kwóngtung really belong? *Kók íp* every possession, *kók chü* every master, i. e. each and every possession of houses has its appropriate owner.

2. *Wóng t‘ò* is the royal domain, a classical expression, in which *wóng* a king, is applied to the emperor. *Hung k‘ai* is, literally, ‘red deed’, so called because the document is stamp-

| | | |
|---|---|---|
| 3. When people have purchased these houses, what rate of interest do they gain? | 是則置買房屋<br>賺息有幾多 | Shí$^2$ tsak, chí$^3$ ʻmái ˏfóng uk,, chán$^2$ sik, ʻyau ʻkí ˏtó? |
| The highest is twelve per cent., the lowest nine and a half per cent., annually. | 多則一分少則<br>八厘 | ˏTó tsak, yat, ˏfan; ʻshiú tsak, pát, ˏlí. |
| 4. Is there any tax levied or not?<br>There is. | 要納稅唔要呢<br>要咯 | Íú$^3$ náp$_2$ shui$^3$, ˏ'm íú$^3$ ˏní?<br>Íú$^3$ lók,. |
| 5. Is this tax paid every year, or every month? | 分每年納抑或<br>分每月呢 | ˏFan ʻmúi ˏnín náp$_2$, yik, wák$_2$ ˏfan ʻmúi üt$_2$ ˏní? |
| It is paid once every year. | 每年納一次 | ʻMúi ˏnín náp$_2$ yat, ts'z$^3$. |
| 6. What is the amount of the tax?<br>It is levied according to the extent and quality of the ground, and is called the ground rent. | 納幾多爲額呢<br>量地多寡良歹<br>而納又名納地<br>租 | Náp$_2$ ʻkí ˏtó ˏwai ngák$_2$ ˏní?<br>Léung$^2$ tí$^2$ ˏtó ʻkwá ˏléung ʻtái ˏí náp$_2$; yau$^2$ ˏming náp$_2$ tí$^2$ ˏtsò. |
| 7. Suppose a person wishes to hire a house, where must he go to find one? | 假如有人想租<br>屋向邊處埋呢 | ʻKá ˏü ʻyau ˏyan ʻséung ˏtsò uk,, héung$^3$ ˏp'ín ch'ü$^3$ ˏmái ˏní? |
| The landlord having pasted up a card giving notice that he has a house to rent, the lessee either goes in person and makes inquiries and agrees on the terms, or employs another person to go and do this for him. | 業主將租帖標<br>起承賃者或自<br>行問到議租或<br>托來人來問 | Íp$_2$ ʻchü ˏtséung ˏtsò t'íp, ˏpíú ʻhí, ˏshing yam$^2$ ʻché wák$_2$ tsz$^2$ ˏhang man$^2$ tò$^3$ ʻí ˏtsò, wák$_2$ t'ók, ˏloi ˏyan ˏloi man$^2$. |
| 8. After an agreement has been made for the amount of rent, how is it attested? | 既議定租後以<br>何爲憑 | Kí$^3$ ʻí ting$^2$ ˏtsò hau$^2$ ʻí ˏhó ˏwai ˏp'ang? |
| The lessee must have some one to be surety for him, and the lessor must open a rent book. | 承賃者有擔保<br>業主亦設租簿 | ˏShing yam$^2$ ʻché ʻyau ˏtám ʻpò; íp$_2$ ʻchü yik$_2$ ch'ít, ˏtsò pò$^2$. |

ed with red ink: the *k'ai* is a formal paper, and puts the holder in perpetual possession of the land, provided he pays the taxes, and conform to the laws of the empire respecting the occupation of land.

3. This amount of interest, paid for the money invested in houses, is diminished by expenditure for repairs, taxes, &c.; *yat fan* or one candareen is one hundredth part of a tael, which is paid for each month, making twelve per cent. annually: eight *lí* or cash is four fifths of that sum, or nine and a half per cent.

7. The *ts'ò típ* is precisely like the advertisements for letting houses among ourselves, and is usually pasted upon the door or wall of the house to be leased, and directs the inquirer where to find the landlord.

9. What is written in the rent book?

租簿裏頭點樣
寫呢

‹Tsò pò$^{2}$ ʻlui ‚t'au ʻtím yéung$^{2}$ ʻsé ‹ní?

The writing is in the form of a lease, with the difference of its being entered in a book, thus:—

The family of Wingch'ün, of the clan Ch'an, hereby certifies that it has a house, situated in the Eighteenth ward, extending four rooms in breadth, and three entries in depth, each room measuring twenty-one ridges of tiles; the partitions, doors, kitchen, and well, all complete; which house is now rented to the family of Kingshan of the clan Yü for a private family residence. Nothing illegal may be transacted therein. It is distinctly understood, that the rent shall be thirty taels per month, besides two dollars annually for shoe money;—the rent to be paid every month; if arrears accumulate, the security shall be responsible for the same. When the time for removing from the house arrives, the whole of the rent must be paid, and the house delivered over to the landlord, it shall not be lawful to underlet it to any other person. Witness this agreement.

好似批咁樣不
過寫明落簿頭
立明據人陳穎
川堂有屋一所
坐落十八甫平
排四間深三進
每間二十一桁
板障門扇廚井
一切俱全今租
與敬愼堂余住
居宅眷不得私
設違禁之事言
明每月租銀三
十兩另每年鞋
金銀二元按月
清租如有拖欠
爲擔保是問臨
遷之日租銀清
結將屋交回業
主不得轉租別
人此據

ʻHò ʻts'z' ‹p'ai ʻkóm yéung$^{2}$, pat› kwó' ʻsé ‚ming lók$_{2}$ pò$^{2}$ ‚t'au.

Lap$_{2}$ ‚ming kü' ‚yan ‚Ch'an Wing$^{2}$ ‹ch'ün ‚t'óng, ʻyau uk› yat› ʻshó, tsó$^{2}$ lók$_{2}$ Shap$_{2}$ pát› ʻpò, ‚p'ing ‚p'ái sz$^{2}$ ‹kán, ‹sham ‹sám tsun', ʻmúi ‹kán í$^{2}$ shap$_{2}$ yat› ‹háng; ʻpán chéung$^{2}$, ‚mún shín', ‚ch'ü, ʻtsing, yat› ts'ít› ‹k'ü ‚ts'ün; ‹kam ‹tsò ʻü King' shan$^{2}$ ‚t'óng ‚Yü chü$^{2}$ ‹kü chák$_{2}$ kün'. Pat› tak› ‹sz' ch'ít› ‚wai kam' ‹chí sz$^{2}$. ‚Ín ‹ming ʻmúi üt$_{2}$ ‹tsò ‚ngan ‹sám ‚shap$_{2}$ ʻléung, líng$^{2}$ ʻmúi ‚nín ‚hái ‹kam ‚ngan í$^{2}$ ‚ün, ón' üt$_{2}$ ‹ts'ing ‹tsò, ‚ü$^{c}$ yau ‹t'o hím' ‚wai ‹tám ʻpò shí$^{2}$ man$^{2}$. ‚Lam ‹ts'ín ‹chí yat$_{2}$, ‹tsò ‚ngan ‹ts'ing kít›, ‹tséung uk› ‹káu ‚úi íp$_{2}$ ʻchü, pat› tak› ʻchün ‹tsò pít$_{2}$ ‚yan, ʻts'z' kü'.

The rent is to commence from the date of this agreement, being the fifteenth day of the eighth month, in the eighteenth year of Tòkwóng.

道光十八年八
月十五日起租
立據

Tò$^{2}$ ‹kwóng shap$_{2}$ pát› ‚nín, pát› üt$_{2}$, shap$_{2}$ ʻʻng yat$_{2}$, ʻhí ‹tsò lap$_{2}$ kü'.

9. This writing is abridged, the usual forms being much more extended and minute, specifying the length and breadth of the several apartments, &c. *Ch'an* is the *sing* or surname of the clan or tribe; *Wingch'ün t'óng* is the name of a specific branch of the clan.

The 'shoe money' is a fee to the collector of the rent, and is so called, because it is suppos-

| | | |
|---|---|---|
| 10. If we take the houses in the city of Canton, what may be the monthly rent for those of the largest class, for those of the second, and for those of the smallest kind? | 以廣東省城之屋而論至大者每月收租銀有幾多次等者有幾多至小者又有幾多 | ʿI ʿKwóng ˌtung ʿshang ˌshing ˌchí uk˒ ˏí lun², chí˒ tái¹ ʿché ʿmúi üt˒ ˌshau ˌtsò ˌngan ʿyau ʿkí ˌtó, ts'z" ʿtang ʿché ʿyau ʿkí ˌtó, chí˒ ʿsíú ʿché yau˒ ʿyau ʿkí ˌtó? |
| For the largest, the rent does not exceed forty or fifty taels per month;—these are for the most part occupied by official people; for houses of the second size, six or seven dollars are paid; while for the smallest, the rent is not more than one or two mace. There are, however, some houses still larger; but most of these, being very large, are either rented to several persons, or are occupied by the landlords themselves. | 至大者每月不過四五十兩其中公館居多次等者六七元至小者一二錢然屋更大者非無惟過大非分賃則業主自居者居多 | Chí˒ tái¹ ʿché ʿmúi üt˒ pat˒ kwó˒ sz˒ ʿ'ng shap˒ ʿléung, ˌk'í ˌchung ˌkung ʿkún ˌkü ˌtó; ts'z" ʿtang ʿché luk˒ ts'at˒ ˏün; chí˒ ʿsíú ʿché yat˒ í² ˏts'ín: ˏín uk˒ kang˒ tái¹ ʿché ˌfí ˏmò, ˏwai kwó˒ tái¹ ˌfí ˌfan yam², tsak˒ íp˒ ʿchü tsz"² ˌkü ʿché ˏkü ˌtó. |

ed to be expended on an extra pair of shoes, required in running after the rent. Charges, which bear a similar aspect of extortion, often occur in the transactions of the Chinese.

10. Large numbers of officers are often waiting in the capital for appointments in the province, and while thus waiting they have to provide houses for themselves.

## Section Second.

## OF APARTMENTS OF HOUSES.

## 房屋類第二章

ˌFóng uk˒ lui²; tai² í² ˌchéung.

| | | |
|---|---|---|
| 1. The *inner apartments* are not to be entered irregularly. | 內室不許亂進 | Noi² shat˒ pat˒ ʿh'ü lün² tsun˒. |

### *Notes and Explanations.*

THIS section includes, together with the names of the common apartments of houses, those of such other parts as are frequently spoken of in domestic affairs. The names, in this and a few of the succeeding sections, are italicized, and arranged alphabetically.

廣東方言讀本



| | | |
|---|---|---|
| 2. If there had been no *balustrade*, I should have fallen down. | 若係冇欄杆我就跌落去 | Yéuk˳ hai² ʻmò ˏlán ˓kón, ʻngó tsau² tít˒ lók˳ h‘ü’. |
| 3. The thieves, even without lifting up the *bar* across the doors, burst them open. | 個賊冇撓起門閂咁就開門 | Kó’ ts‘ak˳ ʻmò ‘tau ‘hí ˏmún ˓shán, ‘kóm tsau² ˓hoi ˏmún. |
| 4. The wind is very boisterous, and you must put the *bars* in the windows. | 翻風太要落窓壓 | ˓Fán ˓fung ˓t‘ái íú’ lók˳ ˓ch‘éung át˒. |
| 5. The water in the *bathing-room* is ready. | 洗身房水便嚹 | ‘Sai ˓shan ˏfóng ‘shui pín² lá’. |
| 6. Is there any fire in the *bedroom* fireplace? | 瞓房火爐有火冇呀 | Fan’ ˏfóng ‘fó ˏlò ʻyau ‘fó ʻmò á’? |
| 7. Open the Venetian *blinds* in the front veranda, and fasten them open. | 開正面天臺嘅牛百葉窓鈎住 | ˓Hoi ching’ mín² ˓t‘ín ˏt‘oi ké’ ˏngau pák˒ íp˳ ˓ch‘éung, ˓kau chü². |
| 8. Shut the Venetian *blinds*. | 閂埋板簾窓門 | ˓Shán ˏmái ‘pán ˏlím ˓ch‘éung ˏmún. |
| 9. The *ceiling* needs to be swept. | 要掃吓天花板 | Íú’ sò’ ‘há ˓t‘ín ˓fá ‘pán. |
| 10. Let us repair to the *guest chamber* to converse. | 請到客廳叙話 | ‘Ts‘ing tò’ hák˒ ˓t‘ing tsui² wá². |
| 11. The *chimney* is clogged, the smoke does not ascend. | 烟通塞唔上烟 | ˓Ín ˓t‘ung sak˒, ˏ’m ʻshéung ˓ín. |
| 12. Put that pair of shoes away in the *closet*. | 個對鞋擠房仔 | Kó’ túi’ ˏhái ˓chai ˏfóng ‘tsai. |
| 13. Spacious *cow-houses* are the best. | 牛槽闊的致好 | ˏNgau ˓ts‘ò fút˒ tí˒ chí’ ‘hò. |
| 14. The *dining-room* is too small to accommodate so large a number of people. | 大飡樓細唔坐得咁多人 | Tái² ˓ts‘án ˏlau sai’ ˏ’m tsó² tak˒ kóm’ ˓tó ˏyan. |
| 15. The *door* was closed, but not locked. | 房門虛掩未關 | ˏFóng ˏmún ˓h‘ü ‘ím, mí² ˓kwán. |
| 16. From the *side door* he turned and went away. | 在橫門轉過去 | Tsoi² ˏwáng ˏmún ‘chün kwó’ h‘ü’. |
| 17. The *great door* is always shut in the daytime. | 大門日裏常關 | Tái² ˏmún yat˳ ʻlui ˏshéung ˓kwán. |

1. This is an appropriate term for the retired apartments of females, whether married or unmarried, old or young.
3. *Tau* is a local word, not found in lexicons; its import is like that of *hí*, to lift, or raise.
6. *Lò* is a place to contain fire, and, with or without *fó* preceding it, may be translated either, a furnace, a stove, a fireplace, or grate.
7. *T‘ín t‘oi* is applied both to verandas and to terraces; *ngau pák íp*, 'cow's hundred leaves' is an allusion to the internal folds of the omasum or manyplus, the third stomach of the cow; the cavity of this stomach is much contracted by numerous and broad duplicatures of the internal coat, which lie lengthwise, vary in breadth in a regular alternate order, and amount to about one hundred; thus showing the appropriateness of this singular allusion for describing the Venetian blinds: *ch‘éung* is a window, and is usually followed by *mún*, the two words retaining the same meaning.

| | | |
|---|---|---|
| 18. Open the *middle door* to receive the guests. | 打開中門接客 | 'Tá ˏhoi ˏchung ˏmún tsipˎ hákˎ. |
| 19. The *low door* is a short door. | 矮門即短門也 | 'Ai ˏmún tsikˎ 'tün ˏmún 'yá. |
| 20. Stop at the *inner door* and call. | 宅門止步揚聲 | Chák₂ ˏmún 'chí pò² ˏyéung ˏshing. |
| 21. Bamboos were planted about the *round door*. | 月門外皆種竹 | Ut₂ ˏmún ngoi² ˏkái chung' chukˎ. |
| 22. That apartment has a small *dressing-room* belonging to it. | 個間房裏頭有間替身房仔 | Kó' ˏkán ˏfóng 'lui ˏt'au 'yau ˏkán t'ai' ˏshan ˏfóng 'tsai. |
| 23. He took leave of the guest in the *entry*. | 送客出門官廳 | Sung' hákˎ ch'utˎ ˏmún ˏkún ˏt'ing. |
| 24. Make a fire in that *fireplace*. | 起着個火爐龕 | 'Hí chéukˎ kó' 'fó ˏlò ham'. |
| 25. Call the coolie to wipe the *floor*. | 叫管店抹樓板 | Kíú' 'kún tím' mútˎ ˏlau 'pán. |
| 26. The bars of the *grate* ought not to be made very close to each other. | 火爐嘅鐵柱唔好密 | 'Fó ˏlò ké' t'itˎ 'chü ˏ'm 'hò mat₂. |
| 27. The *great hall* is full of noble friends. | 大廳高朋滿座 | Tái² ˏt'ing ˏkò ˏp'ang 'mún tsó². |
| 28. He passed over to the *side hall*. | 轉過橫廳個邊 | 'Chün kwó' ˏwáng ˏt'ing kó' ˏpín. |
| 29. He went to the middle of the *second hall*. | 入到二廳堂中 | Yap₂ tò' í² ˏt'ing ˏt'óng ˏchung. |
| 30. Brush together and take away the ashes from the *hearth*. | 拂火爐底個的灰去 | Fatˎ 'fó ˏlò 'tai kó' tikˎ ˏfúi h'ü'. |
| 31. The *hen-house* is in the garden. | 鷄欄喺園裏嚟 | ˏKai ˏlán 'hai ˏün 'lui ˏlai. |
| 32. The *jambs* are on each side of the fireplace. | 火爐兩傍柱躉 | 'Fó ˏlò 'léung ˏp'óng 'chü 'tan. |

18. In the principal houses, just within the great door, there is a triple doorway; of which the central one is only opened for such guests as arrive in sedans or on horseback. Those who come on foot enter the side doors, right and left.

19. The low door is close on the outer side of the great front door, and to about one half the height of it, allowing the breeze to pass over it, when the great door is open.

20. This is the door which leads into the inner apartments, which are occupied by the female members of the house.

21. This is literally the moon gate, being made perfectly round like the full moon; it usually leads into the garden or some open area.

23. This entry is a small space between the great door and the middle door, and is called *mún kún ting*, 'court of the guardians of the door', because of certain images which are usually placed in niches on each side of the door, as its protectors.

24. *Ham* is properly a shrine, usually made in Chinese houses in the walls, and in its form bears some resemblance to our fireplaces or grates.

27. This is the principal room of the house, in which levees are held, and large parties are assembled: the *hák t'ing* is inferior to it, being generally a *wáng t'ing* or side apartment: the *tái t'ing* is in the middle of the house, and in the rear of it, the *í t'ing* or second hall is situated.

30. *Fó lò tai* denotes beneath the fireplace, and not the hearth itself, of which there is none in the native houses of Canton.

廣東方言讀本

| | | |
|---|---|---|
| 33. Order the fire in the *kitchen* to be extinguished. | 吩咐廚房熄火 | ‹Fan fú' ˏch'ü ˏfóng sik› 'fó |
| 34. Lift up the *latch* [of the sliding bolt], and then you can open the door. | 挑起門鬼致開<br>得門 | ‹T'iú 'hí ˏmún 'kwai chí' ‹hoi tak› ˏmún. |
| 35. The pencils and ink in the *library* are scattered about. | 書房筆硯縱橫 | ‹Shü ˏfóng pat› ín² ‹tsung ˏwáng. |
| 36. The *lintel* is a bar across the top of the door. | 門楣戶頂橫木 | ˏMún ˏmí ú² 'ting ˏwáng muk₂. |
| 37. *Lock* that door. | 鎖埋個度房門 | 'Só ˏmái kó' tò² ˏfóng ˏmún. |
| 38. The *mantle-piece* of that fireplace is made of stone. | 火爐額個塊係<br>石板 | 'Fó ˏlò ngák₂ kó' fái' hai² shek₂ 'pán. |
| 39. She did not go three steps from the *nursery*. | 三步不出閨門 | ‹Sám pò² pat› ch'ut› ‹kwai ˏmún. |
| 40. Is there an *oven* belonging to the kitchen? | 廚房有局爐有<br>冇呀 | ˏCh'ü ˏfóng 'yau kuk₂ ˏlò 'yau 'mò á'? |
| 41. The *pantry* is very spacious. | 管事房好闊落 | 'Kún sz'² ˏfóng 'hò fút› lók₂. |
| 42. That little child looked through the seams of the *partition*, to see if its father was within or not. | 個個細蚊仔喺<br>板障罅裝吓睇<br>老子喺處唔喺 | Kó' kó' sai' ˏman 'tsai 'hai 'pán chéung' lá' ‹chóng 'há, 't'ai 'lò 'tsz' 'hai ch'ü' ˏ'm 'hai. |
| 43. Walking to and fro in the *piazza*. | 徘徊兩廊之間 | ˏP'úi ˏúi 'léung ˏlóng ‹chí ‹kán. |
| 44. The *privy* ought to be kept clean. | 廁所更宜潔净 | Ts'z'² 'shó kang' ˏí kít› tsing². |
| 45. Putting the hand on the *rail*, he ascended the stairs. | 噤住扶手致上<br>樓梯 | Kam² chü² ˏfú 'shau chí' 'shéung ˏlau ‹t'ai. |
| 46. The *roof* of this house is damaged, call the mason to repair the leak. | 屋背爛叫泥水<br>佬執漏 | Uk› púi' lán², kíú' ˏnai 'shui 'lò chap› lau². |
| 47. Call the coolie here to brush down the spider's webs in this *room*. | 叫管店黎撩呢<br>間房嘅蜘蛛網 | Kíú' 'kún tím' ˏlai 'líú ‹ni ‹kán ˏfóng ké' ‹chí ‹chü 'móng. |

34. The *mún kwai* is a catch sometimes attached to the *shán* (No. 3) or large sliding bolt which passes across the doors withinside, for the purpose of fastening the bar more securely.

39. *Kwai* is composed of *door* and *sceptre; kwai mún* is nearly the same as *noi shat*, and is applied to the apartments of females who are young and unmarried: the term is also applied to the harems of the rich.

45. This rail, or hand-support, denotes those balusters which are placed on the side of stairs, and not those of verandas and terraces.

47. *Kún tím*, overseer of a shop, is applied to those who labor in warehouses, factories, &c., in carrying burdens, and in doing severe labor; *coolie*, here used as a translation of it, is an Indian word, and is now in common use among foreigners in Canton.

| | | |
|---|---|---|
| 48. The *basement rooms* are usually damp. | 地下嘅房總帶濕的 | Tí[2] há[2] ké' ˏfóng ʻtsung tái' shap› tí›. |
| 49. Fasten up the *glass sash*. | 頂起玻璃蕩窗 | ʻTing ʻhí ‹pó ˏlí t'óng' ‹ch'éung. |
| 50. Fix that shell *sky-light*. | 整的明瓦天窗 | ʻChing tik› ˏming ʻngá ‹t'ín ‹ch'éung. |
| 51. Has this house a *stable* for horses? | 呢間屋有馬房冇呀 | ‹Ní ‹kán uk› ʻyau ʻmá ˏfóng ʻmò á'? |
| 52. He ascended the *stairs* step by step. | 一步步上樓梯 | Yat› pò[2] pò[2] ʻshéung ˏlau ‹t'ai. |
| 53. The *stair-case* is quite too dark. | 樓梯房黑過頭 | ˏLau ‹t'ai ˏfóng hak› kwó' ˏt'au. |
| 54. This house is two *stories* high. | 呢間屋兩層高 | ‹Ní ‹kán uk› ʻléung ˏts'ang ‹kò. |
| 55. Together ascend the *terrace* to enjoy the moonlight. | 共登天臺玩月 | Kung[2] ‹tang ‹t'ín ˏtoi ún[2] üt[2]. |
| 56. He sat on the *threshold* of the door. | 佢喺門棖黎坐 | ʻKü ʻhai ˏmún ˏch'án ˏlai tsó[2]. |
| 57. Stanzas written on the plastering of the *wall*. | 喺粉壁上題詞 | ʻHai ʻfan pik› ʻshéung ˏt'ai ˏtsz'. |
| 58. That *well* is not very deep. | 個個井冇幾深 | Kó' kó' ʻtsing ʻmò ʻkí ‹sham. |
| 59. Open the *glass windows*. | 掩開玻璃窗門 | ʻÍm ‹hoi ‹pó ˏlí ‹ch'éung ˏmún. |
| 60. Do not open the *windows*. | 唔好推開窗門 | ˏ'M ʻhò ‹t'ui ‹hoi ‹ch'éung ‹mún. |

49. These are the windows which are made to slide up and down like a sash, the word *t'óng* denoting that motion.
56. This is a raised threshold, common at the principal entrances of large houses, temples, &c., being from three to six or eight inches high.

## Section Third.

## OF THE FURNITURE OF HOUSES.

器用類第三章
Hí' yung[2] lui[2]; tai[2] ‹sám ‹chéung.

| | | |
|---|---|---|
| 1. Call the coolie to roll up the *bamboo awning*. | 叫管店扯竹簾 | Kiú' ʻkún tím' ‹ch'é chuk› ˏlím. |
| 2. Open the *cloth awning* to shade from the sun's glare. | 開布帳遮日晒 | ‹Hoi pò' chéung' ‹ché yat› shái'. |

### *Notes and Explanations.*

THE articles of household furniture, enumerated in this section, are, like those in the preceding, arranged alphabetically and their names are italicized, and when repeated with different

| | | |
|---|---|---|
| 3. The *barometer* is an index of the wind and rain. | 風雨針指風雨 | ‹Fung ʻü ‹cham ʻchí ‹fung ʻü. |
| 4. The water leaks from that *barrel.* | 個琵琶桶漏水 | Kóʼ ‹p'í ‹p'á ʻt'ung lauʼ ʻshui. |
| 5. Scour that copper *wash hand-basin* bright. | 睄净個銅面盤 | ʻSháng tsingʼ kóʼ ‹t'ung mínʼ ‹p'ún. |
| 6. The *baskets* are all made of bamboo. | 筐皆以竹爲之 | ‹Kóng ‹kái ʻí chuk› ‹wai ‹chí. |
| 7. A servant girl carrying a *covered basket* on her arm. | 妹仔挽盒籮嚟 | ‹Múi ʻtsai ʻwán hóp› ‹ló ‹lai. |
| 8. Take the *market basket* on your arm and go and buy some provisions. | 挽弓籃去買送 | ʻWán ‹kung ‹lám h'üʼ ʻmái sungʼ. |
| 9. Take and carry away this *basket of money.* | 擰呢籮仔銀去 | ‹Ning ‹ní ‹ló ʻtsai ‹ngan h'üʼ. |
| 10. Shoulder the *peddling baskets* and go to the market. | 擔擔籮去趂墟 | ‹Tám támʼ ‹ló h'üʼ ch'anʼ ‹h'ü. |
| 11. Open the *partition basket* and bring it here. | 開食格籃拈嚟 | ‹Hoi shik› kák› ‹lám ‹ním ‹lai. |
| 12. Burn the paper in the *refuse-paper basket.* | 燒字紙笠嘅紙 | ‹Shíú tszʼ ʻchí lap› kéʼ ʻchí. |
| 13. All kinds of *rattan baskets* on sale. | 各欵藤籃寄賣 | Kók› ʻfún ‹t'ang ‹lám kíʼ máiʼ. |
| 14. Buy that *open-worked rattan basket.* | 買個疎眼藤笠 | ʻMái kòʼ ‹shó ʻngán ‹t'ang lap›. |
| 15. Use a *tray basket* to hang it up. | 使隻筲挂起佢 | ʻShai chik› ‹lí kwáʼ ʻhí ʻk'ü. |
| 16. Put some water into the *bathing-tub.* | 打水落洗身盤 | ʻTá ʻshui lók› ʻsai ‹shan ‹p'ún. |
| 17. Replace the catches in this *carrying beam.* | 釘番昴落擔杆 | ‹Ting ‹fán ʻmáu lók› támʼ ‹kón. |
| 18. Ring the *hand bell* and call him here. | 搖鐘仔叫佢嚟 | ‹Íú ‹chung ʻtsai kíúʼ ʻk'ü ‹lai. |

adjectives or modifying words, those are also distinguished in the same way. It includes those articles which are moveable and commonly found in houses, without endeavoring to specify all the varieties that fancy and fashion have invented.

5. *P'ún*, a vessel, is usually joined with some other word, which modifies its meaning; thus, *mín p'ún*, face basin or a basin used in washing the face and hands; *sai shan p'ún*, a a bath or bathing-tub.

8. *Sung* includes meat, fish, vegetables, preserved articles, and whatever else may be eaten with rice, as an accompaniment to give it relish. *Wán* expresses the action of carrying a basket on the elbow by putting the arm through the handle.

10. The *tám ló* are usually in pairs; two baskets are suspended, one from each end of a light beam balanced on the shoulder of the man, who goes to the market, or who carries small articles about the streets for sale.

11. This basket, usually made of bamboo, is constructed of several parts, like little drawers, placed in a series one upon another: into each of these partitions different kinds of food, and other articles are placed.

15. This is a light open worked basket, having a broad bottom and narrow sides and two loops to suspend it resembling a wooden tray; hence its name.

17. This is the beam on which the peddling baskets are carried, as well as almost every other kind of burden; it is ordinarily about six feet long, two inches broad, and an inch thick, having short catches near each end to prevent the baskets, or whatever is suspended thereon, from slipping off; these frets or catches are also called *má* as well as *máu.*

18. This word *íú*, to shake, is in use for *ngò*, which is commonly used in speaking, but for which there is no written character.

| | | |
|---|---|---|
| 19. Work the *bellows* to make the fire burn. | 扯風箱使火猛 | ꜂Ch‘é ꜀fung ꜀séung ꜂shai ꜂fó ꜃mang. |
| 20. Shut the doors of that *book-case.* | 掩埋個書櫃門 | ꜂Ím ꜁mái kó꜄ ꜀shü kwai꜅ ꜁mún. |
| 21. Move away this *book-stand.* | 移開呢個書架 | ꜁Í ꜀hoi ꜀ní kó꜄ ꜀shü ká꜄. |
| 22. Arrange those *wine bottles* in good order. | 擠好個的酒罇 | ꜀Chai ꜂hò kó꜄ tik꜆ ꜂tsau ꜀tsun. |
| 23. Wipe this *bowl* dry. | 抹乾呢隻碗瓈 | Mút꜆ ꜀kón ꜀ní chik꜆ ꜂ün ꜁lai. |
| 24. As large as a *dessert bowl.* | 如氷盤咁大隻 | ꜁Ü ꜀ping ꜁p‘ún kóm꜄ tái꜅ chik꜆. |
| 25. Ten *soup bowls* make one set. | 一筒湯碗十隻 | Yat꜆ ꜁t‘ung ꜀tóng ꜂ün shap꜇ chik꜆. |
| 26. Large and small *lacquered boxes* for sale. | 漆箱大小出賣 | Ts‘at꜆ ꜀séung tái꜅ ꜂síú ch‘ut꜇ mái꜅. |
| 27. A lacquered *partition box* is not strong. | 漆文具唔主固 | Ts‘at꜆ ꜁man kü꜅ ꜁’m ꜂chü kú꜄. |
| 28. Arrange the things in the *rattan box.* | 執好藤盒嘅嘢 | Chap꜆ ꜂hò ꜁t‘ang hóp꜇ ké꜄ ꜃yé. |
| 29. A *work-box* with ivory fixtures. | 工夫箱有牙器 | ꜀Kung ꜀fú ꜀séung ꜃yau ꜁ngá hí꜄. |
| 30. Sediment is easily removed with a *bamboo broom.* | 竹掃易去泥積 | Chuk꜆ sò꜄ í꜅ h‘ü꜄ ꜁nai tsik꜆. |
| 31. A *coir broom* for removing oily deposits. | 椰衣掃去油氣 | ꜁Yé ꜀í sò꜄ h‘ü꜄ ꜁yau hí꜄. |
| 32. A *straw broom* for sweeping the floor. | 禾稈掃掃樓淨 | ꜁Wó ꜂kón sò꜄ sò꜄ ꜁lau tsing꜅. |
| 33. The *clothes' brush* is made of hog's bristles. | 衣服擦猪鬃做 | ꜀Í fuk꜇ tsát꜆ ꜀chü ꜀tsung tsò꜅. |
| 34. Let the *bucket* down into the well. | 放個吊桶落井 | Fóng꜄ kó꜄ tíú꜄ ꜂t‘ung lók꜇ ꜂tsing. |
| 35. Hang up the *bird-cage* in the gateway. | 掛雀籠在門口 | Kwá꜄ tséuk꜆ ꜁lung tsoi꜅ ꜁mún ꜂hau. |
| 36. Bring the oil *can* and fix the lamp. | 拈油瓶來整燈 | ꜀Ním ꜁yau ꜁p‘ing ꜁loi ꜂ching ꜀tang. |
| 37. Scour that *candlestick* bright. | 擦靚個蠟燭盤 | Ts‘át꜆ ling꜄ kó꜄ láp꜇ chuk꜆ ꜁p‘ún. |
| 38. A silver *candlestick* is easily burnished. | 銀燭檯易打磨 | ꜁Ngan chuk꜆ ꜁t‘oi í꜅ ꜂tá ꜁mó. |

22, 23. *Chai* is sometimes pronounced *tsai;* and *mút* is almost invariably read *mát:* either may be used, though *chai* and *mút* are the best.

27. This is made of wood in a manner similar to that in No. 11, but is less strong and more elegant; it is often used, as its name imports, (*man kü* literary collectanea,) for carrying the apparatus for writing and studying.

28. *Chap hò* means literally to hold fast, or hold good; the phrase is here used to express the act of placing the contents of the box in due order; *chap* is used in the same sense in the phrase *chap tsz'*, to set types, or a printer's composing.

29. *Kung fú séung* is the lady's work-box, and the *ngá hí* are the various articles for winding silk, &c., &c., with which it is supplied. The box in which carpenters keep their nails, chisels, and other tools, is also called by this name.

31. Called *yé í sò* cocoa-nut clothes broom, because it is made of the outer covering of the cocoa nut; this substance is employed by the Chinese in manufacturing not only brooms, but ropes, cordage, cables, rain-cloaks, and other articles.

34. *Tíú t‘ung*, 'suspended bucket,' is that which is used for drawing water from wells; *tíú* denotes to suspend, suspended, hanging.

| | | |
|---|---|---|
| 39. Put out the light on the *candlestick.* | 熄蠟燭盞嘅火 | Sik˒ láp˳ chuk˒ ʻtan ké˒ ʻfo. |
| 40. Rub the glass *candle-shade* clean. | 抹淨玻璃燈罩 | Mút˒ tsing˳ ˏpó ˏlí ˏtang cháu˒. |
| 41. Every description of leaden *tea canisters.* | 各樣鉛茶葉罐 | Kók˒ yéung˳ ˏün ˏch'á íp˳ kún˒. |
| 42. Spread down the *carpet* in the parlor. | 鋪番地毡落廳 | ˏP'ò ˏfán tí˳ ˏchín lók˳ ˏt'ing. |
| 43. Bargained for a new *castor.* | 定新樣五味架 | Ting˳ ˏsan yéung˳ ʻng mí˳ ká˒. |
| 44. A set of new tin *censers.* | 一副新錫香案 | Yat˒ fú˒ ˏsan sik˒ ˏhéung ón˒. |
| 45. Twelve *easy chairs.* | 十二張學士椅 | Shap˳ í˳ ˏchéung hók˳ sz'˳ ʻí. |
| 46. Arrange a dozen of *chairs.* | 擺一副燈掛椅 | ʻPái yat˒ fú˒ ˏtang kwá˒ ʻí. |
| 47. Open the *camp-chair* at the gate. | 開馬极喺門口 | ˏHoi ʻmá cháp˳ ʻhai ˏmún ʻhau. |
| 48. A set of lacquered *arm-chairs.* | 一堂漆圈手椅 | Yat˒ ˏt'óng ts'at˒ ˏhün ʻshau ʻí. |
| 49. Bring an *elbow-chair* and place it near me. | 擰張交椅埋黎 | ˏNing ˏchéung ˏkáu ʻí ˏmái ˏlai. |
| 50. Foreign *chandeliers* are very brilliant. | 洋枝燈份外光 | ˏYéung ˏchí ˏtang fan˳ ngoi˳ ˏkwóng. |
| 51. An iron *treasure chest* is safer than a wooden one. | 鐵甲萬矜過木 | T'ít˒ káp˒ mán˳ ˏkam kwó˒ muk˳. |
| 52. All the tea in the *tea chest* is consumed. | 茶箱茶葉食晒 | ˏCh'á ˏséung ˏch'á íp˳ shik˳ sái˒. |
| 53. Bamboo *chopsticks* are not good looking. | 竹快子唔好睇 | Chuk˒ fái˒ ʻtsz' ˏ'm ʻhò ʻt'ai. |
| 54. A *churn* is used to make butter. | 牛油銃整牛油 | ˏNgau ˏyau ch'ung˒ ʻching ˏngau ˏyau. |
| 55. Wood is easily split with a heavy *cleaver.* | 柴刀重易破柴 | ˏCh'ái ˏtò chung˳ í˳ p'ó˒ ˏch'ái. |
| 56. Wind up the *clock.* | 上番時辰鐘鍊 | ʻShéung ˏfán ˏshí ˏshan ˏchung lín˳. |
| 57. It is hard to repair a broken *coffee-mill.* | 架啡磨爛難整 | Ká˒ ˏfí mó˳ lán˳ ˏnán ʻching. |
| 58. Without a *corkscrew* it is difficult to draw a cork. | 冇酒鑽難開[illegible] | ʻMò ʻtsau tsün˒ ˏnán ˏhoi chat˒. |

37—39. These three candlesticks differ from each other; the first has a broad base like a dish on which the snuffers are placed; the second is tall and slender; and the third one is but little more than a wooden block into which the stick running through the candle is thrust.

45—49. The first of these, the *hók sz' í* (a term that may also be rendered 'the professor's chair,') is a large, easy chair, made for show as well as convenience. The *tang kwá í* lamp suspended chair is the common backed chair, so called from its resemblance to a wall lamp stand which is hung against the wainscot. The camp chair is a light and strong chair, with a leathern seat made so that it can be easily folded up and carried from place to place; it is used by military officers in field reviews, and is common in boats, &c. The *hün shau í* rounded arm chair has the supports at the side somewhat curved, so that both sides form an elliptical figure, and is the proper elbow-chair. The last name, *káu í*, is a generic term for all chairs, as well as a specific one for those which have supports at the side; the two last terms as well as the first are often used interchangeably for arm-chairs.

53. *Fái tsz'*, literally, nimble ones, take the place of knife and fork with the Chinese, and are made of various materials; those of bamboo are the most common.

57. *Ká fí* is intended to denote the foreign name of coffee, the Chinese themselves having



廣東方言讀本

| | | |
|---|---|---|
| 59. A *couch* with a bottom of woven rattans. | 交子床藤織底 | ‹Káu 'tsz' ˏch'óng ˏt'ang chik› 'tai. |
| 60. A hundred large and small tin *covers*. | 大小錫蓋一百 | Tái' 'síú sik› koi' yat› pák›. |
| 61. A *cup* is used for drinking and drawing water. | 缶飲器汲水器 | ‹Fau 'yam hí' kap› 'shui hí'. |
| 62. Make a new *butter cup*. | 打番個牛油盅 | 'Tá ‹fán kó' ˏngau ˏyau ‹chung. |
| 63. *Custard cups* are not very large. | 吉時杯冇乜大 | Kat› ˏshi ‹púi 'mò mat› tái'. |
| 64. A *milk cup* with one spout. | 牛乳盅一筒嘴 | ˏNgau 'yü ‹chung yat› ˏt'ung 'tsui. |
| 65. Shut the doors of the *cupboard*. | 閂埋碗碟櫃門 | ‹Shán ˏmái 'ún típˎ kwai' ˏmún. |
| 66. Roll up this silk *curtain*. | 扯開呢塊綢簾 | 'Ch'é ‹hoi ‹ní fái' ˏch'au ˏlím. |
| 67. A chair *cushion*, one side rattan and the other cloth. | 藤絨兩面椅墊 | ˏT'ang ˏyung 'léung mín' 'í tín'. |
| 68. A flat *cutting-board* is the best for use. | 砧板平好切肉 | ‹Cham 'pán ˏp'ing 'hò ts'ít› yukˎ. |
| 69. A glass *decanter* is transparent. | 玻璃酒罇通照 | ‹Pó ˏlí 'tsau ‹tsun ‹t'ung chíú'. |
| 70. Turn the key in the *writing desk*. | 扭埋寫字箱話 | 'Nau ˏmái 'sé tsz'' ‹séung wá'. |
| 71. Take and bring this tray of *dessert plates*. | 抽呢盤菓碟嚟 | ‹Ch'au ‹ní ˏp'ún 'kwó típˎ ˏlai. |
| 72. Bring a *cocoa-nut dipper* to bail some water. | 拈椰殼揔水嚟 | ‹Ním ˏyé hók› fat› 'shui ˏlai. |
| 73. Let the crumbs remain for the *beggar's dish*. | 食剩等乞鉢嚟 | Shikˎ shing' 'tang h'at› pút› ˏlai. |
| 74. The *dish* for fish-sauce is not very high. | 魚油盅冇乜高 | ˏU ˏyau ‹chung 'mò mat› ‹kò. |
| 75. Bring a *dish-cloth* and wipe this plate clean. | 擰謭布撟净碟 | ‹Ning 'tsín pò' 'kíú tsing' típˎ. |
| 76. Bring a *dust board* to take up this refuse. | 拈揔斗揔擸㩋 | ‹Ním fat› 'tau fat› lápˎ sáp›. |
| 77. A *dust basket* is needed when sweeping the ground. | 掃地須用竹篸 | Sò' tí' ˏsü yung' chuk› 'ch'ám. |
| 78. Use the rattan handled feather *duster*. | 使藤柄鷄毛掃 | 'Shai ˏt'ang ping' ‹kai ˏmò sò'. |
| 79. Wipe that silver *egg-cup*. | 抹過個銀蛋盅 | Mút› kwó' kó' ˏngan tán' ‹chung. |
| 80. Call the silversmith to make a new *egg-cup stand*. | 叫銀匠打蛋架 | Kíú' ˏngan tséung' 'tá tán' ká'. |
| 81. *Fenders* made close are the best. | 火爐圍密嘅好 | 'Fó ˏlò ˏwai matˎ ké' 'hò. |
| 82. Bring the *finger-bowls* quickly. | 快擰洗手盅嚟 | Fái' ‹ning 'sai 'shau ‹chung ˏlai. |

no name for this article. So *kat shí* cups for custard cups, *sám pín púi* for champagne glasses, and other phrases.

70. *Nau* expresses the wringing motion of the hand in locking a bolt, turning a screw, &c.; *mái* added to it in this connection implies that the lock must be secured; *wá* is to order.

72. The dipper made of the cocoa-nut shell, *yé hók*, is called by the same name; with a handle of bamboo fitted to them they are used for dipping water, oil, &c.

81. This refers to fenders which are made of wires, those being regarded the most safe which have the wires in the net-work close together.

廣東方言讀本



| | | |
|---|---|---|
| 83. As high as a *footstool.* | 脚踏櫈咁高嘅 | Kéuk› táp, tang' kóm' ‹kò ké'. |
| 84. Pass it along with a silver *fork.* | 使銀鈫釵過嚟 | 'Shai ‚ngan ‹ch'á ‹ch'á kwó' ‚lai. |
| 85. An antique *flower-pot* is priceless. | 古老花瓶冇價 | 'Kú 'lò ‹fá ‚p'ing 'mò ká'. |
| 86. An iron *frying-pan* is made use of in frying cakes. | 用鐵鍋哩炕餅 | Yung$^2$ t'ít› ‹wó ‚lé hóng' 'ping. |
| 87. It is hard to light a fire in a wet *furnace.* | 濕風爐難着火 | Shap› ‹fung ‚lò ‚nán chéuk› 'fó. |
| 88. Things in a *gallipot* do not lose their flavor. | 勘盅擠唔漏氣 | Hóm$^2$ ‹chung ‹chai ‚'m lau$^2$ hí'. |
| 89. *Champagne glasses* are very high. | 三鞭酒杯最高 | ‹Sám ‹pín 'tsau ‹púi tsui' ‹kò. |
| 90. Hand me here a *claret glass.* | 遞隻紅酒杯嚟 | Tai$^2$ chik› ‚hung 'tsau ‹púi ‚lai. |
| 91. A *grate* placed in the wall is extremely warm. | 入墻火爐極暖 | Yap, ‚ts'eung 'fó ‚lò kik, 'nün. |
| 92. A *grater* is required for rasping ginger. | 取薑汁要薑擦 | 'Ts'ü ‹kéung chap› iú' ‹kéung ts'át›. |
| 93. Move away a little that *gravy dish.* | 移開吓個汁盅 | ‚I ‹hoi 'há kó' chap› ‹chung. |
| 94. An even fire is needed when using a *gridiron.* | 燒鐵鈀火要勻 | ‹Shiú t'ít› ‚p'á 'fó iú' ‚wan. |
| 95. Use a *hearth-brush* to clean the fireplace. | 用灰掃整淨爐 | Yung$^2$ ‹fúi sò' 'ching tsing$^2$ ‚lò. |
| 96. A *heater* must be used in cold weather. | 天寒必用火鍋 | ‹T'in ‚hón pít› yung$^2$ 'fó ‹wó. |
| 97. The tub's *hoops* have burst and the water leaks. | 桶箍咆了漏水 | 'T'ung ‹fú páu' 'líú lau$^2$ 'shui. |
| 98. Flour is stored in *kegs.* | 琵琶桶仔裝麵 | ‚P'í ‚p'á 't'ung 'tsai ‹chóng mín$^2$. |
| 99. It is easy to boil water in a copper *kettle.* | 銅煲煲水易滾 | ‚T'ung ‹pò ‹pò 'shui í$^2$ 'kwan. |
| 100. Two *keys* will make a noise. | 兩條匙就有聲 | 'Léung ‚t'íú ‚shí tsau$^2$ 'yau ‹shing. |
| 101. An iron *kettle* is made use of in boiling food. | 使大鐵鑊烚野 | 'Shai tái$^2$ t'ít, wók, shap, 'yé. |
| 102. Split some *kindlings* to make the fire burn. | 破柴花好熡爐 | P'ó' ‹ch'ái ‹fá 'hò lau$^2$ ‚lò. |
| 103. Change that *carving knife.* | 換過張大餐刀 | Ún$^2$ kwó' ‹chéung tái$^2$ ‹ts'án ‹tò. |
| 104. Do not scour the *case knives* so thin. | 牛肉刀莫磨薄 | ‚Ngau yuk, ‹tò mók, ‚mó pók,. |

83. This is said in derision of persons without learning or merit, but who amply supply their deficiencies with pretensions, upstarts inflated with pride and who are easily seen through by their neighbors. "As high as my ankle," is another phrase to the same purpose.

87. This piece of furniture is usually called a fogong by foreigners in Canton; it is made of burnt clay, and is in universal use among the natives.

96. The utensil here called a heater is a copper tube in which coals are placed, and which opens beneath into a pan or hearth of the same metal; it is inserted in the middle of a large tin vessel that contains the victuals, and is kept constantly supplied with coals. The utensil is most frequently found in taverns and public eating-houses.

100. This is an expression used by the Chinese, when they speak of the difference between company and solitude; one wife, say they, and the house is quiet, but two make a continual jingling; so in intercourse with friends, or play among children.

| | | |
|---|---|---|
| 105. With a *vegetable knife* it is cut very even. | 菜刀切過咁齊 | Ts'oi' ‹tò ts'it› kwó' kóm' ‹ts'ai. |
| 106. Pass me the *fish-knife*. | 遞一張魚刀嚟 | Tai² yat› ‹chéung ‹ü ‹tò ‹lai. |
| 107. A *pen-knife* with two blades. | 摺鉸刀仔兩開 | Chíp› káu' ‹tò 'tsai 'léung ‹hoi. |
| 108. A board is fitted to scour *dessert knives*. | 菓刀使板磨好 | 'Kwó ‹tò 'shai 'pán ‹mó 'hò. |
| 109. Nine *jars* and ten covers. | 九個甖十個噂 | ‹Kau kó' ‹áng shap› kó' 'ts'un. |
| 110. His belly is like an unglazed *jar*. | 眞好似塔咁肚 | ‹Chan 'hò 'tsz' táp› kóm' 't'ò. |
| 111. I will give you a *jar* for a gall-bladder. | 俾甕缸你做膽 | 'Pí ung' ‹kóng 'ní tsò² 'tám. |
| 112. Go and bring two *jugs* of spring water. | 去擔兩埕山水 | H'ü' ‹tám 'leung ‹ch'ing ‹shán 'shui. |
| 113. When lighting a high lamp use a *ladder*. | 點高燈用梯櫈 | 'Tím ‹kò ‹tang yung² ‹t'ai tang'. |
| 114. Copper *ladles* are easily scoured. | 銅殼容易打抹 | ‹T'ung hók› ‹yung í² 'tá mút›. |
| 115. Bring a *soup ladle* to serve out the soup. | 擰湯殼擾湯嚟 | ‹Ning ‹t'ong hók› 'iú ‹t'ong ‹lai. |
| 116. Wooden *ladles* are made of cross-grained wood. | 橫紋木做木殼 | ‹Wáng ‹man muk› tsò² muk› hók›. |
| 117. A *helmet-shaped lamp* hanging in the great hall. | 大堂吊盔頭燈 | Tái² ‹t'óng tiú' ‹kw'ai ‹t'au ‹tang. |
| 118. Light the *globular lamp*. | 點着金魚缸燈 | 'Tím chéuk› ‹kam ‹ü ‹kóng ‹tang. |
| 119. Relight the *water-lamp*. | 點番着個琉璃 | 'Tím ‹fán chéuk› kó' lau² ‹lí. |
| 120. This *lamp-stand* fell down and is out of order. | 跌攣呢枝燈檯 | Tít› ‹lün ‹ní ‹chí ‹tang ‹t'oi. |
| 121. Use a *lamp-chimney* and you need not fear the wind. | 使燈筒唔怕風 | 'Shai ‹tang ‹t'ung ‹'m p'á' ‹fung. |
| 122. *Lampwicks* are made of cotton thread. | 棉紗繩做燈心 | ‹Mín ‹shá ‹shing tsò² ‹tang ‹sam. |
| 123. If the *rush lampwick* be small the oil hardly ascends. | 燈草細惡上油 | ‹Tang 'ts'ò sai' ók› 'shéung ‹yau. |

109. This phrase is employed to denote a deficiency, as in case of income and expenditure, where the latter exceeds the former.

111. The gall-bladder is supposed, by the Chinese, to be the seat of courage: the phrase is used to excite an adversary.

117. *Kw'ai t'au* is a wire covering for the head of a conical shape, a kind of helmet, which this lamp, often called a hall lamp, somewhat resembles; when hung up in lanes, or at the entrance of houses, it is called *lò tang*, a way lamp.

118. Literally, 'the gold-fish bowl lamp,' so called because the globular bowl in which the *lau lí* or water lamp is suspended is often used by the Chinese as an ornamental vessel, in which gold-fish are kept alive.

119. The *lau lí* or water lamp is a small glass cup, partly filled with water, and the oil is poured upon its surface; the wick, made of rush pith, is suspended in the vessel by means of wires, and burns till the oil is consumed. The Chinese have no specific names for the many fashions of lamps in use among foreigners, but give descriptive names which frequently differ among themselves: an Argand lamp-globe is called *ü ngán wat*, from its resemblance to the crystaline lens of a fish's eye; a table stand lamp is named *sán tang*, umbrella lamp; and a desk lamp with a tin shade is termed *ché tang*, a parasol lamp.

| | | |
|---|---|---|
| 124. Light the *lantern* to go into the street. | 點燈籠去出街 | 'Tím ‹tang ‹lung h'ü' ch'ut› ‹kái. |
| 125. I cannot open this *lock*. | 呢把鎖唔開得 | ‹Ní 'pá 'só ‹'m ‹hoi tak›. |
| 126. In warm weather, change the rattan *chair mats*. | 暑天換過藤墊 | 'Shü ‹t'in ún$^2$ kwò' ‹t'ang tin$^2$. |
| 127. Rattan *dish mats* are used at dinner. | 藤碟墊大餐用 | ‹T'ang típ› tín$^2$ tái$^2$ ‹tsán yung$^2$. |
| 128. Spread the *rush matting* in the hall. | 用草蓆鋪大廳 | Yung$^2$ 'ts'ò tsik$_2$ ‹pò tái$^2$ ‹t'ing. |
| 129. Cover the floor with *matting* from Línt'án. | 連灘草蓆墊樓 | ‹Lín ‹t'án 'ts'ò tsik$_2$ tín$^2$ ‹lau. |
| 130. Rice *measures* are made of bamboo tubes. | 捭竹筒做米升 | 'Pí chuk› ‹t'ung tsò' 'mai ‹shing. |
| 131. Working the *mill* till one's hands are tired. | 推石磨手唅倦 | ‹T'úi shik$_2$ mó$^2$ 'shau 'úi kün$^2$. |
| 132. *Mops* are used to wash floors. | 洗大樓用布嘜 | 'Sai tái$^2$ ‹lau yung$^2$ pò' mak›. |
| 133. Bring a *mortar* and pestle to pound sugar candy. | 擡舂砍舂氷糖 | ‹T'oi ‹chung 'hóm ‹chung ‹ping ‹t'óng. |
| 134. Wash out that *mustard pot*. | 洗吓個芥末盅 | 'Sai 'há ko' kái' mút$_2$ ‹chung. |
| 135. This *napkin* is very dirty. | 呢條茶布汚漕 | ‹Ní ‹tiú ‹ch'á pò' ‹ú ‹tsò. |
| 136. Use a *padlock* to secure it. | 使盒鑼鎖主固 | 'Shai hóp$_2$ ‹lò 'só 'chü kú'. |
| 137. Shoulder a pair of *pails* and come here. | 擔一擔水桶嚟 | ‹Tám yat› tám' 'shui 't'ung ‹lai. |
| 138. The *pan* is a utensil for boiling meat. | 鑊乃煮肉之器 | Wók$_2$ 'nái 'chü yuk$_2$ ‹chí hí'. |
| 139. Glaze another *pane* of glass [in this window]. | 鑲過塊玻璃片 | ‹Séung kwò' fái' ‹pó ‹lí p'ín'. |
| 140. The top of the *pepper box* is pierced with holes. | 胡椒罇蓋漏眼 | ‹Ú ‹tsíú ‹tsun koi' lau$^2$ 'ngán. |
| 141. A heavy *pestle* is ill fitted for use. | 舂杵重唔好使 | ‹Chung 'ch'ü chung$^2$ ‹'m 'hò 'shai. |
| 142. Open the *piano*. | 揭開八音琴蓋 | K'ít› ‹hoi pát› ‹yam ‹k'am koi'. |
| 143. The *picture-frame* must be made like the pattern. | 整畫架要合式 | 'Ching wá$^2$ ká' íú' hóp$_2$ shik›. |
| 144. Wipe down that *pier-glass*. | 抹吓個照身鏡 | Mút› 'há kò' chíú' ‹shan king'. |

124. *Ch'ut kái* is an idiomatic phrase for to go out, or to go abroad,—without reference necessarily to the streets.

131. The mill here referred to is the small one made of two stones, and worked by hand, commonly seen in houses; it is mostly employed in grinding rice or pulse, though the hand mill is probably not as much used by the Chinese as by the Hindoos.

132. Here is another instance of an attempt to give the sound of the foreign article; this is indicated by placing *mouth* by the side of *mik*, without which it means to seek, to search after.

142. The reference here is to the foreign instrument, the piano-forte, called by the Chinese *pát yam k'am*, or eight sounding harp: this, however, may not be the most appropriate term, the phrase *pát yam* eight sounds, is often used as a general appellation for musical instruments.

144. This term is applied not only to those which hang between windows, or against piers but to large mirrors generally, which will *chíú shan*, reflect the whole person, such as are set above a fireplace, or mounted on a frame.

| | | |
|---|---|---|
| 145. Bring a *pipe* and follow on after me. | 擰烟筒跟人尾 | ‹Ning ‹ín ‹t'ung ‹kan ‹yan ʿmí. |
| 146. Commenced life with only a *fire pipe*. | 係吹火筒出身 | Hai$^2$ ‹ch'ui ʿfó ‹t'ung ch'ut› ‹shan. |
| 147. Replace a bowl in that *pipe-stem*. | 鑲起個烟筒斗 | ‹Séung ʿhí kó' ‹ín ‹t'ung ʿtau. |
| 148. It is easy to pour water from a large full *pitcher*. | 銚缸裝水好斟 | Tiú$^2$ ‹kóng ‹chóng ʿshui ʿhò ‹cham. |
| 149. Change the *plate* and bring a clean one. | 替過隻淨碟黎 | T'ai' kwó' chik› tsing$^2$ típ$_2$ ‹lai. |
| 150. *Lacquered plates* cannot be long used. | 漆碟唔使得耐 | Ts'at› típ$_2$ ‹'m ʿshai tak› noi$^2$. |
| 151. Push away that large silver *plate*. | 推開隻大銀碟 | ‹T'úi ‹hoi chik› tái$^2$ ‹ngán típ$_2$. |
| 152. Take off the cover from this *platter*. | 揭起呢冚兜蓋 | K'ít› ʿhí ‹ní ʿk'am ‹tau koi'. |
| 153. The *poker* is placed by the fireside. | 火爐邊嘅火杵 | ʿFó ‹lò ‹pín ké' ʿfó ʿch'ü. |
| 154. Put the bills in the *portfolio*. | 將單放在書挾 | ‹Tséung ‹tán fóng' tsoi$^2$ ‹shü káp$_2$. |
| 155. Call the coolie to pull the *punkah*. | 叫管店扯風扇 | Kíú' ʿkún tím' ʿch'é ‹fung shín'. |
| 156. A *rolling pin* is used to roll out pastry. | 使麵棍開麵薄 | ʿShai mín$^2$ kwan' ‹hoi mín$^2$ pók$_2$. |
| 157. The shoes were brushed upon the *rug*. | 在地毡擦過鞋 | Tsoi$^2$ tí$^2$ ‹chín tsát› kwó' ‹hái. |
| 158. Put what remains of the food in a *safe*. | 紗風燈擠宿肉 | ‹Shá ‹fung ‹tang ‹chai suk› yuk$_2$. |
| 159. The new fashioned *salt-cellars* are very elegant. | 時興塩盅精緻 | ‹Shí ‹hing ‹ím ‹chung ‹tsing chí'. |
| 160. In serving up tea, use a *saucer*. | 奉茶要用茶碟 | Fung$^2$ ‹ch'á íú' yung$^2$ ‹ch'á típ$_2$. |
| 161. The *saucer boat* is dented, and needs mending. | 茶船凹要整番 | ‹Ch'á ‹shün nap› íú' ʿching ‹fán. |
| 162. The rat fell into the *scales* [to weigh himself]. | 老鼠跌落天平 | ʿLò ʿshü tít› lók$_2$ ‹t'ín ‹p'ing. |
| 163. The *pan* of the *scales* is hung too high. | 天平盤吊得高 | ‹T'ín ‹p'ing ‹p'ún tíú' tak› ‹kò. |
| 164. Grind the *scissors* sharp to cut out clothes. | 磨利鉸剪裁衣 | ‹Mó lí$^2$ káu' ʿtsín ‹ts'oi ‹í. |

146. This phrase is employed to denote the condition of one who has risen from extreme penury,—a cook's assistant, capable only of blowing the fire with a bamboo pipe,—to affluence and high respectability: the *fó t'ung* is a hollow stick of bamboo, and is used like a blowpipe.

155. The word punkah is, in Canton, usually defined to mean the large boards with fringes which are suspended above tables, and swung to and fro during a meal.

157. The word *chín* is used for hearth rugs, door mats, carpets, and so forth, made of wool, hair, coir, or other materials. The Chinese in this region use matting to preserve or adorn the floors of their dwellings.

160, 161. That is, do not present a cup of tea without placing it upon a saucer. The kind of saucer used by the Chinese is a sort of saucer boat,—a small dish made of metal, somewhat in the shape of a boat, in which the tea-cup is placed, and thus handed to guests. The character *nap* is intended to represent an indented surface; characters that are carved below the surface are called *nap tsz'*.

162. This phrase is applied to self-conceited persons who stand high in their own estimation: the *t'ín p'ing* are the common scales.

| | | |
|---|---|---|
| 165. It is well to keep scissors in a *scissor-case.* | 剪有匣好收藏 | ʻTsín ʻyau háp$_2$ ʻhò ‹shau ˏts'óng. |
| 166. Behind the *screen* he listened to their words. | 屏風後聽佢講 | ˏP'ing ‹fung hau$^2$ ‹t'ing ʻk'ü ʻkóng. |
| 167. Open the *folding screen* to set off an apartment. | 開圍屏閘間房 | ‹Hoi ˏwai ˏp'ing cháp$_2$ ‹kán ˏfóng. |
| 168. A new *steaming screen* gives a taste of bamboo. | 新蒸籠有竹氣 | ‹San ‹ching ˏlung ʻyau chuk› hí'. |
| 169. He has gone in a *sedan* to repay visits. | 擡乘轎去拜會 | ˏToi shing$^2$ kíú$^2$ h'ü' pái' úi$^2$. |
| 170. A black *lacquered server* is substantial. | 黑漆托盤老實 | Hak› ts'at› t'ók› ˏp'ún ʻlò shat$_2$. |
| 171. A *bamboo settee* is very cool in warm weather. | 竹床暑天貪涼 | Chuk› ˏch'óng ʻshü ‹t'ín ‹t'ám ˏléung. |
| 172. *Shears* should shut close together. | 大鉸剪要哈口 | Tái$^2$ káu$^2$ ʻtsín íú' kóp› ʻhau. |
| 173. The *betel-nut shears* will not cut it open. | 梹榔鋏鋏唔開 | ‹Ping ˏlóng cháp$_2$ cháp$_2$ ˏ'm ‹hoi. |
| 174. Nail a *shelf* in the corner of the wall. | 墻角釘狗髀架 | ˏTs'éung kók› ‹ting ʻkau ʻpí ká'. |
| 175. Use the *shovel* to take away the ashes. | 使火鏟去爐灰 | ʻShai ʻfó ʻch'án h'ü' ˏló ‹fúi. |
| 176. The *rice shovel* can be used on either side. | 鑊鏟致轉得便 | Wók$_2$ ʻch'án chí' ʻchün tak› pín$^2$. |
| 177. An iron *skimmer* takes the scum from the broth. | 鐵漏殼起湯糜 | T'ít› lau$^2$ hók› ʻhí ‹t'ong ˏmí. |
| 178. Use a *sieve* to winnow the chaff from the rice. | 使篩箕簸米糠 | ʻShai ‹shai ‹kí pó' ʻmai ‹kóng. |
| 179. A *sieve* is required to sift rice flour. | 米粉用羅斗篩 | ʻMai ʻfan yung$^2$ ˏló ʻtau ‹shai. |
| 180. On the *oil slings* it is easily upset. | 油絡安佢唔穩 | ˏYau lók› ‹ón ʻk'ü ˏ'm ʻwan. |
| 181. A pair of the *twine slings* is lost. | 失去一對線絡 | Shat› h'ü' yat› túi' sín' lók›. |
| 182. *Snuffers* prevent the candle from becoming dim. | 燭剪唔怕火暗 | Chuk› ʻtsín ˏ'm p'á' ʻfó óm'. |
| 183. A *sofa* of horse hair is pleasant to recline upon. | 馬尾睡椅好瞓 | ʻMá ʻmí shui$^2$ ʻí ʻhò fan'. |
| 184. Bargained for a new fashioned *soy-stand.* | 定新樣豉油架 | Ting$^2$ ‹san yéung$^2$ shí$^2$ ˏyau ká'. |
| 185. Take the *spoon* away and wash it clean. | 擰匙羹去洗净 | ‹Ning ˏhí ‹kang h'ü' ʻsai tsing$^2$. |
| 186. I have not seen the *sugar spoon.* | 唔見減枝糖羹 | ˏ'M kín' ʻkám ‹chí ˏt'óng ‹kang. |
| 187. Put the *salt spoon* back in its place. | 擠番枝塩羹處 | ‹Chai ‹fán ‹chí ˏím ‹kang ch'ü'. |

168. This utensil is used in cooking food by means of steam; the food, usually rice, is put into a wooden vessel, and a fine screen or net of bamboo placed upon the top; it is now inverted over a pan of boiling water, and stands upon the steaming sticks (No. 192), by which means it is exposed to the aqueous vapor.

176. The *wók ch'án* is not much unlike an apothecary's spatula; it is thicker and heavier, and like it, may be used with either side up.

180, 181. The *yau lók* is made of rattans or bamboos, in the form of a four cornered frame or basket, within and upon which the articles to be carried are placed. The *sín lók* is made of twine; it is a network, with broad meshes, in the form of a sachel; small boxes and other light articles are carried in it.

| | | |
|---|---|---|
| 188. Change this *gravy spoon.* | 換過呢枝汁羹 | Ún$^{2}$ kwó' ꜀ní ꜀chí chap꜁ ꜀kang. |
| 189. Make another *rice spoon.* | 打番一枝飯羹, | 'Tá ꜀fán yat꜁ ꜀chí fán$^{2}$ ꜀kang. |
| 190. *Egg-green spoons* are in common use. | 蛋青調羹通用 | Tán$^{2}$ ꜀ts'ing ꜂t'iú ꜀kang ꜀t'ung yung$^{2}$. |
| 191. It is easy to go up and down upon a *step-ladder.* | 用板梯易上落 | Yung$^{2}$ 'pán ꜀t'ai í$^{2}$ 'shéung lók$_{2}$. |
| 192. *Steaming-sticks* are used in pairs. | 烝箸須用一對 | ꜀Ching chü$^{2}$ ꜀sui yung$^{2}$ yat꜁ túi'. |
| 193. The *steelyards* are not at all too large. | 司碼秤冇大的 | ꜀Sz' 'má ꜂ch'ing 'mò tái$^{2}$ tik꜁. |
| 194. The thing is as square as a *stool.* | 似斗方椅咁正 | 'Ts'z' 'tau ꜀fóng 'i kóm' ching'. |
| 195. *Earthen stools* are cool to sit upon. | 好貪凉坐瓦鼓 | 'Hò ꜀t'ám ꜂léung 'tsó$^{2}$ 'ngá 'kú. |
| 196. *Bamboo stools* are cooler than wooden ones. | 竹椅凉過木嘅 | Chuk꜁ 'i ꜂léung kwó' muk꜀ ké'. |
| 197. Eight *stone bottomed stools.* | 八張石面馬瓠 | Pát꜁ ꜀chéung shik꜁ mín$^{2}$ 'má ꜂ú. |
| 198. Take away the *sugar bowl.* | 搬開冰糖盅去 | ꜀Pún ꜀hoi ꜀ping ꜂tóng ꜀chung h'ü'. |
| 199. The whole family eating at one *table.* | 大家同檯食飯 | Tái$^{2}$ ꜀ká ꜂t'ung ꜂t'oi shik꜀ fán$^{2}$. |
| 200. Change the top of the *stone table.* | 換過塊石枱面 | Ún$^{2}$ kwó' fái' shik꜀ ꜂t'oi mín$^{2}$. |
| 201. A *bamboo table* is light and easily moved. | 竹枱輕容易搬 | Chuk꜁ ꜂t'oi ꜀hing ꜂yung í$^{2}$ ꜀pún. |
| 202. Lay the *table-cloth* straight on the table. | 大枱布要齊整 | Tái$^{2}$ ꜂t'oi pò' iú' ꜂ts'ai 'ching. |
| 203. Brush those *tea-poys.* | 掃過個張茶机 | Sò' kwó' kó' ꜀chéung ꜂ch'á ꜀kí. |
| 204. Engaged to have a *tea-strainer* made ready. | 定打便個茶漏 | Ting$^{2}$ 'tá pín$^{2}$ kó' ꜂ch'á lau$^{2}$. |
| 205. Use a *tea-kettle* to boil medicine. | 使茶煲做藥煲 | 'Shai ꜂ch'á ꜀pò tsò$^{2}$ yéuk꜀ ꜀pò. |
| 206. The tin *tea-kettle* goes with the dowry. | 錫茶提隨嫁用 | Sik꜁ ꜂ch'á ꜂t'ai ꜂ts'ui ká' yung$^{2}$. |
| 207. Use a *tea-spoon* to stir it up. | 使茶匙攪起佢 | 'Shai ꜂ch'á ꜂shí 'káu 'hí 'k'ü. |
| 208. All kinds of tin *tea-pots.* | 各欵錫器茶壺 | Kók꜁ 'fún sik꜁ hí' ꜂ch'á ꜂ú. |
| 209. The covered *tea-cup* is inferior to the tea pot. | 局盅唔似茶壺 | Kuk꜀ chung ꜂'m 'ts'z' ꜂ch'á ꜂ú. |

190. These spoons, somewhat larger than table spoons, are made of earthenware of a dull pale green color, and the bowls are not much unlike in shape to the transverse segment of an egg-shell.

192. The sticks are laid one across the other in the boiler, so as to form a rack or grate, on which the wooden tub or other vessel containing the provisions is placed in order to be cooked.

193. These steelyards are those used by the government, or like them: the public offices are called *sz'*; and *má* denotes the weights, with which the steelyards are poised: hence *sz' má*, official weights. The implement is also called a dotchin, and is in general use to weigh heavy articles as well as those where a delicate balance is required.

195. The *ngá kú*, earthen drums are the garden seats commonly exported from China. They are named from the resemblance in form of the generality of them to drums.

| | | |
|---|---|---|
| 210. The *tea-cup* with a single handle. | 茶杯有單耳嘅 | ꜁Ch'á ꜀púi 'yau ꜀tán 'í ké'. |
| 211. With a *tea-tray*, the table will not be wet. | 有茶盤唔濕檯 | 'Yau ꜁ch'á ꜁p'ún ꜁'m shap꜆ ꜁t'oi. |
| 212. One tin *tea-canister*. | 一個錫茶葉罇 | Yat꜆ kó' sik꜆ ꜁ch'á íp꜇ ꜀tsun. |
| 213. If you cannot see, then use a *telescope*. | 唔見打千里鏡 | ꜁'M kín' 'tá ꜀ts'ín 'lí king'. |
| 214. How does the *thermometer* stand? | 寒暑針到幾度 | ꜁Hón 'shü ꜀cham tò' 'kí tò'? |
| 215. Lost a *toast-rack*. | 失一個多時架 | Shat꜆ yat꜆ kó' ꜀tó ꜁shí ká'. |
| 216. A coal has jumped out, take it up quickly in the *tongs*. | 炭射出快鉗去 | T'án' shé' ch'ut꜆ fái' ꜁kím h'ü'. |
| 217. Fasten some bait on the rat *trap*. | 綁的餌在鼠挾 | 'Póng tik꜆ ní' tsoi' 'shü káp꜆. |
| 218. Carry the presents in an *eating tray*. | 擡食箱去送禮 | ꜁T'oi shik꜇ ꜀séung h'ü' sung' 'lai. |
| 219. A lacquered *tray* well gilded is wanted. | 漆托盤要好金 | Ts'at꜆ t'ók꜆ ꜁p'ún íú' 'hò ꜀kam. |
| 220. Put it into the *tray-basket*, and place it in the sun. | 窩籃裝起去晒 | ꜀Wó ꜁lám ꜀chóng 'hí h'ü' shái'. |
| 221. Take care of that *clothes' trunk*. | 提防吓個衣箱 | ꜁T'ai ꜁fóng 'há kó' ꜀í ꜀séung. |
| 222. A *leathern trunk* is light and easily carried. | 皮槓輕出門便 | ꜁P'í 'lung ꜀hing ch'ut꜆ ꜁mun pín'. |
| 223. A *low tub* for washing clothes. | 扁身洗衣服盤 | 'Pín ꜀shan 'sai ꜀í fuk꜇ ꜁p'ún. |
| 224. A *high tub* for washing jackets. | 高身嘅洗衫盤 | ꜀Kò ꜀shan ké' 'sai ꜀shám ꜁p'ún. |
| 225. Bring me a *tumbler* of cold water. | 擰一杯凍水嚟 | ꜀Ning yat꜆ ꜀púi tung' 'shui ꜁lai. |
| 226. Find a *tunnel* to put in the wine. | 搵漏斗嚟入酒 | 'Wan lau' 'tau ꜁lai yap꜇ 'tsau. |
| 227. A chinaware soup *tureen* with two handles. | 磁器兩耳湯兜 | ꜁Ts'z' hí' 'léung 'í ꜀t'óng ꜀tau. |
| 228. Artificial flowers put into a flower *vase*. | 紙蓪花插花瓶 | 'Chí ꜀t'ung ꜀fá ch'áp꜆ ꜀fá ꜁p'ing. |
| 229. A *well rope* with buckets on each end. | 兩頭繩綁吊桶 | 'Léung ꜁t'au ꜁shing 'póng tíú' 't'ung. |
| 230. Be careful of that *wine glass*. | 小心吓隻脚杯 | 'Síú ꜀sam 'há chik꜆ kéuk꜆ ꜀púi. |
| 231. A low *wine jar* with an even top. | 平蓋矮身酒壺 | ꜁P'ing koi' 'ai ꜀shan 'tsau ꜁ú. |
| 232. A *whetstone* should be very smooth. | 磨刀石要幼凍 | ꜁Mó ꜀tò shik꜇ íú' yau' tung'. |

213. If unable to see an object at a distance with the naked eye, then use the thousand *lí* glass: *ts'ín lí king* is applied to the common telescope.

216. In this phrase, the word *kím* is used as a verb; *fái* quickly, *kím* tong it, *h'ü* back, is the literal rendering; *shé ch'ut* is an allusion to the starting of an arrow from the bow.

218. The *shik séung* resembles a case of shallow drawers placed upon each other, to the number of four, five, or more; these are filled with food, and fitted into a frame, in which they are carried.

220. The *wó lám* is a circular bamboo utensil, made shallow like a tray, with a low rim around the edge, in which grain and other articles are sometimes exposed for sale; there is another still flatter and smaller, but similar in shape, in common use.

## Section Fourth.

## ARTICLES OF DRESS.

### 首飾衣服類第四章

'Shau shik, ‹í fuk$_2$ lui$^2$; tai$^2$ sz'' ‹chéung.

| | | |
|---|---|---|
| 1. Tie on an *apron.* | 勒番條帷裙咋 | Lak$_2$ ‹fán ‚t'iú ‚wai ‚kw'an chá'. |
| 2. Ancient *court bonnets* were made of leather. | 古視朝以皮弁 | 'Kú shí$^2$ ‚ch'iú 'í ‚p'í pín$^2$. |
| 3. All the ancient *bonnets* were black. | 凡古冠皆用玄 | ‚Fán 'kú ‹kún ‹kái yung$^2$ ‚ün. |
| 4. Modern hats are the ancient *bonnets.* | 今帽即古冠弁 | ‹Kam mò$^2$ tsik, 'kú ‹kún pín$^2$. |
| 5. Fasten back that *bonnet-ring.* | 釘番個帽圈咋 | ‹Ting ‹fán kó' mò$^2$ ‹hün chá'. |
| 6. The straps which are tied beneath the chin are called *bonnet-strings.* | 綁住下耙底下個條叫做帽攀 | 'Póng chü$^2$ há$^2$ ‚p'á 'tai há$^2$, kò' ‚t'iú kíú' tsò$^2$ mò$^2$ p'án'. |
| 7. The button is fitted into the *bonnet-cylinder.* | 安帽頂係帽籠 | ‹Ón mò$^2$ 'ting hai$^2$ mò$^2$ ‹lung. |
| 8. Put the *bonnet* in the bandbox. | 擠丨落帽盒嚟 | ‹Chai mò$^2$ lók$_2$ mò$^2$ h'óp$_2$ ‚lai. |
| 9. Brush that pair of *boots* clean. | 擦乾凈個對靴 | Ts'át, ‹kón tsing$^2$ kó' túi' ‹h'éu. |
| 10. In cold weather we must put on *leather boots.* | 天冷要着皮靴 | ‹T'ín 'lang íú' chéuk, ‚p'í ‹h'éu. |
| 11. In warm weather we must put on *satin boots.* | 天熱要着絲靴 | ‹T'ín ít$_2$ íú' chéuk, ‹sz' ‹h'éu. |
| 12. Expose that *breast-pin.* | 打出枝胸針來 | 'Tá ch'ut, ‹chí ‹hung ‹cham ‚loi. |

## *Notes and Explanations.*

SHAUSHIK are ornaments for the head; *ífuk* are garments; the two together include every description of dresses, plain and ornamental, for men and women. The actual difference between the articles which appropriately come under this and the next section is so little that some may be searched for in one, that are placed in the other. It has been the design in arranging them to place those articles which more strictly appertain to the usual dress in this section, while those employed in ornamenting or cleansing the person will be found in the following.

2—4. There were many sumptuary laws established by the ancient dynasties to regulate the forms of headdresses, by which in this, as in other countries, rank was designated; the *pín* was made in different forms, some of which resembled the trencher cap of European universities, and others a tiara or mitre; the *kún* was worn by inferior officers: they may be indifferently rendered caps or bonnets.

5. *Mò hün*, bonnet-ring, or ring of the bonnet, is a small band of cloth, so fitted on the inside of those bonnets which are made of hard and stiff material and in a conical form, that it serves to make them set easy and firm upon the head.

7. *Mò lung*, bonnet-cylinder, or cylinder of the bonnet, is a bit of wood, or other hard substance, in the apex of the bonnet, having a spiral groove, into which the button or knob is screwed.

| | | |
|---|---|---|
| 13. *Breeches* come down to the knees. | 牛頭褲到膝頭 | ˏNgau ˏt'au fú' tò' sat, ˏt'au. |
| 14. I do not find the *buckle* of the hatband. | 唔見個帽帶扣 | ˏ'M kín' kó' mò$^2$ tái' k'au'. |
| 15. Fasten the *button* in the button-hole. | 扣番鈕入鈕門 | K'au' ˌfán 'nau yap$_2$ 'nau ˏmún. |
| 16. Where have you put that small *cap?* | 擠頂小帽去邊 | ˌChai 'ting 'síú mò$^2$ h'ü' ˌpín? |
| 17. The child's *cap* is furnished with a tassel. | 細蚊仔拖帽繸 | Sai' ˏman 'tsai ˌt'ó mò$^2$ sui$^2$. |
| 18. When the snow falls we must put on *cloaks.* | 落雪要着大褸 | Lók$_2$ süt, íú' chéuk, tái$^2$ ˌlau. |
| 19. In wet weather we must wear *clogs.* | 落雨天穿屐鞋 | Lók$_2$ 'ü ˌt'ín ˌch'ün k'ik, ˏhái. |
| 20. What is the cost of a *great coat?* | 幾多銀買長袍 | 'Kí ˌtó ˏngan 'mái ˏch'éung ˏpáu? |
| 21. That *coat* is quite too short. | 個件大衫太短 | Kó' kín$^2$ tái$^2$ ˌshám t'ái' 'tün. |
| 22. In cold weather a *long coat* is comfortable. | 天冷着長衫好 | ˌT'ín 'lang chéuk, ˏch'éung ˌshám 'hò. |
| 23. A black *woolen collar* is in good style. | 黑絨風領致着 | Hak, ˏyung ˌfung 'ling chí' chéuk,. |
| 24. The *costumes* of nations are unlike. | 各國衣服唔同 | Kók, kwók, ˌí fuk$_2$ ˏ'm ˏt'ung. |
| 25. This *cravat* is unfit for use. | 呢條頸帶唔着 | ˌNí ˏt'íú 'king tái' ˏ'm chéuk,. |
| 26. Ancient *crowns* had pendants before and behind. | 古冕前後有旒 | 'Kú 'mín ˏts'ín hau$^2$ 'yau ˏlau. |
| 27. Sow up again the seam of that *cuff.* | 挑番袖口綫步 | ˌT'íú ˌfán tsau$^2$ 'hau sín' pò$^2$. |
| 28. *Flannel drawers* are very warm. | 絨裏褲實首暖 | ˏYung 'lui fú' shat$_2$ 'shau 'nün. |
| 29. Bring a pair of *cotton drawers.* | 拈棉布裏褲嚟 | ˌNím ˏmín pò' 'lui fú' ˏlai. |
| 30. The *dresses* of the upper and lower classes of the people, likewise, are different. | 上下各等人嘅衣服亦係唔同 | Shéung$^2$ há$^2$ kók, 'tang ˏyan ké' ˌí fuk$_2$ yik$_2$ hai$^2$ ˏ'm ˏt'ung. |
| 31. *Dresses* need not be very costly; that they are clean and comely is the important point. | 衣裳唔論貴總要乾净嘅就好 | ˌÍ ˏshéung ˏ'm lun$^2$ kwai', 'tsung íú' ˌkón tsing$^2$ ké' tsau$^2$ 'hò. |

13. The *ngau t'au fú*, cow's head trowsers, is worn by laborers in summer, constituting their entire dress; it is equivalent to the sarong or waistcloth of the Malays, into which it frequently passes.

19. This description of clogs are made in the same fashion as the common shoes, with a thick wooden sole, and are usually worn in rainy seasons; they are also called *shui hái* water shoes, and *muk hái* wooden shoes.

21, 22. *Táishám* is used in Canton to denote the upper garment, the coat worn by foreigners, and also a loose outer one worn by the Chinese, a kind of frock; the *ch'éung shám* is long, descends nearly to the ankles, and resembles a gown.

26. The form of these crowns was that of a richly ornamented cap fitting close to the head, with jewels hanging from the margins of a flat board on the top before and behind, which made a tinkling as the person walked; the number of these pendants designated the rank of the wearer; the emperor is said to have had two hundred and eighty-eight of them. They are not now worn.

| | | |
|---|---|---|
| 32. Arrange the *dress* of that doll. | 裝好公仔衣服 | ˏChóng ʻhò ˏkung ʻtsai ˏí fuk[2]. |
| 33. An *earpick* is useful to take wax from the ear. | 要耳挖取耳屎 | Iʻú ʻí watˎ ʻtsü ʻí ʻshí. |
| 34. This is a very good *fan*. | 呢把扇實首好 | ˏNí ʻpá shínʼ shat[2] ʻshau ʻhò. |
| 35. Buy for inspection several *fans*, of *ivory*, *feather*, *paper*, and *leaf*, one of each kind. | 牙毛紙葵各等扇買把番嚟睇 | ˏNgá ˏmò ʻchí ˏkwʻai kókˎ ʻtang shínʼ ʻmái ʻpá ˏfán ˏlai ʻtʻai. |
| 36. Hang the *fancase* on the girdle, and arrange it in its proper place. | 駝番個扇插落腰帶襯吓罷囉 | ˏTʻó ˏfán kóʼ shínʼ chʻápˎ lók[2] ˏíú táiʼ chʻunʼ ʻhá ʻpá ˏló. |
| 37. Put a *fob* into the pantaloons. | 整個標袋落褲 | ʻChing kóʼ ˏpíú toi[2] lók[2] fúʼ. |
| 38. Grasscloth *frocks* are very good. | 夏布大衫致好 | Há[2] pòʼ tái[2] ˏshám chíʼ ʻhò. |
| 39. Purchase a pair of *gaiters*. | 買對脚掹番嚟 | ʻMái túiʼ kéukˎ ˏmáng ˏfán ˏlai. |
| 40. I purchased a pair of new *garters*. | 我買對新襪帶 | ʻNgó ʻmái túiʼ ˏsan mat[2] táiʼ. |
| 41. A leathern *girdle* is worn around the waist. | 皮帶係束腰物 | ˏPʻí táiʼ hai[2] chʻukˎ ˏíú mat[2]. |
| 42. My pair of *gloves* is ragged. | 我對手笠爛咯 | ʻNgó túiʼ ʻshau lapˎ lán[2] lókˎ. |
| 43. I like *grasscloth handkerchiefs*. | 我中意夏布巾 | ʻNgó ˏchung íʼ há[2] pòʼ ˏkan. |
| 44. This *hat* is made of wool. | 呢頂帽羊毛嘅 | ˏNí ʻting mò[2] ˏyéung ˏmò kéʼ. |
| 45. Put on a *rain-hat* to shelter from the rain. | 戴件雨帽遮雨 | Táiʼ kín[2] ʻü mò[2] ˏché ʻü. |
| 46. *Felt hats* are very good. | 毡毛做〡更好 | ˏChím ˏmò tsò[2] mò[2] kangʼ ʻhò. |
| 47. The *summer hat* is made of bamboo splints. | 凉帽用竹絲胎 | ˏLéung mò[2] yung[2] chukˎ ˏszʼ ˏtʻoi. |
| 48. *Straw hats* are worn in summer. | 草〡天熱戴着 | ʻTsʻò mò[2] ˏtʻin ít[2] táiʼ chéukˎ. |
| 49. Orders to change and put on the *winter hat*. | 牌示換戴暖帽 | ˏPʻái shí[2] ún[2] táiʼ ʻnün mò[2]. |
| 50. The *red hat* is worn on ceremonial occasions. | 有事致戴紅〡 | ʻYau szʼ[2] chíʼ táiʼ ˏhung mò[2]. |
| 51. The seam of the *jacket* is broken open. | 中衫甩了線步 | ˏChung ˏshám latˎ ʻlíú sínʼ pò[2]. |

35. The variety and elegance displayed by the Chinese in their fans is well known; it is an indispensable article of dress with all classes, and they are made of almost every material that can be easily employed.

37. The Chinese carry their watches suspended from the girdle in a case, which just exposes the face; their's is literally a *píú toi*, watch pocket.

42. The Chinese have no covering for the hands like gloves; the *lap* is a broad brimmed hat laid upon the head to defend it from the rain, and is by usage applied to gloves.

49. This phrase occurs in the Canton Court Circular, in spring and autumn, in which it is stated that, on a given day, orders were issued by the chief provincial officer for changing caps, from the summer to the winter, or *vice versâ* according to the season.

50. The cap is in the shape of a cone, and is called the *hung mò* because of a red fringe, usually made of dyed hair or fine silk which, from the apex, depends on every side.

| | | |
|---|---|---|
| 52. A cloth *riding jacket* is a convenient dress. | 絨馬褂係便服 | ꜀Yung ʿmá ʿkw'á hai² pín² fuk꜀. |
| 53. With *kneepads* it is not painful to kneel. | 纜包膝跪唔痛 | Lám² ꜀páu sat꜀ kwai² ꜀'m t'ung'. |
| 54. A nicely turned *lappet* looks well. | 歛好衫襟好睇 | ʿLím ʿhò ꜀shám ꜀k'am ʿhò ʿt'ai. |
| 55. Make a pair of *leggins* lined with cotton. | 做棉套褲黎着 | Tsò² ꜀mín t'ò' fú' ꜀lai chéuk꜀. |
| 56. Bring me a *neckcloth*. | 掂條頸巾黎我 | ꜀Ním ꜀t'íú ʿking ꜀kan ꜀lai ʿngó. |
| 57. Where are my *pantaloons?* | 我大褲在邊處 | ʿNgó tái² fú' tsoi² ꜀pín ch'ü' ? |
| 58. The ancient *pattens* had only one strap. | 古人屐一條面 | ʿKú ꜀yan k'ek꜀ yat꜀ ꜀t'íú mín². |
| 59. The many plaited *petticoat* is a ceremonial dress. | 百褶裙係禮服 | Pák꜀ chíp꜀ ꜀kw'an hai² ʿlai fuk꜀. |
| 60. Bid him make a *pocket* in the vest. | 吩咐背心做袋 | ꜀Fan ꜀fú púi' ꜀sam tsò² toi². |
| 61. Put on a *rain cloak*, and go to put out the fire. | 褸蓑衣去救火 | ꜀Lau ꜀só ꜀í h'ü' kau' ʿfó. |
| 62. The garment opened before and behind, with the cuffs of the sleeves like a horse's hoof, is called a *robe*. | 前後開衩左右<br>馬蹄袖謂之袍 | ꜀Ts'ín hau² ꜀hoi ch'á' ʿtsó yau² ʿmá ꜀t'ai tsau² wai² ꜀chí ꜀p'ò. |
| 63. The courier's *sandals* have leathern soles. | 千里馬皮底鞋 | ꜀Ts'ín ʿlí ʿmá ꜀p'í ʿtai ꜀hái. |
| 64. *Sandals* are bound on with cords. | 草鞋使繩綁緊 | ʿTs'ò ꜀hái ʿshai ꜀shing ʿpóng ʿkan. |
| 65. Throw on an embroidered *shawl*. | 褸條花搭膊巾 | ꜀Lau ꜀t'íú ꜀fá táp꜀ pók꜀ ꜀kan. |
| 66. He has put on his *shirt*. | 佢着件貼身衫 | ʿK'ü chéuk꜀ kín² t'íp꜀ ꜀shan ꜀shám. |
| 67. Has the *shirt* been washed or not? | 汗衫洗了唔曾 | Hón² ꜀shám ʿsai ʿlíú ꜀'m ꜀ts'ang? |
| 68. Brush that pair of *shoes* clean. | 擦乾淨個對鞋 | Ts'át꜀ ꜀kón tsing² kó' túi' ꜀hái. |
| 69. Do not go out with *shoes* down at the heel. | 撻踭鞋唔出街 | Tát꜀ ꜀chang ꜀hái ꜀'m ch'ut꜀ ꜀kái. |
| 70. Ladies' small tricolored *shoes* are handsome. | 纏脚鞋三鑲好 | ꜀Ch'ín kéuk꜀ ꜀hái ꜀sám ꜀séung ʿhò. |
| 71. The *sleeves* of the robe of a priest trail on the ground. | 和尚袍袖拖地 | ꜀Wò shéung² ꜀p'ò tsau² ꜀t'ó tí². |

51. This is an outside garment made large and short, furnished with short sleeves; it is seen in a great variety of patterns, is worn by all classes of people, and on almost all occasions.

59. The apron of No. 1. is also called *kw'an*, and this garment partakes of the form of an apron, being tied around the waist, and open behind. It is worn when going abroad and on occasions of ceremony, over the common loose trowsers, and underneath the gown, and reaches nearly to the ground, just so as to allow the tiny feet to be seen. The plaits are on the sides, leaving a flat section before and behind, on which flowers are embroidered; the garment is sometimes made very rich and elegant.

61. This is an excuse used by a man to avoid helping his neighbor; the *só í* is made of rush or bamboo leaves stitched together, and would quickly catch fire on approaching a burning dwelling; wherefore he had better keep at a distance.

62. This is the dress of honor with the Chinese, and its shape differs but little from the *ch'éung shám:* the sleevos being very long, the cuffs are folded inward to allow the free use of the hands, and the fold is supposed to be blunt like a horse's hoof.

| | | |
|---|---|---|
| 72. The pantaloons should be long when *socks* are worn. | 着襪頭落褲脚 | Chéuk꜀ mat꜀ ꜁t'au lók꜀ fú' kéuk꜀. |
| 73. Crystal *spectacles* preserve the eyes. | 水晶眼鏡養眼 | ʻShui ꜀tsing ʻngán king' ʻyéung ʻngán. |
| 74. A *stock* is worn round the neck. | 頸帶係圍頸嘅 | ʻKing tái' hai' ꜁wai ʻking ké'. |
| 75. Give me a pair of *woolen stockings.* | 俾對毡襪過我 | ʻPí túi' ꜀chín mat꜀ kwò' ʻngó. |
| 76. In Canton *silk stockings* are cheap. | 省城絲襪係平 | ʻShang ꜁shing ꜀sz' mat꜀ hai' ꜁p'ing. |
| 77. When taking off the shirt put on a *stomacher.* | 脫衫要纜暖肚 | Tüt꜀ ꜀shám iú' lám' ʻnün ʻtò. |
| 78. [Priests] put on a *surplice* when sitting at the altar. | 披袈裟坐正壇 | ꜀P'í ꜀ká ꜀shá tsó' ching' ꜁tán. |
| 79. *Suspenders* are cross bands. | 褲帶即十字帶 | Fú' tái' tsik꜀ shap꜀ tsz' tái'. |
| 80. My *trowsers* need to be washed. | 我條褲要洗嘞 | ʻNgó ꜁t'iú fú' iú' ʻsai lá'. |
| 81. Women ought to wear *turbans.* | 女人應纜頭帕 | ʻNü ꜁yan ꜀ying lám' ꜁t'au p'á'. |
| 82. Gauze *veils* are in use among foreigners. | 外國有障面紗 | Ngói' kwók꜀ ʻyau chéung' mín' ꜀shá. |
| 83. Women wore *veils* in the time of Hón. | 漢時婦有面衣 | Hón' ꜁shí ʻfú ʻyau mín' ꜀í. |
| 84. Make a *vest.* | 做件背心嚟着 | Tsò' kín' púi' ꜀sam ꜁lai chéuk꜀. |
| 85. Bring a new *waistcoat.* | 擰件新背心嚟 | ꜀Ning kín' ꜀san púi' ꜀sam ꜁lai. |
| 86. The *wallet* is used as a purse. | 荷包擠錢銀嘅 | ꜁Hó ꜀páu ꜁chai ꜁ts'ín ꜁ngan ké'. |

77. Careful mothers put this garment upon their children to keep, (as its name imports,) the belly warm; adults also sometimes wear it.

## Section Fifth.

## OF THE TOILET.

### 粧扮類第五章

꜀Chóng pán' lui'; tai' ʻ'ng ꜀chéung.

| | | |
|---|---|---|
| 1. Hang the *amulets* on the collar. | 駝香包落襟頭 | ꜁T'ó ꜀héung ꜀páu lók꜀ ꜀k'am ꜁t'au. |
| 2. Put on again that pair of *anklets.* | 戴番對脚鈪咋 | Tái' ꜀fán túi' kéuk꜀ ák꜀ chá'. |

### *Notes and Explanations.*

CHÓNGPAN is a phrase, meaning to dress, and includes all the various operations connected with dressing, such as bathing, cutting or shaving the hair and beard, &c. A few articles of furniture and clothing, enumerated in the two preceding sections, are here repeated, usually in connection with some act belonging to the toilet.

1. The amulets are usually small bags, filled with aromatic substances, sometimes merely

| | | |
|---|---|---|
| 3. Tell the *barber* to come to-morrow morning at early dawn, to cut my hair and shave my beard. | 叫剃頭佬聽早<br>天朦朧黎同我<br>剪髮剃鬚 | Kiú' t'ai' ˏt'au ˈlò ˏt'ing ˈtsò ˏt'ín ˏmung ˏlung ˏlai ˏt'ung ˈngó ˈtsín fát˒ t'ai' ˏsò. |
| 4. The water in the *bath* is too cold, pour in a little warm water and stir it up. | 洗身水凍侵的<br>熱水和吓添 | ˈSai ˏshan ˈshui tung' ˏts'am tik˒ ít˒ ˈshui wó' ˈhá ˏtím. |
| 5. I am going to the sea-shore to *bathe*, bring me my *bathing-dress*. | 我想去海邊洗<br>身擰洗身衫黎 | ˈNgó ˈséung h'ü' ˈhoi ˏpín ˈsai ˏshan, ˏning ˈsai ˏshan ˏshám ˏlai. |
| 6. Bring a string of *court beads*, and hang them carefully on my neck. | 拈串朝珠小心<br>掛落我頸 | ˏNím ch'ün' ˏch'íú ˏchü ˈsíú ˏsam kwá' lók˒ ˈngó ˈking. |
| 7. Put on again quickly the string of *aromatic beads*. | 快馱番串香珠 | Fái' ˏt'ó ˏfán ch'ün' ˏhéung ˏchü. |
| 8. He wets himself in eating, you must put a *bib* on him. | 食野流濕身共<br>佢着番口水肩 | Shik˒ ˈyé ˏlau shap˒ ˏshan ˈkung ˈk'ü chéuk˒ ˏfán ˈhau ˈshui ˏkín. |
| 9. Just try on this *bonnet* and see if it will suit you. | 你試吓個件帽<br>睇中意唔中意 | ˈNí shí' ˈhá kó' kín' mò' ˈt'ai ˏchung í' ˏ'm ˏchung í'. |
| 10. Look at this pair of *boots* of mine, and see if they are well made. | 你睇我呢對靴<br>好工作唔好呵 | ˈNí ˈt'ai ˈngó ˏní túi' ˏh'éu ˈhò ˏkung tsók˒ ˏ'm ˈhò ˏó. |
| 11. Have you a *boot-jack?* | 有脫靴板冇呀 | ˈYau t'üt˒ ˏh'éu ˈpán ˈmò á'? |
| 12. Where are my *bracelets?* | 我的釧在邊處 | ˈNgó tik˒ ch'ün' tsoi' ˏpín ch'ü'? |

for the purpose of guarding one's person from any offensive fumes, but oftener to ward off imaginary evils; the character *t'ó* is not here used in its common acceptation of a camel, but as a provincial term for suspending.

3. The barber is called *t'ai t'au lò*, because his chief business here is to shave the head. The Chinese generally shave their heads four, five, or six times a month; some of them much oftener.

5. *Hoi pín*, side of the sea, is constantly used also for smaller portions of water, such as rivers: 'I am going to bathe in the river, or by the river-side,' may be used by one going to the river, or to the sea.

6. The court beads are so called because they form a part of the court dress. The string is a yard and a half or two yards long, containing 108 beads, about the size of acorns; they are made of hard wood, and are separated, on the string, into four or more divisions, by smaller balls made of pearl, ivory, or metal.

7. These are much smaller than the court beads, and are on strings about a foot long; they are not, like the court beads, hung over the neck, but are attached to a button of the outer dress, on the right side, two or three inches below the chin. They are usually made of an aromatic composition; and, in regard to size, are of two kinds; a string of the larger contains only eighteen, usually worn by men, as the fragrant bag, mentioned above, is by females.

12, 13. The *ch'ün* and *ák* are the same, the former is not as colloquial as the second; which, to distinguish it from the anklets, (No. 2.) is sometimes called *shau ák;* both are worn

| | | |
|---|---|---|
| 13. Bring my *bracelets* and put them on for me. | 擰鈪嚟同我戴 | ‹Ning ák› ˏlai ˏt'ung ʿngó tái'. |
| 14. Brush the dust from my coat with the *clothes' broom*. | 衣服掃掃衫塵 | ‹Í fuk₂ sò' sò' ‹shám ˏch'au. |
| 15. The *shaving brush*, dipped in soap, is used to lather the beard. | 鬚擦沗梘搽鬚 | ‹Sò ts'át› ʿt'ím 'kán ˏch'á ‹sò. |
| 16. Give me a *tooth-brush* to clean my teeth. | 捭牙擦我擦牙 | 'Pí ˏngá ts'át› ʿngò ts'át› ˏngá. |
| 17. Brush your head with a *hair-brush*. | 使髮亅擦頭髮 | 'Shai fát› ts'át› ts'át› ˏt'au fát›. |
| 18. Your coat does not set well, *unbutton* and set it right, and then *button* it again. | 你件衫唔齊整除鈕着好佢致扣番鈕啦 | ʿNí kín² ‹shám ˏ'm ˏts'ai 'ching ; ˏch'ü ʿnau, chéuk› 'hò ʿk'ü, chí' k'au' ‹fán ʿnau ‹lá. |
| 19. Do you use a *cane* when you go in the streets? | 遊街用鞭杆唔 | ˏYau ‹kái yung² ‹pín ‹kón ˏ'm? |
| 20. Put the cards in the *card box*. | 擠帖落帖盒囉 | ‹Chai t'íp› lók₂ t'íp› hóp₂ ló'. |
| 21. The jewels are in the *casket*. | 珠寶喺首飾箱 | ‹Chü 'pò 'hai 'shau shik› ‹seung. |
| 22. Help me to fasten this *clasp* again. | 幫我扣番帶扣 | ‹Póng ʿngó k'au' ‹fán tái' k'au'. |
| 23. Hang the dresses on the *clothes' horse*. | 掛衣服落衣架 | Kwá' ‹í fuk₂ lók₂ ‹í ká'. |
| 24. Is the *collar* of the coat in its place? | 衫領齊整唔呀 | ‹Shám ʿling ˏts'ai 'ching ˏ'm á'? |
| 25. Comb the head smooth with a *comb*. | 使梳梳光頭髮 | 'Shai ‹shó ‹shó ‹kwóng ˏt'au fát›. |
| 26. The teeth of the *comb* are so close they hardly enter the hair. | 篦齒密難入髮 | Pí² 'ch'í mat₂ ˏnán yap₂ fát›. |
| 27. Put the *tortoise-shell comb* in my hair. | 插玳瑁梳落頭 | Ch'áp› toi² múi² ‹shó lók₂ ˏt'au. |
| 28. Do not put on a *corset* to-day. | 今日莫纜捫胸 | ‹Kam yat₂ mók₂ lám² ˏmán ‹hung. |
| 29. Is the *cosmetic* well applied? | 水粉搽勻唔呀 | 'Shui 'fan ˏch'á ˏwan ˏ'm á'? |
| 30. Tie my *cravat* properly for me. | 同我綁好頸巾 | ˏT'ung ʿngó 'póng 'hò 'king ‹kan. |

by Chinese females, old and young, rich and poor, and the bracelets are worn not unfrequently by men also; they are made of silver, tin, and various kinds of precious stones, usually plain, but sometimes gilt and slightly ornamented.

15. *T'ím* is used to denote the act of dipping a pencil in paints or ink, and for filling the brush with soap for lathering the beard; but the word does not occur with this sense in lexicons, and there are different modes of writing it.

25, 26. The *shó* is a coarse toothed comb, and the *pí* has the teeth very close, and usually on both sides; it is made of wood.

29. This cosmetic is manufactured in great quantities from limestone, which is reduced to powder by stones fitted and worked like those employed in grinding grain, the use of it being almost universal among one half of the Chinese people. The process is quite like that of pulverizing gypsum for agricultural purposes.

31. The cue requires plaiting every morning. All the hair which is not shaven close to the head, is allowed to grow to its full length, and when in good condition often reaches to the

| | | |
|---|---|---|
| 31. Early in the morning wash the face and plait the *cue*. | 清晨洗面打辮 | ˏTs'ing ˏshan 'sai mín' 'tá ˏpín. |
| 32. Empty and cleanse the *cuspidor*. | 倒乾淨個痰罐 | 'Tò ˏkón tsing' kó' ˏt'ám kún'. |
| 33. Lock that case of *drawers*. | 鎖埋衣服櫃桶 | 'Só ˏmái ˏí fukˎ kwai' 't'ung. |
| 34. See whether this *dress* fits me well or not? | 你睇我件衣服着齊整未 | 'Ní 't'ai 'ngó kín' ˏí fukˎ chéukˎ ˏts'ai 'ching mí'? |
| 35. Will you allow me to set your *dress* to rights for you? | 等我同你扯正吓個件衣服唉 | 'Tang 'ngó ˏt'ung 'ní 'ch'é ching' 'há kó' kín' ˏí fukˎ ˏé? |
| 36. Give me a *dressing gown*. | 𢬿頭髮衫過我 | 'Pí ˏt'au fátˎ ˏshám kwó' 'ngó. |
| 37. Have you put my *dressing table* in order yet? | 你擺好我個張梳頭檯唔曾呀 | 'Ní 'pái 'hò 'ngó kó' ˏchéung ˏshó ˏt'au ˏt'oi ˏ'm ˏts'ang á'? |
| 38. Open my *dressing case*. | 撐開我個鏡粧 | ˏCh'ang ˏhoi 'ngó kó' king' ˏchóng. |
| 39. Take these *earrings* from my ears. | 同我除對耳環 | ˏT'ung 'ngó ˏch'ü túi' 'í ˏwán. |
| 40. Is there water in that *ewer*? | 個水罌有水冇 | Kó' 'shui ˏang 'yau 'shui 'mò? |
| 41. Char some sprigs of willow, and let me give a good black color to your *eyebrows*. | 燒的柳枝炭我畫好個對眼眉 | ˏShiú tikˎ 'lau ˏchí t'án' 'ngó wákˎ 'hò kó' túi' 'ngán ˏmí. |
| 42. I forgot to put the *fan* in its case. | 忘記唊番扇插 | ˏMóng kí' ngápˎ ˏfán shín' ch'ápˎ. |
| 43. My dress must be according to the *fashion*. | 我衣服要時興 | 'Ngó ˏí fukˎ íú' ˏshi hing'. |
| 44. Put that *fingerring* on my little finger. | 套隻戒指落我個隻尾指處嚟 | T'ò' chikˎ kái' 'chí lókˎ 'ngó kó' chikˎ 'mí 'chí ch'ü' ˏlai. |
| 45. Bring a cluster of *flowers* to put on my head. | 擰朵花戴落頭 | ˏNing 'tó ˏfá tái' lókˎ ˏt'au. |
| 46. Bring the *girdle* and put it on. | 擰腰帶嚟束腰 | ˏNing ˏíú tái' ˏlai ch'ukˎ ˏíú. |
| 47. Cut the *hair* on the left side of my head a little shorter. | 同我剪短吓左邊個的長頭髮 | ˏT'ung 'ngó 'tsín 'tün 'há 'tsó ˏpín kó' tikˎ ˏch'éung ˏt'au fátˎ. |
| 48. Put in order your flowing *locks of hair*. | 挑好個的髯呵 | ˏT'iú 'hò kó' tikˎ ˏyam ˏó. |

calves of the legs; those who have a sparse head of hair frequently eke out their cues with false hair.

41. Chinese ladies are remarkably fond of adorning their heads with flowers; these are usually worn in sprigs, instead of wreaths; and there is a silver or golden pin often worn in the hair, with a tube in one end of it for the insertion of flowers.

48. *Yam* designates the locks of hair of young girls, which are often allowed to hang down round the forehead and on both sides of the face, not in ringlets, but in the manner of a fringe.

| | | |
|---|---|---|
| 49. The golden *hair-pin* fell down beside the pillow. | 金釵墜落枕邊 | ˏKam ˏch'ái chui3 lòk2 'cham ˏpín. |
| 50. Shake clean the *handkerchief.* | 抰乾净條手巾 | 'Yéung ˏkón tsing2 ˏt'iú 'shau ˏkan. |
| 51. The *handkerchief* is tucked under the girdle. | 腰帶映條襯巾 | ˏI'ú tái3 ngápˎ ˏt'iú ch'an3 ˏkan. |
| 52. That lady's *headdress* is handsome. | 姑娘梳粧好睇 | ˏKú ˏnéung ˏshó ˏchóng 'hò 't'ai. |
| 53. A pouch and *knife* hung [one] on each side. | 兩邊襯袋佩刀 | 'Léung ˏpín ch'an3 toí2 p'úi3 ˏtò. |
| 54. Bring a small *knife* to pare your nails. | 拈刀仔批指甲 | ˏNím ˏtò 'tsai ˏp'ai 'chí kápˎ. |
| 55. Put the *looking-glass* on the dressing table. | 擠個照面鏡喺<br>個張梳頭檯嚟 | ˏChai kó3 chíú3 mín2 king3 'hai kó3 ˏchéung ˏshó ˏt'au ˏt'oi ˏlai. |
| 56. The *looking-glass* stand should be well fastened. | 鏡架要準頭好 | King3 ká3 íú3 'sun ˏt'au 'hò |
| 57. Use a hand *mirror* to give a double reflection. | 使手鏡能映照 | 'Shai 'shau king3 ˏnang 'yéung chíú3. |
| 58. Where is my *necklace?* | 我個條頸鍊呢 | 'Ngó kó3 ˏt'íú 'king lín2 ˏní? |
| 59. Thread a *needle* and sew this garment. | 穿管針聯衣服 | ˏChün 'kún ˏcham ˏlín ˏí fuk2. |
| 60. When the sun is hot you should carry a *parasol.* | 日頭猛要擔遮 | Yat2 ˏt'au 'máng íú3 ˏtám ˏché. |
| 61. Have you any *perfumery* for me? | 有香物我搽冇 | 'Yau ˏhéung mat2 'ngó ˏch'á 'mò? |
| 62. Bring a *pin* and fasten the cuff. | 擰鼓槌針攜袖 | ˏNing 'kú ˏch'ui ˏcham 'kíú tsau2. |
| 63. Go and buy a *pin-case.* | 去買個針筒嚟 | H'ü3 'mái kó3 ˏcham ˏt'ung ˏlai. |
| 64. What has become of that *pin-box?* | 個針箱去邊處 | Kó3 ˏcham ˏséung h'ü3 ˏpín ch'ü3? |
| 65. Where has the *pin-cushion* gone to? | 個針毡去邊處 | Kó3 ˏcham ˏchín h'ü3 ˏpín ch'ü3? |
| 66. Where is my *pomatum?* | 我個的香油呢 | 'Ngó kó3 tikˎ ˏhéung ˏyau ˏní? |
| 67. The *razor* is dull and needs honeing. | 剃鬚刀斷要磨 | T'ai3 ˏsò ˏtò tün2 íú3 ˏmó. |
| 68. Give me a *razor-strop* to sharpen the edge of this razor. | 捭喝刀皮喝吓<br>個張刀口嘅鋒 | 'Pí hótˎ ˏtò ˏp'í hótˎ 'há kó3 ˏchéung ˏtò 'hau ké3 ˏfung. |
| 69. Have you yet found those *ribbons?* | 絲帶仔搵番未 | ˏSz' tái3 'tsai 'wan ˏfán mí2? |

51, 53. The *ch'an kan* and *ch'an toi* are usually attached to the girdle, one hanging on each side; *ch'an* has the sense of personal, near to; it means also those garments which are under the outer dress. A watch encased in a pocket, a fancase, a pair of chopsticks, or, as in the present example, a knife, are worn in the same manner: the knife resembles the short-dagger of Europeans, but is never, like it, worn for purposes of defense.

59, 62—65. The Chinese have no pins; the *cham* is a needle, but in these examples, it is indifferently applied to the various cases in which both pins or needles are kept; the *kú ch'ui cham*, or drumstick needle, is strictly a pin.

66. *Héung yau* may be applied to any kind of oleaginous or greasy perfume, as well as to pomatm.

| | | |
|---|---|---|
| 70. Have you any *oil of roses?* | 你有梅桂油冇 | ˊNí ˊyau ˏmúi kwaiˋ ˏyau ˊmò? |
| 71. Rub a little *rouge* on the lips. | 口唇搽的胭脂 | ˊHau ˏshun ˏch'á tikˎ ˏín ˏchí |
| 72. Bring me a pair of *scissors.* | 拈把鉸剪嚟我 | ˏNím ˊpá káuˋ ˊtsín ˏlai ˊngó. |
| 73. A *tongue scraper* made of pure silver. | 打枝高銀利刮 | ˊTá ˏchí ˏkò ˏngan lí² kwátˎ. |
| 74. Open my *shaving case.* | 揭開個剃鬚箱 | K'ítˎ ˏhoi kóˋ t'aiˋ ˏsò ˏséung. |
| 75. Moisten the *shavings* for smoothing my hair. | 淥刨花我抆頭 | Lukˎ ˏpáu ˏfá ˊngó ˊman ˏt'au. |
| 76. Give me a *cotton shirt.* | 俾棉布汗衫我 | ˊPí ˏmín pòˋ hón² ˏshám ˊngó. |
| 77. Tie up my *shoe strings.* | 綁起我條鞋帶 | ˊPong ˊhí ˊngó ˏt'íú ˏhái táiˋ. |
| 78. Give me some *perfumed soap.* | 拈的香鹼嚟我 | ˏNím tikˎ ˏhéung ˊkán ˏlai ˊngó. |
| 79. Moisten the *sponge* with cold water, and bring it to wipe my forehead. | 捭凍水濕水泡<br>拈嚟我抹額頭 | ˊPí tungˋ ˊshui shapˎ ˊshui ˊpò ˏním ˏlai ˊngó mútˎ ngák² ˏt'au. |
| 80. *Talismans,* worn on the collar, expel evil influences. | 襟頭符驅邪物 | ˏK'am ˏt'au ˏfú ˏk'ü ˏts'é mat². |
| 81. Put on the *thimble* to baste this garment. | 帶針頂行衣服 | Tái² ˏcham ˊting ˏhóng ˏí fuk². |
| 82. Untie a silken *thread* and hem this coat. | 解子絲線挑衫 | ˊKái ˊtszˋ ˏszˋ sínˋ ˏt'íú ˏshám. |
| 83. A set of *toothpicks,* etc., hung on the collar. | 襟頭一副牙籤 | ˏK'am ˏt'au yatˎ fúˋ ˏngá ˏts'ím. |
| 84. Open a new box of *tooth-powder.* | 開個新牙灰盒 | ˏHoi kóˋ ˏsan ˏngá ˏfúi hóp². |
| 85. Take away this *towel.* | 拈呢條面巾去 | ˏNím ˏní ˏt'íú mín² ˏkan h'üˋ. |
| 86. The legs of my *trowsers* are too large. | 外褲脚係太闊 | Ngoi² fúˋ kéukˎ hai² t'áiˋ fútˎ. |
| 87. With *tweezers* pulling the hairs even on the forehead. | 鑷鉗撍齊額毛 | Nípˎ ˏk'ím ˏts'ím ˏts'ai ngák² ˏmò. |
| 88. Open the *umbrella* and give it me. | 開個把遮俾我 | ˏHoi kóˋ ˊpá ˏché ˊpí ˊngó. |
| 89. Pray *unrobe* and sit down. | 請寬衣埋位坐 | ˊTs'ing ˏfún ˏí ˏmái wai² tsó². |
| 90. Put on again that *vandyke.* | 披番個雲肩吖 | ˏP'í ˏfán kóˋ ˏwan ˏkín ˏá. |
| 91. Put the *veil* in the bureau. | 擠障面紗落櫃 | ˏChai chéung² mín² ˏshá lók² kwai². |

73. The tongue scraper is a very thin sheet or strip of silver, say one third of an inch in breadth, and eight or ten inches long.

75. These shavings are used by Chinese females to give smoothness and glossiness to their hair. They are cut from resinous wood, and by being dipped in a little warm water the gum is drawn out and diluted, and thus by applying them to the hair the object is effected.

80. The Chinese have many of these *fú*, differing in their form and use. Those worn on the collar, those here specified, often consist of metal, but are also made of wood, or cloth.

81, 82. To join two pieces of cloth together is called *lín;* (No. 59.) to do so in an open light manner or to baste is termed *kóng;* and to sew a seam down a second time on the inside is called *t'íú:* to embroider is *sau.*

| | | |
|---|---|---|
| 92. Open the *wardrobe* and lay out my woolen dress. | 開衣服櫃擰我個的絨衣服來 | ‹Hoi ‹í fuk₂ kwai² ‹ning ʿngó kó' tik› ˏyung ‹í fuk₂ ˏloi. |
| 93. Pour a little *water* on my hands. | 斟的水落我手 | ‹Cham tik› ʻshui lók₂ ʿngó ʻshau. |
| 94. I wish to shave, go quickly and bring me some *hot water*. | 我愛剃鬚快去拈的熱水嚟我 | ʿNgó oi' t'ai' ‹sò fái' h'ü' ‹ním tik› ít₂ ʻshui ˏlai ʿngó. |
| 95. Place the soap on the *wash-stand*. | 擠梘落面盤架 | ‹Chai ʻkán lók₂ mín² ˏp'ún ká'. |
| 96. Have you yet found the *workbag*? | 搵着針線包冇 | ʻWan chéuk₂ ‹cham sín' ‹páu ʿmò? |

95. The stand called by this name is a kind of tripod on which the basin is placed; when large and square it is called a *t'oi* or table.

## Section Sixth.

## OF THE BEDROOM.

## 瞓房類第六章
Fan' ˏfóng lui²; tai² luk₂ ‹chéung.

| | | |
|---|---|---|
| 1. Where is my bedroom? | 我個間瞓房喺邊處呀 | ʿNgó kó' ‹kán fan' ˏfóng ʻhai ‹pin ch'ü' ‹á? |
| It is in the third story. | 喺第三層樓處 | ʻHai tai² ‹sám ˏts'ang ˏlau ch'ü'. |
| 2. How many windows are there in the room? | 房裏頭有幾多度窓門呢 | ˏFóng ʿlui ˏt'au ʿyau ʻkí ‹tó tò² ‹ch'éung ˏmún ‹ní? |
| There are two. | 兩度啫 | ʿLéung tò² ‹ché. |
| 3. Can the morning sun shine into the room? | 朝頭早熱頭晒得入房唔呀 | ‹Chíú ˏt'au ʻtsò ít₂ ˏt'au shái' tak› yap› ˏfóng ˏ'm á'? |

### *Notes and Explanations.*

THE beds of the Chinese are constructed and furnished somewhat different from those of Europeans. Instead of the bedstead with high posts, they have one with a frame and pannels, which are often carved. Boards also are used in the place of sacking. With the common people, a few plain boards placed on two wooden forms, serve for a bedstead, light bamboos being erected for a tester on which to suspend the curtains, which are indispensable in Canton as a security against musketoes.

1. *Fan* is a local word in common use, and having no character to represent it, one of the same sound is borrowed, and *muk*, an eye, is added to it for the purpose of indicating in some degree its new meaning.

| | | |
|---|---|---|
| It cannot; because one window is on the south, and one on the north side. | 唔晒得着一度喺南一度喺北 | ˌ'M shái' tak˒ chéuk˒, yat˒ tò² 'hai ˌnám yat˒ tò² 'hai pak˒. |
| 4. Is the room, clean, cool, and pleasant? | 個間房乾净凉爽唔呀 | Kó' ˓kán ˌfóng ˓kón tsing², ˌléung, 'shóng, ˌ'm á'? |
| It is a fine airy room, and also admits the wind on two sides. | 房裏頭好氣息兩頭又有風黎 | ˌFóng 'lui ˌt'au 'hò hí' shik˒ 'léung ˌt'au yau² 'yau ˓fung ˌlai. |
| 5. Is the room supplied with furniture? | 房內嘅野齊備唔呀 | ˌFóng noi² ké' 'yé ˌts'ai pí² ˌ'm á'? |
| The bed, bedding, and curtains, are all complete. | 床鋪被帳俱全 | ˌCh'óng ˓p'ò 'p'í chéung' ˓k'ü ˌts'ün. |
| 6. Is there a matress on the bed? | 個張床有褥有冇呀 | Kó' ˓chéung ˌch'óng 'yau yuk₂ 'yau 'mò á'? |
| There is one, filled with rattan shavings. | 有張係藤絲嘅 | 'Yau ˓chéung hai² ˌt'ang ˓sz' ké'. |
| 7. Can you find a feather bed for me? | 你同我搵張鷄毛嘅呵 | 'Ní ˌt'ung 'ngó 'wan ˓chéung ˓kai ˌmò ké' ˓ó? |
| The Chinese have none. | 唐人冇喉 | ˌT'óng ˌyan 'mò ˓é. |
| 8. Have you had the room opened and aired? | 你有打開間房吹吓冇呀 | 'Ní 'yau 'tá ˓hoi ˓kán ˌfóng ˓chui 'há 'mò á'? |
| Yes; to-day the windows have been kept open all day long. | 有今日的窓門成日打開處 | 'Yau ˓kam yat₂ tik˒ ˓ch'éung ˌmún ˌshing yat₂ 'tá ˓hoi ch'ü'. |
| 9. Have you made my bed this morning? | 你今早鋪好我個張床唔曾呀 | 'Ní ˓kam 'tsò ˓p'ò 'hò 'ngó kó' ˓chéung ˌch'óng ˌ'm ˌts'ang á'? |
| I have not yet made it, for the sheets have just now come back from being washed, and are a little damp. | 唔曾喇被單正話洗完番嚟都重濕濕地 | ˌ'M ˌts'ang lé'; 'p'í ˓tán ching' wá² 'sai ˌün ˓fán ˌlai ˓tò chung² shap˒ shap˒ ti². |

5. *Yé ts'ai pí*, things fully prepared, is a phrase expressing that all is in order; *yé* means articles, things, &c. *Ch'óng* is the bedstead; *p'ò* is the coverlet; *p'í* denotes sheets and blankets; and *chéung* the musketoe curtains. The phrase is intended to include whatever is necessary to render the bed complete.

9. Here *p'ò* is used as a verb, and means to spread out, to make or put in order; and *ch'óng* denotes the bed: thus they often say, in the language of command, *p'ò ch'óng*, make the bed. *Tí*, the earth, here loses its common signification, and has the sense of a little—damp in a slight degree.

| | | |
|---|---|---|
| 10. Have you put them in the sun, where they will dry? | 你有擠佢喺熱頭嚟晒冇呀 | ꜂Ní ꜂yau ‹chai ꜂k'ü ʻhai ít› ꜀t'au ꜀lai shái' ꜂mò á' ? |
| No, but I have hung them up before the kitchen fire to dry. | 冇我不過晾倒厨房嚟焙啫 | ꜂Mò, ꜂ngó pat› kwó' lóng' ʻtò ꜀ch'ü ꜀fong ꜀lai púi$^2$ ‹ché. |
| 11. Has the tailor brought back the coverlet? | 個裁縫擰番張花被面嚟未呀 | Kó' ꜀ts'oi ꜀fung ‹ning ‹fán ‹chéung ‹fá ꜂p'í mín$^2$ ꜀lai mí$^2$ á' ? |
| No, not yet, but he promised to bring it this evening. | 唔曾佢話挨晚至擰嚟和 | ꜀'M ꜀ts'ang ꜂k'ü wá$^2$ ‹ái ꜂mán chí' ‹ning ꜀lai wó'. |
| 12. Change that pair of sheets, take away the dirty ones, and put on a clean pair. | 換過個兩張被單拈開兩張污糟嘅捭過兩張乾淨嘅嚟 | Ún$^2$ kwó' kó' ꜂léung ‹chéung ꜂p'í ‹tán ‹ním ‹hoi ꜂léung ‹chéung ‹ú ‹tsò ké', ʻpí kwó' ꜂léung ‹chéung ‹kón tsing$^2$ ké' ꜀lai. |
| I have already changed them. | 我已經換咯 | ꜂Ngó ꜂í ‹king ún$^2$ lók›. |
| 13. Bring a bolster. | 拈過一個長枕頭嚟 | ‹Ním kwó' yat› kó' ꜀ch'éung ʻcham ꜀t'au ꜀lai. |
| I have just now brought one. | 我而家就至拈㨢個嚟咋 | ꜂Ngó ꜀í ‹ká tsau$^2$ chí' ‹ním ʻkám kó' ꜀lai chá'. |
| 14. Have you also changed the pillow-cases? | 你有換過枕頭布冇呀 | ꜂Ní ꜂yau ún$^2$ kwó' ʻcham ꜀t'au pò' ꜂mò á' ? |
| Yes. | 換咯 | Ún$^2$ lók›. |
| 15. Are there any blankets in the house? | 屋裏頭有白氈冇呀 | Uk› ꜂lui ꜀t'au ꜂yau pák› ‹chín ꜂mò á' ? |
| There are some new ones. | 有的新過嘅處 | ꜂Yau tik› ‹san kwó' ʻhai ch'ü'. |
| 16. Call the tailor to mend the musketoe curtains. | 叫個裁縫補番個張蚊帳呀 | Kíú' kó' ꜀ts'oi ꜀fung ʻpò ‹fán kó' ‹chéung ‹man chéung' á'. |
| 17. When you make the bed, do not let any musketoes get inside of the curtains. | 鋪床囉咪捭蚊的趯入去呀 | ‹P'ò ꜀ch'óng ‹ló ꜂mai ʻpí ‹man tik› yap› h'ü' á'. |

12. The phrase *꜂í‹king* expresses the past tense, and is in common use for saying that a command has been obeyed, or a duty performed.

| | | |
|---|---|---|
| 18. Put these dirty clothes in the basket. | 擠呢的𧓍揸衣<br>服落笠呵 | ꜀Chai ꜀ní tik꜂ lá$^{3}$ ꜂chá ꜀í fuk$_{2}$ lók$_{2}$ lap꜂ ꜀ó. |
| 19. One cannot turn in the bed, it is so narrow. | 床窄冇定轉身 | ꜁Ch'óng chák꜂ ꜂mò ting$^{3}$ ꜂chün ꜀shan. |
| 20. Have you a sleeping-gown that you can give me? | 有睡袍俾過我 | ꜂Yau shui$^{3}$ ꜁p'ò ꜂pí kwó$^{3}$ ꜂ngó? |
| 21. The bed is supported by a pair of forms. | 一對條櫈扛床 | Yat꜂ túi$^{3}$ ꜁t'iú tang$^{3}$ ꜀hóng ꜁ch'óng. |
| 22. In a cradle children easily go to sleep. | 搋床孩子易瞓 | ꜁Ngò ꜁ch'óng ꜁hoi ꜂tsz' í$^{2}$ fan$^{3}$. |
| 23. The curtains adorned with poetry and pictures. | 蚊帳𢇞寫詩畫 | ꜁Man chéung$^{3}$ ꜁yam ꜂sé ꜀shí wá$^{2}$. |
| 24. The curtains hung up on the tenter hooks. | 亻帳鈎掛蚊帳 | ꜁Man chéung$^{3}$ ꜀kau kwá$^{3}$ ꜁man chéung$^{3}$. |
| 25. Hang the musketoe whip upon the curtain hook. | 挂枝蚊拂在帳<br>鈎處 | Kwá$^{3}$ ꜀chí ꜁man fat꜂ tsoi$^{2}$ chéung$^{3}$ ꜀kau ch'ü$^{3}$. |
| 26. Tell the coolie to put the chamber-pot under the bed, and place the chamber lamp by the side of the fire-place. | 叫管店擠個便<br>壺落床下底又<br>放盞暗燈喺火<br>爐邊嚟 | Kíú$^{3}$ ꜂kún tím$^{3}$ ꜀chai kó$^{3}$ pín$^{2}$ ꜁ú lók$_{2}$ ꜁ch'óng há$^{2}$ ꜂tai; yau$^{2}$ fong$^{3}$ ꜂chán om$^{3}$ ꜀tang ꜂hai ꜂fó ꜁lò ꜀pín ꜁lai. |
| 27. There are too many clothes on the bed, take off a blanket. | 床上衣服多得<br>嚌拈減張毡去 | ꜁Ch'óng shéung$^{2}$ ꜀í fuk$_{2}$ ꜀tó tak꜂ tsai$^{2}$ ꜀ním ꜂kám ꜀chéung ꜀chín h'ü$^{3}$. |
| 28. Will this do? | 咁做得未呀 | ꜂Kóm tsò$^{2}$ tak꜂ mí$^{2}$ á$^{3}$? |
| It will do. | 做得咯 | Tsò$^{2}$ tak꜂ lók꜂. |
| 29. Call me to-morrow morning at five o'clock. | 聽朝五點鐘叫<br>醒我起身吓 | ꜀T'ing ꜀chíú ꜂'ng ꜂tím ꜀chung kíú$^{3}$ ꜂sing ꜂ngó ꜂hí ꜀shan ꜂há. |
| 30. There was so much noise in the street last night that I could not sleep at all. | 昨晚街咁嘈整<br>得我成夜都瞓<br>唔着 | Tsók$_{2}$ ꜂mán ꜀kái kóm$^{3}$ ts'ò$^{3}$ ꜂ching tak꜂ ꜂ngó ꜁shing yé$^{2}$ ꜀tò fan$^{3}$ ꜁'m chéuk꜂. |

23. The Chinese hang stripes of cloth or silk around the top of the tester, answering to a fringe, on which flowers are painted or poetry is written.

25. This is a whip made from the hair of a horse's tail, and is used as a switch to kill musketoes.

## Section Seventh.

# ARTICLES OF FOOD.

## 食物類第七章
Shik$_2$ mat$_2$ lui$^2$; tai$^2$ ts'át› ‹chéung.

| | | |
|---|---|---|
| 1. If you wish to have good *anchovy sauce* it is necessary to keep [the fish] six or seven months, when it will be fit for use. | 欲糟魚解得味必須六七個月咁耐然後做得 | Yuk$_2$ ‹tsò ˏü ʻkái tak› mí$^2$, pít› ‹sü luk$_2$ ts'át› kó' ùt$_2$, kóm' noi$^2$, ˏín hau$^2$ tsò$^2$ tak›. |
| 2. We want some *dried apples.* | 要幾件乾平果 | Íú' ʻkí ʻkín$^2$ ‹kón ˏp'ing ʻkwó. |
| 3. *Beans* taken with ham improve its flavor. | 火腿得荳角更加一味 | ʻFó ʻt'úi tak› tau$^2$ kók› kang' ‹ká yat$_2$ mí$^2$. |
| 4. Fry some plantains covered with *batter.* | 熠蕉外搽麵料 | Cháu' ‹tsíú ngoi$^2$ ˏch'á mín$^2$ líú$^2$. |
| 5. The flesh of slaughtered cattle is called *beef.* | 牛劏後名牛肉 | ˏNgau ‹t'óng hau$^2$, ˏming ˏngau yuk$_2$. |
| 6. I want some *boiled beef* for dinner. | 大餐使烚牛肉 | Tái$^2$ ‹ts'án ʻshai shap$_2$ ˏngau yuk$_2$. |
| 7. Tell the cook to *roast* some *beef.* | 呌厨子燒牛肉 | Kíú' ˏch'ü ʻtsz' ‹shíú ˏngau yuk$_2$. |
| 8. Taste a little of this *rolled beef.* | 嘗吓捲筒牛肉 | ˏShéung ʻhá ʻkün ˏt'ung ˏngau yuk$_2$. |
| 9. On board ship [at sea] *salt beef* is eaten. | 行船食鹹牛肉 | ˏHang ˏshün shik$_2$ ˏhám ˏngau yuk$_2$. |
| 10. Change this for *beef-steak.* | 改轉鐵耙牛肉 | ʻKoi ʻchün tít› ˏp'á ˏngau yuk$_2$. |
| 11. In roasting *birds* string them on a spit. | 燒雀仔穿成串 | ‹Shíú tséuk› ʻtsai ‹ch'ün ˏshing ch'ün'. |
| 12. *Biscuit* will keep a long time. | 麵餅乾安得耐 | Mín$^2$ ʻping ‹kón ‹ón tak› noi$^2$. |
| 13. Go and buy two loaves of *bread,* and also three loaves of *bran bread.* | 去買麵頭二個麥糠麵頭三個 | H'ü' ʻmái mín$^2$ ˏt'au í$^2$ kó', mak$_2$ ‹hóng mín$^2$ ˏt'au ‹sám kó'. |

## *Notes and Explanations.*

UNDER the head of *shik mat* the Chinese arrange all kinds of edibles. Those enumerated in this section, constitute no inconsiderable portion of the common articles of food, excepting fish and vegetables, most of which are here omitted, as they belong more appropriately to another chapter. The different modes of cooking provisions, the ingredients of dishes, condiments used at table, names of sauces, and other preparations which the skill of the cook produces, will for the most part be found in this section.

10. This mode of cooking derives its name from the utensil on which it is broiled, the *tít p'á* iron rake or gridiron; and meat or vegetables, when sliced and cooked by broiling, bear the same name.

13. *Mín t'au* is, literally, wheaten-flour head; *mín* is used to designate the flour which is made from wheat; brown or unbolted bread is literally, wheat bran wheaten-flour head.

| | | |
|---|---|---|
| 14. Good *beer* is very lively. | 好啤酒氣性猛 | ‘Hò ‹pé ‘tsau h‘í’ sing’ ‘máng. |
| 15. In winter, then drink [hot] *broth.* | 冬日則飲湯 | ‹Tung yat$_2$ tsak› ‘yam ‹t‘óng. |
| 16. It is necessary to use *butter.* | 必須用牛奶油 | Pít› ‹sü’ yung$^2$ ‹ngau ‘nái ‹yau. |
| 17. *Cabbage* is palatable whether it be eaten raw, or boiled, or pickled [as sour crout]. | 椰菜擰嚟生食熟食醋醃都好 | ‹Yé ts‘oi’ ‹ning ‹lai ‹shang shik$_2$, shuk› shik$_2$, ts‘ò’ ‹ím, ‹tò ‘hò. |
| 18. Bring a wheaten *cake* here. | 攞一個麵餅嚟 | ‘Ló yat› kó’ mín$^2$ ‘ping ‹lai. |
| 19. All kinds of *cakes* are prepared [here]. | 各色餅食俱全 | Kók› shik› ‘ping shik$_2$ ‹k‘ü ‹ts‘ün. |
| 20. *Wine cake* requires poached egg upon it. | 酒餅要落蛋泡 | ‘Tsau ‘ping íú’ lók$_2$ tán$^2$ ‘p‘ò. |
| 21. A *capon* should be hung up [a few days] to make it tender, and also more delicate when roasted. | 騸鷄弔鬆重要燒得嫩 | Sín’ ‹kai tíú’ ‹sung chung$^2$ íú’ ‹shíú tak› nün$^2$. |
| 22. *Carrots* require boiling a full hour before they become fit to be eaten. | 紅蘿蔔要烚得一點鐘正食得 | ‹Hung ‹lò pák$_2$ íú’ sháp$_2$ tak› yat› ‘tím ‹chung ching’ shik$_2$ tak›. |
| 23. *Celery* when prepared in pickle is very tender. | 塘蒿醃過甚脆 | ‹T‘óng ‹hò ‹ím kwó’ sham$^2$ ts‘ui’. |
| 24. It is easy to get intoxicated with *champagne.* | 三鞭酒易飲醉 | ‹Sám ‹pín ‘tsau í$^2$ ‘yam tsui’. |
| 25. I am fond of good *cheese.* | 愛上好牛奶餅 | Oi’ shéung$^2$ ‘hò ‹ngau ‘nái ‘ping. |
| 26. I wish to have a *chicken* cooked cased in paper. | 要辦味紙袋鷄 | Í’ú’ pán$^2$ mí$^2$ ‘chí toi$^2$ ‹kai. |
| 27. Cook a *boned chicken.* | 弄一隻撻骨鷄 | Lung$^2$ yat› chik› t‘an’ kwat› ‹kai. |
| 28. Prepare some *chocolate* for supper. | 晚茶使揸古聿 | ‘Mán ‹ch‘á ‘shai ‹chá ‘kú lut$_2$. |
| 29. To make *chowder,* take fish, pork, onions, dried biscuit, pepper, flour, and | 做魚羹須用魚猪肉葱頭乾餅 | Tsò$^2$ ‹ü ‹kang ‹sü yung$^2$ ‹ü, ‹chü yuk$_2$, ‹ts‘ung ‹t‘au, ‹kón ‘ping, ‹ú ‹tsíú, mín$^2$ ‘fan, |

16. *Ngau nái yau,* cow's milk oil, is used by the Chinese to denote both cream and butter, neither of which are much used by themselves: for butter they frequently say simply *ngau yau,* and sometimes attempt to imitate cream by *kilím.*

18. The Chinese have a great variety of cakes, made of different substances and in many shapes, most of which are included under the term *ping* or *peng,* and distinguished from each other by appropriate terms; stalls for the sale of them are to be seen at every corner in the streets of their towns.

20. Wine cake generally denotes, among the Chinese, a cake in the form and size of a small square tile an inch thick, used by distillers to produce fermentation: here it is used to designate what is sometimes called ‘tipsey cake,’ or ‘brandy pudding.’

25. *Ngau nái ping,* milk cake, is used to denote cheese, of which the Chinese have none, and in speaking of it they commonly try to imitate the sound of the word by saying *chíshí.*

27. *Lung* means to play with, to toss in the hands, and here alludes to the preparation of a fowl by, *t‘an kwat,* retracting or pulling out the bones from the flesh; the word *t‘an* expresses the motion of pulling the arm within the sleeve, which the loose dress of the Chinese so easily permits.

| | | |
|---|---|---|
| salt, and boil them all together, and the chowder is made. | 胡椒麵粉鹽等烹而爲羹 | ˏím, ‘tang ‹p‘ang ˏí ˏwai ‹kang. |
| 30. The taste of *cider* is a little sour. | 平菓酒味道酸 | ˏP‘ing ‘kwó ‘tsau mí² tò² ‹sün. |
| 31. The fringe of your hat is made of *cives.* | 韭菜係你帽纓 | ‘Kau ts‘oi’ hai² ‘ní mò² ‹ying. |
| 32. *Claret* is a very fine beverage. | 紅酒甚是好飲 | ˏHung ‘tsau sham² shí² ‘hò ‘yam. |
| 33. *Coffee* must be thoroughly roasted to be good. | 架啡炒焦致好 | Ká’ ‹fí ‘ch‘áu ‹tsiú chí’ ‘hò. |
| 34. Pure hot *congee* always ready. | 明火白粥常便 | ˏMing ‘fó pák₂ chuk› ˏshéung pín². |
| 35. *Cream* collects on milk set in pans. | 牛乳捭碟凝油 | ˏNgau ‘yü ‘pí típ₂ ˏking ˏyau. |
| 36. Poor people make their relish of *bean curd.* | 貧窮荳腐做送 | ˏP‘an ˏk‘ung tau² fú² tsò² sung’. |
| 37. *Curry stuff* may be used for seasoning. | 黃薑材料辦菜 | ˏWóng ‹kéung ˏts‘oi líú² pán² ts‘oi’. |
| 38. Boil four cups of *custards.* | 燉四杯吉時嚟 | Tun’ sz’ ‹púi kat› ˏshí ˏlai. |
| 39. Do you know how to prepare fowl *cutlets?* | 你識辦吉烈雞唔呀 | ‘Ní shik› pán² kat› lít₂ ‹kai ˏ’m á’? |
| 40. *Deer's sinews* thoroughly boiled are nourishing. | 鹿筋煲腍有益 | Luk₂ ‹kán ‹pò ˏnam ‘yau yik›. |
| 41. *Ducks* are dried in the northerly winds of winter. | 北風天晒臘鴨 | Pak› ‹fung ‹t‘ín shái’ láp₂ áp›. |
| 42. This *roast duck* has no stuffing in it. | 呢隻燒鴨都冇釀肚嘅 | ‹Ní chik› ‹shíú áp› ‹tò ‘mò yéung² ‘t‘ò ké’. |
| 43. Both boiled and fried *eggs* are good. | 雞蛋炒烚都好 | ‹Kai tán² ‘ch‘áu sháp₂ ‹tò ‘hò. |
| 44. Beautiful as a [boiled] *egg* when the shell is taken off. | 雞春剝殼咁靚 | ‹Kai ‹ch‘un mók› hók› kóm’ ‘ling’. |
| 45. *Cow's feet* when thoroughly boiled are good food. | 牛腳煲腍好食 | ˏNgau kéuk› ‹pò ˏnam ‘hò shik₂. |

31. *Kau ts‘oi*, &c., is used by the people of Canton to reproach one whose wife is suspected of being unfaithful to him.

34. *Pák chuk* is the pure congee, which has nothing else cooked with it: *ming fó* indicates that the fire, by which it is cooked, is never allowed to be extinguished, which is equivalent to saying that the congee is always kept on hand hot, ready for use.

36. *Tau fú*, literally ‘pulse jam’, is made of peas or beans, which after being soaked a few hours are ground to powder in a hand-mill, and then pressed like a cheese curd, which the preparation very much resembles. There is another condiment made from pulse called *fú yü*, curd milk, which is more expensive than this, made by introducing the saturated dregs of rice spirit into the *tau fú*, and putting the whole aside for a month, after which it is eaten.

41. *Láp* is a term for the twelfth month. In olden times people slaughtered no animals for three days after new year; instead of fresh meat, they ate that which was pickled or dried. The bodies of ducks are often prepared in the latter way, by being split open and stretched out so as to be quite thin; hence the origin of its application to dried ducks.

44. This is a complimentary phrase applied to youth of both sexes when their personal beauty or fair complexion attract the admiring praises of friends.

| | | |
|---|---|---|
| 46. In roasting that *fillet of pork*, do'nt overdo it. | 燒猪朏砧莫燶 | ‹Shíú ‹chü ‘pí ‹cham mók, ‹nung. |
| 47. From the *fish* and prawns in the water I select fresh ones at pleasure. | 水上魚蝦任我採鮮 | ‘Shui shéung² ‹ü ‹há yam² ‘ngó ‘ts‘oi ‹sín. |
| 48. Foreign *salt fish* has an unusually good flavor. | 來路鹹魚分外野味 | ‹Loi lò² ‹hám ‹ü fan² ngoi² ‘yé mí². |
| 49. The best *flour* is used for making pastry. | 使標麵做點心 | ‘Shai ‹píú mín² tsò² ‘tím ‹sam. |
| 50. In roasting *fowls* do not crack their skins. | 燒雞莫燒裂皮 | ‹Shíú ‹kai mók, ‹shíú lít, ‹p‘í. |
| 51. The skin of this *fricasseed fowl* is fried very tough. | 呢的佛蘭晒嘅雞煼硬皮 | ‹Ní tik› fat, ‹lán ‹sai ké’ ‹kai cháu’ ngáng² ‹p‘í. |
| 52. Roast a *rabbit fowl.* | 燒一隻老鼠雞 | ‹Shíú yat› chik› ‘lò ‘shü ‹kai. |
| 53. In procuring various kinds of *fruits*, select those which are the most thoroughly ripe. | 辦幾樣菓子要熟嘅 | Pán² ‘kí yéung² ‘kwó ‘tsz’ íú’ shuk, ké’. |
| 54. Every body dislikes the smell of *garlic.* | 青蒜氣逢人厭 | ‹Ts‘ing sün’ h‘í’ ‹fung ‹yan ím’. |
| 55. Bid him prepare a *giblet pie.* | 呌整好鵞頭龜 | Kíú’ ‘ching ‘hò ‹ngó ‹t‘au ‹kwai. |
| 56. Can you roast a *goose* with stuffing in it? | 喴釀燒鵞唔喴 | ‘Ui yéung² ‹shíú ‹ngó ‹’m ‘úi? |
| 57. The roasted flesh of the *wild goose* is very tough. | 燒鴈鵞肉極肕 | ‹Shíú ngán² ‹ngó yuk, kik, yan’. |
| 58. Go and buy some *grape wine.* | 去買葡萄酒嚟 | H‘ü’ ‘mái ‹p‘ò ‹t‘ò ‘tsau ‹lai. |
| 59. That which drips from roast meat is called *gravy.* | 熟肉餘水曰汁 | Shuk, yuk, ‹ü ‘shui üt, chap›. |
| 60. Boil some *rice gruel* to feed the baby. | 煮米糊嚟餵仔 | ‘Chü ‘mai ‹ú ‹lai wai’ ‘tsai. |
| 61. *Hams* thoroughly boiled are very good. | 火腿烚透至好 | ‘Fó ‘t‘úi sháp, t‘au’ chí’ ‘hò. |
| 62. Keep the beef till to-morrow and make a *hash* of it. | 留番聽日做乞食牛肉 | ‹Lau ‹fán ‹t‘ing yat, tsò² hat› shik, ‹ngau yuk,. |

47. This is said by fishermen, and tropically by others also, who, as they themselves procure what they use, can select whatever suits their palate.

49. *Tím sam* is used to denote not only pastry, but confectionary, and almost every variety of made dishes; it is commonly applied to dessert dishes, and to those which are taken between the principal meals, as luncheon, tiffin, &c.

55. *Kwai*, here used for pie, is the name of the tortoise. The Chinese make no pies for themselves; and the term *kwai* may have been selected to denote a pie on account of its back being round and flat like a pie.

62. *Hat shik*, like the words *chákúlut*, *chíshí*, *katlít*, *pé* for beer, *katshí* for custards, *chélí* for jelly, and several others, which being altogether unknown in Chinese cookery, the characters are used merely to denote the sound of a foreign word, their sense being entirely disregarded: of course the meaning of such words cannot be very extensively known.

| | | |
|---|---|---|
| 63. There is not enough for a *haunch of mutton.* | 唔够一邊羊肉 | ˏ'M kau' yatˎ ˓pín ˏyéung yukˎ. |
| 64. Flatulence is most to be feared in eating *honey.* | 食蜜糖最忌風 | Shikˎ matˎ ˏt'óng tsui' kí' ˓fung. |
| 65. Give me a little whampe *jam.* | 挑的黄皮膏我 | ˓Tíú tikˎ ˏwóng ˏp'í ˓kò 'ngó. |
| 66. Pig's foot *jelly* is eaten in winter. | 冬天食猪脚凍 | ˓Tung ˓t'ín shikˎ ˓chü kéukˎ tung'. |
| 67. *Jellies* will not acquire consistence in warm weather. | 天暖車厘唔埋 | ˓T'ín 'nün ˓ch'é ˏlí ˏ'm ˏmái. |
| 68. If *lard* is used there will be no oily taste. | 使猪油冇油益 | ˓Shai ˓chü ˏyau 'mò ˏyau yikˎ. |
| 69. *Laichis* dried by fire are not so good as those which are dried in the sun. | 火焙荔枝乾唔似生曬嘅 | 'Fó púi' lai' ˓chí ˓kón ˏ'm 'ts'z' ˓shang shái' ké'. |
| 70. Open that bottle of *Madeira* for use. | 開罇白酒嚟飲 | ˓Hoi ˓tsun pákˎ 'tsau ˏlai 'yam. |
| 71. His beard is as long as the silk of *maize.* | 一包粟咁長鬚 | Yatˎ ˓páu sukˎ kóm' ˏch'éung ˓sò. |
| 72. *Indian meal* spoils if kept a long time. | 粟米粉耐漚壞 | Sukˎ 'mai 'fan noi' au' wái'. |
| 73. He is like a large winter *melon.* | 佢似個大冬瓜 | 'K'ü 'ts'z' kò' tái' ˓tung ˓kwá. |
| 74. I wish some *milk* poured into my tea. | 愛牛奶嚟撞茶 | Oí' ˏngau 'nái ˏlai chóng' ˏch'á. |
| 75. *Molasses* is spread upon eatables. | 桔水糖點野食 | Katˎ 'shui ˏt'óng 'tím 'yé shikˎ. |
| 76. Do not make the *mulligatawny* so hot. | 黄薑湯莫整咁辣噃 | ˏWóng ˓kéung ˓t'óng mókˎ 'ching kóm' látˎ pó'. |
| 77. *Mustard* is eaten with beef. | 食牛肉用芥末 | Shikˎ ˏngau yukˎ yung' kái' mútˎ. |
| 78. Without getting any *mutton* to eat, you may become frowzy therewith. | 唔得羊肉食惹得一身臊 | ˏ'M takˎ ˏyéung yukˎ shikˎ, 'yé takˎ yatˎ ˓shan ˓sò. |
| 79. The *mutton* steak is not yet ready. | 鐵耙羊肉未整 | T'ítˎ ˏp'á ˏyéung yukˎ mí' 'ching. |
| 80. To roast a *leg of mutton* much care is needed. | 燒羊髀要用心 | ˓Shíú ˏyéung 'pí íú' yung' ˓sam. |
| 81. Boil a joint of *nelumbium root* by itself. | 白焓一節蓮藕 | Pákˎ shápˎ yatˎ tsítˎ ˏlín 'ngau. |
| 82. Bring some of the best *nutmegs.* | 拈上好荳蔻嚟 | ˓Ním shéung' 'hò tau' k'au' ˏlai. |
| 83. *Sweet oil* is eaten fresh. | 生菜油生食嘅 | ˓Shang ts'oi' ˏyau ˓shang shikˎ ké'. |

71. This is a simile employed when speaking in complimentary terms of the flowing beard of an old man.

73. This comparison is used to describe a thick headed fellow who has no tact for anything, one who needs to be directed in all he undertakes, or who, like a round melon, will go no further than he is kicked; it is also applied to very corpulent persons.

78. This phrase expresses, what often happens in China, the implication of people in such a manner that they become sufferers (or get tainted or frowzy,) without obtaining any good object, or any reward.

| | | |
|---|---|---|
| 84. The flavor of *Sesamum oil* is exceedingly fragrant. | 芝蔴油味極香 | ‹Chí ‚má ‚yau mí² kik‚ ‹héung. |
| 85. Foreign *onions* are tender and sweet. | 來路葱頭爽甜 | ‚Loi lò² ‹ts'ung ‚t'au 'shóng ‚t'ím. |
| 86. Bake the *oyster pie* so that [the pastry] will become light and tender. | 局蠔麵龜要起好酥 | Kuk‚ ‚hò mín² ‹kwai iú' 'hí 'hò ‹sò. |
| 87. To fry the *liver* of beef a good deal of skill is necessary. | 煎牛肝必要好手勢 | ‹Tsín ‚ngau ‹kón pít‚ iú' 'hò 'shau shai'. |
| 88. Rice *pancakes* should be fried till they are brown. | 飯班戟要煎嫩 | Fán² ‹pán kik‚ iú' ‹tsín nün². |
| 89. I wish to buy some *parsley*. | 我要買旱芹菜 | 'Ngó iú' 'mái 'hón ‚kan ts'oi'. |
| 90. The body of a *partridge* is warm when dead. | 鷓鴣身死重暖 | Ché' ‹kú ‹shan 'sz' chung² 'nün. |
| 91. *Pastry* should be made tender and fine. | 麵食弄幼細的 | Mín² shik‚ lung² yau' sai' tik‚. |
| 92. *Green peas* put into the water for a while will presently sprout. | 菉荳俾水淋就出芽菜 | Luk‚ tau² 'pí 'shui ‚lam tsau² ch'ut‚ ‚ngá ts'oi'. |
| 93. Black *pepper* is not so pungent as Cayenne. | 胡椒唔似花椒咁辣 | ‚Ú ‹tsíú ‚'m 'ts'z' ‹fá ‹tsíú kóm' lát‚. |
| 94. A baked *pig* retains the entire flavor. | 局猪豚極全味 | Kuk‚ ‹chü ‚tün kik‚ ‚ts'ün mí². |
| 95. Bring a bottle of *pickles*. | 拈罇酸菓埋嚟 | ‹Ním ‹tsun ‹sün 'kwó ‚mái ‚lai. |
| 96. Take care how you roast the *pigeons*. | 俾心機燒班鳩 | 'Pí ‹sam ‹kí ‹shíú ‹pán ‹kau. |
| 97. *Pigeon's eggs* stewed with birdsnests. | 白鴿蛋會燕窩 | Pák‚ kóp‚ tán² úi² ín' ‹wó. |
| 98. Make the *pigeon pie* tender and crisp. | 做個鬆酥白鴿麵龜 | Tsò² kó' ‹sung ‹sò pák‚ kóp‚ mín² ‹kwai. |
| 99. I wish to have a *pilau*. | 要整盤波羅飯 | Íú' 'ching ‚p'ún ‹pó ‚ló fán². |
| 100. I wish for some *pork chops* to eat. | 愛食燒猪排骨 | Oi' shik‚ ‹shíú ‹chü ‚p'ái kwat‚. |
| 101. Taste a little of this *fried pork*. | 試吓小炒猪肉 | Shí' 'há 'síú 'ch'áu ‹chü yuk‚. |
| 102. *Salt pork* must be first soaked in water when it will be ready for boiling. | 鹹猪肉先浸水致好焓 | ‚Hám ‹chü yuk‚ ‹sín tsam' 'shui chí' 'ho sháp‚. |
| 103. Pour out a full glass of *Port* for me. | 斟滿杯砵酒我 | ‹Cham 'mún ‹púi pút‚ 'tsau 'ngó. |
| 104. Baked *potatoes* should be a little brown. | 局薯仔要黃淨 | Kuk‚ ‚shü 'tsai íú' ‚wong tsing². |

84. The oil of the Sesamum orientale, and also of the Ricinus communis or castor oil plant, are both used by the Chinese in cooking; the latter is used to the greatest extent in

| | | |
|---|---|---|
| 105. The *potatoe* has fallen into the ash-hole of the furnace to be roasted! | 畨薯跌落竈窟該煨 | ‹Fán ˏshü tít› lók² tsò’ fat› ‹koi ‹úi! |
| 106. The slices of *sweet potatoes* should be thin. | 鐵耙紅薯切薄 | T‘ít› ˏp‘á ˏhung ˏshü ts‘it› pok². |
| 107. The tavern is furnished with wines and *provisions*. | 高樓酒菜麵食 | ‹Kò ˏlau ‘tsau ts‘oi’ mín² shik². |
| 108. Boil a *bread pudding*. | 燉個麵頭布顛 | Tun’ kó’ mín² ˏt‘au pò’ ‹tín. |
| 109. I cannot make stewed *rabbit*. | 唔噲做會兎子 | ˏ’M ‘úi tsò² úi² t‘ò’ ‘tsz’. |
| 110. In making the rice pudding put some *raisins* into it. | 整飯布顛落菩提子 | ‘Ching fán² pò’ ‹tín lók² ˏpò ˏt‘ai ‘tsz’. |
| 111. *Old man's rice* is glutinous when thoroughly done. | 糯米煮熟膠煉 | Nò² ‘mai ‘chü shuk² ‹káu lín². |
| 112. The price of *rice* at present is high. | 現在米價高昂 | Ín² tsoi² ‘mai ká’ ‹kò ˏngóng. |
| 113. When one has eaten fully of *rice*, he forgets hunger. | 飯飽却就忘饑 | Fán² ‘páu k‘éuk› tsau² ˏmóng ‹kí. |
| 114. You ought to remember that not a grain of *rice* or a drop of congee comes without toil. | 一粥一飯當思來處不易 | Yat› chuk› yat› fán² ‹tóng ‹sz’ ˏloi ch‘ü’ pat› í². |
| 115. Eat a bowl of *sago* for tiffin. | 食碗西米做晏 | Shik² ‘ún ‹sai ‘mai tsò² án’. |
| 116. Add a pecul of *salt* and it will still be tasteless. | 落擔塩都冇味 | Lók² tám’ ˏím ‹tò ‘mò mí². |
| 117. *Sausages* are dried in the northerly winds. | 北風晒臘猪腸 | Pak› ‹fung shái’ láp² ‹chü ˏch‘éung. |
| 118. In roasting *snipes* they should not be opened. | 燒沙椎唔開肚 | ‹Shíú ‹shá ‹chui ˏ’m ‹hoi ‘t‘ò. |
| 119. Make *beef soup* this evening. | 今晚做牛肉湯 | ‹Kam ‘máu tsò² ˏngau yuk› ‹t‘óng. |
| 120. To-day make *mutton soup*. | 今日整羊肉湯 | ‹Kam yat² ‘ching ˏyéung yuk² ‹t‘óng. |
| 121. Boiled *turtle soup* is strengthening. | 燉脚魚湯有補 | Tan’ kéuk› ˏü ‹t‘ong ‘yau ‘pò. |
| 122. *Souse* should be stewed till it is tender. | 猪利脚要會腍 | ‹Chü lí² kéuk› íú’ úi² ˏnam. |
| 123. Cut for me a little of the *spare rib*. | 斬的猪尾龍黎 | ‘Chám tik› ‹chü ‘mí ˏlung ˏlai. |

the northern parts of the empire. The process of cooking appears to deprive them both in a great measure of their detergent qualities.

105. This comparison is employed by one who is involved in difficulties, and in danger of making shipwreck of all his interests, and that too in a good degree by reason of his own folly and mismanagement.

107. *Kò lau* is the tavern, inn, or hotel, of the Chinese; for the two latter terms, however, *hit tím*, resting or stopping place, is the most common and appropriate phrase. The *kò lau*, or lofty room, is strictly a victualing-house, furnished with, *tsau* wines, and *ts‘oi mín shik* vegetable and wheaten provisions; i. e. (the two terms taken together,) with all kinds of provisions.

112, 113. *Mai* is the grain of rice as it comes into the market; and *fán* is the term for the same article after it has been cooked, which is usually done by boiling. With the Chinese rice is "the staff of life."

廣東方言讀本



| | | |
|---|---|---|
| 124. He will by and by take away all your *soy* from you. | 當豉油都嗆點乾你 | Tóng꜅ shí꜅ ꜁yau ꜀tò ꜂úi ꜂tím ꜀kón ꜂ní. |
| 125. *Stockfish* and green vegetables are the common family dishes. | 鹹魚青菜係家常送 | ꜁Hám ꜁ü ꜀ts'ing ts'oi꜄ hai꜅ ꜀ká ꜁shéung sung꜄. |
| 126. Really as sweet as *sugar candy*. | 眞正冰糖咁甜 | ꜀Chan ching꜄ ꜀ping ꜁t'óng kóm꜄ ꜁t'ím. |
| 127. Beef *suet* is used in making puddings. | 牛骨髓做布顛 | ꜁Ngau kwat꜆ ꜂sui tsò꜅ pò꜄ ꜀tín. |
| 128. Bring the *sweetmeats* here. | 拈蜜餞糖菓嚟 | ꜀Ním mat꜇ tsín꜄ ꜁t'óng ꜂kwó ꜁lai. |
| 129. Boil the *taro* till it is mealy. | 烚熟芋頭鬆嘅 | Sháp꜇ shuk꜇ ú꜅ ꜁t'au ꜀sung ké꜄. |
| 130. Cut me a piece of the carambola *tart*. | 切一塊三捻噠 | Ts'it꜆ yat꜆ fái꜄ ꜀sám ním꜅ tát꜆. |
| 131. Tell him to prepare some *tea*. | 叫佢冲壺茶嚟 | Kíú꜄ ꜂k'ü ꜀ch'ung ꜁ú ꜁ch'á ꜁lai. |
| 132. You must not make the *toast* so hard. | 炕多時勿嘅烘 | Hóng꜄ ꜀tó ꜁shí mat꜇ ké꜄ hóng꜄. |
| 133. The *beef's tongue* is too salt, tell him to boil it till it is more fresh. | 鹹牛利叫佢烚淡的嚟 | ꜁Hám ꜁ngau lí꜅, kíú꜄ ꜂k'ü sháp꜇ tám꜅ tik꜆ ꜁lai. |
| 134. Order a *turkey* to be roasted. | 吩咐使燒火鷄 | ꜀Fan fú꜅ ꜂shai ꜀shíú ꜂fó ꜀kai. |
| 135. It is not necessary to have any *veal*. | 不必使牛仔肉 | Pat꜆ pít꜆ ꜂shai ꜁ngau ꜂tsai yuk꜇. |
| 136. While boiling dried *venison*, occasionally try it. | 烚塊鹿脯試試 | Sháp꜇ fái꜄ luk꜇ ꜂fú shí꜄ shí꜄. |
| 137. Put some *vermicelli* into the boiling soup. | 要落粉絲滾湯 | Íú꜄ lók꜇ ꜂fan ꜀sz꜄ ꜂kwan ꜀t'óng. |
| 138. Provide plenty of *victuals* when you voyage. | 行船多辦火食 | ꜁Hang ꜁shün ꜀tó pán꜅ ꜂fó shik꜇. |
| 139. They both have been drinking *vinegar*. | 兩個食起醋嚟 | ꜂Léung kó꜄ shik꜇ ꜂hí ts'ò꜄ ꜁lai. |
| 140. Pour out a tumbler of *spring water* for me. | 去倒杯山水嚟 | H'ü꜄ ꜂tò ꜀púi ꜀shán ꜂shui ꜁lai. |
| 141. The tea in this pot is very strong, pour in some *boiling water* to make it weaker. | 呢盅茶濃到刧冲滾水和淡吓 | ꜀Ní ꜀chung ꜁ch'á ꜁yung tò꜄ kíp꜆, ꜀ch'ung ꜂kwan ꜂shui wó꜅ ꜂tám ꜂há. |
| 142. Come let us go together and take some *wine*. | 相請去飲燒酒 | ꜀Séung ꜂ts'ing h'ü꜄ ꜂yam ꜀shíú ꜂tsau. |
| 143. *Yams* when boiled soft are very mealy. | 大薯甑腍極鬆 | Tái꜅ ꜁shü tsang꜄ ꜁nam kik꜇ ꜀sung. |
| 144. To make bread it is necessary to put *yeast* into it. | 發麵包須落酵 | Fát꜆ mín꜅ ꜀páu ꜀sü lók꜇ káu꜄. |

124. This is a piece of advice to a poor man not to be too fond of associating with rich men, lest they take away his all; he must furnish his share of an entertainment, and thus go far beyond his means, which will soon dry up his [soy or] limited resources. The allusion is to a poor and rich man eating at the same table, and the latter dips his morsel of meat into the poor man's soy, who cannot repay the compliment by dipping his dish into the other's.

## Section Eighth.

## OF THE STEWARD.

### 買辦類第八章
ʻMái pán' lui'; tai' pát, ˏchéung.

| | | |
|---|---|---|
| 1. Steward, what is your name? | 買辦你呌做乜名呀 | ʻMái pán', ʻní kíú' tsò' mat, ˏming á'? |
| My name is *Aloi*. | 我呌做阿來 | ʻNgó kíú' tsò' Á' ˏloi. |
| 2. What wages do stewards commonly receive [monthly]? | 買辦平時受幾多工錢呢 | ʻMái pán' ˏp'ing ˏshí shau' ʻkí ˏtó ˏkung ˏtsín ˏní? |
| There is no fixed rate; sometimes they receive ten or twenty [dollars], or it may be less than these sums. | 唔定有時一二十個或者少的 | ˏ'M ting'; ʻyau ˏshí yat, í' shap, kó', wák, ʻché ʻshíú tik,. |
| 3. Do stewards receive any perquisites in addition to their wages? | 除人工外買辦有賞有冇呢 | ˏCh'ü ˏyan ˏkung ngoi' ʻmái pán' ʻyau ʻshéung ʻyau ʻmò ˏní? |
| I think they do. | 我睇得有 | ʻNgó ʻt'ai tak, ʻyau. |
| 4. What is the amount of these annually? | 每年有幾多呢 | ʻMúí ˏnín ʻyau ʻkí ˏtó ˏní? |
| It is not fixed, but varies according as the business is great or small. | 唔定睇事幹大小嚟凑 | ˏ'M ting'; ʻt'ai sz'' kón' tái' ʻshíú ˏlai ch'au'. |
| 5. Are stewards required to make any presents? | 買辦使送禮孝敬人唔使呢 | ʻMái pán' ʻshai sung' ʻlai hau' king' ˏyan, ˏ'm ʻshai ˏní? |
| They are, and these are not a few. | 使呀而且多呀 | ʻShai á', ˏí ʻch'é ˏtó á'. |

### *Notes and Explanations.*

THE duties of this person do but partially appear from his designation, *máipán*, the literal meaning of which is purveyor, or, following the Portuguese nomenclature which is commonly used in Canton, comprador. In commercial establishments, he adds to the duties of mere purveyor, those of treasurer, and keeper of small stores, and also of steward in the domestic department,—procuring and standing responsible for all the native servants of the house, keeping them in order, &c.

2. In large establishments the wages of stewards constitute only a very small fraction of their income, arising not only from a heavy percentage on provisions purchased, but also from the mercantile transactions, and money payments, of the house. In fact, they are often regarded less as hired servants, than as agents, or brokers between the foreigner and the native. They usually have their own servants and employés, the latter of whom are well designated *máipán cháu*, the comprador's claws.

5. These presents are made to the local magistrate, from whom they obtain their license to

| | | |
|---|---|---|
| 6. How many persons have you employed in the house? | 呢行內一總有幾多人呀 | ‹Ní ‹hóng noi² yat› ʽtsung ʽyau ʽkí ‹tó ‹yan á²? |
| Nine persons. | 九個 | ʽKau kó². |
| 7. How are they employed? | 做乜野嘅呀 | Tsò² mat› ʽyé ké² á²? |
| Three are personal servants, three are coolies, one is a cowkeeper, one a porter, and one is a cook. | 三個事仔三個管店一個看牛一個看門一個做厨 | ‹Sám kó² sz²² ʽtsai, ‹sám kó² ʽkún tím², yat› kó² hón² ‹ngau, yat› kó² hón² ‹mún, yat› kó² tsò² ‹ch'ü. |
| 8. What wages do they receive? | 佢哋受幾多工錢呢 | ʽK'ü tí² shau² ʽkí ‹tó ‹kung ‹ts'ín ‹ní? |
| The personal servants receive each five dollars; the coolies and porter, each four dollars; the cook, seven; and the cowkeeper, three; making a total sum of forty dollars, monthly wages. | 事仔每人五個銀錢管店看門每人四個做厨七個看牛三個每月共支工銀四十元 | Sz²² ʽtsai ʽmúi ‹yan ʽʽng kó² ‹ngan ‹ts'ín; ʽkún tím² hón² ‹mún ʽmúi ‹yan sz²² kó², tsò² ‹ch'ü ts'át› kó², hón² ‹ngau ‹sám kó²; ʽmúi üt₂ kung² ‹chí ‹kung ‹ngan sz²² shap₂ ‹ün. |
| 9. When do they receive their wages? | 各人幾時支人工呢 | Kók› ‹yan ʽkí ‹shí ‹chí ‹yan ‹kung ‹ní? |
| On the first day of each month they receive the wages for the preceding month. | 每月一號支上月嘅銀 | ʽMúi üt₂ yat› hò² ‹chí shéung² üt₂ ké² ‹ngan. |
| 10. Have they any perquisites? | 佢哋有賞冇呢 | ʽK'ü tí² ʽyau ʽshéung ʽmò ‹ní? |

act as stewards, and to the police, etc; in addition, they are also subjected to various irregular extortions from officers of government, which are exacted whenever a pretense can be found for so doing; and which coming upon them at uncertain seasons, and from different causes usually beyond their control, accounts in a measure for their timidity.

6. These nine are exclusive of his own personal servants and claws. Those natives who are attached to the factories are thought to demean themselves by attending on the orders of foreigners; and hence, to avoid the appearance of lowering their character, a somewhat singular nomenclature has come into vogue, derived from the shop, and not from the family. These personal servants call themselves, and are called, 'children of the business,' or subordinates, while their masters are styled, 'heads of the business,' or principals. And the coolies,—servants who do all manner of work,—are named 'overseers of the shop.'

10. This reply must be limited to those employers who transact little or no commercial business, for where extensive dealings are carried on either in money or barter, by the 'principal,' the 'subordinate' usually manages also to secure something for himself.

| English | Chinese | Romanization |
|---|---|---|
| They have, but not of any considerable amount. | 有吖總係冇幾多啫 | 'Yau ,á, 'tsung hai 'mò 'ki ,tò ,ché. |
| 11. Do you keep an account of the daily expenses of the house? | 行內嘅日用有上數冇呀 | ,Hóng noi ké yat yung 'yau 'shéung shò 'mò á? |
| Yes, I keep a daily account with my own hand. | 有日日我都親手上 | 'Yau, yat yat 'ngó ,tò ,ts'an 'shau 'shéung. |
| 12. Bring yesterday's account for examination. | 擰昨日數嚟對 | ,Ning tsók yat shò ,lai túi. |
| I have already brought it, and here it is. | 已經擰定喺呢處嚟嘑 | 'Í ,king ,ning ting 'hai ,ní ch'ü ,lai lá. |
| 13. What are the items of it? | 有的乜野呢 | 'Yau tik mat 'yé ,ní? |
| Do you, sir, wish me to read it to you? | 東家你要我念過你聽呀 | ,Tung ,ká 'ní íú 'ngó ním kwò 'ní ,t'ing ,mé? |
| 14. Yes, and read it very slowly and distinctly. | 係慢慢念得伶伶俐俐的嚟 | Hai, mán mán ním tak ,ling ,ling lí lí tik ,lai. |

[It is as follows:]

| | Catty. | | Can. | | T. m. c. |
|---|---|---|---|---|---|
| Rice, | 2½ | at | 4 | is | 0 1 0 |
| Beef, | 4 | " | 9 | " | 0 3 6 |
| Sugar, | 10 | " | 8 | " | 0 8 0 |
| Flour, | 8 | " | 5 | " | 0 4 0 |
| Eggs, | 12 | " | 5 cash | | 0 0 6 |
| | | | | Total, | 1 7 2 |

白米二斤半四算銀一錢
牛肉四斤九算銀三錢六分
冰花糖十斤八算銀八錢
白麵八斤五算銀四錢
鷄蛋十二隻五算銀六分
共銀一両七錢二分

Pák 'mai, í ,kan pún, sz" sün, ,ngan yat ,ts'ín;
,Ngau yuk, sz" ,kan, 'kau sün, ,ngan ,sám ,ts'ín [luk ,fan;
,Ping ,fá ,t'óng, shap ,kan, pát sün, ,ngan pát ,ts'ín;
Pák mín, pát ,kan, "ng sün, ,ngan sz" ,ts'ín;
,Kai tán, shap í chik, "ng sün, ,ngan luk ,fan;
Kung ,ngan, yat 'léung, ts'át ,ts'ín, í ,fan.

13. *Tungká*, the east of the house, being in large establishments the peculiar residence of the master, has, by metonymy, come to mean 'master.'

14. This is given merely as a specimen of the manner and matter of the daily account which the steward brings forward, for provisions; it commences on the right hand side, and reads downward in the usual mode of Chinese writing.

| | | |
|---|---|---|
| 15. I think you have made a mistake in the reckoning, bring the abacus and let me see you reckon it again. | 我睇你計唔準<br>擰算盤再覆過<br>我看 | 'Ngó 't'ai 'ní kai' ,'m 'sun, ,ning sün' ,p'ún tsoi' fuk, kwó' 'ngó hon'. |
| It is unnecessary, for I have already repeated the reckoning two or three times. | 不用囉我已經<br>再三算眞咖囉 | Pat, yung' ,lo; 'ngó 'í ,king tsoi' ,sám sün' ,chan ,ká ,ló. |
| 16. What is the amount of this sum in dollars and cents? | 咁多係幾元零<br>幾多個先士呢 | Kóm' ,tó hai[2] 'kí ,ün ,ling 'kí ,tó kó' ,sín sz'[2] ,ní? |
| Reckoning each dollar at seven mace and two candareens, for each one hundred cents, the whole amounts to two dollars and twenty-nine cents. | 以每元七錢二<br>分每元一百個<br>先士計總共二<br>元二毫九先士 | 'Í 'múi ,ün ts'át, ,ts'ín í[2] ,fan, 'múi ,ün yat, pák, kó' ,sín sz'[2], kai' 'tsung kung[2] í[2] ,ün í[2] ,hò 'kau ,sín sz'[2]. |
| 17. For breakfast to-morrow morning, get some fish, eggs, and rice, with coffee, tea, and toast. | 聽朝整的魚雞<br>蛋白飯冲的架<br>啡茶炕的麵包<br>嚟做早餐 | ,T'ing ,chiú 'ching tik, ,ü, ,kai tán[2], pák, fán[2] ,ch'ung tik, ká' ,fí ,ch'á, h'óng' tik, mín[2] ,páu ,lai tsò[2] 'tsò ,ts'án. |
| 18. Do you wish for anything else? | 重要的乜野添<br>唔要呀 | Chung[2] iú' tik, mat, 'yé ,t'ím, ,'m iú' á'? |
| No, only take care to have the articles which I named to you made ready; those are enough; and see that the breakfast is prepared at eight o'clock. | 唔要嚹總係用<br>心整好我話過<br>你知個的野就<br>做得嚹〇八點<br>鐘就好整便嚹<br>係咯 | ,'M iú lá'; 'tsung hai[2] yung[2] ,sam 'ching 'hò 'ngó wá[2] kwó' 'ní ,chí kó' tik, 'yé tsau[2] tsò[2] tak, lá'. Pát, 'tím ,chung tsau[2] 'hò 'ching pín[2] lá' hai[2] lók,. |
| 19. For how many, Sir, shall I make tea to-morrow morning? | 事頭聽早做幾<br>多個人茶嚹 | Sz'[2] ,t'au ,t'ing 'tsò tsò[2] 'kí ,tó kó' ,yan ,ch'á lá'? |
| Besides the three members of the family, which you count, I have invited three other gentlemen. | 你打算自家屋<br>三位另外請三<br>位添 | 'Ní 'tá sün' tsz'[2] ,ká uk, ,sám wai[2], ling[2] ngoi[2] 'ts'ing ,sám wai[2] ,t'ím. |

19. *Ling ngoi* is the usual phrase for besides, over and above; *wai*, composed of *man* and

20. The master of a family [in China, among those who are affluent, usually] has four personal servants; two grown men, who wait upon him at meals, take care of his clothes, and attend to all such matters; and two younger persons, to follow him when he goes abroad, to carry his pipe, to fan him, and to present his cards.

一個東家有四個跟班兩個大的伺候東家食飯料理衣服·各樣事兩個細的跟東家出街要裝烟打扇遞帖

Yat› kó' ‹tung ‹ká 'yau sz" kó' ‹kan ‹pán; 'léung kó' tái2 tik›, tsz'2 hau2 ‹tung ‹ká shik, fán2, liú2 'lí ‹í fuk,, kók, yéung2 sz'2; 'léung kó' sai' tik›, ‹kan ‹tung ‹ká ch'ut› ‹kái iú' ‹chóng ‹ín, 'tá shín', tai' t'íp›.

He has also four domestics; the older carry water, and go to the bazars; the younger sweep the floors, light the lamps, and wipe the chairs and tables.

有四個住年㡳大的要擔水買野細的要掃地點燈抹枱椅

'Yau sz" kó' chü2 ,nín 'tai; tái2 tik› iú' ‹tám 'shui 'mái 'yé, sai' tik› iú' sò' tí2, 'tím ‹tang, mút› ,t'oi 'í.

21. The mistress of a family has four waiting maids; the older ones, to take care of her clothes, and to attend on her when eating; the younger ones, to follow her when she goes out, to hand her tea and tobacco, to fan her, &c. These waiting maids are [not unfrequently] slaves, whom she has purchased for herself.

一個東主娘有四個使妹大的料理衣服伺候東主娘食飯細的跟東主娘出街遞茶裝烟打扇個的使妹係自己買來用嘅丫頭

Yat› kó' ‹tung 'chü ,néung 'yau sz" kó' 'shai múi': tai2 tik›, liú2 'lí ‹í fuk,, tsz'2 hau2 ‹tung 'chü ,néung shik, fán2; sai' tik› ‹kan ‹tung 'chü ,néung ch'ut› ‹kái, tai' ,ch'á, ‹chóng ‹ín, 'tá shín'; kó' tik› 'shai múi' hai2 tsz" 'kí 'mái ,loi yung2 ké' ‹á ,t'au.

Besides these, she hires several housemaids; [as] one to dress her hair, one to cook her food, one to wash her clothes, and one to follow her when she goes abroad.

另又僱幾個亞媽一個梳頭一個煮飯一個洗衣裳一個跟出街

Ling2 yau2 kú' 'kí kó' á' 'má; yat› kó' ‹shó ,t'au, yat› kó' 'chü fán2, yat› kó' 'sai ‹í ,shéung, yat› kó' ‹kan ch'ut› ‹kái.

*to establish* is the common term of respect for strangers, or others, and corresponds in its usual acceptation to the word gentleman.

20. It will be noted that here and in the next paragraph, the terms used for personal servants are different from those in No. 7 above. Those here employed are the ones in common use with the Chinese.

## Section Ninth.

# OF THE BREAKFAST TABLE.

## 早膳類第九章

'Tsò shín² lui²; tai² 'kau ‹chéung.

| | | |
|---|---|---|
| 1. *Ásám*, is breakfast ready? | 阿三早茶便未曾呀 | Á' ‹sám, 'tsò ‹ch'á pín mí² ˏts'ang á'? |
| It is all ready, Sir. | 齊備晒咯 | ˏTs'ai pí² sái' lòk›. |
| 2. Don't you see that this table is not set in a proper manner? Put it to rights quickly. | 你睇鋪呢張檯唔着咁擺設快的鋪過囉 | 'Ní 't'ai ‹p'ò ‹ní ‹chéung ˏt'oi ˏ'm chéuk› 'kóm 'pái ch'ít›? Fái' tik› ‹p'ò kwó' ‹ló. |
| 3. Go and invite the gentlemen to come to breakfast. | 去請齊的人嚟食囉 | H'ü' 'ts'ing ˏts'ai tik› ˏyan ˏlai shik₂ ‹ló. |
| Yes, Sir. | 呀好咧 | Á² 'hò ‹lé. |
| 4. Take off the dish covers from the curry and rice. | 揭起個碟黃薑同飯嘅冚盖 | K'ít› 'hí kó' típ₂ ˏwóng ‹kéung ˏt'ung fán² ké' 'k'am koi'. |
| 5. Give this plate to the gentleman nearest to me on my right hand. | 俾呢碟過我右邊至得近個個人客唉 | 'Pí ‹ní típ₂ kwó' 'ngó yau² ‹pín chí' tak› kan² kó' kó' ˏyan hák› ‹é. |
| 6. Bring the eggs and the butter cup. | 擰個的鷄蛋同牛油盅嚟 | ‹Ning kó' tik› ‹kai tán² ˏt'ung ˏngau ˏyau ‹chung ˏlai. |
| 7. That gentleman's napkin seems dirty, change it for another. | 個位人客嘅抹手巾怕污糟換轉條嚟 | Kó' wai² ˏyan hák› ké' mut› 'shau ‹kan pá' ‹ú ‹tsò, ún² 'chün ˏt'íú ˏlai. |

### *Notes and Explanations.*

THE character *shín* is composed of *flesh* placed on the left of good or *excellent*, and has the sense of meal, or a good meal. The Chinese usually have their breakfast served up about ten o'clock; but among laborers in the field, and artisans whose work is severe, as carpenters, masons, &c., it is brought on the table at an earlier hour, as these classes have an intervening meal about noontide. They often call it *tsò ch'á*, and *tsò ts'án*, both of which terms convey nearly the same meaning as the phrase here given.

| | | |
|---|---|---|
| 8. Carry away these dishes, and bring the fish. | 擰呢隻碟去替個的魚嚟 | ‹Ning ‹ní chik› típ$_{2}$ h‘ü’ t‘ai’ kó’ tik› ˏü ˏlai. |
| 9. Bring the castor here. | 拈個五味架嚟 | ‹Ním kó’ ˏ’ng mí$^{2}$ ká’ ˏlai. |
| 10. Have you prepared any toast? | 你有炕定的多時唔曾呀 | ʿNí ʿyau hòng’ ting$^{2}$ tik› ‹tó ˏshí ˏ’m ˏts‘ang á’? |
| I have not yet. | 唔曾 | ˏ’M ˏts‘ang. |
| 11. Put a little more tea into the teapot, and pour in some hot water also. | 擠的茶葉落茶壺嚟冲的滾水添 | ‹Chai tik› ˏch‘á íp$_{2}$ lók$_{2}$ ˏch‘á ˏú ˏlai, ‹ch‘ung tik› ʿkwan ʿshui ‹t‘ím. |
| 12. Ask that gentleman if his tea is agreeable or not. | 問吓個位人客睇吓佢嫌茶濃唔嫌 | Man$^{2}$ ʿhá kó’ wai$^{2}$ ˏyan hák›, ʿt‘ai ʿhá ʿk‘ü ˏím ˏch‘á ˏyung ˏ’m ˏím. |
| 13. Which gentleman? | 邊位人客呀 | ‹Pín wai$^{2}$ ˏyan hák› á’? |
| The one opposite to me. | 我對面個個呢 | ʿNgó túi’ mín$^{2}$ kó’ kó’ ‹ní. |
| He says it is agreeable. | 佢話啱咯 | ʿK‘ü wá$^{2}$ ‹ngám lók›. |
| 14. Ask this lady if she wishes for an egg or not. | 問呢位阿娘愛雞蛋唔吖 | Man$^{2}$ ‹ní wai$^{2}$ á’ ˏnéung oi’ ‹kai tán$^{2}$ ˏ’m ‹á? |
| 15. Bring a cup of tea, and some sugar, for her. | 拈一杯茶同的糖遞過佢 | ‹Ním yat› ‹púi ˏch‘á ˏt‘ung tik› ˏt‘óng tai$^{2}$ kwó’ ʿk‘ü. |
| 16. Put a little more milk into my tea. | 捭的牛乳落我杯茶添 | ʿPí tik› ˏngau ʿyü lók› ʿngó ‹púi ˏch‘á ‹t‘ím. |
| 17. Remove the table-cloth, and bring the finger-bowls. | 收檯布去擰洗手盅嚟 | ‹Shau ˏt‘oi pò’ h‘ü’, ‹ning ʿsai ʿshau ‹chung ˏlai. |
| 18. After the gentlemen have retired from the table, bid the coolie to rub it down. | 人客散之後叫管店擦乾淨個張枱嚟 | ˏYan hák› sán’ ‹chí hau$^{2}$, kíú’ ʿkún tím’ ts‘át› ‹kón ts‘ing$^{2}$ kó’ ‹chéung ˏt‘oi ˏlai. |

廣東方言讀本

## Section Tenth.

# OF THE DINNER TABLE.

## 大餐類第十章

Tái' ꜀ts'án lui'; tai' shap, ꜀chéung.

| | | |
|---|---|---|
| 1. *Álun*, make ready the dinner to-day at three o'clock. | 阿倫今日三點鐘齊備大餐喇 | Á' ꜂lun, ꜀kam yat, ꜀sám 'tím ꜀chung ꜂ts'ai pí' tái' ꜀ts'án lá'. |
| 2. Is the dinner ready? | 大餐便唔曾呀 | Tái' ꜀ts'án pín' ꜂'m ꜂ts'ang á'? |
| 3. Request the gentlemen to come to dinner. Take your seats!—take your seats. | 請列位入席請呀請呀 | 'Ts'ing lít, wai' yap, tsik,. 'Ts'ing á'! 'ts'ing á'! |
| 4. This crab soup has the appearance of being good, who will like some of it? | 呢的蟹湯似得幾好乜誰要唔呢 | ꜀Ní tik, 'hái ꜀t'óng 'ts'z' tak, 'kí 'hò, mat, ꜂shui iú' ꜂'m ꜀ní? |
| 5. I will thank you to send me a little of it. | 我請你遞的過我吖 | 'Ngó 'ts'ing 'ní tai' tik, kwó' 'ngó ꜀á. |
| 6. Remove this soup tureen, and bring that plate of roast beef. | 擰呢個湯兜去拈個碟燒牛肉嚟 | ꜀Ning ꜀ní kó' ꜀t'óng ꜀tau h'ü', ꜀ním kó' típ, ꜀shiú ꜂ngau yuk, ꜂lai. |
| 7. This beef cuts very good; allow me to send you a slice of it? | 呢的牛肉切開實守好等我遞塊過你阿 | ꜀Ní tik, ꜂ngau yuk, ts'ít, ꜀hoi shat, 'shau 'hò; 'tang 'ngó tai' fái' kwó' 'ní ꜀ó? |

### *Notes and Explanations.*

GENERAL custom among the Chinese authorizes three meals a day, but the hours at which they are taken varies among different classes. The *táits'án* is, as its name signifies, the principal meal with them, and is served up, usually, not earlier than four, nor later than seven o'clock P. M. Among the poorer classes it consists of boiled rice, with the addition of a few vegetables, and occasionally a small dish of fish or pork; rice is seldom eaten alone. The middling classes usually have a good supply of all these; while with the rich, the list is increased till it includes a large assortment of the best articles found in the markets. At the banquets of the most wealthy, the number of dishes is often extravagent, and some of them are very costly. Some of the phrases comprised in this, as well as in the preceding and following, sections, may at first appear to be more stiff and formal than those commonly used; but when they have become a little familiar by practice, it will be easy to abbreviate and improve them, and also add to their number, *pro re natâ*.

| | | |
|---|---|---|
| 8. If you please. | 隨便啦 | ,Ts'ui pín$^{2}$ ‹lá. |
| 9. I beg you will carve that capon. | 請你割開個隻刬鷄呵 | 'Ts'ing 'ní kót› ‹hoi kó' chik› sín' ‹kai ‹ó. |
| 10. Bring that dish of sauce. | 拈個汁盅黎 | ‹Ním kó' chap› ‹chung ,lai. |
| 11. Bring a salt cellar. | 拈個塩盅丨 | ‹Ním kó' ,ím ‹chung ,lai. |
| 12. Do you prefer beef which is roasted rare, or that which is thoroughly done? | 食牛肉你愛燒得嫩嘅還是中意老嘅𠺝 | Shik$_{2}$ ,ngau yuk$_{2}$, 'ní oi' ‹shíú tak› nün$^{2}$ ké', ,wán shí$^{2}$ ‹chung í' 'lò ké' lá'? |
| 13. Take away those knives and forks. | 收個的刀釵去 | ‹Shau kó' tik› ‹tò ‹ch'á h'ü'. |
| 14. I will thank you to send me some of the boiled fowl. | 請你遞的白焓鷄來我 | 'Ts'ing 'ní tai$^{2}$ tik› pák$_{2}$ sháp› ‹kai ,loi 'ngó. |
| 15. Are you, Sir, a good carver? | 你好手勢割野唔好呀 | 'Ní 'hò 'shau shai' kót› 'yé, ,'m 'hò á'? |
| 16. I will thank you to cut up that duck, and help my friend *Man* to a slice of it. | 請你摵個隻鴨來切開一塊塊遞塊過文哥呵 | 'Ts'ing 'ní 'kái kó' chik› áp› ,loi, ts'ít› ‹hoi yat› fái' fái', tai$^{2}$ fái' kwó' ,Man ‹kó ‹ó. |
| 17. Take a little of the ginger to sharpen your appetite. | 食的薑開吓個胃呵 | Shik$_{2}$ tik› ‹kéung ‹hoi 'há kó' wai$^{2}$ ‹ó. |
| 18. Help me to a little pepper to sprinkle [on my food.] | 幫我滲的椒末添吖 | ‹Póng 'ngó 'sham tik› ‹tsíú mút$_{2}$ ‹t'ím ‹á. |
| 19. Do you think that pastry fried in fat is good? | 好食油熠麵食唔呢 | 'Hò shik› ,yau ch'áu' mín shik$_{2}$ ,'m ‹ní? |
| 20. It is palatable enough, but quite indigestible. | 個的係利口唔利腹嘅 | Kó' tik› hai$^{2}$ lí$^{2}$ 'hau ,'m lí$^{2}$ fuk› ké'. |
| 21. I beg you will take more food, for we shall have nothing to eat with our tea this evening. | 請你再用晚茶冇乜食設𠺝 | 'Ts'ing 'ni tsoi' yung$^{2}$, 'mán ,ch'á 'mò mat› shik› ch'ít› lá'. |

17. 'Eat a little ginger to open the stomach,' is a recommendation similar to our own to take a whet; a number of vulgar expressions, among which are *sai wai*, wash the stomach, and *sáng wai* scour the stomach, are also used by the common people to denote the same thing.

| | | |
|---|---|---|
| 22. Very well, I will see to that; indeed, I usually take only two meals a day. | 呀我自己哈打理平時我一日都係食兩餐睹 | Á' ˊngó tsz'² ˊkí ˊúi ˊtá ˊlí; ˏp'ing ˏshi ˊngó yatˎ yat₂ ˏtò hai² shik₂ ˊléung ˏts'án ˏché. |
| 23. Formerly, I was accustomed to eat an evening meal, and then was unable to sleep, and was restless and disturbed all night long. | 先日我都食夜餐整得我成夜都瞓唔着俺俺惗惗咁 | ˏSín yat₂ ˊngó ˏtò shik₂ yé² ˏts'án, ˊching takˎ ˊngó ˏshing yé² ˏtò fan' ˏ'm chéuk₂, ˏím ˏím ˏchim ˏchim ˊkóm. |
| 24. Why is it, Sir, that you utterly forbear to take any wine? | 乜咁量貴總唔肯飲啲 | Matˎ kóm' léung² kwai' ˊtsung ˏ'm ˊhang ˊyam pò'? |
| 25. It is because I have lately been unwell, and have adopted a close regimen. | 爲因近來唔爽飲食所以節戒 | Wai² ˏyan kan² ˏloi ˏ'm ˊshóng ˊyam shik₂ ˊshó ˊi tsítˎ kái'. |
| 26. You really eat but a very little; allow me to send you some of this stewed beef? | 乜你咁細食嘅呀等我遞的會牛肉過你添呵 | Matˎ ˊní kóm' sai' shik₂ ké' á'? ˊtang ˊngó tai² tikˎ úi' ˏngau yuk₂ kwó' ˊní ˏt'ím ˏò? |
| 27. I thank you, I am reserving my appetite for a wing of that turkey. | 多謝咯我食開隻火鷄翼處 | ˏTó tsé² lòkˎ, ˊngó shik₂ ˏhoi chikˎ ˊfó ˏkai yik₂ ch'ü'. |
| 28. May I ask you to help me to a slice of that ham? | 請你遞塊火腿嚟我吖 | ˊTs'ing ˊní tai² fái' ˊfo ˊt'úi ˏlai ˊngó ˏá? |
| 29. With much pleasure; do you prefer the fat, or that which is lean? | 好喇愛肥嘅吖抑或要瘦嘅呢 | ˊHò lé'; oi' ˏfí ké' ˏá, yikˎ wák₂ íú' shau' ké' ˏní? |
| 30. A part of both, if you please. | 半肥瘦啦 | Pún' ˏfí shau' lá'. |
| 31. Shall I add a little of this gravy? | 揔的汁你攞吓食呀 | Fatˎ tikˎ chapˎ ˊní ˏlo ˊhá shik₂ á'? |
| 32. I fear it is not well boiled. | 我怕唔曾焓得好呀 | ˊNgó p'á' ˏ'm ˏts'ang shápˎ takˎ ˊhò á'. |
| 33. Allow me to send you some of that partridge. | 等我遞的鷓鴣過你罷啦 | ˊTang ˊngó tai² tikˎ ché' ˏkú kwó' ˊní pá' lá'. |

24. 'What such ability of your honor,' is a literal rendering of the first four words in this sentence; *léung* is an ability or capacity to drink much, to do which is considered as praiseworthy, and it is complimentary to tell a guest that he can drink largely.

| | | |
|---|---|---|
| 34. Which do you prefer a leg, or a wing? | 你中意髀吖定中意翼呢 | ʿNí ‹chung í' ʻpí ‹á, pí' ‹chung í' yik$_{2}$ ‹ní? |
| 35. It is quite immaterial. | 都係一樣啫 | ‹Tò hai$^{2}$ yat› yéung$^{2}$ ‹ché. |
| 36. How do you like it? | 好食唔好吖 | ʻHò shik$_{2}$ ‚'m ʻhò ‹á? |
| 37. It is really very fine, and has also an excellent flavor. | 眞正好兼之又好味道添 | ‹Chan ching' ʻhò, ‹kím ‹chí yau$^{2}$ ʻhò mí$^{2}$ tò' ‹t'ím. |
| 38. What is there in that dish? | 裝個碟係乜野呀 | ‹Chóng kó' típ$_{2}$ hai$^{2}$ mat› ʿyé á'? |
| 39. There are some snipes. | 係沙椎嚟 | Hai$^{2}$ ‹shá ‹chui ‚lai. |
| 40. Send me one. | 遞隻過我呀 | Tai$^{2}$ chik› kwó' ʿngó á'. |
| 41. I will thank you to send me one of the smallest. | 請你遞隻至細嘅嚟我 | ʻTs'ing ʿní tai$^{2}$ chik› chí' sai' ké' ‚lai ʿngó. |
| 42. Allow me to send you a little of this flour pudding. | 等我遞呇的麪粉布顛過你呵 | ʻTang ʿngó tai$^{2}$ ‹fán tik› mín$^{2}$ ʻfan pò' ‹tín kwó' ʿní ‹ó? |
| 43. None of it, I thank you, I have already taken quite sufficient. | 好咯多謝咯我够算咯 | ʻHò lók›, ‹tó tsé$^{2}$ lók›, ʿngó kau$^{2}$ sün' lók›. |
| 44. I beg you will take one of these very light custards. | 請飲杯稀稀哋吉時呵 | ʻTs'ing ʻyam ‹púi ‹h'í ‹h'í tí$^{2}$ kat› ‚shí ‹ó. |
| 45. Will you join me in taking a glass of claret? | 請你面杯飲呢杯紅酒 | ʻTs'ing ʿní mín$^{2}$ ‹púi ʻyam ‹ní ‹púi ‚hung ʻtsau? |
| 46. I thank you, I have taken enough already, and dare not drink any more to-day. | 好咯多謝咯今日不敢領 | ʻHò lók›, ‹tó tsé$^{2}$ lók›, ‹kam yat$_{2}$ pat› ʻkóm ʿlíng. |

45. *Mín púi yam* is to drink face to face in the usual manner. There are two other modes of taking wine or strong drink, common among the Chinese. The first is the *kwó púi yam*, in which case two friends, having filled each his glass and holding it in his right hand, one extends his glass to the mouth of the other, who in return extends his to the mouth of the first, and thus they drink from each other's glasses. The second is called *ch'ái múi*, which resembles the *micare digitis* of the Romans; two persons, having furnished themselves with a quantity of spirits, and each a small cup or glass filled, simultaneously raise the right hand closed; they then, both at the same moment, bring down the same hand before them, each person opening one or more of his fingers, and uttering the word ten or one of the nine digits: if one calls out seven, and the sum of the number of fingers which he and the other both opened is seven, then the latter must drink a glass of wine; in case neither hits the exact number, or both hit it, then neither is required to drink, and the trial is repeated.

廣東方言讀本

| | | |
|---|---|---|
| 47. Oh no, you may venture to take a little. | 唔係飲少的喉 | ₅'M hai², 'yam 'shíú tik, ₅é. |
| 48. I have taken enough already; I will thank you for a tumbler of water. | 好喀請你俾杯水過我罷咯 | 'Hò lák,, 'ts'ing 'ní 'pí 'púi 'shui kwó' 'ngó pá² lók,. |
| 49. Take away these things, and bring on the dessert. | 收呢的野去拈菓子嚟咯 | ₍Shau ₍ní tik, 'yé h'ü', ₍ním 'kwó 'tsz' ₅lai lók,. |
| 50. This is most excellent fruit. | 呢的菓子實守好呀 | ₍Ní tik, 'kwó 'tsz' shat₂ 'shau 'hò á'. |
| 51. Please eat freely of the fruit before you, at your pleasure. | 隨意食的生菓都好吖 | ₅Tsui í' shik₂ tik, ₍shang 'kwó ₍tò 'hò ₍á. |
| 52. Which kind do you prefer? | 你中意邊的呢 | 'Ní ₍chung í' ₍pín tik, ₍ní? |
| 53. They are all alike very good. | 𪚩𠾴哈都係一樣嘅 | Ham² páng² láng² ₍tò hai² yat, yéung² ₍ché. |
| 54. Bring the finger bowls; and after we have used them, remove all the things from the table. | 拈洗手盅嚟洗手就設檯罅 | ₍Ním 'sai 'shau ₍chung ₅lai, 'sai 'shau tsau² ch'ít, ₅t'oi lá'. |

53. The phrase *ham páng láng*, or as it is always abbreviated *hampaláng*, is in constant use to express a collected quantity or a number of things when taken together; in Macao, the word *tò tò*, from the Portuguese *todo*, is frequently employed.

## Section Eleventh.

## OF THE TEA TABLE.

### 晚茶類第十一章

'Mán ₅ch'á lui²; tai² shap₂ yat, ₍cheung.

| | | |
|---|---|---|
| 1. *Álung*, make ready the tea this evening at eight o'clock. | 阿蕹今晚八點鐘預便晚茶罅 | Á' ₍lung, ₍kam 'mán, pát, 'tím ₍chung ü² pín² 'mán ₅ch'á lá'. |
| 2. Is the tea ready? | 晚茶便唔曾呀 | 'Mán ₅ch'á pín² ₅'m ₅ts'ang á'? |

### *Notes and Explanations.*

THOUGH the Chinese sometimes take three meals in a day; yet tea, which they drink at all hours, is never served up for them with the formalities of the European tea table.

| | | |
|---|---|---|
| 3. Place the tea-tray on the table at my right hand. | 擠呢個托茶嘅盤喺檯上我右手便嚟 | ‹Chai ‹ní kó' t'ók› ꜀ch'á ké' ꜀p'ún 'hai ꜀t'oi shéung² 'ngó yau² 'shau pín² ꜀lai. |
| 4. Bring the tea-canister. | 擰個茶葉罇嚟 | ‹Ning kó' ꜀ch'á íp₂ ‹tsun ꜀lai. |
| 5. Take the lid off the tea-canister. | 揭開茶葉罇個蓋囉 | K'ít› ‹hoi ꜀ch'á íp₂ ‹tsun kó' koi' ‹ló. |
| 6. Pour a little tea into this cup. | 倒的茶葉喺隻杯嚟 | 'Tò tik› ꜀ch'á íp₂ 'hai chik› ‹púi ꜀lai. |
| 7. Take off the lid from the tea-pot, and put the tea into it. | 揭開個茶壺蓋擠的茶葉落去 | K'ít› ‹hoi kó' ꜀ch'á ꜀ú koi' ‹chai tik› ꜀ch'á íp₂ lók₂ h'ü'. |
| 8. Bring some boiling water, and fill the tea-pot half full. | 擰的滾水嚟冲半壺咁多 | ‹Ning tik› 'kwan 'shui ꜀lai ‹ch'ung pún' ꜀ú kóm' ‹tó. |
| 9. That is enough. | 咁多夠咯 | Kóm' ‹tó kau² lók›. |
| 10. What kind of tea do you prefer? | 你中意乜野嘅茶呢 | 'Ní ‹chung í' mat› 'yé ké' ꜀ch'á ‹ní? |
| 11. I fear, Sir, your tea is too strong. | 我睇得你杯茶濃估呀 | 'Ngó 't'ai tak› 'ní ‹púi ꜀ch'á ꜀yung 'kú á'. |
| 12. *Álung*, see if that gentleman wishes some hot water in his tea. | 阿聾睇吓個位人客要滾水唔 | Á' ꜀lung, 't'ai 'há kó' wai² ꜀yan hák› íú' 'kwan 'shui ꜀'m. |
| 13. May I add a little water to your tea? | 等我冲的滾水喺呢處添嗾 | 'Tang 'ngó ‹ch'ung tik› 'kwan 'shui 'hai ‹ní ch'ü' ‹t'ím ‹é? |
| 14. My tea is too weak, change it for another cup. | 我杯茶淡得濟擰過一杯嚟囉 | 'Ngó ‹púi ꜀ch'á tám² tak› tsai², ‹ning kwò' yat› ‹púi ꜀lai ‹ló. |
| 15. Bring another tea saucer. | 擰過隻茶碟嚟 | ‹Ning kwò' chik› ꜀ch'á típ₂ ꜀lai. |
| 16. This tea has really an excellent flavor. | 呢的茶眞正係香咯 | ‹Ní tik› ꜀ch'á ‹chun ching' hai² ‹héung lók›. |

8. The use of *kwan* to express boiling water is a provincialism; it is derived, by a catachresis not at all uncommon, from the strict definition, which is to roll or to surge, as waves do, from comparing the appearance of the surfaces of water when boiling, and when agitated by the wind.

| | | |
|---|---|---|
| 17. Is your tea agreeable? | 你的茶啱唔呀 | ʻNí tik˒ ˏchʻá ꜀ngám ˏʻm á'? |
| 18. *Álung*, bring me the milk-cup. | 阿聾拈呢盅牛乳嚟我 | Á' ˏlung, ꜀ním ꜀ní ꜀chung ˏngau ʻyü ˏlai ʻngó. |
| 19. Take some of this warmed bread along with your tea. | 你掝的炕麵包嚟送茶呵 | ʻNí ʻkái tik˒ hóng' mín$^{2}$ ꜀páu ˏlai sung' ˏchʻá ꜀ó. |
| 20. This preserved ginger is very good; will you try some of it? | 呢的糖薑實守好你試吓好啩 | ꜀Ní tik˒ ˏtʻóng ꜀kéung shat$_{2}$ ʻshau ʻhò, ʻní shí' ʻhá ʻhò kwá'? |
| 21. I beg you will take a little honey with your bread. | 請你食的蜜糖共麵頭呵 | ʻTsʻing ʻní shik$_{2}$ tik˒ mat$_{2}$ ˏtʻóng kung$^{2}$ mín$^{2}$ ˏtʻau ꜀ó? |
| 22. I think you will rather prefer some cake, will you not? | 我睇得你中意麵餅估呀 | ʻNgó ʻtʻai tak˒ ʻní ꜀chung í' mín$^{2}$ ʻping ʻkú á'? |
| 23. These preserved peaches are from abroad, help yourself to some of them, and see if they are good. | 呢的係來路嘅蜜餞糖桃嚸你擰的試吓呵 | ꜀Ní tik˒ hai$^{2}$ ˏloi lò$^{2}$ ˏlai ké' mat$_{2}$ tsín' ˏtʻóng ˏtʻò pó', ʻní ꜀ning tik˒ shí' ʻhá ꜀ó. |
| 24. Will you take another cup of tea? | 用過杯茶唉 | Yung$^{2}$ kwó' ꜀púi ˏchʻá ꜀é? |
| 25. Yes, if you please. | 好咯隨便咯 | ʻHò lók$_{2}$, ˏtsʻui pín$^{2}$ lók˒. |
| 26. Allow me to send you another cup. | 等我遞杯你唉 | ʻTang ʻngó tai$^{2}$ ꜀púi ʻní ꜀é. |
| 27. I thank you, two cups are quite sufficient. | 多謝嚹兩杯够有凸嚹 | ꜀Tó tsé$^{2}$ lá', ʻléung ꜀púi kau$^{2}$ ʻyau tat$_{2}$ lá'. |
| 28. When you have drank tea, does it ever produce unpleasant sensations of dizziness? | 你飲茶有見昏昏沌咁冇呀 | ʻNí ʻyam ˏchʻá, ʻyau kín' ꜀wan ꜀wan tan' kóm' ʻmò á'? |
| 29. Never, because tea is not injurious, but on the contrary, a very wholesome beverage. | 冇因爲茶冇乜害而且係最好飲之物 | ʻMò, ꜀yan wai$^{2}$ ˏchʻá ʻmò mat˒ hoi$^{2}$, ˏí ʻchʻé hai$^{2}$ tsui' ʻhò ʻyam ꜀chí mat$_{2}$. |
| 30. Do the Chinese use milk and sugar with their tea? | 唐人有掝牛乳共糖嚟攪茶有冇呢 | ˏTʻóng ˏyan ʻyau ʻkái ˏngau ʻyü kung$^{2}$ ˏtʻóng ˏlai ʻkáu ˏchʻá ʻyau ʻmò ꜀ní? |

27. The character *tat* is supposed to resemble characters cut in relief, as *áu*, its opposite, with the upper part sunk in, is like those cut in intaglio; *tat* here means a sufficiency.

31. No; they all much prefer to drink pure tea.

有都係飲清茶
多啫

ʻMò, ͵tò hai$^2$ ʻyam ͵tsʻing ͵chʻá ͵tò ͵ché.

32. When do they drink tea?

佢哋幾時正飲
茶呢

ʻKʻü tí$^2$ ʻkí ͵shí ching$^3$ ʻyam ͵chʻá ͵ní?

33. Several times a day sometimes more, and sometimes less, frequently.

一日飲幾回有
時多有時少

Yatˏ yatˎ ʻyam ʻkí ͵úi, ʻyau ͵shí ͵tó, ʻyau ͵shí ʻshíú.

34. Do they ever experience any injury from it?

飲了有壞冇呢

ʻYam ʻlíú ʻyau wái$^2$ ʻmò ͵ní?

35. I have seen them drink it freely at all times, but have never yet heard of its producing any injurious effects.

我見佢哋都係
時時隨便飲唔
曾聽見話有飲
壞過嘅

ʻNgò kín$^3$ ʻkʻü tí$^2$ ͵tò hai$^2$ ͵shí ͵shí ͵tsʻui pín$^2$ ʻyam, ͵ʻm ͵tsʻang ͵tʻing kín$^3$ wá$^2$ ʻyau ʻyam wái$^2$ kwó$^3$ ké$^3$.

## Section Twelfth.

## RULES OF VISITING.

## 交接儀容類第十二章

͵Káu tsípˏ ͵í ͵yung lui$^2$; tai$^2$ shapˎ í$^2$ ͵chéung.

1. Supposing that a person is going to visit a friend, what are the forms of etiquette to be observed?

設有一人往拜
客當如何儀注

Chʻítˏ ʻyau yatˏ ͵yan ʻwòng pái$^3$ hákˏ, ͵tong ͵ü ͵hó ͵í chü$^3$?

2. On such an occasion, he procures a card, and on the lower half of it writes, "your friend Chéung King-shan bows his head in salutation." Or, he simply writes his name on the upper half of the card at the [right] side,

於是用一帖在
下半截書愚弟
張敬慎頓首拜
或於帖上截傍

͵Ü shí$^2$, yung$^2$ yatˏ tʻípˏ, tsoi$^2$ há$^2$ pún$^3$ tsitˎ ͵shü, ͵U tai$^2$ ͵Chéung King$^3$ shan$^2$ tun$^3$ ʻshau pái$^3$; wákˎ ͵ü tʻípˏ shéung$^2$ tsítˎ ͵pʻóng ͵pín,

*Notes and Explanations.*

VISITING is conducted by the Chinese with great formality, blended with much urbanity. The subject naturally forms a branch of domestic affairs, since it is intimately connected with household regulations. This section affords a specimen of what is required from those who move in the middle classes of society.

1. The phrase *í chü* includes all the ceremonies requisite in paying and receiving visits, which are varied, however, in many minor particulars, according to age and rank.

2. These cards are made of bright red paper cut about ten inches long, four and a half wide, and are either single or folded—the latter four, six, or eight times.

or in place of writing it, he may have the same stamped.

邊書一名卽印的亦可

‹shü, yat› ˏming tsik› yan' tik› yik^2 ʻhó.

3. He then puts on his robes and cap, takes his seat in a sedan, or mounts his horse, or perhaps goes on foot, and proceeds to pay his visit.

於是穿衣帽或打轎或配馬或步行往拜

ˏÜ shí^2 ‹ch'ün ‹í mò^2, wák^2 ʻtá kíú^2, wák^2 p'úi' ʻmá, wák^2 pò^2 ˏhang, ʻwóng pái'.

4. If he has a servant in attendance, the servant precedes him, and knocking at the gate, says aloud, "The gentleman Chéung King-shan has come to pay a visit," at the same time presenting his master's card.

若有小子相隨則小子先至扣門說道張敬愼老爺親到拜將名帖遞進

Yéuk^2 ʻyau ʻsíú ʻtsz' ‹séung ˏts'ui, tsak› ʻsíú ʻtsz' ‹sín chí' k'au' ˏmún, shüt› tò^2, ‹Chéung King' shan^2 ʻlò ˏyé, ‹ts'an tò' pái', ‹tséung ˏming t'íp› tai^2 tsun'.

5. The servant of the host then receives the card, and goes into the house, and presents it to his master, who, if he does not wish to receive company, says, "Stay the gentleman's approach." His servant immediately goes out, and standing beside the visitor's sedan, [returning the card, and] bending the knee, says, "Stay the gentleman's approach."

6. The visitor, accordingly, turns and goes back.

其時主家亦有小子接帖入內稟明其主如不欲會說道擋駕則小子出而在客轎前打一千說道擋駕客卽回去

‹K'í ˏshí ʻchü ‹ká yik^2 ʻyau ʻsíú ʻtsz' tsip› t'íp›, yap^2 noi^2 ʻpan ˏming ˏk'í ʻchü, ˏü pat› yuk^2 úi^2, shüt› tò^2, ʻtóng ká'. Tsak› ʻsíú ʻtsz' ch'ut›, ˏí tsoi^2 hák› kíú^2 ˏts'ín, ʻtá yat› ‹ts'ín, shüt› tò^2, ʻtóng ká'.

Hák› tsik› ˏúi h'ü'.

7. But if the master says, "Invite him to come in," the servant goes out and commands the middle door to be opened. The gentleman then comes forth to receive the visitor, bows, and invites him to enter. They ascend the hall together, and take their seats, as host and guest.

如主曰請小子出吩咐開中門主人出迎揖客入升堂分賓主而坐

ˏÜ ʻchü üt^2, ʻts'ing, ʻsíú ʻtsz' ch'ut›, ‹fan fú' ‹hoi ‹chung ˏmún. ʻChü ˏyan ch'ut› ˏying yap› hák› yap^2 ‹shing ˏt'óng ‹fan ‹pan ʻchü ˏí tsó^2.

---

3. Among the common people the sedan is borne by two men. Inferior magistrates are allowed four bearers, and the highest provincial officers may employ eight. Foreigners are not permitted the use of sedans in Canton,—nor even in Macao, with Chinese bearers. In quiet times, however, this regulation is not observed in Macao.

5. *Tá yat ts'ín* is used to denote the bending, half way to the ground, of one knee. There are occasions (such as when an inferior is seeking to visit a superior, or when the master is absent,) in which the card may be retained; but its being *returned*, as in the present instance, does not prevent the visitor from repeating his call.

7. The left side is the place of honor with the Chinese; in taking seats, therefore, the host will insist on the visitor's taking his place on the left, while he occupies the right.

| | | |
|---|---|---|
| 8. The guest [perhaps] says, "It is a long time since we met, and I have now come Sir, to pay my respects." | 客曰許久不面特來候駕 | Hák› üt₂, 'hü 'kau pat› mín', tak₂ ˌloi hau' ká'. |
| 9. The host replies, "I am unworthy the honor you have taken the trouble to do me. I hope, Sir, you are well." | 主曰豈敢有勞貴步駕上好吖 | 'Chü üt₂, 'hí 'kóm, ˌyau ˌlò kwai' pò'. Ká' shéung' 'hò ‹á? |
| 10. "Very well, I thank you," rejoins the guest. | 客答曰托賴 | Hák› táp› üt₂, t'ók› lái'. |
| 11. At this time the servants present betel and tea, and after these are ended, pipes with tobacco for smoking are brought in. | 斯時小子們奉梹欵茗茶罷繼奉以烟 | ‹Sz' ˌshí, 'síú 'tsz' ˌmún fung' ‹pan, 'fún 'ming ˌch'á, pá' kai' fung' 'i ‹ín. |
| 12. The guest again says, "I beg you will mention my name to her ladyship (your mother), and present my compliments and best wishes." | 客又曰在老太太處代我叱名請安 | Hák› yau' üt₂, tsoi' 'lò t'ái' t'ái' ch'ü', toi' 'ngó ts'ik› ˌming, 'ts'ing ‹ón. |
| 13. The host replies, "I thank you, you are very kind, but [my mother] is unworthy of such attention." | 主曰不敢當多謝有心 | 'Chü üt₂, pat› 'kóm ‹tóng, ‹tó tsé', 'yau ‹sam. |
| 14. "Does your honored mother," (adds the host,) "enjoy good health?" | 令壽堂實守壯健啩 | Ling' shau' ˌt'óng shat₂ 'shau chòng' kín' kwá'? |
| 15. The guest replies, "I am much obliged for your kind inquiries; recently she has been very unwell." | 客答托賴近來病痛多咯 | Hák› táp›, t'ók› lai', kan' ˌloi ping' t'ung' ‹tó lók›. |
| 16. The host says, "This is a matter of course with a person of advanced age; pray, what is the age of your parent?" | 主曰高年人自當如此今年貴庚呢 | 'Chü üt₂, ‹kò ˌnín ˌyan tsz'' ‹tóng ˌü 'tsz'; ‹kam ˌnín kwai' ‹kang ‹ní? |
| 17. "Her age this year is seventy-one." | 今年七十有一 | ‹Kam ˌnín ts'át› shap₂ 'yau yat›. |
| 18. The host further adds, "It was said by the ancients, 'few reach threescore years and ten;' I presume your aged mother has a very good constitution." | 主又曰古云人生七十古來稀算是老當益壯 | 'Chü yau' üt₂, 'kú ˌwan, ˌyan ‹shang ts'át› shap₂ 'kú ˌloi ‹hí.; sün' shi' 'lò ‹tóng yik› chòng'. |
| 19. "Very good indeed, I thank you," says the guest; [and then inquires] "how | 客曰皆藉洪福駕上近來添到 | Hák› üt₂, ‹kái tsik₂ ˌhung fuk›; ká' shéung' kan' ˌloi |

11. Betel, tea, and tobacco, are always presented to the visitor, but he is at liberty to decline them if he pleases, without any breach of good breeding, but this, however, is not often the case. The pipe is used by ladies as well as gentlemen; it is made of a slender bamboo, about two feet long, and has a bowl that holds only a very small pinch of tobacco.

廣東方言讀本



many sons, Sir, have been presented to you?"

幾多個公郎呢

‹t'ím tò' 'kí ‹tó kó' ‹kung ˏlóng ‹ní?

20. The host answers, "I am an unfortunate man, and have had but one poor boy."

主曰命鄙只得
一個小蟲

'Chü üt2, ming2 'p'í, chat› tak› yat› kó' 'síú ˏch'ung.

21. "I remember," says the guest, "that formerly, I came to your house to celebrate the birth of a son; I cannot realize that six years have since elapsed; I suppose the boy is already learning to read."

客曰記得從前
我曾到府飲薑
酒不覺又六年
現在讀書估嚹

Hák› üt2, kí' tak› ˏts'ung ˏts'ín 'ngó ˏts'ang tò' 'fú 'yam ‹kéung 'tsau; pat› kók› yau2 luk2 ˏnín; ín2 tsoi2 tuk2 ‹shü 'kú lá'.

22. "This year," says the host, "he commenced going to school."

主云今年正話
啟蒙啫

'Chü ˏwan, ‹kam ˏnín ching' wá2 'k'ai ˏmung ‹ché.

23. Again it is asked, "Since your son has grown up to boyhood I have not seen him; he must, I think, be very apt in learning, is he not?"

又問公郎大了
我未曾見過讀
書想必伶俐

Yau2 man2, ‹kung ˏlóng tái2 'líú, 'ngó mí2 ˏts'ang kín' kwó'; tuk2 ‹shü 'séung pít› ˏling li2.

24. "He possesses only ordinary abilities," is the reply.

答曰姿質有限

Táp› üt2, ‹tsz' chat› 'yau hán'.

25. The guest says, "I beg you will let me see him."

客曰請來一見

Hák› üt2, 'ts'ing ˏloi yat› kín'.

26. The master of the house then bids a servant go to the study, and ask the lad to make his appearance.

主命小子往書
房請相公回來

'Chü ming2 'síú 'tsz' 'wóng ‹shü ˏfóng, 'ts'ing séung' ‹kung ˏúi ˏloi.

27. The boy follows the servant into the hall, and the host, pointing [to the visitor,] says, "This is my honored friend Chéung, come up before him, make your bow, and ask him how he does."

其兒隨小子登
堂主指曰此位
是張世伯上前
叩頭請安呀

ˏK'í ˏí ˏts'ui 'síú 'tsz' ‹tang ˏt'óng, 'chü 'chí üt2, 'tsz' wai2 shí2 ‹Chéung shai' pák›, 'shéung ˏts'ín, k'au' ˏt'au, 'ts'ing ‹ón á'.

28. The child then turning to him, says, "Honored friend;" and in a hurried manner kneels down before him, and makes a low bow.

子即向前叫一
聲世伯忙即跪
下叩頭

'Tsz' tsik› héung' ˏts'ín, kíú' yat› ‹shing shai' pák›, ˏmóng tsik› kwai2 há2, k'au' ˏt'au.

29. The guest immediately reaches forward, raises him up, and bows in return for his salutation.

客隨扶起回答
一揖

Hák› ˏts'ui ˏfú 'hí ˏúi táp› yat› yap›.

19, 20. A constant endeavor is made in Chinese etiquette to speak slightingly of whatever pertains to one's self, and to exalt or praise all that belongs to the party spoken to; the expressions made use of by both parties in this strife of politeness are frequently very singular for the allusions contained in them. In this instance, the host says his "fate is poor [or niggardly,] only obtained one small worm," referring to his only son, in reply to the guest's inquiry, "how many worthy young gentlemen?" he had.

30. The boy then takes his stand at a respectful distance, with his face turned towards the guest;

其子侍立於下面朝上

ˏK'í 'tsz' shí² lap₂ ˏü há², mín² ˏch'iú shéung²;

31. Who (addressing his father) says, "The boy really possesses superior intelligence and will perpetuate the literary reputation of the family."

客曰果然生得聰慧將來足繼書香

Hák, üt₂, 'kwó ˏín ˏshang tak, ˏts'ung wai², ˏtséung ˏloi tsuk, kai' ˏshü ˏhéung.

32. The host replies, "The reputation of our family is not great, high expectations are not to be entertained of him; if he can only gain a livelihood, it will be enough.

主曰山田福薄不敢妄想但可覓食足矣

'Chü üt₂, ˏshán ˏtín fuk, pók₂; pat, 'kóm móng² 'séung; tán² 'hó mik₂ shik₂ tsuk, 'í.

33. "You are quite too modest," says the guest; "I beg you will let him return to his studies in the school-room."

客曰太謙了請回書房讀書罷

Hák, üt₂, t'ái' ˏhím 'líú, 'ts'ing ˏúi ˏshü ˏfóng tuk₂ ˏshü pá².

34. The boy bows to the guest, saying, "Pray excuse me," and immediately retires.

其子揖客曰少陪遂出

ˏK'í 'tsz' yap, hák, üt₂, 'shíú ˏp'úi; sui² ch'ut,.

35. Then the conversation being ended, the guest rises and announces his departure, and says, "Another day I will come again to receive your counsel."

於是言罷客起告辭曰改日再來領教

ˏÜ shí² ˏín pá², hák, 'hí kò' ˏts'z', üt₂, 'koi yat₂ tsoi' ˏloi 'ling káu'.

36. The guest says, "Ah! you do me too much honor, I rather ought to wait on you to-morrow."

主曰豈敢弟當明日回候

'Chü üt₂, 'hí 'kóm! tai² ˏtóng ˏming yat₂ ˏúi hau².

37. "You are very kind," says the guest; "Good bye."

客曰不敢請呀

Hák, üt₂, pat, 'kóm, 'ts'ing á'!

38. "Good bye," responds the host.

主亻請呀

'Chü üt₂, 'ts'ing á'!

39. The servant now goes out, preceding his master, and orders the sedan to be made ready, which is tilted up behind, and down before, to that the shafts are brought low; the visitor steps in between the shafts, and moves backward and sits down in the sedan, and the bearers raise it up on their shoulders.

此時小子先出吩咐打轎其轎後⿰扌兜起轎前倒下以低其扛客踏入轎扛內退行入轎坐定轎夫起膊

'Ts'z' ˏshí 'síú 'tsz' ˏsín ch'ut, ˏfan fú' 'tá kíú², ˏk'í kíú² hau² ˏtau 'hí, kíú² ˏts'ín 'tò há², 'í ˏtai ˏk'í kóng'; hák, táp₂ yap₂ kíú² kóng' noi², túi' ˏhang yap₂ kíú², tsó² ting², kíú² ˏfú 'hí pók,.

---

34. *Shíú p'úi* means to support or wait upon only for a little time; the lad would intimate that he ought to wait on his father's friend and guest longer, but his studies requiring his return, he begs to be excused in the terms above. Wealthy families in China frequently engage a domestic tutor, who is furnished with a small room in the house fitted up as a

廣東方言讀本

| | | |
|---|---|---|
| 40. The guest, now seated in the sedan, bends forward, gently bowing his head, says, "Pray, Sir, go back, go back." | 客在轎內俯身<br>把頭一低曰請<br>回請回 | Hák, tsoi' kíú' noi' 'fú ,shan, 'pá ,t'au yat, ,tai, üt,, 'ts'ing ,úi, 'ts'ing ,úi. |
| 41. The host, standing [at the door,] his hands joined together, says, "Good bye." | 主立拱手亦曰<br>請呀請呀 | 'Chü lap, 'kung 'shau, yik, üt,, 'ts'ing á'! 'ts'ing á'! |
| 42. The sedan moves off, and the gentleman retires into his house. Such is an outline of the general rules for visiting. | 轎去後主人乃<br>入凡交接儀容<br>大畧做此 | Kíú' h'ü' hau', 'chü ,yan 'nái yap,. ,Fán ,káu tsíp, ,í ,yung, tái' léuk, 'fong 'tsz'. |
| 43. But supposing that guests are to be invited to one's own house for a social visit, or on any similar occasion, then the cards of invitation are prepared on a previous day;—on the right side of the upper half write thus, *On the fifteenth day a light entertainment will await;* in the middle at the top write, *the light [of your presence;]* and at the bottom on the left of the card write, *Ts'ò Chíman's compliments.* Thus prepared the host sends it by the hands of a servant to the persons to be invited. | 又或邀客到家<br>敘慶等事則預<br>日寫一帖寫於<br>上截右傍云十<br>五日薄酌候中<br>頂寫一光字帖<br>下截左邊寫曹<br>治文拜如此吩<br>咐小子送去 | Yau' wák, ,íú hák, tò' ,ká tsü' hing' 'tang sz', tsak, ü' yat, 'sé yat, t'íp,; 'sé ,ü shéung' tsít, yau' ,p'óng, ,wan, Shap, 'ng yat, pók, chéuk, hau'; ,chung 'ting 'sé yat, ,kwóng tsz'; t'íp, há' tsít, 'tsó ,pín 'sé, ,Ts'ò Chí' ,man pái'; ,ü 'ts'z', ,fan fú' 'síú 'tsz' sung' h'ü'. |
| 44. On the appointed day, in his full dress, he awaits the visitor's arrival, when the host goes forth to receive and entertain him, and after the usual salutations and compliments, they take their seats. | 是日衣冠待客<br>客至赴席主人<br>迎入見禮分賓<br>主而坐 | Shi' yat, ,í ,kún toi' hák,, hák, chí' fú' tsik, 'chü ,yan ,ying yap, kín' 'lai, ,fan ,pan 'chü ,í tsó'. |
| 45. The host says, "It is a frugal meal to which you are invited, prepared without attempt at display." | 主曰便飯虛邀<br>毫無敬意 | 'Chü üt,, pín' fán' ,hü ,íú, ,hò ,mò king' í'. |
| 46. The guest replies, "The supply is abundant." | 客曰足領之至 | Hák, üt,, tsuk, 'ling ,chí chí'. |

school room, where he instructs the children of his patron, and it may be one or two more, the school varying from six to eight pupils.

43. These cards of invitation are sometimes written on a smaller paper than those described in No. 2, and are sent under an envelop. The hour of dining may also be written in small characters at the top on the left side of the card. The whole would then read thus: "On the 15th instant a light entertainment will await the light of your presence. [This invitation is sent with] Ts'ò Chíman's compliments. We dine at six o'clock." Instead of *pók chéuk*, they sometimes write *Kít ming*, "I will prepare tea," &c.

| | | |
|---|---|---|
| 47. The servants now present tea, and offer pipes and tobacco to the visitor. | 斯時小子奉茶<br>遞烟 | ‹Sz' ‚shí, 'síú 'tsz' fung' ‚ch'á tai$^2$ ‹ín. |
| 48. The host says, "There is no visitor present except yourself, we are all old acquaintances, I beg you will lay aside your cap and your robes." | 主曰別無他客<br>所有皆屬世好<br>且請卸冠寬衣 | 'Chü üt$_2$, pít$_2$ ‚mò ‹t'á hák›, 'shó 'yau ‹kái shuk$_2$ shai' 'hò, 'ch'é 'ts'ing ‹shing ‹kún ‹fún ‹í. |
| 49. The guest replies, "As there is no distinguished guest present, I will do as you suggest." | 客曰果無嬌客<br>弟當從命 | Hák› üt$_2$, 'kwó ‚mò ‹kíú hák›, tai$^2$ ‹tóng ‚tsung ming$^2$. |
| 50. The master of the house commands his servants to lay the table. | 於是主人吩附<br>小子擺席 | 'Ü shí$^2$ 'chü ‚yan ‹fan fú' 'síú 'tsz' 'pái tsik$_2$. |
| 51. This done, a servant, covering his mouth with his hand, bending by his master's side whispers in his ear, "The table is all ready, be pleased to invite the guest to sit down." | 擺備小子以手<br>掩口附主耳邊<br>低聲曰席已擺<br>好請客入席 | 'Pái pí$^2$, 'síú 'tsz' 'í 'shau 'im 'hau fú$^2$ 'chü 'í ‹pín, ‹tai ‹shing üt$_2$ tsik$_2$ 'í 'pái 'hò, 'ts'ing hák› yap$_2$ tsik$_2$. |
| 52. The gentleman of the house rises and says, "Please to take your seats at table." | 主人起曰請入<br>席請入席 | 'Chü ‚yan 'hí, üt$_2$, 'ts'ing yap$_2$ tsik$_2$, 'ts'ing yap$_2$ tsik$_2$. |
| 53. "I thank you," says the guest. | 客曰多謝 | Hák› üt$_2$, ‹tó tsé$^2$. |
| 54. "You will smile at our fare," says the host. | 主曰見笑之至 | 'Chü üt$_2$, kín' síú' ‹chí chí'. |
| 55. The host and guest, after attempting to yield precedence to each other, take their seats. | 主與客遜謙遜<br>而坐 | 'Chü 'ü hák› sui$^2$ ‹hím sun' ‚í tsó$^2$. |
| 56. The host says, "It is several years since we feasted together, we must now enjoy ourselves to the utmost before you leave. | 主曰不共飲數<br>年務必要盡歡<br>而返 | 'Chü üt$_2$, pat› kung$^2$ 'yam shò' ‚nín, mò$^2$ pít› íú' tsun$^2$ ‹fún ‚í 'fán. |
| 57. The guest says, "I am able to drink very little, yet shall do my best to meet your pleasure, and am exceedingly sorry that you have been at so great expense in providing an entertainment." | 客曰量甚淺狹<br>務盡主人之歡<br>惟是費財太甚<br>實爲過意不去 | Hák› üt$_2$, léung$^2$ sham$^2$ 'ts'ín háp$_2$, mò$^2$ tsun$^2$ 'chü ‚yan ‹chí ‹fún, ‚wai shí$^2$ fai' ‚ts'oi t'ái' sham$^2$, shat$_2$ ‚wai kwó' í' pat› h'ü'. |
| 58. Says the other, "I am quite ashamed that I have | 主答並無佳品 | 'Chü táp›, ping$^2$ ‚mò ‹kái |

48. The ceremonial dress of the Chinese, being somewhat irksome, the upper parts and cap are laid aside when eating, or when politeness does not require them to be retained.

| | | |
|---|---|---|
| only the commonest viands for you; I beg you will drink freely." | 褻瀆之至請飲深的 | 'pan, sít₎ tuk₂ ₍chí chi', 'ts'ing 'yam ₍sham tik₎. |
| 59. "I will try to do my best," says the visitor. | 客曰隨量好咯 | Hák₎ üt₂, ₌ts'ui léung$^2$ 'hò lók₎. |
| 60. "I hope," says the host, "that you are favored of late with a keen appetite." | 主曰近來胃口都甚好嗜 | 'Chü üt₂, kan$^2$ ₌loi wai$^2$ 'hau ₍tò sham$^2$ 'hò ₍chá. |
| 61. "Not so good as formerly, [I am sorry to say,] for if I eat a few bits of fat, or oily food, it overcharges my stomach; I have drank too much wine to-night, and I beg you will allow the rice to be served up." | 唔似上日多食幾件肥膩就似覺會滯今晚酒多了請起晏罷 | ₌'M 'tsz' shéung$^2$ yat₂, ₍to shik₂ 'kí kín$^2$ ₌fí ní$^2$, tsau$^2$ 'tsz' kók₎ 'úi chai$^2$; ₍kam 'mán 'tsau ₍tó 'líú, 'ts'ing 'hí án' pá$^2$. |
| 62. The host immediately orders the rice to be served up; and then says, "A little more wine, after which we will take the rice, and close the dinner." | 主卽吩咐載飯曰少飲然後用飯食畢席散 | 'Chü tsik₎ ₍fan fú' tsoi' fán$^2$, üt₂, 'shíú 'yam ₌ín hau$^2$ yung$^2$ fán$^2$, shik₂ pat₎, tsik₂ sán'. |
| 63. When the visitor says he will take leave, the master of the house accompanies him to the outer gate, where they bow and separate. | 客告辭主人送出門外一揖而別 | Hák₎ kò' ₌ts'z', 'chü ₌yan sung' ch'ut₎ ₌mún ngoi$^2$, yat₎ yap₎ ₌í pít₂. |
| 64. These are the principal rules to be observed in visiting; the others it will always be easy to regulate according to times and circumstances. | 大抵交接儀容不外乎此其餘惟臨時隨機應變而已 | Tái$^2$ 'tai ₍káu tsíp₎ ₌í ₌yung, pat₎ ngoi$^2$ ₌ú 'ts'z', ₌k'í ₌ü, ₌wai ₌lam ₌shí ₌ts'ui ₍kí ying' pín' ₌í 'í. |

61. The number of courses in a formal Chinese dinner is sometimes very great; ten, twenty, thirty, and upwards are not unusual, but the guest is not expected to do more than taste the numerous dishes set before him. The food is, for the most part, prepared in stews, cut up previously to cooking in small bits, in order to accommodate it to the chopsticks, and served up in small saucers, which are placed near each guest. During the dinner, hot spirit is drank in cups not much larger than thimbles, but they are frequently replenished; flowers and fruits are placed upon the table as dessert, and not unfrequently made dishes, elaborately prepared and fancifully arranged, are brought up, which are intended merely to gratify the sight of the already half surfeited guest. Plain boiled rice is the last dish, and always concludes the entertainment.

# CHAPTER VI.

# COMMERCIAL AFFAIRS.

# 貿易篇六

Mau’ yik‚; ‚p‘ín luk‚.

## Section First.

## OF RENTING SHOPS.

### 批賃舖店第一章

‚P‘ai yam’ p‘ò’ tím’; tai’ yat‚ ‚chéung.

| | | |
|---|---|---|
| 1. How are those persons, who have shops to let, denominated? | 有舖出賃嘅人點樣稱呢 | ‘Yau p‘ò’ ch‘ut‚ yam’ ké’ ‚yan, ‘tím yéung’ ‚ch‘ing ‚ní? |
| Some men call them shop-owners, others call them landlords. | 有人吽舖主有人吽業主 | ‘Yau ‚yan kíú’ p‘ò’ ‘chü, ‘yau ‚yan kíú’ íp‚ ‘chü. |
| 2. And what do the landlords style those who have hired their shops? | 業主稱租賃嘅又點呢 | Íp‚ ‘chü ‚ch‘ing ‚tsò yam’ ké’, yau’ ‘tím ‚ní? |
| They call them tenants. | 稱做舖客 | ‚Ch‘ing tsò’ p‘ò’ hák‚. |
| 3. In leasing and hiring, what securities are taken? | 一租一賃有乜凴據呢 | Yat‚ ‚tsò, yat‚ yam’, ‘yau mat‚ ‚p‘ang kü’ ‚ní? |
| A lease and a bond. | 有批有領 | ‘Yau ‚p‘ai, ‘yau ‘ling. |
| 4. What are these two instruments? | 批係點樣領係點樣嘅呢 | ‚P‘ai hai’ ‘tím yéung’, ‘ling hai’ ‘tím yéung’ ké’ ‚ní? |

## *Notes and Explanations.*

Mau yik originally meant to barter, or trade by exchanging commodities, but it now includes all operations of buying and selling. The terms and manner of drafting the conditions of agreement in renting shops, factories, and warehouses, differ somewhat from those used in renting dwelling-houses. These differences will appear on comparing this section with the first in chapter V. *T‘ím* and *p‘ò* are synonyms; and the phraseology employed here in speaking of them is equally applicable to factories and warehouses.

The lease, clearly specifying the conditions on which the shop is rented, is a written document, delivered into the hands of the tenant, who keeps it in witness thereof. The bond, which is made out by the tenant after he has examined the lease, is a writing given in reply thereto, signifying his wish to receive the shop.

批係以文字批明於紙交舖客收執爲據領係看批來意寫回一張領領到他舖之意

‹P'ai hai' ʻí ˏman tsz' ˏp'ai ˏming ‹ü ʻchí, ‹káu p'ò' hák› ‹shau chap› ˏwai kü'. ˏLing hai' hón' ‹p'ai ˏloi í' ʻsé ˏúi yat› ‹chéung ʻling, ʻling tò' ‹t'á p'ò' ‹chí í'.

5. What are the forms to be observed in writing the lease?

個張批點樣寫法呢

Kó' ‹chéung ‹p'ai ʻtím yéung' ʻsé fát› ‹ní ?

You can here see a specimen.

你睇呵

ʻNí ʻt'ai ‹ó.

The family of Wáipún, of the clan Hó, make and issue this lease, hereby declaring, that they are the owners of a shop, situated in the Thirteen Factory street, beyond the Great Peaceful gate, facing the south. It is two entries in depth, and nineteen rows of tiles in breadth; the roof of the building, the rooms, terraces, windows, doors, and counting-room are all complete. It is now leased to Yau Kwóngí, to be opened as a money changer's shop, with the sign Ying Shing. It is distinctly understood that the rent shall be one hundred and twenty taels each year, whole dollars, weighed according to the standard balances of the government; two dollars shall also be paid each year for shoe money; the rent for the intercalary months is to be reckoned the same as that for other months; also a deposit of two hundred taels is to be made. The shop is free from all incumbrances; hereafter, if any small repairs or painting are required, they must all

立發明舖批人懷本堂何有舖一間在太平門外十三行南向深兩進濶十九桁上蓋瓦面週圍樓閣窗扇帳房一應俱全今批與游廣義開張榮盛店找換錢銀生理言明每年租銀一百二十兩正淨元司碼秤兌另每年鞋金銀二元閏月照算又先交押櫃銀二百兩此舖原無頂

Lap› fát› ˏming p'ò' ‹p'ai ˏyan ˏWái ʻpún ˏt'óng ˏHó, ʻyau p'ò' yat› ‹kán, tsoi' T'ái' ˏP'ing ˏmún ngoi', Shap› ‹sám ˏHóng, ˏnám héung'. ‹Sham ʻléung tsun', fút› shap› ʻkau ‹hang; shéung' koi' ʻngá mín', ‹chau ˏwai ˏlau kók›, ‹ch'éung shín' chéung' ˏfóng, yat› ying' ‹k'ü ˏts'ün. ‹Kam ‹p'ai ʻü ˏYau ʻKwóng í', ‹hoi ‹chéung ˏYing ˏShing, tím' ʻcháu ún' ˏts'ín ˏngan ‹shang ʻlí. ˏÍn ˏming ʻmúi ˏnín ‹tsò ˏngan yat› pák› í' shap› ʻléung ‹ching', tsing' ˏün ‹sz' ʻmá ‹p'ing túi'; ling' ʻmúi ˏnín ˏhái ‹kam ˏngan í' ˏün; yun' üt› chíú' sün'; yau' ‹sín ‹káu át› kwai' ˏngan í' pák› ʻléung. ʻTs'z' p'ò' ˏün ˏmò ʻting ʻshau;

6. Shops in China are always known abroad by the *hò* or sign, which is suspended in gilt letters in conspicuous places in and out of the shop.

be done at the charge of the tenant himself; but if the walls happen to be broken down, the bricks, tile, timber, and stone, for repairs, are to be furnished by the landlord; for all the rest, hire of labor, &c., the tenant is to pay, and the landlord shall in no way be accountable. It is agreed, and hereby specified, that the term of lease shall be ten years, which term being completed, the lease shall be renewable. The rent is to be paid quarterly, and punctually as it becomes due. If the tenant engages in any other business [than that specified,] the shop shall then revert to its owner. If the rent is not paid when due, it shall be allowable to make up the deficiency from the deposit; and it shall not be lawful, on plea that the term of the lease has not expired, to keep possession of the shop while the rent is unpaid. From and after the giving of this lease, the business of the shop shall be lawfully conducted; no contraband goods shall be stored therein; nor shall gamblers assemble, or thieves and robbers be concealed, there; nor may any similar illegalities be committed; if they be, the landlord shall be at liberty to take back the house and lease it to another, and the tenant shall not by any means retard or prevent his so doing, or underlet it to any other person.

小鋪牆木出係業十之其清另交任扣期鋪後得物等任另端頂有係遇瓦所皆與批滿之批交倘鋪租兩批據之不貨匪弊回多私倘俱如磚主價理議期新季欠將欠銀以詞賃生禁窩此取得及後飾理稍鋪工辦涉期換四拖業有櫃得爲自營違賭有主無與刷粉自傾乃餘客無爲另分得別如押不滿租分頓聚倘鋪亦阻人手修客壁石其鋪主年日租毋圖回將足未拖安貯及情從租揩別

tsz'² hau² ᶜt'óng ᶜyau ᶜsíú ₍sau ᶜfan shik₎, ₍k'ü hai² p'ò' hák₎ tsz'² ᶜlí; ₌ü yü² ₌ts'éung pik₎ ₍king ₌t'úi, ₍chün, ᶜngá, muk₂, shek₂, ᶜnai p'ò' ᶜchü ᶜshó ch'ut₎; ₌k'í ₌ü ₍kung ká', ₍kái hai² p'ò' hák₎ pán² ᶜlí, ᶜü íp₂ ᶜchü ₌mò shíp₎. ᶜI' ₍p'ai shap₂ ₌nín ₌wai ₌k'í, ₌k'í ᶜmún ₍chí yat₂, ling² ún² ₍san ₍p'ai. ₌K'í ₍tsò ₍fan sz'' kwai' ₍káu ₍ts'ing, ₌mò tak₎ ₍t'ó hím'. ᶜT'óng ling² ₌t'ò pít₂ íp₂, ₍tséung p'ò' ₍káu ₌úi. ₌U ᶜyau hím' ₍tsò, yam² ₍tséung át₎ kwai² ₌ngan ᶜléung k'au' tsuk₎; pat₎ tak₎ ᶜí ₍p'ai ₌k'í mí² ᶜmún ₌wai ₌tsz', kü' p'ò' ₍t'ó ₍tsò. Tsz'² yam² ₍chí hau², ₍ón fan² ₌ying ₍shang, pat₎ tak₎ ᶜchü tun² ₌wai kam' fò' mat₂; kap₂ tsü' ᶜtò ₍wó ᶜfí ᶜtang ₌tsing; ᶜt'óng ᶜyau ᶜts'z' pai², yam² ₌tsung p'ò' ᶜchü ᶜtsü ₌ü ling² ₍tsò, yik₂ ₌mò tak₎ ₍tó ₍tün k'ang' ᶜtsó, ᶜü kap₂ ₍sz' ᶜting pít₂ ₌yan.

These are the terms, on which both the landlord and tenant are agreed, and from which hereafter it shall not be lawful to retract. In witness whereof, I now, desir-

願得憑情不有家後欲二日今係事言此之異

ᶜTs'z' hai² í² ₍ká ₌tsing ün² ₍chí sz'², yat₂ hau² pat₎ tak₎ í² ₌ín. ₍Kam yuk₂ ᶜyau

ing to afford evidence, prepare this lease, and give it to the tenant of the shop YING SHING, to be kept as a testimony of the agreement.

Written this 10th day of the 7th month of the 18th year of Tòkwóng, by Hó, of the family Wáipún, who grants this lease of the shop.

立此舖批一紙
交與榮盛店收
執爲據

道光十八年七
月初十日發舖
批人懷本堂何
宅立

‹p'ang, lap$_2$ 'ts'z' p'ò' ‹p'ai yat› 'chí, ‹káu 'ü ‹Ying ‹Shing tím', ‹shau chap› ‹wai kü'.

Tò' ‹kwóng shap$_2$ pát› ‹nín, ts'át› üt$_2$, ‹chò shap$_2$ yat›, fát› p'ò' ‹p'ai ‹yan ‹Wái 'pún ‹t'óng ‹Hó chák$_2$ lap$_2$.

6. In what manner is the bond written?

Here also you have a formula of it.

Yau Kwóngí, the tenant (or shopman) who makes this bond, has now received a shop, let to him by Hó, of the family Wáipún, which is to be opened under the sign YING SHING, and to be employed as a money-changer's shop. It is distinctly understood that the rent shall be one hundred and twenty taels each year, whole dollars, according to the balances of government; two dollars also shall be paid each year for shoe money; the rent for the intercalary month is to be reckoned the same as that for the other months; and a deposit of two hundred taels is to be made in advance. The shop is free from all incumbrances. And furthermore, the building having been newly repaired, if any small additional repairs or painting are required, they must all be made at the charge of the tenant himself; but if after a lapse of time, the walls become dilapidated, the bricks, tile, timber, and stone, for

領又點樣寫呢
看列於後

立領舖人游廣
義今領到懷本
堂何宅舖一間
開張榮盛字號
找換錢銀生理
言明每年租銀
一百二十兩淨
元司碼另每年
鞋金銀二元閏
月租銀照算先
交押櫃銀二百
兩此舖原無頂
手與及新修堅
固倘有小修粉
飾俱係住舖之
人自理至於日
久牆壁傾頹其

'Ling yau$^2$ 'tím yéung$^2$ 'sé ‹ní?
Hón' lít$_2$ ‹ü hau$^2$.

Lap$_2$ 'ling, p'ò' ‹yan ‹Yau 'Kwóng í$^2$ ‹kam 'ling tò' ‹Wái 'pún ‹t'óng ‹Hó chák$_2$ p'ò' yat› ‹kán, ‹hoi ‹chéung ‹Ying ‹Shing tsz'$^2$ hò$^2$, 'cháu ún$^2$ ‹ts'ín ‹ngan ‹shang 'lí. ‹Ín ‹ming 'múi ‹nín ‹tsò ‹ngan yat› pák› í$^2$ shap$_2$ 'léung, tsing$^2$ ‹ün ‹sz' 'má; ling$^2$ 'múi ‹nín ‹hái ‹kam ‹ngan í$^2$ ‹ün; yun$^2$ üt$_2$ ‹tsò ‹ngan chíú' sün'; ‹sín ‹káu át› kwai$^2$ ‹ngan í$^2$ pák› 'léung. 'Ts'z' p'ò' ‹ün ‹mò 'ting 'shau. 'Ü kap$_2$, ‹san ‹sau ‹kín kú', 't'óng 'yau 'síú ‹sau 'fan shik$_2$, ‹k'ü$^2$ hai$^2$ chü$^2$ p'ò' ‹chí ‹yan tsz'$^2$ 'lí; chí' ‹ü yat$_2$ 'kau ‹tséung pik› ‹king ‹t'úi, ‹k'í

6. The sign-board of a money-changer's shop usually reads, *ts'ín ngan pín ún*, meaning, cash and silver changed at pleasure; to attract the notice of customers more certainly, there are, besides the gay sign-board, three or four wooden cylinders, marked with lines to represent so many strings of cash, suspended over the door.

repairs, are to be furnished at the landlord's expense; for the rest, the hire of labor, &c., the tenant shall be responsible, and shall not be allowed to make any deduction from the rent. The term of lease is ten years, which being completed, the lease may be renewed. If the tenant engages in any other business [than that specified], the shop shall then revert to its owner. If no rent remains unpaid after the lease has expired, then the whole deposit money shall be returned; but if the rent is not paid when due, then it shall be lawful to make up the deficiency from the money in deposit; from this there shall be no dissent. The rent shall be punctually paid quarterly, when it becomes due, without failure. From and after the giving of this deed, the business of the shop shall be lawfully conducted; no contraband goods shall be stored therein; nor shall bands of thieves and gamblers, and such like, assemble, or be concealed, there.

磚瓦木石乃舖
主所出其餘工
價乃舖客自行
辦理毋得將租
扣除以十年爲
限期滿另轉新
批倘另圖別業
將舖交回業主
如不欠租即將
押櫃銀照數交
回倘若欠租任
將押櫃銀扣足
毋得異言其租
銀限分四季交
清斷無拖欠自
領之後安分營
生不得貯頓違
禁貨物及窩匪
聚賭等情

‹chün, ˢngá, muk$_2$, shik$_2$, ˢnái p'ò' 'chü 'shó ch'ut›; ˏk'í ˏü ‹kung ká', ˢnái p'ò' hák› tsz'$^2$ ˏhang pán$^2$ ˢlí, ˏmò tak› ‹tséung ‹tsò k'au' ˏch'ü. ˢÍ shap$_2$ ˏnín ˏwai hán$^2$ ˏk'í ˢmún ling$^2$ 'chün ‹san ‹p'ai. 'T'óng ling$^2$ ˏt'ò pít$_2$ íp$_2$, ‹tséung p'ò' ‹káu ˏúi íp$_2$ 'chü. ˏU pat› hím' ‹tsò, tsik› ‹tséung át› kwai$^2$ ˏngan chíú' shò' ‹káu ˏúi; 't'óng yéuk› hím' ‹tsò, yam$^2$ ‹tséung át› kwai$^2$ ˏngan k'au' tsuk›; ˏmò tak› í$^2$ ˏín. ˏK'í ‹tsò ˏngan hán$^2$ ‹fan sz'$^2$ kwai' ‹káu ‹ts'ing, tün$^2$ ˏmò ‹t'ó hím'. Tsz'$^2$ ˢling ‹chí hau$^2$, ‹ón fan$^2$ ˏying ‹shang; pat› tak› ˢch'ü tun$^2$ ˏwai kam' fó' mat$_2$; kap› ‹wó 'fí tsü$^2$ 'tò 'tang ˏts'ing.

These are the terms of the lease which have been clearly expressed in person, to which landlord and tenant both agree, and from which hereafter it shall not be lawful to retract. In witness whereof, I now desiring to afford evidence, prepare this deed, and give it to the family Wáipún, to be kept as a tesmony of the agreement.

此乃當面言明
二家允肯日後
不得異言今欲
有憑立此舖領
一紙交懷本堂
收執爲據

'Ts'z' ˢnái ‹tóng mín$^2$ ˏín ˏming, í$^2$ ‹ká ˢwan 'hang, yat$_2$ hau$^2$ pat› tak› í$^2$ ˏín. ‹Kam yuk$_2$ ˢyau ˏp'ang, lap$_2$ 'ts'z' p'ò' ˢling yat› 'chí, ‹káu ˏWái 'pún ˏt'óng ‹shau chap› ˏwai kü'.

Written this 15th day of the 7th month in the 18th year of Tòkwóng, by Yau Kwóngí, who makes and gives this deed, in testimony of his having received the lease.

道光十八年七
月十五日立舖
領人游廣義的
筆

Tò$^2$ ‹kwóng shap$_2$ pát› ˏnín, ts'át› üt$_2$, shap$_2$ ˢ'ng yat$_2$, lap$_2$ p'ò' ˢling ˏyan ˏYau 'Kwóng í$^2$ tik› pat›.

| | | |
|---|---|---|
| 7. What is the usual rate of rent for the year or month? | 每年每月租銀幾多呢 | ʻMúi ˏnín, ʻmúi üt₂, ˓tsò ˏngan ʻkí ˓tó ˓ní? |
| The rent varies according to the amount of capital invested, regard being also had to the locality and to the current pay for such property. | 租銀論本取息亦看地與時價然後議租 | ˓Tsò ˏngan lun[2] ʻpún ʻts'ü sik˒, yik₂ hón' tí[2] ʻü ˏshí ká', ˏín hau[2] ʻí ˓tsò. |
| 8. When the money is to be received monthly, in what manner is it paid? | 每月收銀點樣交收呢 | ʻMúi üt₂ ˓shau ˏngan, ʻtím yéung[2] ˓káu ˓shau ˓ní? |
| Every owner of property, who lets a shop, besides the bond received from the tenant, must also be furnished with a small book from him, which he is to keep as a book of rents; and when the time of payment comes, then, on the testimony of this book, it may be received. | 凡租賃舖者除批領外舖客另設一小簿交舖主收執至期則憑此簿收租 | ˏFán ˓tsò yam[2] p'ò' ʻché, ˏch'ü ˓p'ai ʻling ngoi[2], p'ò' hák˒ ling[2] ch'ít˒ yat˒ ʻsíú pò[2], ˓káu p'ò' ʻchü ˓shau chap˒; chí' ˏk'í tsak˒ ˏp'ang ʻts'z' pò[2] ˓shau ˓tsò. |
| 9. What is the deposit money? | 點樣係押櫃呢 | ʻTím yéung[2] hai[2] át˒ kwai[2] ˓ní? |
| The deposit money is a given sum, folded up and deposited in a chest, and is not to be used, unless the rent is not paid when it becomes due, in which case it is to be deducted therefrom. | 押櫃者原係包封押於櫃內而不用倘有欠租在此扣除 | Á't˒ kwai[2] ʻché, ˏün hai[2] ˓páu ˓fung át˒ ˓ü kwai[2] noi[2], ˏí pat˒ yung[2], ʻt'óng ʻyau hím' ˓tsò, tsoi[2] ʻts'z' k'au[2] ˏch'ü. |
| 10. What is the payment called the shoe money? | 乜野叫做係鞋金呢 | Mat˒ ʻyé kíú[2] tsò[2] hai[2] ˏhái ˓kam ˓ní? |
| The person who receives the rent has to travel much; and therefore the tenant, in addition to the rent, must add shoe money, which he pays over to the collector of the rent for the purchase of shoes, as a reward for his trouble in going backwards and forwards; and hence it is called shoe money. | 收租之人多於奔走故舖客於租之外另加鞋金送與收租之人買鞋以謝其往返之勞故曰鞋金 | ˓Shau ˓tsò ˓chí ˏyan, ˓tó ˓ü ˓pan ʻtsau; kú' p'ò' hák˒ ˓ü ˓tsò ˓chí ngoi[2], ling[2] ˓ká ˏhái ˓kam, sung' ʻü ˓shau ˓tsò ˓chí ˏyan ʻmái ˏhái ʻí tsé[2] ˏk'í ʻwóng ʻfán ˓chí ˏlò; kú' üt₂, ˏhái ˓kam. |
| 11. What is the inviting of purchase? | 召頂點解呢 | Chíú[2] ʻting ʻtím ʻkái ˓ní? |

7. The phrase *ts'ü sik* means to collect or gather interest; *pún* is the money originally expended in building the shop.

The *purchase* is simply the purchasing of fixtures, and not of the shop itself. When the tenant has purchased the fixtures, then there is no necessity for his making a deposit of money; because the proceeds of the fixtures, if sold at any time, will liquidate any sum that may be due for rent. *Inviting* is the inviting of persons to take the fixtures.

頂者不過頂其傢伙什物非頂其鋪凡向來有頂手則無押櫃因有頂手之項以清舊租召招也招人頂之意

'Ting 'ché, patˎ kwó' 'ting ˏk'í ˎká 'fó shapˎ mat₂ ˎfí 'ting ˏk'í p'ò'. ˏFán ˏhéung ˏloi 'yau 'ting 'shau, tsakˎ ˏmò átˎ kwai'; ˎyan 'yau 'ting 'shau ˎchí hóng' 'í ˎts'ing kau' ˎtsò. Chíú' ˎchíú 'yá, ˎchíú ˏyan 'ting ˎchí í'.

12. And why is earnest money required?

又定銀點解呢

Yau' ting' ˏngan 'tím 'kái ˎní?

Without earnest money no confidence can be had that the agreement will be kept; besides, at the time of payment it is to be deducted from the rent.

無定不足以取信惟於收租時在租內扣還

ˏMò ting' patˎ tsukˎ 'í 'ts'ü sun'; ˏwai ˎü ˎshau ˎtsò ˏshí tsoi' ˎtsò noi' k'au' ˏwán.

13. What is meant by becoming surety?

點樣係擔保呢

'Tím yéung' hai' ˎtám 'pò ˎní?

*Becoming* denotes the receiving and sustaining of a thing; *surety* signifies the security given that arrears of rent shall not be incurred.

擔者擔承也保是保其無欠租等事

ˎTám 'ché ˎtám ˏshing 'yá; 'pò shí', 'pò ˏk'í ˏmò hím' ˎtsò 'tang sz'.

14. Why is it, that, in addition to the rent, a lease fee is also required from the tenant?

有租爲乜事又要批頭呢

'Yau ˎtsò wai' matˎ sz' yau' iú' ˎp'ai ˏt'au ˎní?

The lease fee is a deduction made from the rent of the shop; when a shop is to be hired it is necessary to have a midsman to propose the contract; the landlord likewise requires some one to take care of his shop. Consequently a lease fee, equaling one month's rent, is taken and divided beween those two men.

批頭乃批鋪之抽頭也原租鋪必有中人說合業主亦有看鋪之人故取一月批頭爲他二人分用

ˎP'ai ˏt'au 'nái ˎp'ai p'ò' ˎchí ˎch'au ˏt'au 'yá; ˏün ˎtsò p'ò' pítˎ 'yau ˎchung ˏyan shüt hóp₂ íp₂; 'chü yik₂ 'yau hón' p'ò' ˎchí ˏyan. Kú' 'tsü yatˎ üt ˎp'ai ˏt'au, ˏwai ˎt'á í' ˏyan ˎfan yung'.

15. Do the landlord and tenant then receive no part of the lease fee?

咁話鋪主鋪客都冇得收呀

'Kóm wà' p'ò' 'chü p'ò' hákˎ ˎtò 'mò takˎ ˎshau á'?

If a man goes himself and makes all the inquiries about

間有自行問到

Kán' 'yau tsz' ˏhang man'

12. This practice of depositing earnest money, in which the Chinese resemble the Turks, is carried into all important transactions of life; even betrothment is not settled without it.

the renting of a shop, without the assistance of a second person; and if the landlord likewise has no need of any one to take care of his shop; then the lease fee is to be equally divided between the landlord and the tenant.

租賃無中人者與及業主亦無看鋪之人則批頭各得一半

tò' ˌtsò yam' ˌmò ˌchung ˌyan ˈché; ˈü kap íp ˈchü yik, ˌmò hón' p'ò' ˌchí ˌyan; tsak ˌp'ai ˌt'au kók tak yat pún'.

16. Again; as the intercalary month is an additional one, why is it that sometimes only half a month's rent is paid, while at others, a full month's rent is paid?

又閏月係多一月爲何有交一半又有照算交嘅呢

Yau' yun' üt hai' ˌtó yat üt, wai' ˌhó ˈyau ˌkáu yat pún', yau' ˈyau chiú' siin' ˌkáu ké' ˌní?

If the lease be for a long time, it may be that only half a month's rent is paid; a full month's rent is the highest; but that nothing be paid is very unusual.

租鋪日久或交一半照算者多不交者少

ˌTsò p'ò' yat ˈkau, wak ˌkáu yat pún'; chiú' sün' ˈché ˌtó; pat ˌkáu ˈché ˈshiú.

17. Why is it that some persons pay the rent every month, and others pay it quarterly?

爲何又有按月清租又有按季嘅呢

Wai' ˌho yau' ˈyau ón' üt ˌts'ing ˌtsò, yau' ˈyau ón' kwai' ké' ˌní?

A monthly payment is made, because, the sum being then small, it is more easily raised; and does not allow the tenant to become deeply involved; but when the landlord has full confidence in the ability of the tenant, and he regards the monthly payment as troublesome, he will in that case prefer quarterly payments.

按月以其數輕易於爲力鋪客少拖欠之弊若知其人必不欠者又見按月紛繁故有分四季

Ón' üt ˈí ˌk'i shò' ˌhing í' ˌü ˌwai lik; p'ò' hak ˈshiú ˌt'ó him' ˌchí pai'; yéuk ˌchí ˌk'i ˌyan pit pat him' ˈché, yau' kín' ón' üt ˌfan ˌfán kú' ˈyau ˌfan sz' kwai'.

16. It is not uncommon when hiring dwelling-houses to lease them by the year, and to pay the same price annually, whether there is an intercalary month or not; but in shops the case is a little different. There is frequently a kitchen attached to shops where apprentices and workmen cook their food, who usually also sleep within the precincts of the building.

17. The rent, whether paid monthly, quarterly, or as is sometimes the case, once in four months, is always paid at the commencement of the term over which the time extends. The phrase *fan fán* or *fan wan* means a confused multiplicity of things or affairs, ensuing upon a large business, which tend unnecessarily to distract the mind.

## Section Second.

# COMMERCIAL ARTICLES AND TERMS.

## 通商名字類第二章
‹T'ung ˏshéung ˏming tsz[2] lui[2]; tai[2] í[2] ‹chéung.

1. *Abatement* is a reduction made by a person who wishes to obtain a speedy payment of money; it is also a reduction of duties, made at the custom-house, on account of the goods being damaged.

減少的如欲人速交銀於我其請如此壞貨請關減稅者亦同

ʿ*Kám* ʿ*shíú* tik›, ˏü yuk› ˏyan ts'uk› ‹káu ˏngan ‹ü ʿngó, ˏk'í ʿts'ing ˏü ʿts'zʾ; wái[2] fóʾ ʿts'ing ‹kwán ʿkám shuiʾ ʿché, yik› ˏt'ung.

2. *Accountants* are those who within the counter have charge of keeping accounts in the account-books.

掌櫃者執掌櫃內賬目數簿也

ʿ*Chéung kwai*[2] ʿché, chap› ʿchéung kwai[2] noi[2] chéungʾ muk› shòʾ pò[2] ʿyá.

3. *Advance* on a contract is the earnest money.

訂據銀即定銀

*Tingʾ kü[2] ˏngan*, tsik› ting[2] ˏngan.

4. *Advertisement* is a public notice of the sale of goods, renting of shops, houses, and such like.

招帖乃出賣貨與出賃舖戶等招人之帖

‹*Chíú t'íp*›, ʿnái ch'ut› mái[2] fóʾ, ʿü ch'ut› yam[2] p'òʾ ú[2] ʿtang, ˏchíú ˏyan ‹chí t'íp›.

5. Letter of *advice* for the payment of a bill; if a man has money which he wishes to have received in another place at a distance, the party who is to pay the money gives him a draft for which the money is to be received on its presentation at that place; the same party also writes a letter of advice, and sends it to the person who is to pay the money.

托代照單交銀信如人有銀欲在別處收回應交者寫一單與他到某處憑單收銀另寫此信寄與交銀之人

T'ok› toi[2] chíúʾ ‹tán ‹*káu ˏngan sun*ʾ; ˏü ˏyan ʿyau ˏngan, yuk› tsoi[2] pít› ch'üʾ ‹shau ˏúi; ‹ying ‹káu ʿché, ʿsé yat› ‹tán ʿü ‹t'á, tò[2] ʿmau ch'üʾ ˏp'ang ‹tán ‹shau ˏngan; ling[2] ʿsé ʿt'szʾ sunʾ kíʾ ʿü ‹káu ˏngan ‹chí ˏyan.

## *Notes and Explanations.*

THIS section is intended to include those words and phrases which are appropriated to commerce as techinal terms, together with the names of the various commodities, which occur in the foreign trade at Canton. As far as practicable, brief definitions are given of the terms, with a view to exhibit their meaning and use. In some instances, commodities are described in a similar manner; but when they are well known, they are, for the most part, spoken of in some way, designed to convey information respecting their uses, manufacture, origen, &c.

2. This sentence includes three terms in common use among the shopmen in Canton—accounts, accountants, and account-books; *chéung muk* are the accounts of goods of any kind; and *chéung muk shò pò* is the account-book.

5. The drawer of a bill or order should always take care that a letter, containing all the

| | | |
|---|---|---|
| 6. In the city of Canton those people who work and traffic in *agates* have established an assembly-hall. | 粵省造賣瑪瑙器者同立會館 | Üt, 'sháng tsò' mái' *'má 'nò* hí' 'ché, ,t'ung lap, úi' 'kún. |
| 7. *Agents* are those who act for, or in the place of, others, [by whom they are commissioned.] | 替身乃代理代辦之人 | *T'ai' ,shan*, 'nái toi' 'lí toi' pán' ,chí ,yan. |
| 8. *Almonds*, both from the north and south, are used as medicine. | 南北杏仁皆屬藥材 | ,Nám pak, *hang' ,yan*, ,kái shuk, yéuk, ,ts'oi. |
| 9. *Aloes-wood* newly arrived, for sale. | 新到沉香發客 | ,San tò' *,ch'am ,héung* fát, hák,. |
| 10. *Alum*,* when put into water, precipitates the smallest impurities contained in it. | 白礬入水其水溦必墜 | *Pák, ,fán* yap, 'shui, ,k'í 'shui ,mí pít, chui'. |
| 11. *Amber;* the price of this is very high in Canton. | 琥珀土價最高 | *'Fú p'ák,;* 't'ò ká' tsui' ,kò. |
| 12. *False amber;*† this is included among the fifty-three articles of import which are interdicted, except only to the hong merchants, who are allowed to buy and sell it. | 蜜珀乃奉禁五十三欵內入口之貨應歸洋商販賣 | *Mat, p'ák,;* 'nái fung' kam' 'ng shap, ,sám 'fún noi' yap, 'hau ,chí fó', ,ying ,kwai ,yéung ,shéung fán' mái'. |
| 13. *Anchor;* this is an iron instrument, which, when the ship is to be anchored in a harbor, is cast down to stop the course of the ship and make her fast. | 錨乃船灣泊時抛下水止船不行者以鐵爲之 | *,Náu;* 'nái ,shün ,wán pók, ,shí, ,p'áu há' 'shui 'chí ,shün pat, ,hang 'ché, 'í t'ít, ,wai ,chí. |
| 14. *Anchorage* is a place of deep water, free from rocks, fitted for the mooring of vessels. | 泊船頭乃水深無石應停舟處 | *Pók, ,shün ,t'au*, 'nái 'shui ,sham ,mò shik,, ,ying ,t'ing ,chau ch'ü'. |

proper particulars of advice, is in the hands of the drawee by the time the bill is to be paid, because for want of such advice the bill is liable to be dishonored.

6. Most of the different classes of people in Canton, who are engaged in the same trade or manufacture, have their respective *úi kún*, in which they assemble for consultation about all such matters as relate to their interests as members of that same trade or branch of manufactures. In these assembly-halls they usually keep the records of their proceedings, &c.

9. In the phrase *fát hák*, which is equivalent to the English term "for sale," *hák* denotes customers, or those to whom goods are offered for sale. The phrase often occurs as the last two characters on sign boards.

10. (*) In July, 1828, a series of regulations were framed and sanctioned by the Chinese government, according to which, twenty-four articles for exportation, and fifty-three for importation, were restricted to the hong merchants. In all articles, excepting these seventy-seven, which are not made contraband by the general laws of the empire, other native merchants were allowed to trade. In order to distinguish those commodities which are monopolized, they are marked in this section, the exports with an asterisk (*), and the imports with a dagger (†), while those free to all are left unmarked.

13. With the Chinese, anchors are for the most part made of a heavy wood, and have their flukes pointed with iron so that they will easily take hold of the ground.

| | | |
|---|---|---|
| 15. ***Annisseed stars;**** these have an aromatic flavor, and the body of each has eight prongs; hence the name. | 八角味香以其體有八角故名 | *Pát, kók,*; mí² ˏhéung ʻí ˏk'í, ʻt'ai ʻyau pát, kók,; kú' ˏming. |
| 16. ***Antelopes' horns*** are used as refrigerant medicine. | 羚羊角藥性凉 | *ˏLing ˏyéung kók,*, yéuk, sing' ˏléung. |
| 17. ***Arrack*** is the name of a foreign spirituous liquor. | 啞叻酒乃外洋之酒名 | *A' lik, ʻtsau,* ʻnái ngoi² ˏyéung ˏchí ʻtsau ˏming. |
| 18. ***Arrow-root;*** this is a fecula made from the inspissated juice of the water lily. | 藕粉即蓮藕汁所凝之粉 | *ʻNgau ʻfan;* tsik, ˏlín ʻngau chap, ʻshó ˏying ˏchí ʻfan. |
| 19. ***Arsenic*** is also called *p'aiséung;* those who swallow it will certainly die. | 信石一名砒霜食者必死 | *Sun' shik,* yat, ˏming *ˏp'ai ˏséung;* shik, ʻché pít, ʻsz'. |
| 20. ***Asafœtida*†** is brought from Persia. | 阿魏出波斯國 | *ˏÓ ngai²* ch'ut, ˏPó ˏsz' kwók,. |
| 21. ***Assets*** are the entire property of all sorts, belonging to a firm, available for the payment of its debts. | 產業乃家產財物可抄償債者 | *ʻCh'án íp,* ʻnái ˏká ʻch'án ˏts'oi mat, ʻhó ˏch'áu ˏch'éung chái' ʻché. |
| 22. ***Auction sale;*** this is done by exhibiting goods to public inspection, and then afterwards selling them to those who offer the highest price. | 出投乃以貨視衆而出價高者得之 | *Ch'ut, ˏt'au* ʻnái ʻí fó' shí² chung' ˏí ch'ut, ká' ˏkò ʻché tak, ˏchí. |
| 23. ***Auction of goods by sending in notes;*** these are paper cards, on which each person silently writes a price; and after being opened and examined, he who has offered the highest price obtains the article. | 落標投貨標者紙單也各默寫價於內後開看價高者得 | *Lók, ˏpíú ˏt'au fó'*, ˏpíú ʻché ʻchí ˏtán ʻyá; kók, mak, ʻsé ká' ˏü noi², hau² ˏhoi hón' ká' ˏkò ʻché tak,. |
| 24. ***Auctioneer*** is the person who invites people to come together for the purchase of goods by auction. | 掌投貨者乃招聚投買賣之人 | *ʻChéung ˏt'au fó' ʻché,* ʻnái ˏchíú tsui² ˏt'au ʻmái mái² ˏchí ˏyan. |
| 25. A ***bale of goods:*** bales are of two kinds, whole bales and half bales. | 一包貨有大包中包兩種 | *Yat, ˏpáu fó'*, ʻyau tái² ˏpáu, ʻchung ˏpáu, ʻléung ʻchung. |

18. The Chinese make preparations, all of which go with foreigners under the general name of arrow-root, from the water chestnut, water caltrops, and caladium, as well as the water lily; all of them are much inferior to that made from the Maranta and Curcuma, or from the Tacca of the Pacific islands. The Chinese have no general name corresponding to arrow-root, but specify each sort.

23. This mode of selling various articles is often resorted to by the Chinese; it is usual on such occasions to name some price below which no bidder is allowed to go.

25. This mode of designating whole and half bales obtains among the native merchants of Canton; and the same mode prevails also for designating chests of ten; thus, *tái séung*, *chung séung*, and *síú séung*, are used for whole, half, and quarter, chests.

| | | |
|---|---|---|
| 26. *Ballast;* lest the ship should be too heavy above and light below, stones or iron are put into her hold as ballast to keep her upright. | 船墜乃恐其船上重下輕故放石或鐵於艙底 | ꜁*Shün chui*$^{2}$; ʻnái ʻhung ꜁k'í ꜁shün shéung$^{2}$ chung$^{2}$ há$^{2}$ ꜀hing, kú' fóng' shik$_{2}$, wák$_{2}$ títˏ ꜀ü ꜀ts'óng ʻtai. |
| 27. *Bamboos* are used to make the handles of umbrellas, the stems of tobacco pipes &c. | 竹杆用作雨傘柄烟筒等項 | *Chukˏ* ꜀*kón*, yung$^{2}$ tsókˏ ʻü sán' ping', ꜀ín ꜁t'ung ʻtang hóng$^{2}$. |
| 28. *Banks*, mints, and the houses of money-changers, are all called money shops; the former are those which take money, and place it out on interest. | 生放傾銷便換俱稱銀舖生放者將銀放出生息之意 | ꜀*Shang fóng*', ꜀k'ing ꜀síú, pín$^{2}$ ún$^{2}$, ꜀k'ü ꜀ch'ing ꜁ngan p'ò'; ꜀shang fóng' ʻché, ꜀tséung ꜁ngan fóng' ch'utˏ ꜀shang sikˏ ꜀chí í'. |
| 29. *Bankruptcy* is this; in the prosecution of commerce, if one is unable to succeed, his capital is wastde, so that his establishment becomes insolvent. | 折本乃生意不遂折耗其本如倒行也 | *Chítˏ ʻpún*, ʻnái ꜀shang í' patˏ sui$^{2}$, chítˏ hò' ꜁k'í ʻpún, ꜁ü ʻtò ꜁hóng ʻyá. |
| 30. *Beads;* these are of several different kinds, as pearl, gem, glass, wood, and such like. | 珠有珍寶料木各等不同 | ꜀*Chü*, ʻyau ꜀chan, ʻpò, líú$^{2}$, muk$_{2}$, kókˏ ʻtang patˏ ꜁t'ung. |
| 31. *Beeswax;* the color of this is a bright yellow; it is a product of the honey bee. | 蜜蠟其色黃潔亦出於蜂 | *Mat*$_{2}$ *láp*$_{2}$, ꜁k'í shikˏ ꜁wóng kítˏ; yik$_{2}$ ch'utˏ ꜀ü ꜀fung. |
| 32. *Betel nut* † is masticated with lime and siri leaf. | 檳榔兼灰荖食 | ꜀*Pan* ꜁*lóng* ꜀kím ꜀fúi ꜀lau shik$_{2}$. |
| 33. *Bezoar* † is produced when the cow is diseased. | 牛黃牛病然後生黃 | ꜁*Ngau* ꜁*wóng*, ꜁ngau ping$^{2}$, ꜁ín hau$^{2}$ ꜀shang ꜁wóng. |
| 34. *Biche de mer,* † black and thin, is the best. | 海參黑薄尤佳 | ʻ*Hoi* ꜀*sham*, hakˏ pók$_{2}$ ꜁yau ꜀kái. |
| 35. *Bill of exchange* is an order, written in explicit terms by the person obligated to pay money, which is to be received on its presentation at a given place. | 會單乃應交銀人寫明一單到某處收回 | *Ui*$^{2}$ ꜀*tán*, ʻnái ꜀ying ꜀káu ꜁ngan ꜁yan ʻsé ꜁ming yatˏ ꜀tán, tò' ʻmau ch'ü' ꜀shau ꜁úi. |
| 36. *Birdsnests* † which are free from feathers are the best, and are called *kún ín*. | 燕窩以毛淨者爲上名曰官燕 | *Ín*$^{2}$ ꜀*wó*, ʻí ꜁mò tsing$^{2}$ ʻché ꜁wai shéung$^{2}$, ꜁ming üt$_{2}$ ʻkún ín$^{2}$. |

32. This nut, which is an article of commerce in all the Archipelago, is the produce of the areca palm, and is called betel nut from its being always eaten in combination with the leaf of the betel pepper; it is usually brought to China with the husk remaining on. The lime used to increase the pungency of the preparation, and it is said, prevent the nut injuring the stomach, is made of small bivalve shells burnt and reduced to an impalpable powder; it is of a red color, and is mixed with water before using.

| | | |
|---|---|---|
| 37. ***Feathery birdsnests*** † are placed among the fifty-three restricted articles, as separate and distinct from the true birdsnests. | 毛燕於奉禁五<br>十三欵內另列<br>與燕窩不同 | ˏ*Mò ín'*, ˓ü fung² kam' ʻ'ng shap ˓sám ʻfún noi² ling² lít, ʻü ín' ˓wó pat˒ ˏt'ung. |
| 38. ***Blacking*** is applied to leathern shoes with a brush, for the purpose of giving them a fine polish. | 墨水用以擦皮<br>鞋其意欲靚也 | *Mak, ʻshui*, yung² ʻí ts'át, ˏp'í ˏhái, ˏk'í í' yuk, tsing' ʻyá. |
| 39. ***Blacklead*** is like coal, but of a much greater specific gravity. | 黑鉛如煤其體<br>最重 | *Hak˒ ˏün*, ˏü ˏmúi, ˏk'í ʻt'ai tsui' chung². |
| 40. ***Bombasin*** † is made of silk, and is brought from beyond sea. | 羽布以絲爲之<br>來自外洋 | ʻ*Ü pò'*, ʻí ˓sz' ˏwai ˓chí, ˏloi tsz'² ngoi² ˏyéung. |
| 41. ***Book-keeping*** is the art of keeping and regulating mercantile accounts in a book. | 司理數目簿乃<br>管理其數目者 | ˓*Sz' ʻlí shò' muk, pò'*, ˏnái ʻkún ʻlí ˏk'í shò' muk, ʻché. |
| 42. ***Bottomry*** is this; the transfer of a ship to other parties by its owner, because he has incurred debts and is without means to liquidate them. | 典船乃船家無<br>資有欠故將船<br>典與別人 | ʻ*Tín ˏshün*, ʻnái ˏshün ˓ká ˏmò ˓tsz' ʻyau hím', kú' ˓tséung ˏshün ʻtín ʻü pít˒ ˏyan. |
| 43. ***Bounty***; if a person brings into the country commodities which are of great value to it, or exports [others for its advantage], not only are the duties thereon remitted, but money is paid as a bounty. | 賞銀如人將國<br>中最要之物帶<br>出入口餉固不<br>納尤賞之以銀 | ʻ*Shéung ˏngan*, ˏü ˏyan ˓tséung kwók˒ ˓chung tsui' iú' ˓chí mat, tái' ch'ut˒ yap, ʻhau, héung' kú' pat˒ náp, ˏyau ʻshéung ˓chí ʻí ˏngan. |
| 44. ***Brass*** is used for the manufacture of rings, hooks, and many kinds of things. | 黃銅用作環扣<br>諸色等物 | ˏ*Wóng ˏt'ung*, yung² tsók˒ ˏwán k'au', ˓chü shik˒ ʻtang mat. |
| 45. ***Brass leaf*** is hammered from small pieces of molten brass. | 銅薄乃銅鎔化<br>鑄片而捶薄也 | ˏ*T'ung pók˒*, ʻnái ˏt'ung ˏyung fá' chü² pín' ˏí ˏch'ui pók, ʻyá. |

36, 37. Those nests that are obtained before the swallows have hatched their young are the best, being free from feathers, shells and other impurities. The inferior sort, obtained after hatching, constitutes much the largest portion of the nests brought to market, and the separation of all the impurities to render them saleable and eatable affords employment for many persons.

38. The term *mak shui*, ink water, is in common use for writing ink; and blacking is usually designated by *hái mak shui;* but in commerce it is as above.

43. An approximation to this is found in China, in the remitting of certain duties on such ships as enter the port of Canton laden only with rice.

45. The manufacture of this article is very extensive; it is used to make *kam fá* or golden flowers, which are ornaments for temples, ancestral tablets, &c., and in many ways are connected with the religious ceremonies of the Chinese.

| | | |
|---|---|---|
| 46. The best *brimstone* is brought in foreign ships. | 硫磺番舶者良 | *Lau wóng*, fán pók ché léung. |
| 47. *Bristles* are made into brushes. | 猪鬃毛用作擦 | *Chü tsung* mò, yung tsók ts'át. |
| 48. *Broadcloth*, † otherwise called woolens, comes [to China] from foreign countries. | 大絨即大呢來自外國 | *Tái yung*, tsik tái ní, loi tsz' ngoi kwók. |
| 49. *Buoys* are made of blocks of wood, which are anchored fast, and placed on the surface of the water, to point where it is deep, and thus to enable one to sail a ship with safety. | 浮桴用一木下墜錨放水面能知水深淺亦能護船而行 | *Fau fú*, yung yat muk, há chui náu, fong 'shui mín nang chí 'shui sham ts'ín, yik nang ú shün í hang. |
| 50. Chain *cables* are made of iron, wrought into links, which are fastened together and attached to the anchor, so that by its being cast into the midst of the sea, the vessel becomes immovable. | 錨練以鐵打成連環相扣於錨身上拋下於海中使船不動 | *Náu lín*, 'í t'ít 'tá shing, lín wán séung k'au' ü náu shan shéung, p'áu há ü 'hoi chung, 'sz' shün pat tung. |
| 51. *Rope cables* are made of coir, and may be used instead of chain cables. | 錨纜以棕打成或用以代鐵練 | *Náu lám*, 'í tsung 'tá shing, wák yung 'í toi t'ít lín. |
| 52. *Camlets* † are articles of foreign manufacture. | 羽紗外洋所製之物 | *'Ü shá*, ngoi yéung 'shó chai' chí mát. |
| 53. *Camlets;* † those called *ütün* are from Holland, while the *üshá* come from England. | 羽緞出荷蘭羽紗出㖈咭唎國 | *'Ü tün*, ch'ut Hó lán; 'ü shá ch'ut Ying kat lí kwók. |
| 54. *Camphor* * † is produced from the camphor tree; it is also called 'ice petals,' 'dragon's brains,' and 'Borneo perfume.' | 樟腦出於樟樹有冰片龍腦波羅香等別名 | *Chéung 'nò*, ch'ut ü chéung shü, 'yau ping p'ín, lung 'nò, Pó ló héung, 'tang pít ming. |
| 55. *Canes* are sometimes made of bamboo, and sometimes of rattan. | 鞭竿或竹或藤爲之 | *Pín kón*, wák chuk, wák t'ang wai chí. |
| 56. Native *cassia* * has a pungent, aromatic taste; the fresh is esteemed the best. | 土桂皮其味辛香鮮者爲佳 | 'T'ò *kwai' p'í*, k'í mí' san héung; sin 'ché wai kái. |
| 57. *Cassia buds* * are purchased in the provincial city Canton, where also they are sold for exportation. | 桂子由粤東省城販賣出洋 | *Kwai' 'tsz'*, yau Üt tung 'sháng shing fán' mái' ch'ut yéung. |

50, 51. Chain cables are very seldom used in Chinese vessels; the cables are sometimes made of hemp, though large junks usually use those made of rattan or coir.

| | | |
|---|---|---|
| 58. *China root* * has a carnation skin, white flesh, and in form resembles ginger. | 茯苓皮赤肉白形如薑 | *Fuk*₂ ˏ*ling*, ˏp'í chik›, yuk₂ pák›, ˏying ˏü ‹kéung. |
| 59. *Chunam* is made by putting the oil of the Jatropha with lime, and beating them thoroughly together. | 桐油灰將桐油入灰舂煉而成 | ˏ*T'ung* ‹*yau* ‹*fúi* ‹tséung ˏt'ung ˏyau yap₂ ‹fúi, ‹chung lín² ˏí ˏshing. |
| 60. *Cigars* are made [by the Chinese] of the tobacco leaf rolled up in paper so as to be smoked; but in making the foreign cigars it is rolled in the leaf itself. | 孖姑烟用紙捲烟葉成筒吹之外洋則以烟葉捲成 | ‹*Má* ‹*kú* ‹*in*, yung² 'chí 'kün ‹in íp₂ ˏshing ˏt'ung, ‹ch'ui ‹chí; ngoi² ˏyéung tsak› 'í ‹in íp₂ 'kün ˏshing. |
| 61. *Cinnamon;* the best is from the frontiers of Cochinchina. | 玉桂以安邊者為佳 | *Yuk*₂ *kwai*', 'í ‹Ón ‹pín 'ché ˏwai ‹kái. |
| 62. *Clocks* report the hours and minutes. | 時辰鐘報時刻 | ˏ*Shí* ˏ*shan* ‹*chung*, pò' ˏshí hak›. |
| 63. All kinds of *cloth piece goods* * can be bought and sold for exportation only by the hong merchants. | 各色布疋可販賣出口惟洋商能之 | Kók› shik› *pò' p'at*›, 'hó fán' mái² ch'ut› 'hau, ˏwai ˏyéung ‹shéung ˏnang ‹chí. |
| 64. *Cloves* * † are of two distinct kinds, male and female. | 丁香有雌雄兩種不同 | ‹*Ting* ‹*héung*, 'yau ‹tsz' ˏhung, 'léung 'chung pat› ˏt'ung. |
| 65. *Cochineal* * † comes from foreign countries, and is used in dyeing. | 呀囒米來自外洋用以染色 | ˏ*Ngá* ‹*lán* '*mai*, ˏloi tsz'² ngoi² ˏyéung, yung² 'í 'ím shik›. |
| 66. *Cocoanuts* are produced in [the island of] Hainan. | 椰子出自海南 | ˏ*Yé* '*tsz'* ch'ut› tsz'² 'Hoi ˏnám. |
| 67. Foreign *coins* are made of copper, silver, and gold. | 番錢銅銀金皆為之 | ‹Fán ˏ*ts'ín*, ˏt'ung, ˏngan, ‹kam, ‹kái ˏwai ‹chí. |
| 68. *Commerce* is a trade extending to all places, far and near. | 貿易有遠近各處通商 | *Mau*² *yik*₂, 'yau 'ün kan², kók› ch'ü' ‹t'ung ‹shéung. |

59. Chunam is an Indian word for lime, but in China it is applied to a mixture of lime and oil, used for caulking boats and junks; the mixture of lime, sand, and oil, which is so commonly used in this country for floors and walks instead of a pavement is called *fúi shá*, or sanded lime.

64. Those cloves that are gathered before the corol of the flower is opened are called male cloves, and those after are termed female cloves.

65. *Ngá lán* is a dark crimson color, nearly the same as that produced from cochineal, and is applied to this article because of the color; *mái*, rice, here has the sense of a kernel or grain alluding to the shape. This, and a few other articles, being both imported and exported, have both marks attached to them.

69. *The compass* is used for determining direction, and distinguishing the four cardinal points.

羅經用以定向而分別四方

꜁*Ló ꜀king*, yung$^{2}$ ʿi ting$^{2}$ héung$^{2}$, ꜁í ꜀fan pít$_{2}$ sz$^{2}$ ꜀fóng.

70. *Contraband;* all nations have prohibitory regulations; whatever is carried in opposition to these is termed contraband.

犯禁凡國皆有例禁悖之者曰犯禁

*Fán$^{2}$ kam$^{2}$;* ꜁fán kwók꜄ ꜀kái ʿyau lai$^{2}$ kam$^{2}$, púi$^{2}$ ꜀chí ʿché, üt$_{2}$ fán$^{2}$ kam$^{2}$.

71. *Convoys* are vessels designed for protective service, to prevent piracies, and plundering of goods, on the high seas.

護貨船恐海中有賊刼貨故設以護之

*Ú$^{2}$ fó$^{2}$ ꜁shün,* ʿhung ʿhoi ꜀chung ʿyau tsák$_{2}$ kíp꜄ fó$^{2}$, kú$^{2}$ chʿít꜄ ʿi ú$^{2}$ ꜀chí.

72. *Foreign copper* † is of a light red color.

番銅其色淡紅

꜀*Fán ꜁tʿung*, ꜁kʿí shik꜄ tám$^{2}$ ꜁hung.

73. *Cordage* is made of hemp twisted together; when small it is called a cord; when large it is called a rope.

纜蔴草攪之小曰繩大曰纜

*Lám$^{2}$*, ꜁má ʿtsʿò ʿkáu ꜀chí; ʿsíu üt$_{2}$ ꜁shing, tái$^{2}$ üt$_{2}$ lám$^{2}$.

74. *Cornelians* (or agates) are of different colors, red, white, yellow, &c.

瑪瑙石有紅白黃等色

ʿ*Má* ʿ*nò* shik$_{2}$, ʿyau ꜁hung, pák$_{2}$, ꜁wóng, ʿtang shik꜄.

75. *Cotton* † from beyond sea, is in great abundance.

棉花外洋最盛

꜁*Mín* ꜀*fá*, ngoi$^{2}$ ꜁yéung tsui$^{2}$ shing$^{2}$.

76. *Crape* is made of silk by weaving, and has a crisped appearance.

縐紗以絲織成縐者也

*Tsau$^{2}$* ꜀*shá*, ʿi ꜀sz$^{2}$ chik꜄ ꜁shing tsau$^{2}$ ʿché ʿyá.

77. *Credit;* goods are said to be on credit, when they are received before the money is paid.

賒無銀而先取貨曰賒

꜀*Shé*, ꜁mò ꜁ngan ꜁í ꜀sín ʿtsʿü fó$^{2}$, üt$_{2}$ ꜀shé.

78. *A creditor* may appeal to government for the recovery of a debt, when the debtor has refused payment for three months after the term of agreement has expired.

債主如展限三月後欠者復不還則禀官押追

*Chái$^{2}$* ʿ*chü*, ꜁ü ʿchín hán$^{2}$ ꜀sám üt$_{2}$ hau$^{2}$, hím$^{2}$ ʿché fuk$_{2}$ pat꜄ ꜁wán, tsak꜄ ʿpan ꜀kún áp꜄ ꜀chui.

79. *Custom-houses* are established in order to prevent the evils of smuggling and the loss of duties.

關口設以查走私漏稅之弊

꜀*Kwán* ʿ*hau*, chʿít꜄ ʿi ꜁chʿá ʿtsau ꜀sz$^{2}$ lau$^{2}$ shui$^{2}$ ꜀chí pai$^{2}$.

80. *Cutch* † is used to dye cloth of an umber color.

兒茶用以染布其色赤

꜁*Í* ꜁*chʿá* yung$^{2}$ ʿi ʿím pò$^{2}$ ꜁kʿí shik꜄ ꜀chik꜄.

78. This regulation is contained in the penal code; but before three months have expired, recourse is often had to violent and oppressive measures for the recovery of debts. When a debtor absconds, it is usual for all his creditors to paste upon his door the bills and accounts which they hold against him. Sometimes the creditor, in lieu of money or goods, takes from the debtor his wives, sons, concubines, and daughters; but this procedure is not allowed by the laws of the empire, and is therefore not carried to a great extent.

81. *Cutlery* consists of iron utensils, which have a sharp edge.

利器即鐵器之利者也

*Lí hí*, tsik t'it hí ‹chí lí 'ché 'yá.

82. *Damaged goods;* all kinds of merchandise which have been drenched in water are called damaged goods.

水漬貨凡貨被水浸濕則曰水漬貨

'*Shui tsik fó*; ‹fán fó' pí 'shui tsam' shap, tsak üt 'shui tsik fó'.

83. *Damar* is used for covering packages of goods to prevent them from being damaged by water.

打嘛油包貨後用此塗上不妨水沾

'*Tá ‹má ‹yau*, ‹páu fó' hau yung 'ts'z ‹tò 'shéung, pat ‹fóng 'shui ‹chím.

84. *Damask* is of two kinds, linen and silk.

布緞皆有大花

Pò' tün ‹kái 'yau *tái ‹fá*.

85. *Day-book* is the blotter in which accounts are daily recorded; and because, like flowing water, it runs on from the beginning to the end of each day, it is therefore called a day-book.

流水簿即每日登記之草簿以其每日自上而下如流水故名

‹*Lau 'shui pò*, tsik 'múi yat ‹tang kí' ‹chí 'ts'ò pò', 'í ‹k'í 'múi yat tsz' shéung ‹í há ‹ü ‹lau 'shui, kú' ‹ming.

86. *Debtors*, who owe money to private individuals, and refuse to pay for three months, contrary to the terms of agreement, and the debts being above five taels, shall be punished with ten blows.

欠主其負欠私債違約不還者五兩以上違三月笞一十

*Hím' 'chü*, ‹k'í fú hím' ‹sz' chái', ‹wai yéuk pat ‹wán 'ché, 'ng 'léung 'í shéung, ‹wai ‹sám üt, ‹ch'í yat shap.

87. *Demurrage* is money paid for the detention [of a ship] beyond a specified time.

逾限銀即過限另加之銀也

*Ü hán ‹ngan*, tsik kwó' hán ling ‹ká ‹chí ‹ngan 'yá.

88. Foreign *dimity* † is so named because the cloth is woven with the figures in a diagonal form.

番斜紋布因經斜織之故

‹*Fán ‹ts'é ‹man pò*' ‹yau ‹king ‹ts'é chik ‹chí kú'.

89. *Discount* is the deduction made from a sum of money; in commercial transactions, when it is agreed that the deduction shall be eight or nine [parts from ten],

扣頭銀即除頭銀也買賣先言明八扣或九扣

*K'au' ‹t'au ‹ngan*, tsik ‹ch'ü ‹t'au ‹ngan 'yá; 'mái mái ‹sín ‹ín ‹ming pát k'au', wák 'kau k'au', ‹k'í ‹ü

---

82. This term, *shui tsik*, is applied to all goods which have been damaged by water while being transported from one place to another.

86. This punishment, according to Chinese law, is to go on increasing one degree each month, till it amounts to forty blows. Also, when the debt is fifty taels, the punishment is twenty blows; when one hundred taels, it is thirty blows.

89. The *pát k'au*, or [ten parts] diminished to eight, according to Chinese phraseology, is equivalent to a discount of twenty per cent.; and *kau k'au*, or nine diminishings, (i. e. ten diminished to nine,) is ten per cent.

| | | |
|---|---|---|
| the difference is called the discount. | 其餘銀則曰扣頭銀 | ngan, tsak, üt, k'au' t'au ngan. |
| 90. *Dividend;* in the prosecution of commerce, whether there be profit or loss, the division is made according to the capital invested. | 均攤貿易中不拘賺折以多少而分也 | *Kwan t'án,* mau yik, chung pat, k'ü chán chít, 'í tó 'shíú í fan 'yá. |
| 91. *Docks* are places in which ships are made fast for the purposes of repairing, for loading and unloading their cargoes. | 橫涌步頭乃修葺船與上落貨船停泊之所 | *Wáng ch'ung pò t'au* 'nái sau ts'ap, shün, 'ü 'shéung lók, fó' shün t'ing pók, chí 'shó. |
| 92. *Drawback;* the repayment of duties on goods which, not being sold, are re-shipped is so called. | 賠還稅銀乃貨未賣帶回故曰賠還 | *P'úi wán shui' ngan,* 'nái fó' mí máí tái' úi, kú' üt, p'úi wán. |
| 93. *Earnest money;* whoever purchases any goods must lay down some money to insure confidence, and to show that the engagement will not be broken. | 定銀凡買貨必落些銀以取信即定而不易意 | *Ting' ngan,* fán 'mái fó' pít, lók, sé ngan 'í 'ts'ü sun', tsik, ting' í pat, yik, í'. |
| 94. *Ebony* † is very hard and heavy. | 烏木而最堅重 | *Ú muk,* í tsui' kín chung. |
| 95. *Engrossing* is effected by buying up the whole amount of any commodity, and then raising the price to sell it at a high rate. | 囤積居奇凡貨必設法買盡然後高擡市價 | *T'ün tsik, kü k'í,* fán fó' pít, ch'ít, fát, 'mái tsun', ín hau' kò t'oi 'shí ká'. |
| 96. *Exports* are those goods which are carried abroad out of the ports of a country. | 出口貨物由本地出海口之貨 | *Ch'ut, 'hau fó' mat,* yau 'pún tí' ch'ut, 'hoi 'hau chí fó'. |
| 97. *Factor* is one who conducts the mercantile business of his friends at a distance. | 代辦商與遠友代辦買賣事者 | *Toi' pán' shéung,* 'ü 'ün 'yau toi' pán' 'mái mái' sz' 'ché. |
| 98. *Fairs* are markets, which are opened once in | 趁墟墟者市也 | *Ch'an' hü;* hü 'ché, 'shí |

90. The phrase *kwan t'án* includes a division of losses as well as profits; whatever is deficient on making up the balance sheet must be supplied by the partners.

92. The Chinese allow no drawback, but levy duties, not only on all exports to foreign countries, but even on goods which are shipped from one port to another in the empire itself; the whole system of drawbacks, bonding, and bounties, has no existence in this country.

95. Rich merchants not unfrequently endeavor to engross the trade in a particular article, by which they hope to realize profit; rice is a commodity very frequently bought up. The Chinese entertain the same prejudices against those who engross the trade in staple articles as the English did in former days, and the government always endeavors to cast odium upon the transaction.

| | | |
|---|---|---|
| several days; when at the appointed seasons people resort to them for the purpose of traffic. | 數日一次趁者及時到墟貿易之意 | 'yá; shò' yat, yat, tsz'' ch'an' 'ché, kap, shí tò' hü mau' yik, chí í'. |
| 99. *Fireworks* are curiously formed into boxes; and when they are set on fire, they are accompanied by crackers. | 烟火以盒載故事燒時有火炮隨之 | *Ín 'fó*, 'í hóp, tsoi' kú' sz'', shíú shí 'yau 'fó páu' ts'ui chí. |
| 100. *Fishmaws*† are among the dainties from the sea. | 魚肚皆是海味 | *Ü 't'ò* kái shí' 'hoi mí'. |
| 101. *Flints*† emit sparks on being struck by iron. | 火石以鐵擊之其火卽射 | *'Fó shik*, 'í t'ít, kik, chí k'í 'fó tsik, sh'é'. |
| 102. *Forestalling* is when one purchases the whole of an article, and then fixes his own price for it. | 壟斷居奇自網盡其貨而勒價 | *'Lung tün' kü k'í*, tsz'' 'móng tsun' k'í fó', í lak, ká'. |
| 103. *Freight* is the money which is paid for the transportation of goods by ship. | 水腳銀用船載貨之使用也 | *'Shui kéuk, ngan*, yung' shün tsoi' fó' chí 'sz' yung' 'yá. |
| 104. *Funds* are the original sums of money laid out in the purchase of goods. | 貨本卽買貨之本錢也 | *Fó' 'pún*, tsik, 'mái fó' chí 'pún ts'ín 'yá. |
| 105. *Furs* are the hairy skins of animals; fur dresses are these sewed into garments. | 皮獸之皮毛也裘則拚而成衣 | *P'í*, shau' chí p'í mò 'yá; k'au, tsak, p'ún í shing í. |
| 106. *Galangal** is produced in the province of Canton. | 良薑產粵東省 | *Léung kéung* 'ch'án Üt, tung 'sháng. |
| 107. *Galbanum* is a fragrant, resinous substance; its color is white, tinged with yellow. | 楓脂香卽白松香色白微黃 | *Fung chí héung*, tsik, pák, tsung héung, shik, pák, mí wóng. |
| 108. *Gall-nuts* have a light shell and break short; they are hollow, and are used, both when green and when dried, for giving black color. | 五棓子殼輕脆而中虛可以染皂或生或炒用 | *'Ng púi' 'tsz'*, hók, hing ts'ui', í chung hü, 'hó 'í 'ím tsò', wák, shang, wák, 'ch'au yung'. |
| 109. *Gambier* is a gelatinous substance used to size fishing-nets, and to dye cloth which is to be made into garments. | 薯莨用膠以漿罟網或膠布以爲衣服 | *Shü léung*, yung' káu 'í tséung 'kú 'móng, wák, káu pò' 'í wai í fuk,. |

99. With the Chinese these 'smoking fires' are worked into a great variety of toys, which have their appropriate names; but when spoken of in the gross, they are usually designated as above.

109. The gambier found in this market is not a product of China itself, being imported

| | | |
|---|---|---|
| 110.[1] *Gamboge* * is used in painting as a pigment. | 藤黃用以塗畫作色 | ˏ*Tʻang ˏwóng* yung[2] ʻí ˏtʻò wá[2] tsók˒ shik˒. |
| 111. *Gentian* has a bitter taste, and a yellow color. | 黃連味苦色黃 | ˏ*Wóng ˏlín* mí[2] ʻfú, shik˒ ˏwóng. |
| 112. Foreign *ginseng;* † that which comes from beyond sea is so designated; it is precisely the same as the native ginseng, differing from it in no way whatever. | 洋參以其由外洋而至故曰洋參實與本土土木人參無異 | ˏYéung ˎ*sham*, ʻí ˏkʻí ˏyau ngoi[2] ˏyéung ˏí chíˀ, kúˀ üt˒ ˏyéung ˎsham; shat˒ ʻü ʻpún ʻtʻò, ʻtʻò muk˒ ˏyan ˎsham ˏmò í[2]. |
| 113. *Glass stuff* † is used to make glass ware, such as tumblers, decanters, and dishes. | 燒料用作玻璃器杯罇器皿 | ˏ*Shíú líú*ˀ yung[2] tsók˒ ˎpó ˏlí híˀ, ˎpúi ˎtsan híˀ ʻming. |
| 114. *Glue* which is clear and translucent is the best. | 牛皮膠以明亮者爲佳 | ˏ*Ngau ˏpʻí ˎkáu* ʻí ˏming léungˀ ʻché ˏwai ˎkai. |
| 115. *Gums* are the juices of trees, obtained by cutting their bark. | 樹膠樹中之汁破皮而取之 | *Shü*[2] *ˎkáu*, shü[2] ˎchung ˎchí chap˒, pʻóˀ ˏpʻí ˏí ʻtsʻü ˎchí. |
| 116. *Gunpowder* is made of saltpetre, sulphur, and pine charcoal. | 火藥以硝磺杉炭爲之 | ʻ*Fó yéuk*[2], ʻí ˎsíú, ˏwóng, chʻámˀ tánˀ, ˏwai ˎchí. |
| 117. *Harbor* (or port) is a place surrounded by land, where houses are crowded together, and merchants assembled in great numbers. | 港口即人烟稠密客商雲集之處水口也 | ʻ*Kóng ʻhau*, tsik˒ ˏyan ˎín ˏchau mat[2], hák˒ ˎshéung ˏwan tsap[2], ˎchí chʻüˀ ʻshui ʻhau ʻyá. |
| 118. *Hardware;* implements and utensils made of iron are so called. | 鐵器以鐵打成器皿故名 | *Tʻít˒ híˀ*, ʻí tʻít˒ ʻtá ˏshing híˀ ʻming; kúˀ ˏming. |
| 119. *Hawkers* are those who go through the street, crying out that they have goods for sale. | 販仔即遊街喊賣貨者 | *Fánˀ ʻtsai*, tsik˒ ˏyau ˎkái hámˀ mái[2] fóˀ ʻché. |
| 120. *Hemp* is both coarse and fine; the former is made into cordage, while the latter is woven into various kinds of grass-cloth. | 胡蔴有粗幼粗則攬繩幼則織夏布等物 | ˏ*Ú ˏmá*, ʻyau ˎtsò yauˀ; ˎtsò, tsak˒ ʻkáu ˏshing; yauˀ, tsak˒ chik˒ há[2] pòˀ ʻtang mat[2]. |

from Singapore and other ports of the Archipelago; it is used by the poor as a cheap dye for coarse fabrics, producing a color resembling iron rust tinged with red.

117. The idea attached to the phrase *kóng hau* is that of a convenient anchorage for ships, where they can lie and receive cargo from the mart on shore, which is supposed to be a small unwalled village or at least not a walled city, and inhabited principally by merchants attracted thither for trade.

| | | |
|---|---|---|
| 121. *Hong* is a mercantile establishment; when a large building it is called a *hong*, when small a shop. | 行貿易之家大稱行小稱店 | ,*Hóng*, mau' yik, ,chí ,ká; tái' ,ching ,hóng, 'síú ,ching tím'. |
| 122. *Imports* are foreign goods. | 入口之貨即洋貨也 | *Yap, 'hau ,chí fó'*, tsik, ,yéung fó' 'yá. |
| 123. Bill of *indemnity*; this is an agreement which one makes, promising, in case he loses another's property, and is unable to return it, to replace its equivalent. | 賠補單如失人財物不能以原物還人則立單言明日賠補單 | ,*P'úi 'pò ,tán*, ,ü shat, ,yan ,ts'oi mat,, pat, ,nang 'í ,ün mat, ,wán ,yan, tsak, lap, ,tán ,ín ,ming, üt, ,p'úi 'pò ,tán. |
| 124. *Indian rubber* is tough and not easily broken, and letters written with a lead pencil can be rubbed out with it. | 抹紙膠肕而難斷鉛書之字抹之即去 | *Mút, 'chí ,káu* ngan', ,í ,nán tün', ,ün ,shü ,chí tsz' mút, ,chí tsik, h'ü'. |
| 125. Native *indigo* is a blue coloring stuff. | 土靛即青黛也 | '*Tò tín'*, tsik, ,ts'ing toi' 'yá. |
| 126. *Insurance companies* exist for securing ships, houses, and human life. | 擔保會乃保人船舍人命等事 | ,*Tám 'pò úi'*, 'nái 'pò ,yan ,shün shé' ,yan ming' 'tang sz'. |
| 127. *Interest* is a certain rate of profit on capital, paid monthly by the borrower for the use of money. | 利息以銀借人每月於本中生息也 | *Li' sik,*, 'í ,ngan tsé' ,yan 'múi üt, ,ü 'pún ,chung ,shang sik, 'yá. |
| 128. *Invoice* is a bill containing the description and prices of goods purchased in trade. | 貨單即買賣所書之貨價單也 | *Fó' ,tán*, tsik, 'mái mái' 'shó ,shü ,chí fó' ká' ,tán 'yá. |
| 129. *Foreign iron* † is as hard and firm as steel; it is made into plates and rods, and other forms. | 洋鐵堅硬如鋼造成板條欵式 | ,*Yéung t'it,* ,kín ngáng' ,ü kóng'; ts'ò' ,shing 'pán ,t'íú 'kún shik,. |
| 130. *Isinglass;* this is made of the sounds of fishes which are boiled till they become glue. | 魚膠取魚肚熬之成膠 | ,*Ü ,káu* 'ts'ü ,ü 't'ò ngò' ,chí ,shing ,káu. |
| 131. *Ivory* † is the tusks of the elephant. | 象牙象獸牙也 | *Tséung' ,ngá* tséung' shau' ,ngá 'yá. |
| 132. *Ivory cuttings* are valued according to their | 牙片價錢相應 | ,*Ngá pín'* ká' ,ts'ín ,séung ,ying. |
| 133. *Gum lac* † is used as a dye, and also for filling up the small crevices in cabinet-work. | 紫梗用和染料或補椅棹小孔 | '*Tsz' 'kang*, yung' ,wó 'ím líú', wák, 'pò 'í chéuk, 'síú 'hung. |

126. Under a despotic government like that of China, there is no sufficient security from governmental exactions, and consequently no mutual confidence among mercantile classes,

| | | |
|---|---|---|
| 134. *Gold and silver lace* is woven of gold and silver thread. | 金銀線帶以金銀線織成帶也 | *‹Kam ˏngan sín' tái'*, ʻí ‹kam ˏngan sín' chik› ˏshing tái' ʻyá. |
| 135. *Lackered ware* comprises such articles of furniture as are lackered, and sometimes gilded. | 漆器以漆抹其器皿外或描金 | *Ts'at› hí'*, ʻí ts'at› mút› ˏk'í hí' ʻming, ngoi$^2$ wák$_2$ ˏmúi ‹kam. |
| 136. *Lapis lazuli;* the color of this mineral is a light blue, and hence its name. | 青金共金之色畧青故名 | *‹Ts'ing ‹kam*, ˏk'í ‹kam ‹chí shik› léuk$_2$ ‹ts'ing, kú' ˏming. |
| 137. *Lead* † is obtained from the hills, and when alloyed with tin, is used in the manufacture of tea-canisters. | 鉛出山中與錫類彷彿用作茶罐等物 | *ˏÜn*, ch'ut› ‹shán ‹chung, ʻü sik› lui$^2$ ʻfóng fat›, yung$^2$ tsók› ˏch'á kún' ʻtang mat$_2$. |
| 138. *Leger* (or General Book) is that into which the accounts of receipts and expenditures, being summed up and brought together, are transferred and preserved. | 總簿即收支截數埋總存貯過數之簿 | *ʻTsung pò$^2$*, tsik› ‹shau ‹chí tsít$_2$ shò', ˏmái ʻtsung ˏts'ün ʻch'ü kwó' shò' ‹chí pò$^2$. |
| 139. *License* is a paper so called, which being examined allows one to proceed (or act). | 牌請驗放行之紙曰牌 | *ˏP'ái*, ʻts'ing ím$^2$ fóng' ˏhang ‹chí ʻchí, üt$_2$ ˏp'ái. |
| 140. *A lighthouse* is a building for ships to see; it is built on the seashore, and resembles a pagoda; a fire is placed within which shines afar, and ships on seeing it know they are near land. | 光樓即船望樓建海傍如塔內設燈火遠照船見以知近岸 | *‹Kwóng ˏlau*, tsik› ˏshün móng$^2$ ˏlau; kín$^2$ ʻhoi ˏp'óng ˏü t'áp›; noi$^2$ ch'ít› ‹tang ʻfo ʻün chíú' ˏshün kín$^2$ ʻí ‹chí kan$^2$ ngón$^2$. |
| 141. *Linen* is the cloth which is woven from hemp. | 蔴布以蔴織成之布也 | *ˏMá pò'*, ʻí ˏmá chik› ˏshing ‹chí pò' ʻyá. |
| 142. *The loadstone* attracts iron; a vulgar name is *shíp shik*. | 磁石能攝鐵俗名攝石 | *ˏTs'z' shik$_2$* ˏnang shíp› t'ít›; suk$_2$ ˏming *shíp› shik$_2$*. |
| 143. *Madder* has a bitter taste and a carnation color. | 丹參味苦赤色 | *‹Tán ‹sham*, mí$^2$ ʻfú, ch'ik› shik›. |
| 144. *Manifests* are given by custom-house officers, signifying that goods, having been examined, may pass. | 牌照官給以爲關隘驗貨放行 | *ˏP'ái chíú'*, ‹kún kap› ʻí ˏwai ‹kwán ái', ím$^2$ fó' fóng' ˏhang. |
| 145. *A market* is a place where all sorts of goods are collected together for sale. | 市乃各貨雲集之所 | *ʻShí*, ʻnái kók› fó' ˏwan tsap$_2$ ‹chí ʻshó. |

both of which are indispensably requisite to establish associations like our insurance companies, and they are of course unknown.

| | | |
|---|---|---|
| 146. ***Mats*** are made of straw or rattans. | 蔗草藤等爲之 | *T'sik*₂ 'ts'ò ,t'ang 'tang ,wai ,chí. |
| 147. ***Molasses*** is made from white sugar; into the sediment which is left from boiling, the *kat* and other fruits are preserved, whence the name. | 桔水糖做白糖<br>剩之糖底以爲<br>浸桔果因爲名 | *Kat*, *'shui ,t'óng* tsò² pák² ,t'óng shing² ,chí ,t'óng 'tai 'í ,wai cham² kat, 'kwó ,yan ,wai ,ming. |
| 148. ***Molasses glue*** is made by melting sugar, and stirring it till it is cold and forms a glue. | 糖膠將糖鎔化<br>攪冷成膠 | *,T'óng ,káu* ,tséung ,t'óng ,yung fá' 'káu 'lang ,shing ,káu. |
| 149. ***Monopoly*** is a traffic carried on by a single party, which is allowed to trade in articles, while others are not allowed so to do. | 獨市生意其貨<br>只自己有而別<br>人無者是也 | *Tuk*₂ *'shí ,shang í'*, ,k'í fò' 'chat tsz'² 'kí 'yau, ,í pít₂ ,yan ,mò 'ché shí² 'yá. |
| 150. ***Mortgage*** houses to other people. | 典當房舍與人 | *'Tín* tóng' ,fóng shé' 'ü ,yan. |
| 151. ***Mother o' Pearl**** is used to make fancy articles. | 雲母殼造玩物 | *,Wan 'mò* hók, ts'ò' ún² mat₂. |
| 152. ***Musk*** is from a species of deer; it is the fragrant navel of the animal. | 麝香麝乃鹿類<br>此獸之香臍也 | *Shé² ,héung;* shé² 'nái luk₂ lui'; 'ts'z' shau' ,chí ,héung ,ts'z' 'yá. |
| 153. ***Myrrh*** † is brought from southern countries; it has a flesh color, and is classed with amber. | 没藥出南洋色<br>赤類琥珀 | *Mút₂ yéuk*₂, ch'ut, ,nám ,yéung, shik, ch'ik,, lui² 'fú pák,. |
| 154. ***Nankeen*** is a carnation colored cloth; it is woven of cotton of that color, and hence its name. | 紫花布即赤布<br>也其綿色紫者<br>織之故名 | *'Tsz' ,fá pò'*, tsik, ch'ik, pò', 'yá; ,k'í ,mín shik, 'tsz' 'ché chik, ,chí, kú' ,ming. |
| 155. ***Nutmegs,**** † also called gem fruit, have a white color; those from abroad are the best. | 荳蔻又名玉菓<br>色白外洋者良 | *Tau² k'au'* yau² ,ming yuk₂ 'kwó, shik, pák,; ngoi² ,yéung 'ché ,léung. |
| 156. ***Nux vomica*** is poisonous, and if eaten by dogs it will certainly cause their death. | 馬前有毒犬食<br>必死 | *'Má ,ts'ín* 'yau tuk₂, 'hün shik₂ pít, 'sz'. |
| 157. ***Olibanum*** † resembles milk; the foreign and transparent is the best. | 乳香形如乳頭<br>外洋明透者艮 | *'Yü ,héung* ,ying ,ü 'yü ,t'au; ngoi² ,yéung ,ming t'au' 'ché ,léung. |

148. This substance is made from the *wóng t'óng* or yellow sugar, which is the purest sugar the Chinese have, by inspissating it till very thick, and then stirring it in the air; it is used in joining lackered ware and other fine work, and is said to resist dampness better than common glue.

154. The English term nankeen is derived from the city of Nanking in the province of Kóngsú, where this cloth is extensively manufactured. It is made of unbleached cotton, *tsz' fá* being an elliptical expression for the flower of the cotton plant, which is the origin of the Chinese name.

| | | |
|---|---|---|
| 158. *Olives*, called the green fruit, are large in the middle, and sharp-pointed at both ends. | 欖一名青菓中大而兩頭尖 | '*Lám*, yat› ꜀ming ‹ts'ing 'kwó, ‹chung tái[2], ꜀í 'léung ꜀t'au ‹tsím. |
| 159. *Opium* is also called *6fúyung;* the flower resembles that of the Hibiscus, whence its name. | 鴉片又名阿芙蓉其花似芙蓉因名之 | ‹*Á p'ín*' yau[2] ꜀ming ‹ó ꜀fú ꜀yung; ꜀k'í ‹fá 'ts'z' ꜀fú ꜀yung, ‹yan ꜀ming ‹chí. |
| 160. *Paper* is made by reducing bamboo to a pulp in a mortar. | 紙以漚爛竹舂而作之 | '*Chí*, ꜀í au' lán[2] chuk› ‹chung ꜀í tsók› ‹chí. |
| 161. *A parcel;* whatever things are bound up together, form a parcel. | 一包各物包束裝成是也 | *Yat› ‹páu;* kók› mat[2] ‹páu chuk› ‹chóng ꜀shing shí' 'yá. |
| 162. *Partner* is the joint owner of capital, which is employed in commerce. | 夥伴者即合本做生意之人也 | '*Fó pún*[2] '*ché*, tsik› hop[2] 'pún tsò[2] ‹shang í' ‹chí ꜀yan 'yá. |
| 163. *Pass* is a place at which goods, &c., must all undergo examination, after which they may pass. | 關津之所必須盤驗而後放行 | ‹*Kwán* ‹*tsun* ‹chí 'shó, pít› ‹sü ꜀pún ím[2] ꜀í hau[2] fóng' ꜀hang. |
| 164. *Passenger* is one who goes as a friend in a ship. | 搭客附船同行之人 | *Táp› hák›*, fú[2] ꜀shün ꜀t'ung, ꜀hang ‹chí ꜀yan. |
| 165. *Passport* is a license bearing the official seals of government. | 紅牌乃有官印之牌照也 | ꜀*Hung* ꜀*p'ái* 'nái 'yau ‹kún yan' ‹chí ꜀p'ái chíú' 'yá. |
| 166. *A pattern*, that is a model or an examplar. | 樣子即規模也 | *Yéung*[2] '*tsz*', tsik› ‹kw'ai ꜀mò 'yá. |
| 167. *A pawnbroker* is one who lends money on a pledge or deposit of goods. | 當舖人以物押然後借銀者 | *Tóng*' *p'ò*' ꜀*yan*, 'í mat[2] át›, ꜀ín hau[2] tsé' ꜀ngan 'ché. |
| 168. *Pearls* are precious beads. | 珍珠珍寶珠也 | ‹*Chan* ‹*chü*, ‹chan 'pò ‹chü 'yá. |
| 169. *Pencils* are used for writing, and are made of bamboo stems and wolf's hair. | 筆書字者也以竹竿狼毛作之 | *Pat*›, ‹shü tsz[2] 'ché 'yá; 'í chuk› ‹kón ꜀lóng ꜀mò tsók› ‹chí. |
| 170. *Pens* (or goosequill pencils) are made of the barrels of goosequills, which being cut down to a point, and tipped with ink are used in writing. | 鵞毛筆以鵞毛管削成貫墨水書之 | ꜀*Ngó* ꜀*mò pat*›, 'í ꜀ngó ꜀mò 'kún séuk› ꜀shing, kún' mak[2] 'shui ‹shü ‹chí. |

163. A *kwán* is a pass on shore, a guard-house on the borders of two provinces, where persons and goods are examined; custom-houses are called *kwán hau*, the mouth or opening to the *kwán; tsun* is a ford, or the narrow entrance of a river, at which persons or vessels arrive on their way to a *kwán:* the phrase here used occurs in the Penal Code to express both internal and external passes.

| | | |
|---|---|---|
| 171. *Pepper* † has an exceedingly acrid taste. | 胡椒其味甚辣 | ꜁*Ú* ꜀*tsiú*, ꜁k'í mí꜅ sham꜅ lát꜇. |
| 172. *Porcelain* is made of earthy substances, and burnt in the fire. | 磁器以土爲之後燒以火 | ꜁*Ts'z' hí*꜄, ꜃í ꜂t'ò ꜁wai ꜀chí, hau꜅ ꜀shíú ꜃í ꜂fó. |
| 173. *Porters* are persons who carry cargo. | 挑夫挑貨之人 | ꜀*T'íú* ꜀*fú*, ꜀t'íú fó꜄ ꜀chí ꜁yan. |
| 174. *Postage* is the money which is paid to the carrier of letters. | 信資以錢謝帶信之人也 | *Sun*꜄ ꜀*tsz*꜄, ꜃í ꜁ts'ín tsé꜅ tái꜄ sun꜄ ꜀chí ꜁yan ꜃yá. |
| 175. *Posting of accounts;* this is taking the accounts of the day-book, and, having arranged them in chronological order, transferring them to a leger. | 過數日中草簿之數隨時分別另抄過大簿也 | *Kwó*꜄ *shò*꜄, yat꜇ ꜀chung ꜂ts'ò pò꜅ ꜀chí shò꜄, ꜁ts'ui ꜁shí ꜀fan pít꜇ ling꜅ ꜀ch'áu kwó꜄ tái꜅ pò꜅ ꜃yá. |
| 176. *Price current* is a paper, which, having the current prices of goods put down in order, is circulated for general information. | 時價紙將貨以現今價錢列紙上派人觀覽 | ꜁*Shí ká*꜄ ꜂*chí*, ꜀tséung fó꜄ ꜃í ín꜅ ꜀kam ká꜄ ꜁ts'ín lít꜇ ꜂chí shéung꜅ p'ái꜄ ꜁yan ꜀kún ꜃lám. |
| 177. *Prussian blue* † is of a delicate blue color, and is manufactured from cowhides. | 洋靛色藍而嬌出於牛皮中 | ꜁*Yéung tín*꜅ shik꜆ ꜁lám ꜁í ꜀kíú, ch'ut꜆ ꜀ü ꜁ngau ꜁p'í ꜀chung. |
| 178. *Putchuck* † has a white color, an aromatic taste, and is used as a medicine. | 木香色白味香可入藥 | *Muk*꜇ ꜀*héung*, shik꜆ pák꜇, mí꜅ ꜀héung, ꜂hó yap꜇ yéuk꜇. |
| 179. *Quicksilver* * † is vulgarly said to be the concrete effluence of the hills. | 水銀俗云山之精而結 | ꜂*Shui* ꜁*ngan*, suk꜇ ꜁wan ꜀shán ꜀chí ꜀ts'ing ꜁í kít꜆. |
| 180. *Raisins* are of two kinds, red and white. | 菩提乾有紫白兩種 | ꜁*P'ò* ꜁*t'ai* ꜀*kón* ꜃yau ꜂tsz' pák꜇, ꜃léung ꜂chung. |
| 181. *Rattans* † are brought from abroad, and are used for binding up packages of goods. | 沙藤來外洋用以綑束貨物 | ꜀*Shá* ꜁*t'ang*, ꜁loi ngoi꜅ ꜁yéung yung꜅ ꜃í ꜂kwan ch'uk꜆ fó꜄ mat꜇. |

174. There is no public post in China except for the use of government, but there are numbers of well-known and trustworthy persons who are employed as letter carriers between towns and villages, and who in a manner supply the absence of a regular post. There are places sometimes appointed where letters can be left for the postman, and he is not unfrequently seen, with a letter bag on his back marked with the place of his destination, passing through the street and calling for letters. The charge for postage is light; between Canton and Macao it will average for single letters about thirty cash.

177. Prussian blue is called the foreign blue dye in distinction from indigo, and because it was formerly imported into China from England. The manufacture of it at Canton was introduced by a Chinese, who frequented the shops in London where it was made and learned the process thoroughly, and on his return established a manufactory, whose products have now entirely superseded the importation.

| | | |
|---|---|---|
| 182. *Receipt* is a paper which a person, who has received money or goods from any one, gives him in return to be kept in evidence thereof. | 收單收到銀兩或貨物寫一紙交來人拿回以爲凭 | ꜀*Shau* ꜀*tán*, ꜀shau tò' ꜁ngan 'léung, wák꜇ fó' mat꜇, 'sé yat꜆ 'chí ꜀káu ꜁loí ꜁yan ꜁ná ꜁úi, ꜃í ꜁wai ꜁p'ang. |
| 183. *Register* of a ship's crew; on leaving the port, this is drawn up and presented to the custom-house officers for examination, to be inspected and verified. | 船丁册出口船錄此呈驗以凭稽核 | ꜁*Shün* ꜀*ting* *ch'ák*꜆; ch'ut꜆ 'hau ꜁shün luk꜇ 'ts'z' ꜁ch'ing ím꜅, ꜃í ꜁p'ang ꜀k'ai hat꜇. |
| 184. *Report of a ship's cargo;* on entering the port this is drawn up and presented to the custom-house officers, that they may know the amount of cargo. | 報貨單入口船錄此呈閱以便知貨多少 | *Pò' fó'* ꜀*tán;* yap꜇ 'hau ꜁shün luk꜇ 'ts'z' ꜁ch'ing üt꜇, ꜃í pín꜅ ꜀chí fó' ꜀tó 'shíú. |
| 185. *Rhubarb* * has a yellow color, and removes disease. | 大黃色黃解毒 | *Tái*꜅ ꜁*wóng* shik꜆ ꜁wóng 'kái tuk꜇. |
| 186. *Rice;* when the paddy is deprived of the husk it is called rice. | 米將穀而碾其皮曰米 | ꜃*Mai*, ꜀tséung kuk꜆ ꜁í 'chín ꜁k'í ꜁p'í, üt꜇ ꜃mai. |
| 187. *Ropes;* these are made either of hemp or grass, by being twisted together. | 繩索或蔴或草攪埋曰繩索 | ꜁*Shing sók*꜆, wák꜇ ꜁má, wák꜇ 'ts'ò 'káu ꜁mai; üt꜇ ꜁shing sók꜆. |
| 188. *Rose maloes,* † if rubbed upon the person, will remove distempers. | 蘇合酒搽之可以敺風 | ꜀*Sú hóp*꜇ ꜃*yau* ꜁ch'á ꜀chí 'hó ꜃í ꜀k'ü ꜀fung. |
| 189. *Rosin* * is the gum of the pine. | 松香即松脂膏 | ꜁*Tsung* ꜀*héung*, tsik꜆ ꜁tsung ꜀chí ꜀kò. |
| 190. *Sago* † is also called *shákuk* grain. | 西米即砂穀米 | ꜀*Sai* ꜃*mai*, tsik꜆ ꜀shá kuk꜆ ꜃mai. |
| 191. *Salt* is made by evaporating salt water to dryness. | 塩以鹹水晒乾作之 | ꜁*Ím*, ꜃í ꜁hám 'shui shái' ꜀kón tsók꜆ ꜀chí. |
| 192. *Saltpetre* is obtained from walls after a long time, which when lixiviated produce it. | 硝牆日久即有煎而後出 | ꜀*Síú*, ꜁tséung yat꜇ 'kau tsik꜆ ꜃yau tsín' ꜁í hau꜅ ch'ut꜆. |
| 193. *Sample* is a pattern after which a thing must be made. | 樣子即規模定式也 | *Yéung*꜅ *'tsz'*, tsik꜆ ꜀kw'ai ꜁mò ting꜅ shik꜆ ꜃yá. |

191, 192. The manufacture and sale of salt is a governmental monopoly, in the hands of a distinct department, whose agents are found in every maritime place to enforce the laws against making it, and to carry on the trade in it; in consequence of its high price, the poorer Chinese endeavor in all possible ways to economize its use. Saltpetre, powder, bows and arrows, cannon, and whatever pertains to military affairs are prohibited as articles of trade in this market.

| | | |
|---|---|---|
| 194. ***Sandal wood*** † is exceedingly fragrant when burnt. | 檀香木燒之極香 | ‚*T'án ‹héung muk*, ‹shiú ‹chí kik, ‹héung. |
| 195. ***Sapan wood*** † is of a red color, and is used as a dyestuff. | 蘇木色赤用作染料 | ‹*Sò muk*, shik, ch'ik, yung² tsók, 'ím líú². |
| 196. ***Seamen*** are the sailors who work the ship. | 水手即駕船之水梢人也 | '*Shui 'shau*, tsik, ká' ‚shün ‹chí 'shui ‹sháu ‚yan 'yá. |
| 197. ***Seaweed*** † is boiled into a glue for use. | 海菜煮成膠用 | '*Hoi ts'oi*' 'chü ‚shing ‹káu yung². |
| 198. A man affording ***security*** is one who is able to stand surety for another, and for whose good conduct he engages to hold himself responsible. | 擔保人乃一力擔當認保其人無不善之事 | ‹*Tám 'pò ‚yan*, 'nái yat, lik, ‹tám ‹tóng, yan² 'pò ‚k'í ‚yan ‚mò pat, shín' ‹chí sz'². |
| 199. ***Settlement of accounts;*** to take an account of that which is owed, and pay it, is so called. | 清數將所欠之賬還足之謂 | ‹*Ts'ing shò'*; ‹tséung, 'shó hím' ‹chí chéung' ‚wáu tsuk, ‹chí wai². |
| 200. ***Shark's fins;*** † are the fins on both sides of the fish by which it propels itself in the water; when washed clean and cooked thoroughly, they are eatable. | 魚翅魚身兩傍之翅藉以棹水洗淨烹調可食 | ‚*Ü ch'í*', ‚ü ‹shan 'léung ‚p'óng ‹chí ch'í', tsik, 'í cháu² 'shui; 'sai tsing² ‹p'ang ‚t'íú 'hó shik,. |
| 201. ***Signboards*** are wooden boards placed on warehouses and shops to invite men to buy and sell goods. | 招牌乃行店招人買賣貨木牌 | ‹*Chíú ‚p'ái*, 'nái ‚hóng tím' ‹chíú ‚yan 'mái mái' fó' muk, ‚p'ái. |
| 202. ***Silks*** * are a general name for satins, crapes, &c. | 絲髮綢紗總名 | ‹*Sz' fát*, ‚chau ‹shá 'tsung ‚ming. |
| 203. Every kind of ***skins*** † are restricted to the hong merchants. | 各項皮張皆歸洋商所辦 | Kók, hóng² ‚p'í ‹chéung ‹kái ‹kwai ‚yéung ‹shéung 'shó pán². |
| 204. ***Smalts*** † have a very deep blue color, and are used to paint flowers upon porcelain. | 大青其色深藍以畫磁器花草 | *Tái² ‹ts'ing* ‚k'í shik, ‹sham ‚lám, 'í wák, ‚ts'z' hí' ‹fá 'ts'ò. |
| 205. ***Snuff*** is fine as dust, and inhaled into the nose. | 鼻烟幼如末以鼻吸之 | *Pí² ‹ín* yau' ‚ü mút, 'í pí² hap, ‹chí. |

201. Great variety is displayed in the signboards of Chinese shops, and some of them are elegant; they are usually hung or placed upright at the side of the street, having the name of the shop at the top, and the list of wares for sale beneath; and by alternation of colors in the characters, or diversity in the style of writing, the shopman endeavors to attract customers.

203. The importation of skins and furs into Canton has fallen off in the last few years, owing rather to the gradual decrease of the supply from abroad, than to any diminished demand. Rabbit, seal, sea and land otter, fox, and beaver skins constitute the greater part of the importations. Lamb skins from Tartary are also much used by the Chinese for dresses.

| | | |
|---|---|---|
| 206. *Soap* comes from foreign countries, and is used in baths for cleansing the body. | 番鹼來外洋浴身極去垢 | *‹Fán ‘kán*, ‹loi ngoi$^{2}$ ‹yéung, yuk$_{2}$ ‹shan kik$_{2}$ h‘ü$^{2}$ ‘kau. |
| 207. *Soy* is made by exposing black [soy] beans in the heat of the sun, and then boiling them in water, and adding aromatics of various sorts, after which the liquid is strained off. | 豉油以黑荳向日晾過熬水再加香料等然後取其湛下之水 | *Shí$^{2}$ ‹yau* ‘í hak› tau$^{2}$ héung$^{2}$ yat$_{2}$ lóng$^{2}$ kwó$^{2}$, ngò$^{2}$ ‘shui tsoi$^{2}$ ‹ká ‹héung líú$^{2}$ ‘tang, ‹sín hau$^{2}$ ‘ts‘ü ‹k‘í sham$^{2}$ há$^{2}$ ‹chí ‘shui. |
| 208. *Spermaceti* is obtained by boiling the blubber of the whale. | 鯨油以鯨脂煎油也 | *‹King ‹yau*, ‘í ‹king ‹chí ‹tsín ‹yau ‘yá. |
| 209. *Spices* are aromatics which are used to improve the taste of food. | 香物以製味之馨香也 | *‹Héung mat$_{2}$*, ‘í chai$^{2}$ mí$^{2}$ ‹chí ‹hing ‹héung ‘yá. |
| 210. *Spirits:* by well mixing yeast cakes in boiled rice, and after the mass has risen, distilling it in an inverted position, the spirit will flow off. | 酒以米飯猜酒餅醱透而蒸其倒汗水即酒也 | *‘Tsau*, ‘í ‘mai fán$^{2}$ ‹ch‘ái ‘tsau ‘ping, fát› t‘au$^{2}$ ‹í ‹ching ‹k‘í tò$^{2}$ hón$^{2}$ ‘shui, tsik› ‘tsau ‘yá. |
| 211. *Steel;* † this is hardened iron. | 鐵鋼鐵之堅者 | *T‘ít› ‹kóng*, t‘ít› ‹chí ‹kín ‘ché. |
| 212. *Sugar** is boiled from the sweet cane. | 糖以甘蔗熬成 | *‹T‘óng*, ‘í ‹kóm ché$^{2}$ ngò$^{2}$ ‹shing. |
| 213. *Sugar candy** is crystalized white like ice. | 冰糖結白似冰 | *‹Ping ‹t‘óng*, kít› pák$_{2}$ ‘ts‘z$^{2}$ ‹ping. |
| 214. *Sulphur;* pulverized brimstone is so called. | 硫磺粉以硫磺研末曰粉 | *‹Lau ‹wóng ‘fan*, ‘í ‹lau ‹wóng ‹ín mút$_{2}$, üt$_{2}$ ‘fan. |
| 215. *Tariff* is a list of goods with the duties required thereon at the customhouse. | 則例關稅貨物之定例銀也 | *Tsak› lai$^{2}$*, ‹kwán shui$^{2}$ fó$^{2}$ mat$_{2}$ ‹chí ting$^{2}$ lai$^{2}$ ‹ngan ‘yá. |
| 216. *Tea** boiled in water affords a beverage. | 茶葉泡滾水然後飲 | *‹Ch‘á íp$_{2}$*, p‘áu$^{2}$ ‘kwan ‘shui ‹sín hau$^{2}$ ‘yam. |
| 217. *Thread* is spun out of silk and hemp. | 線以絲蔴搓成 | *Sín$^{2}$*, ‘í ‹sz ‹má ‹ch‘ó ‹shing. |
| 218. *Gold and silver thread*† is made by winding gold and silver around silk into a thread. | 金銀線以金銀裹絲成線也 | *‹Kam ‹ngan sín$^{2}$*, ‘í ‹kam ‹ngan ‘kwó ‹sz ‹shing sín$^{2}$ ‘yá. |
| 219. *Tin*† is alloyed with copper and iron to make various utensils. | 錫侵銅鐵可作器皿 | *Sik›* ‹ts‘am ‹t‘ung t‘ít› ‘hó tsók› hí$^{2}$ ‘ming. |

207. *Dolichos soja* is the bean usually employed for the principal ingredient of soy, but the variety, and the quantity of the spices which are added accounts in a good degree for the

| | | |
|---|---|---|
| 220. *Tin plates* come from abroad, and are made of tin and iron. | 馬口鐵出自來<br>路以錫鐵而成 | *'Má 'hau t'ít*, ch'ut, tsz'² ˌloi lò² 'í sik, t'ít, ˌí ˌshing. |
| 221. *Tonnage* of a ship is its measurement, taken so as to know how much cargo it will contain. | 艙量丈量其艙<br>知貨多少 | *ˌCh'óng ˌléung*, chéung² ˌléung ˌk'í ˌch'óng ˌchí fò' ˌtó 'shíú. |
| 222. *Tortoiseshell* is from the turtle, whose shell is procured to make articles. | 玳瑁即鼈取其<br>甲以爲器 | *Toi² múi²*, tsik, pít, 'ts'ü ˌk'í káp, 'í ˌwai hí'. |
| 223. *Treaty* is an agreement between two nations, respecting their mutual intercourse. | 相約兩國相約<br>共事也 | *ˌSéung yéuk*, 'léung kwók, ˌséung yéuk, kung² sz'² 'yá. |
| 224. *Trial balance;* in length of time accounts must become complicated, therefore, in order to prevent mistakes and confusions, they ought to be summed up and balanced at short intervals. | 截數數目日久<br>必多恐錯亂難<br>計故以即截止<br>其數而埋總 | *Tsít₂ shò'*, shò' muk₂ yat₂ 'kau pít, ˌtó, 'hung ts'ò' lün' ˌnán kai', kú' 'í tsik, tsít₂ 'chí ˌk'í shò' ˌí ˌmái 'tsung. |
| 225. *Tripang*, [meaning] gems of the sea, is served up as an article of food at feasts. | 海參海珍也用<br>以上筵爲饌 | *'Hoi ˌsham*, 'hoi ˌchun 'yá; yung² 'í 'shéung ˌín ˌwai chán². |
| 226. *Tutenague** is used to make utensils. | 白鉛以作器用 | *Pák₂ ˌün*, 'í tsók, hí' yung². |
| 227. *Verdigris;* when copper remains unused for a long time, verdigris collects upon it. | 銅綠銅貯日久<br>即生綠 | *ˌT'ung luk₂*, ˌt'ung 'ch'ü yat₂ 'kau tsik, ˌshang luk₂. |
| 228. *Vermilion;* * quicksilver is heated until it flakes, and then by triturating, it becomes vermilion. | 硍硃水銀製鍊<br>成塊磨爲硍硃 | *ˌNgan ˌchü*, 'shui ˌngan chai' lín² ˌshing fái', mó² ˌwai ˌngan ˌchü. |
| 229. *Blue vitriol* is made by combining sulphur and copper. | 膽礬乃銅與硫<br>磺合而爲之 | *'Tám ˌfán*, 'nái ˌt'ung 'ü ˌlau ˌwong hop, ˌí ˌwai ˌchí. |
| 230. *Walking sticks* are made of the culms of bamboo. | 竹竿即竹枝幹 | *Chuk, ˌkón*, tsik, chuk, ˌchí kón'. |
| 231. *Watches* are brought from foreign countries. | 時辰標乃外洋<br>所來之物 | *ˌShí ˌshan ˌpíú*, 'nái ngoi² ˌyéung 'shó ˌloi ˌchí mat₂. |
| 232. *Whanghees* are the roots of bamboo beneath the earth. | 竹強即竹頭入<br>地之根 | *Chuk, 'k'éung*, tsik, chuk, ˌt'au yap₂ tí² ˌchí ˌkan. |

great diversity of quality found in this article; annisseed stars are added as one of the aromatics, but soy, among the Chinese, is made by different manufacturers to suit various tastes.

220. This name is given to tin plates from the use made of them in stopping up holes, and binding seams together, the colloquial term for that being *má hau*, quasi, riding the hole.

| | | |
|---|---|---|
| 233. ***Wharf*** is a high bank beside of which boats and ships anchor. | 渡頭渡船所抵之岸 | *Tò$^{2}$ ˏt'au*, tò$^{2}$ ˏshün ‘shó ‘tai ˎchí ngón$^{2}$. |
| 234. ***Wool*** is bought and sold for the manufacture of cloths and blankets. | 綿羊毛販賣與人作呢毡 | *ˏMín ˏyéung ˏmò*, fán’ mái$^{2}$ ‘ü ˏyan tsók˒ ˏní ˎchín. |
| 235. ***Woolens*** † are divided into broad and narrow kinds. | 哆囉絨即大小呢之總名 | *ˎTó ˏló ˏyung*, tsik˒ tái$^{2}$ ‘síú ˏní ˎchí ‘tsung ˏming. |
| 236. ***Zinc***, lead and black-lead are three sorts of metals, and their names are to be distinguished. | 白鉛鉛黑鉛乃三金分而名之 | *Pák$_{2}$ ˏün*, ˏün, hak˒ ˏün, ‘nái ˎsám ˎkam ˎfan ˏí ˏming ˎchí. |

236. Zinc, spelter, and tutenague are all called *pák ün*, the Chinese supposing from the color that they are merely varieties of lead.

## Section Third.

## REGULATIONS RESPECTING PILOTS.

### 引水章程第三章

‘Yan ‘shui ˎchéung ˏching; tai$^{2}$ ˎsám ˎchéung.

| | | |
|---|---|---|
| 1. All merchants who come from other countries to Canton, to engage in commerce, ought, as soon as the ship makes the land, to engage the services of some one who is thoroughly acquainted with the entrance of the river, then they may venture to make their way into the embouchure. It is necessary to obtain an outside pilot, | 各國客商來粵貿易船到見岸必請熟識水路之人方敢進港因山水口深淺不定是以必請 | Kók˒ kwók˒ hák˒ ˎshéung ˏloi Ut$_{2}$ mau$^{2}$ yik$_{2}$, ˏshün tò’ kín’ ngón$^{2}$, pít˒ ‘ts‘ing shuk$_{2}$ shik˒ ‘shui lò$^{2}$ ˎchí ˏyan, ˎfóng ‘kóm tsun’ ‘kóng. ˏYan ˎshán ‘shui ‘hau, ˎsham ‘tsín pat˒ ting$^{2}$, shí$^{2}$ ‘í pít˒ ‘ts‘ing ngoi$^{2}$ ˏyéung tái’ ‘shui. |

### *Notes and Explanations.*

THESE regulations are few and simple. The pilots—usually fourteen in number, but now (Feb. 1839) sixteen—obtain their licenses from the *kwanman fú*, the sub-prefect of Ts‘ínshán or Casa Branca, with the sanction of the governor at Canton, on the payment of eight hundred or a thousand dollars. Most of them live in Macao or its vicinity, but have associates at Canton and Whampoa.

1. In the early periods of the foreign trade to China, it was customary for merchants to come and to return in their ships with their merchandize, as supercargoes; the phraseology is here framed to suit that usage, although the practice of having supercagoes is nearly discontinued, the trade being for the most part conducted by resident merchants.

because the depth of the water among the islands is not uniform. The men, who are now employed as [outside] pilots, are persons engaged in the fishing-smacks.

外洋帶水其帶水之人即今之漁艇是也

K'í tái' 'shui chí yan, tsik kam chí ü 'ting shí' 'yá.

2. The amount of compensation, which they are to receive, ought to be distinctly specified when they are engaged; it may vary from ten or twenty to fifty or more dollars, and should be regulated according to the state of the weather, as it may be fair or foul; but in all cases it should be distinctly agreed on, [by the captain and pilot] in order to prevent subsequent disputes.

至於帶水酬工必須講明銀多少或一二十元不定或五十元不定看其風之順逆而取工價必須船主與他講明免至爭論

Chí' ü tái' 'shui ch'au kung pít sü 'kóng ming ngan tó 'shíú; wák yat 'í shap ün pat ting', wák 'ng shap ün pat ting', hón' k'í fung chí shun' yik sí 'ts'ü kung ká', pít sü shün 'chü 'ü t'á 'kóng ming, 'mín chí' chang lun'.

3. The ship, having passed in through the islands, is anchored, perhaps off Cabreta Point, or beyond the Shallows (off Macao Roads,) or off Lintin. The captain, having brought his ship to an anchor, procures a native boat, or perhaps employing his own gig, and goes to Macao, in order to obtain a passport. He there calls a pilot, who reports [for him to the Chinese authorities], the number of men composing the ship's crew, the number of cannon, muskets, and swords, the quan-

既入了山水口或寄泊鷄頸頭或沙瀝或伶仃船已灣泊即僱艇埋澳或自駕三板到澳叫帶水請牌報明商梢多少大砲多少各項鳥鎗劍

Kí' yap 'líú shán 'shui 'hau, wák kí' pók Kai 'king t'au, wák Shá lek, wák Ling ting, shün 'í pók, tsik kú' 't'ing mái Ó', wák tsz' ká' sám 'pán tò' Ó' kíú' tái' 'shui 'ts'ing p'ai pò' ming shéung shau tó 'shíú, tái' p'áu' tó 'shíú, kók hóng' 'níú

2. The demands made by the outside pilots, for their services are often very extravagant; but if no anxiety is manifested by the commander of the vessel to secure their assistance, and the weather is fair, they will usually soon moderate their demands; and on an average, probaby do not receive more than fifteen or twenty dollars, perhaps not even so much.

3. Near the Chinese custom-house station and landing-place on the Praya Grande, is a *yanshui kún*, or pilot's office, at which application should be made for the pilot by the master or officer of the vessel, or by some one else in his stead. The application should be made immediately after landing, as sometimes a day or more is requisite for obtaining the passport, which, together with almost every other kind of passport or paper issued from an officer under the government, is called by foreigners a *chop*. The following is a translation of a pilot's report, such as are usually made out on the arrival of ships.

"To his honor, the sub-prefect of Ts'ínshán (or Casa Branca) &c. &c.

"A report from the pilot Pò Shángan. The reporter respectfully states that, on the 22d instant, an English merchantman [Victoria, captain] Camden, laden with cotton and other merchandise, arrived off the province of Kwóngtung; and that on examination, it appears the said vessel has no foreign ladies on board. Now, therefore, I, the said pilot, before conduct-

tity of powder and shot, also stating whether the vessel is loaded with rice or other merchandise. The pilot having made his report, and obtained a passport, is then permitted to take the ship within the Bogue.

刀火藥彈子多少或米或貨報明領牌帶水方能引船入虎門

ʾch'éung kím' ˌtò ʿfó yéuk,, ˌtán² ʿtsz' ˌtó ʿshíú, wák, ʿmai, wák, fó'. Pò' ˌming ʿling ˌp'ái, tái' ʿshui ˌfóng ˌnang ʿyan ˌshün yap, ʿFú ˌmún.

4. He now goes on board and directs the ship through the Bogue; for which service, as also for conducting her out of the river, he receives sixty dollars each way, which payment is made in accordance with long established usage.

駕船入虎門此際帶水出入口工銀六十元以循照上日章程也

Ká' ˌshün yap, ʿFú ˌmún, ʿts'z' tsai' tái' ʿshui ch'ut, yap, ʿhau, ˌkung ˌngan luk, shap, ˌün, ʿí ˌts'un chíú' shéung² yat, ˌchéung ˌch'ing ʿyá.

5. When the ship reaches the Bogue, she must anchor, while the pilot goes on shore to the fort, where he presents the passport for examination; and, after it has been clearly ascertained that the ship and cargo correspond to those named in the passport, the pilot returns again on board ship, and she is allowed to pass the Bogue.

若到虎門必須寄泊帶水埋虎門炮台呈驗船牌驗明何國船隻裝何貨物來粤俟帶水回船方能進虎門

Yéuk, tò' ʿFú ˌmún, pít, ˌsü kí' pók,, tái' ʿshui ˌmái ʿFú ˌmún páu' ˌt'oi, ˌch'ing ím² ˌshün ˌp'ái; ím² ˌming ˌhó kwók,, ˌshün chik, ˌchóng ˌhó fó' mat, ˌloi Ut,, tsz'² tái' ʿshui ˌúi ˌshün, ˌfóng ˌnang tsun' ʿFú ˌmún.

6. When some distance within the Bogue, there are shallows, and it is necessary to procure several bar-boats, perhaps some ten or more in number, for each of which a dollar is to be paid. As

入虎門一路亦有深淺必須僱篤水船數隻或十餘隻每隻價

Yap, ʿFú ˌmún yat, lò² yik, ʿyau ˌsham ʿts'ín, pít, ˌsü kú' tuk, ʿshui ˌshün shò' chik,, wák, shap, ˌü chik,, ʿmúi chik, ká' ˌngan yat,

ing the ship to the anchorage at Whampoa where she is to be moored, respectfully report that the following are the number of men and amount of munitions on board, to wit: 60 seamen, 4 cannon, 20 muskets, 20 swords, 100 catties of powder, and 100 balls.

"Tòkwóng, 18th year, 11th month, 26th day."

The sub-prefect, in conjunction with other local officers, immediately forwards a report, including the statements of the pilot, to the chief provincial officers at Canton, and at the same time issues a passport for the ship to proceed up the river.

4. About one half of the sixty dollars for pilotage, which is in all cases paid in advance, before the pilot goes on board, is divided among different officers at Macao, and at the forts and custom-house stations along the river, between Macao and Canton. The pilots holding a license, usually have a few persons who are well acquainted with the navigation of the river, in their employ, to assist them, or to serve in their stead.

5. It is not necessary for the ship to be anchored while the pilot goes on shore; by slacking sail, he may precede the vessel, present the passport, and be in readiness to join her by the time she arrives opposite the fort. No one comes on board ship from the forts to examine the cargo, or to make any inquiries respecting her, but if any trouble should arise after her entry

the ship approaches the shallows at the Second Bar, these boats must go forward and erect some signals to serve as guides, so that the pilot on board ship may easily know where the water is shallow, and thus be able to pass the Second Bar.

蠔必件船處到水物洋淺若篤立號知墪元口豎暗便蠔一淺頭為見過銀墪先以看而

ˏün. Yéukˏ tò' ˏHò ˏtan 'ts'ín 'hau tukˏ 'shui pítˏ ˏsín ˏt'au shü² lapˏ matˏ kín², 'í ˏwai óm' hò² ˏyéung ˏshün hón' kín' pín² ˏchí 'ts'ín ch'ü', ˏí kwó' ˏHò ˏtan.

7. After the ship has passed the shallows of the Second Bar, and arrived at the First Bar, at which place are the Fish-head (or Brunswick) Rocks, it is again necessary for the bar-boats to go ahead and raise signals, by which means she will easily pass by these rocks.

口該亦豎以也淺頭石行號口墪蠔頭先為石蠔大魚水件過過到有篤物於已又處要立便

'Í kwó' ˏHò ˏtan 'ts'ín 'hau yau² tò' Tái² ˏhò ˏt'au ˏkoi ch'ü' 'yau ˏU ˏt'au ˏshikˏ, yikˏ íú' tukˏ 'shui ˏsín ˏhang shü² lapˏ matˏ kín² ˏwai hò², 'í pín² ˏü kwó' shikˏ 'hau 'yá.

8. Immediately after passing these rocks, you reach Whampoa, where the ship is safely anchored. The pilot then leaves the ship and goes to all the custom-house stations and reports that such a ship, of such a nation, has entered the port for trading.

到隻船明口纔船離報進口穩能口隻石泊方關船了埔水各國易過黃帶往何貿

Kwó' 'líú shikˏ 'hau, ˏts'oi tò' ˏWóng 'pò pókˏ 'wan ˏshün chikˏ. Tái' 'shui ˏfóng ˏnang ˏlí ˏshün, 'wóng kókˏ ˏkwán 'hau pò' ˏming, ˏhó kwókˏ ˏshün chikˏ tsun' 'hau mau² yikˏ.

9. When the ship has reached the anchorage, and been moored a day or two, guard boats, belonging to the government, will be stationed to keep watch on both sides of the ship, having in them tide-waiters from the custom-house and deputies from the governor's office.

泊押兩海材灣有押乃督埔必到此總了日艇口役矣進二官艙差等船一船便關官

ˏShün tsun' 'líú 'pò, ˏwán pókˏ yatˏ í² yatˏ, pítˏ 'yau ápˏ ˏshün ˏkún 't'ing tò' ápˏ 'léung pín² ˏts'óng 'hau; 'ts'z' 'nái 'hoi ˏkwán ˏch'ái yikˏ 'tsung tukˏ ˏts'oi ˏkún 'tang 'í.

10. After the ship has obtained a security merchant and linguist, she may discharge her cargo.

商貨保起了能定方船事後通

Hau² ˏshün ting² 'líú 'pò ˏshéung ˏt'ung sz'², ˏfóng ˏnang 'hí fò'.

---

in consequence of illegal freight, the pilot who conducted her in will be endangered because he did not inform the officers at the Bogue.

9. These persons, or some others in their stead, are required by the regulations of the port to join the vessel with the pilot, when he comes off from the port at the Bogue. They are

11. When the cargo is unloaded, a return one received on board, and the ship in readiness for sailing, the security merchants must send a petition to the government requesting two passports; which on their being issued, the security merchant must receive and deliver to the master of the vessel, who receives them.

倘起完貨復落滿貨船將開行保商則先具稟請發紅牌二張其牌發出保商必交與船主收執

'T'óng 'hí ˌün fó' fuk˛ lók˛ 'mún fó˒, ˛shün ˌtséung ˌhoi ˛hang, 'pó ˌshéung tsak˒ ˌsín kü² 'pan 'ts'ing fát˒ ˛hung ˛p'ái í² ˌchéung; ˛k'í ˛p'ái fát˒ ch'ut˒, 'pò ˌshéung pít˒ ˌkáu 'ü ˛shün 'chü ˌshau chap˒.

12. Afterwards, when the ship is ready for sea, the pilot ought to repair on board and conduct her out of port; having passed the Second Bar, and reached the fort at the Bogue, he again goes on shore and presents the passport for examination, after which she is allowed to proceed.

帶水俟船開身回國仍引船出口一路過蠔墊到虎門口帶水亦呈驗紅牌然後放行

Tái' 'shui tsz'² ˛shün ˌhoi ˌshan ˛üi kwók˒, ˛ying 'yan ˌshün ch'ut˒ 'hau; yat˒ lò² kwó' ˛Hò ˌtan tó' 'Fú ˛mún 'hau, tái' 'shui yik˛ ˛ch'ing ím² ˛hung ˛p'ái ˛ín hau² fóng' ˛hang.

13. The ship having now passed the Bogue, and arrived off Lintin, or perhaps off Cabreta Point, the pilot leaves her, while she under full sail returns to her own country.

既出虎門到伶仃或雞頸帶水返然後揚帆回國也

Kí' ch'ut˒ 'Fú ˛mún tò' ˛Ling ˌting, wák˛ ˌKai 'king, tái' 'shui 'fán, ˛ín hau² ˛yéung ˛fán ˛üi kwók˒ 'yá.

called hoppo boats by foreigners, and usually remain attached to the stern of the vessel during the whole time she lies at Whampoa.

11. One of these "two passports" allows the vessel to pass the Bogue, at which place it is left by the pilot; the other is to be retained by the captain; and, in case of his being driven by stress of weather to any other part of the Chinese coast, it will secure for his ship admittance into the port, and if need be serve as a warrant for the local authorities "to refit the ship" and "bestow food and raiment on the sufferers," from the public money. This is "an everlasting law," established by the emperor Kínlung, A. D. 1737. This passport is known by the name of the *grand chop*, and according to law, cannot be given to the captain until all the duties on the cargo, the measurement fee and other port charges, and every demand made by the government, are fairly settled. The system by which the trade is conducted affords every facility for unloading and loading a cargo, and when it is prosecuted without interruption, there are few ports where greater dispatch can be made than at Canton.

12. The same pilot who conducts the ship into the river is on the lookout to ascertain when she is ready for sea, and always carries her out of the river; this is well understood among the pilots, because when a ship obtains an entrance passport, the fees for her pilotage both in and out are paid to the officers by the pilot who conducts her in.

## Section Fourth.

## DIFFERENT KINDS OF TEAS.

## 茶葉類第四章

ˎCh'á íp$_{2}$ lui$^{2}$; tai$^{2}$ sz" ˏchéung.

| | | |
|---|---|---|
| 1. From whence is the tea leaf obtained? | 茶葉出在邊處嚟嘅呢 | ˎCh'á íp$_{2}$ ch'ut› tsoi$^{2}$ ˏpín ch'ü' ˎlai ké' ˏní? |
| Much comes from the Mòí (Bohea) hills in Fukkín; and also from the province of O'nfai, and Wóp'ing [in Kwóngtung]; but there are not more than two general names, the black tea, and the green tea. | 福建武彜嘅多安徽和平都有但係總名不過兩個啫一名黑茶一名綠茶 | Fuk$_{2}$ kín$^{2}$, 'Mò ˎí, ké' ˏtó; ˏO'n ˏfai, ˎWó ˎp'ing, ˏt'ò 'yau; tán$^{2}$ hai$^{2}$ 'tsung ˎming pat› kwó' 'léung kó' ˏché; yat› ˎming hak› ˎch'á, yat› ˎming luk$_{2}$ ˎch'á. |
| 2. From whence are the black teas brought? | 邊處出黑茶呢 | ˏPín ch'ü' ch'ut› hak› ˎch'á ˏní? |
| The greater part comes from the Bohea hills. | 出於武彜嘅多 | Ch'ut› ˏü 'Mò ˎí ké' ˏtó. |
| 3. How many different names are there? | 有幾多名目呢 | 'Yau 'kí ˏtó ˎming muk$_{2}$ ˏní? |

### *Notes and Explanations.*

THE object of this section is to give a brief account of the principal varieties of teas, with some notices of their cultivation, the manner of curing the leaf, packing, and transporting it to Canton. The importance of this export demands for it a more extended notice than other articles found in this market.

1. The botanical name for tea is Thea, and it is intimately allied to the genus Camellia, both of which are called by the same general name of *ch'á* among the Chinese. The flowers of tea are inodorous, less showy than the Camellia, and the plant is seldom cultivated merely for ornament, while its congener is one of the favorite plants of gardeners at home and abroad. The Bohea hills, which name has been introduced into the English through the Fukkín pronunciation of Bú-í, are in lat. 27° 47′ N., and long. 118° 17′ E., bordering on the two provinces of Fukkín and Kóngsai. They include two ranges, one of which is called the Mò hills, and the other the I′ hills, and are situated in the department of Kinnang, and the district of Tsungón, being a part of the chain of mountains which runs through the central parts of the empire. The name given the hills is derived from two brothers, Mò and I′, who were sons of an ancient prince, and when he died refused to succeed him, but retired to settle on these hills far from their patrimony, and built them a dwelling, which after their death was called the palace of Mòí. There is a temple to their memory, in which incense is burnt. The circuit of the hills is 120 *lí*, in all of which the tea is raised. A stream divides the hills, the I′ being on the north side, and the Mò on the south; and the tea from the former is considered the best, probably because of the southerly exposure given to the plants. There are many villages among the hills where the cultivators and the proprietors of tea reside, but the tea itself is for the most part brought for sale to the village of Singtsün, where are shops and warehouses for exposing it, and where the purchasers come to examine and price the different qualities.

A great many; such as 'white hair,' or *Pecco;* 'very fragrant,' or *Orange Pecco;* 'old man's eyebrows,' or *Pecco;* 'carnation hair,' or *Inferior Pecco;* 'red plum [blossom],' or *Hungmuey;* 'nelumbium kernel;' 'sparrow's tongue;' 'fir-leaf pattern;' 'dragon's pellet;' 'dragon's whiskers;' 'small plant,' or *Souchong;* 'folded plant,' or *Powchong;* 'working tea,' or *Congo;* 'autumn dew;' 'pearl flower,' or *Chulán;* 'careful firing,' or *Campoi;* and others, which are names of black tea.

有好多嚹如白
毫上香君眉紫
毫紅梅蓮子心
雀舌松製龍團
龍鬚小種包種
工夫秋露珠蘭
揀焙等就係黑
茶名喇

'Yau 'hò ˏtó lá'; ˏü Pakˀ ˏhò, 'Shéung ˏhéung, ˏKwan ˏmí, 'Tsz' ˏhò, ˏHung ˏmúi, ˏLín 'tsz' ˏsam, Tséukˀ shítˀ, ˏTsung chai', ˏLung ˏt'ün, ˏLung ˏsü, 'Síu 'chung, ˏPáu 'chung, ˏKung ˏfú, ˏTsau lú', ˏChü ˏlán, 'Kán púi', 'tang, tsau' hai' hakˀ ˏch'á ˏming lé'.

4. Where are the green teas produced, and how many kinds are there?

綠茶出於何處
又有幾多名呢

Lukˀ ˏch'á ch'utˀ ˏü ˏhó ch'ü', yau' 'yau 'kí ˏtó ˏming ˏní?

The greater part comes from the province of O'nfai. Their names are 'rains before,' or *Young Hyson;* 'plum petals,' or *Young Hyson;* 'flourish spring,' or *Hyson;* 'flourish skin,' or *Old Hyson;* 'T'ünk'ai tea,' or *Twankay;* 'Tsungló tea,' or *Sunglo;* 'hemp pearl,' or *Gunpowder;* 'great pearl,' or *Imperial;* 'pearl flower,' or *Imperial;* 'skin tea,' or *Hyson Skin;* and others, all of which are green teas.

多出安徽其名
雨前梅片熙春
熙皮屯溪松蘿
蔴珠大珠珠蘭
皮茶等即是綠
茶喇

ˏTó ch'utˀ ˏÓn ˏfai. ˏK'i ˏming 'U ˏts'ín, ˏMúi p'ín', ˏHí ˏch'un, ˏHí ˏp'í, ˏT'ün ˏk'ai, ˏTsung ˏló, ˏMá ˏchü, Tái' ˏchü, ˏChü ˏlán, ˏP'í ˏch'á, 'tang, tsikˀ shí' lukˀ ˏch'á lé'.

5. How is the tea plant cultivated in the Bohea hills?

武彝山裏茶點
樣種呢

'Mò ˏí ˏshán 'lí, ˏch'á 'tím yéung' chung' ˏní?

---

3. There are many varieties of tea among the Chinese, for which there are no foreign names, several of them being comprised under one general term; as for instance, the first eleven kinds on this list, with the exception of Hungmuey, are all included under the two designations of Pecco and Souchong. Many of the terms have some allusion to the shape or color of the leaf, the mode of its preparation, or time of gathering. Pecco is made of the opening leaf buds, while yet there is a white pubescence upon the leaf; Powchong is so called because it is wrapped in small parcels; "autumn dew" alludes to the time when it is picked, in the latter part of the season, in the month of September; Chulan tea is brought to market rolled up in little pellets, and is called *chülán* tea because the flowers of that name are mixed up with the tea for a time to scent it; Congo is explained in No. 7, in this section. The names of tea here printed in italics are the designations by which they are known to foreigners, being in most cases corruptions of the Chinese names.

4. There are not as many varieties of green tea as of black, for it is used to a very limited extent by the Chinese. "Rain before" refers to that tea which is gathered before the *kuk ü tsít*, or "grain rain term," in the third month or April. Hyson and Old Hyson are gathered after spring is well begun, and the leaves have attained some size and thickness; the latter is the inferior portion of the former. Twankay and Sunglo are names of places where these

During the vernal months of the previous year, the seeds of the tea are mixed up with very wet sand in a careful and thorough manner, where they remain until the sprout appears. After the soaking rains of spring are over, and the soil is soft and plastic, then the seeds should be planted with the shoot pointing upward, after which the tea will grow without further care or watering; if it receive the rain from heaven, it will certainly soon become very exuberant. It is important to examine the soil, whether it be fertile or not; if it is rich, then, in a year or upwards, the leaves will be in a condition to gather; but if the soil is poor, two years or so must elapse before the leaves can be picked.

上年春間先將
茶予用沙濕透
和勻待茶子發
芽後春雨淋漓
地土泥滓便將
茶子種下其芽
向上則茶自然
發生不用澆淋
得天雨定然茂
盛但看其土厚
薄地厚則年零
便有收成如地
土薄則必須二
年後纔能有茶
採摘

Shéung[2] ‚nín ˓ch'un ˓kán, ˓sín ˓tséung ‚ch'á 'tsz' yung[2] ˓shá shap˒ t'au[2] wó' ‚wan, toi' ‚ch'á 'tsz' fát[2] ‚ngá. Hau[2] ˓ch'un 'ü ‚lam ‚lí, tí[2] 't'ò ‚nai ˓ning, pín[2] ˓tséung ‚ch'á 'tsz' chung[2] há[2], ‚k'í ‚ngá héung[2] 'shéung; tsak˒ ‚ch'á tsz" ‚ín fát[2] ˓shang, pat˒ yung[2] ˓shíú ‚lam; tak˒ ˓t'ín 'ü ting[2] ‚ín mau' shing[2]. Tán' hon' ‚k'í 't'ò hau[2] pók[2]; tí[2] hau[2] tsak˒ ‚nín ‚ling pín[2] 'yau ˓shau ‚shing; ‚ü tí[2] 't'ò pók[2], tsak˒ pít˒ ˓sü í[2] ‚nín hau[2], ˓tsoi ‚nang 'yau ‚ch'á 'ts'oi chák˒.

In the next place we will speak of the weather. If there is too much rain, then the leaves will become mildewed, and broken, of a yellow color, and not at all flourishing; if the season is very dry, the leaves will be few and small, having many yellow ones among them. But if the rains fall equably, and after the showers a bright sun appears, then the leaves will be abundant and flourishing as well as thick; the flavor will be fragrant, and the aroma also of long continuance; the leaf will be of a bright green color, thick in texture, and will roll up compactly and

其次則論天時
如雨水過多其
葉則霉爛而黃
不旺若天大旱
其葉則稀少而
黃葉多但雨水
調和於大雨後
又有太陽則其
葉繁盛而益壯
味亦香而且長

‚K'í ts'z", tsak˒ lun[2] ˓t'ín ‚shí. ‚U 'ü 'shui kwó' 'tó, ‚k'í íp[2] tsak˒ ‚múi, lán[2], ‚í ‚wóng, pat˒ wóng'; yéuk[2] ˓t'ín tái[2] hón[2], ‚k'í íp[2] tsak˒ ˓hí 'síú, ‚í ‚wóng íp[2] ˓tó. Tán' 'ü 'shui ‚t'íú ‚wó, ‚ü tái[2] 'ü hau[2], yau[2] 'yau t'ái' ‚yéung, tsak˒ ‚k'í íp[2] ‚fán shing[2], ‚í yik˒ chóng'; mí[2] yik[2] ˓héung, ‚í 'ch'é ‚ch'éung,

varieties grow. Individual trees sometimes have particular names, and the tea from them is very celebrated, either by reason of some association, or from its own good quality.

5. The mode of planting and growing the tea shrub may vary in different places, and the account here given is intended to apply principally to the cultivation of black tea in the Bohea hills. In planting, care is taken to insure at least a few shoots by putting several seeds into the hole, as the greater part always prove abortive from their oily nature. The seeds of

look large. Great care should be exercised in selecting the ground; that which is loamy and damp is the best.

色青葉厚條子
結而壯大然以
擇地爲要肥潤
者佳也

shik› ‹ts‘ing, íp$_2$ hau$^2$, ˏt‘íú ‘tsz’ kít$_2$, ˏí chóng’ tái$^2$. ˏÍ‘n ‘í chák$_2$ tí$^2$ ˏwai íú’; ˏfí yan’ ‘ché ‹kai ‘yá.

6. Are there any particular rules for picking the leaf?

採摘有乜方法
冇呢

‘Ts‘oi chák$_2$ ‘yau mat› ‹fóng fát› ‘mò ‹ní?

In picking tea, the most important rule to be observed is to do it in the proper time; when the leaf has a fresh, bright appearance and is fully matured, then it must be gathered. For if only one day too early, then the leaf will be very soft, and the decoction destitute of a good taste or color; and if one day too late, then the leaf will become old and hard, cannot be rolled compactly, and will be inferior in both taste and color.

採茶之法最要
得時如葉色鮮
明長足之日卽
須採摘若早一
日則葉太嫩而
無味無色如遲
一日則葉老硬
做不成條色味
俱不可

‘Ts‘oi ˏch‘á ‹chí fát› tsui’ íú’ tak› ˏshí; ˏü íp$_2$ shik› ‹sín ‹ming ‘ch‘éung tsuk› ‹chí yat$_2$, tsik› ‹sü ‘ts‘oi chák$_2$. Yéuk$_2$ ‘tsò yat› yat$_2$ tsak› íp$_2$ t‘ái’ nün’, ˏí ˏmò mí$^2$, ˏmò shik›; ˏü ˏch‘í yat› yat$_2$, tsak› íp$_2$ ‘lò ngáng$^2$, tsò$^2$ pat› ˏshing ˏt‘íú, shik› mí$^2$ ‹k‘ü pat› ‘hó.

If the weather is gloomy, and it threatens to blow or rain, then the leaves certainly cannot be gathered, but all must wait till the sky is clear and the weather fair, when the people can begin to work. As in planting, it is desirable to select a fruitful soil, so in picking the leaf, to choose good weather is important. When the time to gather has come, first estimate the quantity of leaves, and then engage a proportionate number of workmen,

又天暗而作風
雨切不可採摘
須待天晴氣爽
方可動手是以
種則宜取地利
採亦宜察天時
也然採時觀其
葉之多後定數

Yau$^2$ ‹t‘ín om$^2$, ˏí tsók› ‹fung ‘ü, ts‘ít› pat› ‘hó ‘ts‘oi chák$_2$ ‹sü toi’ ‹t‘ín ˏtsing hí’ ‘shóng, ‹fóng ‘hó tung$^2$ ‘shau. Shí$^2$ ‘í chung$^2$ tsak› ˏí ‘ts‘ü tí$^2$ lí$^2$, ‘ts‘oi yik$_2$ ˏí ch‘át› ‹t‘ín ˏshí ‘yá. ˏÍ‘n ‘ts‘oi ˏshí, ‹kún ˏk‘í íp$_2$ ‹chí ‹tó, hau$^2$ ting$^2$ shò’ yung$^2$ ˏyan, pat› k‘ü

tea usually grow in a triangular capsule, having three partitions, each of which contains a round seed of the size of a rifle bullet; there are sometimes only two seeds in a capsule. In the Ankoi hills, the seeds are planted in the ground without any previous germination, and three years elapse before any leaves can be picked; but this time is no doubt much shortened when diligence in manuring, and richness of soil accelerate the growth of the plant. The soil in those hills is very sandy and barren, and the tea shrubs are planted where nothing else will grow, but this is not the case in the more extensive plantations at the Bohea hills, where the cultivation of the plant is the principal occupation of the inhabitants. The best tea is, however, always produced on the sides of mountains where there can be but little accumulation of vegetable mold, and where the soil is somewhat sandy.

| | | |
|---|---|---|
| either men or women; it is of the highest importance that the work be done quickly, because the chosen day and the proper time must be improved on the instant. | 用人不拘男女<br>總以手快者爲<br>上以其赶日趁<br>時之故 | ˏnám ˊnü; ˊtsung ˊí ˊshau fái' ché' ˏwai shéung², ˊí ˏk'í ˊkón yatˏ ch'au' ˏshí ˏchí kú'. |
| Each workman can on an average collect ten catties of leaves per day, for which he receives five or six cash each catty. He should also carry some dry provision about his person, so that he will not hinder the work by going to and returning [from his meals]. The workmen must be directed not to pick the old leaves, nor those which are very soft. These are the most important particulars regarding the picking of the leaves. | 每人每日約採<br>十餘斤每斤工<br>錢五六文須帶<br>乾糧在身以免<br>往返躭擱又須<br>吩咐不採老葉<br>與太嫩葉此採<br>摘之大畧也 | ˊMúi ˏyan ˊmúi yatˏ, yéukˏ ˊts'oi shapˏ ˏü ˏkan, ˊmúi ˏkan ˏkung ˏts'ín ˊ'ng lukˏ ˏman. ˏSü tai' ˏkón ˏléung tsoi² ˏshan, ˊí ˊmín ˊwóng ˊfán ˏtám kókˏ. Yau² ˏsü ˏfan fú² patˏ ˊts'oi ˊlò ípˏ, ˊü t'ái' nün² ípˏ. ˊTs'z' ˊts'oi chákˏ ˏchí tái² léukˏ ˊyá. |
| 7. When the leaves are picked and brought home, how are they cured? | 摘了番來點樣<br>製造呢 | Chákˏ ˊlíú ˏfán ˏloi, ˊtím yéung² chai' ts'ò' ˏní? |
| After they are gathered and housed, they are again assorted in a careful manner; all the yellow and broken leaves are picked out, and also those which are too old or too young. [The good leaves] are then spread very thin upon bamboo trays, and placed in the wind; for this purpose wooden frames are used, upon each of which ten or more trays can be aired. There they are left until the | 採摘回來再將<br>揀過去淨黃爛<br>過老過嫩等葉<br>然後用竹篙裝<br>載攤薄放於當<br>風下再用木架<br>子每架晾十餘 | ˊTs'oi chákˏ ˏúi ˏloi, tsoi² ˏtséung ˊkán kwó' h'ü' tsing² ˏwóng, lán², kwó' ˊlò, kwó' nün², ˊtang ípˏ. ˏI'n hau², yung² chukˏ ˏwó ˏchóng tsoi² ˏt'án pókˏ, fóng' ˏü ˏtóng ˏfung há'; tsoi² yung² mukˏ ká' ˊtsz', ˊmúi ká' lóng' shapˏ ˊü ˏwó. Lóng' chí' |

6. Inferior tea is frequently gathered by clipping off the small twigs with shears, but the usual mode is to pick the leaves by hand, the finer sorts in a very careful manner, and put them into bamboo trays or shallow baskets. The constant practice of depriving the plant of its natural dress stunts it, and after a few years it is cut down to produce a new growth of branches. The shrubs are also, either through the carelessness of the cultivators, or from the leanness of the soil, after a few years, covered with lichens which dry up their juices, and shorten their lives. The leaves grow very thickly upon the shrub, but the produce of single plants seldom exceeds two catties, and the quantity commonly gathered is from eight taels to a catty. There are there pickings in a season; the first, in which the delicate leaf buds are collected, is in Ts'ingming term, during the middle of the third month, or the first part of April; the second is at the end of the fourth, and beginning of the fifth month, and is technically called the *í ch'un* or second spring; the third, by which time the leaves become thick and coarse, is at the end of the fifth, and beginning of the sixth month, and is called *sám ch'un* or third spring.

leaves begin to be rather soft; and then, while lying on the tray, they are gently rolled and rubbed, until red spots begin to appear, when they are ready. They are then tested by pouring hot water upon them, when the edge of the leaf becomes yellow. In doing this part, they must all be equably and frequently rubbed, for which reason the tea is called [Congo or] workman's tea.

窩晾至其葉一軟便在窩裏細挪細擦務擦至起紅點爲度其後泡水起金邊者其造法在於手勻多擦名曰工夫即此意也

k'í íp yat 'ün; pín tsoi wó 'lí sai nó, sai ch'át, mò ch'át chí 'hí hung 'tím wai tò. K'í hau p'áu 'shui 'hí kam pín 'ché. K'í ts'ò fát tsoi ü 'shau wan tó ch'át, ming üt Kung fú; tsik 'ts'z' í 'yá.

After the leaves are well rolled, they are put into an iron pan to roast, in doing which it is important to observe certain rules. When the pan has become redhot, a handful of leaves are scattered on it, and the workman waits till the leaves are popped alike, when they are hastily taken out at once, for if there is any delay they may be reduced to a cinder. After this, the color and flavor [of the decoction] are tested, which are all the rules to be observed at this stage. The next operation is to prepare a fire for drying the

挪好時放於鐵鍋中炒要得法燒紅鑊取茶一把撒在鑊內待其每粒爆勻快手一撈齊齊取上遲恐成炭後之色味盡於此時得法以後便發焙籠之火則

Nó 'hò shí fóng ü t'ít wó chung 'ch'áu iú tak fát. Shíú hung wók, 'ts'ü ch'á yat 'pá, sát tsoi wók noi, toi k'í 'múi nap páu wan, fái 'shau yat lau, ts'ai ts'ai 'ts'ü 'shéung; ch'í, 'hung shing tán. Hau chí shik mí tsun ü 'ts'z' shí tak fát. 'I hau pín fát púi lung chí 'fo, tsak

7. The curing performed at the hills is not repeated, unless the tea becomes damaged during its passage to Canton. The operation of roasting the leaves is attended with some inconvenience to the workman by reason of a yellowish, acrid fluid which exudes from the leaves, and irritates the hands. Peceo and other fine kinds are not roasted on hot pans, but after having been dried in the wind are placed over the fire in bamboo drying baskets, after which they are carefully packed in leaden canisters for exportation. The leaves which are to be made into Hungmuey are placed under cover for two or three days, until they begin to corrupt, after which they are dried in the sun and cured thoroughly. All tea is packed in boxes or canisters as soon as it is cured, the common kinds in large chests, and the fine sorts in leaden canisters. On its arrival in Canton, it is if required, often repacked in boxes and canisters of different sizes, which are always lined with lead. It is probable that the principal varieties of black or green tea are owing chiefly to the age of the leaf, while subordinate kinds are made by different processes in manufacturing. After the tea has been roasted, it is examined to see if there are any leaves without the yellow edge and red spots, and that have not burst, and they are taken out. Before being placed in the drying baskets, the roasted tea is aired for an hour; and particular care is taken that there be no smoke while drying.

There is is a slight difference in the shape of the leaf of green and black tea, but the principal cause of their diversity is owing to the different modes of curing them; in making green tea a gentle fire is used, and they are simply dried; but the leaves of black tea are roasted

leaves, for which the most compact charcoal is used; when it has become thoroughly ignited, and there is no smoke, it is covered over with ashes, and the basket placed upon the fire to dry the leaves. About ten catties are dried at once, for there must not be too many, lest the fire should not dry them equally. While drying they are unceasingly stirred and turned over by the hand, in order that the tea may be all alike dried; when dried sufficiently, it is immediately packed in boxes.

用堅炭燒透無
烟用火灰蓋火
則放籠下焙以
十斤為度不可
太多多則火色
不勻則不停以
手攪翻令其茶
火色勻透至火
足卽赶裝箱

yung$^{2}$ ‹kín tán$^{2}$; ‹shíú tʻau$^{1}$ ˏmò ‹ín, yung$^{2}$ ʻfó ‹fúi koiʼ ʻfó; tsak› fóngʼ ˏlung há$^{1}$ púi$^{2}$. ʻI shap› ‹kan ˏwai tò$^{2}$, pat› ʻhó tʻáiʼ ‹tó; ‹tó tsak› ʻfó shik› pát› ˏwan. Tsak› pat› ˏting ʻí ʻshau ʻkáu ˏfán, ling$^{2}$ ˏkʻí ˏchʻá ʻfó shik› ˏwan tʻau$^{1}$; chíʼ ʻfó tsuk›, tsik› ʻkón ‹chóng ‹séung.

8. How is the quality of the tea tested?

A quantity of spring water is boiled in an earthen pot and poured upon it; if the water is not boiling hot, the leaves will float, and the color and flavor will not be well developed. Having got boiling water, then put the leaves into a covered cup, and pour the water upon them, when the flavor and color will both appear. In the best qualities of tea, the taste is aromatous and oily, and a clear yet strong fluid is in the cup. The inferior sorts are known by

試茶又點樣呢
則用瓦煲煎滾
山水泡之若水
未滾茶葉必浮
味色皆不出若
滾的將茶放蓋
盅內泡起味色
皆現如上等者
味色香滑清中
帶濃下等者香

Shíʼ ‹chʻá yau$^{1}$ ʻtím yéung$^{2}$ ‹ní?

Tsak› yung$^{2}$ ʻngá ‹pò, ‹tsín ʻkwʻan ‹shán ʻshui ʻpʻáuʼ ‹chí; yéuk› ʻshui mí$^{2}$ ʻkwʻan, ˏchʻá íp› pít› ˏfau, mí$^{2}$ shik› ‹kái pat› chʻut›. Yéuk› ʻkwʻan tik›, ‹tséung ˏchʻá fóngʼ koiʼ ˏchung noi$^{2}$, pʻáuʼ ʻhí mí$^{2}$ shik› ‹kái ín$^{2}$. ˏU shéung$^{2}$ ʻtang ʻché, mí$^{2}$ shik› ‹héung wát›, ‹tsʻing ‹chung taiʼ ˏyung. Há$^{1}$ ʻtang ʻché, ‹héung pít› ʻyé,

on a hot iron until they pop, after which they are again dried, and these processes make the leaves black. The Chinese say that green tea can be made into black by roasting and curing it until it becomes black; but black cannot be made into green, because it is already of a dark color and cannot be changed. Fresh and tender leaves are roasted by a gentle fire, old and thick ones by a fervid heat. Ten things are to be observed in inspecting green tea: the leaf must be green and glabrous; it must be rolled firmly; all the twigs must be separated from the leaves; the texture of the leaf must be thick; no dirt or sticks in it; it must be well roasted; taste of the decoction aromatous; and the liquid clear, without a muddy appearance, which is the most important particular; and it must have an oily taste; leaf of a uniform color. It is also said that in good tea no pellicle floats upon the top of the infusion.

8. It is well known that the Chinese drink the simple decoction of tea without any addition and pour off the infusion almost immediately after the boiling water has been poured on. They also frequently drink the tea from off the leaves; a cup is provided with a cover that fits rather closely, and boiling water is poured upon a few leaves at the bottom, when the cover is immediately placed upon it until ready to drink. There are are also other plants used for tea by the poor Chinese; the leaves of one or two species of Camellia are sometimes employed for this purpose in districts where they are abundant, but these and all other plants are considered as poor substitutes for the true tea by the natives themselves.

an unpleasant smell, and a weak decoction. The leaves, which, when in the water, unroll without tearing, are the best. The other rules need not be detailed minutely; but those persons who are skillful in testing teas, judge according to the current price and demand in settling the value, for there is no fixed rule for examining.

必野清必寡以沉水葉放不闌者爲佳餘法未盡述惟善觀者量時度價而已不可以一律觀

ts'ing pit 'kwá. 'Í ch'am 'shui ip, fong' pat lán 'ché, wai kai. U fát mí tsun shut; wai shín kún 'ché, léung shí, tók ká', í 'í; pat 'hó 'í yat lat kún.

9. Are teas also produced in the province of Canton?

至於粵東有茶出唔呢

Chí' ü Üt tung 'yau ch'á ch'ut 'm ní?

They are, but the whole amount is not much; and those places where they are grown all give their names to the teas produced there. The places which produce the most black tea are Stony Kúlò, and the districts of Ts'ingün, and Wóp'ing. [The district of] Hókshán, Hónám, and Sámtóchuk [in the district of Wóp'ing], are the principal places which afford green tea. There is the Hungkam tea, so named because it grows partly in Námhung [in Kwóngtung], and partly in Kam chau [in Kóngsai]. The Shamk'ai is produced in Kwóngsai, and the O'nk'ai (Ankoi), in Fukkín, province; but of the varieties in the other provinces, it is unnecessary to speak minutely.

亦有總係不甚多惟幾處地方有種皆以此地之名爲名如大石古勞清遠和平俱是以製黑茶又鶴山河南三多竹製爲綠茶又有雄贛因南雄贛州界地所產故也又岑溪乃廣西茶也又安溪福建茶也別省皆有未便盡述

Yik 'yau, 'ts'ung hai pat sham tó; wai 'kí ch'ü' tí fong 'yau chung', kái 'í 'ts'z' tí chí ming, wai ming. U Tái shik 'Kú lò, Ts'ing 'ün, Wó p'ing, k'ü shí 'í chai' hak ch'á. Yau Hók shán, Hó nám, Sám tó chuk, chai' wai luk ch'á. Yau 'yau Hung kam', yan Nám hung, Kam' chau, kái tí 'shó 'chán, kú 'yá. Yau Sham k'ai, 'nái 'Kwóng sai ch'á 'yá; yau O'n k'ai, Fuk kín' ch'á 'yá; pít 'sháng kái 'yau, mí pín tsun shut.

10. What distance in miles is the length of the road [by which the tea comes]?

沿途路程幾多里呢

Ün t'ò lò ching 'kí tó 'lí ní?

9. Both black and green tea are produced in this province, but the quantity is not so great as in Fukkín and O'nfai. The tea plant is found in every province of China, but it is not cultivated for exportation in all of them. The Tartars and other races living on the north and west of China procure their supplies from the western provinces, and it forms an article of trade between Wannám and Burmah. There is a form of tea used by the Tartars called *brick tea*, which is made by softening the leaves and small twigs with boiling water, and then pressing them into large flat cakes resembling tiles.

| | | |
|---|---|---|
| From the provincial city of Kwóngtung to the Mòí hills in Fukkín is reckoned upwards of two thousand, eight hundred and eighty *lí* (or about 900 miles). [From Canton] to Súchau fú in the province of Kóngsú, is reckoned upwards of three thousand, five hundred and eighty-one *lí* (or about 1200 English miles). | 由廣東省城至福建武彝山計程二千八百八十五里至江蘇蘇州府計程三千五百八十有一里 | ‚Yau 'Kwóng ‚tung 'sháng ‚shing chí' Fuk› kín', 'Mò ‚í ‚shán, kai' ‚ching í² ‚tsín, pát› pák›, pát› shap₂ ‚'ng 'lí. Chí' ‚Kóng ‚sú, ‚Sú ‚chau 'fú, kai' ‚ching ‚sám ‚tsín, ‚'ng pák›, pát› shap₂ 'yau yat› 'lí. |
| 11. How are the duties collected at the various passes on the road hither. | 沿途關津稅餉點樣報呢 | ‚Ün ‚t'ò ‚kwán ‚tsun shui² 'héung, 'tím yéung² pò² ‚ní? |
| A report is first written, stating definitely from whence the supercargo [of the tea] has come, what his name is, how many chests of tea he has with him transporting to Canton to be sold there; aud requesting the favor of being examined, that the cargo may pass. After the duty is paid at the pass, the whole is allowed to proceed. | 先寫一稟書明何處人氏某名隨帶茶葉若干箱運回粵東販賣懇恩查驗放行之意納過關稅後能裝回 | ‚Sín 'sé yat› 'pan, ‚shü ‚ming ‚hó ch'ü' ‚yan shí², 'mau ‚ming, ‚tsui tai' ‚ch'á íp₂ yéuk₂ ‚kón ‚séung, wán² ‚úi Ut₂ ‚tung fán² mái²; 'han ‚yan ‚chá ím² fóng' ‚hang ‚chí í'. Nap₂ kwó² ‚kwán shui² hau² ‚nang ‚chóng ‚úi. |
| 12. When the tea reaches Canton, how is it sold to go abroad? | 茶到省點樣發賣別國呢 | ‚Ch'á tò' 'sháng, 'tím yéung² fát› mái² pít› kwók› ‚ní? |
| This commodity is all carried to the hong merchants who manage it among them, for other shops are not permitted to receive and send it out of the port. | 此係歸洋商分辦各鋪戶不能濫辦出口耳 | 'Ts'z' hai² ‚kwai ‚yéung ‚shéung ‚fan pán²; kók› p'ò' ú² pat› ‚nang lám' pán² ch'ut› 'hau 'í. |
| Such are the general particulars concerning the planting, picking, curing, and selling of teas. | 此則種採製販茶之大畧情形乃本乎此 | 'Ts'z' tsak› chung', 'ts'oi, chai', fán², ‚ch'á ‚chí tái² léuk₂, ‚tsing ‚ying 'nái 'pún ‚ú 'ts'z'. |

10. Many streams have their sources in the Bohea hills, a part of which flow to the northwest, emptying themselves into the lakes of Kóngsai. The tea is carried down these streams into the lakes, and then passing around enter the river Kam, a large stream that drains the southwestern parts of Kóngsai, which is ascended as far as the water will permit. The tea is then taken out of the batteaux and carried by porters across the Múi ling, a chain of mountains which lie in the northern part of Kwóngtung, and reshipped on the river Chü, by which it raches Canton. The green tea is brought down to the lakes of Kóngsai by water carriage, from whence its route is the same as the black.

## Section Fifth.

## DIALOGUE ON BUYING WOOLENS.

### 買賣疋頭問答第五章

ˢMái mái$^2$ p'at˃ ˏt'au man$^2$ táp˃; tai˛ ˢ'ng ˓chéung.

| | | |
|---|---|---|
| 1. Are you well, Sir? | 大班好吖 | Tái$^2$ ˓pán, 'hò ˓á? |
| I am well;—and you, are you well? | 好　你好吖 | 'Hò! ˢNí 'hò ˓á? |
| 2. Well! If you only say so, I'm well. | 好　你話過就好咯 | 'Hò! ˢNí wá$^2$ kwò', tsau$^2$ 'hò lók˃. |
| What business have you to-day? | 你今日有乜事幹呢 | ˢNí ˓kam yat˛ ˢyau mat˃ sz'$^2$ kón' ˓ní? |
| 3. I have come to call on you to-day to see if you will patronize me or not. | 我今日嚟探你睇你有乜帮襯我冇 | ˢNgó ˓kam yat˛ ˏlai t'ám' ˢní, 't'ai ˢní ˢyau mat˃ ˓póng ch'an' ˢngó ˢmò. |
| In what way patronize you? Let me know, if you please. | 點樣帮襯你呢你話我知囉 | 'Tím yéung$^2$ ˓póng ch'an' ˢní ˓ní? ˢNí wá$^2$ ˢngó ˓chí ˓lò. |
| 4. I have come to request, that you will be good enough to give me the different colors of your woolens; I wish, at the same time to inquire of you, if any new goods have arrived; for if so, then I will invite some | 我就係嚟請你俾個的大呢嘅花色過我乘機問你有乜新貨 | ˢNgó tsau$^2$ hai$^2$ ˏlai 'ts'ing ˢní 'pí kó' tik˃ tái$^2$ ˏní ké' ˓fá shik˃ kwó' ˢngó; ˏshing ˓kí man$^2$ ˢní ˢyau mat˃ ˓san |

### *Notes and Explanations.*

VERY much of the business of buying and selling in Canton is effected through the agency of native brokers, called *kingkí yan*. This section is designed to show, together with the names of woolen goods, the manner and phraseology in which conversation is sometimes carried on between these brokers and foreign merchants. *Mái mái* means buying and selling; *p'at t'au* is a general term for woolens; and *man táp* are question and answer, or dialogue.

1. The broker commences the dialogue by addressing his foreign friend with the compellative *táipán*, used as a term of respect by the Chinese, when addressing, or speaking of, foreigners. The term was formerly applied to the chief of the foreign factories, as it now is to the respective principals of the commercial houses in Canton.

3. *Póng ch'an* conveys the idea of assisting a merchant, or person of any pursuit, by giving him business or employment, and hence its meaning, patronage or to patronize.

4. *Tái ní* are the common broadcloths, the various colors of which are spoken of collectively under the term *fá-shik*, 'flower-colors.' *Síú ní* is the narrow description of woolens, used in opposition to the *tái ní* or broad kind.

| | | |
|---|---|---|
| merchants to come and purchase, who will give a good price for your goods, so that I may secure a little profit for myself: thus it will be for our mutual advantage. | 到有等我叫人<br>客嚟買出多的<br>價俾你等我又<br>賺的用錢咁都<br>好吖 | fó' tò' 'mò; 'tang 'ngó kiú' ,yan hák, ,lai 'mái, ch'ut, ,tó tik, ká' 'pí 'ní, 'tang 'ngó yau' chán' tik, yung' ,ts'ín; 'kóm ,tò 'hò ,á? |
| Very well! I have here two hundred pieces of woolens. | 好咧我有大呢<br>二百疋 | 'Hò ,lé! 'ngó 'yau tái' ,ní í' pák, p'at,. |
| 5. What kind of goods are they? | 係乜野呀 | Hai' mat, 'yé á'? |
| They are Company's woolens. | 係公司大呢 | Hai' ,Kung ,sz' tái' ,ní. |
| 6. Let me see them, will you? Lackaday! these are very poor goods indeed. Surely they cannot be Company's woolens; I fear they are goods of a second quality. | 俾我睇吓呵唉<br>吔呢的貨吩得<br>嚌唔係公司貨<br>怕係船主貨 | 'Pí 'ngó 't'ai 'há ,ó? ,Ái 'yá! ,ní tik, fó' 'yai tak, tsai'. ,'M hai' ,Kung ,sz' fó'; p'á' hai' ,shün 'chü fó'. |
| Not so, they are really very nice goods, only the mode of packing is not quite what it ought to be. | 唔係貨都係好<br>貨總係裝頭爭<br>的啫 | ,'M hai', fó' ,tò hai' 'hò fó', 'tsung hai' ,chóng ,t'au ,chang tik, ,ché. |
| 7. The body of the article is poor; it is thin; it has no nap upon it. | 身分又唔好又<br>薄又冇毛 | ,Shan fan' yau' ,'m 'hò; yau' pók, yau' 'mò ,mò. |
| You quite mistake, Sir! Wishing to buy cheap, you undertake to say that my goods are bad; but if the same goods were only for sale in your own shop, then you would declare that they were most excellent. | 幾假嘁你想買<br>平貨所以就話<br>我的貨唔好之<br>掣倒你舖頭賣<br>個陣時你就話<br>好嘅之哩 | 'Kí 'ká ,né. 'Ní 'séung 'mái ,p'ing fó', 'shó 'í tsau' wá' 'ngó tik, fó' ,'m 'hò ,chí; ,chai 'tò 'ní p'ò' ,t'au mái', kó' chan' ,shí, 'ní tsau' wá' 'hò ké' ,chí lé'. |

5. These broadcloths are styled *Company's* by the Chinese from the fact of their having been first, and for a long time, imported by the English E. I. Company.

6. *Shün chü fó*, shipmaster's cargo, denotes a second quality of broadcloths, such having been formerly imported by the masters of the Company's ships. *Yai tak tsai* designates very poor and worthless commodities.

7. *Kí ká*, several falsities, is a way of telling another that he is mistaken. The phrase *kó chan shí* or *ní chan shí* is used to denote that instant or this instant, always intending a very short space of time.

8. No such thing; you and I are old acquaintances; surely you cannot suppose that I would impose on you.

唔係咁話你我
都係老相與唔
通重嚟你呀

ˏ'M hai$^2$ 'kóm wá$^2$, 'ní 'ngó ˏtò hai$^2$ 'lò ˏséung 'ü; ˏ'm ˏt'ung chung$^2$ t'am' 'ní ˏmé.

I do not know what your intentions are; neither do I pretend to control you. In a word, if you know how to buy, I also know how to sell; I am an old resident in Canton, and if you think you can take me in, that's not quite so easy, I'd have you know.

我唔知你點心
事我不管你總
係你會買我亦
會賣我係老廣
東你想嚟我亦
唔得咁容易實
在話你知呵

'Ngó ˏ'm ˏchí 'ní 'tím ˏsam sz'$^2$, 'ngó pat 'kún 'ní. 'Tsung hai$^2$ 'ní 'úi 'mái, 'ngó yik$_2$ 'úi mái$^2$; 'ngó hai$^2$ 'lò 'Kwóng ˏtung, 'ní 'séung t'am' 'ngó, yik$_2$ ˏ'm tak kóm' ˏyung í$^2$, shat$_2$ tsoi$^2$ wá$^2$ 'ní ˏchí ˏó.

9. Well, well, Sir, let us have no more of this idle talk. Tell me truly, now, how much money you want a yard for this article?

好嚹好嚹咪講
閒話嚹實在你
要幾多銀一碼
呢

'Hò lá', 'hò lá', 'mai 'kóng ˏhán wá$^2$ lá'. Shat$_2$ tsoi$^2$ 'ní iú' 'kí ˏtó ˏngan yat 'má ˏní?

The true and real price is one dollar and thirty-five cents,—besides the duty.

實價一個三毫
半另餉

Shat$_2$ ká' yat kó' ˏsám ˏhò pún', ling$^2$ 'héung.

10. It does not sell at so high a rate; the current price is by no means so high as this.

唔賣得咁價而
家冇咁行情

ˏ'M mái$^2$ tak 'kóm ká'; ˏí ˏká 'mò kóm' ˏhóng ˏts'ing.

Well, if you talk in this manner, pray tell me what you will give?

咁話你俾乜野
價呢

'Kóm wá$^2$, 'ní 'pí mat 'yé ká' ˏní?

11. Just now the local price, at which the article is selling, is one dollar and a half; from this you must discount three per cent.; and you must also take away the duty, twenty-five cents per yard, with the consoo charge of one dollar per piece. Summing up the whole, the very utmost I can

現在本地價賣
得個半要九七
扣又要除餉二
毫半又除行用
每疋一吱算起
嚟至多俾你一

Ín$^2$ tsoi$^2$ 'pún tí$^2$ ká' mái$^2$ tak kó' pún'; iú' 'kau ts'at k'au'; yau$^2$ iú' ˏch'ü 'héung í$^2$ ˏhò pún'; yau$^2$ ˏch'ü ˏhóng yung$^2$, 'múi p'at yat ˏman. Sün' 'hí ˏlai chí' ˏtó 'pí

8. *T'am* is a local term, used commonly in conversation, having the meaning conveyed by the terms, impose on, take in, deceive, &c. Foreigners who have resided in the country for a long time, are called *lò Kwóngtung* by the people, a phrase which is sometimes translated "an old Cantoner."

| | | |
|---|---|---|
| give you, is one dollar and sixteen cents, to be paid in ready money. | 個一毫六係交現銀 | ʻní yatˀ kóʾ yatˀ ˏhò lukˀ, hai$^2$ ˏkáu ín$^2$ ˏngan. |
| That's too bad! I can never lose so much. | 嚡唔蝕得咁多 | ˏHái! ˏʻm shít, takˀ kómʾ ˏtó. |
| 12. All kinds of woolen goods, which are imported, are selling below their prime cost. | 個的來路疋頭所有都要蝕的本嚹 | Kóʾ tikˀ ˏloi lò$^2$ pʻatˀ ˏtʻau, ʻshó ʻyau ˏtò iú' shít, tikˀ ʻpún láʾ. |
| As for losing money on goods, if it is only a few per cent., it is of no great importance; but when you want me to lose twenty or thirty per cent., how can I ever do that? | 蝕係蝕蝕幾厘就唔相干你要我蝕二三分錢黙做得呢 | Shít, hai$^2$ shít,; shít, ʻkí ˏlí tsáu$^2$ ˏʻm ˏséung ˏkón; ʻní iúʾ ʻngó shít, í$^2$ ˏsám ˏfan ˏtsʻín, ʻtím tsò$^2$ takˀ ˏní? |
| 13. Well, then, since we cannot fix on any price for this article, let us talk about some other. Have you any fine broadcloth on hand? | 噢呢宗唔講得喘又講別樣你有衣着大呢有冇蠘 | Ó, ˏní ˏtsung ˏʻm ʻkóng takˀ, ˏngám, yau$^2$ ʻkóng pít, yéung$^2$. ʻNí ʻyau ˏí chéukˀ tái$^2$ ˏní ʻyau ʻmò ˏné? |
| No, I brought some two years ago, but your people here would not pay what it cost me, and I suffered a loss on it, and therefore I have never brought any more since that time; and moreover, the amount consumed here is very small indeed. | 冇先兩年我都帶嚟總係你的本地人唔出得價要蝕本所以總唔帶嚟況且又唔消得幾多 | ʻMò; ˏsín ʻléung ˏnín ʻngó ˏtò taiʾ ˏlai, ʻtsung hai$^2$ ʻní tikˀ ʻpún tí$^2$ ˏyan ˏʻm chʻutˀ takˀ káʾ, iúʾ shít, ʻpún, ʻshò ʻi ʻtsung ˏʻm taiʾ ˏlai; fóngʾ ʻchʻé yau$^2$ ˏʻm ˏsíú takˀ ʻkí ˏtó. |
| 14. Alas, what a pity! Why, only the day before yesterday, Mr. So-and-so sold upwards of a hundred pieces, at four dollars per yard, including duty,—so good is the price at which this article is now sold. | 唉吔可惜美士某某大前日賣個一百幾疋四個銀錢連餉咋而家賣得咁好價 | ˏÁi ʻyá, ˏʻhó sikˀ! ʻMí sz' ʻMau ʻmau, tái$^2$ ˏtsʻín yat, mái$^2$ kóʾ yatˀ pákˀ ʻkí pʻatˀ, sz' kóʾ ˏngan ˏtsʻín, ˏlín ʻhéung cháʾ; ˏí ˏká mái$^2$ takˀ kómʾ ʻhò káʾ. |
| What kind of stuff was it? | 黙樣嘅貨呀 | ʻTím yéung$^2$ kéʾ fóʾ áʾ? |

13. *Ngám* and *ó*, and also *hái* in No. 11, above, are local terms; they are not always used in precisely the same sense, nor is it possible to translate them in all cases by a single word.

| | | |
|---|---|---|
| 15. It was not of the first quality superfine cloth, it was only of the second quality, in a flowered tillot, that opened at the side. | 又唔係頂上衣着係冲衣着花袋橫開裝嘅 | Yau[2] ꜁'m hai[2] 'ting shéung[2] ꜀í chéuk꜁, hai[2] ꜀ch'ung ꜀í chéuk꜁, ꜀fá toi[3] ꜁wáng ꜀hoi ꜀chóng ké꜃. |
| Do you know whether it was packed in bales, or whether it was put up in wooden boxes? | 你知係包仔裝頭備亻木箱裝頭呢 | 'Ní ꜀chí hai[2] ꜀páu 'tsai ꜀chóng ꜁t'au, pí[2] hai[2] muk꜁ ꜀séung ꜀chóng ꜁t'au ꜀ní? |
| 16. It was put up in wooden boxes, the inside of which were lined with tin, and ten pieces were packed in each box. | 係木箱裝嘅裡頭有馬口鐵礶每箱裝十疋 | Hai[2] muk꜁ ꜀séung ꜀chóng ké꜃, 'lí ꜁t'au 'yau 'má 'hau t'ít꜁ kún꜃, 'múi ꜀séung ꜀chóng shap꜁ p'at꜁. |
| Just now what kinds of goods are in the highest demand in the market? | 而家邊宗貨至好賣呢 | ꜁Í ꜀ká ꜀pín ꜀tsung fó꜃ chí꜃ 'hò mái[2] ꜀ní? |
| 17. Just now the goods highest in demand are the habit cloths, with gold headings; also those put up in tillots, opening at the side. Those also with two dragons on the tillot heads are very good. But those with double wings [on the tillot heads], those loosely put up, white ground tillot heads, elephants and double I on the tillot heads, plain tillots, and those with eagle's heads, are all sold with difficulty. | 而家至好賣係金紙頭橫開月亮其餘龍鳳頭都好總係個的雙翼懶梳粧粉頭象頭雙工字素袋鷄頭都係惡賣的 | ꜁Í ꜀ká chí꜃ 'hò mái[2] hai[2] ꜀kam 'chí ꜁t'au, ꜁wáng ꜀hoi ut꜁ léung[2]. ꜁K'i ꜁ü ꜁lung fung[2] ꜁t'au ꜀tò 'hò. 'Tsung hai[2] kó꜃ tik꜁ ꜀shéung yik꜁, 'lán ꜀shó ꜀chóng, 'fan ꜁t'au, tséung[2] ꜁t'au, ꜀shéung ꜀kung tsz'[2], sü꜃ toi[2], ꜀kai ꜁t'au, ꜀tò hai[2] ok꜁ mái[2] tik꜁. |
| Those narrow woolens, 32½ inches wide (worleys), how are they doing at present? | 個的二尺二小呢點樣呢 | Kó꜃ tik꜁ í[2] ch'ik꜁ í[2] 'síu ꜁ní 'tím yéung[2] ꜀ní? |
| 18. At present they command no price at all. | 而家冇乜價錢 | ꜁Í ꜀ká 'mò mat꜁ ká꜃ ꜁ts'ín. |
| And coarse stuffs (such as baize), how are they? | 粗嘅呢 | ꜀Ts'ò ké꜃ ꜀ní? |
| 19. Nobody wants them. | 冇人愛 | 'Mò ꜁yan oi꜃ |

Attention to the manner and connection in which they are used will usually show their true meaning.

17. What the Chinese, in this instance, call *kai t'au*, are fair pictures of an eagle's head, and are consequently so put in the translation. The same style of giving misnomers occurs in some other instances, such as where the picture of the lion's head is styled *chü t'au*, a hog's head. The character *kung* is used to denote that kind of cloth marked with a double I on the tillots because of the resemblance between the character and the letter, as the Chinese prefer, in most cases, to describe the mark than to transfer it.

| | | |
|---|---|---|
| At the present time what is the best assortment of colors for woolen goods? | 而家個的大呢<br>點樣配色好呢 | ˏÍ ‹ká kóʼ tik› tái$^{2}$ ˏní, ʻtím yéung$^{2}$ pʻúiʼ shik› ʻhò ‹ní? |
| 20. The greater part should consisє of purple, mazarine, scarlet, and black, for these are the best; the other mixed colors are sold at present with great difficulty. You ought to sort them, as they used to be done, formerly, in the times of the Company—this would be the best plan for you. | 總要蒲青寶藍<br>花紅元青配得<br>多就好其餘雜<br>色就惡賣㘓你<br>要配番舊公司<br>個陣時咁樣就<br>好嘞 | ʻTsung íúʼ ˏpʻò ‹tsʻing, ʻpò ˏlám, ‹fá ˏhung, ˏün ‹tsʻing, pʻúi› tak› ‹tó tsau$^{2}$ ʻhò; ˏkʻí ˏü tsáp$_{2}$ shik› tsau$^{2}$ ók› mái$^{2}$ láʼ. ʻNí íúʼ pʻúiʼ ‹fán kau$^{2}$ ˏKung ‹szʼ kóʼ chan$^{2}$ ˏshí; kómʼ yéung$^{2}$ tsau$^{2}$ ʻhò lák›. |
| No doubt of it. | 係咧 | Hai$^{2}$ ‹lé. |
| 21. In reference to your goods, I should like to know how the custom-house officer measured them for duty? | 而家你的貨唔<br>知老太驗算幾<br>長呀 | ˏÍ ‹ká ʻní tik› fóʼ ˏʼm ‹chí ʻlò tʻáiʼ ím$^{2}$ sünʼ ʻkí ˏchʻéung áʼ? |
| Why is it, now, that you trouble me, by asking this question? | 你做乜問起我<br>個的嚟呀 | ʻNí tsò$^{2}$ mat› man$^{2}$ ʻhí ʻngó kóʼ tik› ˏlai áʼ? |
| 22. It is not asked to trouble you, but because on a former occasion I was greatly taken in; not knowing beforehand that he examined and entered them as being so very long [as he did], I had consequently to suffer severely for it: truly I was deceived in the matter. | 唔係因爲我從<br>前上過當嚟我<br>先唔知到佢驗<br>長咁多要我暗<br>蝕咁多銀眞正<br>唔抵 | ˏʼM hai$^{2}$, ‹yan wai$^{2}$ ʻngó ˏtsʻung ‹tsʻín ʻshéung kwóʼ tóngʼ ˏlai; ʻngó ‹sín ˏʼm ‹chí tòʼ ʻkʻü ím$^{2}$ ‹chʻéung kómʼ ‹tó, íúʼ ʻngó ómʼ shít$_{2}$ kómʼ ‹tó ˏngan: ‹chan chingʼ ˏʼm ʻtai. |
| On this occasion you have no cause to fear, for he examined them very favorably indeed, reckoning each piece at fifty cubits. | 呢回唔怕佢都<br>驗得好每疋作<br>五丈算 | ‹Ní ˏúi ˏʼm pʻáʼ; ʻkʻü ‹tò ím$^{2}$ tak› ʻhò ʻmúi pʻat› tsók› ʻʼng chéung$^{2}$ sünʼ? |
| 23. Well, have you on hand any long-ells or not? | 你重有嗶嘰有<br>冇呀 | ʻNí chung$^{2}$ ʻyau pat› ‹kí ʻyau ʻmò áʼ? |

22. Much difficulty has long existed in regard to the measuring of goods in this market, and the cases in which deception is practiced are numerous. The phrase *shéung kwó tóng* alludes to the pawnbroker's occupation, and is used by unfortunate individuals whose necessities oblige them to procure money in this mode, when they think they have been deceived.

| | | |
|---|---|---|
| I have. | 有 | ᶜYau. |
| 24. What assortment of colors are they? | 係乜野配色嘅 | Hai$^2$ mat꜀ ᶜyé p‘úi$^2$ shik꜀ ké$^2$? |
| I'll let you see them, so that you may write down the different colors. | 我俾你睇等你抄花色去阿 | ᶜNgó ᶜpí ᶜní ᶜt‘ai, ᶜtang ᶜní ꜀ch‘áu ꜀fá shik꜀ h‘ü$^2$ ꜀ó. |
| 25. Lackaday! What a motley assortment of colors you have here—too many of green, yellow, and gray—all of which are troublesome to sell. | 唉吔咁雜色嘅嚊都係綠黃灰多咁就費事惡賣 | ꜀Ái ᶜyá! kóm$^2$ tsáp$_2$ shik꜀ ké$^2$ pí$^2$; ꜀tò hai$^2$ luk$_2$, ꜁wóng, ꜀fúi ꜀tó, kóm$^2$ tsau$^2$ fai$^2$ sz'$^2$ ók꜀ mái$^2$? |
| If you will only examine the article, you will find that it is good and strong, though the assortment of colors is somewhat inferior. | 你睇雖然配色唔係好到底身分好又結實 | ᶜNí ᶜt‘ai ꜀sui ꜁ín p‘úi$^2$ shik꜀ ꜁'m hai$^2$ ᶜhò, tò$^2$ ᶜtai ꜀shan fan$^2$ ᶜhò, yau$^2$ kít꜀ shat$_2$. |
| 26. I see, however, that the goods are rather narrow. | 我睇呢個貨窄得的 | ᶜNgó ᶜt‘ai ꜀ní kó$^2$ fó$^2$ chák꜀ tak꜀ tik꜀. |
| If so, I will accordingly reduce the price, that I may sell them to you—indeed I will. | 係窄的我減的價賣過你係咧 | Hai$^2$ chák꜀ tik꜀, ᶜngó ᶜkám tik꜀ ká$^2$ mái$^2$ kwó$^2$ ᶜní, hai$^2$ ꜀lé. |
| 27. Now really and truly, how much money do you want for this article? | 你實在要幾多銀呢 | ᶜNí shat$_2$ tsoi$^2$ íú$^2$ ᶜkí ꜀tó ꜁ngan ꜀ní? |
| I will tell you the true price, the very lowest cash at which I can sell them is seven dollars and a half, you paying duty. | 我話個老實價至少七個半你出餉 | ᶜNgó wá$^2$ kó$^2$ ᶜlò shat$_2$ ká$^2$, chí$^2$ ᶜshiú ts‘at꜀ kó$^2$ pún$^2$, ᶜní ch‘ut꜀ ᶜhéung. |
| 28. I cannot give you so high a price, the very utmost I can give is seven dollars and twenty-five cents. | 我唔俾得咁高至多俾你七個二毫半 | ᶜNgó ꜁'m ᶜpí tak꜀ kóm$^2$ ꜀kò; chí$^2$ ꜀tó ᶜpí ᶜní ts‘at꜀ kó$^2$ í$^2$ ꜁hò pún$^2$. |
| You ought to add a little to your price, then it will do very well. | 你要添起的至做得 | ᶜNí íú$^2$ ꜀t‘ím ᶜhí tik꜀ chí$^2$ tsò$^2$ tak꜀. |
| 29. You ought to abate a little from your price, then it will do very well. | 你又要減的至做得 | ᶜNí yau$^2$ íú$^2$ ᶜkám tik꜀ chí$^2$ tsò$^2$ tak꜀. |

24. *P‘úi* means a class or sort, referring here to cloths of various shades well arranged in separate cases or divisions, and not where there are *tsáp shik*, motley colors.

Well, well, then, let us split the difference.

好唎好唎拗開
佢丨

ʻHò ˓lé, ʻhò ˓lé, ʻáu ˓hoi ʽk'ü ˓lé.

30. Ah! that will do very well. What will be the price, when thus computed?

呀就好唎算係
幾多嘅

Á'! tsau$^{2}$ ʻhò ˓lé. Sün' hai$^{2}$ ʻkí ˓tó ˓né?

When computed at this rate, it will amount to seven dollars and thirty-seven and a half cents; and you must pay me ready money.

算係七個三毫
七絲半你要交
現銀俾我

Sün' hai$^{2}$ ts'at˒ kó' ˓sám ˏhò ts'at˒ ˓sz' pún'; ʽní íú' ˓káu ín$^{2}$ ˏngan ʻpí ʽngó.

31. No, never, I am reckoning it at two month's credit.

冇呀我算兩月
期呀

ʽMò á'; ʽngó sün' ʽléung üt$_{2}$ ˓k'í á'.

This will never do; I want to pay money to the *I'wó hóng* (Howqua's). Do you go now and pay the money over to him, and ask him to put it to my account; and that will answer.

唔係我要俾銀
過怡和你去交
銀過佢呌佢入
我數就係唎

ˏ'M hai$^{2}$; ʽngó íú' ʻpí ˏngan kwó' ˏI' ˏwó. ʽNí h'ü' ˓káu ˏngan kwó' ʽk'ü, kíú' ʽk'ü yap$_{2}$ ʽngó sò'; tsau$^{2}$ hai$^{2}$ ˓lé.

32. Very good; and what other cargo have you on hand?

好唎你重有乜
野貨呢

ʻHò ˓lé; ʽní chung$^{2}$ ʽyau mat˒ ʽyé fó' ˓ní?

I have still a thousand pieces of long-ells, but they are only single seal, and are not double seals; and they have neither double wings nor stars [on the shields]; but they are like the eagle's head, with two wings.

我重有一千疋
單鉛錢嗶嘰唔
係雙鉛錢又唔
係雙翼又唔係
花籃算係鷄頭
兩翼

ʽNgó chung$^{2}$ ʽyau yat˒ ˓ts'ín p'at˒ ˓tán ˏün ˏts'ín pat˒ ˓kí, ˏ'm hai$^{2}$ ˓shéung ˏün ˏts'ín; yau$^{2}$ ˏ'm hai$^{2}$ ˓shéung yik$_{2}$; yau$^{2}$ ˏ'm hai$^{2}$ ˓fá ˏlám, sün' hai$^{2}$ ˓kai ˏt'au ʽléung yik$_{2}$.

33. What a pity! This description of goods must sell still cheaper than before. If they were only the large and small dog-[like figure], or that of the insect, they would do very well. But these eagle heads, and flowered til-

唉吔呢個貨越
法要平比方係
大小狗蚊蟣都
重好的呢個鷄

˓Ái ʽyá! ˓Ní kó' fó' üt$_{2}$ fát˒ íú' ˏp'ing. ʻPí ˓fóng hai$^{2}$ tái$^{2}$ ʻsíú ʻkau, ˓man ˓tsz', ˓tò chung$^{2}$ ʻhò tik˒. ˓Ní kó'

29. The phrase *áu hoi k'ü*, means split open it, i. e. divide the difference in the prices, named by us, into two equal parts, so that each may take an equal share.

31. *K'í* denotes a term of time, a fixed period, and here the context shows the term refers to the time of payment, thus showing how long the term of credit was to be extended.

32. The Chinese having but one coin, apply the word *ts'ín* as a general term for all coins bearing devices, and by a further extension, include stamped seals like those here described.

廣東方言讀本

lots, are sold with extreme difficulty. And I perceive, moreover, that this kind of goods has no substance—they are coarse and loose.

頭花袋至難賣
嘅我睇呢個貨
又冇身分又粗
又鬆

‹kai ˏt‘au ‹fá toi$^{2}$, chí’ ˏnán mái$^{2}$ ké’. ʿNgó ‘t‘ai ‹ní kó’ fó’ yau$^{2}$ ʿmò ‹shan fan$^{2}$, yau$^{2}$ ‹ts‘ò, yau$^{2}$ ‹sung.

Well, granting that they are, will you nevertheless, make me an offer for them?

雖係咁樣你都
俾個價錢我唉

‹Sui hai$^{2}$ ‘kóm yéung$^{2}$, ʿní ‹tò ‘pí kó’ ká’ ˏts‘ín ʿngó ‹é?

34. The very utmost I can give is eight dollars, including the duty.

我至多俾八個
銀錢過你連餉

ʿNgó chí’ ‹tó ‘pí pát› kò’ ˏngan ˏts‘ín kwó’ ʿní, ˏlín ‘héung.

This will never do; so I have only to wait patiently for a while, and see if the price does not rise, then I can sell.

咁樣唔做得只
骨等吓睇試起
的價至賣咯

‘Kóm yéung$^{2}$ ˏ’m tsò$^{2}$ tak›; chat› ‘kún ‘tang ʿhá, ‘t‘ai shí’ ‘hí tik› ká’ chí’ mái$^{2}$ lók›.

35. So indeed! You are then expecting the price will go up, which is not very probable; I conceive it will go down instead of rising. This kind of inferior goods, you ought to sell off immediately; this is the best thing you can do.

唉吔你想起價
唔輕易我睇得
有跌冇起咁嘅
呺貨你要赶快
賣至着

‹Ái ʿyá! ʿNí ‘séung ‘hí ká’ ˏ’m ‹hing í$^{2}$; ʿngó ‘t‘ai tak› ʿyau tít› ʿmò ‘hí. ‘Kóm ké’ ʿyai fó’, ʿní íú’ ‘kón fái’ mái$^{2}$ chí’ chéuk›.

Very well; do you see if there is anybody who will consent to barter tea and other goods for them; if so, then it will be easy to come to an agreement.

好喇你睇有人
肯換茶葉等貨
就易商量的

‘Hò ‹lé, ʿní ‘t‘ai ʿyau ˏyan ‘hang ún$^{2}$ ˏch‘á íp› ‘tang fó’; tsau$^{2}$ í$^{2}$, ‹shéung ˏléung tik›.

36. You ought by all means to write a letter to your correspondents, advising them never again to send any more of this kind of goods having ticket ends; 't is of the utmost importance to do so.

你千萬要寫信
話過你伙計知
唔好辦呢個牌
頭貨嚟至緊至
緊呀

ʿNí ‹ts‘ín mán$^{2}$ íú’ ‘sé sun’ wá$^{2}$ kwó’ ʿní ‘fó kí’ ‹chí, ˏ’m ‘hò pán$^{2}$ ‹ní kó’ ˏp‘ái ˏt‘au fó’ ˏlai; chí’ ‘kan, chí’ ‘kan á’.

So indeed it is, and I thank you much for your

係咯多得多得

Hai$^{2}$ lok›, ‹tó tak›, ‹tó tak›.

36. *Fóki* is a familiar phrase applied by one to his companions, or comrades: *fó* signifies a man who messes with another, or has his food cooked at the same fire with him, compounded of man and fire; *ki* means to calculate, to plan, and here it indicates the character of the Chinese merchant in his plans and calculations for acquiring gain. The phrase has become at Canton among foreigners, in some sort a sobriquet for the Chinese people generally, as John Bull is for the people of England, or Jonathan for those of the United States.

| | | |
|---|---|---|
| advice. I have here some camlets which I must commission you to sell. | 我呢處有羽紗<br>拜托你賣 | ʻNgó ˏní chʻü' ʻyau ʻü ˏshá pái' tʻok, ʻní mái'. |
| 37. Unfortunate indeed! of all things, camlets are the most difficult to sell; now-a-days these goods are not in general consumption. | 唉吔至唔好賣<br>係羽紗而家個<br>宗貨總唔消流 | ˏÁi ʻyá! chí' ˏ'm ʻhò mái' hai' ʻü ˏshá; ˏí ˏká kó' ˏtsung fó' ʻtsung ˏ'm ˏsíú ˏlau. |
| Why is this? | 乜原故呢 | Mat, ˏün kú' ˏní? |
| 38. It is because the northern people for the most part do not wear them, since their own silk camlets are far better, being both more durable and more handsome. | 所有外江都唔<br>興着佢因爲本<br>地綢緞重好又<br>蚙又好睇 | ʻShó ʻyau ngoi' ˏkóng ˏtò ˏ'm ˏhing chéuk, ʻkʻü, ˏyan wai' ʻpún tí' ˏchʻau tün' chung' ʻhò, yau' ˏkʻam, yau' ʻhò ʻtʻai. |
| Well then, see if you can barter them for some commodity or other. | 好喇你睇以貨<br>易貨都好喇 | ʻHò ˏlé, ʻní ʻtʻai ʻí fó' yik, fó' ˏtò ʻhò ˏlé. |
| 39. For what kinds of produce would you like to exchange them? | 你想換乜野貨<br>嚱 | ʻNí ʻséung ún' mat, ʻyé fó' ˏné? |
| Teas, Nankeen, raw silk, rhubarb, and sundry other commodities, are all exchangeable. You may give the holder of the produce a rather high price, that I may be able to sell the camlets more readily. | 茶葉湖絲大黃<br>雜貨都得你俾<br>貨客好的價我<br>的羽紗就易賣 | ˏChʻá íp, ˏú ˏsz', tái' ˏwóng, tsáp, fó', ˏtò tak,. ʻNí ʻpí fó' hák, ʻhò tik, ká', ʻngó tik, ʻü ˏshá tsau' í' mái'. |
| 40. Very good; if you please let me see of what quality they are, and how they are packed. | 好喇俾我睇乜<br>野號乜野裝頭 | ʻHò ˏlé; ʻpí ʻngó ʻtʻai mat, ʻyé hò', mat, ʻyé ˏchóng ˏtʻau. |
| I have got Doubles, Singles, and Second Singles; you may see the foreign letters D, S, and SS, which are distinctly written on the ticket-ends. | 一二三號都有<br>你睇個的番字<br>D S SS 都寫明<br>在牌頭呢 | Yat,, í', ˏsám, hò', ˏtò ʻyau; ʻní ʻtʻai kó' tik, ˏfán tsz'', *de*, *ess*, *double-ess* ˏtò ʻsé ˏming tsoi' ˏpʻái ˏtʻau ˏní. |

38. The phrase *ngoi kóng*, beyond the river, is used by the people of Canton to designate those who come from the middle and eastern provinces to the city to trade, and by extension is also sometimes employed to denote persons from all parts of the empire, except this and the adjoining province of Fukkín.

40. Foreign letters, like D, S, SS., &c., may be often seen on goods in Chinese shops and warehouses. The names of manufacturers, affixed to their goods, sometimes become celebrated. Once, and for a long time, the English E. I. Company's mark was regarded as a sure warrant for a good quality of merchandise.

廣東方言讀本

41. This ticket-end has not the two white fish-eyes, though it has the blue threads; it is only an imitation of the Company's cargo.

呢個牌頭唔係雙白魚眼係個藍間線假裝公司貨

‹Ní kó' ˏp'ái ˏt'au ˏ'm hai[2] ‹shéung pák› ˏü ʻngán, hai[2] kó' ‹lám kán[2] sín', ʻká ‹chóng ‹Kung ‹sz' fó'.

Very true; but only observe the [low] price of the goods, and among them are some having the green fish-eyes.

係咯你睇乜野價錢唉裡頭亦有綠魚眼嘅

Hai[2] lók›; ʻní ʻt'ai mat› ʻyé ká' ˏts'ín ‹é, ʻlí ˏt'au yik› ʻyau luk› ˏü ʻngán ké'.

42. Enough, enough! Have you on hand any Dutch camlets or not?

罷嚹你有荷囒羽緞冇呢

Pá[2] lá'; ʻní ʻyau ˏHó ‹lán ʻü tün[2] ʻmò ‹né?

Of those Dutch camlets, I have sold all I had, but I have still some English imitations of Dutch, would you like them or not?

個的荷囒羽緞賣嘥咯重有的羽緞仔你愛唔愛呢

Kó' tik› ˏHó ‹lán ʻü tün[2] mái[2] sái' lók›, chung[2] ʻyau tik› ʻü tün[2] ʻtsai, ʻní oi' ˏ'm oi' ‹ní?

43. I do not want any of your English imitations of Dutch; nobody will wear them. What other goods have you?

唔愛你的紅毛羽緞冇人着重有乜貨呢

ˏ'M oi', ʻní tik› ˏHung ˏmò ʻü tün[2] ʻmò ˏyan chéuk›; chung' ʻyau mat› fó' ‹ní?

I have got bombazetts, Angola cloths, lastings, figured bombazetts, merinoes, coarse bunting, and worsted thread;—will you purchase or not?

有羽紗仔羽綢羽綾扯花羽綢羽斜羽布毛線買唔買呢

ʻYau ʻü ‹shá ʻtsai, ʻü ˏch'au, ʻü ˏling, ʻch'ó ‹fá ʻü ˏch'au, ʻü ˏts'é, ʻü pò', ˏmò sín'; ʻmái ˏ'm ʻmái ‹ní?

44. These articles of merchandise are, at present, not at all in vogue.

個的貨而家總唔通行

Kó' tik› fó' ˏí ‹ká ʻtsung ˏ'm ‹tung ˏhang.

Though they may not be in vogue, yet they must be sold. Is it possible that nobody will ever want them? According to what you say, my best plan would be to shut up my doors, and wholly desist from business!

唔通行都要賣呀唔通總冇人愛依你咁話不如關了門唔做生意咯

ˏ'M ‹tung ˏhang, ‹tò íú' mái[2] á'. ˏ'M ‹tung ʻtsung ʻmò ˏyan oi'? ‹I' ʻní ʻkóm wá[2], pat› ˏü ‹kwán ʻlíú ˏmún, ˏ'm tsò[2] ‹shang í' lók›.

42. The meaning of *ütün tsai*, in the closing part of this paragraph, is explained in the beginning of the next, by *Hungmò*, a vulgar, but common name, for English.

| | | |
|---|---|---|
| 45. No, I meant no such thing; and only intended to say that, the price being now so very low, I was afraid you would not like to part with your goods. You had better let a few days pass, when the price certainly must rise a little. Have you yet any new goods, which have come to your consignment? | 唔係咁話不過時價冷淡你未必肯甩手不如再過幾日是必起的價你重有乜新貨到冇呀 | ˛'M hai$^{2}$ 'kóm wá$^{1}$; pat› kwó$^{3}$ ˛shí ká$^{3}$ 'lang tám$^{2}$, 'ní mí$^{2}$ pít› 'hang lat› 'shau. Pat› ˛ü tsoi$^{3}$ kwó$^{3}$ 'kí yat˛, shí$^{2}$ pít› 'hí tik› ká$^{3}$. 'Ní chung$^{2}$ 'yau mat› ‹san fó$^{3}$ tò$^{3}$ 'mò á$^{3}$? |
| My long-cloths are still at Whampoa, not having yet been brought up from the ship. Moreover, in the vessels recently arrived, it is very probable there are goods to my consignment; but not having yet received any invoices or samples, I cannot inform you with certainty respecting them. | 我的洋布在黃埔未曾起重有新到個幫船大約我都有貨在內總係未曾收到貨單貨辦唔話得實你知 | 'Ngó tik› ˛yéung pò$^{3}$ tsoi$^{2}$ ˛Wóng pò$^{3}$, mí$^{2}$ ˛ts'ang 'hí. Chung$^{2}$ 'yau ‹san tò$^{3}$ kó$^{3}$ ‹póng ˛shün, tái$^{2}$ yéuk› 'ngó ‹tò 'yau fó$^{3}$ tsoi$^{2}$ noi$^{2}$; 'tsung hai$^{2}$ mí$^{2}$ ˛ts'ang ‹shau tò$^{3}$ fó$^{3}$ ‹tán, fó$^{3}$ pán$^{2}$, ˛'m wá$^{2}$ tak› shat˛ 'ní ‹chí. |
| 46. Very well. So soon as your samples do arrive, will you be so good as to inform me? | 好咧貨辦就到你就通知我囉 | 'Hò ‹lé. Fó$^{3}$ pán$^{2}$ tsau$^{2}$ tò$^{3}$, 'ní tsau$^{2}$ ‹tung ‹chí 'ngó ‹lò? |
| Certainly I will. | 自然咧 | Tsz'$^{2}$ ˛ín ‹lé. |
| 47. Upon this understanding, I'll bid you good bye, wishing you success in your sales. | 咁話請咯你好賣至囉 | 'Kóm wá$^{2}$, 'ts'ing lok›, 'ní 'hò mái$^{2}$ chí$^{3}$ ‹lò. |
| Go in peace! you will, of course, come again and patronize me. | 好行咧再來幫襯 | 'Hò ˛hang ‹lé; tsoi$^{3}$ ˛loi ‹póng ch'an$^{3}$. |
| 48. You are very kind. Good bye! | 好話請 | 'Hò wá$^{2}$. 'Ts'ing! |
| Good bye! | 請 | 'Ts'ing! |

45. *Fópán*, in the dialect prevalent in Canton between foreign and native merchants, is usually translated *muster*; thus there are musters of teas, musters of silks, &c. The names given to cloths of foreign manufacture by the Chinese are not always the same in different places; sometimes persons will learn the foreign names, and call the fabric by it, while others not having heard its original appellation, are obliged to invent a descriptive term for the article, which in places remote from each other, may be also unlike. The same remark applies to other articles of import besides woolens.

## Section Sixth.

# DIALOGUE ON BUYING PIECE GOODS.

## 買賣布疋問答第六章

ʻMái mái$^{2}$ pò' p'at› man$^{2}$ táp›; tai$^{2}$ luk$_{2}$ ‹chéung.

| | | |
|---|---|---|
| 1. You have opened a shop for the sale of all kinds of piece goods, have you not? | 你開一間舖賣各樣布疋係嗎 | ʻNí ‹hoi yat› ‹kán p'ò' mái$^{2}$ kók› yéung$^{2}$ pò' p'at›, hai$^{2}$ ʻmá? |
| Yes, yes. No mistake! | 冇錯冇錯 | ʻMò ts'ó'! ʻmò ts'ó'! |
| 2. Have you foreign long-cloths? | 你有洋布冇呀 | ʻNí ʻyau ͵yéung pò', ʻmò á'? |
| I have both white long-cloths, and gray long-cloths; but those domestics are all sold off. | 有咧白丨元色布都有個的粗丨賣嘥咯 | ʻYau ‹lé; pák$_{2}$ pò', ͵ün shik› pò', ‹tò ʻyau; kó' tik› ‹ts'ò pò' mái$^{2}$ sái' lòk›. |
| 3. If you have samples, will you let me see them? | 你有辦俾我睇吓呵 | ʻNí ʻyau pán$^{2}$ ʻpí ʻngó ʻt'ai ʻhá ‹ó? |
| Here I have some small samples. | 呢處有小辦 | ‹Ní ch'ü' ʻyau ʻsíú pán$^{2}$. |
| 4. Small samples are of no use whatever, for one cannot form a correct opinion from them; pull out a whole piece, and let me look at it. | 小辦唔中用唔睇得清楚摺疋成疋嘅俾我睇 | ʻSíú pán$^{2}$ ͵'m ‹chung yung$^{2}$, ͵'m ʻt'ai tak› ‹ts'ing ʻch'o; ͵tsím p'at› ͵shing p'at› ké' ʻpí ʻngó ʻt'ai. |
| Here is a piece which has a six gold thread end. | 呢處有一疋係六金頭 | ‹Ní ch'ü' ʻyau yat› p'at› hai$^{2}$ luk$_{2}$ ‹kam ͵t'au. |
| 5. I want a seven gold thread end. | 我要七金頭 | ʻNgó íú' ts'at› ‹kam ͵t'au. |
| I have it; I have also three red thread ends, and twelve red thread ends. | 有重有三紅頭十二紅頭 | ʻYau; chung$^{2}$ ʻyau ‹sám ͵hung ͵t'au, shap$_{2}$ í$^{2}$ ͵hung ͵t'au. |

### *Notes and Explanations.*

THIS dialogue is supposed to be held between two natives, one a shopman and the other his customer. The language is designed to correspond with that ordinarily used among the common people, in their daily intercourse for business. Different trades among the Chinese have a great number of slang expressions peculiar to themselves, and shopmen abound in them; there are also many phrases in common use alluding to buying and selling, strikingly characteristic of the trading propensities of this people.

2. It will be seen that nearly all the articles enumerated in this section are cotton; and the names, English and Chinese, are those by which they are commonly known in this market.

| | | |
|---|---|---|
| 6. Very well; bring me also a piece of red and gold crossed end. | 好咧重攞一疋紅夾金嘅 | 'Hò ˏlé; chung² 'ló yatˋ p'atˋ ˏhung kápˋ ˏkam ké'. |
| I have it also here. | 都有 | ˏTò 'yau. |
| 7. Have you also any tape ends? | 你重有素頭嘅 | 'Ní chung² 'yau sú' ˏt'au ké'? |
| No, I have not. | 冇咯 | 'Mò lókˋ. |
| 8. I know the most saleable kind are these tape-ends, but as for those stamped with St. George and the Dragon, nobody wants them. | 我知到素頭係好賣總係個的人馬印就冇人愛嘅咯 | 'Ngó ˏchí tò' sú' ˏt'au hai² 'hò mái², 'tsung hai² kó' tikˋ ˏyan 'má yan' tsau² 'mò ˏyan oi' ké' lákˋ. |
| Right, you're quite right: just now I calculate that the qualities 72s and 66s are the two chiefly in consumption; here I have them both. | 冇錯冇錯而家重算〧〢〦〦兩樣通流呢處都有 | 'Mò ts'ó'! 'mò ts'ó'! ˏí ˏká chung² sün' ts'atˋ-í² lukˏ-lukˏ 'léung yéung² ˏt'ung ˏlau; ˏní ch'ü' ˏtò 'yau. |
| 9. Lackaday! This cloth of yours is all starched as stiff as buckram; if your goods were really taken up soft, it would surely be an improvement in them. Those goods, the long-ells, are they in single or double pieces? | 唉吔個的都係粉漿嘅刮漿嘅如果係淨水布就好你的貨係單疋備係雙疋嘅呢 | ˏÁi 'yá! kó' tikˋ ˏtò hai² 'fan ˏtséung ké', kwátˋ ˏtséung ké'; ˏü 'kwó hai² tsing² 'shui pò', tsau² 'hò. 'Ní tikˋ fó' hai² ˏtán p'atˋ, pí² hai² ˏshéung p'atˋ ké' ˏné? |
| I have some of eighty yards in length, and also of forty yards, which you may have at your pleasure. | 亦有八十碼嘅又有四十碼嘅隨你要啫 | Yikˏ 'yau pátˋ shapˏ 'má ké'; yau² 'yau sz' shapˏ 'má ké'; ˏts'ui 'ní iú' ché.' |
| 10. Give me some of your goods, I wish to see if they are long enough, and broad enough. | 俾呢的貨我睇吓夠長夠闊唔夠啊 | 'Pí ˏní tikˋ fó', 'ngó 't'ai 'há, káu' ˏch'éung kau' fútˋ ˏ'm káu' ˏó. |
| They are full breadth, but they are not quite long | 闊就夠長就唔 | Fútˋ tsau² káu', ˏch'éung |

8. Goods stamped with St. George and the Dragon, are styled by the shopmen, *yan má yan*, or man horse stamp. The phrase *mò ts'ó* is used to express whatever is right, or correctly said, having no confusion or mistake; *ts'ó* originally meant the confused appearance of gold or metal as it occurs in the ore.

10. *Kóm shéung há*, so above below, is a common phrase for expressing about, the medium, so and so, and other similar terms used in conversation.

| | | |
|---|---|---|
| enough, as they fall short about one yard, more or less. | 够爭一碼咁上下處 | tsau$^{2}$ ˏ'm kauʼ, ‹chang yat› ʿmá kómʼ shéung$^{2}$ há$^{2}$ ch'üʼ. |
| 11. How much will you deduct on that account? | 割番幾多銀呢 | Kót› ‹fán ʻkí ‹tó ˏngan ‹ní? |
| Why, when I see what the whole amount will be, then I can tell you how much. | 照數計幾多就割幾多係咧 | Chíúʼ shòʼ kaiʼ ʻkí ‹tó, tsau$^{2}$ kót› ʻkí ‹tó hai$^{2}$ ‹lé. |
| 12. Tell me now, what is the true and real price you want for these goods? | 呢的貨實價要幾多銀呢 | ‹Ní tik› fóʼ, shat$_{2}$ káʼ íúʼ ʻkí ‹tó ˏngan ‹ní? |
| What quantity of goods do you want? | 你要幾多貨 | ʿNí íúʼ ʻkí ‹tó fóʼ? |
| 13. I want 100 pieces of the seven gold thread ends, 200 of the red gold crossed ends, 300 of the 66s and 72s half and half; and see now that you do not charge an exorbitant price. | 我要一百七金頭二百紅夾金三百[七二][六六]對半你莫個開咁大價呀 | ʿNgó íúʼ yat› pák› ts'at› ‹kam ˏt'au, í$^{2}$ pák› ˏhung káp› ‹kam, ‹sám pák› ts'at›-í$^{2}$ luk$_{2}$-luk$_{2}$ túiʼ púnʼ; ʿní mók› kóʼ ‹hoi kómʼ tái$^{2}$ káʼ ‹á. |
| I always set a just price; my merchandise is good, and my price fair. The seven gold thread ends sell at $5.80; the red and gold crossed ends at $5.60; and the 72s and 66s, half and half, sell at $5.40. Lumping them all together and summing up the whole, I make the average price just $5.56, at which price I will sell them to you. | 我講公道價錢貨眞價實個的七金頭賣五個八紅夾金五個六[七二][六六]對半五個四喊嗙呤拉扯算作五個五毫六賣過你 | ʿNgó ʻkóng ‹kung tò$^{2}$ káʼ ˏts'ín, fóʼ ‹chan, káʼ shat$_{2}$. Kóʼ tik› ts'at› ‹kam ˏt'au, mái$^{2}$ ʿ'ng kóʼ pát›; ˏhung káp› ‹kam, ʿ'ng kóʼ luk$_{2}$; ts'at›-í$^{2}$ luk$_{2}$-luk$_{2}$ túiʼ púnʼ, ʿ'ng kóʼ szʼ$^{2}$. Ham$^{2}$ páng$^{2}$ láng$^{2}$ ‹lá ʻch'é sünʼ, tsók› ʿ'ng kóʼ ʿ'ng ˏhò luk$_{2}$, mái$^{2}$ kwóʼ ʿní. |
| 14. Exorbitantly dear! you ought to reduce the price a little; I will give you $5.45 for the whole lot, and that will be quite enough. | 硬得齊你要減的我俾你五個四毫半一罟錨買就係咧 | Ngángʼ tak› tsaiʼ! ʿNí íúʼ ʻkám tik›; ʿngó ʻpí ʿní ʿ'ng kóʼ szʼʼ ˏhò púnʼ, yat› ‹kú ʻnáu ʿmái tsau$^{2}$ hai$^{2}$ ‹lé. |
| That will never do, for it does not equal the prime | 唔做得唔够本 | ˏ'M tsò$^{2}$ tak›; ˏ'm kauʼ ʻpún; |

13. *Túi pún*, half and half, that is, one half of the 66s, and the other half of the 72s.

14. *Yat kú náu* or *yat kú láu*, quasi, one drag of the net, is an expression for averaging the price of a number of things, and taking the whole at a medium rate; *yat kú kwát*, one scrape of the drag, is another mode of expressing the same thing.

| | | |
|---|---|---|
| cost; I will take off the six odd cents, and then it will certainly do. | 我就減個六絲<br>就係喇 | ʿngó tsau' ʿkám kó' luk, ˏsz' tsau' hai' ˏlé. |
| 15. That will suit to a hair. Book the sale, and let there be no backing out of it afterwards. | 咁就咬線憾上<br>簿冇反口嘅嗱 | ʿKóm tsau' ʿngáu sin' h'am'. ʿShéung pò' ʿmò ʿfán ʿhau ké' lá'. |
| Ah! when once a sale is entered in the book, there is indeed no way for recanting. A'mat, bring that chintz, and let the gentleman see it. | 呀一上簿自然<br>唔反悔亞乜擰<br>個的花布嚟俾<br>人客睇 | ˏÁ! yat, ʿshéung pò' tsz' ˏín ˏ'm ʿfán fúi'. A' mat, ˏning kó' tik, ˏfá pò' ˏlai, ʿpí ˏyan hák, ʿt'ai. |
| 16. What kind of chintz have you? | 你有乜野花布 | ʿNí ʿyau mat, ʿyé ˏfá pò'! |
| I have every description; I have five colored chintz, and rich speckled ground chintz, showy flower patterns, and also Turkey red chintz: I will open them all out for your inspection. | 各樣都有有五<br>彩花布有錦地<br>軟枝有洋紅花<br>布擺開你睇 | Kok, yéung' ˏtò ʿyau; ʿyau ʿng ʿts'oi ˏfá pò', ʿyau ʿkam tí' ʿün ˏchí, ʿyau ˏyéung ˏhung ˏfá pò'; ʿpái ˏhoi ʿní ʿt'ai. |
| 17. Lackaday! All these chintzes are taken up soft, they will never do; glazed chintzes are all the rage just now. | 唉吔呢個淨水<br>嘅唔好而家時<br>興都要蠟面嘅 | ˏÁi ʿyá! ˏní kó' tsing' ʿshui ké' ˏ'm ʿhò; ˏí ˏká ˏshí ˏhing ˏtò iú' láp, mín' ké'. |
| In buying these chintzes, pray what use do you intend to make of them? | 你買呢個花布<br>着乜用 | ʿNí ʿmái ˏní kó' ˏfá pò', chéuk, mat, yung'? |
| 18. I am buying them for the purpose of making bed-covers, door-screens, awnings, linings for sedans, chair cushions, and so forth. | 我哋買嚟做被<br>面門簾天遮轎<br>襯椅褥各樣 | ʿNgó tí' ʿmái ˏlai tsò' ʿp'í mín', ˏmún ˏlím, ˏt'ín ˏché, kíú' ch'an', ʿí yuk,, kok, yéung'. |
| If so, then will not this white ground article be just the thing for you? | 咁話呢個白地<br>嘅至好啩 | Kóm' wá', ˏní kó' pak, tí' ké' chí' ʿhò kwá'? |
| 19. It gets dirty very easy. | 容易整污糟 | ˏYung í' ʿching ˏú ˏtsò. |
| This dark mottled ground then, will suit you. | 呢個古銅好 | ˏNí kó' ʿkú ˏt'ung ʿhò. |
| 20. Dark mottled ground will not suit, it makes no sort of display at all. | 古銅又唔好唔<br>得霎 | ʿKú ˏt'ung yau' ˏ'm ʿhò, ˏ'm tak, sháp,. |

17. *Hing* means to rise, and when used with regard to commercial articles is applied to those in general and extensive use, or to those which at the time are very fashionable.

| | | |
|---|---|---|
| This single plate is fine. | 呢個單色好 | ‹Ní kó’ ‹tán shik› ʿhò. |
| 21. This is miserably inferior, it is coarse, and very thin, and the threads are far apart; the article is of no use whatever. | 呢個𠯢過頭又粗又稀削又疎唔着使 | ‹Ní kó’ ˏyai kwó’ ˏt‘au, yau$^2$ ‹ts‘ò, yau$^2$ ‹h‘í shéuk›, yau$^2$ ‹shó ; ˏ’m chéuk$_2$ ʿshai. |
| Miserable indeed! You rigidly exact perfection, I can never come up to your standard. You want your goods better than anybody ever before had them, then they will suit you. | 唉吔你咁師傅骨唔交得你准咯你嘅野要加料嘅至做得 | ‹Ái ʿyá ! ʿNí kóm’ ‹sz’ fú$^2$ kwat›, ˏ’m ‹káu tak› ʿní ʿchun lók›. ʿNí ké’ ʿyé íú’ ‹ká líú$^2$ ké’ chí’ tsò$^2$ tak›. |
| 22. I do not want any of these chintzes. Do you select for me a piece of deep rose colored ground, large flowered pattern, and let me have it for my own private use. | 呢的花布都唔愛你揀一疋彩紅地大花葉俾我做家用 | ‹Ní tik› ‹fá pò’ ‹tò ˏ’m oi’. ʿNí ʿkám yat› p‘at› ʿts‘oi ˏhung tí$^2$ tái$^2$ ‹fá íp$_2$, ʿpí ʿngó tsò$^2$ ‹ká yung$^2$. |
| Here you have it. | 呢處有 | ‹Ní ch‘ü’ ʿyau. |
| 23. This piece is so rumpled, it won't do; pick out another piece for me, one that is spick and span new. | 呢疋咁㗲唔做得搵過一疋新鮮嘅囉 | ‹Ní p‘at› kóm’ ˏch‘áu ˏ’m tsò$^2$ tak›; ʿwan kwó’ yat› p‘at› ‹san ‹sín ké’ ‹ló. |
| Here is a piece for you, which has never before been out of the fold. | 呢處有疋原來頭拿 | ‹Ní ch‘ü’ ʿyau p‘at› ˏün ˏloi ˏt‘au ˏná. |
| 24. How much do you want for it? | 愛點價錢 | Oi’ ʿtím ká’ ˏts‘ín ? |
| Six dollars, ready money. | 六呅現銀 | Luk$_2$ ‹man ín$^2$ ˏngan. |
| 25. I think five and half is enough, is it not? | 五個半都做得估嚹 | ʿ’Ng kó’ pún’ ‹tò tsò$^2$ tak›, ʿkú lá’ ? |
| No, it is not. | 唔做得 | ˏ’M tsò$^2$ tak›. |
| 26. Well, as you say so, then get me another piece. | 咁話搵疋添囉 | ʿKóm wá$^2$, ʿwan p‘at› ‹tím ‹ló. |

21. *Sz' fú kwat*, or schoolmaster's bones, refers to the exactness with which the master or foreman of a shop examines the work of the apprentices, criticising every imperfection, and demanding better work; he is as strict and unfeeling as a bone deprived of its flesh. Slang phrases, like this, are of very frequent occurrence among the common people.

22. *Ká yung*, or family use, is said of goods intended for domestic consumption, in contradistinction to those bought to be resold.

26. *Amat* is not the name of a person, but like the term Mr. So-and-So is used here and elsewhere to indicate the place of one spoken to.

| | | |
|---|---|---|
| Ámat, bring another piece of the same kind as the former. Besides I have twilled cloth, fine linen, coarse linen; but I do not know whether you wish any of them or not. | 亞七照樣攞疋<br>添過嚟重有的<br>斜紋布竹布蔴<br>布唔知你愛唔<br>愛 | Á' mat›, chíú' yéung² 'ló p'at› ‹tím kwó' ‚lai. Chung² 'yau tik› ‚ts'é ‚man pò', chuk› pò', ‚má pò', ‚'m ‹chí 'ní oi' ‚'m oi'. |
| 27. I do not want any of them. Have you on hand any cambrics? | 唔愛你有袈裟<br>布冇蠘 | ‚'M oi'. 'Ní 'yau ‹ká ‹shá pò' 'mò ‹né? |
| I have none. | 冇咯 | 'Mò lók›. |
| 28. Give me a look at some of your checks and stripes, if you have them. | 俾個的棋盤布<br>柳條布我睇吓<br>有 | 'Pí kó' tik› ‚k'í ‚p'ún pò', 'lau ‚t'íú pò' 'ngó 't'ai 'há. |
| Here we have them. | | 'Yau. |
| 29. What a pity! The checks in these checkered goods are far too small; and your stripes are much too broad; they are all unsuitable. | 唉吔呢的棋盤<br>布盤眼太細柳<br>條又闊過頭都<br>唔合式 | ‹Ái 'yá! ‹Ní tik› ‚k'í ‚p'ún pò' ‚p'ún 'ngán t'ái' sai'; 'lau ‚t'íú yau² fút› kwó' ‚t'au; ‹tò ‚'m hóp₂ shik›. |
| Well, if none of these please you, I have another description of goods here—the warp is blue, and the web is red—which I will give you to look at; and if you still say these goods are bad, then it will be of no use for you to seek for any others. | 你唔啱我重有<br>宗藍線經紅線<br>緯俾你睇呢宗<br>都話唔好你就<br>唔使搵買咯 | 'Ní ‚'m ‹ngám, 'ngó chung² 'yau ‹tsung ‚lám sín' ‹king, ‚hung sín' 'wai, 'pí 'ní 't'ai; ‹ní ‹tsung ‹tò wá² ‚'m 'hò, 'ní tsau² ‚'m 'shai 'wan 'mái lók›. |
| 30. Ah, what stuff! why, I'd not take it, if you'd give it to me. Come now, let me look at some of those handkerchiefs. | 唉吔你送過我<br>都唔愛俾的手<br>巾過我睇罷啦 | ‹Ái 'yá! 'ní sung² kwó' 'ngó ‹tò ‚'m oi'. 'Pí tik› 'shau ‹kan kwó' 'ngó 't'ai ‹pá ‹lá. |
| Here, here, here they are, Sir. *(Said aside.)* Oh! you are such a troublesome fellow to sell goods to, that it is no easy matter to deal with you. *(Aloud.)* Do you want rose red? Well look, see if these will suit you. | 有有有你咁惡<br>打發都費事呀<br>要梅紅嘅睇好<br>唔好 | 'Yau, 'yau, 'yau. 'Ní kóm' ók› 'tá fát› ‹tò fai' sz'² á'. Yíú' ‚múi ‚hung ké'? 't'ai 'hò ‚'m 'hò. |

29. The *k'í p'ún* is the chess-board of the Chinese, which is marked into squares like ours, except that there are eighty-one instead of sixty-four squares.

廣東方言讀本

| | | |
|---|---|---|
| 31. This color is so very light, that it looks like water red; certainly it cannot be rose red. | 色水咁淺算係<br>水紅唔係梅紅 | Shik› ʻshui kóm’ ʻts‘ín, sün’ hai$^{2}$ ʻshui ‚hung, ‚’m hai$^{2}$ ‚múi ‚hung. |
| This scarlet then, what do you think if it? | 呢個花紅點呢 | ‹Ní kó’ ‹fá ‚hung, ʻtím ‹ní? |
| 32. Too deep by far; and the flower patterns are by no means handsome. | 深過頭花樣又<br>唔精緻 | ‹Sham kwó’ ‚t‘au; ‹fá yéung$^{2}$ yau$^{2}$ ‚’m ‹tsing chí’. |
| This Turkey red will certainly suit your fancy. | 洋紅嘅你就中<br>意咯 | ‚Yéung ‚hung ké’, ʻní tsau$^{2}$ ‹chung í’ lók›. |
| 33. Tush! This is not really Turkey red. Smell it, why it has no smell whatever; at a single washing, the whole of the color will come out. Come now, don't you try to make game of me, [by showing me such stuff.] | 嗚嘩呢個係假<br>洋紅聞佢都冇<br>隨一洗就甩色<br>嘅咯你咪嚟混<br>我囉 | ‚Ú ‚wá! ‹Ní kó’ hai$^{2}$ ʻká ‚yéung ‚hung. ‚Man ʻk‘ü ‹tò ʻmò ‚ts‘ui, yat› ʻsai tsau$^{2}$ lat› shik› ké’ lók›. ʻNí ʻmai ‚lai wan$^{2}$ ʻngó ló’. |
| Ah me! how unfortunate I am, I have really met with a cruel disappointment. | 唉吔晦氣兜真<br>正撞板 | ‹Ái ʻyá! Fúi’ hí’ ‹tau, ‹chan ching’ chóng$^{2}$ ʻpán. |
| 34. Never mind, never mind! Hand me those [handkerchiefs] with the white ground and two blue patterns, this description; of goods you surely must have of a good quality. | 唔相干俾個的<br>白地二藍花個<br>宗你哋是必有<br>好嘅 | ‚’M ‹séung ‹kón! ʻPí kó’ tik› pák$^{2}$ tí$^{2}$ í$^{2}$ ‚lám ‹fá; kó’ ‹tsung ʻní tí$^{2}$ shí$^{2}$ pít› ʻyau ʻhò ké’. |
| All my articles are good enough; but the whole difficulty is with you, who will never be satisfied; it is hard to tell you [all I think]. | 一的貨都係好<br>嘅總係你冇厭<br>足難講唉 | Yat› tik› fó’ ‹tò hai$^{2}$ ʻhò ké’; ʻtsung hai$^{2}$ ʻní ʻmò ím’ tsuk›; ‚nán ʻkóng ‹é. |
| 35. Now as for these two blue patterns, put them by one side, and let me have yet another look at your three | 呢的二藍花嘅<br>掣開一邊再睇 | ‹Ní tik› í$^{2}$ ‚lám ‹fá ké’, ‹chai ‹hoi yat› ‹pín, tsoi’ ʻt‘ai ‹sám |

33. *Ts'ui* is here used in a local sense, meaning the scent of a thing, or any peculiar smell that marks it; *lat* is also a provincial term for taking out, or depriving of. *Fúi hí*, dusky aspect, refers to the clouded countenance of a man who has suddenly been disappointed, alluding to the dusky appearance of the sky at twilight; *chóng pán* or impinging boards, means in this connection, a discord between two players, or a want of harmony in parties, from one not agreeing with, or disappointing, the other.

35. You afford me no patronage, literally, you are not to me a god, or genius, of wealth. Near the doors of Chinese shops is a small niche, within which is a shrine to Plutus, and by offering incense to it the tradesman hopes to get rich; very often the names of other divinities are inscribed in the niche along with that of the god of wealth.

blues. Ah, these surely are not square, their form is that of a parallelogram; they are of no kind of use whatever.

三藍花嘅唉呢的唔係結方係日字樣嘅唔着使

˓lám ˓fá ké˒. ˓Ái! ˓ní tik˒ ˏ'm hai$^{2}$ kít˒ ˓fóng, hai$^{2}$ yat$_{2}$ tsz'$^{2}$ yéung$^{2}$ ké˒; ˏ'm chéuk$_{2}$ ˊshai.

Well, upon my word, you are a troublesome fellow; looking at you after this fashion, you afford me no patronage, but have thus annoyed me full half a day!

混屁賬睇你個樣都唔係財神足足混我大半日

Wan$^{2}$ p'í˒ chéung˒; ˊt'ai ˊní kó˒ yéung$^{2}$ ˓tò ˏ'm hai$^{2}$ ˏts'oi ˏshan, tsuk˒ tsuk˒ wan$^{2}$ ˊngó tái$^{2}$ pún˒ yat$_{2}$.

36. Have a little patience. Don't get angry!

忍耐吓唔使怒

ˊYan noi$^{2}$ ˊhá; ˏ'm ˊshai nò$^{2}$.

Well, well, all sorts of colors are here mixed together. Come now, select for yourself.

好喀好喀各樣顏色都齊呢處喀你自己揀喀

ˊHò lák$_{2}$! ˊhò lák$_{2}$! kók˒ yéung$^{2}$ ˏngán shik˒ ˓tò ˏts'ai ˓ní ch'ü˒ lák$_{2}$. ˊNí tsz'$^{2}$ ˊkí ˊkám lák$_{2}$.

37. Well done! All sorts of colors, then, amount to just so many old odds and ends of goods! Really and truly, my good Sir, don't you try to play off so many of your tricks on me; but give me the really true and good whites, that I may see what kind of material they are.

嚡各樣顏色都係食飽煎堆嘅咯實的咯事頭咪混我咁多喀俾過的真囒貨我睇罷喀

ˏHái! Kók˒ yéung$^{2}$ ˏngán shik˒ ˓tò hai$^{2}$ shik$_{2}$ ˊpáu ˓ts'ín ˓túi ké˒ lók˒! Shat$_{2}$ tik˒ lók˒, sz'$^{2}$ ˏt'au, ˊmai wan$^{2}$ ˊngo kóm˒ ˓tó lók˒; ˊpí kwó˒ tik˒ ˓chan ˓lán fó˒, ˊngó ˊt'ai p'á˒ lák$_{2}$.

Good articles! Yet I fear that you will not give me the price for them, I do indeed. Here also are these twilled bandana handkerchiefs, I have no fear that you won't find them good, though in price they are rather dear.

好貨又怕你唔出得價錢噃呢的鶴絨巾唔憂唔好咯總係貴的啫

ˊHò fó˒! Yau$^{2}$ p'á˒ ˊní ˏ'm ch'ut˒ tak˒ ká˒ ˏts'ín pó˒. ˓Ní tik˒ hók$_{2}$ ˏyung ˓kan, ˏ'm ˓yau ˏ'm ˊhò lók˒, ˊtsung hai$^{2}$ kwai˒ tik˒ ˓ché.

38. Lackaday! Were they as cheap [as dirt], no man would like them. Come now, let us again talk about those handkerchiefs with the white ground and the two blue pat-

唉吔平都冇人愛好咧就講個的白地二藍花

˓Ái ˊyá! ˏP'ing ˓tò ˊmò ˏyan oi˒. ˊHò ˓lé, tsau$^{2}$ ˊkóng kó˒ tik˒ pák$_{2}$ tí$^{2}$ í$^{2}$ ˏlám ˓fá

37. *Ts'ín túi* are cakes made on the last day of the year for the festivities of the next day; they are thus carried, as it were, from one year to another, and supply the allusion of goods left on hand the last year forming part of the stock of this. *Shik páu*, eaten sufficient, means that the goods have been on hand a long time, and are, like these cakes, still carried over to another year.

廣東方言讀本

terns; what price do you want for them?

I will calculate it, *(he says to himself.)* Each dozen stood me in $1.80 prime cost; then adding thereto charges and expenses, therefore, *(addressing his customer,)* for every handkerchief I ought to reckon one mace and two candareens of silver.

嘅幾多價錢㖭
我打過嗻每打
臣一個八承本
加起盤費使用
每條該銀一錢
二分算

ké'; 'kí ,tó ká' ,ts'in ,né?

'Ngó 'tá kwó' ché'. 'Múi 'tá ,shan yat, kó' pát,, ,shing 'pún; ,ká 'hí ,p'ún fai' 'shai yung[2], 'múi ,t'iú ,koi ,ngan yat, ,ts'in í[2] ,fan sün'.

39. I will give you one mace and one candareen apiece, and I wish to purchase of you a thousand handkerchiefs.

我俾一錢一分
算過你我要買
一千條

'Ngó 'pí yat, ,ts'in yat, ,fan sün' kwó' 'ní; 'ngó íú' 'mái yat, ,ts'in ,t'iú.

Very well, very well; and I will reduce the price five cash; were you even to buy ten thousand, you should have them all at this same [moderate] price.

好喇好喇我就
減個五厘你買
一萬條都係咁
價咯

'Hò ,lé, 'hò ,lé! 'Ngó tsau[2] 'kám kó' ''ng ,lí; 'ní 'mái yat, mán[2] ,t'iú ,tò hai[2] kóm' ká' lók,.

40. Very good; and this you will trust me with, for just now I have no ready money to pay you; do you consent to the bargain or not?

係咯都係賒賬
啫冇現銀俾你
肯唔肯呀

Hai[2] lók,! ,tò hai[2] ,shé chéung' ,ché; 'mò ín[2] ,ngan 'pí 'ní; 'hang ,'m 'hang á'?

I do not consent; as for trusting you, there is no occasion to say a word about it.

唔做得賒就唔
使講咯

,'M tsò[2] tak,; ,shé tsau[2] ,'m 'shai 'kóng lók,.

41. That is very strange, I declare! So then you will not believe me, eh? Whenever you want anything from me, I shall grant it accordingly, and that will be all right.

古怪咯咁都唔
信得呀隨時要
隨時俾你就係
喇

'Kú kwái' lók,! 'Kóm ,tò ,'m sun' tak, ,mé? ,Ts'ui ,shí íú', ,ts'ui ,shí 'pí 'ní, tsau[2] hai[2] ,lé.

It is not that I will not believe you, but only because my capital is small, and I must keep it constantly in circulation. Moreover, as the case is, I cannot collect my outstanding debts; I am daily urging people, and yet I cannot get their accounts

唔係唔信得總
係本錢少要嚟
轉動因爲各賬
都唔收得起日
日係咁催都唔

,'M hai[2] ,'m sun' tak,, 'tsung hai[2] 'pún ,ts'in 'shiú, íú' ,lai chün' tung[2]. ,Yan wai[2] kók, chéung' ,tò ,'m ,shau tak, 'hí; yat, yat, hai[2] kóm'

41. *Ts'ui shí íú, ts'ui shí pí*, according to the time want, according to the time give; *ts'ui shí* are here used as correllative terms, like when and then.

in. And were I now again to grant credit, I should not find a moment's leisure, which would still more prejudice my business.

收得番再要賒
出去個陣日日
唔得閒越法悞
事

‹tsúi ‹tò ‚'m ‹shau tak› ‹fán. Tsoi[2] fú' ‹shé ch'ut› h'ü', kó' chan[2] yat$_{2}$ yat$_{2}$ ‚'m tak› ‚hán, üt$_{2}$ fát› 'ng[2] sz'[2].

42. Well then, if I pay you ready money, what discount ought you to make in your price for the cash down?

好唎我交現銀
過你應扣現幾
多呢

'Hò ‹lé! ‘Ngó ‹káu ín[2] ‚ngan kwó' ‘ní, ‹ying k'au' ín[2] 'kí ‹tó ‹ní?

Make what discount? Why, we arranged at first for paying down the cash.

扣乜現呀本來
講現銀嘅

K'au' mat› ín[2] á'? 'Pún ‚loi 'kóng ín[2] ‚ngan ké'.

43. But observe now;—when I wanted these goods from you, I did it foolishly, not knowing what I was about. Besides, having a poor border, the article is narrow, all of which I said nothing about; and still you are unwilling to make any discount for ready money.

你睇我都係孖
孖夫湊你愛嗻
邊欄又俗貨又
窄我都唔計較
扣現你都重唔
肯咩

‘Ní 't'ai ‘ngó ‹tò hai[2] ‹má ‹má ‹fú, ts'au' ‘ní oi' ‹ché. ‹Pín ‚lán yau[2] suk$_{2}$, fó' yau[2] chák›, ‘ngó ‹tò ‚'m kai' káu'; k'au' ín[2] ‘ní ‹tò chung[2] ‚'m 'hang ‹mé!

Alas for you! My goods are all full thirty-three and a half inches wide, which is just enough, being two cubits and two and a half tenths. And now what more defects will you urge, in order to lower the price? You have already agreed to a bargain, and why now do you recant? However, to end the trouble, I will make, in your favor, a discount of three per cent., which will surely do. Ah, Sir! you are truly a very hard man to trade with; there is no occasion to fear that anybody will get away the profits of your money.

唉吔我的貨都
够三十三個烟
治足够二尺二
寸半你重動乜
擔杆呢你已經
講成有乜反悔
呢幾好處咯俾
個九七現銀過
我就係唎唉吔
眞眞利害唔慌
有人賺得你銀
倒咯

‹Ái ‘yá? ‘Ngó tik› fó' ‹tò kau' ‹sám shap$_{2}$ ‹sám kó' ‹ín chí[2], tsuk› kau', í[2] ch'ik› í[2] ts'ün' pún'. ‘Ní chung[2] tung[2] mat› tám' ‹kón ‹ní? ‘Ní ‘í ‹king 'kóng ‚shing, ‘yau mat› 'fán fúi' ‹ní? 'Kí 'hò ch'ü' lók›, 'pí kó' 'kau ts'at› ín[2] ‚ngan kwó' ‘ngó, tsau[2] hai[2] ‹lé. ‹Ái ‘yá! ‹chan ‹chan lí[2] hoi[2]; ‚'m ‹fóng ‘yau ‚yan chán[2] tak› ‘ní ‚ngan 'tò lók›.

43. *Má má fú* is a doltish, silly person, one who does what others request him to do, without reflecting upon the consequences.

| | | |
|---|---|---|
| 44. You must still get a little more angry than before, for I wish you to make a further discount of four cents per thousand for scales weight. | 你重要嬲〻添我重扣四個秤頭呀 | ʻNí chung$^2$ iú' ˏnau ˏnau ˏt'ím, ʻngó chung$^2$ k'au' sz' kó' ch'ing' ˏt'au á'. |
| Mind you, Sir, this is the way we calculate the prices with foreigners; we Chinese [among ourselves] have no regulation of this sort. | 唉吔呢宗係番人算法我哋本地冇呢宗例 | ˏÁi ʻyá! ˏní ˏtsung hai$^2$ ˏfán ˏyan sün' fát,; ʻngó tí$^2$ ʻpún tí$^2$ ʻmò ˏní ˏtsung lai$^2$. |
| 45. Enough, enough! Have you got any cotton yarn, or any cotton thread? | 罷咧罷咧你有綿線綿紗冇呀 | Pá$^2$ ˏlé! pá$^2$ ˏlé! ʻNí ʻyau ˏmín sín', ˏmín ˏshá, ʻmò ˏá? |
| I have got cotton yarn, but my cotton thread is all sold off. | 綿紗有綿線賣晒咯 | ˏMín ˏshá ʻyau, ˏmín sín' mái$^2$ sái' lók,. |
| 46. Is your cotton yarn water twist, or is it mule twist? | 你的綿紗係水紡備係火紡嘅 | ʻNí tik, ˏmín ˏshá hai$^2$ ʻshui ʻfóng pí$^2$ hai$^2$ ʻfó ʻfóng ké'? |
| I have got both. | 兩樣都有 | ʻLéung yéung$^2$ ˏtò ʻyau. |
| 47. Of what assortment of numbers is it? | 係乜號數呀 | Hai$^2$ mat, hò$^2$ shò' á'? |
| The assortment ranges from Nos. 18 to Nos. 40. | 十八號至四十號止 | Shap$_2$ pát, hò$^2$ chí' sz' shap$_2$ hò$^2$ ʻchí. |
| 48. How many pounds are there packed in a single bale? | 裝幾多磅做一包呢 | ˏChóng ʻkí ˏtó póng' tsò$^2$ yat, ˏpáu ˏní? |
| The bales are each 400 lbs., and the bundles are 10 lbs. exactly. | 大包四百磅包仔十磅 | Tái$^2$ ˏpáu sz' pák, pong', ˏpáu ʻtsai shap$_2$ póng'. |
| 49. Let me look at the article: upon my word, this yarn is very loosely twisted, it is full of lumps, and can never answer for warp, it can only be used for weft, and for nothing else. | 俾我睇吓唉吔呢個貨又鬆又紗節多唔做得絲經只可做棉緯啫 | ʻPí ʻngó ʻt'ai ʻhá; ˏái ʻyá! ˏní kó' fó' yau$^2$ ˏsung, yau$^2$ ˏshá tsít, ˏtó, ˏʻm tsò$^2$ tak, ˏsz' ˏking, ʻchí ʻhó tsò$^2$ ˏmín ʻwai ˏché. |
| And this quality? | 呢宗呢 | ˏNí ˏtsung ˏní? |

45. *Pá lé* or *pá líú* is a common phrase for finishing the discussion of a subject as, it is enough, there's an end of the matter, 'twill do, etc.

48. *Póng* is an attempt to express the English word pound, as *ínchí* is inches, and *táshan* is dozen; these three are in very common use.

| | | |
|---|---|---|
| 50. This quality, although it may be called hard twisted and clean, white and smooth [in the main]; yet after all, it has some seeds and dirt, and you ought to sell it somewhat cheaper. | 呢宗雖然緊淨又係白滑到底重有黑泡紗屎你要平的賣 | ‹Ní ‹tsung, ‹sui ‚ín ʻkan tsingʼ yauʼ haiʼ pák‚ wát‚; tòʼ ʻtai chungʼ ʻyau hak› ‹páu ‹shá ʻshí, ʻní iúʼ ‚p'ing tik› máiʼ. |
| Arranging one number with another, I will put it at thirty-one dollars per pecul. | 拉扯算每擔三十一員 | ‹Lá ʻch'é sünʼ ʻmúi támʼ ‹sám shap‚ yat› ‚ün. |
| 51. Well, well, there is no occasion for so much talk about the matter, say thirty dollars and the bargain is settled at once. | 好咯唔使講咁多咯三十吙就係咯 | ʻHò lók›, ‚'m ʻshai ʻkóng kómʼ ‹tó lók›; ‹sám shap‚ ‹man, tsauʼ haiʼ lók›. |
| Good, good! I will yield the difference, and say no more about it. | 係咯係咯讓俾你係喇 | Haiʼ lók›! haiʼ lók›! yéungʼ ʻpí ʻní haiʼ léʼ. |
| 52. This bale is damaged by sea water, and that is torn; you must, on that account, therefore, make a reduction, and the price will answer. | 呢包有水漬個包又爛你要減咁的至做得呀 | ‹Ní ‹páu ʻyau ʻshui tsik›, kóʼ ‹páu yauʼ lánʼ; ʻní iúʼ ʻkám ʻkóm tik›, chíʼ tsòʼ tak› áʼ. |
| Yes, yes, we will again consult about that, there will be no difficulty on that point. | 係咯再斟酌個的容易 | Haiʼ lók›; tsoiʼ ‹cham chéuk› kóʼ tik› ‚yung íʼ. |
| 53. You must procure me a bill from the hong merchants, and also an invoice of the goods. | 你要攞行單兼開貨單俾我 | ʻNí iúʼ ʻló ‚hóng ‹tán ‹kím ‹hoi fóʼ ‹tán ʻpí ʻngó. |
| To be sure I must. | 自然喇 | Tszʼʼ ‚ín ‹lé. |
| 54. Be seated! | 你坐 | ʻNí tsóʼ! |
| Good luck attend you. (Then aside, he says to himself,) aye, you are a very screw, a perfect skinflint! I would indeed much rather be without your custom than with it. | 好行嚡又係一個芝蔴銼蝦春鈒唔帮襯第一帮襯第二啫 | ʻHò ‚hang. ‚Hái! yauʼ haiʼ yat› kóʼ ‹chí ‚má ts'óʼ, ‹há ‹ch'un cháp‚! ‚'M ‹póng ch'anʼ taiʼ yat›, ‹póng ch'anʼ taiʼ íʼ ‹ché. |

54. *Chí má* is the hemp plant, the seeds of which are proverbially small, but even these his miserly heart wishes to file off, and save the chaff; *há ch'un* are crab's eggs, and these he wishes to cut in two with a pair of shears. The sentence, not patronize is number one, patronize is number two, compares the loss with the obtaining of his custom, and losing it is better than keeping it.

# Section Seventh.

## NATIONAL COINS.

## 國寶類第七章

Kwókˏ ʻpò lui$^{2}$; tai$^{2}$ ts'atˏ ˏchéung.

1. What precious metals are there in common use in your country?

貴處有乜寶貝
時常使得嘅呢

Kwai$^{3}$ ch'ü$^{3}$ ʻyau matˏ ʻpò púi$^{3}$ ˏshí ˏshéung ʻshai takˏ ké$^{3}$ ˏní?

There are gold, silver, and copper coins.

有金銀銅錢

ʻYau ˏkam, ˏngan, ˏt'ung ˏts'ín.

2. For about how much silver can a tael of gold be exchanged? and how many copper pieces can be obtained for a tael of silver?

金每兩約換銀
多少銀每兩又
找錢多少呢

ˏKam ʻmúi ʻléung yéukˏ ún$^{2}$ ˏngan ˏtò ʻshíú? ˏngan ʻmúi ʻléung yau$^{2}$ ʻcháu ˏts'ín ˏtó ʻshíú ˏní?

A tael of gold is exchanged for about seventeen taels of silver; and for a tael of silver fourteen or fifteen hundred pieces of copper are given.

金價每兩約換
銀十七兩銀每
兩找錢一千四
五百文

ˏKam ká$^{3}$ ʻmúi ʻléung yéukˏ ún$^{2}$ ˏngan shap ˏts'atˏ ʻléung; ˏngan ʻmúi ʻléung ʻcháu ˏts'ín yatˏ ˏts'ín sz$^{3}$ ʻʻng pákˏ ˏman.

3. How are these copper pieces prepared for use?

銅錢點樣做嚟
使嘅呢

ˏT'ung ˏts'ín ʻtím yéung$^{2}$ tsò$^{2}$ ˏlai ʻshai ké$^{3}$ ˏní?

These copper pieces are those in constant use, and the new coin is thus cast. From the Board [of Revenue at Peking] models are obtained, and in each provincial city a mint is established, over which a director is appointed. When the mint is to be worked, the director weighs out the proper quantity of copper and delivers it to the workmen to be cast into money, and to be returned ac-

銅錢係常使之
錢新錢鼓鑄規
矩由部頒式各
省城立一錢局
內設一委員於
鑄錢時將銅兌
過斤兩發交鑄

ˏT'ung ˏts'ín hai$^{2}$ ˏshéung ʻshai ˏchí ˏts'ín; ˏsan ˏts'ín ʻkú chü$^{3}$ ˏkw'ai ʻkü. ˏYau Pò$^{2}$ ˏpán shikˏ, kókˏ ʻsháng ˏshing lap$^{2}$ yatˏ ˏts'ín kuk$^{2}$, noi$^{2}$ ch'ítˏ yatˏ ʻwai ˏün. ˏU chü$^{3}$ ˏts'ín ˏshí, ˏtséung ˏt'ung túi$^{3}$ kwò$^{3}$ ˏkan ʻléung, fátˏ

### *Notes and Explanations.*

COINAGE, in the strictest sense of the word, is hardly applicable to the Chinese mode of working the precious metals, as the sequel will show. The term *pò* denotes things which are highly esteemed, and hence it is here used for the precious metals.

3. A *kuk* is a confined place, an oven-like place; a powder manufactory, as well as a mint, is called by this name; because the operations are kept secret, and the workmen restrained in their egress and ingress.

cording to the quantity given; but it often happens that these workmen throw sand into the mold with the metal, and are thus enabled to purloin the copper. When they are about to cast, they take the metal and put it into a furnace to be fused, and afterwards pour it into a clay mold. This mold has a reverse (or back), and an obverse (or face); the face has a device for each dynasty and reign; on the reverse is the name of the reign, with the addition of the two words, current money, being in all four words; thus, *Mánlik's current money*, is an instance in point. Afterwards when the metal has become cold and hard, it is turned out of the mold.

錢之人以爲鑄
成回兌之計但
時人多以小砂
楪內則可竊取
其銅鑄時將銅
放於紅爐內鎔
化後傾於泥印
內其印有底面
面則每朝每代
一式底則爵國
號加上通寶二
字共成四宇如
萬曆通寶四字
便是後至其銅
凍冷然後傾出

káu chü' ts'ín chí yan, 'í wai chü' shing úi túi[2] chí kai'; tán[2] shí yan tó 'í 'síú shá tsáp noi[2], tsak 'hó sít 'ts'ü k'í t'ung. Chü' shí tséung t'ung fóng' ü hung lò noi[2], yung fá'; hau[2] k'ing ü nai yan' noi[2]. K'í yan' 'yau 'tai mín[2]; mín[2] tsak 'múi ch'íú 'múi toi[2] yat shik; 'tai tsak tséung kwók hò[2] ká 'shéung t'ung 'pò í[2] tsz'[2], kung[2] shing sz" tsz'[2]; ü Mán[2] lik t'ung 'pò sz" tsz'[1] pín[2] shí[2]. Hau[2] chí' k'í t'ung tung' 'lang, ín hau[2] k'ing ch'ut.

The weight of each piece of the money is one mace *(ts'ín)*, and hence it is called by the same name; the value fixed by government is the thousandth part of a tael's weight of silver.

每錢一文重一
錢故名之日錢
官價定以一厘
銀作錢一文

'Múi ts'ín yat man, chung[2] yat ts'ín, kú' ming chí üt ts'ín; kún ká' ting' 'í yat lí ngan, tsók ts'ín yat man.

Moreover, the second, fifth, and eighth days of each month are the periods fixed for commencing the work; and the third, sixth, and ninth are the days for weighing the money, and delivering it to the commissioner of finance. The people who work the mint are required to be always in the establishment, not being at liberty to go in

又每月以二五
八日爲期開工
三六九日上藩
司兌交支餉造
錢之人常在局
內不能任意出

Yau[2] 'múi üt 'í í[2] 'ng pát yat wai k'í hoi kung; sám luk 'kau yat 'shéung fán sz' túi[2] káu chí 'héung. Ts'ò' ts'ín chí yan shéung tsoi[2] kuk noi[2], pat nang yam[2] í' ch'ut yap; wai lun

3. The writing on the face of these copper pieces is in the Mantchou character, which is unintelligible to most of the Chinese. The name of the dynasty is placed on the left side, and that of the reigning monarch on the right of the square hole. The value of these *cash*, as they are called by foreigners, has fallen much within a few years, having formerly approximated nearly to the standard. The amount of pure copper contained in them varies almost as much as their value. Tutenague is the principal alloy contained in it.

廣東方言讀本

and out at pleasure; but they are changed in rotation: and, except on the third, sixth, and ninth days, when after they have weighed and delivered the money over to the commissioner of finance, are they permitted to leave the mint, but are required to return on the same evening.

入惟輪班換人
而已獨於三六
九日帶錢上藩
司交兌時然後
出外至晚復回

‹pán ún2 ‹yan ‹í 'í: tuk2 ‹ü ‹sám luk2 'kau yat2, tái' ‹ts'ín 'shéung ‹fán ‹sz' ‹káu túi2 ‹shí ‹ín hau2 ch'ut› ngoi2, chí' 'mán fuk2 ‹úi.

4. This being the way it is made, how is it passed?

咁話點樣使呢

'Kóm wá2, 'tím yéung2 'shai ‹ní?

The newly made coin always passes current with the old money.

同埋古錢撈勻
照常使咯

‹Tung ‹mái 'kú ‹ts'ín ‹lò ‹wan, chíú' ‹shéung 'shai lók›.

5. Where is this copper procured?

個的銅係邊處
嚟嘅

Kó' tik› ‹t'ung hai2 ‹pín ch'ü' ‹lai ké'?

It is found in all the provinces, but the greatest supplies are from Wannám; and in all cases the working of the mines is under the direction of the government.

各省都有惟係
雲南較多惟所
有皆歸官採

Kók› 'sháng ‹tò 'yau, ‹wai hai2 ‹Wan ‹nám káu' ‹tó; ‹wai 'shó 'yau ‹kái ‹kwai ‹kún 'ts'oi.

6. In what manner does silver pass current?

白銀點樣使呢

Pák› ‹ngan 'tím yéung2 'shai ‹ní?

The native sycee silver is used by officers and soldiers, and in the payment of taxes, &c.; but in the markets foreign coins are current, and are exchanged for copper money.

土產嘅紋銀爲
支官兵餉使咯
但市上都係使
洋錢找換啫

'T'ò 'ch'án ké' ‹man ‹ngan, ‹wai ‹chí ‹kún ‹ping 'héung 'shai lók›; tán2 'shí shéung2 ‹tò hai2 'shai ‹yéung ‹ts'ín 'cháu ún2 ‹ché.

7. How is this native silver prepared?

紋銀點樣做呢

‹Man ‹ngan 'tím yéung2 tsò2 ‹ní?

It is manufactured at the shops of native bankers. Suppose, for example, that the officers of the several departments and districts are wishing to pay over [to the heads of the government] the revenue arising from the land-tax, and the various duties on merchandise, they go to the bankers' shops, and obtain the amount in pure silver, making up to the bankers any deficiency there

紋銀係傾銷銀
店做嘅如各府
州縣要解地丁
雜稅則到傾銷
銀店傾足色紋
銀上兌所有低
耗照數補足銀

‹Man ‹ngan hai2 ‹k'ing ‹síú ‹ngan tím' tsò2 ké'. ‹Ü kók› 'fú, ‹chau, ün2, íú' kai' tí2 ‹ting, tsáp2 shui2, tsak› tò' ‹k'ing ‹síú ‹ngan tím' ‹k'ing tsuk› shik› ‹man ‹ngan 'shéung túi2 'shó 'yau ‹tai hò', chíú' shó' 'pò tsuk›.

7. There are a great many of these *ngantím* in Canton; the largest are private banks; the inferior ones are managed by shroffs and money-changers. The term *man* is applied to silver to denote its fineness and purity; *saisz'* or floss silk, from whence comes *sycee*, is another term.

may be between it and the money they bring to their shops. The bankers having paid over into the provincial treasury the money for the officers, bring back a receipt for proof of the same. Besides, those who have to pay the duties on salt, take the money to the bankers who pay its equivalent in pure silver, at a rate one or two per cent. below that arising from the land tax.

店即代爲上庫
取有藩司回照
爲凴其餘塩課
各稅則往領銷
店領足上兌其
色與地丁畧低
一二色

꜀Ngan tím’ tsik› toi$^2$ ꜀wai ‘shéung fú’, ‘ts‘ü ‘yau ꜀fán ‹sz’ ꜀úi chiú’ ꜀wai ꜀p‘ang. ꜀K‘í ꜀ü ꜀ím fó’ kók› shui’, tsak› ‘wóng ‹k‘ing ‹síú tím’, ‹k‘ing tsuk› ‘shéung túi$^2$, ꜀k‘í shik› ‘ü tí$^2$ ‹ting léuk$_2$ ‹tai yat› í$^2$ shik›.

These banks have furnaces, in which the workmen place the silver to fuse it, and then pour it into clay molds, and in this way it is formed into ingots, some of which are large and some are small. After the metal is cold and hard, it is thrown out of the mold,—the ingot having upon it the date of a given year, of a given district, and perhaps also the kind of tax for which it was cast to pay, with the names of the workmen and the shop where it was cast. Then after it has been lodged in the provincial treasury, if found to be debased, inquiries can be made respecting it at the shop.

其店內有銀爐
匠入將銀鎔化
傾入一泥印如
元寶錠有大有
小冷凍後取出
錠面有某年的
年號有某縣或
某餉銀匠某店
字樣然後上庫
倘有低僞爲該
店是問

꜀K‘í tím’ noi$^2$ ‘yau ꜀ngan ꜀lò, tséung$^2$ ꜀yan ‹tséung ꜀ngan ꜀yung fá’, ‹k‘ing yap$_2$ yat› ꜀nai yan’, ꜀ü ꜀ün ‘pò ting$^2$, ‘yau tái$^2$ ‘yau ‘síú. ‘Lang tung’ hau$^2$ ‘ts‘ü ch‘ut›, ting$^2$ mín$^2$ ‘yau ‘mau ꜀nín tik› ꜀nín hò$^2$, ‘yau ‘mau ün$^2$, wák› ‘mau ‘héung, ꜀ngan tséung$^2$ ‘mau tím’ tsz’$^2$ yéung$^2$. ꜀Ín hau$^2$ ‘shéung fú’, ‘t‘óng ‘yau ‹tai ngai$^2$, ꜀wai ‹koi tím’ shí$^2$ man$^2$.

8. Where is the sycee silver found?

紋銀在邊處嚟
嘅呢

꜀Man ꜀ngan tsoi$^2$ ‹pín ch‘ü’ ꜀lai ké’ ‹ní?

Silver mines exist in several parts of the empire, some of which may have been already exhausted, and the working of others prohibited; but the most extensive mines, and those from which the greatest part of the fine silver is obtained, are at Fóshán, on the frontiers of Burmah, belonging to Tséungchau in Wannám, and at Sungsing in Cochin-

內地諸山有銀
礦者或已採盡
或奉封禁惟滇
南匠州有緬屬
之火山廠廣西
邊外有安南之
宋星廠銀礦極

Noi$^2$ tí$^2$ ‹chü ‹shán ‘yau ꜀ngan kw‘óng’ ‘ché, wák$_2$ ‘í ‘ts‘oi tsun$^2$ wák$_2$ fung$^2$ ‹fung kam’; ꜀wai ꜀Tín ꜀nám Tséung$^2$ ‹chau ‘yau ‘Mín shuk$_2$ ‹chí ‘Fó ‹shán ‘ch‘óng, ‘Kwóng ‹sai ‹pín ngoi$^2$ ‘yau ‹Ón ꜀nám ‹chí Sung’ ‹sing ‘ch‘óng ꜀ngan kw‘óng’ kik$_2$

9. The facts here stated, respecting the mines at Fóshán and Sungsing, are obtained from a recent memorial to the throne respecting the exportation of sycee, the state of the finances, &c.

| | | |
|---|---|---|
| china, on the frontiers of Kwóngsai. | 䀡紋銀多由此出 | wóng ₛman ₛngan ₛtó ₛyau 'ts'z' ch'ut. |
| 9. Are these mines open to any who please to work them? | 可是人人能取係唔係呢 | 'Hó shí ₛyan ₛyan ₛnang 'ts'ü hai' ₛ'm hai' ₛní? |
| They are not; but are intrusted to certain merchants who pay duty on them, and are worked by Chinese. At both of the places, some forty or fifty thousand men are constantly employed every year; the quantity obtained does not exceed two millions of taels, which is brought into China. | 唔係乃設商投稅聽內地人採取兩處每歲常役四五萬所得不過二百萬兩賫回內地啫 | ₛ'M hai', 'nái ch'ít, ₛshéung ₛt'au shui', ting' noi' tí' ₛyan 'ts'oi 'ts'ü, 'léung ch'ü' 'múi sui' ₛshéung yik, sz' ''ng mán', 'shó tak, pat, kwó' í' pák, mán' 'léung, ₛtsai ₛúi noi' tí' ₛché. |
| 10. How is it with regard to gold? | 金點樣呢 | ₛKam 'tím yéung' ₛní? |
| The establishments which deal in gold purchase it at the current price, and sell it again in the same manner. | 金店以時價採買番嚟以時價發賣咯 | ₛKam tím' 'í ₛshí ká' 'ts'oi 'mái ₛfán ₛlai 'í ₛshí ká' fát, mai' lók. |
| 11. Is there a large amount of gold in your country? | 你地貴處有幾多金呢 | 'Ní tí' kwai' ch'ü' 'yau 'kí ₛtó ₛkam ₛní? |
| There is but little, and therefore it is dear. | 金係少故此貴 | ₛKam hai' 'shíú, kú' 'ts'z' kwai'. |
| 12. Where is it found? | 在邊處嚟嘅呢 | Tsoi' ₛpín ch'ü' ₛlai ké' ₛní? |
| Some is obtained from copper after it is melted, and some is obtained from sand by washing. | 有在銅內傾出有在砂裏淘出嚟嘅 | 'Yau tsoi' ₛt'ung noi' ₛk'ing ch'ut, 'yau tsoi' ₛshá 'lü ₛt'ò ch'ut, ₛlai ké'. |
| 13. What are the ancient coins? | 古錢點樣嘅呢 | 'Kú ₛts'ín 'tím yéung' ké' ₛní? |
| There are, you see, several kinds of these coin; such as the celestial deity's, that which rained down in Hámyeung, the golden five pearl, &c. &c. Besides these there are several kinds of foreign coin. | 你睇天帝錢咸陽雨錢金五銖錢就係咧其餘又有別國嘅呀 | 'Ní 't'ai ₛt'ín tai' ₛts'ín, ₛHám ₛyéung 'ü ₛts'ín, ₛkam ''ng ₛchü ₛts'ín, tsau' hai' ₛlé. ₛK'í ₛü yau' 'yau pít, kwók, ké' á'. |

12. It may be doubted whether any gold is obtained from copper in China, as here stated; the statement is made on the authority of persons who have had no opportunity to test the matter by experiment. Some of the streams in the western parts of the empire afford gold dust, but the precise localities and the quantity produced are unknown.

| | | |
|---|---|---|
| 14. What description of coins have foreign countries in circulation? | 番國有幾多樣<br>銀使嘅呢 | ‹Fán kwók› 'yau 'kí ‹tó yéung$^{2}$ ‹ngan 'shai ké' ‹ní? |
| There are a good many kinds. | 有好幾樣咧 | 'Yau 'hó 'kí yéung$^{2}$ ‹lé. |
| The 'tribute eagle money' is made in the country of Mexico. | 貢鷹銀乃係覓<br>士哥國鑄的咧 | Kung$^{2}$ ‹ying ‹ngan 'nái hai$^{2}$ Mak› sz'$^{2}$ ‹kó kwók› chü' tik› ‹lé. |
| The 'single eagle money' comes from the United States of America. | 單鷹銀乃咪唎<br>加國出嘅 | ‹Tán ‹ying ‹ngan 'nái Mí' lí$^{2}$ ‹ká kwók› ch'ut› ké'. |
| The 'four I I I I money,' or the 'large petticoat fringes,' or 'the old head' money comes from Spain. | 四工銀即大裙<br>脚又舊頭乃大<br>呂宋銀也 | Sz" ‹kung ‹ngan tsik› tái$^{1}$ ‹kw'an kéuk›, yau$^{2}$ kau$^{2}$ ‹t'au, 'nái Tái$^{2}$ 'Lü sung' ‹ngan 'yá. |
| The 'beautiful tribute money' is that which comes from France. | 考貢銀係佛蘭<br>西國 | 'Háu kung' ‹ngan hai$^{2}$ Fat‹ 'lán ‹sai kwók›. |
| General names for dollars are 'flower edged,' and 'devil's head.' | 又喚之花邊及<br>鬼頭此之總名 | Yau$^{2}$ ún$^{2}$ ‹chí ‹fá ‹pín, kap‹ 'kwai ‹t'au, 'ts'z' ‹chí 'tsung ‹ming. |
| 15. Besides these, the *Sám ts'oi t'ò* also speaks of the coins of the U'-yik-shán-lí country, of the O'n-sik, the Hó, the Kóng, and other countries. | 三才圖云另有<br>烏弋山離國錢<br>安息國錢何國<br>康國等錢就係<br>咧 | ‹Sám ‹ts'oi ‹t'ò ‹wan, ling$^{2}$ 'yau ‹U' yik‹ ‹shan ‹lí kwók› ‹ts'ín, ‹O'n sik› kwók› ‹ts'ín, ‹Hó kwók›, ‹Kóng kwók›, 'tang ‹ts'ín, tsau$^{2}$ hai$^{2}$ ‹lé. |

14. The Chinese are very fastidious in their choice of foreign coins, rejecting some and choosing others merely with regard to the device. Spanish dollars with pillars, especially those issued in the reign of Charles IV. are the most current, often bearing a slight premium; while on the other hand, the coins of all the American states are passed with difficulty, even at a discount of two, three, and even six per cent. Other names, besides those given above, are in use, taken from the various devices on the different coins; *pò koi*, or 'precious cover' is a name given to the crown surmounting the pillars in Carolus dollars; 'the two candlestick dollars' is a term by which the Spanish coin is also known. Bolivian dollars are called *lám t'ung chü*, 'grasping the copper pillar,' from the central figures. 'Precious goose,' 'precious duck,' 'flying hen,' dollars are other appellations given to the coins of the American states.

15. The names of these ancient and foreign coins are taken from the *Sám Ts'oi T'ò*, a Chinese encyclopedia, to which the antiquarian, if disposed, can refer for further information respecting this subject.

## Section Eighth.

# VARIETIES OF SILK.

## 各欵綢緞第八章

Kók, 'kún ,ch'au tün'; tai' pát, ,chéung.

| | | |
|---|---|---|
| 1. The produce of a single silkworm is called a floss, ten of which make a [thread of] silk. The ends taken up and drawn out of the simple cocoons are also called silk. | 一蠶所吐爲忽十忽爲絲抽引精繭出緒亦曰絲 | Yat, ,ts'ám 'shó t'ò' ,wai fat, shap, fat, ,wai ,sz'. ,Chau 'yan ,tsing 'kín ch'ut, 'shü, yik, üt, ,sz'. |
| 2. One piece of silk costs the lives of a thousand silkworms. | 一片之絲千蠶之命 | Yat, p'in' ,chí ,sz' ,ts'ín ,ts'ám ,chí ,ming. |
| 3. The culture of the mulberry and hemp, raising of the silkworm and spinning, commenced with Yünfí. | 桑麻蠶績自元妃而始興 | ,Sóng ,má ,ts'ám chik, tsz' ,Yün ,fí ,í 'chí ,hing. |
| 4. Nanking [raw] silk is that which comes from the department of Uchau; Canton [raw] silk is produced in this province. | 湖絲乃湖州府絲土絲乃本土之絲也 | ,Ú ,sz' 'nái ,Ú ,chau 'fú ,sz'; 't'ò ,sz' 'nái 'pún 't'ò ,chí ,sz' 'yá. |
| 5. The Nanking silk, when woven, is called Nanking senshaw. The native silk, when woven, is called | 湖絲織名喚湖牛郎土絲織名 | ,Ú ,sz' chik, ,ming ún' ,ú ,ngau ,lóng. 'T'ò ,sz' chik, |

## *Notes and Explanations.*

THE names of the principal kinds of silken fabrics, sought by foreigners in this market, are here enumerated. The varieties in color, figure, quality, &c., are very numerous, and constantly changing. Inquiries respecting prices, &c., may be formed at pleasure on the model of phrases given in preceding sections.

1. The words *silk* and *satin*, like the articles themselves, seem to be of Chinese origin. Endeavoring to imitate the word *sz'* or *sze*, the foreigner, whatever language he used, would naturally approximate to the same sound; hence the words serica, seres, &c., and the English word silk. In like manner *sz'tün*, or *szetwan*, would become, in the west, sindon, seda, seta, and satin. Silk was probably first brought to Rome in the time of Pompey and Julius Cæsar; it became common in the fourth century; and in the sixth century, two Persian monks brought eggs of the silkworm from China to Constantinople.

3. Yünfí was consort of the ancient monarch, Wóngtai, the yellow emperor, who lived according to Chinese chronologists, about 4300 years ago.

4. The Nanking raw silk is called *ú sz'* or lake silk, from the name of the department of Úchau in Chítkóng, where some of the finest silk is cultivated, but it is here applied in a wider sense including all the raw silk brought from northern provinces, most of which comes from Chítkóng and Kóngsú. The *ú sz'* is divided in *taysaam* and *tsatlee;* the best quality of the latter is considered to be the finest and whitest silk produced in any part of the world.

| | | |
|---|---|---|
| Canton senshaw; a distinction is made between the two, and they are thus named. | 土牛郎則有兩種分别而名之 | ꜂ming ‘t‘ò ꜂ngau ꜂lóng, tsak꜄ ‘yau ‘léung ‘chung ꜀fan pít꜆ ꜂í ꜂ming ꜀chí. |
| 6. Superior fine wove plain lutestring. | 上等結素薄絹 | Shéung$^{2}$ ‘tang kít꜆ sü’ pók꜆ kün’. |
| 7. Second quality mixed lutestring. | 二等班絹 | I’$^{2}$ ‘tang ꜀pán kün’. |
| 8. My own loom's best flowered lutestring. | 本機上紡彩絹 | ‘Pún ꜂kí shéung$^{2}$ ‘fóng ‘ts‘oi kün’. |
| 9. Yellow flowered lutestring. | 黄色織花絲絹 | ꜂Wóng shik꜄ chik꜄ ꜀fá ꜀sz’ kün’. |
| 10. Light ground lutestring with various colors. | 粉地五色絲丨 | ‘Fan tí’ ꜂’ng shik꜄ ꜀sz’ kün’. |
| 11. Every description of flowered lutestring. | 各式花薄絹 | Kók꜄ shik꜄ ꜀fá pók꜆ kún’. |
| 12. Superior plain satin of every color. | 上頂五色素緞 | Shéung$^{2}$ ‘ting ꜂’ng shik꜄ sü’ tün’. |
| 13. Second quality of flowered striped satin. | 二頂花柳條緞 | I’$^{2}$ ‘ting ꜀fá ‘lau ꜂t‘íú tün’. |
| 14. New and fashionable changeable satin. | 新織時樣閃緞 | ꜀San shik꜄ ꜂shí yéung$^{2}$ ‘shím tün’. |
| 15. Flowered satin of a brownish red color. | 古銅色花局緞 | ‘Kú ꜂t‘ung shik꜄ ꜀fá kúk꜆ tün’. |
| 16. Plain crimson satin with eight threads. | 呀囒素八絲緞 | ꜂Ngá ꜀lán sü’ pát꜄ ꜀sz’ tün’. |
| 17. Figured eight threaded satin with raised flowers on a white ground. | 白地五彩扯起花八絲緞 | Pák꜆ tí$^{2}$ ꜂’ng ‘ts‘oi ‘ch‘é ‘hí ꜀fá pát꜄ ꜀sz’ tün’. |
| 18. Deep blue twilled Levantine satin with five threads. | 深藍斜紋花五絲緞 | ꜀Sham ꜂lám ꜂ts‘é ꜂man ꜀fá ꜂’ng ꜀sz’ tün’. |
| 19. Second quality of cross barred twilled Levantine satin, with five threads. | 次等革斜紋五絲緞 | Ts‘z” ‘tang kik꜄ ꜂ts‘é ꜂man ꜂’ng ꜂sz’ tün’. |
| 20. The satin used by the Chinese officers is of the very best kind. | 漢府緞乃緞之最好者 | Hón$^{2}$ ‘fú tün’ ‘nái tün’ ꜀chí tsü’ ‘hò ‘ché. |
| 21. In camlets, the threads are straight not crossed. | 線縐紋直無斜 | Sín’ tsau$^{2}$ ꜂man chik꜆ ꜂mò ꜂ts‘é. |

13. *Lau t‘íú*, willow lines; the stripes of the cloth are so designated because of their resemblance to the long depending branches of the willow tree, covered with lanceolate shaped leaves.

14. *Shím* is the common word for expressing the flash of lightning, or any quick glancing of light from off a brilliant surface; it is applied to those kinds of silk goods, which by a change of position, are somewhat iridescent, including both changeable and water colored silk; the last is also called *shui pó man* or water waved streaks, which is very near the English term.

20. *Hón fú* is literally officers of Hón, i. e. Chinese officers. The Chinese often call themselves sons of Hón, esteeming it an honor to bear the name of that ancient dynasty; this explanation is doubted by some, who say the term refers to Hónyéung fú, one of the departments in the province of U’pak.

| | | |
|---|---|---|
| 22. Superior plain black camlets. | 上等素黑線縐 | Shéung² ʻtang sü³ hak› sín³ tsau³. |
| 23. There are two kinds of camlets, one packed for foreign, and one for domestic, use. | 洋裝土裝兩等<br>線縐 | ˏYéung ˓chóng ʻtʻò ˓chóng ʻléung ʻtang sín³ tsau³. |
| 24. The *Luk* flowered pongee has a smooth body and raised flowers, which are of many colors, ten or more in variety; it was first woven by a man who was surnamed Luk, whence this sort of pongee has since been thus called. | 陸家花綢身滑<br>而起花其花樣<br>幾種顏色亦十<br>餘色乃陸姓人<br>始織此綢故而<br>名之 | Luk₂ ˓ká ˓fá ˏchʻau ˓shan wát₂ ˏí ʻhí ˓fá, ˏkʻi ˓fá yéung² ʻkí ʻchung ˏngán shik› yik₂ shap₂ ˏü shik›; ʻnái Luk₂ sing³ ˏyan ʻchí chik›, ʻtsʻz³ ˏchʻau, kú³ ˏí ˏming ˓chí. |
| 25. The pongee from Hòngchau fú is very thick and lustrous resembling satin. | 府綢厚結光滑<br>似緞 | ʻFú ˏchʻau hau² kít› ˓kwong wát₂ ʻtsʻz² tün². |
| 26. Sz'chʻüü pongee comes from Sz'chʻüü [province]. | 四川綢出四川 | Sz³ ˓chʻün ˏchʻau chʻut› Sz³ ˓chʻün. |
| 27. Cassia flowered pongee has figures like the flowers of cassia woven into it. | 桂花綢爲其織<br>出桂花 | Kwai³ ˓fá ˏchʻau wai² ˏkʻí chik› chʻut› kwai³ ˓fá. |
| 28. Ornamented pongees are flowered, and used for the inner part of double garments [as lining]. | 錦綢皆有花爲<br>夾納裏用 | ʻKam ˏchʻau ˓kái ʻyau ˓fá ˏwai káp› náp₂ ʻlí yung². |
| 29. The pongee known by the name *puk ün* has no flowers, and is also much used for lining. | 卜原綢無花亦<br>多爲納裏 | Puk› ˏün ˏchʻau ˏmò ˓fá yik₂ ˓tó ˏwai náp₂ ʻlí. |
| 30. Stiff pongee, which is woven of loose threads, is used for summer dresses. | 生綢生紗織皆<br>作夏衣 | ˓Shang ˏchʻau ˓shang ˓shá chik› ˓kái tsók› há² ˓í. |
| 31. Soft pongee has a soft yet solid texture, and is worn in the second and eighth months. | 熟綢身軟熟爲<br>二八月用 | Shuk₂ ˏchʻau ˓shan ʻün shuk₂ ˏwai í² pát› üt₂ yung². |
| 32. Reeled pongee is woven of the best reeled threads, and is the most expensive kind. | 紡綢上紡紗織<br>比之稍貴 | ʻFóng ˏchʻau shéung² ʻfong ˓shá chik› ʻpí ˓chí ˏyau kwai³. |

26.—34. As with other fabrics which are much sought after, so it is with silk among the Chinese, there are numberless varieties depending on the color, texture, or quality, the district in which it is grown, and the mode of weaving, each of which has its appropriate appellation known to those familiar with the trade. In a work of this kind, it would be comparatively of little use to designate the many names indicating all the shades of difference growing out of these causes, since they could hardly be described so as to be recognized, and experience is usually the only means to an acquaintance with them. This is particularly the case with the various sorts of pongee and senshaw, which are much worn by the Chinese.

| | | |
|---|---|---|
| 33. *Ningch'au* pongee is thick and firm, and is much used for ceremonial winter dresses. | 寧紬厚結多爲冬天禮服 | ˏNing ˏch'au hau$^{2}$ kít˒ ˎtó ˏwai ˎtung ˎt'ín ʿlai fuk˓. |
| 34. *Tsiú puk* pongee is woven with raised flowers which resemble those of the pepper. | 椒卜綢織成花如椒點墳起 | ˎTsiú puk˒ ˏch'au chik˒ ˏshing ˎfá ˏü ˎtsiú ʿtím ˏpan ʿhí. |
| 35. Rust colored senshaw is dyed in a jelly, made from gambier, several times, and dried in the sun until the dye appears on the surface in a lustrous rust color. | 薯莨紬以薯莨搗膠染紬染晒數次膠現於面光亮色赤 | ˏShü ˏléung ˏch'au ʿí ˏshü ˏléung ʿtò ˎkáu ʿím ˏch'au ʿím shái' shò' tsz'$^{2}$ ˎkáu ín$^{2}$ ˎü mín$^{2}$ ˎkwóng léung' shik˒ chik˒. |
| 36. Black senshaw is also dyed in a jelly, and then exposed in the sun to make it complete. | 黑膠綢亦用膠染晒而成 | Hak˒ ˎkáu ˏch'au yik˓ yung' ˎkáu ʿím shái' ˏí ˏshing. |
| 37. *Chün* senshaw is woven from Nanking silk, and is the best kind. | 串紬湖絲所織比之猶佳 | Ch'ün' ˏch'au ˏÚ ˎsz' ʿshó chik˒ ʿpí ˎchí ˏyau ˎkai. |
| 38. *Pák wái* senshaw is at first of a white color, and is afterwards dyed of various hues. | 白懷紬原來色白加染各色 | Pák˓ ˏwái ˏch'au ˏün ˏloi shik˒ pák˓ ˎká ʿím kók˒ shik˒. |
| 39. Cotton senshaw is woven of a mixture of cotton and silk, and is dyed of various colors; it is not very lustrous or beautiful. | 棉紬以棉雜絲而織皆染各色不甚光亮亦無嬌艷 | ˏMín ˏch'au ʿí ˏmín tsáp˓ ˎsz', ˏí chik˒ ˎkái ʿím kók˒ shik˒ pat˒ sham$^{2}$ ˎkwóng léung' yik˓ ˏmò ˎkíú yím$^{2}$. |
| 40. The *Sham* senshaw was first woven by a man surnamed Sham; formerly, it was held in high repute. | 沈紬乃沈姓始製古人甚尚之 | ʿSham ˏch'au ʿnái ʿSham sing' ʿchí chai'; ʿkú ˏyau sham$^{2}$ shéung$^{2}$ ˎchí. |
| 41. Crape is so called because the threads are crinkled; there is plain and figured, of many tens of colors, all of which differ among themselves; the tints are very delicate and elegant, and the goods are highly prized. | 縐紗因有縐紋而名有素有花花樣數十種顏色各異惟色最嬌艷人多貴之 | Tsau$^{2}$ ˎshá ˎyan ʿyau tsau$^{2}$ ˏman ˏí ˏming; ʿyau sü' ʿyau ˎfá; ˎfá yéung$^{2}$ shò' shap˓ ʿchung ˏngán shik˒ kók˒ í' ˏwai shik˒ tsü' ˎkíú yím$^{2}$ ˏyan ˎtó kwai$^{2}$ ˎchí. |
| 42. There is fine law with [five threads in a] bar, and another with three [threads in a] bar. | 熟羅有五梭有三梭之名 | Shuk˓ ˏló ʿyau ʿ'ng ˎsó ʿyau ˎsám ˎsó ˎchí ˏming. |

35, 36. This description of silk is worn by the poorer classes of natives very extensively, for summer clothing. It is cheap — a whole suit costing between four and five dollars—and

| | | |
|---|---|---|
| 43. Stiff law is woven of raw threads, and is often used for summer dresses. | 生羅以生絲織<br>以便夏天用 | ‹Shang ‚ló 'í ‹shang ‹sz' chik› 'í pín$^2$ há$^2$ ‹t'ín yúng$^2$. |
| 44. Damask silk is light and thin; its surface is lustrous, and there are plain and figured kinds. | 綾輕薄面而有<br>靚色亦有花素 | ‚Líng ‹hing pók‚ mín$^2$ ‚í 'yau ling$^2$ shik› yik‚ 'yau ‹fá sü'. |
| 45. Hóngchau damask silk has a smooth and brilliant surface; it is woven in the department of Hóngchau. | 杭綾面光滑杭<br>州所出 | ‚Hóng ‚ling mín$^2$ ‹kwóng wát‚; ‚Hóng ‹chau 'shó ch'ut›. |
| 46. Gauze is assorted into the transparent and dark ground varieties. | 紗有通紗有密<br>地紗之分 | ‹Shá 'yau ‹t'ung ‹shá 'yau mat‚ tí$^2$ ‹shá ‹chí ‹fan. |
| 47. Glazed gauze is very lustrous. | 亮丨爲色有亮 | Léung$^2$ ‹shá wai$^2$ shik› 'yau léung$^2$. |
| 48. Spring gauze is so called because it is adapted for wearing in that season. | 春丨謂當春時<br>能着 | ‹Ch'un ‹shá wai$^2$ ‹tóng ‹ch'un ‚shí ‚nang chéuk‚. |
| 49. Watered gauze has the figures like clouds. | 響雲紗其花如<br>雲 | 'Héung ‚wan ‹shá ‚k'í ‹fá ‚ü ‚wan. |
| 50. Musketo curtain gauze is used to make bed curtains. | 蚊帳丨乃爲帳<br>所用 | ‚Man cheung$^2$ ‹shá 'nái ‚wai chéung$^2$ 'shó yung$^2$. |
| 51. Coarse gauze is very thin and light, and is employed for festoons, and for pasting paper upon. | 機紗稀薄以爲<br>結彩裱紙 | ‹Kí ‹shá ‹hí pók‚ 'í ‚wai kít› 'ts'oi 'píú 'chí. |
| 52. Every sort of silk ribands. | 各式絲扁帶 | Kók› shik› ‹sz' 'pín tái'. |
| 53. Embroidered and figured crape handkerchiefs. | 顧繡花縐紗巾 | Kò$^2$ sau$^2$ ‹fá tsau$^2$ ‹shá ‹kan. |
| 54. Floss is made of silk and is dyed of various colors for embroidering. | 絨以絲加染各<br>色爲之顧繡 | ‚Yung 'í ‹sz' ‹ká 'ím kók› shik› ‚wai ‹chí kò$^2$ sau$^2$. |
| 55. [Silk] yarn is spun from raw silk, for making the warp and woof when weaving silk goods. | 紗紡絲成之以<br>作織疋頭經緯 | ‹Shá 'fóng ‹sz' ‚shing ‹chí 'í tsók› chik› pat‚ ‚t'au ‹king 'wai. |
| 56. Velvet is woven from both cotton and silk. | 剪絨以棉與絲<br>而織成之 | 'Tsín ‚yung 'í ‚mín 'ü ‹sz' ‚í chik› ‚shing ‹chí. |

from the color does not show dirt, and is withal very enduring. The two forms of *ch'au* in these two sentences are precisely alike in meaning, and at all times interchangeable.

42, 43. The fine law is a beautiful fabric, about two feet broad, woven with stripes running across, and figures in the body of the cloth. The name law is derived from the Chinese *ló*, and is applied to the fine kinds, which are both plain and figured. The common or stiff law is a coarse fabric, and little of it is exported.

## Section Ninth.

# EDICT FOR THE DELIVERY OF OPIUM.

## 諭令繳鴉片；第九章

U$^{2}$ ling$^{2}$ ‘kiú ‹á pín$^{2}$; tai$^{2}$ ‘kau ‹chéung.

1. Lam, high imperial commissioner of the celestial court, a director of the Board of War, and governor of U'kwóng, issues his commands to the foreigners of every nation for their full information.

2. It is known that the foreign ships which come to Canton for general trade, have obtained very large profits. This is herein evinced; that, while formerly the vessels arriving each year were hardly reckoned by tens, the number of late years has amounted to a hundred and several tens; that whatever commodities they may have brought, none have failed to be disposed of; and that, whatever they may have sought to purchase, there have been none which they could not at once obtain. Let it be asked, whether, between heaven and earth, so advantageous a commercial mart can anywhere else be found? It is because our great emperors, in their universal benevolence, have granted you commercial pri-

天朝欽差大臣
兵部尚書湖廣
總督部堂林諭
各國夷人知悉
照得夷船到廣
通商獲利甚厚
是以從前來船
每歲不及數十
隻近年來至一
百數十隻之多
不論所帶何貨
無不全銷欲置
何貨無不立辦
試問天地間如
此利市馬頭倘
有別處可覓否
我大皇帝一視

‹T‘ín ‹ch‘iú, ‹yam ‹ch‘ái, tái$^{2}$ ‹shan ‹Ping Pò$^{2}$ shéung$^{2}$ ‹shü, ‹U‘ ‘kwóng ‘tsung tuk›, pò$^{2}$ ‹t‘óng, ‹Lam, ü$^{2}$ kók› kwók› ‹í ‹yan ‹chí sik›.

Chiú’ tak› ‹í ‹shün tò’ ‘Kwóng ‹t‘ung ‹shéung, wók$_{2}$ lí$^{2}$ sham$^{2}$ hau$^{2}$. Shí$^{2}$ ‘í ‹ts‘ung ‹ts‘ín ‹loi ‹shün, ‘múi sui’ pat› k‘ap$_{2}$ shò’ shap$_{2}$ chik›; kan$^{2}$ ‹nín ‹loi chí’ yat› pák› shò’ shap$_{2}$ chik› ‹chí ‹tó; pat› lun$^{2}$ ‘shó tái’ ‹hó fó’, ‹mò pat› ‹tsün ‹síú; yuk$_{2}$ chí’ ‹hó fó’ ‹mò pat› lap$_{2}$ pán$^{2}$. Shí’ man$^{2}$ ‹t‘ín tí$^{2}$ ‹kán, ‹ü ‘ts‘z’ lí$^{2}$ ‘shí ‘má ‹t‘au, shéung$^{2}$ ‘yau pít$_{2}$ ch‘ü’ ‘hó mik$_{2}$ ‘fau? ‘Ngó tái$^{2}$ ‹wóng tai’ yat› shí$^{2}$ ‹t‘ung

## *Notes and Explanations.*

THIS edict bearing directly on the commercial and other relations with this country, and being also a specimen of highly finished composition, will not be inappropiate here. Papers of this kind, respecting foreigners, usually come through the hong merchants' hall, where the originals are retained, and copies are sent to the foreigners. On some important occasions they are transmitted through the offices of the local magistrates. In the present case it came directly from his excellency, bearing the seals of his high commission. The word *ü* is employed both as a noun and as a verb; it is a command, an order; or to command, to order; referring always to that which is issued by a superior authority to inferiors, and which by the latter must be regarded as a rule or law for their obedience. *Ling* has something of the same import: *ü ling kiú*, an edict commanding the delivery of *ápín*, opium.

vileges, that you now enjoy these commercial advantages. If once our ports are closed against you, for what profit can your several nations any longer look? Moreover, our tea and rhubarb, without which you foreigners have no means of supporting life, are without stint or grudge granted you year by year for exportation beyond sea. Favors never have been greater.

易貿爾准仁同
利此得沾纔爾
各爾港封一倘
況圖可利何國
夷外黃大葉茶
無卽此得不若
爾聽乃命爲以
洋出運販年年
莫恩惜斬不絕
　　　　焉大

ˏyan ˋchun ˋi mau[2] yik, ˋi ˏts'oi ˏchím tak, ˋts'z' li[2]. ˋT'óng yat, ˏfung ˋkóng ˋi kók, kwók, ˏhó li[2] ˋhó ˏt'ò? Fóng' ˏch'á ip, tái[2] ˏwóng, ngoi[2] ˏi yéuk, pat, tak, ˋts'z', tsik, ˏmò ˋi ˏwai ming', ˋnái t'ing' ˋi ˏnín ˏnín fán' wan[2] ch'ut, ˏyéung, tsüt, pat, kan' sik,. ˏYan mók, tái[2] ˏín.

3. Are you grateful for these favors? Then you ought to fear the laws, and in benefiting yourselves should not do injury to others. Why do you take the drug opium, which is not eaten in your own countries, and bring it into this land to defraud the people of their property, and to injure their lives? I find that with this thing you have deceived and

須卽恩感等爾
可不已利法畏
爾將得何人害
片鴉之食不國
騙地內來帶烟
命人害而財人
此以等爾查乎

ˋi ˋtang ˋhám ˏyan? Tsik, ˏsü wai' fát,, li[2] ˋkí pat, ˋhó hoi[2] ˏyan. ˏHó tak, ˏtséung ˋi kwók, pat, shik, ˏchí ˏá p'ín' ˏín, tái' ˏloi noi[2] ti[2], p'ín' ˏyan ˏts'oi, ˏi hoi[2] ˏyan ming[2] ˏú? ˏCh'á ˋi ˋtang ˋi

1. Lam:—as is usual in official papers of this kind, only his family name is given, and it is placed after his titles, the reverse of western usage. Literally, it reads thus; heavenly dynasty's imperially commissioned great minister, War-Board president *(shéungshü)*, Lake-broad general government office-occupier *(pò-tóng)*, Lam. Foreigner is a mild translation of *i;* there are within the boundaries of the empire numerous tribes of uncivlized mountaineers, who are designated *i yan;* thus there are two classes of *i yan;* those within the empire are called *noi i* and all without the empire are *ngoi i*. The term is used here nearly in the sense in which the Greeks and Romans used the word barbarian. *Chí shik*, fully to know, i. e. for your full information.

2. *Chiú tak* is a technical phrase: *chiú* light shining forth, information respecting any subject, *tak* obtained, appears, or is manifest. *Kwóng* is an abbreviation of Kwóngtung. *Tung shéung* an open market, one accessible to all without distinction. *Shí i* here by, i. e. the fact stated in the preceding clause is confirmed *by this*, what is hereinafter adduced. *Tái wóng tai* may be rendered great august ruler, or dread sovereign; *tái wóng* is an epithet indicative of the highest dignity, applied to great sovereigns, to deities, to heaven, &c. There cannot be, among men on earth, but one *tái wóng tai* at the same time; and to him, as vicegerent of heaven, all other rulers are subordinate. *Tsik mò i wai ming*, then nothing to use for life; if the ports of the empire are once closed, not only will there be an end to your profits; *fóng* but, moreover, and what is still worse, you, *ngoi i* foreign brbarians, not being able to procure tea and rhubarb, will then have nothing to subsist upona

3. *Pat shik chí áp'ín ín*, not eaten of opium smoke, i. e. the smoke of opium which is not

deluded the people of China for tens of years past, and that the unjust hoards thus acquired cannot be numbered. With such conduct the hearts of men are roused to indignation, and heavenly reason cannot deal leniently.

物蠱惑華民已歷數十年所得不義之財不可勝計此人心所共憤亦天理所難容

ʻtsʻzʼ matˏ ʻkú wákˏ ˏWá ˏman, ʻí likˏ shòʼ shapˏ ˏnín, ʻshó takˏ patˏ íʼ ˏchí ˏtsʻoi patˏ ʻhó ˏshing kaiʼ. ʻTsʻzʼ ˏyan ˏsam ʻshó kungʼ ʻfan, yikˏ ˏtʻín ʻlí ʻshó ˏnán ˏyung.

4. Formerly, the prohibitions of the celestial court were comparatively lax; and it was possible clandestinely to penetrate the various ports. Now the great emperor, hearing of this, and roused to indignation, will utterly exterminate it ere he stop. Whoever of the people in this land traffic in opium, or establish houses for smoking the drug, shall instantly be visited with the extreme penalty of the laws; and it is also in contemplation to regard those who smoke as guilty of death. And you, having come to the territories of the celestial court, ought equally with the people of the land to obey its laws and statutes.

從前天朝例禁向寬各口猶可偷漏今大皇帝聞而震怒必盡除之而後已所有內地民人販鴉片開烟館者立即正法吸食者亦議死罪爾等來至天朝地方即應與內地民人同遵法度

ˏTsʻung ˏtsʻín, ˏtʻín ˏchʻiú laiʼ kamʼ shéungʼ ˏfún; kókˏ ʻhau ˏyau ʻhó ˏtʻau lauʼ. ˏKam táiʼ ˏwóng taiʼ ˏman, ˏí chauʼ nòʼ, pítˏ tsunʼ ˏchü ˏchí, ˏí hauʼ ʻí. ʻShó ʻyau noiʼ tíʼ ˏman ˏyan fánʼ ˏá pʻínʼ, ˏhoi ˏín ʻkún ʻché, lapˏ tsikˏ chingʼ fátˏ; kʻapˏ shikˏ ʻché, yikˏ ʻí ʻszʼ tsúiʼ. ʻI ʻtang ˏloi chíʼ ˏtʻín ˏchʻiú tíʼ ˏfóng, tsikˏ ˏying ʻü noiʼ tíʼ ˏman ˏyan ˏtʻung ˏtsun fátˏ tòʼ.

5. I, the commissioner, having my home in the maritime province of Fukkin, had early a profound acquaintance with all the arts

本大臣家居閩海於外夷一切伎倆早皆深悉

ʻPún táiʼ ˏshan ˏká ˏkü ˏMan ʻhoi, ˏü ngoiʼ ˏí yatˏ tsʻitˏ chíʼ ʻléung, ʻtsò ˏkái ˏsham sʻikˏ ˏkʻí ˏtsʻéung.

inhaled. *Noí tí*, inner land, is used by the Chinese with emphasis, and is equivalent to the common phrase, our country; it has originated in the idea that this land is placed in the centre of the world, and that all other kingdoms and lands are placed on the extreme borders, the outer regions, of it. *Wá man*, the adorned people, i. e. the Chinese, the civilized, or the people adorned with learning and virtue.

4. *Lai kam*, laws prohibitive, the prohibitions of the government were, *shéung fún* somewhat lax, so that its, *kók hau* several ports, *yau hó* possibly might admit, *tʻò lau* a clandestine leaking—in of opium, or out of sycee. *Chan nò*, quaking wrath, fearful anger is what causes terror and agitation, like that excited by the falling of a thunderbolt, or the quaking of the earth. *Ching fát*, execute the laws, i. e. inflict capital punishment in conformity to the laws.

5. *Man hoi*, seas of Man; Man is an ancient classical name of Fukkín; the commissioner is from the department of Fukchau, the capital of the province. The terms of his commission run thus, literally; *ping ting* pacifier and settler, *ngoi wák* of the outer regions, *lui tsz'* repeatedly, *lap* established in, *kung chí* meritoriousness, *yam chái* imperial commissioner,

and shifts of the outer barbarians. Hence I have been especially honored by the great emperor, with his grant of, plenipotentiary powers, or *High imperial commissioner, and for repeated services sent to settle the affairs of the frontiers.*

其詳是以特蒙大皇帝頒給平定外域屢次立功之欽差大臣關防前來查辦

Shí 'í tak ˛mung tái ˛wóng tai' ‹pán k'ap› ˛p'ing ting' ngoi' wák, 'lü ts'z' lap ‹kung ‹chí ‹yam ‹ch'ái tái' ˛shan, ‹kwán ˛fóng ˛ts'ín ˛loi ˛ch'á pán'.

6. Should I search closely into the offenses of foreigners, in carrying on for so many years past their traffic, they would be found to be already beyond the bounds of indulgence. But considering that they are men from afar, and hitherto not aware that the prohibitions were so severe, I cannot bear, in carrying out the present plain enforcement of the laws, to cut them off, without first giving instructive admonition.

若追究該夷人積年販賣之罪即已不可姑容惟念究係遠人從前倘未知有此嚴禁今與明申約法不忍不敎而誅

Yéuk ‹chui kau' ‹koi ˛í ˛yan tsik› ˛nín fán' mái' ‹chí tsúi', tsik› 'í pat› 'hó ‹kú ˛yung. ˛Wai ním' kau' hai' 'ün ˛yan, ˛ts'ung ˛ts'ín shéung' mí' ‹chí 'yau 'ts'z' ˛ím kam', ‹kam 'ü ˛ming ‹shan yéuk› fát›, pat› 'yan pat› káu' ˛í ‹chü.

7. I find, that on board the warehousing vessels, which you have now lying at anchor in the Lintin and other offings, there are stored up some tens of thousands of chests of opium, which it is your purpose and desire to sell clandestinely, without ever considering the present severity of the measures for seizing it at every port. How will men dare again to give it escort? And in every province the same severe measures are in operation for seizing it. Where else, then, will any be found who will presume to join in the traffic? At the present time opium is entirely stopped. All men know it to be a nauseous poison. Why then will you be at the trouble of laying

查爾等現泊伶仃等洋之躉船存有鴉片數萬箱意欲私行售賣獨不思海口如此嚴拏豈復有人敢爲護送而各省亦皆嚴拏更有何處敢與銷售此時鴉片禁止不行人人知爲鴆毒何

˛Ch'á 'í 'tang íu' pók› ‹Ling ‹ting, 'tang, ˛yéung ‹chí ‹tun ˛shün, ˛ts'ün 'yau ‹á p'ín' shò' mán' ‹séung, í' yuk› ‹sz' ˛hing kau' mái', tuk› pat› ‹sz' 'hoi 'hau ˛ü 'ts'z' ˛ím ˛ná. 'Hí fuk› 'yau ˛yan 'kóm ˛wai ú' sung'? ˛I' kók› 'shang yik› ‹kái ˛ím ˛ná. Kang' 'yau ˛hó ch'ü' 'kóm 'ü ‹síú kau'? 'Ts'z' ˛shí ‹á p'ín' kam' 'chí, pat› ˛hing. ˛Yan ˛yan ‹chí ˛wai ˛sham tuk›.

*tái shan* high minister. The remaining six characters, *kwán fóng ts'ín loi ch'á pán*, belong to what precèdes the words, ping ting, &c. It is to be construed thus, *pán k'ap . . . . . kwán fóng ts'ín loi ch'á pán*, conferred and gave previleges and powers . . . . . to come forward to examine and act.

6. *Yün yan*, distant men, men from afar; these words often form a convenient and appropriate term for the word foreigner or foreigners.

it up on board your storeships, long detaining them on the high seas, not only expending to no purpose your labor and wealth, but even exposing it to unforeseen dangers from storms and fires.

苦貯在夷躉久
停大洋不獨枉
費工貲恐風火
更不可測也

‹Hó ʻfú ʻch'ü tsoi2 ‚í tun ʻkau ting2 tái2 ‚yéung, pat› tuk2 ʻwóng fai' ‹kung ‹tsz' ʻkung ‹fung ʻfó, kang' pat› ʻhó tsak› ʻyá.

9. Wherefore I proceed to issue my commands. When these reach the foreign merchants, let them immediately take the entire amount of opium in their storeships and deliver it up to government. Let it be ascertained clearly by the hong merchants how many chests are delivered up by each person, and what is the whole amount in catties and taels. Let these particulars be brought together in a clear tabular form, and presented to government for examination, that in strict conformity thereto it may be received and destroyed, to the utter extirpation of the evil. Not the smallest particle must be withheld or concealed.

合行諭飭諭到
該夷商等速即
遵照將躉船鴉
片盡數繳官由
洋商查明何人
名下繳出若干
箱統共若干斤
兩造具清冊呈
官點驗收明燬
化以絕其害不
得絲毫藏匿

Hóp› ‚hing ü2 shik›. Ü2 tò' ‹koi ‚í ‹shéung ʻtang, ‹ts'uk tsik› ‹tsün chiú', ‹tséung ʻtun ‚shun ‹á p'ín' tsun2 shò' ʻk'ú ‹kún. ‚Yan ‚yéung ‚shéung ‚ch'á ‚ming ‚hó ‚yan ‚ming há2 ʻkíú ch'ut› yéuk2 ‹kón ‹séung, ʻt'ung kung' yéuk2 ‹kón ‹kan ʻléung. ʻTsò' kü2 ‹ts'ing ch'ák›, ‚ch'ing ‹kún ʻtím ʻím ‹shau ‚ming ʻwai fá', ʻí tsüt2 ‚k'í hoi'. Pat› tak› ‹sz' ‚hò ‚ch'óng nik›.

10. At the same time let these foreigners give a bond, written jointly in the foreign and Chinese languages, declaring plainly, "That their ships, hereafter resorting hither, will never bring opium; that if they should bring it, as soon as discovered the whole shall be confiscated, and the men suffer the extreme penalty of the laws; and that such punishment will be submitted to willingly."

一面出具夷字
漢字合同甘結
聲明嗣後來船
永不敢夾帶鴉
片如有帶來一
經查出貨盡沒
官人即正法情
甘服罪字樣

Yat› mín2 ch'ut› kü2 ‚í tsz'2 hón' tsz'2 hóp2 ‚t'ang ‹kóm kít2, ‹shing ‚ming, tsz'2 hau2 ‚loi ‚shün, ‚wing pat› ʻkóm káp› tái' ‹á p'ín'; ‚ü ʻyau tái' ‚loi, yat› ‹king ‚ch'á ch'ut›, fò' tsun2 mút2 ‹kún, ‚yan tsik› ching' fát›, ‚ts'ing ‹kóm fuk2 tsúi2 tsz'2 yéung2.

7. *Tun shün*, store-house ships, ships remaining stationary and serving as depôts. *Sham tuk* is a nauseous, deadly, or virulent poison.

9. *Hóp* wherefore — uniting into one view all the particulars which have been narrated and closing the case, forming my judgment and decisions according to those particulars — *hing ü shik* I proceed to issue my commands. *Tím ím* is an examination made of goods according to a list, on which the several items of goods are *tím*, or marked, as soon as they are *ím*, examined and verified. The phrase *wai fá* means utter destruction: *wai* is destruction by fire, and *fá* si a change wrought in the nature of any substance or being. *Yung fá* is another phrase for expressing the same idea.

10. *Kóm Kít*, a sweet knot, a voluntary bond: the phrase is used on all accasion in which the people bind themselves to observe specific regulations.

11. I have heard that you foreigners always attach great importance to the word *good faith*. If then you will really do as I, the commissioner, have commanded, will deliver up the entire amount already here, and assuredly prevent the introduction of that which has not arrived,—thus evincing contrition for guilt and a dread of punishment,—the past need not be investigated. And I, the commissioner, will then, in conjunction with the governor, and lieutenant-governor, address the throne, imploring the great emperor to vouchsafe extraordinary favors, not only to forgive former errors, but also—as we will request—to confer rewards, to encourage a spirit of contrition and fear. After this, commercial intercourse will be enjoyed as formerly; and your character as good foreigners will not be lost. Moreover, by an honorable traffic, you may freely acquire profits and become rich. Will not this be most honorable?

聞該夷平日重
一信字果如本
大臣所諭已來
者盡數呈繳未
來者斷絕不來
是能悔罪畏刑
尙可不追既往
本大臣卽當會
同督部堂撫部
院奏懇大皇帝
格外施恩不特
寬免前愆並請
酌予賞犒以獎
其悔懼之心此
後照常貿易既
不失爲良夷且
正經買賣儘可
獲利致富豈不
體面

ˌMan ˌkoi ˌí ˌp'ing yat, chung yat, *san* tsz'. 'Kwó ˌü 'pún tái ˌshan 'shó ü', 'í ˌloi 'ché tsun shò' ˌch'ing 'kíú, mí ˌloi 'ché tün tsüt, pat, ˌloi, shí ˌnang fúi tsúi wai ˌying, shéung 'hó pat, ˌchui kí 'wóng. 'Pún tái ˌshan, tsik, ˌtóng úi ˌt'ung tuk, pò, ˌt'óng 'fú pò ün' tsau' 'han tái ˌwóng tai' kák, ngoi ˌshí ˌyan, pat, tak, ˌfún 'mín ˌts'in ˌhín, ping' 'ts'ing chéuk, ˌü 'shéung hò', 'í 'tséung ˌk'í fúi kü' ˌchí ˌsam. 'Ts'z' hau' chíú' ˌshéung mau' yik, kí' pat, shat, ˌwai ˌléung ˌí. 'Ch'é ching' ˌking 'mái mái' 'tsun 'hó wók, lí' chí' fú'. 'Hí pat, 't'ai mín'?

12. But if you obstinately adhere to folly, and will not

倘執迷不悟稽

'T'óng chap, ˌmai pat, 'ng;

11. *Man* is used to denote what one hears, as current rumors, reports, &c. *San*, good faith, is truth, verity, or sincerity; one who forfeits his word, *shat san*, loses or breaks his good faith. *Tsau* is used appropriately for all addresses made to the sovereign, as *pan* is for all those which are made to the magistracy; it is used both as a noun and as a verb; it is a memorial, or to memorialize. *Kák ngoi shí yan*, limits beyond extend favors; that is, vouchsafe extraordinary favors. *Shéung hò* are rewards, such as are conferred on heroes and others, who have acted in a manner to merit favor. *I tséung* to encourage, *k'í fúi kü chí sam*, the repentance and fear 's mind; meaning, to develop a spirit of fear and contrition. *Chíú shéung*, according to the ordinary course, or in the usual manner. *T'ai mín* substantial face, respectable, honorable.

12. *T'óng* if you, *chap* adhere to, *mai* your folly or blindness, *pat 'ng* and will not awake, to a sense of duty, *yau* still, *sz'* thinking, *níp* falsely, *pan* to address me. *T'ók ming*, to commit to the name, *shui shau* of seamen, that is, to bring it in under the name of seamen, pretending that the resident merchants have nothing to do with it. *T'óng sik*, to bar and shut up, to bar any inquiry, *í kíú* and deliver, *shap chí yat í* one or two of ten. It is a favorite mode of expressing relations of quantities among the Chinese, to speak of so many tenth

awake; if you yet think, under cover of false representations to continue your illicit traffic; or to pretend that it is brought by seamen, unconnected with the foreign merchants; or deceitfully to declare that it shall be returned to your country, or cast into the sea; or to take occasion to go to other provinces seeking to sell it; or to stifle inquiry by giving up one or two tenths: in all these cases it will be evident that you retain a contumacious and disobedient spirit, upholding vice and unwilling to reform. Then, although the celestial court treats with tenderness and great mildness men from afar, still, as it cannot bear with their scorn and contempt, it will be right to subject you likewise, according to the new law, to the same severe course of punishment.

思揑稟售私或
託名水手帶來
與夷商無涉或
詭稱帶回該國
投入海中或乘
問而赴他省覓
售或搪塞而繳
十之一二是皆
有心違抗怙惡
不悛雖以天朝
柔遠綏懷亦不
能任其藐玩應
即遵照新例一
體從重懲創

ˏyau ˓sz' níp 'pan kau' ˓sz'; wák t'ók ˏming 'shui 'shau tái' ˏloi, 'ü ˏí ˓shéung ˏmò shíp; wák 'kwai ˓ch'ing tái' ˏúi ˓koi kwók, ˏt'au yap 'hoi ˓chung; wák ˏshing ˓kán ˏí fú' ˓t'á 'sháng mik kau'; wák ˏt'óng sik ˏí 'kíú shap ˓chí yat í': shí' ˓kái 'yau ˓sam ˏwai k'óng', fú' ók pat ˓só. ˓Sui 'í ˓t'ín ˏch'íú ˏyau 'ün ˓shü ˏwái, yik pat ˏnang yam' ˏk'í 'míú ún', ˓ying tsik ˓chün chíú' ˓san lai', yat 't'ai ˏts'ung chung' 'ching ch'óng'.

13. On this occasion, I, the commissioner, while at the capital received in person the sacred commands, that wherever law exists, it must be executed. Moreover, having brought these full powers and privileges, enabling me to do whatever seems right—powers with which those ordinarily given for inquiring and acting in regard to other matters cannot be compared: so long as the opium remains unexterminated, so long will I, the

此次本大臣自
京面承聖諭法
在必行且既帶
此關防得以便
宜行事非尋常
查辦他務可比
若鴉片一日未
絕本大臣一日

'Ts'z' ts'z'' 'pún tái' ˏshan tsz'' ˓king mín' ˏshing shing' ü', fát tsoi' pít ˏhing. 'Ch'é kí' tái' 'ts'z' ˓kwán ˏfóng tak 'í pín' ˏí ˏhing sz'', ˓fí ˏts'am ˏshéung ˏch'á pán' ˓t'á mò' 'hó 'pí: yéuk ˓á p'ín' yat yat mí' tsüt, 'pún tái' ˏshan yat yat pat ˏúi.

parts. So much is this the case, that to say *yat í fan*, one or two parts, expresses the same thing as to say *shap chí yat í*, one or two parts of ten. Even qualities are thus compared; a person is said to be so many tenths recovered from illness; and *shap fan*, ten parts, is the most common term used to denote perfection.

13. *Ts'z' king* [coming] from the capital, *mín ching* have face to face received, *shing ü*, the sacred [that is, the emperor's] commands. *Kwán fóng* is a compound term, here meaning powers to prohibit, stop up, and regulate everything pertaining to the traffic. *Ts'am shéung*, searchingly constant, is a common term for the constant and ordinary routine of things, for whatever is common and usual. *Chai* swearing, *ü ts'z' sz'* that in this affair, *séung ch'í chung* [I will] join the beginning and the end, that is, thoroughly investigating it, leaving no part unexamined; the sentence is peculiarly emphatic and terse, and is a good instance of the nervousness of which the language is capable.

commissioner, not return. I swear that I will progress in this business from beginning to end: certainly I will not stop midway in its execution.

不回誓與此事
相始終斷無中
止之理

Chai$^{2}$ ʻü ʻtsʻz’ sz’$^{2}$ ‹séung ʻchʻí ‹chung: tün’ ˏmò ‹chung ʻchí ‹chí ʻlí.

14. Furthermore, I observe the popular feeling is all so roused to public indignation, that, if you foreigners remain insensible to reformation and contrition, continuing to make gain your sole object, there will not only be arrayed against you the martial terrors and powerful energies of our military and naval forces; but the able-bodied of the people, being called on, will be more than sufficient for placing your lives within my power. And moreover, by a temporary embargo, or by a permanent closing of our ports, what difficulty will there be in effectually cutting off the intercourse? Our central empire, comprising a territory of many thousands of miles, and possessing in rich abundance all the products of the soil, derives no profit from your foreign commodities; you may, therefore, well fear that the means of livelihood of your several nations will cease. You, who have come so far for commerce, how is it that you do not perceive the difference between toil and repose, between the power of the many, and that of the few!

況察看內地民
情皆動公憤倘
該夷不知改悔
惟利是圖非但
水陸官兵軍威
壯盛即號召民
間丁壯已足制
其命而有餘而
且暫則封艙久
則封港更何難
絕其交通我中
原數萬里版輿
百產豐盈並不
藉資夷貨恐爾
各國生計從此
休矣爾等遠出
經商豈尚不知
勞逸之殊形與
衆寡之異勢哉

Fóng’ chʻát› hón’ noi$^{2}$ tí$^{2}$ ˏman ˏtsing, ‹kái tung$^{2}$ ‹kung ʻfan, ʻtʻóng ‹koi ˏí pat› ‹chí ʻkoi fúi’, ˏwai lí$^{2}$ shí$^{2}$ ˏtʻò, ‹fí tán$^{2}$ ʻshui luk$_{2}$ ‹kún ‹ping ‹kwan ‹wai chóng’ shing$^{2}$; tsik› hò$^{2}$ chíú$^{2}$ ˏman ‹kán ‹ting chóng’, ʻí tsuk› chai’ ˏkʻí ming$^{2}$ ˏí ʻyau ˏü. ˏI’ ʻchʻé tsám$^{2}$ tsak› ‹fung ‹chʻóng, ʻkau tsak› ‹fung ʻkóng, kang’ ˏhó ˏnán tsüt$_{2}$ ˏkʻí ‹káu ‹tʻung? ʻNgó ‹chung ˏün shò’ mán$^{2}$ ʻlí ʻpán ˏü, pák› ʻchʻán ‹fung ˏying; ping$^{2}$ pat› tsik$_{2}$ ‹tsz’ ˏí fó’; ʻkung ʻí kók› kwók› ‹shang kai’, ˏtsʻung ʻtsʻz’ ‹yau ʻí. ʻI’ ʻtang ʻün chʻut› ‹king ‹shéung, ʻhí shéung$^{2}$ pat› ‹chí ˏlò yat$_{2}$ ‹chí ˏshü ˏying, ʻü chung’ ʻkwá ‹chí í$^{2}$ shai$^{2}$ ‹tsoi!

15. As to those crafty foreigners, resident in the

至夷館中慣販

Chí’ ˏí ʻkún ‹chung kwán’

14. *Hò chíú man kán ting chóng*, by proclamation call out the serviceable and able-bodied from among the people. This designates a kind of *posse comitatus*, formed by levies of such men as the magistrates of districts choose to select from among the able-bodied of the male population, between the ages of sixteen and sixty. All men between these ages are to hold themselves at the service of the state in military emergencies. What the commissioner would express seems to be, that the undisciplined levies would be so strongly actuated by popular feeling against the foreign opium dealers, that they would form a sufficient power unaided by the regular military, to enforce the severest treatment. The words *fung chʻóng* signify only the closing of the holds of ships, but this, in China, implies also the prohibition to leave the port, and forbids them too from entering. Our central empire, or more literally, our central

foreign factories, continually selling opium, I, the commissioner, was early furnished with a list of their names. And those good foreigners, also, who have not sold opium, must not fail to be distinguished. Those who will point out the bad foreigners, compel them to deliver up their opium, and are first to give the bond, are the good foreigners; and I the commissioner, will early and liberally reward them. Weal and woe, honor and disgrace, now remain with you yourselves alone to choose.

鴉片之奸夷本大臣早已備記其名而不賣鴉片之良夷亦不可不爲剖白有能指出奸夷責令呈繳鴉片並首先具結者卽是良夷本大臣必先優加獎賞禍福榮辱惟其自取

fán' ‹á p'ín' ‹chí ‹kán ‹í, 'pún tái$^2$ ‹shan 'tsò 'kí pí$^2$ kí' ‹k'í ‹míng. ‹Í pat› mái$^2$ ‹á p'ín' ‹chí ‹léung ‹í, yik› pat› 'hó pat› ‹wai 'pau pák›. 'Yau ‹nang 'chí ch'ut› ‹kán ‹í, chák› ling$^2$ ‹ch'ing ‹kíú ‹á p'ín' ping$^2$ 'shau ‹sín kü$^2$ kít›, 'ché, tsik› shí$^2$ ‹léung ‹í; 'pún tái$^2$ ‹shan pít› ‹sín ‹yau ‹ká 'tséung 'shéung. Wò$^2$ fuk› ‹wing yuk› ‹wai ‹k'í tsz$^2$ 'ts'ü.

16. Now I am about to command the hong merchants, *'Ng Shíúwing* [or Howqua] and others, to proceed to your factories to instruct you. A term of three days is allowed for your reply; at the same time, let the duly attested bond be given; while you wait for me, in conjunction with the governor and lieutenant-governor to appoint a time for the opium to be received. Indulge no idle expectation, seeking for delay, till repentance will be too late! A special edict.

今令洋商伍紹榮等到館開導限三日內回稟一面取具切實甘結聽候會同督部堂撫部院示期收繳毋得觀望諉延後悔無及特諭

‹Kam ling$^2$ ‹yéung ‹shéung 'Ng Shíú$^2$ ‹wing 'tang, tò' 'kún ‹hoi tò$^2$. Hán$^2$ ‹sám yat› noi$^2$, ‹úi 'pan; yat› mín$^2$ 'ts'ü kü$^2$ ts'ít› shat›, ‹kóm kít›; t'ing' hau$^2$ úi$^2$ ‹t'ung tuk› pò$^2$ ‹t'óng 'fú pò$^2$ ün$^2$ shí$^2$ ‹k'í ‹shau 'kíú. ‹Mò tak› ‹kún móng$^2$ 'wai ‹ín, hau$^2$ fúi' ‹mò k'ap›. Tak› ü$^2$.

Given this 19th year of Tòkwóng, 2d month, 4th day. [March 18th, 1839.]

道光十九年二月初四日

Tò$^2$ ‹kwóng, shap› 'kau ‹nín, í$^2$ üt›, ‹ch'ó sz$^2$ yat›.

place of origin, is a common designation for China, considered as the centre of civilization, if not of the earth, and the birthplace of mankind. *Shò mán lí pán ü*, several myriads of *lí* registered and mapped, *pák ch'án fung ying*, and having a hundred (or all) products in exuberant fullness.

# CHAPTER VII.
# MECHANICAL AFFAIRS.
# 工藝篇七
,Kung ngai$^{2}$; ,p'ín ts'at,.

## Section First.
## NAMES OF ARTIFICERS.
### 名匠第一章
,Ming tséung$^{2}$; tai$^{2}$ yat, ,chéung.

| English | Chinese | Romanization |
| --- | --- | --- |
| 1. *Architects* are those who plan and build all kinds of lodging-places. | 工匠營造起居所類者 | ,*Kung tséung*$^{2}$, ,ying tsò$^{2}$ 'hí ,kü 'shó lui$^{2}$ 'ché. |
| 2. *Armorers* make military implements. | 軍器匠作兵械 | ,*Kwan hí*' *tséung*$^{2}$, tsòk, ,ping hái$^{2}$. |
| 3. *Artificial flowermen* take pith-paper, and skillfully work it into the form of flowers. | 紙蓪花師傅將蓪紙巧造如花 | '*Chí* ,*t'ung* ,*fá* ,*sz'* *fú*$^{2}$, ,tséung ,t'ung 'chí 'háu tsò$^{2}$ ,ü ,fá. |
| 4. *Artisan* is a general name for all skillful handicraftsmen; and whoever is thus skillful in one occupation, confining himself to that alone, is then called this or that artificer, or this or that workman. | 工作者乃手藝人之總名凡藝擅專門則云某匠或曰某師傅 | ,*Kung tsók*, '*ché*, 'nái 'shau ngai$^{2}$ ,yan ,chí 'tsung ,ming; ,fán ngai$^{2}$ shín$^{2}$ ,chün ,mún, tsak, ,wan 'mau tséung$^{2}$, wák$_{2}$ üt$_{2}$ 'mau ,sz' fú$^{2}$. |

## *Notes and Explanations.*

In all those manipulations which are in any great measure dependent on the exact sciences, the Chinese for the most part are poor proficients. The construction of chronometers, thermometers, and such like instruments, they have seldom if ever attempted. In less exact works they succeed better. For example, the *shui ch'é*, 'water carriage,' as they name the fire-engine, introduced among them since the commencement of the nineteenth century, is now manufactured extensively by them, and in such a manner as to show that they are not deficient in imitative skill. *Tséung* denotes simply an artisan or an artificer.

1. *Kung tséung* is literally defined thus, 'build make rising dwelling places kinds the agents;' i. e. *kung tséung*, or architects, are those persons who construct all the kinds of buildings which are required for the various purposes of life.

3. *Sz' fú* is a complimentary term, often applied to workmen, indicating that they possess skill and learning. Tutors and masters are sometimes so denominated.

4. *Tsók* means to do, to make; preceded by *kung* work, and followed by *ché*, it denotes

CHI. CHR. 70

| | | |
|---|---|---|
| 5. An *awning maker*, by using matting, bamboos, and posts, constructs rooms and houses. | 棚匠以篷竹杉<br>搭成樓屋 | *ˏP'áng tséung*ʾ, ʿí ˏp'ung chukˎ, ch'ám', tápˎ ˏshing ˏlau ukˎ. |
| 6. A *baker* is one who makes and bakes bread, and so forth. | 饅頭師傅乃炕<br>造麵飽者 | *Mán*ʾ *ˏt'au ˏsz' fú*ʾ, ʿnái hóng' tsòʾ mínʾ ˏpáu ʿché. |
| 7. *Barbers* are those persons who improve the appearance, and shave the hair. | 剃頭師傅乃整<br>容落髮人也 | *T'ai' ˏt'au ˏsz' fú*ʾ, ʿnái ʿching ˏyung lòkˎ fátˎ ˏyan ʿyá. |
| 8. *Basket makers*, using bamboo splints, weave them into different kinds of baskets. | 竹器師傅以竹<br>篾編織籃笠者 | *Chukˎ hí' ˏsz' fú*ʾ, ʿí chukˎ mítˎ ˏpín chikˎ ˏlám lapˎ ʿché. |
| 9. The *blackletter printer*, first taking a sheet of paper and spreading it upon a stone table, thoroughly wets it; he then with cotton beats the paper into the characters [cut in the stone], and having touched it over with ink, takes it off, thus completing the blackletter characters. | 法帖匠先將紙<br>鋪碑上浸透用<br>棉花搥紙於字<br>中外過墨起之<br>則成法帖字 | *Fátˎ t'ípˎ tséung*ʾ, ˏsín ˏtséung ʿchí ˏp'ò ˏpí shéungʾ tsam' t'au', yungʾ ˏmín ˏfá ʿch'ui ʿchí ˏü tszʾ ˏchung, ngoiʾ kwó' makˎ, ʿhí ˏchí, tsakˎ ˏshing fátˎ t'ípˎ tszʾ. |
| 10. *Blacksmiths* are those who beat and make iron utensils. | 打鐵匠乃打造<br>鐵器者 | *ʿTá t'itˎ tséung*ʾ, ʿnái ʿtá tsòʾ t'itˎ hí' ʿché. |
| 11. A *bookbinder* is one who binds and trims books, prepares stationary, and so forth. | 釘裝匠乃釘裝<br>書籍等物 | *ˏTing ˏchóng tséung*ʾ, ʿnái ˏting ˏchóng ˏshü tsikˎ ʿtang matˎ. |
| 12. Those who make bows and arrows are named *bowmakers*. | 製造弓箭名爲<br>弓箭匠 | Chai' tsòʾ ˏkung tsín', ˏming ˏwai *ˏkung tsín' tséung*ʾ. |
| 13. A *brazier* is one who fuses and casts utensils of brass. | 打銅丨即鍛鍊<br>銅器者 | *ʿTa ˏt'ung tséung*ʾ, tsikˎ tün' línʾ ˏt'ung hí' ʿché. |

the doer of work, a workman, an artisan. *Ngai*, which also means to do, has the additional meaning of order; it is an orderly, a scientific, doing; and hence is applied to the fine arts, such as music, writing, &c. *Shín chün*, taken together, mean to assume the power of acting independently; here, in connection with the words preceding and following them, the shade of meaning is changed: *shín chün mún*, is to select and confine one's self to a single occupation.

5. *P'áng* is applied the most frequently to mere temporary buildings, such as the tents and barracks of soldiers in field service, small mat sheds for victualers in the streets and market-places, and the large temporary structures erected for theatrical exhibitions.

7. *T'ai t'au lò*, shave head old-man, is also a common appellation for the tonsor, whose business it is to shave the hair from the head as well as the beard from the face.

11. *Ting* means to nail; *chóng*, to bind or place in order, here signifies not only putting of the leaves in order, but also the trimming of them with the knife. *Tsik* joined with *shü* implies all kinds of books, letter-paper, &c.

| | | |
|---|---|---|
| 14. *Brickmakers* build furnaces, make and burn bricks and tiles. | 磚瓦師傅結窰<br>燒造磚瓦 | ‹*Chün ʻngá ‹sz' fú*$^{2}$, kít› ‹íú ‹shíú tsò$^{2}$ ‹chün ʻngá. |
| 15. Those who slaughter and dress living animals are named *butchers.* | 宰殺生者名曰<br>屠人 | ʻTsoi shát› ‹shang ʻché, ‹ming üt› ‹*t'ò* ‹*yan.* |
| 16. A *cabinet maker* is one skilled in the manufacture of trunks, boxes, and so forth. | 甲萬師傅精造<br>甲萬櫃箱等物 | *Káp› mán*$^{2}$ ‹*sz' fú*$^{2}$, ‹tsing tsò$^{2}$ káp› mán$^{2}$ ʻlung ‹séung ʻtang mat›. |
| 17. The *calenderer*, by the use of a calendering stone, makes the cloth smooth and glossy. | 碾布師傅以石<br>碾滑其布者也 | *Shín' pò'* ‹*sz' fú*$^{2}$, ʻí shik› shín' wát› ‹k'í pò' ʻché ʻyá. |
| 18. *Carpenters* construct rafters and build houses, lodges, temples, and such like edifices. | 木匠架桁蓋成<br>樓閣祠宇 | *Muk› tséung*$^{2}$, ká' ‹háng k'oi' ‹shing ‹lau kók› ‹ts'z' ʻü. |
| 19. A *cartwright* makes carriages with wheels. | 輿匠造輪輿者 | ‹*Ü tséung*$^{2}$, tsò$^{2}$ ‹lun ‹ü ʻché. |
| 20. A *carver* of *wood* cuts and engraves flowers, and so forth, very finely on all kinds of utensils. | 細花木匠雕刻<br>花草等物幼細<br>器皿 | *Sai' ‹fá muk› tséung*$^{2}$, ‹tíú hak› ‹fá ʻts'ò ʻtang mat› yau' sai' hí' ʻming. |
| 21. A *chandler*, having mixed [vegetable] tallow with oil, dips the wicks and makes candles. | 澆燭師傅以蠟<br>和油澆淋成燭 | ‹*Kíú chuk›* ‹*sz' fú*$^{2}$, ʻí láp› ‹wó ‹yau ‹kíú ‹lam ‹shing chuk›. |
| 22. A *clothes' mender*, when garments have been rent, weaves and mends them the same as before. | 織補師傅衫若<br>破穿織補如故 | *Chik› ʻpò ‹sz' fú*$^{2}$, ‹shám yéuk› p'ò' ‹ch'ün chik› ʻpò ‹ü kú'. |

16. The student will not fail to notice the manner in which *tsò*, to make, is connected with other words: here it is *tsing tsò;* in No. 3, it is *háu tsò;* in No. 6, *hóng tsò;* in No. 10, *tá tsò;* in No. 12, *chai tsò;* and in No. 14, *shíú tsò*, are used. In No. 13, the two terms *tün lín* are nearly synonymous, and may be translated in a similar manner, by the use of two similar terms; they are also used in a metaphorical sense, to denote a magistrate who can shape a case in law into any form he pleases.

17. The stone used in this process, by workmen in Canton, is perhaps four feet long and one foot thick, made like the crooked axletree of a carriage. It is so made as to give a plane surface on the under side about two feet long, while a foot at each end is scolloped out, on a line approximating to a segment of a circle, and rising on the upper side so as to preserve the height of the stone uniform from top to bottom. Several thick planks three feet long, are firmly imbedded in the floor of the shop, having their upper surface made smooth as glass; this surface bends downwards, so that it resembles a section of the inner part of a hollow cylinder; and one end of the piece of cloth to be calendered is spread out upon it; a small cylinder of very hard wood is then laid on the cloth; and the workman, having the stone made ready to fall upon and move the little cylinder as a roller, mounts on top of the stone, placing one foot on each end, and commences a seesaw motion, which carries the little cylinder rapidly and heavily over the cloth for some minutes; he then pitches the stone off on end, moves the cloth forward, and resumes the seesaw. There is a wooden frame above the stone on which he leans when rolling.

| | | |
|---|---|---|
| 23. A *cobbler* is vulgarly called an old shoemender [or an old man who mends shoes]. | 補爛鞋者俗呼<br>爲補鞋佬 | *'Pò lán*[2] *ˏhái 'ché*, suk[2] ˏfú ˏwai 'pò ˏhái 'lò. |
| 24. A *coffin-maker* cuts and makes coffins and cases of longevity. | 鬬壽板師傅製<br>造棺槨長生者 | *Tau' shau*[2] *'pán ˏsz' fú*[2], chai' tsò[2] ˏkún kwók, ˏch'éung ˏshang 'ché. |
| 25. *Colliers* are those who go to the hills and dig coals. | 採煤人入山掘<br>煤炭者 | *'Ts'oi ˏmúi ˏyan*, yap[2] ˏshán kwat[2] ˏmúi t'án' 'chí. |
| 26. Those who are said by the world to make wooden combs are *comb-makers*. | 世號做木梳者<br>爲整梳師傅 | Shai' hò[2] tsò[2] muk[2] ˏshó 'ché, ˏwai *'ching ˏshó ˏsz' fú*[2]. |
| 27. *Compositors* are those who take moveable types, and arrange them into pages for printing. | 擺板人乃執活<br>字擺成書板而<br>印之 | *'Pái 'pán ˏyan*, 'nái chap, út[2] tsz'[2] 'pái ˏshing ˏshü 'pán ˏí yan' ˏchí. |
| 28. A *confectioner* takes green fruit and stews it in sugar. | 蜜餞師傅用糖<br>而煮生菓 | *Mat*[2] *tsín' ˏsz' fú*[2], yung' ˏtóng ˏí 'chü ˏshang 'kwo. |
| 29. The *cooper*, when casks and tubs are about to fall to pieces, binds them together again with hoops. | 箍桶佬桶盆將<br>裂乃以篾箍回 | *ˏFú 't'ung 'lò*, 't'ung ˏp'ún ˏtséung lít[2], 'nái 'í mít[2] ˏfú ˏúi. |
| 30. The *currier* first tans the skins, and then dyes them with colors. | 皮匠先銷其皮<br>後染其色 | *ˏP'í tséung*[2], ˏsín ˏsíu ˏk'í ˏp'í hau[2] 'ím ˏk'í shik, . |
| 31. A *cutler* is one who forges and tempers knives and scissors. | 利器匠乃鋼鍊<br>造刀剪之人 | *Lí*[2] *hí' tséung*[2], 'nái kong' lín[2] tsò[2] ˏtò 'tsín ˏchí ˏyan. |
| 32. A *distiller* is one who distills grain, and makes spirits. | 蒸酒師傅乃蒸<br>米作酒者 | *ˏChing 'tsau ˏsz' fú*[2], 'nái ˏching 'mai tsók, 'tsau 'ché. |
| 33. A *dyer* is one who dyes silks, satins, and piece-goods. | 染房師傅乃染<br>絲髮綢綾布疋 | *'Ím ˏfóng ˏsz' fú*[2], 'nái 'ím ˏsz' fát, ˏch'au, ˏling, pò' p'at, . |

24. Literally, this name means, 'wrangle longevity board master;' *kún*, or *kúntsoi*, is the most common name for coffin; *kwók* is a case occasionally used now, but very often in former times, for inclosing coffins; *ch'éung shang*, 'long life,' is nearly equivalent to *shau pán*: the idea of the four characters, *kún kwók ch'éung shang*, is simply coffin.

27. The Chinese have wooden types, which have however seldom been used for printing books. *Pái pán*, to spread out or arrange these blocks or types, is used, therefore, as equivalent to *chap tsz'*, which is the common and vulgar phrase.

32. The business of distilling is carried on in China to a great extent, but on a limited scale,—the establishments being very small and very numerous. Rice is the only kind of grain employed for this purpose.

| | | |
|---|---|---|
| 34. An *embroiderer* tastefully works variegated devices upon garments, handkerchiefs, and so forth. | 顧繡師傅精繡錦於衣巾等物之中 | *Kú' sau' ‹sz' fú*$^2$, ‹tsing sau' 'kam ‹yü ‹í ‹kan 'tang mat$_2$ ‹chí ‹chung. |
| 35. A *falconer* breeds hawks in order to catch other birds. | 捕雀手畜鷹以攫禽者 | *Pò*$^2$ *tséuk› 'shau*, ch'uk› ‹ying 'í wók$_2$ ‹k'am 'ché. |
| 36. The *fan-maker* constructs all kinds of fans. | 扇工製各欵扇 | *Shín' ‹kung*, chai' kók› 'fún shín'. |
| 37. The *farrier* is a man who cures the diseases of oxen and horses. | 獸醫治牛馬病人也 | *Shau' ‹í*, chí$^2$ ‹ngau 'má ping$^2$ ‹yan 'yá. |
| 38. A *florist* carefully plants and rears all kinds of flowers. | 花王精種花卉者也 | *‹Fá ‹wóng*, ‹tsing chung' ‹fá 'wai 'ché 'yá. |
| 39. A *founder* is one who fuses metal, and casts cannon and brazen tripods. | 鼓鑄手卽鼓鑄大炮銅鼎之人 | *'Kú chü' 'shau*, tsik› 'kú chü' tái$^2$ p'au' ‹t'ung 'ting ‹chí ‹yan. |
| 40. A *glassblower* melts and cuts glass into various articles of furniture. | 吹玻璃師傅燒解玻璃料器等 | *‹Ch'ui ‹pó ‹lí ‹sz' fú*$^2$, ‹shíú 'kái ‹pó ‹lí líú$^2$ hí' 'tang. |
| 41. A *glass-mender* is one who mends broken and cracked porcelain and crockery. | 補瓷缸匠乃補破爛瓷器缸瓦 | *'Pò ‹ts'z' ‹kóng tséung*$^2$, 'nái 'pò p'ó' lán$^2$ ‹ts'z' hí' ‹kóng 'ngá. |
| 42. A *glazier* takes flat pieces of glass, measures and cuts them into panes and glazes them. | 鑲玻璃師傅將玻璃片裁度而鑲之 | *‹Séung ‹pó ‹lí ‹sz' fú*$^2$, ‹tséung ‹pó ‹lí p'ín' ‹ts'oi tók$_2$ ‹í ‹séung ‹chí. |
| 43. The *goldsmith* makes golden ornaments of dress. | 金匠製金首飾 | *‹Kam tséung*$^2$ chai' ‹kam 'shau shik›. |
| 44. A *gunsmith* is one who makes all kinds of firearms. | 鎗銃火器匠乃造各欵火器人 | *‹Ts'éung ch'ung' 'fó hí' tséung*$^2$, 'nái tsò$^2$ kók› 'fún 'fó hí' ‹yan. |
| 45. The *hatter* ingeniously makes fashionable hats of every description. | 裝帽師傅精裝各式時欵帽 | *‹Chóng mò*$^2$ *‹sz' fú*$^2$ ‹tsing ‹chóng kók› shik› ‹shí 'fún mò$^2$. |

34. Both men and women are employed as embroiderers, some of the latter earning ten twenty, or more dollars per month. The elegant products of their needles are well known.

35. The training of hawks was formerly practiced in China to a great extent, and the sports of falconry pursued by the people, but they are now almost wholly neglected.

41. This is usually done by wires; a row of small holes, on both sides of the crack, is drilled partly through the porcelain, and then short clamps are made to span across from side to side, drawing the parts close together. Glass, even when very thin, is mended in the same manner.

| | | |
|---|---|---|
| 46. The *herbalist* is one who collects medicinal plants on hills and sells them to other people. | 採藥先生乃採<br>山藥而賣與人 | *'Ts'oi yéuk2 ˛sín ˛shang*, 'nái 'ts'oi ˛shán yéuk2 ˛í mái2 'ü ˛yan. |
| 47. The master of a hotel or tavern is called an *innkeeper*. | 客寓歇店內之<br>主人日店主 | Hák˒ yü2 hít˒ tím' noi2 ˛chí 'chü ˛yan üt2 *tím' 'chü.* |
| 48. A *jeweler* cuts and carves every description of things which are made of precious stones. | 玉器師傅雕琢<br>各款玉石器皿 | *Yuk2 hí' ˛sz' fú2* ˛tíú téuk˒ kók˒ 'fún yuk2 shik2 hí' 'ming. |
| 49. The *joiner* undertakes the making of windows, doors, and so forth. | 造窓木匠承辦<br>窓門等物 | *Tsò2 ˛ch'éung muk2 tséung2* ˛shing pán2 ˛ch'éung ˛mún 'tang ˛mat. |
| 50. The *lapicide* is one who ingeniously carves from stone every kind of article. | 石器匠乃精琢<br>各項石器者 | *Shik2 hí' tséung2*, 'nái ˛tsing téuk˒ ˛kók˒ hóng2 shik2 hí' 'ché. |
| 51. The *landscape-painter* carefully portrays landscapes, human beings, and all kinds of flowers. | 畫工精寫山水<br>人物花草 | *Wák˒ kung*, ˛tsing 'sé ˛shán 'shui ˛yan mat2 ˛fá 'ts'ò. |
| 52. A *lime burner* takes the shells of oysters and burns them into lime. | 燒灰佬以蠔殼<br>燒而成灰 | *˛Shíú ˛fúi 'lò* 'í ˛hò hók˒ ˛shíú ˛í ˛shing ˛fúi. |
| 53. *Masons* are those persons who undertake to build houses, temples, and other dwellings. | 坭水師傅承接<br>建造樓房祠宇 | *˛Nai 'shui ˛sz' fú2* ˛shing tsíp˒ kín' tsò2 ˛lau ˛fóng ˛ts'z' 'ü. |
| 54. The *matmaker* takes grass, and weaving it together, makes mats. | 織蓆師傅用草<br>編織成蓆 | *Chik˒ tsik2 ˛sz' fú2* yung2 'ts'ò ˛pín chik˒ ˛shing tsik2. |
| 55. *Mirror grinders* are those men who brush and polish old mirrors. | 省鏡匠乃擦磨<br>舊鏡之人 | *'Sháng king' tséung2*, 'nái ts'át˒ ˛mó kau2 king' ˛chí ˛yan. |
| 56. A *mother-of-pearl cutter* turns and makes pearls, and valuable articles for toys. | 車寶匠車造珠<br>寶玩器 | *˛Ch'é 'pò tséung2*, ˛ch'é tsò2 ˛chü 'pò ún2 hí'. |
| 57. A *maker of musical instruments* is one who cuts and forms these instruments. | 作樂師傅調製<br>樂器人也 | *Tsók˒ ngók2 ˛sz' fú2* ˛t'íú chai' ngók2 hí' ˛yan 'yá. |
| 58. *Musicians* play on all kinds of wind and stringed | 童子八音吹彈 | *˛T'ung 'tsz' pát˒ ˛yam* ˛ch'ui |

47. Hotels, except in the large cities, are few in this country, in consequence no doubt of so many travelers going in boats. The names of those who take lodgings in hotels and taverns are registered by the landlord, who is required to keep his list open for the inspection of the magistracy.

55. This is said with reference to metallic mirrors, such as were extensively used in China and Japan; from the latter country fine ones are now sometimes brought.

| | | |
|---|---|---|
| instruments, and also those of percussion, to aid vocal music. | 八音絃索以助<br>唱者 | ꜀t'án pát꜁ ꜀yam ꜀ín sók꜁ ꜂í chó꜃ ch'éung꜃ ꜂ché. |
| 59. The *presser of oil* takes ground-nuts and sesamum seeds, and so forth, and presses them and makes oil. | 榨油師傅將花<br>生芝蔴等物榨<br>成油 | *Chá꜃ ꜀yau ꜀sz' fú꜃* ꜀tséung ꜀fá ꜀shang ꜀chí ꜀má ꜂tang mat꜁ chá꜃ ꜀shing ꜀yau. |
| 60. Those who take glass, to melt and work it into ornaments, are denominated *ornament workers.* | 以料燒作首飾<br>稱爲燒料師傅 | ꜂í líú꜃ ꜀shíú tsók꜁ ꜂shau shik꜁ ꜀ch'ing ꜀wai *꜀shíú líú꜃ ꜀sz' fú꜃.* |
| 61. A *house-painter*, taking oil and varnish, paints and ornaments houses and temples. | 油漆師傅以油<br>漆粉飾屋宇者 | *꜀Yau ts'at꜁ ꜀sz' fú꜃* ꜂í ꜀yau ts'at꜁ ꜂fan shik꜁ uk꜁ ꜂ü ꜂ché. |
| 62. The *portrait-painter* delineates the human form and expression to the very life. | 寫像先生以描<br>繪人容貌爲生 | *꜂Sé tséung꜃ ꜀sín ꜀shang,* ꜂í ꜀míú ꜂fúi ꜀yan ꜀yung máu꜃ ꜀wai ꜀shang. |
| 63. A *paper-maker* is one who manufactures paper. | 紙匠製紙爲工 | *꜂Chí tséung꜃* chai꜃ ꜂chí ꜀wai ꜀kung. |
| 64. A *pedler* first buys articles and then afterwards carries them through the streets for retail. | 販仔先買而後<br>挑上街零賣者 | *Fán꜃ ꜂tsai,* ꜀sín ꜂mái ꜀í hau꜃ ꜀t'íú ꜂shéung ꜀kái ꜀ling mái꜃ ꜂ché. |
| 65. A *pencil-maker* manufactures all kinds of pencils which are of any note. | 筆匠精製各色<br>名筆 | *Pat꜁ tséung꜃* ꜀tsing chai꜃ kók꜁ shik꜁ ꜀ming pat꜁. |
| 66. Those who make pewter utensils of all descriptions, the world denominate *pewterers.* | 打造各式錫器<br>世稱打錫師傅 | ꜂Tá tsò꜃ kók꜁ shik꜁ sik꜁ hí꜃ shai꜃ ꜀ch'ing *꜂tá sik꜁ ꜀sz' fú꜃.* |
| 67. A *potter* makes and burns all descriptions of pots and jars. | 缸瓦師傅燒造<br>各項缸瓦 | *꜀Kóng ꜂ngá ꜀sz' fú꜃* ꜀shíú tsò꜃ kók꜁ hóng꜃ ꜀kóng ꜂ngá. |
| 68. The *printer* spreads ink on the blocks, and then prints from them. | 刋刷匠刷墨於<br>板上而後印之 | *꜂Hón sát꜁ tséung꜃* sát꜁ mak꜁ ꜀ü ꜂pán shéung꜃, ꜀í hau꜃ yan꜃ ꜀chí. |

64. The number of these pedlers is very great, and they engage in all sorts of traffic. Some of them come to the wholesale dealer or to the farmer, and propose to hawk their goods for a certain per centage; others buy them and make as much profit as they can by retail. Poultry, vegetables, fruit, and other eatables are everywhere peddled; earthenware, lackered-ware, &c., are also vended in this manner.

67. Earthen and porcelain vessels for containing liquids are extensively used among the Chinese; some of them are very capacious, and others display the taste of the artist. Stoneware, or coarse earthen jars, are sometimes seen as large as hogsheads; earthen cooking utensils are here employed, which elsewhere are made of iron or wood. Artificial grotto work, images of all kinds, as well as table furniture, are also made by the potter or porcelain burner. In burning the ware, the contrivances to save fuel are sometimes very ingenious, and exhibit the economy of the Chinese.

| | | |
|---|---|---|
| 69. *Quarrymen*, going among the hills, quarry out the rocks. | 採石人入山開<br>鑿取石者 | ‘*Ts‘oi shik* ˏ*yan* yap ˏshán ˏhoi tsók ‘ts‘ü shik ‘ché. |
| 70. *Rope-makers* manufacture ropes from coir, hemp, or grass. | 絞纜師傅以椶<br>或蔴或草絞成 | ‘*Káu lám* ˏ*sz’ fú*, ‘í ˏtsung wák ˏmá, wák ‘ts‘ò ‘káu ˏshing. |
| 71. A *saddler* is one especially engaged in the manufacture of saddles. | 馬鞍師傅專造<br>馬鞍者 | ‘*Má* ˏ*ón* ˏ*sz’ fú*, ˏchün tsò ‘má ˏón ‘ché. |
| 72. *Sail-makers* sew together cloth or matting for sails. | 縫𢃇人或布或<br>草蓆縫之 | ˏ*Fung* ‘*lí* ˏ*yan*, wák pò’ wák ‘ts‘ò tsik ˏfung ˏchí. |
| 73. A *seal-maker* engraves all forms of devices and characters on stone for seals. | 鐫圖章匠刻各<br>體文字圖書上 | *Tsun’* ˏ*t‘ò* ˏ*chéung tséung* hak kók ‘t‘ai ˏman tsz’ ˏt‘ò ˏshü shéung. |
| 74. The *shipwright* carefully constructs vessels of every form and description. | 裝船匠精裝各<br>式船隻 | ˏ*Chóng* ˏ*shün tséung* ˏtsing ˏchóng kók shik ˏshün chik. |
| 75. The *shoemaker* is a manufacturer of shoes. | 鞋匠乃造鞋者 | ˏ*Hái tséung* ‘nái tsò ˏhái ‘ché. |
| 76. The *spectacle-maker* takes quartz crystals, and turning them in a lathe, makes spectacles. | 眼鏡匠以水晶<br>車成如眼鏡 | ‘*Ngán king’ tséung* ‘í ‘shui ˏtsing ˏch‘é ˏshing ˏü ‘ngán king’. |
| 77. The *spinner* takes cotton and spins it into thread (or yarn). | 紡紗人將棉花<br>紡成紗條 | ‘*Fóng* ˏ*shá* ˏ*yan* ˏtséung ˏmín ˏfá ‘fóng ˏshing ˏshá ˏt‘iú. |
| 78. *Hemp-spinners* take hemp and form it into thread by rolling it [like a cobbler]. | 織蔴人以蔴搓<br>成線 | *Chik* ˏ*má* ˏ*yan*, ‘í ˏmá ˏts‘o ˏshing sín’. |
| 79. The *tailor* cuts out, sews and makes garments of apparel. | 裁縫師傅裁剪<br>布帛縫成衣服 | ˏ*Ts‘oi* ˏ*fung* ˏ*sz’ fú* ˏts‘oi ‘tsín pò’ pák ˏfung ˏshing ˏí fuk. |
| 80. The *tinker* takes and mends broken and fractured iron dishes. | 補鑊佬收補破<br>爛鐵鑊 | ‘*Pò wók* ‘*lò*, ˏshau ‘pò p‘o’ lán t‘ít wók. |
| 81. The *tinsel-maker* takes brass, hammers it thin, cuts it | 金花匠以銅鎚 | ˏ*Kam* ˏ*fá tséung* ‘í ˏt‘ung |

73. These seals are often beautiful and very large, but almost always written in the ancient seal character; books are published containing mottoes, devices, &c., from which to select appropriate ones. See page 41.

81. The word tinsel is here applied to those imitations of flowers, persons, &c., which the Chinese make out of iron wire and brass leaf, for religious purposes. Their manufacture employes a separate class of workmen, and they are made to sell from one mace to one hundred dollars and more a pair. Their form somewhat resembles a bundle of plumes; the figures are inserted upon the front, and the appearance is gaudy in the highest degree.

| | | |
|---|---|---|
| into flowers, arranges, and ties it up so as to form branches and twigs for honoring the gods. | 薄剪花找結成枝以敬神 | ˏch'ui pók˒ 'tsín ˏfá 'cháu kít˒ ˏshing ˏchí 'í king' ˏshan. |
| 82. *Typecutters* are those who engrave characters. | 刻書板匠卽雕字者也 | *Hak˒ ˏshü 'pán tséung'*, tsik˒ ˏtiú tsz'² 'ché 'yá. |
| 83. *Washermen* rinse and wash garments to make them clean from dirt and stains. | 洗衣服佬漂洗衫之漬垢者 | *'Sai ˏí fúk˒ 'lò* p'iú' 'sai ˏshám ˏchí tsik˒ 'kau 'ché. |
| 84. The *watchmaker* repairs clocks and watches, and makes them go correctly. | 修標師傅修整時辰鐘標 | ˏ*Sau ˏpíú ˏsz' fú²* ˏsau 'ching ˏshí ˏshan ˏchung ˏpíú. |
| 85. *Weavers* are those who are employed in the business of weaving and making cloth. | 機女以織製布疋爲事者 | ˏ*Kí 'nü*, 'í chik˒ chai' pò' p'at˒ ˏwai sz'² 'ché. |
| 86. *Hired workmen* are those who do [any and] all kinds of work. | 僱工者乃作各樣工夫 | *Kú' ˏkung* 'ché, 'nái tsók˒ kók˒ yéung² ˏkung ˏfú. |

84. The Chinese construct all the parts of a watch except the main spring and hair-spring, which are imported from Europe. They have not yet been able to manufacture time-pieces equal to those imported, and consequently prefer to possess those of foreign workmanship; they are, however, very skillful in cleaning and regulating them.

## Section Second.

## MECHANICAL OPERATIONS.

### 百藝類第二章

Pák˒ ngai² lui²; tai² í² ˏchéung.

| | | |
|---|---|---|
| 1. *Annealing;* whenever glass or other vitreous substances are made, then, while they are still very hot, they are put into an oven, in order that they may gradually | 爁炎凡造料與玻璃等物熱極時另放入局爐 | *Kám' ˏím;* ˏfán tsò² líú² 'ü ˏpó ˏlí 'tang mat˒, ít˒ kik˒ ˏshí, ling² fong' yap˒ kuk˒ |

### *Notes and Explanations.*

SEVERAL of the terms comprised in this section, not being found in native authors, have been formed, and may not therefore always be the best that could be conceived. This may be the case with the phrase *pák ngai lui*, 'the hundred kinds of arts,' used as a general term for mechanical operations. There are, comparatively speaking, but few single characters in this language, whose meaning is generic, including many species, but new terms

become cool and not allowed to cool too rapidly [which would make them brittle and liable to be easily broken].

內令其由漸而冷不逼其凍也

lú noi, ling k'í yau tsím í lang, pat pik k'í tung yá.

2. *Assaying* is performed by taking some of the ore, and carefully separating the valuable from the base, and the true from the false.

傾礦將採出之礦傾辦高低與眞僞

*K'ing kw'óng*; tséung ts'oi ch'ut chí kw'óng, k'ing pán kò tai, ü chan ngai.

3. *Bleaching*; the original color of cotton and hemp is a carnation; but by rinsing in water and sunning them, they are whitened.

漂晒布帛原色赤乃以水漂晒使其白也

*P'iú shái*; pò pák ün shik ch'ik, nái í shui p'iú shái, sz k'í pák yá.

4. *Boring* is done by the use of awls and gimlets, by which round holes are bored out.

錐鑽用錐或鑽以穿圓孔

*Chui tsün*, yung chui wák tsün í ch'ün ün hung.

5. *Bowing of cotton*; cotton being mixed together in disorder and formed into hard bunches, it is therefore beaten into flocks by the use of a bowstring, which is struck with a beater and made to vibrate.

彈棉花棉花亂且實故用一槌刮彈弓之絃而打鬆之

*T'án mín fá*; mín fá lün ch'é shat, kú yung yat ch'ui kwát t'án kung chí ín, í tá sung chí.

6. *Burnishing*; all sorts of gold and silver utensils of a square form, which cannot be renewed by the lathe, are burnished and scraped with knives to make them bright and smooth.

刮削凡金銀方器不能車新故用刀刮削使其光滑

*Kwát séuk*; fán kam ngan fóng hí, pat nang ch'é san, kú yung tò kwát séuk, sz k'í kwóng wát.

7. *Carding* is done by cards, which, moving backwards and forwards, card cotton, flax, wool, and so forth, for the purpose of making them smooth, free from snarls, and clean.

振刷以刷板振作而刷棉蔴羊毛等物梳刷其亂而使其淨

*Chan shát*, í shát pán chan tsók í shat mín, má, yéung mò, tang mat, shó shát k'í lün, í sz k'í tsing.

---

can be formed by the scholar in a similar manner to those here given; in a few cases, the operations described are probably new to the Chinese.

1. *Líú* is one of those peculiar words, which, though often used, are sometimes employed in such a manner as scarcely to admit of an exact translation. It answers to the French word *materièl*, the raw stuff from which utensils are made. That which is here intended is sometimes called *shiú líú*, burning stuff, denoting the various substances employed in the manufacture of glass. It is very commonly applied as a name to a kind of semi-translucent glass, usually tinged green, which is extensively manufactured by the Chinese into hair-pins, bracelets, anklets, etc.

5. Cotton is prepared in this way, by the Chinese, for spinning and for padding of winter garments and bedding. The operation is precisely like that of the hatters in preparing felt for hats.

| | | |
|---|---|---|
| 8. *Casting* is done by fusing metallic substances, and then pouring them into molds, thus forming them into implements and utensils. | 鎔鑄以金銀鎔化傾入模內印成器皿 | ꜀*Yung chü'*, 'í ꜀kam ꜀ngan ꜀yung fá', ꜀k'ing yap, ꜀mò noi', yan' ꜀shing hí' 'ming. |
| 9. *Cementing;* things are joined together by wiping the surfaces [to be brought in contact] with glue, varnish, paste, &c. | 粘貼用膠漆糊等物抹上合貼粘之 | ꜀*Chím t'íp*, yung' ꜀káu, ts'at, ꜀ú, 'tang mat, mút, 'shéung hóp, t'íp, ꜀chím ꜀chí. |
| 10. *Charring* of timber is done by applying fire to it, so as to make it bend, or for the purpose of preserving it from decay when put in the ground. | 燋木以火烙木而曲或入土之不致易爛 | *Tsíú' muk,* 'í 'fó lók, muk, ꜀í huk, wák, yap, 't'ò ꜀chí, pat, chí' í' lán'. |
| 11. *Collating;* this is the taking of leaves after they are printed, and putting them together fit for binding. | 撿篇將印起之書撿齊釘裝 | '*K'ím* ꜀*p'ín*, ꜀tséung yan' 'hí ꜀chí ꜀shü 'k'ím ꜀ts'ai ꜀ting ꜀chóng. |
| 12. *Composing;* procure a good wooden plate, measure the length and the breadth of the page, and then empale it on the four sides: on the left side arrange a full line of characters, placing in against it a dividing line, and fastening the same with a wooden wedge; then, with small pieces of bamboo, carefully adjust and fasten the characters, if they happen to be too short or out of place; when this is done, and the whole body of the page is made smooth and level, then it is ready for printing. | 安字用好板一片量書面大小四圍作欄右邊擺滿安界欄以木揳揳之先作小竹片如字有低邪隨字形襯墊揳之至字體平穩然後刷印 | ꜀*Ón tsz'*; yung' 'hò 'pán yat, p'ín', léung' ꜀shü mín' tai' 'síú, sz' ꜀wai tsók, ꜀lán, yau' ꜀pín 'pái 'mún, ꜀ón kái' ꜀lán, 'í muk, síp, síp, ꜀chí, ꜀sín tsók, 'síú chuk, p'ín', ꜀ü tsz' 'yau ꜀tai ꜀ts'é, ꜀ts'ui tsz' ꜀ying ts'an' tím' síp, ꜀chí, chí' tsz' 't'ai ꜀p'ing 'wan, ꜀ín hau' shat, yan'. |
| 13. *Composing* is the arrangement of movable types so as to form sentences and sections. | 執字將活字疊成章句 | *Chap, tsz'*, ꜀tséung út, tsz' típ, ꜀shing ꜀chéung kü'. |
| 14. *Currying* of leather is performed by covering the skin with oil and causing it | 湛皮以油抹皮面令其毛管湛 | *Chám'* ꜀*p'í*, 'í ꜀yau mút, ꜀p'í mín', ling' ꜀k'í ꜀mò 'kún |

12. This account of composing is abridged from the *Sám T'soi T'ò*, fourth *kün*, under the head of *yan mat*, where may be found brief notices of the *út tsz'* or movable types, which seem never to have been much used or valued by the Chinese.

13. In describing objects or processes, heretofore unknown to them, different Chinese vary a great deal in the terms they employ. The unlettered workman will describe the tools put into hands in his own way, often in vulgar terms, and sometimes in such as have no appropriate characters in the language. When the scholar sits down to write of the same things, he chooses other terms, which he thinks will convey to strangers correct ideas of any

to enter the pores, and then the skin becomes pliable, and does not permit the water to enter and injure it.

入皮身自然軟
熱不致防有透
水之患

chám' yap₂ ꜀p'í ꜀shan, tsz'² ꜀ín ʻün shuk₂, pat₃ chí' ꜀fóng ʻyau t'au' ʻshui ꜀chí wán².

15. *Distributing* types; taking those which have been already used, they are carefully separated and each returned to its proper place.

歸原字先將曾
用之字尋出分
别各歸各號

꜀*Kwai* ꜀*ün* *tsz'*², ꜀sín ꜀tséung ꜀ts'ang yung² ꜀chí tsz'² ꜀ts'am ch'ut₃ ꜀fan pít₂, kók₃ ꜀kwai kók₃ hò².

16. *Dovetailing;* in making boxes and trunks, where the corners are joined, teeth are chiseled so as to interlock and complete the boxes and trunks.

交齒凡造箱櫃
合角處鑿齒互
合而成箱櫃也

꜀*Káu* ʻ*ch'í;* ꜀fán tsò² ꜀séung ʻlung hóp₂, kók₃ ch'ü', tsók₂ ʻch'í ú² hóp₂, ꜀í ꜀shing ꜀séung ʻlung ʻyá.

17. *Drawing* is done by taking the exact outline of landscapes, and so carefully portraying them that their appearance will be as natural as the reality.

描畫乃對山川
景象描繪圖形
儼如真然景物

꜀*Míú wák₂*, ʻnái túi' ꜀shán ꜀ch'ün ʻking tséung², ꜀míú f'úi' ꜀t'ò ꜀ying, ʻím ꜀ü ꜀chan ꜀ín ʻking mat₂.

18. *Dyeing;* all kinds of coloring stuffs are used, which being properly applied to silk and cotton cloths gives them bright, glossy, and unchangeable hues.

繒綵用各色顏
料分染布帛使
各色鮮妍不變

꜀*Tsang* ʻ*ts'oi,* yung² kók₃ shik₃ ꜀ngán líú² ꜀fan ʻím pò' pák₂ ʻsz' kók₃ shik₃ ꜀sín ꜀ín pat₃ pín'.

19. *Enchasing;* because the plate of metal is so thin that the flowers cannot be cut out in relief, therefore by beating on the under surface, the device is made to stand out from it in high relief, and thus the figure is completed.

哽花因金片薄
不能刻凸花故
於底哽花凸出
面而成形影

ʻ*Ang* ꜀*fá;* ꜀yan ꜀kam p'in' pók₂ pat₃ ꜀nang hak₃ tat₂ ꜀fá, kú' ꜀ü ʻtai ʻang ꜀fá tat₂ ch'ut₃ mín² ꜀í ꜀shing ꜀ying ʻying.

20. *Engraving;* this is done by knives and pointed tools, with which all manner of human designs are cut on stone, ivory, wood, and so forth.

雕刻乃用刀械
雕刻各欵人物
等於石牙木之
上者

꜀*Tíú hak₃;* ʻnái yung² ꜀tò kái² ꜀tíú hak₃ kók₃ ʻfún ꜀yan mat₂ ʻtang ꜀ü shik₂, ꜀ngá, muk₂ ꜀chí shéung² ʻché.

21. *Folding* paper is taking that which has been printed, and properly folding it.

摺紙將印起之
紙編摺之

*Chip₃* ʻ*chí;* ꜀tséung yan' ʻhí ꜀chí ʻchí ꜀pín chip₃ ꜀chí.

---

given object or process. These remarks are applicable to several articles in this and other sections. Thus in No. 15, the scholar will write *kwai ün tsz'*, which is correct, while the unlettered workman says *pái tsz'*.

19. The word *fá*, compounded of two characters, one meaning *to transform* and the other denoting *plants*, is of very extensive application; it is used to express whatever is flowery, colored, variegated, fanciful, as carvings, moldings, devices; it is used also in metaphorical senses.

22. *Forging* consists in taking iron and melting and fusing it thoroughly, so as to give it strength as well as purity.

煅煉將鐵鍛鍊其性使其堅且淨也

*Tün' lín*$^2$; ‹tséung t'ít› tün' lín$^2$ ˏk'í sing', 'sz' ˏk'í ‹kín 'ch'é tsing$^2$ 'yá.

23. *Fritting;* take several kinds of metallic substances, and, mixing them together, place them in a dull red heat; wait till they become blended together, then while they are yet soft, but not in a state of fusion, take them out, and they are ready for use.

炕焙將各金湊成放微熱火內待其和埋軟熟而未鎔之際拿出以作物

*Hóng' púi*$^2$; ‹tséung kók› ‹kam ts'au' ˏshing, fóng' ˏmí ít$_2$ 'fó nói$^2$; toi$^2$ ˏk'í wó$^2$ ˏmái, 'yün shuk$_2$ ˏí mí$^2$ ˏyung ‹chí tsai', ˏná ch'ut› 'í tsók› mat$_2$.

24. *Gearing* is effected by having the teeth of a large wheel interlock those of a small one placed by its side, so as to cause the small wheel to revolve simultaneously with it.

撥齒乃以大輪之齒撥傍小輪之齒使小輪相隨轉也

*Pút*$_2$ '*ch'í* 'nái 'í tái$^2$ ˏlun ‹chí 'ch'í, pút$_2$ ˏp'óng 'síú ˏlun ‹chí 'ch'í, 'sz' 'síú ˏlun ‹séung ˏts'ui 'chün 'yá.

25. *Gilding* is done by cementing gold upon the surface of various articles, so as to embellish them with golden ornaments.

鑲金用金鑲於別物之上以成金花

‹*Séung* ‹*kam*, yung$^2$ ‹kam ‹séung ‹ü pít$_2$ mat$_2$ ‹chí shéung$^2$, 'í ˏshing ‹kam ‹fá.

26. *Hooping;* in the manufacture of wooden tubs and casks, either iron or bamboo slats are hooped round them to make them close.

箍束乃造木盤木桶或鐵或篾箍束而成

‹*Fú ch'uk*›; 'nái tsò$^2$ muk$_2$ ˏp'ún muk$_2$ 't'ung, wák$_2$ t'ít›, wák$_2$ mít›, ‹fú ch'uk› ˏí ˏshing.

27. *Imposing* is arranging several pages so that they can be printed all at once.

合板或合數板然後齊印

*Hóp*$_2$ '*pán;* wák$_2$ hóp$_2$ shò' 'pán, ˏín hau$^2$ ˏts'ai yan'.

28. *Japanning;* by varnish being rubbed upon implements and utensils they become bright and smooth.

抹漆以漆抹器皿上取其光潤

*Mút› ts'at›;* 'í ts'at› mút› hí' 'ming shéung$^2$ 'ts'ü ˏk'í ‹kwóng yun$^2$.

29. *Lackering;* this is done by taking different colors and mixing them with varnish, so as to render the different colors fresh, clear, and brilliant.

較漆以各色較入漆內使各色鮮研而明亮

*Káu' ts'at›;* 'í kók› shik› káu' yap$_2$ ts'at› noi$^2$, 'sz' kók› shik› ‹sín ˏín ˏí ˏming léung$^2$.

---

**25.** Menders of old tubs, etc., are often seen in the streets, and at the doors of houses diligently employed in their vocation. They carry a few tools with them, and a supply of bamboo splints, and are always careful to take away with them the refuse of whatever comes into their hands.

**28.** *Ts'at* is applied by the Chinese, not only to the juice of the proper varnish-tree (Vernicia), but to all varnishes, though no other than that one is much used by them. The

30. *Melting;* the metals are melted and transformed by fire.

銷鎔以火鎔化
其金也

‹Síú ‹yung; ʻí ʻfó ‹yung fá' ‹k'í ‹kam ʻyá.

31. *Modeling;* a mold is first carved from wood; then sand and mortar are pressed close around it; and when the mortar has become dry and hard, the wooden mold is removed; by the use of this mold, utensils [of various kinds] are cast.

甄陶以木先刻
成模後以砂坭
塡封待坭乾固
檖出內木將坭
模即鑄成器矣

‹Yan ‹t'ò, ʻí muk ‹sín hak ‹shing ‹mò, hau' ʻí ‹shá ‹nai ‹t'ín ‹fung, toi' ‹nai ‹kón kú', tun' ch'ut noi' muk, ‹tséung ‹nai ‹mò tsik chü' ‹shing hí' ʻí.

32. *Mortising;* at the place where the ends of two timbers meet, a mortise is chiseled to receive the tenon, and they are then framed.

閗榫兩.頭交搭
處鑿孔入榫而
後架也

Tau' ʻsun; ʻléung ‹t'au ‹káu táp ch'ü', tsók ʻhung yap ʻsun, ‹í hau' ká' ʻyá.

33. *Molding* (*lit.* blowing) of glass is done by using a mold, into which the glass, being blown, is placed and again blown; by this blowing the implements and utensils are completed.

吹玻璃用一模
將玻璃吹起放
模內合之復吹
即吹成器皿矣

‹Ch'ui ‹pó ‹lí; yung' yat ‹mò, ‹tséung ‹pó ‹lí ‹ch'ui ʻhí, fóng' ‹mò noi', hóp ‹chí fuk ‹ch'ui, tsik ‹ch'ui ‹shing hí' ʻming ʻí.

34. *Painting* is the overlaying of various kinds of furniture with oil and paints, so as to protect them from moisture.

抹油以各色油
先抹各器之上
以免水漬

Mút ‹yau; ʻí kók shik ‹yau ‹sín mút kók hí' ‹chí shéung', ʻí ʻmín ʻshui tsik.

35. *Painting* of portraits consists in portraying the exact form and attitudes of men; but as it regards their various changes and alterations, these depend upon the imagination of the human mind, and the skillful handling of the pencil; they cannot be exactly delineated.

畫像乃畫人物
規矩至於有時
更變則在乎人
心之巧思手之
運筆不可拘泥

Wák tséung'; ʻnái wák ‹yan mat, ‹kwai ʻkü, chí' ‹ü ʻyau ‹shí ‹kang pín', tsak tsoi' ‹ü ‹yan ‹sam ‹chí ʻháu ‹sz', ʻshau ‹chí wan' pat, pat ʻhó ‹k'ü ní'.

36. *Plating;* silver is spread upon copper and other utensils by a strong heat, for the purpose of giving them the lustre and elegance of silver.

鍍銀以銀燒鎔
敷銅等物上欲
如銀之光彩也

Tò' ‹ngan; ʻí ‹ngan ‹shiú ‹yung ‹fú ‹t'ung ʻtang mat shéung', yuk ‹ü ‹ngan ‹chí ‹kwóng ʻts'oi ʻyá.

genuine lackered-ware, for which the Japanese and Chinese are so noted, is made of the sap of the varnish-tree mixed with lampblack and other ingredients.

35. This definition is abridged for the *Sám Tsai T'ò*, (the same volume that contains the account of movable types,) in which there is a series of plates, intended to exhibit the attitudes of man, the various forms of countenance, and the different expressions which are caused by the working of the passions, &c.

37. *Printing;* this is done by spreading ink upon the pages with a hair-brush, and then laying paper upon them which is printed.

印書乃用毛擦掃墨於板而後鋪紙印之

*Yan*ʼ ꜀*shü;* ʻnái yung$^2$ ꜀mò ts'át꜁ sòʼ mak$_2$ ꜀ü ʻpán, ꜀í hau$^2$ ꜀p'ò ʻchí yanʼ ꜀chí.

38. *Reeling;* the threads of small spools (or quills) is taken, and wound off upon a large frame (or reel), in order to have it ready when wanted in weaving cloth.

蟠紗將小紉之紗條另蟠纏過於大架以便織時用也

꜀*P'ún* ꜀*shá;* ꜀tséung ʻsíu ꜀ts'un ꜀chí ꜀shá ꜀t'íú, ling$^2$ ꜀p'ún ꜀ch'in kwóʼ ꜀ü tái$^2$ káʼ, ʻí pín$^2$ chik꜁ ꜀shí yung$^2$ ʻyá.

39. *Sawing* is done by the use of an iron-toothed saw, sawing the timber, so as to divide it into two parts.

鋸木乃將鐵齒鋸鋸木分而爲二者

*Kü*ʼ *muk*$_2$*;* ʻnái ꜀tséung t'ít꜁ ʻch'í küʼ küʼ muk$_2$, ꜀fan ꜀í ꜀wai í$^2$ ʻché.

40. *Slacking* of lime; all kinds of shells are burned till changed, when they are thoroughly sprinkled with water; by this process, the whole is changed and formed into lime powder, and afterwards sifted.

發灰凡殼燒化即以水洒透於是化成灰粉而後篩之

*Fát*꜁ ꜀*fúi;* ꜀fán hók꜁ ꜀shíú fáʼ, tsik꜁ ʻí ʻshui ʻshá t'auʼ, ꜀ü shí$^2$ fáʼ ꜀shing ꜀fúi ʻfan, ꜀í hau$^2$ ꜀shai ꜀chí.

41. *Sharpening;* all sorts of cutlery which have become so dull and blunt that they can scarcely be ground, are sharpened by a sharpening chisel.

劖磨凡利器厚鈍難磨則先以劖劖之

ʻ*Ch'án* ꜀*mó;* ꜀fán líʼ híʼ hau$^2$ tun$^2$ ꜀nán ꜀mó, tsak꜁ ꜀sín ʻí ʻch'án ʻch'án ꜀chí.

42. *Shroffing* is the separation of the true from the bad coin; sometimes the pieces are bored with an awl so as to examine them more clearly.

睇銀分辨眞僞或時以錐鑽而觀也

ʻ*T'ai* ꜀*ngan;* ꜀fan pín$^2$ ꜀chan ngai$^2$, wák$_2$ ꜀shí ʻí ꜀chui tsünʼ ꜀í ꜀kún ʻyá.

40. Most if not all the lime used by the Chinese is manufactured from shells; the process of preparation is very simple. The kiln is merely a circular space inclosed by a low wall, having a vent-hole in the bottom, through which air from a bellows is conducted by a passage to the fire placed just above the hole. Wood is laid on the bottom of the kiln, and as soon as it is kindled, the shells, previously cleansed and dried, are laid loosely upon the top, and the bellows set agoing. As the lower tier ignites, other shells are piled on, until the kiln is full; when the whole is on fire, the bellows cease, and the shells are soon calcined. One day is sufficient to burn a kiln, and in the night the whole cools, so that the lime is ready to be taken out in the morning to be sifted. In the vicinity of Héungshán, many tens of large boats are constantly employed in dredging for oyster-shells to be burned into lime. The shells of small molluscæ are more carefully calcined for eating with betel-nut.

42. This term is applied to the operation of examining money by a certain class of persons, who in India and other parts of the East are called shroffs; they are paid a small per centage; after their examination, each coin is stamped with the mark of the examiner's employer, as a warranty of its goodness. In some cases, the purity of the metal is tested by the color of the trace left on a Lydian stone; in others by boring.

| | | |
|---|---|---|
| 43. *Smelting* consists in taking the native ore, and fusing it so as to extract the pure metal. | 傾煉將礦燒煉以取足金 | *K'ing lín*, tséung kw'ong' shíú lín, í 'ts'ü tsuk kam. |
| 44. *Soldering;* all metallic substances which are united by their edges, are soldered by the application of solders with a carbonaceous substance in a state of fusion. | 釬口凡五金合口處以百草霜和碎金鎔釬之 | *Hón 'hau;* fán 'ng kam hóp 'hau ch'ü', í pák, 'ts'ò séung wò sü' kam yung hón chí. |
| 45. *Spinning* is the drawing out and making round and firm threads of silk, cotton, and wool. | 紡線以絲棉毛紡成圓結紗條 | *'Fóng sín'*, í sz' mín mò 'fóng shing ün kít shá t'íú. |
| 46. *Steaming;* all kinds of straight bamboos and timbers which it is wished to bend, and those which are crooked that are to be straightened, are heated by fire so as make them flexible. | 屈曲凡直竹木欲製其曲曲者製其直即以火燂屈之 | *Wat huk;* fán chik chuk muk yuk chai' k'í huk, huk 'ché chai' k'í chik, tsik í 'fò tám wat chí. |
| 47. *Tanning;* the skins having been put into lime water and thoroughly soaked, the hair is then easily scraped off, and the flesh cut away, and the skins dried for use. | 淹皮將皮入灰水淹過取易刮毛削肉後晒用 | *Ím p'í;* tséung p'í yap fúi 'shui ím kwó' 'ts'ü í kwát mò séuk yuk, hau shái' yung. |
| 48. *Tawing;* the skins, having been tanned by the use of saltpetre, are afterwards ready for use in the manufacture of garments. | 硝皮以硝硝過其皮然後能用以作裘 | *Síú p'í;* í síú síú kwó' k'í p'í, ín hau nang yung í tsók k'au. |
| 49. *Turning;* in making all kinds of pillars (or round columns) and pearls, they must be placed in a lathe, and turned into their proper shape. | 切磋凡造圓柱圓珠必上車架而車成之 | *Ts'ít ts'ó;* fán tsò ün 'ch'ü ün chü, pít 'shéung ch'é ká', í ch'é shing chí. |
| 50. *Veneering;* in the manufacture of tables [altars, &c.], different kinds of wood are inlaid, in order by the various colors to render the work beautiful. | 鑲線邊凡檯邊用别色木鑲入取其出色可觀 | *Séung sín' pín;* fán t'oi pín yung pít shik muk séung yap, 'ts'ü k'í ch'ut shik 'hó kún. |
| 51. *Warping* is the taking of threads and arranging them on the loom so as to form the warp. | 耕紗以紗佈機上作經 | *Kang shá*, í shá pò' kí shéung tsók king. |
| 52. *Weaving* is the throwing of the shuttle and the moving of the loom so as to make pieces of cloth. | 織布拋杼織成布疋也 | *Chik pò';* p'áu 'ch'ü chik shing pò' p'at 'yá. |

46. The mode of steaming most common among the Chinese is that here described: instead of subjecting the material to a hot steam, the stick is bent while placed in the smoke.

## Section Third.

# MECHANICAL IMPLEMENTS.

## 器具第三章
**Hí' kü²; tai² ˏsám ˏchéung.**

| | | |
|---|---|---|
| 1. An *adz* has a curved handle so as to cut level. | 釿曲柄砍平之 | ˏ*Kan*, huk, ping' 'hóm ˏp'ing ˏchí. |
| 2. The modern name of an *anvil* is the iron washblock. | 鑕今名之鐵砧 | *Chat*, ˏkam ˏming ˏchí t'it, ˏcham. |
| 3. An *auger* has, upon its upper end, a cross-piece of wood fastened, and is turned by both hands in boring holes. | 螺絲鑽於頭鑲橫木兩手鑽孔 | ˏ*Ló ˏsz' tsün'* ˏü ˏt'au ˏséung ˏwáng muk₂, 'léung 'shau tsün' 'hung. |
| 4. Hung his head from a beam pierced his thigh with an *awl*. | 頭懸梁錐刺股 | ˏT'au ˏün ˏléung, ˏ*chui* sik, 'kú. |
| 5. An *axe* is an instrument for felling timber. | 斧頭代柯之器 | '*Fú ˏt'au* fat₂ ˏó ˏchí hí'. |
| 6. Wheel and *axle* are for raising and lowering [things]. | 絞軸輪使收放 | 'Káu *chau²* ˏlun 'sz' ˏshau fong'. |
| 7. A *band* is a cord which by passing over one wheel, causes another one to revolve. | 拖線前轉拖後轉之線也 | ˏ*T'ó sín'* ˏts'ín 'chün ˏt'ó hau² 'chün ˏchí sín' 'yá. |
| 8. A *barber's call* is an instrument by the twang of which the barber announces his calling. | 鑼引剃頭者响之以爲報號 | ˏ*Ló 'yan*, t'ai' ˏt'au 'ché 'héung ˏchí 'í ˏwai pò' hò², |
| 9. A *fish basket* is a thing for holding fish. | 魚笈盛魚之具 | ˏ*Ü káp*, shing² ˏü ˏchí kü². |
| 10. The *bevel* (square-measure's corner) is named from its form, and is used in making corners. | 斗角象形而名製方角器也 | '*Tau kók*, tséung² ˏying ˏí ˏming chai' ˏfóng kók, hí' 'yá. |

## *Notes and Explanations.*

THIS section is intended to include the names of tools of various sorts used by artificers in their mechanical operations. *Hí kü* is a phrase denoting things that are prepared for use, and includes all manner of tools and utensils employed by handicraftsmen in their various works.

2. The shape of the Chinese anvil corresponds nearly to that in use among Europeans; its 'modern name' seems to have been suggested from the practice of washermen, who wash their clothes by beating them upon a stone; standing in a stream, where the rocks rise a little above the surface of the water, they take hold of one end of an article, which is to be washed, and commence beating the other by bringing it down upon the rock, as the blacksmith does his hammer upon the anvil.

4. This sentence is quoted from the Sám Tsz' King, see line 140; the reference is to two sleepy students; one of whom, in order to drive away sleep, suspended his head by the hair from a beam, so that the slightest nod would rouse him; the other made a shoemaker's awl serve the same purpose.

8. This implement resembles a pair of long iron tweezers, having the connecting part made thin and broadish, so as that when twanged, the tines will prolong the vibration.

| | | |
|---|---|---|
| 11. A *blowpipe* is used to blow with in soldering. | 燈吹用吹釺口 | ‹*Tang* ‹*ch'ui* yung$^{2}$ ‹ch'ui hón$^{2}$ ‘hau. |
| 12. A *bodkin* is used for pulling and changing types. | 鋏攝攝換活字 | *Káp*› *níp*$_{2}$ níp$_{2}$ ún$^{2}$ út$_{2}$ tsz'$^{2}$. |
| 13. A *cotton bow* is the bow used to flock cotton. | 彈弓彈棉花弓 | ˏ*T'án* ‹*kung* ˏt'án ˏmín ‹fá ‹kung. |
| 14. A *lacker bowl* is used for containing lacker. | 漆盆用爲載漆 | ‹*Ts'at*› ˏ*p'ún* yung$^{2}$ ˏwai tsoi’ ts'at›. |
| 15. A *paint bowl* is used in grinding paints. | 顏色砵擂顏色 | ˏ*Ngán shik*› *pút*› ˏlúi ˏngán shik›. |
| 16. A *paint box* contains all sorts of colors. | 研色盆載各色 | ˏ*I'n shik*› ˏ*p'ún* tsoi’ kók› shik›. |
| 17. A *painter's box* contains paints, oils, lackers, and so forth, with his various implements. | 油漆箱載顏料油漆等器 | ˏ*Yau ts'at*› ‹*séung* tsoi’ ˏngán líú$^{2}$ ˏyau ts'at› ‘tang hí’. |
| 18. A *brick-knife* is one which is used to trim bricks, so as to make them work into their proper places. | 磚刀削改青磚入砌者 | ‹*Chün* ‹*tò* séuk› ‘koi ‹ts'ing ‹chün yap$_{2}$ ts'ai’ ‘ché. |
| 19. A *hemp-root broom* is used for priming. | 蔴薑掃用打底 | ˏ*Má* ‘*kéung* sò’ yung$^{2}$ ‘tá ‘tai. |
| 20. A *brass-wire brush* is used for brushing ornamental articles, which have been washed with gold. | 銅絲擦打磨鍍金首飾 | ˏ*T'ung* ‹*sz'* *ts'at*› ‘tá ˏmó tò$^{2}$ ‹kam ‘shau shik›. |
| 21. A *priming brush* is used to lay on clear oil. | 絲根用上明油 | ‹*Sz'* ‹*kan* yung$^{2}$ ‘shéung ˏming ˏyau. |
| 22. A *small priming brush* is a small plated brush, which is used for laying on lacker. | 小刷上漆刷之小者 | ‘*Síú* ‹*shán* ‘shéung ts'at› ‹shán ‹chí ‘síú ‘ché. |
| 23. A *lacker priming brush* is made of bristles. | 漆刷猪鬃毛作 | *Ts'at*› ‹*shán* ‹chü ‹tsung ˏmò tsók›. |
| 24. An *agate burnisher* is an instrument used to burnish articles, after they have been gilded. | 瑪瑙研鍍金後以其研光 | ‘*Má* ‘*nò* ˏ*ín*, tò$^{2}$ ‹kam hau$^{2}$ ‘í ˏk'í ˏín ‹kwóng. |
| 25. An *iron burnisher* is an instrument used to lay on the gilding, and then to rub it bright. | 鍍金棒凡鍍起之後研之使耀 | *Tò*$^{2}$ ‹*kam* ‘*páng*, ˏfán tò$^{2}$ ‘hí ‹chí, hau$^{2}$ ˏín ‹chí ‘sz’ íú$^{2}$. |
| 26. The *calendering stone* is like the ingot of sycee. | 碾布石如銀錠 | *Shín*’ *pò*’ *shik*$_{2}$ ˏü ˏngan ting$^{2}$. |
| 27. A *calendering roll* calenders cloth smooth. | 光布軸碾光布 | ‹*Kwóng pò*’ chau$^{2}$ shín’ ‹kwóng pò’. |
| 28. In the large *cases* for [Chinese] types, each of the several classes of characters is arranged in order. | 列字大架將每字佈列其中 | *Lít*$_{2}$ *tsz'*$^{2}$ *tái*$^{2}$ *ká*’, ‹tséung ‘múi tsz'$^{2}$ pò’ lít$_{2}$ ˏk'í ‹chung. |
| 29. A *case* is divided into apartments for holding types. | 字盤間隔裝字 | *Tsz'*$^{2}$ ˏ*p'ún*, kán’ kák› ‹chóng tsz'$^{2}$. |

11. The blowpipe is frequently seen in the mouths of silversmiths and whitesmiths, but among hundreds that may be seen using it, not one has learned the mode of keeping up a constant blast: its form is like the common one used by mineralogists. *Hau* here means the edges of the pieces of metal to be soldered, a use of the word that is applied to many things.

| | | |
|---|---|---|
| 30. A *centre-bit* is worked by a cord, wound around it. | 繩鑽繩纏車之 | ,*Shing tsün*' ,shing ,ch'ín ,ch'é ,chí. |
| 31. *Chains* are made of iron, which is beaten into links and locked together one into another in a series. | 鐵鍊用鐵打成<br>連環扣也 | *T'ít, lín*² yung² t'ít, 'tá ,shing ,lín ,wán k'au' 'yá. |
| 32. The *chalk-line* is for making a straight line; it is the same as the "black-measure-line." | 繩為直制度墨<br>斗線同之 | ,*Shing*, ,wai chik, chai' tò², mak, 'tau sín' ,t'ung ,chí. |
| 33. A *chase* embraces the characters as they are formed into pages, so that afterwards they may be printed. | 埋板架埋字成<br>板而後印之 | ,*Mái 'pán ká*', ,mái tsz'² ,shing 'pán, ,í hau² yan' ,chí. |
| 34. A *large chisel* is for making holes in wood. | 大鑿木中開孔 | *Tái*² *tsók*, muk, ,chung ,hoi 'hung. |
| 35. A *stone chisel* is an instrument used to chisel stone level and smooth. | 石鑿擊石以取<br>平滑 | *Shik, tsók*, kik, shik, 'í 'ts'ü ,p'ing wát,. |
| 36. With a *flower chisel* ornamental work is carved. | 花鑿雕刻花草 | ,*Fá tsók*, ,tíú hak, ,fá 'ts'ò. |
| 37. The *tile chisel* is used to trim tiles. | 堦磚鑿用以裁<br>堦甎 | ,*Kái ,chün tsók*, yung² 'í ,ts'oi ,kái ,chün. |
| 38. When any kind of tubs and bowls are broken in pieces, iron *clamps* are used to bind them together again. | 馬釘凡盤砵破<br>裂用此馬回 | '*Má ,ting*, ,fán ,p'ún pút, p'ò' lít,, yung² 'ts'z' 'má ,úi. |
| 39. *Compasses* are used for describing circles; they are now called, in vulgar language, hedge shears. | 規以造圓基剪<br>今之俗名 | ,*Kw'ai*, 'í tsò² ,ün ,kí 'tsín ,kam ,chí tsuk, ,ming. |
| 40. A *composing-stick* is for containing lines and sentences as the types are set. | 執字架執字疊<br>成行句於此者 | *Chap, tsz*'² *ká*', chap, tsz'² típ, ,shing ,hang kü' ,ü 'ts'z' 'ché. |
| 41. A *crucible* is made of clay, and in form resembles a small bell. | 鎔銀鍋以坭作<br>成如小銅鐘樣 | ,*Yung ,ngan ,wó*, 'í ,nai tsók, ,shing ,ü 'síú ,t'ung ,chung yéung². |
| 42. A *copper crucible* is used in fusing copper. | 銅鍋用以鎔銅 | ,*T'ung ,wó* yung² 'í ,yung ,t'ung. |
| 43. A *sand dish* has scores within it. | 砂盤內有牙齒 | ,*Shá ,p'ún* noi² 'yau ,ngá 'ch'í. |
| 44. A *hand drum* has two buttons attached to it by cords one on each side; it is beaten to cry wares. | 轆鼓左右兩鈕<br>齊調擊報雜貨 | *Luk*, '*kú*, 'tsó yau² 'léung nau² ,ts'ai tíú², kik, pò' tsáp, fó'. |

32. Chinese carpenters make a black line on their boards with a line marked with writing ink, by drawing it through cotton soaked with a solution of ink; the term *mak tau sín* is therefore descriptive of the tool.

39. The compasses in use among the Chinese are without legs; the instrument consists of a straight stick, having a pin in each end; one of which serves as a pivot, while the other set at any given distance describes the circle.

| | | |
|---|---|---|
| 45. The *small copper drum* is beaten to cry bean-curd soup for sale. | 小銅鼓擊報賣荳腐花 | *'Síú ˌt'ung 'kú*, kik˒ pò' mái[2] tau[2] fú[1] ˓fá. |
| 46. *Dyeing jars* are earthen vessels to contain a blue dye. | 靛缸載靛瓦缸 | *Tín[2] ˓kóng*, tsoi' tín[2] 'ngá ˓kóng. |
| 47. *Dyeing rods* are for bleaching dyed cloth. | 晒布棚晒染布 | *Shái' pò' ˌp'ang* shái' 'ím pò'. |
| 48. An *ear-brush* is made of duck's down tied together. | 消塞鴨絨扎成 | *˓Síú sak˒* áp˒ ˌyung chát˒ ˌshing. |
| 49. An *ear-spoon* is for cleansing the ears. | 耳挑爲之取耳 | *'I ˓t'íú*, ˌwai ˓chí 'ts'ü 'í. |
| 50. *Ear-tweezers* are used for taking cerumen out of the ears and cleaning them. | 耳鉗用捻耳中垢漬 | *'Í ˌk'ím* yung[2] níp[2] 'í ˓chung 'kau tsik˒. |
| 51. *Eye-pearls* are used for washing the eyes. | 眼珠用以洗眼 | *'Ngán ˓chü* yung[2] 'í 'sai 'ngán. |
| 52. A *file* is a tool used to smooth iron. | 銼以銼滑鐵器 | *Ts'ó'* 'í ts'ó' wát[2] t'ít˒ hí'. |
| 53. A *three-cornered file* is so named from its shape. | 三角銼名象形 | *˓Sám kók˒ ts'ó'* ˌming tséung[2] ˌying. |
| 54. The *rat-tail file* is named from its shape, and is used for the same purposes as other files. | 鼠尾銼象形而名所用皆同 | *'Shü 'mí ts'ó'* tséung[2] ˌying ˌí ˌming, 'shó yung[2] ˓kái ˌt'ung. |
| 55. The *fleam* is but little used [by Chinese]. | 放馬血刀少用 | *Fóng' 'má hüt˒ ˓tò* 'shíú yung[2]. |
| 56. A *frisket* is for retaining and separating paper. | 隔紙揿隔紙用 | *Kák˒ 'chí 'k'am* kák˒ 'chí yung[2]. |
| 57. A *tinman's furnace* is used in fusing tin. | 打錫爐用煮錫 | *'Tá sik˒ ˌlò*, yung[2] 'chü sik˒. |
| 58. [The printer's] *furniture* binds the pages' sides. | 夾板枋夾板旁 | *Káp˒ 'pán 'fóng* káp˒ 'pán ˌp'óng. |
| 59. A *gally* is employed for holding composition. | 安字板備列此 | *˓On tsz'[2] 'pán* pí[2] lít[2] 'ts'z'. |
| 60. A *gimlet* bores holes for nails. | 手鑽穿孔入釘 | *'Shau tsün'* ˓ch'ün 'hung yap[2] ˓ting. |
| 61. The *hand gong* is struck to announce the purchase of the fragments of miscellaneous things. | 蘇鑼擊報收買、零碎什物 | *˓Sú ˌló*, kik˒ pò' ˓shau 'mái ˌling sui' shap[2] mat[2]. |
| 62. A *semicircle-gouge* is in the shape of a crescent. | 月鏟形如灣月 | *Üt[2] 'ch'án* ˌying ˌü ˓wán üt[2]. |
| 63. The *eyebrow-gouge* opens round holes. | 蛾眉鑿開圓孔 | *ˌNgó ˌmí tsók[2]* ˓hoi ˌün 'hung. |
| 64. *Fish grains* are made with five prongs. | 魚叉造成五齒 | *ˌÜ ˓ch'á* tsò[2] ˌshing 'ng 'ch'í. |

44, 45. The hand drum is about four inches in diameter, and two in thickness; it has a handle, by which it is twirled, and thus strikes the two buttons alternately on one side and the other. The copper drum is simply a plate of copper suspended in one hand by a cord, and violently struck with a stick by the other.

48.—51. These four articles belong to the barber's profession. The ear-brush resembles the globular flower of the Acacia, and is used after the ear-spoon; which is usually a thin slip of horn. The eye-pearl is a small pellet of coral fastened on the end of a slip of horn, and is passed under the eyelid to remove superfluous matter, and often doubtless to the injury of the eye.

廣東方言讀本

| | | |
|---|---|---|
| 64. The *grindstone*, by turning round and round like a wheel, grinds things sharp. | 磨刀石輪攪其輪轉而磨之 | *ˏMó ꜀tò shik$_2$ ˏlun* ʻkáu ˏkʻí ˏlun ʻchün ˏí ˏmó ꜀chí, |
| 65. A *gauge* is an instrument for marking wood so as to saw it into dovetails. | 交齒揦畫木以鋸交齒 | *꜀Káu ʻchʻí lát$_2$* wák$_2$ muk$_2$ ʻí küʼ ꜀káu ʻchʻ í. |
| 66. A *stone-hammer* is an implement used to strike the chisel in working stone. | 石鎚打鑿而擊石者 | *Shik$_2$ ˏchʻui* ʻtá tsók$_2$ ˏí kik꜄ shik$_2$ ʻché. |
| 67. A *shoe-hammer* is used by shoemakers. | 鞋槌造鞋所用 | *ˏHái ˏchʻui* tsò$^2$ ˏhái ʻshó yung$^2$. |
| 68. A *pile-hammer*; when walls are to be raised on new ground, it is required to drive piles of fir into the ground in order to make it firm and solid. | 打庄槌新土築垣必打杉入土爲庄以取堅固 | *ʻTá ꜀chóng ˏchʻui* ꜀san ʻtʻò chuk꜄ ˏún, pít꜄ ʻtá chʻámʼ yap$_2$ ʻtʻò ˏwai ꜀chóng, ʻí ʻtsʻü ꜀kín kúʼ. |
| 69. A *tinman's hammer* has a curved handle. | 打錫槌其柄曲 | *ʻTá sik꜄ ˏchʻui* ˏkʻí pingʼ huk꜄. |
| 70. The *harness* divides the warp into upper and lower. | 綜上下經交隔 | *꜀Tsung* shéung$^2$ há$^2$ ꜀king ꜀káu kák꜄. |
| 71. The present name of a *harpoon* is fish spear. | 矟今之爲魚標 | *꜀Sáu*, ꜀kam ꜀chí ˏwai ˏü ꜀píu. |
| 72. A *helve* is the handle of an axe. | 柯乃斧柄也 | *꜀Ó*, ʻnái ʻfú pingʼ ʻyá. |
| 73. A *hod* is filled with mortar. | 灰斗盛灰坭者 | *꜀Fúi ʻtau* shing$^2$ ꜀fúi ˏnai ʻché. |
| 74. A *basket-hod* is used for holding mortar. | 灰簍載灰坭用 | *꜀Fúi ʻtsʻám* tsoiʼ ꜀fúi ˏnai yung$^2$. |
| 75. *Hooks*, both great and small, are made of brass and iron, and vary according to circumstances. | 鈎銅鐵所作大小各用不同 | *꜀Kau*, ˏtʻung tʻít꜄ ʻshó tsók꜄ tái$^2$ ʻsíú, kók꜄ yung$^2$ pat꜄ ˏtʻung. |
| 76. An *ink-cup* is for holding ink. | 墨升以爲裝墨 | *Mak$_2$ ꜀shing* ʻí ˏwai ꜀chóng mak$_2$. |
| 77. An *ink-roller* is for rolling out ink upon a table. | 墨轆開墨於檯 | *Mak$_2$ luk꜄* ꜀hoi mak$_2$ ꜀ü ˏtʻoi. |
| 78. *Ink-shovel* is a bamboo for taking out ink. | 墨挑挑墨竹也 | *Mak$_2$ ꜀tʻíu*, ꜀tʻíu mak$_2$ chuk꜄ ʻyá. |
| 79. An *ink-table* is for distributing the ink. | 丨檯轆勻墨者 | *Mak$_2$ ˏtʻoi* luk꜄ ˏwan mak$_2$ ʻché. |
| 80. *Pottery-kiln* is a place where articles of pottery are made and burnt. | 瓦窰結爐燒瓦器處 | *ʻNgá ˏíú* kít꜄ ˏlò ꜀shíú ʻngá híʼ chʻüʼ. |
| 81. A *lime-kiln* burns shells into lime. | 灰爐燒殼成灰 | *꜀Fúi ˏlò* ꜀shíú hók꜄ ˏshing ꜀fúi. |

69. The pile-hammer is usually a large and heavy block of wood, with a strong handle on two sides, so that it can be raised and brought down by the united strength of two men.

70. In the manufacture of figured cloth, a second workman is employed, who sits upon the top of the loom, and whose business it is to pull the harness up and down.

76—79. All these several articles are used in foreign printing-offices, and not by Chinese workmen.

| | | |
|---|---|---|
| 82. A *beveled knife* has an angular edge. | 劖刀刀口斜落 | *Tsám*$^2$ ‹*tò*, ‹tò ʻhau ˏts'é lók$_2$. |
| 83. A *drawing-knife* has crooked handles on both ends. | 刀剷兩頭曲柄 | ‹*Tò* ʻ*chá'n* ʻléung ˏt'au huk› ping'. |
| 84. A *scraping-knife* is a knife which is used for scraping things bright and clean. | 刮刀打磨光亮之刀也 | *Kwát*› ‹tò, ʻtà ˏmó ‹kwóng léung$^2$ ‹chí ‹tò ʻyá. |
| 85. A *last* is a mold on which shoes are made. | 鞋楦造鞵模也 | ˏ*Hái hün*' tsò$^2$ ˏhái ˏmò ʻyá. |
| 86. *Tinman's lathe;* whatever tin utensils are of a round form, must be put in a lathe and turned. | 錫車凡圓樣錫器必上架車之 | *Sik*› ‹*ch'é* ˏfán ˏün yéung$^2$ sik› hí' pít› ʻshéung ká' ‹ch'é ‹chí. |
| 87. *Leads* are for separating lines [of types]. | 鉛間隔分行數 | ˏ*Ün kán*' *kák*› ‹fan ˏhang shò'. |
| 88. A *lever* is for raising stones. | 動鍬鍬起石者 | *Tung*$^2$ ‹*chiú* ‹chiú ʻhí shik$_2$ ʻché. |
| 89. *Links* are bent and joined together. | 連環扣圈相拖 | ‹*Lín* ˏ*wán kau*$^2$ ‹kün ‹séung tó'. |
| 90. A *loom* is a frame made of wood, upon which yarn is spread and woven into cloth. | 機以木造架一座佈紗而織之 | ‹*Kí*, ʻí muk$_2$ tsò$^2$ ká' yat› tsó$^2$, pò' ‹shá ˏí chik› ‹chí. |
| 91. A *mallet* drives the quoins of furniture. | 木槌打尖書板 | *Muk*$_2$ ˏ*ch'ui* ʻtá ‹tsím ‹shü ʻpán. |
| 92. A *marking line* is the same as the ink measure line. | 間尺即墨斗線 | *Kán*' *chik*› tsik› mak$_2$ ʻtau sín'. |
| 93. *Marking lines* are shaved thin for marking black. | 籤竹削扁間墨 | ‹*Ts'am chuk*› séuk› ʻpín kán' mak$_2$. |
| 94. A *tin mold* is a matrix used in manufacturing utensils from molten tin. | 錫模鎔鑄錫器之印 | *Sik*› ˏ*mò* ˏyung chü' sik› hí' ‹chí yan'. |
| 95. A *lime mortar* contains lime for pounding. | 灰坎載灰舂之 | ‹*Fúi* ʻ*hóm* tsoi' ‹fúi ‹chung ‹chí. |
| 96. A *physic-mortar* is for rolling the medicine to a powder; its present name is the rolling vessel. | 藥碾研藥爲末今名之曰研船 | *Yéuk*› ʻ*chín* ˏín yéuk$_2$ ˏwai mút$_2$ ‹kam ˏming ‹chí üt$_2$ ˏín ˏshün. |
| 97. A *muller;* the crude paints are put into a basin or bowl, and are ground fine by rubbing them with this stone. | 研色石顏色粗放砵內以此石圍扨之 | ˏ*Ín shik*› *shik*$_2$; ˏngán shik› ‹ts'ò fóng' pút› noi$^2$ ʻí ʻts'z' shik$_2$ ʻü yau' ‹chí. |
| 98. A *nail* is wrought of iron to nail things. | 釘鐵鑄釘什物 | ‹*Ting*, t'ít› chü' ‹ting shap$_2$ mat$_2$. |
| 99. A *net* is woven of hemp, and daubed with the white of duck's eggs, which serves for bait. | 網以蔴織成鴨蛋白漿之爲餌 | ʻ*Móng*, ʻí ˏmá chik› ˏshing áp› tán$^2$ pák$_2$ ‹tséung ‹chí ˏwai ní$^2$. |

96. This somewhat resembles the half of a very flat hollow spheroid; it is made of cast iron with four short legs, so as to be firm. It is said to have been introduced from India. That which serves for the pestle is an iron wheel with a long axle for a handle, and made sharp on the periphery; it rather cuts than triturates what is put into the mortar.

| | | |
|---|---|---|
| 100. A *drag net* is drawn by two boats, separated from each other, so as to catch fish. | 罟以二船分牽捕魚者 | *'Kú*, 'í í² shün fan hín pò² ü 'ché. |
| 101. A *lifting net* is an apparatus of net work fastened to bamboos, by raising which the fish are taken up. | 罾繫竹牽抝魚之器 | *Tsang* hai² chuk hín 'áu ü chí hí'. |
| 102. *Crab nets* are woven of bamboo in such a manner that fish can enter but not go out of them. | 倒鬚籠竹織成魚入而不能出 | *'Tò sü lung* chuk chik shing ü yap², 'í pat nang ch'ut. |
| 103. An *oil-press* is used to press fresh oil. | 榨用榨生油者 | *Cha'*, yung² chá' shang yau 'ché. |
| 104. A *pallet* is a board on which colors are placed, and mixed, so as to see if they are prepared in due proportion and with proper tints. | 較色板以各色放板上和勻較試深淺 | *Káu' shik 'pán*, 'í kók shik fóng' 'pán shéung² wó² wan, káu' shí' sham 'ts'ín. |
| 105. *Paste-bowl* is for holding paste. | 糊盤載糊之盤 | *Ú p'ún*, tsoi' ú chí p'ún |
| 106. A *paste-brush* is for pasting paper. | 漿糊掃以裱紙 | *Tséung ú* sò' 'í 'píu 'chí. |
| 107. *Pasting table* is for spreading paper on for pasting. | 裱床鋪畫裱之 | *'Píu ch'óng* p'ò wá² 'píu chí. |
| 108. A *spread pencil* is made fo several bound together. | 排筆數枝貫成 | *P'ái pat* shò' chí kún' shing. |
| 109. A *gilding pencil* is one which is used to brush off the gold after it has been laid [on a surface]. | 掃金筆差金後以掃餘金 | *Sú' kam pat*, ts'z' kam hau² 'í sò' ü kam. |
| 110. *Pestles* are used in mixing lime and mortar. | 舂杵搗鍊灰坭 | *Chung 'ch'ü* 't'ò lín² fúi nai. |
| 111. A *plane* is a tool for leveling and smoothing wood. | 鉋平滑木之器 | *P'áu*, p'ing wát² muk² chí hí'. |
| 112. A *bead plane* raises a on the edge of the line board. | 線鉋木邊起線 | *Sín' p'áu*, muk² pín 'hí sín'. |
| 113. A *gouge plane* is used for planing crooked things. | 灣亻曲用此鉋 | *Wán p'áu* huk yung² 'ts'z' p'áu. |
| 114. A *sash plane* is used for cutting a deep line. | 柳亻起深線者 | *'Lau p'áu* 'hí sham sín' 'ché. |
| 115. *Smoothing plane* is a small plane used after one planing to give a greater smoothness. | 光亻畧小鉋後再以此畧亻光 | *Kwóng p'áu* léuk² 'síu p'áu hau² tsoi' 'í 'ts'z' léuk² p'áu kwóng. |
| 116. *Casting plates* are for forming sheets of lead. | 倒錫板鑄錫片 | *'Tò sik 'pán'* chü sik p'í'n'. |
| 117. *Paper poles* are used for drying wet paper. | 晾紙竹晾濕紙 | *Léung² 'chí chuk* léung² shap 'chí. |
| 118. A *fish pole* has a hook strung to it for fishing. | 釣竿繫鈎釣魚 | *Tíú' kón* hai² kau tíú' ü. |
| 119. *Bookbinder's press* is for pressing books. | 攪盤攪夾書者 | *'Káu p'ún* 'káu káp shü 'ché. |

116. These are merely two large tiles covered with several thicknesses of paper; the melted lead or pewter is poured upon the lower one, and the upper instantly let down upon it, thus

| | | |
|---|---|---|
| 120. A *printing press* is made of iron in such a manner as to print several pages at once. | 印書架鐵爲之<br>一印數板 | *Yan' ˌshü ká'*, t'ít ˌwai ˌchi, yat yan' shò' 'pán. |
| 121. In a *proof*, the writing may be complete, yet not without errors; it is therefore desired for correction. | 書稿文雖成而<br>格未定欲改者 | *ˌShü 'kò;* ˌman ˌsui ˌshing, ˌí kák mí' ting', yuk 'koi ˌché. |
| 122. *Quoins* are used for compressing the pages. | 木尖以廹實板 | *Muk ˌtsím*, 'í pik shat 'pán. |
| 123. A *rasp* is a large iron implement with which things are filed smooth. | 大銼鐵器也以<br>此銼滑之 | *Tái' ts'ó'* t'ít hí' 'yá, 'í 'ts'z' ts'ó' wát ˌchí. |
| 124. A *reel* is a revolving bamboo for winding thread. | 撥拊運竹捲紗 | *Pút fú'* wan' chuk 'kün ˌshá. |
| 125. A *cocoon reeler* is for winding silk from cocoons. | 繰車絞繭出絲 | *'Tsò ˌk'ü* 'káu 'kín ch'ut ˌsz'. |
| 126. A *horizontal reel* is also used for reeling silk. | 絡柅亦理捲絲 | *Lók ˌní* yik 'lí 'kün ˌsz'. |
| 127. A *rivet* is a nail, that has its two heads nearly alike. | 鉸釘兩頭畧大而 | *Káu'*, ˌting 'léung ˌt'au léuk tái'. |
| 128. A *rule* is to put between the lines [in composing types], to separate them. | 銅片隔間行而<br>疊砌之 | *ˌT'ung p'ín' kák* kán' ˌhang ˌí típ ts'ai' ˌchí. |
| 129. A *small saw's* teeth separate to the right and left. | 小鋸齒分左右 | *'Síú kü'* 'ch'í ˌfan 'tsó yau'. |
| 130. A *great saw* is used for cutting wood in two. | 大鋸解木爲二 | *Tái' kü'* kái' muk ˌwai í'. |
| 131. A *hand saw* has its blade set obliquely. | 手鋸其肉斜鑲 | *'Shau kü'* ˌk'í yuk ˌts'é ˌséung. |
| 132. A *scoop* is used for taking fish out of the net. | 攩網在罾撈魚 | *T'óng' 'móng* tsoi' ˌtsang ˌlò ˌü. |
| 133. A *tinman's shears* are for cutting sheets and strips. | 錫剪裁片成條 | *Sik 'tsín* ˌts'oi p'ín' ˌshing ˌt'íú. |
| 134. A *shooting-stick* drives up the wooden quoins. | 木撞槌撞尖木 | *Muk chóng' ˌch'ui* chóng' ˌtsím muk. |
| 135. The *shuttle* is used to shoot the woof in weaving. | 杼藏緯以抛織 | *'Ch'ü ˌch'óng* 'wai 'í ˌp'áu chik. |
| 136. *Sieve pearls* are both great and small; and when used for washing fancy buttons, are put into a bag with them to scour them, so that not the smallest speck of surface remains which is not polished. | 漏珠大小不等<br>洗花鈕時同放<br>袋內擦之毋使<br>罅隙有不耀意 | *Lau' ˌchü* tái' 'síú pat 'tang, 'sai ˌfá 'nau ˌshí ˌt'ung fóng' toi' noi' ts'át ˌchí, ˌmò 'sz' lá' kwik 'yau pat íú' í'. |

forming an even sheet. The lining of tea-chests, and sheet lead for other purposes, is made in this manner.

131. The blade and the frame of a saw are usually in different planes; the angle of the blade being such as to allow a larger piece of wood to be sawed without interfering with the frame than could otherwise be done. The Chinese have no saw-mills worked by water power, but all their boards, planks, and other wood work, is sawed by human labor, and as might be supposed employs hundreds and thousands of hands. The log, when small, is firmly placed in a vertical position to be sawed.

| | | |
|---|---|---|
| 137. The *slaie* confines the warp like a comb. | 筬夾經如梳者 | *ˏShing*, káp› ‹king ˏü ‹shó ‘ché. |
| 138. A *lime spatula* holds mortar for pointing bricks. | 灰板載灰抆磚 | *‹Fúi ‘pán* tsoi’ ‹fúi ‘man ‹chün. |
| 139. A *spinning wheel* is a machine by which threads are made from silk and cotton. | 紡車乃紡絲棉作紗者 | *‘Fóng ‹ch‘é* ‘nái ‘fóng ‹sz’ ˏmín tsók› ‹shá ‘ché. |
| 140. A *spool* is a bamboo stick on which to wind thread. | 竽以竹竿捲紗 | *‹Fú* ‘í chuk› ‹kón ‘kün ‹shá. |
| 141. A *square* is used for forming right angles. | 矩凴以製方者 | *‘Kü*, ˏp‘ang ‘í chai’ ‹fóng ‘ché. |
| 142. A *square* is used for making square corners. | 墨殼方角間墨 | *Mak₂ hók›* ‹fóng kók› kán’ mak₂. |
| 143. A *lime stick;* when lime is thick and hard, a lime stick is then used to stir it up. | 灰剷灰實即以剷丨之 | *‹Fúi ‹ch‘ú* ‹fúi shat₂ tsik› ‘í ‹ch‘ú ‹ch‘ú ‹chí. |
| 144. A clicking of *bamboo sticks* announces meat cakes. | 竹策報賣雲吞 | *Chuk› ch‘ák›* pò’ mái² ˏwan ‹t‘an. |
| 145. A *Lydian stone* is used for testing silver. | 磨銀石辨銀色 | *ˏMó ‹ngan shik₂* pán² ˏngan shik›. |
| 146. A *straight-edge* shows what is level and straight. | 準能定其平正 | *‘Chun*, ˏnang ting² ˏk‘í ˏp‘ing ching’. |
| 147. A *striker* levels the grain when measuring it. | 斗刮量米刮平 | *‘Tau kwát›* ˏléung ‘mai kwát› ˏp‘ing. |
| 148. An *imposing table* is used for arranging pages. | 字板檯埋書板 | *Tsz’² ‘pán ˏt‘oi* ˏmái ‹shü ‘pán. |
| 149. The *ting-tóng* is twirled and struck to announce that cloth is for sale. | 叮鐺轉調擊報賣布 | *‹Ting ‹tóng* ‘chün ˏt‘íú kik› pò’ mái² pò’. |
| 150. The *small ting-tóng* is for selling floss and thread. | 小叮鐺賣絨線 | *‘Síú ‹ting ‹tóng* mái² ˏyung sín’. |
| 151. A *round ting*, struck by blind persons, announces that they will tell fortunes; they also use bamboo sticks. | 月叮瞽者擊報占算或兩竹片 | *Ut₂ ‹ting*, ‘kú ‘ché kik› pò’ ‹chím sün’; wák₂ ‘léung chuk› p‘ín’. |
| 152. The *tóng-tóng* announces that fish are to be sold. | 鐺鐺報賣魚生 | *‹Tóng ‹tóng* pò’ mái² ˏü ‹shang. |
| 153. A *trowel* is used for spreading mortar on bricks. | 灰匙抆灰磚口 | *‹Fúi ˏsh‘í* ‘man ‹fúi ‹chün ‘hau. |
| 154. *Tympan;* the paper is spread upon it, then it is folded over, and the paper is printed. | 印字撿鋪紙其上後捡下印之 | *Yan’ tsz’² ‘k‘am* ‹p‘ò ‘chí ˏk‘í shéung², hau² ‘k‘am há² yan’ ‹chí. |
| 155. Metallic movable *types;* all the characters are | 鉛活字每字以 | *ˏÜn út₂ tsz’²* ‘múi tsz’² ‘í ˏün |

145. Lydian stone or basanite is sometimes used by the Chinese to test the purity of silver; but in doubtful cases other more decisive tests are resorted to for ascertaining its purity.

149. The *ting-tóng* resembles the *luk kú* or hand-drum in design; it is a plate of copper hung by four sides within a hoop, which, as it is twirled by a handle, sets in motion a button suspended on the side to strike the copper.

151. The round or *üt ting* is a circular piece of copper, hung by two strings to a stick; a second stick is hung between the strings, and as the blind man perambulates the streets, he strikes the pendulous stick against the copper.

engraved on separate bodies of lead, and these are arranged into pages by words and sentences for printing.

156. A *vice* is for holding metallic articles securely in order to file them.

157. *Well-sweeps* are used for drawing water.

158. A *winder* is used for winding thread into balls.

159. *Iron-wire* is iron drawn out into threads.

160. A *wrench* is used for drawing spikes.

161. A *wrench* is an instrument which is used for taking out screws.

鉛條刻備照章
句叠成板印之
老鼠砧爲實鋏
鉗器以銼作之
桔槔用以汲水
㩁車理紗纏績
鐵線鐵造如線
千斤用拔大釘
螺絲擰用以開
螺絲者

ˏt'iú hak˒ pí' chiú' ˓chéung kü' típ˒ ˏshing 'pán yan' ˓chí.

*'Lò 'shü ˓cham* ˏwai shat˒ kíp˒ ˓kam hí' 'í ts'ò' tsok˒ ˓chí.

*Kat˒ ˓kò*, yung' 'í k'ap˒ 'shui.

*Tsui' ˓kü* 'lí ˓shá ˏch'in chik˒.

*T'it˒ sín'* t'it˒ tsò' ˏü sín'.

*˓Ts'in ˓kan*, yung' pát˒ tái' ˓ting.

*ˏLó ˓sz' ning'* yung' 'í ˓hoi ˏló ˓sz' 'ché.

160. The implement called *ts'in kan*, or 'thousand catties', is simply an iron rod or staple with a broad ring attached to it; the head of the spike is caught between the rod and ring, and pulled out on the principle of the lever.

## Section Fourth.

## NAMES OF COLORS.

## 顏色名第四章

ˏNgán shik˒ ˏming; tai' sz' ˓chéung.

The names of all colors were at first obtained from observing the color of some one thing, which was an exact image of the given color; hence, therefore, for the names to designate colors we refer to the names of

凡顏色之初得
名者皆由觀一
物色而象是色
故指物爲名色

ˏFán ˏngán shik˒ ˓chí ˓ch'o tak˒ ˏming 'ché, ˓kái ˏyau ˓kún yat˒ mat˒ shik˒, ˏí tséung' shí' shik˒; kú' 'chí mat˒ ˏming ˏwai shik˒ ˏming

### *Notes and Explanations.*

THE solar beam is divisible into seven primary colors, viz. violet, indigo, blue, green, yellow, orange, red — white being the mixture, and black the privation, of all of them. Three of these — blue, red, and yellow — by their intermixture are capable of producing all the rest. Those five which the Chinese call primary or true colors, are *ts'ing*, *wóng*, *ch'ik*, *pák*, *hak*, i. e. azure, yellow, carnation, white, and black. The single characters standing for other colors, such as *'luk* green, *lám* blue, &c., were, it is said, appropriated to this use, their primary sense not being that of color.

things. From of old, there were five primary colors; the rest are produced by a mixture of these colors.

名呼之自古以五色爲正色餘即爲間色

‹fú ‹chí. Tsz'$^2$ 'kú 'í ''ng shik› ‹wai ching' shik›, ‹yü tsik› ‹wai kán' shik›.

At present, by taking several colors and combining and mixing them together, new and brilliant tints are produced, so that the names of all the colors cannot be enumerated. If a person happens not to know the name of a color, then he takes the name of one of the five colors and adds to it another term—as light, dark, rich, dull, mellow, soft, delicate, changeable, glistening, cloudy, plain, marbled, &c., and by the use of these several terms gives the appropriate names; and these are so numerous that it is impracticable to gain a perfect knowledge of them.

茲將數色較和以爲新奇故色之名不可勝計或有不識其名者即將五色名加以淺深濃淡老嫩嬌閃靚啞素雜此數字而呼之皆多而不能盡識之故也

‹Tsz' ‹tséung shò' shik› káu' wó$^2$, 'í ‹wai ‹san ‹k'í, kú' shik› ‹chí ‹ming pat› 'hó ‹shing kai'. Wák$_2$ 'yau pat› shik› ‹k'í ‹ming 'ché, tsik› ‹tséung ''ng shik› ‹ming ‹ká 'í 'ts'ín, ‹sham, ‹nung, tám$^2$, 'lò, nün$^2$, ‹kíú, 'shím, ling$^2$, 'á, sò', tsáp$_2$; 'ts'z', shò' tsz'$^2$ ‹í ‹fú ‹chí, ‹kái ‹tò ‹í pat› ‹nang tsun$^2$ shik› ‹chí kú' 'yá.

1. *Ash color.* — 灰色 — ‹Fúi shik›

2. Purplish ash. — 鴿灰 — Kóp› ‹fúi

3. *Bister* (or pig's liver color). — 猪肝色 — ‹Chü ‹kón shik›

4. *Black* is sometimes designated sombre, dark, and raven, all of which are one and the same color. — 有時黑號玄皂烏皆同一色 — 'Yau ‹shí hak› hò$^2$ ‹ün, tsò$^2$, ‹ú, ‹kái ‹t'ung yat› shik›.

5. Hair-black color (color of Chinese hair). — 髮色 — Fát› shik›.

6. Ink black. — 京墨 — ‹King mak$_2$.

7. Soot black. — 油烟 — ‹Yau ‹ín.

8. Blue black. — 老藍 — 'Lò ‹lám.

1. *Ash* color or *fúi shik* is a very common tint among the Chinese, and the various shades of it are not well defined. *Kóp shik* dove color, is the shade on the necks of white doves.

3. *Bister* is prepared from common soot of wood, by pulverizing and washing. The soot of the beech is said to afford the best.

4. *Blacks.* Lampblack is a light carbonaceous substance, thrown off during the combustion of resinous and oily substances. The chips of fir and pine trees are burnt under tents, to the inside of which the lampblack adheres. In China, the article for making ink is obtained from oil, burned by lighted wicks in a vessel, over which a funnel-shaped cover is hung to receive the smoke or lampblack; and this, mixed with gluten, and made into paste, is formed into little cakes, and becomes the far famed, but misnamed, Indian ink. It is a little singular how the idea should have become so prevalent that this ink, of which tons are annually consumed in China and Japan, was made of the black secretion of the cuttle-fish.

| | | |
|---|---|---|
| 9. *Blue.* | 藍 | ˌLám. |
| 10. Sky blue. | 三青 | ˏSám ˏts'ing. |
| 11. Smaltz blue. | 佛頭青 | Fatˌ ˌt'au ˏts'ing. |
| 12. Azure blue. | 天青 | ˏT'ín ˏts'ing. |
| 13. Deep blue. | 元青 | ˌÜn ˏts'ing. |
| 14. Pure blue. | 二青 | Íˌ ˏts'ing. |
| 15. Light azure blue. | 玉藍 | Yukˌ ˌlám. |
| 16. *Brown.* (Coir brown.) | 椶色 | ˏTsung shikˎ. |
| 17. Rust brown. | 鐵椶 | T'ítˎ ˏtsung. |
| 18. Reddish brown. | 紅椶 | ˌHung ˏtsung. |
| 19. Chestnut brown. | 栗色 | Lutˌ shikˎ. |
| 20. Spanish brown (or sheep's liver color). | 羊肝色 | ˌYéung ˏkón shikˎ. |
| 21. *Carmine.* | 金魚紅 | ˏKam ˌü ˌhung. |
| 22. *Carnation.* | 赤色 | Ch'ikˎ shikˌ. |
| 23. *Cinnabar.* | 硃砂 | ˏChü ˏshá. |
| 24. *Cochineal color.* | 呀囒色 | ˌNgá ˏlán shikˎ. |
| 25. *Crimson* (or rouge red). | 胭脂 | ˏÍn ˏchí. |
| 26. *Gray.* | 褐色 | Kótˎ shikˎ. |
| 27. Yellowish gray. | 原色 | ˌÜn shikˎ. |
| 28. Reddish gray. | 紫色 | 'Tsz' shikˎ. |
| 29. Bluish gray. | 淡灰色 | Tám' ˏfúi shikˎ. |
| 30. *Green.* | 綠色 | Lukˌ shikˎ. |
| 31. Plant green. | 青色 | ˏTs'ing shikˎ, |

9. *Blue. Lám* is the common term for those blue colors that are dark and tinged with red. For the light blues, as azure and mountain blue, the word *ts'ing* is employed. There is, however, more discrepancy among the Chinese concerning the color intended by *ts'ing* than any other color; it is both the color of the sky and of trees; and even the color of ether is called *ts'ing*. The term may, perhaps, be defined, the color of nature, or the natural heavens; and this vague term is applied by different persons in a different manner, and to diverse objects.

16. *Tsung* is the net-like bark of the Cycas, from which the Chinese make ropes, brooms, &c.; it is taken by them as the pure shade of brown.

26. *Kót* is the color of hemp, before it has been bleached; *ün skik* means the "original

| | | |
|---|---|---|
| 32. Green bice. | 虎綠 | ʻFú luk$_2$. |
| 33. Sap green. | 墨綠 | Mak$_2$ luk$_2$. |
| 34. Blackish green (unripe lemon green). | 檬綠 | ꜀Mung luk$_2$. |
| 35. Emerald green. | 二綠 | Í$^2$ luk$_2$. |
| 36. Pea green. | 豆青 | Tau$^2$ ꜀ts'ing. |
| 37. Leek green. | 葱綠 | ꜀Ts'ung luk$_2$. |
| 38. Olive green. | 欖青 | ʻLám ꜀ts'ing. |
| 39. *Indigo.* | 洋藍 | ꜁Yéung ꜁lám. |
| 40. *Orange.* | 黄丹 | ꜁Wóng ꜀tán. |
| 41. *Purple.* | 紫粉 | ʻTsz' ʻfan. |
| 42. Iris purple. | 蒲青 | ꜁P'ò ꜀ts'ing. |
| 43. *Prussian blue.* | 洋靛 | ꜁Yéung tín$^2$. |
| 44. *Red.* | 紅色 | ꜁Hung shik꜄. |
| 45. Brownish red. | 赭石 | ʻChé shik$_2$. |
| 46. Lake red. | 番紅 | ꜀Fán ꜁hung. |
| 47. Copper red. | 古銅色 | ʻKú ꜁t'ung shik꜄. |
| 48. Rose red. | 銀紅 | ꜁Ngan ꜁hung. |
| 49. Orange red. | 紫丹 | ʻTsz' ꜀tán. |
| 50. Peach red. | 桃紅 | ꜁T'ò ꜁hung. |
| 51. Brick red. | 青蓮 | ꜀Ts'ing ꜁lín. |
| 52. Light red. | 宮粉 | ꜀Kung ʻfan. |
| 53. Hyacinth red. | 金飛紅 | ꜀Kam ꜀fí ꜁hung. |
| 54. Lightish red. | 粉紅 | ʻFan ꜁hung. |
| 55. *Scarlet.* | 花紅 | ꜀Fá ꜁hung. |
| 56. *Sepia.* | 雅灰 | ʻNgá ꜀fúi. |
| 57. *Snuff* color. | 鼻烟色 | Pí$^2$ ꜀ín shik꜄. |
| 58. *Verdigris* green. | 銅綠 | ꜁T'ung luk$_2$. |

color," and the term is principally applied to the color of raw silk; while *tsz' shik* is appropriated to the reddish-yellow gray of Nankeen cloth.

CHI. CHR. 77

| | | |
|---|---|---|
| 59. *Vermilion* red. | 硍硃 | ˏNgan ‹chü. |
| 60. *White.* | 白色 | Pák, shik›. |
| 61. Grayish white. | 淺灰 | ˋTs'ín ‹fúi› |
| 62. Quicksilver white. | 乳銀 | ˋYü ˏngan. |
| 63. Spanish white. | 鉛粉 | ˏÜn ˋfan. |
| 64. Snow white. | 雪白 | Süt› pák,. |
| 65. Ivory white. | 牙黃 | ˏNgá ˏwóng. |
| 66. Pearl white. | 珠色 | ‹Chü shik›. |
| 67. Bluish white. | 札藍 | Chát› ˏlám. |
| 68. *Yellow.* | 黃色 | ˏWóng shik›. |
| 69. Brass yellow. | 乳金 | ˋYü ‹kam. |
| 70. Amber yellow. | 碧色 | Pik› shik›. |
| 71. Honey yellow. | 雄黃 | ˏHung ˏwóng. |
| 72. Lemon yellow. | 粉黃 | ˋFan ˏwóng. |
| 73. Oker yellow. | 坭黃 | ˏNai ˏwóng. |
| 74. Almond yellow. | 杏黃 | Hang² ˏwóng. |
| 75. Sulphur yellow. | 石黃 | Shik, ˏwóng. |
| 76. Yolk yellow. | 蛋黃 | Tán² ˏwóng. |
| 77. Brown-brass yellow. | 青金 | ‹Ts'ing ˏkam. |
| 78. Canary yellow. | 辰時雀黃 | ˏShí ˏshan tséuk› ˏwóng. |
| 79. Gamboge yellow. | 籐黃 | ˏT'ang ˏwóng. |

49. Red ink is made from vermilion, and this color is often used by the emperor, or others at his dictation, in writing edicts, which are then called *chü pat*, or writings in vermilion; his majesty's replies, when written by officers in waiting, are called *chú pí*, or replies [written in] vermilion. Magistrates also use this color in punctuating their edicts. *Tán* and *chü* are nearly synonymous in common use; *tán* is, however, a lighter, orange-red than vermilion.

# CHAPTER VIII.

# ARCHITECTURE.

# 工匠務篇八

‹Kung tséung$^{2}$ mú$^{2}$; ‹p'ín pát›.

## Section First.

## VARIOUS KINDS OF EDIFICES.

## 宮室類第一章

‹Kung shat› lui$^{2}$; tai$^{2}$ yat› ‹chéung.

1. In the remotest ages of antiquity, caves in desert places were the habitations of the people: during winter, they lived in holes dug in the ground; and in summer, they dwelt in thatched huts. In subsequent times, their chieftains made dwelling places of wood and earth; and very soon afterwards they also constructed regular houses, with beams and pillars, for protection against winds and rains.

上古之世穴居而野處冬則居營窟夏則居橧巢後世聖入以木處而顛土處而病然後爲之宮室上棟下宇以待風雨

Shéung$^{2}$ 'kú ‹chí shai$^{2}$, hüt› ‹kü ‹í 'yé 'ch'ü; ‹tung tsak› ‹kü ‹ying fat›; há$^{2}$ tsak› ‹kü ‹tsang ‹ch'áu. Hau$^{2}$ shai$^{2}$, shing$^{2}$ ‹yan 'í muk› 'ch'ü ‹í ‹tín 't'ò 'ch'ü; ‹í ping$^{2}$ ‹ín hau$^{2}$ ‹wai ‹chí ‹kung shat›, shéung$^{2}$ tung$^{2}$ há$^{2}$ 'ü 'í toi$^{2}$ ‹fung 'ü.

2. See the General Account of buildings, in the Illustrations of the Four Books.

見四書圖考宮室總畧

Kín$^{2}$ Sz$^{2}$ ‹Shü ‹T'ò 'háu, ‹Kung shat› 'tsung léuk›.

### *Notes and Explanations.*

Literally, *kung tséung mú* denotes the operations of architects, or those who construct all kinds of buildings, together with vessels and land carriages of every description.

1. These *shing yan* are known to the Chinese only by tradition, as distinguished benefactors of their nation, who lived in the remotest antiquity; they are perhaps identical with Tubal-cain and others mentioned in the first book of Moses. *Kung* and *shat*, often used as distinct terms for different ideas, are here synonymous and express the simple idea of house, or the abodes of man. *Shéung tung, há ü*, are the framework and covering of the house. The first inhabitants of the land, as here described, seem to have been troglodytes, rather than nomads

2. These Illustrations are comprised in twelve small octavo volumes, with plates, all executed in the best style of Chinese printing and engraving.

| | | |
|---|---|---|
| 3. An *academy* is the village school-house. | 社學本鄉學館 | '*Shé hók* 'pún ‹héung hók 'kún. |
| 4. The *imperial academy* is a public hall for the residence of those who, having attained the rank of *hónlam*, have not become magistrates. | 翰林院乃初中未任民情之官署也 | *Hón' ˏlam ün'* 'nái ‹ch'o chung' mí yam' ˏman ˏts'ing ‹chí ‹kún 'shü 'yá. |
| 5. The 'golden horse' and 'gemmeous court' are terms for the *imperial academy*. | 金馬玉堂翰林院宇 | ‹Kam 'má yuk ˏtong, *hón' ˏlam ün'* 'ü. |
| 6. The *altars* for the vernal and autumnal sacrifices to the gods of the land and grain are placed right and left. | 社稷壇右社左稷春秋令祭之 | '*Shé tsik* ˏ*tán*, yau' 'shé, 'tsó tsik, ‹ch'un ‹ts'au ling' tsai' ‹chí. |
| 7. The *altars of the people* are shaded by trees, and offerings are made in spring and autumn for fruitful seasons. | 民社樹以木春秋時酧豐年也 | ˏ*Man 'shé* shü' 'í muk ‹ch'un ‹ts'au ˏshí ˏch'au ‹fung ˏnin 'yá. |
| 8. An *arbor*, in a garden, is built high, in order that it may be cool and afford a fine prospect. | 凉亭於園內高建爲納凉眺望 | ˏ*Léung ˏt'ing*, ‹ü ˏün noi' ‹kò kín' ˏwai náp ˏléung tíú' móng'. |
| 9. A *wayside arbor* has no walls, but only pillars. | 亭無垣而有柱 | ˏ*T'ing* ˏmò ˏhün ˏí 'yau 'chü. |
| 10. An *arsenal* is a depository of arms. | 軍器局貯兵器 | ‹*Kwan hí' kuk* 'ch'ü ‹ping hí'. |
| 11. A *barrier* is built on the frontiers, in order to guard and protect the boundary. | 關閘邊塞建關以爲界限防守 | ‹*Kwán cháp* ‹pín sui' kín' ‹kwán 'í ˏwai kái' han' ˏfong 'shau. |
| 12. A *bridge* is a traveler's passage over a river. | 橋爲水渡行人 | ˏ*Kíú* ká' 'shui tò' ˏhang ˏyan. |
| 13. A *floating bridge* may be made of boats. | 浮橋或舟爲之 | ˏ*Fau ˏkíú* wák ‹chau ˏwai ‹chí. |
| 14. *Suspension bridges* are made of the Anagyris and elm, and are constructed like other bridges. | 釣橋造以榆槐之木其製如橋 | *Tíú' ˏkíú* tsò' 'í ˏü ˏkwai ‹chí muk, ˏk'í chai' ˏü ˏkíú. |
| 15. 'Green windows' are poor women's *cabins*. | 綠窗是貧婦室 | Luk ‹ch'óng shí' ˏpan fú' *shat*. |
| 16. A *caravansary* is a resting-place on the highway. | 驛中途駐足所 | *Yik* ‹chung ˏt'ò chü' tsuk 'shò. |
| 17. A *city* is walled for the prince's defense. | 城乃築以衛君 | ˏ*Shing* 'nái chuk 'í wai' ‹kwan. |
| 18. The *colleges* of princes were called 'p'únkung.' | 諸侯學曰泮宮 | ‹Chü ˏhau hók üt *p'ún' ‹kung*. |

5. The term *pák má* alludes to two brazen images of horses placed in the doorway of the academy by the emperor Mú of the Hón dynasty about the year 140 B. C. The characters *yuk tóng* are placed above the gate of the academy, and correspond, in this usage, to similar fanciful designations for public institutions in western lands.

14. A bridge of this kind is figured and described in the *Sám Ts'oi T'ò*, and resembles very much the suspension bridges of Europe.

16. These in China are established by government, and seem to be for the sole use of those who are employed on public service.

廣東方言讀本

| | | |
|---|---|---|
| 19. The *college* of the emperor was called 'p'ikyung.' | 天子學曰辟雍 | ‚T'ín 'tsz' hók₂ üt₂ *p'ik₃ ‚yung.* |
| 20. *Colleges* are everywhere established for the support and education of men of genius and talent. | 書院各屬設建<br>得以教育英才 | *‚Shü ün'* kók₃ shuk₂ ch'ít₃ kín² tak₃ 'í káu' yuk₂ ‚ying ‚ts'oi. |
| 21. *Imperial colleges;* officers are commissioned by the emperor and sent thither to select the talented. | 貢院朝廷命官<br>到此考取文才 | *Kung' ün'* ‚ch'iú ‚ting ming² ‚kún tò' 'ts'z' 'háu 'ts'ü ‚man ‚ts'oi. |
| 22. A *cantonment* is a small encampment of troops for the purpose of guarding the frontiers. | 寨乃屯兵之小<br>城以防守邊塞 | *Chái²* 'nái ‚t'ün ‚ping ‚chí 'síú ‚shing 'í ‚fóng 'shau ‚pín sui'. |
| 23. The Taouists reside in their own *convents.* | 觀中道士隱居 | *Kún'* ‚chung Tò² sz'² 'yan ‚kü. |
| 24. *Cottages* are covered with thatch. | 茅屋茅草蓋成 | *‚Máu uk₃* ‚máu 'ts'ò koi' ‚shing. |
| 25. *Council chambers* are for deliberative assemblies. | 公所集議之所 | *‚Kung 'shó* tsáp₂ 'í ‚chí 'shò. |
| 26. *Exchanges* are established by all the several trades, for the purpose of united deliberation. | 會舘各行商賈<br>設爲會衆議事 | *Úi² 'kún* kók₃ ‚hóng ‚shéung 'ká ch'ít₃ ‚wai úi² chung' 'í sz'². |
| 27. *Farm-houses* are constructed of reeds, and have doors made of rushes and coarse grass. | 廬屋以蒲蔣扉<br>以蘧蒢 | *‚Lú uk₃* 'í ‚pò 'tséung ‚fí 'í ‚k'ü ‚ch'ü. |
| 28. In a *fort,* guns are placed for defense. | 砲臺置砲防守 | *P'áu' ‚t'oi* chí' p'áu' ‚fóng 'shau. |
| 29. *Granaries* are places for storing grain. | 倉乃藏穀之處 | *‚Ts'óng* 'nái ‚ch'óng kuk₃ ‚chí ch'ü'. |
| 30. A *kw'an* is a round granary. | 囷乃倉之圓者 | *‚Kw'an* 'nái ‚ts'óng ‚chí ‚ün 'ché. |
| 31. A *king* is a square granary. | 京乃倉之方者 | *‚King* 'nái ‚ts'óng ‚chí ‚fóng 'ché. |
| 32. A granary having bins is called *pan.* | 倉之有屋曰廩 | ‚Ts'óng ‚chí 'yau uk₃ üt₂ *'pan.* |
| 33. A *grocery* has oil, sugar, spirits, rice, and other miscellaneous articles for sale. | 雜貨舖油糖酒<br>米雜貨沽之 | *Tsáp₂ fò' p'ò'* ‚yau ‚t'óng 'tsau 'mai tsáp₂ fò' ‚kú ‚chí. |

18—21. For colleges, academies, and minor schools, and for the buildings in which they are established, a great variety of names have been, and are still, employed, the principal of which are given in this section. *P'ikyung* and *p'únkung* are now disused. Beautiful plates of them both may by seen in the Illustrations of the Four Books: the former was entirely surrounded by water; the latter, as its name indicates, had water only around one half.

25, 26. The *kung shó,* or public places, are established in streets and villages, and the gentry and elders assemble in them for the transaction of all their public business; they are equivalent to town-halls and town-houses, in some western states. The *úi kún,* or assembly halls, have already been noticed on page 199; they differ from modern European exchanges in each one's being limited to a single trade, but resemble in all their principal features the ancient guilds of Europe, approaching as near to a corporation as the nature of the supreme government will permit.

29—32. Public granaries seem to have existed in this country from time immemorial, and they have assumed a great variety of forms. Among the Chinese, the practice of storing grain in the earth has long since ceased.

| | | |
|---|---|---|
| 34. A *guard-house* is for protecting important passes. | 卡以爲防險要 | *Ká'* ʻí ,wai ,fóng ʻhím iú'. |
| 35. The term *hall* was first used by the emperor Wóng. | 堂之名肇黃帝 | ,*T'óng* ,chí ,ming shü' ,Wóng tai'. |
| 36. *Halls of science* are temples of the sages, and every department and district has one of its own. | 學宮聖廟也府州縣各有建立 | *Hók*, ,*kung* shing' míú' ʻyá; ʻfú ,chau ün' kók, ʻyau kín' lap,. |
| 37. A *hermitage* is the dwelling of a retired man. | 衡門隱逸之宅 | ,*Hang* ,*mún* ʻyan yat, ,chí chák,. |
| 38. A *hospital* is a place for healing the sick. | 醫館治病之居 | ,*I'* ʻ*kún* chí' ping' ,chí ,kü. |
| 39. A *foundling hospital* is erected in a town for nurturing and bring up orphan children, who reside there from infancy. | 育嬰堂乃邑中建育無父母撫養嬰兒居也 | *Yuk*, ,*ying* ,*t'óng* ʻnái yap, ,chung kín' yuk, ,mò, fú' ʻmò ʻfú ʻyéung, ,ying ,í ,kü ʻyá. |
| 40. The mansion for visitors is called a *hotel.* | 待賓之舍曰館 | Toi' ,pan ,chí shé' üt, ʻ*kún*. |
| 41. A *public hotel* is where officers put up. | 公館官之寓所 | ,*Kung* ʻ*kún* ,kún ,chí ü' ʻshó. |
| 42. The 'white house' is a poor man's *hut.* | 白屋布衣之家 | *Pák*, *uk*, pò' ,í ,chí ,ká. |
| 43. A *kitchen* is a house for cooking provisions. | 庖厨烹調火食 | ,*P'áu* ,*ch'ü* ,p'ang ,t'íú ʻfó shik,. |
| 44. A *lodge* is a thatch for watching grain. | 守舍看禾廬也 | ʻ*Shau shé'* hón' ,wó ,lú ʻyá. |
| 45. A *snail's lodge* is a modest term for one's house. | 蝸廬自謙屋小 | ,*Wó* ,*lú* tsz' ,h'ím uk, ʻsíú. |
| 46. '*Red lofts*' are rich women's houses. | 紅樓乃富女居 | ,*Hung* ,*lau* ʻnái fú' ʻnü ,kü. |
| 47. A *magazine* is a depository of powder. | 火藥局制火藥 | ʻ*Fó yéuk*, *kuk*, chai' ʻfó yéuk,. |
| 48. A *magistrate's office* is the abode of officers. | 廨百官之所居 | *Kái'* pák, ,kún ,chí ʻshó ,kü. |
| 49. A *mansion*, with five acres of land, is surrounded by a wall, which is called the palace-wall. | 五畝之宅外環以墻謂之宮墻 | ʻ'Ng ʻmau ,chí *chák*, ngoi' ,wán ʻí ,ts'éung wai' ,chí ,kung ,ts'éung. |
| 50. In the *market*, provisions are bought and sold, for which purpose all kinds of shops are opened there. | 市井買賣食物各鋪建設之處 | ʻ*Sh'í* ʻ*tsing* ʻmái mái' shik, mat, kók, p'ò' kín' ch'ít, ,chí ch'ü'. |
| 51. A *menagerie* is where wild animals are reared. | 苑所以養禽獸 | *Ün'* ʻshó ʻí ʻyéung ,k'am shau'. |

40, 41. For an account of the more common inns or taverns, see page 282; these buildings are also called *ü*, and *ü shó*, i. e. lodgings, or lodging-places.

42. The meaning of *pák* is unfurnished, unadorned, and alludes to the poor but honest man, whose poverty is still further expressed in this sentence by *pò í*, cotton clothes, which he wears.

43. The *p'áu ch'ü* differs from a *ch'ü fóng* or cooking-room (chap. V. sec. 2: 33); the latter is a single apartment of a house occupied solely for cooking; while the former is usually a separate building, attached to temples, monasteries, &c.

45. The allusion here is to the smallness of the house, and the straitened circumstances of the owner, who, in the oriental style of mock humility, disparagingly likens his tenement to the contracted lodgment of a snail.

50. In early times, the market was called *sh'í sz'*, of which a plan may be seen in the Illustra-

| | | |
|---|---|---|
| 52. A *military post* is the same as a guard-house. | 官堆亦卽卡也 | ‹*Kún* ‹*túi* yik, tsik, ká' 'yá. |
| 53. *Monasteries* are the abodes of the Budhists, first erected in the reign of Ming of the Hón dynasty. | 寺漢明帝時始創乃僧人所居 | *Shí'* Hón' ‚Ming tai' ‚shí, 'chí 'ch'óng, 'nái ‹Tsang ‚yan 'shó ‹kü. |
| 54. Priestesses of Budha dwell in *nunneries*. | 庵內女尼奉佛 | ‹*Ím* noi$^2$ 'nü ‚ní fung$^2$ Fat,. |
| 55. *Observatories* are so called, because on them you can look abroad and take observations. | 觀之言可以觀望於其上也 | *Kún'* ‹chí ‚ín 'hó 'í ‹kún móng$^2$ ‚ü ‚k'í shéung$^2$ 'yá. |
| 56. King Man of Chau built the *imperial observatory*. | 周文王作靈臺 | ‹Chau ‚Man ‚wóng tsók, ‚*ling* ‚*t'oi*. |
| 57. *Public offices* are those of the magistrates. | 衙署亦卽廨也 | ‚*Ngá* '*shü* yik, tsik, kái' 'yá. |
| 58. The 'fir-platform' and 'rookery,' are also terms for the *censor's office*. | 柏臺烏府御史衙門云爾 | Pák, ‚t'oi ‹ú 'fú *ü*$^2$ '*sz'* ‚*ngá* ‚*mún* ‚wan 'í. |
| 59. The *orbate temple*; if one has no posterity, his tablet is placed and worshiped in this temple. | 無祠壇若無後祠者牌位祀此 | ‚*Mò sz'*$^2$ ‚*t'án*; yéuk, ‚mò hau$^2$ sz'$^2$ 'ché ‚pái wai$^2$ sz'$^2$ 'ts'z'. |
| 60. A *pagoda* is sometimes several stories and tens of feet high, with windows on all the six sides. | 塔或高數丈數重窗通六面 | *T'áp*, wák, ‹kò shò' chéung$^2$ shò' ‚ch'ung ‹ch'óng ‹t'ung luk, mín$^2$. |
| 61. The *literary pagodas* are two or three stories high, and in them sacrifices are offered to the god of letters. | 文閣高二三層祀文星於其上 | ‚*Man kók*, ‹kò í$^2$ ‹sám ‚ts'ang sz'$^2$ ‚man ‹sing ‹ü ‚k'í shéung$^2$. |
| 62. When the ancients built houses high and majestic, they usually denominated them *palaces*. | 古制屋之高嚴通呼爲殿 | 'Kú chai$^2$ uk, ‹chí ‹kò ‚ím ‹t'ung ‹fú ‚wai *tín*$^2$. |
| 63. A *palace* is the house of an emperor or king. | 大內帝王之屋 | *Tái*$^2$ *noi*$^2$ tai' ‚wóng ‹chí uk,. |
| 64. The *honorary portal* emblazons good deeds; it is also called 'páifong.' | 牌樓旌表善行又謂牌坊 | ‚*Pái* ‚*lau* ‹sing 'píú shín' hing'; yau$^2$ wai' ‚pái ‹fong. |
| 65. A *prison* is for incarcerating notorious offenders. | 監牢以囚重犯 | ‹*Kám* ‚*lò* 'í ‚ch'au chung$^2$ fán$^2$. |

tions of the Four Books: for explanations of *sz'* and *sh'í*, see pages 121 and 211. In the *Sám Ts'oi T'ò*, the *sh'í tsing* is represented as a collection of buildings, forming an extensive market.

58. The first of these terms arose, it appears, from a very large fir-tree which grew in an inclosure near the front of the censor's office in Peking; the second derived its origin from the rookery of crows that occupied the branches of this tree. *Ngá mún* is a common term for public offices, synonymous with *ngá shü*, in the preceding sentence.

59. This building is sometimes attached to a large temple, and contains the tablets of those who left no descendants to perpetuate their name, and offer sacrifices to their manes; the number collected in them is often very great.

64. The *páilau*, whether of wood or of stone, have been called triumphal arches: arches however, they are not; nor are they like an arch; nor have they usually any claim whatever to be denominated triumphal. In shape, they resemble the posts of a gate with a very broad lintol or beam; often they have two beams, one above the other, with a tablet between them.

| | | |
|---|---|---|
| 66. The *family residence* of a statesman is called 't'án fú.' | 潭府仕宦之家 | *ˏT'án ˊfú* sz'ˀ wánˀ ˏchí ˏká. |
| 67. The 'pearly door' is the *seat* of a rich man. | 朱門富豪之第 | ˏ*Chü ˏmún* fú' ˏhò ˏchí taiˀ. |
| 68. A *seraglio* is the secluded residence of imperial ladies. | 內宮妃嬪深居 | *Noiˀ ˏkung* ˏfí pan' ˏsham ˏkü. |
| 69. By *signal posts* an enemy's approach is announced. | 烽墪設以禦敵 | ˏ*Fung ˏtun* ch'ít, ˊí üˀ tik. |
| 70. A *souterrain* has a small mouth and is very capacious; grain is deposited through a hole in its side. | 竇口小腹大或竅通旁以藏粟 | *Tauˀ* ˊhau ˊsíú fuk, táiˀ, wák, kíú' ˏt'ung ˏp'ong ˊí ˏch'óng suk,. |
| 71. A *káu* is a place in the earth for storing grain. | 窖地中藏穀處 | *Káu*' tíˀ ˏchung ˏch'óng kuk, ch'ü'. |
| 72. The *vegetable stall* exposes vegetables for sale. | 瓜菜攤擺賣菜 | ˏ*Kwá* ts'oi' ˏ*t'án* ˊ*pái* mái' ts'oi'. |
| 73. The *store-house* is for storing up goods. | 棧爲貯放貨物 | *Chán*ˀ ˏwai ˊshü fóng' fó' mat. |
| 74. Swine are domesticated in a *sty*. | 圈畜牛豕者是 | ˏ*Hün* ch'uk, ˏngau ˊshí ˊché shíˀ. |
| 75. A *temple* contains images of the gods, and has priests ordained to offer sacrifices. | 廟爲祀神靈乃設司祝者奉祀 | *Míú*ˀ ˏwai szˀ ˏshan ˏling ˊnái ch'ít, ˏsz' chuk, ˊché fung' szˀ. |
| 76. In the *temple of ancestors* their tablets are placed, and there sacrifices are offered to them. | 祠堂立祖宗牌位而祭祀之處 | ˏ*Sz'* ˏ*t'óng* lap, ˊtsò ˏtsung ˏpái waiˀ ˏí tsai' szˀ ˏchí ch'ü'. |
| 77. *Tents* are coverings made of cloth for the purpose of affording lodging-places to soldiers. | 營盤以布搭蓋以爲屯宿軍士 | ˏ*Ying* ˏ*p'ún* ˊí pò' táp, koi' ˊí ˏwai ˏt'ün shuk, ˏkwan szˀ. |
| 78. The *general's tent* is the station of the general. | 帥府主帥所居 | *Sz'*' ˊ*fú* ˊchü sz'ˀ ˊshó ˏkü. |
| 79. *Treasuries* are built for depositing money. | 庫設以藏金銀 | *Fú*' ch'ít, ˊí ˏch'óng ˏkam ˏngan. |
| 80. *Victualing-houses* are buildings which are furnished with wine and meat for entertainment. | 高樓舖內有點心酒肉 | ˏ*Kò* ˏ*lau* p'ò' noiˀ ˊyau ˊtím ˏsam ˊtsau yuk. |

The two principal posts are, say twenty feet high, and stand about twenty feet apart. Outside of these two posts, are usually two shorter ones, each connected by a short beam to the larger ones. On all these posts, beams, and tablet are inscriptions, to emblazon and to commemorate the virtuous actions of those for whose honor they are erected.

70, 71. These are of two kinds, and were frequently constructed so as to preserve valuable jewels, treasure, books, and other things which the owner wished to lay up secure from theft and mold. The *káu* was made much smaller than the *tau*, and provided with a small pent-roof to keep the rain from soaking the covering.

75. Temples in China, like churches and chapels in western countries, have a great variety of names, and afford some of the finest specimens of architecture that are to be seen in the country. They are generally constructed of the best materials, and in superior style. Poor villages often have rich temples; while those built by affluent persons, by officers, or by members of the imperial family, are very costly and beautiful, and sometimes superb.

廣東方言讀本

## Section Second.

# THE PARTS OF BUILDINGS.

## 宮室物料類第二章

‘Kung shat˒ mat$_2$ líú$^2$ lui$^2$; tai$^2$ í$^2$ ˓chéung.

| | | |
|---|---|---|
| 1. An *arch* is made by placing stones in a circular form either over a door, or under a bridge. | 拱乃砌圓拱於門或造於橋下 | ‘*Kung* ˢnái ts‘ai˒ ˏün ‘kung ˓ü ˏmún, wák$_2$ tsò$^2$ ˓ü ˏk‘íú há$^2$. |
| 2. The *audience-hall* is the place where the monarch assembles his ministers, to deliberate with them in person. | 殿堂乃王者會羣臣朝議之也 | *Tín$^2$ ˏt‘óng* ˢnái ˏwóng ‘ché úi$^2$ ˏkw‘an ˏshan ˏch‘íú ˢí ˓chí ˢyá. |
| 3. An *avenue* is the strait path which leads from the principal outer gate to the front door of the house. | 㰯道乃頭門直達二門之道也 | ‘*Yung tò$^2$* ˢnái ˏt‘au ˏmún chik$_2$ tát$_2$ í$^2$ ˏmún ˓chí tò$^2$ ˢyá. |
| 4. The *balistic platform* is erected to discharge crossbows. | 弩臺設以發弩 | ˓*Nú ˏt‘oi* ch‘ít˒ ˢí fát˒ ˏnú. |
| 5. *Base* is the present name of a column's pedestal. | 礎乃今之柱墪 | ‘*Ch‘ó* ˢnái ˓kam ˓chí ˢch‘ü ˓tun. |
| 6. The *empress' bed-room* is called the 'pepper-chamber.' | 椒房王后所居 | ˓*Tsíú ˏfóng* ˏwóng hau$^2$ ‘shó ˓kü. |
| 7. A *belfry* is a high part of a building, in which the bell is hung and struck to announce the hour of the day. | 鐘樓高數丈懸鐘撞以報時辰 | ˓*Chung ˏlau* ˓kò shò˒ chéung$^2$ ˏün ˓chung chóng$^2$ ˢí pò$^2$ ˏshí ˏshan. |
| 8. A *brace;* a beam being inserted into a post, then another short piece of timber (i. e. a brace) is let into the post, rising diagonally to support the beam. | 掙角柱鑲橫木另加短木於柱斜掙之 | ˓*Chang kók*˒ ˢch‘ü ˓séung ˏwáng muk$_2$, ling$^2$ ˓ká ‘tün muk$_2$ ˓ü ˢch‘ü ˏts‘é ˓chang ˓chí. |
| 9. *Bricks* are used for constructing walls. | 青甎用築垣墻 | ˓*Ts‘ing ˓chün* yung$^2$ chuk˒ ˏún ˏts‘éung. |
| 10. *Capital* is the top of the column, on which flowers are | 柱碟卽柱頭刻 | ˢ*Ch‘ü típ$_2$* tsik˒ ˢch‘ü ˏt‘au |

## *Notes and Explanations.*

THE principal apartments of houses were enumerated in chap. V., sec. 2., with such parts as are frequently spoken of in domestic affairs. The style of Chinese architecture differs so much from Egyptian, Greek, Roman, Gothic, or any more modern one, that the definitions and descriptions of parts must necessarily differ in some degree accordingly.

6. According to the *Kú Sz' King Lam*, in the times of the Hón dynasty, the walls of the harem were plastered with pepper, from the notion that its pungent properties would dispel or neutralize all noxious vapors in the rooms. From this practice, the phrase is now used to denote the apartments of the empress in the palace.

7. The temples of the Chinese are usually furnished with bells; and they are almost always hung on low frames, so as to be only some six or eight feet from the ground.

9. Sometimes, the Chinese merely dry their bricks in the sun, but they are generally burned sufficiently hard, that when kept out of water, the wall is preserved from rapid decay. Their color is usually a light slate blue, or as the Chinese describe them, *ts‘ing chün*, azure bricks.

| | | |
|---|---|---|
| carved; it rises and spreads out like a plate, at the place where it meets the entablature. | 花起托如碟直<br>接至線盤之處 | hak, ‹fá ʻhí tʻók, ‹ü típ, chik, tsíp, chíʼ sínʼ ‹pʻún ‹chí chʻüʼ. |
| 11. *Cells* are the dormitories of Budhistic priests. | 禪房僧人寢室 | ‹*Shín* ‹*fóng* ‹Tsang ‹yan ʻtsʻam shat,. |
| 12. At the principal gate of the imperial palaces and of temples, four *columns* are erected on stylobates. | 宮殿廟宇頭門<br>四柱竪於地臺 | ‹Kung tínʼ míúʼ ʻü . ‹tʻau ‹mún szʼ ʻ*chʻü* shüʼ ‹ü tíʼ ‹tʻoi. |
| 13. *Cornice* is a narrow piece of carved work, nailed to the wall close adjoining the ceiling. | 花板脚雕花邊<br>釘墻接近花板 | ‹*Fá* ʻ*pán kéuk*, ‹tíú ‹fá ‹pín ‹ting ‹tsʻéung tsíp, kanʼ ‹fá ʻpán. |
| 14. A *cornice* is before and beneath the eaves, extending in a line upon the wall of the house. | 簷口線簷前下<br>出線於墻 | ‹*Ím* ʻhau sínʼ ‹ím ‹tsʻín háʼ chʻut, sínʼ ‹ü ‹tsʻéung. |
| 15. A *court* is opened in front of a hall; it is made for the admission of light and fresh air. | 天井乃堂前開<br>以透光而納凉 | ‹*Tʻín* ʻ*tsing* ʻnái ‹tʻóng ‹tsʻín ‹hoi ʻí tʻauʼ ‹kwóng ‹í náp, ‹léung. |
| 16. In the *palace court*, all the officers were arranged. | 丹墀陳列百官 | ‹*Tán* ‹*chʻí* ‹chʻan lit, pák, ‹kún. |
| 17. The *court yard* is between the hall and gate. | 庭是堂下至門 | ‹*Tʻing* shíʼ ‹tʻóng háʼ chíʼ ‹mún. |
| 18. A *ditch* is a stream of water surrounding the wall of the city, and affording a free ingress into it. | 濠水繞城外可<br>通運入內 | ‹*Hʻò* ʻshui ʻíú ‹shing ngoiʼ ʻhò ‹tʻung wanʼ yap, noiʼ. |
| 19. *Ditch-gate* (or lock) is a gate in the ditch where the water enters the city. | 水關濠水通城<br>之門也 | ʻ*Shui* ‹*kwán* ‹hʻò ʻshui ‹tʻung ‹shing ‹chí ‹mún ʻyá. |
| 20. A *dome* upon the roof of a house is constructed in shape resembling an inverted boiler. | 鑊底頂屋背上<br>造成形如覆鑊 | *Wák,* ʻ*tai* ʻting uk, púiʼ shéungʼ tsòʼ ‹shing ‹ying ‹ü fuk, wák,. |
| 21. *Dome-balls* are made round like pearls, and are placed as mountings on the top of the roof. | 屋頂乃作圓珠<br>置瓦背上爲頂 | *Uk,* ʻ*ting* ʻnái tsók, ‹ün ‹chü chíʼ ʻngá púiʼ shéungʼ ‹wai ʻting. |
| 22. *Door-pivots* are the wooden tenons of the door. | 門樞即木門斗 | ‹*Mún* ‹*shʻü* tsik, muk, ‹mún ʻtau. |
| 23. *Door-posts* are the timbers on the sides of the door. | 門枋門旁之木 | ‹*Mún* ‹*fóng* ‹mún ‹pʻóng ‹chí muk,. |

13. This *fápán kéuk* is within the house; but the term *fápán* might be applied to the frieze, and *fápán kéuk* to the cornice, above the architrave, or rather the lower part of the entablature, in the front of a building.

16. This is the floor of the audience hall, which is said to be sanded with native cinnabar, and where the emperor collects his ministers for consultations.

18. Most, if not all, of the walled cities in China have moats dug around them; but during the long respite which the country has enjoyed from war, they have become in many places obliterated, except where the inhabitants use them as canals. A part of the ditch on the northern side of Canton is used as a rice field, and on the west and east as a thoroughfare for boats.

22. The *door-pivots* are like tenons, one at the top and one at the bottom of the door, and serve instead of hinges on which the door is turned.

| | | |
|---|---|---|
| 24. ***Shop door-posts*** are the small round posts placed erect in the door of the shop to close it up. | 門論子鋪門之企柱以住之 | ˏ*Mún lun*$^{2}$ '*tsz*ʾ p'òʾ ˏmún ꜀chí ˢk'í ˢch'ü ˢí chü$^{2}$ ꜀chí. |
| 25. ***Door-sill*** is also called the threshold. | 閾亦名之門限 | *Kók*$_{2}$ yik$_{2}$ ˏming ꜀chí ˏmún han$^{2}$. |
| 26. ***Door-shutters;*** these shutters are employed, in order to close up the front windows of a shop. | 鋪窓板爲閂鋪窓加以此板 | *P'ò*ʾ ꜀*ch'éung* '*pán* ˏwai ꜀shán p'òʾ ꜀ch'éung ꜀ká ˢí 'ts'zʾ 'pán. |
| 27. The ***eaves*** are at the lower edge of the roof. | 檐屋瓦口之處 | ˏ*Ím* ukʾ ˢngá 'hau ꜀chí ch'üʾ. |
| 28. The ***flying eaves*** are the four corners of the roof of the house, which are made to curl up. | 飛簷乃屋上造成四角捲起 | ꜀*Fí* ˏ*ím* ˢnái ukʾ shéung$^{2}$ tsò$^{2}$ ˏshíng szʾ kókʾ 'kün 'hí. |
| 29. The ***embrasures*** are in the parapet of a wall, and are the places where cannon are set and worked. | 女墻卽城上雉堞亦駕砲之處 | ˢ*Nü* ˏ*ts'éung*ʾ tsikʾ ˏshing shéung$^{2}$ chí$^{2}$ típ$_{2}$ʾ yik$_{2}$ káʾ p'áuʾ ꜀chí ch'üʾ. |
| 30. The ***entablature*** is the wall at the summit of the columns, where it is connected with them. | 線盤乃柱頂之墻起線接柱 | *Sín*ʾ ˏ*p'ún* ˢnái ˢch'ü 'ting ꜀chí ˏts'éung 'hí sínʾ tsípʾ 'ch'ü. |
| 31. A ***fence*** is made of bamboos stuck in the ground, around gardens of flowers and trees. | 籬以竹插地圖種花木 | ˏ*Lí*, ˢí chukʾ ch'ápʾ tí$^{2}$ ˏt'ò chungʾ ꜀fá muk$_{2}$. |
| 32. In ***fish-pools***, the spring water is clear and green. | 池塘春水清綠 | ˏ*Ch'í* ˏ*t'óng* ꜀ch'un 'shui ꜀ts'ing luk$_{2}$. |
| 33. ***Flag-staffs*** are erected without the gate. | 旗杆竪立門外 | ˏ*K'í* ꜀*kón* shü$^{2}$ lap$_{2}$ ˏmún ngoi$^{2}$. |
| 34. A ***foundation*** is now called the 'foot of the wall.' | 基今名爲墻脚 | ꜀*Kí*, ꜀kam ˏming ˏwai ˏts'éung kéukʾ. |
| 35. ***Foundation-stones*** are beneath the steps. | 砌乃階下之石 | *Ch'ai*ʾ ˢnái ꜀kái há$^{2}$ ꜀chí shik$_{2}$. |
| 36. ***Frame of a roof*** is the top of the house; it is framed like the character 金; and also like a dog's thigh, for supporting the purlins. | 狗髀乃屋頂旁頭架金字亦如狗髀以爲承桁 | '*Kau* '*pí* ˢnái ukʾ 'ting ˏp'óng ˏt'au, káʾ ꜀kam tsz$^{2}$, yik$_{2}$ ˏü 'kau 'pí, ˢí ˏwai ˏshing ꜀háng. |

28. In the flying eaves, the resemblance to a tent—the model of the Chinese style of architecture—is seen; these are, however, considered rather as ornaments to the roof, than as component parts, and are most frequently seen on temples, and other large buildings, where it is intended to construct a finished edifice. What are called wings, fishes, dragons, and so forth, (according to the taste of the architect,) may sometimes be seen on the ridge, as well as corners, of the roof.

33. A pair of these flag-staffs may be seen standing before the principal door of almost every magistrate's office and large temple; and sometimes also at the doors of private gentlemen, holding nominal rank, or who have held office in the government. A single post now and then may be seen instead of the two.

36. On account of the great weight of the tiles, Chinese carpenters endeavor to have the expanse of the roof as small as possible, and consequently their large houses are almost always covered with hipped roofs, where the four sides are oblique. They also make the purlins much larger, and place them closer, than is usual in European buildings in order to assist in supporting the tiles at right angles with their courses.

| | | |
|---|---|---|
| 37. A *frieze* is a raised border above the columns upon the entablature. | 腰線乃柱碟上之起線 | ,*Iú sín*' 'nái 'ch'ü típ, shéung² ,chí 'hí sín². |
| 38. A *furnace* for cooking is made of bricks and mortar, and chaldrons are set in it for cooking food. | 竈以磚泥結成置鑊烹煮食物 | *Tsò*' 'í ,chün ,nai kít, ,shing chí' wák, ,p'ang 'ch'ü shik, mat,. |
| 39. *Gables* are the walls on the ends of houses. | 屋飛樓上旁墻 | *Uk*, ,*fí* ,lau shéung² ,p'óng ,ts'éung. |
| 40. The *gable-ears* rise high above the roof of the house on the two ends, and turn up like ears. | 夫捲耳高出瓦上兩傍如捲耳 | ,Fú '*kün* 'í ,kò ch'ut, 'ngá shéung², 'léung ,p'óng ,yü 'kün 'í. |
| 41. A *garden* is for cultivating all kinds of plants and curious flowers in order to sell to the curious. | 園爲栽植百卉奇花以供遊賞 | ,*Ün* ,wai ,ts'oi chik, pák, 'wai ,k'í ,fá 'í 'kung ,yau 'shéung. |
| 42. A *walled garden* is surrounded by a wall, and is designed for the production of fruit-trees. | 圍築墻圍之以種果木也 | ,*Wai* chuk, ,ts'éung ,wai ,chí 'í chung² 'kwó muk, 'yá. |
| 43. The *gate* of a village is called a 'lü.' | 閭乃鄉黨之門 | ,*Lü* 'nái ,héung 'tóng ,chí ,mún. |
| 44. *Go-downs* are the rooms in the basement story. | 土庫卽樓下房 | '*T'ò fú*' tsik, ,lau há² ,fóng. |
| 45. The 'flowery-hall' in an office is the *guest chamber*. | 花廳官家待客 | ,*Fá ,t'ing* ,kún ,ká toi² hák,. |
| 46. The *gutter* is a trough, which is attached to the channels formed by the tiles of the roof. | 水漕乃接瓦坑之水路 | '*Shui ,tsò* 'nái tsíp, 'ngá ,háng ,chí 'shui lò². |
| 47. The *harem* is the utmost interior of the palace, the entrance to which is strictly forbidden. | 禁院宮殿深居封禁不得擅進 | *Kam*² *ün*² ,kung tín² ,sham ,kü ,fung kam² pat, tak, shín² tsun'. |
| 48. *Hinges* of the door are made of brass and iron. | 門較銅鐵造成 | ,*Mún káu*' ,t'ung t'ít, tsò² ,shing. |
| 49. A *magistrate's hall* is a court of justice. | 宮堂治民之堂 | ,*Kung ,t'óng* chí' ,man ,chí ,t'óng. |
| 50. *King-posts* are set upright in the framework of a roof, in order to support the ridge-tree. | 矮仔豎於狗肶架中以助頂梁 | '*Ai 'tsai* shü² ,ü 'kau 'pí ká' ,chung 'í chó² 'ting ,léung. |
| 51. A *knocker* consists of two rings, nailed on the front of the door, to call for it to be opened. | 門環造兩圈釘門面叫門敲之 | ,*Mún ,wán* tsò² 'léung ,ün ,ting ,mún mín² kíú' ,mún ,kò ,chí. |

42. The walled gardens often include extensive orchards of fruit trees, in some parts of the country consisting of the pear, apple, peach, &c. The walls are raised eight or ten feet from the ground, most frequently built of brick; but often too a stockade or ditch surrounds the garden.

43. Gates are constructed over the principal thoroughfare, where it enters the precincts of the village, defining the limits of the place; the sides and lintel are usually ornamented with inscriptions.

44. These go-downs, as they are called in the east, are store-rooms, in which merchandise, provisions, and similar articles are deposited; they are generally spacious, and are sometimes fitted up for offices or counting-rooms in mercantile houses.

| | | |
|---|---|---|
| 52. *Lathing* is made of strips of wood, a little separated from each other, and nailed on the upper part of the room; on these mortar is spread smooth in order to serve in the place of a ceiling made of boards. | 天籠子以木條間踈釘室上加灰蕩滑以代天花板 | *T'ín lung 'tsz'* 'í muk t'íú kán', shó ting shat shéung, ká fúi tóng wát 'í toi t'ín fá 'pán. |
| 53. A *loft* is an upper story of a house; a gallery. | 樓重屋卽閣也 | *Lau* ch'ung uk tsik kók 'yá. |
| 54. A *mold-board* is a raised board, nailed on the sides of the floor close against the walls. | 墻脚線樓板邊貼墻釘木起線 | *Ts'éung kéuk sín'*, lau 'pán pín t'íp ts'éung ting muk 'hí sín'. |
| 55. *Pannels* are set in the middle of doors and windows. | 窓門心鑲凸鼓 | Ch'éung mún sam séung *tut 'kú*. |
| 56. A *park* is where storks, deer, and similar animals are kept and fed. | 囿以爲豢養鶴鹿等物 | *Yau* 'í wai wán 'yéung hók luk 'tang mat. |
| 57. *Pediments;* the plain parts at the ends of the roofs of houses are called the pediments [or honorary portal, Sec. 1:64, page 311]; they are also called *kam tsz'*. | 牌樓屋瓦上旁頭之處曰牌樓一名金字 | *P'ái lau;* uk 'ngá shéung p'óng t'au chí ch'ü, üt p'ái lau; yat ming kam tsz'. |
| 58. A *pillar* is a column of a palace. | 楹乃殿堂之柱 | *Ying* 'nái tín t'óng chí 'ch'ü. |
| 59. A *plate* is the timber which is placed horizontally on the top of the walls, in order to support the rafters. | 水古墻頭上橫木用以承釘桷 | *'Shui 'kú*, ts'éung t'au shéung wáng muk, yung 'í shing ting kók. |
| 60. *Porches* extend all round the outside of the palace. | 廊廡殿下周廊 | *Lóng 'mú* tín há chau lóng. |
| 61. *Purlins* are timbers parallel with the ridge-tree. | 桁乃梁旁橫木 | *Háng* 'nái léung p'óng wáng muk. |
| 62. *Rafters* are placed on the purlins to support the tiles. | 桷駕桁上承瓦 | *Kók* ka háng shéung shing 'ngá. |
| 63. *Inner rafters* are placed beneath the others for their support, on which the roof is built. | 斜角內承桁以爲盖瓦 | *Ts'é kók* noi shing háng 'í wai ko'i 'ngá. |
| 64. For a *summer residence*, a very cool and airy place is selected, in order to escape the summer's heat. | 謝暑軒最凉處夏熱避暑之所 | *Tsé 'shü hín*, tsüi léung ch'ü, há ít pí 'shü chí 'shó. |
| 65. A *retreat* is a place for dwelling at ease in retirement. | 齋乃燕居之所 | *Chái* 'nái ín kü chí 'shó. |
| 66. The *ridge* of a house is covered with tiles. | 屋脊盖梁瓦㼧 | *Uk tsik* k'oi léung 'ngá t'ung. |
| 67. The *ridge-tree* is the timber in the top of the house. | 梁乃屋之正梁 | *Léung*, 'nái uk chí ching léung. |

60. These correspond to the covered walks or porticos which were sometimes built by the Greeks and Jews in front of their great buildings; in this country, they are attached to temples, palaces and other large governmental buildings, and sometimes to private houses.

65. This retreat is sometimes the study of literati; but more commonly it is the residence of wealthy gentlemen who seek for relaxation, by retiring for a time, from the bustle of public life.

| | | |
|---|---|---|
| 68. The 'warm gallery' is a noble lady's *dressing-room*. | 暖閣命婦粧樓 | *'Nün kók*, ming' 'fú ˌchóng ˌlau. |
| 69. A *reading-room* is a place for visitors to read. | 館待賓讀書所 | *'Kún* toi' ˌpan tuk, ˌshü 'shó. |
| 70. A *retiring-room* is a place for the king to retire. | 偏殿王者閒居 | *ˌP'ín tín'* ˌwóng 'ché ˌhán ˌkü. |
| 71. A *screen* is for the support of the monarch. | 屏為人君倚立 | *ˌP'ing* ˌwai ˌyan ˌkwan 'í lap. |
| 72. A *sewer* is a passage for the water, which is poured down beneath a house. | 溝渠乃屋下放水之路 | *ˌKau ˌk'ü* 'nái uk, há' fóng' 'shui ˌchí lò'. |
| 73. The *shaft* is the main body of a column, and sometimes it is fluted for the sake of ornament. | 柱棟即柱身或造成瓜晰 | *'Ch'ü tung'* tsik, 'ch'ü ˌshan wák, tsò' ˌshing ˌkwá chát,. |
| 74. A *shrine* is where idols are placed to be worshiped. | 神龕祀神於內 | *ˌShan ˌhóm* tsz'' ˌshan ˌü noi'. |
| 75. The 'lotus seat' is now called a *shrine* because Budha was seated on carved lotus petals. | 蓮坐今之神位因佛座刻蓮瓣 | *ˌLín tsó'* ˌkam ˌchí ˌshan wai', ˌyan Fat, tsó' hak, ˌlín pín'. |
| 76. The *lares' shrine* is erected in the hall; a small shelf is made to place the images on, where also the ancestral tablets are placed at their side. | 神樓於廳上建小樓祀神或旁奉祖先於其上 | *ˌShan ˌlau*; ˌü ˌt'ing shéung' kín' 'síú ˌlau tsz'' ˌshan; wák, ˌp'ŏng fung' 'tsò ˌsín ˌü ˌk'í shéung'. |
| 77. A *sink* is a railing of bricks built up in a kitchen into which water is thrown. | 水圍以磚築欄於厨內放水 | *'Shui ˌwai*, 'í ˌchün chuk, ˌlán ˌü ˌch'ü noi' fóng' 'shui. |
| 78. A *sink-drain* is a hole in the house into which water is thrown to run off into the sewer. | 滲井乃家內放水落渠之穴 | *Sham' 'tsing* 'nái ˌká noi' fóng' 'shui lók, ˌk'ü ˌchí üt,. |
| 79. *Sleepers* are the timbers which are laid horizontally to support the boards of the floor. | 樓鎮即承樓板之橫木 | *ˌLau chan'* tsik, ˌshing ˌlau 'pán ˌchí ˌwáng muk,. |
| 80. The *water-spout* is a tube attached to the gutter of a roof for conducting off the water. | 水管接水漕之水而流下 | *'Shui 'kún* tsíp, 'shui ˌts'ò ˌchí 'shui ˌí ˌlau há'. |
| 81. A *study* is denominated the 'rue windows.' | 芸窗號曰書齋 | ˌWan ˌch'éung hò' üt, *ˌshü ˌchái*. |
| 82. The *stylobate* (or pedestal) supports the pillar's base. | 地臺以承柱礎 | *Tí' ˌt'oi* 'í ˌshing 'ch'ü 'chó. |

73. Columns are common in Chinese buildings; they are made round, square, &c., of wood, bricks, and stone. The base is small in proportion to the height, and the top is seldom ornamented with a capital, but the plain shaft passes directly from the base to the roof or entablature. The pillars in temples very frequently have inscriptions cut lengthwise upon the shaft in a very elegant manner; such are also engraved upon gateways.

81. The flower here called *wan* is considered by the Chinese as a preservative of books against insects, especially the Lepisma or bookworm; it would be accordingly found among the books of a careful student; *ch'éung* a window is employed in this phrase, because the student

| | | |
|---|---|---|
| 83. The *summer* is a timber placed above the lintel, in order to support the bricks and mortar. | 責泥門楣上承磚泥之木 | *Chak,* ,*nai* ,mún ,mí shéung$^{2}$ ,shing ,chün ,nai ,chí muk,. |
| 84. The *tie-beam* is a timber which is laid horizontally, from the front to the rear walls. | 扯鎮乃前後墻上之橫木 | ‘*Ch‘é chan*’ ‘nái ,ts‘ín hau$^{2}$ ,ts‘éung shéung$^{2}$ ,chí ,wáng muk,. |
| 85. *Tiles* are used for the covering of a house; some are with a concave, and others with a convex, surface. | 瓦以蓋屋上有丨瓪瓦㼧之別 | ‘*Ngá,* ‘í k‘oi’ uk, shéung$^{2}$; ‘yau ‘ngá ‘pán ‘ngá ,t‘ung ,chí pít,. |
| 86. The *green* [glazed] *tiles* are those which are used for covering imperial palaces and temples. | 綠瓦宮殿廟宇能蓋之 | *Luk,* ‘*ngá,* ,kung tín$^{2}$ míú$^{2}$ ‘ü ,nang k‘oi’ ,chí. |
| 87. *Square tiles* turn red after having been burned. | 堦磚燒後轉紅 | ,*Kái* ,*chün* ,shíú hau$^{2}$ ‘chün ,hung. |
| 88. *Turrets* are for watching and guarding against fire; the ‘battle tent’ is made in the same manner. | 敵樓望陣防火戰棚製一用 | *Tik,* ,*lau,* móng$^{2}$ chan$^{2}$ ,fóng ‘fó; chín’ ,p‘áng chai’ yat, yung$^{2}$. |
| 89. A *vestibule,* a vacancy; on both sides of the [principal] door are vacancies, which serve as entrances. | 闕缺也門兩邊缺然爲道者也 | *Hüt,* hüt, ‘yá; ,mún ‘léung ,pín hüt, ,ín ,wai tò$^{2}$ ‘ché ‘yá. |
| 90. The *ún* is a low, and the *ts‘éung* a high, *wall,* surrounding houses; the *pik* is also a wall. | 垣卑墻高屋之圍墻壁亦墻也 | ,*Ün* ,pí, ,ts‘éung ,kò, uk, ,chí ,wai ,*ts‘éung;* pik, yik, ,ts‘éung ‘yá. |
| 91. The *emblazoned wall* is that which is directly in front of temples and magistrates’ offices. | 照壁衙署祠廟之對面墻也 | *Chíú’ pik,* ,ngá ‘ch‘ü ,tsz’ míú$^{2}$ ,chí túi’ mín$^{2}$ ,ts‘éung ‘yá. |
| 92. A *wattle* is made of bamboos framed into trellises, built around gardens. | 籓以竹交加作眼亦爲圍種 | ,*Fán,* ‘í chuk, ,káu ,ká tsók, ‘ngán, yik, ,wai ,wai chung’. |
| 93. *Watch-towers* are high; and there the watchmen beat the hour of the night. They are also named lookout-houses. | 更樓高築晚上巡更又名望樓 | ,*Kang* ,*lau* ,kò chuk, ‘mán shéung$^{2}$ ,tsun ,kang, yau$^{2}$ ,ming móng$^{2}$ ,lau. |
| 94. A *watch-tower* is built very high, for the accommodation of a single watchman. | 白露屋高建中容一人爲候望 | *Pák, lò$^{2}$ uk,* ,kò kín’, ,chung ,yung yat, ,yan ,wai hau$^{2}$ móng$^{2}$. |
| 95. *Shop windows* are horizontal windows, opened on the sides of the door, where goods are exposed for sale. | 鋪窓開橫窓於門旁擺賣貨物 | *P‘ò’* ,*ch‘éung* ,hoi ,wáng ,ch‘éung ,ü ,mún ,p‘óng, ‘pái mái$^{2}$ fò’ mat,. |

sets his table near the window, on account of the light. This is a poetical expression first used by the famous poet Sú Tungpó.

94. This is described in the *Sám Ts‘oi T‘ò* as a small turret-like place, made of bamboo, and covered with hides and lime to protect it from fire-arrows, and elevated on poles inside of the city to several times the height of the wall, for the purpose of watching the approach of enemies without, and the breaking out of fires within, the city.

## Section Third.

# OF SHIPS AND THEIR APPENDAGES.

## 舟楫類第三章

‚Chau chíp‚ lui²; tai² ‚sám ‚chéung.

| | | |
|---|---|---|
| 1. Approaching the shore, *cast anchor* fast in the harbor. | 抵岸拋錨灣泊 | ʻTai ngón² ‚p'áu ‚náu ‚wán pók‚. |
| 2. Soon we shall wish to *weigh anchor*. | 不久就要絞錨 | Pat‚ ʻkau tsau² íú² ʻkáu ‚náu. |
| 3. An *anchor-buoy;* a piece of wood is tied to the anchor, and floating on the surface indicates its position. | 錨泡錨入水繫<br>木浮水面為號 | ‚Náu p'áu², ‚náu yap‚ ʻshui hai² muk‚ ‚fau ʻshui mín² ‚wai hò². |
| 4. The *apron* is within to strengthen the stem. | 頭枕內助頭鰲 | ‚T'au ʻcham noi² chó² ‚t'au ‚ngò. |
| 5. An *awning* is raised to screen off wind and heat. | 篷船上擋風熱 | ‚P'ung ‚shün shéung² ʻtóng ‚fung ít‚. |
| 6. If the ship leaks, quickly *bale* out the water. | 船漏速即戽水 | ‚Shün lau² ts'uk‚ tsik‚ fú² ʻshui. |
| 7. *Ballast* consists of stones which are put into the hold of the ship, in order to prevent it from being overturned. | 壓艙石以石放<br>艙底無傾覆患 | Át‚ ‚ts'óng shik‚ ʻí shik‚ fóng² ‚ts'óng ʻtai, ‚mò ‚k'ing fuk‚ wán². |
| 8. *Bilge water* is the water which leaks into the ship. | 水漬船漏水入 | ʻShui tsik‚ ‚shün lau² ʻshui yap‚. |
| 9. The *binnacle* is near where the pilot [or helmsman] stands in order to guide the helm. | 船尾棚梢公在<br>此把舵 | ‚Shün ʻmí ‚p'áng ‚sháu ‚kung tsoi² ʻts'z' ʻpá ‚t'ó. |
| 10. A *small* [tanka] *boat* carries passengers back and forth. | 細艇渡客往來 | Sai² ʻt'ing tò² hák‚ ʻwóng ‚loi. |
| 11. A *rice boat* is used by agriculturists. | 剗船田家所用 | ʻCh'án ‚shün ‚t'ín ‚ká ʻshó yung². |
| 12. The *dragon boats* are made like a dragon; and on the 5th of the 5th month they engage in the races. | 龍船制如龍形<br>端陽競渡之戲 | ‚Lung ‚shün chai² ‚ü ‚lung ‚ying, ‚tün ‚yéung king² tò² ‚chí hí². |
| 13. *Tanka-boat people* are born and live on the water. | 蛋家水生水養 | Tán² ‚ká ʻshui ‚shang ʻshui ʻyéung. |

### *Notes and Explanations.*

BESIDES the names of ships and boats, and the various implements connected with them, this section also contains some of the terms and phrases peculiar to a seafaring occupation, and to the art of navigation. Some terms, therefore, given in former sections are repeated here. That science which enables the navigator, by the aid of chronometers and celestial observations, to shape his course and determine his position at sea, is quite unknown to the Chinese.

12. The circumstances in which this festival originated are given on page 121. These boats vary in length from fifty to a hundred feet, and are worked by men with short paddles; more than a hundred men may sometimes be seen in a single boat.

13. The term *tán ká*, literally egg families, is derived from the shape of the boats in which these watermen and waterwomen live; they are not unlike eggs in their general contour. These people, by a metonymy not at all unusual in Chinese, are characterized by the buildings they

| | | |
|---|---|---|
| 14. The *skin boats* are made of raw cow-hide in the shape of a trunk [or chest]. | 皮船以生牛皮制如箱形 | ˏ*P'í* ˏ*shün* 'í ˎshang ˏngau ˏp'í chai' ˏü ˎséung ˏying. |
| 15. *Ferry-boats* are those which are employed to carry passengers across from one to the other side of a river. | 橫水渡渡客橫過對岸者 | ˏ*Wáng* '*shui* *tò*2 tò2 hákˎ ˏwáng kwò' túi' ngón2 'ché. |
| 16. *Lodging-boats* are hired out to travelers. | 紫洞艇供遊客 | '*Tsz'* *t'ung*2 '*t'ing*, ˎkung ˏyau hákˎ. |
| 17. *Píntán boats* are the cargo boats for Macao. | 便單澳門載貨 | *Pín*2 ˎ*tán* 'Ó ˏmún tsoi' fó'. |
| 18. A *pleasure-boat* is one for parties of pleasure. | 槎乃遊樂之船 | ˏ*Ch'á* 'nái ˏyau lókˎ ˎchí ˏshün. |
| 19. The *fast-boats* are propelled rapidly by many oars. | 快艇多槳捷走 | *Fái'* '*t'ing* ˎtó 'tséung tsítˎ 'tsau. |
| 20. *Flower-boats* have the delights of beauty and wine. | 花艇花酒宴樂 | ˎ*Fá* '*t'ing* ˎfá 'tsau ín' lókˎ. |
| 21. *Passage-boats* carry passengers to a distance. | 渡船以渡遠客 | *Tò*2 ˏ*shün* 'í tò2 'ün hákˎ. |
| 22. The *post-boats* are used by officers of government. | 站丨官府所坐 | *Chám*2 ˏ*shün* ˎkún 'fú 'shó tsó2. |
| 23. *Fishing-boats* drag nets to catch fish. | 罟丨牽罟捕魚 | '*Kú* ˏ*shün* ˎhín 'kú pò2 'ü. |
| 24. *Salt-boats* are loaded with salt for transportation. | 鹽丨載鹽來往 | ˏ*Ím* ˏ*shün* tsoi' ˏím ˏloi 'wóng. |
| 25. The *sín boats* are somewhat more flat and shallow than the post-boats, and are let to travelers. | 仙丨比站船畧匾而淺供遊客 | ˎ*Sín* ˏ*shün* 'pí chám2 ˏshün léukˎ 'pín ˏí 'ts'ín, ˎkung ˏyau hákˎ. |
| 26. The *crab boats* have many oars, and are very swift. | 快蟹槳多極快 | *Fái'* '*hái* 'tséung ˎtó kikˎ fái'. |
| 27. The *beams* are horizontal rafters for supporting the planking of the deck. | 櫃鎮承船板之橫桁 | *Kwai*2 *chan'* ˏshing ˏshün 'pán ˎchí ˏwáng ˎháng. |
| 28. The *bows* of a junk are vulgarly named 'long lips'. | 船頭俗名暢嘴 | ˏ*Shün* ˏ*t'au* tsukˎ ˏming ch'éung' 'tsui. |
| 29. The *bowsprit* is the mast in the stem. | 頭弼船頭之桅 | ˏ*T'au* *pak*ˎ ˏshün ˏt'au ˎchí wai2. |
| 30. The *bowsprit bumpkin* is a horizontal timber, through which ropes are reeved. | 頭弼橫擔通繩之橫木 | ˏ*T'au* *pak*ˎ ˏ*wáng* ˎtám ˎt'ung ˏshing ˎchí ˏwáng mukˎ. |
| 31. A boat is *breamed* by burning straw beneath it. | 燂船以草灼底 | '*Tám* ˏ*shün* 'í 'ts'ò chéukˎ 'tai. |
| 32. Two masted vessels (or *brigs*), and three masted vessels (or ships), are foreign vessels. | 兩枝桅船三枝桅船亦番舶也 | '*Léung* ˎ*chí* ˏ*wai* ˏ*shün*, ˎsám ˎchí ˏwai ˏshün, yikˎ ˎfán pókˎ 'yá. |

occupy; they are generally poor and illiterate, and those living ashore affect to hold them in contempt. They get their living by ferryage and fishing.

17. These boats are in every respect like other lighters; the name is apparently a local one, for which no other reason can be found than the caprice of the proprietors.

20. These are sometimes occupied by those who have a good reputation for sobriety and chastity; those of an opposite character are, however, their most common occupants,—being places of dissipation, and the retreats of the abandoned.

| | | |
|---|---|---|
| 33. The *bulwarks* are boards built up one story high on the side to defend against the waves. | 旱旁另作板旁<br>一層以防浪 | ʻ*Hón ˏpʻóng* lingˀ tsók, ʻpán ˏpʻóng yat, ˏtsʻang ʻí ˏfóng lóngˀ. |
| 34. The *cabin* is the place where the captain or passengers or supercargoes reside. | 船尾房乃船主<br>客商所居 | ˏ*Shün ʻmí ˏfóng* ʻnái ˏshün ʻchü hák, ˓shéung ʻsho ˓kü. |
| 35. The *cable* is attached to the anchor in the water. | 錨纜繫錨下水 | ˏ*Náu lám*ˀ haiˀ ˏnáu háˀ ʻshui. |
| 36. The *cap* is a plank made with two holes to join two masts closely together. | 桅帽以木造穿<br>二圈為駁二喘 | ˏ*Wai mò*ˀ ʻí muk, tsòˀ ˓chʻün íˀ ˓hün ˏwai pók, íˀ ʻchʻün. |
| 37. The *capstan* is placed in the middle of the ship's [deck], either for the purpose of raising heavy things, or for hoisting the yards, or similar uses. | 絞盤置船之中<br>或起重物及帆<br>杠等 | ʻ*Káu ˏpʻún* chíʼ ˏshün ˓chí ˓chung, wák, ʻhí chungˀ mat,, kap, ˏfán kóngʼ ʻtang. |
| 38. The ship's *captain* is the person who has the general control in the ship. | 船主乃船中統<br>理之人 | ˏ*Shün ʻchü* ʻnái ˏshün ˓chung ʻtʻung ʻlí ˓chí ˏyan. |
| 39. *Cat-heads;* when the anchor is hove up, these are for supporting and hanging it. | 錨拮起錨得以<br>挂之 | ˏ*Náu kat,* ʻhí ˏnáu tak, ʻí kwáʼ ˓chí. |
| 40. For *caulking*, bamboo shavings are used. | 打捍乃用竹絲 | ʻ*Tá ˓cháng* ʻnái yungˀ chuk, ˓sz'. |
| 41. The *chains* are the planks below the dead-eyes. | 鷄翼三星下木 | ˓*Kai yik,* ˓sám ˓sing háˀ muk,. |
| 42. *Cruizers* go out to reconnoitre smugglers. | 巡船出海緝私 | ˏ*Tsʻun ˏshün* chʻut, ʻhoi tsʻap, ˓sz'. |
| 43. The *cut-water* is on the bow of the ship at the point where the waves are divided. | 鵝膝船頭破浪<br>之處 | ˏ*Ngó sò*ʼ ˏshün ˏtʻaupʻóʼ lóngˀ ˓chí chʻüʼ. |
| 44. *Davits* are for suspending the boat. | 拮鷄為吊三板 | ˓*Kat ˓kai* ˏwai tíúʼ ˓sám ʻpán. |
| 45. *Dead-eyes* are below the gunwale; laniards are secured to them, which have ratlines thickly spread upon them. | 三星在大根下<br>繫繩密佈成梯 | ˓*Sám ˓sing,* tsoiˀ táiˀ ˓kan háˀ haiʼ ˏshing, mat, pòʼ ˏshing ˓tʻai. |
| 46. The *deck* consists of the planks on the top of the ship. | 櫃面船面之板 | *Kwai*ˀ *mín*ˀ ˏshün mínˀ ˓chí ʻpán. |

31. This is a very common operation performed upon Chinese vessels of all sizes. Old custom, strong as the laws of the country, forbids the bottoms to be coppered or sheathed, and consequently filth collects very rapidly, and even in despite of the greatest care soon destroys the vessel.

37. Many of the terms in this chapter for the parts of a ship are known only to those conversant with foreign vessels; the capstan is an instance, no native vessels having them.

42. These vessels are of a beautiful model for rowing boats, being fifty to seventy feet long, sharp in the bows, and low in the middle; they carry a small gun on the bow. When pulled by fifty or sixty oarsmen, they will advance probably at the rate of ten or fifteen miles an hour. The fast-crab boats are similar to them in shape, &c., and are used in this region principally by smugglers and fishermen.

| | | |
|---|---|---|
| 47. A ship's *deck* consists of the boards which are on the upper part of the vessel, covering the hold. | 艙板乃船面盖<br>艙之板 | *Ts'óng 'pán* 'nái shün mín k'oi ts'óng chí 'pán. |
| 48. The *gun-deck* and the lowest deck are both within the hold of the vessels as two decks, being made like stories. | 二層櫃三層櫃<br>即倉內間爲二<br>層如樓也 | *Í ts'ang kwai*, sám ts'ang kwai, tsik ts'óng noi kán wai í ts'ang ü lau 'yá. |
| 49. The *fashion-piece* is scarfed into the stern-post as a brace to secure it to the keel. | 尾枕鑲於尾鰲<br>之角並助底骨 | '*Mí 'cham* séung ü 'mí ngò chí kók ping chó 'tai kwat. |
| 50. A *fid* is for joining two masts that the upper one may stand firmly. | 桅枷以爲續二<br>喘高竪 | *Wai ká* 'í wai tsuk í 'ch'ün kò shü. |
| 51. The *figure-head* is a painting of a tiger's head upon the bow in order to decline seeing the god of the sea. | 免朝牌舡首虎<br>頭牌海神免朝 | '*Mín chíú pái* shün 'shau 'fú t'au pái 'hoi shan 'mín ch'íú. |
| 52. *Flags;* the Chinese have no national flag to distinguish their vessels, but every vessel may hoist a flag of its own, for a mark of distinction. | 船旗唐國本無<br>旗號各船或豎<br>乃自立亻號耳 | *Shün k'í;* T'óng kwók 'pún mò k'í hò, kók shün wák shü 'nái tsz' lap shün hò 'í. |
| 53. The *flag-pole* is hung upon the mast. | 横纛懸於檣間 | *Wáng tuk* ün ü ts'éung kán. |
| 54. The *foot-waling* is in the ship's hold, nailed on as a ceiling upon the ribs. | 隔水旁在船肚<br>內釘蓋彎柴 | *Kák 'shui p'óng* tsoi shün 't'ò noi ting k'oi wán ch'ái. |
| 55. The *gangway* is where the ladder is placed, and is the opening for ascending and descending. | 水仙門置梯上<br>落之門 | '*Shui sín mún* chí t'ai 'shéung lók chí mún. |
| 56. The *gangway-ladder* is for getting up and down. | 船梯渡人上落 | *Shün t'ai tò* yan 'shéung lók. |
| 57. An *eight-oared gig* is only for reconnoitering and carrying men; it is not for attacking pirates. | 八槳船但可供<br>哨探不能擊賊 | *Pát 'tséung shün* tán 'hó kung shau t'ám, pat nang kik ts'ák. |
| 58. A *grappling-iron* is an anchor; it is made with four flukes, for easily anchoring fast the vessel. | 錠亦錨也制成<br>四鈎泊船易定 | *Ting* yik náu 'yá; chai shing sz' kau, pók shün í ting. |

51. The tiger's head is most distinctly seen upon the bows of small governmental cruizers, but it is depicted, either in part or whole, upon nearly all large vessels; it answers to the figure-head upon foreign ships. The superstitious mariner, dreading a visit from the Neptune of his imagination, depicts a tiger's head upon his bows, in order to terrify him, and thus, *mín ch'íú*, decline an audience.

53. The streamers and weather-vanes attached to junks and other vessels are run up the mast as usual, but when the flag bears an inscription, it is fastened to a pole, that is suspended from the mast head about half way down, and secured by another line passing from its handle to the mast, so that the flag hangs obliquely, and blows out with the least wind.

| | | |
|---|---|---|
| 59. The *gunwale* is the large timber on the side of the ship. | 大根爲船旁之大木 | *Tái kan* wai shün p'óng chí tái muk. |
| 60. *Halliards* are for raising and lowering sails. | 哩纜絞哩上落 | *Lí lám* 'káu 'lí 'shéung lók. |
| 61. *Hatchways* are covered by hatches. | 艙口蓋以揜艙 | *Ts'óng 'hau* k'oi' 'í 'k'am ts'óng. |
| 62. In order to turn the vessel's head, turn the *helm*. | 舟轉頭卽攀柁 | Chau 'chün t'au tsik 'pán *t'ó*. |
| 63. The *main hold* of the ship is the hold near the mast, in which the goods are stored. | 桅夾艙近桅之艙爲裝載貨物 | *Wai káp ts'óng* kan wai chí ts'óng, wai chóng tsoi' fó' mat. |
| 64. An *hourglass* is for determining the ship's progress. | 沙漏以訂船行 | *Shá lau* 'í ting' shün hang. |
| 65. The *hull* is the empty body of a ship. | 船殼乃空丨身 | *Shün hók* 'nái hung shün shan. |
| 66. The *jib-boom* is the second mast [which is placed in the bowsprit]. | 頭弼標乃第二節也 | *T'au pak píú* 'nái tai í tsít 'yá. |
| 67. The *flying jib-boom* is the third mast [in the bowsprit]. | 三嘴頭弼標乃第三節也 | *Sám 'ch'ün t'au pak píú* 'nái tai sám tsít 'yá. |
| 68. *Junks* are able to pass on the high seas. | 艚船能過重洋 | *Ts'ò shün* nang kwó' ch'ung yéung. |
| 69. The *keel* is the timber at the bottom of a vessel. | 底骨船底之木 | *'Tai kwat* shün 'tai chí muk. |
| 70. The *kelson* is let down close to the keel in order to secure and strengthen the ribs. | 裡籠貼近以夾助彎柴 | *'Lí lung* t'íp kan 'í káp chó wán ch'ái. |
| 71. The *knight-heads* are for clasping and securing the bowsprit. | 將軍柱以爲夾堅頭弼 | *Tséung kwan* 'ch'ü 'í wai káp shü t'au pak. |
| 72. *Leechlines* are fastened to the sail to hold it in sailing; [an order is] "hold the leechlines slack, and not clue them." | 繚絲繫哩牽駛揸生繚勿死繚 | *Líú* sz' hai 'lí hín 'shai, chá shang líú, mat 'sz' líú. |
| 73. *Lighters* are used for transporting goods. | 西瓜扁以駁貨 | *Sai kwá 'pín* 'í pók fó'. |

64. The Chinese junks that go to the islands of the Archipelago are often navigated by Portuguese of Macao, the Chinese themselves having no charts or instruments of any value, excepting the compass and hourglass.

68. The word junk is of eastern origin, now exclusively applied to the largest vessels of the Chinese and Japanese. The Chinese junks are known by the high stern, split open half its length, and without a stern-post, and by the lip-like bows, with a large eye pointed or carved on each side. The model from which a junk was first derived is said by the Chinese to have been a monstrous fish; the fancied resemblance is kept up in the eyes, the mouth, and teeth painted on the bow, a frisking tail in the high stern, &c. The registered tonnage of the largest which come to this port does not probably exceed five hundred tons.

72. The leechlines are numerous, a line being fastened to each fold of the sail, and each one joined at different angles to two large ropes, leading aft to the rudder, so that the helmsman can shift the sail according to the wind.

| | | |
|---|---|---|
| 74. The *sounding line* is used to ascertain the depth of the water; it is now called the sounding lead. | 龍純用試水深淺今名爲沁鉈 | ˏ*Lung* ˏ*shün* yung$^{2}$ shíʼ ʻshui ˓sham ʻtsʻín; ˓kam ˏming ˏwai tsamʼ ˏtʻó. |
| 75. The *martingal* is morticed into the bowsprit for the purpose of leading the ropes through to the jib-boom. | 倒吊鑲於頭弼中引繩通標尾 | ʻ*Tò tíú*ʼ ˓séung ˓ü ˏtʻau pat$_{2}$ ˓chung ʻyan ˏshing ˓tʻung ˓píú ʻmí. |
| 76. Sails are spread on the *mast* to take the wind; a *wai* is the sail-pole of a small vessel. | 檣掛帆使風者桅小舟帆竿也 | ˏ*Tsʻéung* kwáʼ ˏfán ʻshai ˓fung ʻché; ˏwai ʻsíú ˓chau ˏfán ˓kón ʻyá. |
| 77. *Fore-mast*, *main-mast*, and *mizzen-mast*, are the names of the masts in foreign ships. | 頭桅大桅尾桅乃番船之桅名 | ˏ*Tʻau* ˏ*wai*, *tái*$^{1}$ ˏ*wai*, ʻ*mí* ˏ*wai*$_{1}$, ʻnái ˓fán ˏshün ˓chí ˏwai ˏming. |
| 78. *Masts* in foreign vessels have three divisions, joined together and standing; each division has its own name, making the topmast, topgallant-mast and royal-mast. | 番桅有三節纘豎每節分呼爲二三四喘而名 | ˓Fán ˏ*wai* ʻyau ˓sám tsít$_{1}$, tsuk$_{2}$ shü$^{2}$; ʻmúi tsít$_{1}$ ˓fan ˓fú ˏwai í$^{2}$ ˓sám sz$^{1}$ ʻchʻün ˏí ˏming. |
| 79. Lower the *mast*, and there is no fear of running under. | 落桅不防駛低 | Lók$_{2}$ ˏ*wai* pat$_{1}$ ˏfóng ʻshai ˓tai. |
| 80. The *chief mate* is at the head of the sailors, and is thoroughly acquainted with the channels and courses of the waters. In large ships, there are two or three mates, and they are, therefore, designated first mate, second mate, and third mate. | 伙長即梢公熟識水道船大用二三名故叉有大伙二伙三伙之稱 | ʻ*Fó* ʻ*chéung*, tsik$_{1}$ ˓shau ˓kung, shuk$_{2}$ shik$_{1}$ ʻshui tò$^{2}$. ˏShün tái$^{1}$ yung$^{2}$ í$^{2}$ ˓sám ˏming, kúʼ yau$^{2}$ ʻyau tái$^{1}$ ʻfó, í$^{2}$ ʻfó, ˓sám ʻfó ˓chí ˓chʻing. |
| 81. Tanka boats require *bow mats* to screen them. | 小艇要蓋頭篷 | ʻSíú ʻtʻing íúʼ kʻoiʼ ˏ*tʻau* ˏ*pʻung*. |
| 82. *Measure* the dimensions of the ship. | 丈量船之大小 | *Chéung*$^{2}$ ˏ*léung* ˏshün ˓chí tái$^{1}$ ʻsíú. |
| 83. Cruisers are likewise called *men-of-war*, and also designated military vessels. | 師船又曰戰船兵丨也 | ˓Szʼ ˏshün yau$^{2}$ üt$_{2}$ *chínʼ* ˏ*shün*, ˓ping ˏshün ʻyá. |
| 84. The *ship's name* is written on her stern. | 船名寫於船尾 | ˏ*Shün* ˏ*ming* ʻsé ˓ü ˏshün ʻmí. |
| 85. *Oars* are rowed to propel the boat. | 槳棹船以渡水 | ʻ*Tséung* cháu$^{2}$ ˏshün ʻí tò$^{1}$ ʻshui. |
| 86. The *oar-tie* is fitted upon the *oar-post*. | 丨耳扣住槳椏 | ʻ*Tséung* ʻí kʻauʼ chü$^{1}$ ʻ*tséung* ˓*á*. |

79. The foot of the mast in Chinese vessels is usually let into a socket in the deck; on each side of this hole, a thick plank or timber is firmly morticed into the deck, both of them forming a stock, which, with the addition of pins or boards crosswise, inclose the mast. By taking out the after pins, the mast can easily and quickly be let down upon deck.

84. Not only does the stern of Chinese merchantmen bear the name of the vessel, but it is often decorated with paintings of flowers, a phœnix standing on one leg, pictures of demigods, &c.; or with short sentences indicative of the hap-hazard nature of seafaring occupations: as, "May favorable winds attend you;" "With fair winds make profit;" "Fair winds are a great happiness;" &c.

| | | |
|---|---|---|
| 87. *Oiling* the bottom of a boat makes her sail well. | 哨油船底好駛 | *Shâu*' ꜀*yau* ꜀shün ʿtai ʿhò ʿshai. |
| 88. *Paddles* are shorter than an oar, and they are used in boats by grasping them with the hand to paddle. | 扒短於槳三板中用手持以扒 | ꜀*P'á* ʿtün ꜀ü ʿtséung ꜀sám ʿpán ꜀chung yung$^{2}$ ʿshau ꜀ch'í ʿí ꜀p'á. |
| 89. The *pilot* is the man at the helm. | 梢公把柁之人 | ꜀*Shau* ꜀*kung* ʿpá ꜀t'ó ꜀chí ꜀yan. |
| 90. A *pinnace* (or gig) carries goods off and on. | 三板駁貨開埋 | ꜀*Sám* ʿ*pán* pók꜇ fò' ꜀hoi ꜀mai. |
| 91. The *pintles* are for hooking the rudder. | 柁鈎以爲勾者 | ꜀*T'ó* ꜀*kau* ʿí ꜀wai ꜀kau ʿché. |
| 92. A *poop-railing* is built up at the stern in order to lean against and look abroad. | 欄河船尾加欄以爲凭眺 | ꜀*Lán* ꜀*hó* ꜀shün ʿmí ꜀ká ꜀lán ʿí ꜀wai ꜀p'ang t'iú'. |
| 93. *Port-holes* are opened in the bulwarks. | 炮門開在旱旁 | *Páu*' ꜀*mún* ꜀hoi tsoi$^{2}$ ʿhón ꜀p'óng. |
| 94. A *pully* is secured to the mast for hoisting the sail. | 轆轤繫桅扯悝 | *Luk*꜇ ꜀*ló* hai$^{2}$ ꜀wai ʿch'é ʿlí. |
| 95. The *pump* by working is used to raise the water in the ship's hold. | 拖水嘜用以絞船底上水 | ꜀Tó ʿshui *póm*', yung$^{2}$ ʿí ʿkáu ꜀shün ʿtai ʿshéung ʿshui. |
| 96. The *quarter-pieces* are joined to the gunwale, and are crooked timbers scarfed into the transom. | 曲爭縛大根而曲鑲爲尾旁 | *Huk*꜇ ꜀*chang* pók꜇ tái$^{2}$ ꜀kan ꜀í huk꜇ ꜀séung ꜀wai ʿmí ꜀p'óng. |
| 97. A *raft* is the name of the modern bamboo float. | 竹筏今之竹排 | Chuk꜇ *fat*꜇ ꜀kam ꜀chí chuk꜇ ꜀p'ái. |
| 98. In sailing, lookout for sand-banks and *rapids*. | 駛船最怕炕灘 | ʿShai ꜀shün tsui' p'á' hóng' ꜀*tán*. |
| 99. Write the *register* of her tonnage. | 寫載位運貨物 | ʿSé *tsoi*' *wai*$^{2}$ wan$^{2}$ fò' mat꜇. |
| 100. The *ribs* are the crooked timbers within the ship. | 彎柴船內曲木 | ꜀*Wán* ꜀*ch'ái* ꜀shün noi$^{2}$ huk꜇ muk꜇. |
| 101. At sunset, rock a boat and *row* an oar. | 日落泛舟棹槳 | Yat꜇ lók꜇ fán' ꜀chau *cháu*' ʿtséung. |
| 102. A ship answers as she is turned by a *rudder*. | 尾柁轉運憑之 | ʿ*Mí* ꜀*t'ó* ʿchün wan$^{2}$ ꜀p'ang ꜀chí. |
| 103. The *rudder-ropes* extend from the stern to the bow clasping the sides of the vessel, and are fastened to the rudder. | 勒肚自首至尾勒船肚而繫舵 | *Lak*꜇ ʿ*t'ò* tsz'$^{2}$ ʿshau chí' ʿmí lak꜇ ꜀shün ʿt'ò ꜀í hai$^{2}$ ʿt'ó. |
| 104. The *sails* are bent for sailing. | 悝揚掛駛船行 | ʿ*Lí* ꜀*yéung* kwá' ʿshai ꜀shün ꜀hang. |

89. This *shaukung*, who answers somewhat nearly to the chief mate in European vessels, corresponds very exactly to the *gubernator* of the Romans. He sets at the helm, gives orders for managing the sails, oars, &c.; he frequently hires the crew, and always receives higher wages than the other sailors. It is his part to know the signs of the weather, currents, ports, &c.

104. The character *li* is a vulgar one, used in this region to denote sails; *p'ang* is the term for those made of matting. The matting is made from the culms of different kinds of rushes, at first woven in pieces about three feet square, and then sowed together in one sail. In order to support the body of the sail, several light bamboos are secured to it, each of which passes through a traveler or rope that surrounds the mast, thus preventing the sail from beating to pieces in the wind, and keeping it close to the wind in sailing. In small boats, there are no bamboos attached to the sail, except as yards above and below.

| | | |
|---|---|---|
| 105. If the wind is high, *take in sail*, and you can go on. | 風猛減哩能行 | Fung máng *kám lí* nang hang. |
| 106. With a fair wind, *hoist sail* and start off. | 順風扯哩開身 | Shun fung *ché lí* hoi shan. |
| 107. *Wear sail* so as to take the side wind. | 轉篷爲駛橫風 | *Chün p'ung* wai shai wáng fung. |
| 108. A *sprit-sail* is a small sail for use in light winds, it is set forward of the bow. | 頭緝船頭外之小風帆也 | *T'au ts'ap*, shün t'au ngoi chí síú fung fán yá. |
| 109. *Sailors* are the workmen on board of a ship; they are likewise called "water-hands." | 梢船上工人亦名水手 | *Shau* shün shéung kung yan; yik ming shui shau. |
| 110. *Wild scow;* whoever wishes to pass a river in it, uses a long line by which he pulls to the opposite bank. | 野航但渡水用長索牽扺彼岸 | *Yé hóng* tán tò shui yung, ch'éung sók hín tai pí ngón. |
| 111. *Sculls* are worked on the quarters instead of a rudder. | 船旁橈櫓代柁 | Shün p'óng íú lò toi t'ó. |
| 112. Add a *bow scull*, and it will be easy to turn the boat. | 加頭梢易轉動 | Ká *t'au shau* í chün tung. |
| 113. The scull is worked upon the *scull-pin*. | 櫓率貫櫓橈之 | *Lò sut*, kún lò íú chí. |
| 114. *Scuppers* are those places where the water runs off. | 水仙門放水處 | *Shui sín mún* fóng shui ch'ü. |
| 115. Entice a man aboard, then take up the *shore-board*. | 騙人上船拔跳 | P'ín yan shéung shün pát *t'íú*. |
| 116. *Fishing smacks* cast their nets on the broad ocean. | 拖船大海拖網 | *T'ó shün* tái hoi t'ó móng. |
| 117. The *spanker-boom* is the lower yard of the sail. | 尾送哩下之木 | *Mí sung* lí há chí muk. |
| 118. *Splicing of ropes* is done by joining two ropes together in such a manner as to make one. | 續纜以兩纜續而爲一 | *Tsuk lám* í léung lám tsuk í wai yat. |
| 119. *Stanchions* are set up to support the boards of the side. | 企柱豎夾板旁 | *K'í ch'ü* shü káp pán p'óng. |
| 120. The *steamboat* has wheels; these are set in motion by steam, and turning in the water, move it rapidly. | 烟船有輪烟熏輪轉攪水速行 | *In shün* yau lun; in fan lun chün, káu shui ts'uk hang. |
| 121. The *stem* is inclined and scarfed into the keel. | 頭鰲直貫底骨 | *T'au ngò* chik kún tai kwat. |
| 122. The *sternpost* is the inclined timber in the ship's stern, and it extends down to the keel. | 尾鰲夾船尾之直木通至底骨 | *Mí ngò* káp shün mí chí chik muk, t'ung chí tai kwat. |
| 123. *Stocks* are the timbers which support the mast. | 桅夾夾桅之木 | *Wai káp* káp wai chí muk. |

106. This sail is sometimes seen in large junks, bent to a yard which is run out upon a kind of movable bowsprit, and having the sheets fastened to the lips of the bow. It is made of canvas, and very seldom used.

112. The scull in the bows of a boat differs from those in the stern, in being longer and larger, and is only used for the purpose of guiding the boat.

115. This is a proverb, meaning to deceive one; invite a person aboard, and then pull in the shore-board, when he must either go with the crew, or run the risk of drowning in jumping ashore.

| | | |
|---|---|---|
| 124. ***Studding-sails*** are set on both sides of the ship, when there are light winds. | 左右插花加悝<br>於旁細風卽用 | ꜂Tsó yau[2] *chʻáp*, *꜀fá* ꜀ká ꜂lí ꜀ü ꜀pʻóng, sai[3] ꜀fung tsik, yung[2]. |
| 125. The *taffrail-rail* is a frame made of bamboo, placed on the stern, or on the two quarters. | 船架揦以竹欄<br>丨尾或兩旁 | *꜀Shün kʻá[3] lát,* ꜂í chuk, ꜀lán ꜀shün ꜂mí wák[2] ꜂léung ꜀pʻóng. |
| 126. The *tank* contains the water in a ship. | 水櫃盛水於船 | *꜂Shui kwai[2]* shing[2] ꜂shui ꜀ü ꜀shün. |
| 127. The full *tide* in the morning is called *chʻiú*. | 朝水漲卽爲潮 | ꜀Chʻíú ꜂shui chéung[3] tsik, ꜀wai *꜀chʻíú*. |
| 128. The full *tide* in the evening is called *tsik*. | 晚水長乃曰汐 | ꜂Mán ꜂shui ꜂chéung ꜂nái üt[2] *tsik[2]*. |
| 129. When it is *high tide*, the vessel can be floated. | 水大順水推船 | *꜂Shui tái[2]* shun[2] ꜂shui ꜀tʻúi ꜀shün. |
| 130. With an *ebb tide* running contrary, it is hard to go. | 水乾逆流難行 | *꜂Shui ꜀kón* yik[2] ꜀lau ꜀nán ꜀hang. |
| 131. The *tiller* is a stick which is fitted into the rudder-post, to take hold of in steering the ship. | 柁杠橫鑲而用<br>得以揸手攀駛 | *꜀Tʻó kóng[3]* ꜀wáng ꜀séung ꜀í yung[2], tak, ꜂í ꜀chá ꜂shau ꜀pʻán ꜂shai. |
| 132. In the *tops* is the place where marines are concealed, in order to discharge arrows against the enemy. | 桅盤舟師伏於<br>其上放箭攻敵 | *꜀Wai ꜀pʻún* ꜀chau ꜀sz[3] fuk[2] ꜀ü ꜀kʻí shéung[2], fóng[3] tsín[3] ꜀kung tik[2]. |
| 133. A *topsail* is the sail of the upper yards in a Chinese vessel. | 頭巾頂唐船頭<br>喘悝也 | *꜀Tʻau ꜀kan ꜂ting* ꜀Tʻóng ꜀shün ꜀tʻau ꜂chʻün ꜂lí ꜂yá. |
| 134. *Tow a boat*; when the boat cannot move, then use another one, to which being fastened by a rope she is draged forward, and so made to advance. | 嚹船船不能行<br>用別丨繫纜牽<br>導而行 | *Nái[3] ꜀shün;* ꜀shün pat, ꜀nang ꜀hang, yung[2] pít[2] ꜀shün hai[2] lám[2] ꜀hín tò[2] ꜀í ꜀hang. |
| 135. When it is calm, *track* the boat with ropes. | 無風牽纜行船 | ꜀Mò ꜀fung *꜀hín lám[2]* ꜀hang ꜀shün. |
| 136. When the water is shallow use *tracking-poles*. | 篙水淺卽撑之 | *꜀Kò* ꜂shui ꜂tsʻín tsik, ꜀chʻáng ꜀chí. |
| 137. The *transoms* are below the gunwale, and attached close to the stern. | 尾當貼近船尾<br>大根之下 | *꜂Mí ꜀tóng* tʻíp, kan[2] ꜀shün ꜂mí tái[2] ꜀kan ꜀chí há[2]. |

125. This is a strong frame, made for the purpose of containing boxes, spears, provisions, and other loose articles, and is placed upon both quarters, and on the stern like a gallery. It projects over the side two or three feet; there are sometimes two, one above the other.

132. In ancient times, the Chinese had vessels of war furnished with spearmen and archers, and some of the latter were placed in the tops. Bows and arrows may sometimes be seen in ships at the present day.

133. This sail is usually made of canvas, and rigged at the top of the main or fore-mast upon a light spar, like a gaff-sail. Topsails and those above them in foreign vessels are named from the yards; as *tai sám fán kóng lí*, the topgallant-sail, and so for the others.

135. Tracking is very common among the Chinese, when traveling on canals and rivers. Instead of horses, human strength is employed. Long lines, at one end fastened to the tops of the masts, are taken hold of at the other by men and boys on the banks of the stream, by which means, without wind or tide, boats are easily moved at the rate of three or four miles an hour.

| | | |
|---|---|---|
| 138. A *weather-vane* is placed on the top of the mast. | 風信旗竪桅尾 | ‹*Fung san*' ‹*k'i* shü[2] ‹wai ʿmí. |
| 139. *Wales* are the horizontal timbers laid upon the ribs. | 旁爲横架彎柴 | ‹*P'óng* ‹wai ‹wáng ká' ‹wán ‹ch'ái. |
| 140. *Wheel* [rudder] of a ship; when the rudder is to be raised up high, then this is used to elevate it. | 柁絞起高柁即用絞之 | ‹*T'ó ʿkáu*; ʿhí ‹kò ‹t'ó, tsik, yung[2] ʿkáu ‹chí. |
| 141. *Whirlpools* are places that ought to be avoided. | 攪流處要關防 | ʿ*Káu* ‹*lau* ch'ü' íú' ‹kwán ‹fong. |
| 142. Let no *head winds* be met by you. | 莫遇係頂頭風 | Mók[2] yü[2] hai[2] ʿ*ting* ‹*t'au* ‹*fung*. |
| 143. Assuredly *fair winds* will attend you. | 必定順風相送 | Pít, ting[2] *shun*[2] ‹*fung* ‹séung sung'. |
| 144. With a *foul wind* you must reduce the sail. | 逆風駕駛勾篷 | *Yik*[2] ‹*fung* ká' ʿshai ‹kau ‹p'ung. |
| 145. The *windlass* is secured in the bow of the ship for heaving up the anchor. | 猪籠絞置船頭以爲絞錨 | ‹*Chü* ‹*lung* ʿ*káu* chí' ‹shün ‹t'au ʿí ‹wai ʿkáu ‹náu. |
| 146. *Yards* are the horizontal spars supporting the sails; there are three tiers of sails, and therefore these are named main, topsail, and topgallant, yards. | 帆杠乃駕帆横木有帆三層即分名爲大二三嘴帆杠 | ‹*Fán kóng*' ʿnái ká' ‹fán ‹wáng muk[2]; ʿyau ‹fán ‹sám ‹ts'ang, tsik, ‹fan ‹ming ‹wai tái[2], í[2], ‹sám ʿch'ün ‹fán kóng'. |

139. The channel wale of a junk is a very large timber, laid upon the outside of the ribs, often projecting from the side of the hull so much as to give it a flattened apprearance. In Chinese men-of-war, the upper wales are smaller, and do not project so much as in junks; the largest and upper wale is the *tái kan* (No. 59) or gunwale of the vessel.

140. The rudder of a junk is very large, compared with that of a ship; it takes the place in a great measure of a keel in keeping the vessel to the wind, and is managed by a tiller proportionably large; it is hoisted by a wheel in shallow water. The rudder itself has numerous rhomboidal holes cut in it, from a notion that the eddying of the water through them causes more resistance than a plain board.

## Section Fourth.

## OF CARRIAGES AND SEDANS.

### 車輿類第四章

‹Kü ‹yü lui[2]; tai[2] sz' ‹chéung.

| | | |
|---|---|---|
| 1. The *axletree* is a horizontal timber for joining the naves. | 軸横木以貫轂 | *Chau*[2] ‹wáng muk[2] ʿí kún' kuk,. |

### *Notes and Explanations.*

WHEELED CARRIAGES are but little used in China, especially in the southern and eastern parts, and in the vicinity of the large rivers, where boats are made to serve in their stead; most of those

| | | |
|---|---|---|
| 2. *Poles of the axle* are its two ends in the nave. | 轊軸兩頭貫轂 | *Wai² chau²* ˢléung ˏt'au kún' kukˌ. |
| 3. The *axle-cheeks* are also called *puk*, and likewise *fuk*; they are placed on the axle-tree on the right and left. | 伏兎又名轐名輹在軸上左右 | *Fukˌ t'ò²* yau² ˏming *pukˌ*, ˏming *fukˌ*; tsoi² chau' shéung² ˋtsó yau². |
| 4. *Bells of horses* are the brazen bells on their necks. | 馬鈴頸下銅鈴 | *ˢMá ˏling* ˋking há² ˏt'ung ˏling. |
| 5. *Bit* is the iron in the horse's mouth. | 銜馬口含之鐵 | *ˏHám* ˢmá ˋhau ˏhám ˏchí t'itˌ. |
| 6. A *brace* is a horizontal wood at the end of the thills. | 輗轅端上橫木 | *ˏNgai* ˏün ˏtün shéung² ˏwáng mukˌ. |
| 7. Luktín says, 'that in riding a frantic horse, you must use a whip to master him; and in riding a rampant horse, you must use a *bridle* to control him.' | 陸佃曰御駑馬以鞭爲主御駻馬以轡爲主 | Lukˌ tín² ütˌ, yü² ˏnò ˢmá, ˢí ˏpín ˏwai ˋchü; yü² ˋhón ˢmá ˢí *pí²* ˏwai ˋchü. |
| 8. A *sword-car* has swords in its back, and is placed at the breaches in walls to obstruct them. | 刀車後出鎗刄城壞以其塞之 | ˏ*Tò ˏkü* hau² ch'utˌ, ˏts'éung yan², ˏshing wái² ˢí ˏk'í sakˌ ˏchí. |
| 9. The *great car* is the emperor's carriage; there are five sorts differing from each other. | 大輅天子輦也有五式之別 | *Tái² lókˌ*, ˏt'ín ˋtsz' ˢlín ˢyá; ˢyau ˢ'ng shikˌ ˏchí pítˌ. |
| 10. A *scaling-car* is one used in approaching walls to throw scaling ladders, so as to climb up and take the city. | 絞車爲逼城拋鉤索登城攻敵 | *ˋKáu ˏkü* ˏwai pikˌ ˏshing ˏp'áu ˏkau sókˌ, ˏtang ˏshing ˏkung tikˌ. |
| 11. The *carriage-box* is also called *pan fuk*. | 車箱又名牝服 | ˏ*Kü ˏséung* yau² ˏming *ˢpan fukˌ*. |
| 12. The *imperial carriage* is moved by men. | 丨輦人步輓車 | ˏ*Kü ˢlín* ˏyan pò² ˢwán ˏkü. |
| 13. A *sedan carriage* has the upper part like a sedan, with wheels underneath by which it advances. | 馬車轎上如轎下有車輪轉行 | *ˢMá ˏkü kiú²* shéung² ˏü kiú², há² ˢyau ˏkü ˏlun ˋchün ˏhang. |
| 14. A *cart* (or field carriage) is one which is fitted for carrying heavy burdens in the fields. | 下澤丨田間任載之丨 | *Há² chákˌ ˏkü* ˏt'ín ˏkán yam² tsoi² ˏchí ˏkü. |
| 15. A *shoulder-chair* is the present sedan. | 肩輿卽今轎也 | ˏ*Kín ˏyü* tsikˌ ˏkam kiú² ˢyá. |
| 16. A *basket-chair* is a basket woven of bamboo, having one pole by which it is carried. | 籃輿以竹織籃使一挑而扛之 | *ˏLám ˏyü* ˢí chukˌ chikˌ ˏlám ˋsz' yatˌ ˏt'íú ˏí ˏkóng ˏchí. |

that are employed have but two wheels, and are very rude in their construction. Several of those described in this section are ancient ones, now quite disused, like those once in use among the Romans. Some very good pictures of the ancient carriages may be seen in the Illustrations of the Four Books.

3. These "sleeping rabbits," as the Chinese call them, appear to have been intended to ease the roughness of the road; they were mere blocks of wood, with a flat top, placed on the axle, and having the box of the carriage resting upon them.

15. Sedans are in use by all classes, the only restriction being the means of the individual; some of the sedans of officers are elegant, others are poor, being made of bamboo.

| | | |
|---|---|---|
| 17. A *war-chariot* is one used in war. | 兵車出兵車也 | ꜀*Ping* ꜀*kü* ch'ut꜁ ꜀ping ꜀kü ꜂yá. |
| 18. A *general's war-chariot* has ten horses, and is the chariot of the general in the van. | 戎丨十乘乃先軍之戎車者也 | ꜀*Yung* ꜀*kü* shap꜁ shing꜃, ꜂nái ꜀sín ꜀kwan ꜀chí ꜀yung ꜀kü ꜂ché ꜂yá. |
| 19. The *charioteer* holds the reins and guides the horses. | 御馬執綏使馬 | *Yü*꜃ ꜂má chap꜁ ꜀shui ꜂shai ꜂má. |
| 20. An *easy coach* has four wheels, and is so constructed that one can lean forwards or backwards. | 安車四輪前可憑後可倚 | ꜀*Ón* ꜀*kü* sz꜃ ꜀lun ꜀ts'ín ꜂hó ꜀p'ang, hau꜃ ꜂hó ꜂í. |
| 21. A *stage-coach* is a foreign carriage; it is used instead of a passage-boat and carries passengers. | 渡車番國車也如渡船而運客 | *Tò*꜃ ꜀*kü* ꜀fán kwók꜁ ꜀kü ꜂yá, ꜀ü tò꜃ ꜀shün ꜀í wan꜃ hák꜁. |
| 22. The *crupper* is the strap upon the horse's rump. | 鞦乃馬後之帶 | ꜀*Ts'au* ꜂nái ꜂má hau꜃ ꜀chí tái꜃. |
| 23. The *felly* is the outside circular part of a wheel; anciently, it was called the 'tooth,' and also the 'rim.' | 輞輪外圓古名曰牙又名曰渠 | ꜂*Móng* ꜀lun ngoi꜃ ꜀ün, ꜂kú ꜀ming üt꜁ ꜀ngá, yau꜃ ꜀ming üt꜁ ꜀k'ü. |
| 24. The *fire-engine* is used to extinguish fires. | 水車救火所用 | ꜂*Shui* ꜀*ch'é* kau꜃ ꜂fó ꜂shó yung꜃. |
| 25. The *girth* is a strap fastened under the horse's belly. | 馬肚帶繫馬肚 | ꜂*Má* ꜂*t'ò* *tái*꜃ hai꜃ ꜂má ꜂t'ò. |
| 26. A *headstall* is the strap fastened upon the head of the horse. | 馬籠頭繫馬頭之帶 | ꜂*Má* ꜀*lung* ꜀*t'au* hai꜃ ꜂má ꜀t'au ꜀chí tái꜃. |
| 27. The *housings* are also called spatterdashes; they are made of bear or deer's skin, and are fastened upon the back of the horse. | 韂又名障泥以熊鹿皮爲之勒於馬後 | ꜀*Shim* yau꜃ ꜀ming chéung꜃ ꜀nai; ꜂í ꜀hung luk꜁ ꜀p'í ꜀wai ꜀chí lak꜁ ꜀ü ꜂má hau꜃. |
| 28. The *linchpin* is a cross pin in the end of the axletree. | 轄軸頭之橫閂 | *Hat*꜁ chau꜃ ꜀t'au ꜀chí ꜀wáng ꜀shán. |
| 29. The *nave* is the wood in the centre of the wheel. | 轂乃輪心之木 | *Kuk*꜁ ꜂nái ꜀lun ꜀sam ꜀chí muk꜁. |
| 30. The *nave-box* in the largest end is called *ín*. | 賢內大穿之名 | ꜀*Ín* noi꜃ tái꜃ ꜀ch'ün ꜀chí ꜀ming. |
| 31. The *nave-box* in the smallest end is called *chat*. | 軹內小穿之名 | *Chat*꜁ noi꜃ ꜂síú ꜀ch'ün ꜀chí ꜀ming. |
| 32. A *noose* is an iron bored into the nose of an ox, to which a cord is tied to lead him along. | 桊以鐵穿牛鼻繫繩牽之 | *Kün*꜃ ꜂í t'ít꜁ ꜀ch'ün ꜀ngau pí꜃ hai꜃ ꜀shing ꜀hín ꜀chí. |
| 33. *The reins* are the lines held by one in the carriage. | 綏挽以上車索 | ꜀*Shui* ꜂wán ꜂í ꜂shéung ꜀kü sók꜁. |

24. The second character in this sentence is read *ch'é*; it is identical with that read *kü* in No. 20; though some distinguish the two by making the upper and lower strokes of different lengths.

32. In the meadows along the banks of the rivers, and on the uplands where herds of cattle graze, boys may often be seen riding on the backs of oxen or buffaloes, which they control and guide by a noose; the ox is often managed in the same way when harnessed to the plough.

33, 34. The first of these are the long reins held in the hand when driving a carriage; the second are the shorter reins of a bridle.

| | | |
|---|---|---|
| 34. The *reins* are the cords used for checking the horse. | 繮乃兜馬韁繩 | ‚*Kéung* 'nái ‚tau 'má ‚kéung ‚shing. |
| 35. To *ride* a horse is to amble pleasurably and slowly. | 騎馬緩行遊樂 | ‚*K'í 'má* ún[2] ‚hang ‚yau lók‚. |
| 36. A *saddle* is used to set upon in riding to shoot. | 鞍用以坐騎射 | ‚*Ón* yung[2] 'í tsó[2] ‚k'í shé[2]. |
| 37. A *saddle-pad* is the protecting pad laid upon the back of the horse. | 馬鎧馬脊之披<br>甲也 | '*Má 'hoi* 'má tsik‚ ‚chí ‚p'í káp‚ 'yá. |
| 38. A *sedan*, having no wheels, is carried by poles. | 輿無輪以程代 | ‚*Yü* ‚mò ‚lun 'í ‚ch'ing toi[2]. |
| 39. An *imperial sedan* is used within the palace. | 輦宮內擡行者 | '*Lín* ‚kung noi[2] ‚t'oi ‚hang 'ché. |
| 40. An *open sedan* is a chair for resting the body, and has two poles, it is borne like the common sedan. | 兜即凴身椅貫<br>兩程如轎扛之 | ‚*Tau* tsik‚ ‚p'ang ‚shan 'í, kún' 'léung ‚ch'ing ‚ü kíú[2] ‚kóng ‚chí. |
| 41. *Sedan bearers* are those who carry the sedan—one before and one behind—on their shoulders. | 轎夫擡轎者前<br>後一人以肩擡 | *Kíú*[2] ‚*fú* ‚t'oi kíú[2] 'ché, ‚ts'in hau[2] yat‚ ‚yan 'í ‚kín ‚t'oi. |
| 42. The *snaffle* is fastened on both sides of the bit, for the purpose of making fast the reins. | 鑣連銜夾口旁<br>以爲繫繩執之 | ‚*Píú* ‚*lín* ‚*hám* káp‚ 'hau ‚p'óng, 'í ‚wai hai[2] ‚shing chap‚ ‚chí. |
| 43. The *spokes* are the thirty sticks within the felly. | 輻輞中木三十 | *Fuk*‚ 'móng ‚chung muk‚ ‚sám shap‚. |
| 44. The *stirrups* are used in mounting the horse. | 馬踏鐙上馬用 | '*Má táp*‚ *tang*' 'shéung 'má yung[2]. |
| 45. A *support* is for leaning upon, being a resting-board. | 軾可凴即按板 | *Shik*‚ 'hó ‚p'ang tsik‚ ón' 'pán. |
| 46. The *thills* are the shafts for guiding the carriage. | 轅駕馬之車杠 | ‚*Yün* ká' 'má ‚chí ‚kü kóng'. |
| 47. The *tongue* is the crooked timber in front, let into the axle for drawing the vehicle. | 輈車前曲木貫<br>軸中拖車行者 | ‚*Chau* ‚kü ‚ts'ín huk‚ muk‚, kún' chau[2] ‚chung ‚t'ó ‚kü ‚hang 'ché. |
| 48. A *waggon* is a vehicle for transporting goods on level ground. | 大車平地任載<br>之丨也 | *Tái*[2] ‚*kü* ‚p'ing tí[2] yam[2] tsoi' ‚chí ‚kü 'yá. |
| 49. The carriage rests upon the *wheels*, which turn round. | 輪丨凴其轉行 | ‚*Lun* ‚kü ‚p'ang ‚k'í 'chün ‚hang. |
| 50. A *whip* is for beating the horse to make him go. | 鞭撻馬使速行 | ‚*Pín* t'át‚ 'má 'sz' ts'uk‚ ‚hang. |
| 51. A *hair-whip* is used for switching the horse, or for driving away the musquitoes. | 拂塵用拂馬身<br>或用以拂蚊者 | *Fat*‚ ‚*ch'an* yung[2] fat‚ 'má ‚shan, wák‚ yung[2] 'í fat‚ ‚man 'ché. |
| 52. A *yoke* is a transverse stick at the end of the tongue. | 衡曲輈上橫木 | ‚*Hang* huk‚ ‚chau shéung[2] ‚wáng muk‚. |

35. There are other expressions for riding besides *k'í má;* thus, a slow pace is expressed by *líú má*, and racing in the manner of jockies, by standing in the stirrups, is called *páu má;* but *k'í má* is the common expression for riding, whether slow or fast.

49. Wheels of various sizes and shapes are figured in the Chinese books, the number of spokes differing from few to many; there are also truck wheels.

# CHAPTER IX.

# AGRICULTURE.

# 耕農篇九
꜀Kang ꜁nung; ꜀p'ín ꜂kau.

## Section First.

## IMPLEMENTS OF AGRICULTURE.

## 農器類第一章
꜁Nung hí' lui²; tai² yat› ꜀chéung.

| | | |
|---|---|---|
| 1. An *aqueduct* is made of bamboos to conduct water. | 連筒以竹通水 | ꜁*Lín* ꜁*t'ung* ꜃í chuk› ꜀t'ung ꜂shui. |
| 2. The *base of a plough* is the piece of wood which is close upon the ground, and supports the share. | 犂底貼地推鑱之木 | ꜁*Lai* ꜂*tai* t'íp› tí² ꜀t'úi ꜁ts'ám ꜀chí muk₂. |
| 3. The *round osier-basket* is for containing grain. | 𥬠盛穀之器也 | ꜁*T'ün* shing² kuk› ꜀chí hí' ꜃yá. |
| 4. A *splint-basket* is made of split bamboos to hold grain. | 篅判竹以盛穀 | ꜀*Ch'ün* p'ún' chuk› ꜃í shing² kuk›. |
| 5. The *round splint-basket* is another name for the two preceding; there are large and small, and nearly alike. | 篨𥬠篅別名大小有差 | *Ch'ü'* ꜁t'ün ꜀ch'ün pít₂ ꜁ming; tái² ꜂síú ꜃yau ꜀ts'z'. |
| 6. An *eared basket* resembles the pedler's, though flatter. | 䇦籮屬比籮匾 | ꜀*Ts'ó* ꜁ló shuk₂ ꜂pí ꜁ló ꜂pín. |
| 7. The *wheat-basket* is for containing reaped wheat. | 麥籠盛芟麥器 | *Mak₂* ꜁*lung* shing² ꜀shám mak₂ hí'. |
| 8. The *sprout-basket* is for holding sprouted grain. | 篠盛種之器也 | ꜃*T'iú* shing² ꜂chung ꜀chí hí' ꜃yá. |

### *Notes and Explanations.*

Agriculture holds a very high rank in the estimation of the Chinese, and the implements which they have invented to facilitate its operations have been very numerous. This chapter contains, besides the names of various utensils employed by the husbandman, questions respecting his principal operations, especially in the cultivation of rice, and a discourse on the importance of tillage to the wellbeing of the state. The first section is designed to contain the names of the principal implements, both ancient and modern, used in the various departments of agriculture. Some, here enumerated, are now disused; but being often referred to in their ancient books, ought not to be omitted.

1. The *lín tung*, connected tubes of bamboo, form a very simple and durable aqueduct, for temperate latitudes where there is no exposure to frosts. Large bamboos are taken, their knots bored through, and then several pieces joined together to any extent desired.

| | | |
|---|---|---|
| 9. The *sunning-basket* is of bamboo for drying grain. | 曬槃曝穀竹器 | *Shái'* ˏ*p'ún* puk, kuk, chuk, hí'. |
| 10. The *tall sprout-basket* is also for containing grain; it differs from the preceding, whether large or small. | 簣亦盛〻器與<br>篠大小異形 | *Kwai'* yik, shing' kuk, hí' ʻü ˏt'iú tái' ʻsiú í' ˏying. |
| 11. A *globular basket* is made of bamboo to hold sprouts. | 種簟盛種竹器 | *ʻChung ʻt'ím* shing' ʻchung chuk, hí'. |
| 12. The *beam* of a plough is the long timber in its front. | 犂轅犂前長木 | ˏ*Lai* ˏ*ün* ˏlai ˏts'ín ˏch'éung muk,. |
| 13. A *beetle* is used for leveling the ground. | 櫌摩田之器也 | ˏ*Yau* ˏmó ˏt'ín ˏchí hí' ʻyá. |
| 14. The *water-bellows* is furnished with a leathern bag to blow the fire; wooden fans are now used instead. | 水排以韋囊吹<br>火今代以木扇 | *ʻShui* ˏ*p'ái* ʻí ʻwai ˏnóng ˏch'ui ʻfó, ˏkam toi' ʻí muk, shín'. |
| 15. The *round strait besom* differs in form from the *flat besom*, but their uses are the same. | 掃箒與條箒形<br>異而制用同 | *Sò' ʻchau* ʻü· ˏ*t'iú ʻchau* ˏying í' ˏí chai' yung' ˏt'ung. |
| 16. A *bill-hook* is an instrument for cutting grain. | 銍穫禾穗刄也 | *Chat,* wók, ˏwó sui' yan' ʻyá. |
| 17. The *crooked bill-hook* is a blade for cutting grain. | 翳鐮刈禾穗刄 | *Ai'* ˏ*lím* ngái' ˏwó sui' yan'. |
| 18. A *hedge-bill* is crooked at the end with a straight handle. | 鍥上彎而下直 | *Kít,* shéung' ˏwán ˏí há' chik,. |
| 19. *Cow blankets* are rudely woven of coarse hemp. | 牛衣編亂麻作 | ˏ*Ngau* ˏ*í* ˏpín lün' ˏmá tsók,. |
| 20. The *bolt* is fastened between the beam and regulator. | 犂建抳轅與評 | ˏ*Lai kín'* ní' ˏün ʻü ˏp'ing. |
| 21. The *irrigating bucket* consists of a pail with cords fastened to it, so that two men can dip up water upon a field. | 戽斗以繩繫桶<br>二人戽水落田 | *Fú' ʻtau* ʻí ˏshing hai' ʻt'ung, í' ˏyan fú' ʻshui lók, ˏt'ín. |
| 22. The *chaff-cutter* resembles shears, for cutting grass. | 鏩如鈒切草器 | *Ch'at,* ˏü cháp, ts'ít, ʻts'ò hí'. |
| 23. The *coulter-plough* is a blade for turning up the soil. | 劙刀開墾之刄 | *Lai'* ˏtò ˏhoi ʻhan ˏchí yan'. |
| 24. A *crow-bar* is for the purpose of raising heavy stones. | 動釗爲起重石 | *Tung'* ˏ*ch'iú* ˏwai ʻhí chung' shik,. |
| 25. A *dam* is made of separate timbers to obstruct water. | 水柵排木障水 | *ʻShui cháp,* ˏp'ái muk, chéung' ʻshui. |
| 26. The *drag* is framed together of several pieces of wood, for the purpose of leveling the ground. | 耮用條木編之<br>以摩田也 | ˏ*Lò* yung' ˏt'iú muk, ˏpín ˏchí ʻí ˏmó ˏt'ín ʻyá. |

14. This *shui p'ái* is represented as a pair of bellows, invented in the time of the Hón dynasty for the purpose of saving human strength—called *shui p'ái* because it was worked by the power of water; it was employed in furnaces.

16. The *chat* differs but little from a sickle; the blade of the *kít* may be a foot long, and is curved like a snipe's bill at one end, while at the other it is fastened on a straight wooden handle of about the same length as the blade. Of the *ai lím*, there are two forms; one differs from the *kít* only in having the blade much bent near the handle, and being straight and square at the end; the other has a scythe-like blade fitted into a handle at right angles.

23. The common plough of the Chinese is without a colter; and the colter-plough seems to have been used to break up hard and uncultivated ground, to prepare it for the common plough; it is like a broad colter fastened to a handle, and having a beam by which to draw it.

| | | |
|---|---|---|
| 27. The *square drag* has its teeth set in two beams. | 方耙兩程齒離 | ‹*Fóng* ˏ*p'á* ʻléung ˏch'ing ʻch'í ˏlí. |
| 28. A *bush-drag* is for leveling the ground. | 撻打田攣者也 | *T'át*, ʻ*tá* ˏt'ín wai' ʻché ʻyá. |
| 29. The *gourd-drill* holds seed for sowing in fields. | 瓠種貯種播田 | ˏ*Ú* ʻ*chung* ʻch'ü ʻchung pó' ˏt'ín. |
| 30. A *winnowing fan* separates chaff from the grain. | 箕簸米去糠者 | ‹*Kí* p'ó' ʻmai h'ü' ‹hóng ʻché. |
| 31. The *winnowing fan*, holding chaff and broken kernels mixed, turns them up to the wind, to become clean. | 颺籃糠粃相雜 向風擲乃得淨 | ˏ*Yéung* ˏ*lám* ‹hóng ngat, ‹séung tsáp, héung' ‹fung chák, ʻnái tak, tsing'. |
| 32. The *fanning-mill*, being worked, winnows out the chaff, and the grain falls into the trough below. | 風櫃攪之殼吹 出米從槽而下 | ‹*Fung kwai'* ʻkáu ‹chí hók, ‹ch'ui ch'ut, ʻmai ˏts'ung ˏts'ò ˏí há'. |
| 33. The teeth of an *iron feeler* are sharp and partly bent. | 鐵搭齒銳微鈎 | *T'ít, táp*, ʻch'í yui' ˏmí ‹kau. |
| 34. A *flail* is an implement for thrashing grain. | 連耞打禾之器 | ˏ*Lín* ‹*ká* ʻtá ˏwó ‹chí hí'. |
| 35. A *rice-fluke* is a tool for gathering grain. | 禾鈎斂禾具也 | ˏ*Wó* ‹*kau* ʻlím ˏwó kü' ʻyá. |
| 36. The *fore-brace* of the plough extends from the stud-brace to the base of the plough, and passes through it. | 犁箭自策額達 亅底縱而貫之 | ˏ*Lai tsín'* tsz' ch'ák, ngák, tát, ˏlai ʻtai tsung' ˏí kún' ‹chí. |
| 37. A *fork* is an implement for taking up grain. | 杈箝禾之具也 | ‹*Ch'á* ˏk'ím ˏwó ‹chí kü' ʻyá. |
| 38. A *grain-bin* is a square box for for containing grain. | 穀匣盛穀方匣 | *Kuk, háp*, shing' kuk, ‹fóng háp,. |
| 39. The *triangular harrow* is made like the character 人 farmers use it in harrowing. | 人字杷如人字 齊民鈀田要術 | ˏ*Yan tsz'* ˏ*p'á* ˏü ˏyan tsz'; ˏts'ai ˏman ˏp'á ˏt'ín íú' shat,. |
| 40. The *long-toothed harrow* is for loosening the ground. | 耖爲疏通田坭 | *Ch'au'* ˏwai ‹shó ‹t'ung ˏt'ín ˏnai. |
| 41. A *drill-harrow* is for sowing grain. | 耬車下種之器 | *Lau'* ‹*kü* há' ʻchung ‹chí hí'. |
| 42. The *square-harrow* derives its name from its form. | 方杷形方故名 | ‹*Fóng* ˏ*p'á* ˏying ‹fóng kú' ˏming. |
| 43. *Pók* is a *weeding-hoe*, an utensil for removing grass. | 鎛即耨除草物 | *Pók*, tsik, *nau'* ˏch'ü ʻts'ò mat,. |
| 44. The *weeding-hoe* removes weeds to help the grain. | 耰耝去莠助苗 | ‹*Yau tsui'* h'ü' ʻyau chó' ˏmíú. |
| 45. The *rice-jar* is a vessel for preserving rice. | 儋貯米之器也 | ‹*Tám*, ʻch'ü ʻmai ‹chí hí' ʻyá. |
| 46. A *wooden ladle* is used for watering fields. | 木勺拂水淋田 | *Muk, shéuk*, fat, ʻshui ˏlam ˏt'ín. |
| 47. A *leveler* resembles a rake without teeth. | 朳似無齒之耙 | ˏ*P'á* ʻts'z' ˏmò ʻch'í ‹chí ˏp'á. |

29. This is a gourd, having a tube passing through it lengthwise, and sharp at the bottom, where are also several holes through which the grain contained in the gourd is strown on the field.

41. This machine is drawn by a yoke, and is so contrived that the grain, which is held in baskets on the top of the frame, falls into the furrows made by the teeth of the harrow underneath; there are four or five large teeth, with a supply of grain above each.

39—42. Chinese husbandmen make great use of the harrow in breaking the clods, and reducing the soil of the rice-fields, where they are very wet, to a fine mesh.

48. A *lock* is a wooden barrier constructed in a river, to stop the course of the water.
河閘於河間設
木閘阻水往來
ˏ*Hó cháp*2 ˏü ˏhó ˏkán ch'it3 muk2 cháp2 'tsò 'shui 'wóng ˏloi.

49. A *thrashing-mat* preserves the falling grain.
摜稻簟承遺稻
*Kwán*' *tò*2 '*t'ím* ˏshing ˏwai tò2.

50. A *mattoc* is smaller than a pickaxe, and has its edge overlaid and defended with iron.
鎊口鋤頭之小
者其口以鐵鑲
ˏ*Póng* 'hau ˏ*ch'ó* ˏ*t'au* ˏchí 'sıú - 'ché, ˏk'í 'hau 'í t'ít3 ˏséung.

51. The *water bolting-mill* sifts the flour rapidly.
水打籮篩麵速
'*Shui* '*tá* ˏ*lò* 'shai mín2 ts'uk3.

52. The *skinning-mill* has a vase for a mortar.
堈碓以堈作臼
ˏ*Kóng túi*' 'í ˏkóng tsok3 'kau.

53. The *wooden mill* is worked to hull the grain.
礱礧穀以去殼
'*Lung* 'lui kuk3 'í h'ü' hók3.

54. The *stone mill* is sometimes worked by animal strength, and sometimes by water power.
磨多用畜力輓
行或用水力
*Mó*2 ˏtó yung2 ch'uk3 lik2 'wán ˏhang, wák2 yung2 'shui lik2.

55. The *wooden* and *stone water-mills*, and the *vertical wheel-mortar*, all have their wheels turned by water, and are worked for the purpose of grinding rice and wheat.
水磨及水礱水
碾皆水轉輪而
運行以礫穀麥
'*Shui mó*2 kap2 '*shui* '*lung*, '*shui* '*chín*, ˏkái 'shui 'chün ˏlun ˏí wan2 ˏhang, 'í lik3 kuk3 mak2.

56. The *vertical wheel-mortar* has a round stone to grind.
碾以石碣礫穀
'*Chín* 'í shik2 ˏkwó lik3 kuk3.

57. The *wheel-skinning mortar* is turned by water.
機碓即水碓也
ˏ*Kí túi*' tsik3 'shui túi' 'yá.

58. A *bird-net* is stretched out in order to catch birds, and a stool-pigeon being fastened [close by the net], induces the birds to come down so that they are taken in it.
羅張之以捕飛
禽繫囮誘而入
擒之
ˏ*Ló*, ˏchéung ˏchí 'í pò2 ˏfí ˏk'am, hai2 ˏngó, 'yau ˏí yap2, ˏk'am ˏchí.

59. The *plough* is an implement for opening up the soil.
犁乃開田之器
ˏ*Lai* 'nái ˏhoi ˏt'ín ˏchí hí'.

60. The *plough-handle* is the tail of the plough.
丨梢即犁尾也
ˏ*Lai* ˏ*shau* tsik3 ˏlai 'mí 'yá.

61. The *ploughshare* is the iron edge of the plough.
丨鑱即丨口鐵
ˏ*Lai* ˏ*ts'ám* tsik3 ˏlai 'hau t'ít3.

62. The *bamboo-rake* is used in thrashing-floors, and is employed for the purpose of raking off refuse matter.
竹杷場圃間用
以扒餘物
*Chuk*3 ˏ*p'á* ˏch'éung 'p'ò ˏkán yung2 'í ˏp'á ˏü mat2.

55. Mills and mortars for hulling, pounding, and grinding exist in several forms among the Chinese; those worked by water power, however, are very few; some are worked by hand; but for the most part they are turned by oxen, mules, and horses.

59. The plough of the Chinese, though very simple in its construction, has at different times assumed a variety of shapes; one of their best, described in the Sám Ts'oi T'ò, consists of eleven parts, namely, the base, share, mold-board, beam, handle, fore-brace, regulator, bolt, stud-brace, share-brace, whipple-tree or ear. There is no colter, and the mold-board is of iron. The fore-brace is called 'the arrow' of the plough; it seems never to be mortised into the beam, but to be fastened to it by a withe or thong, while another one passes around it and the handle, (about half-way between the base and beam,) lashing them together; this latter one, the regulator, is contracted or loosened by the bolt, by which it is twisted or untwisted.

| | | |
|---|---|---|
| 63. Both the *large rakes* and *small rakes* have straight handles and transverse heads. | 大杷小杷皆直柄橫首 | *Tái$^2$ ˏp'á 'síu ˏp'á*, ˓kái chik˒ ping' ˏwáng 'shau. |
| 64. The *harrow-rake* is a long rake for gathering wheat. | 拖杷樓麥長杷 | ˓*T'ó ˏp'á* ˏlau mak$_2$ ˏch'éung ˏp'á. |
| 65. The *grain-rake* is used to spread out grain to dry. | 穀杷用攤晒穀 | *Kuk˒ ˏp'á* yung$^2$ ˓tán shái' kuk˒. |
| 66. The *weeding-rake* is used for weeding rice. | 耘杷用耘稻禾 | ˏ*Wan ˏp'á* yung$^2$ ˏwan tò˒ ˏwó. |
| 67. The *reaping-basket* (or cradle) is for gathering wheat. | 麥綽杪麥之器 | *Mak$_2$ ch'éuk˒* ch'áu' mak$_2$ ˓chí hí'. |
| 68. A *reaping-rod* is a bamboo for raising the grain. | 抄竿扶麥之竹 | ˓*Ch'áu ˓kón* ˏfú mak$_2$ ˓chí chuk˒. |
| 69. The *regulator* of the plough gauges the fore-brace. | 犂評用以定箭 | ˏ*Lai ˏp'ing* yung$^2$ 'í ting$^2$ tsín'. |
| 70. *Grain-ricks* are frames made of wood and bamboo. | 麥笐竹木成架 | *Mak$_2$ k'óng'* chuk˒ muk$_2$ ˏshing ká'. |
| 71. A *roller* revolves and beats down grass and shrubs. | 輥軸輥碾草木 | ˓*Kwan chau$_2$* ˓kwan 'chín 'ts'ò muk$_2$. |
| 72. The *fluted roller* resembles a muskmelon, suspended [by its two ends] in a square frame. | 磟碡方架內如懸瓜 | *Luk$_2$ tuk$_2$* ˓fong ká' noi$^2$ ˏü ˏün ˓kwá. |
| 73. The *wheeled roller* has stone wheels. | 砘車砘石碢也 | ˏ*Tün ˓kü* ˏtün shik$_2$ ˓kwó 'yá. |
| 74. A *toothed stone roller* is made like the fluted roller; but it has teeth arranged on the outside. | 石礰礋與磟碡制同但外列齒 | *Shik$_2$ lik$_2$ chák$_2$* 'ü luk˒ tuk$_2$ chai$^2$ ˏt'ung, tán$^2$ ngoi$^2$ lít$_2$ 'ch'í. |
| 75. The *bill-knife* is a knife for cutting hemp. | 刈刀穫麻刄也 | *Ngái$^2$ ˓tò* wák$_2$ ˏmá yan$^2$ 'yá. |
| 76. A *salmon-leap* is for catching fish; it consists of bamboos arranged close together on the water's surface, with a fire on it, and the fish seeing the light, leap upon it. | 魚梁捕魚竹牌置河面另燃火魚見光即躍上 | ˏ*Ü ˏléung* pò$^2$ ˏü chuk˒ ˏp'ái, chí' ˏhó mín$^2$, ling$^2$ ˏín 'fó, ˏü kín' ˓kwóng, tsik˒ yéuk˒ 'shéung. |
| 77. A *scarecrow* is a thing made like a man, standing in the field, in order to frighten away the birds. | 案山子作物如人立田以逐禽 | *Ón' ˓shán 'tsz'* tsók˒ mat$_2$ ˏü ˏyan lap$_2$ ˏt'ín, 'í chuk$_2$ ˏk'am. |
| 78. A *scraper* is a tool for scraping the ground. | 刮板剗土具也 | *Kwát˒ 'pán* 'ch'án 't'ò kü$^2$ 'yá. |
| 79. A *mud scraper* is used for leveling down the soil. | 平板用平田坭 | ˏ*P'ing 'pán* yung$^2$ ˏp'ing ˏt'ín ˏnai. |

67. This implement resembles a basket-scoop, having a broad handle, by which it is turned over, and the blade on the side brought against the grain; as the grain is cut, it falls over into the basket, and is immediately put into the cart.

71—74. There are rollers of various kinds figured in the *Sám Ts'oi T'ò*, some of which combine the roller and the harrow, being armed with large, short, teeth. The *luk tuk* has the grooves running lengthwise, and is of an egg shape. In the cultivation of rice, however, little or no use is made of rollers, as the ground is too wet.

77. Various contrivances are resorted to by the farmers in China, as well as elsewhere, to preserve the growing grain from the depredations of birds; sometimes lines are stretched across the field, with things attached to them to jingle in the wind; at others, fantastic human forms are made. Watchmen are also frequently stationed to guard the field.

| | | |
|---|---|---|
| 80. A *hand-scraper* is an implement to level the ground. | 田盪均坭田器 | *ˏT'ín t'óng'* ˓kwan ˏnai ˏt'ín hí'. |
| 81. The *scythe* is a crooked instrument, for the purpose of cutting grass. | 芒鐮刃曲以爲割草 | *ˏMóng ˏlím yan* huk, ʿí ˏwai kót, ʿts'ò. |
| 82. A *sieve* is square inside, and round without, and is used for sifting grain. | 籭內方外圓用篩穀之物 | *Lí* noi ˓fóng ngoi ˏün, yung ˓shai kuk, ˓chí mat. |
| 83. The *share-brace* is under the share and moldboard. | 壓鑱鑱辟底木 | *Át, ˏts'ám* ˏts'ám pik, ʿtai muk. |
| 84. A *shovel* is that with which ditches are opened. | 臿所以開渠者 | *Ch'áp,* ʿshó ʿí ˓hoi ˏk'ü ʿché. |
| 85. The *sickle* is the modern cutting-bill. | 艾卽今之钩鐮 | *Ngái* tsik, ˓kam ˓chí ˓kau ˏlím. |
| 86. A *corn-sickle* is a blade for cutting ears of grain. | 栗截禾穎刃也 | *Lut* tsít ˏwó wing yan ʿyá. |
| 87. The *wheeled sickle* has a blade for cutting grain. | 推鐮斂禾之刃 | *˓T'úi ˏlím* ʿlím ˏwó ˓chí yan. |
| 88. A *wheat sickle* is a blade for cutting wheat. | 麥釤芟麥之丨 | *Mak shám'* ˓shám mak ˓chí yan. |
| 89. A *sluice* is a gate constructed in the side of a field, to allow the high tides to run into the fields. | 竇門於田壆設閘放潮水入田 | *Tau ˏmún* ˓ü ˏt'ín pók, ch'ít, cháp, fóng' ˏch'íú ʿshui yap ˏt'ín. |
| 90. A *screen-sluice* is constructed with a bamboo sieve, or a basket sieve. | 水簩竹箕也又籠也 | *ʿShui ˏp'óng* chuk, ˓kí ʿyá, yau ˏlung ʿyá. |
| 91. A *spade* has a metallic edge, which is very sharp. | 鋒共金口甚銳 | *˓Fung,* ˏk'í ˓kam ʿhau sham yui. |
| 92. A *share-spade* is thrust into the ground with the foot. | 長鑱踏田器也 | *ˏCh'éung ˏts'ám* táp ˏt'ín hí' ʿyá. |
| 93. The *wooden spade*, the *iron shod spade*, and the *basket-spade*, are all agricultural implements. | 木杴與鐵刃杴竹揚杴皆田器 | *Muk ˓h'ím,* ʿü *t'ít, yan ˓h'ím, chuk, ˏyéung ˓h'ím,* ˓kái ˏt'ín hí'. |
| 94. A *weeding-spade* is a tool for removing weeds. | 鐙鋤剗穢器也 | *˓Tang ˏch'ó* ʿchán wai' hí' ʿyá. |
| 95. The *garden-spade* is for leveling and trimming. | 鏟平削之剷也 | *ʿCh'án* ˏp'ing séuk, ˓chí ʿch'án ʿyá. |

81. The scythe and sickle, as well as the plough and all the other implements and tools here used in agriculture, are remarkably simple, yet for the most part answering their end admirably. The names by which the Chinese terms in this section are rendered do not always, however, describe an implement of precisely the same form, size, and construction as those used in western lands, but rather their equivalents—tools that are employed to do the same service; and although they answer the same purposes very well, still the most of them are roughly made, and destitute of any great degree of finish.

90. This screen-sluice is designed to prevent sticks, grass, weeds, and other rubbish from being carried on to the fields of rice while the grain is young, which otherwise might overspread and destroy it.

91—96. The spade is much used by Chinese farmers and gardeners, and the forms which it has taken are very numerous; it is generally made of hard wood, and the edge of the blade guarded with iron, but sometimes the whole blade is iron. The basket-spade is used in the provinces of Chítkóng and Kóngsai; it is made of bamboo, and constructed to dig up and carry away light rubbish.

| | | |
|---|---|---|
| 96. The *ancient wooden spade* was a hand plough; the crooked handle was called *loi*, the iron was called *tsz'*. | 耒耜手耕器曲<br>木曰耒金曰耜 | *Loi*2 *tsz'*2 'shau ‚kang hí' ; huk› muk2 üt2 *loi*2, ‚kam üt2 *tsz'*2. |
| 97. A *stack* is an accumulation of dried grass (or hay) formed like a barrow; its common name is a straw heap. | 積苫堆稈草成<br>墪俗曰禾稈墪 | *Tsik›* ‚*chím* ‚túi ‚kón 'ts'ò ‚shing ‚tun; tsuk› üt2 ‚wó 'kón ‚tun. |
| 98. The *stud-brace* affords support to the moldboard. | 策額可以扦鐴 | *Ch'ák› ngák*2 'hó 'í hón2 pik›. |
| 99. *Traces* are the lines by which the plough is drawn. | 耕索以輓犁也 | ‚*Kang sók›* 'í 'wán ‚lai 'yá. |
| 100. A *frame trough* is a wooden watering trough. | 架槽木架水槽 | *Ká*' ‚*ts'ò* muk2 ká' 'shui ‚ts'ò. |
| 101. The *paddle-trough* is for scooping up water upon a field; it is turned by treading upon a wheel. | 翻車刮水上田<br>以脚踏輪而轉也 | ‚*Fán* ‚*ch'é* kwát› 'shui 'shéung ‚t'ín; 'í kéuk› táp2 ‚lun ‚í 'chün. |
| 102. *Earthen tubes* are water spouts. | 瓦竇泄水器也 | '*Ngá tau*2 sít› 'shui hí' 'yá. |
| 103. The *water-gate* can be employed for watering the fields, and when closed the fish [within] may be caught. | 閘闌亦放水入<br>田者閂可捕魚 | *Cháp*2 ‚*lán* yik2 fong' 'shui yap2 ‚t'ín 'ché, ‚shán 'hó pò2 ‚ü. |
| 104. The *grinding and spinning water-wheel* can be used both for grinding grain, and spinning thread. | 水轉大紡車可<br>磨亦可績紡 | '*Shui* '*chün tái*2 '*fóng* ‚*ch'é* 'hó mò2 yik2 'hó chik› 'fóng. |
| 105. The *high chain bucket wheel* has a frame at both ends, and each of them has a wheel. | 高轉筒車上下<br>架木各豎一輪 | ‚*Kò* '*chün* ‚*t'ung* ‚*ch'é* shéung2 há2 ká' muk2, kók› shü2 yat› ‚lun. |
| 106. The *wheel-barrow* is for carrying things in the field. | 手車搬運田器 | '*Shau* ‚*ch'é* ‚pún wan2 ‚t'ín hí'. |
| 107. The *whipple-tree* is a cross bar which is fixed upon the end of the beam of the plough. | 犁槃橫於轅之<br>前末 | ‚*Lai* ‚*p'ún* ‚wáng ‚ü ‚ün ‚chí ‚ts'ín mut2. |
| 108. A *winnowing machine* is for cleaning grain. | 颺扇搧穀糠粞 | ‚*Yéung shín*' shín' kuk› ‚hóng ‚sai. |
| 109. The *ox yoke* is an implement for restraining the ox, and is made large or small according to his size. | 牛軛服牛具隨<br>牛大小制之 | ‚*Ngau ák›* fuk2 ‚ngau kü2 ‚ts'ui ‚ngau tái2 'síú chai' ‚chí. |

101. This is described and figured in Staunton's Embassy, and is much used to elevate water; the paddles are attached to a rope that runs through a long trough, which is turned at its upper end by a wheel.

105. The chain bucket wheel is a series of small buckets attached to a rope, passing over two large wheels; one of them is placed in, and turned by, a current of water, the other is placed upon a frame in the field; the buckets, forty or fifty in number, are attached to a rope passing over the two wheels, and as the wheel in the stream turns, the buckets are filled, pass up, and empty themselves upon the field.

## Section Second.

# AGRICULTURAL OPERATIONS.

## 農事類第二章

ˏNung sz'$^{2}$ lui$^{2}$; tai$^{2}$ í$^{2}$ ˓chéung.

| | | |
|---|---|---|
| 1. What grade of men are agriculturalists? | 農夫係邊流人 | ˏNung ˓fú hai$^{2}$ ˓pín ˏlau ˏyan? |
| A very honorable one, being considered as the second of the four classes of the people. | 其大名係入四民之二 | ˏK'í tái$^{2}$ ˏming, hai$^{2}$ yap$_{2}$ sz'$^{2}$ ˏman ˓chí í$^{2}$. |
| 2. What are these four classes of the people? | 乜野叫四民呢 | Mat˒ 'yé kíú' sz'$^{2}$ ˏman ˓ní? |
| They are scholars, husbandmen, mechanics, merchants. | 係士農工商咯 | Hai$^{2}$ sz'$^{2}$, ˏnung, ˓kung, ˓shéung, lók˒. |
| 3. In the cultivation of rice, what is the first process? | 種禾點起首呢 | Chung' ˏwó 'tím 'hí 'shau ˓ní? |
| The ground is to be ploughed, manures are to be applied, and water is to be let in upon the fields. | 犂鬆地落肥料兼放水咯 | ˏLai ˓sung tí$^{2}$, lók$_{2}$ ˏfí líú$^{2}$, ˓kím fóng' 'shui lók$_{2}$. |
| 4. When the fields have been first duly prepared, is the seed then sown directly upon them? | 田先預備停當係候撒種唔呢 | ˏT'ín ˓sín ü$^{2}$ pí$^{2}$ ˏt'ing tóng', hai$^{2}$ hau$^{2}$ sát˒ 'chung ˏ'm ˓ní? |
| It is unnecessary to sow the whole ground, for it is far better to prepare thoroughly a small plat, and sow it very thickly for the production of young shoots. | 唔使盡撒務須預將一小畝多撒種做秧係咧 | ˏ'M 'shai tsun$^{2}$ sát˒, mò$^{2}$ ˓sü ü$^{2}$ ˓tséung yat' 'síú 'mau, ˓tò sát˒ 'chung tsò$^{2}$ ˏyéung hai$^{2}$ ˓lé. |
| 5. How is the seed, that is to be sown, made to sprout? | 撒嘅種點發呢 | Sát˒ ké' 'chung 'tím fát˒ ˓ní? |
| The seed is first soaked for a time until it sprouts, after which it is taken and sown. | 將種先浸等發芽然後擰嚟播 | ˓Tséung 'chung ˓sín tsam' 'tang fát˒ ˏngá, ˏín hau$^{2}$ ˓ning ˏlai pó'. |
| 6. After the sowing of the seed, how long must you wait before the shoots will do to transplant? | 撒種後等幾耐至做得秧插呢 | Sát˒ 'chung hau$^{2}$ 'tang 'kí noi$^{2}$ chí' tsò$^{2}$ tak˒ ˓yéung ch'áp˒ ˓ní? |

### *Notes and Explanations.*

AGRICULTURAL operations are performed by the Chinese without much regard to science, or much help from any mechanical agency. The various processes are simple, requiring only small outlays of stock, and are, with but few exceptions, conducted throughout by manual labor. The culture of rice forms a very important branch of labor. Some of the implements and processes described in Loudon's Encyclopædia of Agriculture, as once existing among the Egyptians and people of western Asia, may be now seen among the Chinese.

3. The *Oryza sativa*, of which there are many varieties, is called by different names at the different stages of its growth. The ripe grain is called *wó* by the Chinese, and sometimes among foreigners paddee, both before and after it has been thrashed. The names will appear in the sequel.

廣東方言讀本



| | | |
|---|---|---|
| Generally about ten days are required, at which time they may be taken and transplanted. | 大約總要十幾日至擰得嚟插 | Tái$^{2}$ yéuk, ʻtsung íú' shap$_{2}$ ʻkí yat$_{2}$ chí' ˏning tak, ˏlai ch'áp,. |
| 7. What is the very best method of transplanting the young shoots? | 實在揷嘅法點樣呢 | Shat$_{2}$ tsoi$^{2}$ ch'áp, ké' fát,, ʻtím yéung$^{2}$ ˏní? |
| The shoots, being taken up with a small spade (or shovel), are held in one hand, while with the other they are planted in rows, and at short intervals. | 將秧鏟起一手執一手插行行離疏種下 | ˏTséung ˏyéung ʻch'án ʻhí, yat, ʻshau chap,, yat, ʻshau ch'áp,, ˏhóng ˏhóng ˏlí ˏshó chung' há$^{2}$. |
| 8. How far apart must they be separated? | 要離幾濶呢 | Íú' ˏlí ʻkí fút, ˏní? |
| Each plant may be about six inches from the others. | 各子離六寸咁 | Kók$_{2}$ ʻtsz' ˏlí luk$_{2}$ ts'ün' ʻkóm. |
| 9. While the young plants are growing, is there anything to be done to them? | 秧生起又做乜事呢 | ˏYéung ˏshang ʻhí yau$^{2}$ tsò$^{2}$ mat, sz'$^{2}$ ˏní? |
| The diligent farmer plucks out the weeds, thins the young grain, and likewise lets in water upon his fields; but when the rice has become thoroughly ripe, the water is then drawn off. | 勤力農夫耨草攕秧兼共放水入田到禾熟時放水流去 | ˏK'an lik$_{2}$ ˏnung ˏfú nau$^{2}$ ʻts'ò, líp$_{2}$ ˏyéung ˏkím kung$^{2}$ fóng' ʻshui yap$_{2}$ ˏt'ín; tò' ˏwó shuk$_{2}$ ˏshí fóng' ʻshui ˏlau h'ü'. |
| 10. In what months are the young shoots planted, and in what months does the grain become ripe? | 係乜月份插秧呢乜月穀成熟呢 | Hai$^{2}$ mat, üt$_{2}$ fan$^{2}$ ch'áp, ˏyéung, mat, üt$_{2}$ kuk, ˏshing shuk$_{2}$ ˏní? |
| The planting of the young shoots is done during the second and seventh months, and the grain becomes fully ripe in the sixth and tenth months. | 插秧在二月七月穀熟應在六月十月咯 | Ch'áp, ˏyéung tsoi$^{2}$ í$^{2}$ üt$_{2}$ ts'at, üt$_{2}$; kuk, shuk$_{2}$ ˏying tsoi$^{2}$ luk$_{2}$ üt$_{2}$ shap$_{2}$ üt$_{2}$ lók,. |
| 11. In what manner is the rice reaped? | 割禾又點樣呢 | Kót, ˏwó yau$^{2}$ ʻtím yéung$^{2}$ ˏní? |
| When the grain is ripe, it is cut with a sickle close to the ground. | 禾熟用鐮貼地割咯 | ˏWó shuk$_{2}$ yung$^{2}$ ˏlím t'íp, tí$^{2}$ kót, lók,. |
| 12. And what is to be done with the rice after it has been reaped? | 禾割了又點樣做呢 | ˏWó kót, ʻlíú, yau$^{2}$ ʻtím yéung$^{2}$ tsò$^{2}$ ˏní? |

6. Though they may be ready for transplanting in ten days, twice that time, and more, may elapse before the period is passed, when they become unfit to be removed.

7. Rice-shoots are sometimes made an article of sale, though farmers usually sow their own; about six roots are set out in the same spot, and the work is done with a good degree of regularity.

10. It is not always that two crops of rice are taken from the same field in one year. From the richest lands in the southern and eastern parts of the empire, however, which are well manured and watered, two crops may be, and generally are, gathered.

| | | |
|---|---|---|
| When the rice has been thoroughly dried, it is either thrashed out with a flail, or it is beaten into a tub, by which means the grain falls out. | 將禾晒乾或用<br>連耞打或拍落<br>桶務使其穀落 | ꜀Tséung ꜁wó shái' ꜀kón, wák, yung' ꜁lín ꜀ká 'tá, wák, p'ák, lók, 't'ung mò' 'sz' ꜁k'í kuk, lók. |
| 13. The grain being thrashed, what becomes of the straw? | 旣落稈又點呢 | Kí' lók,, 'kón yau' 'tím ꜀ní? |
| It is taken and dried, and having been bound up into separate sheaves, it is sunned and dried for fuel. | 將稈扎起一束<br>束晒乾作柴燒 | ꜀Tséung 'kón chát, 'hí yat, ch'uk,, ch'uk, shái' ꜀kón tsók, ꜁ch'ái 'shíú. |
| 14. And after the thrashing, what further remains to be done with it? | 穀落咯還有乜<br>法子做呢 | Kuk, lók, lók,, ꜁wán 'yau mat, fát, 'tsz' tsò' ꜀ní? |
| It is put into a fanning-mill upon the thrashing-floor, and fanned, in order to remove the bad grain and the chaff. | 將穀用風櫃在<br>塲上攪去嘢嘅<br>共糠咯 | ꜀Tséung kuk, yung' ꜀fung kwai' tsoi' ꜁ch'éung shéung', 'káu h'ü' p'án' ké' kung' ꜀hóng lók,. |
| 15. What are thrashing-floors, and where and how are they constructed? | 塲係乜野又在<br>邊處呢 | ꜁Ch'éung hai' mat, 'yé, yau' tsoi' ꜀pín ch'ü' ꜀ní? |
| A level piece of ground is selected, near at hand, which, covered with lime and sand, is pounded hard; its vulgar name is 'earth-palace;' and this is the place which is used for thrashing the rice, and drying the grain. | 擇附近平地用<br>灰砂舂實俗名<br>地堂卽打禾曬<br>穀所用之處 | Chák, fú' kan' ꜁p'ing tí', yung' ꜀fúi ꜀shá ꜀chung shat,, tsuk, ꜁ming *tí' ꜁t'óng;* tsik, 'tá ꜁wó shái' kuk,, 'shó yung' ꜀chí ch'ü'. |
| 16. And how is the manure used? | 個的糞點用呢 | Kó' tik, fan' 'tím yung' ꜀ní? |
| Manure, that has been a long time in a state of fermentation in the vats, is taken and formed into cakes and thoroughly dried; these are bought for two or three taels per pecul; and, being pounded fine with a pestle, are spread upon the field; this process is called 'dropping fatness.' | 將糞在氹漚久<br>作成糞餅曬乾<br>每担約銀二三<br>兩買囬舂碎撒<br>下田名曰落肥 | ꜀Tséung fan' tsoi' ꜀tam au' 'kau, tsók, ꜁shing fan' 'ping, shái' ꜀kón; 'múi tám' yéuk, ꜁ngan í' ꜀sám 'léung; 'mái ꜁úi ꜀chung sui', sát, há' ꜁t'ín, ꜁ming üt, lók, ꜁fí. |
| 17. When farmers hire fellow-laborers to assist them in doing their work, about how much money do they want for each day's work? | 農夫請伙計做<br>工每日約要幾<br>多銀呢 | ꜁Nung ꜀fú 'ts'ing 'fó kí' tsò' ꜀kung, 'múi yat, yéuk, íú' 'kí ꜀tó ꜁ngan ꜀ní? |

13. Brooms, mats, and thatches are made of rice-straw, and it is also ploughed in as manure; but much of it is used as fuel.

16. Great care is exercised by the Chinese in the preparation and application of manures. Their usual degree of simplicity is seen is both these processes, and more than an ordinary share of economy in collecting whatever can be converted into fertilizing matter.

For each day's work a mace of money, perhaps eight candareens, with three meals of victuals; ploughing and harrowing the fields is done at a given rate by the acre, the price for the labor on each being between one mace and eight candareens, and also three meals of victuals.

每日工銀一錢或八分供三飡犂田耙田以畝數計每畝工銀一錢八分之間亦食三飡

ʻMúi yat, ˌkung ˏngan yat, ˏtsʻín, wák, pát, ˌfan, ˌkung ˏsám ˌtsʻán; ˏlai ˏtʻín, ˏpʻá ˏtʻín, ʻí ʻmau shò kai; ʻmúi ʻmau ˌkung ˏngan yat, ˏtsʻín pát, ˌfan ˌchí ˌkán, yik, shik, ˌsám ˌtsʻán.

18. For those who transplant, and weed, and cut the grain, what is the amount of wages?

插秧耨草割禾點工價呢

Chʻáp, ˌyéung nau ʻtsʻò kót, ˏwó ʻtím ˌkung ká ˌní?

For transplanting the young shoots, the best wages are three or four mace; one mace is the common price; the very lowest must be seven candareens [for a day's work]; for weeding and reaping the amount of wages is the same. But for reaping, the pay may be something different: for reaping a single day, two *tau* of grain are required; sometimes also the arrangement is made that for each pecul twelve catties shall be given; and moreover, in all these several cases, from the first ploughing till the harvest, the laborers receive three meals per day.

插秧好價錢三四銀平價一錢至平都要七分耘草割禾工價一樣其中割禾或有唔同嘅割得一日要穀二斗另有講割得一担要穀十二斤至于日供三飡所有開田嘅人都係咯

Chʻáp, ˌyéung ʻhò ká ˏtsʻín ˌsám sz ˏngan; ˏpʻing ká yat, ˏtsʻín; chí ˏpʻing ˌtò iú tsʻat, ˌfan; ˏwan ʻtsʻò kót, ˏwó, ˌkung ká yat, yéung. ˏKʻí ˌchung kót, ˏwó, wák, ʻyau ˏʻm ˏtʻung ké; kót, tak, yat, yat, iú kuk, í ʻtau; ling ʻyau ʻkóng kót, tak, yat, tám, iú kuk, shap, í ˌkan; chí ˌü yat, ˌkung ˌsám ˌtsʻán, ʻshó ʻyau ˌhoi ˏtʻín ké ˏyan ˌtò hai lók.

19. What are the customs and usages to be observed when a farmer hires a field?

農夫領田納租規矩又點樣呢

ˏNung ˌfú ʻling ˏtʻín, náp, ˌtsò, ˌkwʻai ʻkü yau ʻtím yéung ˌní?

When making out the papers for the lease, it is clearly stated how much grain or money shall be paid for each acre annually; sometimes also the produce is equally divided; and after the particulars are explained, they are written down in papers to be kept as evidence of the agreement.

批領時言明每畝每年納穀或銀若干亦有均分穀的言明後寫於批領為憑

ˌPʻai ʻling ˏshí, ˏín ˏming ʻmúi ʻmau, ʻmúi ˏnín, náp, kuk, wák, ˏngan yéuk, ˌkón; yik, ʻyau ˌkwan ˌfan kuk, tik, ˏín ˏming hau ʻsé ˌü ˌpʻai ʻling ˏwai ˏpʻang.

18. It is not to be supposed that the amount of wages, here specified, can be more than an approximation to that actually paid at different times and places; generally the price of labor is very low.

| | | |
|---|---|---|
| **20.** In what manner do the landholders pay their rent in kind and their taxes to the government? | 佃戶點樣輸糧<br>納稅呢 | Tín² ú² ʿtím yéung² ˏshü ˏléung náp₂ shui˒ ˏní? |
| In the winter of each year, they repair to the office of the district magistrate, where, in the gabel department, are recorded the names of the township, the village, the neighborhood, the tything, the family to which one belongs, and what member of the family he is; the tax on each acre is levied at seven candareens in silver, besides one *shing* and one *kóp* of rice. The value of the grain is converted into silver, and an allowance must also be made for refining and stamping it: when all this is done, [the landholder] receives a duplicate receipt that it has been paid. | 每年冬到縣衙<br>糧房處錄某司<br>某都某啚某甲<br>戶丁某名完某<br>戶該每畝納銀<br>七分另米一升<br>一合將米折銀<br>另將銀補回火<br>耗納訖有執照<br>二張領回 | ʿMúi ˏnín ˏtung, tò˒ ün² ˏnga ˏléung ˏfong ch'ü˒, luk₂ ʿmau ˏsz', ʿmau ˏtò, ʿmau ˏt'ò, ʿmau káp˒ ú² ˏting ʿmau ˏming, ˏün ʿmau ú²; ˏkoi ʿmúi ʿmau náp₂ ˏngan ts'at˒ ˏfan, ling² ʿmai yat˒ ˏshing yat˒ kóp˒; ˏtséung ʿmai chít˒ ʿngan, ling² ˏtséung ˏngan ʿpò ˏúi ʿfó hò˒; náp₂ kat₂, ʿyau chap˒ chíú˒ í² ˏchéung ʿling ˏúi. |
| **21.** What kind of fields are the best for the cultivation of rice? | 禾田點樣嘅係<br>好呢 | ˏWó ˏt'ín ʿtím yéung² ké˒ hai² ʿhò ˏní? |
| Elevated fields, where there are springs of water above them, so that the water can be brought down upon them, having a rich soil and a degree of moisture, are the best. | 田高上有山水<br>下可放水坭腴<br>澤潤就好啫 | ˏT'ín ˏkò, shéung² ʿyau ˏshán ʿshui, há² ʿhó fong˒ ʿshui, ˏnai ˏyü chák₂ yun², tsau² ʿhò ˏché. |
| **22.** What kinds of animals are domesticated? | 乜野禽獸係養<br>得嘅呢 | Mat˒ ʿyé ˏk'am shau˒ hai² ʿyéung tak˒ ké˒ ˏní? |
| Poultry, ducks, cattle, sheep, horses, swine, and so forth, are all domesticated. | 雞鴨牛羊馬豕<br>等類皆可養 | ˏKai, áp˒, ˏngau, ˏyéung, ʿmá, ʿch'í ʿtang lui² ˏkái ʿhó ʿyéung. |
| **23.** How large a proportion of the whole country do you suppose is cultivated? | 通國計地田居<br>幾多呢 | ˏT'ung kwók˒ kai˒ tí² ˏt'ín ˏkü ʿkí ˏtó ˏní? |

20. In the southern provinces, the tax in kind is commuted for silver, as the transportation of grain to Peking would be too expensive. The rate of taxation varies according to the fertility of the soil, and in many instances is less than the sum here mentioned. When new lands are brought under cultivation, the government often does not assess them until the cultivator has been partly repaid for his outlay; the tax on such fields as are reclaimed from the banks of rivers and marshes is called *ü yau*, or fish-wandering; for the first or second year, when the tax is raised, it is termed *hók lap* or stork-standing.

21. Not high lands or hills, but plains or upland meadows, so situated that at all times a good supply of fresh water may be let in upon them at pleasure.

22. Beef is not much used by the Chinese, and horse flesh still less. Droves of sheep are sometimes brought to the south. Pork, poultry, and fish, are the staple articles of animal food.

| | | |
|---|---|---|
| The amount of cultivated land may be about one eighth. | 田居八份一啱 | ˏT'ín ‹kü pát› fan$^2$ yat› ‘kóm. |
| 24. How large a part is wild and uncultivated? | 荒野有幾多呢 | ‹Fóng ˢyé ˢyau ‘kí ‹tó ‹ní! |
| A like proportion, probably about one eighth, more or less. | 都係八份一啱上下 | ‹Tò hai$^2$ pát› fan$^2$ yat›, ‘kóm shéung$^2$ há$^2$. |
| 25. How much of it is forest? | 有幾多樹木呢 | ˢYau ‘kí ‹tó shü$^2$ muk$_2$ ‹ní? |
| The population of China being very dense, the forests cannot be extensive. | 中國人烟稠集樹木無多 | ‹Chung kwók› ˏyan ‹ín ˏch'au tsáp$_2$, shü$^2$ muk$_2$ ˏmò ‹tó. |
| 26. How much grazing land is used for pasturing horses, cattle, and sheep? | 有幾多馬牛羊臥食嘅草披呢 | ˢYau ‘kí ‹tó ˢmá, ˏngau, ˏyéung, ngó$^2$ shik$_2$ ké’ ‘ts'ò ‹p'í ‹ní? |
| It is uncertain, but there is quite enough. | 冇底數使為止 | ˢMò ‘tai, kau’ ‘shai ˏwai ‘chí. |
| 27. How many sorts of fences and wattles are there, and how are they constructed? | 藩籬有幾多樣又點做嘅呢 | ˏFán ˏlí ˢyau ‘kí ‹tó yéung$^2$, yau$^2$ ‘tím tsò$^2$ ké’ ‹ní? |
| They are made either of rattans, or rushes, or bamboos, and are interlaced with interstices. | 或籐或蘆荻或竹交加間搭嘅 | Wák$_2$ ˏt'ang, wák$_2$ ˏlò tik$_2$, wák$_2$ chuk›, ‹káu ‹ká kán’ táp› ké’. |
| 28. How are flowers and fruit-trees grafted? | 花菓點駁枝呢 | ‹Fá ‘kwó ‘tím pók› ‹chí ‹ní? |
| The scions are cut out in spring, and earth is bound about the place where they are inserted. | 春季折枝駁口處包坭 | ‹Ch'un kwai’ chít› ‹chí, pók› ‘hau ch'ü’ ‹páu ‹nai. |
| 29. What proportion of the land throughout the whole empire is occupied with the mulberry-tree? | 通國計有幾多桑地呢 | ‹T'ung kwók› kai’ ˢyau ‘kí ‹tó ‹sóng tí$^2$ ‹ní? |
| The land occupied with the mulberry-tree does not equal one eighth of the rice fields. | 桑地不敷禾田八份之一 | ‹Sóng tí$^2$ pat› ‹fú ˏwó ˏt'ín pát› fan$^2$ ‹chí yat›. |
| 30. How large a part of the whole country is occupied with orchards? | 菓木地總共計有多少 | ‘Kwó muk$_2$ tí$^2$, ‘tsung kung$^2$ kai’ ˢyau ‹tó ‘shíú? |
| Compared with the mulberry-trees, the fruit-trees are the most numerous, and their grounds the most extensive. | 菓木比桑畧多量其地亦畧廣 | ‘Kwó muk$_2$ ‘pí ‹sóng léuk$_2$ ‹tó, léung$^2$ ˏk'í tí$^2$ yik$_2$ léuk$_2$ ‘kwóng. |

24. Statistics doubtless exist sufficient to form a very exact estimate on this subject, but they seem never to have been collected and compared; and the statement here made is simply a conjecture. The principal object of this and a few of the following questions is merely to serve as examples of the manner of prosecuting similar inquiries.

27. Fences made of boards, or posts and rails, and stone walls, are not much used. Small orchards and gardens are often surrounded with walls. Hurdles and wattles are common, and on low lands ditches—which serve to separate the lands belonging to different persons.

| | | |
|---|---|---|
| 31. What extent of fields and lands are possessed by single individuals? | 每人有幾多田地呢 | ˢMúi ˏyan ˢyau ˢkí ˏtó ˏt'ín tí² ˏní? |
| The rich possess hundreds and thousands of acres, but the poor are without any at all. | 富者千百頃貧無半斗升 | Fú' ˢché ˏts'ín pák, ˢk'ing, ˏp'an ˏmò pún' ˢtau ˏshing. |
| 32. How are the field-walks built? | 田基點樣築呢 | ˏT'ín ˏkí ˢtím yéung² chuk, ˏní? |
| The foundations are formed by posts driven down, with earth piled on them, made hard and solid. | 基脚打樁培泥擣而實之 | ˏKí kéuk, ˢtá ˏchóng ˏpúi ˏnai ˢt'ò ˏí shat₂ ˏchí. |
| 33. How is the water let in upon the fields? | 田水點樣放呢 | ˏT'ín ˢshui ˢtím yéung² fóng' ˏní? |
| If the fields are near the hills, gullies are formed for the water, and the banks are opened to let it on to them. | 田近高山堵截水路開基放入 | ˏT'ín kan² ˏkò ˏshán ˢtò tsít₂ ˢshui lò², ˏhoi ˏkí fóng' yap₂. |
| 34. When are farmers most at leisure? | 農夫幾時閒呢 | ˏNung ˏfú ˢkí ˏshí ˏhán ˏní? |
| They have but a very little leisure, merely the short intervals between the seasons. | 得閒甚少不過係農隙個陣啫 | Tak, ˏhán sham² ˢshíú, pat, kwó' hai² ˏnung kwik, kó' chan² ˏché. |
| 35. In what parts of the country are sheep the most numerous? | 通國以邊處爲至多羊呢 | ˏT'ung kwók, ˢí ˏpín ch'ü' ˏwai chí' ˏtó ˏyéung ˏní? |
| In the northern regions, beyond the Great Pass, they are the most numerous and the best. | 以北方潼關外爲多爲好 | ˢÍ pak, ˏfóng ˏTung ˏKwán ngoi² ˏwai ˏtó ˏwai ˢhò. |
| 36. How many kinds of gardens are there? | 園有幾多樣呢 | ˏÜn ˢyau ˢkí ˏtó yéung² ˏní? |
| There are gardens for flowers, fruits, melons, vegetables, &c. | 有花菓瓜菜等各園 | ˢYau ˏfá ˢkwó, ˏkwá, ts'oi' ˢtang kók, ˏün. |
| 37. What do the Chinese use to make their spirituous liquors? | 中國用乜野蒸酒呢 | ˏChung kwók, yung² mat, ˢyé ˏching ˢtsau ˏní? |
| Rice is used for the common, and particular ingredients for particular kinds. | 常酒用米其餘飲何酒用何物 | ˏShéung ˢtsau' yung² ˢmai, ˏk'í ˏü yuk, ˏhó ˢtsau yung² ˏhó mat₂. |

32. The fields of the Chinese are often divided from each other by raised walks and embankments of different degrees of stability. Small plats of ground are separated by mere footwalks, covered with sod; while larger portions are divided by walks paved with stone, and frequently shaded with trees; in the latter case, they are the roads between towns and villages.

33. The manner of irrigating rice-fields is adapted, for the most part, to their position and locality; in many cases, rivulets from a neighboring hill are led down into the fields, passing from one to the other, until they empty into a creek or river; at other positions, tanks are dug, as reservoirs to supply the fields. When near a river or creek, sluice-gates are made in the bank to let the water upon the grain, which are stopped as it ripens; fields are also watered by hand.

| | | |
|---|---|---|
| 38. In what manner are animals fattened and made fit for slaughter? | 點能養得肥畜嚟劏呢 | 'Tím ˏnang ˊyéung takˎ ˏfí ch'ukˎ ˏlai ˏt'óng ˏní? |
| Only let them be kept in good places, be fed at the proper times, and with suitable food, and assuredly there will be no difficulty in their becoming fat. | 養得其地食得其時又得其物何患不肥 | ˊYéung takˎ ˏk'í tí², shik₂ takˎ ˏk'í ˏshí, yau² takˎ ˏk'í mat₂ ˏhó wán² patˎ ˏfí. |
| 39. Are fishermen allowed to take fish in whatever places they please? | 漁人能隨處捕魚唔呢 | ˏÜ ˏyan ˏnang ˏts'ui ch'ü' pò² ˏü, ˏ'm ˏní? |
| In the great rivers, which do not belong to any particular persons, people may fish at pleasure. | 大江中非人屬地方·可任意 | Tái² ˏkóng ˏchung ˏfí ˏyan shuk₂ tí², ˏfóng ˊhó yam² í'. |

39. Fisheries are very extensive and very productive, and are open to all as here stated. No tax seems to be levied on them in any way. There are, however, small lakes and ponds, the property of individuals, subject of course to their control.

## Section Third.

# ON THE IMPORTANCE OF AGRICULTURE.

## 農本第三章

ˏNung ˊpún; tai² ˏsám ˏchéung.

| | | |
|---|---|---|
| The Sacred Commands say, Give importance to agriculture and the mulberry, and so provide enough food and raiment. | 聖諭云重農桑以足衣食 | Shing' Yü² ˏwan, Chung² ˏnung ˏsóng, ˊí tsukˎ ˏí shik₂. |
| 2. We have heard that food and raiment constitute the essential supports of a people. Agriculture and the mulberry-tree are the sources from whence these are derived. If a man does not plough, he may very likely suffer hunger; if a woman does not weave, she may very likely suffer cold. | 朕聞養民之本在於衣食農桑者衣食所由出也一夫不耕或受之饑一女不織或受之寒 | Cham² ˏman ˊyéung ˏman ˏchí ˊpún, tsoi² ˏü ˏí shik₂. ˏNung ˏsóng ˊché, ˏí shik₂ ˊshó ˏyau ch'utˎ ˊyá. Yatˎ ˏfú patˎ ˏkang, wák₂ shau² ˏchí ˏkí; yatˎ ˊnü patˎ chikˎ, wák₂ shau² ˏchí ˏhón. |

### *Notes and Explanations.*

OF the sixteen maxims, *Shing Yü*, or Sacred Commands, of Hónghí, the sentence contained in the first paragraph is the fourth; and the remainder of the section contains the whole of the amplification of it, by his imperial son, Yungching, comprising six hundred and sixty-one characters. It affords some data for forming a tolerably correct idea of the estimation in which

3. In ancient times, the emperors ploughed the lands, and the empresses cultivated the mulberry. Though the most honorable, they did not disdain to toil and labor, as examples to the whole empire, in order to induce all the people to seek these essential supports.

古者天子親耕
后親桑躬爲至
尊不憚勤勞爲
天下倡凡爲兆
姓圖其本也

ʻKú ʻché, ˏtʻín ʻtsz' ˏtsʻan ˏkang, hau² ˏtsʻan ˏsóng. ˏKung ˏwai chí' ˏtsün, pat˒ tán² ˏkʻan ˏlò, ˏwai ˏtʻín há² ˏchʻéung, ˏfán ˏwai chíú² sing' ˏtʻò ˏkʻí ʻpún ʻyá.

4. In the economy of food and raiment, which are produced from the ground, nurtured by the seasons, gathered by human strength—articles essentially important—a want of exertion is equivalent to sitting still, and waiting for poverty. Therefore, if diligent, the farmer will have a superabundance of grain, and the housewife a superabundance of cloth; but if negligent, then on the one hand, you will not have enough to serve your parents, nor on the other, sufficient to feed your wives and children. This rule is most certain.

夫衣食之道生
於地長於時而
聚於力本務所
在稍不自力坐
受其困故勤則
男有餘粟女有
餘帛不勤則仰
不足事父母俯
不足畜妻子其
理然也

ˏFú ˏí shik₂ ˏchí tò², ˏshang ˏü tí², ʻchéung ˏü ˏshí, ˏí tsü² ˏü lik₂, ʻpún mò² ʻshò tsoi², ʻsháu pat˒ tsz'² lik₂, tsó² shau² ˏkʻí kwʻan'. Kú' ˏkʻan tsak˒ ˏnám ʻyau ˏü suk˒, ʻnü ʻyau ˏü pák₂; pat˒ ˏkʻan, tsak˒ ʻyéung pat˒ tsuk˒ sz'² fú² ʻmò, ʻfú pat˒ tsuk˒ chʻuk˒ ˏtsʻai ʻtsz'. ˏKʻí ʻlí ˏín ʻyá.

5. Although the northern and southern parts of the country differ in being high or low, dry or wet; yet the high and the dry are suitable for millet and rye, the low and wet for the different varieties of rice. The soils on which these provisions are produced vary, while the agricultural labors are identical.

彼南北地土雖
有高下燥濕之
殊然高燥者宜
黍稷下濕者宜
秔稻食之所出
不同其爲農事
一也

ʻPí ˏnám pak˒ tí² ʻtʻò, ˏsui ʻyau ˏkò há², tsʻò' shap˒ ˏchí ˏshü; ˏín ˏkò tsʻò' ʻché, ˏí ʻshü tsik˒, há² shap˒ ʻché ˏí kʻóng' tò². Shik₂ ˏchí ʻshò chʻut˒ pat˒ ˏtʻung, ˏkʻí ˏwai ˏnung sz'² yat˒ ʻyá.

agriculture is held by the rulers of this country. The division into paragraphs does not exist in the original, and is introduced into the translation solely for the sake of convenience.

4. In the phrase *í shik chí tò*, the economy of food and raiment, the word *tò* denotes "the regular operations of nature in the generation, nutrition, and preservation of animals and plants."

5. The study of the mineral kingdom and of the atmosphere have never been carried to any great extent among the Chinese. Experience has taught them many useful lessons, only a few of which, however, seem ever to have been reduced to writing. There are no doubt, useful treatises on this subject, but they are not much valued by the common farmer, who generally prefers to take his lessons from his father and grandfather, and is contented with the small stock of traditional knowledge which is transmitted to him by them. The idea of the royal commentator in this paragraph appears to be that those lands lying northward are high and dry, while the southern parts of the empire would necessarily be low and wet; this, however, is not the case, the surface of the country being very low in some parts of the northern provinces.

廣東方言讀本

6. For the culture of the mulberry-tree, and rearing of the silkworm, excepting Kóng-nám, Chítkóng, Sz'ch'ün, and Úpak, the other provinces are not very well adapted, though they are fit for the production of hemp and cotton, either for rolling or spinning thread. Thus the materials from which garments are made are various, while their labor is identical with the culture of the mulberry-tree.

樹桑養蠶除江浙四川湖北外餘省多不相宜然植麻種棉或績或紡衣之所出不同其事與樹桑一也

Shü2 ꜀sóng ˋyéung ˏts'ám, ˏch'ü ꜀Kóng, Chít,, Sz'' ꜀ch'ün, ˏU pak, ngoi2, ˏü ˋsháng ꜀tó pat, ꜀séung ˏí; ˏín chik, ˏmá chung' ˏmín, wák2 chik,, wák2 ˋfong. ꜀I' ꜀chi ˋshó ch'ut, pat, ˏt'ung, ˏk'í sz'2 ˋü shü2 ꜀sóng yat, ˋyá.

7. We desire our people to exercise all their strength on agriculture and the mulberry-tree: do not love indolence, and hate toil; do not be diligent at first, and afterwards idle; do not, because a season of dearth may sometimes happen, lightly abandon your fields and gardens; do not covet extraordinary and exorbitant rates of profits, and hastily change your old occupations. If you give due weight to fundamentals, although from one year's income, after liquidating public and private accounts, there remain only a very small surplus; yet by daily and monthly increase and augment, it will become a very rich and affluent patrimony, and by sons and grandsons preserved from age to age, will afford an inexhaustible source of productive support: if you do not so, but seek the end without the essential means, how can such supports be long continued?

願吾民盡力農桑勿好逸惡勞勿始勤終惰勿因天時偶歉而輕棄田園勿慕奇贏倍利而輒改故業苟能重本務雖一歲所入公私輸用而外羨餘無幾而日積月累以至身家饒裕子孫世守則利賴無窮不然而捨本逐末豈能若是之緜遠乎

Ün2 ˏ'ng ˏman tsun2 lik2 ˏnung ꜀sóng; mat2 hò' yat2 ú' ˏlò; mat2 ˋch'í ˏk'an ꜀chung to'; mat2 ꜀yan ꜀t'ín ˏshí ˋngau híp,, ˏí ˏhing hí' ˏt'ín ˏün; mat2 mò2 ˏk'í ˏying ˋp'úi lí2, ˏí ch'íp, ˋkoi kú' íp2. ˋKau ˏnang chung2 ˋpún mò2; ꜀sui yat, sui' ˋshó yap2, ꜀kung ꜀sz' ꜀shü yung2 ˏí ngoi2, sín2 ˏü ˏmò ˋkí; ˏí yat2 tsik, üt2 lui2, ˋí chí' ꜀shan ꜀ká ˏíú ü2, ˋtsz' ꜀sün shai' ˋshau, tsak, lí2 lái2 ˏmò ˏk'ung: pat, ˏín, ˏí ˋshé ˋpún, chuk2 mút2, ˋhí ˏnang yéuk2 shí2 ꜀chí ˏmín ˋün ˏú?

8. You soldiers, in the ranks of the army, not engaged in agriculture, try to realize that the monthly disburse-

至爾兵隸在戎伍不事農桑試

Chí' ˋí ꜀ping tai2 tsoi2 ˏyung ˋ'ng, pat, sz'2 ˏnung ꜀sóng,

6. Silk, like tea, is probably cultivated to some extent in all the provinces of the empire, but as was observed in chap. VII., sect. 8, some provinces produce it in much higher perfection than others. The amount produced in the province of Canton is known to be large in some districts, as is also that of cotton. *Chik* means to spin or roll hempen threads on the knee by the hand.

7. It has been somewhere said that the Chinese never change their profession or occupation of life; but their being here admonished by the emperor not to do so *hastily*, presents another view of the case.

ments of money, with the rice dealt out from the granaries, are all distributed from the revenues which are paid in by the people, for the support of yourselves and your families; there is not one floss of silk, nor one kernel of grain, which is not the product of agriculture and the mulberry-tree. Enjoying these their profits, you ought to live in mutual peace with them, by all means protecting them, so that they may exhaust all their strength on agriculture and the culture of the mulberry-tree, then your supplies of food and raiment will never fail, and thus also you will have [a source of food and raiment] whereon you can confidently depend.

之之納各一農其安農爾不賴
給放輸等絲自享相使力遠有
分支姓爾一出既此衛盡永重
有有百給家不等彼扞得食亦
月倉皆散身莫爾當方俱衣則
思餉米以贍粒桑利多桑輩匱焉

shí' ‚sz' üt, 'yau ‚fan k'óp, ‚chí 'héung, ‚ts'ong 'yau ‚chí fóng' ‚chí 'mai, ‚kái pák, sing' ‚shü náp, 'í sán' k'óp,; 'í 'tang kók, ‚chím ‚shan ‚ká; yat, ‚sz' yat, nap,, mók, pat, ch'ut, tsz', ‚nung ‚sóng. 'I 'tang kí' 'héung ‚k'í lí', ‚tóng 'pí 'ts'z' ‚séung ‚ón, ‚tó ‚fóng hón' wai', 'sz' ‚nung ‚sóng ‚k'ü tak, tsun' lik,, 'í púi' ‚í shik,, 'wing 'ün pat, kwai', tsak, yik, chung' 'yau lái' ‚ín.

9. You likewise, local, civil and military officers, whose bounden duty it is to urge on their tasks, do not rob the people of their time, nor impede their business; correct the unsteady and idle, and encourage the diligent and laborious; let none of the lands lie waste; let there be no vagrants in the villages; let no husbandman throw aside his plough and hoe; nor any housewife put away her silkworms and weaving; likewise, let the products of the hills, marshes, orchards, and gardens, and the increase of poultry, pigs, dogs, and swine, be all nourished in a proper manner, and gathered in due season, in order to

官之勿者勞曠農婦卽之之
武課時惰者無民耜織圃彘
文勸民浮苦野游耒蠶園狗
方有奪事勤使無其其澤豚
地俱勿民之務邑捨休山鷄
若僚責妨懲之土無無至利

Yéuk, tí' ‚fóng ‚man 'mò ‚kún ‚líú, ‚k'ü 'yau hün' fó' ‚chí chak,, mat, tüt, ‚man ‚shí, mat, ‚fóng ‚man sz'; ‚fau tó' 'ché 'ch'ing ‚chí, ‚k'an 'fú 'ché lò' ‚chí; mò' 'sz' 'yé ‚mò kw'óng' 't'ò; yap, ‚mò ‚yau ‚man, ‚nung ‚mò 'shé ‚k'í loi' tsz'; 'fú ‚mò ‚yau ‚k'í ‚ts'ám chik,; tsik, chí' ‚shán chák, ‚ün 'p'ò ‚chí lí', ‚kai ‚t'ün 'kau chí' ‚chí

8. In all the provinces, the imperial troops are stationed in small parties in the principal towns and districts of the empire,—and receive their pay and rations from the local magistracy by orders from the commissariat in each provincial city. Being thus spread all over the country, it is in their power to give much protection or annoyance to the people, according as they are disposed. How they act depends, nevertheless, very much on the character of the magistracy. Their pay ordinarily, in times of peace, is small; and not unfrequently they have recourse to labor, in agriculture or mechanics, in order to provide for themselves and their families. In this way, in agricultural districts, they become identified with the yeomanry of the country. But sometimes, under a bad magistracy, they are troublesome neighbors.

supply the deficiencies of agriculture and the mulberry-tree; and if the proper diligence be bestowed on these essential employments, the sources of food and raiment will be kept full.

畜亦皆養之有
道取之有時以
佐農桑之不逮
庶幾克勤本業
而衣食之源溥
矣

ch'uk›, yik, ‹kái ˁyéung ‹chí ˁyau tò, ‘ts'ü ‹chí ˁyau ˏshí, ˁí tsó’ ˏnung ‹sóng ‹chí pat› tai, shü’ ‹kí hak› ˏk'an ‘pún íp, ˏí ‹í shik, ‹chí ˏün, ˏp'ò ˁí.

10. It is to be feared, that in years of full harvest, you will neglect to store up the surplus; and that there will be an unnecessary use of cloth when it is abundant; so that the evils of prodigality will equal those of idleness. And it is still more to be feared, that gold and gems will be esteemed, while vegetables and grain are neglected; that labor will be bestowed on embroidery, while the silkworm and mulberry-tree are disregarded; and that the habits of following light fashions and gaudy shows will be acquired;—against these you, both people and soldiers, ought especially to guard.

所慮年穀豐登
或忽於儲蓄布
帛充贍或侈於
費用不儉之弊
與不勤等甚且
貴金玉而忽菽
粟工文繡而廢
蠶桑相率為紛
華靡麗之習尤
爾兵民所當深
戒者也

‘Shó lui ˏnín kuk› ‹fung ‹tang, wák fat› ‹ü ˏch'ü ch'uk›; pò’ pák ‹ch'ung ‹chím, wák ‘ch'í ‹ü fai’ yung, pat› kím ‹chí pai, ˁü pat› ˏk'an ‘tang. Sham ‘ch'é kwai’ ‹kam yuk; ˏí fat› shuk suk›, ‹kung ˏman sau’, ˏí fai’ ˏts'ám ‹sóng, ‹séung sut› ˏwai ‹fan ˏwá ‘mí lai ‹chí tsáp, ˏyau ˁí ‹ping ˏman ‘shó ‹tóng ‹sham kái’ ‘ché ˁyá.

11. From ancient times, in the reign of prosperous kings, the aged wore silks and ate flesh, and the people suffered neither hunger nor cold; those kings enjoyed an abundance of people and wealth, and a renovating influences went abroad: this, in like manner, resulted from the same causes [diligence and economy].

自古盛王之世
老者衣帛食肉
黎民不饑不寒
亨庶富之盛而
致教化之興其
道胥由乎此

Tsz’ ‘kú shing ˏwóng ‹chí shai’, ˁlò ‘ché ‹í pák shik yuk, ˏlai ˏman pat› ‹kí pat› ˏhón, ‘héung shü’ fú’ ‹chí shing: ˏí chí’ káu’ fá’ ‹chí ‹hing: ˏk'í tò ‹sü ˏyau ˏú ‘ts'z’.

9. In ancient times the magistracy—the local, civil, and military officers—were wont to call on the people *ad libitum*, to work for them; at present, except in cases of emergency, the laws and usages of the country secure to the people the entire command of their time. The *yau-man*, vagrants or sauntering people, are very numerous in these degenerate times. Efforts are often made by the government to remove them from the large cities and towns, and to fix them in regular employments on waste lands. These efforts usually succeed but poorly.

11. This maxim, that the aged only should live on flesh and be clothed with silk, finds a place in the popular creed of the day, but in practice it has not much effect.

12. The work here referred to, called *Kang Chik T'ò*, or Plates illustrating Agriculture and Weaving, is a large quarto, containing forty-six leaves, done in the best style of Chinese printing, and having the imperial dragon surrounding each page of letter-press. There are twenty-three

| | | |
|---|---|---|
| 12. Our sacred predecessor, the august emperor Pious, anxiously concerned for the people, caused a book of plates, on agriculture and the manufacture of cloth, to be printed and circulated far and near, thereby evincing great regard for the people's support. | 我聖祖仁皇帝念切民依嘗刊耕織圖頒行中外所以敦本阜民者甚 | ʽNgó shing' ʽtsò ˏYan ˏwòng tai', ním' ts'ít, ˏman ˏí, ˏshéung ʽhón ˏkang chik, ˏt'ò ˏpán ˏhang ˏchung ngoi', ʽshó ʽí ˏtun ʽpún fau' ˏman ʽché sham'. |
| 13. And we, looking up to and considering his sacred instructions, anxious for the most important affairs of the people, have fully explained it, admonishing you to exert all your strength upon the essential supports of life. I, the one man, clothed and fed by the revenues of the state, desire that all in the empire may be equally filled and warmed. | 至朕仰惟聖諭念民事之至重廣爲詮解勸爾等力於本務余一人衣租食稅願與天下共飽煖也 | Chí' cham' ʽyéung ˏwai shing' ü', ním' ˏman sz' ˏchí chí' chung', ʽkwóng ˏwai ˏsün ʽkái, hün' ʽí ʽtang lik, ˏü ʽpún mò'. ˏU yat, ˏyan ˏí ˏtsò shik, shui', ün' ʽü ˏt'ín há' kung' ʽpáu ʽnün ʽyá. |
| 14. Six hundred and sixty-one characters. | 六百六十一字 | Luk, pák, luk, shap, yat, tsz'. |

plates illustrating the different operations of agriculture, and the same number exhibiting the various manipulations in raising silkworms and weaving cloth. The descriptions are in poetry, and for the most part, far beyond the scholarship of those for whom they were designed. The subjects of the twenty-three plates on agriculture are as follows, beginning with the first:—soaking the grain in water, previous to sowing it; ploughing the rice-grounds; harrowing them, and reducing the soil to a mesh; harrowing a second time, with a harrow-rake; rolling the fields, with a toothed roller; sowing the grain; observing the shoots, just above the ground; manuring them with liquid manure; pulling up the shoots for transplanting; transplanting the shoots; thinning and weeding the growing grain for the first time; a second weeding and thinning; a third weeding; irrigating the growing grain; reaping the ripe grain; carrying the sheaves to the thrashing-floor; thrashing the grain with flails; hulling the paddee in mortars; sifting the grain; winnowing it in fans; grinding it in a wooden mortar, which takes off the skin of the kernel; storing it in granaries; and lastly, returning thanks to the agricultural gods for the harvest. The subjects of the remaining plates are on rearing the silkworm, and weaving, as follows: washing the eggs of the worms; spreading them out on trays in racks; hatching the eggs; bringing leaves to feed the worms; cleaning the trays after the worms have eaten; removing the trays to different situations; picking mulberry leaves; covering the trays with branches for the worms to roll their coccoons; smoking the trays over a fire; weighing the coccoons; assorting the coccoons; sealing them in jars for about ten days, until the moth is hatched; reeling off the coccoons; the moths laying eggs; returning thanks to the gods for the crop of silk, and offering a part; reeling off the spools of single floss to form threads; weaving plain cloth; reeling and spinning thread; making the warp; dyeing the thread; weaving figured cloth; cutting cloth for garments; and lastly, making garments. The plates are among the best that Chinese art has produced, the perspective being tolerably good, and the filling up of the design often exhibiting many little sketches of rural life; and, were not the price of the book so high as to place it beyond the reach of common laborers, it might be useful to them.

14. The Chinese, like the Hebrews, often number the words of their sacred books. There are editions of all their classics, in which the number of the characters is marked at the end of each book, part, or section, as in the present instance.

# CHAPTER X.

# THE LIBERAL ARTS.

# 六藝篇十

Luk$_2$ ngai$^2$; ˏp'ín shap$_2$.

## Section First.

## OF CEREMONIAL RITES.

## 禮儀類第一章

ˤLai ˏí lui$^2$; tai$^2$ yat, ˓chéung.

| | | |
|---|---|---|
| 1. I have heard people speak of six liberal arts; what now [I desire to ask] are these six arts? | 吾聞人稱六藝究竟是何六藝 | ˏ'Ng ˏman ˏyan ˓ch'ing luk$_2$ ngai$^2$, kau' ˋking shí$^2$ ˏhó luk$_2$ ngai$^2$? |
| They are, it may be said in reply, etiquette, music, archery, charioteering, writing, and arithmetic. | 答曰禮樂射御書數是也 | Táp, üt$_2$, ˤlai, ngók$_2$, shé$^2$, yü$^2$, ˓shü, shò', shí$^2$ ˤyá. |
| 2. May I presume to ask what is etiquette? | 敢問何謂禮 | ˋKóm man$^2$ ˏhó wai$^2$ ˤlai? |
| Etiquette may be described, as including the forms and modes required by divine law, with the rules and observances imposed by human society. | 曰禮也者天理之節文人事之儀則也 | Üt$_2$, ˤlai ˤyá ˋché, ˓t'ín ˤlí ˓chí tsít, ˏman, ˏyan sz'$^2$ ˓chí ˏí tsak, ˤyá. |
| 3. And how is it in regard to common etiquette? | 曰常禮又如何 | Üt$_2$ ˏshéung ˤlai yau$^2$ ˏü ˏhó? |
| It is concerned with marriage, mourning, offering sacrifices, saluting and taking leave, answering and replying to one another. Nothing is without its ceremonies. | 曰婚姻喪祭進退應對之間無不以禮 | Üt$_2$, ˓fan ˓yan, ˓sóng tsai', tsun' t'úi', ying' túi' ˓chí ˓kán. ˏMò pat, ˤí ˤlai. |

### *Notes and Explanations.*

**Here**, as in other countries, the liberal arts are not very distinctly separated from the mechanical, or even from the sciences. Formerly in the west, grammar, dialectics, rhetoric, music, arithmetic, geometry, and astronomy, were styled the fine arts; more recently, and by a more correct nomenclature, those whose object is not utility, such as sculpture, architecture, painting, poetry, music, etc., have been so designated. In what estimation the six arts are held by the Chinese, the sequel will show.

2. The word *lai* has different shades of meaning in different places; its primary sense seems

| | | |
|---|---|---|
| 4. If so, where then can a thorough knowledge of both their principles and forms be obtained? | 然則禮義之本末何由得而知 | Ín tsak, lai i chí pún mút, hó yau tak, í chí? |
| There are the Ritual of Chau, the Ceremonial Forms, and the Book of Rites, three entire and lucid codes. | 曰有周禮儀禮禮記三亻詳言 | Üt, yau Chau Lai, Í Lai, Lai Kí, sám lai ts'éung ín. |
| 5. What is the Ritual of Chau? | 周禮者何也 | Chau Lai ché, hó yá? |
| The Ritual of Chau is the work of the prince of that line, whose family name was Kí, son of king Man, and younger brother of king Mò. This work, the Ritual of Chau, was framed in order to establish, for the several officers of that family, their respective duties. | 周亻周公所作公姓姬氏文王子武王弟也周禮一書爲周家一代設官分職之制 | Chau Lai Chau kung shó tsók, kung sing, Kí shí, Man wóng tsz, Mò wóng tai yá. Chau Lai yat, shü, wai Chau ká yat, toi, ch'ít, kún fan chik, chí chai. |
| 6. What is that called the Ceremonial Forms? | 何謂儀禮 | Hó wai Í Lai? |
| The rules and canons, comprising the Ceremonial Forms, are the production of the sages, a digest of the laws and canons of king Man and the prince of Chau, and derived from the same source as the Ritual of Chau. The Ritual of Chau may be regarded as the supplement, and the Ceremonial Forms as the body [of one work]. | 儀禮之制度文爲出於聖人文王周公之法度粗具與周禮一原周禮爲末儀禮則其本也 | Í Lai chí chai, tò man wai, ch'ut, ü shing, yan, Man wóng, Chau kung chí fát, tò ts'ò kü, ü Chau Lai yat, ün. Chau Lai wai mút, Í Lai tsak, k'í pún yá. |
| 7. And what is the Book of Rites? | 亻記又何如 | Lai Kí yau hó ü? |
| Tái Tak, a philosopher of the Hón dynasty, collected all the ancient ceremonial and musical writings, one hundred and eighty, and reduced them to eighty-five chapters, now | 漢儒戴德集古禮樂諸書一百八十篇刪定爲 | Hón yü, Tái Tak, tsáp, kú lai ngók, chü shü, yat, pák, pát, shap, p'ín, shán ting |

to be that of prescribed form,—which is to be observed, and extended so as to regulate the mode of every action. It also means whatever is according to the order of nature, as the *propriety* of the social relations, or that fitness of things which is felt to be right; *í* is external ceremony alone, but *lai* appears to include both internal and external.

5. In this work is found the origin of the *Luk Pò* or Six Boards; the work is divided into six parts, one for each Board; and is often found on the same shelf with the Five Classics.

6. In its present shape, the Ritual of Chau, though regarded as supplementary, seems, nevertheless, to be the most esteemed, being more copious and methodical than the Ceremonial Forms.

7. The Book of Rites has already (in Chap. I. sect. 3: 74—77.) been mentioned. It is highly valued by the Chinese, and is appealed to by them as an infallible standard in all matters relating to civil and religious rites, etiquette, etc. Of its forty-nine chapters, two have been taken to form parts of the Four Books; viz. chap. 31. the Chung Yung, and chap. 42. the Tái Hók, both good specimens of the Lai Kí.

called the Book of Rites by the Elder Tái. The Younger Tái still further abridged this, and formed a complete work in forty-nine chapters. The Ritual of the Elder Tái is no longer extant; and the Book of Rites by the Younger Tái is placed among the Five Classics. This Younger Tái, son of Tak's elder brother, was called Tái Shing.

八十五篇今名
大戴禮記小戴
更爲裁定成書
四十九篇大戴
禮今不行惟小
戴禮記列於五
經小戴者則德
兄子丨聖也

ˏwai pátˎ shapˎ ʻʼng ˏpʻín, ˏkam ˏming Táiˎ Táiʼ ʻLai Kíʼ. ʻSíú Táiʼ kangʼ ˏwai ˏtsʻoi tingˎ ˏshing ˏshü Szʼʼ shapˎ ʻkau ˏpʻín. Táiˎ Táiʼ ʻLai, ˏkam patˎ ˏhang; ˏwai ʻSíú Táiʼ ʻLai Kíʼ lítˎ ˏü ʻʼNg ˏKing. ʻSíú Táiʼ ʻché, tsakˎ Takˎ ˏhing ʻtszʼ Táiʼ Shingʼ ʻyá.

8. In the Illustrations of Rites it is said, Never be disrespectful, but grave and considerate, and let your words be calm and determined, then you will tranquilize the people!

曲禮曰毋不敬
儼若思安定辭
安民哉

Hukˎ ʻLai ütˎ, ˏmò patˎ kingʼ, ʻím yéukˎ ˏszʼ, ˏón tingˎ ˏtszʼ, ˏón ˏman ˏtsoi!

9. From birth till ten years of age, [man] is called a child, and then begins to learn; till twenty, he is called a youth, and is then capped; to thirty, he is in his manhood, and may marry; at forty, he is full of strength, and may enter the magistracy; at fifty, he becomes gray, and may serve in the high offices of state; at sixty, he becomes advanced in years, and may direct affairs; at seventy, he becomes an old man, and may retire from business; at eighty and ninety, he becomes infirm and forgetful. Till seven the child is an object of compassion, and both he and the man at seventy and eighty are not liable to punishment when guilty of crimes. When an hundred years, then he must be fed.

人生十年日幼
學二十日弱冠
三十日壯有室
四十日強而仕
五十日艾服官
政六十日耆指
使七十日老而
傳八十九十日
耄七年日悼悼
與耄雖有罪不
加刑焉百年日
期頤

ˏYan ˏshang shapˎ ˏnín ütˎ yauʼ, hókˎ; íˎ shapˎ ütˎ yéukˎ, künʼ; ˏsám shapˎ ütˎ chóngʼ, ʻyau shatˎ; szʼʼ shapˎ ütˎ ˏkéung, ˏí szʼˎ; ʻʼng shapˎ ütˎ ngáiˎ, fukˎ ˏkún chingʼ; lukˎ shapˎ ütˎ ˏkʻí, ʻchí ʻszʼ; tsʻatˎ shapˎ ütˎ ʻlò, ˏí ˏchʻün; pátˎ shapˎ ʻkau shapˎ ütˎ mòˎ. Tsʻatˎ ˏnín ütˎ tòˎ, tòˎ ʻü mòˎ, ˏsui ʻyau tsúiˎ, patˎ ˏká ˏying ˏín. Pákˎ ˏnín ütˎ ˏkʻí, ˏhí.

8. This is the first sentence of the first chapter of the Book of Rites; and though brief, it presents a fair example of the style of the work, which is for the most part laconic and didactic.

9. This is also from the first chapter of the Book of Rites. The term *kún* here denotes the ceremony of putting on the cap, which is performed at the age of twenty, and introduces the youth to the honors of manhood. They may and do enter office much earlier than at the periods here specified; and they also remain longer in office.

## Section Second.

## MUSICAL INSTRUMENTS.

### 樂器類第二章

Ngók₂ hí' lui²; tai² í² ,chéung.

1. Music ranks as second of the six liberal arts. There are various methods of playing on the different kinds of musical instruments; some are played by blowing, others by thrumming, or sucking, striking and bowing; there are also several notes *hó, sz', í, sháng, ch'é, kung, fán, líú, ú*, used in concert with the tones of the singer's voice, whether high or low, long or short; and thus music is made to contribute to man's pleasure and joy.

樂入六藝之次諸樂奏法不同有吹彈呼打挫等法仍用合士乙上尺工凡六五等音使合歌者之聲高低長短相同能助人喜樂也

Ngók₂ yap₂ luk₂ ngai² ,chí ts'z'. ,Chü ngók₂ tsau' fát, pat, ,t'ung; 'yau ,ch'ui, ,t'án, ,fú, 'tá, ts'ó', 'tang fát,; ,ying yung² *,hó, sz'², ,í, sháng'*, *,ch'é, ,kung, fán', ,líú, ,ú*, 'tang ,yam, 'sz' hóp, ,kó 'ché ,chí ,shing,, ,kó ,tai ,ch'éung 'tün ,séung ,t'ung, ,nang chó² ,yan 'hí lók₂ 'yá.

2. When playing on the lute or harp, there are other rules to be observed; to show the order of moving the fingers, they employ such terms as mean *to snap, to strike, to hook, to push*, etc., indicated by the [contracted] characters, *tíú, mút, kau, t'ik*, &c. For instance, [in the combined cha-

至於琴瑟則另有他法以指分次第用挑抹勾剔等法乚木勹乃是也如函則

Chí' ,ü ,k'am shat,, tsak, ling² 'yau ,t'á fát,; 'í 'chí ,fan ts'z' tai², yung² ,t'íú mút₂. ,kau, t'ik,, 'tang fát,, ,tíú, mút₂, ,kau, t'ik,, shí² 'yá.

### *Notes and Explanations.*

VOLUMES would be necessary to contain a complete and full account of the musical instruments and musical art of the Chinese. Little beside a brief enumeration of their principal instruments is contained in this section. As lovers of pleasure, they have always had great respect for music, one of its principal promoters; and for tones and rhythm, the two essential elements of music and of song, they manifest great fondness. Allied to music, they have something that resembles dancing—it is termed *mò* or posture making, and is of two kinds, civic and martial. In the Sám Ts'oi T'ò, there is a series of plates, exhibiting the various attitudes of the performer. Their writings on the subject of music, though hard to be understood, are very numerous; and they contain records of the art, in the earliest periods of their history, accompanied with drawings and descriptions of their instruments. Many of the most ancient are now disused. Often the instruments differ from any that are found in the west; and it must not be supposed, therefore, that in all cases where the same names have been adopted, the instruments are identical.

1. These nine characters are the names of the notes in Chinese music, corresponding to the *do, ri, mi, si*, &c.; the sounds of the characters are changed to accommodate them to this use. In writing vocal music, these characters are merely set down one after the other, which, when thus written, indicate only the pitch of the notes in a certain scale, leaving out altogether the two important particulars of length and absolute pitch, which are to be learned from the teacher's voice. The order of the notes in the Chinese scale is as given in the text. If the first or low-

racter here given,] the thumb of the left hand is to be placed on the fifth string, while the sixth string is snapped with the right hand. After this same manner, are all the other combined characters to be explained.

用左手大指按
五絃右手則挑
第六絃以此類
推餘皆倣此

ˏÜ —— tsakˎ yung² ʻtsó ʻshau tái² ʻchí ón' ʻʼng ˏin, yau² ʻshau tsakˎ ˏtʻiú tai² luk₂ ˏin: ʻí ʻtsʻz' lui² ˏtʻúi, ˏyü ˏkái ʻfong ʻtsʻz'.

§ INSTRUMENTS OF PERCUSSION.

樂器打類

§ Ngók₂ hí' ʻtá lui².

3. The *drum* is made of wood in the form of a cylinder, bulging in the middle, and covered at each end with skin; large and small ones are made in the same manner.

鼓以木作一鼓
腹之圍底面皮
捫大小同

ʻ*Kú* ʻí muk₂ tsókˎ yatˎ ʻkú fukˎ ˏchí ˏwai, ʻtai mín² ˏpʻí ˏmún, tái² ʻsíú ˏtʻung.

4. The *battle drum* is made of wood, its body is flat, and its two ends are covered with skin; it is now used in archery, and to announce the watches of the night.

戰鼓木作身扁
底面皮捫今用
以報射報更

*Chin'* ʻ*kú* muk₂ tsókˎ, ˏshan ʻpín, ʻtai mín² ˏpʻí ˏmún, ˏkam yung² ʻí pò' shé² pò' ˏkang.

5. *Base drums;* the small base drum is called *ying*, the large ones are called *fan*.

鼖鼓鼓之小者
曰應大者曰鼖

ˏ*Fan* ʻ*kú;* ʻkú ˏchí ʻsíú ʻché üt₂ *ying'*, tái² ʻché üt₂ ˏ*fan*.

6. The *tsun, pí, tsʻik,* and *kò* are four sorts of drums, all of which were made in ancient times, but are now disused.

晉鼙鼜鼛四鼓
皆古制今不用

*Tsun'*, ˏ*pí*, *tsʻik*ˎ, ˏ*kò*, sz'' ʻkú ˏkái ʻkú chai', ˏkam patˎ yung².

7. The *leading drum* is the leader of the *ying* drum.

𢅥鼓應鼓之引

*Lát*ˎ ʻ*kú* ying' ʻkú ˏchí ʻyan.

---

est be taken as the tonic, then they form a diatonic octave, with the addition of the ninth, or one note more than an octave, making *hó* an octave below *líú*, and *ú* an octave above *sz'*. There then would be no difference between this scale and that of Europe. But *í* and *fán* seem to be little used, and hence it loses its diatonic character.

2. The rules for writing instrumental music among the Chinese change somewhat according to the instrument employed; thus the lute requires a very different system of notation from the guitar; and both from the rebeck. In the notation adopted for the lute, "each note is a cluster of characters; one denotes the string, another the stud, a third informs you in what manner the fingers of the right hand are to be used, a fourth does the same in reference to the left, a fifth tells the performer in what way he must slide the hand before or after the appropriate sound has been given, and a sixth says, perhaps, that two notes are to be struck at the same time." It is partly on account of this clumsy mode of notation that so few Chinese learn to play the lute scientifically. These four, *tiú, mút, kau* and *tʻik*, are some of the characters employed technically to describe the various movements of the hands; the contractions used in the notes are written immediately underneath them in the text; and in the note introduced into the text, which is a very simple one, the first contracted character, *tiú*, is written at the bottom. There are works published, containing rules for playing the *kam* or lute, with diagrams showing the positions of the hands, &c., and also various tunes for the player. The *Kam Pò tái shing*, or Complete Treatise for playing on the lute, is regarded as one of the most perfect works on that subject.

3. The drum has received a great variety of forms and sizes among the Chinese. The largest and best are seen in their temples. Most of them are of wood, hollow and cylindrical, with skin or vellum stretched over one or both heads, and but seldom provided with braces by which they can be tightened or relaxed.

7. There was an ancient instrument of this name, made long and slender, bulging a little in the middle; the one now in use is hemispherical, small and almost solid, having skin stretched tight over its whole upper surface.

| | | |
|---|---|---|
| 8. The *Súchau drum* is made of wood, its body is very thick, and the skin covers it entirely. | 蘇鼓木作極厚皮捫至脚 | ꜀*Sú* ꜂*kú* muk꜇ tsók꜆, kik꜇ hau꜅, ꜁p'í ꜀mún chí꜄ kéuk꜆. |
| 9. The *pillar drum* is supported by a pillar in its centre. | 楹鼓中植以柱 | ꜁*Ying* ꜂*kú* ꜀chung chik꜇ ꜃í ꜃ch'ü. |
| 10. The *double drum* is employed for the purpose of rejoicing (i. e. conjuring) men and spirits. | 路丨以爲降人鬼之樂 | *Lò*꜅ ꜂*kú* ꜃í ꜁wai kóng꜄ ꜁yan ꜂kwai ꜀chí ngók꜇. |
| 11. The *concert drum* i made of wood, the body is flattish, the top covered with skin, and the bottom hollow. | 梆鼓木爲身畧匾面捫皮底空 | ꜀*Póng* ꜂*kú* muk꜇ ꜁wai, ꜀shan léuk꜇ ꜂pín, mín꜅ ꜀mún ꜁p'í, ꜂tai ꜀hung. |
| 12. The *loaf-shaped drum* is of wood, the face is covered with skin, the bottom is small, and the belly hooped. | 饅頭鼓木作面捫皮底尖箍腰 | *Mán*꜅ ꜁*t'au* ꜂*kú* muk꜇ tsók꜆, mín꜅ ꜀mún ꜁p'í, ꜂tai ꜀tsím, ꜀fú ꜀iú. |
| 13. The *flat drum* is made of thick wood, with a flat body, and skin stretched over both ends. | 懷鼓厚木作身匾底面捫皮 | ꜁*Wái* ꜂*kú* hau꜅ muk꜇ tsók꜆, ꜀shan ꜂pín, ꜂tai mín꜅ ꜀mún ꜁p'í. |
| 14. The *waist drum* has large heads, a small barrel, and the two ends, being beaten, respond to each other. | 腰鼓頭大腰小兩頭擊聲相應 | ꜀*Iú* ꜂*kú*, ꜁t'au tái꜅ ꜀iú ꜂síú, ꜃léung ꜁t'au kik꜆ ꜀shing ꜀séung ying꜄. |
| 15. The *tamborine* and the *rattle drum*, have six faces. | 靈鼓靈鼗六面 | ꜁*Ling* ꜂*kú* ꜁ling ꜁t'ò luk꜇ mín꜅. |
| 16. The *twirling drum* has a small barrel, with a stick running through it, and it has two clappers. | 鼗鼓身小以木貫之有兩耳 | ꜁*T'ò* ꜂*kú* ꜀shan ꜂síú, ꜃í muk꜇ kún꜄ ꜀chí, ꜃yau ꜃léung ꜃í. |
| 17. Both ends of the *tamborine drum* may be struck; they are made of the skins of the chamois. | 羯鼓兩頭可擊以戎羯爲之 | *Ít*꜆ ꜂*kú* ꜃léung ꜁t'au ꜂hó kik꜆; ꜃í ꜁yung ít꜆ ꜁wai ꜀chí. |

8. This, which derives its name from the famous city of Súchau, is small and flat, has but one head, and is much used at present on the stage in theatrical amusements. The concert drum is often used in its stead.

9. Pillar drums are still to be seen in temples, and some of them are large and elegant; they usually stand on a single pillar, elevated six or eight feet from the ground. They are beaten with a single mallet, at the hours of devotion, for the double purpose of summoning together the worshipers, and of arousing the attention of the gods. The diameter of the largest of these drums cannot be less than three feet.

10. The *lò kú* has two barrels, sometimes placed parallel to each other, and sometimes across each other; it was sometimes suspended from a wooden frame, and sometimes placed on a single pillar. The purposes to which they were applied are not very apparent; and they seem to have gone entirely into disuse at the present time.

12. This is a small instrument, used in religious processions; its diameter may be about one foot, and it gives a grave sound like the base drum.

13. This is much used by blind singers, who saunter through the streets in the night; as an accompaniment to their voices, and a regulator of the time, it has a good effect. These singers are also the tellers of old stories. Many of them are poor female children, early trained to this business, by which they procure support for their parents, sometimes, as well as for themselves.

15, 16. Both the tamborine and twirling drums have balls suspended from the barrels which strike the heads when twirled; their shapes varied, and some of the *ling kú* were made with several drums attached to a central frame, and struck only on one head.

廣東方言讀本

| | | |
|---|---|---|
| 18. The *hand tamborine* is flat and small, with a handle; singers hold it in the left, and strike it with the right hand. | 手鼓匾小有柄<br>歌者左執右擊 | *'Shau 'kú* 'pín 'síú 'yau ping', ꜀kó 'ché 'tsó chap, yau' kik,. |
| 19. The *equestrian drum* is used on horseback. | 提鼓馬上鼓也 | ꜁*T'ai 'kú* 'má shéung' 'kú 'yá. |
| 20. The *earthen drum* is an ancient instrument. | 土丨古樂器也 | *'T'ò 'kú* 'kú ngók, hí' 'yá. |
| 21. The *fish tamborine* is made of a joint of bamboo, its head is covered with skin, and two fingers are used to play upon it. | 魚丨截竹爲筩<br>以皮冒首用兩<br>指擊之 | ꜁*Ü 'kú* tsít, chuk, ꜁wai ꜁t'ung, 'í ꜁p'í mò' 'shau, yung' 'léung 'chí kik, ꜀chí. |
| 22. The *great gong* is cast of copper, in the shape of a platter; it is suspended by a string and struck. | 大鑼銅鑄形如<br>盤繩貫吊擊之 | *Tái' ꜁lò* ꜁t'ung chü', ꜁ying ꜁ü ꜁p'ún, ꜁shing kún' tíú' kik, ꜀chí. |
| 23. The *small gong* is made of very thick copper, a pair of them is always required for playing. | 单打厚銅爲之<br>每打用一對 | ꜀*Tán 'tá* hau' ꜁t'ung ꜁wai ꜀chí, 'múi 'tá yung' yat, túi'. |
| 24. The *drum gong* is like a waterman's hat, with a convex centre, and is struck with a mallet. | 銅鼓形若蛋家<br>帽中突用槌擊 | ꜁*T'ung 'kú* ꜁ying yéuk, tán' ꜀ká mò', ꜀chung tut,, yung' ꜁ch'úi kik,. |
| 25. The *gong from Súchau* is shaped like a boiler; and being suspended by the finger, is beaten with the corner of a small billet of wood. | 蘇鑼形如鍋以<br>指頭頂起用木<br>片之角擊之 | ꜀*Sú ꜁lò* ꜁ying ꜁ü ꜀kwó, 'í 'chí ꜁t'au 'ting 'hí, yung' muk, p'ín' ꜀chí kók, kik, ꜀chí. |
| 26. The *watch-gong;* this was anciently used to strike the hours; it is now a common instrument, used in concert with the drum gong, and is called the watch-gong. | 點子卽古之更<br>點今俗樂以之<br>配銅鼓曰點子 | *'Tím 'tsz'*, tsik, 'kú ꜀chí ꜀kang 'tím; ꜀kam tsuk, ngók, 'í ꜀chí p'úi' ꜁t'ung 'kú, üt, 'tím 'tsz'. |
| 27. *A frame of gongs;* thirteen small gongs, made of copper, are fitted into a frame, which is furnished with a long handle on its lower part. | 雲鑼以銅爲小<br>鑼十三同一木<br>架下有長柄 | ꜁*Wan ꜁lò* 'í ꜁t'ung ꜁wai 'síú ꜁lò shap, ꜀sám, ꜁t'ung, yat, muk, ká', há' 'yau ꜁ch'éung ping'. |
| 28. *Cymbals* are both large and small; in shape they are like a rain hat, and they are vulgarly called, the 'great clang,' and the 'little clang.' | 鈸有大小形若<br>雨帽俗號爲大<br>鈔小吵 | *Pút,* 'yau tái' 'síú; ꜁ying yéuk, 'ü mò', tsuk, hò' ꜁wai tái' 'ch'áu, 'síú 'ch'áu. |

22. This instrument is a simple metallic plate, in very general use in processions, in the army, the navy, on board of merchant vessels, &c. It is of various sizes, from a few inches to two or three feet in diameter.

24. The proper gongs or *lò* have flat faces, but this instrument has a protuberance in the centre which makes it resemble a waterman's hat; they are smaller than the common gong, and are used on the stage in concert with the watch-gong, as well as elsewhere.

28. These cymbals are much used on the stage; they are thin metallic plates, used in pairs;

| | | |
|---|---|---|
| 29. The *great bell* is composed of six parts of copper, and one part of tin, in order to make it very sonorous. | 鐘六分其銅而錫居一使聲響 | ˏ*Chung* luk₂ ˏfan ˏk'i ˏt'ung, ˏí. sik, ˏkü yat, 'sz' ˏshing 'héung. |
| 30. *Long bells* are like the the great bell; they differ in having metallic or wooden tongues. | 鐸形如鐘內懸金木舌之別 | *Tók*₂ ˏying ˏü ˏchung, noi² ˏün ˏkam muk₂ shít₂ ˏchí pít₂. |
| 31. *Wind bells* have long streamers hung upon the tongue, which strike as they are waved by the wind. | 風鈴外拖長幅於舌觸風而動 | ˏ*Fung ˏling* ngoi² ˏt'ó ˏch'éung fuk, ˏü shít₂, chuk, ˏfung ˏí tung². |
| 32. The *sistrum bell* resembles the great bell, and small round bells are suspended in it, for a tongue. | 金錞形象鐘內懸鈴子鈴銅舌 | ˏ*Kam ˏshun* ˏying tséung² ˏchung, noi² ˏün ˏling 'tsz', ˏling ˏt'ung shít₂. |
| 33. The *sacred king* is made of stone, and is suspended in order that it may be struck. | 磬以石作懸而擊之 | *Hing*' 'í shik₂ tsók,, ˏün ˏí kik, ˏchí. |
| 34. The *pitch-note king* was employed in the palace, as a leading instrument of music. | 天球以爲堂上首樂 | ˏ*T'in ˏk'au* 'í ˏwai ˏt'óng shéung² 'shau ngók₂. |
| 35. *Oblong plates* are made of iron, and are used [as musical instruments] instead of the king. | 方響鐵爲之以代磬 | ˏ*Fóng 'héung*, t'ít, ˏwai ˏchí 'í toi² hing'. |
| 36. *Upright supports* are used for hanging bells and king. | 簴用以懸鐘磬 | *Kü*² yung² 'í ˏün ˏchung hing'. |
| 37. *Wind glasses*, also called 'a hibiscus suspended by golden threads,' consist of small pieces of glass, suspended by silken threads; these being driven back and forth by the wind strike against each other, and so emit sound. | 响碼一名金線弔芙蓉以線弔玻璃片使觸風相撲而鳴 | '*Héung 'má*, yat, ˏming ˏ*kam sin' tiú' ˏfú ˏyung*, 'í sín' tiú' ˏpó ˏlí p'ín', 'sz' chuk, ˏfung ˏséung p'ók, ˏí ˏming. |
| 38. *Musical cups* or vases; twelve of these vases are taken, and into them more or less water is poured, and then they are played on with slender iron rods. | 甄卽甌也用十二甌施加減水以鐵筋擊之 | ˏ*Yan* tsik, ˏau 'yá; yung² shap₂ í² ˏau, ˏshí ˏká 'kám 'shui, 'í t'ít, chü² kik, ˏchí. |

the performer, holding one in each hand, strikes and rattles them together with great clatter and clangor, that has given them their vulgar name, well deserved.

29. With the ancient Chinese, this bell was "the regulator of the harmonic scale." A full description of it may be found in the imperial edition of the Book of Rites, and in the Illustrations of the Four Books. It is always made without a tongue, and is struck with a stick upon the rim.

33. This might be called the *right-angle*, since in shape it represents the two sides of a right-angled triangle, which form the right-angle; it is sometimes made with one of its legs more than twice the length of the other, in other instances, the legs are of the same length.

35. Ten of these were suspended, in two rows, upon a small wooden frame. They were played on in the same manner, and for the same purpose, as the instrument for which they were substituted.

37. These constitute a common ornament in summer houses, verandahs, &c., where the wind will gently hit them together; between ten and twenty pieces are usually hung from one hoop.

39. The *sounding vase* is made of porcelain and is hollow; when struck, the sound issues from its centre.

古缶瓦器中虛擊之聲自中出

'Kú ˏfau ˋngá hí', ˏchung ˏhü, kik, ˏchí, ˏshing tsz'² ˏchung ch'ut,.

40. The *musical box* was made of wood, like a lacker-box; in the middle, a wooden clapper, called a stopper, was fastened, attached to the bottom, by which it was worked.

柷以木作如漆桶中設椎柄連底挏之柄名止

*Chuk,* ˋí muk₂ tsók,, ˏü ts'at, ˋt'ung, ˏchung ch'ít, ˏch'ui ping', ˏlín ˋtai, tung² ˏchí, ping' ˏming ˋchí.

41. The *finale box* resembled a tiger couchant; its head was struck with a bundle of bamboos, and then run reversely across the back in order to stop the music.

敔狀類伏虎以籈擊其首而逆戛之以止樂

ˋYü chóng² lui² fuk₂ ˋfú, ˋí ˏyan kik, ˏk'í ˋshau, ˏí yik₂ át, ˏchí ˋí ˋchí ngók₂.

42. *Castanet boards* are billets of wood; there are in all three pieces, two of which are joined as one, and are beaten by the other piece.

拍板木片也共三片以二片合爲一單片拍之

*P'ák,* ˋpán, muk₂ p'ín' ˋyá, kung² ˏsám p'ín', ˋí i² p'ín' hóp₂ ˏwai yat,, ˏtán p'ín' p'ák, ˏchí.

43. The *Budhistic fish* is made of wood, it has a horizontal opening in its side, and its middle is hollowed out.

卜魚木爲之邊開橫口中挖空

*Puk,* ˏü muk₂ ˏwai ˏchí, ˏpín ˏhoi ˏwáng ˋhau, ˏchung wát, ˏhung.

44. The *wooden fish* is carved from wood in the shape of a fish, hollow in the middle, and rings when struck.

木魚刻木爲魚形中空敲有聲

*Muk₂* ˏü hak, muk₂ ˏwai ˏü ˏying, ˏchung ˏhung, ˏháu ˋyau ˏshing.

45. *Chaff balls* are like leathern bags, stuffed with chaff; they are struck in order to mark time in music.

拊狀如革囊實以糠擊以節樂

ˋFú chóng² ˏü kák, ˏnóng, shat₂ ˋí ˏhóng, kik, ˋí tsít, ngók₂.

46. The *copper-wire harmonicon* has copper nails at each end, upon which some ten or more copper threads are stretched, which are beaten by slips of bamboo.

洋琴兩頭有銅釘扯銅絃十數條小竹片打之

ˏYéung ˏk'am ˋléung ˏt'au ˋyau ˏt'ung ˏting, ˋch'é ˏt'ung ˏín shap₂ shò' ˏt'íú, ˋsíú chuk, p'ín' ˋtá ˏchí.

39. Its dimensions are very nearly those of a common sized tea-urn, which it somewhat resembles in shape.

40, 41. The first of these was used by the ancient Chinese in their musical entertainments, both civic and religious, to announce the time of commencing, and the second, of stopping, the music. The *chuk* resembled a square box, having the *stopper* attached to the bottom, and rattled from one side to the other through a hole in the front by means of a stick. The *yü* probably produced a rattling sound, from the sticks in the back of the tiger reverberating through the hollow body when struck. The names of these, and other ancient instruments, are introduced into this section, because they frequently occur in books, although they are now nearly disused.

42. These, differing very little from this description, may frequently be seen in the hands of musicians at the present day, used for the purpose of marking time.

43. This *puk ü*, "divining fish," is used in the recitation of prayers, both private and public, by the Budhistic priests, for the purpose of marking time. The *muk ü* is like it in shape.

46. The board of this instrument resembles the frustrum of a triangle, and the strings decrease in length from the base upward, being fastened securely upon the nails. There are two sets of strings, made by placing the bridges at different distances from the pegs, and causing the wires from one side to pass over one bridge, and under the other.

| | | |
|---|---|---|
| 47. The *seven stringed harmonicon* is like a lute, with seven strings, and is played on with a bamboo. | 篸與箏似七絃<br>用竹軋之 | *Sau'* ʿü ‹chang ʿts'z', ts'at, ‹ín, yung' chuk, chát, ‹chí. |
| §§ STRINGED INSTRUMENTS FOR THRUMMING. | 樂器彈類 | §§ Ngók, hí' ‹t'án lui'. |
| 48. The *scholar's lute* is made of wood, it is hollow within, and has seven strings on its face. | 琴以木爲之中<br>空面有七絃 | *‹K'am* ʿí muk, ‹wai ‹chí, ‹chung ‹hung, mín' ʿyau ts'at, ‹ín. |
| 49. The *many stringed lute* is like the scholar's lute, but while the latter has nuts, this has bridges. | 瑟與琴同惟琴<br>有軫瑟有柱 | *Shat,* ʿü ‹k'am ‹t'ung, ‹wai ‹k'am ʿyau ʿch'an, shat, ʿyau ʿch'ü. |
| 50. The *flat lute* is smaller than the many stringed one, has thirty strings, and is played on with a plectrum. | 箜篌小於瑟二<br>十三絃用撥彈 | *‹Hung ‹hau* ʿsíú ‹ü shat,, í' shap, ‹sám ‹ín, yung' pút, ‹t'án. |
| 51. The *small flat lute* has thirteen strings, its top is round, its bottom flat, and its middle hollow. | 箏十三絃上圓<br>下平中空 | *‹Chang* shap, ‹sám ‹ín, shéung' ‹ün, há' ‹p'ing, ‹chung ‹hung. |
| 52. The *three-stringed guitar* has the drum covered with snake's skin; the bridge is the support of the three strings. | 三絃蛇皮捫鼓<br>柱即三絃之碼 | *‹Sám ‹in* ‹shé ‹p'í ‹mún ʿkú, ʿch'ü, tsik, ‹sám ‹ín ‹chí ʿmá. |
| 53. The *balloon-shaped guitar* has a body like a goose-egg, and the four strings are thrummed with the fingers. | 琵琶身形如鵝<br>卵四絃指撥之 | *‹P'i ‹p'á* ‹shan ‹ying ‹ü ‹ngó ʿlun, sz' ‹ín, ʿchí pút, ‹chí. |
| 54. The *moon guitar* is like the full moon in shape, and its sounds resemble those of the lute; and hence its name. | 月琴以其形若<br>月聲似琴故名 | *Üt, ‹k'am* ʿí ‹k'í ‹ying yéuk, üt,, ‹shing ʿts'z' ‹k'am; kú' ‹ming. |

48. The *kam* (or *kin*) is justly more esteemed than any other musical instrument of the Chinese. A native writer says its name is synonymous with the term *kam*, which means to prohibit, and is so called because "it restrains and checks evil passions, and corrects the human heart." It is indeed a beautiful instrument, and 'discourses most excellent music.' It is about four feet long, convex above and plane below. Its strings are of silk, and differ a little in their relative diameter; they pass over the smaller end, and distribute themselves upon two pegs below. A bridge, near the wider end, gives them the proper elevation. The length of the sounding board is divided by thirteen studs of nacre as a guide to the performer. They are placed so that the length of the strings is divided into "aliquot parts of eight, with the omission of the seventh." A more extended description of the *kam* by G. T. Lay esq., can be seen in the Chinese Repository, vol. VIII., page 38.

52. This has a drum-shaped, hollow cylindrical body, with a very long neck and head. Its strings are tuned as fourths to each other; its sounds are low and dull, and it is played as an accompaniment to the *p'ip'á*.

53. This is nearly three feet long, and differs from the *sám ín* by having four strings, and a body which is nearly a foot in diameter. It is one of the most common accompaniments to the voice of ballad singers.

54. The *üt kam* is so called because the body is circular like the full moon; it resembles the theorbo or arch-lute of Europe in its general contour, but the number of strings does not exceed four, while that has ten or more. There are a number of raised frets upon the neck for the convenience of the player in fingering. The strings are of silk, and stand in two pairs, which are tuned as fifths to each other; they are struck forcibly by a plectrum or the nail, and in the hands of a good player emit very agreeable sounds.

海上絲綢之路文獻集成 科技與文化編

廣東方言讀本



55. The *four-stringed guitar* is like, but smaller than, the *üt kam*, and is played with a horn plectrum.

阮咸如月琴畧細以角撥彈之

*'Yün ,hám* ,ü üt, ,k'am, léuk, sai', 'í kók, pút, ,t'án ,chí.

56. The *bamboo guitar* is made of a large joint of bamboo [like a corn-stalk fiddle].

竹銅鼓截大竹爲之

*Chuk, ,t'ung 'kú* tsít, tái' chuk, ,wai ,chí.

§§§ WIND INSTRUMENTS.

樂器吹類

§§§ Ngók, hí' ,ch'ui lui'.

57. The *brazen trumpet* was anciently made of wood, but has in modern times been exchanged for copper.

銅角古以木作今變以銅

*,T'ung kók,* 'kú 'í muk, tsók, ,kam pín' 'í ,t'ung.

58. The *funeral pipe* is made of copper, and has a single hole; it is blown vertically, the tube is small, but the bell is very broad, resembling the brazen trumpet.

喇叭制以銅一竅直吹身細尾口殊敞似銅角

*,Lá pát,* chai' 'í ,t'ung, yat, híú', chik, ,ch'ui, ,shan sai', 'mí 'hau ,shü 'chóng, 'ts'z' ,t'ung kók,.

59. The *clarion* is formed from a sheet of copper into a crooked pipe; it encloses a small copper tube, which is drawn out when it is to be blown.

札角銅片製成曲筒內套小銅管吹時扯出

*Chát, kók,* ,t'ung p'ín' chai' ,shing huk, ,t'ung, noi' t'ò' 'síú ,t'ung 'kún, ,ch'ui ,shí 'ch'é ch'ut,.

60. The *trombone trumpet* is made of wood, and is blown in the same manner as the clarion.

號筒以木作吹法同札角

*Hò' ,t'ung* 'í muk, tsók,, ,ch'ui fát, ,tung chát, kók,.

61. The *hour horn* is used in the army, for the purpose of regulating the morning and evening hours.

晝角軍中置之以司晨昏

*Wú' kók,* ,kwan ,chung chí' ,chí, 'í ,sz' ,shan ,fan.

62. The *copper clarinet* is like the funeral pipe, it has seven holes, the ends are of brass, the barrel of wood.

瑣吶如喇叭七孔首尾銅木管

*'Só nát,* ,ü ,lá pát,, ts'at, 'hung, 'shau 'mí ,t'ung, muk, 'kún.

63. The *flageolet* is made of a reed; it is also called the *pat lut*.

笳以蘆爲之又名篳篥

*,K'á* 'í ,lò ,wai ,chí, yau' ,ming *pat, lut,*.

64. The *flageolet pipe* is a single wooden pipe; it has six holes, and is inserted at the mouth into a copper bell.

响笛一木筒六孔下貫一銅圈

*'Héung tik,*, yat, muk, ,t'ung; luk, 'hung, há' kún' yat, ,t'ung ,hün.

65. The *whistle* is used on board foreign ships to call the seamen.

銀鷄番國船上吹而傳人

*,Ngan ,kai* ,fán kwók, ,shün shéung' ,ch'ui ,í ,ch'ün ,yan.

---

56. This is made by cutting four or five strings in the cuticle of the bamboo, and elevating them by nuts as tense as possible; it is a childish instrument, like the plaything of lads in America to which it is likened.

57. Generally speaking, the wind instruments of the Chinese are inferior in sweetness of tone to their stringed instruments. This remark applies to the trumpets and pipes, which have the bodies short and usually straight, the bell made of thin copper, and the mouth-piece of a reed; the whole instrument being at once difficult to play upon, and very shrill in its tones.

| English | Chinese | Romanization |
|---|---|---|
| 66. The *clarinet* is blown at the end. | 竪笛直而吹之 | *Shü tik* chik, í ch'ui chí. |
| 67. The *conch* is a large sea-shell. | 海螺螺大殼也 | '*Hoi ló* ló tái hók 'yá. |
| 68. The *flute* has only seven holes; one is blown into with the mouth, and six are covered with the fingers. | 笛不過七孔口吹一孔按六孔 | *Tik* pat kwó ts'at 'hung, 'hau ch'ui yat 'hung, on luk 'hung. |
| 69. The *fife* is made of bamboo, it has three holes, and it is used to harmonize all kinds of sounds. | 籥以竹爲之三孔所以和衆聲 | *Yéuk* 'í chuk wai chí, sám 'hung, 'shó 'í wo chung shing. |
| 70. Large and small *fifes* are made of bamboo. | 大小篪竹爲之 | Tái 'síú *chí* chuk wai chí. |
| 71. The *pandean pipe* is analagous to the double pandean; it has twelve pipes, six base and six tenor. | 律如簫類六陽六陰共十二管 | *Lut* ü síú lui, luk yéung luk yam, kung shap í 'kún. |
| 72. The *double pandean pipes* are made of bamboos, and whether large or small, the number of pipes may vary. | 簫竹爲之或大或小管數不同 | *Síú* chuk wai chí, wák tái wák 'síú, 'kún shò pat t'ung. |
| 73. The *wooťung pipe* is blown by children. | 梧桐角兒童吹 | *'Ng t'ung kók* í t'ung ch'ui. |
| 74. The *earthen cone* is made of earth like a steelyards' weight, and whether large or small has six holes. | 塤象秤錘以土作大小皆六孔 | *Hün* tséung p'ing ch'ui, 'í 't'ò tsók, tái 'síú kái luk 'hung. |
| 75. In the *organ* (or seraphine) the foot works the bellows, causing the wind to enter the pipes and emit sound. | 風琴脚踏風箱使風入管而响 | *Fung k'am* kéuk táp fung séung, 'sz' fung yap 'kún í 'héung. |
| 76. *Small music boxes* are furnished with steel springs, and when wound up will emit sound. | 小風琴內有鐵線轉其機而响 | '*Síú fung k'am*, noí 'yau t'it sín 'chün k'í kí í 'héung. |
| §§§§ STRINGED INSTRUMENTS FOR BOWING. | 樂器挫類 | §§§§ Ngók hí ts'ó lui. |
| 77. A *two stringed fiddle* is a modern instrument, and is played by a bowstring of horse hair. | 二絃時樂以馬尾弓挫弦發聲 | *Í ín* shí ngók, 'í 'má 'mí kung ts'ó ín fát shing. |

67. The shells employed are large turbinated volutes, with the apex bored; they are often blown by private watchmen "for the purpose," as the Chinese say, "to let thieves know that the house is guarded."

68. This is also called *wáng tik* or the horizontal flute, to distinguish it from the *shü tik* or straight flute, i. e. the clarinet. It is made of bamboo, without joints or keys, and is a very shrill instrument compared with the German flute. Between the mouth-hole and the first finger-hole, there is an eighth one, covered with a film.

71, 72. The pipes of the *lut*, like the pandean pipes of Europe, decrease regularly from one end to the other, while those of the proper *síú* are longest in the middle, decreasing alike both ways; both kinds are, however, called *síú*. It is a very ancient instrument among the Chinese, as well as among the Egyptians, and not an uncommon one. Some are highly ornamented.

74. This is made of porcelain, not unlike a pear in shape, and adorned with figures. There are six round holes in the body, and one at the apex, but it is difficult to understand how the sound was produced from the instrument, nor do the books afford a satisfactory explanation; it was used in religious services at the temples and elsewhere.

| | | |
|---|---|---|
| 78. The *bass fiddle* is like a two-stringed fiddle, and a cocoanut shell serves for its drum. | 啼琴如二絃惟下貫椰殼 | ˌ*T'ai* ˌ*k'am* ˌü i² ˌín, ˌwai há² kún' ˌyé hok˒. |
| 79. A *violin* is like a two-stringed fiddle, and is played with a bow; it is a foreign instrument. | 四絃如二絃以弓挫外國所用 | *Sz'* ˌ*ín* ˌü i², ˌín ˊí ˌkung ts'o'; ngoi² kwok˒ ˊshó yung². |
| §§§§§ INSTRUMENTS FOR SUCKING. | 樂器呼類 | §§§§§ Ngók˒ hí' ˌfú lui². |
| 80. The *reed organ* is made of a gourd, into the middle of which thirteen reeds are arranged in order; its mouth-piece is called *wóng*. | 笙以瓠爲之十三管列瓠中其嘴曰簧 | ˌ*Shang* ˊí ˌú ˌwai ˌchí, shap₂ ˌsám ˊkún lít₂ ˌú ˌchung; ˌk'i ˊtsui üt₂ ˌ*wóng*. |
| 81. The *h'ü* belongs to the same class as the reed organ; in most points it is the same, but is a little different. | 竽亦笙類大同而小異 | ˌ*H'ü* yik˒ ˌshang lui², tái² ˌt'ung ˌí ˊsíú í². |
| 82. A *plectrum* is used to strike the strings. | 撥用以撥絃者 | *Pút₂* yung² ˊí pút₂ ˌín ˊché. |
| 83. The *nail plectrum* is for playing on such instruments as the three stringed guitar, it is put on the fingers as false nail. | 套甲即彈三絃等指頭套之甲 | *T'ò' káp*˒ tsik˒ ˌt'án ˌsám ˌín ˊtang, ˊchí ˌt'au t'ò' ˌchí káp˒. |
| 84. A *nut* is the wood in the head of the *p'ip'á* and similar instruments, to shorten and relax the strings. | 軫即琵琶等頭收放絃之木 | ˊ*Ch'an* tsik˒ ˌp'í ˌp'á ˊtang, ˌt'au ˌshau fóng' ˌín ˌchí muk₂. |
| 85. A *bridge* is a support; all stringed instruments employ them to elevate the strings. | 柱即碼也凡絃樂皆用以頂之 | ˊ*Ch'ü* tsik˒ ˊmá, ˊyá; ˌfán ˌín ngók₂ ˌkái yung² ˊí ˊting ˌchí. |

77, 78. These are almost the only instruments among the Chinese that are played with a bow. The first is as rude in appearance as it is unmusical in sound, being in outline merely a stick of bamboo, passing through a hollow cylinder of the same material. The bow passes between the strings which are tightened or relaxed by nuts upon the top of the stick, and elevated by a bridge set upon the sounding-board. The second emits sounds still more coarse and gruff than the first.

80, 81. The Chinese play upon these two instruments by sucking the mouth-piece, but sounds can be produced also by blowing. This mouth-piece is inserted into the gourd or wooden ball, which composes the barrel or wind chest, and connects it with the tubes; the latter are all of different lengths, having ventiges near the base to prevent their sounding, except at the will of the performer, thus giving the essential parts of an organ, with the stops. It is, at present, but seldom used by the Chinese, though it is one of the most ancient of their musical instruments.

N. B. A full account of the ancient music of the Chinese is contained in the Illustrations of the Four Books. The *'ng shing, pát yam, 'ng yam séung shang, luk lut*, &c., are there fully explained and illustrated by diagrams. That which represents the *genesis* of the five notes gives them thus; *kung*, the leading note,=81; *shéung*,=72; *kók*=64; *chí*=54; *ü*=48. "These five notes," says the commentator, "are produced from the *wóng chung*, which gives *kung*, the leading note; and a reed (or tube, *kún*) nine inches long, doubled nine times gives the number 81; from *kung* take one third, and it produces *chí*, whose number is 54; to *chí* add one third, and it produces *shéung*, whose number is 72; from *shéung* take one third, and it produces *ü*, whose number is 48; to *ü* add one third, and it produces *kók*, whose number is 64."

## Section Third.

## RULES OF ARCHERY.

### 射法類第三章
Shé$^2$ fát, lui$^2$; tai$^2$ ‚sám ‚chéung.

| | | |
|---|---|---|
| 1. The ancients practiced archery, in order to develop their virtue, causing their internal faculties to become correct, and their external demeanor upright. | 古者射以觀德使其內志正外體直 | ‘Kú ‘ché, shé$^2$ ‘í ‚kǔn tak,, ‘sz’ ‚k‘í noi$^2$ chí’ ching’, ngoi$^2$ ‘t‘ai chik$_2$. |
| 2. His spirit roused, the archer bends the bow, with great strength and bowstring opened wide; it checked, he lets fly the arrow, with mind settled and thoughts collected. | 怒氣開弓力雄而引滿息氣放箭心定而慮周 | Nò$^2$ hí’ ‚hoi ‚kung, lik$_2$ ‚hung ‚í ‘yan ‘mún; sik, hí’ fóng’ tsín’, ‚sam ting$^2$ ‚í lui$^2$ ‚chau. |
| 3. Estimate your strength, and make the bow; estimate the bow, and then make the arrows. | 量力調弓量弓制矢 | Léung$^2$ lik$_2$, ‚t‘íú ‚kung; léung$^2$ ‚kung, chai’ ‘ch‘í. |
| 4. In grasping the bow, it is necessary that the thumb should press firmly upon the middle fingers. | 把弓須以大指壓中指 | ‘Pá ‚kung, ‚sü ‘í tái$^2$ ‘chí át, chung’ ‘chí. |
| 5. The strong bow, it is especially required, should be stretched to nine tenths of its utmost bent. | 馬弓決要開至九分滿 | ‘Má ‚kung, k‘üt, íú’ ‚hoi chí’ ‘kau ‚fan ‘mún. |
| 6. In shooting the arrow, it is better it should go high and beyond, than too low and not reach, the mark. | 發矢寧高而過愼勿低而不及 | Fát, ‘ch‘í, ‚ning ‚kò ‚í kwó’, shan$^2$ mat$_2$ ‚tai ‚í pat, k‘ap$_2$. |
| 7. In practicing archery on horseback, the eyes must not roll about, nor the person sit in a leaning posture. | 騎射目勿瞬視身勿倨坐 | ‚K‘í shé$^2$, muk$_2$ mat$_2$ ‘shun shí$^2$, ‚shan mat$_2$ kü’ tsó$^2$. |
| 8. In practicing archery on foot, first learn to bend the bow wide and shoot far, afterwards by degrees seek to come nearer and nearer the mark. | 步射先學扯滿射遠然後自近求準 | Pò$^2$ shé$^2$, ‚sín hók, ‘ch‘é ‘mún, shé$^2$ ‘ün, ‚ín hau$^2$ tsz’$^2$ kan$^2$ ‚k‘au ‘chan. |

### *Notes and Explanations.*

ARCHERY has always, from very remote times, been held in high estimation and much cultivated by the Chinese. It is now, however, looked upon as rather an elegant accomplishment for gentlemen and military men, like fencing among some Europeans, than as a means of defense or offense in actual warfare, when recourse is had to firearms and swords. The bow is used in hte army, on board ship, and in gymnastic exercises.

7. Practicing archery on horseback is regarded as a high attainment, and is described with care in books treating of tactics.

廣東方言讀本



9. Rules for placing the feet: the forward leg is to be placed like a post, and the hinder one in a flexible position; when the direction of the arrow is to be changed, it is to be effected by moving the hinder foot; the tip of the left shoulder must be exactly opposite the right foot; they must not be placed like the letter T, nor like the letter A; if shooting to the left, change to the right, and vice versâ.

足法前腿似橛
後腿似瘸隨箭
改移只在後脚
左肩尖直對右
脚尖丁字不成
八字不就射右
改左射左改右

Tsuk, fát,, ,ts'ín 't'úi 'ts'z' k'üt,, hau² 't'úi 'ts'z' ,kwan; ,ts'ui tsín' 'koi ,í, chat, tsoi² hau² kéuk,; 'tsó ,kín ,tsím, chik, túi' yau² kéuk, ,tsím, ,ting tsz'² pat, ,shing, pát, tsz'² pat, tsau², shé² yau² 'koi 'tsó, shé² 'tsó 'koi yau².

10. The rule for the eyes: never look at the thumb-ring.

眼法不許看扣

'Ngán fát,, pat, 'hü hón' k'au'.

11. Rules for the arms: let the forward arm be as if pushing over a mountain, and the hinder (i. e. the right) one as if grasping hold of a tiger's tail.

手法前手如推
太山後手如握
虎尾

'Shau fát,, ,ts'ín 'shau ,ü ,t'ui t'ái' ,shán, hau² 'shau ,ü ák, 'fú 'mí.

12. Rules for the body: let the cheeks avoid hanging downwards; let the head avoid nodding; let the breast avoid swelling out forwards, and the back from being humped.

身法頤惡傍引
頭惡却垂胸惡
前凸背惡後偃

,Shan fát,, ,hí ú' ,p'óng 'yan, ,t'au ú' k'éuk, ,shui, ,hung ú' ,ts'ín tut,, púi' ú' hau² 'ín.

13. Finger-cots: these are made of leather, and are worn on the three fingers of the left hand; they are useful in handling the string.

極以朱韋爲之
所以韜右三指
利放絃也

Kik, 'í ,chü 'wai ,wai ,chí, 'shó 'í ,tò yau² ,sám 'chí, lí² fóng' ,ín 'yá.

14. The quiver is vulgarly called the arrow-bag.

[illegible]俗名爲箭袋

,Ch'á, tsuk, ,ming ,wai tsín' toi².

15. The bow: the body of it is made of cow's horn; its strings are made of sinews, and its shape is crooked.

弓以牛角作身
筋作弦其形曲

,Kung, 'í ,ngau kók, tsók, ,shan; ,kan tsok, ,ín, ,k'í ,ying huk,.

16. The bull's-eye is the red spot in the target's centre.

的垛中之紅心

Tik, 'tó ,chung ,chí ,hung ,sam.

17. Bow glove is another name for the finger-cots.

韘即極之别名

Tít, tsik, kik, ,chí pít, ,ming.

18. The bracer is bound on the arms to ease the shooting.

韝縛臂以便射

,Kau pók, p'í² 'í pín² shé².

19. The thumb-ring is made of ivory, and fitted to

決象骨爲之著

K'üt, tséung² kwat, ,wai ,chí

10. If in action with an enemy or a pirate, the eyes must be riveted on them, or on the target if practicing merely for acquiring knowledge and ability in the art.

15. The bow is not made entirely of horn; the horn is wrought into, and bound fast on, those parts which give the instrument its elasticity and power. The longest bows exceed six feet and six inches, and are beautifully made. When unstrung, the ends of the bow bend back, making it like a ⌒ in shape; this gives it greater force when strung.

18. In the Encyclopedia Britannica, art. Archery, there is a description of what is called a *bracer:* "to prevent the bowstring from striking the left arm, the arm is covered with a piece of smooth leather, fastened on the outside of the arm:" in Chinese this is called *kau.*

the thumb of the right hand; by it the string is held and the bow bent; it is commonly called *pán chí* [i. e. the finger's regulator].

於布巨指所以
鉤弦而開者也
俗謂之班指

chéuk, ü yau' kü' 'chí, 'shó 'í ˛kau ˛ín ˛í ˛hoi 'ché 'yá: tsuk, wai' ˛chí ˛pán 'chí.

20. The bow-case, also called a greave, is made of leather; it is for protecting the string.

遂韔也以韋爲
之所以遂弦也

Sui' ˛kau 'yá, 'í 'wai ˛wai ˛chí, 'shó 'í sui' ˛ín 'yá.

21. The target resembles a modern screen; it is made of leather, and varnished.

乏似今之屏風
以牛革鞔漆之

Fat, 'ts'z' ˛kam ˛chí ˛p'ing ˛fung, 'í ˛ngau kák, ˛mún ts'at, ˛chí.

20. This case is little more than half the length of the bow, and is made firm and strong, so that both bow and string are protected when placed in it. When marching, it is hung on the soldier's back, or under his left arm.

21. The target in use among the Chinese is made of a number of concentric rings, hung in a piece of canvas, and so contrived that when the innermost one is hit, all will fall out; but when an outer one is hit, none of the inner ones will fall. The arrows used in practicing have the heads bored with holes to produce a twanging sound as they fly.

## Section Fourth.

## CHARIOTEERING ILLUSTRATED.

### 御考第四章

Yü' 'háu; tai' sz' ˛chéung.

1. In the Book of Rites it is said, among the accomplishments are six liberal arts; charioteering is one. Accordingly, the controler-general instructed all people in it; and in it the royal tutors instructed the eldest sons of the emperor and his officers. The Odes regard 'managing the reins as silken cords' an excellence; Confucius esteemed

禮書曰禮有六
藝御居一焉故
司徒以之教萬
民保氏以之教
國子詩以執轡
如組爲賢孔子

'Lai ˛Shü üt, 'lai 'yau luk ngai', yü' ˛kü yat, ˛ín. Kú' ˛sz' ˛t'ò 'í ˛chí káu' mán' ˛man. 'Pò shí' 'í ˛chí káu' kwók, 'tsz'. ˛Shí 'í chap, pí' ˛ü 'tsò ˛wai ˛ín. 'Hung 'tsz'

### Notes and Explanations.

CHARIOTS and carriages of various kinds have been already described, in chapter tenth, section fourth. *Yü* is used to denote, according to its position, either the person who directs the chariot and horses, the *auriga* of the Latins, or the business itself of managing the horses and chariot. Sometimes a single horse was harnessed to a carriage; and sometimes two, four, and even six, all abreast. Oxen were sometimes used instead of horses.—The descriptions and representations of Egyptian chariots and charioteers, as given by J. G. Wilkinson, are in many particulars not unlike those of the ancient Chinese.

廣東方言讀本

'managing the chariot' an accomplishment. In Chau's list of officers, the duties of the great charioteer, martial charioteer, field charioteer, and equal charioteer, were all performed by great men, and superior scholars: thus charioteering was no mean business.

以執御爲能而周官大馭戎僕田僕齊僕之官皆大夫上士爲之則御非賤者之事

ʿí chap, yü' ˏwai ˏnang. ˏí ˓Chau ˓kún tái' yü', ˏyung puk,, ˏt'ín puk,, ˏts'ai puk, ˓chí ˓kún, ˓kái tái' ˓fú shéung' sz'' ˏwai ˓chí: tsak, yü' ˓fí tsín' ʿché ˓chí sz''.

2. Accordingly there were those of equal rank who acted as charioteers; there were those of inferior rank who acted as charioteers; there were scholars who, for their master, acted as charioteers; and there were persons of high degree who acted as charioteers for those of low degree.

故有以同等爲之僕者有以降等爲之僕者有以弟子爲師之僕者有以貴者爲賤人之僕者

Kú' ʿyau ʿí ˏt'ung ʿtang ˏwai ˓chí puk, ʿché; ʿyau ʿí kóng' ʿtang ˏwai ˓chí puk, ʿché; ʿyau ʿí tai' ʿtsz' ˏwai ˓sz' ˓chí puk, ʿché; ʿyau ʿí kwai' ʿché ˏwai tsín' ˏyan ˓chí puk, ʿché.

3. In the Book of Rites it is said, 'if the charioteers are of an inferior rank, receive them, but not if otherwise.' This is said of charioteers of equal and inferior ranks.

禮曰若僕降等則受不然則否此同等降等者之爲僕也

ʿLai üt,, yéuk, puk, kóng' ʿtang tsak, shau', pat, ˏín tsak, ʿfau. ʿTs'z' ˏt'ung ʿtang kóng' ʿtang ʿché ˓chí ˏwai puk, ʿyá.

4. If the sovereign commands, although they be persons of low degree, the great men and scholars must of necessity act for them as charioteers: this illustrates 'persons of high degree acting as charioteers for those of low degree.'

君命召雖賤人大夫士必自御之此貴者爲賤人之僕也

˓Kwan ming' chíú', ˓sui tsín' ˏyan tái' ˓fú sz'' pít, tsz'' yü' ˓chí; ʿts'z' kwai' ʿché ˏwai tsín' ˏyan ˓chí puk, ʿyá.

5. In the Dialogues of Confucius, sometimes Í'myau is spoken of as charioteer, and sometimes Fánch'í is so denominated: and this illustrates, 'scholars acting for their masters as charioteers.'

論語或稱冉有僕或稱樊遲御此弟子爲師之僕也

ˏLun ʿYü wák, ˓ch'ing ʿÍm ʿyau puk,, wák, ˓ch'ing ˏFán ˏch'í yü'; ʿts'z' tai' ʿtsz' ˏwai ˓sz' ˓chí puk, ʿyá.

6. In charioteering, why speak of rank or degree!

僕何可論乎哉

Puk, ˏhó ʿhó lun' ˏú ˓tsoi!

---

1. *Lai*, in this first line, is used in its widest and most general sense, and therefore rendered accomplishments. *Sz' t'ò* and *pò shí* were ancient officers, whose duties are fully described in the Chau Kún, a part of the Chau Lai.

6. This exclamatory sentence is added to the text by a commentator. Since equals may serve each other as charioteers, scholars their masters, and those of high degrees of rank serve those of low degree, there need be no discussion in this case about superiority.

## Section Fifth.

## ON WRITING.

### 書寫類第五章

꜀Shü ꜂sé lui$^2$; tai$^2$ ꜂'ng ꜀chéung.

| | | |
|---|---|---|
| 1. At what age do the children of the Chinese commence learning to write? | 中國孩童以幾歲初學書寫呢 | ꜀Chung kwók꜁ ꜀hoi ꜀t'ung ꜂í ꜂kí sui꜄ ꜀ch'ó hók$_2$ ꜀shü ꜂sé ꜀ní? |
| In ancient times, at the age of eight years they commenced their primary studies, and were taught the six liberal arts; now also [they are taught] in the same manner. | 古者八歲入小學教以六藝茲亦如之 | ꜂Kú ꜂ché pát꜁ sui꜄ yap$_2$ ꜂síú hók$_2$, káu꜄ ꜂í luk$_2$ ngai$^2$; ꜀tsz' yik$_2$ ꜀ü ꜀chí. |
| 2. Well, as this is the case, what apparatus is required for use in writing? | 然則用何物而書呢 | ꜀ín tsak꜁ yung$^2$ ꜀hó mat$_2$ ꜀í ꜀shü ꜀ní? |
| The four precious articles of the study—the pencil, ink, paper, and ink-stone—are required for writing. | 以文房四寶之筆墨紙硯而書 | ꜂í ꜀man ꜀fong sz'꜄ ꜂pò ꜀chí pat꜁, mak$_2$, ꜂chí, ín$^2$ ꜀í ꜀shü. |
| 3. With regard to the rules for writing, what are held in the highest estimation? | 書法以何者爲高呢 | ꜀Shü fát꜁ ꜂í ꜀hó ꜂ché ꜀wai ꜀kò ꜀ní? |
| The copy-plates of Wong Yaukwan are esteemed the best: see chapter first, sections five and six. | 以王右軍筆陣圖爲上見一篇五六章 | ꜂í ꜀Wóng Yau$^2$ ꜀kwan pat꜁ chan$^2$ ꜀t'ò ꜀wai shéung$^2$; kín꜄ yat꜁ ꜀p'ín, ꜂'ng luk$_2$ ꜀chéung. |
| 4. With whom did writing commence? | 書寫始自誰呢 | ꜀Shü ꜂sé ꜂ch'í tsz'$^2$ ꜀shui ꜀ní? |
| In high antiquity, knotted cords were used in government; in after ages, the sages exchanged them for writing, and in the time of Ts'óng Kat, the written characters were fully and perfectly formed. | 上古結繩而治後世聖人易之以書契迨至倉頡字於是大備 | Shéung$^2$ ꜂kú kít꜁ ꜀shing ꜀í chí$^2$; hau$^2$ shai꜄ shing꜄ ꜀yan yik$_2$ ꜀chí ꜂í ꜀shü k'ai꜄, ꜂t'oi chí꜄ ꜀Ts'óng Kat꜁, tsz'$^2$ ꜀ü shí$^2$ tái$^2$ pí$^2$. |
| 5. And with regard to paper and pencils, who were the first makers of them? | 至紙筆又何人始創嘅呢 | Chí꜄ ꜂chí pat꜁ yau$^2$ ꜀hó ꜀yan ꜂ch'í ch'óng꜄ ké꜄ ꜀ní? |

*Notes and Explanations.*

1. Rules for writing, with an account of the six styles in vogue among the Chinese, have already been given, as referred to in the third answer in this section.

4. The exact period at which writing was commenced, and the persons with whom it originated, are not well ascertained—*kái mò tsung kai háu yá*. See the Kóng Kám I' Chí.

| | | |
|---|---|---|
| Pencils are attributed to Mung T'ím, paper to Ts'oi Lun; the Thousand Character Classic says thus, T'ím [made] pencils, and Lun paper. | 筆稱蒙恬紙號<br>蔡倫千字文謂<br>恬筆倫紙是也 | Pat, ch'ing Mung T'ím; chí hò Ts'oi Lun; Ts'ín Tsz' Man wai T'ím pat, Lun chí, shí yá. |
| 6. Where are the most accomplished portrait painters to be found? | 善於寫真者何<br>處方有 | Shín ü sé chan ché, hó ch'ü fóng yau? |
| They are in each and all of the provinces; if reference be had only to the province of Canton, many, who were the most distinguished, are deceased; those at present in the metropolis, such as Chung Námshán, Lái Ts'ingchan, &c., are however favored with a respectable share of business. | 各省皆有以廣<br>東而論稱妙手<br>者多已物故現<br>如省之鍾南山<br>賴清真等亦不<br>過應酬而已 | Kók sháng kái yau, í Kwóng tung í lun, ch'ing míú shau ché, tó kí mat kú; ín ü sháng chí Chung Nám shán Lái Ts'ing chan tang, yik pat kwó ying ch'au í í. |
| 7. Is this class of portrait painters held in high esteem by the people generally or not? | 其寫像者世俗<br>還尙他否 | K'í sé tséung ché, shai tsuk, wán shéung t'á fau? |
| Of those who live by the pencil and ink, they are none that are not addressed as *sín-shang;* and by the people generally they are held in high estimation. | 筆墨生涯罔不<br>號爲先生世俗<br>未嘗不尙 | Pat, mak, shang ngai, móng pat, hò wai sín shang; shai tsuk, mí shéung pat, shéung. |
| 9. What kinds of paintings do the people most esteem? | 世所尙者何畫 | Shai shó shéung ché hó wá? |
| The landscape paintings; for by them are seen the thoughts cherished in the human breast, and therefore they are esteemed. | 亦山水也以其<br>足見人之胸懷<br>故也 | Yik, shán shui yá; í k'í tsuk, kín yan chí hung wái, kú yá. |
| 18. Are there any books of pictures which are printed from plates? | 畫有刊刷之圖<br>本否 | Wá yau hón sát, chí t'ò pún fau? |
| The books of pictures printed from plates are by no means few. | 世之圖本不一<br>而足 | Shai chí t'ò pún, pat, yat, í tsuk. |
| 11. And what kinds of pictures printed from plates are regarded as the most elegant? | 又以何圖本爲<br>最佳呢 | Yau í hó t'ò pún wai tsui kai ní? |

5. The first flourished in the reign of Tsun Chíwóng, the great destroyer of books; the second lived soon after in the time of the Hau Hón dynasty.

6, 7. The phrases *sé chan ché*, and *sé tséung ché*, are synonymous. Their delineations of the human countenance are not always so *true* as the first phrase would seem to indicate; but the Chinese paint insects, fishes, flowers, fruit, &c., admirably; and often group with taste and effect.

At present the pictures forming the Garden of Kale are regarded as the most superb.

現以芥子園畫譜爲妙

Ín$^{2}$ 'í Kái' 'Tsz' ,Ün wá$^{2}$ 'p'ò ,wai míú$^{2}$.

12. What materials are used to make the plates for these pictures?

其圖板用何物而作呢

,K'í ,t'ò 'pán yung$^{2}$ ,hó mat$_{2}$ ,í tsók, ,ní?

There are plates of brass and stone, but those of wood are by far the most numerous.

板或有銅石第以木做者尤多

'Pán wák$_{2}$ 'yau ,t'ung shik$_{2}$, tai$^{2}$ 'í muk$_{2}$ tsò$^{2}$ 'ché ,yau ,tó.

13. When commencing learning to read, are books with pictures and names attached to them used or not?

初習讀時有用左圖右字書否

,Ch'ó tsap$_{2}$ tuk$_{2}$ ,shí, 'yau yung$^{2}$ 'tsó ,t'ò yau$^{2}$ tsz$^{2}$' ,shü 'fau?

Although there are books of this kind, they are never used in learning to read.

雖有此書然習讀者却不用

,Sui 'yau 'ts'z' ,shü, ,ín tsap$_{2}$ tuk$_{2}$ 'ché k'éuk, pat, yung$^{2}$.

12. Etching, engraving on steel, and so forth, are arts which are scarcely known in this country, and have not been employed at all in illustrating books. Stone plates are little used, and lithography is entirely unknown.

13. It has been said that there are books of pictures, giving representations of animals, things and actions, with their appropriate names, for the use of children when learning to read; drawings of a few common things are sometimes introduced into the native almanacs, with the names written beneath them, but the plan does not seem to have been carried into use in instruction.

## Section Sixth.

## ON ARITHMETIC.

### 數目類第六章

Shò' muk$_{2}$ lui$^{2}$; tai$^{2}$ luk$_{2}$ ,chéung.

1. One is the beginning of numbers; ten is the completion of numbers; they advance up to one hundred which is a multiple of ten. Ten reduplicated and multiplied ten times makes one hunded; one hundred reduplicated and mutiplied ten times, makes a thousand; a thousand

一者數之始十者數之終至於百者十之盈也十累而盈滿十則爲百百累而

Yat, 'ché shò' ,chí 'ch'í, shap$_{2}$ 'ché shò' ,chí ,chung; chí' ,yü pák, 'ché, shap$_{2}$ ,chí ,ying 'yá. Shap$_{2}$ 'lui ,í ,ying, 'mún shap$_{2}$ tsak, ,wai pák,;

### *Notes and Explanations.*

THE paragraphs, composing this short section, will at once serve to complete the view of the iber al arts, and form an appropriate introduction to the next chapter.

reduplicated and multiplied ten times, makes a myriad. Passing this, and advancing onwards, numbers are without any assignable limit, incapable of being exhausted.

盈滿十則爲千千累而盈滿十則爲萬也過此以往數無紀極莫之能窮

pák, 'lui ,í ,ying, 'mún shap, tsak, ,wai ,ts'ín; ,ts'ín 'lui, ,í ,ying, 'mún shap, tsak, ,wai mán' 'yá. Kwó' 'ts'z' 'í 'wóng, shò' ,mò 'kí kik,, mók, ,chí ,nang ,k'ung.

2. With regard to the fractional numbers—tenths, hundredths, thousandths, and tens of thousandths,—they all decrease by tens. All numbers without exception are reckoned in this manner.

至小數之分厘毫絲忽皆滿十而推凡數莫不有也

Chí' 'síú shò' ,chí ,fan, ,lí, ,hò, ,sz', fat,, ,kái 'mún shap, ,í ,t'úi. ,Fán shò' mók, pat, 'yau 'yá.

3. How did numbers originate? They originated with drawings and writing. Fukhí, obtaining them, drew his eight diagrams; Yü the Great, obtaining them, measured off the lands for cultivation. By these same means the sages arranged things into classes and completed their works. Of all the celestial officers, terrestrial magistrates, music, signs, soldiers, taxes, extending to the minutest points and the smallest fractions, there is not one with which numbers are not concerned; accordingly there is nothing which, in its original principles, is not included in the Book of Changes.

數何肇其肇自圖書乎伏羲得之以畫八卦大禹得之以序疇列聖得之以門物成務凡天官地員律曆兵賦以及纖悉抄忽莫不有數則莫不本於易範

Shò' ,hó shíú'? ,K'í shíú' tsz' ,t'ò ,shü ,ú. Fuk, ,hí tak, ,chí 'í wák, pát, kwá'; Tái' 'Yü tak, ,chí 'í tsü' ,ch'au. Lít, shing' tak, ,chí 'í ,mún mat, ,shing mò'. ,Fán ,t'ín ,kún, tí' ,ün, lut,, lik,, ,ping, fú', 'í k'ap, ,ts'ím, shik,, ,ch'au, fat,; mók, pat, 'yau shò'; tsak, mók, pat, 'pún ,yü Yik, fán'.

4. The Book of Changes is one entire work; its diagrams are those originally drawn by Fukhí; its explanations are those which were added by king Man and the prince of Chau; and likewise there are some by Confucius: and in it are comprised the principles

易經一書其卦本伏羲所畫其辭乃文王周公所繫并孔子所作其中變化之

Yik, ,King yat, ,shü; ,k'í kwá' 'pún Fuk, ,hí 'shó wák,; ,k'í ,ts'z' 'nái ,Man ,wóng ,Chau ,kung 'shó hai'; ping' 'Hung 'tsz' 'shó tsók,; ,k'í ,chung pín' fá' ,chí 'lí,

1. This paragraph is quoted entire from the commentary on the Trimetrical Classic. See chapter first, section third, page 11.

3. This paragraph forms the exordium of Ching Yüsz' Arithmetic. According to tradition, on a certain time, a seamonster, or *lung-má*, came up from the abyss, bearing on his back some drawings, or *tó;* Fukhí obtaining possesion of these, formed from them his diagrams. On another occasion, a tortoise, or *kwai*, coming on land from a river, Yü the Great discovered certain characters on his back, and hence devised a system for laying out lands. And hence too, came writing and arithmetic! The origin and history of the lung-má or dragon-horse are not explained. Pictures of the animal may be seen in the Chinese arithmetics and almanacs.

of all changes, which extend to all concerns, and to all things, without exception.

理萬事萬物無不出乎其中

mán' sz'' mán' mat, ,mò pat, ch'ut, ,ú ,k'í ,chung.

5. In ancient times, children when eight years of age commenced their primary studies, and when fifteen they entered on the higher branches; and those of the present age, though not rigidly conforming to these periods, yet by cutting off excess, and supplying deficiency, also do not deviate far from the same general standard.

古者八歲而入小學十五而入大學當今之世雖不决於其時然截長補短亦不外如斯

'Kú 'ché pát, sui' ,í yap, 'síú hók, shap, 'ng ,í yap, tái' hók,; ,tóng ,kam ,chí shai', ,sui pat, k'üt, ,yü ,k'í ,shí, ,ín tsít, ,ch'éung 'pò 'tün, yik, pat, ngoi' ,ü ,sz'.

6. With regard to books on numbers, they are everywhere to be found; but if you seek for the most general and important, the most methodical and best arranged, there is indeed no one book so well prepared every way, as the General Comprehensive Arithmetic.

夫數一書靡不有之而提綱挈要纏柝支分則又不如算法統宗一書之為大備也

,Fú shò' yat, ,shü, 'mí pat, 'yau ,chí, ,í ,t'ai ,kóng k'ít, íú' 'lui ts'ik, ,chí ,fan, tsak, yau' pat, ,ü sün' fát, 'T'ung ,Tsung yat, ,shü ,chí ,wai tái' pí' 'yá.

7. The general Comprehensive Arithmetic is the compilation of Ching Yüsz' of the Ming dynasty: the work is well arranged, comprising in one summary view, extending from the most remote times, whatever has been said respecting the higher branches, and downwards to all the fundamental rules inclusive; and a thorough acquaintance with it, will make the student perfect master of the subject.

算法統宗乃明萬歷間程汝思所輯其書具在一寓目而千古所謂方田以下旁要以上九數云者靡不了了於胸中

Sün' fát, 'T'ung ,Tsung, 'nái ,Ming Mán' lik, ,kán, ,Ch'ing 'Yü ,sz' 'shó ts'ap,; ,k'í ,shü kü' tsoi', yat, yü' muk, ,í ,ts'in 'kú 'shó wai' ,fóng ,t'ín 'í há', ,p'óng ,íú 'í shéung', 'kau shò' ,wan 'ché, 'mí pat, 'líú 'líú ,ü ,hung ,chung.

5. This arithmetic is comprised in five duodecimo volumes; it is an elementary treatise, and comprises much useful matter; and besides the fundamental rules, it contains some general views of mensuration, astronomy, &c. Among the Chinese, arithmetic does not receive much attention; their youth, who aspire to preferment and honor in the state, give their undivided attention to classical learning; and arithmetic is studied only for practical purposes, in order to facilitate the common transactions of life. Such fundamental principles as are acquired by the child, are usually taught as a part of domestic education. The arithmetical operations are performed on the counting board, described in the sequel.

# CHAPTER XI.

# MATHEMATICS.

# 數學篇十一

**Shò' hók₂; ‹p'ín shap₂ yat›.**

## Section First.

## NUMERICAL CHARACTERS.

### 數字類第一章

**Shò' tsz'² lui²; tai² yat› ‹chéung.**

| | | |
|---|---|---|
| 1. The *worked factor* is the given number. | 實者本數也 | *Shat₂* 'ché, 'pún shò' ʿyá. |
| 2. The *working factor* is the supposed number. | 法者樣數也 | *Fát›* 'ché, yéung² shò' ʿyá. |
| 3. Suppose you now have two hundred and sixty taels, three mace, and two candareens, to be divided among six men; the question is, how much will each man receive of the said money? | 假如今有銀二百六十両三錢二分作六人分之問每人該銀若干 | 'Ká ‚ü, ‹kam ʿyau ‚ngan pák› luk₂ shap₂ ʿléung, ‹sám ‚ts'ín, í² ‹fan, tsók› luk₂ ‚yan ‹fan ‹chí; man² ʿmúi ‚yan ‹koi ‚ngan yéuk₂ ‹kón? |
| 3. Answer: forty-four taels, two mace, and two candareens. | 答曰四十四両二錢二分 | Táp› üt₂, sz'' shap₂ sz'' ʿléung₂ í² ‚ts'ín, í² ‹fan. |
| 4. The method [for its solution) is this; the money laid down, 260. 3. 2. is the *worked factor;* and the 6, the | 法曰置銀二六三二爲實以六 | Fát› üt₂, chí' ‚ngan í² luk‹ ‹sám í² ‚wai shat₂; ʿí luk₂ ‚yan |

## *Notes and Explanations.*

SHÒ HÓK, meaning literally 'the science of numbers,' corresponds very nearly to the term Mathematics; and so it is regarded, by the Chinese, as the science which treats of numbers and magnitude, or of whatever can be numbered or measured.

*Shò tsz'* corresponds to the phrase, 'mathematical definition:' and as the foundation of all knowledge of this science depends on definitions, it is requisite that these should be first explained. In Ching's arithmetic, noticed in the last section, is a list of definitions, some of which are here quoted. The Chinese systems of notation are very clumsy and not easily comprehended.

1, 2. These terms are used both in multiplication and division: in the first, for the multiplicand and multiplier; in the second, for the dividend and divisor.

| | | |
|---|---|---|
| number of men, is the ***working factor:*** six is the number by which the given number is to be divided. | 人爲法用六歸算之則合 | ˏwai fátˎ; yung² lukˎ, ˏkwai sün' ˏchí, tsakˎ hóp₂. |
| 5. ***Addition*** is to augment and increase. | 加者增添也 | ˏ*Ká* 'ché, ˏtsang ˏt'ím 'yá. |
| 6. ***Subtraction*** is to diminish and lessen. | 減者除少也 | '*Kám* 'ché, ˏch'ü 'shíú 'yá. |
| 7. ***Multiplication*** is the junction of the worked and working factors so as to produce another number. | 乘者法實合變數也 | ˏ*Shing* 'ché, fátˎ shatˎ hópˎ pín' shò' 'yá. |
| 8. ***Division*** is the resolution of numbers. | 歸入已之數也 | ˏ*Kwai*, yap₂ 'kí ˏchí shò' 'yá. |
| 9. ***Reduction*** is the rule by which (any thing, such as) catties, for instance, are reduced to taels. | 折者以斤折兩是也 | *Chít*ˎ 'ché, 'í ˏkan chítˎ 'léung shí² 'yá. |
| 10. ***Reduplication*** is the doubling of a number. | 倍加上倍數也 | '*P'úi*, ˏká 'shéung 'p'úi shò' 'yá. |
| 11. ***Coupling*** is the joining together of two numbers. | 併者二數相合 | *Ping*² 'ché, í² shò' ˏséung hóp₂. |
| 12. ***Separation*** is cutting off and taking away. | 截者割斷也 | *Tsít*₂ 'ché, kótˎ tün² 'yá. |
| 13. ***Original*** numbers are those first given. | 原者初數也 | ˏ*Ün* 'ché, ˏch'ó shò' 'yá. |
| 14. ***Difference*** is when the numbers are unlike, one being greater or less than the other. | 差者多少不同數也 | ˏ*Ch'á* 'ché, ˏtó 'shíú patˎ ˏt'ung shò' 'yá. |
| 15. The ***sum total*** is the sum of the united numbers. | 通者會同其數 | ˏ*T'ung* 'ché, úi² ˏt'ung ˏk'í shò'. |
| 16. ***Involution*** is the multiplication of numbers into themselves, and repeated a second time. | 再乘者自乘之而又乘也 | *Tsoi*' ˏ*shing* 'ché, tsz'² ˏshing ˏchí, ˏí yau² ˏshing 'yá. |
| 17. A ***Remainder*** is that which is left after any given part whatever has been taken away. | 剩者除去尙存之餘 | *Shing*² 'ch'é, ˏch'ü h'ü' shéung² ˏts'un ˏchí ˏyü. |
| 18. All numbers, whether in long measure, dry measure, or weights, from ***units*** ascend to ***tens, hundreds, thousands, tens of thousands, hundreds of thousands, millions, tens of millions, hundreds of millions, billions, tens of billions,***—units occupying the first place, tens the second, hundreds the third, and so forth. | 凡度量衡自単位以上則曰十百千萬億兆京垓秭穰單爲一位十爲二位百爲三位云云 | ˏFán tók₂, ˏléung, ˏhang, tsz'² ˏtán wai² 'í shéung², tsakˎ ütˎ shap₂, pákˎ, ˏts'ín, mán², yikˎ, chíú², ˏking, ˏhoi, 'tsz', ˏyéung; ˏtán ˏwai yatˎ wai², shap₂ ˏwai í² wai², pákˎ ˏwai ˏsám wai² ˏwan, ˏwan. |

10, 11. The first of these is simply a multiplication of any number by two; the second is adding together any two numbers.

18. The fundamental law of numeration, that *a removal, of one place, towards the left increases the value of a figure ten times*, is here recognized. *Cypher*, or the omission of any place, is denoted by the word *ling*, literally 'remainder.'

19. *Fractions:* if, in long measure, for example, a *chéung* is made unit, then the *ch'ik*, *ts'ün*, *fan*, &c., are all fractions (or broken numbers).

奇零如度法命
丈爲單位則尺
寸分皆爲奇零

꜀K'í ꜀ling, ꜀ü tók꜆ fát꜆, ming' chéung² ꜀wai ꜀tán wai², tsak꜆ ch'ik꜆, ts'ün', ꜀fan, ꜀kái ꜀wai ꜀k'í ꜀ling.

20. Moreover, there are simple and complex numbers, also a species of short-hand. [Thus,]

另有淺數深數
與及花碼

Ling² ꜂yau ꜂ts'ín shò', ꜀sham shò' ꜂ü k'ap꜆ ꜀fá ꜂má.

| | | | | | | | | |
|---|---|---|---|---|---|---|---|---|
| I | *one* | 1 | 一 | 壹 | 〡 | yat꜆ | yat꜆ | yat꜆ |
| II | *two* | 2 | 二 | 貳 | 〢 | í² | í² | í² |
| III | *three* | 3 | 三 | 叁 | 〣 | ꜀sám | ꜀sám | ꜀sám |
| IV | *four* | 4 | 四 | 肆 | 〤 | sz" | sz" | sz" |
| V | *five* | 5 | 五 | 伍 | 〥 | ꜂'ng | ꜂'ng | ꜂'ng |
| VI | *six* | 6 | 六 | 陸 | 〦 | luk꜇ | luk꜇ | luk꜇ |
| VII | *seven* | 7 | 七 | 柒 | 〧 | ts'at꜆ | ts'at꜆ | ts'at꜆ |
| VIII | *eight* | 8 | 八 | 捌 | 〨 | pát꜆ | pát꜆ | pát꜆ |
| IX | *nine* | 9 | 九 | 玖 | 〩 | ꜂kau | ꜂kau | ꜂kau |
| X | *ten* | 10 | 十 | 拾 | 什 | shap꜇ | shap꜇ | shap꜇ |

21. Now in reckoning numbers, we stop at myriads, and although there are hundreds of thousands, millions, and other [higher] numbers, they are not very much employed. For instance, Three hundred and sixty-two millions, four hundred and forty-seven thousand, one hundred and eighty-three (362,447,183), is read three myriads, six thousand, two hundred and forty-four myriads, seven thousand one hundred and eighty-three.

今人算數以萬
爲止雖有億兆
等數多不用如
三垓六京二兆
四億四萬七千
一百八十三則
曰三萬六千二
百四十四萬七
千一百八十三

꜀Kam ꜁yan sün' shò' ꜂í mán² ꜁wai ꜂chí, ꜀sui ꜂yau yik꜆, chíú², ꜂tang shò', ꜀tó pat꜆ yung². ꜁Ü ꜀sám ꜀hoi, luk꜇ ꜀king, í² chíú², sz" yik꜆, sz" mán², ts'at꜆ ꜀ts'ín, yat꜆ pák꜆, pát꜆ shap꜇ ꜀sám, tsak꜆ üt꜇ ꜀sám mán², luk꜇ ꜀ts'ín, í² pák꜆ sz" shap꜇ sz" mán², ts'at꜆ ꜀ts'ín yat꜆ pák꜆ pát꜆ shap꜇ ꜀sám.

20. The figures in the first column are used in books and documents; those in the middle column are employed in mercantile accounts, drafts, &c., to prevent any change being easily made in the sum; and the contracted forms, in the last column, are used in letters, and the transactions of every-day life. The characters in the middle column, except the first three, also have other meanings than numerical; they are employed for this purpose partly from the similarity of sound, and partly from a resemblance to the figures themselves.

21. This number (362,447,183), introduced here to illustrate the Chinese system of notation, gives the total population of the empire in 1812, as stated in an edition of the Ta Tsing Ui Tín, published in 1828.

## Section Second.

## RULES OF ARITHMETIC.

### 算法類第二章
Sün' fát, lui²; tai² í² ꜀chéung.

1. For all calculations of numbers, the four fundamental rules of *addition*, *subtraction*, *division*, and *multiplication*, are necessarily the first used; and are all performed on the counting-board.

凡算法必先以加減歸乘四法爲要而皆以算盤習之

꜁Fán sün' fát, pít, ꜀sín ꜂í ꜀ká, ꜂kám, ꜀kwai, ꜁shing, sz'' fát, ꜁wai íú' ; ꜁í ꜀kái ꜂í sün' ꜁p'ún tsáp, ꜀chí.

2. The *rule of addition* is exemplified thus: if to each tael of money, you add interest three candareens, and, without breaking the original sum, you increase it by three, you have the operation which is called addition.

加法謂如每銀一両加利三分不破本身以三增之故謂之加

꜀Ká fát, wai² ꜁ü ꜂múi ꜁ngan yat, ꜂léung ꜀ká lí² ꜀sám ꜀fan, pat, p'ó' ꜂pún ꜀shan, ꜂í ꜀sám ꜀tsang ꜀chí, kú' wai² ꜀chí ꜀ká.

3. The *rule of subtraction* is exemplified thus: the capital and interest of money is four taels, and each tael is to be diminished by taking away three mace; you have then only to triple the three and subtract the nine, and you will obtain a remainder of three taels, with a fraction of one mace.

減法謂如本利銀四両每両減去三錢只呼三三除減九錢得本銀三両零一錢之類

꜂Kám fát, wai² ꜁ü ꜂pún lí² ꜁ngan sz'' ꜂léung, ꜂múi ꜂léung ꜂kám h'ü' ꜀sám ꜁ts'ín, chat, ꜀fú ꜀sám ꜀sám ꜁ch'ü ꜂kám ꜂kau ꜁ts'ín, tak, ꜂pún ꜁ngan ꜀sám ꜂léung ꜁ling yat, ꜁ts'ín ꜀chí lui².

## *Notes and Explanations.*

NUMBERS, being employed to denote things of almost every kind and magnitude, have been subjected to a great variety of rules, of which the four here named are the most simple and useful. Ching's Manual will furnish the student with a great number of others; some of them are curious, and are expressed in rhyme, like the old stanza:

Thirty days hath September,
April, June, and November;
All the rest have thirty-one
February twenty-eight alone,
But in leap year twenty-nine.

1. This abacus is in universal use among the Chinese. It consists of an oblong frame of wood, with a bar running lengthwise forming two compartments; through this bar, at right angles, are usually placed seventeen (but sometimes more) small pins, having on each seven balls; five on one side, and two on the other side, of the bar. Any ball in the larger compartment, being placed against the bar, is called unity; and on the left of this they increase, and on the right they decrease, by tens, hundredths, &c; the corresponding balls, in the smaller compartment, increase or decrease by fifths, fiftieths, &c. By this means, all numbers, in the common transactions of business integral or decimal, are computed with much ease and rapidity.

4. The *rule of multiplication* is thus exemplified: there are four hundred and twenty-five pieces of cloth, and each piece costs two mace and five candareens; it is asked, what will be the amount of the money required for the whole [of the said cloth]?

乘法謂如有布
四百二十五疋
每疋價銀二錢
五分問共該銀
若干

ˏShing fát˰, waiˀ ˏü ˋyau pòˀ szˀ pák˰ íˀ shap˲ ˋng p'at˰; ˋmúi p'at˰ káˀ ˏngan íˀ ˏts'ín ˋng ˏfan; manˀ kungˀ ˏkoi ˏngan yéuk˲ ˏkón?

The answer is, one hundred and six taels, two mace and five candareens.

答曰一百零六
兩二錢五分

Táp˰ üt˲ yat˰ pák˰ ˏling luk˲ ˋléung, íˀ ˏts'ín, ˋng ˏfan.

The operation is performed thus: the cloth is taken as the multiplicand, and the price of each piece of cloth, two mace and five candareens, as the multiplier; then by multiplying them together, the product is obtained.

法曰置布爲實
以每疋價二錢
五分爲法乘之
則得

Fát˰ üt˲, chíˀ pòˀ ˏwai shat˲ ˋí ˋmúi p'at˰ káˀ íˀ ˏts'ín, ˋng ˏfan ˏwai fát˰, ˏshing ˏchí tsak˰ tak˰.

**MULTIPLICATION TABLE.** 九九合數 ˋKau ˋkau hŏp˲ shòˀ.

一一如一
一二如二 二二如四
一三如三 二三如六 三三如九
一四如四 二四如八 三四一十二 四四一
十六
一五如五 二五得一十 三五一十五 四五
得二十 五五二十五
一六如六 二六一十二 三六一十八 四六
二十四 五六得三十 六六三十六
一七如七 二七一十四 三七二十一 四七
二十八 五七三十五 六七四十二 七七四
十九
一八如八 二八一十六 三八二十四 四八
三十二 五八得四十 六八四十八 七八五
十六 八八六十四
一九如九 二九一十八 三九二十七 四九
三十六 五九四十五 六九五十四 七九六
十三 八九七十二 九九八十一

4. This table, commencing on the left at the top, reads thus: $1\times1=1$, or literally, one one as one; the second column is $1\times2=2$; $2\times2=4$; the third column in the same way, $1\times3=3$,

| | | |
|---|---|---|
| 5. The *rule of division* is exemplified thus: there are twenty stone of rice, which is to be divided equally among fifty thousand men; it is asked, how much of this rice will each man have? | 歸法謂如有米<br>二十石作五萬<br>人分之問每人<br>該米若干 | Kwai fát, wai ü yau mai í shap shik, tsók ng mán yan fan chí; man múi yan koi mai yéuk kón? |
| The answer is, four *chéuk.* | 答曰四勺 | Táp üt, sz' chéuk. |
| The operation is thus: the given rice is made the dividend, and the five thousand men taken as a divisor; the sum being thus divided, the quotient is obtained. | 法曰置米爲實<br>以人五萬爲法<br>歸之則得 | Fát üt, chí' mai wai shat, í yan ng mán wai fát, kwai chí tsak tak. |

and so on to the end, $9 \times 9 = 81$. In its arrangement, this is less simple and easy than that usually called the table of Pythagoras, though in principle it is identical with it. The Chinese have no algebraic system, and are without any mathematical signs or symbols like those used in algebra.

5. This and the three preceding rules are abridged from the work of Ching, in which they are illustrated, by very numerous examples.

## Section Third.

## MEASURES OF LENGTH.

## 度法類第三章

Tók fát lui; tai sám chéung.

| | | |
|---|---|---|
| 1. Long measure is that by which the length of piece-goods, bamboos, timber, and such like articles is determined. The terms used are these: | 度者所以分别<br>布疋竹木等物<br>長短即 | Tók 'ché, 'shó 'í fan pít pò' p'at, chuk, muk, 'tang mat, ch'éung 'tün. Tsik,— |
| 1 grain is one *fan;* | 一粒爲一分 | Yat nap wai yat fan; |
| 10 *fan* make one *ts'ün;* | 十分爲一寸 | Shap fan wai yat ts'ün'; |
| 10 *ts'ün* make one *ch'ik;* | 十寸爲一尺 | Shap ts'ün' wai yat ch'ik; |

### *Notes and Explanations.*

LIKE the people of all other nations, the Chinese have had great trouble and perplexity in trying to fix a standard of weights and measures. Without any permanent standard—"established by nature and accessible at all places on the earth," like the French *metre*, one 40 millionth part of a meridian of the earth, or 39⅓ English inches nearly—the Chinese made the *wóng chung* the foundation of all their measures. A certain number of kernels of grain—whether disposed lengthwise or crosswise is disputed—was assumed for a starting point, like so many

| | | |
|---|---|---|
| 10 *ch'ik* make one *chéung;* | 十尺爲一丈 | Shap꜇ ch'ik꜆ ꜁wai yat꜆ chéung꜅; |
| 10 *chéung* make one *yan.* | 十丈爲一引 | Shap꜇ chéung꜅ ꜁wai yat꜆ ꜂yan. |
| 2. It is also employed for determining geographical distances; in these terms: | 又分别土地遠近以 | Yau꜅ ꜀fan pít꜇ ꜂t'ò ti꜅, ꜃ün kan꜅; ꜃í— |
| Half a *ts'ün* is one *lí;* | 半寸爲一厘 | Pún꜄ ts'ün꜄ ꜁wai yat꜆ ꜁lí; |
| 5 *ts'ün* make one *fan;* | 五寸爲一分 | ꜃'Ng ts'ün꜄ ꜁wai yat꜆ ꜀fan; |
| 5 *ch'ik* make one *pò;* | 五尺爲一步 | ꜃'Ng ch'ik꜆ ꜁wai yat꜆ pò꜅; |
| 360 *pò* make one *lí;* | 三百六十步爲一里 | ꜀Sám pák꜄ luk꜇ shap꜇ pò꜅ ꜁wai yat꜆ ꜃lí; |
| 250 *lí* make one *tò.* | 二百五十里爲一度 | Í꜅ pák꜆ ꜃'ng shap꜇ ꜃lí ꜁wai yat꜆ tò꜅. |
| 3. What is the length of an English mile? | 英國一里有幾長呢 | ꜀Ying kwók꜆ yat꜆ ꜃lí ꜃yau ꜂kí ꜁ch'éung ꜀ní? |
| It is a little less than three Chinese miles. | 唐三里畧减些 | ꜁T'óng, ꜀sám ꜃lí léuk꜇ ꜂kám ꜀sé. |
| 4. How many *ch'ik* make a Chinese mile? | 唐里有幾尺呢 | ꜁T'óng ꜃lí ꜃yau ꜂kí ch'ik꜆ ꜀ní? |
| One thousand eight hundred and twenty-six feet make one *lí* (or mile). | 一千八百二十六丨爲一里 | Yat꜆ ꜀ts'ín pát꜆ pák꜆ í꜅ shap꜇ luk꜇ ch'ik꜆ ꜁wai yat꜆ ꜃lí. |
| 5. How many feet make one English mile? | 英國一里有幾多尺呢 | ꜀Ying kwók꜆ yat꜆ ꜃lí, ꜃yau ꜂kí ꜀tó ch'ik꜆ ꜀ní? |
| Five thousand, two hundred and eighty feet make one English mile. | 五千二百八十尺爲一里 | ꜃'Ng ꜀ts'ín í꜅ pák꜆ pát꜆ shap꜇ ch'ik꜆ ꜁wai yat꜆ ꜃lí. |

*drams, grains,* and *barley-corns,* in English tables. The *ch'ik,* (cubit, covid, or foot) fixed by the Mathematical Board at Peking, is 13.125 English inches; that used by tradesmen in Canton varies from 14.625 inches to 14.81 and that employed by the engineers of public works is 12.7 inches; and that by which distances is usually measured is 12.1 nearly. The *lí,* or mile is 1897½ English feet; and 192½ *lí* were reckoned for a degree of latitude or longitude. But the European mathematicians at the capital, deviating from their predecessors, divided the degree into 250 *lí,* reducing it to 1826 English feet, or the tenth part of a French league; and this, at present, is the established measure. Accordingly, the *lí* is a little *more* than one third of an English mile.

1. These terms do not correspond exactly with those in use by any Europeans. The *fan* may, however, be taken as equivalent to a line, in rough calculations; it is (calling the *ch'ik* 14.625 in.) exactly 1.015625 of the twelfth of an inch. The *ts'ün* is called *punt* or *punto* in Canton, and is equal to 1.21875 of an inch, or one inch and one fifth. The *chéung* is frequently used by carpenters and other artisans in measuring their work; the length of course corresponds to the *ch'ik* employed, but it is usually about 14.3.5 feet. The *yan* is not much used.

| | | |
|---|---|---|
| 6. How do the Chinese and English inches compare with each other in length? | 唐英兩寸相較點樣呢 | ˏT'óng ˏYing 'léung ts'ün' ˏséung káu' 'tím yéung² ˏní? |
| According to the measure of the Astronomical Board, ten Chinese inches are nearly equal to thirteen and a half English inches; but according to the usage in Canton, they are nearly equal to fourteen inches and six tenths. | 遵欽天監制度唐十寸即英國十三寸半照廣東規矩將十四寸六 | ˏTsun ˏyam ˏt'ín kám' chái' tò² ˏT'óng shap₂ ts'ün', tsik, ˏYing kwók, shap₂ ˏsám ts'ün' pún'; chíú' 'Kwóng ˏtung ˏkw'ai 'kü, ˏtséung shap₂ sz' ts'ün' luk₂. |
| 7. Now there are of cloth forty-eight *chéung*, six feet, and three inches, to be divided equally between two men: It is asked, How much of the said cloth will each of the men receive? | 今有布四十八丈六尺三寸以二人分之問每人該幾多 | ˏKam 'yau pò' sz' shap₂ pát, chéung², luk₂ ch'ik, ˏsám ts'ün', 'í í² ˏyan ˏfan ˏchí; man² 'múi ˏyan ˏkoi 'kí ˏtó? |
| The answer is, each man will receive twenty-four *chéung*, three feet, one inch, and five tenths. | 答曰每人各得二十四丈三尺一寸五分 | Táp, üt₂, 'múi ˏyan kók, tak, í² shap₂ sz' chéung², ˏsám ch'ik, yat, ts'ün', 'ng ˏfan. |
| 8. The circumference of the earth is three hundred and sixty degrees, which gives a total [on the equator] of ninety thousand [Chinese] miles; these being converted into paces [*pó*] give thirty-two millions and four hundred thousand; the paces being reduced to feet [*ch'ik*], give one hundred and sixty-two millions of feet. | 地球週圍三百六十度共得地九萬里變計即三千二百四十萬步以尺易步則一萬六千二百萬尺 | Tí² ˏk'au ˏchau ˏwai ˏsám pák, luk₂ shap₂ tò², kung² tak, tí² 'kau mán² 'lí; pín' kai' tsik, ˏsám ˏts'ín, í² pák, sz' shap₂ mán² pò²; 'í ch'ik, yik₂ pò², tsak, yat, mán² luk₂ ˏts'ín í² pák, mán² ch'ik. |

7, 8. These are given merely as examples of the manner in which the terms are used in the transaction of business. The most common implement for measuring is a small rule, called a *ch'ik*, from its length; it is made of a slip of bamboo, neatly divided into *ts'ün* and *fan* by brass pins. There is no supervision exercised by the government over the manufacture of the measures of length, and the extremes of length in a large number promiscuously collected are as much as half or three fourths of a *fan*. The *ch'ik* of tailors, carpenters, &c., is called *pái ts'ín ch'ik*, in distinction from the shorter one used by masons, which is called *chau tung ch'ik*, and which is 12.7 inches in length. They also measure their work with a *chéung* or pole, ten of these *ch'ik* in length; this *chéung* is not far from eleven English feet.

## Section Fourth.

# MEASURES OF CAPACITY.

## 量法類第四章

ˏLéung' fát˒ lui²; tai² sz'' ˓chéung.

| | | |
|---|---|---|
| 1. Whenever the quantity of rice, maize, pease, or other grain is to be determined, they are measured by these rules, which are as follows: | 凡分别米粟豆<br>穀多寡皆以量<br>爲法其量則以 | ˏFán ˓fan pít₂ ʿmai, suk˒, tau², kuk˒ ˓tó ʿkwá, ˓kái ʿí ˏléung ˏwai fát˒, ˏk'í ˏléung tsak˒ ʿí: |
| 1 grain of maize is a *suk*; | 一粒之粟爲粟 | Yat˒ nap˒ ˓chí suk˒ ˏwai suk˒; |
| 6 *suk* make one *kwai*; | 六粟爲一圭 | Luk₂ suk˒ ˏwai yat˒ ˓kwai; |
| 10 *kwai* make one *ts'üt*; | 十圭爲一撮 | Shap₂ ˓kwai ˏwai yat˒ ts'üt˒; |
| 10 *ts'üt* make one *ch'áu*; | 十撮爲一抄 | Shap₂ ts'üt˒ ˏwai yat˒ ˓ch'áu; |
| 10 *ch'áu* make one *chéuk*; | 十抄爲一勺 | Shap₂ ˓ch'áu ˏwai yat˒ chéuk˒; |
| 5 *chéuk* make one *yéuk*; | 五勺爲一龠 | ʿ'Ng chéuk˒ ˏwai yat˒ yéuk₂; |
| 2 *yéuk* make one *kóp*; | 兩龠爲一合 | ʿLéung yéuk₂ ˏwai yat˒ kóp˒; |
| 10 *kóp* make one *shing*; | 十合爲一升 | Shap₂ kóp˒ ˏwai yat˒ ˓shing; |
| 10 *shing* make one *tau*; | 十升爲一斗 | Shap₂ ˓shing ˏwai yat˒ ʿtau; |
| 5 *tau* make one *hók*; | 五斗爲一斛 | ʿ'Ng ʿtau ˏwai yat˒ hók₂; |
| 2 *hók* make one *shik*; | 兩斛爲一石 | ʿLéung hók₂ ˏwai yat˒ shik₂; |
| 1 *fú* is equal to 6 *tau* and 4 *shing*; | 釜則六斗四升 | ʿFú tsak˒ luk₂ ʿtau sz'' ˓shing; |
| 1 *yü* is equal to 16 *tau*; | 庾十六斗 | ˏYü shap₂ luk₂ ʿtau; |
| 1 *ping* is equal to 16 *hók*. | 秉十六斛 | ʿPing shap₂ luk₂ hók₂. |
| 2. Now, if you have forty-six thousand, seven hundred and fifty-one stone of rice, and to every stone you add | 今有米四萬六<br>千七百五十一 | ˓Kam ʿyau ʿmai sz'' mán² luk₂ ˓ts'ín, ts'at˒ pák˒, ʿ'ng |

## *Notes and Explanations.*

MEASURES of capacity are used chiefly in buying and selling small quantities of rice, wheat, and other grain; for large quantities are usually bought and sold by weight.

1. There are only four of these fourteen measures which are actually in common use among the Chinese, the others are imaginary; these are the *kóp*, the half *shing*, the whole *shing*, and the *tau*. The first three are made of the cylindrical joints of the bamboo; and the *tau* is made of wood in the shape of the frustrum of a pyramid, neatly bound with brass, and having a handle across the top. There are two sizes of the *tau* and *shing*; one, called *shí tau*, or the current *tau*, contains just ten catties weight of rice, and is also called *shap kan tau*, from this fact;

| | | |
|---|---|---|
| for tare seven *shing*; what will be the whole amount of the rice? | 石每石加耗七<br>升問共米若干 | shap, yat, shik,, ˢmúi shik, ˛ká hò' ts'at, ˛shing,; man' kung' ˢmai yéuk, ˛kón? |
| 3. Answer: the whole amount of the original and that added for tare, is five thousand and twenty-three stone, five *tau*, and seven *shing*. | 答曰正耗共五<br>萬零二十三石<br>五斗七升 | Táp, üt,, ching' hò' kung' ˢ'ng mán' ˛ling í' shap, ˛sám shik,, ˢ'ng 'tau, ts'at, ˛shing. |
| 4. Again, [suppose] you have one thousand and thirty-eight stone of pease, which are to be equally divided among one hundred and seventy-three men; How many stone will each man receive? | 又有豆一千零<br>三十八石作一<br>百七十三人分<br>問每人該若干 | Yau' ˢyau tau' yat, ˛ts'in ˛ling ˛sám shap, pát, shik,, tsók, yat, pák, ts'at, shap, ˛sám ˛yan ˛fan; man' ˢmúi ˛yan ˛koi yéuk, ˛kón. |
| 5. Answer: six stone. | 答日六石 | Tap, üt,, luk, shik,. |

the corresponding *shing* is named in a similar manner, and contains one catty of rice. The *shik* is in this proportion, and is bought and sold as a pecul. The second size of the *tau* is the *ts'óng tau* or granary *tau*, and holds about six and a half catties of rice; it measures 309.57148 cubic inches (including the handle), and is commonly used in retail shops. The *shing*, called also *ts'óng shing*, is proportionate, and contains 30.43415 cubic inches. The half *shing* and *kóp* are in proportion, but in consequence of the inaccuracy of the bamboo joints, their capacities vary considerably; the *kóp* is also called *fan* and *mak* by the common people. The English pint measures $35\frac{3}{8}$ cubic inches nearly; the gallon is $277\frac{1}{4}$ cubic inches nearly. The *tau* measure often has the name of the local magistrate engraven on its side, showing that it has been officially examined and its accuracy proved; the smaller measures are not stamped in this manner.

## Section Fifth.

## WEIGHTS.

## 衡法類第五章

˛Hang fát, lui'; tai' ˢ'ng ˛chéung.

| | | |
|---|---|---|
| 1. In order to ascertain the amount of things by weight, it is necessary first to know the weights, to wit: | 蓋拼秤物輕重<br>須先知衡法以 | K'oi' pín' ch'ing' mat, ˛hing chung', ˛sü ˛sín ˛chí ˛hang fát,, ˢí: |
| 1 kernel of grain is one *shü*; | 一粒黍為一黍 | Yat, nap, 'shü ˛wai yat, 'shü: |
| 10 *shü* make one *lui*; | 十黍為一累 | Shap, 'shü ˛wai yat, ˢlui: |

### *Notes and Explanations.*

ALMOST everything, among the Chinese, is sold by weight, not excepting timber, liquids, and live stock.

廣東方言讀本



| | | |
|---|---|---|
| 10 *lui* make one *chü;* | 十絫為一銖 | Shap₂ ʿlui ˏwai yat˒ ˓chü; |
| 24 *chü* make one *léung;* | 二十四銖為兩 | Í² shap₂ sz'' ˓chü ˏwai ʿleung; |
| 16 *léung* make one *kan;* | 十六兩為一斤 | Shap₂ luk₂ ʿléung ˏwai yat˒ ˓kan; |
| 2 *kan* make one *yin;* | 二斤為一引 | Í² ˓kan ˏwai yat˒ ˤyan; |
| 30 *kan* make one *kwan;* | 三十斤為一鈞 | ˓Sám shap₂ ˓kan ˏwai yat˒ ˓kwan; |
| 100 *kan* make one *tám;* | 百斤為一擔 | Pák˒ ˓kan ˏwai yat˒ tám'; |
| 120 *kan* make one *shik;* | 百二十斤為石 | Pák˒ í² shap₂ ˓kan ˏwai shik₂. |
| 2. But at present, everything less than a tael, is denoted by *ts'in, fan, lí, hò, sz', fat,* and so forth. | 第今兩以下惟用錢分厘毫絲忽而已 | Tai² ˓kam ʿléung ˤí há², ˏwai yung² ˏts'ín, ˓fan, ˏlí, ˏhò, ˓sz', fat₂, ˏí ˤí. |
| 3. There are three instruments for weighing; one is called *a balance;* one is called a *steelyard;* and one a *money scales;* all are fixed by standard weights, granted by the imperial Board [at Peking]. The balance requires weights, of which the tael is the greatest [denomination], and the *lí* is the smallest. The steelyard and the money scales both require a counterpoise. On the beam, there are small stars, and by moving the counterpoise, the beam is balanced. According to the steelyard, sixteen taels make a catty, and it ascends to a pecul, which is the greatest weight, while the *ts'ín* is the smallest. By the money scales, the tael is the largest, and the *lí* is the smallest [weight]. | 衡物有三曰天平曰秤曰戥皆以部頒法碼為定天平用碼以兩為首以厘為末秤與戥皆用錘杆身上點星移錘就之秤以十六兩作斤以擔為首以錢為末戥以兩為首以厘為末 | ˏHang mat₂ ˤyau ˓sám, üt₂ ˓t'ín ˏp'ing, üt₂ ch'ing', üt₂ tang²; ˓kái ˤí Pò² ˓pán fát˒ ˤmá ˏwai ting². ˓T'ín ˏp'ing yung² ˤmá, ˤí ʿléung ˏwai ʿshau, ˤí ˏlí ˏwai mút₂. Ch'ing' ˤü tang² ˓kái yung² ˏch'ui. ˓Kón ˓shan shéung² ʿtím ˓sing, ˏí ˏch'ui tsau² ˓chí. Ch'ing' ˤí shap₂ luk₂ ʿléung tsók˒ ˓kan; ˤí tám' ˏwai ʿshau, ʿi ˓ts'in ˏwai mút₂. Tang² ˤí ʿléung ˏwai ʿshau, ˤí ˏlí ˏwai mút₂. |

1. The first three of these denominations, with the *yan, kwan,* and *shik,* are nominal; the *tael* weighs 1⅓oz. av.; the *catty* 1⅓lb. av., and the *pecul* 133⅓ lbs. av. The pecul is distinguished by the Portuguese into three kinds; the *pecul balança* or common pecul of 100 catties, the *pecul seda* of 111.15 catties = 148 lbs., and the *pecul chapa* of 150 catties = 200 lbs.

2. The *ts'ín* is the same aliquot part of the *léung* (one tenth) in weights as in money, and bears the same name of mace; the *fan* is also called candareen, and the *lí* cash.

3. The *t'in p'ing* is used to weigh valuable articles, as drugs, gems, &c., and is made of various sizes; articles weighed by it are reckoned in *léung,* and its subdivisions of *ts'ín, fan,* &c., and the weights are made from one cash up to a hundred taels in convenient sizes, the larger of brass, the smaller of ivory. The *ch'ing* is the most common instrument for weighing, and is made of hard wood like a steelyard, neatly marked off into peculs, catties, taels, &c.: the counterpoise is usually of stone. The *tang* is made on the same principle as the *ch'ing,* of an ivory rod, and is called money scales from its most common use.

CHI. CHR. 97

## Section Sixth.

## LAND MEASURES.

### 畝法類第六章

ˢMau fát˒ lui²; tai² luk₂ ˓chéung˒

| | | |
|---|---|---|
| 1. Land measure is that by which the length and breadth of lands are measured; the following terms are used: | 畝法所以分別<br>田地濶狹則有 | ˢMau fát˒ ʿshó ˢí ˓fan pít₂ ˛tʻín tí² fút˒ háp₂; tsak˒ ˢyau: |
| 5 *ch'ik* make 1 *pò* (or pace); | 五尺爲一步 | ʿ'Ng chʻik˒ ˛wai yat˒ pò²; |
| 24 *pò* make one *fan;* | 二十四步爲分 | Í² shap₂ sz'' pò² ˛wai ˓fan; |
| 60 *pò* make one *kók;* | 六十步爲一角 | Luk₂ shap₂ pò² ˛wai yat˒ kók˒; |
| 4 *kók* make one *mau;* thus making one *mau* equal to 240 *pò;* | 四角爲一畝即<br>二百四十步也 | Sz'' kók˒ ˛wai yat˒ ˢmau; tsik˒, í² pák˒, sz'' shap₂ pò² ˢyá; |
| 100 *mau* make one *k'ing.* | 百畝爲一頃 | Pák˒ ˢmau ˛wai yat˒ ʿkʻing. |
| 2. But, at present, from the *mau* downwards, the denominations are *fan, lí, hò, sz', fat;* and sometimes they are called *shik, tau,* and *shing;* and whether the plats of ground be square or round, irregular or oblong, crooked or straight, although the same terms for the measurement are employed, the method for each kind of plat is different. | 惟今自畝以下<br>則曰分厘毫絲<br>忽或曰石斗升<br>即方圓斜橫曲<br>直之田丈量雖<br>同而法則各異 | ˛Wai ˓kam tsz'² ˢmau ˢí há², tsak˒ üt₂ ˓fan, ˛lí, ˛hò, ˓sz', fat˒; wák₂ üt₂ shik₂, ʿtau, ˓shing; tsik˒ ˓fóng, ˛ün, ˛tsʻé, ˛wáng, huk˒, chik₂ ˓chí ˛tʻín, chéung² ˛léung ˓sui ˛tʻung, ˛í fát˒ tsak˒ kók˒ í². |
| 3. Question; what is the area of a right-angled triangular piece of ground, whose perpendicular (or longest side) is sixty *pò,* and its base (or shortest side) thirty *pò?* | 問句股田股長<br>六十步句濶三<br>十步得田幾何 | Man² ˓kau ʿkú ˛tʻín, ʿkú ˛chʻéung luk₂ shap₂ pò², ˓kau fút˒ ˓sám shap₂ pò², tak˒ ˛tʻín ʿkí ˛hó? |
| 4. Answer; three *mau,* seven *fan,* and five *lí* (or 3.75 acres). | 答曰三畝七分<br>五厘 | Táp˒ üt₂; ˓sám ˢmau, tsʻat˒ ˓fan, ˢ'ng ˛lí. |

## *Notes and Explanations.*

MAU is used in two senses; one denoting a plat of ground of any dimensions; the other, a specific area, anciently including one hundred *pò,* but now two hundred and forty.

1. The *fan* here given must not be confounded with the *fan* among the measures of length, the latter being only a fractional part of a *ch'ik.* The measure here is *square* measure: 240 square *pò* = 1 mau or Chinese acre.

2. It will be seen from the many different measures and weights into which the terms *fan, lí, hò,* &c., enter, that they are not proper, but common terms, answering exactly to decima

5. Rule: take the perpendicular, sixty *pò*, and the base, thirty *pò*; then multiply them together, and a product will be obtained, one thousand eight hundred *pò*; take away one half, and there are nine hundred *pò*, which being reduced according to the land measure, the answer is obtained.

法以股六十步句三十步相乘得積一千八百步折半得九百步畝法除之卽得

Fát,, 'í 'kú luk, shap, pò', ,kau ,sám shap, pò', ,séung ,shing tak, tsik, yat, ,ts'ín pát, pák, pò'; chít, pún' tak, 'kau pák, pò', 'mau fát, ,ch'ü ,chí, tsik, tak,.

(*a*) The base and perpendicular of the triangle multiplied together produce a parallelogram; but the shape of the right-angled triangle is only half a parallelogram; therefore by taking away one half, the true product is obtained.

句股相乘成一長方積句股形得長方之半故折半定積

,Kau 'kú ,séung ,shing ,shing yat, ,ch'éung ,fóng tsik,, ,kau 'kú ,ying, tak, ,ch'éung ,fóng ,chí pún', kú' chít, pún' ting' tsik,.

(*b*) If you take the length sixty *pò*, and cut off one half, you have thirty *pò*, which, with the breadth, thirty *pò*, being multiplied together, the same product is obtained. [Again —]

若以長六十步折半得三十步與闊三十步相乘得積同

Yéuk, 'í ,ch'éung luk, shap, pò' chít, pún' tak, ,sám shap, pò', 'ü fút, ,sám shap, pò', ,séung ,shing tak, tsik, ,t'ung.

(*c*) If you take the breadth thirty *pò*, and cut off one half, you have fifteen *pò*, which, with the length, sixty *pò*, being multiplied together, the same product is again obtained.

若以闊三十步折半得十五步與長六十步相乘得積亦同

Yéuk, 'í fút, ,sám shap, pò', chít, pún' tak, shap, 'ng pò', 'ü ,ch'éung luk, shap, pò', ,séung ,shing, tak, tsik, yik, ,t'ung.

6. The square of any number is the product of that number multiplied into itself: the square of three is nine.

數自乘之積三自乘之積爲九

Shò' tsz' ,shing ,chí tsik,; ,sám tsz' ,shing ,chí tsik, ,wai 'kau.

7. In land measure, if one acre of land be taken, and its contents be computed in square feet [Chinese], it will give six thousand feet.

畝法若以一畝自方五尺計之積六千尺也

'Mau fát,, yéuk, 'í yat, 'mau tsz' ,fóng, 'ng ch'ik, kai' ,chí, tsik, luk, ,ts'ín ch'ik, 'yá.

---

fractions, and should be read here tenths, hundredths, &c. Whenever used by a Chinese, their meaning is so many tenths or hundredths of the integer mentioned before the *fan*; as, 15 catties, 6 taels, 8 mace, 3 candareens, and 9 cash, is equal to 15 catties, 6.839 taels.

3. This problem is introduced for the sake of the terms employed, and not for the illustration of geometrical principles; most of the terms, being used in a definite mathematical sense, are easily understood. For a further account of the *mau fát*, see the fifth volume of the ***Ts'uimí shán Fóng Shòhók***, or the "Mathematics of the Lagerstrœmia hill Institution."

## Section Seventh.

# MEASURES OF TIME.

## 曆法類第七章
Lik$_2$ fát$_2$ lui$^2$; tai$^2$ ts'at$_2$ ꜀chéung.

1. The celestial sovereign invented the ten stems, *viz.*, *káp*, *üt*, *ping*, *ting*, *mò*, *kí*, *kang*, *san*, *yam*, and *kwai*; and the twelve branches, *viz.*, *tsz'*, *ch'au*, *yan*, *mau*, *shan*, *tsz'*, *'ng*, *mi*, *shan*, *yau*, *sut*, and *hoi*. Afterwards, Náu the Great, taking the first of the stems and branches, joined them together in pairs, and formed a cyclic nomenclature for the years, months, and days; and by drawing it in continuation downwards, it requires sixty years [to complete the series of changes], after which the process is recommenced and repeated. Thus, for example, are joined *káptsz'*, *ütch'au*, and so forth; by degrees the progression is carried on through the whole series of the stems and branches; and

天皇氏制十干甲乙丙丁戊已庚辛壬癸十二支子丑寅夘辰巳午未申酉戌亥迨至大撓則以干支之首配合而年月日爲之號拖連而下必須六十載然後可復始如甲子乙丑之類由

꜀T'ín ꜁wóng shí$^2$ chai' shap$_2$ ꜀kón, káp$_2$, üt$_2$, 'ping, ꜀ting, mò$^2$, 'kí, ꜀kang, ꜀san, ꜁yam, kwai'; shap$_2$ í$^2$ ꜀chí, 'tsz', 'ch'au, ꜁yan, ꜂mau, ꜀shan, tsz'$^2$ ꜂'ng, mí$^2$, ꜀shan, 'yau, sut$_2$, hoi$^2$. 'T'oi chí' Tái$^2$ ꜁Náu tsak, 'í ꜀kón ꜀chí ꜀chí 'shau, p'úi' hóp$_2$ ꜁í ꜁nín üt$_2$ yat$_2$ ꜁wai ꜀chí hò$^2$; ꜀t'ó ꜁lín ꜁í há$^2$, pít$_2$ ꜀sü luk$_2$ shap$_2$ tsoi', ꜁ín hau$^2$ 'hó fuk$_2$ 'ch'í. ꜁Yü káp$_2$ 'tsz', üt$_2$ 'ch'au, ꜀chí lui$^2$;

TABLE OF THE CYCLE OF SIXTY YEARS, OR FÁ KÁP TSZ'.

| | | | | | |
|---|---|---|---|---|---|
| 1804 甲子 | 1814 甲戌 | 1824 甲申 | 1834 甲午 | 1844 甲辰 | 1854 甲寅 |
| 1805 乙丑 | 1815 乙亥 | 1825 乙酉 | 1835 乙未 | 1845 乙巳 | 1855 乙夘 |
| 1806 丙寅 | 1816 丙子 | 1826 丙戌 | 1836 丙申 | 1846 丙午 | 1856 丙辰 |
| 1807 丁夘 | 1817 丁丑 | 1827 丁亥 | 1837 丁酉 | 1847 丁未 | 1857 丁巳 |
| 1808 戊辰 | 1818 戊寅 | 1828 戊子 | 1838 戊戌 | 1848 戊申 | 1858 戊午 |
| 1809 已巳 | 1819 已夘 | 1829 已丑 | 1839 已亥 | 1849 已酉 | 1859 已未 |
| 1810 庚午 | 1820 庚辰 | 1830 庚寅 | 1840 庚子 | 1850 庚戌 | 1860 庚申 |
| 1811 辛未 | 1821 辛巳 | 1831 辛夘 | 1841 辛丑 | 1851 辛亥 | 1861 辛酉 |
| 1812 壬申 | 1822 壬午 | 1832 壬辰 | 1842 壬寅 | 1852 壬子 | 1862 壬戌 |
| 1813 癸酉 | 1823 癸未 | 1833 癸巳 | 1843 癸夘 | 1853 癸丑 | 1863 癸亥 |

accordingly it is called, *The cycle of sixty.*

漸而下名之日
六十花甲子

꜁yau tsím꜅ ꜁í há꜅, ꜁ming ꜀chí üt꜇, luk꜇ shap꜇ ꜀fá káp꜆ ‘tsz’.

2. The tropical year is divided into *four seasons*, called Spring, Summer, Autumn, and Winter; the first, second, and third months make the spring season; the fourth, fifth, and sixth months make the summer season; the seventh, eighth, and ninth months make the autumnal season; the tenth, the eleventh, and twelfth, make the winter season.

週歲分以四季
日春夏秋冬以
正二三月爲春
季四五六月爲
夏季七八九月
爲秋季十十一
十二爲冬季

꜀Chau sui꜄ ꜀fan ꜃í sz꜄ kwai꜄, üt꜇ ꜀ch'un há꜅ ꜀ts'au ꜀tung; ꜃í ꜀ching í꜅ ꜁sám üt꜇ ꜁wai ꜀ch'un kwai꜄; sz꜄, ꜃'ng luk꜇ üt꜇ ꜁wai há꜅ kwai꜄; ts'at꜆ pát꜆ ‘kau üt꜇ ꜁wai ꜀ts'au kwai꜄; shap꜇, shap꜇ yat꜆, shap꜇ í꜅ ꜁wai ꜀tung kwai꜄.

3. *Twelve months* make one year; in five years there are two *intercalary* months. Sometimes thirty days make one month; and sometimes twenty-nine days make one month.

十二月爲一年
五年內兩閏或
三十日爲一月
或二十九日爲
一月

Shap꜇ í꜅ üt꜇ ꜁wai yat꜆ ꜁nín, ꜃'ng ꜁nín noi꜅ ꜃léung yun꜅. Wák꜇ ꜀sám shap꜇ yat꜇ ꜁wai yat꜆ üt꜇; wák꜇ í꜅ shap꜇ ‘kau yat꜇ ꜁wai yat꜆ üt꜇.

## *Notes and Explanations.*

HOROLOGY, or the art of measuring time, early engaged the attention of the Chinese, who, like other nations, have devised various methods for marking its progress by distinct periods. The choice of these periods and their order of arrangement constitute what is called the *Calendar*.

1. According to tradition, *Tái Náu* was one of the ministers of Wóng tai, and flourished 2637 years B. C., at which time, by the commands of his sovereign, he formed the cycle of sixty, which was immediately adopted; accordingly, 1840 is the 37th year of the 75th cycle. The twelve characters used to designate the *chí*, or branches, have certain animals appropriated to them, by which they are frequently alluded to in poetical and other writings; the ten *kón*, or stems, have certain inanimate things appropriated to them in like manner. Thus, the twelve *chí*:—

| | | | | | | | |
|---|---|---|---|---|---|---|---|
| *tsz'* | 子 | is represented by *shü*, | 鼠 a rat; | *'ng* | 午 | is represented by *má*, | 馬 a horse; |
| *ch'au* | 丑 | " by *ngau*, | 牛 a cow; | *mí* | 未 | " by *yéung*, | 羊 a sheep; |
| *yan* | 寅 | " by *fú*, | 虎 a tiger; | *shan* | 申 | " by *hau*, | 猴 a monkey |
| *mau* | 卯 | " by *t'ò*, | 兎 a rabbit; | *yau* | 酉 | " by *kai*, | 鷄 a cock; |
| *shan* | 辰 | " by *lung*, | 龍 a dragon; | *sut* | 戌 | " by *hün*, | 犬 a dog; |
| *tsz'* | 巳 | " by *shé*, | 蛇 a snake; | *hoi* | 亥 | " by *chü*, | 猪 a boar. |

The ten *kón* are connected with the five elements, according to the cosmogony of the Chinese; *káp* and *üt* are allied to wood, which is figured as the *yam* and *yéung* wood, or a fir and a bamboo; *ping* and *ting* are allied to fire, divided in the same manner into coal-fire and incense-fire; *mò* and *kí* to earth, as hills and plains; *kang* and *san* to metal; and *yam* and *kwai* to water; each of which produces its successor, and destroys its predecessor. N. B. In order to distinguish *mò*, *sut*, and *shü* (another similar character), the Chinese use the following verse: *Wáng sut, tím shü, mò chung hung;* i. e. cross *sut*, point *shü*, and leave open the middle of *mò*.

2. In the Trimetrical Classic there is a commentary on the four seasons, intended to illustrate their order, and the mode in which, by the alternation of cold and heat, &c., they operate for

4. Ten days make a *decade*, of which in a month there are three, the first, middle, and last decades.

5. A year is divided into *twenty-four terms:* the spring season consists of—opening-spring, rain-water, excited-insects, vernal-equinox, pure-brightness, grain-rains; six terms. The summer season consists of—opening-summer, [ears of grain] little-filled, spiked-grain, summer-solstice, little-heat, and great-heat; six

十日一旬月內
分上中下三旬
歲中共二十四
節春季得立春
雨水驚蟄春分
清明穀雨六節
夏季得立夏小
滿芒種夏至小

Shap, yat, yat, ,ts'un, üt, noi' ,fan shéung', ,chung, há', ,sám ,ts'un.

Sui' ,chung kung' i' shap, sz' tsít,; ,ch'un kwai' tak, lap, ,ch'un, 'ü 'shui, ,king chat,, ,ch'un ,fan, ,ts'ing ,ming, kuk, 'ü, luk, tsít,. Há' kwai' tak, lap, há', 'síú 'mún, ,móng 'chung, há'

the production of trees and vegetables of all kinds. See Chap. I., sec. 2., No. 29. The interval of time employed by the sun between two successive returns to one and the same point in the ecliptic makes a complete year, usually called the *tropical year*. Its duration has always been a subject of interest. The true mean year, as given by the last tables of M. Delambre, is 365d. 5h. 48′ 51″.61.

3. The Chinese year, which is *luni-solar*, consists of 12 months, except when, by this mode of reckoning, the lunar time falls behind the solar time one whole revolution of the moon; then an intercalary month is added, by the following rule; if, during any *lunar* month, the sun does not enter any sign of the zodiac, that month is intercalary, and the year consequently contains thirteen months. The intercalary year contains 384 days, and the common year 354 days; the 1st, 3d, 4th, 8th, and 12th months have 29 days. The month of 30 days is called *tái üt*, that of 29, is called *síú üt;* the greater and the lesser months.

5. These twelve terms express the periods of the sun's passage through the 12 signs of the zodiac: in their meaning there is a reference to the season of the year. The terms are applied to the day that the sun is in the first and fifteenth degree of a sign of the zodiac; consequently in reckoning by the lunar year, their places in the calender will change every year, but in the solar year of Europeans, they will fall more uniformly upon the same day, in successive years. When an intercalary month occurs, the terms continue to be reckoned as usual, an arrangement that sometimes brings the first term into the twelfth moon, making 25 terms in a year, but most usually it falls in the first month. Some of the terms are sixteen days in length, and some are fourteen, but the average is fifteen; and they correspond to our months nearly as follows, falling in the signs here given.

| | | | | | | | |
|---|---|---|---|---|---|---|---|
| Feb. 6. | 立春 | Lap ch'un. | ☉ 15° in Aquarius. | Aug. 7. | 立秋 | Lap ts'au. | In Leo. |
| Feb. 20. | 雨水 | Ü shui. | In Pisces. | Aug. 23. | 處暑 | Chü shü. | In Virgo. |
| March 5. | 驚蟄 | King chat. | | Sept. 8. | 白露 | Pák lú. | |
| Mar. 20. | 春分 | Ch'un fan. | In Aries. | Sept. 23. | 秋分 | Ts'au fan. | In Libra. |
| April 5. | 清明 | Ts'ing ming. | | Oct. 8. | 寒露 | Hón lú. | |
| April 20. | 谷雨 | Kuk ü. | In Taurus. | Oct. 23. | 霜降 | Séung kóng. | In Scorpio. |
| May 5. | 立夏 | Lap há. | | Nov. 7. | 立冬 | Lap tung. | |
| May 21. | 小滿 | Síú mún. | In Gemini. | Nov. 22. | 小雪 | Síú süt. | In Sagittarius. |
| June 6. | 芒種 | Móng chung. | | Dec. 7. | 大雪 | Tái süt. | |
| June 21. | 夏至 | Há chí. | In Cancer. | Dec. 22. | 冬至 | Tung chí. | In Capricornus. |
| July 7. | 小暑 | Síú shü. | | Jan. 6. | 小寒 | Síú hón. | |
| July 23. | 大暑 | Tái shü. | In Leo. | Jan. 21. | 大寒 | Tái hón. | ☉ enters Aquarius. |

terms. The autumnal season consists of—opening-autumn, abated-heat, white-dew, autumnal-equinox, cold-dew, descending-hoarfrost; six terms. The winter season consists of—opening winter, little-snow, great snow, winter-solstice, little-cold, great-cold; six terms.

暑大暑六節秋季得立秋處暑白露秋分寒露霜降六節冬季得立冬小雪大雪冬至小寒大寒六節

chí', 'síú 'shü, tái$^2$ 'shü, luk$_2$ tsít,. ˏTs'au kwai' tak, lap$_2$ ˏts'au, ch'ü' 'shü, pák$_2$ lú$^2$, ˏts'au ˏfan, ˏhón lú$^2$, ˏséung kóng', luk$_2$ tsít,. ˏTung kwai' tak, lap$_2$ ˏtung, 'síú süt,, tái$^2$ süt,, ˏtung chí', 'síú ˏhón, tái$^2$ ˏhón, luk$_2$ tsít,.

6. Every and each period of a day and night together includes ninety-six quarters, which are arranged into twelve periods of time, marked by the twelve branches; one period includes eight quarters, each of which consists of fifteen minutes; half a period makes one hour, or sixty minutes. Thus, in the day time, eleven o'clock, according to the common mode of speaking, is called *káu-'ng*; half-past two o'clock, in like manner, is called *mí ching í hak.*

凡每日晝夜共九十六刻分十二時辰即十二支一時共八刻每刻十五分半時爲一點即六十分如日十一點即俗所謂交午一點半則日未正二刻

ˏFán 'múi yat$_2$ chau' yé$^2$ kung$^2$ 'kau shap$_2$ luk$_2$ hak,, ˏfan shap$_2$ í$^2$ ˏshí ˏshan, tsik, shap$_2$ í$^2$ ˏchí, yat, ˏshí kung$^2$ pát, hak, 'múi hak, shap$_2$ ''ng ˏfan; pún' ˏshí ˏwai yat, 'tím, tsik, luk$_2$ shap$_2$ ˏfan. ˏU yat$_2$ shap$_2$ yat, 'tím, tsik, tsuk$_2$ 'shó wai$^2$ ˏkáu ''ng; yat, 'tím pún', tsak, üt$_2$ mí$^2$ ching' í$^2$ hak,.

7. The brazen *clepsydra* is formed of six water-pots, arranged in successive order one above another, and from which through small perforations the water gradually

蓋銅壺滴漏者乃以六盤疊次滲水而出至末

K'oi' ˏt'ung ˏú tik, lau$^2$ 'ché 'nái 'í luk$_2$ ˏp'ún típ$_2$ ts'z' sham' 'shui ˏí ch'ut,. Chí'

6. *Hak* is a section, a notch, a small division of time; as it corresponds in duration with the fourth part of an hour, it may be rendered *quarter*. The day among the Chinese commences at eleven o'clock P. M. according to European reckoning. The hours are designated by the 12 *chi*, which from this use have been sometimes translated horary characters; and are thus applied.

| | | | |
|---|---|---|---|
| From 11 to 1 A. M. (3d 三更 watch.) is | 子 | From 11 to 1 P. M. 正午 is noon. | 午 |
| " 1—3 (4th 四更 watch.) is | 丑 | " 1—3 下午 is afternoon. | 未 |
| " 3—5 (5th 五更 watch.) is | 寅 | " 3—5 . . . . . . . . . . . . . . . | 申 |
| " 5—7 . . . . . . . . . . . . . . . | 卯 | " 5—7 . . . . . . . . . . . . . . . | 酉 |
| " 7—9 . . . . . . . . . . . . . . . | 辰 | " 7—9 (1st 初更 watch.) | 戌 |
| " 9—11 上午 is forenoon. | 巳 | " 9—11 (2d 二更 watch.) | 亥 |

7. Clepsydras are still in use; they have varied in their construction at different periods. The water-pots seem originally to have been made of brass, and the term *t'ung* is still retained, although wood only is now used. In the city of Canton, there is a building called *kung pak lau*, "bowing northward loft;" it serves partly as an observatory, and partly as a watch-house, and is maintained by the government.

drops. The extreme lower vessel, which receives the water, has a wooden cover, and through it a hole is cut; and into it an index, marked with periods of time, is inserted. Then as the water in the vessel fills one degree, the index, floating on its surface, rises one quarter. The periods of time, and the watches, are all indicated by this means.

用板蓋一盤以
接其水板面開
孔插一時辰尺
於內若壺水滿
一分則尺浮高
一刻時辰更籌
皆以此報

mút, yung' 'pán k'oi' yat, ,p'ún, 'í tsíp, ,k'í 'shui, 'pán mín' ,hoi 'lung, ch'áp, yat, ,shí ,shan ch'ik, ,ü noi'. Yéuk, ,ú 'shui 'mún yat, ,fan, tsak, ch'ik, ,fau ,kò yat, hak,. ,Shí ,shan ,kang ,ch'au, ,kái 'í 'ts'z' pò'.

8. Also there are *incense sticks* which are employed to indicate periods of time; being lighted, the true time is indicated by the progress of the fire.

又有時辰香以
報時刻點以火
所到爲準

Yau' 'yau ,shí ,shan ,héung 'í pò' ,shí hak,; 'tím 'í 'fó 'shó tò' ,wai 'chun.

9. The *sun-dial* was devised for the purpose of observing the time, by the progress of the sun; a line is stretched due south so that the rays of the sun will fall on it; by the shadow of this line the true time of the day is indicated.

制日晷以觀日
行所到之時立
線向南太陽照
之以線影所指
處爲眞

Chai' yat, 'kwai 'í 'kún yat, ,hang 'shó tò' ,chí ,shí; lap, sín' héung' ,nám, t'ái' ,yéung chíú' ,chí, 'í sín' 'ying 'sho 'chí ch'ü' ,wai ,chan.

10. The whole night is divided into five *watches*, and commencing at 7 P. M. are announced as follows; *Káu sut* is announced as the opening watch, the first watch;
*Káu hoi* is announced as the second watch;
*Káu tsz'* is announced as the third watch;
*Káu ch'au* is announced as the fourth watch;
*Káu yan* is announced as the fifth watch.
The methods of announcing the watches are various: sometimes they are announced by the gong; sometimes by the drum, and afterwards by the gong, in concert. In villages, and in streets and market-places, hollow bamboos and sticks are chiefly used for announcing the watches.

通夜以五更報
之如交戌報以
初更卽一更也
交亥報以二更
交子報以三〡
交丑報以四〡
交寅報以五〡
報更不一或鼓
報或鑼報或先
鼓後鑼同報閭
閻市井以竹木
筒敲報者尤甚

,T'ung yé' 'í 'ng ,kang pò' ,chí; ,ü ,káu sut, pò' 'í ,ch'ó ,kang, tsik, yat, ,kang 'yá;

,Káu hoi', pò' 'í í' ,kang;

,Káu 'tsz', pò' 'í ,sám ,kang;

,Káu 'ch'au, pò' 'í sz' ,kang;

,Káu ,yan, pò' 'í 'ng ,kang.

Pò' ,kang pat, yat,; wák, 'kú pò', wák, ,ló pò', wák, ,sín 'kú hau' ,ló ,t'ung pò'. ,Lui ,ín 'shí 'tsing, 'í chuk, muk, ,t'ung ,háu pò' 'ché ,yau sham'.

10. *Káu sut* is the time when the watch is set or commences, and is beat as the first watch till *káu hoi*, on the opening of the second; and so of the others till 5 o'clock A. M., when the watch breaks up with a reveille, which the Chinese call *sánlui*.

廣東方言讀本



## Section Eighth.

# GEOMETRY AND TRIGONOMETRY.

## 方田弧角類第八章

‹Fóng ˏt'ín ˏú kók› lui$^{2}$; tai$^{2}$ pát› ‹chéung.

| | | |
|---|---|---|
| 1. In the first place lay down the terms of a *problem*, and afterwards state the method for finding the *solution*. | 先設爲幾何之<br>分然後立相求<br>之法 | ‹Sín ch'ít› ˏwai ʻkí ˏhó ‹chí ‹fan, ˏín hau$^{2}$ lap$_{2}$ ‹séung ˏkau ‹chí fát›. |
| 2. That which has length without breadth is called a *line:* a line is formed of points. | 有長無濶者謂<br>之線線成於點 | ʻYau ˏch'éung ˏmò fút› ʻché, wai$^{2}$ ‹chí sín›: sín› ˏshing ‹ü ʻtím. |
| 3. The two ends of a line are *points*. | 線之兩端卽點 | Sín› ‹chí ʻléung ‹tün, tsik› ʻtím. |
| 4. A point is without length or shortness, breadth or narrowness, thickness or thinness whereof to speak; but by one point being drawn out and lengthened till another point is attained and made the stopping-place, a line is formed. | 點無長短濶狹<br>厚薄可論然自<br>一點引而長之<br>至又一點止則<br>成線 | ʻTím ˏmò ˏch'éung ʻtün, fút› háp$_{2}$, hau› pók$_{2}$, ʻhó lun$^{2}$; ˏín tsz'$^{2}$ yat› ʻtím ʻyan, ˏí ˏch'éung ‹chí, chí› yau$^{2}$ yat› ʻtím ʻchí, tsak› ˏshing sín›. |
| 5. Lines are of two kinds, *rectilineal* and *curvilinear*. | 線有直曲兩種 | Sín› ʻyau chik$_{2}$ huk›, ʻléung ʻchung. |
| 6. A *surface* is formed of lines. | 面成於線 | Mín$^{2}$ ˏshing ‹ü sín›. |
| 7. A *solid* is formed of surfaces. | 體成於面 | ʻT'ai ˏshing ‹ü mín$^{2}$. |
| 8. If one end of a line is made a *centre;* and the other end of the same line, taken as a limit, be carried in a circumference, then it will form a *circle*. | 若線之一端爲<br>樞復以此線之<br>一端爲界旋轉<br>一周卽成一圜 | Yéuk$_{2}$ sín› ‹chí yat› ‹tün ˏwai ‹shü, fuk$_{2}$ ʻí ʻts'z' sín› ‹chí yat› ‹tün ˏwai kái›, ˏsün ʻchün yat› ‹chau tsik› ˏshing yat› ˏwán. |

## *Notes and Explanations.*

For most of their knowledge of mathematics, both pure and mixed, the Chinese are indebted to foreigners. Mohammedans first, and subsequently Jesuits, translated into their language treatises on the various branches of this science. This section, containing a few of the definitions and first principles of geometry and trigonometry, affords a specimen of the phraseology used in treating of these subjects.

1. A *problem* is something to be done: frequently, the object of inquiry is not the demonstration of any truth, but the performing of some operation, such as extracting the cube root, or inscribing a circle in a square; this is called *solving* a problem.

8. *Shü* is the pivot at the bottom of a door on which it turns, and is here used as synonimous with *sam*, a heart, which is the proper term for the centre of a circle.

9. A *square* is a figure which has its four sides of equal length, and the measure of its angles also equal.

正方形有四邊線度等而角度亦等者

Ching' ꜀fóng ꜁ying ꜂yau sz' ꜀pín sín' tò' ꜂tang, ꜁í kók, tò' yik, ꜂tang ꜂ché.

10. When all the surfaces are severally equal, and all the sides are similar and equal, if the angles are all equal, it is a *cube* (*lit.* an even-face-perfect-square-solid).

各面俱等各邊相等所成各角等平面正方體

Kók, mín' ꜀k'ü ꜂tang, kók, ꜀pín ꜀séung ꜂tang, ꜂shó ꜁shing kók, kók, ꜂tang, ꜁p'ing mín' ching' ꜀fóng ꜂t'ai.

11. Whenever one straight line is drawn to meet another [straight] line, if the angles which it makes with it are right angles, this line is called a *perpendicular line:* for the two lines [being prolonged] will divide the circle into four equal parts.

凡畫一直線交於别線其所成之角若直此線謂之垂線蓋其兩線平分還界爲四

꜁Fán wák, yat, chik, sín' ꜀káu ꜀ü pít, sín', ꜁k'í ꜂shó ꜁shing ꜀chí kók, yéuk, chik, ꜂ts'z' sín' wai' ꜀chí ꜁shui sín'; k'oi' ꜁k'í ꜂léung sín' ꜁p'ing ꜀fan ꜁wán kái' ꜁wai sz'.

12. Whenever the *arc* which is opposite an angle is one fourth part of the circumference of a circle, this angle must be straight; therefore it is called a *right angle*.

凡角相對之弧得圜界四分之一者此角必直故謂之直角

꜁Fán kók, ꜀séung túi' ꜀chí ꜁ú, tak, ꜁wán kái' sz' ꜀fan ꜀chí yat, ꜂ché, ꜂ts'z kók, pít, chik,; kú' wai' ꜀chí chik, kók,.

13. The circumference of a circle which is opposite to an angle is called its *arc;* and the arc which is opposite that angle is called its *measure* (i.e. the measure of the angle).

圜界以所對之角而命其弧而角又以所對之弧而命其度

꜁Wán kái' ꜂í ꜂shó túi' ꜀chí kók, ꜁í ming' ꜁k'í ꜁ú; ꜁í kók, yau' ꜂í ꜂shó túi' ꜀chí ꜁ú ꜁í ming' ꜁k'í tò'.

14. Every triangle which has one right angle is a *right-angled triangle*.

凡三角形一角直者爲直角三角形

꜁Fán ꜀sám kók, ꜁ying yat, kók, chik, ꜂ché ꜁wai chik, kók, ꜀sám kók, ꜁ying.

15. The three angles of every triangle taken together must be equal to two right angles.

凡三角形之三角度相併必與二直角度等

꜁Fán ꜀sám kók, ꜁ying ꜀chí ꜀sám kók, tò' ꜀séung ping', pít, ꜂yü i' chik, kók, tò' ꜂tang.

11. This and the preceding definitions differ, but not essentially, from those given in European books, from which they seem (at least some of them) to have been translated. Thus Euclid; "a line is length without breadth;" "the extremities of lines are points;" "a circle is a plane figure contained by one line, which is called the circumference, and is such that all straight lines drawn from a certain point within the figure to the circumference are equal to one another."

16. The *base* and *perpendicular* of a right-angled triangle severally multiplied into themselves, are together equal to the square of the *hypotenuse*. (Euclid, Book I. 45.)

勾股各自乘之積相弦而與弦自乘之積等

꜁Kau ꜂kú kók꜄ tsz'꜇ ꜁shing ꜀chí tsik꜄ ꜀séung ꜁ín, ꜁í ꜂yü ꜁ín tsz'꜇ ꜁shing ꜀chí tsik꜄ ꜂tang.

17. From the square of the side subtending a right angle, subtract the square of the longer side of that angle, and the square of the shorter side is obtained.

弦之自乘積內減股自乘之積得勾自乘之積

꜁Ín ꜀chí tsz'꜇ ꜁shing tsik꜄ noi꜇ ꜂kám, ꜂kú tsz'꜇ ꜁shing ꜀chí tsik꜄, tak꜄ ꜀kau tsz'꜇ ꜁shing ꜀chí tsik꜄.

18. If from one circumference of a circle a straight line be drawn through its centre to the opposite side, then that line will be the *diameter* of the circle.

自一界過圜心至相對之界畫直線則是圜徑

Tsz'꜇ yat꜄ kái' kwó' ꜁wán ꜀sam chí' ꜀séung túi' ꜀chí kái' wák꜅ chik꜅ sín', tsak꜄ shí꜇ ꜁wán king'.

19. If from the middle of the diameter [of a circle] another straight line be drawn as a *radius*, and not equally dividing the circumference of the semicircle, then it will make one *acute* angle, and one *obtuse* angle.

自圜徑中心復畫一輻線而不平分半圜之界則成一銳角一鈍角

Tsz'꜇ ꜁wán king꜇ ꜀chung ꜀sam fuk꜅ wák꜅ yat꜄ fuk꜅ sín', ꜁í pat꜄ ꜁p'ing ꜀fan pún' ꜁wán ꜀chí kái', tsak꜄ ꜁shing yat꜄ yui꜇ kók꜄ yat꜄ tun꜇ kók꜄.

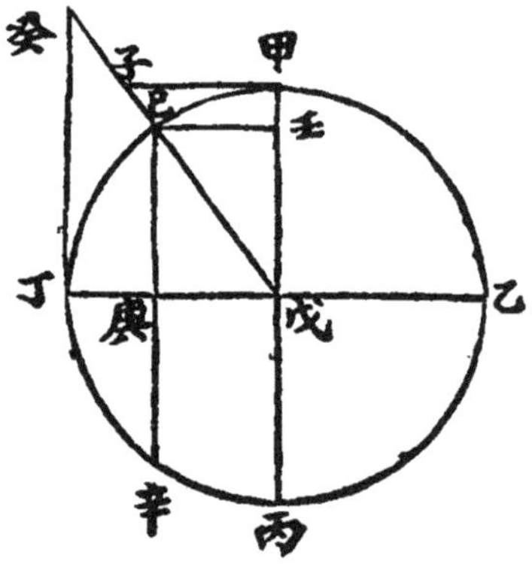


20. Suppose, in the figure, *káp üt ping ting* be a complete circle; *káp üt ping* is a semicircle; *káp üt* is a quadrant; *üt ting* is a whole diameter; *ting mò* is the semidiameter;

如圖甲乙丙丁爲全圜甲乙丙爲半周甲乙爲象限乙丁爲全徑丁戊爲半徑

꜁Yü ꜁t'ò, káp꜄ üt꜅ ꜂ping ꜀ting ꜁wai ꜁tsüin ꜁wán; káp꜄ üt꜅ ꜂ping ꜁wai pún' ꜀chau; káp꜄ üt꜅ ꜁wai ts'éung꜇ hán꜇; üt꜅ ꜀ting ꜁wai ꜁ts'üin king꜄; ꜀ting mò꜇ ꜁wai pún' king'; ꜂kí ꜀ting

20. The sine and cosine, the versed sine with the versed sine of the complement, the tangent and the cotangent, the secant and cosecant, form the *pát sín*, or eight lines of the Chinese.

*kí ting* is a given arc; *káp kí* is its complement; *kí san* is a chord; *kí kang* is a sine; *kí yam* is the cosine; *ting kang* is the versed sine; *káp yam* is the versed sine of the complement; *üt kang* is the versed sine of the supplement; (i. e. the versed sine of *üt mò kí* is *üt kang*=*üt mò* and *kang mò*;) *ting kwai* is the tangent; *káp tsz'* is the cotangent; *mò kwai* is the secant; *mò tsz'* is the cosecant.

已丁爲本弧甲已爲餘弧已辛爲通弦已庚爲正弦已壬爲餘弦丁庚爲正矢甲壬爲餘矢乙庚爲大矢丁癸爲正切甲子爲餘切戊癸爲正割戊子爲餘割

ˏwai ʻpún ˏú; káp, kí[2] ˏwai ˏü ˏú ʻkí ˏsan ˏwai ˏtʻung ˏín; ʻkí ˏkang ˏwai chingʼ ˏín; ʻkí ˏyam ˏwai ˏü ˏín; ˏting ˏkang ˏwai chingʼ ʻchʻí; káp, ˏyam ˏwai ˏü ʻchʻí; üt, ˏkang ˏwai tái[2] ʻchʻí; ˏting kwaiʼ ˏwai chingʼ tsʻít,; káp, ʻtszʼ ˏwai ˏü tsʻít,; mò[2] kwaiʼ ˏwai chingʼ kót,; mò[2] ʻtszʼ ˏwai ˏü kót,.

21. The Mathematics of the Tsʻuimí Hill Institution.

22. The logarithmic tables are the work of a western scholar, John Napier (Jeŏ-wang Nă-pĭh-urh).

翠薇山房數學

對數比例乃西士若往納白爾所作

Tsʻuiʼ ˏmí ˏShán ˏFong Shòʼ hók$_2$.

Túiʼ shòʼ ʻpí lai[2] ʻnái ˏsai szʼ[2] Yéuk$_2$ ʻwóng Náp$_2$ pák$_2$ ʻí ʻshó tsók,.

21. *Tsʻuimí* is the flower of the *Lagerstrœmia Indica*, and the name is here employed like those sometimes given to books in the west; as, the Cambridge system of Physics, the Bridgewater Treatises, &c. The work is comprised in thirty-six (sometimes in 38) octavo volumes; and forms a complete course, including geometry, plain and spherical trigonometry, mensuration, astronomy, etc. It contains a table of natural signs and tangents, and also a table of logarithmic sines, tangents, secants, &c., for every degree and minute.

## Section Ninth.

## OF ASTRONOMY.

## 天文類第九章

ˏTʻín ˏman lui[2]; tai[2] ʻkau ˏchéung.

1. The body of the heavens is [apparently] spherical like a globe. Its breadth is immeasurable. The terrestrial

天體渾圓如球其廣莫測地球

ˏTʻín ʻtʻai wan[2] ˏün ˏü ˏkʻau. ˏKʻí ʻkwóng mók$_2$ chʻák,. Tí[2] ˏkʻau ˏün ˏü

### *Notes and Explanations.*

Astronomy seems to have been studied by the Chinese chiefly for astrological purposes. Complete systems of this science, however, have been compiled and translated into their language,

globe is suspended in its midst; and about [the earth, as a centre] are several concentric spheres, to which the sun, moon, and stars are attached. Hence is the name, celestial sphere.—See the first volume of Plates Illustrative of the Heavens, drawn and described by Ts'ingloi Lí Ming-ch'ít, under the patronage of Yün Yün of Íching, [a district in the province of Kóng-sú.]

懸於當中外面數重包裏內則日月星辰繫焉故名渾天見儀徵阮元鑒定青來李明徹述圓天圖說上卷

‹tóng ‹chung; ngoi$^2$ mín$^2$ shò' ˏchung ‹páu ʿkwó, noi$^2$ tsak› yat$_2$, üt$_2$, ‹sing ˏshan hai$^2$ ˏin. Kú' ˏming wan$^2$ ‹t'ín.—Kin' ˏÍ ‹ching ʿYün ˏYün kám' ting$^2$, ‹Ts'ing ˏloi ʿLí ˏMing ch'ít› shut$_2$ ˏWán ‹t'ín ˏT'ò Shüt›, shéung$^2$ ʿkün.

2. The body of the celestial sphere (or heavenly system) has two extremes, north and south, which are the poles of the heavens; the heavens revolve, but the poles are immovable. Directly opposite and centrically between the two poles, dividing equally the heavenly body into two halves, is the place of a circle occupying this central division; this is the equator (*lit.* the bright or flesh colored path). All computations are referred to and depend on this fixed line. The whole circumference of the equator (or equinoctial line) is graduated into 360 degrees; thirty degrees form a sign (or house), and each of the degrees are divided into twelve periods [of 24 hours each].

渾天之體有南北二極為天之樞紐天動而極不動從二極正對當中平分天體為兩半其中分之一圈處是為赤道凡推測者皆賴此為準繩赤道周圍列三百六十度三十度為一宮每度分十二時

Wan$^2$ ‹t'ín ‹chí ʿt'ai, ʿyau ˏnám pak› í$^2$ kik$_2$ ˏwai ‹t'ín ‹chí ‹shü ʿnau; ‹t'ín tung$^2$, ˏí kik$_2$ pat› tung$^2$. ˏTs'ung í$^2$ kik$_2$ ching' túi' ‹tóng ‹chung, ˏp'ing ‹fan ‹t'ín ʿt'ai ˏwai ʿléung pún', ˏk'í ‹chung ‹fan ‹chí yat› ‹kün ch'ü', shí$^2$ ˏwai ch'ik› tò$^2$. ˏFán ‹t'úi ch'ák› ʿché, ‹kái lái' ʿts'z' ˏwai ʿchun ˏshing. Ch'ik› tò$^2$ ‹chau ˏwai lít$_2$ ‹sám pák› luk$_2$ shap$_2$ tò$^2$; ‹sám shap$_2$ tò$^2$ ˏwai yat› ‹kung; ʿmúi tò$^2$ ‹fan shap$_2$ í$^2$ ˏshí.

by Europeans. Probably the best work of this kind is found in the *Lut Lik Ün Ün*, a work comprised in one hundred volumes, "a few of which illustrate the theory of music, with the European mode of notation; the others contain the principles of mathematics, spherics, the calculation of eclipses, with tables of the sun and moon's mean motions, nodes, and anomalies, with tables of all the necessary equations," &c. See Morrison's Dictionary, Part II., Vol. I., p. 1064.

1. The work here referred to is in five volumes, containing an epitome of astronomy and geography. The author, who died in the vicinity of Canton only a few years since, was educated by Europeans, and derived most of his knowledge from their books. With that which is true, he has blended much that is ideal and erroneous, as will be seen from this, and the several paragraphs which follow, selected from his work. He makes the heavens to consist of ten concentric hollow spheres or envelops: the first contains the moon's orbit; the second that of Mercury; those of Venus, the Sun, Mars, Jupiter, Saturn, and the twenty-four constellations follow; the ninth envelops and binds together the eight interior ones, and revolves daily; the tenth "is the abode of the celestial sovereign, the Great Ruler, with all the gods and sages, where they enjoy eternal tranquillity." The author's patron (Yün Yün) was for sometime governor of Canton, and has since been one of the principal ministers of state, from which office he retired in 1838 to his paternal estates in the province of Kóngsú.

3. There are two north and two south poles, those of the equator and those of the ecliptic. The poles of the ecliptic regulate the varied machinery of the heavenly revolutions, and turn round unceasingly. The poles of the equator are the pivots of the primitive celestial body, and remain permanently unmoved. What are called the two poles, therefore, are really not stars, but two immovable points, in the north and in the south.

南北二極各有二赤極黃極是也黃極主天旋之化機運行不息赤極乃天元本體之樞居所不動名爲二極實非星也乃南北二點不動處

꜀Nám pak꜁ í꜃ kik꜁ kók꜁ ꜂yau í꜃, ch'ik꜁ kik꜁ ꜀wóng kik꜁ shí꜃ ꜂yá. ꜀Wóng kik꜁ ꜂chü ꜀t'ín ꜀sün ꜂chí fá꜃ ꜀kí, wan꜃ ꜀hang pat꜁ sik꜁. Ch'ik꜁ kik꜁ ꜂nái ꜀t'ín ꜀ün ꜂pún ꜂t'ai ꜀chí ꜀shü, ꜀kü ꜂shó pat꜁ tung꜃. ꜀Ming ꜀wai í꜃ kik꜁, shat꜁ ꜀fí ꜀sing ꜂yá, ꜂nái ꜀nám pak꜁ í꜃ ꜂tím pat꜁ tung꜃ ch'ü꜃.

4. The centre of the terrestrial globe is the place towards which the whole of the surrounding parts gravitate; and therefore the hills, the seas, men, and all things do not fall upside down into ruins.

地球中心爲周圍重性所趨處故山海人物皆爲無傾倒之虞

Tí꜃ ꜀k'au ꜀chung ꜀sam ꜀wai ꜀chau ꜀wai chung꜃ sing꜃ ꜂shó ꜀ts'ü ch'ü꜃; kú꜃ ꜀shán ꜂hoi ꜀yan mat꜁, ꜀kái ꜀wai ꜀mò ꜀k'ing ꜂tò ꜀chí ꜀yü.

5. Always on the recurrence of new moon, the sun and moon move together in the same course; at the time of full moon they are in direct opposition, and distant from each other half a circle.

凡遇朔時日月共躔一度望時日月相對各遠半周

꜀Fán yü꜃ shók꜁ ꜀shí, yat꜁ üt꜁ kung꜃ ꜀ch'ín yat꜁ tò꜃; móng꜃ ꜀shí yat꜁ üt꜁ ꜀séung túi꜃, kók꜁ ꜂ün pún꜃ ꜀chau.

6. The ecliptic's greatest southern boundary is twenty-three degrees and a half from the equator (or equinoctial line).

黃道最南之界在赤道緯度二十三度半

꜀Wóng tò꜃ tsui꜃ ꜀nám ꜀chí kái꜃, tsoi꜃ ch'ik꜁ tò꜃ ꜂wai tò꜃ í꜃ shap꜁ ꜀sám tò꜃ pún꜃.

7. In the twentieth year of the reign of Tòkwóng, in the second month, and on the first day of the month, there was an eclipse of the sun. (March 4th, 1840.)
Beginning of the eclipse, 10 h. 20 m., A. M.
Middle of the eclipse, 11 h. 30 m.
End of the eclipse, 0 h. 54 m., P. M.

道光二十年二月初一日日蝕初虧已正初刻五分蝕甚午初二刻無分復圓午正三刻九分

Tò꜃ ꜀kwóng, í꜃ shap꜁ ꜀nín, í꜃ üt꜁ ꜀ch'ó yat꜁ yat꜁, yat꜁ shik꜁. ꜀Ch'ó ꜀fai tsz꜃ ching꜃ ꜀ch'ó hak꜁ ꜂'ng ꜀fan; shik꜁ sham꜃ ꜂'ng ꜀ch'ó í꜃ hak꜁ ꜀mò ꜀fan; fuk꜁ ꜀ün ꜂'ng ching꜃ ꜀sám hak꜁ ꜂kau ꜀fan.

7. This is copied from a native almanac, published in Canton. The time of the eclipse corresponds to the 3d of March, on the other side of the globe, and it is accordingly so noted in the almanacs of Europe and America.

The Chinese name their five planets by the five elements; thus, Venus is the star of gold, or the star that is allied to gold; Mercury is the star of water; Saturn, that of earth; Mars, that of fire; and Jupiter that of wood.

# CHAPTER XII.

# GEOGRAPHY.

# 地理志篇十二

Tí$^{2}$ ʿlí chí'; ꜀p'ín shap꜇ í$^{2}$.

## Section First.

## SHAPE OF THE EARTH.

### 地形類第一章

T'í$^{2}$ ꜁ying lui$^{2}$; tai$^{2}$ yat꜇ ꜀chéung.

| | | |
|---|---|---|
| 1. The earth is a sphere situated in the midst of the celestial sphere: and the heavens surround the earth, just as [the white of] an egg surrounds the yolk. | 地本正圓居天<br>圓之中天包地<br>外如卵裹黄 | Tí$^{2}$ ʿpún ching' ꜁yün, ꜀kü ꜀t'ín ꜁yün ꜀chí ꜀chung; ꜀t'ín ꜀páu tí$^{2}$ ngoi$^{2}$, ꜁ü ʿlun ʿkwó ꜁wóng. |
| 2. The body of the sun is one million, three hundred and eight thousand times greater than the earth. If viewed from the sun, the earth would appear like a small speck; but the sun, viewed from the earth, appears as large as the wheel of a carriage. | 日體大地一百<br>三十八萬倍自<br>日視地僅小如<br>彈丸自地球視<br>日則大如車輪 | Yat꜇ ʿt'ai tái$^{2}$ tí$^{2}$ yat꜇ pák꜇ ꜀sám shap꜇ pát꜇ mán$^{2}$ ʿp'úi. Tsz'$^{2}$ yat꜇ shí$^{2}$ tí$^{2}$ ʿkan ʿsíú ꜁ü ꜁tán ꜁ün; tsz'$^{2}$ tí$^{2}$ ꜁k'au shí$^{2}$ yat꜇, tsak꜇ tái$^{2}$ ꜁ü ꜀kü ꜁lun. |
| 3. If the earth were a square solid body, then the sun, moon, and all the stars, would not have the varied appearances of rising and sitting. | 若地爲方體者<br>則日月諸星不<br>當有隱顯各異 | Yéuk꜇ tí$^{2}$ ꜁wai ꜀fong ʿt'ai ʿché, tsak꜇ yat꜇ üt꜇ ꜀chü ꜀sing pat꜇ ꜀tóng ʿyau ʿyan ʿhín kók꜇ í$^{2}$. |

### *Notes and Explanations.*

Unassisted by foreigners, the Chinese have done very little in the study of geography, or, as they term it, *tí lí chí*, the Records of the earth's principles. Nor of the knowledge brought from abroad, on this subject, have they made much use. Geography is not with them regarded as a branch of education; and only a few, even of their literati, understand the first principles of the science. Ts'ingloi Lí Mingch'ít, in his work just noticed (page 379), has given an outline of geography, illustrated with plates. See his *Wán T'ín T'ò Shüt*, volume III, from which most of the phraseology of this section is selected.

3. That the earth is not only not square, but is not an immense stationary plain, is the idea which the native author here wishes to combat.

4. If two ships in Europe on the same day take their departure together, one sailing towards the east, and one sailing towards the west, they will afterwards meet in Uttung (or Canton); but that which sailed to the east will, at the time of her arrival, have gained half a day, while that which sailed to the west will have lost half a day; which computed together will give a difference of one whole day. If that ship which came eastward to Canton, again goes eastward to Europe, and that ship which came westward to Canton again goes westward to Europe, then their time when computed together will give a difference of two whole days.

若二船在歐邏巴同日解維一向東行一向西往後遇於粵東其東行者到時是上半日西行者到時是下半日合計者約差一日矣其東來之船在粵東復東行至歐邏巴其西來之船在粵東復西行至歐邏巴合計者僅差兩日而矣

Yéuk, í' ˏshün tsoi' ˏAu ˏlò ˏpá ˏt'ung yat, 'kái ˏwai, yat, héung' ˏtung ˏhang, yat, héung' ˏsai 'wóng, hau' ü' ˏü Ut, ˏtung; ˏk'í ˏtung ˏhang 'ché tò' ˏshí shí' shéung' pún' yat,; ˏsai ˏhang 'ché tò' ˏshí shí' há' pún' yat,; hóp, kai' 'ché yéuk, ˏch'á yat, yat, 'í. ˏK'í ˏtung ˏloi ˏchí ˏshün tsoi' Ut, tung, fuk, ˏtung ˏhang chí' ˏAu ˏlò ˏpá, ˏk'í ˏsai ˏloi ˏchí ˏshün tsoi' Ut, ˏtung fuk, ˏsai ˏhang chí' ˏAu ˏlò ˏpá, hóp, kai' 'ché, 'kan ˏch'á 'léung yat, ˏí 'í.

5. One fixed immovable line, passing through the centre and extending from the north pole to the south pole, is called the axis of the earth.

一定不易貫心線自北極至南極曰地之直距

Yat, ting' pat, yik, kún' ˏsam sín', tsz' pak, kik, chí' ˏnám kik,, üt, tí' ˏchí chik, 'k'ü.

6. The two poles are the extremities of the axis, the north pole and the south pole.

兩極即直距尾之北極南極

'Léung kik, tsik, chik, 'k'ü 'mí ˏchí pak, kik, ˏnám kik,.

7. From the north pole to the south pole, passing through the centre of the globe, the distance is about eight thousand English miles.

在北丨至南極貫球心照英國約八千里

Tsoi' pak, kik, chí' ˏnám kik, kún' ˏk'au ˏsam chiú' ˏYing kwok, yéuk, pát, ˏts'ín 'lí.

8. The equator is one fixed line, which divides the earth

赤道者一定線

Ch'ik, tò' 'ché yat, ting' sín'

---

4. This paragraph is abridged from the work of Ts'ingloi, where it is illustrated by a diagram, rude indeed, but sufficiently clear to make the subject intelligible. A ship sails from Macao on a Monday the first day of a month, and on Monday the eighth arrives in Manila, where the inhabitants are regarding the day as the Sabbath, the seventh of the week and month; thus to the people in the ship two Sabbath days come together. The reckoning of time at Macao is that of those who came from the west, at Manila it is that of those who came from the east, around cape Horn. European navigators usually change their reckoning on reaching the 180° from the meridian of Greenwich.

8. The summer solstice, they aptly call *há chí*, or summer's limit, and *tung chí* is winter's

in twain, so that the equator is equally distant from the north and south poles.

破地爲二故赤
道往南北同遠

pó' tí' ˏwai í', kú' ch'ik, tò 'wóng ˏnám pak, ˏt'ung 'ün.

9. By the lines (or parallels) of latitude extending from east to west, the length of the world is reckoned; by the lines of longitude (or meridians), extending from north to south, the breadth of the world is reckoned. Take the equinoctial line and make it the middle line for the parallels of latitude; then from this middle line (the equator) reckoning up to the north pole, will make the northern hemisphere; and from this middle line (the equator), reckoning down to the south pole, will make the southern hemisphere.

東西緯線是數
天下之長南北
經線是數天下
之寬以晝夜平
線定緯度中線
從中線往上數
至北極爲北方
從中線往下數
至南極爲南方

ˏTung ˏsai ˏwai sín', shí' 'shò ˏt'ín há' ˏchí ˏch'éung; ˏnám pak, ˏking sín', shí' shò' ˏt'ín há' ˏchí ˏfún. 'Í chau' yé' ˏp'ing sín', ting' ˏwai tò' ˏchung sín'; ˏts'ung ˏchung sín' 'wóng shéung' 'shò chí' pak, kik,, ˏwai pak, ˏfong: ˏts'ung ˏchung sín' 'wóng há' 'shò ˏchí ˏnám kik,, ˏwai ˏnám ˏfong.

10. Now we employ this reckoning in order to show the elevation of each pole above the earth; for the number of degrees any place is distant from the equinoctial line, and the number of degrees the pole is elevated at that place, are equal to each other; but in the southern [hemisphere] then it will be according to the elevation of the south pole; in the northern, it will be according to the elevation of the north pole. Therefore, seeing that the capital of China is forty degrees from the equator, we know that at that place the elevation of the north pole is forty degrees above the earth.

卽用此數以著
各極出地多寡
盖離晝夜平線
度數與極出地
度數相等但在
南則若南極出
地之數在北則
若北極出地之
數故視京師隔
中線四十度卽
知京師北極出
地四十度

Tsik, yung' 'ts'z' shò', 'í chü' kók, kik, ch'ut, tí' ˏtó 'kwá; k'oi' ˏlí chau' yé' ˏp'ing sín' tò' shò', 'ü kik, ch'ut, tí' tò' shò', ˏséung 'tang; tán' tsoi' ˏnám, tsak, yéuk, ˏnám kik, ch'ut, tí' ˏchí shò'; tsoi' pak,, tsak, yéuk, pak, kik, ch'ut, tí' ˏchí shò'. Kú' shí' ˏking ˏsz' kák, ˏchung sín' sz' shap, tò', tsik, ˏchí ˏking sz' pak, kik, ch'ut, tí' sz' shap, tò'.

11. On modern maps, ten degrees are allowed for each line, in order that they may be more distinctly and easily inspected. The parallels of latitude, dividing the north

今圖內十度爲
一格使簡約便
覽共緯度自晝

ˏKam ˏt'ò noi' shap, tò' ˏwai yat, kák,; 'sz' 'kán yéuk, pín' 'lám. ˏK'í ˏwai

---

limit, or the winter solstice. So zenith and nadir, and other terms, are expressed by words or phrases whose literal meanings are equivalent to the technical terms in use among Europeans.

11. The writer, Ts'ingloi, is here describing and referring to a small map of the world, presenting the two hemispheres, the eastern and western; on which, as on European maps of the same size, the only lines of latitude and longitude are those marked by the numbers, 10, 20, 30, &c.

and south poles from the equinoctial line, are longitudinal degrees; and as they gradually near the poles, in like manner the circles gradually become smaller, and cease in the ninetieh degree.

夜平線分南北兩極係橫度漸近極則圈漸小而盡於九十度

tò, tsz' chau' yé ˏp'ing sín' ˎfan ˏnám pak, ˊléung kik, hai ˏwáng ˊtò; tsim kan kik, tsak, ˎhün tsim ˊsíú, ˏí tsun ˎü ˊkau shap, tò.

12. At the capital city, in the department of Shunt'ín, the elevation of the north pole is forty degrees; and this [city] is taken to be the first meridian line.

京都順天府北極出地四十度即爲中線

ˎKing ˎtò, Shun ˎt'in ˊfú, pak, kik, ch'ut, tí sz' shap, tò; tsik, ˏwai ˎchung sín'.

13. In Shingking, at the city of Fungt'ín (or Moukden), the elevation of the north pole is forty-two degrees; and its eastern longitude is seven degrees.

盛京奉天府北極出地四十二度偏東七度

Shing ˎking, Fung ˎt'ín ˊfú, pak, kik, ch'ut, tí sz' shap, í tò; ˎp'ín ˎtung ts'at, tò.

14. In Kwóngtung, the city of Kwóngchau (or Canton), is in [north] latitude twenty-three degrees and twenty minutes, and in west longitude three degrees and thirty minutes.

廣東廣州府二十三度二十分偏西三度三十分

ˊKwóng ˎtung, ˊKwóng ˎchau ˊfú, í shap, ˎsám tò í shap, ˎfan; ˎp'ín ˎsai ˎsám tò ˎsám shap, ˎfan.

15. In [the province of] Wannám, the city of Wannám is in [north] latitude twenty-five degrees and twenty minutes, west longitude thirteen degrees and forty minutes.

雲南雲南府二十五度二十分偏西十三度四十分

ˏWan ˏnám, ˏWan ˏnám ˊfú, í shap, ˊ'ng tò í shap, ˎfan; ˎp'ín ˎsai shap, ˎsám tò sz' shap, ˎfan.

16. In ancient times men did not perceive that the earth was a round ball, and therefore nothing was said respecting it. Subsequently, after more deep researches, they understood that the divisions, Asia, Europe, America, Africa, and New Holland, were five great continents; and that besides them there were also several other small islands, rising between those continents.

昔人未覺地如渾球故無從指說迨後詳究則知分亞細亞歐邏巴亞非利加美理哥新荷蘭爲五大州其外尙餘各小海洲出乎其間

Sik, ˏyan mí kók, tí ˏü wan ˏk'au, kú' ˏmò ˏts'ung ˊchí shüt,. ˊToi hau ˏtséung kau', tsak, ˎchí ˎfan A' sai' á', ˎAu ˏlò ˎpá, A' ˎfí lí ˎká, ˊMí ˊlí ˎkó, ˎSan ˏHó ˎlan, ˏwai ˊ'ng tái ˎchau; ˏk'í ngoi' shéung ˏü, kók, ˊsíú ˊhoi ˎchau ch'ut, ˏú ˏk'í ˎkán.

12—15. The latitude and longitude of these places are copied from Ts'ingloi's work. The foreign factories in Canton, situated a few rods southwest from the walls of the city, are in latitude 23 degrees, 7 minutes, 10 seconds north, and in longitude 113 degrees, 14 minutes, 30 seconds east of Greenwich.

廣東方言讀本

## Section Second.

# METEOROLOGY.

## 氣奇象類第二章

Hí' ˏk'í tséung² lui²; tai² í² ˓chéung.

---

1. *Air* is that which is exhaled and inhaled by all creatures. It possesses varieties in rarity and density, elasticity and pliability, humidity and aridity, heat and cold. The earth, moreover, is surrounded by and enveloped in it, just as the white of the egg encompasses the yolk on all sides.

氣者萬物之呼吸也有輕重爽膩濕燥冷熱不同地球亦包涵於氣內如雞卵之白藏其黃也

*Hí'* ˊché, mán² mat˳ ˓chí ˓fú k'ap˒ ˊyá. ˊYau ˓hing chung², ˊshóng ní², shap˒ ts'ò², ˊlang ít˳, pat˒ ˏt'ung. Tí² ˏk'au yik˳ p'áu ˏhám ˏü hí' noi², ˏü ˓kai ˊlun ˓chí pák˳ ˏts'óng ˏk'í ˏwóng ˊyá.

2. *Clouds:* the humid vapors, rising from the hills, the streams, rivers, and seas, ascend and collect in the midst of the firmament, and form the clouds, which are borne along and moved by the wind.

雲者山川河海蒸濕之氣騰結空中而成雲候風送而行也

ˏ*Wan* ˊché: ˓shán ˓ch'ün ˏhó ˊhoi ˓ching shap˒ ˓chí hí', ˏtang kít˒ ˓hung ˓chung, ˏí ˏshing ˏwan; tsz'² ˓fung sung' ˏí ˏhang ˊyá.

3. *Dew* and hoarfrost are fundamentally of the same class. When the wind is calm, and the atmosphere warm, then the dew falls; when the wind is calm and the atmosphere cold, then hoarfrost is deposited.

露霜本一類也風靜而天氣暖則露下風靜而天氣寒則霜下

*Lò²* ˓séung ˊpún yat˒ lui² ˊyá. ˓Fung tsing² ˏí ˓t'ín hí' ˊnün, tsak˒ lò² há²; ˓fung tsing² ˏí ˓t'ín hí' ˏhón, tsak˒ ˓séung há².

4. *Earthquake:* when the watery and fiery vapors confined in the earth are unable to get vent, then by their agitations they cause the earth to quake.

地震蓋因地中水火之氣不舒是以激致地震

*Tí² chan'*: k'oi' ˓yan tí² ˓chung ˊshui ˊfo ˓chí hí', pat˒ ˓shü, shí² ˊí kik˒ chí' tí² chan'

## *Notes and Explanations.*

Meteorology, that department of science which makes us acquainted with the properties and relations of the atmosphere surrounding the earth, occupies the principal part of the fifth and last volume of Ts'ingloi's work, from which the following paragraphs are abridged. Exactness in such a science is hardly attainable, even by the ablest masters. Ts'ingloi has often used words in a technical sense, and without the requisite definitions being attached; it is, therefore, sometimes impossible to determine their meaning. In such cases only their literal meaning can be given.

1. The word *hí* is used to express very diverse ideas, relating to matter and mind, things physical, spiritual, and imaginary. Here it evidently denotes simply the atmospheric air; with many of the operations and properties of which the Chinese are familiar, though they seem to have nó idea of its constituent parts as a compound fluid, consisting of oxygen gas, and nitrogen or azote.

5. *Fog* is a light vapor arising from humidity; when there is not wind and heat of the sun sufficient to cause its dispersion, it collects together and forms fog.

霧者濕之輕氣因無風太陽飄散致結爲霧也

*Mò*² 'ché, shap˃ ‹chí ‹hing hí˃: ‹yan ˏmò ‹fung t'ái² ˏyéung ‹píú sán˃, chí˃ kít˃ ˏwai mò² ˢyá.

6. *Hail* is a species of ice; when the drops of rain descending downwards, happen to meet with intense cold, they congeal and become solid.

雹即冰之類乃雨水下降忽遇極寒而凝實也

‹*P'áu* tsik˃ ‹ping ‹chí lui²: ˢnái ˢü 'shui há² kóng², fat˃ ü² kik₂ ˏhón, ˏí ˏying shat₂ ˢyá.

7. *Halo* of the sun: this is caused by the cloudy vapor of the sky coming in direct contact with the sun's light, thus forming a ring surrounding the sun's disc.

日暈者乃空中之雲氣直逼日之光圍抱成環

*Yat*₂ *wan*² 'ché: ˢnái ‹hung ‹chung ‹chí ˏwan hí˃, chik₂ pik˃ yat₂ ‹chí ‹kwóng, ˏwai ˢp'ò ˏsháng ˏwan.

8. *Hoarfrost* is dew congealed.

霜者露所結也

‹*Séung* 'ché lò² 'shó kit˃ ˢyá.

9. *Ice* is formed by cold air acting on water. In the first of winter the ice begins to form; in the middle of winter it becomes more firm; and in the end of winter it is most perfect.

冰者寒氣藉水而成故孟冬冰始結仲冬冰益壯季冬冰方盛

‹*Ping* 'ché, ˏhón hí² tsik₂ 'shui ˏí ˏshing. Kú˃ mang² ‹tung ‹ping 'ch'í kít˃ chung² ‹tung ‹ping yik˃ chóng˃; kwai˃ ‹tung ‹ping ‹fong shing².

10. *Light* proceeds forth from the sun, and in making its descent to the earth, takes only about eight minutes, its velocity being nearly thirty-six millions of miles each minute.

光者由日出而臨於地僅計八分而每分可行三千六百萬里

‹*Kwóng* 'ché, ˏyau yat₂ ch'ut˃ ˢí ˏlam ‹ü tí², 'kan kai˃ pát˃ ‹fan ˏí ˢmúi ‹fan 'hó ˏhang ‹sám ‹ts'ín luk₂ pák˃ mán² ˢlí.

The moon is originally without light, always borrowing the light with which she shines, from the sun.

月本無光恒借太陽光以爲光

Üt₂ 'pún ˏmò ‹kwóng, ˏhang tsé˃ t'ái˃ ˏyéung ‹kwóng ˢí ˏwai ‹kwóng.

11. *Lightning*: when the aqueous vapor from the earth collects and carries along subtle matter, small as the cinders of saltpetre, a fiery heat is developed; when this reaches the bright clouds, and the subtle material comes in contact, it flashes forth in lightnings.

電者因水土氣挾帶微質略如硝炱火熱發越適映雲際逢其質氣閃爲電光

*Tín*² 'ché, ‹yan 'shui 't'ò hí˃ káp₂ tái˃ ˏmí chat˃, léuk₂ ˏü ‹síú ˏt'oi, 'fó ít₂ fát˃ üt₂, shik˃ 'ying ˏwan chái˃, ˏfung ˏk'í chat˃ hí˃ 'shím ˏwai tín² ‹kwóng.

9. The terms *mang*, *chung*, and *kwai*, are employed where only a triad is spoken of, and denote the first, second, and third, like *shéung*, *chung*, and *há*. The *icicle* the Chinese call *ping ch'ü*, a column of ice.

11. The electricity of the atmosphere is very imperfectly understood, even by European philosophers. The terms here employed are those in common use among the Chinese when speaking of, or describing electrical phenomena. There are also many superstitious notions concerning the cause of lightning, current among the people, which involve the agency of spirits, gods, &c.

12. *Parhelia* and *paraselenæ* (mock sun & moon) described.

日月重見說

Yat$_2$ *üt*$_2$ *chung*$^2$ *kín*ʼ shüt.

13. *Rain:* clouds collect in the heavens, and after they become thick and dense the rain falls.

雨者雲聚於天
積重然後雨落

‚Ü ʻché, ‚wan ts'ü$^2$ ‚ü ‚t'ín tsik, chung$^2$, ‚ín hau$^2$ ʻü lók$_2$.

14. A *rainbow* is a certain evidence of the presence of rain. The clouds are situated on one side, and the sun on the other side [of the observer]: the solar rays, in contact with the rain from the clouds, are refracted and reflected back; and it is by these rays, reflected from the rain of the clouds, that the rainbow is formed.

虹者乃雨際之
徵雲在一邊日
又在一邊日光
與雲雨斜對抵
住是映射之雲
雨所以成虹也

‚*Hung* ʻché, ʻnái ʻü tsaiʼ ‚chí ‚ching. ‚Wan tsoi$^2$ yat ‚pín; yat$_2$ yau$^2$ tsoi$^2$ yat ‚pín; yat$_2$ ‚kwóng ʻyü ‚wan ʻü ‚ts'é túiʼ ʻtai chü$^2$; shí$^2$ ʻying shé$^2$ ‚chí ‚wan ʻü, ʻshó ʻí ‚shing ‚hung ʻyá.

15. *Sleet:* by the intense cold of winter the humid air ascends, and forms conglomerated vapors; which meeting with the cold air congeal with frost, and so are formed into distinct globules; these globules are sleet. They are also called *pearl-snow;* and they are accompanied also with drops of rain.

霰者乃隆冬濕
氣升即成圓雲
遇冷凝沍悉成
散圓散圓即霰
也又名珠雪亦
兼同雨點

*Sán*ʼ ʻché, ʻnái ‚lung ‚tung shap hí ‚shing, tsik ‚shing ‚ün ‚wan, ü$^2$ ʻlang ‚ying ú$^2$; sik, ‚shing sánʼ ‚ün; sánʼ ‚ün tsik sán ʻyá. Yau$^2$ ‚ming ‚*chü süt*; yik$_2$, ‚kím ‚t'ung ʻü ʻtím.

16. *Snow* and rain have precisely the same rationale; and the drops of rain on meeting the cold air congeal in flakes and descend to the ground.

雪與雨其理並
同雨滴遇寒氣
凝片而下地

*Süt*, ʻyü ʻü ‚k'í ʻlí ping$^2$ ‚t'ung; ʻü tik ü$^2$ ‚hón híʼ ‚ying p'ínʼ ‚í há$^2$ tí$^2$.

17. *Thunder* is caused by lightning as it bursts forth; accordingly at the time of the lightning's flash, there is the sound of thunder.

雷者由電而發
故閃電之際而
有雷之聲也

‚*Lui* ʻché, ‚yau tín$^2$ ‚í fát; kúʼ ʻshím tín$^2$ ‚chí tsaiʼ, ‚í ʻyau ‚lui ‚chí ‚shing ʻyá.

18. *Tides* described. These consist of an alternate rise and fall of the water. The water continues to rise during six hours' time, after which it falls; and the fall also continues during six hours' time, after which the water again rises; if at twelve o'clock it is at its height then it will turn and ebb till six.

潮汐說水有長
退長必三時之
久然後退退亦
三時之久然後
復長如子時長
則夘時退也

‚*Ch'iú tsik*$_2$ shüt. ʻShui ʻyau ʻchéung t'úiʼ. ʻChéung pít ‚sám ‚shí ‚chí ʻkau, ‚ín hau$^2$ t'úiʼ; t'úiʼ yik$_2$ ‚sám ‚shí ‚chí ʻkau, ‚ín hau$^2$ fuk$_2$ ʻchéung; ‚ü ʻtszʼ ‚shí ʻchéung, tsak ʻmau ‚shí t'úiʼ ʻyá.

---

14. The rainbow is said by the Chinese to be caused by an effluence resulting from the union of the dual powers, *yam* and *yéung*. It is known by various names, as *hung ní*, *tái tung*, and *t'ín hung*, which last is the most common term.

CHI. CHR. 102

19. *Wind:* in those regions where the heat of the sun is powerful, the air becoming rarified ascends; and the cold air acting on this heated air produces wind. In the equatorial regions, if there are thin fleecy clouds, then there will be a tyfoon. Whirlwinds are occasioned by the sun's proximity.

風者太陽所曝之處則氣炎而騰及凍氣激之而成風赤道之下有片雲卽有颶風以日近故有旋風

‚*Fung* ʻché, tʻái' ‚yéung ʻshó puk, ‚chí chʻü', tsak, hí' ‚ím ‚í ‚tang; kʻap, tung' hí' kik, ‚chí ‚í ‚shing ‚fung. Chʻik, tò' ‚chí há' ʻyau pʻín' ‚wan. tsik, ʻyau kü' ‚fung. ʻI' yat, kan' kú' ʻyau ‚sün ‚fung.

19. *Fung* is one of the radicals of the Chinese language; 183 characters are comprised under it, the greater part of which designate various modes and operations of the wind. Tyfoons, or *tái fung*, as the Chinese often call the *kü fung*, occur on the southern coasts of their country.

## Section Third.

## NATIONS OF ASIA.

### 亞細亞國第三章

A' sai' á' kwók,; tai' ‚sám ‚chéung.

1. *Arabia* on the north is conterminous with Turkey; on the east it joins upon Persia; on the south it extends to the Indian ocean; and on the west borders upon the Red sea.

亞喇伯北接土耳基東連波斯南至印度海西接紅海

Á' ‚lá pák,, pak, tsíp, ʻTʻò ʻí ‚kí; ‚tung ‚lín ‚Pó ‚sz'; ‚nám chí' Yan' tò' ʻhoi; ‚sai tsíp, ‚Hung ʻhoi.

2. *Burmah* on the north is conterminous with Wannám; on both the east and south it borders upon Siam; and its western boundaries are the British possessions. Míntín belongs to Burmah (or Ava).

阿瓦北接雲南東南皆連暹邏西界英國屬地緬甸屬阿瓦國

‚Á ʻwá pak, tsíp, ‚Wan ‚nám; ‚tung ‚nám ‚kái ‚lín Tsím' ‚lò; ‚sai kái' ‚Ying kwók, shuk, tí'. ʻMín tín' shuk, ‚A' ʻwá kwók,.

### *Notes and Explanations.*

THE names of the different countries comprised in this and the four following sections will come nearer their true sounds if pronounced according to the court dialect. Most of them, especially the names of European and Asiatic countries, are borrowed from Tsʻingloi and other native authors, and are arranged in alphabetical order.

2. The whole Burman empire seems to be now known to the Chinese under the name of *A'wá*, while Míntín is applied by them to a small region, the northwest of Burmah.

3. *The Chinese empire* on the north is conterminous with Russia; east it extends to the Pacific ocean; south it borders on Cochinchina, Burmah, Nípál, and so forth; and its western boundaries are several small Mohammedan states.

大清國北接俄羅斯東至平洋南連越南阿瓦廓爾喀等處西界回疆外諸邦

*Tái²* ‹*Ts'ing* kwók›, pak› tsíp› ꜂Ngó ꜂ló ‹sz'; ‹tung chí' ꜂P'ing ꜂yéung; ꜂nám ꜂lín Ut꜄ ꜂nám, ‹A' 'wá Kwók› 'í hák›, 'tang ch'ü'; ‹sai kái' ꜂Ui ‹kéung ngoi² ‹chü ‹p'áng.

4. The king of *Cochinchina* is styled Mingming; this country on the north is conterminous with the Chinese empire; on both the east and south it extends to the ocean; and its western boundary is Siam. *Tungking*, *Champa*, and *Camboja* are now included in and form a part of the kingdom.

越南國王號明命其地北接大清東南皆至於洋西界暹邏內有東京占城東埔寨附之

*Üt*꜄ ꜂*nám* kwók›, ꜂wóng hò² ꜂Ming ming²; ꜂k'í tí² pak› tsíp› Tái² ‹Ts'ing; ‹tung ꜂nám ‹kái chí' ‹ü ꜂yéung; ‹sai kái' Tsím' ꜂lò. Noi² 'yau ‹Tung ‹king, Chím' ꜂shing ‹Tung 'pò chái² fú² ‹chí.

5. *Corea* is a small country, situated between the Chinese empire and Japan.

朝鮮小國間於大清日本之中

‹*Ch'iú* '*sín* ‹síú kwók› kán' ‹ü Tái² ‹Ts'ing, Yat꜄ 'pún ‹chí ‹chung.

6. The greatest part of *India* is the territory of the English, and is under the control of a governor-general. The principal province is called *Bengal;* its capital city is *Calcutta*, and its port is *Kedgeree*. The second city is *Madras;* the third is *Bombay;* and the fourth *Agra:* and each of them is a provincial capital. On the north, India is bounded by Nípál, and the frontiers of numerous Mohammedan states; east it joins on Burmah; south it extends to the Indian ocean; and its western boundaries are the countries of the Afghâns and Bilúchís.

天竺大半爲暎國屬地以總督管之首省名明呀喇省城曰咕哩噶噠其港口曰葛支里其次省名曼噠喇薩又次曰孟買又其次阿古剌各爲省會北界廓爾喀及回回諸邦東連阿瓦南至印度海西界阿付干及卑路治之國

‹*T'ín chuk*› tái² pún' ꜂wai ‹Ying kwók› shuk꜄ tí², 'í 'tsung tuk› 'kún ‹chí. 'Shau 'sháng ꜂ming *Ming' ꜂ngá lá²*; 'sháng ꜂shing üt꜄ '*Kú* '*li kat› tát*꜄; ꜂k'í 'kóng 'hau üt꜄ *Kat› ‹chí* '*li*. ꜂K'í ts'z' 'sháng ꜂ming *Mán' tát*꜄ ‹*lá sát*꜄; yau² ts'z' üt꜄ *Mang'* '*mái*; yau² ꜂k'í ts'z' ‹*A'* '*kú* ‹*lá;* kók› ꜂wai 'sháng úi². Pak› kái' Kwók› 'í hák꜄, k'ap꜄ ꜂Ui ꜂úi ‹chü ‹páng; ‹tung ꜂lín ‹A' 'wá; ꜂nám chí' Yan' tò² 'hoi; ‹sai kái' ‹A' fú² ‹kón, k'ap꜄ ‹Pí lò² chí² ‹chí kwók›.

3—5. China is also called Chung kwók; Cochinchina is also called Ónnám; Corea, Kòlí;

| | | |
|---|---|---|
| 7. *Persia* on the north extends to the *Caspian sea;* east it borders on the two countries of the Afghâns and Bilúchís; south it extends to the ocean; and west it is conterminous with Arabia. | 波斯北至裏海<br>東連阿付干卑<br>路治兩國南至<br>洋西接亞喇伯 | ‚*Pó* ‚*sz'*, pak‚ chí' '*Lí* '*hoi;* ‚tung ‚lín ‚A' fú' ‚kón k'ap‚ ‚Pí lò' chí' 'léung kwók‚; ‚nám chí' ‚yéung; ‚sai tsíp‚ A'' ‚lá pák‚. |
| 8. In the north of Asia is the territory of *Russia,* whose sovereign is called an emperor; his name is *Nicholas.* This territory on the north extend to the Icy seas; on the east it reaches to the Pacific ocean; its southern boundary is the Chinese empire; and on the west it joins upon Europe. | 亞細亞北方俄<br>羅斯之地國君<br>稱皇帝其號尼<br>可勞地北則冰<br>海東至平洋南<br>界大清西連歐<br>邏巴 | Á' sai' á' pak‚ ‚fong ‚*Ngó* ‚*ló* ‚*sz'* ‚chí tí'; kwók‚ ‚kwan ‚ch'ing ‚wóng tai', ‚k'í hò' ‚*Ní* '*kó* ‚*lò*. Tí' pak‚ tsak‚ ‚Ping 'hoi; ‚tung chí' ‚P'ing ‚yéung; ‚nám kái' Tái' ‚Ts'ing; ‚sai ‚lín ‚Au ‚lò ‚pá. |
| 9. *Siam* on the north is conterminous with Wannám; on the east it borders on Cochinchina; southward it stretches out to the sea; and has Burmah on the west. | 暹邏北接雲南<br>省東連越南南<br>至海西界阿瓦 | *Tsím'* ‚*lò*, pak‚ tsíp‚ ‚Wan ‚nám 'sháng; ‚tung ‚lín Ut‚ ‚nám; ‚nám chí' 'hoi; ‚sai kái' ‚A' 'wá. |
| 10. *Turkey* on the north extends to the *Black sea;* east it borders on Persia; its southern boundary is Arabia; and to the west it extends to the *Mediterranean sea.* | 土耳基北至黑<br>海東連波斯南<br>界亞喇伯西至<br>地中海 | '*T'ò* '*í* ‚*ki*, pak‚ chí' *Hak‚* '*hoi*; ‚tung ‚lín ‚Pó ‚sz'; ‚nám kái' A'' ‚lá pák‚; ‚sai chí' *Tí'* ‚*chung* '*hoi*. |
| 11. Malacca, Pondicherry, Travancore, Cochin, Goa, Mahratta, Surat, &c., are names of places. | 麻六呷笨支里<br>打冷莽柯固貞<br>小西洋嗎喇他<br>蘇辣等地名 | ‚Má luk‚ káp‚, Pan' ‚chí 'lí, 'Tá 'lang 'móng ‚hó, Kú' ‚ching, 'Síú ‚Sai ‚yéung, 'Má ‚lá ‚tá, ‚Sú lát‚, 'tang tí' ‚ming. |
| 12. Besides these there are several tens of other countries. Among them, some have kings, and others have chiefs, who govern them; full descriptions of which it is impossible to give. | 此外有國數十<br>其中或有王或<br>諸侯管轄不等<br>未能盡述也 | 'Ts'z' ngoi' 'yau kwók‚ shò' shap‚. ‚K'í ‚chung wák‚ 'yau ‚wóng, wák‚ ‚chü ‚hau 'kún hat‚ pat‚ 'tang; mí' ‚nang tsun' shut‚ 'yá. |

and India, Yantú, or Yintoo kwók, the country of the Hindús. *Kwók í hák* is strictly Ghorka or the name of the reigning family of Nípál.

12. Chinese travelers and voyagers (for a few such there have been,) have given to their countrymen descriptions of the principal seaports of Asia, from Japan to the Red sea; and have added thereto notices of their inhabitants and articles of commerce.

## Section Fourth.

## NATIONS OF EUROPE.

## 歐邏巴國第四章.

‹Au ˏlò ‹pá kwók›; tai² sz²' ‹chéung.

1. This section summarily mentions the principal nations of Europe, together with the names of their sovereigns; other small countries are not noticed. The territories of Europe extend from north to south about forty or fifty thousand miles; and from east to west they extend nearly an equal distance.

此章略言歐邏巴之大國並君號另小國未有悉記其疆域自北至南約四五萬里東至西大略相同

ʻTs'zʼ ‹chéung léuk₂ ˏsín ‹Au ˏlò ‹pá ‹chí tái² kwók›, ping² ‹kwan hò²; ling² ʻsíú kwók› mí² ʻyau sik› kí². ˏK'í ‹kéung wák₂ tsz'² pak› chí' ˏnám, yéuk› sz'' ʻʻng mán² ʻlí; ‹tung chí' ‹sai, tái² léuk₂ ‹séung ˏt'ung.

2. *Europe* on the north extends to the Icy sea; east it borders on Asia; south it extends to the Black sea and the Mediterranean; west it reaches to the waters of the Atlantic.

歐邏巴北至冰海東連亞細亞南至黑海及地中海西至壓蘭的海

‹*Au* ˏ*lò* ‹*pá* pak› chí' ‹Ping ʻhoi; ‹tung ˏlín A'' sai' á'; ˏnám chí' Hak› ʻhoi, k'ap₂ Tí² ‹chung ʻhoi; ‹sai chí' A't› ˏlán tik› ʻhoi.

3. The sovereign of *Austria* has the title of emperor, his name is Ferdinand, and his capital is called Vienna.

墺地哩亞國君稱皇帝其號非耳地難建都城曰美衍

*Ó' tí² ʻlí á'* kwók› ‹kwan ‹ch'ing ˏwóng tai'; ˏk'í hò² ‹Fí ʻí tí² ˏnán; kín' ‹tò ˏshing üt₂ ʻMí ʻín.

4. *Bavaria*, of which Louis is king.

巴尾哩亞王號璐義

‹*Pá* ʻ*wá* ʻ*lí á'* ˏwóng hò² Lúi² í².

5. *Belgium*, of which Leopold is king.

比里朕國者王號勒阿撥

ʻ*Pí* ʻ*lí cham*² kwók›, ʻché, ˏwóng hò² Lak₂ ‹ó pút₂.

### *Notes and Explanations.*

EVEN the names of some of the nations of Europe, as well as those of their sovereigns, are unknown to the Chinese; accordingly some new combinations of characters have been required to express these names. In such cases it is a rule with the Chinese to select the characters which will best express the sound of the names.

3. The rule to express the sound of the foreign name is not always observed: sometimes a prominent national characteristic is employed for naming a country. Thus Austria is known to the

| | | |
|---|---|---|
| 6. ***Denmark***, of which Christian VII. is king. | 大尼國者王號基士陣第七傳 | *Tái*' ,*ní* kwók, 'ché, ,wóng hò' ,Kí sz'' chan', tai' ts'at, ,ch'ün. |
| 7. ***Great Britain***, or ***England***, of which Victoria is queen, and whose capital is called London. | 大暎即暎咭唎國者女王號威哆哩建都城曰倫敦 | *Tái*' ,*Ying*, tsik, ,*Ying kat*, *li*' kwók, 'ché, 'nü ,wóng hò' ,Wai 'tó 'lí; kín' ,tò ,shing üt, ,Lun ,tun. |
| 8. ***France***, of which Louis Philippe is king, and whose capital is called Paris. | 法蘭西者王號璐義腓立建都城曰巴犂 | *Fát*, ,*lán* ,*sai* 'ché, ,wóng hò' Lú' í' 'Fí lap,, kín' ,tò ,shing üt, ,Pá ,lai. |
| 9. The families of *Germany* (i. e. the Germanic states) are divided into several kingdoms, which, though they are called Germany, have separate names. | 阿理曼族類分立幾國仍稱阿理曼另有國名 | ,*Á* '*li mán*' tsuk, lui' ,fan lap, 'kí kwók, ,ying ,ch'ing ,A' 'lí mán' ling' 'yau kwók, ,ming. |
| 10. ***Greece***, of which Otho is king. | 希獵國者王號阿士 | ,*Hí líp*, kwók, 'ché, ,wóng hò' ,O' 't'ò. |
| 11. ***Holland***, of which William is king. | 荷蘭國者王號威廉 | ,*Hó* ,*lán* kwók, 'ché, ,wóng hò' ,Wai ,lím. |
| 12. The capital of modern *Italy* is called Rome. | 今之以大利國其京城名羅馬 | ,Kam ,chí '*í tái*' *li*' kwók,, ,k'í ,king ,shing ,ming ,Ló 'má. |
| 13. ***Portugal***, also named Western Ocean, of which Maria II. is queen. | 葡萄牙一名西洋國者女王號馬利亞第二傳 | ,*Pò* ,*tò* ,*ngá*, yat, ,ming ,Sai ,Yéung kwók, 'ché; 'nü ,wóng hò' 'Má lí' á' tai' í' ,ch'ün. |
| 14. ***Prussia*** of which Frederic William III. is king. The Chinese call this country Tánying (or Single Eagle). | 破魯西國者王號非得勒威廉第三傳唐人呼其國曰單鷹 | ,*P'ó* '*lú* ,*sai* kwók, 'ché ,wóng hò' ,Fí tak, lak, ,Wai ,lím tai' ,sám ,ch'ün. ,T'óng ,yan ,fú ,k'í kwók, üt, ,Tán ,Ying. |

people of Canton by the name *Má Ying* or *Shéung Ying kwók*, The Double Eagle country, because, as the Chinese say, 'on its white flag is painted the double head of a bird.'

6. Denmark is usually known among the Chinese of Canton as the *Wóng Kí kwók*, the country with the Yellow Flag. This inclination of the Chinese to designate foreign countries, by descriptive epithets, rather than by terms which merely express the sound of their names, is owing partly to the nature of their language, and partly to their ignorance of the true names, when the inhabitants of those countries first appeared in China.

廣東方言讀本

| | | |
|---|---|---|
| 15. The people of *Rome*, in ancient times, used the Latin written language. | 羅馬國人古時用拉體納文字 | ˏ*Ló* '*má* kwókˎ ˏyan 'kú ˏshí yung² ˏLá 't'ai nápˎ ˏman tsz'². |
| 16. *Russia;* half of this country is situated in Europe, and half is situated in Asia. | 俄羅斯國其地半在歐邏巴半在亞細亞 | ˏ*Ngó* ˏ*ló* ˏ*sz'* kwókˎ; ˏk'í tí² pún' tsoi² ˏAu ˏlò ˏpá, pún' tsoi² A'' sai' á'. |
| 17. *Sardinia*, of which Albert is king. | 撒顛牙國者王號亞里弼 | *Sát*ˎ ˏ*tín* ˏ*ngá* kwókˎ 'ché, ˏwóng hò² A'' 'lí patˎ. |
| 18. *Saxony*, of which Frederic is king. | 撒所尼國者王號非得勒 | *Sát*ˎ '*shó* ˏ*ní* kwókˎ 'ché, ˏwóng hò² ˏFí takˎ lakˎ. |
| 19. *Spain*, of which Isabella II. is queen. | 西班牙國者女王號以散比喇第二傳 | ˏ*Sai* ˏ*pán* ˏ*ngá* kwókˎ 'ché, 'nü ˏwóng hò² 'Í sán' 'pí ˏlá tai² í² ˏch'ün. |
| 20. *Sweden* and *Norway*, of which Charles XIV. is king. | 瑞典那華兩國者王號搽理第十四傳 | *Sui*² '*tín*, '*Nó* ˏ*wá* 'léung kwókˎ 'ché, ˏwóng hò² ˏChá 'lí, tai² shapˎ sz'' ˏch'ün. |
| 21. *Switzerland* is situated between Germany, France, and Italy. | 瑞西國在阿理曼法蘭西以大利等國中間 | *Sui*² ˏ*sai* kwókˎ tsoi² ˏÁ 'lí mán², Fátˎ lan² ˏsai, 'Í tái² lí², 'tang kwókˎ ˏchung ˏkán. |
| 22. *Turkey;* half of this country is in Europe, and half is in Asia. | 土耳基國者其國半在歐邏巴半在亞細亞 | '*T'ò* '*í* ˏ*kí* kwókˎ 'ché; ˏk'í kwókˎ pún' tsoi² ˏAu ˏlò ˏpá, pún' tsoi² A'' sai' á'. |
| 23. The whole number of states in Europe is about fifty; and they have different governments; among them some are governed by emperors, some by kings and queens, or by other persons of noble rank. | 歐邏巴內共五十餘國其國政各異中或皇帝或王后或尊爵者管轄不等 | ˏAu ˏlò ˏpá noi² kung² 'ng shapˎ ˏü kwókˎ; ˏk'í kwókˎ ching' kókˎ í², ˏchung wákˎ ˏwóng tai', wákˎ ˏwóng hau², wákˎ ˏts'ün tséukˎ 'ché, 'kún hatˎ patˎ 'tang. |

19. Among the Chinese, Spain is usually called *Tái Luisung*, or Great Luçon, in contradistinction to the Philippines which they call Small Luçon.

## Section Fifth.

## NATIONS OF AFRICA.

### 亞非利加國第五章

A' ˏfí lí' ˏká kwók, ; tai' ʻng ˏchéung.

1. Africa extends from north to south more than ten thousand miles, and from east to west more than nine thousand miles.

亞非利加由北而南一萬幾千里自西而東九千幾百里

A' ˏfí lí' ˏká ˏyau pak, ˏí ˏnám, yat, mán' ˏkí ˏts'ín ʻlí; tsz' ˏsai ˏí ˏtung ʻkau ˏts'ín ˏkí pák, ʻlí.

2. On the north, its boundary is the Mediterranean sea; on the west its boundary is the Atlantic; its southern boundary is the Southern ocean; and the Red sea and Indian ocean form its eastern boundary.

北以地中海爲界西以壓蘭的海爲界南以南海爲界東以紅海印度海爲界

Pak, ʻí Tí' ˏchung ʻhoi ˏwai kái'; ˏsai ʻí A't, ˏlán tik, ʻhoi ˏwai kái'; ˏnám ʻí ˏNám ʻhoi ˏwai kái'; ˏtung ʻí ˏHung ʻhoi Yan' tò' ʻhoi ˏwai kái'.

3. At the northeast, there is a narrow neck of land (an isthmus), by which it is connected with Asia.

東北區紅海處有微地與亞細亞相連

ˏTung pak, ˏk'ü ˏHung ʻhoi ch'ü' ʻyau ˏmí tí', ʻü A' sai' á' ˏséung ˏlín.

4. On the northwest, at the straits of the Mediterranean sea, that narrow channel connects it with Spain in Europe.

西北地中海界首廹狹而接歐邏巴之西班牙

ˏSai pak, Tí' ˏchung ʻhoi kái' ʻshau pik, háp, ˏí tsíp, ˏAu ˏlò ˏpá ˏchí ˏSí ˏpán ˏngá.

5. The whole continent is divided by the equator, so that about three tenths of the continent are on the north of the line, and about seven tenths are on the south of it. In the centre of the continent are wild and desert lands. Its extreme southern point is called the Cape.

統計其地以赤道橫分而論南得其三北居其七中惟荒野地其南極處日呷

ʻTung kai' ˏk'í tí' ʻí ch'ik, tò' ˏwáng ˏfan ˏí lun', ˏnám tak, ˏk'í ˏsám, pak, ˏkü ˏk'í ts'at,. ˏChung ˏwai ˏfong ʻyé tí'. ˏK'í ˏnám kik, ch'ü' üt, Káp,.

## *Notes and Explanations.*

AFRICA and its inhabitants and productions are also quite unknown to the Chinese. Ts'ingloi barely names the country, which he calls *Lí-pí-á*, or Libya, as written by the Jesuits; but gives no description of its several parts. The Cape, and the possessions of the Portuguese, are mentioned by a modern traveler, Tsé Tingkò, who says that there are many native states, some of which are Mohammedans, and that "the people are as black as lacker; ivory, rhinoceros' horns, grain, and melons, are the products."

6. Along all the coast there are settlements; and on the south are several regions of country which belong to the English and Portuguese.

沿海皆有民居
南且有數方屬
大𠸄與葡萄牙

ˏÜn ˋhoi ˏkái ˋyau ˏman ˏkü ˏnám ˋch'é ˋyau shò' ˏfong shuk, Tái² ˏYing ˋü ˏPò ˏtò ˏngá.

7. On the north are several states, as Morocco, Algiers, Tunis, Tripoli, &c.

北有數國曰麻
囉哥安遮耳都
尼士脫破利等

Pak, ˋyau shò' kwok, üt, ˏMá ˏló ˏkó, ˏO'n ˏché ˋí, ˏTò ˏni sz'², Túi' p'ó' lí², ˋtang.

8. Egypt is situated at the northeastern part, bordering on the Red sea.

東北附紅海處
有麥西國

ˏTung pak, fú² ˏHung ˋhoi ch'ü' ˋyau Mák, ˏsai kwok,.

8. In the manners and customs of the ancient Egyptians there are points of resemblance to the modern usages of the Chinese; and it is by no means improbable that some intercourse once existed between the two nations. Satisfactory evidence of this, however, seems to be wanting.

## Section Sixth.

## NATIONS OF AMERICA.

## 美理哥國第六章

ˋMí ˋlí ˏkó kwók,; tai² luk, ˏchéung.

1. Were the globe of the earth opened and spread out, and were Asia, and Europe, and Africa, made to constitute one hemisphere, then America would be opposite to it.

推佈地球以亞
細亞歐邏巴亞
非利加爲正面
美理哥爲背面

ˏT'úi pò' ti² ˏk'au, ˋí Á' sai' á', ˏAu ˏlò ˏpá, A' ˏfí lí² ˏká, ˏwai ching' min², ˋMí ˋlí ˏkó ˏwai púi' min².

2. In high antiquity, it was not known that the earth was round and revolved; subsequently it was perceived that the whole world was divided into three parts; but yet it was not known that there were still people residing in the farthest west. At length there

上古不知地如
球轉後覺天下
中列作三分然
猶未知西極尚
有民居及有智

Shéung² ˋkú pat, ˏchí ti² ˏü ˏk'au ˋchün; hau² kók, ˏt'in há² ˏchung lít, tsók, ˏsám ˏfan; ˏín ˏyau mí² ˏchí ˏsai kik, shéung² ˋyau ˏman ˏkü. K'ap, ˋyau chí' ˋché, ˏming

### *Notes and Explanations.*

AMERICA is known to the Chinese generally as the country of the citizens of the United States; with the people from other American states, they have never had much intercourse. The word America is written with different characters, but those which are here given appear to be preferable, from their coming nearest to the sound of Amerigo's name. In names, the Chinese often

was a very learned man, called Copernicus, who supposed that the earth must be round like a globe and revolve; however there was no certain evidence of this, and accordingly it was not believed.

者名個班匿固
料地必如球而
旋動第無徵而
不信焉

Kó' ,pán néuk, kú', líú[2] tí[2] pít, ,ü ,k'au ,í ,sün tung[2]: tai[2] ,mò ,ching ,í pat, sun' ,ín.

3. In the reign of Hungchí of the Ming dynasty, *Columbus*, an Italian, sailed on a voyage, and went thither (to America) in person.

明弘治年間以
大理之個倫布
者由是日解維
身歷於斯

,Ming, ,Hung chí[2] ,nín ,kán 'í tái[2] 'lí ,chí Kó' ,lun pò' 'ché, ,yau shí[2] yat, 'kai ,wai ,shan lik, ,ü ,sz'.

4. Several years subsequently, the voyage was repeated by *Amerigo*, who having purchased a ship again went to this country, where for a time he resided; on his return home he drew maps of the new country, and hence the country came to be generally called *America*. It is also called the New World, and likewise designated the western continent.

後數年復有美
理哥者買舟再
赴久住於此歸
本國描畫新國
地圖俗因名之
曰美理哥又曰
新地且號西方

Hau[2] shò' ,nín fuk, 'yau *'Mí 'lí ,kó* 'ché, 'mái ,chau tsoi' fú[2], 'kau chü[2] ,ü 'ts'z': ,kwai 'pún kwók, ,míú wák, ,san kwók, tí[2] ,t'ò, tsuk, ,yan ,ming ,chí, üt, 'Mí 'lí ,kó. Yau[2] üt, ,San Tí[2], 'ch'é hò[2] ,sai ,fóng.

5. This land is divided into North and South; about eight degrees north of the equator there is a narrow piece of land, which is called *Darien*, by which the southern regions are connected [with the north]; hence the continent is divided into North and South America.

其地爲分南北
以其於赤道出
北八度處有微
地曰爹哩現與
南極下地相連
故分南北

,Kí tí[2] ,wai ,fan ,Nám Pak,: 'í ,k'í ,ü ch'ik, tò[2] ch'ut, pak, pát, tò[2] ch'ü' 'yau ,mí tí[2] üt, ,*Té 'lí ín*[2] 'ü ,nám kik, há[2] tí[2] ,séung ,lín; kú' ,fan ,Nám Pak,.

6. On the north of America are the *Canadas*, lands belonging to the English. On the northwest are wild regions which belong to Russia. In the middle [of North America] are the United States, called by the Chinese, Spangled

北美理哥之北
有干拿大國屬
暎土西北荒野
屬俄羅斯中美

Pak, 'Mí 'lí ,kó ,chí pak, 'yau ,*Kón ,ná tái*[2] kwók, shuk, ,Ying 't'ò. ,Sai pak, ,fóng 'yé shuk, ,Ngó ,ló ,sz'.

drop the first syllable *a*; *r* they change into *l*, and confound *g* with *k*; thus for Amerigo, they would choose to say *Mí-lí-kó* or Meleko.

3. Christopher Columbus, sailing in search of a shorter passage to the *east*, landed on one of the *West* India islands in 1492. Amerigo Vespucci, a native of Florence, followed him in 1499; in 1508 he was appointed principal pilot by the king of Spain, and his duties were to prepare charts and prescribe routes for vessels leaving for the New World, and in this way the continent soon received his name.

Banner. In the twentieth year of Tòkwóng, the number of states was twenty-six. The capital of the United States is called Washington. The country has no king, but a president and a vice-president, who hold their offices for four years, and who receive salaries for their personal support. In their language, manners, and customs, the people of this country are quite like those of Great Britain, inasmuch as most of their ancestors originally came from thence.

理哥合省國華人號曰花旗道光二十年共計二十六省京城號華盛頓國無王而有正副首領四年一任廉俸自支其國言語規矩與大英一類因其宗祖本由大英而來

‹Chung ʻMí ʻlí ‹kó Hóp› ʻSháng kwók›, ‚Wá ‹yan hòʼ üt› ‹Fá ‚kí. Tòʼ ‹kwóng, íʼ shap› ‚nín kungʼ kaiʼ íʼ shap› luk› ʻsháng. ‹King ‚shing hòʼ ‚Wá shingʼ tunʼ. Kwók› ‚mò ‚wóng ‚í ʻyau chingʼ fúʼ ʻshau ʻling, szʼ ‚nín yat› yamʼ ‚lím ʻfung tszʼ ‹chí. ‚K'í kwók› ‚ín ʻyü ‹kw'ai ʻkü ʻü Táiʼ ‹Ying yat› luiʼ ʻyan ‚k'í ‹tsung ʻtsò ʻpún ‚yau Táiʼ ‹Ying ‚í ‚loi.

7. On the south of the United States are the two countries of *Mexico* and *Texas*.

合省國之南有墨息哥滴些士二國

Hóp› ʻSháng kwók› ‹chí ‚nám ʻyau *Mak› sik›* ‹*kó*, *Tik›* ‹*sé szʼ*, íʼ kwók›.

8. In South America are the states of *Columbia, Brazil, Peru, Bolivia, Chili,* and *La Plata*, and so forth.

南美理哥中有個倫布亞庇理些離飄而魯破理華支離臘巴打等國

‚Nám ʻMí ʻlí ‹kó ‹chung ʻyau *Kó ‚lun pòʼ áʼ*, *Píʼ ʻlí*, ‹*sé ʻlí*, ‚*Piú ‚í ʻlú*, *Póʼ ʻlí ‚wá*, ‹*Chí ‚lí*, *Láp› ‹Pá ʻtá*, ʻtang kwók›.

9. In the narrow regions between North and South America are numerous islands, of which *Cuba* and *Hayti* are the largest.

美理哥南北夾道之中有海島數十處其最大者古巴哈地等

ʻMí ʻlí ‹kó ‚nám pak› háp› tòʼ ‹chí ‹chung ʻyau ʻhoi ʻtò shòʼ shap› ch'üʼ; ‚k'í tsuiʼ táiʼ ʻché, *ʻKá ‹pá*, ‹*Há tiʼ* ʻtang.

9. In writing the names of foreign countries, cities, persons, &c., it is very desirable that the same characters should always be chosen; uniformity is especially important in those names which are mentioned in the Scriptures, and they should conform to the received version.

## Section Seventh.

## ISLANDS OF THE SEA.

### 海洲類第七章
'Hoi ‹chau lui²; tai² ts'at› ‹chéung.

1. *Acheen* is situated on the north-west point of Sumatra; and is a city.

亞齊在蘇門答
剌之西角乃一
城也

*Á'* ˏ*tsai* tsoi² ‹Sú ˏmún tap› ‹lá ‹chí ‹sai pak› kók›, 'nái yat› ˏshing 'yá.

2. *Batavia*, or Ká-lau-pá, is a city situated on the north-west side of the island of Java.

噶喇巴即加留
巴在爪哇洲之
西北邊一城也

‹*Ká* ‹*lá* ‹*pá*, tsik› ‹Ká ˏlau ‹pá, tsoi² ‹Kwá ‹wá ‹chau ‹chi ‹sai pak› ‹pín, yat› ˏshing 'yá.

3. *Borneo*, or the island of Póló, is situated on both sides of the equator; from north to south it extends about two thousand and five hundred miles, and from east to west about two thousand.

文萊即婆羅洲
中間赤道自北
而南二千五百
里由東而西二
千里

ˏ*Man* ˏ*loi* tsik› ˏPò ˏló ˏchau, ‹chung ‹kán ch'ik› tò²; tsz'² pak› ˏí ˏnám í² ‹ts'ín ''ng pák› 'lí, ˏyau ‹tung ˏí ‹sai í² ˏts'ín 'lí.

4. The island of *Celebes* is situated east of Borneo; along the sea-coast the native inhabitants are tribes of Malays. Besides them, there is one other tribe, called Bugis; the rich take their families with them to engage in trade, and

細利窪洲在文
萊之東沿海土
番爲無來由種
類別有一種名
舞吉子富者攜
眷經商所至即

*Sai' lí²* ‹*wá* ‹chau tsoi² ˏMan ˏloi ‹chí ‹tung; ˏün 'hoi 't'ò ‹fán ˏwai ˏMò ˏloi ˏyau 'chung lui². Pít› 'yau yat› chung' ˏming 'Mò kat› 'tsz'; fú' ‹ché, ˏkwai kün' ‹king ‹shéung, 'sho

## *Notes and Explanations.*

LARGE islands are hardly distinguished by the Chinese from continents. Of such islands as Borneo, Java, Sumatra, etc., they seem not to have any just notions regarding either their form, size, or their situation. Indeed they seem not to know whether they be islands or not. The distance from one place to another they express only by the number of days usually occupied in sailing the distance.

1. By some Chinese, two places are mentioned of this name, one called Great Acheen, and the other Little Acheen. Others speak of only one, which is the modern town or city of Acheen. The names of Acheen, Batavia, and few other cities, are entered on this list, because of their being so often referred to.

3. Manloi and Póló were most likely the names, originally, of towns or settlements; and it is doubtful whether they are, or ever were, applied by the Chinese to the island as one whole—for as such they seem not to know it.

to whatever place they come there they abide, without any thought of their ancient lands, and without any permanent abode, when they are poor, then many of them become thieves and robbers.

安無故土之思
亦無一定之寓
貧者則多爲盗
劫

chí' tsik ‹ón ‹mò kú', 'tò ‹chí ‹sz', yik, ‹mò yat, tíng² ‹chí yü'; ‹pan 'ché, tsak, ‹tó ‹wai tò' kíp,.

5. The *Fiji* islands are in the South Pacific ocean, and yield abundance of birds-nests.

匪支島在平洋
之南多出燕窩

'*Fí ‹chí* 'tò tsoi² ‹P'ing ‹yeung ‹chí ‹nám, ‹tó ch'ut, ín' ‹wo.

6. Off in the Pacific ocean are four islands, which form the empire of *Japan*.

平洋外四洲而
成國者曰日本

‹P'ing ‹yéung ngoi² sz" ‹chau ‹í ‹shing kwok, 'ché, üt, *Yat, 'pún*.

7. The island of *Java* is situated in south latitude more than six degrees south [of the equator]. From east to west it extends one thousand eight hundred miles; from north to south three hundred miles. The number of inhabitants is about seven or eight millions. The island belongs to the Dutch.

爪哇洲南極出
地六度餘西至
東一千八百里
北至南三百里
人約七八百萬
亦荷蘭所屬

‹*Chau ‹wá* ‹chau ‹nám kik, ch'ut, tí² luk, tò² ‹ü. ‹Sai chí' ‹tung yat, ‹ts'ín pát, pák, 'lí; pak, chí' ‹nám ‹sám pák, 'lí. ‹Yan yéuk, ts'at, pát, pák, mán². Yik, ‹Hó ‹lán 'sho shuk,.

8. South of Japan, off at some distance in the ocean, is the little kingdom of *Lew-chew*.

日本南洋而外
有琉球小國

Yat, 'pún ‹nám ‹yéung ‹í ngoi², 'yau ‹*Lau* ‹*kau* 'siú kwok,.

9. *Luçonia* (or the Philippines) is situated south-east from Macao; and [from thence] with a fair wind it may be reached in seven or eight days. It includes more than ten islands, which belong to Spain. By law it has no king, a governor-general being chief; the city in which he resides is called *Manila*.

呂宋在澳之東
南順風七八日
可到中有十餘
洲皆屬西班牙
例不立主以總
督爲首居城曰
馬呢喇

'*Lui sung*' tsoi² O' ‹chí ‹tung ‹nám; shun² ‹fung ts'at, pát, yat, 'hó tò'. ‹Chung 'yau shap, ‹ü ‹chau, ‹kái shuk, ‹Sai ‹pán ‹ngá. Lai² pat, lap, 'chü; 'í 'tsung tuk, ‹wai 'shau; ‹kü ‹shing üt, '*Má ‹ní lá*.

10. In the Researches in the East and West it is said, that in the reign of Wing-lók (about A. D. 1420), there were certain Franks, who traded with the people of Luçon. On the king's birthday they made him presents

東西洋考云永
樂年間有佛郎
機與呂宋互市
因上黃金爲呂

‹Tung ‹Sai ‹yéung 'Háu ‹wan, 'Wing lók, ‹nín ‹kán, 'yau Fat, ‹lóng ‹kí, 'ü 'Lui sung' ú² 'shí. ‹Yan 'shéung ‹wóng

10. *Fat lóng kí* should not be confounded with *Fát lán sai*, as it sometimes has been both by foreigners and Chinese. The first is applied to all foreigners from Europe, the second only to the French.

of gold, and begged of him a piece of ground as large as a cow's skin, whereon to build a house. The king believing them sincere promised it, but the Franks took the cow's skin, cut it into strips and then joined them together, and therewith encircled a square, and begged for the ground corresponding to it. At this the king was greatly troubled, but dreading to break his promise to the foreigners, he finally gave them the land.

宋王壽乞地如牛皮大蓋屋王信而許之佛郎機乃取牛皮剪而相續之以爲四圍乞地稱是王難之然重失信遠夷竟予地

˛kam ˛wai ʿLui sungʾ ˛wóng shau², hat, tí² ˛ü ˛ngau ˛pʿí tái², kʿoiʾ uk,. ˛Wóng sunʾ ˛í ʿhü ˛chí; Fat, ˛lóng ˛kí ʿnái ʿtsʿü ˛ngau ˛pʿí, ʿtsín ˛í ˛séung tsuk, ˛chí, ʿí ˛wai szʾ ˛wai, hat, tí² ˛chʿing shí². ˛Wóng ˛nán ˛chí, ˛ín chung² shat, sunʾ ʿün ˛í, ʿking ʿü tí².

11. *Macassar* is situated on the south-west of the Celebes; it is a mart (or commercial town).

茫咖薩在細利窪之西南乃一埠也

˛Móng ˛ká sát, tsoi² Saiʾ lí² ˛wá ˛chí ˛sai ˛nám, ʿnái yat, fau² ʿyá.

12. *Madagascar* is situated in the Indian sea, on the east of Africa; its population is about two millions.

馬帝加士架在印度海亞非利加之東人約二百萬餘

ʿMa taiʾ ˛ká szʾ káʾ tsoi² Yanʾ tò² ʿhoi, Aʾ ˛fí lí² ˛ká ˛chí ˛tung; ˛yan yéuk, í² pák, mán² ˛ü.

13. *Mauritius* is an island, and is also situated in the Indian sea. It is several tens of miles in circumference, and is under the government of England.

妙理士亦在印度海中島嶼也周圍數十里爲嘆咭唎所轄

Míú² ʿlí sz² yik, tsoi² Yanʾ tò² ʿhoi ˛chung, ʿtò ʿsü ʿyá. ˛Chau ˛wai shòʾ shap, ʿlí, ˛wai ˛Ying kat, lí² ʿshó hat,.

14. The *Moluccas*, or the Mí-luk-hóp, include more than ten islands, situated east of Celebes.

美洛居即米六合中有十餘洲在細利窪之東

ʿMí lók, ˛kü, tsik, ʿMai luk, hóp,, ˛chung ʿyau shap, ˛ü ˛chau, tsoi² Saiʾ lí² ˛wá ˛chí ˛tung.

15. *Nias* is an island situated north-west from Padang, in the midst of the sea, rising in one solitary hill; the people resemble the Chinese but are smaller.

呢是島在叭當之西北海中獨峙一山民似中國而小

˛Ní shí² ʿtò tsoi² Pát, ˛tóng ˛chí ˛sai pak,; ʿhoi ˛chung tuk, shí² yat, ˛shán, ˛man ʿtsʿz ˛Chung kwók, ˛í ʿsíú.

11, 14, 15. To these places Chinese vessels have often found their way; formerly in considerable numbers, but recently their number has decreased.

12, 13. To Madagascar and Mauritias, Chinese vessels are not known ever to have gone: though the places have been visited by Chinese, who have gone, as they frequently do, in the capacity of servants on board foreign vessels.

| | | |
|---|---|---|
| 16. The *Nicobars* are situated north-west from the extreme point of Acheen. | 呢咕吧拉在亞齊盡處之西北 | ‹*Ní* ‹*kú* ‹*pá* ‹*lá* tsoi[2] Á' ˏtsai tsun[2] ch'ü' ‹chí ‹sai pak›. |
| 17. *New Holland;* this country belongs to Great Britain; it is distant south from Papua, by sea, three degrees; in extent it is nearly equal to Europe. | 新荷蘭地屬大英由吧布阿之南越洋三度而至廣若歐邏巴 | ‹*San* ˏ*Hó* ˏ*lán;* tí[2] shuk› Tái[2] ‹Ying; ˏyau ‹Pá pò' ‹á ‹chí ˏnám üt› ˏyéung ‹sám tò[2] ˏí chí'; 'kwóng yéuk› ‹Au ˏlò ‹pá. |
| 18. *New Zealand* is distant from New Holland about fifteen degrees. | 新西蘭由新荷蘭東越洋約十五度而至 | ‹*San* ‹*Sai* ˏ*lán* ˏyau ‹San ˏHó ˏlán ‹tung üt› ˏyéung yéuk› shap› 'ng tò[2] ˏí chí'. |
| 19. *Padang* is a harbor on the west of Sumatra. | 叭當港口在蘇門塔喇之西 | *Pát›* ‹*tóng* 'kóng 'hau tsoi[2] ‹Sú ˏmún táp› lá' ‹chí ‹sai. |
| 20. *Papua* is situated south-west from the Moluccas. | 吧布阿在美洛居之東南 | ‹*Pá pò'* ‹*á* tsoi[2] 'Mí lók› ‹kü ‹chí ‹tung ˏnám. |
| 21. *Pínang* is an island in the midst of the sea; it is also called Púlo Pínang. In all Malayan countries, there are two kinds of fruit; one is called the durion, in shape like the pine apple, having many warts, and the pulp exceedingly fragrant and pleasant; the other is called the mangostan, or the mangostan chestnut, in shape like the persimmon, with a rind, and like the other of a rich, juicy taste. | 新埠海中島也一名布路檳榔凡無來由所居地有果二種一名流連子形似波羅蜜而多刺肉極香甜一名茫姑生又名茫栗形如柿而有殼味亦清甜 | ‹*San Fau*[2] 'hoi ‹chung 'tò 'yá; yat› ˏming Pò' lò[2] ‹Pan ˏlóng. ˏFán ˏMò ˏloi ˏyau 'shó ‹kü tí[2], 'yau 'kwó í[2] chung'; yat› ˏming ‹lau ˏlín 'tsz'[2], ‹ying 'ts'z' ‹pó ˏlò mat›, ˏí ‹tó tsz", yuk› kik› ‹héung ˏt'ím. Yat› ˏming ˏmóng ‹kú ‹shang, yau[2] ˏming ‹móng lut›; ‹ying ‹ü ‹tsz', ˏí 'yau hók›, mí' yik› ‹ts'ing ˏt'ím. |
| 22. The *Sandwich Islands* are situated eighty degrees due east from Canton; they are thirteen in number; the largest of them is called *Hawaii.* | 檀香山由粵省正東八十度餘中有十三洲一名阿哇希最大 | ˏ*Tán* ‹*Héung* ‹*shán* ˏyau Üt› 'sháng ching' ‹tung pát› shap› tò[2] ˏü; ‹chung 'yau shap› ‹sám ‹chau; yat› ˏming ‹*Á* ‹*wá* ‹*hí* ts'ü' tái[2]. |

16. The Nicobars are described by Tsé Ts'ingkò, together with another place in its vicinity, (perhaps the Andamans,) the latter, he says "have inhabitants with faces like the horse, who eat men, and nobody dares to go among them."

23. *Singapore*, or San-ká-pó, belongs to Great Britain; it has several schools, and is the residence of many English and Chinese.

息辣即新嘉坡地屬大暎中建數書院英華人多集於斯

*Sik, lát,* tsik,, ,San ,ká ,pó, tí² shuk,, Tái² ,Ying; ,chung kín' shò' ,shü ün² ,Ying ,Wá ,yan ,tó tsap, ,ü ,sz'

24. The *Súlú* islands are situated on the north-east of Borneo, and are more than ten in number.

蘇祿在文萊之東北中十餘島

,*Sú luk,* tsoi² ,Man ,loi ,chí ,tung pak,, ,chung shap, ,ü 'tò.

25. *Sumatra* is situated west from Borneo, distaht about ten degrees.

蘇門答喇在文萊之西約十度

,*Sú ,mún táp, lá'* tsoi² ,Man ,loi ,chí ,sai, yéuk, shap, tò².

26. *Timor* is situated south east from the Celebes, and is under the government of the Portuguese.

地問在細利漥之東南地歸西洋管轄

*Tí² man²* tsoi² Sai' lí² ,wá ,chí ,tung ,nám, tí² ,kwai ,Sai ,yéung 'kún hat,.

27. If you desire to understand the situation and form of the seas and lands throughout the world, you are requested to examine (1) the *Researches in the East and West*, written by Wóng Hítsung of Kamling; also (2) the *Notices of the Seas*, by Yéung Píngnám of the department of Káying in Kwóngtung; (3) the *Notices of things Heard and Seen in Maritime Countries*, by Chan Lunkwing of the district Tungón in Fukkín; with (4) the *Memoranda of the Foreign tribes on the New Frontiers* by Chʻunyün of Chiktai. From these works some distinct information may be obtained.

欲識天下水陸形勢請覽金陵王起宗所著東西洋考並廣東嘉應州楊炳南之海錄福建同安縣陳倫烱之海國聞見錄直隸椿園之新疆外藩紀畧亦頗得其詳矣

Yéuk, shik, ,tʻín há' 'shui luk, ,ying shai', 'tsʻing 'lám ,Kam ,ling ,Wóng 'Hí ,tsung 'shó chü', ,Tung ,Sai ,Yéung 'Háu; ping² 'Kwóng ,tung ,Ká ying' ,chau, ,Yéung 'Ping ,nám ,chí 'Hoi Luk,; Fuk, Kín' ,Tʻung ,ón ün², ,Chan ,Lun 'kwing ,chí 'Hoi Kwok, ,Man Kín' Luk,; Chik, tai² ,Chʻun ,yün ,chí ,San ,Kéung Ngoi² ,Fán 'Kí Léuk,. Yik, 'pʻó tak, ,kʻí ,tséung 'í.

27. (1) The Researches in the East and West is in six volumes, octavo; it was written about two centuries ago, near the close of the Ming dynasty; the first volume contains some very rude charts, intended to show the situation and form of foreign countries.

(2) The Notices of the Seas is in one volume octavo. Its author obtained his information from his townsman, Tsé Tsingkò who, when his ship was wrecked at sea, was himself saved by the people on board a foreign vessel. After continuing abroad fourteen years, voyaging from country to country, he returned to China, and became blind, after which he was engaged as interpreter in Macao, where Yéung Pingnám meeting with him obtained the materials of his book.

(3) The Notices of things Heard and Seen in Foreign Countries are comprised in two small duodecimo volumes, written about a century ago. The second volume contains a chart of the whole Chinese coast.

(4) The Memoranda of the Foreign Tribes form four small octavo volumes, and were published in the reign of Kínlung of the present dynasty.

廣東方言讀本

# Section Eighth.

# THE IMPERIAL DOMINIONS.

## 皇輿略第八章

ˏWóng ˏyü léuk$_2$; tai$^2$ pát$_3$ ‹chéung.

| | | |
|---|---|---|
| 1. *Chilí* forms the capital province of the Chinese empire, and was anciently called Yú and Yen. | 直隸爲中華首省古稱幽燕 | *Chik$_2$ tai$^2$* ˏwai ‹Chung ˏwá ‘shau ‘sháng, ‘kú ‹ch‘ing ‹Yau, I′n’. |
| 2. *Shántung,* i. e. east of the hills, was anciently called Tsí and Lú. Confucius, the sage, was born in this province. | 山東乃山之東古稱齊魯孔聖生於此省 | ‹*Shán ‹tung* ‘nái ‹shán ‹chí ‹tung, ‘kú ‹ch‘ing ˏTs‘ai, ˏLò. ‘Hung shing’ ‹shang ‹ü ‘ts‘z’ ‘shing. |
| 3. *Shánsi,* i. e. west of the hills, was anciently called Tsin and Cháu. | 山西乃山之西古稱晉趙 | ‹*Shán ‹sai* ‘nái ‹shán ‹chí ‹sai, ‘kú ‹ch‘ing Tsun’, Chiú$^2$. |
| 4. *Honán* forms the centre of the Chinese empire, south of the Yellow river, is designated the Centre-region, and was anciently called Yen and Yü. | 河南爲華夏之中黄河之南號中州古稱兗豫 | ˏ*Hó ˏnám* ˏwai ˏWá há$^2$ ‹chí ‹chung, ‹Wóng ˏhó ‹chí ˏnám, hò$^2$ ‹Chung ‹chau, ‘kú ‹ch‘ing ‘Hín, Yü$^2$. |
| 5. *Kiángnán* is now divided into two provinces *Kiángsú* and *A′nhwui.* The ancient Nánking constitutes the modern city Kiángning, otherwise designated Kinling. | 江南今分江蘇安徽二省古南京在今江寧府别號金陵 | ‹*Kóng ˏnám* ‹kam ‹fan ‹*Kóng ‹sú*, ‹*O′n ‹fai*, í$^2$ ‘sháng. ‘Kú ˏNám ‹king tsoi$^2$ ‹kam ‹Kóng ˏning ‘fú, pít$_2$ hò$^2$ ‹Kam ˏling. |
| 6. *Kiángsí,* otherwise denominated Yücháng, is also called Wúsí. | 江西别號豫章又曰吳西 | ‹*Kóng ‹sai* pít$_2$ hò$^2$ Yü$^2$ ‹chéung, yau$^2$ üt$_2$ ˏ’Ng ‹sai. |
| 7. *Chekiáng* was originally the country of Yue. | 浙江原爲越國 | *Chít$_3$ ‹kóng* ˏyün ˏwai Yüt$_2$ kwók$_3$. |

## *Notes and Explanations.*

IMPERIAL dominions is a term which, by the native reader, can be applied to nothing but the *Chunghwá*, the centre of wealth and civilization, the *Tái Ts‘ing Kwók* or ‘empire of the Great Pure Dynasty,’ which stretches from lat. 18° to 55° N., and from lon. 70° to 140° E., and includes about 3,010,400 square miles, in extent exceeding the whole of Europe. This section includes the names of the provinces, and also some of the principal rivers, lakes, and mountains.

N. B. Throughout the section the orthography, in the left hand column, indicates the sound of the names when pronounced according to the court dialect.

1. The term China is probably derived from *Tsin*, one of the ancient dynasties. Each of the eighteen provinces, into which China Proper is now divided, is often designated in writing by the ancient name of the same region. The modern names of many of the provinces, as Shántung, Shánsí, Chekiáng, Húnán, Húpa, &c., is derived from their geographical position, or from some other circumstance connected with their topography.

| | | |
|---|---|---|
| 8. *Fukien* was anciently called Min. *Formosa* and the *Piscadore* islands both belong to it. | 福建古稱閩臺<br>灣彭湖皆所屬 | *Fuk, kin'* 'kú ꜀ch'ing ꜁Mán. ꜁*T'oi* ꜀*wán*, ꜁*P'áng* ꜁*ú* ꜀kái 'shó shuk₂. |
| 9. *Húkwáng* was anciently called Sántsú; because it had many lakes, it was therefore called Húkwáng; it is now divided into two provinces, called *Húnán*, and *Húpa*. | 湖廣古稱三楚<br>因其多湖故名<br>湖廣今分兩省<br>曰湖南湖北 | ꜁Ú *'kwóng* 'kú ꜀ch'ing ꜀Sam 'Ch'ó; ꜀yan ꜁k'í ꜀tó ꜁ú, kú' ꜁ming ꜁U' 'kwóng; ꜀kam ꜀fan ꜁léung 'sháng üt₁ ꜁*U'* ꜁*nám* ꜁*U' pak*. |
| 10. *Shènsí*, otherwise designated Kingcháu, was anciently called Kwánchung. | 陝西別號京兆<br>古稱關中 | *'Shim* ꜀*sai* pít₂ hò' ꜀King chiú' 'kú ꜀ch'ing ꜀Kwán ꜀chung. |
| 11. *Kánsu* was separated from the province of Shènsí. | 甘肅陝西分省 | ꜀*Kóm suk*, 'Shím ꜀sai ꜀fan 'sháng. |
| 12. *Sz'chuen* was anciently called Sishu. | 四川古稱西蜀 | *Sz'* ꜀*ch'ün* 'kú ꜀ch'ing ꜀Sai shuk₂. |
| 13. *Kwángtung* is also called Yuetung. | 廣東亦稱粵東 | *'Kwóng* ꜀*tung* yik₂ ꜀ch'ing Üt₂ ꜀tung. |
| 14. *Kwángsi* is also called Yuesi. | 廣西亦稱粵西 | *'Kwóng* ꜀*sai* yik₂ ꜀ch'ing Üt₂ ꜀sai. |
| 15. *Yunnán* was anciently called Tien. | 雲南古稱曰滇 | ꜁*Wan* ꜁*nám* 'kú ꜀ch'ing üt₂ ꜁T'ín. |
| 16. *Kweichau* was anciently called the land of Kien. | 貴州古稱黔地 | *Kwai'* ꜀*chau* 'kú ꜀ch'ing ꜁Kím tí'. |
| 17. Of *Mantchúria*, the provinces are three, namely, *Shingking* (or Moukden) *Kirin*, and *Tsitsihar*, or Halungkiáng. These are called the three eastern provinces. On the north, Mantchúria is bounded by the Russian territory, from which the Hingán (the Daourian) mountains separate it: on the east it reaches to the sea; on the south it is bounded by Corea; on the west it is conterminous with the tribes of Mongolia, and on the south-west with the province of Chilí. | 滿洲之省有三<br>曰盛京曰吉林<br>曰濟濟哈爾即<br>黑龍江謂之東<br>三省北界鄂羅<br>斯地由興安嶺<br>相分焉東至海<br>南界朝鮮西連<br>蒙古各部落西<br>南連直隸省 | ꜁*Mún* ꜀*chau* ꜀chí 'sháng, 'yau ꜀sám, üt₂ *Shing'* ꜀*king*, üt₂ *Kat*, ꜁*lam*, üt₂ *Tsai' tsai'* ꜀*há* ꜁í, tsik, Hak, ꜁lung ꜀kóng. Wai' ꜀chí ꜀tung ꜀sám 'sháng. Pak, kái' Ngók₂ ꜁ló ꜀sz' tí', ꜁yau ꜀Hing ꜀on ꜁ling ꜀séung ꜀fan ꜀ín; ꜀tung chí' 'hoi: ꜁nám kái' ꜁Ch'íú 'sín; ꜀sai ꜁lín ꜁Mung 'kú kók, pò' lók,: ꜀sai ꜁nám ꜁lín Chik, tai' 'sháng. |

1—16. Of this list, Chilí, Shántung, Shánsí, and Honán may be regarded as the northern provinces; Kiángnán (or Kiángsú and A'nhwui), Kiángsí, Chekiáng, and Fukien, the eastern: Húkwáng (or Húnán and Húpa), the central; Shènsí, Kánsu, and Sz'chuen, the western: and Kwángtung, Kwángsí, Yunnán, and Kweichau, the southern. These eighteen provinces are situated between lat. 18° and 41° N., and between long. 98° and 123° E., from Greenwich, and include about 1,298,000 square miles.

17. The extent of Mantchúria, from north to south, is about twelve degrees, and about sixteen from east to west. It is mountainous, little cultivated, and thinly peopled. The name is derived from its inhabitants, the Manchús, who four centuries ago were only a few wandering tribes, but are now masters of China.—*Ngók* and *Ngó* are both used in writing the name Russia.

18. The territory of ***Mongolia***, on the east is conterminous with Mantchúria, on the south is bounded by the provinces Chilí, Shánsí, Shènsí, and Kánsu; on the west, it is conterminous with Í'lí. It is divided into four parts: 1. The ***Inner Mongols***, 24 tribes, situated on the north of the four provinces above named, and on the south of the Shámo or desert of Gobi; 2. The ***Outer Mongols***, the tribes of the four Kalka khans, on the north of Shámo, and conterminous with Russia: 3. ***Ouliasutai*** and its subject places, Gobdo, &c., on the west of the Outer Mongols: and 4. ***Koko-nor***, or the Azure sea, on the south of Kánsu and the west of Shènsí.

蒙古之地東連
滿洲南界直隸
山西陝西甘肅
各省西連伊犁
分作四段一曰
內蒙古二十四
部落在四省之
北沙漠即戈壁
之南一曰外蒙
古格爾格四汗
之部在沙漠之
北與俄羅斯界
連一曰烏里雅
蘇台及所屬科
布多等處在外
蒙古之西一曰
庫庫腦兒即青
海在甘肅之南
陝西之西

*ˏMung ʻkú* ˎchí tí$^{2}$, ˎtung ˏlín ʻMún ˎchau; ˏnám kái$^{3}$ Chik$_{2}$ tai$^{2}$, ˎShán ˎsai, ʻShím ˎsai, ˎKóm suk$_{3}$, kók$_{3}$ ʻsháng; ˎsai ˏlín ˎÍ' ˏlai. ˎFan tsók$_{3}$ sz$^{3}$ tün$^{2}$: yat$_{3}$ üt$_{2}$ Noi$^{2}$ ˏMung ʻkú, ʻí$^{2}$ shap$_{2}$ sz$^{3}$ pò$^{2}$ lók$_{2}$, tsoi$^{2}$ sz$^{3}$ ʻsháng ˎchí pak$_{3}$, ˎShá mók$_{2}$ tsik$_{3}$ ˎKó pik$_{3}$ ˎchí ˏnám; yat$_{3}$ üt$_{2}$ Ngoi$^{2}$ ˏMung ʻkú, Kák$_{3}$ ʻí kák$_{3}$ sz$^{3}$ hón$^{2}$ ˎchí pò$^{2}$, tsoi$^{2}$ ˎShá mók$_{2}$ ˎchí pak$_{3}$, ʻü ˏNgó ˏló ˎsz' kái$^{3}$ ˏlín: yat$_{3}$ üt$_{2}$ ˎU ʻlí ʻngá ˎsú ˏtʻoi, kʻap$_{2}$ ʻshó shuk$_{2}$ ˎKó pò$^{3}$ ˎtó ʻtang chʻü$^{3}$: tsoi$^{2}$ Ngoi$^{2}$ ˏMung ʻkú ˎchí ˎsai; yat$_{3}$ üt$_{2}$ Kó$^{3}$ kó$^{3}$ ʻnó ˏí, tsik$_{3}$ ˎTsʻing ʻhoi, tsoi$^{2}$ ˎKóm suk$_{3}$ ˎchí ˏnám, ʻShím ˎsai ˎchí ˎsai.

19. ***Íli*** is divided into two provinces (or Roads). The northern Road is on the north of the ***Celestial mountains*** (Tien shán), conterminous with Russia, and is the origi-

伊犁分作兩路
北路在天山之
北界連俄羅斯
原爲準噶爾地

ˎÍ ˏlai ˎfan tsók$_{3}$ ʻléung lò$^{2}$. Pak$_{3}$ lò$^{2}$ tsoi$^{2}$ ˎTʻin ˎshán ˎchí pak$_{3}$, kái$^{3}$ ˏlín ˏNgó ˏló ˎsz', ˏün ˏwai ʻChun kót$_{3}$ ʻí tí$^{2}$;

---

18. The boundary lines of Mongolia are not very accurately defined. The ***Mungkú***, or Mongols, are not confined to its limits, but are scattered over the whole Chinese empire: in the eighteen provinces, they are divided into eight standards; in Mantchúria, they are shepherds, as they are for the most part in Mongolia; in Í'lí and Tibet they appear almost as strangers, settled by force of arms rather than of free will. In Inner Mongolia are 24 tribes, divided into 49 standards; in Outer Mongolia are 4 tribes, divided into 86 standards; similar divisions and subdivisions exist in Ouliasutai and Koko-nor. Mongolia is an elevated tract of country, and is considered as the first of the Chinese colonies.

19. ***Hwuiyuen*** (***ching***) is the capital of Í'lí, and the first canton; ***Tarbagatae*** (Táp-í-pá-háp-tái) is the second, and ***Kour-khara-ousou*** (Kú-í-hák-láp-ú-sú) is the third. ***Bárkoul*** (Pá-lí-kwan) now called ***Chinsí fú***, or the department of Chinsí (Chan-sai), and ***Oroumtchi*** (U-lò-muk-tsai)

nal Soungaria; on its west are the pastoral tribes of the Hassáks (or Cossacks). The southern Road lies on the south of the Celestial mountains, and the north of the Kwanlun mountains; it is the New Territory called that of the 'eight Mohammedan cities.' The minister charged with the general control of affairs in the Mohammedan territory resides at Yárkand. Westward are situated the several [independent] Mohammedan tribes.

其西爲哈薩克
遊牧南路在天
山之南崑崙之
北回回八城新
疆總理回疆事
務大臣駐劄葉
爾羌西則回回
諸部分住

꜁k'í ꜀sai ꜁wai ꜀Há sát꜄ hak꜄ ꜁yau muk$_2$. ꜁Nám lò$^2$ tsoi$^2$ ꜀T'ín ꜀shán ꜀chí ꜁nám, ꜀Kwan ꜁lun ꜀chí pak꜄, ꜁U'i ꜁úi pát꜄ ꜁shing ꜀San ꜀Kéung. 'Tsung ꜂lí ꜂úi ꜀kéung sz'$^2$ mò$^2$ tái$^2$ ꜁shan, chü$^2$ cháp꜄ Í'p$_2$ ꜂í ꜀kwai. ꜀Sai tsak꜄ ꜁U'i ꜁úi ꜀chui pò$^2$ ꜀fan chü$^2$.

20. *Tibet* is on the west of Sz'chuen province, and is divided into Anterior and Ulterior Tibet; there is in each a Minister resident in Tibet, in order to regulate the affairs of the lámás.

西藏在四川省
之西分作前藏
後藏各置駐藏
大臣以理喇嘛
之事

꜀*Sai Tsóng*$^2$ tsoi$^2$ Sz'$^2$ ꜀ch'ün 'sháng ꜀chí ꜀sai, ꜀fan tsók꜄ ꜁Ts'ín Tsóng$^2$, Hau$^2$ Tsóng$^2$; kók꜄ chí$^2$ chü$^2$ tsóng$^2$ tái$^2$ ꜁shan, ꜂í ꜂lí ꜀lá ꜁má ꜀chi sz'$^2$.

21. Those by whom the yellow religion (Shámanism) is maintained among the Mongols and Tangouths are called lámás.

以黃教行於蒙
古唐古特者曰
喇嘛

꜂Í ꜁wóng káu' ꜁hang ꜀yü ꜁Mung 'kú ꜁T'óng 'kú tak꜄ 'ché, üt$_2$ ꜀lá ꜁má.

22. *Anterior Tibet* is divided into two territories, *Kham* and *Wei*, the chief city being Lassa, which is the residence of the great teacher of the yellow religion, the dalaï lámá.

前藏分作康衛
二地其首城拉
撒爲黃教大師
達賴喇嘛住所

꜁*Ts'ín Tsóng*$^2$ ꜀fan tsók꜄ ꜁*Hóng Wai*$^2$ í$^2$ tí$^2$, ꜁k'í 'shau ꜁shing ꜀Lá sát꜄, ꜁wai ꜁wóng káu' tái$^2$ ꜀sz', tát$_2$ lái$^2$ ꜀lá ꜁má chü$^2$ ꜀shó.

23. *Ulterior Tibet* is also divided into two territories, namely *Tsáng* and *'Ari*; westward is *Ladák*, and southward is *Ghorka* (or Nipál).

後藏亦分二地
曰藏曰阿里西
則喇達克南則
郭爾喀

*Hau*$^2$ *Tsóng*$^2$ yik$_2$ ꜀fan í$^2$ tí$^2$, üt$_2$ *Tsóng*$^2$, üt$_2$ ꜀*O'* ꜂*li*, ꜀sai tsak꜄ ꜀*Lá tát*$_2$ *hak*꜄, ꜁nám tsak꜄ *Kwók*꜄ ꜂*í hák*꜄.

now called *Tihwá chau*, or the department of *Tihwá* (Tai-fá), with their dependencies, belong to Kánsu. The Hassaks are better known as Kirghís, i. e. "robbers of the deserts." The cantons *Hami* (Há-mat) and *Turfan* (Tú-lí-fan) are the ancient possessions of Turkish tribes, situated in the southern regions. The eight Mohammedan cities are, *Harashar* (or Hák-lá-shá-í), *Kootché* (Fú-ché); *Aksou* (O'-hak-sú); *Oushi* (U'-shap); *Kashgar* (Hák-shap-kót-í); *Yengi-hissar* (Ying-kat-shá-ó); *Yárkand* (Í'p-í-kéung); and *Khoten* (Wó-tín).

20. The name Tibet is said to be derived from *Tou-p'ho*, afterwards corrupted into Toubet. The country is also called Tangout: the Chinese now usually designate it, as above, *Sí Tsáng* or the Western Tsáng.

| | | |
|---|---|---|
| 24. Mungtíen of the Tsin dynasty built the *Great wall* (i. e. the wall of ten thousand miles); it commences at Lintáu and extends to Liáutung, more than 10,000 *lí* in length. | 秦蒙恬築萬里<br>長城起臨洮至<br>遼東遠萬餘里 | ˏTs'un ˏMung ˊt'im chuk, *mán² ˊli ˏch'éung ˏshing*; ˊhi ˏLam ˏt'ò chí' ˏLiú ˏtung, ˊün mán² ˏü ˊli. |
| 25. The *Yellow river*, taking its rise in the Sea of Constellations, among the Kwanlun mountains, enters the sea at Fauning in Kiángsú. | 黃河出崑崙山<br>星宿海至江蘇<br>阜寧而出於海 | ˏ*Wóng ˏhó* ch'ut, ˏKwan ˏlun ˏshán, ˏSing suk, ˊhoi, chí' ˏKóng ˏsú Fau² ˏning, ˏi ch'ut, ˏü ˊhoi. |
| 26. The *Yángtsz' kiáng*, taking its rise to the westward of the Sea of Constellations, enters Yunnán, passes through Húkwáng, and enters the ocean at the island of Sungming. | 洋子江起於星<br>宿海之西入雲<br>南經湖廣至崇<br>明洲而入於海 | ˏ*Yéung ˊtsz' ˏkóng* ˊhi ˏü ˏSing suk, ˊhoi ˏchí ˏsai, yap₂ ˏWan ˏnám, ˏking ˏÚ ˊkwóng chí' ˏShung ˏming ˏchau, ˏi yap₂ ˏü ˊhoi. |
| 27. The *Grand Canal* was dug under Kiálú's direction, by command of the emperor Shuntí of the Yuen dynasty. | 運河元順帝命<br>賈魯督挖 | *Wan² ˏHó* ˏYün Shun² tai' ming² ˊKá ˊlò tuk, wát,. |
| 28. The eastern mountain *Tái Shán* is situated in the department *Tsinán* in Shántung. | 東嶽泰山在山<br>東濟南府 | ˏTung ngók₂ *Tai' ˏShán* tsoi² ˏShán ˏtung Ts'ai' ˏnám ˊfú. |
| 29. The western mountain *Hwá Shán* is siuated in the department Sí'án of Shènsí. | 西嶽華山在陝<br>西西安府 | ˏSai ngók₂ ˏ*Wá ˏShán* tsoi² ˊShím ˏsai ˏSai ˏón ˊfú. |
| 30. The southern mountain *Háng Shán* is situated in the department Hángchau in Húkwáng. | 南嶽衡山在湖<br>廣衡州府 | ˏNám ngók₂ ˏ*Hang ˏShán* tsoi² ˏÚ ˊkwóng ˏHang ˏchau ˊfú. |
| 31. The northern mountain *Hang Shán* is situated in the department Chinting in Chilí. | 北嶽恒山在直<br>隸真定府 | Pak, ngók₂ ˏ*Hang ˏShán* tsoi² Chik₂ tai² ˏChan ting' ˊfú. |
| 32. The central mountains *Sung Shán* are situated in the department Honán in Honán. | 中嶽嵩山在河<br>南河南府 | ˏChung ngók₂ ˏ*Sung ˏShán* tsoi² ˏHó ˏnám ˏHó ˏnám ˊfú. |
| 33. The lake *Poyáng* is situated in the department Jáuchau in Kiángsí. | 鄱陽湖在江西<br>饒州府 | *Pó' ˏyéung ˏú* tsoi² ˏKóng ˏsai ˏI'ú ˏchau ˊfú. |
| 34. The lake *Tsingtsáu* is situated in the department Yochau in Húkwáng. | 青草湖在湖廣<br>岳州府 | ˏ*Ts'ing ˊts'ò ˏú* tsoi² ˏÚ ˊkwóng Ngók₂ ˏchau ˊfú. |

26. Writers on Chinese geography have differed in their opinions respecting the orthography of the name of this river; that here given, meaning the child of the ocean, seems the most apposite, and is now the most commonly used.

28—32. These five mountains are chiefly deserving of notice, only on account of their being frequently mentioned in the ancient books of the Chinese.

| | | |
|---|---|---|
| 35. The lake *Tányáng* is situated in the department Junchau in Kiángnán. | 丹陽湖在江南<br>潤州府 | ‹*Tán* ˛*yéung* ˛ú tsoi² ‹Kóng ˛nám ‘Yun ‹chau fú². |
| 36. The lake *Tái* is situated in the department Súchau in Kiángsú. | 太湖在江蘇蘇<br>州府 | *T‘ái*² ˛ú tsoi² ‹Kóng ‹sú ‹Sú ‹chau ‘fú. |
| 37. The lake *Tungting* is situated in the department Wúcháng in Húkwáng. | 洞庭湖在湖廣<br>武昌府 | *Tung*² ˛*t‘ing* ˛ú tsoi² ˛ú ‘kwóng ˛Mò ‹ch‘éung ‘fú. |

32—37. The Tungt‘ing is said to be about 220 miles in circumference. The Póyéung is of somewhat less extent. They both discharge their waters into the Yéungtsz' kóng. Like the five mountains, mentioned above, these five lakes are often spoken of collectively in the Chinese classics.

## Section Ninth.

## PROVINCE OF KWANGTUNG.

### 廣東省第九章

‘Kwóng ‹tung ‘sháng; tai² ‘kau ‹chéung.

| | | |
|---|---|---|
| 1. The districts comprised in the department of Kwángchau are Nánhái, Puányü, Shunta, Tungkwán, Hiángshán, Sinhwui, Sánshui, Tsunghwá, Lungman, Tsangching, Sinning, Tsingyuen, Sin'án, and Hwá. | 廣州府之縣南<br>海番禺順德東<br>莞香山新會三<br>水從化龍門增<br>城新寧清遠新<br>安花縣 | ‘Kóng ‹chau ‘fú ‹chí yun², ˛Nám ‘hoi, ‹P‘ún ˛yü, Shun tak², ‹Tung ‘kún, ‹Héung ‹shán, ‹San úi², ‹Sám ‘shui, ˛Ts‘ung fá', ˛Lung ˛mún, ‹Tsang ˛shing, ‹San ˛ning, ‹Ts‘ing ‘ün, ‹San ‹ón, ‹Fá ün². |
| 2. In the department of Shauchau, the districts are Kiukiáng, Locháng, Jinhwá, Jüyuen, Ungyuen, and Yingta. | 韶州府之縣曲<br>江樂昌仁化乳<br>源翁源英德 | ˛Shíú ‹chau ‘fú ‹chí yun². Huk² ‹kóng, Lók² ‹ch‘éung, ˛Yan fá', ‘Yü ˛ün, ‹Yung ˛ün, ‹Ying tak². |

### *Notes and Explanations.*

This section affords a specimen of the territorial subdivisions of the eighteen provinces. The province of Kwóngtung is estimated to contain 79,456 square miles; and, like the other provinces, is divided into *fú*, *chau*, *t‘ing*, and *yün*. The *fú*, or department, is the largest of these subdivisions; there are nine of them in this province. Of the *chau*, there are two kinds; the one, independent of any other subdivision—its chief officers being directly answerable to the provincial authorities, like those of the *fú*—is called an inferior department, or *chiktai chau*, an independent *chau*. The other, whose chief officers are subordinate to the prefect of a depart-

| | | |
|---|---|---|
| 3. In the department of Hwuichau, they are Kweishen, Polò, Chángning, Yung'án, Háifung, Lufung, Lungchuen, Hoyuen, Hoping, and the superior district (*chau*) named Lienping. | 惠州府之縣歸善博羅長寧永安海豐陸豐龍川河源和平連平州 | Wai² ꜀chau ꜂fú ꜀chí yün², ꜀Kwai shín², Pók꜁ ꜁ló, ꜁Ch'éung ꜁ning, ꜂Wing ꜀ón, ꜂Hoi ꜀fung, Luk꜁ ꜀fung, ꜁Lung ꜀ch'ün, ꜁Hó ꜁ün, ꜀Wó ꜁p'ing, ꜁Lín ꜁p'ing ꜀chau. |
| 4. In the department of Cháuchau, the districts are, Háiyáng, Fungshun, Cháuyáng, Kieyáng, Jáuping, Hwuilái, Tápú, Chinghái, and Púning. | 潮州府之縣海陽豐順潮陽揭陽饒平惠來大埔澄海普寧 | ꜁Ch'iú ꜀chau ꜂fú ꜀chí yün², ꜂Hoi ꜁yéung, ꜀Fung shun², ꜁Ch'iú ꜁yéung, K'ít꜁ ꜁yéung, ꜁Ú ꜁p'ing, Wai² ꜁loi, Tái² ꜂pò, ꜁Ch'ing ꜂hoi, ꜀P'ò ꜁ning. |
| 5. Those in the department of Sháuking are, Káuyáu, Sz'hwui, Sinhing, Yángchun, Yángkiáng, Káuming, 'Anping, Kwángning, Káiping, Hoshán, Fungchuen, Káikien, and the superior district named Taking. | 肇慶府之縣高要四會新興陽春陽江高明恩平廣寧開平鶴山封川開建德慶州 | Shíú² hing² ꜂fú ꜀chí yün², ꜀Kò ꜀iú, Sz² úi², ꜀San ꜀hing, ꜁Yéung ꜀ch'un, ꜁Yéung ꜀kóng, ꜀Kò ꜁ming, ꜀Yan ꜁p'ing, ꜂Kwóng ꜁ning, ꜀Hoi ꜁p'ing, Hók꜁ ꜀shán, ꜀Fung ꜀ch'ün, ꜀Hoi kín², Tak꜁ hing² ꜀chau. |
| 6. In the department of Káuchau, there are the districts, Mauming, Tienpa, Sin'í, Úchuen, and Shiching, and the superior district Hwá. | 高州府之縣茂名電白信宜吳川石城化州 | ꜀Kò ꜀chau ꜂fú ꜀chí yün², Mau² ꜁ming, Tín² pak꜁, Sun² ꜁í, ꜁'Ng ꜀ch'ün, Shik꜁ ꜁shing, Fá² ꜀chau. |
| 7. These are the districts of the department Lienchau, Hopú and Lingshán, and the superior district Kin. | 廉州府之縣合浦靈山欽州 | ꜁Lím ꜀chau ꜂fú ꜀chí yün², Hóp꜁ ꜂p'ò, ꜁Ling ꜂shán, ꜀Yam ꜀chau. |
| 8. In the department of Lúichau, they are these, Háikáng, Suikí, and Süwan. | 雷州府之縣海康遂溪徐聞 | ꜁Lui ꜀chau ꜂fú ꜀chí yün², ꜂Hoi ꜀hóng, Sui² ꜀k'ai, ꜁Ts'ui ꜁man. |
| 9. The department of Kiungchau (or island of Háinán) comprises these districts, Kiungshán, Ching- | 瓊州府之縣瓊山澄邁定安文 | ꜁K'ing ꜀chau ꜂fú ꜀chí yün², ꜁K'ing ꜀shán, ꜁Ch'ing mái². |

ment, like those of the *yün*, is called a superior district: of the first kind there are four, and of the second seven, in this province. The four *chiktai chau* are subdivided into districts, but as one of these districts always retains the name of the *chau*, it may also be regarded as a superior district: of these there are four. Thus the *chiktai chau* may be either an inferior department, or a superior district. The *yün* is a subdivision of both the *fú* and the superior (*chiktai*) *chau*, and is called a district. The *t'ing*, in extent of territory, resembles the *yün*, but being like the *chiktai chau* independent of any other subdivision, takes the same rank, and may also be called an inferior department; of these there are two, while there is one (Námò), which ranks with the *yün*. Thus there are in all 15 departments. And, including the 78 *yün*, the 7 *chau* of the

| | | |
|---|---|---|
| mái, Ting'án, Wancháng, Hwuitung, Lohwui, Linkáu Chánghwá, Lingshui Kán-'an, and the superior districts, Yái, Wán, and Tán. | 昌會同樂會臨高昌化陵水感恩崖州萬州儋州 | Ting$^2$ ‹ón, ‚Man ‹ch'éung, Ui$^2$ ‚t'ung, Lók‚ úi$^2$, ‚Lam ‹kò, ‹Ch'éung fá', ‚Ling ʻshui, ʻKam ‹yan, ‚Ngái ‹chau, Mán$^2$ ‹chau, ‹Tám ‹chau. |
| 10. The divisions of the inferior department (*chili chau*) of Loting are the superior district Loting, and the districts Tung'án and Sining. | 羅定直隸州之分羅定州東安西寧兩縣 | ‚Ló ting$^2$ chik‚ tai$^2$ ‹chau ‹chí ‹fan, ‚Ló ting$^2$ ‹chau, ‹Tung ‹ón, ‹Sai ‚ning, ʻléung, yün$^2$. |
| 11. The divisions of the inferior department Lienchau are Lienchau and the district Yángshán. | 連州直隸州之分連州陽山縣 | ‚Lín ‹chau chik‚ tai$^2$ ‹chau ‹chí ‹fan ‚Lín ‹chau ‚Yéung ‹shán, yün$^2$. |
| 12. The divisions of the inferior department Nánhiung are the superior district Nánhiung, and the district of Chíhing. | 南雄直隸州之分南雄州始興縣 | ‚Nám ‚hung chik‚ tai$^2$ ‹chau ‹chí fan$^2$ ‚Nám ‚hung ‹chau, Chí ‹hing yün$^2$. |
| 13. The divisions of the inferior department Kiáying are, the superior district Kiáying, with the districts Hingning, Chánglo, Pingyuen, and Chinping. | 嘉應直隸州之分嘉應州興寧長樂平遠鎮平縣 | ‹Ká ying' chik‚ tai$^2$ ‹chau ‹chí ‹fan ‹Ká ying' ‹chau. ‹Hing ‚ning, ‚Ch'éung lòk‚, ‚P'ing ʻün, Chan' ‚p'ing, yün$^2$. |
| 14. The inferior department (*ting*) Fakáng is on the north of the department Kwángchau, and is governed by a sub-prefect. | 佛岡直隸廳在廣州府之北同知理之 | Fat‚ ‹kóng chik‚ tai$^2$ ‹t'ing tsoi$^2$ ʻKwóng ‹chau ʻfú ‹chí pak‚, ‚t'ung ‹chí ʻlí ‹chí. |
| 15. The inferior department, Lienshán Suiyáu, also called Liyáu, is situated on the west of Lienchau. | 連山綏猺直隸廳亦名理猺廳在連州之西 | Lín' ‹shán ‹Sui ‚iú chik‚ tai$^2$ ‹t'ing, yik‚ ‚ming ʻLí ‚iú ‹t'ing, tsoi$^2$ ‚Lín ‹chau ‹chí ‹sai. |
| 16. The inferior department of Nánau (Namoh) pertains half to Kwángtung, and half to Fukien. | 南澳廳半屬廣東半福建 | ‚Nám ò' ‹t'ing pún' shuk‚ ʻKwóng ‹tung, pún' Fuk‚ kín'. |
| 17. Macao is situated on the south of the district Hiángshán; it is under the government of a sub-prefect, and is the residence of an inferior magistrate of Hiángshán. | 澳門在香山縣之南同知所轄香山左堂駐此 | Ò' mún tsoi$^2$ ‹Héung ‹shán ‹chí ‚nám; ‚t'ung ‹chí ʻshò hat‚; ‹Héung ‹shán ʻtsò ‹tong chü$^2$ ʻts'z'. |

rank of *yün*, with the 4 superior districts, and the 3 *t'ing*, gives a total of 92 districts. Besides these divisions, there are some others both larger and smaller than the *yün*, over which there are proper officers.

# CHAPTER XIII.

# MINERALOGY.

# 石論篇十三

Shik, lun' ; ,p'ín shap, ,sám.

---

## Section First.

## MINERALS.

### 玉石等類第一章

Yuk, shik, 'tang lui': tai' yat, ,chéung.

1. The productions of the earth are distributed into three great divisions (or kingdoms). The first division is called the inanimate, comprising such as minerals, coal, earths, &c. The second comprises those which are animate, but have no breath or blood, such as flowers, trees, vegetables, grasses, &c. The third consists of those animate objects which have breath and blood, as finny and shelly animals, crawling and flying insects, birds and beasts, which move upon the face of the earth. These three kingdoms combined constitute the whole body of the globe, and there is nothing else, besides what is comprised in them.

蓋天下生物分
三大類一曰死
者如石煤土等
是也一曰生而
無氣血者花木
蔬草等是也一
曰生而有氣血
者鱗介昆虫禽
獸遊行地面者
是也三者積聚
成一地球捨此
而外更無他耳

K'oi' ,t'in há' ,shang mat, ,fan ,sám tái' lui'. Yat, üt, 'sz' 'ché, ,ü shik, ,múi, 't'ò, 'tang shí' 'yá. Yat, üt, ,shang ,í ,mò hí' hüt, 'ché, ,fá, muk,, ,shó, 'ts'ò, 'tang shí' 'yá. Yat, üt, ,shang ,í 'yau hí' hüt, 'ché, ,lun, kái', ,kwan ,ch'ung, ,k'am, shau', ,yau ,hang tí' mín' 'ché, shí' 'yá. ,Sám 'ché tsik, tsüi' ,shing yat, tí' ,k'au, 'shé 'ts'z' ,í ngoi', kang' ,mò ,t'á 'í.

## *Notes and Explanations.*

Natural History has been studied, among the Chinese, chiefly by physicians, and for the most part in an empirical manner. Attempts have been made, indeed, to classify the productions of the earth, and systematists have offered their various plans of arrangement. The most complete system of classification is that of Lí Shíchan, as exhibited in the *Pún Ts'ò* or Materia Medica, an elaborate compendium of Chinese medical knowledge, by several authors, of whom he is the principal. In this work, inorganic substances are arranged under the several heads of water, fire, earth, metals, gems, and stones. Water is divided into ærial and terrestrial water,

| | | |
|---|---|---|
| 2. Agate. | 白瑪瑙 | Pák$_2$ ˊmá ˊnò. |
| 3. Almagatholite. | 圖書石　粉石 | ˏT'ò ˏshü shik$_2$. ˊFan shik$_2$. |
| 4. Alum. | 白礬 | Pák$_2$ ˏfán. |
| 5. Alum, crystals of. | 鏡礬 | King' ˏfán. |
| 6. Amber. | 琥珀 | ˊFú p'ák$_2$. |
| 7. Amethyst. | 藍寶石 | ˏLám ˊpò shik$_2$. |
| 8. Amethystine spar, crystalized. | 紫石英 | ˊTsz' shik$_2$ ˎying. |
| 9. Argillite. | 老坑石 | ˊLò ˎháng shik$_2$. |
| 10. Asbestos. | 陽起丨 | ˏYéung ˊhí shik$_2$. |
| 11. Borax. | 硼砂 | ˎP'ang ˎshá. |
| 12. Brimstone. | 琉璜 | ˏLau ˏwóng. |
| 13. Burning wells. | 火井 | ˊFó ˊtsing. |
| 14. Calcareous spar. | 寒水石　鹽精石 | ˏHón ˊshui shik$_2$. ˏÍm ˎtsing shik$_2$. |
| 15. Chalk. | 火石粉 | ˊFó shik$_2$ ˊfan. |
| 16. Chrysoprase. | 翡翠玉 | ˊFi ts'ui' yuk$_2$. |
| 17. Coal. | 煤　石炭 | ˏMúi. Shik$_2$ ˎtán. |
| 18. Conglomerate (or pudding stone). | 蠻石 | ˏMán shik$_2$. |
| 19. Coral, red, precious. | 珊瑚 | ˎShán ˏú. |
| 20. Coral, white, branching. | 石花 | Shik$_2$ ˎfá. |
| 21. Coral, madrepore. | 瑯玕 | ˏLóng ˎkón. |
| 22. Cornelian. | 紅瑪瑙 | ˏHung ˊmá ˊnò. |

or that from the clouds, and that from springs, the ocean, &c. Fire is considered under eleven species, among which are the flame of coals, bamboo, &c. The division of earth comprises the secretions from various animals, as well as soot, ink, etc; that of metals includes metallic substances and their common oxyds; and gems are found in the next division. The sixth and last head combines whatever could not be placed in the preceding divisions. No principle of arrangement runs through any of them, and the heterogenous collection under some of the heads causes no little trouble to the student.—This section comprises mineral substances, not metallic; and includes whatever, in the present limited opportunities of becoming acquainted with the productions of China, has been with any certainty ascertained by foreigners.

9. This is the mineral of which the Chinese ink-stones are made, and also the *shik ping* or stone screens,—carved stones used as ornaments in Chinese houses. It more nearly resembles argillite or shale than any other mineral, but its geological position is not known.

16. *Fí ts'ui*, the name of a small parrot with a green changeable plumage, is applied not only to chrysoprase, but also to some varieties of serpentine, jade, and even colored vitreous compound substances.

| | | |
|---|---|---|
| 23. Diamond. | 金鋼石 | ‹Kam ‹kóng shik$_2$. |
| 24. Emery. | 鑽石 | Tsün' shik$_2$. |
| 25. Flint. | 火丨 | ‘Fó shik$_2$. |
| 26. Glauber's salts (sulphate of soda). | 玄明粉 | ˏHün ˏming ‘fan. |
| 27. Granite. | 花缸青 | ‹Fá ‹kóng ‹ts‘ing. |
| 28. Gypsum. | 石羔 | Shik$_2$ ‹kò. |
| 29. Jade (or nephrite). | 玉 | Yuk$_2$. |
| 30. Jade, clouded. | 碧牙犀 | Pik› ˏngá ‹sai. |
| 31. Jasper, green. | 青碧 | ‹Ts‘ing pik›. |
| 32. Jet. | 不灰木 | Pat› ‹fúi muk$_2$. |
| 33. Kaolin. | 高嶺石 | ˏKó ‘ling shik$_2$. |
| 34. Lapis lazuli. | 青金 | ‹Ts‘ing ‹kam. |
| 35. Lava. | 温石 | ‹Wan shik$_2$. |
| 36. Lime. | 灰 | ‹Fúi. |
| 37. Limestone (or marble). | 粉石 | ‘Fan shik$_2$. |
| 38. Limestone is used to make artificial rockwork. | 英丨用作假山 | ‹Ying shik$_2$ yung$^2$ tsók› ‘ká ‹shán. |
| 39. Marble, blue clouded. | 雲丨　大理石 | ˏWan shik$_2$. Tăi$^2$ ‘lí shik$_2$. |
| 40. Marble, red breccia. | 花蕊石 | ‹Fá yui$^2$ shik$_2$. |
| 41. Mica, friable. | 金星丨 | ‹Kam ‹sing shik$_2$. |
| 42. Mica, foliated. | 千層紙 | ‹Ts‘ín ˏts‘ang ‘chí. |
| 43. Mica, decomposed, coarse. | 蠓石 | ‹Mung shik$_2$. |
| 44. Naptha. | 石腦油石漆 | Shik$_2$ ˏnò ‘yau. Shik$_2$ ts‘at›. |

27. The most common kinds of rock used in Canton and its vicinity for building, paving, and other like purposes, are granite and sandstone. There are several varieties of both these valuable minerals, differing to some extent in their color and fineness, and in the proportion of their ingredients. Among the people, these varieties give rise to different names, most of which are derived from the localities of the sort in question. This remark is likewise applicable to other minerals, and in some cases, perhaps, the names here given may not be those most in use.

29. The term *yuk* is one of very common and extensive application; it is the name of a family of minerals, of which fine jade is the type, and serpentine, prase, chrysoprase, &c., are some of the species; and it is also extended to include all gems, and whatever else (as malachite and jet,) can be used for ornaments or jewelry.

40. This variety of marble is employed in making tables and ornamental articles for opulent Chinese. It is said to be brought from Shíúhing fú in the western part of this province. *Shíúhing shik* is applied to a sort of black marble, brought from the same place.

| | | |
|---|---|---|
| 45. Ochery. | 赭石 | ʿChé shik$_2$. |
| 46. Opal. | 貓兒眼 | ꜀Máu ꜀í ʿngán. |
| 47. Ore of gems. | 璞 | Pʿuk$_2$. |
| 48. Pebbles, milky, quartzy. | 鵝卵石 | ꜀Ngó ʿlün shik$_2$. |
| 49. Petrified pecten. | 石燕 | Shik$_2$ ʿín. |
| 50. Petrified crabs. | 丨蟹 | Shik$_2$ ʿhái. |
| 51. Petrified orthocera. | 石蛇 | Shik$_2$ ꜀shé. |
| 52. Petuntse. | 白不子 | Pák$_2$ ʿtun ʿtsz'. |
| 53. Potash. | 鹹砂 | ꜀Hám ꜁shá. |
| 54. Pumice. | 浮石 | ꜀Fau shik$_2$. |
| 55. Quartz, crystals of. | 白丨英 | Pák$_2$ shik$_2$ ꜁ying. |
| 56. Quartz, clear, crystalized. | 水晶 | ʿShui ꜁tsing. |
| 57. Quartz, smoky. | 墨晶 | Mak$_2$ ꜁tsing. |
| 58. Quartz, smoky, (Cairngoram or tea stone.) | 茶晶 | ꜀Chʿá ꜁tsing. |
| 59. Quartz, rose. | 紅晶 | ꜀Hung ꜁tsing. |
| 60. Quartzy pebbles. | 石春 | Shik$_2$ ꜁chʿun. |
| 61. Quartz, yellowish. | 蠟石 | Láp$_2$ shik$_2$. |
| 62. Ruby. | 紅寶石 | ꜀Hung ʿpò shik$_2$. |
| 63. Sal Ammoniac. | 硇砂 | ꜀Náu ꜁shá. |
| 64. Salt. | 白鹽 | Pák$_2$ ꜀ím. |
| 65. Salt, crystals of. | 戎鹽 | ꜀Yung ꜀ím. |
| 66. Saltpetre (or nitre). | 硝 | ꜁Síú. |
| 67. Saline springs. | 鹽池 | ꜀Ím ꜀chʿí. |
| 68. Sandstone. | 紅坭石 | ꜀Hung ꜀nai shik$_2$. |
| 69. Schistose stone. | 越砒丨 | Yüt$_2$ ꜁pí shik$_2$. |

49—51. These and other petrifactions are considered by the Chinese as wonderful things, lusus naturæ that are inexplicable: petrified crabs are found in the island of Hainan, and are often sold at extravagant prices as panaceas.

55, 56. These are the same minerals, but the latter name is applied to the quartz when made into spectacle-glasses, and the former is the name of the quartz crystal.

61. This is called *láp shik* or wax stone, from its color, which is caused by varnishing it; it is made into ornamental and fanciful shapes.

| | | |
|---|---|---|
| 70. Soapstone. | 滑石 | Wát₂ shik₂. |
| 71. Soda. | 青鹽 | ‹Ts'ing ‹ím. |
| 72. Stalactite. | 石鐘乳 | Shik₂ ‹chung ʾyü. |
| 73. Stalagmite. | 石牀 | Shik₂ ‹ch'óng. |
| 74. Sulphur. | 硫磺粉 | ‹Lau ‹wóng ʿfan. |
| 75. Tabasheer. | 竹黃 | Chuk› ‹wong. |
| 76. Talc. | 雲母石 | ‹Wan ʿmò shik₂. |
| 77. Warm springs. | 温泉 | ‹Wan ‹ts'üu. |
| 77. Whetstone. | 礪石 | Lai² shik₂. |

72. Lí Shíchan, in the *Pún Ts'ò*, speaking of stalactites, says, "In the *Íyung* hill, near Kwailam (in Kwóngsai), there is a cave containing a great number of stalactites; on looking up where the percolation issues forth, you see stalactites white as snow. The moisture on the stone solidifies, forming them like so many little pinnacles upside down; the apex is pointed and sharp; they are about as long as icicles, hollow in the middle like a goose's quill; the milky water drops unceasingly, concreting as it falls; it is very clear, and is caught in bamboo tubes."

## Section Second.

## METALS.

### 五金類第二章
ʿ'Ng ‹kam lui²; tai² í² ‹chéung.

| | | |
|---|---|---|
| 1. Metal is a general term for gold, silver, copper, iron, tin, &c.; there are reckoned to be in all forty-two sorts. Of all substances in nature, metals are the heaviest. | 金者乃金銀銅鐵錫等總名共計四十二種萬物中惟金最重 | ‹Kam ʿché, ʿnái ‹kam, ‹ngan ‹t'ung, t'ít›, sik›, ʿtang ʿts'ung ‹ming; kung² kai² sz² shap₂ í² ʿchung. Mán² mat₂ ‹chung, ‹wai ‹kam tsui² chung². |
| 2. Arsenic. | 砒霜信石生信 | ‹Pí ‹séung. Sun² shik₂. ‹Shang sun². |
| 3. Black lead. | 黑鉛 | Hak› ‹ün. |
| 4. Brass leaf. | 銅薄 | ‹T'ung pók₂. |

### *Notes and Explanations.*

In the term *'ng kam*, the Chinese comprehend metals in generals, though they do not seem to have any distinct idea of metallic bodies as distinguished from other minerals. In the popular system of physics, the five metals are associated with the five colors, five planets, five viscera, five elements, &c., and between these the Chinese suppose there is constant action and reäction, but

| | | |
|---|---|---|
| 5. Cinnabar. | 硃砂 丹砂 | ‹Chü ‹shá. ‹Tán ‹shá. |
| 6. Cinders. | 鐵屎 | T'ít› 'shí. |
| 7. Copper is also called the red metal. | 銅卽赤金也 | ‚T'ung, tsik› ch'ik› ‹kam 'yá. |
| 8. Virgin copper. | 自然銅 | Tsz'² ‚ín ‚t'ung. |
| 9. Sulphate of copper (or blue vitriol). | 膽礬 | 'Tám ‚fán. |
| 10. White copper. | 白銅 | Pák₂ ‚t'ung. |
| 11. Copperas. | 皂礬 青礬 | Tsò² ‚fán. ‹Ts'íng ‚fán. |
| 12. Gold, if laid by for a long time, will not gather rust, nor will a hundred fusings lessen it. | 黄金久埋不生衣百陶不輕 | ‚Wóng ‹kam 'kau ‚mai pat› ‹shang ‹í, pák› ‚t'ò pat› ‹hing. |
| 13. Gold dust. | 水金 | 'Shui ‹kam. |
| 14. Gold leaf. | 金薄 | ‹Kam pók₂. |
| 15. Hæmatitic iron ore. | 代赭石 | Toi² 'ché shik₂. |
| 16. Iron, otherwise called the black metal, is the most abundant of all metals. | 鐵卽黑金也五金以鐵爲最多 | T'ít› tsik› hak› ‹kam 'yá: ‚'ng ‹kam 'í t'ít› ‚wai tsui' ‹tó. |
| 17. Lead, i. e. the clear metal. | 鉛卽青金也 | ‚Ün tsik› ‹ts'ing ‹kam 'yá. |
| 18. White lead. | 鉛粉 | ‚Ün 'fan. |
| 19. Litharge. | 蜜佗僧 | Mat₂ ‹t'ó ‹sang. |
| 20. Loadstone. | 攝石 磁石 閃石 | Shíp› shik₂. ‚Tsz' shik₂. 'Shím shik₂. |
| 21. Malachite. | 石綠 綠青 | Shik₂ luk₂. Luk₂ tsing. |
| 22. Minium. | 鉛丹 | ‚Ün ‚tán. |
| 23. Orpiment (or hartall). | 雄黄 | ‚Hung ‚wóng. |

in what manner they cannot tell. The mineral treasures of China have not been explored to a very great extent, and some of the gold and silver mines once opened are not now worked.

7—10. Copper, according to the Materia Medica, occurs in all the western provinces. "The etymology of the character, 'the metal the same as gold,' is given to it because its color is like that of gold." The Chinese do not use pure copper so much as its alloys, of which they have one or two not known in other countries. *Pák t'ung*, or white copper, is said by Lí Shíchan to be made by fusing copper ore with arsenical ore. Henry's Chemistry gives, as its constituents, iron, copper, zinc, and nickel; others say it contains some silver, but the composition is not accurately known, and probably varies in different specimens, as the alloy is made by fusing ores. It is used for dish-covers and other domestic utensils, and when new looks almost as well as silver.

16. Iron is said to be found in all the eastern provinces, and the Chinese are skilled in smelting the ores. As repositories of facts in natural history, the works of natives, who have written upon the subject, are not unworthy of notice; and they frequently describe what they have seen with tolerable accuracy; as in the *Pún Ts'ò*, where, in this instance, the varieties and principal uses of iron are detailed with much accuracy. But when they attempt to theorize, their

廣東方言讀本

| | | |
|---|---|---|
| 24. All metals are taken from *mines* in the hills. When first dug they are termed *ore*, and then they also combine other substances; as there is copper ore which combines lead and silver, and there is pure copper without any admixture. All ore, when dug, is first put into a kiln to be roasted, and then into a furnace to be smelted, in order to clear it of scoria, and obtain the coarse metal: afterwards it is once and again smelted to make it pure. | 五金皆由山坑採出初出曰礦而礦中亦有夾他物者如銅礦有夾鉛銀者有純銅不雜者凡採璞先設爐竈鍛鍊去其滓成鈹然後再三鼓鍊方成也 | ˈ'Ng ˌkam ˌkái ˏyau ˌshán, ˌ*háng* ˈts'oi ch'ut˳. ˌCh'o ch'ut˳ üt˳ ˈ*kwóng*, ˏí ˈkwóng ˌchung yik˳ ˏyau káp˳ ˌt'á mat˳ ˈché; ˏü ˏt'ung ˈkwóng ˏyau káp˳ ˏün ˏngan ˈché, ˏyau ˏshun ˏt'ung pat˳ tsáp˳ ˈché. ˏFán ˈts'oi p'ók˳ ˌsín ch'ít˳ ˏlò tsò' tün' lín', h'ü' ˏk'í ˈtsz', ˏshing ˌpí; ˏín hau' tsoi' ˌsám ˈkú lín', ˌfóng ˏshing ˈyá. |
| 25. Pyrites, coarse. | 青蒙石 | ˌTs'ing ˏmung shik˳. |
| 26. Quicksilver. | 水銀 汞 | ˈShui ˏngan. Hung'. |
| 27. Rust of iron. | 鐵銹 | T'ít˳ sau'. |
| 28. Silver, or the white metal. | 銀即白金也 | ˏNgan, tsik˳ pák˳ ˌkam ˈyá. |
| 29. Smalts. | 大青 | Tái' ˌts'ing. |
| 30. Sublimate of mercury. | 輕粉 | ˌHing ˈfan. |
| 31. Spelter (or tutenague). | 白鉛 | Pak˳ ˏün. |
| 32. Steel. | 鋼 | ˌKóng. |
| 33. Tin. | 錫 | Sik˳. |
| 34. Block tin. | 斗錫 花錫 | ˈTau sik˳. ˌFá sik˳. |
| 35. Verdigris. | 銅綠 | ˏT'ung luk˳. |
| 36. Vermilion. | 硍硃 | ˏNgan ˌchü. |

writings are more amusing than instructive, as the introduction to the chapter on metals and stones in that work will show. Lí says, "Stones are the kernels of the atmosphere, and the bones of the earth; when large, they form mountains and cliffs, when small, sand and dust: their pure parts form metals and gems; their noxious, barytes and arsenic. When the atmosphere coagulates, being solid, it forms sands of various sorts; when it permutes, being liquid, it becomes salt or quicksilver. In its commutations, it may sometimes change from soft to hard, as when percolations and saline drippings become stone; at other times, animate things become immovable, as when plants and grass petrify. Or when birds and beasts, which breathe, petrify, then that which had life becomes inanimate; or when thunder, earthquakes, stars, and meteors, are transformed, then what was formless takes a shape. Metals and minerals, when well smelted and thoroughly prepared, greatly assist mankind; although they are like rubbish, still they make and change things to an unlimited extent. Moreover, they are available as property, and are used medicinally to strengthen the body; although they are called inanimate things, still their profitable uses are unlimited."

# CHAPTER XIV.

# BOTANY.

# 草木篇十四

ʻTsʻò mukₐ; ‹pʻín shapₐ szʼʼ.

## Section First.

## PARTS OF PLANTS.

## 草木百體第一章

ʻTsʻò muk$_2$ pák› ʻtʻai; taiʼ yat› ‹chéung.

| | | |
|---|---|---|
| 1. The *bark* is the covering of the branches and trunk. | 樹皮枝幹外衣 | *Shü*$^2$ ‹*pʻí* ‹chí kónʼ ngoi$^2$ ‹i. |
| 2. *Branches* grow from the sides of trees. | 枝樹木傍生也 | ‹*Chí* shü$^2$ muk$_2$ ‚pʻóng ‹shang ʻyá. |
| 3. A *flower bud* is one whose petals are unexpanded; it is also called *púi.* | 蕾花瓣未開也<br>亦曰蓓 | ‚*Lui*, ‹fá fánʼ mí$^2$ ‹hoi ʻyá; yik$_2$ üt$_2$ *púi*ʼ. |
| 4. A *leaf bud* is the first sprouting of the bud when yet tender. | 薳乃枝上初生<br>至嫩之處 | ʻ*Ün*, ʻnái ‹chí shéung$^2$ ‹chʻo ‹shang chíʼ nün$^2$ ‹chí chʻüʼ. |
| 5. The *calyx* is that which supports the flower's petals. | 萼托花瓣者也 | *Ngók*$_2$ tók› ‹fá fánʼ ʻché ʻyá. |
| 6. A *catkin* is the silken flowers of a willow. | 柳絮柳之絲也 | ʻ*Lau* ʻ*sui* ʻlau ‹chí ‹szʼ ʻyá. |
| 7. *Corol* is a general term for the petals of a flower. | 葩花瓣總稱也 | ‹*Pá* ‹fá fánʼ ʻtsung ‹chʻing ʻyá. |
| 8. A *crotch* of a branch is where it is divided. | 椏枝之分岐處 | ‹*Á* ‹chí ‹chí ‹fan ‚kʻí chʻüʼ. |
| 9. A *culm* is the erect stem of a grass. | 莖草之正幹也 | ‚*King* ʻtsʻò ‹chí chingʼ kónʼ ʻyá. |

### *Notes and Explanations.*

BOTANY, in the scientific sense of the word, is wholly unknown to the Chinese. Physicians and herbalists have, however, done much in describing plants; and the study of their medical properties, from the time of the renowned Shannung, 'the divine husbandman,' to the present day, has not been neglected. This personage, the Esculapius of Chinese medicine, is reported to have tested the virtues of all the plants he described, and their effects upon his system were observed by him as they passed through his bowels! His supposed observations have been the foundation upon which his successors have built the present received system as exhibited in the *Pún Tsʻò*. In this work, plants are comprised in twenty-seven chapters or *kün*, (which are here wholly arbitrary,) arranged under five divisions or *pò*; viz., *tsʻò pò* herbs, *kuk pò* grains, *tsoi pò* vegeta-

| | | |
|---|---|---|
| 10. The *beard* of the grain grows from the glume. | 穀鎗穀皮所生 | *Kuk*, *‹ts'éung* kuk, ‹p'í 'sho ‹shang. |
| 11. *Chaff* is the husky skin of rice. | 穅米之皮殼也 | ‹*Hóng* 'mai ‹chí ‹p'í hók, 'yá. |
| 12. The *chorion* is the incomplete grain, when it is as yet but a small kernel. | 秕不成穀而成小粒者也 | ‹*P'í*, pat, ‹shing kuk,, ‹í ‹shing 'síú nap, 'ché 'yá. |
| 13. A *cupule* is the receptacle of an acorn. | 梂櫟之房實也 | ‹*K'au* lik, ‹chí ‹fóng shat, 'yá. |
| 14. *Faggots;* wood cleaved down and cut up for cooking is called *faggots* and *billets*. | 薪伐下之木炊爨曰薪曰柴 | ‹*San* fat, há' ‹chí muk, ‹ch'ui 'ts'ün, üt, ‹*san*, üt, ‹*ch'ái*. |
| 15. A *fruit* is the seed of a tree. | 菓乃木實也 | '*Kwó* 'nái muk, shat, 'yá. |
| 16. A *gourd* is the hard covering of a melon. | 匏瓠瓜硬殼也 | ‹*Páu* ‹ú ‹kwá ngáng' hók, 'yá. |
| 17. A *graft* is the term by which a plant is designated when grafted into another plant. | 挨枝別種寄生之稱 | ‹*Ai* ‹*chí* pít, 'chung kí' ‹shang ‹chí ‹ch'ing. |
| 18. *Gum* is the viscid sap of the trunks of trees, which, when the skin cracks, exudes and concretes. | 樹膠乃樹身之潤液裂皮而出積成也 | *Shü'* ‹*káu* 'nái shü' ‹shan ‹chí yun' yik,, lít, ‹p'í ‹í ch'ut, tsik, ‹shing 'yá. |
| 19. *Juice* is the water in the pulp of fruits. | 菓汁菓肉之槳 | '*Kwó chap*, 'kwó yuk, ‹chí ‹tséung. |

bles, *kwó pò* fruits, and *muk pò* trees. These are still further divided into *lui* or families, which, however, as there are no settled principles of classification, frequently include many plants that have no family resemblance. The lowest term in the scale is *chung*, which is sometimes includes a genus of plants, but oftener corresponds to a species, or even a variety. There is nothing in the *Pún Ts'ò*, that indicates any knowledge of what constitutes a genus or a species.

I. The division of herbs contains nine *lui:* viz., 1. *shán ts'ò*, hill plants, such as grow wild, e. g. liquorice, ginseng, narcissus, has 70 *chung*, or species; 2. *fóng ts'ò*, odoriferous plants, such as mowtan, mint, tumeric, has 56 species; 3. *shap ts'ò*, marshy plants, such as Indian shot, plantago, chrysanthemum, has 126 species; 4. *tuk ts'ò*, poisonous or noxious plants, such as rhubarb, day-lily, balsam, has 27 species; 5. *mán ts'ò*, creeping plants, such as convolvulus, China root, honeysuckle, cucumber, has 73 species; it has also a sub-family containing 19 species of scandent plants; 6. *shui ts'ò*, aquatic plants, such as azolla, acorus, confervæ, has 22 species; 7. *shik ts'ò*, plants growing in stony places, as sedum, ferns, saxifrage, has 19 species; 8. *toi lui*, family of mosses, as lichens, &c., has 16 species, and seems intended to comprise all plants whose parasitic habitat is old walls, rocks, &c.; 9. *tsáp ts'ò*, miscellaneous plants, and plants not used in medicine, in all 162 species. In this classification, the habitat is the most influential principle of arrangement for the families; the division for the most part includes herbs, and whatever is not eaten or used in the arts, or does not attain to the consideration and magnitude of a tree.

II. The division of grains contains four families: 1. *má mak tò lui*, the family of hemp, wheat, rice, &c., has 12 species; 2. *tsik suk lui*, the family of millet, maize, &c., has 18 species; 3. *shuk tau lui*, the family of leguminous plants, has 14 species; 4. *tsò néung lui*, family of what can be fermented, such as bean curd, boiled rice, wine, yeast, bread, congee, has 29 species. The first three families comprehend all those plants which are cultivated for their edible seeds, and form three tolerably well defined families; the fourth is added on account of the medical nature of the work, and in a strictly scientific work would of course be left out.

III. The division of edible vegetables, or kitchen herbs, contains five families: 1. *fan san lui*, offensive, pungent plants, such as leeks, garlic, mustard, ginger, has 22 species; 2. *yau*

| | | |
|---|---|---|
| 20. A *kernel* is the flesh inside of a nut. | 仁菓核內之肉 | ‹*Yan* ‘kwó wat$_2$ noi$^2$ ‹chí yuk$_2$. |
| 21. *Knot* is the place where the branches of trees grow out: a *joint* is where the internodes of a bamboo are joined. | 節樹出枝之處又竹筒接續處 | *Tsít*› shü$^2$ ch‘ut› ‹chí ‹chí ch‘ü’; yau$^2$ chuk› ‹t‘ung tsíp› shuk$_2$ ch‘ü’. |
| 22. *Leaves* grow upon the branches and make a shade. | 葉枝上生成遮陰者 | *Íp$_2$* ‹chí shéung$^2$ ‹shang ‹shing ‹ché ‹yam ‘ché. |
| 23. The *midrib* is that which appears on the surface of the leaf, as the roots of the veins. | 葉根葉上現紋之根 | *Íp$_2$* ‹*kan* íp$_2$ shéung$^2$ ín$^2$ ‹man ‹chí ‹kan. |
| 24. A *nut* is contained within the pulp of the fruit. | 核在菓肉之內 | *Wat$_2$* tsoi$^2$ ‘kwó yuk$_2$ ‹chí noi$^2$. |
| 25. A *parasite* is another plant that enters the branches [of a tree] and grows. | 寄生別種入枝而生 | *Kí*’ ‹*shang* pit$_2$ ‘chung yap$_2$ ‹chí ‹í ‹shang. |
| 26. A *peduncle* grows beneath the calyx. | 蒂生於萼下者 | ‘*T‘ai* ‹shang ‹ü ngók$_2$ há$^2$ ‘ché. |
| 27. *Petals* are the flakey parts of the blossom. | 瓣花之片片也 | *Fán*’, ‹fá ‹chí p‘ín’ p‘ín’ ‘yá. |
| 28. The *petiole* grows under the leaf. | 梗生於葉下者 | ‘*Káng* ‹shang ‹ü íp$_2$ há$^2$ ‘ché. |
| 29. *Pistils* are the beard inside of the flower. | 蕊花心之鬚也 | *Yui*$^2$, ‹fá ‹sam ‹chí ‹sú ‘yá. |
| 30. The *pith* is the heart of the trunk. | 蓪即樹心也 | ‹*T‘ung* tsik› shü$^2$ ‹sam ‘yá. |
| 31. A *pod* is the shell of pulse. | 筴荳殼也 | *Káp*› tau$^2$ hók› ‘yá. |
| 32. A *receptacle* is the head of the peduncle. | 花房蒂之頭也 | ‹*Fá* ‹*fóng* ‘t‘ai ‹chí ‹t‘au ‘yá. |
| 33. *Roots* are the feet of plants which enter the earth. | 根樹脚入坭者 | ‹*Kan* shü$^2$ kéuk› yap$_2$ ‹nai ‘ché. |

*wat lui*, soft and smooth plants, such as are mucilaginous and juicy, as dandelions, lilies, bamboo sprouts, has 41 species; 3. *lò ts‘oi*, vegetables producing fruit on the ground, such as tomatoes, melons, has 11 species; 4. *shui ts‘oi*, aquatic vegetables, as fuci, algæ, has 6 species; 5. *chí í*, mushrooms and fungi, has 15 species.

IV. The division of fruits contains six families: 1. *’ng kwó*, the five fruits, such as plum, peach, date, has 11 species; 2. *shán kwó*, wild (or uncultivated) fruits, such as orange, pear, citron, acorn, persimmon, has 34 species; *i kwó*, foreign fruits, as the cocoa-nut, areca, fig, laichí, carambola, has 32 species; 4. *mí lui*, family of aromatics, as pepper, tea, has 14 species; 5. *lò lui* fruits produced on the ground, as water-melon, grape, sugar-cane, 9 species; 5. *shui kwó* aquatic fruits, as water caltrops, water lily, water chestnut, caladium, has 6 species, with a sub-family of 23 species not used in medicine.

V. The division of trees contains six families: 1. *héung muk*, aromatic trees, as pine, cassia, rose, assafœtida, champhor, aloes, has 35 species; 2. *kiú muk*, stately trees, as the willow, dryandra, tamarix, sapindus, varnish tree, elm, croton, has 52 species; 3. *kwan muk*, luxuriant growing trees, as mulberry, gardinia, paper tree, cercis, cotton tree, has 50 species; 4. *ü muk*, attached to trees, as parasites, amber, has 12 species; 5. *páu muk*, flexible plants, as bamboo, has 4 species; 6. *tsáp muk*, miscellaneous trees, has 7 species, and a sub-family containing 20 species. A synopsis of the whole gives 5 divisions, 30 families, and 1094 species.

The drawings of plants in the *Pún Ts‘ò* are exceedingly rude and inaccurate, rendering it almost impossible to recognize even the most common and well marked flowers. In this respect, it is excelled by the plates in the *Sám Ts‘oi T‘ò*, six volumes of which work is filled with figures

34. *Sap* is the juice of trees. 樹液即樹津也 *Shü' yik*, tsik, shü' tsun 'yá.

35. [*Seeds*;] a *tsz'* is the flower setting and before the fruit is perfected. A *shat* is also a general name for the fruit; *yéung* are the seeds of melons; *kwó* are the seeds of plants which ripen on the ground. 子乃花初結而未成菓也實亦菓總名瓤亦瓜實也蓏草之實 *'Tsz'* 'nái fá ch'ó kít, í mí' shing 'kwó 'yá. *Shat*, yik, 'kwó 'tsung ming. *Yéung'* yik, kwá shat, 'yá. *'Kwó* 'ts'ò chí shat,.

36. The *sheath* of the leaf in grasses is where they clasp the stem. 莢草葉裹莖而生也 *Káp*, 'ts'ò íp, 'lui king í shang 'yá.

37. The *sheath* of the joint in bamboos is its covering. 籜竹節之衣也 *T'ók*, chuk, tsít, chí í 'yá.

38. A *spathe* is a leaf which surrounds the yet unopened flowers. 花衣花未開時所包之葉 *Fá í* fá mí' hoi shí 'shó páu chí íp,.

39. A *spike*; the head of grain or millet, where the seeds are congregated is so called. 穗禾稻結實成串而言 *Sui'* wó tò' kít, shat, shing ch'ün' í ín.

40. *Spines* grow upon the branches like thorns. 花艻枝上生如刺者 *Fá lik*, chí shéung' shang ü tsz' 'ché.

41. A *sprout*; that which first of plant and herbs shoots forth is called a sprout. 芽草木初萌之物曰芽 *Ngá*; 'ts'ò muk, ch'ò ming chí mat, üt, ngá.

42. *Sprouts of bamboo* are their first growth. 筍竹之初生也 *'Sun* chuk, chí ch'ó shang 'yá.

43. A *stem*; in grasses is called a *culm*; in the bamboo a *stalk*; in trees a *trunk*; and in grain a *culm*. 幹若草曰莖竹曰箇木曰枚禾曰稾 *Kón'*; yéuk, 'ts'ò üt, *king*; chuk, üt, *kó'*; muk, üt, *múi*; wó üt, *'kò*.

44. A *stump* enters the earth, bearing roots. 樹頭入地生彊 *Shü' t'au* yap, tí' shang 'k'éung.

45. *Tendrils* are like those of rattans and vines. 萁如籐蔓者亦曰萁 *Kí*; ü tang mán' 'ché yik, üt, kí.

46. A *trunk* is the original body of the tree. 幹樹之本身也 *Kón'* shü' chí 'pún shan 'yá.

47. *Twigs* are the end of the branches ascending to the sky; they are also called *sáu*. 杪枝尾叅天曰杪亦曰梢 *M'iú*; chí 'mí ts'ám t'ín üt, *m'iú*, yik, üt, *sháu*.

48. *Vines* drag along and thus grow. 蔓牽連而生也 *Mán'* hín lín í shang 'yá.

of plants arranged into 12 *kün* or chapters, under the same five heads of herbs, trees, vegetables, flowers, and fruits. There are also monographs on the most important productions, as tea, bamboo, &c., to which, as well as the *Pún Ts'ò*, the student is referred for information concerning the knowledge of the Chinese on these subjects.

## Section Second.

## FOREST TREES.

### 喬木類第二章
,K'iú muk, lüi'; tai' í' ,chéung.

| | | |
|---|---|---|
| 1. Amboyna wood. | 影木 | 'Ying muk,. |
| 2. Areca palm. | 梹榔 | ,Pan ,lông. |
| 3. Ash tree. | 槐樹 | ,Wái shü'. |
| 4. Bamboo. | 竹樹 | Chuk, shü'. |
| 5. Black bamboo. | 紫竹 | 'Tsz' chuk,. |
| 6. Whanghee bamboo. | 佛肚竹 | Fat, 't'ò chuk,. |
| 7. Pencil-tube bamboo. | 茅竹 | ,Máu chuk,. |
| 8. Jointless bamboo. | 無節竹 虎邱竹 | ,Mò tsít, chuk,. 'Fú ,yau chuk,. |
| 9. Empress' bamboo. | 湘妃竹 | ,Séung ,fí chuk,. |
| 10. Banian fig. *Ficus.* | 榕樹 | ,Yung shü'. |
| 11. Camphor. *Laurus.* | 樟木 楠木 | ,Chéung muk,. ,Nám muk,. |
| 12. Cassia tree. | 桂樹 | Kwai' shü'. |
| 13. Cinnamon. *Laurus.* | 玉桂 | Yuk, kwai'. |
| 14. Clove tree. | 丁香 | ,Ting ,héung. |
| 15. Coir palm. | 椶樹 | ,Ts'ung shü'. |
| 16. Cotton plant. *Gossypium.* | 棉丨 | ,Mín shü'. |
| 17. Cotton tree. *Bombax.* | 木棉樹 | Muk, ,mín shü'. |
| 18. Cycas. | 畨利市錢 | ,Fán lí' 'shí ,ts'ín. |
| 19. Cypress. *Cupressus.* | 柏樹 | P'ák, shü'. |
| 20. Flat leaved cypress. | 扁栢 | 'Pín p'ák,. |

## *Notes and Explanations.*

BY the term *k'iú muk*, the Chinese intend to include tall, stately trees, of which pines and firs are the types. Trees of all sizes are, however, comprehended in the family, so that it might more accurately be defined timber trees, or those not cultivated for their fruit. The number and variety of forest trees in China is not very great, if the spare use of wood for domestic uses, and the few drawings in botanical works can be taken as evidence. Some of the woods used in cabinet-work are elegant and durable.

廣東方言讀本

| | | |
|---|---|---|
| 21. Dryandra. | 梧桐 | ꜁'Ng ꜁t'ung. |
| 22. Ebony. | 烏木 | ꜀Ú muk$_{2}$. |
| 23. Ebony-like wood. | 酸枝 | ꜀Sün ꜀chí. |
| 24. Echites. | 山羊角樹 | ꜀Shán ꜁yéung kok› shü$^{2}$. |
| 25. Elm. | 榆樹 | ꜁Ü shü$^{2}$. |
| 26. Erythrina. | 古抱樹 | 'Kú 'p'ò shü$^{2}$. |
| 27. Eugenia. | 白飯子 | Pák$_{2}$ fán$^{2}$ 'tsz'. |
| 28. Fagara | 山介樹 | ꜀Shán kái' shü$^{2}$. |
| 29. Fir. | 松樹 | ꜀Ts'ung shü$^{2}$. |
| 30. Iron pear wood. | 鐵梨木 | T'ít› ꜁lí muk$_{2}$. |
| 31. Jatropha. | 桐柚樹 | ꜁T'ung ꜁yau shü$^{2}$. |
| 32. Lagerstrœmia. | 紫薇丨 | 'Tsz' ꜁mí shü$^{2}$. |
| 33. Magnolia yulan. | 玉蘭 | Yuk$_{2}$ ꜁lán. |
| 34. Maple. | 楓樹 | ꜀Fung shü$^{2}$. |
| 35. Mimosa. | 肥皂 | ꜁Fí tsò$^{2}$. |
| 36. Mountain ebony. *Bauhinia.* | 鱗甲 | ꜁Lun káp›. |
| 37. Mulberry. *Morus.* | 桑樹 | ꜀Sóng shü$^{2}$. |
| 38. Oak. | 櫟樹 橡樹 | Lik$_{2}$ shü$^{2}$. Séung$^{2}$ shü$^{2}$. |
| 39. Oak (with smooth acorns). | 槲樕 | Huk$_{2}$ ts'uk›. |
| 40. Palm. | 棕櫚 | ꜀Tsung 'lü. |
| 41. Pandanus. | 蘆兜樹 | ꜁Lò ꜀tau shü$^{2}$. |
| 42.. Paper tree. *Broussonetia.* | 楮樹 | 'Chü shü$^{2}$. |
| 43. Pine. | 杉 | Ch'ám'. |
| 44. Pride of India. *Melia.* | 森木 苦楝 | ꜀Sham muk$_{2}$. 'Fú lín$^{2}$. |

23. This wood is employed in the manufacture of musical instruments, and fine articles of furniture, and is carved into stands for curiosities; it is nearly as black and heavy as ebony.

32. The bark of the paper tree is used very extensively in Japan for making paper, but the Chinese principally employ the bamboo for that purpose.

43. All the cone-bearing trees found in China are great favorites with the people. Pines and firs frequently cover the sides of mountains forming forests, and constitute the greatest part of the wood used for fuel and building; they are also cultivated for these latter purposes. The arbor vitæ, (*Thuja orientalis*) or flat leaved cypress, is a common ornament in parterres and gardens, and is employed in religious ceremonies.

| | | |
|---|---|---|
| 45. Rattans. *Calamus.* | 沙籐 | ˏShá ˏt'ang. |
| 46. Robinia. | 過山蹲 | Kwó' ˏshán 'tsun. |
| 47. Rose wood. | 花梨木 | ˏFá ˏlí muk₂. |
| 48. Sandal-wood tree. | 檀香 | ˏT'án ˏhéung. |
| 49. Sapan wood. | 蘇木 | ˏSú muk₂. |
| 50. Sapindus. | 無患樹木患子 | ˏMò wán² shü². Muk₂ wán² 'tsz'. |
| 51. Sterculia. | 蘋婆 〃 | ˏP'an ˏp'ó shü². |
| 52. Sideroxylon. | 山欖 〃 | ˏShán 'lám shü². |
| 53. Tallow tree. *Stillingia.* | 桕樹 | ˏKung shü². |
| 54. Tamarix. | 垂絲柳 | ˏShui ˏsz' 'lau. |
| 55. Taxus. | 羅漢松 | ˏLó hon' ˏts'ung. |
| 56. Varnish tree. | 漆樹 | Ts'at₁ shü². |
| 57. Willow. | 楊柳 | ˏYéung 'lau. |
| 58. Weeping willow. | 檉樹雨絲絲柳 | Shing' shü². 'Ü ˏsz'. ˏSz' 'lau. |

50. The seeds of this tree are used for their detergent properties, and the nuts are employed by the Budhists to make rosaries; they say, "you should string together 108 soap berries and always wear them about your person. The wood of this tree is what all demons are afraid of:" it has therefore been named *mò wán shü*, or the preventative of evil.

## Section Third.

## FRUIT TREES.

### 菓木類第三章

'Kwó muk₂ lui²; tai² ˏsám ˏchéung.

| | | |
|---|---|---|
| 1. Aleurites. | 石栗 | Shik₂ lut₂. |
| 2. Almonds. | 杏仁 | Hang² ˏyan. |

### *Notes and Explanations.*

A considerable proportion of the food of the Chinese consists of fruit, which is, at least in the southern parts of the empire, both cheap and abundant. Fruit-stalls line the sides of the streets, and baskets-full fill the doorways of shops. The variety is not so great as in western countries, where exotic fruits are added to the indigenous, nor is the flavor of Chinese fruits as a whole

廣東方言讀本

| | | |
|---|---|---|
| 3. Apple. | 平菓 | ꜁P‘ing ‘kwó. |
| 4. Apricot. *Prunus.* | 黃梅 | ꜁Wóng ꜁múi. |
| 5. Bullace. | 柰 | Noi꜅. |
| 6. Carambola, *Averrhoa.* | 三捻 楊桃 | ꜀Sám ním꜅. ꜁Yéung ꜁t‘ò. |
| 7. Chestnut. | 風栗 | ꜀Fung lut꜇. |
| 8. Citron. *Citrus.* | 佛手 香橼 | ꜁Fat ‘shau. ꜀Héung ꜁ün. |
| 9. Cocoa-nut. | 椰子 | ꜁Yé ‘tsz’. |
| 10. Custard apple. *Bromelia.* | 番荔枝 | ꜀Fán lai꜅ ꜀chí. |
| 11. Dates. *Rhamnus.* | 白棗 | Pák꜇ ‘tsò. |
| 12. Red dates. | 紅棗 | ꜁Hung ‘tsò. |
| 13. Dates of the palm. | 波斯子 無漏子 | ꜀Pó ꜀sz’ ‘tsz’. ꜁Mò lau꜅ ‘tsz’. |
| 14. Euonymus. | 山柚柑 | ꜀Shán ꜁yau ꜀kóm. |
| 15. Fig. | 無花菓 | ꜁Mò ꜀fá ‘kwó. |
| 16. Grape. | 葡萄 | ꜁P‘ò ꜁t‘ò. |
| 17. Ground nut. *Arachis.* | 花生 | ꜀Fá ꜀shang. |
| 18. Guava. *Psidium.* | 番石榴 雞屎菓 | ꜀Fán shik꜇ ꜁lau. ꜀Kai ‘shí ‘kwó. |
| 19. Hazle nut. | 榛子 | ꜃P‘áng ‘tsz’. |
| 20. Long hazle nut. | 榧子 | ‘Fí ‘tsz’. |
| 21. Hovenia. | 枳椇 | Chat꜆ kü꜅. |
| 22. Jack fruit. | 波羅蜜 | ꜀Pó ꜁ló mat꜇. |
| 23. Kæmpferia. | 山柰 | ꜀Shán noi꜅. |
| 24. Lemon or lime. | 檸檬 | ꜁Ning ꜁mung. |
| 25. Líchí. *Dimocarpus.* | 荔枝 | Lai꜅ ꜀chí. |
| 26. Common líchí. | 玉荷包 大造 | Yuk꜇ ꜁hó ꜀páu. Tái꜅ tsò꜅. |
| 27. Black leaved líchí. | 黑葉荔枝 | Hak꜆ íp꜇ lai꜅ ꜀chí. |
| 28. Small, late líchí. | 槐枝〡〡 | ꜁Wái ꜀chí lai꜅ ꜀chí. |
| 29. Thorny-skinned líchí. | 火山〡枝 | ‘Fó ꜀shán lai꜅ ꜀chí. |

equal to that of lands where skill and science have combined to improve the productions of nature.

8. Budhá's hand, the meaning of *Fat shau*, is applied to this fruit by the Chinese on account of its singular digitate appearance, which is caused artificially; and converts the greatest part

| | | |
|---|---|---|
| 30. Greenish líchí. | 掛綠丨枝 | Kwá' luk, lai' ,chí. |
| 31. Small stone líchí. | 香荔丨枝 | ,Héung lai' lai' ,chi. |
| 32. Egg-shaped líchí. | 進鳳丨丨 | Tsun' fung' lai' ,chí. |
| 33. Viscid líchí. | 糯米栫丨枝 | Nó' 'mai ,ts'z' lai' ,chi. |
| 34. Dried líchí. | 荔枝乾 | Lai' ,chí ,kón. |
| 35. Longan. *Dimocarpus.* | 龍眼 | ,Lung 'ngán. |
| 36. Loquat. *Eriobotrya.* | 琵琶菓 蘆橘 | ,P'í ,p'á 'kwó. ,Lò kwat,. |
| 37. Mango. *Mangifera.* | 芒菓 | ,Móng 'kwó. |
| 38. Medlar. | 枸杞子 | 'Kau 'kí 'tsz'. |
| 39. Olive. *Cannarium.* | 橄欖 | ,Kóm 'lám. |
| 40. Coolie orange. *Citrus.* | 橙 | ,Ch'áng. |
| 41. Mandarin orange. | 硃砂桔 | ,Chü ,shá kat,. |
| 42. Coolie-mandarin orange. | 柑 | ,Kóm. |
| 43. Kumkwat orange. | 金橘 | ,Kam kwat,. |
| 44. Nutmeg orange. | 四季桔 | Sz' kwai' kat,. |
| 45. Gold nutmeg orange. | 金錢桔 | ,Kam ,ts'ín kat,. |
| 46. Sweet orange. | 甜橙 | ,T'ím ,ch'áng. |
| 47. Thin skinned orange. | 茶枝柑 | ,Ch'á ,chí ,kóm. |
| 48. Dark skinned orange (from Sz'úi). | 四會柑 | Sz' úi' ,kóm. |
| 49. Papaw. *Carica.* | 木瓜 | Muk, ,kwá. |
| 50. Peach. | 桃 | ,T'ò. |
| 51. Hami peach. | 哈蜜桃 | ,Há mat, ,t'ò. |
| 52. Sweet peach. | 英桃 | ,Ying ,t'ò. |

of the fruit into rind; when ripe it is much sought after on account of its agreeable perfume, one specimen being sufficiently powerful to scent a large room.

25—36. The varieties of this fruit are tolerably well defined, arising chiefly from situation and care. It is not found in the northern provinces, but has been introduced into the Archipelago from China. The longan (or lungyen) is inferior in size, and the flavor is very unlike that of the líchí; there are also several varieties of it.

39. This has been called the Chinese olive, merely from the color and shape somewhat resembling that from the Levant; it is a very ordinary fruit, and usually pickled.

40—48. The Chinese have no general name for the orange, each variety bearing a different one. The fruit is very abundant in the winter season, and speceies of the genus, especially the citron and the kumkwat, are raised in pots as ornamental shrubs.

廣東方言讀本



| | | |
|---|---|---|
| 53. Pointed peach. | 鸚嘴桃 | ‹Ying ‘tsui ˛tʻò. |
| 54. Bitter peach. | 冷飯桃 | ˢLang fán² ˛tʻò. |
| 55. Flat peach. | 扁桃 | ‘Pín ˛tʻò. |
| 56. Pear. | 梨 | ˛Lí. |
| 57. Russet pear. | 沙梨 | ‹Shá ˛lí. |
| 58. Shántung pear. | 雪梨 | Süt› ˛lí. |
| 59. Persimmon. *Diospyrus.* | 柿　鷄心柿 | ˛Tsʻz’. ‹Kai ‹sam ˛tsʻz’. |
| 60. Persimmon cakes. | 柿乾 | ˛Ts’z’ ‹kón. |
| 61. Pine apple. | 波羅 | ‹Pó ˛ló. |
| 62. Pine seeds. | 松子　柏子仁 | ‹Tsʻung ‘tsz’. Pʻák› ‘tsz’ ˛yan. |
| 63. Plantain, common. | 生蕉　香牙蕉 | ‹Shang ‹tsíú. ‹Héung ˛ngá ‹tsíú. |
| 64. Green plantain. | 芭蕉 | ‹Pá ‹tsíú. |
| 65. Triangular plantain. | 鼓槌蕉 | ‘Kú ˛chʻui ‹tsíú. |
| 66. Thin skinned plantain. | 阿婆〡 | Á› ˛pʻó ‹tsíú. |
| 67. Short plantain. | 新婦〡 | ‹San ˢfú ‹tsíú. |
| 68. Plum. | 梅 | ˛Múi. |
| 69. Sour plum. | 酸梅 | ‹Sün ˛múi. |
| 70. Red plum. | 紅梅 | ˛Hung ˛múi. |
| 71. Black plum. | 烏梅 | ‹Ú ˛múi. |
| 72. Dark red plum. | 杏 | Hang². |
| 73. Small yellow plum. | 李 | ˢLí. |
| 74. Red heart plum. | 紅心李 | ˛Hung ‹sam ˢlí. |
| 75. Juicy plum. | 鵝膏李 | ˛Ngó ‹kò ˢlí. |
| 76. Nánhwá plum. | 南華李 | ˛Nám ˛wá ˢlí. |

50—55. The peach is one of the best fruits found in China, though it is not usually allowed to attain its full maturity on the tree. This practice of picking fruits, before they are fully ripe, is very common in China, and is often the chief reason of their insipidity. The peach tree is a great favorite with the Chinese, and its budding leaves, opening flowers, and general beauty, furnish an abundance of metaphors to their poets.

56—58. The pears of China often grow to a large size, but their flavor, as well as that of the apple, is far inferior to the same fruits in England and elsewhere. The cause of this inferiority is found in the ignorance of Chinese gardeners of the methods of improving the quality of fruit by grafting and careful cultivation.

| | | |
|---|---|---|
| 77. Green plum. | 青竹李 | ,Ts'ing chuk, 'lí. |
| 78. Pomegranate. *Punica.* | 石榴 | Shik, ,lau. |
| 79. Prunus. (A cherry?) | 櫻子 | ,Ying 'tsz'. |
| 80. Pumelo. *Citrus.* | 柚 | ,Yau. |
| 81. Flat pumelo. | 斗柚 | 'Tau ,yau. |
| 82. Ribbed pumelo. | 桑麻柚 | ,Sóng ,má ,yau. |
| 83. Oblong pumelo. | 陽額柚 | ,Yéung ngák, 'yau. |
| 84. Quince. | 萬壽菓 木瓜 | Mán' shau' 'kwó. Muk, ,kwá. |
| 85. Raisins. | 葡提子 | ,P'ò ,t'ai 'tsz'. |
| 86. Rubus, or Raspberry. | 苺 覆盆子 | ,Múi Fuk, ,p'ún 'tsz'. |
| 87. Salisburia seeds. | 銀杏 白菓 | ,Ngan hang'. Pák, 'kwó. |
| 88. Seeds of *Hovenia.* | 卍字菓 | ,Mán tsz' 'kwó. |
| 89. Strawberry tree. *Arbutus.* | 楊梅 | ,Yéung ,múi. |
| 90. Walnuts. | 核桃 | Hat, ,t'o. |
| 91. Large walnuts (Juvia, or Brazil nut.) | 盒桃 胡桃 | Hóp, ,t'ò. ,Ú ,t'ò. |
| 92. Whampe. *Cookia.* | 黃皮 | ,Wóng ,p'í. |

84. The quince and the papaw are both called 'tree melon;' the former bears another name, 'the fruit of ten thousand ages,' given to it from its unwithering nature.

87. The seeds of the Salisburia resemble almonds in taste, and somewhat in appearance, from whence the Chinese have transferred the name of its seeds to the almonds brought from abroad. The leaves of the Salisburia are used by the Japanese to put between the leaves of their books to preserve them from the depredations of insects.

88. This, the more common name for the fleshy peduncles of the Hovenia, was omitted in its proper place; the fruit is sold in apothecaries' shops, attached to the peduncle, and is used to increase the flavor of wine. The character *mán* is meant to imitate the form of the peduncle; it is the Vitruvian scroll or the Indian Swastica, and is identical in meaning with the character *mán*, a myriad.

## Section Fourth.

# VEGETABLES AND GRAINS.

## 禾菜類第四章

ˏWó ts'oi' lui$^2$; tai$^2$ sz'' ˏchéung.

| | | |
|---|---|---|
| 1. Bamboo shoots. | 竹笋 | Chuk, 'sun. |
| 2. Barley. | 大麥　麰麥 | Tái$^2$ mak$_2$. ˏMau mak$_2$. |
| 3. Fragrant basil. *Ocimum.* | 紫蘇 | 'Tsz' ˏsú. |
| 4. Beans. | 蠶荳 | ˏTs'ám tau$^2$. |
| 5. Long beans. *Dolichos.* | 荳角 | Tau$^2$ kók,. |
| 6. Soy beans. | 白荳 | Pák$_2$ tau$^2$. |
| 7. Red beans. | 紅荳 | ˏHung tau$^2$. |
| 8. Black beans. | 黑荳 | Hak, tau$^2$. |
| 9. Small red bean. | 赤小豆 | Ch'ik, 'síú tau$^2$. |
| 10. Broad bean. | 藊豆 | 'Pín tau$^2$. |
| 11. Ensiform bean. | 刀豆 | ˏTò tau$^2$. |
| 12. Betel leaf. | 蒟葉　蔞葉 | ˏLau íp$_2$. ˏLau íp$_2$. |
| 13. Brassica (or petsae). | 白菜　菘菜 | Pák$_2$ ts'oi'. ˏS'ung ts'oi'. |
| 14. Buckwheat. | 三角麥　蕎麥 | ˏSám kók, mak$_2$. ˏKíú mak$_2$. |
| 15. Cabbage. | 椰菜 | ˏYé ts'oi'. |

## *Notes and Explanations.*

CHINESE agriculturalists excel in the cultivation of kitchen herbs and vegetables, of which they raise a great variety and an abundant supply. Their forte lies in this branch of gardening; and in the amount of vegetables produced from a single acre probably no people exceed them. By constant manuring, transplanting, and forcing, three, four, and even five crops of vegetables are obtained from the same bed in a twelvemonth. This section contains the names of the most common vegetables found in the markets; but the minor varieties in this neighborhood, and the sorts found elsewhere in China, are not yet accurately ascertained; many of them have never been examined by foreigners.

4—11. Leguminous plants, comprising the numerous species and varieties of pulse, fitches, &c., are included under the general term of *tau;* they are objects of considerable attention to the Chinese gardener. The seeds are used in making soy, bean-curd, and other condiments; the pods, seeds and tender leaves form important articles of food, and the sprouts, germinated artificially, are also used for the same purpose.

13. This is the most common of the vegetables used by the Chinese; it is called 'white greens' from the leaf-stalks being blanched.

| | | |
|---|---|---|
| 16. Caladium. | 蕬菇 茨菰 | ‹Tsz’ ‹kú. ‹Tsz’ ‹kú. |
| 17. Caraway. *Carum.* | 胡荽 芫茜 | ͵Ú ‹sui. ͵Ün ‹sai. |
| 18. Carrot. | 紅蘿蔔 | ͵Hung ͵ló pák$_2$. |
| 19. Cauliflower. | 花椰菜 | ‹Fá ͵yé ts‘oi’. |
| 20. Cayenne pepper. | 辣椒 番椒 花椒 | Lát$_2$ ‹tsíú. ‹Fán ‹tsíú. ‹Fá ‹tsíú. |
| 21. Celery. | 塘蒿 | ͵T‘óng ‹hò. |
| 22. Chives. | 薤 | Hái’. |
| 23. Cress. | 水芹 | ‘Shui ͵k‘an. |
| 24. Cucumber. | 黃瓜 | ͵Wóng ‹kwá. |
| 25. Egg plant, or brinjal. | 苦瓜 | ‘Fú ‹kwá. |
| 26. Garlic. | 青蒜 | ‹Ts‘ing sün’. |
| 27. Ginger. | 薑 | ‹Kéung. |
| 28. Gourd-squash. | 瓠 | ͵Ú. |
| 29. Snake gourd. *Tricosanthes.* | 絲瓜 | ‹Sz’ ‹kwá. |
| 30. Bottle gourd. *Cucurbita.* | 葫蘆 | ͵Ú ͵lò. |
| 31. Grain, growing. | 禾 | ͵Wó. |
| 32. Grain in the chaff. | 穀 | Kuk$_2$. |
| 33. Greens. | 菜 | Ts‘oi’. |
| 34. Water greens. | 蕹菜 | Ang’ ts‘oi’. |
| 35. Winter coarse greens. | 菠菜 赤根菜 | ‹Pó ts‘oi’. Ch‘ik$_2$ ‹kan ts‘oi’. |
| 36. Smooth leaved greens. | 籐菜 | ͵T‘ang ts‘oi’. |
| 37. Narrow leaved greens. | 金針菜 | ‹Kam ‹cham ts‘oi’. |

17. Caraway and sweet basil are both cultivated for seasoning food; the seeds and leaves of the former are both used, but only the leaves of the latter.

30. The bottle gourd is cultivated both for food, and for its horny shell; the latter is employed in the kitchen as a dipper, and on board boats, where it is tied to the backs of infants to enable them to float when they fall overboard.

31. *Wó* is both a general and a particular term; it is applied to growing rice in common conversation, and in books its meaning is sometimes extended to include other edible grasses.

33. The word *ts‘oi* denotes a family of plants, corresponding in English to the terms greens, kitchen vegetables, sallads, &c., meaning those plants which are chiefly cultivated for their leaves. This definition is not, however, very strictly adhered to, for there are several plants not found in it whose leaves are eaten. The number of sorts of *ts‘oi* known, and the quantity cultivated by Chinese gardeners, is very great; hardly a beggar is so poor that he cannot procure some greens to serve as a relish to eat with his rice.

| | | |
|---|---|---|
| 38. Winter greens. | 觀達菜 猪乸菜 | ‹Kún tát˛ ts'oi'. ‹Chu 'na ts'oi'. |
| 39. Pickled greens. | 鹹菜 | ˛Hám ts'oi'. |
| 40. Bean-sprout greens. | 大豆芽菜 | Tái' tau' ˛ngá ts'oi'. |
| 41. Pea-sprout greens. | 細豆芽菜 | Sai' tau' ˛ngá ts'oi'. |
| 42. Lettuce. | 生菜 | ‹Shang ts'oi'. |
| 43. Maize. | 粟米 | Suk› 'mai. |
| 44. Melon. | 瓜 | ‹Kwá. |
| 45. Millet, *Setaria*. | 粟 | Suk›. |
| 46. Barbadoes millet. *Holcus*. | 粱 | ˛Léung. |
| 47. Panicled millet. *Milium*. | 稷 | Tsik›. |
| 48. Grand millet. *Sorghum*. | 黍 | 'Shü. |
| 49. Sz'ch'üen millet. | 蜀黍 | Shuk˛ 'shü. |
| 50. Small mushrooms. | 香信 | ‹Héung sun'. |
| 51. Black, edible mushrooms. | 木耳 | Muk˛ 'í. |
| 52. Muskmelon. | 香瓜 金瓜 | ‹Héung ‹kwá. ‹Kam ‹kwá. |
| 53. Mustard. | 芥菜 | Kái' ts'oi'. |
| 54. Coarse mustard. | 芥蘭 | Kái' ˛lán. |
| 55. Onions. | 葱頭 | ‹Ts'ung ˛t'au. |
| 56. Small onions. | 胡葱 | ˛Ú ‹ts'ung. |
| 57. Paddee. | 稻子 | Tò' 'tsz'. |
| 58. Parsley. | 旱芹菜 | 'Hon ˛k'an ts'oi'. |
| 59. Pearl barley. | 薏苡米 | Í' 'í 'mai. |
| 60. Peas. | 荷蘭豆 | ˛Ho ‹lán tau'. |
| 61. Green (colored) peas. | 綠豆 | Luk˛ tau'. |

45—49. Millet constitutes a larger proportion of the food of the people in the northern provinces than in the southern; the sorts here mentioned are the principal ones, but native botanical works on this subject mention many varieties which cannot be accurately discriminated without an examination of the plants.

55. Onions, garlic, and all other edible alliaceous plants, are consumed by the Chinese in large quantities, so much so, in some instances, as to taint their persons with the odor. There are several varieties, the principal of which are here enumerated.

59. Pearl barley is made from the seeds of the *Coix lachryma*, or Job's tears: the leaves of this grass are used in weaving the mat sails of Chinese vessels.

| | | |
|---|---|---|
| 62. Green peas. | 青豆 | ꜀Ts‘ing tau꜅. |
| 63. Black pepper. | 胡椒 | ꜁Ú ꜀tsiú. |
| 64. Chinese pepper. | 川椒 | ꜀Ch‘ün ꜀tsiú. |
| 65. Long pepper. | 蓽檖子 | Pat꜆ pút꜆ ꜂tsz꜄. |
| 66. Irish potato. | 荷蘭薯 | ꜁Hó ꜀lán ꜁shü. |
| 67. Sweet potato. | 紅薯 番薯 | ꜁Hung ꜁shü. ꜀Fán ꜁shü. |
| 68. Pulse. | 菽 | Shuk꜇. |
| 69. Pumpkin. | 冬瓜 | ꜀Tung ꜀kwá. |
| 70. Flat yellow pumpkin. | 番〃 南瓜 | ꜀Fán ꜀kwá. ꜁Nám ꜀kwá. |
| 71. Purslane. | 猪仔菜 耳脾菜 | ꜀Chü ꜂tsai ts‘oi꜄. ꜃Í ꜁p‘ai ts‘oi꜄. |
| 72. Radish. | 紅蘿蔔 | ꜁Hung ꜁ló pák꜇. |
| 73. Rice. | 米 | ꜃Mai. |
| 74. Old man's rice (or glutinous rice). | 糯米 | Nó꜅ ꜃mai. |
| 75. Common rice. | 粘米 | ꜀Chim ꜃mai. |
| 76. Unhulled rice. | 糙米 | Ts‘ò꜄ ꜃mai. |
| 77. Red rice. | 紅谷米 | ꜁Hung kuk꜆ ꜃mai. |
| 78. White rice. | 白米 | Pák꜇ ꜃mai. |
| 79. Sago. | 西谷米 | ꜀Sai kuk꜆ ꜃mai. |
| 80. Scallions. | 韭菜 | ꜂Kau ts‘oi꜄. |
| 81. Sea-weed. | 海菜 | ꜂Hoi ts‘oi꜄. |
| 82. Sesamum. | 芝蔴 胡蔴 | ꜀Chí ꜁má. ꜁Ú ꜁má. |
| 83. Sonchus or sow thistle. | 苦菜 | ꜂Fú ts‘oi꜄. |
| 84. White spinage. *Amaranthus.* | 白莧菜 | Pák꜇ ín꜅ ts‘oi꜄. |
| 85. Red spinage. | 紅莧菜 | ꜁Hung ín꜅ ts‘oi꜄. |
| 86. Long leaved spinage. | 馬齒莧 | ꜃Má ꜂ch‘í ín꜅. |
| 87. Long crooked squash. | 水瓜 | ꜂Shui ꜀kwá. |

68. *Shuk* is the general name for pulse, and *tau* is the term for the edible seeds, as peas beans, &c.

73. The cultivation of rice is briefly described in Chap. IX., Sect. 2. The number of varieties is very great, and the distinctions between them minute and unimportant; those mentioned here are the most common.

| | | | |
|---|---|---|---|
| 88. Reddish crooked squash. | 矮瓜 | | ʻAi ˓kwá. |
| 89. White cucumber. | 白〡 | | Pák$_2$ ˓kwá. |
| 90. Bottle squash. | 𦽃芋 | | ˓Kóng ú$^2$. |
| 91. Hairy squash. | 節瓜 | | Tsít$_3$ ˓kwá. |
| 92. Sugar cane. | 甘蔗 | | ˓Kóm ché'. |
| 93. Hot sugar cane. | 熱蔗 | | Ít$_2$ ché'. |
| 94. Taro. | 芋頭 | | Ú$^2$ ˛t'au. |
| 95. Tomatoes. *Solanum.* | 番茄 | | ˓Fán ˛k'é. |
| 96. Turnips. | 蘿蔔 | 蕪菁 | ˛Ló pák$_2$. ˛Mò ˓ts'ing. |
| 97. Watermelon. | 西瓜 | | ˓Sai ˓kwá. |
| 98. Water caltrops. *Trapa bicornis.* | 菱角 | | ˛Ling kók$_3$. |
| 99. Water chestnut. *Eleocharis tuberosus.* | 馬蹄 | 荸薺 | ʻMá ˛tai. Pút$_2$ ˛tsz'. |
| 100. Water lily seeds. | 蓮子 | 蓮米 | ˛Lín 'tsz'. ˛Lín ʻmai. |
| 101. Water lily roots. | 蓮藕 | | ˛Lín ʻngau. |
| 102. Wheat. | 麥 | | Mak$_2$. |
| 103. Yam. *Dioscorea.* | 大薯 | | Tái$^2$ ˛shü. |

88. *Kwá*, like *ts'oi*, *tau*, *kuk*, and other words, indicates a family of plants, viz., that of the cucurbitaceæ, or gourds. An attempt has been made to arrange them under their common English names, but perhaps not altogether successfully, the same name being applied to different species, and the same sort, moreover, sometimes having two or more names.

98, 99. Both these plants are cultivated in the vicinity of Canton as common articles of food; they usually form the winter crop in rice fields, after the second crop of rice has been harvested. The latter is a pleasant and wholesome vegetable, with a crisp taste, something like that of the artichoke.

## Section Fifth.

## ORNAMENTAL FLOWERS.

### 名花類第五章
˛Ming ˓fá lui$^2$; tai$^2$ ʻng ˓chéung.

| | | |
|---|---|---|
| 1. Acacia. | 銷塞花 | ˓Síú sak$_3$ ˓fá. |

### *Notes and Explanations.*

Ornamental flowers, or *ming fá*, are cultivated by the Chinese to such an extent as fairly to

| | | |
|---|---|---|
| 2. Agapanthus. | 百子蓮 | Pák, 'tsz' ,lín. |
| 3. Aglaia odorata. | 三葉蘭 | ,Sám íp$_2$ ,lán. |
| 4. Aglaia odorata. *var.* | 五葉蘭 | 'Ng íp$_2$ ,lán. |
| 5. Air-plant. *Ærides* and *Vanda.* | 吊蘭　風蘭 | Tíú' ,lán. 'Fung ,lán. |
| 6. Alpinia nutans. | 鴨脚花 | Áp,-kéuk, ,fá. |
| 7. Azalea Indica. | 杜鵑花 | Tò$^2$ ,kün ,fá. |
| 8. Bæckia frutescens. | 榕篩花 | ,Yung ,shai ,fá. |
| 9. Begonia discolor. | 春海棠 | ,Ch'un 'hoi ,t'óng. |
| 10. Bignonia grandiflora. | 凌雪花 | ,Ling süt, ,fá. |
| 11. Bletia hyacinthina. | 紫蘭 | 'Tsz' ,lán. |
| 12. Bletia Tankervilliæ. | 鶴頂花 | Hók$_2$ 'ting ,fá. |
| 13. Variegated Camellia. | 蜀茶 | Shuk$_2$ ,ch'á. |
| 14. Laich'un Camellia. | 麗春茶 | Lai$^2$ ,ch'un ,ch'á. |
| 15. Cercis siliquastrum. | 紫荊 | 'Tsz' ,hing. |
| 16. Chimonanthus fragrans. | 蠟梅花 | Láp$_2$ ,múi ,fá. |
| 17. Chloranthus inconspicuus. | 鷄爪蘭　珠蘭 | ,Kai 'chau ,lán. ,Chü ,lán. |
| 18. Chloranthus monostachys. | 白珠蘭 | Pák$_2$ ,chü ,lán. |
| 19. ~~Chrysanthemum Sinense.~~ aster sinensis / Chrysanthemum indicum | 菊花 / 菊 | Kuk, ,fá. / Kuk$_3$ |

indicate a general taste for flowers. Ladies wear them in their hair, and pots of the common sorts adorn the door-way or terraces; a tree or shrub is planted in the inner court of the house or temple, and flowers are hawked about the streets, in bouquets, festoons, and garlands, at all seasons. Their floriculture is conducted with a success depending more on practice than the deductions of science, and confined to the most popular favorites, as camellias, chrysanthemums, oranges, &c., in these, being all indigenous plants, they succeed very well, and they have produced a great number of varieties. The practice of dwarfing forest trees is common, and considered as a test of the gardener's skill; bamboos, cypresses, oranges, and trees, are thus treated; and when well stunted and contorted, these victims of fashion often bear extravagant prices. The *Fá tí*, or Flower gardens near Canton afford a good idea of Chinese horticulture, both useful and ornamental; and in number of species and varieties it is probably not exceeded by any in the country, as the patronage of foreign customers has drawn to it plants from all parts of China.

8. This plant is very abundant upon the rocky hills near Whampoa and Macao, continuing in flower all the summer; it is frequently gathered to make brooms, and is also found among the herbseller's stock.

13, 14. *Ch'á fá* is the common term for both Camellia and Thea. The varieties of the former are numerous, cultivated both for use and beauty, and the flower is as great a favorite in its native land as in western countries.

19. The term *kuk* is a general one for all large and gay syngenesious flowers, of which the Chrysanthemum is the type. This species is a favorite plant with Chinese gardeners, who are very successful in its cultivation, and enumerate more than a hundred varieties.

| | | |
|---|---|---|
| 20. Chrysanthemum, or China aster. | 江南菊花 | ˎKóng ˏnám kukˎ ˎfá. |
| 21. Clerodendrum squamatum & Bryophyllum calcynum | 燈籠花 | ˎTang ˏlung ˎfá. |
| 22. Cockscomb. - *Celosia cristata.* | 鷄冠花 | ˎKai ˎkún ˎfá. |
| 23. Commelina. | 淡竹葉 鴨跖 | Tám$^{2}$ chukˎ íp$_{2}$. Ápˎ tsik$_{2}$. |
| 24. Cotyledon serrata. | 刀傷藥 | ˎTò ˎshéung yéuk$_{2}$. |
| 25. Crinum Asiaticum. | 文樹蘭 | ˏMan shü$^{2}$ ˏlán. |
| 26. Cymbidium. | 玉蝶蘭 | Yuk$_{2}$ típ$_{2}$ ˏlán. |
| 27. Daphne odora. | 瑞香 | Sui$^{2}$ ˎhéung. |
| 28. Dracæna ferrea. | 鐵樹花 | Tʻítˎ shü$^{2}$ ˎfá. |
| 29. Enkianthus quinqueflora, or new-year's bell flower. | 弔鐘花 | Tíú$^{3}$ ˎchung ˎfá. |
| 30. Epidendrum. | 蘭花 | ˏLán ˎfá. |
| 31. Gardenia florida. | 白蟾花 黃梔 | Pák$_{2}$ ˏshím ˎfá. ˏWóng ˎchí. |
| 32. Gardenia spinosa. | 對面芀 | Túi$^{3}$ mín$^{2}$ lik$_{2}$. |
| 33. Geranium, or crane's bill. | 香葉 | ˎHéung íp$_{2}$. |
| 34. Holly-leaved geranium. | 洋葵 | ˏYéung ˏkwʻai. |
| 35. Gomphrena globosa, or bachelor's button. | 百日紅 | Pákˎ yat$_{2}$ ˏhung. |
| 36. Hedysarum (*Zornia*) pulchellum. | 阿婆錢 | Á$^{3}$ ˏpʻó ˏtsʻín. |
| 37. Hibiscus okro. | 黃蜀葵 | ˏWóng shuk$_{2}$ ˏkwʻai. |
| 38. Hibiscus mutabilis. | 芙蓉 | ˏFú ˏyung. |
| 39. Hibiscus rosa-sinensis. | 紅花 | ˏHung ˎfá. |
| 40. Double buff Hibiscus. | 旦青硃錦 | Tán$^{3}$ ˎtsʻing ˎchü ˊkam. |
| 41. Double white Hibiscus. | 宮粉佛桑 | ˎKung ˊfan fat$_{2}$ ˎsóng. |
| 42. Double red Hibiscus. | 大紅佛桑 | Tái$^{2}$ ˏhung fat$_{2}$ ˎsóng. |
| 43. Purple Hibiscus. | 紫佛桑 | ˊTsz fat$_{2}$ ˎsóng. |
| 44. Holly leaved acanthus. *Acanthus ilicifolius.* | 莨花芀 | ˏLóng ˎfá lik$_{2}$. |
| 45. Honeysuckle. *Lonicera periclymenum.* | 金銀花 | ˎKam ˏngan ˎfá. |

29. This pretty flower is sold in the markets at the new-year, it being much sought after to grace the apartments of houses and shops; cuttings are put into vases of water, and by a little care, made to throw out an abundance of flowers, covering the otherwise naked branches.

30. *Lán* is a general term for gynandrous plants like the Epidendrum, Malaxis, Vanda, &c., and for those of other genera whose flowers resemble them in their general contour, as the

| | | |
|---|---|---|
| 46. Hoya carnosa. | 玉綉球 | Yuk, sau' ͵k'au. |
| 47. Hydrangea hortensis. | 洋綉球 | ͵Yéung sau' ͵k'au. |
| 48. Hypericum monogynum. | 金絲海棠 | ͵Kam ͵sz' 'hoi ͵t'ong. |
| 49. Impatiens cristata (?) or touch-me-not. | 燈盞花急性子 | ͵Tang 'chán ͵fá. Kap, sing' 'tsz'. |
| 50. Impatiens balsamina. | 鳳仙花 | ͵Fung ͵sín ͵fá. |
| 51. Indian shot. *Canna indica.* | 筆管子水蕉花 | Pat, 'kún 'tsz'. 'Shui ͵tsiú ͵fá. |
| 52. Ipomæa quamoclit. | 白錦屏風 | Pák, 'kam ͵p'ing ͵fung. |
| 53. Ipomæa maratima. | 鱟籐 | Hau' ͵t'ang. |
| 54. Ipomæa grandiflora. | 大葉錦屏風 | Tái' íp, 'kam ͵p'ing ͵fung. |
| 55. Iris. | 杜若 | Tò' yéuk,. |
| 56. Iris, or fleur-de-lis. | 蝴蝶花　馬蘭 | ͵Ú típ, ͵fá. 'Má lun'. |
| 57. Ixora coccinea. | 牡英丹花 | 'Mau ͵ying ͵tán ͵fá. |
| 58. White jasmine. | 茉莉花 | Mút, lí' ͵fá. |
| 59. Common white jasmine. *Jasminum officinale.* | 素馨花 | Sú' ͵hing ͵fá. |
| 60. Lawsonia purpurea. | 指甲花 | 'Chí káp, ͵fá. |
| 61. Lilium concolor. | 朱頂花 | ͵Chü 'ting ͵fá. |
| 62. Tiger-spotted lily. *Lilium tigrinum.* | 捲丹 | 'Kün ͵tán. |
| 63. White lily. | 百合花 | Pák, hóp, ͵fá. |
| 64. White day lily. *Hemerocallis Japonica.* | 玉簪 | Yuk, ͵tsám. |
| 65. Yellow day lily. *Hemerocallis fulva.* | 萱草 | ͵Hün 'ts'ò. |
| 66. Lychnis coronata. | 虞美人 | ͵Ü 'mí ͵yan. |
| 67. Magnolia pumila. | 夜合花 | Yé' hóp, ͵fá. |
| 68. Magnolia fuscata. | 含笑花 | ͵Hóm síú' ͵fá. |
| 69. Magnolia purpurea. | 辛荑花 | ͵San ͵í ͵fá. |
| 70. Malaxis. | 雀舌蘭 | Tséuk, shít, ͵lán. |
| 71. Marvel of Peru. *Mirabilis Jalapa.* | 胭脂花 | ͵Ín ͵chí ͵fá. |
| 72. Marygold. *Tagetes patula.* | 萬壽菊 | Mán' shau' kuk,. |

Chloranthus, Crinum, &c. There are many orchideous genera found in China, whose gay flowers early drew the admiring notice of the people, and they are consequently very common in gardens.

55, 56. There are several species of Iris found in China, but their native names are not

| | | |
|---|---|---|
| 73. Melastoma. | 鷄芝拈 | ‹Kai ‹chí ‹ním. |
| 74. Michelia champaca. | 洋狗牙 | ˏYéung ʻkau ˏngá. |
| 75. Murraya exotica. | 九里香 | ʻKau ˏʻlí ‹héung. |
| 76. Mussænda Chinensis. | 山白蟾 白葉茶 | ‹Shán pák, ˏshím. Pák, íp, ˏchʻá. |
| 77. Myrtus tomentosa. | 烏拈 | ‹Uʻ ‹ním. |
| 78. Narcissus tazetta. | 水仙花 | ʻShui ‹sín ‹fá. |
| 79. Nasturtion, or Indian cress. *Tropæolum.* | 荷葉蓮 | ˏHó íp, ˏlín. |
| 80. Oleander. *Nerium oleander.* | 夾竹桃 | Káp, chuk, ˏtʻò. |
| 81. White olive. *Olea fragrans.* | 桂花 丹桂花 | Kwaiʼ ‹fá. ‹Tán kwaiʼ ‹fá. |
| 82. Reddish olive. *var.* | 木樨花 | Muk, ‹sai ‹fá. |
| 83. Orchis. | 石仙桃 | Shik, ‹sín ˏtʻò. |
| 84. Pæderia fetida. | 鷄屎籐 | ‹Kai ʻshí ˏtʻang. |
| 85. Passion flower. *Passiflora.* | 風車花 西番蓮 | ‹Fung ‹chʻé ‹fá. ‹Sai ‹fán ˏlín. |
| 86. White double flowering peach. | 碧桃花 | Pik, ˏtʻò ‹fá. |
| 87. Flowering almond. | 緋桃 | ‹Fí ˏtʻò. |
| 88. Small pæony. *Pæonia albiflora.* | 芍藥花 | Chʻéuk, yéuk, ‹fá. |
| 89. Mowtan pæony. *Pæonia moutan.* | 牡丹花 花王 | ˏʻMau ‹tán ‹fá. ‹Fá ˏwóng. |
| 90. Pentapetes phœnicia. | 午時花 | ˏʻNg ˏshí ‹fá. |
| 91. Pergularia odoratissima. | 夜來香 | Yéʼ ˏloi ‹héung. |
| 92. Chinese pink. *Dianthus.* | 剪邊蘿 | ʻTsín ‹pín ˏló. |
| 93. Early pink. | 剪春蘿 | ʻTsín ‹chʻun ˏló. |
| 94. Late pink. | 剪秋蘿 | ʻTsín ‹tsʻau ˏló. |
| 95. Variegated pink. | 番石竹 | ‹Fán shik, chuk,. |
| 96. Pitcher plant. (?) *Nepenthes.* | 猪籠草 | ‹Chü ˏlung ʻtsʻò. |
| 97. Pittosporum tobira. | 海童花 | ʻHoi ˏtʻung ‹fá. |
| 98. Plumbago. | 雁來紅 | Ngánʼ ˏloi ˏhung. |

definitely ascertained; *ú tip*, or butterfly-flower is applied to two or three flowers as well as to the Iris. In truth, it may be observed that the names of plants and flowers are generally learned traditionally, and consequently, much discrepancy is found between them, as given by different persons; moreover, the characters employed to write the same name are, if anything, more diverse than the names themselves, thus rendering it difficult to ascertain which is right.

| | | |
|---|---|---|
| 99. Plumieria acuminata. | 鷄蛋花鷄春花 | ˏKai tán² ˏfá. ˏKai ˏch'un ˏfá. |
| 100. Poinciana pulcherrima. | 金鳳花 | ˏKam fung² ˏfá. |
| 101. Primrose. *Primrose.* | 蓮馨花 | ˏLín ˏhing ˏfá. |
| 102. Double flowering prunus. | 賀正梅 | Hó² ˏching ˏmúi. |
| 103. Red double prunus. | 紅梅花硃砂梅 | ˏHung ˏmúi ˏfá. ˏChü ˏshá ˏmúi. |
| 104. White double flowering prunus. | 白梅花 | Pák₂ ˏmúi ˏfá. |
| 105. Flowering pyrus. | 紅鐵海棠花 | ˏHung t'ít, 'hoi ˏt'óng ˏfá. |
| 106. Quisqualis indica. | 使君子 | Sz² ˏkwan 'tsz'. |
| 107. Rose. *Rosa.* | 玫瑰花 | ˏMúi kwai² ˏfá. |
| 108. Seven sisters. | 七姊妹 | Ts'at, 'tsz' múi². |
| 109. Red monthly rose. | 胭脂蝶 | ˏÍn ˏchí típ₂. |
| 110. Monthly rose. | 月瑰 | Üt₂ kwai². |
| 111. Cinnamon rose. | 薔薇 | ˏTséung ˏmí. |
| 112. Roses of various sorts. | 紅鐵海 棠鶯 脂粉團 荼薇 醉楊妃 | ˏHung t'ít, 'hoi. ˏT'ong ˏang. ˏChí 'fan ˏt'ün. ˏT'ò ˏmí. Tsui² ˏyéung ˏfí. |
| 113. Serissa fetida. | 滿天星 | 'Mún ˏt'ín ˏsing. |
| 114. Spiræa crenata. | 碎玉 | Sui² yuk₂. |
| 115. Sunflower. *Helianthus.* | 向日葵 | Héung² yat₂ ˏkw'ai. |
| 116. Sunflower. | 照葵 | Chíú² ˏkw'ai. |
| 117. Tabernæmontana coronaria. | 狗牙花 | 'Kau ˏngá ˏfá. |
| 118. Tuberose. *Polianthes.* | 細葉玉簪花 | Sai² íp₂ yuk₂ ˏtsám ˏfá. |
| 119. Uvaria. (*Artabotrys*) uncata. | 鷹爪 | ˏYing 'cháu. |
| 120. Vinca rosea. | 四時春 | Sz² ˏshí ˏch'un. |
| 121. Violet. | 堇菜 | 'Kan ts'oi². |
| 122. Water lily. *Nelumbium.* | 蓮花 | ˏLín ˏfá. |
| 123. Golden edged water lily. | 金邊蓮 | ˏKam ˏpín ˏlín. |

107—112. Twenty species of roses are known to be natives of China, besides the multiplied varieties of the most popular. The *Rosa Banksia* grows wild near Canton.

# Section Sixth.

## MISCELLANEOUS PLANTS.

## 百草類第六章
Pák˒ ‛ts‘ò lui˒; tai˒ luk˒ ˓chéung.

| | | |
|---|---|---|
| 1. Abrus precatorius. | 紅相思 | ˏHung ˓séung ˓sz'. |
| 2. Acorus calamus, or sweet flag. | 菖蒲 劍蘭 | ˓Ch‘éung ˏp‘ò. Kím' ˏlan. |
| 3. Actæa aspera. | 錫葉 | Sik˒ íp˒. |
| 4. Adiantum, or maiden hair. | 黑骨芒 | Hak˒ kwat˒ ˏmóng. |
| 5. Agar agar. | 紫菜 | ‛Tsz' ts‘oi'. |
| 6. Agaricus. | 草菇 蕈 菌 | ‛Ts‘ò ˓kú. ‛Tsam. ‛Kw‘an. |
| 7. Ajuga. | 老虎鬚 | ‛Lò ‛fú ˓sú. |
| 8. Aloes. | 覇王鞭 火殃竻 | Pá' ˏwóng ˓pín. ‛Fo ˓ying lik˒. |
| 9. Hemp aloes. | 波羅麻 | ˓Pó ˏló ˏmá. |
| 10. Amarantus spinosus. | 假莧菜 | ‛Ká ín' ts‘oi'. |
| 11. Argemone Mexicana. | 老鼠竻 | ‛Lò ‛shü lik˒. |
| 12. Artemisia, or mugwort. | 艾草 艾旗 | Ngái' ‛ts‘ò. Ngái' ˏki. |
| 13. Arundo. | 莨草 | ˏLóng ‛ts‘ò. |
| 14. Arundo. | 芒 | ˏMóng. |
| 15. Boletus. | 木耳 | Muk˒ ‛í. |
| 16. Cactus, night blooming cereus, or prickly pear. | 神僊掌 | ˏShan ˓sín ‛chéung. |
| 17. Conferva. | 海藻 | ‛Hoi ‛ts‘ò. |
| 18. Coreopsis. | 九里明 | ‛Kau ‛lí ˏming. |
| 19. Croton tiglium. | 芭荳 | ˓Pá tau'. |

### *Notes and Explanations.*

THIS section comprises such herbs and plants as are not entitled to a place among ornamental flowers, or vegetables used for food. The lower families of plants, or those included under the comprehensive terms of weeds, mosses, grasses, &c., seem never to have drawn much of the attention of Chinese herbalists, and the names of such as have been described are applied in a general manner, one term frequently including all plants of the same habit and appearance.

5. This is the Malay name for the tenacious jelly or glue made from the *Gigartina tenax*, a marine fucus; it is brought to China from the Indian Archipelago, and is also made in this country, and is applied to many useful purposes. The bamboo lattice work of lanterns and windows is covered with it; and when preserved with sugar it is eaten.

| | | |
|---|---|---|
| 20. Dandelion. *Leontodon Chinensis.* | 蒲公英 | ꜁Pʻò ꜀kung ꜀ying. |
| 21. Datura metel. | 鬧陽花 | Nau$^2$ ꜁yéung ꜀fá. |
| 22. Dodder. *Cuscuta.* | 無葉籐 | ꜁Mò íp$_2$ ꜁tʻang. |
| 23. Equisetum, or scouring rush. | 木賊 | Muk$_2$ tsʻák$_2$. |
| 24. Eriocaulon. | 穀精草 | Kuk$_3$ ꜀tsing ʻtsʻò. |
| 25. Fallopia nervosa. | 薢寶葉 後山茶 | Hái$^2$ ʻpò íp$_2$. Hau$^2$ ꜀shán ꜁chʻá. |
| 26. Ferns. *Pteris* or *Asplenium.* | 鳳尾草 | Fung$^2$ ʻmí ʻtsʻò. |
| 27. Edible ferns. | 蕨 | Kʻüt$_3$. |
| 28. Ferns. *Acrostichum.* | 石韋 | Shik$_2$ ʻwai. |
| 29. Unexpanded ferns. | 狗脊 | ʻKau tsik$_3$. |
| 30. Fungus. | 芝栭 | ꜀Chí ꜁í. |
| 31. Fungi on bamboo. | 竹蓐 | Chuk$_3$ yuk$_2$. |
| 32. Grass. | 草 | ʻTsʻò. |
| 33. Hay. | 乾草 | ꜀Kón ʻtsʻò. |
| 34. Hemp. *Sida tiliæfolia.* | 蔴 | ꜁Má. |
| 35. Hemp. | 苧 | ʻChʻü. |
| 36. Ipomea tuberosa, seeds of the. | 牽牛子 | ꜀Hín ꜁ngau ʻtsz'. |
| 37. Laminaria (?) or edible algæ. | 昆布 海帶 | ꜀Kwan pò'. ʻHoi ʻtai. |
| 38. Lampwick grass. | 燈心草 | ꜀Tang ꜀sam ʻtsʻò. |
| 39. Leaf used for painting. | 菩提紗 | ꜁Pò ꜁tʻai ꜀shá. |
| 40. Lemna, Azolla, or duck weed. | 萍 蒲蕎 | ꜁Pʻing. ꜁Pʻò ꜁kíú. |
| 41. Lichen. | 石耳 石蕊 | Shik$_2$ ʻí. Shik$_2$ ʻyui. |
| 42. Liquorice. | 甘草 | ꜀Kóm ʻtsʻò. |
| 43. Lycoperdon, or puff balls. | 灰菰 牛屎菇 | ꜀Fúi ꜀kú. ꜁Ngau ʻshí ꜀kú. |
| 44. Lycopodium. | 絲芒 | ꜀Sz' ꜁móng. |
| 45. Lycopodium. | 萬年松 卷栢 | Mán$^2$ ꜁nín ꜁tsʻung. ʻKün pʻák$_3$. |

25. The plant bears this name in Loureiro's Flora. It is found wild on the islands near Macao, and the leaves are gathered by the Chinese as a substitute for tea.

40. *Pʻing* means small plants of any sort floating on the surface of pools. A species of duck-weed of a reddish color is found in fish tanks, where it covers the surface, and affords food to the fish by becoming the resort of many insects.

| | | |
|---|---|---|
| 46. Mat grass. | 藺 | Lun$^{2}$. |
| 47. Mosses. | 苔　蘚 | ꜀T'oi. ʻSín. |
| 48. Mushroom. | 鷄蹤　土菌 | ꜀Kai ꜀tsung. ʻT'ò ʻkw'an. |
| 49. Poppy. | 阿芙蓉　罌粟 | ꜀Ó ꜀fú ꜀yung. ꜀Ying suk꜀. |
| 50. Palma Christi. *Ricinus.* | 萆蔴草 | ꜀Pí ꜀má ʻts'ò. |
| 51. Pigeon grass, or cat's tail grass. | 莠　狗尾草 | ʻYau. ʻKau ʻmí ʻts'ò. |
| 52. Plantago. | 車前草 | ꜀Ch'é ꜀ts'ín ʻts'ò. |
| 53. Polygonum. | 葒 | ꜀Hung. |
| 54. Polygonum tinctorium. | 藍草 | ꜀Lám ʻts'ò. |
| 55. Polygonum. | 人葉 | ꜀Yan íp꜀. |
| 56. Aquatic polygonum. | 水蓼 | ʻShui líú$^{2}$. |
| 57. Rubia cordifolia (?) | 茜根 | ꜀Sai ꜀kan. |
| 58. Rush, or aquatic grasses. | 葦 | ʻWai. |
| 59. Quickset grass, or the couch grass. | 茅草 | ꜀Máu ʻts'ò. |
| 60. Saxifraga sarmentosa. | 老虎耳 | ʻLò ʻfú ʻí. |
| 61. Scirpus. | 草菰 | ʻTs'ò ꜀kú. |
| 62. Solanum, wild species of. | 顛茄 | ꜀Tín ꜀k'é. |
| 63. Solanum indicum. | 黄茄花 | ꜀Wóng ꜀k'é ꜀fá. |
| 64. Spinifex squarrosus. | 老鼠芀 | ʻLò ʻshü lik꜀. |
| 65. Thistle. | 小薊 | ʻSíú kai$^{3}$. |
| 66. Tobacco. | 烟草 | ꜀Ín ʻts'ò. |
| 67. Turmeric. | 薑黄 | ꜀Kéung ꜀wóng. |
| 68. Typha, reed mace, or cat's tail. | 蒲 | ꜀P'ò. |
| 69. Weeds. | 薉 | Wai$^{3}$. |

50. The oil from this plant is employed in cooking, but not to a very great extent in this part of the country; animal fat is much preferred when it can be obtained.

62. The resemblance of the noxious fruit of the wild Solanum to the wholesome tomato has given rise to a proverb; *t'ung ngan mái t'ín k'é, léung há tau fún hí*; "With a copper dollar to buy a wild mad-apple, both parties chuckle with pleasure;" meaning that each is pleased in trying to cheat his fellow.

64. This and the Argemone are popularly known by the same name, one instance out of many of the confusion in the names of plants.

## CHAPTER XV.

# ZOOLOGY.

# 生物篇十五

‚Shang mat₂; ‚p'ín shap₂ ˢ'ng.

---

### Section First.

## PARTS OF ANIMALS.

### 生物百體第一章

‚Shang mat₂ pák, 't'ai; tai² yat, ‚chéung.

| | | |
|---|---|---|
| 1. The *air-bladder* of fishes is their *sound;* it is a bag in their bellies, and by means of it they can rise and fall. | 膠即鰾也乃魚肚中之胞藉此而浮沉也 | ‚*Káu*, tsik, '*piú* ˢyá; ˢnái ‚u ˢt'ò ‚chung ‚chí ‚páu, tsik₂ 'ts'z' ‚í ‚fau ‚sh'am ˢyá. |
| 2. *Antennæ* are these things which insects employ to touch objects. | 鬚昆虫藉以探物也 | ‚*Sú* ‚kwan ‚ch'ung tsik₂ ˢí t'ám' mat₂ ˢyá. |
| 3. A *beak* (or bill) is that with which birds peck. | 嘴飛禽藉以啄物也 | '*Tsui* ‚fí ‚k'am tsik₂ ˢí téuk, mat₂ ˢyá. |
| 4. A *burrow* (or den) is the place where animals retreat. | 穴走獸藏身之所也 | *Üt₂* 'tsau shau' ‚ts'óng ‚shan ‚chí 'shó ˢyá. |

### *Notes and Explanations.*

Animated nature is a free rendering of the phrase *shang mat.* Of zoölogy as a science, the Chinese know nothing; their observations being confined to species. Their classification of animals is, however, better than that of plants, as the marks by which the former are grouped in popular classifications are much less recondite than in the latter. An old and popular arrangement of the whole animal world by the Chinese is into five divisions; that of feathered, hairy, naked, shelly, and scaly, animals; at the head of each of these divisions stands a type, technically called *ch'éung*, chief or superior. The phænix, unicorn, man, tortoise, and dragon, are the respective types of these divisions, and in themselves comprise all the good qualities of all the other 360 species found in it. The arrangement followed in the *Pún Ts'ò* is more elaborate than the popular one, and exhibits more study than that found in any other work; animals are there assorted into groups sufficiently natural, but as there are no settled principles of arrangement, it still comprises many anomalies; as, for instance, the bat and flying squirrel are said to be the only birds with hairy wings, and the pangolin the only fish that has legs! The number of *pò*,

| | | |
|---|---|---|
| 5. *Carapace;* the shell of crabs is called a carapace. | 介蟹有甲者曰<br>介 | *Káiʾ;* ˢhái ˢyau káp, ‘che üt, káiʾ. |
| 6. *Chrysalis;* the lodging of flying insects before they are produced is called a chrysalis (or aurelia); the chrysalis of a mantis is called *piú siú.* | 繭乃飛虫未出<br>其房曰繭惟螳<br>螂之繭曰螵蛸 | ‘*Kin* (or ‘*kán*), ˢnái ˓fi ˏch‘ung míʾ ch‘ut, ˏk‘i ˏfóng üt, ‘kin; ˏwai ˏt‘óng ˏlóng ˓chi ‘kin üt, ‘*piú* ˓*siú.* |
| 7. *Claws* are used by birds and beasts to seize objects. | 爪禽獸用以攫<br>物也 | ‘*Chau* ˏk‘am shauʾ yungʾ ‘i ˓ying mat, ˢyá. |
| 8. A *comb* is the fleshy crest upon the head of gallinaceous birds. | 冠鷄類頂上之<br>肉髻也 | ˓*Kún* ˓kai luiʾ ‘ting shéungʾ ˓chí yuk, kaiʾ ˢyá. |
| 9. A *crest* is the elegant feathers upon the crown of birds. | 髻乃鳥頂上所<br>鬆之毛 | *Kaiʾ* ˢnái ˢníú ‘ting shéungʾ ‘shó ˓sung ˓chí ˏmò. |
| 10. *Crown-line* is a marked line upon the top of the head of birds. | 頂線鳥頭上之<br>一線紋也 | ‘*Ting sinʾ* ˢníú ˏt‘au shéungʾ ˓chí yat, sínʾ ˏman ˢyá. |
| 11. A *dewlap* is the flesh pendent from the neck of bovine animals. | 胡牛類頸下垂<br>肉也 | ˏ*Ú* ˏngau luiʾ ‘king háʾ ˏshui yuk, ˢyá. |
| 12. A *dew-claw* (or toe) is the posterior claw in the feet of cows, hogs, &c. | 距乃牛豕之後<br>趾也 | ‘*Kü* ˢnái ˏngau ‘ch‘i ˓chí hauʾ ‘chí ˢyá. |

or divisions (or more properly orders) are five; viz., I. *ch'ung pò,* or insects; II. *lun pò* or scaly animals; III. *kái pò,* or shelly animals; IV. *k'am pò,* birds; V. and *shau pò,* quadrupeds; man succeeds, and forms an order by himself. Each of these are subdivided, as in botany, into *lui* families or tribes, and *chung* genera or species.

I. The order of *ch'ung* or insects comprises four *lui* or families: 1. *lun shang,* or born from eggs, numbering twenty-three species, contains but little else than the two tribes of bees and silkworms; 2. also called *lun shang,* numbers twenty-two species, and is filled with spiders, butterflies, &c.; 3. *fá shang,* the family of those produced by metamorphosis, contains thirty-one species, as bugs, glow-worms, mole-crickets, cockroaches, &c.; 4. *shap shang,* or aquatic born, has twenty-three species, among which are toads, frogs, centipedes, &c.

II. The order of scaly animals contains four families: 1. *lung,* the dragons, comprising also the manis, has nine species; 2. *shé,* snakes, has seventeen species; 3. *ü lui,* or family of fishes, has thirty-one species; 4. *mò lun ü,* fishes without scales, as the eel, cuttle-fish, prawns, ray, &c., has twenty-eight species, with a sub-family of nine species, which includes miscellaneous marine things used in medicine, as the roe and fat of fishes, &c.

III. Animals with shells are divided into two families: 1. *kwai pit lui,* tortoises and turtles, making seventeen species; 2. *páng kóp,* bivalve and univalve shells, including star-fish, echinus, and the hermit-crab, making twenty nine species.

IV. Birds are arranged into four families: 1. *shui k'am* or water-fowl, as storks, herons, ducks, kingfishers, &c., comprising twenty-three species; 2. *üin k'am* or heath fowl, as pheasants, partridges, sparrows, &c., has also twenty-three species; 3. *lam k'am,* forest birds, as magpies, pigeons, crows, &c., has seventeen species; 4. *shán k'am,* birds of the mountains, as owls, eagles, hawks, &c., has twelve species.

| | | |
|---|---|---|
| 13. A *dorsal spinous fin* is the fin on the back of a fish. | 鰭鱗魚脊上之<br>鬣也 | ꜀*Shi* ꜀lun ꜀ü tsik꜀ shéung² ꜀chi líp꜀ ʿyá. |
| 14. *Eggs* or *tán*; whatever is borne from the womb of birds, upon which they set, and from which their young come forth, is an egg. | 卵即蛋凡由鳥<br>胎中生下哺鬪<br>而仔出者也 | ʿ*Lun* tsik꜀ tán²; ꜀fán ꜀yau ʿníú ꜀tʻoi ꜀chung ꜀shang há² pò² tau', ꜀í ʿtsai chʻut꜀ ʿché ʿyá. |
| 15. The *elytra* are upon the outside of the bodies of insects in order to cover their wings. | 硬翼在虫身外<br>以盖予翼也 | *Ngáng² yik꜀* tsoi² ꜀chʻung ꜀shan ngoi² ʿí kʻoi' ʿtsz' yik꜀ ʿyá. |
| 16. *Exuviæ* are the cast off skins, etc., which cicada, snakes, &c., throw off. | 蛻乃蟬蛇等類<br>退下之脫皮也 | *Túi*' ʿnái ꜀shín ꜀shé ʿtang lui² tʻúi' há² ꜀chí tʻüt꜀ ꜀pʻí ʿyá. |
| 17. *Feathers* are the small pinions of birds. | 毛羽之小者也 | ꜀*Mò* ʿü ꜀chí ʿsíú ʿché ʿyá. |
| 18. *Pan* is the *female* of birds and beasts; the vulgar name is *ná*. *Tsz'* is the female of birds. | 牝禽獸之母也<br>俗名曰乸雌鳥<br>母也 | ʿ*Pan* ꜀kʻam shau' ꜀chí ʿmò ʿyá; tsuk꜀ ꜀ming üt꜀ ʿ*ná*. ꜀*Tsz'* ʿníú ʿmò ʿyá. |
| 19. *Fins*; those appendages on the belly and sides of fish with which they throw aside the water are so called; large fins are called *wings*. | 翅即魚腹下兩<br>邊擺水曰翅大<br>翅曰翼 | *Chʻí*' tsik꜀ ꜀ü fuk꜀ há² ʿléung ꜀pín ʿpái ʿshui üt꜀ chʻí'; tái² chʻí' üt꜀ *yik꜀*. |
| 20. *Gills* are the lungs of fishes. | 鰓魚之肺也 | ꜀*Soi* ꜀ü ꜀chí fai' ʿyá. |
| 21. *Hair* is the covering of quadrupeds. | 毛走獸之衣也 | ꜀*Mò* ʿtsau shau' ꜀chí ꜀i ʿyá. |
| 22. *Hallux* is the posterior toe in the claws of birds. | 後趾鳥爪中之<br>後指也 | *Hau*² ʿ*chí* ʿníú ʿchau ꜀chung ꜀chí hau² ʿchí ʿyá. |
| 23. *Horns* are the antlers upon the top of the head. | 角獸頭上之觡 | *Kók꜀* shau' ꜀tʻau shéung² ꜀chi ꜀chʻá. |

V. Beasts are likewise arranged into four families: 1. *chʻuk*, or domesticated animals, contains twenty-eight species; in this family, besides the nine domestic animals, are enumerated a great number of animal products, as milk, skin, blood, &c.; 2. *shau*, or wild animals, as the lions, deer, hare, otter, &c., has thirty-eight species; 3. *shü*, or rats, including also the squirrels and hedgehogs, has twelve species; 4. *ü kwái*, monkeys and fairies, numbering eight species.

In this classification, there are five orders, eighteen families, and 391 species, but the actual number of objects described is about 330, the remainder being made up of miscellaneous animal substances employed in medicine. Three volumes of the *Sám Tsʻoi Tʻò* are taken up with animated nature, arranged into six sections: birds and beasts fill two volumes, and men shelly and scaly animals, with insects and worms, occupy the third. The whole is a fair speci- of the ignorance and credulity of Chinese authors on such subjects, for the most ill-founded accounts of birds with six heads, others with one leg, or with a human face, horned horses, flying wolves, hoofed monkeys, and other chimera, are mixed up with descriptions and tolerable drawings of those objects that really have an existence. The descriptions are very brief, and much inferior to those in the *Pún Tsʻò*.

| | | |
|---|---|---|
| 24. *Hoofs* are the horny feet of cows, horses, &c. | 蹄牛馬等之甲<br>足也 | ˏT'ai ˏngau ˊmá ˋtang ˏchí káp, tsuk, ˊyá. |
| 25. *Máu* is the *male* of birds and beasts; the vulgar name is *kung*. *Hung* is the male of birds. | 牡鳥獸之公也<br>俗名曰公雄即<br>鳥牡也 | ˊ*Máu* ˊníú shau' ˏchí ˏ*kung* ˊyá; tsuk, ˏming üt, ˏ*kung*. ˏ*Hung* tsik, ˊníú ˊmáu ˊyá. |
| 26. The *mane* is the long hair on the necks of horses, lions, &c. | 鬣馬獅等頸之<br>長毛也 | *Tsung'*, ˊmá ˏsz' ˋtang ˋking ˏchí ˏch'éung ˏmò ˊyá. |
| 27. *Metatarsus* is the place separating the claws from the leg. | 跖爪足分界之<br>處也 | *Tsik*, ˋchau tsuk, ˏfan kái' ˏchí ch'ü' ˊyá. |
| 28. *Nests* are the habitations of birds upon trees. | 巢乃鳥居樹之<br>所 | ˏ*Ch'áu* ˊnái ˊníú ˏkü shü' ˏchí ˋshó. |
| 29. *Nests* are habitations of birds and animals upon the ground. | 窩鳥獸居地之<br>所 | ˏ*Wó* ˊníú shau' ˏkü tí' ˏchí ˋshó. |
| 30. *Nictitating membrane* is the thin eyelid of birds. | 鳥眼膜眼之薄<br>蓋也 | ˊNíú ˊ*ngán mók*, ˊngán ˏchí pók, k'oi' ˊyá. |
| 31. The *operculum* of shells is the scale upon the orifice. | 螺厴螺頭之甲 | ˏ*Ló* ˋ*ím* ˏló ˏt'au ˏchí káp,. |
| 32. An *ovipositor* is that which proceeds from the tail of female insects, either long or short, and is used to store up her eggs. | 尾鎗凡虫毋尾<br>所出或長或短<br>乃藏櫄之物 | ˊ*Mí ˏtséung* ˏfán ˏch'ung ˊmò ˊmí ˋshó ch'ut,, wák, ˏch'éung wák, ˋtün, ˊnái ˏts'óng ˏch'un ˏchí mat,. |

The classification of natural objects in the Chinese language itself should be mentioned in connection with this of the *Pún Ts'ò*. The language is admirably adapted to the arrangement of natural objects in a natural method, by taking the left part called the radical as the genus, and the right half as the species. The most familiar objects, such as the tiger, horse, dog, &c., being first named, were afterwards taken as types of classes; then, when any new object was found, a name was given to it comprising that type to which it bore the greatest resemblance, and another character indicating some specific characteristic of the new object. But this idea has been carried out very imperfectly, partly, no doubt, from the impossibility of directing the formation of the character by any fixed rules, and partly from the difficulty, in doubtful cases, or in exotic species, of referring the new object to its appropriate type. There are sixteen radicals, out of the 214, which are appropriated to zoölogy, eleven to the vegetable world, and five to the mineral. Of the sixteen zoölogical radicals, nine denote mammalia; of these the tiger, dog, and leopard, stand for carnivorous animals; the rat for rodent; the ox, sheep, and deer for ruminant, the horse and hog for pachydermatous; birds are all comprised under two radicals, birds generally and short-tailed birds; the tortoise, dragon, and toad make three families; fishes form one, and insects one. The first and fourteenth, or the tiger and the toad, are confined to the type; the second and third, and the tenth and eleventh, are interchangeable, and some of the others include many strange anomalies. The eleven botanical radicals are principally esculent plants; trees, herbs, bamboo, and hemp are exceptions; the two first comprise nine tenths

| | | |
|---|---|---|
| 33. *Paw* is the sole of the foot of beasts; the paw of a bear is its palm. | 蹯獸足掌也熊蹯即熊掌也 | ˏ*Pún* shauʾ tsukˎ ʿchéung ʿyá; ˏhung ˏpún tsikˎ ˏhung ʿchéung ʿyá. |
| 34. The *pincers of crabs* are their nippers, or the two large claws. | 蟹螯即蟹鉗蟹之兩大爪也 | ʿ*Hái* ˏ*ngáu* tsikˎ ʿhái ˏkim ʿhái ˏchí ʿléung táiʾ ʿchau ʿyá. |
| 35. A *pinion* is the feathery wing of a bird. | 羽鳥之翅毛也 | ʿ*Ü* ʿníú ˏchí chʿíʾ ˏmò ʿyá. |
| 36. *Proboscis* is the long nose of the elephant with which he seizes things and bends them into his mouth. | 象拔乃象之長鼻取物以捲入口也 | *Tséungʾ patˎ* ʿnái tséungʾ ˏchí, ˏchʿéung píʾ ʿtsʿü matˎ ʿí ʿkün yapˎ ʿhau ʿyá. |
| 37. *Quill* of a feather is its barrel. | 毛管毛之筒也 | ˏ*Mò* ʿ*kún* ˏmò ˏchí ˏtʿung ʿyá. |
| 38. *Roe* is the young of fishes or their eggs. | 鯤即魚子魚蛋 | ˏ*Kwan*, tsikˎ ˏü ʿtszʾ, ˏü tánʾ. |
| 39. *Scales* are the outer covering of the bodies of fishes. | 鱗即魚身上之衣也 | ˏ*Lun* tsikˎ ˏü ˏshan shéungʾ ˏchí ˏí ʿyá. |
| 40. *Shell* is the hard covering of turtles and tortoises. | 甲龜鱉之殼也 | *Káp*ˎ ˏkwai pítˎ ˏchí hókˎ ʿyá. |
| 41. *Shell* is the hard covering of oysters and clams. | 殼如蠔蜆之硬皮也 | *Hók*ˎ ˏü ˏhò ʿhín ˏchí ngángʾ ˏpʿí ʿyá. |
| 42. *Spines* are the hard hair of hedgehogs. | 刺蝟之硬毛也 | *Tszʾ* waiʾ ˏchí ngángʾ ˏmò ʿyá. |
| 43. *Spots* or stripes, are the marks upon the bodies of tigers and pards. | 斑即文也虎豹身上之紋是也 | ˏ*Pán* tsikˎ ˏman ʿyá; ʿfú pʿáuʾ ˏshan shéungʾ ˏchí ˏman shíʾ ʿyá. |
| 44. *Spur* is the thorn of a fowl, that posterior claw which does not touch the ground. | 雞踼雞距也腳之後爪不到地者也 | ˏ*Kai tʿik*ˎ ˏkai ʿkü ʿyá; kéukˎ ˏchí hauʾ ʿchau patˎ tòʾ tíʾ ˏché yá. |
| 45. A *sting* is also called *chák*; it is the needle of a bee. | 蠆即螫乃蜂之針也 | *Chaiʾ* tsikˎ *chák*ˎ ʿnái ˏfung ˏchí ˏcham ʿyá. |
| 46. *Tail* is the posterior appendage of birds, beasts, fishes, insects, &c. | 尾鳥獸魚虫皆有後梢也 | ʿ*Mí*, ʿníú shauʾ, ˏü, ˏchʿung, ʿkái ʿyau hauʾ ˏsháu ʿyá. |

of all plants. Millet, wheat, rice, and growing grain form four families; and leguminous, cucurbitaceous, and alliaceous plants each make one. The mineral kingdom is arranged under the five heads of gems, stones, metals, earths, and salts.

33. The paws of bears are considered by Chinese epicures as a very delicate dish; they are said to be brought from Manchouria for the table.

40, 41. *Káp* is strictly applied to the marbled carapace of the turtle; *hók* has a much more extended meaning.

廣東方言讀本

| | | |
|---|---|---|
| 47. *Ling* are the *tail feathers* in gallinaceous birds. | 翎鷄類尾之長毛也 | ꜀*Ling* ꜀kai lui$^{2}$ ʻmi ꜀chí ꜀chʻeung ꜀mò ʻyá. |
| 48. *Tusks* are the teeth which grow from the mouths of elephants. | 象牙即象口所出者 | *Tséung*$^{2}$ ꜀*ngá* tsik꜄ tséung$^{2}$ ʻhau ʻshó chʻut꜄ ʻché. |
| 49. The *voices* of birds and beasts are all unlike; (as for instance,) it is said that hens cackle, horses neigh, birds generally sing, scream, or carol; cows bellow, cicadas chirrup, tigers roar, sheep bleat, cranes cry, parrots sing, dragons howl, frogs croak, and swallows chatter. | 各鳥獸所鳴不同鷄曰啼馬曰嘶鳥曰鳴曰叫曰唱貓曰喊犬曰吠牛曰吼蟬曰噪虎曰嘯羊曰咩鶴曰嗥鶯曰歌龍曰吟蛙曰鬧燕曰語 | Kók꜄ ʻníú shauʼ ʻshó ꜀*ming* pat꜄ ꜀tʻung; ꜀kai üt$_{2}$ ꜀tʻai, ʻmá üt$_{2}$ ꜀szʼ, ʻníú üt$_{2}$ ꜀ming, üt$_{2}$ kíúʼ, üt$_{2}$ chʻéungʼ, ꜀miú üt$_{2}$ hámʼ, ʻhün üt$_{2}$ faiʼ, ꜀ngau üt$_{2}$ ʻhau, ꜀shín üt$_{2}$ tsʻòʼ, ʻfú üt$_{2}$ síúʼ, ꜀yéung üt$_{2}$ ꜀mé, hók$_{2}$ üt$_{2}$ lui$^{2}$, ꜀ang üt$_{2}$ ꜀kó, ꜀lung üt$_{2}$ ꜀yam, ꜀wá üt$_{2}$ náu$^{2}$, ínʼ üt$_{2}$ ʻü. |
| 50. *Wattles* are fleshy caruncles hanging below both cheeks in fowls. | 下冠鷄之兩頰垂肉也 | *Há*$^{2}$ ꜀*kún* ꜀kai ꜀chí ʻléung háp꜄ ꜀shui yuk$_{2}$ ʻyá. |
| 51. *Web* is the skin joining the tarsi, as in the feet of geese. | 掌有皮相連其指如鵞之掌也 | ʻ*Chéung* ʻyau ꜀pʻí ꜀séung ꜀lín ꜀kʻí ʻchí, ꜀ü ꜀ngó ꜀chí ʻchéung ʻyá. |
| 52. A *web* is the silk that spiders spin and form into a net. | 網乃蜘蛛吐絲而結成網 | ʻ*Móng* ʻnái ꜀chí ꜀chü tʻòʼ ꜀szʼ ꜀í kít꜄ ꜀shing ʻmóng. |
| 53. *Whiskers* are the rigid hairs surrounding the mouth of wild beasts. | 鬚獸之環口硬毛也 | ꜀*Sü* shauʼ ꜀chí ꜀wán ʻhau ngáng$^{2}$ ꜀mò ʻyá. |
| 54. *Wings* are used by birds in flying. | 翼鳥用能飛也 | *Yik*$_{2}$ ʻníú yung$^{2}$ ꜀nung ꜀fi ʻyá. |
| 55. *Young* is the tender offspring of birds, beasts, &c., which they bear. | 子鳥獸等所生之幼者 | ʻ*Tsz*ʼ ʻníú shauʼ ʻtang ʻshó ꜀shang ꜀chí yauʼ ʻché. |

47. The tail feathers of the peacock are used by the emperor to confer upon worthy officers as badges of honor equivalent in a degree to titles of nobility in western lands.

49. The Chinese do not attempt to discriminate between the various sounds of animals, a few terms serving to express them all. Many of those in this sentence are not in common use, though they will all be understood from the connection in which they here stand.

## Section Second.

## MAMMALIA.

## 走獸類第二章
'Tsau shau' lui$^{2}$; tai$^{2}$ í$^{2}$ ‚chéung.

1. Quadrupeds (or mammiferous animals) comprise all those animals which are born from the womb, and nourished by milk; they are divided into seven orders. The first order consists of monkeys; they have four hands, by all of which they can seize objects. The second consists of carniverous animals, with pointed (or canine) teeth, and sharp claws; such as the tiger, cat, &c. The third comprises rats and squirrels, which gnaw with their teeth, and subsist on fruits and grain. The fourth order consists of edentata, which eat insects, ants, &c., such as the pangolin. Those of the fifth [ruminate, that is ] eat grass, bring it up from the stomach, chew and swallow it again, such as cows, deer, &c. The sixth comprises the pachydermata (or thick skinned) and four hoofed, such as the elephant, horse, &c. The seventh consists of amphibious animals, which have fore legs, but no hind ones, and which swim; of which the porpoise is an instance.

凡走獸皆屬胎
生乳哺仍分七
類一曰禺類則
四掌皆可攫物
也一類食肉牙
尖而爪利如虎
貓是也一曰鼠
貂以齒嚙物而
食糧肉一類無
牙而食虫蟻穿
山甲是也一類
食草翻胃而噬
吞之牛鹿是也
一類皮厚四蹄
如象馬是也一
類水獸有前脚
而無後脚可以
遊水河豚是也

‚Fán 'tsau shau' ‚kái shuk, ‚t'oi ‚shang 'yü ‚pò, ‚ying ‚fan ts'at, lui$^{2}$. Yat, üt, ‚yü lui$^{2}$, tsak, sz' 'chéung ‚kái 'hó ‚ying mat, 'yá. Yat, lui$^{2}$ shik, yuk, ‚ngá ‚tsím, ‚í 'chau lí$^{2}$, ‚ü 'fú ‚míú shí$^{2}$ 'yá. Yat, üt, 'shü ‚tíú, 'í 'ch'i ngít, mat, ‚í shik, ‚léung yuk,. Yat, lui$^{2}$ ‚mò ‚ngá, ‚í shik, ‚ch'ung 'ngai, ‚ch'ün ‚shán káp, shí$^{2}$ 'yá. Yat, lui$^{2}$ shik, 'ts'ò, 'fán wai$^{2}$ ‚í ít, ‚t'un ‚chí, ‚ngau luk, shí$^{2}$ 'yá. Yat, lui$^{2}$ ‚p'í hau$^{2}$, sz' ‚t'ai, ‚ü tséung$^{2}$ 'má shí$^{2}$ 'yá. Yat, lui$^{2}$ 'shui shau', 'yau ‚ts'ín kéuk, ‚í 'mò hau$^{2}$ kéuk, 'hó 'í ‚yau 'shui, ‚hó ‚t'ün shí$^{2}$ 'yá.

### *Notes and Explanations.*

MAMMALIA is the equivalent term for *tsau shau*, rather than a literal translation of it; it is a common term in Chinese books, meaning four footed animals or quadrupeds. In popular usage, animals are subdivided into four classes; viz., *ch'uk*, or domestic animals, of which there are nine, the horse, cow, camel, hog, sheep, dog, goat, ass, and mule; *shau*, or wild beasts; *shü*, rats or small animals generally, which are described as being expert in thieving; and *yü* or the monkey tribes. In this introductory paragraph, a slight outline is given of the classification of animals for the use of the Chinese student. The zoölogy of the Chinese empire is but partially known, nor do native works and drawings afford much aid in determining what are new from those already ascertained. Large animals, it is said by the Chinese themselves, are of rare oc-

| | | |
|---|---|---|
| 2. Antelope, or pigmy deer. | 麞　麕 | ꜀Chéung. ʿKwan. |
| 3. Antilope gutturosa. | 黄羊 | ˏWóng ˏyéung. |
| 4. Ape or tailless monkeys. | 猿　猨 | ˏÜn. ˏÜn. |
| 5. Ass. | 驢 | ˏLò. |
| 6. Bat. | 蝙蝠　飛鼠 | ꜀Pín fuk꜆. ꜀Fí ʿshü. |
| 7. Bear. | 熊 | ˏHung. |
| 8. White bear. | 羆 | ꜀P'í. |
| 9. Bitch. | 狗牸　狗母 | ʿKau tsz'². ʿKau ˢmò. |
| 10. Boar. | 猪公 | ꜀Chü ꜀kung. |
| 11. Wild boar. | 野猪　豪猪 | ˢYé ꜀chü. ˏHò ꜀chü. |
| 12. Buck. | 麚 | ꜀Ká. |
| 13. Buffalo. | 水牛 | ʿShui ˏngau. |
| 14. Bull. | 牛牯　牛公 | ˏNgau ʿkú. ˏNgau ꜀kung. |
| 15. Calf. | 牛仔　犢 | ˏNgau ʿtsai. Tuk₂. |
| 16. Camel. | 駱駝　橐駝 | Lók꜆ ˏt'ó. T'ók꜆ ˏt'ó. |
| 17. Cat. | 猫　家狸 | ˏMíú. ꜀Ká ˏlí. |
| 18. Chamois. | 麢羊　羚羊 | ˏLing ˏyéung. ˏLing ˏyéung. |
| 19. Civet (?) | 靈猫 | ˏLing ˏmíú. |
| 20. Colt. | 馬仔　駒　騑 | ˢMá ʿtsai. ꜀K'ü. ˏFí. |
| 21. Cow. | 黄牛 | ˏWóng ˏngau. |
| 22. Deer. | 鹿 | Luk₂. |
| 23. Musk deer. | 麝　香麞 | Shé². ꜀Héung ꜀chéung. |
| 24. Mouse deer. | 黄麖 | ˏWóng ꜀king. |
| 25. Spotted deer, or axis. | 金錢鹿 | ꜀Kam ˏts'ín luk₂. |
| 26. Doe. | 麀 | ꜀Yau. |

currence in their country; but there are probably, among the descriptions and drawings in works on natural history, species hitherto unknown to western naturalists.

7, 8. The bear; "an animal that hybernates in the winter;" so the Chinese describe it. The white bear has been seen, they say, in Leaoutung, but it is probably a rare visitant there.

19. This animal is described as possessing an odor like that of the musk deer; it may not be the true civet, though that animal is sometimes seen in Macao.

29. Elephants are at present not used by the Chinese either for war or for purposes of state, if

| | | |
|---|---|---|
| 27. Dog. | 犬　狗 | ‘Hün. ‘Kau. |
| 28. Shaggy dog. | 㺜犬 | ˏNung ‘hün. |
| 29. Elephant. | 象 | Tséung². |
| 30. Fawn. | 麑　麛 | ˏÍ. Ní². |
| 31. Flying squirrel. | 鼯　鸓鼠 | ˏ’Ng. ‘Lui ‘shü. |
| 32. Fox. | 狐狸 | ˏÚ ˏlí. |
| 33. Gelding. | 騸馬 | Shín² ‘má. |
| 34. Gibbon, or long armed ape. | 烏猿 | ˏÚ ˏün. |
| 35. Goat. | 山羊　草羊 | ˏShán ˏyéung. ‘Ts‘ò ˏyéung. |
| 36. Guinea pig. | 荷蘭猪 | ˏHó ˏlán ˏchü. |
| 37. Hog. | 豕　豬　彘 | ‘Ch‘í. ˏChü. Chi². |
| 38. Horse. | 馬 | ‘Má. |
| 39. Dappled horse. | 驄馬 | ˏTs‘ung ‘má. |
| 40. Bay horse. | 赤馬 | Ch‘ik, ‘má. |
| 41. White horse. | 白馬　騮 | Pák, ‘má. ˏLau. |
| 42. Wild horse. | 野馬 | ‘Yé ‘má. |
| 43. Piebald horse. | 駁馬 | Pók, ‘má. |
| 44. Kid. | 山羊仔 | ˏShán ˏyéung ‘tsai. |
| 45. Kitten. | 貓仔 | ˏMíú ‘tsai. |
| 46. Lamb. | 羊仔　羔 | ˏYéung ‘tsai. ˏKò. |
| 47. Leopard. | 豹 | P‘áu². |
| 48. Lion. | 獅子 | ˏSz’ ‘tsz’. |

we except a few in Peking which have been given to the emperor by neighboring princes. It is said to be still found in the provinces of Wannám and Sz’ch‘üen.

31. The place for the flying squirrel and the bat has been as great a puzzle to Chinese systematists as the duck-billed platypus of Australia has been to European naturalists. Some have placed them among squirrels and others among birds; the *Pún Ts‘ò* and *I' Ngá* rank them among birds that have hairy wings.

32. Two different animals are described by these two characters in the *Pún Ts‘ò*, but the racoon-faced dog or Chinese fox (*Canis procyonoides* of Gray) is called by this name when brought to Canton; its hair is used to make pencils.

49. The figures given of this animal differ very much, for it appears to be a mere creature of imagination. One drawing of it partly resembles the fabled griffon of the Greeks; a spinous fin upon the back, a large horn upon the forehead, the claws and teeth of a lion, with the skin of a tiger, are its usual outlines.

| | | |
|---|---|---|
| 49. Lion-unicorn. | 獬豸 | ʿHái ʿchí. |
| 50. Manis or pangolin. | 穿山甲 鯪鯉 | ˏCh'ün ˏshán káp˳. ˏLing ʿlí. |
| 51. Mare. | 牝馬 草馬 騇 | ʿPan ʿmá. ʿTs'ò ʿmá. ʿShé. |
| 52. Marmot. | 土撥鼠 | ʿT'ò pút˳ ʿshü. |
| 53. Mole. | 田鼠 鼴鼠 | ˏTín ʿshü. Án' ʿshü. |
| 54. Monkey. | 獼猴 馬騮 | ˏNí ˏhau. ʿMá ˏlau. |
| 55. Proboscis monkey. | 果然 [illegible]獨 | ʿKwó ˏín. ʿHái tuk˳. |
| 56. Mouse. | 鼫鼠 | Shik˳ ʿshü. |
| 57. Shrew mouse. | 臊鼠 | ˏTsò ʿshü. |
| 58. Mule. | 騾 | ˏLui. |
| 59. Orang outang. | 狒狒 猩猩 | ʿFí ʿfí. ˏSing ˏsing. |
| 60. Otter. | 水獺 | ʿShui chát˳. |
| 61. Sea otter. | 海獺 | ʿHoi chát˳. |
| 62. Ox. | 閹牛 | ˏÍm ˏngau. |
| 63. Pig. | 猪仔 豚 | ˏChü ʿtsai. ˏT'un. |
| 64. Porcupine or hedgehog. | 蝟 箭猪 | Wai'. Tsín' ˏchü. |
| 65. Porpoise. | 河豚 魨 | ˏHó ˏt'un. ˏT'un. |

50. The scaly ant-eater or manis is common in China; the people say it is a fish with legs, that lives both on land and in water. The hairy scales and other parts of the body are thought to be powerful medicines by Chinese doctors, the saving efficacy of whose prescriptions in some cases appears to be in direct ratio to the strangeness of their ingredients.

54. The family of *ü* or monkeys in the *Pún Ts'ò* contains eight species, but the descriptions are too vague to identify them. The common monkey is said to be common in the mountains of Ukwóng and Fukkín; it is often brought to Canton by strolling mountebanks.

55. The first name *kwó ín* here given to the proboscis monkey is from the *Pún Ts'ò*, the second *hái tuk* is from Taberd's Annamese Dictionary. This animal is described from a specimen in Paris as of a "reddish brown color, the face black, and with a nose of extraordinary length." The Chinese account says "its nose is turned upwards, and the tail very long and forked at the end, and that whenever it rains, the animal thrusts the two forks into its nose. It goes in herds, and lives in friendship; when one dies, the rest accompany it to burial." The account goes on to state its activity, which is so great that it runs its head against the trees; its fur is soft and gray, the face black, and the body about three cubits high.

59. There appears to be two distinct animals described by these two names, but the accounts are not very precise; the principal difference between them consists in the mane or long hair from the head which covers the back of the *fífí*, and in its lips, which are so long as to cover its eyes when it laughs. The *singsing* is found on the west of China, is smaller than the former, and more nearly resembles a man in its hair and erect gait. It may be akin to the chimpanse, while the *fífí* is more nearly allied to the orang outang, both being perhaps new species of quadrumana.

66. This is the name given to a large cetaceous animal very common in the shallow waters of

| | | |
|---|---|---|
| 66. White porpoise. | 白鱀 | Pák꜀ ꜁kí. |
| 67. Rabbit. | 兔 | Tʻò꜄. |
| 68. Ram. | 牡羊　羊公 | ꜂Máu ꜁yéung. ꜁Yéung ꜀kung. |
| 69. Rat. | 老鼠　耗子 | ꜂Lò ꜂shü. Hò꜄ ꜂tsz꜄. |
| 70. Bamboo rat. | 竹丨 | Chuk꜆ ꜂shü. |
| 71. Granary rat. | 倉丨 | ꜀Tsʻong ꜂shü. |
| 72. Water rat. | 渠丨 | ꜁Kʻü ꜂shü. |
| 73. Rhinoceros. | 犀牛　兕 | ꜀Sai ꜁ngau. ꜁Tsz꜄. |
| 74. Seal. | 膃肭獸　海狗 | Út꜀ ꜀tò shau꜄. ꜂Hoi ꜂kau. |
| 75. Fur seal. | 芝蔴貂 | ꜀Chí ꜁má ꜀tíú. |
| 76. Sheep. | 綿羊 | ꜁Mín ꜁yéung. |
| 67. Sow. | 猪乸　猪母 | ꜀Chü ꜂ná. ꜀Chü ꜂mò. |
| 78. Squirrel. | 鬆鼠　黃鼠 | ꜀Sung ꜂shü. ꜁Wong ꜂shü. |
| 79. Stag. | 麋 | ꜁Mí. |
| 80. Stallion. | 牡馬　騭 | ꜂Máu ꜂má. Chʻat꜀ |
| 81. Tapir. | 貘　白豹 | Mak꜀. Pák꜆ pʻáu꜄. |
| 82. Tiger. | 老虎 | ꜂Lò ꜂fú. |
| 83. Benevolent tiger. | 騶虞 | ꜀Tsau ꜁ü. |
| 84. Unicorn. | 麒麟 | ꜁Kʻí ꜁lun. |
| 85. Weasel. | 鼬鼠 | ꜁Yau ꜂shü. |
| 86. Whale. | 鯨 | ꜁Kʻing. |
| 87. Wolf. | 豺狼 | ꜁Chʻái ꜁lóng. |
| 88. Yak or grunting ox. | 犛牛 | ꜁Máu ꜁ngau. |
| 89. Zebu. | 犎牛 | ꜁Fung ꜁ngau. |

the Pearl river below the Bogue. It is regarded with superstitious reverence by the fishermen, who release it whenever it gets entangled in their nets, a respect which may have originated in distaste of its oily flesh and its great strength. From a sight of it in the water, it appears to be a species of Delphinapterus. The snout is long and tapering, color of the skin like that of a scalded hog, and the body from six to eight feet in length.

83. This, like the lion-unicorn, is a fabulous animal, endowed with a disposition so benevolent that it never treads on living objects. It is introduced into this list, together with the unicorn, phœnix, and other imaginary creatures, on account of the comparisons drawn from their supposed qualities by Chinese writers.

## Section Third.

## BIRDS.

### 飛禽類第三章
꜀Fí ꜁k'am lui²; tai² ꜀sám ꜀chéung.

1. All birds are produced from eggs which are set upon till the young are hatched; they are divided into five orders according to their bills and claws.| The first order consists of falcons (or accipitres), which have crooked bills, sharp talons, and eat flesh; such as eagles and ospreys.|| The second order comprises sparrows (or passerinæ), which have straight bills, weak feet, and eat fruit and insects; such as crows and thrushes.||| Appended to the sparrows, is a small order, which have three claws before and one behind, and are expert in climbing trees; such as the parrot and woodpecker.|||| The third order consists of fowls (or gallinaceæ), whose legs are large, with a spur behind, and the wings small; such as the silver pheasant and the quail.一 The fourth order is composed of cranes (or the waders), which have long, naked legs, and the bill and neck proportionably long, and eat snakes and reptiles; such as the egret and stork.二 The fifth order comprises the ducks (or web-footed), whose feet are formed into a palm, and placed behind, to adapt them for swimming easily; such as the goose and duck.

蛋子分類食也直虫是類善啄鷄距鶉類頸如日生如
屬生仍鷹而是嘴果眉小一哥曰後鵰鶴嘴蛤一掌水
皆而爪曰利鳶類食畫有後鷄一有如曰而蛇也成遊也
禽鬪嘴一爪鷲雀而鴉雀三如也大短一長食是脚利是
飛捕其類曲如曰弱鳥附前樹是脚翼也裸長鷺類後鴨
凡生依五嘴肉一爪如也趾登木類而是脚配鸛鳧過鵝

꜁Fán ꜀fí ꜁k'am ꜀kái shuk₂ tán² ꜀shang, pò² tau' ꜁í 'ch'án 'tsz'; ꜀í ꜁k'í 'tsui 'cháu, ꜁ying ꜀fan ꜂'ng lui².| Yat꜄ üt₂ ꜀ying lui², 'tsui huk꜄, 'cháu lí², ꜁í shik₂ yuk₂; ꜁ü tsau², ꜁ün shí² ꜂yá. Yat꜄ üt₂ tséuk꜄ lui², 'tsui chik₂, 'cháu yéuk₂, ꜁í shik₂ 'kwó ꜁ch'ung; ꜁ü ꜀ú ꜀á, wá² ꜁mí shí² ꜂yá.|| Fú² tséuk꜄, ꜂yau 'síú lui², 'chí ꜁ts'ín ꜀sám hau² yat꜄, shín² ꜀tang shü²; ꜁ü ꜀ying ꜀kó, téuk꜄ muk₂ shí² ꜂yá. Yat꜄ üt₂ ꜀kai lui², kéuk꜄ tái², ꜂yau hau² kü² ꜁í yik₂ 'tün; ꜁ü ꜁hán ꜀shun shí² ꜂yá.一 Yat꜄ üt₂ hók₂ lui², kéuk꜄ 'kwó ꜁ch'éung, ꜁í 'tsui, 'king p'úi' ꜁ch'éung, shik₂ ꜁shé kóp꜄, ꜁ü kún' lò² shí² ꜂yá.二 Yat꜄ üt₂ ꜁fú lui², kéuk꜄ ꜁shing 'chéung ꜀shang kwó' hau² lí² ꜁yau 'shui; ꜁ü ꜁ngó áp꜄ shí² ꜂yá.

## *Notes and Explanations.*

BIRDS are not arranged by Chinese naturalists into different groups under certain conspicuous examples as animals are, but are classified according to their habitat, into water, earth or fountain,

| | | |
|---|---|---|
| 2. Avedavat, brown with red spots. | 梅花雀 | ˏMúi ˎfá tséukˏ. |
| 3. Avedavat, red and black with red spots. | 小紅娘 | ʻSíú ˏhung ˏnéung. |
| 4. Blackbird. | 山烏 | ˎShán ˎú. |
| 5. Bird of paradise. | 雀皇 | Tséukˏ ˏwóng. |
| 6. Canary-bird. | 時辰雀 白燕 | ˏShí ˏshan tséukˏ. Pákˎ in'. |
| 7. Capon. | 𠝹鷄 | Sín' ˎkai. |
| 8. Cardinal. | 高髻冠 | ˎKò kai' ˎkún. |
| 9. Chaffinch. | 金絲夾鵲 | ˎKam ˎsz' ˏtsʻz' tséukˏ. |
| 10. Chicken. | 鷄仔 | ˎKai ʻtsai. |
| 11. Cock. | 鷄公 | ˎKai ˎkung. |
| 12. Bantam (or short legged) cock. | 矮鷄 | ʻAi ˎkai. |
| 13. Silken cock. | 絲毛鷄 竹絲鷄 | ˎSz' ˏmò ˎkai. Chukˏ ˎsz' ˎkai. |
| 14. Fishing cormorant. | 鸕鷀 | ˏLò ˎtsz'. |
| 15. White crane. | 鸛 | Kún'. |
| 16. Red headed crane. | 鶴 | Hókˎ. |
| 17. Crockotoa. | 白鶯哥 | Pákˎ ˎying ˎkó. |
| 18. Crow. | 烏 烏鴉 鴉鵲 | ˎÚ. ˎÚ ˎá. ˎÁ tséukˏ. |
| 19. Crow-pheasant. | 芒公 | ˏMóng ˎkung. |

forest, and hill, birds. The introduction to the *kʻam pò*, order of birds, in the *Pún Tsʻò* exhibits their ideas upon the habits of birds generally: "Lí Shíchan says, 'what has two legs and feathers is called a (*kʻam*) bird.' Sz'kwóng says, 'The plumage of the 360 kinds of feathered beings (i. e. all birds) harmonises with the four seasons, and their hues correspond to the five quarters. Hill birds roost on cliffs, earth birds live on the ground; forest birds sing at dawn, water birds cry at night. The beaks of land birds are short, and their tails adorned; the bills of water birds are long, and their tails abbreviated. Birds are produced by laying eggs from under the wing, or by a change in the same class, (as when hawks become pigeons); or by transformation from different orders (as when moles become quails); or lastly by changing into lifeless beings (as sparrows turning into shells). Truly, if the laws of beings are so various as this, how diligent must the student be if he wishes to know them?" This section contains the English names of the most common birds, without endeavoring to refer them to their scientific genera. The terms employed in the first paragraph to indicate the orders of birds have been chosen on account of their being used in Chinese works as references for birds less common, and so far employed by them as types of families. The paragraph will afford to the Chinese student a sketch of modern classification in ornithology, and enable him to perceive the principles on which it is founded.

5. This significant name has been given to the bird of paradise by Mr. Beale of Macao; and it is now generally so called among the Chinese.

18. The character *ú* first applied to the crow now also means black or blackness; instances of this sort are frequent in the Chinese language.

廣東方言讀本



| | | |
|---|---|---|
| 20. Black crane. | 鶬鷄　鶬鴰 | ˬTs'ong ˬkai. ˬTs'ong k'ût˰. |
| 21. Dove. | 白鴿 | Pák˱ kóp˰. |
| 22. Drake. | 鴨公 | Áp˰ ˬkung. |
| 23. Duck. | 鴨　鶩 | Áp˰. Muk˱ |
| 24. Mandarin duck. | 鴛鴦　黃鴨鴠 | ˬÜn ˬyéung. ˱Wong áp˰ p'at˱. |
| 25. Wild duck, or mallard. | 水鴨　鳧 | ʻShui áp˰. ˱Fú. |
| 26. Eagle. | 鷲　神鷹 | Tsau². ˱Shan ˬying. |
| 27. Lammergyr eagle. | 皂鵰 | Tsò² ˬtiú. |
| 28. Egret. | 鷺鷥 | Lò² ˬtsz'. |
| 29. Falcon. | 鵻　白鷹 | ʻChun. Pák˱ ˬying. |
| 30. Hunting falcon. | 雀鵵 | Tséuk˰ ˬsung. |
| 31. Finches. | 黃雀 | ˱Wóng tséuk˰. |
| 32. Fish-hawk. | 鶚　魚鷹 | Ngók˱. ˱Ü ˬying. |
| 33. Flycatcher. | 京燕 | ˬKing in'. |
| 34. Fowls, or gallinaceous birds. | 鷄類 | ˬKai lui². |
| 35. Gander. | 鵝公 | ˱Ngo ˬküng. |
| 36. Goatsucker (?) | 杜鵑 | Tò² ˬkün. |
| 37. Goose. | 草鵞 | ʻTs'ò ˱ngó. |
| 38. Wild goose. | 鴻鴈　鴈鵞 | ˱Hung ngán². Ngan² ˱ngó. |
| 39. Goshawk, or buzzard. | 鶻 | Fuk˱. |
| 40. Wattled grackle. | 了哥　八哥 | ʻLiú ˬkó. Pát˰ ˬkó. |
| 41. Spotted grackle (or pie.) | 鵯 | Pat˱. |

24. The word 'mandarin' applied to this bird, denotes, as it does in a few other instances, its superiority over other ducks, and has no allusion to appropriation by officers of government; here, the superiority consists in its gay and grotesque coloring; at other times, as in the mandarin orange, the superiority consists in the flavor. There is nothing in the original to correspond to this term. The mandarin duck *(Anas galericulata)* occurs, according to the *Pún Ts'ò*, in the lakes of southern China, but it is not widely diffused. It is an emblem of conjugal fidelity among the Chinese, of which a singular instance once occurred at Mr. Beale's aviary in Macao: a drake was stolen from the inclosure, and during his absence, his mate received very marked attentions from another drake, to which she was obliged to submit, and which were all reported to her lord on his unexpected return, who thereupon avenged himself by pecking the unfortunate drake to death.

25. Under the name of *shui áp*, there are included many kinds of the wild water fowl, which frequent the shallows and inlets at the mouth of the Pearl river.

| | | |
|---|---|---|
| 42. Grebe. | 水奴 | 'Shui ˎnò. |
| 43. Grouse (?) | 雉鳩 | Chí² ˏkau. |
| 44. Gull. | 鷗 | ˏAu. |
| 45. Hawfinch. | 蠟嘴禾鵠 | Láp₂ 'tsui ˎwó kuk₃. |
| 46. Hawk. | 鷹 | ˏYing. |
| 47. Imperial or horned hawk. | 御鷹 角鷹 | Yü² ˏying. Kók₃ ˏying. |
| 48. Hen. | 鷄乸 | ˏKai 'ná. |
| 49. Heron. | 蒼鷺 艨艟 | ˏTs'óng lò². ˎMung ˎt' ung. |
| 50. Jacana. | 白勝鷄 | Pák₂ shing' ˏkai. |
| 51. Jay. | 鵲 | Tséuk₃. |
| 52. Reddish jay, with mottled wings. | 山和尙 | ˏShán ˎwó shéung². |
| 53. Kingfisher. | 魚狗 鴗 釣魚郎 | ˎÜ 'kau. Láp₂. Tíú' ˎü ˎlóng. |
| 54. Variegated kingfisher. | 翡翠 | 'Fí ts'ui'. |
| 55. Kite. | 怪鴟 | Kwái' ˏch'í. |
| 56. Crested lark. | 角䴇 | Kók₃ ˎling. |
| 57. Singing lark. | 百䴇 百鴒 | Pák₃ ˎling. Pák₃ ˎling. |
| 58. Wood lark. *Alauda.* | 山麻鵲 | ˏShán ˎmá tséuk₃. |
| 59. Magpie. | 四喜鵲 | Sz" 'hí tséuk₃. |
| 60. Blue magpie, with two long tail feathers. | 練鵲 | Lín² tséuk₃. |
| 61. Magpie, with a gradated tail. | 山喜鵲 | ˏShán 'hí tséuk₃ |
| 62. Mango bird. | 黃鶯 | ˎWóng ˏang. |
| 63. Owl. | 梟 貓兒頭鷹 | ˏHíú. ˎMíú ˎí ˎt'au ˏying. |
| 64. Horned owl. | 角鴟 鴟鵂 | Kók₃ ˏch'í. ˏCh'í ˏyau. |
| 65. Paddy bird. | 禾鵠 | ˎWó kuk₃. |
| 66. Parrot. | 鸚哥 鸚鵡 | ˏYing ˏkó. ˏYing 'mò. |
| 67. Partridge. | 鷓鴣 | Ché' ˏkú. |
| 68. Peacock. | 孔雀 | 'Hung tséuk₃. |

54. This most elegant little bird, of green and red plumage, is very common in the vicinity of Macao. The feathers are sometimes employed by artists to lay upon wires and frames in forming little grotto work and landscapes.

廣東方言讀本



| | | |
|---|---|---|
| 69. Pelican. | 塘鵝 | ˏT'óng ˏngó. |
| 70. Penguin. | 企鵝 | ʻK'í ˏngó. |
| 71. Common pheasant. | 山雞 | ˎShán ˎkai. |
| 72. Argus pheasant. | 鸞雞 | ˏLün ˎkai. |
| 73. Medallion pheasant. | 吐綬雞　鷊 | T'ò' shau$^{2}$ ˎkai. Yik$_{2}$. |
| 74. Silver pheasant. | 白鷴 | Pák$_{2}$ ˏhán. |
| 75. Golden pheasant. | 錦雞　鷩雉 | ʻKam ˎkai. Pít, chí$^{2}$. |
| 76. Tartar pheasant. | 雉雞 | Chí$^{2}$ ˎkai. |
| 77. Peacock pheasant. | 金錢雞 | ˎKam ˏts'ín ˎkai. |
| 78. Phœnix. | 鳳凰　鷰鳳 | Fung$^{2}$ ˏwóng. Ín' fung$^{2}$. |
| 79. Pigeon. | 班鳩 | ˎPán ˎkau. |
| 80. Brown pigeon. | 鴟鳩 | ˎCh'í ˎkau. |
| 81. Pullet. | 雞項 | ˎKai hóng$^{2}$. |
| 82. Quail. | 鵪鶉 | ˎAm ˏshun. |
| 83. Rail or wedge tailed partridge. | 竹雞 | Chuk, ˎkai. |
| 84. Red headed rail. | 白面雞 | Pák$_{2}$ mín$^{2}$ ˎkai. |
| 85. Rain harbinger. | 天天雀 | ˎT'ín t'ín tséuk,. |
| 86. Raven. | 鸚鵒　八哥 | ˎYing kuk,. Pát, ˎkó. |
| 87. Ringed raven. | 老鴉 | ʻLò ˎá. |
| 88. Robin. | 桂林相思 | Kwai' ˏlam ˎséung ˎsz'. |
| 89. Roc. | 鵬 | ˏP'ang. |

71—77. The splendid plumage and graceful motions of the pheasants found in China have long been the admiration of mankind. The gay and variegated vestment of the golden pheasant, and the beauty of the black and white silver pheasant, have caused them to be much sought after by the Chinese.

78. The argus pheasant appears to have been taken as the model for the Chinese phœnix, which, as a kind of form, they have bedecked with every natural and moral excellence. For notices of Chinese descriptions of the phœnix, unicorn, and other animals, the student is referred to several articles in the VIIth volume of the Chinese Repository.

82. The quail is used by the Chinese as a game bird, and great pains are bestowed upon its training, and large sums betted upon its prowess.

83. These two birds are thought to be sufficiently alike by the Chinese to have the same name, though their habits are very dissimilar. Instances of the sort are not uncommon, and perhaps others may occur in the section.

89. This bird corresponds sufficiently with the roc of Arabian history; it is fabled to be changed into a bird from the *kwan* fish, a monster of many miles in length.

| | | |
|---|---|---|
| 90. Sandpiper. | 秧鷄 | ˛Yéung ˛kai. |
| 91. Secretary, or snake eater. | 鴆 | ʻSham. |
| 92. Shrike or butcher bird. | 鵙　伯勞　伯鷯 | K'í'. Pák, ˛lò. Pak, ˛liú. |
| 93. Snipe. | 鷸　沙錐 | Kwat,. ˛Shá ˛chui. |
| 94. Hill snipe, brown back, gray spotted, tail short. | 山錐 | ˛Shán ˛chui. |
| 95. Sparrow. | 雀　麻雀 | Tséuk,. ˛Má tséuk,. |
| 96. Java sparrows. | 紅嘴 | ˛Hung ʻtsui. |
| 97. Sparrow hawk. | 鳶 | ˛Ün. |
| 98. Stork. | 鵁鶄 | ˛Káu ˛ts'ing. |
| 99. Rock swallow. | 胡燕 | ˛Ú ín'. |
| 100. Swallow or martin. | 燕 | Ín'. |
| 101. Swan. | 鵠　天鵞 | Kuk,. ˛T'ín ˛ngó. |
| 102. Tailor bird. | 巧婦鳥 | ʻHáu ʻfú ʻníú. |
| 103. Teal. | 小水鴨 | ʻSíú ʻshui áp,. |
| 104. Thrush. | 白畫眉 | Pák, wá' ˛mí. |
| 105. White eyed, gray thrush. | 畫眉 | Wá' ˛mí. |
| 106. Singing thrush. | 烏屎吉　豬屎偽 | ˛Ú ʻshí kat,. ˛Chü ʻshí chá'. |
| 107. Turkey. | 火鷄　駝鳥 | ʻFó ˛kai. ˛T'ó ʻníú. |
| 108. Turtle dove, ringed. | 鴟鳩 | ˛Ch'í ˛kau. |
| 109. Wagtail. | 鶺鴒 | Tsik, ˛ling. |
| 110. Warbler, a kind of robin. | 藍相思 | ˛Lám ˛séung ˛sz'. |
| 111. Warbler, a kind of nightingale or lark. | 鸎 | ˛Ying. |
| 112. Widgeon. | 鸊鷉 | Pik, ˛ch'í. |
| 113. Woodpecker. | 啄木鳥 | Téuk, muk, ʻníú. |
| 114. Wren. | 鷦鷯 | ˛Tsíú ˛líú. |

91. The body, feathers, and all that appertains to this bird are thought by the Chinese to be deadly poisons; its habits, as described, indicate its affinity to the secretary falcon of Africa.

98. The stork, crane, egret, and other shore birds are favorites of the Chinese; the crane is an emblem of longevity; and similes are taken from the soaring flight, periodical migrations, nightly screams, and other habits of these birds.

## Section Fourth.

## REPTILES.

### 鱗介類第四章

ˏLun kái' luiˎ; taiˎ sz' ˏchéung.

| | | |
|---|---|---|
| 1. All scaly and shelly [reptiles] are produced from eggs, which are not hatched by incubation; their blood is cold when fresh. They are divided into four orders according to the shape of their bodies. The first comprises tortoises, whose bodies are covered by their carapace; such as turtles. The second consists of lizards, whose bodies are scaly, and have four legs, such as crocodiles. The third consists of snakes, which have no legs, and their bodies are cylindrical and long; such as the boa. The fourth consists of frogs, whose bodies have no hair or scales; such as the toad. | 凡鱗介皆屬蛋生不捕鬪而出其血鮮冷因其身形仍分四類一曰龜類身以介盖如鼈是也一曰蠕蜓類身鱗四足如鱷魚是也一曰蛇類無足身圓且長如蟒是也一曰蛙類體無鱗毛如蟾蜍是也 | ˏFán ˏlun kái' ˏkái shuk, tánˎ ˏshang pat, pòˎ tau', ˏí ch'ut,; ˏk'í hüt, ˏsín ʻlang. ˏYan ˏk'í ˏshan ˏying, ˏying ˏfan sz' luiˎ. Yat, üt, ˏkwai luiˎ, ˏshan ʻí kái' k'oi', ˏü, pít, shiˎ ʻyá. Yat, üt, ʻín ˏt'ing luiˎ, ˏshan ˏlun, sz' tsuk,, ˏü ngok, ˏü shíˎ ʻyá. Yat, üt, ˏshé luiˎ, ˏmò tsuk,, ˏshan ˏün ʻch'é ˏch'éung, ˏü ʻmóng, shiˎ ʻyá. Yat, üt, ˏwá luiˎ, ʻt'ai ˏmò ˏlun ˏmò, ˏü ˏshím ˏshü shíˎ ʻyá. |
| 2. Adder. | 蝮 | Fuk,. |
| 3. Amphisbena. | 兩頭蛇 | ʻLéung ˏt'au ˏshé. |
| 4. Black snake. | 烏蛇 | ˏÚ ˏshé. |
| 5. Boa of Yunnan. | 蟒 巨蛇 | ʻMóng. Küˎ ˏshé. |
| 6. Cobra di capello. | 樸箕簏 | P'ók, ˏkí háp,. |
| 7. Crocodile. | 鱷魚 鼉龍 | Ngók, ˏü. ˏTò ˏlung. |

## *Notes and Explanations.*

REPTILES are not recognized as a separate class of animals in Chinese works; the title of this section means literally, the scaly and shelly class, and the introductory paragraph will indicate its restrictive sense as here used. Foreigners possess very little knowledge of the species comprised in this division of vertebrated animals, partly owing to their uninviting aspect or dangerous powers preventing their being brought by natives as objects of curiosity and sale, and partly to there having been no particular attention paid to them.

5. The *móng* appears to be the same as the anaconda of India, being very similar to it in size and habits. The *ím shé* (No. 21) is perhaps only another name for it, for Chinese writers on these

| | | |
|---|---|---|
| 8. Dragon of the sky. | 龍 | ˏLung. |
| 9. Dragon of the mountains. | 蛟 | ‹Káu. |
| 10. Dragon of the deep. | 螭 | ˏLí. |
| 11. Frog. | 蛙 鼃 田 鷄 蛤 乸 | ‹Wá. ‹Wá. ˏT'ín ‹kai. Kóp› ‘ná. |
| 12. Tree frog! | 山 蛤 | ˏShán kóp›. |
| 13. Striped frog. | 蝦 蟆 | ‹Há ˏmá. |
| 14. Gecko. | 雷 公 蛇 | ˏLui ‹kung ˏshé. |
| 15. Common lizard. | 蟾 蛇 | ˏShím ˏshé. |
| 16. House lizard. | 蝘 蜓 守 宮 壁 虎 | ‘Ín ˏt'ing. ‘Shau ‹kung. Pik› ‘fú. |
| 17. Livid earth lizard. | 蜥 蜴 石 龍 子 | Sik› yik›. Shik› ˏlung ‘tsz’. |
| 18. Red spotted lizard. | 蛤 蚧 | Kóp› kái’. |
| 19. Water lizard. | 蠑 螈 | ˏWing ˏün. |
| 20. Newt. | 鯑 | ˏT'ai. |
| 21. Large snake. | 蚺 蛇 南 蛇 | ˏÍm ˏshé. ˏNám ˏshé. |
| 22. Water snake. | 水 蛇 | ‘Shui ‹shé. |
| 23. Spotted snake. | 白 花 蛇 | Pák› ‹fá ˏshé. |
| 24. Tadpole. | 蝌 蚪 嚶 盎 仔 | ‹Fó ‘tau. ‹Ying óng’ ‘tsai. |
| 25. Toad. | 蟾 蜍 黽 | ˏShím ˏshü. ‘Mín. |
| 26. Tortoise. | 龜 | ‹Kwai. |
| 27. Shell tortoise. | 玳 瑁 龜 | Toi’ múi’ ‹kwai. |
| 28. Turtle. | 鱉 | Pít›. |
| 29. Green turtle. | 脚 魚 | Kéuk› ˏü. |

subjects exercise so little discrimination in their quotations, that they are easily led astray by a different name. Even in those objects which might be supposed most familiar, it is surprising how many names they bear among the common people, thereby causing no little trouble to ascertain which is the most correct.

8—10. The dragon of the sky, or the *lung*, is the most celebrated of all those fabulous beings, which the Chinese have invested with extraordinary attributes of a physical and moral nature. The dragon is considered as the emblem of imperial power and majesty, it is emblazoned on the dress of the emperor, surrounds all edicts that appertain to himself, the title pages of books printed by his authority, and more than anything else, may be regarded as the national coat of arms of the Chinese empire.

# Section Fifth.

## FISHES.

## 魚類第五章

ˏÜ lui$^{2}$; tai$^{2}$ ˏ'ng ꜀chéung.

1. All fishes are produced from eggs (or roe) scattered upon the banks of the ocean, from which the young afterwards are hatched of themselves. They are divided into two great classes, according as their bones are hard or soft. Soft boned (or cartilaginous) fishes are such as the eel, the shark, the sturgeon, &c. Hard boned (or osseous) fishes are arranged into nine orders according to their fins: as the dorsal fin being spinous makes one order, if flexible makes another order, &c.

凡魚類皆屬散
春於海傍而後
自出則以其骨
之剛柔而分二
大類骨之柔者
如鯶鯋鱘龍等
是也骨之剛者
以其翅而分九
類如背翅之刺
剛者爲一類柔
者爲一類

ˏFán ˏü lui$^{2}$ ꜀kái shuk, sán' ꜀ch'un ꜀ü 'hoi ˏp'óng ˏí hau, tsz'$^{2}$ ch'ut,. Tsak, 'í ˏk'i kwat, ꜀chí ꜀kóng ˏyau, ˏí ꜀fan í$^{2}$ tái$^{2}$ lui$^{2}$. Kwat, ꜀chí ˏyau 'ché, ˏü ˏshín, ꜀shá, ˏtsam ˏlung 'tang shí$^{2}$ 'yá. Kwat, ꜀chí ꜀kóng 'ché, 'í ˏk'í ch'í' ˏí ꜀fan 'kau lui$^{2}$; ˏü púi' ch'í' ꜀chí ts'z" ꜀kóng 'ché, ˏwai yat, lui$^{2}$, ˏyau 'ché ˏwai yat, lui$^{2}$.

### *Notes and Explanations.*

THE original form of the character *ü* somewhat resembled a fish, but in its present contracted shape, the similarity is nearly lost. Fish compose two tribes of the class *lun pò*, or scaly animals, in the *Pún Ts'ò*. Lí Shíchan, in his introduction to this class, says, "there are two orders of scaly animals, the aquatic and terrestrial, and although they are very unlike [in many things], still both are alike scaly; for dragons and snakes are sagacious animals, but the numerous families of fishes are nourished in the water: although the two classes differ, still they mutually pass into each other in their metamorphosis; for, if their bodies do vary greatly, they are affected in the same manner. The tribes of scaly animals are all produced from eggs, though the adder is born from the womb. The eyes of fishes do not close, though porpoises can move their eyes. The tail of the blue snake is a remedy for the poison of its head; and the skin of the shark removes all the concretions (or accumulations) of minced fish."

There are thirty-one sorts of scaly fishes, and twenty-eight of scaleless fishes, crabs, prawns, crawfish, &c., described. Under the radical *ü* in the Imperial Dictionary, the principal families of fishes are assorted by their most common species, though as might be supposed with no very great exactitude. The fishes in this section are chiefly those found in the waters about Canton and Macao, though they are not, probably, more than a moiety of them, so numerous are the species in these markets; their native names were obtained from drawings in the possession of Mr. Beale of Macao, which he kindly loaned for examination. They were all painted from the life, under the constant inspection of a foreigner, and as far as external characters go, the genus can be ascertained, though the teeth and gill membranes are in many cases necessary to determine them accurately. The brief descriptions here given are intended to be supplementary to the fuller one given to the genus in ichthyological works, to which reference should be made for a complete account. The generic names, which are principally those of groups or tribes, are from Cuvier's large work on fishes.

| | | |
|---|---|---|
| 2. Anchovy; body silvery, back high, anal long, pectoral long, before the ventral *Thryssa.* | 馬鮆 | ʻMá ʻtsai. |
| 3. Anchovy; first pectoral rays free, anal joined to caudal, long tapering body. *Thryssa.* | 鳳尾 | Fung² ʻmi. |
| 4. Anchovy; hairy processes behind gills, belly serrate, dorsal far back. *Engraulis?* | 青狐 | ˏTsʻing ˏkú. |
| 5. Band-fish; no caudal fin, reddish yellow, body thin tapering. *Cepola.* | 紅帶 | ˏHung tái². |
| 6. Barbel; four cirri, brown and yellowish, no spines, fins short. *Barbus.* | 嘉魚 | ˏKá ˏü. |
| 7. Blenny; green cylindrical body, red ring on the tail, 2 cirri. *Blennius?* | 烏魚 | ˏÚ ˏü. |
| 8. Bream; broad body, no cirri, pectoral small, dorsal long, spines weak. *Cyprinus.* | 鯽魚 | Tsik, ˏü. |
| 9. Bream; body broad, no cirri, 2 dorsal spines, anal long. *Cyprinus.* | 扁魚 | ʻPín ˏü. |
| 10. Bream; broad, angular, silvery green, one dorsal spine, no cirri. *Gobio?* | 扁魚 | ʻPín ˏü. |
| 11. Carp; general name for oblong cyprini with large fins and cirri. | 鯉魚 | ʻLí ˏü. |
| 12. Carp; dark red fins thin and large, spine jagged, 4 cirri, dark brown. *Cyprinus.* | 芙蓉鯉 | ˏFú ˏyung ʻli. |
| 13. Carp; 4 cirri, body broad, greenish brown, fins small, reddish. *Cyprinus.* | 綠鯉 | Luk₂ ʻlí. |
| 14. Carp; 4 cirri, reddish fins, body whitish brown, spines jagged. *Cyprinus.* | 塘｜ | ˏTʻóng ʻlí. |
| 15. Carp; 4 cirri, tail black, broad body, head somwhat emarginate. *Cyprinus.* | 黑｜ | Hak, ʻlí. |
| 16. Carp; 2 cirri, greenish, red tail, broad, dorsal spine jagged. *Cyprinus.* | 海｜ | ʻHoi ʻlí. |
| 17. Carp; 2 cirri, tail red, body angular, spines notched. *Cyprinus.* | 上海鱲 | Shéung² ʻhoi láp₂. |
| 18. Carp; 4 cirri, body reddish green, caudal and pectoral fins red. *Cyprinus.* | 火鯉 | ʻFó ʻlí. |
| 19. Carp; 4 cirri, back spotted, body angular, fins colored. *Cyprinus.* | 展鯉 | Kik₂ ʻlí. |
| 20. Carp; fins dark brown, body blunt, and spine serrate. *Cyprinus.* | 縮骨鯽 | Shuk, kwat, tsik,. |
| 21. Carp; body broad, angular, light green, mouth very small. *Cyprinus.* | 展魚 | Kik₂ ˏü. |
| 22. Carp; yellowish red, ventral before dorsal, tail reddish banded. *Cyprinus.* | 金鯽 | ˏKam tsik,. |
| 23. Chætodon; green and yellow banded, black spot on dorsal, body round. *Chætodon.* | 尖嘴鱲 | ˏTsím ʻtsui láp₂. |
| 24. Chætodon; two inches long, greenish spotted black. *Chætodon.* | 金鼓 | ˏKam ʻkú. |
| 25. Chætodon; yellow, black band across the head and tail, mouth turned up. *Chætodon.* | 荷包金 | ˏHó ˏpáu ˏkam. |
| 26. Chætodon; long finned, body broader than long, brown banded. *Platax.* | 飛翼 | ˏFí yik₂. |

11.—22. The carp is one of the most common fishes in China. Some of the species are raised in tubs and tanks, where the water is constantly flowing, and grow to a very large size; others are raised in fish-ponds. Carp are generally hawked about the streets alive, while lying in shallow water.

23.—26. The Chinese names of fishes are sometimes very descriptive. 'Tapering beaked perch,' 'golden drum,' 'golden money-pouch,' 'flying wings,' &c., are some of the expressive names given to species of chætodon.

| | | |
|---|---|---|
| 27. Chætodon; silvery ash color, body roundish with irregular dark spots. *Chætodon.* | 銀扁魚 | ꜀Ngan ꜂pín ꜀ü. |
| 28. Chætodon; greenish with dark stripes, fleshy fins small, 11 dorsal spines. *Chætodon.* | 柴魚 | ꜀Ch'ái ꜀ü. |
| 29. Chætodon; blackish spotted, operculum scaly, back fins square. *Pimelepterus.* | 黑石鱲 | Hak꜆ shik꜆ láp꜆. |
| 30. Chætodon; body roundish, banded greenish, dorsal spines freeish. *Ephippus.* | 銀拱 | ꜀Ngan ꜂kung. |
| 31. Dace; tail yellow, 2 dorsal spines, no anal spine, no cirri, fins small. *Leuciscus.* | 黃尾鯪 | ꜀Wóng ꜂mí ꜀ling. |
| 32. Dace; no spines or cirri, greenish yellowish, 8 dorsal, 14 anal, rays. *Leuciscus.* | 鱅魚 | ꜀Yung ꜀ü. |
| 33. Dace; broad, whitish, blue spots near gills, ventral behind dorsal. *Leuciscus.* | 土鯪 | ꜂T'ò ꜀ling. |
| 34. Diodon; with a globular prickly body. *Diodon.* | 竻泡 | Lik꜇ p'áu꜄. |
| 35. Dory; silvery white, head depressed; body rhomboidal, ventrals long. *Scyris.* | 長翼芒 | ꜀Ch'éung yik꜇ ꜀móng. |
| 36. Dory; silvery, fins short, head oblique, dorsal and anal rays long. *Scyris.* | 白鬚公 | Pák꜇ ꜀sú ꜀kung. |
| 37. Dory; body clouded, oval, anal spinous, dorsal continuous. *Amphacanthus?* | 黎猛 | ꜀Lai ꜂máng. |
| 38. Dog-fish; ashy, with black spotted bands; 18 inches long. *Scyllium ornatum.* | 跌墮沙 | Tít꜆ tò꜅ ꜀shá. |
| 39. Dragon-weever; brown back, purple belly, black dorsal, 2 large gill spines. *Percis.* | 角魚 | Kók꜆ ꜀ü. |
| 40. Dragonet; umber, head $\frac{1}{3}$ of length, dorsals separate, 12 anal rays. *Platycephalus.* | 沙甲 | ꜀Shá káp꜆. |
| 41. Dragonet; belly greenish, back umber, flat, head 4 rows of spines. *Platycephalus.* | 刀甲 | ꜀Tò káp꜆. |
| 42. Dried fish from Bombay, called Bombay ducks. | 狗吐乾 | ꜂Kau t'ò꜄ ꜀kòn. |
| 43. Eel; no pectoral, umber, with black spots, 2 cirri, mouth deeply cleft. *Muræna.* | 鱲鎚 | Láp꜇ ꜀chui. |
| 44. Eel; general name for those with fins and spiracles. | 鱓　鰌 | ꜀Shín. ꜀Yau. |
| 45. White or light colored eel. Yellow eel. | 白鱔　黃鱓 | Pák꜇ ꜀shín. ꜀Wóng ꜀shín. |
| 46. Red eel. Large eel. | 血〡　骨〡 | Hüt꜆ ꜀shín. Kwat꜆ ꜀shín. |
| 47. Conger eel; pectorals large. *Anguilla.* | 鰻鱺 | Mán꜅ lai꜅. |
| 48. File-fish; back slate colored, yellow pectoral and tail, 2 ventral spines. *Balistes.* | 剝皮洋 | Mók꜆ ꜀p'í ꜀yéung. |
| 49. File-fish; large, body reddish gray, no ventrals, dorsal spine very small. *Aluteres.* | 沙猛 | ꜀Shá ꜂máng. |
| 50. File-fish; blackish, tail banded, lateral line angular, spine jagged. *Monocanthus.* | 黑皮洋 | Hak꜆ ꜀p'í ꜀yéung. |
| 51. Fishing-frog; dark ashy color, with cutaneous cirri; four dorsal spines. *Lophius.* | 震麻魚　虎魚 | Chan꜄ ꜀má ꜀ü. ꜂Fú ꜀ü |
| 52. Fistularia; body and fins red, mouth at end of a long tube, teeth large. *Fistularia.* | 馬鞭 | ꜂Má ꜀pín. |
| 53. Flounder; reddish brown, eyes left, teeth large. *Platessa.* | 左口撻沙 | ꜂Tsó ꜂hau tát꜆ ꜀shá. |

42. *Kau t'ò* is the name of a small species of salmon about the same size, to which the Chinese term refers.

43—47. The number of species of eels found in the markets exceeds what are here men-

| | | |
|---|---|---|
| 54. Flounder; reddish, with many dark spots, eyes right, fins yellowish. *Platessa.* | 破篷 | Pʻóʼ ˏpʻung. |
| 55. Fluke; marbled brown, fins lighter spotted, eyes right and others left. *Platessa.* | 花正鼻 | ˎFá chingʼ pʻíʼ. |
| 56. Flying-fish; pectorals very long reaching to the caudal. *Exocetus.* | 飛魚 鰩 | ˎFí ˏü. ˏÍú. |
| 57. Gar-pike; green back, silvery belly, long snout, anal longer than dorsal. *Belone.* | 鶴浸 | Hók, tsamʼ. |
| 58. Gar-pike; small, silvery, black spot on tail, dorsal near tail. *Belone.* | 鶴浸 | Hók, tsamʼ. |
| 59. Garoupa; marbled dusky red, fins banded, 11 dorsal spines, head smooth. *Merra?* | 石斑魚 | Shik, ˎpán ˏü. |
| 60. Tortoise-shell garoupa; marked in angular spots, reddish. *Chrysophris?* | 玳瑁斑 | Toiʼ mòʼ ˎpán. |
| 61. Garoupa; brick red spots on a brown ground, operculum 2 points. *Chrysophris?* | 花石斑 | ˎFá shik, ˎpán. |
| 62. Garoupa; dark red marbled, lower jaw projects, preoperculum serrate. *Centropristis?* | 花斑魚 | ˎFá ˎpán ˏü. |
| 63. Gilt-head; marked in squares of yellow and blue, dorsal yellow striped. *Dentex?* | 鶯哥鯉 | ˏAng ʻkó ʻlí. |
| 64. Gilt-head; head blue, body reddish brown, fins red, head smooth. *Dentex?* | 紅鶯哥 鯉 | ˎHung ˏang ˎkó ʻlí. |
| 65. Gilt-head; yellowish green with blue stripes, fins spotted blue. *Dentex?* | 花鶯紅 | ˎFá ˎang ʻkó. |
| 66. Gilt-head; back bright red, fins yellowish red, upper ray of tail long. *Sparus.* | 紅杉 | ˏHung ˎshám. |
| 67. Gilt-head; head smooth, two first rays of dorsal filamentous. *Pagrus?* | 錦鮹 牛尼鮹 | ʻKam ˎshau. ˏNgau ʻmí ˎshau |
| 68. Gilt-head; head purplish, body brown and yellow striped, operculum scaly. *Sparus.* | 畫眉鱭 | Wáʼ ˏmí ˏtsʻò. |
| 69. Gilt-head; blackish, 2 greenish bands, tail whitish, belly yellow. *Amphiprion?* | 海金魚 | ʻHoi ˎkam ˏü. |
| 70. Gold fish; body golden red, fins large, dorsal often wanting. *Cyprinus.* | 金魚 | ˎKam ˏü. |
| 71. Gudgeon; 3 inches long, spotted umber back, belly purple, dorsal entire. *Gobius.* | 擗口狗 | Mák, ʻhau ʻkau. |
| 72. Gudgeon; 5 inches, brown back, blue belly, spotted, first dorsal small. *Gobius.* | 趕鷄棒 | ʻKón ˎkai ʻpʻáng. |
| 73. Gudgeon; green back, dingy belly, first dorsal 5 rayed, ventral large. *Gobius.* | 白蛤 | Pák, kóp,. |
| 74. Gudgeon; anal and 2d dorsal nearly equal, brown back, belly lighter. *Gobius.* | 長腰稔 | ˏChʻéung ˎíú ʻnam. |
| 75. Gudgeon; brown, spotted, 1st dorsal 6, second 9 rayed, ventral large. *Gobius.* | 筍殼 | ʻSun hók,. |
| 76. Gudgeon; 1st dorsal 6 rayed, fins rounded, large, spotted brown body. *Gobius.* | 稔魚 | ʻNam ˏü. |
| 77. Gudgeon; spotted green, 1st dorsal 5 rays, partly free. *Periopthalmus.* | 花亻 彈塗 | ˎFá ˏü. ˏTán ˏtò. |

tioned; some of them are so much like water snakes in external appearance, that those reptiles have been added by travelers to the list of strange viands found on the tables of the Chinese. The *tʻang shin*, or rattan eel, so called from its small size and yellowish color; the *mún shín* or large murena; the *shá líú*, or sand borer, and others, also occur.

59—62. Under the name of *shik pán ü*, or *pán ü*, the Chinese include such fish as have dark red marbled bodies, small scales, and spinous fins. There appears to be several genera comprised under this name, whose distinctive differences are not well ascertained. The first in the list is the species commonly brought upon the tables of foreigners.

61.—69. The gobies or gudgeons are seen in abundance in the markets, where by sprinkling

| | | |
|---|---|---|
| 78. Gurnard; large blue pectoral, 2 dorsals, body red and green, fins red. *Trigla.* | 藍翼魚 | ꜁Lám yik$_{2}$ ꜁ü. |
| 79. Gurnard; body reddish, 2 spines projecting beyond mouth, 2 fleshy cirri. *Trigla.* | 紅角 | ꜁Hung kók꜄. |
| 80. Hemiramphus; light bluish silvery, ventral near tail, anal short. *Hemiramphus.* | 長短浸 | ꜁Ch'éung ꜂tün tsam꜄. |
| 81. Herring; greenish white, anal fin long, ventrals small, belly trenchant. *Clupea.* | 鰽白 | ꜁Ts'ò pák$_{2}$. |
| 82. Herring; dark green, body broad, belly trenchant, dorsal and ventral opposite. *Clupea.* | 青鱗 | ꜀Ts'ing ꜁lun. |
| 83. Herring; greenish white, mouth small, anal near tail, ventral with 4 rays. *Gobio.* | 長腰鱗 | ꜁Ch'éung ꜀íú ꜁lun. |
| 84. Herring; greenish, mouth small, belly smooth, ventrals opposite dorsal. *Clupea?* | 黃澤 | ꜁Wóng chák$_{2}$. |
| 85. Herring; small, body silvery, belly smooth, ventrals near anal. *Clupea?* | 海河 | ꜂Hoi ꜁hó. |
| 86. Herring; lateral line large, dorsal emarginate, behind the pectoral. *Megalops.* | 忌魚 | Kí$^{2}$ ꜁ü. |
| 87. Herring; yellowish green, belly dentated, 6 spots on the back. *Chatoessus.* | 黃亻 | ꜁Wóng ꜁ü. |
| 88. Herring; bluish silvery, last ray of dorsal shortish, lateral line large. *Megalops.* | 坑鰽白 | ꜀Háng ꜁ts'ò pák$_{2}$. |
| 89. Herring; body long, silvery, fins small, dorsal ray long. *Megalops.* | 水滑 | ꜂Shui wát$_{2}$. |
| 90. Herring; upper jaw emarginate, teeth exsert, body silvery green. *Chirocentrus.* | 布刀 | Pò꜄ ꜀tò. |
| 91. Herring; body broad, silvery, anal low, ventrals small. *Megalops.* | 黃魚海 | ꜁Wóng ꜁ü ꜂hoi. |
| 92. Herring; belly serrate, ventral small, rays 7, partly free. *Clupea.* | 三黎 | ꜀Sám ꜁lai. |
| 93. Holocentrum; head red, body with 5 red stripes, spines large. *Holocentrum.* | 將軍甲 | ꜀Tséung ꜀kwan káp꜄. |
| 94. Holocentrum; striped dark and light red, tail cleft, 3 gill spines. *Holocentrum.* | 金鱗甲 | ꜀Kam ꜁lun káp꜄. |
| 95. Labrus; gray, back and fins spotted black, lips large, operculum acute. *Labrus.* | 花軟唇 | ꜀Fá ꜂ün ꜁shan. |
| 96. Labrus; reddish brown, with black scales, fins green, anal scaly 3 spines. *Labrus.* | 軟唇鱲 | ꜂Ün ꜁shan láp$_{2}$. |
| 97. Labrus; tail red, body banded gray and brown, 11 dorsal spines. *Crenilabrus.* | 石刼鱲 | Shik$_{2}$ kíp꜄ láp$_{2}$. |
| 98. Labrus; body and fins yellowish, mouth vertical, dorsal 7 spinous rays. *Crenilabrus.* | 黃皮頭石首魚 | ꜁Wóng ꜁p'í ꜁tau, Shik$_{2}$ ꜂shau ꜁ü. |
| 99. Labrus; body yellowish-greenish, lateral line crooked, tail rounded. *Labrus.* | 黃畫 | ꜁Wóng wák$_{2}$. |
| 100. Labrus; reddish green spotted, operculum scaly, one ventral spine. *Crenilabrus.* | 金絲衲 | ꜀Kam ꜀sz' náp$_{2}$. |
| 101. Labrus: lateral line wavy, silvery gray, back elevated, operculum acute. *Labrus?* | 亂皮鱲 | Yan$^{2}$ ꜁p'í láp$_{2}$. |
| 102. Labrus; dorsal continuous, mouth small, prolonged, head smooth. *Julis.* | 石刼 | Shik$_{2}$ kíp꜄. |

a little water upon them they are kept alive for two or three days. As seen in the markets, wriggling in the watery slime which keeps them alive, the gobies appear very repulsive as an article of food.

95.—103. The first two species in this list are undoubtedly true labri, and the others belong to that extensive group of fishes, but perhaps the sub-genera to which they are referred may not be correct, for, so many generic marks are derived from the teeth, the number of gill-rays, and the minute dentations of the operculum, preoperculum, and other parts about the gills, which

| | | |
|---|---|---|
| 103. Labrus; long even dorsal and anal, smooth head, red eyes, greenish. *Julis?* | 海龍 | ʻHoi ˌlung. |
| 104. Loche; 4 cirri, umber, spotted, pectoral 5 rayed, opposite the dorsal. *Cobitis.* | 沙錐 | ˏShá ˏchui. |
| 105. Mackerel; five finlets, marbled green, no carina, dorsals separate. *Auxis.* | 花鯕 | ˏFá ˏchʻi. |
| 106. Mackerel; fusiform, row of black spots on back, 5 finlets both sides. *Auxis.* | 花鯕 | ˏFá ˏchʻi. |
| 107. Mackerel; first dorsal blackish, body greenish, no horizontal spine. *Caranx?* | 方丨 | ˏFòng ˏchʻí. |
| 108. Mackerel; greenish, dorsals near, pectorals yellow, line mailed. *Caranx.* | 蝦丨 | ˏHá ˏchʻí. |
| 109. Mackerel; lateral line carinated, prominent, 8 finlets, pectorals long. *Orcynus.* | 扁甲鯕 | ʻPín káp, ˏchʻí. |
| 110. Mackerel; 9 finlets above, 7 below, no caudal carina, dorsals near. *Auxis.* | 赤甲鯕 | Chʻik, káp, ˏchʻí. |
| 111. Mackerel; one dorsal, equaling anal, one finlet, line mailed, silvery green. *Auxis?* | 鯕魚 | ˏChʻí ˌü. |
| 112. Mackerel; yellowish-green, 1st dorsal a spine, dorsal and anal long. *Caranx?* | 黃乳 | ˌWóng ʻyü. |
| 113. Mackerel: names of Scomberoides in books. | 鯖　馬鮫 | ˏTsing. ʻMá ˏkáu. |
| 114. Mango-fish; silvery slate color, dorsals separate, filaments 6, short. *Polynemus.* | 馬鮫郎 | ʻMá ˏkáu ˌlóng. |
| 115. Mango-fish; slate, 4 filaments, fins black, first dorsal 7 rays. *Polynemus.* | 馬友　馬母 | ʻMá ʻyau. ʻMá ʻmò. |
| 116. Moon-gazer; reddish brown, clouded, many cirri, pectorals broad. *Blepsias.* | 石獅子 | Shik, ˏsz' ʻtsz'. |
| 117. Mullet; light green, scales on back marked, fins and tail yellowish. *Mugil.* | 黃尾鰶 | ˌWòng ʻmi ʻtsai. |
| 118. Mullet; tail purplish, body silvery green, angular muzzle reddish. *Mugil.* | 白鰶 | Pák, ʻtsai. |
| 119. Mullet; silvery, striped with brown, ventral forward, dorsal and anal equal. *Mugil.* | 烏頭 | ˏÚ ˌtʻau. |
| 120. Mullet; back angular, silvery, head blunt, anal large, one spined. *Mugil.* | 蜆魚 | ʻHín ˌü. |
| 121. Ophicephalus; dorsal long, body cylindrical clouded, tail round. *Ophicephalus.* | 生丨 | ˏShang ˌü. |
| 122. Parrot-fish; dusky green above, yellow belly, dorsal 9 spiny rays. *Scarus.* | 翠鱗錐 | Tsʻui' ˌlun ˏchui. |
| 123. Parrot-fish; darkl green, fins and mouth blue edged, scales large. *Scarus.* | 青衣 | ˏTsʻing ˏí. |
| 124. Parrot-fish; dark slate, banded, fins yellow, tail spotted white. *Scarus.* | 雞公魚 | ʻKai ˏkung ˌü. |
| 125. Parrot-fish; blue stripes, fins edged blue, belly yellow, teeth notched. *Scarus.* | 碎牙 | Tsui' ˌngá. |

cannot be ascertained from drawings, that it is not unlikely some of them may be referred to the wrong genus. The same remark applies to the groups included under the English names of gilt-head, garoupa, mackerel, perch and dory.

114, 115. The second of these is a delicate fish, and much sought after, by the Chinese; it is called salmon by foreigners, upon whose tables it is no stranger. The first is much smaller, and considered by some to be superior. A common saying in the market of Macao runs thus: *Tai yat móng, tai í tsóng, tai sám má káu lóng,* "First the silure, then the pomfret, and third, the small polynemus." This fish, also called bynni-carp, is common in the river Nile.

121. *Shang ü,* or living fish, is a very appropriate name for the ophicephalus, whose power of living for a long time out of water by means of the peculiar mechanism of its gills is so well known. It is hawked about the streets in shallow tubs, and cut up alive as it is sold.

| | | |
|---|---|---|
| 126. Pegasus; snout salient, body mailed, pectorals large, wing like. *Pegasus.* | 飛魚　鷹魚 | ‹Fí ‚ü. ‹Ying ‚ü. |
| 127. Perch; dorsal emarginate, opposite the ventral and pectoral, head blunt. *Perca?* | 鰄頭 | Wák$_2$ ‚t'au. |
| 128. Perch; dark reddish brown, gills unarmed, scaly, dorsal emarginate. *Anthias?* | 黑鰽 | Hak$_3$ ‚ts'ò. |
| 129. Perch; operculum scaly, body silvery, yellowish lower fins. *Anthias?* | 白花 | Pák$_2$ ‹fá. |
| 130. Perch; light green, spotted opercular spine large, scales minute. *Therapon?* | 釘公魚 | ‹Ting ‹kung ‚ü. |
| 131. Perch; body yellowish green, mouth prolonged, operculum acute. *Mesoprion?* | 石角鯽 | Shik$_2$ kók$_3$ tsik$_3$. |
| 132. Perch; dark red, back wavy, operculum scaly, teeth hooked. *Mesoprion.* | 火鰽 | ʻFó ‚ts'ò. |
| 133. Perch; body silvery, fins reddish, operculum dentated, dorsal scaly. *Corvina?* | 黃丨 | ‚Wóng ‚ts'ò. |
| 134. Perch; 2d anal spine large, top of head and tail red, body greenish. *Pelates.* | 頭鱸 | ‚T'au ‚lò. |
| 135. Perch; body brown-silvery, operculum scaly, acute. *Serranus?* | 白鱸 | ‹Pák ‚lò. |
| 136. Perch; small, gills scaly, acute, body green, striped brown. *Serranus?* | 唱歌婆 | ‹Ch'éung ʻko ‚p'ó. |
| 137. Perch; body reddish brown, clouded, head rough, 12 dorsal spines. *Myripristis?* | 石狗公 | Shik$_2$ ʻkau ‹kung. |
| 138. Perch; mouth large, body brown, banded, first dorsal 8 spiny rays. *Ambassis?* | 黑石班 | Hak$_3$ shik$_2$ pán. |
| 139. Perch; eyes large, back and dorsal red, mouth vertical, tail rayed. *Priacanthus.* | 大眼鱲 | Tái$^2$ ʻngán láp$_2$. |
| 140. Perch; preoperculum smooth, serrate, body brown, mouth projecting. *Crenilabrus?* | 頭鱸 | ‚T'au ‚lò. |
| 141. Perches, or other similar fishes with spinous fins. | 鯛　鮸 | ‹Tíú. ʻMín. |
| 142. Perch-pike; 3 hooked front teeth, back brown, belly silvery. *Lucio-perca.* | 三牙 | ‹Sám ‚ngá. |
| 143. Pilot-fish; fusiform, 8 free dorsal spines, purplish black, striped. *Elacates.* | 黑鮫 | Hak$_3$ ‹káu. |
| 144. Pipe fish; head like a horse's, body mailed. *Syngnathus.* | 海馬 | ʻHoi ʻmá. |
| 145. Plaice; eyes right, dark brown spotted, fins bluish, pectorals red. *Platessa.* | 花破篷 | ‚Fá p'ó' ‚p'ung. |
| 146. Plaice; ashy with lighter spots, fins bluish, eyes left, dorsal short. *Platessa.* | 正鼻 | Ching' pí$^2$. |
| 147. Plaice; dark reddish brown, teeth large, tail broad, distinct. *Platessa.* | 左口 | ʻTsó ʻhau. |
| 148. Pomfret; body broad, no dorsal spines, greenish, fins equal. *Stromateus.* | 蒼魚　鯧 | ‹Ts'óng ‚ü. ‹Ch'éung. |
| 149. Pomfret; purplish greenish, long pectorals, lateral line silvery. *Stromateus.* | 黑蒼 | Hak$_3$ ‹ts'óng. |
| 150. Pomfret; 5 dorsal & 3 anal spines, body broad, yellowish, ventrals small. *Kurtus.* | 黃蠟蒼 | ‚Wóng láp$_2$ ‹ts'óng. |
| 151. Pomfret; oval, first dorsal 6 rayed, silvery, tail small. *Caranx?* | 花蒼 | ‹Fá ‹ts'óng. |

127.—140. The remarks upon the genus Labrus apply with equal force to the fishes grouped under perch, Sciæna, and Sparus, most of the distinctions between which consist in the position of the teeth, dentations of the gill-covers, and number of rays in the gills, which cannot be accurately ascertained from drawings. Many of them are among the most common fishes in these markets.

| | | |
|---|---|---|
| 152. Pomfret; blunt head, body oval, reddish-green, dorsal long, few spines. *Equula?* | 瓜子蒼 | ‹Kwá ‘tsz’ ‹ts‘ong. |
| 153. Pomfret; ventrals long, body purplish green, anal and dorsal equal. *Vomer.* | 跳板魚 | Tíú’ ‘pán ˏü. |
| 154. Ray; 3 rows of spines on back, head broad, spotted white. *Rhina acylostoma.* | 琵琶沙 | ˏP‘í ‹p‘á ‹shá. |
| 155. Ray; tail spinous, back umber, spotted, few spines, nose sharp, belly purple. *Raia.* | 冰紗鯆 | ‹Ping ‹shá ‹po. |
| 156. Ray; reddish brown, spines arranged like a T, 2 dorsals on tail. *Raia.* | 黃點丨 | ˏWong ‘tím ‹pò. |
| 157. Ray; head projecting, body reddish brown, tail thrice as long as body. *Myliobates.* | 張鶯 | ‹Chéung ‹ang. |
| 158. Ray; broad, greenish brown, spotted, tail long and slender like a whip. *Myliobates.* | 花點張鶯 | ‹Fá ‘tím ‹chéung ‹ang. |
| 159. Ray; dark reddish green, body semicircular, tail short. *Anacanthus.* | 鯆荖 | ‹Pò ‘lò. |
| 160. Ray; comprising such as are broad. | 鱝 海鷂魚 | ‘Fan. ‘Hoi ˏíú ˏü. |
| 161. Roach; fusiform, brownish green, red eyes, dorsal and ventrals opposite. *Leuciscus.* | 蠢魚 | ‘Ch‘un ˏü. |
| 162. Roach; fusiform, greenish, lateral line flexuous, one dorsal spine. *Leuciscus.* | 藍刀 | ˏLám ‹tò. |
| 163. Roaches, or other similar cyprini. | 鰣 鰱 鱒 | ˏShí. ˏLín. ‘Ts‘ün. |
| 164. Salmon; speckled reddish, pectorals black, ventral and dorsal opposite. *Salmo.* | 狗吐魚 | ‘Kau t‘ò’ ˏü. |
| 165. Salmon; brown back, silvery belly, mouth deeply cleft, head smooth. *Osmerus?* | 錦鱗鎚 | ‘Kam ˏlun ‹chui. |
| 166. Sciæna; operculum scaly, ventral and pectoral opposite, body silvery. *Sciæna?* | 鰽魚 | ˏTs‘ò ˏü. |
| 167. Sciæna; body and fins red, green spot on back, dorsal and gills scaly. *Hæmulon?* | 雄丨 | ˏHung ˏü. |
| 168. Sciæna; silvery brown, preoperculum serrated, tail reddish at the end. *Pristiproma?* | 鷄丨 | ‹Kai ˏü. |
| 169. Sciæna; body reddish orange, dorsal rays freeish, weak, operculum scaly. *Lobotes?* | 黃鰲 | ˏWóng ˏngò. |
| 170. Sciæna; first dorsal 6 rayed, head smooth greenish brown, 2 anal spines. *Sciæna?* | 洋梭鮦 | ˏYéung ‹shó ˏó. |
| 171. Sciæna; small, fins red, 2 dorsals near, large eyes, body brown striped. *Sciæna?* | 紅梳丨 | ˏHung ‹shó ˏo. |
| 172. Sciæna; long, yellowish, dorsal emarginate, teeth hooked, anal spine. *Otolithus?* | 花鱸 | ‹Fá ˏlò. |
| 173. Sciæna; dark green, fins yellowish, anal scaly, operculum acute. *Diagramma?* | 海鰽 | ‘Hoi ˏts‘ò. |
| 174. Sciæna; dark brown, spotted, gills scaly, dorsal emarginate. *Sciæna?* | 鰵魚 | ‘Man ˏü. |
| 175. Sciæna; one cirrus on the lower jaw, dorsal emarginate, rays freeish. *Umbrina?* | 生鬚鰔 | ‹Shang ‘sú wák. |
| 176. Sciæna; or a spinous finned thoracic fish, with a large ear stone. | 鯼 石首魚 | ‹Tsung. Shik ‘shau ˏü. |

148.—153. The first of this group is the fish commonly known as the pomfret, or pampel: the others resemble it in their general contour, from whence the Chinese call them *ts‘ong*.

154.—159. Both sharks and rays are eaten by the Chinese, at all stages of their growth: even the young are taken from the mother for the table. There are other species not enumerated here brought to market, some of them so large as to require two or three men to carry them. The *Zygæna* or hammer-headed shark is often seen in the market at Macao, but compared with other species of shark it is commonly small, not exceeding three feet in length.

| | | |
|---|---|---|
| 177. Scorpæna; blackish, many cirri on lower jaw, ventrals united. *Scorpæna.* | 老虎魚 | ‘Lò ‘fú ˏü. |
| 178. Scorpæna; reddish, free rays of pectoral reach to the tail, dorsal rays free. *Pterois.* | 龍鬚丨 | ˏLung ˏsú ˏü. |
| 179. Scorpæna; pectorals and tail yellow spotted, spines free, body dark clouded. *Pelor.* | 黃豹魚 | ˏWóng p‘áu’ ˏü. |
| 180. Scorpæna; rays of dorsal and pectorals free, feathery, body banded red. *Pterois.* | 鰲魚 | ˏNgò’ ˏü. |
| 181. Scorpæna; pectorals 2 free rays, body spotted, umber color, smooth. *Pelor.* | 貓丨 | ˏMáu ˏü. |
| 182. Scorpæna; or gurnard, or one of the mailed fishes. | 螣　鯄 | ˏT‘ang. ˏK‘au. |
| 183. Shad; abdomen serrated, anal fin near tail, ventral very small. *Clupea.* | 三黎 | ˏSám ˏlai. |
| 184. Common shark; brown back, nose sharp, fins small, 2d dorsal small. *Carcharias.* | 沙魚　魦　鯊 | ˏShá ˏü. ˏShá. ˏShá. |
| 185. Shark; a spine on each dorsal, body banded black and gray. *Cestracion zebra.* | 貓兒沙 | ˏMáu ˏí ˏshá. |
| 186. Shark; snout sharp, 2 small dorsals, dull gray, marbled. *Rhinobatus.* | 犂頭沙 | ˏLai ˏt‘au ˏshá. |
| 187. Shark; black fins, whitish beneath, back greenish, anal near tail. *Carcharias.* | 烏翼沙 | ˏÚ yik˒ ˏshá. |
| 188. Shark; fins and back dirty green, belly white, head blunt. *Carcharias.* | 齊頭沙 | ˏTs‘ai ˏt‘au ˏshá. |
| 189. Hammer-headed shark; dirty green, eyes protruding, front of head thin. *Zygæna.* | 公子帽沙 | ˏKung ‘tsz’. mò² ˏshá. |
| 190. Silure; marbled brown, 4 cirri, fins particolored, single dorsal small. *Silurus.* | 黃骨魚 | ˏWóng kwat˒ ˏü. |
| 191. Silure; back dusky green, one small dorsal, 4 cirri, mouth turned up. *Silurus.* | 鰜魚 | ˏLím ˏü. |
| 192. Silure; dusky green, spotted black, 6 cirri, spines jagged. *Bagrus.* | 鰔丨 | ‘Kóm ˏü |
| 193. Silure; dull green, small 2d dorsal, 6 cirri, spines stout, jagged. *Bagrus.* | 鰜丨 | ˏLím ˏü. |
| 194. Silure; dark green, fins reddish, dorsal spine smooth, 6 short 2 long cirri. *Bagrus.* | 牛丨 | ˏNgau ˏü. |
| 195. Silure; small silvery green, 6 cirri, spines jagged, dorsal 6 rayed. *Bagrus.* | 芒仔 | ˏMóng ‘tsai. |
| 196. Silure; purplish back, spotted black, 8 cirri, second dorsal long. *Bagrus.* | 花鰔 | ˏFá ‘kóm. |
| 197. Silure; pectoral spine stout, 2d dorsal and anal joined, mottled green. *Plotosus.* | 庵丁 | ˏÓm ˏting. |
| 198. Silure; 8 cirri, body dark green, one dorsal, pectoral spine large *Heterobranchus.* | 塘虱 | ˏT‘óng sat˒. |
| 199. Silure; 4 upper and 4 lower cirri, body brown marbled, head sharp. *Pimelodus.* | 黃龍 | ˏWóng ˏlung. |
| 200. Silure; or bull-head, or a species of mud fish. | 鮧　鮎 | ˏI. ˏNím. |
| 201. Silver-fish; a variety in color, of the gold fish when young. *Cyprinus.* | 珠鱗金魚 | ˏChü ˏlun ˏkam ˏü. |
| 202. Smelt; greenish, dorsals near, mouth small, head smooth, anal long, soft. *Atherina.* | 沙鑽 | ˏShá tsün’. |
| 203. Guava leaf sole; brown, spots large, eyes right and others left; small. *Solea.* | 拈葉仔 | ˏNím íp˒ ‘tsai. |

177.—181. Some of these fishes are considered to be poisonous by the Chinese, an idea that has no doubt partly arisen from their forbidding aspect. The *ngò ü* is marked with bright reddish bands, with cirri pendent from each eye, while the feathery fins, marked in brown bands

| | | |
|---|---|---|
| 204. Sole; yellow spotted ring on tail, body banded, eyes left, pectoral whitish. *Solea.* | 花撻沙 | ‹Fá t'át› ‹shá. |
| 205. Sole; small, uniform reddish brown, eyes right, dorsal reaches the muzzle. *Achirus.* | 細鱗撻沙 | Sai' ˛lun t'át› ‹shá. |
| 206. Sole; scales large, umber, eyes right, dorsal ends opposite the mouth. *Achirus.* | 密鱗撻沙 | Mat› ˛lun t'át› ‹shá. |
| 207. Sole; uniform reddish brown, dorsal reaches gills, fins ashy, eyes right. *Achirus.* | 黑鱗撻沙 | Hak› ˛lun t'át› ‹shá. |
| 208. Sole; brown, fins reddish yellow, eyes right, dorsal reaches muzzle. *Achirus.* | 金邊撻沙 | ‹Kam ‹pín t'át› ‹shá. |
| 209. Sole; reddish spotted brown, dorsal extends to the muzzle, eyes right. *Achirus.* | 花點撻沙 | ‹Fá 'tím t'át› ‹shá. |
| 210. Sole; reddish, black spots, fins yellowish green, eyes right. *Achirus.* | 黑點撻沙 | Hak› 'tím t'át› ‹shá. |
| 211. Sole fish; other general names for the genus *Pleuronectes.* | 鰈鞋底比目魚 | T'áp›. ˛Hái 'tai 'Pí muk$_2$ ˛ü. |
| 212. Sparus; reddish, spotted blue, teeth large, operculum acute. *Sargus?* | 金絲鱲 | ‹Kam ‹sz' láp$_2$. |
| 213. Sparus; body oval, light red, dorsal continuous, 24 rays, operculum scaly. *Sargus?* | 紅鱲 | ˛Hung láp$_2$. |
| 214. Sparus; spotted red on gray body, narrow at the tail, dorsal spotted. *Sargus?* | 凹尾 | Yap› 'mí. |
| 215. Sparus; head square, body reddish, dorsal even, teeth numerous. *Boops?* | 方頭魊 | ‹Fóng ˛t'au wák$_2$. |
| 216. Sparus; body oval, back brown, belly light, head smooth, eyes blue. *Boops?* | 瓜子鱲 | ‹Kwá 'tsz' láp$_2$. |
| 217. Sparus; dorsal deeply cleft, ventral behind pectoral, brown spotted. *Boops?* | 班鱸 | ‹Pán ˛lò. |
| 218. Sparus; head tapering, greenish back, mouth projecting, small. *Pagelus?* | 鑽嘴 | Tsün' 'tsui. |
| 219. Sparus; body brownish red, operculum scaly, acute, dorsal fin striped. *Pagelus?* | 素哥 | Sú' ‹kó. |
| 220. Sparus; reddish brown, black spot on flank, operculum scaly. *Dentex?* | 火點鰽 | 'Fó 'tím ˛ts'ò. |
| 221. Sparus; fins yellow, dorsal and body silvery blue, teeth large. *Dentex?* | 黃翼 | ˛Wóng yik$_2$. |
| 222. Sparus; head scaly, lower fins yellow, body greenish, tail green and yellow. *Pagrus?* | 金絲鱲 | ˛Kam ‹sz' láp$_2$. |
| 223. Sparus; head smooth, mouth small, 9 dorsal spinous rays, anal scaly. *Sparus?* | 海鯽 | 'Hoi tsik›. |
| 224. Sphyræna; 2d dorsal opposite anal, greenish, first dorsal five rayed. *Sphyræna.* | 竹簽 | Chuk› ‹tsím. |
| 225. Sturgeon; back with a row of plates. *Accipenser.* | 鱘龍魚 | ˛Tsam ˛lung ˛ü. |
| 226. Sturgeon; has three rows of plates on the back. | 鱣　鱑魚 | ‹Chín. ˛Wong ˛ü. |
| 227. Surgeon-fish; dusky green, 4 caudal spines, eyes blue, anal long. *Acanthurus.* | 黑將軍蒼 | Hak› ˛tséung ‹kwan ‹ts'óng. |

upon a slate colored ground, and the large eyes, add to its singular and brilliant appearance. The *wóng p'áu ü* is one of the most hideous of fishes.

203.—210. Flounder, fluke, plaice, and sole, are English terms for fishes of the old genus Pleuronectes, several species of which are very abundant in the shallow waters of the Pearl river. The sole is called *pí muk ü*, or the fish with corresponding eyes, because, as the Imperial Dictionary says, "if their eyes do not correspond they cannot swim;" consequently they are drawn in pairs, one of which looks to the right and the other to the left.

226. These characters, and those under Nos. 113, 141, 160, 163, 176, 182, 200, 211, and 239, are taken from Chinese books; the figures in them are so rude and misshapen, that it is

| | | |
|---|---|---|
| 228. Surmullet; broad, reddish, with back brown, lips large, fins red. *Mullus.* | 飛啼鵲 | ‹Fí ‚t'ai tséuk›. |
| 229. Surmullet; dark green back, spotted, belly silvery, tail banded. *Mullus.* | 洋鑽 | ‚Yéung tsün'. |
| 230. Tænioides; body dark red, long, head smooth, eyes concealed. *Tænioides.* | 紅鱺 硃筆魚 | ‚Hung lái². ‹Chü pat› ‚ü. |
| 231. Tænioides; brick red, mouth turned up, dorsal long, tail distinct. *Tænioides.* | 蛇更 | ‚Shé ‹kang. |
| 232. Tench; dark green, brown fins, ventrals and dorsal spiny, opposite. *Leuciscus.* | 鯇魚 | ʻWán ‚ü. |
| 233. Tench; blackish, long, fins whitish, lateral line white, no cirri. *Leuciscus.* | 黑鯇 | Hak› ʻwán. |
| 234. Tench; head depressed, mouth vertical, silvery, no anal spine. *Leuciscus.* | 拗頸 | Áu' ʻking. |
| 235. Tench; fusiform, brown back, green, belly, red eyes, dorsal 9 rayed. *Leuciscus.* | 紅眼筍 | ‚Hung ʻngán ʻsun. |
| 236. Tench; fins reddish, body dusky green, head tapering, fins jagged. *Leuciscus.* | 黑石鯇 | Hak› shik₂ ʻwán. |
| 237. Tench; fusiform, bluish green, ventral and dorsal opposite. *Leuciscus.* | 鰔魚 | ʻKóm ‚ü. |
| 238. Tench; or other cyprini, with and without cirri. | 鯔 鱮 鰤 | ‹Tsz'. ‚Ü ‚Í. |
| 239. Tetraodon; spineless, clouded, spotted white, 4 nasal tubercles. *Tetraodon.* | 燈籠泡 | ‹Tang ‚lung p'áu'. |
| 240. Torpedo; head round, 2 dorsals on tail, body dark reddish, spotted. *Torpedo.* | 木勺鯆 | Muk₂ chéuk› ‹pò. |
| 241. Trichiurus; body thin, long, white, belly serrate, no caudal or ventral. *Trichiurus.* | 白帶 矢幹魚 | Pák₂ tái'. ʻCh'i kón' ‚ü. |
| 242. Trunk-fish; body globular. plated with hexagonal plates. *Ostracion.* | 海牛 | ʻHoi ‚ngau. |
| 243. Tunny; spotted green back, 7 finlets, dorsals separate, three carina. *Thynnus.* | 鮫魚 | ‹Káu ‚ü. |
| 244. White rice fish; body diaphanous, fins small, head pointed. *Leucosoma.* | 白飯魚 | Pák₂ fán² ‚ü. |
| 245. Wolf-fish; cylindrical, brown banded with white spots, reddish belly. *Anarrhicas* | 井公魚 | ʻChing ‹kung ‚ü. |
| 246. Wolf-fish; brown and red banded, green head, anal low, long. *Anarrhicas.* | 雷公魚 | ‚Lui ‹kung ‚ü. |

impossible to do more than ascertain the order, and even this in many cases is impracticable. The *wóng ü*, or *chín*, is a native of the Yellow river; it is spoken of by Du Halde and other writers in high terms, and from the description in the *Pún Ts'ò* of its habits and appearance it is evidently a sturgeon. The sturgeon is now and then seen in these markets.

230, 231. These two fishes are akin to the gobies or gudgeons. They are remarkable for the manner in which the eyes are concealed in the skin, and for the length of the under jaw, which is everywhere convex, and ascends in front of the upper jaw, presenting a singular profile. The first species is the *Tænioides hermannien* of Lacepede.

244. This singular fish is nearly transparent, and the scientific name, meaning white body, expresses this characteristic. It belongs to the salmons, and is esteemed a delicate fish for the table. Of the fish found in these markets, and of which this list contains only a part, the garoupa, pomfret, marbled mackerel, polynemus or salmon, sole, and mullet, with the *lung tan ü*, are the most esteemed for the table. The Chinese, however, eat nearly all sorts of fish, and the contrivances they employ for capturing them, from the smack that ventures out 50 or 100 miles from the coast, to the simple hook and net of the *tánká* woman, barely suffice to supply the demand.

## Section Sixth.

# CRUSTACEA AND MOLLUSCA.

## 蟹蚌類第六章

'Hái 'p'óng lui'; tai' luk, ,chéung.

| | | |
|---|---|---|
| 1. All animals are divided into two great classes, viz., those with backbones (or vertebrated), and those without backbones (or invertebrated). Vertebrated animals are such as birds, beasts, tortoises, frogs, snakes, fishes, &c. Invertebrated animals are divided into three classes; the first consists of shells (or mollusca), the second of insects and crabs (or articulata), and the third of star-fish and sea-urchins (or radiata). The first class is subdivided into two orders; the second into five orders; and the third also into five orders. | 凡生物統分二大部曰有脊曰無脊有脊者如禽獸龜蛙蛇魚是也無脊者列類有三一曰螺蚌二曰蟲蟹三曰海膽海燕是也且首類中分二小類次類中分五小類又次類中亦分五小類 | ,Fán ,shang mat, 't'ung ,fan í' tái' pò', üt, 'yau tsik,, üt, ,mò tsik,. 'Yau tsik, 'ché, ,ü ,k'am, shau', ,kwai, ,wá, ,shé, ,ü shí' 'yá. ,Mò tsik, 'ché, lit, lui' 'yau ,sám; yat, üt, ,ló 'p'óng; í' üt, ,ch'ung 'hái; ,sám üt, 'hoi 'tám, 'hoi ín', shí' 'yá. 'Ch'é 'shau lui' ,chung ,fan í' 'síú lui'; ts'z' lui' ,chung ,fan 'ng 'síú lui'; yau' ts'z' lui' ,chung yik, ,fan 'ng 'síú lui'. |
| 2. Arca nodulosa. | 瓦屋子　螄堪 | 'Ngá uk, 'tsz'. ,Sz' ,hóm. |
| 3. Clams, an ebible species of Mactra. | 沙白 | ,Shá pák,. |
| 4. Cockle, or spiral univalves. | 螺螄 | ,Ló ,sz'. |
| 5. Cones, or round pyramidal shells. | 珂　雞心螺 | ,Ó. ,Kai ,sam ,ló. |
| 6. Cowries. | 貝子 | Púi' 'tsz'. |
| 7. Crab. | 蟹　蟛蟹　螃蟹 | 'Hái. ,P'áng 'hái. ,P'ong 'hái. |
| 8. Hairy crab. | 生支蟹 | ,Shang ,chí 'hái. |

### *Notes and Explanations.*

THIS section contains not only crustaceous and molluscous animals, but all the classes of invertebrata, except insects. The introductory paragraph is a very slight outline of their division into mollusca, articulata, and radiata, but as the Chinese have very partially investigated the small beings composing these classes, and often apply the same name to many species widely differing from one another, it is difficult to quote instances of the several orders, and therefore no attempt has been made to describe the several orders.

| | | |
|---|---|---|
| 9. Smooth shelled swimming crab. | 蠘　花娘蠏 | Tsít,. ꜀Fá ꜁néung ʿhái. |
| 10. Rough shelled swimming crabs, or Pilumnus? | 蟳　老虎丨 | ꜁Tsʻam. ʿLò ʻfú ʿhái. |
| 11. Hermit crab, or Pagurus. | 寄蟲　寄居蟲 | Kíʾ ꜀chʻung. Kíʾ ꜀kü ꜁chʻung. |
| 12. Edible crab. | 肉蠏 | Yuk, ʿhái. |
| 13. Spider crab. | 蜘蛛蠏 | ꜀Chí ꜀chü ʿhái. |
| 14. Crawfish, or large sea prawns. *Palinurus.* | 龍蝦　鰝 | ꜁Lung ꜁há. Hòʾ. |
| 15. Crevette, or broad sea-shrimp. | 蝦姑 | ʿHá ʻkú. |
| 16. Cuttle-fish. | 烏賊　墨魚 | ꜀Ú tsák,. Mak, ꜁ü. |
| 17. Cuttle-fish bone. | 海螵蛸 | ʻHoi ꜀píú ꜀síú. |
| 18. Eight armed cuttle fish, or Octopus. | 章舉 | ꜀Chéung ʻkü. |
| 19. Cypræa. | 紫貝　貝子 | ʻTszʾ púiʾ. Púiʾ ʻtszʾ. |
| 20. Dolium shell. | 琵琶螺 | ꜁Pʻí ꜁pʻá ꜁ló. |
| 21. Ear-shell, or Haliotis. | 鰒　石決明 | Fuk,. Shik, küt, ꜁ming. |
| 22. Horsehoof, or king crab. | 鱟 | Hauʾ. |
| 23. Leech, or bloodsucker. | 馬蟥蜞　蜞乸<br>水蛭　牛丨 | ʿMá ꜁wóng ꜁kʻí. ꜁Kʻí ʿná.<br>ʻShui chat,. ꜁Ngau ꜁kʻí. |
| 24. Lobsters? | 大頭蝦 | Táiʾ ꜁tʻau ꜀há. |
| 25. Mother of pearl shell. | 雲母殼 | ꜁Wan ʻmò hók,. |
| 26. Murex, or trumpet shell. | 響螺　吹螺 | ʻHéung ꜁ló. ꜀Chʻui ꜁ló. |
| 27. Murex muriatacus? | 長指螺 | ꜁Chʻéung ʻchí ꜁ló. |
| 28. Murex longicauda? | 欖核丨 | ʻLám wat, ꜁ló. |
| 29. Murex, a spinous species. | 長嘴竻丨 | ꜁Chʻéung ʻtsui lik, ꜁ló. |
| 30. Murex, a large unarmed edible species. | 辣蠃 | Lát, ꜁ló. |
| 31. Edible Mytilus, a small gibbous species. | 沙蜆 | ꜀Shá ʿhín. |
| 32. Nerita, two species of. | 沿歌麽　鷹歌嘴 | ꜁Ün ꜀kó ʿmò. ꜀Ying ꜀kó ʻtsui. |

7.—13. The word *hái* means crabs, comprising such species of the genus Cancer as are somewhat square; *há* denotes those which are long, as crawfish, prawns, &c. There are more than twenty species of *há* known here, most of them found in salt water, and about fifteen different kinds of *hái;* all of them form articles of food. The *wóng há*, *shá há*, and *ming há* among shrimps, and the *yuk hái* among crabs are the most esteemed.

22. The king crab, or Monoculus polyphemus, is eaten by the Chinese, and the shells are dried and formed into water ladles.

| | | |
|---|---|---|
| 33. Oysters. | 蠔 牡蠣 | ˏHò. ˋMau lai². |
| 34. Pectens, or eared oysters. | 車渠 | ˏCh'é ˏk'ü. |
| 35. Prawns. | 明蝦 | ˏMing ˏhá. |
| 36. Razor sheath, or Solen. | 蟶 沙螺 | ˏChing. ˏShá ˏló. |
| 37. Sand-hoppers, or sea-fleas. *Gammarus.* | 水甲由 蝦虱 | ˏShui ˏká chát₃. ˏHá sat₃. |
| 38. Sea-urchin, or Echinus. | 海膽 | ˋHoi ˋtám. |
| 39. Sea-wing, or Pinna. | 玉珧 | Yuk₂ ˏtíú. |
| 40. Sea-qualm, or Medusa. | 水母 | ˋShui ˋmò. |
| 41. Bivalve shells, thick and furrowed, as Arca. | 蚶 魁蛤 | ˏKóm. ˏFúi kóp₃. |
| 42. Bivalve shells, thin and colored, as Tellina, Cardium. | 蛤 | Kóp₃. |
| 43. Bivalve shells, thick and smooth, as Mya, Mytilus, &c. | 蜆 扁螺 | ˋHín. ˋPín ˏló. |
| 44. Fresh water bivalves, broad and thin, as Unio. | 蚌 | ˋP'óng. |
| 45. Univalve spiral shells. | 螺 螄 | ˏLó. ˏSz'. |
| 46. Shrimps. | 河蝦 蔴蝦 | ˏHó ˏhá. ˏMá ˏhá. |
| 47. Sea shrimps or Crangons. | 沙蝦 銀蝦 | ˏShá ˏhá. ˏNgan ˏhá. |
| 48. Slugs. | 蛞蝓 | Út₃ ˏü. |
| 49. Land snail or Helix. | 蝸牛 蜆蠃虫 | ˏKwá ˏngau. ˏHín ˏló ˏch'ung. |
| 50. Lymnea, or fresh water snails. | 田螺 | ˏT'ín ˏló. |
| 51. Sponge. | 水泡 | ˋShui ˋpò. |
| 52. Star-fish, or asteria. | 海燕 雞爪魚 | ˋHoi ín². ˏKai ˋchau ˏü. |
| 53. Strombus. | 戒指螺 | Kái² ˋchí ˏló. |
| 54. Tellina. | 玳瑁蜆 交文蜆 | Toi² mò² ˋhín. ˏKáu ˏman ˋhín. |
| 55. Trochus niloticus. | 亞婆髻 | A² ˏp'ó kai². |
| 56. Wentletrap, or Scalaria pretiosa. | 珍瓏絲螺 | ˏChan ˏlung ˏsz' ˏló. |

41.—45. Shell-fish form no inconsiderable portion of the food of the people in this region. Oysters are abundant, though by foreigners they are regarded as inferior; clams of several sizes, small muscles of four or five genera, species of Murex, Helix, and Arca, besides others, are constantly seen in the markets.

56. This elegant shell is often seen in the shops of Canton, where also are found many other species, some of them brought in junks from the Indian Archipelago, and others collected on the coasts. Fresh water shells, of the genera Unio, Mytilus, Cyclas, and others are sometimes met with, but as the Chinese think the gayest shells are the most valuable, they do not collect fluviatic species.

# Section Seventh.

## INSECTS.

## 昆蟲類第七章

ˏKwʻan ˏchʻung lui²; tai² tsʻat͵ ˏchéung.

| | | |
|---|---|---|
| 1. Ant. | 蟻 | ˊNgai. |
| 2. White ant. | 白蟻 | Pák₂ ˊngai. |
| 3. Large red spotted ant. | 蠪 朾螘 | ˏLung. ˏChʻáng ˊoi. |
| 4. Winged ant. | 螱 飛蟻 翼蟻 | Wai². ˏFi ˊngai. Yik ˊngai. |
| 5. Bed bug, and other fetid bugs, as Cimex. | 臭虫 | Chʻau² ˏchʻung. |
| 6. Honey bee. | 蜜蜂 蠭 | Mat₂ ˏfung. ˏFung. |
| 7. Queen bee. | 蜂王 | ˏFung ˏwóng. |
| 8. Drone of a beehive. | 蜜奴 | Mat₂ ˏnò. |
| 9. Cells of a hive. | 窩蜜 | ˏWo mat₂. |
| 10. Beetle. | 猪仔虫 | ˏChü ʻtsai ˏchʻung. |
| 11. Gold green beetle, as Cetonia. | 金龜子 | ˏKam ˏkwai ʻtsz'. |
| 12. Book worm. | 蠹蟲 蠹魚 | Tò² ˏchʻung. Tò² ˏü. |
| 13. Bugs found in wood. | 木虱 | Muk₂ shat͵. |
| 14. Butterfly. | 蝴蝶 蛺蝶 | ˏÚ típ₂. Kap͵ típ₂. |
| 15. Large or Atlas butterfly. | 花羅大極 | ˏFá ˏlo tái² kik͵. |
| 16. Caterpillars on trees. | 蠹蟲 蝎 | Tò² ˏchʻung. Hít͵. |
| 17. Smooth caterpillars, as the larvæ of the sphinx. | 芋蠋 青虫 | ˏÚ chuk₂. ˏTsʻing ˏchʻung. |
| 18. Hairy caterpillar. | 蛄蟖 狗毛虫 | ˏÍm ˏsz'. ʻKau ˏmò ˏchʻung. |

### *Notes and Explanations.*

THE greatest part of the characters under the radical *chʻung* are names of insects, or, with a few exceptions, the group corresponds to the Linnæan order of *Vermes*. Many of them exhibit in their combinations some striking characteristic either of the shape, habits, or color, of the insect intended; thus *ngai*, an ant, means the 'orderly insect;' *fung*, a bee, is the 'needle insect;' *ying* a fly, is the 'thread insect,' alluding to the spinning like mode of brushing its legs; *man*, a musketo, is the 'letter insect,' referring to the white lines upon its body; and so of many others. Speaking of insects, Lí Shíchan says, "Insects are the smallest of animals; their tribes are exceedingly multifarious, for which reason the character *chʻung* is tripled to embody this idea. According to the Memoir of Ingenious Works, 'some insects have bones outside, and others have them inside; some go backwards and others sideways; some in a file and others zigzag. They sing with

CHI. CHR. 124

| | | |
|---|---|---|
| 19. Centipede, a Scolopendra. | 蜈蚣 蝍蛆 百足 | ˏ'Ng ‹kung. Tsik› ‹tsʻü. Pák› tsuk›. |
| 20. Centipede with angular legs, a Scutigera. | 蚰蜒 蠙螢 蛈蠷 | ‹Yau ˏín. ˏYan ˏín. ˏChʻéung ‹shí. |
| 21. Cerambyx, elytra blackish, with white spots. | 牛蜋 | ˏNgau ˏlóng. |
| 22. Chrysalis of the silkworm. | 繭 | ʻKán. |
| 23. Cicada, or broad locust. | 蟬 蜩 | ˏShím. ˏTíú. |
| 24. Cockchaffer, or dorrbeetle, a Melolontha. | 黃砂蝸 | ˏWóng ‹shá ʻná. |
| 25. Cockroach. | 行夜 甴甲 蜚蠊 滑蟲 | ˏHang yé². ‹Ká chát›. ˏFí ˏlím. Wát› ˏchʻung. |
| 26. Cricket. | 蟋蟀 蛬 | Tsik› tsut›. ʻKung. |
| 27. Hearth cricket, a large species, small wings. | 竈馬 | Tau³ ʻmá. |
| 28. Dragon fly or Libellula (Æshna). | 蜻蛉 蜻蜓 蜻蜓 | ‹Tsing ˏling. ‹Tsing ˏtʻing. ‹Tsing ˏtʻing. |
| 29. Dragon needle, a slender black species, an Agrion. | 赤卒 紺蠜 | Chik› sut›. Kóm³ ‹fán. |
| 30. Dung fly. | 大屎烏蠅 | Tái² ʻshí ʻú ˏying. |
| 31. Earthworm. | 蚯蚓 | ‹Yau ʻyan. |
| 32. Ephemera fly. | 蜉蝣 | ˏFau ˏyau. |
| 33. Fire-fly. | 螢火 飛螢 | ˏYing ʻfó. ‹Fí ˏying. |
| 34. Flea. | 跳虱 蚤 狗虱 | Tíú³ shat›. ʻTsʻò. ʻKau shat›. |
| 35. Flies found near stagnant water. | 蠛蠓 | Mít² ʻmung. |
| 36. House fly. | 烏蠅 蒼蠅 | ‹Ú ˏying. ‹Tsʻóng ˏying. |
| 37. Gad-fly, or breeze. | 蜚虻 | Fí³ ˏmóng. |
| 38. Gally-worm, or Julus. | 百足 馬陸 山蛩 | Pák› tsuk›. ʻMá luk². ‹Shán ˏkʻung. |
| 39. Geometrical worms. | 尺蠖 | Chʻik› wók². |
| 40. Glow worm. | 螢蛆 蠲 | ˏYing ‹tsʻü. ʻKün. |
| 41. Gnat. | 蚋 蜹 | Yui². Yui². |

the thorax, mouth, sides, wings, belly, or breast; all these are called the tribes of small insects.' These beings, if they are minute, must not be confounded with reptiles, birds, or fishes, although their bodies are feathery, hairy, scaly, shelly, or naked." Most of the names in this section are obtained from books, as it is difficult to ascertain the very vulgar term for any except the most common insects.

23. It is an amusement of boys to capture this insect, and tie it up in such a manner as to excite it to sing. Its stridulous noise is so loud as to overpower the voice when near by.

26. Crickets are collected by the Chinese in large quantities, and sold in the markets for fighting. Two of them are placed in a basin, and irritated by a straw, when they attack each

| | | |
|---|---|---|
| 42. Grasshopper. | 蛗螽　斯草蜢 | Fau² ‹chung. ‹Sz' 'ts'ò 'mang. |
| 43. Green headed grasshopper, a Truxalis. | 螇蚸 | ‚Hai ‚k'í. |
| 44. Grubs, or large larva found in the earth. | 蠐螬 | ‚Ts'ai ‚ts'ò. |
| 45. Horse fly. | 馬蜂 | 'Má ‹fung. |
| 46. Lady bug. | 班蝥　花金龜 | Pán› ‚máu. ‹Fá ‹kam ‹kwai. |
| 47. Lantern fly, or Fulgora. | 龍眼鵞 | ‚Lung ‚ngán ‚ngó. |
| 48. Lepisma. | 白魚　蟫　鉗蟲 | Pák₂ ‚ü. ‚Yam. ‚K'im ‚ch'ung. |
| 49. Locust. | 蝽蟓　螽斯 | ‹Chung chü'. ‹Chung ‹sz'. |
| 50. Locust, or Acrydium. | 蛗螽　蚱蜢 | Fau² ‹chung. Chák› 'mang. |
| 51. Migratory locust. | 蝗蚱 | ‚Wóng chák›. |
| 52. Migratory locust. | 青軌蜢 | ‹Ts'ing 'kwai 'mang. |
| 53. Large winged locust. | 蠻虫 | ‚Lün ‚ch'ung. |
| 54. Long legs. | 琴勞 | ‚K'am ‹lò. |
| 55. Louse. | 虱乸　虱子　蝨 | Shat› 'ná. Shat› 'tsz'. Shat›. |
| 56. Wood louse. | 木虱 | Muk₂ shat›. |
| 57. Maggots in flesh. | 蛆 | ‹Ts'ü. |
| 58. Maggots in grain. | 蛑虫 | ‚Mai ‚ch'ung. |
| 59. Praying mantis. | 螳螂　馬江蜋 | ‚T'óng ‚lóng. 'Má ‹kóng ‚lóng. |
| 60. Mole cricket. | 土狗　螻蛄 | 'T'ò 'kau. ‚Lau ‹kú. |
| 61. Large moth, as Sphinx or Phalæna. | 蛾 | ‚Ngó. |
| 62. Candle moth. | 燈蛾 | ‹Tang ‚ngó. |
| 63. Silkworm moth. | 蠶蛾 | ‚Ts'ám ‚ngó. |
| 64. Phalena atlas, or Atlas moth. | 羅浮蝶公 | ‚Ló 'fau típ› ‹kung. |
| 65. Musketo. | 蚊 | ‚Man. |
| 66. Larva of musketoes. | 孑孓 | K'ít› k'ít›. |

other with great violence, though the combat does not usually end in the death of one, but in its retreat. Hundreds of dollars are staked on the result of these miniature conflicts, and large sums are often paid for victorious warriors.

55. *Shat* is a generic term for parasitic insects, for small bugs, and for the larvæ of Aphides or plant lice. *Tsui*, a maggot, *ngó*, a moth, *fung*, a Vespa, *ying*, a fly, and many others, are similar terms for tribes. These constitute, however, but a small portion of the whole, the greatest number of insects being named by specific characters.

| | | |
|---|---|---|
| 67. Nit. | 蟣 | ˛Kí. |
| 68. Ptinus, or small insects in books. | 蛀 | Chü'. |
| 69. Scarabus, species of. | 黃蟲 勒皮象 | ˛Wóng ˛ch'ung. Lik˒ ˛p'í tséung². |
| 70. Scarabus carnifex. | 奔屎蟲 | ˛Pan 'shí ˛ch'ung. |
| 71. Scorpion. | 蠍 蠆尾虫 | Kít˒. ˛Chái ˢmí ˛ch'ung. |
| 72. Sea snail. | 泥龜 | ˛Nai ˛kwai. |
| 73. Silkworm. | 蠶 | ˛Ts'ám. |
| 74. Sow bug, mud lice, or Asellus. | 地溥 地珠 土鱉 | Tí² 'pò. Tí² ˛chü. 'T'ò pít˒. |
| 75. Large sow bug, or Oniscus. | 蛜蝛 鼠婦 蟅蟲 | ˛Í ˛wai. 'Shü 'fú. Ché' ˛ch'ung. |
| 76. Spider. | 蜘蛛 蟧蝸 蠿蟊 | ˛Chí ˛chü. ˛Lau ˛ü. Chüt˒ ˛mau. |
| 77. Large spider, yellow spotted. | 壁錢 壁鏡 | Pik˒ ˛ts'ín. Pik˒ king'. |
| 78. Many spotted spider. | 五色琴勞 | ˢ'Ng shik˒ ˛k'am ˛lò. |
| 79. Burrowing spider. | 螲蟷 土蜘蛛 | Chat₂ ˛tóng. 'T'ò ˛chí ˛chü. |
| 80. Field spider. | 草蜘蛛 蟢 | 'Ts'ò ˛chí ˛chü. 'Hí. |
| 81. Water spider. | 水蜘亅 | 'Shui ˛chí ˛chü. |
| 82. Tape worm. | 蚘蟲 蛔 蛕 | ˛Yau ˛ch'ung. ˛Wúi. ˛Wúi. |
| 83. Tumble dung, or Aleochara. | 蛣蜣 蜣蜋 | K'ít˒ ˛kéung. ˛Kéung ˛lóng. |
| 84. Wasp. | 黃蜂 | ˛Wóng ˛fung. |
| 85. Slender waisted, or solitary wasp, or Sphex. | 蠮螉 細腰蠭 | Ít˒ ˛yung. ˛Sai ˛iú ˛fung. |
| 86. Water beetle, or Dytiscus. | 山龍虱 水金龜 | ˛Shán ˛lung shat˒. 'Shui ˛kam ˛kwai. |
| 87. Weevil. | 米牛 | ˢMai ˛ngau. |
| 88. Worms or larva in liquids. | 蠹蟲 | Tò² ˛ch'ung. |

85. Singular notions are entertained concerning this insect, which is supposed to have no mate, but to take the young of another insect to transform into its own. See Chinese Repository, Vol. VII., page 488.

86. The Dytiscus is common in the pools of Macao, and is sometimes captured for food. Silkworms (after they have spun the coccoon,) are also fried in oil for the table: and in some seasons, locusts are served up in the same manner.

# CHAPTER XVI.

# MEDICINE.

# 醫學篇十六

‹Í hók$_2$; ‹p'ín shap$_2$ luk$_2$.

## Section First.

## CONVERSATION ON MEDICINE.

## 醫學論語第一章

‹Í hók$_2$ lun$^2$ 'ü; tai$^2$ yat$_>$ ‹chéung.

| | | |
|---|---|---|
| 1. What is the object of medical science? | 何為醫學 | ‚Hó ‚wai ‹í hók$_2$? |
| It is to protect and preserve human life; hence it is necessary to know the nature of medicines, and the origin of diseases, together with the laws of treating them. | 乃保全人命者故須知藥性與病源及治之法 | 'Nái 'pò ‚ts'ün ‚yan ming-'ché; kú' ‹sü ‹chí yéuk$_2$ sing', 'ü ping$^2$ ‚ün, k'ap$_2$ chí' ‹chi fát$_>$. |
| 2. In what estimation is medicine held by the Chinese? | 中土視醫輕否 | ‹Chung 't'ò shí$^2$ ‹í ‹hing 'fau? |
| Medicine, designed to protect and prolong human life, has been called the benevolent art; and therefore is esteemed second only to the literary profession. | 醫乃保全人命仁術稱焉故書家之外則推醫 | ‹Í 'nái 'pò ‚ts'ün ‚yan ming$^2$. ‚yan shut$_2$ ‹ch'ing ‚in; kú' ‹shü ‹ká ‹chi ngoi$^2$, tsak$_>$ ‹t'ui ‹í. |

### *Notes and Explanations.*

MEDICAL science among the Chinese is in a very different state from that to which it has been advanced by modern practitioners in the west. It is where it was centuries ago: many diseases are regarded as incurable, for which modern improvement has devised sure and speedy remedies. However, a more thorough investigation of the healing art, as understood by this people, may yet be of essential advantage to the science. It would probably be found, were the subject sufficiently examined, that the Chinese, as a nation, enjoy as good a degree of health, and on an average attain to as great an age, as any other people.

1. Preventive medicine, or *hygiene*, is a part of the benevolent art to which the Chinese pay great, but evidently not too much, attention; they say, truly, "Prevention is better than cure." The words ***pò ts'ün***, as here used, are quoted from an imperial work, and indicate that the primary object of the science is to preserve and to protect men from illness, rather than to heal their diseases, or to cure their maladies.

3. The phrase *í li*, or institutes of medicine, may be understood as comprising the general physiological, hygienic, and therapeutical relations of medicine, or the general and fundamental principles of the science.

3. What is requisite in order to enter the profession?

You must seek for some celebrated practitioner, and become his pupil. In order to search into the principles of the science, and investigate the nature of remedies, select several medical authors for study; and peruse them until the principles are understood, and your knowledge is extensive, then you may read all the professional writers.

進醫門事何事
拜訪名師投於
門下追求醫理
深究藥性擇數
醫本熟讀待理
明識廣然後遍
覽諸家

Tsun' ˏí ˏmún sz' ˏhó sz'?

Pái' 'fong ˏming ˏsz', ˏt'au ˏü ˏmún há. ˏChui ˏk'au ˏí 'li, ˏcham kau' yéuk sing', chák shò' ˏí 'pún shuk tuk, toi' 'lí ˏming shik 'kwóng, ˏin hau p'ín' 'lám ˏchü ˏká.

4. Are there any medical schools?

There are none in all the country; but at Peking there has been established a Great Medical College; and persons most thoroughly acquainted with medicine, and possessing an unblemished character, are after examination selected to enter the college, to fill its offices, and to practice therein. This Great Medical College has one principal director, and also one of a secondary, and another of a subordinate, rank, who superintend and examine the treatment of all the nine classes of diseases, and who direct all those who are intrusted with the business of the institution. Fifteen members of the college hold the rank of imperial physicians; thirty are overseers; forty are masters of medicine; and thirty rank as bachelors of medicine.

有教習醫館否
通國皆無惟京
城立太醫院考
選通曉亅理身
無過犯者入院
補缺以習焉其
太醫院院使一
人左院判一人
右院判一人掌
考九科之術率
其屬以供醫事
御醫十有五人
吏目三十人醫
士四十人醫生
三十人

'Yau káu' tsap ˏí 'kún 'fau?

ˏT'ung kwok ˏkái ˏmò, ˏwai ˏKing ˏshing lap T'ái' ˏI' Yün, 'háu 'sün ˏt'ung 'hiú ˏí 'lí, ˏshan ˏmò kwò' fán' 'ché, yap yün 'pò küt, 'í tsap ˏín. ˏK'i T'ái' ˏI' Yün yün sz' yat ˏyan, 'tso yün p'ún' yat ˏyan, yau' yün p'ún' yat ˏyan, 'chéung 'háu 'kau ˏfó ˏchí shut, sut, ˏk'i shuk 'í ˏkung ˏí sz'. Yü' ˏí shap 'yau 'ng ˏyan; lí' muk ˏsám shap ˏyan; ˏí sz' sz' shap ˏyan; ˏí ˏshang ˏsám shap ˏyan.

5. Who are some of the ancient eminent physicians?

The earliest were the emperors Ím and Wóng: next

昔精醫者爲誰
始於炎黃旣

Sik ˏtsing ˏí 'ché ˏwai ˏshui?

'Ch'í ˏü ˏÍm ˏWóng: ki'

5. Ím tai—Yen te, or the emperor Yen,—is otherwise called Shannung, the divine husbandman, and the father of medicine. The emperor Wóng was his successor, and with him K'ípák was cotemporary. Pákkò lived about the same time. Mohàn, Ts'óngkung, with his pupil Píntséuk, lived prior to our era. Wát'ò is the physician said to have laid bare and scraped a bone of the hero Kwán, and so saved him from the fatal effects of a poisoned arrow: one is now styled a god of medicine, and the other of war. Popular tradition says, that Wát'ò was decapitated at the instigation of Tsò Tsò, for having proposed to trepan that famous general with a view to cure him of an affection of the brain. Shunyü I' lived near the same time. Wóng Shukwó is known by his work on the pulse, epitomized in Du Halde. Ch'an Kwai is said to have remov-

were K'ipák, and Pákkò; and after them followed Mòhám, Ts'óngkung, Píntséuk, Wát'ò, Shunyü I', Wóng Shukwó, Ch'an Kwai, Hü Háutsung, Lí Shíchan; and also there were Chéung Chungking, Lau Shauchan, Lí Tungún, and Chü Tánk'ai, designated the four great and renowned physicians, who are even to this day much esteemed.

岐伯伯高迨後
則巫咸倉公扁
鵲華陀淳于意
王叔和陳桂許
孝宗李時珍又
張仲景劉守眞
李東垣朱丹溪
號爲四大名家
至今猶尙

ü K'í pák, Pák kò; t'oi hau' tsai, Mò hám, Ts'óng kung, 'Pín tséuk, Wá t'ò, Shun yü I', Wóng Shuk wó, Ch'an Kwai', 'Hü Háu' tsung, 'Lí Shí chan; yau' Chéung Chung' 'king, Lau 'Shau chan, 'Lí Tung ún, Chü Tán k'ai, hò' wai sz' tái' ming ká, chí' kam yau shéung'.

6. What are the best medical books?

醫書何爲至善

Í shü hó wai chí' shín'?

The medical books cannot be severally considered; for every branch having its own authors, the doing so would only perplex the student. But for matter and method none equal the 'Golden Mirror of Eminent Authors,' and the 'Comparative Compendium of Medical Writers.'

醫書不能枚舉
各自成家反足
惑人而善言大
備莫如醫宗金
鑑醫書匯叅等

Í shü pat nang múi 'kü; kók tsz' shing ká, 'fán tsuk, wák yan. Í shín' ín tái' pí', mók ü Í Tsung Kam Kám', Í Shü Ui' Ts'ám, 'tang.

7. How are diseases to be treated?

又如何臨症呢

Yau' ü hó lam ching' ní?

Always in treating diseases, whether they be internal or external, it is necessary in all cases to examine into the origin of the malady by inspection, by hearing, by interrogation, and by feeling the pulse.

臨症時無論內
外科皆以望聞
問切四字審明
病源爲要

Lam ching' shí, mò lun' noi' ngoi' fó, kái 'í móng', man, man', tsít, sz' tsz' 'sham ming ping' ün, wai íú'.

8. Are there any hospitals for gratuitous practice?

有週濟醫館否

'Yau chau tsai' í 'kún 'fau?

Sometimes only there have been such.

不過時有時無

Pat kwò' shí 'yau shí mò.

9. At the apothecary's shop, in what manner are medicines sold, and how are they compounded?

藥店如何發售
如何泡製

Yéuk tím' ü hó fát shau', ü hó p'áu' chai'?

Medicines, in a crude or prepared state, are purchased

各省生熟藥販

Kók 'sháng shang shuk

---

ed diseased viscera. Of Lí Shíchan, who flourished in the reign of Mánlik of the Ming dynasty, it is enough to say he is the compiler and principal author of the *Pún Ts'ò*. There are also many other physicians, ancient and modern, who are highly celebrated.

6. Besides these, there are many others in high repute and extensively used. In the sixth volume of the *Pún Ts'ò*, there is a list of 276 medical works quoted by Lí Shíchan; and likewise a list of 440 miscellaneous works, historical, biographical, &c., from which he made extracts for his materia medica.

from all the provinces, and are either cut in pieces or preserved whole; and then they are measured out according to recipes, sometimes several kinds being compounded together, at others they are formed into ointments, pills, or powders, or steeped in spirits, and retailed in small quantities.

回或裁碎或原
身看來方多少
或將數味製成
膏丹丸散或浸
水酒零沽

yéuk, fán' ,úi, wák, ,tsʻoi sui' wák, ,ün ,shan; hon' ,loi ,fong ,to 'shiú, wák, ,tséung shò' mí' chai' ,shing ,kò, ,tán, ,ün, sán', wák, tsam' 'shui 'tsau ,ling ,kú.

10. Does the Penal Code speak on this subject?

律例曾言醫否

Lut, Lai' ,tsʻang ,in ,i 'fau!

It speaks respecting physicians: 'On injuring or killing persons by an unskillful practitioner,' it thus decrees:

律例言醫者因
庸醫殺傷人故
例載凡庸醫為

Lut, Lai' ,in ,í 'ché: ,Yan, ,yung ,í shát, ,shéung ,yan, kú' lai' tsoi':

"Whenever an unskillful practitioner, in administering medicines, or using the puncturing needle, proceeds contrary to the established forms, and thereby causes the death of a patient, the magistrate shall call in other practitioners to examine the medicine or the wound, and if it appears that the injury done was unintentional, the practitioner shall then be treated according to the statute for accidental homicides, and shall not be allowed any longer to practice medicine. But if designedly he departs from the established forms, and deceives in his attempts to cure the malady, in order to obtain property, then according to its amount he shall be treated as a thief; and if death shall ensue from his malpractice, then for having thus used medicine with intent to kill, he shall be beheaded."

人用藥針刺誤
不如本方因而
致死者責令別
醫辨驗藥餌穴
道如無故害之
情者以過失殺
人論不許行醫
若故違本方詐
療疾病而取財
物者計贓准竊
盜論因而致死
及因事故用藥
殺人者斬

,Fán ,yung ,í, ,wai ,yan yung' yéuk, ,cham tsʻz', 'ng' pat, ,ü 'pún ,fong, ,yan ,í chi' 'sz' 'ché, chák, ling' pít, ,i pín' ím' yéuk, ní' yüt, tò'; ,ü ,mò kú' hoi' ,chí ,tsʻing 'ché, 'í kwó' shat, shát, ,yan lun', pat, 'hü ,hing ,í. Yéuk, kú' ,wai 'pún ,fong, chá' ,liú tsat, ping', ,í 'tsʻü ,tsʻoi mat, 'ché, kai' ,tsóng 'chun sit, tò' lun'; ,yan ,í chi' 'sz', kap, ,yan sz'', kú' yung' yéuk, shát, ,yan 'ché 'chám.

10. This law, here quoted, forms the 297th section of the Penal Code, and seems to be the only reference made therein to the medical profession. For engaging in the practice of medicine no license is required; but the physician must be ware, lest his medicines fail to have the desired effect.

# Section Second.

## NOSOLOGY.

### 百病類第二章
Pák› ping² lui²; tai² í² ‹chéung.

| | | |
|---|---|---|
| 1. The Great Medical College has 9 classes [of diseases]. | 太醫院凡九科 | T'ái² ‹Í Yün² ‚fán ʻkau ‹fo. |
| First class; diseases affecting the pulse violently. | 一曰大方脈科 | Yat› üt₂, tái² ‹fóng mak› ‹fo. |
| Second class; diseases affecting the pulse slightly. | 二曰小方脈科 | Í² üt₂, ʻsíú ‹fóng mak› ‹fo. |
| Third class; diseases arising from cold. | 三曰傷寒科 | ‹Sám üt₂, ‹shéung ‚hón ‹fó. |
| Fourth class; diseases of females. | 四曰婦人科 | Sz'² üt₂, ʻfú ‚yan ‹fo. |
| Fifth class; ulcers and cutaneous diseases. | 五曰瘡瘍科 | ʻ'Ng üt₂, ‹ch'óng ‚yéung ‹fo. |
| Sixth class; diseases needing the acupuncture and cautery. | 六曰鍼灸科 | Luk₂ üt₂, ‹cham chik₂ ‹fo. |
| Seventh class; diseases of the eyes. | 七曰眼科 | Ts'at› üt₂, ʻngán ‹fo. |
| Eighth class; diseases of the mouth and teeth. | 八曰口齒科 | Pát₂ üt₂, ʻhau ʻch'í ‹fó. |
| Ninth class; diseases of the bones. | 九曰正骨科 | ʻKau üt₂, ching² kwat› ‹fo. |
| 2. The book [entitled] *A Sure Guide containing Ten Thousand Recipes* is the work of doctor Ts'oi Kínchái of Shányam. Considering that the chapters and pages in the Materia Medica were very numerous, and all the recipes were promiscuously inserted under the names of the medicines, he designed this book to be a true guide to that | 萬方鍼線一書<br>山陰蔡繭齋先<br>生作也以本草<br>卷篇繁賾凡方<br>散載乎藥品之<br>下思此爲針線 | Mán² ‹Fóng ‹Kám Sín² yat› ‚shü, ‹Shán ‚yam Ts'oi² ʻKín ‹chái ‹sín ‹shang tsók› ʻyá. ʻÍ ʻPún ʻTs'ò ʻkün ‹p'ín ‚fán chak›, ‚fán ‹fóng sán² tsoi² ‚ú yéuk₂ ʻpan ‹chí há², ʻsz² ʻts'z² ‚wai ‹cham sín² ‹chí ʻyá. ‹Fan |

## *Notes and Explanations.*

THE phrase 'hundred diseases,' *pák ping*, is nearly equivalent to nosology. The literal term, *ping lun*, would perhaps be intelligible, but it seems never to have been used by the Chinese.

1. Synoptical views of diseases,—arranged into classes and orders, like those of Linnæus, Cullen, Vogel, Sagar, Macbride, and Good,—are common with the Chinese, and may be found in most of their medical works. The Medical College at Peking formerly arranged all diseases into eleven classes, having a separate one for diseases of the throat, which are now included in the eighth, and another for cutaneous diseases, at present combined with those under the second class: for each of these eight classes, medical officers are appointed, all of whom are Chinese, and some of them are in constant attendance on the emperor and his family.—The doctrine of the pulse is treated of at great length and minutely by the Chinese: there are three places on each wrist, at each of which they distinguish 24 different kinds of diseases. See Indo-Chinese Gleaner, vol. III., p. 129. Most acute diseases, such as originate from checked perspiration, are comprised in the third class. Ulcers and cutaneous diseases, and diseases of the eyes, are in Canton and its vicinity more prevalent than any of the other classes.

| | | |
|---|---|---|
| work. Arranged in their due order,—under the several classes of diseases, general and particular—there are in number about fifteen or sixteen thousand recipes. By the help of this Guide, all the recipes, which are scattered through the *Pún Ts'ò*, may be easily referred to for use, and there will be no necessity for any other book of recipes. | 之也分門析類<br>兼理卌門約得<br>方一萬五六千<br>之數有此則本<br>草所載之方皆<br>以適用而更不<br>必具方書云 | ₍mún sik› lui[2], ‹kím ʿlí ‹chün ₍mún, yéuk› tak› ‹fóng yat› mán[2] ʿ'ng luk₂ ‹ts'ín ‹chí shò[2]. ʿYau 'ts'z', tsak› 'Pún 'Ts'ò 'shó tsoi' ‹chí ‹fóng, ‹kái ʿí shik› yung[2], ₍í ‹kang pat› pít› kü[2] ‹fóng ₍shü ‹wan. |
| 3. Abortion. Abortio. | 小產 | 'Síú 'ch'án. |
| 4. Abscess. Abscessio. | 膿瘡 | ₍Nung ‹ch'óng. |
| 5. Ague, or febris intermittens. | 瘧疾 | Yéuk₂ tsat₂. |
| 6. Albugo, leucoma, or opacity of the cornea. | 眼瘼 | ʿNgán mók₂. |
| 7. Amaurosis, or gutta serena. | 發睛光 | Fát› ‹tsing ‹kwóng. |
| 8. Amenorrhœa. | 閉經 | Pai' ‹king. |
| 9. Anasarca, or cellular dropsy. | 水種 | 'Shui 'chung. |
| 10. Aphonia, or loss of the voice. | 失音 | Shat› ‹yam. |
| 11. Ascaris, or ascarides, or worms in the bowels. | 胃腸小虫 | Wai[2] ₍ch'éung 'síú ₍ch'ung. |
| 12. Ascites, or dropsy of the belly. | 水蠱 蠱脹 | 'Shui 'kú. 'Kú chéung'. |
| 13. Asthma. | 哮喘 | ‹Háu 'ch'ün. |
| 14. Blindness. | 瞽 盲眼 | 'Kú. ₍Máng ʿngán. |

2. This book of recipes is comprised in three small volumes; and the references to all the recipes are arranged in order under those diseases for the cure of which they are intended.

| | | |
|---|---|---|
| General diseases are divided into | - - - | 53 classes. |
| Diseases of the upper extremities are divided into | - | 9 classes. |
| Diseases of the middle regions are divided into | - | 8 classes. |
| Diseases of the lower extremities are divided into | | 15 classes. |
| Diseases peculiar to female children are divided into | | 8 classes. |
| Diseases peculiar to grown up females are divided into | | 8 classes. |
| Diseases peculiar to children are divided into | - | 4 classes. |

Under these one hundred and five classes, are specified several thousands of diseases; under each of them its symptoms are first briefly detailed, and then the references are made to the work of Lí Shíchan, in which at a given chapter and page, recipes for the disease will be found. Sometimes references are made to several recipes, from which the patient may take his choice. This Guide now usually forms the third, fourth, and fifth volumes of the *Pún Ts'ò*.

3. The diseases, the names of which are given in alphabetical order in this list, are for the most part, those which have come under the notice of foreign practitioners: often the name is descriptive of the disease; but sometimes it is not so, having been adopted from some incidental or local circumstance and not from any characteristic of the malady itself. In numerous instances, both the common and the technical names are given.

| | | |
|---|---|---|
| 15. Day blindness. | 畏日眼 | Wai' yat, 'ngán. |
| 16. Night blindness. | 畏夜眼 | Wai' yé' 'ngán. |
| 17. Bronchocele, or goitre. | 鵞喉　喉痺 | ꜁Ngó ꜁hau. ꜁Hau pí'. |
| 18. Bubo. | 魚口 | ꜁Ü 'hau. |
| 19. Burns. Ambustio. | 火傷　火灼　火炙 | 'Fó ꜀shéung. 'Fó chéuk,. 'Fó chik,. |
| 20. Cancer of the breast. | 乳癰 | 'Yü ꜀yung. |
| 21. Carbuncle. Anthrax. | 癰疽　夜明珠 | ꜀Yung ꜀tsü. Yé' ꜁ming ꜀chü. |
| 22. Cataract. Cataracta. | 綠水灌瞳人 | Luk, 'shui kún' ꜁t'ung ꜁yan. |
| 23. Catamenia. | 經水　月水 | ꜀King 'shui. Üt, 'shui. |
| 24. Catarrh. | 傷風 | ꜀Shéung ꜀fung. |
| 25. Cerumen excessive. | 濕耳 | Shap, 'í. |
| 26. Cerumen defective. | 乾耳 | ꜀Kón 'í. |
| 27. Cholera. | 霍亂　吐瀉 | Fok, lün'. T'ò' sé'. |
| 28. Cholic. Cholica. | 心腹絞痛 | ꜀Sam fuk, 'káu t'ung'. |
| 29. Conjunctivitis, or inflammation of the conjunctiva. | 眼蓋內膜赤熱 | 'Ngán 'k'oi noi' mók, ch'ik, ít,. |
| 30. Consumption. Phthisis. | 癆症 | ꜁Lò ching'. |
| 31. Contusion, or bruise. | 損傷 | 'Sün ꜀shéung. |
| 32. Constipation. | 大便秘 | Tái' pín' pai'. |
| 33. Contagion. | 瘟疫 | ꜀Wan yik,. |
| 34. Convulsions. | 癇 | ꜁Hán. |
| 35. Convulsions of the hands and feet. | 手足瘛瘲 | 'Shau tsuk, tsít, tsung'. |
| 36. Cough. Tussis. | 咳嗽 | ꜀K'at sau'. |
| 37. Croup. Cynanche, or sore throat. | 哮㗇 | ꜀Háu ꜀ká. |
| 38. Curvature of the spine. | 曲脊 | Huk, tsik,. |
| 39. Cutaneous diseases. | 皮病 | ꜁P'í ping'. |

27. Among the Chinese at the straits of Malacca, the cholera broke out in 1819, and raged violently, as it did subsequently in other places in its westward course. In Canton, cases are said to occur almost every year; but the disease is not known ever to have raged here, or in any part of China, with that dreadful mortality so common to it in Europe and in Western Asia.

39. Diseases of the skin are very numerous among the Chinese. Their mode of dressing, and the little use made of the bath, are two of the principal reasons for their frequency. The *shirt* is unknown to the Chinese; and their under dress, of whatever description it may be, is

| | | |
|---|---|---|
| 40. Cystitis, or inflammation of the bladder. | 膀胱熱 | ꜀P'óng ꜀kwóng ít$_2$. |
| 41. Dandrif. Pityriasis. | 頭枯皮 | ꜀T'au ꜀kú ꜀p'í. |
| 42. Deafness. Surditas. | 耳聾 | ꜂Í ꜀lung. |
| 43. Dementia, or madness. | 顛狂症　發顛 | ꜀Tín ꜀kw'óng ching'. Fát, ꜀tín. |
| 44. Dentition. | 乳牙 | ꜂Yü ꜀ngá. |
| 45. Diabetes. | 發尿淋 | Fát, níú$^2$ ꜀lam. |
| 46. Acute disease. | 初起之病 | ꜀Ch'ó ꜂hí ꜀chí ping$^2$. |
| 47. Chronic disease. | 痼疾　固病 | Kú' tsat$_2$. Kú' ping$^2$. |
| 48. Dislocation, or luxation. | 跌出骨 | Tít, ch'ut, kwat,. |
| 49. Dumbness. Mutitas. | 啞 | ꜂Á. |
| 50. Dysentery, or flux. | 痢症　紅白痢 | Lí$^2$ ching'. ꜀Hung pák$_2$ lí$^2$. |
| 51. Earache. Disease of the ear. | 耳痛　耳病 | ꜂Í t'ung'. ꜂Í ping$^2$. |
| 52. Ectropium, or turning out of the eyelids. | 顴毛反出 | ꜀K'ün ꜀mò ꜂fán ch'ut,. |
| 53. Enteritis, or inflammation of the intestines. | 腸熱 | ꜀Ch'éung ít$_2$. |
| 54. Entropium, or turning in of the eyelashes. | 顴毛倒插 | ꜀K'ün ꜀mò ꜂tò ch'áp,. |
| 55. Epilepsy. | 發痒吊 | Fát, ꜀yéung tíú'. |
| 56. Eruptions. | 瘢疹 | ꜀Pán ꜂ch'an. |
| 57. Erysipelas. Ignis sacer. | 天泡瘡 | ꜀T'ín ꜀p'ò ꜀ch'óng. |
| 58. Fainting, or syncope. | 失口 | Shat, ꜂hau. |
| 59. Fever. Febris. | 燒病　身熱　瘢症 | ꜀Shíú ping$^2$. ꜀Shan ít$_2$. ꜀Pán ching'. |
| 60. Intermittent fever. Febris intermittens. | 寒熱往來 | ꜀Hón ít$_2$ ꜂wóng ꜀loi. |
| 61. Remittent fever. Febris remittens. | 發冷發熱　瘧疾 | Fát, ꜂lang, fát, ít$_2$. Yéuk, tsat$_2$. |
| 62. Glaucoma, or greenness of the vitreous humor. | 眼珠變綠 | ꜂Ngán ꜀chü pín' luk$_2$. |
| 63. Gonorrhœa. | 白濁 | Pák$_2$ shuk$_2$. |
| 64. Gout. Arthritis, or Podagra. | 酒風脚 | ꜂Tsau ꜀fung kéuk,. |
| 65. Granulations. | 肉芽 | Yuk$_2$ ꜀ngá. |

seldom changed. In their ancient literature, there is mention made of the bathing-tub, on which the sages had their maxims engraved; but public baths seem never to have existed in this country, and private ones are not common, nor much frequented.

59. The kinds of fevers enumerated by Chinese nosologists are numerous, but it is almost impossible to denote their differences so as to distinguish the several species.

| | | |
|---|---|---|
| 66. Gravel, calculus, or stone. | 砂淋 | ˏShá ˏlam. |
| 67. Hepatitis, or inflammation of the liver. | 肝熱 | ˏKón ít$_2$. |
| 68. Hernia. | 跌打出腸 | Tít˒ ˋtá chʻut˒ ˏchʻéung. |
| 69. Hernia. | 小腸氣 | ˋSíú ˏchʻéung híˊ. |
| 70. Hiccup. Singultus. | 打咽 | ˋTá ít˒. |
| 71. Hœmoptysis, or spitting of blood. | 痰有血　吐血 | ˏTʻám ˋyau hüt˒. Tʻòˊ hüt˒. |
| 72. Humpbacked. | 駝背　傴者 | ˏTʻó púiˊ. ˋÜ ˋché. |
| 73. Hydrocele, or dropsy of the scrotum. | 卵脬水脹 | ˋLun ˏfú ˋshui chéungˊ. |
| 74. Hydrophobia. Rabies canina. | 狂犬傳染症 | ˏKwʻóng ˋhün ˏchün ˋím chingˊ. |
| 75. Ichthyosis, or scaly skin. | 生蛇皮　魚鱗皮 | ˏShang ˏshé ˏpʻí. ˏÜ ˏlun ˏpʻí. |
| 76. Idiotism. | 不省人事 | Pat˒ ˋsing ˏyan sz$^2$. |
| 77. Imperforate meatus auditorus. | 無竅耳 | ˏMò kíúˊ ˋí. |
| 78. Incontinence of urine. | 尿急症 | Níú$^2$ kap˒ chingˊ. |
| 79. Indigestion. | 不消化 | Pat˒ ˏsíú ˏfá. |
| 80. Inflammation of the iris. Iritis. | 眼黑睛赤熱 | ˋNgán hak˒ ˏtsing chʻik˒ ít$_2$. |
| 81. Inflammation of the cornea. Corneitis. | 眼外睛赤熱 | ˋNgán ngoi$^2$ ˏtsing chʻik˒ ít$_2$. |
| 82. Itch. | 乾癩　癩瘡 | ˏKón láiˊ. Láiˊ ˏchʻóng. |
| 83. Jaundice. Icterus. | 發黃症 | Fát˒ ˏwóng chingˊ. |
| 84. Lameness. | 跛脚 | ˏPai kéuk˒. |
| 85. Leprosy. Lepra. | 痲瘋　發瘋 | ˏMá ˏfung. Fát˒ ˏfung. |
| 86. Leuce, Alphus, or Lepra. | 白食 | Pák$_2$ shik$_2$. |
| 87. Leucorrhœa. | 流白帶 | ˏLau pák$_2$ táiˊ. |
| 88. Lichen simplex, or the tetter. | 火疔瘡 | ˋFó ˏting ˏchʻóng. |
| 89. Lippitudo, or blear-eyedness. | 爛眼邊 | Lán$^2$ ˋngán ˏpín. |
| 90. Loss of memory. | 症痺　怔忡 | Chingˊ ˏchʻung. Chingˊ ˏchʻung |
| 91. Madness. Mania. | 顛狂症　顛戇症 | ˏTín ˏkwʻóng chingˊ. ˏTín óng$^2$ chingˊ. |
| 92. Mania potu, or delirium tremens. | 發酒顛 | Fát˒ ˋtsau ˏtín. |

74. Hydrophobia seems to be almost unknown among the Chinese. Somewhere among the clauses or notes which accompany the Penal Code, there is mention made of the *kwʻóng hün*, or mad dog. But instances of canine madness, few in this part of the country have ever witnessed.

| | | |
|---|---|---|
| 93. Miasmatic contagion. | 瘴癘 | ,Chéung lai². |
| 94. Measles. Rubeola. | 痲症 | ,Lam ching'. |
| 95. Menses, or Menstruation. | 經水　月水 | ,King 'shui. Üt, 'shui. |
| 96. Menorrhagia. | 血山崩 | Hüt, ,shán ,pang. |
| 97. Muscæ volitantes. | 眼花 | 'Ngán ,fá. |
| 98. Nebulæ, cloudy spots on the corners of the eye. | 蘿蔔花 | ,Ló pák, ,fá. |
| 99. Neuralgia (?) or disease of the nerves. | 筋病 | ,Kan ping². |
| 100. Odontalgia, or toothache. | 牙症 | ,Ngá ching'. |
| 101. Ophthalmia. | 眼〡 | 'Ngán ching'. |
| 102. Acute ophthalmia. | 新患眼 | ,San wán² 'ngán. |
| 103. Chronic ophthalmia. | 遠年患眼 | 'Ün ,nín wán² 'ngán. |
| 104. Purulent ophthalmia. | 眼膠 | 'Ngán ,káu. |
| 105. Rheumatic ophthalmia. | 瘵瀝眼疾 | 'Ló lik, 'ngán tsat,. |
| 106. Scrofulous ophthalmia. | 眼風病 | 'Ngán ,fung ping². |
| 107. Gonorrhœal ophthalmia. | 色眼 | Shik, 'ngán. |
| 108. Otorrhœa, or a discharge from ear. | 生耳睜 | ,Shang 'í tsing². |
| 109. Palpitation of the heart. | 心跳 | ,Sam t'íú'. |
| 110. Palsy. Paralysis. | 癱瘓 | 'T'án ún². |
| 111. Pestilence. | 瘟疫　疫症 | ,Wan yik,. Yik, ching'. |
| 112. Petechiæ. | 瘢症 | ,Pán ching'. |
| 113. Piles. Hœmorrhoids. | 痔瘡 | Chí² ,ch'óng. |
| 114. Pneumonia, or inflammation of the lungs. | 癆疾 | ,Lò tsat,. |
| 115. Polypus of the ear. | 耳花 | 'í ,fá. |
| 116. Nasal polypus. | 鼻中瘜肉 | Pí² ,chung sik, yuk,. |
| 117. Pox, or syphilis. | 疔 | ,Ting. |
| 118. Small-pox. | 痘　出痘 | Tau². Ch'ut, tau². |

93. The phrase, *chéung lai* is used to denote both the disease, miasmatic contagion, and the miasma from which it originates. Other phrases are to be found used in the same manner.

99. Though *kan ping* may be the proper and the best term to denote disease or pain of the nerves, yet it is exceedingly doubtful whether the term is generally understood as applying only to this class of diseases.

| | | |
|---|---|---|
| 119. Chicken-pox. Varicella. | 水泡 | ʻShui pʻáuʼ. |
| 120. Prickly heat. | 熱痱　痱子 | Ít˳ faiʼ. Faiʼ ʻtszʼ. |
| 121. Prolapsus recti. | 脫肛之症 | Tʻüt˳ ˏkóng ˏchí chingʼ. |
| 122. Prolapsus uteri. | 小產落胎下胎 | ʻSíú ʻchʻán. Lók˳ ˏtʻoi. Há˳ ˏtʻoi. |
| 123. Pterygium, or excrescence upon the eye. | 老肉扳睛 | ʿLò yuk˳ ˏpʻán ˏtsing. |
| 124. Ptosis, or inability to raise the eyelid. | 睛皮墜下 | ˏTsing ˏpʻí chui˳ há˳. |
| 125. Closed pupil, with deposition of lymph. | 瞳人閉合 | ˏTʻung ˏyan paiʼ hóp˳. |
| 126. Quinsy. Cynanchea tonsillaris. | 喉嚨痛 | ˏHau ˏlung tʻungʼ. |
| 127. Rheumatism. | 風濕 | ˏFung shap˳. |
| 128. Ringworm, or Tinea capitis. | 金錢癬 | ˏKam ˏtsʻín ʻsín. |
| 129. Scorbutus, or scurvy. | 生疽 | ˏShang ˏtsü. |
| 130. Scrofula. | 瘰癧 | ʻLó lik˳. |
| 131. Sea-sickness. | 運浪　嘔浪 | Wan˳ lóng˳. ʻAu lóng˳. |
| 132. Near-sightedness. | 近視眼 | Kan˳ shí˳ ʿngán. |
| 133. Far-sightedness. | 遠視眼 | ʿYün shí˳ ʿngán. |
| 134. Shingles, or Herpes zoster. | 腰帶癬　圍腰癬 | ˏÍú táiʼ ʻsín. ˏWai ˏíú ʻsín. |
| 135. Sleepiness of the foot. | 脚痺 | Kéuk˳ píʼ. |
| 136. Stammering, or stuttering. | 口吃 | ʻHau kat˳. |
| 137. Staphyloma, or projection of the cornea. | 凸眼珠　大眼珠 | Tat˳ ʿngán ʻchü. Tái˳ ʿngán ʻchü. |
| 138. Strabismus, crosseyed, or squinting. | 斜視眼 | ˏTsʻé shí˳ ʿngán. |
| 139. Strangury. | 小便熱痛 | ˏSíú ʻpín ít˳ tʻungʼ. |
| 140. Stone. | 膀胱大砂淋 | ˏPʻóng ˏkwóng tái˳ ˏshá ˏlam. |
| 141. Suffocation by drowning. | 溺水痰壅 | Nik˳ ʻshui ˏtʻám ʻyung. |
| 142. Syphilis. | 生疔 | ˏShang ˏting. |
| 143. Tetanus, or lockjaw. | 口噤　牙關緊閉 | ʻHau kamʼ. ˏNgá ˏkwán ʻkan paiʼ. |

147. Vaccination appears to have been entirely unknown to the Chinese, until introduced in 1805, by Alexander Pearson, esq., surgeon of the East India Company's factory, who both vaccinated numbers himself, and wrote a small tract in explanation of the theory and art: it was translated into Chinese by sir George Staunton. From that time to the present, an efficient vaccine establishment has been maintained at Canton, first under the care of doctor Pearson, and subsequently under a native gentleman, He qua, who was initiated and well instructed in the business by the founder of the institution. From Canton, the practice has spread into

| | | |
|---|---|---|
| 144. Tinnitus aurium, or ringing in the ears. | 耳鳴 | ʿI ˏming. |
| 145. Tumors. | 肉瘤 | Yuk₂ ˏlau. |
| 146. Ulcers and sores. | 瘡 | ˏCh'óng. |
| 147. Vaccination. | 種痘 | Chung² tau². |
| 148. Venereal ulcers. | 楊梅瘡 | ˏYéung ˏmúi ˏch'óng. |
| 149. Vertigo, or giddiness. | 頭運眼花 | ˏT'au wan² ʿngán ˏfá. |
| 150. Warts and corns. | 雞眼 | ˏKai ʿngán. |
| 151. Worms. | 虫 胃虫 | ˏCh'ung. Wai² ˏch'ung. |
| 152. Wounds. | 傷處 傷 | ˏShéung ch'ü². ˏShéung. |
| 153. Xeroma, or dryness of the eyes. | 無淚眼 乾眼 | ˏMò lui² ʿngán. ˏKon ʿngán. |

several, if not most, of the provinces of the empire, and the tract has also been widely circulated, the Chinese publishers carefully suppressing its foreign origin.

152. External diseases, and especially those injuries which are caused by violence, called *shéung*, do not usually form a distinct class with the Chinese. And surgery, or chirurgery, as a distinct science, a separate branch of the healing art, is quite unknown to native physicians; there is not, probably, one in the empire who would venture to attempt to open a vein, or to amputate a finger.

## Section Third.

## MATERIA MEDICA.

### 百藥類第三章
Pák₃ yéuk₂ lui²; tai² ˏsám ˏchéung.

| | | |
|---|---|---|
| 1. Whatsoever things are produced in the world,—birds, beasts, creeping things, and fishes, which are generated, and have blood and breath; likewise flowers and trees, which are generated, but are without blood and breath; | 凡天下生物飛獸虫魚生而血氣者也如草如木生無血氣者 | ˏFán ˏt'ín há² ˏshang mat₂, ˏfí shau³, ˏch'ung, ˏü, ˏshang ˏí hüt₃ hí³ ʿché ʿyá. ˏYü ʿts'ò, ˏyü muk₂ ˏshang ˏmò hüt₃ |

### *Notes and Explanations.*

THE Materia Medica of Lí Shíchan, often mentioned and quoted in the preceding pages, is comprised in forty octavo volumes, divided into fifty-two chapters. The 1st and 2d chapters consist of introductory matters; and with them are included the *Mán Fóng Kám Sín*, noticed in the preceding section;—the whole filling seven volumes. The 3d and 4th contain lists of medicines for the cure of all diseases, which fill three volumes and a half. The 5th chapter treats of

and also inanimate objects, such as rocks and hard iron,—all these can be used as healing medicines. Those examined in the Materia Medica of Lí Shichan, amount to one thousand, eight hundred, and seventy-one kinds.

也頑然如石堅然如鐵者皆可作爲醫藥也攷諸李時珍本草得一千八百七十一種

hí' ʻché ʻyá. ˏWán ˏin ˏü shik₂, ˏkín ˏin ˏü t'ít, ʻché, ˏkái ʻhó tsók, ˏwai ˏí yéuk₂ ʻyá. ʻHáu ˏchü ʻLí ˏShi ˏchan ʻPún ʻTs'ò tak, yat, ts'ín pát, pák, ts'at, shap, yat, ʻchung.

2. The notable arrangement in the work of Shannung.

3. Of the first class of medicines there are 120 kinds, which are sovereign, and the chief supporters of human life, thereby resembling heaven. They are not poisonous, and however freely or constantly used they are harmless. If you would exhilirate the body, and improve the breath, and retard the approach of age, use this first class of medicines.

神農本經名例

上藥一百二十種爲君主養命以應天無毒多服久服不傷人欲輕身益氣不老延年者本上經

ˏShan ˏnung ʻpún ˏking ˏming lai².

Shéung² yéuk₂ yat, pák, i² shap₂ ʻchung, ˏwai ˏkwan, ʻchü ʻyéung ming², ʻí ying' ˏt'ín. ˏMò tuk₂ ˏtò fuk₂ ʻkau fuk₂ pat, ˏshéung ˏyan. Yuk₂ ˏhing ˏshan yik, hí', pat, ʻlò ˏín ˏnín ʻché, ʻpún shéung² ˏking.

4. Of the second class there are 120 kinds, which are ministering servants, and the chief supporters of human nature, thereby resembling man. Some are poisonous and some not, and they ought to be used with caution. If you wish to check disease, and restore those who are thin and emaciated, use the second class of medicines.

中藥一百二十種爲臣主養性以應人無毒有毒斟酌其宜欲遏病補虛羸者本中經

ˏChung yéuk₂ yat, pák, i² shap₂ ʻchung, ˏwai ˏshan, ʻchü ʻyéung sing', ʻí ying' ˏyan. ˏMò tuk₂ ʻyau tuk₂, ˏcham chéuk, ˏk'í ˏí. Yuk₂ át, ping², ʻpò ˏh'ü ˏlúi ʻché, ʻpún ˏchung ˏking.

waters; the 6th, of fires; the 7th, of earths. In chapters 8, 9, 10, and 11, metals and rocks are described. Chapters 12 to 37 inclusive, are devoted to the vegetable kingdom. The 38th treats of garments and domestic utensils. The remaining chapters, from the 39th to the 52d, treat of the various tribes in the animal kingdom. The preceding chapters fill thirty-nine volumes; the fortieth is filled with dissertations and notices respecting the pulse. The properties of the articles discussed are considered in a very methodical manner, so that the student can immediately turn to a plant or mineral, and ascertain its virtues by a moment's inspection. Thus, the properties of the various parts of a horse are treated of under twenty-four heads, in which the qualities and efficacy of the viscera, hair, hoofs, &c., &c., are described. See Chinese Repository, Vol. VII., page 393.

The shop of an apothecary in Canton is said to contain usually not less than three hundred medicines; yet the most intelligent of the Chinese affirm that forty or fifty only are absolutely necessary in medical practice. In the streets and markets, there are numerous stalls in which are exposed for sale a great many fresh and dried vegetable substances, which have never been received into any European pharmacopœia. Most of these, together with whatever other articles can be gleaned from the kingdoms of nature, and are used in the materia medica of the Chinese, may be found enumerated in the chapters on natural history.

5. There are 125 kinds of medicines of the third class, which are assistants and agents, curing diseases, thereby resembling earth. They are poisonous, and ought not to be much used. If you wish to remove cold or heat, correct bad breath, or break up congestion, or cure disease, use the medicines comprised in this class.

下藥一百二十
五種爲佐使主
治病以應地多
毒不可久服欲
除寒熱邪氣破
積聚愈疾者本
下經

Há2 yéuk2 yat, pák, í2 shap2 'ng 'chung, ,wai tsó' sz". 'chü chí2 ping2 'í ying' tí2. ,To tuk2 pat, 'hó 'kau fuk2. Yuk2 ,ch'ü ,hón ít2, ,ts'é hí'. p'ó' tsik, tsü2 ü2 tsat, 'ché. 'pún há2 ,king.

6. These three kinds being united make three hundred and sixty-five, corresponding [in number] to the three hundred and sixty-five degrees into which the zodiac is divided, one degree answering to one day, and so completing a year. This number doubled, will give seven hundred and thirty names.

三品合三百六
十五種法三百
六十五度一度
應一日以成一
歲倍其數合七
百三十名也

,Sám 'pan hop2 ,sám pák, luk2 shap2 'ng 'chung, fát, ,sám pák, luk2 shap2 'ng tò2, yat, tò2 ying' yat, yat2 'í ,shing yat, sui'. 'P'úi ,k'i shò' hóp2 ts'at, pák, ,sám shap, ,ming 'yá.

7. Medicines have sovereigns, ministers, assistants, and agents, by which they promulge and receive. An harmonic union ought to have one sovereign, two ministers, three assistants, and five agents; also one sovereign, three ministers, and nine assistants and agents, is a good combination.

藥有君臣佐使
以相宣攝合和
宜一君二臣三
佐五使又可一
君三臣九佐使
也

Yéuk2 'yau ,kwan, ,shan, tsó'. sz", 'í ,séung ,ssün shíp, hóp2 ,wo ,í yat, ,kwan, í2 ,shan, ,sám tsó', 'ng sz"; yau2 'hó yat, ,kwan, ,sám ,shan, 'kau tsó' sz" 'yá.

8. There are medicines which are to be used alone; others must be used together; some are to be employed as agents; some stand in awe of each other; and among some

藥有單行者有
相須者有相使
者有相畏者有

Yéuk2 'yau ,tán ,hang 'che: 'yau ,séung ,sü 'ché; 'yau ,séung sz" 'ché; 'yau ,séung wai' 'ché; 'yau ,séung ú'

2—6. This arrangement—by tradition attributed to Shannung—is more curious and fanciful than rational or useful; it is here introduced, from the sixth volume of the Materia Medica, as a specimen of those imaginary systems, which are still adhered to by the Chinese as tenaciously as they ever were by western physicians of olden times.

7. What may have been, or what can ever be, the advantage of such a distribution of medicines, the Chinese physicians do not explain, nor is it easy to imagine. The theory is founded on the constitution of the state, but the relation in numbers is not very well maintained, there being only two or three ministers for a sovereign. There are other systems of a somewhat similar nature, in which the domestic relations of father and son, elder and younger brothers, &c., are introduced.

8. Of the 365 kinds of medicines forming the system of the celebrated Shannung, 71 are to be used alone, 12 are to be used with each other, 90 are employed as agents, 78 stand in awe of each other, 60 are repulsive or hate each other, 18 are opposites, and 36 neutralize each other.

there is mutual repulsion; others there are which are opposites; and also some neutralize each other. Whenever medicines with these seven natures are to be mixed together for use, it will be well to employ those which associate and assist each other; but you must not employ those which repel and are opposites one to the other. If a malignant case is to be treated, employ those which stand in awe of or neutralize one another; otherwise you must not use the medicines together.

相惡者有相反者有相殺者凡此七情合和時之當用相須相使者良勿用相惡相反者若有毒宜制可用相畏相殺者不爾勿合用也

'ché; 'yau ,séung 'fán 'ché; 'yau ,séung shát, 'ché. ,Fán 'ts'z' ts'at, 'tsing hóp, ,wó shí' ,chí ,tóng yung' ,séung ,sü ,séung sz' 'ché ,léung; mat, yung' ,séung ú' ,séung 'fán 'ché. Yéuk, 'yau tuk, ,í chai' 'hó yung' ,séung wai' ,séung shát, 'ché, pat, 'í mat, hóp, yung' 'yá.

9. Medicines have acidity, saltness, sweetness, bitterness, and acridness, which are their five tastes: there is the acidity of vinegar; the saltness of salt; the sweetness of liquorice; the bitterness of rhubarb; and the acridness of pepper.

藥有酸鹹甘苦辛藥之五味醋之酸食鹽之鹹甘草之甘大黃之苦花椒之辛

Yéuk, 'yau ,sün, ,hám, ,kóm, 'fú, ,san, yéuk, ,chí 'ng mí': ts'ò' ,chí ,sün; shik, ,ím ,chí ,hám; ,kóm 'ts'ò ,chí ,kóm; tái' ,wóng ,chí 'fú: ,fá ,tsíú ,chí ,san.

10. They also have the properties of cold and heat, of warmth and coolness: for example, the cold of gypsum; the heat of cassia; the warmth of oily nuts; and the coolness of the oil of peppermint.

又有寒熱溫涼性如石膏之寒桂皮之熱半夏之溫薄荷之涼

Yau' 'yau ,hón, ít,, ,wan, ,léung, sing': ,ü shik, ,kò ,chí ,hón; kwai' ,p'í ,chí ít,; pún' há' ,chí ,wan; pók, ,hó ,chí ,léung.

11. There are the four smells of fragrant, fetid, frowzy, and rank; thus aloes, sandal-wood and musk have a fragrant smell; garlic and assafetida have a fetid smell; fowls, fish, ducks, snakes, &c.,

香臭腥臊四氣如沉檀麝則其氣香蒜與阿魏則其氣臭雞魚

,Héung, ch'au', ,sing, ,tsò, sz' hí': ,ü ,ch'am, ,t'án, shé', tsak, ,k'í hí' ,héung; sün' ,ü ,ó ngai', tsak, ,k'í hí' ch'au';

These *seven natures*,—properties, qualities, or passions—are apparently imaginary; they have never been recognized in European books, nor can they be very accurately described.

9. Tastes, with the Chinese as with Europeans, are very numerous, and vary in kind and strength to an extent almost interminable. An accurate classification of them is impracticable. Those here enumerated are easily understood and recognized, and, with the subdivisions, they quite sufficient for all useful purposes. There is another distinction, that of agreeable and disagreeable, instinctively recognized by brute animals; the first being for the most part wholesome and nutritious, while those composing the second are hurtful.

10. These qualities are constantly referred to in Chinese medical works; the third and fourth appear to be merely modifications of the first and second,—being the same in kind and differing only in degree.

11. *Héung* and *ch'au* are common words to denote such smells as are grateful or offensive, whatsoever may be their source. *Sing* is the smell which proceeds from animals when disem-

have a frowzy smell; foxes, have a rank smell.

鴨蛇則其氣腥狐貍則其氣臊

kai, ü, áp, shé, tsak, k'i hí' sing; ú lí tsak, k'i hí' tsò.

12. Medicines operate three ways, by causing perspiration, vomiting, and purging.

有三治曰汗曰吐曰下

'Yau sám chí', üt, hon', üt, t'ò', üt, há'.

13. There are six incurable cases. The self-indulgent and the profligate, unreasonably violating propriety, is the 1st case; the inconstant and the covetous, is the 2d case; the unsuitably clothed and fed, is the 3d case; the constitution which has its functions deranged, is the 4th case; the emaciated who is unable to take medicines, is the 5th; and the believer in enchantments, who has no faith in physicians, is the 6th case.

有六不治驕恣不論干理一不治輕身重財二不治衣食不適三不治陰陽臟氣不定四不治形羸不能服藥五不治信巫不信醫六不治

'Yau luk, pat, chí'. Kiú ts'z' pat, lun' kòn 'lí, yat, pat, chí'; hing shan chung' ts'oi, í' pat, chí'; í shik, pat, shik, sám pat, chí'; yam yéung tsóng' hí' pat, ting', sz' pat, chí'; ying lúi pat, nang fuk, yéuk, 'ng pat, chí'; sun' mò pat, sun' í, luk, pat, chí'.

14. Disease may prove fatal in six ways;—in the 1st place, by its not being examined; in the 2d, by its not being acknowledged; in the 3d, by its being neglected; in the 4th, by the bad choice of a physician; in the 5th, by his not understanding the disease: if there exist one of these six causes of failures, then the cure will be difficult.

病有六失失于不審失于不信失于不過時失于不擇醫失于不識病六失有一即爲難治

Ping' 'yau luk, shat,: shat, ü pat, 'sham; shat, ü pat, sun'; shat, ü pat, kwò' shí; shat, ü pat, chák, í; shat, ü pat, shik, ping'; luk, shat, 'yau yat, tsik, wai nán chí'.

15. The nature of medicines requires that some of them be used as pills, others ought to be used as powders, others boiled in water, others should be steeped in wine, and others fried in fat; and there may also be materials that re-

藥性有宜丸者宜散者宜水煮者宜酒漬者宜膏煎者亦有一

Yéuk, sing' 'yau í ün 'ché; í sán' 'ché, í 'shui 'chü 'ché, í 'tsau tsik, 'ché, í kò tsín 'ché, yik, 'yau yat, mat,

bowelled; *tsò* is the rank, strong, effluvia from animals in heat, and the peculiar odor given off by some of the canine animals.

14. This is quoted from the sixth volume of the *Pún Ts'ò*, page 50; and appears to be a fragment of some one of the ancient authors, who had named *six ways* in which disease might prove fatal; but in the book from which it is quoted, no reason is assigned for the omission of one of the six.

15. The Chinese have their treatises on regimen, in which are rules for the attainment of long life. One of these is divided into four parts; the 1st treats of the heart and affections, the 2d treats of food, the 3d of business, and the 4th of rest by sleep. These treatises comprise, with some things that are fanciful, many very useful remarks, which are evidently the result of careful observation and long experience.

| | | |
|---|---|---|
| quire a combination of these modes. Some there may be which cannot be used with hot water or wine. Always have regard to the nature of the medicine, that it may not be resisted or disregarded. | 物兼宜者亦有<br>不可入湯酒者<br>並隨藥性不得<br>違越 | ˌkím ˌı ˈché. Yik˒ ˈyau pat˒ ˈhó yap˒ ˌt'óng ˈtsau ˈche. Ping˒ ˌts'ui yéuk˒ sing˒, pat˒ tak˒ ˌwai üt˒. |
| 16. Because all things may be used in the materia medica, it is unnecessary to enumerate them in detail; but some of them are taken and compounded and mixed so as to form a new medicine, which is then known by a new name. Of such the following are the most important. | 萬物皆可作藥<br>石用也不消繁<br>敘乃有以之泡<br>製埋劑斯成妙<br>藥名以新方此<br>以下凡最重者 | Mán² mat˒ ˌkái ˈhó tsok˒ yéuk˒ shik˒ yung² ˈyá, pat˒ ˌsíu ˌfán tsü²; ˈnái ˈyau ˈi ˌchí p'áu˒ chai˒ ˌmái ˌtsai, ˌsz˒ ˌshing míu˒ yéuk˒, ˌming ˈi ˌsan ˌfong. ˈTsz˒ ˈi há˒ ˌfán tsui˒ chung² ˈché. |
| 17. Absorbents. | 滲濕收濇之劑 | ˈSham shap˒. ˌShau shik˒ ˌchí ˌtsai. |
| 18. Acetous. | 有醋的 | ˈYau ts'ò˒ tik˒. |
| 19. Aliments. | 食物　養物 | Shik² mat². ˈYéung mat². |
| 20. Aromatics. | 味類 | Mí² lui². |
| 21. Octo-genii, or octo-angelic cakes. | 八仙糕 | Pát˒ ˌsín ˌkò. |

16. The articles—mineral, animal, and vegetable—comprised in the Materia Medica of Lí Shíchan, are severally described in the following order. Taking for an example, *táiwóng*, or rhubarb, which is the 1st article in the 4th family of the 1st order of vegetable productions, in vol. xx, chap. 17; it is treated under eight distinct heads, the whole description occupying seven leaves, or 14 octavo pages. Under the 1st head, *shik ming*, the Chinese scientific name and the synonyms by which it is known are explained. Under the 2d, *tsáp kái*, there is a collection of explanations, comprising the history and botanical description of the plant. Under the 3d, *ching 'ng*, are corrections of errors, and instructions for preventing the improper use of the article as a medicine. Under the 4th, *sau ch'i*, the mode of preparing it for use is detailed. Under the 5th, *hí mí*, its taste, smell, etc., are noticed. Under the 6th, *chü chí*, its masterly operations, i. e. its specific virtues as a medicine, are enumerated. Under the 7th, *fát ming*, is given a clear exposition of its uses, in other words, its rationale. Under the 8th and last head, *fú fnóg*, there is a list of recipes, with the names of the maladies for which it is a remedy. There is some variety in the mode of describing different articles; thus, the roots, branches, flowers, secretions and fruit of a tree, if each is to be used separately as a medicine, will have its own description. So in describing animals; the various organs and secretions are treated of under separate heads, enabling the student immediately to refer to any part he wishes to examine. In the main, however, the above order is preserved throughout the book.

17. These two terms, *sham shap*, and *shau shik chí tsai*, are applied to those medicinal substances which have the faculty of withdrawing moisture from the atmosphere, or any object to which they are applied. They seem also to be applied sometimes to those medicines which have no acrimony in themselves and neutralize acidity in the stomach and bowels, such as magnesia, prepared chalk, &c. The word *tsai* is, in its correct application, confined to compounded medicines.

18. The words *yau tik*, belonging to, or possessing the quality of, occurring in the phrase *yau ts'ò tik*, is a common mode of expressing a quality or nature, indicated in English by *ous*, *ish*, &c. This phrase may serve as a model for forming or rendering other similar sentences.

| | | |
|---|---|---|
| 22. Carbonaceous powders. | 百草霜 | Pák, 'ts'ò ,séung. |
| 23. Cathartic. | 泄瀉之劑 | Sít, sé' ,chí ,tsai. |
| 24. Caustic. | 艾茸 | Ngái$^{2}$ ,yung. |
| 25. Chemist, or druggist(?) | 丹家 | ,Tán ,ká. |
| 26. Cinchona bark. | 金鷄勒 | ,Kam ,kai lak$_{2}$. |
| 27. Diuretic. | 動小便的藥 | Tung$^{2}$ 'síú pín$^{2}$ tik, yéuk$_{2}$. |
| 28. Emetic. | 嘔吐之劑 | 'Au 't'ò ,chí ,tsai. |
| 29. Enema. | 以藥硬納便道中 | 'Í yéuk$_{2}$ ngáng' náp$_{2}$ pín$^{2}$ tò$^{2}$ ,chung. |
| 30. Ferment. | 釀 | Yéung$^{2}$. |
| 31. Hartshorn. | 鹿茸 | Luk$_{2}$ ,yung. |
| 32. Iron filings. | 鐵屑 | T'ít, sít,. |
| 33. Liquor of divine healing. | 聖愈湯 | Shing' yü$^{2}$ ,t'óng. |
| 34. Lixivium. | 堅水 | ,Kín 'shui. |
| 35. Lotions. | 洗藥　洗滌 | Sai' yéuk$_{2}$. 'Sai tik$_{2}$. |
| 36. Medicine. | 藥 | Yéuk$_{2}$. |
| 37. Myrrh. | 没藥 | Mút$_{2}$ yéuk$_{2}$. |
| 38. Ointment. | 膏 | ,Kò. |
| 39. Oil of peppermint. | 薄荷油 | Pók$_{2}$ ,hó ,yau. |
| 40. Panacea. | 藥萬病 | Yéuk$_{2}$ mán$^{2}$ ping$^{2}$. |
| 41. Pill. | 藥丸　丹 | Yéuk$_{2}$ ,ün. ,Tán. |
| 42. Plaster. | 膏藥 | ,Kò yéuk$_{2}$. |
| 43. Potion for warming the stomach. | 温胃飲 | ,Wan wai' 'yam. |
| 44. Powder. | 粉　散 | 'Fan. Sán'. |
| 45. Prescription. | 藥方子 | Yéuk$_{2}$ ,fong 'tsz'. |
| 46. Refrigerants. | 清熱的藥 | 'Ts'ing ít$_{2}$ tik, yéuk$_{2}$. |
| 47. Sudorific medicines. | 發表之劑 | Fát, 'píú ,chí ,tsai. |

33. Recipes for many kinds of cakes, liquors, lotions, pills, powders, plasters, etc., with sundry directions for using them, may be found in the Golden Mirror; see chap. LXII.

## Section Fourth.

## ANATOMY.

### 骨節臟腑第四章
Kwat, tsít, tsóng' 'fú; tai' sz' ‚chéung.

| | | |
|---|---|---|
| 1. Abdomen; the part below the diaphragm is called the abdomen, or vulgarly the belly: the part below the umbilicus is called the small abdomen. | 腹者膈之下曰腹俗名曰肚臍之下曰小腹 | Fuk, 'ché, kák, ‚chí há' üt, fuk,, tsuk, ‚ming üt, 't'ò; ‚ts'z' ‚chí há' üt, 'síú fuk,. |
| 2. Acetabulum, the cup-like cavity of the os innominatum. | 髀樞環跳穴處 | ‚P'í ‚sh'ü, ‚wán t'íú' üt, ch'ü'. |
| 3. Adipose substance, or the fat. | 膏肉 | ‚Kò yuk,. |
| 4. Alveolar process. | 牙藏骨 | ‚Ngá ‚ch'óng kwat,. |
| 5. Ankle; below the bones of the leg, and above the top of the foot, on the two sides, there projects out a high bone; the one on the outside is the externus malleolus, and the one on the inside is the internus malleolus. Vulgarly, they are called the foot's eyes. | 踝者胻骨之下足附之上兩旁突出高骨在外爲外踝在內爲內踝俗曰脚眼 | Wá' 'ché, ‚hang kwat, ‚chí há' tsuk, fú' ‚chí shéung' 'léung ‚p'óng tat, ch'ut, ‚kò kwat,; tsoi' ngoi' ‚wai ngoi' wá', tsoi' noi' ‚wai noi' wá'. Tsuk, üt, kéuk, 'ngán. |
| 6. Anus. | 肛門　穀道 | ‚Kung ‚mún. Kuk, tò'. |
| 7. Arms is the general designation of the two large limbs on the upper part of the | 臂者上身兩大肢之通稱也一 | Pí' 'ché, shéung' ‚shan 'léung tái' ‚chí ‚chí ‚t'ung ‚ch'ing |

### *Notes and Explanations.*

WHILE anatomy is admitted by western physicians to be the basis of medical science, it is by the Chinese almost wholly unknown and neglected. The single fact that dissection is seldom if ever attempted in this country is evidence enough to prove that there cannot be any very accurate knowledge of the human frame and its functions. Animal physiology is of course, but partially understood. This section comprises, with few exceptions, only such terms as are in use among the Chinese, and well-understood by them. From the nature of the case, it is very limited—those names being for the most part excluded from it which, though well-known by foreigners, are not recognized by the Chinese, and *vice versâ*. A very few new terms have been admitted, and where much doubt exists as to the correctness of any such it is indicated by a point of interrogation. Some account of the human body has already been given on preceding pages; see chapter II. In the Golden Mirror, noticed on page 499, human anatomy occupies several chapters, commencing with the 80th, in which the principal parts of the osseous system are named, and the names anatomically defined. A similar list of terms and definitions occurs in the *Lui King*, or Medical Cyclopedia, by Chéung, vol. XVII.

1, 7. These definitions of the abdomen and arms are copied verbatim from the Golden Mirror. The latter definition, though it is very deficient and even erroneous in regard to the position and size of the ulna and radius, yet clearly points to them in the *ching fú í kwat*, as the primary and secondary bones of the fore-arm.

| | | |
|---|---|---|
| body; they are also called *kwang*, and vulgarly, *yikp'ók*. The joint in the middle of the arm, where the bones in the upper and lower part of the arm are joined together, is called the elbow. The bone above the elbow is called the humerus. The bones below the elbow are called the fore-arm: the bones of the fore-arm are two, a primary and a secondary; the secondary (or the *ulna*) is joined above, is short, small, and inclined outwards; the primary (or *radius*) is articulated at the lower end, is long, large, and inclined inwards. At the lower extremity they both join the bones of the wrist. | 名曰肱俗名肐髆肐髆中節上下骨交接處名曰肘肘上之骨曰臑骨肘下之骨曰臂骨臂、有正輔二骨輔骨在上短細偏外正骨居下長大偏內俱下接腕骨也 | 'yá; yat, ,ming üt, ,kwang, tsuk, ,ming yik, p'ók,. Yik, p'ók, ,chung tsít, shéung² há² kwat, ,káu tsíp, ch'ü', ,ming üt, 'chau. 'Chau shéung² ,chí kwat, üt, ,nò kwat,. 'Chau há² ,chí kwat, üt, pí² kwat,; pí² kwat, 'yau ching' fú², fú² kwat, tsoi² shéung² 'tün sai' ,p'ín ngoi²; ching' kwat, ,kü há² ,ch'éung tai² ,p'ín noi². ,Kü há² tsíp, 'ún kwat, 'yá. |
| 8. Arteries. (?) | 脈筋 | Mak, ,kan. |
| 9. Articulations; place that can be bent and straightened. | 鉸可曲可直處 | Káu'; 'hó huk, 'hó chik, ch'ü'. |
| 10. Astragalus, ankle-bone, or sling bone. (?) | 核骨 | Hat, kwat,. |
| 11. Auditory foramen. | 耳吼 | 'Í ,lung. |
| 12. Axilla; vulgarly called the arm-pit. | 腋俗名肐肢窩 | Yik, tsuk, ,ming yik, ,chí ,wó. |
| 13. Basilar process of the temporal bone. | 完骨 | ,Ün kwat,. |
| 14. The gall-bladder. | 胆 | 'Tám. |
| 15. The urinary bladder. | 膀胱 | ,P'óng ,kwóng. |
| 16. Blood vessels. (?) | 經絡經脈絡脈 | ,King lók,. ,King mak,. Lók, mak,. |
| 17. Bones of the head. | 頭骨 | ,T'au kwat,. |
| 18. The brain is the marrow of the head. | 腦者頭骨之髓 | 'Nò 'ché, ,t'au kwat, ,chí 'tsui. |
| 19. Internal canthus, or inner corner of the eye. | 眼頭 內眥 | 'Ngán ,t'au. Noi² ts'z'. |
| 20. External canthus, or outer corner of the eye. | 眼尾 外眥 | 'Ngán 'mí. Ngoi² ts'z'. |
| 21. Capillaries. (?) | 小血筋 | 'Síú hüt, ,kan. |
| 22. Capsule of the lens. | 眼珠胎 | 'Ngán ,chü ,t'oi. |
| 23. Cardiac orifice of the stomach. | 胃管口 賁門 | Wai² 'kún 'hau. ,Pan ,mún. |

17. Terms for designating the bones of the head, bones of the back, and those of all other parts of the body, are formed by joining the word *kwat* to these several parts respectively; an enumeration of them, therefore, is unnecessary.

| | | |
|---|---|---|
| 24. Carpal bones are those small bones situated where the hand and the wrist are joined together. | 碎骨者在掌腕交接處 | Súi' kwat, 'ché, tsoi' 'chéung 'ún ˏkáu tsíp, ch'ü'. |
| 25. Cartilages (literally, flexible bones). | 脆骨 | Ts'ui' kwat,. |
| 26. Ensiform cartilage of the sternum, or the bone covering the heart. This substance is a cartilaginous bone, and is situated at the bottom of the sternum, and between the divisions of that appendage. | 鳩尾者即蔽心骨也其質係脆亻在胸骨之下岐骨之間 | ˏKau 'mí 'ché, tsik, pai' ˏsam kwat, 'yá. ˏK'í chat, hai' ts'ui' kwat, tsoi' ˏhung kwat, ˏchí há' ˏk'í kwat, ˏchí ˏkán. |
| 27. Caruncula lachrymalis, gland in the corner of the eye. | 眼頭肉 | 'Ngán ˏt'au yuk,. |
| 28. Cellular tissue, or the texture of animal organs. | 網膏 | ˏMóng ˏkò. |
| 29. Cerebellum, or little brain. | 小腦漿 | 'Síú 'nò ˏtséung. |
| 30. Cerebrum, or brain. | 腦漿 | 'Nò ˏtséung. |
| 31. Cerumen, or ear-wax. | 耳臘 | 'Í láp,. |
| 32. Chamber of the eye, anterior. (?) | 眼前方 | 'Ngán ˏts'ín ˏfóng. |
| 33. Chamber of the eye, posterior. (?) | 眼後方 | 'Ngán hau' ˏfóng. |
| 34. Cheeks. | 頰 | Káp,. |
| 35. Cheek-bones (or the ossa malarum) are the prominent square bones which form the upper part of the cheeks. | 顴者面兩旁高起之大骨也 | ˏK'ün 'ché mín' 'léung ˏp'óng ˏkò 'hí ˏchí tái' kwat, 'yá. |
| 36. Chin. | 下把 | Há' 'pá. |
| 37. Covering or base of the chin. | 頦者即下把殼 | ˏHoi 'ché, tsik, há' 'pá hok,. |
| 38. Choroid coat, or second tunic of the eye. (?) | 眼睛內黑皮 | 'Ngán ˏtsing noi' hak, ˏp'í. |
| 39. Cilia, or the eyelashes. | 顴毛 | ˏK'ün ˏmò. |
| 40. Clavicle is a bone outside of the top-ridge of the sternum, above the cartilages of the ribs, commonly called the collar-bone. Interiorly it joins on the upper ribs, externally it joins upon the top of the shoulder joint. | 拄骨者膺上缺盆之外俗名鎖子骨也內接横骨外接肩解也 | ˏCh'ü kwat, 'ché ˏying shéung' hüt, ˏp'ún ˏchí ngoi'. tsuk, ˏming 'só 'tsz' kwat, 'yá. Noi' tsíp, ˏwáng kwat,, ngoi' tsíp, ˏkín 'kái 'yá. |
| 41. Cochlea, or spiral bone of the ear. | 耳內螺骨 | 'Í noi' ˏló kwat,. |

26. *Kau mí* literally signifies dove's tail, which this cartilage resembles, and from which it derives its name. *Ts'ui kwat* is the white elastic substance growing to the bones, commonly called gristle; *k'í kwat* is a forked bone.

40. *Ch'ü kwat* is a transverse bone, and is commonly called by the Chinese, as in Europe, the *só tsz' kwat*, or the key bone; *hüt p'ún* seems to denote the upper ridge of the sternum.

| | | |
|---|---|---|
| 42. Concha, or trumpet of the ear. | 蔽者耳門也 | Pai' 'ché ʻí ˏmún ʻyá. |
| 43. Condyles of the femur. | 連骸 | ˏLín ˏhoi. |
| 44. Conjunctiva oculi. | 眼睛膜 | ʻNgán ˏtsing mók₂. |
| 45. Conjunctiva corneæ. | 眼盖內膜 | ʻNgán k'oi' noi² mók₂. |
| 46. Conjunctiva palpebræ. | 眼外睛膜 | ʻNgán ngoi² ˏtsing mók₂. |
| 47. Cornea, or anterior transparent convex part of the eye. | 眼外亅 | ʻNgán ngoi² ˏtsing. |
| 48. Crystalline lens. | 眼睛珠 | ʻNgán ˏtsing ˏchü. |
| 49. Dermis. | 網皮 | ˏMóng ˏp'í. |
| 50. Diaphragm. | 膈者 | Kák, 'ché. |
| 51. Nasal duct. | 鼻管 | Pí² 'kún. |
| 52. Lachrymal duct. | 眼淚管 | ʻNgán lui² 'kún. |
| 53. Lactiferous duct. | 出乳管 | Ch'ut, ʻyü 'kún. |
| 54. Dura mater, or thick membrane around the brain. | 腦漿韌膜 | ʻNò ˏtséung yan' mók₂. |
| 55. Elbow. | 手拗 | 'Shau áu'. |
| 56. Enamel. (?) | 牙皮 | ˏNgá ˏp'í. |
| 57. Epidermis, or scarf-skin. | 薄皮 | Pók₂ ˏp'í. |
| 58. Epiglottis. | 會厭者 | Úi' ím' 'ché. |
| 59. Eyeball. | 眼睛 | ʻNgán ˏtsing. |
| 60. Eyelids. | 目胞 | Muk₂ ˏpáu. |
| 61. Fauces, (?) or larynx. | 喉嚨 | ˏHau ˏlung. |
| 62. Fibula, or long bone of the leg. | 成骨　骭骨 | ˏShing kwat,. Kón' kwat,. |
| 63. Finger bones. | 指亅 | 'Chí kwat,. |
| 64. Fontanelle; this is in the front part of the skull. In infant children when just born, before the bone is closed up, it is called the fontanelle; but | 頭之前顖門也生初兒小名曰顖門未闔 | Sun' ˏmún ˏtín ˏts'in ˏchi ˏt'au kwat, ʻyá. 'Síú ˏi ˏch'o ˏshang mí² hóp₂, ˏming ut₂ |

47. Of the internal structure of the eye, it is generally believed by Europeans, that the Chinese have no very extensive or accurate knowledge; the terms, therefore, which are used in this section to designate internal parts of that organ, must be received with caution. The statement somewhere advanced, that Chinese physicians many centuries ago operated for the cure of the cataract seems incredible, and unsupported by any good authority.

63. Under the head of *chí kwat*, the Chinese arrange not only the phalanges of the fingers, but also the metacarpal bones.

廣東方言讀本



| | | |
|---|---|---|
| after it is closed it is called the fontanelle bone, i. e. the covering of the celestial spirit. | 已闔名日囟骨即天靈蓋 | sunʼ ˏmún ; ʻí hóp$_2$ ˏming üt$_2$ sunʼ kwatˎ, . tsikˎ ˏtʻín ˏling kʻoiʼ. |
| 65. Foramina, or small openings. | 吼 | ˏLung. |
| 66. Fossa, sinuses, or small cavities and depressions. | 穴 | Üt$_2$. |
| 67. Frontal bone, or highest bone of the head. | 顚者頭頂也 | ˏTín ʻché, ˏtʻau ʻting ʻyá. |
| 68. Frontal eminences. | 頭角 | ˏTʻau kókˎ. |
| 69. Frontal line. | 額顱 | Ngák$_2$ ˏlò. |
| 70. Gizzard of a fowl. | 鷄腎 | ˏKai ʻshan. |
| 71. Lachrymal glands. | 眼淚核 | ʻNgán lui$^2$ hat$_2$. |
| 72. Meibomian glands of the eye. | 眼邊小核 | ʻNgán ˏpín ʻsíú hat$_2$. |
| 73. Parotid glands. | 牙鉸下丨 | ˏNgá káuʼ há$^2$ hat$_2$. |
| 74. Submaxillary glands. | 寢核 | ʻTsʻam hat$_2$. |
| 75. Salivary glands. | 口水核 | ʻHau ʻshui hat$_2$. |
| 76. Sublingual glands. | 舌下丨 | Shít$_2$ há$^2$ hat$_2$. |
| 77. The glenoid cavity of the scapula. | 肩胛骨頭臼 | ʻKín kápˎ kwatˎ ˏtʻau ʻkʻau. |
| 78. Gums. | 口齗所生之骨 | ʻHau ˏkan ʻshó ˏshang ˏchí kwatˎ. |
| 79. Hair on the head. | 髮 | Fátˎ. |
| 80. Hair on the body. | 毛 | ˏMò. |
| 81. Hair on the upper lip, or mustaches. | 髭 | ˏTszʼ. |
| 82. Hair on the temples. | 鬢 | Panʼ. |
| 83. Hair on the cheeks, or whiskers. | 髯 鬍鬚 | ˏÍm. ˏÚ ˏsü. |
| 84. Hair on the chin, or beard. | 鬚 | ˏSü. |
| 85. Ham, or hollow under the knee. | 膝凹 膕 腿凹 | Tsatˎ áuʼ. Kwókˎ. ʻTúi áuʼ. |

66. The term *üt* is not confined to this single meaning, but is very often employed to denote certain parts of the body, supposed to be under the particular influence of one of the dual principles *yam* and *yéung*.

71.—76. The glands of the human body are but little understood, and but poorly described by Chinese physicians; there may be other names for them besides those here given, and further investigations may show that *hat* is not the best term for gland.

86. The heart and its appendages are described and illustrated at considerable length in the Golden Mirror; see chap. 82, which is wholly occupied with this one subject. The heart is there considered as the seat of human intelligence, fulfilling the functions of sovereign lord in the empire of the human system. The other principal organs of the body are also described at length in the same work.

| | | |
|---|---|---|
| 86. Heart. | 心 | ‹Sam. |
| 87. Heel of the foot. | 脚踭 | Kéuk› ‹chang. |
| 88. Os calcis, or he elbone. | 跟骨 | ˏKan kwat›. |
| 89. Helix, or rim of the ear. | 耳郭者耳輪也 | ˢÍ kwók› ˋché ˢí ˏlun ˢyá. |
| 90. Ilium, or haunch bone. | 腰髁骨 | ‹Iú wá› kwat›. |
| 91. Incus, or anvil-bone of the ear. | 耳內砧骨 | ˢÍ noi² ‹cham kwat›. |
| 92. Instep. | 脚背　跗骨 | Kéuk› púi›. Fú› kwat›. |
| 93. Small and great intestines. | 小腸　大腸 | ˋSíú ˏch'éung. Tái› ˏch'éung. |
| 94. Iris, or colored part of the eye. | 瞳人外黑睛 | ˏT'ung ˏyan ngoi² hak› ‹tsing. |
| 95. Ischium, or hip-bone. | 楗骨 | Kín› kwat›. |
| 96. Jawbone. | 頰車 | Háp› ‹ch'é. |
| 97. Upper jawbone, or superior maxillary bone. | 上牙藏牙骨 | Shéung² ˏngá ˏch'óng ˏnga kwat›. |
| 98. Under jawbone, or inferior maxillary bone. | 下牙較牙丨 | Há² ˏngá káu› ˏngá kwat›. |
| 99. Kidneys. | 內腎 | Noi² ˢshan. |
| 100. Knee-joint. | 膝解 | Tsat› ˋkái. |
| 101. Knee-pan, or patella. | 膝盖骨 | Tsat› k'oi› kwat›. |
| 102. Lachrymal sack. | 淚管袋 | Lui² ˋkún toi². |
| 103. Leg. | 胻骨　脚梗 | ˏHang kwat›. Kéuk› ˋkwang. |
| 104. Calf of the leg. | 脚囊 | Kéuk› ˏnóng. |
| 105. Liver. | 肝 | ‹Kón. |
| 106. Parenchyma of the liver. | 肝眼 | ‹Kón ˢngán. |
| 107. Loins. | 胕 | ‹Cháu. |
| 108. Lungs. | 肺 | Fai›. |
| 109. Malleus, or hammer bone of the ear. | 耳內錘骨 | ˢÍ noi² ˏch'ui kwat›. |
| 110. Mammæ or the breasts. | 奶　乳 | ˢNái. ˢYü. |
| 111. Angle of the inferior maxillary process. | 曲骨 | Huk› kwat›. |
| 112. Medulla spinalis, or spinal marrow. | 脊髓 | Tsik› ˋsui. |

103. The parts of the leg, and especially the tibia and fibula, like the principal parts of the arm, are described in the medical works of the Chinese; in which, attempts are sometimes made to give the dimensions, shape, and weight, of the bones.

| | | |
|---|---|---|
| 113. Membrana tympani, or tympan of the ear. | 耳膜 | ˋÍ mók2. |
| 114. Muscles. (?) | 肉筋 | Yuk2 ˏkan. |
| 115. Muscles of the eye. | 眼肉筋 | ˋNgán yuk2 ˏkan. |
| 116. Nails of the fingers. | 手甲 | ˋShau káp3. |
| 117. Nameless bones. Ossa innominata. | 臀骨 | ˏT'ün kwat3. |
| 118. Nares anterior, or outer nostril. | 外鼻吼 | Ngoi2 pí2 ˏlung. |
| 119. Nares posterior. | 內鼻丨 | Noi2 pí2 ˏlung. |
| 120. Nates, or buttocks. | 屁股 | Pí3 ˋkú. |
| 121. Navel, or umbilicus. | 臍 | ˏTs'z'. |
| 122. Nerves. (?) | 筋 | ˏKan. |
| 123. Olfactory nerves. (?) | 聞氣筋 | ˏMan hí3 ˏkan. |
| 124. Optic nerves. (?) | 眼總筋　目系 | ˋNgán ˋtsung ˏkan. Muk2 hai2. |
| 125. Nerves of the eye. (?) | 眼內筋 | ˋNgán noi2 ˏkan. |
| 126. Occipital bone, or bone on the back of the head. | 後枕骨 | Hau2 ˋch'am kwat3. |
| 127. Occipital bones. | 腦後丨 | ˋNò hau2 kwat3. |
| 128. Occipital protuberance. | 枕骨 | ˋCh'am kwat3. |
| 129. Œsophagus, or gullet. | 咽者飲食之路 | Ít3 ˋché ˋyam shik2 ˏchí lò2. |
| 130. Orbicular bone, or round bone in the ear. | 耳內樞骨 | ˋÍ noi2 ˏsh'ü kwat3. |
| 131. Orbital foramen, or socket of the eye. | 眼吼 | ˋNgán ˏlung. |
| 132. Os pubis. | 下橫骨　橫骨 | Há2 ˏwáng kwat3. ˏWáng kwat3. |
| 133. Os coccygis. | 尾閭　骶端 | ˋMí ˏlü. Tai3 ˏtün. |
| 134. Palate, or velum palatinum. | 懸雍垂　即　碓嘴 | ˏÜn ˏyung ˏshui, tsik3 ˏchúi ˋtsui. |
| 135. Palpebræ. | 眼蓋 | ˋNgán k'oi3. |
| 136. Parietal bones, or bones on the sides of the head. | 頂骨 | ˋTing kwat3. |
| 137. Pelvis. | 波羅蓋骨 | ˏP'ó ˏló k'oi3 kwat3. |

114. The Chinese appear to be entirely ignorant of the muscles, unaware that there are in the human body distinct portions of the flesh, which, susceptible of contraction and relaxation, are in their natural healthy state subject to the will.

122. Of the nerves also the Chinese are ignorant, excepting in such respects as a knowledge of them is obtainable without dissection. It should be remembered, however, (and it may be here once for all remarked,) that with regard to the exact extent of the knowledge actually possessed by the Chinese, foreigners are but poorly informed.

| | | |
|---|---|---|
| 138. Pericardium, the bag that surrounds the heart. | 心包絡 | ‹Sam ‹p'áu lók›. |
| 139. Pharynx, or top of the gullet. | 咽喉 | Ít› ‹hau. |
| 140. Pia mater, or soft covering of the brain. | 腦漿脆膜 | ‘Nò ‹tséung ts'ui' mók›. |
| 141. Pleura. | 肺膜 | Fai' mók›. |
| 142. Pomum Adami, or Adam's apple. | 喉欖 | ‹Hau ‘lám. |
| 143. Puncta lachrymale. | 淚吼尖 | Lui$^{2}$ ‹lung ‹tsím. |
| 144. Pupil. | 瞳人 | ‹T'ung ‹yan. |
| 145. Pylorus, or inferior opening of the stomach. | 幽門 闌門 | ‹Yau ‹mún. ‹Lán ‹mún. |
| 146. Rectum. | 臟督 直腸 | Tsòng$^{2}$ tuk›. Chik› ‹ch'éung. |
| 147. Retina. | 眼網 | ‘Ngán ‘móng. |
| 148. Ribs, or costæ. | 脇肋骨 | Híp› lak› kwat›. |
| 149. False ribs. | 季脇 | Kwai' híp›. |
| 150. First ribs. | 上橫骨 | Shéung$^{2}$ ‹wáng kwat›. |
| 151. Cartilages of the ribs. (?) | 膺 | ‹Ying. |
| 152. Sacrum. | 尾龍骨 尻骨 | ‘Mí ‹lung kwat›. ‹Kú kwat›. |
| 153. Sclerotica, or white of the eye. | 眼白 | ‘Ngán pák›. |
| 154. Shoulder blade, or scapula. | 飯匙骨 | Fán' ‹shí kwat›. |
| 155. Shoulder bone, or humerus. | 臑骨 | ‹Nò kwat›. |
| 156. Human skeleton. | 人骨 | ‹Yan kwat›. |
| 157. Anterior view of the human skeleton. | 正面骨度部位圖 | Ching' mín$^{2}$ kwat› to$^{2}$ po$^{2}$ wai$^{2}$ ‹t'ò. |
| 158. Posterior view of the human skeleton. | 背面骨度部位圖 | Púi' mín$^{2}$ kwat› to$^{2}$ pò$^{2}$ wai$^{2}$ ‹t'ò. |
| 159. Skull, or cranium. | 骷髏 | ‹Kú ‹lau. |
| 160. Sole of the foot. | 脚板膛 | Kéuk› ‘pán ‹t'ong. |
| 161. The back is the general designation given to the back part of the body, from the principal vertebræ downwards and above the loins; | 背者後身大椎以下腰以上之通稱也脊者脊 | Púi' ‘ché hau$^{2}$ ‹shan tái$^{2}$ ‹ch'ui ‘í há$^{2}$ ‹íú ‘í shéung$^{2}$ ‹chí ‹t'ung ‹ch'ing ‘yá; tsik› ‘ché tsik› |

157. Most of the Chinese works on medicine have pictoral illustrations of the human body; but these are exceedingly rude, and for the most part very inaccurate, not excepting those published by the Medical College at Peking.

161. A more detailed account of the spine may be found in the Golden Mirror; see chap. 89. The general divisions correspond pretty nearly with those in European books.

| | | |
|---|---|---|
| the backbone is the vertebral column; and is commonly called the ridge-pole of the back (or the spine). | 膂骨也俗名脊樑丨 | 'lü kwat, 'yá; tsuk, ,ming tsik, ,léung kwat,. |
| 162. Stapes, or stirrup-bone of the ear. | 耳內馬蹬骨 | 'í noi' 'má tang' kwat,. |
| 163. Sternum, or breast bone. | 胸骨 | ,Hung kwat,. |
| 164. Stomach. | 胃 | Wai'. |
| 165. Tarsus, or instep. | 脚背骨 | Kéuk, púi' kwat,. |
| 166. Tarsus, or cartilage of the eyelids. | 目綱 | Muk, ,kóng. |
| 167. Superior tarsi. (?) | 眼上脆骨 | 'Ngán shéung' ts'ui' kwat,. |
| 168. Inferior tarsi. (?) | 眼下脆丨 | 'Ngán há' ts'ui' kwat,. |
| 169. Teeth are commonly called *ngá*. | 齒者俗名曰牙 | 'Ch'í 'ché tsuk, ,ming üt, ,ngá. |
| 170. Canine teeth. | 虎牙 | 'Fú ,ngá. |
| 171. Incisor teeth. | 門牙 | ,Mún ,ngá. |
| 172. Molar teeth. | 大牙 槽牙 | Tái' ,ngá. ,Ts'ò ,ngá. |
| 173. Crown of the tooth. | 牙頂 | ,Ngá 'ting. |
| 174. Body of the tooth. | 牙身 | ,Ngá ,shan. |
| 175. Fang of the tooth. | 牙脚 | ,Ngá kéuk,. |
| 176. Temporal bone, or bone on the corners of the head. | 魂精骨 鬢骨 | ,Wan ,tsing kwat,. Pan' kwat,. |
| 177. Temporal ridges. | 額顱 | Ngák, ,lò. |
| 178. The thighs is the general name given to the two great limbs which form the lower extremities of the body; they are vulgarly called the thigh and the leg. The middle joint, where the upper and lower bones are joined together, is called the knee-joint. The bone above the knee is called the os femoris, or great bone of the thigh; the bones below the knee are called the leg bones (tibia and fibula) or the great bones of the leg. | 股者下身兩大肢之通稱也俗名大腿小腿中節上下交接處名曰膝膝上之骨曰髀骨股之大骨也膝下之骨曰胻骨脛之大骨也 | 'Kú 'ché, há' ,shan 'léung tái' ,chí ,chí ,t'ung ,ch'ing 'yá; tsuk, ,ming tái' 'túi, 'siú 'túi. ,Chung tsít, shéung' há' ,káu tsip, ch'ü' ,ming üt, tsat,. Tsat, shéung' ,chí kwat, üt, 'pí kwat,, 'kú ,chí tái' kwat, 'yá; tsat, há' ,chí kwat, üt, ,hang kwat,, king' ,chí tái' kwat, 'yá. |

169. Teeth are seldom extracted by the Chinese, unless they are in such a state that they can be easily removed without the use of forceps,—to which recourse is had only in extreme cases. As dentists, native physicians have very little skill.

| | | |
|---|---|---|
| 179. The thigh bone (or os femoris) is the great bone above the knee. The upper head of it is like a pestle, and is received into the acetabulam; the lower head is like a mallet, and is articulated with the bones of the leg. | 髀者膝上之大骨也上端如杵接於髀樞下端如鎚接於胻骨 | 'Pí 'ché, tsat, shéung² ˌchí tái² kwat, 'yá. Shéung² ˌtün ˌü 'ch'ü tsíp, ˌü 'pí ˌsh'ü; há² ˌtün ˌü ˌch'úi tsíp, ˌü ˌhang kwat,. |
| 180. Thorax, or chest, is a collective designation of the bones of the breast. | 髑骭者胸之衆骨名也 | Ót, kón' 'ché, ˌhung ˌchí ˌchung kwat, ˌming 'yá. |
| 181. Tibia, or bone of the leg. | 脚梗骨 | Kéuk, 'kwang kwat,. |
| 182. Ureter, or duct leading from the kidneys to bladder. | 內腎管通膀胱 | Noi² 'shan 'kún ˌt'ung ˌp'óng ˌkwóng. |
| 183. Uvea, or posterior lamina of the iris. | 瞳人內黑睛皮 | ˌT'ung ˌyan noi² hak, ˌts'ing ˌp'í. |
| 184. Veins. | 血筋 | Hüt, ˌkan. |
| 185. Vertebral column, or backbone. | 脊骨 | Tsik, kwat,. |
| 186. Vertebræ. | 脊丨節　椎 | Tsik, kwat, tsít,. ˌCh'ui. |
| 187. Cervical vertebræ. | 頸丨 | 'King kwat,. |
| 188. Three upper cervical vertebræ. | 項丨 | Hóng² kwat,. |
| 189. Dorsal vertebræ. | 背丨 | Púi' kwat,. |
| 190. Lumbar vertebræ. | 腰丨 | ˌÍú kwat,. |
| 191. Vitreous humor of the eye. | 眼睛內之水 | 'Ngán ˌtsing noi² ˌchí 'shui. |
| 192. Vomer is the beam (or partition) of the nose, i. e. the 'root of the hill.' | 頞者鼻梁即山根也 | Át, 'ché pí² ˌléung, tsik, ˌshán ˌkan 'yá. |
| 193. Windpipe, or trachea. | 喉者通聲息路 | ˌHau 'ché ˌt'ung ˌshing sik, lò². |
| 194. Wrist; this is so named because that part where the fore-arm and bones of the hand are joined together, easily bends and turns. | 腕者臂掌骨接交處以其宛屈故名也 | 'Ún 'ché pí' 'chéung kwat, tsíp, ˌkáu ch'ü', 'í ˌk'í 'ún wat,, kú' ˌming 'yá. |

184. Veins and arteries are not distinguished by the Chinese—at least foreigners have not been able hitherto to ascertain that they make any distinction between them: *lŏk mak*, and *king mak*, seem to include the whole system of blood vessels, without indicating that it is twofold—having a system of arteries for carrying the blood outward, and a system of veins for returning it back to the heart.

廣東方言讀本

# Section Fifth.

## SURGERY.

## 外治法第五章
Ngoi2 chí2' fát,; tai2 'ng ͵chéung.

1. The term chirurgery denotes an application of the hands to bones and tendons which have been injured, so as to cause restoration to their former state. But since the injuries may be slight or severe, they severally require appropriate modes of treatment; and the slowness or rapidity with which they may heal, also whether or not any disease or escars supervene and remain, all depend on the securing appropriate modes of chirurgical treatment, which appropriate modes may be wholly wanting, or they may be defective in their application.

夫手法者謂以兩手安置所傷之筋骨使仍復於舊也但傷有輕重而手法各有所宜其痊可之遲速及遺留殘疾與否皆關乎手法之所施得宜或失其宜或未盡其法也

͵Fú ʻshau fát, ʻché, wai2 ͵í ʻléung ʻshau ͵ón chí' ʻshó ͵shéung ͵chí ͵kan kwat,. ʻsz' ͵ying fuk2 ͵yü kau2 ʻyá. Tán2 ͵shéung ʻyau ͵hing chung2, ͵í ʻshau fát, kók, ʻyau ʻshó ͵í; ͵k'í ͵sün ʻhó ͵chí ͵ch'í tsuk,, kap2 ͵wai ͵lau ͵ts'án tsat, ʻyü ʻfau, ͵kái ͵kwán ͵ú ʻshau fát, ͵chí ʻshó ͵shí tak, ͵í, wák2 shat, ͵k'í ͵í, wák2 mi2 tsun2 ͵k'í fát, ʻyá.

2. Explanations of the eight chirurgical operations.

手法釋義有八

ʻShau fát, shik, í2 ʻyau pát,.

3. The first is called feeling. Feeling is the very careful use of both hands, in rubbing them on the parts which are injured, in order to ascertain whether bones are broken, or are splintered into small pieces, whether they are

一曰摸法摸者用手細細摸其所傷之處或骨斷骨碎骨歪骨

Yat, üt2 mók2 fát,. Mók2 ʻché, yung2 ʻshau sai' sai' mók2 ͵k'í ʻshó ͵shéung ͵chí ch'ü', wak2 kwat, ʻtün, kwat, súi', kwat,

## *Notes and Explanations.*

THESE quotations, from the 87th chapter of the Golden Mirror, will afford a variety of technical phraseology appropriate to the department of surgery, and will show at the same time how limited and how defective is the knowledge of the Chinese on this subject. *Ngoi chí* means external practice,—surgery, or that branch of the healing art which has for its object the healing of external diseases. In the practice of midwifery, among the Chinese, the accoucheur's functions are always performed by women, and usually by those who from experience and success in the art have acquired celebrity.

1. Chirurgery is a fair equivalent for *shau fát*, which literally means, *hands' laws;* or more freely, the methods of applying the hands, and hence the operations performed by the hands, which they reduce to eight.

3. The examination of the body, as here described, is always restricted to its external surface; and even in the dead subject no attempts are made to acquire a knowledge of the internal structure of the system, or of the character of the diseases by which it is attacked and destroyed.

in or out of place, or whether they have become too weak or too hard; or whether the tendons are too stiff or too limber, whether they are in place or not, or whether they have been broken or have been distorted, or are enlarged, or are reversed, or affected with cold or heat; also whether the injury be deep or superficial, light or serious, likewise whether the injury be recent or of long standing. Having first by feeling ascertained whether the injury has been caused by a fall, or by a sprain, or by a blow, then apply the remedy according to the diagnosis.

筋筋丨丨虛新或錯慹
硬歪走寒裏之其爲撞之
骨筋筋丨表患摸或打治
輭柔斷翻及所先撲爲法
骨筋筋丨以並也跌或依
正強正粗熱實舊爲閃後

‹wái, kwat› ching’, kwat› ʿün, kwat› ‘ngáng; ‹kan ˏkéung, ‹kan ˏyau, ‹kan ‹wái. ‹kan ching’, ‹kan ʿtün, ‹kan ‘tsau, ‹kan ‹ts‘ú, ‹kan ‹fán, ‹kan ˏhón, ‹kan ít$_2$; ʿí kap$_2$ ‘píú, ʿlü, ‹h‘ü, shat$_2$, ping ‘shó wán$^2$ ‹chí ‹san kau$^2$ ʿyá. ‹Sín mók$_2$ ˏk‘í wák$_2$ ˏwai tít$_2$ pók›, wák$_2$ ˏwai tsók› ‘shím. wák$_2$ ˏwai ‘tá chóng$^2$, ˏín hau$^2$ ‹í fát› chí$^2$ ‹chí.

4. The second is the reduction of fractures. This is defined to be the causing of bones broken asunder, after being brought together and made fast in one place, to return again to their former state. Whenever there is a dislocation of a bone caused by a fall or injury,—whether it be broken into two distinct parts, or whether it be fractured and drops down, or be divided into numerous small parts and scattered, or split into a fork and protrudes out upon the side,—carefully consider its form and appearances, and then very gradually reduce it: thus cause that which was broken to reünite, that which was fallen down to reäscend, that which was divided into small pieces to coalesce and consolidate, and that which was elevated to be restored to its former level. Whether the operation is to be performed with the hands or with instruments alone, or

者骨歸之斷而散突徐復碎復或法而
接之復骨或拆而傍徐者起者法手後
法斷處凡落或碎而勢斷復突手或先
接已一也錯分或岐形使者完用具分
日使攏舊傷兩下或其之陷復或器具
二謂合於跌而陷亂相接續者平用器

í$^2$ üt$_2$ tsíp› fát›. Tsíp› ‘ché wai$^2$ ‘sz’ ʿí ʿtün ‹chí kwat›. hóp$_2$ ʿlung yat› ch‘ü’, fuk$_2$ ‹kwai ‹ü kau$^2$ ʿyá. ˏFán kwat› ‹chí tít› ‹shéung tsók› lók$_2$, wák$_2$ ʿtün ˏí ʿléung ‹fan. wák$_2$ chít› ˏí hám$^2$ há$^2$, wák$_2$ súi’ ˏí sán’ lün$^2$, wák$_2$ ˏk‘í ˏí ˏp‘óng tut$_2$; séung’ ˏk‘í ˏying shai’, ˏch‘ü ˏch‘ü tsíp› ‹chí ‘sz’ ʿtün ‘ché fuk$_2$ tsuk$_2$; hám$^2$ ‘ché fuk$_2$ ‘hí; súi’ ‘ché fuk$_2$ ˏün; tut$_2$ ‘ché fuk$_2$ ˏp‘ing. Wák$_2$ yung$^2$ ‘shau fát›, wák$_2$ yung$^2$ hí’ kü$^2$, wak$_2$ ‘shau fát› hí’ kü$^2$, ‹fan ‹sín hau$^2$ ˏí

4. The word *tsíp* here indicates what kind of reduction is intended by the phrase *tsíp fát*. rules of joining,—i. e. the reduction of bones which have been not simply displaced, and only need to be restored, but of such as have been so ruptured or broken as to need to be (*tsíp*) joined or reünited. There may be numerous cases in which perfect success attends the reduction of fractures performed by native practitioners, but the cases of failure are not few, and in some instances the injury is rendered incurable and fatal through their malpractice; some of them are a sad comment on the surgical skill of the "profession" in this country.

with both, first one and then the other, or both together, must be left to the surgeon's discretion.

兼用之是在醫者之通達也

꜀kím, yung꜃ ꜀chí, shí꜃ tsoi꜃ ꜀í ꜂ché ꜀chí ꜀t'ung tát꜁ ꜂yá.

5. The third is the reduction of dislocations. In performing this kind of reduction, with one or both hands grasp fast hold of the part which is to be reduced, and then mindful of the character of the injury light or severe, either from below bring up the bone to its place, or from outwards move it inwards to its position, either in a straight or a transverse direction [according to its natural situation]. For when the bones have been removed from their natural situation, they must be reduced by exertion of the hands; then without any long lapse of time, the bones will regain their points and be united. They ought to be neither flattened nor projected, and then when healed there will be no deformity from their being too long or too short, or at all uneven.

三曰端法端者或用兩手一手擒定應端之處酌其重輕或從下往上端或從外向內托或直端斜端也蓋骨離其位必以手法端之則不待曠日遲久而骨縫即合仍須不偏不倚庶愈後無長短不齊之患

꜀Sám üt꜁ ꜀tün fát꜁. ꜀Tün ꜂ché wák꜁ yung꜃ ꜂léung ꜂shau yat꜁ ꜂shau ꜀k'am ting꜃ ꜀ying ꜀tün ꜀chí ch'ü꜃, chéuk꜁ ꜀k'í chung꜃ ꜀hing, wák꜁ ꜀tsung há꜃ ꜂wóng shéung꜃ ꜀tün, wák꜁ ꜀tsung ngoi꜃ héung꜃ noi꜃ t'ók꜁, wák꜁ chik꜁ ꜀tün ꜀tsé ꜀tün ꜂yá. K'oi꜃ kwat꜁ ꜀lí ꜀k'í wai꜃ pít꜁ ꜂í ꜂shau fát꜁ ꜀tün ꜀chí, tsak꜁ pat꜁ toi꜃ kwóng꜃ yat꜁ ꜀ch'í ꜂kau, ꜀í kwat꜁ ꜀fung tsik꜁ hóp꜁. ꜀Ying ꜀sü pat꜁ ꜀pín pat꜁ ꜂í shü꜃ yü꜃ hau꜃ ꜀mò ꜀ch'éung ꜂tün pat꜁ ꜀ts'ai ꜀chí wán꜃.

6. The fourth is the elevation of depressed bones. By this is meant the raising up and restoring to its proper place a bone that has fallen down. The rules for doing this are not uniform. Sometimes both hands are employed to elevate it; sometimes a cord or a bandage is used to fasten it up to some high place; and after it has been elevated, an apparatus is used to support it, to prevent its again falling down. It is necessary to consider whether the injury is light or severe, superficial or deep, and then to regulate the treatment accordingly. If the injury is severe and the

四曰提法提者謂陷下之骨提出如舊也其法非一有用兩手提者有用繩帛繫高處提者有提後用器具輔之不致仍陷者必量所傷之輕重淺深然後施

Sz" üt꜁ ꜀t'ai fát꜁. ꜀T'ai ꜂ché wai꜃ hám꜃ há꜃ ꜀chí kwat꜁, ꜀t'ai ch'ut꜁ ꜀yü kau꜃ ꜂yá. ꜀K'í fát꜁ ꜀fí yat꜁. ꜂Yau yung꜃ ꜂léung ꜂shau ꜀t'ai ꜂ché; ꜂yau yung꜃ ꜀shing pák꜁ hai꜃ ꜀kò ch'ü꜃ ꜀t'ai ꜂ché; ꜂yau ꜀t'ai hau꜃ yung꜃ hí꜃ kü꜃ fú꜃ ꜀chí, pat꜁ chí꜃ ꜀ying hám꜃ ꜂ché. Pít꜁ leung꜃ ꜂shó ꜀shéung ꜀chí ꜀hing chung꜃, ꜂ts'ín ꜀sham, ꜀ín hau꜃ ꜀shí chí꜃.

5. The reduction of a dislocation, or 'the displacement of the articulatory portion of a bone, from the surface on which it was naturally received,' seems here intended. Cases of luxation, as might be expected in the hands of the Chinese surgeon, fare no better than those of fracture. Usually and for the most part both are miserably treated; and many times, slight injuries, by being neglected or ill-treated, are never cured.

elevation is slight, then the malady cannot be cured. If the injury be slight and the elevation great, then, although the old complaint may be removed or cured, yet still a new one will supervene.

治倘重者輕提則病莫能愈輕者重提則舊患雖去而又增新患矣

'T'óng chung² 'ché ˌhing ˏt'ai tsak, ping² mók, ˏnang yu², ˌhing 'ché chung² ˏt'ai tsak, kau² wán² ˌsui hü', ˏí yau' ˌtsang ˌsan wán² 'í.

7. The fifth is the depression of elevations; this is done by moving the hands downwards, so as to press the part in that direction.

五曰按法按者謂以手往下抑之也

ˏ'Ng üt, ón' fát,; ón' 'ché wai² 'í 'shau 'wóng há² yik, ˌchi 'yá.

8. The sixth is trituration, which may be defined a gradual moving and rubbing of the hands.

六曰摩法摩者謂徐徐揉摩之

Luk, üt, ˌmó fát,; ˏmó 'che wai² ˌch'ü ˏch'ü ˏyau ˏmó ˌchi.

9. The seventh is protrusion. This may be defined a pushing outwards with the hands, so as to cause any part [out of place] to be restored.

七曰推法推者謂以手推之使還舊處也

Ts'at, üt, ˌtúi fát,; ˌtúi 'ché wai² 'í 'shau ˌtúi ˌchí 'sz' ˏwán kau² ch'ü' 'yá.

10. The eighth is grasping or tension. This may be defined the taking hold with one or both hands of the injured parts, and then, with due regard to the condition of the wound, gradually reduce them to their former situation.

八曰拿法拿者或兩手一手捏定患處酌其宜輕宜重緩緩焉以復其位也

Pát, üt, ˏná fát,; ˏná 'ché wák, 'léung 'shau yat, 'shau níp, ting² wán² ch'ü', chéuk, ˏk'í ˏí ˌhing ˏí chung² ún² ún² ˏín 'í fuk, ˏk'í wai² 'yá.

11. General observations on surgical apparatus. In cases of bruises, contusions, laceration, and other wounds, although you do employ the hands to dress them, it may yet be feared lest, all not being done which is necessary, that the pain of the cure will not be less than if no cure were attempted; in such cases it cannot be said that the principles of the healing art are clearly understood.

器具總論跌撲損傷雖用手法調治恐未盡得其宜以致有治如未治之苦則未可云醫理之周詳也

Hí' kü² 'tsung lun². Tít, pók, 'süin ˌshéung, ˌsui yung² 'shau fát, ˏtíú chí², 'hung mi² tsun² tak, ˏk'í ˏí, 'í chí² 'yau chí² ˏyü mí² chí' ˌchí 'fú; tsak, mí² 'hó ˏwan ˌí 'lí ˌchi ˌchau ˏtséung 'yá.

3—10. These eight explanations are, as they here stand, somewhat abridged; the student is therefore referred to the Mirror for a fuller account of the chirurgical operations of the Chinese. In the original, however, the compilers do not pretend to give more than an outline of the subject.

11. Surgical apparatus is here limited and poor, and poorly applied, in the hands of Chinese doctors. Necessity has extorted from them some few articles, but they are very badly designed and executed. Ten, mentioned and described in the Golden Mirror, seem to constitute the circle of their chirurgical apparatus, and are noticed in the sequel.

12. Wherefore, according to the shape of the body in all its various parts, respectively and separately considered, prepare apparatus properly adapted to these parts, so as to supply that which cannot be effected by the hands; and by these means, that which is displaced will be restored; that which is high will be brought to its proper level; and that which has fallen down will be raised up to its place. Then the alarming prognosis may turn and become quieting; and the wounds which were dangerous will be viewed with unconcern.

爰因身體上下正側之象製器以正之用輔手法之所不逮以冀分者復合欹者復正高者就其平陷者升其位則危證可轉於安重傷可就其輕

ˏÜn ˓yan ˓shan ‘t‘ai shéung‘ há$^2$ ching’ chak˒ ˓chí tséung‘, chai’ hí’ ‘í ching’ ˓chí, yung$^2$ fú$^2$ ‘shau fát˒ ˓chí ‘shó pat˒ tai’; ‘í k‘í’ ˓fan ‘ché fuk$_2$ hóp$_2$; ˓k‘í ‘ché fuk$_2$ ching’: ˓kò ‘ché tsau$^2$ ˏk‘í ˏp‘ing: hám$^2$ ‘ché, ˓shing ˏk‘í wai’. Tsak˒ ˏngai ching’ ‘hò ‘chün ˓yü ˓ón; chung$^2$ ˓shéung ‘hò tsau$^2$ ˏk‘í ˓hing.

13. And in the second place you must avail yourself of the efficacy of medical remedies; and also direct that there be paid a strict regard to regimen. Then the ways and means of curing the bones will be perfect.

再施以藥餌之功更示以調養之善則正骨之道全矣

Tsoi’ ˓shí ‘í yéuk$_2$ ní$^2$ ˓chí ˓kung; kang’ shí$^2$ ‘í ˏt‘íú ‘yéung ˓chí shín$^2$. Tsak˒ ching’ kwat˒ ˓chí tò$^2$ ˏts‘ün ‘í.

14. Bandages are made of white cloth. When the nature of the wound is such that it admits no other dressings, it is then requisite to bind it up with cloth; dressings of this form having come into vogue, they were accordingly named bandages. Their size long or short, broad or narrow, must be gauged according to the nature of the wound.

裹帘以白布爲之因患處不宜他器只宜布纏始爲得法故名裹帘其長短濶狹量病勢用之

‘Kwó ˏlím ‘í pák$_2$ pò’ ˏwai ˓chí. ˓Yan wán$^2$ ch‘ü’ pat˒ ˏí ˓t‘á hí’, chat˒ ˏí pò’ ˏch‘ín: ‘chí ˏwai tak˒ fát˒, kú’ ˏming ‘kwó ˏlím. ˏK‘í ˏch‘éung ‘tün, fút˒ háp$_2$, léung$^2$ ping$^2$ shai$^2$ yung$^2$ ˓chí.

15. Beater; this is a wooden cudgel, one foot and a half long, in diameter about an inch; or if it be of the dimensions of a baker's roller it will suffice.

振梃即木棒也長尺半圓如錢大或麵杖亦可

Chan’ ‘ting; tsik˒ muk$_2$ ‘páng ‘yá, ˏch‘éung chik˒ pún’, ˏün ˏyü ˏts‘ín tái$^2$, wák$_2$ mín$^2$ ch‘éung$^2$ yik$_2$ ‘hó.

16. The broad supporter consists of a piece of cowhide, five inches long and three inches broad, and with

披肩用熟牛皮一塊長五寸寬

˓P‘í ˓kín yung$^2$ shuk$_2$ ˏngau ˏp‘í yat˒ fái’, ˏch‘éung ‘’ng

14. These ten articles, viz., bandages, beaters, broad supporters, climbing cords, piled bricks, back splints, lumbar splints, suspensory bandages, pine compresses, and knee caps; with the nine needles mentioned in No. 25, constitute the whole assortment of Chinese surgical apparatus.

15. In the Golden Mirror, short explanations for the use, follow the description of these several articles. The beater is to be applied to the soles of the feet; and, after this is done, if the patient is favorably affected, he may be expected to recover; but if he remains insensible to the application his case is to be regarded as hopeless.

two holes opened at each end. Being placed on the wounded part, cotton strings are passed through the holes, and they are drawn very tight, so as to make it fast. This bandage compared with splints is much the most soft and pliable.

三寸兩頭各開
二孔夾於傷處
以綿繩穿之緊
緊縛定較之木
板稍覺柔活

ts'ün', ‹fún ‹sám ts'ün', ʿléung ‹t'au kók› ‹hoi í² ʿhung. Káp› ‹yü ‹shéung ch'ü', ʿí ‹mín ‹shing ‹ch'ün ‹chí, ʿkan ʿkan fók› ting². Káu' ‹chi muk› ʿpán, ʿsháu kok› ‹yau út›.

17. Climbing cords are prepared by suspending cords from a high place, on which both hands take hold, as in the attitude of climbing.

攀索者以繩掛
於高處用兩手
攀之也

‹Pán sók› ʿché, ʿí ‹shing kwá' ‹yü ‹kò ch'ü', yung² ʿléung ʿshau ‹pán ‹chi ʿyá.

18. Piled bricks; six bricks are taken and piled up three in a pile, the two separated one on the right and one on the left, upon which the two feet are to be placed for the purpose of straightening the body.

疊甎者以甎六
塊分左右各疊
置三塊兩足踏
於其上也

Típ› ‹ch'ün ʿché; ʿí ‹ch'ün luk› fái', ‹fan ʿtsó yau² kok› típ›, chí' ‹sám fái', ʿléung tsuk› táp› ‹yü ‹k'i shéung² ʿyá.

19. Back splint. For making this, you take a piece of pine timber, three inches in breadth, and two inches in thickness, having its length extending up from the loins an inch or more above the shoulders; the outer surface is made smooth; and in the inner surface, where it is to fit to the spine, grooves are cut, so that it may set close to the flesh upon the backbone.

通木者用杉木
寬三寸厚二寸
其長自腰起上
過肩一寸許外
面平整向脊背
之內面刻凹形
務與脊骨膂肉
吻合

‹T'ung muk› ʿché; yung² ch'ám' muk›, ‹fún ‹sám ts'ün', hau² í² ts'ün', ‹k'i ‹ch'éung tsz'² ‹iú ʿhí shéung² kwó' ‹kín yat› ts'ün' ʿhü; ngoi² mín² ‹p'ing ʿching, héung' tsik› púi' ‹chí noi² mín² hak› áu' ‹ying, mò² ʿyü tsik› kwat› ʿlü yuk› ʿman hòp›.

20. Splints for the loins consist of four pieces of thin wood of the pine tree, made like a flat carrying beam, an inch thick, with length suited to the several dimensions of

腰柱者以杉木
四根製如扁擔
形寬一寸厚五
分長短以患處

‹Iú ʿch'ü ʿché, ʿí ch'ám' muk› sz'² ‹kan, chai' ‹yü ʿpin tám' ‹ying, ‹fún yat› ts'ün', hau² ʿng ‹fan, ‹ch'éung ʿtün ʿí

17, 18. In the original, this is illustrated by a diagram; a beam is erected on poles a few inches above the utmost reach of the patient, and round it are placed two short cords to serve as handles; the patient then steps upon the bricks, having three under one foot, and three under the other, and firmly grasps the cords; after this is done, the bricks, one after another, are gradually removed; the operation brings, or is designed to bring, the decrepid patient to his natural shape. See Golden Mirror.

20. These splints are like the frame-work of a corset. The cords run through near each end of the several pieces, and serve to bind them upon the body, which is by this means supported and strengthened.

| | | |
|---|---|---|
| the wound; holes are then bored though the sides of these splints, and small cords run through them. | 患處爲度俱自側面鑽孔以繩聯貫之也 | wán' ch'ü' ,wai tò'; ,kü tsz' chak, mín' tsün' 'hung, 'i ,shing ,lün kún' ,chí 'yá. |
| 21. The suspensory bandage is a cool bandage, for use in summer. Take the dimensions of the injured part, in its length and breadth, &c., and then cut the bandage so as to suit it. | 竹簾者即夏月涼簾也量患處之大小長短裁取之 | Chuk, ,lím 'ché, tsik, há' üt, ,léung ,lím 'yá. Léung' wán' ch'ü' ,chí tái' 'síú ,ch'éung 'tün, ,ts'oi 'ts'ü ,chí. |
| 22. The pine compresses are articles for closing and compressing. Measure the length, breadth, and figure, with the elevations and depressions of the wounded parts, in their exact configurations, and then according to these make the compresses of pine wood. | 杉籬者複逼之器也量患處之長短濶狹曲直凸凹之形以杉木爲之 | Ch'ám' ,lí 'ché, fuk, pik, ,chí hí' 'yá. Léung' wán' ch'ü' ,chí ,ch'éung, 'tün, fút, háp,, huk,, chik,, tat,, áu', ,chí, ,ying, 'í ch'ám' muk, ,wai ,chí. |
| 23. Knee cap; this consists of a bamboo ring, furnished with four feet [or clasps]. | 抱膝者有四足之竹圈也 | 'P'ò sat, 'ché; 'yau sz'' tsuk, ,chí chuk, ,hün 'yá. |
| 24. Compresses are made of cloth, variously folded; they are laid on above plasters, [lint, &c.] and are then bound close with rollers and bandages. | 貼布者以布摺疊爲之壓膏藥上然後以裹帘裹之 | T'íp, pò' 'ché, 'í pò' tsíp, típ, ,wai ,chí, át, ,kò yéuk, shéung', ,ín hau' 'í 'kwó ,lím 'kwó ,chí. |
| 25. The nine needles are, the arrowheaded, blunt, puncturing, spear-pointed, ensiform, round, capillary, long, and great. | 九鍼鑱員鍉鋒鈹員利毫長大鍼也 | 'Kau ,cham, ,ts'ám, ,ün, ,tai, ,fung, ,pí, ,ün lí', ,hò, ,ch'éung, tái', ,cham 'yá. |
| 26. Amputating instruments. | 割斷器 | Kót, 'tün hí'. |
| 27. Sharp-pointed bistoury. | 彎口尖刀 | ,Wán 'hau ,tsím ,tò. |

21. This bandage is made of rattan or bamboo matting, and is used chiefly for suspending the hand or arm, after the dressings have been applied.

22. These pine compresses resemble the lumbar splints described in No. 20; they are made of narrow splints of wood, arranged parallel to each other, and are strung upon cords, by which they are bound upon the body or limbs so as to close up and compress the wound.

23. The object of the knee cap is to give strength and firmness to the joint, and the cap is so made and bound on as to accomplish this.

24. The description of these compresses, made of cloth, is not taken from the Mirror, but has been written out by a native student, from drawings and descriptions found in European books.

25. These nine are the only instruments described in the Golden Mirror, and are merely needles or fine lancets, designed for puncturing the skin, &c.

| | | |
|---|---|---|
| 28. Catling. | 劍刀 | Kím' ꜀tò. |
| 29. Canula for passing ligatures. | 導線銀管 | Tò² sín' ꜂ngan 'kún. |
| 30. Director. | 導刀鍼 | Tò² ꜀tò ꜀cham. |
| 31. Elevator. | 開骨器 | ꜀Hoi kwat, hí'. |
| 32. Forceps. | 鐵鑷 | T'ít, níp₂. |
| 33. Curved forceps. | 彎 〡 | ꜀Wán níp₂. |
| 34. Crooked forceps for extracting teeth. | 曲牙鉗 | Huk, ꜂ngá ꜂kím. |
| 35. Tooth scaling instrument. | 刮牙器 | Kwát, ꜂ngá hí'. |
| 36. Abscess knife. | 膿瘡刀 | ꜂Nung ꜀chóng ꜀tò. |
| 37. Ligature. | 綁脈筋線 | 'Póng mak₂ ꜀kan sín'. |
| 38. Bullet scoup. | 炮彈挖 | Páu' tán² wát,. |
| 39. Stylet. | 插鼻鍼 | Ch'áp, pí² ꜀cham. |
| 40. Brass syringe. | 銅水捷 | ꜂T'ung 'shui tsít,. |
| 41. Ivory syringe. | 象牙水捷 | Tséung² ꜂ngá 'shui tsít₂. |
| 42. Scalpel. | 圓口刀 | ꜂Ün 'hau ꜀tò. |
| 43. Spatula. | 開藥刀 | ꜀Hoi yéuk₂ ꜀tò. |
| 44. Stethescope. | 聞症筒 | ꜂Man ching' ꜂t'ung. |
| 45. Trochar for paracenties. | 蠱脹鍼 | 'Kú ch'éung' ꜀cham. |
| 46. Tenaculum. | 鋼鈎 | Kóng' ꜀kau. |
| 47. Tourniquet. | 截血帶 | Tsít₂ hüt, tái'. |
| 48. Truss for hernia. | 揑腸夾 | Níp₂ ꜂ch'éung káp,. |

26—48. These names have been framed by foreign practitioners, aided by native assistants; by use in the hospitals at Canton and Macao, they have gained some degree of currency, and are therefore here introduced. They may or they may not be the best terms for specifying the several instruments which they designate.

# CHAPTER XVII.

# GOVERNMENTAL AFFAIRS.

# 王制篇十七

꜀Wóng chai'; ꜀p'ín shap$_{2}$ ts'at꜀.

---

## Section First.

## THE PENAL CODE.

## 律例第一章

Lut$_{2}$ lai$^{2}$; tai$^{2}$ yat꜀ ꜀chéung.

---

| §1. General Laws. | 名律例 | ꜀*Ming lut$_{2}$ lai$^{2}$.* |
|---|---|---|
| 1. The five modes of punishment. | 五刑 | ꜂Ng ꜀ying. |
| 2. The ten great offenses, or crimes of great enormity. | 十惡 | Shap$_{2}$ ók꜀. |
| 3. The eight classes privileged to enjoy deliberation. | 八議 | Pát꜀ ꜄í. |

### *Notes and Explanations.*

Royal rule is the literal meaning of *wóng chai*, the sovereign power; the phrase is here used to denote those affairs which are regulated by the highest national authority. The *lut lai* include the whole penal code, which had its origin in very remote times, and has undergone many changes. The original statutes were termed *lut;* and the new clauses, introduced to limit, explain, and alter them, were called *lai*. Such was the Penal Code under the late Ming dynasty. Soon after the present family ascended the throne, its first monarch Shunchí ordered a revision of that code, which was published under imperial authority in 1647, in seven divisions, and 436 sections, under an equal number (436) of separate heads, which are here given as they stand in the original, according to an edition in 28 vols, published at Peking in 1830. A new edition is published by authority every five years. The first of the seven divisions is in 46 sections, consisting of general laws, comprising principles and definitions applicable to the whole code.

1. From 10 to 50 blows with the lesser bamboo is the first kind of punishment; from 50 to 100 with the greater bamboo is the second; transportation to any distance not exceeding 500 *li* is the third; perpetual transportation is the fourth; and death either by strangulation or decollation is the fifth. The bamboo, the cangue or movable pillory, the iron chain, handcuffs, and fetters, are the common instruments of punishment. The bamboo is 5 *chik* 5 *ts'ün* in length: the lesser is 1½ *ts'ün* broad by 1 thick, weighing 1½ catties; the larger is 2 by 1½, and weighs 2 catties. The cangue is 3 *chik* long by 2 *chik* 9 *ts'ün*, and ordinarily weighs 25 catties.

2. Rebellion, disloyalty, desertion, parricide, massacre, sacrilege, impiety, discord, insubordination, and incest, are the ten great offenses, so designated on account of their enormity.

3. The privileges of imperial blood and connections, of long service, of illustrious actions, of extraordinary wisdom, of great abilities, of zeal and assiduity, or nobility, and of birth, form these eight classes. See Chinese Repository, Vol. IV., page 15.

| | | |
|---|---|---|
| 4. Offenses of the [eight] privileged classes. | 應議者犯罪 | ꜀Ying ꜂í ꜂ché fán꜅ tsúi꜅. |
| 5. Offenses committed by the father or grandfather of persons belonging to the eight privileged classes. | 應議者之父祖有犯 | ꜀Ying ꜂í ꜂ché ꜀chí fú꜅ ꜂tso ꜃yau fán꜅. |
| 6. Offenses of persons holding office. | 職官有犯 | Chik꜆ ꜀kún ꜃yau fán꜅. |
| 7. Public offenses of civil and military officers. | 文武官丨公罪 | ꜁Man ꜃mò ꜀kún fán꜅ ꜀kung tsúi꜅. |
| 8. Private offenses of civil and military officers. | 文武官丨私罪 | ꜁Man ꜃mò ꜀kún fán꜅ ꜀sz' tsúi꜅. |
| 9. Offenders who are not to be transported. | 犯罪免發遣 | Fán꜅ tsúi꜅ ꜃mín fát꜆ ꜂hín. |
| 10. Offenses of those who belong to the military classes. | 軍籍有犯 | ꜀Kwan tsik꜇ ꜃yau fán꜅. |
| 11. Cases of mitigation of punishment. | 犯罪得累減 | Fán꜅ tsúi꜅ tak꜆ lui꜅ ꜂kám. |
| 12. Removal from office without disgrace. | 以理去官 | ꜃Í ꜃lí hü꜄ ꜀kún. |
| 13. Offenses committed before entering office. | 無官犯罪 | ꜁Mò ꜀kún fán꜅ tsúi꜅. |
| 14. Those dismissed from office liable to service. | 除名當差 | ꜁Ch'ü ꜁ming ꜀tóng ꜀chái. |
| 15. The relations of those who are transported. | 流囚家屬 | ꜁Lau ꜁ch'au ꜀ká shuk꜇. |
| 16. Persons who are not to be included in general pardon. | 常赦所不原 | ꜁Chéung shé꜄ ꜂shó pat꜆ ꜁un. |
| 17. Effect of general pardons on those being transported. | 流犯在道會赦 | ꜁Lau fán꜅ tsoi꜅ tò꜅ úi꜅ shé꜄. |
| 18. Offenders detained to serve their parents. | 犯罪存留養親 | Fán꜅ tsúi꜅ ꜁tsün ꜁lau yéung꜅ ꜀ts'an. |
| 19. Offenses committed by astronomers. | 天文生有犯 | ꜀T'ín ꜁man ꜀shang ꜃yau fán꜅. |
| 20. Offenses committed by artisans, musicians [in the employ of government], and women. | 工樂戶及婦人犯罪 | ꜀Kung ngók꜇ ú꜅ kap꜇ ꜃fú ꜁yan fán꜅ tsúi꜅. |
| 21. On second offenses of transported convicts. | 徒流人又犯罪 | ꜁Tò ꜁lau ꜁yan yau꜅ fán꜅ tsúi꜅. |
| 22. Ransom to be paid by the old, young, and disabled. | 老小廢疾收贖 | ꜃Lò síú꜄ fai꜄ tsat꜇ ꜀shau tsuk꜇. |
| 23. Offenses committed before becoming old & disabled. | 犯罪時未老疾 | Fán꜅ tsúi꜅ ꜁shí mí꜅ ꜃lò tsat꜇. |
| 24. Restitution and forfeiture of goods. | 給没贓物 | K'ap꜆ mút꜇ ꜀tsóng mat꜇. |
| 25. Criminals surrendering themselves to justice. | 犯罪自首 | Fán꜅ tsúi꜅ tsz'꜅ ꜂shau. |

7, 8. "The offenses denominated *private*, in fact comprehend almost all cases of direct criminality, whereas those denominated *public*, are cases of liability to punishment solely from the official responsibility of the party implicated." *Sir G. T. Staunton*. See his translation of the Penal Code—constant reference to which, and to a manuscript by Dr. Morrison, has been made in preparing this section.

15. As no criminal is sent out of the country, transportation seems to be a more appropriate term for *lau* than banishment, for denoting a removal from one place to another.

20. In favor of all these the severity of the law is mitigated,—in the first and second because of their services, and in the third because of their personal character.

| | | |
|---|---|---|
| 26. Repeated offenses to be judged with severity. | 二罪俱發以重論 | ,Í² tsúi² ,kü fát, ʽí chung² lun². |
| 27. Offenders all making their escape. | 犯罪共逃 | Fán² tsúi² kung² ,t'ò. |
| 28. Official associates committing a public offense. | 同僚犯公罪 | ,T'ung ,líú fán² ,kung tsúi². |
| 29. Errors or failures in public proceedings. | 公事失錯 | ,Kung sz'₂ shat, ts'ók,. |
| 30. Distinction between the leader and accomplices. | 共犯罪分首從 | Kung² fán² tsúi² ,fan ʽshau tsung². |
| 31. Proceedings when one of the offenders has escaped. | 犯罪事發在逃 | Fán² tsúi² sz'² fát, tsoi² ,t'ò. |
| 32. Kindred concealing the offenses of each other. | 親屬相爲容隱 | ,Ts'an shuk₂ ,séung ,wai ,yung ʽyan. |
| 33. Punishment of deserters from the army. | 處決叛軍 | ʽCh'ü küt, pún² ,kwan. |
| 34. Offenses of foreigners who have been naturalized. | 化外人有犯 | Fá² ngoi² ,yan ʽyau fán². |
| 35. Particular cases where the law appears contradictory. | 本條別有罪名 | ʽPún ,t'íú pít₂ ʽyau tsúi² ,ming. |
| 36. Rules for increasing and diminishing punishment. | 加減罪例 | ,Ká ʽkám tsúi² lai². |
| 37. Privileges and distinction of imperial rank. | 稱乘輿車駕御 | ,Ch'ing ,shing, ,yü, ,kü, ká² yü². |
| 38. Relations of the first degree defined. | 稱期親祖父母 | ,Ch'ing ,kí ,ts'an ʽtsò fú² ʽmò. |
| 39. The phrase 'partaker of the same crime' defined. | 稱與同罪 | ,Ch'ing ʽyü ,t'ung tsúi². |
| 40. The terms 'superintendent and keeper' defined. | 稱監臨主守 | ,Ch'ing ,kám ,lam chü² ʽshau. |
| 41. A day is defined to be a hundred quarters. | 稱日者以百刻 | ,Ch'ing yat₂ ʽché ʽí pák, hak,. |
| 42. Rules for the priests and nuns of the Taou sect. | 稱道士女冠 | ,Ch'ing Tò² sz'² ʽnü ,kún. |
| 43. On the decision of cases by new laws. | 斷罪依新頒律 | Tün² tsúi² ,í ,san ,pán lut₂. |

28. This refers to cases where the parties become associates to some illegality, through ignorance, error of judgment, &c., without any sinister or selfish motive.

34. This law ordains, that the naturalized subject shall, like the native, be amenable to the laws, and equally enjoy their protection. It does not include the foreign residents in Canton, but such as the Mongols who have become subjects. It has, however, been quoted by the provincial authorities with special reference to cases of homicide in Canton and Macao.

35. Crimes specifically provided for in the subsequent part of the code, must be decided on according to the general principles in this division: and if they appear to differ, preference must be given to the latter.

37. These five appellatives are to be used instead of the explicit term emperor, empress, empress-mother, and empress-grandmother, in order to avoid the frequent use of sacred majesty.

38. The terms *kí ts'an*, &c., refer to the nine classes of kindred, (see Chap. I, sec. 3: 45.) which are to be mourned for, and this section defines their use in the code.

42. The priests and priestesses of Budha are specified in and subject to the same laws: both sects are tolerated by the government, but derive all their support from private sources—their own funds or voluntary contributions.

43, 44. New laws are to take effect from the day of their promulgation. As laws are necessarily limited while crimes are infinitely varied, cases for which there are no specific laws must be decided from analogy.

| | | |
|---|---|---|
| 44. On the decision of cases not provided for by law. | 斷罪無正條 | Tün' tsúi$^2$ ˛mò ching' ˛t'ʻiú. |
| 45. Places of temporary and perpetual transportation. | 徒流遷徙地方 | ˛Tò ˛lau ˓ts'ín ʻsái tí$^2$ ˓fóng. |
| 46. Places of extraordinary transportation. | 充軍地方 | ˓Ch'ung ˓kwan tí$^2$ ˓fóng. |
| §2. CIVIL LAWS. | 吏律 | *Lí$^2$ lut$_2$.* |
| 47. Successor to hereditary offices and titles. | 官員襲廕 | ˓Kún ˛ün tsap$_2$ yam'. |
| 48. Ministers of state are not to confer appointments. | 大臣專擅選官 | Tái$^2$ ˛shan ˓chün shín$^2$ ʻsün ˓kún. |
| 49. Civilians (or high officers) are not allowed to solicit titles of nobility (except in extraordinary cases). | 文官不許封公侯 | ˛Man ˓kún pat˒ ʻhü ˓fung ˓kung ˛hau. |
| 50. On the appointment of supernumerary officers. | 濫設官吏 | Lám$^2$ ch'ít˒ ˓kún lí$^2$. |
| 51. On warrants granted to the police. | 信牌 | Sun' ˛p'ái. |
| 52. On the appointment of improper persons. | 貢舉非其人 | Kung' ʻkü ˓fí ˛k'í ˛yan. |
| 53. Recommendtaion of offenders once dismissed. | 舉用有過官吏 | ʻKü yung$^2$ ʻyau kwo' ˓kún lí$^2$. |
| 54. On the quitting of office without leave. | 擅離職役 | Shín$^2$ ˛lí chik˒ yik$_2$. |
| 55. On delays in entering upon the duties of office. | 官員赴任過限 | ˓Kún ˛ün fú' yam$^2$ kwo' hán$^2$. |
| 56. Non-attendance daily in their place at court, or at the public offices in the provinces. | 無故不朝參公座 | ˛Mò kú' pat˒ ˛chíú ˓ts'ám ˓kung tsò$^2$. |
| 57. Interference with subordinate magistrates. | 擅勾屬官 | Shín$^2$ ˓kau shuk$_2$ ˓kún. |
| 58. Malicious cabals, or state intrigues. | 姦黨 | ˓Kán ʻtóng. |
| 59. Collusion of provincial and court officers. | 交結近侍官員 | ˓Káu kít˒ kan$^2$ shí$^2$ ˓kún ˛ün. |
| 60. Address in favor of great officers of state. | 上言大臣德政 | Shéung$^2$ ˛ín tái$^2$ ˛shan tak˒ ching'. |
| 61. Thorough knowledge of the laws required. | 講讀律令 | ʻKóng tuk$_2$ lut$_2$ ling$^2$. |
| 62. Non-execution of imperial edicts. | 制書有違 | Chai' ˓shü ʻyau ˛wai. |
| 63. Destroying imperial edicts and seals of office. | 棄毀制書印信 | Hí' ʻwai chai' ˓shü yan' sun'. |

45, 46. Temporary transportation must not exceed 500 *li*; there are three degrees of perpetual transportation, first, 2000, second, 2500, third, 3000 *li*; of the extraordinary, or transportation to the army, there are degrees of 2000, 2500, 3000, and 4000 *li*. The severest is to Ílí for life.

§2. The *lí lut*, or laws for the regulation of the civil service, are 28; fourteen (from Nos. 47 to 60,) refer to the *shik chai*, or system of government; and fourteen (61 to 74) to the *kung shik*, or the conduct of magistrates.

48. High provincial officers are constantly in the habit of filling vacancies, both civil and military, that occur within their jurisdiction; this, however, is only done by special permission, ad interim, till the pleasure of the emperor can be signified.

61. Not only are all officers of government required to make themselves acquainted with the laws of the empire, but such knowledge is deemed meritorious in husbandmen and artisans.

| | | |
|---|---|---|
| 64. Errors in public documents and memorials. | 上書奏事犯諱 | ꜃Shéung ꜀shü tsau’ sz’꜅ fán’ ꜃wai. |
| 65. On failure to make due reports to the emperor. | 事應奏不奏 | Sz’꜅ ꜀ying tsau’ pat› tsau’. |
| 66. Non-return of warrant after its execution. | 出使不復命 | Chʻut› ‘sz’ pat› fuk꜇ ming꜅. |
| 67. Delay in transmitting governmental dispatches. | 官文書稽程 | ꜀Kún ꜁man ꜀shü ꜀kai꜁ chʻing. |
| 68. Examination and preservation of records. | 照刷文卷 | Chíú’ shát› ꜁man ‘kün. |
| 69. On the examination of official documents. | 磨勘卷宗 | ꜁Mó hóm’ ‘kün ꜀tsung. |
| 70. On official persons acting in concert and writing and signing documents for each other. | 同僚代判署文案 | ꜁Tʻung ꜁líú tòi꜅ pún’ ‘shü ꜁man ón’. |
| 71. Adding to or abridging official papers. | 增減官文書 | ꜀Tsang ‘kám ꜀kún ꜁man ꜀shü. |
| 72. On the use and keeping of public seals. | 封掌印信 | ꜀Fung ‘chéung yan’ sun’. |
| 73. Omitting to use or improperly using public seals. | 漏使印信 | Lau꜅ ‘sz’ yan’ sun’. |
| 74. On using the public seals to call out the military. | 擅用調兵印信 | Shín꜅ yung꜅ tíú꜅ ꜀ping yan’ sun’. |
| §3. Fiscal Laws. | 戶律 | *Ú꜅ lut꜇.* |
| 75. Omitting to register families and individuals. | 脫漏戶口 | Tʻüt› lau꜅ ú꜅ ‘hau. |
| 76. The registry of persons to be according to profession. | 人戶以籍爲定 | ꜁Yan ú꜅ ꜃í tsik꜇ ꜁wai ting꜅. |
| 77. Temples and monasteries not to be built, nor any person enter the priesthood, without permission of government. | 私捌菴院及私度僧道 | ꜀Sz’ chʻóng’ ꜀óm ün꜅ kap꜇ ꜀sz’ tò꜅ ꜀sang tò꜅. |
| 78. On the appointment of an heir. | 立嫡子違法 | Lap꜇ tik› ‘tsz’ ꜁wai fát›. |
| 79. On receiving and detaining stray children. | 收留迷失女子 | ꜀Shau ꜁lau ꜁mai shat› ꜃nü ‘tsz’. |
| 80. On inequality in taxes and personal service. | 賦役不均 | Fú’ yik꜇ pat› ꜀kwan. |
| 81. Unequal treatment of persons in the public service. | 丁夫差遣不平 | ꜀Ting ꜀fú ꜀chái ꜃hín pat› ꜁pʻing. |
| 82. Clandestine connections with the civil service. | 隱蔽差役 | ‘Yan pai’ ꜀chái yik꜇. |
| 83. Against assuming the office of constables, &c. | 禁革主保里長 | Kam’ kák› ‘chü ‘pò ‘li ‘chʻéung. |
| 84. Evasion of public service by desertion. | 逃避差役 | ꜁Tʻò pí꜅ ꜀chái yik꜇. |

§3. Fiscal laws, or the regulations concerning the population and revenue, are 82;—fifteen (Nos. 75 to 89,) refer to the *ú yik* or enrolment of the people; eleven (90 to 100) to *tʻin chák* or lands and tenements; seventeen (101 to 117) to *wan yan* or marriage; twenty-three (118 to 140) to *tsʻóng fú* or granaries and treasuries; eight (141 to 148) to *fó chʻing* or duties and customs; three (149 to 151) to *tsʻin chái* or money loans; five (152 to 156) to *shí chín* or markets and shops.

76. According to this statute, persons and families are not only required truly to represent their profession in life, but in whatever that may be (the agricultural, mechanical, or any other), therein they must remain fixed for ever: *shai shai pat tak koi í*, 'generation after generation they must not change or alter it.'

| | | |
|---|---|---|
| 85. Police-men appointed to be guards of prisons. | 點差獄卒 | ʻTím ꜀chái yuk꜆ tsut꜆. |
| 86. Employing people and artisans on private service. | 私役部民夫匠 | ꜀Sz' yik꜆ pòʼ ꜁man ꜀fú tséungʼ. |
| 87. On the separation of registry and property. | 别籍異財 | Pít꜆ tsik꜆ íʼ ꜁tsʻoi. |
| 88. On the use of property by inferiors and youth. | 卑幼私擅用財 | ꜀Pí yauʼ ꜀szʼ shínʼ yungʼ ꜁tsʻoi. |
| 89. On provision for the bereaved and aged. | 收養孤老 | ꜀Shau ʻyéung ꜀kú ʻlò. |
| 90. Fraudulent misrepresentations of landed property. | 欺隱田糧 | ꜀Hí ʻyan ꜁tʻín ꜁léung. |
| 91. Personal inspection of lands injured by calamities. | 檢踏災傷田糧 | ʻKím táp꜆ ꜀tsoi ꜀shéung ꜁tʻín ꜁léung. |
| 92. Lands of meritorious ministers. | 功臣田土 | ꜀Kung ꜁shan ꜁tʻín ʻtʻò. |
| 93. Usurpation of lands and tenements. | 盜賣田宅 | Tòʼ máiʼ ꜁tʻín chák꜆. |
| 94. Purchases of lands and tenements by office-bearers. | 任所置買田宅 | Yamʼ ʻshó chíʼ ʻmái ꜁tʻín chák꜆. |
| 95. Mortgaging of lands and tenements. | 典買田宅 | ʻTín ʻmái ꜁tʻín chák꜆. |
| 96. On usurping public or private land fraudulently. | 盜耕種官民田 | Tòʼ ꜀kang chungʼ ꜀kún ꜁man ꜁tʻín. |
| 97. On abandoning registered lands. | 荒蕪田地 | ꜀Wóng ꜁mú ꜁tʻín tíʼ. |
| 98. On casting away and destroying good utensils, harvests, &c. | 棄毀器物稼穡等 | Híʼ ʻwai híʼ mat꜆ káʼ shik꜆ ʻtang. |
| 99. On taking the productions of gardens and orchards. | 擅食田園瓜菓 | Shínʼ shik꜆ ꜁tʻín ꜁ün ꜀kwá ʻkwò. |
| 100. Private employmen of public carriages and boats. | 私借官車船 | ꜀Szʼ tséʼ ꜀kún ꜀kü ꜁shün. |
| 101. Marriage of males and females, how regulated. | 男女婚姻 | ꜁Nám ʻnü ꜀wan ꜀yan. |
| 102. On mortgaging a wife or daughter. | 典雇妻女 | ʻTín kúʼ ꜀tsʻai ʻnü. |
| 103. On disregarding the rank of wife and concubine. | 妻妾失序 | ꜀Tsʻai tsʻíp꜆ shat꜆ tsüʼ. |

89. This law requires that all poor destitute widowers and widows, the fatherless and childless, the helpless and the infirm, shall receive a needful support from the magistrates of their native district or city, provided they are without relations on whom they can depend for support. The foundling hospitals and those for the aged are designed to meet the requirements of this law.

90. It is worthy of remark, under this head, that both literary and religious institutions are exempt from the tax on tenements.

91. Officers of government are the guardians of the people, and stand to them in the relation of parents; and as the emperor's servants, they are by him held responsible for maintaining and protecting and governing the people: hence, when any natural calamities befall the people, it becomes the duty of the magistrates to examine the effects of the same in person, so that they may faithfully report them to his master.

92. The lands of meritorious officers especially granted to them by imperial patent, are exempt from taxation, while their private lands are subject like all others to the land-tax.

101—117. The right of controling marriages rests with parents and grandparents, or those who stand in their stead. The *tsʻai* or wife is the husband's equal; the *tsʻip* holds an inferior rank: the one honorable, the other mean: to confound their rank would be to destroy propriety, and to rebel against social order.

| | | |
|---|---|---|
| 104. Ejecting a son-in-law, and marrying the girl again. | 逐婿嫁女 | Chuk꜇ sai꜄ ká꜄ ꜂nü. |
| 105. On marrying during the period of mourning. | 居喪嫁娶 | ꜀Kü ꜀sóng ká꜄ ts‘ü꜄. |
| 106. Marriage interdicted during parents' imprisonment. | 父母囚禁嫁娶 | Fú꜅ ꜂mò ꜁ch‘au kàm꜄ ká꜄ ts‘ü꜄. |
| 107. Marriage of those of the same family name. | 同姓爲婚 | ꜁T‘ung sing꜄ ꜁wai ꜀wan. |
| 108. Marriage between the honorable and the mean. | 尊卑爲婚 | ꜀Tsün ꜀pí ꜁wai ꜀wan. |
| 109. On marrying a wife or concubine's relations. | 娶親屬妻妾 | Ts‘ü꜄ ꜀ts‘an shuk꜇ ꜀ts‘ai ts‘íp꜆. |
| 110. Official persons marrying as wives or concubines the wives or daughters of families under their jurisdiction. | 娶部民婦女爲妻妾 | Ts‘ü꜄ pò꜅ ꜁man ꜂fú ꜂nü ꜁wai ꜀ts‘ai ts‘íp꜆. |
| 111. On marrying with those who have absconded. | 娶逃走婦女 | Ts‘ü꜄ ꜁t‘ò ꜂tsau ꜂fú ꜂nü. |
| 112. Forcible marriage of freemens' wives and daughters. | 強占良家妻女 | ꜁Kéung chím꜄ ꜁léung ꜀ká ꜀ts‘ai ꜂nü. |
| 113. On marrying female musicians. | 娶樂人爲妻妾 | Ts‘ü꜄ ngók꜇ ꜁yan ꜁wai ꜀ts‘ai ts‘íp꜆. |
| 114. On the marriage of priests. | 僧道娶妻 | ꜀Sang tò꜅ ts‘ü꜄ ꜀ts‘ai. |
| 115. On marriage between free persons and slaves. | 良賤爲婚姻 | ꜁Léung tsín꜅ ꜁wai ꜀wan ꜀yan. |
| 116. On the regulations for divorce. | 出妻 | Ch‘ut꜆ ꜀ts‘ai. |
| 117. When marriages are contracted contrary to law, both the controler and the go-between are responsible. | 嫁娶違律主婚媒人罪 | Ká꜄ ts‘ü꜄ ꜁wai lut꜇ ꜂chü ꜀wan ꜁múi ꜁yan tsúi꜅. |
| 118. Regulations concerning coinage. | 錢法 | ꜁Ts‘ín fát꜆. |
| 119. Periods for receiving taxes in kind not to be passed. | 收糧違限 | ꜀Shau ꜁léung ꜁wai hán꜅. |
| 120. Impartiality in collecting the revenue in kind. | 多收稅糧斛面 | ꜀Tó ꜀shau shui꜄ ꜁léung huk꜇ mín꜅. |
| 121. On concealing or wasting the revenue whether consisting of grain or other commodities. | 隱匿費用稅糧課物 | ꜂Yan nik꜆ fai꜄ yung꜅ shui꜄ ꜁léung fó꜄ mat꜇. |
| 122. On monopolizing the payment of taxes. | 攬納稅糧 | ꜂Káu náp꜇ shui꜄ ꜁léung. |
| 123. On granting false receipts at the storehouses. | 虛出通關硃鈔 | ꜀Hü ch‘ut꜆ ꜀t‘ung ꜀kwán ꜀chü ꜀cháu. |
| 124. Of excess in receipts; all private appropriation forbidden, and a faithful report required. | 附餘錢糧私下補數 | Fú꜅ ꜁ü ꜁ts‘ín ꜁léung ꜀sz꜄ há꜅ ꜂pò shò꜄. |
| 125. On clandestine lending or using the revenue. | 私借錢糧 | ꜀Sz꜄ tsé꜄ ꜁ts‘ín ꜁léung. |

104, 105. Priests are forbidden to marry, or to have concubines. However, the priests of the Taou sect often violate this law. Marriage between free persons and slaves is strictly interdicted.

116. There are seven causes for putting away a wife, and there are three considerations which interfere to prevent such an act: these are specified in Chap. III. sec. 4. page 96.

| | | |
|---|---|---|
| 126. On clandestine lending or using public property. | 私借官物 | ‹Sz’ tsé’ ‹kún mat$_2$. |
| 127. On the transfers, expenditures, and receipts. | 那移出納 | ꜁Nó ꜁í chʻut› náp$_2$. |
| 128. On frauds by workmen in the storehouses. | 庫秤雇役侵欺 | Fú’ ꜁pʻing kú’ yik$_2$ ‹tsʻam ‹hi. |
| 129. On fraud in the distribution of rations. | 冒支官糧 | Mò$^2$ ‹chí ‹kún ꜁léung. |
| 130. Revenue officers answerable for each other. | 錢粮互相覺察 | ꜁Tsʻín ꜁léung ú$^2$ ‹séung kok› chʻát›. |
| 131. On thefts in the granaries and storehouses. | 倉庫不覺被盜 | ‹Tsʻong fú’ pat› hók› pí$^2$ tò$^2$. |
| 132. On the duties of the receivers and the distributors of property which belongs to the government. | 守支錢粮及擅開官封 | ‘Shau ‹chí ꜁tsʻín ꜁léung kap$_2$ shín$^2$ ‹hoi ‹kún ꜁fung. |
| 133. Fraud in the issues and receipts of public stores. | 出納官物有違 | Chʻut, náp$_2$ ‹kún mat$_2$ ‘yau ꜁wai. |
| 134. On detention and annoyance in receiving revenue. | 收支留難 | ‹Shau ‹chí ꜁lau ꜁nán. |
| 135. Purity of the gold and silver delivered to government. | 起解金銀足色 | ‘Hí kái’ ‹kam ꜁ngan tsuk› shik›. |
| 136. On the damaging of governmental stores. | 損壞倉庫財物 | ‘Sün wái$^2$ ‹tsʻong fú’ ꜁tsʻoi mat$_2$. |
| 137. On the transmission of governmental stores. | 轉解官物 | ‘Chün kái’ ‹kún mat$_2$. |
| 138. On the distribution of confiscated property. | 擬斷贓罰不當 | ‘Í tün’ ‹tsóng fát$_2$ pat› tóng’. |
| 139. On the safe keeping of confiscated property. | 守掌在官財物 | ‘Shau ‘chéung tsoi$^2$ ‹kún ꜁tsʻoi mat$_2$. |
| 140. Concealment of such property or of persons. | 隱瞞入官家產 | ‘Yan ꜁mún yap› ‹kún ‹ká ‘chʻán. |
| 141. Regulation of the salt department. | 鹽法 | ꜁Ím fát›. |
| 142. On the avails obtained by the superintendents. | 監臨勢要中鹽 | ‹Kám ꜁lam shai’ íú’ ‹chung ꜁ím. |
| 143. On the preservation of the regulations on salt. | 阻壞鹽法 | ‘Chó wái$^2$ ꜁ím fát›. |
| 144. On the smuggling of tea. | 私茶 | ‹Sz’ ꜁chʻá. |
| 145. On the smuggling of alum. | 私礬 | ‹Sz’ ꜁fán. |
| 146. Evasion of duties of any kind. | 匿稅 | Nik› shui’. |
| 147. On the concealment of goods by merchant vessels. | 舶商匿貨 | Pák$_2$ ‹shéung nik› fó’. |
| 148. Arrears in the payment of duties and customs. | 人戶虧兌課程 | ꜁Yán ú$^2$ ‹fai túi$^2$ fó’ ꜁chʻing. |
| 149. On taking unlawful interest. | 違禁取利 | ꜁Wai kam’ ‘tsü li$^2$. |

141—148. Duties and customs are regulated by these laws. The trade in salt is one of the principal sources of revenue, and is under the control of government, in the hands of licensed merchants; and both the manufacture and the transportation of the article, as well as the sale of it, are also regulated by government.

149, 151. Private property, and money loans, *tsʻín chái*, are regulated by these laws. The maximum rate of interest is 30 per cent. per annum, but in no length of years can the interest exceed the principal.

| | | |
|---|---|---|
| 150. Breach of trust in keeping property. | 費用受寄財產 | Fai' yung' shau' kí' ,ts'oi 'ch'án. |
| 151. On finding things that have been lost. | 得遺失物 | Tak, ,wai shat, mat,. |
| 152. On clandestinely opening factories and warehouses. | 私充牙行埠頭 | ,Sz' ,ch'ung ,ngá ,hóng fau' ,ta'n. |
| 153. On the valuation of goods by factors. | 市司評物價 | 'Shí ,sz' ,ping mat, ká'. |
| 154. On combinations of factors and traders. | 把持行市 | 'Pá ,ch'í ,hóng 'shí. |
| 155. On false weights, measures, and scales. | 私造斛斗秤尺 | ,Sz' tsò' huk, 'tau ch'ing' ch'ik,. |
| 156. On manufacturing utensils and silk stuffs in a manner unsanctioned by usage. | 器用布絹不如法 | Hí' yung' pò' kün' pat, ,ü fát,. |
| §4. RITUAL LAWS. | 禮律 | *'Lai lut,.* |
| 157. Administration of sacred rites. | 祭享 | Tsai' 'héung. |
| 158. On destroying the altars for the great sacrifices. | 毀大祀邱壇 | 'Wai tái' tsz'' ,yau ,t'án. |
| 159. Sacrifices and offerings to local divinities. | 致祭祀典神祇 | Chí' tsai' tsz'' 'tín ,shan ,k'í. |
| 160. Concerning the tombs of ancient emperors and kings. | 歷代帝王陵寢 | Lik, toi' tai' ,wóng ,ling 'ts'am. |
| 161. On doing dishonor to the gods. | 褻瀆神明 | Sít, tuk, ,shan ,ming. |
| 162. Prohibition of magicians and depraved arts. | 禁止師巫邪術 | Kam' 'chí ,sz' ,mò ,ts'é shut,. |
| 163. On preparing medicines for the emperor. | 合和御藥 | Hóp, ,wó yü' yéuk,. |
| 164. Care of the imperial equipage and wardrobe. | 乘輿服御物 | ,Shing ,yü fuk, yü' mat,. |
| 165. On keeping and concealing interdicted books. | 收藏禁書 | ,Shau ,ts'óng kam' ,shü. |
| 166. On the transmission of imperial presents. | 御賜衣物 | Yü' ts'z'' ,í mat,. |
| 167. Neglects and errors in congratulations at court. | 失誤朝賀 | Shat, 'ng' ,chíú hó'. |
| 168. On neglect of the appointed ceremonies. | 失儀 | Shat, ,í. |

152—156. These *ngá hóng* are establishments for the exchange of commodities, approved of and sanctioned by government; and the agents in charge of them are allowed only a fixed per centage on the goods they ship or exchange. By the 154th section, these agents are forbidden to forestal the markets so as to raise or depress the prices of goods.

§4. The ritual laws, or those which are designed to regulate the performance of religious duties, are only 26 in number; of which six (157 to 162) refer to *tsai tsz'*, or sacrifices and offerings, and twenty (163 to 182) to *í chai*, or ceremonial rules. In the religion of state, the emperor and his officers all bear a part; the son of heaven is high priest of the empire, and it is his sole perogative to offer the great sacrifices to the Most High, to heaven, to earth, ancestors, &c. All the officers have their appointed duties in this legal service. See Chinese Repository, Vol. III. page 49.

157—162. These six laws have special reference to *tsai tsz'* or sacrifices and offerings; there must be no remissness or error in the worshipers, nor defects in the victims. According to the 161st section, private individuals are forbidden to worship the great divinities; and by the 162d, heterodoxy of all kinds is interdicted.

| | | |
|---|---|---|
| 169. Breach of order in responding to the emperor. | 奏對失序 | Tsau' túi' shat, tsü$^{2}$. |
| 170. On preventing or impeding imperial audiences. | 朝見留難 | ˎChíú kín' ˏlau ˏnán. |
| 171. Addresses on public affairs. | 上書陳言 | ʽShéung ˎshü ˏchʻan ˏín. |
| 172. On the erecting of monuments by officers to commemorate their own acts. | 見任官輙自立碑 | Kín' yam$^{2}$ ˎkún chíp, tsz'$^{2}$ lap$_{2}$ ˎpí. |
| 173. Interdicts on receiving and taking leave of officers. | 禁止迎送 | Kam' ʽchí ˏying sung'. |
| 174. Against official messengers behaving rudely towards provincial officers. | 公差人員欺陵長官 | ˎKung ˎchái ˏyan ˏün ˎhí ˏling ʽchʻéung ˎkún. |
| 175. Sumptuary laws respecting dress, houses, &c. | 服舍違式 | Fuk$_{2}$ shé' ˏwai shik,. |
| 176. Respect to parents from the priesthood. | 僧道拜父母 | ˎSang tò$^{2}$ pái' fú$^{2}$ ʽmò. |
| 177. Neglecting to note celestial phenomena. | 失占天象 | Shat, ˎchím ˎtʻín tséung$^{2}$. |
| 178. On the predicting of weal and woe by magicians. | 術士妄言禍福 | Shut$_{2}$ sz'$^{2}$ móng$^{2}$ ˏín wó$^{2}$ fuk,. |
| 179. Concealment of deaths by proper mourners. | 匿父母夫喪 | Nik, fú$^{2}$ ʽmò ˎfú ˎsóng. |
| 180. On neglect of parents by office-bearers. | 棄親之任 | Hí' ˎtsʻan ˎchí yam$^{2}$. |
| 181. Regulations for interment and funeral rites. | 喪葬 | ˎSóng tsóng'. |
| 182. Regulations for village festivals. | 鄉飲酒禮 | ˎHéung ʽyam ʽtsau ʽlai. |
| §5. MILITARY LAWS. | 兵律 | *ˎPing lut$_{2}$.* |
| 183. Unauthorizedly entering the imperial temples. | 太廟門擅入 | Tʻái' míú$^{2}$ ˏmún shín$^{2}$ yap$_{2}$. |
| 184. Unauthorizedly entering the imperial palace. | 宮殿門擅入 | ˎKung tín$^{2}$ ˏmún shín$^{2}$ yap$_{2}$. |
| 185. Imperial guards not allowed by night or day to obtain any substitutes without leave. | 宿衛守衛人私自代替 | Suk, wai$^{2}$ ʽshau wai$^{2}$ ˏyan ˎsz' tsz'$^{2}$ toi$^{2}$ tʻai'. |
| 186. On the imperial retinue failing in attendance. | 從駕稽違 | ˏTsung ká' ˎkai ˏwai. |
| 187. Trespass on the imperial roads. | 直行御道 | Chik$_{2}$ ˏhang yü$^{2}$ tò$^{2}$. |
| 188. On the employment of substitutes for the workmen in the imperial palaces. | 內府工作人匠替役 | Noi$^{2}$ ʽfú ˎkung tsók, ˏyan tséung$^{2}$ tʻai' yik$_{2}$. |

§5. These laws are 71 in number; sixteen (183—198) referring to *kung ngá* or the protection of the palace; twenty-one (199—219) to *kwan ching*, or the government of the army; seven (220—226) to *kwán tsun* or boundaries and passes; eleven (227—237) to *chau muk*, or the governmental herds; sixteen (238—253) to *yau yik*, or posts and expresses.

183, 184. Reference is made in these to the imperial mausolea, gardens, parks, &c. The apartments of the empress, empress-mother, and empress-grandmother enjoy the same protection as those of the emperor.

| | | |
|---|---|---|
| 189. On the non-departure of workmen after completing their work in the imperial palaces. | 宮殿造作罷不出 | ꜀Kung tín꜅ tsò꜅ tsók꜆ pá꜅ pat꜆ ch‘ut꜆. |
| 190. On irregularly going in and out of the palaces. | 輒出入宮殿門 | Chíp꜆ ch‘ut꜆ yap꜇ ꜀kung tín꜅ ꜁mún. |
| 191. On keeping a guard when employés enter & depart. | 關防內使出入 | ꜀Kwán ꜁fóng noi꜅ sz꜅ ch‘ut꜆ yap꜇. |
| 192. On shooting arrows towards the imperial palaces. | 向宮殿射箭 | Héung꜄ ꜀kung tín꜅ shé꜅ ts‘ín꜄. |
| 193. The noctnrnal guards are not to lay down their arms. | 宿衛人兵仗 | Suk꜆ wai꜅ ꜁yan ꜀ping chéung꜅. |
| 194. Convicted persons and their relatives forbidden to serve on the night guards. | 禁經斷人充宿衛 | Kam꜄ ꜀king ꜂tün ꜁yan ꜀ch‘ung suk꜆ wai꜅. |
| 195. Incroachments on the imperial retinue. | 衝突儀仗 | ꜀Chung tat꜇ ꜁í chéung꜅. |
| 196. Entering the imperial cantonment. | 行宮營門 | ꜁Hang ꜀kung ꜁ying ꜁mún. |
| 197. On passing over the wall of the imperial city. | 越城 | Üt꜇ ꜁shing. |
| 198. On closing and locking gates of cities. | 門禁鎖鑰 | ꜁Mún kam꜄ ꜂só yéuk꜇. |
| 199. Against moving troops without due authority. | 擅調官軍 | Shín꜅ tíú꜅ ꜀kún ꜀kwan. |
| 200. Military operations to be duly reported. | 申報軍務 | ꜀Shan pò꜅ ꜀kwan mò꜅. |
| 201. On sending expresses concerning military affairs. | 飛報軍情 | ꜀Fí pò꜄ ꜀kwan ꜁ts‘ing. |
| 202. On betraying the secrets of the army. | 漏泄軍情大事 | Lau꜅ sít꜆ ꜀kwan ꜁ts‘ing tái꜅ sz꜅. |
| 203. Application for military supplies on the frontiers. | 邊境申索軍需 | ꜀Pín ꜂king ꜀shan sók꜆ ꜀kwan ꜀sü. |
| 204. Failures and errors in military affairs. | 失誤軍事 | Shat꜆ ꜃ng꜅ ꜀kwan sz꜅. |
| 205. On delays in advancing according to orders. | 從征違期 | ꜁Tsung ꜀ching ꜁wai ꜁kí. |
| 206. On soldiers serving as substitutes. | 軍人替役 | ꜀Kwan ꜁yan t‘ai꜄ yik꜇. |
| 207. Unfaithfulness in commanders-in-chief. | 主將不固守 | ꜂Chü tséung꜄ pat꜆ kú꜄ ꜂shau. |
| 208. On allowing the army to kidnap and plunder. | 縱軍擄掠 | Tsung꜄ ꜀kwan ꜃lú léuk꜇. |
| 209. On neglect of exercise and discipline. | 不操練軍事 | Pat꜆ ꜀tsò lín꜅ ꜀kwan sz꜅ |
| 210. On provoking peaceable people to insurrection. | 激變良民 | Kik꜆ pín꜄ ꜁léung ꜁man. |
| 211. Clandestine sale of war horses. | 私賣戰馬 | ꜀Sz꜄ mái꜅ chín꜅ ꜂má. |
| 212. On clandestine sale of arms and accoutrements. | 私賣軍器 | ꜀Sz꜄ mái꜅ ꜀kwan hí꜄. |

198. The cities are regarded as fortifid places, and their gates are required to be locked at a specified time at night, and ordinarily are not to be opened until a specified hour in the morning.

199—219. These all refer to *kwan ching*, the government of the army. According to the 207th section, if an officer, in chief command of any city or fortress, is surprised and unable to defend his post, he shall suffer death by decapitation.

| | | |
|---|---|---|
| 213. On destroying or abandoning the same. | 毀棄軍器 | 'Wai hí' ‹kwan hí'. |
| 214. On secretly keeping prohibited arms. | 私藏應禁軍器 | ‹Sz' ‚ts'óng ‹ying kam' ‹kwan hí'. |
| 215. On allowing soldiers leave of absence. | 縱放軍人歇役 | Tsung' fóng' ‹kwan ‚yan hít› yik$_2$. |
| 216. Noblemen secretly employing governmental troops. | 公侯私役官軍 | ‹Kung ‚hau ‹sz' yik$_2$ ‹kún ‹kwan. |
| 217. Against leaving or running away from the army when called on to perform service. | 從征守禦官軍逃 | ‚Tsung ‹ching 'shau yü$^2$ ‹kún ‹kwan ‚t'ò. |
| 218. Favors to those who belong to the army. | 優恤軍屬 | ‹Yau sut› ‹kwan shuk$_2$. |
| 219. Regulations for nocturnal police. | 夜禁 | Yé$^2$ kam'. |
| 220. On crossing a barrier without a passport. | 私越冒度關津 | ‹Sz' üt$_2$ mò$^2$ tò$^2$ ‹kwán ‹tsun. |
| 221. Granting passports on false pretenses. | 詐冒給路引 | Chá' mò$^2$ kap› lò$^2$ 'yan. |
| 222. On detentions and annoyances at barriers. | 關津留難 | ‹Kwán ‹tsun ‚lau ‚nán. |
| 223. On assisting the wives and daughters of deserters to go forth from the cities or fortified towns. | 遞送逃軍妻女出城 | Tai$^2$ sung' ‚t'ò ‹kwan ‹ts'ai 'nü ch'ut› ‚shing. |
| 224. On discovering and seizing spies. | 盤詰姦細 | ‚P'ún kít› ‹kán sai'. |
| 225. On passing secretly the frontiers, and on going out to sea contrary to the regulations. | 私出外境及違禁下海 | ‹Sz' ch'ut› ngoi$^2$ 'king kap$_2$ ‚wai kam' há$^2$ 'hoi. |
| 226. Private employment of public archers. | 私役弓兵 | ‹Sz' yik$_2$ ‹kung ‹ping. |
| 227. Concerning the improper management of the herds and flocks belonging to government. | 牧養畜產不如法 | Muk$_2$ 'yéung ch'uk› 'ch'án pat› ‚yü fát›. |
| 228. On the breeding of horses for government. | 孳生馬匹 | ‹Tsz' ‹shang 'má pat›. |
| 229. Unfaithfulness in the examination of animals. | 驗畜產不以實 | Ím$^2$ ch'uk› 'ch'án pat› 'í shat$_2$. |
| 230. On failing to feed and doctor lean and sick animals according to prescribed rules. | 養療瘦病畜產不如法 | 'Yéung ‚líú shau' ping$^2$ ch'uk› 'ch'án pat› ‚yü fát›. |

218. In case a soldier dies or is killed in the army, the local officers are required to provide for the surviving relations with temporary means of subsistence, and of returning to their native place, if absent from their families.

220—226. These laws refer to boundaries and passes both by sea and land. A clause under the 224th section forbids the Chinese inhabiting the small islands along the coast. This law however is not enforced, and multitudes inhabit the islands.

230. The veterinary art has received no inconsiderable attention from the Chinese, as the *Ma King*, or Memoir on Horses, a work in four volumes containing recipes for curing the diseases of not only horses but cattle and camels, sufficiently testifies. Horses, horned cattle, camels, mules, and asses, are the several kinds of animals specified in this law, which refers only to those kinds of animals that belong to the government, or are designed for its service.

廣東方言讀本



| | | |
|---|---|---|
| 231. On using the cattle of government in such a manner as to injure their backs or necks. | 乘官畜脊破領穿 | ˏShing ˏkún ch'ukˏ tsikˏ p'o' ˈling ˏch'ün. |
| 232. Improper training of governmental horses. | 官馬不調習 | ˏKún ˈmá patˏ ˏt'iú tsápˏ. |
| 233. On slaughtering or killing horses and cattle. | 宰殺馬牛 | ˈTsoi shátˏ ˈmá ˏngau. |
| 234. On cattle biting and injuring people. | 畜產咬踢人 | Ch'ukˏ ˈch'án ˈngáu tikˏ ˏyan. |
| 235. On concealing the increase of cattle and horses which belong to the government. | 隱匿孳生官畜產 | ˈYan nikˏ ˏtsz' ˏshang ˏkún ch'ukˏ ˈch'án. |
| 236. Privately lending animals belonging to government. | 私借官畜產 | ˏSz' tsé' ˏkún ch'ukˏ ˈch'án. |
| 237. Concerning the public messengers improperly compelling the loan of horses. | 公使人等索借馬匹 | ˏKung sz'' ˏyan ˈtang sokˏ tsé' ˈmá p'atˏ. |
| 238. On the conveyance of governmental dispatches. | 遞送公文 | Tai² sung' ˏkung ˏman. |
| 239. On intercepting dispatches of government. | 邀取實封公文 | ˏÍú ˈtsü shat₂ ˏfung ˏkung ˏman. |
| 240. Post-offices must not be allowed to go out of repair. | 鋪舍損壞 | P'ò' shé' ˈsün wái². |
| 241. Private employment of the office-soldiers. | 私役鋪兵 | ˏSz' yik₂ p'ò' ˏping. |
| 242. Delays of the expresses in carrying dispatches. | 驛使稽程 | Yik₂ sz'' ˏkai ˏch'ing. |
| 243. On exceeding the number of horses allowed. | 多乘驛馬 | ˏTó ˏshing yik₂ ˈmá. |
| 244. On granting an excess of rations. | 多支廩給 | ˏTó ˏchí ˈlam kapˏ. |
| 245. On refusing to furnish post-horses, for conveying dispatches, when they are due. | 文書應給驛而不給 | ˏMan ˏshü ˏying kapˏ yik₂ ˏí patˏ kapˏ. |
| 246. Delay in the transmission of governmental effects. | 公事應行稽程 | ˏKung sz'² ˏying ˏhang ˏkai ˏch'ing. |
| 247. On occupying the principal apartments of post offices. | 占宿驛舍上房 | Chim' sukˏ yik₂ shé' shéung² ˏfóng. |
| 248. On carrying private property on post-horses. | 乘驛馬齎私物 | ˏShing yik₂ ˈmá ˏtsai ˏsz' mat₂. |
| 249. Officers forcing the people to carry their sedans. | 私役民夫抬轎 | ˏSz' yik₂ ˏman ˏfú ˏt'oi kíú². |

231. This law was made in consideration of government and for its benefit, and not in mercy to the brute creation; however, in its operation it is most favorable to the 'dumb ass and ox.' The Chinese generally seem not to be cruel to their brute beasts; and much of the labor borne by the ox and the horse in other countries is here sustained by man.

233. This law ordains that, 'whoever, without the permission of government kills his own horses and horned cattle shall be punished with 100 blows.' Swine and sheep are also included in this law, and the killing of them without license is forbidden.

238—253. These sixteen laws regulate the *yau yik*, or post-offices and expresses for the transmission of governmental dispatches. The ordinary rate of dispatches is 300 *li* per day; in cases of great moment they are called fire dispatches, and are carried 500 *li* per day, arriving in Canton from the capital in twelve or thirteen days.

| | | |
|---|---|---|
| 250. The families of deceased officers are to be removed to their homes at the expense of government. | 病故官家屬還鄉 | Ping꜆ kú' ꜀kún ꜀ká shuk꜇ ꜁wán ꜀héung. |
| 251. Committing to others the care of conveying property. | 承差轉雇寄人 | ꜁Shing ꜀chái ʻchün kú' kí' ꜁yan. |
| 252. On the conveyance of private property by the cattle, carts, or vessels of government. | 乘官畜產車船附私物 | ꜁Shing ꜀kún chʻuk꜅ ʻchʻán ꜀kü ꜁shün fú꜆ ꜀sz' mat꜇. |
| 253. On privately lending the post-horses of government. | 私借驛馬 | ꜀Sz' tsé' yik꜇ ʻmá. |
| §6. CRIMINAL LAWS. | 刑律 | ꜁*Ying lut꜇*. |
| 254. High treason, or concerting high rebellion. | 謀反大逆 | ꜁Mau ʻfán tái꜆ yik꜇. |
| 255. Concerting revolt or desertion. | 謀叛 | ꜁Mau pún꜆. |
| 256. On making strange (or wicked) books or speeches. | 造妖書妖言 | Tsò꜆ ʻíú ꜀shü ʻíú ꜁ín. |
| 257. Stealing things used by the emperor in sacrifices. | 盜大祀神御物 | Tò꜆ tái꜆ tsz'꜆ ꜁shan yü꜆ mat꜇. |
| 258. Stealing documents written by the emperor. | 〃制書 | Tò꜆ chai' ꜀shü. |
| 259. Stealing the seals of government. | 〃印信 | Tò꜆ yan' sun'. |
| 260. Stealing from the imperial palace. | 〃內府財物 | Tò꜆ noi꜆ ʻfú ꜁tsoi mat꜇. |
| 261. Stealing the keys of city gates. | 〃城門鑰 | Tò꜆ ꜁shing ꜁mún yéuk꜇. |
| 262. Stealing of military weapons. | 〃軍器 | Tò꜆ ꜀kwan hí'. |
| 263. Stealing timber from gardens and mausolea. | 〃園陵樹木 | Tò꜆ ꜁ün ꜁ling shü꜆ muk꜇. |
| 264. Superintendents and keepers stealing provisions and money from the treasuries and storehouses. | 監守自盜倉庫錢糧 | ꜀Kám ʻshau tsz'꜆ tò꜆ ꜀tsʻóng fú' ꜁tsʻín ꜁léung. |
| 265. Common people stealing provisions and money from the treasuries and storehouses. | 常人盜倉庫錢糧 | ꜁Shéung ꜁yan tò꜆ ꜀tsʻóng fú' ꜁tsʻín ꜁léung. |
| 266. Robbery, or stealing by violence. | 強盜 | ꜁Kéung tò꜆. |
| 267. Releasing prisoners by violence. | 刼囚 | Kíp꜅ ꜁chʻau. |
| 268. On committing robbery in open daylight. | 白晝搶奪 | Pák꜇ chau' ʻtséung tüt꜇. |

§6. The criminal laws are 170, extending from Nos. 254 to 423, and are comprised in eleven subdivisions: twenty-eight (254 to 281) refer to *tò tsʻák* or theft and robbery; twenty (282 to 301) to *yan ming* or loss of human life; twenty-two (302 to 323) to *tau au*, or quarreling and fighting; eight (324 to 331) to *má lai* or abusive language; twelve (332 to 343) to *sú chung* or litigations; eleven (344 to 354) to *shau chóng* or bribery; eleven (355 to 365) to *chá ngai* or frauds and forgery; ten (366 to 375) to *fán kán* or illicit intercourse; eleven (376 to 386) to *tsáp fán* or miscellaneous offenses; eight (387 to 394) to *pò móng* or arrest and escapes; twenty-nine (395 to 423) to *tün yuk* or imprisonments.

256. This law interdicts prophetic sayings, such as the foretelling of national prosperity or adversity, and also the publication of obscene and heterodox books.

| | | |
|---|---|---|
| 269. Stealing, or taking property by stealth. | 竊盜 | Sít, tò$^{2}$. |
| 270. On stealing horses and other domestic animals. | 盜馬牛畜產 | Tò$^{2}$ 'má ˏngau ch'uk, 'ch'án. |
| 271. On stealing grain and the products of the fields. | 丨田野穀麥 | Tò$^{2}$ ˏt'ín 'yé kuk, mák$_{2}$. |
| 272. On stealing from kindred and relations. | 親屬相盜 | ‹Ts'an shuk$_{2}$ ‹séung tò$^{2}$. |
| 273. On obtaining property by alarms and threats. | 恐嚇取財 | 'Hung hák, 'tsü ˏts'oi. |
| 274. Obtaining public or private property fraudulently. | 詐欺官私取財 | Chá' ‹hí ‹kún ‹sz' 'tsü ˏts'oi. |
| 275. On kidnapping and selling persons to be slaves. | 畧人畧賣人 | Léuk$_{2}$ ˏyan léuk$_{2}$ mái$^{2}$ ˏyan. |
| 276. On opening graves [to rob the dead]. | 發塚 | Fát, 'chung. |
| 277. Causelessly entering houses by night. | 夜無故入人家 | Yé$^{2}$ ˏmò kú' yap$_{2}$ ˏyan ‹ká. |
| 278. On harboring thieves and robbers. | 盜賊窩主 | Tò$^{2}$ tsák$_{2}$ ‹wó 'chü. |
| 279. Concerning those who abet plans for robbery. | 共謀爲盜 | Kung$^{2}$ ˏmau ˏwai tò$^{2}$. |
| 280. The publicly taking [by force], and the secretly obtaining of property are both alike to be regarded as robbery. | 公取竊取皆爲盜 | ‹Kung 'tsü sít, 'tsü ‹kái ˏwai tò$^{2}$. |
| 281. On the defacing of branded marks. | 起除刺字 | 'Hí ˏch'ü sik, tsz'$^{2}$. |
| 282. On concerting the killing of a person. | 謀殺人 | ˏMau shát, ˏyan. |
| 283. On concerting the murder of an imperial envoy, or a magistrate under whom one lives. | 謀丨制使及本管長官 | ˏMau shát$_{2}$ chai' sz' kap$_{2}$ 'pún 'kún 'ch'éung ‹kún. |
| 284. On killing with malice prepense, father or mother, grandfather or grandmother. | 謀殺祖父母父母 | ˏMau shát, 'tsò fú$^{2}$ 'mò fú$^{2}$ 'mò. |
| 285. On killing an adulterer by the husband. | 殺死姦夫 | Shát, 'sz' ‹kán ‹fú. |
| 286. Killing one's deceased husband's father and mother. | 謀殺故夫父母 | ˏMau shát, kú' ‹fú fú$^{2}$ 'mò. |
| 287. On killing three persons in one family. | 殺一家三人 | Shát, yat, ‹ká ‹sám ˏyan. |

273. Cases of this kind are not unfrequent; the plunderers, feigning themselves to be official persons, enter the shops or premises of those whom they know to be obnoxious to justice, and behave as if they were going to seize persons or property; but overtures being made for settlement they accept money and move off before the deception is detected. Redress is then too late. Such impositions are punishable with death.

276. The opening of graves and the disturbing of the dead are viewed by the Chinese as acts of great enormity, and as equally offensive to gods and to men, to the living and to the dead. These acts are sometimes committed for the sake of plunder, and sometimes in retaliation for deeds done by the living. Cases of the latter often occur in prosecuting family feuds.

280. The legal term robbery is applied to the acts of all those who publicly with open violence or clandestinely take, or attempt to take, the property of other people.

285. The husband who kills the adulterer or adulteress or both, when discovered by him in the very act, shall not be punishable.

| | | |
|---|---|---|
| 288. On cutting to pieces human beings. | 採生折割人 | 'Ts'oi ˏshang chít, kót, ˏyan. |
| 289. On preparing animal poisons to kill people. | 造畜蠱毒殺人 | Tsò' ch'uk, 'kú tuk, ˏshát ˏyan. |
| 290. On fighting and intentionally killing people. | 鬬毆及故丨人 | Tau' 'au kap, kú' shát, ˏyan. |
| 291. On depriving people of food and raiment. | 屏去人服食 | ˏPing hü' ˏyan fuk, shik,. |
| 292. On killing or maiming persons in playing with them, or by mistake, or by simple accidents. | 戲殺誤殺過失殺傷人 | Hí' shát,' ng' shát, kwó' shat, shát, ˏshéung ˏyan. |
| 293. On a husband's beating to death a wife or concubine, who is obnoxious to punishment. | 夫毆死有罪妻妾 | ˏFú 'au 'sz' 'yau tsúi' ˏts'ai tsí'p,. |
| 294. On killing a child or grandchild, or a male or female slave, and charging the crime on others. | 殺子孫及奴婢圖賴人 | Shát, 'tsz' ˏsün kap, ˏnú 'pí ˏt'ò lái' ˏyan. |
| 295. On wounding persons by shooting arrows, &c. | 弓箭傷人 | ˏKung ts'ín' ˏshéung ˏyan. |
| 296. On killing or wounding by carriages or horses. | 車馬殺傷人 | ˏKü 'má shát, ˏshéung ˏyan. |
| 297. On injuring or killing by improper use of medicine. | 庸醫丨傷人 | ˏYung ˏí shát, ˏshéung ˏyan. |
| 298. On killing or wounding by pitfalls or traps. | 窩弓丨傷人 | ˏWó ˏkung shát, ˏshéung ˏyan. |
| 299. On causing the death of persons by cruel annoyances. | 威逼人致死 | ˏWai pik, ˏyan chí' 'sz'. |
| 300. On the heads of families compromising or concealing the murder of children or dependents. | 尊長爲人丨私和 | ˏTsün 'ch'éung wai' ˏyan shát, ˏsz' ˏwó. |
| 301. Interference in cases of intended injury. | 同行知有謀害 | ˏT'ung ˏhang ˏchí 'yau ˏmau hoi'. |
| 302. On quarreling and fighting in ordinary cases. | 鬬毆 | Tau' 'au. |
| 303. Period of responsibility for consequences of injury. | 保辜限期 | 'Pò ˏkú hán' ˏkí. |
| 304. Angry contentions in the imperial palaces. | 宮內忿爭 | ˏKung noi' 'fan ˏcháng. |
| 305. Cases in which members of the imperial family, near or remote, are beaten or injured. | 宗室覺羅以上親被毆 | ˏTsung shat, kók, ˏló 'í shéung' ˏts'an pí' 'au. |

288. This law has reference to cutting in pieces the human body in revenge, and also for magical purposes. Those who are found guilty of this crime must suffer death by 'the slow and painful process.'

291. By this statute, the applying of any noxious thing to the mouth, nose, or other natural outlets of the body, in such a manner as to cause injury or death, is forbidden.

298. This law requires all persons, who dig pitfalls, or conceal springes and traps, etc., for the purpose of taking game, to give notice of such pits by erecting flags, or stretching cords around the dangerous spot.

301. This law requires those, who know of any injury intended to any one, to endeavor in the first place to prevent it; and if unsuccessful, then, in the second place, to report the matter to the magistrates.

| | | |
|---|---|---|
| 306. On beating an imperial envoy, or any officer or magistrate under whom one is living. | 毆制使及本管長官 | 'Au chai' 'sz' kap, 'pún 'kún 'ch'éung ,kún. |
| 307. Inferior officers striking or injuring their superiors under whose orders they are residing. | 佐職統屬毆長官 | Tsó' chik, 't'ung shuk, 'au 'ch'éung ,kún. |
| 308. Officers in superior stations quarreling or fighting with those under their own authority. | 上司官與統屬官相毆 | Shéung' ,sz' ,kún 'yü 't'ung shuk, ,kún ,séung 'au. |
| 309. Officers of the ninth degree of rank striking those of the third degree and upwards. | 九品以上官毆長官 | 'Kau 'pan 'í shéung' ,kún 'au 'ch'éung ,kún. |
| 310. On striking persons employed in public service. | 拒毆追攝人 | 'Kü 'au ,chui shíp, ,yan. |
| 311. Scholars and apprentices striking their masters. | 毆受業師 | 'Au shau' íp, ,sz'. |
| 312. On binding and confining persons by the powerful. | 威力制縛人 | ,Wai lik, chai' fok, ,yan. |
| 313. On free persons and slaves beating each other. | 良賤相毆 | ,Léung ts'ín' ,séung 'au. |
| 314. On male and female slaves striking their masters. | 奴婢毆家長 | ,Nò 'pí 'au ,ká 'ch'éung. |
| 315. Wives and concubines striking their husbands. | 妻妾丨夫 | ,Ts'ai ts'íp, 'au ,fú. |
| 316. On kindred fighting with each other. | 同姓親屬相毆 | ,T'ung sing' ,ts'an shuk, ,séung 'au. |
| 317. The mean and young members of a family striking those who are honorable and aged. | 毆大功以下尊長 | 'Au tái' ,kung 'í há' ,tsün 'ch'éung. |
| 318. Young members striking the elder members. | 毆期親尊長 | 'Au ,kí ,ts'an ,tsün 'ch'éung. |
| 319. Children striking their parents or grandparents. | 丨祖父母父母 | 'Au 'tsò fú' 'mò fú' 'mò. |
| 320. Wives and concubines who strike the kindred and relations of their husbands. | 妻妾與夫親屬相毆 | ,Ts'ai ts'íp, 'yü ,fú ,ts'an shuk, ,séung ,au. |
| 321. Striking the children of a wife's former husband. | 毆妻前夫之子 | 'Au ,ts'ai ,ts'ín ,fú ,chí 'tsz'. |
| 322. Wives and concubines striking the father and mother of a deceased husband. | 妻妾毆故夫父母 | ,Ts'ai ts'íp, 'au kú' ,fú fú' 'mò. |
| 323. On a father or grandfather being beaten. | 父祖被毆 | Fú' 'tsò pí' 'au. |
| 324. On using abusive language. | 罵人 | Má' ,yan. |

313. The slave who strikes a free person is to be punished one degree more severely than an ordinary person, and is to suffer death if the consequences of the beating prove to be fatal, or even very serious.

314. This, if done designedly, is a capital crime, and all engaged in it, without distinction between principals and accessories, shall suffer death by decapitation.

| | | |
|---|---|---|
| 325. On abusing an imperial envoy, or an officer under whose jurisdiction one is living. | 罵制使及本管長官 | Má$^{2}$ chai' sz'‘ kap, ‘pún ‘kún ‘ch‘éung ˏkún. |
| 326. An inferior officer in any department using abusive language towards his superiors. | 佐職統屬罵長官 | Tsó' chik, ‘t‘ung shuk, má$^{2}$ ‘ch‘éung ˏkún. |
| 327. Male or female slaves abusing their masters. | 奴婢罵家長 | ˏNò ‘pí má$^{2}$ ˏká ‘ch‘éung. |
| 328. On abusing the honorable and aged of a family. | 罵尊長 | Má$^{2}$ ˏtsün ‘ch‘éung. |
| 329. On abusing parents or grandparents. | 罵祖父母父母 | Má$^{2}$ ‘tsò fú$^{2}$ ‘mò fú$^{2}$ ‘mò. |
| 330. Wives and concubines using abusive language towards the elder kindred of a husband. | 妻妾罵夫期親尊長 | ˏTs‘ai ts‘íp, má$^{2}$ ˏfú ˏkí ˏts‘an ˏtsün ‘ch‘éung. |
| 331. Wives and concubines using abusive language to the father and mother of a deceased husband. | 妻妾罵故夫父母 | ˏTs‘ai ts‘íp, má$^{2}$ kú' ˏfú fú$^{2}$ ‘mò. |
| 332. Passing the proper and complaining to a higher officer. | 越訴 | Üt, sò'. |
| 333. Concerning those who put forth anonymous documents impeaching others of crimes. | 投匿名文書告人罪 | ˏTau nik, ˏming ˏman ˏshü kò' ˏyan tsúi$^{2}$. |
| 334. On neglecting to receive appeals. | 告狀不受理 | Kò' chóng$^{2}$ pat, shau$^{2}$ ‘lí. |
| 335. Cases in which magistrates must retire. | 聽訟迴避 | T‘ing' tsung$^{2}$ ˏúi pí$^{2}$. |
| 336. On bringing forward false accusations. | 誣告 | ˏMò kò'. |
| 337. Accusations against one's own kindred. | 干名犯義 | ˏKón ˏming fán$^{2}$ í$^{2}$. |
| 338. When children and grandchildren disobey orders. | 子孫違犯教令 | ‘Tsz' ˏsün ˏwai fán$^{2}$ káu' ling$^{2}$. |
| 339. Prisoners in confinement cannot accuse others (except it be their keepers in case of ill usage). | 見禁囚不得告舉他事 | Kín' kam' ˏch‘au pat, tak, kò' ‘kü ˏt‘á sz'$^{2}$. |
| 340. On exciting and seducing people to litigations. | 教唆詞訟 | Káu' ˏsó ˏtsz' tsung$^{2}$. |
| 341. Mode of trial in cases of those enrolled as soldiers. | 軍民約會詞訟 | ˏKwan ˏman yéuk, úi$^{2}$ ˏtsz' tsung$^{2}$. |

333. Whoever placards, or brings before government, an anonymous document falsely accusing others of crimes, shall, according to this law, be strangled; and, although what he declares be true, he shall yet be convicted. Notwithstanding the severity of this law, persons who feel themselves aggrieved, have recourse to placards; and so bold are the people, that sometimes they post up their complaints on the very walls of the magistrate's office. Recourse is also had to anonymous letters.

335. These are cases in which the kindred or relations of the magistrate are brought to his court or tribunal; whenever this happens the officer must retire before the trial can proceed—it being supposed that in such cases he will not act with impartiality.

337. Children who accuse their parents, and wives and concubines who accuse their husbands, shall receive 100 blows, even if the charge be true; and death shall be the punishment, if it be false in only one particular.

| | | |
|---|---|---|
| 342. Litigations in behalf of officers of government are to be managed by their domestics. | 官吏詞訟家人訴 | ‹Kún lí$^{2}$ ˏtsz' tsung$^{2}$ ‹ká ˏyan sò'. |
| 343. On being sentenced to the army, or transported for bringing forward false accusations. | 誣告充軍及遷徙 | ˏMò kò' ‹ch'ung ‹kwan kap$_{2}$ ‹ts'ín ʻsái. |
| 344. On officers of government receiving bribes. | 官吏受財 | ‹Kún lí$^{2}$ shau$^{2}$ ˏts'oi. |
| 345. On bestowal of property that may lead to crime. | 坐贓致罪 | Tsó$^{2}$ ‹ch'óng chí' tsúi$^{2}$. |
| 346. On receiving a bribe after an act is done. | 事後受財 | Sz'$^{2}$ hau$^{2}$ shau$^{2}$ ˏts'oi. |
| 347. On magistrates listening to promises of bribes. | 官吏聽許財物 | ‹Kún lí$^{2}$ ting' ʻhü ˏts'oi mat$_{2}$. |
| 348. On seeking aid by bribes when in trouble. | 有事以財請求 | ʻYau sz'$^{2}$ ʻí ˏts'oi ʻts'ing ˏkau. |
| 349. Concerning the extortion of loans by those who are in the service of government. | 在官求索借貸人財物 | Tsoi$^{2}$ ‹kún ˏkau sók$_{2}$ tsé' t'ái' ˏyan ˏts'oi mat$_{2}$. |
| 350. Extortion of loans by an officer's domestics. | 家人求索 | ‹Ká ˏyan ˏkau sók$_{2}$. |
| 351. Reception of bribes by high and influential officers. | 風憲官吏犯贓 | ‹Fung hín' ‹kún lí$^{2}$ fán$^{2}$ ‹ch'óng. |
| 352. Levying contributions on pretexts of public service. | 因公科斂 | ‹Yan ‹kung ‹fó ʻlím. |
| 353. On retaining stolen goods recovered by the police. | 尅留盜贓 | Hak$_{2}$ ˏlau tò$^{2}$ ‹ch'óng. |
| 354. The military receiving presents from the nobility. | 私受公侯財物 | ‹Sz' shau$^{2}$ ‹kung ˏhau ˏts'oi mat$_{2}$. |
| 355. On forging an imperial document. | 詐爲制書 | Chá' ˏwai chai' ‹shü. |
| 356. On falsely promulgating imperial orders. | 丨傳詔旨 | Chá' ˏchün chíú' ʻchí. |
| 357. On giving false replies to inquiries which are made by the emperor. | 對制上書詐不以實 | Túi' chai' ʻshéung ‹shü chá' pat$_{2}$ ʻí shat$_{2}$. |
| 358. Against counterfeiting governmental seals, and the imperial kalenders. | 僞造印信時憲書等 | Ngai$^{2}$ ts'ò$^{2}$ yan' sun' ˏshí hín' ‹shü ʻtang. |
| 359. Against the private casting of copper money. | 私鑄銅錢 | ‹Sz' chü' ˏt'ung ˏts'ín. |
| 360. Falsely pretending to be officers of government. | 詐假官 | Chá' ʻká ‹kún. |

344. No officer or other person in the employment of government is allowed, *shau ts'oi*, to receive property, as gifts or bribes; those who do so shall be immediately deprived of their honors and office, dismissed from service, and be punished according to the value of the gift: if it be in value one ounce or less of silver, 60 blows shall be the punishment; if 120 ounces or more, death. The penalties of this law are often evaded; and presents to a very large amount, in one way or another, reach the hands of official persons.

351. These high officers, governors, lieutenant-governors, commissioners of justice, of finance, &c., and high ministers of state who are guilty of these crimes, are to be punished two degrees more severely than those who are only of the rank of prefects.

| | | |
|---|---|---|
| 361. Pretending to be high officers of state. | 詐稱內使等官 | Chá' ‹ch'ing noi[2] sz'' 'tang ‹kún. |
| 362. High officers feigning to hold secret commissions. | 近侍詐稱私行 | Kan[2] shí[2] chá' ‹ching ‹sz' ‚hang. |
| 363. Pretending that there are felicitous omens. | 詐爲瑞應 | Chá' ‚wai sui[2] ying'. |
| 364. On pretending sickness or death to avoid business. | 丨病死傷避事 | Chá' ping[2] 'sz' ‹shéung pí[2] sz'[2]. |
| 365. Deceitfully persuading people to transgress the law. | 丨教誘人犯法 | Chá' káu' 'yau ‚yan fán[2] fát‚. |
| 366. On illicit sexual intercourse. | 犯姦 | Fán[2] ‹kán. |
| 367. Conniving at illicit conduct of wife or concubine. | 縱容妻妾犯姦 | Tsung' ‚yung ‹ts'ai ts'íp‚ fán[2] ‹kán. |
| 368. Incest, or illicit intercourse between relations. | 親屬相姦 | ‹Ts'an shuk‚ ‹séung ‹kán. |
| 369. Falsely accusing a husband's father of incest. | 誣執翁姦 | ‚Mò chap‚ ‹yung ‹kán. |
| 370. Slaves or hired domestics having illicit intercourse with the master's wife. | 奴及雇工人姦家長妻 | ‚Nò kap‚ kú' ‹kung ‚yan ‹kán ‹ká 'chéung ‹ts'ai. |
| 371. Illicit intercourse with people's wives and daughters. | 姦部民妻女 | ‹Kán pò[2] ‚man ‹ts'ai 'nü. |
| 372. Illicit intercourse by those who are in mourning, or by the priests of Budha and of the Taou sect. | 居喪及僧道犯姦 | ‹Kü ‹sóng kap‚ ‹sang tò[2] fan[2] ‹kán. |
| 373. Illicit intercourse between free persons and slaves. | 良賤相姦 | ‚Séung ts'ín[2] ‹séung ‹kán. |
| 374. Officers of government frequenting brothels. | 官吏宿娼 | ‹Kún lí[2] suk‚ ‹ch'éung. |
| 375. On buying free persons to be prostitutes. | 買良爲娼 | 'Mái ‚léung ‚wai ‹ch'éung. |
| 376. On defacing or destroying public monuments. | 拆毀申明亭 | Chúk‚ 'wai ‹shan ‚ming ‚ting. |
| 377. On procuring medical aid for laborers and soldiers in the public service. | 夫匠軍士病給醫藥 | ‹Fú tséung' ‹kwan sz'[2] ping[2] kap‚ ‹í yéuk‚. |
| 378. Laws for the suppression of gambling. | 賭博 | 'Tò pók‚. |
| 379. Eunuchs [forbidden to all but titular kings]. | 閹割火者 | ‹Ím kót‚ 'fó ché. |
| 380. Soliciting malversation in public business. | 囑託公事 | Chuk‚ tók‚ ‹kung sz'[2]. |

364. Leave of absence is very often obtained on plea of illness; and cases are not infrequent in which the illness is feigned.

366—375. These laws, and the clauses under them, evince a most horrible state of crime, while they show also how wisely reasonable men, with no other guide than conscience, can legislate: having not the Divine law, they are a law unto themselves.

376. The *shan ming ting* are halls or courts in which the names of bad people are exposed; and they might be called halls of exposure.

378. There are nineteen clauses under this law, the last of which was enacted in 1819. The government disallows all sorts of gambling, lotteries, &c., and often severely punishes those who transgress these laws; still the evil practice in one form or another prevails to a great extent among almost all classes of the people.

| | | |
|---|---|---|
| 381. On privately hushing up public crimes. | 私和公事 | ‹Sz' ˏwó ‹kung sz'$^2$. |
| 382. Laws respecting accidental fires. | 失火 | Shat› 'fó. |
| 383. On willfully or maliciously setting fire to the houses of other people. | 放火故燒人房屋 | Fóng' 'fó kú' ‹shíú ˏyan ˏfóng uk›. |
| 384. Laws respecting theatrical representations. | 搬做雜劇 | ‹Pún tsò$^2$ tsáp$_2$ kik$_2$. |
| 385. On disobedience to the orders of government. | 違令 | ˏWai ling$^2$. |
| 386. On doing what ought not to be done. | 不應爲 | Pat› ‹ying ˏwai. |
| 387. On the duty of police-officers in pursuing and apprehending thieves. | 應捕人追捕罪人 | ‹Ying pò$^2$ ˏyan ‹chui pò$^2$ tsúi$^2$ ˏyan. |
| 388. Criminals resisting officers of the police. | 罪人拒捕 | Tsúi$^2$ ˏyan 'kü pò$^2$. |
| 389. On escaping from prison by stealth, and on breaking it open by violence. | 獄囚脫監及反獄在逃 | Yuk$_2$ ˏch'au t'üt› ‹kám kap$_2$ 'fán yuk$_2$ tsoi$^2$ ˏt'ò. |
| 390. On the escaping of transported convicts. | 徒流人逃 | ˏT'ò ˏlau ˏyan ˏt'ò. |
| 391. On delays in transporting convicts. | 稽留囚徒 | ‹Kai ˏlau ˏch'au ˏt'ò. |
| 392. Keepers not observing the escape of prisoners. | 主守不覺失囚 | 'Chü 'shau pat› kók› shat› ˏch'au. |
| 393. Concealing criminals, while aware of their crimes. | 知情藏匿罪人 | ‹Chí ˏts'ing ˏts'óng nik› tsúi$^2$ ˏyan. |
| 394. Limited term of apprehending thieves and robbers. | 盜賊捕限 | T'ò$^2$ ts'ak$_2$ pò$^2$ hán$^2$. |
| 395. On neglecting to confine prisoners. | 囚應禁而不禁 | ˏCh'au ‹ying kam' ˏí pat› kam'. |
| 396. Maliciously imprisoning or torturing innocent men. | 故禁故勘平人 | Kú' kam' kú' hóm' ˏp'ing ˏyan. |

381. Evasions of this law, by compromising offenses, and withdrawing them from the cognizance of the officers to whose notice they have been brought, are very frequent among the Chinese. Few magistrates will refuse to allow this when the temptation is sufficiently strong, and few offenders are slow to resort to it when they have the means of making the temptation so strong as to effect their purpose, and 'shove by justice.' Consequently, when one high in rank is known to have passed through his office clean-handed, he is proportionably lauded by the people—a reward highly prized by some Chinese statesmen.

382. This law subjects the master of any house, which is accidentally or any other way set on fire, to punishment by the bamboo, and to death if the fire chance to extend to any of the imperial temples.

384. By this law, actors are precluded from representing, in any of their performances, empresses, famous princes, ministers, and generals of former ages; it is not however intended to prohibit fictitious characters, if they be just and upright men, chaste wives, or pious and obedient children. These very characters, by this law prohibited, are the most usual and constant ones seen upon the Chinese stage. The theatre here, a favorite place of resort, is far from being an unexceptionable 'school of virtue.'

395. Prison discipline in China is in a very low state, the condition of the prisons wretched in the extreme, and the abuses enormous. The regulations for the management of prisons are often allowed to remain dormant, and the sufferings of the inmates are horrible beyond description.

| | | |
|---|---|---|
| 397. Unjustly protracting imprisonment. | 淹禁 | ‹Ím kam'. |
| 398. On the ill treatment of prisoners. | 陵虐罪囚 | ‹Ling yéuk, tsúi' ‹ch'au. |
| 399. On giving prisoners tools to effect their release. | 與囚金刃解脫 | 'Yü ‹ch'au ‹kam yan' 'kái t'üt,. |
| 400. Keepers exciting prisoners to reverse a confession. | 主守教囚反異 | 'Chü 'sh'au káu' ‹ch'au 'fán í'. |
| 401. On the raiment and food of prisoners. | 獄囚衣糧 | Yuk, ‹ch'au ‹í ‹léung. |
| 402. On permitting the kindred of statesmen once meritorious to visit them when prisoners. | 功臣應禁親人入視 | ‹Kung ‹shan ‹ying kam' ‹ts'an ‹yan yap, shí'. |
| 403. Condemned criminals procuring their own death. | 死囚令人自殺 | 'Sz' ‹ch'au ling' ‹yan tsz'' shát,. |
| 404. Age and youth not to be examined by torture. | 老幼不拷訊 | 'Lò yau' pat, ‹háu sun'. |
| 405. Cases in which prisoners are to be confronted. | 鞫獄停囚待對 | Kuk, yuk, ‹ting ‹ch'au toi' túi'. |
| 406. Examination to be confined to the indictment. | 依告狀鞫獄 | ‹I' kò' chóng' kuk, yuk,. |
| 407. Against the disallowing of the return of plaintiff or accusers after the case is finished. | 原告人事畢不放回 | ‹Ün kò' ‹yan sz'' pat, pat, fóng' ‹úi. |
| 408. Prisoners falsely accusing innocent persons. | 獄囚誣指平人 | Yuk, ‹ch'au ‹mò 'chí ‹p'ing ‹yan. |
| 409. On palliating or magnifying a prisoner's offense. | 官司出入人罪 | ‹Kún ‹sz' ch'ut, yap, ‹yan tsúi'. |
| 410. On clearing up cases of false accusation. | 辯明冤枉 | Pín' ‹ming ‹ün 'wóng. |
| 411. Sentences determined by competent authorities. | 有司決囚等第 | 'Yau ‹sz' k'üt, ‹ch'au 'tang tai'. |
| 412. Against all fallacious practices in holding an inquest on a dead body. | 檢驗屍傷不以實 | 'Kím ím' ‹shí ‹shéung pat, 'í shat,. |
| 413. Adjudging punishment which is illegal. | 決罰不如法 | K'üt, fát, pat, ‹ü fát,. |
| 414. Offenses of high officers and imperial envoys. | 長官使人有犯 | 'Ch'éung ‹kún sz'' ‹yan 'yau fán'. |
| 415. In giving decisions, the law must be quoted. | 斷罪引律令 | Tün' tsúi' 'yan lut, ling'. |

404. By the provisions of this law, those who are above the age of 70, or under the age of 15, are exempt from torture.

405. Magistrates, at whose tribunal a case has been brought, are allowed to demand the attendance of associates and accomplices in it, who may be in the custody of other magistrates, and the demand must be complied with in three days.

409. Magistrates acting as judges, by intentionally extenuating or aggravating the guilt of prisoners—in other words, who designedly pronounce and execute any unjust sentence,—expose themselves to the penalties of this law, and "in every such case, the member of the court who stands first in point of responsibility, shall suffer punishment equal in degree with that which was, when it ought not to have been, or was not, when it ought to have been, inflicted."

415. Under this head reference is made to common as well as to statute law: 'old custom,' or well supported and well defined precedents, are no mean or infrequent authorities among the Chinese.

| | | |
|---|---|---|
| 416. Criminals allowed to confess and to protest. | 獄囚取服辯 | Yuk, ,ch'au 'tsü fuk, pín'. |
| 417. Effect of a pardon on a foregoing sentence. | 赦前斷罪不當 | Shé' ,ts'ín tün' tsúi' pat, tóng'. |
| 418. He who on the hearing of a general pardon commits a crime [shall receive heavier punishment]. | 聞有恩赦而故犯 | ,Man 'yau ,yan shé' ,í kú' fán'. |
| 419. Transported convicts refusing to work. | 徒囚不應役 | ,T'ò ,ch'au pat, ,ying yik,. |
| 420. On offenses committed by females. | 婦人犯罪 | 'Fú ,yan fán' tsúi'. |
| 421. Waiting the report of cases from the emperor. | 死囚覆奏待報 | 'Sz' ,ch'au fuk, tsau' toi' pò'. |
| 422. On passing erroneous sentences. | 斷罪不當 | Tün' tsúi' pat, tóng'. |
| 423. Clerks writing confessions for others. | 吏典代寫招草 | Lí' 'tín toi' 'sé ,chíú 'ts'ò. |
| §7. Public Works. | 工律 | ,*Kung Lut*,. |
| 424. On assuming to effect public works. | 擅造作 | Shín' ts'ò' tsók,. |
| 425. On waste or expenditure of time and wages on materials that are unfit for use. | 虛費工力採取不堪用 | ,H'ü fai' ,kung lik, 'ts'oi 'tsü pat, ,hóm yung'. |
| 426. On buildings or manufactures not according to law. | 造作不如法 | Tsò' tsók, pat, ,ü fát,. |
| 427. Misapplication of the public property. | 冒破物料 | Mò' p'ó' mat, líú'. |
| 428. Misapplication of the governmental silks. | 帶造段疋 | Tái' ts'ò' tün' p'at,. |

416. When a prisoner is sentenced to death, or to be transported, he must according to this law have his case stated to him, so that be may either confess or dispute it; and his kindred, within 300 *li*, must be summoned to attend the trial.

417. By the provisions of this law, an erroneous sentence passed immediately after a general pardon, may be so far corrected or reversed, as to be included in such general pardon.

420. Except in capital cases and those of adultery, females are not to be imprisoned, but kept in the custody of their husbands or other kindred.

421. Ordinarily, provincial authorities, after reporting a criminal case to the throne, must wait for the imperial rescript before proceeding to inflict capital punishment. In certain cases, however, these formalities are dispensed with, and a criminal is led away to execution in a few hours after his apprehension. For this end, there is lodged with the *fúyün*, or lieutenant-governor of each province, a symbol of authority, called *wóng ming*. The criminal being judged and sentenced, the presiding officer, even if it be the *fúyün* himself, goes in state, and, with prescribed formalities, requests the delivery of the *wóng ming;* and being taken from the place where it is kept deposited, it is borne with great pomp and solemnity before the criminal to the fatal spot, where in its presence the victim kneels toward the emperor's palace, and by a single stroke of the executioner's sword expires in the attitude of giving thanks to him for the dispensation of justice! The phrase *wóng ming*, literally 'king's order,' is equivalent to *death-warrant*, and is often so translated; it is supposed to be derived from high antiquity, before the use of the word emperor, and hence the name king's order is still retained.

§7. These laws are thirteen in number, and refer chiefly to manufactures, and the construction of buildings, for government.

428. This law is intended to prevent any one from mixing his own private materials with those of the government, in its manufactories of silks, &c.

| | | |
|---|---|---|
| 429. Against weaving or manufacturing interdicted patterns of the dragon, phœnix, &c. | 織造違禁龍鳳文叚疋 | Chik, ts‘ò$^{2}$ ,wai kam’ ,lung fung$^{2}$ ,man tün$^{2}$ p‘at,. |
| 430. On exceeding the limited time for work. | 造作過限 | Ts‘ò$^{2}$ tsók, kwó’ hán$^{2}$. |
| 431. On repairing granaries and storehouses. | 脩理倉庫 | ,Sau ‘lí ,ts‘óng fú’. |
| 432. Concerning officers, and those in the employment of government, not residing in their offices. | 有司官吏不住公廨 | ‘Yau ,sz’ ,kún lí$^{2}$ pat, chü$^{2}$ ,kung kái’. |
| 433. On breaking down embankments. | 盜決河防 | T‘ò$^{2}$ k‘üt, ,hó ,fóng. |
| 434. On failure in the time for repairs. | 失時不脩隄防 | Shat, ,shí pat, ,sau ,t‘ai ,fóng. |
| 435. Encroachments on streets and highways. | 侵占街道 | ,Tsam chím’ ,kái tò$^{2}$. |
| 436. Concerning repairs of bridges and roads. | 脩理橋梁道路 | ,Sau ‘lí ,k‘íú ,léung tò$^{2}$ lò$^{2}$. |

## TABLE I.

This table is an abstract of the principal articles of the laws specially provided for the protection of public and private property. The grade of punishments here exhibited are for crimes committed against the statutes in the first and sixth subdivisions of the criminal laws, viz. Nos. 254—281, and Nos. 343—354. By this table, it appears on inspection, that whoever is guilty of any species of pecuniary malversation, to the extent of 20 taels of silver, shall, generally speaking, be liable, at the least to a punishment of 40 blows: that whoever is guilty of a theft of private property, or of receiving a bribe for an object in itself lawful, to the same extent, is punishable with 80 blows: that whoever is guilty to the same extent of a theft of public property, or of receiving a bribe for an object in itself unlawful, is punishable with 60 blows, and banishment for the space of one year: and, lastly, that whoever is guilty of embezzling much of the public property, will be punishable with 100 blows, and perpetual banishment to the distance of 2000 *lí*. (See Sir G. T. Staunton's Translation of the Penal Code.)

**SCALE OF PUNISHMENT FOR OFFENSES AGAINST PUBLIC AND PRIVATE PROPERTY.**

| Punishment. | Pecuniary Malversation. | Theft. | Bribery for a lawful Object. | Bribery for an unlawful Object. | Theft of Public Property. | Embezzlement of public property. |
|---|---|---|---|---|---|---|
| | Taels. | Taels. | Taels. | Taels. | Taels. | Taels. |
| 20 blows with the bamboo | 1 or less | | | | | |
| 30 blows | 1 to 10 | | | | | |
| 40 blows | 20 to 30 | | | | | |
| 50 blows | 30 to 40 | | | | | |
| 60 blows | 40 to 50 | 1 or less | 1 or less | | | |
| 70 blows | 50 to 60 | 10 — | 10 — | 1 or less | 1 or less | |
| 80 blows | 60 to 70 | 20 — | 20 — | 1 to 5 tls. | 1 to 5 tls. | 1 or less |
| 90 blows | 70 to 80 | 30 — | 30 — | 10 — | 10 — | 1 to 2½ |
| 100 blows | 80 to 90 | 40 — | 40 — | 15 — | 15 — | 5 |
| 60 blows and 1 year's banishment | 100 to 200 | 50 — | 50 — | 20 — | 20 — | 7½ |
| 70 blows and 1½ year's banishment | 200 to 300 | 60 — | 60 — | 25 — | 25 — | 10 |
| 80 blows and 2 years' banishment | 300 to 400 | 70 — | 70 — | 30 — | 30 — | 12½ |
| 90 blows and 2½ years' banishment | 400 to 500 | 80 — | 80 — | 35 — | 35 — | 15 |
| 100 blows and 3 years' banishment | 500 & up'ds | 90 — | 90 — | 40 — | 40 — | 17½ |
| 100 blows and perpet. banish. 2000 *lí*. | —— | 100 — | 100 — | 45 — | 45 — | 20 |
| 100 blows and perpet. banish. 2500 *lí*. | —— | 110 — | 110 — | 50 — | 50 — | 25 |
| 100 blows and perpet. banish. 3000 *lí*. | —— | 120 — | 120 — | 55 — | 55 — | 30 |
| Death,—to be strangled | —— | Upwards of 120 taels. | Upwards of 120 taels. | 80 or 120 If an inferior Officer. | 80 in extreme cases. | |
| Death,—to be beheaded | —— | —— | —— | —— | —— | 80 in extreme cases. |

廣東方言讀本

## TABLE II.

### SCALE OF THE PECUNIARY REDEMPTION OF NECESSARILY REDEEMABLE PUNISHMENTS.

| Punishment. | If well able to pay. | If not altogether destitute. | If aged, or under Age. | Females in certain cases. | Killing or wounding accidentaly | Females in general: Days confin't. | Females in general: Dec. of taels. |
|---|---|---|---|---|---|---|---|
| | T. m. c. c. | T. m. c. c. | T. m. c. c. | T. m. c. c. | T. m. c. c. | | |
| 10 blows with the bamboo | 2 5 | 3 | 7 5 | 1 | —— | 20 and | 105 |
| 20 blows | 5 | 4 5 | 1 8 | 2 | 3 5 4 | 25 and | 135 |
| 30 blows | 7 5 | 6 | 2 2 5 | 3 | 3 3 2 | 30 and | 165 |
| 40 blows | 1 | 6 5 | 3 | 4 | 7 9 | 35 and | 195 |
| 50 blows | 1 2 4 | 9 | 3 7 5 | 5 | 8 8 7 | 40 and | 225 |
| 60 blows | 3 | 1 2 | 4 5 | 6 | —— | 50 and | 3 |
| 70 blows | 3 5 | 1 3 5 | 5 2 5 | 7 | —— | 55 and | 3375 |
| 80 blows | 4 | 1 5 | 6 | 8 | 1 4 1 9 | 60 and | 375 |
| 90 blows | 4 5 | 1 6 5 | 6 7 5 | 9 | —— | | |
| 100 blows | 5 | 1 8 | 7 5 | 1 1 0 | 1 7 7 4 | | |
| 1 year's banishment | 7 5 | 3 6 | 1 5 | 1 7 5 | 3 5 4 8 | | |
| 1½ year's banishment | 10 | 5 4 | 1 8 7 5 | 1 1 1 25 | —— | | |
| 2 years' banishment | 12 5 | 7 2 | 2 2 7 | 1 1 5 | 5 3 2 2 | | |
| 2½ years' banishment | 15 | 9 | 2 6 2 5 | 1 1 8 75 | —— | | |
| 3 years' banishment | 17 5 | 10 8 | 3 | 1 2 2 50 | 7 0 9 7 | | |
| 4 years' banishment | 20 | 14 4 | 4 | —— | —— | | |
| 5 years' banishment | 25 | 18 | 4 | —— | —— | | |
| Perpetual banishment to 2000 *li*. | —— | —— | —— | 1 3 | —— | | |
| Perpetual banishment to 2500 *li*. | —— | —— | —— | 1 3 3 75 | —— | | |
| Perpetual banishment to 3000 *li*. | —— | —— | —— | 1 3 7 5 | 10 6 4 6 | | |
| Death,—to be strangled<br>Death,—to be beheaded | —— | —— | —— | 1 45 | 12 4 2 | | |

## TABLE III.

Scale of pecuniary redemption in such cases as are not legally excluded from the benefit of general acts of grace and pardon, and which, though not necessarily redeemable, have, by an edict of the eighth year of the emperor Kínlung (1744), been made redeemable upon petition.

| *Rank of the Offender.* | *Sentence.* | *Commutation.* |
|---|---|---|
| An officer above the fourth rank | Death by strangulation or decollation. | 12,000 taels. |
| An officer of the fourth rank | | 5,000 taels. |
| An officer of the fifth or sixth rank | | 4,000 taels. |
| An officer of the seventh, or any inferior rank, or a Master of Arts | | 2,500 taels. |
| A graduate, licenciate, or a Bachelor of Arts | | 2,000 taels. |
| A private individual | | 1,200 taels. |
| An officer above the fourth rank | Perpetual banishment. | 7,200 taels. |
| An officer of the fourth rank | | 3,000 taels. |
| An officer of the fifth or sixth rank | | 2,400 taels. |
| An officer of the seventh, or any inferior rank, or a Master of Arts | | 1,500 taels. |
| A graduate, licenciate, or a Bachelor of Arts | | 1,200 taels. |
| A private individual | | 720 taels. |
| An officer above the fourth rank | Temporary banishment, or blows with the bamboo. | 4,800 taels. |
| An officer of the fourth rank | | 2,000 taels. |
| An officer of the fifth or sixth rank | | 1,600 taels. |
| An officer of the seventh, or any inferior rank, or a Master of Arts | | 1,000 taels. |
| A graduate, licenciate, or a Bachelor of Arts | | 800 taels. |
| A private individual | | 480 taels. |

## TABLE IV.—DEGREES OF PUNISHMENT.

| Deg. | Nominaly | Reduced. | Dimensions of the Bamboo. | Deg. | Nominally | Reduced. | Together with Banishment. |
|---|---|---|---|---|---|---|---|
| 1 | 10 | 4 blows | Inflicted with a Bamboo 5 *chik* 5 *tsün*. 1½ *tsün* by 1 *tsün* broad at the ends. Weight 1½ catties. | 11 | 60 | 20 blows | For one year to a distance of 500 *li*. |
| 2 | 20 | 5 " | | 12 | 70 | 25 " | For one year and a half.....500 *li*. |
| 3 | 30 | 10 " | | 13 | 80 | 30 " | For two years..............500 *li*. |
| 4 | 40 | 15 " | | 14 | 90 | 35 " | For two years and a half.....500 *li*. |
| 5 | 50 | 20 " | | 15 | 100 | 40 " | For three years..........500 *li*. |
| 6 | 60 | 20 " | 2 *tsün* by 1½ broad at the ends. Weight 2 catties. | 16 | 100 | 40 " | For life..................2000 *li*. |
| 7 | 70 | 25 " | | 17 | 100 | 40 " | For life..................2500 *li*. |
| 8 | 80 | 30 " | | 18 | 100 | 40 " | For life..................3000 *li*. |
| 9 | 90 | 35 " | | 19 | Death by strangulation. | | |
| 10 | 100 | 40 " | | 20 | Death by decollation. | | |

## Section Second.

## IMPERIAL TITLES.

### 皇王畧說第二章

ˏWóng ˏwóng ʻlʼ shüt,; tai² ʻí² ˏchéung.

| | | |
|---|---|---|
| 1. August is resplendent. Complete virtue is very resplendent, and there is no place which it does not illumine. | 皇煌也盛德煌煌無所不照也 | ˏWóng, ˏwóng ʻyá. Shing tak, ˏwóng ˏwóng, ˏmò ʻshó pat, chíú' ʻyá. |
| 2. August sovereign is an appellation of one possessing complete virtue and able to act on heavenly principles. | 皇帝有盛德而能行天道之稱 | ˏWóng tai' ʻyau shing² tak, ˏí ˏnang ˏhang ˏtʻín tò² ˏchí ˏchʻing. |
| 3. August emperor is one very resplendent and complete in virtue, who is above the people (i. e. is emperor). | 皇上煌煌盛德爲民之上者 | ˏWóng shéung², ˏwóng ˏwóng shing² tak,, ˏwai ˏman ˏchí shéung² ʻché. |
| 4. August heaven (the emperor) is he who because of his complete virtue and great splendor, is great as heaven. | 皇天以其盛德煌煌如天大意 | ˏWóng ˏtʻín, ʻí ˏkʻí shing² tak, ˏwóng ˏwóng, ˏü ˏtʻín tái² í'. |
| 5. The words of the august sovereign are silken sounds. | 皇帝言曰綸音 | ˏWóng tai' ˏín üt, ˏlun ˏyam. |
| 6. The august sovereign's car is the gemmeous carriage. | 皇帝車曰玉輦 | ˏWóng tai' ˏkü üt, yuk, ʻlím. |
| 7. The august sovereign's seal is the gemmeous signet. | 皇帝印曰玉璽 | ˏWóng tai' yan' üt, yuk, ʻsái. |
| 8. The commands of the august sovereign are the imperial commands, or the phœnix (the incomparable) mandate. | 皇帝之諭曰上諭又曰鳳詔 | ˏWóng tai' ˏchí yü² üt, shéung² yü², yau² üt, fung² chíú'. |
| 9. The decree of the august sovereign is the revered decree, and is otherwise called the sacred will. | 皇帝之命曰欽命又曰聖旨 | ˏWóng tai' ˏchí ming² üt, ˏyam ming², yau² üt, shing' ʻchí. |

## *Notes and Explanations.*

IMPERIAL titles have been variously written at different periods. *Wóng*, the august or the august one, was first applied to the three ancient sovereigns—Fukhí, Shannung, and Wóngtai. In the *Yik Shi*, or 'Unravelment of History,' *kün í, pín yat*, it is said: "*Wóng* or august is heaven: heaven speaks not, yet the four seasons follow in regular succession, and all things spring forth. So the three august ones descended in state, and without even uttering a word, the people bowed to their sway. Their virtue was inscrutable and boundless, like august heaven; and therefore were they called august," or the august ones. Commonly *wóng*, august, is composed of *wóng*, a king or ruler, surmounted by *pák*, clear or bright; in the *Yik Shi*, the *wóng* is surmounted by *tsz'* or self, thus indicating *self-king*, *self-ruler*, or one ruling alone and supreme.

2. *Wóngtai*, august sovereign or emperor, is a very common appellation of the reigning monarch: and, when speaking of him, it is used as an equivalent for H. I. M. or his imperial majesty. The five immediate successors of the three august ones were called *tai*; and sometimes the three august ones, with their next successors *Yau* and *Shun*, were called the five *tai*.

9. The word *yam* denotes that which is grand, majestic, and worthy to be revered; and is applied particularly to what belongs to the emperor; and hence *yam chái*, *yam ming*, and *yam*

| | | |
|---|---|---|
| 10. The celestial august one; indicating great splendor and perfect virtue like those of heaven. | 天皇煌煌盛德有如天大之意 | ꜀T‘ín ꜀wóng; ꜀wóng ꜀wóng shingʼ tak꜁, ʻyau ꜀yü ꜀t‘ín táiʼ ꜀chí íʼ. |
| 11. The wise and august, is one infinite in knowledge, complete in virtue, and very resplendent. | 聖皇於事無不通盛德煌煌也 | Shingʼ ꜀wóng, ꜀yü szʼ ꜀mò pat꜁ ꜀t‘ung,ʼ shingʼ tak꜁, ꜀wóng ꜀wóng ʻyá. |
| 12. The once august is the designation of one deceased. | 先皇已崩之稱 | ꜀Sín ꜀wóng, ʻí ꜀p‘ang ꜀chí ꜀ch‘ing. |
| 13. Sovereign or a judger; one able to act on celestial principles, and in the service of heaven execute judgment. | 帝諦也能行天道事天審諦也 | Taiʼ, taiʼ ʻyá; ꜀nang ꜀hang ꜀t‘ín tòʼ, szʼ ꜀t‘ín ʻsham taiʼ ʻyá. |
| 14. Sovereign king is one able to act on celestial principles, and to whom the empire goes and submits. | 帝王能行天道而天下歸往焉 | Taiʼ ꜀wóng; ꜀nang ꜀hang ꜀t‘ín tòʼ, ꜀í ꜀t‘ín háʼ ꜀kwai ʻwóng ꜀ín. |
| 15. Celestial sovereign is one able to act on celestial principles, and to whom the whole empire submits. | 天帝能行天道而天下歸之也 | ꜀T‘ín taiʼ, ꜀nang ꜀hang ꜀t‘ín tòʼ, ꜀í ꜀t‘ín háʼ ꜀kwai ꜀chí ʻyá. |
| 16. The sacred sovereign is one able to act on heavenly principles, who is thoroughly acquainted with all things. | 聖帝能行天道且於事無不通 | Shingʼ taiʼ, ꜀nang ꜀hang ꜀t‘ín tòʼ, ʻch‘é ꜀ü szʼ ꜀mò pat꜁ ꜀t‘ung. |
| 17. The genealogical books of the sovereign's descendents are named the gemmeous pages (or pearly tablets). | 帝胄之譜名爲玉牒 | Taiʼ chauʼ ꜀chí ʻpò, ꜀ming ꜀wai yuk꜁ típ꜁. |
| 18. King is to go; meaning that all the empire goes and submits to him [who is so styled their king]. | 王往也天下所歸往之意 | ꜀Wóng, ʻwóng ʻyá; ꜀t‘ín háʼ ʻshó ꜀kwai ʻwóng ꜀chí íʼ. |
| 19. The celestial king is a designation given by the Chinese, denoting one to whom all the empire submits. | 天王諸夏所稱意謂天下歸往 | ꜀T‘ín ꜀wóng ꜀chü háʼ ʻshó ꜀ch‘ing, íʼ waiʼ ꜀t‘ín haʼ ꜀kwai ʻwóng. |
| 20. A wise king is one whose knowledge is unbounded, and to whom the whole empire submits. | 聖王事無不通而天下歸往也 | Shingʼ ꜀wóng szʼ ꜀mò pat꜁ ꜀t‘ung, ꜀í ꜀t‘ín háʼ ꜀kwai ʻwóng ʻyá. |
| 21. Aged king is the designation of the king's father. | 老王王父之稱 | ʻLò ꜀wóng ꜀wóng fúʼ ꜀chí ꜀ch‘ing. |

*fung*, are rendered, 'imperial commissioner,' 'imperial decree,' and 'that which is or ought to be received with reverence.' Works published by imperial authority are styled *yam ting*, i. e. with the emperor's sanction, or by the emperor's permission.

12. The phrase *sín wóng* is applied only to emperors after they are deceased. Their demise is expressed by *p‘ang*, which denotes the fall of anything high and massive, or honorable and great, like the fall of a mountain, or the death of one who possesses great power and is highly honored and revered, as is always supposed to be the case with an emperor.

13—17. These several sentences show the meaning which is attached to this word *tai*, both when used alone and in connection with others. Sovereign, ruler, potentate, and so forth, are terms which may be used as equivalents for it.

18. This term has been used by the Chinese as the title of their sovereign. They say "heaven cannot have two suns, nor the people two *wóng* or kings," i. e. sovereign rulers. One says that 'he who can keep the three powers, heaven, earth, and man in union, is a *wóng*.' At present there are in the imperial family different orders of kings, all inferior to the emperor.

| | | |
|---|---|---|
| 22. Honored king is one to whom the hearts of all people submit, and to whom the whole empire shows obedience. | 君王羣下歸心<br>天下趨向歸往 | ‹Kwan ‚wóng, ‚kwan há$^2$ ‹kwai ‹sam, ‹t'ín há$^2$ ‹tsü héung' ‹kwai ‘wóng. |
| 23. The nation's king is the prince; one to whom the people of a nation submit, and hence the name. | 國王君也一國<br>之民歸往故名 | Kwók›, ‚wóng, ‹kwan ‘yá; yat› kwók› ‹chí ‚man ‹kwai ‘wóng, kú' ‚ming. |
| 24. The lone king is a modest appellation of a prince used by himself, denoting that he is poor. | 孤王君自卑而<br>稱孤陋之人意 | ‹Kú ‚wóng, ‹kwan tsz'$^2$ ‹pí ‚í ‹ch'ing ‹kú lau$^2$ ‹chí ‚yan í'. |
| 25. A retired or ex-king is one who was once king, but has on account of age resigned in favor of his son. | 太上王前曾爲<br>王辭老王父 | T'ái' shéung$^2$ ‚wóng, ‚ts'in ‚tsang ‚wai ‚wóng, ‚ts'z' ‘ló ‚wóng fú$^2$. |
| 26. Prince is a multitude; the term indicates one to whom the hearts of the multitude submit. | 君羣也羣下歸<br>心之意 | ‹Kwan ‚kwan ‘yá; ‚kwan há$^2$ ‹kwai ‹sam ‹chí í'. |
| 27. Prince of the country is a phrase indicating one to whom the hearts of the people of the country submit. | 國君國民歸心<br>之意 | Kwók› ‹kwan, kwók› ‚man ‹kwai ‹sam ‹chí í'. |
| 28. Solitary prince is an appellation of a prince used only by himself, meaning that he is without virtue. | 寡君君自稱意<br>謂寡德也 | ‘Kwá ‹kwan, ‹kwan tsz'$^2$ ‹ch'ing, í' wai$^2$ ‘kwá tak› ‘yá. |
| 29. Wise prince is one whose knowledge is infinite, and to whom the hearts of the multitude submit. | 聖君事無不通<br>而羣下歸心也 | Shing' ‹kwan, sz'$^2$ ‚mò pat› ‹t'ung, ‚í ‚kwan há$^2$ ‹kwai ‹sam ‘yá. |
| 30. The solitary man is a modest appellation of a prince applied to himself as one possessed of few virtues. | 寡人君自謙爲<br>寡德之人也 | ‘Kwá ‚yan, ‹kwan tsz'$^2$ ‹hím ‚wai ‘kwá tak› ‹chí ‚yan ‘yá. |
| 31. The son of heaven is lord of the whole empire, and is so called because heaven is his father and earth his mother. | 天子天下之主<br>父天母地之謂 | ‹T'ín ‘tsz' ‹t'ín há$^2$ ‹chí ‘chü, fú$^2$ ‹t'ín ‘mò tí$^2$ ‹chí wai$^2$. |
| 32. The wise son of heaven is one who is born of heaven and whose knowledge is infinite. | 聖天子天之所<br>生事無不通也 | Shing' ‹t'ín ‘tsz', ‹t'ín ‹chí ‘shó ‹shang, sz'$^2$ ‚mò pat› ‹t'ung ‘yá. |
| 33. The face of the son of heaven (i.e. the emperor's face) is called the dragon's face. | 天子之面曰龍<br>顏 | ‹T'ín ‘tsz' ‹chí mín$^2$ üt› ‚lung ‚ngán. |

24. This is rather affected than real poverty: in modern times Chinese kings possess but little power, and are in no way comparable to the *wóng tai*, who alone is supreme; they are usually, if not always, members of the imperial house.

28. Here the meaning of *kwá* is like *kú* in No. 24; both are used to express humility and lowliness, and are also employed as a designation of one's self, when a sovereign is speaking in the first person. *Kwá* also means a widow, and *kú* an orphan.

31. This high—too high—title, for mortal man, is in very common use. The notice of its origin, as here explained, is taken from the archæological work called *Kú Sz' Ts'am Yün*.

33. The emperor's person is also called the dragon's body, and his throne, the dragon's throne. Moreover, as elsewhere explained, his coat of arms is the dragon.

| | | |
|---|---|---|
| 34. The effects and furniture (i. e. the chattels) of the emperor are called the imperial chattels. | 天子之物曰御物 | ,T'ín 'tsz' ,chí mat$_2$ üt$_2$ ü$^2$ mat$_2$. |
| 35. Whatever place is reached by the carriage or the car of the son of heaven is said to be blessed. | 天子車駕所至曰幸 | ,T'ín 'tsz' ,kü ká' 'shó chí' üt$_2$ hang$^2$. |
| 36. The place of residence for the emperor is called, hall of audience, golden palace, the ninth entrance, vermilion avenue, vermilion hall, rosy hall, forbidden hall, the crimson and forbidden place, gemmeous steps, golden steps, meridian portal, gemmeous avenue, celestial steps, celestial court, forbidden palace, great interior, the maple pavilion, and royal house. | 天子所居之處曰朝廷金殿九重丹墀丹庭彤庭禁庭紫禁玉堦金堦午門玉墀天丨天庭禁宮大內楓宸王室 | ,T'ín 'tsz' 'shó ,kü ,chí ch'ü', üt$_2$ ,ch'íú ,t'ing, ,kam tín$^2$, 'kau ,chung, ,tán ,chí, ,tán ,t'ing, ,tung ,t'ing, kam' ,t'ing, 'tsz' kam', yuk$_2$ ,kái, ,kam ,kái, 'ng ,mún, yuk$_2$ ,chí, ,t'ín ,kái, ,t'ín ,t'ing, kam' ,kung, tái$^2$ noi$^2$, ,fung ,shan, ,wóng shat$_2$. |
| 37. Wise lord; his knowledge of things is infinite, and he lords it over the country and rules the people. | 聖主事無不通而主國治民者 | Shing' 'chü, sz'$^2$ ,mò pat, ,t'ung, ,í 'chü kwók, chí$^2$ ,man 'ché. |
| 38. Lord paramount is one who holds and regulates those affairs which are above the people. | 主上執掌爲民上之事也 | 'Chü shéung$^2$, chap, 'chéung ,wai ,man shéung$^2$ ,chí sz'$^2$ 'yá. |
| 39. Our master is a common appellation given to the monarchs of the present dynasty by officers in conversation. | 主子本朝文武恒談而稱君者 | 'Chü 'tsz', 'pún ,ch'íú ,man 'mò ,hang ,tám ,í ,ch'ing ,kwan 'ché. |
| 40. Lord of the country is the prince, so called because by him is exercised the lordship over the country. | 國主君也以其爲一國之主也 | Kwók, 'chü, ,kwan 'yá; 'í ,k'í ,wai yat, kwók, ,chí 'chü 'yá. |
| 41. Sole potentate is an appellation of the highest honor, employed by the prince, denoting WE, US, OUR, &c. | 朕至尊之稱君自謂言我也 | Cham$^2$ chí' ,tsün ,chí ,ch'ing ,kwan tsz'$^2$ wai$^2$ ,ín 'ngo 'yá. |

36. The origin of each of these terms is capable of explanation, and some of them are explained in several ways: thus, *chíú t'ing* is the hall of light, so called because there at *early dawn* the emperor is wont to see his ministers, or because there they are permitted to see the *light* of his countenance: again, there are nine successive gates or doorways to the palace, each opening into a new suit of apartments; the emperor usually resides within the ninth, and hence the term *kau chung:* the term 'maple' is employed, some say because around the palace were planted many maple trees which overshadowed it, others say because it is built of maple timber. The other terms are explained in a similar way.

41. This word *cham* was originally used for the first person by all classes; but having been employed by the first universal monarch of China as the peculiar designation of royalty, it came to be, and is now, the proper appellation of the sovereign, when speaking of himself; it is used by the emperor in the sense of *ngó*, as employed by the people. The term frequently occurs in imperial edicts.

| | | |
|---|---|---|
| 42. Footstool is the term used by the ministers of state in direct address to the emperor. | 陛下尊稱皇帝陛言爾也 | Pai$^2$ há$^2$, ˏtsün ˏchʻing ˌwóng tai$^3$, ˌín ʻí ʻyá. |
| 43. Ten thousand years is an appellation of the emperor. | 萬歲稱呼皇帝 | Mán$^2$ sui$^3$, ˏchʻing ˏfú ˌwóng tai$^3$. |
| 44. The empress is one who continues the prince's succession; she bows and submits to him, and hence the name. | 后繼體君也揖讓受於君故名 | Hau$^2$, kai$^3$ ʻtʻai ˏkwan ʻyá; yap, yéung$^2$ shau$^2$ ˏü ˏkwan, kú$^3$ ˌming. |
| 45. The august empress mother is the emperor's mother. | 皇太后王母也 | ˌWóng tʻái$^3$ hau$^2$ ˌwóng ʻmò ʻyá. |
| 46. She is also called the great one of the nation. | 國太王母之稱 | Kwók, tʻái$^3$, ˌwóng ʻmò ˏchí ˏchʻing. |
| 47. The great empress is also an appellation given to the emperor's mother by the ministers of state and the people. | 太后亦臣民之稱王母者 | Tʻái$^3$ hau$^2$, yik$_2$ ˌshan ˌman ˏchí ˏchʻing ˌwóng ʻmò ʻché. |
| 48. The august empress is a title of the prince's consort. | 皇后君妻之稱 | ˌWóng hau$^2$, ˏkwan ˏtsʻai ˏchí ˏchʻing. |
| 49. The queen of a country is a title of a prince's consort. | 國后稱君之妻 | Kwók, hau$^2$ ˏchʻing ˏkwan ˏchí ˏtsʻai. |
| 50. Princess is the designation given to the prince's consort by his ministers and people. | 娘娘臣民而稱君妻者 | ˌNéung ˌnéung ˌshan ˌman ˌí ˏchʻing ˏkwan ˏtsʻai ʻché. |
| 51. Imperial lady is the title of the prince's concubine. | 后妃稱君之妾 | Hau$^2$ ˏfí ˏchʻing ˏkwan ˏchí tsʻíp,. |
| 52. Imperial consort is the title given to her by the prince. | 御妻君自稱謂 | Yü$^2$ ˏtsʻai ˏkwan tsz'$^2$ ˏchʻing wai$^2$. |
| 53. The orders of the august empress are called her excellent pleasure. | 皇后之命謂之懿旨 | ˌWóng hau$^2$ ˏchí ming$^2$, wai$^2$ ˏchí í$^3$ ʻchí. |
| 54. The empress' room is called the pepper-chamber. | 椒房皇后所居 | ˏTsʻíú ˌfóng ˌwóng hau$^2$ ʻshó ˏkü. |
| 55. Chief palace; the palace is divided into eastern and western, which are the apartments of the royal consort. | 正宮宮分東西正者乃妻所居 | Ching$^3$ ˏkung; ˏkung ˏfan ˏtung ˏsai, ching$^3$ ʻché ʻnái ˏtsʻai ʻshó ˏkü. |
| 56. Eastern palace and western palace both are apartments which are occupied by the prince's concubines. | 東宮西宮皆君妾所居 | ˏTung ˏkung, ˏsai ˏkung, ˏkái ˏkwan tsʻíp, ʻshó ˏkü. |
| 57. August honorable ladies are the titles given to the concubines of the prince. | 皇貴妃稱君之妾也 | ˌWóng kwai$^3$ ˏfí, ˏchʻing ˏkwan ˏchí tsʻíp, ʻyá. |

42. *Pai há* denotes primarily the footsteps beneath the place where the monarch is seated. There his personal attendants stood to hear and to report to him the requests and complaints of others; and hence to report to those ministers, standing on the steps beneath the throne, came to be equivalent to addressing the throne, or him that sat thereon.

43. *Mán sui* is often used in the sense of *vive le roi*, expressing the wish that the monarch's life may be greatly prolonged. *Mán sui yé*, *father of* 10,000 *years* is also a common phrase. It resembles the Hebrew phrase מלכא לעלמין חיי O king live for ever! and is used in a similar manner when approaching to and addressing the sovereign.

58. The oldest son has the title of heir apparent.
太子號曰儲君
T'ái' 'tsz' hò² üt₂ ꜁chü ꜀kwan.

59. Elder brother is the title of the emperor's sons.
阿哥君子之稱
꜀Á ꜀kó ꜀kwan 'tsz' ꜀chí ꜀ch'ing.

60. The heir apparent's residence is called green palace.
太子居曰青宮
T'ái' 'tsz' ꜀kü üt₂ ꜀tsi'ng ꜀kung.

61. Congratulations of the heir apparent on his birthday are expressed by the phrase, 'thousand autumns.'
祝太子壽曰千秋
Chuk, t'ái' 'tsz' shau² üt₂ ꜀ts'ín ꜀tsau.

62. Lord of the palace; when the emperor gives a daughter in marriage, he does not himself direct its ceremonies, but employs one of the same family to do it, who is therefore called lord of the palace.
宮主天子嫁女不自主婚使諸侯同姓者主之故曰宮主
꜀Kung 'chü: ꜀t'ín 'tsz' kà' 'nü, pat, tsz'² 'chü ꜀wan, 'sz' ꜀chü ꜁hau ꜁t'ung sing' 'che 'chü ꜀chí, kú' üt₂ ꜀kung 'chü.

59. This usage seems to have been introduced by, and to be confined to, the reigning family: the oldest is called *Akó*, the next is called *í Akó*, the third *sám Akó*, and so on.

## Section Third.

## IMPERIAL FAMILY.

## 宗人類第三章

꜁Tsung ꜁yan lui² tai² ꜀sám ꜀chéung.

1. Our primeval progenitor, the emperor Origin.
肇祖原皇帝
Shíú² 'tsò ꜁Yün ꜁wóng tai'.

2. Our prosperous progenitor, the sovereign Dispatch.
興祖直皇帝
꜀Hing 'tsò Chik₂ ꜁wóng tai'.

3. Our luminous progenitor, the sovereign Benign.
景祖翼皇帝
'King 'tsò Yik₂ ꜁wóng tai'.

4. Our illustrious progenitor, the sovereign Munificent.
顯祖宣皇帝
'Hín 'tsò ꜀Sün ꜁wóng tai'.

### *Notes and Explanations.*

THE imperial family, now ruling over the Chinese empire, by endeavoring to conceal their recent origin as an independent state, has blended fables and facts in their early history, and thus attempted to deduce their descent from the gods. The Mantchou nation was evidently formed of several Tongouse tribes, situated on the north of Corea, along the banks of the Amour. In the time of the Sung dynasty, they were known as the *kam ch'ú*, or golden court, and subdued several districts of northern China. For a while their progress was checked by the Mongols, who were led on by a grandson of Genghis, and who, destroying both the Sung dynasty and its enemies, founded the Yün in 1279, which continued down to A. D. 1367, a period of 89 years. The Ming family then came to the throne, from whom, after a reign of 276 years, it was wrested by the Mantchou line, A. D. 1643-44. (See Companion to the Anglo-Chinese Kalendar for 1832.)

1—6. These are neither the proper names of the sovereigns, nor of those periods during which each in succession held the supreme authority; they are the *míú hò*, 'temple designations,' or posthumous titles conferred on the monarchs by their descendents, and written upon their monu-

| | | |
|---|---|---|
| 5. Our magnanimous progenitor, the sovereign Noble. | 太祖高皇帝 | T'ái' 'tsò ‹Kò ‚wóng tai'. |
| 6. Our magnanimous ancestor, the emperor Accomplished. | 太宗文皇帝 | T'ái' ‹tsung ‚Man ‚wóng tai'. |
| 7. Our immortal progenitor, the monarch Brilliant. | 世祖章皇帝 | Shai' 'tsò ‹Chéung ‚wóng tai'. |
| 8. Our sacred progenitor, the emperor Pious. | 聖祖仁 丨 帝 | Shing' 'tsò ‚Yan ‚wóng tai'. |
| 9. Our immortal ancestor, the emperor Excellent. | 世宗憲 丨 帝 | Shai' ‹tsung Hín' ‚wóng tai'. |
| 10. Our exalted ancestor, the emperor Pure. | 高宗純 丨 帝 | ‹Kò ‹tsung ‚Shun ‚wóng tai'. |
| 11. Our benevolent ancestor, the emperor Discreet. | 仁宗睿皇帝 | ‚Yan ‹tsang Yui$^{2}$ ‚wóng tai'. |
| 12. Rules for all posthumous titles: the several characters, examined and defined, are entered in the register. | 凡諡法各考其<br>字義而著於冊 | ‚Fán shí$^{2}$ fát,: kók, 'háu ‚k'í tsz'$^{2}$ í$^{2}$, ‚í chü$^{2}$ ‹ü chák,. |
| 13. Several terms selected for the ancestral temples. | 列聖廟號取焉 | Lít$_{2}$ shing' míú$^{2}$ hò$^{2}$ 'tsü ‹ín. |
| 14. *Primeval*, a divine and martial founder. | 神武創業曰肇 | ‚Shan 'mò chóng$^{2}$ íp$_{2}$ üt$_{2}$ shíú$^{2}$. |
| 15. *Prosperous*, wise to devise and great to effect. | 聖圖丕振曰興 | Shing' ‚t'ò ‹pí chan' üt$_{2}$ ‹hing. |
| 16. *Luminous*, having authority with ample resources. | 光有令緒曰景 | ‹Kwóng 'yau ling$^{2}$ 'sui üt$_{2}$ 'king. |
| 17. *Illustrious*, conspicuous for merit, virtue and diligence. | 功德懋著曰顯 | ‹Kung tak, mau$^{2}$ chü' üt$_{2}$ 'hín. |
| 18. *Magnanimous*, shedding down light on a thousand ages. | 光啟千禩曰太 | ‹Kwóng 'kai ‹ts'ín tsz'$^{2}$ üt$_{2}$ t'ái'. |
| 19. *Immortal*, giving protection to all posterity. | 貽庥奕葉曰世 | ‚I' ‹yau yik$_{2}$ íp$_{2}$ üt$_{2}$ shai'. |

ments or tablets in the ancestral temple and in the annals of the country. The first, second, third, and fourth in this list, were mere chieftains; the fifth, having become confederate with the family of Ming, ruled over several tribes of Mongols and Mantchous, and in 1616 took, for the title of his reign, the words *T'ín-ming*; in 1627 he was succeeded by T'ín-tsung. These six chieftains and kings all reigned in Mantchouria.

7—11. These are the posthumous titles of their successors; who have reigned in China, as the Tá Ts'ing chíú, or Great Pure dynasty; the following are their *kwók hò*.

7. Shunchí, (Shun-chí) who ruled 18 years, commencing in 1644;
8. Hónghí, (Káng-hí) who ruled 61 years, commencing in 1662;
9. Yungching, (Yung-ching) who ruled 13 years, commencing in 1723;
10. Kínlung, (Kien-lung) who ruled 60 years, commencing in 1736;
11. Káhing, (Keá-king) who ruled 25 years, commencing in 1796;

and ending in 1821; at which time he was succeeded by his imperial majesty, Tòkwóng (Táu-kwáng), then in the 39th year of his age; who in figure, is said to be tall, thin, and of a dark complexion: and in the business of government, diligent, and economical. Some have reported him to be mild and generous in his disposition; others have represented him as being unkind and cruel even to his own children.

12. These rules are contained in the second volume of the Tá Tsing Úi Tín, a "Collection of Statutes of the great Pure dynasty." Some one or two hundred characters have been selected and defined, (as in the examples Nos. 14 to 21, and 23 to 33,) and arranged for use into several classes, according to the rank and station of the persons to whom they are to be given as titles. *Shíú*, *hing*, *king*, &c. from No. 14 to 21, are selected from the first class. Those commencing with No. 22, are from the second class of these selected characters.

14. He who like a divinity and like a warrior lays the foundations of an empire is, or may be, called, *shíú*, a patriarch, or one of primitive and primeval character.

| | | |
|---|---|---|
| 20. ***Wise,*** having great virtue continually exhibited. | 峻德垂統曰聖 | Tsun' tak, ˏshui ˋt'ung üt, shing'. |
| 21. ***Exalted,*** with rising merit carried to the utmost. | 肇紀立極曰高 | Shíú² ˋkí lap, kik, üt, ˏkò. |
| 22. Selection of posthumous names. | 列聖尊謚取焉 | Lít, shing' ˏtsün shí² ˋtsü ˏín. |
| 23. ***Origin,*** planting virtue laid a foundation. | 植德開基曰原 | Chik, tak, ˏhoi ˏkí üt, ˏün. |
| 24. ***Dispatch,*** begining with diligence perfected his work. | 肇敏行成曰直 | Shíú² ˋman ˏhang ˏshing üt, chik,. |
| 25. ***Benign,*** loved the people and ruled them well. | 愛民好治曰翼 | Oi' ˏman hò' chí² üt, yik,. |
| 26. ***Munificent,*** dispensed and that without selfishness. | 施而不私曰宣 | ˏShí ˏí pat, ˏsz' üt, ˏsün. |
| 27. ***Noble,*** had merits and virtue in full greatness. | 功德盛大曰高 | ˏKung tak, shing² tái² üt, ˏkò. |
| 28. ***Accomplished,*** so as to span heaven and measure earth. | 經天緯地曰文 | ˏKing ˏt'ín ˋwai tí² üt, ˏman. |
| 29. ***Benevolent,*** loving all living creatures as heaven. | 如天好生曰仁 | ˏÜ ˏt'ín hò' ˏshang üt, ˏyan. |
| 30. ***Brilliant,*** i.e. respectful, faithful, elevated, clear. | 敬愼高明曰章 | King' shan² ˏkò ˏming üt, ˏchéung. |
| 31. ***Excellent,*** rewarding the good, punishing the bad. | 賞善罰奸曰憲 | ˋChéung shín² fat, ˏkán üt, hín'. |
| 32. ***Pure,*** one whose inmost soul was pure and single. | 內心和一曰純 | Noi² ˏsam ˏwó yat, üt, ˏshun. |
| 33. ***Discreet,*** wise and deeply and minutely learned. | 聖知通微曰睿 | Shing' ˏchí ˏt'ung ˏmí üt, yui². |
| 34. All the emperor's kindred, as more or less nearly related, are called either the *imperial family* or *gioro.* The birth of children must be duly announced, and their names entered on the family register; for adopted children, the same must be done; for the sons-in-law and daughters-in-law, the same must be done; and so also it must be with the conferment or withdrawal of honors. Every ten years these must be entered on the gemmeous tables. | 凡皇族別以近遠曰宗室曰覺羅生子則以告而書於冊繼嗣亦如之婚嫁亦如之爵秩始末亦如之十年則登於玉牒 | ˏFán ˏwóng tsuk, pít, ˋí kan² ˋyün, üt, ˏtsung shat,, üt, kók, ˏló. ˏShang ˋtsz' tsak, ˋí kò' ˏí ˏshü ˏü chák,; kai' tsz'² yik, ˏü ˏchí, ˏwan ká' yik, ˏü ˏchí; tséuk, tít, ˋchí mút, yik, ˏü ˏchí. Shap, ˏnín tsak, ˏtang ˏü yuk, típ,. |

23—25. In these there is supposed to be a reference to the order of succession: there is first, Origin, or the one who laid the foundation of the dynasty; next is Dispatch, or the one who succeeded and carried forward—dispatching in order and with promptness—that which the first had commenced; and then comes the Benign to give finish and completeness to the structure. As in European states, the epithets and the posthumous names are intended by the Chinese to exhibit the character of those illustrious personages to whom they are given.

29. On a preceding page (see Chap. III. Sec. 1. No. 42.), *yan* was rendered Pious; Benevolent, however, seems to be the proper translation. In the list of words, contained in the Collection of Statutes, three different definitions are given to this single character *yan*; it is not quite certain whether or not the definition here given was intended for Honghí; it is, however, sufficiently appropriate, and may be regarded accordingly, at least till the contrary is known.

34. The imperial family wear a golden yellow sash, and the gioro a red one; when degraded, the former take a red sash, and the latter a carnation one.

| | | |
|---|---|---|
| 35. The descendants of the illustrious progenitor the august Munificent, in a direct line, constitute the 'imperial family;' the descendants of his uncles and brothers constitute the gioro (or *kóklό*). | 顯祖宣皇帝本支爲宗室伯叔兄弟之支爲覺羅 | 'Hín 'tsò ‹Sün ˏwóng tai' 'pún ‹chí ˏwai ‹tsung shat›, pák› shuk› ‹hing tai$^2$ ‹chí ‹chí ˏwai kók› ˏló. |
| 36. The titles, conferred on members of the imperial family, are divided into twelve orders: | 凡宗室封爵之等十有二曰 | ˏFán ‹tsung shat› ‹fung tséuk› ‹chí 'tang shap$_2$ ˏyau í$^2$ üt$_2$ : |
| (*a*) The mild, eminent, kindred king. | 和碩親王 | ˏWó shik$_2$ ‹ts'an ˏwóng. |
| (*b*) The extolled, elegant, noble king. | 多羅郡王 | ‹Tó ˏló kwan$^2$ ˏwóng. |
| (*c*) The extolled, elegant, honorable knight. | 多羅貝勒 | ‹Tó ˏló púi' lak$_2$. |
| (*d*) The firm, elevated, honorable prince. | 固山貝子 | Kò' ‹shán púi' 'tsz'. |
| (*e*) High honorary state protector duke. | 奉恩鎮國公 | Fung$^2$ ‹yan chan' kwók› ‹kung. |
| (*f*) High honorary state supporter duke. | 奉恩輔國公 | Fung$^2$ ‹yan fú$^2$ kwók› ‹kung. |
| (*g*) Secondary state protector duke. | 不入八分鎮國公 | Pat› yap$_2$ pát› ‹fan chan' kwók› ‹kung. |
| (*h*) Secondary state supporter duke. | 不入八分輔國公 | Pat› yap$_2$ pát› ‹fan fú$^2$ kwók› ‹kung. |
| (*i*) State protector general. | 鎮國將軍 | Chan' kwók› ‹tséung ‹kwan. |
| (*j*) State supporter general. | 輔國將軍 | Fú$^2$ kwók› ‹tséung ‹kwan. |
| (*k*) High state general. | 奉國將軍 | Fung$^2$ kwók› ‹tséung ‹kwan. |
| (*l*) High honorary general. | 奉恩將軍 | Fung$^2$ ‹yan ‹tséung ‹kwan. |
| 37. If without titles, then rank is conferred. | 無爵則給以品 | ˏMò tséuk› tsak› k'ap› 'í 'pan. |

35. "Among the chiefs of their tribes was one Aisin Keŏlo, or *Gioro*, whom the Mantchous make the son of a divine virgin, who became pregnant of him by eating a fruit brought to her in the bill of a magpie: this Aisin Gioro at first ruled over three tribes, but afterwards others submitted to him, and he became king of a nation, to which he gave the name Mantchou (*mánchau*), which in Chinese signifies, thé full (or well-peopled) country." These gioro are those who have descended collaterally from Aisin Gioro.

36. These titles of nobility are confined to the male branches of the imperial house; there are, however, several others which are conferred on the female members, all of whom seem to have titles of nobility or degrees of rank. *Wó shik, tó ló, tó ló púi lák, kò shán púi tsz'*, are Mantchou words,—the *meaning* of which may or may not be (probably it is not) correctly expressed by the Chinese characters.

(*g, h.*) In the time of Shunchí's grandfather, T'ínming, who reigned in Mantchouria, there were appointed eight *wó-shik* and *púi-lak* to deliberate and consult together on the affairs of government; of each of the two there were four, each having his appropriate duties; hence the *pát fan*, which may be regarded as secondary orders of nobility.

38. The titles with which the eldest sons are invested are two, one is syled 'perpetual prince,' and the other is styled 'elevated prince.'

嫡子之受封者
其等二曰世子
曰長子

Tik, 'tsz' ,chí shau[2] ,fung 'ché ,k'í 'tang í[2], üt, shai' 'tsz', üt, 'ch'éung 'tsz'.

39. All the titles of nobility are either meritorious titles, or honorary titles, or hereditary titles, or titles which are conferred on examination.

凡封爵有功封
有恩封有襲封
有考封

,Fán ,fung tseuk,, 'yau ,kung ,fung, 'yau ,yan ,fung, 'yau tsap, ,fung, 'yau 'háu ,fung.

40. Whenever any titles are conferred, or any posthumous names are decreed to the kindred and noble kings, these are all determined and fixed by order of precedence.

凡親王郡王封
則賜號歿則予
諡皆定以班

,Fán ,ts'an ,wóng kwan[2] ,wóng, ,fung tsak, tsz'' hò[2], mút, tsak, 'ü shí[2], ,kái ting[2] 'í ,pán.

41. Government of the imperial family: there are (1st) a president, (2d) a left assistant director, (3d) a right assistant director, (4th) a left assistant, and (5th) a right assistant,—which officers hold the government and direction of the imperial kindred.

宗人府宗令一
人左宗正一人
右宗正一人左
宗人一人右宗
人一人掌皇族
之政令

,Tsung ,yan 'fú; ,tsung ling[2] yat, ,yan, 'tsó ,tsung ching' yat, ,yan, yau[2] ,tsung ching' yat, ,yan, 'tsó ,tsung ,yan yat, ,yan, yau[2] ,tsung ,yan yat, ,yan; 'chéung ,wóng tsuk, ,chí ching' ling[2].

38. The title of *shai tsz'* is conferred on the eldest son of the *ts'an wóng*, and that of *ch'éung tsz'* on the eldest son of the *kwan wóng*; and in this way the direct line of each is continued.

41. These five officers are all selected from among the members of the imperial clan: the president must be either a *ts'an wóng* or a *kwan wóng*; and the second and third officers must be from one of the first six ranks noticed in No. 36.

## Section Fourth.

## INNER COUNCIL.

### 內閣第四章
Noi[2] kók,; tai[2] sz' ,chéung.

1. The high chancellors of the Inner Council, two Mantchous and two Chinese, [with two]—

內閣大學士滿
洲二人漢二人

Noi[2] kók, tái[2] hók, sz'[2], 'Mún ,chau í[2] ,yan, Hón' í[2] ,yan—

### *Notes and Explanations.*

THE word *kók* denotes a pavilion, a court, or council-chamber, and by metonomy those who

2. Joint adjutant high chancellors—

協辦大學士

Híp, pán[2] tái[2] hók, sz'[1]—

3. Deliberate on the government of the empire, proclaim abroad the imperial pleasure, regulate the canons of state together with the whole administration of the great balance of power, thus aiding the emperor in directing the affairs of state. Whenever the great solemnities [are to be celebrated], they then bring forward all the officers to take part.

掌議天下之政宣布絲綸釐治憲典總鈞衡之任以贊上理庶務凡大典禮則率百寮以將事

'Chéung ˊí ˏt'ín há[2] ˏchí ching', ˏsün pò' ˏsz' ˏlun, ˏlí chí[2] hín' 'tín, 'tsung ˏkwan ˏhang ˏchí yam[2], ˊí tsán' shéung[2] ˊlí shü' mò[2]; ˏfán tái[2] 'tín ˊlai, tsak, sut, pák, ˏlíú ˊí ˏtséung sz'[3].

4. Whenever the imperial pleasure is to be promulged, whether by an order, a declaration, a proclamation, or a warrant, in all cases their forms must be decided on and introduced [for H. I. M.'s inspection]; so also with the sacrificial liturgy; so too with congratulatory cards, if they contain any phrases. Whenever they receive the emperor's pleasure in commands to be promulgated, if it be an answer given to a memorial, and has already been sent down, they must consign it to the appropriate department to be copied.

凡綸音之下達者曰制曰詔曰誥曰勅皆擬其式而進焉祝辭亦如之進賀表若致辭亦如之凡承宣諭旨若章奏之批答者既下乃布於百司而抄焉

ˏFán ˏlun ˏyam ˏchí há[2] tát, 'ché, üt, chai', üt, chíú', üt, kò', üt, ch'ik, ˏkái ˊí ˏk'í shik, ˏí tsun' ˏín; chuk, ˏts'z' yik, ˏü ˏchí; tsun' hò[2] 'píú, yéuk, chí' ˏts'z', yik, ˏü ˏchí. ˏFán ˏching ˏsün yü[2] 'chí, yéuk, ˏchéung tsau' ˏchí ˏpai táp, 'ché, kí' há[2], 'nái pò' ˏyü pák, ˏtsz' ˏí ˏcháu ˏín.

5. The announcement of all great solemnities to those in office is made by an *order*.

凡大典禮宣示百寮則有制辭

ˏFán tái[2] 'tín ˊlai, ˏsün shí[2] pák, ˏlíú tsak, 'yau chai' ˏts'z'.

occupy such a place: the *Noi Kók* is the emperor's cabinet or privy council. There are also in this council ten *hók sz'*, who are ex-officio members of the Board of Rites, of whom four are Chinese, four are Mantchous, and two Mongols. Besides these, there are eight *shítuk hóksz'*, of whom four are Mantchous, two Mongols, and two are Chinese; also sixteen *shítuk*, ten of them being Mantchous, three Mongols, and three Chinese. Next are six *tíntsik*, two Mantchous and four Chinese. Then there are ninety-two *chung shü*, of whom sixty-eight are Mantchous, sixteen Mongols, and eight Chinese, with about eighty or ninety more under-secretaries, and so forth. For further particulars respecting this Council, see the Chinese Repository, vol. IV., page 137; and also the Chinese Court Calender, or Red Book.

1. Literally *tái hók sz'*, great learned scholars; they are the highest and principal officers in the executive department of the state, in daily intercourse with H. I. M., to whom they are prime ministers—what in other countries is intrusted to one is here lodged in the hands of these four ministers, some one or more of whom, however, are often absent from the capital, acting either as governors or special envoys.

3. The phrase *pák líú* is equivalent to *pák kún*, and includes all the high officers who are associated in the administration of the government.

4. Among the first duties of the high chancellors of state are those which appertain to the ritual observances, coronations, &c., on all which occasions they have to preside and direct. Next to these duties are those here specified, which constitute their principal daily business.

| | | |
|---|---|---|
| 6. The publication of all great governmental affairs to ministers and people, and the promulgation of imperial laws and ordinances, are made by *declaration* or *proclamation*. | 大政事布告臣民垂示彝憲則有詔有誥 | Tái ching' sz', pò' kò' shan man, shui shí í hín', tsak yau chíú' yau kò'. |
| 7. When by special favor there are conferred the fifth and higher degrees of rank in office, or orders of perpetual hereditary nobility, it is done by *proclamation decree* (or is proclaimed by decree). | 覃恩封贈五品以上官及世爵承襲罔替者曰誥命 | Tám yan fung ts'ang 'ng 'pan í shéung kún, kap shai' tséuk shing tsap móng tai' 'ché, üt kò' ming. |
| 8. The investiture is made abroad by warrant: when by special favor are conferred the sixth and lower degrees of rank in office, or the orders of limited hereditary nobility, both are done by *warrant decree*. | 敕封外藩覃恩封贈六品以下官及世爵有襲次者曰敕命 | Chik fung ngoi fán, tám yan fung ts'ang luk 'pan í há kún, kap shai' tséuk 'yau tsap tsz' 'ché, üt chik ming. |
| 9. When an edict is to be promulgated in the colonies, or a warrant is to be held by a colonial officer, or is to be transmitted by him, it is done by a *warrant edict*. | 諭告外藩及外任官坐名敕傳敕曰敕諭 | Yü kò' ngoi fán, kap ngoi yam kún tsó ming chik, chün chik, üt chik yü. |
| 10. These must be early prepared and presented, and respectfully delayed for the imperial decision thereon. | 皆先期撰擬呈進恭候欽定 | Kái sín kí chán í ching tsun', kung hau yam ting. |
| 11. The manner of introducing documents to H. I. M. | 定進本之式 | Ting tsun' 'pún chí shik. |
| 12. All documents, whether they be from the dispatch office, or from the other local offices, must before presentation be submitted to the Council, and duplicates of them all must be prepared. If there are plans, or schedules, or bills, or billets attached, these must accompany the documents. | 凡本有通本有部本先期以達於閣皆備其副若圖若冊若單若夾簽皆附焉 | Fán 'pún, 'yau t'ung 'pún, 'yau pò 'pún, sín kí 'í tát ü Kók, kái pí kʻí fú'. Yéuk t'ò, yéuk chák, yéuk tán, yéuk káp tsím, kái fú in. |

5—9. The *chai* or order, *chiú* or declaration, *kò* or proclamation, *kò ming* or proclamation decree, and the *chik yü* or warrant edict, are similar to the proclamations, letters-patent, &c., among western nations. They are all state papers, and the occasions and manner of their use will best explain their specific character. It is not always easy—perhaps not exactly possible—to mark, by any corresponding term in our language, the distinctions which exist, and are carefully maintained among the Chinese. The word *pan* (*pin* in the court dialect) is a case in point, and illustrates this difficulty; it means petition, address, report, &c.

8. The words *ngoi fán* here refer to those portions of the Chinese empire which are situated beyond the eighteen provinces. See Chap. XII., Sec. 8., Nos. 17—23.

11. The outline of the manner of introducing state papers to the emperor is given in the following numbers, from the 12th to the 16th. In the original work, under this head, certain days are specified on which no papers can be presented; these amount to some fifty or more in a year, being days sacred to the memory of distinguished ancestors, the worship of gods, &c.

| | | |
|---|---|---|
| 13. The proposed decisions being settled, billets are prepared; when there are two proposals, two billets are made; if three, then three; if four, four; all being prepared, they must be kept in waiting for the decision of the emperor thereon. | 票擬則繕簽有<br>兩擬者繕雙簽<br>若三簽若四簽<br>皆備擬以候欽<br>定 | Píú' 'í tsak, shín' ,tsím, 'yau 'léung 'í 'ché shín' ,shéung ,tsím, yéuk, ,sám ,tsím, yéuk, sz' ,tsím, ,kái pí' 'í 'í hau' ,yam ting'. |
| 14. The reasons for the decisions are stated in codicils and H. I. M.'s pleasure being obtained respecting the proposals, the documents are sent to the six notary-offices. | 申以說帖得旨<br>則批本乃發於<br>六科 | ,Shan 'í shüt, típ, tak, 'chí tsak, ,pai 'pún; 'nái fát, ,ü luk, ,fò. |
| 15. On the emperor's approach to the audience gate to hear of the government, open documents are then presented. | 御門聽政則進<br>折本 | Ü' ,mún ting' ching', tsak, tsun' chák, 'pún. |
| 16. The decisions made in the imperial presence, and at the autumnal assizes, being brought forward, those to be executed are marked off according to H. I. M.'s pleasure. | 朝審秋審之勾<br>决者得旨則予<br>勾 | ,Ch'íú 'sham ,tsau 'sham ,chí ,kau küt, 'ché, tak, 'chí tsak, 'ü ,kau. |
| 17. All the documents which are presented, after two days are returned; if they have special reference to matters requiring haste they are returned the same day. | 凡進本逾二日<br>乃下焉其即下<br>者不越日 | ,Fán tsun' 'pún, ü' í' yat, 'nái há' ,ín; ,k'í tsik, há' 'ché pat, üt, yat,. |
| 18. The emperor's seals are deposited in the palace of Peace; they are twenty-five in number. | 貯御寶於交泰<br>殿凡二十有五 | 'Chü ü' 'pò ,ü ,Káu tái' tín': ,fán í' shap, 'yau 'ng. |
| 19. The *first* is called the seal under which the Great Pure dynasty received its decree (or commission) to reign. | 一日大清受命<br>之寶 | Yat, üt, Tái' ,Ts'ing shau' ming' ,chí 'pò. |

12—13. The *plans* here referred to are those of public buildings, such as courts, palaces, granaries, forts, bridges, &c., which are to be constructed at the expense of government. The *schedules* and *bills* are similar documents, both referring to public works. The *billets* are small cards, or slips of paper, attached to those documents, respecting which a variety of decisions—two, three, four, or more—are proposed: they contain brief answers, such as it is supposed the emperor may please to give: the object of them is to economise time when in his presence, for then a stroke of the vermilion pencil on the one he prefers, is decisive.

14. The *shüt tip*, or card of explanation, is a kind of *codicillus*, in which the reasons for the several decisions are briefly noted, so that they may be ready at hand in case they are called for by the emperor.

15. This gate is that called *Kín Ts'ing*, or Heavenly Purity; and thither his majesty ascends and sits down to listen to the affairs of *t'ín há*, or all those beneath the heavens—his empire.

16. The cases of certain state criminals who have been condemned to capital punishment by the provincial officers, are annually referred to the emperor in autumn.

18. The high chancellors of the Inner Council are charged with the keeping of the imperial seals, which when not in use are laid up in the palace called *Káutái tín*, which, for a more convenient term, is rendered 'palace of Peace.'

| | | |
|---|---|---|
| 20. The *second* is called the seal under which the august sovereign receives his celestial authority. | 二曰皇帝奉天之寶 | I' üt, ,wóng tai' fung' ,t'ín ,chí 'pò. |
| 21. The *third* is called the seal under which the Great Pure dynasty perpetuates its emperors. | 三曰大清嗣天子寶 | ,Sám üt, Tái' ,Ts'ing sz'' ,t'ín 'tsz' 'pò. |
| 22. The *fourth* is the seal of the august sovereign. | 四曰皇帝之寶 | Sz'' üt, ,wóng tai' ,chí 'pò. |
| 23. The *fifth* is also called the seal of the august sovereign. | 五亦曰皇帝之寶 | ,'Ng yik, üt, ,wóng tai' ,chí 'pò. |
| 24. The *sixth* is called the emperor's seal. | 六曰天子之寶 | Luk, üt, ,t'ín 'sz' ,chí 'pò. |
| 25. The *seventh* is called the seal of the honorable kindred of the august sovereign. | 七丨皇帝尊親之寶 | Ts'at, üt, ,wóng tai' ,tsün ,ts'an ,chí 'pò. |
| 26. The *eighth* is called the seal of the august emperor's near relations. | 八曰皇帝親親之寶 | Pát, üt, ,wóng tai' ,ts'an ,ts'an ,chí 'pò. |
| 27. The *ninth* is the seal for the sovereign's acts. | 九曰皇帝行寶 | 'Kau üt, ,wóng tai' ,hang 'pò. |
| 28. The *tenth* is the seal for the sovereign's credentials. | 十丨皇帝信寶 | Shap, üt, ,wóng tai' sun' 'pò. |
| 29. The *eleventh* is called the seal of the emperor's acts. | 十有一曰天子行寶 | Shap, 'yau yat, üt, ,t'ín 'tsz' ,hang 'pò. |
| 30. The *twelfth* is called the seal of the emperor's credentials. | 十有二曰天子信寶 | Shap, 'yau í' üt, ,t'ín 'tsz' sun' 'pò. |
| 31. The *thirteenth* is called the seal by which heaven is honored and the people made (or commanded to be) diligent. | 十有三曰敬天勤民之寶 | Shap, 'yau ,sám üt, king' ,t'ín ,kan ,man ,chí 'pò. |

19. It is evident from the names of some of these seals that they are not often required for use; nor is it easy to understand what mortal could use this first, inasmuch as the investiture is (or would fain appear to be) from heaven.

20. This is the seal used on the occasion of a new succession to the throne; and of course has been required only six successive times since the rise of the present dynasty, during a period of nearly two hundred years.

25, 26. These two seals seem to be nearly or quite the same, as are also the fourth and fifth; the reason for having two of the same kind, in either instance, does not appear, nor is it easy to conjecture.

27. The meaning of *hang*, here and in No. 29, is obscure and doubtful: but for the twentieth, it would be natural to suppose it was intended for the emperor's *traveling* seal, and possibly such may be the right interpretation of it; this being designed for his common excursions, and that for those of a particular kind.

28. The same must be said of the word *sun*; it may refer to his private documents, if any such as ordinary letters or private correspondence be allowed: it seems, however, to refer to the seal which is used in communications to tributary or foreign states, or on such occasions as those when the emperor grants investiture to the kings of Corea, &c. So of the 12th.

| | | |
|---|---|---|
| 32. The *fourteenth* is called the seal of orders and proclamations (i. e. seals used when issuing orders), &c. | 十有四曰制誥之寶 | Shap$_2$ ʻyau sz$^3$ üt$_2$ chai$^3$ kò$^2$ ˏchí ʻpò. |
| 33. The *fifteenth* is called the seal of the warrant decree. | 十有五曰勅命之寶 | Shap$_2$ ʻyau ʻng üt$_2$ chik$_3$ ming$^2$ ˏchí ʻpò. |
| 34. The *sixteenth* is called the seal under which instruction is sent down. | 十有六曰垂訓之寶 | Shap$_2$ ʻyau luk$_2$ üt$_2$ ˏshui fan$^3$ ˏchí ʻpò. |
| 35. The *seventeenth* is called the seal of decreed virtue (i. e. of his appointment to rule in righteousness). | 十有七曰命德之寶 | Shap$_2$ ʻyau tsʻat$_3$ üt$_2$ ming$^2$ tak$_3$ ˏchí ʻpò. |
| 36. The *eighteenth* is called the seal for imperial papers. | 十有八曰欽文之寶 | Shap$_2$ ʻyau pát$_2$ üt$_2$ ˏyam ˏman ˏchí ʻpò. |
| 37. The *nineteenth* is called the seal for manifests, classics, and histories. | 十有九曰表章經史之寶 | Shap$_2$ ʻyau ʻkau üt$_2$ ʻpíú ˏchéung ˏking ʻsz$^3$ ˏchí ʻpò. |
| 38. The *twentieth* is called the seal for patroling and guarding the empire. | 二十曰巡狩天下之寶 | Í$^2$ shap$_2$ üt$_2$ ˏtsun shau$^3$ ˏtʻín há$^2$ ˏchí ʻpò. |
| 39. The *twenty-first* is called the seal of punishing crimes and quieting the people (the one used in criminal cases). | 二十一曰討罪安民之寶 | Í$^2$ shap$_2$ yat$_3$ üt$_2$ ʻtʻò tsúi$^2$ ˏón ˏman ˏchí ʻpò. |
| 40. The *twenty-second* is called the seal for regulating and controling the army. | 二十二曰制馭六師之寶 | Í$^2$ shap$_2$ í$^2$ üt$_2$ chai$^3$ ü$^2$ luk$_2$ ˏsz$^3$ ˏchi ʻpò. |
| 41. The *twenty-third* is called the seal of warrant for keeping in order all nations. | 二十三曰勅正萬邦之寶 | Í$^2$ shap$_2$ ˏsám üt$_2$ chik$_3$ ching$^3$ mán$^2$ ˏpóng ˏchí ʻpò. |
| 42. The *twenty-fourth* is called the seal of warrant for keeping in order all people. | 二十四曰勅正萬民之寶 | Í$^2$ shap$_2$ sz$^3$ üt$_2$ chik$_3$ ching$^3$ mán$^2$ ˏman ˏchí ʻpò. |
| 43. The *twenty-fifth* is called the seal of broad revolutions. | 二十五曰廣運之寶 | Í$^2$ shap$_2$ ʻng üt$_2$ ʻkwóng wan$^2$ ˏchí ʻpò. |

32, 33. These are, apparently, the common seals of state, or those which his majesty employs on all ordinary occasions.

36, 37. There are numerous historical and statistical works, which are published by the government alone, others are issued by imperial sanction; these are all called imperial editions.

38. It used to be customary for the emperor once in the year, or oftener, to proceed on hunting excursions—which was done partly for the purpose of exercising and reviewing his troops: it was on these excursions that this seal was used.

43. Here again the meaning is obscure: the *kwóng wan*, broad revolutions, or extensive circulations, seems to refer to a favorite idea of universal empire.

| | | |
|---|---|---|
| 44. Whenever the emperor's pleasure is to be proclaimed, his chancellors request the seals, and use them; when he goes on a tour, they receive them and follow him. At the end of the year they are laid up. Those at Moukden (the Affluent Capital) are kept carefully in deposit. | 凡宣綸音皆請寶而用焉巡幸則奉以從歲終乃洗寶其貯盛京者備尊藏焉 | ˏFán ˌsün ˏlun ˌyam, ˌkái ˊtsʻing ˊpò ˏí yung² ˏín; ˏtsun hang² tsak˒ fung² ˊí ˏtsung. Sui³ ˌchung, ˊnái ˊsai ˊpò. ˏKʻí ˊchü Shing² ˌking ˊché, pí² ˌtsün ˏtsʻóng ˏín. |

44. The materials of which the seals are made, and their dimensions, are all specified in the original. Most of them are made of gem-stone, green, white, black, clouded, &c.; one or two are made of fragrant wood. They are all square, and vary from two to six inches in the length of their sides; and are one inch or more thick. They are all ornamented with the figure of the dragon. Those at Moukden are only ten in number and apparently are seldom, if ever, taken for use from their place of deposit—their use being superseded by those in Peking.

## Section Fifth.

## GENERAL COUNCIL.

### 軍機處第五章

ˌKwan ˌkí chʻü³; tai² ˊ'ng ˌchéung.

| | | |
|---|---|---|
| 1. Court for managing the machinery of state. Its great ministers superintend the preparation of imperial edicts and commands, together with the essential interests of the army and nation, thus assisting the emperor's administration. | 軍處機書之要務辦理軍機大臣掌書諭旨綜軍國之要以贊上治 | Pán² ˊlí ˌKwan ˌKí chʻü³. ˌKwan ˌKí tái² ˏshan ˊchéung ˌshü ü² ˊchí, ˌtsung ˌkwan kwók˒ ˌchí íú³, ˊí tsán³ shéung² chí² ˌkí mò³. |
| 2. The great ministers of the several councils, consisting of an indefinite number of Mantchou and Chinese of- | 軍機大臣於滿漢大學士尚書 | ˌKwan ˌKí tái² ˏshan ˌü ˊMún ˊHón tái² hók˒ sz'² shéung² |

## *Notes and Explanations.*

GENERAL Council is rather an equivalent for, than a translation of, the phrase *Kwan Kí Chʻü*: *chʻü* means a place, and here denotes a court or council, including all those servants of the emperor who are appointed to deliberate on the machinery of the army. The general government of this country partakes more of the military character than of the civil; and hence *kwan*, army, is used as an equivalent for state; and machinery of the army, instead of council of state, or general council of the nation.

Under this and the Inner Council, and under all the principal Boards and offices in the capital, there are a great number of subordinate departments for carrying on the various details of business: these are filled by clerks, under-writers, supervisors, inspectors, keepers of seals, recorders, &c.

2. In this, as in most of the other principal councils and courts of the capital, there is a division of the office-bearers, nearly one half being allotted to the Mantchous, and the other half to the Chinese and Mongols: the number of Mongols, however, is very small.

| | | |
|---|---|---|
| ficers, are selected from among the high chancellors, presidents, and vice-presidents in the metropolitan courts. | 侍郎京堂內特<br>簡無定員 | ˏshü shí² ˏlóng ˏking ˏtóng noi² tak₂ ʻkán, ˏmò ting² ˏün. |
| 3. On all ordinary days, they repair to the forbidden palace, and there wait to be summoned to audience. | 常日直禁庭以<br>待召見 | ˏChéung yat₂ chik₂ kam' ˏting ʻí toi² chíú² kín'. |
| 4. The hall of the General Council is situated within the gate of Eminent Ancestors: daily, between the hours of 5 and 6 o'clock, the great ministers of state repair thither. After the completion of business, and when the eunuchs of the palace in attendance have communicated the imperial pleasure for their dispersion, they straightway retire. There are no fixed times for audiences; sometimes they are summoned once, and sometimes repeatedly on the same day; on approaching his majesty's presence, they place a mat on the ground, and are permitted to sit. | 軍機堂在隆宗<br>門內每日寅時<br>軍機大臣入直<br>於此至辦事畢<br>內奏事太監傳<br>旨令散乃下直<br>召見無時或一<br>次或數次軍機<br>大臣至上前豫<br>敷席於地賜坐 | ˏKwan ˏKí ˏtóng tsoi² ˏLung ˏtsung ˏmún noi²; ʻmúi yat₂ ˏyan ˏshí, ˏKwan ˏKí tái² ˏshan yap₂ chik₂ ˏü ˏts'z'; chí' pán² sz'² pat₂, noi² ts'au' sz'² t'ái' kám' ˏchün ʻchí ling² sán'. ʻnái há² chik₂. Chíú² kín' ˏmò ˏshí, wák₂ yat₂ ts'z', wák₂ shò' ts'z'; ˏkwan ˏkí tái² ˏshan chí' shéung² ˏts'ín ü². ˏfú tsik₂ ˏü tí², tsz' tsó². |
| 5. Whenever edicts or the pleasure of the emperor are openly sent down, after being duly served by them, the papers are transmitted to the Inner Council. | 凡諭旨明降者<br>既述則下於內<br>閣 | ˏFán ü² ʻchí ˏming kóng' ʻché, kí' shut₂, tsak₂ há² ˏü Noi² Kók₂. |
| 6. Papers originating with the emperor are called *edicts*; those which are sent down as answers to addresses to the throne, are called *the sovereign's pleasure*; if however these answers are to be proclaimed and promulgated to all far and near, then also they are called *edicts*. Their | 特降者爲諭因<br>所奏請而降者<br>爲旨其或因所<br>奏請而卽以宣<br>示中外者亦爲 | Tak₂ kóng' ʻché ˏwai ü²; ˏyan ʻshó ts'au' ʻts'ing ˏí kóng' ʻché ˏwai ʻchí; ˏk'í wák₂ ˏyan ʻshó ts'au' ʻts'ing ˏí tsik₂ ʻí ˏsün shí² ˏchung ngoi² ʻché, yik₂ |

3—4. In the original of the Collection of Statutes from which these paragraphs are selected, par. No. 4. is an explanation of No. 3; and in like manner No. 2. above is an explanation of No. 1. The Nos. 1 and 3 are in large type, and Nos. 2 and 4 are in small type, one half the size of the former, as explanatory notes. *T'ái kám*, literally 'the great overseers,' are the personal attendants of the emperor, and keepers of the inner gates of the palace. Throughout the empire, as well as in the capital, the ministers and servants of the emperor are expected to be at their posts and in the performance of their duties early in the morning.

5. *Shut* means to narrate, to tell, to rehearse, to arrange, &c; in this instance, it seems to denote a compound act; the papers are to be revised, have their proper dates inserted, and then, after being reported or rehearsed to the emperor, are transmitted to the Inner Council to be made public, or otherwise disposed of, according to the nature of the respective documents.

6. This paragraph also appears in the original as a note, explanatory of the preceding paragraph; and so in the sequel, the 8th is explanatory of the 7th, and the 10th of the 9th.

style is thus: an edict is called, *'An edict received from the Inner Council;'* the other, thus; *'The imperial pleasure is received.'*

諭其式諭曰內
閣奉上諭旨曰
奉旨

ˌwai ü. ˌK'í shik, ü üt, Noi Kók, fung shéung ü; 'chí üt, fung 'chí.

7. Whenever an edict is to be carried into effect by the ministers of the General Council, after being duly served by them, it is sealed and dispatched.

諭軍機大臣行
者旣述則封寄
焉

Ü ˌKwan ˌKí tái ˌshan ˌhang 'ché, kí shut, tsak ˌfung kí ˌsín.

8. If the edict either requires haste or is a secret one, it is called a *palace dispatch*, and is not openly sent down to pass through the Inner Council, but goes directly from the General Council sealed, and is delivered to the express office of the Board of War, to be forwarded; and according to the urgency of the case or otherwise, it is hastened by couriers, traveling at the rate of four hundred, or five hunded, or six hundred, and, in very important cases, even more than six hundred *lí* per day.

或速諭或密諭
不由內閣明降
者爲廷寄徑由
軍機處封交兵
部捷報處遞往
視事之緩急或
馬上飛遞或四
百里或五百里
或六百里或六
百里加緊

Wák tsuk ü, wák mat ü, pat ˌyau Noi Kók, ˌming kóng 'ché, ˌwai ˌting kí; king ˌyau ˌKwan ˌKí ch'ü ˌfung ˌkáu ˌPing Pò tsít, pò ch'ü tai 'wong; shí sz' ˌchí ún kap; wák 'má shéung ˌfí tai, wák sz' pák 'lí, wák 'ng pák 'lí, wák luk pák 'lí, wák luk pák 'lí ˌká 'kan.

9. When H. I. M.'s pleasure is to be kept in remembrance, it is put upon record and laid aside; and at the proper time it is brought forward and presented.

凡有旨存記者
皆書於冊而藏
之屆時則提奏

ˌFán 'yau 'chí ˌtsün kí 'ché, ˌkái ˌshü ˌü chák, ˌí ˌts'ông ˌchí; kái ˌshí tsak, ˌtai ts'au.

10. A memorandum book is prepared, and whenever the imperial pleasure concerning any affair is received, and is to be kept in remembrance, it is in his majesty's presence written in the book; and at the proper time it is brought forward and presented, and his further pleasure requested; if it be of a nature requiring secrecy, then as such the memorandum is sealed; and at the proper moment the seal is broken, and the business receives attention.

設存記簿凡奉
旨存記事件皆
以面奉諭旨書
於簿至應行時
提奏請旨其應
密存事件則密
封存記亦於屆
時拆封辦理

Chít ˌtsün kí pò; ˌfán fung 'chí ˌtsün kí sz' kín, ˌkái 'í mín fung ü 'chí ˌshü ˌü pò; chí ˌying ˌhang ˌshí ˌtai ts'au 'ts'ing 'chí; ˌk'í ˌying mat ˌtsün sz' kín, tsak mat ˌfung ˌtsün kí, yik ˌü kái ˌshí chák, ˌfung pán 'lí.

8. These dispatches are commonly called 'fire dispatches;' they seldom, however, exceed the rate of four hundred Chinese (or about 130 English) miles a day. The 'express-office' is supplied with a large number of couriers, ready at all times for dispatch.

## Section Sixth.

# THE SIX SUPREME BOARDS.

## 六部第六章

Luk$_{2}$ Pò$^{2}$; tai$^{2}$ luk$_{2}$ ‹chéung.

1. The presidents of the *Board of Civil Office*, a Mantchou and a Chinese; the left vice-presidents, a Mantchou and a Chinese; and the right vice-presidents, a Mantchou and a Chinese—have the government and direction of all the various officers in the civil service of the empire, and thereby they assist the emperor to rule all people.

吏部尙書滿洲一人漢一人左侍郎滿洲一人漢一人右侍郎滿洲一人漢一人掌天下文職官吏之政令以贊上治萬民

Lí$^{2}$ Pò$^{2}$ shéung$^{2}$ ‹shü, ‘Mún ‹chau yat› ‚yan, Hón’ yat› ‚yan; ‘tsó shí$^{2}$ ‚lóng, ‘Mún ‹chau yat› ‚yan, Hón’ yat› ‚yan; yau$^{2}$ shí$^{2}$ ‚lóng, ‘Mún ‹chau yat› ‚yan, Hón’ yat› ‚yan; ‘chéung ‹t‘ín há$^{2}$ ‚man chik› ‹kún lí$^{2}$ ‹chí ching’ ling$^{2}$, ‘í tsán’ shéung$^{2}$ chí$^{2}$ mán$^{2}$ ‚man.

2. Whatever appertains to the plans of selecting and arranging rank and gradation; to the rules of determining degradation and promotion; to the ordinances for granting investitures and rewards; and to the laws for fixing schedules and furloughs—are reported to the Board by the appropriate officers; and the presidents and the vice-presidents with those under them deliberate thereon; if important affairs they are reported to the throne, otherwise they are dispatched at once; thus supplying the civil service.

凡品秩銓敘之制考課黜陟之方封授策賞之典定籍終制之法百司以達於部尙書侍郎率其屬以定議大事上之小事則行以布邦職

‚Fán pan’ tít$_{2}$ ‚tsün tsü$^{2}$ ‹chí chai’; ‘háu fó’ chut› · chik› ‹chí ‹fong; ‹fung shau$^{2}$ chák› ‘chéung ‹chí ‘tín; ting$^{2}$ tsik$_{2}$ ‹chung chai’ ‹chí fát›; pák› ‹sz’ ‘í tát$_{2}$ ‹ü Pò$^{2}$, shéung$^{2}$ ‹shü shí$^{2}$ ‚lóng sut› ‚k‘í shuk$_{2}$ ‘í ting$^{2}$ ‘í, tái$^{2}$ sz’$^{2}$ shéung$^{2}$ ‹chí, ‘síú sz’$^{2}$ tsak› ‚hang, ‘í pò’ ‹póng chik›.

### *Notes and Explanations.*

THESE six supreme Boards are, (1) the Board of Civil Office, (2) the Board of Revenue, (3) the Board of Rites, (4) the Board of War, (5) the Board of Punishments, and (6) the Board of Works. The duties of the Inner and General Councils are of a general nature, and refer directly to the emperor and his family, or to all the departments of state; and they serve to connect the supreme head with the subordinate branches of the administration—of which these six are the principal and have cognizance of all that appertains to the civil service in the eighteen provinces. See Chinese Repository, vol. IV., page 139; and also the Collection of Statues,—from which the several paragraphs of this section are extracted.

1. The general duties of this Board—indicated by its name—consist in the arrangement and distribution of those who are employed in the civil offices throughout the provinces. They have also to direct the introduction of these officers to the imperial presence. The number and order of those employed in the civil service are all specified.

3. The presidents of the *Board of Revenue*, a Mantchou and a Chinese; the left vice-presidents, a Mantchou and a Chinese; and the right vice-presidents, a Mantchou and a Chinese,—direct the territorial government of the empire, and keep the lists of population, in order to aid the emperor in nourishing all people.

戶部尚書滿洲一人漢一人左侍郎滿洲一人漢一人右侍郎滿洲一人漢一人掌天下之地政與其版籍以贊上養萬民

Ú² Pò² shéung² ‹shü, ꜂Mún ‹chau yat› ꜂yan, Hón' yat› ꜂yan; 'tsó shí² ꜂lóng, ꜂Mún ‹chau yat› ꜂yan, Hón' yat› ꜂yan; yau' shí² ꜂lóng, ꜂Mún ‹chau yat› ꜂yan, Hón' yat› ꜂yan, 'chéung ‹t'ín há² ‹chí tí² ching', ꜂ü ꜂k'í 'pán tsik₂, ꜂í tsán' shéung² 'yéung mán² ꜂man.

4. Whatever appertains to the regulations for levying and collecting duties and taxes; to the plans for distributing salaries and allowances; to the rates for receipts and disbursements at the granaries and treasuries; and to the rights for transportation both by land and water—are reported to this Board by the appropriate officers; and the presidents, &c. deliberate thereon; if important affairs they are reported to the throne, otherwise they are at once dispatched; in this way sufficient supplies for the country are provided.

凡賦稅徵課之則俸餉須給之制倉庫出納之數川陸轉運之宜百司以達於部尚書侍郎率其屬以定議大事上之小事則行以足邦用

꜂Fán fú² shui' ‹ching fó' ‹chí tsak›, 'fung 'héung ‹pán kap› ‹chí chai'; ‹ts'óng fú' ch'ut› náp₂ ‹chí shò'; ‹ch'ün luk₂, 'chün wan² ‹chí ꜂í; pák› ‹sz' ꜂í tát₂ ‹ü Pò², shéung² ‹shü shí² ꜂lóng sut› ꜂k'í shuk₂ ꜂í ting² ꜂í; tái² sz'² shéung² ‹chí, 'síú sz'² tsak› ꜂hang, ꜂í tsuk› ‹póng yung².

2. The special duties of each of the six Boards are drawn out, in the Collection of Statutes precisely in the same form, and are, as in this one, arranged under four distinct heads. In the phrase *háu fó*, *háu* seems to have reference to the reasons and considerations, upon the examination of which the degradation and promotion of officers is determined; it therefore qualifies *fó*, and indicates the manner of determining, viz., by examination. The *tsik* appear to be lists or schedules, containing the names of officers for civil service; and the *chung chai* are grants of temporary retirement from office, which are allowed in order to attend upon the aged, the sick, and to mourn for the dead.

3. The fiscal laws of the empire are enumerated in Sec. 1. §3. of this chapter. The details of this department of the government fill six volumes of the Collection of Statutes, including chapters 10 to 18. This Board directs concerning the emperor's ploughing and sowing, which are done annually as patterns for all the people of the empire. Formerly four furrows used to be turned by the emperor, now the number is reduced to three. The admeasurement and surveying of the empire is done under the direction of this Board, which regulates its divisions into provinces, departments, districts, &c. In the eleventh chapter of the Collection of Statutes there is given a complete census of the whole empire—the number in each province, and in each of the colonial dependencies being enumerated separately.

4. The chief and the most important duties of the Board of Revenue are indicated, in four distinct branches. Attached to this Board are fourteen subordinate departments, charged with the supervision of the revenue of the empire,—which for this purpose is arranged into the same number of territorial departments. Each of them has also to attend to particular portions of the general business of the Board. In addition to these fourteen, there are several other minor offices;—a court of appeal on disputes respecting property and succession; various minor treasuries

5. The presidents of the *Board of Rites*, a Mantchou and a Chinese; the left vice-presidents a Mantchou and a Chinese; and the right vice-presidents, a Mantchou and a Chinese—examine and direct concerning the performance of the five kinds of ritual observances, and make proclamation thereof to the whole empire; thus aiding the emperor in guiding all people.

禮部尚書滿洲一人漢一人左侍郎滿洲一人漢一人右侍郎滿洲一人漢一人掌考五禮之用達於天下以贊上導萬民

'Lai Pò' shéung' ,shü, 'Mún ,chau yat, ,yan, Hón' yat, ,yan; 'tsó shí' ,lóng ,Mún ,chau yat, ,yan, Hón' yat, ,yan; yau' shí' ,lóng 'Mún ,chau yat, ,yan, Hón' yat, ,yan; 'chéung 'háu 'ng 'lai ,chí yung', tát, ,ü ,t'ín há'; 'í tsán' shéung' tò' mán, ,man.

6. Whatever appertains to the ordinances for regulating precedence and literary distinctions; to the canons for maintaining religious honor and fidelity; to the orders respecting intercourse and tribute; and to the forms of giving banquets and granting bounties—are reported to the Board by the appropriate officers; and the presidents, &c. deliberate thereon; if important affairs they report them to the throne, otherwise they at once dispatch them; in this way promoting national education.

凡班制論材之典達誠致愼之經會同職貢之政燕饗餼廩之式百司以達於部尚書侍郎率其屬以定議大事上之小事則行以布邦教

,Fán ,pán chai' lun' ,tsoi 'chí 'tín; tát, ,shing chí' shan' ,chí ,king; úi' ,t'ung chik, kung' ,chí ching'; ín' 'héung hí' 'lam ,chí shik,; pák, ,sz' 'í tát, ,ü Pò'; shéung' ,shü shí' ,lóng sut, ,k'í shuk, 'í ting' 'í; tái' sz'' shéung' ,chí, 'síú sz'' tsak, ,hang; 'í pò' ,pong káu'.

for supplying the expenses, or attending to the receipts arising from particular branches of the affairs of the Board; a mint under the direction of two vice-presidents; an office having under its charge depositories of metals, silks, and coloring materials; an office for providing supplies of grain in and about the capital; &c.

5. Eight volumes,—the 13th to 20th inclusive—of the Collected Statutes are filled with the details of the duties of this Board, comprising 14 chapters. The five kinds of ritual observances are the following, (1) *kat lai*, felicitous, or those which relate to festivals and sacrifices in honor of gods, departed heroes, and so forth, extending to 123 varieties; (2) *ká lai*, joyous, or those which relate to new accessions to the throne, state congratulations, &c., 74 in variety; (3) *kwan lai*, martial, or those which have reference to military affairs, the review of troops, preparations for war, and such like, comprising 18 in variety; (4) *pan lai*, or those of a hospitable nature, such as are required at the entertainment of guests, both domestic and foreign, 20 in number; and (5) *hung lai*, infelicitous, or those which are appropriate to mournful occasions, 15 in number; being of all the five kinds, 250 varieties.

6. The four subordinate departments of the Board of Rites, for carrying on its general business are: the (1) *I'chai sz'*, or the department of ceremonial forms and regulations; "it has the regulation of the etiquette to be observed at court, on ordinary and extraordinary occasions, on congratulatory attendance, in the performance of ministerial and official duties, &c.; also the regulation of dresses, caps, &c., as to figure, size, color, and the nature of their ornaments; of carriages and their riding accoutrements, their form, &c., with the number of followers, and the insignia of rank; it has also the direction of the entire ceremonial of personal intercourse between the various ranks of peers, minutely defining the number of bows and degrees of attention which each is to pay to the other, when meeting in official capacities, according as they are on terms of equality or

7. The presidents of the *Board of War*, a Mantchou and a Chinese; the left vice-presidents, a Mantchou and a Chinese; the right vice-presidents,—have the government and direction of all the officers within and without the provinces employed in the military service of the empire, for the purpose of aiding the emperor in protecting all people.

兵部尚書滿洲一人漢一人左侍郎滿洲一人漢一人右侍郎滿洲一人漢一人掌中外武職官之政令以贊上衛萬民

‚Ping Pò² shéung² ‚shü, ‘Mún ‚chau yat‚ ‚yan, Hón’ yat‚ ‚yan; ‘tsó shí² ‚lóng, ‘Mún ‚chau yat‚ ‚yan, Hón’ yat‚ ‚yan; yau² shí² ‚lóng, ‘Mún ‚chau yat‚ ‚yan, Hón’ yat‚ ‚yan; ‘chéung ‚chung ngoi² ‘mò chik‚ ‚kún ‚chí ching² ling², ‘í tsán’ shéung² wai² mán² ‚man.

8. Whatever appertains to the ordinances for taking away, giving, and granting office, or inheriting rank; to the plans of the post-office department; to the rules of military examination and discipline; and to the rates of enrolment and actual service—are reported to the Board by the appropriate officers; and the presidents, &c., with those under them, deliberate thereon; if important, report them to the throne, but if otherwise, they at once dispatch them, thus regulating the hinge of state.

凡除授封蔭之典乘載郵傳之制甄覈簡練之方士籍軍實之數百司以達于部尚書侍郎率其屬以定議大事上之小事則行以整邦樞

‚Fán ‚ch‘ü shau² ‚fung yam’ ‚chí ‘tín; ‚shing tsoi’ ‚yau ‚chün ‚chí chai’; ‚yan hat‚ ‘kán lín’ ‚chí ‚fong; sz’² tsik‚ ‚kwan shat‚ ‚chí shò’; pák‚ ‚sz’ ‘í tát‚ ‚ü Pò², shéung² ‚shü shí² ‚lóng sut‚ ‚k‘í shuk‚ ‘í ting² ‘í; tái² sz’² shéung² ‚chí, ‘síú sz’² tsak‚ ‚hang; ‘í ‘ching ‚póng ‚sh‘ü.

otherwise. It has also to direct the forms of their written official intercourse, including the forms to be observed in addresses to and from foreign states. It has further to attend to the establishment of governmental schools and academies; and the regulation of the public literary examinations; the number of the graduates, the distinction of their classes, the forms of their selection, and the privileges of the successful candidates;" &c., &c. The (2) *Tsaitsz' sz'*, or the department for sacrificial rites, &c. The (3) *Chühák sz'*, or the department for regulating the intercourse of hosts and guests, &c. And the (4) *Ts'ingshín sz'*, or the department for the preparation of food, &c.

7. The military laws of the Penal Code are enumerated in the 1st section of this chapter. In the Collection of Statutes, the details of this Board fill five volumes, the 22d to the 26th inclusive, comprising the chapters 35 to 40. The general regulations of the army are under the control of this Board; its presidents introduce to his majesty's presence all military officers, who are on such occasions required to appear armed with the bow. The Board keeps lists of all the military officers in the empire, grants commissions, honors, rank, &c., and withdraws them at the emperor's pleasure. It also superintends the posts and expresses for the transmission of orders and commands, and takes care of the arsenals and all military stores.

8. The hinge of state, here mentioned, is the army, the essential part, the mainspring in the government of the empire. Of the four subordinate branches of this Board, the 1st is the *Mòsün sz'*, an office, at the head of which are eight Mantchous, four Chinese, and one Mongolian, whose duties are—the adjustment of the rank and grade of military officers, the examination of their skill in tactics, the regulation of their duties in the camp, &c. The degrees of rank in the army are nine, the same as in the civil service, each of which is divided into a primary and a secondary, making in fact eighteen degrees. The 2d subordinate branch is the *Chikfóng sz'*, an

9. The presidents of the *Board of Punishments*, a Mantchou and a Chinese; the left vice-presidents, a Mantchou and a Chinese; the right vice-presidents, a Mantchou and a Chinese—have the government and direction of the punishments throughout the empire, for the purpose of aiding the emperor in correcting all people.

刑部尙書滿洲一人漢一人左侍郎滿洲一人漢一人右侍郎滿洲一人漢一人掌天下刑罰之政令以贊上正萬民

ˏYing Pò' shéung' ˏshü, 'Mún ˏchau yatˎ ˏyan, Hón' yatˎ ˏyan; 'tsó shí' ˏlóng, 'Mún ˏchau yatˎ ˏyan, Hón' yatˎ ˏyan; yau' shí' ˏlóng, 'Mún ˏchau yatˎ ˏyan, Hón' yatˎ ˏvan; 'chéung ˏt'ín há' ˏying fátˎ ˏchí ching' lıng', 'í tsán' shéung' ching' mán' ˏman.

10. Whatever appertains to the measures of applying the laws with leniency or severity; to the task of hearing evidence and giving decisions; to the rights of granting pardons, reprieves, or otherwise; and to the rate of fines and interest—are all reported by the several officers to the Board; and the presidents and the vice-presidents with those under them deliberate thereon; if important, they report them to the throne, otherwise they dispatch them at once; thus aiding in giving dignity to national manners.

凡律例輕重之適聽斷出入之孚決宥緩速之宜贓罰追貸之數各司以達于部尙書侍郎率其屬以定議大事上之小事則行以肅邦紀

ˏFán lutˎ lai' ˏhing chung' ˏchí shikˎ; ting' tün' ch'ütˎ yapˎ ˏchí ˏfú; kütˎ yau' ún' tsukˎ ˏchí ˏí; ˏchong fátˎ ˏchui toi' ˏchí shò'; kókˎ ˏsz' 'í tátˎ ˏü Pò', shéung' ˏshü shí' ˏlóng sutˎ ˏk'í shukˎ 'í ting' 'í; tái' sz'' shéung' ˏchí, 'síú sz'' tsakˎ ˏhang, 'í sukˎ ˏpóng 'kí.

office, at the head of which are eight Mantchous, five Chinese, and two Mongolians, whose duties are the investigation of the merits and demerits of officers, the examination of their claims for favors, the trial of their talents and qualifications, the supervision of their discipline, their instruction, mock battles, and such like. The 3d is the department *Chémá*, at the head of which are four Mantchous, two Chinese, and one Mongolian, who are charged with the especial care of the horses and chariots of the army; they have the supervision of the cavalry, waggons, posts, and the express office, or literally, 'the office for the announcement of victories.' The 4th is the *Mòfú sz'*, an office at the head of which are four Mantchous, two Chinese, and one Mongolian, whose duties are the inspection of the rolls and the general direction of the military stores, and all the munitions of war.

9. The criminal laws of this Board are enumerated in the 1st section of this chapter; its details fill only two volumes, the 27th and 28th, in the Collection of Statutes, comprising the sections 41 to 44. The principal duties of this Board are—the settlement of penal laws, the decision of appeals, the confirmation or reversal of sentences, the regulation of fines and mulcts. In all cases of capital crimes, with a few particular exceptions, there are assembled the *sám fát sz'*, three law offices, in one joint assembly, which comprises the leading members of this and those of the two other criminal courts, the *Tòchát yüu*, and the *Táli sz'*. For deliberating on the criminal cases which come up from all the provinces annually in autumn, there are collected in joint assembly *kau hing*, nine bodies of ministers, one from this and each of the other supreme Boards, and one from each of the three offices, the *Tòchát yüu*, the *Tungching sz'*, and the *Táli sz'*. The object of these joint assemblies is to prevent malversation in the administration of justice, in cases where human life is involved. The provisions of the law, to secure the impartial administration of justice in this country, have been made with no ordinary degree of consideration; and when the offender goes unpunished, or the innocent is made to suffer, it must be more the fault of the executors of the laws than of their makers.

11. The presidents of the *Board of Works*, a Mantchou and a Chinese; the left vice-presidents, a Mantchou and a Chinese; and the right vice-presidents, a Mantchou and a Chinese—have the government and direction of the public works throughout the empire, together with the current expenses of the same, for the purpose of aiding the emperor to keep all people in a state of repose.

工部尚書滿洲一人漢一人左侍郎滿洲一人漢一人右侍郎滿洲一人漢一人掌天下造作之政令與共經費以贊上奠萬民

‹Kung Pò[2] shéung[2] ‹shü ʻMún ‹chau yat› ˏyan, Hón’ yat› ˏyan; ʻtsó shí[2] ˏlóng ʻMún ‹chau yat› ˏyan, Hón’ yat› ˏyan; yau[2] shí[2] ˏlóng ʻMún ‹chau yat› ˏyan, Hón’ yat› ˏyan; ʻchéung ‹tʻín há[2] tsʻò[2] tsók› ‹chí ching’ ling[2] ʻü ˏkʻí ‹king fai’, ʻí tsán’ shéung[2] tín[2] mán[2] ˏman.

12. Whatever appertains to plans for buildings of wood or earth; to the forms of useful implements; to the laws for stopping up or opening channels; and to the ordinances for constructing mausolea and temples—are all reported to the Board by the appropriate officers; and the presidents and vice-presidents deliberate thereon; if important, they report them to the throne, otherwise they at once dispatch them, thus perfecting the national works.

凡土木興建之制器物利用之式渠堰疏障之法陵寢供億之典百司以達於部尚書侍郎率其屬以定議大事上之小事則行以飭邦事

ˏFán ʻtʻò muk₂ ˏhing kín’ ‹chí chai’; hí’ mat₂ lí[2] yung[2] ‹chí shik›; ˏkü ʻín ‹shó chéung’ ‹chí fát›; ˏling ʻtsam ‹kung yik› ‹chí ʻtín; pák› ‹sz’ ʻí tát₂ ‹ü Pò[2]—shéung[2] ‹shü shí[2] ˏlóng sut› ˏkʻí shuk₂ ʻí ting[2] ʻí; tái[2] sz[2]’ shéung[2] ‹chí, ʻsíú sz’[2] tsak› ‹hang ʻí shik› ‹póng sz’[2].

10. The five kinds and the several degrees of punishment have been enumerated in the first section of this chapter.

11. The laws respecting public works are enumerated in the first section of this chapter. In the Collection of Statutes, the details of this Board fill three volumes, the 29th, 30th, and 31st, comprising sections 45th to 48th inclusive.

12. Literally, these four leading clauses read thus: (1) all earth wood raise build 's plans; (2) utensil things fitting use 's fashion; (3) gutter stop up open dike 's laws; (4) tombs temples arrange contrive 's ordinances. The subordinate departments are similar to those of the other Boards; and it has cognizance of all public works—such as the constructing of governmental offices, temples, palaces, &c., belonging to the state; it has the charge of preparing all implements of war, tents, carriages, shot, &c.; confiscated property, consisting of buildings, also comes under its care; it regulates the construction of all weights and measures; dikes and canals, highways and bridges, dock-yards, &c., all come under its supervision, and also the mint, with several minor offices.

## Section Seventh.

# THE COLONIAL OFFICE.

## 理藩院第七章

ʻLí ˏfán yün²; tai² tsʻat˒ ˓chéung.

1. The president of the Colonial Office, a Mantchou; the left vice-president, a Mantchou; the right vice-president a Mantchou; with one supernumerary vice-president, a Mangolian—have the government and direction of the colonial states, order their honors and emoluments, appoint their visits to court, and regulate their punishments; upon all these various branches of business, the presidents and vice-presidents, with those under them, deliberate; if important they report them to the throne, otherwise they dispatch them at once, thus displaying the majesty and virtue of the state.

理藩院尚書滿洲一人左侍郎滿洲一人右侍郎滿洲一人額外侍郎蒙古一人掌外藩之政令制其爵祿定其朝會正其刑罰尚書侍郎率其屬以定議大事上之小事則行以布國之威德

ʻLí ˏFán Yün², shéung² ˓shü, ʻMún ˓chau yat˒ ˏyan; ʻtsó shí² ˏlóng, ʻMún ˓chau yat˒ ˏyan; yau² shí² ˏlóng, ʻMún ˓chau yat˒ ˏyan; ngák˒ ngoi² shí² ˏlóng, ˏMung ʻkú yat˒ ˏyan—ʻchéung ngoi² ˏfán ˓chí ching² ling², chai² ˏkʻí tséuk˒ luk₂, ting² ˏkʻí ˏchʻiú úi², ching² ˏkʻí ˏying fát₂; shéung² ˓shü shí² ˏlóng shut˒ ˏkʻí shuk₂ ʻí ting² ʻí; tái² sz²² shéung² ˓chí, ʻsiú sz²² tsak˒ ˏhang, ʻí pò² kwók˒ ˓chí ˓wai tak˒.

2. The officers in the department for the military rolls are, a Mantchou and two Mongolian secretaries; a member of the imperial house a Mantchou, and two Mongolian

旗籍清吏司郎中滿洲一人蒙古二人員外郎

ˏKʻí tsik₂ ˓tsʻing lí² ˓sz², ˏlóng ˓chung, ʻMún ˓chau yat˒ ˏyan, ˏMung ʻkú í² ˏyan; ˏün ngoi²

### *Notes and Explanations.*

LITERALLY, *li fán yün* means a board or court for the government of foreigners—subjected and tributary tribes, situated on the west of China Proper. For the geographical position of these, see Chap. XII. Sec. 8. No. 18, and the sequel. This office regulates the government of the nomads, and defines their boundaries. What of the government in the 18 provinces is intrusted to the six supreme Boards, is in the western states of the empire intrusted to this Colonial or Foreign Office. Its duties are, of course, multifarious and arduous, and of no small importance, whether they be viewed with reference either to the people who inhabit those western states or to the supreme head the emperor—between which two, the lord paramount and his liege subjects, the *Lí Fán Yün* forms the connecting link, the bond of union.

2. Literally, this reads thus, *flag roll pure officers department:* it has charge of the boundaries of the country, and the allotment of lands, the rank and succession of the princes and nobles, the appointment of subordinate officers, taxation of the people, their arrangement into tribes, review of the troops, and so forth. *Chát sát hak* is a Mongolian term, used apparently with different shades of meaning, and differently applied, analagous to *kún* or *kún chik;* here *noi chát*

廣東方言讀本



under-secretaries; with one Mantchou director: these have to examine and give direction to whatever appertains to the territory of the inner chieftains, to the regulation of their honors, and of their census. All the affairs respecting the officers, the clansmen, their alliances, the army, and the posts, the whole they direct; as they do also the nomads who are in or connected with their territories.

宗室一人滿洲
一人蒙古二人
主事滿洲一人
掌考內扎薩克
之疆理斂其封
爵與其譜系凡
官屬部衆會盟
軍旅鄉傳之事
皆掌之掌遊牧
之內屬者

ˏlóng, ˓chung shat˒ yat˒ ˏyan, ˢMún ˓chau yat˒ ˏyan, ˏMung ‘kú í[2] ˏyan, ‘chü sz’[2], ˢMún ˓chau yat˒ ˏyan; ‘chéung ‘háu noi[2] chát˒ sát˒ hak˒ ˓chí ˓kéung ˢlí, chü[2] ˏk‘í ˓fung tséuk˒ ˢü ˏk‘í ‘pò hai[2]. ˏFán ˓kún shuk₂, pò[2] chung’, úi[2] ˏmang, ˓kwan ˢlü, ˏyau ˏchün ˓chí sz’[2], ˓kái ‘chéung ˓chí; ‘chéung ˏyau muk₂ ˓chí noi[2] shuk₂ ‘ché.

3. The officers connected with the department for imperial audiences, are a Mantchou and two Mongolian secretaries; two Mantchou and three Mongolian under-secretaries; with two Mongolian directors: these have to regulate the distribution of emoluments among the inner chieftains, their visits to court, their tribute, with the banquets and grants which are made to them.

王會清吏司郎
中滿洲一人蒙
古二人員外郎
滿洲二人蒙古
三人主事蒙古
二人掌須祿於
內扎薩克而治
其朝貢燕饗賚
予之事

ˏWóng úi[2] ˓ts‘ing lí[2] ˓sz’, ˏlóng ˓chung, ˢMún ˓chau yat˒ ˏyan, ˏMung ‘kú í[2] ˏyan; ˏün ngoi[2] ˏlóng, ˢMún ˓chau í[2] ˏyan, ˏMung ‘kú ˓sám ˏyan; ‘chü sz’[2], ˏMung ‘kú í[2] ˏyan: ‘chéung ˓pán luk₂ ˓ü noi[2] chát˒ sát˒ hak˒, ˏí chí[2] ˏk‘í ˏch‘íú kung’ ín’ ‘héung loi[2] ˢü ˓chí sz’[2].

4. Rule for the conferment of emoluments upon those foreigners. The gifts which they receive consist of both money and silken fabrics; and in all are arranged into seven classes: (*a*) their kindred kings receive each two thou-

制外藩之祿有
俸銀有俸幣其
等各有七外藩
親王俸銀二千

Chai’ ngoi[2] ˏfán ˓chí luk₂. ˢYau ‘fung ˏngan, ˢyau ‘fung pai[2]; ˏk‘í ‘tang kók˒ ˢyau ts‘at˒; ngoi[2] ˏfán ˓ts‘an ˏwóng, ‘fung ˏngan í[2] ˓ts‘ín ‘léung,

---

*sát hak* seems to mean literally the *inner military chieftains;* the word is sometimes written *dsassak* or *dzassak*. According to Timkowski, "a dzassak is the hereditary chief of a *kouchoun* or division, generally composed of two thousand families." These divisions are not always equally numerous. Sometimes the term seems to be used in a more general sense, denoting not the chiefs merely, but the whole divisions over which they exercise their authority.

3. The salaries and whatever appertains to the emoluments of the several grades of officers in Inner Mongolia are regulated by this department: literally *wóng úi* is a royal assembly, or a meeting of kings. These high personages, who pay court to the emperor their master, do it in regular succession, and for this purpose they are divided into several divisions or courses, one of which repairs to Peking annually. Their retinue and guards are specified and fixed by statute, under the cognizance and direction of the several officers of this department.

sand taels in money and twenty-five pieces of silk; (*b*) their noble kings receive one thousand and two hundred taels in money, and fifteen pieces of silk; (*c*) their honorable knights receive eight hundred taels in money and thirteen pieces of silk; (*d*) the honorable princes receive each five hundred taels in money and ten pieces of silk; (*e*) the state protector dukes receive each three hundred taels in money and nine pieces of silk; (*f*) the state supporter dukes receive two hundred taels and seven pieces of silk; and (*g*) the secondary and last of these titular nobles receive each one hundred taels in money, and four pieces of silk.

兩俸緞二十五
疋郡王俸銀一
千二百兩俸緞
十五疋貝勒俸
銀八百兩俸緞
十三疋貝子俸
銀五百兩俸緞
十疋鎮國公俸
銀三百兩俸緞
九疋輔國公俸
銀二百兩俸緞
七疋扎薩克台
吉塔布囊俸銀
一百兩俸緞四
疋

'fung tün² í² shap₂ ₛ'ng pat,; kwan² ₛwóng, 'fung ₛngan yat, ₜts'ín í² pák, 'léung, 'fung tün² shap, ₛ'ng pat,; púi² lak₂, 'fung ₛngan pát, pák, 'léung, 'fung tün² shap₂ ₜsám pat,; púi² 'tsz', 'fung ₛngan ₛ'ng pák, 'léung, 'fung tün² shap₂ pat,; chan² kwók, ₜkung, 'fung ₛngan ₜsám pák, 'léung, 'fung tün² 'kau pat,; fú² kwók, ₜkung, 'fung ₛngan í² pák, 'léung, 'fung tün² ts'at, pat,; chát, sát, hak, ₛtoi kat, táp, pò² ₛnóng 'fung ₛngan yat, pák, 'léung, 'fung tün² sz'' pat,.

5. The officers in the department for what is connected with the established ordinances, are two secretaries, a Mantchou and a Mongolian; two Mantchou and six Mongolian, under-secretaries; with two, a Mantchou and a Mongolian, directors: these have to examine and regulate the affairs of the tribes and soldiers of the outer chieftains, and to control their posts and relays: and also with regard to fairs and markets they pro-

典屬清吏司郎
中滿洲一人蒙
古一人員外郎
滿洲二人蒙古
六人主事滿洲
一人蒙古一人
掌轄外扎薩克
部旗之事治其

'Tín shuk₂ ₜts'ing lí² ₜsz', ₛlóng ₜchung, 'Mún ₜchau yat, ₛyan, ₛMung 'kú yat, ₛyan; ₜün ngoi² ₛlóng, 'Mún ₜchau í² ₛyan, ₛMung 'kú luk₂ ₛyan; 'chü sz'² 'Mún ₜchau yat, ₛyan, ₛMung 'kú yat, ₛyan: 'chéung hat₂ ngoi² chát, sát, hak, pò² ₛk'í ₜchí sz'², chí²

5. The meaning of *tín shuk* here seems be *what belongs to governmental affairs*, referring to the general government of the country. This department exercises the same, or nearly the same control over the *Outer* Mongolian tribes, as the first one (the *K'ítsik sz'*) does over the Inner tribes. Merchants going to its territories must be provided with licenses from the foreign office. Officers connected with this department have the oversight and regulation of the commercial intercourse carried on between Russia and China at Kiachta. The officers of this department have to fix the limits to the territories of the several tribes, supervise their governments, regulate their rank and succession, arrange their people into corps or divisions, superintend their ways of communication, and regulate all their intercourse. The order of succession among the lamas is regulated by the 'son of heaven' through the functionaries of this office.

mulge the regulations: whatever appertains to the lamas both far and near, the whole they regulate, as they do also all the nomads who are within or belong to their territories.

郵驛互市則頒其禁令凡內外之喇嘛皆掌之掌遊牧之內屬者

꜁k'í ꜁yau yik꜀: ú$^{2}$ 'shí tsak꜀ ꜀pán ꜁k'í kam' ling$^{2}$; ꜁fán noi$^{2}$ ngoi$^{2}$ ꜀chí ꜀lá ꜁má ꜀kái 'chéung ꜀chí, 'chéung ꜁yau muk꜀ ꜀chí noi$^{2}$ shuk꜀ 'ché.

6. The officers in the department for the mild treatment of those from afar are, one secretary, a member of the imperial house, with two Mantchou, and five Mongolian under-secretaries, and one Mongolian director: these have the regulation of whatever appertains to the emoluments, visits to court, tribute, &c., among the Outer Mongolian lamas.

柔遠清吏司郎中宗室一人員外郎滿洲二人蒙古五人主事蒙古一人掌外扎薩克喇嘛祿廩朝貢之事

꜁Yau 'ün ꜀ts'ing lí$^{2}$ ꜀sz', ꜁lóng ꜀chung ꜀tsung shat꜀ yat꜀ ꜁yan, ꜁ün ngoi$^{2}$ ꜁lóng, 'Mún ꜀chau í$^{2}$ ꜁yan, ꜁Mung 'kú 'ng ꜁yan, 'chü sz'$^{2}$ ꜁Mung 'kú yat꜀ ꜁yan: 'chéung ngoi$^{2}$ chát꜀ sát꜀ hak꜀ ꜀lá ꜁má luk꜀ 'lam ꜁ch'iú kung' ꜀chí sz'$^{2}$.

7. The officers in the department for those drawn from afar are, one Mongolian secretary, two Mantchou and three Mongolian under-secretaries, with two Mongolian directors: these have the government and direction of the begs and chiefs of the Mohammedan tribes among the Mongolians: whatever appertains to the annual visits of the Mohammedans is regulated by them: they also regulate their visits and their tribute paid to court.

徠遠清吏司郎中蒙古一人員外郎滿洲二人蒙古三人主事蒙古二人掌回部扎薩克伯克之政令凡回番之年班皆掌之掌外裔之朝貢

꜁Loi 'ün ꜀ts'ing lí$^{2}$ ꜀sz', ꜁lóng ꜀chung, ꜁Mung 'kú yat꜀ ꜁yan; ꜁ün ngoi$^{2}$ ꜁lóng, 'Mún ꜀chau í$^{2}$ ꜁yan, ꜁Mung 'kú ꜀sám ꜁yan; 'chü sz'$^{2}$, ꜁Mung 'kú í$^{2}$ ꜁yan: 'chéung ꜁Ui pò$^{2}$ chát꜀ sát꜀ hak꜀, pák꜀ hak꜀, ꜀chí ching' ling$^{2}$, ꜁fán ꜁Ui ꜀fán ꜀chí ꜁nín ꜀pán ꜀kái 'chéung ꜀chí, 'chéung ngoi$^{2}$ yui$^{2}$ ꜀chí ꜁ch'iú kung$^{2}$.

8. The officers in the department for penal discipline are, two Mongolian secretaries, two Mantchou, and four

理刑清吏司郎中蒙古二人員

'Lí ꜁ying ꜀ts'ing lí$^{2}$ ꜀sz', ꜁long ꜀chung, ꜁Mung 'kú í$^{2}$ ꜁yan;

6. The literal meaning of the title of this department is the *mild distant pure officers department;* i. e. the department whose pure functionaries extend the imperial kindness and favor to those who dwell far remote from the court. The king, his imperial majesty's liege servant, called *khán*; his annual emoluments are, from the emperor annually, 2500 taels of silver, with 40 pieces of silk; the gifts to be conferred on the khán's officers are also specified, so likewise are the articles and the amount of tribute; the periods for their visits to Peking are also fixed. The *lamas*, here and elsewhere mentioned, form no small nor uninfluential class; they take rank among the chiefs and princes of the state.

7. This is literally, come or *drawn remote pure officers department;* and besides the Mohammedan princes or *kháns*, and the *pák hak* or begs, it controls in a measure the Kassaks and Turkomans on the remote frontiers of the Chinese empire. See Chinese Repository, Vol. IV., page 148.

| | | |
|---|---|---|
| Mongolian under-secretaries, with one Mongolian director: these have the direction and control of whatever appertains to penal discipline among the several tribes of these remote foreigners. | 外郎滿洲二人<br>蒙古四八主事<br>蒙古一人掌外<br>藩各部刑罰之<br>事 | ˌün ngoiˀ ˌlóng, ˈMún ˌchau í ˌyan, ˌMung ˈkú szˀ ˌyan; ˈchü szˀ, ˌMung ˈkú yat, ˌyan: ˈchéung ngoiˀ ˌfán kók, pòˀ ˌying fát, ˌchí szˀ. |

8. *Regulate punishment pure officers department;* the ordinary and most common punishments awarded by this department are fines, which are estimated and paid in cattle and horses.

## Section Eighth.

## OFFICIAL TITLES.

### 職分類第八章
Chik, fan² lui²; tai² pát, ˌchéung.

| | | |
|---|---|---|
| 1. Governor; *lit.* ruling tribunal, or H. E. the governor. | 制臺 | Chaiˀ ˌtʻoi. |
| 2. Commissioner or master of the police. | 制置使 | Chaiˀ chíˀ szˀ.* |
| 3. Police-runners. | 差役 | ˌChái yik,. |
| 4. Protector, protectorate, or protectorship. | 鎮 鎮臺 鎮守 | Chanˀ. Chanˀ ˌtʻoi. Chanˀ ˈshau. |
| 5. The protector's subalterns, or staff. | 鎮標 | Chanˀ ˌpíú. |
| 6. Major-general of the protectorate. | 鎮守揔兵 | Chanˀ ˈshau ˈtsung ˌping. |
| 7. Keeper of the palace, or master of the palace. | 執金吾 | Chap, ˌkam ˌ'ng.* |
| 8. Canal commissioners and keepers of passes. | 閘官 | Cháp, ˌkún. |
| 9. Shepherd of a department, i. e. its chief magistrate. | 州牧 | ˌChau muk,. |
| 10. An assistant magistrate of a department or district. | 州同 | ˌChau ˌtʻung. |
| 11. A subordinate magistrate of a district. | 州判 | ˌChau púnˀ. |

## *Notes and Explanations.*

UNDER the head of *chik fan* are arranged the titles of the functionaries of the government, both civil and military. The order of arrangement here adopted is the alphabetical, according to the Chinese pronunciation in the provincial dialect. The list is intended to include the titles of all the principal officers, of ancient and modern times; those not now in use are marked with an asterisk. In addition to the titles, the names of several offices, schools, &c., are enumerated.

8. There are many of these inferior officers; and they are stationed at the locks on canals, at the passes through the country, at gateways, &c.

| | | |
|---|---|---|
| 12. Chief secretary of state, or prime-minister. | 掌書記 | ‘Chéung ‹shü kí’.* |
| 13. Master of the privy council. | 知樞密院 | ‹Chí ‹sh‘ü mat, ün$^2$.* |
| 14. Examiner of literary graduates. | 知貢舉 | ‹Chí kung’ kü’.* |
| 15. Prefect (chief civil officer) of a department. | 知府 | ‹Chí ‘fú. |
| 16. Prefect of a minor department. | 知州 | ‹Chí ‹chau. |
| 17. Magistrate (chief civil officer) of a district. | 知縣 | ‹Chí ün$^2$. |
| 18. Master attendant, or under-secretary. | 知事 | ‹Chí sz’$^2$. |
| 19. Sub-agent, or assistant manager. | 支使 | ‹Chí sz”.* |
| 20. Keeper of records, or a clerk in the interior. | 治中 | Chí$^2$ ‹chung.* |
| 21. Chief secretary, and censor in waiting. | 治書侍御史 | Chí$^2$ ‹shü shí$^2$ ü$^2$ ‘sz’.* |
| 22. Commissioner in the grain department. | 治粟內史 | Chí$^2$ suk› noi$^2$ ‘sz’.* |
| 23. Supervisor in the Office of Supervisors. | 詹事府詹事 | ‹Chím sz’$^2$ ‘fú ‹chím sz’$^2$. |
| 24. Subordinate supervisor in the same. | 詹事府少詹事 | ‹Chím sz’$^2$ ‘fú shíú’ ‹chím sz’$^2$. |
| 25. Keeper of records in the same. | 丨事府主簿 | ‹Chím sz’$^2$ ‘fú ‘chü pò’. |
| 26. Recorder or clerk in the same. | 詹事府錄事 | ‹Chím sz’$^2$ ‘fú luk, sz’$^2$. |
| 27. Chief or principal (in an office or department). | 正堂 | Ching’ ‹tóng. |
| 28. Honorary nobles. | 徹侯 | Chít› ‹hau.* |
| 29. School for polite literature. | 昭文館 | ‹Chíú ‹man kún’.* |
| 30. Commissioner for suppressing rebellion. | 招討使 | ‹Chíú ‘tò sz”.* |
| 31. Courtier's sons and grandsons. | 朝官子孫 | ‹Ch‘íú ‹kún ‘tsz’ ‹sün*. |
| 32. Court nobles, or courtiers. | 朝侯 | ‹Ch‘íú ‹hau.* |
| 33. Keeper of the seals, *lit.* elucidator and examiner. | 照磨 | Chíú’ ‹mó. |
| 34. Under-secretary. | 照廳 | Chíú’ ‹ting. |
| 35. Chief of the literati. | 狀元 | Chóng$^2$ ‹yün. |
| 36. General and chief presidents. | 諸曹尚書 | ‹Chü ‹ts‘ò shéung$^2$ ‹shü.* |
| 37. General and chief vice-presidents. | 諸曹郎官 | ‹Chü ‹ts‘ò ‹lóng ‹kún.* |

18. The *chisz’*, *chíúmó*, *kinglik*, *kingching* and *chíúting*, are nearly of the same grade, all of them being of the lowest rank.

35. The first on the list of graduates of the three highest literary ranks is called *yün*; the *chóng yün* is the highest, or the first on the list of the Hanlin, a rank acquired only after a long course of study, and consequently highly honorable.

| | | |
|---|---|---|
| 38. General and chief military inspector. | 諸曹參軍 | ‹Chü ¸ts'ò ‹tsám ‹kwan.* |
| 39. General overseer of the herds. | 諸牧監 | ‹Chü muk› ‹kám.* |
| 40. Nobles, chiefs, princes, or marquises. | 諸侯 | ‹Chü ¸hau.* |
| 41. Director, agent, or manager. | 主事 | ‘Chü sz’². |
| 42. Chief examiner (at the provincial examinations). | 主考 | ‘Chü ‘háu. |
| 43. Chief or principal secretary. | 主書 | ‘Chü ‹shü. |
| 44. Keeper of records. | 主簿 | ‘Chü pò². |
| 45. Gentleman usher of the palace. | 主客郎中 | ‘Chü hák› ¸lóng ‹chung.* |
| 46. Chief secretary in the military department. | 主管機宜文字 | ‘Chü ‘kún ‹kí ¸í ¸man tsz’².* |
| 47. Gentleman annalist, or composer of history. | 著作郎 | Chü’ tsók› ‹lóng.* |
| 48. Commissionor for transports. | 轉運使 | ‘Chün wan² sz’. |
| 49. Great assistant, or prime minister. | 冢相 | ‘Chung séung’. |
| 50. Great ruler, or prime minister. | 冢宰 | ‘Chung ‘tsoi. |
| 51. Assistant of the inner court. | 中相 | ‹Chung séung’. |
| 52. Inner director. | 中正 | ‹Chung ching’. |
| 53. Inner secretary. | 中書 | ‹Chung ‹shü. |
| 54. Inner governor, i. e. *shéung shü*, or president. | 中臺 | ‹Chung ¸t'oi.* |
| 55. Inner assistant. | 中丞 | ‹Chung ¸shing. |
| 56. Guardian of the prince's manners. | 中允 | ‹Chung ‘wan.* |
| 57. Minister of state, *lit.* inner supporter. | 中當 | ‹Chung ¸tóng. |
| 58. A military secretary. | 中軍 | ‹Chung ‹kwan. |
| 69. Aid-de-camp. | 中協 | ‹Chung híp›. |
| 60. Inner gentleman usher and general. | 中郎將 | ‹Chung ¸lóng tséung’.* |
| 61. Keepers of H. I. M.'s papers. | 中書科 | ‹Chung ¸shü ‘fó. |
| 62. Inner secretary and director. | 中書令 | ‹Chung ¸shü ling².* |
| 63. Inner secretary and overseer. | 中書監 | ‹Chung ¸shü kám’.* |

40. Of these *chü hau* there were several in the time of the Hón dynasty; they were feudal chiefs, at the head of departments or little principalities into which the empire was divided.

42. At the triennial examinations in the provincial capitals, two individuals, from among the members of the Imperial Academy, are appointed to preside, a principal or *chü háu*, and a secondary or *fú háu*, also called *fú chü háu*.

| | | |
|---|---|---|
| 64. Inner secretary, overseer and director. | 中書監令 | ꜀Chung ꜀shü kám' ling$^2$.* |
| 65. Inner secretary of secondary rank, i. e. clerk. | 中書舍人 | ꜀Chung ꜀shü shé' ꜁yan.* |
| 66. Imperial body-guard, wearing peacock's feathers. | 花翎侍衛 | ꜀Fá ꜁ling shí$^2$ wai$^2$. |
| 67. District instructor. | 訓導　教諭 | Fan' tò$^2$. Káu' yü$^2$. |
| 68. Translators. | 分掌繙繹 | ꜀Fan 'chéung ꜀fán yik$_2$. |
| 69. Lieutenant (in the army). | 分府　分守 | ꜀Fan 'fú. ꜀Fan 'shau. |
| 70. Provincial treasurer, or commissioner of finance. | 藩臺 | ꜁Fán ꜁t'oi. |
| 71. Commissioner for defense of the state. | 防禦使 | ꜁Fóng yü$^2$ sz'.* |
| 72. Lieutenant-governor, or controling officer. | 撫院　撫臺 | 'Fú yün$^2$. 'Fú ꜁t'oi. |
| 73. Lieutenant-governor's staff or subalterns. | 撫標 | 'Fú ꜀píú. |
| 74. Lieutenant-governor's civil aid-de-camp. | 撫院文巡捕 | 'Fú yün$^2$ ꜁man ꜁tsun pò$^2$. |
| 75. Lieutenant-governor's military aid-de-camp. | 院撫武巡捕 | 'Fú yün$^2$ 'mò ꜁tsun pò$^2$. |
| 76. Veteran general and gentleman usher. | 虎賁中郎將 | 'Fú ꜀pan ꜀chung ꜀lóng tséung'.* |
| 77. Lieutenant-general. | 副都統 | Fú' ꜀tò 't'ung. |
| 78. Deputy (or assistant) censor. | 副都御史 | Fú' ꜀tò yü$^2$ 'sz'. |
| 79. Second examiner of literary candidates. | 副主考 | Fú' 'chü 'háu. |
| 80. Second commissioner. | 副使 | Fú' sz'. |
| 81. Colonel, or commander of a regiment. | 副將 | Fú' tséung'. |
| 82. Secondary leader, or field-martial. | 副元帥 | Fú' ꜁yün shui'. |
| 83. Treasury department, or board of exchequer. | 庫部 | Fú' pò$^2$. |
| 84. Chief keeper of the treasury. | 庫大使 | Fú' tái$^2$ sz'. |
| 85. Keeper of the imperial signets (or seals). | 符寶郎符節令 | ꜁Fú 'pò ꜁lóng. ꜁Fú tsít, ling$^2$.* |
| 86. Assistant leader of the horse guards. | 附馬都尉 | Fú$^2$ 'má ꜀tò wai'.* |
| 87. Supporter general, (*lit.* support country lead army). | 輔國將軍 | Fú$^2$ kwók, ꜀tséung ꜀kwan. |
| 88. Provincial commissioners of finance. | 行臺省 | ꜁Hang ꜁t'oi 'sing.* |
| 89. Traveling censors, or board of circuit censors. | 行御史臺 | ꜁Hang yü$^2$ 'sz' ꜁t'oi.* |

67. The *fan tò*, 'admonitor and guide,' is the chief literary officer in a *yün* or district; he is usually a literary graduate, and always paid by the government. In each district, the government has a high-school or academy, over which he presides.

73. The *fú píú* includes the whole of the military officers and soldiers, under the control of the lieutenant-governor.

| | | |
|---|---|---|
| 90. General leader of the cavalry. | 行軍司馬 | ˏHang ˏkwan ˏsz' 'má.* |
| 91. Inspector-general, (*lit.* walk army teach give). | 行軍教授 | ˏHang ˏkwan káu' shau'.* |
| 92. Master-controler of the army. | 行軍校尉 | ˏHang ˏkwan káu' wai'.* |
| 93. Marquis, (*lit.* marquis nobility, or rank of marquis). | 候爵 | ˏHau tséukˌ. |
| 94. Examiner of merits and gentleman-usher. | 考功郎中 | 'Hau ˏkung ˏlóng ˏchung.* |
| 95. Gentleman of distinction; (*lit.* dutiful and pure). | 孝廉 | Hau' ˏlím.* |
| 96. Recorder of H. I. M.'s words and actions. | 起居注 | 'Hí ˏkü chü'. |
| 97. Sub-recorders of the same. | 起居舍人 | 'Hí ˏkü shé' ˏyan. |
| 98. Colonel of a regiment. | 協鎭協臺協守 | Hípˌ chan'. Hípˌ ˏt'oi. Hípˌ 'shau. |
| 99. Joint adjutant high chancellor of state. | 協辦大學士 | Hípˌ pán² tái² hókˌ sz'². |
| 100. Governor general of rivers and canals. | 河道揔督 | ˏHó tò² 'tsung tukˌ. |
| 101. Staff of the governor of the rivers. | 河標 | ˏHó ˏpíú. |
| 102. Overseer of the boats on the river at Canton. | 河泊所 | ˏHó pókˌ 'shó. |
| 103. Magistrate of the dwellers on the river. | 河政廳 | ˏHó ching' ˏt'ing. |
| 104. Commissioner of maratime customs. | 海關 | 'Hoi ˏkwán. |
| 105. Chancellor of state, or chief minister of state. | 學士 | Hókˌ sz'². |
| 106. Literary chancellor, or director of learning. | 學院學臺學政 | Hókˌ yün². Hókˌ ˏt'oi. Hókˌ ching'. |
| 107. The Imperial Academy, (*lit.* pencil forest court). | 翰林院 | Hón² ˏlam yün². |
| 108. Chancellors and directors of the members of the Imperial Academy. | 翰林院掌院學士 | Hón² ˏlam yün² 'chéung yün² hókˌ sz'². |
| 109. Chancellors, receivers of the emperor's pleasure, and members of the Imperial Academy. | 翰林院學士承旨 | Hón² ˏlam yün² hókˌ sz'² ˏshing 'chí. |
| 110. Chancellors, readers to his majesty, and members of the Imperial Academy. | 翰林院侍讀學士 | Hón² ˏlam yün² shí² tukˌ hókˌ sz'². |

96. These recorders accompany the emperor when he goes abroad, or appears in public, and it is their duty to record all his words.

102, 103. These are interior officers; one is stationed in the vicinity of Canton, (where are a large number of people constantly living on the water,) and the others (two or three only) are in the eastern provinces.

107. This academy is the emperor's principal laboratory for state papers. Official documents and all national literary works, are prepared for publication either by, or under the direction of, the members of this institute. There are several subordinate branches of the institution, with their appropriate officers.

廣東方言讀本

| | | |
|---|---|---|
| 111. Chancellors, lecturers to his majesty, and members of the Imperial Academy. | 翰林院侍講學士 | Hón$^2$ ꜁lam yün$^2$ shí$^2$ ‘kóng hók$_2$ sz'$^2$. |
| 112. President of the Court of Ceremonies. | 鴻臚寺卿 | ꜁Hung ꜁lò tsz'$^2$ ꜀hing. |
| 113. Vice-president of the Court of Ceremonies. | 鴻臚寺少卿 | ꜁Hung ꜁lò tsz'$^2$ shíú' ꜀hing. |
| 114. Department for the transport of salt. | 鹽運司 | ꜁Ím wan$^2$ ꜀sz'. |
| 115. Commissioner for the transport of salt. | 鹽運使 | ꜁Ím wan$^2$ sz'$^3$. |
| 116. Servant-archers and reporters to H. I. M. | 謁者僕射 | Ít$_3$ ‘ché puk$_2$ yik$_2$. |
| 117. Commissioner of justice. | 臬司　臬臺 | Ít$_2$ ꜀sz'. Ít$_2$ ꜁t‘oi. |
| 118. Board for the imperial carriages. | 駕部 | Ká' pò$^2$.* |
| 119. Superintendent of the papers of the court. | 架閣 | Ká' kók$_3$.* |
| 120. Domestics, or official servants of the hoppo. | 家人 | ꜀Ká ꜁yan. |
| 121. Chief of the second rank of literati, or of A. M. | 解元 | Kái' ꜁ün. |
| 122. Office for care of the highways. | 街道衙門 | ꜀Kái tò$^2$ ꜁ngá ꜁mún. |
| 123. Board of exchequer, or treasury department. | 金部 | ꜀Kam pò$^2$.* |
| 124. His imperial majesty's body-guard. | 錦衣衛 | ‘Kam ꜀í wai$^2$.* |
| 125. Military inspector, (*lit.* inspect army). | 監軍 | ꜀Kám ꜀kwan.* |
| 126. President of a college, or collegiate inspector. | 監院 | ꜀Kám yün$^2$. |
| 127. Porter, or keeper of the palace gate. | 監門 | ꜀Kám ꜁mún. |
| 128. Commissioner for inspecting the army. | 監軍使 | ꜀Kám ꜀kwan sz'$^3$.* |
| 129. Inspector and examining censor. | 監察御史 | ꜀Kám chát$_3$ yü$^2$ ‘sz'.* |
| 130. Under-graduate, or a graduate of the lowest rank. | 監生 | Kám' ꜀shang. |
| 131. His excellency, the imperial councellor. | 諫議大夫 | Kán' ꜁í tái$^2$ ꜀fú.* |
| 132. Messengers to his imperial majesty. | 給事中 | K‘ap$_3$ sz'$^2$ ꜀chung. |
| 133. Literary officers, (*lit.* magistrates of instruction). | 教官 | Káu' kún'. |
| 134. Teacher of a department (*lit.* instruction giver). | 教授 | Káu' shau$^2$. |
| 135. Master-controller, (*lit.* compare-tranquilize). | 校尉 | Káu' wai'. |
| 136. Ministers of state, (*lit.* spring balances). | 機衡 | ꜀Kí ꜁hang.* |

115. The commissioner for the transportation of salt is at the head of the gabel department, or *ím wan sz'*, and takes rank with the two commissioners, the *pò ching sz'*, and the *ón chát sz'*; he has numerous assistants, clerks, &c., under him.

| | | |
|---|---|---|
| 137. General controller of the cavalry. | 騎都尉 | ꜁Kí ꜀tò wai꜄. |
| 138. Prefect's secretary, (*lit.* arranger and controler). | 檢校 | ꜂Kím káu꜅. |
| 139. Professor of belles-lettres, (*lit.* classic lore officers). | 經筵官 | ꜀King ꜁ín ꜀kún. |
| 140. Erudite professor of polite literature. | 經筵博士 | ꜀King ꜁ín pók꜆ sz꜅. |
| 141. Chief general of military operations. | 經畧大將軍 | ꜀King léuk꜇ tái꜅ ꜀tséung ꜀kwan. |
| 142. Commissioner for military operations. | 經畧使 | ꜀King léuk꜇ sz꜅. |
| 143. Clerk, or under-secretary. | 經歷 經廳 | ꜀King lik꜇. ꜀King ꜀t'ing. |
| 144. Metropolitan officers, or magistracy of the capital. | 京尹 京兆尹 | ꜀King ꜂wan. ꜀King ch'iú꜅ ꜂wan. |
| 145. Commissioner for admonishing other officers. | 警巡院使 | ꜂King ꜁tsun yün꜅ sz꜅.* |
| 146. Under-secretary, or copyist. | 稿公 | ꜂Kò ꜀kung. |
| 147. Chancellor of the Inner Council. | 閣學士 | Kók꜆ hók꜇ sz꜅. |
| 148. A graduate of the second degree, or A. M. | 舉人 | ꜁Kü ꜁yan. |
| 149. General of the armed chariots and light-horse. | 車騎將軍 | ꜀Kü ꜁kí ꜀tséung ꜀kwan.* |
| 150. Commissioner for observation and inspection. | 觀察使 | ꜀Kún chát꜆ sz꜅.* |
| 151. Officers: civil officers; and military officers. | 官府文官武官 | ꜀Kún ꜂fú: ꜁man ꜀kún; ꜂mò ꜀kún. |
| 152. Duke; marquis; earl; viscount; and baron. | 公 侯 伯 子 男 | ꜀Kung; ꜁hau; pák꜆; ꜂tsz; ꜁nám.* |
| 153. Officer for recording merits and demerits. | 功曹叅軍 | ꜀Kung ꜁ts'ò ꜀ts'ám ꜀kwan. |
| 154. Great ministers of state. | 軍機大臣 | ꜀Kwan ꜀kí tái꜅ ꜁shan. |
| 155. Military teacher, or a fencing-master. | 軍中教習 | ꜀Kwan ꜀chung káu꜄ tsáp꜇. |
| 156. Inspector of military implements. | 軍器監 | ꜀Kwan hí꜄ ꜀kám. |
| 157. Sub-prefect. | 軍民府 | ꜀Kwan ꜁man ꜂fú. |
| 158. Military leader. | 軍師 | ꜀Kwan ꜀sz'. |
| 159. Military subalterns. | 軍標 | ꜀Kwan ꜀píú. |
| 160. Controller, a controller of a district or department. | 郡尉 | Kwan꜅ wai꜄. |
| 161. Local magistrates; officers of a district. | 郡官 | Kwan꜅ ꜀kún. |

152. These *titles of nobility* are of ancient date, and are explained as indicative of certain qualities in those to whom they were given: *kung* had regard to *public* good; *hau*, expelled for their virtues, *waited* for better times; *pák* were *bright-men* of distinguished intelligence: *tsz* were capable of *training* others; and *nám* were those who were capable of *sustaining* important and responsible duties.

157. This officer exercises civil and military authority, having control over both soldiers and people; one bearing this title resides at Tsínshán or Caza Branca, near Macao.

| | | |
|---|---|---|
| 162. Magistrate of a district; local magistrate. | 郡丞　郡佐 | Kwan$^{2}$ ˏshing. Kwan$^{2}$ tsóʾ.* |
| 163. H. E. the chief superintendent of customs. | 貴監督 | Kwaiʾ ‹kám tuk›. |
| 164. Commissioner of customs. | 関部 | ‹Kwán pò$^{2}$. |
| 165. Principals of the national college. | 國子監祭酒 | Kwók› ʻtszʾ kámʾ ts$^{ʻ}$aiʾ ʻtsau. |
| 166. Professors of the national college. | 國子監司業 | Kwók› ʻtszʾ kámʾ ‹szʾ íp$_{2}$. |
| 167. Principal director of the Banqueting House. | 光祿寺卿 | ‹Kwóng luk$_{2}$ tszʾ$^{2}$ ‹hing. |
| 168. Vice-director of the Banqueting House. | 光祿寺少卿 | ‹Kwóng luk$_{2}$ tszʾ$^{2}$ shíúʾ ‹hing. |
| 169. Principal overseer of the Banqueting House. | 光祿寺署正 | ‹Kwóng luk$_{2}$ tszʾ$^{2}$ $^{s}$shü chingʾ. |
| 170. Secondary overseer in the Banqueting House. | 光祿寺署丞 | ‹Kwóng luk$_{2}$ tszʾ$^{2}$ $^{s}$shü ˏshing. |
| 171. Imperial body guard with blue peacock's feathers. | 藍翎侍衛 | ˏLám ˏling shí$^{2}$ wai$^{2}$. |
| 172. Commissary or collector of grain. | 糧道 | ˏLéung tò$^{2}$. |
| 173. Commissioners for the collection of grain. | 糧儲道 | ˏLéung ˏchü tò$^{2}$. |
| 174. Deputed officers, or official attendants. | 吏員 | Lí$^{2}$ ˏüin. |
| 175. Chief attendant, head officer, magistrate's secretary. | 吏目 | Lí$^{2}$ muk$_{2}$. |
| 176. Secretary to the commissioner of finance. | 理問 | ʻLí man$^{2}$. |
| 177. General and commander-in-chief. | 領軍將軍 | $^{s}$Lìng ‹kwan ‹tséung ‹kwan.* |
| 178. Gentleman usher (*lit.* pavilion centre). | 郎中 | ˏLóng ‹chung. |
| 179. Secretary in the army. | 錄事參軍 | Luk$_{2}$ szʾ$^{2}$ ‹ts$^{ʻ}$ám ‹kwan.* |
| 180. Officers in the field service, or military officers. | 陸路官 | Luk$_{2}$ lò$^{2}$ ‹kún. |
| 181. Keepers of seals, or sub-censors. | 六科 | Luk$_{2}$ ‹fó. |
| 182. Office of the imperial guards. | 鑾儀衛 | ˏLün ˏí wai$^{2}$. |
| 183. Chief commissioner of the imperial guards. | 鑾儀衛冠軍使 | ˏLün ˏí wai$^{2}$ kúnʾ ‹kwan szʾ. |
| 184. Law-professors, or the professors of jurisprudence. | 律學博士 | Lut$_{2}$ hók$_{2}$ pók› szʾ$^{2}$.* |

164. This is the officer who, by the foreigners in Canton, is called the *hoppo*; he is also called *hoi kwán* (No. 104); he is addressed by the title *kwai kám tuk* (163); a petition or written address to him is superscribed, *Yüt hoi kwán, kwán tuk tái yan, ón pan.*

165. The branches taught in this school are belles-lettres, the classics, mathematics, &c.; and attached to it are departments for the education of Russians, Lewchewans, &c. There is a long list of instructors, with their appropriate titles, professors, tutors, lecturers, &c.

167. Literally, *kwóng luk tsz'* means a temple of glory and emoluments; it is designed for feasting the meritorious, and banqueting the deserving; and its officers are charged with providing victims for the imperial sacrifices.

172, 173. The duties of these commissioners for collecting grain are in six of the provinces performed by the *ónchát sz'*.

| | | |
|---|---|---|
| 185. Directors of the horse, or of the horse department. | 馬司 | 'Má ,sz'.* |
| 186. Commissioner & commander-in-chief of the cavalry. | 馬軍都指麾使 | 'Má ,kwan ,tò 'chí ,fai sz".* |
| 187. Director of the military stores. | 武庫令 | 'Mò fú' ling$^{2}$.* |
| 188. General and military protector. | 武衛將軍 | 'Mò wai$^{2}$ ,tséung ,kwan.* |
| 189. Watchman at the palace gate. | 門下省 | ,Mún há$^{2}$ 'sing.* |
| 190. Chief officers of the five Boards. | 五部督郵 | ''Ng Pò$^{2}$ tuk, ,yau.* |
| 191. Inspectors of polite literature. | 藝文監 | Ngai$^{2}$ ,man ,kám.* |
| 192. Sub-sergeant, or corporal in the army. | 額外外委 | Ngák, ngoi$^{2}$ ngoi$^{2}$ 'wai. |
| 193. Sergeant. | 外委 | Ngoi$^{2}$ 'wai. |
| 194. Minister in the capital, or metropolitan officer. | 內史 | Noi$^{2}$ 'sz'.* |
| 195. Overseers of the imperial household. | 內寺省 | Noi$^{2}$ tsz'$^{2}$ 'sing.* |
| 196. Department for regulating H. I. M.'s household. | 內務府 | Noi$^{2}$ mò$^{2}$ 'fú. |
| 197. Commissioner for judicial trials, or judge. | 按察使 | Ón' chát, sz". |
| 198. Ensign in the army. | 把摠 | 'Pá 'tsung. |
| 199. Ministers of state (*lit.* bowing assistants). | 拜相 | Pái' séung'. |
| 200. Begs, or Mongolian and Mohammedan princes. | 伯克 | Pák, hak,. |
| 201. There are nine official ranks, subdivided into eighteen degrees, (9) principal, and (9) subordinate. | 品有九其級十<br>有八分正從 | 'Pan 'yau 'kau; ,k'í kap, shap, 'yau pát,; ,fan ching' tsung$^{2}$. |
| 202. Board of accountants, or financial department. | 比部 | 'Pí pò$^{2}$.* |
| 203. Keeper of national archives. | 秘書監秘書令 | Pí' ,shü kám'.* Pí' ,shü ling$^{2}$.* |
| 204. Under-secretary, or copyist. | 筆帖式 | Pat, típ, shik,. |
| 205. Chief minister of state. | 平章事 | ,P'ing ,chéung sz'$^{2}$.* |
| 206. Assistant commissary. | 兵備道 | ,Ping pí$^{2}$ tò$^{2}$. |
| 207. Aid-de-camp (*lit.* another carriage). | 别駕 | Pít, ká'.* |
| 208. General of the light-horse, or leader of the cavalry. | 驃騎將軍 | ,Píu ,k'í ,tséung ,kwan.* |

196. Literally *inner business house*, or department, the object of which is to control the government of a class of the imperial slaves or domestics in the palace. The department is filled with an indefinite number of 'great ministers,' under whose supervision and direction are placed all the financial, civil, ritual, military, penal, and operative, affairs of H. I. M.'s household.

201. Officers of the first rank, both principal and subordinate, are distinguished by a red precious stone ball on the top of their caps; the 2d wear a red coral; 3d, a blue precious stone: 4th, a dark blue or purple; 5th, a crystal; 6th, an opaque white or jade stone; 7th, 8th, and 9th,

| | | |
|---|---|---|
| 209. Supporter to H. I. M. (*lit.* supply deficiency). | 補闕 | ‘Pò hüt›.* |
| 210. Commissioner for regulating the civil government. | 布政司 | Pò’ ching’ ‹sz’. |
| 211. Constables, or village justices of the peace. | 捕廳 | Pò² ‹ting. |
| 212. Servant-archer, or ministers of state. | 僕射 | Puk₂ yik₂.* |
| 213. Four ministers directing official appointments. | 西曹主吏 | ‹Sai ‚ts‘ò ‘chü lí².* |
| 214. Assistant secretaries to the four ministers. | 西曹書佐 | ‹Sai ‚ts‘ò ‹shü tsó’.* |
| 215. Three minor dukes (guardians of the prince). | 三少 | ‹Sám shíú’. |
| 216. Three guardians (i. e. guardians of the prince). | 三省 | ‹Sám ‘sing.* |
| 217. Three dukes (guardians of the prince). | 三公 | ‹Sám ‹kung. |
| 218. Three commissioners, of justice, finance, and excise. | 三司 | ‹Sám ‹sz’. |
| 219. Imperial attendants on horseback. | 散騎常侍 | Sán’ ‚k‘í ‚shéung shí².* |
| 220. Principal and secondary keepers of seals attached to the monastery of the priests of Budha. | 僧錄司正印副印 | ‹Sang luk₂ ‹sz’ ching’ yan’ fú’ yan’. |
| 221. Right and left chief instructors attached to the monastery of the priests of Budha. | 僧錄司左右善世 | ‹Sang luk₂ ‹sz’ ‘tsó yau² shín² shai’. |
| 222. Teachers and commentators of the monastery. | 僧錄司闡教 | ‹Sang luk₂ ‹sz’ ‘chín káu’. |
| 223. Officiating priests in the monastery. | 僧錄司講經 | ‹Sang luk₂ ‹sz’ ‘kóng ‹king. |
| 224. Chief director of the inferior monasteries. | 僧綱司副都綱 | ‹Sang ‹kóng ‹sz’ fú’ ‹tò ‹kóng. |
| 225. Director of the inferior monasteries. | 僧綱司僧正 | ‹Sang ‹kóng ‹sz’ ‹sang ching’. |
| 226. Fellow of the inferior monasteries. | 僧綱司僧會 | ‹Sang ‹kóng ‹sz’ ‹sang úi². |
| 227. College of revisors, to prepare official documents. | 脩書院 | ‹Sau ‹shü ün².* |
| 228. Board for preparing official papers. | 脩文館脩文尋 | ‹Sau ‚man ‘kún.* ‹Sau ‚man ‚tsam.* |
| 229. First literary degree (equivalent to A. B.). | 秀才 | Sau’ ‚ts‘oi. |
| 230. Advisers (*lit.* embroidered clad straight pointers). | 繡衣直指 | Sau’ ‹í chik₂ ‘chí.* |
| 231. Ministers of state (*lit.* assistants of the state). | 相國 | Séung’ kwók›.* |
| 232. Admonitors (*lit.* supplying deficiency) to H. I. M. | 拾遺 | Shap₂ ‚wai.* |

worked gold. Officers who have not entered, or attained to, the nine ranks are designated the *mí yap lau.*

197, 210. These two officers, by way of eminence, are often called the two commissioners,—one is at the head of the judicial, and the other is at the head of the territorial and financial, department of the provincial government: they are two of the *sám sz’* (218).

| | | |
|---|---|---|
| 233. Prime-minister. | 首相 | ‘Shau séung’.* |
| 234. Captain. | 守備　守府 | ‘Shau pí$^{2}$. ‘Shau ‘fú. |
| 235. Overseers of H. I. M.'s medicine. | 尙藥 | Shéung$^{2}$ yéuk$_{2}$.* |
| 236. President, or the chief secretary (of state). | 尙書 | Shéung$^{2}$ ꜀shü. |
| 237. Chief president and principal secretary. | 尙書令　尙書臺 | Shéung$^{2}$ ꜀shü ling$^{2}$.* Shéung$^{2}$ ꜀shü ꜁t‘oi.* |
| 238. President and examiner. | 尙書省 | Shéung$^{2}$ ꜀shü ‘sing.* |
| 239. Gentleman president. | 尙書郎 | Shéung$^{2}$ ꜀shü ꜁lóng.* |
| 240. Presidents and first and second ministers of state. | 尙書左右丞 | Shéung$^{2}$ ꜀shü ‘tsó yau$^{2}$ ꜁shing.* |
| 241. Directing president and historiographer. | 尙書史令 | Shéung$^{2}$ ꜀shü ‘sz’ ling$^{2}$.* |
| 242. President and director (at court). | 尙書都事 | Shéung$^{2}$ ꜀shü ꜀tò sz’$^{2}$.* |
| 243. Overseers of the imperial wardrobe. | 尙衣監 | Shéung$^{2}$ ꜀í kám’.* |
| 244. Imperial chamberlain: gent. of the bedchamber. | 尙寢局 | Shéung$^{2}$ ‘ts‘am kuk$_{2}$.* |
| 245. Perpetual and privy councilor. | 常機密 | ꜁Shéung ꜀kí mat$_{2}$.* |
| 246. Vice-president, or under-secretary (of state). | 侍郎 | Shí$^{2}$ ꜁lóng. |
| 247. Servants of the emperor. | 侍中 | Shí$^{2}$ ꜀chung.* |
| 248. Readers to his imperial majesty. | 侍讀 | Shí$^{2}$ tuk$_{2}$. |
| 249. Lecturers to his imperial majesty. | 侍講 | Shí$^{2}$ ‘kóng. |
| 250. Imperial body guard. | 侍衛 | Shí$^{2}$ wai$^{2}$. |
| 251. Office for directing the servants of the emperor. | 侍中寺 | Shí$^{2}$ ꜀chung tsz’$^{2}$.* |
| 252. Censors in attendance on the emperor. | 侍御史 | Shí$^{2}$ yü$^{2}$ ‘sz’.* |
| 253. Commanders of the horse body guard. | 侍衛馬軍司 | Shí$^{2}$ wai$^{2}$ ‘má ꜀kwan ꜀sz’.* |
| 254. Commanders of the infantry body guard. | 侍衛步軍司 | Shí$^{2}$ wai$^{2}$ pò$^{2}$ ꜀kwan ꜀sz’.* |
| 255. Board superintending the emperor's table. | 膳部 | Shín$^{2}$ pò$^{2}$.* |
| 256. Minister of state (*lit.* helper and assistant). | 丞相 | ꜁Shing séung’. |
| 257. Gentleman and keeper of the seals. | 丞領符璽郎 | ꜁Shing ‘ling ꜁fú ‘sái ꜁lóng.* |
| 258. Department for promulging governmental dispatches. | 承宣布政司 | ꜁Shing ꜀sün pò$^{2}$ ching$^{2}$ ꜀sz’. |

236. The *shéung shü* are the high officers who stand at the head of several of the principal departments of state; one or more of them the emperor places over each of the six Boards. President and secretary seem to be the best terms yet proposed as equivalents for *shéung shü*.

246. ‘Waiting gentleman’ is a literal rendering of *shí lóng*, and is perhaps well enough expressed by the term vice-president or under-secretary.

| | | |
|---|---|---|
| 259. Master-controller of the city gates. | 城門校尉 | ꜁Shing ꜁mún káu’ wai’*. |
| 260. High priest in the temple of Confucius. | 聖廟啟事 | Shing’ míú$^{2}$ ‘kai sz’$^{2}$. |
| 261. Master of the band in the temple of Confucius. | 聖廟司樂 | Shing’ míú$^{2}$ ꜀sz’ ngók$_{2}$. |
| 262. Minor master, secondary guardian of the prince. | 少師 | Shíú’ ꜀sz’. |
| 263. Minor tutor, secondary guardian of the prince. | 少傅 | Shíú’ fú$^{2}$. |
| 264. Minor protector, secondary guardian of the prince. | 少保 | Shíú’ ‘pò. |
| 265. Vice president, or under-secretary. | 少常伯 | Shíú’ ꜁shéung pák$_{3}$.* |
| 266. Ministers of state (*lit.* pivot springs). | 樞機 | ꜀Sh‘ü ꜀kí.* |
| 267. Privy council (consisting of eunuchs). | 樞密院 | ꜀Sh‘ü mat$_{2}$ yün$^{2}$.* |
| 268. Commissioner of the privy council. | 樞密使 | ꜀Sh‘ü mat$_{2}$ ‘sz’.* |
| 269. Professor of general literature. | 書學博士 | ꜀Shü hók$_{2}$ pók$_{2}$ sz’$^{2}$.* |
| 270. Naval officers, or officers of the marine. | 水師官 | ‘Shui ꜀sz’ ꜀kún. |
| 271. Admiral, or naval commander-in-chief. | 水師提督 | ‘Shui ꜀sz’ ꜁t‘ai tuk$_{3}$. |
| 272. Commissioner for soothing the people. | 宣撫使 | ꜀Sün ‘fú sz’.* |
| 273. Commissioner for admonishing the people. | 宣諭使 | ꜀Sün ü$^{2}$ sz’.* |
| 274. Gentlemen and recommenders of persons for office. | 選舉郎 | ‘Sün ‘kü ꜁lóng.* |
| 275. Professor of mathematical sciences. | 算學博士 | Sün’ hók$_{2}$ pók$_{2}$ sz’$^{2}$.* |
| 276. Private secretaries to officers of government. | 師爺 | ꜀Sz’ ꜁yé. |
| 277. Superintendent of the manufactures of cloth. | 司服 | ꜀Sz’ fuk$_{2}$. |
| 278. Superintendent of the treasury. | 司庫 | ꜀Sz’ fú’. |
| 279. Jailors, or keepers of prisons. | 司獄 | ꜀Sz’ yuk$_{2}$. |
| 280. Superintendent of learning (*lit.* control multitude). | 司徒 | ꜀Sz’ ꜁tò.* |
| 281. Leader or controler of cavalry. | 司馬 | ꜀Sz’ ‘má.* |
| 282. Directors of work (to be done by those at leisure). | 司空 | ꜀Sz’ ꜀hung.* |
| 283. Superintendent of malefactors. | 司寇 | ꜀Sz’ kau’.* |

260. In the capital, each of the three prevailing religious sects has its own public institutions, enjoying the patronage of the government, and especially consecrated for the service of the emperor and his ministers. *Shing míú* is the temple of Confucius.

270, 271. The titles of the naval officers are the same as those of the land or field service; thus there is a *luk lò t‘ai tuk* a commander-in-chief of the field service, a generalissimo; and there is also a *shui sz’ t‘ai tuk* a commander-in-chief of the water service, an admiral. The chief naval officers ordinarily reside on shore.

| | | |
|---|---|---|
| 284. Professors, or professional masters. | 司業 | ‹Sz' íp,. |
| 285. Directors (of the receipt and dispatch of papers). | 司務 | ‹Sz' mò'. |
| 286. Board of Agriculture and Husbandry. | 司農司 | ‹Sz' ˛nung ‹sz'.* |
| 287. Ministers superintending agriculture. | 司農卿 | ‹Sz' ˛nung ˛hing.* |
| 288. Vice-president, under-secretary, or clerk. | 司郎中 | ‹Sz' ˛lóng ‹chung.* |
| 289. Vice-president directing investitures. | 司封郎中 | ‹Sz' ‹fung ˛lóng ‹chung.* |
| 290. Vice-president directing acknowledged favors. | 司勲郎中 | ‹Sz' ‹fán ˛lóng ‹chung.* |
| 291. Master-controller and inspector-general. | 司隸校尉 | ‹Sz' tai' káu' wai'.* |
| 292. Under-secretary and examiner of merits. | 司功書佐 | ‹Sz' ‹kung ‹shü tsó'.* |
| 293. Officers superintending the merits of others. | 司功參軍 | ‹Sz' ‹kung ‹ts'ám ‹kwan.* |
| 294. Officers superintending the grain department. | 司倉參軍 | ‹Sz' ‹ts'óng ‹ts'ám ‹kwan.* |
| 295. His excellency the director of the horse. | 司馬大夫 | ‹Sz' ˢmá tái' ‹fú.* |
| 296. His excellency the director of the army. | 司戎大夫 | ‹Sz' ˛yung tái' ‹fú.* |
| 297. His excellency the director of the chariots. | 司輿大夫 | ‹Sz' ˛yü tái' ‹fú.* |
| 298. His excellency the director of sacrifices. | 司禋大夫 | ‹Sz' ‹yan tái' ‹fú.*. |
| 299. His excellency the director of banquets. | 司烹大夫 | ‹Sz' ‹páng tái' ‹fú.* |
| 300. Vice-president of the Board of Office. | 司列少常伯 | ‹Sz' lít, shíú' ˛shéung pák,.* |
| 301. Vice-president of the Board of Revenue. | 丨元少常伯 | ‹Sz' ˛yün shíú' ˛shéung pák,.* |
| 302. Vice-president of the Board of Rites. | 丨禮少常伯 | ‹Sz' ˢlai shíú' ˛shéung pák,.* |
| 303. Vice-president of the Board of War. | 丨戎少常伯 | ‹Sz' ˛yung shíú' ˛shéung pák,.* |
| 304. Vice-president of the Board of Punishments. | 丨刑少常伯 | ‹Sz' ˛ying shíú' ˛shéung pák,.* |
| 305. Vice-president of the Board of Works. | 丨平少常伯 | ‹Sz' ˛p'ing shíú' ˛shéung pák,.* |
| 306. General and commander-in-chief. | 四征將軍 | Sz'' ‹ching ‹tséung ‹kwan.* |
| 307. General and commander-in-chief. | 四平將軍 | Sz'' ˛p'ing ‹tséung ‹kwan.* |
| 308. Four high ministers of state. | 四曹 | Sz'' ˛ts'ò.* |
| 309. Historiographers, or imperial annalists. | 史官 | ‘Sz' ‹kún. |

284. The word *ip* denotes an employment, manual or mental, followed for either amusement or to gain a livelihood: *hók íp* is a literary employment, the profession of letters: *sz' ip* is a phrase of wider import, applicable to the proficient in any of the useful or ornamental branches.

300—305. These terms *lít*, *yün*, *lai*, *yung*, *ying*, *p'ing*, were once used to designate the six Supreme Boards; other terms have, at various times, been employed for the same purpose.

廣東方言讀本



| | | |
|---|---|---|
| 310. Chief controller, or great tranquillizer. | 太尉 | T'ái' wai'.* |
| 311. Chief censor, or president of the historiographers. | 太史 | T'ái' 'sz'.* |
| 312. Prime minister of state. | 太宰 | T'ái' 'tsoi.* |
| 313. Chief guardian, or great protector. | 太守 | T'ái' 'shau.* |
| 314. Chief overseers, or principal directors (eunuchs). | 太監 | T'ái' kám'. |
| 315. Ministers and overseers of the excchequer. | 太府監太府卿 | T'ái' 'fú kám'.* T'ái' 'fú ,hing.* |
| 316. Director of the historiographers. | 太史令 | T'ái' 'sz' ling².* |
| 317. Director of the chief musicians. | 太樂令 | T'ái' ngók₂ ling².* |
| 318. The six guardians of the prince. | 太子六傅 | T'ái' 'tsz' luk₂ fú². |
| 319. Great master of the prince, i. e. his guardian. | 太子太師 | T'ái' 'tsz' t'ái' ,sz'. |
| 320. Great tutor to the prince, i. e. his guardian. | 太子〡傅 | T'ái' 'tsz' t'ái' fú². |
| 321. Great protector to the prince, i. e. his guardian. | 太子〡保 | T'ái' 'tsz' t'ái' 'pò. |
| 322. Junior master to the prince. | 太子少師 | T'ái' 'tsz' shíú' ,sz'. |
| 323. Junior tutor to the prince. | 太子少傅 | T'ái' 'tsz' shíú' fú². |
| 324. Junior protector to the prince. | 太子少保 | T'ái' 'tsz' shíú' 'pò. |
| 325. Groom to the prince or heir-apparent. | 太子洗馬 | T'ái' 'tsz' 'sai 'má.* |
| 326. Overseer of the prince's clepsydra. | 太子率使更 | T'ái' 'tsz' sut, 'sz' ,kang.* |
| 327. Directors of the prince's body guard. | 太子左右衛率 | T'ái' 'tsz' 'tsó yau' wai² sut,.* |
| 328. President of the office for regulating H. I. M.'s stud. | 太僕寺卿 | T'ái' puk₂ tsz'² ,hing. |
| 329. Book-keeper in the office of H. I. M.'s stud. | 太僕寺主簿 | T'ái' puk₂ tsz'² 'chü pò². |
| 330. Imperial servant and master of the herds. | 太僕牧師 | T'ái' puk₂ muk₂ ,sz'.* |
| 331. President of the Sacrificial Court. | 太常寺卿 | T'ái' ,shéung tsz'² ,hing. |
| 332. Assistant minister of the Sacrificial Court. | 太常寺少卿 | T'ái' ,shéung tsz'² shíú' ,hing. |
| 333. Principal director of the Great Medical College. | 太醫院院使 | T'ái' ,í yün² yün² 'sz'. |
| 334. Secretaries and principal ministers of state. | 太傅錄尙書事 | T'ái' fú² luk₂ shéung² ,shü sz'².* |
| 335. Great person, i. e. his honor, or his excellency. | 大夫　大人 | Tái² ,fú. Tái² ,yan. |

328. This office for regulating H. I. M.'s stud is charged with the rearing of horses, taking account of their increase and the training of them for service; it is under the direction of two principal and two secondary ministers, aided by many minor officers, and is in some degree subservient to the Board of War. This stud supplies horses for the imperial cavalry; and extensive lands beyond the Great Wall are occupied for pastures.

| | | |
|---|---|---|
| 336. High chancellor, great minister of state. | 大學士 | Tái$^{2}$ hók$_{2}$ sz'$^{2}$. |
| 337. Great prime minister of state. | 大冢宰 | Tái$^{2}$ 'chung 'tsoi.* |
| 338. Minister of the Board of Officers. | 大銓衡 | Tái$^{2}$ ˏtsün ˏhang. |
| 339. Great manager of official rank. | 大司列 | Tái$^{2}$ ‹sz' lít$_{2}$. |
| 340. Director of the Board of Office. | 大提衡 | Tái$^{2}$ ˏt'ai ˏhang. |
| 341. Great director of honors. | 大司績 | Tái$^{2}$ ‹sz' chik$_{3}$. |
| 342. Great director of investitures. | 大丨封 | Tái$^{2}$ ‹sz' ‹fung. |
| 343. Great director of imperial honors. | 大丨勳 | Tái$^{2}$ ‹sz' ‹fan. |
| 344. Great director of the host. | 大丨徒 | Tái$^{2}$ ‹sz' ˏtò. |
| 345. Great director of agriculture. | 大丨農 | Tái$^{2}$ ‹sz' ˏnung. |
| 346. Great director of the multitude (of the people). | 大丨元 | Tái$^{2}$ ‹sz' ˏyün. |
| 347. Great director of measures. | 大丨度 | Tái$^{2}$ ‹sz' tò$^{2}$. |
| 348. Great director of the granaries. | 大丨儲 | Tái$^{2}$ ‹sz' ˏchü. |
| 349. Great director of the stores. | 大丨庾 | Tái$^{2}$ ‹sz' ˏü. |
| 350. Great director of the exchequer. | 大丨金 | Tái$^{2}$ ‹sz' ‹kam. |
| 351. Great director of the mint. | 大丨圜 | Tái$^{2}$ ‹sz' ˏwán. |
| 352. Great director of the currency. | 大丨泉 | Tái$^{2}$ ‹sz' ˏtsün. |
| 353. Great regulator of ceremonies. | 大秩宗 | Tái$^{2}$ tít$_{2}$ ‹tsung. |
| 354. Great lord of the sacrifices. | 大主禋 | Tái$^{2}$ 'chü ‹yan. |
| 355. Great master of ceremonies. | 大典賓 | Tái$^{2}$ 'tin ‹pan. |
| 356. Minister of the Supreme Court of Judicature. | 大理寺卿 | Tái$^{2}$ ˏlí tsz'$^{2}$ ‹hing. |
| 357. Assistant minister of the Sup. Court of Judicature. | 大理寺少卿 | Tái$^{2}$ ˏlí tsz'$^{2}$ shíú' ‹hing. |
| 358. Examiners in the Supreme Court of Judicature. | 大理寺評事 | Tái$^{2}$ ˏlí tsz'$^{2}$ ˏping sz'$^{2}$. |
| 359. Commanders-in-chief, or major-generals. | 提督　提臺 | ˏT'ai tuk$_{3}$. ˏT'ai ˏt'oi. |
| 360. Staff (or subalterns) of the commander-in-chief. | 提標 | ˏT'ai ‹píú. |
| 361. A superintendent (regulator of the price) of grain. | 提舉 | ˏT'ai 'kü. |
| 362. Chief provincial director of education. | 提督學政 | ˏT'ai tuk$_{3}$ hók$_{2}$ ching'. |

356. Lit. *great justice temple*, i. e. the Temple of Supreme Justice. This was mentioned on page 580, in connection with the Board of Punishments. It is a high court of appeals, the duty of which is, by statute, "to adjust all criminal punishments in the empire."

| | | |
|---|---|---|
| 363. Overseer of the revenues arising from shipping. | 提舉市舶 | ‚T'ai ʻkü ʻshí pók$_{2}$.* |
| 364. Circuit commissioners of justice. | 提刑按察使 | ‚T'ai ‚ying ón' chát› sz'. |
| 365. Third of the highest rank, Hónlam (or LL. D.). | 探花 | T'ám' ‹fá. |
| 366. Sole dictator, monarch, or sovereign. | 單于 | ‹Tán ‹yü.* |
| 367. Commander-in-chief of national infantry and horse. | 天下兵馬元帥 | ‹T'ín há$^{2}$ ‹ping ʻmá ‚yün shui'.* |
| 368. Under-secretaries, or clerks. | 典籍 | ʻTín tsik$_{2}$.* |
| 369. Director of the police, or justice of the peace. | 典吏 | ʻTín lí$^{2}$. |
| 370. Director and keeper of the imperial signets. | 典瑞掌節 | ʻTín sui$^{2}$ ʻchéung tsít›.* |
| 371. Clerk to the secretary of a district. | 典郡書佐 | ʻTín kwan$^{2}$ ‹shü tsó'.* |
| 372. Chancellor of the imperial palace. | 殿學士 | Tín$^{2}$ hók$_{2}$ sz'$^{2}$. |
| 373. Censor attending on H. I. M. in the palace. | 殿中侍御史 | Tín$^{2}$ ‹chung shí$^{2}$ yü$^{2}$ ʻsz'.* |
| 374. Inspector general of the body-guard. | 殿前都檢點司 | Tín$^{2}$ ‚ts'ín ‹tò ʻkím ʻtím ‹sz'*. |
| 375. A general, commander-in-chief. | 都督 | ‹Tò tuk›. |
| 376. General, commander-in-chief (*lit.* all director). | 都統 | ‹Tò ʻt'ung. |
| 377. General soother. | 都尉 | ‹Tò ʻwai.* |
| 378. Major. | 都司都府都閫 | ‹Tò ‹sz'. ‹Tò ʻfú. ‹Tò ʻkw'an. |
| 379. Leader of the van guards. | 都指揮 | ‹Tò ʻchí ‹fai.* |
| 380. Keeper of the imperial pleasure grounds. | 都水使者 | ‹Tò ʻshui sz' ʻché. |
| 381. Left censor of the Board of Censors, or Censorate. | 都察院左都御史 | ‹Tò chát› yün$^{2}$ ʻtsó ‹tò yü$^{2}$ ʻsz'. |
| 382. Right censor of the Board of Censors, or Censorate. | 都察院右都御史 | ‹Tò chát› yün$^{2}$ yau$^{2}$ ‹tò yü$^{2}$ ʻsz'. |
| 383. An intendant of circuit. | 道臺　巡道 | Tò$^{2}$ ‚t'oi. ‚Ts'un tò$^{2}$. |
| 384. A chief priest in the school of the Rationalists. | 道錄司正一 | Tò$^{2}$ luk$_{2}$ ‹sz' ching' yat›. |

381. This Board of Censors, or Censorate, is one of the principal courts of the capital, intrusted with "the care of manners and customs, the investigation of all public offices within and without the capital, the discrimination between the good and the bad performance of the business thereof, and between the uprightness and depravity of the officers employed therein; taking the lead of the other censors, and uttering each his sentiments and reproofs, in order to cause officers to be diligent in attention to their daily duties, and render stable the government of the empire." On most state occasions, some of the members of this court attend by the side of the emperor, and are usually permitted to express to him their opinions openly. They usually take the lead in bringing new subjects for legislation before the emperor and his ministers.

| | | |
|---|---|---|
| 385. Professors attached to the school of the Rationalists. | 道錄司演法 | Tò' luk, ꜀sz' ʻhín fát,. |
| 386. Masters attached to the school of the Rationalists. | 道錄司至靈 | Tò' luk, ꜀sz' chí' ꜁ling. |
| 387. Superintendents, superintending the school. | 道紀司都紀 | Tò' ʻkí ꜀sz' ꜀tò ʻkí. |
| 388. Colonel. | 叅將 參府 | ꜀Ts'ám tséung'. ꜀Ts'ám ʻfú. |
| 389. A councillor, or an adviser. | 參謀 | ꜀Ts'ám ꜁mau.* |
| 390. An adviser in the national councils. | 參知政事 | ꜀Ts'ám ꜀chí ching' sz''.* |
| 391. Court of assembled worthies. | 集賢院 | Tsap, ꜁ín yün'.* |
| 392. Assembled worthies and chancellors of the palace. | 集賢殿學士 | Tsap, ꜁ín tín', hók, sz''.* |
| 393. General, leader of the army, a commandant. | 將軍 | ꜀Tséung ꜀kwan. |
| 394. Overseer of the imperial works. | 將作監 | ꜀Tséung tsók, kám'.* |
| 395. Lieutenant. | 千總 | ꜀Ts'ín ʻtsung. |
| 396. Leader of the van, or vanguards. | 前部先鋒 | ꜁Ts'ín pò' ꜀sín ꜀fung. |
| 397. Commanders-in-chief of the van, rear, left, and right. | 前後左右將軍 | ꜁Ts'ín, hau', ʻtsó, yau', ꜀tséung ꜀kwan.* |
| 398. Commissioners for preserving the imperial rule. | 節度使 | Tsít, tò' sz''.* |
| 399. Right and left admonitors to H. I. M. | 左右司諫 | ʻTsó yau' ꜀sz' kán'.* |
| 400. Ministers of state (*lit.* left right help assistants). | 左右丞相 | ʻTsó yau' ꜁shing séung'. |
| 401. Right and left pillars of state. | 左右柱國 | ʻTsó yau' ʻch'ü kwók,.* |
| 402. Right and left officers of the palace. | 左右內史 | ʻTsó yau' noi' ʻsz'.* |
| 403. Right and left attendants in the palace. | 左右春坊庶子 | ʻTsó yau' ꜀ch'un ꜀fong shü' ʻtsz'. |
| 404. Secondary right and left attendants in the palace. | 左右春坊中允 | ʻTsó yau' ꜀ch'un ꜀fong ꜀chung ʻwan. |
| 405. Right and left generals of the body-guards. | 左右衛將軍 | ʻTsó yau' wai' ꜀tséung ꜀kwan. |
| 406. Sub-magistrate, or under-magistrate. | 左堂 | ʻTsó ꜁t'ong. |
| 407. Minister of state (*lit.* ruling assistant). | 宰相 | ʻTsoi séung'. |
| 408. Corn department (*lit.* granary board). | 倉部 | ꜀Ts'ong pò'.* |
| 409. Director general of the imperial granaries. | 倉場總督 | ꜀Ts'ong ꜁ch'éung ʻtsung tuk,. |
| 410. Literary graduate of the third degree. | 進士 | Tsun' sz''. |

384, 387. The members of this institution, with those attached to the *sang luk sz'* (Nos. 222, 226), and to the *shing míú* (Nos. 260, 261), form the *sám káu* of the Chinese. The patronage which these three religious sects enjoy seems to be limited to the capital; and the respective officers, in those several religious houses, schools, and temples which are there dedicated to the emperor's use, are appointed by government.

| | | |
|---|---|---|
| 411. Circuit justices of the peace. | 巡檢司 巡捕官 | ˏTs'un ʿkím ꜀sz'. ˏTs'un pò$^2$ ꜀kún. |
| 412. Lieutenant-governor ex-officio member of B. W. | 巡撫部院 | ˏTs'un ʿfú pò$^2$ yün$^2$. |
| 413. Governor, or governor-general. | 總督 | ʿTsung tuk꜄. |
| 414. Governor of the imperial canal. | 總漕 | ʿTsung ˏts'ò. |
| 415. Governor of (the great) rivers. | 總河 | ʿTsung ˏhó. |
| 416. Major-general, or commander-in-chief. | 總兵 | ʿTsung ꜀ping. |
| 417. General (or the chief) standard-bearer. | 總旗 | ʿTsung ˏk'í.* |
| 418. Department for the direction of manufactures. | 摠理織造府 | ʿTsung ʿlí chik꜄ ts'ò$^2$ ʿfú. |
| 419. General directors of the army and state. | 摠知軍國事 | ʿTsung ꜀chí ꜀kwan kwók꜄ sz'$^2$.* |
| 420. Under-secretary, or clerk. | 從事 | ˏTs'ung sz'$^2$.* |
| 421. The Board of Sacrifices, or sacrificial department. | 祠部 | ˏTs'z' pò$^2$.* |
| 422. Court-martial (*lit.* investigating officers). | 推官 | ꜀T'úi ꜀kún.* |
| 423. The governor's staff or subalterns. | 督標 | Tuk꜄ ꜀píú. |
| 424. Chief director of the commissariate. | 督糧道 | Tuk꜄ ˏléung tò$^2$. |
| 425. Local magistrate, justice of the peace. | 通守 通判 | ꜀T'ung ʿshau.* ꜀T'ung p'ún'.* |
| 426. Court of Representation. | 通政司 | ꜀T'ung ching' ꜀sz'. |
| 427. Commissioner of the Court of Representation. | 通政使 | ꜀T'ung ching' sz''. |
| 428. Deputy-commissioners of the Court of Representation. | 通政副使 | ꜀T'ung ching' fú' sz''. |
| 429. Councillors of the Court of Representation. | 通政司參議 | ꜀T'ung ching' ꜀sz' ꜀ts'ám ʿí. |
| 430. Secretaries of the Court of Representation. | 通政司經歷 | ꜀T'ung ching' ꜀sz' ꜀king lik$_2$. |
| 431. Under-secretaries of the Court of Representation. | 通政司知事 | ꜀T'ung ching' ꜀sz' ꜀chí sz'$^2$. |
| 432. Sub-prefect, under, or joint magistrate. | 同知 | ˏT'ung ꜀chí. |
| 433. Chief of the third literary degree. | 會元 | Úi$^2$ ˏyün. |
| 434. Under-secretaries, or clerks. | 員外郎 | ˏÜn ngoi$^2$ ˏlóng. |
| 435. Chief director of the imperial guards. | 衛尉卿 | Wai$^2$ ʿwai ꜀hing. |
| 436. Lieutenant of the imperial guards. | 衛千摠 衛分府 | Wai$^2$ ꜀ts'ín ʿtsung. Wai$^2$ ꜀fan ʿfú. |
| 437. Secretary to the imperial guards. | 衛經歷 | Wai$^2$ ꜀king lik$_2$. |

426. This court receives appeals from the people and memorials from the officers in the provinces, and places them before the Inner Council; it has charge also of the great drum at the palace gate.

| | | |
|---|---|---|
| 438. General of the imperial body guards. | 衞將軍 | Wai$^{2}$ ꜀tséung ꜀kwan. |
| 439. Instructor and defender of learning. | 衞學教授 | Wai$^{2}$ hók$_{2}$ káu꜃ shau$^{2}$. |
| 440. Deputies, officers who are deputed. | 委員 | ꜂Wai ꜁ün. |
| 441. School of literature, or royal academy. | 弘文舘 | ꜁Wang ꜁man ꜂kún.* |
| 442. Officers attached to a royal duke. | 王侯官屬 | ꜁Wóng ꜁hau ꜀kún shuk$_{2}$. |
| 443. Imperial commissioner, or envoy. | 欽差 | ꜀Yam ꜀ch'ái. |
| 444. President of the Imperial Astronomical Board. | 欽天監監正 | ꜀Yam ꜀t'ín kám꜃ ꜀kám ching꜃. |
| 445. Right and left vice-presidents of the Imperial Astronomical Board. | 欽天監左右監副 | ꜀Yam ꜀t'ín kám꜃ ꜂tsó yau$^{2}$ ꜀kám fú꜃. |
| 446. Magistrate of a district or city. | 邑宰 | Yap꜄ ꜂tsoi.* |
| 447. Assistant magistrate of a district. | 邑尉 邑曹 | Yap꜄ ꜂wai.* Yap꜄ ꜁ts'ò.* |
| 448. Lieutenant-colonel. | 遊擊 遊府 | ꜁Yau kik꜄. ꜁Yau ꜂fú. |
| 449. Sub-magistrate, or under-magistrate. | 右堂 | Yau$^{2}$ ꜁t'óng. |
| 450. Keepers of the imperial post-offices. | 驛丞 | Yik$_{2}$ ꜁shing.* |
| 451. Censors, or imperial historiographers. | 御史 | Yü$^{2}$ ꜂sz'. |
| 452. The tribunal of the censors, or Censorate. | 御史臺 | Yü$^{2}$ ꜂sz' ꜁t'oi.* |
| 453. His excellency the censor. | 御史大夫 | Yü$^{2}$ ꜂sz' tái$^{2}$ ꜀fú.* |
| 454. Keeper of records in the Censorate. | 御史主簿 | Yü$^{2}$ ꜂sz' ꜂chü pò$^{2}$. |
| 455. Imperial guard in waiting. | 御前侍衞 | Yü$^{2}$ ꜁ts'ín shí$^{2}$ wai$^{2}$. |
| 456. Principal director in the school of Confucius. | 儒學正堂 | ꜁Yü hók$_{2}$ ching꜃ ꜁t'óng. |
| 457. Secondary director in the school of Confucius. | 儒學副堂 | ꜁Yü hók$_{2}$ fú꜃ ꜁t'óng. |
| 458. Board for the regulation of the imperial gardens. | 虞部 | ꜁Yü pò$^{2}$.* |
| 459. Under-magistrate of a district. | 縣令 | Yün$^{2}$ ling$^{2}$. |
| 460. Director of the police of a district. | 縣尉 | Yün$^{2}$ wai꜃.* |
| 461. Sub-magistrate. | 縣丞 | Yün$^{2}$ ꜁shing. |
| 462. Military leader, generalissimo of the army. | 元帥 | ꜁Yün shui꜃. |

451. These officers form the *Tòchát yün* (No. 381); the governors of provinces are ex-officio principal censors, and the lieutenant governors are ex-officio secondary censors.

# GENERAL INDEX.

*Note.*—This Index is intended to guide the student to all the things and subjects treated of or named in the first column, and, consequently, it contains proportionably a greater number of nouns, than of adjectives, verbs, or adverbs, though these classes of words have by no means been overlooked. The words given in the second column of the index are the translations of the corresponding English words; but it has sometimes happened that the English words, found in the first column of the body of the work, could not be inserted in this index because there were no corresponding Chinese terms for them, and vice versâ. Many of the words here given are not used in conversation, other and more colloquial terms being employed, or a periphrasis used; some of these terms do not occur in the index. It will, however, to a good degree, serve the purpose of a vocabulary; and it will be advantageous to refer to the body of the work to see the connection in which a word or phrase is used before employing it, as well as to learn what are its proper characters. The first column of figures refers to the page, and the second to the number of the paragraph; an *n* after the English word denotes that it is explained in a note.

廣東方言讀本

廣東方言讀本

廣東方言讀本

廣東方言讀本

廣東方言讀本

廣東方言讀本

廣東方言讀本

廣東方言讀本

廣東方言讀本

廣東方言讀本

# INDEX OF CHINESE PROPER NAMES

*ARRANGED ACCORDING TO THE CHINESE SOUNDS.*

---

CHI. CHR. 175

国家出版基金项目
NATIONAL PUBLICATION FOUNDATION

# 海上絲綢之路文獻集成

總主編　陳支平　陳春聲

## 科技與文化編 97

主編　王揚宗　葉　農

海峽出版發行集團
THE STRAITS PUBLISHING & DISTRIBUTING GROUP
福建人民出版社

# 本册目次

# 初學階

（*Ch'o Hok Kai: A Handbook of the Canton Vernacular of the Chinese Language: Being a Series of Introductory Lessons, for Domestic and Business Purposes*）

〔英〕德呢克（Nicholas Belfield Dennys）編

《初學階》，英國德呢克編。德呢克（Nicholas Belfield Dennys，一八三九—一九〇〇），又名戴尼斯，英國在華公務員，新聞記者。著有《通商口岸與中國民俗》、《中日商埠志》等。此書專供粵方言之學習，前有序言、導言及發音，正文設六十課，皆以漢文居中，英譯居左，羅馬字注音居右，間有詳細解說。書末附詞彙表。據一八七四年香港版影印。

初學階

# 初學階

CH'O HOK KAI.

A

# HANDBOOK

OF

# THE CANTON VERNACULAR

OF THE

# CHINESE LANGUAGE.

BEING A SERIES OF INTRODUCTORY LESSONS, FOR DOMESTIC AND BUSINESS PURPOSES.

By N. B. DENNYS, M.R.A.S., &c.

LONDON:
TRÜBNER & CO.

HONGKONG: "CHINA MAIL" OFFICE,
1874.
G

PRINTED AT THE "CHINA MAIL" OFFICE, HONGKONG.

# PREFACE.

The want of any work which even attempts to impart in a systematic way a knowledge of the Canton Vernacular, will, it is hoped, be a sufficient excuse for the publication of the following pages. That there is no "Royal Road" to acquiring any of the spoken languages of China is a fact verified by the lengthened experience of many European students: but that their acquisition can be facilitated or retarded, according to the means used, is an obvious truism. To no vernacular is the application of system, by those who study it, more necessary than to Cantonese, and to none has less systematic effort been applied to smooth the path of beginners. Numerous works have, indeed, made their appearance since Dr. Morrison first placed in the hands of his countrymen a tolerably effective key to the study of the written language, but, valuable as they nearly all are, two only—those of Bridgman and Williams—were even designed to furnish progressive lessons on any intelligible plan.

The author is conscious of his temerity in thus venturing upon a task which so many better qualified have declined; the more so as the time at his disposal for the compilation of the work has been restricted to the brief intervals of leisure allowed by more pressing avocations. Those, however, who best know its difficulties, will, probably, be most lenient in judging him, and most ready to recognize whatever of good there may be in the effort. He is of course largely indebted to all who have previously treated the subject, and to particularize would be to simply name every writer who has ever dealt with the Canton vernacular. In so far as this attempt may be held to have failed, more competent hands may find hints for fresh efforts. The lessons herein given make no pretence of being more than introductory for those who intend to make a study of the language the business of their lives; but they will probably be found sufficient for those who desire only to obtain a mere every-day acquaintance with Cantonese for business and domestic purposes. That numerous errors will be found in these pages —especially in the tones, regarding which there exists an endless diversity of opinion,—is highly probable, but it has not been deemed necessary to make a table of errata for those detected.

The Author most warmly acknowledges the valuable aid he has received from Mr. F. Stewart, M.A. the Inspector of Government Schools, both in his encouragement to attempt the publication of the work, and in his kind revision of the proof sheets. To the Rev. E. J. Eitel Ph.D., to whose scholarly advice and help is due the absence of far more numerous errors than are even now apparent, his obligations are of the deepest nature. His thanks are also due to his brother, Mr. H. L. Dennys, for assistance in the preparation of the sentences which form the examples to each lesson, and to Mr. Chun Ayin for similar aid in the Chinese manuscript. In conclusion he would beg students to point out to him what they deem faulty, as, though perfection in such a work is almost unattainable, hints towards improvement will be most valuable should a second edition be called for.

Hongkong, November, 1874.

# INTRODUCTION.

Under the belief that a few brief remarks upon the most striking characteristics of the Chinese language generally, and of the Canton dialect more particularly, will be of service to intending students, they are hereunder subjoined.

THE SPOKEN LANGUAGES of China, which embrace four strongly marked divisions known as the Mandarin, Fuhkien, Cantonese and Hakka *Vernaculars*, are reputed to include some 360 *dialects*, many of which present but very slight differences of word or idiom. The Vernaculars, on the other hand, are to all intents and purposes, distinct languages, connected together only by the common use of the same *written* character and idiom. A popular, but very mistaken, notion is prevalent, on the part of those unacquainted with Chinese, that a sentence of Cantonese, written as it is spoken, is necessarily intelligible to a native of another part of the Empire. This is by no means the case, but as Cantonese and Tartars alike use a style of written composition understood by all, men who cannot understand a word of each others' *speech* can at once understand each others' letters or dispatches. They therefore possess a common literature, which justifies us in talking of "Chinese" as if the term referred to but one language, possessing only different *dialects*. It is here unnecessary to enter into any disquisition upon the genius of this written language, which must form the subject of a separate work. It will be sufficient to say that the characters used to represent words consist of various combinations of certain signs, a vast proportion of which, now-a-days arbitrary, can be traced to an original hieroglyphic or ideographic representation of the object alluded to. Under the system now in use 214 of these signs, usually termed "radicals," have been selected as the "keys" under which every character in the language is ranged. They therefore take the place of western alphabets, with the serious difference that they do not by any means neccssarily indicate the *sound* of the characters found under them. The acquisition of the written or "book" language, as it is for convenience termed, hence becomes a very serious effort of memory to the majority of students.

The present work is intended primarily for those who desire in the first instance to acquire a knowledge of the vernacular only, the Chinese type being used, chiefly, to allow a native teacher to correct the student's pronunciation; and the author strongly recommends a preliminary six months *oral* study of the language before the written character is attacked. Many eminent scholars, however, recommend a contrary course, and maintain that no word should be deemed as learnt until the character expressing it is mastered also. The objections to this are, that as many characters have a different sense in the colloquial to that they possess in the "book" style, some confusion is therefore likely to arise in the student's mind; while the difficulties of mastering the characters will probably so retard him in his study of the colloquial, that the enthusiasm of a beginner is apt to become unduly damped. There is, however, nothing to prevent any one so minded from studying both simultaneously. The only necessary caution is that in Chinese every step must be *thoroughly* mastered. Superficial work is essentially *wasted* work.

THE STRUCTURE of the vernaculars of China has, like the written language, been the subject of much misconception. The Chinese is one of a group of tongues which, numerically few, are nevertheless spoken by a third of the world's inhabitants. This group—which includes Chinese, Annamese, Burmese, Siamese and Shyan—is usually denominated by philologists "monosyllabic," meaning that nearly every word is in them expressed by a monosyllable. This definition, while fairly applicable to the written forms, is, however, by no means applicable to the colloquials. Owing to causes we need not here stop to discuss Chinese, at a very early date, appears to have stopped short in that process of combining sounds which gives to western tongues their variety and adaptability, and hence possesses only some five hundred syllables in each vernacular. It is obvious that under such circumstances a vast number of words possessing no likeness to each other in our own language must be pronounced alike in Chinese. Some ingenuity has been, however, displayed in extending this slender stocks of syllables by giving to each a different mode of pronunciation, by means of tones. In this way the Cantonese have contrived to distinguish some three thousand vocables. But even this leaves an enormous number of words exactly similar in pronunciation, the entire written language numbering some forty thousand significatives. So long as the written language alone was to be dealt with, this was comparatively unimportant. It was far otherwise with the colloquials, and necessity soon led to an improvement, which, while it made their acquisition and use far more easy, hopelessly cut off that intimate connection between the written and the spoken languages which obtains with western tongues. Words were introduced which, combined with the vocables dealt with, at once rendered their meaning clear to the listener. It was as if we had a hundred words in English all pronounced like the word *air*, and in order to distinguish them we called them *breath-air*, *son-heir*, *time-e'er*, &c. Hence the vernaculars of China cannot be deemed monosyllabic.

It is customary to assert that Chinese has no Grammar, and, if by that it be meant that its construction outrages western ideas of grammar, the assertion is true. The same word constantly does duty for various parts of speech—just as if we, taking the word "*ambition*," used it as a noun, adjective, adverb, verb, &c, as convenient, and were to say "he likes *ambition*," "he is an *ambition* man," "he did it *ambition*," "he *ambition* that post." Now we do, with such a word, use it very much in that way (ambition, ambitious, ambitiously &c,) but we *inflect* it. The Chinese do not; and moreover they use almost any word in a similar manner. But to assert that they have "no Grammar" is to assert a manifest absurdity, as no language can exist without some *custom* of forming sentences, which in time becomes the grammarian's rule.

In these remarks no pretence has been made of doing more than very briefly sketching the *nature* of the language the student is about to essay. Most of the dictionaries, Williams' "Middle Kingdom," and other works will give ample information on the subject. In conclusion, the author can only quote the oft repeated dictum "*Patientia omnia vincit*"—even Chinese.

---

The following remarks should be thoroughly mastered by the student before proceeding to the lessons.

### On The Tones.

The vernaculars of China differ from almost all other spoken tongues* in possessing certain peculiarities which to Europeans render the task of acquiring them one of extreme difficulty. These are usually termed *tones*, or inflections of the voice which give to each spoken word a sound not dissimilar to that which, with us, conveys a sense of some emotion—such as suprise, joy, grief, etc—on the part of the speaker. Many and various have been the attempts made by writers on the Chinese language to convey, by means of illustrations drawn from our own, some idea of their nature. It must be candidly confessed that, at best, these efforts have been only partially successful, nor can we hope in these pages to arrive at a much more satisfactory result. Attention to the following remarks will however, ensure a tolerable comprehension of the general meaning of the tonal system. Every spoken word in any language may of course be pronounced in more than one way, though our perception of that fact is somewhat deadened by our own custom of confining differences of intonation to expressions of emotion. The least tutored ear will detect the difference between the word *when*, in the sentence, "When he comes back, ask him," and the same word enquiringly ejaculated—as for instance if you tell a man that his son went away yesterday, and he angrily responds *When?* The drawn-out,

* Burmese, Siamese, and Shyan possess something resembling tones, but they are far less in number and consequently less embarrassing than in Chinese.

anxious, surprised tone in which the same word may be pronounced in answer to some unexpected statement, will also be perceived to differ from either of the foregoing. The following short dialogue, which is taken, with a slight alteration, from Mr. Wade's Mandarin Course, will perhaps best convey the idea of the four fundamental tones to the learner's mind. The words italicised are pronounced very nearly like the four tones of the mandarin dialect. Three persons, A, B, & C., are supposed to be speaking.

A. (1). Poor X died this morning

B. (2). (suddenly and emphatically)—*Died?*

C. (3). (somewhat sadly and slowly—evidently moved) W-h-a-t?

A. (4). (the first speaker, abruptly, as if not wishing to say any more) Yes!

Taking the line A. B. hereunder to represent the normal modulation of the voice, these tones would be symbolically expressed as follows:—

A..........1st tone...—........2nd tone.../........3rd tone...◟........4th tone...\\..........B

| 1st tone | 2nd tone | 3rd tone | 4th tone |
|---|---|---|---|
| even. | rising. | falling questioning. | abrupt and slightly falling. |

Now, Cantonese possesses eight tones, which may be described as two sets of four, each set being very similar to the above. The distinction between them is that the one set is pronounced with the voice pitched nearly a fourth of the musical octave higher than that used for the other. They are thus named and arranged:—

| | 1 | 2 | 3 | 4 |
|---|---|---|---|---|
| Upper Series— | *sheung-ping* | *sheung-sheung'* | *sheung-hü`* | *sheung-yap.* |
| Lower Series— | ha-ping | ha-sheung' | ha-hü` | ha-yap. |

It must be remembered that these tones are often quite independent of the emotion to be expressed, so that words pronounced in a surprised way do not necessarily express any surprise on the part of the speaker. The tones doubtless took their origin in the paucity of original vocables, the list of which, by some singular accident, has remained almost as restricted as it was two thousand years ago. It does not appear that the same vocables have always retained the same tones, but any dissertation on that subject would here be out of place. Suffice it to say that the tones present a stumbling-block to the student which must be manfully attacked at the outset, until ear and tongue are alike accustomed to detect and pronounce each method of intonation. But one rule for acquiring them can be given to the student—to observe the habit of *constant practice.*

In the following lessons the tone of each word given in the vocabularies is carefully marked according to the plan given above. This has not, however, been done with the illustrative sentences, inasmuch as the pronunciation in roman type is intended simply as an *aid* to the student's memory. The correct rythm and tone of each individual sentence must be independently and accurately learned by the student, as a matter of memory, if he would acquire facility in speaking.

# PRONUNCIATION.

---

The consonants in the romanized pronunciation given to each word are to be pronounced as in English. The vowels should be sounded as follows:—

*a*, and *a* final as in *father*

*ȧ*, not final, as *o* in *company*

*ai* as *y* in *fly*

*au*, as *ow* in *now*

*e*, as in they

*eu*, as *eyo* in *beyond*

*i*, as in *machine*, but before *ng* and *k* as in *king*

*iu*, as *ee* with *ou* in *see-you*, almost as *ew* in *yew*

*o*, final, as in *no*, and not final, as in *hop*

*ö*, as in *Göethe*

*oh*, as *o* in *folding* (sometimes nearly as *ho* in *horn*)

*oi*, as *oy* in *boy*

*sze* or *sz* like *si* in *sibilant*, or *si* in *sir*

*u*, as *oo* in school

*ü*, as in *Trübner*

*ui*, nearly as in *Louis* or *ooi* in *cooing*

# LESSON I.

The following tables should be repeated carefully after a native teacher some twenty times; nor should the pupil neglect to similarly repeat at least one of them daily, until he has reached the 20th or 30th lesson. Words in the upper tone series will, throughout this work, be printed in *italics*, those in the lower series being in roman type.* *Unaccented* words, whether italic or roman, are to be pronounced in the *first* or *even* tone. *Second tone* words will be distinguished by an *acute accent*, thus: *nau'*. *Third tone* words will be marked with a *grave accent*; thus *lin`*. All words ending in *k. p.* or *t.* are *fourth tone* words. It must be noted that very few syllables (as we term them) run through the whole eight tones. The student need not trouble himself about the meaning of the characters subjoined.

TABLE I.

UPPER SERIES.

| 1. *Sheung p'ing* | 2. *Sheung sheung'*. | 3. *Sheung hü`*. | 4. *Sheung yap*. |
|---|---|---|---|
| *Sin* 先 | *sin'* 鮮 | *sin`* 綫 | *sit* 屑 |
| *Tung* 東 | *tung'* 董 | *tung`* 凍 | *tuk* 篤 |
| *Ying* 英 | *ying'* 影 | *ying`* 應 | *yik* 益 |
| *Kong* 剛 | *kong'* 講 | *kong`* 降 | *kok* 角 |

LOWER SERIES.

| 1. Ha p'ing. | 2. Ha Sheung'. | 3. Ha hü`. | 4. Ha yap. |
|---|---|---|---|
| Lin 連 | lin' 璉 | lin` 鍊 | lit 列 |
| Yung 容 | yung' 勇 | yung` 用 | yuk 欲 |
| Ling 靈 | ling' 領 | ling` 令 | lik 力 |
| Wong 王 | wong' 往 | wong` 旺 | wok 鑊 |

* This simple yet satisfactory mode of indicating the tone in type was first applied by the Rev. J. Chalmers in his "English and Cantonese Pocket Dictionary." For manuscript the student will probably find it handier to use figures, with a dash under them for the *upper series*: e.g. sin 1, kong 2, fan 3, taug 4, or adopt the method followed by Dr. Williams in which a ͻ for the upper, and a ͻ for the lower series denotes the tone by its position at either corner of the word.

初學階



### TABLE II.

In this the English pronunciation of the *sheung* and ha p'ing will alone be given.

| | | | | | | | | | |
|---|---|---|---|---|---|---|---|---|---|
| *Tăng* | 登 | 等 | 凳 | 德 | Mang | 盟 | 猛 | 孟 | 墨 |
| *Kăm* | 金 | 錦 | 禁 | 急 | Yăm | 吟 | 衽 | 任 | 入 |
| *Kim* | 兼 | 檢 | 劍 | 刧 | Im | 嚴 | 染 | 驗 | 業 |
| *Tsun* | 津 | 贐 | 進 | 卒 | Lun | 倫 | 卵 | 論 | 律 |
| *Kam* | 緘 | 減 | 鑒 | 甲 | Lam | 藍 | 覽 | 纜 | 蠟 |
| *Fan* | 翻 | 反 | 泛 | 發 | Lan | 闌 | 懶 | 爛 | 辣 |
| *Kun* | 官 | 管 | 貫 | 括 | Mun | 門 | 滿 | 悶 | 末 |
| *Kon* | 干 | 趕 | 幹 | 割 | Hon | 寒 | 旱 | 翰 | 褐 |
| *Kom* | 甘 | 敢 | 紺 | 蛤 | Hom | 含 | 頷 | 憾 | 合 |

### TABLE III.

Particular care must be taken to distinguish between words which contain an *aspirate* (expressed by an inverted comma, as in ch'ü,) and those which do not. The teacher's voice must be most carefully imitated. Most aspirated words are of the lower tone series.

| | | | | | | | |
|---|---|---|---|---|---|---|---|
| *Wai* | 威 | 偉 | 畏 | Mai | 迷 | 米 | 袂 |
| *Ki* | 幾 | 紀 | 記 | I | 宜 | 議 | 貳 |
| *Chü* | 諸 | 主 | 著 | Ch'ü | 除 | 佇 | 處 |
| *Sau* | 修 | 叟 | 秀 | Lau | 留 | 柳 | 陋 |
| *Chiu* | 朝 | 沼 | 照 | Liu | 寮 | 了 | 料 |
| *Ku* | 孤 | 古 | 故 | Mu | 無 | 母 | 務 |
| *Tsoi* | 栽 | 宰 | 載 | T'oi | 臺 | 殆 | 代 |
| *Fo* | 火 | 科 | 貨 | Ngo | 鵝 | 我 | 臥 |

---

## LESSON II.

| | | | | | |
|---|---|---|---|---|---|
| Water | 水 | *shui'* | Bring | 拎—嚟, 來 | *ning*—lai, (or) loi |
| Tea | 茶 | ch'a | Do. | 拈—嚟, 來 | *nim*—lai, (or) loi |
| I or me | 我 | ngo' | Do. | 攞* | *loh'* |
| You | 你 | ni' | Give me tea | 俾茶我 | *pi'* ch'a ngo' |
| Have | 有 | yau' | To want (like) | 要, 愛 | *iu`* (or) *oi`* |
| Give | 俾 | *pi'* | Interog. particles at end of a question. | 啞, 呢, 咩, 冇, 麽. | *ă*, *ni*, *me*, mo', and *mo* (*mo* only follows yau; it is contraction of 'm yau.) |
| Sugar (white) | 白糖 | pak-t'ong | | | |
| Bread | 麵飽 | min`-*pau* | | | |
| Tea-cup | 茶杯 | ch'a-*pui* | | | |

* See page 10.

The interrogative particles are respectively used rather in observance of custom than because of any marked difference in value, though MO seems more generally than the others to imply a belief on the part of the speaker that the answer will be affirmative. Two are sometimes used together.

There being no case inflections in Chinese, the same word answers for *I* or *me*, according to its place in the sentence. Thus "I give" is NGO PI 我俾 "give me" is PI NGO 俾我.

There is, strictly speaking, no article* in Chinese though the numeral "one" or a demonstrative pronoun frequently supplies its place.

The mood and tenses of verbs are not marked by inflections, particles being used in their place.

In ordinary colloquial, the copulative conjunction is often replaced by the verb when several nouns are coupled as, what we should term, nominatives or accusatives of a verb. Thus: *give me tea sugar and milk* may be translated, *give tea, give sugar, give milk, me.*

The word *bring* is, literally, *carry come* (NING LOI 擰來) in Chinese. *Take away* is, similarly, *carry go*, as will be seen hereafter.

In the following sentences words in brackets are not expressed in the Chinese. With the exception of the article they will be so marked in this and the two following lessons.

| | | |
|---|---|---|
| 1 Bring (some) bread | 擰麵飽來 | ning min-pau loi |
| 2 Bring (some) water | 擰水來 | ning shui loi |
| 3 Bring me (some) tea | 擰茶來我 | ning ch'a loi ngo |
| 4 Bring a tea-cup | 擰茶杯來 | ning ch'a-pui loi |
| 5 Give me sugar | 俾白糖我 | pi pak-t'ong ngo |
| 6 Have you (any) sugar? | 你有白糖冇呀 | ni yau pak-t'ong mo à? |
| 7 I have sugar | 我有白糖 | ngo yau pak-t'ong |
| 8 Give me tea (and) sugar | 俾茶俾白糖我 | pi ch'a, pi pak-t'ong ngo |
| 9 Give me bread (and) water | 俾麵飽俾水我 | pi min-pau, pi shui ngo |
| 10 Bring sugar (and) water | 擰白糖擰水來 | ning pak-t'ong, ning shui loi |
| 11 Have you tea? | 你有茶呢 | ni yau ch'a ni? |
| 12 I have tea | 我有茶 | ngo yau ch'a |
| 13 Have you water? | 你有水麼 | ni yau shui mo? |
| 14 I have sugar | 我有白糖 | ngo yau pak-t'ong |
| 15 Have you (any) bread? | 你有麵飽呀 | ni yau min-pau à? |
| 16 I have tea-cups | 我有茶杯 | ngo yau ch'a-pui |
| 17 Give me tea-cups | 俾茶杯我 | pi ch'a-pui ngo |
| 18 Give me water, sugar (and) tea | 俾水,俾白糖,俾茶我 | pi shui, pi pak-t'ong, pi ch'a, ngo |

* See Lesson XVIII.

| | | |
|---|---|---|
| 19 Have you (any) sugar? | 你有白糖呀 | ni yau pak-t'ong à? |
| 20 I have sugar; have you tea? | 我有白糖，你有茶呢 | ngo yau pak-t'ong; ni yau ch'a ni? |
| 21 Have you tea, bread (and) water? | 你有茶，有麵飽，有水呀 | ni yau ch'a, yau min-pau, yau shui à? |
| 22 I have bread, sugar (and) tea | 我有麵飽，有白糖，有茶 | ngo yau min-pau, yau pak-t'ong, yau ch'a |
| 23 I want tea (and) sugar | 我要茶，要白糖 | ngo iu ch'a, iu pak-t'ong |
| 24 You want tea-cups | 你要茶杯 | ni iu ch'a-pui |
| 25 I have tea-cups; have you tea? | 我有茶杯，你有茶呢 | ngo yau ch'a-pui; ni yau ch'a ni? |

# LESSON III.

Most Chinese nouns signifying objects take before them a syllable or word usually termed by foreigners a classifier* or numerative. This is, to a certain extent, generic; i.e. a similar word applies to a large number of nouns having some analogy to each other. Thus the word CHI, meaning a branch, is applied to pens, candles, whips, pencils, muskets, and other straight things; e.g. *a pen*, YAT CHI PAT, 一枝筆; *a whip*, YAT CHI MA PIN, 一枝馬鞭.

The adjective comes between the classifier and its noun, when following a numeral; thus, *a large pen*, YAT CHI TAI PAT, 一枝大筆.

The classifiers are distinguished in the vocabularies of these lessons by being placed within brackets.

| | | | | | |
|---|---|---|---|---|---|
| Kuife (table) | 張刀 | (*cheung*) *to* | This | 呢，呢個. | *ni*, *ni-ko`*. |
| Wine | 酒 | *tsau'* | These | 呢啲 | *ni-ti* |
| Tumbler | 水杯 | *shui'-pui* | That | 啯，啯個. | *ko'*, *ko'-ko`* |
| Plate | 隻碟 | (*chek*) tip | Those | 個啲 | *ko`-ti* |
| Fork | 枝叉 | (*chi*) *ch'a* | No | 唔係 | 'm hai` |
| Spoon | 隻匙羹 | (*chek*) shi-*kang* | Not, neg. part. | 唔，冇，不 | 'm, mo', *pat*. |

* Note.—Althongh I have here adopted the conventional term applied by foreiguers to a large number of words which are constantly used in combination with nouns, it may be well to point out that the designation thus used is to a great extent a misnomer. There are, strictly speaking, but eight or nine "classifiers," i.e. words which have no analogous terms in our own language. It is obviously absurd to denominate such words as pair, flock, frame, lump, string, suit, cluster, &c. "classifiers," they being in reality either simple nouns or nouns of multitude. The term, being, however, convenient, is adhered to, with this protest against possible misconception.

| | | | | | |
|---|---|---|---|---|---|
| Rice (used to express food generally) | 飯 | fan`* | Yes | 係 | hai` |
| Wine-glass | 酒杯 | *tsau'-pui* | Large | 大 | tai` |
| Is, it is, are | 係 | hai` | Small | 細 | *sai`* |

Ni-ti 呢啲 ko-ti 個啲, though properly plural forms, are used for *this* and *that* before words signifying fluids, or matter consisting of small particles such as sand, dust, flour, &c., and occasionally before other words.

*Yes* and *no* are expressed by the verb *to be*, joined, in the case of *no*, to a negative particle; thus, *yes* is expressed by *it is*, and *no* by *it is not.*

Adjectives precede the substantives they qualify, as in English.

| | | |
|---|---|---|
| 1 Bring a plate | 拎隻碟來 | ning chek tip loi |
| 2 Give me the knife | 俾張刀我 | pi cheung to ngo |
| 3 Have you the fork (and) spoon? | 你有枝叉，有匙羹呀 | ni yau chi ch'a, yau shi-kang a? |
| 4 I have the plate (and) the fork | 我有隻碟，有枝叉 | ngo yau chek tip, yau chi ch'a |
| 5 (It) is wine | 係酒 | hai tsau |
| 6 I want a wine-glass | 我要酒杯 | ngo iu tsau-pui |
| 7 This (is) large | 呢個大 | ni ko tai |
| 8 This is large tea-cup | 呢個係大茶杯 | ni ko hai tai ch'a-pui |
| 9 Get the sugar spoon | 拎白糖羹來 | ning pak-t'ong kang loi |
| 10 Have you (any) wine? | 你有酒冇 | ni yau tsau mo? |
| 11 I have wine, I (have) no tumbler | 我有酒，我冇水杯 | ngo yau tsau, ngo mo shui-pui |
| 12 This is a tumbler, that is a wine-glass | 呢個係水杯，個啲係酒杯 | ni ko hai shui-pui, ko ti hai tsau-pui |
| 13 Bring tea, (and) a spoon | 拎茶拈匙羹來 | ning ch'a, nim shi-kang loi |
| 14 Give me (some) water | 俾水我 | pi shui ngo |
| 15 Have you a wine-glass? | 你有酒杯冇 | ni yau tsau-pui mo? |
| 16 I (have) no wine-glass, (I) have a tea-cup | 我冇酒杯，有茶杯 | ngo mo tsau-pui, yau ch'a-pui |
| 17 Is that tea? | 個啲係茶咩 | ko ti hai ch'a me? |
| 18 Yes, (it) is tea | 係；係茶 | hai; hai ch'a |
| 19 The large fork, the small spoon | 大枝叉，細匙羹 | tai chi ch'a, sai shi-kang |
| 20 Get me the sugar spoon | 拎白糖羹俾我 | ning pak-t'ong kang pi ngo |
| 21 Bring me wine (and) water | 拎酒，拎水來俾我 | ning tsau, ning shui loi pi ngo |
| 22 Have you the plate? I have the plate | 你有隻碟呀，我有隻碟 | ni yau chek tip à? ngo yau chek tip |

* See remark p. 28.

| | | |
|---|---|---|
| 23 Have you a wine-glass? yes | 你有酒杯冇，有 | ni yau tsau-pui mo? yau |
| 24 No; I have not a wine-glass, I have a tumbler | 冇；冇酒杯，有水杯 | mo; mo tsau-pui, yau shui-pui |
| 25 A large plate; a small fork | 大隻碟；細枝叉 | tai chek tip; sai chi ch'a |
| 26 This plate; that spoon; this fork; that tea-cup | 呢隻碟；個隻羹；呢枝叉；個隻茶杯 | ni chek tip; ko chek kang; ni chi ch'a; ko chek ch'a-pui |
| 27 It is not a tea-cup; it is a tumbler | 唔係茶杯；係水杯 | 'm hai ch'a-pui; hai shui-pui |
| 28 No; it is a wine-glass | 唔係，係酒杯 | 'm hai; hai tsau-pui |
| 29 It is a large fork | 係大枝叉 | hai tai chi ch'a |
| 30 No, it is not; it is a knife | 唔係；係張刀 | 'm hai; hai cheung to |

---

# LESSON IV.

| | | | | | |
|---|---|---|---|---|---|
| Basin (lit. face pan.) | 面盆 | min\` p'un | Bad (not good) | 唔好 | 'm-*ho'* |
| | | | Very well! | 好咯 | *ho' lok* |
| Towel (lit. face napkin.) | 面巾 | min\`-*kän* | Good | 好 | *ho'* |
| | | | Put | 放 | *fong\`* |
| He, she, it | 佢 | k'ü' | Go | 去 | *hü\`* |
| We | 我哋 | ngo'-ti\` | Here (this place) | 呢處 | *ni-ch'ü\`: ni-shü\`* |
| His | 佢嘅 | k'ü'-*ke\`* | There (that ,, ) | 嗰處 | *ko'-ch'ü: ko'-shü\`* |
| Come | 嚟，來 | lai, loi | Above, upon | 上高 | sheung-*ko* |
| Our, ours | 我哋嘅 | ngo'-ti\`-*ke\`* | Below, beneath | 下底 | ha\`-*tai'* |
| My, mine | 我，我嘅 | ngo', ngo'-*ke* | At or on (also meaning *to be* at or on.) | 在 | tsoi\` |
| You | 你，你嘅 | ni', ni'-*ke\`* | | | |

The verb *to be* may often be omitted if TSOI 在 be used, unless it be desired to emphasize the fact of a thing being in a given situation.

CH'Ü 處 is sometimes used by itself to express *here*, more especially when it merely means *in place*.

Possessives are formed from nouns and personal pronouns by the addition of KE 嘅, but in every-day speech no distinction is observed between the nominative and possessive; e.g. *my plate*, NGO CHEK TIP, 我隻碟. There is no distinction of gender.

The plurals *our, your, their,* are formed by adding TI 哋

The plurals of nouns are formed by altering the classifiers to 啲 TI ; as NI KO YAN 呢個人, *this man,* becomes NI TI YAN, 呢啲人, *these men.*

The possessive form of pronouns is seldom used in practice. Thus, instead of NGO KE CHEK TIP 我嘅隻碟 NGO CHEK TIP, 我隻碟 is more usual.

LOK 咯 is frequently added at the end of sentences for the sake of euphony.

*And,* as a copulative for substantives, (rendered by KUNG 共 and KĀP 及) is not of very frequent use, and will not be translated in the first few lessons.

| | | |
|---|---|---|
| 1 My knife ; your fork | 我張刀，你枝叉 | ngo cheung to, ni chi ch'a |
| 2 His plate ; my wine | 佢隻碟，我嘅酒 | k'ü chek tip, ngo-ke tsau |
| 3 A good basin ; bad tea ; good water | 好面盆；唔好茶；好水 | ho min-p'un ; 'm ho ch'a ; ho shui |
| 4 Have you my good sugar? | 你有我嘅好白糖呀 | ni yau ngo ke ho pak-t'ong à? |
| 5 No ; I have not good sugar | 冇，我冇好白糖 | mo ; ngo mo ho pak-t'ong |
| 6 Come here ; bring my towel | 來呢處，擰我面巾來 | lai ni ch'ü ; ning ngo min-kàn loi |
| 7 Have you the basin (and) towel? | 你有面盆面巾冇 | ni yau min-p'un min-kăn mo ? |
| 8 I have a wine-glass (and) tumbler | 我有酒杯水杯 | ngo yau tsau-pui shui-pui |
| 9 Put the tea there | 放茶個處 | fong ch'a ko ch'ü |
| 10 Go (and) bring me a large fork | 去擰枝大叉來我 | hü, ning chi tai ch'a loi ngo |
| 11 Get (a) tea-cup, tea (and) sugar | 拈茶杯拈茶拈白糖來 | nim ch'a-pui, nim ch'a, nim pak-t'ong loi |
| 12 Is that his? is it ours? | 嗰啲係佢嘅咩係我哋嘅唔係 | ko ti hai k'ü ke me? hai ngo ti ke 'm hai ? |
| 13 It is mine ; it is hers | 係我嘅，係佢嘅 | hai ngo ke, hai k'ü ke |
| 14 It is above ; it is below | 在上，在下低 | tsoi sheung ; tsoi ha-tai |
| 15 We (are) above ; they (are) below | 我哋在上高，佢哋下低 | ngo-ti tsoi sheung-ko : k'ü-ti tsoi ha-tai |
| 16 These (are) yours | 呢啲你嘅 | ni ti ni ke |
| 17 Yours (are) above ; mine (are) below | 你嘅在上高，我嘅在下低 | ni ke tsoi sheung-ko, ngo ke tsoi ha-tai |
| 18 Put the towel in the basin | 放面巾在面盆 | fong min-kán tsoi min-p'un |
| 19 Go there ; bring a large fork | 去個處拈枝大叉來 | hü ko ch'ü ; nim chi tai ch'a lai |
| 20 Is this a large spoon? | 呢隻係大羹咩 | ni chek hai tai kang me ? |

| | | |
|---|---|---|
| 21 Is this tea good? No; it is not | 呢啲茶好唔呢, 唔好 | ni ti ch'a ho 'm ni? 'm ho |
| 22 Is that his bad basin? | 個啲係佢嘅唔好面盆咩 | ko ti hai k'ü ké 'm ho min-p'un me? |
| 23 No; it is his good plate | 唔係; 係佢隻好碟 | 'm hai; hai k'ü chek ho tip |
| 24 Do you want tea? | 你愛茶唔愛 | ni oi ch'a 'm oi? |
| 25 No; I want a basin, a towel (and) a spoon | 唔愛, 我愛面盆, 面巾, 匙羹 | 'm oi; ngo oi min-p'un, min-kăn, shi-kang |
| 26 These towels (are) good, those (are) bad | 呢啲面巾好, 個啲唔好 | ni ti min-kăn ho; ko ti 'm ho |
| 27 These basins (are) large; those forks (are) small | 呢啲面盆大, 個啲义細 | ni ti min-p'un tai; ko ti ch'a sai |
| 28 That wine (is) bad; this tea (is) good | 個啲酒唔好, 呢啲茶好 | ko ti tsau 'm ho; ni ti ch'a ho |
| 29 I (am) good; he (is) bad; it (is) large | 我好, 佢唔好, 係大 | ngo ho; k'ü 'm ho; hai tai |
| 30 This tea (is) good | 呢啲茶好 | ni ti ch'a ho |
| 31 Very well; have you a tea-spoon? | 好咧, 你有茶羹冇 | ho le; ni yau ch'a-kang mo? ko |

---

# LESSON V.

| | | | | | |
|---|---|---|---|---|---|
| In, to go in | 入 | yăp | One | 一 | *yat* |
| Within | 裡頭 | lüi'-t'au | Two | 二 | yi\` |
| Inside | 裡邊 | lüi'-*pin* | Three | 三 | *sam* |
| Out, outside | 外邊 | ngoi\`-*pin* | Four | 四 | *sze*\` |
| Downstairs | 樓下, 底下 | lau-ha\`, *tai'*-ha\` | Five | 五 | 'ng' |
| Chair | 椅 | i', Jang | Six | 六 | lūk |
| Table | 檯 | t'oi | Seven | 七 | *ts'at* |
| Ice, for the table | 冰, 雪 | properly *ping* but erroneously named in colloquial *süt* (snow.) | Take away | 拈去, 搬去 | *nim hü*\`, *pun hü* |
| | | | Upstairs | 樓上 | lau-sheung\` |
| Where | 邊處 | *pin-ch'ü* | There | 嗰處 | *ko'-ch'ü* |

To bring, when used of any article taken between the finger and thumb is 拈 *nim.**

With certain words "*upon*" is expressed by MIN 面; thus *upon the table, upon the ship's deck*, are T'OI MIN, 檯面, SHÜN MIN 船面.

The word used for *stairs* in down-stairs, up-stairs, is properly *a story*; *stairs* are KAI KUP 階級.

*Where, when, who*, and similar words do not usually require an interrogative particle (such as NI, MO, &c.,) but the rule is not invariable.

The word PIN 邊 literally denotes *side* or *place*, but in interrogative adverbs it answers to *who, which*, or *what?* as PIN CH'Ü 邊處 *what place* (that is, *where?*)

| | | |
|---|---|---|
| 1 Bring me a chair; two chairs | 拈一張椅來我，兩張椅 | nim yat cheung i loi ngo; leung cheung i |
| 2 I have three plates, and four knives | 我有三隻碟，四張刀 | ngo yau sam chek tip, sze cheung to |
| 3 Where is the good wine? | 嗰啲好酒喺邊處 | ko ti ho tsau hai pin ch'ü? |
| 4 It is on the large table | 喺大檯面 | hai tai t'oi min |
| 5 I want one basin and two towels | 我要一個面盆，兩條面巾 | ngo iu yat ko min-p'un, leung t'iu min-kăn |
| 6 There are no good spoons | 冇好匙羹 | mo ho shi-kang |
| 7 Very well, bring five chairs | 好唎，拈五張椅來 | ho le, nim 'ng cheung i loi |
| 8 The chair is upon the table | 嗰張椅在檯面 | ko cheung i tsoi t'oi min |
| 9 The ice is beneath the table | 嗰啲雪在檯下低 | ko ti süt tsoi t'oi ha tai |
| 10 Where are those seven tea-cups? | 嗰七隻茶杯喺邊處 | ko ts'at chek ch'a-pui hai pin ch'ü? |
| 11 They are upstairs | 喺樓上 | hai lau-sheung |
| 12 Those chairs are downstairs | 嗰啲椅喺下低 | ko ti i hai ha tai |
| 13 Bring seven forks and one plate | 擰七枝叉，一隻碟嚟 | ning ts'at chi ch'a, yat chek tip lai |
| 14 That ice is in the basin | 嗰啲冰喺面盆裡頭 | ko ti ping hai min p'un lui t'au |
| 15 Where is our table? | 我哋嗰張檯喺邊處 | ngo ti ko cheung t'oi hai pin ch'ü? |
| 16 Your good tumbler is here | 你嘅好水杯喺呢處 | ni ke ho shui-pui hai ni ch'ü |
| 17 That bread is bad; is it yours? | 嗰的麵飽唔好嘅，係你嘅唔係 | ko ti min-pau 'm ho ke, hai ni ke 'm hai? |
| 18 It is not mine, it is his | 唔係我嘅，係佢嘅 | 'm hai ngo ke, hai k'ü ke |

* *Nim* 拈 appears however to be frequently used in place of *ning*, 擰.

| | | |
|---|---|---|
| 19 That ice is ours: this table is mine | 啲嘞雪係我哋嘅，呢張檯係我嘅 | ko ti süt hai ngo ti ke: ni cheung t'oi hai ngo ke |
| 20 Where is my tea-cup? | 我隻茶杯喺邊處 | ngo chek ch'a pui hai pin ch'ü? |
| 21 Here it is; have you any tea? | 喺呢處，你有茶冇 | hai ni ch'ü, ni yau ch'a mo? |
| 22 No, I have no tea, I have wine | 冇，我冇茶，有酒啫 | mo, ngo mo ch'a, yau tsau ché |
| 23 Bring two chairs, three tea-cups and five knives | 擰兩張椅，三隻茶杯，五張刀來 | ning leung cheung i, sam chek ch'a-pui, 'ng cheung to loi |
| 24 Take away that wine | 擰啲的酒去 | ning ko ti tsau hü |
| 25 Where shall I put it? | 放在邊處好 | fong tsoi pin ch'ü ho? |
| 26 Put it on the large table | 放在大檯面 | fong tsoi tai t'oi min |
| 27 Very well: where is the table? | 好唎，啲張檯喺邊處呢 | ho le, ko cheung t'oi hai pin ch'ü ni? |
| 28 It is downstairs | 喺下低 | hai ha tai |
| 29 Bring the tea upstairs | 擰茶上來 | ning ch'a sheung loi |
| 30 Take the ice and wine downstairs | 擰雪擰酒去下底 | ning süt ning tsau hü ha tai |

---

# LESSON VI.

| | | | | | |
|---|---|---|---|---|---|
| Thanks (lit. "don't deserve") | 唔該 | 'm *koi* | Coolie (house) | 管店 | *kun'*-tim` |
| | | | Cook | 火頭 | *fo'*-t'au |
| Please, if you please | 請，多煩 | *ts'ing'*, (or) *to* fan | Nine | 九 | *kau'* |
| | | | To go away | 咀，去 | *ch'é*, *hü`* |
| Don't | 咪，唔好，唔使 | mai`, 'm *ho'*, 'm *shai'* | That will do (sufficient) | 够咯，做得咯 | *kau`* *lok*, (or) tso` *tak lok* |
| Man (i.e. male) | 男人 | nam-yan | Ten | 十 | shap |
| Eight | 八 | *pat* | Eleven | 十一 | shap *yat* |
| To call | 呌 | *kiu`* | Chair coolie | 轎夫，檯轎佬 | kiu'-*foo*, (or) t'oi kiu' *lo'* |
| Very | 最，十分 | tsui`, (or) shap *fän* | | | |
| Woman (a female) | 女人 | nüi'-yan | Gone | 去了 | *hü`* liu |

The verb *to have* is sometimes expressed by inverting the sentence and placing the nominative between the words HAI 喺 and CH'Ü 處; e.g. *the man has the basin* becomes: *the basin is* (at) *the man's place* 面盆喺男人處 MIN P'UN HAI NAM YAN CH'Ü.

The word *call* and *tell* (order) are expressed by the same word in Chinese: e.g. KIU K'Ü 叫佢 is either *tell him* or *call him*. A distinction is sometimes made by the use of the words WA K'Ü T'ING 話佢聽 to signify *tell him*, (lit. tell him to know.)

The past participle is formed by the addition of KWO 過, or HIU 曉; thus *to go* is HÜ 去; *gone* is HÜ KWO or HÜ HIU, 去過, 去曉. The past form, however, is often dispensed with in actual practice, the context being deemed sufficient to shew that it is implied.

Ho 好 *good*, is frequently prefixed to adjectives to express *very*; e.g. HO TAI 好大 *very large*.

The plural forms of *this* and *that*, NI TI 呢啲 KO TI 啗啲 are frequently used when speaking of liquids, or with words which take no distinction of number, such as weather, &c.

| | | |
|---|---|---|
| 1 Where is that man? | 啗個人喺邊處 | ko ko yan hai pin ch'ü? |
| 2 He is upstairs | 佢喺樓上 | k'ü hai lau sheung |
| 3 That table is very large | 啗張檯好大 | ko cheung t'oi ho tai |
| 4 That man is good; that woman is very bad | 啗個人好,啗個女人十分唔好 | ko ko yan ho, ko ko nüi-yan shap-fan 'm ho |
| 5 Call the chair coolie | 叫抬轎佬來 | kiu t'oi kiu-lo loi |
| 6 Please bring nine large tea-cups | 多煩拎九隻大茶杯來 | to fan ning kau chek tai ch'a-pui loi |
| 7 I want ten chairs | 我要十張椅 | ngo iu shap cheung i |
| 8 Is the good table here? | 啗張好檯喺呢處唔係呢 | ko cheung ho t'oi hai ni ch'ü 'm hai ni? |
| 9 These men are good; those women are bad | 呢啲男人好,啗的女人唔好 | ni ti nam-yan ho, ko ti nüi-yan 'm ho |
| 10 Where is the cook? | 火頭喺邊處呢 | fo-t'au hai pin ch'ü ni? |
| 11 He is gone to call the house-coolie | 佢去叫管店來 | k'ü hü kiu kun-tim loi |
| 12 Don't take away the tea | 咪拎啗啲茶去 | mai ning ko ti ch'a hü |
| 13 Put nine tea-cups inside | 放九隻茶杯在裡頭 | fong kau chek ch'a-pui tsoi lüi t'au |
| 14 Put the large basin on the table | 放啗個大面盆在檯面 | fong ko ko tai min-p'un tsoi t'oi min |

初學階

| | | |
|---|---|---|
| 15 Here are ten towels | 呢處有十條面巾 | ni ch‘ü yau shap t‘iu min-kăn |
| 16 These chairs are very good | 呢啲椅至好 | ni ti i chi ho |
| 17 Your ice is very bad | 你個啲雪十分唔好 | ni ko ti süt shap fan ’m ho |
| 18 Bring me eleven tea-cups | 擰十一隻茶杯來我 | ning shap yat chek ch‘a-pui loi ngo |
| 19 That will do. Thanks | 夠咯, 唔該呀 | kau lok, ’m koi a |
| 20 One man, two women and three coolies | 一個男人, 兩個女人, 三個轎佬 | yat ko nam-yan, leung ko nüi-yan, sam ko kiu-lo |
| 21 Dont bring any wine | 唔好擰酒來 | ’m ho ning tsau loi |
| 22 That cook is downstairs | 嗰個火頭喺下低 | ko ko fo-t‘au hai ha tai |
| 23 Call the man upstairs | 叫嗰個人上來 | kiu ko ko yan sheung loi |
| 24 Put nine chairs inside | 放九張椅裡邊 | fong kau cheung i lüi pin |
| 25 The woman has the basin | 嗰個面盆喺個女人處 | ko ko min-p‘un hai ko nüi-yan ch‘ü |
| 26 That man has the towels | 個啲面巾喺嗰個男人處 | ko ti min-kăn hai ko ko nam-yan ch‘ü |
| 27 That house coolie has gone away | 嗰個管店咀嘵咯 | ko ko kun-tim ché hiu lok |
| 28 Eight men and eleven women | 八個男人, 十一個女人 | pat ko nam-yan, shap yat ko nüi-yan |
| 29 Our cook is inside | 我哋嘅火頭喺裡邊 | ngo ti ke fo-t‘au hai lüi pin |
| 30 Nine women are downstairs | 九個女人喺下低 | kau ko nüi-yan hai ha tai |

## LESSON VII.

| | | | | | |
|---|---|---|---|---|---|
| Paper | 紙 | *chí* | Tea-pot | 茶壺 | ch‘a-oo |
| Pen | 枝筆 | (*chi*) *păt* | Water-bottle | 水罇 | *shuí tsun* |
| Ink (foreign) | 墨水 | măk-*shuí* | To use | 使用 | *shaí* (or) yung` |
| Book | 部書 | (po`) *shü* | With | 同 | t‘ung |
| Clothes-brush | 衣擦 | *i ts‘ăt* | Twelve | 十二 | shap yi` |
| Tell, (order) | 話, 叫 | wa`, *kiu`* | Twenty | 二十 | yi` shap |

| | | | | | |
|---|---|---|---|---|---|
| Hair-brush | 擦頭掃 | *ts'at*-t'*au-so* | Fifty | 五十 | 'ng' shap |
| Broom | 掃把 | *so'-pa'* | Much, many | 多 | *to* |
| To sweep | 掃 | *so'* | How many? | 幾多 | *ki' to?* |
| Floor | 樓板 | lau-*pan'* | | | |

The numbers from eleven to nineteen form regularly, as: ten-one (11), ten-two (12), &c. From twenty to ninety they form similarly, as: two-ten (20), three-ten (30), and so on.

WA—CHI 話一知 is used for *tell*, when that word is intended to be used in a non-imperative sense.

KI 幾 in KI TO 幾多, *how many*, is literally *a few, several.* The two words in conjunction are, however, not always used in an interrogative sense, but sometimes answer to "a certain number;" as NGO MO KI TO, 我冇幾多, *I have not many.*

| | | |
|---|---|---|
| 1 Bring a broom | 拎把掃把來 | ning pa so-pa loi |
| 2 Sweep the floor | 掃樓板 | so lau pan |
| 3 Give me pen and ink | 俾筆俾墨水我 | pi pät pi mak-shui ngo |
| 4 Get a clothes-brush | 拎衣擦來 | ning i-ts'at loi |
| 5 Have you a book? | 你有一部書冇 | ni yau yat po shü mo? |
| 6 Tell the house coolie to bring paper | 叫管店拎紙來 | kiu kun-tim ning chi loi |
| 7 I want a tea-pot | 我要茶壺 | ngo iu ch'a-oo |
| 8 I have no tea-cup | 我冇茶杯 | ngo mo ch'a-pui |
| 9 Have you a water-bottle? | 你有水樽冇 | ni yau shui tsun mo? |
| 10 I have ten chairs | 我有十張椅 | ngo yau shap cheung i |
| 11 Where is that hair brush? | 嗰個擦頭掃喺邊處 | ko ko ts'at-t'au-so hai pin ch'ü? |
| 12 There are twenty books on the table | 檯面有二十部書 | t'oi min yau yi shap po shü |
| 13 I want fifty chairs | 我要五十張椅 | ngo iu 'ng shap cheung i |
| 14 How many tables have you? | 你有幾多張檯呢 | ni yau ki to cheung t'oi ni? |
| 15 I have not many; I have only six | 我冇幾多；有六張啫 | ngo mo ki to; yau luk cheung ché |
| 16 There are twenty house-coolies | 有二十個管店 | yau yi shap ko kun-tim |
| 17 Those house-coolies have no tea | 個啲管店冇茶 | ko ti kun-tim mo ch'a |
| 18 Fourteen men and six women | 十四個男人，六個女人 | shap sze ko nam-yan, luk ko nü-yan |

| | | |
|---|---|---|
| 19 Five water bottles and fifty books | 五個水樽,五十簿書 | 'ng ko shui-tsun, 'ng shap po shü |
| 20 How many house-coolies are there? | 有幾多個管店呢 | yau ki to ko kun-tim ni? |
| 21 Don't tell that man to come | 唔好叫個个人來 | 'm hò kiu ko ko yan loi |
| 22 Tell the house-coolie to sweep the floor | 叫管店掃樓板 | kiu kun-tim so lau-pan |
| 23 How many books have you? | 你有幾多簿書 | ni yau ki to po shü? |
| 24 Have you much ice? | 你有好多雪麼 | ni yau ho to süt mo? |
| 25 No; I have no ice: I have pens, paper and ink | 冇,我冇雪,我有筆,有紙,有墨水 | mo; ngo mo süt; ngo yau păt, yau chi, yau măk-shui |
| 26 Where is the teapot? | 嗰個茶壺放在邊處呢 | ko ti ch'a-oo fong tsoi pin ch'ü ni? |
| 27 The tea is in the teapot | 茶喺茶壺 | ch'a hai ch'a-oo |
| 28 Where is that cook? | 嗰個火頭喺邊處 | ko ko fo-t'au hai pin ch'ü |
| 29 He is upstairs; where is that woman? | 佢喺樓上;嗰個女人喺邊處呢 | k'ü hai lau sheung; ko ko nü-yan hai pin ch'ü ni |
| 30 She is downstairs | 佢喺下低 | k'ü hai ha tai |
| 31 Tell her to come here | 叫佢來呢處 | kiu k'ü loi ni ch'ü |

# LESSON VIII.

| | | | | | |
|---|---|---|---|---|---|
| Bottle | 樽 | *tsun* | To brush | 擦 | *ts'ăt* |
| Beer | 啤酒 | *pi tsau* | Boots (a pair of) | 一對靴 | *yat (tui) hö* |
| Table napkin | 條茶巾 | (t'iu) ch'a-*kăn* | To take off | 除,脫 | ch'ü, *t'üt* |
| Soda water | 嗬囒水 | ho *lan shui* | Shoes (a pair of) | 一對鞋 | *yat (tui)* hai |
| Comb | 梳 | *sho* | Slippers | 撻踭鞋 | *t'at tsang* hai |
| To put on | 著,戴 | *cheuk; tai* | Stick | 鞭杆 | *pin kon* |
| Clothes | 衣服 | *i* fuk | Coat | 件衫 | (kin) *sham* |

| | | | | | |
|---|---|---|---|---|---|
| Cap or hat | 頂帽 | (*teng'*) mo' | To put away | 收埋, 擠 | *shau* mai, *tsai* |
| To put on clothes | 着衣服 | *cheuk i* fuk | | 埋 | mai |
| To put on a hat | 戴帽 | *tai* mo' | To (lit. to pass over) | 過 | *kwo'* |
| Box | 箱 | *seung* | | | |
| Looking glass | 面鏡 | min' *keng'* | To be able, can | 得, 能 | *tăk*, nang |

CH'Ü 處, place, is often added at the end of sentences indicating locality; e.g HAI T'OI MIN CH'Ü 喺檯面處, *it is on the table.* PI TSAU 啤酒 like many other compounds, such as KA LI 咖喱 *curry*, KA FEI 咖非 *coffee* &c. are bastard words intended to express the foreign sound of the article named. Several such words are unavoidably introduced in these exercises, on account of their being current amongst native servants. I FOOK 衣服 means *clothes* generally; KO KIN SHAM 啲件衫 *the coat* and *visible parts of a suit.*

| | | |
|---|---|---|
| 1 One bottle of beer | 一樽啤酒 | yat tsün pi tsau |
| 2 I want to put on clothes | 要着衣服 | iu cheuk i fook |
| 3 Where is the comb? | 梳喺邊處 | sho hai pin ch'ü? |
| 4 It is on the looking glass | 在鏡面處 | tsoi keng min ch'ü |
| 5 Brush my boots | 擦我對靴 | ts'at ngo tui hö' |
| 6 Take off your clothes | 除衣服 | ch'ü i fook |
| 7 Bring my slippers | 拈我對撻䏲鞋來 | nim ngo tui t'at tsang hai loi |
| 8 Put away my boots | 擠埋我對靴 | tsai mai ngo tui hö |
| 9 Have you good boots? | 你有好靴冇 | ni yau ho hö mo? |
| 10 How many table napkins have you? | 你有幾多條茶巾 | ni yau ki to t'iu ch'a kăn? |
| 11 I have six | 我有六條 | ngo yau luk t'iu |
| 12 Put them in the box | 擠入箱喇 | tsai yap seung la |
| 13 Put away my coat | 擠埋我件衫 | tsai mai ngo kin sham |
| 14 Do you want a stick? | 你要鞭杆唔要 | ni iu pin kon 'm iu |
| 15 Where is my hat? | 我頂帽喺邊處 | ngo teng mo hai pin ch'ü? |
| 16 Here it is on the tablo | 喺檯面處 | hai t'oi min ch'ü |
| 17 Please give it me | 請你俾過我 | ts'ing ni pi kwo ngo |
| 18 Tell the house-coolie to brush my boots | 叫管店擦我對靴 | kiu kun-tim ts'at ngo tui hö |
| 19 Bring soda water | 拈荷蘭水來 | nim ho-lan-shui loi |
| 20 Get my shoes and clothes | 拈我對鞋及衣服來 | nim ngo tui hai kap i fook loi |

| | | |
|---|---|---|
| 21 Put away that beer | 擠埋啁啲啤酒 | tsai mai ko ti pi tsau |
| 22 He has fifty hats and thirty sticks | 佢有五十頂帽，三十枝鞭杆 | k'ü yau ng shap teng mo, sam shap chi pin-kon |
| 23 Do you want beer? | 要啤酒唔要 | iu pi-tsau 'm iu? |
| 24 No; I like soda-water | 唔要，我中意荷蘭水 | 'm iu; ngo chung i ho-lan-shui |
| 25 Bring me a large hair brush | 拈一個大擦頭掃來我 | nim yat ko tai ts'at-t'au-so lai ngo |
| 26 These are good clothes | 呢啲衫好 | ni ti sham ho |
| 27 That is a bad coat | 啁件衫唔好 | ko kin sham 'm ho |
| 28 Put on your hat | 戴帽 | tai mo |
| 29 Where are the paper, pens, and ink? | 紙筆同墨水喺邊處 | chi, păt, t'ung măk-shui hai pin ch'ü? |
| 30 The paper is upstairs, the ink is here | 紙喺樓上，墨水喺呢處 | chi hai lau sheung măk-shui hai ni ch'ü |

---

# LESSON IX.

| | | | | | |
|---|---|---|---|---|---|
| Candle (lit. wax candle) | 蠟燭 | lap *chuk* | Needle (lit. eye pin) | 眼針 | ngan-*chăm* |
| | | | Pencil (lead) | 鉛筆 | ün-*păt* |
| Lantern | 手燈 | *shau' tăng* | What (thing)? | 乜野 | *măt*-ye' |
| Ink (Chinese) | 墨 | măk | Thread | 綫 | *sin*` |
| Ink-slab | 墨硯 | măk in` | Pin | 大頭針 | tai t'au *chăm* |
| To rub | 磨 | moh | Write | 寫 | *se'* |
| Penknife | 刀仔 | *to tsai'* | Scissors | 鉸剪 | *kau`-tsin'* |
| To light | 點 | *tim'* | To cut (with a knife) | 切 | *ts'it* |
| Lamp | 盞燈 | (*chăn*) *tăng* | Umbrella | 把遮 | (*pa'*) *che* |
| Characters (words) | 字 | tsz` | To cut (with scissors) | 剪 | *tsin'* |
| To call | 叫 | *kiu*` | And | 及 | kap |
| Handkerchief | 條手巾 | (t'iu) *shau' kăn* | Can, to be able | 噲 | ui' |
| Trowsers | 條褲 | (t'iu) *fu*` | | | |

It will be seen that compound words are not unfrequent, and that the *monosyllabic* character of the spoken language is by no means so strongly marked as is sometimes imagined. All compound words are hyphened in these exercises.

The particle TI 的 before a noun signifies *some, a little.*

The word TSO 做 *to do* or *make,* is often added to other verbs as an intensive particle; e.g. *It is called "to,"* KIU TSO TO 叫做刀.

曉 HIU, *to understand, "to know how to"* is often used in place of UI 噲, where in English we should use the words *can, to be able*: e.g. *Can you write?* NI HIU SE TSZ MO? 你曉寫字麼.

| | | |
|---|---|---|
| 1 Don't take away that ink | 唔好拈个的墨水去 | 'm ho nim ko-ti măk-shui hü |
| 2 Very well, I will put it here | 好咯;我放在呢處 | ho lok, ngo fong tsoi ni ch'ü |
| 3 Bring ink, I want to write | 拈墨水來,我要寫字 | nim măk-shui loi, ngo iu se tsz |
| 4 Put the candle on the table | 放蠟燭在檯面 | fong lap-chuk tsoi t'oi min |
| 5 Light the lamp | 點個盞燈 | tim ko chăn-tăng |
| 6 Bring a pen and an ink-slab | 拈筆墨硯來 | nim păt măk-in loi |
| 7 Rub me some ink | 磨的墨我 | moh ti măk ngo |
| 8 Get a pair of scissors and cut that handkerchief | 拈把較剪來,剪個條手巾 | nim pa kau-tsin loi, tsin ko t'iu shau-kăn |
| 9 Get me a handkerchief and my umbrella | 拈條手巾,拈把遮來我 | nim t'iu shau-kăn, nim pa che loi ngo |
| 10 Light the candle and take it up-stairs | 點蠟燭拈上去 | tim lap chuk, nim sheung hü |
| 11 Brush my trowsers | 擦我條褲 | ts'at ngo t'iu fu |
| 12 Where are the needle and thread? | 個眼針線喺邊處 | ko ngan chăm, sin hai pin ch'ü? |
| 13 It is down-stairs | 喺下低 | hai ha tai |
| 14 Get me a pin and the scissors | 拈大頭針,拈較剪來我 | nim tai t'au chăm, nim kau-tsin loi ngo |
| 15 Fetch the lantern | 拈手燈來我 | nim shau tăng loi ngo |
| 16 Have you a penknife | 你有刀仔冇 | ni yau to-tsai mo? |
| 17 No! but I have a pencil | 冇!我有鉛筆 | mo! ngo yau ün-păt |
| 18 What is this called? | 呢的叫乜野 | ni ti kiu măt-ye? |
| 19 It is called a penknife | 叫做刀仔 | kiu tso to-tsai |
| 20 Can you write characters? | 你曉寫字麼 | ni hiu se tsz moh? |
| 21 I cannot write characters | 我唔噲寫字 | ngo 'm ui se tsz |

初學階

| | | |
|---|---|---|
| 22 Come (*lit.* go) with me; fetch the lantern | 同我去;拈手燈黎 | t'ung ngo hü; nim shau-tăng lai |
| 23 Where are my coat, boots and cap? | 我件衫,我對靴,我頂帽喺邊處呢 | ngo kin sham, ngo tui hö, ngo teng mo, hai pin ch'ü ni |
| 24 They are put away | 擠埋喳 | tsai mai cha |
| 25 Bring me a bottle of soda-water | 拈一樽荷蘭水來我 | nim yat tsun ho-lan-shui loi ngo |
| 26 I want a pencil to write characters | 我要一枝筆寫字 | ngo iu yat chi păt se tsz |
| 27 Get paper, pens, ink, and an ink-slab | 拈紙筆墨水,及墨硯黎 | nim chi, păt, măk-shui kap măk-in, lai |
| 28 Sweep the floor; that will do! | 掃樓板,好咯 | so lau-pan; ho lok! |
| 29 Where is my penknife? | 我張刀仔喺邊處呢 | ngo cheung to-tsai hai pin ch'ü ni? |
| 30 Cut the handkerchief with the scissors | 使較剪剪手巾 | shai kau-tsin tsin shau-kăn |
| 31 Put on your trowsers and coat | 着褲着衫 | cheuk fu, cheuk sham |
| 32 Get my book and stick | 拈我簿書及我枝鞭杆來 | nim ngo po shü, kap ngo chi pin-kon loi |

# LESSON X.

| | | | | | |
|---|---|---|---|---|---|
| Chinese (adj.) | 唐人嘅 | t'ong yan *ke*` | Bell | 鐘 | *chung* |
| To break | 整爛 | *ching*' lan` | Quickly | 快啲 | *fai*` *ti*' |
| To tear | 撕破 | *sze p'o*` | To ring (a bell) | 打鐘,拏鐘 | *ta*' *chung*, ngo *chung* |
| To mend | 補翻 | *po*' fan | | | |
| To make | 整 | *ching*' | To send for and call | 使人叫 | *shai*' yan *kiu*` |
| To buy | 買 | mai' | A tailor | 裁縫佬 | ts'oi-fung *lo*' |
| To sell | 賣 | mai` | A needle-woman | 補衫婆 | *po*' *sham* p'oh |
| Watch | 時辰鏢 | shi-shăn-*piu* | | (*lit.* mend clothes old woman.) | |
| Corkscrew | 酒鑽 | *tsau*' *tsün*` | Socks | 襪,襪頭 | măt, măt-t'au |

The student will note that several words, when used in sentences, very frequently take the *second* instead of their proper tones; e.g. yan, *a man*, lan', to break, tan', an egg, etc., become yan', lan', tan', etc.

*For* (*on account of*) may be expressed by KWO 過 as MAI KWO NGO, 買過我, *buy for me.* It is not however always expressed in Chinese; e.g. *Tell the coolie to buy that table for me,* is KIU KUN TIM MAI KO CHEUNG T'OI NGO 叫管店買個張檯我.

The future, both positive and interrogative, is formed by making use of SEUNG 想 *think* or *intend.* Thus *will you* or *do you like to go?* NI SEUNG HÜ 'M NI 你想去唔呢. *Will you sell?* NI SEUNG MAI 'M NI 你想賣唔呢.

Several words are used by the Cantonese to designate themselves and their country. The most common is that given above; others are CHUNG-KWOK YAN 中國人 (central-kingdom man) PUN-TI YAN 本地人 (native soil man) PUNTI is used amongst themselves in contradistinction to HAKKA and HOKLO, (vide Introduction.)

| | | |
|---|---|---|
| 1 Mend the clothes | 補衣服 | po i fuk |
| 2 I want to buy a watch | 我要買個時辰鏢 | ngo iu mai ko shi-shăn-piu |
| 3 Come quickly and brush my boots | 快啲來，擦我對靴 | fai ti loi ts'at ngo tui hö |
| 4 Sell me your umbrella | 你把遮賣過我拉 | ni pa ché mai kwo ngo la |
| 5 I want to buy a bell and a lamp | 我要買一個鐘，一盞燈 | ngo iu mai yat ko chung, yat chăn tăng |
| 6 Are you making a book? | 你係整一簿書唔係 | ni hai ching yat po shü 'm hai? |
| 7 I am mending clothes | 我補衣服 | ngo po i fuk |
| 8 Don't break the bottle | 唔好整爛嗰個罇 | 'm ho ching lan ko ko tsun |
| 9 It is a Chinese bottle | 係唐人罇 | hai t'ọng yan tsun |
| 10 Is it a Chinese watch? | 係唐人時辰鏢唔係 | hai t'ong yan shi-shăn-piu 'm hai? |
| 11 No it is not, it is mine | 唔係，係我嘅 | 'm hai, hai ngo ke |
| 12 Ring the bell | 打鐘 | ta chung |
| 13 Send (*lit.* make somebody call) for the coolie | 使人叫管店來 | shai yan kiu kun-tim loi |
| 14 Tell a Chinaman to mend this | 叫個唐人補翻呢的 | kiu ko t'ong yan po fan ni ti |
| 15 Call the cook; tell him to come quickly | 叫廚夫叫佢快啲黎 | kiu ch'ü fu, kiu k'ü fai ti lai |
| 16 Will you buy a stick? | 你想買枝鞭干唔呢 | ni seung mai chi pin-kon 'm ni? |
| 17 Will you sell that cork-screw? | 你想賣個的酒鑽唔呢 | ni seung mai ko ti tsau-tsun 'm ni |

| | | |
|---|---|---|
| 18 No, I will sell the bell | 唔係,我想賣個鐘啫 | 'm hai, ngo seung mai ko chung ché |
| 19 How many watches have you? | 你有幾多個時辰鏢呢 | ni yau ki to ko shi-shăn-piu ni? |
| 20 I have nineteen pairs of socks | 我有十九對襪 | ngo yau shap-kau tui măt |
| 21 Where is the tailor? | 裁縫佬喺邊處呢 | ts'oi fung lo hai pin ch'ü ni? |
| 22 He has gone away | 佢扯咯 | k'ü ch'o lok |
| 23 Tell a needle-woman to come | 叫個補衣服婆黎 | kiu ko po-i-fuk-p'oh lai |
| 24 She is tearing the coat | 佢撕破㗎件衫 | k'ü sze p'o ko kin sham |
| 25 I want to mend the shoes | 我要補翻㗎對鞋 | ngo iu po-fan ko tui hai |
| 26 Mend these shoes for me | 補翻呢對鞋過我 | po-fan ni tui hai kwo ngo |
| 27 Do you want to break the stick? | 你要整爛個枝鞭杆咩 | ni iu ching-lan ko chi pin-kon me? |
| 28 Make a coat for me | 整一件衫過我 | ching yat kin sham kwo ngo |
| 29 Buy a candle for me | 買枝蠟燭過我 | mai chi lap-chuk kwo ngo |
| 30 Are you a Chinaman? | 你係唐人唔係 | ni hai t'ong yan 'm hai? |
| 31 I am not a Chinaman; what are you? | 我唔係唐人,你係邊處人呢 | ngo 'm hai t'ong yan; ni hai pin ch'ü yan ni? |
| 32 I am a tailor | 我做裁縫嘅 | ngo tso ts'oi fung ke |

# LESSON XI.

| | | | | | |
|---|---|---|---|---|---|
| Visiting card | 拜帖 | *pai`* *t'ip* | White | 白色 | pak-*shik* |
| To pay a visit | 探 | *t'am`* | Red | 紅色 | hung-*shik* |
| Good morning | 早晨 | *tso'* shan | Blue | 藍色 | lam-*shik* |
| Good bye | 好行 | *ho'* hang | Yellow | 黃色 | wong-*shik* |
| Spectacles | 眼鏡 | ngan' *keng`* | A word | 一句說話 | *yat kü` shüt wa`* |
| Waistcoat (lit. back heart) | 背心 | *pui`-săm* | Somebody, one | 人,有人 | yan, yau yan |
| | | | Cannot mend | 唔補得翻 | 'm *po' tăk fan* |
| Beef | 牛肉 | ngau-yuk | Buy a little for me | 買啲過我 | mai' *ti'* kwo ngo' |
| Mutton | 羊肉 | yeung-yuk | | | |

| | | | | | |
|---|---|---|---|---|---|
| Pork | 猪肉 | *chü*-yuk | I am going to; intend to | 我想 | ngo' *seung'* |
| Veal | 牛仔肉 | ngau-*tsai'*-yuk | | | |
| Soup | 湯 | *t'ong* | Have you bought (it)? | 你有買冇 | ni' yau mai' *mo*? |
| Vegetables | 菜 | *ts'oi`* | | | |
| Fruit | 菓子 | *kwoh'-tsz'* | I have torn (it) | 我撕破嘵 | ngo' *sze p'o`* hiu |
| Black | 黑色 | *hak-shik* | | | |

The word YAN 人 *man, one, somebody* is used somewhat like the German *man* or the English *one*; e.g. *one says* (*man sagt*) YAN WA 人話.

*Good morning* and *good bye* are in Chinese (as are similar phrases in most languages) idiomatic expressions to which custom has affixed their peculiar meaning. TSO SHAN 早晨 is literally *early time*, and HO HANG 好行 *good walk*.

| | | |
|---|---|---|
| 1 I want to put on my coat and trowsers | 我要着衫褲 | ngo iu cheuk sham fu |
| 2 Have you a visiting card? | 你有個拜帖冇 | ni yau ko pai-t'ip mo |
| 3 I have a white visiting card | 我有個白拜帖 | ngo yau ko pak pai-t'ip |
| 4 Are you going to pay a visit? | 你想去探人咩 | ni seung hü t'am yan me? |
| 5 Yes; good bye | 係, 好行喳 | hai; ho hang cha |
| 6 Good morning; have you a watch to sell? | 早晨, 你有時辰鏢賣冇 | tso shan; ni yau shi-shan-piu mai mo? |
| 7 I have no watch to sell | 我冇時辰鏢賣 | ngo mo shi-shan-piu mai |
| 8 Where are my spectacles? | 我對眼鏡在邊嘘呢 | ngo tui ngan-keng tsoi pin ch'ü ni |
| 9 (They are) on the black table | 在黑色檯面 | tsoi hak-shik t'oi min |
| 10 Mend my white waistcoat | 補我件白背心 | po ngo kin pak pui-säm |
| 11 Buy beef and mutton | 買牛肉羊肉嚟 | mai ngau-yuk, yeung-yuk lai |
| 12 Write the characters for soup and veal | 寫湯字牛仔肉字 | se t'ong tsz, ngau-tsai yuk, tsz |
| 13 Send for some red thread | 使人拈紅線黎 | shai yan nim hung sin lai |
| 14 Don't tear the yellow handkerchief | 唔好撕爛個條黃手巾 | 'm ho sze lan ko t'iu wong shau-kan |
| 15 Have you a blue coat? | 你有件藍衫冇 | ni yau kin lam sham mo? |
| 16 I have not a blue coat; I have black shoes | 我冇藍衫, 有對黑鞋啫 | ngo mo lam sham, yau tui hak hai che |
| 17 Have you bought the bread? | 你有買麵飽冇 | ni yau mai min-pau mo? |

| | | |
|---|---|---|
| 18 Very well; good bye, come soon | 好咯，好行喇，早啲翻黎啵 | ho lok: ho hang la, tso ti fan lai po |
| 19 Red visiting cards | 紅拜帖 | hung pai-t‘ip |
| 20 He has torn the red visiting card | 佢撕爛嘵嗰個紅拜帖 | k‘ü sze lan hiu ko ko hung pai-t‘ip |
| 21 This is a bad waistcoat | 呢件唔好嘅背心 | ni kin 'm ho ke pui-săm |
| 22 He cannot mend the waistcoat | 佢唔補得翻個件背心 | k‘ü 'm po tak fan ko kin pui-săm |
| 23 Buy me a pair of white socks | 買對白襪過我 | mai tui pak măt kwo ngo |
| 24 Light a candle and then bring me a pen and ink | 點蠟燭，然後拈筆拈墨水黎我 | tim lap-chuk, in hau nim păt, nim măk-shui lai ngo |
| 25 Where are you taking that umbrella to? | 你拈個把遮去邊處呢 | ni nim ko pa che hü pin ch‘u ni? |
| 26 I am taking it to the tailor's | 我拈去裁縫佬處 | ngo nim hü ts‘oi-fung lo ch‘u |
| 27 Do you like vegetables? | 你中意菜唔中意 | ni chung i ts‘oi 'm chung i? |
| 28 No, I like veal | 唔中意，我中意牛仔肉 | 'm chung i; ngo chung i ngau-tsai-yuk |
| 29 Good bye, I am going to buy a penknife | 好行啫，我去買張刀仔 | ho hang che, ngo hü mai cheung to-tsai |
| 30 Send somebody for a needle-woman to mend my handkerchief | 使人去叫個補衫婆黎，補翻我條手巾 | shai yan hü kiu ko po-shăm-p‘oh lai, po-fau ngo t‘iu shau-kăn |

# LESSON XII.

| | | | | | |
|---|---|---|---|---|---|
| Trees | 樖樹 | *p‘oh* shü' | Together, with, and | 共 | kung |
| Leaves | 樹葉 | shü' ip | Fish | 魚 | ü |
| Green | 綠色，青 | luk *shik*, *ts‘ing* | Fowl | 雞 | *kai* |
| Brown | 棕色 | *tsung shik* | Ham | 火腿 | *foh' t‘ui'* |
| Children | 仔女 | *tsai'* nü' | Milk | 牛奶 | ngau-nai' |

| | | | | | |
|---|---|---|---|---|---|
| Girl | 女仔 | nü' *tsai'* | Price | 價錢 | *ka'* tsʻin |
| Boy | 男仔 | nam *tsai'* | Make (cause to be done) | 整 | *ching'* |
| To look for, to fetch | 搵 | *wan'* | Make (to do) | 做 | tso\` |
| Potatoes | 薯仔 | shü-*tsai'* | Catty ($1\frac{1}{3}$ lb.) | 斤 | *kăn* |
| Do. (lit. Holland root) | 荷蘭薯 | ho-lan-shü | Cents | 仙士 | sin sze |
| | | | Houseboy | 事仔 | sze\` *tsai'* |
| Eggs | 鷄蛋 | *kai* tan\` | | | |

NAM TSAI 男仔 *a boy* is literally *a male child.*

The word SIN SZE 仙士 for *cent* is merely an attempt to reproduce the English expression.

Particular attention must be paid to the accent of the words SZE TSAI 事仔 *house-boy*; if the emphasis be thrown on the first word it means a dead child.

Note the distinction between "make" cause to be done, and "make" meaning simply *to do.*

When girls and boys are spoken of antithetically in the same sentence NÜ and TSAI only need be used.

| | | | |
|---|---|---|---|
| 1 | Trees have green leaves | 樹有青葉 | shü yau tsʻing ip |
| 2 | Have you potatoes? | 你有薯仔冇 | ni yau shü-tsai mo? |
| 3 | I have two children | 我有兩個仔女 | ngo yau leung ko tsai nü |
| 4 | Have you boys and girls? | 你有仔女冇 | ni yau tsai nü mo? |
| 5 | I have one boy and one girl | 我有一個仔一個女 | ngo yau yat ko tsai, yat ko nü |
| 6 | The boy likes fish | 個仔愛魚 | ko tsai oi ü |
| 7 | Make some fish curry | 整啲咖喱魚 | ching ti ka li ü |
| 8 | Get me some veal and ham | 拈啲牛仔肉共火腿來我 | nim ti ngau-tsai-yuk kung foh-tʻui loi ngo |
| 9 | Buy me some milk and eggs | 買啲牛奶, 買啲鷄蛋我 | mai ti ngau-nai, mai ti kai-tan ngo |
| 10 | I want fowls, eggs, and vegetables | 我要鷄, 鷄蛋, 共菜 | ngo iu kai, kai-tan, kung tsʻoi |
| 11 | What is the price of potatoes? | 薯仔係乜野價錢呢 | shü tsai hai măt yé ka tsʻin ni? |
| 12 | They are three cents a catty | 係三個仙士一斤 | hai sam ko sin-sze yat kăn |
| 13 | Send for six catties | 使人買六斤 | shai yan mai luk kăn |
| 14 | Buy me four catties of vegetables | 買四斤菜我 | mai sze kăn tsʻoi ngo |

| | | |
|---|---|---|
| 15 Tell the girl to fetch a needle-woman | 叫個女仔去,叫個補衫婆來 | kiu ko nü-tsai hü kiu ko po-sham-p'oh loi |
| 16 Make some vegetable soup | 整的菜湯 | ching ti ts'oi-t'ong |
| 17 That boy is good, that girl is bad | 個男仔好,個女仔唔好 | ko nam-tsai ho, ko nü-tsai 'm ho |
| 18 Have you fish to sell? | 你有魚賣冇 | ni yau ü mai mo? |
| 19 No, the girl has fish to sell | 冇,個女仔有魚賣 | mo; ko nü-tsai yau ü mai |
| 20 Mend my white socks | 補翻我對白襪 | po fan ngo tui pak-măt |
| 21 Brush my brown clothes | 擦我的棕個色衣服 | ts'at ngo ko ti tsung-shik i-fuk |
| 22 Tea leaves are green and black | 茶葉有青色,有黑色嘅 | ch'a ip yau ts'ing-shik, yau hak-shik ke |
| 23 How many eggs have you to sell? | 你有幾多鷄蛋賣 | ni yau ki to kai-tan mai? |
| 24 Ring the bell to call the boy | 揫鐘叫事仔來 | ngo chung kiu sze-tsai loi |
| 25 This fish is bad; take it away | 呢的魚唔好,擰佢去喇 | ni ti ü 'm ho, ning k'ü hü la |
| 26 Get me some good soup beef | 搵啲好湯肉來我 | wan ti ho t'ong yuk loi ngo |
| 27 What have you there? | 你嗰處有乜野 | ni ko ch'ü yau măt ye |
| 28 I have ham and veal | 我有火腿有牛仔肉 | ngo yau foh t'ui, yau ngau-tsai-yuk |
| 29 These are very large trees | 呢啲樹好大裔 | ni ti shü ho tai p'oh |
| 30 Are these good eggs? | 呢的鷄蛋好唔呢 | ni ti kai-tan ho 'm ni? |
| 31 No, they are bad eggs, I have some good milk | 唔係,個的唔好鷄蛋我有啲好牛奶 | 'm ho: ko ti 'm ho kai-tan; ngo yau ti ho ngau-nai |

---

# LESSON XIII.

| | | | | | |
|---|---|---|---|---|---|
| Biscuit | 餅干 | *peng'-kon* | Breakfast | 小飡,早飯 | *siu' ts'an, tso'* fan\` |
| To bake | 烘,局 | *hong\`*, kuk | | | |
| To boil | 煲,烚 | *po*, shăp | Dinner | 大飡,晚飡 | tai\` *ts'an*, man\` *ts'an* |
| Cabbage | 白菜 | pak-*ts'oi\`* | | | |

| | | | | | |
|---|---|---|---|---|---|
| Cake | 餅 | *peng'* | Tiffin | 小食, 食 | *siu'* shik, shik |
| Mustard | 芥末 | *kai'*-mut | | 晏, 食 | *an'*, shik |
| Pepper | 胡椒末 | u-*tsiu*-mut | | 晏晝 | *an' chau'* |
| A slice | 一塊 | *yat fai'* | Ready | 齊備, 便 | ts'ai-pi', pin |
| Vinegar | 醋 | *ts'o'* | Take care | 小心 | *siu' săm* |
| Pastry | 餅食 | *peng'*-shik | A piece | 一啲 | *yat ti* |
| To hand (at table) | 俾 | *pi'* | Gold | 金 | *kăm* |
| | | | Silver | 銀 | ngăn |
| A meal | 一飱 | *yat ts'an* | To eat | 食, 吃 | shik, *yak* |
| thus, (adv. of quality) then, in this case | 噉, 就 | kom, tsau | To like | 中意 | *chung-i'* |
| | | | Or | 嘅 | *chi'* |

*Breakfast* and *dinner* are simply the "*little*" and the "*great meal.*"

*To take care* is literally "*little heart,*" caution, it is supposed, inducing a contraction of that organ.

*To "hand"* a thing is rendered by PI 俾 *to give.*

*Or* is sometimes rendered by 嘅 CHI. The Chinese prefer however to alter the construction of the phrase when it implies antithesis (see sentence 17 *infra.*)

| | | | |
|---|---|---|---|
| 1 | Do you like to eat fowl? | 你中意食鷄唔呢 | ni chung i shik kai 'm ni? |
| 2 | No, I don't like fowl, I like eggs | 唔中意吃鷄, 我中意鷄蛋 | 'm chung i yak kai; ngo chung i kai-tan |
| 3 | Boil the soup quickly | 快啲焓湯 | fai ti shăp t'ong |
| 4 | I want you to bake this cake | 要你局呢的餅 | iu ni kuk ni ti peng |
| 5 | Green cabbage is good | 青菜好吃 | ts'eng ts'oi ho yak |
| 6 | Hand me the mustard | 俾芥末過我 | pi kai-mut kwo ngo |
| 7 | Bring me some vinegar | 拈啲醋我 | nim ti ts'o ngo |
| 8 | What pastry have you? | 你有乜野餅食呢 | ni yau măt ye peng-shik ni? |
| 9 | Buy me a piece of cake | 買一塊餅過我 | mai yat fai peng kwo ngo |
| 10 | Hand me some water | 俾的水我 | pi ti shui ngo |
| 11 | Breakfast is ready | 小餐便咯 | siu ts'an pin lok |
| 12 | When will dinner be ready? | 大餐幾時便呢 | tai ts'an ki shi pin ni? |
| 13 | It will be ready directly (quickly) | 就便咯 | tsau pin lok |
| 14 | Bring the tiffin | 拈小食來 | nim siu shik loi |
| 15 | This makes a good meal | 呢的噉就係一飱好飯 | ni ti kom tsau hai yat ts'an ho fan |

初學階

| | | |
|---|---|---|
| 16 Are you ready? | 你齊備唔曾 | ni ts'ai-pi 'm ts'ang |
| 17 Take care, or you will (*lit.* don't if not, then you) break that bottle | 小心呀，唔係你就打爛嗰個罇咯 | siu săm a, 'm hai ni tsau ta lan ko ko tsun lok |
| 18 I have torn my handkerchief | 我撕爛曉我條手巾 | ngo szc lan hiu ngo t'iu shau-kăn |
| 19 A gold pin and a silver teapot | 一枝金針，一個銀茶壺 | yat chi kăm chăm, yat ko ngăn ch'a-oo |
| 20 A piece of bread | 一塊麵飽 | yat fai min-pau |
| 21 Get my slippers | 拈我對撻踭鞋來 | nim ngo tui t'at chang hai loi |
| 22 Those boots are very large | 个對靴好大 | ko tui hö ho tai |
| 23 This pastry is very good | 呢的餅食十分好 | ni ti peng-shik shap-făn ho |
| 24 That vinegar is bad | 個啲醋唔好 | ko ti ts'o 'm ho |
| 25 Is that a silver or a golden lamp? | 個盞燈係銀嘅，噉係金嘅呢 | ko chăn tăng hai ngăn ke chi hai kăm ke ni |
| 26 It is a large silver lamp | 係一盞大銀燈 | hai yat chăn tai ngăn tăng |
| 27 Mustard, pepper, and vinegar are good | 個啲芥末胡椒末係好嘅 | ko ti kai-mut, oo-tsiu-mut, tso, hai ho ke |
| 28 This biscuit is very large | 呢個餅干好大 | ni ko peng-kon ho tai |
| 29 That child has come (comes) to dinner | 个個細紋仔來吃大餐 | ko ko sai-man-tsai loi yak tai ts'an |
| 30 Do you want a meal? | 你愛吃餐咩 | ni oi yak ts'an me? |

---

## LESSON XIV

| | | | | | |
|---|---|---|---|---|---|
| Cigars | 呂宋烟 | lü'-*sung*`-*in* | To eat enough (full) | 吃飽 | *yak pau'* |
| Pipe | 烟筒 | *in*-t'ung | Saucepan | 鑊 | wok |
| Tobacco | 烟餅 | *in-peng'* | Copper | 銅 | t'ung |
| To smoke (a pipe) | 食烟 | shik *in* | Directly | 即刻 | *tsik hak* |
| All | 㗎嘭唥，晒 | ham`-pang`-lang`, *sai*` | Sausage | 釀腸 | yeung` ch'eung |
| | | | Shrimps | 蝦 | *ha* |

| | | | | | |
|---|---|---|---|---|---|
| Iron | 鐵 | *t'it* | Flowers | 花 | *fa* |
| Banana | 蕉 | *tsiu* | To gather flowers | 摘花 | chak *fa* |
| Custard Apple | 番荔枝 | *fan* lai`-*chi* | To plant | 種 | *chung`* |
| Lychee | 荔枝 | lai`-*chi* | A ten cent piece | 一個豪子 | *yat* ko ho-tsz' |
| Whampee | 黃皮 | wong-p'i | | | |
| Orange (small) | 桔仔, 柑 | *kat-tsai, kom,* | Thing | 野 | ye' |
| Coolie orange | 橙 | ch'ang | Dollar | 銀錢 | ngăn-ts'in |

*To smoke tobacco* is literally "*eat smoke*,"—an expression to be found in some other languages also.

*Rice*, as given above, refers to the cooked grain.

*And* may be rendered by 共 KUNG when coupling substantives, 零 LING being used between numerals. Neither, however, is very frequently used.

| | | |
|---|---|---|
| 1 Boil some rice directly | 即刻煲飯 | tsik hak po fan |
| 2 Have you any cigars to sell? | 你有呂宋烟賣冇 | ni yau lü-sung-in mai mo? |
| 3 I want to buy a pipe | 我要買枝烟筒 | ngo iu mai chi in-t'ung |
| 4 Do you smoke tobacco? | 你食烟唔食 | ni shik in 'm shik? |
| 5 I like bananas and custard apples | 我愛蕉共番荔枝 | ngo oi tsiu kung fan lai-chi |
| 6 The lychees are good, the whampees bad | 荔枝好黃皮唔好 | lai-chi ho, wong-p'i 'm ho |
| 7 Get me fifty oranges (small) | 拈五十個桔仔來我 | nim 'ng shap ko kăt-tsai loi ngo |
| 8 Boil the sausage | 烚個啲釀腸 | shăp ko ti yeung-ch'eung |
| 9 Take away those shrimps | 拈個啲蝦去 | nim ko ti ha hü |
| 10 Do you like to gather flowers? | 你愛摘花唔愛 | ni oi chak fa 'm oi? |
| 11 Go and plant those vegetables | 去種個啲菜 | hü chung ko ti ts'oi |
| 12 This is a silver watch | 呢個時晨錶係銀嘅 | ni ko shi-shăn-piu hai ngăn ke |
| 13 That is a copper bell | 個的鐘銅嘅 | ko ti chung t'ung ke |
| 14 I want to buy an iron cork-screw | 我要買個鐵酒鑽 | ngo iu mai ko t'it tsau-tsün |
| 15 What is this thing? | 呢的係乜野 | ni ti hai măt ye? |
| 16 It is an iron saucepan | 係鐵鑊 | hai t'it wok |
| 17 All are here | 喊嘭哈喺處 | ham-pang-lang hai ch'ü |

| | | |
|---|---|---|
| 18 What is the price of that gold watch? | 啲個金時晨鏢係乜價錢呢 | ko ko kăm shi-shăn-piu hai măt ka ts'in ni? |
| 19 The price is fifty dollars | 五十個銀錢 | 'ng-shap ko ngăn-ts'in |
| 20 I will give you forty-five dollars | 我俾四十五銀錢你 | ngo pi sze shap 'ng ngăn ts'in ni |
| 21 Take care, you'll break that pipe directly (*lit.* wait and you'll break &c.) | 小心呀，等吓你會打爛個枝烟筒 | siu săm a, tăng ha ni ui ta lan ko chi in-t'ung |
| 22 This is very good tobacco; where did you get it? | 呢的烟餅十分好，喺邊處得來嘅呢 | ni ti in-peng shap-făn ho; hai pin ch'ü tăk loi ke ni? |
| 23 Both the rice and bread are enough | 飯共麵飽，兩樣都够咯 | fan kung min-pau leung yeung to kau lok |
| 24 Boil the meat in the saucepan (*lit.* give that saucepan and boil &c.) | 俾個鑊嚟烚個啲肉 | pi ko wok lai shăp ko ti yuk |
| 25 Is it baked enough? | 局好唔曾 | kuk ho 'm ts'ang? |
| 26 Are all the handkerchiefs mended? | 㗎𠵱唅個啲手巾補好嗮唔曾 | ham-pang-lang ko ti shau-kăn po ho sai 'm ts'ăng? |
| 27 Bring dinner directly | 快的搬晚餐來 | fai-ti pun man ts'an loi |
| 28 Put the flowers on the table | 個的花放檯面處 | ko ti fa fong t'oi min ch'ü |
| 29 How many dollars have you? | 你有幾多個銀錢呢 | ni yau ki to ko ngăn-ts'in ni? |
| 30 I have sixteen dollars, forty cents | 我有十六個銀錢零四豪子 | ngo yau shap luk ko ngăn-ts'in ling sze ho-tsz |

---

# LESSON XV.

| | | | | | |
|---|---|---|---|---|---|
| To add up | 計 | kai | A period (time) | 耐，一時 | noi, *yat* shi |
| To alter | 改 | *koi'* | must; really | 必 | *pit* |
| To begin | 起首 | *hi' shau'* | To count | 數 | *sho'* |
| To blow out | 吹息 | *ch'ui sik* | To die | 死 | *sze'* |
| A letter (postal) | 封信 | (*fung*) *săn`* | To do | 做 | tso` |

| | | |
|---|---|---|
| An account (bill) | 單 | *tan* |
| Do. money statement of any sort. | 數目 | *sho`* muk |
| To burn | 燒 | *shiu* |
| To change (cash) | 找 | *chau'* |
| To clean | 整乾淨 | *ching' kon* tseng` |
| To copy | 抄寫 | *ch'au se'* |
| To dwell (live in) | 住 | chü` |
| Conversation | 講話, 商酌 | *kong'* wa`, *sheung* cheuk |
| Gold dollar | 金仔 | *kăm-tsai'* |
| So or "thus" (adv. of quantity.) See lesson XIII for same word as adv. of quality | 咁 | *kom`* |

### CONJUGATION OF NON-COMPOUND VERBS.

The Chinese word expressing a verb undergoes no change or inflexion on account of mood or tense.

The nominative, when expressed, precedes it as in English. In order to express the time of action (i.e. the different shades of meaning dependent on what we term moods and tenses) other words are added, or the verb is so placed in the sentence that the context sufficiently shews the intention of the speaker. The following table shews the principal parts of the active verb:—

| | | | |
|---|---|---|---|
| Infinitive | To WALK | 行 | hang |
| Present | *I walk* | 我行 | ngo hang |
| Imperfect | *I walked* | 我行過 | ngo hang kwo |
| Perfect | *I have walked* | 我已經行咯, 我有行曉 | ngo i king hang lok: ngo yau hang hiu |
| Potential | *I can walk* | 我行得 | ngo hang tăk |
| ,, | *I may or can walk* | 我噲行 | ngo ui hang |
| Subjunctive | *If I walk* | 我若係行 | ngo yeuk hai hang |
| Future | *I shall or will walk* | 我將來行 | ngo tseung loi hang |
| ,, | *I will* (have an intention to) *walk* | 我想行 | ngo seung hang |

The Chinese call a verb UT TSZ 活字 i.e. the "living" or "active" character. Note that the accusative or accusative phrase frequently precedes the verb.

The intensive particle 啫 CHE is frequently found following a verb. It is not translated.

| | | |
|---|---|---|
| 1 Have you tobacco to sell? | 你有烟餅賣冇 | ni yau in-peng mai mo? |
| 2 No; I have tobacco to smoke | 冇, 我有烟食啫 | mo; ngo yau in shik che |
| 3 Will you begin to smoke? | 你起首食烟唔呢 | ni hi shau shik in 'm ni |
| 4 Is breakfast ready? | 早餐便唔曾 | tso ts'an pin 'm ts'ăng |

| | | |
|---|---|---|
| 5 Blow out the candle | 吹息蠟燭 | chʻui sik lap-chuk |
| 6 Bring me your bill | 拈你張單來我 | nim ni cheung-tan loi ngo |
| 7 Alter this bill | 改呢張單 | koi ni cheung tan |
| 8 I will not alter this bill | 我唔想改呢張單 | ngo 'm seung koi ni cheung-tan |
| 9 Add up the account | 計數目 | kai sho muk |
| 10 Burn it all | 燒𠯢 | shiu sai |
| 11 I wish to alter the bill | 我想改嗰張單 | ngo seung koi ko cheung-tan |
| 12 Buy me some cigars | 買的呂宋烟過我 | mai ti Lü-Sung in kwo ngo |
| 13 Will you sell me some oranges? | 你想賣的柑我唔呢 | ni seung mai ti kăm ngo 'm ni? |
| 14 I have bought some lychees | 我買得啲荔枝咯 | ngo mai tăk ti lai-chi lok |
| 15 Have you bought any flowers? | 你買曉花未 | ni mai hiu fa me? |
| 16 Clean the saucepan | 整乾凈嗰個鑊 | ching kon-tseng ko ko wok |
| 17 Please change this for me | 請找呢的過我 | tsʻing chau ni ti kwo ngo |
| 18 Will you copy characters? | 你想抄字唔想 | ni seung chʻau tsz 'm seung? |
| 19 He may die | 或者佢會死 | wak che kʻü ui sze |
| 20 Count all those things | 數過𠯢个啲野 | sho kwo sai ko ti ye |
| 21 If he smoke he may die | 佢食烟怕會死 | kʻü shik in pʻa ui sze |
| 22 Can you do this for me? | 你替我做得呢的唔呢 | ni tʻai ngo tso tăk ni ti 'm ni? |
| 23 Where do you reside? | 你喺邊處住 | ni hai pin-chʻü chü? |
| 24 I had a conversation with him | 我有同佢講過說話咯 | ngo yau tʻung kʻü kong kwo shüt wa lok |
| 25 Begin to count | 起首數 | hi shau sho |
| 26 Buy me that cake | 買個啲餅我 | mai ko-ti peng ngo |
| 27 Sell me that rice | 賣個啲米過我 | mai ko-ti mai kwo ngo |
| 28 I like gold dollars | 我中意金仔 | ngo chung i kăm tsai |
| 29 Where is the bill? | 個張單在邊處呢 | ko cheung tan tsoi pin-chʻü ni? |
| 30 A good long conversation | 講好耐說話 | kong ho noi shüt wa |
| 31 I began it upstairs | 我喺樓上起首先 | ngo hai lau-sheung hi shau sin |
| 32 Clean the boots downstairs | 落下低擦靴 | lok ha tai tsʻat hö |
| 33 Take care, you will burn it | 小心唔好燒着佢 | siu săm 'm ho shiu cheuk kʻü |
| 34 I have blown it out | 我吹息曉佢咯 | ngo chʻui sik hiu kʻü lok |
| 35 I have not blown it out | 我未曾吹息佢 | ngo mi tsăng chʻui sik kʻü |

| | | |
|---|---|---|
| 36 It will burn the cake | 必燒烘個啲餅嘅 | pit shiu nung ko ti peng ke |
| 37 Change this silver dollar for me | 找呢個銀錢過我 | chau ni ko ngăn-ts'in kwo ngo |
| 38 Copy this letter for me | 抄呢封信過我 | ch'au ni fung săn kwo ngo |
| 39 He sells shrimps | 佢賣蝦 | k'ü mai ha |
| 40 Buy some mustard and pepper for me | 買的芥末共椒末過我 | mai ti kai-mut kung tsiu-mut kwo ngo |

# LESSON XVI.

| | | | | | |
|---|---|---|---|---|---|
| To empty | 整空 | *ching' hung* | To lend | 借 | *tse`* |
| To employ | 請, 使, 用 | *ts'ing', shai',* yung` | A dog | 隻狗 | (chek) *kau'* |
| | | | Parents | 父母 | fu` mo' |
| To feed | 喂 | *wai`* | Everywhere | 處處 | *ch'ü'-ch'ü'* |
| To learn | 學 | hok | To interpret | 傳話, 繙譯 | ch'ün-wa`, *fan* yik |
| A door | 門 | mun | | | |
| At | 在 | tsoi` | To keep (retain) | 留翻 | lau *fan* |
| A friend | 朋友 | p'ang yau' | To kill | 打死 | *ta' sze'* |
| To find | 搵着 | *wan'* cheuk | To know (be acquainted with) | 識 | *shik* |
| To finish | 做完 | tso` ün | | | |
| To heat | 燒熱 | *shiu* it | To lock | 鎖 | *soh'* |
| To hurt | 傷 | *sheung* | True, really | 實 | shat |

The verb as given in these lists of words is to be regarded as in the infinitive mood. Thus *I wish to learn*, NGO CHUNG I HOK 我中意學.

Participle:—The present participle is often expressed either by the infinitive alone, or by its combination with an adverb of time. In other cases the word HAI 係 *to be—is*, is used, as in English, before the infinitive and adverb; e.g. "*He is eating*," is either *he eats*, K'Ü HAI YAK KĂN 佢係吃緊, or *he eats at this time*, K'Ü I KA YAK 佢而家吃.

The potential *may* is sometimes rendered by HO 好.

The past participle is expressed by the adverb of time, the particle KE 嘅 sometimes following the verb, e.g., *He was beaten,* K'Ü PI YAN KO CHAN SHI TA TS'AN KE 佢被人个陣時打親嘅, *The door was locked* KO TO MUN KO CHAN SHI SOH MAI KE 嗰度門个陣時鎖埋嘅.

| | | |
|---|---|---|
| 1 Do you eat oranges? | 你吃柑唔吃 | ni yak kom 'm yak? |
| 2 Lend me a saucepan | 借一個鑊過我 | tsé yat ko wok kwo ngo |
| 3 Will you employ that man? | 你想用嗰个人咩 | ni seung yung ko ko yan me? |
| 4 The dog begins to walk | 個隻狗起首行 | ko chek kau hi shau hang |
| 5 Will you add up the account or not? | 你肯計呢張單唔肯 | ni hàng kai ni cheung tan 'm hàng? |
| 6 Find me that bill | 搵着呢張單過我 | wăn cheuk ko cheung tan kwo ngo |
| 7 Have you finished learning? | 你學完唔曾 | ni hok ün 'm ts'ăng? |
| 8 Empty that pipe for me | 整空個枝烟筒過我 | ching hung ko chi in-t'ung kwo ngo |
| 9 Have you changed that money? | 你有找个的錢唔曾 | ni yau chau ko ti ts'in 'm ts'ăng? |
| 10 Feed those children | 喂嗰啲仔女 | wai ko ti tsai nü |
| 11 Where is he? | 佢在邊處 | k'ü tsoi pin-ch'ü? |
| 12 He is at his parents' | 佢在父母處 | k'ü tsoi fu mo ch'ü |
| 13 Lock the door | 鎖門 | soh mun |
| 14 Do you know that man? | 你識个個人唔識 | ni shik ko ko yan 'm shik? |
| 15 I do not know that man | 我唔識佢 | ngo 'm shik k'ü |
| 16 He has killed his parents | 佢有打死佢父母 | k'ü yau ta sze k'ü fu mo |
| 17 He has friends everywhere | 佢邊處都有朋友咯 | k'ü pin ch'ü to yau p'ang yau lok |
| 18 Where do you keep (i.e. where is) your dog? | 你隻狗在邊處呢 | ni chek kau tsoi pin ch'ü ni |
| 19 Can you interpret Chinese characters | 唐字你噲翻譯唔噲 | t'ong tsz ni ui fan yik 'm ui? |
| 20 I have interpreted Chinese characters | 我有翻譯過唐字 | ngo yau fan yik kwo t'ong tsz |
| 21 Is that man hurt? | 個个人有傷冇 | ko ko yan yau sheung mo? |
| 22 Heat me some water | 燒熱的水我 | shiu it ti shui ngo |
| 23 I have finished eating | 我吃完咯 | ngo yak ün lok |
| 24 He may lend a dollar | 佢可以借一個銀錢 | k'ü ho i tse yat ko ngan ts'in |
| 25 Has he learned those characters? | 個的字佢學過唔曾 | ko ti tsz k'ü hok kwo 'm ts'ăng? |

| | | |
|---|---|---|
| 26 He has locked the door | 佢有鎖門 | k'u yau soh mun |
| 27 Tell him to interpret | 叫佢傳話 | kiu k'ü ch'ün wa |
| 28 Does he like to gather flowers? | 佢中意擇花唔呢 | k'ü chung i chak fa 'm ni? |
| 29 He has found a copper saucepan | 佢揾着一个銅水煲 | k'ü wăn cheuk yat ko t'ung shui-po |
| 30 Will he keep (retain) it? | 佢想留翻唔想 | k'ü seung lau fan 'm seung? |
| 31 No, he will bring it directly | 唔想佢就拈來 | 'm seung k'ü tsau nim loi |

# LESSON XVII.

| | | | | | |
|---|---|---|---|---|---|
| To see, look at | 睇見 | *t'ai' kin`* | To punish (a fault) | 責罰 | *chak*-fat |
| To marry (said of a man) | 娶老婆 | *ts'o`* lo'-p'oh | Goods | 貨物 | *fo`*-măt |
| | | | To make (compel) | 監, 勉强 | *kam*; min' k'eung' |
| To marry (said of a woman) | 出嫁 | *ch'ut ka`* | | | |
| | | | Afterwards | 然後, 後來 | in-hau`, hau`-loi |
| To move (shake) | 郁動 | *yuk* tung` | | | |
| To open | 開 | *hoi* | Friend | 朋友 | p'ang-yau' |
| Always | 時時 | shi-shi | To put down | 放下 | *fong`* ha` |
| Family | 家眷 | *ka-kun`* | To quarrel | 爭論, 嗌交 | *chang*-lun', *ai`-kau* |
| To owe | 欠 | *him`* | | | |
| To pay (give) | 俾 | *pi'* | To read (recite) | 睇書, 讀 | *t'ai' shü*, tuk |
| To play | 反 | *fan'* | To remember | 記得 | *ki` tak* |
| To pour out | 斟出 | *cham ch'ut* | Towards | 向 | *heung`* |
| To fill | 斟滿 | *cham* mun' | Far | 遠 | ün' |
| To punish (officially) | 治罪 | chi` tsui` | Near | 近 | kan` |
| | | | To be willing | 肯 | *hăng'* |

The formation usually termed by grammarians "second future" (*shall have done* so and so) may be expressed by TSEUNG LOI 将來, though this construction is very seldom availed of; e.g. *I shall have walked,* NGO TSEUNG LOI HANG 我将來行.

The Perfect (*have walked*) and Pluperfect (*had walked*) are sometimes shewn by the context, but are frequently expressed in the form following; e.g. *he has gone away*, K'Ü HÜ KWO LOK 佢去過咯; *I had* (*just*) *gone out* NGO (NGAM NGAM) I KING CH'UT MUN 我(啱啱)已經出門.

The following adverbs: FONG 方 *place, thereon*, TSOI 在 *still* or *at*, CHING 正 *direct*, CHING KAN 正間 *just now*, CHING TSOI 正在, TSAU CHING 就正 *just now*, with others, express the pluperfect tense when used in a sentence following (or in reply to) another expressing past action; e.g. (in reply to "Had he eaten that fruit?") *He had eaten the fruit*, K'Ü CHAU CHING YAK KWO KWOH LOK 佢就正吃過菓咯.

TO LOK 到咯 follows certain verbs to express the perfect participle; e.g. SHAU TO LOK 收到咯 *received*.

In some cases TO 到 is used alone; e.g. TUK TO 讀到, *read*.

| | | |
|---|---|---|
| 1 I looked at that man | 我有睇見個个人 | ngo yau t'ai kin ko-ko yan |
| 2 He has made the door | 佢整好個度門囉 | k'ü ching ho ko to mun lo |
| 3 He has finished the account | 佢計完數 | k'ü kai ün sho |
| 4 That woman had married him | 個个女人嫁過佢 | ko-ko nü yan ka kwo k'ü |
| 5 He had married two wives | 佢娶過兩個老婆 | k'ü ts'o kwo leung ko lo-p'o |
| 6 I have moved away those flowers | 我有拈去个的花 | ngo yau nim hü ko-ti fa |
| 7 Had he opened the door? (*lit* was it he who opened the door?) | 係佢有開門冇 | hai k'ü yau hoi mun mo? |
| 8 He had just paid it | 佢啱啱已經俾過 | k'ü ngam ngam i king pi kwo |
| 9 We owed him money formerly | 我哋舊時欠佢銀 | ngo-ti kau-shi him k'ü ngăn |
| 10 Take care; he will not pay you | 小心，佢唔肯俾錢你 | siu săm; k'ü 'm hăng pi ts'in ni |
| 11 I wish to go to play | 我愛去反 | ngo oi hü fan |
| 12 I wish he had poured it out | 我想佢有斟出佢 | ngo seung k'ü yau chau ch'ut k'ü |
| 13 Please fill that saucepan | 請斟滿個个鑊 | ts'ing chăm mun ko-ko wok |
| 14 Do not punish my friend | 唔好責罰我嘅朋友 | 'm ho chak fat ngo ke p'ang-yau |
| 15 I am going towards Hongkong | 我向香港去 | ngo heung Heung-Kong hü |
| 16 Has he quarreled with his | 佢有同佢嘅家眷爭 | k'ü yau t'ung k'ü ke ka-kün chang |

| | | |
|---|---|---|
| family? | 論 (or 嗌交) 冇 | lun (*or* ai kau) mo? |
| 17 He put it down afterwards | 佢後來放落去 | k'ü hau-loi fong lok hü |
| 18 Does he read books always? | 佢係時時睇書嘅咩 | k'ü hai shi-shi t'ai shü ke me? |
| 19 I cannot remember | 我唔記得 | ngo 'm ki tak |
| 20 Had he heated the water? | 個的水係佢煲熱嘅 | ko ti shui hai k'ü po it ke? |
| 21 He has employed a coolie | 佢請嘵一個管店咯 | k'ü ts'ing hiu yat ko kun-tim lok |
| 22 Had he emptied the saucepan | 佢有整空个個鑊冇 | k'ü yau tsing hung ko-ko wok mo? |
| 23 No; he had heated the water | 冇; 佢煲熱水 | mo; k'ü po it-shui |
| 24 Shall I punish the coolie? | 我責罰個管店好唔好 | ngo chak fat ko kun-tim ho 'm ho? |
| 25 He received and read it | 佢收到又讀過佢咯 | k'ü shau-to yau tuk-kwo k'ü lok |
| 26 Did you get those goods? | 你有收到个的貨物冇 | ni yau shau-to ko-ti fo-măt mo? |
| 27 No; my friend received them | 冇; 我朋友收倒咯 | mo; ngo p'ang-yau shau-to lok |
| 28 Is his family here, or not? | 佢嘅家眷在呢處唔呢 | k'ü ke ka-kün tsoi ni ch'ü 'm ni? |
| 29 Yes; and a good many of his friends | 係咯, 重有好多佢嘅朋友喺處 | hai lok, chung yau ho to k'ü-ke p'ang-yau hai ch'ü |
| 30 She married him afterwards | 佢後來嫁佢 | k'ü hau loi ka k'ü |
| 31 Where does the house-boy owe money? | 個个事仔欠邊處嘅銀呢 | ko ko sze-tsai him pin-ch'ü ke ngăn ni? |
| 32 I can't remember; I think it is for eggs | 唔記得咯我估係雞蛋錢 | 'm ki-tak lok; ngo ku hai kai-tan ts'in |
| 33 Had he emptied the basin? | 佢有整空嗰個面盤麽 | k'ü yau ching-hung ko-ko min-p'un mo? |
| 34 He had not emptied (the basin); he had poured out water | 佢唔係整空佢斟落去啫 | k'ü 'm hai ching-hung k'ü; chăm lok hu che |
| 35 Did you punish him afterwards? | 你後來有責罰佢冇 | ni hau-loi yau chak-fat k'ü mo? |
| 36 I did not punish him afterwards I paid him | 我後來冇責罰佢, 我俾嘵銀佢 | ngo hau-loi mo chak-fat k'ü; ngo pi hiu ngăn k'ü |
| 37 Did you make him pay you? | 你係監佢俾銀你唔係 | ni hai kam k'ü pi ngăn ni 'm hai? |

# LESSON XVIII.

| | | | | | |
|---|---|---|---|---|---|
| To repair | 修整 | *sau ching'* | City (walled) | 城 | shing |
| To row (with oars) | 棹槳 | chau` *tseung'* | Foreign | 外國 | ngoi kwok |
| To shave | 剃 | *t'ai`* | To return | 翻來 | *fan* loi |
| To sign (one's name) | 簽名 | *ts'im* meng | To look for | 搵 | *wăn'* |
| | | | To say or speak | 話 | wa` |
| Mountain | 山 | *shan* | To separate | 別開 | pit-*hoi* |
| Music | 音樂 | *yăm* ngok | To shew | 俾—睇 | *pi'*—*t'ai'* |
| To ride | 騎馬 | k'e ma' | Matches (lucifers) | 火柴 | *foh'*-ch'ai |
| To sail (a ship) | 駛船 | *shai'* shün | People | 百姓 | *pak-sing`* |
| To send | 寄—去 | *ki`*—*hü`* | Native | 本地 | *pun'*-ti` |
| To sew | 聯 | lün | To tell | 話—知 | wa`—*chi* |
| Weather | 天氣 | *t'in-hi`* | A boat | 三板 | *sam-pan'* |

The following characters are used to express the perfect tense: TS'ANG 曾 "*have*" "*done,*" HIU 曉 "*have,*" LIU 了 "*have,*" I 已 "*just*" *done* and I KING 已經 *already*; KWO 過 *past action*, "*beyond.*" LOK 咯, LA 喇, LO 囉 and PA LO 罷囉 also express the perfect when used affirmatively or responsively; e.g., *I have left* NGO HÜ LIU 我去了; *I have walked,* NGO HANG KWO 我行過; *I have copied it,* NGO CH'AU LOK 我抄咯; *He has died,* K'Ü SZ HIU 佢死曉.

As will have been seen, the demonstrative pronoun frequently supplies the place of the definite article. It is generally so used when the sense admits of it, but the rule is by no means invariable.

| | | |
|---|---|---|
| 1 Have you repaired the box? | 你脩整好個个箱未曾 | ni sau ching ho ko-ko seung mi ts'ang? |
| 2 Did you row the boat? | 你棹曉三板唔呢 | ni chau hiu sam-pan 'm ni? |
| 3 I have seen many men | 我見過好多人 | ngo kin kwo ho to yan |
| 4 Tell the man to shave me | 呌嗰個人同我剃面 | kiu ko-ko yan t'ung ngo t'ai min |
| 5 Make him sign his name | 强佢簽名 | k'eung k'ü ts'im meng |
| 6 Can you see the mountain? | 你睇得見嗰個山唔得 | ni t'ai tăk kin ko-ko shan 'm tăk? |
| 7 I want to go to my parents | 我要去父母處 | ngo iu hü fu mo ch'ü |

| | | |
|---|---|---|
| 8 Do you like music? Can you ride? | 你中意音樂唔呢,你噲騎馬唔噲 | ni chung-i yăm-ngok 'm ni; ni ui k'e ma 'm ui? |
| 9 I have never ridden | 我唔會騎馬 | ngo 'm ts'ăng k'e ma |
| 10 Can the ship sail well? | 個隻船駛得好唔呢 | ko chek shün shai-tăk ho 'm ni? |
| 11 Send me a seamstress | 使一個補衫婆來 | shai yat ko po-sham-p'oh loi |
| 12 The weather has been very good | 天氣已經十分好 | t'in-hi i-king shap-fău ho |
| 13 We had bad weather but now it is good | 先時唔好天,現時好 | sin shi 'm ho t'in; in shi ho |
| 14 Is that a foreign man? | 啊個係外國人唔係 | ko ko hai ngoi kwok yan 'm hai? |
| 15 That was a large city formerly | 啊個舊時係好大嘅城 | ko ko kau shi hai ho tai ke shing |
| 16 I have been to a foreign city | 我去過一個外國嘅城 | ngo hü kwo yat ko ngoi kwok ke shing |
| 17 Will you return and tell me? | 你肯翻來話我聽嗎 | ni hăng fan-loi wa ngo t'eng ma? |
| 18 Does he speak well? | 佢講得好咩 | k'ü kong-tăk ho me? |
| 19 I cannot separate them | 我唔擺得開佢哋 | ngo 'm pai-tăk hoi k'ü-ti |
| 20 Shew me those matches | 俾個的火柴我睇 | pi ko-ti fo-ts'ai ngo t'ai |
| 21 Is he a native or not? | 佢係本地人唔係 | k'ü hai pun-ti yan 'm hai? |
| 22 The people are everywhere | 百姓處處都有 | pak-sing ch'ü-ch'ü to yau |
| 23 Does he intend to marry? | 佢係想娶老婆唔係 | k'ü hai seung ts'o lo-p'oh 'm hai? |
| 24 He cannot pay the money | 佢唔俾得銀 | k'ü 'm pi tăk ngăn |
| 25 Will he return to his family? | 佢想翻去佢嘅家眷唔想 | k'ü seung fan hü k'ü ke ka-kün 'm seung? |
| 26 That, I can not say, really | 個啲我唔話得實 | ko ti ngo 'm wa tăk shat |
| 27 He was always a good friend | 佢時時係做好朋友 | k'ü shi shi hai tso ho p'ang yau |
| 28 They have said so | 佢哋有噉話 | k'ü ti yau kom wa |
| 29 Is the weather in the city good? | 城裡頭天氣好唔呢 | shing lui t'au t'in hi ho 'm ni |
| 30 Had you repaired the box? | 你修整嘵個个箱未 | ni sau ching hiu ko-ko seung mi? |
| 31 He looks everywhere | 佢處處都搵 | k'ü ch'ü-ch'ü to wăn |
| 32 I will go out boat sailing (to sail) afterwards | 我想後來駛三板 | ngo seung hau loi shai sam-pan |
| 33 Will you return those matches? | 你想俾翻個的火柴咩 | ni seung pi fan ko-ti foh-ts'ai me? |

| | | |
|---|---|---|
| 34 I have shewn him the city | 個的城我有同佢睇 | ko ti shing ngo yau t'ung k'ü t'ai |
| 35 What do all the people say? | 百姓點話呢 | pak-sing tim wa ni? |
| 36 They say he has gone away to ride | 佢哋話佢去嘵騎馬 | k'ü-ti wa k'ü hü hiu k'e ma |
| 37 I have ridden, and you have sailed | 我有騎馬你駛嘵三板 | ngo yau k'e ma, ni shai hiu sam-pan |
| 38 He had returned, and will send a man | 佢已經翻來就使人來咯 | k'ü i-king fan loi, chau shai yan loi lok |
| 39 Where is the mountain in the foreign city | 响個外國城邊處有山 | ko-ko ngoi-kwok shing, pin-ch'ü yau shan |
| 40 The people cannot say; the weather is too bad to see it | 百姓唔話得；天氣唔好唔睇得見 | pak-sing 'm wa tăk; t'in hi 'm ho, 'm t'ai tăk kin |

---

# LESSON XIX.

| | | | | | |
|---|---|---|---|---|---|
| A receipt | 收單 | *shau-tan* | Sometimes | 有時 | yau' shi |
| To give a receipt | 俾收單 | *pi' shau-tan* | Then (at that time) | 個陣時 | *ko*\` chan\` shi |
| Rent | 租銀 | *tso* ngăn | | | |
| To pay rent | 納租銀 | năp *tso*-ugăn | When | 幾時 | *ki'* shi |
| Sail (a) | 㨫帆 | (*teng'*) li' | To sleep | 瞓 | *făn*\` |
| To hoist a sail | 扯𢃇 | *ch'e'* li' | To smell (with the nose) | 聞 | măn |
| To set sail (depart) | 開身 | *hoi shăn* | | | |
| To go sailing | 駛𢃇 | *shai'* li' | Smell (as of a flower) | 香 | *heung* |
| Formerly | 先時 | *sin* shi | | | |
| Now | 現時 | in\` shi | To sit down | 坐 | tsoh\` |
| Never | 總冇 | *tsung'* mo' | To spoil | 整壞 | *ching'* wai\` |
| Not yet | 唔曾 | 'm ts'ang | To stand up | 企起身 | k'i' *hi' shăn* |
| Often | 好多回 | *ho' to* ui | To steal | 偷 | *t'au* |
| To observe | 聞見 | măn *kin*\` | | | |

### AUXILIARY VERBS.

As in all other languages, certain verbs in frequent use are auxiliary to others.

Of these the most useful in Chinese (in which the strictly auxiliary uses of "*to have*" and "*to be*" are not found,) are the following:— TAK 得 *to be able, can*; CHEUK 着 implying *action*; SHAI 使 *to bid*; LING 令 *to make* or *cause*; and PI 俾 *to give, cause, make*, or *let.*

PIT 必 *must* and SÜ 須 *necessary* (with other expressions of which they are components) meaning *must, ought to*, may be deemed auxiliaries; as may also several others which will be given in the lessons immediately following.

肯 HÀNG, *to be willing, to assent to*, is used to express the future tense when intention is implied. (*Vide* sentence 4, &c.)

| | | |
|---|---|---|
| 1 Send that man for a receipt | 使啲個人去攞收單 | shai ko ko yan hü lo shau-tan |
| 2 Tell him he must pay the rent | 話佢知是必要納租銀 | wa k'ü chi shi pit iu nap tso-ngăn |
| 3 He can't give a receipt | 佢唔俾得收單 | k'ü 'm pi tăk shau-tan |
| 4 He will not give a receipt yet | 佢唔肯現時開收單 | k'ü 'm hăng in shi hoi shau-tan |
| 5 Has he ever set a sail in a boat? | 佢有在過三板扯㡳唔曾 | k'ü yau tsoi kwo sam-pan ch'é li 'm ts'ăng? |
| 6 He did so formerly | 佢先時做過 | k'ü sin-shi tso kwo |
| 7 He is going to row now | 佢現時想去棹槳 | k'ü in-shi seung hü chau tseung |
| 8 I never signed my name | 我唔曾簽過名 | ngo 'm ts'ang ts'im kwo meng |
| 9 She often sews clothes | 佢好多囘聯衣服咯 | k'ü ho to ui lün i-fuk lok |
| 10 Sometimes he pays and sometimes he does'nt | 佢有時俾銀有時唔俾 | k'ü yau shi pi ngăn, yau shi 'm pi |
| 11 Did he set sail then? | 佢係個陣時開身唔係 | k'ü hai ko chan shi hoi shăn 'm hai |
| 12 When he gave the receipt he had no money | 佢開收單時冇銀 | k'ü hoi shau-tan shi mo ngăn |
| 13 We do not often sleep there | 我地冇幾多囘喺個處瞓 | ngo ti mo ki to ui hai ko-ch'ü făn |
| 14 I observe that the flowers smell very well | 我聞見啲啲花好香 | ngo măn kin ko-ti fa ho heung |
| 15 Will he sit down now or not? | 佢現時肯坐低唔肯 | k'ü in-shi hăng tso tai 'm hăng? |

| | | |
|---|---|---|
| 16 Had he spoiled the cake? | 佢有整壞個的餅冇 | k'ü yau ching wai ko-ti peng mo? |
| 17 Stand up and tell me the price | 企起身話我知幾多價錢 | ki hi shăn wa ngo chi ki to ka-ts'in |
| 18 Who is the man that stole that cup? | 邊個人偷啗个杯 | pin-ko yau t'au ko-ko pui? |
| 19 The leaves of trees are sometimes large | 樹葉有時好大 | shü ip yau-shi ho tai |
| 20 Did he formerly give a receipt | 佢先時有開收單冇 | k'ü sin shi yau hoi shau-tan mo? |
| 21 We never slept there at that time | 個時我哋總冇喺個處瞓 | ko shi ngo-ti tsung-mo hai ko-ch'ü fan |
| 22 That cabbage smells very badly | 个啲白菜聞得十分唔好 | ko ti pak-ts'oi măn tăk shap-făn 'm ho |
| 23 The music was formerly good; now it is bad | 音樂先時好, 現時唔好 | yăm-ngok sin-shi ho; in-shi 'm ho |
| 24 Have you set down the child? | 你有放落個个仔唔曾 | ni yau fong lok ko-ko tsai 'm ts'ăng? |
| 25 He stole the bread and wine | 佢偷曉啗啲麵飽共酒咯 | k'ü t'au hiu ko-ti min-pau kung tsau lok |
| 26 You have not yet bought the boat | 你未曾買啗隻三板 | ni mi ts'ang mai ko chek sam-pan |
| 27 I often go out boat sailing | 我好多回駛悝出去 | ngo ho to ui shai li ch'ut hü |
| 28 We sometimes sail there | 我哋有時喺個處駛悝 | ngo ti yau-shi hai ko ch'ü shai li |
| 29 Will you give me a receipt now? | 你現時開收單我唔呢 | ni in-shi hoi shau-tan ngo 'm ni? |
| 30 Does he sometimes shave the man? | 佢有時剃啗个人嘅頭唔呢 | k'ü yau-shi t'ai ko-ko yan ke t'au 'm ni? |
| 31 He does not often do so; he did so formerly | 佢冇幾多回咁做, 佢先時有做 | k'ü mo ki to ui kom tso, k'ü sin shi yau tso |
| 32 When does he sleep at that place? | 佢幾時喺个處瞓 | k'ü ki shi hai ko-ch'ü fan? |
| 33 I cannot not say for certain; he has not yet returned | 我唔話得實, 佢未曾翻 | ngo 'm wa tăk shat; k'ü mi ts'ăng fan |

| | | |
|---|---|---|
| 34 He is a bad man; he never pays his rent | 佢唔好人，佢總唔納租銀嘅 | k'ü 'm ho yan; k'ü tsung 'm nap tso ngăn ke |
| 35 Do those flowers smell good or bad? | 啲啲花聞得好唄唔好 | ko-ti fa măn tăk ho chi 'm ho? |
| 36 Those flowers smell very good; but that beef smells bad | 啲啲花聞得好，啲啲牛肉聞得唔好 | ko ti fa măn tăk ho; ko-ti ngau-yuk măn tăk 'm ho |
| 37 Does he often steal anything (things) | 佢好多回偷野嘅咩 | k'ü ho to ui t'au ye ke me? |

# LESSON XX.

| | | | | | |
|---|---|---|---|---|---|
| To steer (a boat or ship) | 把舦，揸舦 | pa' t'ai', *cha* t'ai | Debt | 欠債 | *him'-chai'* |
| | | | To pay debts | 還錢 | wan ts'in |
| To stop (obstruct) | 攔住 | lan chü' | Both | 兩個 | leung' *ko'* |
| To taste (as food) | 嘗，餂 | sheung, t'im' | A ship | (隻) 船 | (*chek*) shün |
| Cotton cloth | 棉布 | min-*po'* | To think; guess | 想，估 | *seung'*; *ku'* |
| Danger | 危險 | ngai-*him'* | To throw down | 擗 | p'ek |
| About (nearly) | 差不多 | *ch'a-pat-to* | To throw away | 擗去 | p'ek *hü'* |
| | 大約 | tai-*yeuk* | To tie up | 綁住 | *pong'* chü' |
| To study (i.e. to read aloud, as Chinese boys study) | 讀書 | tuk *shü* | Sun | 日 | yat |
| | | | Moon | 月 | üt |
| To sweep clean | 掃乾淨 | *so'* *kon*-tseng' | Either—or | 抑—或 | *yik*—wak |
| To swear to | 誓愿 | shai'-ün' | Bad (wicked) | 惡 | *ok* |

Negatives should precede the verb, and the auxiliary the adverb, in sentences where an adverbial formation expresses the tense of the verb; e.g. *He cannot write quickly* 佢唔寫得快 K'Ü 'M SÉ TĂK FAI. *He cannot do it properly* 佢唔做得好 K'Ü 'M TSO TĂK HO.

*May* (or *must* in its non-intensive sense) is expressed by HOH 可.

CHEUK 着 (see lesson 16) rather completes than intensifies the sense of any verb with which it is used. Experience and practice alone can determine the words with which it is compounded.

KAU 教 *to cause*, is often used in an auxiliary way, implying *to teach, shewing how to act*, or *letting one know*; e.g. *Let me shew you*, 等我教你呀 TĂNG NGO KAU NI A.

| | | | | | |
|---|---|---|---|---|---|
| Sit down | 坐喇 | tso la | Teacher, Sir (lit. elder born) | 先生 | sin shăng |
| Many thanks | 多謝 | to tsé | | | |
| Light the lamp | 點燈 | tim tăng | All | 齊嚟 | ts'ai *sai* |

都 TO, *all, complete*, frequently follows a phrase expressing number, to intensify the sense (Vide sentence 20.)

| | | |
|---|---|---|
| 1 Can you steer this boat? | 呢隻三板你會揸軚唔會 | ni chek sam-pan ni ui cha t'ai 'm ui? |
| 2 Will you taste that fruit? | 你想嘗个啲菓子唔呢 | ni seung sheung ko-ti kwo-tsz 'm ni? |
| 3 Sit down; there is no danger | 坐喇唔係危險嘅 | tso la! 'm hai ngai him ke |
| 4 Good morning; when do you sail? | 早晨, 你幾時開身 | tso shan! ni ki shi hoi shăn? |
| 5 Good bye! I am going to study (See vocab.) | 好行喇, 我去讀書 | ho hang la! ngo hü tuk shü |
| 6 Sweep it all away | 掃嚟去喇 | so sai hü la |
| 7 He has paid the debt; give him a receipt | 佢還淸錢咯, 俾張收單佢喇 | k'ü wan ts'ing ts'in lok; pi cheung shau tan k'ü la |
| 8 Tell him to pay | 叫佢還錢 | kiu k'ü wan ts'in |
| 9 Don't stop him: he will throw it away | 唔好攔住佢, 佢想擗佢出去 | 'm ho lan chü k'ü; k'ü seung p'ek k'ü ch'ut hü |
| 10 It smells very bad; bring it here | 聞得十分唔好, 拈來呢處 | măn tăk shap-făn 'm ho; nim loi ni ch'ü |
| 11 Light the lamp; tie the dog up | 點燈綁住隻狗 | tim tăng; pong-chü chek kau |
| 12 The teacher thinks it is good | 個先生估係好嘅 | ko sin-shang ku hai ho ke |
| 13 Can you see the sun now? | 你現時見得個日頭唔見得呢 | ni in-shi kin tăk ko yat t'au 'm kin tăk ni? |

| | | |
|---|---|---|
| 14 No, but I can see the moon | 唔得，但係我見得個月 | 'm tăk: tan hai ngo kin tak ko üt |
| 15 Bring either beer or foreign wine | 拈悲酒或洋酒來 | nim pi tsau wak yeung tsau loi |
| 16 What is that made of? | 個啲係乜野做嘅 | ko ti hai măt ye tso ke? |
| 17 It is made of good cotton cloth | 係好棉布做嘅 | hai ho min-po tso ke |
| 18 Make him stand up; he has stolen a fork | 監佢企起身，佢偷過一枝义 | kam k'ü ki hi shăn: k'ü t'au kwo yat chi cha |
| 19 Throw it down here | 擗落呢處 | p'ek lok ni ch'ü |
| 20 Both the men have slept there | 兩個人都喺个處瞓過咯 | leung ko yan to hai ko ch'ü fan kwo lok |
| 21 When did they swear to that? | 佢哋幾時誓愿嗰件事 | k'ü-ti ki shi shai-ün ko kin sze? |
| 22 Before they went away, (lit. They first swore; [they] afterwards went away) | 佢哋先時誓愿，然後正咀 | k'ü-ti sin-shi shai-ün; in-hau ching ch'e |
| 23 Formerly they had a quarrel | 佢哋舊時嗌過交 | k'ü ti kau-shi ai kwo kau |
| 24 There are about six of them | 大約有六個處 | tai yeuk yau luk ko ch'ü |
| 25 He likes to read books | 佢中意睇書 | k'ü chung-i t'ai shü |
| 26 Who told you so? Was it the teacher? | 乜誰噉話你知：係先生唔係 | măt-shui kom wa ni chi? hai sin-shang 'm hai? |
| 27 No, it was the houseboy | 唔係，係事仔 | 'm hai; hai sze-tsai |
| 28 What did he say afterwards? | 佢後來點話呢 | k'ü hau loi tim wa ni? |
| 29 He said both the men were bad | 佢話兩個都係惡人 | k'ü wa leung ko to hai ok yan |
| 30 Why did he not stop them? | 佢做乜唔攔住佢哋呢 | k'ü tso măt 'm lan-chü k'ü ti ni? |
| 31 They had tied him up | 佢哋綁曉佢 | k'ü ti pong hiu k'ü |
| 32 Tell the coolie to sweep the floor | 叫管店掃樓板 | kiu kun-tim so lau-pan |
| 33 He had not paid his rent | 佢唔曾俾租銀 | k'ü 'm ts'ang pi tso-ngăn |
| 34 It has often been so | 時時都係咁 | shi-shi to hai kom |

# LESSON XXI.

| | | | | | |
|---|---|---|---|---|---|
| To day | 今日 | *kăm* yat | To walk | 行路 | hang-loˋ |
| Tomorrow | 聽日 | *tʻeng* yat | To warm | 整煖 | *chingˊ*-nünˊ |
| Day after to-morrow | 後日 | hauˋ yat | To wash | 洗 | *saiˊ* |
| | | | Face | 面 | minˋ |
| Yesterday | 昨日 | tsok yat | Hands | 手 | *shauˊ* |
| This month | 呢个月 | *niˊ ko*ˋ üt | To work | 打工 | *taˊ-kung* |
| Last month | 上個月 | sheungˋ *ko*ˋ üt | The body | 身 | *shăn* |
| Next year | 明年 | ming nin | In the midst of | 中間 | *chung-kan* |
| Next month | 第二个月，下月 | taiˋ iˋ *ko*ˋ üt, haˋ üt | Too (much or little &c.) | 得嚌 | *tăk*-tsaiˋ |
| This year | 今年 | *kăm* nin | Altogether | 總共 | *tsungˊ* kungˋ |
| Last year | 舊年 | kauˋ nin | Although | 雖然 | *sui*-in |
| To touch | 摩着 | *moh*-cheuk | Because | 因爲 | *yan*-waiˋ |
| To translate | 翻譯 | *fan*-yik | Consequently | 所以 | *shohˊ*-iˊ |
| To understand | 明白 | ming-pak | It | 若 | yeuk |
| To upset | 打倒 | *taˊ-to*ˋ | Therefore | 所以 | *shohˊ*-iˋ |

Several words in addition to those already given are, by some grammarians, described as auxiliary verbs, their only claim to that title, however, being the frequency with which they occur in compound verbal phrases. Such are CHUNG-I 中意 *to like*, KOM 敢 *to dare*, &c.

*To have*, YAU 有, is frequently used (much as in German) for *to be*; e.g. *to be ill* is YAU PENG 有病 "*to have illness.*" (*comp.* hunger, durst haben, &c.)

| | | | | | |
|---|---|---|---|---|---|
| Right | 着 | cheuk | Is that right or wrong | 啲個着唔着 | ko ko cheuk 'm cheuk |
| Wrong | 唔着 | 'm cheuk | | | |

| | | |
|---|---|---|
| 1 Where is he to-day? | 佢今日喺邊處 | k'ü kăm yat hai pin ch'ü? |
| 2 I don't dare say | 我唔敢講 | ngo 'm kom kong |
| 3 Do you go tomorrow or the day after? | 你聽日或後日去咩 | ni tʻeng-yat wak hau-yat hü me? |
| 4 I went there yesterday | 我昨日去个處 | ngo tsok-yat hü ko ch'ü |

| | | |
|---|---|---|
| 5 Will you translate both of those books? | 個兩部書你想翻譯唔呢 | ko leung po shü ni seung fan-yik 'm ni? |
| 6 No, I don't understand them | 唔想，我唔明白佢 | 'm seung, ngo 'm ming pak k'ü |
| 7 He does not like to touch them | 佢唔中意摩着佢 | k'ü 'm chung-i moh cheuk k'ü |
| 8 He stopped him last month | 佢上個月攔住佢 | k'ü sheung ko üt lan-chü k'ü |
| 9 Will he walk much this month? | 佢呢個月行得多唔呢 | k'ü ni-ko üt hang tăk to 'm ni? |
| 10 He upset the table | 佢打倒个張檯 | k'ü ta to ko cheung t'oi |
| 11 Will you tell him to warm the water? | 你想叫佢整煖水咩 | ni seung kiu k'ü ching nün shui me? |
| 12 Make him wash his face and hands | 強佢洗面洗手 | k'eung k'ü sai min sai shau |
| 13 Has he not yet done so? | 佢唔曾噉做咩 | k'ü 'm ts'ăng kom tso me? |
| 14 Next month he intends to work | 佢第二個月想打工 | k'ü tai i ko üt seung ta kung |
| 15 Will he go out sailing this year? | 佢今年去行船唔呢 | k'ü kăm nin hü hang shün 'm ni? |
| 16 I don't know; he went last year | 我唔知，佢舊年去過 | ngo 'm chi, k'ü kau nin hü kwo |
| 17 He must work a good deal next year | 佢明年是必要做好多工夫 | k'ü ming nin shi-pit iu tso ho to kung fu |
| 18 Why does he write thus? | 佢爲乜野係噉寫 | k'ü wai măt ye hai kom sé? |
| 19 He wishes to take a bath (wash the body) | 佢要洗身 | k'ü iu sai shăn |
| 20 He is in the midst of friends | 佢在朋友中間 | k'ü tsoi p'ăng-yau chung-kan |
| 21 He does not entirely understand | 佢唔明白得嗮 | k'ü 'm ming-pak tăk sai |
| 22 Is that too big for you? | 係噉大得嚌唔呢 | hai kom tai tăk tsai 'm ni? |
| 23 Although he is good, the woman is bad | 佢雖然好，但個女人唔好 | k'ü sui-in ho, tan ko nü yan 'm ho |
| 24 That is altogether wrong | 個啲總唔着 | ko ti tsung 'm cheuk |
| 25 Why is it wrong? | 爲乜野唔着 | wai măt ye 'm cheuk? |
| 26 Because it wants finishing | 因爲唔曾整起 | yan-wai 'm ts'ăng ching hi |
| 27 Then it is consequently bad | 噉所以唔好 | kom shoh i 'm ho |
| 28 No, if it were finished it would be good | 唔係，若係整起就好嘅咯 | 'm hai, yeuk hai ching hi chau ho ke lok |

| | | |
|---|---|---|
| 29 He told me he had finished it | 佢話我知佢整起咯 | k'ü wa ngo chi k'ü ching hi lok |
| 30 He does'nt like to do it? | 佢唔中意做 | k'ü 'm chung i tso |
| 31 Tell him it must be done | 話佢知，是必要做 | wa k'ü chi shi-pit iu tso |
| 32 When? tomorrow, or the next day? | 幾時呢，聽日或後日 | ki shi ni, t'eng-yat wak hau-yat? |
| 33 Next year will also do | 明年都做得 | ming nin to tso tak |
| 34 I shall do it to-day | 我想今日做 | ngo seung kam-yat tso |

# LESSON XXII.

| | | | | | |
|---|---|---|---|---|---|
| Of course | 自必然 | tsz'-*pit*-in | To lay or make a fire | 打火爐 | *ta' fo'* lo |
| Only: but | 但係，啫 | tan' hai', *che* | To extinguish (fire) | 熄 | *sik* |
| In the first place | 首先， | *shau'-sin*, | To go out (of a house) | 出 | *ch'ut* |
| (firstly) | 第一件 | tai *yat* kin' | | | |
| Pretty well | 幾，幾好 | *ki, ki' ho'* | To kill | 打死 | *ta' sze'* |
| Regularly (always) | 常時 | sheung-shi | Cockroach | 甴甲 | kat-tsat |
| | | | To knock at | 拍 | *p'ak* |
| Slowly | 慢慢 | man'-man' | To break, (prize) | 打開， | *ta' hoi*, |
| Suppose that | 譬如 | *p'i'* ü | open | 撬開 | kiu' *hoi* |
| Compradore | 買辦 | mai'-pan' | To leave open | 打開 | *ta' hoi* |
| Weak (physically) | 軟弱 | ün'-yeuk | To shut | 掩埋，閂 | *im'* mai, *shan* |
| Ready | 便 | pin' | A long time | 好久 | *ho' kau'* |
| To make a bed | 鋪牀 | *p'o* ch'ong | So long a time | 咁耐 | *kom'* noi' |

Several words besides HAI 係 are used to express "*to be*"; such as SHI 是, WAI 爲, NAI 乃, and TSOI 在.

| | | |
|---|---|---|
| To let (one) do it | 許一做 | hü—tso, 由得 yau tăk, 任得 yăm tăk |
| To let go | 放手 | fong shau |
| To let (it) down | 放下 | fong ha |
| To let off (release) | 釋放 | shik fong |

| | | | | | |
|---|---|---|---|---|---|
| I beg pardon | 唔該 | 'm koi | Try it once | 試一試, | shi yat shi, |
| Lazily | 懶惰 | lan-to | | 試吓 | shi ha |
| I am engaged | 我有事 | ngo yau sze | A good plan | 好計 | ho kai |
| That is right | 噉着咯 | kom cheuk lok | To have leisure | 得閒 | tăk han |
| Lastly | 收尾 | shau mi | More than | 過頭, | kwo t'au, |
| Stop! | 罷咯, | pa lok, | | 多過 | to kwo |
| | 停止 | t'ing chi | There is some good (in it) | 有的好 | yau ti ho |
| Don't speak so fast | 唔好講咁快 | 'm ho kong kom fai | | | |

| | | |
|---|---|---|
| 1 Will you break that open to-day? | 你係今日打開个啲唔係 | ni hai kăm-yat ta hoi ko-ti 'm hai? |
| 2 I cannot; in the first place I am not ready | 唔得; 第一件我唔曾齊備 | 'm tăk; tai yat kin ngo 'm ts'ang ts'ai pi |
| 3 He makes a bed pretty well | 佢幾噲鋪牀 | k'ü ki ui p'o ch'ong |
| 4 Does he light the lamp regularly? | 佢常時點燈咩 | k'ü sheung shi tim tăng me? |
| 5 He does not dare touch the lamp | 佢唔噉摩個盞燈 | k'ü 'm kom moh ko chan tăng |
| 6 Did he leave the door open? | 佢係打開度門唔係 | k'ü hai ta hoi to mun 'm hai? |
| 7 Suppose he had; did you tell him to shut it? | 譬如佢係, 你有叫佢掩埋冇呀 | p'i ü k'ü hai, ni yau kiu k'ü im mai mo a? |
| 8 I beg your pardon, give it to me | 唔該你俾過我 | 'm koi, ni pi kwo ngo |
| 9 Why does he kill that cockroach? | 佢爲乜野打死個隻甴曱 | k'ü wai-măt-ye ta sze ko chek kat-tsat? |
| 10 I don't know; he kills them regularly | 我唔知, 佢常時打死佢 | ngo 'm chi; k'ü sheung shi ta sze k'ü |
| 11 Tell him to make a fire and afterwards shut the door | 叫佢打火爐, 然後掩埋門 | kiu k'ü ta fo-lo, in hau im mai mun |
| 12 Of course he is not ready | 自必然佢唔齊備 | tsz-pit-in k'ü 'm ts'ai pi |
| 13 He does things so slowly | 佢做野咁慢嘅 | k'ü tso ye kom man ke |
| 14 Did you knock at the door? | 係你拍門唔係 | hai ni pak mun 'm hai? |
| 15 No, I broke it open | 唔係, 我打開佢 | 'm hai; ngo ta hoi k'ü |

| | | | |
|---|---|---|---|
| 16 | Did he let the book go? | 佢放開手個部書麽 | k‘ü fong hoi shau ko po shü mo? |
| 17 | No, not for a long time | 冇,佢好耐都冇放手 | mo, k‘ü ho noi to mo fong shau |
| 18 | The compradore is very weak | 個買辦好軟弱嘅 | ko mai-pan ho ün yeuk ke |
| 19 | He is a coolie | 佢係做管店嘅啫 | k‘ü hai tso kun-tim ke che |
| 20 | Extinguish that candle directly | 即刻熄個啲蠟燭 | tsik hak sik ko ti lap-chuk |
| 21 | It's only a candle | 單係蠟燭 | tan hai lap-chuk |
| 22 | Is it therefore to be thrown away? | 因咁所以擗佢去係唔係 | yan kom shoh-i p‘ek k‘ü hü hai 'm hai? |
| 23 | No, light it again | 唔係,再點着佢 | 'm hai; tsoi tim cheuk k‘ü |
| 24 | Are you busy? have you leisure? | 你有事冇,得閒唔呢 | ni yau sze mo? tăk han 'm ni? |
| 25 | No, I am engaged; don't speak so fast | 唔得閒,我有事,唔好講咁快 | 'm tăk han; ngo yau sze; 'm ho kong kom fai |
| 26 | I intend to go tomorrow | 我想聽日去 | ngo seung t‘eng yat hü |
| 27 | That's right; its a good plan | 噉着咯眞好計 | kom cheuk lok; chan ho kai |
| 28 | Are there more than fifty of them? | 佢哋係多過五十唔係 | k‘ü ti hai to kwo 'ng shap 'm hai? |
| 29 | I cannot say, I have not counted them | 唔知得眞,我冇數過佢 | 'm chi tăk chăn; ngo mo sho kwo k‘ü |
| 30 | Try to count them, and tell me how many there are | 你試數吓佢就話過我聽有幾多 | ni shi sho ha k‘ü; tsau wa kwo ngo t‘eng yau ki to |
| 31 | There are more than a hundred | 多過一百咯 | to kwo yat pak lok |
| 32 | Don't let him leave the door open | 唔好俾佢打開度門 | 'm ho pi k‘ü ta hoi to mun |
| 33 | If he does I won't let him off | 若係佢噉做,我唔放過佢 | yeuk hai k‘ü kom tso, ngo 'm fong kwo k‘ü |
| 34 | There is some good in him, but I don't like him | 佢有的好處,但係我唔中意佢 | k‘ü yau ti ho ch‘ü; tan hai ngo 'm chung i k‘ü |

# LESSON XXIII.

| | | | | | |
|---|---|---|---|---|---|
| To return | 翻黎 | *fan* lai | A fragment, a bit | 碎, 片 | *sui` p'in`* |
| What | 乜野 | *măt-ye'* | To live, reside | 住 | chü` |
| To know (be aware of) | 知到 | *chi-to`* | Any longer (in time) | 耐的 | noi` *ti* |
| To set (a table) | 擠好 | *chai ho'* | Exactly | 正正 | *ching`-ching`* |
| To be tired | 癐, 倦 | kui`, kün` | Not quite | 爭的 | *chang ti* |
| With | 同 | t'ung | Name (given after birth) | 名 | ming |
| To save (put by) | 剩翻 | shing` *fan* | | | |
| To waste | 多費 | *to fai`* | To be in an employ | 替, 打工, 有工打 | *t'ai`, ta' kung*, yau' *kung ta'* |
| Expensive (dear) | 貴 | *kwai`* | | | |
| Fire | 火 | *foh'* | | | |

PARTICLES.

The vernaculars of Chinese abound in untranslatable particles, of which the student will come across several examples in this and following exercises. They are never found at the beginning of a phrase, but seldom in the middle of it, and generally at the end. They are called by the people LI YAM 脷音 or "tongue sounds" and probably owe their origin to the difficulties experienced by Chinese in checking their utterance of certain final sounds,—as exemplified in "pidgin" English in which *like* becomes likee, *catch*, catchee, &c. They have now, however, acquired specific values as intensifying the affirmation, question, or doubt expressed by the sentences in which they occur.

The following are those most commonly used, the second character, where two are given, being more intensive than the first.

| | | | | | | | |
|---|---|---|---|---|---|---|---|
| 1. Imperative particle - | *la* | 喇 | *la`* | 罅 | | |
| 2. Responsive particle in answering questions | *lok* | 咯 | *lo* | 囉 | | |
| 3. Interrogative particle - | *ni* | 呢 | *a* | 呀 | *a`* | 亞 |

NI 呢, is occasionally used as responsive.

| | | |
|---|---|---|
| 1 Tell him to return | 叫佢翻黎喇 | kiu k'ü fan lai la |
| 2 He says he is tired | 佢話癐咯 | k'ü wa kui lok |
| 3 What has he been doing? | 佢做過乜野嚟呢 | k'ü tso-kwo măt-ye lai ni? |
| 4 I really don't know | 我唔知得實咯 | ngo 'm chi-tăk shat lok |
| 5 He works very slowly | 佢做工夫係好慢嘅 | k'ü tso kung-fu hai ho man ke |

初學階

| | | |
|---|---|---|
| 6 Does he know how to set a table? | 佢噲擠好檯啲野唔噲呢 | k'ü ui chai-ho t'oi ti ye 'm ui ni? |
| 7 Yes, pretty well but not very well | 噲咯, 幾好, 但唔係十分好啫 | ui lok, ki ho; tan 'm hai shap-fan ho che |
| 8 Tell him to save that meat | 叫佢剩翻个的肉 | kiu k'ü shing-fan ko-ti yuk |
| 9 He broke open the box | 佢撬開曉個个箱 | k'ü kiu-hoi hiu ko-ko seung |
| 10 Has he left the door open? | 佢有打開個度門冇呀 | k'ü yau ta hoi ko to-mun mo a? |
| 11 No; he shut it at once | 冇, 佢即刻閂埋嚹 | mo; k'ü tsik hak shan mai la |
| 12 Will he waste that sugar? | 佢想多費个的白糖唔呢 | k'ü seung to-fai ko ti pak-t'ong 'm ni? |
| 13 No; it is too expensive | 唔咯, 貴過頭 | 'm lok; kwai kwo t'au |
| 14 Where does he reside? | 佢喺邊處住呢 | k'ü hai pin-ch'ü chü ni? |
| 15 He lives with me | 佢同我住咯 | k'ü t'ung ngo chü lok |
| 16 Will he live with you any longer? | 佢想同你住耐啲麼 | k'ü seung t'ung ni chü noi ti mo? |
| 17 He will live several years with me | 佢想同我住數年 | k'ü seung t'ung ngo chü sho nin |
| 18 He has not been here quite a year | 佢喺處爭啲一年 | k'ü hai ch'ü chăng-ti yat nin |
| 19 It is eleven months exactly | 正正十一個月咯 | ching-ching shap yat ko üt lok |
| 20 How long have they been in your employ? | 佢哋喺你處做曉幾耐呢 | k'ü ti hai ni ch'ü tso hiu ki noi ni? |
| 21 All last year and part of this | 舊年成年; 又今年幾個月 | kau nin shing niu; yau kăm nin ki-ko üt |
| 22 What is the name of that man? | 個个人叫乜名呢 | ko ko yan kiu mat ming ni? |
| 23 I don't know, I think it is A-yau | 我唔知, 我估係亞有 | ngo 'm chi; ngo ku hai A-yau |
| 24 I am very tired, I have been studying | 我十分瘖咯, 我讀書嚟 | ngo shap-făn kui lok; ngo tuk shü lai |
| 25 How long have you been studying? | 你讀書幾耐呢 | ni tuk shü ki noi ni? |
| 26 Several hours; I study regularly | 讀曉幾點鐘啫, 我時時讀咯 | tuk hiu ki tim chung che; ngo shi-shi tuk lok |

| | | |
|---|---|---|
| 27 Have you a piece of bread here? | 呢處有碎麵飽冇 | ni ch'ü yau sui min-pau mo? |
| 28 No, I have wine, coffee, and rice | 冇咯，我有酒架啡同飯啫 | mo lok! ngo yau tsau, ka-fe, t'ung fan che |
| 29 Send that man away | 吽個个人咀喇 | kin ko-ko yan c'he la |
| 30 Why does he not sweep the room? | 佢乜唔掃个間房呢 | k'ü mät 'm so ko kan fong ni? |
| 31 He cannot sweep it quickly | 佢唔掃得快啫 | k'ü 'm so-täk fai che |
| 32 Why not? He understands | 乜唔得呢，佢識得 | mät 'm täk ni? k'ü shik täk |
| 33 No, he does not, I will teach him | 佢唔識得，我教佢啫 | k'ü 'm shik täk, ngo kau k'ü che |
| 34 He must not remain any longer | 佢唔好等啲添咯 | k'ü 'm ho täng noi ti t'im lok |
| 35 Good bye, I am going out* | 坐喳，我出去咯 | tso cha! ngo ch'ut hü lok |
| 36 If you are going out buy me a pen | 你若係出去買枝筆過我喇 | ni yeuk hai ch'ut hü, mai chi pat kwo ngo la |

---

# LESSON XXIV.

A very large number of verbs used in the Chinese vernaculars are compound, their invariable use in this way indeed, by itself justifying the assertion, already made, that the spoken vernaculars are not monosyllabic. The words with which they are most frequently compounded are as follows.

| | | | | | |
|---|---|---|---|---|---|
| *K'euk* | 却 | to stop (a causative particle) | Mai | 埋 | to conceal, connect with |
| Chü' | 住 | to dwell | *Ch'ut* | 出 | to go out |
| *Hi'* | 起 | to rise | *Hü'* | 去 | to go |
| *To'* | 到 | to arrive at | Loi | 來 | to come |
| *To'* | 倒 | to fall down | *Ta'* | 打 | to strike |

And a few others. Of all of these numerous examples will occur in future lessons.

* When "good bye" is used by one leaving a house, the Chinese term is "tso cha," (*lit.* sit down,) i.e. as much as to say, "Will you please sit down; You need not accompany me out."

| | | | | | |
|---|---|---|---|---|---|
| To put on | 着住 | *cheuk* chü` | To look on | 望住 | mong` chü` |
| To wear | 戴住 | *tai`* chü` | To refuse | 推却 | *t‘ui k‘euk* |
| To lock | 鎖住 | *soh'* chü` | To drink up | 飲嗺 | *yăm' sai`* |
| To fear | 怕到 | *pa` to`* | To copy | 抄起 | *ch‘au hi`* |
| To live at | 居住 | *kü* chü` | To forget | 忘却 | mong *k‘euk* |
| To become annoyed | 怒起 | no` *hi'* | To assist | 扶起，帮助 | fu *hi'*, *pong* choh` |

PARTICLES (CONTINUED.)

4. Affirmative particles — *Li* 哩 *Le`* 咧
5. Interrogative and Responsive particle often conveying an idea of disapprobation — *Me* 咩
6. Restrictive particles often used in answers but seldom in questions — *Che* 啫, Chü` 咄
7. Doubting particle expressing doubt — *Kwa`* 啩
8. Desiderating particle expressing desire — *Ai* 唉
9. Admonishing or directing particles, not so intense as to convey the idea of command — *Po`* 嚩, *O* 呵

In some cases two of these are conjoined: thus LO' PO' (Nos. 2. & 9.) have the force of a strongly declarative expression.

| | | |
|---|---|---|
| 1 Good morning Sir! look at that hill | 早晨呀先生，望吓嗰個山 | tso-shan a sin-shang; mong ha ko-ko shan |
| 2 What sort of a coat have you put on? | 你着住點樣嘅衫呢 | ni cheuk chü tim yeung ke sham ni? |
| 3 I am wearing a blue coat | 我着藍衫 | ngo cheuk lam-sham |
| 4 Is it a blue or a brown coat? | 係藍色只係棕色衫呢 | hai lam shik chi hai chung shik ni? |
| 5 Assist me to carry this book | 帮助我抬呢部書 | pong choh ngo t‘oi ni po shü |
| 6 Tell him to lock the door | 叫佢鎖門囉 | kiu k‘ü soh mun lo |
| 7 Where did you say he lived? | 你話佢喺邊處住呢 | ni wa k‘ü hai pin-ch‘ü chü ni? |
| 8 He lives at Hongkong | 佢喺香港居住嘅 | k‘ü hai Heung-kong kü chü ke |
| 9 Does he ever quarrel with you? | 佢有時同你嗌交冇 | k‘ü yau-shi t‘ung ni ai-kau mo? |
| 10 No, he fears to do so | 冇，佢唔敢嘅 | mo; k‘ü 'm kom ke |
| 11 I don't think he lives here | 我估佢唔喺呢處住 | ngo ku k‘ü 'm hai ni-ch‘ü chü |

| | | |
|---|---|---|
| 12 I wish he did so | 我中意佢有噉做咯 | ngo chung-i k'ü yau kom tso lok |
| 13 Tell your friend to drink this wine | 叫你朋友飲呢啲酒喇 | kiu ni p'ăng-yau yăm ni-ti tsau la |
| 14 He may not like to drink it | 或者佢唔中意飲呢 | wak che k'ü 'm chung i yăm ni |
| 15 I want you to copy this | 我要你抄呢啲野 | ngo iu ni ch'au ni-ti ye |
| 16 What? all this; it is too much | 乜野呀？咁多，多過頭咯 | mat ye a? kom to, to kwo t'au lok |
| 17 You cannot refuse to do it | 你推却唔做得咯 | ni t'ui k'euk 'm tso tăk lok |
| 18 I have forgotten how to write | 我唔記得點樣寫咯 | ngo 'm ki tăk tim-yeung se lok |
| 19 You are very lazy, I fear | 我怕你係好懶惰嘅 | ngo p'a ni hai ho lan-to ke |
| 20 No; but I have been working the whole day | 唔係，我成日做工夫 | 'm hai; ngo shing-yat tso kuug fu |
| 21 Although you have worked you must write this | 雖然你有做工夫，亦必要寫呢的字 | sui-in ni yau kung-fu, yik pit iu se ni-ti tsz |
| 22 It will take too long a time | 要好耐正做得咯 | iu ho noi ching tso tăk lok |
| 23 It won't take long if you understand it | 若係你明白，就唔使幾耐啫 | yeuk hai ni ming-pak, tsau 'm shai ki noi che |
| 24 Have you been for a walk? | 你係出街行嚟咩 | ni hai ch'ut kai hang lai me? |
| 25 Yes, and I saw several people | 係咯，我見過好多人喇 | hai lok, ngo kin kwo ho to yan la |
| 26 When was that? yesterday or to-day? | 係幾時呀，係昨日只今日 | hai ki shi a? hai tsok-yat chi kam-yat |
| 27 I have forgotten; I am very tired | 我唔記得咯，我好癐 | ngo 'm ki-tăk lok; ngo ho kui |
| 28 Don't wear those clothes to-morrow | 聽日唔好着嗰的衫袍 | t'eng-yat 'm ho cheuk ko-ti sham po |
| 29 Very well; shall I leave the door open? | 好咧，我打開門好唔好呢 | ho le! ngo ta-hoi mun ho 'm ho ni? |
| 30 Yes! leave it open | 好咯，離開佢喇 | ho lok; li hoi k'ü la |
| 31 When did the compradore go out? | 買辦係幾時出去呢 | mai-pan hai ki shi ch'ut hü ni? |
| 32 He went out this morning | 佢係今朝出去嘅 | k'ü hai kăm chiu ch'ut hü ke |
| 33 Does he always go out like this? | 佢時時係噉出去咩 | k'ü shi-shi hai kom ch'ut hü me? |
| 34 He always locks the door | 佢時時鎖門嘅 | k'ü shi-shi soh mun ke |

# LESSON XXV.

### CLASSIFIERS.

Attention has already been drawn to the Classifiers, and their use explained. (Vide Lesson III and note.) As a perfect knowledge of them is a great aid to correct speaking, the learner will do well to commit to memory the lists given in this and following lessons.

1. *Ko`* 個, *a thing*, is, strictly speaking, applied to *men* and KO 箇, *a bamboo stalk*, to *inanimate objects*; the latter may often be used with other substantives when the correct classifier is unknown; the contracted form of 箇 is 个 and it is usually so written in manuscript.
2. *Chek* 隻, *single*, is applied to boats or ships, birds, quadrupeds and the limbs of the body.
3. *Tui`* 對, *a pair*, is applied to all articles necessarily used in pairs; such as shoes, stockings, &c.
4. *Sheung* 雙, *a couple*, is applied to articles not necessarily pairs but dual; TUI 對 and SHEUNG 雙 are sometimes interchanged.
5. *Pa'* 把, *to grasp*, is applied to articles that can be grasped, such as a knife, umbrella, &c.
6. *Cheung* 張, *to spread out*, is applied chiefly to things that are spread out, such as sheets, table-covers, mats, &c.

The classifier invariably follows the numeral and precedes the adjective, in sentences where both are expressed; e.g. *One good man* YAT KO HO YAN 一個好人.

### GENDER.

Gender is only expressed when it is desired to distinguish the sexes. The words used are as follows.

| | | | | | | |
|---|---|---|---|---|---|---|
| For mankind | nam | 男 male | nü' | 女 female | | |
| ,, animals (generally) | *kung* | 公 ,, | *na'* | 乸 ,, | | |
| ,, birds | hung | 雄 ,, | *ts'z* | 雌 ,, | | |
| and | *kung* | 公 ,, | mo' | 母 ,, | are also used | |
| ,, quadrupeds | mau' | 牡 ,, | p'an' | 牝 ,, | | |

| | | | | | |
|---|---|---|---|---|---|
| A cock | 一隻鷄公 | *yat chek kai-kung* | A pig | 一隻猪公 | *yat chek chü-kung* |
| A hen | 一隻鷄乸 | *yat chek kai-na'* | A sow | 一隻猪乸 | *yat chek chü-na'* |

| | | | | | |
|---|---|---|---|---|---|
| A bull | 一隻牛公 | *yat chek* ngau-*kung* | A horse | 一隻馬公 | *yat chek* ma'-*kung* |
| A cow | 一隻牛㚻 | *yat chek* ngau-*na'* | A mare | 一隻馬㚻 | *yat chek* ma'-*na'* |
| A boat | 一隻艇 | *yat chek* t'eng' | Anything | 野, 物件 | ye', mät kin' |
| A bird | 一隻雀 | *yat chek tseuk* | At home | 家住 | *ka* chü' |
| A pair of sheets | 一對被單 | *yat tui'* p'i'-*tan* | Mats | 蓆 | tsek |
| | | | Sort of | 樣 | yeung' |
| Animals | 畜生 | ch'uk-*shäng* | Certain | 定 | ting' |
| Daily | 日日 | yat-yat | Difficult | 難 | nan |

| | | |
|---|---|---|
| 1 That man and that bird | 嗰个人個隻雀 | ko ko yan ko chek tseuk |
| 2 Have you seen that boat of mine? | 我隻艇你有見過冇呀 | ngo chek t'eng ni yau kin kwo mo a? |
| 3 I have not seen it; this man has it | 我未見過, 呢個人有 | ngo mi kin kwo; ni ko yan yau |
| 4 Have you my pair of boots? | 你有我對靴冇呀 | ni yau ngo tui hö mo a? |
| 5 I have not your pair of boots, I have your knife | 我冇你對靴, 有你張刀啫 | ngo mo ni tui hö, yau ni cheung to che |
| 6 Will you buy a mat for me? | 你肯買張蓆過我麼 | ni hang mai cheung tsek kwo ngo moh? |
| 7 No; but I will buy a pair of stockings for you | 唔肯, 但我買一對襪過你喇 | 'm hang; tan ngo mai yat tui mat kwo ni la |
| 8 He wants to sell one cock and two hens | 佢想賣一隻鷄公及兩隻鷄㚻 | k'ü seung mai yat chek kai-kung kap leung chek kai-na |
| 9 I thought he had only hens | 我估佢淨有鷄㚻啫 | ngo ku k'ü tsing yau kai-na che |
| 10 He tells me he has a pair of horses | 佢話我知佢有一雙馬 | k'ü wa ngo chi, k'ü yau yat sheung ma |
| 11 That is a very good sort of sampan | 個隻三板好樣嘅 | ko chek sam-pan ho yeung ke |
| 12 Is that a horse or a mare? | 個隻係馬公只馬㚻呢 | ko chek hai ma-kung, chi ma-na ni? |
| 13 I think it is a horse, I am not certain | 我估係馬公但唔話得定 | ngo ku hai ma-kung; tan 'm wa täk ting |
| 14 Will the man or the woman come? | 係男人嚟只女人嚟 | hai nam-yan lai chi nü-yan lai? |

初學階

| | | |
|---|---|---|
| 15 The woman will come, and the two girls also | 嗰個女人嚟，共兩個女仔添 | ko-ko nü-yan lai, kung leung ko nü-tsai t'im |
| 16 Does he want to buy anything? | 佢想買野麽 | k'ü seung mai ye mo? |
| 17 Yes; he wants to buy a great many animals | 係咯，佢想買好多畜生 | hai lok; k'ü seung mai ho to ch'uk-shăng |
| 18 What animals does he want to buy? | 買乜畜生呢 | mai mat ch'uk-shăng ni? |
| 19 He wants a bull, a cow, a pig and a sow | 佢想買一隻牛公，一隻牛母，一隻猪公，一隻猪母 | k'ü seung mai yat chek ngau-kung, yat chek ngau-mo, yat chek chü-kung, yat chek chü-mo |
| 20 Does he want nothing more? | 唔愛乜野添羅咩 | 'm oi mat-ye t'im lo me? |
| 21 Nothing more to-day; to-morrow he will want something | 今日佢唔愛乜野添喇，聽日佢正愛咯 | kăm-yat 'm oi mat-ye t'im la; t'eng-yat k'ü ching oi lok |
| 22 Has that coolie made a fire yet? | 嗰个管店點着火爐唔曾 | ko-ko kun-tim tim cheuk foh-lo 'm ts'ăng? |
| 23 He has extinguished the fire | 佢整熄个火爐 | k'ü ching sik ko foh-lo |
| 24 Is he not ready to make the bed? | 佢未整便去鋪牀咩 | k'ü mi ching-pin hü p'o ch'ong me? |
| 25 Suppose he is not here | 或者佢唔喺處 | wak che k'ü 'm hai ch'ü |
| 26 How long a time will he remain? | 佢等幾耐呀 | k'ü tăng ki noi a? |
| 27 About a year or two years | 約一年或兩年 | yeuk yat nin, wak leung nin |
| 28 I cannot translate these lessons | 呢啲課文，我唔會繙譯 | ni ti fo-măn ngo 'm ui fan yik |
| 29 Are they too difficult? Tell me | 係難過頭唔呢，你話我聽 | hai nan kwo t'au 'm ni? ni wa ngo t'eng |
| 30 No, not altogether; but they are too long | 唔係淨難，但係長過頭啫 | 'm hai tsing nan; tan hai ch'eung kwo t'au che |
| 31 Well, you must study constantly | 好剌，你必要時時讀書 | ho la; ni pit iu shi-shi tuk shü |
| 32 But I cannot study constantly | 但我唔做得時時讀書 | tan ngo 'm tso tăk shi-shi tuk shü |

| | | |
|---|---|---|
| 33 How many months in the year do you study? | 一年內你有幾多個月讀書呢 | yat nin noi ni yau ki to ko üt tuk shü ni? |
| 34 Oh! nine months; I am at home three months | 唉, 九個月, 我在家三個月啫 | ai! kau ko üt; ngo tsoi ka sam ko üt che |
| 35 That is too long a time | 噉耐過頭 | kom noi kwo t'au |
| 36 You must study daily | 你是必日日要讀 | ni shi-pit yat-yat iu tuk |

# LESSON XXVI.

| | | | | | |
|---|---|---|---|---|---|
| To be careful (lit. little heart) | 小心 | *siu' săm* | People (all men) | 人人 | yan yan |
| | | | Weak (as a decoction) | 淡 | tam\` |
| Do. | 好聲 | *ho' sheng* | Strong (do.) | 濃 | yung |
| To wait | 等 | *tang'* | Strong (as an essence) | 揞 | *k'ang'* |
| Wait a little | 等吓 | *tăng'* ha' | Strong (in muscle) | 有力 | yau' lik |
| Daily (all days) | 日日 | yat yat | | | |

Number, like gender, is in Chinese only expressed when distinctness is required, the same word being ordinarily used to signify either singular or plural. To form specific plurals the noun is, in some few cases, repeated as above; in other cases TĂNG 等 and TI 哋 are suffixed.

| | | |
|---|---|---|
| Men | 人哋 | yan ti\` |
| Us | 我等, 我哋 | ngo'-*tăng'*, ngo'-ti\` |
| You | 你等, 你哋 | ni'-*tăng'*, ni'-ti\` |

Note that the noun very seldom has a plural suffix, even when it is desired to speak of more than one object, if a demonstrative pronoun in the plural form precedes it.

| | | |
|---|---|---|
| Those tables | 個啲檯 | *ko\` ti* t'oi |
| These plates | 呢啲碟 | *ni' ti* tip |

The classifier is less often used with a plural pronoun than when the singular form only is used.

| | | |
|---|---|---|
| Good morning | 早晨* | *tso'*-shan |
| Sit down! (to equals) | 請坐 | *ts'ing'* ts'oh' |
| Do. (to inferiors) | 坐囉 | t'soh' *lo* |
| How do you do to-day? | 你今日好呀 | ni' *kăm*-yat *ho'* *a*? |
| I am quite well - | 託賴平安 | *t'ok*-lai' p'ing-*on* |
| I am very unwell | 我十分唔自然 | ngo' shap-*făn* 'm tsz-in |
| Are you quite well, Sir? | 閣下十分好呀 | *kok*-ha' shap-*făn* *ho'* *a*? |

KOK HA 閣下 is only used by literati.

| | | |
|---|---|---|
| You (from employè to master) | 東家, | *tung ka* |
| You (polite form) | 駕上 | *ka'* sheung' |
| Comfortable | 舒服, | *shü* fuk |
| Well | 平安 | p'ing *on* |
| To hold (lead with a cord, as a horse, &c.) | 牽住 | *hin* chü' |
| To put on | 着住 | *cheuk* chü' |
| To drink | 飲 | *yăm* |
| To be hungry | 肚餓 | t'o' ngo' |
| Do. thirsty | 頸渴 | *keng'* *hot* |
| Do. sleepy | 眼瞓 | ngan' *fan'* |
| Intelligible | 明白 | ming pak |
| To smoke tobacco | 食烟 | shik *in* |
| On the side | 側邊 | *chak pin* |
| Sickness | 病 | peng' |
| Oil | 油 | yau |
| To sit in | 坐住 | ts'oh' chü' |
| To stop | 止住 | *chi'* chü' |
| To ascend | 上去 | sheung' *hü'* |
| To brush | 擦起 | *ts'ot hi'* |
| To lift up (as a chair) | 抬起 | t'oi *hi'* |
| To carry (do.) | 抬住 | t'oi chü' |
| Very | 實首 | shat *shau'* |

| | | |
|---|---|---|
| 1 Good morning; wait a little | 早晨, 等吓 | tso-shăn; tăng ha |
| 2 How do you do? sit down | 你好呀. 請坐 | ni ho a? ts'ing ts'oh |
| 3 Be careful, I am very unwell | 小心我十分唔自然 | siu-săm; ngo shap-făn 'm tsz-in |
| 4 Is that tea weak or strong | 個的茶係淡只濃呢 | ko-ti ch'a hai tam chi yung ni? |
| 5 People say it is very weak | 人哋話好淡嘅 | yan-ti wa ho tam ke |
| 6 Are you all quite well? | 你哋咁多位都好呀 | ni-ti kom to wai to ho a? |
| 7 We are not very well | 我哋不甚好啫 | ngo-ti păt shăm ho che |
| 8 Tell that man to wait for us | 叫嗰個人等我哋 | kiu ko-ko yan tăng ngo-ti |
| 9 Whose are these tables and those plates? | 個張檯共的碟, 係乜人嘅呢 | ko cheung t'oi kung ti tip hai măt yan ke ni? |
| 10 They belong to us; are you hungry? | 個的野係我哋嘅, 你見肚餓唔呢 | ko-ti ye hai ngo-ti ke; ni kin t'o ngo 'm ni? |

* *Note.* The lessous following No. XXV will be found to contain most of the short sentences given in works hitherto published.

| | | |
|---|---|---|
| 11 No; but I am thirsty and sleepy | 唔見，净係見頸渴眼瞓啫 | 'm kin; tsing hai kin keng hot ngan-fan che |
| 12 Are they very sleepy | 佢哋係實首眼瞓麼 | k'ü-ti hai shat-shau ngan-făn mo? |
| 13 I don't know; I see they are comfortable | 我唔知，我見佢哋好舒服 | ngo 'm chi; ngo kin k'ü-ti ho shü fuk |
| 14 I think that horse is well | 我睇個隻馬都幾好 | ngo t'ai ko p'ăt ma to ki ho |
| 15 Will you hold that mare for me | 請你牽住啲隻馬乸 | ts'ing ni hin chü ko chek ma-na |
| 16 Does he drink tea or wine? | 佢飲茶只飲酒呢 | k'ü yăm ch'a chi yăm tsau ni? |
| 17 He does not drink wine; he smokes | 佢唔飲酒，食烟啫 | k'ü 'm yăm tsau; shik in che |
| 18 Why does he not put on his clothes? | 做乜佢唔着衫呢 | tso măt k'ü 'm cheuk sham ni? |
| 19 He is sick, and must be assisted to put them on | 佢有病，要人同佢着 | k'ü yau peng, iu yan t'ung k'ü cheuk |
| 20 What sort of sickness has he? | 佢有乜病呢 | k'ü yau măt peng ni? |
| 21 He is very tired and cannot do anything | 佢十分瘡，唔做得事 | k'ü shap-fan kui, 'm tso tăk sze |
| 22 Are those words intelligible or not? | 个句話明白唔呢 | ko kü wa ming-pak 'm ni? |
| 23 Do you mean those written outside the box | 你問啲个箱外邊嘅字咩 | ni măn ko-ko seung ngoi-pin ke tsz me? |
| 24 No; I mean those in the book he is carrying | 唔係，我問佢挾住個部書嘅字 | 'm hai; ngo măn k'ü kip chü ko po shü ke tsz |
| 25 Take that candle and set it there | 拈個枝蜡燭放埋呢啲啲處 | nim ko chi lap-chuk fong mai ni ti ko-chü |
| 26 Tell all the people to wait together | 呌各人等埋一齊 | kiu kok yan tăng mai yat ts'ai |
| 27 What are they to do? | 佢哋做乜野 | k'ü-ti tso măt ye? |
| 28 Tell them to look at those cows and pigs | 話佢哋知，睇吓个的牛共猪 | wa k'ü-ti chi; t'ai ha ko ti ngau kung chü |
| 29 Will he ascend if he is told? | 你呌佢上去，你估佢肯上唔呢 | ni kiu k'ü sheung hü, ni ku k'ü hăng sheung 'm ni? |

| | | |
|---|---|---|
| 30 We don't know; he is in the boat | 我啲唔知，佢在三板嚟呢 | ngo-ti 'm chi; k'ü tsoi sam-pan lai ni |
| 31 Tell him to brush my clothes | 叫佢擦我嘅衣裳 | kiu k'ü ts'at ngo ke i-sheung |
| 32 Are you quite well to-day? | 你今日實首好呀 | ni kăm-yat shat-shau ho a? |
| 33 Yes, but I was very unwell yesterday | 係咯，但係昨日十分唔自然 | hai lok, tan hai tsok-yat shap-fău 'm tsz-in |
| 34 Sit down and listen to me | 你坐處等我話你知 | ni tsoh chü, tăng ngo wa ni chi |
| 35 Is that a cock or a hen? | 個隻鷄係公只係乸呢 | ko chek kai hai kung chi hai na ni? |
| 36 I don't know anything of birds | 我唔曉得分雀公雀乸嘅 | ngo 'm hiu tăk fan tseuk-kung tseuk-na ke |
| 37 You are not looking at them | 你都唔係睇住佢 | ni to 'm hai t'ai chü k'ü |
| 38 I think it is a hen; but I don't know | 我估係乸，但唔知得實 | ngo ku hai na; tan 'm chi tăk shat |
| 39 Where can I get a pair of sheets? | 我去邊處攞得倒一對被單呢 | ngo hü pin-chü lo tăk to yat tui p'i-tan ni? |
| 40 You (polite form) can get them upstairs | 駕上上樓攞得倒咯 | Ka sheung sheung lau lo tăk to lok |

## LESSON XXVII.

| | | | | | |
|---|---|---|---|---|---|
| To fill it up | 裝滿佢， | *tsong* mun' k'ü', | To reflect | 思想 | *sze seung* |
| | 斟滿 | *tsam* mun' | To forget | 忘却， | mong *k'euk*, |
| To carry (between two) | 扛起， | *kong hi*, | | 忘記 | mong *ki`* |
| | 抬起 | t'oi *hi'* | To refuse | 推却 | *t'ui k'euk* |
| To carry by turns | 輪流抬 | lun lau t'oi | To diminish | 減小 | *kam' shiu'* |
| To carry (with a pole) | 担起 | *tam hi'* | To throw away | 丟去 | *tiu hü`* |

The genitive or, possessive case is expressed by TI 啲 or, more commonly, by KE 嘅, though the position of a word in the sentence frequently makes its case so clear that the particle may be dispensed with; e.g. *The stars of heaven*, T'IN SING 天星 or T'IN KE SING 天嘅星.

CLASSIFIERS (CONTINUED.)

7. *Chi* 枝 a branch: applied to slender long round objects such as pencils pens, &c.
8. T'iu 條 a branch or twig: applied to similar objects as No. 7, and more frequently used. It is also applied to the divisions or articles of a code, and snakes, roads, whips, girdles, &c., take t'iu before them.
9. *Kan* 間 a crevice or interval: applied to buildings, rooms, &c. (fong kan 房間 in the rooms; ha kan 下間 below; yat nin kan 一年間 within one year.)
10. Tsoh' 座 a seat or throne: applied to buildings, hills, cities, pagodas, seats, &c.
11. To' 度 to pass, a limit: applied to places through, or over, which one can pass; such as doors, bridges, &c.
12. *Fuk* 幅 a strip of cloth: applied to maps, pictures, and similar things that are rolled up or stretched out.

| | | | | | |
|---|---|---|---|---|---|
| A hall of meeting | 一間敘會堂 | *yat kan* tsü' ui' t'ong | A map | 一幅地理圖 | *yat fuk* ti' li' t'o |
| A pair of chopsticks | 一對快子 | *yat tui' fai'* *tsz'* | A snake | 條蛇 | (t'iu) she |
| A house (building) | 間屋 | (*kan*) *uk* | A bridge | 度橋 | (to') k'iu |

| | | |
|---|---|---|
| To try | 試 | *shi* |
| To try once | 試吓, 試一吓 | *shi'* ha', *shi' yat* ha |
| To worship spirits | 拜神 | *pai'* shăn |
| A scheme, plan | 計, 計謀 | *kai'*, *kai'* mau |
| I have no leisure | 我唔得閒 | ngo' 'm *tak* han |
| Immediately - - | 即刻, 立刻 | *tsik hak* (or) lap *hak* (the former also means "straight on.") |
| To be engaged | 有事, 唔得閒 | yau' sze', 'm *tak* han |
| More than - | 多過 | *to kwo'* |
| Unlimited | 無限 | mo han' |

"A little" shorter, longer, narrower, wider, &c. is formed by adding TI 啲 to the adjective, e.g.

初學階

| | | |
|---|---|---|
| A little longer | 長啲 | ch'eung *ti* |
| Add a little | 添啲 | *t'im ti* |
| Take a little off | 減啲 | *kam' ti* |

*What*, in the sense of *that which*, is rendered by SHOH—KE 所—嘅.

| | | |
|---|---|---|
| 1 I wish he would fill up the man's cup | 我想佢斟滿嗰個人嘅杯 | ngo seung k'ü chăm mun ko-ko yan ke pui |
| 2 Reflect upon what you are doing | 思想吓你所做嘅事 | sze-seung ha ni shoh tso ke sze |
| 3 Try it again once more; it's a good plan | 試一吓添，係好計嚟啞 | shi yat ha t'im; hai ho kai lai a |
| 4 What good plan do you speak of? | 你講乜野好計啞 | ni kong măt-ye ho kai a? |
| 5 A plan to kill the snake | 打死條蛇嘅計囉 | ta sze t'iu she ke kai lo |
| 6 She is going there to worship spirits | 佢去個處拜神 | k'ü hü ko-ch'ü pai shan |
| 7 I have no leisure to go to worship | 我唔得閒去拜 | ngo 'm tăk han hü pai |
| 8 This is the hall (of the house) | 呢處係廳 | ni-ch'ü hai t'eng |
| 9 Is this a map of the bridge? | 呢幅係嗰度橋嘅圖唔係呢 | ni fuk hai ko to k'iu ke t'o 'm hai ni? |
| 10 No; it is a map of the hall | 唔係，係廳嘅圖啫 | 'm hai; hai t'eng ke t'o che |
| 11 This is the man's son's chop-sticks | 呢對筷子係嗰个人嘅仔嘅 | ni tui fai-tsz hai ko-ko yan ke tsai ke |
| 12 Did you forget to throw it away? | 你忘記丟佢去咩 | ni mong-ki tiu k'ü hü me? |
| 13 No; he refused to throw it away | 唔係，佢唔肯丟佢去 | 'm hai; k'ü 'm hăng tiu k'ü hü |
| 14 The people at that place have diminished a little | 個的人喺嗰處減少啲咯 | ko-ti yan hai ko-ch'ü kăm siu ti lok |
| 15 Are you engaged now? | 你如今有事咩 | ni ü kăm yau sze me? |
| 16 No; but we are going out immediately | 唔係，但係我哋即刻就去街咯 | 'm hai; tan hai ngo-ti tsik-hak tsau hü kai lok |
| 17 Are there more than four hundred people? | 嗰處多過四百人係唔係呢 | ko-ch'ü to kwo sze pak yan hai 'm hai ni? |

| | | |
|---|---|---|
| 18 I cannot say for certain; there are many women | 我唔話得定，嗰處有好多女人 | ngo 'm wa tăk ting; ko ch'ü yau ho to nü-yan |
| 19 Can't you make it a little longer? | 你整長啲佢做得唔呢 | ni ching ch'eung ti k'ü tso tăk 'm ni? |
| 20 It cannot be made longer; it is the man's | 唔整得長咯，係嗰個人嘅 | 'm ching tăk ch'eung lok; hai ko-ko yan ke |
| 21 Were all the people there? | 喊嘭唥咁多人在處咩 | ham-pang-lang kom to yan tsoi ch'ü me? |
| 22 Yes; and the woman's daughter was there | 係，嗰個女人嘅女都在處 | hai; ko-ko nü-yan ke nü to tsoi ch'ü |
| 23 She said she was very uncomfortable | 佢話佢十分唔安樂 | k'ü wa k'ü shap-făn 'm on-lok |
| 24 There are more than forty persons there | 嗰處有多過四十人在處 | ko ch'ü yau to kwo sze-shap yan tsoi chü |
| 25 Take a little of that soup and give it to her | 擰啲咁多湯俾過佢 | ning ti kom to t'ong pi kwo k'ü |
| 26 Who made that map? | 乜誰整嗰个圖嘅呢 | măt-shui ching ko-ko t'o ke ni? |
| 27 The compradore made it | 嗰個買辦整嘅 | ko-ko mai-pan ching ke |
| 28 He must have made it very slowly | 佢是必係慢慢整嘅咯 | k'ü shi-pit hai man-man ching ke lok |
| 29 He worked at it regularly, but slowly | 佢都係照常咁做，但係做得慢啲 | k'ü to hai chiu sheung kom tso; tan hai tso tăk man ti |
| 30 Suppose that he had not done it? | 若係佢冇做得嚟呢 | yeuk hai k'ü mo tso tăk lai ni? |
| 31 He took a long time about it | 佢用嘵好多時候做佢嘅咯 | k'ü yung hiu ho to shi-hau tso k'ü ke lok |
| 32 He was looking at it too long | 佢睇嘵好久 | k'ü t'ai hiu ho kau |
| 33 Tell him to put on those clothes immediately | 叫佢即刻着嗰啲衣服 | kiu k'ü tsik-hak cheuk ko-ti i-fuk |
| 34 Whose clothes? those of the man's son? | 乜誰嘅衣服呀，嗰個人嘅仔的 | măt shui ke i-fuk a? ko-ko yan ke tsai tik |
| 35 Is that a house or a hall? | 嗰間係屋呀只係廳呢 | ko kan hai uk a, chi hai t'eng ni? |

| | | | |
|---|---|---|---|
| 36 | It is a house; it stands (*lit.* is erected) by the side of the bridge | 係屋嚟,建在嗰度橋邊嘅呢 | hai uk lai; kin tsoi ko to k'iu pin ke ni |
| 37 | I want some men to translate for me | 我要人同我譒繹 | ngo iu yan t'ung ngo fan-yik |
| 38 | They must not be English but Chinese | 唔係要英人,要唐人啫 | 'm hai iu ying-yan; iu t'ong-yan che |
| 39 | Tell her I don't want him any longer | 話佢知,我唔要佢耐啲添喇 | wa k'ü chi; ngo 'm iu k'ü noi ti t'im la |
| 40 | He comes here very regularly | 佢常常喺呢邊來 | k'ü sheung-sheung hai ni-pin loi |
| 41 | Of course he does; he is a friend | 自必然係喇,佢係朋友啫 | tze-pit-in hai la; k'ü hai p'ăng-yan che |
| 42 | When he comes I wish to have some conversation with him | 佢嚟時,我想同佢講吓說話 | k'ü lai shi, ngo seung t'ung k'ü kong ha shüt wa |

---

# LESSON XXVIII.

| | | | | | |
|---|---|---|---|---|---|
| An altar | 一个神壇 | *yat koˋ* shăn-t'an | A mountain pass | 一幅山峽 | *yat fuk shan-*hap |
| A waterfall | 一座水景 | *yat* tsoˋ *shuiˊ-kingˊ* | A place, locality | 一處地方 | *yat ch'üˋ* tiˋ-*fong* |
| A carriage | 一駕馬車 | *yat kaˋ* maˊ-*ch'e* | Things, goods | 物件 | măt-kinˋ |
| A wall | 一幅墻 | *yat fuk* ts'eung | To set out | 起程 | *hiˊ* ch'ing |
| A road | 一條路 | *yat* t'iu loˋ | | | |
| A pagoda | 一座塔 | *yat* tsoˋ *t'ap* | | | |

The words used to express *to* and *with* are T'UNG 同 KWO 過 and MAI 埋, e.g.

| | | |
|---|---|---|
| Give it to him | 俾過佢 | *piˊ kwoˋ* k'üˊ |
| Speak with him | 你同佢講 | niˊ t'ung k'üˊ *kongˊ* |
| Put it close to him | 放埋近佢 | *fongˋ* mai kanˋ k'üˊ |

T'UNG 同 *with*, frequently supplies the English word *for*; e.g. *buy that for me*, NI T'UNG NGO MAI KO-KO 你同我買啯個.

| | | | | | |
|---|---|---|---|---|---|
| To remove entirely | 除去 | c'hü *hü*\` | To press between | 夾住 | kap chü\` |
| To live together | 同住 | t'ung chü\` | To discourse | 講論 | *kong'* lun\` |
| To store away | 貯住 | ch'ü' chü\` | To decline | 辭去 | ts'z *hü*\` |
| To obstruct | 攔住 | lan chü\` | To collect | 收起 | *shau ki'* |

| | | |
|---|---|---|
| What time is it? | 幾多點鐘呢 | *ki' to tim' chung ni?* |
| Elder brother | 大佬 | tai\` *lo'* |
| Younger brother - | 細佬 | *sai*\` *lo'* |

CHUNG 鐘, lit. *a bell*, has passed into use as the word for *clock*; TIM 點 is literally *a dot, a point*.

| | | |
|---|---|---|
| What is your family name? (polite form) | 你高姓呀 | ni' *ko sing*\` *a?* (*ko* 高 meaning lofty) |
| Do. (to an inferior) | 你姓乜野 | ni' *sing*\` *măt*-ye' ? |
| What is this called? | 呢啲叫乜野呢 | *ni'-ti kiu*\` *măt*-ye' *ni?* |
| My name is Ch'ăn (polite form) | 我小姓陳 | ngo' *siu' sing*\` ch'ăn |
| Do. (to equals) | 我姓陳 | ngo' *sing*\` ch'ăn |
| What Ch'ăn is that? | 係乜陳呢 | hai\` *măt* ch'ăn *ni?* |
| It is the character ch'ăn in "p'o ch'ăn" (to seat in order) | 係鋪陳嘅陳字 | hai\` *p'o*-ch'ăn *ke*\` ch'ăn tsz\` |
| Speak slowly | 慢慢講 | man\`-man\` *kong'* |
| It is finished | 做完咯 | tso\` ün *lok* |
| Is that native or foreign? | 啯個係本地只來路嘅呢 | *ko'-ko*\` hai\` *pun'*-ti\` chi' loi-lo\` *ke*\` *ni?* |
| It is not enough | 唔得夠 | 'm *tăk kau*\` |
| Please say it again | 請再講過 | *ts'ing' tsoi*\` *kong' kwo*\` |
| It is uncertain | 唔得定 | 'm *tăk* ting\` |
| A Newspaper | 新聞紙 | *săn*-măn-*chi'* |
| Question and answer | 問答 | măn\` *tap* |

---

1 Do you go by this road? 你喺呢條路去咩 ni hai ni t'iu lo hü me?

2 I am going to the large pagoda 我去啯座大番塔處 ngo hü ko tso tai fan-t'ap ch'ü.

初學階

| | | |
|---|---|---|
| 3 Do you go in a carriage? No | 你坐馬車去咩. 唔係 | ni tso ma-ch'e hü me? 'm hai |
| 4 Is there an altar in the pagoda? | 嗰座番塔有一个神壇咩 | ko tso fan-t'ap yau yat ko shăn-t'an me? |
| 5 No; the altar is outside the wall | 唔係, 嗰度神壇係在个幅墻外 | 'm hai; ko to shăn-t'an hai tsoi ko fuk ch'eung ngoi |
| 6 Have you a map of the place? | 你有嗰處嘅地圖冇呢 | ni yau ko ch'ü ke ti-t'o mo ni? |
| 7 If you have a map give it to me | 你若係有幅地圖, 俾過我喇 | ni yeuk hai yau fuk ti-t'o, pi kwo ngo la |
| 8 People speak of a mountain pass there | 人哋話嗰處有幅山峽啝 | yan ti wa ko-ch'ü yau fuk shan-hap woh |
| 9 It is all written in the letter | 嗰封信一啲都寫晒嘅咯 | ko fung-sän yat ti to se sai ke lok |
| 10 Does the letter speak of a waterfall? | 信內有講到一座水景冇呢 | sän noi yau kong to yat tso shui-king mo ni? |
| 11 The letter is incomplete | 嗰封信唔得全備 | ko fung-săn 'm tăk ts'ün pi |
| 12 Do those men live together? | 嗰啲人係同埋一處住唔係呢 | ko-ti yan hai t'ung mai yat ch'ü chü 'm hai ni? |
| 13 Yes! he lives there with his elder brother | 係, 佢同埋佢嘅大佬住 | hai, k'ü t'ung mai k'ü ke tai lo chü |
| 14 Is his younger brother hungry? | 佢嘅細佬係肚餓唔係呢 | k'ü ke sai lo hai t'o ngo 'm hai ni? |
| 15 No; but he is very unwell | 唔係, 但係佢好唔自然 | 'm hai; tan hai k'ü ho 'm tsz-in |
| 16 Why do they obstruct those men? | 佢哋爲乜事幹攔住嗰啲人呢 | k'ü-ti wai-măt sz-kon lan-chü ko-ti yan ni? |
| 17 They do not want them to finish the house | 佢哋唔中意佢哋起好嗰間屋 | k'ü-ti 'm chung-i k'ü-ti hi ho ko kan uk |
| 18 Will the compradore collect money? | 嗰個買辦肯去收銀唔呢 | ko-ko mai-pan hăng hü shau ngăn 'm ni? |
| 19 He would not let him pass | 佢唔肯俾佢過去 | k'ü 'm hăng pi k'ü kwo hü |

| | | |
|---|---|---|
| 20 What time is it? Has it struck ten? | 幾多點鐘，打曉十點未呢 | ki to tim chung? ta hiu shap tim mi ni? |
| 21 He declines to answer | 佢唔肯答 | k'ü 'm hăng tap |
| 22 I wish those people would remove it entirely | 我想啲啲人搬曬佢去啫 | ngo seung ko-ti yan pun sai k'ü hü che |
| 23 His elder brother is speaking (discoursing) | 佢嘅大佬講僅一件事幹 | k'ü ke tai lo kong kan yat kin sze-kon |
| 24 I wish you to speak slowly | 我想你慢慢講 | ngo seung ni man-man kong |
| 25 Bring some to her, to us, and to them | 拧啲俾佢，一啲我哋，又一啲佢哋 | ning ti pi k'ü, yat ti ngo-ti, yau yat ti k'ü-ti |
| 26 You have not bought enough | 你唔曾買得够 | ni 'm ts'ăng mai tăk kau |
| 27 At what hour do you set out? | 你幾多點鐘起程呢 | ni ki to tim chung hi ch'ing ni? |
| 28 It is quite uncertain, I cannot say positively | 十分唔定，我唔話得實 | shap-făn 'm ting; ngo 'm wa tăk shat |
| 29 What time was it when he started? | 佢起程時，幾多點鐘呢 | k'u hi ch'ing shi, ki to tim chung ni? |
| 30 It was about half past eleven | 啲陣時，大約十一點半 | ko chăn shi, tai yeuk shap-yat tim pun |
| 31 Is that a Chinese or an English newspaper? | 啲張係唐字新聞紙，或英字新聞紙呢 | ko cheung hai t'ong tsz săn-man-chi wak ying tsz săn-man-chi ni? |
| 32 Where is the book I gave you? | 我俾你啲本書喺邊處 | ngo pi ni ko pun shü hai pin-ch'ü? |
| 33 It is downstairs, shall I (suppose I) fetch it? | 喺樓下嚟，我去拧唔呢 | hai lau ha lai; ngo hü ning 'm ni? |
| 34 Never mind, tell me the name of the book, and it will do | 唔使咯，話啲本書名過我知就做得喇 | 'm shai lok; wa ko pun shü meng kwo ngo chi, tsau tso tăk la |
| 35 Is it a native or a foreign book? | 係唐書只係外國嘅書呢 | hai t'ong shü chi hai ngoi-kwok ke shü ni? |
| 36 It is a foreign book but has a Chinese name | 係外國嘅書，但係有個唐人名字 | hai ngoi-kwok ke shü; tan hai yau ko t'ong-yan ming-tsz |

| | | |
|---|---|---|
| 37 You have not told me its name | 你冇話啁個名過我知啞 | ni mo wa ko-ko ming kwo ngo chi a |
| 38 I will tell it you to-morrow | 我明日話你知 | ngo ming-yat wa ni chi |
| 39 Where shall I put this knife? | 我擠埋呢張刀仔在邊處好呢 | ngo chai mai ni cheung to-tsai tsoi pin-ch'ü ho ni? |
| 40 Put it close to him | 放埋近住佢啁處 | fong mai kan chü k'ü ko-ch'ü |

---

# LESSON XXIX.

The accusative or objective case (as we term it) generally follows the verb in simple phrases, but in long sentences occasionally precedes it.

What we should in other languages term the ablative is rendered either by the prepositions TSZ 自, YAU 由, &c.; by using words, not properly prepositions, in that sense; or by transposing the sentence; e.g.

| | | |
|---|---|---|
| He comes from Hongkong | 佢喺香港來 | k'ü' hai *Heung-kong'* loi |
| He comes by ship | 佢搭船來 | k'ü' tap shün loi |
| Killed by a sword | 用刀殺人 | yung' *to shat* yan (*lit.* us-[ing] a sword, killed one) |

| | | | | | |
|---|---|---|---|---|---|
| A sheet of paper | 一張紙 | *yat cheung chí* | To seal | 封住 | *fung* chü' |
| A sedan chair | 一頂轎 | *yat ting'* kiu' | To connect | 連住 | lin chü' |
| To envelop (wrap up) | 包起 | *pau hí* | To guard | 守住 | *shau'* chü' |
| To draw to pull up | 楸起 | *ts'au hí* | To bar | 關住 | *kwan* chü' |
| The heavens, sky | 天 | *t'in* | A village | 條村 | t'iu *ts'ün* |

Diminutives are expressed by SIU 小 (already given) or SAI 細 *small*, preceding the noun, and TSAI 仔 following it; e.g., *a small house*, SIU KAN UK; or YAT KAN UK-TSAI, 小間屋或一間屋仔; *a small knife*, TO-TSAI 刀仔.

CLASSIFIERS.

13. Chan' 陣 to range, is applied to a gust, puff, dash, shower, cloud, beam of light, &c.

14. *Nap* 粒 a grain, is applied to seeds and grains, buttons, sand.

15. Ch'eung 場 a fit, spell, is applied as No. 13 but implies longer duration.

16. Tui` 隊 a crowd, is applied to a party or group of people, body of soldiers, &c.

17. Kw'an 羣 a company, is applied to a herd, flock, drove.

18. *Tat* 笪 a patch, daub, is applied to spots or irregular marks.

| | | |
|---|---|---|
| What noise is that? . . . . . | 個啲係乜野聲音呢 | *ko'-ti* hai` *mat*-ye' *shing-yăm ni?* |
| He has just gone out . . . . . | 佢就至去啫 | k'ü' tsan` *chi`* *hü`* *che* |
| Do you want this any longer . | 你重要呢個唔要呢 | ni' chung` *iu`* *ni-ko`* 'm *iu`* *ni?* |
| What is your name? (the name conferred after birth) | 你叫乜野名呢 | ni' *kiu`* *măt*-ye' meng *ni?* |
| Who are you working for? . . | 你同乜人打工呢 | ni' t'ung *măt* yan *ta'* *kung* *ni?* |
| Take this letter to the Post office | 拎呢封信去書信館 | *ning ni fung-sän`* *hü`* *shü-săn`-kun* |
| Ask if there is an answer? . . | 你問吓有囘音冇 | ni' măn` ba' yau' ui-*yăm* mo? |
| Wait a little, I am busy . . . | 等吓喳，我有事幹 | *tăng'* ha' *cha`*, ngo' yau' sze`-*kon`* |

| | | | | | |
|---|---|---|---|---|---|
| Printing office | 印字館 | *yan`*-tze`-*kun'* | Dispensary | 藥房 | yeuk-fong |
| Chapel | 禮拜堂 | lai'-*pai`*-t'ong | Barracks | 兵房 | *ping*-fong |
| Post office | 書信館 | *shu-săn`-kun'* | Shop | 舖頭 | *p'o`*-t'au |
| Dwelling house | 屋舍 | *uk-she`* | Godowns | 貨倉 | *fo`-ts'ong* |
| Pawnbroker's shop | 當舖 | *tong`-p'o`* | Prison | 監房 | *kăm*-fong |
| Mandarin office | 衙門 | nga-mun | Hotel | 客店 | *hak-tim`* |
| Custom house | 關口 | *kwan-hau'* | Market | 街市 | *kai*-shi' |
| Police station | 差館 | *ch'ai-kun'* | School | 書館 | *shü-kun'* |
| House of business | 行 | hong | Temple | 廟 | miu` |

*Do you* (they, etc) *do* so and so, is expressed by adding HAI 'M HAI 係唔係 to the end of the sentence.

嗳 AI, an expression of doubt, is frequently affixed to sentences rendered in English by *suppose* (v. sentence 8. etc.)

| | | |
|---|---|---|
| 1 Do you come from the Post office? | 你喺書信館來嘅係唔係 | ni hai shü-săn-kun loi ke hai 'm hai? |
| 2 No; I come from the Police station | 唔係，我喺差館來嘅 | 'm hai, ngo hai ch'ai-kun loi ke |
| 3 Do they guard those barracks? | 佢哋守住嗰間兵房係唔係 | k'ü-ti shau-chü ko kan ping-fong hai 'm hai? |

初學階

| | | |
|---|---|---|
| 4 They guard the barracks and the prison | 佢哋守住嗰間兵房共監房 | k'ü-ti shau-chü ko kan ping-fong kung kam-fong |
| 5 There is a market in the little village | 嗰條村仔有個街市 | ko t'iu ts'ün-tsai yau ko kai-shi |
| 6 Is there a custom house there also? | 嗰處有間關口添咩 | ko-ch'ü yau kan kwan-hau t'im me? |
| 7 He came from the Chapel; I came from the school | 佢喺禮拜堂來，我由書館來 | k'ü hai lai-pai-t'ong loi; ngo yau shü-kun loi |
| 8 Suppose we go to the dispensary? | 我哋去藥房噯 | ngo ti hü yeuk-fong ai? |
| 9 Is that a Pawnbroker's shop or a printing office? | 嗰間係當舖只係印字館呢 | ko kan hai tong-p'o chi hai yan-tsz-kun ni? |
| 10 It is a mandarin's office | 嗰間係衙門 | ko kan hai nga-mun |
| 11 Seal this letter for me | 同我封起呢封信 | t'ung ngo fung-hi ni fung-săn |
| 12 A puff of wind opened the door | 一陣風吹開嗰度門 | yat chăn fung ch'ui hoi ko to mun |
| 22 Take this sedan chair and go back to the house | 抬呢頂轎翻去屋 | t'oi ni ting kiu fan hü uk |
| 14 Wrap this up in a sheet of paper (i e. use paper to &c.) | 俾張紙包起佢 | pi cheung chi pau hi k'ü |
| 15 Where did he put the goods? | 佢擠啲貨在邊處呢 | k'ü chai ti fo tsoi pin-ch'ü ni? |
| 16 He put them in the godown | 佢擠佢在貨倉嚟 | k'ü chai k'ü tsoi fo-ts'ong lai |
| 17 Why does he bar the door? | 爲乜事佢關埋度門 | wai-mat-sze k'ü kwan mai to mun? |
| 18 Connect those carriages together | 連埋嗰幾駕馬車 | lin mai ko ki ka ma-ch'e |
| 19 That is a small shop, this is a large one | 嗰間舖頭仔，呢間大舖頭 | ko kan p'o-t'au-tsai, ni kan tai p'o-t'au |
| 20 Why don't you go to the hotel? | 爲乜你唔去客店呢 | wai-mat ni 'm hü hak-tim ni? |
| 21 Because I have to go to my house of business | 因爲我要去行有事 | yan-wai ngo iu hü hong yau sze |
| 22 What do they do at the temple? | 佢哋在廟做乜野呢 | k'ü-ti tsoi miu tso măt-ye ni? |

| | | |
|---|---|---|
| 23 I forget what they do there | 我唔記得佢哋在嗰處做乜野 | ngo 'm ki-tăk k'ü-ti tsoi ko-ch'ü tso màt-ye |
| 24 The sky is all blue | 個天青曬 | ko t'in ts'ing sai |
| 25 Did he come from Hongkong by ship? | 佢喺香港搭船來係唔係 | k'ü hai Heung-kong tap shün loi hai 'm hai? |
| 26 Yes, he came in a large ship | 係,佢搭隻大船來嘅 | hai, k'ü tap chek tai shün loi ke |
| 27 Who killed that man? | 乜誰殺死嗰個人 | măt-shui shat-sze ko-ko yan? |
| 28 Four men killed him with swords | 四個人俾刀殺死佢 | sze ko yan pi to shat-sze k'ü |
| 29 A large party of people were there | 一隊人响處 | yat tui yan heung ch'ü |
| 30 A puff of wind came suddenly | 一陣風忽然間吹來 | yat chăn fung fat-in-kan ch'ui loi |
| 31 Take this letter and bring an answer | 帶呢封信去攞回音翻來 | tai ni fung-săn hü lo ui-yăm fan loi |
| 32 Who gave you this answer? | 乜誰俾回音過你呢 | măt-shui pi ui-yăm kwo ni ni? |
| 33 If he is not at his office, go to his house | 若係佢唔在寫字樓,就去佢嘅屋 | yeuk hai k'ü 'm tsoi se-tsz-lau, tsau hü k'ü ke uk |
| 34 I don't want you any longer | 我唔使用你啲咁耐添咯 | ngo 'm shai yung ni ti kom noi t'im lok |
| 35 Tell him to wait, I am very busy | 叫佢等吓,我十分唔得閒 | kiu k'ü tăng ha, ngo shap-fân 'm tăk han |
| 36 Go and see (ask) what that noise is | 去問吓做乜野咁嘈 | hü màn ha tso-măt-ye kom ts'o |
| 37 It is a little boy making a noise | 嗰個細紋仔嘈呢 | ko-ko sai-màn-tsai ts'o ni |
| 38 Tell him he will be punished | 話佢知,等吓責罰佢 | wa k'ü chi, tăng ha chak-fat k'ü |
| 39 Have you walked to the school? | 你有行路去書館冇 | ni yau hang lo hü shü-kun mo? |
| 40 No, I went in a carriage | 唔係,我坐馬車去嘅 | 'm hai, ngo tso ma-ch'e hü ke |

# LESSON XXX.

| | | | | | |
|---|---|---|---|---|---|
| An account (bill) | 一條數 | *yat* t'iu *sho*` | To reckon up | 計起 | *kai*` *hi*' |
| A church | 福音堂 | *fuk-yăm*-t'ong | To know | 知到 | *chi to*` |
| To dislike | 唔中意 | 'm *chung-i*` | To waken | 叫醒 | *kiu*` *sing*' |
| To choose, select | 揀擇 | *kàn*'-chak | Moreover | 而且 | i-*ch'e*' |
| To anchor | 抛錨 | *p'au* nau | The mind (heart) | 心 | *săm* |
| A (street) barrier | 街閘 | *kai*-chap | Troops | 兵 | *ping* |
| To stop up | 塞住 | *sak* chü` | To level | 平 | p'ing |
| To follow | 跟住 | *kan* chü` | Rope | 繩 | shing |

Adjectives usually precede, or follow, the nouns they qualify as in English; e g., *a good horse*, YAT P'AT HO MA 一匹好馬; *this horse is good*, NI P'AT MA HO, 呢匹馬好.

Many adjectives are formed from nouns by the addition of TI 啲; e.g., *better* HO TI 好啲, *worse, inferior*, YAI-TI 𠵱啲. As, however, TI 啲 when following an adjective expressing form, quality, colour, or space, usually signifies the comparative degree (as in SAI-TI 細啲 *smaller*, TAI-TI 大啲 *larger*, etc.) KE 嘅 is more frequently used for such adjectives in their positive sense, though TI 啲 is sometimes retained for the sake of euphony. When two adjectival words come together, TI 啲 or KE 嘅 is generally omitted; e.g., *a rich man* FU-KWAI YAN 富貴人, or TS'OI-CHÜ LO 財主佬.

| | | | | | | | | |
|---|---|---|---|---|---|---|---|---|
| Beautiful | 好睇 | *ho*' *t'ai* | Clean | 乾凈 | *kon*-tseng` | Poor | 窮 | k'ung |
| Do. | 華美 | wa-mi' | Wrong | 錯 | *ts'oh*` | Old | 老 | lo' |
| Rich | 財主 | ts'oi-*chü*' | Short | 短 | *tün*' | Hot | 熱 | it |

| | | |
|---|---|---|
| That is middling | 呴個係中中嘅啫 | *ko*'-*ko*` hai` *chung-chung ke*` *che* |
| Read that book aloud | 大聲讀呴簿書 | tai` *shing* tuk *ko*' po` *shü* |
| I want to go to sleep | 我愛去瞓咯 | ngo' *oi*` hü` *făn*` *lok* |
| I dare not do it | 我唔敢做 | ngo' 'm *kom*' tso` |
| I dare not presume | 我唔敢當 | ngo' 'm *kom*' *tong* |
| Wake him up | 叫醒佢 | *kiu*` *sing*' k'ü' |
| Give a little more | 俾啲添 | *pi*' *ti t'im* |

| | | |
|---|---|---|
| To accompany friends | 送朋友 | *sung'* p‘ăng-yau' |
| You are very good (kind) | 你有心 | ni' yau' *săm* |
| Wait for an answer | 等回音 | *tăng'* ui-*yăm* |
| Speak loudly | 大聲講 | tai` *shing kong'* |
| Wherefore?—what for? | 爲乜野 | wai`-*măt*-ye' |
| To visit a person | 探人 | *t‘am`* yan |

| | | | | | |
|---|---|---|---|---|---|
| Dining-room | 大餐房 | tai`-*ts‘an*-fong | Scaffolding (bamboo) | 竹棚 | *chuk*-p‘ăng |
| Bath-room | 洗身房 | *sai'*-*shăn*-fong | Study or library | 書房 | *shü*-fong |
| Bed-room | 瞓房 | *făn`*-fong | Flower-garden | 花園 | *fa*-ün |
| Steps | 階級 | *kai-k‘ăp* | Drawing-room | 客廳 | *hak-t‘eng* |
| Lock | 把鎖 | *pa'-soh'* | Foundation | 地脚 | ti`-*keuk* |
| Key | 鎖匙 | *soh'*-shi | Brick wall | 磚牆 | *chün* ts‘eung |
| Hinges | 較 | *kau`* | Mud wall | 坭牆 | nai ts‘eung |
| Wall | 牆 | ts‘eung | God (the Creator) | 上帝 | sheung` *tai`* |

Considerable discussion—extending to the publication of entire volumes devoted to the subject—has arisen as to the best Chinese equivalent for the word "God." That above given is now adopted by the majority of sinologues.

*All*, when used substantively in the sense of a relative pronoun, is idiomatically expressed by YAT KO TO 一個都.

*Both*——*and* are expressed by YAU 又——YAU 又; e.g., *they are all both old and poor*, YAT KO TO HAI YAU LO YAU K‘UNG 一個都係又老又窮.

| | | |
|---|---|---|
| 1 Are those steps short or long? | 啯啲階級係長只短呢 | ko-ti kai-k‘ăp hai ch‘eung chi tün ni? |
| 2 Where did the boat anchor? | 啯隻船抛在邊處 | ko chek shün p‘au tsoi pin-ch‘ü? |
| 3 He went to the beautiful garden | 佢去啯間華美嘅花園處 | k‘ü hü ko kan wa-mi ke fa-ün ch‘ü |
| 4 It was very hot yesterday; to-day it is warm | 昨日好熱，今日煖啫 | tsok-yat ho it; kăm-yat nün che |
| 5 Why do you dislike the people? | 爲乜事你唔中意人哋呢 | wai-măt-sze ni 'm chung-i yan ti ni? |
| 6 Tell him to reckon up the bill | 叫佢計起啯張單 | kiu k‘ü kai-hi ko cheung tan |
| 7 My house has a dining-room and a bed-room | 我嘅屋有間大餐房共間瞓房 | ngo ke uk yau kan tai-ts‘an-fong kung kan făn-fong |

| | | |
|---|---|---|
| 8 Make him always keep the bath-room clean | 叫佢時時整乾凈個洗身房 | kiu kʻü shi-shi ching kon-tseng ko sai-shăn-fong |
| 9 Carry those things into my study | 抬嗰啲野入去我嘅書房 | tʻoi ko-ti ye yap hü ngo ke shü-fong |
| 10 The foundation is not level | 嗰啲地脚唔係平嘅 | ko-ti ti-keuk 'm hai pʻing ke |
| 11 He does his work wrongly | 佢做錯佢嘅工夫咯 | kʻü tso tsʻoh kʻü ke kung-fu lok |
| 12 She is old and poor | 佢又老又窮 | kʻü yau lo yau kʻung |
| 13 Does he worship God at the Church? | 佢去福音堂拜上帝唔拜呢 | kʻü hü fuk-yăm-tʻong pai sheung-tai 'm pai ni? |
| 14 There is a barrier at that place | 個處有度街閘 | ko-chʻü yau to kai-chap |
| 15 Get some rope; there is no lock there | 揾啲繩嚟；嗰處冇鎖 | wan ti shing lai; ko-chʻü mo soh |
| 16 Tell the coolie to follow the troops | 話個管店知跟住嗰啲兵 | wa ko kun-tim chi kan-chü ko-ti ping |
| 17 His heart is bad, but he fears me | 佢嘅心唔好，但係佢怕我 | kʻü ke săm 'm ho, tan hai kʻü pʻa ngo |
| 18 There is a scaffolding by the side of the brick wall | 嗰幅磚墻邊有个竹棚 | ko fuk chün tsʻeung pin yau ko chuk-pʻang |
| 19 It is not a brick wall, it is a mud wall | 嗰幅唔係磚墻，係坭墻啫 | ko fuk 'm hai chün-tsʻeung, hai nai-tsʻeung che |
| 20 Get the key for this lock | 揾呢把鎖嘅鎖匙嚟 | wan ni pa-soh ke soh-shi lai |
| 21 Why do you want to stop up the door? | 爲乜野你要塞住嗰度門口 | wai-măt-ye ni iu sak chü ko to-mun-hau |
| 22 It has no hinges, and besides, it's broken | 佢冇較嘅，而且又爛曉咯 | kʻü mo kau ke, i-chʻe yau lan hiu lok |
| 23 Choose the good ones quickly | 快快揀啲好嘅 | fai-fai kăn ti ho ke |
| 24 Why should I do it quickly? | 爲乜我要咁快做啫 | wai-măt ngo iu kom fai tso che |
| 25 Because I want to pay a visit to a person | 因爲我要去探一個人 | yan-wai ngo iu hü tʻam yat ko yan |
| 26 Tell the boy to read it aloud | 叫個細紋仔大聲讀 | kiu ko sai-man-tsai tai shing tuk |
| 27 He does not like to read aloud | 佢唔中意大聲讀 | kʻü 'm chung-i tai shing tuk |

| | | |
|---|---|---|
| 28 Why? does he want to go to sleep? | 爲乜事呢，佢係想去瞓咩 | wai-măt-sz ni? k‘ü hai seung hü fan me? |
| 29 No, he wants to accompany his friends | 唔係，佢想去送朋友啫 | ’m hai, k‘ü seung hü sung p‘ăng-yau che |
| 30 He cannot accompany them; call him here | 佢唔去送得，叫佢嚟呢處 | k‘ü ’m hü seung tăk; kiu k‘ü lai ni ch‘ü |
| 31 Why won’t you give a little more? | 乜野你唔俾啲添呢 | măt-ye ni ’m pi ti t‘im ni? |
| 32 I have not enough money; I dare uot do it | 我唔够銀；唔敢做咯 | ngo ’m kau ngău; ’m kom tso lok |
| 33 Suppose I give it to you? | 若係我俾啲你呢 | yeuk hai ngo pi ti ni ni? |
| 34 You are very good; I thank you | 你眞正好咯，我多謝你 | ni chăn ching ho lok; ngo to tse ni |
| 35 I wish you would go and wake him up | 我想你去叫醒佢啫 | ngo seung ni hü kiu sing k‘ü che |
| 36 He has not come here for a long time | 佢唔曾來呢處好久咯 | k‘ü ’m ts‘ăng loi ni-ch‘ü ho kau lok |
| 37 Is there any body in the drawing-room? | 個客廳有人喺處冇 | ko hak-t‘eng yau yan hai ch‘ü mo? |
| 38 There are a good many people | 嗰處有好多人 | ko-ch‘ü yau ho to yan |
| 39 Are they all rich people? | 一總都係財主佬唔係呢 | yat tsung to hai ts‘oi-chü lo ’m hai ni? |
| 40 No, they are all both old and poor | 唔係，一個都係又老又窮嘅 | ’m hai, yat ko to hai yau lo yau k‘ung ke |

# LESSON XXXI.

| | | | | | |
|---|---|---|---|---|---|
| To work in (as gold, &c.) | 打起 | *ta' hi'* | To reach with the hands | 伸到 (or) 擙到 | *shăn to`* (or) *o to`* |
| To pull or haul on | 扭住 | *ch'e'* chü` | To pacify | 安住 (or) 和息 | *on* chü` (or) woh *sik* |
| To haul or drag | 扭起 | *ch'e' hi'* | To run after | 追到 | *chui to`* |
| To send (transmit) | 寄到 | *ki` to`* | | | |
| To heap up | 推起 | *t'ui hi'* | | | |
| To prevent | 阻住 | *cho'* chü` | | | |

Words signifying nouns are often converted into adjectives by placing YAU 有 before and KE 嘅 after them; as *a wealthy man* YAU TS'IN KE YAN, 有錢嘅人; *a sick man* YAU PENG KE YAN 有病嘅人.

| | | |
|---|---|---|
| Bad language | 唔好嘅說話 (or) 爛口話 | 'm *ho ke` shüt* wa` (or) lan` *hau'* wa` |
| A crafty man | 乖滑嘅人 | *kwai* wăt *ke`* yan |
| Detestable | 可惡 | *ho' u`* |
| Amiable | 可愛 | *ho' oi`* |
| Hateful | 可恨 | *ho'* han` |

CLASSIFIERS (*continued.*)

19. *Fu`* 副 to assist, is used as the classifier of lots, sets, beads, tools, &c.
20. Kin` 件 to divide, is applied to goods, affairs of business, articles of dress, &c.
21. *Fai`* 塊 a piece of, is applied to portions of stone, metal, earth, wood, cloth, &c
22. T'ün 團 a lump, is applied to earth, dough, clay, &c.
23. T'ong 堂 a hall, is applied to screens, curtains, ladders, sails, (seldom used.)
24. Hong 行 a series, is applied to a row of characters, or objects, such as trees ships, &c.

| | | | | | |
|---|---|---|---|---|---|
| A mosquito curtain | 一堂蚊帳 | *yat* t'ong *măn-cheung`* | Earth (mud) | 坭 | nai |
| A willow tree | 一頜柳樹 | *yat p'o* lau'-shü` | Dough | 麵 | min` |
| A ladder | 一堂梯 | *yat* t'ong *t'ai* | | | |

| | | |
|---|---|---|
| I've finished writing | 我寫完咯 | ngo' *se'* üu *lok* |
| Assist me | 帮助我 | *pong* cho` ngo' |
| Don't trouble me | 咪混我 | mai' wan` ngo' |

| | | |
|---|---|---|
| Tea is ready | 茶便咯 | ch'a pin` *lok* |
| Let it alone | 咪鬥佢 | mai' *tau*` k'ü' |
| Don't injure him (or it) | 咪害佢 | mai' hoi` k'ü' |
| Don't fear | 唔使怕 | 'm *shai*' *p'a*` |
| Step aside a little | 行開啲 | hang *hoi ti* |
| Don't fall down | 咪跌倒 | mai' *tit to*' |
| I am afraid to speak | 我怕講 | ngo' *p'a*` *kong*' |
| Of no use | 冇用嘅 | mo' yung` *ke*` |
| To put on again | 着番 | *cheuk fan* |

| | | | | | |
|---|---|---|---|---|---|
| Office | 寫字房 | *se*'-tsz`-fong | Window | 窗門 | *ch'eung*-mun |
| Ceiling | 天花板 | *t'in-fa-pan*' | Horse-whip | 馬鞭 | ma'-*pin* |
| Blinds | 百葉窗 | *pak*-ip-*ch'eung* | A saddle | 馬鞍 | ma'-*on* |
| The floor | 地台板 | ti`-t'oi-*pan*' | Bridle | 馬韁 | ma'-*keung* |
| Stirrup | 馬踏橙 | ma'-tap-*tang*` | Roof | 瓦背 | nga'-*poi*` |
| Partition | 板帳 | *pan*'-*cheung*` | Do. | 瓦面 | nga'-min` |
| Kitchen | 廚房 | ch'ü-fong | Window | 窗 | *ch'eung* |
| Chimney | 烟通 | *in-t'ung* | Tiles | 瓦 | nga' |

The accusative (objective) following an active verb is sometimes preceded by TSEUNG 將 (here meaning *to take*) and is then placed first in the sentence; e.g., *put that horse-whip down there* TSEUNG KO CHI MA-PIN FONG HA KO-CH'Ü 將嗰枝馬鞭放下個處.

| | | |
|---|---|---|
| 1 Assist me to pacify that man | 帮助我和息嗰個人 | pong cho ngo woh sik ko-ko yan |
| 2 We cannot prevent his doing it so | 我哋不能阻住佢噉做 | ngo-ti păt năng choh chü k'ü kom tso |
| 3 Go and pull on that rope | 去扭住個條繩 | hü ch'e chü ko t'iu shing |
| 4 Does he work in silver or gold? | 佢打金只打銀呢 | k'ü ta kăm chi ta ngăn ni? |
| 5 Has your office a chimney? | 你嘅寫字房有個烟通冇 | ni ke se-tsz-fong yau ko in-t'ung mo? |
| 6 No, my kitchen has a chimney and two windows | 唔係, 我嘅廚房有個烟通及兩度窗門 | 'm hai, ngo ke ch'ü-fong yau ko in-t'ung k'ap leung to ch'eung-mun |

初學階

| | | |
|---|---|---|
| 7 You must have some blinds | 你是必有的百葉窓 | ni shi-pit yau ti pak-ip-ch'eung |
| 8 There are a good many tiles on the roof | 瓦背面有好多瓦 | nga-pui min yau ho to nga |
| 9 Tell the coolie to sweep the floor | 叫個管店掃啲個地台板 | kiu ko kun-tim so ko-ko ti-t'oi-pan |
| 10 Can you reach it with your hands | 你用手可以攞得到唔呢 | ni yung shau ho i o tăk to 'm ni? |
| 11 I want a saddle and a bridle | 我要個馬鞍及馬韁 | ngo iu ko ma-on k'ap ma-keung |
| 12 Run after that man and get my stirrups | 追到啲個人攞番我嘅馬踏橙 | chui to ko-ko yan lo fan ngo ke ma-tap-tăng |
| 13 Send my horsewhip to me | 寄我嘅馬鞭嚟我 | ki ngo ke ma-pin lai ngo |
| 14 The horses drag the carriage | 馬拉車 | ma lai ch'e |
| 15 He is a wealthy man, but not amiable | 佢係有錢嘅人,但唔係可愛嘅 | k'ü hai yau ts'in ke yan, tan 'm hai ho oi ke |
| 16 Here are some lumps of earth | 呢處有幾堆坭 | ni-ch'ü yau ki tui nai |
| 17 There are several willows there | 個處有幾翕柳樹 | ko-ch'ü yau ki p'o lau-shü |
| 18 Has that boat a sail? | 個隻艇有堂悝冇 | ko chek t'ing yau t'ong li mo? |
| 19 I must buy a mosquito curtain | 我要買堂蚊帳 | ngo iu mai t'ong măn-cheung |
| 20 He uses very bad language | 佢用十分爛口 | k'ü yung shap-fan lan hau |
| 21 That is of no use | 啲的冇用嘅 | ko-ti mo yung ke |
| 22 He is a hateful man; but don't injure him | 佢係一個可恨嘅人;但唔好害佢 | k'ü hai yat ko ho-ban ke yan; tan 'm ho boi k'ü |
| 23 His language is detestable | 佢出啲說話可惡得嚌 | k'ü ch'ut ti shüt wa bo u tăk tsai |
| 24 Tell me when the tea is ready | 茶便時話我知 | ch'a pin shi wa ngo chi |
| 25 Don't trouble me; wait till I've finished writing | 咪混我,等我寫完字喳 | mai wan ngo; tăng ngo se ün tsz cha |
| 26 He is a crafty man, but don't fear | 佢係一個詭滑嘅人,但唔使怕 | k'ü hai yat ko kwai-wăt ke yan, tan 'm shai p'a |
| 27 Look at the ceiling; tell me if it will do | 睇吓啲的天花板;話我聽做得未 | tai ha ko-ti t'in-fa-pan; wa ngo t'ing tso tăk mi |

| | | |
|---|---|---|
| 28 Open the window door (French window) a little | 開啲度窗門一的咁多 | hoi ko to ch'eung-mun yat tik kom to |
| 29 Take care! don't fall down | 子細吓，咪跌倒 | tsz sai ha ! mai tit to |
| 30 Have you put your boots on again | 你有着翻你對靴未曾呀 | ni yau cheuk fan ni tui hö mi ts'ăng a? |
| 31 No, I put on my shoes | 冇，我着鞋啫 | mo, ngo cheuk hai che |
| 32 At what time do you go to school? | 你幾多點鐘去書館 | ni ki to tim chung hü shü-kun? |
| 33 I go when I come from the shop | 我喺舖頭番來就去咯 | ngo hai p'o-t'au fan loi chau hü lok |
| 34 Did you see any one at the Post office? | 書信館啲處你見有人冇呀 | shü-săn-kun ko-ch'ü, ni kin yau yan mo a? |
| 35 No, I saw several people in the market | 冇，我見街市有幾個人 | mo, ngo kin kai-shi yau ki ko yan |
| 36 What are you doing with that lump of dough? | 你揸啲團麵粉做乜野呢 | ni ning ko t'ün min-făn tso măt ye ni? |
| 37 I am going to make bread of it | 我將佢嚟整麵包 | ngo tseung k'ü lai ching min-pau |
| 38 Fetch me a ladder quickly | 快啲担把梯來 | fai-ti tam pa-t'ai loi |
| 39 It was very wrong to do so | 噉做係十分錯咯 | kom tso hai shap-făn ts'oh lok |
| 40 Bring your bill to me to-morrow | 明日你揸單嚟喇 | ming-yat ni ning tan lai la |

# LESSON XXXII.

| | | | | | |
|---|---|---|---|---|---|
| To be seated in | 坐倒 | tso' *to'* | Nothing | 冇乜野 | mo'-*mat*-ye' |
| To seize up on | 拉住 | *lai* chü' | To care for (like) | 料理 | liu' li' |
| To sleep on | 瞓倒 | *făn'* *to'* | To have rather | 寧愿 | ning ün' |
| To think on | 想起 | *seung'* *hi'* | To tie a knot | 打結 | *ta'* *kit* |
| To hang up | 掛起 | *kwa'* *hi'* | Wages | 人工 | yan-*kung* |
| To stir up | 攪起 | *kau* *hi'* | To go home | 去歸 | *hü'* *kwai* |

The ordinary comparison of adjectives in the Canton vernacular is very simple, the word KĂNG 更 for the comparative, and CHI 至, TING 頂, KIK 極, or TAI YAT 第一 for the superlative, being prefixed to the word; e.g. *good* HO 好, *better* KĂNG HO 更好, *best* CHI HO 至好. (See Lesson XXX, p. 73, upon forming the comparative by TI 啲.)

Another way of forming the comparative is to use KWO after the adjective; e.g. *He is better than I*, K'Ü HAI HO KWO NGO 佢係好過我; *This is better than that*, NI-KO HO KWO KO-KO 呢個好過嗰個.

The comparative is also formed by placing KWO Ü 過於 after the adjective, e.g. *Older than I*, TAI KWO Ü NGO 大過於我.

When two comparatives occur together, the word ÜT 越 is placed before each; e.g. *The slower the better*, ÜT MAN ÜT HO 越慢越好.

| | | | | | |
|---|---|---|---|---|---|
| Deceitful | 奸詐嘅 | *kan-cha*\` *ke*\` | Cold | 凍 (or) 冷 | *tung*\` (or) lang' |
| Fresh (as meat) | 新鮮 | *săn-sin* | Empty | 空 | *hung* |
| Faithful | 忠直 | *chung*-chik | Cool | 涼 | leung |
| Carefully | 子細 | *tze*'-*sai*\` | Dry | 乾 | *kon* |
| Upright | 正直 | *ching*\`-chik | Salted | 鹹 | ham |
| Fine (not coarse) | 幼 | *yau*\` | Easy | 易 | i\` |
| Fresh (water) | 淡 | tam\` | | | |

| | | |
|---|---|---|
| To turn inside out | 翻轉裡便出嚟 | *fan-chün*\` li'-pin\` *ch'ut* lai |
| ,, upside down - | 翻轉底上嚟 | *fan-chün*\` *tai*' sheung' lai |
| Dont be in such a hurry | 唔使咁快吔 | 'm *shai*' *kom*\` *fai*\` chi\` |
| I don't believe you | 我唔信你 | ngo' 'm *sun*\` ni' |
| Stay here | 在呢處等 | tsoi\` *ni ch'ü*\` *tăng*' |
| It is useless | 係冇用嘅 | hai\` mo'-yung\` *ke*\` |
| Come directly | 就嚟咯 | tsau\` lai *lok* |
| There is but little difference | 争有限 | *chang* yau' han\` |
| He has gone home | 佢去歸 | k'ü' *hü*\` *kwai* |
| Not a bit of it | 并無有 | ping\` mo yau' |
| Empty it - | 搬空佢 | *pun hung* k'ü' |
| Mix it together | 攪埋佢 | *kau*' mai k'ü' |
| Get out of the way | 行開 | hang-*hoi* |

| | | | | | |
|---|---|---|---|---|---|
| Blacking brush | 鞋墨掃 | hai-mak-*so`* | Starch | 米漿 | mai'-*tseung* |
| Blacking | 鞋墨水 | hai-mak-*shui'* | Birdcage | 雀籠 | *tseuk*-lung |
| Cooking pots | 沙煲 | *sha-po* | Dust pan | 拂斗 | *fat-tau'* |
| Lamp wick | 燈心 | *tăng-săm* | Soap | 番梘 | *fan-kan'* |
| Lamp oil | 生油 | *shăng*-yan | Frying pan | 鑊 | wok |
| Charcoal | 煤炭 | mui-*t'an`* | Firewood | 柴 | ch'ai |
| Coals | 京炭 | *king-t'an`* | Basket | 籃 | lam |
| Tongs | 火鉗 | *foh*-k'im | | | |

| | | |
|---|---|---|
| 1 Charcoal is better than firewood | 京炭好過煤炭 | king t'an ho kwo mui-t'an |
| 2 Are not coals better than charcoal? | 煤炭唔係好過京炭咩 | mui-t'an 'm hai ho kwo king-t'an me? |
| 3 To-day is colder than yesterday | 今日冷過昨日 | kàm-yat lang kwo tsok-yat |
| 4 This man is faithful; that man is deceitful | 呢個人忠直，嗰個人奸詐 | ni-ko yan chung-chik; ko-ko yan kan-cha |
| 5 This cotton cloth is finer than that | 呢啲棉布幼細過嗰啲 | ni-ti min-po yau sai kwo ko-ti |
| 6 Do you like salt meat? | 你中意鹹肉唔呢 | ni chung-i ham-yuk 'm ni? |
| 7 No, I don't like it; I like fresh meat regularly (generally) | 唔中意；我常常中意新鮮肉 | 'm chung-i; ngo sheung-sheung chung-i săn sin yuk |
| 8 The weather is very cool | 天時十分凉 | t'in-shi shap-făn leung |
| 9 Is not this month cooler than last? | 呢個月唔係凉過先個月咩 | ni-ko üt 'm hai leung kwo sin-ko üt me? |
| 10 No; but it is a good deal drier | 唔係，但係天時乾好多 | 'm hai; tan hai t'in-shi kon ho to |
| 11 Is it easy or difficult to tie a knot? | 打個結易只難呢 | ta ko kit (*or* lit) i chi nan ni? |
| 12 I have never thought about it | 我未曾有想過 | ngo mi ts'ăng yan seung kwo |
| 13 What has the cook done with the frying pan and pots? | 嗰個火頭擰啲嗰啲鑊共沙煲去曉邊處 | ko-ko fo-t'au ning ko-ti wok kung sha-po hü hiu pin-ch'ü? |
| 14 He has put them in the basket | 佢擠佢在個籃嚟 | k'ü chai k'ü tsoi ko lam lai |
| 15 Tell the boy to buy some blacking to black my boots | 叫個事仔去買啲鞋墨水擦淨我對靴 | kiu ko sze-tsai hü mai ti hai mak-shui ts'at tseng ngo tui hö |

| | | |
|---|---|---|
| 16 Is the birdcage empty? | 嗰個雀籠空嘅咩 | ko-ko tseuk-lung hung ke me? |
| 17 Does he sleep on the floor? | 佢喺樓板瞓咩 | k'ü hai lau-pan fán me? |
| 18 He does not do so now; but did last year | 如今佢唔係噉做咯, 但舊年係啫 | ü-kăm k'ü 'm hai kom tso lok; tan kau-nin hai che |
| 19 The weather is very cold | 天時十分冷 | t'in-shi shap-fán lang |
| 20 For me the colder the better | 我就越冷越好 | ngo tsau üt lang üt ho |
| 21 What was he seated in? | 佢坐住乜野呢 | k'ü tso chü măt-ye ni? |
| 22 He was seated in the carriage | 佢坐在馬車嚟 | k'ü tso tsoi ma-ch'e lai |
| 23 I thought he was seated in a boat | 我估佢坐在艇嚟 | ngo ku k'ü tso tsoi t'ing lai |
| 24 Hang up that birdcage on the wall | 掛起個雀籠在個墻上嚟 | kwa hi ko tseuk-lung tsoi ko ts'eung sheung lai |
| 25 Buy some lamp oil and wick for me | 買啲燈心共油過我 | mai ti tăng-săm kung yau kwo ngo |
| 26 Did he seize upon those people? | 佢[illegible]住嗰啲人咩 | k'ü lai chü ko-ti yan me? |
| 27 Yes; but it was no use | 係, 但唔濟事咯 | hai, tan 'm tsai sze lok |
| 28 I had rather he had not done so | 我寗愿佢唔曾噉做喇 | ngo ning-ün k'ü 'm ts'ăng kom tso la |
| 29 Don't let him stir it up | 咪俾佢攪起佢 | mai pi k'ü kau-hi k'ü |
| 30 Why won't he go home? | 爲乜事佢唔肯去歸呢 | wai-măt-sze k'ü 'm hăng hü kwai ni? |
| 31 He does not care to; he has no wages | 佢唔多想啫, 佢冇人工嘅 | k'ü 'm to seung che, k'ü mo yan-kung ke |
| 32 Is there anything there? | 嗰處有野冇呢 | ko-ch'ü yau ye mo ni? |
| 33 No; there is nothing | 冇, 嗰處冇野 | mo, ko-ch'ü mo ye |
| 34 I don't believe it; go and see | 我唔信, 去睇吓喇 | ngo 'm săn, hü t'ai ha la |
| 35 Get out of the way; a sedan is coming | 行開, 有乘轎來[illegible] | hang hoi; yau shing kiu loi la. |
| 36 Why don't you like to stay here? | 爲乜你唔中意喺呢處呢 | wai-măt ni 'm chung-i hai ni-ch'ü ni? |
| 37 It is useless; I had rather go | 冇用呀, 我寗愿去罷咯 | mo yeung a; ngo ning-ün hü pa lok |
| 38 He says he will come directly | 佢話佢就來咯 | k'ü wa k'ü tsau loi lok |

39 Not a bit of it; he won't come 一的都唔係；佢唔來嘅咯 yat tik to 'm hai; k'ü 'm loi ke lok

40 Tell him to mix those things together carefully 叫佢仔細的攪勻呴啲野 kiu k'ü tsz-sai tik kau-wăn ko-ti ye

---

# LESSON XXXIII.

| | | | | | |
|---|---|---|---|---|---|
| Good | 好 | *ho'* | Bad | 惡 | *ok* |
| Better | 更好 | *kăng' ho'* | Worse | 更惡 | *kăng' ok* |
| Best | 至好 | *chi' ho'* | Worst | 至惡 | *chi' ok* |
| Short | 短 | *tün'* | White | 白 | pak |
| Shorter | 更短 | *kăng' tün'* | Whiter | 更白 | *kăng'* pak |
| Shortest | 至短 | *chi' tün'* | Whitest | 至白 | *chi'* pak |
| Much | 多 | *to* | Little | 少 | *siu'* |
| More | 重多 | chung' *to* | Less | 更少 | *kăng' siu'* |
| Most | 至多 | *chi' to* | Least | 至少 | *chi' siu'* |

To form the superlative KE 嘅 is sometimes used after the adjective, which takes CHI 至 or TAI YAT 大一, before it; e.g. *The most distant mountain* CHI ÜN KE SHAN 至遠嘅山.

Other ways of forming the superlative are:—

(*a*) By placing TĂK TSAI 得嚌 KWO T'AU 過頭 or PĂT SHING 不勝 after the adjective.

(*b*) By placing KIK 極 before, and KE 嘅, after the adjective.

SHAP-FĂN 十分 and SHEUNG' 上 are also used to express *very*, *the highest.*

CLASSIFIERS (*continued*)

25. *Ka'* 架 a wooden frame, is applied to stands, fire-engines, &c.

26. *To'* 朶 hanging branches, is applied to flowers, fire, flames, etc.

27. *P'in'* 片 a slip or fragment, is applied to slices, slips, bits, etc. of various articles.

28. Tsek 蓆 a mat, is applied to spots of ground, feasts, conversations, &c. (Seldom used, but included in most lists of classifiers.)

29. *Pau* 包 a bundle, is applied to bales, bundles, or packages of goods.

30. *Chăt* 札 do., is applied, similarly to No. 29, to rolls or packages of small articles.

| | | |
|---|---|---|
| This side up | 擠呢便上嚟 | *chai ni* pin` sheung′ lai |
| Do it now | 如今做咯 | ü-*kàm* tso` *lok* |
| As I like | 隨我中意 | ts'ui ngo′ *chung-i*` |
| How do you do it? | 你點樣做 | ni′ *tim*′ yeung` tso` |
| Do it secretly | 偷偷的做 | *t'au-t'au-tik* tso` |
| No occasion | 唔使咯 | 'm *shai*′ *lok* |
| No matter | 唔相干 | 'm *seung kon* |
| No help for it | 冇奈何 | mo′ noi` ho |
| Never mind | 唔使咯 | 'm *shai*′ *lok* |
| Put it back | 放番落 | *fong*` *fan* lok |
| Oblige me by — | 拜託你 | *pai*` *t'ok* ni′ — |

| | | | | | |
|---|---|---|---|---|---|
| Blacksmith | 打鐵師傅 | *ta′-t'it-sze*-fu` | Captain (sea) | 船主 | shün-*chü*′ |
| Do. | 打鐵佬 | *ta′-t'it-lo*′ | Emperor | 皇帝 | wong-*tai*` |
| Bookbinder | 釘書師傅 | *teng-shü-sze*-fu` | Beggar | 乞兒 | *hat*-i |
| Do. | 釘書佬 | *teng-shü-lo*′ | Flowerpot | 花盆 | *fa*-p'un |
| Apothecary | 藥材舖佬 | yeuk-ts'oi-*p'o*` *lo*′ | Flowerpot stand | 花架 | *fa-ka*` |
| Bookseller | 賣書人 | mai`-*shü*-yan | Awning | 天遮 | *t'in-che* |
| Consul | 領事官 | ling′-sze`-*kun* | Bench | 張凳 | (*cheung*) *tăng*` |
| Clerk | 寫字人 | se′-tsz`-yan | Time (occasion) | 勻 | wàn |
| Barber | 剃頭佬 | *t'ai*`-t'au-*lo*′ | Do. | 回 | ui |

| | | |
|---|---|---|
| 1 This is good, but that is better | 呢啲好，嗰個更好 | ni-ti ho, ko-ko kăng ho |
| 2 These are the best mats | 呢啲蓆係至好嘅 | ni-ti tsek hai chi ho ke |
| 3 Do you think that bench is too short? | 你估嗰張凳短唔呢 | ni ku ko cheung tăng tün 'm ni? |
| 4 That awning is very white | 嗰個天遮十分白 | ko-ko t'in-che shap-făn pak |
| 5 Has the barber the smallest lantern? | 嗰個剃頭佬有個蓋至細嘅燈係唔係 | ko-ko t'ai-t'au-lo yau ko chan chi sai ke tăng, hai 'm hai? |

| | | |
|---|---|---|
| 6 Give these books to the book-binder; tell him to bind them very well | 俾呢啲書過個釘書佬；叫佢釘得好好 | pi ni-ti shü kwo ko teng-shü-lo; kiu k‘ü teng tăk ho ho |
| 7 The bookseller has the smallest house | 個釘書佬有間極細嘅屋 | ko teng-shü-lo yau kan kik sai ke uk |
| 8 Has the Captain gone on board the ship? | 啁個船主落船未曾 | ko-ko shün-chü lok shün mi ts‘ăng? |
| 9 No, he is very unwell | 未曾，佢十分唔自然 | mi ts‘ăng, k‘ü shap-făn ’m tsz-in |
| 10 Is he a Consul or a clerk? | 佢係個領事官只寫字人呢 | k‘ü hai ko ling-sz-kun chi se-tsz-yan ni? |
| 11 I don’t know; he is a very rich man | 我唔知，佢係個十分財主嘅人 | ngo ’m chi; k‘ü hai ko shap-făn ts‘oi-chü ke yan |
| 12 Is he older than the blacksmith? | 佢大過啁個打鐵佬係唔係 | k‘ü tai kwo ko-ko ta-t‘it-lo hai ’m hai? |
| 13 What was the blacksmith doing? | 啁個打鐵佬做乜野呢 | ko-ko ta-t‘it-lo tso măt-ye ni? |
| 14 He works in iron daily | 佢日日都係打鐵嘅 | k‘ü yat-yat to hai ta t‘it ke |
| 15 Has he seen the Emperor? | 佢有見過皇帝冇呢 | k‘ü yau kin kwo wong-tai mo ni? |
| 16 No, nobody can see the Emperor | 冇，冇人見得皇帝嘅 | mo, mo yan kin tăk wong-tai ke |
| 17 Did they go to the apothecary’s shop? | 佢哋有去啁間藥材舖冇 | k‘ü-ti yau hü ko kan yeuk-ts‘oi-p‘o mo? |
| 18 No, there were too many beggars there | 冇，啁處好多乞兒 | mo, ko-ch‘ü ho to hat-i |
| 19 I want you to buy me some flower-pots | 我要你同我買啲花盆 | ngo iu ni t‘ung ngo mai ti fa-p‘un |
| 20 Do you want some flower-pot-stands also? | 你要花盆架添唔呢 | ni iu fa-p‘un-ka t‘im ’m ni? |
| 21 No, they are too dear; they are dearer than flower-pots | 唔要咯，太貴得嚌，貴過花盆啤 | ’m iu lok, t‘ai kwai tăk tsai; kwai kwo fa-p‘un pe |
| 22 Clean this lantern | 整乾淨呢盞燈 | ching kon-tseng ni chan-tăng |
| 23 Oblige me by doing that at once | 多煩你即刻同我做 | to-fan ni tsik-hak t‘ung ngo tso |

初學階

| | | | |
|---|---|---|---|
| 24 | Put it back where you got it from | 你喺邊處攞嚟嘅，就擠翻个處喇 | ni hai pin-ch‘ü lo lai ke, tsau chai fan ko-ch‘ü la |
| 25 | Never mind now; it will do as it is | 如今唔使喇，就噉做得咯 | ü-kàm ’m shai la; tsau kom tso tàk lok |
| 26 | That is not as I like it; it is unfinished | 我唔中意噉樣；都未曾做完 | ngo ’m chung-i kom yeung; to mi ts‘ăng tso ün |
| 27 | Do whatever you like, but don’t do it secretly | 你做乜野都好，但唔好偷偷的做 | ni tso măt-ye to ho, tan ’m ho t‘au-t‘au-tik tso |
| 28 | Tell me how you do it | 話我聽你點樣做嘅喇 | wa ngo t‘eng ni tim yeung tso ke la |
| 29 | There is no help for it; it must be done | 冇奈何呀，一定要做嘅咯 | mo noi ho a; yat ting iu tso ke lok |
| 30 | What is the name of the farthest (most distant) mountain? | 嗰個至遠嘅山叫乜名呢 | ko-ko chi ün ke shan kiu măt ming ni? |
| 31 | It is called Lung-shan; have you been there? | 叫做龍山，你去過未曾呀 | kin tso Lung-shan; ni hü kwo mi ts‘ăng a? |
| 32 | No, I have never been there | 未曾，我未有去過 | mi ts‘ăng, ngo mi yau hü kwo |
| 33 | It is higher than the Kwăn-lun mountain | 高過昆侖山 | ko kwo Kwăn-lun shan |
| 34 | Tell the gardener to bring me some flowers | 叫個花王拈啲花嚟我 | kin ko fa-wong nim ti fa lai ngo |
| 35 | The compradore has bought six bundles of goods | 嗰個買辦買曉六包貨 | ko-ko mai-pan mai hiu luk pan foh |
| 36 | Buy me a small bundle of pens | 買一細札筆過我 | mai yat sai chat pat kwo ngo |
| 37 | Get a slice of cake for the child | 搦一塊餅過個細紋仔 | ning yat fai peng kwo ko sai-măn-tsai |
| 38 | This is considerably better than that | 呢啲好過嗰個好多 | ni-ti ho kwo ko-ko ho to |
| 39 | I wish you would listen to what I say; do it now | 我想你聽我噉話，如今做喇 | ngo seung ni t‘ing ngo kom wa ü-kàm tso la |
| 40 | As it’s the first time, never mind | 呢轉第一回，唔使咯 | ni chün tai yat ui, ’m shai lok |

# LESSON XXXIV.

| | | | | | |
|---|---|---|---|---|---|
| To travel by land | 打路去 | *ta'* lo' *hü'* | The world; empire | 天下 | *t'in*-ha' |
| Do. | 行遊 | hang-yau | Profit (money) | 利 | li' |
| Interest (of money) | 利息 | li'-*sik* | To invite | 請 | *ts'ing'* |
| A stove-bed | 炕床 | *hong'*-ch'ong | To worship | 拜 | *pai'* |
| News | 新聞 | *sün*-man | Ghosts | 鬼 | *kwai'* |
| Guest | 人客 | yan-*hak* | | | |

Owing to the previously existing ignorance of Chinese geographers regarding foreign countries, most of words used to express both them and their inhabitants are "bastard," i.e. attempts for the most part to reproduce the sounds of the names phonetically or descriptively. The following are those most commonly used:—

| | | | | | |
|---|---|---|---|---|---|
| Englishman | 英吉利人 | *ying-kat*-li' yan | Annamite | 安南人 | *on*-nam yan |
| German | 日耳曼人 | yat-i'-man yan | Macaoese | 澳門人 | o'-mun yan |
| Frenchman | 佛蘭西人 | fat-*lan-sai* yan | Parsee | 白頭人 | pak-t'au yan |
| Spaniard | 呂宋人 | lü'-*sung'* yan | American | 花旗人 | *fa*-k'i yan |
| Portuguese | 西洋人 | *sai*-yeung yan | | | |

By substituting KWOK 國 for YAN 人 the name of the country is expressed, KWOK 國 meaning a state, country, kingdom. The word "world" above given, is in the Chinese classics used only to designate China, or *the* empire *par excellence.*

| | | |
|---|---|---|
| To stay at on in | 在處住 | tsoi' *ch'ü'* chü' |
| To sneeze | 打嚇㖤 | *ta' hat-ch'i* |
| To gape | 打喊露 | *ta' ham'* lo' |
| To sail to | 駛去 | *shai' hü'* |
| To go to | 開去 | *hoi hü'* |
| To leave a place | 離開 | li-*hoi* |

| | | |
|---|---|---|
| I wear spectacles | 我帶眼鏡 | ngo' *tai'* ngan'-*keng'* |
| I am taking tiffin - | 我食晏晝 | ngo' shik *an'-chau'* |
| It is a dissyllable - | 係蜆殼字 | hai' *hin'-hok*-tsz' |

| | | |
|---|---|---|
| Go to the Post office - | 去書信館 | *hu*\` *she-sün*\`*-kun*′ |
| He comes by ship | 佢打船來 | k‘u′ *ta*′ shün loi |
| It is so generally | 大概係噉 | tai\`-*k‘oi*′ hai\` *kom*′ |
| Present it to him | 送過佢 | *sung*\` *kwo*\` k‘ü′ |
| Within the town | 城裡頭 | shing lui′-t‘au |
| Stop working | 收工喇 | *shau kung la* |
| Open (your) mouth | 擘大口 | *mak* tai\` *hau*′ |
| I fear it is so | 都怕係 | *to p‘a* hai\` |
| Fill it full | 斟滿佢 | *chăm* mun′ k‘ü′ |

| | | | | | |
|---|---|---|---|---|---|
| Crockery-mender | 補瓷器人 | *po*′-ts‘z-*hi*\` yan | Executioner | 殺手佬 | *shat-shau*′*-lo*′ |
| Gentleman | 人客 | yan-*hak* | Fisherman | 攞魚人 | *loh*′-ü-yau |
| Farmer | 耕田佬 | *kang*-t‘in-*lo*′ | Desk | 寫字檯 | *se*′-tsz\`-t‘oi |
| Do. | 農夫 | nung-*fu* | Governor | 總督 | *tsung*′*-tuk* |
| Gambler | 賭博佬 | *to*′*-pok-lo*′ | Engraver | 雕匠 | *tiu*-tseung |
| Do. | 賭錢佬 | *to*′-ts‘in-*lo*′ | Almanac | 通書 | *t‘ung-shü* |
| Gardener | 園丁 | ün-*ting* | Bookcase | 書櫃 | *shü*-kwai\` |
| Do. | 花王 | *fa*-wong | Envelope | 信封 | *sun*\`*-fung* |
| Blank book | 簿 | po\` | Ferryman (master of a passage boat) | 渡主 | to\`-*chü* |

*Neither*———*nor* is rendered by ’M HAI 唔係———YAU ’M HAI 又唔係; e.g. *They are neither good nor bad,* ’M HAI HO YAU ’M HAI ’M HO 唔係好又唔係唔好.

| | | | |
|---|---|---|---|
| 1 | Are those men Frenchmen or Portuguese? | 嗰啲係佛蘭西人只西洋人呢 | ko-ti hai Fat-lan-sai yan, chi Sai-yeung yan ni? |
| 2 | They are Englishmen and Germans | 佢哋係英吉利人共日耳曼人 | k‘ü-ti hai Ying-kat-li yan kung Yat-i-man yan |
| 3 | Is there news from Annam? | 安南有新聞冇呢 | On-nam yau săn-măn mo ni? |
| 4 | Is he a Chinese or Macaoese? | 佢係唐人只澳門人呢 | k‘ü hai T‘ong-yan chi O-mun yan ni? |
| 5 | They are neither Parsees nor Americans | 佢哋唔係白頭人,又唔係花旗人 | k‘ü-ti ’m hai Pak-t‘au yan, yau ’m hai Fa-k‘i yan |

| | | |
|---|---|---|
| 6 Where does that man intend to travel? | 嗰個人想打路去邊處遊呢 | ko-ko yan seung ta lo hu pin-chʻü yau ni? |
| 7 He intends to travel in China | 佢想去中國遊 | kʻü seung hü Chung-kwok yau |
| 8 Do you think he will first worship the spirits? | 你估佢先拜神係唔呢 | ni ku kʻü sin pai shăn hai 'm ni? |
| 9 I suppose so; he sails to-morrow | 斷估都係喇，佢聽日開身 | tün ku to hai la; kʻü tʻing-yat hoi shăn |
| 10 Did the executioner kill the man? | 個殺手佬殺嗰個人咩 | ko shat-shau-lo shat ko-ko yan me? |
| 11 The Governor ordered him to kill the farmer | 個總督命佢殺嗰個耕田佬 | ko tsung-tuk ming kʻü shat ko-ko kang-tʻin lo |
| 12 He paid the money, principal and interest | 佢連本帶利都還清咯 | kʻü lin pun tai li to wan-tsʻing lok |
| 13 There is no news from America | 花旗國冇新聞 | Fa-kʻi kwok mo săn-măn |
| 14 Did he invite many guests? | 佢請好多人客咩 | kʻü tsʻing ho to yan-hak me? |
| 15 No; all of them had left the place | 唔係；佢哋喊嘭唥都離嘵嗰笪地方咯 | 'm hai; kʻü-ti ham-pang-lang to li hiu ko tat ti-fong lok |
| 16 Is the ferryman also a fisherman? | 嗰個渡主又係攞魚佬唔係呢 | ko-ko to-chü yau hai loh-ü-lo 'm hai ni? |
| 17 That gentleman wishes to see the general | 嗰位人客想見將軍 | ko wai yan-hak seung kin tseung-kwăn |
| 18 When will that gentleman leave? | 嗰個人客幾時至去呢 | ko-ko yan-hak ki shi chi hü ni? |
| 19 The Portuguese will stay there some time | 嗰個西洋人住好耐至去嘅咯 | ko-ko Sai-yeung yau chu ho noi chi hü ke lok |
| 20 Did you put the almanac in the bookcase? | 你擠本通書在書櫃係唔係 | ni chai pun tʻung-shü tsoi shü-kwai hai 'm hai? |
| 21 No, I fear it is on the stove bed | 唔係，我怕佢在個張炕床嚟 | 'm hai, ngo pʻa kʻü tsoi ko cheung hong-chʻong lai |
| 22 Why did you put it there? | 爲乜你擠嗰處嚟呢 | wai-mat ni chai ko-chʻü lai ni? |
| 23 It is generally put there | 常時都係擠嗰處嘅咯 | sheung-shi to hai chai ko-chʻü ke lok |

| | | |
|---|---|---|
| 24 Do the Chinese wear spectacles? | 唐人帶眼鏡唔呢 | t'ong-yan tai ngan-keng 'm ni? |
| 25 They wear spectacles to read books | 佢哋帶眼鏡嚟讀書 | k'ü-ti tai ngan-keng lai tuk shü |
| 26 Why do you open your mouth so? | 爲乜野你擘個口咁大呢 | wai-măt-ye ni mak ko hau kom tai ni? |
| 27 I fear I was gaping | 我怕我打喊露 | ngo p'a ngo ta-ham-lo |
| 28 Look at that Spaniard; he wants to sneeze! | 睇吓嗰個呂宋人，佢想打嚇哆 | t'ai ha ko-ko Lü-sung yan, k'ü seung ta hat-ch'i |
| 29 Did he come here by ship or by road? | 佢打船只打路來嘅呢 | k'ü ta shün chi ta lo loi ke ni? |
| 30 How many guests came with him? | 幾多個人客同埋佢來呢 | ki to ko yan-hak t'ung mai k'ü loi ni? |
| 31 I think some Annamites came with him | 我估有幾個安南人同佢來 | ngo ku yau ki ko On-nam yan t'ung k'ü loi |
| 32 If the guest comes tell him I am taking tiffin | 若係個人客來到，就話佢知我食僅晏晝 | yeuk hai ko yan-hak loi to, tsau wa k'ü chi ngo shik kăn an-chau |
| 33 Are these Englishman gamblers? | 嗰啲英吉利人係賭博佬唔係呢 | ko-ti Ying-kat-li yan hai to-pok-lo 'm hai ni? |
| 34 No, the Americans and the Annamites are gamblers | 唔係，嗰啲花旗人共安南人係賭博佬 | 'm hai, ko-ti Fa-k'i yan kung On-nam yan hai to-pok-lo |
| 35 Did he sail to France? | 佢駛去佛蘭西咩 | k'ü shai hü Fat-lan-sai me? |
| 36 No, he did not go there; he stayed here | 唔係，佢冇去嗰處，响呢處啫 | 'm hai, k'ü mo hü ko-ch'ü, heung ni-ch'ü che |
| 37 Did he sneeze very much | 佢打好多嚇哆咩 | k'ü ta ho to hat-ch'i me? |
| 38 No, he gaped and said he was sleepy | 唔係，佢打喊露又話眼瞓添 | 'm hai, k'ü ta ham-lo yau wa ngan-făn t'im |
| 39 Is he generally so bad? | 佢時常都係咁盻嘅咩 | k'ü shi-sheung to hai kom yai ke me? |
| 40 I fear so, he is a lazy man | 我怕係，佢係好懶惰嘅人 | ngo p'a hai, k'ü hai ho lan-to ke yan |

# LESSON XXXV.

| | | | | | |
|---|---|---|---|---|---|
| To insert | 放入 | *fong`* yap | To arrest, apprehend (seize) | 捉住 | *chuk* chü |
| To kick | 踢起 | *t'ek hi'* | | 拿住 | na chü` |
| To lock up | 鎖起 | *soh' hi'* | To cover | 蓋住 | *k'oi`* chü` |
| To leap or jump | 跳起 | *t'iu` hi'* | To descend | 落去 | lok *hü`* |
| To lift up | 攪起 | *tau hi'* | To fly away | 飛去 | *fi hü`* |
| To carry (children) | 抱住 | p'o' chü` | A play (drama) | 戲 | *hi`* |
| To rest from | 歇住 | *hit* chü` | To hope | 望 | mong` |
| To reflect upon | 顧住 | *ku`* chü` | | | |

The verb *to rest from* is applied to the agent and not to the act; e.g., *to rest from work* is "*to cease with the hand*" HIT CHÜ SHAU 歇住手; *to stop eating* HIT CHÜ HAU 歇住口 (*rest the mouth.*)

| | | | | | |
|---|---|---|---|---|---|
| An affair | 一宗事 | *yat tsung* sze` | A flagstaff | 旗杆 | k'i-*kon* |
| A map | 地理圖 | ti`-li'-t'o | The legs | 大髀 | tai`-*pi'* |
| A weight | 稱, 枰 | *ch'ing`*, p'ing | An enemy | 仇敵 | ch'au-tik |
| Children (babies; more generally applied to males) | 孩兒 | hoi-i | Robbers | 賊匪 | ts'ak-*fi'* |
| | | | The eyes | 眼 | ngan' |

In addition to the forms of personal and possessive pronouns already given in previous lessons, there are several substitues in polite colloquial. A person speaking of his own relations uses either a descriptive or depreciatory phrase. Of the former the following are examples.

| | | |
|---|---|---|
| My father | 父親 | fu`-*ts'an* |
| Do.. | 家父 | *ka*-fu` |
| My elder brother | 家兄 | *ka-hing* |
| My younger (cottage) brother | 舍弟 | *she`*-tai` |
| My wife | 老婆 | lo'-p'oh |
| Do. | 內人 | noi`-yan |
| Do. | 內室 | noi`-*shat* |

KA-FU 家父 can also be used for *your father*; SAI-LO 細佬 is the every day term used for *younger brother*; FU-YAN 夫人 is the ordinary term for *your wife*.

| | | |
|---|---|---|
| Delay a little | 遲啲咁耐 | ch'i *ti kom*` noi` |
| Not equal to original cost | 唔够本 | 'm *kau*` *pun*' |
| To despise others - | 輕忽人 | *hing fat* yan |
| Do. | 睇小人 | *t'ai*' *siu*' yan |
| A rich man - | 財主佬 | ts'oi-*chü*'-*lo*' |
| Very well flavoured | 好味道 | *ho*' mi`-to` |
| To eat one's fill | 吃飽囉 | *yak pau*' *lo* |
| To play the organ | 揞風琴 | *om*' *fung*-k'ăm |
| Do. guitar | 彈琵琶 | t'an p'i-p'a |
| Do. fiddle | 彈三絃 | t'an *sam*-in |
| To make a mistake | 做錯 | tso` *t'soh*` |

| | | | | | |
|---|---|---|---|---|---|
| Magistrate | 審事官 | *shăm*'-sze`-*kun* | Law clerk | 師爺 | *sze-ye* |
| Judge | 按察司 | *on*`-*ch'at-sze* | Merchant | 商人 | *sheung*-yan |
| Money changer | 找錢佬 | *chau*'-ts'in-*lo*' | Groom | 馬夫 | ma'-*fu* |
| Mason | 坭水佬 | nai-*shui*'-*lo*' | Coolie | 姑厘* | *ku-li* |
| Lady | 師奶 | *sze-nai* | Nurse | 亞媽 | *a*`-*ma* |
| Lawyer | 狀師 | chong`-*sze* | Wet-nurse) | 奶媽 | nai'-*ma* |

* This is a bastard word.

| | | |
|---|---|---|
| 1 Do those coolies carry babies? | 嗰啲姑厘抱孩子嘅唔呢 | ko-ti ku-li p'o hoi-tsz ke 'm ni? |
| 2 They carry the babies of my younger brother | 佢哋抱我舍弟嘅孩子 | k'ü-ti p'o ngo she-tai ke hoi-tsz |
| 3 At what time will they rest from work? | 佢哋幾時正歇工呢 | k'ü-ti ki shi ching hit kung ni? |
| 4 When did they lock up the house? | 佢哋幾時鎖好嗰間屋呢 | k'ü-ti ki shi soh ho ko kan uk ni? |
| 5 Is he a farmer or fisherman? | 佢係耕田佬只攞魚佬呢 | k'ü hai kang-t'in-lo chi loh-ü-lo ni? |
| 6 He is only a gardener | 佢係一個花王啫 | k'ü hai yat ko fa-wong che |
| 7 Have you been to see that play? | 你有去睇過嗰班戲冇呢 | ni yau hü t'ai kwo ko pan-hi mo ni? |

| | | |
|---|---|---|
| 8 Yes, but I made a mistake; it was fininlshed when I got there | 有，但我記錯，我去到時都已經做完咯 | yau, tan ngo ki ts'oh; ngo hü to shi to i-king tso-ün lok |
| 9 Does the excutioner arrest robbers? | 個殺手佬捉賊嘅唔呢 | ko shat-shau-lo chuk ts'ak ke 'm ni? |
| 10 No; he kills bad men | 唔捉，佢殺惡人嘅嗻 | 'm chuk; k'ü shat ok-yan ke che |
| 11 He is the Governor's groom | 佢係總督嘅馬夫 | k'ü hai tsung-tuk ke ma-fu |
| 12 Did he leave off kicking him? | 佢有歇脚踢佢冇 | k'ü yau hit keuk t'ek k'ü mo? |
| 13 He jumped up very high | 佢跳起好高 | k'ü t'iu hi ho ko |
| 14 Tell him to stop eating | 叫佢歇口食 | kiu k'ü hit hau shik |
| 15 He has not eaten his fill | 佢未食飽 | k'ü mi shik pau |
| 16 Did you insert that in the book? | 你有放入嗰啲落個本書嚟冇呢 | ni yau fong yap ko-ti lok ko pun shü lai mo ni? |
| 17 He cannot lift up that weight | 佢唔舉得起咁重 | k'ü 'm kü tăk hi kom ch'ung |
| 18 The fowls all flew away | 個啲雞喊嘭唥飛嘥去咯 | ko-ti kai ham-pang-lang fi sai hü lok |
| 19 Bid him descend at once | 吩咐佢即刻落去 | fān-fu k'ü tsik hak lok hü |
| 20 I hoped you would reflect a little | 我望你想過吓正好 | ngo mong ni seung kwo ha ching ho |
| 21 Use your eyes more, and stop talking | 俾對眼睇吓添，然後歇口咪講 | pi tui ngan t'ai ha t'im, in-hau hit hau mai kong |
| 22 The lawyer and the judge were both there | 嗰個狀師共個按察司兩個都响處 | ko-ko chong-sze kung ko on-ch'at-sze leung ko to heung ch'ü |
| 23 My father was taken before the magistrate | 我家父被攋去官府處 | ngo ka-fu pi lai hü kun-fu ch'ü |
| 24 My elder aud younger brother are both ill | 我家兄共舍弟兩個都病 | ngo ka-hing kung she-tai leung-ko to peng |
| 25 Don't buy any more of those | 唔好買嗰啲添咯 | 'm ho mai ko-ti t'im lok |
| 26 The merchant gave me this map | 嗰個商人俾個地理圖過我 | ko-ko sheung-yan pi ko ti-li-t'o kwo ngo |
| 27 Has he any business (affairs) to do? | 佢有事業做冇呢 | k'ü yau sze-yip tso mo ni? |

| | | |
|---|---|---|
| 28 No, he has ceased to do anything | 冇，佢歇手唔做事幹咯 | mo, k‘ü hit shau 'm tso sze-kon lok |
| 29 Tell the wet nurse to carry that baby | 叫個奶媽抱嗰個孩子 | kiu ko nai-ma p‘o ko-ko hoi-tsz |
| 30 Some ladies came with him | 有幾個同師奶佢來 | yau ki ko sze-nai t‘ung k‘ü loi |
| 31 How many gentlemen are coming to-night? | 今晚有幾多個人客來呢 | kăm-man yau ki to ko yan-hak loi ni? |
| 32 I don't know; ask the boy (servant) | 我唔知問事仔喇 | ngo 'm chi; măn sze-tsai la |
| 33 It is wrong to despise others | 輕忽人係唔着嘅 | hing-fat yan hai 'm cheuk ke |
| 34 He is very rich man, people say | 人哋話，佢係一個十分財主嘅人 | yan-ti wa k‘ü hai yat ko shap-făn ts‘oi-chü ke yan |
| 35 He does nothing but play the guitar | 佢乜都唔做，獨係彈琵琶 | k‘ü măt to 'm tso, tuk hai t‘an p‘i-p‘a |
| 36 I thought he played the fiddle | 我估佢彈三絃 | ngo ku k‘ü t‘an sam-in |
| 37 You are mistaken; he does neither (does not play either) | 你估錯咯，佢兩樣都唔彈 | ni ku ts‘oh lok; k‘ü leung yeung to 'm t‘an |
| 38 Send for an engraver to do that | 叫個彫匠做嗰啲喇 | kiu ko tiu-tseung tso ko-ti la |
| 39 Is the fruit well flavoured? | 嗰啲生菓好味道唔呢 | ko-ti shang-kwo ho mi-to 'm ni? |
| 40 No, it is not at all well flavoured | 唔係，唔係好味道得啫 | 'm hai, 'm hai ho mi-to tăk che |

---

## LESSON XXXVI.

Following out the idea explained in the previous lesson, self depreciatory phrases are constantly used by the Chinese in referring to their own relations, designations and possessions. Thus *my wife* is expressed by TSIN FONG 賤房 "*the mean one within the house*;" TUK FU 獨婦 "*the lonely woman*;" SHAN TS‘AI 山妻 "*(my) rustic* (lit. *mountain*) *wife*."

| | | | |
|---|---|---|---|
| My house | 敝屋 | pai` *uk* | (vile dwelling) |
| My country | 敝國 | pai` *kwok* | (vile country) |
| My surname | 賤姓 | tsin` *sing`* | (mean surname) |
| Son | 小兒 | *siu'*-i | (little child) |

It is of course on ceremonious occasions only that such words as are given above are much used. The speaker at such times is expected, on the other hand, to use complimentary phrases when alluding to the relations, &c. of the person addressed. Of these examples will be found in the next lesson.

| | | | | | |
|---|---|---|---|---|---|
| To hold a horse | 牽住匹馬 | *hin* chü` *p'at* ma' | To be safe | 穩咯 | *wăn'* *lok* |
| To wash one's hands | 洗手 | *sai'* *shau'* | To mistake | 記錯 | *ki`* *tsoh`* |
| To guess, think, believe | 估 | *ku'* | (remember wrongly) | | |

CLASSIFIERS (*continued.*)

31. *Fung* 封 to seal, is applied to letters and despatches.
32. *To* 刀 a knife, ,, quires of paper.
33. *Pun'* 本 a root, ,, volumes of books, acts of a play, &c.
34. *T'o* 套 a wrapper, ,, sets of books, plays, suits of cloths, &c.
35. Po` 部 a class, ,, to single volumes of books (more commonly used than *pun'*.)
36. *P'at* 匹 to unite, ,, to horses, boards, &c.

| | | |
|---|---|---|
| Will this do? | 噉樣做得未呢 | *kom'* yeung` tso` *tăk* mi` *ni*? |
| It is certainly right | 必定係着咯 | *pit*-ting` hai` cheuk *lok* |
| Who can do it? | 乜人噲做呢 | *măt* yan ui' tso` *ni*? |
| Not well done | 做得唔好 | tso` *tăk* 'm *ho'* |
| Quite done | 做起嘥咯 | tso` *hi'* *sai`* *lok* |
| Look for that thing | 尋啯啲野 | ts'am *ko'*-*ti* ye' |
| Idle talk | 閒談說話 | han t'am *shut* wa` |
| Don't get in the light | 莫遮住 | mok *che* chü` |

| | | | | | |
|---|---|---|---|---|---|
| Pastrycook | 麵食師傅 | min` shik *sze*-fu` | Ink stone cover | 墨硯蓋 | mak-in-*k'oi`* |
| Do. | 做餅食人 | tso` *peng'* shik yan | Ink stone tray | 墨硯盤 | mak-in-p'un |
| Pawnbroker | 當舖佬 | *tong`*-*p'o`*-*lo'* | Ink stand | 墨水甇 | mak-*shui'*-*ang* |
| Pilot | 帶水人 | *tai`*-*shui'*-yan | Ink stone box | 墨硯盒 | mak-in-hap |

| | | | | | |
|---|---|---|---|---|---|
| Newspaper | 新文紙 | *săn*-măn-*chi'* | Physician | 醫生 | *i-shăng* |
| Pilferer | 三隻手 | *sam-chek-shau'* | Pirate | 海賊 | *hoi'*-ts'ak |
| Do. | 小手 | *siu'-shau'* | Pleased | 歡喜 | *fun-hi'* |
| Letter | 書信 | *shü-sun`* | Very, extremely | 極 | kik |

| | | |
|---|---|---|
| 1 I shall be very pleased to see you at my house | 我極歡喜在我嘅屋見你 | ngo kik fun-hi tsoi ngo-ke uk kin ni |
| 2 Of what country is that man? | 咰個人係乜國嘅呢 | ko-ko yan hai măt kwok ke ni? |
| 3 He is a countryman of mine | 佢係我同國嘅人 | k'ü hai ngo t'ung kwok ke yan |
| 4 My (humble) surname is Ho | 小姓何 | siu sing Ho |
| 5 Did he bring a letter? | 佢有帶封信來冇呢 | k'ü yau tai fung-sun loi mo ni? |
| 6 Yes; he gave it to your father | 有, 佢俾嘵你嘅父親咯 | yau; k'ü pi hiu ni ke fu-ts'ăn lok |
| 7 How many quires of paper have you? | 你有幾多刀紙呢 | ni yau ki to to chi ni? |
| 8 I have no paper, I have six volumes of books | 我冇紙, 有六部書啫 | ngo mo chi, yau luk po shü che |
| 9 Have you seen two plays? | 你睇嘵兩套戲咩 | ni t'ai hiu leung t'o-hi me? |
| 10 I saw two plays; did your brother see them? | 我睇嘵兩套戲; 你嘅兄弟有睇冇 | ngo t'ai hiu leung t'o hi; ni ke hing-tai yau t'ai mo? |
| 11 Will the boy (servant) hold my horse? | 咰個事仔肯同我牽住匹馬唔呢 | ko-ko sze-tsai hăng t'ung ngo hin chü p'at ma 'm ni? |
| 12 Bring the ink and inkstand, I want to write | 拈墨共墨硯來, 我要寫野 | nim mak kung mak-in loi, ngo iu se ye |
| 13 Has the inkstone no box or cover? | 咰個墨硯冇盒或冇蓋嘅咩 | ko-ko mak-in mo hap wak mo k'oi ke me? |
| 14 Yes; they are on the inkstone tray | 有, 個的喺墨硯盆嚟 | yau; ko-tik hai mak-in-p'un lai |
| 15 That is a foreign inkstand; I want an inkstone | 咰個係來路嘅墨水甖; 我要個墨硯 | ko-ko hai loi-lo ke mak-shui-ang; ngo iu ko mak-in |
| 16 I am going to write two letters now | 我如今要寫兩封信 | ngo ü-kăm iu se leung fung-sun |

| | | |
|---|---|---|
| 17 The pilot is on board the ship | 個帶水人喺船嚟 | ko tai-shui-yan hai shün lai |
| 18 Do they not fear pirates? | 佢哋唔怕海賊咩 | k'ü-ti 'm p'a hoi-ts'ak me? |
| 19 The police seized the pilferer | 啲啲差役捉倒個小手 | ko-ti ch'ai-yik chuk to ko siu-shau |
| 20 This man is very ill; call a doctor | 呢個人病十分重；請個醫生嚟喇 | ni-ko yan peng shap-făn chung; ts'ing ko i-shăng lai la |
| 21 Take these things to the pawnbroker | 拎呢啲野去個當舖佬處 | ning ni-ti ye hü ko tong-p'o-lo ch'ü |
| 22 Does the pastrycook make cakes? | 啲個麵食師傅噲整餅唔呢 | ko-ko mio-shik-sze-fu ui ching peng 'm ni? |
| 23 Look for that book of mine | 尋着我嘅本書 | ts'ăm-cheuk ngo ke pun shü |
| 24 Hang those clothes up for me | 同我掛起啲啲衣服 | t'ung ngo kwa-hi ko-ti i-fuk |
| 25 Let me (*lit.* wait till I) wash my hands here | 等我在呢處洗吓對手 | tăng ngo tsoi ni-ch'ü sai ha tui shau |
| 26 Does the bookseller sell many books? | 啲個賣書佬賣好多書咩 | ko-ko mai-shü-lo mai ho to shü me? |
| 27 He has only sold one volume | 佢獨係賣曉一本啫 | k'ü tuk hai mai hiu yat pun che |
| 28 Don't get in the light; I want to read (aloud) | 咪遮住啲啲光；我要讀書 | mai che chü ko ti kwong; ngo iu tuk shü |
| 29 What do you want to write? | 你要寫乜野呢 | ni iu se măt-ye ni? |
| 30 He doesn't want to write anything | 乜野佢都唔想寫 | măt-ye k'ü to 'm seung se |
| 31 Is that affair quite finished? | 啲件事喊嘭唥完曉囉咩 | ko kin sze ham-pang-lang ün hiu lo me? |
| 32 It is not yet finished | 未曾完 | mi ts'ăng ün |
| 33 It should have been finished yesterday | 昨日應該做完嘅喇 | tsok-yat ying-koi tso-ün ke la |
| 34 It is finished, but it is not well done | 做完咯，但係唔做得好 | tso-ün lok, tan hai 'm tso tăk ho |
| 35 Can any man do it well? | 有人可以做得好唔呢 | yau yan ho-i tso tak ho 'm ni? |
| 36 You had better go and ask | 你去問吓好啫 | ni hü măn ha ho che |

| | | |
|---|---|---|
| 37 This is my horse; that is your mare | 呢匹馬係我嘅，嗰匹馬乸係你嘅 | ni p'at ma hai ngo-ke; ko p'at ma-na hai ni-ke |
| 38 Have you many of that sort? | 你有好多噉樣嘅咩 | ni yau ho to kom yeung ke me? |
| 39 Don't make so many mistakes | 咪整錯咁多嗏 | mai ching tsoh kom to cha |
| 40 Come and stay in my house | 來；去我間屋住喇 | loi; hü ngo kan uk chü la |

---

# LESSON XXXVII.

| | | | | | |
|---|---|---|---|---|---|
| To hoist (as a flag) | 扯起 | *ch'e' hi'* | To lead forth | 帶出 | *tai' ch'ut* |
| To roll up | 捲起 | *kün' hi'* | To discourse | 講出 | *kong' ch'ut* |
| To run | 走起 | *tsau' hi'* | To pour out | 倒出 | *to' ch'ut* |
| To pursue | 趕起 | *kon' hi'* | Do. | 斟出 | *chăm ch'ut* |
| To write out | 寫出 | *se' ch'ut* | To write on | 寫住 | *se'* chü' |
| To invent | 想出 | *seung' ch'ut* | To enter | 入去 | yăp *hü'* |
| To divulge | 露出 | lo' *ch'ut* | | | |

The synonyms for "*your*" when addressing superiors, or equals when one desires to be ceremonious, are: LING 令 *excellent*, KWAI 貴 *honourable*, FONG 芳 *fragrant*, and KO 高 *lofty*.

| | | | | | |
|---|---|---|---|---|---|
| Your surname | 高姓 | *ko sing'* | Your mother | 令壽堂 | ling'-shau'-t'ong |
| Your age | 貴庚 | *kwai' kăng* | Your father | 令尊 | ling'-*tsün* |
| Your pre-name | 芳名 | *fong* ming | Your son | 令郎 | ling'-long |
| Your name | 大號 | tai' ho' | Your daughter | 令愛 | ling'-*oi'* |
| Your country | 貴國 | *kwai' kwok* | Your wife | 令正 | ling'-*ching'* |

The demonstrative pronouns *this* and *that* have been given in earlier lessons. As the student will have noticed the TI 啲 and KO 嗰 of KO-TI 嗰啲 NI-TI 呢啲 NI-KO 呢個, &c., are often replaced by the classifier when a noun is specified; e.g., *he entered that shop* K'Ü YÀP KO KAN P'O-T'AU 佢入嗰間舖頭.

| | | |
|---|---|---|
| Take it easy | 修柔做喇 | *sau*-yau tso` *la* |
| A ferry boat - | 橫水渡 | wang-*shui*´-to` |
| To be thirsty | 覺頸渴 | *kok keng*´-*hot* |
| To fly a kite | 放紙鷂 | *fong*` *chi*´-iu` |
| A sudden shower - - | 白撞雨 | pak-chong-ü |
| To blow heavily | 打大風 | *ta*´ tai` *fung* |
| Too low | 矮得嚌 | *ai*´ *tăk*-tsai` |
| Too high | 高得嚌 | *ko tăk*-tsai` |
| Too far - | 遠得嚌 | ün´ *tăk*-tsai` |
| Open the umbrella | 開遮喇 | *hoi che la* |
| At that time | 嗰陣時 | *ko*´ chan` shi |
| It is raining | 落雨咯 | lok ü´ *lok* |

| | | | | | |
|---|---|---|---|---|---|
| Silversmith | 打銀師傅 | *ta*´-ngăn-*sze*-fu` | Priest (Buddhist) | 和尙 | woh-sheung` |
| Do. | 首飾匠 | *shau*´-*shik*-tseung | Priest (Tauist) | 道士 | to`-sze` |
| Shoemaker | 做鞋師傅 | tso`-hai-*sze*-fu` | Sailor | 水手 | *shui*´-*shau*´ |
| Porter | 看門公 | *hon*-mun-*kung* | Pencil rest | 筆架 | *păt-ka*` |
| Scholar | 學生 | hok-*shăng* | Pencil cover | 筆筒 | *păt*-t'ung |
| Do. (classical) | 學者 | hok-*che*´ | Pencil cup | 筆升 | *păt-shing* |
| Shopkeeper | 舖主 | *p'o*`-*chu*´ | Scales | 天秤 | *t'in*-p'ing |
| Do. | 舖家 | *p'o*`-*ka* | To weigh | 秤 | *ch'ing*` |
| Policeman | 差役 | *ch'ai*-yik | Scales (for small money) | 厘戥 | li-*tang*´ |
| Do. | 綠衣 | luk-*i* (*lit.* green coat) | | | |

| | | |
|---|---|---|
| 1 What is your father's age this year? | 令尊今年貴庚呢 | ling-tsün kăm-nin kwai kăng ni? |
| 2 What is your son's name? | 令郎叫乜大號呀 | ling-long kiu măt tai ho a? |
| 3 My son's name is A-chăn | 小兒叫做亞鎮 | sui-i kiu tso A-chăn |
| 4 Are your son and daughter coming? | 令郎及令愛來唔來呢 | ling-long k'ap ling-oi loi 'm loi ni? |
| 5 Did *you* pour out that tea? | 係你斟出嗰啲茶咩 | hai ni chăm-ch'ut ko-ti ch'a me? |
| 6 He has written many characters on it | 佢寫曉好多個字喺處 | k'ü se hiu ho to ko tsz hai ch'ü |
| 7 Did he write out the whole? | 佢寫起嗮喊彭唥係唔係呢 | k'ü se hi sai ham-pang-lang hai 'm hai ni? |

| | | |
|---|---|---|
| 8 Why did they not roll up the map? | 爲乜事佢哋唔捲起嗰地圖 | wai-măt-sze k‘ü-ti ’m kün-hi ko ti-t‘o? |
| 9 They had run fast | 佢哋走得好快 | k‘ü-ti tsau tăk ho fai |
| 10 Let them enter if they wish | 佢哋若係想入由得佢喇 | k‘ü-ti yeuk hai seung yăp yau tăk k‘ü la |
| 11 Who invented that chair? | 乜誰想出嗰張椅樣嚟呢 | măt-shui seung-ch‘ut ko cheung i yeung lai ni? |
| 12 He discoursed with all of them | 佢同佢哋大衆講論 | k‘ü t‘ung k‘ü-ti tai-chung kong-lun |
| 13 Did the General lead the soldiers? | 嗰個將軍帶嗰啲兵出咩 | ko-ko tseung-kwăn tai ko-ti ping ch‘ut me? |
| 14 Do you think that man is a sailor? | 你估嗰個人係水手唔係呢 | ni ku ko-ko yan hai shui-shau ’m hai ni? |
| 15 What did he say when he saw you? | 佢見你時有乜野講呢 | k‘ü kin ni shi yau măt-ye kong ni? |
| 16 He said: What is your name and pre-name? | 佢問你尊姓芳名 | k‘ü măn: ni tsün-sing fong-ming? |
| 17 Did he ask your age? | 佢有問你尊庚冇呢 | k‘ü yau măn ni tsün-kăng mo ni? |
| 18 No; he said, is your father in Hong-kong? | 冇, 佢話你嘅令尊在香港唔呢 | mo; k‘ü wa ni ke ling-tsün tsoi Heung-kong ’m ni? |
| 19 Has the shoemaker repaired the shoes? | 嗰個做鞋佬修整好對鞋唔曾 | ko-ko tso-hai-lo sau-ching-ho tui hai ’m ts‘ăng? |
| 20 Yes; (he has repaired them) he gave them to the shop-keeper | 修整好咯; 佢俾轉過個間鋪頭佬 | sau-ching-ho lok; k‘ü pi chün kwo ko kan p‘o-t‘au-lo |
| 21 What does the silversmith do? | 嗰個打銀師傅做乜野呢 | ko-ko ta-ngăn-sze-fu tso măt-ye ui? |
| 22 He works iu gold and silver | 佢打金及打銀嘅 | k‘ü ta kăm k‘ap ta ngăn ke |
| 23 I am going to write; put the pencil-cup, rest, and cover all here | 我就要寫字, 放好個筆升, 筆架共筆筒一一在呢處 | ngo tsau iu se tsz; fong ho ko păt-sing, păt-ka kung păt-t‘ung yat yat tsoi ni-ch‘ü |
| 24 What sort of paper is that? | 嗰啲係乜野紙呢 | ko-ti hai măt-ye chi ni? |
| 25 It is English paper; it is very dear | 係英國嘅紙; 十分貴的 | hai Ying-kwok ke chi; shap-făn kwai tik |

| | | |
|---|---|---|
| 26 Do you weigh meat in these scales? | 你俾天秤秤肉嘅咩 | ni pi t'in-p'ing ch'ing yuk ke me? |
| 27 No; I use small scales to weigh dollars | 唔係，我用厘戥秤銀 | 'm hai, ngo yung li-tăng ch'ing ngăn |
| 28 Go and call a policemen | 去叫個差役來 | hü kiu ko ch'ai-yik loi |
| 29 Do you want to arrest the porter? | 你要拉個看門公咩 | ni iu lai ko hon-mun-kung me? |
| 30 What is that Buddhist priest doing there? | 响個和尚喺處做乜野呢 | ko-ko woh-sheung hai ch'ü tso măt-ye ni? |
| 31 He is not a Buddhist; he is a Tauist priest | 佢唔係和尚；係道士啫 | k'ü 'm hai woh-sheung; hai to-sze che |
| 32 You have put those flowers too high | 你擠响啲花高得嚌 | ni chai ko-ti fa ko tăk tsai |
| 33 Are you going to Kow-loong to-day? | 你今日去九龍係唔係呢 | ni kăm-yat hü Kau-lung hai 'm hai ni? |
| 34 No, it is too far; I am going to-morrow | 唔係，遠得嚌，我明日正去 | 'm hai, ün tăk tsai; ngo ming-yat ching hü |
| 35 Do you go by the ferry boat? | 你搭橫水渡去咩 | ni tap wang-shui-to hü me? |
| 36 Yes; if it does not rain I shall go | 係，若係唔落雨就去咯 | hai, yeuk hai 'm lok ü tsau hü lok |
| 37 You had better take an umbrella with you | 你帶把遮去好啫 | ni tai pa-che hü ho che |
| 38 Give this to your mother from me | 同我俾呢啲過你嘅令壽堂 | t'ung ngo pi ni-ti kwo ni ke ling-shau-tong |
| 39 Did he fly that kite high? | 佢放响個紙鷂放得高唔呢 | k'ü fong ko-ko chi-in fong tăk ko 'm ni? |
| 40 No, a sudden shower come on and he went away | 唔係高得啫，一陣白撞雨來，佢就去咯 | 'm hai ko tăk che, yat chan pak-chong-ü loi, k'ü tsau hü lok |

# LESSON XXXVIII.

| | | | | | |
|---|---|---|---|---|---|
| To revive | 翻生 | *fan shăng* | To scheme, plan | 出計 | *ch'ut kai'* |
| To return | 翻去 | *fan hü'* | To be surprised | 出奇 | *ch'ut*-k'i |
| To pass over | 過去 | *kwo' hü'* | To take a walk | 出街 | *ch'ut kai* |

The relative pronoun is in Cantonese expressed by the insertion of the particle KE 嘅 after the relative phrase; e.g., *those who study this are good men*, is, literally, "*study this*-KE (嘅) *are good men*," HOK NI-TI KE HAI HO YAN 學呢啲嘅係好人. *The house I was born in was built long since*, NGO CH'UT SHAI KO KAN UK HAI HI HIU HO KAU KE LOK 我出世啯間屋係起嘵好久嘅咯. *The men I require are these*, NGO SHAI KO-TI YAN HAI NI-TI KE LOK 我使啯啲人係呢啲嘅咯.

The reflective pronouns *self, selves*, are expressed by TSZ-KI 自已, and TSZ-KA 自家.

| | | | | | |
|---|---|---|---|---|---|
| Himself | 佢自已 | k'ü'-tsz'-*ki'* | Each other, one another | 對, | *tui'* |
| Do. | 自家 | tsz'-*ka* | | 毎 | mui' |
| Self, oneself | 自已 | tsz'-*ki'* | Mutual | 相 | *seung* |

CLASSIFIERS (*continued.*)

37. Ha' 吓 a time, a while, is applied to blows with a hand or stick; (*strike one blow:* TA YAT HA SHAU 打一吓手.)

38. *Ch'ün'* 串 to connect, „ things strung together such as beads, &c.

39. Shing' 乘 to ride, „ to chairs (sedans) and carriages (TING 頂, is also used for sedan chairs.)

40. *T'üt* 脫 a pattern, „ suits of clothes.

41. *Ku'* 股 a share, proportion, „ heads of an essay, shares in business.

42. Kuk 局 a chessboard square, „ games of chess and chess boards.

It must be understood by the student that the meanings placed against the classifiers are in many cases but some of several significations attached to the characters, which are not only classifiers but independent words.

| | | |
|---|---|---|
| Mind your own business | 理你自已事罷喇 | li' ni' tsz'-*ki'* sze' pa' *la* |
| To guard the door - - | 把守住門口 | *pa'*-*shau'*-chü' mun-hau' |
| To get on (in life) | 發達起嚟 | *fat*-tat *hi'* lai |
| Sit still - - - | 靜靜坐落 | tsing'-tsing' tso' lok |

| | | |
|---|---|---|
| Suddenly | 忽然間 | fat-in-kan |
| All given away | 派晒咯 | p'ai` sai` lok |
| Very clever | 好手勢 | ho' shau'-shai` |
| A good speculation | 好打算 | ho' ta' sün` |
| To count on an abacus | 打算盤 | ta' sün`-p'un |
| Fine flavoured | 好滋味 | ho' tsz mi` |
| Much better | 越法好 | üt fat ho' |
| Counted wrongly | 計唔眞 | kai` 'm chăn |
| Hook it up | 鈎起嚟 | kau hi' lai |
| To go to the (mountain) peak | 上山頂 | sheung' shan-teng' |
| Go first | 先去 | sin hü` |

| | | | | | |
|---|---|---|---|---|---|
| Umbrella-maker | 做遮師傅 | tso`-che-sze-fu` | Pen (quill) | 鵝毛筆 | ngo-mo-păt |
| Watchmaker | 整鏢師傅 | ching-piu-sze-fu` | Slate pencil | 石筆 | shek-pát |
| Tinsmith | 打錫師傅 | ta'-sek-sze-fu` | Pen-knife | 刀仔 | to-tsai' |
| Washerman | 洗衣服人 | sai'-i-fuk-yan | Queen | 皇后 | wong-hau` |
| Surgeon | 外科醫生 | ngoi`-fo-i-shăng | Soldier | 兵人 | ping-yan |
| Weaver | 機房佬 | ki-fong-lo' | Table boy | 事仔 | sze`-tsai' |
| Printer | 印字人 | yan`-tsz`-yan | Do. | 侍仔 | shi`-tsai' |
| Watchman | 看更佬 | hon-kăng-lo' | Thief | 賊仔 | ts'ak-tsai' |
| Do. | 更練 | kăng-lin` | | | |

| | | | |
|---|---|---|---|
| 1 | These are the men who do it | 係呢啲人做嘅 | hai ni-ti yan tso ke |
| 2 | Did they do it themselves? | 係佢哋自已做嘅咩 | hai k'ü-ti tsz-ki tso ke me? |
| 3 | Did he strike you a blow? | 佢打你一吓咩 | k'ü ta ni yat ha me? |
| 4 | They struck one another | 佢哋對打 | k'ü-ti tui ta |
| 5 | Are these what you wanted? | 呢啲係你要嘵嘅咩 | ni-ti hai ni iu hiu ke me? |
| 6 | Those who did so are bad men | 做噉樣嘅係唔好人 | tso kom-yeung ke hai m ho yan |
| 7 | Were those the tailor's clothes? | 啯啲係裁縫佬嘅衣服麼 | ko-ti hai ts'oi-fung-lo ke i-fuk moh? |
| 8 | Did the printer print these books? | 呢啲書係啯個印字人印嘅咩 | ni-ti shü hai ko-ko yan-tsz-yan yan ke me? |
| 9 | At what hour did the washerman bring these clothes? | 幾多點鐘啯個洗衣服佬拈呢啲衣服嚟嘅呢 | ki-to tim chung ko-ko sai-i-fuk-lo nim ni-ti i-fuk lai ke ni? |

| | | |
|---|---|---|
| 10 Are they mutual friends? | 佢哋係相好朋友唔係呢 | k'ü-ti hai seung ho pang-yau 'm hai ni? |
| 11 Did the watchmaker mend the watch? | 啲個整鏢佬整好個鏢嘅咩 | ko-ko ching-piu-lo ching ho ko piu ke me? |
| 12 The soldier came in a chair | 啲個兵坐轎來嘅 | ko-ko ping tso kiu loi ke |
| 13 Where did you put that pen-knife and slate pencil? | 你擠啲張刀仔共石筆喺邊處 | ni chai ko cheung to-tsai kung shek-pät hai pin-ch'ü? |
| 14 The teacher tells me he is a thief | 啲個先生話我知,佢係賊仔 | ko-ko sin-shang wa ngo chi, k'ü hai ts'ak-tsai |
| 15 Does the watchman want to go away? | 啲個看更佬係要去咩 | ko-ko hon-käng-lo hai iu hü me? |
| 16 He says he will certainly kill himself | 佢話佢是必殺死自已 | k'ü wa k'ü shi-pit shat-sze tsz-ki |
| 17 They did it themselves | 佢哋自已做嘅 | k'ü-ti tsz-ki tso ke |
| 18 Those who make this are weavers | 整呢啲嘅係織布人 | ching ni-ti ke hai chik-po-yan |
| 19 Tell the tinsmith to mend this for me | 叫個打錫師傅同我補好佢 | kiu ko ta-sek-sze-fu t'ung ngo po-ho k'ü |
| 20 Are those the things you want mended? | 啲啲野係你要補嘅咩 | ko-ti ye hai ni iu po ke me? |
| 21 The Queen is unwell I hear | 我聞得皇后唔自然 | ngo măn tăk ko Wong-hau 'm tsz-in |
| 22 Send your boy to call a surgeon | 使你嘅事仔去請個外科先生嚟 | sai ni ke sze-tsai hü ts'ing ko ngoi-fo-sin-shăng lai |
| 23 Do you think that is a good speculation? | 你估啲啲係好打算唔呢 | ni ku ko-ti hai ho ta sün 'm ni? |
| 24 I have'nt counted it up (on the abacus) yet | 我未曾打算盤咁 | ngo mi ts'ăng ta sün-p'un chi |
| 25 Try again; he has counted it wrongly | 試過,佢算錯嘵咯 | shi kwo; k'ü sün ts'oh hiu lok |
| 26 Sit still there and don't move | 坐定啲處唔好郁 | tso ting ko-ch'ü 'm ho yuk |
| 27 Is this the pen you sent for? | 呢枝筆係你叫寄嚟嘅咩 | ni chi pät hai ni kiu ki lai ke me? |

| | | |
|---|---|---|
| 28 He won't get on in life that way | 佢噉樣唔發達得嘅 | k'ü kom yeung 'm fat-tat tăk ke |
| 29 Have you ever been up to the peak? | 你有上過山頂冇呢 | ni yau sheung kwo shan-teng mo ni? |
| 30 Mind your own business and go away | 理你自已嘅事罷咯，去喇 | li ni tsz-ki ke sze pa lok, hü la |
| 31 Why do you send away me so suddenly? | 爲乜你忽然間噉就打發我去呢 | wai-măt ni fat-in-kan kom tsau ta-fat ngo hü ni? |
| 32 He was killed; they could not revive him | 佢俾人殺死嘵，佢哋不能翻生得佢 | k'ü pi yan shat sze hiu; k'ü-ti păt năng fan-shăng tăk k'ü |
| 33 Do you think he will return? | 你估佢翻嚟唔呢 | ni ku k'ü fan lai 'm ni? |
| 34 It is very uncertain. If he does I shall be surprised | 十分唔得定，若係佢翻嚟我見奇怪咯 | shap-făn 'm tăk ting, yeuk hai k'ü fan lai ngo kin k'i-kwai lok |
| 35 That plan is not a very good one | 响條計唔係十分好嘅 | ko t'iu kai 'm hai shap-făn ho ke |
| 36 He is a very clever (handicrafts) man | 佢係一個十分好手勢嘅人 | k'ü hai yat ko shap-făn ho shau-shai-ke yan |
| 37 I think I shall go and take a walk | 我想去街行吓正得 | ngo seung hü kai hang ha ching tăk |
| 38 Shall you pass over that bridge? | 你喺响度橋過去咩 | ni hai ko to k'iu kwo hü me? |
| 39 I do not know; I am not going far | 我唔知；我唔去幾遠啫 | ngo 'm chi; ngo 'm hü ki ün che |
| 40 Take that pen and write what I tell you | 拈响枝筆嚟，照我噉話你就噉寫喇 | nim ko chi păt lai, chiu ngo kom wa ni tsau kom se la |

# LESSON XXXIX.

| | | | | | |
|---|---|---|---|---|---|
| To run away | 走去 | *tsau'*-*hü'* | To make money | 賺來 | chan'-loi |
| To let go | 放去 | *fong'*-*hü'* | To row (a boat) | 棹來 | chau'-loi |
| To fill up | 塡埋 | t'in-mai | To pluck | 摘來 | *chak*-loi |
| To wrap up | 包埋 | *pau*-mai | To dress | 打扮 | *ta'*-pan' |
| To keep | 擠埋 | *chai*-mai | To reward | 打賞 | *ta'*-*sheung'* |
| To put away | 擺埋 | *pai'*-mai | To despatch | 打發 | *ta'*-*fat* |
| To level | 掘平 | kwăt-p'ing | To break | 打爛 | *ta'*-lan' |

The force of MAI 埋 as a verbal compound is generally that of *up, into, with* or *at*, while in other cases it simply means a past or completed action (see Williams Cant. Dic. ch. MAI 埋.) That of HÜ 去 and LOI 來 is sufficiently evident from their colloquial meanings. TA 打 denotes action and (while the others follow) always precedes the verb with which it is compounded.

| | | | | | |
|---|---|---|---|---|---|
| A blanket | 一張氈 | *yat cheung chin* | An ornament (in a room) | 玩器 | un'-*hi'* |
| A hole | 一個孔 | *yat ko' hung'* | | | |
| Messenger | 來使 | loi-*sze'* | Fruit | 生菓 | *shăng-kwoh'* |
| Official do. | 公使 | *kung-sze'* | A hill | 山 | *shan* |

| | | |
|---|---|---|
| Do you live here? | 你在呢處住咩 | ni' tsoi' *ni-c'hü'* chü' *me?* |
| It goes too fast (as a clock) | 行得實手快 | hang *tăk* shat *shau' fai'* |
| Do. slow do. - | 行得實手慢 | ,, ,, ,, ,, man' |
| Three o'clock - | 三點鐘 | *sam tim' chung* |
| Past half past three o'clock | 三點半過鐘 | *sam tim' pun' kwo' chung* |
| Past three o'clock - | 三點過鐘 | *sam tim' kwo' chung* |
| A mistaken affair - - | 一宗誤事 | *yat tsung* ng' sze' |
| It is just so - - | 就係噉樣 | tsau' hai' *kom'* yeung' |
| He is not in - - - | 佢唔在處 | k'ü' 'm tsoi' *ch'ü'* |
| Four hours - - - | 兩個時辰 | leung' *ko'* shi-shăn |
| Two hours - | 一個時辰 | *yat ko'* shi-shăn |
| Do. - - - | 兩點鐘 | leung' *tim' chung* |

| | | |
|---|---|---|
| Gone out | 出街去 | *ch'ut kai hü`* |
| It rains - - | 落雨 | lok ü' |
| It rains hard | 落大雨 | lok tai` ü' |
| It (the clock) does not go | 唔行 | 'm hang |

| | | | | | |
|---|---|---|---|---|---|
| Feather-brush | 鷄毛掃 | *kai-mo-so`* | Screen (folding) | 圍屏 | wai-p'ing |
| Candlestick | 蠟燭檯 | lap-*chuk*-t'oi | Lamp shade | 燈罩 | *tăng-chau`* |
| Snuffers | 蠟燭剪 | lap-*chuk-tsin'* | Mirror frame | 鏡架 | *keng`-ka`* |
| Footstool | 脚踏凳 | *keuk*-tap-*tăng`* | Chair cushion | 坐褥 | tso`-yuk |
| Fender | 火爐圍 | *foh'*-lo-wai | Carpet | 地氈 | ti`-*chin* |
| Flowers, a bunch of (nosegay) | 一球花 | *yat* k'au *fa* | Fan | 把扇 | *pa'-shin`* |
| | | | Shovel | 鏟 | *ch'an'* |
| Flower vase | 花瓶 | *fa*-p'eng | Picture | 畫 | wa` |
| Screen (fire) | 火遮 | *foh'-che* | Screen | 遮 | *che* |
| Fire place | 火爐 | *foh'*-lo | | | |

| | | |
|---|---|---|
| 1 He let it go and ran away | 佢放佢去就走嘵 | k'ü fong k'ü hü tsau tsau biu |
| 2 Will he not lend it to you? | 佢唔肯借過你咩 | k'ü 'm hăng tse kwo ni me? |
| 3 He filled up the whole | 佢塡埋晒喊嘭唥 | k'ü t'in-mai sai ham-pang-lang |
| 4 He wrapped it up in a blanket | 佢俾張氈包埋佢 | k'ü pi cheung-chin pau-mai k'ü |
| 5 Put the lampshade on the lamp | 擠個燈罩在嗰盞燈𥗽 | chai ko tăng-chau tsoi ko chan-tăng lai |
| 6 Are you fond of pictures? | 你好中意畫咩 | ni ho chung-i wa me? |
| 7 Put away that screen | 擺埋嗰個圍屏 | pai-mai ko-ko wai-p'ing |
| 8 Where do you keep the shovel? | 你擠埋個鏟喺邊處呢 | ni chai-mai ko chan hai pin-ch'ü ni? |
| 9 It is in the fender | 在火爐圍嗰處 | tsoi fo-lo-wai ko-ch'ü |
| 10 Is that a fire screen or a folding screen? | 嗰個係火爐遮只圍屏呢 | ko-ko hai foh-lo-che chi wai-p'ing ni? |
| 11 Tell them not to pluck the fruit | 叫佢哋唔好摘個啲生菓 | kiu k'ü-ti 'm ho chak ko-ti shăng-kwo |
| 12 When did your son return from school? | 你嘅仔幾時喺書館番來 | ni ko tsai ki-shi hai shü-kun fan loi? |
| 13 I think that messenger makes money | 我估嗰個來使賺錢啫 | ngo ku ko-ko loi-sze chan ts'in che |

初學階

| | | |
|---|---|---|
| 14 Who were rowing in the boat? | 乜誰棹艇呀 | mät-shui chau t'eng a? |
| 15 Two men and one women were rowing | 兩個男人一個女人棹 | leung ko nam-yan yat ko nü-yan chau |
| 16 Did she dress the child? | 佢有打扮個細蚊仔冇呢 | k'ü yau ta-pan ko sai-män-tsai mo ni? |
| 17 Send some men to go and plant trees | 使啲人去種樹 | shai ti yan hü chung shü |
| 18 Put the candlestick on the table | 擠枝蠟燭檯在檯面 | chai chi lap-chuk-t'oi tsoi t'oi min |
| 19 Don't break that fan | 咪整爛嗰把扇 | mai ching-lan ko pa-shin |
| 20 I have a large bunch of flowers in the vase | 我有大球花在個花瓶嚟 | ngo yau tai k'au fa tsoi ko fa-p'ing lai |
| 21 Is that an ornament near the fire-place? | 近火爐圍處嗰個係玩器麼 | kän fo-lo-wai ch'ü ko-ko hai un-hi moh? |
| 22 No, it is a very pretty feather brush | 唔係，係一個十分精緻嘅毛掃 | 'm hai, bai yat ko shap-fän tsing-chi ke mo-so |
| 23 Why have you no carpet in your room? | 爲乜你嘅房冇地氈呢 | wai-mät ni ke fong mo ti-chin ni? |
| 24 I don't make money enough to buy a carpet | 我唔得够銀嚟買張地氈 | ngo 'm täk kau ngän lai mai cheung ti-chin |
| 25 He despatched ten men to help him | 佢打發十個人去帮助佢 | k'ü ta-fat shap ko yan hü pong choh k'ü |
| 26 I want to have that hill levelled | 我要掘平嗰個山 | ngo in kwät p'ing ko-ko shan |
| 27 What's o'clock? Is it three o'clock yet? | 幾多點鐘，有三點鐘冇呀 | ki to tim chung? yau sam tim chung mo a? |
| 28 It's nearly half past three | 上吓三點半咯 | sheung-ha sam tim pun lok |
| 29 Your watch is wrong, it goes too fast | 你個錶唔準，行得太快 | ni ko piu 'm chun, hang täk t'ai fai |
| 30 It was two hours fast yesterday | 昨日快兩點鐘 | tsok-yat fai leung tim chung |
| 31 Do you think it's a mis-taken affair? | 你估係一宗誤事唔係呀 | ni ku hai yat tsung ng-sze 'm hai a? |
| 32 I fear it is just so | 我怕就係噉 | ngo p'a tsau hai kom |

| | | |
|---|---|---|
| 33 Does your friend live here? | 你慨朋友喺呢處住咩 | ni ke p'ang-yau hai ni-ch'ü chü me? |
| 34 Yes, but he's just gone out | 係，但係佢就正去街啫 | hai, tan hai k'ü tsau-ching hü kai che |
| 35 I see it is raining; what bad weather! | 我見落雨；幾唔好天時呢 | ngo kin lok ü; ki 'm ho t'in-shi ni? |
| 36 It always rains hard in the fourth month | 四月常時都係落大雨嘅 | sze üt sheung-shi to hai lok tai ü ke |
| 37 Did it rain when you went to visit the school? | 你去探書館時有雨落冇呢 | ni hü t'am shü-kun shi yau ü lok mo ni? |
| 38 I did not go to the school; I went to row in a boat | 我冇去書館，去棹艇啫 | ngo mo hü shü-kun; hü chau t'eng che |
| 39 Have you told them to let go the rope? | 你有話佢哋聽放手個條繩冇呢 | ni yau wa k'ü-ti t'eng fong-shau ko t'iu shing mo ni? |
| 40 I told them to let it go in two hours' time | 我話佢哋聽過一個時辰放手 | ngo wa k'ü-ti t'eng kwo yat ko shi-shăn fong-shau |

# LESSON XL.

The interrogative pronouns chiefly used are as follow. Although several have been already given they are here repeated for convenience of reference:—

| | | | | | |
|---|---|---|---|---|---|
| What? (business) | 爲乜事幹 | wai\`-*măt*-sze\`-*kon*\`? | Which? | 邊個 | *pin-ko*\`? |
| Of which, whom, of whose? | 邊個人嘅 | *pin-ko*\`-yau-*ke*\`? | Where? | 邊處 | *pin-ch'ü*\`? |
| | 乜誰嘅 | *măt*-shui-*ke*\`? | Do. | 何處 | ho-*ch'ü*\`? |
| Why, for what reason? | 爲乜野 | wai\`-*măt*-ye'? | Why? | 爲何 | wai\`-ho? |
| | | | Who? | 乜誰 | *măt*-shui? |
| What? | 乜野 | *măt*-ye'? (contracted into *me*'a?) | How? (classical) | 如何 | ü-ho? |
| | | | What? (do) | 何 | ho? |
| Whence? (from what place) | 邊處 | *pin-ch'ü*\`? | What? (in the sense of "how many?") | 幾 | *ki*'? |

初學階

CLASSIFIERS (*continued.*)

43 *Kon* 竿 a pole, is applied to bamboos, sticks, etc.

44 *Chü'* 炷 a wick, „ a cluster of incense sticks, pencils, or small pencil-like articles.

45 *Fo'* 夥 an associate, „ parties, bands, companies, etc.

46 Măn 文 lines, spots, „ cash, and may rather be considered as an independent word than a classifier. It however precedes TS'IN 錢 in the phrase "*how much money.*"

47 Mun 門 a door, „ pieces of artillery.

48 *Hau'* 口 a mouth, & Ham 喊 all, „ pistols, revolvers, and small-arms.

| | | |
|---|---|---|
| To look out a radical | 查字部 | ch'a tsz' po' |
| To explain clearly - - - | 解明白 | *kai'* ming-pak |
| What is its meaning? | 點解呢 | *tim' kai' ni?* |
| Say it again - | 再講過 | *tsoi' kong' kwo'* |
| I'll trouble you to—— - | 多煩你 | *to*-fan ni' |
| Hot weather | 熱天 | it *t'in* |
| Much rain | 雨多 | ü' *to* |
| Good morning! | 早晨 | *tso'*-shăn |
| Excuse my disrespect | 失敬 | *shat king'* |
| Many thanks! | 多謝 | *to*-tse' |
| Permit me | 容我 | yung ngo' |
| As you please - | 隨便 | tsui-pin' |

| | | | | | |
|---|---|---|---|---|---|
| A carpenter | 木匠 | muk-tseung' | Square | 曲尺 | *huk-ch'ek* |
| Tools (generally) | 器具 | *hi'*-kü' | Screw | 螺絲 | lo-*sze* |
| Tool chest | 鐵器箱 | *t'it-hi'-seung* | Awl | 錐 | *chui* |
| Hone | 磨刀石 | mo-*to*-shek | Chisel | 鑿 | tsok |
| Screw-driver | 螺絲鑽 | lo-*sze-tsün'* | Drill | 鑽 | *tsün'* |
| Do. | 螺絲搒 | lo-*sze*-ning' | File | 銼 | *ts'oh'* |
| Hammer | 鐵鎚 | *t'it*-ch'ui | Nail | 釘 | *teng* |
| Pincers | 鐵鉗 | *t'it*-k'im | Plane | 刨 | p'au |
| Axe | 斧頭 | *fu'*-t'au | Rule | 尺 | *ch'ek* |
| Gimlet | 手鑽 | *shau'-tsün'* | Saw | 鋸 | *kü'* |

| | | | |
|---|---|---|---|
| 1 | What sort of weather have you at Canton? | 你喺省城時天氣點樣呀 | ni hai shang-shing shi t‘in-hi tim yeung a? |
| 2 | For half the month we have hot weather; afterwards much rain | 半個月天熱，然後多雨 | puu ko üt t‘in-it; iu-han to ü |
| 3 | Why don't you buy some good pencils? | 爲乜野你唔買啲好筆呢 | wai-măt-yo ni ’m mai ti ho păt ni? |
| 4 | Which is the better of these two books? | 呢兩部書邊部好呢 | ni leung po shü pin po ho ni? |
| 5 | What do you say? | 佢點話呢 | ni tim wa ni? |
| 6 | I asked you which was the better book | 我問你邊部書好啫 | ngo măn ni pin po shü ho che |
| 7 | Where did you get them from? | 你喺邊處得嚟嘅 | ni hai pin-ch‘ü tăk lai ke? |
| 8 | Who told you to buy them? | 乜誰叫你買嘅呢 | măt-shui kiu ui mai ke ni? |
| 9 | The writer told me to buy them | 個寫字人叫我買嘅 | ko se-tsz-yan kiu ngo mai ke |
| 10 | He said he wanted books to write in | 佢話佢要書嚟寫字嘅 | k‘ü wa k‘ü iu shü lai se tsz ke |
| 11 | Did he clearly explain what he wanted? | 佢有解明你聽佢要乜野冇呢 | k‘ü yau kai-ming ni t‘eng k‘ü iu măt-ye mo ni? |
| 12 | You are mistaken; he does not want this sort of book | 你錯咯；佢唔要噉樣嘅書 | ni tsoh lok; k‘ü ’m iu kom yeung ke shü |
| 13 | May I trouble you to explain this character? | 我可以煩你解呢個字麼 | ngo ho-i fan ni kai ni ko tsz moh? |
| 14 | What is the meaning of that word? | 嗰句說話點解呢 | ko kü shüt-wa tim kai ui? |
| 15 | I did not hear you; please say it again | 我唔聽見；多煩你再話過喇 | ngo ’m t‘eng kin; to-fan ni tsoi wa kwo la |
| 16 | You must look out its radical | 你要查字部正得嘅 | ni iu ch‘a tsz po ching tăk ke |
| 17 | I don't understand; what is a radical? | 我唔明白字部係乜野 | ngo ’m ming-pak; tsz po hai măt-ye? |
| 18 | It is the root of a character | 即係字種啫 | tsik hai tsz chung che |

| | | |
|---|---|---|
| 19 Why did he buy that stick? | 爲乜野佢買嗰枝鞭杆呢 | wai-măt-ye kʻü mai ko chi pin-kon ni? |
| 20 He bought it to beat the horse with | 佢買嚟打個匹馬嘅 | kʻü mai lai ta ko pʻat ma ke |
| 21 Has the carpenter plenty of tools? | 嗰個木匠有好多器具咩 | ko-ko muk-tseung yau ho to hi-kü me? |
| 22 Are his tools foreign or native? | 佢嘅器具係來路只本地嘅呢 | kʻü ke hi-kü hai loi-lo chi pun-ti ke ni? |
| 23 They are all native; he keeps them in a tool-chest | 一的都係本地嘅；佢放好在鐵器箱內 | yat ti to hai pun-ti ke; kʻü fong-ho tsoi tʻit-hi-seung noi |
| 24 What are the largest tools he has? | 佢有乜野至大嘅器具呢 | kʻü yau măt-ye chi tai ke hi-kü ni? |
| 25 The axe and the saw are the largest | 個斧頭共把鋸係至大嘅 | ko fu-tʻau kung pa kü hai chi tai ke |
| 26 Do Chinese carpenters use the native rule and square? | 唐人木匠用唐人尺共曲尺咩 | tʻong-yan muk-tseung yung tʻong-yan chʻek kung huk-chʻek me? |
| 27 Yes; but they use foreign nails and screws | 係，但佢哋用來路釘共螺絲 | hai; tan kʻü-ti yung loi-lo teng kung lo-sze |
| 28 Did he say good morning when he came in? | 佢入來時有話早晨冇呢 | kʻü yăp loi shi yau wa tso-shăn mo ni? |
| 29 No; he said nothing. I asked him where he came from | 冇，佢冇出到聲，我問佢邊處來嘅 | mo; kʻü mo chʻut to shing. ngo măn kʻü pin-chʻü loi ke |
| 30 Did he tell you immediately? | 佢係卽刻答你咩 | kʻü hai tsik-hak tap ni me? |
| 31 He asked me whose servant I was | 佢問我係乜誰嘅事仔 | kʻü măn ngo hai măt-shui ke sze-tsai |
| 32 What did you say then? | 你點話呢 | ni tim wai ni? |
| 33 I said I was Mr. Chʻan's servant | 我話我係陳先生嘅事仔 | ngo wa ngo hai Chăn sin-shăng ke sze-tsai |
| 34 What was his business in Hongkong? | 佢喺香港做乜野生意呢 | kʻü hai Heung-kong tso măt-ye shăng-i ni? |
| 35 I think he was a carpenter | 我估係做木匠嘅 | ngo ku hai tso muk-tseung ke |

| | | |
|---|---|---|
| 36 People say he sold arms | 人哋話佢賣軍器嘅 | yan-ti wa k'ü mai kwăn-hi ke |
| 37 It may be so; I never asked him | 或者係都唔定；我未曾問過佢 | wak che hai to 'm ting; ngo mi ts'ăng măn kwo k'ü |
| 38 Foreign tools look better than native tools | 來路器具好睇過本地器具 | loi-lo hi-kü ho t'ai kwo pun-ti hi-kü |
| 39 Yes; but the Chinese drill is much the best | 係，但唐人鑽係至好嘅 | hai; tan T'ong-yan tsün hai chi ho ke |
| 40 I don't think so, (I say it's not so) though some people do (so say) | 我話唔係，雖然人哋噉話啫 | ngo wa 'm hai, sui-in yan-ti kom wa che |

# LESSON XLI.

| | | | | | |
|---|---|---|---|---|---|
| A bunch of keys | 一楸鎖匙 | *yat ts'au soh-* shi | To let (a house) | 出賃 | *ch'ut*-yăm' |
| To make a bundle | 綑埋 | *kw'ăn'*-mai | To wonder at | 出奇 | *ch'ut*-k'i |
| To shut up | 閂埋 | *shan*-maī | To go out | 出去 | *ch'ut-hü'* |
| To finish | 做完 | tso'-ün | To push away | 推去 | *t'ui-hü'* |
| To pick up | 執起 | *chop-hi'* | A prison | 監房 | *kam-fong* |
| Conduct (subs.) | 行爲 | hang-wai | A street | 街 | *kai* |

The use of an auxiliary with certain verbs to convert them into dissyllabic words, whenever possible, will be found advantageous by the student, and it may be noted that the natives themselves often prefer to avoid the risk of being misunderstood by using a redundancy of expression. The following are examples of words forming trisyllables in ordinary colloquial.

| | | | | | |
|---|---|---|---|---|---|
| To consider thoroughly | 想眞嚟 | *seung'-chan* lai | Official records (law cases, precedents) | 案牘 | *on'*-tuk |
| To hold it fast | 揸實嚟 | *cha*-shat lai | A despatch (inferior to superior) | 公文 | *kung*-măn |
| To overtake | 追到嚟 | *chui-to'* lai | | | |
| To separate | 分開嚟 | *făn-hoi* lai | | | |

| | | | | | |
|---|---|---|---|---|---|
| To paste on (book) covers | 打書皮 | ta' shü-pʻi | A despatch (sup. to inf.) | 文書 | măn-shü |
| To grind the teeth | 打齧牙 | ta'-ngit-nga | A governor (of a province) | 巡撫 | tsʻun-fu' |
| To make a bed | 打鋪蓋 | ta' pʻo-kʻoiˋ | A magistrate | 官府 | kun-fu' |
| To cheat | 打斧頭 | ta'-fu'-tʻau | A viceroy | 總督 | tsung'-tuk |
| Do. | 阨騙 | ngak-pʻinˋ | | | |
| A courtroom | 公堂 | kung-tʻong | | | |

| | | |
|---|---|---|
| This will do | 呢個做得咯 | ni koˋ tsoˋ tăk lok |
| Who are you? | 你係乜誰 | ni' haiˋ măt-shui? |
| What's the news? | 有乜新聞 | yau' măt săn-măn? |
| What's the matter? | 有乜事幹 | yau' măt sze'-konˋ? |
| I think (guess) it's so | 我估係噉 | ngo' ku' haiˋ kom' |
| You must do it | 你必要做 | ni' pit iuˋ tsoˋ |
| Do it now | 而家做喇 | i-ka tsoˋ la |
| He is dead | 佢過身咯 | kʻü' kwoˋ shăn lok |
| Go with me | 嚟同我去 | lai tʻung ngo' hüˋ |
| How do you know? | 你點知得 | ni' tim' chi-tăk? |

| | | | | | |
|---|---|---|---|---|---|
| Table (card) | 紙牌檯 | chi'-pʻai-tʻoi | Steelyards (for weighing money) | 厘戥 | li-tăng' |
| Seal (wax) | 火漆印 | foh'-tsʻat-yanˋ | Umbrella stand | 遮架 | che-kaˋ |
| Telescope | 千里鏡 | tsʻin-li'-kengˋ | Water cup (for writing) | 水池 | shui'-chʻi |
| Wafer | 火漆片 | foh'-tsʻat-pʻinˋ | Sofa | 睡椅 | shuiˋ-i' |
| Wax (sealing) | 火漆 | foh-tsʻat | String | 線 | sinˋ |
| Hat-stand | 帽架 | moˋ-kaˋ | Do. | 繩 | shing |
| Weights | 銅碼 | tʻung-ma' | Steelyards (for weighing heavy articles) | 秤 | chʻingˋ |
| Paste | 漿糊 | tseung-u | | | |
| A slate | 石板 | shek-pan' | | | |
| Tea-poys | 茶機 | chʻa-ki | | | |

| | | |
|---|---|---|
| 1 Do you want to let that house? | 你啲間屋想出賃咩 | ni ko kan uk seung chʻut-yăm me? |
| 2 I don't want to let it | 我唔要出賃佢 | ngo 'm iu chʻut-yăm kʻü |
| 3 At what time will he go out? | 佢幾時正出街呢 | kʻü ki shi ching chʻut kai ni? |
| 4 People all wondered at that affair | 人人都見啲宗事奇怪咯 | yau-yan to kin ko tsung sze kʻi-kwai lok |

| | | |
|---|---|---|
| 5 Let him enter; don't push him away | 由佢入；唔好推佢出去 | yau k'ü yăp; m' ho t'ui k'ü ch'ut hü |
| 6 Have they shut up the yamun? | 佢哋有閂埋嗰度衙門冇呢 | k'ü-ti yau shan-mai ko to nga-mun mo ni? |
| 7 He picked it up in the street | 佢喺街執倒嘅 | k'ü hai kai chăp-to ke |
| 8 What did he do with the sticks when he picked them up? | 佢執起嗰啲鞭竿時將佢嚟點樣用呢 | k'ü chăp hi ko-ti pin-kon shi, tseung k'ü lai tim-yeung yung ni? |
| 9 He made a bundle of them | 佢將佢嚟綑埋一札 | k'ü tseung k'ü lai kw'ăn-mai yat chat |
| 10 If such be his conduct he must go to prison | 佢嘅行爲若係噉樣就要坐監咯 | k'ü ke hang-wai yeuk hai kom yeung tsau iu tso kam lok |
| 11 Have they finished copying those despatches? | 佢哋抄起嗰啲文書唔曾呢 | k'ü-ti ch'au hi ko-ti măn-shü 'm ts'ăng ni? |
| 12 It was not possible to overtake him | 不能追得倒佢 | pat năng chui tăk to k'ü |
| 13 Is that the Viceroy's seal? | 嗰個印係總督嘅咩 | ko-ko yan hai tsung-tuk ke me? |
| 14 The Governor sent the man to the magistrate | 個巡撫使個人去個官府處 | ko ts'un-fu shai ko yan hü ko kun-fu ch'ü |
| 15 He was cheating people; therefore the policemen took him | 佢阸騙人；所以個差役攞佢 | k'ü ngak-p'in yan; sho-i ko ch'ai-yik lai k'ü |
| 16 The Judge has the official records in the court | 個按察司有啲案牘在公堂 | ko on-ch'at-sze yau ti on-tuk tsoi kung t'ong |
| 17 The Viceroy sent a despatch about the affair | 個總督行一封文書講論呢宗事嘅 | ko tsung-tuk hang yat fung măn-shü kong-lün ni tsung sze ke |
| 18 Can the coolie make the bed? | 個管店噲鋪床唔呢 | ko kun-tim ui p'o ch'ong 'm ni? |
| 19 Tell the binder to bind the book | 叫釘書佬釘起呢本書 | kiu teng-shü-lo teng hi ni pun shü |
| 20 He is fond of cheating people | 佢好中意阸騙人 | k'ü ho chung-i ngak-p'in yan |
| 21 The boy uses the slate | 個細文仔用個石板 | ko sai-măn-tsai yung ko shek-pan |
| 22 Get me a long piece of string | 揾一條長線過我 | wăn yat t'iu ch'eung sin kwo ngo |
| 23 Have you telescopes in China? | 在中國你有千里鏡冇呢 | tsoi Chung-kwok ni yau ts'in-li-keng mo ni? |

| | | |
|---|---|---|
| 24 You can buy telescopes in Hongkong | 喺香港你可以買得千里鏡喇 | hai Heung-kong ni ho-i mai tăk ts'in-li-keng la |
| 25 Do the Chinese use a wafer or sealing-wax | 唐人用火漆片只火漆呢 | T'ong-yan yung foh-ts'at-p'in chi foh-ts'at ni? |
| 26 They use paste generally (*lit.* much paste) | 佢哋用漿糊多 | k'ü-ti yung tseung-u to |
| 27 Do you use those weights with the steelyard? | 你使秤用個啲銅碼唔用呢 | ni shai ch'ing yung ko-ti t'ung-ma 'm yung ni? |
| 28 Yes; we use them to weigh meat | 用；我哋用佢嚟秤肉 | yung; ngo-ti yung k'ü lai ch'ing yuk |
| 29 Is there any news to-day? | 今日有乜新聞呢 | kăm-yat yau măt săn-măn ni? |
| 30 There is not much news to-day; the man is dead | 今日冇乜新聞啫；個人死嘵咯 | kăm-yat mo măt săn-măn che; ko yan sze hiu lok |
| 31 How do you know that he is dead? | 你點知佢死嘵呢 | ni tim chi k'ü sze hiu ni? |
| 32 A friend wrote and told me in a letter | 有朋友寫信嚟話我知嘅 | yau p'ang-yau se sun lai wa ngo chi ke |
| 33 Are you not afraid of his cheating you? | 你唔怕佢阨騙你咩 | ni 'm p'a k'ü ngak-p'in ni me? |
| 34 How do you know he will cheat me? | 你點知佢噲阨騙我呢 | ni tim chi k'ü ui ngak-p'in ngo ni? |
| 35 I consider him a thoroughly bad man | 我筭佢係全唔好嘅人 | ngo sün k'ü hai ts'ün 'm ho ke yan |
| 36 If he is bad you should take him before the magistrate | 若係佢唔好,你應該逮佢去見官 | yeuk hai k'ü 'm ho, ni ying-koi lai k'ü hü kin kun |
| 37 That would be of no use. The office is closed | 唔中用呀·衙門都閂埋咯 | 'm chung yung a. nga-mun to shan-mai lok |
| 38 I wish you would do it now | 我想你而家做啫 | ngo seung ni i-ka tso che |
| 39 Do it to-morrow, that will be sufficient | 聽日正做,就可以得咯 | t'ing-yat ching tso, tsau ho-i tăk lok |
| 40 How long has that man been dead? | 嗰個人死嘵幾耐呢 | ko-ko yan sze hiu ki noi ni? |

# LESSON XLII.

## Indefinite Pronouns.

The indefinite pronouns are as follow:—

| | | |
|---|---|---|
| Everybody, everyone | 各人 | *kok* yan |
| Do. | 每人 | mui' yan |
| Both, a pair of | 兩個 | leung' *ko`* |
| Do. | 雙 | *sheung* |
| One another | 各人 | *kok* yan |
| Do. | 大家 | tai` *ka* |
| Very many, most | 大多 | tai` *to* |
| Certain men | 或人 | wak yan |
| Somebody | 有人 | yau' yan |
| Several (indefinite) | 幾個 | *ki' ko`* |
| Few (do.) | 幾個 | „ |
| None, not any | 無 | mo |
| Each, every | 每 | mui' |
| Little | 少 | *shiu'* |

| | | |
|---|---|---|
| One and all | 一齊 (一總) 咁多人 | *yat* ts'ai (or *yat tsung'*) *kom`* *to* yan |
| One (as an indefinite pronoun) | 一 | *yat* |
| Everything | 各件 | *kok* kin` |
| Nothing | 無野 | mo ye' |
| Such | 噉樣 | *kom'* yeung` |
| Either | 或 | wak |
| Do. (classical) | 是但 | shi` tan` |
| "A certain one" can be expressed verbally; e.g. A certain man | 有人 | yau' yan |

The word "*people*" is expressed by YAN 人 (one, certain persons). Most of the above are used as in English, many being interchangeable. Thus *several* and *few* are at times used indifferently to convey the idea of an indefinite number of people.

### Classifiers (*continued*)

49. *Fong* 方 a square, is applied to squares of ink, inkstones, junkets of beef, mutton, pork, &c.

50. *P'at* 疋 a piece, „ cloth or silk; its proper meaning is a piece of 40 yards.

51. *Fo`* 顆 a clod, „ pearls, beads and similar articles.

52. Tün` 段 a fragment, „ sentences, paragraphs, parts or pieces (e.g. a piece of news—a piece of ground.)

53. *Fun'* 欵 a class, „ sections or articles of laws, treaties, petitions, business, news, &c.

54. Wai` 位 a seat, „ respectable persons e.g., YAT WAI HAK, 一位客, a visitor.

| | | |
|---|---|---|
| Place it on the table | 擠倒檯面嚟 | *chai to'* t'oi min' lai |
| Is it aspirated? (said of a word) | 有噴氣冇呢 | yau' *p'ün'-hi'* mo *ni*? |
| Don't wait so long | 咪等咁耐 | mai' *tăng' kom'* noi' |
| He won't come | 佢唔肯來 | k'ü' 'm *hăng'* loi |
| Try once more | 再試一吓 | *tsoi' shi' yat* ha' |
| What tone has it? | 係乜聲呢 | hai' *măt shing ni*? |
| Retain one (of them) | 留翻一個 | lau-*fan yat ko'* |
| Exert yourself | 盡力做剌 | tsun' lik tso' *la* |
| He speaks Chinese | 佢講唐話 | k'ü' *kong'* T'ong wa' |
| Not yet seen | 唔曾見 | 'm ts'ăng *kin'* |
| The wind is fair | 係順風 | hai' shun' *fung* |

| | | | | | |
|---|---|---|---|---|---|
| Counterpane | 白花被 | pak-*fa*-p'i | Clothes-horse | 衣架 | *i-ka'* |
| Pillow-case | 枕頭布 | *chăm'*-t'au-*po'* | Mattress | 墊褥 | *tsin'*-yuk |
| Bolster | 長枕頭 | ch'eung-*chăm*-t'au | Blanket | 洋氈 | yeung-*chin* |
| Pillow | 枕頭 | *chăm'*-t'au | Couch | 睡椅 | shui'-*i'* |
| Musquito curtain | 蚊帳 | *măn-cheung'* | Quilt | 棉被 | min-p'i' |
| Cot or hammock | 吊床 | *tiu'*-ch'ong | Bedding | 床鋪 | ch'ong-*p'o* |
| Bedpost | 床柱 | ch'ong-ch'ü' | Bedstead | 床 | ch'ong |

| | | |
|---|---|---|
| 1 Has that person a pair of horses? | 啲個人有雙馬冇呢 | ko-ko yan yau sheung ma mo ni? |
| 2 Each bed has two blankets and two pillows | 每張床有兩張氈共兩個枕頭 | mui cheung ch'ong yau leung cheung chin, kung leung ko chăm-t'au |
| 3 Everybody uses chairs | 人人都用椅嘅 | yan yan to yung i ke |
| 4 Nothing more was heard of him | 冇聽聞佢嘅消息添咯 | mo t'ing măn k'ü ke siu sik t'im lok |
| 5 Several men said they had seen him | 幾個人話佢哋有見過佢咯 | ki ko yan wa k'ü-ti yau kin kwo k'ü lok |
| 6 One and all were willing to go | 一總咁多人都愿去 | yat tsung kom to yan to ün hü |
| 7 People ought to love one another | 衆人應該大家相愛 | chung yan ying-koi tai-ka seung-oi |
| 8 He came to look for somebody | 佢來搵人 | k'ü loi wăn yan |

| | | |
|---|---|---|
| 9 Certain people took him and beat him | 有人捉倒佢嚟打 | yau yan chuk to k'ü lai ta |
| 10 Either of the couches will do | 或係一張睡椅都做得咯 | wak hai yat cheung shui-i to tso tăk lok |
| 11 He has a few friends, and but little to eat | 佢有幾個朋友，但係好少野食啫 | k'ü yau yi ko pang-yau, tan hai ho shiu ye shik che |
| 12 Most of the men had gone | 大多人都去咯 | tai to yan to hü lok |
| 13 Such people as this must be punished | 噉樣嘅人必要受責罰咯 | kom yeung ke yan pit iu shau chak-fat lok |
| 14 Get me an inkstone; I don't want it for long | 搵個墨硯過我，我要使佢冇耐啫 | wan ko măk-in kwo ngo; ngo iu shai k'ü mo noi che |
| 15 How much does one piece of cloth cost? | 一疋布要幾多錢呢 | yat p'at po iu ki to ts'in ni? |
| 16 His letter was written in paragraphs | 佢封信係分開一段段寫嘅 | k'ü fung sun hai făn-hoi yat tün tün se ke |
| 17 I have had no visitors to-day | 今日我冇人客嚟到 | kăm-yat ngo mo yan-hak lai to |
| 18 Put the pillow-case on the pillow | 擠個枕頭布在個枕頭嚟 | chai ko chăm-t'au-po tsoi ko chăm-t'au lai |
| 19 Make the bed and put sheets and blanket on it | 鋪牀就擠被單共氈在呴處 | p'o ch'ong tsau chai p'i-tan kung chin tsoi ko-ch'ü |
| 20 I have no bed, I have only a hammock | 我冇牀，獨有張吊牀啫 | ngo mo ch'ong, tuk yau cheung tiu-ch'ong che |
| 21 Do you use a mosquito curtain? | 你用蚊帳唔用呢 | ni yung măn-cheung 'm yung ni? |
| 22 Yes, I use one every summer | 用，年年天熱時我都用嘅 | yung, nin nin t'in it shi ngo to yung ke |
| 23 Do you use it each night? | 你每晚用佢唔呢 | ni mui man yung k'ü 'm ni? |
| 24 It is put over the bed each night | 每晚用嚟蓋住張牀 | mui man yung lai k'oi-chü cheung ch'ong |
| 25 Is this character aspirated? | 呢個字有噴氣聲冇 | ni-ko tsz yau p'an-hi shing mo? |
| 26 Please tell me what tone it has | 多煩話我聽係乜野聲喇 | to-fan wa ngo t'eng hai măt-ye shing la |
| 27 That has the "sheung yăp" tone | 呴個係上入聲嘅 | ko-ko hai sheung yăp shing ke |

| | | |
|---|---|---|
| 28 You must exert yourself to read | 你是必要盡力讀書嚁 | ni shi-pit iu tsun-lik tuk shü poh |
| 29 You will find it difficult to learn Chinese | 你將來就知得學唐話係難咯 | ni tseung-loi tsau chi tăk hok T'ong-wa hai nan lok |
| 30 Who gave you those chairs? | 乜誰俾啲啲椅過你嘅呢 | măt-shui pi ko-ti i kwo ni ke ni? |
| 31 A certain friend of mine gave them to me | 有一個朋友俾過我嘅 | yau yat ko p'ang-yau pi kwo ngo ke |
| 32 Have you not yet seen him? | 你未曾見過佢咩 | ni mi ts'ăng kin kwo k'ü me? |
| 33 I have seen him a few times only | 我見過佢幾次啫 | ngo kin kwo k'ü ki ts'z che |
| 34 Have many visitors come to-day? | 今日有好多人客來咩 | kam-yat yau ho to yan-hak loi me? |
| 35 Not many to day; I expect a great many to-morrow | 今日冇幾多啫；聽日怕多啲 | kam-yat mo ki to che; t'eng-yat p'a to ti |
| 36 Exert yourself to do that properly | 盡力做妥當啲啲 | tsun-lik tso t'oh tong ko-ti |
| 37 There is nothing said about him | 冇乜野話到佢呀 | mo măt-ye wa to k'ü a |
| 38 Such conduct is most improper | 噉樣嘅行爲係極唔合嘅 | kom yeung ke hang-wai hai kik 'm hop ke |
| 39 Every thing is exactly as I like it | 各樣都係十分中我意嘅咯 | kok yeung to hai shap-făn chung ngo i ke lok |

# LESSON XLIII.

| | | | | | |
|---|---|---|---|---|---|
| To have no leisure | 唔得閒 | m' *tăk* han | To hasten | 趕快 | *kon'-fai`* |
| To know | 識得；知 | *shik-tăk*; *chi* | Business | 事幹 | sze`-*kon`* |
| An answer | 囘音 | ui-*yăm* | Upright | 忠直 | *chung*-chik |
| To stay | 等，住 | *tăng'*, chü` | Faithful | 信實 | *sun`*-shat |

| | | | | | |
|---|---|---|---|---|---|
| Salary (*lit.* firewood and water) | 俸祿 | *fung'*-luk | Deceit | 詭譎 | *kwai'-kwăt* |
| | | | Wages | 人工 | yan-*kung* |
| To get out of the way | 行開 | hang-*hoi* | To hurry | 急 | *kăp* |
| | | | Late | 遲 | ch'i |

NUMERALS.

With the ordinary numerals the student is already familiar. These are however *written* in two other ways besides the forms already given, and those who are studying the character will find it advantageous to acquire them from a teacher. The mode here adopted is that usually found in books. The more complicated form is used in important documents to lessen the chance of fraud; and the other is a contracted form used in arithmetical computations and current accounts.

In counting from 100 to 110 the character LING 零 is introduced before the additional uumber; e.g., 100=YAT PAK 一百; 110=YAT PAK LING SHAP 一百零十.

The word signifying *ten* is often omitted after the hundred; e.g. 150=YAT PAK 'NG 一百五; 1000=YAT TS'IN 一千; a myriad=一萬 YAT MAN.

The numerals enter into a large number of phrases in common use and in which their actual numerical signification is lost sight of. In most cases, however, this is easily traceable

IDIOMATIC USES of. *One*, YAT 一.

| | | | | | |
|---|---|---|---|---|---|
| Disagreement (*lit.* not of one mind) | 心不一 | *săm pat yat* | One by one | 一一 | *yat ya* |
| | | | Whilst | 一面 | *yat* min' |
| Glance at it | 睇一吓 | *t'ai' yat* ha' | Addicted | 專一 | *chün yat* |
| The whole life | 一生 | *yat shăng* | As soon as | 一經 | *yat king* |
| As soon as he left | 一往 | *yat* wong' | | | |

| | | |
|---|---|---|
| I can't put it there | 唔擠得啲處 | 'm *chai tăk ko'-ch'ü'* |
| A heavy cargo - | 好重嘅貨物 | *ho'* chung' *ke' foh'*-măt |
| There is no room | 冇地方 | mo' ti'-*fong* |
| A head wind | 頂頭風 | *ting'* t'au *fung* |
| A fair wind - . | 順風 | shun' *fung* |
| A fair tide | 順水 | shun' *shui* |
| A head tide - | 逆水 | yik *shui* |

| | | |
|---|---|---|
| Ebb tide | 水乾 | *shui´ kon* |
| Flood tide - | 水大 | *shui´* tai` |
| A cabin | 廂房 | *seung*-fong |
| A ship's deck | 船面 | shün-min` |
| To tack ship | 摳篷 | *k‘au* p‘ung |

| | | | | | |
|---|---|---|---|---|---|
| Dressing room | 修飾房 | *sau-shik*-fong | Scented soap | 香梘 | *heung-kan´* |
| Do. table | 梳粧檯 | *sho-chong*-t‘oi | Sponge | 水泡 | *shui`*-p‘o´ |
| Do. case | 鏡粧 | *keng`-chong* | Razor | 剃刀 | *t‘ai`-to* |
| Tooth powder | 牙灰 | nga-*fui* | Glass-box | 鏡箱 | *keng`-seung* |
| Do. box | 牙灰盒 | nga-*fui*-hap | Hat box | 帽盒 | mo`-hap |
| Clothes trunk | 衣箱 | *i-seung* | Drawer | 櫃桶 | kwai`-*t‘ung´* |
| Do. press | 衣櫃 | *i*-kwai` | | | |

| | | |
|---|---|---|
| 1 What are his wages per month? | 佢受幾多人工一個月呢 | k‘ü shau ki to yan-kung yat ko üt ni? |
| 2 He gets a hundred and thirty dollars | 佢受一百三十員 | k‘ü shau yat pak sam-shap ün |
| 3 That makes one thousand five hundred and sixty a year | 噉樣一年共計一千五百六十員 | kom yeung yat nin kung kai yat ts‘in ’ng pak luk-shap ün |
| 4 How many thousands make a myriad? Ten | 幾多千爲一萬呢，十千咯 | ki to ts‘in wai yat man ni? shap ts‘in lok |
| 5 Tell him to answer immediately | 叫佢卽刻囘音 | kiu k‘ü tsik-hak ui yăm |
| 6 There is no hurry; bring the men one by one | 唔使噉急；帶啲人一個一個嚟 | ’m shai kom kăp; tai ti yan yat-ko yat-ko lai |
| 7 He has been busy his whole life | 佢一生都係唔得閒嘅 | k‘ü yat-shăng to hai ’m tăk han ke |
| 8 I knew he would not stay | 我知佢唔等嘅咯 | ngo chi k‘ü ’m tăng ke lok |
| 9 His salary was not sufficient | 佢嘅俸祿唔够 | k‘ü ke fung-luk ’m kau |
| 10 Had he any disagreement with you? | 佢同你有心不一冇呢 | k‘ü t‘ung ni yau săm-pat-yat mo ni? |
| 11 As soon as he left he hastened away | 佢一出就趕快去咯 | k‘ü yat ch‘ut tsau kon-fai hü lok |
| 12 I had rather he had stayed | 我寧愿佢喺處 | ngo ning-ün k‘ü hai ch‘ü |

| | | |
|---|---|---|
| 13 As soon as you have finished get out of the way | 你做完嘥就行開剌 | ni tso-ün sai tsau hang hoi la |
| 14 He is upright and faithful in business | 佢做事幹忠直又信實 | k'ü tso sze-kon chung-chik yau shun-shat |
| 15 Do you use a razor daily? | 你每日用剃刀嘅咩 | ni mui yat yung t'ai-to ke me? |
| 16 No, but as soon as I return I shall use it | 唔係，但我一翻嚟就用咯 | 'm hai, tan ngo yat fan-lai tsau yung lok |
| 17 Give a glance at that dressing table | 睇吓嗰張鏡粧檯 | t'ai ha ko cheung keng-chong-t'oi |
| 18 A sponge, towel, and soap are wanted to wash the face with | 水泡面巾共香梘係用嚟洗面嘅 | shui-p'o, min-kăn, kung heung-kan hai yung lai sai min ke |
| 19 Is the tooth powder in the box? | 嗰啲牙灰喺個箱嚟咩 | ko-ti nga-fui hai ko seung lai me? |
| 20 What is the meaning of a "glass-box?" | 個鏡箱係點解嘅呢 | ko "keng-seung" hai tim kai ke ni? |
| 21 It is a box with a small looking glass in it | 係一個箱有個小鏡喺裏頭嘅 | hai yat ko seung yau ko siu-keng hai lui-t'au ke |
| 22 Are those drawers in the clothes press? | 嗰櫃桶喺個衣櫃嚟咩 | ko kwai-t'ung hai ko i-kwai lai me? |
| 23 The clothes' trunk is in the dressing-room | 嗰個衣箱係在個粧飭房嚟 | ko-ko i-seung hai tsoi tsong-shik fong lai |
| 24 Shall you stay at Hongkong? | 你喺香港等吓咩 | ni hai Heung-kong tăng ha me? |
| 25 No, I shall leave as soon as there's a fair wind | 唔係，一順風我就去咯 | 'm hai, yat shun-fung ngo tsau hü lok |
| 26 How is the tide? is it ebb or flood? | 潮水如何呀，水乾只水大呢 | ch'iu-shui ü-ho a? shui-kon chi shui tai ni? |
| 27 It is flood: that is a head tide for us | 係水大；我哋遇逆水咯 | hai shui tai; ngo-ti ü yik shui lok |
| 28 Do you think we shall have a fair wind? | 你估我哋遇啱順風唔呢 | ni ku ngo-ti ü-ngam shun-fung 'm ni? |
| 29 I fear we shall have a head wind | 我怕我哋遇頂頭風哩 | ngo p'a ngo-ti ü ting-t'au fung li |

初學階

| | | |
|---|---|---|
| 30 Whilst I go, you observe him | 我一面去，你睇住佢喇 | ngo yat min hü, ni t'ai chü k'ü la |
| 31 Put the sponge in the hot water | 擠個水泡落熱水嚟 | chai ko shui-p'o lok it-shui lai |
| 32 There is some disagreement between those men | 嗰的人唔同一心嘅 | ko-ti yan 'm t'ung yat săm ke |
| 33 Is the box on the ship's deck? | 個箱喺船面咩 | ko seung hai shün-min me? |
| 34 Is he addicted to breaking things? | 佢好打爛野嘅咩 | k'ü ho ta-lan ye ke me? |
| 35 That ship has a very heavy cargo | 嗰隻船載有好重嘅貨 | ko chek shün tsoi yau ho chung ke foh |
| 36 There is no room for more | 冇地方載多啲添咯 | mo ti-fong tsoi to ti t'im lok |
| 37 Put some of the things in the cabin | 擠啲野在個廂房嚟 | chai ti ye tsoi ko seung-fong lai |
| 38 I'm not able to! there are too many men there | 我不能，嗰處已經有好多人咯 | ngo păt năng! ko ch'ü i-king yau ho to yan lok |
| 39 More than I ever saw in my whole life | 多過我一生所見嘅 | to kwo ngo yat shăng sho kin ke |
| 40 Tell him he ought to tack ship | 話佢知；佢應該摳篷嘑 | wa k'ü chi; k'ü ying-koi k'au p'ung la |

---

# LESSON XLIV.

IDIOMATIC USES of *two* I 二 OR LEUNG 兩.

Double minded 二心 i` *sam* The parents 兩親 leung' *tsăn*

Plaintiff and defendant 兩造 leung' tso`

OF *three* SAM 三.

A thief 三隻手 *sam-chek-shau'* A crossway 三丫路 *sam-a-lo`*

### OF *four* SZE 四.

| | | |
|---|---|---|
| A little (as; he knows a little) | 四四六六 | *sze*` *sze*` luk luk |
| Travelled, worldly wise | 四海嘅人 | *sze*` *hoi*' *ke*` yan |
| A person wearing spectacles | 四眼佬 | *sze*`-ngan'-*lo*' |
| China, the world | 四海 | *sze*`-*hoi*' |
| On every side | 四面 | *sze*`-min` |
| Everywhere | 四處 | *sze*`-*ch'ü*` |
| All about | 四下 | *sze*`-ha' |
| Anyway | 四路 | *sze*`-lo` |

### OF *five* 'NG 五.

The four points of the compass and the centre, 五方 'ng *fong*

### OF *ten* SHAP 十.

*Very* or *perfectly* is expressed by shap-*făn* 十分 lit. *ten divisions*; all weights and measures in China being decimal, ten divisions = *the whole*; i.e. *perfection.*

### CLASSIFIERS (CONTINUED.)

55. Ün 圓 (or 員) a circle, a ball, is applied to things round or circular, such as dollars, coin, &c.

56. Ün 員 to circulate, is applied to officers of the government

57. Ts'ăng 層 a tier, ,, the floors or stories of houses

58. Ip 頁 the head, ,, strips or leaves of paper

59. To` 道 a way, ,, documents written, commands of the Emperor, and, sometimes, to men

60. *T'ip* 貼 to paste up, ,, adhesive substances such as plasters, small paper packages, &c.

| | | |
|---|---|---|
| What are you laughing at? - | 你笑乜野呢 | ni` *siu*` *măt*-ye' *ni*? |
| It is deep water | 係深水 | hai` *shăm shui*' |
| Begin to row | 落槳 | lok *tseung*' |
| To pull an oar | 棹槳 | chau` *tseung*' |
| To hoist a sail (set sail) | 扯悝 | *ch'e*' li' |
| To lower a sail | 落悝 | lok li' |
| To cast anchor | 拋錨 | *p'au* nau |
| To get up anchor - | 起錨 | *hi*' nau |
| To steer - - - - | 駛艜 | *sai*' t'ai' |

初學階

| | | |
|---|---|---|
| A steamer | 火船 | *foh'*-shun |
| A merchantman | 貨船 | *foh`*-shün |
| A man of war | 兵船 | *ping*-shün |
| A blockhead | 蠢人 | *ch'ăn'* yan |

| | | | | | |
|---|---|---|---|---|---|
| Wash-hand stand | 面盆架 | min`-p'un-*ka`* | Tooth-brush | 牙刷 | nga-*shat* |
| Bathing tub | 洗身桶 | *sai'-shăn-t'ung'* | Hair-brush | 髮掃 | *fat-so`* |
| Shaving-brush | 水抆掃 | *shui'*-măn'-*so`* | Clothes-brush | 衣掃 | *i-so`* |
| Nail-brush | 指甲掃 | *chi'-kap-so`* | Shoe-brush | 鞋掃 | hai-*so`* |
| Water-goblet | 水壺 | *shui'*-u | Comb (coarse) | 梳 | *sho* |
| Wooden tub | 木盆 | muk-p'un | Comb (fine) | 篦 | pi` |

| | | |
|---|---|---|
| 1 Are his parents living there? | 佢嘅兩親喺呾處居住咩 | k'ü ke leung-ts'ăn hai ko-ch'ü kü chü 'me? |
| 2 I fancy he's a double minded man | 我估佢係一個二心嘅人 | ngo ku k'ü hai yat ko i-sam ke yan |
| 3 Plaintiff and defendant both went to the yamun | 兩造都去嘵衙門咯 | leung tso to hü hiu nga-mun lok |
| 4 He's a regular thief | 佢正係一個三隻手 | k'ü ching hai yat ko sam-chek-shau |
| 5 There are thieves found every where | 四處都有賊匪 | sze-ch'ü to yau ts'ak-fi |
| 6 You are a wearer of spectacles, are you! | 四眼佬就係你咯 | sze-ngan-lo tsau hai ni lok |
| 7 You know very little about it | 你知得四四六六啫 | ni chi tăk sze-sze-luk-luk che |
| 8 He's quite a travelled man | 佢係一個十分四海嘅人 | k'ü hai yat ko shap-făn sze hoi ke yan |
| 9 Yes, but he's a great block-head | 係, 但佢係十分蠢呆嘅 | hai, tan k'ü hai shap-făn ch'ăn-ngoi-ke |
| 10 He knows every place (lit. the four places) | 佢四處都識得 | k'ü sze-ch'ü to shik tăk |
| 11 Bad weather prevails on every side | 四面都唔好時氣 | sze-min to 'm ho shi-hi |
| 12 He's very hard working | 佢十分勤力 | k'ü shap-făn k'ăn-lik |
| 13 Go straight on and you'll come to a cross-way | 你直去就行到一條三丫路咯 | ni chik hü tsau hang to yat t'iu sam-a-lo lok |

| | | |
|---|---|---|
| 14 The price of that book is two dollars | 啲本書要銀兩圓 | ko pun shü iu ngan leung un |
| 15 How many stories has that house? | 啲間樓有幾多層呢 | ko kau lau yau ki to ts'ăng ni? |
| 16 Buy me a dozen strips of paper | 買十二頁紙過我 | mai shap i ip chi kwo ngo |
| 17 Get me a brush and comb | 拈個掃共梳嚟我 | nim ko so kung sho lai ngo |
| 18 Do you mean a toothbrush? | 你要個牙刷咩 | ni iu ko nga-shat me? |
| 19 No, a hairbrush and the fine comb | 唔係, 要個髮掃共隻篦 | 'm hai, iu ko fat-so kung chek pi |
| 20 Put water in the bathing tub | 擠啲水在個洗身桶嚟 | chai ti shui tsoi ko sai-shăn-t'ung lai |
| 21 Don't put any in the wooden tub; its not large enough | 唔好擠落個木桶, 佢係唔够大嘅 | 'm ho chai lok ko muk-t'ung; k'ü hai 'm kau tai ke |
| 22 Are you fond of going about in boats? | 你中意駛艇四下去咩 | ni chung-i sai t'ing sze-ha hü me? |
| 23 I can steer, but I cannot pull an oar | 我噲駛艕; 但唔噲掉槳 | ngo ui sai t'ai; tan 'm ui chau tseung |
| 24 Hoist the sail when you get a fair wind | 好風時你就要扭幃喇 | ho fung shi ni tsau iu ch'e li la |
| 25 When he anchors he lowers the sail | 佢抛錨時就落幃咯 | k'ü p'au nau shi tsau lok li lok |
| 26 Is that a merchantman or a man of war? | 啲隻係貨船只兵船呢 | ko chek hai foh-shün chi ping-shün ni? |
| 27 It is a steamer—a merchant steamer I think | 係火船, 我估係生意嘅火船 | hai foh-shün, ngo ku hai shăng-i ke foh-shün |
| 28 What are you laughing at? I said it was a steamer | 你笑乜野呢? 我話係火船咯 | ni siu măt-ye ni? ngo wa hai foh-shün lok |
| 29 Do you use foreign towels in bathing? | 你洗身用來路面巾咩 | ni sai-shăn yung loi-lo min-kăn me? |
| 30 I sometimes use foreign, and sometimes native towels | 我有時用來路面巾有時本地嘅 | ngo yau-shi yung loi-lo min-kăn, yau shi pun-ti ke |
| 31 Does the barber use a shaving brush? | 個剃頭佬用個水抆掃咩 | ko t'ai-t'au-lo yung ko shui-măn so me? |

| | | |
|---|---|---|
| 32 He uses a shaving brush when he shaves people | 佢同人剃頭時，用個水抆掃 | k'ü t'ung yan t'ai t'au shi yung ko shui-măn-so |
| 33 What goods are on board the merchant vessel? | 啲隻貨船載有乜野貨呢 | ko chek foh-shün tsoi yau măt-ye foh ni? |
| 34 She has guns and ammunition (ma'-tsz') | 佢有鎗砲共碼子 | k'ü yau ts'eung p'au kung ma-tsz |
| 35 Are there many Spaniards at that place? | 啲處有好多呂宋人咩 | ko ch'ü yau ho to Lü-sung yan me? |
| 36 No, but there are several Chinese and Englishmen | 冇，但有幾個唐人共英國人啫 | mo, tan yau ki ko T'ong-yan kung Ying-kwok yan che |
| 37 Did all the birds fly away? | 咁多雀都飛曬去咩 | kom to tseuk to fi sai hü me? |
| 38 You should have taken more care | 你應該子細啲 | ni ying-koi tsz-sai ti |
| 39 There is a disagreement between these two men | 啲兩個人嘅心十分不一 | ko leung ko yan ke sam shap-făn pat yat |
| 40 A whole life is not enough to do it in | 一世都唔做得曬嘅 | yat shai to 'm tso tăk sai ke |

---

# LESSON XLV.

| | | | | | |
|---|---|---|---|---|---|
| To use one ill | 刻薄待人 | *hak*-pok toi` yan | To mix together | 攪埋 | *kau'*-mai |
| No help for it | 冇奈何 | mo'-noi`-ho | To empty | 倒空 | *to'-hung* |
| Oblige me | 爲吓我 | wai` ha' ngo' | To turn out | 倒出 | *to'-ch'ut* |
| Secretly | 私私啲 | *sze-sze-ti* | Fireworks | 烟火 | *in-foh'* |
| To turn inside out | 翻裏面 出嚟 | *fan'* li'-min` *ch'ut* lai | To let off fireworks | 燒烟火 | *shiu in-foh'* |
| | | | To look after | 看住 | *hon*-chü` |
| To turn upside down | 倒轉 | *to'-chün`* | To care for | 睇顧 | *t'ai'-ku`* |
| A mosquito net | 蚊袋 | *măn*-toi` | Do. | 照料 | *chiu`*-liu` |
| The least bit | 至少 | *chi` shiu'* | Do. | 顧住 | *ku`*-chü` |

The word PAK 百, *one hundred*, is frequently used to express a collective quality or quantity; e.g., PAK-SING 百姓 (lit. the hundred names) *the people*; PAK MUK 百木 *all the trees*; PAK TS'IN MAN 百千萬 *an immense number*.

MAN 萬 *a myriad* is used in the same sense; e.g. MAN-KWOK 萬國 *all nations*; MAN-FONG 萬方 *all parts of the world*; MAN-SUI 萬歲 *for all years*. The Emperor is addressed as MAN-SUI-YE 萬歲爺 (*thousand years' sire!*) *a million* is expressed by YAT PAK MAN 一百萬, or YAT CHIU 一兆.

ORDINAL NUMBERS.

The ordinal numbers are expressed by prefixing TAI 第 before the cardinal numbers; e.g. *the first* TAI YAT 第一, *the second* TAI I 第二, &c.

*The first who* is expressed by SIN 先———KE 嘅; e.g. *the first who arrived*, SIN TO KE 先到嘅.

*The last who* is expressed by SHAU MI 收尾———KE 嘅; e.g. *the last who arrived* SHAU MI TO KE 收尾到嘅.

When used to express the quality of goods the words *first* and *second* are rendered by SHEUNG 上 and CHUNG 中; e.g. *first quality of rice* SHEUNG MAI 上米; *second do.* CHUNG MAI 中米.

*Firstly* and *secondly* (or *then*) as applied to actions, are expressed by the simple ordinals.

| | | |
|---|---|---|
| They forgot it | 佢哋忘記咯 | k'ü'-ti' mong-*ki' lok* |
| We took medicine | 我哋食曉藥 | ngo'-ti' shik *hiu* yeuk |
| Have you any more? | 你重有冇呢 | ni' chung' yau' mo' *ni*? |
| Anything will do | 乜野都好 | *măt*-ye' *to ho'* |
| Don't trouble me | 咪煩我喇 | mai' fan ngo' *la* |
| Useless | 冇乜用嘅 | mo' *măt* yung' *ke'* |
| It can't last long | 不能長久 | *pat* năng ch'eung *kau'* |
| Of no importance | 冇乜相干 | mo' *măt seung-kon* |
| Does it pain you? | 令你痛咩 | ling' ni' *t'ung' me*? |
| Is it swollen? | 有瘇冇呀 | yau' *chung'* mo' *a*? |
| It leaks there | 响處漏水 | *ko'-ch'ü'* lau' *shui'* |
| Look in the dictionary | 查字典 | ch'a tsz'-*tin'* |

| | | | | | |
|---|---|---|---|---|---|
| Dressing-gown | 修飾衫 | *sau-shik-sham* | Button hole | 鈕扣 | *nau'-k'au'* |
| Night-gown | 墊瞓衫 | *tin'-fan'-sham* | Garters | 襪帶 | mat-*tai'* |
| Pin | 鼓槌針 | *ku'*-ch'ui-*cham* | Gloves | 手笠 | *shau'-lap* |

| | | | | | |
|---|---|---|---|---|---|
| Head dress | 首飾 | *shau'-shik* | Petticoat | 裙 | kw‘ăn |
| Night cap | 瞓帽 | *fŭn`*-mo` | Button | 鈕 | *nau'* |
| Pocket | 衣袋 | *i*-toi` | Bag | 袋 | toi` |
| Apron | 圍裙 | wai-kw‘ăn | | | |

| | | |
|---|---|---|
| 1 The people use him ill | 個啲百姓刻薄待佢 | ko-ti pak-sing hak-pok toi k‘ü |
| 2 Does he care for his friends? | 佢顧住佢嘅朋友唔呢 | k‘ü ku-chü k‘ü ke p‘ang-yau ’m ni? |
| 3 He emptied the wooden tub | 佢倒清嗰個木桶 | k‘ü to-ts‘ing ko-ko muk-t‘ung |
| 4 Tell him to mix the medicine | 叫佢攪勻嗰啲藥 | kiu k‘ü kau-wăn ko-ti yeuk |
| 5 Turn the box upside down | 倒轉個箱底向上 | to-chün ko seung tai heung sheung |
| 6 Turn the bag inside out | 翻轉個袋裏面出嚟 | fan-chün ko toi li-min ch‘ut lai |
| 7 Don't spoil that hat | 咪整壞個頂帽 | mai ching-wai ko ting mo |
| 8 Put the mosquito net over the bed | 擠個蚊袋在床上 | chai ko măn-toi tsoi ch‘ong-sheung |
| 9 All nations use clothes | 萬國都用衣服嘅 | man-kwok to yung i-fuk ke |
| 10 I am afraid there is no help for it | 我怕冇奈何咯 | ngo p‘a mo-noi-ho lok |
| 11 Oblige me by doing this | 爲吓我做呢啲喇 | wai ha ngo tso ni-ti la |
| 12 Men wear coats, and women wear petticoats | 男人着長衫, 女人着裙 | nam-yan cheuk ch‘eung-sham, nü-yan cheuk kw‘ăn |
| 13 You should not do that secretly | 你私私啲做唔合理 | ni sze-sze-ti tso ’m hop li |
| 14 You have written all those characters wrong | 你寫錯嗁個啲字咯 | ni se ts‘oh sai ko-ti tsz lok |
| 15 Tell the boy to hold my horse | 叫個事仔牽住我匹馬 | kiu ko sze-tsai hin chü ngo p‘at ma |
| 16 Do they let off fireworks? | 佢哋燒烟火咩 | k‘ü-ti shiu in-foh me? |
| 17 Which (man) arrived first? | 乜誰先到呢 | măt-shui sin to ni? |
| 18 The first who arrived was your brother | 到先嗰個係你嘅兄弟 | to sin ko-ko hai ni ke hing-tai |
| 19 I heard he was the last who arrived | 我聞得佢係至收尾到嘅 | ngo măn tăk k‘ü hai chi shau-mi to ke |

| | | |
|---|---|---|
| 20 Is this rice first or second quality? | 呢啲米係第一等只第二等嘅呢 | ni-ti mai hai tai yat tăng, chi tai i tăng ke ni? |
| 21 Do women wear aprons? | 女人着圍裙嘅咩 | nü-yan cheuk wai-kw'ăn ke me? |
| 22 Chinese women do not; Foreign women wear them | 唐人女人唔着；外國女人着啫 | T'ong-yan nü-yan 'm cheuk; ngoi-kwok nü-yan cheuk che |
| 23 Have you gold buttons on your clothes? | 你嘅衣服有金鈕冇呢 | ni ke i-fuk yau kom nau mo ni? |
| 24 How many sorts of caps are there? | 有幾多樣帽呢 | yau ki to yeung mo ni? |
| 25 Nearly all caps come from Canton (i.e. the provincial city) | 差不多咁多帽都係省城來嘅 | ch'a-pat-to kom to mo to hai Shăng-shing loi ke |
| 26 They are all first quality caps | 一啲帽都係第一等嘅 | yat ti mo to hai tai yat tăng ke |
| 27 The gloves I bought last are the best | 我收尾買個對手笠係至好嘅 | ngo shau-mi mai ko tui shau-lap hai chi ho ke |
| 28 Do they sell Japanese (Yat pun ke) dressing gowns (here)? | 佢地賣日本嘅修飾衫咩 | k'ü-ti mai Yat-pun ke sau-shik-sham me? |
| 29 They sell English handkerchiefs | 佢哋賣英國嘅手巾 | k'ü-ti mai Ying-kwok ke shau-kăn |
| 30 That head-dress is very handsome | 個啲首飾係十分好睇 | ko-ti shau-shik hai shap-făn ho t'ai |
| 31 Does that house leak much? | 嗰間屋好漏嘅咩 | ko kan uk ho lau ke me? |
| 32 It leaks a great deal when it rains | 落雨時就十分漏咯 | lok ü shi tsau shap-făn lau lok |
| 33 Do you think that is useless? | 你估嗰啲係冇用嘅咩 | ni ku ko-ti hai mo yung ke me? |
| 34 It is of no great importance | 唔係十分交關啫 | 'm hai shap-făn kau-kwan che |
| 35 How many sorts of pins have you? | 你有幾多樣嘅大頭針呢 | ni yau ki to yeung ke tai-t'au-chăm ni? |
| 36 I have several in my pocket | 我嘅袋有幾眼啫 | ngo ke toi yau ki ngan che |
| 37 That affair should be quickly finished | 嗰件事應該趕快做完喇 | ko kin-sze ying-koi kon-fai tso ün la |

| | | |
|---|---|---|
| 38 Does your head pain you? | 你嘅頭令你痛咩 | ni-ke t'au ling ni t'ung me? |
| 39 Not very much; but I am unwell | 唔係十分痛啫，但係我唔精神 | 'm hai shap-făn t'ung che; tan hai ngo 'm tsing-shăn |
| 40 You will have to take some medicine | 你要吃葯正做得咯 | ni iu yak yeuk ching tso tăk lok |

# LESSON XLVI.

"*Times*" (or *turns*) is translated by PIN 𠹺 as well as by UI 囘; e.g. *how many times?* KI TO PIN NI 幾多𠹺呢.

*Constantly* is translated by SHEUNG-SHI 常時 or SHI-SHI 時時; e.g. *he constantly does it* K'Ü SHI-SHI TSO 佢時時做.

| | | | | | |
|---|---|---|---|---|---|
| One quarter | 一角 | *yat kok* | One third | 三分有一 | *sam* fan' yau' *yat* |
| | 四分有一 | *sze*' făn' yau' *yat* | Two thirds | 三分有二 | *sam* făn' yau' i' |
| Three quarters | 三角 | *sam kok* | One half | 一半 | *yat pun*' |
| | 四分有三 | *sze*' făn' yau' *sam* | Double | 雙 (contracted to 双) | *sheung* |

TIME.

| | | | | | |
|---|---|---|---|---|---|
| New year's day | 正月初一 | *ching* üt *ch'oh yat* | Quarter of an hour | 點鐘之一角 | *tim chung chi yat kok** |
| The first month of the year | 正月 | *ching* üt | Hour (equal to 2 European hours) | 時辰 | shi-shăn |
| The first day of the month | 初一 | *ch'oh yat* | Afternoon | 下午 | ha'-ng'* |
| | | | Do. | 下晝 | ha'-*chau*' |
| The intercalary month | 閏月 | yun' üt | Forenoon | 上午 | sheung'-ng'* |
| | | | Do. | 上晝 | sheung'-*chau*' |
| Minute | 分時 | *făn* shi | Noon | 正午 | *ching*'-ng'* |
| Do. (bastard word) | 𠺘尼 | *min-ni*' | Do. | 晏晝 | *an*'-*chau*' |

How old are you? (*lit.* your honourable age) 貴庚 *kwai*' *kăng*

How old is he? - 佢有幾多歲呀 k'ü yau' *ki*' *to sui*' *a*?

* These phrases are rather book language than colloquial, but are frequently used.

### Classifiers.

61. *Tim'* 點 a spot or dot, is applied to dots, spots, moments, hours of the clock, etc.

62. *Tam`* 担 to bear, „ burdens, weights of material, &c.

63. Ch'ung 重 to repeat, „ a series or succession of objects.

64. Lat 剌 a row, „ rows or objects, with interstices between them, such as balustrades, trees, &c.

65. *Hou'* 口 a mouth, an opening, „ things with sharp edges, swords, &c.

66. Min` 面 a surface, the face, „ gongs, looking-glasses, banners, &c.

| | | |
|---|---|---|
| We have all kinds of goods | 我哋各樣貨都有 | ngo'-ti *kok* yeung` *foh`* *to* yau' |
| He asks too high a price | 佢要得價高 | k'ü' *iu tăk ka`* *ko* |
| What's the price? | 幾多價錢呢 | *ki'* *to ka`* ts'in *ni*? |
| How much is it worth? | 値得幾多呢 | chik *tăk ki'* *to ni*? |
| What colour? - | 乜野顏色呢 | *măt*-ye' ngan-*shik ni*? |
| All colours | 各樣顏色 | *kok* yeung` ngan-*shik* |
| I can't afford it | 我唔出得 | ngo' 'm *ch'ut tăk* |
| I can't help it - | 我不得已 | ngo' *pat tăk* i' |
| Best quality | 上等嘅 | sheung` *tăng'* *ke`* |
| Middling quality | 中等嘅 | *chung tăng'* *ke`* |
| Low quality | 下等嘅 | ha` *tăng'* *ke`* |
| It won't suit | 唔啱咯 | 'm *ngam lok* |

| | | | | | |
|---|---|---|---|---|---|
| Visiting card case | 拜帖盒 | *pai`-t'ip*-hop | Bell (hand) | 手鐘 | *shau'*-*chung* |
| Snuff-bottle | 鼻烟壺 | pi`-*in*-u | Watch chain | 錶鍊 | *piu*-lin` |
| Snuff-box | 鼻烟盒 | pi`-*in*-hop | Watch key | 錶匙 | *piu*-shi |
| Purse | 腰屏袋 | *iu*-p'ing-toi` | Necktie | 頸帶 | *keng'*-*tai`* |
| Shirt or chemise | 汗衫 | hon`-*sham* | Glass | 玻璃 | *po*-li |
| Rings (finger) | 戒指 | *kai`-chi'* | To put on (said of neckties, and similar small articles) | 攬 | lam` |
| Rings (ear) | 耳環 | i'-wan | | | |
| Thimble | 針頂 | *chăm-ting'* | | | |

1 How many times have you been there? 你去啯處幾多𨈇呀 ni hü ko ch'ü ki to pin a?

2 I go there constantly 我時時去啯處 ngo shi-shi hü ko-ch'ü

3 Did you stay a half day there? 你喺啯處成半日咩 ni hai ko-ch'ü shing pun-yat me?

| | | |
|---|---|---|
| 4 I stay one third of the time at Canton and two thirds at Hongkong | 我在省三分有一咁耐，在香港三分有二咁耐 | ngo tsoi Shăng sam făn yau yat kom noi, tsoi Heung-kong sam făn yau i kom noi |
| 5 Is tomorrow new year's day? | 聽日係年初一咩 | t‘ing-yat hai nin ch‘oh yat me? |
| 6 No, it is the first day of the intercalary month | 唔係，係閏月初一啫 | 'm hai, hai yun üt ch‘oh yat che |
| 7 He came here about noon; and went in the afternoon | 佢上下晏晝來；下午就去曉咯 | k‘ü sheung ha an-chan loi; ha-'ng tsau hü hiu lok |
| 8 What o'clock was it when he came? | 佢來時幾多點鐘呢 | k‘ü loi shi ki to tim chung ni? |
| 9 It was a quarter past two | 係兩點一個角 | hai leung tim yat ko kok |
| 10 There were six rows of trees in the garden | 個花園有六刺樹 | ko fa-ün yau luk lat shü |
| 11 He has a very fine looking-glass | 佢有一個面鏡十分好嘅 | k‘ü yau yat ko min-keng shap-făn ho ke |
| 12 Women wear earrings; men wear finger rings | 女人帶耳環，男人帶戒指 | nü-yan tai i-wan; nam-yan tai kai-chi |
| 13 Put the money in your purse | 擠個啲銀在你嘅腰瓶袋 | chai ko-ti ngan tsoi ni ke iu-p‘ing-toi |
| 14 The needle-woman makes shirts | 個補衫婆做汗衫 | ko po-sham-p‘oh tso hon-sham |
| 15 Do you require spectacles? | 你要帶眼鏡咩 | ni iu tai ngan-keng me? |
| 16 Do Foreigners and Chinese take snuff? | 外國人共唐人都食鼻烟咩 | ngoi-kwok yan kung T‘ong-yan to shik pi-in me? |
| 17 Yes, Foreigners use snuff-boxes; Chinese use snuff bottles | 係，外國人用鼻烟盒，唐人用鼻烟壺 | hai; ngoi-kwok yan yung pi-in-hop; T‘ong-yàn yung pi-in-u |
| 18 Women do not wear neck-ties | 女人唔攬頸帶嘅 | nü-yau 'm lam keng-tai ke |
| 19 Neckties are of all colours | 頸帶有各樣色嘅 | keng-tai yau kok yeung shik ke |
| 20 Did he want to buy a sword? | 佢要買張劍咩 | k‘ü iu mai cheung kim me? |
| 21 No, he wanted to buy all sorts of goods | 唔係，佢要買各樣嘅貨 | 'm hai, k‘ü iu mai kok yeung ke foh |

| | | |
|---|---|---|
| 22 Has that shop best quality goods? | 啯間舖頭有上等嘅貨咩 | ko kan p'o-t'au yau sheung tăng ke foh me? |
| 23 No. It does not sell goods, it is a watchmaker's | 冇, 佢唔賣貨嘅, 係整鏢佬啫 | mo, k'ü 'm mai foh ke, hai ching piu lo che |
| 24 Is your watch-key on your watch-chain? | 你嘅鏢匙喺你嘅鏢鍊嚟咩 | ni ke piu-shi hai ni ke piu-lin lai me? |
| 25 Are these things first or middling quality? | 呢啲野係第一等只中等嘅呢 | ni-ti ye hai tai yat tăng chi chung tăng ke ni? |
| 26 They are all of low quality | 佢哋一啲都係下等嘅 | k'ü-ti yat ti to hai ha tăng ke |
| 27 He has cloth to sell of all colours | 佢有各樣色嘅布出賣 | k'ü yau kok yeung shik ke po ch'ut mai |
| 28 What's the price of that red cloth? | 啯啲紅布乜野價錢呢 | ko-ti hung-po măt-ye ka ts'in ni? |
| 29 He asks a dollar and quarter for that piece | 啯疋佢要一圓零一角 | ko p'at k'ü iu yat ün ling yat kok |
| 30 That is too dear; I can't afford it | 太貴得嚌, 我唔出得 | t'ai kwai tăk tsai; ngo 'm ch'ut tăk |
| 31 How old is your son? | 令郎貴庚呀 | ling-long kwai kăng a? |
| 32 My son is very young: only sixteen years | 小兒十分後生; 十六歲啫 | siu-i shap-făn hau shăng, shap luk sui che |
| 33 I've not seen your father for a whole year | 成年都未曾見過你令尊咯 | shing nin to mi ts'ăng kin kwo ni ling-tsün lok |
| 34 You will see him when he comes this afternoon | 佢今日下晝來, 你就見佢咯 | k'ü kam-yat ha-chau loi, ni tsau kin k'ü lok |
| 35 The price of that is seventy-five dollars | 啯啲要七十五員 | ko-ti iu ts'at shap 'ng un |
| 36 How many times did you ring the bell? | 你撳鐘幾多𠹌呢 | ni ngo chung ki to pin ni? |
| 37 Is that bottle made of glass? | 啯個樽係玻璃整嘅咩 | ko-ko tsun hai po-li ching ke me? |
| 38 How many more times will you come here? | 你重喺呢處幾多𠹌添呀 | ni chung hai ni-ch'ü ki to pin t'im a? |

| | | |
|---|---|---|
| 39 I cannot say, because I don't know | 我唔話得定，因為我唔知得 | ngo 'm wa tăk ting, yan wai ngo 'm chi tăk |
| 40 That sort of cloth won't suit me | 啯樣布唔合我用嘅 | ko yeung po 'm hop ngo yung ke |

---

## LESSON XLVII.

| | | | | | |
|---|---|---|---|---|---|
| What's o'clock? | 幾多點鐘呢 | *ki' to tim'* *chung ni?* | To get in one's light | 遮黑 | *che-hak* |
| | | | I beg pardon | 唔該 | 'm-*koi* |
| Excuse me | 算我唔着 | *sün`* ngo' 'm cheuk | To live at | 住在 | chü`-tsoi |
| | | | To rain | 落雨 | lok ü' |
| One o'clock | 一點鐘 | *yat tim' chung* | Permit me!. | 容我 | yung-ngo' |
| Half past two | 兩點半 | leung' *tim' pun`* | To be mistaken | 錯 | *ts'oh`* |
| To go fast (as a clock) | 行快 | hang *fai`* | To search for | 尋 | ts'ăm |
| To make a mistake | 整錯 | *ching' ts'oh`* | | | |

### Passive verbs.

The passive voice of Chinese verbs may be formed by adding certain particles to the root or infinitive; but most sentences which take a passive form in English are preferentially rendered in Chinese by the active form of the verb, and a corresponding change in the sentence. Thus "*I have been beaten by him*" would be rendered by "*He has beaten me*" 佢打親我 K'Ü TA TS'ĂN NGO. The tendency of Chinese colloquial is towards simplification, and this is aided by the habit of making sentences as short as possible, thus to a great extent dispensing with passive formations, relatives, etc. As the student, however, should be acquainted with the passive voice, an example is given hereunder, the formative particles being in brackets. These formations are not, strictly speaking, colloquial, but are perfectly well understood, and are at times used, by educated Cantonese.

| | | |
|---|---|---|
| I am beaten | 我（被打）親 | ngo' (pi` *ta'*) *ts'ăn* |
| I am hated | 我（被見）惡 | ngo' (pi` *kin`*) *u`* |
| I was beaten - | 我（曾被）打親 | ngo' (ts'ăng pi`) *ta' ts'ăn* |
| I was cheated - | 我（曾被）騙 | ngo' (ts'ăng pi`) *p'in`* |

| | | |
|---|---|---|
| I may be loved | 我(或者見)愛 | ngo' (wak *che' kin*\`) *oi*\` |
| He may be hated | 佢(或者見)惡 | k'ü' (wak *che' kin*\`) *u*\` |
| I might be taught | 我(或者可蒙)教 | ngo' (wak *che' ho'* mung) *kau*\` |
| He might be pitied | 佢(或者可蒙見)憐 | k'ü' (wak *che' ho'* mung) lin |
| If I listen | (若係)我聽 | (yeuk hai\`) ngo' *t'eng* |
| If he teaches - | (若係)佢教 | (yeuk hai\`) k'ü' *kau*\` |
| If we spoke | (若係)我哋(有)講 | (yeuk hai\`) ngo'-ti\` (yau') *kong'* |
| If they exerted themselves | (若係)佢哋(肯)用力 | (yeuk hai\`) k'ü'-ti\` (*hăng'*) yung\` lik |
| Would that he could go! | (願不得)佢去 | (üu\` *pat tăk*) k'ü' *kü*\` ! |

| | | |
|---|---|---|
| None of is it clear (comprehensible) | 冇啲明白嘅 | mo' *ti* ming-pak *ke*\` |
| Just like that | 同啪個一樣 | t'ung *ko'-ko*\` *yat* yeung\` |
| I'm sure of it | 我知眞嘅咯 | ngo' *chi chăn ke*\` *lok* |
| What is it good for? | 做乜使好呀 | tso\` *măt shai' ho' a*? |
| It is neither | 兩個都唔係 | leung' *ko*\` *to* 'm hai\` |
| It cost nine cash | 買曉九個錢 | mai' *hiu kau' ko*\` ts'in |
| Not worth a cash | 唔值一個錢 | 'm chik *yat ko*\` ts'in |
| I had rather | 我寧願—— | ngo' ning-üu\` |
| Not worth so much | 唔值咁多 | 'm chik *kom*\` *to* |
| Commence work to day | 今日開工 | *kăm*-yat *hoi kung* |
| It's the market price - | 係時價 | hai\` shi-*ka*\` |
| She would not allow it | 佢唔准 | k'ü' 'm *chun'* |

| | | | | | |
|---|---|---|---|---|---|
| Castor-stand | 五味架 | 'ng'-mi\`-*ka*\` | Gravy dish | 汁盅 | *chăp-chung* |
| Ladle | 調羹,殼 | t'iu-*kang*, *hok* | Punkah | 風扇 | *fung-shin*\` |
| Table-cloth | 檯布 | t'oi-*po*\` | Cork | 樽枳 | *tsun-chut* |
| Small plate | 碟仔 | tip-*tsai'* | Cupboard | 碗櫃 | *un'*-kwai\` |
| Small knife or penknife | 刀仔 | *to-tsai'* | Bowl | 碗 | *un'* |

| | | |
|---|---|---|
| 1 Did you haug up the punkah? | 你掛起個把風扇未呢 | ni kwa hi ko pa fung-shin mi ni? |
| 2 Tell him to search for those chopsticks | 叫佢尋着個啲快子 | kiu k'ü ts'ăm cheuk ko-ti fai-tsz |

| | | |
|---|---|---|
| 3 He is always getting in my light | 佢常時遮黑我 | k'ü sheung-shi che-hak ngo |
| 4 You make a mistake; it is not worth so much | 你整錯咯;唔値咁多 | ni ching ts'oh lok; 'm chik kom to |
| 5 What do you guess is the market price? | 你估乜野時價呢 | ni ku măt-ye shi ka ni? |
| 6 I think it is two dollars. I may be mistaken | 我估係兩員.或者我錯 | ngo ku hai leung ün. wak che ngo ts'oh |
| 7 That cannot be guessed | 唔估得中嘅 | 'm ku tăk chung ke |
| 8 I had rather go if he wishes it | 若佢中意,我寧願去咯 | yeuk k'ü chung-i ngo ning ün hü lok |
| 9 Did he ask you what's o'clock? | 佢有問你幾多點鐘冇呢 | k'ü yau măn ni ki to tim chung mo ni? |
| 10 He might have asked; I don't remember | 佢或者有問;我唔記得咯 | k'ü wak che yau măn; ngo 'm ki tăk lok |
| 11 He was first cheated, and then beaten | 佢先被人騙,後被打親 | k'ü sin pi yan p'in, hau pi ta ts'ăn |
| 12 If we spoke to him he exerted himself | 若我哋對佢講,佢就用力咯 | yeuk ngo-ti tui k'ü kong, k'ü tsau yung lik lok |
| 13 Did they never live at Hong-kong? | 佢哋冇喺香港住過咩 | k'ü-ti mo hai Heung-kong chü kwo me? |
| 14 Permit me to ask its price | 容我問吓乜野價錢 | yung ngo măn ha măt-ye ka-ts'in |
| 15 If they had exerted themselves they would have finished it | 若係佢哋有用心,就已經做完嘅咯 | yeuk hai k'ü-ti yau yung sam, tsau i-king tso ün ke lok |
| 16 Did it rain here daily in this way? | 呢處日日係噉落雨嘅咩 | ni-ch'ü yat yat hai kom lok ü ke me? |
| 17 It would be a good thing if it did (would that it did!) | 寧可噉做就好喇 | ning ho kom tso tsau ho la |
| 18 Your o'clock goes a great deal too fast | 你嘅鐘行得太快 | ni ke chung hang tăk t'ai fai |
| 19 Is that man hated by people? | 嗰個人被人憎惡咩 | ko-ko yan pi yan tsăng-u me? |
| 20 He might be loved if he were good | 佢若係好嘅或者爲人所愛 | k'ü yeuk hai ho ke wak che wai yan shoh oi |

| | | |
|---|---|---|
| 21 People say he is much to be pitied | 人哋話佢係十分可憐嘅 | yan-ti wa k'ü hai shap-făn ho lin ke |
| 22 He uses a corkscrew to open that bottle | 佢用個酒鑽嚟開嗰個樽 | k'ü yung ko tsau-tsün lai hoi ko-ko tsun |
| 23 Did you put the table cloth on the table? | 你放張檯布在檯上嚟咩 | ni fong cheung t'oi-po tsoi t'oi sheung lai me? |
| 24 Has he get a ladle and a gravy dish? | 佢有個壳共隻汁盅咩 | k'ü yau ko hok kung chek chap-chung me? |
| 25 That small knife of his is not worth a cash | 佢嗰張細刀仔唔值一個錢 | k'ü ko cheung sai to-tsai 'm chik yat ko ts'in |
| 26 If he washed the bowl it would be clean | 若係佢洗過隻碗就乾凈嘅咯 | yeuk hai k'ü sai kwo chek un tsau kon-tsing ke lok |
| 27 They would not allow it to be washed | 佢哋唔肯俾佢洗 | k'ü-ti 'm hăng pi k'ü sai |
| 28 Do you understand the sentences given above? | 上高所寫個啲句語你識得唔呢 | sheung ko shoh se ko-ti kü ü ni shik tăk 'm ni? |
| 29 They are not very clear | 佢哋唔係十分明白 | k'ü-ti 'm hai shap-făn ming-pak |
| 30 Chinese and English people are not quite alike | 唐人共英國人唔係十分相同 | T'ong-yan kung Ying-kwok yan 'm hai shap-făn seung t'ung |
| 31 If yon liked you might be taught | 若係你中意，你或者可蒙教 | yeuk hai ni chung-i, ni wak che ho mung kau |
| 32 If we spoke Chinese daily we should learn quickly | 若係我哋日日講唐話就學得快咯 | yeuk hai ngo-ti yat yat kong T'ong-wa tsau hok tăk fai lok |
| 33 Are you quite sure of what you said? | 你所講嘅；你知得眞唔呢 | ni shoh kong ke; ni chi tăk chan 'm ni? |
| 34 I am sure of it; every body says so | 我知得眞咯；人人都噉話 | ngo chi tăk chăn lok; yan yan to kom wa |
| 35 Excuse me! I think you are mistaken | 筭我唔着喇，我估你錯哩 | sün ngo 'm cheuk la! ngo ku ni ts'oh li |
| 63 Permit me to say you are wrong! | 容我講你唔着喇 | yung ngo kong ni 'm cheuk la |

| | | |
|---|---|---|
| 37 If the teacher says so, it cannot be wrong | 若係先生噉話就冇錯嘅咯 | yeuk hai sin shăng kom wa tsau mo ts'oh ke lok |
| 38 You may not hear rightly what he says | 或者你聽唔眞佢話啫 | wak che ni t'eng 'm chăn k'ü wa che |
| 39 If he speaks plainly we shall understand | 若係佢講得明白我哋就識得咯 | yeuk hai k'ü kong tăk ming-pak ngo-ti tsau shik tăk lok |
| 40 Let us all commence to-day | 等我哋咸嘭唥今日開工 | tăng ngo-ti ham-pang-lan kom-yat hoi kung |

---

# LESSON XLVIII.

The following words are of frequent use with the conditional word.

| | | | | | |
|---|---|---|---|---|---|
| Suppose that | 倘若 | *t'ong'*-yeuk | Unless | 若唔係 | yeuk 'm hai` |
| For instance | 譬如 | *p'i`*-ü | Do. | 除非 | ch'ü *fi* |
| Do. | 設使 | *ch'it-sze'* | Perhaps | 或者 | wak *che'* |
| Possibly | 可以 | *ho'*-i' | If | 若係 | yeuk hai` |
| Do. | 能 | năng | | | |

## Adverbs of Place.

Variations of the renderings given in former lessons will be found in the following list.

| | | | | | |
|---|---|---|---|---|---|
| At what place? | 乜地方 | *măt* ti`-*fong*? | Far, far off | 遠, 遠處 | ün', ün' *ch'ü`* |
| Do. | 何處呢 | ho *ch'ü ni*? | Near | 近, 附近 | kăn`, fu` kăn` |
| Where? | 邊吓呢 | *pin* ha' *ni*? | Abroad | 在外國 | tsoi` ngoi` *kwok* |
| To the right | 在右便 | tsoi` yau` pin` | Outside | 在外出 | tsoi` ngoi` *ch'ut* |
| To the left | 在左便 | tsoi` *tsoh'* pin` | Hither | 在呢處 | tsoi` *ni ch'ü`* |
| Downwards | 在下便 | tsoi` ha` pin` | Whither | 在啯處 | tsoi` *ko' ch'ü`* |
| Backwards | 背後便 | *pui`* hau` pin` | Above | 在上高 | tsoi` sheung` *ko* |
| Behind | 在後便 | tsoi` hau` pin` | Below | 在下底 | tsoi` ha` *tai* |

| | | | | | |
|---|---|---|---|---|---|
| Aside | 在一便 | tsoi` *yat* pin` | Round about | 週圍 | *chau* wai |
| Here | 在呢便 | tsoi` *ni* pin` | Upwards | 在上 | tsoi` sheung` |
| Do. | 在呢處 | tsoi` *ni ch'ü`* | Before | 在前 | tsoi` ts'in |
| Yonder | 在開頭 | tsoi` *hoi* t'au | There 咰處 | 咰處 | *ko'-sh'ü`* |

| | | |
|---|---|---|
| You are very smart | 你好底手嘅 | ni' *ho' tai' shau' ke`* |
| To study (*lit.* read aloud) diligently | 勤力讀書 | k'ăn lik tuk *shü* |
| To exert oneself | 出力做咯 | *ch'ut* lik tso *lok* |
| To shut both eyes | 眯埋雙眼 | *mi* mai *sheung* ngan' |
| Quite harmonious | 一團和氣 | *yat* t'ün woh *hi`* |
| Don't worry me | 咪厭悶我 | mai' *im`* mun` ngo' |
| To sent a messenger | 打發人去 | *ta'-fat* yan *hü`* |
| Pour in a little more oil | 斟的油添 | *chăm ti* yau *t'im* |
| Pour out a little tea | 斟的茶嚟 | *chăm ti* ch'a lai |
| So well dressed | 咁好粧扮 | *kom`* *ho'* *chong*-pan` |
| Dressed like a Chinese | 扮唐人粧 | pan` T'ong-yan *chong* |
| He skipped a page (in reading) | 瀨曉一篇 | lai *hiu yat p'in* |

One advantage of the deficiencies (as Europeans are apt to consider them) of Chinese grammar, is that there is no such thing as an irregular verb, while nouns are "declined," if that term can be used, in a simple and unvarying way. This very simplicity, however, obliges rigid adherence to precise form in framing sentences, and the student will do well to commit every example given to memory.

| | | | | | |
|---|---|---|---|---|---|
| Cheese (a bastard word) | 之時餅 | *chi*-shi-*peng'* | Teacup (large) | 茶盅 | ch'a-*chung* |
| | | | Table napkin | 茶巾 | ch'a-*kăn* |
| Chicken pie | 鷄仔麵龜 | *kai-tsai'*-min-*kwai* | Small waiter | 茶盤 | ch'a-p'un |
| | | | Slop basin | 茶碗 | ch'a-*un'* |
| Tea board (waiter) | 托盆 | *t'ok*-p'un | Tea strainer | 茶漏 | ch'a-lau` |
| Chicken | 鷄仔 | *kai-tsai'* | Tooth pick | 牙簽 | nga-*ts'im* |
| Capon | 𫑋鷄 | *sin`-kai* | Soup ladle | 湯殼 | *t'ong-hok* |
| Crab | 蟹 | hai' | Table mat | 碟墊 | tip-*tsin`* |

| | | |
|---|---|---|
| 1 Where did you send the messenger to? | 你打發個人去邊處呢 | ni ta-fat ko yan hü pin-ch'ü ni? |
| 2 Suppose that he does not return? | 設使佢唔翻嚟呢 | ch'it sze k'ü 'm fan lai ni? |

| | | |
|---|---|---|
| 3 Perhaps, he will not exert himself | 或者佢唔肯出力 | wak che k'ü 'm hang ch'ut lik |
| 4 Unless he studies diligently he will be punished | 若唔係佢勤力讀書，佢就受責罰咯 | yeuk 'm hai k'ü k'ăn-lik tuk shü, k'ü tsau shau chăk-fat lok |
| 5 How can he possibly study? he has no time | 佢点能讀書啫佢冇時候哩 | k'ü tim năng tuk shü che? k'ü mo shi-hau li |
| 6 Tell me, for intance, if he is lazy | 話我知，譬如佢懶惰啞 | wa ngo chi, p'i-ü 'kü lan-to a |
| 7 At what place is his house? | 佢嘅屋在邊處呢 | k'ü ke uk tsoi pin ch'ü ni? |
| 8 First turn to the right, and then to the left | 先轉過右，後轉過左 | sin chün kwo yau, hau chün kwo tsoh |
| 9 Walk round about the town | 嗰個城週圍行過咯 | ko-ko shing chau-wai hang kwo lok |
| 10 Is that a man or a boy yonder? | 在開頭處嗰個係大人只細文仔呢 | tsoi-hoi-t'au ch'ü ko-ko hai tai yan chi sai-măn-tsai ni? |
| 11 I can't see; it is too far off | 我睇唔見；遠得嚌 | ngo t'ai 'm kin; ün tăk tsai |
| 12 Does he live above or below the road? | 佢在路上只路下居住呢 | k'ü tsoi lo sheung chi lo ha kü chü ni? |
| 13 He lives behind the barracks | 佢在兵房後便住 | k'ü tsoi ping-fong hau pin chü |
| 14 Has your father ever been abroad? | 你令尊有出過外冇呢 | ni ling-tsün yau ch'ut kwo ngoi mo ni? |
| 15 Smoke goes upwards; water flows downwards | 烟從上去；水望下流 | in ts'ung sheung hü; shui mong ha lau |
| 16 Had you ever seen him before? | 你從前有見過佢冇呢 | ni ts'ung ts'in yau kin kwo k'ü mo ni? |
| 17 Possibly I have seen him once | 或者我有見過佢都未定 | wak che ngo yau kin kwo k'ü to mi ting |
| 18 Put the table mat on the table | 放塊檯墊在張檯面嚟 | fong fai t'oi-ts'in tsoi cheung t'oi min lai |
| 19 Take care not to break the soup ladle | 子細咪打爛個隻湯壳 | tsz-sai mai ta-lan ko chek t'ong hok |
| 20 Bring the cups here on a tea-board | 俾個托盆拈啲杯嚟呢處 | pi ko t'ok-p'un nim ti pui lai ni-ch'ü |
| 21 Pour the tea into the slop basin | 倒啲茶落個茶碗嚟 | to ti ch'a lok ko ch'a-un lai |
| 22 What is the use of a tooth-pick? | 牙簽做乜用嘅呢 | nga-ts'im tso măt yung ke ni? |

| | | | |
|---|---|---|---|
| 23 | It is used by Chinese to pick the teeth | 唐人用嚟簽牙嘅 | T'ong-yan yung lai ts'im nga ke |
| 24 | What is that? a capon or a chicken | 咺隻係乜野呀，㓾雞只雞仔呢 | ko chek hai măt-ye a? sin kai chi kai-tsai ni? |
| 25 | It is a chicken which I am going to use for a pie | 係雞仔，我將嚟整麪龜嘅 | hai kai tsai, ngo tseung lai ching min-kwai ke |
| 26 | Where are crabs found? | 蟹喺邊處有呢 | hai hai pin-ch'ü yau ni? |
| 27 | They are found at Hongkong sometimes | 香港有時都有 | Heung-kong yau shi to yau |
| 28 | What is the distinction between a *t'ok-pun* and a *ch'a-pun*? | 托盆共茶盆有乜分別呢 | t'ok-p'un kung ch'a-p'un yau măt făn-pit ni? |
| 29 | The one is a large, the other a small waiter | 一個大啲，一個細啲 | yat ko tai ti, yat ko sai ti |
| 30 | Does the coolie put oil in the lamp? | 個管店斟油落個盞燈嚟咩 | ko kun-tim chăm yau lok ko tsan tăng lai me? |
| 31 | He puts oil in it; but he wants a little more | 佢斟油落去咯，但佢要啲添 | k'ü chăm yau lok hü lok, tan k'ü iu ti t'im |
| 32 | One should read books slowly and carefully | 人人讀書要慢慢又要留心正好 | yan yan tuk shü iu man-man yau iu lau-sam ching ho |
| 33 | Is that person well dressed? | 咺個人係好粧扮唔呢 | ko-ko yan hai ho chong-pan 'm ni? |
| 34 | Not so well dressed as we are | 冇我哋咁好粧扮 | mo ngo-ti kom ho chong-pan |
| 35 | Did he skip a page in reading that book? | 佢讀書嚹嘵一篇咩 | k'ü tuk shü lai-hiu yat p'in me? |
| 36 | He skipped several pages | 佢嚹嘵幾篇咁多咯 | k'ü lai-hiu ki p'in kom to lok |
| 37 | Is he dressed like a Chinese or Foreigner? | 佢扮唐人粧只外國人粧呢 | k'ü pan T'ong-yan chong chi ngoi kwok yan chong ni? |
| 38 | He is dressed like an Annamese | 佢打扮好似一個安南人噉樣 | k'ü ta pan ho tsz yat ko On-nam yan kom yeung |
| 39 | Is that place very far off? | 咺處好遠咩 | ko-ch'ü ho ün me? |
| 40 | It is not very far off; It is very near | 唔係十分遠嘅；好近啫 | 'm hai shap-făn ün ke; ho kăn che |

初學階

# LESSON XLIX.

### Adverbs of Place (Continued.)

| | | | | | |
|---|---|---|---|---|---|
| Whence? | 由邊處 | yau *pin-ch'ü'*? | Everywhere | 處處 | *ch'ü' ch'ü'* |
| Thence | 由嗰處 | yau *ko'-ch'ü'* | Anywhere | 各處 | *kok ch'ü'* |
| Hence | 離呢處 | li *ni-ch'ü'* | Inwards | 在內 | tsoi' noi' |
| Nowhere | 冇邊處 | mo' *pin-ch'ü'* | Outwards | 在外 | tsoi'n goi' |

### Classifiers (*continued*)

67. *Tsung* 宗 a matter, is applied to affairs, court cases, business matters, etc. (—of infrequent occurrence.)

68. T'oi 檯 a table, stage, „ plays and theatrical performances.

69. Mi 尾 the tail, „ fishes.

| | | | | | |
|---|---|---|---|---|---|
| To speak Chinese | 講唐話 | *kong'* T'ong-wa' | A radical (of a character) | 字部 | tsz'-po' |
| To trouble one | 煩勞人 | fan lo yan | | 字母 | tsz'-mo' |
| A port clearance | 放行紙 | *fong'*-hang-*chi'* | A steamer | 火船 | *foh'*-shün |
| Meaning (of a word) | 意思 | *i'-sze'* | Climate | 水土 | *shui'-t'o'* |
| Writing | 寫字 | *se'* tsz' | | | |

The student will not have failed to remark the way in which adverbs are formed from nouns, adjectives, and verbs. In some cases the adverbial form is given by repeating the adjective and affixing TI 啲 or KE 嘅; e.g., *slowly* MAN MAN TI 慢慢啲.

### Weights and Measures, 1.

| | | | | | |
|---|---|---|---|---|---|
| 1 Kernel | is | 1 *Shü'* | 黍 | |
| 10 *Shü'* | = | 1 Lui' | 纍 | |
| 10 Lui' | = | 1 *Chü* | 銖 | |
| 24 *Chü* | = | 1 *Leung'* | 兩 | tael (or ounce |
| 10 *Leung'* | = | 1 *Kän* | 斤 | catty (of $1\frac{1}{3}$ lb.) |
| 2 *Kän* | = | 1 Yan' | 引 | of $2\frac{2}{3}$ lb. |
| 30 *Kän* | = | 1 *Kwăn* | 鈞 | of 40 lb. |
| 100 *Kän* | = | 1 Tam' | 担 | picul (of $133\frac{1}{3}$ lb.) |
| 120 *Kän* | = | 1 Shek | 石 | of 166 lb. |

| | | |
|---|---|---|
| But little difference—very much alike | 大同小異 | taiˋ tʻung *siuˊ* iˋ |
| The climate does not suit | 唔服水土 | 'm fuk *shuiˊ-tʻoˊ* |
| I have everything | 乜野都有 | *măt*-yeˊ *to* yauˊ |
| Done all well | 做好晒咯 | tsoˋ *hoˊ saiˋ lok* |

| | | | | | |
|---|---|---|---|---|---|
| Curried fowl | 架喱鷄 | *kaˋ-li-kai* | Beefsteak | 鐵耙牛肉 | *tʻit*-pʻa-ngau-yuk |
| Do. | 黃羌鷄 | wong-*keung-kai* | | | |
| Egg (dove's) | 白鴿蛋 | pak-*kap*-tanˋ | Baked | 局熟 | kuk-shuk |
| Egg (duck's) | 鴨蛋 | *ap*-tanˋ | Boiled | 烚熟 | shap-shuk |
| Egg (hen's) | 鷄蛋 | *kai*-tanˋ | Fired | 煎熟 | *tsin*-shuk |
| Egg (boiled) | 烚蛋 | shap tanˋ | Minced | 免治 | minˊ-chiˋ* |
| Beche de mer | 海參 | *hoi-shăm* | Hashed | 乞食 | *hăt*-shik* |
| Butter | 牛油 | ngau-yau | Do. | 雜膾 | tsap-uiˊ |
| Duck (wild) | 水鴨 | *shuiˊ-ap* | Roasted | 燒 | *shiu* |
| Eel | 鱔魚 | shinˊ-ü | Stewed | 膾 | uiˋ |
| Egg (fired or poached) | 煎蛋 | *tsin* tanˋ | Duck | 鴨 | *ap* |

* Bastard words.

| | | |
|---|---|---|
| Either——or | 或——或 | wak——wak |
| Either this or that | 或呢個或嗰個 | wak *ni koˋ* wak *koˊ koˋ* |
| Neither——nor - | 唔係——又唔係 | 'm haiˋ——yauˋ 'm haiˋ |
| Neither this nor that - | 唔係呢個又唔係嗰個 | 'm haiˋ *ni koˋ* yauˋ 'm haiˋ *koˊ koˋ* |
| To prefer | 寧願 | ning-ünˋ |

| | | |
|---|---|---|
| 1 Is that ship going inwards or outwards? | 嗰隻船出口或入口嘅呢 | ko chek shün chuʻt hau wak yap hau ke ni? |
| 2 I don't think she is going any where | 我估佢處處都唔去 | ngo ku kʻü chʻü-chʻü to 'm hü |
| 3 Whence come all those people? | 咁多人由邊處嚟嘅呢 | kom to yan yau pin-chʻü lai ke ni? |
| 4 I can find those books nowhere | 我冇邊處搵得着嗰啲書 | ngo mo pin-chʻü wan tăk cheuk ko-ti shü |
| 5 It is not your business to look for books | 搵書唔係你嘅事幹 | wăn shü 'm hai ni ke sze-kon |
| 6 I will not trouble you to look for them | 我唔煩勞你搵咯 | ngo 'm fan-lo ni wăn lok |

| | | |
|---|---|---|
| 7 What sort of climate has Canton? | 省城水土點樣呢 | Shăng-shing shui-t'o tim yeung ni? |
| 8 Not very good; the climate does not suit me | 唔係十分好；個水土唔合我嘅 | 'm hai shap-făn ho; ko shui-t'o 'm hop ngo ke |
| 9 The ship goes on the ebb tide, but with a fair wind | 嗰隻船趁水乾時去又遇順風 | ko chek shün ts'ăn shui kon shi hü, yau ü shun fung |
| 10 The Captain of the ship is on deck | 船主在船面嚟 | shün-chü tsoi shün-min lai |
| 11 Has that steamer anchored yet? | 嗰隻火船拋錨未曾呢 | ko chek foh-shün p'au nau mi ts'ăng ni? |
| 12 She will hoist sail as soon as she has her port clearance | 佢一有放行紙就扯哩咯 | k'ü yat yau fong-hang-chi, tsau ch'e li lok |
| 13 Do you speak Chinese? I speak it sometimes | 你噲講唐話咩，我有時都講 | ni ui kong T'ong-wa me? ngo yau shi to kong |
| 14 What is the meaning of that radical? | 嗰個字母係點解呢 | ko-ko tsz-mo hai tim kai ni? |
| 15 Put it in writing for me to make it plain (ming-pak) | 寫落字使我明白 | se lok tsz shai ngo ming-pak |
| 16 Is that your business? | 嗰啲係你嘅工夫咩 | ko-ti hai ni ke kung-fu me? |
| 17 It is not my business; I have to do with plays | 唔係我嘅事，我有份做戲啫 | m' hai ngo ke sze, ngo yau făn tso hi che |
| 18 Are there many fish in that sea? | 嗰個海有好多魚咩 | ko-ko hoi yau ho to ü me? |
| 19 Where does Beche-de-mer come from? | 海參喺邊處來嘅呢 | hoi-shăm hai pin-ch'ü loi ke ni? |
| 20 Are beef-steaks roasted or stewed? | 牛肉鈀係煎嘅或膾嘅呢 | ngau-yuk-p'a hai tsin ke wak ui ke ni? |
| 21 They are always fired | 喊嘭哈都係煎嘅多 | ham-pang-lang to hai tsin ke to |
| 22 Do you like curried fowl or curried duck? | 你中意架哩雞或架哩鴨呢 | ni chung-i ka-li-kai wak ka-li-ap ni? |
| 23 I do not like either, I prefer eggs | 兩樣我都唔中意，我中意蛋啫 | leung yeung ngo to 'm chung-i, ngo chung-i tan che |
| 24 Do you like eggs boiled or poached? | 你中意烚蛋或煎蛋呢 | ni chung-i shap tan wak tsin tan ni? |

| | | | |
|---|---|---|---|
| 25 | I prefer duck's eggs if they are boiled | 若係烚嘅我中意鴨蛋 | yeuk hai shap ke ngo chung-i ap-tan |
| 26 | Did you ever eat salted hen's eggs? | 你有食鹹雞蛋冇呢 | ni yau shik ham kai-tan mo ni? |
| 27 | What are salted eggs? I never heard of them | 鹹蛋係乜野呢，我未曾聞過 | ham tan hai măt-ye ni? ngo mi tsʻăng măn kwo |
| 28 | All Chinese eat salted eggs | 喊嘭唥唐人都食鹹蛋嘅 | ham-pan-lan Tʻong-yan to shik ham-tan ke |
| 29 | I have not seen them anywhere | 我處處都冇見過佢哋 | ngo chʻü-chʻu to mo kin kwo kʻü-ti |
| 30 | Buy me a catty of beef-steaks | 買一斤牛肉鈀過我 | mai yat kăn ngau-yuk-pʻa kwo ngo |
| 31 | Had I not better buy one pound? | 我唔係買一磅咩 | ngo 'm hai mai yat pong me? |
| 32 | Beche-de-mer is sold by the picul | 海參係成担賣嘅 | hoi-shăm hai shing tam mai ke |
| 33 | How many ounces make a catty? | 幾多兩爲一斤呢 | ki to leung wai yat kăn ni? |
| 34 | Sixteen Chinese ounces make one catty | 唐人十六兩爲一斤 | Tʻong-yan shap-luk leung wai yat kăn |
| 35 | How many catties make a picul? | 幾多斤爲一担呢 | ki to kăn wai yat tam ni? |
| 36 | A picul contains one hundred catties | 一担即係一百斤 | yat tam tsik hai yat pak kăn |
| 37 | A *shik*, then, is more than a picul? | 一石多過一担咩 | yat shek to kwo yat tam me? |
| 38 | A *shik* is one hundred and twenty catties | 一石即係一百零二十斤 | yat shek tsik hai yat pak ling i-shap kăn |
| 39 | There is then but little difference between the two? | 兩樣都係唔同嘅咩 | leung yeung to hai 'm tʻung ke me? |
| 40 | There is a difference of twenty catties | 爭二十斤唔同 | chăng i-shap kăn 'm tʻung |

# LESSON L.

### Adverbs and Adverbial Expressions of Present Time.

| | | | | | |
|---|---|---|---|---|---|
| In the morning | 朝頭早 | *chiu*-t'au-*tso'* | To this day | 至到今日 | *chi' to' kăm*-yat |
| At night | 夜晚黑 | ye'-man'-*hak* | Day-time | 日頭 | yat-t'au |
| This morning | 今朝 | *kăm-chiu* | By day | 日間 | yat-*kan* |
| This evening | 今晚 | *kăm*-man' | Now, at present | 如今 | ü-*kăm* |
| To-night | 今夜 | *kăm*-ye' | Now-a-days | 近來 | kăn-loi |
| Mid-night | 半夜 | *pun*-ye' | This time | 呢陳 | *ni*-chăn' |
| By night | 夜間 | ye'-*kan* | | | |

---

| | | |
|---|---|---|
| A processsion | 出遊 | *ch'ut*-yau |
| A tube | 筒 | t'ung |

70. *Pan'* 板 a board, slab, is applied to processions, shallow vessels of wood, &c.
71. *Chü* 株 a trunk, & *Kăn* 根 a root, are ,, trees.
72. *Kun'* 管 a reed, is ,, tubes (chiefly those of bamboo)

A thorough acquaintance with the auxiliary parts of speech, such as adverbs, prepositions, etc., is of the highest importance to the student who would learn to accurately express those shades of meaning implied in English by the tenses of verbs. Copious vocabularies of such words are therefore given in these lessons.

### Measures of Length.

| | | | | | | |
|---|---|---|---|---|---|---|
| 1 *Nap* | 粒 | or grain | = | 1 *Făn* | 分 | or division |
| 10 *Făn* | 分 | | = | 1 *Ts'ün'* | 寸 | or inch |
| 10 *Ts'ün'* | 寸 | | = | 1 *Ch'ek* | 尺 | or foot |
| 10 *Ch'ek* | 尺 | | = | 1 Cheung' | 丈 | or rod |
| 10 Cheung' | 丈 | | = | 1 Yan' | 仞 | of eight cubits |

It will be observed that the decimal system forms the basis both of this and of the preceding table given.

| | | |
|---|---|---|
| What makes you think so? | 爲乜噉想呀 | wai'-*măt kom' seung' a*? |
| I won't be done by you | 唔聽你嚤咯 | 'm *t'eng* ni' *t'am' lok* |
| Not very good | 唔係甚好嘅 | 'm hai' shăm' *ho' ke'* |
| Is that all? | 係咁多咩 | hai' *kom' to me*? |
| Understand all | 明白嗮咯 | ming-pak *sai' lok* |
| No matter what sort | 唔論邊樣 | 'm lun' *pin* yeung' |
| Had it before | 先日有過 | *sin* yat yau *kwo'* |
| I will buy it all | 隴總買嗮 | *lung'-tsung'* mai' *sai'* |
| I've no more | 我冇曉咯 | ngo' mo' *hiu lok* |
| Exactly suits me | 正合我嘅 | *ching* hop ngo' *ke'* |

| | | | | | |
|---|---|---|---|---|---|
| Mutton broth | 羊肉湯 | yeung-yuk-*t'ong* | Cuttle fish | 墨魚 | mak-ü |
| Mutton chops | 羊排骨 | yeung-p'ai-*kwat* | Turtle | 脚魚 | *keuk*-ü |
| Lobster | 龍蝦 | lung-*ha* | Shell-fish | 鮑魚 | *pau*-ü |
| Lard | 猪油 | *chu*-yau | Salted fish | 鹹魚 | ham-ü |
| Goose (wild) | 鴈鵝 | ngan'-ngo | Fins | 魚翅 | ü-*ch'i'* |
| Goose | 鵝 | ngo | Jelly | 凍 | *tung'* |

| | | |
|---|---|---|
| 1 Have you been to his house to-day? | 你今日有去過佢嘅屋冇呢 | ni kăm-yat yau hü kwo k'ü ke uk mo ni? |
| 2 I went there this morning early | 我今朝好早去咯 | ngo kăm-chiu ho tso hü lok |
| 3 Will he come again this evening? | 今晚佢重來唔呢 | kăm-man k'ü chung loi 'm ni? |
| 4 They will all be here to-night | 佢哋喊唪呤今夜來 | k'ü-ti ham-pan-lan kăm ye loi |
| 5 Tell the carpenter to come early in the morning | 吽個木匠佬朝頭早早的來 | kiu ko muk-tseung-lo chiu t'au tso tso ti loi |
| 6 I don't like to be away at night | 我夜晚黑唔中意出去 | ngo ye man hak 'm chung-i ch'ut hü |
| 7 Do you read books in the fore-noon or afternoon? | 你上晝只下晝讀書呢 | ni sheung-chau chi ha-chau tuk shü ni? |
| 8 Twelve o'clock is the same as noon | 十二點鐘即係晏晝咯 | shap-i tim chung tsik hai an-chau lok |
| 9 At midnight people are all asleep | 半夜人人都瞓嗮喇 | pun-ye yan-yan to făn sai la |

| | | |
|---|---|---|
| 10 Things are very dear now-a-days | 近日物件十分貴 | kän-yat mat-kin shap-fān kwai |
| 11 I will not punish him this time | 呢陳我唔責罰佢 | ni chăn ngo 'm chak-fat k'ü |
| 12 That tree is there to this day | 嗰稐樹至到今日都重喺處 | ko p'oh shü chi to kăm-yat to chung hai ch'ü |
| 13 What is the difference between the expression "day-time" and "by day" | 日頭日間兩句話有分乜別呢 | "yat-t'au" "yat-kan" leung kü wa yau mat fān-pit ni? |
| 14 There is very little difference between the expressions | 嗰兩句說話好少分別啫 | ko leung kü shüt-wa ho shiu fān-pit che |
| 15 He does work both by day and by night | 佢日夜都做工夫 | k'ü yat ye to tso kung-fu |
| 16 Is he now working for you? | 佢如今同你做工夫咩 | k'ü ü-kăm t'ung ni tso kung-fu me? |
| 17 How many inches long is that? | 有幾多寸長呢 | yau ki to ts'ün ch'eung ni? |
| 18 It is nearly a foot long | 一尺長差不多 | yat ch'ek ch'eung ch'a-pat-to |
| 19 How many inches go to a foot? | 幾多寸成一尺 | ki to ts'ün shing yat ch'ek? |
| 20 A foot has ten Chinese and twelve foreign inches | 唐人十寸爲一尺；外國人十二寸爲一尺 | T'ong-yau shap ts'ün wai yat ch'ek; ngoi-kwok yau shap i ts'ün wai yat ch'ek |
| 21 Did that comprador buy a fowl and a wild goose? | 嗰個買辦買嘵一隻雞共一隻鴈鵝咩 | ko-ko mai-pan mai hiu yat chek kai kung yat chek ngan-ngo me? |
| 22 No, he only bought lobsters and fish | 冇，佢獨係買得龍蝦共魚啫 | mo, k'ü tuk hai mai tăk lung-ha kung ü che |
| 23 Do you want to buy salt fish or shell fish? | 你要買鹹魚只鮑魚呢 | ni iu mai ham-ü chi pau-ü ni? |
| 24 No matter what sort, but buy some to-day | 唔論邊樣但係今日買嘅 | 'm lun pin yeung tan hai kăm-yat mai ke |
| 25 Did you ever get milk from that man? | 你舊時有同嗰個人買牛奶冇呢 | ni kau-shi yau t'ung ko-ko yan mai ngau-nai mo ni? |
| 26 I got it formerly. I don't get it now-a-days | 我舊日有啫，近日總冇咯 | ngo kau yat yau che, kăn yat tsung mo lok |

| | | |
|---|---|---|
| 27 What I buy is not very good | 我所買嘅邊啲唔係十分好 | ngo shoh mai ke pin ti 'm hai shap-fān ho |
| 28 Did you even taste fish-fin soup? | 你有食過魚翅羹冇呢 | ni yau shik kwo ü-ch'i kang mo ni? |
| 29 No; they only gave me mutton broth | 冇，佢哋獨係俾羊肉湯過我啫 | mo, k'ü-ti tuk hai pi yeung-yuk-t'ong kwo ngo che |
| 30 What did he say when you took that ham? | 你擰個隻火腿時，佢點話呢 | ni ning ko chek foh-t'ui shi, k'ü tim wa ni? |
| 31 He said, "I won't be done by you" | 佢話，我唔俾你噤 | k'ü wa, "ngo 'm pi ni t'ām" |
| 32 What makes you think pigs feet jelly unfit (not good) to eat? | 你爲乜野話猪脚凍唔好食呢 | ni wai-măt-ye wa chü-keuk tung 'm ho shik ni? |
| 33 I think it unfit to eat because it was not made to-day | 我估佢唔好食，因爲唔係今日整嘅 | ngo ku k'ü 'm ho shik, yan-wai 'm hai kăm-yat ching ke |
| 34 Did all those people walk in the procession? | 喊嘭唥咁多人都係出遊嘅咩 | ham-pang-lan kom to yan to hai ch'ut yau ke me? |
| 35 A good many walked; not all of them | 有好多係；但唔係喊嘭唥嘅 | yau ho to hai; tan 'm hai ham-pang-lan ke |
| 36 Bamboo tubes are used for many things | 竹筒用嚟整好多野 | chuk-t'ung yeung lai ching ho to ye |
| 37 They are used to make pens and sticks | 用嚟整筆共鞭竿 | yeung lai ching pat kung pin-kon |
| 38 Does the cook use lard in cooking mutton chops? | 個火頭煎羊排骨用猪油唔呢 | ko foh-t'au tsin yeung-p'ai-kwat yeung chü-yau 'm ni? |
| 39 Tell him I don't like him to use that | 話佢聽我唔中意佢用嗰啲 | wa k'ü t'ing ngo 'm chung-i k'ü yeung ko-ti |
| 40 Ask him why he does not do as he is told? | 問吓佢爲乜事唔照依佢吩咐噉樣做呢 | măn ha k'ü, wai-măt-sze 'm chiu i k'ü făn-fu kom yeung tso ni? |

初學階

# LESSON LI.

Loi 來 frequently conveys the sense of coming *from*; e.g. "*He comes from America*," K'ü HAI FA-K'I LOI KE 佢喺花旗來嘅 (花旗 FA-K'I *lit.* "flower flag" used by metonomy for the United States.)

### Common Adverbs and Adverbial Expressions of Past time.

| | | | | | |
|---|---|---|---|---|---|
| A fortnight ago | 前兩個禮拜 | ts'in leung' ko' lai'-pai' | Last evening | 昨晚 | tsok-man' |
| | | | Last night | 昨夜 | tsok-ye' |
| Last week | 先個禮拜 | sin ko' lai'-pai' | Just now | 正今 | ching'-kám |
| | | | Already | 已經 | i'-king |
| Until now | 至今日 | chi' kăm-yat | Formerly | 前時 | ts'in-shi |
| A short time since | 不久 | păt kau' | Of old | 舊時 | kau-shi |
| The other day | 往日 | wong'-yat | Recently | 近日 | kăn-yat |
| Do. | 先日 | sin-yat | Do. | 近來 | kăn-loi |
| Yesterday | 昨日 | tsok-yat | Day before yesterday | 前日 | ts'in-yat |
| Do. | 往日 | wong'-yat | | | |
| Of late | 近來 | kăn-loi | | | |

---

| | | | | | |
|---|---|---|---|---|---|
| To return home | 返去歸 | fan' hü' kwai | To go fishing (with nets) | 攞魚 | loh' ü |
| To extinguish fire | 打烏火 | ta' u foh' | | | |
| Do. | 整熄火 | ching' sik foh' | To go shooting (birds) | 打雀 | ta' tseuk |
| To draw a tooth | 脫牙 | t'üt nga | | | |
| To lock up | 關埋 | kwan mai | To draw water | 打水 | ta' shui' |
| To abscond | 逃去 | t'o hü' | To fight | 打交 | ta'-kau |
| Do. | 走路 | tsau' lo' | To whip | 鞭打 | pin ta' |
| To contain | 載去 | tsoi' hü' | To turn over | 返轉 | fan' chün' |
| Do. | 載有 | tsoi' yau' | To revive | 翻生 | fan shăng |

| | | |
|---|---|---|
| It's all a lie | 係一片浮言 | hai' yat p'in' fau in |
| Consider the matter well | 細想啲件事 | sai' seung' ko' kin' sze' |
| This would'nt do | 呢件唔啱 | ni kin' 'm ngam |

| | | |
|---|---|---|
| How was it at last? | 到底點樣呢 | to` tai' tim' yeung` ni? |
| Everything is agreeable | 件件都啱 | kin` kin` to ngam |
| Love others as yourself | 愛人如已 | oi' yan ü ki' |
| Afraid it can't be attained | 怕都唔得 | p'a` to 'm tăk |
| Very wet and dirty | 濕濕濇濇 | shăp-shăp nap-nap |
| To throw one's whole heart into | 一片苦心 | yot p'in' fu'-săm |
| Rather indisposed | 唔多舒服 | 'm to shü-fuk |
| It is so | 係噉嘅 | hai` kom' ke` |
| Do. | 有噉嘅 | yau' kom' ke` |
| All sorts | 樣樣 | yeung` yeung` |

| | | | | | |
|---|---|---|---|---|---|
| Anchorage | 拋船地方 | p'au shün ti-fong | Auction (to sell by) | 投賣 | t'au-mai` |
| | | | Do. | 夜冷 | ye`-lang |
| Do. | 埠頭 | fau`-t'au | Arrow | 箭 | tsin` |
| To square an account | 算賬目 | sün` cheung`-muk | To let fly an arrow | 射箭 | she`-tsin` |
| | | | To give alms | 施捨 | shi-she' |
| To cash a cheque | 支銀單 | chi ngăn-tan | Do. | 貧窮 | p'ăn-k'ung |
| Ball (shot) | 彈子 | tan`-tsz' | Alarm | 驚慌 | king-fong |
| To cast cannon balls | 鑄彈子 | chü` tan`-tsz' | Air | 天氣 | t'in-hi` |
| Bachelor | 未娶親 | mi` ts'ui` ts'ăn | Arms | 軍器 | kwăn-hi` |
| Barrel | 琵琶桶 | p'i-p'a-t'ung' | Do. | 器械 | hi`-hai` |
| Battle | 打仗 | ta'-cheung` | Bankruptcy | 報窮 | po`-k'ung |
| To lose a battle | 打輸 | ta'-shü | Baggage | 行李 | hang-li' |
| To win a battle | 打贏 | ta'-yeng | Ant | 蟻 | ngai' |
| Ball (for play) | 毬 | k'au | Yellow ants | 黃蟻 | wong-ngai' |
| To play at ball | 打毬 | ta' k'au | White ants | 白蟻 | pak-ngai' |

| | | |
|---|---|---|
| 1 Has that person come from France? | 咱個人喺佛蘭西國來嘅咩 | ko-ko yan hai Fat-lan-sai kwok loi ke me? |
| 2 He came from France the day before yesterday | 佢前日由佛蘭西國來嘅 | k'ü ts'in-yat yau Fat-lan-sai kwok loi ke |
| 3 Did you see those people recently? | 你近日有見個啲人冇呢 | ni kăn-yat yau kin ko-ti yan mo ni? |
| 4 I have not seen them until now | 我未曾見過佢哋如今正見啫 | ngo mi ts'ăng kin kwo k'ü-ti u-kăm ching kin che |

初學階

| | | |
|---|---|---|
| 5 That poor man was formerly a compradore | 嗰個窮佬前時係做買辦嘅 | ko-ko k'ung-lo t'sin shi hai tso mai-pan ke |
| 6 He used to square all old accounts | 佢往日嘅賬目總算清咯 | k'ü wong-yat ke cheung-muk tsung sün ts'ing lok |
| 7 Have you already had your tooth drawn? | 你有脫去你嘅牙冇呢 | ni yau t'üt hü ni ke nga mo ni? |
| 8 I had it drawn just now, before I went to draw water | 我先脫嘵後正去打水 | ngo sin t'üt hiu hau ching hü ta shui |
| 9 Did he go a-fishing (with nets) last week? | 佢先個禮拜有去攞魚冇呢 | k'ü sin ko lai-pai yau hü loh ü mo ni? |
| 10 He did not go a-fishing; he went shooting | 佢冇去攞魚；去打雀啫 | k'ü mo hü loh ü; hü ta tseuk che |
| 11 Why does that man whip that horse so much? | 爲乜嗰個人鞭打嗰隻馬咁多呢 | wai-măt ko-ko yan pin ta ko chek ma kom to ni? |
| 12 They had a fight and several men were killed | 佢哋打交打死幾個人 | k'ü-ti ta-kau ta sze ki ko yan |
| 13 Did that happen before you returned home? | 嗰啲事幹係你未曾返去歸時做出嚟嘅咩 | ko-ti sze-kon hai ni mi ts'ăng fan hü kwai shi tso ch'ut lai ke me? |
| 14 It happened a short time since;—about a fortnight ago | 先冇幾耐做出嚟—大約前兩個禮拜啫 | sin mo ki noi tso ch'ut loi—tai yeuk ts'in leung ko lai-pai che |
| 15 If you want to revive that man you must give him air | 你想整翻生嗰個人，你要整佢抖氣 | ni seung ching fan-shăng ko-ko yan, ni iu ching k'ü t'au hi |
| 16 Soldiers use arms in battle | 兵人打仗係用軍器嘅 | ping-yan ta cheung hai yung kwăn-hi ke |
| 17 Does that book contain many pages? | 個本書載有好多篇咩 | ko pun shü tsoi yau ho to p'in me? |
| 18 I wish you would have that book bound for me | 我要你釘我嗰本書咯 | ngo iu ni t'eng ngo ko pun shü lok |
| 19 Do you want that done before your return home? | 你想整起嗰啲正返去歸咩 | ni seung ching hi ko-ti ching fan hü kwai me? |

| | | |
|---|---|---|
| 20 Yes; I want to put it in my baggage | 係；我想放在我嘅行李嚟 | hai; ngo seung fong tsoi ngo ke hang-li lai |
| 21 Children play at ball. Men go to auctions | 細紋仔打毬，男人去投賣館 | sai-mān-tsai ta k'au. nam-yan hü t'au-mai-kun |
| 22 Is the ship lying in the anchorage? | 個隻船拋在埠頭嚟咩 | ko chek shün p'au tsoi fau-t'au lai me? |
| 23 What sort of ants are in the house?—white or red ants? | 乜野蟻喺屋嚟呢，白蟻或紅蟻呀 | māt-ye ngai hai uk lai ni? pak-ngai wak hung-ngai a? |
| 24 Formerly we had white ants; but there are none now | 前時有白蟻；如今冇咯 | ts'in-shi yau pak-ngai; ü-kām mo lok |
| 25 Why does not he cash the cheque for me? | 為乜佢唔支啲張銀單過我呢 | wai-māt k'ü 'm chi ko cheung ngān-tan kwo ngo ni? |
| 26 He has gone into bankruptcy and has no money to pay | 佢報曉窮咯，冇錢還債 | k'ü po hiu k'ung lok, mo ts'in wan chai |
| 27 Did you feel much alarm at the fire? | 火燭你十分驚慌咩 | foh-chuk ni shap-fān king-fong me? |
| 28 No, it was quickly extinguished | 唔係；即刻整熄火咯 | 'm hai; tsik-hak ching sik foh lok |
| 29 Does that man come from England? | 啲個人喺英國來嘅咩 | ko-ko yan hai Ying-kwok loi ke me? |
| 30 He come last week and has already gone again | 佢先個禮拜來嘅，如今又去曉咯 | k'ü sin ko lai-pai loi ke, ü-kām yau hü hiu lok |
| 31 People give alms when asked | 人問到時就施捨喇 | yan mān to shi tsau shi-she la |
| 32 Chinese soldiers discharge arrows in battle | 唐兵打仗時射箭 | T'ong-ping ta cheung shi she tsin |
| 33 Tell the boy to go to market and buy some bread | 叫個事仔去街市買的麵包返嚟 | kiu ko sze-tsai hü kai-shi mai ti min-pau fan lai |
| 34 I will consider the matter and let you know | 我想過然後話你知 | ngo seung kwo, in-hau wa ni chi |
| 35 Is every thing as agreeable as before? | 件件事都係好似舊時咁自然咩 | kin-kin sze to hai ho ts'z kau-shi kom tsz-in me? |

| | | |
|---|---|---|
| 36 No; of late they have been rather disinclined to work | 唔係，近日佢哋好似唔多愿做工夫 | 'm hai; kăn yat k'ü-ti ho ts'z 'm to ün tso kung-fu |
| 37 What sort of weather had you last week | 先個禮拜天氣點樣呢 | sin ko lai-pai t'in-hi tim yeung ni? |
| 38 It was very wet and dirty; one could not go out | 十分濕濕湆湆唔出得街 | shap-făn shap-shap nap-nap 'm ch'ut tăk kai |
| 39 I am very sorry to hear it; you must go out now | 我聽聞噉樣十分閉翳；你如今要出去咯 | ngo t'eng măn kom yeung shap-făn pai-ai; ni ü-kăm iu ch'ut hü lok |
| 40 Both English and Chinese have an old saying, "Love others as yourself" | 唐人共外國人都有句古語，愛人如已 | T'ong-yan kung ngoi-kwok yan to yan kü ku-ü, "oi yan ü ki" |

# LESSON LII.

| | | | | | |
|---|---|---|---|---|---|
| To ask too much | 要得太多 | *iu' tăk t'ai' to* | To be sure of anything | 知得眞 | *chi tăk chăn* |
| I can't help it | 我無奈何 | ngo' mo-noi'-ho | To be worth | 値得 | chik *tăk* |
| | | | To afford | 出得 | *ch'ut tăk* |
| Best quality | 至上等 | *chi'* sheung' *tăng'* | To be useless | 冇用 | mo' yeung' |
| Good quality | 上等 | sheung' *tăng'* | To be like | 同樣 | t'ung yeung' |
| Medium quality | 中等 | *chung tăng'* | Market price | 時價 | shi-*ka'* |
| Low quality | 下等 | ha' *tăng'* | Cheap | 平 | p'ing |
| To buy goods | 買貨 | mai' *foh'* | | | |

CLASSIFIERS.

73. *Chan'* 盞 a saucer, is applied to lamps.

74. *Kü'* 句 a stop, an expression, ,, sentences, phrases, &c.

75. *Ting'* 頂 the top, summit, ,, Chinese hats, caps, sedan chairs and other articles with pointed tops.

The foregoing conclude the list of classifiers. Many of them are only occasionally used, while others form unvarying compounds with the words they qualify. A perfect acquaintance with them is invaluable to the foreign speaker of Chinese, their correct application often ensuring comprehension when a mistake is made in the tone of a word.

### MEASURES OF CAPACITY.

| | | | | |
|---|---|---|---|---|
| 1 *Kop* | 合 | = | nearly 1 English gill | |
| 10 *Kop* | 合 | = | 1 *Shing* 升 | or Chinese pint |
| 10 *Shing* | 升 | — | 1 *Tau'* 斗 | or Chinese peck (bushel) |
| 10 *Tau'* | 斗 | — | 1 Shek 石 | or dry & liquid measure of 100 & 120 catties |

| | | |
|---|---|---|
| He owes you how much money? | 佢欠你幾多銀呢 | k'ü *him`* ni' *ki'* *to* ngăn *ni*? |
| The scales are incorrect | 嗰把戥唔準咯 | *ko' pa' tăng'* 'm *chun' lok* |
| Ten dollars a peck - | 十個銀錢一斗 | shap *ko`* ngăn-ts'in *yat tau'* |
| Send it to my house | 送到屋裡去噃 | *sung` to` uk* li' *hü` poh'* |
| Make you out the bill - | 寫貨單過你 | *se' foh`-tan kwo`* ni' |
| Give me a receipt | 寫收單過我 | *se' shau-tan kwo`* ngo' |
| No place to put it | 冇地方放咯 | mo' ti`-*fong fong` lok* |
| Wrap it up | 包起嚟喇 | *pau hi'* lai *la* |
| Weigh the goods | 秤貨 | *ch'ing` foh`* |
| Measure the goods - | 量貨 | leung *foh`* |

| | | | | | |
|---|---|---|---|---|---|
| Cargo | 船貨 | shün-*foh`* | Cards (playing) | 紙牌 | *chi'*-p'ai |
| The ship has a miscellaneous cargo | 船裝雜貨 | shün *chong* tsap-*foh`* | Playing at cards | 打紙牌 | *ta' chi'*-p'ai |
| | | | Cat | 貓 | *miu* |
| Cannon | 大炮 | tai`-*p'au`* | A rat-hunting cat | 捉鼠貓 | *chuk-shü'-miu* |
| A great cannonade | 大炮轟天 | tai`-*p'au` kwăng t'in* | Canal | 運河 | wăn`-ho |
| | | | The canal is shallow | 運河淺 | wăn`-ho *ts'in'* |
| Canvas (sail cloth) | 悝布 | li'-*po`* | | | |
| An awning of canvas | 悝布天遮 | li'-*po` t'in-che* | Grave | 棺材窟 | *kun*-ts'oi-*fat* |
| | | | Do. | 墳墓 | făn-mo` |
| Character, disposition | 皮氣 | p'i-*hi`* | Unsafe | 唔主固 | 'm-*chü'-ku`* |
| A gentle disposition | 心水温良 | *săm-shui' wăn* leung | Favourable wind | 順風 | shun` *fung* |
| | | | Calm | 無風 | mo *fung* |
| Cape (point of land) | 海角 | *hoi'-kok* | Birds | 雀鳥 | *tseuk*-niu' |
| The horizon | 天涯 | *t'in*-ngai | | | |

| | | |
|---|---|---|
| 1 Those goods are not worth the market price | 嗰啲貨照時價唔值咯 | ko-ti foh chiu shi-ka 'm chik lok |
| 2 If of good quality they are very cheap | 若係上等貨就平咯 | yeuk hai sheung tăng foh tsau p'eng lok |
| 3 There is no wind to-day on the sea | 今日海上冇風 | kăm-yat hoi sheung mo fung |
| 4 I should like to go through the canal | 我中意由運河過 | ngo chung-i yau wàn-ho kwo |
| 5 Can you get all the cargo through? | 你可以寄得嘥嗰啲船貨唔呢 | ni ho-i ki tăk sai ko-ti shün-foh 'm ni? |
| 6 Will you take the canvas down? | 你肯放低啲悝布唔呢 | ni hàng fong tai ti li-po 'm ni? |
| 7 Have you been to my house? | 你去過我間屋未曾呢 | ni hü kwo ngo kan uk mi ts'ăng ni? |
| 8 No; I went to the grave | 冇，我去墳墓嚟啫 | mo, ngo hü făn-mo lai che |
| 9 Did you ever play cards? | 你有打過紙牌冇呢 | ni yau ta kwo chi-p'ai mo ni? |
| 10 Yes, but I do not shoot birds | 有，但係我冇打雀 | yau, tan hai ngo mo ta tseuk |
| 11 There is a large cannon in that ship | 嗰隻船有口大炮 | ko chek shün yau hau tai p'au |
| 12 Weigh all the cargo, and tell me how much it is | 秤過嘥个的貨話我知幾多 | ch'ing kwo sai ko ti foh wa ngo chi ki to |
| 13 Do not cheat me; I won't have it | 唔好騙我嬏；我唔要噉嘅 | 'm ho p'in ngo poh; ngo 'm iu kom ke |
| 14 Measure everything that he has bought | 佢買嚟嗰啲野，你量過嘥正好 | k'ü mai lai ko-ti ye, ni leung kwo sai ching ho |
| 15 My cat is very small but very clever | 我嘅貓好細但好伶俐 | ngo ke mau ho sai, tan ho ling-li |
| 16 Pick her up and show her to me | 拾起佢俾我睇吓 | shap hi k'ü pi ngo t'ai ha |
| 17 I'm afraid she is not strong (in health) | 我怕佢唔係十分好身子 | ngo p'a k'ü 'm hai shap-făn ho shăn-tsz |
| 18 I hear he has a very bad disposition | 我聞得佢十分唔好皮氣 | ngo măn tăk k'ü shap-făn 'm ho p'i-hi |

| | | |
|---|---|---|
| 19 He did not give the receipt to me very quietly | 佢唔係靜靜俾收單過我嘅 | k'ü 'm hai tsing-tsing pi shau-tan kwo ngo ke |
| 20 Did you ask him if the scales were correct? | 你有問佢嗰啲秤係準嘅唔呢 | ni yau măn k'ü ko-ti ch'ing hai chun ke 'm ni? |
| 21 I had no time to ask everything | 我唔得閒逐件問過咯 | ngo 'm tăk han chuk kin măn kwo lok |
| 22 What is the quality of that cloth? | 嗰啲布係屬邊等嘅呢 | ko-ti po hai shuk pin tăng ke ni? |
| 23 I cannot tell for certain; I think it is first quality | 我唔話得實; 我估係上等嘅 | ngo 'm wa tăk shat; ngo ku hai sheung tăng ke |
| 24 Have you seen the Gunboat? | 你有見過嗰隻砲船冇呢 | ni yau kin kwo ko chek p'au-shün mo ni? |
| 25 I have seen the sea several times | 我見過大海幾次咯 | ngo kin kwo tai hoi ki ts'z lok |
| 26 Does your cat hunt rats? | 你嘅貓捉老鼠唔呢 | ni ke mau chuk lo-shü 'm ni? |
| 27 No, she is afraid to hunt them | 唔捉, 佢怕捉佢哋嘅 | 'm chuk, k'ü p'a chuk k'ü-ti ke |
| 28 I am going away; it is useless to bring goods | 我就去咯, 送貨嚟唔中用嘅喇 | ngo tsau hü lok, sung foh lai 'm chung-yung ke la |
| 29 That is of no importance; you had better bring them | 冇緊要, 你帶埋去喇 | mo kăn iu; ni tai mai hü la |
| 30 But I have no money to buy anything with! | 但係我冇銀買野呀 | tan hai ngo mo ngăn mai ye a |
| 31 You can go to my house and stay there | 你可以去我嘅屋居住 | ni ho-i hü ngo ke uk kü-chü |
| 32 I am going to sail to-morrow or next day | 我明日或後日就開身咯 | ngo ming-yat wak hau-yat tsau hoi shăn lok |
| 33 Are you sure it is in the cemetery (yăm shing)? | 你知得眞喺個陰城裡便咩 | ni chi tăk chăn hai ko yăm-shing li pin me? |
| 34 That bird is very like a fowl | 嗰隻雀十分似一隻雞 | ko chek tseuk shap-făn ts'z yat chek kai |
| 35 That boat is very unsafe | 嗰隻艇十分唔主固 | ko che t'eng shap-făn 'm chü-ku |

| | | |
|---|---|---|
| 36 I cannot afford so much; the price is too dear | 我唔出得咁多錢,價錢太貴 | ngo 'm ch'ut tăk kom to ts'in; ka-ts'in t'ai kwai |
| 37 (It is only) three dollars a bushel | 三個銀錢一斗啫 | sam ko ngăn-ts'in yat tau che |
| 38 Did the compradore go away to worship the graves? | 啲個買辦去曉拜山咩 | ko-ko mai-pan hü hiu pai shan me? |
| 39 I don't know? I think he went last month | 我唔知;我估佢先個月去嘅咯 | ngo 'm chi; ngo ku k'ü sin ko üt hü ke lok |
| 40 Why are you always so very lazy? | 爲乜野你時時咁懶惰呢 | wai-măt-ye ni shi-shi kom lan-to ni? |

---

# LESSON LIII.

## Adverbs and Adverbial Expressions of Future Time.

*When* is rendered by SHI 時 *time*, preceded by the sign of the possessive CHI 之, if used in a positive sense, and preceded by KI 幾 *how much, how many*, when used interrogatively.

| | | |
|---|---|---|
| e.g. When they were going out | 佢哋去街之時 | k'ü'-ti' *hü*' *kai chi* shi |
| When are you coming back? | 你幾時翻來呢 | ni' *ki*' shi *fan* loi *ni*? |

*Whenever* is expressed by the sentence MO LUN KI SHI 無論幾時 (lit. no matter what time.)

| | | | | | |
|---|---|---|---|---|---|
| As soon as | 有咁快 | yau' *kom*'-*fai*' | Early to-morrow | 明早 | ming-*tso*' |
| | 得咁快 | *tăk kom*'-*fai*' | Betime, early | 早時 | *tso*'-shi |
| A week hence | 後一個 | hau' *yat ko*' | Afterwards | 將來 | *tseung*-loi |
| | 禮拜 | lai'-*pai*' | Thereafter | 後來 | hau'-loi |
| Henceforward | 自後 | tsz'-hau' | By and by | 慢慢 | man'-man' |
| Alternately | 輪流 | lun-lau | | | |

Many of the above expressions have several equivalents, but they are not given, as it is better not to burden the student's memory with too many words at a time. A reference to the vocabulary at the end of the book will frequently furnish synonyms, or a native teacher can readily supply them if desired; but some caution must be observed in accepting all phrases from such a source, many teachers using book sentences to an undue extent.

The phrase "*as soon as*" is often expressed by an idiom very similar to one found in English; e.g. "*As soon as he heard it he went*" is, literally, "one hear, then (he) went." YAT T'ENG TSAU HÜ 一聽就去. The English phrase "*one blow, and all was over*" embodies a similar elision, answering as it does to "(as soon as) *one blow* (had been struck) *all was over*."

| | | |
|---|---|---|
| What's the whole amount? | 共計幾多呢 | kung` *kai`* *ki'* *to ni?* |
| Returned not long ago | 返來冇耐啫 | *fan'* loi mo' noi` *che* |
| To respect paper that has been written on | 敬惜字紙 | *king`* *sik* tsz`-*chi'* |
| Difficult to distinguish gems and stones | 玉石難分 | yuk shek nau *făn* |
| No fixed time | 冇乜定期 | mo' *măt* ting` k'i |
| I don't require you | 我唔使你 | ngo' 'm *shai* ni' |
| Don't ask so many questions | 咪問咁多 | mai' măn *kom`* *to* |
| He has not come back | 佢未翻來 | k'ü' mi' *fan* loi |
| Don't let people pass | 咪俾人行 | mai' *pi'* yan hang |
| He is well informed | 佢好博覽 | k'ü' *ho'* *pok*-lam' |
| Be careful of fire | 小心火燭 | *siu'* *săm* *foh'*-*chuk* |
| He likes to cheat | 佢好阨騙 | k'ü' *ho`* *ngak*-*p'in`* |
| Has undeserved celebrity (lit. has a reputation but without reality) | 有名無實 | yau' ming mo shat |

| | | |
|---|---|---|
| To converse about pleasant old times | 相叙舊好 | *seung* tsü` kau`-*ho'* |
| Compass (mariner's) | 指南針 | *chi'*-nam-*chăm* |
| Do. | 羅經 | lo-*kăng* |
| Class of men | 人類 | yan-lui` |
| There are many classes of men | 人類衆多 | yan-lui` *chung`* *to* |
| Country | 地方 | ti`-*fong* |
| An out-of-the-way place | 偏僻地方 | *p'in*-*p'ik*-ti`-*fong* |

| | | |
|---|---|---|
| Conversation | 講說話 | *kong'* *shüt*-wa` |
| Do. | 叙談 | tsü`-t'am |
| Chop (merchandise) | 字號 | tsz`-ho` |
| To assault a city | 攻城 | *kung* shing |
| Commerce | 貿易 | mau`-yik |
| Courage | 好胆 | *ho'*-*tam'* |
| East | 東 | *tung* |
| South | 南 | nam |
| West | 西 | *sai* |
| North | 北 | *pak* |

| | | | | | |
|---|---|---|---|---|---|
| Cold | 寒凍 | hon-*tung*` | North-East | 東北 | *tung-pak* |
| Cold weather | 天時寒凍 | *t'in*-shi hon-*tung*` | North-West | 西北 | *sai-pak* |
| To weave cotton cloth | 織綿花布 | *chik* min-*fa*-*po*` | South-East | 東南 | *tung*-nam |
| Great merchants | 大商賈 | tai` *sheung-ku*' | South-West | 西南 | *sai*-nam |
| | | | Cloud | 雲 | wăn |

| | | |
|---|---|---|
| 1 It will be very cold to-morrow | 明日好冷 | ming-yat ho lăng |
| 2 Tell me whenever you go to the city | 無論幾時你去城就話我知 | mo lun ki shi ni hü shing tsau wa ngo chi |
| 3 When did he kill that cockroach? | 佢幾時打死嗰隻曱甴呢 | k'ü ki shi ta sze ko chek kat-tsat ni? |
| 4 He killed it when he was going out | 佢出街嗰時打死佢嘅 | k'ü ch'ut kai ko shi ta sze k'ü ke |
| 5 It has been a very cold season | 有一季天時十分冷 | yau yat kwai t'in-shi shap-fău lăng |
| 6 Finish your conversation as soon as you can | 有咁快得咁快好講完你嘅說話喇 | yau kom fai tăk kom fai ho kong ün ni ke shüt-wa la |
| 7 We will finish it immediately if we can | 若可以做得我哋即刻就做完咯 | yeuk ho i tso tăk ngo-ti tsik hak tsau tso ün lok |
| 8 How much cotton have you bought lately? | 你近日買嘵幾多棉花呢 | ni kăn-yat mai liu ki to min-fa ni? |
| 9 I have bought none; I shall buy some a week hence | 我冇買到；歇一個禮拜添我就買啲 | ngo mo mai to; hit yat ko lai-pai t'im ngo tsau mai ti |
| 10 To-morrow will be Sunday, therefore no business will be done | 明日係禮拜日，所以唔做工夫 | ming-yat hai lai-pai yat, shoh-i 'm tso kung-fu |
| 11 He will cheat you if possible | 佢阨得你過就阨你咯 | k'ü ngak tăk ni kwo tsau ngak ni lok |
| 12 I shall go to the city by and by | 我將來慢慢去城 | ngo tseung-loi man-man hü shing |
| 13 He visits his friends alternately | 佢輪流探佢嘅朋友 | k'ü lun-lau t'am k'ü ke p'ang-yau |

| | | |
|---|---|---|
| 14 The clouds are very dark to-day | 今日嗰的雲十分黑 | kăm-yat ko-ti wăn shap-făn hak |
| 15 That is because the wind is from the north | 因爲嗰啲風由北邊吹來 | yan wai ko-ti fung yau pak-pin ch‘ui loi |
| 16 I shall go away immediately | 我卽刻就去咯 | ngo tsik hak tsau hü lok |
| 17 They are a very bad class of men | 佢哋係一班十分唔好嘅人 | k‘ü-ti hai yat pan shap-făn 'm ho ke yan |
| 18 The country is very beautiful | 嗰的地方係十分華美 | ko-ti ti-fong hai shap-făn wa-mi |
| 19 It is a place seldom visited | 嗰處地方係冇乜人到嘅 | ko-ch‘ü ti-fong hai mo măt yan to ke |
| 20 Whenever you go let me know | 無論你幾時去就話我知喇 | mo lun ni ki shi hü tsau wa ngo chi la |
| 21 Henceforward I shall go at no fixed time | 自今以後我冇定期去 | tsz-kăm i-hau ngo mo ting k‘i hü |
| 22 Did you require it afterwards? | 你後來要用咩 | ni hau-loi iu yung me? |
| 23 He intends to return early to-morrow | 佢想聽朝早返來 | k‘ü seung t‘ing-chiu-tso fan loi |
| 24 As soon as he saw him he struck him | 佢一見佢就打佢咯 | k‘ü yat kin k‘ü tsau ta k‘ü lok |
| 25 Do you steer the boat by the compass? | 你用羅經嚟駛嗰隻船咩 | ni yung lo-kăng lai shai ko chek shün me? |
| 26 Yes; I am steering north-west | 係，我向西北駛去 | hai; ngo heung sai-pak shai hü |
| 27 What cargo has that ship on board? | 嗰隻船載有乜貨物呢 | ko chek shün tsoi yau măt foh-mat ni? |
| 28 She has a cargo of cotton and goods | 佢有棉花共貨物 | k‘ü yau min-fa kung foh-mat |
| 29 Did you always pay the market price? | 你常時都係照時價俾咩 | ni sheung-shi to hai chiu shi-ka pi me? |
| 30 No; I could not afford it always | 唔係，我時常唔出得咁多錢 | 'm hai, ngo shi-sheung 'm ch‘ut tăk kom to ts‘in |
| 31 How much does he owe you already? | 佢已經欠你幾多錢呢 | k‘ü i king him ni ki to ts‘in ni? |

| | | | |
|---|---|---|---|
| 32 | The soldiers will assault the city the day after to-morrow | 啯啲兵後日就攻城 | ko-ti ping hau-yat tsau kung shing |
| 33 | What do those great merchants buy and sell? | 啯的大商賈買賣乜野呢 | ko-ti tai sheung-ku mai mai măt-ye ni? |
| 34 | They constantly buy and sell chops of tea | 佢哋時時買賣幾號茶 | k'ü-ti shi-shi mai mai ki ho ch'a |
| 35 | The business of merchants is commerce | 生意人嘅事幹就係貿易喇 | shăng-i yan ke sze-kon tsau hai mau-yik la |
| 36 | Where do they weave cotton cloth? | 佢哋喺邊處織棉布呢 | k'ü-ti hai pin-ch'ü chik min-po ni? |
| 37 | They weave it in the neighbourhood of Canton | 佢哋喺省城左近織嘅 | k'ü-ti hai Shăng-shing tsoh kăn chik ke |
| 38 | What is the whole amount he owes you? | 佢總共欠你幾多呢 | k'ü tsung kung him ni ki to ni? |
| 39 | Is he fond of reading books? | 佢中意讀書咩 | k'ü chung-i tuk shü me? |
| 40 | Yes; he is an extremely well-informed man | 係, 佢係一個極博學嘅人 | hai, k'ü hai yat ko kik pok-hok ke yan |

# LESSON LIV.

### Adverbs and Adverbial Expressions of Number and Order.

The word CH'O 初 *to begin, commence,* enters into certain combinations expressing "*first*" and is specially used with the first ten numbers of a series, such as the days of the month etc.; e.g., CH'O YAT 初一 *the first,* CH'O I 初二 *the second*; CH'O KIN 初見 *the first interview.*

ÜN 元 *original,* is also used for the first day, month, year, &c.: ÜN-TAN 元旦 *new year's day.*

| | | | | | |
|---|---|---|---|---|---|
| Every other day | 每第二日 | mui' tai' i' yat | Firstly | 一來 | *yat* loi |
| | | | Secondly | 二來 | i' loi |

| | | | | | |
|---|---|---|---|---|---|
| Every other day | 間日 | *kan*\` yat | Several times | 幾囘 | *ki*′ ui |
| Once | 一吓 | *yat* ha′ | The last, end | 收尾 | *shau*-mi′ |
| Once more | 多一吓 | *to yat* ha′ | One by one | 一一 | *yat yat* |
| Many times | 好多囘 | *ho*′ *to* ui | Every day | 每日 | mui′ yat |
| Ten times | 十吓 | shap ha′ | Again | 又,再 | yau\`, *tsoi*\` |
| In order (arranged) | 次序 | *ts*‘z\`-tsü\` | Collectively | 合同 | hop t‘ung |
| Turn and turn (by turns) | 輪流 | lun-lau | Do. | 同埋 | t‘ung mai |
| | | | Thereupou | 就 | tsau\` |

| | | |
|---|---|---|
| The first born son | 寵子,長子 | *ch*‘*ung*′-*tsz*′, *cheung*′-*tsz*′ |
| At most; at least | 至多;至少 | *chi*\` *to*; *chi*\` *shiu*′ |
| To talk at random | 亂講 | lün\`-*kong*′ |

TIMES.

| | | |
|---|---|---|
| A period of ten days | 一旬 | *yat* ts‘un |
| Three decades (=1 month) | 三旬 | *sam* ts‘un |
| Within ten days | 旬內 | ts‘un noi\` |
| More than ten days | 旬外 | ts‘un ngoi\` |
| An intercalary month | 閏月 | yun\`-üt |
| A watch (of two hours) | 一更 | *yat kăng* |

| | | |
|---|---|---|
| He is very attentive | 佢十分用心 | k‘ü shap-*făn* yung\` *săm* |
| See if they agree | 睇吓對唔對 | *tai*′ ha′ *tui*\` 'm *tui*\` |
| Extremely beautiful | 十分華美 | shap-*făn* wa-mi′ |
| Can't believe it | 心唔信得 | *săm* 'm *sun*′ *tăk* |
| Tie the string tight | 綁緊的繩 | *pong*′ *kăn*′ *ti* shing |
| Can't get it back | 唔攞得番 | 'm *loh*′ *tak* *fan* |
| Brougbt it very far | 好遠担來 | *ho*′ ün′ *tam* loi |
| Only several hundred | 不過幾百 | *pat kwo*\` *ki*′ *pak* |
| More than 100,000 | 十多萬 | shap *to* man\` |

| | | | | | |
|---|---|---|---|---|---|
| Eclipse (solar) | 日蝕 | yat-shik | To burn fire-works | 燒烟火 | *shiu in-foh*′ |
| There is an eclipse ("*lit.* the Heavenly dog devours the sun") | 天狗食日 | *t*‘*in-kau*′ shik yat | Duty (Custom-house) | 餉銀 | *heung*′-ngăn |

| | | | | | |
|---|---|---|---|---|---|
| Lunar eclipse | 月蝕 | üt-shik | To pay duties | 納餉銀 | nap *heung'*-ngăn |
| There is a lunar eclipse | 天狗食月 | *t'in-kau'* shik üt | Elephant | 象 | tseung` |
| | | | Ivory ball | 象牙毬 | tseung`-nga-k'au |
| Enemy | 仇敵 | ch'au-tik | Evidence | 口供 | *hau'-kung* |
| To resist an enemy | 抵擋仇敵 | *tai' tong'* ch'au-tik | Famine | 饑荒 | *ki-fong* |
| | | | Dust | 泥塵 | nai-ch'ăn |
| Ferry boat | 橫水渡 | wang-*shui'*-to` | A family or clan | 宅 | chak |
| The landing place of a ferry | 橫水渡頭 | wang-*shui'*-to` t'au | To agree with (as testimony) | 符 | fu |
| The price of grain is rising | 穀米騰貴 | *kuk* mai' t'ang *kwai`* | Field | 田 | t'in |
| | | | To weed a field | 耘田 | wăn t'in |
| Emoluments (official) | 養廉，養廉銀 | yeung'-lim, yeung'-lim-ngăn | Fire | 火 | *foh'* |

| | | | |
|---|---|---|---|
| 1 | To-morrow will be the first day of the Month | 明日係初一 | ming-yat hai ch'o yat |
| 2 | Then to-day is the last of this month | 今日就係呢個月收尾嘅日 | kăm-yat tsau hai ni-ko üt shau-mi ke yat |
| 3 | Have you seen him only once? | 你獨係見過佢一次咩 | ni tuk hai kin kwo k'ü yat ts'z me? |
| 4 | I have seen him very many times | 我見過佢好多次咯 | ngo kin kwo k'ü ho to ts'z lok |
| 5 | You are talking at random; he only came to-day | 你亂講嘅；佢今日正來過啫 | ni lün kong ke; k'ü kăm-yat ching loi kwo che |
| 6 | At most you can only have seen him once | 你至多見過佢一次啫 | ni chi to kin kwo k'ü yat ts'z che |
| 7 | What did they do when they came? | 佢哋來嗰時做乜野呢 | kü-ti loi ko shi tso măt-ye ni? |
| 8 | Firstly they came here to see you; and secondly they went to the city to buy things | 一來佢哋來呢處探你，二來佢哋去城買野 | yat loi k'ü-ti loi ni-ch'ü t'am ni; i loi k'ü-ti hü shing mai ye |
| 9 | Do you only pay Customs duties once? | 你獨係納餉一次咩 | ni tuk hai nap heung yat ts'z me? |

| | | |
|---|---|---|
| 10 No: they have to be paid several times | 唔係，要納幾次嘅 | 'm hai, iu nap ki ts'z ke |
| 11 What do you go there for every day? | 你日日去嗰處做乜野呢 | ni yat-yat hü ko-ch'ü tso măt-ye ni? |
| 12 I go to my family every other day | 我間日翻去我嘅住家 | ngo kan-yat fan hü ngo ke chü-ka |
| 13 That flower garden is extremely beautiful | 嗰個花園十分華美 | ko-ko fa-ün shap-făn wa-mi |
| 14 Are these the things you want? | 呢啲係你要嘅野咩 | ni-ti hai ni iu ke ye me? |
| 15 This is the first, and the others follow in order | 呢啲係第一，其餘照次序跟住喇 | ni-ti hai tai yat, k'i ü chiu ts'z-tsü kăn chü la |
| 16 Those men are working turn and turn about | 嗰啲人輪流做工夫 | ko-ti yan lun-lau tso kung-fu |
| 17 There is a great deal of dust to-day | 今日好多泥塵 | kăm-yat ho to nai-ch'ăn |
| 18 What is the price of those fireworks collectively? | 嗰啲烟火共埋幾多錢呢 | ko-ti in-foh kung mai ki to ts'in ni? |
| 19 Do you want to let off fireworks to night? | 今晚你中意燒烟火咩 | kăm-man ni chung-i shiu in-foh me? |
| 20 The boat has gone to the landing place | 嗰隻艇埋嘵渡頭咯 | ko chek t'eng mai hiu to-t'au lok |
| 21 The women are weeding the fields | 嗰啲女人耘田 | ko-ti nü-yan wăn t'in |
| 22 Do they fear famine? | 佢哋怕饑荒唔呢 | k'ü-ti p'a ki-fong 'm ni? |
| 23 Have you ever seen a solar eclipse? | 你有見過日蝕冇呢 | ni yau kin kwo yat-shik mo ni? |
| 24 No, there was a lunar eclipse last month | 冇，先個月月蝕啫 | mo, sin ko üt üt-shik che |
| 25 Those balls are all made of ivory | 嗰啲毬係象牙整嘅 | ko-ti k'au hai tseung-nga ching ke |
| 26 The emoluments were not sufficient; he thereupon left | 廉俸唔够；所以佢去咯 | lim-fung 'm kau; shoh-i k'ü hü lok |
| 27 I hope he will come back again | 我望佢翻來 | ngo mong k'ü fan loi |

| | | |
|---|---|---|
| 28 Was there any evidence against that man ? | 有乜口供証㖭個人有呢 | yau măt hau-kung ching ko-ko yan mo ni? |
| 29 The Lü family gave evidence against him | 呂宅嚟供佢 | Lü chak lai kung k'ü |
| 30 Did what they said agree? | 佢哋所講嘅符合唔呢 | k'ü-ti shoh kong ke fu-hop 'm ni? |
| 31 He buys it for his first-born son | 佢買嚟俾佢嘅長子嘅 | k'ü mai lai pi k'ü ke cheung-tsz ke |
| 32 I can't believe it; they are bad men | 我唔信得, 佢哋係唔好人 | ngo 'm sun tăk ; k'ü-ti hai 'm ho yan |
| 33 I wish he wouldn't ring that bell | 我恨不得佢唔打㖭個鐘 | ngo hăn pat tăk k'ü 'm ta ko-ko chung |
| 34 It is rung every other day at this time | 間日係呢個時候打嘅 | kan-yat hai ni-ko shi-hau ta ke |
| 35 Have you been playing at cards with them? | 你有同佢哋打紙牌有呢 | ni yau t'ung k'ü-ti ta chi-p'ai mo ni? |
| 36 Yes, and I have lost money | 有, 我輸嘵錢咯 | yau, ngo shü hiu ts'in lok |
| 37 You are writing a very long sentence | 你寫一句好長嘅喇 | ni se yat kü ho ch'eung ke la |
| 38 Are you going to Peking once again? | 你又想去北京一次添咩 | ni yau seung hü Pak-king yat ts'z t'im me? |
| 39 I may go and I may not | 我或去又或唔去 | ngo wak hü yau wak 'm hü |
| 40 He said a good deal about sickness and so forth | 佢講好多話病云云 | k'ü kong ho to wa peng wăn wăn |

---

# LESSON LV.

## Adverbs of Quality

| | | | | | |
|---|---|---|---|---|---|
| More | 多啲 | *to ti* | Suddenly | 忽然 | *fat*-in |
| Very much | 十分多 | shap-*făn to* | Generally | 大概 | tai`-*k'oi*` |
| Do. | 好多 | *ho' to* | Do. | 常時 | sheung-shi |

| | | | | | |
|---|---|---|---|---|---|
| As much as | 咁多 | *kom*` *to* | Accidentally | 偶然 | ngau'-in |
| Not right | 唔着 | 'm cheuk | Extremely | 得嚌 | *tăk*-tsai` (affix) |
| Otherwise | 別樣 | pit yeung` | Do. | 極 | kik |
| Willingly | 甘心 | *kom-săm* | Scarcely | 僅 | *kăn'* |
| Peaceably | 平安 | p'ing-*on* | Rather | 頗 | *p'oh'* |
| Nearly | 將近 | *tseung*-kăn` | Only | 獨 | tuk |

| | | |
|---|---|---|
| So far: so near | 咁遠，咁近 | *kom*` ün; *kom*` kăn` |
| I came by land | 我打路來 | ngo' *ta'* lo' loi |
| I came in a ship | 我搭船來 | ngo' *tap* shün loi |
| Perhaps it is not | 或者唔係 | wak *che'* 'm hai` |
| Do it gradually | 漸漸做 | tsim` tsim` tso` |
| You are making money | 你如今發財咯 | ni' ü-*kăm fat*-ts'oi *lok* |
| I can't distinguish them | 我唔分得開 | ngo' 'm *făn tăk hoi* |
| That agrees best | 嗰個至合式 | *ko'-ko*` *chi*` hop *shik* |
| Don't you feel ashamed? | 你唔見醜咩 | ni' 'm *kin*` *ch'au'* *me*? |
| Do the whole again | 一總做過咯 | *yat tsung'* tso` *kwo*` *lok* |
| Don't be so violent | 好唔咁躁暴 | 'm *ho' kom*` *ts'o*`-po` |
| Whose fault is it? | 乜誰嘅錯呢 | *măt*-shui *ke*` *ts'oh*` *ni*? |
| He desires too much | 佢愛多得嚌 | k'ü *oi*` *to tăk* tsai` |
| Don't be so hasty | 唔好咁頻㕭 | 'm *ho' kom*` p'ăn-lăn |
| Paid all debts | 還清債咯 | wan *ts'ing chai*` *lok* |
| Obtain great profits | 賺得重咯 | chan` *tăk* ch'ung' *lok* |
| I'm sorry to trouble you | 我唔該你 | ngo' 'm *koi* ni' |
| It is too large | 係大過頭 | hai` tai` *kwo*` t'au |
| I think so too | 我都噉想 | ngo' *to kom' seung'* |
| A very little | 的咁多 | *tik kom*` *to* |

| | | | | | |
|---|---|---|---|---|---|
| A mender of crockery-ware | 補花碗佬 | *po-fa-un'*-*lo'* | Scent | 花露水 | *fa*-lo`-*shui'* |
| | | | Crape | 縐紗 | *tsau*`-*sha* |
| A pressing crowd | 好逼人 | *ho' pik* yan | Crockery | 磁器 | ts'*z-hi*` |
| Dollar | 一員銀 | *yat* ün ngăn | Dew | 露水 | lo`-*shui'* |
| ,, Spanish | 呂宋銀 | Lü'-*sung*` ngăn | Dancing | 跳舞 | *t'iu*` mo' |
| ,, Mexican | 鷹銀 | *ying*-ngăn | Darkness | 暗 | *om*` |
| ,, Ferdinand | 勾銀 | *kau*-ngăn | Death | 死 | *sze'* |

初學階

| | | | | | |
|---|---|---|---|---|---|
| ¾ of a dollar | 五錢四 | ng‵ ts‘in sze‵ | Hunting dog | 獵狗 | lip-*kau′* |
| ½ ,, | 三錢六 | *sam* ts‘in luk | Deer | 鹿 | luk |
| ¼ ,, | 錢八 | ts‘in *pat* | A crowd | 堆 | *tui* |

| | | |
|---|---|---|
| 1 When did you find it out? | 你幾時尋出嘅呢 | ni ki shi ts‘ăm ch‘ut ke ni? |
| 2 I have not yet paid all my debts | 我未曾還清債 | ngo mi ts‘ăng wan ts‘ing chai |
| 3 I would willingly do it over again | 我甘心再做過 | ngo kom-săm tsoi tso kwo |
| 4 I must not be so violent | 我唔着咁躁暴 | ngo ’m cheuk kom ts‘o-po |
| 5 If I could only make some money I would pay you | 若係我賺得啲錢我就還你咯 | yeuk hai ngo chan tăk ti ts‘in, ngo tsau wan ni lok |
| 6 It is always very little that I can do | 我時時都係做得的咁多啫 | ngo shi-shi to hai tso tăk tik kom to che |
| 7 It is as much as it cost when new | 新時至多都係值得咁多錢啫 | săn shi chi to to hai chik tăk kom to ts‘in che |
| 8 It is more than I would pay | 多過我所愿出嘅咯 | to kwo ngo shoh ün ch‘ut ke lok |
| 9 I very much regret not having seen you before | 我可惜唔曾見過你 | ngo ho-sik ’m ts‘ăng kin kwo ni |
| 10 It is only a quarter to five | 爭個骨五点啫 | chăng ko kwat ng tim che |
| 11 They would rather I did not go | 佢哋寧愿我唔去重好 | k‘ü-ti ning-ün ngo ’m hü chung ho |
| 12 He is certain to be there | 佢實係在個處嘅咯 | k‘ü shat hai tsoi ko-ch‘ü ke lok |
| 13 When will it be finished? | 幾時正做得完呢 | ki shi ching tso tăk ün ni? |
| 14 There is not nearly enough for dinner | 未有來得够做大餐啲 | mi yau loi tăk kau tso tai ts‘an chi |
| 15 Do you think he will come peaceably? | 你估佢係平安來唔呢 | ni ku k‘ü hai p‘ing-on loi ’m ni? |
| 16 I can scarcely tell; he is generally good tempered | 我都難話, 佢時常係好品性嘅 | ngo to nan wa; k‘ü shi-sheung hai ho păn-sing ke |
| 17 There has been extremely bad weather all this month | 呢個月天時全係唔好嘅 | ni ko üt t‘in-shi ts‘ün hai ’m ho ke |
| 18 He cannot row very well | 佢唔係十分噲棹 | k‘ü ’m hai shap-făn ui chau |

| | | |
|---|---|---|
| 19 Will you come? Otherwise I shall go away | 你來唔呀，唔係我就去咯 | ni loi 'm a? 'm hai ngo tsau hü lok |
| 20 He must have died very suddenly | 佢是必係忽然死嘅咯 | k'ü shi-pit hai fat-in sze ke lok |
| 21 His horse fell down quite accidentally | 佢嘅馬偶然間跌倒嘅 | k'ü ke ma ngau-in-kan tit to ke |
| 22 Those people generally go by land | 嗰啲人時常打路去嘅多 | ko-ti yan shi-sheung ta lo hü ke to |
| 23 It is very well done, it is worth three dollars (Mexican) | 整得十分好，値得三個鷹銀 | ching tăk shap-făn ho, chik tăk sam ko ying-ngăn |
| 24 He always wants to gain a great deal of money | 佢時時都要賺好多銀 | k'ü shi-shi to iu chan ho to ngăn |
| 25 That is why he came by land | 因係噉佢打路來 | yan hai kom k'ü ta lo loi |
| 26 That is not your fault, you came in a ship | 唔係你嘅錯過，你搭船來嘅 | 'm hai ni ke ts'oh kwo, ni tap shün loi ke |
| 27 If you come to stay you must not be violent | 若係你來住唔好作惡蟠 | yeuk hai ni loi chü 'm ho tsok ok poh |
| 28 I shall finish this gradually after dinner | 吃完大餐我就漸漸做完佢 | yak ün tai ts'an ngo tsau tsim-tsim tso ün k'ü |
| 29 If you were not so violent you would do it better | 若你唔係咁躁暴，是必做得好啲 | yeuk ni 'm hai kom ts'o-po, shi-pit tso tăk ho ti |
| 30 Perhaps it will not be so bad by and by | 或者慢慢冇咁[口兮] | wak che man-man mo kom yai |
| 31 When are you going over it again? | 你幾時再做過呀 | ni ki shi tsoi tso kwo a? (a somewhat slang expression) |
| 32 I think I shall do it when I have plenty of time | 我有大把時候時正做 | ngo yau tai pa shi-hau shi ching tso |
| 33 The crape long coat was not always worn by him | 個件縐紗長衫佢唔係時時着嘅 | ko kin tsau-sha ch'eung-sham k'ü 'm hai shi-shi cheuk ke |
| 34 His uncle died very suddenly | 佢嘅亞叔忽然間就死嘅 | k'ü ke a shuk fat-in-kan tsau sze ke |
| 35 That crockery was very nicely coloured | 嗰啲磁器十分好色澤 | ko-ti ts'z-hi shap-făn ho shik-chak |

初學階

| | | |
|---|---|---|
| 36 There was a very large crowd to see it | 好逼人去睇 | ho pik yan hü t'ai |
| 37 He says there is no danger of fire | 佢話啯處唔怕火燭 | k'ü wa ko-ch'ü 'm p'a foh-chuk |
| 38 It is very dark, I cannot see the dog | 十分黑,我唔睇得見啯隻狗 | shap-făn hak, ngo 'm t'ai tăk kiu ko chek kau |
| 39 They had been to see the dancing | 佢哋去睇過人哋跳舞咯 | k'ü-ti hü t'ai kwo yan-ti t'iu-mo lok |
| 40 Have you heard of that person's death? | 你有聞得啯個人死嘵冇呢 | ni yau măn tăk ko-ko yan sze hiu mo ni? |
| 41 Do Chinese use scent? | 唐人用花露水唔呢 | T'ong-yan yung fa-lo-shui 'm ni? |
| 42 They generally do not use such a scent (water) | 佢哋平日唔多用啯啲噉嘅香水 | k'ü-ti p'ing-yat 'm to yung ko-ti kom ke heung-shui |

## LESSON LVI.

| | | | | | |
|---|---|---|---|---|---|
| Future events | 未來嘅事 | mi` loi *ke`* sze` | Unitedly | 合埋 | hop-mai |
| Neighbouring | 隔籬 | *kak*-li | Lastly | 收尾 | *shau*-mi' |
| Separately | 隔開 | *kak-hoi* | Confusedly | 亂 | lün` |

Intensity of assertion is conveyed by the use of such words as CHI 至, TAI 大, HOH 可, TS'IT 切, MAN 萬, KÜT 决, TSUNG 總, HAM 噉, CHĂN 眞, PIT 必, &c., with PAT 不 or MO 冇 for the negation; e.g., *most decidedly not* 决然唔係 KÜT IN 'M HAI; *I really cannot do it* 我眞係唔做得 NGO CHĂN HAI 'M TSO TĂK; *he will certainly come* 佢是必來 K'Ü SHI-PIT LOI; *he is surely mad* 佢眞正係顚 K'Ü CHĂN CHING HAI TIN.

| | | | | | |
|---|---|---|---|---|---|
| A circle | 一個圈 | *yat ko` hün* | Memory | 記性 | *ki`-sing`* |
| One-eyed | 單眼嘅 | *tan*-ngan` *ke`* | Fault | 錯 | *ts'oh`* |

| | | | | | |
|---|---|---|---|---|---|
| Powder (medicine) | 藥散 | yeuk-*san*' | To pronounce (as a tone) | 話聲 | wa'-*sheng* |
| Arrange (to) | 整齊 | *ching*'-ts'ai | Stroke (of a character) | 畫 | wak |
| Moonlight | 月光 | üt-*kwong* | Deep | 深 | *shăm* |
| Headache | 頭痛 | t'au-*t'ung*' | Tone | 音 | *yăm* |
| To turn over (as the leaves of a book) | 翻轉 | *fan-chün*' | | | |

Ke 嘅, answers to "=ed" in cases where nouns are used as adjectives to qualify other nouns; e.g., *is that a one-eyed man?* 佢係單眼嘅唔係呢. K'Ü HAI TAN-NGAN KE 'M HAI NI?

| | | |
|---|---|---|
| Whose turn is it to read? | 輪到邊個讀呢 | lun *to*' *pin ko*' tuk *ni*? |
| I cannot lift it | 我唔搾得起 | ngo' 'm *ning tăk hi*' |
| It must be true | 必定係眞嘅 | *pit* ting' hai' *chăn ke*' |
| You talk too much | 你講多得嚌 | ni' *kong*' *to tăk* tsai' |
| As hard as stone | 好似石咁硬 | *ho*' ts'z' shek *kom*' ngang' |
| Has it the same tone? | 同音唔同呢 | t'ung *yăm* 'm t'ung *ni*? |
| I don't feel very well | 我唔多自然 | ngo' 'm *to* tsz-in |
| How many strokes has it? | 有幾多畫呢 | yau' *ki*' *to* wak *ni*? |
| Arrange those books | 整齊個啲書 | *ching*' ts'ai *ko*'-*ti shü* |
| It will certainly be advantageous | 是必有益嘅 | shi'-*pit* yau' *yik ke* |
| Take (eat) this powder | 食呢啲藥散 | shik *ni-ti* yeuk-*san*' |
| Do you feel giddy? | 有頭暈冇呢 | yau' t'au-wăn mo' *ni*? |
| He is deaf | 佢係耳聾嘅 | k'ü hai' i'-lung *ke*' |
| He died of small pox | 佢出痘死嘅 | k'ü' *ch'ut* tau' *sze*' *ke*' |
| I am considerably better (*lit.* I am more than half cured) | 好翻大半喇 | *ho*' *fan* tai' *pun*' *la* |

| | | | | | |
|---|---|---|---|---|---|
| Gunpowder | 火藥 | *foh*'-yeuk | Heavens | 天, 天堂 | *t'in*, *t'in*-t'ong |
| To make gunpowder | 整火藥 | *ching*' *foh*'-yeuk | Landlord (of a shop) | 舖主 | *p'o*'-*chü*' |
| Law | 律法 | lut-*fat* | Landlord (of a house) | 屋主 | *uk-chü*' |
| To keep the law | 守律法 | *shau*' lut-*fat* | Gratitude | 知恩 | *chi yăn* |
| Leisure | 閒暇 | han-ha' | Catalogue | 張單 | *cheung-tan* |
| Do. | 閒時候 | han-shi-hau' | | | |
| Gauze (watered) | 響雲紗 | *heung*'-wăn-*sha* | | | |

| | | | | | |
|---|---|---|---|---|---|
| Thermomoter | 寒暑針 | hon-*shü'-chăm* | Flagstaff | 旗杆 | k'i-*kon* |
| Freight (cost of) | 水脚銀 | *shui'-keuk*-ngăn | Ivory | 象牙 | tseung'-nga |
| Glue | 牛皮膠 | ngau-p'i-*kau* | Intimate | 心腹 | *săm-fuk* |
| To draw up a list | 開列 | *hoi* lit | Landing place (wharf) | 渡頭 | to'-t'au |
| Lackered ware | 漆器 | *ts'at-hi'* | | | |
| Fire-crackers | 爆像 | *pau*-tseung' | Light (the) | 光 | *kwong* |
| Grass-cloth | 夏布 | ha'-*po'* | Handle | 柄 | *ping'* |
| Goat | 草羊 | *ts'o'*-yeung | Frost | 霜 | *seung* |
| Do. | 山羊 | *shan*-yeung | Fog | 霧 | mo' |
| Flea | 狗虱 | *kau'-shat* | Grass | 草 | *ts'o'* |
| Fly | 烏蠅 | *u*-ying | Heat | 熱 | it |

| | | |
|---|---|---|
| 1 What flag is that on the high flagstaff? | 啲枝高旗杆頂嘅旗係乜野旗呢 | ko chi ko k'i-kon teng ke k'i hai măt-ye k'i ni? |
| 2 There are certainly some flowers in that garden now | 啲個花園現時是必有花 | ko-ko fa-ün in-shi shi-pit yau fa |
| 3 The Chinese are very fond of fire-crackers | 唐人好中意爆像 | T'ong-yan ho chung-i pau-tseung |
| 4 Yesterday there was frost and now there is a fog | 昨日有霜, 如今有霧 | tsok-yat yau seung, ü-kăm yau mo |
| 5 When the heat comes there will be flies and fleas | 天時熱, 就有烏蠅共狗虱 | t'in-shi it, tsau yau u-ying kung kau-shat |
| 6 Those flowers in the grass are very beautiful | 草內個啲花十分精緻 | ts'o noi ko-ti fa shap-făn tsing-chi |
| 7 I want some glue to use for this chair | 我要的牛皮膠嚟整呢張椅 | ngo iu tik ngau-p'i-kau lai ching ni cheung i |
| 8 My friend is the landlord of a large garden | 我嘅朋友係啲一間大花園嘅主人 | ngo ke p'ang-yau hai ko yat kan tai fa-ün ke chü-yan |
| 9 What amount of freight does that ship earn? | 啲隻船載貨有幾多水脚銀呢 | ko chek shün tsoi foh yau ki to shui-keuk ngăn ni? |
| 10 She will most likely bring ivory and lackered-ware | 大槪載好多象牙共漆器 | tai-k'oi tsoi ho to tseung-nga kung ts'at-hi |
| 11 Bring me a light; I want to see the landing place (wharf) | 拈個火嚟我, 我要睇吓渡頭 | nim ko foh lai ngo; ngo iu t'ai ha to-t'au |

| | | |
|---|---|---|
| 12 What kind of gauze is that? | 個啲係乜野紗呢 | ko-ti hai măt-ye sha ni? |
| 13 The sky is (Heavens are) very light | 天十分光 | t'in shap-făn kwong |
| 14 That man has a large amount of gratitude | 嗰個人好知恩嘅 | ko-ko yan ho chi yan ke |
| 15 I shall go out shooting when I have leisure | 我得閒時就去打雀 | ngo tăk han shi, tsau hü ta tseuk |
| 16 Have you any gunpowder here with you? | 你呢處有火藥冇呢 | ni ni-ch'ü yau foh-yeuk mo ni? |
| 17 Who was that touched the handle of the door? | 乜誰摩嗰個門柄呢 | măt-shui mo ko-ko mun-ping ni? |
| 18 This grass-cloth is very good | 呢啲夏布十分好 | ni-ti ha-po shap-făn ho |
| 19 When will you get that thermometer? | 你幾時正攞得嗰枝寒暑針呢 | ni ki shi ching loh tăk ko chi hon-shü-chăm ni? |
| 20 I do not know; I cannot tell you | 我唔知得,唔話得你知 | ngo 'm chi tăk; 'm wa tăk ni chi |
| 21 How do you expect the list will be arranged? | 你估嗰張單點樣開列呢 | ni ku ko cheung tan tim yeung hoi lit ni? |
| 22 You have written that separately | 你分開寫嗰啲 | ni făn hoi se ko-ti |
| 23 You would have done it better unitedly | 你應該合埋做好啲呀 | ni ying-koi hop-mai tso ho ti a |
| 24 Of late it was done very confusedly | 近日整得好亂 | kăn-yat ching tăk ho lün |
| 25 What tone did he say it in? | 佢講乜野聲音呢 | k'ü kong măt-ye sheng-yăm ni? |
| 26 I entirely forget; I have a bad memory | 我總忘記晒咯,我唔好記性 | ngo tsung mong-ki sai lok, ngo 'm ho ki-sing |
| 27 How many strokes were there in the character? | 嗰個字有幾多畫呢 | ko-ko tsz yau ki to wak ni? |
| 28 I only saw it by moonlight | 我獨係月光時睇見 | ngo tuk hai yüt-kwong shi t'ai kin |
| 29 Is that pool of water deep or shallow | 嗰個塘嘅水深或淺呢 | ko-ko t'ong ke shui shăm wak ts'in ni? |

| | | |
|---|---|---|
| 30 That man is one-eyed, but it is not his fault | 嗰個人係單眼嘅，但唔係佢嘅錯 | ko-ko yan hai tan-ngan ke, tan 'm hai k'ü ke ts'oh |
| 31 When did you turn over the leaves of that book? | 你幾時翻轉個本書頁呀 | ni ki shi fan-chün ko pun shü-ip a? |
| 32 I really do not remember when I saw it | 我眞唔記得幾時見過 | ngo chăn 'm ki tăk ki shi kin kwo |
| 33 That man is very deaf | 嗰個人耳十分聾 | ko-ko yan i shap-fān lung |
| 34 When were you last not very well? | 你先邊幾時唔多自然呀 | ni sin pin ki shi 'm to tsz-in a? |
| 35 About nine months ago when I had small pox | 大約九個月前我出痘嗰時 | tai-yeuk kau ko üt ts'in ngo ch'ut tau ko shi |
| 36 What time is it by the clock now? | 如今個鐘幾多點呢 | ü-kăm ko chung ki to tim ni? |
| 37 I much wish the time would not go so quickly | 我眞正想時候咪去咁快 | ngo chăn ching seung shi-hau mai hü kom fai |
| 38 I think it is not yet twelve o'clock | 我估未有十二點咍 | ngo ku mi yau shap-i tim chi |
| 39 There are six flags up now on the flagstaff | 如今旗杆頂有六枝旗 | ü-kăm k'i-kon ting yau luk chi k'i |
| 40 They will presently fire some gunpowder | 佢哋就燒啲火藥咯 | k'ü-ti tsau shiu ti foh-yeuk lok |

# LESSON LVII.

## PREPOSITIONS.

| | | | | | |
|---|---|---|---|---|---|
| About (just going to) | 將 | *tseung* | Besides | 另外 | ling' ngoi' |
| About (concerning) | 及 | k'ap | Do. | 而且 | i-*ch'e* |
| About (nearly) | 上吓 | sheung'-*ha'* | Amongst } | 中間 | *chung-kan* |
| Across | 橫，過 | wang, *kwo'* | Amidst } | 中 | *chung* |
| Below | 下便 | ha'-pin' | Beyond | 格外 | *kak*-ngoi' |

| | | | | | |
|---|---|---|---|---|---|
| According to | 照依 | *chiu`-i* | After (*lit.* to fallow) | 跟 | *kăn* |
| At present | 現在 | in`-tsoi | Against | 逆 | ngak |
| At home | 在家 | tsoi` *ka* | Beyond | 過 | *kwoh* |

| | | |
|---|---|---|
| By what means? | 用乜法呢 | yung` *măt fat ni*? |
| To sell by the catty | 論斤賣 | lun` *kăn* mai` |

### Itinerary Measures.

| | | | | | | |
|---|---|---|---|---|---|---|
| Half a *ts'ün`* | 寸 | or inch | = | 1 | 釐 | li |
| 5 *ts'ün`* | 寸 | | = | 1 | 分 | *făn* |
| 5 *ch'ek* | 尺 | | = | 1 | 步 | po`, or *pace* |
| 368 po` | 步 | | = | 1 | 里 | li' or Chinese mile |
| 3 li' | 里 | | = | 1 | | *English mile* (nearly) |
| 10 li' | 里 | | = | 1 | 塘汛 | t'ong-*sun`* or *league* |
| 250 li' | 里 | | = | 1 | 度 | to`, or *degree* |

The fullest information on the weights and measures of China will be found in William's *Commercial Guide* p. 278 *et seqq.*

| | | |
|---|---|---|
| Don't soak the brush (pencil) so much | 咪點咁淰嗰枝筆 | mai' *tim' kom`* nam *ko' chi păt* |
| A friend gave it to me - | 朋友送過我嘅 | p'ang-yau' *sung` kwo`* ngo' *ke`* |
| Not sufficient room - - | 地方唔够使 | ti`-*fong* 'm *kau` shai'* |
| Wounded many people - | 打傷好多人 | *ta' sheung ho' to* yan |
| It is about to rain | 上吓有雨落 | sheung`-*ha'* yau' ü' lok |
| Roll up that painting | 捲埋嗰幅畫 | *kün'* mai *ko' fuk* wa` |
| Fold up the picture | 摺埋嗰幅畫 | *chip* mai *ko' fuk* wa` |
| Bring warm water for washing | 俾煖水嚟洗 | *pi'* nün-*shui'* lai *sai'* |
| He is very affable - - | 佢係好相與 | k'ü' hai` *ho' seung*-ü' |
| There was a fire last night - | 昨晚有火燭 | tsok-man' yau' *foh'-chuk* |
| To-night I want a coverlet - | 今晚要唫被 | *kăm*-man' *iu` k'ăm'*-p'i' |
| Worthless articles (utensils) - | 唔成器皿 | 'm shing *hi`*-ming' |

| | | | | | |
|---|---|---|---|---|---|
| Port clearance | 船放行紙 | shün *fong`*-hang-*chi'* | To stick up a placard | 出標紅 | *ch'ut piu*-hung |
| Opium pipe | 鴉片烟筒 | *a-p'in`-in* t'ung | To play (at a theatre) | 做戲 | tso` *hi`* |
| Mother of pearl | 雲母殼 | wăn-mo'-*hok* | To play (make music) | 造樂 | tso` ngok |
| Money changer | 找錢佬 | *chau'*-ts'in-*lo'* | | | |

| | | |
|---|---|---|
| To mark goods | 落暗號 | lok *om*\`-ho\` |
| Revolver (pistol) | 六口連 | luk-*hau*'-liu |
| Muslin | 袈裟布 | *ka-sha-po*\` |
| A muster (pattern) | 樣子 | yeung\`-*tsz*' |
| Do. | 辦 | pan\` |
| Oar | 槳 | *tseung*' |
| To pull the oars | 棹槳 | chau\` *tseung*' |
| Fowling piece | 鳥鎗 | niu'-*ts'eung* |
| Marriage | 嫁娶 | *ka*\` *ts'ü*\` |
| Trade | 生意 | *shăng-i*\` |
| Pistol | 手鎗 | *shau*'-*ts'eung* |
| An ignoramus | 山佬 | *shan-lo*' |
| Do. | 山毒 | *shan*-tuk |
| Placard | 標紅 | *piu*-hung |
| Do. | 街招 | *kai-chiu* |
| To make verses | 吟詩 | yăm *shi* |
| Politeness | 禮貌 | lai'-mau\` |
| Do. (rules of) | 禮數 | lai'-*sho*\` |
| Mud fort | 坭城 | nai-shing |
| Ocean | 洋海 | yeung-*hoi*' |
| Mouse | 石鼠 | shek-*shü*' |
| Bat | 飛鼠 | *fi-shü*' |
| Postage | 信資 | *sun*\`-*tsz* |
| Monkey | 馬溜 | ma'-*lau* |
| Do. (a slang term) | 亞三 | *a*\`-*sam* |
| Mosquito | 蚊 | *măn* |
| Poetry | 詩 | *shi* |
| Poison | 毒 | tuk |
| Net | 網 | mong' |

| | | | |
|---|---|---|---|
| 1 | I hear that there is a monkey at that place | 我聞得嗰處有隻馬溜 | ngo măn tăk ko-ch'ü yau chek ma-lau |
| 2 | About how much will it cost to feed it? | 大約要幾多錢正養得佢呢 | tai yeuk iu ki to ts'in ching yeung tăk k'ü ni? |
| 3 | Will you go to see it? | 你去睇嗰啲咩 | ni hü t'ai ko-ti me? |
| 4 | That will be according to the weather | 照依天時嚟湊 | chiu-i t'in-shi lai ts'au |
| 5 | Do you know whether you will be at home? | 你知到你在屋裡嚟唔呀 | ni chi to ni tsoi uk li lai 'm a? |
| 6 | I shall be for the present; besides, I cannot miss the music | 現時在，而且我失嗰啲樂音唔好 | in-shi tsoi; i-ch'e ngo shat ko-ti ngok-yăm 'm ho |
| 7 | I want to write to him because of the mistake | 我要寫信過佢因爲嗰啲錯處 | ngo iu se sun kwo k'ü yan-wai ko-ti ts'oh ch'ü |
| 8 | You must not let the mud get on your clothes | 你唔好俾啲泥整親你嘅衫 | ni 'm ho pi ti nai ching ts'ăn ni ke sham |
| 9 | Send a muster of these goods to my house | 寄呢的貨辦去我嘅屋嚟 | ki ni-ti foh-pan hü ngo ke uk lai |

| | | |
|---|---|---|
| 10 The moon is behind the mountaius | 個月在嗰個山後便嚟 | ko üt tsoi ko-ko shan hau-pin lai |
| 11 What is that writing below the private mark? | 嗰個暗號下底寫乜野字嚟呢 | ko-ko om-ho ha-tai se măt-ye tsz lai ni? |
| 12 That remark might have been without meaning | 或者嗰句係冇乜意思嘅 | wak-che ko kü hai mo măt i-sz ke |
| 13 The Chinese do a good deal of money-changing | 唐人好多做找換嘅生意 | T'ong-yan ho to tso chau-un ke shăng-i |
| 14 The moon is always bright just now | 呢陣時個月常時係好光 | ni-chăn shi ko üt sheung-shi hai ho kwong |
| 15 The mosquitos are very trouble-some; I must use a net | 個啲蚊係十分煩擾,我要用個網 | ko-ti măn hai shap-făn fan-iu; ngo iu yung ko mong |
| 16 England is situated beyond the ocean | 英國係在洋海外 | Ying-kwok hai tsoi yeung hoi ngoi |
| 17 Why do they stick up placards about it? | 佢哋爲乜野貼街招呢 | k'ü-ti wai-măt-ye t'ip kai-chiu ni? |
| 18 Because they come from the sea | 因爲佢哋由海上來嘅 | yan-wai k'ü-ti yau hoi sheung loi ke |
| 19 While I was smoking my pipe, I saw a mouse | 我食僅烟時見一隻石鼠 | ngo shik kău in shi kin yat chek shek-shü |
| 20 There is not sufficient room to sit down here | 呢處唔够地方坐 | ni-ch'ü 'm kau ti-fong tso |
| 21 Can you pull two oars at one time? | 你一齊掉得兩枝槳唔呢 | ni yat ts'ai chau tăk leung chi tseung 'm ni? |
| 22 I did so when I was working in a boat | 我先日在艇打工時有用 | ngo sin-yat tsoi t'ing ta kung shi yau yung |
| 23 They use a great deal of paste to stick up the placards | 佢哋用好多漿糊貼嗰啲街招 | k'ü-ti yung ho to tseung-u t'ip ko-ti kai-chin |
| 24 Do you ever smoke opium? It is very bad | 你有食過鴉片烟冇呢;係十分唔好 | ui yau shik kwo a-p'in-in mo ni? hai shap-făn 'm ho |
| 25 I used to have a revolver; you had only a common pistol | 我先時有枝六口連,你有枝平常手鎗啫 | ngo sin-shi yau chi luk-hau-lin; ni yau chi p'ing-sheung shau-ts'eung che |

| | | |
|---|---|---|
| 26 I was very fond of play when I was a boy | 我細蚊仔時好反斗嘅 | ngo sai-măn-tsai shi ho fan-tau ke |
| 27 Do you like poetry? I sometimes make verses | 你中意詩唔呢, 我有時吟詩 | ni chung-i shi 'm ni? ngo yau-shi yăm shi |
| 28 No; I do not, though many people do | 唔中意, 唔噲, 雖係好多人噲 | 'm chung-i; 'm ui, sui hai ho to yau ui |
| 29 Have you ever seen a man take poison? | 你有見過人服毒藥冇呢 | ni yau kin kwo yan fuk tuk-yeuk mo ni? |
| 30 The Chinese are very polite (to each other) | 唐人大家十分好禮數 | T'ong-yan tai-ka shap-făn ho lai-sho |
| 31 Have you received your port clearance yet? | 你有接到放行紙冇呢 | ni yau tsip to fong-hang-chi mo ni? |
| 32 No; they would not give it me | 冇, 佢哋唔肯俾我 | mo, k'ü-ti 'm hăng pi ngo |
| 33 What is the postage of a letter to England? | 寄封信去英國要幾多信資呢 | ki fung sun hü Ying-kwok iu ki to sun-tsze ni? |
| 34 I think it is about thirty cents, perhaps it may be more | 我估要三十個先士, 或者重要多啲都唔定 | ngo ku iu sam-shap-ko sin-sz, wak che chung iu to ti to 'm ting |
| 35 Has there been any fire lately in Hong-kong? | 香港近日有火燭冇呢 | Heung-kong kăn-yat yau foh-chuk mo ni? |
| 36 There was a small one last night | 昨夜有小小火燭啫 | tsok-ye yau siu-siu foh-chuk che |
| 37 Do you use warm water for washing your face now? | 如今你重用煖水洗面唔呢 | ü-kăm ni chung yung nün-shui sai min 'm ni? |
| 38 Yes; but I shall not use it much longer | 要, 但係我唔用幾耐咯 | iu; tan hai ngo 'm yung ki noi lok |
| 39 There was a fight last night, and they wounded several people | 昨晚响處打交, 打傷幾個人 | tsok-man ko-ch'ü ta-kau, ta sheung ki ko yan |
| 40 Do you put a private mark on your boxes? | 你有落個暗號在你嘅箱面冇呢 | ni yau lok ko om-ho tsoi ni ke seung min mo ni? |

# LESSON LVIII.

| | | | | | |
|---|---|---|---|---|---|
| Contrary to | 相反 | *seung-fan'* | Opposed to | 相反 | *seung-fan* |
| During | 當時 | *tong*-shi | Opposite | 對面 | *tui'*-min' |
| Do. | 之耐 | *chi*-noi' | Long since | 好久 | *ho' kau'* |
| In, within | 在內 | tsoi' noi' | To (unto) | 對 | *tui'* |
| Into | 入內 | yap noi' | Through | 通 | *t'ung* |
| Since | 之後 | *chi*-hau' | Except | 除 | ch'ü |
| Do. | 自從 | tsz'-ts'ung | Till | 等 | *tang'* |
| For (instead of) | 代 | toi' | | | |

**Land Measures.**

| | | | | | | |
|---|---|---|---|---|---|---|
| 5 *c'hek* | 尺 | make one | po' | 步 | or *kung* 弓 | (=30.3234 sq. feet) |
| 24 po' | 步 | " | *făn* | 分 | | |
| 60 po' | 步 | " | *kok* | 角 | | (=202.56 sq yards) |
| 4 *kok* | 角 | " | mau' | 畝 | or Chinese acre | (=27.23 sq. poles) |
| 100 mau' | 畝 | " | *k'ing'* | 頃 | | (=16.7 acres) |

The "mau" is, at most of the ports, roughly reckoned as one sixth of an English acre.

| | | |
|---|---|---|
| Can you secure his safety? | 你保得佢平安唔呢 | ni' *po' tàk* k'ü' p'ing-*on* 'm *ni*? |
| What evidence have you? | 有乜野憑據呢 | yau' *măt*-ye' p'ăng-*kü'* *ni*? |
| It looks better than formerly | 更好睇過舊時 | *kăng' ho' t'ai' kwo'* kau'-shi |
| That suits very well | 啲個至啱咯 | *ko'-ko' chi' ngam lok* |
| The streets are very wet | 街上好濕嘅 | *kai*-sheung' *ho' shap ke'* |
| This year's almanack | 今年嘅通書 | *kăm*-nin *ke' t'ung-shü* |
| I know nothing about it | 我都唔知到 | ngo' *to* 'm *chi to'* |
| Never mind of he doesn't believe it | 佢唔信就罷 | k'ü' 'm *sun'* tsau' pa' |
| At last it will break | 日子耐噲爛 | yat-*tsz'* noi' ui' lan' |
| Has he brought any? | 有帶來冇呢 | yau' *tai'* loi mo' *ni*? |
| No need of disturbing him | 唔使驚動佢 | m *shai' king* tung' k'ü' |

| | | |
|---|---|---|
| You should get a little more angry! | 重要嬲嬲添 | chung` iu` *nau nau t'im* |
| That colour is good | 啲啲顏色好 | *ko'-ti* ngan-*shik ho'* |
| Have you got an answer? | 有回音冇呢 | yau' ui-*yăm* mo' *ni*? |
| The harvest is good - | 好收成 | *ho' shau*-shing |
| Do not censure him (don't blow him up) | 唔好責鬧佢 | 'm *ho' chak* nau` k'ü' |

| | | |
|---|---|---|
| Proclamation | 告示 | *ko`*-shi` |
| To issue a proclamation | 出告示 | *ch'ut ko`*-shi` |
| Passage-boat | 渡船 | to`-shün |
| To embark in a passage boat | 搭渡船 | *tap* to`-shün |
| Riches | 財帛 | ts'oi-pak |
| To covet riches | 貪財帛 | *t'am* ts'oi-pak |
| Tanka boat | 三板 | *sam-pan'* |
| Do. | 蛋家艇 | tan`-*ka*-t'eng' |
| Rag | 布碎 | *po`-sui`* |
| Do. | 什碎布 | shap-*sui`-po`* |
| Do. | 爛布 | lan`-*po`* |
| Rope of a sail | 繂大繚 | lut tai` liu |
| Satin | 漢府緞 | *hon`-fu'*-tün` |
| Ocean | 洋海 | yeung-*hoi'* |
| A man-of-war | 兵船 | *ping*-shün |
| Foresail | 頭幃 | t'au li' |
| Mainsail | 大幃 | tai` li' |
| Mizen (after sail) | 尾幃 | mi' li' |
| Province | 省 | *shang'* |
| Provincial city (applied in the South to Canton and in other provinces to the local metropolis) | 省城 | *shang'*-shing |
| Remainder | 有剩 | yau' shing` |
| Rainbow | 天虹 | *t'in*-hung |
| Rattan | 沙籐 | *sha*-t'ăng |
| River | 江, 河 | *kong*, ho |
| Highway | 大路 | tai` lo` |
| Rocks | 磐石 | p'un-shek |
| Hidden rocks | 暗石 | *om`*-shek |
| Security | 包管 | *pau-kun'* |
| Do. | 擔保 | *tam-po'* |
| Promise | 應承 | *ying*-shing |
| Do. | 應許 | *ying-hü'* |
| Salary | 俸祿 | *fung'*-luk |
| Do. | 辛俸 | *săn-fung'* |
| Do. | 人工 | yan-*kung* |
| Riot | 作亂 | *tsok* lün` |
| Do. | 鬧事 | nau` sze` |
| Small boat | 細艇 | *sai`* t'eng' |
| Fast-boat | 快艇 | *fai`*-t'eng' |
| Mast | 枝桅 | *chi* wai |
| Rain | 雨水 | ü'-*shui'* |
| Do. | 雨 | ü' |
| Broad | 闊 | *fut* |
| Sea | 海 | *hoi'* |

1 He made a promise to visit me at the provincial city — 佢應承在省城探我 — k'ü ying-shing tsoi shang-shing t'am ngo

2 The mandarin issued a pro- — 官府出告示話 — kun-fu ch'ut ko-shi wa ko-ti

| | | |
|---|---|---|
| clamation to say it was contrary to law | 嗰啲係唔合例嘅 | hai 'm hop lai ke |
| 3 He has nothing on whatever but rags | 佢冇乜野着獨有爛布啫 | k'ü mo măt-ye cheuk tuk yau lan-po che |
| 4 It has rained all day of late | 近來成日落雨 | kăn-loi shing-yat lok u |
| 5 Is there any difference between a small boat and a Tan-ka boat? | 艇仔共蛋家艇有分別冇呢 | t'eng-tsai kung Tan-ka-t'eng yau fán-pit mo ni? |
| 6 There is a very great difference; both sorts are (found) on the river | 十分大分別，兩樣都係在河面嚟 | shap-făn tai făn-pit; leung yeung to hai tsoi hoh min lai |
| 7 This is a very dirty road you are taking me | 你帶我行一條汚糟嘅路 | ni tai ngo hang yat t'iu u-tso ke lo |
| 8 There were thieves round about Canton | 省城週圍有賊 | Shang-shing chau-wai yau ts'ak |
| 9 Did the rat eat the rope on board the ship? | 老鼠食船上嗰啲繩唔呢 | lo-shü shik shün sheung ko-ti shing 'm ni? |
| 10 How broad is that sea? | 嗰個海幾闊呢 | ko-ko hoi ki fut ni? |
| 11 It is nearly as large as the province of Kwang-tung | 差不多好似廣東省咁大 | ch'a-pat-to ho ts'z Kwong-tung-shang kom tai |
| 12 What sorts of boats are to be seen going towards Hong-kong? | 向香港駛去嘅艇係乜樣子嘅呢 | heung Heung-kong shai hü ke t'eng hai măt yeung-tsz ke ni? |
| 13 There are fast boats, passage boats and men-of-war going through Cap-shui-mun | 有快艇有渡船共兵船向急水門駛去 | yau fai-t'eng, yau to-shün, kung ping-shün heung Kap-shui-mun shai hü |
| 14 From what city does this satin chiefly come? | 呢啲漢府緞由邊個城來得多呢 | ni-ti hon-fu-tün yau pin-ko shing loi tăk to ni? |
| 15 Have you often seen a rainbow in the sky? | 你有見天上嘅天虹有呢 | ni yau kin t'in sheung ke t'in-hung mo ni? |
| 16 Not very often. It so seldom rains here | 冇幾何，呢處甚少有雨落 | mo ki ho; ni-ch'ü shăm shiu yau ü lok |

初學階

| | | |
|---|---|---|
| 17 A riot took place not far from here | 離呢處冇幾遠有鬧事 | li ni-ch'ü mo ki ün yau nau-sze |
| 18 I do not like people who covet riches | 貪財帛嘅人,我唔中意嘅 | t'am ts'oi-pak ke yan, ngo 'm chung-i ke |
| 19 He put the remainder of that bread away long since | 佢擠埋所剩下嗰啲麵包好耐咯 | k'ü chai mai shoh shing-ha ko-ti min-pau ho noi lok |
| 20 She is a three-masted American ship | 佢係一隻三枝桅嘅花旗船 | k'ü hai yat chek sam chi wai ke Fa-k'i shün |
| 21 Has she set her foresail and mainsail? | 佢有掛起頭悝共大悝冇呢 | k'ü yau kwa hi t'au-li kung tai li mo ni? |
| 22 The passage boat he embarked in was opposite my house | 佢所落嘅渡船係在我屋對面嚟 | k'ü shoh lok ke to-shün hai tsoi ngo uk tui-min lai |
| 23 The compradore says he can give full security | 個買辦有話可以盡力担保佢 | ko mai-pan yau wa ho-i tsun-lik tam-po k'ü |
| 24 There are a good many rocks in that sea | 嗰個海有好多石 | ko-ko hoi yau ho to shek |
| 25 Rattans are used at Canton to make chairs | 省城用籐嚟做椅嘅 | Shang-shing yung t'ăng lai tso i ke |
| 26 What salary does your teacher get monthly? | 你嘅先生每月受幾多脩金呢 | ni ke sin-shăng mui üt shau ki to sau-kăm ni? |
| 27 He gets a very good salary as he is a good man | 佢嘅脩金十分好,因佢係個好人 | k'ü ke sau-kăm shap-făn ho, yan k'ü hai ko ho yan |
| 28 Can you secure his being industrious? | 你能担保佢勤力唔呢 | ni nang tam-po k'ü k'ăn-lik 'm ni? |
| 29 That is always a difficult matter | 嗰啲時常係好難嘅 | ko-ti shi-sheung hai ho nan ke |
| 30 You ought not to have to censure him very often | 你唔應該責鬧佢咁多 | ni 'm ying-koi chak nau k'ü kom to |
| 31 The ship ran upon a hidden rock five days since | 五日前個隻船駛埋一嚿暗石 | ng yat ts'in ko chek shün shai mai yat kau om-shek |
| 32 How many were drowned in consequence? | 噉就有幾多人沉死呢 | kom tsau yau ki to yan chăm sze ni? |

| | | |
|---|---|---|
| 33 I know nothing about it; all I have heard is that this ship struck | 我乜都唔知，獨係聞得啲隻船碰着石啫 | ngo mät to 'm chi, tuk hai măn tăk ko chek shün p'ung cheuk shek che |
| 34 Shall I find things about the weather in this year's almanack? | 你估我在今年通書可以揾得論天時嘅事唔呢 | ni ku ngo tsoi kăm-nin ke t'ung-shü ho-i wăn tăk lun t'in-shi ke sze 'm ni? |
| 35 I believe so; but I have not a copy of the book | 我信係噉；但係我冇噉嘅書 | ngo sun hai kom; tan hai ngo mo kom ke shü |
| 36 Tell that man people should never get angry | 話過嗰個人知，衆人總唔着嬲怒 | wa kwo ko-ko yan chi, chung yan tsung 'm cheuk nau no |
| 37 Do not censure him; he is a well meaning man | 咪鬧佢，佢係好心地嘅人 | mai nau k'ü, k'ü hai ho sam-ti ke yan |
| 38 It is long since I have seen him in the province | 我喺省見過佢好耐咯 | ngo hai shang kin kwo k'ü ho noi lok |
| 39 He is here because it is a Poussa's birth day | 佢在呢處，因爲今日係菩薩誕 | k'ü tsoi ni-ch'ü, yan wai kăm-yat hai p'o-sat tan |
| 40 I suppose he will go to the temple to burn incense | 我估佢等吓去廟燒香 | ngo ku k'ü tăng-ha hü miu shiu heung |

---

# LESSON LIX.

| | | | | | |
|---|---|---|---|---|---|
| With respect to | 論及 | lun` k'ap* | And | 另 | ling` |
| Regarding | 至於 | *chi` ü** | Do. (with) | 與 | ü'* |
| Naturally | 自然 | tsz`-in | Without | 冇 | mo' |
| Yet, still | 仍然 | ying in* | Also | 又 | yau` |
| As if | 好似 | *ho'*-ts'z' | As | 如 | ü |
| Together with | 連 | lin | | | |

* These are not strictly speaking colloquial phrases but are frequently used by well educated Chinese.

初學階

### TEAS 茶 CH‘A.

| | | |
|---|---|---|
| A "chop" - - - | 號, 字號 | ho`, tsz`-ho` |
| Gunpowder tea - | 芝珠茶 | *chi-chü*-ch‘a |
| Imperial tea - | 圓珠茶 | ün-*chü*-ch‘a |
| Caper - „ - - | 珠蘭茶 | *chü*-lan-ch‘a |
| Black - „ - - | 黑茶 | *hak*-ch‘a |
| Suchong „ | 小種 | *siu'-chung'* |
| Pekoe „ - | 白毫 | pak-ho |
| Green „ | 綠茶 | luk-ch‘a |
| Hyson - „ | 正茶 | *ching*`-ch‘a |

### COMMON DISEASES, &c.

| | | | | | |
|---|---|---|---|---|---|
| Dislocation | 跌錯較骨 | *tit ts‘oh` kau`-kwat* | Contusion | 瘀傷 | *ü`-sheung* |
| | | | Blindness | 盲眼 | mang-ngan' |
| Hiccough | 打思臆 | *ta'-sze-yik* | Deafness | 耳聾 | i'-lung |
| Inflammation | 腫熱 | *chung'*-it | Cough | 咳嗽 | *k‘at-sau*` |
| Dumbness | 啞口 | *a'-hau'* | Fracture | 拆骨 | *chit-kwat* |
| Dysentery | 疴痢 | *oh*-li` | Asthma | 氣緊 | *hi`-kăn'* |
| Diarrhœa | 肚疴 | t‘o'-*oh* | Cholera | 時症 | shi-*ching*` |
| Eruption | 癍疹 | *pan-ch‘ăn'* | Corns | 鷄眼 | *kai*-ngan' |
| Fainting | 失魂 | *shat*-wăn | Fever | 發熱 | *fat*-it |
| Abscess (boil) | 瘡 | *ch‘ong* | Ague | 發冷 | *fat*-lang' |

| | | |
|---|---|---|
| He has a broken fore-arm - | 佢隻手肘拆曉咯 | k‘ü' *chek shau'-chau' chit hiu lok* |
| I cannot cure you - - | 我唔能醫得你咯 | ngo' 'm nang *i tăk* ni' *lok* |
| How long have you been ill? | 你病嘵幾耐呢 | ni' peng` *hiu ki'* noi` *ni*? |
| He has sprained his ancle - | 佢扭着脚眼骨 | k‘ü' *nau'* cheuk *keuk*-ngan'-*kwat* |
| I am indisposed - | 我見唔自在咯 | ngo' *kin*` 'm tsz`-tsoi` *lok* |
| What is the matter (sickness) with you? | 你有乜野病呢 | ni' yau' *măt*-ye' peng *ni*? |
| It is necessary to operate - | 是必要割咯 | shi-*pit iu*` *kot lok* |
| Have you pain? - - | 你痛唔呀 | ni' *t‘ung*` 'm *a*? |

| | | | | | |
|---|---|---|---|---|---|
| European | 歐羅巴人 | *Au*-lo-*pa*-yan | Story (tale) | 古 | *ku'* |
| | | | Do. | 古仔 | *ku'-tsai'* |
| Style | 文理 | măn-li' | Do. | 花話 | *fa*-wa` |

| | | | | | |
|---|---|---|---|---|---|
| Spider | 蟾蟧 | k'ăm-lo | Shop | 舖頭, 店 | *p'o'*-t'au, *tim'* |
| Do. web | 蟾蟧網 | k'ăm-lo-mong' | Sunshine | 日頭處 | yat-t'au *ch'ü'* |
| Cabin | 船尾房 | shün-mi'-fong | Rudder | 船舦 | shün-tai' |
| Sun | 日頭 | yat-t'au | Hold | 船艙 | shün-*ts'ong* |
| The sun is very hot | 日頭烘 | yat-t'au *hung'* | Storm | 大風 | tai' *fung* |
| | | | Do. | 風颶 | *fung*-kü' |
| To put in a mast | 豎桅 | shü wai | Stars | 天星 | *t'in sing* |
| Mainmast | 大桅 | tai wai | Signboard | 招牌 | *chiu*-p'ai |
| Foremast | 頭桅 | t'au-wai | Supper | 晚餐 | man' *ts'an* |
| Mizenmast | 尾桅 | mi'-wai | Tariff | 稅則 | *shui'-tsak* |
| Sycee silver | 紋銀 | măn-ngăn | Tax | 錢糧 | ts'in-leung |
| To quarry stone | 鑿石 | tsok shek | Do. | 稅銀 | *shui'*-ngăn |
| Stone | 石 | shek | | | |

| | | |
|---|---|---|
| 1 Did he speak to you regarding his asthma? | 佢有對你講及佢嘅氣緊冇呀 | k'ü yau tui ni kong k'ap k'ü ke hi-kăn mo a? |
| 2 He put a fore, main, and mizen mast into the ship | 佢豎一枝頭桅中桅共尾桅落隻船嚟 | k'ü shü yat chi t'au-wai, chung-wai, kung mi-wai lok chek shün lai |
| 3 The merchant sent one chop of black and one chop of green teas | 個商人寄一號黑茶共一號綠茶嚟 | ko sheung-yan ki yat ho hak-ch'a kung yat ho luk-ch'a lai |
| 4 Were they both put in the hold of the vessel? | 佢哋兩個都係擠入船艙裡頭咩 | k'ü-ti leung ko to hai chai yap shün-ts'ong li-t'au me? |
| 5 The tea shops at Canton have red and gold sign-boards | 省城嘅茶行有紅色共金色嘅招牌 | Shang-shing ke ch'a-hong yau hung-shik kung kăm-shik ke chiu-p'ai |
| 6 How long has your father had that cough? | 你嘅父親有噉嘅咳嗽幾耐呢 | ni ke fu-ts'ăn yau kom ke k'at-sau ki noi ni? |
| 7 He has had it ever since he had the fever | 佢自從有發熱症時就有咯 | k'ü tsz-ts'ung yau fat-it ching shi tsau yau lok |
| 8 Do the Chinese use spider's web as a medicine? | 唐人有用蟾蟧網做藥材冇呢 | T'ong-yan yau yung k'ăm-lo-mong tso yeuk-ts'oi mo ni? |

初學階



| | | |
|---|---|---|
| 9 The stone struck the woman and gave her a contusion | 啁偺石打襯個女人打瘀傷曉 | ko kau-shek ta ts'ăn ko nü-yan ta ü-sheung hiu |
| 10 The child fell down by the Chapel and broke its arm | 個細紋仔喺個間禮拜堂處跌折隻手 | ko sai-măn-tsai hai ko kan lai-pai-t'ong ch'ü tit chit chek shau |
| 11 Do you think it will be necessary to operate? | 你估要割唔呢 | ni ku iu kot 'm ni? |
| 21 I do not think so: I think it is only a dislocation | 我睇唔使,我估係跌錯較骨啫 | ngo t'ai 'm shai; ngo ku hai tit ts'oh kau-kwăt che |
| 13 Deaf and dumb people abound (are many) in China | 聾人啞人中國有好多 | lung-yan a-yan Chung-kwok yau ho to |
| 14 The sun is very hot in the streets just now | 而今街上日頭十分烘 | i-kăm kai-sheung yat-t'au shap-făn hung |
| 15 The moon and stars were visible last night | 昨夜睇得見啁個月共啲星 | tsok-ye t'ai tăk kin ko-ko üt kung ti sing |
| 16 While he was telling a story he was seized with a fainting fit | 佢講僅古啁陣時就失魂起嚟 | k'ü kong kăn ku ko chăn-shi, tsau shat-wăn hi lai |
| 17 Children suffer from eruptions in the summer | 天時熱細紋仔噲生痱疹 | t'in-shi-it sai-măn-tsai ui shăng pau-ch'ăn |
| 18 Do Chinese ever get corns on the feet? | 唐人脚上有生鷄眼冇呢 | T'ong-yan keuk sheung yau shăng kai-ngan mo ni? |
| 19 No; because their shoes are not of the same sort as those of Europeans | 冇,因爲佢哋所着嘅鞋唔同歐羅巴人嘅 | mo, yau-wai k'ü-ti shoh cheuk ke hai 'm t'ung Au-lo-pa yan ke |
| 20 Hiccough is very uncomfortable, although not serious | 打思噎係十分唔自然嘅,雖然唔係交關 | ta-sze-yik hai shap-făn 'm tsz-in ke, sui-in 'm hai kau-kwan |
| 21 Dysentery is certainly worse than diarrhœa | 痾痢自然係交關過肚痾喇 | o-li tsz-in hai kau-kwan kwo t'o-o la |
| 22 Cholera is a more dangerous disease than any other | 時症係險過各樣嘅症候 | shi-ching hai him kwo kok yeung ke ching-hau |

| | | |
|---|---|---|
| 23 Boils are very common amongst foreigners | 外國人好慣生瘡嘅 | ngoi-kwok yan ho kwan shăng ch'ong ke |
| 24 How did you manage to sprain your ankle? | 你點樣扭得着你嘅脚眼呢 | ni tim yeung nau-tăk cheuk ni ke keuk-ngan ni? |
| 25 The Doctor says he cannot cure you | 醫生有話佢唔醫得你咯 | i-shăng yau wa k'ü 'm i tăk ni lok |
| 26 I will come, together with my brother, after supper | 我等吓食完晚餐就同我嘅兄弟來 | ngo tăng-ha shik ün man t'an tsau t'ung ngo-ke hing-tai loi |
| 27 The storm last week was very heavy (great) | 先個禮拜個塲風颶好大 | sin ko lai-pai ko ch'eung fung-kü ho tai |
| 28 It was not nearly so bad as that of last night | 未有唻似昨夜嗰塲咁弊咍 | mi-yau-loi ts'z tsok-ye ko ch'eung kom pai chi |
| 29 Do those books contain tales? | 嗰啲書有載古仔嘅咩 | ko-ti shü yau tsoi ku-tsai ke me? |
| 30 No, their style is too good for story books | 唔係. 嗰啲文理好過古仔嘅書 | 'm hai, ko-ti măn-li ho kwo ku-tsai ke shü |
| 31 Do they quarry those stones in Hong-kong? | 佢哋喺香港鑿個啲石嘅咩 | k'ü-ti hai Heung-kong tsok ko-ti shek ke me? |
| 32 They quarry them here but they polish them in Hongkong | 佢哋喺呢處鑿, 但喺香港打嗟咯 | k'ü-ti hai ni-ch'ü tsok, tan hai Heung-kong ta sai lok |
| 33 Do not let the children go in the sunshine | 咪俾個啲細紋仔走去日頭處 | mai pi ko-ti sai-măn-tsai tsau hü yat-t'au ch'ü |
| 34 Have you sycee silver as well as dollars? | 你有紋銀共銀錢冇呢 | ni yau măn-ngăn kung ngăn-ts'in mo ni? |
| 35 They use broken silver as if it was money in Canton | 省城嘅人用碎銀好似銀錢一樣 | Shang-shing ke yan yung sui-ngăn ho-ts'z ngăn-ts'in yat yeung |
| 36 That is because they have no silver dollars | 個啲係因爲佢哋冇銀錢啫 | ko-ti hai yan-wai k'ü-ti mo ngăn-ts'in che |
| 37 The tariff on goods is fixed very high | 貨物稅則係十分高 | foh-mat shui-tsak hai shap-făn ko |

初學階

| | | |
|---|---|---|
| 38 They pay all the taxos there in sycee | 佢哋喺呴處納稅都係用紋銀 | k'ü-ti hai ko-ch'ü nap shui to hai yung măn-ngăn |
| 39 Do the shops have to pay heavy taxes? | 舖頭係要納好重嘅稅唔呢 | p'o-t'au hai iu nap ho ch'ung ke shui 'm ni? |
| 40 They pay taxes but they are not very heavy | 佢哋要納稅, 但唔係十分重 | k'ü-ti iu nap shui, tan 'm hai shap fan ch'ung |

# LESSON LX.

| | | | | | |
|---|---|---|---|---|---|
| Either—or | 或, 一或, | wak,—wak | No sooner | 一見 | *yat kin`* |
| Do. | 唔係 | 'm hai` | Unless | 若不 | yeuk-*pat* |
| Than | 過, 過於 | *kwo`*, *kwo`-ü* | When | 當 | *tong* |
| Then | 方, 然後 | *fong*, in-hau` | Even | 連 | lin |
| Neither—nor | 不—不 | *pat, pat* | Only | 祇 | *chi'* |
| Not—but | 不—乃 | *pat,* nai' | | | |

[Nearly all of the foregoing are more classical than colloquial but they are generally understood and used by all natives with any pretensions to education.]

### Common Diseases &c. (continued.)

| | | | | | |
|---|---|---|---|---|---|
| Squinting | 扭視眼 | *ch'e'*-shi`-ngan' | Small pox | 出痘 | *ch'ut* tau` |
| Consumption | 內傷 | noi`-*sheung* | Wounds | 損傷 | *sün' sheung* |
| Rheumatism | 瘋濕 | *fung-shap* | Leprosy | 痳瘋 | ma-*fung* |
| Sea-sickness | 暈浪 | wăn-long` | Measles | 出痳 | *ch'ut* ma |
| Stammering | 謭牙 | na'-nga | Palsy | 瘋癱 | *fung-t'an'* |
| Lameness | 跛脚 | *pai-keuk* | Itch | 生瀨 | *shăng lai`* |
| Vomiting | 嘔吐 | *au'-t'o`* | Ulcer | 癰 | *yung* |
| Insanity | 發顚 | *fat-tin* | | | |

### Silk, Raw and Manufactured.

| | | |
|---|---|---|
| Velvet - | 天鵝絨 | *t'in*-ngo-yung |
| Refuse - - | 亂絲頭 | lün *sze*-t'au |

| | | |
|---|---|---|
| Canton raw silk | 土絲 | *to'-sze* |
| Cocoons | 蠶繭 | ts'am-*kan'* |
| Thread - | 絲線 | *sze-sin`* |
| Satin | 絲緞 | *sze*-tün` |
| Crape | 縐紗 | *tsau`-sha* |
| Gauze | 紗 | *sha* |
| Floss | 絨 | yung |

The terms used by silk merchants to express the different qualities of silk are mostly pure Chinese—such as TSAT-LI, TAI-SAM &c.

| | | |
|---|---|---|
| Of what is this made? | 呢的係乜野做嘅呢 | *ni-ti* hai` *măt*-ye' tso` *ke`* *ni*? |
| I have heard some-one say so | 我聽聞有噉話 | ngo' *t'eng*-măn yau' *kom'* wa` |
| Give an answer to what I say | 回答我說話 | ui-*tap* ngo' *shüt*-wa` |
| I can't bear it any longer | 我唔抵得住 | ngo' 'm *tai'-tăk*-chü` |
| To please myself I would not go | 我情愿唔去 | ngo' ts'ing-ün` 'm *hü`* |
| I don't quite understand it | 我唔曉得晒 | ngo' 'm *hiu'* *tăk* *sai`* |
| What means are there of doing it? | 有乜法子呢 | yau' *măt făt-tsz'* *ni*? |
| I can't reach up to it - | 我唔攞得到 | ngo' 'm *o tăk to`* |
| He's not a foolish person - | 佢唔係呆人 | k'ü' 'm hai` ngoi-yan |

| | | | | | |
|---|---|---|---|---|---|
| Weather cock | 風信旗 | *fung-sun`*-k'i | The world (i.e. everywhere) | 世間 | *shai`-kan* |
| Thunder | 雷,雷公 | lui, lui-*kung* | | | |
| Villain | 奸狡人 | *kan-kau'*-yan | Market town | 墟市 | *hü*-shi' |
| Woollen cloth | 呢 | ni | Victuals | 伙食 | *foh'*-shik |
| Do. | 小呢絨 | *siu'*-ni-yung | Victory | 戰勝 | *chin`-shing`* |
| Value (fixed price) | 實價 | shat-*ka`* | Do. | 打贏 | *tă'*-yeng |
| To get mouldy | 生霉 | *shăng* mui | Witness | 証人 | *ching`*-yan |
| Do. | 發毛 | *fat* mo | Village | 村鄉 | *ts'un-heung* |
| Weight (gross) | 毛重 | mo ch'ung` | Valley | 山谷 | *shan-kuk* |
| Do. (nett) | 凈重 | tsing` ch'ung` | Wages | 工錢 | *kung*-ts'in |
| To get damp | 翻潮 | *fan*-ch'iu | Ware | 器 | *hi`* |
| Wax | 蠟 | lap | Do. | 器用 | *hi`*-yung` |
| Yellow wax | 黃蠟 | wong-lap | Wave | 海浪 | *hoi'*-long` |
| White wax | 白蠟 | pak-lap | Well (a) | 井 | *tseng* |

初學階

| | | |
|---|---|---|
| 1 He must either do as he is told or go away | 佢要照佢話噉做，唔係就扭喇 | k'ü in chiu k'ü wa kom tso, 'm hai tsau ch'e la |
| 2 People in Hongkong suffer from rheumatism | 香港嘅人都患瘋濕 | Heung-koug ke yan to wan fung-shap |
| 3 He cannot be cured unless he goes to a doctor | 佢唔好得嘅咯，除非去醫生處醫啫 | k'ü 'm ho tăk ke lok, ch'ü fi hü i-shăng ch'ü i che |
| 4 Insanity is worse than consumption | 發顛交關過內傷 | fat-tin kau kwan kwo noi-sheung |
| 5 The leper was suffering from palsy | 個發瘋佬又患瘋癱病添 | ko fat-fung-lo yau wan fung-t'an peng t'im |
| 6 He finally left the town and went to the village | 佢收尾離墟市去鄉村 | k'ü shau-mi li hü-shi hü heung-ts'ün |
| 7 Did you hear it thunder on Wednesday? | 禮拜三你有聽聞行雷冇呢 | lai-pai sam ni yau t'eng-măn hang lui mo ni? |
| 8 No, I only saw it rain; I was at home then | 冇，我祇見落雨啫，我個陣時喺屋裡 | mo, ngo chi kin lok ü che; ngo ko chăn-shi hai uk-li |
| 9 Those goods have got damp and their weight has increased | 個啲貨濕嘵，所以重啲 | ko-ti foh shap hiu, shoh-i ch'ung ti |
| 10 The weather has been bad and the woollen cloth has got mouldy | 天時唔好，個啲絨發毛 | t'in-shi 'm ho, ko-ti yung fat mo |
| 11 No sooner had he commenced to speak, than he became ill | 佢一講啫，就病起嚟咯 | k'ü yat kong che, tsau peng hi lai lok |
| 12 It was not the weather but want of care | 唔關天時，係冇子細啫 | 'm kwan t'in-shi, hai mo tsz-sai che |
| 13 What is the value of that wax? | 個啲蠟值得幾多錢呢 | ko-ti lap chik tăk ki to ts'in ni? |
| 14 It costs a dollar a catty. That is very dear | 要一個銀錢一斤，係十分貴嘅 | iu yat ko ngăn-ts'in yat kăn, hai shap-făn kwai ke |
| 15 What is the use of a weather vane? | 風信旗係做乜野用嘅呢 | fung-sun-k'i hai tso măt-ye yung ke ni? |
| 16 It is used to show the direction of the wind | 用嚟測風向邊便嘅 | yung lai ts'ak fung heung pin-pin ke |

| | | |
|---|---|---|
| 17 The soldiers won the victory but many received wounds | 嗰啲兵打勝，但好多受傷 | ko-ti ping ta shing, tan ho to shau sheung |
| 18 Did the witness appear before the mandarin? | 個証人有到堂見官冇呢 | ko ching-yan yau to t'ong kin kun mo ni? |
| 19 That box is neither pretty nor useful | 嗰個箱唔好睇又冇用嘅 | ko-ko seung 'm ho t'ai yau mo yung ke |
| 20 When you went to the village did you see the villain? | 你去個條村有見個奸狡人冇呢 | ni hü ko t'in ts'ün yau kin ko kan-kau yan mo ni? |
| 21 No sooner had I seen him than he ran away | 我一見佢，佢就走咯 | ngo yat kin k'ü, k'ü tsau tsau lok |
| 22 Is that iron or wood ware? | 個啲係鐵器或木器呢 | ko-ti hai t'it-hi wak muk-hi ni? |
| 23 It is difficult to cure people of squinting | 扭矿眼好難醫嘅 | ch'e-shi-ngan ho nan i ke |
| 24 Do you often meet Chinese who stammer? | 你常遇見唐人諁牙冇呢 | ni sheung ü kin T'ong-yan na-nga mo ni? |
| 25 No, but I have often seen natives who have had the small pox | 冇，但係我常見本地人有出痘啫 | mo, tan hai ngo sheung kin pun-ti yan yau ch'ut tau che |
| 26 Please tell me the weight of that raw silk | 多煩話我知個啲生絲幾重呢 | to-fan wa ngo chi ko-ti shăng-sze ki ch'ung ni? |
| 27 We don't weigh it here; I cannot tell you | 我哋呢處唔秤嘅；唔話得你知 | ngo-ti ni-ch'ü 'm ch'ing ke; 'm wa tăk ni chi |
| 28 What wages do those men receive per month? | 個啲人一個月受幾多工錢呢 | ko-ti yan yat ko üt shau ki to kung-ts'in ni? |
| 29 They get six dollars apiece a year | 每人一年六個銀錢 | mui yan yat nin luk ko ngan-ts'in |
| 30 There were not victuals enough for so many soldiers | 嗰啲火食唔夠咁多兵用 | ko-ti foh-shik 'm kau kom to ping yung |
| 31 I want to buy six yards of yellow satin | 我要買六碼黃緞 | ngo iu mai luk ma wong-tün |
| 32 Yellow satin is only used by the Emperor | 獨係皇帝正用黃緞啫 | tuk hoi wong-tai ching yung wong-tün che |

| | | |
|---|---|---|
| 33 I am anxious to buy some blue silk gauze | 我十分中意買啲藍紗 | ngo shap-fàn chung-i mai ti lam-sha |
| 34 What is the difference between gauze and crape? | 紗共縐紗有乜分別呢 | sha kung tsau-sha yau măt făn-pit ni? |
| 35 One is much thicker and stronger than the other | 一樣厚嘅及主固過啲樣 | yat yung hau ke kap chü-ku kwo ko yeung |
| 36 The nett weight of that floss silk is but trifling | 個的絲絨凈重係爭有限啫 | ko-ti sze-yung tsing ch'ung hai chang yau hau che |
| 37 What means have you of weighing it | 你有乜野方法秤佢呢 | ni yau măt-ye fong-fat ch'ing k'ü ni? |
| 38 We use scales and weights made of copper | 我哋用秤共銅做嘅碼子 | ngo-ti yung ch'ing, kung t'ung tso ke ma-tsz |
| 39 I can't bear this illness any longer | 我唔抵得住噉嘅病添咯 | ngo 'm tai tăk chü kom ke peng t'im lok |
| 40 There are a great many illnesses to be met with in the world | 世間有好多病症碰着嘅 | shai-kan yau ho to peng-ching p'ung cheuk ke |

FINIS.

# APPENDIX

## VOCABULARY OF WORDS USED IN THE FOREGOING LESSONS.

A, an, (one) (一 *yat*, used in conjunction with the classifier) the most common being 個 *koh`*, as 一個人 *yat koh`* yan, "one man" or "a man," 一條魚 *yat* t'iu ü, "a fish."

Abacus, or counting frame, 算盤 *sün`*-p'un.

Abcess, (boil), 瘡 *ch'ong*.

Ability, 才能 ts'oi-nang.

Able, 得 *tăk*, 能 nang, 噲 ui'.

About, (round-) 周圍 *chau*-wai, all about 四吓 *sze`* ha`, (nearly) 約 *yeuk*, 大約 tai`-*yeuk*, (about to) 將近 *tseung*-kăn` (k'ăn'), (concerning) 論及 lun`-k'ăp.

Above, 上 sheung', 在上高 tsoi` sheung` *ko*.

Abroad, 外 ngoi`, 在外國 tsoi` ngoi`-*kwok*.

Abscond, 逃去 t'o *hü`*, 走路 *tsau'* lo`.

Absent, 唔在 'm tsoi`.

Abundant, 豐阜 *fung*-fau`.

Accept, 收納 *shau*-nap.

Accidentally, 偶然 ngau'-in, 意外 i-ngoi`.

Accompany, 同埋 t'ung-mai, 陪 p'ui, 送 *sung`*.

According to, 照依 *chiu`-i*.

Accordingly, 噉就 *kom'*-tsau`.

Account, (money) 單 *tan*, 條數 t'iu *sho`*.

Acre, (Chinese) 畝 mau' ($6\frac{1}{2}$ = 1 Eng.)

Across, 橫 wang, 過 *kwoh`*.

Act, 做 tso`, 行 hang.

Add, 加 *ka*, 添 *t'im*, 計 *kai`*.

Addicted to, 專一 *chün yat*.

Advantageous, 贏 yeng, 益 *yik*.

Affable, 好相與 *ho' seung*-ü'.

Affair, 事幹 sze`-*kon`*.

Afford, 出得 *ch'ut tăk*, 供給 *kung-k'ăp*.

Afraid, 恐怕 *hung'-p'a`*.

After, 跟 *kăn*, 後 hau`.

Afternoon, 下午 ha`-'ng', 下晝 ha`-*chau`*.

Afterwards, 然後 in-hau`, 將來 *tseung*-loi.

Again, 番 *fan*, 再 *tsoi`*, 又再 yau` *tsoi`*.

Against, 逆 yik or ngak.

Age, 年紀 nin-*ki'*, (what is your?) 你有幾多歲 ni' yau' *ki toh sui*`, 貴庚呢 *kwai*`-*kang ni?*

Agree, 符 fu, 合式 hop-*shik*, (suit) 對 *tui*`.

Agreeable, 啱 *ngam*.

Air, (atmosphere) 天氣 *t'in-hi*`.

Alarm, 驚慌 *king-fong*.

All, 攏總 lung'-*tsung'*, 晒 *sai*`, 喊嘭唥 ham`-pang`-lang`.

Almanac, 通書 *t'ung-shu*.

Almost, 差不多 *ch'a-pat-toh*.

Alms, (to give) 施捨 *shi-she'*, 貧窮 p'ăn-k'ung.

Aloud, 大聲 tai` *sheng*.

Already, 已經 i'-*king*.

Also, 又 yau`.

Altar, 神壇 shăn-t'an.

Alter, 改 *koi'*.

Alternately (in succession) 輪流 lun-lau.

Although, 雖然 *sui*-in.

Altogether, 總共 *tsung'*-kung`, 喊嘭唥 ham`-pang`-lang`, 一片 *yat p'in*`.

Always, 時時 shi-shi.

Am, (I) 我係 ngo' hai`.

America, 亞美利加 *A*`-mi'-li`-*ka*.

American, 花旗人 *Fa*-k'i-yan.

Amiable, 可愛 *hoh'* oi`

Among, amidst, 中 *chung*, 中間 *chung-kan*.

Anchor, (to) 抛錨 *p'au* nau.

Anchorage, 埠頭 fau`-t'au, 抛船地方 *p'au* shün ti`-*fong*.

And, 及 k'ăp, 共 kung`, 與 ü', 又 yau`, 另 ling`.

Angry, 嬲嬲 *nau nau*.

Animals, 生靈 *shăng*-ling, 畜牲 *ch'uk-shăng*.

Ankle, 脚眼骨 *keuk*-ngan'-*kwăt*.

Annamese, 安南人 *On*-nam-yan.

Annoyed, (to be) 怒起 no` *hi'*.

Answer, 答 *tap*, 囘音 ui-*yăm*, (to) 囘覆 ui-*fuk*.

Ant, 蟻 ngai'.

Anything, 野 ye'.

Any way, 四路 *sze*`-lo`.

Anywhere, 邊處 *pin-ch'ü*` or *pin shü*.

Apothecary, 藥材舖佬 yeuk-ts'oi-*p'o*`-*lo'*.

Apron, 圍裙 wai-kw'ăn.

Are, 係 hai`.

Arm, (fore) 手肘 *shau'-chau'*, (whole) 肩膀 *kin-pong'*.

Arms, 軍器 *kwăn-hi*`, 器械 *hi*`-hai`.

Arrange, 整齊 *ching'*-ts'ai.

Arrest, 捉 *chuk*, 拿住 na-chü`.

Arrive, 到 *to*`.

Arrow, 箭 *tsin*`, to shoot an arrow, 射箭 she`-*tsin*`.

As, 如 ü, 隨 ts'ui.

Ascend, 上 sheung', 上去 sheung'-*hü*`.

Ashamed, 見醜 *kin*`-*ch'au'*.

Aside, 在一邊 tsoi` *yat pin*, (step aside) 行開 hang-*hoi*.

Ask, 問 măn`.

Aspirate, 噴氣 *p'ăn*`-*hi*`.

Assault, 攻 *kung*.

Assist, 扶起 fu-*hi'*.

At, 在 tsoi\`.

Asthma, 氣緊 *hi\`-kăn'*.

Attain, 得到 *tăk-to\`*.

Attentive, 用心 yung\`-*sàm*.

Auction, 投 t'au, 夜冷 ye\`-lang'.

Awl, 錐 *chui*.

Awning, 天遮 *t'in-che*.

Axe, 斧頭 *fu'*-t'au.

B

Baby, 孩兒 hoi-i.

Bachelor, 未娶親 mi\` *ts'ü' ts'ăn*.

Backwards, 背後便 *pui\`* hau\` pin\`.

Bad, 唔好 'm *ho'*, (language) 爛口 lan\`-*hau'*.

Bag, 袋 toi\`.

Baggage, 行李 hang-li'.

Bake, 炕 *hong\`*, 局 kuk, 局熟 kuk-shuk.

Ball, (a) 毬 k'au, (cannon) 彈子 tan\`-*tsz'*, (to play at ball) 打毬 *ta'* k'au.

Bamboo, 竹 *chuk*.

Banana, 蕉 *chiu*.

Bankruptcy, 報窮 *po\`* k'ung.

Bar, (to) 關住 *kwan*-chü\`.

Barber, 剃頭佬 *t'ai\`*-t'au-*lo'*.

Barracks, 兵房 *ping*-fong.

Barrel, 琵琶桶 p'i-p'a-*t'ung'*.

Barrier, 街閘 *kai*-chap.

Basin, 盤 p'un, (washing basin) 面盤 min\`-p'un.

Basket, 籃 lam.

Bat, 飛鼠 *fi-shü'*.

Bathe, 洗身 *sai'-shăn*.

Bathroom, 洗身房 *sai'-shăn*-fong.

Bathtub, 洗身桶 *sai'-shăn-t'ung'*.

Battle, (a) 打仗 *ta'*-cheung\`.

Bear, 抵住 *tai'*-chü\`.

Beat, 打 *ta'*.

Beautiful, 華美 wa-mi'.

Because, 因為 *yăn*-wai\`.

Beche-de-mer, 海參 *hoi'-shăm*.

Bed, 牀 ch'ong, (to make a) 鋪牀 *p'o* ch'ong.

Bedpost, 牀柱 ch'ong-ch'ü'.

Bed-chamber, 瞓房 *făn\`*-fong.

Beef, 牛肉 ngau-yuk.

Beef-steak, 鐵耙牛肉 *t'it*-p'a-ngau-yuk.

Beer, 啤酒 *pe-tsau'*.

Before, 前 ts'in, 先時 *sin*-shi, 先日 *sin*-yat.

Beggar, 乞兒 *hat*-i.

Begin, 開手 *hoi-shau'*, 起首 *hi'-shau'*.

Behind, 後便 hau\`-pin\`.

Believe, 信 *sun\`*.

Bell, 鐘 *chung*, hand bell 手鐘 *shau'-chung*.

Below, 在下底 tsoi\` ha\` *tai'*, 下便 ha\` pin\`.

Bench, 長櫈 ch'eung-*tăng\`*.

Beneath, 在下 tsoi\` ha\`, 下底 ha\` *tai'*.

Besides, 另外 ling\`-ngoi\`, 而且 i-*c'he'*.

Best, 至好 *chi\` ho'*.

Betimes, 早時 *tso'*-shi.

Better, 更好 *kăng\`-ho'*.

Beyond, (to go) 過 *kwoh`*, 格外 *kak*-ngoi`.

Bill, (paper) 貨單 *foh`-tan*.

Bind, (pasting covers on) 打書皮 *ta' shü*-p'i.

Bird, 雀鳥 *tseuk*-niu', bird-cage 雀籠 *tseuk*-lung.

Birth-day, 生日 *shăng*-yat, (of a god) 誕 *tan`*.

Biscuit, 餅乾 *peng'-kon*.

Black, 黑色 *hak-shik*.

Blacking, (shoe-) 鞋墨水 hai-mak-*shui'*.

Black-brush, 鞋墨掃 hai-mak-*so`*.

Black-smith, 打鐵佬 *ta'-t'it-lo'*.

Blank book, 簿 po`.

Blanket, 張氊 *cheung chin*, 洋氊 yeung-*chin*.

Blindness, 盲眼 mang-ngan'.

Blinds, 百葉窗 pak-ip-*ch'eung*.

Blockhead, 四方木 *sze`-fong*-muk.

Blow, (strike) 打 *ta'*, 打一吓 *ta' yat* ha', (out) 吹 *ch'ui*.

Blue, 藍色 lam-shik.

Boat, 艇 t'eng', 三板 *sam-pan'*.

Body, 身 *shăn*.

Boil, 煲 *po*, 烚 shap, 烚熟 shap-shuk.

Bolster, 長枕頭 ch'eung-*chăm'*-t'au.

Book, 書 *shü*, (a) 一部書 *yat* po` *shü*.

Bookbinder, 釘書人 *teng-shü*-yan, (or 佬 *lo'*, or 師傅 *sze*-fu`.)

Book case, 書櫃 *shü*-kwai`.

Bookseller, 賣書人 mai`-*shü*-yan.

Boot, 靴 *hö*.

Both, 兩個 leung' *koh`*, (a pair of) 雙 *sheung*.

Both—and, 又—又 yau`—yau`.

Bottle, 罇 *tsun*.

Bowl, 碗 *un'*.

Box, 箱 *seung*.

Boy, 男仔 nam-*tsai'*, (servant-) 事仔 sze`-*tsai'*.

Bread, 麵包 min`-*pau*.

Break, 打爛 *ta'*-lan`, 整爛 *ching'*-lan`, 折 *chit*, (open) 打開 *ta'-hoi*, 撬開 kiu`-*hoi*.

Breakfast, 早飯 *tso'*-fan`, 小餐 *siu' ts'an*, 早餐 *tso'-ts'an*.

Brick, 磚 *chün*.

Bridge, 度橋 to`-ki'u.

Bridle, 馬韁 ma'-*keung*.

Bring, 拧一來 *ning*—loi, 拈一來 *nim*—loi.

Broad, 闊 *fut*.

Broom, 把掃 *pa'-so`*.

Brother, (elder) 兄 *hing*, 家兄 *ka-hing*, 大佬 tai'-*lo'*, (younger) 弟 tai`, 細佬 *sai`-lo'*, 舍弟 *she`*-tai`.

Brown, 棕色 *tsung-shik*.

Brush, 擦 *ts'at*, (pencil) 筆 *păt*.

Bull, 牛公 ngau-*kung*.

Bunch of keys, 一揪鎖匙 *yat ts'au soh'*-shi.

Bundle, 包 *pau*, 札 *chat*; make a bundle 綑埋 *kw'ăn'*-mai.

Burn, (to) 燒 *shiu*.

Business, 事幹 *sze`-kon`*.

But, 但 tan`, 乃 nai'.

Butter, 牛油 ngau-yau.

Button, 鈕 nau', button hole, 鈕扣 nau'-kau`.

Buy, 買 mai'.

By and bye, 慢慢 man`-man`

## C

Cabbage, 白菜 pak-ts'oi`.

Cabin, (ship's) 船尾房 shün-mi'-fong, 廂房 seung-fong.

Cake, 餅 peng'.

Call, 叫 kiu`.

Calm, (without wind) 無風 mo' fung.

Can, 得 tăk, 噲 ui', 做得 tso`-tăk.

Canal, 運河 wan`-ho.

Candle, 蠟燭 lap-chuk.

Candle-stick, 蠟燭臺 lap-chuk-t'oi.

Cannon, 大炮 tai`-p'au`.

Cannot, 唔得 'm-tăk.

Canvas, 帆布 li'-po`.

Cap, (a) 頂帽 teng'-mo`.

Cape, (of land) 海角 hoi'-kok.

Capon, 騸鷄 sin`-kai.

Captain, 船主 shün-chü'.

Card, (playing) 紙牌 chi'-p'ai, (card table) 紙牌檯 chi'-p'ai-t'oi.

Care, (to) 料理 liu`-li'; care for 看住 hon-chü`, 睇顧 t'ai'-ku`, 照料 chiu`-liu`, 顧住 ku`-chü`.

Careful, 小心 siu'-săm.

Carefully, 仔細 tsze'-sai`.

Cargo, 船貨 shün-foh, 貨物 foh-mat.

Carpenter, 木匠 muk-tseung`.

Carpet, 地氈 ti`-chin.

Carriage, (a) 駕馬車 ka` ma'-ch'e.

Carry, (on a pole) 擔 tam, (between two) 抬 t'oi, 抬起 t'oi-hi', (in the arms) 抱住 p'o'-chü`.

Cash, 錢 ts'in; cash a cheque 支銀單 chi ngăn-tan.

Cast, 鑄 chü`.

Castor stand, 五味架 'ng'-mi'-ka`.

Cat, 貓 mau or miu.

Catalogue, 張單 cheung-tan.

Catch, 捉 chuk.

Catty, 斤 kăn.

Ceiling, 天花板 t'in-fa-pan'.

Celebrity, 名聲 ming-shing.

Cemetery, 陰城 yăm-sheng.

Censure, to 責鬧 chak-nau`.

Cent, 先士 sin-sze`.

Certain, 定 ting`, a certain man 有人 yau' yan, certain men 或人 wak yan.

Certainly, 必定 pit-ting`, 自然 tsz`-in.

Chair, (a) 張椅 cheung-i'.

Chair coolie, 轎夫 kiu`-fu, 抬轎佬 t'oi-kiu`-lo', chair cushion 坐褥 tso`-yuk.

Change, 改 koi'.

Changer, (money-) 找錢人 chau'-ts'in-yan.

Chapel, 禮拜堂 lai'-pai`-t'ong.

Character, 品行 păn'-hang`, (a letter) 字 tsze`.

Charcoal, 京炭 king-t'an`.

Cheap, 平 p'eng.

Cheat, 呃騙 ngak-p'in`, 打斧頭 ta' fu' t'au.

Cheese, 之時餅 *chi-shi-peng*

Chicken, 雞仔 *kai-tsai'*.

Child, 細蚊仔 *sai'-man-tsai'*.

Children, 仔女 *tsai'*-nü', (young) 孩兒 hoi-i.

Chimney, 烟通 *in-t'ung*.

China, 中國 *Chung-kwok*.

Chinese, (a) 唐人 T'ong-yan, (language) 唐話 T'ong-wa'.

Chisel, 鑿 tsok.

Cholera, 時症 shi-*ching'*.

Choose, 揀擇 *kan'*-chak.

Chop, (a mark) 字號 tsze'-ho'.

Chop-sticks, 快子 *fai'-tsze'*.

Church, 福音堂 *fuk-yam*-t'ong.

Cigar, 呂宋烟 Lü'-*sung'-in*.

Circle, 圈 *hün*.

City, 城 sheng.

Class, 類 lui'.

Clean, 乾凈 *kon*-tseng'.

Cleanse, 做乾凈 tso' *kon*-tseng'.

Clear, (comprehensible) 清 *ts'ing*; clearly, 明白 ming-pak.

Clearance, (port) 放行紙 *fong'*-hang-*chi'*

Clerk, 寫字人 *se'*-tsze'-yan.

Clever, 手勢 *shau'*-shai'.

Climate, 水土 *shui'*-*t'o'*.

Clock, 鐘 *chung*, (o'clock) 點鐘 *tim' chung*.

Close, (near) 近 kan', k'an'.

Cloth, 布 *po'*.

Clothes, 衣服 *i*-fuk.

Clothes-brush, 衣擦 *i-ts'at*, 衣掃 *i-so'*.

Clothes-horse, 衣架 *i-ka'*.

Clothes-press, 衣櫃 *i*-kwai'.

Cloud, 雲 wān.

Coal, 煤炭 mui-*t'an*.

Coat, 大衫 tai'-*sham*, 件衫 kin' *sham*

Cock, 鷄公 *kai-kung*.

Cockroach, 甴曱 kat-tsat.

Cold, 凍 *tung'*, 寒凍 hon-*tung'*.

Cold season, 天時寒凍 *t'in*-shi hon-*tung'*.

Collect, 收起 *shau-hi'*.

Collectively, 合同 hop t'ung, 同埋 t'ung mai.

Colour, 色 *shik*, 顏色 ngan-*shik*.

Comb, (a) 隻梳 *chek shoh*, (fine) 篦 pi'.

Come, 來 loi, (COL) 嚟 lai.

Comfortable, 平安 p'ing-*on*, 舒服 *shü*-fuk

Commerce, 貿易 mau'-yik.

Compass, 羅經 lo-*kung*, 指南針 *chi'*-nam-*cham*. Four points and centre 五方 'ng'-*fong*.

Compel, 强 k'eung'.

Compradore, 買辦 mai'-pan'.

Conceal, 埋 mai.

Conduct, 行爲 hang-wai.

Confusedly, 亂 lün'.

Connect, 連住 lin-chu'.

Consequently, 所以 *shoh'*-i'.

Consider, 思想吓 *sze-seung'*-ha'; consider thoroughly, 想眞來 *seung'-chan*-loi.

Considerable, 越發 üt-*fat*.

Consul, 領事官 ling'-sze'-*kun*.

Consumption, (disease) 肺勞症 *fai'*-lo-*ching'*, 內傷 noi'-*sheung*.

Contain, 載去 *tsoi`* *hü`*, 載有 *tsoi`* yau'.

Contrary, to 唔合 'm hop.

Contusion, 瘀傷 *ü'-sheung.*

Converse, 相叙 *seung*-tsui`.

Conversation, 叙談 tsui`-t'am, 講說話 *kong' shüt*-wa`, 相酌話 *seung cheuk* wa`.

Cook, 火頭 *foh'*-t'au.

Cooking-pot, 沙煲 *sha-po.*

Cool, 凉 leung.

Coolie, 管店 *kun'-tim`*, (street) 挑夫 *t'iu-fu.*

Copper, 銅 t'ung.

Copy, (to) 抄 *ch'au*, 抄起 *ch'au-hi'*.

Cork, (a) 樽枳 *tsün-chat.*

Cock-screw, 酒鑽 *tsau'-tsün`*.

Corn, (on the toe) 鷄眼 *kai*-ngan'.

Correct, 正 *ching`*.

Cot or hammock, 吊床 *tiu`*-ch'ong.

Cotton, (raw) 棉花 min-*fa.*

Cotton cloth, 布 *po`*.

Couch, 睡椅 shui`-*i'*.

Cough, 咳嗽 *k'at-sau`*.

Count, (to) 數 *sho`*, 計 *kai`*.

Counterpane, 白花被 pak-*fa*-p'i'.

Country, 國 *kwok*, 地方 ti`-*fong.*

Courage, 好胆 *ho'-tam'*.

Course, (of course) 自然 tsz`-in.

Court, 公堂 *kung*-t'ong.

Cover, 蓋 *k'oi`*, to cover 蓋住 *k'oi`*-chü`.

Coverlet, 衿被 *k'äm'*-p'i'.

Covet, 貪 *t'am.*

Cow, 牛 ngau, 牛乸 ngau-*na'*.

Crab, 蟹 hai'.

Crafty, 詭滑 *kwai'*-wat.

Crape, 縐紗 *tsau`-sha.*

Crockery, 磁器 ts'ze-*hi`*, crockery mender 補磁器人 *po'*-ts'ze-*hi`*-yan, or 補花碗佬 *po'-fa-un' lo'*.

Cross way, 三丫路 *sam-a*-lo`.

Crowd, 一堆 *yat tui*; pressing crowd 好逼人 *ho' pik* yan.

Cup, 盃 *pui*, (for writing ink) 池 ch'i.

Cup-board, 碗櫃 *un'*-kwai`.

Cure, 醫好 *i-ho'*, 好翻 *ho'-fan.*

Curry-powder, 黃薑粉 wong-*keung-fan'*, 架厘粉 *ka`*-li-*făn'*.

Curtain, 蚊帳 *măn-cheung`*

Custard-apple, 番荔枝 *fan*-lai`-*chi.*

Custom, (house) 關口 *kwan-hau'*

Cut, 切 *ts'it*, with scissors 剪 *tsin'*.

Cuttlefish, 墨魚 măk-u.

## D

Daily, 日日 yat-yat.

Damp, 翻潮 *fan*-ch'iu.

Dancing, 跳舞 *t'iu`*-mo'.

Danger, 危險 ngai-*him'*.

Dare, 敢 *kom'*.

Dark, 暗 *om`*.

Daughter, (your) 令愛 ling`-*oi`*.

Day, 日 yat; the other day 往日 *wong'*-yat, 先日 *sin*-yat; to this day 至到今日 *chi` to`* *kăm*-yat.

Daytime, 日頭 yat-t'au, by day 日間 yat-*kan*

Dead, 死了 *sze'*-liu', 過身 *kwoh`-shan.*

Deafness, 耳聾 i'-lung.

Dear, 貴 *kwai`.*

Death, 死 *sze'.*

Debt, 欠債 *him`-chai`.*

Decade, 旬 ts'un.

Deceit, 詭譎 *kwai'-kwăt.*

Deceitful, 奸詐嘅 *kan-cha` ke`.*

Deck, 船面 shün-min`.

Decline, (to) 辭却 ts'ze-*k'euk.*

Deep, 深 *shàm.*

Deer, 鹿 luk.

Degree, (measure) 度 to`.

Delay, 遲 ch'i.

Descend, 落去 lok-*hü`.*

Desire, 欲 yuk, want 愛 *oi`.*

Desist, (from work) 收工 *shau-kung.*

Desk, 寫字檯 *se'*-tsze`-t'oi.

Despatch, (to) 打發 *ta'-fat.*

Despatch, a, (inf. to sup.) 公文 *kung*-măn, (sup. to inf.) 文書 măn-*shü.*

Despise, 輕忽 *hing-făt,* 睇小 *t'ai'-siu'.*

Destestable, 可惡 *ho'-u`.*

Dew, 露水 lo`-*shui'.*

Diarrhœa, 肚痾 t'o'-*oh.*

Dictionary, 字典 tsze`-*tin'.*

Die, (to) 死 *sze'.*

Different, 異 i`.

Difficult, 難 nan.

Diligent, 勤力 k'ăn-lik.

Diminish, 減少 *kăm'-shiu'.*

Dinner, 大餐 tai' *ts'an,* 晚餐 man' *ts'an.*

Dining room, 大餐房 tai`-*ts'an*-fong.

Directly, 就 tsau`, 卽刻 *tsik-hak*

Dirty, 唔乾淨 'm kon-tsing`, 汚糟 *u-tso.*

Disagreement, 心不一 *săm pat yat.*

Discourse, 講出 *kong'-ch'ut,* 講論 *kong'*-lun`.

Dislike, 唔中意 'm *chung-i`.*

Dislocations, 跌錯鉸骨 *tit ts'oh` kau`-kwăt.*

Disrespectful, 唔恭敬 'm *kung-king`.*

Disyllable, 蜆殼字 *hin'-hok*-tsze`.

Distinguish, 分別 *făn-pit,* 分開 *făn-hoi.*

Disturb, 驚動 *king*-tung`.

Divulge, 露出 lo`-*ch'ut.*

Do, 做 tso`.

Dog, 狗 *kau',* hunting dog, 獵狗 lip-*kau'.*

Dollar, (see lesson 55 for varieties) 銀錢 ngăn-ts'in.

Don't, 咪 mai', 唔好 'm *ho',* 唔使 'm shai'.

Door, 門 mun, 門口 mun-*hau'.*

Double, 雙 (cont. 双) *sheung.*

Double minded, 二心 i`-*săm.*

Dough, 麵 min`.

Dove, 鴿 *kop.*

Downstairs, 樓下 lau-ha`, 底下 *tai'*-ha`, 在下便 tsoi`-ha`-pin`.

Draw, a tooth 脫牙 *t'üt*-nga, (water) 打 *ta',* (pull up) 揪起 *ts'au hi'.*

Drawer 櫃桶 kwai`-*t'ung'.*

Drawing-room, 客廳 *hak-t'eng.*

Dress, 裝扮 *chong*-pan`, 打扮 *ta'*-pan`, (to) 着衣服 *cheuk i*-fuk.

Dressing-case, 鏡粧 *keng`-chong.*

Dressing-gown, 修飾衫 *sau-shik-sham.*

Dressing-room, 修飾房 *sau-shik*-fong.

Dressing-table, 梳粧檯 *shoh-chong*-t'oi.

Drill, (to) 鑽 *tsün`*, 鑽子 *tsün`-tsze'*.

Drink, 飲 *yăm'*.

Dry, 乾 *kon*.

Duck, 鴨 *ap*, (wild) 水鴨 *shui'-ap*.

Dumb, 瘂口 *a'-hau'*.

During, 之耐—— *chi*-noi`, 之時—— *chi*-shi.

Dust, 泥塵 nai-ch'ăn, dust-pan 拂斗 *fat-tau'*.

Duty, (customs) 餉銀 *heung'*-ngăn, (to pay) 納餉銀 nap *heung'*-ngăn.

Dwell, 住 chü`.

Dwelling house, 屋舍 *uk-she`*.

Dysentery, 疴痢 *oh*-li`.

## E

Each, 每 mui', 對 *tui`*, 各 *kok*.

Early, 早時 *tso'*-shi.

Earth, 地 ti`, (matter) 坭土 nai-*t'o'*.

East, 東 *tung*.

Easy, 易 i`, take it easy 修柔做喇 *sau* yau tso` *la*.

Eat, 食 shik, 吃 *yak*.

Eau de Cologue, (*lit.* flower-dew water) 花露水 *fa*-lo`-*shui'*.

Ebb, 水乾 *shui'-kon*.

Eclipse, solar 日蝕 yat-shik, lunar 月蝕 üt-shik.

Eel, 鱔魚 shin'-ü.

Egg, 蛋 tan`.

Eight, 八 *pat*.

Either, 是但 shi`-tan`, 或 wak, 一係唔係 *yat* hai` 'm hai`.

Elephant, 象 tseung`.

Eleven, 十一 shap-*yat*.

Embark, 搭 *tap*.

Emoluments, (official) 養廉 yeung'-lim,

Emperor, 皇帝 wong-*tai`*.

Empire, (the world) 天下 *t'in*-ha`.

Employ, 請 *ts'eng'*, 使 *shai'*, to be in an employ, 打 *ta'*, 打工 *ta'-kung*.

Empty, 空 *hung*, (to) 整空 *ching'-hung*, 倒空 *to'-hung*, 搬空 *pun-hung*.

End, 收尾 *shau*-mi'.

Enemy, 仇敵 ch'au-tik.

Englishman, 英吉利人 *Ying-kat*-li`-yan.

Engraver, 雕匠 *tiu*-tseung`.

Enough, 够 *kau`*.

Enter, 入去 yăp *hü`*.

Entirely, 齊晒 ts'ai-*sai`*.

Envelop, 包起 *pau-hi'*.

Envelope, 信封 *sun`-fung*.

Eruption, (on the skin) 瘢疹 *pan-ch'an'*.

Even, (also) 連 lin.

Evening, 晚 man', this evening 今晚 *kăm*-man'.

Event, 事 sze`.

Everybody, 各人 *kok* yan, 每人 mui' yan.

Everyday, 每日 mui' yat.

Everything, 各件 *kok* kin`, 乜野 *măt*-ye'.

Everywhere, 處處 ch'ü`-ch'ü`, 便便 pin`-pin`, 四處 sze`-ch'ü`, on every side 四面 sze`-min`.

Evidence, 口供 hau'-kung, 憑據 p'ang-kü`.

Exact, 合 hop, 正 ching`, 啱啱 ngam-ngam.

Exactly, 正正 ching`-ching`.

Except, 除 ch'ü.

Excuse me (I am sorry) 箕我唔着 sün` ngo 'm cheuk.

Executioner, 殺手 shat-shau'.

Exert, 用力 yeung`-lik, 出力 ch'ut-lik, 盡力 tsun`-lik.

Expensive, 貴 kwai`.

Explain, 解 kai'.

Extiuguish, 熄 sik, 打烏火 ta'-u-foh', 整熄火 ching'-sik-foh'.

Extremely, 極 kik, 得濟 tak-tsai`.

Eye, 眼 ngan', one eyed 單眼嘅 tan-ngan' ke`.

# F

Face, 面 min`.

Faint, (to) 失魂 shat-wăn.

Fair, (-wind) 順風 shun`-fung.

Faithful, 忠直 chung-chik, 信實 sun`-shat.

Fall down, 跌倒 tit-to'.

Family, 家眷 ka-kün`.

Famine, 饑荒 ki-fong.

Fan, (a) 把扇 pa'-shin`.

Far, 遠 ün', 遠處 ün'-ch'ü`.

Farmer, 農夫 nung-fu, 耕田佬 kang-t'in-lo'.

Fast, (quick) 快 fai`, (boat) 快艇 fai`-t'eng', to go fast (as a clock) 行快 hang-fai`.

Father, 尊父 tsün-fu`, 家父 ka-fu`, 父親 fu`-ts'an.

Fault, 錯 ts'oh`.

Favourable, 順 shun`, by your favour, 託賴 t'ok-lai`.

Fear, 怕 p'a`.

Feather, 鷄毛 kai-mo.

Feed, to 餵 wai`.

Fender, 火爐圍 foh'-lo-wai.

Ferry, (landing place) 渡頭 to`-t'au.

Ferry-boat, 橫水渡 wang-shui'-to`.

Ferry-man, 渡主 to`-chü'.

Fever, 發熱 fat-it, 發冷 fat-lăng'.

Few, a few (indef) 幾個 ki' koh`.

Field, 田 t'in.

Fifty, 五十 'ng shap.

Fight, 打交 ta'-kau.

File, 銼 ts'oh`.

Fill, 斟滿 chăm-mun', fill up 填埋 t'in-mai.

Fin, 魚翅 ü-ch'i`.

Finally, 收尾 shau-mi'.

Find, 搵着 wăn'-cheuk.

Fine, 幼 yau`.

Finish, 做完 tso`-ün, 做埋 tso`-mai.

Fire, 火 foh', conflagration 火燭 foh'-chuk, make a fire 打火爐 ta' foh'-lo, fire place 火爐 foh'-lo.

Fire-crackers, 炮像 *p'au'*-tseung'.

Fire-wood, 柴 ch'ai.

Fire-works, (to burn) 燒烟火 *shiu in-foh'*.

First, 先 *sin*, firstly 一來 *yat* loi, first day of the month 初一 *ch'o-yat*, in the first place 先處 *sin-ch'ü'*.

Fish, 魚 ü, (to) 打魚 *ta'*-ü, salt-fish 鹹魚 ham-yü.

Fisherman, 攞魚人 *loh'*-ü-yan.

Five, 五 'ng'.

Fix, 定實 ting'-shat.

Flag, (a) 旗 k'i, staff 旗杆 k'i-*kon*.

Flavoured, 滋味 *tsz*-mi', 氣味道 *hi'*-mi'-to'.

Flea, 狗虱 *kau'-shat*.

Flood-tide, 水大 *shui'*-tai'.

Floor, 樓板 lau-*pan'*, (ground-) 地檯板 ti'-t'oi-*pan'*.

Flower, 花 *fa*, flower vase 花瓶 *fa*-p'ing, -pot stand 花架 *fa-ka'*, flower pot 花盆 *fa*-p'un, bunch of flowers 一球花 *yat*-k'au-*fa*.

Fly away, 飛去 *fi*-hü', fly a kite 放 *fong'*, (a) 烏蠅 *u*-ying.

Fog, 曚霧 mung-mo'.

Fold (to) 摺埋 *chip*-mai.

Follow, 跟住 *kan*-chü'.

Foolish, 呆 ngoi.

Foot, 脚 *keuk*, (measure) 尺 *ch'ek*, footstool 脚踏櫈 *keuk*-tap-*tăng'*.

For, (prep.) 代 toi'.

Foreign, 來路 loi-lo'; (the Cantonese call foreigners 番人 *fan*-yan.)

Forenoon, 上晝 sheung'-*chau'*, 上午 sheung'-ng'.

Foresail, 頭幃 t'au-li'.

Forget, 忘記 mong-*ki'*, 忘却 mong-*k'euk*.

Fork, (a) 枝叉 *chi-ch'a*.

Formerly, 先時 *sin*-shi, 舊時 kau'-shi, 前時 ts'in-shi.

Fort, 炮臺 *p'au'*-t'oi, 城 sheng.

Fortnight, 兩個禮拜 leung'-*koh'* lai'-*pai'*

Foundation, 地基 ti'-*ki*.

Four, 四 *sze'*.

Fowl, 鷄 *kai*,

Fowling-piece, 鳥鎗 niu'-*ts'eung*.

Fracture, 拆骨 *chit-kwat*.

Freight, 水脚銀 *shui'-keuk*-ngăn.

Frenchman, 佛蘭西人 Fat-lan-*sai*-yan.

Fresh, 新鮮 *san-sin*, (water) 淡 tam'.

Friend, 朋友 p'ang-yau'.

From, 由 yau, 自 tsze'.

Frost, 霜 *seung*.

Fruit, 菓子 *kwoh'-tsz'*, 生菓 *shang-kwoh'*.

Fry, 煎 *tsin*, 煎熟 *tsin*-shuk.

Frying-pan, 鑊 wok.

Full, 滿 mun', (in eating) 飽 *pau'*.

Future, 來 loi, (-events) 未來嘅事 mi'-loi-*ke'*-sze'.

## G

Gambler, 賭博佬 *to'-pok-lo'*, 賭錢佬 *to'*-ts'in-*lo'*.

Gape, 打喊露 *ta'-ham'*-lo'.

Garden, 園 ün.

Gardener, 園丁 ün-*ting*, 花王 *fa*-wong.

Garter, 襪帶 mat-*tai*`.

Gather, (flowers) 摘 *chak*.

Gauze, 響雲紗 *heung'*-wăn-*sha*.

Gem, 玉 yuk.

Generally, 大概 tai`-*k'oi*`.

Gentle, 温良 *wăn*-leung.

Gentleman, 位人客 wei`-yan-*hak*.

German, 日耳曼人 Yat-i'-man'-yan.

Get on, (in life) 發達起 *fat*-tat-*hi'*.

Ghost, 鬼 *kwai'*.

Giddy, 頭暈 t'au-wăn.

Gill, (measure) 合 *kop*.

Gimlet, 手鑽 *shau'-tsun*.

Girl, 女仔 nü'-*tsai'*.

Give 俾 *pi'*,

Give away, distribute 派 *p'ai*`.

Glance, (at) 睇一吓 *t'ai'-yat-ha*.

Glass, 玻璃 *poh*-li.

Glass, (a tumbler) 玻璃杯 *poh*-li-*pui*.

Gloves, 手笠 *shau'-lap*.

Glue, 牛皮膠 ngau-p'i-*kau*.

Go, (as a clock) 行 hang, (go out) 出去 *ch'ut-hü*, (go away) 扯 *ch'e'*

Goat, 草羊 *ts'o'*-yeung.

Goblet, 水壺 *shui'*-u.

GOD, 上帝 Sheung`-*Tai*`.

Godown, 貨倉 *foh*`-ts'ong.

Gold, 金 *kum*.

Gone, 去了 *hü*-liu', 去曉 *hü*-*hiu*, 去過 *hü*`-*kwoh*`.

Good bye, 好行 *ho'*-hang.

Goods, 貨 *foh*`, 貨物 *foh*`-măt, 物件 măt-kin`.

Goose, 鵝 ngoh, (wild) 鴈鵝 ngan`-ngoh.

Governor, (general) 總督 *tsung'-tuk*, (of a province) 巡撫 *ts'un-fu'*.

Gradually, 漸漸 tsim`-tsim`.

Grass, 草 *ts'o'*.

Grass-cloth, 夏布 ha`-*po*`.

Gratitude, 承惠 shing-wai`, 知恩 *chi-yăn*.

Grave, 棺材窟 *kun*-ts'oi-*fat*.

Gravy dish, 汁盅 *chăp*-chung.

Green, 青綠 *ts'ing*-luk.

Grind the teeth, 打齧牙 *ta'-ngit*-nga.

Groom, 馬夫 ma'-*fu*.

Guard, 守住 *shau'*-chü`.

Guess, 估 *ku'*.

Guest, 人客 yan-*hak*.

Gun-powder, 火藥 *foh'*-yeuk.

## H

Hair, 毛 mo (of the head) 頭髮 t'au-*fat*.

Hair-brush, 頭掃 t'au-*so*`, 髮掃 *fat-so*`.

Half, 半 pun`.

Hall, 堂 t'ong.

Ham, 火腿 *foh'-t'ui'*.

Hammer, 鐵鎚 *t'it*-ch'ui.

Hand, (to) at table 手俾 *shau'-pi'*, 遞轉 tai`-*chün*`.

Handkerchief, 手巾 *shau'-kun*.

Handle, (a) 柄 *ping*`.

Hang, (up) 掛起 *kwa*`-*hi'*.

Hard, 硬 ngang`.

Harmonious, 和氣 *woh-hi*\`.

Harvest, 收成 *shau*-shing.

Hash, (to) 乞食 *hăt*-shik 雜膾 tsap-ui\`.

Hasten, 趕快 *kon*′-*fai*\`, 快趨 *fai*\`-*ts'ü*.

Hasty, 頻 p'ăn.

Hat, 帽 mo\`, hat-stand 帽架 mo\`-*ka*\`.

Hate, 見惡 *kin*\`-*u*\`, 可恨 *ho*′-han\`.

Haul on, 扯起 *ch'e*′-*hi*′.

Have, 有 yau′.

He, 佢 k'ü′.

Head, 頭 t'au.

Headache, 頭痛 t'au-*t'ung*\`.

Head-dress, 首飾 *shau*′-*shik*,

Head wind, 頂頭風 *ting*′-t'au-*fung*.

Heap, (to) 堆起 *tui-hi*′.

Hear, 聽 *t'eng*.

Heart, 心 *săm*.

Heat, 熱 it, (to) 燒熱 *shiu*-it

Heaven, 天 *t'in*, (the abode) 天堂 *t'in*-t'ong.

Heavy, 重 chung\`.

Help, 帮助 *pong*-choh\`, (no) 無奈何 mo-noi\`-hoh.

Hen, 鷄乸 *kai-na*′.

Hence, 離呢處 li-*ni-ch'ü*\`.

Henceforth, 自今以後 tsz\`-*kăm*-i′-hau\`, 自後 tsz\`-hau\`.

Here, 呢處 *ni-ch'ü*\`, 呢便 *ni*-pin\`.

Hereafter, 後來 hau\`-loi.

Hiccough, 打嘶嗌 *ta*′-*sze-yik*.

Hidden, 暗 *om*\`.

High, 高 *ko*.

Highway, 大路 tai\`-lo\`.

Hill, 山 *shan*.

Himself, 自家 tsz\`-*ka*.

Hinge, 鉸 *kau*\`.

His, 佢嘅 k'ü′-*ke*\`.

Hither, 在呢處 *tsoi*\`-*ni-ch'ü*\`.

Hoist, (a sail) 扯起 *ch'e*′-*hi*′.

Hold, (a horse) 牽住 *hin*-chü\`, (fast) 揸實來 *cha*-shat-loi.

Hold, (ship's) 艙 *ts'ong*.

Home, (at) 在家 tsoi\`-*ka*, (go) 歸 *kwai*, 家主 *ka-chü*′.

Hone, 磨刀石 mo-*to*-shek.

Honourable, 貴 *kwai*\`.

Hook up, 鈎起 *kau-hi*′.

Hope, 望 mong\`.

Hongkong, 香港 *Heung-kong*′.

Horizon, 天涯 *t'in*-ngai.

Horse, 馬 ma′, (a) 一隻馬 *yat-chek*-ma′.

Horse-whip, 馬鞭 ma′-*pin*.

Hot, 熱 it, (as the sun) 烘 hung.

Hotel, 客店 *hak-tim*\`.

Hour, 點鐘 *tim*′-*chung*, Chinese hour=2 European hours 時辰 *shi-shăn*.

House, 屋 *uk*, 間屋 *kan-uk*.

Houseboy, 事仔 sze\`-*ts'ai*′.

How? 點 *tim*′, 點樣 *tim*′-yeung\`, 如何 ü-hoh.

How many? 幾多 *ki*′-*toh*.

Hungry, 肚餓 t'o′-ngoh\`.

Hurry, 急 *kăp* 快啲 *fai*\`-chi\`.

Hurt, 傷 *sheung*, (to give pain) 痛 *t'ung*\`.

# I

I, 我 ngo'.

Ice, 冰 *ping*, 雪 *suet* (*lit.* snow).

Idle, 閒 han.

If, 若 yeuk, as if 好似 *ho'*-ts'z'.

Ignoramus, 山佬 *shan-lo'*, 山毒 *shan-*tuk.

Ill, (bad) 唔好 'm-*ho'*, treat ill 刻薄待人 *hak*-pok-toi'-yan.

Immediately, 立刻 làp-*hak*, 卽刻 *tsik-hak*.

In, (into) 入 yăp, 在內 tsoi'-noi'.

Inch, 寸 *ts'ün'*.

Incorrect, 唔準嘅 'm-*chun'-ke'*.

Indisposed, 唔自在 'm-tsze'-tsoi', (unwell) 唔舒服 'm-*shü*-fuk.

Inflammation, 腫熱 *chung'*-it.

Ink, 墨水 mak-*shui'*.

Ink-stand, 墨水罌 mak-*shui'-ang*.

Ink-stone, 墨硯 mak-in', (-tray) 盤 p'un.

Ink-stone box, 墨硯盒 mak-in'-hop.

Ink-stone cover, 墨硯蓋 mak-in'-*k'oi'*.

Insane, (-ity) 發癲 *fat-tin*.

Insert, 放入 *fong'*-yăp.

Inside, 裏頭 lui'-t'au 內便 noi'-pin', to turn inside out 翻裏便出來 *fan'*-lui'-pin' *ch'ut*-loi.

Instance, (for) 比如 *pi'*-ü, 設使 *ch'it-sze'*.

Intend, 想 *seung'*.

Intercalary, 閏 yun'.

Interest, 利息 li'-*sik*.

Interpret, 傳話 ch'ün-wa', 番譯 *fan*-yik.

Interrogative particles 呢, 吖, 冇 *ni*, *a*, mo'.

Intimate, 心腹 *săm-fuk*.

Into, 入內 yăp-noi'.

Invent, 想出 *seung'-ch'ut*.

Invite, 請 *ts'eng'*.

Inwards 在內 tsoi'-noi'.

Iron, 鐵 *t'it*.

Is, 係 hai', 是 shi'.

It, 佢 k'ü', it is 係 hai'.

Itch, 生癩 *shăng-lai'*.

Ivory, 象牙 tseung'-nga.

# J

Jelly, 凍 *tung'*.

Judge, 按察司 *on'-ch'at-sze*.

Just so, 噉樣 *kom'*-yeung'.

Just now, 正今 *ching'-kăm*, 就 tsau'.

# K

Keep, 擠埋 *chai*-mai, 守 *shau'*.

Key, 鎖匙 *soh'*-shi.

Kick, 踢起 *t'ek-hi'*.

Kill, 殺 *shat*, 打死 *ta'-sze'*.

Kitchen, 廚房 ch'ü-fong.

Kite, (paper) 紙鷂 *chi'*-iu, (to fly) 放紙鷂 *fong'-chi'*-iu.

Knife, 刀 *to*, pen knife 張刀仔 *cheung-to-tsai'*.

Knock, 打 *ta'*, 拍 *p'ak*.

Knot, 打纈 *ta'-lit*.

Know, 知 *chi*, 知到 *chi-to'*, 識得 *shik-tăk*.

# L

Lacker-ware, 漆器 *ts'at-hi'*.

Ladder, 堂梯 t'ong-*t'ai*.

Ladle, 湯羹 *t'ong-kang*, 殼 *hok*.

Lady, 奶奶 *nai-nai*, little lady (said to a child) 亞娘仔 *a'*-neung-*tsai'*.

Lame, (-ness) 跛脚 *pai-keuk*.

Lamp, 盞燈 *chan'-tăng*.

Lamp-oil, 生油 *shăng*-yau.

Lamp-shade, 燈罩 *tăng-chau'*.

Lamp-wick, 燈心 *tăng-săm*.

Landing-place, 渡頭 to'-t'au.

Landlord, 屋主 *uk-chü'*, (shop) 舖主 *p'o'-chü'*.

Lantern, 手燈 *shau'-tăng*.

Lard, 猪油 *chü*-yau.

Large, 大 tai'.

Last, 收尾 *shau*-mi', 舊 kau', at last 畢竟 *pat-king'*, 到底 *to'-tai'*, lastly 輪到 lun-*to'*.

Late 遲 ch'i.

Lately, of late, 近來 kan'-loi.

Law, 律法 lut *fat*, (to keep the) 守律法 *shau*-lut-*fat*.

Law clerk, 師爺 *sze*-ye.

Lawyer, 狀師 chong'-*sze*.

Lay a fire, 打火爐 *ta'-foh'*-lo.

Lazy, 懶惰 lan'-toh'.

Lead, (to) 帶出 *tai'-ch'ut*.

Leaf, 葉 ip, (of a book) 篇 *p'in*.

League, (10 *li*.) 塘汎 t'ong-*sun'*.

Leak, 漏水 lau'-*shui'*.

Leap, 跳起 *t'iu-hi'*.

Learn, 學 hok.

Least, 至小 *chi'-siu'*.

Leave, (to) 離別 li-pit, (open) 離開 li-*hoi*.

Left, 左 *tsoh'*, 左便 *tsoh'*-pin'.

Leg, 大髀 tai'-*pi'*.

Leisure, 閒 hau, 閒時候 han-shi-hau', 閒暇 hau-ha', (no-) 唔得閒 'm-*tăk*-han.

Lend, 借去 *tse'-hü'*, 借過 *tse'-kwoh'*.

Leprosy, 痳瘋 ma-*fung*.

Less, 更小 *kăng'-siu'*.

Let, 俾 *pi'*, let go 放去 *fong' hü'*, (rent) 出賃 *ch'ut* yăm'.

Let-go, 任去 yăm' *hü'*, let do 去做 *hü'* tso', let down, 放下 *fong'* ha'.

Letter, 封信 *fung-sun'*, 書信 *shü-sun'*.

Level, 平 p'ing, to level, 掘平 kwat-p'ing.

Library, 書房 *shü*-fong.

Lie, (a) 浮言 fau-in.

Life, 生 *shăng*, the whole life 一生 *yat-shăng*.

Lift, 擰起 *ning-hi'*, (up) 撓起 *tau-hi'*.

Light, (the light) 光 *kwong*, get in the light 遮黑 *che hak*, to light 點 *tim'*. (not heavy) 輕 *hing*.

Like, (to) 中意 *chung-i'*, 愛 *oi'*, to be like 同樣 t'ung yeung'.

Limited, 有限 yau'-han'.

List, 條目 t'iu muk, to draw up a catalogue 開列 *hoi*-lit.

Listen, 細聽 *sai'-t'eng.*

Little, 細 *sai'*, 小 *siu'*, (in a depreciatory sense) 四四六六 *sze' sze'* luk luk.

Live, (dwell) 住 chü', live at 住在 chü' tsoi', live together 同住 t'ung chü'.

Load, (to) 裝貨 *chong foh'.*

Lobster, 龍蝦 lung-*ha.*

Lock, (a) 把鎖 *pa'-soh'*, (to) 鎖 *soh'*, to lock up, 關埋 *kwan*-mai, 鎖住 *soh'*-chü', 鎖起 *soh'-hi'.*

Long, (in time) 耐 noi', 重 chung', a long time 好久 *ho' kau'*, so long a time 咁耐 *kom'*-noi', any longer 耐啲 noi' *ti*, how long? 幾耐 *ki'* noi'.

Look, 睇 *t'ai'*, look at 望住 mong'-chü', 睇見 *t'ai' kin'*, look for 搵 *wăn'*, 尋 ts'ăm.

Looking-glass, 面鏡 min'-*keng'.*

Look out, (in a dictionary) 查 ch'a.

Lose, 失 *shat*, lose a battle 打輸 *ta' shü.*

Love, 見愛 *kin' oi'.*

Low, 低 *tai*, 矮 *ai'.*

Lower, (to) 落 lok.

Lychees, 荔枝 lai'-*chi.*

## M

Macao, 澳門 O'-mun.

Macaoese, 澳門人 O'-mun-yan.

Magistrates, 官府 *kun-fu'*, 審事官 *sham'*-sze'-*kun.*

Mainsail, 大帆 tai' li'.

Make, 做 tso', 整 *ching'*, (compel) 監 *kam*, 強 k'eung', make money 賺來 chan' loi, (a bed) 打鋪蓋 *ta' p'o-k'oi'.*

Male, 男 nam, animals (generally), 公 *kung* birds 雄 hung and 公 *kung*, quadrupeds 牡 mau'.

Man, 人 yan, men 衆人 *chung'* yan.

Man-of-war, 兵船 *ping*-shun.

Many, 多 *toh*, very many, 大多 tai' *toh.*

Map, 圖 t'o.

Mare, 馬母 ma'-mu'.

Mark, (to put a private mark on goods) 打暗號 *ta' om'*-ho'.

Market, 街市 *kai*-shi'.

Market-place, 市頭 shi'-t'au, (town) 墟市 *hü*-shi'.

Market-price, 時價 shi-*ka'.*

Marriage, 嫁娶 *ka' ts'ü'.*

Marry, (said of a man) *ts'ü'* lo'-p'oh 娶老婆, (of a woman) *ch'ut ka'* 出嫁.

Mason, 泥水佬 nai-*shui'-lo'.*

Mast, 枝桅 *chi*-wai, to put in a mast 豎桅 shü'-wai, mainmast 大桅 tai' wai, foremast 頭桅 t'au-wai, mizenmast 尾桅 mi'-wai.

Mat, 席 tsek.

Match, 火柴 *foh'*-ch'ai.

Matter, 事幹 sze'-*kon'*, (no) 唔論 'm-lun'.

Mattress, 墊褥 tin'-yuk.

May, (can) 可以 *hoh'*-i'.

Me, 我 ngoh'.

Meal, (a) 餐 *ts'an*.

Mean, (base) 賤 tsin'.

Meaning, 意思 *i'-sze'*.

Means, 法子 *fat-tsze'*.

Measles, 出痲 *ch'ut* ma.

Measure, (to) 量度 leung' tok, (a) 量 leung'.

Medicine, 藥 yeuk.

Memory, 記性 *ki'-sing'*.

Mend, 補 *po'*, 補翻 *po'-fan*.

Merchant, 商賈 *sheung-ku'*, 商人 *sheung*-yan.

Merchant vessel, 貨船 *foh'*-shün.

Messenger, 來使 loi-*sze'*, (official) 公使 *kung-sze'*.

Middle, 中 *chung*.

Middling, 中中 *chung-chung*.

Midnight, 半夜 *pun'*-ye'.

Midst of, 中間 *chung-kan*.

Mile, (Chinese; $\frac{36}{100}$ of an English) 里 li'.

Milk, 牛嬭 ngau-nai'.

Mince, 免治 min'-chi' (bast.)

Mind, 心 *săm*, to mind (i.e. look after) 理 li'.

Minute, 喕尼 *min-ni'* (bast.)

Mirror, 面鏡 min'-*keng'*.

Mirror, frame 鏡架 *keng'-ka'*.

Miscellaneous, 雜 tsap.

Miss, (to) 嚫 lai.

Mistake, (to) 記錯 *ki'-ts'oh'*, to make a 整錯 *ching' ts'oh'*.

Mistaken, 宗誤 *tsung* 'ng'.

Mix, 摳埋 *k'au*-mai.

Mizen sail, 尾幔 mi'-li'.

Money, 錢 ts'in, to make money (grow rich) 發財 *fat*-ts'oi.

Money changer, 換錢 un' ts'in, 找錢佬 *chau'*-ts'in-*lo'*

Monkey, 馬騮 ma'-lau, 亞三 *a'-sam* (slang.)

Month, 月 üt, this month 呢个月 *ni koh* üt, last month 上個月 sheung' *koh'* üt, next month 第二个月 tai' i' *koh'* üt, 下月 ha' üt.

Moon, 月 üt, 月光 üt-*kwong*.

More, 多啲 *toh ti*, 重多 chung'-*toh*.

Moreover, 而且 i-*ch'e'*.

Morning, 早 *tso'*, (good) 早辰 *tso'*-shăn, this morning 今朝 *kăm-chiu*, in the morniug 朝頭早 *chiu*-t'au-*tso'*.

Mosquito, 蚊 *măn*.

Mosquito-curtain, (a) 一堂蚊帳 *yat* t'ong *măn-cheung'*, 蚊袋 *măn*-toi'.

Most, 至多 *chi' toh*.

Mother, 母親 mu'-*ts'ăn*, your—令壽堂 ling'-shau'-t'ong.

Mother o'pearl, 雲母殼 wăn-mu'-*hok*.

Mouldy, 發 *fat*, 生霉 *shăng* mui.

Mountain, 山 *shan*.

Mouse, 臊鼠 *so-shü'*.

Move, 郁動 *yuk*-tung', (remove) 搬 *pun*.

Much, 多 *toh*, as much as 咁多 *kom' toh*.

Mud, 坭 nai.

Music, 音樂 *yăm*-ngok, to make music 造樂 tso' ngok.

Muslin, 袈裟布 *ka-sha-po'*.

**Must,** 必 *pit,* 必定 *pit*-ting', 必要 *pit-iu'*, 是必 shi'-*pit,*

**Mustard,** 芥末 *kai'*-mut.

**Muster,** (a) 𨐌 pan', 樣子 yeung'-*tsze'*.

**Mutton,** 羊肉 yeung-yuk, mutton broth 羊肉湯 yeung-yuk-*t'ong*, mutton chops 羊排骨 yeung-p'ai-*kwat.*

**Mutual,** 相 *seung.*

**My, mine,** 我嘅 ngo'-*ke'*, my father 父親 fu'-*ts'ăn*, my father 家父 *ka*-fu' my elder brother 家兄 *ka-hing*, my younger (cottage) brother 舍弟 *she'*-tai', my wife 老婆 lo'-p'oh, 內人 noi'-yan, my house 敝屋 pai' *uk*, my country 敝國 pai' *kwok*, my surname 賤姓 tsin' *sing'*.

**Myriad** (10,000), 萬 man'.

## N

**Nail,** 釘 *teng*, (finger- &c.) 甲 *kap*, -brush 指甲掃 *chi'-kap-so'*.

**Name,** 名 meng, your 大號 tai'-ho', pre-name (polite form) 芳名 *fong*-meng, family name 姓 *sing'*.

**Napkin,** 茶巾 ch'a-*kan.*

**Native,** 本地 *pun'*-ti.

**Near,** 近 kăn', 附近 fu'-kăn'.

**Nearly,** 將近 *tseung*-kăn', 爭 *chang*, 差不多 *ch'a-pat-toh.*

**Necessary,** 必要 *pit-iu'*, 是必 shi'-*pit.*

**Necktie,** 頸帶 *keng'-tai'*.

**Needle,** 眼針 ngan'-*chim.*

**Needlewoman,** 鋪衫婆 *po'-sham*-p'oh.

**Needless,** 唔使 'm *shai'*.

**Neglect,** 失 *shat.*

**Neighbouring,** 隔離 *kak*-li.

**Neither——nor** 不——不 *pat——pat*, 唔係——又唔係 'm-hai'——yau'-'m-hai'.

**Net,** 網 mong'.

**Never,** 總無 *tsung'*-mo, never mind 就罷 tsau'-pa'.

**News,** 新聞 *săn*-măn.

**Newspaper,** 新聞紙 *săn*-măn-*chi'*.

**New year's day,** 正月初一 *ching* üt *ch'oh yat.*

**Night,** 夜晚 ye'-man', at night 夜晚黑 ye'-man'-*hak*, by night 夜間 ye'-*kan*, last night 昨夜 tsok-ye'.

**Night-dress,** 墊瞓衫 tin'-*făn'-sham*, night-cap 瞓帽 *făn'*-mo'.

**Nine,** 九 *kau'*.

**No,** 唔係 'm hai'.

**Noise,** 聲音 *shing yăm.*

**None,** 冇 mo'.

**Noon,** 晏晝 *an'-chau'*, 正午 *ching'*-'ng'.

**North,** 北 *pak*, (N.E. &c.) 東北 *tung-pak.*

**Nosegay,** (a) 一球花 *yat* k'au *fa.*

**Not,** 唔 'm, 咪 mai'.

**Not——but,** 不——但 *pat*——tan'.

**Nothing,** 冇乜野 mo'-*măt*-ye', 冇野 mo'-ye'.

**Now,** 如今 ü-*kăm*, 而家 i-*ka*, 現時 in'-shi.

Nowhere, 冇邊處 mo' *pin ch'ü*`.

Now-a-days, 近來 kău`-loi.

Nurse, 亞媽 *a*`-*ma*, (wet-) 奶媽 nai'-*ma*.

# O

Oar, 枝槳 *chi-tseung'*.

Oblige, to (compel) 監 *kam*, 强 k'eung'.

Oblige me, 爲吓我 wai` ha' ngo', 拜託你 *pai`-t'ok* ni'.

Obtsruct, 攔住 lan-chü`.

Occupation, (trade) 生意 *shăng-i*`.

Ocean, 大洋海 tai` yeung-*hoi'*.

Office, 寫字房 *se'*-tszc`-fong, (Mandarin's) 衙門 nga-mun.

Often, 好多囘 *ho' toh* ui.

Oil, 油 yau.

Old, 老 lo', of old 舊時 kau`-shi, 昔時 *sik*-shi.

Once, 一吓 *yat* ha', once more 多一吓 *toh yat* ha'.

One, 一 *yat*, one by one, 一一 *yat yat*, one another 各人 *kok* yau, 大家 tai` *ka*, one and all 一齊咁多人 *yat* ts'ai *kom*` *toh* yan, oneself 自已 tsze`-*ki'*.

Only, 單 *tan*, 獨 tuk, 但 tan`, 不過 *pat kwoh*`.

Open, 開 *hoi*, 擘 *mak*.

Opium, 片鴉 *a-p'in*`.

Opposite, 對面 *tui*`-min`, opposed to 相反 *seung-fan'*.

Orange, 橙 ch'ang, (loose skinned) 柑 *kom*, (small smooth) 桔 *kăt*, 桔仔 *kăt-tsai'*.

Order, (in order) 次序 *ts'ze*`-tsü`.

Original, 本 *pun'*.

Ornament, (in a room) 玩器 uu`-*hi*`.

Otherwise, 別樣 pit-yeung`.

Ounce, (Chinese) 兩 *leung'*.

Our, 我哋嘅 ngoh'-ti`-*ke*`.

Outside, 外便 ngoi`-pin`, 在外出 tsoi` ngoi` *ch'ut*.

Out of the way, 偏僻 *p'in-p'ik*.

Outwards, 在外 tsoi` ngoi`.

Overtake, 追到來 *chui to*` loi.

Owe, 欠 *him*`.

# P

Pace, 步 po`.

Pacify, 和息 wo-*sik*, 安住 *on*-chü`.

Pagoda, 枝塔 *chi-t'ap*.

Pain, 痛 *t'ung*`.

Painting, (a) 幅畫 *fuk* wa`.

Pair, 對 *tui*`, 雙 *sheung*.

Palsy, 瘋癱 *fung-t'an'*.

Paper, 紙 *chi'*.

Pardon, (I beg) 唔該 'm-*koi*.

Parents, 父母 fu`-mu', 兩親 leung'-*ts'ăn*.

Parsee, 白頭人 pak-t'au-yan.

Partition, 板帳 *pan'-cheung*`.

Pass, (to) 過去 *kwoh' hü*`.

Pass, (mountain) 度山峽 to` *shan*-hap.

Passage boat, 渡船 to`-shün.

Paste, 漿糊 *tseung*-u.

Pastry, 麵食 min`-shik, 餅食 *peng*´-shik, pastry cook 做餅食人 tso` *peng*´-shik yan, 麵食師傅 min`-shik *sze*-fu`.

Pawn-broker, 當舖佬 *tong*`-*p*'*o*`-*lo*´.

Pawn-shop, 當舖 *tong*`-*p*'*o*`.

Pay, 還 wan, 俾 *pi*´, pay rent 納租銀 nap *tso*-ngăn, pay off 還淸 wan-*ts*'*ing*, pay debts 欠債還錢 *him*` *chai*` wan t'sin.

Peaceably, 安然 *on*-in.

Peck, (a) 斗 *tau*´.

Pen, pencil, 枝筆 *chi păt*, lead- 鉛筆 ün-*păt*, slate 石筆 shek-*păt*, -rest 筆架 *păt-ka*`, -cover 筆筒 *păt*-t'ung, -cup 筆升 *păt-shing*, quill pen 鵝毛筆 ngoh-mo-*păt*.

Penknife, 刀仔 *to-tsai*´.

People, 百姓 *pak-sing*`, 人人 yan yan.

Pepper, 椒末 *tsiu*-mut.

Perhaps, 或者 wak-*che*´.

Permit, 容 yung.

Petticoat, 裙 kw'ăn.

Physician, 醫生 *i-shăng*.

Pick up, 執起 *chăp-hi*´.

Picture, 畫 wa`.

Picul, 擔 *tam*`.

Pie, (pastry) 麵龜 min`-*kwai*.

Piece, 塊 *fai*`, 的 *tik*.

Pig, 猪 *chü*, (a) 隻猪 *chek chü*.

Pilferer, 三隻手 *sam-chek-shau*´, 小手 *siu*´-*shau*´.

Pillow, 枕頭 *chăm*´-t'au, -case 枕頭布 *chăm*´-t'au-*po*`.

Pilot, 帶水佬 *tai*`-*shui*´-*lo*´.

Pin, 頭針 t'au-*chăm*, 鼓槌針 *ku*´-ch'ui-*chăm*.

Pincers, 鐵鉗 *t'it*-k'im.

Pint, (a) 升 *shing*.

Pipe, 筒 t'ung, tobacco- 烟筒 *in*-t'ung.

Pirate, 海賊 *hoi*´-ts'ak.

Pistol, 手鎗 *shau*´-*ts*'*eung*.

Pity, 憐 lin.

Placard, 標紅 *piu*-hung, 街招 *kai-chiu*.

Place, 處 *ch'ü*`, 地方 *ti*`-*fong*, (to) 擠 *chai*.

Plaintiff and defendent, 兩造 leung´ tso`.

Plane, (tool) 刨 p'au.

Plant, (a) 草 *ts'o*´, (to) 種 *chung*`.

Plate, (a) 碟 tip, 隻碟 *chek* tip.

Play, 反斗 *fan*´-*tau*´, a play 戲 *hi*`, to play 做戲 tso`-*hi*`, -the organ, &c. 揞 *om*´, -the guitar, &c. 彈 t'an.

Please, 請 *ts'eng*´, (as you) 隨便 ts'ui-pin`.

Pleased, 歡喜 *fun-hi*´.

Pluck, (to) 摘來 chak loi.

Poach, (eggs) 煎 *tsin*.

Pocket, 衣袋 *i*-toi`.

Poetry, 詩 *shi*, write or make verses 吟詩 yăm-*shi*.

Poison, 毒 tuk.

Police, 差役 *ch'ai*-yik, (in Hongkong) 綠衣 luk-*i* (*lit.* green clothes).

Police station, 差館 *ch'ai-kun*´.

Politeness, 禮貌 lai´-mau`, 禮數 lai´-*sho*`.

Poor, 窮 k'ung.

初學階

Pork, 猪肉 *chü*-yuk.

Port-clearance, 船放行紙 shün-*fong*'-hang-*chi*'.

Porter, (at a gate) 看門公 *hon*-mun-*kung*.

Portuguese, 西洋人 *Sai*-yeung-yan.

Possibly, 可以 *hoh*'-i', 萬一 man'-*yat*.

Postage, 信資 *sun*'-*tsze*.

Post-office, 書信館 *shü-sun*'-*kun*'.

Pot, 壺 u.

Potatoe, 荷蘭薯 Hoh-lan-shü, 薯仔 shü-*tsai*'.

Pour out, 斟 *chăm*, 倒出 *to*'-*ch'ut*, 斟出 *chăm-ch'ut*.

Powder, (medicine) 藥散 yeuk-*san*', (gun-) 火藥 *foh*'-yeuk.

Prefer, 寧愿 ning-ün', 情愿 ts'ing-ün'.

Present, (at) 現在 in'-tsoi', (to) 送 *sung*'.

Press between, 夾住 kap-chü'.

Presume, 敢當 *kom' tong*.

Pretty, 好睇 *ho*'-*t'ai*', 美 mi', (-well) 幾好 *ki*' *ho*'.

Prevent, 阻住 *choh*'-chü'.

Price, 價錢 *ka*'-ts'in, 價 *ka*'.

Priest, (Bud.) 和尚 wo-sheung', (Tau.) 道士 to'-sze'.

Printer 印字人 *yăn*'-tsze'-yan.

Printing office, 印字館 *yăn*'-tsze'-*kun*',

Prison, 監房 *kam*-fong.

Procession, (idolatrous) 出遊 *ch'ut*-yau.

Proclamation, (a) 告示 *ko*'-shi', to issue a proclamation 出告示 *ch'ut ko*'-shi'.

Profit, 利益 li'-*yik* (to) 賺 chan', 利 li'.

Promise, 應承 *ying*-shing, 應許 *ying-hü*'.

Pronounce, (as a tone) 話聲 wa'-*sheng*.

Province, 省 *shang*', provincial city, 省城 *shang*'-shing.

Pull, (on) 扯住 *ch'e*'-chü', pull an oar, 棹 chau'.

Punish, 治罪 chi'-tsui'.

Punkah, 風扇 *fung-shin*'.

Purse, 腰瓶袋 *iu*-p'eng-*toi*'.

Pursue, 趕起 *kon*'-*hi*'.

Push, (away) 推去 *t'ui-hü*'.

Put, 放 *fong*', -down 放落 *fong*'-lok, 擠 *chai*, -on 着 *cheuk*, (put away) 收埋 *shau*-mai, 擺埋 *pai*'-mai, put by 剩翻 shing'-*fan*.

# Q

Quality, 等 *tăng*', best 至上 *chi*' sheung', good 上等 sheung'-*tăng*', medium 中等 *chung-tăng*', low 下等 ha'-*tăng*'.

Quarrel, 爭論 *chang*-lun'.

Quarry, 鑿石 tsok shek.

Quarter, (a) 四分之一 *sze*' făn' *chi yat*, 一角 *yat kok*, (of an hour) 點鐘之一角 *tim' chung chi yat kok*.

Queen, 皇后 wong-hau'.

Question, 問 măn'.

Quick, 快 *fai*', 快快 *fai*'-*fai*', 快啲 *fai*'-*ti*.

Quilt, 綿被 min-p'i'.

Quite, 一團 *yat* t'ün, 嗤 *sai*', (not quite) 爭啲 *chang-ti*.

# R

Radicals, 字部 tsze' po', 字母 tsze' mu'.

Rag, 布碎 po'-sui', 揸碎布 sàp-sui'-po'.

Rain, 雨 ü', (to) 落雨 lok ü', (-water) 雨水 ü'-shui'.

Rainbow, 天虹 t'in-hung.

Rat, 鼠 shü'.

Rather, 頗 p'oh', had rather 寧愿 ning-ün'.

Rattan, 沙籐 sha-t'ang

Razor, 剃刀 t'ai'-to.

Reach, 襖到 o-to', 伸到 shàn-to'.

Read, 讀 tuk, (in silence) 睇住 t'ai' chü'.

Ready, 齊備 ts'ai-pi'.

Really, 實 shat, 幷 ping'.

Receipt, 收單 shau-tan.

Receipt, to give a 開收單 hoi shau-tan.

Recently, 近來 kän'-loi, 近日 kän'-yat.

Reckon up, 計起 kai hi'.

Records, (office) 案牘 on'-tuk.

Red, 紅 hung.

Reflect, 思想 sze-seung', 顧住 ku'-chü'.

Refuse, 推却 t'ui-k'euk.

Regarding, 至於 chi'-ü.

Regularly, 常時 sheung-shi.

Release, 釋放 shik-fong'.

Remainder, 有剩 yau' shing'.

Remember, 記得 ki'-tăk.

Remove, (put away) 除去 ch'ü-hü', (entirely) 除却 ch'ü-k'euk.

Rent, 租銀 tso-ngăn, to pay, 納租銀 nap tso-ngăn.

Repair, 修整 sau-ching', 補好 po'-ho'.

Require, (to want) 要 iu', 使 shai'.

Resist, 抵擋 tai'-tong'.

Respect, (to) 敬惜 king'-sik, with respect to 論及 lun'-k'ăp.

Rest, 息 sik, to rest from 歇住 hit chü'.

Retain, 留翻 lau-fan.

Return, 翻去 fan-hü', 翻來 fan-loi.

Return home, 翻去歸 fan-hü'-kwai.

Revive, 翻生 fan-shăng.

Revolver, 六口連鎗 luk-hau'-lin-ts'eung.

Reward, (to) 打賞 ta' sheung'.

Rheumatism, 風濕 fung-shăp.

Rice, (boiled) 飯 fan'.

Rich, 財主 ts'oi-chü'.

Riches, 財帛 ts'oi-pak.

Ride, (a horse) 騎馬 k'i ma'.

Right, 着 cheuk, (side) 右便 yau'-pin'.

Ring, 環 wan, (ear-) 耳環 i'-wan, (finger) 戒指 kai'-chi', (to ring a bell) 打鐘 ta' chung.

Riot, 鬧事 nau'-sze', 作亂 tsok-lün'.

Rise, 起 hi'.

River, 河 hoh, 江 kong.

Road, 條路 t'iu lo'.

Roast, 燒 shiu.

Robber, 賊匪 ts'ak-fi'.

Rock, 磐石 p'un-shek.

Rod, (a measure) 丈 cheung'.

Roll, (up) 捲埋 kün'-mai, 捲起 kün'-hi'.

Roof, 屋背 uk-pui'.

Room, 房 fong, 地方 ti`-fong.

Rope, 繩 shing, of a sail 繂大繚 lut tai` liu.

Row, (to) 櫂來 chau`-loi, 棹槳 chau`-tseung'.

Rub, 磨 moh.

Rudder, 舦 t'ai',

Rule, (carpenter's) 尺 ch'ek.

Run, 走起 tsau'-hi', 走去 tsau'-hü`, run after 追到 chui-to`, run away, 避 pi`.

# S

Saddle, 馬鞍 ma'-on.

Safe, 穩咯 wăn' lok.

Sail, 𢃇 li', (to) 駛 sai', (set-) 開身 hoi-shăn, 扯𢃇 ch'e' li'.

Sailor, 水手 shui'-shau'.

Salary, 俸祿 fung'-luk, 薪水 săn-shui'.

Salt, 鹽 im, (salted) 鹹 ham.

Satin, 漢府緞 hon`-fu'-tün`.

Sauce-pan, 水煲 shui'-po.

Sausage, 猪腸 chü-ch'eung, (force-meat) 肉丸 yuk-ün.

Save (put by) 剩 shing`.

Saw, 把鋸 pa'-kü`.

Say, 話 wa`.

Scaffold, 棚 p'ang.

Scales, (for weighing) 把戥 pa'-tăng', 天平 t'in-p'ing, money scales 厘戥 li-tăng'.

Scarcely, 僅 kăn'.

Scent, 香 heung.

Scheme, 計謀 kai`-mau, to scheme 出計 ch'ut kai`.

Scholar, 學生 hok-shăng, 學者 hok-che'.

School, 書館 shü-kun'.

Scissors, 鉸剪 kau`-tsin'.

Screen, (a) 遮 che, fire screen 火遮 foh'-che, folding screen 圍屏 wai-p'ing.

Screw, 螺絲 loh-sze.

Screw-driver, 螺絲擰 loh-sze-ning`.

Sea, 海 hoi'.

Sea-sickness, 暈浪 wăn-long`.

Seal, (to) 封住 fung-chü`.

Sealing-wax, 火漆 foh'-ts'at, (wax) 火漆印 foh'-ts'at-yăn`.

Search, 查 ch'a, search for 尋 ts'ăm.

Seat 坐 tso`, to be seated in 坐倒 tso` to'.

Secondly, 二來 i`-loi.

Secretly, 私私哋 sze sze ti, 偷偷哋 t'au t'au ti.

Secure, (guaranted) 保 po'.

Security, 擔保 tam-po', 包管 pau-kun'.

Sedan-chair, 頂轎 ting'-kiu`, 乘轎 shing-kiu`.

See, 見 kin`, 睇見 t'ai' kin`.

Seize, 捉 chuk, seize upon 拉住 lai-chü`.

Self, 自己 tsze`-ki', 己 ki'.

Sell, 賣 mai`.

Send, 寄去 ki`-hü`, (a person) 送 sung`, 打發 ta'-fat, 使 shai', transmit 寄到 ki`-to`.

Separate, 別開 pit-hoi, 分開 făn-hoi,

Separately 隔開 kak-hoi.

Set out, 起程 *hi'*-ch'ing.

Seven, 七 *ts'at.*

Several, 幾個 *ki' koh`.*

Sew, 聯 lün.

Shallow, 淺 *ts'in'.*

Shave, 剃 *t'ai`.*

Shaving brush, 水抆掃 *shui'*-män'-*so`.*

She, he, or it, 佢 k'ü'.

Sheet, (of a bed) 被單 p'i'-*tan*, of (paper) 張 *cheung.*

Shell-fish, 鮑魚 *pau*-ü.

Ship, 船 shün.

Shirt, 汗衫 hon`-*sham.*

Shoe, 鞋 hai, (pair of shoes) 對鞋 *tui`* hai.

Shoe brush 鞋掃 hai-*so`.*

Shoemaker, 做鞋師傅 tso` hai *sze*-fu`.

Shoot birds, 打雀 *ta' tseuk.*

Shop, 舖頭 *p'o`*-t'au, 店 *tim`.*

Shopkeeper, 舖家 *p'o`-ka,* 舖主 *p'o`-chü'.*

Short, 短 *tün'.*

Shovel, 鏟 *ch'an'.*

Show, 俾——睇 *pi'——t'ai'.*

Shower, 陣雨 chăn`-ü'.

Shrimp, 蝦 *ha.*

Shut, (up) 閂埋 *shan*-mai, 掩埋 *im'*-mai, (-eye) 眯埋 *mi*-mai.

Sickness, 病 peng`.

Side, 側邊 *chak-pin.*

Sign, (one's name) 簽名 *ts'im*-meng.

Signboard 招牌 *chiu*-p'ai.

Silk, (material) 絲 *sze,* Canton raw silk 土絲 *t'o'-sze,* cocoons 蠶繭 ts'am-*kan',* thread 絲線 *sze-sin`,* satin 絲緞 *sze*-tün`, crape 縐紗 *tsau`-sha,* gauze 紗 *sha,* floss 絨 yung.

Silver, 銀 ngăn, silversmith 首飾匠 *shau' shik*-tseung`, 打銀師傅 *ta'* ngăn *sze*-fu`.

Since, 自從 tsz`-ts'ung, (—seeing that) 既然 ki`-in, short time since 不久 *pat-kau',* long since 好久 *ho' kau'.*

Six, 六 luk.

Skip, 喇 lai.

Sky, 天 *t'in.*

Slate, 石版 shek-*pan'.*

Sleep, 瞓 *făn`,* sleep upon 眠倒 min-*to'.*

Sleepy, 眼瞓 ngan-*făn`.*

Slice, 塊 *fai`.*

Slippers, 睡鞋 shui`-hai.

Slop-basin, 茶碗 ch'a-*un'.*

Slowly, 慢慢 man`-man`.

Small, 細 *sai`,* 小 *siu',* 仔 *tsai'.*

Small-pox, 出痘 *ch'ut* tau`.

Smart, 底手嘅 *tai'-shau' ke`.*

Smell, 聞 măn.

Smoke, (to, tobacco &c.) 食烟 shik-*in.*

Snake, (a) 條蛇 t'iu-she.

Sneeze, 打嚇咳 *ta'-hat-ch'i.*

Snuff, 鼻烟 pi`-*in,* snuff box 鼻烟盒 pi`-*in*-hop.

Snuffers 蠟燭剪 lap-*chuk-tsin'.*

So, 咁 *kom`,* (in kind) 噉 *kom',* (so and so) 某某 mau'-mau', (so forth) 云云 wăn-wăn.

Soak, 淰 năm`.

Soap, 番鹼 *fan-kan'*.

Socks, 襪頭 mät-t'au.

Soda-water, 荷蘭水 hoh-lan-*shui*.

Sofa, 睡椅 shui'-*i'*.

Soldier, 兵丁 *ping-ting*.

Somebody, one 人 yan, 有人 yau' yan.

Sometimes, 有時 yau'-shi.

Son, 子 *tsze'*, 仔 *tsai'*, (your) 令郎 ling'-long, (my) 小兒 *siu'*-i.

Soon, as soon as 一經 *yat-king*, 有咁快得咁快 yau' *kom' fai' tak kom' fai'*, no sooner, 一見 *yat kin'*.

Sort, 樣 yeung'.

Soup, 湯 *t'ong*, ladle 湯殼 *t'ong-hok*.

South, 南 nam, (S.E. &c.) 東南 *tung*-nam.

Sow, (a) 猪乸 *chü-na'*.

Spain, 呂宋 Lü'-*sung'*, Spaniard 呂宋人 Lü'-*sung'* yan.

Speak, 講 *kong'*.

Spectacles, 眼鏡 ngan'-*keng'*.

Spectacles, one who wears 四眼佬 *sze'*-ngan-*lo'*.

Speculation, 打算 *ta'-sun'*.

Spider, 蟾蟧 k'ám-lo.

Spider's web, 蟾蟧網 k'ám-lo-mong'.

Spirit, 神 shăn.

Spoil, 整壞 *ching'* wai'.

Sponge, 水泡 *shui'*-p'o'.

Spoon, 匙羹 shi-*kang*.

Sprain, 扭 *nau'*, (to) 扭着 *nau'*-cheuk.

Square, 方 *fong*.

Square an account (to), 算賬目 *sun' cheung'*-muk.

Square, (a tool) 曲尺 *kuk*-ch'ek.

Squinting, 狙視眼 *ch'e'*-shi'-ngan'.

Stairs, 樓梯 lau-*t'ai*.

Stammering, 詉牙 na'-nga.

Stand, (up) 起身 *hi'-shăn*, 企起 k'i'-*hi'*.

Star, 天星 *t'in-sing*.

Starch, 米漿 mai'-*tseung*.

Stay, (to) 等 *tăng'*, 住 chü'.

Steal, 偷 *t'au*.

Steamer, 火船 *foh'*-shün.

Steelyard, 把稱 *pa'-ch'ing'*, (money-) 釐戥 li-*tang'*.

Steer, (to) 揸舦 *cha*-t'ai', 把舦 *pa'*-t'ai', 駛舦 *sai'*-t'ai'.

Step, 行 hang, (in a stair) 階級 *kai-k'ăp*.

Stew, (to) 會 ui'.

Stick, (a) 鞭杆 *pin-kon*.

Stick up, (a placard) 貼 *t'ip*.

Still, (quiet) 靜靜 *tsing'*-tsing'

Stir, (to) 攪起 *kau'-hi'*.

Stirrup, 馬踏機 ma'-tap-*tăng'*.

Stone, 石 shek.

Stop, (to) 却 *k'euk*, (up) 塞住 *sak*-chü', 罷咯 pa'-*lok*, (obstruct) 攔住 lan-chü'.

Store, (away) 貯住 *ch'ü'*-chü'.

Storm, 大風 tai'-*fung*, 風颶 *fung*-kü'.

Story, (tale) 花話 *fa*-wa', 唔正經嘅話 'm *ching' king ke'* wa'.

Stove bed, 炕床 *hong'*-ch'ong.

Street, 街 *kai*.

Strike, 打 *ta'*.

String, 繩 shing, 線 *sin'*.

Stroke, (line) 畫 wak.

Strong, 有力 yau'-lik, (as tobacco) 揹 *kang'*, (as tea &c.) 濃 yung.

Study, (to) 讀書 tuk-*shü*, (a) 書房 *shü*-fong.

Style, 文理 măn-li'.

Such, 噉樣 *kom'*-yeung'.

Sudden, 白撞 pak-chong'.

Suddenly, 忽然 *fat*-in.

Sufficient, 㝅 *kau'*.

Sugar, 糖 t'ong, white do. 白糖 pak-t'ong.

Suit, (to) 合 hop, 啱 *ngam*.

Sun, 日 yat, 日頭 yat-t'au.

Sunshine, 日晒 yat *sai'*.

Supper, 晚餐 man'-*ts'an*.

Suppose, 估 *ku'*.

Suppose that, 比如 *pi'*-ü, 倘若 *t'ong'*-yeuk, (a particle at the end of a sentence signifying doubt) 嘪 *ai*.

Sure, to be 知得眞 *chi tăk chăn*.

Surgeon, 外科醫生 ngoi'-*foh-i-shăng*.

Surname, 姓 *sing'*.

Surprising (to be surprised,) 出奇 *ch'ut*-k'i.

Swear, 誓愿 shai'-ün'.

Sweep, 掃 *so'*, -clean 掃乾凈 *so' kon*-tseng'.

Swollen, 瘇 *chung'*.

Sword, 劍 *kim'*.

Sycee, 紋銀 măn-ngăn.

T

Table, 張檯 *cheung*-t'oi.

Table boy, 事仔 sze'-*tsai'*, 侍仔 shi'-*tsai'*.

Table cloth, 檯布 t'oi-*po'*.

Table mat, 碟墊 tip-tin'.

Table napkin, 茶巾 ch'a-*kăn*.

Tack, (in sailing) 摳篷 *k'au*-p'ung.

Tael, 兩 *leung'*.

Tailor, 裁縫 ts'oi-fung.

Take, 拧 *ning*, (with the finger and thumb) 拈 *nim*.

Take away, 拧去 *nim-hü'*.

Take care, 小心 *siu'-săm*.

Take off, 除 ch'ü.

Talk, 講 *kong'*, 話 wa'.

Tanka, 蛋家 tan'-*ka*.

Tanka boat, 三板 *sam-pan'*.

Tariff, 則例 *tsak*-lai'.

Taste, 味道 mi'-to', (to) 嚐 sheung.

Tax, 錢糧 ts'in-leung, 稅銀 *shui'*-ngăn.

Tea, 茶 ch'a, gunpowder tea 芝珠茶 *chi*-*chü*-ch'a, imperial tea 圓珠茶 ün-*chü*-ch'a, caper tea 珠蘭茶 *chü*-lan-ch'a, black tea 黑茶 *hak*-ch'a, su-chong tea 小種 *siu'-chung'*, pekoe tea 白毫 pak-ho, green tea 綠茶 luk-ch'a, hyson tea 正茶 *ching'*-ch'a.

Tea-cup, 茶杯 ch'a-*pui*, (large) 茶盅 ch'a-*chung*.

Tea-pot, 茶壺 ch'a-u.

Teapoys, 茶機 ch'a-*ki*.

Tea-strainer, 茶漏 ch‘a-lau‵.

Teach, 教 *kau‵*.

Tear, (to) 撕破 *sze-p‘oh‵*.

Telescope, 千里鏡 *ts‘in-li′-keng‵*.

Tell, 話 wa‵, 話——聽 wa‵——*t‘eng*, (order) 叫 *kiu‵*.

Temple, 廟 miu‵.

Ten, 十 shăp, ten cent piece 毫子 ho-*tsze′*.

Than, 過於 *kwoh‵-ü*, 於 *ü*.

Thanks, 謝 tse‵, 多謝 *toh*-tse‵, 唔該 ’m-*koi*.

That, 啯個 *koh′-koh‵*, 個 *koh‵*, 個啲 *koh‵-ti*.

Then, 方 *fong*, (afterwards) 然後 in-hau‵, 就 tsau‵.

Thence, 由啯處 yau *koh′-ch‘ü‵*.

There, 個處 *koh′-ch‘ü‵*, 便處 *pin-ch‘ü‵*.

Thereupon, 就 tsau‵.

Therefore, 所以 *shoh′*-i′.

Thermometer, 寒暑針 hon-*shü′-chăm*.

These, 呢的 *ni-ti*.

They, 佢哋 k‘ü′-ti‵.

Thief, 賊佬 ts‘ak-*lo′*, 賊匪 ts‘ak-*fi′*, 賊仔 ts‘ak-*tsai′*, 三隻手 *sam-chek-shau′*.

Thimble, 針頂 *chăm-ting′*.

Thing, 物件 măt-kin‵, 野 ye′.

Think, 思想 *sze-seung′*, (guess) 估 *ku′*, (on) 想起 *seung′-hi′*.

Thirst, 頸渴 *keng′-hot*, thirsty 口渴 *hau-hot*.

This, 呢個 *ni-koh‵*, these 呢啲 *ni-ti*.

Those, 個的 *koh-ti*.

Thousand, 千 *ts‘in*.

Thread, 線 *sin‵*.

Three, 三 *sam*.

Through, 通 *t‘ung*.

Throw, 擗 p‘ek, (away) 擗去 p‘ek-*hü‵*.

Thunder, 雷 lui, 雷公 lui-*kung*.

Tide, 潮水 ch‘iu-*shui′*, head tide 逆水 yik-*shui′*.

Tie, (to) 綁 *pong′*, 綁住 *pong′*-chü‵, (a knot) 打結, 縭, *ta′-kit*, (*lit*).

Tiffin, 晏晝 *an‵-chau‵*, 小食 *siu′*-shik.

Tight, 緊 *kăn′*.

Tile, 瓦 nga′.

Till, 等 *tang′*.

Time, 時 shi, (set) 期 k‘i, (hour) 點鐘 *tim′-chung*.

Times, (occasions) 吓 ha′, 囘 ui, 次 *ts‘ze‵*, 匀 wan, (this time) 呢轉 *ni-chün′*.

Tinsmith, 打錫師傅 *ta′ sek sze-fu‵*.

To, 過 *kwoh‵*, 埋 mai, 對 *tui‵*, 同 t‘ung.

Tobacco, 烟餅 *in-peng′*.

To-day, 今日 *kăm*-yat.

Together with, 連 lin.

Tomorrow, 聽日 *t‘eng*-yat, 明日 ming-yat, day after 後日 hau‵-yat.

Tone, 音 *yăm*, 聲 *shing*.

Tongs, 火鉗 *foh′*-k‘im.

To-night, 今晚 *kăm*-man′, 今夜 *kăm*-ye‵.

Too, 過頭 *kwoh‵*-t‘au, 得嚌 *tăk*-tsai‵, (also) 都 *tu*.

Tool, 器具 *hi‵*-kü‵, tool chest, 鉄器箱 *t‘it-hi‵-seung*.

Tooth-brush, 牙刷 nga-shat.

Tooth-pick, 牙簽 nga-ts'im.

Tooth-powder, 牙灰 nga-fui, tooth-box 牙灰盒 nga-fui-hop.

Torn, 裂了 lit-liu'.

Touch, 掂 tim', 摩 moh, 鬥 tau`.

Towards, 向 heung`.

Towel, 面巾 min`-kăn.

Town, (walled) 城 shing.

Translate, 繙譯 fan-yik.

Travel, by land 打路去 ta' lo` hü`.

Traveled, 四海嘅 sze`-hoi'-ke`.

Tree, (a) 翕樹 p'oh-shü`.

Troops, 兵士 ping-sze`.

Trouble, 煩勞 fan-lo, (to) 混 wan`, 煩 fan, (I will—you) 多煩 toh-fan.

Trouser, 條褲 t'iu-fu`.

True, 眞 chăn, 實 shat.

Try, 試吓 shi`-ha', 試一試 shi`-yat-shi`.

Tub, 木盤 muk-p'un.

Tube, 筒 t'ung.

Tumbler, (glass) 玻璃杯 poh-li-pui, 水杯 shui'-pui.

Turn out, 倒出 to'-ch'ut, turn over 打轉 ta'-chün', 翻轉 fan-chün'.

Turns, 輪流 lun-lau.

Turtle, 脚魚 keuk-ü.

Twelve, 十二 shăp-i`.

Twenty, 二十 i`-shăp.

Two, 二 i`, 兩 leung'.

# U

Ulcer, 癰 yung.

Umbrella, 把遮 pa'-che. [fu`.

Umbrella maker, 做遮師傅 tso` che sze-

Umbrella stand, 遮架 che-ka`.

Uncertain, 唔得定 'm-tăk-ting`, 不定 pat-ting`.

Understand, 曉 hiu', 明白 ming-pak.

Undeserved, 無實 mo shat.

Unimportant, 無乜相干 mo'-măt-seung-kon.

Unitedly, 合埋 hop-mai.

Unless, 若不 yeuk-pat, 除非 ch'ü-fi.

Unlimited, 冇限 mo'-han`.

Unsafe, 唔主固 'm chü'-ku`.

Unsuitable, 唔服 'm-fuk.

Until now, 至今日 chi`-kăm-yat.

Unwell, 唔自然 'm tsze`-in, 唔舒服 'm-shü-fuk.

Upon, 在 tsoi`.

Upright, (just) 正直 ching`-chik, 忠直 chung-chik.

Upset, (to) 打倒 ta'-to'.

Upside down, (to turn) 倒轉 to'-chün', 翻轉底上嚟 fan-chün'-tai'-sheung' [lai.

Upstairs, 樓上 lau-sheung`.

Upwards, 在上 tsoi`-sheung`.

Use, 使 shai', 用 yung`.

Useless, 冇用嘅 mo'-yung`-ke`, 冇乜用處 mo'-măt-yung`-ch'ü`.

Utensil, 器皿 hi`-ming'.

## V

Valley, 山谷 *shan-kuk.*

Value, 實價 shat-*ka'.*

Veal, 牛仔肉 ngau-*tsai'*-yuk.

Vegetable, 菜 *ts'oi'.*

Very, 實首 shat-*shau'*, 十分 shap-*fan*, 好 *ho'*, 甚 sham', 極 kik, 最 *tsui'.*

Viceroy, 總督 *tsung'-tuk.*

Victory, 打贏 *ta'*-yeng, 戰勝 *chin'-shing'.*

Victuals, 伙食 *foh'*-shik.

Vile, 僘 pai'.

Village, (a) 條村 t'iu-*ts'ün*, 村鄉 *ts'ün-heung.*

Villain, 奸狡人 *kan-kau'*-yan.

Vinegar, 醋 *ts'o'.*

Violent, 操 *ts'o.*

Visit, 探見 t'*am'-kin'.*

Visiting-card, 拜帖 *pai'-t'ip.*

Visiting-case, 拜帖盒 *pai'-t'ip*-hop.

Vomit, 嘔吐 *au'-t'o'.*

## W

Wafer, 火漆片 *foh'-ts'at-p'in'.*

Wages, 工錢 *kung*-ts'in, 人工 yan-*kung.*

Waistcoat, 背心 *pui'-sam.*

Wait, 等 *tang'*, 等吓 *tang'*-ha'.

Waiter, for cups &c. 托盤 *t'ok*-p'un, small waiter, 茶盤 ch'a-p'un.

Waken, 叫醒 *kiu'-seng'.*

Walk, (to) 行 hang, 行路 hang-lo', 行街 hang-*kai.*

Wall, 牆 ts'eung.

Wampee, 黃皮 wong-p'i.

Want, 要 *iu'*, 愛 *oi'.*

Ware, 器 *hi'*, 器用 *hi'*-yung'.

Warm, 煖 nün', 整煖 *ching'* nün'.

Wash, 洗 *sai'*, (the hands) 洗手 *sai'-shau'.*

Washerman, 洗衣服人 *sai'-i*-fuk-yan.

Wash-stand, 面盤架 min'-p'un-*ka'.*

Waste, (to) 費 *fai'.*

Watch, (at night) 更 *kang.*

Watch, (a time piece) 時辰鏢 shi-shan-*piu.*

Watch chain, 鏢鏈 *piu*-lin'.

Watch key, 鏢匙 *piu*-shi.

Watchman, 更鍊 *kang*-lin', 看更佬 *hon-kang-lo'.*

Watchmaker, 整鏢師傅 *ching'-piu-sze*-fu'.

Water, 水 *shui'.*

Water-fall, 度水景 to'-*shui'-king'.*

Wave, 浪 long'.

Wax, 蠟 lap, (white) 白蠟 pak-lap.

Way, 道路 to'-lo', 方法 *fong-fat*, (get out of the-) 行開 hang-*hoi.*

We, 我地 ngoh'-ti'.

Weak, 軟弱 ün'-yeuk, (watery) 淡 tam'.

Wealthy, 有錢嘅 yau' ts'in *ke'.*

Wear, 戴 *tai'*, 着 *cheuk.*

Weather, 天氣 *t'in-hi'*, (hot) 天時熱 *t'in*-shi-it.

Weather-cock, 風信旗 *fung-sun'*-k'i.

Weave, 織 *chik*, weaver, 機房佬 *ki-fong-lo'*.

Weed, (to) 耘 wăn.

Week, 禮拜 lai'-*pai`*, 先個禮拜 *sin koh`* lai'-*pai`*.

Weigh, 稱 *ch'ing`*.

Weights, 法碼 *fat*-ma', 銅碼 t'ung-ma'.

Weight (gross), 毛重 mo-chung`, weight (net) 凈重 tsing`-chung`.

Well, (a) 井 *tseng'*.

Well, 自然 tsz`-in, to be well, 有心 yau' *săm*, pretty well 幾好 *ki' ho'*, not well (adverb) 唔着 'm cheuk.

Well informed, 博覽 *pok*-lam'.

West, 西 *sai*.

Wet, 濕 *shăp*.

What? 乜 *măt*, 乜野 *măt*-ye'? (mea) 所——旣 *shoh'*——*ki`*, how many 何 ho, 幾 *ki'*.

When? 幾時 *ki'*-shi.

When, ——个時 ——*koh`*-shi, 當 *tong*.

Whence? 由邊處 yau *pin-ch'ü`*? 邊處 *pin-ch'ü`*?

Where? 邊處 *pin-ch'ü`*? 邊吓 *pin*-ha'? 何處 ho-*ch'ü`*?

Wherefore? 爲乜野 wai`-*măt*-ye'.

Which? 邊個 *pin-koh`*?

Whilst, 一面 *yat*-min`.

Whip, (to) 鞭打 *pin-ta'*.

Whither? 在嗰處 tsoi` *koh'-ch'ü`*.

White, 白色 pak-*shik*.

Who? 乜誰 *măt*-shui.

Whole, 一總 *yat-tsung'*, 共 kung`, 喊嘭唥 ham`-pang`-lang`.

Whose? 邊個人嘅 *pin-koh'* yan *ke*? 乜誰嘅 *măt*-shui *ke`*?

Why? (what business?) 爲乜 wai`-*măt*? 爲乜野 wai`-*măt*-ye'? 爲何 wai`-hoh?

Wife, 老婆 lo'-p'oh, (my) 內人 noi`-yan, 內室 noi`-*shat*, (your) 夫人 *fu*-yan, 令正 ling`-*ching`*.

Willing, 肯 *hang'* 中意 *chung-i`*.

Willingly, 甘心 *kom-săm*.

Willow, 柳樹 lau'-shü`.

Win, (a battle) 打贏 *ta'*-yeng.

Wind, (the) 風 *fung*,

Window, 窓 *ch'eung*, 窓門 *ch'eung*-mun.

Wine, 酒 *tsau'*.

Wine glass 酒杯 *tsau'-pui*.

With, 同埋 t'ung-mai.

Within, 裏頭 lui'-t'au, 在內 tsoi`-noi`.

Without, 外頭 ngoi`-t'au (wanting), 冇 mo'.

Witness, (a) 証人 *ching`*-yan.

Woman, 女人 nui'-yan.

Wonder (at) 出奇 *ch'ut*-k'i.

Woollen cloth, 呢 ni, 小呢絨 *siu'*-ni-yung.

Word, 話 wa`, 個字眼 *koh`*-tsze`-ngan'.

Work, 打工 *ta'-kung*, (in) 打起 *ta'-hi'*.

World, 四海 *sze`-hoi'*, 天下 *t'in*-ha`.

Worry, 厭悶 *im`*-mun`.

Worst, 至惡 *chi`*-ok, 更惡 *kăng*-ok.

Worship, 拜 *pai`*.

Worth, 値得 chik-*tăk*.

Worthless, 唔成 'm-shing.

Wound, 損傷 *sün'-sheung*.

Wrap up, 包埋 *pau*-mai, 包起 *pau-hi'*.

Write, 寫 *se'*, (write on) 寫住 *se'*-chü', write out 寫出 *se'-ch'ut*.

Wrong, 錯 *ts'oh'*.

Wrongly, 唔真 'm-*chăn*.

## Y

Year, 年 nin, 歲 *sui'*, this year 今年 *kăm*-nin, last year 舊年 kau'-nin, next year 明年 ming-nin.

Yellow, 黃 wong, 黃色 wong-*shik*.

Yes, 係 hai', 係咯 hai' *lok*.

Yesterday, 昨日 tsok-yat, 往日 wong'-yat, (day before-) 前日 ts'in-yat.

Yesternight, 昨晚 tsok-man'.

Yet, (still) 重 chung', 仍然 ying-in, (not-) 未曾 mi'-ts'ăng, 唔曾 'm-ts'ăng.

Yonder, 在開頭 tsoi'-*hoi*-t'au.

You, 你 ni', 駕上 *ka'*-sheung', 閣下 *kok*-ha' (used only by literati.)

Your, 你嘅 ni' *ke'*, your surname 高姓 *ko-sing'*, your age 貴庚 *kwai'-kăng*, your pre-name 芳名 *fong*-ming, your name 大號 tai'-ho', your couutry 貴國 *kwai'-kwok*, your mother 令壽堂 ling'-shau'-t'ong, your father 令尊 ling'-*tsün*, your son 令郎 ling'-long, your daughter 令愛 ling'-*oi'*, your wife 令正 ling'-*ching'*.

# 易學廣東話

（*How to Speak Cantonese: Fifty Conversations in Cantonese Colloquial; With the Chinese Character, Free and Literal English Translations, and Romanised Spelling with Tonic and Diacritical Marks, &c*）

〔美〕波乃耶（James Dyer Ball）編

《易學廣東話》，美國波乃耶編。波乃耶（James Dyer Ball，一八四七—一九一九），美國公理會傳教士。生於廣州，被譽爲香港最識廣州話之外國人，亦旁通其他方言多種。著有《中國風土人民事物記》、《潮州語》、《順德話》、《如何書寫中文》等。此書前設五課，皆爲常用單詞，後設對話五十則。全書排版，雙數頁爲廣東話及英譯，單數頁爲羅馬字注音及英文逐詞翻譯，頗便對照學習。據一九〇二年香港版影印。

# How to Speak Cantonese:

## FIFTY CONVERSATIONS IN CANTONESE COLLOQUIAL;

WITH THE CHINESE CHARACTER, FREE AND LITERAL ENGLISH TRANSLATIONS, AND ROMANISED SPELLING WITH TONIC AND DIACRITICAL MARKS, &c.

PRECEDED BY FIVE SHORT LESSONS OF ONE, TWO, AND THREE WORDS.

SECOND EDITION,

Revised and Corrected.

By

J. DYER BALL, M.R.A.S., ETC.

[illegible] MAJESTY'S CIVIL SERVICE, HONGKONG.

*And Author of 'Things Chinese,' 'Cantonese Made Easy,' 'The Cantonese Made Easy Vocabulary,' 'The English-Cantonese Pocket Vocabulary,' 'Readings in Cantonese Colloquial,' 'Easy Sentences in the Hakka Dialect with a Vocabulary,' 'Hakka Made Easy,' 'How to Write the Radicals,' 'How to Write Chinese,'*

*&c., &c., &c.*

HONGKONG:

MESSRS. KELLY & WALSH.

1902.

# HOW TO SPEAK CANTONESE.

## *By the same Author.*

**The 'Cantonese-Made-Easy' Series, and other Works, as follows:—**

| | |
|---|---|
| 'THINGS CHINESE,' 3rd Edition........................................................ | 6.50 |
| 'CANTONESE MADE EASY,' 3rd Edition. (In the Press.)......... ........... | |
| 'READINGS IN CANTONESE COLLOQUIAL.' ........................................ | 3.00 |
| 'THE CANTONESE-MADE-EASY VOCABULARY.' ....... ......................... | 1.00 |
| 'EASY SENTENCES IN THE CANTONESE DIALECT, with a VOCABULARY,' being the first part of 'CANTONESE-MADE EASY,' and the whole of the Cantonese-Made-Easy Vocabulary bound in one volume. (Out of Print.) ........ | |
| 'AN ENGLISH-CANTONESE POCKET VOCABULARY.'............................... | 0.75 |
| 'EASY SENTENCES IN THE HAKKA DIALECT, with a VOCABULARY.' ........ | 1.00 |
| 'HAKKA MADE EASY,' Part I. ....................................................... | 2.00 |
| 'HOW TO WRITE THE RADICALS.' ........................................ ........... | 0.75 |
| 'HOW TO WRITE CHINESE,' Part I. (Out of Print.) .......................... | |
| 'THE SAN WÚI DIALECT.' .. ......................................................... | 0.50 |
| 'THE TUNG KWÚN DIALECT.' (Out of Print.) ............................... | |
| 'THE HŌNG SHÁN, or MACAO DIALECT.' ........................................ | 0.50 |
| 'THE SHUN TAK DIALECT.'................. ........................................ | 1.00 |
| 'THE ENGLISH-CHINESE COOKERY BOOK' 2nd Edition. (In the Press.)... | |
| 'QUOTATIONS FROM THE CHINESE CLASSICS IN COLLOQUIAL USE.' (In the Press.) | |

# PREFACE TO FIRST EDITION.

There being a desire for more lessons in Cantonese Colloquial than the fifteen contained in 'Cantonese Made Easy,' the Author has prepared this book. It has been his endeavour to make it practical. Conversations which those desirous of speaking Cantonese are likely to wish to engage in have been compiled. It is no doubt a difficult matter to launch *in medias res*, especially with a language like Chinese; the learner will, however, find that in this book he need not expect to have his breath taken away by a sudden plunge, as the first few conversations are as easy as it is almost possible to make them while endeavouring at the same time to ensure consecutiveness, to keep the idea of a conversation up, and not to present merely scraps of sentences.

This book is intended as a companion volume to 'Cantonese Made Easy.' All the tones, tonic marks, spelling of Chinese words in English, and diacritical marks are fully explained in the Introduction to that book; and the numbers attached to the finals refer to the list of finals near the end of that book.

The learner may find the first five or ten conversations in this book easier than the first few lessons in 'Cantonese Made Easy.' If so, it might, therefore, be a good plan for him to take these first few lessons and learn them thoroughly before beginning the first lessons in the other book. After learning thoroughly the fifty lessons in this and the fifteen in the other book, the learner ought to find himself the master of a pretty good vocabulary, as well as possess the knack of stringing Chinese words together on the thread of Chinese ideas—a thread which he must remember will snap if he tries to strain it and stretch it out according to English ideas.

A glance at the table of contents will show that the conversations run over a variety of subjects, and it has been the author's endeavour to prevent them from being as dry as dust, and on the contrary to render them interesting, while, at the same time, they shall be lifelike, so that pleasure and profit may be the result. If they should lighten the toil of the foreign traveller along the unknown paths of Chinese ideas, and render the acquisition of the faculty of Chinese speech and thought easier to him, one great object of the book will have been accomplished. Trusting that it will meet with as great success as its predecessor and companion volume, 'Cantonese Made Easy,' the author thus sends it forth on its trial.

J. DYER BALL.

HONGKONG, 13*th February*, 1889.

# PREFACE TO SECOND EDITION.

The author has much pleasure in being able at last to bring his labours on this edition of 'How to Speak Cantonese' to a conclusion; for the book has been out of print for some time and many enquiries have been made for it.

The whole book has been most carefully gone through and revised and corrected. The 'variant tones,' as they have been styled, are marked. The learner is referred to the Introduction of 'Cantonese Made Easy' for a description of these tones and an explanation of the tonic marks used for them in this series of books. In most cases the method of calling attention to them consists in reversing the usual tonic marks and the use of an asterisk. The learner should turn a deaf ear to all statements by those who try to make out that these tones are of little moment; for those who attempt to minimise the importance of the Cantonese 'variant tones' are simply ignorant on the subject. One instance alone will suffice to show that attention must be paid to them. To say, for example, that a man has ꜀tsaú lò² höü꜆ when one should say that he has ꜀tsaú lò⁵* höü꜆ does not convey the meaning intended at all; the latter is 'to abscond,' and the former 'to go by road.' The omission of the variants often causes misapprehension: sometimes the listener may make a guess at the meaning of the foreigner; at other times he is left entirely in the dark as to his intention.

The English type used in this edition is larger than in the former and will doubtless prove more pleasant to the eye and less fatiguing.

J. DYER BALL.

1st January, 1902.

# CONTENTS.

# ABBREVIATIONS USED IN THIS BOOK.

[C.] = Classifier.

[S. of p. t.] Sign of past time.

Lit. — Literally.

* Indicates that the tone of the word in Colloquial, as marked in this book, is different from the tone in the book-language.

† Means that the pronunciation of the word, as given in this book, is different from that given to it in the book-language.

The figures denote the final, which is used in the Chinese. The numbers correspond with the numbers of the List of Finals towards the end of 'Cantonese Made Easy.'

The Chinese Characters in brackets are words which may be used with the other character or characters preceding them, or not. It will be seen that in the literal English rendering the English words within the brackets explain these extra characters.

The hyphen between two or more English words in the literal translation shows that these words represent one Chinese Character.

# LESSON I.

PRELIMINARY—SINGLE WORDS.

| | | |
|---|---|---|
| 1. | Come. | 嚟、 |
| 2. | Go. | 去、 |
| 3. | Walk. | 行、 |
| 4. | Run. | 走、 |
| 5. | Go up. | 上、 |
| 6. | Go down. | 落、 |
| 7. | Let go, *or* Set down (as a chair). | 鬆、 |
| 8. | Strike. | 打、 |
| 9. | Very good. | 好、 |
| 10. | Yes. | 係、 |
| 11. | Do it. | 做、 |
| 12. | Open. | 開、 |
| 13. | Shut. | 閂、 |
| 14. | Lock. | 鎖、 |
| 15. | Be off. | 擠、 |
| 16. | Give. | 俾、 |
| 17. | To present, *or* give. | 送、 |
| 18. | Pull (as a punkah). | 搖、 *or* 扯、 |
| 19. | Pull (as a jinrickshaw). | 拉、 |
| 20. | Chair! (Sedan). | 轎、 |
| 21. | Boat! | 艇、 |
| 22. | Jinrickshaw! | 車(仔)、 |
| 23. | Take it. | 拧、 |
| 24. | Thief. | 賊、 |
| 25. | Dear (in price). | 貴、 |
| 26. | Cheap. | 平、 |
| 27. | Cash. | 錢、 |
| 28. | I. | 我、 |
| 29. | You. | 你、 |
| 30. | He, *or* She, *or* It. | 佢、 |
| 31. | There are. | 有、 |
| 32. | There are none. | 冇、 |

易學廣東話



# LESSON I.

## Preliminary—single words.

| | | |
|---|---|---|
| 1. | ꜁Lai. | Come. |
| 2. | Höü꜄. | Go. |
| 3. | ꜀Háng.† | Walk. |
| 4. | ꜂Tsau. | Run. |
| 5. | ꜃Shöng. | Up. |
| 6. | Lok꜆. | Down. |
| 7. | ꜀Sung. | Let go. |
| 8. | ꜂Tá. | Strike. |
| 9. | ꜂Hò. | Good. |
| 10. | Hai꜅. | It-is. |
| 11. | Tsò꜅. | Do. |
| 12. | ꜀Hoi. | Open. |
| 13. | ꜀Shàn. | Shut. |
| 14. | ꜂So. | Lock. |
| 15. | ꜂Ch'e. | Off. |
| 16. | ꜂Péi. | Give. |
| 17. | Sung꜄. | Give. |
| 18. | ꜀Mang.† *or* ꜂ch'e. | Pull. |
| 19. | ꜀Lai. | Drag. |
| 20. | ꜂Kiú.* | Sedan-chair. |
| 21. | ꜃T'eng.† | Boat. |
| 22. | ꜀Ch'e (꜂tsai). | Vehicle (a diminutive). |
| 23. | ꜀Ning. | Take. |
| 24. | Ts'ák꜆. | Thief. |
| 25. | Kwai꜄. | Dear. |
| 26. | ꜀P'eng.† | Cheap. |
| 27. | ꜃Ts'in.* | Cash. |
| 28. | ꜃Ngo. | I. |
| 29. | ꜃Néi. | You. |
| 30. | ꜃K'öü. | He, or She, or It. |
| 31. | ꜃Yau. | There-are. |
| 32. | ꜃Mo. | There-are-none. |

# LESSON II.

PRELIMINARY—SHORT PHRASES AND SENTENCES FORMED WITH 'COME.'

| | | |
|---|---|---|
| 1. | Come. | 嚟， |
| 2. | Come in. | 入嚟， |
| 3. | Come up. | 上嚟， |
| 4. | Will not come. | 唔嚟， |
| 5. | Come down. | 落嚟， |
| 6. | Will you come or not ? | 嚟唔嚟， |
| 7. | I am coming. | (我)嚟， |
| 8. | You come. | 你嚟， |
| 9. | He is coming. | 佢嚟， |
| 10. | Coming too slowly. | 嚟慢， |
| 11. | Coming quickly. | 嚟快， |
| 12. | Comes flying. | 飛嚟， |
| 13. | Comes running. | 走嚟， |
| 14. | Comes steaming. | 車嚟， |
| 15. | Coming. | 嚟緊， |
| 16. | Come out. | 出嚟， |
| 17. | Come back. | 翻嚟， |
| 18. | Do not come. | 咪嚟， *or* 唔好嚟， |
| 19. | I cannot come. | 唔嚟得， |
| 20. | The horse is coming. | 馬嚟， |
| 21. | The rain is coming. | 雨嚟， |
| 22. | Comes blowing, *or* Blown here. | 吹嚟， |
| 23. | The boat comes. | 艇嚟， |
| 24. | Came. | 嚟咀， |
| 25. | Came. | ‘嚟咯， |
| 26. | A man comes. | 人嚟， |
| 27. | The water comes. | 水嚟， |
| 28. | The official comes. | 官嚟， |
| 29. | The wind comes. | 風嚟， |
| 30. | The dog comes. | 狗嚟， |
| 31. | Comes to strike. | 嚟打， |
| 32. | Struck. | 打嚟， |

易學廣東話



# LESSON II.

PRELIMINARY—SHORT PHRASES AND SENTENCES FORMED WITH 'COME.'

| | | |
|---|---|---|
| 1. | ꜁Laí. | Come. |
| 2. | Yap꜇ ꜁laí. | In come. |
| 3. | ꜃Shöng ꜁laí. | Up come. |
| 4. | ꜁M ꜁laí. | Not come. |
| 5. | Lok꜇ ꜁laí. | Down come. |
| 6. | ꜁Laí ꜁m ꜁laí. | Come, not come? |
| 7. | (꜃Ngo) ꜁laí. | (I) come. |
| 8. | ꜃Néí ꜁laí. | You come. |
| 9. | ꜃K'öü ꜁laí. | He comes. |
| 10. | ꜁Laí mán꜅. | Comes slowly. |
| 11. | ꜁Laí faí꜄. | Comes quickly. |
| 12. | ꜀Féí ꜁laí. | Flying comes. |
| 13. | ꜂Tsau ꜁laí. | Running comes. |
| 14. | ꜀Ch'e ꜁laí. | Steaming comes. |
| 15. | ꜁Laí ꜂kau. | Coming. |
| 16. | Ch'ut꜆ ꜁laí. | Out comes. |
| 17. | ꜁Fán ꜁laí. | Back comes. |
| 18. | ꜃Maí ꜁laí, *or* ꜁m ꜂hò ꜁laí. | Do-not come, *or* Not good come. |
| 19. | ꜁M ꜁laí tak꜆. | Not come can. |
| 20. | ꜃Má ꜁laí. | Horse coming. |
| 21. | ꜃Yü ꜁laí. | Rain coming. |
| 22. | ꜀Ch'uí ꜁laí. | Blowing comes. |
| 23. | ꜃T'eng† ꜁laí. | Boat comes. |
| 24. | ꜁Laí ꜂cho. | Came. [S. of p. t.] |
| 25. | ꜁Laí lok꜆. | Came. 32. |
| 26. | ꜁Yan ꜁laí. | Man comes. |
| 27. | ꜂Shuí ꜁laí. | Water comes. |
| 28. | ꜀Kwún ꜁laí. | Officer comes. |
| 29. | ꜀Fung ꜁laí. | Wind comes. |
| 30. | ꜂Kau ꜁laí. | Dog comes. |
| 31. | ꜁Laí ꜂tá. | Come to-strike. |
| 32. | ꜂Tá ꜁laí. | Striking comes. |

# LESSON III.

PRELIMINARY—SHORT PHRASES AND SENTENCES FORMED WITH 'GO.'

| | | |
|---|---|---|
| 1. | Go. | 去、 |
| 2. | Go up. | 上去、 |
| 3. | Go down. | 落去、 |
| 4. | Go in. | 入去、 |
| 5. | Gone. | 去咽、 |
| 6. | Gone. | 去曉、 |
| 7. | Gone out. | 出去、 |
| 8. | Do not go. | 咪去、 |
| 9. | Do not go. | 唔好去、 |
| 10. | Better go. | 好去、 |
| 11. | Better not go. | 唔好去、 |
| 12. | Go again. | 再去、 |
| 13. | Going again. | 又去、 |
| 14. | Did go, *or* Have gone. | 有去、 |
| 15. | Did not go, *or* Have not gone. | 冇去、 |
| 16. | No one goes, *or* No one has gone. | 冇人去、 |
| 17. | There are people going, *or* Some one has gone. | 有人去、 |
| 18. | It is well to go. | 去好、 |
| 19. | As soon as gone. | 一去、 |
| 20. | As soon as I went. | 我一去、 |
| 21. | Went first, *or* Go first. | 先去、 |
| 22. | Went afterwards. | 後去、 |
| 23. | Have you been yet? | 去未、 |
| 24. | I have not been yet. | 未去、 |
| 25. | Go early. | 早去、 |
| 26. | Go late (at night). | 夜去、 |
| 27. | Carry it away (by one man, slung on to the two ends of a pole). | 擔去、 |
| 28. | Carry it away (between two men, on a pole). | 抬去、 |
| 29. | Carry it away (resting on one's shoulder, &c.). | 托去、 |
| 30. | Take it away. | 揸去、 |
| 31. | Go and get it. | 去揸、 |
| 32. | Go and get it. | 去攞、 |

# LESSON III.

PRELIMINARY—SHORT PHRASES AND SENTENCES FORMED WITH 'GO.'

| | | |
|---|---|---|
| 1. | Höüʾ. | Go. |
| 2. | ᶜShöng höüʾ. | Up go. |
| 3. | Lok$_2$ höüʾ. | Down go. |
| 4. | Yap$_2$ höüʾ. | In go. |
| 5. | Höüʾ ᶜcho. | Gone. (S. of p. t.) |
| 6. | Höüʾ ꜀lúi.* | Gone (S. of p. t.) |
| 7. | Ch'ut$_{\supset}$ höüʾ. | Out go. |
| 8. | ᶜMaí höüʾ. | Do-not go. |
| 9. | ꜀M ᶜhò höüʾ. | Not good go. |
| 10. | ᶜHò höüʾ. | Good go. |
| 11. | ꜀M ᶜhò höüʾ. | Not good go. |
| 12. | Tsoíʾ höüʾ. | Again go. |
| 13. | Yau$^2$ höüʾ. | Again go. |
| 14. | ᶜYau höüʾ. | Have go. |
| 15. | ᶜMò höüʾ. | Not go. |
| 16. | ᶜMò ꜀yan höüʾ. | No one goes. |
| 17. | ᶜYau ꜀yan höüʾ. | Have man go. |
| 18. | Höüʾ ᶜhò. | To-go good. |
| 19. | Yat$_{\supset}$ höü. | Once gone. |
| 20. | ᶜNgo yat$_{\supset}$ höüʾ. | I once gone. |
| 21. | ꜀Sín höüʾ. | First went. |
| 22. | Han$^2$ höüʾ. | After went. |
| 23. | Höüʾ méi$^2$ ? | Gone yet ? |
| 24. | Méi$^2$ höüʾ. | Not-yet gone. |
| 25. | ᶜTsò höüʾ. | Early go. |
| 26. | Ye$^2$ höüʾ. | Late (at night) go. |
| 27. | ꜀Tàm höüʾ. | Carry away. |
| 28. | ꜀T'oí höüʾ. | Carry away. |
| 29. | T'ok$_{\circ}$ höüʾ. | Carry away. |
| 30. | ꜀Ning höüʾ. | Take away. |
| 31. | Höüʾ ꜀ning. | Go take. |
| 32. | Höüʾ ᶜlo. | Go get. |

# LESSON IV.

PRELIMINARY—SHORT PHRASES AND SENTENCES FORMED WITH 'DOWN.'

| | | |
|---|---|---|
| 1. | It rains. | 落雨, |
| 2. | It snows. | 落雪, |
| 3. | It hails. | 落雹, |
| 4. | To fall. | 跌落, |
| 5. | Come down. | 落嚟, |
| 6. | Go down. | 落去, |
| 7. | Exert yourself. | 落力, |
| 8. | To pay bargain money. | 落定, |
| 9. | To put in capital. | 落本, |
| 10. | Commence writing. | 落筆, |
| 11. | To go on board. | 落船, |
| 12. | To take in cargo. | 落貨, |
| 13. | To go into the water. | 落水, |
| 14. | Mix with sand. | 落沙, |
| 15. | The sun is going down. | 日落, |
| 16. | The moon is setting. | 月落, |
| 17. | To give anyone the sack. | 落箱, |
| 18. | To go down the street. | 落街, |
| 19. | To go down into the street. | 落街, |
| 20. | To go downstairs. | 落樓, |
| 21. | To go down the hill. | 落山, |
| 22. | Go down. | 落, |
| 23. | To go down. | 落去, |
| 24. | To put down. | 丟落, |
| 25. | To put down. | 放落, |
| 26. | Place it down. | 擠落, |
| 27. | To throw down. | 泵落, |
| 28. | To carry down. | 擔落, |
| 29. | To carry down. | 抬落, |
| 30. | Take it down. | 捊落, |
| 31. | Take care how you go down. | 細心落, |
| 32. | Take care how you go down. | 好聲落, |

# LESSON IV.

PRELIMINARY—SHORT PHRASES AND SENTENCES FORMED WITH 'DOWN.'

| | | |
|---|---|---|
| 1. | Lok$_2$ ᶜyü. | Down rain. |
| 2. | Lok$_2$ süt꜀. | Down snow. |
| 3. | Lok$_2$ pok$_2$. | Down hail. |
| 4. | Tit꜀ lok$_2$. | Fall down. |
| 5. | Lok$_2$ ꜀lai. | Down come. |
| 6. | Lok$_2$ höüᵓ. | Down go. |
| 7. | Lok$_2$ lik$_2$. | Down (with your) strength. |
| 8. | Lok$_2$ teng$^2$†. | (Pay) down bargain (money). |
| 9. | Lok$_2$ ᶜpún. | Down capital. |
| 10. | Lok$_2$ pat$_2$. | Down pen. |
| 11. | Lok$_2$ ꜀shün. | (To go) down (on) ship. |
| 12. | Lok$_2$ foᵓ. | (To put) down goods. |
| 13. | Lok$_2$ ᶜshöü. | Down (into) water. |
| 14. | Lok$_2$ ꜀shá. | Down sand. |
| 15. | Yat$_2$ lok$_2$. | Sun down. |
| 16. | Yüt$_2$ lok$_2$. | Moon down. |
| 17. | Lok$_2$ ꜀söng. | Down box. |
| 18. | Lok$_2$ ꜀kái. | Down street. |
| 19. | Lok$_2$ ꜀kái. | Down street. |
| 20. | Lok$_2$ ᶜlau.* | Down story. |
| 21. | Lok$_2$ ꜀shán. | Down hill. |
| 22. | Lok$_2$. | Down. |
| 23. | Lok$_2$ höüᵓ. | Down go. |
| 24. | ꜀Tíú lok$_2$. | Put down. |
| 25. | Fongᵓ lok$_2$. | Place down. |
| 26. | ꜀Chai lok$_2$. | Place down. |
| 27. | ᶜTám lok$_2$. | Throw down. |
| 28. | ꜀Tám lok$_2$. | Carry down. |
| 29. | ꜀T'oi lok$_2$. | Carry down. |
| 30. | ꜀Ning lok$_2$. | Take down. |
| 31. | Saiᵓ ꜀sam lok$_2$. | Small heart go-down. |
| 32. | ᶜHò ꜀sheng† lok$_2$. | Very carefully go-down. |

# LESSON V.

PRELIMINARY—SHORT PHRASES AND SENTENCES FORMED WITH 'STRIKE.'

| | | |
|---|---|---|
| 1. | Strike (the rallying call in a street fight.) | 打、 |
| 2. | Strike him. | 打佢、 |
| 3. | To fight. | 打交、*or* 打架、 |
| 4. | To strike me. | 打我、 |
| 5. | I will strike you. | 我打你、 |
| 6. | To kill. | 打死、 |
| 7. | To work in iron. | 打鐵、 |
| 8. | To work in copper. | 打銅、 |
| 9. | To throw open. | 打開、 |
| 10. | To shoot birds. | 打雀、 |
| 11. | Hit. | 打親、*or* 打着、 |
| 12. | Cannot hit it. | 打唔倒、 |
| 13. | Do not fight. | 唔好打、 |
| 14. | To cut stone. | 打石、 |
| 15. | To go by road. | 打路、 |
| 16. | To fetch, (*or* draw) water. | 打水、 |
| 17. | Struck by lightning. | 雷打、 |
| 18. | To send a telegram. | 打電線、 |
| 19. | To spy. | 打探、 |
| 20. | To fight a battle. | 打仗、 |
| 21. | To win. | 打贏、 |
| 22. | To wound. | 打傷、 |
| 23. | To be defeated. | 打輸、 |
| 24. | To commit highway robbery. | 打脚骨、 |
| 25. | To sneeze. | 打嚇哆、 |
| 26. | To yawn. | 打喊露、 |
| 27. | To pierce. | 打穿、 |
| 28. | To play cards. | 打紙牌、 |
| 29. | To play at dominoes. | 打骨牌、 |
| 30. | To play 'Heaven's Nine' (a game at dominoes). | 打天九、 |
| 31. | To work. | 打工、 |
| 32. | To play shuttlecock. | 打燕、 |

# LESSON V.

PRELIMINARY—SHORT PHRASES AND SENTENCES FORMED WITH 'STRIKE.'

| | | |
|---|---|---|
| 1. | ᶜTá. | Strike. |
| 2. | ᶜTá ᶜk'öü. | Strike him. |
| 3. | ᶜTá ꜀kaú, *or* ᶜtá ká'. | To fight. |
| 4. | ᶜTá ᶜngo. | Strike me. |
| 5. | ᶜNgo ᶜtá ᶜnéi. | I strike you. |
| 6. | ᶜTá ᶜsz. | Strike to-death. |
| 7. | ᶜTá t'ít꜀. | Strike iron. |
| 8. | ᶜTá ꜀t'ung. | Strike copper. |
| 9. | ᶜTá ꜀hoi. | Throw open. |
| 10. | ᶜTá tsök꜀. | Strike bird. |
| 11. | ᶜTá ꜀ts'an, *or* ᶜTá chök$_2$. | Strike. |
| 12. | ᶜTá ꜀m ᶜtò. | Struck not reach. |
| 13. | ꜀M ᶜhò ᶜtá. | Not good strike. |
| 14. | ᶜTá shek$_2$. † | Strike stone. |
| 15. | ᶜTá ꜀lò. | To-go-by road. |
| 16. | ᶜTá ᶜshöü. | Fetch water. |
| 17. | ꜀Löü ᶜtá. | Thunder struck. |
| 18. | ᶜTá tin$^2$-sin'. | Send telegram. |
| 19. | ᶜTá t'am'. | To spy. |
| 20. | ᶜTá chöng'. [1] | To fight. |
| 21. | ᶜTá ꜀yeng. † | To win. |
| 22. | ᶜTá ꜀shöng. | To-be wounded. |
| 23. | ᶜTá ꜀shü. | Defeated. |
| 24. | ᶜTá kök꜀ kwat꜀. | Strike feet bones. |
| 25. | ᶜTá hat꜀ ꜀ch'i. | Sneeze (onomatopoetic). |
| 26. | ᶜTá hám' lò$^2$. | Yawn. |
| 27. | ᶜTá ꜀ch'ün. | Strike through. |
| 28. | ᶜTá ᶜchi ᶜp'ái.* | Play paper tickets. |
| 29. | ᶜTá kwat꜀ ᶜp'ái.* | Play bone tickets. |
| 30. | ᶜTá ꜀t'in ᶜkau. | Play 'heaven's nine.' |
| 31. | ᶜTá ꜀kung. | Work. |
| 32. | ᶜTá ᶜyin. [In book language yin'.] | Strike shuttlecock. |

1. Note.—In the book Language this is 下去 ha$^2$ hui', chöng$^2$; but in the Colloquial it is pronounced as above. This does not seem to have been noticed by anyone before. At all events the Dictionaries do not call attention to it.

B 2

## CONVERSATION 1st.—PUTTING OFF.

| | |
|---|---|
| 1. Do you understand? | 你曉嗎, |
| 2. I do. | 曉咯, |
| 3. Go and do it. | 去做喇, |
| 4. I will do it by and by. | 慢慢做, |
| 5. Do it now. | 而家做, |
| 6. I will do it to-morrow. | 聽日做, |
| 7. Do it to-day. | 今日做, |
| 8. I have no time. | 唔得閒, |
| 9. Why? | 做乜呢, |
| 10. There are too many things *or* Too much business (to be done). | 野多吖, *or* 事多吖, |
| 11. No. | 唔係, |
| 12. I will do it when I come back. | 翻嚟做, |
| 13. Where are you going? | 去邊, *or* 去邊處, |
| 14. Going out. | 出街一陣(間), |
| 15. You need not go. | 唔使去, |
| 16. It is very important. | 好緊要, |
| 17. How long will you be out? | 去幾耐, |
| 18. Not long. | 冇耐者, |
| 19. Oh! Very well. | 悟, 好喇, |
| 20. I am going now. | 而家去, |
| 21. Do not go yet. | 咪去自, |
| 22. Why? | 做乜呢, |
| 23. I am engaged. | 我有事, |
| 24. I will wait a while. | 我等吓, |
| 25. Wait for what? | 等乜呢, |
| 26. You need not wait. | 唔使等, |
| 27. I will wait. | 我等呀, |
| 28. How kind you are. | 咁好心, |
| 29. Oh, no. | 唔係吖, |
| 30. I think you are. | 我算係, |
| 31. Why? | 點解呢, |
| 32. To wait for me. | 等我咯, |

## CONVERSATION 1st.—PUTTING OFF.

| | | |
|---|---|---|
| 1. | ᶜNéi ᶜhiú maᵓ ? | You understand, eh ? 35 |
| 2. | ᶜHiú lok . | Understand. 32 |
| 3. | Höüᵓ tsò$^{2}$ ꜀lá. | Go do. 21. |
| 4. | Mán$^{2}$ ᶜmán* tsò$^{2}$. | Slow slow do. |
| 5. | ꜀Yí-꜀kai tsò$^{2}$. | Now do. |
| 6. | ꜀T'ing-yat꜋ tsò$^{2}$. | To-morrow do. |
| 7. | ꜀Kam yat꜋ tsò$^{2}$. | Now-day do. |
| 8. | ꜀M tak꜋ ꜀hán. | Not able (to have) leisure (to do it). |
| 9. | Tsò$^{2}$ mat꜋ ꜀ni ? | Why, eh ? 51 |
| 10. | ᶜYe ꜀to ꜀á, *or* Sz$^{2}$ ꜀to ꜀á. | Things many. 1, *or* Business much. 1. |
| 11. | ꜀M hai$^{2}$. | Not is. |
| 12. | ꜀Fán ꜀lai tsò$^{2}$. | Back come do. |
| 13. | Höüᵓ ꜀pín ? *or* Höüᵓ ꜀pín shöüᵓ ? | Go where ? *or* Go what place ? |
| 14. | Ch'ut꜋ ꜀kai yat꜋ chan$^{2}$ ꜀kán. | Go-out street one short (space). |
| 15. | ꜀M ᶜshai hüiᵓ. | Not need go. |
| 16. | ᶜHò ᶜkan yíuᵓ. | Very pressing need. |
| 17. | Höüᵓ ᶜkéi ᶜnoi.?* | Go how long ? |
| 18. | ᶜMò ᶜnoi* ꜀che (*or* ꜀che). | Not long only. 7 |
| 19. | ꜀Ng. ᶜhò ꜀lá. | Well, good. 21 |
| 20. | ꜀Yí-꜀kai höüᵓ. | Now go. |
| 21. | ᶜMai höüᵓ tsz$^{2}$. | Don't go yet. |
| 22. | Tsò$^{2}$ mat꜋ ꜀ni ? | Do what, eh ? 53 |
| 23. | ᶜNgo ᶜyan sz$^{2}$. | I have business. |
| 24. | ᶜNgo ᶜtang ᶜhá. | I wait a-bit. |
| 25. | ᶜTang mat꜋ ꜀ni ? | Wait (what) thing eh ? 53 |
| 26. | ꜀M ᶜshai ᶜtang. | Not need wait. |
| 27. | ᶜNgo ᶜtang aᵓ. | I wait. 2. |
| 28. | Kòmᵓ ᶜhò ꜀sam. | So good heart. |
| 29. | ꜀M hai$^{2}$ ꜀á. | Not is. 1 |
| 30. | ᶜNgo sünᵓ hai$^{2}$. | I thing is. |
| 31. | ᶜTím ᶜkái ꜀ni? (*or* more decidedly ꜀ni). | How explain, eh ? 53 (51) |
| 32. | ᶜTang ᶜngo lok꜋. | Wait me. 32 |

## CONVERSATION 2ND.—COME AND HELP ME.

| | | |
|---|---|---|
| 1. | Come and help me. | 嚟帮我、 |
| 2. | To do what? | 做乜野、 |
| 3. | To lift that trunk. | 抽個櫃、 |
| 4. | Why? | 做乜呢、 |
| 5. | I have let something fall. | 跌啲野、 |
| 6. | What have you let fall? | 跌乜呢、 |
| 7. | Keys. | 鎖匙、 |
| 8. | How many? | 幾多條、 |
| 9. | A bunch. | 一昤、 |
| 10. | Where? | 喺邊處、 |
| 11. | Behind the trunk. | 櫃後便、 |
| 12. | Dear me! How heavy it is! | 嗾、咁重、 |
| 13. | It is very heavy. | 好重呀、 |
| 14. | What is in it? | 裝乜野、 |
| 15. | Books. | 書咯、 |
| 16. | And that one? | 嗰個呢、 |
| 17. | Clothes. | 衣裳咯、 |
| 18. | That is light. | 嗰個輕、 |
| 19. | Of course it is light. | 輕定喇、 |
| 20. | How is that? | 點解呢、 |
| 21. | There is nothing in it. | 冇野咯、 |
| 22. | Oh! indeed! | 係咩、 |
| 23. | Take them out. | 攞出嚟、 |
| 24. | There is nothing. | 冇野吖、 |
| 25. | Those books. | 個啲書、 |
| 26. | Where shall I put them? | 擠邊處、 |
| 27. | Place them on the table. | 放檯上、 |
| 28. | Which table? | 邊張檯、 |
| 29. | The marble table. | 雲石檯、 |
| 30. | There is no room. | 冇地方、 |
| 31. | Move the things off. | 搬開野、 |
| 32. | That will do. | 噉得咯、 |

## CONVERSATION 2ND.—COME AND HELP ME.

| | | |
|---|---|---|
| 1. | ꜀Lai ꜀pong ᶝngo. | Come help me. |
| 2. | Tsò² ꜀mi ᶜye? | Do what thing? |
| 3. | ꜀Ch'ún koᵓ ᶝlung. | Lift that trunk. |
| 4. | Tsò² mat꜄ ꜀ni? | Do what, eh? 53 |
| 5. | Titᵕ-ᶜcho ᶝye. | Fallen things. |
| 6. | Titᵕ mat꜄ ꜀ni? | Fallen what, eh? 53? |
| 7. | ᶜSo ꜀shí. | Lock keys. |
| 8. | ᶜKéi ꜀to ꜀t'iú? | How many [C.]? |
| 9. | Yat꜄ lungᵓ. | One bunch. |
| 10. | ᶜHai ꜀pín (shüᵓ)? | At what (place)? |
| 11. | ᶝLung hau² pín². | Trunk behind side. |
| 12. | ꜀Ai! Kòmᵓ ᶝch'úng! | Oh! How heavy! |
| 13. | ᶜHò ᶝch'úng áᵓ. | Very heavy. 2 |
| 14. | ꜀Chong ꜀mi ᶝye? | Hold what things? |
| 15. | ꜀Shü lokᵕ. | Books. 32 |
| 16. | ᶜKo-koᵓ ᵕni? | That eh? 54 |
| 17. | ꜀Yí-꜀shöng lokᵕ. | Clothing. 32 |
| 18. | ᶜKo-koᵓ ᵕheng*†. | That light. |
| 19. | ₒHeng*† ᶜting* ꜀lá. | Light certainly. 21 |
| 20. | ᶜTím ᶜkái ꜀ni? (*or* ₒni) | How explain, eh? 53 (*or* 54) |
| 21. | ᶝMò ᶝye lokₒ. | Not anything. 32 |
| 22. | Hai² ꜀me? (*or* ₒ me) | Yes, eh? 39. |
| 23. | ꜀Ning ch'ut꜄ ꜀lai. | Bring out come. |
| 24. | ᶝMò ᶝye ꜀á. | Not anything. 1 |
| 25. | Koᵓ-꜀ti ꜀shü. | Those books. |
| 26. | ꜀Chai-pín shüᵓ? | Place what place? |
| 27. | Fongᵓ ᶜt'oi* shöng². | Place table on. |
| 28. | ꜀Pín ꜀chöng ᶜt'oi?* | Which [C.] table? |
| 29. | ꜀Wan shek꜄† ᶜt'oi.* | Cloud stone table. |
| 30. | ᶝMò téi²-꜀fong. | No room. |
| 31. | ꜀Pún ꜀hoi-ᶝye. | Move off things. |
| 32. | ᶜKòm tak꜄ lokᵕ. | So can. 32 |

## CONVERSATION 3RD.—THE SICK MAN.

| | | |
|---|---|---|
| 1. | It is too fierce. | 猛過頭、 |
| 2. | What is fierce? | 乜野猛、 |
| 3. | The fire. | 火咯、 |
| 4. | Oh, no! | 唔係吖、 |
| 5. | I feel it hot. | 我見熱、 |
| 6. | Open the window. | 開窗門、 |
| 7. | You open it. | 你開喇、 |
| 8. | How is that? | 噉好嗎、 |
| 9. | It is better. | 好啲咯、 |
| 10. | It would be well to open the door. | 開門好、 |
| 11. | It would be well. | 都好吖、 |
| 12. | I will open it. | 我開喇、 |
| 13. | I still feel hot. | 都見熱、 |
| 14. | It is not hot. | 唔係熱、 |
| 15. | I say it is hot. | 我話熱、 |
| 16. | You are perhaps ill. | 你病嘞、 |
| 17. | I am not ill. | 唔係病、 |
| 18. | I am afraid you are. | 怕係嘞、 |
| 19. | I am ill? | 我病咩、 |
| 20. | Certainly you are. | 病定喇、 |
| 21. | I am not. | 唔係嘅、 |
| 22. | I think you are. | 我咕係、 |
| 23. | You are mistaken. | 你咕錯、 |
| 24. | I am not. | 唔係錯、 |
| 25. | You are a fool. | 你呆嘅、 |
| 26. | It can be seen. | 見得出、 |
| 27. | It—can—be—seen. | 見得出、 |
| 28. | You won't believe it. | 你唔信、 |
| 29. | Believe what? | 信乜呢、 |
| 30. | What I say. | 我所講、 |
| 31. | I do not. | 唔信咯、 |
| 32. | You will by and by. | 等吓信、 |

## CONVERSATION 3RD.—THE SICK MAN.

| | | |
|---|---|---|
| 1. | ᶜMáng kwoˀ ꜀t'au. | Fierce over much (lit. over head). |
| 2. | ꜀Mi ᶜye ᶜmáng? | What thing fierce? |
| 3. | ᶜFo lok꜀. | Fire. 32 |
| 4. | ꜀M hai² ꜀á. | Not is. 1 |
| 5. | ᶜNgo kínˀ yít₂. | I feel hot. |
| 6. | ꜀Hoí ꜀ch'öng-꜀mún. | Open window. |
| 7. | ᶜNéi ꜀hoí ꜀lá. | You open. 21 |
| 8. | ᶜKòm ᶜhò máˀ? | So, good, eh? 35 |
| 9. | ᶜHò-꜀tí lok꜀. | Better. 32 |
| 10. | ꜀Hoí ꜀mún ᶜhò. | Open door good. |
| 11. | ꜀Tò ᶜhò ꜀á. | Also good. 1 |
| 12. | ᶜNgo ꜀hoí ꜀lá. | I open. 21 |
| 13. | ꜀Tò kínˀ yit₂. | Yet feel hot. |
| 14. | ꜀M hai² yit₂. | Not is hot. |
| 15. | ᶜNgo wá² yít₂. | I say hot. |
| 16. | ᶜNéi peng²† kwáˀ. | You ill, I-suppose. 18 |
| 17. | ꜀M hai² peng²†. | Not am ill. |
| 18. | P'áˀ hai² kwáˀ. | Fear are likely. 18 |
| 19. | ᶜNgo peng²† ꜀me (*or* ꜀me)? | I ill, eh? 39 |
| 20. | Peng²† ᶜting* ꜀lá. | Ill certainly. 21. |
| 21. | ꜀M hai² keˀ. | Not am. 15 |
| 22. | ᶜNgo ᶜkwú hai². | I think it-is-so. |
| 23. | ᶜNéi ᶜkwú ts'oˀ. | You think wrong. |
| 24. | ꜀M hai² ts'oˀ. | Not am wrong. |
| 25. | ᶜNéi ꜀ngoi keˀ. | You foolish. 15 |
| 26. | Kínˀ tak꜀ ch'ut꜀. | See can out. |
| 27. | Kínˀ—tak꜀—ch'ut꜀. | See—can—out. |
| 28. | ᶜNéi ꜀m sunˀ. | You not believe. |
| 29. | Sunˀ mat꜀ ꜀ni? | Believe what, eh? 53 |
| 30. | ᶜNgo ᶜsho ᶜkong. | I what speak. |
| 31. | ꜀M sunˀ lok꜀. | Not believe. 32 |
| 32. | ᶜTang ꜀há* sunˀ. | Wait a-bit believe. |

C

## CONVERSATION 4TH.—COME, GET UP.

| | | |
|---|---|---|
| 1. | Come, get up. | 起身喇、 |
| 2. | Why? | 做乜呀、 |
| 3. | It is six o'clock. | 六點咯、 |
| 4. | Well! all right. | 俉、好喇、 |
| 5. | Be quick. | 快啲喇、 |
| 6. | By and by. | 等吓、 |
| 7. | That will not do. | 唔做得、 |
| 8. | It will do. | 做得、 |
| 9. | It will not. | 唔得、 |
| 10. | Why not? | 點解呀、 |
| 11. | I will not explain. | 唔解咯、 |
| 12. | I want you. | 我要你、 |
| 13. | I will not come. | 唔嚟咯、 |
| 14. | Come here. | 嚟呢處、 |
| 15. | What do you want? | 你要乜、 |
| 16. | You. | 你呀、 |
| 17. | Tell him to come. | 叫佢嚟、 |
| 18. | I cannot. | 唔做得、 |
| 19. | You cannot call him? | 唔叫得、 |
| 20. | Yes. | 係哩、 |
| 21. | Rubbish! | 發譫話、 |
| 22. | It is not. | 唔係呀、 |
| 23. | I say it is. | 我話係、 |
| 24. | You do not know. | 你唔識、 |
| 25. | Do I not? | 唔識咩、 |
| 26. | You do not. | 係哩、 |
| 27. | How do I not know? | 點唔識、 |
| 28. | He is deaf. | 佢耳聾、 |
| 29. | No, he is not. | 唔係、 |
| 30. | Yes, he is. | 係哩、 |
| 31. | You are deceiving me. | 你嚛我、 |
| 32. | You will not believe. | 你唔信、 |

## CONVERSATION 4TH.—COME, GET UP.

| | | |
|---|---|---|
| 1. | ᶜHéi ꜀shan ꜀lá. | Raise body. 21 |
| 2. | Tsò$^{2}$ mat꜆ áᵓ? | Do what, eh? 2 |
| 3. | Luk$_{2}$ ᶜtím lok꜄. | Six strokes. 32 |
| 4. | ꜀Ng, ᶜhò ꜀lá. | Well! good. 21 |
| 5. | Fáiᵓ-ₒtí ꜀lá. | Quickly. 21 |
| 6. | ᶜTang ₒhá*. | Wait bit. |
| 7. | ꜀M tsò$^{2}$ tak꜆. | Not do can. |
| 8. | Tsò$^{2}$ tak꜆. | Do can. |
| 9. | ꜀M tak꜆. | Not can. |
| 10. | ᶜTím ᶜkái áᵓ? | How explain, eh? 2 |
| 11. | ꜀M ᶜkái lok꜄. | Not explain. 32 |
| 12. | ᶜNgo yíúᵓ ᶜnéi. | I want you. |
| 13. | ꜀M ꜀lai lok꜄. | Won't come. 32 |
| 14. | ꜀Lai ₒni shüᵓ. | Come this place. |
| 15. | ᶜNéi yíúᵓ mat꜆? | You want what? |
| 16. | ᶜNéi áᵓ. | You. 2 |
| 17. | Kíúᵓ ᶜk'öü ꜀laí. | Call him come. |
| 18. | ꜀M tsò$^{2}$ tak꜆. | Not do can. |
| 19. | ꜀M kíúᵓ tak꜆? | Not call can? |
| 20. | Haí$^{2}$ ꜀le (*or* ₒle.) | Yes. 24 |
| 21. | Fátₒ-ngámᵓ wá$^{2}$. | Nonsense! |
| 22. | ꜀M haí$^{2}$ áᵓ. | Not is. 2 |
| 23. | ᶜNgo wá$^{2}$ haí$^{2}$. | I say is. |
| 24. | ᶜNéi ꜀m shik꜆. | You not understand. |
| 25. | ꜀M shik꜆ ꜀me (*or* ₒme?) | Not know, eh? 39 |
| 26. | Haí$^{2}$ ꜀le (*or* leₒ.) | Yes. 24 |
| 27. | ᶜTím ꜀m shik꜆? | How not know? |
| 28. | ᶜK'öü ᶜyí-꜀lung. | He deaf. |
| 29. | ꜀M haí$^{2}$. | Not is. |
| 30. | Haí$^{2}$ ꜀le (*or* ₒle.) | Yes. 24 |
| 31. | ᶜNéi t'amᵓ ᶜngo. | You deceive me. |
| 32. | ᶜNéi ꜀m sunᵓ. | You not believe. |

海上絲綢之路文獻集成 科技與文化編

## CONVERSATION 5TH.—IN A HURRY.

| | | |
|---|---|---|
| 1. | Please sit down. | 請坐、 |
| 2. | Sit down. | 坐喇、 |
| 3. | I will not sit down. | 我唔坐、 |
| 4. | Why not? | 做乜唔坐呢、 |
| 5. | I cannot. | 唔坐得噱、 |
| 6. | Why not? | 點解唔坐得呢、 |
| 7. | I have not time. | 唔得閒、 |
| 8. | Are you going? | 你去咩、 |
| 9. | Yes, I wish to go. | 係吖、想去咯、 |
| 10. | Do not go. Go by and by. | 唔好去呀、等吓至去喇、 |
| 11. | I must go. I must go now. | 要去呀、而家要去、 |
| 12. | Must you certainly go? | 你是必要去咩、 |
| 13. | I have business. | 我有事、 |
| 14. | It does not matter; it is not [important. | 唔相干、唔相干嘅、 |
| 15. | Is'nt it important? | 唔相干、 |
| 16. | It is very important. | 好緊要嘅、 |
| 17. | No, it is not; is it? | 唔係啩、 |
| 18. | It really is. | 眞正係呀、 |
| 19. | Oh! indeed. | 係咩、 |
| 20. | Yes, there is no mistake about it. | 係呀、冇錯呀、 |
| 21. | Then you won't sit down? | 噉你唔坐噱咩、 |
| 22. | How can I? | 點做得呢、 |
| 23. | I wish to talk with you. | 我想同你講咯、 |
| 24. | What do you wish to talk about? | 想講乜野呢、 |
| 25. | A great many things. | 想講好多野咯、 |
| 26. | I have not time. | 唔得閒呀、 |
| 27. | You never have time. | 你時時都唔得閒、 |
| 28. | I have not time to-day. | 我今日唔得閒、 |
| 29. | Good bye (by the host). | 好行吖、 |
| 30. | Good bye (by the guest). | 坐吖、 |
| 31. | Walk slowly. | 慢慢行喇、 |
| 32. | Sit down. | 坐喇、 |

## CONVERSATION 5TH.—IN A HURRY.

| | | |
|---|---|---|
| 1. | ᶜTs'eng† ᶝts'o*†. | Invite (you) sit-down. |
| 2. | ᶝTs'o*† ꜀lá. | Sit-down. 21 |
| 3. | ᶝNgo ꜁m ᶝts'o*†. | I not sit-down. |
| 4. | Tsò$^2$-mat꜆ ꜁m ᶝts'o*† ꜀ni (*or* ˳ni)? | Why not sit-down, eh? 53 |
| 5. | ꜁M ᶝts'o*† tak꜆ láʾ. | Not sit can. 22 |
| 6. | ᶜTím ᶜkái ꜁m ᶝts'o*† tak꜆ ꜀ni? | How explain not sit can, eh? 53 |
| 7. | ꜁M tak꜆ ꜁hán. | Not possess leisure. |
| 8. | ᶝNéi hőüʾ ꜀me (*or* ˳me)? | You go, eh? 39 |
| 9. | Hai$^2$ ꜀á, (*or* ꜀á) ᶜsöng hőüʾ lok˳. | Yes, I, wish to-go. 32 |
| 10. | ꜁M ᶜhò hőüʾ áʾ. ᶜTang ꜀há* (*or* ꜀ha) chíʾ hőüʾ ꜀lá. | Not good go. 2 Wait while before go. 21 |
| 11. | Yíúʾ hőüʾ áʾ. ꜁Yí-꜀ká* yíúʾ hőüʾ. | Want go. 2 Now want go. |
| 12. | ᶝNéi shí$^2$-pít꜆ yíúʾ hőüʾ ꜀me (*or* ˳me)? | You certainly must go, eh? 39 |
| 13. | ᶝNgo ᶝyan sz$^2$. | I have business. |
| 14. | ꜁M ꜀söng-꜀kon; ꜁m ꜀söng-꜀kon keʾ. | No matter; no importance. 15 |
| 15. | ꜁M ꜀söng-˳kon? | Not important? |
| 16. | ᶜHò ᶜkan-yíúʾ keʾ. | Very pressing. 15 |
| 17. | ꜁M hai$^2$ kwáʾ. | Not is, I-think? 18 |
| 18. | ꜀Chan-chingʾ hai$^2$ áʾ. | Truly is. 2 |
| 19. | Hai$^2$ ꜀me (*or* ˳me)? | Is-it, eh? 39 |
| 20. | Hai$^2$ áʾ. ᶝMò ts'oʾ áʾ. | It-is 2 No mistake. 2 |
| 21. | ᶜKòm ᶝnéi ꜁m ᶝts'o*† láʾ ꜀me (*or* ˳me)? | Then you not sit-down? 22, 39 |
| 22. | ᶜTím tsò$^2$ tak꜆ ꜀ni (*or* ˳ni)? | How do can, eh? 53 |
| 23. | ᶝNgo ᶜsöng ꜁t'ung ᶝnéi ᶜkong lok˳. | I wish with you speak. 32 |
| 24. | ᶜSöng ᶜkong mat꜆ ᶝye ꜀ni (*or* ˳ni)? | Wish speak what thing, eh? 53 |
| 25. | ᶜSöng ᶜkong ᶜhò ꜀to ᶝye lok˳. | Wish speak very many things. 32 |
| 26. | ꜁M tak꜆ ꜁hán áʾ. | Not possess leisure. 2 |
| 27. | ᶝNéi ꜁shí ꜁shí ꜀to ꜁m tak꜆ ꜁hán. | You time (after) time also not possess [leisure. |
| 28. | ᶝNgo ꜀kam-mat꜇ ꜁m tak꜆ ꜁hán. | I to-day not possess leisure. |
| 29. | ᶜHò ꜁hàng ꜀á. | Well walk. 1 |
| 30. | ᶝTs'o*† ꜀á (*or* ꜀á). | Sit-down (Do sit-down). 1 |
| 31. | Mán$^2$-ᶝmán* ꜁háng ꜀lá. | Slowly walk. 21 |
| 32. | ᶝTs'o ꜀lá (*or* ˳lá). | Sit-down. 21 |

## CONVERSATION 6TH.—A SHORT CONVERSATION.

| | |
|---|---|
| 1. Come. | 嚟、 |
| 2. Come here. | 嚟呢處、 |
| 3. Come up. | 上嚟、 |
| 4. It is nice here. | 呢處好、 |
| 5. No, it is not. | 唔係、 |
| 6. I say it is: what do you say? | 我話係叮、你話、 |
| 7. You think so. | 你估係唄、 |
| 8. I know it is. | 我知到係呀、 |
| 9. You do not know. | 你唔知叮、 |
| 10. Why should not I know? | 做乜唔知呢、 |
| 11. You do not understand. | 你唔識嘅、 |
| 12. I do understand. | 我識叮、 |
| 13. How do you understand? | 你點識呢、 |
| 14. I understand everything. | 我樣樣都識嘅、 |
| 15. How strange! | 咁出奇嘅、 |
| 16. You do not believe it, eh? | 你唔信啩、 |
| 17. Certainly, I do not. | 唔信定喇、 |
| 18. You ought to believe it. | 你應該信呀、 |
| 19. Why should I? | 做乜應該信呢、 |
| 20. It is true. | 眞係嘅、 |
| 21. Oh! no. | 唔係、唔係、 |
| 22. You are telling lies. | 你講大話、 |
| 23. Do not say that. | 唔好噉講、 |
| 24. I beg your pardon. | 唔該呀、 |
| 25. Granted. | 好話、 |
| 26. I was very angry. | 我好嬲、 |
| 27. You need not be angry. | 唔使嬲、 |
| 28. He was angry with me. | 佢嬲我咯、 |
| 29. Good friends. | 好朋友、 |
| 30. I know you: you know me. | 我識你、你識我、 |
| 31. Acquainted. | 相識、 |
| 32. Mutually acquaintedy. | 兩家相識、 |

## CONVERSATION 6TH.—A SHORT CONVERSATION.

| | | |
|---|---|---|
| 1. | ꜁lai. | Come. |
| 2. | ꜁Lai ˳ni shü꜄. | Come this place. |
| 3. | ꜃Shöng ꜁lai. | Up come. |
| 4. | ꜀Ni shü꜄ ꜂hò. | This place good. |
| 5. | ꜁M hai$^2$. | Not is. |
| 6. | ꜃Ngo wá$^2$ hai$^2$ ꜀á; ꜃nei ꜂wá* ? | I say it-is 1; you say? |
| 7. | ꜃Néi ꜂kwá hai$^2$ ꜀che. | You think it-is only (you think so.) 7 |
| 8. | ꜃Ngo ꜀chi-tò꜄ hai$^2$ á꜄. | I know it-is. 2 |
| 9. | ꜃Néi ꜁m ꜀chi ꜀á? | You not know. 1 |
| 10. | Tsò$^2$-mat꜆ ꜁m ꜀chi ꜀ni? | Why not know, eh? 53 |
| 11. | ꜃Néi ꜁m shik꜆ ke꜄. | You not know-about is. 15 |
| 12. | ꜃Ngo shik꜆ ꜀á. | I know. 1 |
| 13. | ꜃Néi ꜂tim shik꜆ ꜀ni? | You how know, eh? 53 |
| 14. | ꜃Ngo yöng$^2$ yöng$^2$ ˳tò shik꜆ ke꜄. | I thing (upon) thing even know. 15 |
| 15. | Kòm꜄ ch'ut꜆-꜁k'éi ke꜄. | So extraordinary. 15 |
| 16. | ꜃Néi ꜁m sun꜄ kwá꜄? | You not believe I-suppose? 18 |
| 17. | ꜁M sun꜄ ꜂ting* ꜀lá? | Not believe certainly. 21 |
| 18. | ꜃Néi ꜀ying-꜀koi sun꜄ á꜄? | You ought to-believe. 2 |
| 19. | Tsò$^2$-mat꜆ ꜀ying-꜀koi sun꜄ ꜀ni? | Why ought to-believe, eh? 53 |
| 20. | Hai$^2$ ꜀chan ke꜄. | It is true. 15 |
| 21. | ꜁M hai$^2$, ꜁m hai$^2$. | Not is, not is. |
| 22. | ꜃Néi ꜂kong tái$^2$ wá$^2$. | You speak large words. |
| 23. | ꜁M ꜂hò ꜂kòm ꜂kong. | Not good so say. |
| 24. | ꜁M ꜀koi á꜄. | Not proper. 2 |
| 25. | ꜂Hò wá$^2$. | Good words. |
| 26. | ꜃Ngo ꜂hò ꜀nau. | I very angry. |
| 27. | ꜁M ꜂shai ꜀nau. | Not need to-be-angry. |
| 28. | ꜃K'öü ꜀nau (˳nau) ꜃ngo lok˳. | He is angry (has been angry) with-me. 32 |
| 29. | ꜂Hò ꜁p'ang-꜃yau. | Good friends. |
| 30. | ꜃Ngo shik꜆ ꜃néi; ꜃néi shik꜆ ꜃ngo. | I know you; you know me. |
| 31. | ꜀Söng shik꜆. | Mutually acquainted. |
| 32. | ꜃Löng ꜀ká ꜀söng shik꜆. | Two persons mutually acquainted. |

## CONVERSATION 7TH.—THE SEARCH.

| | | |
|---|---|---|
| 1. | I do not see it. | 唔見呀. |
| 2. | What is it? | 乜野呢、 |
| 3. | Nothing much. | 少少野嘸、 |
| 4. | Is it lost? | 唔見嘞咩、 |
| 5. | I am afraid so. | 怕係呀、 |
| 6. | Have you looked for it? | 去搵未呀、 |
| 7. | I have. | 搵嚟咯、 |
| 8. | And you cannot find it? | 搵唔倒咩、 |
| 9. | I cannot find it. | 搵唔倒咯、 |
| 10. | Look again. | 再搵吓喇、 |
| 11. | I cannot. | 唔得呀、 |
| 12. | Why not? | 做乜唔得呢、 |
| 13. | It is dark. | 黑咯、 |
| 14. | Not yet. | 唔曾吖、 |
| 15. | Nearly. | 上吓喇、 |
| 16. | Not quite. | 唔曾齊黑、 |
| 17. | I cannot see. | 唔睇得見、 |
| 18. | I can. | 我睇得見吖. |
| 19. | Your eyes are good. | 你眼好、 |
| 20. | And yours? | 你嘅呢、 |
| 21. | Not very good. | 唔多好、 |
| 22. | Light a lamp. | 點燈、 |
| 23. | It is outside. | 喺外頭、 |
| 24. | Go and get it. | 去攞、 |
| 25. | Very well, I will go. | 悟、我去喇、 |
| 26. | Come back again. | 翻嚟吖、 |
| 27. | I will come by and by. | 等吓翻嚟咯、 |
| 28. | Come back when you have lighted the [lamp. | 點嘞燈翻嚟、 |
| 29. | All right. | 好哩、 |
| 30. | I will help you. | 我帮你、 |
| 31. | What will you help me do? | 帮我做乜、 |
| 32. | To look for the things. | 搵野咯、 |

易學廣東話



## CONVERSATION 7TH.—THE SEARCH.

| | | |
|---|---|---|
| 1. | ꜁M kin꜄ á꜄. | Not see. 2 |
| 2. | ꜀Mi ꜂ye ꜀ni (*or* ꜀ni)? | What thing, eh? 53 |
| 3. | ᶜShiú-ᶜshiú ꜂ye ꜀che (*or* ꜀che). | Little-little thing only. 7 |
| 4. | ꜁M kin꜄-ᶜcho ꜀me (*or* ꜀me)? | Not seen, eh? (*i.e.*, lost to sight.) 39 |
| 5. | P'á꜄ hai² á꜄. | Afraid is. 2 |
| 6. | Höü꜄ ᶜwan méi² á꜄? | Gone looked (for it) yet, eh? 2 |
| 7. | ᶜWan-꜁lai lok꜆. | Looked. 32 |
| 8. | ᶜWan ꜁m ᶜtò ꜀me (*or* ꜀me)? | Looked not found, eh? 39 |
| 9. | ᶜWan ꜁m ᶜtò lok꜆. | Looked not found. 32 |
| 10. | Tsoi꜄ ᶜwan ꜂há ꜀lá. | Again look a-bit. 21 |
| 11. | ꜁M tak꜆ á꜄. | Not can. 2 |
| 12. | Tso²-mat꜆ ꜁m tak꜆ ꜀ni (*or* ꜀ni)? | Why not can, eh? 53 |
| 13. | Hak꜆ lok꜆. | Dark. 32 |
| 14. | ꜁M ꜁ts'ang ꜀á (*or* ꜀á). | Not yet. 1 |
| 15. | Shöng²-꜂há ꜀lá (*or* ꜀lá). | Almost. 21 |
| 16. | ꜁M ꜁ts'ang ꜁ts'ai hak꜆ ꜀á (*or* ꜀á). | Not yet completely dark. 1 |
| 17. | ꜁M ᶜt'ai tak꜆ kin꜄. | Cannot see (so as) to-be-able to-perceive. |
| 18. | ꜂Ngo ᶜt'ai tak꜆ kin꜄ ꜀á (*or* ꜀á). | I see can-to-arrive-at perceiving. 1 |
| 19. | ꜂Néi ꜂ngán ᶜhò. | Your eyes good. |
| 20. | ꜂Néi-ke꜄ ꜀ni (*or* ꜀ni)? | Yours, eh? 53 |
| 21. | ꜁M ꜀to ᶜhò. | Not much good. |
| 22. | ᶜTim ꜀tang. [1] | Light lamp. |
| 23. | ᶜHai ngoi²-꜁t'au. | Is outside. |
| 24. | Höü꜄ ᶜlo. | Go fetch. |
| 25. | ꜁Ng, ꜂ngo höü꜄ ꜀lá. | Well, I go. 21 |
| 26. | ꜀Fán ꜁lai ꜀á (*or* ꜀á). | Back come. 1 |
| 27. | ᶜTang ꜀lai* ꜀fán ꜁lai lok꜆. | Wait a-while back come. 32 |
| 28. | ᶜTim-ᶜcho ꜀tang ꜀fán ꜁lai. | Lighted lamp back come. |
| 29. | ᶜHò ꜀le (*or* ꜀le). | Good. 24 |
| 30. | ꜂Ngo ꜀pong ꜂néi. | I help you. |
| 31. | ꜀Pong ꜂ngo tsò² mat꜆? | Help me do what? |
| 32. | ᶜWan ꜂ye lok꜆. | Look for things. 32 |

1. NOTE.—In some cases this character is put into the tone, ꜀tang, but not in this connection.

D

## CONVERSATION 8TH.—CURIOSITY AND THE TEASE.

| | | |
|---|---|---|
| 1. | I have it. | 我有咯、 |
| 2. | What have you got? | 你有乜野、 |
| 3. | These. | 呢啲、 |
| 4. | What are these? | 呢啲係乜野、 |
| 5. | What do you think they are? | 你估係乜野呢、 |
| 6. | I do not know. | 唔知、 |
| 7. | I will tell you; shall I? | 我話你知、睺、 |
| 8. | Very good. | 好吖、 |
| 9. | I will not tell you; don't you know? | 我唔話你知咯、你唔知、 |
| 10. | Is that the way you do? | 噉嘅咩、 |
| 11. | Yes. | 係咯、 |
| 12. | I do not like it. | 我唔中意、 |
| 13. | It does not matter; Does it not matter? | 冇相干、冇相干、 |
| 14. | That is not nice. | 噉唔好呀、 |
| 15. | Probably it is not. | 大槪唔好咯、 |
| 16. | Then why do you do so? | 係噉、做乜噉做呢、 |
| 17. | I am tired. | 我瘖咯、 |
| 18. | If you are, you need not act so. | 瘖都唔使噉做嘅、 |
| 19. | I will give them to you. | 我俾過你喇、 |
| 20. | Many thanks. | 多謝、 |
| 21. | Do you want to know what they are? | 你想知係乜野嗎、 |
| 22. | Certainly I do. | 想定喇、 |
| 23. | Do not you know? | 你都唔知咩、 |
| 24. | How do I know? | 我點知吖、 |
| 25. | I will let you see them. | 我俾你睇吓呀、 |
| 26. | Let me see. | 俾我睇喇、 |
| 27. | By and by. | 等吓咋、 |
| 28. | No, now. | 唔好、而家好、 |
| 29. | There is nothing. | 冇野嘅、 |
| 30. | There is something. | 有野嘅、 |
| 31. | There, look at them. | 拿、睇吖、 |
| 32. | Why! they are the kittens. | 唉、係貓仔哋、 |

## CONVERSATION 8TH.—CURIOSITY AND THE TEASE.

| | | |
|---|---|---|
| 1. | ꜂Ngo ꜂yau lok꜀. | I have. 32 |
| 2. | ꜂Néi ꜂yau ꜀mi ꜂ye? | You have what thing? |
| 3. | ꜀Ni-ₒti. | These. |
| 4. | ꜀Ni-ₒti hai$^2$ mat꜆ ꜂ye? | These are what things? |
| 5. | ꜂Néi ᶜkwú hai$^2$ mat꜆ ꜂ye ꜀ni (*or* ꜀ni)? | You think are what things, eh? 53 |
| 6. | ꜁M ꜀chí. | Not know. |
| 7. | ꜂Ngo wá$^2$ ꜂néi ꜀chí, ꜀e? | I say to-you to-know, eh? 12 |
| 8. | ᶜHò ꜀á. | Good. 1. |
| 9. | ꜂Ngo ꜁m wá$^2$ ꜂néi ꜀chí lok꜀; néi | I not say to-you to-know. 32 You don't |
| 10. | ᶜKòm keᵓ ꜀me (*or* ꜀me)? [꜁m ꜀chí? | So-fashion, eh? 15, 39 [know? |
| 11. | Hai$^2$ lokₒ. | Is. 32 |
| 12. | ꜂Ngo ꜁m ꜀chung-yíᵓ. | I not like. |
| 13. | ꜂Mò ꜀söng-꜀kon; ꜂Mò ꜀söng ꜀kon? | No matter. It-does-not matter? |
| 14. | ᶜKòm ꜁m ᶜhò áᵓ. | So not good. 2 |
| 15. | Tái$^2$-ᶜk'oi* ꜁m ᶜhò lok꜀. | Probably not good. 32 |
| 16. | Hai$^2$ ᶜkòm, tsò$^2$ mat꜆ ᶜkòm tsò$^2$ ꜀ni | Is so, do what (*i.e.* why) so do, eh? 53 |
| 17. | ꜂Ngo kwúi$^2$ lok꜀. [(*or* ꜀ni)? | I am-tired. 32 |
| 18. | Kwúi$^2$ ₒtò ꜁m ᶜshai ᶜkòm tsò$^2$ keᵓ. | Tired even not need so do. 15 |
| 19. | ꜂Ngo ᶜpéi kwoᵓ ꜂néi ꜀lá (*or* ꜀lá). | I give to you. 21 |
| 20. | ꜀To tse$^2$. | Many thanks. |
| 21. | ꜂Néi ᶜsöng ꜀chí hai$^2$ mat꜆ ꜂ye ꜂má? | You wish to-know are what things, eh? 37 |
| 22. | ᶜSöng ᶜting* ꜀lá (*or* ꜀lá). | Wish certainly. 21 |
| 23. | ꜂Néi ₒtò ꜁m ꜀chí ꜀me? | You even not know, eh? 39 |
| 24. | ꜂Ngo ᶜtím ꜀chí ꜀á? | I how know? 1 [to-you). 2 |
| 25. | ꜂Ngo ᶜpéi ꜂néi ᶜtaʻi ꜂há áᵓ. | I give to-you to-see a-bit (*i.e.* I will show |
| 26. | ᶜPéi ꜂ngo ᶜtaʻi ꜀lá. (*or* ꜀lá). | Give to-me to-see. 21 [them |
| 27. | ᶜTang ꜀há* cháᵓ. | Wait a-while before. 6 |
| 28. | ꜁M ᶜhò, ꜁yí-꜀ká (*or* ꜁yí-꜀ká) ᶜhò. | Not good, now good. |
| 29. | ꜂Mo-꜂ye keᵓ. | Nothing. (lit. no thing). 15 |
| 30. | ꜂Yau ꜂ye keᵓ. | Have-got thing (*i.e.*, Something). 15 |
| 31. | Ná$^2$, ᶜt'aí ꜀á. | There, look. 1 |
| 32. | ꜀Ai (*or* ₒAi)! hai$^2$ ꜀máú-ᶜtsai ꜀che. | Oh! are kittens only. 7 |

## CONVERSATION 9TH.—SOMETHING TO DRINK.

| | | |
|---|---|---|
| 1. | Bring it to me. | 擰俾我、 |
| 2. | What shall I bring to you? | 擰乜野俾你呢、 |
| 3. | A cup; a cup of tea. | 一隻杯、一杯茶、 |
| 4. | I do not want sugar. | 唔要糖、 |
| 5. | It is very strong. | 好濃呀、 |
| 6. | It is too strong. | 濃過頭、 |
| 7. | Bring some hot water. | 擰啲熱水嚟、 |
| 8. | Pour it in. | 倒落去、 |
| 9. | Fill the cup up. | 斟滿個杯、 |
| 10. | The water is cold. | 個啲水凍、 |
| 11. | Make it hot again. | 整翻熱、 |
| 12. | Do you want water? | 你要水咩、 |
| 13. | I do. | 要咯、 |
| 14. | Bring a glass of water. | 擰一玻璃杯水嚟、 |
| 15. | Give me some iced water. | 俾啲雪水我、 |
| 16. | Give it to him (*or* her.) | 俾佢、 |
| 17. | He wishes to drink it. | 佢想飲、 |
| 18. | Let him drink it. | 俾佢飲喇、 |
| 19. | What water is it? | 係乜野水呢、 |
| 20. | Soda water. | 荷蘭水咯、 |
| 21. | Bring some ice. | 擰啲雪嚟、 |
| 22. | Bring two or three pieces. | 擰兩三嚿嚟、 |
| 23. | The water is bad. | 水唔好、 |
| 24. | That water is bad. | 個啲水唔好、 |
| 25. | It is broken. | 爛咗咯、 |
| 26. | What did you say? | 你話乜野、 |
| 27. | I said the water bucket was broken. | 我話水桶爛咯、 |
| 28. | Mend it. | 整翻好喇、 |
| 29. | I want spring water. | 我要山水、 |
| 30. | Without spring water, the tea is not good. | 冇山水、茶唔好、 |
| 31. | It is bad tea; this is good tea. | 唔好茶、 |
| 32. | This tea is good; this is good tea. | 呢啲茶好、呢的係好茶、 |

## CONVERSATION 9TH.—SOMETHING TO DRINK.

| | | |
|---|---|---|
| 1. | ꜀Ning ᶜpéi ᶝngo. | Bring give me. |
| 2. | ꜀Ning ꜀mi ᶝye ᶜpéi ᶝnéi ꜀ni (*or* ₒni)? | Bring what thing give you, eh? 53 |
| 3. | Yat꜄ chek꜄ ₒpúi: yat꜄ ꜀púi ꜁ch'á. | A [class.] cup; a cup of-tea. |
| 4. | ꜁M yiúᵓ ꜁t'ong. | Not want sugar. |
| 5. | ᶜHò ꜁yung áᵓ. | Very strong. 2 |
| 6. | ꜁Yung ᶜkwo* ꜁t'an. | Strong over much. |
| 7. | ꜀Ning ꜀ti yít꜅ ᶜshöü ꜁laí. | Bring some hot water come. |
| 8. | ᶜTò lok꜅ höüᵓ. | Pour down away. |
| 9. | ꜀Cham ᶝmúün koᵓ ꜀púí. | Fill full that cup. |
| 10. | Koᵓ- ti ᶜshöü tungᵓ. | That water cold. |
| 11. | ᶜChing ꜀fán yit꜅. | Make back-again hot. |
| 12. | ᶝNéi yiúᵓ ᶜshöü ꜀me (*or* ₒme)? | You want water, eh? 39 |
| 13. | Yiúᵓ lok꜅. | Want. 32 |
| 14. | ꜀Ning yat꜄ ꜀po-꜀léi* ₒpúí ᶜshöü ꜁laí. | Bring one glass cup of-water come. |
| 15. | ᶜPéi ₒti süt꜄ ᶜshöü ᶝngo. | Give some ice water to-me. |
| 16. | ᶜPéi ᶝk'öü. | Give to-him. |
| 17. | ᶝK'öü ᶜsöng ᶜyam. | He wishes to-drink. |
| 18. | ᶜPéi ᶝk'öü ᶜyam ꜀lá (*or* ₒlá). | Give him to-drink. 21 |
| 19. | Hai² mat꜅ ᶝye ᶜshöü ꜀ni (*or* ₒni)? | Is what thing water, eh? 53 |
| 20. | ꜁Ho-꜀lán* ᶜshöü lok꜅. | Holland water. 32 |
| 21. | ꜀Ning ti süt꜄ ꜁laí. | Bring some ice come. |
| 22. | ꜀Ning ᶝlöng ꜀sám kan² ꜁laí. | Bring two three pieces come. |
| 23. | ᶜShöü ꜁m ᶜhò. | Water not good. |
| 24. | Koᵓ- ti ᶜshöü ꜁m ᶜhò. | That water not good. |
| 25. | Lán²-ᶜcho lok꜅. | Broken. 32 |
| 26. | ᶝNéi wa² ꜀mi ᶝye? | You say what thing? |
| 27. | ᶝNgo wa² ᶜshöü ᶜt'ung lán² lok꜅. | I say water bucket broken. 32 |
| 28. | ᶜChing ꜀fán ᶜhò ꜀lá (*or* ₒlá). | Make back good. 21 |
| 29. | ᶝNgo yiúᵓ ꜀shán ᶜshöü. | I want mountain water. |
| 30. | ᶝMo ꜀shán ᶜshöü, ꜁ch'á ꜁m ᶜhò. | No hill water, tea not good. |
| 31. | ꜁M ᶜhò ꜁ch'á. | Not good tea. |
| 32. | ꜀Ni-ₒti ꜁ch'á ᶜhò. | This tea good. |

## CONVERSATION 10TH.—SOMETHING TO DO.

| | | |
|---|---|---|
| 1. | To do anything. | 做野、 |
| 2. | He did it. | 佢做嘅、 |
| 3. | He did (it) well. | 佢做好、 |
| 4. | He did not know how to do it. | 佢唔曉做、 |
| 5. | Did not you (pl.) know how to do it? | 你哋唔曉做咩、 |
| 6. | I cannot do it. | 我唔噲做、 |
| 7. | Why cannot you? | 做乜唔噲呢、 |
| 8. | It is very difficult. | 好難做嘅、 |
| 9. | What are we doing? | 我哋做乜野呢、 |
| 10. | It is hard to say. | 難講咯、 |
| 11. | I am not doing anything. | 我冇做野吖、 |
| 12. | They have nothing to do. | 佢哋冇野做咯、 |
| 13. | What a pity. | 可惜咯、 |
| 14. | They might do something. | 佢哋可以做野、 |
| 15. | I will find something for them to do. | 我揾野俾佢(哋)做、 |
| 16. | There is no need. [selves. | 唔使咯、 |
| 17. | They cannot find anything them- | (佢哋)自已唔揾得嘅、 |
| 18. | They do not want to; that is all. | 唔想揾係噉咫、 |
| 19. | I do not know as to that. | 個啲我又唔知、 |
| 20. | But I do. | 但係我知吖、 |
| 21. | You do, do you? | 你知囉咩、 |
| 22. | Yes, I do. No, I don't. [about it. | 知咯、唔知咯、 |
| 23. | Then there is nothing to be said | 噉唔使講喇、 |
| 24. | That is what I have said all along. (See note) | 我一流都係噉講吖、 |
| 25. | I thought it was only that they could not find any work. | 我估唔揾得頭路咫、 |
| 26. | No indeed; that was not it. | 唔係、至好唔揾得、 |
| 27. | It is hard to find work. | 難揾工打嘅、 |
| 28. | It depends upon what it is. | 睇嚟渏、 |
| 29. | Yes, that is so. | 係呀、冇錯、 |
| 30. | Some work is difficult. | 有啲工夫難做嘅、 |
| 31. | Then few know how to do it. | 噉冇幾多人曉做、 |
| 32. | You had better find some work soon. | 你快啲揾啲工夫做至好、 |

NOTE.—In the book language it is in the ha² ꜀p'ing tone, ꜀lau. In pure Cantonese colloquial as above. In Whampoa dialect 嘍 ꜂lau.

## CONVERSATION 10TH.—SOMETHING TO DO.

| | | |
|---|---|---|
| 1. | Tsò[2] ᶜye. | To-do anything. |
| 2. | ᶜK'öü tsò[2] keᵓ. | He did (it). 15 |
| 3. | ᶜK'öü tsò[2] ᶜhò. | He did (it) well. |
| 4. | ᶜK'öü ꜀m ᶜhiú tsò[2]. | He not understand to-do. |
| 5. | ᶜNéi-téi[2] ꜀m ᶜhiú tsò[2] ꜀me (or ꜀me)? | You (pl.) not know to-do, eh? 39 |
| 6. | ᶜNgo ꜀m ᶜwúi tsò[2]. | I not able to-do. |
| 7. | Tsò[2]-matᵓ ꜀m ᶜwúi ꜀ni (or ꜀ni)? | Why not able, eh? 53 |
| 8. | ᶜHò ꜀nán tsò[2] keᵓ. | Very difficult to-do. 15 |
| 9. | ᶜNgo-téi[2] tsò[2] ꜀mi ᶜye ꜀ni (or ꜀ni)? | We do what thing, eh? 53 |
| 10. | ꜀Nan ᶜkong lok. | Difficult to-say. 32 |
| 11. | ᶜNgo ᶜmò tsò[2] ᶜye ꜀á (or ꜀á). | I not do anything. 1 |
| 12. | ᶜK'öü-téi[2] ᶜmò-ᶜye tsò[2] lok꜀. | They nothing to-do. 32 |
| 13. | ᶜHo sikᵓ lok꜀. | To-be pitied. 32 |
| 14. | ᶜK'öü-téi[2] ᶜho-ᶜyí tsò[2] ᶜye. | They might do something. |
| 15. | ᶜNgo ᶜwan ᶜye ᶜpéi ᶜk'öü (téi[2]) tsò[2]. | I find something give them to-do. |
| 16. | ꜀M ᶜshai lokᵓ. | Not need. 32 |
| 17. | (ᶜK'öü téi[2]) tsz[2]-ᶜkéi ꜀m ᶜwan takᵓ keᵓ. | (They) themselves not find able. 15 |
| 18. | ꜀M ᶜsöng ᶜwan, hai[2] ᶜkòm ꜀che (or ꜀che). | Not wish to-find; is so only. 7 |
| 19. | Koᵓ-꜀ti ᶜngo yau[2] ꜀m ꜀chí. | That I also not know. |
| 20. | Tán[2]-hai[2] ᶜngo ꜀chí ꜀á (or ꜀á). | But I know. 1 |
| 21. | ᶜNéi ꜀chí (or ꜀chí) loᵓ ꜀me? | You know, eh? 31, 39 |
| 22. | ꜀Chí (or ꜀chí) lok꜀: ꜀m ꜀chí lok꜀. | Know, (certainly already know): not know. 32 |
| 23. | ᶜKòm ꜀m ᶜshai ᶜkong ꜀lá (or ꜀lá). | Then not need to-talk. 21 |
| 24. | ᶜNgo yatᵓ ᶜlau (꜀lau*) ꜀tò hai[2] ᶜkòm ᶜkong ꜀á (or ꜀á). | I all along also have so said. 1 |
| 25. | ᶜNgo ᶜkwú ꜀m ᶜwan takᵓ ꜀t'an-lò[2] ꜀che (or ꜀che). | I thought not find able work only. 7 |
| 26. | ꜀M hai[2]. Chíᵓ-ᶜhò ꜀m ᶜwan takᵓ. | Not is. Best (*compare English ironically* 'that is good, I must say') not find able. |
| 27. | ꜀Nán ᶜwan ꜀kung ᶜtá keᵓ. | Difficult find work to-do. 15 |
| 28. | ᶜT'ái ꜀lai ts'anᵓ. | That depends upon-circumstances. (Seeing how things are then you come to the position of being able to estimate the probabilties.) |
| 29. | Hai[2] áᵓ, ᶜmò ts'oᵓ. | Yes, 2 no mistake. |
| 30. | ᶜYau ꜀ti ꜀kung-꜀fú ꜀nán tsò[2] keᵓ. | Have some work difficult to-do. 15 |
| 31. | ᶜKòm ᶜmò ᶜkéi-꜀to ꜀yan ᶜhiú tsò[2]. | Then not many people understand to-do. |
| 32. | ᶜNéi fáiᵓ-꜀ti ᶜwan ꜀ti ꜀kung-꜀fú tsò[2] chíᵓ-ᶜhò. | You quickly find some work (in-order-to) do (it) best (thing). |

## CONVERSATION 11TH.—THE RAIN.

| | | |
|---|---|---|
| 1. | It rains. | 落雨、 |
| 2. | There is rain. | 有雨、 |
| 3. | Yes, there is rain. | 係吖、有雨、 |
| 4. | It is raining. | 落緊雨、 |
| 5. | It is raining now. | 而家有雨落、 |
| 6. | You are right, it is raining now. | 冇錯、而家落緊雨、 |
| 7. | It rained last night. | 昨晚落雨、 |
| 8. | I was asleep: I do not know. | 我瞓 (*or* 瞓咗) 唔知咯、 |
| 9. | Do not you know whether it did, or not? | 你都唔知有雨落冇、 |
| 10. | How could I when I was asleep? | 我瞓着點知吖、 |
| 11. | Did you not wake? | 冇醒咩、 |
| 12. | Wake in the middle of the night? No. | 半夜醒咩、冇、 |
| 13. | Then you sleep well. | 噉你好瞓咯、 |
| 14. | I sleep very soundly. | 我瞓得好稔嘅、 |
| 15. | Well, the rain woke me. | 個啲雨整醒我、 |
| 16. | Did it rain very heavily? | 落好大雨咩、 |
| 17. | It did rain heavily indeed. | 大雨咯、大雨咯、 |
| 18. | It is strange. | 出奇咯、 |
| 19. | Why strange? | 做乜出奇呢、 |
| 20. | It was such good weather last evening. | 昨晚咁好天呢、 |
| 21. | There were some slight showers during the day. | 昨日有啲落雨嘛 (*or* 噭) 呀、 |
| 22. | I remember. | 記得咯、 |
| 23. | What do you remember? | 記得乜野呀、 |
| 24. | There was a passing shower at noon. | 晏晝有過雲雨喇、 |
| 25. | I was out at the time. | 我個陣 (*or* 陣時) 出街咯、 |
| 26. | Did you get wet? | 濕身嗎、 |
| 27. | I was wet through. | 濕嗮身咯、 |
| 28. | It was an April shower. | 係白撞雨、 |
| 29. | To-day it rains again. | 今日又落雨咯、 |
| 30. | It is a drizzling rain to-day. | 今日微絲雨、 |
| 31. | Do not go out. | 唔好出街、 |
| 32. | I am afraid I must. | 我怕要出街、 |

## CONVERSATION 11TH.—THE RAIN.

| | | |
|---|---|---|
| 1. | Lok꜇ ꜃yü. | Falling rain. |
| 2. | ꜃Yau ꜃yü. | Have rain. |
| 3. | Hai꜅ ꜀á, (*or* ₒá) ꜃yau ꜃yü. | Yes (1), have rain. |
| 4. | Lok꜇-꜂kau ꜃yü. | Falling rain. |
| 5. | ꜁Yí-꜀ká (*or* ꜁yí-ₒká) ꜃yau ꜃yü lok꜇. | Now have rain fall. |
| 6. | ꜃Mò ts'o꜄, ꜁yí-꜀ká (*or* ꜁yí-ᵕká) lok꜇-[꜂kau ꜃yü. | No mistake, now falling rain. |
| 7. | Tsok꜇ ꜃mán lok꜇ ꜃yü. | Last night fell rain. |
| 8. | ꜃Ngo ꜂fan* (*or* fan꜄ ꜂cho); ꜁m ꜀chí lokₒ. | I was-asleep (*or* asleep had-fallen) : not [know. 32 |
| 9. | ꜃Néi ꜀to ꜁m ꜀chí ꜃yau ꜃yü lok꜇ ꜃mò ꜀me (*or* ꜀me)? | You even not know have rain fall (or) not, eh? 39 |
| 10. | ꜃Ngo ꜂fan*-chök꜇ ꜂tím ꜀chí ꜀á (*or* ₒá)? | I asleep, how know, eh? 1 |
| 11. | ꜃Mò ꜂seng† ꜀me (*or* ₒme)? | Not waked? 39 |
| 12. | Pún꜄-ye꜅ ꜂seng† ꜀me (*or* ₒme)? ꜃Mò. | Mid-night wake, eh? 39 No! |
| 13. | ꜂Kòm ꜃néi ꜂hò fan꜄ lokₒ. | Then you good sleep. 32 |
| 14. | ꜃Ngo fan꜄ tak꜆ ꜂hò nam꜅ ke꜄. | I sleep able very soundly. 15 |
| 15. | Ko꜄-ₒti ꜃yü ꜂ching ꜂seng† ꜃ngo. | The rain made wake me (*i.e.* made me wake.). |
| 16. | Lok꜇ ꜂hò tái꜅ ꜃yü ꜁me (*or* ₒme)? | Fell very great rain, eh? 39 |
| 17. | Tái꜅ ꜃yü lokₒ; tái꜅ ꜃yü lokᵕ. | Great rain 32, great rain. 32 |
| 18. | Ch'ut꜆-꜁k'éi lokₒ. | Extraordinary. 32 |
| 19. | Tsò꜅-mat꜆ ch'ut꜆-꜁k'éi ꜀ni (*or* ₒni)? | Why extraordinary, eh? 53 |
| 20. | Tsok꜇ ꜃mán kòm꜄ ꜂hò ꜀t'ín ꜀ni. | Last night so good weather (*lit.* sky). 53 |
| 21. | Tsok꜇-yat꜇ ꜃yau ꜀ti lok꜇ ꜃yü ꜁méi á꜄. | Yesterday have some fall rain fine. 2 |
| 22. | Kéi꜄-tak꜆ lokₒ. | Remember. 32 |
| 23. | Kéi꜄-tak꜆ ꜀mi ꜃ye á꜄? | Remember what thing, eh? 2 |
| 24. | Án꜄-chau꜄ ꜃yau kwo꜄ ꜁wan ꜃yü ꜀lá. | Noon have passing shower rain. 21. |
| 25. | ꜃Ngo ko꜄ ꜂chau* (*or* chau꜅ ꜁shí) ch'ut꜆ ꜀kái lokₒ. | I that period (*or* period of-time) go-out street. 32 |
| 26. | Shap꜆ ꜀shan má꜄? | Wet body, eh? 35 |
| 27. | Shap꜆ sái꜄ ꜀shan lokₒ. | Wet all (*or* whole) body. 32 |
| 28. | Hai꜅ pák꜇-chong꜅ ꜃yü. | Was shower-amidst-sunshine rain. |
| 29. | ꜀Kam-yat꜇ yau꜅ lok꜇ ꜃yü lokₒ. | To-day again falls rain. 32 |
| 30. | ꜀Kam-mat꜆ ꜁méi-꜀sz ꜃yü. | To-day drizzling rain. |
| 31. | ꜁M ꜂hò ch'ut꜆ ꜀kái. | Not good go-out street. |
| 32. | ꜃Ngo p'á꜄ yíú꜄ ch'ut꜆ ꜀kái. | I fear must go-out street. |

E

## CONVERSATION 12TH.—THE WRONG MAN.

| | | |
|---|---|---|
| 1. | How are you? | 你好呀、 |
| 2. | I am well, and you? | 好呀、你好呀、 |
| 3. | I am well. | 好呀、 |
| 4. | I have not seen you for a long time. | 好耐唔見你、 |
| 5. | I have been to Shanghai. | 我去上海、 |
| 6. | Oh! Have you? | 阿、係咩、 |
| 7. | You have had a good time of it, eh? | 好世界吖、 |
| 8. | Only middling. | 嘛嘛哋𠺝 (*or* 哾)、 |
| 9. | You have made money. | 發財喇、 |
| 10. | No, I have not. | 冇錢撈、 |
| 11. | How is that? | 點解呢、 |
| 12. | I have failed in business. | 賠本咯、 |
| 13. | Failed? | 賠本咩、 |
| 14. | Yes. | 賠本咯、 |
| 15. | I heard you had made a lot of money. | 我聽聞你發大財啝、 |
| 16. | It is not so. | 唔係嘅、 |
| 17. | That is what was said. | 人哋係噉講囉、 |
| 18. | They made a mistake. | 講錯咯、 |
| 19. | Perhaps they made a mistake. | 怕佢哋聽錯咯、 |
| 20. | Perhaps they did. | 怕係都唔定、 |
| 21. | They said it was you. | 佢話係你啝、 |
| 22. | It was not I. | 唔係我、 |
| 23. | Who was it? | 係邊個呢、 |
| 24. | My elder brother. | 我大佬𠺝 (*or* 哾)、 |
| 25. | Oh! that was it, was it? | 阿、噉咩、 |
| 26. | It must have been. | 是必係喇、 |
| 27. | Then you have come back now? | 噉你而家翻嚟囉咩、 |
| 28. | Yes, I have. | 翻嚟咯、 |
| 29. | What are you going to do? | 想做乜野呢、 |
| 30. | I want to get something to do. | 想揾啲世界做吓咯、 |
| 31. | Well, very good, good bye. | 吾、好吖、好行喇、 |
| 32. | Good bye. | 好行喇、 |

## CONVERSATION 12TH.—THE WRONG MAN.

| | | |
|---|---|---|
| 1. | ꜃Néi ʿhò áʾ ? | You well? 2 |
| 2. | ʿHò áʾ ꜃néi ʿhò áʾ ? | Well 2, you well? 2 |
| 3. | ʿHò áʾ. | Well. 2 |
| 4. | ʿHò noi$^2$ ꜁m kínʾ ꜃néi. | Very long not seen you. |
| 5. | ꜃Ngo höüʾ Shöng$^2$-ʿhoí. | I gone Shanghai. |
| 6. | O$^2$, Hai$^2$ ꜁me (*or* $_o$me)? | O! It-is-so, eh? 39 |
| 7. | ʿHò shaiʾ káiʾ ꜁á (*or* $_o$á)? | Good world-of-it, eh? 1 |
| 8. | ꜁Má-ʿmá*-tei$^2$ ꜀che (*or* chek͵). | Middling only. 7 |
| 9. | Fát$_o$ ꜀ts'oi ꜁lá (*or* $_o$lá). | Made wealthy. 21 |
| 10. | ꜃Mò ꜃ts'ín* lòʾ. | No cash to-get-on-with. |
| 11. | ʿTím ʿkái ꜀ni (*or* ꜀ni)? | How explain, eh? 53 |
| 12. | Shít$_2$ ʿpún lok$_o$. | Lost my-money-put-into-business (*i.e.*, |
| 13. | Shít$_2$ ʿpún ꜁me (*or* ꜀me)? | Lost capital, eh? 39 [capital.) 32. |
| 14. | Shít$_2$ ʿpún lok$_c$. | Lost capital. 32. |
| 15. | ꜃Ngo ꜀t'eng†-man$^2$ ꜃néi fát$_o$ tái$^2$ | I heard you got very wealthy, so-they- |
| 16. | ꜁M hai$^2$ keʾ. [꜁ts'oí woʾ. | Not is. 15 [said. 64. |
| 17. | ꜁Yan-téi$^2$ hai$^2$ ʿkòm ʿkong káʾ. | People did so speak. 14 |
| 18. | ʿKong ts'oʾ lok$_c$. | Spoke wrong. 32. |
| 19. | P'áʾ ꜃k'öü-téi$^2$ ꜀t'eng† ts'oʾ lok$_c$. | Afraid they heard wrong. 32 |
| 20. | P'áʾ hai$^2$ $_o$tò ꜁m ting$^2$. | Afraid it-was even not certain (*i.e.*, it may be |
| 21. | ꜃K'öü wá$^2$ hai$^2$ ꜃néi woʾ. | They said it-was you, said-they. 64 [so.) |
| 22. | ꜁M hai$^2$ ꜃ngo. | Not was I. |
| 23. | Hai$^2$ ꜀pín koʾ ꜀ni? | Was which one, eh? 53 |
| 24. | ꜃Ngo tái$^2$ ʿlò ꜀che (*or* chek͵). | My elder brother only. 7 |
| 25. | Oʾ, ʿkòm ꜁me (*or* ꜀me)? | O! so, eh? 39 |
| 26. | Shí$^2$-pít͵ hai$^2$ ꜁lá. | Certainly was. 21 |
| 27. | ʿKòm ꜃néi ꜁yí-꜀ká (*or* ꜁yi $_o$ká) ꜀fán | Then you now back come, eh? 31. 39. |
| 28. | ꜀Fán ꜃laí* lok$_o$. [꜁laí loʾ ꜀me? | Back come. 32 |
| 29. | ʿSöng tsò$^2$ ꜀mi ꜃ye ꜀ni (*or* ꜀ni)? | Wish to-do what thing, eh? 53 |
| 30. | ʿSöng ʿwan ꜀ti shaiʾ-káiʾ tsò$^2$ ꜃hai lok$_o$. | Wish to-find some employment to-do |
| 31. | ꜁Ng, ʿhò ꜀á (*or* $_o$á). ʿHò ꜁háng ꜀lá | Well, good 1, well walk. 21 [a-bit 32. |
| 32. | ʿHò ꜁háng ꜀lá (*or* $_o$lá). (*or* ꜀lá). | Well walk. 21 |

## CONVERSATION 13TH.—MY MOTHER IS ILL.

| | | |
|---|---|---|
| 1. | I am off. | 我去咯、 |
| 2. | Where are you going? | 去邊處呀、 |
| 3. | Up to Canton. | 上城、 |
| 4. | Going to Canton are you? | 上城咩、 |
| 5. | Yes, I am going to Canton. | 係吖、上城呀、 |
| 6. | You went a few days ago. | 你先幾日都上城嚟喇、 |
| 7. | Yes, I do. | 係、冇錯、 |
| 8. | But why do you want to go again? | 做乜又要去呢、 |
| 9. | I have some business. | 我有啲事、 |
| 10. | What business? | 乜野事幹、 |
| 11. | Important business. | 緊要事呀、 |
| 12. | Cannot you say what it is? | 唔話得乜野事咩、 |
| 13. | My mother is ill. | 老母病咯、 |
| 14. | Ill eh? | 病咩、 |
| 15. | Serious ill. | 好重病呀、 |
| 16. | She was ill a while ago. | 佢先排都病過嚟咯、 |
| 17. | Yes, she was. | 係吖、 |
| 18. | And she is ill now again? | 佢而家又病咯、 |
| 19. | Yes; so ill, she is having a very hard time of it. | 係呀、病到好關係、 |
| 20. | I thought she was dead. | 我估佢過咀身咯、 |
| 21. | No; she is not dead. | 唔係、唔係死嘅、 |
| 22. | Why, you told me so. | 你都話佢死咯、 |
| 23. | No; it was not I that said so. | 唔係、唔係我話嘅、 |
| 24. | It really was you that said it. | 實係你講嘅、 |
| 25. | I did not say so. When did I say so? | 我冇噉話、我幾時講呀、 |
| 26. | If it was not you, who was it? | 唔係你、係邊個呢、 |
| 27. | My younger brother probably said so. | 大概我細佬係噉話呎、 |
| 28. | Why did he say so? | 做乜佢噉話呢、 |
| 29. | He told a lie. | 佢講大話咯、 |
| 30. | I know; but why? | 知到囉、做乜講大話呢、 |
| 31. | He tells lies. | 佢講大話嘅、 |
| 32. | You must scold him. | 你要鬧佢、 |

## CONVERSATION 13TH.—MY MOTHER IS ILL.

| | | |
|---|---|---|
| 1. | ꜂Ngo höü’ lok˳. | I go. 32 |
| 2. | Höü’ ˳pín shü’ á’? | Go what place, eh? 2 |
| 3. | ꜂Shöng ꜂sheng*† (*or* ꜀sheng*.) [˳me?) | Up-to city. |
| 4. | ꜂Shöng ꜂sheng*† ꜀me (*or* ꜀sheng* | Up-to city, eh? 39 |
| 5. | Haí$^2$ ꜀á (*or* ˳á.): ꜂shöng ꜂sheng*† (*or* ꜀sheng*) á’. | Yes. 1 Up-to city. 2 |
| 6. | ꜂Néi ꜀sin (*or* ˳sin) ꜂kéi yat˳ ˳tò ꜂shöng ꜂sheng*† (*or* ꜀sheng*) ꜀laí ꜀lá (*or* ˳lá.) | You before several days also went-up-to city did. 21 |
| 7. | Haí$^2$, ꜂mò ts‘o’. [˳ni ?) | Yes, no mistake. |
| 8. | Tsò$^2$-mat˳ yau$^2$ yíú’ höü’ ꜀ni (*or* | Why again want to-go, eh? 53 |
| 9. | ꜂Ngo ꜂yau ˳ti sz$^2$. | I have some business. |
| 10. | ꜀Mi-꜂ye sz$^2$-kon’? | What business? |
| 11. | ꜂Kan-yíú’ sz$^2$ á’. | Important business. 2 |
| 12. | ꜀M wá$^2$ tak˳ ꜀mi-꜂ye sz$^2$ ꜀me (*or* ˳me)? | Not say able what business, eh? 39 |
| 13. | ꜂Lò-꜂mò peng$^2$† lok˳. | Mother ill. 32 |
| 14. | Peng$^2$† ꜀me (*or* ˳me?) | Ill, eh? 39 |
| 15. | ꜂Hò ꜂ch‘ung*† peng$^2$† á’. | Very heavy illness. 2 |
| 16. | ꜂K‘öü ꜀sin (*or* ˳sin) ꜂p‘ái* ˳tò peng$^2$† | She before time also ill over did be. 32 |
| 17. | Haí$^2$ ꜀á (*or* ˳á.) [kwo’ ꜀laí lok˳. | Yes. 1 |
| 18. | ꜂K‘öü ꜀yi-꜀ká (*or* ꜀yi ˳ká) yau$^2$ peng$^2$† lok˳? | She now again ill? 32 |
| 19. | Haí$^2$ á’, peng$^2$† tò’ ꜂hò ꜀kwán-haí$^2$. | Yes, 2, ill to very serious. [other) body. 32. |
| 20. | ꜂Ngo ꜂kwú ꜂k‘öü kwo’ ꜂cho ꜀shan lok˳. | I thought she passed-over already (into an- |
| 21. | ꜀M haí$^2$; ꜀m haí$^2$ ꜂sz ke’. | Not is; not is dead. 15 [32 |
| 22. | ꜂Néi ˳tò wá$^2$ ꜂k‘öü ꜂sz lok˳. | You even (it was, who) said she was-dead. |
| 23. | ꜀M haí$^2$; ꜀m haí$^2$ ꜂ngo wá$^2$ ke’. | Not was, not was I said-it. 15 |
| 24. | Shat˳ haí$^2$ ꜂néi ꜂kong ke’. | Really was you said. 15 |
| 25. | ꜂Ngo-꜂mò ꜂kòm wá$^2$. ꜂Ngo ꜂kéi ꜀shí ꜂kong á’? | I not so said. I what time said? 2 |
| 26. | ꜀M haí$^2$ ꜂néi, haí$^2$ ˳pín ko’ ꜀ni? | Not was you, was what one eh? 53 |
| 27. | Táí$^2$-꜂k‘oi ꜂ngo saí’-꜂lò haí$^2$ ꜂kòm wá$^2$ (chek˳.) [˳ni ?) | Probably my younger brother did so say only. 7 |
| 28. | Tsò$^2$-mat˳ ꜂k‘öü ꜂kòm wá$^2$ ꜀ni (*or* | Why he so said, eh? 53 |
| 29. | ꜂K‘öü ꜂kong táí$^2$-wá$^2$ lok˳. [(*or* ˳ni)? | He spoke lie. 32. |
| 30. | ꜀Chi-tò’ lo’, tsò$^2$-mat˳ ꜂kong taí$^2$ wá$^2$ ꜀ni | Know, 31, why speak lies? 53 |
| 31. | ꜂K‘öü ꜂kong táí$^2$-wá$^2$ ke’. | He speaks lies. 15 |
| 32. | ꜂Néi yíú’ náu$^2$ ꜂k‘öü. | You must scold him. |

## CONVERSATION 14TH.—AN IMPORTANT CONVERSATION.

| | | |
|---|---|---|
| 1. | I saw you yesterday. | 我昨日見你吖、 |
| 2. | Where? | 喺邊處呀、 |
| 3. | In the street. | 喺街上、 |
| 4. | I did not see you. | 我唔見你吖、 |
| 5. | You were walking. | 你行緊路吖、 |
| 6. | With whom? | 同邊個行緊路呢、 |
| 7. | With a friend. | 同朋友咯、 |
| 8. | I do not know him. | 我唔識佢嘅、 |
| 9. | You do not know him at all. | 你喊都唔識佢嘅、 |
| 10. | I thought at first I knew him. | 我先頭估識佢、 |
| 11. | I do not think you do. | 我斷估你唔識佢嘅、 |
| 12. | Who was he? | 佢係乜誰呢、 |
| 13. | A school-mate. [time? | 書友咯、 |
| 14. | Then you have known him a long | 噉你識佢好耐啩、 |
| 15. | I have known him a long time. | 識佢好耐咯、 |
| 16. | You had a long talk with him. | 你同佢講好耐呀、 |
| 17. | Only for a short time. | 冇耐嗻 (*or* 呮)、 |
| 18. | You need not say that. | 你唔使噉講、 |
| 19. | Why need not I say that? | 做乜唔使噉講呢、 |
| 20. | Because I saw you. | 我見你嚊、 |
| 21. | We did not have much to say. | 冇乜野講嘅嗻 (*or* 呮)、 |
| 22. | I supposed you had a great deal to say. | 我斷估你有好多野講嘅、 |
| 23. | It was only an ordinary conversation. | 講閒談說話嗻 (*or* 呮)、 |
| 24. | Your friend was speaking in an excited manner. [weather. | 你嘅朋友講到好生硬、 |
| 25. | Oh, no! We were speaking about the | 唔係、講天時呮、 |
| 26. | And yet you did not see me pass. | 噉都唔見我經過、 |
| 27. | Did you pass us? | 你係行過咩、 |
| 28. | Close by you too. [there. | 行埋好近添呀、 |
| 29. | I could not suppose you would be | 我唔估得到你喺處、 |
| 30. | I wished to see you. | 我想見你添、 |
| 31. | Why did you not speak to me? | 做乜唔呌聲我呢、 |
| 32. | I saw you had a friend there. | 我見你有個朋友喺處、 |

## CONVERSATION 14TH.—AN IMPORTANT CONVERSATION.

| | | |
|---|---|---|
| 1. | ᶝNgo tsokₒ-yat꜆ kín꜄ ᶝnéi ꜀á (*or* ₒá.) | I yesterday saw you. 1 |
| 2. | ᶜHai ꜀pín shü꜄ á꜄ ? | At what place? 2 |
| 3. | ᶜHai ꜀kái shöng$^2$. | In street upon. |
| 4. | ᶝNgo ꜀m kín꜄ ᶝnéi ꜀á (*or* ₒá.) | I not see you. 1 |
| 5. | ᶝNéi ꜀háng-ᶜkan lò$^2$ ꜀á (*or* ₒá.) | You were-walking road. 1 |
| 6. | ꜀T'ung ₒpin ko꜄ ꜀háng-ᶜkan lò$^2$ ꜀ni | With what [C.] walking road, eh? 53 |
| 7. | ꜀T'ung ꜀p'ang-ᶝyau lokₒ. [(*or* ₒni?) | With friend. 32. |
| 8. | ᶝNgo ꜀m shik꜆ ᶝk'öü ke꜄. | I not know him. 15 |
| 9. | ᶝNéi ꜀hám ₒtò ꜀m shik꜆ ᶝk'öü ke꜄. | You entirely also not know him. 15 |
| 10. | ᶝNgo sín ꜀t'au ᶜkwú shik꜆ ᶝk'öü. | I first place thought knew him. |
| 11. | ᶝNgo tün꜄-ᶜkwú ᶝnéi ꜀m shik꜆ ᶝk'öü ke꜄. | I suppose you not know him. 15 |
| 12. | ᶝK'öü hai$^2$ mat꜆ ᶜshöü* ꜀ni (*or* ₒni?) | He was what person, eh? 53 |
| 13. | ꜀Shü ᶝyau lokₒ. | Book friend. 32 |
| 14. | ᶜKòm ᶝnéi shik꜆ ᶝk'öü ᶜhò noi$^2$ kwá꜄? | Then you know him very long? 18 |
| 15. | Shik꜆ ᶝk'öü ᶜhò noi$^2$ lokₒ. | Know him very long. 32 |
| 16. | ᶝNéi ꜀t'ung ᶝk'öü ᶜkong ᶜhò noi$^2$ á꜄. | You with him speak very long. |
| 17. | ᶝMò ᶜnoi* ꜀che (*or* chek꜆.) | Not long. 7 |
| 18. | ᶝNéi ꜀m ᶜshai ᶜkòm ᶜkong. (*or* ꜀ni?) | You not need so say. |
| 19. | Tsò$^2$ mat꜆ ꜀m ᶜshai ᶜkòm ᶜkong ꜀ni | Do what not need so speak, eh? 53 |
| 20. | ᶝNgo kín꜄ ᶝnéi pe$^2$. [chek꜆.) | I saw you, you-see. 59 |
| 21. | ᶝMò mat꜆-ᶝye ᶜkong ke꜄ ꜀che (*or* | No much (*or* nothing) speak. 15, 7 |
| 22. | ᶝNgo tün꜄-ᶜkwú ᶝnéi ᶝyau ᶜhò ꜀to ᶝye ᶜkong ke꜄. [chek꜆.) | I supposed you had very many things speaking-about. 15 |
| 23. | ᶜKong ꜀hán-꜀t'ám shüt꜆-wá$^2$ ꜀che (*or* | Speak chit-chat words only. 7 |
| 24. | ᶝNéi-ke꜄ ꜀p'ang-ᶝyau ᶜkong tò꜄ ᶜhò ꜀sháng-ngáng$^2$. | Your friend spoke until (he spoke) very excitedly. |
| 25. | ꜀M hai$^2$; ᶜkong ꜀t'in-꜀shí chek꜆. | Not was; speaking weather only. 7 |
| 26. | ᶜKòm ₒtò ꜀m kín꜄ ᶝngo ꜀king-kwo꜄. | Then also not see me passing. |
| 27. | ᶝNéi hai$^2$ ꜀háng kwo꜄ ꜀me (*or* ₒme?) | You did walk past, eh? 39 |
| 28. | ꜀Háng ꜀mái ᶜhò ᶝk'an ꜀t'im á꜄. | Walk near very near also. 2 [place. |
| 29. | ᶝNgo ꜀m ᶜkwú tak꜆ tò꜄ ᶝnéi ᶜhai shü꜄. | I not think able to-arrive-at you at the- |
| 30. | ᶝNgo ᶜsöng kín꜄ ᶝnéi ꜀t'ím. [(*or* ₒni?) | I wished to-see you too. [53 |
| 31. | Tsò$^2$-mat꜆ ꜀m kín꜄ ꜀sheng† ᶝngo ꜀ni | Why not call-out with-a-sound to-me, eh? |
| 32. | ᶝNgo kín꜄ ᶝnéi ᶝyau ko꜄ ꜀p'ang-ᶝyau ᶜhai shü꜄. | I saw you had a friend at the-place. |

## CONVERSATION 15TH.—THE SHUT DOOR.

| | | |
|---|---|---|
| 1. | Open it. | 開喇、 |
| 2. | It will not open. | 唔開得、 |
| 3. | Who shut it? | 邊個閂呢、 |
| 4. | Who shut it? | 乜誰閂嘅、 |
| 5. | Yes, who shut it? | 係乜人閂呢、 |
| 6. | The woman. | 個女人咯、 |
| 7. | It was she, was it? | 係佢咩、 |
| 8. | Certainly it was. | 係佢定喇、 |
| 9. | Can she shut the door. | 佢閂得門嘅、 |
| 10. | She can shut the door. | 佢噲閂門嘅、 |
| 11. | I am speaking about the front door, the main door. | 我講前門卽大門呢、 |
| 12. | We are both speaking of the chief door, the street door. | 我哋兩個都係講正門、街門呀、 |
| 13. | The side door is also a street door. | 橫門都係街門、 |
| 14. | Whose house is that? | 個間屋係乜誰嘅、(or 邊個嘅、or 乜人嘅) 呢、 |
| 15. | Which house? | 邊間呀、 |
| 16. | That one. | 個間呢、 |
| 17. | Do you mean the one opposite? | 係對面個間唔係呀、 |
| 18. | No, the one nearly opposite. | 唔係、係斜對面個間、 |
| 19. | It is mine. | 係我嘅、 |
| 20. | I did not know it was yours. | 我都唔知係你嘅、 |
| 21. | My father gave it to me. | 我(嘅)老豆俾過我嘅、 |
| 22. | Was it his? | 係佢嘅咩、 |
| 23. | He bought it. | 佢買嘅、 |
| 24. | From whom did he buy it? | 同邊個買呢、 |
| 25. | From your family. | 同你家人買嘅、 |
| 26. | It was theirs. | 係佢哋嘅、 |
| 27. | They did not want it. | 佢哋唔要、 |
| 28. | So sold it. | 所以賣嘅、 |
| 29. | It would have been better if they had given it to you. | 俾過我重好咯、 |
| 30. | They sold it to a neighbour. | 賣俾隔離、 |
| 31. | I say it was not right to sell it to him. | 我話唔着賣過你、 |
| 32. | That is what I say. | 我都係噉話咯、 |

## CONVERSATION 15TH.—THE SHUT DOOR.

| | | |
|---|---|---|
| 1. | ꜀Hoí ꜀lá (*or* ˳lá). | Open. 21 |
| 2. | ꜁M ꜀hoí tak꜆. | Not open able. |
| 3. | ˳Pín ko꜄ ꜀shán ꜀ni (*or* ˳ni)? | What person [C.] shut, eh? 53 |
| 4. | Mat꜆ ꜂shöü* ꜀shán ꜀ni? | What person shut eh? 5, |
| 5. | Haí꜅ mat꜆ ꜂yan* ꜀shán ꜀ni (*or* ˳ni)? | It was what person shut, eh? 53 |
| 6. | Ko꜄ ꜃nöü-꜂yan* lok˳. | The woman. 32 |
| 7. | Haí꜅ ꜃k'öü ꜀me (*or* ˳me)? | It-was she, was-it? 39 |
| 8. | Haí꜅ ꜃k'öü ꜂ting ꜀lá (*or* ˳lá). | It-was she certainly. 21 |
| 9. | ꜃K'öü ꜀shán tak꜆ ꜁mún ke꜄? | She shut able door? 15 |
| 10. | ꜃K'öü ꜃wúí ꜀shán ꜁mún ke꜄. | She able shut door. 15 |
| 11. | ꜃Ngo ꜂kong ꜁ts'in ꜁mún, tsik꜆ taí꜅ ꜁mún ꜀ni. | I speak front door, just-the large door. 53 |
| 12. | ꜃Ngo-téí꜅ ꜃löng ko꜄ ˳tò haí꜅ ꜂kong ching꜄ ꜁mún, ꜀kaí ꜁mún á꜄. | We two individuals [C.] also are talking-about chief door, street door. 2 |
| 13. | ꜁Wáng ꜁mún ˳tò haí꜅ ꜀kaí ꜁mún. | Side door also is street door. |
| 14. | Ko꜄ ꜀kán uk꜆ haí꜅ mat꜆ ꜂shöü*-ke꜄ (*or* ˳pín ko꜄-ke꜄, *or* mat꜆ ꜂yan*-ke꜄) ꜀ni (*or* ˳ni)? | That [C.] house was what person's (*or* which person's, [C.] *or* what man's), eh? 53 |
| 15. | ˳Pín ꜀kán á꜄? | Which [C.]? 2 |
| 16. | Ko꜄ ꜀kán ꜀ni. | That [C.] there. 53 |
| 17. | Haí꜅ töü꜄-mín꜅ ko꜄ ꜀kán ꜁m haí꜅ á꜄? | Is opposite that [C.] not is, eh? 2 |
| 18. | ꜁M haí꜅, haí꜅ ꜁ts'e töü꜄-꜂mín ko꜄ ꜀kán. | Not is, is slanting opposite that [C]. |
| 19. | Haí꜅ ꜃ngo-ke꜄. | Is mine. [15 S. of Poss] |
| 20. | ꜃Ngo ˳tò ꜁m ꜀chí haí꜅ ꜃néí-ke꜄. | I also not know is yours. |
| 21. | ꜃Ngo (ke꜄) ꜃lò-taú꜅ ꜂péi kwo꜄ ꜃ngo ke꜄. | My father gave to me. [15 S. of Poss] |
| 22. | Haí꜅ ꜃k'öü-ke꜄ ꜀me (*or* ˳me)? | Was his, eh? 39 |
| 23. | ꜃K'öü ꜃máí ke꜄. | He bought. 15 |
| 24. | ꜁T'ung ˳pín ko꜄ ꜃máí ꜀ni (*or* ˳ni)? | From which [C.] bought, eh? 53 |
| 25. | ꜁T'ung ꜃néí ꜀ká ꜁yan ꜃máí ke꜄. | From your family persons bought. 15 |
| 26. | Haí꜅ ꜃k'öü-téí꜅ ke꜄. | Was theirs. [15 S. of Poss] |
| 27. | ꜃K'öü-téí꜅ ꜁m yíú꜅. | They not want. |
| 28. | ꜂Sho-꜂yí máí꜅ ke꜄. | Therefore sold. 15 |
| 29. | ꜂Péi kwo꜄ ꜃néí chung꜅ ꜂hò lok˳. | Give to you still better. 32 |
| 30. | Máí꜅ ꜂péi kák˳-꜁léí. | Sold to neighbour. |
| 31. | ꜃Ngo wá꜅ ꜁m chök꜇ maí꜅ kwo꜄ ꜃k'öü. | I say not right sell to him. |
| 32. | ꜃Ngo ˳tò haí꜅ ꜂kòm wá꜅ lok˳. | I also do so say. 32 |

## CONVERSATION 16TH.—OFF IN A BOAT.

| | | |
|---|---|---|
| 1. | Boat ! | 三板呀、 |
| 2. | Do you want a boat ? | 你要艇嗎、 |
| 3. | Yes, I do. You call one. | 要呀、叫隻艇嚟喇、 |
| 4. | That one will not do ; it is dirty. | 個隻唔做得、汚糟咯、 |
| 5. | This one is clean. | 呢隻乾淨嘅、 |
| 6. | It will do. | 做得咯、 |
| 7. | Where are you going ? | 去邊處呀、 |
| 8. | I want to go off to a vessel. | 要櫂開船、 |
| 9. | Which one ? | 邊隻係呀、 |
| 10. | That one out there. | 開頭個隻(係咯)、 |
| 11. | Very well : that will do. | 吾、好咯、做得咯、 |
| 12. | Sit in the centre. | 坐中間喇、 |
| 13. | How few rowers you have. | 咁少人櫂槳嘅、 |
| 14. | We will call another one or two to help us. | 叫多一兩個嚟幫櫂喇、 |
| 15. | Very well : do so. | 好喇、叫喇、 |
| 16. | Pull away. | 櫂起嚟喇、 |
| 17. | The tide is against us. | 𠽌水咯、 |
| 18. | Is it ebb, or flood tide ? | 水大水乾呢、 |
| 19. | The tide is on the turn (*or* rather slack tide.). | 水慢、 |
| 20. | Why do you not use the sail ? | 唔使{巾里}、 |
| 21. | There is no need ; the wind is contrary. | 唔使{巾里}、風𠽌吖、 |
| 22. | Is it a head wind ? | 係頂頭風咩、 |
| 23. | Yes. | 係哩、 |
| 24. | This is not the vessel. | 唔係呢隻吖、 |
| 25. | Then which one is ? | 噉、邊隻係呢、 |
| 26. | Not this one in here ; that one straight off there. | 唔係埋頭呢隻、一對開個隻係咯、 |
| 27. | The one next to the blue funnel one is it. | 藍烟通第二隻係咯、 |
| 28. | Which side of the vessel shall we go alongside ? | 埋邊邊呢、 |
| 29. | The visitors' side. | 人客個邊咯、 |
| 30. | Shall we wait or not ? | 使等唔使呀、 |
| 31. | Yes, you must wait. | 係呀、要等呀、 |
| 32. | I shall go back soon. I shall go in a short time. | 就翻去咯、冇耐翻去咯、 |

易學廣東話

## CONVERSATION 16TH.—OFF IN A BOAT.

| | | |
|---|---|---|
| 1. | ꜀Sám-꜂pán á꜄. | Sampan. 2 |
| 2. | ꜃Néi yiú꜄ ꜃t'eng† má꜄? | You want boat eh? 35 |
| 3. | Yiú꜄ á꜄; kiú꜄ chek$_o$ ꜃t'eng ꜁lai ꜀lá (*or* $_o$lá). | Want 2; call [C.] boat come. 21 |
| 4. | Ko꜄ chek$_o$ ꜁m tsò$^2$ tak꜆, ꜀o-꜀tsò lok$_o$. | That one [C.] not do can, dirty. 32 |
| 5. | ꜀Ni chek$_o$ ꜀kon-tseng$^2$† ke꜄. | This one [C.] clean. 15 |
| 6. | Tsò$^2$ tak꜆ lok$_o$. | Do can. 32 |
| 7. | Höü꜄ $_o$pín shü꜄ á꜄? | Go what place, eh? 2 |
| 8. | Yiú꜄ cháú$^2$ ꜀hoi ꜁shün. | Want row out-to vessel. |
| 9. | $_o$Pín chek$_o$ hai$^2$ ꜀á (*or* $_o$a)? | Which one [C.] (is? 1) |
| 10. | ꜀Hoi-꜁t'aú ko꜄ chek$_o$ (꜀hai$^2$ lok$_o$.) | Outside that one [C.] is. 32 |
| 11. | ꜁Ng, ꜂hò lok$_o$, tsò$^2$ tak꜆ lok$_o$. | Well, good 32, do can. 32 |
| 12. | ꜃Ts'o*† ꜀chung-꜀kán (*or better and more usually* $_o$kán) ꜀la (*or*$_o$ lá). | Sit middle. 21 |
| 13. | Kòm꜄ ꜂shiú ꜁yan cháú$^2$ ꜂tsöng ke꜄. | So few men row oars. 15 |
| 14. | Kiú꜄ ꜀to yat꜆ ꜃löng ko꜄ ꜁lai ꜀pong cháú$^2$ ꜀lá (*or* $_o$lá). | Call more one two [C.] come assist row. 21 |
| 15. | ꜂Hò ꜀lá (*or* $_o$lá); kiú꜄ ꜀lá (*or* $_o$lá). | Good 21; call. 21 |
| 16. | Cháú$^2$ ꜂héi ꜁lai ꜀lá (*or* $_o$lá). | Row up come. 21 |
| 17. | Ngák$_2$ ꜂shöü lok$_o$. | Contrary wind. 32 |
| 18. | ꜂Shöü tái$^2$, ꜂shöü ꜀kon ꜀ni? | Water great, water dried, eh? 53 |
| 19. | ꜂Shöü mán$^2$. | Water slow. |
| 20. | ꜁M ꜂shai ꜃léi? | Not use sail? |
| 21. | ꜁M ꜂shai ꜃léi; ꜀fung ngák$_2$ ꜀á (*or* $_o$á). | Not need sail; wind contrary. 1 |
| 22. | Hai$^2$ ꜂ting ꜁t'aú ꜀fung ꜀me (*or* $_o$me)? | Is against the head (of the boat) wind, eh? 39 |
| 23. | Hai$^2$ ꜀le (*or* $_o$le). | Yes. 24 |
| 24. | ꜁M hai$^2$ ꜀ni chek$_o$ ꜀á (*or* $_o$á). | Not is this one. 1 |
| 25. | ꜂Kòm, $_o$pín chek$_o$ hai$^2$ ꜀ni? | Then, which one [C.] is, eh? 53 |
| 26. | ꜁M hai$^2$ ꜁mái-꜁t'au ꜀ni chek$_o$, yat꜆ töü꜄ ꜀hoi ko꜄ chek$_o$ hai$^2$ lok$_o$. | Not is near this one, [C.] straight opposite out that one [C.] is. 32 |
| 27. | ꜁Lám ꜀yín-꜁t'ung tai$^2$-yi$^2$ chek$_o$ hai$^2$ [lok$_o$. | Blue funnel number two one [C.] is. 32 |
| 28. | ꜁Mái $_o$pín pín$^2$ ꜀ni? | Approach which side, eh? 53 |
| 29. | ꜁Yan-hák$_o$ ko꜄ pín$^2$ lok$_o$. | Visitors that side. 32 |
| 30. | ꜂Shai ꜂tang ꜁m ꜂shai á꜄? | Need wait not need, eh? 2 |
| 31. | Hai$^2$ a꜄, yiú꜄ ꜂tang á꜄. [höü꜄ lok$_o$. | Yes, 2 want wait. 2 |
| 32. | Tsaú$^2$ ꜀fán höü꜄ lok$_o$; ꜃mò ꜂noi* ꜀fán | Just back go; 32 not long back go. 32 |

## CONVERSATION 17TH.—HONGKONG THEN AND NOW.

| | | |
|---|---|---|
| 1. | What part of the country are you | 你係邊處人、 |
| 2. | I am a Höng Shán man. [from? | 我係香山人、 |
| 3. | From the Höng Shán District? | 香山縣人嗎、 |
| 4. | From Höng Shán city. | 係香山城嘅、 |
| 5. | You have been in Hongkong a long | 你喺、(*or* 嚟) 香港好耐咯、 |
| 6. | A long time. [time. | 嚟 (*or* 喺處) 好耐咯、 |
| 7. | How long a time? | 有幾耐呢、 |
| 8. | I came when I was young. | 細個嗰時嚟咯、 |
| 9. | Hongkong is not the same as it was in olden times. | 香港唔似舊時噉、 |
| 10. | No; it is not the same. | 唔似咯、 |
| 11. | It is very different, I suppose. | 爭好遠啩、 |
| 12. | It is very different. | 爭好遠咯、 |
| 13. | There were few people then. | 個時人少咯、 |
| 14. | There were very few people. | 好少人咯、 |
| 15. | Not many houses either. | 又冇乜屋添、 |
| 16. | There were no houses or shops then. | 個陣時冇屋冇舖咯、 |
| 17. | None at all? | 喊都冇咩、 |
| 18. | I did not say that. | 唔係噉話、 |
| 19. | Then there were a few, more or less. | 噉都有多少咯、 |
| 20. | There were only a few. | 有幾間呮、 |
| 21. | Only one here and there; that was all. | 呢處一兩間、嗰處一兩間噉嘅呮、 |
| 22. | Now there are many people. | 呢排人多、 |
| 23. | There are that. | 眞正係咯、 |
| 24. | And streets and wharves and temples and gardens. | 又有街、又有馬頭、又有廟、又有花園、 |
| 25. | You have not said all. | 你唔曾講哓、 |
| 26. | I know that. | 我知到咯、 |
| 27. | How do you go to Höng Shan? | 點去香山呢、 |
| 28. | You can go by passoge boat from Hongkong. [from Macao? | 喺香港搭渡(去)又得、 |
| 29. | And you can go by passage boat | 喺澳門搭渡又得嚟嗎、 |
| 30. | Yes. | 係哩、 |
| 31. | It is not a long journey, I suppose. | 冇幾耐水路啩、 |
| 32. | Not very long. | 冇幾耐呮、 |

## CONVERSATION 17TH.—HONGKONG THEN AND NOW.

| | | |
|---|---|---|
| 1. | ˋNéi hai$^2$ ₒpín shüᵓ ꜀yan ? | You are what place man ? |
| 2. | ꜂Ngo hai$^2$ ꜀Höng ꜀Shán ꜀yan. | I am Höng Shán man. |
| 3. | ꜀Höng ꜀Shan yün$^2$ ꜀yan ꜀má ? | Höng Shán District man, eh ? 33 |
| 4. | Hai$^2$ ꜀Höng ꜀Shán ᶜshéng* keᵓ. | Is Höng Shán city belong-to. 15 |
| 5. | ꜂Néi ᶜhai (*or* ꜀lai) ꜀Höng-ᶜkong ᶜhò ᶜnoi* lokₒ. | You at (*or* come), Hongkong very long. 32 |
| 6. | ꜀Lai (*or* ᶜhai shüᵓ) ᶜhò noi$^2$* lokₒ. | Come (*or* been here) very long. 32 |
| 7. | ꜂Yaú ᶜkéi ᶜnoi* ꜀ni ? | Have how long, eh ? 53 |
| 8. | Saiᵓ koᵓ ᶜko ꜀shí ꜀lai lokₒ. | Little one that time come. 32 |
| 9. | ꜀Höng-ᶜkong ꜀m ꜂ts'z kaú$^2$ ꜀shí ᶜkòm. | Hongkong not like old time so. |
| 10. | ꜀M ꜂ts'z lokₒ. | Not like. 32 |
| 11. | ꜀Cháng ᶜhò ꜂yün kwáᵓ. | Differ very far I-suppose. 18 |
| 12. | ꜀Cháng ᶜhò ꜂yün lokₒ. | Differ very much. 32 |
| 13. | Koᵓ ꜀shí ꜀yan ᶜshíú lokₒ. | That time men few. 32 |
| 14. | ᶜHò ꜂shíú ꜀yan lokₒ. | Very few men. 32 |
| 15. | Yaú$^2$ ꜂mò mat꜄ uk꜄ ꜀t'ím. | Besides not many houses also. [32 |
| 16. | Koᵓ chan$^2$ ᶜshí ꜂mò uk꜄ ꜂mò p'òᵓ lokₒ. | That period [C.] time no houses, no shops. |
| 17. | ꜀Hám ₒtò ꜂mò ꜀me (*or* ꜀me) ? | Entirely also none, eh ? 39 |
| 18. | ꜀M hai$^2$ ᶜkòm wá$^2$. | No is so say. |
| 19. | ᶜKòm, ₒtò ꜂yaú ꜀to ᶜshíú lokₒ. | Then also have more less. 32 |
| 20. | ꜂Yaú ᶜkéi ꜀kán ꜀che. | Have several buildings only. 7 |
| 21. | ꜀Ni shüᵓ yat꜄ ꜂löng ꜀kán, ᶜko shüᵓ yat꜄ ꜂löng ꜀kán ; ᶜkòm-keᵓ ꜀che. | This place one two [C.]; that place one two ; [C.] so only. 15, 7 |
| 22. | ꜀Ni ᶜp'ái* ꜀yan ꜀to. | This time men many. |
| 23. | ꜀Chan chingᵓ hai$^2$ lokₒ. | Truly really it-is-so. 32 |
| 24. | Yaú$^2$ ꜂yaú ꜀kái; yaú$^2$ ꜂yaú ꜂má-ᶜt'au*; yaú$^2$ ꜂yaú ᶜmíú*; yaú$^2$ ꜂yaú ꜀fá-ᶜyün*. | Also have streets ; also have jetties ; also have temples ; also have gardens. |
| 25. | ꜂Néi ꜀m ꜀ts'ang ᶜkong sáiᵓ. | You not yet said all. |
| 26. | ꜂Ngo ꜀chí-tòᵓ lokₒ. | I know. 32 |
| 27. | ᶜTím höüᵓ ꜀Höng ꜀Shán ꜀ni ? | How go Höng Shán, eh ? 53 |
| 28. | ᶜHaí ꜀Höng-ᶜKong tápₒ ᶜtò* (höüᵓ) yaú$^2$ tak꜄. [máᵓ ? | At Hongkong go-on-board passage-boat (go) also can. [can ? 22, 33. |
| 29. | ᶜHaí Òᵓ ꜀Mún tápₒ ᶜtò* yaú$^2$ tak꜄ láᵓ | At Macao go-on-board passage-boat also |
| 30. | Hai$^2$ ꜀le (*or* ₒle). | Yes. 24 |
| 31. | ꜂Mò ᶜkéi ᶜnoi ᶜshöü lò$^2$ kwáᵓ. | Not very long water road I-suppose. 18 |
| 32. | ꜂Mo ᶜkéi ᶜnoi* ꜀che. | Not very long only. 7 |

## CONVERSATION 18TH.—OH! THOSE LAWYERS.

| | | |
|---|---|---|
| 1. | Oh! Those lawyers. | 唉吔、個啲狀師、 |
| 2. | What is the matter now? | 而家有乜事呢、 |
| 3. | I have lost my case. | 我輸案咯、 |
| 4. | Did you retain a lawyer? | 你有請狀師冇呀、 |
| 5. | No, I did not. | 冇、我冇請呀、 |
| 6. | Who did then? | 噉、邊個請呢、 |
| 7. | They did. | 佢個頭咯、 |
| 8. | Did you win or lose? I suppose you lost. | 你輸噉贏呢、冇贏啩、 |
| 9. | I did not. | 冇咯、 |
| 10. | Why did not you have a lawyer? | 做乜你冇請呢、 |
| 11. | I have no money. | 冇銀吖、 |
| 12. | But if you had won, they would have had to pay your lawyer's costs. | 你係贏呢佢個頭要出狀師使用吖、 |
| 13. | They would have had to pay my lawyer's costs to me! | 佢個頭要俾翻我呢頭狀師使費過我、 |
| 14. | It often is so. | 好多賬係噉、 |
| 15. | I did not know; if I had, I would have got not one, but two or three. | 唉、我唔知、我係知、就請狀師、唔止請一個添、請兩三個都好咯、 |
| 16. | I cannot help laughing at what you say. | 你講個啲說話令我好笑咯、 |
| 17. | What are you laughing at? | 笑乜野呢、 |
| 18. | Laughing at you wishing to retain so many lawyers. | 笑你想請咁多狀師嘅、 |
| 19. | Why should not I? It is most important to win. | 做乜唔請呀、至謹係要贏嘅喇、 |
| 20. | With such a small case one would be enough. | 咁少案一個够咯、 |
| 21. | I do not consider it a small matter. | 我唔算係小事、 |
| 22. | But the judge might think it was unnecessary. | 大人或者估唔使咁多呀、 |
| 23. | The judge would not trouble about it I suppose. | 大人唔打理啩、 |
| 24. | Why not? | 做乜唔打理呀、 |
| 25. | Why should he? I thought he would not attend to such things. | 做乜打理吖、我估佢唔打理噉嘅事、 |

## CONVERSATION 18TH.—OH! THOSE LAWYERS.

| | | |
|---|---|---|
| 1. | ꜀Ai ꜀yá (*or* ꜀aí ꜀yá)! koᵓ-ₒti chong$^2$-ₒsz. | Dear me! Those lawyers. |
| 2. | ꜀Yí-꜀ká (*or* ꜀yí-ₒká) ᶜyaú mat꜄ sz$^2$ ꜀ni? | Now have what matter, eh? 53 |
| 3. | ᶜNgo ₒshü onᵓ lokₒ. | I lost [ₒshü = S. of P. T.] case 32 |
| 4. | ᶜNéi ᶜyaú ᶜts'eng† chong$^2$-ₒsz ᶜmò áᵓ? | You have retained lawyer not, eh? 2 |
| 5. | ᶜMò, ᶜngo ᶜmò ᶜts'eng† áᵓ. | No, I not engage. 2 |
| 6. | ᶜKòm ₒpín koᵓ ᶜts'eng† ꜀ni (*or* ₒni)? | Then who [C.] engaged, eh? 53 |
| 7. | ᶜK'öü koᵓ ꜀t'aú lokₒ. [kwáᵓ. | They that side, 32 |
| 8. | ᶜNéi ꜀shü pe$^2$ ꜀yeng† ꜀ni? ᶜmò ꜀yeng† | You win or lose? Not win probably. 18 |
| 9. | ᶜMò lokₒ. [ₒni? | No. 32 |
| 10. | Tsò$^2$ mat꜄ ᶜnéi ᶜmò ᶜts'eng† ꜀ni (*or* | What thing you not retain, eh? 53 |
| 11. | ᶜMò ꜀ngan* ꜀á (*or* ₒá). | No money. 1 |
| 12. | ᶜNéi hai$^2$ ꜀yeng† ꜀ni, ᶜk'öü koᵓ ꜀t'aú yíúᵓ ch'ut꜄ chong$^2$-ₒsz ᶜshaí yung$^2$ ꜀á (*or* ₒá). | You had won 53, they that side (would) need issue lawyers fees. 1 |
| 13. | ᶜK'öü koᵓ ꜀t'aú yíúᵓ ᶜpéi ꜀fán ᶜngo ꜀ni ꜀t'aú chong$^2$-ₒsz ᶜshaí faiᵓ kwoᵓ ᶜngo! | They that side (would) need to-give back my that side lawyer's expenses to me! |
| 14. | ᶜHò ꜀to chöngᵓ hai$^2$ ᶜkòm. | Very many times is so. |
| 15. | ꜀Ai! ᶜngo ꜀m ꜀chí, ᶜngo hai$^2$ ꜀chí, tsaú$^2$ ᶜts'eng† chong$^2$-ₒsz, ꜀m ᶜchí ᶜts'eng† yat꜄ koᵓ ꜀t'ím, ᶜts'eng† ᶜlöng ꜀sàm koᵓ ₒtò ᶜhò lokₒ. | Oh! I not know, I had known then retain lawyers, not only engage one [C.], besides engage two three [C.] also good. 32 |
| 16. | ᶜNéi ᶜkong koᵓ-ₒti shüt꜄-wá$^2$ ꜀ling ᶜngo ᶜhò síúᵓ lokₒ. | You speak those words make me very (much) to-laugh. 32 |
| 17. | Síúᵓ mat꜄ ᶜye ꜀ni (*or* ₒni)? | Laugh-at what thing? 53 |
| 18. | Síúᵓ ᶜnéi ᶜsöng ᶜts'eng† kòmᵓ ꜀to chong$^2$-ₒsz keᵓ. | Laugh-at you wishing to-retain so many lawyers. 15 |
| 19. | Tsò$^2$ mat꜄ ꜀m ᶜts'eng† áᵓ? Chíᵓ ᶜkan hai$^2$ yíúᵓ ꜀yeng† keᵓ ꜀lá. | Do what not retain? 2. Most pressing is must win. 15, 21 |
| 20. | Kòmᵓ ᶜshíú ònᵓ yat꜄ koᵓ kaúᵓ lokₒ. | Such small case one [C.] sufficient. 32 |
| 21. | ᶜNgo ꜀m sünᵓ hai$^2$ ᶜsíú sz$^2$. | I not consider is small matter. |
| 22. | Tái$^2$-꜀yan wák꜄-ᶜche ᶜkwú ꜀m ᶜshaí kòmᵓ ꜀to áᵓ. | His-Lordship perhaps (would) think not need so many. 2 |
| 23. | Tái$^2$-꜀yan ꜀m ᶜtá-ᶜléi kwáᵓ. | His-Lordship not attend-to, probable. 18 |
| 24. | Tsò$^2$ mat꜄ ꜀m ᶜtá-ᶜléi áᵓ? | (For) what thing not trouble-about, eh? 2 |
| 25. | Tsò$^2$ mat꜄ ᶜtá-ᶜléi ꜀á (*or* ₒá)? ᶜNgo ᶜkwú ᶜk'öü ꜀m ᶜtá-ᶜléi ᶜkòm keᵓ sz$^2$. | (For) what thing trouble-about, eh? 1 I thought he not trouble-about such matters. |

### CONVERSATION 18TH.—OH! THOSE LAWYERS.—*(Continued.)*

| | | |
|---|---|---|
| 26. | Indeed! would not he though? | 至好唔打理咯、 |
| 27. | Yes! what would he probably do? | 係咩、 佢大概點理呢、 |
| 28. | He would probably consider one solicitor sufficient in such a case. | 佢大概筭噉嘅案件一個細狀師夠咯、 |
| 29. | And what then? | 噉點呢、 |
| 30. | He might decide that you were to have your barrister's costs, but not your solicitor's. | 佢或者斷你要出自已小狀師使用、佢個頭要出你大狀師使費、 |
| 31. | Oh, indeed. | 啊、係咩、 |
| 32. | Yes. | 係哩、 |

### CONVERSATION 19TH.—KOW LUNG CITY.

| | | |
|---|---|---|
| 1. | Have you been to Kow Lung City? | 你去過九龍城唔曾呢、 |
| 2. | I have been. | 去過咯、 |
| 3. | How do you go? | 點去呢、 |
| 4. | By steam launch. | 搭火船仔咯、 |
| 5. | Where do you start from? | 喺邊處開身呢、 |
| 6. | From the Praya. | 海旁咯、 |
| 7. | When does it start? | 幾時開身呢、 |
| 8. | There is no time fixed. [they go? | 冇限定幾時開身嘅、 |
| 9. | In that case how do you know when | 噉點知到幾時去呢、 |
| 10. | You go on board the launch, sit down, and wait till— | 你落火船仔坐等到— |
| 11. | What till wh n? | 等到幾時呀、 |
| 12. | Till they start. | 等佢開身咯、 |
| 13. | How long is it before they start? | 佢幾耐至開身呢、 |

## CONVERSATION 18TH.—OH! THOSE LAWYERS.—(*Continued.*)

| | | |
|---|---|---|
| 26. | Chí$^{2}$-ᶜhò ꜀m ᶜtá-ᶜléi lok꜄. | *lit.* Best not trouble-about 32. (ironical, which means, *Will not he though?*) |
| 27. | Hai$^{2}$ ꜀me (*or* me): ᶜk'öü tai$^{2}$-ᶜk'oi ᶜtím ᶜᶜléi ꜀ni (*or* ꜀ni)? | Indeed 39; he probably how attend-to eh? 35 |
| 28. | ᶜK'öü tai$^{2}$ ᶜk'oi sün ᵓ ᶜkòm-keᵓ onᵓ-kin$^{2}$, yat꜄ koᵓ saiᵓ chong$^{2}$-sz kauᵓ lok꜀. | He probably (would) consider such case one [C] solicitor enough, 32 (The force of the 嘅 keᵓ will be shewn if the words are transposed, as follows, *a case of such a kind*). |
| 29. | ᶜKòm ᶜtim ꜀ni (*or* ni,? | Then how, eh? 53 |
| 30. | ᶜK'öü wák꜄-ᶜche tünᵓ ᶜnéi yiuᵓ ch'ut꜄ tsz$^{2}$-ᶜke tái$^{2}$ chong$^{2}$-sz ᶜshai-yung$^{2}$, ᶜk'öü koᵓ ꜀t'au yiuᵓ ch'ut꜄ ᶜnéi ᶜsiu chong$^{2}$-sz keᵓ ᶜshai-faiᵓ. | He perhaps (would) decide (that) you would pay-out your own big lawyer's fees, they that side would need to pay-out your little lawyer's fees. |
| 31. | O$^{2}$, hai$^{2}$ ꜀me (*or* me)? | Oh, indeed? 39 |
| 32. | Hai$^{2}$ ꜀le (*or* ꜀le). | Yes, 24 |

---

## CONVERSATION 19TH.—KOW LUNG CITY.

| | | |
|---|---|---|
| 1. | ᶜNéi höüᵓ ᶜKau ꜀Lung ꜀shengᵗ ꜀m ꜀ts'ang ꜀ni (*or* ni)? | You been-to Kau Lung city not yet, eh? 53 |
| 2. | Höüᵓ kwoᵓ lok꜄. | Been, 32 |
| 3. | ᶜTim höüᵓ ꜀ni (*or* ni)? | How go, eh? 53 |
| 4. | Táp꜀ ᶜfo-꜀shün-ᶜtsai lok꜄. | On-board steam launch (*lit* little fire ship). |
| 5. | ᶜHai ꜀pín shüᵓ ꜀hoi-꜀shan ꜀ni? | At what place start, eh? 53 [32 |
| 6. | ᶜHoi ꜀p'ong lok꜄. | Sea side, 32 |
| 7. | ᶜKéi ꜀shi ꜀hoi-꜀shan ꜀ni? [keᵓ. | What time start, eh? 53 |
| 8. | ᶜMò hán$^{2}$ ting$^{2}$ ᶜkéi ᶜshí* ꜀hoi-꜀shan | No limit certain what time start, 15 |
| 9. | ᶜKòm ᶜtím ꜀chi-toᵓ ᶜkéi ᶜshi* höüᵓ ꜀ni? [ᶜtang toᵓ— | Then how know what time go, eh? 53 [till— |
| 10. | ᶜNéi lok꜄ ᶜfo-shün-ᶜtsai ᶜts'o*†. | You go-down-into steam launch sit wait |
| 11. | ᶜTang toᵓ ᶜkéi ᶜshi* áᵓ? | Wait till what time, eh? 2 |
| 12. | ᶜTang ᶜk'öü ꜀hoi-꜀shan lok꜄. [ni)? | Wait till it starts, 32 |
| 13. | ᶜK'öü ᶜkéi ᶜnoi* ꜀hoi-꜀shan ꜀ni (*or* | It how long before start, eh? 53 |

### CONVERSATION 19TH.—KOWLUNG CITY.—(Continued.)

| | | |
|---|---|---|
| 14. | That is uncertain. | 個啲唔定咯、 |
| 15. | Cannot you say? | 你唔話得咩、 |
| 16. | How can I? | 我點話得你、 |
| 17. | I do not know, I am asking you. | 我唔知、我問下你吖、 |
| 18. | And I do not know. | 我都唔知咯、 |
| 19. | How strange! | 咁出奇嘅、 |
| 20. | What is strange? | 乜野出奇呀、 |
| 21. | Is it not strange? You have been there and you do not know anything about it. | 唔係出奇咩、你又去過、你噉都唔知嘅、 |
| 22. | No one knows. | 冇人知嘅、 |
| 23. | That is still more strange. | 噉、越發奇咯、 |
| 24. | You think it very strange. | 你見好怪、 |
| 25. | It is very strange. | 好奇怪咯、 |
| 26. | The steersman even does not know. | 梢工都唔知呀、 |
| 27. | And the Captain? | 船主呢、 |
| 28. | He does not know. | 佢都唔知呀、 |
| 29. | You are talking nonsense. | 你講發譫話咯、 |
| 30. | I am not. How can they know when the passengers will all come? | 唔係呀、佢點知個啲客幾時嚟齊噠呢、 |
| 31. | They wait till there are sufficient passengers before they start; is that it? | 佢等有夠人客至開身咩、係噉唔係呀、 |
| 32. | Of course. Would they go if there were no passengers? | 定喇、冇搭客佢哋去喇咩、 |

### CONVERSATION 20TH.—THE PEAK.

| | | |
|---|---|---|
| 1. | Have you been to the Peak yet? | 你去山頂唔曾呢、 |
| 2. | Not yet. | 未曾呀、 |
| 3. | Not yet? | 唔曾去、 |
| 4. | No. | 未 |
| 5. | You have been in Hongkong so long, and yet have not been? | 你嚟香港咁耐、唔曾去山頂嘅、 |
| 6. | There is no use going. | 冇用去吖、 |

## CONVERSATION 19TH.—KOW LUNG CITY.—(Continued.)

| | | |
|---|---|---|
| 14. | Ko-꜀ti ꜀m ting[2] lok꜀. | That not certain. 32 |
| 15. | ᶜNéi ꜀m wá[2] takʾ ꜀me (or ꜀me)? | You not say able, eh? 39 |
| 16. | ᶜNgo ᶜtim wá[2] takʾ ꜀ni (or ꜀ni)? | I how say able? 53 |
| 17. | ᶜNgo ꜀m ꜀chí; ᶜngo ᶜman* ᶜlá ᶜnéi | I not know: I ask a-bit you. 1 |
| 18. | ᶜNgo ꜀tò ꜀m ꜀chí lok꜀. [꜀á (or ꜀á). | I also not know. 32 |
| 19. | Kòmʾ ch'utʾ-꜀k'éi keʾ! | So strange! 15 |
| 20. | ꜀Mi ᶜye ch'utʾ-꜀k'éi áʾ? | What thing strange, eh? 2 |
| 21. | ꜀M hai[2] ch'utʾ-꜀k'éi ꜀me (or ꜀me)? ᶜNéi yau[2] höüʾ-kwoʾ, ᶜnéi ꜀hám ꜀tò ꜀m ꜀chí keʾ. | Not is strange, eh? 39 You also have-been, you altogether also not know, 15 |
| 22. | ᶜMò ꜀yan ꜀chí keʾ. | No man knows, 15 |
| 23. | ᶜKòm, yütʾ-fát ꜀k'éi lok꜀. | Then, still-more strange. 32 |
| 24. | ᶜNéi kínʾ ᶜhò ᶜkwái*? | You think very extraordinary? [This is in |
| 25. | ᶜHò ꜀k'éi-kwáiʾ lok꜀. | Very strange, 32 [a kind of rising tone.] |
| 26. | ꜀Shai (꜀ch'áü)-꜀kung tò ꜀m ꜀chí | Steersman also not know, 2 |
| 27. | ꜀Shün ᶜchü ꜀ni (or ꜀ni)? [áʾ. | Ship's lord, eh? 53 |
| 28. | ᶜK'öü ꜀tò ꜀m ꜀chí áʾ. | He also not know, 2 |
| 29. | ᶜNéi ᶜkong fát꜀-ngám[2] wá[2] lok꜀. | You speaking nonsensical words, 32 |
| 30. | ꜀M hai[2] áʾ: ᶜk'öü ᶜtím ꜀chí ko-꜀ti hák ᶜkéi ᶜshí* ꜀lai ꜀ts'aí saí ꜀ni (or ꜀ni)? | Not is 2; they how know those passengers what time come together all, eh? 53 |
| 31. | ᶜK'öü ᶜtang ᶜyaú kauʾ ꜀yan-hák꜀ chíʾ ꜀hoi-꜀shan ꜀me (or ꜀me)? Hai[2] ᶜkòm ꜀m hai[2] áʾ? | They wait have enough passengers before starting, eh? 39 Is so, not is? 2 |
| 32. | ᶜTing* ꜀lá. (or ꜀lá) ᶜMò tap꜀-hák꜀ ᶜk'öü-téi[2] höüʾ láʾ ꜀me (or ꜀me?) | Certainly 21. No passengers they would-go, eh? 22, 39 |

## CONVERSATION 20TH.—THE PEAK.

| | | |
|---|---|---|
| 1. | ᶜNéi höüʾ ꜀shán-ᶜteng† ꜀m ꜀ts'ang | You go hill-top not yet, eh? 53 |
| 2. | Méi[2] ꜀ts'ang áʾ. [꜀ni (or ꜀ni?) | Not yet, 2 |
| 3. | ꜀M ꜀ts'ang höüʾ? | Not yet gone? |
| 4. | Méi[2]. | Not-yet. |
| 5. | ᶜNéi ꜀lai ꜀Hông ᶜKong kòmʾ noi[2] ꜀m ꜀ts'ang höüʾ ꜀shán-ᶜteng† keʾ? | You come Hongkong so long, [This keeps its original tone] not yet go hill-top? 15 |
| 6. | ᶜMò yung[2] höüʾ ꜀á (or ꜀á). | No use go. 1 |

## CONVERSATION 20TH.—THE PEAK.—(*Continued.*)

| | | |
|---|---|---|
| 7. | We English are very fond of climbing hills. | 我哋英人好與遊山嘅、 |
| 8. | What is the good of it? | 有乜益呢、 |
| 9. | There is great profit in it. | 冇大益、 |
| 10. | Oh! indeed! | 係咩、 |
| 11. | You exercise your legs when you go for a walk along the hill roads. | 去逛山路、就噲行鬆吓脚步、 |
| 12. | But hill roads are difficult to walk on. | 山路難行、 |
| 13. | That is true; but there are a great many things hard to do in this world. | 冇錯、天下有好多野難做、 |
| 14. | But if a thing is hard to do, does it follow that you must do it? | 因一件野難做、噉人哋是必要做囉咩、 |
| 15. | That is not it. | 唔係噉話、 |
| 16. | Then what do you say? | 噉你點講呢、 |
| 17. | I say it gives you strength to climb hills. | 我話𨅝上山、噲令身子壯健、 |
| 18. | It makes me very tired. | 我𨅝山就見好癐、 |
| 19. | But you feel better afterwards. | 後來見好啲喇、 |
| 20. | No. Even the next day, I do not feel in good spirits. | 唔係、第二日都唔見精神、 |
| 21. | It is only because you are not accustomed to it. | 睺、你唔行慣唄、 |
| 22. | Beside it is cool at the Peak. | 山頂又凉咯、 |
| 23. | It is tolerably cool down below. | 下底都幾凉呀、 |
| 24. | I do not think it cool. | 我話唔凉、 |
| 25. | There are a number of summer residences at the Peak. | 山頂有好多凉亭、 |
| 26. | If you go to the flag staff on a clear day, you can see a long way off. | 去扯旗杆好天好遠都望得到、 |
| 27. | I suppose you can see as far as Kowlung city. | 大概望得到九龍城、 |
| 28. | Further than that. | 唔止咁遠、 |
| 29. | You see the sea all round; do you not? | 周圍都係見海嗎、 |
| 30. | Yes, and a great many islands. | 係吖、有睇得見大多海島、 |
| 31. | There is a fine view I suppose. | 都幾好睇嘅、 |
| 32. | Yes. It is beautiful; you had better go up and see it. | 係呀、好好睇呀、你上去睇好呀、 |

## CONVERSATION 20TH.—THE PEAK.—(*Continued.*)

| | | |
|---|---|---|
| 7. | ˢNgo-téi$^2$ ꜀Ying-꜀yan ᶜhò ꜀hing ꜀yaú ꜀shán keᵓ. | We Englishman very fond-of rambling-on hills, 15 |
| 8. | ˢYaú mat꜀ yik꜀ ꜀ni (*or* ꜀ni)? | Have what profit, eh? 53 |
| 9. | ˢYaú tái$^2$ yik꜀. | Have great profit. |
| 10. | Hai$^2$ ꜀me (*or* ꜀me)? | Yes, eh? 39 |
| 11. | Hööiᵓ k'wángᵓ ꜀shán lò$^2$, tsaú$^2$ ˢwúi ꜀hàng† ꜀sung ˢhai kök꜀-pò$^2$. | Go ramble hill roads, then able walk loose a-bit footsteps. |
| 12. | ꜀Shán lò$^2$ ꜀nán ꜀hàng†. | Hill roads hard to-walk-on. |
| 13. | ˢMò ts'oᵓ, ꜀t'in há$^2$ ˢyaú ᶜhò ꜀to ˢye ꜀nán tsò$^2$. | No mistake, heaven's under have very many things difficult to-do. |
| 14. | ꜀Yan yat꜀ kín$^2$ ˢye ꜀nán tsò$^2$, ᶜkòm ꜀yan-téi$^2$ ꜀shí-pít꜀ yiùᵓ tsò$^2$ lòᵓ | Because a [C.] thing difficult to-do, then people certainly must do (it). |
| 15. | ꜀M hai$^2$ ᶜkòm wá$^2$. [꜀me (*or* ꜀me)? | Not do so say. [eh? 31, 39 |
| 16. | ᶜKòm ˢnéi ᶜtím ᶜkong ꜀ni (*or* ꜀ni)? | Then you how say, eh? 53 |
| 17. | ˢNgo wá$^2$ k'am$^2$ ˢshöng ꜀shán, ˢwúi ling$^2$ ꜀shan-ᶜtsz chongᵓ-kín$^2$. | I say climb up hills can make (*or* cause) (the) body (to be) robust. |
| 18. | ˢNgo k'am$^2$ ꜀shán tsaú$^2$ kínᵓ ᶜhò | I climb hills then feel very tired. |
| 19. | Haú$^2$-꜀loí kínᵓ ᶜhò-ti ꜀lá. [kwúi$^2$. | Afterwards feel better, 21 |
| 20. | ꜀M hai$^2$: tai$^2$-yí$^2$ yat꜀ ꜀tò ꜀m kínᵓ ꜀tsing ꜀shan. [꜀che. | Not is; next day also not feel clear spirits. |
| 21. | ꜀Ai! ˢnéi ꜀m ꜀háng kwánᵓ ꜀che (*or* | Oh! You not walk accustomed only, 7 |
| 22. | ꜀Shán ᶜteng† yaú$^2$ ꜀löng lok꜀ | Hill top also cool, 32 |
| 23. | Há$^2$-ᶜtai ꜀tò ᶜkéi ꜀löng áᵓ. | Below also pretty cool. 2 |
| 24. | ˢNgo wá$^2$ ꜀m ꜀löng. [ᶜt'ing* | I say not cool. |
| 25. | ꜀Shán ᶜteng† ˢyaú ᶜhò ꜀to ꜀löng | Hill top have very many cool arbours. |
| 26. | Hööiᵓ ᶜch'e (*or* ᶜch'e) ꜀k'éi ꜀kon ᶜhò ꜀t'in ᶜhò ˢyün tò mong$^2$ tak꜀ tòᵓ. | Go hoist flagstaff (*i.e.* the staff where a flag is hoisted); (in) good weather, very far also see able reach. |
| 27. | Tái$^2$-ᶜk'oi* mong$^2$ tak꜀ tòᵓ ᶜKaú ꜀Lung ꜀sheng†. | Probably see able to-reach Kow Lung city. |
| 28. | ꜀M ᶜchí (kòmᵓ ˢyün). | Not only (so far). |
| 29. | ꜀Ch'aú-꜀wai ꜀tò hai$^2$ kínᵓ ᶜhoi máᵓ? | All-around also is see sea, eh? 35 |
| 30. | Hai$^2$ ꜀á, (*or* ꜀á), yaú$^2$ ᶜt'ai tak꜀ kínᵓ tái$^2$ ꜀to ᶜhoi-ᶜtò'. | Yes, 1, also looking able to-see great many islands. |
| 31. | ꜀Tò ᶜkéi ᶜhò ᶜt'ai kwáᵓ. | Also pretty good see, I-suppose, 18 |
| 32. | Hai$^2$ áᵓ, ᶜhò ᶜhò ᶜt'ai áᵓ. ˢNéi ˢshöng hööiᵓ ᶜt'ai ᶜhò áᵓ. | Yes 2, good good see 2. You up go see good. 2 |

## CONVERSATION 21ST.—MY TEACHER.

| | | |
|---|---|---|
| 1. | Do you know my teacher? | 你識我嘅先生唔識呀、 |
| 2. | I do not. | 唔識呀、 |
| 3. | You saw him here the other day. | 你先幾日喺呢處見佢嚟呀、 |
| 4. | I have seen him several times. | 我見佢幾勾吖、 |
| 5. | And you said you did not know him. | 你又話唔識佢嘅、 |
| 6. | That is true. I am not acquainted with him. | 冇錯 我唔識佢嘅、 |
| 7. | Well, you know who he is. | 你知到佢係乜誰喇、 |
| 8. | I do. | 知呀、 |
| 9. | Does he speak Cantonese properly? | 佢講正城話唔講呢、 |
| 10. | He speaks the correct Cantonese of the Western suburbs. | 佢講正西關話、 |
| 11. | There is no danger in copying him then. | 學翻佢講唔怕嘞、 |
| 12. | You need not fear to do so. If you copy him, you will be most correct. | 唔怕嘅、學翻佢講、就噲至正嘅咯、 |
| 13. | He does not pronounce his words as the dictionary has them. | 佢又唔照依字典講嘅囉噃、 |
| 14. | The dictionary is probably wrong then. He is not. | 字典大概有啲錯咯、佢唔錯嘅、 |
| 15. | I suppose his tones and the sounds of his words are right? | 佢個啲聲音啱啩、 |
| 16. | They are altogether so. | 啱嗮咯、 |
| 17. | He came to me highly recommended. | 佢嚟我處薦得好硬、 |
| 18. | A number of people recommended him, I suppose? | 好多人舉薦佢啩、 |
| 19. | They did: and his testimonials were first class. | 係吖、佢嘅薦紙係第一好嘅咯、 |
| 20. | You should be well satisfied with him. | 你個心應要好足至得咯 |
| 21. | I cannot find any fault with him | 我唔話得佢有乜錯嘅、 |
| 22. | What do you pay him a month? | 一個月俾幾多書金佢呢、 |
| 23. | Fifteen dollars a month. | 十五個銀錢個月、 |
| 24. | How many hours do you study a day? | 一日讀幾多點鐘書呢、 |

## CONVERSATION 21ST.—MY TEACHER.

| | | |
|---|---|---|
| 1. | ˢNéi shik˒ ˢngo-ke˒ ˓Sín-˓shángt ˓m shik˒ á˒? | You acquainted-with my (sign of poss.) teacher, not acquainted-with, eh? 2 |
| 2. | ˓M shik˒ á˒. | Not acquainted-with, 2 |
| 3. | ˢNéi ˓sín (or ˓sín) ʿkéi yat2 ʿhaí ˓ni shü˒ kín˒ ˢk'öü ˓lai á˒. | You before several days at this place seen him already, 2 |
| 4. | ˢNgo kín˒ ˢk'öü ʿkéi ˓wan ˓á (or ˓á). | I have-seen him several times, 1 [15 |
| 5. | ˢNéi yaú2 wá2 ˓m shik˒ ˢk'öü ke˒? | You yet said not acquainted-with him? |
| 6. | ˢMò ts'o˒, ˢngo ˓m shik˒ ˢk'öü ke˒. | No mistake, I not acquainted-with him. |
| 7. | ˢNéi ˓chi-tò˒ ˢk'öü haí2 mat˒ ʿshöü* | You know he is what person, 21 [15 |
| 8. | ˓Chi á˒. [˓lá (or ˓lá) | Know, 2 |
| 9. | ˢK'öü ʿkong cheng˒† ʿsheng*† ʿwá* ˓m ʿkong˓ ni (or ˓ni)? [ʿwá*. | He speak correct city words not speak, eh? 53 |
| 10. | ˢK'öü ʿkong cheng˒† ˓Saí-˓kwán | He speaks correct Western-suburbs words. |
| 11. | Hok2 ˓fán ˢk'öü ʿkong ˓m p'á˒ kwá˒? | Copy again his speaking no fear, eh? 18 |
| 12. | ˓M p'á˒ ke˒. Hok2 ˓fán ˢk'öü ʿkong, tsaú2 ʿwúi* chí˒ cheng˒† ke˒ lok˓. | No fear 15. Copy again him speaking, then can most correct, 15, 32 |
| 13. | ˢK'öü yaú2 ˓m chiú˒-˓yí tsz2-ʿtín ʿkong ke˒ lo˒ po˒. | He also not according-to dictionary speak, 15, 31, 60 |
| 14. | Tsz2-ʿtín taí2-ʿk'oi* ˢyaú ˓ti ts'o˒ lok˓; ˢk'öü ˓m ts'o˒ ke˒. | Dictionary probable have some mistakes, 32; he not mistake, 15 |
| 15. | ˢK'öü ko˒-˓ti ˓shengt ˓yam ˓ngám (or ˓ngám) kwá˒? | His those tones sounds right probably, Right altogether, 32 [eh? 18 |
| 16. | ˓Ngám (or ˓ngám) saí˒ lok˓. | He come-to my place recommended to-the-extent-of very strongly (*lit.* hard). |
| 17. | ˢK'öü ˓laí ˢngo shü˒, tsín˒ tak˒ ʿho ngáng2. | Very many persons recommended him probably? 18 |
| 18. | ʿHò ˓to ˓yan ʿköü-tsín˒ ˢk'öü kwá˒? | |
| 19. | Haí2 ˓á, (or ˓á) ˢk'öü-ke˒ tsín˒-ʿchí haí2 taí2 yat˒ ʿhò ke˒ lok˓. | Yes, 1. His testimonials are No. 1 good. 15, 32 |
| 20. | ˢNéi ko˒ ˓sam ˓ying-yiú˒ ʿhò tsuk˒ chí˒-tak˒ lok˓. [ts'o˒ ke˒. | Your [C] heart should-be very satisfied in-order-to-be right, 32 |
| 21. | ˢNgo ˓m wá2 tak˒ ˢk'öü ˢyaú mat˒ | I not say can (*i.e.*, I can't say) he has any mistakes, 15 |
| 22. | Yat˒ ko˒ yüt2 ʿpéi ʿkéi ˓to ˓shü-˓kam ˢk'öü ˓ni (or ˓ni)? | One [C.] month give how much book-gold him, eh? 53. |
| 23. | Shap2-ˢng ko˒ ˓ngan-ʿtsín* ko˒ yüt2. | Fifteen [C.] dollars a month. |
| 24. | Yat˒ yat2 túk2 ʿkéi ˓to ʿtím ˓chung ˓shü ˓ni (or ˓ni)? | One day read how many hours (of the) clock books, eh? 53 |

## CONVERSATION 21ST.—MY TEACHER.—(*Continued.*)

| | | |
|---|---|---|
| 25. | It depends upon whether I have time or not. | 睇吓有得閒冇呢、 |
| 26. | On the average how many a day? | 一日通扯計讀幾耐書呢、 |
| 27. | On an average about two or three hours a day. | 一日拉扯計讀有兩三點鐘書喇、 |
| 28. | That is pretty good. | 噉到幾好呀、 |
| 29. | I wish to learn quickly. | 我想快啲學、 |
| 30. | Do you find it easy, or difficult? | 你見易啵難學呢、 |
| 31. | At first it was very difficult: now it is not so difficult. | 大早見好難、而家呢、冇咁難咯、 |
| 32. | That follows as a matter of course. | 自然喇、 |

## CONVERSATION 22ND.—STREET HAWKERS.

| | | |
|---|---|---|
| 1. | What are those who sell things in the street called? | 個啲行街賣野叫做乜野呢、 |
| 2. | Hawkers. | 小販咯、 |
| 3. | There are a great many of them. | 都有好多咯、 |
| 4. | A great many. | 大多咯、 |
| 5. | How are they called? | 個啲小販一樣一樣點叫法呢、 |
| 6. | From the names of the things they sell. | 就賣個樣叫個樣啫 就照、依噉叫啫、 |
| 7. | How? | 點呢、 |
| 8. | Some sell fish, and they are called sellers of fish. | 有啲賣魚嘅、叫做賣魚嘅、 |
| 9. | Is that the way? | 噉嘅咩、 |
| 10. | Yes: how would it be but in that way? | 係哩、唔係噉點呢、 |
| 11. | Are there not some who have a name besides by which they are called? It seems to me as if I had heard some of the names. | 唔係有啲重有名叫法、我好似聽過啲名、 |
| 12. | What do you mean? Everybody has a name. | 點呀、人人都有名吖、 |
| 13. | I am not speaking of that | 唔係講個啲、 |

## CONVERSATION 21ST.—MY TEACHER.

| | | |
|---|---|---|
| 25. | ᶜT'ai ᶜha *ᶜyaü tak,-꜀han ᶜmò ꜀ni? | See a-bit have leisure not, just-is 53. |
| 26. | Yat, yat, t'ung-ᶜche kai' tük, ᶜkéi ᶜnoi* ꜀shü ꜀ni? | One day average reckoning read how long books, eh? 53. |
| 27. | Yat, yat, ꜀lau ᶜche kai' tuk, ᶜyaü ᶜlöng ꜀sam ᶜtım chung ꜀shü ꜀lá.? | One day average reckoning read have two three [C] hours books. 21. |
| 28. | ᶜKom tò ᶜkéi ᶜhò á'.? | So (is) also pretty good. 2. |
| 29. | ᶜNgo ᶜsöng fai'- ti hok,. | I wish quickly learn. |
| 30. | ᶜNéi kın' yi², péi² ꜀nán hok, ꜀ni? | You feel easy, or difficult to-learn eh? 53. |
| 31. | Tai²-ᶜtso kın' ᶜhò ꜀nan, ꜀yi- ka ꜀ni, ᶜmò kom' ꜀nán lok. | At-the-beginning feel very difficult, now then, 53, not so difficult. 32. |
| 32. | Tsz²-꜀yın ꜀la.? | Of course. 21. |

## CONVERSATION 22ND.—STREET HAWKERS.

| | | |
|---|---|---|
| 1. | Ko' -ti ꜀hang kái mái² ᶜye kiu' tsò² mat, ᶜye ꜀ni? | Those walk street sell things called what thing, eh? 53. |
| 2. | ᶜSiu ᶜfan* lok. | Hawkers, 32. |
| 3. | ꜀Tò ᶜyaü ᶜhò ꜀to lok. | Also have very many, 32. |
| 4. | Tái² ꜀to lok. | Great many, 32. |
| 5. | ꜀Ko-ti ᶜsiu-* ᶜfán yat, yöng² yat, yöng² ᶜtim kiu'-fát ꜀ni? | Those hawkers one kind one kind how called, eh? 53. |
| 6. | Tsaü² mái² ko' yöng² kiu' ko' yöng² ꜀che.? or Tsaü² chiu'-꜀yi ᶜkom kiu' ꜀che.? | Just sell that kind called that kind only, 7. or Just according-to so called only, 7. |
| 7. | ᶜTim ꜀ni? | How, eh? 53. |
| 8. | ᶜYaü ti mái² ᶜyü* ke', kiu' tsò² mai² ᶜyü* ke'. | Have some sell fish, 15, called to-be sell fish those-who, 15, (i.e. sellers of fish). |
| 9. | ᶜKom ke' ꜀me? | So, 15, eh? 39. |
| 10. | Hai² ꜀le; ꜀m hai² ᶜkom, ᶜtim ꜀ni? | Yes, 21, not is so, how, eh? 53. |
| 11. | ꜀M hai² ᶜyau ꜀ti chung² ᶜyau ᶜmeng*† kiu' fát? ᶜNgo ᶜhò-ᶜtsz ꜀teng† kwo' ti ᶜmeng*†. | Not is have some besides have names called? I very like heard over some names. |
| 12. | ᶜTim á'? ꜀Yan ꜀yan tò ᶜyaü ᶜmeng*† ꜀á.? | How. 2? Man man (i e. all men) also have names, 1. |
| 13. | ꜀M hai² ᶜkong ko'- ti. | Not am speaking-about that. |

2. Attention having already been sufficiently called to the fact that some of the finals, such as *ni* and *la* may be either ꜀ni or ꜀ni or ꜀lá or la, &c., instead of repeating them in every case a figure 2 will be put after them when both forms can be used.

## CONVERSATION 22ND.—STREET HAWKERS.—(*Continued.*)

| | | |
|---|---|---|
| 14. | Then I do not know what you are speaking about. | 噉、唔知你講乜野咯、 |
| 15. | There, there is one now. | 拏、而家都有個拏、 |
| 16. | Which one? | 邊個呀、 |
| 17. | That one who is walking past making a rattling sound; what is he called? He has a name, I remember that: but I am sorry to say I do not remember what it is. | 行過去嗰個呢、摝摝聲、叫乜野呢、佢係有個名叫嘅、我記得嘅咯、但可惜唔記得乜野名、 |
| 18. | Luk Kwú Lò. | 摝鼓佬咯、 |
| 19. | Ah! yes, that is it. | 呵係咯、冇錯咯、 |
| 20. | There now, that man with two baskets slung to a pole over his shoulder. That is he; what is he called? | 拏、嗰個擔兩個籮、嗰個係咯、人哋點叫法佢呢、 |
| 21. | Oh, he is a marine hawker. | 呵、佢係收買爛銅爛鐵嘅 |
| 22. | Now you know what I mean, tell me some other names. | 拏、你而家明白我個意思講出啲第二啲名過我聽、 |
| 23. | There are none. | 都冇叻、 |
| 24. | There are none? | 冇嘅、 |
| 25. | No: that is about all. | 冇、都係噉上下啫、 |
| 26. | Well, I heard a man say the other day he was a carrier of melons &c., and a seller of vegetables; what does that mean? | 我、先幾日我聽見一個人話、佢係做挑瓜賣菜、個句點解呢、 |
| 27. | Just that he was a hawker of melons and vegetables. | 即係喺街上擔瓜菜嚟賣啫、 |
| 28. | Is that the meaning of it? | 係噉嘅意思咩、 |
| 29. | Yes; and street coolies, who carry burdens, not those who carry chairs, are called ˓t'iú ˓fú. | 係哩、街咕哩擔野嘅呢、唔係抬轎嘅呢、係叫做挑夫、 |

易學廣東話

## CONVERSATION 22ND.—STREET HAWKERS.—(*Continued.*)

| | | |
|---|---|---|
| 14. | ᶜKóm, ꜀m ꜀chi ᶜnéi ᶜkong mat꜁ ᶜye lok . | Then not know you speaking-about what thing, 32. |
| 15. | ꜀Ná, ꜀yí-꜀ká tò ᶜyaú koᵓ, ꜀ná. | There, now also have [C.], there. |
| 16. | Pín koᵓ áᵓ ? | Which [C.] ? 2. |
| 17. | ꜀Háng kwoᵓ höüᵓ ᶜko koᵓ ꜀ni, luk꜁ luk꜁ ꜀sheng† : kiúᵓ mat꜁ ᶜye ꜀ni ?² ᶜK'öü hai² ᶜyaú koᵓ ᶜmeng*† kiúᵓ keᵓ. ᶜNgo kéiᵓ-tak꜁ keᵓ lok . tán² ᶜho-sik꜁ ꜀m kéiᵓ-tak꜁ ꜀mi ᶜye ᶜmeng*†. | Walk over gone that [C.] 53, rattle rattle sound: called what thing eh? 23. He does have [C.] name (by which he is) called, 15. I remember, 15, 32, but, it-is to-be pitied (i.e. alas) not remember what thing name. |
| 18. | Luk꜁-ᶜkwú-ᶜTsʼ lok . | Rattle-drum-fellow, 32. |
| 19. | ꜀O, hai² lok , ᶜmò tsʼoᵓ lok꜁ . | Oh, is, 32, no mistake, 32. |
| 20. | ꜀Ná, ᶜko koᵓ ꜀tám ᶜlöng koᵓ ꜀lo, ᶜko koᵓ ha.² lok : ꜀yan-téí² ᶜtím kiú-fát ᶜk'öü ꜀ni ?² | There that [C.] carry two [C.] baskets, that [C.] is, 32. People how call manner (i.e. In what way is he called ?) him eh ? 53. |
| 21. | ꜀O, ᶜk'öü hai² ꜀shaú ᶜmái lán² ꜀t'ung lán² t'it꜁ keᵓ. | Oh, he is collect (and) buy broken copper broken iron, 15. |
| 22. | ꜀Na, ᶜnéi ꜀yí-꜀ka ꜀ming pak꜁ ᶜngo koᵓ yíᵓ-szᵓ, ᶜkong ch'ut꜁ ti tai²-yí² ꜀ti ᶜmeng*† kwoᵓ ᶜngo ꜀t'eng†. | There you now understand my [C.] meaning, speak out some other names for me to-hear. |
| 23. | ꜀Tò ᶜmò ꜀á.² | Also none, 1. |
| 24. | ᶜMò keᵓ ? | None ? 15. |
| 25. | ᶜMò ; tò hai² ᶜkóm shöng²-ᶜhá* ꜀che² | None: also are about-that more-or-less [only, 7. |
| 26. | ꜀Ng, ꜀sín (*or better* ꜀sín) ᶜkéi yat꜁ ᶜngo ꜀t'eng†-kiúᵓ yat꜁ koᵓ ꜀yan wá² ᶜk'öü hai² tsò² ꜀t'iú ꜀kwá mái² ts'oiᵓ (*or* ᶜts'oi*): koᵓ köüᵓ ᶜtím ᶜkái ꜀ni ?² | Well, before several days I heard one [C.] man say, he was doing the business of carrying melons, selling vegetables; that sentence how explain eh ? 53. |
| 27. | Tsik꜁ hai² ᶜhai ꜀kái shöng² ꜀tám ꜀kwá ts'oiᵓ ꜀lai mái² ꜀che.² | Just is in street on carry melons (and) vegetables in-order-to sell only, 7. |
| 28. | Hai² ᶜkóm keᵓ yíᵓ-szᵓ ꜀me ?² | Is such, 15, (the) meaning, eh ? 39. |
| 29. | Hai² ꜀le² ; ꜀kái (*or* ꜀kái꜁) kwú-kéi, ꜀tám ᶜye keᵓ ꜀ni, ꜀m hai² ꜀t'oi ᶜkiú* keᵓ ꜀ni, hai² kiúᵓ-tsò² ꜀t'iú-꜀fú. | Yes, 24; street coolies carry things, 15, 53, not are carry chairs, 15, 53, are called ꜀t'iú-꜀fú. |

### CONVERSATION 22ND.—STREET HAWKERS.—(*Continued.*)

| | | |
|---|---|---|
| 30. | Well, I have learned several new words to-day. | 嗷，我今日都學幾句新話頭咯， |
| 31. | You, Sir, have learned a great deal of Chinese. | 先生都學倒好多唐話咯， |
| 32. | But there is a great deal to learn yet. | 都有好多未學到呀， |

### CONVERSATION 23RD.—WHAT SHALL I DO?

| | | |
|---|---|---|
| 1. | Alas! What an unfortunate affair! What shall I do? | 𠺝吔，弊傢伙咯，點做好呢， |
| 2. | What is the matter? | 乜野事幹呢， |
| 3. | I have lost every thing. | 唔見曬野咯， |
| 4. | How did that happen? | 點失𠱁呢， |
| 5. | I came from the country. | 我喺鄉下落嚟嘅， |
| 6. | Why did you come? | 落嚟做乜野呢， |
| 7. | I wanted to go abroad. | 想過埠， |
| 8. | Did you bring money with you? | 有帶銀嚟冇呀， |
| 9. | I borrowed from my friends as well as bringing my own. | 同朋友借添吖， |
| 10. | And have you lost it all? | 失曬囉咩， |
| 11. | I have. Hard lines. | 失曬咯，陰功咯， |
| 12. | How did you lose it? | 點失㗎呢， |
| 13. | I do not know. | 唔知咯， |
| 14. | You stupid fellow! What do you mean? | 咁𡃶頭嘅咩，唔見野都唔知點唔見嘅， |
| 15. | Yes, stupid, stupid, senseless. | 係咯，呆咯，呆咯，冇見識咯， |
| 16. | Speaking like that will not get it back again. | 係噉講都唔攞得翻嘅， |
| 17. | Yes, Sir, I know it. I am very stupid. | 係咯，先生，我知咯，我好愚蠢咯， |
| 18. | Well, tell me about it, I do not know how it happened. | 講過我聽，我唔知來歷嘅， |
| 19. | It was stolen by some one. | 俾人偷去咯， |

### CONVERSATION 22ND.—STREET HAWKERS.—*Continued.*

| | | |
|---|---|---|
| 30. | ᶜKóm. ᶝngo ꜀kam-mat$_2$ tò hok$_2$ ᶜkéi köüᵓ ꜀san wá$^2$-꜁tʻaú lok. | So. I to-day also learn several sentences (of) new words, 32. |
| 31. | ꜀Sin-꜀shàng† (*or short* a) tò hok$_2$ ᶜtò ᶜhò ꜀to ꜀Tʻong-ᶜwa* lok. | (You) Sir, also having-learned have-arrived-at very many Chinese words, 32. |
| 32. | Tò ᶝyaú ᶜhò ꜀to méi$^2$ hok$_2$ tòᵓ aᵓ. | Also have very many not-yet learned arrived-at. 2. |

### CONVERSATION 23RD.—WHAT SHALL I DO?

| | | |
|---|---|---|
| 1. | ꜀A-꜁yà! (*or* ꜀Aí-yà!). Paiᵓ-꜀kái-ᶜfo lok! ᶜTím tsò$^2$ ᶜhò ꜀ni?$^2$ | Dear-me! How-unfortunate! 32. How do good, eh? 53. |
| 2. | ꜀Mi ᶝye sz$^2$-kónᵓ ꜀ni?$^2$ | What thing business, eh? 53. |
| 3. | ꜁M kínᵓ saíᵓ ᶝye lok. | Not see (*consequently* lost) all things, 32. |
| 4. | ᶜTím shat꜄ saíᵓ ꜀ni?$^2$ | How lose all, eh? 53. |
| 5. | ᶝNgo ᶜhai ꜀höng-ᶜhá* lok$_2$ ꜁laí keᵓ. | I am country down come, 15. |
| 6. | Lok$_2$ ꜁laí tsò$^2$ ꜀mi ᶝye ꜀ni?$^2$ | Down come do what thing, eh? 53. |
| 7. | ᶜSöng kwoᵓ faú$^2$. | Wanted go-to ports (i.e. foreign ports). |
| 8. | ᶝYaú taíᵓ ᶜngan* ꜁laí ᶝmò aᵓ? | Have bring money come not, eh? 2. |
| 9. | ꜁Tʻung ꜁pʻang-ᶝyaú tséᵓ ꜀tʻím ꜀á.$^2$ | From friends borrow as well (as having some of my own). 1. |
| 10. | Shat꜄ saíᵓ loᵓ ꜀me.$^2$ | Lost all? 31, 39. |
| 11. | Shat꜄ saíᵓ lok. ꜀Yam ꜀kung lok. | Lost all, 32. Infernal work, 32. |
| 12. | ᶜTím shat꜄-ᶜcho ꜀ni?$^2$ | How lost, eh? 53. |
| 13. | ꜁M ꜀chí lok. | Not know, 32. |
| 14. | Kómᵓ tsʻaúᵓ-꜁tʻaú keᵓ ꜀me$^2$, ꜁m-kínᵓ ᶝye tò ꜁m ꜀chí ᶜtím ꜁m-kínᵓ keᵓ. | Such blockhead, 15, 39, lose things also not know how lost, 15. |
| 15. | Hai$^2$ lok, ꜁ngoi lok, ꜁ngoi lok, ᶝmò kínᵓ shik꜄ lok. | Yes, 32. stupid, 32, stupid, 32, no seeing knowing, 32. |
| 16. | Hai$^2$ ᶜkóm ᶜkong tò ꜁m ᶜlo tak꜄ ꜀fan keᵓ. | Do so speak also not get able back, 15. |
| 17. | Hai$^2$ lok, ꜀Sin-꜀shàng† (*or short* a), ᶝngo ꜀chí lok. ᶝNgo ᶜhò ꜁yü-ᶜchʻun lok. | Yes, 32. Sir, I know, 32. I very foolish, 32. |
| 18. | ᶜKong kwoᵓ ᶝngo ꜀tʻeng†, ᶝngo ꜁m ꜀chí ꜁loi-lik$_2$ keᵓ. | Speak over to-me to-hear, I not know history-of-it, 15. |
| 19. | ᶜPéi ꜁yan ꜀tʻaú (*or* tʻaú) tʻauᵓ lok. | Have by-some-one stolen away, 32. |

CONVERSATION 23RD.—WHAT SHALL I DO?—(*Continued.*)

20. How was it stolen? 點偷去呢、
21. That is what I do not know. 個啲我又唔知咯、
22. You will not tell me about it. 你唔講出嚟嘅呪、
23. How can I, when I do not know about it? 我點講得出嚟嘅、我都唔知點偷嘅、
24. But where did you put it? 你擠邊處嚟呢、
25. Did you have it on your person: where did you place it? 擠身上啵丟邊處嚟、
26. Oh! In a pillow box. 呵、俾個枕箱裝嚟嘅、
27. Where did you put the pillow box? 枕箱丟邊處呢、
28. At the head of my bed. 擠牀頭個處咯、
29. If you were in the room, who could steal it? 你喺房邊個偷得呢、
30. I went out only for a moment, and when I came back it was not there. The box and all was gone. 我行出去一陣呪、翻嚟唔喺個、連箱都唔喺處咯、
31. And you did not lock your door when you went out? 你行出去、又唔鎖埋門嘅、
32. I have newly arrived, and did not know that thieves would go in and steal. 我新嚟嘅、唔知賊噲行入去偷野嘅、

CONVERSATION 24TH.—JEWELLERY.

1. Chinese women are fond of wearing jewellery, are they not? 唐人女人中意戴首飾、係唔係呢、
2. Yes, women are very fond of jewellery. 係呀、女人好歡喜首飾、
3. Even poor women have bangles, both for their wrists and ankles. 貧窮女人都戴鈪嘅、手鈪又有、脚鈪又有、
4. Yes, every one has them. 係呀、個個都有呀、
5. I see every woman has earrings. 我睇見個個女人都係有耳環嘅、
6. It is absolutely necessary to wear earrings. 是必要戴耳環嘅、
7. What if they go without them? 冇戴點呢、
8. There is no such thing. 冇噉嘅、
9. Why not? 點解呢、

易學廣東話

## CONVERSATION 23RD.—WHAT SHALL I DO?—(*Continued.*)

| | | |
|---|---|---|
| 20. | ꜂Tim ꜀tʻau höü꜄ ꜀ni?ᶾ | How stolen away, eh? 53. |
| 21. | Ko꜄-꜆ti ꜃ngo yau꜅ ꜁m ꜀chí lok꜆. | That I also not know, 32. |
| 22. | ꜃Nei ꜁m ꜂kong chʻut꜆ ꜁lai ke꜄ chek꜆. | You not speak out come, 15, 7. |
| 23. | ꜃Ngo ꜂tím ꜂kong tak꜇ chʻut꜆ ꜁lai ke꜄? ꜃Ngo ꜆tò ꜁m ꜀chí ꜂tím ꜀tʻau ke꜄. | I how speak can out come? 15. I also not know how stolen, 15. |
| 24. | ꜃Nei ꜀chai ꜆pin shü꜄-꜁lai ꜀ni?ᶾ [꜁lai? | You put what place, eh? 53. |
| 25. | ꜀Chai ꜀shan shöng꜅ pei꜅ ꜀tiu ꜆pin shü꜄? | Put person on, or place what place at? |
| 26. | ꜁O, ꜂pei ko꜄ ꜂cham-꜆söng ꜀chong ꜁lai | Oh! Put [C.] pillow-box in at, 15. |
| 27. | ꜂Cham-꜆söng ꜀tiu ꜆pin shü꜄ ꜀ni?ᶾ [ke꜄. | Pillow-box place what place, eh? 53. |
| 28. | ꜀Chai ꜁chʻong-꜁tʻau ko꜄ shü꜄ lok꜆. | Put bed-head that place, 32. |
| 29. | ꜃Nei ꜂hai ꜂fong*, ꜆pin ko꜄ ꜀tʻau tak꜆ ꜀ni?ᶾ | You in room, who [C.] steal can, eh? 53. |
| 30. | ꜃Ngo ꜂hang*† chʻut꜆ höü꜄ yat꜆ chan꜅ chek꜆; ꜀fán ꜁lai ꜁m ꜂hai ko꜄. ꜁Lin ꜆söng ꜆tò ꜁m ꜂hai shü꜄ lok꜆. | I walk out go one short-space-of-time (꜂chan* would do) only, 7: back come not at place. With box also not at place, 32. |
| 31. | ꜃Nei ꜁hang† chʻut꜆ höü꜄, yau꜅ ꜁m ꜂so ꜁mai ꜁mún ke꜄? | You walk out go also not lock up door? 15. |
| 32. | ꜁Ngo ꜀san ꜁lai ke꜄, ꜁m ꜀chí tsʻak꜇ ꜃wüi ꜁hang† yap꜇ höü꜄, ꜀tʻau ꜃ye ke꜄. | I newly come, 15, not know thieves could walk in, go steal things, 15. |

## CONVERSATION 24TH.—JEWELLERY.

| | | |
|---|---|---|
| 1. | ꜁Tʻong-꜁yan ꜃nöü-꜂yan* ꜀chung-yi꜄ tai꜄ ꜂shau-shik꜆, hai꜅ ꜁m hai꜅ ꜀ni?ᶾ | Chinese women like to-wear jewellery, is not is, eh? 53. |
| 2. | Hai꜅ a꜄, ꜃nöü-꜂yan* ꜂hò ꜀fun-꜂hei ꜂shau-shik꜆? | Is, 2, women very happy (*or* pleased-with) jewellery. |
| 3. | ꜁Pʻan-꜁kʻung ꜃nöü-꜂yan* tò tai꜄ ꜂ak* ke꜄: ꜂shau-꜂ak* yau꜅ ꜃yau; kök꜆-꜂ak* yau꜅ ꜃yau. | Poor women even wear bangles, 15: bracelets have also: anklets have also. [Note that *ak* is always put into a rising tone in conversation.] |
| 4. | Hai꜅ a꜄. ko꜄ ko꜄ ꜆tò ꜃yau a꜄. | Yes, 2. every [C] also have, 2. |
| 5. | ꜃Ngo ꜂tʻai-kin꜄ ko꜄ ko꜄ ꜃nöü-꜂yan* tò hai꜅ ꜃yau ꜃yi-꜂wan* ke꜄. | I see every [C] woman even does have earrings, 15. |
| 6. | Shi꜅-pit꜆ yiu꜄ tai꜄ ꜃yi-꜂wan* ke꜄. | Certainly must wear earrings, 15. |
| 7. | ꜃Mò tai꜄ ꜂tím ꜀ni?ᶾ | Not wear how, eh? 52. |
| 8. | ꜃Mò ꜂kom ke꜄. | Not so, 15. |
| 9. | ꜂Tím ꜂kái ꜀ni?ᶾ | How explain, eh? 53. |

## CONVERSATION 24TH.—JEWELLERY.—(*Continued.*)

| | |
|---|---|
| 10. It is considered impolite to be without them. | 噉冇、就算係失禮人咯、 |
| 11. I see the seamstress at the street corner has a silver ring on. Is that a marriage ring? | 我見坐街邊嗰個補衫婆戴個銀戒指、係嫁個陣時戴嘅嗎、 |
| 12. No; the Chinese have no such custom. | 唔係、唐人冇噉規矩、 |
| 13. Why does she have it on? | 做乜戴呢、 |
| 14. Because she chooses to do so. | 中意戴唄、 |
| 15. If she were rich, I suppose she would wear a gold one. | 佢係財主、大概戴個金嘅咯、 |
| 16. Certainly. | 有錢嘅、是必係喇、 |
| 17. And what is that thing like a long pin in her hair? | 佢頭髮嗰支野、係似長針、個支係乜野呢、 |
| 18. A Chinese hair-pin. | 係簪咯、 |
| 19. That is also made of silver. | 個支都係銀整嘅、 |
| 20. Hers is. | 佢個支係喇、 |
| 21. Are there other kinds? | 有第二樣嘅咩、 |
| 22. There are a great many kinds. | 有好多樣嘅咯、 |
| 23. Tell me what they are. | 講出嚟俾我聽喇、 |
| 24. Some are jade-stone ones; some are made of gold. | 有啲係玉石嘅、有啲金整嘅、 |
| 25. They would be very pretty. | 噉、好睇咯、 |
| 26. Some are really very pretty. | 有啲實首好睇嘅、 |
| 27. What is that ornament which Chinese women wear at the back of their coiffure? | 唐人女人、喺髻中間戴嗰個係乜野呢、 |
| 28. It is a hair-press. | 嗰個係髻押咯、 |
| 29. I suppose these different articles are what women generally wear. What jewellery do men have? | 大概個啲幾樣野係女人平常戴嘅、男人戴乜首飾呢 |
| 30. What men wear is not called jewellery (shaú shik) by the Chinese. | 男人所戴嘅、唐人唔係叫做首飾、 |

## CONVERSATION 21TH.—JEWELLERY.—(*Continued.*)

| | | |
|---|---|---|
| 10. | ᶝMò ; ᶜkòm tsaú² sün' haí² shat, ᶝlaí (꜀yan) lok꜀. | No ; then just considered to-be lose politeness-towards (people), 32. |
| 11. | ᶝNgo kín' ᶝt'so ꜀kái (*it may be* ꜀kái) ꜀pín ᶜko ko' ᶜpò ꜀shám ᶜp'o*taí' ko' ᶜngan* kaí'-ᶜchí. Haí² kà' ko' chan²-ᶜshí*taí' ke' ᶝmá ? | I see sitting street side that [C.] mend jacket woman wear [C.] silver ring. Is marry that time wear ? 15, 38. |
| 12. | ꜀M haí² ; ꜀T'ong-꜀yan ᶝmò ᶜkòm ꜀k'waí-ᶜköü. | Not is ; Chinese have-not such custom. |
| 13. | Tsò²-mat, taí' ꜀ni ?² | Why wear, eh ? 53. |
| 14. | ꜀Chung-yí' taí' chek,. | Like wear only, 7. |
| 15. | ᶝK'öü haí² ꜀ts'oí-ᶜchü, taí²-ᶜk'oí* taí' ko' ꜀kam ke' lok꜀. | She were rich, probably wear [C.] gold, 15, 32. |
| 16. | ᶝYaú ᶜts'in* ke', shí²-pít, haí² ꜀lá.² | Have money, 15, certainly is, 21. |
| 17. | ᶝK'öü ꜀t'aú-fát, ᶜkò ꜀chí ᶝye, haí² ts'z' ꜀ch'öng ꜀cham ; ko' ꜀chí haí² mat, ᶝye ꜀ni ?² | Her hair that [C.] thing, is like long pin ; that is what thing, eh ? 53. |
| 18. | Haí² ꜀tsám lok꜀. | Is (Chinese) hair-pin, 32. |
| 19. | Ko'-꜀chí ꜀tò haí² ᶜngan* ᶜching ke'. | That [C.] also is silver made, 15. |
| 20. | ᶝK'öü ko'-꜀chí haí² ꜀lá.² | Hers that [C.] is, 21. |
| 21. | ᶝYaú taí²-yí² yöng² ke' ꜀me ?² | Have other kinds ? 15, 39. |
| 22. | ᶝYaú ᶜhò ꜀to yöng² ke' lok꜀. [꜀lá.² | Have very many kinds, 15, 32. |
| 23. | ᶜKong ch'ut, ꜀laí ᶜpéi ᶝngo ꜀t'eng† | Speak out come give me to-hear, 21. |
| 24. | ᶝYaú꜀ti haí² yuk, ᶜshek* ke' ; ᶝyaú ꜀ti ꜀kam ᶜching ke'. | Have some are jade stone, 15 ; have some gold made, 15. |
| 25. | ᶜKòm ᶜhò ᶜt'aí lok꜀. | So good looking, 32. |
| 26. | ᶝYaú ꜀ti shat,-ᶜshaú ᶜhò ᶜt'aí ke'. | Have some really good looking, 15. |
| 27. | ꜀T'ong-꜀yan ᶝnöü-ᶜyan*, ᶜhaí kaí' ꜀chung-꜀kán taí' ᶜko-ko' haí² mat, ᶝye ꜀ni ?² | Chinese women at coiffure middle wear that is what thing, eh ? 53. |
| 28. | ᶜKo-ko' haí² kaí'-ᶜát* lok꜀. | That is coiffure-press, 32. |
| 29. | Taí²-ᶜk'oí*ko'-꜀ti ᶜkéi yöng² ᶝye, haí² ᶝnöü-ᶜyan* ꜀p'ing-꜀shöng taí' ke'. ꜀Nám-ᶜyan* taí' mat, ᶜshaú-shik, ꜀ni ?² | Probably those several kinds-of things are woman commonly wear, 15. Men wear what jewellery, eh ? 53. |
| 30. | ᶝNám-꜀yan ᶜsho taí' ke', ꜀T'ong-꜀yan ꜀m haí² kiú' tsò² ᶜshaú-shik,. | Males what wear, 15, Chinese not do call jewellery. |

### CONVERSATION 24TH.—JEWELLERY.—*(Continued.)*

| | | |
|---|---|---|
| 31. | But I have seen Chinese with diamond rings on. | 我都見過唐人男人戴鑽石戒指、 |
| 32. | Quite so; but what men put on is not called (shau shik) jewellery. | 冇錯、但係男人戴嘅、唔係叫做首飾、 |

### CONVERSATION 25TH.—I DO NOT KNOW WHAT TO DO.

| | | |
|---|---|---|
| 1. | Well, I do not know what to do. | 都唔知點筭好咯、 |
| 2. | What about? | 爲乜事呢、 |
| 3. | I have done my best, and he is not pleased with it. | 我做到至好咯、佢都唔中意咯、 |
| 4. | You said he was not pleased with it; who is 'he'? | 你話佢唔中意呀、佢係乜人呢、 |
| 5. | A customer. | 人客咯、 |
| 6. | What did he tell you to do? | 佢叫你做乜野呀、 |
| 7. | This picture. | 呢幅畫咯、 |
| 8. | Have you finished it? | 做完唔曾呀、 |
| 9. | Yes; I finished it, and he said he would not have it. | 做完咯、佢話唔要喎、 |
| 10. | What fault did he find with it? | 佢話有乜野錯呢、 |
| 11. | Everything is wrong about it. | 乜野都錯卵、 |
| 12. | Everything is not wrong about it surely. | 樣樣都唔係錯嚉、 |
| 13. | That is what he says. | 佢係噉話、 |
| 14. | Oh, I do not believe it. | 唉、我唔信咯、 |
| 15. | He is very troublesome. | 佢好懨尖嘅、 |
| 16. | Doubtless he wanted a good picture. | 大概佢要一幅好畫、 |
| 17. | Certainly. And did not I want to paint a good picture too; and is not that a good one? | 定喇、我都唔想畫幅好畫咩、個幅畫唔係好咩、 |
| 18. | Yes; there is good work in that. | 係呀、個幅好手勢、 |
| 19. | Then how is it he does not want it? | 噉、點解佢唔要呢、 |
| 20. | Did he give you a photograph to copy? | 佢係俾個相過你抄係唔係呢、 |
| 21. | Yes; this is the photograph. | 係哩、呢幅相係呀、 |
| 22. | What did he say was wrong? | 佢話有乜錯呢、 |
| 23. | He said the mouth was not the same as in the photograph. | 佢話個口唔同喎、 |

### CONVERSATION 24TH.—JEWELLERY.—(Continued.)

| | | |
|---|---|---|
| 31. | ᶜNgo ₒtò kín꜄-kwo꜄ ꜁T'ong-꜁yan ꜁nám-꜁yan* tái꜄tsün꜄-shek꜆kái꜄-ᶜchí. | I also have-seen Chinese men wear diamond rings. |
| 32. | ᶜMò ts'o꜄; tán꜅-hai꜅꜁nám-꜁yan* tái꜄ ke꜄, ꜁m hai꜅ kíú꜄-tsò꜅ ᶜshaú-shik꜆. | No mistake, but males wear, 15, not is called head ornaments. |

### CONVERSATION 25TH.—I DO NOT KNOW WHAT TO DO.

| | | |
|---|---|---|
| 1. | ₒTò ꜁m ꜁chí ᶜtím sün꜄ ᶜhò lok꜆. | Even not know how consider good, 32. |
| 2. | Wai꜅ mat꜆ sz꜅ ꜁ni ? | About what thing, eh? 53. [32. |
| 3. | ᶜNgo tsò꜅ tò꜄ chí꜄-ᶜhò lok꜆. ᶜk'öü ₒtò ꜁m ꜁chung-yí꜄ lok. | I have-done to-best, 32, he also not pleased, |
| 4. | ᶜNéí wá꜅ 'ᶜk'öü ꜁m ꜁chung-yí꜄ á꜄;' 'ᶜk'öü' hai꜅ mat꜆-꜁yan* ꜁ni ? | You say 'he not pleased', 2, 'he' is what man? 53. |
| 5. | ꜁Yan-hák꜆ lok꜆. | Customer, 32. |
| 6. | ᶜK'öü kín꜄ ᶜnéí tsò꜅ ꜁mi-ᶜye á꜄ ? | He told you do what thing? 2. |
| 7. | ꜁Ni fuk꜆ wá* lok꜆. | This [C.] picture, 32. |
| 8. | Tsò꜅ ꜁yün ꜁m ꜁ts'ang á꜄ ? [ᶜwá. | Do finished, (i e. done) not yet, eh? 2. |
| 9. | Tsò꜅ ꜁yün lok꜆, ᶜk'öü wá꜅ ꜁m yíú꜄ | Done finished, 32, he says not want, so-he-says, 63. |
| 10. | ᶜK'öü wá꜅ ᶜyaú ꜁mi-ᶜye ts'o꜄ ꜁ni ? | He said have what thing wrong, eh? 53. |
| 11. | ꜁Mi-ᶜye ₒtò ts'o꜄ ᶜwo. | Everything even wrong so-he-says, 64. |
| 12. | Yöng꜅ yöng꜅ ₒtò ꜁m hai꜅ ts'o꜄ kwá꜄. | Everything even not is wrong probably, 18. |
| 13. | ᶜK'öü hai꜄ ᶜkòm wá꜅. | He does so say. |
| 14. | ꜁Ai, ᶜngo ꜁m sun꜄ lok꜆. | Oh! I not believe, 32. |
| 15. | ᶜK'öü ᶜhò ꜁yím-꜁tsím ke꜄. [wá*. | He very troublesome, 15. |
| 16. | Tái꜅ ᶜk'oí* ᶜk'öü yíú꜄ yat꜆ fuk꜆ ᶜhò | Probably he wanted a [C.] good picture. |
| 17. | Ting* ꜁lá, ᶜngo ₒtò ꜁m ᶜsöng wák꜆ fuk꜆ ᶜhò wá* ꜁me; ko꜄ fuk꜆ wá* ꜁m hai꜅ ᶜhò ꜁me ? | Certainly, 21, I also not want paint [C.] good picture, eh, 39; that [C.] picture not is good, eh? 39. |
| 18. | Hai꜅ á꜄, ko꜄ fuk꜆ ᶜhò ᶜshaú-shai꜄ á꜄. | Is 2, that [C.] good hand-work, 2. |
| 19. | ᶜKòm, ᶜtím ᶜkái ᶜk'öü ꜁m yíú꜄ ꜁ni ? | Then how explain he not want, eh? 53. |
| 20. | ᶜK'öü hai꜅ ᶜpéí ko꜄ ᶜsöng* kwo꜄ ᶜnéí ꜁ch'áú; hai꜅ ꜁m hai꜅ ꜁ni ? | He did give a [C] photograph (or rather likeness) to you to-copy; is not is, eh? |
| 21. | Hai꜅ ꜁le, ꜁ni fuk꜆ ᶜsöng* hai꜅ á꜄. | Did, 24, this [C.] likeness is, 2. [53. |
| 22. | ᶜK'öü wá꜅ ᶜyaú mat꜆ ts'o꜄ ꜁ni ? | He say have what wrong, eh? 53. |
| 23. | ᶜK'öü wá꜅ ko꜄ ᶜhaú ꜁m ꜁t'ung ᶜwá. | He said the mouth not same so-he-said, 63. |

1.—The learner by this time should know that the rising variant tones into which different words are put are not always the same. In future therefore they will be distinguished as described in the Preface.

## CONVERSATION 25TH.—I DO NOT KNOW WHAT TO DO.—(*Continued.*)

| | |
|---|---|
| 24. Well, there is a little difference; you look. | 噲 爭啲唔同喇，你睇吓， |
| 25. Only a little. | 的咁多啫， |
| 26. But that makes him have a sorrowful—almost a bitter expression, whereas the photograph has a pleasant expression. | 但噉令個畫形容憂愁，爭啲苦容，睇個相嘅面，係有個笑容呢， |
| 27. Well, I will alter that. | 噉，我改過喇， |
| 28. What else was wrong? | 重有乜野錯呢， |
| 29. He told me the hair was to be yellow, golden he said; and now I have done it, he says it is not good. | 佢話個啲頭髮要黃色，金噉嘅色話，我而家做呢，佢又話唔啱話， |
| 30. Ask him to get you some of the hair and show you. | 問佢攞啲個啲頭髮嚟睇吓， |
| 31. He said he could not, as the person lived at home in England. | 佢話唔攞得話，個人喺英國祖家住嘅， |
| 32. I will ask him by and by, and see if he has any friends here whose hair is about the same colour. There was nothing else wrong, except some trifles, which I can easily alter. | 我等問吓佢睇吓佢或喺呢處有啲朋友有頭髮都係咁上下嘅冇呀，冇乜第二樣錯，硬爭幾箇有少少錯啫，個啲我好易改過嘅， |

## CONVERSATION 26TH.—GOING TO PEKING.

| | |
|---|---|
| 1. I am thinking of getting leave to go to Peking. | 我想告假上去北京， |
| 2. Oh, indeed! Are you going up for an examination? | 呀，係咩，係上去考試唔係呀， |
| 3. No; I want to go up and see the place. | 唔係，想上去睇地方啫， |
| 4. It is a nice place. | 地方都幾好呀， |

## CONVERSATION 25TH.—I DO NOT KNOW WHAT TO DO.—*(Continued.)*

24. ꜀Na, ꜀cháng ꜀ti ꜀m ꜀t'ung ꜀lá,² ˁnéi ᶜt'ai ˁhá. — There, wanting a-little not same, 21, look a-bit.

25. Tik꜇ kòmᵓ ꜀to ꜀che.² — A-little so much only, 7.

26. Tán² ᶜkòm ling² koᵓ wá²* ꜀ying-꜀yung ꜀yaú-꜀shaú, ꜀cháng ꜀ti ᶜfú-꜀yung. ᶜT'ai koᵓ ᶜsöng* keᵓ mín², hai² ˁyaú koᵓ síúᵓ-꜀yung-꜀ni. — But so causes the (*or* C.) picture expr ssion sorrowful, wanting a-little bi··er expression. Look that (*or* C.) likeness' face, is have a smiling-expression, 53.

27. ᶜKòm, ˁngo ᶜkoi kwoᵓ ꜀lá.² — Then, (i.e. that being case,) I change over,

28. Chung² ˁyaú mat꜇-ˁye ts'oᵓ ꜀ni ?² — Besides have what thing wrong, eh? 53. [21.

29. ˁK'öü wá² koᵓ-꜀ti ꜀t'aú-fát yúᵓ ꜀wong shik꜇, ꜀kam ᶜkòm keᵓ shik꜇ ˁwá, ˁngo ꜀yi-꜀ká tsò² ꜀ni, ˁk'öü yaú² wá² ꜀m ꜀ngám ˁwá. — He said that hair want yellow colour, gold such colour, so-he-said, 63, I now done 53, he further said not right, so-he-said, 61.

30. Man² ˁk'öü ᶜlo ꜀ti koᵓ-꜀ti ꜀t'aú fát ꜀lai ᶜt'ai ˁhá. — Ask him get some-of that head's hair come look a-bit.

31. ˁK'öü wá² ꜀m ᶜlo tak꜇ ˁwá: koᵓ ꜀yan ᶜhai ꜀Ying Kwok꜇ ᶜts'o ꜀ká chüᵓ keᵓ. — He said not get can, so-he-said: that man in English country ancestral home live, 15.

32. ˁNgo ᶜtang ꜀há man² ˁk'öü, ᶜt'ai ˁhá ˁk'öü wák꜇ ᶜhai ꜀ni shüᵓ ˁyaú ti ꜀p'ang-ˁyaú ˁyaú ꜀t'aú-fát tò hai² kòmᵓ shöng² ˁhá keᵓ ˁmò áᵓ. ˁMò-mat꜇ tai²-yi² yöng² t'soᵓ, ngáng² ꜀cháng ᶜkéi tát ˁyaú ᶜshiú ᶜshiú tsoᵓ ꜀che,² koᵓ-꜀ti ˁngo ᶜhò yi² ᶜkoi tak꜇ kwoᵓ keᵓ. — I wait a-bit ask him, look a-bit he perhaps at this place have some friends have hair also is so up down's, 15, (i.e. about) not, 2. No much other kind wrong, only wanting several places have little little mistake only, 7, those I very easily alter over, 15.

## CONVERSATION 26TH.—GOING TO PEKING.

1. ˁNgo ᶜsöng koᵓ-káᵓ ˁshöng höüᵓ Pak꜇-꜀king. — I wish apply-for-leave up go Peking.

2. ꜀Á, hai² ꜀me ?² Hai² ˁshöng höüᵓ ᶜháú-shiᵓ ꜀m hai² áᵓ ? — Ah! Is eh? 39. Is up go examinations not is, eh? 2.

3. ꜀M hai²; ᶜsöng ˁshöng höüᵓ ᶜt'ai téi²-꜀fong ꜀che.² — Not is; wish up go see place only, 7.

4. Téi²-꜀fong ꜀tò ᶜkéi ᶜhò áᵓ. — Place also pretty good, 2.

## CONVERSATION 26TH.—GOING TO PEKING.—*(Continued.)*

| | | |
|---|---|---|
| 5. | I have some friends who went up last year, and they have asked me to come up and see them. | 我有啲朋友舊年上去，佢哋吽我上去見佢， |
| 6. | That would be nice: it would be well to go up. | 好吖，上去都好呀， |
| 7. | I do not know whether I can go. | 唔知去得唔去得呢， |
| 8. | Why not? | 做乜唔去得呀， |
| 9. | There is no one to do the work. | 冇人做工夫呀， |
| 10. | Cannot you get a friend to do it for you? | 唔吽得朋友同你做咩， |
| 11. | I am afraid there is no one willing to do it. | 我慌冇人肯做呀， |
| 12. | I suppose you will go up by steamer. | 大概搭火船上去喇， |
| 13. | Yes, it will be best to go by steamer. | 係哩，搭火船好嘅， |
| 14. | What is the passage money. | 幾多水脚呢， |
| 15. | I do not know. | 唔知呢， |
| 16. | Even to Shanghai it is some tens of dollars. | 去上海都係幾十文嘅， |
| 17. | At Shanghai you change into another steamer and go to Tientsin. | 喺上海轉過第二隻火船去天津， |
| 18. | And what at Tientsin? | 去到天津點呢， |
| 19. | You go by railway. | 坐火車咯， |
| 20. | And before the railway was made? | 舊時呢，未有火車路呢， |
| 21. | You could do as you liked. You could go in a cart, or in a boat, as there is a small river there. | 由得你點去都得呀，坐車又得，坐艇又得，有條小河喺個處， |
| 22. | I have heard it is hard work riding in those carts. | 我聽聞個啲車都幾難坐咯， |
| 23. | Yes, so they say. | 係話， |
| 24. | The roads are not very good, are they? | 路又唔係十分好，係唔係呢， |
| 25. | You are right. And you are jolted about in the cart. | 冇錯，坐車又踊高又踊低， |

## CONVERSATION 26TH.—GO TO PEKING.—(*Continued.*)

| | | |
|---|---|---|
| 5. | ᶜNgo ᶜyaú ti ꜀p'ang-ᶜyaú kaú[2] ꜀nin* ᶜshöng höüᵓ, ᶜk'öü-tei[2] kiúᵓ ᶜngo ᶜshöng höüᵓ kinᵓ ᶜk'öü. | I have some friends last year up went, they call me up go see them. |
| 6. | ᶜHò ꜀á,[2] ᶜshöng höüᵓ tò ᶜhò áᵓ. | Good, 1, up go also good, 2. |
| 7. | ꜀M ꜀chí höüᵓ takᵓ ꜀m höüᵓ takᵓ ꜀ni.[2] | Not know go able not go able, 53. |
| 8. | Tsò[2] matᵓ ꜀m höüᵓ takᵓ áᵓ. | Do what not go able, eh ? 2. |
| 9. | ᶜMò ꜀yan tsò[2] ꜀kung-꜀fú áᵓ. | No man do work, 2. |
| 10. | ꜀M kiúᵓ takᵓ ꜀p'ang-ᶜyaú ꜀t'ung ᶜnéi tsò[2] ꜀me ?[2] | Not call can friend for you do, eh ? 39. |
| 11. | ᶜNgo ꜀fong ᶜmò ꜀yan ᶜhang tsò[2] áᵓ. | I afraid no man willing do, 2. |
| 12. | Taí[2]-ᶜk'oi* tàp ᶜfo-꜀shün ᶜshöng höüᵓ ꜀lá.[2] | Probably by steamer up go, 21. |
| 13. | Hai[2] ꜀le,[2] tàpₒ ᶜfo-꜀shün ᶜhò ᶜke*. | Yes, 24, by steamer good, 15. |
| 14. | ᶜKéi to ᶜshöü-kök ꜀ni ?[2] | How much fare (*lit.* water-foot), eh ? 53. |
| 15. | ꜀M ꜀chí ꜀ni. | Not know, 53. |
| 16. | Höüᵓ Shöng[2]-ᶜhoi tò hai[2] ᶜkéi shapₒ ꜀man keᵓ. | Go Shanghai also is several tens-of dollars, 15. |
| 17. | ᶜHai Shöng[2]-ᶜhoi ᶜel ün* kwoᵓ tai[2]-yí[2] chekₒ ᶜfo-꜀shün höüᵓ ꜀T'in-꜀tsun. | At Shanghai change another [C.] steamer go Tien-tsin. |
| 18. | Höüᵓ tòᵓ ꜀T'ín-꜀tsun ᶜtim ꜀ni ?[2] | Go to Tien-tsin how, eh ? 53 (i.e. when you get to Tien-tsin). |
| 19. | ᶜTs'o*† ᶜfo-꜀ch'e lok . | Sit fire-carriage, 32. |
| 20. | Kaú[2] ꜀shí* ꜀ni ?[2] Méi[2] ᶜyaú ᶜfo-꜀ch'e-lò[2] ꜀ni ?[2] | Old time eh ? 53. Not yet have fire-carriage-road, eh ? 53. |
| 21. | Yaú[2]-takᵓ ᶜnéi ᶜtím höüᵓ ꜀tò takᵓ áᵓ. Ts'o*† ꜀ch'e yaú[2] takᵓ, ᶜts'o*† ᶜt'eng† yaú[2] takᵓ. ᶜYaú ꜀t'iú ᶜsiú ꜀ho ᶜhai koᵓ shüᵓ. | Allow you how go also can, 2. Sit carriage also can; sit boat also can. Have [C.] small river at that place. |
| 22. | ᶜNgo ꜀t'eng†-꜀man koᵓ-ti ꜀ch'e ꜀tò kéiᵓ ꜀nán ᶜts'o*† lokₒ. | I have-heard those carriages also pretty difficult to-sit. 32. |
| 23. | Hai[2] ᶜwá. | Is-so, it-is-said, 61. |
| 24. | Lò[2] yaú[2] ꜀m hai[2] shapₒ ꜀fan ᶜhò; hai[2] ꜀m hai[2] ꜀ni ?[2] | Road also not is ten parts good; is not is [i.e. Is this the case ?], eh ? 53. |
| 25. | ᶜMò ts'oᵓ, ᶜts'o*† ꜀ch'e yaú[2] ᶜyung ꜀kò, yaú[2] ᶜyung ꜀tai. | No mistake, sit carriage jump up also jump down. |

### CONVERSATION 26TH.—GOING TO PEKING.—(*Continued.*)

| | |
|---|---|
| 26. And your bones ache with the shaking you get. | 郁得咁多、成身個啲骨都痛咯、 |
| 27. The best way is to take a mattress with you. | 至好就帶埋牀褥呀、 |
| 28. What do you do with the mattress? | 使個牀褥做乜野呢、 |
| 29. You sit on it, and it is not so bad. | 使嚟坐咯、噉冇咁辛苦呀、 |
| 30. That is a good idea. | 噉、好法子咯、 |
| 31. How long will it take you? | 要幾耐去得(到呢、 |
| 32. Oh! two or three weeks. | 兩三個禮拜喇、 |

### CONVERSATION 27TH.—SHOPS.

| | |
|---|---|
| 1. When I take a walk I see a number of different shops. Probably each kind has a name. | 我行街見好多樣舖頭、大概每樣有名嘅、 |
| 2. It has. | 有嘅、 |
| 3. Those at the corners, which have a great many things for sale, such as provisions, brooms, clogs, besides many odds and ends— | 角頭個啲賣好多樣野嘅、食物呀、掃把呀、屐呀、重有好多摣摣雜雜噉嘅野、 |
| 4. Those are called grocer's, or chandler's shops. | 個啲叫做雜貨舖咯、 |
| 5. What do they call the shops where cloth is sold? | 賣布個啲舖叫做乜野呢、 |
| 6. The shops in which cloth is sold by the piece are called piece goods shops. | 賣成疋嘅叫做疋頭舖、 |
| 7. And what are those which do not sell by the piece called? | 唔係一疋一疋賣嘅呢、 |
| 8. Those are drapers. | 蘇杭舖咯、 |
| 9. There are shops which sell paper; what are those? | 有啲舖賣紙嘅、個啲呢、 |
| 10. Stationers.' | 紙料舖咯 〔係呢、 |
| 11. Chinese call everything a shop do they not? | 唐人樣樣都叫做舖、係唔 |

## CONVERSATION 26TH.—GOING TO PEKING.—(*Continued.*)

| | | |
|---|---|---|
| 26. | Yuk tak kom to, sheng† shan ko-ti kwat to t'ung lok. | Move can so much, whole body those bones also sore, 32. |
| 27. | Chí-hò tsaú tái mái ch'ong yuk* höü á. | Best then take along mattress go, 2. |
| 28. | Shaí ko ch'ong-yuk* tsò mi-ye ni? | Use the mattress do what thing, eh? 53. |
| 29. | Shaí lai ts'o*† lok. Kòm mò kòm san-fú á. | Use in-order-to sit-on, 32, so not so painful, 2. |
| 30. | Kòm hó fát-tsz lok. | So good plan, 32. |
| 31. | Yiú kéi noi* höü tak (tò) ni? | Want how long go able to, eh? 53. |
| 32. | Löng sám ko lai-pai lá. | Two three [C.] weeks, 21. |

## CONVERSATION 27TH.—SHOPS.

| | | |
|---|---|---|
| 1. | Ngo háng† kai kín hò to yöng p'ò-t'aú*. Tai-k'oi* múi yöng yaú meng* ke. | I walk street see very many kinds-of shops. Probably each kind has name, 15. |
| 2. | Yaú ke. | Has, 15. |
| 3. | Kok-t'aú ko-ti mái hò to yöng ye ke, shik-mat á, sò-pá á, k'ek á, chung yaú hó to láp-láp tsáp tsáp kòm ke ye— | Corners those sell very many kinds things, 15, eatables, 2, brooms, 2, clogs, 2, besides have very many odds and ends such things— |
| 4. | Ko-ti kiú-tsò tsáp-fo p'o* lok. | Those called miscellaneous-goods shop, 32. |
| 5. | Mái pò ko-ti p'ò kiú-tsò mat-ye ni? | Sell cloth those shops called what thing, eh? 53. |
| 6. | Mái sheng† p'at ke kiú-tsò p'at-t'aú p'ò*. | Sell whole piece, 15, called piece-goods shop. |
| 7. | M hai yat p'at yat p'at mái ke ni? | Not is one piece, one piece sell, 15, eh? 53. Drapers, 32. |
| 8. | Sò-hong-p'ò* lok. | Have some shops sell paper, 15, those, eh? 53. |
| 9. | Yaú ti p'ò mái chí ke, ko-ti ni? | Stationers' shops, 32. |
| 10. | Chí-lún* p'ò* lok. | |
| 11. | T'ong-yan yöng yöng tò kiú-tsò p'ò, hai m hai ni? | Chinese every kind also call shops; is not is eh? 53. |

## CONVERSATION 27TH.—SHOPS.—*(Continued.)*

| | |
|---|---|
| 12. A great many are called shops. There are also a great many called tim; those in a large way of business are called hongs. | 有好多叫做鋪、都有好多叫做店呀、大生意嘅叫做行、 |
| 13. Which are called tims? | 邊啲叫做店呢、 |
| 14. Washermen's shops, inns, lodging houses, wine shops, luncheon rooms. | 洗衣店、歇店、客店、酒店、晏店、 |
| 15. Are there any other names? | 有第啲名咩、 |
| 16. Oh! yes, there are. | 都有吖、 |
| 17. What are they? | 點叫呢、 |
| 18. There are pawn shops, large and small, tea houses, roast and dried meat shops. | 有當鋪、有小押、有茶居、有燒臘鋪、 |
| 19. What do they sell in the roast and dried meat shops? | 燒臘鋪賣乜野呢、 |
| 20. They deal in roast and dried meats. | 賣燒味、臘味咯、 |
| 21. Which are roast meats, and which dried meats? | 邊啲叫做燒味、邊啲叫做臘味呢、 |
| 22. Roast meats are roast pork, roast duck, and roast goose. | 燒味就係燒猪呀、燒鴨呀、燒鵝呀、 |
| 23. And the others? | 個啲呢、 |
| 24. Are you speaking of dried meats? | 係講臘味唔係呀、 |
| 25. Yes. | 係哩、 |
| 26. Those are dried ducks, dried sausages, and dried rats. | 個啲就係臘鴨呀、臘腸呀、臘老鼠呀、 |
| 27. Dear me! Have you eaten rats? | 唉吔、你食過老鼠未呀、 |
| 28. I do not eat them. | 我唔食嘅、 |
| 29. How is that? | 點解呢、 |
| 30. They are filthy things. | 骯髒鮓、 |
| 31. Who do eat them? | 邊啲人食呢、 |

## CONVERSATION 27TH.—SHOPS.—(*Continued.*)

| | | |
|---|---|---|
| 12. | Yaú 'hò to kiú'-tsò$^2$ p'ò'; tò yaú 'hò to kiú'-tsò$^2$ tím' á'; táí$^2$ shäng†-yi' ke' kiú'-tsò$^2$* hong*. | Have very many called shops; also have very many called shops, 2; large business, 15, called hongs. |
| 13. | Pin-ti kiú'-tsò$^2$ tím' ni?$^2$ | Which called tím (shops), eh? 53. |
| 14. | 'Sai-yi tím', hit-tím', hák-tím', 'tsaú tím', áu' tím'. | Washermen's, inns, lodging houses, wine shops, luncheon rooms. |
| 15. | Mo tai$^2$-ti meng* me?$^2$ | No other names, eh? 39. |
| 16. | Tò yaú á.$^2$ | Also have, 1. |
| 17. | 'Tim kiú' ni?$^2$ | How called, eh? 53. |
| 18. | Yaú tong'-'p'ò', yaú 'siú át$_5$*, yaú ch'á köü, yaú shíú láp 'p'ò.* | Are pawn-shops, are small pawns, are tea houses, are roast (and) dried shops. |
| 19. | Shíú láp 'p'ò,* máí$^2$ mat, 'ye ni?$^2$ | Roast (and) dried shops sell what things, eh? 53. |
| 20. | Máí$^2$ shíú méí$^5$*, láp$_2$-méí$^5$* lok. | Sell roast dainties, dried dainties, 32. |
| 21. | Pin-ti kiú'-tsò$^2$ shíú méí$^5$*; pin-ti kiú'*-tsò$^2$ láp$_2$ méí$^5$* ni?$^2$ | Which called roast titbits; which called dried delicacies, eh? 53. |
| 22. | Shíú méí$^5$* tsaú$^2$ hai$^2$ shíú chü á', shíú áp$_3$* á', shíú ngo* á'. | Roast relishes just are roast pig, 2, roast duck, 2, roast goose, 2. |
| 23. | Ko'-ti ni?$^2$ | Those, eh? 53. |
| 24. | Hai$^2$ 'kong láp$_2$ méí$^5$* m hai$^2$ á'? | (You) are speaking dried relishes not are, eh? 2. |
| 25. | Hai$^2$ le.$^2$ | Yes, 24. |
| 26. | Ko'-ti tsaú$^2$ hai$^2$ láp$_2$ áp$_3$* á', láp$_2$ ch'öng* á', láp$_2$ 'lò'shü á'. | Those just are dried ducks, 2, dried sausages, 2, dried rats, 2. |
| 27. | Ai-yá (*or* Ai-yá) 'néí shik$_2$ kwo' 'lò-'shü méí$^2$ á'? | Dear me! You eat have rats not-yet, eh? 2. |
| 28. | Ngo m shik$_2$ ke'. | I not eat. 15. |
| 29. | 'Tim 'káí ni. | How explain, eh? 53. |
| 30. | Yim' lá'-'chá. | Consider dirty. |
| 31. | Pin-ti yan (*or* yan*) shik$_2$ ni?$^2$ | Who man eat, eh? 53. |

## CONVERSATION 27TH.—SHOPS.—(*continued.*)

| | |
|---|---|
| 32. Some people eat them. Respectable people do not as a rule eat rats, cats, or dog; as regards the three, respectable people eat dog's flesh more than they would eat rats or cats. Country people are most accustomed to eat dog's flesh. | 有啲人食嘅、斯文家冇幾何食老鼠呀、貓呀、狗呀、講個三樣、斯文人食狗肉多過食老鼠呀、貓呀、至多與食狗肉嘅係鄉下人咯、 |

## CONVERSATION 28TH.—FRUITS.

| | |
|---|---|
| 1. What fruit is there in the market? | 街市有乜菓子呢、 |
| 2. There is not much (*or* no) fruit: there will be more a few months later. | 冇乜菓子咯、遲幾個月噲多啲咯、 |
| 3. When I went out this morning, I saw persimmons, plantains, and carambolas: and I also saw a hawker with some really beautiful custard apples, but he had sold them. | 我今朝出街見柿、蕉、共楊桃、又見一個小販、有啲實手好番荔枝、但係佢賣嗮咯、 |
| 4. I told him to bring some to-morrow. He said he would: and if those he brings to-morrow are as good as those he had to-day, I will certainly buy them. | 我吽佢聽日摔啲嚟、佢話摔嚫、佢聽日或摔今日咁好嘅嚟、我是必買咯、 |
| 5. When shall we get Amoy pumeloes? I like them very much. The Siamese ones are not as good, and the Cantonese are very bad. | 幾時有厦門波碌呢、我好中意食囉、暹羅嘅冇咁好、本地: 又好吟嘅、 |
| 6. They will come in season by and by, they are not ripe yet, when they come in there will be a great many. | 遲吓致有、而家唔曾熟、一有就有好多、 |
| 7. And the pine apples, are there none? | 波羅呢、冇囉咩、 |
| 8. There are none; there have been none for some time. Are there any pine apples now? Why no! | 冇咯、冇曉好耐咯、而家重有波羅咩、唉、冇嘅、 |

## CONVERATION 27.—SHOPS.—(*continued.*)

32. ʿYaú ͵ti ͵yau shik₂ keʾ, ͵sz-͵man kaʾ ʿmò ʿkéi ͵ho shik₂ ʿlò-ʿshü áʾ, máú áʾ, ʿkaú áʾ: ʿkong koʾ ͵sam yöng², ͵sz-͵mán ͵yau shik₂ ʿkaú-yuk₂ ͵to kwoʾ shik₂ ʿlo-ʿshü áʾ, maú áʾ; chiʾ-͵to ͵hing shik₂ ʿkaú-yuk₂ keʾ hai² ͵höng-ʿha ͵yan lok .

Have some people eat, 15, respectable families not very often eat rats, 2, cats, 2, dogs, 2 : speaking-about those three kinds, respectable people eat dog's flesh more than eat rats, 2, cats, 2 : Most like eat dog's flesh, 15, are country people, 32.

## CONVERSATION 28TH. —FRUITS.

1. ͵Kai ʿshi ʿyau mat₃ ʿkwo-ʿtsz ͵ni ?²

Street market have what fruit, eh? 53.

2. ʿMò mat₃ ʿkwo-ʿtsz lok , ͵chʿi ʿkéi koʾ yüt₂ ʿwúi ͵to-͵ti lok .

Not much fruit, 32, later several months will-be more, 32.

3. ʿNgo ͵kam ͵chiú chʿut₃ ͵kai (*or* kái) kínʾ tsʿzʾ*, tsui, kung² ͵yöng-͵tʿòʾ. Yaú² kínʾ yat₃ koʾ ʿsiú-ʿfanʾ ʿyaú ti shat₃-ʿshaú ʿhò ͵fán-lai²-chí, tan²-hai² ʿkʿöü mai² ʿcho lok .

I this morning went-out street saw persimmons, plantains, and carambolas. Besides saw one [C.] hawker had some really good custard-apples, but he had-sold (sign of p. t.) (them), 32.

4. ʿNgo kmʾ ʿkʿöü ͵tʿing-yat₂ ͵ning ti ͵lai. ʿKʿöü wa² ͵ning ʿwá. ʿKʿöü ͵tʿing-yat₂ wak₂ ͵ning ͵kam-yat₂ kómʾ ʿhò keʾ ͵lai, ʿngo ͵shi-pit₃ ʿmái lok .

I told him to-morrow bring some come. He said he-would-bring, said-he, 61. He to-morrow if brings to-day so good, 15, I certainly buy, 32.

5. Kéiʾ ͵shi* ʿyaú Ha²-͵mun ͵po-luk₃ ͵ni ?² ʿNgo ʿhò ͵chung-yiʾ shik₂ káʾ. Tsʿimʾ-͵lo* keʾ ʿmò kómʾ ʿhò : ʿpún-teiʾ* yaú² ʿhò ͵yai keʾ.

What time have Amoy pumeloes, eh ? 53. I much like to-eat, 14. Siamese's (15) not so good : native also very inferior, 15.

6. ͵Chʿi-ʿhá chiʾ ʿyaú, ͵yi-͵ká ͵m-͵tsʿang shuk₂. Yat₃ ʿyaú, tsaú² ʿyaú ʿhò ͵to.

Later before have, now not yet ripe. Once have, then have great many.

7. ͵Po-͵lo ͵ni, ʿmò ͵lo ͵me ?²

Pineapples, eh ? 53. None, 31, eh ? 39.

8. ʿMo lok ; ʿmò-͵hiú ʿhò noi² lok . ͵Yi-͵ka chung² ʿyaú ͵po-͵lo ͵me ?² ͵Ai ! ʿmò keʾ.

None, 32 : none have very long, 32. Now still have pineapples, eh 39 ? Why! there-are-none, 15.

## CONVERSATION 28TH.—FRUITS.—(*Continued.*)

| | | |
|---|---|---|
| 9. | Do you like li-chees? There were very few this year. | 你中意荔枝唔呢、今年好少吖、 |
| 10. | Yes, very much. I like the third crop li-chees best; the stones are small, and the fruit is sweet. | 係、好中意呀、我至中意黑葉荔枝、核又細、肉又甜、 |
| 11. | I do not like lung-ngans, they are tasteless things. | 龍眼我唔中意、冇味道嘅、 |
| 12. | Yes; they are rather tasteless; but the Chinese like them. | 係、都係淡嘅、唐人中意食、 |
| 13. | How many kinds of plantains are there? | 有幾多樣蕉呢、 |
| 14. | There are several kinds: there are large and small; there are cheap and dear; there are good and bad. | 有好幾樣、有大有細、有平有貴、有好有醜、 |
| 15. | I am not speaking of that. Are there not several different names for plantains? | 我唔係講個啲吖、蕉唔係有幾樣名咩、 |
| 16. | Oh! you are speaking about the names of plantains. | 啊、你講蕉名咩、 |
| 17. | Certainly. What else am I talking about I should like to know? | 定喇、唔係講蕉名、係講乜野呢、 |
| 18. | Plantains have several names: there are the dragon tusks, the fragrant plantains, the large plantains, the over-the-mountains plantains; and there are several other kinds. | 蕉有幾樣名嘅、有龍牙蕉、有香蕉、有大蕉、有過山香、重有幾樣添、 |
| 19. | When I went out this morning, I saw some red fruit like a fowl's egg. What fruit was it? | 我今朝出街見啲菓係紅色嘅、好似雞蛋噉嘅、係乜野菓呢、 |
| 20. | Those you saw were small persimmons. Those you have had the last few days are the large persimmons. | 你見個啲係雞心柹、呢幾日你食個啲係牛心柹、 |
| 21. | What fruit is there in winter? | 天冷有乜菓子呢、 |
| 22. | There are loose-skinned oranges, coolie oranges, kat-tsais, mandarin oranges, and Tientsin grapes. | 有柑、有橙、有桔仔、有硃砂桔、有天津葡提子、 |

## CONVERSATION 28TH.—FRUITS.—(*Continued.*)

| | | |
|---|---|---|
| 9. | ᶜNei ꜀chung-yiˀ ᶜlai-꜀chi ꜀m ꜀ni ?² Kam ꜀nin ᶜhò ᶜshiú ꜀á.² | You like li-chees not, eh ? 53. This year very few. 1. |
| 10. | Hai²; ᶜhò ꜀chung-yiˀ á². ᶜNgo chiˀ ꜀chung-yiˀ hak꜀-yíp꜀* lai²-꜀chi; wat꜀ yaú² saiˀ, yuk꜀ yaú² ꜀t'ím. | Yes; much like, 2. I most like black-leaved li-chees, stones also small, fruit also sweet. |
| 11. | ꜀Lung-ᶜngán* ᶜngo ꜀m ꜀chung-yiˀ. ᶜMò méi²-tò² keˀ. | Lung-ngans I not like. No taste, 15. |
| 12. | Hai², tò hai² tám⁵*† keˀ. ꜀T'ong-꜀yan ꜀chung-yiˀ shik꜀. | Yes, also are tasteless, 15. Chinese like to-eat. |
| 13. | ᶜYaú ᶜkéi ꜀to yöng² ꜀tsiú ꜀ni ?² | Have how many kinds plantains, eh ? 53. |
| 14. | ᶜYaú ᶜhò ᶜkéi yöng²: ᶜyaú tai² ᶜyaú saiˀ; ᶜyaú ꜀p'eng† ᶜyaú kwai; ᶜyaú ᶜhò ᶜyaú ᶜch'aú. | Have a-good few sorts: have large have small: have cheap have dear; have good have bad. |
| 15. | ᶜNgo ꜀m-hai² ᶜkong koˀ-ti ꜀a. ꜀Tsiú ꜀m-hai² ᶜyaú ᶜkéi yöng² ꜀meng* ꜀me ?² | I not speak-about these, 1. Plantains not have several kinds names, eh? 39. |
| 16. | ꜀O ! (*or* ꜀O!) ᶜNei ᶜkong tsiú ᶜmeng ꜀me ?² | Ah ! You speak-about plantains' names, eh ? 39. |
| 17. | Ting² ꜀lá.² ꜀M-hai² ᶜkong ꜀tsiú ꜀meng*, hai² ᶜkong mat꜀ ᶜye ꜀ni?² | Certainly, 21. (If) not speak-about plantains' names, are speaking-about what thing, eh ? 53. |
| 18. | ꜀Tsiú ᶜyaú ᶜkéi yöng² ꜀meng* keˀ. ᶜYaú ꜀lung-꜀ngá tsiú, ᶜyaú ꜀höng ꜀tsiú, ᶜyaú tai² tsiú, ᶜyaú ᶜkwo-꜀shán (*or* ꜀shán) ꜀höng. Chung² ᶜyaú ᶜkéi yöng² ꜀t'im. | Plantains have several kinds names, 15. Have dragon-tooth plantains, have fragrant plantains, have large plantains, have over the-hills fragrant (plantains). Besides have several sorts more. |
| 19. | ᶜNgo ꜀kam ꜀chíu ch'ut꜀ ꜀kai (*or* ꜀kai) kínˀ ti ᶜkwo, hai² ꜀hung shik꜀ keˀ, ᶜhò ᶜts'z ꜀kai tán⁵* ᶜkòm keˀ. Hai² ꜀mi ᶜye ᶜkwo ꜀ni ?² | I this morning go-out street saw some fruit was red colour, 15, very like fowl's egg so, 15. Is what thing fruit, eh ? 53. |
| 20. | ᶜNei kínˀ koˀ-꜀ti hai² ꜀kai-꜀sam ts'z⁵*. ꜀Ni ᶜkéi yat꜀ ᶜnei shik꜀ koˀ-꜀ti hai² ꜀ngaú-꜀sam ts'z.⁵* | You saw those are chicken-heart persimmons. These few days you eat those were cow's-heart persimmons. |
| 21. | ꜀T'ín ᶜláng ᶜyaú mat꜀ ᶜkwo-ᶜtsz ꜀ni ?² | Weather cold, have what fruit, eh ? 53. |
| 22. | ᶜYaú ꜀kòm, ᶜyaú ꜀ch'áng*, ᶜyaú k'at꜀-ᶜtsai, ᶜyaú ꜀chü-꜀shá-kat꜀, ᶜyaú ꜀T'in-꜀tsun ꜀p'ò-꜀t'ai-ᶜtsz. | Have loose-skinned-oranges, have coolie-oranges, have kat-tsais, have mandarin-oranges, have Tien-tsin grapes. |

## CONVERSATION 28TH.—FRUITS.—(*Continued.*)

| | | |
|---|---|---|
| 23. | Are pears good to eat? There are two kinds, are there not, or are they both the same? | 沙梨雪梨好食嗎、係有兩樣係唔係呢、抑或同埋一樣呢、 |
| 24. | There are two kinds: the süt-léis and the shá-léis: they are not the same. | 有兩樣、雪梨還雪梨。沙梨還沙梨、係唔同嘅、 |
| 25. | Where do they come from? | 喺邊處嚟嘅呢、 |
| 26. | The süt-léis come from Tien-tsin, and the shá-léis grow here. | 雪梨喺天津嚟嘅、沙梨係本處出嘅、 |
| 27. | Besides there are whampees, guavas, roseapples, and a great many other kinds. | 另外有黄皮、番石榴、葡萄菓、重有好多別樣添、 |
| 28. | Where is the fruit market? Is it inside or outside the city? I have never seen it. | 菓欄喺邊處呢、喺城內𠻹城外呢、我唔曾見呀、 |
| 29. | Shall I take you to see it now? It is worth seeing. There are not only fruits, but many other things there as well. | 我而家帶你去睇吓、好好睇呀、唔止擺菓子賣、重有好多樣野、 |
| 30. | There are walnuts, and chestnuts, and pickles, and sweetmeats, and toys. | 有核桃、有風栗、有酸菓、有甜菓、有公仔、 |
| 31. | Where do all these things come [from? | 咁多野喺邊處嚟呢、 |
| 32. | Some from the North, and some from Tien-tsin, and some the South, and some from foreign countries. | 有啲喺北邊嚟嘅、有啲喺天津嚟嘅、有啲喺南邊嚟嘅、又有啲喺外國嚟嘅、 |

## CONVERSATION 29TH.—THE TYPHOON.

| | | |
|---|---|---|
| 1. | I think there will be a strong blow to-night. | 我估今晚打大風咯、 |
| 2. | I do not think so. | 我估冇、 |
| 3. | Oh, yes, there will be. | 有嘅、 |

## CONVERSATION 28TH.—FRUITS.—(*Continued.*)

| | | |
|---|---|---|
| 23. | ꜀Shá-꜁léi*, süt꜆-꜁léi ꜂hò shik꜇ ꜃má ? Hai2 ꜃yaú ꜃löng yöng2, hai2 ꜁m hai2 ꜀ni,* ? Yik꜇-wák꜇ ꜁t'ung-꜁mái yat꜆ yöng2 ꜀ni ?* | Russet-pears, Tientsin (*lit* snowy)-pears good to-eat, eh? 53. Is-it that-there-are two kinds, is not is, eh ? 53. Or is together one sort, eh ? 53. |
| 24. | ꜃Yaú ꜃löng yöng2: süt꜆-꜁léi ꜁wán süt꜆-꜁léi, ꜀shá-꜁léi ꜁wán ꜀shá-꜁léi (*or the* ꜁léi *in all four may be in the variant tone.*) Hai2 ꜁m ꜁t'ung ke꜄.* | There-are two kinds : Tientsin-pears belong Tientsin pear (variety); russet-pear belong russet-pear (variety). They-are not same, 15. |
| 25. | ꜂Hai ꜀pín shü꜄ ꜁lai ke꜄ ꜀ni ? | From what place come, eh ? 15, 53. |
| 26. | Süt꜆-꜁léi ꜂hai ꜀T'in-꜀tsun ꜁lai ke꜄*; ꜀shá-꜁léi* (*or* ꜁léi) hai2 ꜂pún shü꜄ ch'ut꜆ ke꜄. | Tientsin-pears from Tientsin come, 15 ; russet-pears at this place produced. 15 |
| 27. | Ling2-ngoi2 ꜃yaú ꜁wong-꜁p'éi*, ꜀fán-shek꜇-꜁laú*, ꜁p'ò-꜁t'ò-꜂kwo, chung2 ꜃yaú ꜂hò ꜀to pit꜇ yöng2* ꜀t'ím. | Besides have whampees, guavas, roseapple fruit, besides have very many other kinds more. |
| 28. | ꜂Kwo-꜀lán ꜂hai ꜀pín shü꜄ ꜀ni? ꜂Haí ꜁sheng†noi2, péi2 ꜁sheng†ngoi2 ꜀ni?* ꜃Ngo ꜁m ꜁ts'ang kín꜄ á꜄. | Fruit-market at what place, eh ? 35. In city interior, or city outside, eh ? 35. I not yet seen, 2. |
| 29. | ꜃Ngo ꜁yí-ká tái꜄ ꜃néi höü꜄ ꜂t'aí á? ꜂Hò hò ꜂t'aí á꜄. ꜁M ꜂chí ꜂pái ꜂kwo-꜂tsz mái2, chung2 ꜃yaú ꜂hò ꜀to yöng2 ꜃ye. | I now take you go see, eh? 1. Very good see, 2. Not only spread fruit for-sale, besides have very many kinds of-things. |
| 30. | ꜃Yaú hòp꜇-꜁t'ò*, ꜃yaú fung-lut꜇*, ꜃yaú ꜀sün-꜂kwo, ꜃yaú ꜀t'ím-꜂kwo, ꜃yaú ꜀kung-꜂tsai. | Have walnuts, have chestnuts, have pickles, have sweetmeats, have toys. |
| 31. | Kòm꜄ ꜀to ꜃ye ꜂hai ꜀pín-shü꜄ ꜁lai ni?* | So many things from what place come, eh ? 53. |
| 32. | ꜃Yaú ꜀ti ꜂hai pak꜆ pín2 ꜁lai ke꜄: ꜃yaú ꜀ti ꜂hai ꜀T'in-꜀tsun ꜁lai ke꜄: ꜃yaú ꜀ti ꜂hai ꜁Nám-pín2 ꜁lai ke꜄; yau2 ꜃yaú ꜀ti ꜂hai ngoi2 kwok꜆ ꜁lai ke꜄. | Have some from North side come, 15; have some from Tientsin come, 15 ; have some from South side come, 15 ; yet have some from outside countries come, 15. |

## CONVERSATION 29TH.—THE TYPHOON.

| | | |
|---|---|---|
| 1. | ꜃Ngo ꜂kwú ꜀kam-꜃mán ꜂tá tái2 ꜀fung lok꜇. | I think to-night strike big wind. 32. |
| 2. | ꜃Ngo ꜂kwú ꜃mò. | I think not. |
| 3. | ꜃Yaú ke꜄. | Have, 15. |

## CONVERSATION 29TH—THE TYPHOON.

| | | |
|---|---|---|
| 4. | Why do you say that? The sky does not look windy. | 做乜你噉講呢，天色都唔似有風噉嘅， |
| 5. | One reason is that it has been intensely hot for the last few days. | 一樣呢就係因近來呢幾日天好熱， |
| 6. | It is summer now, and it is always hot. | 現時係天熱嘅時候，時時都係熱嘅咯， |
| 7. | It has been hotter than usual. | 重熱過平常， |
| 8. | There is no certainty about the heat. The weather is changeable. | 佢啲冇定嘅，一時熱一時凍都有嘅， |
| 9. | But for a few days before a typhoon it is usually very hot. Is that not the case? | 唔曾打風颶之前個幾日常時天都係好熱嘅，係唔係呢， |
| 10. | It is. | 係哩， |
| 11. | Besides the sky has been highly coloured at sunset for several nights. | 另外呢幾晚，日落個時，天變好多色水咯， |
| 12. | Oh, indeed! | 係咩， |
| 13. | Have you not seen it? | 你冇見咩， |
| 14. | I have not noticed it. | 我冇覺眼， |
| 15. | The thermometer is high, and the barometer is low. | 寒暑針高，風雨針低， |
| 16. | How high has the thermometer risen? | 寒暑針升幾多度呢， |
| 17. | It has risen six degrees. | 升六度咯， |
| 18. | And the barometer has risen as well. | 風雨針都升高咯， |
| 19. | No, indeed! When there is rain or wind, the barometer falls. | 唔係，有風雨風雨針就跌低咯， |
| 20. | I said so. | 我都係噉講呀， |
| 21. | No; you said it had risen. | 你唔係噉講，你話升高， |
| 22. | Oh! I only made a mistake. | 啊，我講錯啫， |
| 23. | There is also another way of knowing a typhoon is coming. | 重有個緣故所以知有風颶嚟， |
| 24. | Is there? What is it? | 係咩，有乜緣故呀， |
| 25. | There is a telegram. | 有電線咯， |

## CONVERSATION 29TH.—THE TYPHOON.—(*Continued.*)

| | | |
|---|---|---|
| 4. | Tsò$^2$ mat, ꜃néi ꜂kòm ꜂kong ꜁ni ?$^2$ ꜁T‘ín shik, ꜀tò ꜁m ꜃t‘sz ꜃yaú ꜀fung ꜂kòm ke’. | Do what you so speak, eh, 53? Heaven's colour also not like have wind so. 15. |
| 5. | Yat, yöng$^2$ ꜁ni, tsaú$^2$ hai$^2$ ꜀yau kan$^2$-꜁loí* ꜁ni ꜂kéi yat$_2$ ꜀t‘ín ꜂hò yít$_2$. | One thing, 53, just is because near come these several days heaven very hot. |
| 6. | ꜁Yín-꜁shí hai$^2$ ꜀t‘ín yít$_2$ ke’ ꜁shí haú$^2$, ꜁shí ꜁shí ꜀tò hai$^2$ yít$_2$. | At present is heaven's hot season, always also is hot, 15, 32. |
| 7. | Chung$^2$ yít$_2$ kwo’ ꜁p‘íng-꜁shöng. | More hot than usual. |
| 8. | Ko’-꜀tí ꜃mò ting$^2$ ke’. Yat, ꜁shí yít$_2$, yat, ꜁shí tung’ ꜀tò ꜃yaú ke’. | That no certainly, 15. One time hot, one time cold, also have, 15. |
| 9. | ꜁M ꜀ts‘ang ꜂tá ꜀fung-kaú$^2$ ꜀chí ꜁ts‘ín, ko’ ꜂kéi yat$_2$, ꜁shöng-꜁shí ꜀t‘ín ꜀tò hai$^2$ ꜂hò yít$_2$ ke’; hai$^2$ ꜁m hai$^2$ ꜁ni ?$^2$ | Not yet strike typhoon before those several days, always heaven also is very hot, 15, is not is, eh? 53. |
| 10. | Hai$^2$ ꜀lé.$^2$ | Yes, 24. |
| 11. | Ling$^2$-ngoi$^2$ ꜁ni ꜂kéi ꜃mán, yat, (*or* yat$_2$*) lok$_o$ ko’ ꜁shí, ꜀t‘ín pín’ ꜂hò ꜀to shik,-꜂shöü lok$_o$. | Besides these several nights, sun down that time, heaven change very many colours, 32. |
| 12. | Hai$^2$ ꜁me ?$^2$ | Yes, eh? 39. |
| 13. | ꜃Néi ꜃mò kín’ ꜁me ?$^2$ | You not see, eh? 39. |
| 14. | ꜃Ngo ꜃mò kok$_o$ ꜃ngán. | I not notice. |
| 15. | ꜁Hòn-꜂shü-꜀cham ꜀kò; ꜀fung-꜃yü-꜀cham ꜀taí. | Thermometer high; barometer low. |
| 16. | ꜁Hòn-꜂shü-꜀cham ꜀shing ꜂kéi ꜀to tò$^2$ | Thermometer rise how many degrees, |
| 17. | ꜀Shing luk$_2$ tò$^2$ lok$_o$. [꜁ni ?$^2$ | Rise six degrees, 32. [eh? 53. |
| 18. | ꜀Fung-꜃yü-꜀cham ꜀tò ꜀shing ꜀kò lok$_o$. | Barometer also rise high, 32. |
| 19. | ꜁M hai$^2$, ꜃yaú ꜀fung ꜃yü, ꜀fung-꜃yü-꜀cham tsaú$^2$ tít$_o$ ꜀taí lok$_o$. | Not is, have wind rain, barometer then fall low, 32. |
| 20. | ꜃Ngo ꜀tò hai$^2$ ꜂kòm ꜂kong á’. | I also am so speaking, 2. |
| 21. | ꜃Néi ꜁m hai$^2$ ꜂kòm ꜂kong. ꜃Néi wá$^2$ ꜀shing ꜀kò. | You not did so speak. You said rise high. |
| 22. | O$^2$! ꜃ngo ꜂kong ts‘o’ ꜀che.$^2$ | Oh! I spoke wrong only, 7. |
| 23. | Chung$^2$ ꜃yaú ko’ ꜁yün-kwú’ ꜂sho-꜃yi ꜀chí ꜃yaú ꜀fung-kaú$^2$ ꜁laí. | Besides have a reason wherefore know have typhoon come. |
| 24. | Hai$^2$ ꜁me? ꜃Yaú mat, ꜁yün-kwú’ á’ ? | Yes, eh 32? Have what reason, eh? 2. |
| 25. | ꜃Yaú tín$^2$-sín’ ꜁laí. | Have telegram come. |

## CONVERSATION 29TH.—THE TYPHOON.

| | |
|---|---|
| 26. A telegram! I do not understand. What has a telegram to do with a typhoon? Does a typhoon come if there is a telegram? Then telegrams must be rather dangerous. | 電線、我唔曉得咯、電線關風颶乜事呀、有電線嗽就有風颶咩、嗽電線都幾險咯、 |
| 27. What are you speaking about? There is no danger in telegrams. | 你講乜呀、電線唔係危險呀、 |
| 28. I was only joking. | 我講笑啫、 |
| 29. But I am not. | 我唔係呀、 |
| 30. What are you not doing? | 你唔係乜野呀、 |
| 31. Jesting. It is a reality. When a typhoon is coming, notice is sent to people elsewhere in order that they may prepare for it. | 唔係講笑咯、係確實真事咯有風颶嚟呢、就打電線報別處人知、等佢可以躲避咯、 |
| 32. That is good. | 個啲好咯、 |

## CONVERSATION 30TH.—THE VISIT.

| | |
|---|---|
| 1. A Ling, tell the coolies to get out the chair. I am going out calling. | 亞靈、叫咕喱出轎、我出街拜客、 |
| 2. The coolies are having their rice. | 咕喱食飯盯、 |
| 3. Well, tell them to be quick. They should take it before going down to bring me up from office. I cannot wait for them. | 悟、叫佢快啲嚟、佢唔曾落寫字樓、抬我翻上嚟、應該大早食喇、我唔等得佢嘘 |
| 4. How long will they be? | 幾耐食得完呢、 |
| 5. I do not know. | 唔知呢 |
| 6. How can I wait for them? I want to go at once. I always tell them to have their dinner earlier. Why do not they do it? | 點等得佢呢、我要即刻去、我時時叫佢早啲食飯、做乜佢唔做呢、 |
| 7. Now, coolies, have you had your dinner? | 嗱、咕喱食飯喇嗎、 |
| 8. Yes; we have, thank you. | 食嚹、唔該吖、 |
| 9. That is well. How you had a hearty meal? I want to go a long way. | 好嘞、食飽飯未呢、要去好遠路呀、 |

## CONVERSATION 29TH.—THE TYPHOON.—(*Continued.*)

| | | |
|---|---|---|
| 26. | Tín²-sin'! ˤngo ˛m ˤhiu tak˒ lok˳. Tín²-sin' ˛kwán ˛fung-kaú² mat˒ sz² á'? ˤYaú tín²-sin', ˤkòm tsaú² ˤyaú ˛fung-kaú² ˛me?³ ˤKòm tín²-sin' ˳tò ˤkéi ˤhim lok˳. | Telegram! I not understand can, 32. Telegram concern typoon what business, eh? 2. Have telegram then have typhoon, eh? 32. So telegrams also rather dangerous, 32. |
| 27. | ˤNéi ˤkong mat˒ á'? Tín²-sin' ˛m hai² ˛ngai-ˤhim á'. | You speak what, eh? 2. Telegrams not are dangerous. 2 |
| 28. | ˤNgo ˤkong ˤsiú* ˛che.³ | I speaking laughing only. 7 |
| 29. | ˤNgo ˛m hai² á'. | I not am. 2 |
| 30. | ˤNéi ˛m hai² mat˒ ˤye á'? | You not are what thing, eh? 2 |
| 31. | ˛M hai² ˤkong-ˤsiú* lok˳. Hai² k'ok˳-shat˒ ˛chan sz² lok˳. ˤYaú ˛fung-kaú² ˛lai ˛ni, tsaú² ˤtá tín²-sin' pò' pit˒ shü' ˛yan ˛chí, ˤtang ˤk'öü ˤho-ˤyi ˤto-péi² lok˳. | Not am speak laughing 32. Is really true matter, 32. Have typhoon come, 53, then send telegram report other places people know, so they can shelter, 32. |
| 32. | Ko'-˳ti ˤhò lok˳. | That good. 32 |

## CONVERSTION 30TH.—THE VISIT.

| | | |
|---|---|---|
| 1. | Á'-˛ling, kiú' ˛kwá-˳léi ch'ut˒ kiú⁵*. ˤNgo ch'ut˒ ˛kái pái'-hák˳. | A Ling, call coolie get-out chair. I go-out street visiting. |
| 2. | ˛Kwú-˳léi shik˒ fán² ˛á.³ | Coolies eat rice, 1. |
| 3. | Ng², kiú' ˤk'öü fái' ˳ti ˛laí. ˤK'öü ˛m ˛ts'ang lok˒ ˤse-tsz²-˛laú, ˛t'oi ˤngo ˛fán ˤshöng ˛lai, ˛ying-˛koi tai²-ˤtsò shik˒ ˛la. ˤNgo ˛m ˤtang tak˒ ˤk'öü lá'. | Well. Tell them quickly come. They not yet go-down office, carry me back up come, ought early (before that) eat, 21. I not wait able for-them. 22. |
| 4. | ˤKéi noi⁵* shik˒ tak˒ ˛yün ˛ni?³ | How long eat able finish, eh? 53. |
| 5. | ˛M ˛chí ˛ni. | Not know. 53. |
| 6. | ˤTím ˤtang tak˒ ˤk'öü ˛ni? ˤNgo yiú' tsik˒-hak˒ höü'. ˤNgo ˛shí-˛shí kiú' ˤk'öü ˤtsò-˳ti shik˒ fán². Tsò²-mat˒ ˤk'öü ˛m tsò² ni?³ | How wait able for-them, eh, 35? I want immediately go. I constantly tell them earlier eat rice. Why they not do, eh? 53. |
| 7. | ˛Ná, ˛kwú-˳léi shik˒* fán² ˤlá' ˤmá? | Now, coolies eaten rice, eh? 21, 33. |
| 8. | Shik˒* lo', ˛m ˛koi ˛á.? | Eaten, 31, beg pardon, 1, (i.e. *for having eaten before you have*). |
| 9. | ˤHò lo'. Shik˒ ˤpiú fán² méi² ˛ni?³ Yiú' höü' ˤhò ˤyün lò' á'. | Well, 31. Eat full rice not-yet, eh? 53. Want go very long road, 2. |

### CONVERSATION 30TH.—THE VISIT.—(*Continued.*)

| | | |
|---|---|---|
| 10. | Yes, we have. | 食飽囉 |
| 11. | Slowly. A little slower. You need not go so slowly. Do not go very slowly. Quicker. | 慢慢行、慢慢啲、唔使咁慢、唔好十分慢、快啲、 |
| 12. | Stop. Set down the chair. Ring the bell and give the boy this card to take in. Yes, Sir. | 等吓、鬆、*or* 鬆轎、搖鐘俾帖過事仔揸入去、好喇先生、 |
| 13. | Master and mistress have both gone out. | 事頭 (*or* 東家) 事頭婆 (*or* 女東家) 兩個都出街囉、 |
| 14. | When the gentleman and lady come in, give the cards to them. | 先生師奶翻嚟、你俾帖佢喇、 |
| 15. | Please take a seat. It is a long time since I have seen you. Are you well? | 請坐、好耐唔曾見先生、你好吖、 |
| 16. | I heard that you had a fall a while ago. Are you quite recovered from the effects of it? | 我聽見先生、先排跌親、現時好翻嗻未呢、 |
| 17. | You are very kind. I am quite well again. | 你有心、好翻嗻咯、 |
| 18. | And your father and mother, are they also well? | 令尊與及令(壽)堂納福呀、 |
| 19. | I hope your elder brother has been prosperous in business. | 願你大佬做生意發大財、 |
| 20. | The business has not succeeded. I am afraid he will fail. | 生意不前、慌倒灶咯、 |
| 21. | I have a small matter I want to ask your help in. I have a son who knows English. I beg you, Sir, to find him some work. If you could recommend him for an appointment in a foreign office, that would be the best. | 我有少少事想拜託先生爲我做吓、我有個仔識英話、我求先生搵啲路頭俾佢做、可以薦佢入洋行寫字樓、係十分好咯、 |

## CONVERSATION 30TH.—THE VISIT.—(*Continued.*)

10. Shik꜆ ꜂paú lo꜄. — Eat, full, 31.

11. Mán$^{2}$-mán$^{5}$* ꜁háng. Mán$^{2}$-mán$^{5}$* ꜂téi. ꜁M ꜂shai kòm꜄ man$^{2}$. ꜁M ꜂hò shap$_{2}$ ꜀fan man$^{2}$. Fai꜄ ꜀ti. — Slowly walk. Slower. Not need so slow. Not good ten parts slow. Quicker.

12. ꜂Tang ꜃hai. ꜀Sung, *or* ꜀sung꜄ kín$^{5}$*, ꜀Mang ꜀chung, ꜂péi t‘íp꜆ kwo꜄sz$^{2}$-꜂tsai ꜀ning yap$_{2}$ höü꜄. ꜂Hò ꜀lá,$^{2}$ ꜀Sin ꜀sháng† (*or short* a). — Wait a bit. Loosen, *or* let-down chair. (꜀Sung is used more by the chair-bearer, 坐 tsò$^{2}$ is used more by the rider) Pull bell, give card to Boy to-take enter go. Good, 21, Sir. [31.

13. Sz$^{2}$-꜁t‘aú* (*or* politely ꜁Tung-꜀ka) sz$^{2}$-꜁t‘aú-꜁p‘o (*or politely* ꜃Nöü ꜀tung ꜀ká) ꜃löng ko꜄ tò ch‘nt꜆ ꜀kai lo꜄. — Master, mistress two [C.] both [C.] also gone out street. (Different titles should be used according to the position of the people. See Titles of Respect in ‘Cantonese Made Easy’ II Part).

14. ꜀Sin-꜀sháng, ꜀sz-꜀nai ꜀fán ꜁lai, ꜃néi ꜂péi t‘íp꜆* ꜃k‘öü ꜀lá.$^{2}$ — Gentleman, lady back come, you give cards them, 21. (See do. do.)

15 ꜂Ts‘eng† ꜃ts‘o*. ꜂Hò noi$^{2}$ (*or* noi$^{5}$*) ꜁m ꜁ts‘ang kín꜄ ꜀Sin ꜀sháng. ꜃Néi ꜂hò ꜀á?$^{2}$ — Invite sit. Very long not yet see, Sir. You well, eh? 1.

16. ꜃Ngo ꜀t‘eng†-kín꜄ ꜀Sin-꜀sháng ꜀sin-꜁p‘ai* tít꜆-꜀t‘san. Yin$^{2}$-꜁shi (*or* ꜁shi$^{5}$*) ꜂hò ꜀fán sai꜄ méi$^{2}$ ꜀ni?$^{2}$ — I heard, Sir, a-while-since fell. At-present well again all not-yet, eh? 53.

17. ꜃Néi ꜃yau ꜀sam. ꜂Hò ꜀fán sai꜄ lo꜄. — You have heart. Well again entirely, 31.

18. Ling$^{2}$-꜀tsün ꜃yü-k‘ap$_{2}$ Ling$^{2}$-(shaú$^{2}$)-꜁t‘ong nap$_{2}$ fuk꜆ á꜄? — Father and mother enjoy happiness, eh? 2.

19. Yün$^{2}$ ꜃néi$^{2}$ tai$^{2}$-꜂lò tsò$^{2}$ ꜀sháng-yí꜄ fát꜆ tai$^{2}$ ꜁ts‘oi. — Hope your elder-brother doing business made large wealth.

20. ꜀Sháng-yí꜄ pat꜆ ꜁ts‘in. ꜀Fong ꜂tò-tsò꜄ lok꜆. — Business not succeeding. Afraid (he) will fail, 32.

21. ꜃Ngo ꜃yau ꜂shiú-꜂shiú sz$^{2}$, ꜂söng pai꜄-t‘ok꜆ ꜀Sin-꜀sháng wai$^{2}$ ꜃ngo tsò$^{2}$ ꜃hai. ꜃Ngo ꜃yau ko꜄ ꜂tsai shik꜆ ꜀Ying-wá$^{5}$*. ꜃Ngo ꜁k‘aú ꜀Sin-꜀sháng ꜂wan ꜀ti ꜁t‘aú-lò$^{2}$ ꜂péi ꜃k‘öü tsò$^{2}$. ꜂Ho ꜃yí tsín$^{2}$ ꜃k‘öü yap$_{2}$ ꜁yöng ꜀hong ꜂sé-tsz$^{2}$-꜀lau*, hai$^{2}$ shap$_{2}$-꜀fan ꜂hò lok꜆. — I have trifling matter wish beg, Sir, for me do a-bit. I have a son knows English. I beg, Sir, find some work give him do. Able to-recommend him enter foreign firm's office would-be very good, 32.

CONVERSATION 30TH.—THE VISIT —(Continued.)

| | |
|---|---|
| 22. At present there is no one who wishes to engage a novice. If I hear of anyone wishing to engage a Chinese clerk, I shall certainly remember your son. | 現時冇人請新手嘅、我若聽聞有人想請唐人寫字我是必記起你嘅仔嚟、 |
| 23. I congratulate you. I heard a few days ago that you had a grandson. | 我恭喜你、我先幾日聽聞你得個孫咯、 |
| 24. I hear you are going to Swatow shortly. I wish you a pleasant voyage. If you should meet any old friends there, remember me kindly to them. Take care of yourself on board ship. A pleasant voyage. | 我聽聞你遲日想去汕頭、我願你順風、你或見啲舊朋友代我問候佢喇、坐穩船喇、順風喇、 |
| 25. Good bye. We will meet again. We will see each other again. Take care how you go. | 好行喇、後會有期咯、後來致相見喇、慢慢行喇、 |
| 26. Where is that coolie of mine now? Dear me! He is always off. I went in and only stayed a short time, and when I come out again he is not here. Go and look for him. | 我嘅個咕喱呢、睇吔、佢時時都唔喺處嘅、我入去坐一陣、翻出嚟佢就唔喺處咯、去搵佢嚟、 |
| 27. He is coming, Sir, he is coming. | 嚟咯、先生嚟咯、 |
| 28. Why are you always running away? Another time I shall call a street coolie, and you will have to pay him. | 做乜你時時走去嘅呢、我大回就叫個街嘅咕喱、就要你出錢嘅㗎、 |
| 29. I did not think, Sir, that you would come out again so quickly. I only ran over to the next street to buy a piece of sugar-cane. | 我唔估得先生咁快脆出嚟嘅、我就走過隔籬街買一轆蔗食唄、 |
| 30. I waited for you a long time. You bought a piece of sugar-cane, did you? When you came back you were not eating sugar-cane. | 我等你好耐咯、買轆蔗咩、你翻緊嚟又唔見食蔗呢、 |

## CONVERSATION 30TH.—THE VISIT.—(*Continued.*)

| | | |
|---|---|---|
| 22. | Yin²-꜀shí (*or* ꜀shi*) ᶜmò ꜀yan ᶜts'eng† ꜀san ᶜshaú keᵓ. ᶜNgo yök꜄ ꜀t'eng†-man² ᶜyaú ꜀yan ᶜsöng ᶜts'eng† ꜀T'ong-꜀yan ᶜsé-tsz⁵*, ᶜngo ꜀shi-pit꜄ keiᵓ ᶜhéi ᶜnéi-keᵓ ᶜtsai ꜀lai. | At present no man engages new hands, 15. I, if hear have man wish engage Chinese writer, I certainly remember (*or* recall up, *compare* treasure up in my memory) your son. |
| 23. | ᶜNgo ꜀kung-ᶜhéi ᶜnéi. ᶜNgo ꜀sin (*or* ꜀sin) ᶜkéi yat꜄ ꜀t'eng†-man²-ᶜnéi tak꜄ koᵓ ꜀sün lok꜀. | I congratulate you. I before several days heard you obtained a grandson, 32. |
| 24. | ᶜNgo ꜀t'eng†-man² ᶜnéi ꜀ch'i yat꜄ ᶜsöng höüᵓ Shánᵓ-꜀t'aú. ᶜNgo yün² ᶜnéi shun² ꜀fung. ᶜNéi wák꜄ kinᵓ ꜀ti kaú² ꜀p'ang-ᶜyaú, toi² ᶜngo man² haú² ᶜk'öü ꜀lá. ᶜT'so* ᶜwan ꜀shün ꜀lá. Shun² ꜀fung ꜀lá. | I hear you later date wish go Swatow. I hope you (will have) prosperous wind. You perhaps see some old friends for me ask welfare of-them, 21. Sit steady on-board-ship, 21. Prosperous gales, 21. |
| 25. | ᶜHo ꜀háng ꜀lá. Haú² wöüᵓ ᶜyaú ꜀k'éi lok꜀. Haú²-꜀loi chíᵓ ꜀söng kinᵓ ꜀lá. Mán²-mán⁵* ꜀háng ꜀lá.² | Well walk, 21. Afterwards can have date, 32. Afterwards till each see, 21. Slowly walk, 21. |
| 26. | ᶜNgo ᶜko koᵓ kwú-꜀léi ꜀ni? Ai.² ꜀yá²! ᶜK'öü ꜀shi-꜀shi ꜀tò ꜀m ᶜhai shüᵓ keᵓ. ᶜNgo yap꜄ höüᵓ ᶜts'o* yat꜄ chan², (*or* chan⁵* *if a very short time*), ꜀fán ch'ut꜄ ꜀lai, ᶜk'öü tsaú² ꜀m ᶜhai shüᵓ lok꜀. Höüᵓ ᶜwan ᶜk'öü ꜀lai. | My that [C.] coolie, eh, 53? Dear me! He always also not at place, 15. I went in sat one moment, back out come, he then not at place, 32. Go find him come. |
| 27. | ꜀Lai lok꜀. ꜀Sin-꜀sháng, ꜀lai lok꜀. | Coming, 32, Sir, coming, 32. |
| 28. | Tsò²-mat꜄ ᶜnéi ꜀shi-꜀shi ᶜtsau höüᵓ keᵓ ꜀ni?² ᶜNgo tái² (*a rapid pronunciation of* 第二 tai² yi²) ꜀wái tsaú² kiúᵓ ᶜkoᵓ ꜀kái keᵓ ꜀kwú-꜀léi, tsaú² yiúᵓ ᶜnéi ch'ut꜄ ꜀ts'in* keᵓ láᵓ. | Why you constantly run go away, 15, eh? 53. I another time just call a street coolie, then want you pay-out money. [15, 22. |
| 29. | ᶜNgo ꜀m ᶜkwú tak꜄, ꜀Sin-꜀sháng, kòmᵓ fáiᵓ-ts'öüᵓ ch'ut꜄ ꜀lai keᵓ. ᶜNgo tsaú² ᶜtsaú kwoᵓ kák꜀-꜀léi ꜀kái ᶜmái yat꜄ luk꜄ cheᵓ shik꜄ ꜀ché.² | I not think able, Sir, so quickly out come, 15. I just ran go-over neighbouring street buy one piece sugar-cane eat only, 7. |
| 30. | ᶜNgo ᶜtang ᶜnéi ᶜhò noi² (*or* noi⁵*) lok꜀. ᶜMái luk꜄ cheᵓ ꜀me?² ᶜNéi ꜀fán ᶜkan ꜀lai yaú² ꜀m kinᵓ shik꜄ cheᵓ ꜀ni? | I wait you very long, 32. Buy piece sugar-cane, eh? 39. You back in-the-act-of coming yet not see eat sugar-cane, eh? 53. |

## CONVERSATION 30TH.—THE VISIT.—(*Continued.*)

| | | |
|---|---|---|
| 31. | I saw you coming, so I ran quickly back. How could I eat sugar-cane when I was running? | 我見先生嚟、所以我快脆啲走翻嚟、走緊路點食得蔗呢、 |
| 32. | Be quiet. When I go in to call, you should wait for me, and not run away elsewhere. | 咪出聲咯、我入去坐你應該要等我翻出嚟嘅、唔好走去第二處、 |

## CONVERSATION 31ST.—MILITARY.

| | | |
|---|---|---|
| 1. | Is there any fear of war at present? | 現時慌打仗唔慌呢、 |
| 2. | I think there is no need to be afraid at present of war. | 我估呢陣都唔使怕有仗打咯、 |
| 3. | All countries have many soldiers, and they are constantly wanting to fight. | 萬國兵多常時想打仗咯、 |
| 4. | It would be much better if there was universal peace. | 天下太平越發好咯、 |
| 5. | In Western countries there are many soldiers always congregated together ready for fighting. | 在西國有大多兵時時聚埋預備打仗、 |
| 6. | Large sums of money are spent every year in these matters. | 每年使大把錢爲呢啲事嘅咯、 |
| 7. | In olden times soldiers in the West used bows and arrows, or spears, as the Chinese do. | 古時西國兵又用弓箭或札嘴嚟打、好似中國人噉樣、 |
| 8. | But, Sir, do you not know that for some years past the Chinese have been copying the people of your respected country, by using foreign firearms? | 但係先生你唔知近來幾年間、唐人學先生貴國人使洋鎗咩、 |
| 9. | Yes, I know that; and not only that, but they are also making use of torpedoes. | 係吖、我知咯、又唔止用洋鎗、又使水雷炮、 |
| 10. | Have you been, Sir, to the parade ground, and seen the soldiers parade? | 先生去過較塲見操兵唔曾呢、 |
| 11. | I have been several times. It is a fine sight. It is really a fine sight. | 去過有幾次咯、好睇咯、眞正好睇咯、 |

CONVERSATION 30TH.—THE VISIT.—(*Continued.*)

| | | |
|---|---|---|
| 31. | ᶜNgo kinᵓ ꜀Sín-꜀sháng ꜀laí, ᶜsho-ᶜyí ᶜngo fáì²-tsʻöüᵓ-ₒti ᶜtsaú ꜀fán ꜀laí. ᶜTsaú-ᶜkan lò² ᶜtim shik₂ tak₃ cheᵓ ꜀ni? | I saw, you Sir, coming, therefore I quickly run back come. Running road how eat can sugar-cane, eh? 53. |
| 32. | ᶜMaí chʻut₃ ꜀sheng† lok꜀. ᶜNgo yap₂ höüᵓ ᶜtsʻo* ᶜnéi ꜀ying-꜀koi yínᵓ ᶜtang ᶜngo ꜀fán chʻut₃ ꜀laí keᵓ. ꜀M ᶜhò ᶜtsaú höüᵓ taí²-yí² shüᵓ. | Do-not issue sound, 32. I enter go sir, you ought must wait I back out come, 15. Not good run go another place. |

CONVERSATION 31ST.—MILITARY.

| | | |
|---|---|---|
| 1. | Yín² ꜀shí ꜀fong ᶜtá-chöngᵓ* ꜀m ꜀fong ꜀ni?² | Present time fear fighting not fear, eh? 53. |
| 2. | ᶜNgo ᶜkwú ꜀ni chan³* tò ꜀m ᶜshaí pʻáᵓ ᶜyaú chöngᵓ* ᶜtá lok꜀. | I think this time also not need fear have battles fought, 32. |
| 3. | Máń² kwok ꜀ping ꜀to, ꜀shí-shöng² ᶜsöng ᶜtá-chöngᵓ lok꜀. [lok꜀. | All (*lit.* myriad) countries soldiers many, constantly wish to-fight, 32. [32. |
| 4. | ꜀Tʻín há² tʻáìᵓ ꜀pʻing yüt₂-fát ᶜhò | Heaven's beneath great peace more better, |
| 5. | Tsoi² ꜀Saí kwok꜀ ᶜyaú taí² ꜀to ꜀ping ꜀shi-꜀shí (*or* ꜀shí*) tsöü²-꜀maí yü²-pét² ᶜtá-chöngᵓ*. | In Western countries have great many soldiers constantly gathered together, ready to fight. |
| 6. | ᶜMúi ꜀nn ᶜshaí tháí² ᶜpá ꜀tsʻni* waí² ꜀ni- ti sz² keᵓ lok. | Each year spend large handfuls money on-account-of these matters. 15, 32. |
| 7. | ᶜKwú ꜀shí ꜀Saí kwok ꜀ping yaú² yung² ꜀kung, tsmᵓ, wák₂ chát -ᶜtsöü ꜀laí ᶜtá, ᶜhò ᶜtsʻz ꜀Chung-kwok꜀ ꜀yan ᶜkóm yöng³*. | Olden times Western countries' soldiers also used bows, arrows, or spears to fight like Chinese (*lit.* Middle kingdom) men so fashion. |
| 8. | Tán²-haí² ꜀Sín-꜀sháng, ᶜnéi ꜀m ꜀chi kan²-꜀loi* ᶜkéi ꜀nín ꜀kán, ꜀Tʻong ꜀yan hok₂ ꜀Sín-꜀sháng kwaiᵓ kwok ꜀yan ᶜshaí ꜀yöng ꜀tsʻöng ꜀me?² | But, Sir, you not know lately several years time Chinese (*lit.* Tʻong Dynasty) men copy Sir's honourable country's men use foreign firearms, eh? 39. |
| 9. | Haí² ꜀á, ᶜngo ꜀chí lok꜀; yaú² ꜀m ᶜchí yung² ꜀yöng ꜀tsʻöng, yaú² ᶜshaí ᶜshöü-꜀löü-(pʻáuᵓ). | Yes I, I know, 32; also not only use foreign firearms, also use water-thunder guns. |
| 10. | ꜀Sín-꜀sháng höüᵓ-kwoᵓ kaúᵓ-꜀chʻöng* kínᵓ ꜀tsʻò ꜀ping ꜀m ꜀tsʻang ꜀ni?² | Sir gone parade-ground seen parading soldiers not yet, eh? 53. |
| 11. | Höüᵓ-kwoᵓ ᶜyaú ᶜkéi, tsʻzᵓ lok꜀. ᶜHò ᶜtʻaí lok꜀. ꜀Chan chingᵓ ᶜhò ᶜtʻaí lok꜀. | Gone have several times, 32. Good to-see, 32. Truly good to-see, 32. |

## CONVERSATION 31st.—MILITARY.—(*Continued.*)

| | | |
|---|---|---|
| 12. | The General was riding a large black horse, while the Colonel was on one as white as snow. | 將軍騎住一匹大黑馬、個參將騎一隻雪咁白嘅、 |
| 13. | At first there was a regiment of infantry, and some artillery-men. I did not see any cavalry. | 先頭有一營步兵喺處、又有啲炮手、我唔見馬兵、 |
| 14. | Afterwards the volunteers came, and they fought together. | 後來民兵嚟、噉大家相打、 |
| 15. | Which side won, the soldiers, or the other side? | 邊頭贏呢、係官兵抑或嗰頭呢、 |
| 16. | The volunteers were not strong enough to withstand the soldiers. They fought for an hour when they were beaten. | 民兵唔够打、打有成點鐘噉就輸咯、 |
| 17. | Have you seen the new forts yet? There are a great many large guns in them. | 見過新炮台唔曾呢、有好多大炮喺裏頭噃、 |
| 18. | I want to ask you something. Very good. Please tell me what a breach-loading gun is. | 我想問先生一句、好吖、請你話我知後膛炮係乜傢伙呢、 |
| 19. | A breach-loading gun is not the same as the common gun. The cartridge is inserted at the breach of the gun, and not at the muzzle. | 後膛炮呢、唔同平常嘅、在炮尾入炮碼、唔係在炮口入嘅、 |
| 20. | Then that is the same as a revolver. | 噉就同六口連一樣咯、 |
| 21. | Yes, about the same, but there is some difference. | 係、都係咁上下、但係有啲分別嘅、 |
| 22. | And moreover a revolver (*or* pistol) is only a small firearm. | 而且對面笑不過係細鎗啫、 |
| 23. | You are right. When a cannon is let off the whole earth trembles, but when a small firearm is fired there is not much noise. | 冇錯咯、放炮個時成地都震嘵、但燒細鎗冇幾大聲咯、 |
| 24. | I like to see the bayonets. They glitter in the sunlight. | 我中意睇鎗頭劍、日頭晒佢就發光咯、 |
| 25. | Yes, they appear very bright. | 係咯、見好光嗷、 |

## CONVERSATION 31ST.—MILITARY.—(*Continued.*)

12. ꜀Tsöng-꜀kwan ꜀k'e chü$^{2}$ yat꜄ p'at꜄ tái$^{2}$ hak꜄ ᶜmá, koͻ ꜀ts'ám-tsöngͻ ꜀k'e yat꜄ chek꜄ süt꜀ kòmͻ pak꜄ keͻ.
General rode on one [C.] large black horse, the Colonel rode one [C.] snow as white, 15.

13. ꜀Sin-꜀t'ań ᶜyań yat꜄ ꜀ying pò$^{2}$ ꜀ping ᶜhai shü$^{2}$: Yań$^{2}$ ᶜyań ꜀ti p'áńͻ ᶜshań. ᶜNgo ꜀m kinͻ ᶜmá ꜀ping.
First there-was one regiment infantry soldiers at the-place, also have some gun hands. I not see horse soldiers.

14. Hań$^{2}$-꜀hoi ꜀man-꜀ping ꜀lai, ᶜkòm tai$^{2}$-kai ꜀söng ᶜtá.
Afterwards people's soldiers come, then altogether together fought.

15. ꜀Pin ꜀t'ań ꜀yeng† ꜀ni ?$^{2}$ Hai$^{2}$ ꜀kwún ꜀ping, yik꜄-wák꜄ ᶜko ꜀t'ań ꜀ni ?$^{2}$
Which side won, eh, ? 53. Was official soldiers, or that side, eh ? 53.

16. ꜀Man ꜀ping ꜀m kańͻ ᶜtá, ᶜtá ᶜyaú ꜀sheng† ᶜtím chung, ᶜkòm tsań$^{2}$ shü lok꜄.
People's soldiers not sufficient to-fight. Fight have fully an hour, so then lost, 32.

17. Kinͻ-kwoͻ ꜀san p'áńͻ-꜀toi* ꜀m ꜀ts'ang ꜀ni ? ᶜYaú ᶜhò ꜀to tai$^{2}$ p'áńͻ ᶜhai ᶜlöü-꜀t'au kaͻ.
Seen new forts not yet, eh ? 53. Have great many large guns in interior, 14.

18. ᶜNgo ᶜsöng man$^{2}$ ꜀Sin-꜀shàng† yat꜄ köüͻ. ᶜHò ꜀á$^{2}$. ᶜTseng† ᶜnéi wá$^{2}$ ᶜngo ꜀chí, hań$^{2}$-꜀t'ong* p'áńͻ hai$^{2}$ mat꜄ ꜀ká-ᶜfo ꜀ni ?$^{2}$
I wish ask Sir one sentence. Very-good. 1 Invite you tell me to-know breach-loading guns are what articles, eh ? 53.

19. Hań$^{2}$-꜀t'ong* p'áńͻ ꜀ni, ꜀m ꜀t'ung ꜀p'ing-꜀shöng keͻ. Tsoi$^{2}$ p'áńͻ ᶜméi yap꜄ kip꜄-ᶜmá,* ꜀m hai$^{2}$ tsoi$^{2}$ p'áńͻ ᶜhań yap꜄ keͻ.
Breach-loading guns, 53, not same ordinary, 15. At gun's end enter cartridge, not is at gun's month entered, 15.

20. ᶜKòm tsań$^{2}$ ꜀t'ung luk꜄-ᶜhań-꜀lin* yat꜄ yöng$^{2}$ lok꜄.
Then just with six-barrelled revolver one same, 32.

21. Hai$^{2}$, ꜀tò hai$^{2}$ kòmͻ shöng$^{2}$-ᶜha, tán$^{2}$-hai$^{2}$ ᶜyaú ꜀ti ꜀fan-pit꜄ ke꜄.
Yes, also is about the-same, but have some difference, 15.

22. ꜀Yí-ᶜch'e töüͻ-mín$^{2}$-ᶜsiú* pat꜄-kwoͻ hai$^{2}$ saiͻ ꜀ts'öng ꜀che.$^{2}$
Besides revolver only is small firearm only, 7.

23. ᶜMò ts'oͻ lok꜄. Fongͻ p'áńͻ koͻ ꜀shi ꜀sheng† téi$^{2}$ ꜀tò chanͻ-꜀hín, tan$^{2}$ ꜀shiń saiͻ ꜀ts'öng ᶜmò ᶜkéi tai$^{2}$* ꜀sheng† lok꜄.
No mistake, 32. Let-off gun that time whole earth also trembles, but fire small firearm not much great sound, 32.

24. ᶜNgo ꜀chung-yíͻ ᶜt'ai ꜀ts'öng-꜀t'ań-kimͻ. Yat꜄ ꜀t'ań* shaiͻ, ᶜk'öü tsań$^{2}$ fat꜄ ꜀kwong lok꜄.
I like to-see bayonets. Sun shining-on-them they then produce light, 32.

25. Hai$^{2}$ lok꜄, kinͻ ᶜhò ꜀kwong ᶜkòm.
Yes, 32, see very bright so.

## CONVERSATION 31ST—MILITARY.—(*Continued.*)

| | | |
|---|---|---|
| 26. | The officers carry swords, and some ride on horseback. | 兵總馱劍、有啲騎馬添、 |
| 27. | How do you distinguish between a sword and dagger? | 劍同刀有乜分别呢、 |
| 28. | The Chinese call a sword one with two edges, and a one-edged one a knife or dagger. | 唐人啲叫嘅、兩邊口嘅就係劍、一邊口嘅叫做刀、 |
| 29. | I picked up a pair of daggers at the side of the road one day when I was out for a walk. They had been thrown away by thieves, who were afraid of being arrested. | 有一日我行街、喺路邊執倒一孖刀、係賊佬嘅、佢怕差人捉佢啲就掕嘵嘅、 |
| 30. | Oh! did you, and have you still got them? | 係咩、重喺處嗎 (or 重有冇呀、) |
| 31. | Yes, I have. | 重喺處呀 (or 重有咯、) |
| 32. | Let me see them. | 俾我睇喇、 |

## CONVERSATION 32ND.—THE GARDENER.

| | | |
|---|---|---|
| 1. | Tell the gardener to come here. I want to see him. | 叫花王嚟、我要見佢、 |
| 2. | Very well, Sir. | 好喇、先生、 |
| 3. | How is it there are no flowers in my garden? | 點解我花園冇花呢、 |
| 4. | The flowers have not come out yet. | 花唔曾出呀、 |
| 5. | I do not see any buds even. | 花啉都唔見呀、 |
| 6. | There will be some by and by. | 慢慢有咯、 |
| 7. | I bought several China firs last night, and want you to plant them. | 我昨晚買幾兜松樹要你種、 |
| 8. | Shall I plant them where the turf has been laid down? | 種係草披個處好嗎、 |
| 9. | You are stupid. Do you think I want holes dug in the turf? | 你呆嘅、你估我要掘啲窿在草披嚟種咩、 |
| 10. | The leaves on those bamboos are growing too thick together. | 個幾篇竹樹生得葉多、 |
| 11. | And that branch of the tree should be cut off. | 個篇樹嘅樹枝、應該斬斷致得、 |

## CONVERSATION 31st.—MILITARY.—(*Continued.*)

| | | |
|---|---|---|
| 26. | ꜀Ping-꜂tsung ꜀t'o kím꜃, ꜂yaú ꜁ti ꜀k'e ꜂má ꜀t'ím. | Officers carry swords, have some ride horses besides. |
| 27. | Kím꜃ ꜀t'ung ꜀tò ꜂yaú mat꜁ ꜀fan-pit꜁ ꜀ni? | Swords from knives have what distinction, eh? 53. |
| 28. | ꜀T'ong-꜀yan ꜂kòm kiú꜃ ke꜃: ꜂léung ꜀pín ꜂haú ke꜃, tsaú꜄ hai꜄ kím꜃: yat꜁ ꜀pín ꜂haú ke꜃, kiú꜃-tsò꜄ ꜀tò. | Chinese so call, 15: two sides edges, 15, then is sword; one side edge, 15, called knife. |
| 29. | ꜂Yaú yat꜁ yat꜁ ꜂ngo ꜀háng ꜀kái (*better* kái) ꜂haí lò꜄ ꜀pín (better pín) chap꜁-꜂tò yat꜁ ꜀má ꜀tò, hai꜄ ts'ák꜁ ꜂lo ke꜃, k'öü p'á꜃ ꜀ch'ai-꜀yan chuk꜁ ꜂k'öü, ꜂kòm tsaú꜄ ꜀wing-꜀hiú ke꜃. | Have one day I walk street, at road side picked-up one pair knives. Was thief fellows', 15, they afraid police catch them, so then throw-away, 15. |
| 30. | Hai꜄ ꜀me!* Chung꜄ ꜂haí shü꜃ ꜂má? (*or* Chung꜄ ꜂yaú ꜂mò á꜃?) | Indeed! 32. Still at place, eh? 53. (*or* Still have or not, eh? 2.) |
| 31. | Chung꜄ ꜂haí shü꜃ á꜃ (*or* Chung꜄ ꜂yaú lok꜁.) | Still at place. 2, (*or* Still have, 32.) |
| 32. | ꜂Péi ꜂ngo ꜂t'ai ꜀la.* | Give me to-see, 21. |

## CONVERSATION 32nd.—THE GARDENER.

| | | |
|---|---|---|
| 1. | Kiú꜃ ꜀fá ꜀wong ꜀lai. ꜂Ngo yiú꜃ kín꜃ ꜂k'öü. | Call flower prince come. I want see him. |
| 2. | ꜂Hò ꜀lá,* ꜀Sin-꜀sháng†. | Good, 21, Sir. |
| 3. | ꜂Tím ꜂kái ꜂ngo ꜀fá-꜀yün* ꜂mò fá ꜀ni? | How explain my flower-garden no flowers. [eh? 53. |
| 4. | ꜀Fá ꜀m ꜀ts'ang ch'ut꜁ á꜃. | Flowers not yet (come) out, 2. |
| 5. | ꜀Fá (*or* ꜀Fá) ꜀lam ꜁tò ꜀m kín꜃ á꜃. | Flower buds also not see, 2. |
| 6. | Mán꜄-mán꜄* ꜂yaú lok꜁. | Slowly-slowly have. 32. |
| 7. | ꜂Ngo tsok꜁ ꜂man ꜂mái ꜂kéi ꜀taú ꜀ts'ung-shü꜄ yiú꜃ ꜂néi chung꜃. | I last night bought several [C.] fir-trees want you plant. |
| 8. | Chung꜃ ꜂haí ꜂ts'ò-꜀p'éi ko꜃ shü꜃ ꜂hò má꜃? | Plant at turfed that place good, eh? 32. |
| 9. | ꜂Néi ꜀ngoi ke꜃. ꜂Néi ꜂kwú ꜂ngo yiú꜃ kwat꜁ ꜁ti ꜀lung tsoi꜄ ꜂ts'ò-꜀p'éi ꜀lai chung꜃ ꜀me? | You stupid, 15. You think I want dig some holes in turf in-order-to plant, eh? 32. |
| 10. | Ko꜃ ꜂kéi ꜀p'o chuk꜁ shü꜄ ꜀sháng† tak꜁ yip꜁ ꜀to. | Those several [C.] bamboo trees grow have-been-able-to leaves many. |
| 11. | Ko꜃ ꜀p'o shü꜄-ke꜃ shü꜄-꜀chí ꜀ying-꜀koi ꜂chám ꜂t'ün chí꜃-tak꜁. | That [C.] tree's tree branch ought cut short in-order-to do. |

海上絲綢之路文獻集成　科技與文化編

CONVERSATION 32ND.—THE GARDENER.—(*Continued.*)

| | |
|---|---|
| 12. Do you wish those few pots of lotus put into the pond? | 你係要個幾盤蓮花種落塘、係唔係呀、 |
| 13. Yes, certainly. | 係定喇、 |
| 14. A seller of flowers brought a number of roses. He left them here for your approval. | 賣花佬擔啲玫瑰花嚟、佢丟處等你或中意就要、 |
| 15. Let me see them by and by. | 等吓俾我睇喇、 |
| 16. Where have you put all those narcissi we had at Chinese new year? | 唐人新年咁多水仙花、丟嗻邊處呀、 |
| 17. I have put them by, some other kinds will grow next year. | 擠埋咯、出年又噲生出別啲花、 |
| 18. I know that. I wanted you to put them by carefully. | 個啲我都知到叮、我要你收好佢、 |
| 19. Are there any empty flower-pots? | 有啲空花盤有冇呀、 |
| 20. If there are. I want you to plant these seeds in them | 有呢、就要你種呢啲花仁、 |
| 21. These trees need pruning. | 呢啲樹要省枝葉致得、 |
| 22. That plant is dead. Pull it up, and put another in. | 個窩死阻咯、搣出嚟種過第窩、 |
| 23. If I put a dog's tooth flower* in, it will look well. | 我種窩狗牙花都幾好睇、 |
| 24. I want some new plants put on the verandah every week. | 每個禮拜要擺啲新花喺騎樓致得、 |
| 25. Have you watered these flowers? | 你淋呢啲花唔曾呀、 |
| 26. I watered them this morning. | 我今朝淋阻咯、 |
| 27. How is it they are so dry? | 點解咁乾呢、 |
| 28. The sun was very hot to-day. | 今日熱頭晒得好猛、 |
| 29. I want to buy some flowers. What had I better buy? | 我要買啲花、邊啲好買、 |
| 30. There are a great many flowers that it would be well to buy. | 有好多花好買、 |
| 31. I only want to buy a few. | 我淨係要買幾蔸啫、 |
| 32. Then buy some dahlias, sun-flowers, camellias, tuberoses, and that will be enough. | 噉、買啲芍藥花、向日葵、茶花、玉簪花、噉就够咯、 |

* **Note.—The name in the text is a translation of the Chinese name. There would appear to be no common name for it in English. The Botanical name is Tabernœmontana Coronaria, flore plena.**

## CONVERSATION 32ND.—THE GARDENER.—*(Continued.)*

| | | |
|---|---|---|
| 12. | ᶜNéi hai² yiúʾ koʾ ᶜkéi ꜀p'ún ꜀lín ꜀fá chungʾ lok꜀ ꜀t'ong; hai² ꜀m hai² áʾ? | You do want those several pots lotus flower plant down into pond; is not is? 2. |
| 13. | Hai² ting⁵ᵃ ꜀lá.² | Yes, certainly, 21. |
| 14. | Mai² ꜀fá ᶜlò ꜀tám ꜀ti ꜀múi-kwaiʾ-꜀fá ꜀lai. ᶜK'öü ꜀tiú shüʾ ᶜtang ᶜnéi wák꜀ ꜀chung-yiʾ, tsaú² yiúʾ. | Sell flower fellow carry some roses come. He placed here wait you perhaps like, then want. |
| 15. | ᶜTang ꜀há ᶜpéi ᶜngo ᶜt'ai ꜀lá.² | Wait a-while give me to-see, 21 (i.e. Show them to me). |
| 16. | ꜀T'ong-꜀yan ꜀san ꜀nín kòmʾ ꜀to ꜀shöü-꜀sin fá, ꜀tiú sáiʾ ꜀pín shüʾ áʾ? | Chinese new year so many water-genii flowers, place all what place, eh? 2. |
| 17. | ꜀Chai ꜀mái lok꜀, ch'ut꜀ ꜀nín yau² ᶜwúi ꜀shàng† ch'ut꜀ pit꜀-꜀ti fá. | Place together, 32, coming year it also can grow out other kinds flowers. |
| 18. | Koʾ-꜀ti ᶜngo ꜀tò ꜀chí tòʾ ꜀á. ᶜNgo yiúʾ ᶜnéi ꜀shau ᶜhò ᶜk'öü. | That I also know, 1. I want you put-by well them. [eh? 2. |
| 19. | ᶜYaú ꜀ti ꜀hung ꜀fá-꜀p'ún ᶜyaú ᶜmò áʾ? | Have some empty flowers-pots have not, |
| 20. | ᶜYaú ꜀ni, tsaú² yiúʾ ᶜnéi chungʾ ꜀ni-꜀ti ꜀fá ꜀ngan. | Have, 53, then want you plant these flowers seeds. |
| 21. | ꜀Ni-꜀ti shü² yiúʾ ᶜsháng-꜀chi-yíp꜀ chíʾ tak꜀. | These trees want pruning in-order-to do. |
| 22. | Koʾ ꜀p'o ᶜsz ᶜcho lok꜀, ꜀mang ch'ut꜀ ꜀lai chungʾ kwoʾ tai² ꜀p'o. | That [C.] dead, 32, pull out come plant over another [C.] |
| 23. | ᶜNgo chungʾ ꜀p'o ᶜkaú-꜀ngá ꜀fá tó ᶜkéi ᶜhò ᶜt'ai. | I plant [C.] dog's-tooth-flower also pretty good see, |
| 24. | ᶜMúi koʾ ᶜlai-páiʾ yiúʾ ᶜpái ꜀ti ꜀san ꜀fá ᶜhai ꜀k'e-꜀laú* chíʾ tak꜀. | Each [C.] week want spread-out some new flowers at verandah in-order-to do. |
| 25. | ᶜNéi ꜀lam ꜀ni-꜀ti ꜀fá ꜀m-꜀ts'ang áʾ? | Have-you watered these flowers yet, eh? 2. |
| 26. | ᶜNgo ꜀kam ꜀chiú ꜀lam-ᶜcho lok꜀. | I this morning watered. 32. |
| 27. | ᶜTím ᶜkái kòmʾ ꜀kòn ꜀ni?² | How explain so dry, eh? 53. |
| 28. | ꜀Kam-yat꜀ yit꜀-꜀t'aú* sháiʾ tak꜀ ᶜhò ᶜmáng. [ᶜmái? | To-day sun shine was-able-to very fierce. [buy? |
| 29. | ᶜNgo yiúʾ ᶜmái ꜀ti ꜀fá. ꜀Pin-꜀ti ᶜhò | I want buy some flowers. Which good |
| 30. | ᶜYaú ᶜhò ꜀to ꜀fá ᶜhò ᶜmái. | Have good many flowers good buy. |
| 31. | ᶜNgo tsing²-hai² yiúʾ ᶜmái ᶜkéi ꜀taú ꜀che.² | I only am wanting buy several [C.] only, 7. |
| 32. | ᶜKòm, ᶜmái ꜀ti chök꜀-yök꜀ ꜀fá, höngʾ-yat꜀ ꜀kw'ai, ꜀chá ꜀fá, yuk꜀-꜀tsám ꜀fá, ᶜkòm tsaú² kaúʾ lok꜀. | Then buy some dahlias, sun-flowers, camellias, tuberoses, so then enough, 32. |

## CONVERSATION 33RD.—MAIL LETTERS.

| | |
|---|---|
| 1. A gun has gone at the Peak; the mail is coming in. | 山頂燒砍炮咯、祖家船埋緊頭呀、 |
| 2. Yes; What flag is hoisted? | 係咩、扯乜野旗呢、 |
| 3. It looks like the English flag; I cannot see clearly. | 好似英國嘅、唔睇得眞、 |
| 4. Is there a ball up at the mast-head? | 旗杆尾有毬冇呀、 |
| 5. There is, at the very top is the English flag, in the middle the ball, and below a small flag. | 有、至高個係英旗、中間有個毬、下底有枝細旗、 |
| 6. What flag? | 乜野旗呢、 |
| 7. I cannot see. | 睇唔出咯、 |
| 8. You know how far the vessel is off by the small flag. | 睇個枝細旗、就知個隻船有幾遠、 |
| 9. The small flag is down. | 落細旗咯、 |
| 10. It is only hoisted at first. | 不過初初扯細旗呮、 |
| 11. I want the coolie to go for the letters when the steamer comes. | 火船埋頭要管店去攞信、 |
| 12. Let me know when you see the steamer lying along side the wharf. | 見個隻火船拍埋馬頭就話我知呀、 |
| 13. Very good. | 好咯、 |
| 14. It will probably be two hours before she arrives, as it is a clear day, and, there are no mists. | 大概有兩點鐘咁耐至到、因爲今日好天冇山霧、 |
| 15. Now, coolie, I have written a paper for you to go down to the Post Office, to get the mail letters. | 拿、咕喱我寫張紙你落去書信館攞祖家信嚟、 |
| 16. I do not know where the Post Office is. | 唔知書信館喺邊處呢、 |
| 17. It is next to the Clock Tower, in Queen's Road. | 大鐘樓隔離、在大馬路、 |
| 18. Take the paper down and you will see some windows at the side next the Clock Tower. | 拎個張紙落去就見有啲窓門喺大鐘樓個便、 |

## CONVERSATION 33RD.—MAIL LETTERS.

| | | |
|---|---|---|
| 1. | ꜀Shán ʿteng† ꜀shüi ʿham p'áuʾ lok꜄, ʿtsò-꜀ká ꜀shün ꜁mái ʿkan ꜁t'aú áʾ. | Hill top fire [C.] gun 32, ancestral-family-seat vessel arriving. |
| 2. | Hai² ꜀me ?ʾ ʿCh'e ꜀mi ʿye ꜁k'éi ꜀ni? | Is (so), eh ? 39. Hoist what thing flag, eh ? 53. |
| 3. | ʿHò ʿts'z ꜀Ying-kwok꜄ keʾ; ꜁m ʿt'aí tak꜄ ꜀chan. | Very like English-country's 15, not see able true. |
| 4. | ꜁K'éi ꜀kon ʿméi ʿyaú ꜁k'aú* ʿmò áʾ? | Flag staff end have ball not, eh ? 2. |
| 5. | ʿYaú, chiʾ ꜀kò koʾ haiʾ ꜀Ying ꜁k'éi, ꜀chung-꜀kán ʿyaú koʾ ꜁k'aú,* há²-ʿtaí ʿyaú ꜀chi saíʾ ꜁k'éi. | Have most high that is English flag, middle have [C.] ball ,below have [C.] small flag. |
| 6. | Mat꜄ ʿye ꜁k'éi ꜀ni ?ʾ. | What thing flag, eh ? 53. |
| 7. | ʿT'aí ꜁m ch'ut꜄ lok꜄. | See not out. 32. |
| 8. | ʿT'ai koʾ ꜀chi ꜀saí ꜁k'éi, tsaú² ꜀chí koʾ chek꜄ ꜁shün ʿyaú ʿkéi ʿyün.* | Look-at that [C.] small flag then know that [C.] vessel have how far. |
| 9. | Lok꜄ saíʾ ꜁kéi lok꜄. [chek꜄. | Down small flag, 32. [only, 7. |
| 10. | Pat꜄ kwoʾ ꜀ch'o-꜀ch'o ʿch'e saíʾ ꜁k'éi. | Not more than-at first hoist small flag |
| 11. | ʿFo-shün꜁mái-꜁t'aú꜁yiúʾʿkwún-ʿtím* höüʾ ʿlo sunʾ. | Steamer arrive want coolie go get letters. |
| 12. | Kinʾ koʾ chek꜄ ʿfo-꜁shün p'ák꜄ ꜁mái ʿmá-꜁t'aú tsaú² wá² ʿngo ꜀chí áʾ. | See that [C.] steamer lie close-to wharf then say to-me to-know, 2. |
| 13. | ʿHò lok꜄. | Good, 32. |
| 14. | Táí²-k'oíʾ* ʿyaú ʿlöng ʿtím ꜀chung kòmʾ noíʾ* chíʾ tòʾ, ꜀yan-꜁waí ꜀kam mat꜄ ʿhò ꜀t'in ʿmò ꜀shán mò². | Probably have two [C.] hours so long till arrive, because this day good weather, no mountain mist. |
| 15. | Ná², ꜀kwú-꜁léi ʿngo ʿse ꜀chöng ʿchí ʿnéi lok꜄ höüʾ ꜀shú-sunʾ ʿkwún ʿlo ʿtsò-꜀ká sunʾ ꜁laí. | There-now coolie I have-written a-piece [C.] of-paper for-you to-go down away to- Post Office to-bring mail letters come (*to bring-come*, i.e. *to fetch*). |
| 16. | ꜁M ꜀chí ꜀shü-sunʾ-ʿkwún ʿhaí pin shüʾ ꜀ni.ʾ | Not know Post-Office at what place, 32. |
| 17. | Táí²-꜀Chung-꜁Laú* kák꜄-꜁léi, tsoi² Táíʾ ʿMá ꜁Lò. | Large Clock Loft neighbouring, in Large Horse Road. |
| 18. | ꜀Ning koʾ ꜀chöng ʿchi lok꜄ höüʾ, tsaú² kínʾ ʿyaú ꜀ti ꜀ch'öng-꜁mún (*or* ꜀ch'öng ꜁mún*) ʿhaí ʿTáí꜄ Chung ꜁Laú* koʾ pin². | Take that piece [C.] of-paper down go, then see have some windows at Large Clock Tower that side. |

## CONVERSATION 33RD.—MAIL LETTERS.—(*Continued.*)

| | | |
|---|---|---|
| 19. | There are a number of people waiting at the windows to get letters. | 有好多人喺窓門個便等攞信、 |
| 20. | When the windows are opened you show this paper to the people inside, and they will hand you the letters. | 窓門開呢、就俾呢張紙過裏頭個啲人睇、佢就交信出嚟俾你、 |
| 21. | As soon as they are handed to you, you must come up quickly. | 一交信過你、你快脆啲翻上嚟至得、 |
| 22. | Very good, Sir. | 好喇、先生、 |
| 23. | Go at once. | 卽刻去、 |
| 24. | I have come back, Sir. There are three letters and four newspapers. | 先生、翻嚟咯、有三封信、四張新聞紙、 |
| 25. | Very good. Give them to me. | 好喇、俾我喇、 |
| 26. | There are only two letters here, and you said there were three. How is that? | 呢處淨係有兩封信、你又話有三封、點解呢、 |
| 27. | The man told me there was a registered letter, which he would not give me. | 個人話我聽有一封擔保信、佢唔俾我嘅、 |
| 28. | Then he only gave you two letters. | 噉、佢淨係俾兩封你咯、 |
| 29. | Yes, and I had to pay ten cents on this one before he would give it to me. | 係哩、呢封佢又要我俾十個先至交俾我、 |
| 30. | Why was that? | 做乜呢、 |
| 31. | He said the postage was not enough. | 佢話信資唔够嗻、 |
| 32. | All right, that will do. | 好咯、做得咯、 |

## CONVERSATION 34TH.—GEOGRAPHY.

| | | |
|---|---|---|
| 1. | I have bought a new map to-day. Would you like to see it? | 我今日買一幅新地理圖、你想睇唔呀、 |
| 2. | Oh! Indeed? I would. | 呵、係咩、想吖、 |

## CONVERSATION 33RD.—MAIL LETTERS.—(*Continued.*)

| | | |
|---|---|---|
| 19. | ᶝYaú ᶜhò ͺto ͺyan* ᶜhai ͺch'öng-ͺmún (or as above) koʾ pin$^2$ ᶜtang ᶜlo sunʾ. | Have very many people at windows that side waiting to-get letters. |
| 20. | ͺCh'öng-ͺmún (or better as above) ͺhoi ͺni, tsaú$^2$ ᶜpéi ͺni ͺchöng ᶜchi kwoʾ ᶝlöü-ͺt'aú koʾ-ͺti ͺyan ᶜt'aí, ᶝk'öü tsaú$^2$ ͺkaú sunʾ ch'ut, ͺlaí ᶜpéi ᶝnéi. | Windows open, 53, then give this piece-of [C.] paper to inside those men to look-at, they thereupon hand letters out come give you. |
| 21. | ͺYat ͺkaú sunʾ kwoʾ ᶝnéi, ᶝnéi faíʾ-ts'öüʾ-tí ͺfán ᶝshöng ͺlaí chíʾ tak. | Once handed letters over to-you, you quickly back up come in-order-to [do. |
| 22. | ᶜHò ͺlá,$^2$ ͺSin-ͺsháng. | Good, 21, Sir. |
| 23. | Tsik-hak höüʾ. | Immediately go. |
| 24. | ͺSin-ͺsháng†, ͺfán ͺlai* lok, ᶝyaú ͺsám ͺfung sunʾ, szʾ ͺchöng ͺsan-ͺman-ᶜchí. | Sir, back come, 32, have three [C.] letters, four [C.] newspapers. |
| 25. | ᶜHò ͺlá,$^2$ ᶜpéi ᶝngo ͺlá.$^2$ | Good, 21, give to-me, 21. |
| 26. | ͺNi shüʾ tsing$^2$-hai$^2$ ᶝyaú ᶝlöng ͺfung sunʾ, ᶝnéi yaú$^2$ wá$^2$ ᶝyaú ͺsám ͺfung; (This becomes a variant tone as it is in a questioning tone). ᶜTím ᶜkaí ͺni ?$^2$ | This place only have two [C.] letters, you also say have three [C.]. How explain, eh ? 53. |
| 27. | Koʾ ͺyan* wá$^2$ ᶝngo ͺt'eng† ᶝyaú yat ͺfung ͺtám-ᶜpò sunʾ, ᶝk'öü ͺm ᶜpéi ᶝngo keʾ. | The man said to-me to-hear there-was one [C.] registered letter, he not give to-me, 15. |
| 28. | ᶜKòm ᶝk'öü tsing$^2$ hai$^2$ ᶜpéi ᶝlöng ͺfung ᶝnéi lok. | Then he only did give two [C.] to-you, 32. |
| 29. | Hai$^2$ ͺle,$^2$ ͺni ͺfung ᶝk'öü yaú$^2$ yíúʾ ᶝngo ᶜpéi shap koʾ ͺsín chʾi ͺkaú ᶜpéi ᶝngo. | Yes, 24, this [C.] he also required me to-give ten [C] cents before hand-over [give me. |
| 30. | Tsò$^2$ mat ͺni ?$^2$ | Do what, eh ? 53. |
| 31. | ᶝK'öü wá$^2$ sunʾ-tsz ͺm kaúʾ ᶝwá. | He said postage not sufficient so-he-said, |
| 32. | ᶜHò lok, tsò$^2$ tak lok. | Good 32, do can, [i.e., can do] 32. [61. |

## CONVERSATION 34TH.—GEOGRAPHY.

| | | |
|---|---|---|
| 1. | ᶝNgo ͺkam-yat ᶝmái yat fuk ͺsan téi$^2$-ᶝléi-ͺt'ò. ᶝNéi ᶜsöng ᶜt'ai ͺmáʾ? | I to-day buy one [C.] new map. You wish see not, eh ? 2. |
| 2. | ͺO ! hai$^2$ ͺme ?$^2$ ᶜSöng ͺá.$^2$ | Oh ! Is-it-so, eh ? 39. Wish, 1. |

## CONVERSATION 34TH.—GEOGRAPHY.—(*Continued.*)

| | |
|---|---|
| 3. I take it this large place in the centre of the map is China. | 我睇得地理圖中間呢笪大地方係中國啩、 |
| 4. Oh no, thatis Europe, Asia, and Africa. | 唔係、個笪係歐羅巴亞細亞、及亞非利加啫、 |
| 5. Then where is China? I do not see it at all. | 噉、中國喺邊處呢、喊都唔見到咯、 |
| 6. There it is. | 喺個臐咯、 |
| 7. No, you are joking. The Eighteen Provinces so small? | 唔係、先生講笑話咯、十八省咁細嘅咩、 |
| 8. It is not that China is small. China is very large, but the whole world is very much larger than China; It is not only China that is in the world, there are a great many countries in it. | 唔係話中國細、唐山好大地方、但係通天下計埋重大得多過中國咯、天下唔止獨係中國、有好多國嚹、 |
| 9. How strange! It is truly strange! Where are England, and America? | 咁出奇嘅、眞正奇咯、英國美國喺邊處呢、 |
| 10. How do you Western people come to China? | 你哋西國人點嚟中國呢、 |
| 11. There are several routes. From America you come by steamer from California to Yokohama in Japan, and afterwards you come straight to Shanghai, or Hongkong. The whole voyage takes about a month. | 有幾條路嚟嘅、喺美國嚟、就喺舊金山搭火船、嚟到日本橫濱、然後一直駛到上海、或香港、成條水路嚟計約嘆要一個月度、 |
| 12. There are several routes by which you can come from England. | 喺英國有幾條路可以嚟得嘅、 |
| 13. First you start from London, which is the capital of England, or from some other English port. | 第一就喺英國京城倫敦開身、或者喺英國別個埠頭起行、 |

1. It will be noticed two names are given in Chinese for Gibraltar.

CONVERSATION 34TH.—GEOGRAPHY.—(*Continued.*)

| | | |
|---|---|---|
| 3. | ᶜNgo ᶜt'ai takˀ téi2-ᶜléi-꜀t'o ꜀chung-꜀kán ꜀ni tát꜀ tái2 téi2-꜀fong hai2 ꜀Chung-kwok꜀ kwáˀ. | I see able (i.e. I apprehend) map's centre this spot large place is Middle Kingdom I-suppose, 18. |
| 4. | ꜀M hai2, koˀ tát hai2 ꜀Áu-꜀lo-꜀pá, Áˀ-꜀sai-áˀ, kap꜀ Áˀ-꜀féi-léi2-꜀ká ꜀che. | Not is, that spot is Europe, Asia, and Africa, only, 7. |
| 5. | ᶜKóm, ꜀Chung-kwok꜀ ᶜhai ꜀pín shüˀ ꜀ni? Hám2 ꜀tò ꜀m kínˀ tòˀ lok꜀. | Then Middle Kingdom is-at what place, eh? 53. Altogether also not see reach, 32. (Do not arrive at seeing it.) |
| 6. | ᶜHaí koˀ shüˀ lok꜀. | At that place, 32. |
| 7. | ꜀M hai2, ꜀Sín-꜀shàng† ᶜkong síuˀ-wáˀ* lok꜀. Shap꜀-pát꜀ ᶜShàng kómˀ saiˀ keˀ ꜀me? | Not is. Sir speaks laughing words, 32. Eighteen Provinces (i.e., China Proper) so small, eh? 15, 39. |
| 8. | ꜀M hai2 wá2 ꜀Chung-kwok꜀ saiˀ. ꜀T'ong꜀Shán ᶜhò tái2 téi2-꜀fong, tán2-hai2 ꜀t'ung ꜀t'ín-há2 kaiˀ ꜀mái chung2 tái2 tak꜀ ꜀to kwoˀ ꜀Chung-kwok꜀ lok꜀. ꜀T'ín-há2 ꜀m ᶜchí tuk꜀ hái2 ꜀Chung-kwok꜀, ᶜyaú ᶜhò ꜀to kwok꜀ káˀ. | Not do say Middle Kingdom small. China very large place; but all Heaven's Under calculated together still larger able-to-be much than China, 32. World not simply only is China, have great many countries, 14. |
| 9. | Kómˀ ch'ut꜀-꜀k'éi keˀ! ꜀Chan chingˀ ꜀k'éi lok꜀! ꜀Ying-kwok꜀, ᶜMéi-kwok꜀ ᶜhai ꜀pín (shüˀ) ꜀ni? | So extraordinary! 15. Truly really strange! 32. England, America at where, eh? 53. |
| 10. | ᶜNéi-téi2 ꜀Sai-kwok꜀ ꜀yan ᶜtím ꜀lai ꜀Chung-kwok꜀ ꜀ni? | You Western-country men how come-to China, eh? 53. |
| 11. | ᶜYaú ᶜkéi ꜀t'íu lò2 ꜀lai keˀ, ᶜhai ᶜMái-kwok꜀ ꜀lai, tsaú2 ᶜhai Kań2 ꜀Kam-꜀Shán táp꜀ ᶜfo-꜀shün, ꜀lai tòˀ Yat꜀-ᶜpún, ꜀Wáng-꜀pan, ꜀yín-haú2 yat꜀ chik꜀ ᶜshaí tòˀ Shöng2-ᶜhoi wák꜀ ꜀Höng-ᶜkong. ꜀Sheng† ꜀t'íu ᶜshöü-lò2 ꜀lai kaiˀ yök꜀-mok꜀* yiúˀ yat꜀ koˀ yüt꜀ ᶜtò. | Have several lengths-of road come, 15. from America come, then in Old Gold Hills get-on fire-ship come arrive-at Japan, Yokohama. Afterwards one straight sail arrive Shanghai, or Hongkong. All length of water-road come calculate approximately must require one [C.] month about. |
| 12. | ᶜHai ꜀Ying-kwok ᶜyaú ᶜkéi ꜀t'íu lò2 ᶜho-ᶜyí ꜀lai tak꜀ keˀ. | From England have several lengths road come able-to, 15. |
| 13. | Tai2 yat꜀ tsaú2 ᶜhai ꜀Ying-kwok ꜀king-꜀sheng† ꜀Lun-꜀tun (*or* ꜀Lun ꜀tun) ꜀hoi-꜀shan, wák꜀-ᶜche ᶜhai ꜀Ying-kwok꜀ pít꜀ koˀ fau2-꜀t'aú ᶜhéi ꜀háng†. | No. 1 then from England capital city London start, or from England other [C.] port begin to-go. |

## CONVERSATION 34TH.—GEOGRAPHY.—*(Continued.)*

| | |
|---|---|
| 14. You can reach Gibraltar, a fortress and port in the south of Spain, and belonging to England in four, five, or six days, according to the speed of the steamer. | 睇火船行快或慢嘅、五六日就可以到日巴拉大，英國埠頭炮臺、在大呂宋南邊、 |
| 15. Seen either by day or night, Gibraltar is rather like Hongkong. | 唔論日夜支伯拉德·幾似香港噉嘅、 |
| 16. Four or five days' sail in the Mediterranean, and you reach Malta, an English colony, where after staying a day or two you again start for Egypt. | 喺地中海駛船有四五日咁耐就到馬爾達英國屬島、歇一兩日又開身去埃及、 |
| 17. A few days, and you arrive there, and, without changing steamers, you go through the country from North to South by a canal, taking a day for the journey. | 幾日就到咯、又唔使過船就打運河喺國北便駛通到南便、一日水程、 |
| 18. After that you go down the Red Sea for four or five days, and arrive at Aden, an English settlement; here the sun is scorching, and there is little water to drink, much sand, and very little vegetation. | 然後使落紅海四五日到亞丁英國埠頭、喺個處周年極熱、冇乜水飲、有好多沙漠、好少草木、 |
| 19. Then in about ten days' steaming the vessel arrives at Colombo. This is a port in Ceylon, which is a large island at the South of India, belonging to England. | 噉火船駛七日度就到葛蘭巴埠、呢個埠喺錫蘭海島、在印度南便係屬英國嘅、 |
| 20. After seven or eight day's journey you arrive at Penang, and a day or two after at Singapore. These two ports are also English Colonies and there are a great many Chinese engaged in agriculture and business in both. | 然後七八日水路就到庇嚨（卽新埠）及星架波、呢兩個埠頭都係英國屬土、有好多唐人喺處耕田、做生意嘅、 |

易學廣東話



## CONVERSATION 34TH.—GEOGRAPHY.—(*Continued.*)

| | |
|---|---|
| 14. ᶜT'ai ᶜfo-꜀shün ꜀hàng fàiˀ wàk꜀ mán$^2$ keˀ, ᶜng-luk꜀ yat꜀ tsaú$^2$ ᶜho-ᶜyí tòˀ Yat꜀-꜀pà-꜀lai-tàí$^2$, ꜀Ying-kwok fau$^2$-꜀t'aú, p'aúˀ-꜀t'oi, tsoi$^2$ Tái$^2$-ᶜLöü-sung' ꜀nám pín$^2$. | See steamer go fast or slow, 15, five six days then able-to arrive Gibraltar, English port, fort, at Great Luzon (which-is Spain) south side. |
| 15. ꜀M ꜀lun yat꜀ ye$^2$ ᶜChi-pàk꜀-꜀lai-tak꜀,' ᶜkéi ᶜts'z ꜀Höng-ᶜkong ᶜkòm keˀ. | Not speaking (i.e. it does not matter whether you speak of seeing it) day (or) night, Gibraltar rather like Hongkong so, 15. |
| 16. ᶜHai Téi$^2$-꜀Chung-ᶜHoi ᶜshai ꜀shün ᶜyaú szˀ ᶜng yat꜀ kòmˀ noi$^{5*}$ tsaú$^2$ tòˀᶜMà-꜀yi-tát꜀, ꜀Ying-kwok꜀ shuk꜀ ᶜt'òt, lut꜀ yat꜀ ᶜlöng yat꜀ yaú$^2$ ꜀hoi-꜀shan höüˀ ꜀Oi-k'ap꜀. | In Mediterranean Sea sail ship, have four five days so long, then arrive Malta, English belonging island. Stop one two days again start go Egypt. |
| 17. ᶜKéi yat꜀ tsaú$^2$ tòˀ lok꜀, yaú$^2$ ꜀m ᶜshai kwoˀ ꜀shün, tsaú$^2$ ᶜtá wan$^2$-꜀ho ᶜhai kwok꜀ pak꜀ pín$^2$ ᶜshai ꜀t'ung tòˀ ꜀nám pín$^2$ yat꜀ yat꜀ ᶜshöü ꜀ch'ing. | Several days then arrive, 32, further not need cross-over-to (another) ship, then by canal from country's north side going through to south side one day's water journey. |
| 18. ꜀Yin-haú$^2$ ᶜshai lok꜀ ꜀Hung-ᶜHoi szˀ ᶜng yat꜀tòˀ Àˀ-꜀ting ꜀Ying-kwok꜀ fau$^2$-꜀t'aú$^2$; ᶜhai koˀ shüˀ ꜀chaú ꜀nín kik꜀ yít꜀ ᶜmò mat꜀ ᶜshöü ᶜyam, ᶜyaú ᶜhò꜀to ꜀shá mok꜀. ᶜhò ᶜshíú ᶜts'ò muk꜀. | Afterwards sail down Red Sea four five days, arrive Aden, English port. At this (place) throughout year extremely hot, not much (*or* none-at-all) water to-drink, have very much sand desert, is very little grass, wood. |
| 19. ᶜKòm, ᶜfo-꜀shün ᶜshai ts'at꜀ yat꜀ tòˀ$^{5*}$ tsaú$^2$ tòˀ Kòt꜀-꜀lün-꜀pá fau$^2$. ꜀Ni koˀ fau$^2$ ᶜhai Sik꜀-꜀lán ᶜhoi-ᶜtò, tsoi$^2$ Yauˀ-tò$^2$ ꜀nám pín$^2$, hai$^2$ shuk꜀ Ying-kwok꜀ keˀ. | Then steamer sails seven days about, then arrives Colombo port. This [C.] port in Ceylon island, at India south side, belong England's, 15. |
| 20. ꜀Yin-haú$^2$ ts'at꜀ pát yat꜀ ᶜshöü lò$^2$ tsaú$^2$tòˀ Péiˀ-꜀nang (tsik꜀꜀San-fau$^2$) k'ap꜀ ꜀Sing-꜀kà-꜀po. ꜀Ni ᶜlöng koˀ fau$^2$-꜀t'aú tò hai$^2$ ꜀Ying-kwok꜀ shuk꜀ᶜt'òt.ᶜyaú ᶜhò ꜀to ꜀T'ong-꜀yan ᶜhai shüˀ ꜀kang ꜀t'in, tsò$^2$ ꜀shàng†-yiˀ keˀ. | After seven eight days water journey then arrive Penang (which-is New Port) and Singapore. These two [C.] ports also are English belong countries, have very many Chinese at place cultivate fields, do business, 15. |

Note.—If will be noticed that there are two renderings for Gibraltar in Chinese.

## CONVERSATION 34TH.—GEOGRAPHY.—(*Continued.*)

| | |
|---|---|
| 21. Five or six days more and you reach Hongkong, from which place the steamer goes on to Shanghai. You go on board another to go to Nagasaki and Yokohama. | 五六日添就到香港咯、喺香港火船去上海、又搭第二隻火船喺香港去長崎橫濱、 |
| 22. This is the route of the English mail steamer. But there are several ways of going. | 呢啲係英國祖家船所行嘅路程、重有幾條路行得嘅、 |
| 23. What do the mail steamers carry? How often do they come to Hongkong in a year? | 祖家船裝乜野嘅呢、一年間嚟香港有幾多賬呢、 |
| 24. The mail steamers take letters, and carry goods and passengers. Each month there are two English, two French, two American, and two German mail steamers come and go. | 祖家船帶信來往及裝貨共人客、每月有兩隻英國祖家船、兩隻法蘭西祖家船、兩隻花旗祖家船及兩隻雜港(*or* 德國)祖家船埋頭開身嘅、 |
| 25. By travelling in this way you see a great many countries. The languages and dialects differ in each country, I suppose, and the customs probably as well. Is the scenery fine? | 噉樣來往就見得好多國、各國說話土談兼及風俗唔同嘞、山水好睇嗎、 |
| 26. In some places the scenery is really very fine. In every place the people and things are strange, and the customs as well: the difference between one country and another is as great as it is possible to imagine. | 有啲地方山水實首好睇、各處人物出奇、風俗規矩奇怪、一國一國唔同、差有天地咁遠咯、 |
| 27. I have heard it said that in a voyage to England there are many days during which you do not see land. Is that so? | 我聽過搭船去英國有好多日都唔見山、係唔係呢、 |

CONVERSATION 34TH.—GEOGRAPHY.—(*Continued.*)

21. ˤNg-luk˭ yat˭ ˛t'ín tsaú² tò˒ ˛Höng-ˤkong lok˭, ˤhaí ˛Höng-ˤkong ˤfo-˛shün höü˒ Shöng²-ˤhoí. Yaú² táp˯ taí² yí² chek˯ ˤfo-˛shün, ˤhaí ˛Höng-ˤkong höü˒ ˛Ch'öng-˛k'éí, ˛Wáng-˛pan.

Five six days more then arrive Hongkong, 32, from Hongkong steamer go Shanghai (*lit.* super mare). Again go-on No. 2 [C.] steamer from Hongkong go Nagasaki and Yokohama.

22. ˛Ni-˛ti haí² ˛Ying-kwok˯ ˤtsò-˳kà ˛shün ˤsho ˛hàng† ke˒ lò²-˛ch'ing, chung² ˤyaú ˤkéi ˛t'ú lò² ˛hàng† tak˭ ke˒.

These are English ancestral-family (i.e. home) vessel which it-goes, 15, journeys, besides have several lengths road go can, 15.

23. ˤTsò-˳kà ˛shün ˛chong mat˭ ˤye ke˒ ˛ni? Yat˭ ˛nín ˛kán ˛laí ˛Höng-ˤkong ˤyaú ˤkéi ˳to chöng˒ ˛ni?

Ancestral-home vessel contains what things, 15, eh? 53. One year period come Hongkong have how many times, eh? 53.

24. ˤTsò-˳kà ˛shün taí˒ sun˒ ˛loí ˤwong, k'ap˭ ˛chong fo˒, kung² ˛yan-hák˯. ˤMúi yüt˭ ˤyaú ˤlöng chek˯ ˛Ying-kwok˯ ˤtsò-˳kà ˛shün, ˤlöng chek˯ Fàt˭-˛làn-˳saí ˤtsò-˳kà ˛shün, ˤlöng chek˯ ˛Fá-˛k'éí ˤtsò-˳kà ˛shün, k'ap˭ ˤlöng chek˯ Tsáp˭-˛kong (*or* Tak˭ Kwok˯) ˤtsò-˳kà ˛shün ˛maí-˛t'aú, ˛hoí-˛shan ke˒.

Ancestral-home vessels bring letters come go and carry goods with passengers. Each month have two [C.] England ancestral-home vessels, two [C.] French ancestral-home vessels, two [C.] American ancestral-home vessels, and two German ancestral-home vessels arrive, leave, 15.

25. ˤKòm yöng˒* ˛loi ˤwong tsaú² kín˒ tak˭ ˤhò ˛to kwok˯. Kok˯ kwok˯ shüt˭-wá² ˤt'ò-˛t'àm ˛kím-k'ap˭ ˛fung tsuk˭ ˛m ˛t'ung kwá˒. ˛Shán-ˤshöü ˤhò ˤt'aí ˤmaí?

So fashion coming going, then see able great many countries. Each country, speech, dialects, and customs not same I-suppose. Mountain-water good see, eh? 35.

26. ˤYaú ˛ti téi²-˛fong ˛shán-ˤshöü shat²-ˤshan ˤhò ˤt'aí. Kok˯ shü˒ (*or* ch'ü˒) ˛yan mat˭* ch'ut˭-˛k'éí, ˛fung-tsuk˭ ˛kwai-ˤköü ˛k'éi-kwaí˒: yat˭ kwok˯ yat˭ kwok˯ ˛m ˛t'ung: ˛ch'á ˤyaú ˛t'ín téi² kòm˒ ˤyün lok˯.

Have some places scenery really fine to-see. Each place men (and) things strange, customs (and) manners remarkable: one country, one country not same; distinct have heaven earth so far, 32.

27. ˤNgo ˛t'eng† kwo˒ táp˯ ˛shün höü˒ ˛Ying-kwok˯ ˤyaú ˤhò ˛to yat˭ ˳tò ˛m kín˒ ˛shán. Haí² ˛m haí² ˛ni?

I heard have go-on ship go England have very many days also not see hills. Is not is, eh? 53.

CONVERSATION 34TH.—GEOGRAPHY.—(Continued.)

| | | |
|---|---|---|
| 28. | Yes, there are many days on which you do not see land. There is the ocean all round, and sometimes you do not even see birds. | 係、有好多日唔見得岸、周圍有大海、有時連雀都唔見添、 |
| 29. | There being so many fish in the ocean, you will probably every now and then have fish to eat. | 大海咁多魚、耐不耐有魚食啩、 |
| 30. | No, there is no time; there is no time to stop to catch fish. | 唔係、唔得閒、唔得閒停車嚟捉魚、 |
| 31. | How is that? | 點解呢、 |
| 32. | Steamers go too quickly. Besides there are times when you never see any fish at all. | 火船行得快、另外有時㖭都唔見到魚、 |

CONVERSATION 35TH.—THE LOST CHIT BOOK.

| | | |
|---|---|---|
| 1. | A-kam, where is my chit book? | 亞金、我個信部呢、 |
| 2. | I do not know. | 唔知呀、 |
| 3. | You ought to know. | 你應該知呀、 |
| 4. | I have not seen it for several days. | 幾日都唔見呀、 |
| 5. | Have you looked for it? | 搵唔曾呀、 |
| 6. | I have. | 搵嚟咯、 |
| 7. | Ask the coolies for it. | 問咕喱喇、 |
| 8. | Very well. | 好喇、 |
| 9. | Do the coolies know where it is? | 咕喱知喺邊處唔知呀、 |
| 10. | The coolies says when a chit was taken out last night, it was not brought back. | 咕喱話昨晚拎信唔曾 (or 咯) 拎翻嚟、 |
| 11. | Why was it not brought back? | 做乜冇拎翻嚟呢、 |
| 12. | The gentlemen had gone out to dinner, and he left it for him to sign when he returned. | 個事頭出街食餐、佢丟處等佢翻嚟簽名、 |
| 13. | The boy could sign. | 事仔簽得、 |
| 14. | The boy was unwilling to sign. | 事仔唔肯簽字呀、 |
| 15. | He could have signed in Chinese, and given the letter to his master when he came back. | 佢簽唐字得喇、等事頭翻嚟交信俾佢、 |

## CONVERSATION 34TH.—GEOGRAPHY.—(*Continued.*)

| | | |
|---|---|---|
| 28. | Hai$^2$ ᶜyaú ᶜhò ꜀to yat$_2$ ꜀m kín꜄ tak꜀ ngòn$^2$. ꜀Chaú-꜀wai (*or* ꜀chaú ꜀wai) ᶜyaú tái$^2$ ᶜhoi. ᶜyaú ꜀shí ꜀lin tsök꜀* tò ꜀m kin꜄ ꜀t'ím. | It is (the case that you do) have very many days, not see able shore. All round have great sea, have times including birds also not see, too. |
| 29. | Tái$^2$ ᶜhoi kòm꜄ ꜀to ꜀yü* (*or* ꜀yü), noi$^2$ pat꜀ noi$^{5*}$ ᶜyaú ꜀yü* shik$_2$ kwá꜄. | Large ocean so many fish, now and then have fish eat I-suppose, 18. |
| 30. | ꜀M hai$^2$; ꜀m tak꜀ ꜀hán: ꜀m tak꜀ ꜀hán ꜀t'ing ꜀ch'e ꜀lai chuk꜀ ꜀yü*. | Not is, not have leisure; not have leisure stop engine to catch fish. |
| 31. | ᶜTim ᶜkái ꜀ni ? | How explain, eh ? 53. |
| 32. | ᶜFo-꜀shün ꜀hàng† tak꜀ fai꜄. Ling$^2$-ngoi$^2$ ᶜyaú ꜀shí hàm$^2$ ꜀tò ꜀m kin꜄ tò꜄ ꜀yü* | Steamer go can quick. Besides have times altogether also not see fish. |

## CONVERSATION 35TH.—THE LOST CHITBOOK.

| | | |
|---|---|---|
| 1. | Á-꜀kam, ᶜngo ko꜄ sun꜄-pò$^{5*}$ ꜀ni ?$^2$ | A-kam, my that letter-book, eh ? 53. |
| 2. | ꜀M ꜀chi á꜄. | Not know, 2. |
| 3. | ᶜNéi ꜀ying-꜀koi ꜀chí á꜄. | You ought to-know, 2. |
| 4. | ᶜKéi yat$_2$ ꜀tò ꜀m kín꜄ á꜄. | Several days also not see, 2. |
| 5. | ᶜWan ꜀m ꜀ts'ang á꜄ ? | Looked-for not yet ? 2. |
| 6. | ᶜWan ꜀lai lok꜀. | Looked-for have, 32. |
| 7. | Man$^2$ ꜀kwú-꜀léi ꜀lá.$^2$ | Ask coolies, 21. |
| 8. | ᶜHò ꜀lá.$^2$ [꜀chi á꜄ ? | Very good, 21. [eh ? 2. |
| 9. | ꜀Kwú-꜀léi ꜀chí ᶜhai ꜀pín shü꜄ ꜀m | Coolies know at what place not know, |
| 10. | ꜀Kwú-꜀léi wá$^2$ tsok$_2$ ᶜmán ꜀ning sun꜄ ꜀m ꜀ts'ang (*or* ꜀meng) ꜀ning fán ꜀lai. | Coolies say last night took letter not yet bring back come. |
| 11. | Tsò$^2$ mat꜀ ᶜmò ꜀ning ꜀fán ꜀lai ꜀ni ?$^2$ | Do what not brought back come, eh ? 53. |
| 12. | Kò꜄ sz$^2$-꜀t'aú* ch'ut꜀ ꜀kái (*or* ꜀kái) shik$_2$ ꜀ts'án, ᶜk'öü ꜀tiú (*or* ꜀tíú) shü꜄ ᶜtang ᶜk'öü ꜀fán ꜀lai ꜀ts'ím | The master go-out street eat meal, he placed (it) there wait he back come sign name. |
| 13. | Sz$^2$-ᶜtsai ꜀ts'ím tak꜀. [꜀meng*†. | Boy sign can. [2. |
| 14. | Sz$^2$-ᶜtsai ꜀m ᶜhang ꜀ts'ím-tsz$^2$ á꜄. | Boy not willing sign (lit. sign characters). |
| 15. | ᶜK'öü ꜀ts'ím ꜀T'ong-tsz$^2$ tak꜀ ꜀lá,$^2$ ᶜtang sz$^2$-꜀t'aú* ꜀fán ꜀lai ꜀kaú sun꜄ ᶜpéi ᶜk'öü. | He sign Chinese can, 21, wait master back come hand letter give him. |

## CONVERSATION 35TH.—THE LOST CHIT BOOK.—*(Continued.)*

| | | |
|---|---|---|
| 16. | The coolie says those boys are very saucy and will not let you speak, they will not let you even say a word. | 咕喱話個啲事仔好沙塵嘅、唔許你講嘅、一句都唔准你講嘅、 |
| 17. | You tell the coolie that, unless I say the chit is very important, and must be signed by the master himself, the boy's signature will do. | 你話咕喱聽、我唔係話個信係好緊要嘅是必要事頭簽名、事仔簽字可以做得咯、 |
| 18. | The coolies also said that he thought there was money in the letter, as it was so thick and heavy. | 咕喱又話佢見個封信係咁厚、咁重、佢估是必係銀信、 |
| 19. | You tell him what I have said. | 我所講個啲說話、你講翻出嚟俾佢聽、 |
| 20. | I am writing a letter now, and, when I have finished it, I want the coolie to take it to West Point. | 我而家寫一張信、寫完要咕喱拎去西營盤、 |
| 21. | But I want him first to go and get the chit book. | 先要佢去攞翻個信部、 |
| 22. | There is an answer to this letter | 呢封信有回音嘅、 |
| 23. | You must wait for an answer. | 要等回音、 |
| 24. | Take this parcel down to the office. | 呢包野拎落去寫字樓、 |
| 25. | Come back quickly. There is some work to do in the house. | 快啲翻嚟、屋踰有啲工夫做、 |
| 26. | There is no ink in the inkstand; pour some into it. The pen nib is broken; put a new nib into the pen-holder. | 墨水罌冇墨水、倒(*or* 斟)啲落去、筆嘴又爛、(*or* 安插)個新筆嘴入筆竿、 |
| 27. | This note-paper is damp. When you write, the writing is blurred. That envelope is blotted with ink. I cannot use it. | 呢啲信紙腍寫字腍筆咯、個信筒俾墨水整鋍鲊咯、唔使得咯、 |

## CONVERSATION 35TH.—THE LOST CHIT BOOK.—(*Continued.*)

16. ꜀Kwú-꜀léí wá[2] koᵓ-ti sz[2]-ᶜtsaí ᶜhò ꜀shái-꜀ch'an keᵓ, ꜀m ᶜhöü ᶜnéí ᶜkong keᵓ, yat꜆ köüᵓ tò ꜀m ᶜchun ᶜnéí ᶜkong keᵓ. — Coolie says those boys very saucy, 15. not allow you speak, 15, one sentence even not allow you speak, 15.

17. ᶜNéí wá[2] ꜀kwú-꜀léí ꜀t'eng† ᶜngo ꜀m haí[2] wá[2] koᵓ sunᵓ haí[2] ᶜhò ᶜkan-yíúᵓ keᵓ, shí[2]-pit꜆ yíúᵓ sz[2]-꜀t'aú* ꜀ts'ím ꜀meng*†, sz[2]-ᶜtsaí ꜀ts'ím-tsz[2] ᶜho-ᶜyí tsò[2]-tak꜆ lok꜆. — You speak-to coolie (for him) to-hear I not do say that letter is very important, 15, (and) must-certainly want master sign name, boy sign can do, 32.

18. ꜀Kwú-꜀léí yaú[2] wá[2] ᶜk'öü kínᵓ koᵓ ꜀fung sunᵓ haí[2] kòmᵓ ᶜhaú*, kòmᵓ ᶜch'ung,* ᶜk'öü ᶜkwú shí[2]-pít꜆ haíᵓ ꜀ngan sunᵓ. — Coolie further says he saw the [C.] letter was so thick so heavy, he thought must-certainly be money letter.

19. ᶜNgo ᶜsho ᶜkong koᵓ-꜀ti shüt꜆-wá[2] ᶜnéí ᶜkong ꜀fán ch'ut꜆ ꜀lai ᶜpéí ᶜk'öü ꜀t'eng.† — I whatever say those words you speak back out come give him to-hear.

20. ᶜNgo ꜀yí-꜀ká ᶜse yat꜆ ꜀chong sunᵓ, ᶜse ꜀yün, yíúᵓ ꜀kwú ꜀léí ꜀ning höüᵓ Saí-꜀ying-꜀p'ún. — I now write a [C.] letter, write finished, want coolie take go West Point.

21. ꜀Sín yíúᵓ ᶜk'öü höüᵓ ᶜlo ꜀fán koᵓ sunᵓ pòᵓ*. — First want him go get back (fetch) that letter book.

22. ꜀Ni ꜀fung sunᵓ ᶜyaú ꜀wúí-꜀yam keᵓ. — This [C.] letter have reply, 15.

23. Yíúᵓ ᶜtang ꜀wúí-꜀yam. — Must wait-for answer.

24. ꜀Ni ꜀paú ᶜye ꜀ning lok꜆ höüᵓ ᶜse-tsz[2]-꜀laú*. (*or* ꜀laú.) — This bundle-of things take down go office.

25. Faíᵓ-꜀ti ꜀fán ꜀lai, uk꜆-ᶜk'éí ᶜyaú ꜀ti ꜀kung-꜀fú tsò[2]. — Quickly back come. house have some work to-do.

26. Mak꜆-ᶜshöü-꜀áng ᶜmò mak꜆-ᶜshöü; ᶜtò (*or* ꜀cham) ꜀ti lok꜆ höüᵓ. Pat꜆-ᶜtsöü yaú[2] lán[2]; ꜀òn (*or* ch'áp꜆ *or* ꜀òn ch'áp꜆) koᵓ ꜀san pat꜆-ᶜtsöü yap꜆ pat꜆-꜀kòn. — Ink-water-jar no ink-water: pour some down go. Pen-nib also broken; place (*or* stick-in or place and stick-in) a new pen-nib in penholder.

27. ꜀Ni-꜀ti sunᵓ ᶜchí ꜀nam. ᶜSe-tsz[2] nam[2] pat꜆ lok꜆. Koᵓ sunᵓ-꜀t'ung* ᶜpéí mak꜆-ᶜshöü ᶜching ᶜlá-ᶜchai lok꜆, ꜀m ᶜshai tak꜆ lok꜆. — This letter (*or* note) paper damp, writing damp pen, 32. The envelope with ink-water make dirty, 32, not use able, 32.

CONVERSATION 35TH.—THE LOST CHIT FOOK.(*Continued.*)

| | | |
|---|---|---|
| 28. | My lead-pencil is gone. Has it fallen on the floor, or have you taken it? | 我枝鉛筆唔喺個、係跌落地（*or* 樓板）、或你係有揦冇呢 |
| 29. | I have not taken it. I used the slate and slate pencil to put down some accounts. | 我冇揦到呀、我使個塊石板、石筆、嚟上啲數、 |
| 30. | Why do you not take Chinese pen and ink to do that? They are here as well as ink, slab, and paper, all ready. | 做乜你唔用唐筆墨嚟寫呢、呢處有吖、又有墨硯唐人紙、一啲都齊嘥（喺處）咯、 |
| 31. | It is troublesome to grind the ink. | 費事磨個啲墨呀、 |
| 32. | Why, how lazy you are! | 唉、你咁懶惰嘅咩、 |

CONVERSATION 36TH.—DIPLOMATIC.

| | | |
|---|---|---|
| 1. | Many Western countries have made treaties with China. | 好多西國同中國立和約、 |
| 2. | Those who make the treaties are generally ambassadors. | 立和約嘅人平常係欽差定嘅、 |
| 3. | The Chinese have also lately sent ambassadors to foreign countries. | 近來中國打發欽差過外國、 |
| 4. | Ambassadors reside at the capital cities, and consult about governmental matters with ministers of state. | 欽差在京城住、同大臣議國事嘅、 |
| 5. | Consuls reside at other cities to attend to matters relating to their countrymen. | 領事官住別處嘅城、嚟打理佢本國人嘅事幹、 |
| 6. | Despatches are letters sent by officials on government business | 文書係官所附嘅信、講皇家嘅事 |
| 7. | A different style is used in writing them to that which is commonly employed. | 寫文書嘅文法、唔同平常所用嘅、 |

CONVERSATION 35TH.—THE LOST CHIT BOOK.—*(Continued.)*

| | | |
|---|---|---|
| 28. | ˢNgo ꜀chí ꜀yün-pat˒ ꜀m ᶜhaí ko˒. Hai$^{2}$ tit$_{o}$ lok$_{2}$ téi$^{2}$ (*or* ꜀laú*-ᶜpán); wák$_{2}$ ˢnéi hai$^{2}$ ˢyaú ꜀ning ˢmò ꜀ni ?[2] | My [C.] lead-pencil not is at-that. Has-it fallen down ground (*or* is floor); or you did have take not, eh ? 53. |
| 29. | ˢNgo ˢmò ꜀ning-tò˒ á˒. ˢNgo ᶜshaí ko˒ fái˒ shek$_{2}$-ᶜpán, shek$_{2}$-pat˒; ꜀lai ˢshöng ꜀ti sho˒. | I not take, 2. I use the [C.] stone-board, stone-pencil in-order-to put-down some accounts. |
| 30. | Tsò$^{2}$ mat˒ ˢnéi ꜀m yung$^{2}$ ꜀T'ong pat˒ mak$_{2}$ ꜀lai ᶜse ꜀ni? ꜀Ni shü˒ ˢyaú ꜀á, yaú$^{2}$ ˢyaú mak$_{2}$-yín$^{3}$*, ꜀T'ong- ꜀yan ᶜchí, yat˒ ꜀ti ꜀tò ꜀ts'ai sái˒ (ᶜhaí shü˒) lok$_{o}$. | Do what-thing you not use Chinese pen ink in-order-to write, eh ? 53. This place have, 1, also have ink-slab, Chinese paper, each to-the-smallest-item even ready all (at place), 32. |
| 31. | Fai˒-sz$^{2}$ ꜀mo ko˒-꜀ti mak$_{2}$ á˒. | Troublesome grind that ink, 2. |
| 32. | ꜀Ái, (*or* ꜀Ái) ˢnéi kòm˒ ˢlán-to$^{2}$ ke˒ ꜀me ?[2] | Oh ! you so lazy, 15, eh ? 39. |

CONVERSATION 36TH.—DIPLOMATIC.

| | | |
|---|---|---|
| 1. | ᶜHò-꜀to ꜀Sai-kwok$_{o}$ ꜀t'ung ꜀Chung-kwok$_{o}$ láp$_{2}$ ꜀wo-yök$_{o}$. | Many Western-countries with Central-Kingdom made treaties. |
| 2. | Láp$_{2}$ ꜀wo-yök$_{o}$ ᶜke ꜀yan ꜀p'ing-꜀shöng hai$^{2}$ ꜀yam-ch'ái ꜀ting ke˒. | Make treaties those persons usually are ambassadors settle-them, 15. |
| 3. | Kan$^{2}$-꜀loí* ꜀Chung-kwok$_{o}$ ᶜtá-fát$_{o}$ ꜀yam-꜀ch'ái kwo˒ ngoí$^{2}$ kwok$_{o}$. | Lately Central-Kingdom sent ambassadors to outside countries. |
| 4. | ꜀Yam-꜀ch'ái tsoí$^{2}$ ꜀king ꜀sheng† chü$^{2}$, ꜀t'ung taí$^{2}$-꜀shan ˢyí kwok$_{o}$ sz$^{2}$ ke˒. | Ambassadors in capital cities live, with ministers-of-state consult country's business, 15. |
| 5. | ˢLing-sz$^{2}$-꜀kwún chü$^{2}$ pít$_{2}$ shü˒ ke˒ ꜀sheng† ꜀lai ᶜtá-ˢléi ˢk'öü ᶜpún kwok$_{o}$ ꜀yan ke˒ sz$^{2}$-kón˒. | Consuls live-in other places, 15, cities in-order-to attend-to their own country's people's business. |
| 6. | ꜀Man-꜀shü hai$^{2}$ ꜀kwún ᶜsho fú$^{2}$ ke˒ sun˒, ᶜkong ꜀Wong-꜀ká[1] ke˒ sz$^{2}$. | Despatches are officials sent letters speaking-about Governmental matters. |
| 7. | ᶜSe ꜀man-꜀shü-ke˒ ꜀man-fát$_{o}$, ꜀m ꜀t'ung ꜀p'ing-꜀shöng ᶜsho yung$^{2}$ ke˒, (*or better* ke$^{1}$*). | Writing despatches' style, not similar (to-that) usually what employed, 15. |

Note.—1. This is the common term in use amongst the Chinese in Hongkong and has classical sanction; another term is 國家 Kwok$_{o}$ ꜀ká.

## CONVERSATION 36TH.—DIPLOMATIC.—(*Continued.*)

| | |
|---|---|
| 8. It is necessary to know all the different modes of addressing different persons. | 要識所有各樣方法嚟稱呼各人、 |
| 9. I have heard there is a report that the Viceroy is going to Peking. | 我聽聞有聲氣制台去北京、 |
| 10. Yes, every one in the streets says so. | 係哩、街上人人都係噉講咯、 |
| 11. I do not know whether it is true or false. You cannot believe everything that is said in the streets. | 唔知係眞嘅假呢、街上所講嘅、唔信得晒嘅、 |
| 12. Probably there is some truth in it, but I do not know certainly. | 大槪都有啲眞嘅、但係唔知得實咯、 |
| 13. Is the new Intendant of Circuit well spoken of? | 人哋講嗰個新道台、好唔好呢、 |
| 14. He has a good name; and is said to be an upright and just official. | 佢有好名聲、人地話佢係正直公道嘅官、 |
| 15. It is a pity that so many Chinese officials extort money from the populace. | 可惜咁多唐官都係勒索百姓嘅、 |
| 16. It is very rarely that such a thing happens in England; but when it does severe punishment follows. | 英國冇幾何有噉嘅事、若係有、一定嚴辦、 |
| 17. At present the District Magistrate is a good man, and tries cases very clearly. | 現時個縣官好人審事好明白、 |
| 18. The different ranks of Chinese are clearly distinguished by buttons; and there are other ways by which you can discover them. | 唐官等級有頂易得分開、又有第二樣法子可以睇得出嘅、 |

## CONVERSATION 36TH.—DIPLOMATIC.

| | |
|---|---|
| 8. Yiú᾽ shik˒ ᶜsho ᶜyaú kok˓ yöng$^{2}$ ꜀fong-fát˓ ꜀laí ꜀ch'ing-꜀fú kok꜀ ꜀yan. | Must know whatever there-is of each sort of methods to address-politely each person. |
| 9. ᶜNgo ꜀t'eng† ꜀man ᶜyaú ꜀sheng†-héi᾽ Chi$^{2}$-꜀t'oi höü᾽ Pak˒-꜀king. | I hearing heard there-is report Viceroy going-to Northern-capital. |
| 10. Haí$^{2}$ ꜀le, ꜀kái (*or better* ꜀kái) shöng$^{2}$ ꜀yan ꜀yan ꜀tò haí$^{2}$ ᶜkòm ᶜkong lok꜀. | Yes, 24, street on, man (and) man also have so say, 32. |
| 11. ꜀M ꜀chí (*or better* ꜀chí) haí$^{2}$ ꜀chan péí$^{2}$ ᶜká ꜀ni. ꜀Kái shöng$^{2}$ ᶜsho ᶜkong ke᾽ ꜀m sun᾽ tak˒ sáí᾽ ke.᾽* | Not know (is) true or false, 53. Street on what is said, 16, not believe can all, 15. |
| 12. Táí$^{2}$-k'oí᾽* ꜀tò ᶜyaú ꜀ti ꜀chan ke᾽, tán$^{2}$-haí$^{2}$ ꜀m ꜀chí tak˒ shat˒ lok. | Probably also have little truth, 15, but not know able certainly, 32. |
| 13. ꜀Yan-téí$^{2}$ ᶜkong ᶜko-ko᾽ ꜀san Tò$^{2}$-꜀t'oí ᶜhò ꜀m ᶜhò ꜀ni ?$^{2}$ | People say that new Intendant-of-Circuit good not good eh ? 53. |
| 14. ᶜK'öü ᶜyaú ᶜhò ꜀meng†-꜀sheng† (*or* ꜀ming-꜀shing ; ꜀yan-téí$^{2}$ wá$^{2}$ ᶜk'öü haí$^{2}$ ching᾽-chik˒ ꜀kung-tò$^{2}$ ke᾽ ꜀kwún. | He has good report; people say he is upright just's official. |
| 15. ᶜHo-sik˒ kòm᾽ ꜀to ꜀T'ong ꜀kwún ꜀tò haí$^{2}$ lák˒-sok꜀ pák˒-sing᾽ ke᾽*. | To-be-pitied so many Chinese officials also do extort-from (the) hundred surnames. |
| 16. ꜀Ying-kwok꜀ ᶜmò-ᶜkéi-꜀ho ᶜyaú ᶜkòm ke᾽ sz$^{2}$; yök˒ haí$^{2}$ ᶜyaú, yat˒-ting$^{2}$ ꜀yím pán$^{2}$. | England, 15, not-often have such a thing; if it-is-so-that there-is, to-a-certainty severely punished. |
| 17. Yín$^{2}$-꜀shí (*or* yín$^{2}$ ꜀shí*) ko᾽ Yün$^{2}$ ꜀kwún ᶜhò ꜀yan, ᶜsham-sz$^{2}$ ᶜhò ꜀ming-pák꜀. | At present the District Magistrate good man, try cases very clearly. |
| 18. ꜀T'ong ꜀kwún ᶜtang-k'ap˒ ᶜyaú ᶜteng†*, yí$^{2}$-tak˒ ꜀fan-꜀hoí ; yaú$^{2}$ ᶜyaú taí$^{2}$-yí$^{2}$ yöng$^{2}$ fát꜀-ᶜtsz ᶜho-ᶜyi ᶜt'aí tak˒ ch'ut˒ ke᾽*. | Chinese official ranks have buttons, easy able to-divide-apart: also have other kinds-of methods able to-see can out, 15. |

## CONVERSATION 36TH.—DIPLOMTIC.—(*Continued.*)

| | | |
|---|---|---|
| 19. | English officials dress like the people, without any difference, just the same as those who are not officials. | 英官粧扮百姓一樣、冇分別、好似閒人一樣嘅、 |
| 20. | Court dress is sometimes worn by some high officials. | 有啲大官有時着朝廷衣服嘅、 |
| 21. | Do Chinese officials use torture when trying cases? | 唐人官(府)審案有行刑冇呢、 |
| 22. | They do. Do not foreigners employ torture? | 有、西人唔使咩、(*or*) 西人冇行刑咩、 |
| 23. | No, they did in olden times; but now the lowest and poorest individual when tried in court cannot be compelled to acknowledge his guilt. | 冇、古時有、但而家至賤、至貧窮嘅人到堂審、官不能勉强得佢認罪、 |
| 24. | Good, Western customs are good. Chinese customs are good; but unfortunately Chinese officials are sometimes bad. | 好吖、西國規矩好咯、唐人規矩都好吖、但係可惜唐人官有時唔好、 |
| 25. | There are a great many good things amongst the Chinese, but there is one thing not good. Shall I tell you what it is? Chinese officials do not receive an adequate salary. | 唐人有好多好處、但有一樣唔好咯、我講過你聽啊、唐官俸祿唔够使、 |
| 26. | That is right; those words are true. A high official will only receive a few hundred taels as salary, while his expenses are by the thousands. | 冇錯、個啲說話係眞、大官不過得幾百兩銀做俸祿、佢使費唔止咁少、想計起嚟要斷千或萬兩至做得嘅、 |

## CONVERSATION 36TH.—DIPLOMATIC.—(*Continued.*)

| | |
|---|---|
| 19. ᶜHò-꜀to ꜁Ying ꜀kwún ꜀chong-pán˒ pák꜀-sing˒ yat˒ yöng², ᶜmò ꜀fan-pít꜀, ᶜhò-ᶜts'z ꜁hán ꜁yan yat˒ yöng² ke˒. | Many English officials dress people one same, no difference, like unofficial people one same, 15. |
| 20. ᶜYaú ꜀ti tái² ꜀kwún ᶜyaú ꜁shí (*or* ꜁shí*) chök꜀ ꜁ch'iú-꜁t'ing ꜀yí-fuk˒ ke˒ (*or* ke.¹*) | Have some great officials have times wear Court dress, 15. |
| 21. ꜁T'ong-꜁yan ꜀kwún (ᶜfú) ᶜsham òn˒ ᶜyaú ꜁hang-꜁ying ᶜmò ꜀ni ?² | Chinese officials try cases have use-torture not, eh ? 35. |
| 22. ᶜYaú, ꜀Saí ꜁yan ꜁m ᶜshaí ꜀me ?² *or* ꜀Saí ꜁yan ᶜmò ꜁hang-꜁ying ꜀me ?² | Have, Western men no use, eh ? 39, *or* Western men no employ torture, eh ? 39. |
| 23. ᶜMò, ᶜkwú ꜁shí ᶜyaú; tán² ꜁yí-꜀ká chí˒ tsín², chí˒ ꜁p'an-꜁k'ung ke˒ ꜁yan tò˒ ꜁T'ong ᶜsham, ꜀kwún pat˒ ꜁nang ᶜmín-ᶜk'öng tak˒ ᶜk'öü ying²-tsöü². | No: old times have; but now most low, most poor, 15, person arrive-at Court to-try, officials not able compel can acknowledge-guilt. |
| 24. ᶜHò ꜀á. ꜀Saí kwok꜀ ꜀kw'ai-ᶜköü ᶜhò lok꜀. ꜁T'ong-꜁yan ꜀kw'ai-ᶜköü ꜀tò ᶜhò ꜀á, tán² haí² ᶜho-sik˒ ꜁T'ong-꜁yan ꜀kwún ᶜyaú-꜁shí (*or better* ꜁shí*) ꜁m ᶜhò. | Good 1, Western country customs good, 32. Chinese customs also good, 1, but it-is (a thing) to-be-pitied Chinese officials sometimes not good. |
| 25. ꜁T'ong-꜁yan ᶜyaú ᶜhò ꜀to ᶜhò ch'ü˒, tán² ᶜyaú yat˒ yöng² ꜁m ᶜhò lok꜀. ᶜNgo ᶜkong kwo˒ ᶜnéi ꜀t'eng† ꜀o? ꜁T'ong ꜀kwún ᶜfung-luk˒ ꜁m kaú˒ ᶜshaí. | Chinese have very many good points, but have one kind not good, 32. I tell to you to-hear, eh ? 55. Chinese official's salary not enough for-use. |
| 26. ᶜMò ts'o˒; ko˒-꜀ti shüt꜀-wá² haí² ꜀chan. Táí² ꜀kwún pat˒-kwo˒ tak˒ ᶜkéi pák꜀ ᶜlöng tsò² ᶜfung-luk˒; ᶜk'öü ᶜshaí-faí˒ ꜁m ᶜchí kòm˒ ᶜshiú, ᶜsöng kaí˒ ᶜhéi ꜁laí yiú˒ tün˒ ꜀ts'in wák˒ mán² ᶜlöng chí˒ tsò² tak˒ ke˒. | No mistake; those words are true. Great officials only get several hundreds-of taels of money for salary; their expenses not only so little, wish to-calculate up come must by thousand or myriad taels in-order-to do able, 15. |

## CONVERSATION 36TH.—DIPLOMATIC.—(*Continued.*)

| | |
|---|---|
| 27. And, therefore, as he has to spend the money, he must find some means to get it. If good means can be devised, all the better. If not, still the money must be obtained. It would be be impossible to do without it. | 個啲銀是必要使嘅、唔夠使呢、就要想起啲法子嚟揾致得、有好法子越發好、或冇好法子都要揾咯、唔係點做得呢、 |
| 28. But, Sir, I have heard that in your honourable country there are some hundreds of officials in the House of Commons who are paid no salary. Is that also bad? | 但係我聽聞先生貴國、下議院有幾百官冇俸祿食、個啲都唔係好咩、 |
| 29. They are not officials. The people appoint them to be Members of Parliament. Probably it would be better to give them salaries, because at present it is only men with money who can be Members of Parliament. Very few men of no means can become Members of Parliament. | 佢哋唔係做官嘅、百姓設立佢做國會參議、大概俾修金過佢越發好、因爲呢陣時淨係財主佬致做得、甚少冇錢人可以做得嘅、 |
| 30. All countries have good and bad customs. Some are good in one way, and some in another. | 各國有啲好規矩、有啲唔好嘅、有啲國呢樣好、有啲國個樣好、 |
| 31. Each country should copy the good things of other countries. | 每國應學翻別國嘅好處、 |
| 32. Yes; and abstain from any faults of their own. | 冇錯、兼及要戒免自己過失、 |

## CONVERSATION 37TH.—A MISUNDERSTANDING.

| | |
|---|---|
| 1. I do not understand what the words ts'an ts'ik mean. | 我唔曉親戚兩個字點解嘅、 |
| 2. Then in the first place it is necessary to explain the two characters ts'an ts'ik. | 噉、第一要解親戚個兩個字致得、 |

## CONVERSATION 36TH.—DIPLOMATIC.—(*Continued.*)

| | | |
|---|---|---|
| 27. | Koʾ-˳ti ꜀ngan* ꜀shí pít꜁ yiúʾ ᶜshaí keʾ, ꜀m kaúʾ ᶜshai ꜀ni, tsaú$^2$ yiúʾ ᶜsöng-ᶜhéí ˳ti fát˳-ᶜtsz ꜀laí ᶜwan chíʾ tak꜁. ᶝYaú ᶜhò fát꜁-ᶜtsz yüt꜁-fát˳ ᶜhò. Wák꜁ ᶝmò ᶜhò fát꜁-ᶜtsz, ˳tò yiúʾ ᶜwan lok˳. ꜀M hai$^2$ ᶜtím tsò$^2$ tak꜁ ꜀ni ?$^2$ | The money certainly must need-to-be used, 15, not sufficient to-use, 53, then must think-up some means to find (it) in-order-to do. Have good means, more better. If not good means, also must find, 32. Not is (so) how do can, eh ? |
| 28. | Tán$^2$-hai$^2$ ᶝngo ꜀t'eng†-꜀man ꜀sin-꜀shéng† (*or* short a) kwaíʾ kwok˳ Há$^2$-ᶝYí ᶜYün ᶝyaú ᶜkéí pák꜁ ꜀kwún ᶝmò ᶜfung-luk꜁ shik꜁. Koʾ-˳ti ˳tò ꜀m hai$^2$ ᶜhò ꜀me ?$^2$ | But I heard Sir's honourable country House-of-Commons have several hundred officials no salary receive. (lit eat). That also is not good, eh ? 39. |
| 29. | ᶝK'öü-téí$^2$ ꜀m hai$^2$ tsò$^2$ ꜀kwún keʾ. Pák꜁-singʾ ᶝch'ít˳-láp꜁ ᶝk'öü tsò$^2$ Kwok˳-Wúí$^2$ ꜀Ts'ám-ᶝYí. Taí$^2$-k'oí$^1$* ᶜpéí ꜀saú-˳kam kwoʾ ᶝk'öü yüt꜁-fát˳ ᶜhò, ꜀yan-꜀waí ꜀ni chan$^2$ ꜀shí* ꜀ts'ing$^2$-hai$^2$ ꜀ts'oi-ᶜchü ᶜlò chíʾ tsò$^2$ tak꜁. Sham$^2$ ᶜshiú ᶝmò ꜀ts'in* ꜀yan ᶜho-ᶝyí tsò$^2$ tak꜁ keʾ. | They not are being officials, 15. People appoint them to-be Members-of Parliament. Probably give salary to them more good, because at this time only are wealthy men only do able. Very few no money men able to-do can, 15. |
| 30. | Kok˳ kwok˳ ᶝyaú ˳ti ᶜhò ꜀k'wai-ᶜköü, ᶝyaú ˳ti ꜀m ᶜhò keʾ, ᶝYaú ˳ti kwok˳ ꜀ni yöng$^2$ ᶜhò, ᶝyaú ˳ti kwok koʾ yöng$^2$ ᶜhò. | Each country has some good customs, have some not good, 15. Have some countries this sort good, have some countries that sort good. |
| 31. | ᶝMúí kwok˳ ꜀ying hok꜁-꜀fán pít꜁ kwok˳ keʾ ᶜhò ch'üʾ. | Each country ought learn-back other country's good things (i.e. spots, *or* places, in which they are good). |
| 32. | ᶝMò ts'oʾ, ꜀kím-k'ap꜁ yiúʾ kaíʾ-ᶝmín tsz$^2$-ᶜkéí kwoʾ-shat꜁. | No mistake, and must abstain-from self's faults. |

## CONVERSATION 37TH.—A MISUNDERSTANDING.

| | | |
|---|---|---|
| 1. | ᶝNgo ꜀m ᶜhiú ꜀ts'an-ts'ik꜁ ᶝlöng koʾ tsz$^2$ ᶜtím ᶜkáí keʾ, (*or* ke$^1$*). | I not understand ts'an tsik two [C.] characters how to-be-explained, 15. |
| 2. | ᶜKòm, taí$^2$ yat꜁ yiúʾ ᶜkáí ꜀ts'an-ts'ik꜁ koʾ ᶝlöng koʾ tsz$^2$ chíʾ tak꜁. | Then No. 1 must explain ꜀ts'an ts'ik꜁ those two [C.] characters in-order-to do. |

## CONVERSATION 37TH.—A MISUNDERSTANDING.

| | | |
|---|---|---|
| 3. | There is no explanation is there? They stand for relation, I suppose? | 冇乜解法喇嗎、都係親戚喇嘞、 |
| 4. | Wait till I tell you. | 等我講你聽嗜、 |
| 5. | Very well, tell me. | 吾、講喇、 |
| 6. | Ts'an refers to those in the position of ts'an; ts'ik refers to those in the position of ts'ik. | 親還親戚還戚、 |
| 7. | How can I learn if you teach me in that way? I want to know what the words mean. 'Ts'an refers to those in the position of ts'an, and ts'ik refers to those in the position of ts'ik' has no meaning. | 你係噉教我、我點學得嚫、我想知個啲字點解致得吖、親還親、戚還戚、冇意思嘅、 |
| 8. | It has; there is a great deal of meaning in it. Ts'an refers to those in the position of ts'an, ts'ik—— | 有嘅、有大意思嘅、親還親、戚—— |
| 9. | There you are at it again. Do not go back to it again. | 又講過、咪翻轉頭講喇、 |
| 10. | If I do not go back to it again, how can I go on? | 唔係翻轉頭講點得呀、 |
| 11. | After once saying it there is no need of saying it again Say what you have to say straight on. | 一講咽唔使講過、你有乜講一直講落嚟咯、 |
| 12. | I must explain it. | 我要解致得吖、 |
| 13. | Explain it by all means; no one will hinder you. That is just what I wish to hear you do—explaining it. | 解喇、解喇、冇人唔俾你解嚅、我就係想聽你解咯、 |
| 14. | And yet, if you will not let me explain it, how can I? | 你又唔俾我解、我點解得呢、 |
| 15. | I will not let you explain it? Who will not let you explain it? That is really good! Not let you explain it! You need not be afraid of that. I only want to make you explain it, but I do not know how. | 我唔俾你解、邊個唔俾你解呀、至好唔俾你解咯、唔使慌、硬想勉强你解、但唔知有乜法子、 |

## CONVERSATION 37TH.—A MISUNDERSTANDING.—*(Continued.)*

| | | |
|---|---|---|
| 3. | Mò mat, kái-fát lá má? Tò haí ts'an ts'ik, lá kwá? | No particular explanation, 21, 35? Also is relation, I suppose? 21, 18. |
| 4. | Tang ngo kong néí t'eng† chá. | Wait I speak you hear, 7. |
| 5. | Ng, kong lá.* | Well, speak, 21. [ts'ik. |
| 6. | Ts'an wán ts'an; ts'ik wán ts'ik. | Ts'an relates-to ts'an, ts'ik relates-to |
| 7. | Néí haí kòm kán ngo, ngo tím hok tak ká? Ngo söng chí ko-ti tsz tím kái chí tak á.* Ts'an wán ts'an, ts'ik wán ts'ik mò yí-sz ke. | You do so teach me I how learn can, 14? I want to-know those words how explain in-order-to do, 1. Ts'an relates-to ts'an, ts'ik relates-to ts'ik no meaning, 15. |
| 8. | Yaú ke; yaú taí yí-sz ke; ts'an wán ts'an, ts'ik—— | It-has, 15; it-has great meaning, 15; ts'an relates-to ts'an, tsik—— |
| 9. | Yaú kong kwo. Maí fán chün* (*or* chün) t'aú kong lá.* | Again saying over. Do-not back turn head speak, 21. |
| 10. | M haí fán chün t'aú kong tím tak á? | Not do back turn head speak how can? 2. |
| 11. | Yat kong cho m shaí kong kwo. Néí yaú mat kong, yat chik kong lok laí lok. | Once talk done not need speak over. You have what speak, one straight speak down come, 32. |
| 12. | Ngo yíú kái chí tak á.* | I must explain in-order-to do, 1. |
| 13. | Kái lá;* kái lá; mò yan m péí néí kái ká.* Ngo tsaú haí söng t'eng† néí kái lok. | Explain 21, explain 21; no man not let you explain, 14. I just do want hear you explain, 32. |
| 14. | Néí yaú m péí ngo kái; ngo tím kái tak ni?* | You yet not allow me explain; I how explain can, eh? 53. |
| 15. | Ngo m péí néí kái?* Pín ko m péí néí kái á? Chí-hò m péí néí kái lok! M shaí fong. Ngáng söng mín-köng néí kái, tán m chí yaú mat fát-tsz. | I not let you explain? Who [C.] not permit you explain? 2. Best not let you explain! 32. Not need fear [No fear.]. Only wish force you to-explain, but not know have what means. |
| 16. | Sín-sháng† nán-waí ngo lok. | (You), Sir, oppress me, 32. |

## CONVERSATION 37TH.—A MISUNDERSTANDING.—*(Continued.)*

| | | |
|---|---|---|
| 17. | No. | 唔係、 |
| 18. | It seems like it. | 好似係噉、 |
| 19. | It is not so. | 唔係噉嘅、 |
| 20. | I think it is. | 我估係呀、 |
| 21. | Why? | 點解呢、 |
| 22. | Because when I wish to explain it, you, Sir, will not let me explain it. | 因我想解、先生又唔俾我解咯、 |
| 23. | It is not so. I wish you to explain clearly what that character ˓ts‘an means, that is, when it is used. The character ts‘ik, what does it mean; that is, when is ts‘ik˒ used? | 唔係噉、我想你解明個親字點解、即係幾時使用嘅、個戚字點解、即係幾時用呢個戚字、 |
| 24. | That is just what I wanted to say; but you would not let me speak. | 我就係想講個啲、你唔俾我講啫、 |
| 25. | Wait till I have finished. | 等我講完、 |
| 26. | Well; very good; finish what you have to say. | 唔、好喇、先生講埋喇、 |
| 27. | But you would not tell me, you used the word to explain the word itself. I did not know what the word meant, and, if you used the word to explain the word itself, how could you make the meaning clear to me? | 你又唔講過我聽、你使嗰個字嚟解嗰個字、我唔識個字點解、你又使個字嚟解個字、點表得明個意思過我曉呢、 |
| 28. | Oh, now I understand you; I will explain it to you. The word ts‘an is used in speaking of those who belong to your family, that is, of those of the same surname. | 呵、我而家明白你意思、噉我講你聽、親字係使嚟講論所屬歸自已家嘅、即係個啲同姓嘅、 |

## CONVERSATION 37TH.—A MISUNDERSTANDING.—(*Continued.*)

| | | |
|---|---|---|
| 17. | ˓M haí$^{5}$*. | Not is. |
| 18. | ᶜHò ˁts'z haí$^{2}$ ᶜkòm. | Very like is so. |
| 19. | ˁM haí$^{2}$ ᶜkòm keʾ. | Not is so, 15. |
| 20. | ˁNgo ᶜkwú haí$^{2}$ áʾ. | I think is, 2. |
| 21. | ᶜTím ᶜkáí ˓ni ?$^{3}$ | How explain, eh ? 53. |
| 22. | ˓Yan ˁngo ᶜsöng ᶜkáí, ˓Sín-˓sháng yaú$^{2}$ ˓m ᶜpéi ˁngo ᶜkáí lok˳. | Because I wish explain, (you) Sir, also not allow me (*i.e.* give me the opportunity) explain, 32. |
| 23. | ˓M haí$^{2}$ ᶜkòm. ˁNgo ᶜsöng ˁnéi ᶜkáí ˓ming koʾ ˓ts'an tsz$^{2}$ ᶜtím ᶜkáí, tsik˒ haí$^{2}$ ᶜkéi ˓shí ᶜshaí-yung$^{2}$ ᶜke*. Koʾ ts'ik˒ tsz$^{2}$ ᶜtím ᶜkáí ; tsik˒-haí$^{2}$ ᶜkéi ˓shí yung$^{2}$ ᶜni-koʾ ts'ik˒ tsz$^{2}$ ? | Not is so. I wish you explain clearly that ˓ts'an character how explain, that is what time use, 15. That ts'ik˒ word how explain ; that is, what time use this [C.] ts'ik˒ character ? |
| 24. | ˁNgo tsaú$^{2}$ haí$^{2}$ ᶜsöng ᶜkong koʾ-˳ti ; ˁnéi ˓m ᶜpéi ˁngo ᶜkong ˓che. | I just was wishing to-speak that ; you not let me speak only, 7. |
| 25. | ᶜTang ˁngo ᶜkong ˓yün. | Wait I speak finished. |
| 26. | ˓Ng ; ᶜhò ˓lá ;$^{3}$ ˓Sín-˓sháng† ᶜkong ˓máí ˓lá.$^{3}$ | Well ; good, 21 ; Sir, speak finished, 21. |
| 27. | ˁNéi yaú$^{2}$ ˓m ᶜkong kwoʾ ˁngo ˓t'eng†, ˁnéi ᶜshaí ᶜko-koʾ tsz$^{2}$ ˓laí ᶜkáí ᶜko-koʾ tsz$^{2}$. ˁNgo ˓m shik˒ koʾ tsz$^{2}$ ᶜtím ᶜkáí, ˁnéi yaú$^{2}$ ᶜshaí koʾ tsz$^{2}$ ˓laí ᶜkáí koʾ tsz$^{2}$ ; ᶜtím ᶜpíú tak˒ ˓ming koʾ yíʾ-szʾ kwoʾ ˁngo ᶜhíú ˓ni ?$^{3}$ | You yet not speak to me to-hear, you use that word in-order-to explain that word. I not understand that word how explain, you yet use that word in-order-to explain that word (itself); how show-out can clearly that meaning to me to-understand, eh ? 53. |
| 28. | ˓O, ˁngo ˓yí-˳ká ˓ming-pák$_{2}$ ˁnéi yíʾ-szʾ ; ᶜkòm, ˁngo ᶜkong ˁnéi ˓t'eng†. ˓Ts'an tsz$^{2}$ haí$^{2}$ ᶜshaí ˓laí ᶜkong ˓lun ᶜsho shuk$_{2}$- ˓kwaí tsz$^{2}$-ᶜkéi ˓ká keʾ, ts'ik˒ haí$^{2}$ koʾ-˳ti ˓t'ung singʾ keʾ. | Oh, I now understand your meaning ; Now, I speak to-you to-hear. ˓Ts'an character is used in-order-to speak concerning what belongs-appertains-to one's-own family, 15, just is those same surname, 15. |

## CONVERSATION 37TH.—A MISUNDERSTANDING.—*(Continued.)*

| | | |
|---|---|---|
| 29. | Those on the father's side of the family then. | 就係歸於父親個便、 |
| 30. | Yes, belonging to the father's side—those of the same surname. | 係哩、入父親個頭嘅咯、同姓嘅就係喇、 |
| 31. | The word ts'ik, is used in speaking of those on the mother's side, whose surnames differ; combined the two words refer to all those nearly related to us. But fathers and mothers, sisters and brothers are not called ts'an ts'ik. They are called related persons only. | 戚字、係用嚟講個啲母親個頭嘅、卽係唔同姓嘅、合埋講嘅就係講所有親近嘅人、但係父母兄弟姊妹、冇人稱佢哋係親戚嘅、個的叫做親人啫、 |
| 32. | Now, I know the meaning. | 我而家曉個意思咯、 |

## CONVERSATION 38TH.— THE SEAMSTRESS, &C.

| | | |
|---|---|---|
| 1. | You are the seamstress, are you? | 你係揸針嘅係嗎、 |
| 2. | I am. Have you got some work for me to do, Ma'am? | 係吖、你係有啲工夫俾我做吖、師奶、 |
| 3. | I have a lot of work for you, but can you sew well? | 係吖、有好多工夫俾你做、你噲聯好、*or* 你聯得好嗎、 |
| 4. | Yes, I can, I work for a great many ladies. | 噲吖、我同好多師奶聯衫嘅、 |
| 5. | Very well, first sew these buttons on these jackets. Then I want you to mend these stockings, and then darn this hole in my dress. | 唔、好喇、先要釘翻呢啲鈕喺呢啲衫、後來我要你補翻呢啲襪、噉就喺我衫織翻好呢個窿?、 |
| 6. | Very good, Ma'am. Did you knit these stockings yourself? They are very closely knitted, and thick and warm. | 好喇、師奶、呢啲襪係師奶自已織嘅嗎、咁密咁厚咁煖嘅、 |

## CONVERSATION 37TH.—A MISUNDERSTANDING.—(*Continued.*)

| | | |
|---|---|---|
| 29. | Tsaú$^2$ haí$^2$ ꜀kwai-꜀yü fú$^2$-꜀ts'an ko꜄ pín$^2$. | Just is belongs-to father that side. |
| 30. | Haí$^2$ ꜀le,$^*$ yap꜆ fú$^2$-꜀ts'an ko꜄ ꜁t'aú ke꜄ lok꜆—꜁t'ung sing꜄ ke꜄ tsaú$^2$ haí$^2$ ꜀lá.$^*$ | Yes, 24, enter father that side, 15, 32, —same surname, 15, just is, 21. |
| 31. | Ts'ik꜆ tsz$^2$ haí$^2$ yung$^2$ ꜁laí ꜂kong ko꜄-꜀ti ꜃mò-꜀ts'an ko꜄ ꜁t'aú ke꜄, tsik꜆ haí$^2$ ꜁m ꜁t'ung sing꜄ ke꜄; hòp꜆-꜁mái ꜂kong ke꜄ tsaú$^2$ haí$^2$ ꜂kong ꜂sho ꜃yaú ꜀ts'an kan$^2$ ke꜄ ꜁yan; tán$^2$-haí$^2$ fú$^2$-꜃mò, ꜀hing-taí$^2$ ꜂tsz-múí$^2$ ꜃mò ꜁yan ꜀ch'ing ꜃k'öü-teí$^2$ haí$^2$ ꜀ts'án ts'ik꜆ ke꜄. Ko꜄-꜀ti kíú꜄ tsò$^2$ ꜀ts'an ꜁yan chek꜆. | Ts'ik꜆ character is employed in-order-to speak-about those mother's that side, 15, just is not similar surname's, 15; united-together speak, 15, just is speak-about whatever have related nearly's, 15, persons; but parents, brothers, sisters, no man calls them to-be ts'an ts'ik, 15. These called to-be ts'an yan only, 7. |
| 32 | ꜃Ngo ꜁yí-꜀ká ꜂híú ko꜄ yí꜄-sz꜄ lok꜆. | I now know the meaning, 32. |

## CONVERSATION 38TH.—THE SEAMSTREES, &C.

| | | |
|---|---|---|
| 1, | ꜃Néi haí$^2$ ꜀chá-꜀cham-ke꜄, haí$^2$ ꜃má? | You are hold-needle-one, 15, are you, eh? |
| 2. | Haí$^2$ ꜀á;$^*$ ꜃néi haí$^2$ ꜃yaú ꜀tí ꜀kung-꜀fú ꜂péi ꜃ngo tsò$^2$ á$^2$, ꜀Sz-꜀naí? | Yes, 1, You are having some work to-give me to-do, eh? 2, Ma'am? [35. |
| 3. | Haí$^2$ ꜀á,$^*$ ꜃yaú ꜂hò ꜀to ꜀kung-꜀fú ꜂péi ꜃néi tsò$^2$. ꜃Néi ꜃wúi ꜁lün ꜂hò, *or* ꜃Néi ꜁lün tak꜆ ꜂hò má꜄? | Yes 1, have very much work give you to-do. You can sew well, *or* You sew can well eh? 35. |
| 4. | ꜃Wúi ꜀á. ꜃Ngo ꜁t'ung ꜂hò ꜀to ꜀Sz-꜀naí ꜁lün ꜀shám (*or* ꜀shám) ke꜄. | Can 1, I for very many ladies sew clothes, 15. |
| 5. | ꜁Ng, ꜂hò ꜀lá,$^*$ ꜀sín yíú꜄ ꜀teng†-꜀fán ꜀ni-꜀ti ꜀naú* ꜂haí ꜂ni-꜀ti ꜀shám. Haú$^2$-꜁loí ꜃ngo yíú꜄ ꜃néi ꜂pò-꜀fán ꜀ni-꜀ti mat꜆. ꜂Kòm-tsaú$^2$ ꜂haí ꜃ngo ꜀shám (*or* ꜀shám) chik꜆-꜀fán ꜂hò ꜀ni-ko꜄ ꜀lung. | Well good, 21. First must sew back these buttons on these jackets. Afterwards I want you mend-back these stocks. Then in my dress (*or* jacket) darn back good this [C.] hole. |
| 6. | ꜂Hò ꜀lá,$^*$ ꜀Sz-꜀naí. ꜀Ni-꜀ti mat꜆ haí$^2$ ꜀Sz-꜀naí tsz$^2$-꜂kéi chik꜆ ke꜄ má꜄? Kòm꜄ mat꜆, kòm꜄ ꜃haú*, kòm꜄ ꜃nün ke꜄. | Good, 21, ma'am. These stockings are madam herself knit ones 15, eh? 35. So close, so thick, so warm, 15. |

## CONVERSATION 38TH.—THE SEAMSTRESS, &c.

| | | |
|---|---|---|
| 7. | When you have done all these things, I want you to fold them up and put them by. | 做完嘅呢啲、收尾要你摺好擠埋、 |
| 8. | I have some handkerchiefs, that I want you to hem to-morrow. | 我有啲手巾要你聽日挑（*or* 尖） |
| 9. | Do not do them to-day, for, if you have time, I want you to stitch this collar. | 今日唔好做、因爲你今日得閒、我要你鈎密（*or* 鈎密針）呢個頸領、 |
| 10. | You must fasten the ends of your thread very firmly. | 線尾要釘好實致得、 |
| 11. | The stitches are too long. Make the stitches very small. Do not pucker it up. Make it smooth. | 針步長過頭、要聯細步、唔好縮埋、整好滑、 |
| 12. | Baste this seam. When you have done it, give it to me, and I will machine it. | 呢條骨要攤線、做完俾我、我就使車聯、 |
| 13. | Have you seen my thimble? I put it on the dressing table with the pair of scissors. | 你見我頂針冇呀、我同埋個對鉸剪放在鏡粧檯咯、 |
| 14. | Oh! that thread is too thick. You must use finer thread to do this work. | 啊、個啲線粗過頭、做呢啲工夫要用幼細啲線至得、 |
| 15. | Have you made the button holes yet? I want you to put Chinese button loops on this jacket. | 聯個啲鈕門（*or* 鈕口）唔曾呢、呢件衫要你整啲唐人鈕耳喺嘧、 |
| 16. | You must gather this skirt into the band. | 你要縮埋呢個裙喺個裙帶嗰嘧、 |
| 17. | I have picked out this sleeve from the dress, I want you to stitch it into the jacket again. | 我喺個件衫拆嚫呢個（*or better* 筒）衫袖、我要你聯翻入去、 |

易學廣東話



CONVERSATION 38TH.—THE SEAMSTRESS, &C.—(*Continued.*)

| | | |
|---|---|---|
| 7. | Tsò$^{2}$-꜁yün sáiᵓ ꜀ni-ₒti, ꜀shaú-ₒméi yiúᵓ ˤnéi chipₒ ᶜhò ꜀chai ꜁mái. | Done-finished all these, at-the-end want you fold well put by. |
| 8. | ˤNgo ˤyaú ₒti ᶜshaú-ₒkan yiúᵓ ˤnéi ₒt'ing-yat$_{2}$ ꜀t'iú (*or* ꜀tsím). | I have some handkerchiefs wish you to-morrow hem. |
| 9. | ꜀Kam-mat$_{2}$ ꜁m ᶜhò tsò$^{2}$; ꜁yan-wai$^{2}$ ˤnéi ꜀kam-mat$_{2}$ tak꜄-꜁hán ꜁ngo yiúᵓ ˤnéi ꜀k'aú (*or* k'aúᵓ) mat$_{2}$ (*or* ꜀k'aú, *or* mat$_{2}$ ꜀cham) ꜀ni-koᵓ ᶜkeng†-ˤleng†. | To-day not good do; because you to-day have leisure, I want you stitch (*or* stitch) this collar. |
| 10. | Sínᵓ ˤméi yiúᵓ ꜀teng† ᶜhò shat$_{2}$ chíᵓ tak꜄. | Thread end must fasten very firmly in-order to-do. |
| 11. | ꜀Cham-pò$^{2}$ ꜁ch'öng kwoᵓ* ꜁t'aú. Yiúᵓ ꜁lün saiᵓ pò$^{2}$. ꜁M ᶜhò shuk꜄-꜁mái. ᶜChing ᶜhò wát$_{2}$. | Stitches long over much. Must sew small stitches. Not good pucker-together, make very smooth. |
| 12. | ꜀Ni ꜁t'iú kwatᵓ yiúᵓ nánᵓ-sínᵓ. Tsò$^{2}$ ꜁yün ᶜpéi ˤngo, ˤngo tsaú$^{2}$ ᶜshai ꜀ch'e ꜁lün. | This length (of) seam must baste. Done finished give me, I then use machine sew. |
| 13. | ˤNéi kínᵓ ˤngo ᶜting-꜀cham ˤmò áᵓ? ˤNgo ꜁t'ung-꜁mái koᵓ töüᵓ káuᵓ-ᶜtsín fongᵓ tsoi$^{2}$kengᵓ†-ₒchong-꜁t'oi* lokₒ. | You see my thimble not, eh? 2, I with that pair scissors placed on dressing-table, 32. |
| 14. | ꜀O! ꜀ni- ₒti sínᵓ ꜀ts'ò kwoᵓ (*or* kwoᵓ*) ꜁t'aú. Tsò$^{2}$ ꜀ni-ₒti ꜀kung-꜀fú yiúᵓ yung* yaúᵓ-saiᵓ-ₒti sínᵓ chíᵓ tak꜄. | Oh! this coarse over much. Doing this work must use finer thread before (it) can (do). |
| 15. | ꜁Lün koᵓ-ₒti ˤnaú*-꜁mún (*or* ˤnaú*-ᶜhaú) ꜁m ꜁ts'ang ꜀ni? ꜀Ni kínᵓ ₒshám yiúᵓ néi ᶜching ₒti ꜁T'ong-꜁yan ˤnaú*-ˤyí ᶜhai shüᵓ. | Sew those button-doors (*or* button mouths) not yet, eh? 53. This article [C.] jacket want you make some Chinese button- ears on it. |
| 16. | ˤNéi yiúᵓ shuk꜄-꜁mái ꜀ni-koᵓ ꜁k'wan, ᶜhai koᵓ ꜁k'wan-táiᵓ ᶜko shüᵓ. | You must gather-together this skirt at the skirt-band that place. |
| 17. | ˤNgo ᶜhai koᵓ kínᵓ ₒshám (*or* ꜀shám) ch'ákₒ-ᶜcho ꜀ni-koᵓ (*or* ꜀ni ꜁t'ung) ꜀shám-tsaúᵓ, ˤngo yiúᵓ ˤnéi ꜁lün ꜀fán yap$_{2}$ höüᵓ. | I at that [C.] dress picked out this [*or* C.] dress-sleeve. I want you sew back in go. |

## CONVERSATION 38TH.—THE SEAMSTRESS, &c.—(*Continued.*)

| | | |
|---|---|---|
| 18. | Back stitch this seam. | 呢條骨要鈎 (*or* 要鈎唔使鈎密)、 |
| 19. | Run up the seam of this flannel, and then herring-bone it. I want you to bind it round the edge. | 呢啲佛囒仁、要聯骨噉就掇骨、我要你綑個啲邊、 |
| 20. | Slip-stitch this cross-cut piece all round the jacket. | 呢啲衫個啲斜紋布要捅線、 |
| 21. | Can you embroider? | 你噲繡花唔噲呢、 |
| 22. | The tailor has brought back the clothes you gave him to sew last week. | 你先個禮拜俾衣服過個裁縫聯佢而家揦翻嚟咯。 |
| 23. | Tailor, why have you been so long in bringing back these clothes? You said that if I gave them to you to take home to make, you would get them done sooner than here. | 裁縫佬吖、做乜你咁耐噎揦啲衫翻嚟、你話我俾你揦翻去做你聯得快過喺呢嘩做嘅、 |
| 24. | Yes, ma'am, but I have been ill. For several days I was very seriously ill. Really I was in great pain, and had a hard time of it. I could not get up, and I could not take my meals. | 係吖、師奶、但我有病、有幾日病得好交關、眞正係凉凄咯、好辛苦咯、又唔起得身、飯又唔食得咯、 |
| 25. | Well, in that case, being a little late does not matter. I gave you some thread. I gave six reels to you. Where is what is left? | 噉就遲啲都唔相干咯、我俾啲線你吖、我俾六轆線過你咯、餘剩個啲呢、 |
| 26. | Here it is. If you have any more work in future, I hope you will think of me. | 喺喥拿、將來重有啲工夫做、望師奶睇顧我咯、 |

* * * *

CONVERSATION 38TH.—THE SEAMSTRESS,—*(Continued.)*

| | | |
|---|---|---|
| 18. | ꜀Ni-꜁t'iú kwat꜄ yiúᵓ k'aúᵓ (*or* yiúᵓ k'aúᵓ ꜁m ᶜshaí k'aúᵓ mat꜆).— | This length seam [C.] want back-stitch. |
| 19. | ꜀Ni-ₒti fat꜆-ₒlán*-꜁yan[1]* yiúᵓ ꜁lün kwat꜄, ᶜkòm tsaú² kákₒ kwat꜄. ᶜ̱Ngo yiúᵓ ᶜ̱néí ᶜk'wan koᵓ-ₒti ꜀pín. | This flannel want run-up seam, when-so then herring-bone seam. I want you bind the edge. |
| 20. | ꜀Ni-ₒti ꜀shám (*or* ₒshám) koᵓ-ₒti ꜁ts'e꜁man* pòᵓ yiúᵓ ᶜt'ung-sínᵓ. | This jacket that cross-cut cloth want slip-stitch. |
| 21. | ᶜ̱Néí ᶜ̱wúi saúᵓ-fá ꜁m ᶜ̱wúi ꜀ni ?² | You can embroider, not can, eh ?, 53. |
| 22. | ᶜ̱Néí ₒsín (*or* ꜀sín) koᵓ ᶜ̱laí-páíᵓ ᶜpéí ꜁yí-fuk꜆ kwoᵓ koᵓ ꜁ts'oí-꜀fung* ꜁lün, ᶜ̱k'öü ꜁yí-ₒká ꜀ning ꜀fán ꜁laí lokₒ. | You before that week give clothes to that tailor sew, he now bring back come, 32. |
| 23. | ꜁Ts'oí-꜁fung ᶜlò ꜀á,² tsò²-mat꜄ ᶜ̱néí kòmᵓ noí² chíᵓ ꜀ning koᵓ-ₒti ꜀shám (*or* ₒshám) ꜀fán ꜁laí? ᶜ̱Néí wá² ᶜ̱ngo ᶜ̱péí ᶜ̱néí ꜀ning ꜀fán höüᵓ tsò², ᶜ̱néí ꜁lün tak꜄ fáíᵓ kwoᵓ ᶜhaí ꜀ni shüᵓ tsò² keᵓ. | Tailor man, 1, why you so long before bring those clothes back come? You said (if) I let you take back go make, you sew can quicker than at this place do, 15. |
| 24. | Haí² ꜀á,² ꜀Sz-ₒnáí, tán² ᶜ̱ngo ᶜ̱yaú peng²†. ᶜ̱Yaú ᶜkéí yat꜆ peng²† tak꜄ ᶜhò ꜀káú-꜀kwán. ꜀Chan chingᵓ haí² ꜀ts'aí-꜁löng lokₒ, ᶜhò ꜀san- ᶜfú lokₒ. Yaú² ꜁m ᶜhéí tak꜄ ꜀shan, fán² yaú² ꜁m shik꜆ tak꜄ lokₒ. | Yes, 1, ma'am, but I have sick. Have several days ill, to-the-extent-of-being very seriously (ill). Truly really was painful, 32. Very is hard, 32. Also not get-up could body, rice also not eat can, 32. |
| 25. | ᶜKòm tsaú² ꜁ch'í-ₒti ₒtò ꜁m ꜀söng-꜀kòn lokₒ. ᶜNgo ᶜpéí ₒti sínᵓ ᶜ̱néí ꜀á.² ᶜ̱Ngo ᶜpéí luk꜆ luk꜆ sínᵓ kwoᵓ ᶜ̱néí lokₒ. ꜁Yü-shing² koᵓ-ₒti ꜀ní ?² | So then later also not important, 32. I give some thread you, 1. I gave six reels thread to you, 32. Left that, (where is it) eh ? 53. |
| 26. | ᶜHaí shüᵓ ꜁ná, ꜀tsöng-꜁loí chung²-ᶜ̱yaú ₒti ꜀kung-꜀fú tsò², mong² ꜀Sz-ₒnáí ᶜt'aí-kwúᵓ ᶜ̱ngo lokₒ. * * * * | At place, there! In-future besides have some work to-do, I-hope ma'am will-see-after me, 32. * * * * |

1. When said rapidly this sounds like fá-lán-yan ; and the second syllable always goes into the variant tone of the upper even.

## CONVERSATION 38TH.—THE SEAMSTRESS, &c.

| | | |
|---|---|---|
| 27. | Why, you do not do your work well. I told you to dust this room, and see what a quantity of dust there is on that table. Do you think that that will do? | 唉、你做工夫都唔做得好嘅、我叫你喺呢間房抹烟塵、你睇吓個張檯咁多烟塵喺嘸嘅、你估噉做得嘅咩、 |
| 28. | There is no duster. It has gone to pieces. I took the feather brush to do it with. | 冇抹烟塵布咯、爛咗咯、我使鷄毛掃嚟拂啫、 |
| 29. | Why did you not tell me? I would have given you a new one. Did you dust the room first, or did the coolies sweep it first? | 又唔話我聽、我就俾塊新嘅過你咯、你先抹烟塵𠵱咕喱先掃呢、 |
| 30. | I always dust it first, and then the coolies sweep the floor and wash it. It is the same every day. | 我時時都係先抹烟塵、然後咕喱就掃地、抹㯼板、日日都係噉、 |
| 31. | You should wait till the coolies have swept the floor before you dust it. | 你應等咕喱掃完地致抹烟塵吖、 |
| 32. | Very well, Ma'am. | 吾、好喇、師奶、 |

## CONVERSATION 39th.—THE NEW CHAIR COOLIE.

| | | |
|---|---|---|
| 1. | Why was there such a noise in the kitchen this morning? It was a dreadful noise. | 今朝做乜廚房咁嘈、𡁵咁嘈吧噉嘞、 |
| 2. | It was only a bill collector, who had come to the wrong house. | 係收銀嘅嚟錯屋啫、 |
| 3. | Why need he made such a noise? | 使乜咁嘈呢、 |
| 4. | He said the cook's mate was saucy. | 佢話火鷄撐沙塵嗻、 |
| 5. | And who is that now? Tell him to be quiet. | 而家嗰個呢、係乜誰呢、叫佢咪嘈、 |

## CONVERSATION 39TH.—THE NEW CHAIR COOLIE.—(*Continued.*)

| | | |
|---|---|---|
| 27. | ꜀Ai ! (*or* ₒAi), ᶜnéi tsò² ꜀kung-꜀fú ₒtò ꜀m tsò² takᵓ ᶜhò keᵓ. ᶜNgo kíúᵓ ᶜnéi ᶜhaí ꜀ni ꜀kán ꜁fong* mátₒ (*or* mútₒ) ꜀yín-꜁ch'an. ᶜNéi ᶜt'aí ᶜhá koᵓ ꜀chöng ꜁t'oi* kòmᵓ ꜀to ꜀yín-꜁ch'an ᶜhaí shüᵓ keᵓ. ᶜNéi ᶜkwú ᶜkòm tsò² takᵓ keᵓ ꜀me ?² | Why, you do work also not do can well, 15. I told you in this [C.] room wipe dust. You look-a-bit that [C.] table so much dust on place, 15. You think so do can, eh ? 15, 30. |
| 28. | ᶜMò mátₒ-꜀yín-꜁ch'an-pòᵓ lokₒ. Lán² ᶜcho lokₒ. ᶜNgo ᶜshaí ꜀kai-꜁mò sò,ᴶ* laí² fatᵓ ꜀che. | No wipe-dust-cloth, 32. Torn, 32, I use fowl's-feather broom to flop (it with), only, 32. |
| 29. | Yaú² ꜁m wá² ᶜngo ꜀t'eng† ? ᶜNgo tsaú² ᶜpéi fáiᵓ ꜀san keᵓ kwoᵓ ᶜnéi lokₒ. ᶜNéi ꜀sín mátₒ ꜀yín-꜁ch'an, péi² ꜀kwú-ₒléi ꜀sín sòᵓ ꜀ni ?² | Yet not say for-me to-hear? I then give piece new, 15, to you, 32. You first wipe dust, or coolie first sweep, eh ? 53. |
| 30. | ᶜNgo ꜁shí-꜁shí ₒtò haí² ꜀sín mátₒ ꜀yín-꜁ch'an, yín²-haú² ꜀kwú-ₒléi tsaú² sòᵓ téi², mátₒ ꜁laú*-ᶜpán. Yat₂-yat₂ ₒtò hai² ᶜkòm. | I always also do first wipe dust, afterwards coolies then sweep floor, wipe floor boards. Day-by-day also is so. |
| 31. | ᶜNéi ꜀ying ᶜtang ꜀kwú-ₒléi sòᵓ ꜀yün téi² chíᵓ mátₒ ꜀yín-꜁ch'an ꜀á.² | You ought to-wait coolies sweep finish floor before wipe dust, 1. |
| 32. | ꜁Ng, ᶜhò ꜀lá, ꜀Sz-ₒnái. | Well, good, 21, Ma'am. |

## CONVERSATION 39TH.—THE NEW CHAIR COOLIE.

| | | |
|---|---|---|
| 1. | ꜀Kam ꜀chíú tsò²-matᵓ ꜁ch'ü-꜁fong* kòmᵓ ꜁ts'ò ? ₒHöü kòmᵓ ꜁ts'o, ꜀pá kòmᵓ paíᵓ. | This morning why cook-room so noisy ? Market so noisy. |
| 2. | Hai² ꜀shaú ꜁ngan*-keᵓ ꜁laí ts'oᵓ ukᵓ chekᵓ. | Is receive money's come wrong house only, 7. |
| 3. | ᶜShaí matᵓ kòmᵓ ꜁ts'ò ꜀ní ?² | Need why such noise, eh ? 53. |
| 4. | ᶜK'öü wá² ᶜfo-ₒkaí-ch'ángᵓ ꜀shá-꜁ch'an ᶜwá. | He said cook's-mate saucy, so-he-said 61. |
| 5. | ꜁Yí-ₒká ᶜko-koᵓ꜀ni ; hai² matᵓ-꜁shöü* ꜀ni ? Kíúᵓ ᶜk'öü ᶜmaí ꜁ts'ò. | Now that [C.], eh ? 53 ; is who, eh ? 53. Tell him not to-be-noisy. |

## CONVERSATION 39TH.—THE NEW CHAIR COOLIE.

| | |
|---|---|
| 6. Probably it is the new coolie who has come. | 大概係新咕喱嚟咯、 |
| 7. Tell him to come in. | 㪽佢入嚟喇、 |
| 8. Sir, I heard that you want to engage some one to carry the chair. | 先生、我聽聞 (*or better* 聞得) 你要請人抬轎、 |
| 9. Yes, that is so. Where have you been at work before? Have you any testimonials? | 係、冇錯、你喺邊處打過工呢、你有薦紙冇呢、 |
| 10. I have no testimonials; but I will thank you, Sir, to be so good as to write and ask my old master, Mr. Flowers, the head of Messrs. Smith and Brown's about me, he will be happy to answer you. He recommended me to come here. | 我冇薦紙、但係唔該先生好心同我寫封信問我舊事頭、花先生、司馬巴琉伍洋行嘅大班、佢好歡喜寫信舉薦我、係佢舉薦我嚟嘅、 |
| 11. Very well, when I see him to-day, I shall ask him if you did well or not. | 好咯、我今日見佢、我就問佢、你做得好唔好、 |
| 12. How long did you work with him? | 你同佢打幾耐工呢、 |
| 13. I was with him four or five years. He was a good master; and you, Sir, speak Chinese so well, that I am pleased to come and work for you. | 我同佢打四五年工咁耐咯、佢係好事頭、先生又講得唐話咁好、我中意嚟同你打工嚿、 |
| 14. Very well. You come back to-morrow, and I will give you an answer. But how is it you left such a good master's employ? | 好喇、你聽朝翻嚟我俾聲氣你喇、做乜事頭咁好你又唔同佢打工呢、 |

CONVERSATION 39TH.—THE NEW CHAIR COOLIE.—(*Continued.*)

| | | |
|---|---|---|
| 6. | Táí[2]-k'oí꜄* haí[2] ꜀san ꜀kwú-˳léí ꜁laí lok˳. | Probably is new coolie come, 32. |
| 7. | Kíú꜄ ꜃k'öü yap꜆ ꜁laí ꜀lá.[2] | Call him enter come, 21. |
| 8. | ꜀Sín-꜀sháng, ꜃ngo ꜀t'eng-꜁man (*or* ꜁man-tak꜆) ꜃néí yíú꜄ ꜂ts'eng† ꜁yan ꜁t'oí kíú꜄*. | Sir, I hear you want engage men carry chair. |
| 9. | Haí[2], ꜃mò꜄ t'so꜄. ꜃Néí ꜂haí ˳pín-shü꜄ ꜂tá-kwo꜄-˳kung ꜀ni?[2] ꜃Néí ꜃yaú tsín꜄ ꜂chí ꜃mò ꜀ni?[2] | Yes, no mistake. You at what-place have-worked, eh? 53. You have testimonial paper not, eh? 53. |
| 10. | ꜃Ngo ꜃mò tsín꜄-꜂chí, tán[2]-haí[2] ꜁m-꜀koí ꜀Sín-꜀sháng ꜂hò ꜀sam ꜁t'ung ꜃ngo ꜃se ꜀fung-sun꜄ man[2] ꜃ngo kaú[2] sz[2]-꜁t'aú* ꜀Fá ꜀Sín-꜀sháng, ꜀Sz-꜃má ꜀Pá-꜁laú-꜃ng ꜁yöng-꜁hong-ke꜄ táí[2]-˳pán. ꜃K'öü ꜂hò ꜀fún-꜂héí ꜂se sun꜄ ꜂k'öü-tsín꜄ ꜃ngo. Haí[2] ꜃k'öü ꜂köü-tsín꜄ ꜃ngo ꜁laí ke꜄. | I have-not testimonial, but trouble-you, Sir, with-a good heart, for me write letter ask my old master, Flowers Mr., Smith, Brown foreign-firm's head. He very pleased write letter recommend me. It-was he recommended me to-come, 15. |
| 11. | ꜂Hò lok˳. ꜃Ngo ꜀kam-yat꜆ kíú꜄ ꜃k'öü, ꜃ngo tsaú[2] man[2] ꜃k'öü ꜃néí tso[2] tak꜆ ꜂hò ꜁m ꜂hò. | Very well, 32. I to-day see him, I then ask him you do can well, not well. |
| 12 | ꜃Néí ꜁t'ung ꜃k'öü ꜂tá ꜂kéí noí꜄* ˳kung ꜀ni? | You with him work how long labour, eh? 53. |
| 13. | ꜃Ngo ꜁t'ung ꜃k'öü ꜂tá sz꜄ ꜃ng ꜁nín ˳kung kòm꜄ noí꜄* lok˳. ꜃K'öü haí[2] ꜂hò sz[2]-꜁t'aú*; ꜀Sín-꜀sháng yaú[2] ꜂kong tak꜆ ꜁T'ong-wá꜄* kòm꜄ ꜂hò, ꜃ngo ꜀chung-yí꜄ ꜁laí ꜁t'ung ꜃néí ꜂tá-˳kung ká꜄. | I with him do four, five years work so long, 32. He is good master; Sir, also speak able Chinese language so well, I pleased come with you do-work, 14. |
| 14. | ꜂Hò ꜀lá,[2] ꜃néí ꜀t'ing†-꜀chíú ꜀fán ꜁láí ꜃ngo ꜂péí ꜀sheng†-héí꜄ ꜃néí ꜀lá.[2] Tsò[2]-mat꜆ sz[2]-꜁t'aú* kòm꜄ ꜂hò ꜃néí yaú[2] ꜁m ꜁t'ung ꜃k'öü ꜂tá˳kung꜀ni[2]? | Good 21, you to-morrow-morning back come I give answer you, 21. Why master so good you also not with him do work, eh? 53. |

CONVERSATION 39TH.—THE NEW CHAIR COOLIE.—(*Continued.*)

| | | |
|---|---|---|
| 15. | It was this way, Sir. I will tell you about it. It was not that I did not want to work for him. He went home to England last year, and so I was thrown out of employment. | 生先、係噉嚒、我講過你聽、唔係唔想同佢打工嘅、事頭舊年翻去歸祖家、係噉我就冇工打咯、 |
| 16. | What was I to do when I had no work? I went home to the country for a few months. I have come back now, and, as I am out of work, I want to find some employment. | 冇工打做乜野呢、我翻去歸鄉下幾個月(頭)、而家𠵱出嚟冇乜野做、想搵啲頭路、 |
| 17. | Are you strong? Can you carry the chair, and pull the jinricksha? | 你有力冇吖、噲抬轎、噲拉車仔唔呢、 |
| 18. | I can, I can. Shall I carry you to-day, and let you try me? | 噲吖、噲吖、我今日抬先生等你試過我有力冇呀、 |
| 19. | Oh! there is no need for that. Come to-morrow and I will speak with you. | 呵、唔使咯、聽日嚟同我講喇、 |
| 20. | Well, you have come, have you? That is right. I saw your old master yesterday; and he said you were a very good chair bearer; but you were always going out. | 呵、你嚟囉咩、好咯、我昨日見你舊事頭、佢話你抬得轎好、但係你時時出街㖞、 |
| 21. | Oh! no. I do not go out. The man who went out was my fellow chair coolie. I never went out. I only went out sometimes to buy some vegetables, or rice, or food. That was all. | 唔係、我冇出街嘅、出街嗰個係我伙記呮、我喊冇出街嘅、我净係有時出吓街買啲菜、糴吓米呀、買啲餸、噉嘅呮、 |

## CONVERSATION 39TH.—THE NEW CHAIR COOLIE.—(*Continued.*)

| | |
|---|---|
| 15. ꜀Sín-꜀sháng, hai$^2$ ʿkòm ká꜃. ꜂Ngo ʿkong kwo꜃ ꜂néi ꜀t'eng†. ꜀M hai$^2$ ꜀m ʿsöng ꜀t'ung ꜂k'öü ʿtá ˳kung ke꜃. Sz$^2$-꜀t'aú* kaú$^2$ ꜀nín (*or* ꜁nín*) ꜀fán höü꜃ ꜀kwai ʿtsò-˳ká, hai$^2$ ʿkòm ꜂ngo tsaú$^2$ ꜂mò ˳kung ʿtá lok꜄. | Sir, it is so, 14. I talk over you hear, It-not was not wish with him do work, 15. Master last year back went home ancestral-family-home, was so I just no work do, 32. |
| 16. ꜂Mò ˳kung ʿtá tsò$^2$ mat꜄ ꜂ye ꜀ni ?$^2$ ꜂Ngo ꜀fán höü꜃ ꜀kwai ꜀höng-꜂há ʿkéi ko꜃ yüt꜄ (꜀t'aú). ꜀Yí-˳ká ꜀fán ch'ut꜄ ꜀laí ꜂mò mat꜄ ꜂ye tsò$^2$, ʿsöng ʿwan ˳ti ꜀t'aú-lò$^2$. | No work to-work-at do what thing, eh ? 53. I back went home country several [C.] months, now back come out no thing to-do, wish to-find some work. |
| 17. ꜂Néi ꜂yaú lik꜄ ꜂mò ꜀á ?$^2$ ꜂Wúí ꜀t'oí kíú$^5$*, ꜂wúí ꜀lái ˳ch'e-ʿtsai ꜀m ꜁ni ? | You have strength not, eh ? Can carry chair, can pull jinricksha not, eh ? 53. |
| 18. ꜂Wúí ꜀á,$^2$ ꜂wúí ꜀á.$^2$ ꜂Ngo ꜀kam-mat꜄ ꜀t'oí ꜀Sín-꜀sháng ʿtang ꜂néi shí꜃ kwo꜃ ꜂ngo ꜂yaú lik꜄ ꜂mò á꜃ ? | Can 1, can 1. I to-day carry Sir, wait you try over I have strength not, 2. |
| 19. ꜀O, ꜀m ʿshaí lok˳. ˳T'ing-yat꜄ ꜀laí, ꜀t'ung ꜂ngo ʿkong ꜀lá.$^2$ | Oh ! not need, 32. To-morrow come with me speak, 21. |
| 20. ꜀O ! ꜂néi ꜀laí lo꜃ ꜀me ?$^2$ ʿHò lok˳. ꜂Ngo tsok꜄-yat꜄ kín꜃ ꜂néi kaú$^2$ sz$^2$-꜁t'aú* ; ꜂k'öü wá$^2$ ꜂néi ꜀t'oí tak꜄ kíú$^5$* ʿhò, tán$^2$- hai$^2$ ꜂néi ꜀shí-꜀shí ch'ut꜄-꜀kái (*better in its own proper tone*) ꜂wo. | Ah ! you come, 32, eh ? 39. Very-well ; 32. I yesterday saw your old master, he said you carry can chair well, but you constantly out street said-he, 64. |
| 21. ꜀M hai$^2$, ꜂ngo ꜂mò ch'ut꜄ ˳kái (*better in variant tone*) ke꜃. Ch'ut꜄ ꜀kái ʿko ko꜃ hai$^2$ ꜂ngo ʿfo-kéi꜃ chek꜄. ꜂Ngo ꜀hám ꜂mò ch'ut꜄ ꜀kái (*or* ꜀kái) ke꜃. ꜂Ngo tsing$^2$-hai$^2$ ꜂yaú ꜁shí* ch'ut꜄ ꜂há ˳kái ꜂mái ˳ti ts'oí꜃, tek꜄ ꜂há ꜂maí, ꜂mái ˳ti sung꜃, á꜃, ʿkòm ke꜃ chek꜄. | Not is, I not out street, 15. Out street that [C.] was my fellow-servant only, 7. I at-all never out street, 15. I only have times out a-bit street buy some vegetables, buy a-bit rice, buy some meat, 1, so only, 7. |

CONVERSATION 39TH.—THE NEW CHAIR COOLIE.—(*Continued.*)

22. Very well. If you are my coolie, before you go out, you must get leave to do so. If you do not get permission, you must not go out. Do you understand?

係、好喇、你係同我做咕哩、你唔好出街䟃、你要出街先要攞人情致得、唔係唔做得、你明白嗎、

23. I understand. Let it be as you say, Sir. I do not go out.

曉得咯、就依先生嘅話喇、我冇出街嘅、

24. Do you not want to engage another coolie, Sir? I have a clansman (*or* brother), who wishes to learn to be a chair coolie.

先生唔想請個咕哩添咩、我有個兄弟想學做抬轎嘅、

25. Yes, I want to engage another coolie. As one coolie has left me, the other says he is going as well.

係、我想請第二個咕哩、一個辭兩個都要辭嗻、

26. Then I will tell my brother to come. He is a good man. I will teach him, and in a short time he will be able to do everything.

噉、我叫我細佬嚟喇、佢好人吖、我教佢喇、冇幾耐佢樣樣都噲做咯、

27. Do not be in such a hurry. He may be a good man; but how do I know that he will be able to carry the chair. It is not every one that can carry a chair; they need to learn; and some can never learn.

咪咁快嗻、佢或者都係好人、點知佢噲抬轎唔噲呢、唔係人人噲抬轎嘅、要學過致噲嘅、有啲嘁都唔學得嚅、

28. If the chair-bearers do not keep step, the whole chair jumps up and down; and, if they do not walk steadily, the chair rocks from side to side, and is very disagreeable. I cannot stand it.

唔合脚步、乘轎啱啱吓、唔行得穩、轎噲兩邊擺、坐得好辛苦、唔抵得住咯、

## CONVERSATION 39TH.—THE NEW CHAIR COOLIE.—(*Continued.*)

| | | |
|---|---|---|
| 22. | ꜀Ng, ᶜhò ꜀lá.$^{2}$ ᶜNéí hai$^{2}$ ꜀t'ung ᶜngo tsò$^{2}$ ᶜkwú-ₒléí, ᶜnéí ꜀m ᶜhò ch'utᵓ ₒkái láᵓ; ᶜnéí yíúᵓ ch'utᵓ ꜀kái ꜀sín yíúᵓ ᶜlo ꜀yan-꜀ts'ing chíᵓ takᵓ. ꜀M hai$^{2}$, ꜀m tsò$^{2}$ takᵓ. ᶜNéí ꜀ming-pák$_{2}$ ᶜmá? | Yes, very-well 21. (If) you do with me be coolie, you not good out street, 22. You want go-out street, first must get permission in-order-to do. Not do-so, not do can. You understand, eh? 35. |
| 23. | ꜀Híú-takᵓ lokₒ. Tsaú$^{2}$ ꜀yí ꜀Sín-꜀sháng ᶜkòm wá$^{2}$ ꜀lá.$^{2}$ ᶜNgo ᶜmò ch'utᵓ ꜀kái (*or* ₒkái) keᵓ. | Understand, 32. Just according-to Sir so speak, 21. I not go-out street, 15. |
| 24. | ꜀Sín-꜀sháng ꜀m ᶜsöng ᶜts'eng† koᵓ ꜀kwú-ₒléí ꜀t'ím ꜀me?$^{2}$. ᶜNgo ᶜyaú koᵓ ꜀hing-tai$^{2}$ ᶜsöng hok$_{2}$ tsò$^{2}$ ꜀t'oí kíú$^{5}$*keᵓ. | Sir, not want engage [C.] coolie besides, eh? 39. I have [C.] brother wishes learn to-be carry chair one, 15. |
| 25. | Hai$^{2}$, ᶜngo ᶜsöng ᶜts'eng† tai$^{2}$-yí$^{2}$ koᵓ ꜀kwú-ₒléí. Yatᵓ koᵓ ꜀t'sz, ᶜlöng koᵓ ₒtò yíúᵓ ꜀t'sz ᶜwá. | Yes, I wish engage another [C.] coolie. One [C.] left, two [C.] also want leave they-say, 61. |
| 26. | ᶜKòm, ᶜngo kíúᵓ ᶜngo saíᵓ-ᶜlò ꜀laí ꜀lá.$^{2}$ K'öü ᶜhò ꜀yan ꜀á.$^{2}$ ᶜNgo kíúᵓ ᶜk'öü ꜀lá.$^{2}$ ᶜMò ᶜkéí noí$^{5}$* ᶜk'öü yöng$^{2}$-yöng $^{2}$ₒtò ᶜwúí tsò$^{2}$ lokₒ. | So, I call my younger-brother come, 21. He good man, 1. I will-teach him, 21. Not very long he everything also can-do, 32. |
| 27. | ᶜMaí kòmᵓ faíᵓ ꜀chá (*or* ᶜchá). ᶜK'öü wák$_{2}$-ᶜche ₒtò hai$^{2}$ ᶜhò ꜀yan; ᶜtím ꜀chí ᶜk'öü ᶜwúí ꜀t'oí kíú$^{5}$* ꜀m ᶜwúí ꜀ni. ꜀M hai$^{2}$ ꜀yan ꜀yan ᶜwúí ꜀t'oí kíú$^{5}$* keᵓ; yíúᵓ hok$_{2}$ kwoᵓ chíᵓ ᶜwúí keᵓ; ᶜyaú ₒti ꜀hám ₒtò ꜀m hok$_{2}$ takᵓ káᵓ. | Do-not-be so fast, 4. He perhaps although is good man; how know he can carry chair not can, eh? 53. Not is every man can carry chair, 15; must learn over before can, 15; have some not-at-all also not learn can, 14. |
| 28. | ꜀M hòp$_{2}$ kökₒ-pò$^{2}$, sheng$^{2}$† kíú$^{5}$* ngap$_{2}$ ngap$_{2}$ ᶜhá; ꜀m ꜀háng takᵓ ᶜwan, kíú$^{5}$* ᶜwúí ᶜlöng ꜀pín ᶜpáí, ᶜts'o*-takᵓ ᶜhò ꜀san-ᶜfú. ꜀M ᶜtaí takᵓ chü$^{2}$ lokₒ. | Not united footsteps whole chair jumps jumps about; not walk can steadily, chair will two sides move, sit very difficult. Not stand able, 32. |

## CONVERSATION 39TH.—THE NEW CHAIR COOLIE.

| | |
|---|---|
| 29. Well, you come on the first of the month. I shall give you eight dollars a month. If you can get a good chair bearer, accustomed to the work, bring him along with you; and I will see as to engaging him. | 唔、你一號嚟喇、我俾八個銀錢一個月、你揾得好人、熟手抬轎嘅、帶埋佢嚟、我就睇請唔請喇、 |
| 30. I wish to tell you plainly that you must do whatever I tell you. You must not say, 'It is not my work.' | 我要講明過你聽、我叫你做乜野是必要你做、你唔好話、唔係我工夫吖、 |
| 31. It is the same with all the servants in the house. If I tell anyone to do anything, he does it; if not, I dismiss him at once. | 成間屋咁多使喚人都係一樣、我叫人做乜野、佢就做咯、唔係、我即刻辭曉佢咯、 |
| 32. Very well, Sir. I am obedient. I will come to-morrow; and my wages will begin to count from to-morrow, as to-morrow is the first of the English month. Good bye, Sir. | 好咯、先生、我聽話嘅、我聽日嚟喇、人工由聽日起首計咯、因聽日係一號喇、請致咯、先生、 |

## CONVERSATION 40TH.—MOVING HOUSE.

| | |
|---|---|
| 1. Well, Sir, I have brought all the furniture up; but I do not know how you want the articles placed. | 拿、先生、我搬嗮個啲家私什物上嚟、但(係)唔知你想點擠法呢、 |
| 2. Put the table in the centre of the room, or it might be placed there on that side. | 檯就擠在房中心、或擠個便都好呀、 |
| 3. Put the chairs about the room, one here and there. | 個啲椅就擠、一張呢處、一張嗰處、噉嘅、 |
| 4. I have already placed the two arm chairs one on each side of the fire-place. | 個兩張交椅、我已經放在火爐兩邊、 |
| 5. That will do. | 噉都好呀、 |

## CONVERSATION 39TH.—THE NEW CHAIR COOLIE.—(*Continued.*)

| | | |
|---|---|---|
| 29. | Ng, néi yat, hò lai lá.2 Ngo péi pát ko ngan-ts'ín* yat, ko yüt. Néi wan tak, hò yan, shuk,-shaú t'oi kiú3* ke, tái mái k'öü lai; ngo tsaú2 t'ai ts'eng† m ts'eng† lá.2 | Well, you first day come, 21. I give eight [C.] dollars one [C.] month. You find can good man, accustomed-hand carry chair, 15, bring along him come; I then see engage, not engage, 21. |
| 30. | Ngo yiú kong ming kwo néi t'eng†. Ngo kiú néi tsò2 mat,-ye, shi-pít, yiú néi tsò2. Néi m hò wá2, 'M hai2 ngo kung-fú á.2' | I want speak clearly for you to-hear. I tell you do what thing, certainly require you to-do. You not good say, 'Not is my work,' 1. |
| 31. | Sheng† kán uk, kòm to shai-fún2-yan tò hai2 yat, yöng2. Ngo kiú yan tsò2 mat,-ye, k'öü tsaú2 tsò2 lok; m hai2, ngo tsik,-hak, ts'z-híú k'öü lok. | Whole [C.] house so many servants also are one same. I tell anyone do anything he then does, 32; (if) not does, I immediately dismiss him, 32. |
| 32. | Hò lok, Sín-sháng, ngo t'eng†-wá2 ke1*. Ngo t'ing-yat, lai lá.2 Yan-kung yaú2 t'ing-yat, héi-shaú kai lok. T'ing-yat, hai2 yat, hò2 lá.2 Ts'ing-chí lok, Sín-sháng. | Very good, 32, Sir, I listen words, 15. I to-morrow come, 21. Wages from to-morrow begin reckon, 32. To-morrow is first number, 21. Good-bye, 32, Sir. |

## CONVERSATION 40TH.—MOVING HOUSE.

| | | |
|---|---|---|
| 1. | Ná, Sín-sháng†, ngo pún sái ko-ti ká-sz-shap,-mat, shöng lai, tán2-(hai2) m chí néi söng tím chai fát ni. | Well, Sir, I have-moved all the furniture up come; but not know you wish how put method, 53. |
| 2. | T'oi* tsaú2 chai tsoi2 fong* chung-sam, wák, chai ko pín2 tò hò á. | Table just put in room centre, or put that side also good, 2. |
| 3. | Ko-ti yí tsaú2 chai yat, chöng ni shü, yat, chöng ko shü, kòm ke. | Those chairs just put one [C.] this place, one [C.] that place so, 15. |
| 4. | Ko löng chöng kaú-yí, ngo yí-king fong tsoi2 fo lò löng pín. | Those two [C.] arm chairs, I already placed at fire furnace two sides. |
| 5. | Kòm tò hò á. | So also good, 2. |

## CONVERSATION 40TH.—MOVING HOUSE.—(*Continued.*)

| | | |
|---|---|---|
| 6. | Do you want carpet, or matting laid down in this room? | 呢間房要鋪地氈啵鋪蓆呢、 |
| 7. | Put down the carpet which I bought yesterday at the auction; the new matting is to be put in the front room up stairs. | 我昨日、喺喊夜冷投倒個張氈、就鋪在呢間房、個啲新蓆鋪喺樓上前房、 |
| 8. | Get four men to carry in the piano and place it against the wall. | 叫四個人嚟抬個琴入嚟、擠個幅牆個處、 |
| 9. | Shall I put the canterbury beside the piano? | 安個琴書架在琴側邊、(*or* 便)好唔好呀、 |
| 10. | Yes, that will do, and put the stool before the piano. What is the use of putting it over there? | 好呀、做得呀、個凳擠琴前便個處致得呀、擠歸個頭有乜用呢、 |
| 11. | I have arranged the vases on the mantelpiece. | 個啲花罇、我擠好在個火爐頭、 |
| 12. | That will do. It would be well to put some flowers in them. | 噉做得呀、插啲花入去都好呀、 |
| 13. | I told the coolies this morning to brush the fender; and when they had done so to bring it in with the fire-irons as well, and place them neatly before the fire-place (*or* stove). | 我今朝叫咕喱擦火爐圍、擦完連(埋)火棒、火鏟、火鉗、喊唪唥揨㗳入嚟、擺好喺火爐前便、 |
| 14. | The davenport is to be placed between the two windows. | 寫字檯、要擠個兩個窓門之中間個處、 |
| 15. | There is no room there. | 個處冇地方擠呀、 |
| 16. | Oh, Yes, there is. | 有、乜冇、 |
| 17. | I meant to shake and sun the hearth rugs to-day, but it has been raining and I could not. | 我想今日抰個啲火爐氈、晒吓佢、但係落雨唔做得、 |

## CONVERSATION 40TH.—MOVING HOUSE.—(*Continued.*)

6. ꜀Ni ꜀kán ꜁fong* yiúᵓ ꜀p'ò téi²-ₒchín péi² ꜀p'ò tsek꜇† ꜀ni? — This [C.] room want spread carpet or spread matting, eh? 53.

7. ꜃Ngo tsok꜇-yat꜇ ꜂hai hámᵓ-yeᵓ-ₒlán ꜁t'aú-꜂tò koᵓ ꜀chöng ₒchín, tsaú² ꜀p'ò tsoi² ꜀ni ꜀kán ꜁fong*; koᵓ-ₒti ꜀san tsek꜇† ꜀p'ò ꜂hai ꜁laú-shöng² ꜁ts'ín ꜁fong*. — I yesterday at auction bought [*lit* bid-for and got] that [C.] carpet just spread in this [C.] room; that new matting spread in upstairs front room.

8. Kiúᵓ szᵓ koᵓ ꜀yan ꜁lai ꜀t'oi koᵓ ꜀k'am yap꜇ ꜁lai, ꜀chai koᵓ fuk꜆ ꜁ts'öng koᵓ shüᵓ. — Call four [C.] men come carry that piano in come, put that [C.] wall that place.

9. ꜀On koᵓ ꜀k'am-꜀shü-káᵓ* (Káᵓ *will do*) tsoi² ꜀k'am chak꜆-ₒpin (*or* pín² *or even* ꜀pín) ꜂hò ꜁m ꜂hò áᵓ? — Place that piano-book-rack at piano side, good not good, eh? 2.

10. ꜀Hò áᵓ, tsò² tak꜆ áᵓ. Koᵓ tangᵓ ꜀chai ꜀k'am ꜁ts'ín pín² koᵓ shüᵓ chíᵓ-tak꜆ áᵓ. ꜀Chai ꜀kwai koᵓ ꜁t'aú ꜃yaú mat꜆ yung² ꜀ni?² — Good, 2, do can, 2. That stool place piano front side that place in-order-to-do can, 2. Place at that side have what use, eh? 53.

11. Koᵓ-ₒti ꜀fá ₒtsun, ꜃ngo ꜀chai ꜂hò tsoi² koᵓ ꜂fo-꜁lò-꜁t'aú. — Those flower vases, I place properly on the fire-place-head.

12. ꜂Kòm, tsò² tak꜆ áᵓ. Ch'áp꜆ ꜀ti ₒfá yap꜇ höüᵓ ₒtò ꜂hò áᵓ. — So, do can, 2. Stick-in some flowers in go also good, 2.

13. ꜃Ngo ꜀kam ꜀chiú kiúᵓ ꜀kwú-ₒléi ts'át꜆ ꜂fo-꜁lò ꜁wai; ts'át꜆ ꜁yün, ꜁lín (꜁mái) ꜂fo-꜃p'áng, ꜂fo-꜂ch'án, ꜂fo-꜁k'ím hám²-pá²-láng² ꜀ning sáiᵓ yap꜇ ꜁lai, ꜂pái ꜂hò ꜂hai ꜂fo-꜁lò ꜁ts'ín pín². — I this morning told coolies brush fire-furnace fender, brush finish, including poker, shovel, tongs, all bring all in come, spread-out good at fire-furnace front side.

14. ꜂Se-tsz²-꜁t'oi*, yiúᵓ ꜀chai koᵓ ꜃löng koᵓ ₒch'öng ꜁mún*-꜀chí ꜀chung-꜀kán koᵓ shüᵓ. — Writing-table want place those two [C.] window's middle that place.

15. Koᵓ shüᵓ ꜃mò téi²-꜀fong ꜀chai áᵓ. — That place no room to-place, 2.

16. ꜃Yaú; mat꜆ ꜃mò? — Have, why not?

17. ꜃Ngo ꜂söng ꜀kam-mat꜆ ꜂yöng koᵓ-ₒti ꜂fo-꜁lò ꜀chínᵓ, sháiᵓ꜃há ꜃k'öü, tán²-hai² lok꜇ ꜃yü ꜁m tsò² tak꜆. — I wished to-day shake the fire-furnace rugs, dry-in-sun a-bit them, but fall rain not do can.

## CONVERSATION 40TH.—MOVING HOUSE. (*Continud.*)

| | |
|---|---|
| 18. Well, it does not matter; you can do it another day. Nail up the brackets as they were before. | 呵、冇相干、第二日做得咯、釘好個啲古玩架、好似舊時一樣咯、 |
| 19. The over-mantel requires to be placed right and fastened. | 個面有架嘅大鏡、要安好、釘好致得、 |
| 20. The bath-tub is so heavy that two men cannot carry it up. | 個洗身桶咁重、兩個人唔抬得上去、 |
| 21. Well, tell the four who carry the piano to carry it as well. | 噉、叫抬琴個四個抬埋個洗身桶喇、 |
| 22. Is the hat-stand to be put in the passage? | 個帽架係擠冷巷係唔係呢、 |
| 23. Certainly; if you do not put it there, where are you going to put it? | 定喇、唔係擠個處、擠邊處呢、 |
| 24. I do not know; I was only asking you. | 我唔知、我問吓你啫、 |
| 25. The pictures are not broken, are they? | 個幾幅畫冇整爛嗎、 |
| 26. Oh no, I brought them over very carefully. | 冇、我好小心揼過嚟嘅、 |
| 27. The stair carpet is mouldy. | 個樓梯氈發毛咯、 |
| 28. Yes; it has been raining so much lately. | 係呀、呢排落雨多呀、 |
| 29. Where is the bed-room furniture, | 瞓房家私呢、 |
| 30. Some of it has been brought up, and some of it not. The mattresses and mirrors, large and small, have not been brought for fear the rain would wet them. | 有啲揼上嚟、有啲唔曾搬過嚟、牀褥呀、大鏡、鏡屏呀、慌雨整濕冇抬嚟、 |

易學廣東話



CONVERSATION 40TH.—MOVING HOUSE.—(*Continued.*)

| | | |
|---|---|---|
| 18. | ˓O, ˏmò ˏsöng-ˏkòn ; tai$^2$ yí$^2$ yai$_2$ tsò$^2$ tak$_ɔ$ lok$_o$. ˏTeng† ˋhò ko$^ɔ$-ˏti ˋkwú-ˋwún-ˋká*, (ká$^ɔ$ *will do*) ˋhò-ˏt'sz kaú$^2$-ˏshí (*or* ˏshí*) yat$_ɔ$ yöng$^2$ lok$_o$. | Oh, no matter; No. 2 day do can, 32. Nail properly those old-bowl-stands, like old-time one same, 32. |
| 19. | Ko$^ɔ$ mín$^2$ ˏyaú ká$^ɔ$ (*or* ká$^ɔ$*) ke$^ɔ$ tái$^2$ keng$^ɔ$†, yíú$^ɔ$ ˏon ˋhó, ˏteng† ˋhò chí$^ɔ$-tak$_ɔ$. | That [C] have framework, 15, large mirror, want place right, nail well in-order-to-do can. |
| 20. | Ko$^ɔ$ ˋsaí-ˏshan-ˋt'ung kòm$^ɔ$ ˏch'ung† ˏlöng ko$^ɔ$ ˏyan ˏm ˏt'oi tak$_ɔ$ ˏshöng höü$^ɔ$. | That wash-body-tub so heavy two [C.] men not carry can up go. |
| 21. | ˋKòm, kíú$^ɔ$ ˏt'oi ˏk'am ko$^ɔ$ sz$^ɔ$ ko$^ɔ$ ˏt'oi ˏmái ko$^ɔ$ ˋsai-ˏshan-ˋt'ung ˏlá.$^2$ | Then call carry piano those four [C. for men] carry as-well that bath-tub, 21. |
| 22. | Ko$^ɔ$ mò$^5$*-ká$^ɔ$ (*or* ká$^5$*) hai$^2$ ˏchaí ˏláng*-hong$^5$*, (*or* ˏláng hong$^5$*) hai$^2$ ˏm hai$^2$ ˏni ?$^2$ | The hat-stand is placed passage, is not is, eh? 53. |
| 23. | ˋTing ˏlá$^2$ ; ˏm hai$^2$ ˏchai ko$^ɔ$ shü$^ɔ$, ˏchaí ˏpín shü$^ɔ$ ˏni ?$^2$ | Certainly, 21, not is place that spot, put what place, eh? 53. |
| 24. | ˏNgo ˏm ˏchi, ˏngo (*or* man$^5$*) ˏhá ˏnéí ˏche.$^2$ | I not know. I asked you a-bit only, 7. |
| 25. | Ko$^ɔ$ ˋkéí fuk$_ɔ$ wá$^5$* ˏmò ˋching lán$^2$ má$^ɔ$ ? | Those several [C.] pictures not make break, eh? 35. |
| 26. | ˏMò, ˏngo ˋhò ˋsíú-ˏsam ˏning kwo$^ɔ$ ˏlai ke$^ɔ$. | Not, I very carefully brought over come, 15. |
| 27. | Ko$^ɔ$ ˏlaú-ˏt'aí ˏchín fát$_o$-ˏmò* lok$_o$. | The stair carpet got-mouldy, 32. |
| 28. | Hai$^2$ á$^ɔ$ ; ˏni ˏp'ái* lok$_2$ ˏyü ˏto á$^ɔ$. | Yes 2, this time fall rain much, 2. |
| 29. | Fan$^ɔ$-ˏfong* ˏká-ˏsz ˏni ?$^2$ | Sleep-room furniture, eh? 53. |
| 30. | ˏYaú ˏti ˏning ˏshöng ˏlai, ˏyaú ˏti ˏm ˏts'ang ˏpún kwo$^ɔ$ ˏlai. ˏCh'ong-yuk$_5$* á$^ɔ$, tái$^2$ keng$^ɔ$†, keng$^ɔ$† ˏp'ing* á$^ɔ$, ˏfong ˏyü ˋching shap$_c$ ˏmò ˏt'oi ˏlai. | Have some take up come; have some not yet moved over come,—bed-mattress, 2, full-length-large glass-mirror, and looking glass 2, afraid rain make wet not carry come. |

## CONVERSATION 40TH.—MOVING HOUSE.—(*Continued.*)

| | | |
|---|---|---|
| 31. | Wait till I see what is here—beds, basin-stands, dressing-tables, clothes-horses, towel-racks, wardrobes. There are only a few wanting. | 等我睇有乜野喺處呀、牀呀、洗面檯呀、梳粧檯呀、衣架、面巾架、衣櫃、爭冇幾多野啫、 |
| 32. | Yes, that is so—bookcases, dining table, dinner-wagons, what-nots, couches. There has not been time to bring them over. | 係哩、冇錯、書櫃呀、大餐檯呀、盃架、古玩架、交椅牀、唔曾有得閒抬過嚟、 |

## CONVERSATION 41ST.—THE RAILWAY.

| | | |
|---|---|---|
| 1. | What news is there in the papers? | 新聞紙有乜新聞呢、 |
| 2. | There is no news. | 冇乜新聞、 |
| 3. | The Chinese are buying a uumber of ironclad war-ships. | 唐人買好多鐵甲兵船咯、 |
| 4 | Oh! indeed, I have heard so too. | 係咩、我都聽見噉話吖、 |
| 5. | It would be better if they would use the money to construct railways. | 我估至好使個啲銀嚟整鐵路、 |
| 6. | How is that? What are railways? | 點解呢、鐵路係乜野呢、 |
| 7. | Why roads for railway carriages. | 就係火車路咯、 |
| 8. | I do not know that either. | 我都唔識得呀、 |
| 9. | I will explain it to you. In Western countries there are iron roads made for railway carriages to run on; because railway carriages cannot run on the ordinary roads. | 我講過你聽吖、在西國有鐵路整成嚟俾火車行嘅、因為火車不能行平常行個啲路嘅、 |

## CONVERSATION 40TH.—MOVING HOUSE.—*(Concluded.)*

| | | |
|---|---|---|
| 31. | ᶜTang ˢngo ᶜt‘ai ˢyan mat꜄ ˢye ᶜhai shü꜆ á꜆,—꜀ch‘ong á꜆, ᶜsai-mín$^2$-꜂t‘oi* á꜆, ꜀sho-꜀chong-꜂t‘oi* á꜆, ꜀yí-ká꜆, (*or* ꜀yi ká$^1$*, *not so good*) mín$^2$-˳kan-ká꜆, (*or* mín$^2$-˳kan ká$^1$*) ꜀yi-kwai$^2$, ꜀cháng ˢmò ᶜkéi ꜀to ˢye ꜀che. | Wait I see have what thing at place, 2, bed, 2, wash-face-table, 2, dressing-table, 2, clothes-rack, face-cloth-rack, 2, clothes-press, wanting not very many things only, 7. |
| 32. | Hai$^2$ ꜀le ;$^2$ ˢmò ts‘o꜆—꜀shü-kwai$^2$ á꜆. tái$^2$-˳ts‘án ꜂t‘oi* á꜆, ˳pöü-ká꜆, (*or better* ˳pöü ká$^1$*) ᶜkwú-ᶜwún-ká꜆, (*or better* ᶜkwú ᶜwún ká$^1$*) ꜀káu-ᶜyí-꜂ch‘ong. ꜂M ꜂ts‘ang ꜂yaú tak꜄-꜂hán ꜂t‘oi kwo꜆ ꜂lai. | Yes, 24; no mistake,—bookcase, 2, dinner-table, 2, glass stand, curio stand, armed chair-bed, not yet have leisure carry over come. |

## CONVERSATION 41ST.—THE RAILWAY.

| | | |
|---|---|---|
| 1. | ꜀San-꜂man-ᶜchí ˢyaú mat꜄ ꜀san-꜂man* ꜀ni ?$^2$ | Newspapers have what news, eh ? 53. |
| 2. | ˢMò mat꜄ ꜀san-꜂man.* | No news. |
| 3. | ꜂T‘ong-꜂yan ˢmái ꜀hò ꜀to t‘it꜄-káp˳ ꜀ping ꜂shün lok꜄. | Chinese buy very many ironclad soldier ships, 32. |
| 4. | Hai$^2$ ꜀me ?$^2$ ˢNgo ˳tò ꜀t‘eng†-kín꜆ ᶜkòm wá$^2$ ꜀á$^2$. | Yes, eh ? 39. I also heard so said, 1. |
| 5. | ˢNgo ᶜkwú chí꜆ ᶜhò ᶜshai ko꜆-˳ti ꜂ngan* ꜂lai ᶜching t‘it˳ lò$^2$. | I think most good use that money to make iron roads. |
| 6. | ᶜTím ᶜkái ꜀ni ?$^2$ T‘it˳ lò$^2$ hai$^2$ mat꜄ ˢye ꜀ni ?$^2$ | How explain, eh ? 53. Iron roads are what things, eh ? 53. |
| 7. | Tsaú$^2$ hai$^2$ ᶜfo-꜀ch‘e-lò$^2$ lok˳. | Just are fire-carriage-roads, 32. |
| 8. | ꜀Ngo ˳tò ꜂m shik꜄ tak꜄ á꜆. | I also not understand can, 2. |
| 9. | ˢNgo ᶜkong kwo꜆ ˢnéi ꜀t‘eng† ꜀á. Tsoi$^2$ ꜀Sai kwok˳ ˢyaú t‘it˳ lò$^2$ ᶜching ꜂sheng† ꜂lai ᶜpéi ᶜfo ꜀ch‘e ꜂háng ke꜆, ꜀yan-wai$^2$ ᶜfo ꜀ch‘e pat꜄ ꜂nang ꜂háng ꜀p‘ing-꜂shöng ꜂háng ko꜆-˳ti lò$^2$ ke꜆. | I speak for you to-hear, 1. In Western countries have iron roads made complete in-order for fire carriages run, 15. Because fire carriages not able walk usual walk those roads, 15. |

CONVERSATION 41ST.— THE RAILWAY.—*(Continued.)*

| | |
|---|---|
| 10. Suppose now it was desired to construct a railway from Canton to Fat-shan. | 假使間想喺城整一條鐵路去佛山、 |
| 11. Very well. How would it be done? | 好喇、點整呢、 |
| 12. First men are sent to look at the country between Canton and Fat-shan, and see what hills there are, whether large or small; to see what rivers or what water-ways there are, and what villages and other places; and what roads there are; and afterwards the easiest and best way is selected for it. | 先打發人去睇過省城到佛山個啲地方有乜山、或大、或細、有乜河海(吖江河)或水路、有乜村鄉等處、有乜道路、然後揀出至易、至好嘅地方嚟整、 |
| 13. That seems very simple; but in the West can roads be made anywhere? Supposing now a man should say, 'This place is mine, you shall not make your road through it.' | 噉都好似幾易嘅、但係西國隨便邊處都整得路咩、倘若有人話呢笪地方係我嘅、唔准你整一條路通過去、 |
| 14. I am only telling you about it in a general way. I am not entering into full details about it. Of course if a man's land is taken, money is given to him for it. If too much money is wanted, there are officials to decide the matter. | 我不過大概講過你聽嘅嗜、唔係詳細講嚨出嚟嘅、攞人哋嘅自然俾翻銀佢、譬喻間人哋要得多銀、有官判斷、 |
| 15. Then who constructs the railway? I should think it must cost a great deal of money. | 噉、邊個整個啲鐵路呢、我估要使好多銀整咯、 |

## CONVERSATION 41ST.—THE RAILWAY.—(*Continued.*)

| | | |
|---|---|---|
| 10. | ᶜKá-ᶜsz-꜀kán ᶜsöng ᶜhaí ꜁Sheng*† ᶜching yatᵓ ꜁t'íú t'ít꜀-lò[2] höüᵓ Fatᵓ-꜀shán. | Supposing wish at city make one length iron road go Fat-shan. |
| 11. | ᶜHò ꜁lá.[2]. ᶜTím ᶜching ꜀ni ?[2] | Good, 21. How make, eh ? 53 |
| 12. | ꜀Sín ᶜtá-fát꜀ ꜁yan höüᵓ ᶜt'aí kwoᵓ ᶜShing-꜁sheng† tòᵓ Fat꜀-꜀shán koᵓ-꜀ti téí[2]-꜀fong ᶜyaú matᵓ ꜀shán, wákᵓ táí[2], wákᵓ saíᵓ ; ᶜyaú matᵓ ꜁ho-ᶜhoí, (*or better* ꜀kong-꜁ho) wákᵓ ᶜshöü-lò[2] ; ᶜyaú matᵓ ꜀ts'ün-꜀höng ᶜtang ch'üᵓ, ᶜyaú matᵓ tòᵓ lò[2] ꜁yín-haú[2] ᶜkán ch'utᵓ chíᵓ yí,[2] chíᵓ ᶜhò keᵓ téí[2]-꜀fong ꜁laí ᶜching. | First send men go look over provincial city to Fat-shan that place have what hills whether large small : have what rivers or water-roads ; have what villages, other places ; have what roads ; afterwards pick out most easy, most good, 15, place to make. |
| 13. | ᶜKóm ꜀tò ᶜhò ts'zᵓ ᶜkéí yí[2] keᵓ ; tán[2]-haí[2] ꜀Saí-kwok꜀ ꜁ts'öü-pín,[5]* ꜀pín-shüᵓ ꜀tò ᶜching takᵓ lò[2] ꜀me ?[2] ᶜT'ong-yökᵓ ᶜyaú ꜁yan wá[2], 'Ni tát꜀ téí[2]-꜀fong haí[2] ᶜngo keᵓ, ꜁m ᶜchun ᶜnéí ᶜching yatᵓ ꜁t'íú lò[2] ꜀t'ung-kwoᵓ höüᵓ.' | Then also very like rather easy, 15 ; but Western countries any how, any place also make can roads, eh ? 39, Supposing have man say, 'This [C.] place is mine, 15. Not allow you make one length road through go.' |
| 14. | ᶜNgo patᵓ-kwoᵓ táí[2]-k'oí[2]* ᶜkong kwoᵓ ᶜnéí ꜀t'eng† keᵓ ꜀che.[2] ꜁M haí[2] ꜁ts'öng-saíᵓ ᶜkong saíᵓ ch'utᵓ ꜁laí ke.[1]* ᶜLo ꜁yan-téí[2]-keᵓ tsz[2]-꜁yin ᶜpéí ꜀fán ꜁ngan* ᶜk'öü. P'éíᵓ-꜁yü-꜀kán ꜁yan-téí[2] yíúᵓ-takᵓ ꜀to ꜁ngan*, ᶜyaú ꜀kwún p'únᵓ-tünᵓ. | I only generally speak for you to-hear only, 7. Not is minutely tell all out come, 15. Take people's (land) as-a-matter-of-course give back money them. Supposing people want-obtain (too) much money have officals try-decide. |
| 15. | ᶜKóm, ꜀pín koᵓ ᶜching koᵓ-꜀tí t'ít꜀-lò[2] ꜀ni ?[2] ᶜNgo ꜀kwú yíúᵓ ᶜshaí ᶜhò ꜀tò ꜁ngan* ᶜching lokᵓ. | Then which [C.] makes the iron road, eh ? 53. I think must use very much money make, 32. |

## CONVERSATION 41ST.—THE RAILWAY—. (*Continued.*)

| | | |
|---|---|---|
| 16. | Certainly, it costs a great deal of money. They are to be found everywhere in Western countries. In some countries the Government make them, and if there is a profit the Government gets it; in some countries the people make them. | 定喇、使好多錢嘅、在西國到處都有嘅、有處係皇家整嘅、有錢賰皇家收嘅咯、有處係百姓自已整嘅、 |
| 17. | How can the people make them? I can understand the Government constructing them. | 百姓點整得呢、皇家整嘅我可以明白、 |
| 18. | A number of people join together and form a company. They get permission from Parliament to construct the railway; and certain regulations are made to which the Company have to adhere. | 有大多人合埋做成公司、佢哋同議政國會攞人情做個條鐵路、又設立章程、規條、個公司各樣事、要照依個啲章程嚟做、 |
| 19. | How are the iron roads made? Probably there is a great deal of work required over them. | 個啲鐵路點整呢、大概要好多工夫做啩、 |
| 20. | You are right. There is a great deal of work about them. First a road has to be made with stones and earth; and the more level it is the better. The surface must be smooth; and if it can also run in a straight line, it is also well. | 冇錯、要好多工夫嘅、先頭要俾石共坭整一條路、越平越好、上面又要光滑、個條路可以一直去、重好過彎曲嘅、 |
| 21. | Well, what then? I am very much interested in hearing about it. If there should be high mountains obstructing the road, what is done? | 呵、噉點呢、我好中意聽呀、倘若有大山阻攔嗰條路點算好呢、 |

易學廣東話



CONVERSATION 41ST.—THE RAILWAY.—(*Continued.*)

| | |
|---|---|
| 16. ˓Ting* ˏlá,² ˓shaí ˓hò ˏto ˏts'ín* ke˒. Tsoi² ˏSaí kwok˳ tò˒ ch'ü˒ ˳tò ˓yaú ke˒. ˓Yaù shü˒ haí² ˏWong-ˏká ˓ching ke˒, ˓yaú ˏts'ín* chán² ˏWong-ˏká ˏshaú ke˒ lok˳; ˓yaú shü˒ haí² pák˳-sing˒ tsz²-˓kéi ˓ching ke˒. | Certainly, 21, use very much money, 15. In Western countries all places also have, 15. Have places is Government make 15, have money made Government receives, 15, 32; have places is hundred surnames (i.e. the people) themselves make, 15. |
| 17. Pák˳-sing˒ ˓tím ˓ching tak˒ ˏni ?² ˏWong-ˏká ˓ching ke˒ ˓ngo ˓ho-˓yí ˏming-pák˒. | The-people how make can, eh? 53. Government make 15, I can understand. |
| 18. ˓Yaú taí²-ˏto ˏyan hòp˒-ˏmái tsò² ˏsheng† ˏkung-˳sz. ˓K'öü-téi² ˏt'ung ˓Yí-Ching˒-Kwok˳-Wúí² ˓lo ˏyan-ˏts'ing tsò² ko˒ ˏt'íú t'ít˳-lò²; yaú² ch'ít˳-láp˒ ˏchöng-ˏch'ing, ˏkw'aí-ˏt'íú. Ko˒ ˏkung-˳sz kok˳ yöng² sz² yiú˒ chíú˒-ˏyi ko˒-˳ti ˏchöng-ˏch'ing ˏlai tsò². | Have great many (people) join-together make completed company. They from parliament get permission make that length iron-road; also make regulations customs. That company each kind matter must according-to those regulations come to-do. |
| 19. Ko˒-˳ti t'ít˳-lò² ˓tím ˓ching ˏni ?² Tái² ˓k'oi¹*, yiú˒ ˓hò ˏto ˏkung-ˏfú tsò² kwá˒. | Those iron roads how make, eh? Probably must very much work make I-suppose, 18. |
| 20. ˓Mò ts'o˒. Yiú˒ ˓hò ˏto ˏkung-ˏfú ke˒. ˏSín ˏt'aú yiú˒ ˓péi shek˒† kung² ˏnai ˓ching yat˒ ˏt'íú lò²; yüt˒ ˏp'ing yüt˒ ˓hò. Shöng² mín¹* yaú² yiú˒ ˏkwong-wát˒. Ko˒ ˏt'íú lò² ˓ho-˓yí yat˒ chik˒ höü˒ chung² ˓hò kwo˒ ˏwán k'nk˒ ke˒. | No mistake. Require very much work, 15. First place (*lit.* Fore front) must put stones and earth make one length road; more level more better. Top face also must-be bright smooth. That length road can one straight go more good than winding crooked, 15. |
| 21. ˏO! ˓kòm ˓tím ˏni ? ˓Ngo ˓hò ˏchung-yí˒ ˏt'eng† á˒. ˓T'ong-yök˒ ˓yaú tái² ˏshán ˓cho-ˏlán ˓ko ˏt'íú lò², ˓tím sün˒ ˓hò ˏni ?² | Well! How, eh? 53. I very pleased hear, 2. Suppose have large hills obstruct that length road, how consider good, eh? 53. |

## CONVERSATION 41ST.—THE RAILWAY—(*Continued.*)

| | | |
|---|---|---|
| 22. | Supposing the mountains do not cover much ground, the railway can circle round them. If that cannot be done, then a tunnel can be made through to the other side, and the railway passes through the mountain. | 譬喻間大山唔伸得幾遠、火車路可以運大山去、若係唔做得就可以整通個山、鐵路喺山通過去、 |
| 23. | If the hill is not high or large, they prefer to make a cutting through it. If there is high ground or low hills, the railway can ascend on a gradient to the top and then descend again. | 若個山唔喺高大、佢哋寧願喺頂掘斷個座山、有高地或矮山、鐵路可以斜斜上頂、然後斜斜翻落嚟、 |
| 24. | If there is marshy ground, an embankment is made, like a path through a rice field; but much wider, and the iron road is on the top of it. | 或有低濕地就整一條基、好似田基一樣、但闊過田基好多、鐵路喺個條基上面過、 |
| 25. | How do people get out of, and go into, the carriages? | 人哋點上落呢啲車呢、 |
| 26. | There are stations at the principal cities, marts, towns, and villages through which the railway passes. Passengers go into the train, and get out of it, at these stations. The hours are fixed for departure and arrival. The passengers buy the tickets early, and when the train arrives, they go into the carriages and shut the doors. | 鐵路所通嘅大城、墟市、埠頭、村鄉、各處有火輪車嘅站頭、在個處搭客可以上落車嘅、限定時候起行停車、搭客大早買車票、車到就上車閂埋門、 |

## CONVERSATION 41ST.—THE RAILWAY.—(*Continued.*)

| | | |
|---|---|---|
| 22. | P'éi$^{3}$-꜁yü-꜀kán tái$^{2}$ ꜀shán ꜁m ꜀shan tak꜄ ᶜkéi ᶝyün*, ᶜfo-꜀ch'e-lò$^{2}$ ᶜho-ᶝyí ꜁wan tái$^{2}$ ꜀shán höü꜄. Yök$_{2}$-hai$^{2}$ ꜁m tsò$^{2}$ tak꜄, tsaú$^{2}$ ᶜho-ᶝyí ᶜching ꜀t'ung ko꜄ ꜀shán, t'it$_{o}$-lò$^{2}$ ᶜhai ꜀shán ꜀t'ung kwo꜄ höü꜄. | Suppoising large hill not stretch able very far, fire-carriage-road may round large hill go. If not do can, then can make through the hill, iron road in hill penetrate through go. |
| 23. | Yök$_{2}$ ko꜄ ꜀shán ꜁m hai$^{2}$ ꜀kò tái$^{2}$, ᶝk'öü-téi$^{2}$ ꜁ning-yün$^{3}$* ᶜhai ᶜteng† kwat$_{2}$ ᶝt'ün ko꜄ tso$^{2}$ ꜀shán. ᶝYaú ꜀kò téi$^{2}$, wák$_{2}$ ᶜai ꜀shán, t'it$_{o}$-lò$^{2}$ ᶜho-ᶝyí ꜁ts'e ꜁tse* ᶝshöng tò꜄ ᶜteng†, ꜁yín-haú$^{2}$ ꜁ts'e ꜁tse* ꜀fán lok$_{2}$ ꜁laí. | If the hill not is high large, they prefer at (*i.e.* from) top cut through that [C.] hill. If high ground, or low hill, iron road can sloping ascend to top, afterwards sloping back down come. |
| 24. | Wák$_{2}$ ᶝyaú ꜀taí shap꜄ téi$^{2}$, tsaú$^{2}$ ᶜching yat꜄ ꜁t'iú ꜀kéi, ᶜhò-ts'z꜄ ꜁t'ín ꜀kéi yat꜄ yöng$^{2}$; tán$^{2}$ fút$_{o}$ kwo꜄ ꜁t'ín ꜀kéi ᶜhò ꜀to. T'it$_{o}$ lò$^{2}$ ᶜhai ko꜄ ꜁t'iu ꜀kéi shöng$^{2}$ mín$^{3}$* kwo꜄. | If there-is low wet land then make one length embankment, like field embankments one same; but broader than field embankments very much. Iron road on that length [C.] embankment upper face pass-along. |
| 25. | ꜁Yan-téi$^{2}$ ᶜtím ᶝshöng lok$_{2}$ ꜀ni-$_{o}$ti ꜀ch'e ꜀ni$^{2}$? | People how ascend descend these carriages, eh? 53. |
| 26. | T'it$_{o}$-lò$^{2}$ ᶜsho ꜀t'ung ke꜄ tái$^{2}$ ꜁sheng†, ꜀höü ᶝshí, faú$^{2}$-꜁t'aú, ꜀ts'ün-꜀höng, kok$_{o}$ shü꜄ ᶝyaú ᶜfo-꜁lun ꜀ch'e-ke꜄ chám$^{2}$-꜁t'áú. Tsoí$^{2}$ ko꜄ shü꜄ táp$_{o}$-hák$_{o}$ ᶜho-ᶝyí ᶝshöng lok$_{2}$ ꜀ch'e ke꜄. Hán$^{2}$-ting$^{2}$ ꜁shí-haú$^{2}$ ᶜhéi ꜁háng ꜁t'ing ꜀ch'e. Táp$_{o}$-hák$_{o}$ tái$^{2}$-ᶜtsò ᶝmáí ꜀ch'e p'iú꜄ (*or* $_{o}$piú, *or* $_{o}$féi.) ꜀Ch'e tò꜄ tsaú$^{2}$ ᶝshöng ꜀ch'e, ꜀shán ꜁mái ꜁mún. | Iron-road whatever pass-through, 15, large cities, markets, towns, ports, villages, every place have fire-wheel carriage's, 15, stations. At those places passengers can ascend descend carriages, 15. Fixed times commence go stop carriages. Passengers early buy carriage tickets. Carriages arrive then ascend-into carriages shut to door. |

CONVERSATION 41ST.—THE RAILWAY.—*(Concluded)*

| | |
|---|---|
| 27. There are two things I want to ask you about:—You call them 'fire carriages.' Why do you call them that, and besides do they go quickly? | 有兩樣野、我想問吓你、你叫佢做火車、做乜嘢叫呢、另外行得快嗎、 |
| 28. At the front of the train there is an engine with machinery, fire, and furnaces like a steamer. This engine pulls the whole train of carriages whether there be few or many. Sometimes there are two or three carriages, sometimes there are quite a number. There are passenger carriages, luggage vans, and goods wagons; some carry coals, and some carry cattle and sheep. | 個剌火車前便有駕車、有機器在內、有火、有爐差不多同火船一樣、呢乘車拖成剌車、唔論多少、有時有兩三乘、有時有幾十乘、有啲車裝人客嘅、有啲車裝櫃箱行李、又有車裝貨、有啲裝煤炭嘅、有啲裝牛羊嘅、 |
| 29. As regards speed, some go quickly, and some go slowly. The fastest go about one hundred and fifty *li* an hour; the slow trains can go fifty or sixty *li* an hour. | 講行快慢呢、有啲行快、有啲行慢嘅、至快就係一點鐘行一百五十里左右、行慢嘅、一點鐘都行得五六十里嘅、 |
| 30. Truly it is wonderful. I happen just to have some business, so I cannot stay any longer. Good bye, Sir. | 眞正出奇咯、我啱啱有啲事幹、所以唔坐得咯、先生請致咯、 |
| 31. Walk slowly. | 慢慢行喇、 |
| 32. Good bye. | 請呀、 |

## CONVERSATION 41ST.—THE RAILWAY.—(*Concluded.*)

27. ᶜYaú ᶜlöng yöng$^{2}$ ᶜye, ᶜngo ᶜsöng man$^{2}$ (*or* man$^{5}$*) ᶜhá ᶜnéi :—ᶜNéi kiúᵓ ᶜk'öü tsò$^{2}$ ᶜfo-꜀ch'e. Tsò$^{2}$-mat꜄ ᶜkòm kiúᵓ ꜀ni ? Ling$^{2}$-ngoí$^{2}$ ꜀háng tak꜄ fáiᵓ ᶜmá ?

Have two kind things, I wish ask a-bit you:—You call them to-be fire carriages. Why so call, eh ? Besides go can quickly, eh ? 35.

28. Kòᵓ lát꜄ ᶜfo-꜀ch'e ꜀ts'ín pín$^{2}$ ᶜyaú káᵓ ꜀ch'e, ᶜyaú ꜀kéi-héíᵓ tsoí$^{2}$ noí$^{2}$, ᶜyaú ᶜfo, ᶜyaú ꜀lò, ꜀ch'á-pat꜄-꜀to ꜀t'ung ᶜfo-꜀shün yat꜄ yöng.$^{2}$ ꜀Ni shing$^{2}$ ꜀ch'e ꜀t'o ꜀shing (*or* ꜀sheng†) lát꜄ ꜀ch'e, ꜀m lun$^{2}$ ꜀to ᶜshiú. ᶜYaú ꜀shí ᶜyaú ᶜlöng ꜀sám ꜀shing, ᶜyaú ꜀shí ᶜyaú ᶜkéi shap꜄ ꜀shing. ᶜYaú ꜀ti ꜀ch'e ꜀chong ꜀yan-hák꜀ keᵓ ; ᶜyaú ꜀ti ꜀ch'e ꜀chong ᶜlung-꜀söng, ꜀hang-ᶜléi ; yaú$^{2}$ ᶜyaú ꜀ch'e ꜀chong foᵓ ; ᶜyaú ꜀ti ꜀chong ꜀múi-t'ánᵓ keᵓ ; ᶜyaú ꜀ti ꜀chong ꜀ngaú, ꜀yöng keᵓ.

That line fire-carriages front side have one [C.] carriage, have machinery in interior, have fire, have furnaces, differ-not-much-from fire-ship one same. This. [C.] carriage pulls whole row carriages, no matter more less. There-are times (when) there-are two three [C.], there-are times (when) there-are several tens [C.]. Have some carriages carry passengers, 15 ; have some carriages carry trunks-boxes, luggage ; besides have carriages carry goods ; have some carry coal, 15 ; have some carry cows, sheep, 15.

29. ᶜKong ꜀háng fáiᵓ mán$^{2}$ ꜀ni, ᶜyaú ꜀ti ꜀háng fáiᵓ ; ᶜyaú ꜀ti ꜀háng mán$^{2}$ keᵓ. Chíᵓ fáiᵓ tsaú$^{2}$ haí$^{2}$ yat꜄ ᶜtím꜀chung ꜀háng yat꜄ pák꜀ ᶜng-shap꜄ ᶜléi ᶜtso yaú$^{5}$* ; ꜀háng mán$^{2}$ keᵓ yat꜄ ᶜtím ꜀chung ꜀tò ꜀háng tak꜄ ᶜng lúk꜄ shap꜄ ᶜléi keᵓ.

Speaking-about going fast slow, 53. have some go quickly, have some go slowly, 15. Most quick just is one [C.] hour clock go one hundred fifty léi left (or) right ; go slowly, 15, one [C.] hour also go can five six tens léi, 15.

30. ꜀Chan chingᵓ ch'ut꜄-꜀k'éi lok꜀. ᶜNgo ꜀ngám-꜀ngám ᶜyaú ꜀ti sz$^{2}$-konᵓ ᶜsho-ᶜyi ꜀m ᶜts'o tak꜄ lok꜀. ꜀Sín-꜀sháng, ᶜtseng† chíᵓ lok꜀.

Truly really extraordinary. 32. I just have little business therefore not sit can, 32. Sir, good bye for-the-present 32.

31. Mán$^{2}$ ꜀mán (*or* mán$^{5}$*) ꜀háng† ꜀lá.

Slow slow walk, 21.

32. ᶜTseng† áᵓ.

Good-bye, 2.

## CONVERSATION 42ND.—TRADESMEN, &c.

| | |
|---|---|
| 1. The tailor has come. He says you met him in the street yesterday, and you told him to come up this morning. | 裁縫佬嚟咯、佢話你昨日喺街上遇着佢、叫佢今朝上嚟啊、 |
| 2. I have just returned from England, and I have a full supply of everything. I only want some white coats and trousers. | 我就正喺英國翻出嚟、樣樣都齊備㗎咯、我淨係要啲白衫褲啫、 |
| 3. I can make some for you. Let me measure you, and see what size to make the clothes for you. | 我噲同你整、等我度過你身、睇吓你着嗰啲要幾長、幾闊嘅、 |
| 4. I am stouter than I was. You must make them a little easier than those I am wearing. | 我呢陣肥過舊時、要做鬆啲過我而家着個啲噎得、 |
| 5. In a few days I will bring a coat and jacket for you to try on, and see if they are right. They can be easily altered then if necessary. | 我遲幾日拎一件衫、一條褲俾你着過、睇吓啱唔啱、就好易整鬆、或窄啲都得嘅、 |
| 6. Very well. Make me a dozen white coats, the same as this, and six pairs of white linen trousers, and six pairs of white cotton ones. | 好喇、同我做十二件(*or* 一打)白衫、好似呢件一樣、又整六條(*or* 半打)白麻布褲、白布褲、六條、 |
| 7. When can you finish them? I have only just enough to go on with, and no more. | 幾時整得完呢、因為我衣服慳慳够使啫、 |

## CONVERSATION 42ND.—TRADESMEN, &C.

| | |
|---|---|
| 1. ꜁Ts'oí-꜁fung ᶜlò ꜁laí lok$_o$. ˢK'öü wá$^2$ ˢnéí tsok$_2$-yat$_2$ ᶜhai ꜀káí shöng$^2$ yü$^2$-chök$_2$ ˢk'öü, kiúᵓ ˢk'öü ꜀kam ꜀chiú ˢshöng ꜁lai woᵓ. | Tailor fellow come, 32. He says you yesterday in street surface met him, told him this morning up come, he-says, 64. |
| 2. ˢNgo tsaú$^2$-chingᵓ ᶜhai ꜀Ying-kwok$_o$ ꜀fán ch'ut$_ɔ$ ꜁laí, yöng$^2$-yöng$^2$ (*or* yöng$^2$-yöng$^5$*) $_o$tò ꜁ts'ai-péí$^2$ sáiᵓ lok$_o$. ˢNgo tsing$^2$-haí$^2$ yiúᵓ $_o$ti pák$_o$ $_o$shám fúᵓ ꜀che.$^3$ | I just from England back out come, everything also prepared fully, 32. I only want some white coats trousers only, 7. |
| 3. ˢNgo ˢwúí ꜁t'ung ˢnéí ᶜching. ᶜTang ˢngo tok$_o$ kwoᵓ ˢnéí ꜀shan, ᶜt'aí ˢhá ˢnéí chök$_o$ koᵓ-$_o$ti yiúᵓ ᶜkéí ꜁ch'öng,* ᶜkéi fút$_{o_3}$* keᵓ. | I can for you make. Wait (till) I measure over your body, see a-bit you wear those, want how long, how wide, 15. |
| 4. ˢNgo ꜀ni chan$^2$ ꜁féí kwoᵓ kaú$^2$꜁shí,* Yiúᵓ tsò$^2$ ꜀sung-$_o$ti kwoᵓ ˢngo ꜁yí-$_o$ká chök$_o$ koᵓ-$_o$ti cheᵓ tak$_ɔ$. | I this time stouter than old time. Must make looser than I now wear those, in-order-to do. |
| 5. ˢNgo ꜁ch'í ᶜkéí yat$_2$ ꜀ning yat$_ɔ$ kín$^2$ $_o$shám, yat$_ɔ$ ꜁t'iú fúᵓ ᶜpéí ˢnéí chök$_o$ kwoᵓ, ᶜt'aí ˢhá ꜀ngám (*or* $_o$ngám) ꜁m ꜀ngám (*or* $_o$ngám). Tsaú$^2$ ᶜhò yíᵓ ᶜching ꜀sung, wák$_2$ chák$_2$-$_o$ti $_o$tò tak$_ɔ$ keᵓ. | I later several days bring one article (*or* C.) jacket, one pair (*lit.* length, *the* C.) trousers give you put-on (s. of p. t.), see a-bit right not right. Just very easy make loose, or tighter also can, 15. |
| 6. ᶜHò ꜁lá.$^3$ ꜁T'ung ˢngo tsò$^2$ shap$_2$-yí$^2$ kín$^2$ (*or* yat$_ɔ$ $_o$tá) pák$_o$ $_o$shám, ᶜhò-ts'zᵓ ꜀ni kín$^2$ yat$_ɔ$ yöng$^2$, yaú$^2$ ᶜching luk$_2$ ꜁t'iú (*or* púnᵓ$_o$tá) pák$_o$-꜁má-pòᵓ fúᵓ, pák$_2$pòᵓ fúᵓ, luk$^2$ ꜁t'iú. | Well, 21. For me make twelve articles [*i. e.* C.] (*or* one dozen) white coats, like this article (*i.e.* C.) one same, also make six [C.] (*or* half dozen) white linen trousers, white cotton trousers, six pairs. |
| 7. ᶜKéí ꜁shí* ᶜching tak$_ɔ$ ꜁yün ꜀ni? ꜀Yan-꜁wai ˢngo ꜀yí-fuk$_2$ ꜀hán$_o$hán kaúᵓ ᶜshaí ꜀che. | What time make can finish, eh? 53. Because my clothes only just sufficient to-use only, 7. |

## CONVERSATION 42ND.—TRADESMEN, &c.—(*Continued.*)

| | |
|---|---|
| 8. I will make them quickly for you. Do you not want a pith hat? I have a number in the shop, and will bring them up for you to see. | 我同你快啲做喇、你唔要個藫帽咩、我在舖頭有好多、等吓搽上嚟俾你睇、 |
| 9. Yes, I want one; my old one is worn out. | 要呀、我舊帽爛嘥咯、 |
| 10. Do you not want some collars, or neckties, or handkerchiefs, or cinglets, or socks, Sir? | 先生唔要啲頸領呀、頸帶呀、手巾呀、過頭笠呀、襪呀咩、 |
| 11. The shoe-maker is waiting outside. He has brought a new pair of shoes. | 做鞋師傅喺外頭等咯、佢搽對新鞋嚟咯、 |
| 12. Tell him to come in. | 叫佢入嚟喇、 |
| 13. Ah! You have brought my new shoes, have you? Where is the shoe-horn? Oh! they are too small; I cannot put them on. | 呵、你搽我對新鞋嚟囉咩、鞾抽呢、唉、唔着得嘅、細過頭、 |
| 14. I think you can. The leather is stiff, that is all. Let me help you. | 我估做得、皮硬啫、等我帮你嗻、 |
| 15. Ah! there it is on, but it is too tight. It pinches my toes. | 呵、着咯、但係窄過頭呀挾住我脚趾(骨)嘅、 |
| 16. I will take them back, and put them on the lasts, and stretch them. | 我搽翻去、俾鞋楦楦闊啲、 |
| 17. I think they are too short; but if you will bring them back again after stretching them, I will try them once more. | 我估短過頭、楦闊之後、搽翻嚟我再試過喇、 |

## CONVERSATION 42ND.—TRADESMEN, &c.—*(Continued.)*

| | |
|---|---|
| 8. ꜃Ngo ꜁t'ung ꜃néí fáí꜄-°ti tsò² ꜀lá.² ꜃Néí ꜁m yiú꜄ ko꜄ °t'ung mò꜄* ꜀me? ꜃Ngo tsoí² p'ò꜄-꜁t'aú* ꜃yaú ꜂hò ꜀to, ꜂tang ꜃há (*or* °há) ꜀ning ꜃shöng ꜁laí ꜂péí ꜃néí ꜂t'ai. | I for you quickly make, 21. You not want a pith hat, eh? 39. I in shop have great many, wait a-bit bring up come give you see. |
| 9. Yiú꜄ á꜄. ꜃Ngo kaú² mò꜄* lán² ꜂cho lok°. | Want, 2. My old hat broken, (s. of p. t.) 32. |
| 10. ꜀Sín-꜀sháng ꜁m yiú °ti ꜂keng†-꜃leng†. á꜄, ꜂keng-táí꜄* á꜄; ꜂shaú-°kan á꜄, kwo꜄-꜁t'aú-lap꜆ á꜄, mat꜇ á꜄, ꜀me?² | Sir, not want some collars, 2, neckties, 2, handkerchiefs, 2, cinglets, 2, socks, eh? 2, 39. |
| 11. Tsò²-꜁háí ꜀sz-fú꜄* ꜂haí ngoí²-꜁t'aú ꜂tang lok°. ꜃K'öü ꜀ning töü꜄ ꜀san ꜁háí ꜁laí lok°. | Make shoe workman at outside wait, 32. He bring pair new shoes come, 39. |
| 12. Kiú꜄ ꜃k'öü yap꜇ ꜁laí ꜀lá.² | Call him enter come, 21. |
| 13. ꜁O! ꜃Néí ꜀ning ꜂ngo töü꜄ ꜀san ꜁háí ꜁laí lo꜄ ꜀me?² ꜁Háí-°ch'aú ꜀ni?² ꜀Aí (*or* °Aí), ꜁m chök° tak꜆ ke꜄, (*or* ke꜄*); saí꜅ kwo꜄* ꜁t'aú. | Ah! You brought my pair new shoes come? 31, 39. Shoe-lifter, eh? 53. Oh! not put-on can, 15; small over much. |
| 14. ꜃Ngo ꜂kwú tsò² tak꜆. ꜁P'éí* ngáng² ꜀che.² ꜂Tang ꜃ngo ꜀pong ꜃néí chá꜄. | I think do can. Leather stiff only, 7. Wait I assist you, 6. |
| 15. ꜁O! Chök°* lok°; tán²-haí² chák꜆ kwo꜄* ꜁t'aú á꜄. Kíp꜇-chü² ꜃ngo kök°-꜂chí-kwat꜆ (*or* kök°-꜂chí) ke꜄. | Ah! Put-on, 32; but tight over much, 2. Pinch my toe-bones (*or* toes.) 15. |
| 16. ꜃Ngo ꜀ning ꜀fán höü꜄, ꜂péí ꜁háí-hün꜄ hün꜄ fút°-°ti. | I take back go, give shoe-lasts last wider. |
| 17. ꜃Ngo ꜂kwú ꜂tün kwo꜄* ꜁t'aú꜄; hün꜄ fút° ꜀chí-haú², ꜀ning ꜀fán ꜁laí, ꜃ngo tsoi꜄ shí꜄ kwo꜄ ꜀lá.² | I think short over much; last wider afterwards, bring back come, I again try over, 21. |

CONVERSATION 42ND.—TRADESMEN &C,—(*Continued.*)

| | |
|---|---|
| 18. I want this pair of boots mended. I want them reheeled and resoled. | 呢對靴要補翻好、要打掌呀、即係要整新鞋踭鞋底、 |
| 19. I am afraid these will not last well. | 我怕呢啲鞋底唔聆使嘅、 |
| 20. The pair of patent leather shoes you made for me have cracked. I said the leather was not good when you made them for me, and they had only been worn a short time when the soles were worn through. | 你同我整個對漆皮鞋都裂咽、你整個陣時我都話唔好皮、着冇耐鞋底又爛添、 |
| 21. Has the washerman brought the clothes in yet? | 洗衣服佬擰衫翻嚟唔曾呢、 |
| 22. He has. There are three articles short—a white waistcoat and two shirts. | 交咯、佢交少三件、一件就係白背心、嗰兩件係汗衫呀、 |
| 23. He must find them again. If not, he will have to buy new ones, the same as those lost; or I will cut him when I pay him. | 佢要搵翻噎得、唔係、要買新嘅、照依失咽個啲一樣、唔係呢、我就剷佢人工咯、 |
| 24. Oh, dear me! You must take more care. Do not be so rough. You have knocked over the birdcage and frightened the bird to death. | 唉、弊家伙、心機啲噎得嚿、咪咁躁暴、你打轉個雀籠、嚇死個隻雀咯、 |

## CONVERSATION 42ND.—TRADESMEN, &c.—(*Continued.*)

| | | |
|---|---|---|
| 18. | ꜀Ni töü꜂ ꜀hö (Note 1) yiú꜂ ꜁pò-꜀fán ꜁hò, yiú꜂ ꜁tá-꜁chöng á꜂. Tsik꜃-hai$^2$ yiú꜂ ꜁ching ꜀san ꜄hái ꜀cháng, ꜄hái ꜁tai, | This pair boots want mend back good, want resoling. That-is want make new shoes' heel, shoes' sole |
| 19. | ꜅Ngo p'á꜂ ꜀ni-꜀ti ꜄hái ꜁tai ꜄m ꜀k'am ꜁shai ke꜂. | I fear these shoes' soles not durable use, 15. |
| 20. | ꜅Néi ꜄t'ung ꜅ngo ꜁ching ko꜂ töü꜂ ts'at꜃ ꜄p'éi ꜄hái ꜀tò lit$_2$ ꜁cho. ꜅Néi ꜁ching ko꜂ chan$^2$ ꜄shí*, ꜅ngo ꜀tò wá$^2$ ꜄m ꜁hò ꜄p'éi*, chök꜃* ꜅mò noí,$^2$ (*or* noí$^5$*) ꜄hái ꜁tai yaú$^2$ ꜄lán ꜀t'ím. | You for me make that pair patent leather shoes also cracked (s. of p. t.). You make that period time, I said also not good leather, wear not long, shoes' sole also break too. |
| 21. | ꜁Sai-꜀yi-fuk꜃-꜁lò ꜀ning ꜀shám ꜀fán ꜄lai ꜄m ꜄ts'ang ꜀ni? | Wash-clothes-fellow bring clothes back come not yet, eh? 53. |
| 22. | ꜀Káu (Note 2) lok꜀. ꜅K'öü ꜀káu ꜁shiú ꜀sám kín꜂;—yat꜃ kín$^2$ tsaú$^2$ hai$^2$ pák꜃ púi꜂-꜀sam, ꜁ko ꜅löng kín$^2$ hai$^2$ hòn$^2$-꜀shám á꜂. | Handed-over, 32. He handed-over short three articles—one article just was white waist-coat, those two articles were shirts, 2. |
| 23. | ꜅K'öü yiú꜂ ꜁wan ꜀fán che꜂ tak꜃. ꜄M hai$^2$, yiú꜂ ꜅mái ꜀san ke꜂, chíú꜂-꜀yí shat꜃-꜁cho ko꜂-꜀ti yat꜃ yöng$^2$; ꜄m hai$^2$ ꜀ni, ꜅ngo tsaú$^2$ kot꜀ ꜅k'öü ꜄yan-꜀kung lok꜀. | He must find back before-it will-do. Not do (so), must buy new ones, according-to lost those one same; not do-(so), 53, I then cut him wages, 32. |
| 24. | ꜀Aí, (*or* ꜀Ai) Pai$^2$-꜀ká- ꜁fo! ꜀Sam-꜁kéi ꜀ti che꜂ tak꜃ ká꜂. ꜅Mai kòm꜂ ts'ò꜂-pò$^2$. ꜅Néi ꜁tá-꜁chün ko꜂ tsök꜀*-꜄lung, hák꜀ ꜁sz ko꜂ chek꜀ tsök꜀* lok꜀. | Oh! Alas! Carefully more only can, 14. Do-not-be so rough. You struck-turn-over that bird-cage, frighten to-death the [C.] bird, 32. |

1. This is the same sound as in 香 ꜀höng; the only difference being that no consonants follow the 靴 ꜀hö; consequently it is pronounced longer, the voice rests longer on the ö than when followed by consonants.

2. The variant upper even tone shows the past tense.

## CONVERSATION 42ND.—TRADEMEN, &c.—(*Concluded.*)

| | |
|---|---|
| 25. Have you brushed the clothes this morning, that I had on when I went to dinner last night? | 我昨晚着個啲衫出街食餐，你今朝擦咽唔曾呢， |
| 26. Yes, I have, I have folded them up, and put them in the drawer in the chest of drawers. | 擦咽咯，叉摺埋，擠入五桶櫃個櫃桶咯， |
| 27. You have not brushed my shoes well this morning; they do not shine. | 你今朝擦我鞋，冇擦到靚曬， |
| 28. There is no blacking. It is all used up. | 冇擦鞋墨水，使嗮咯， |
| 29. Get some more from the compradore. Give me the pass book, and I will put it down. | 同買辦攞啲喇，俾個部仔我，等我上住咯， |
| 30. Very well. I will go and get it. But what if he has none? | 好喇，我去攞喇，或者冇呢， |
| 31. Go to another shop and buy it. | 去第二間買咯， |
| 32. Very well. | 唔，好喇， |

## CONVERSATION 43RD.—THE BOY PUT INTO AUTHORITY.

| | |
|---|---|
| 1. Now, Boy, I hand over the silverware for you to look after. | 拿，事仔，我交帶個啲銀器過你理， |
| 2. How many articles are there? | 有幾多件呢， |
| 3. Two dozen large spoons and forks. There is one small fork lost, but, barring that, there are as many small forks and spoons. | 兩吋大羹叉，叉有一枝細羹失咽，爭個一枝，細叉羹都係大叉羹咁多， |

## CONVERSATION 42ND.—TRADESMEN, &c.—(*Concluded.*)

| | | |
|---|---|---|
| 25. | ᶜNgo tsok$_2$ ᶜmán chök$_o$ ko'-$_o$ti $_o$shám ch'ut, ꜀kái shik$_2$ $_o$ts'án, ᶜnéí ꜀kam ꜀chíú ts'át$_o$-ᶜcho ꜀m ꜀ts'ang ꜀ni ?$^3$ | I last night wore those clothes go-out streets (*i.e.* to go out) eat meal, you this morning brushed not yet, eh ? 53. |
| 26. | Ts'át$_o$-ᶜcho lok$_o$. Yaú$^2$ chíp$_o$ máí$^2$, ꜀chaí ꜀yap$_2$ ᶜng-ᶜt'ung-kwaí$^2$ ko' kwaí$^2$-ᶜt'ung lok$_o$. | Brushed, 32. Also folded together place in five-drawers-cupboard that drawer, 32. |
| 27. | ᶜNéí ꜀kam ꜀chíú ts'át$_o$ ᶜngo ꜀háí, ᶜmò ts'át$_o$ tò' leng'† ká'. | You this morning brushed my shoes, not brush till bright, 14. |
| 28. | ᶜMò ts'át$_o$ ꜀háí mak$_2$ ᶜshöü. ᶜShaí sáí' lok$_o$. | No brush shoe ink water. Use all, 32. |
| 29. | ꜀T'ung ᶜmáí-pán$^3$* ᶜlo $_o$ti ꜀lá$^2$. ᶜPéí ko' pò$^5$* ᶜtsaí ᶜngo, ᶜtang ᶜngo ᶜshöng-chü$^2$ lok$_o$. | With compradore get some, 21. Give that book little (i.e., little book), to me, till I enter, 32. |
| 30. | ᶜHò ꜀lá.$^2$ ᶜNgo höü' ᶜlo ꜀lá.$^2$ Wák$_2$-ᶜche ᶜmò ꜀ni ?$^3$ | Well, 21. I go get, 21. Perhaps none, eh ? 53. |
| 31. | Höü' taí$^2$ ꜀kán ᶜmáí lok.$_o$ | Go another [the two words are run into one] [C.] buy, 32. |
| 32. | ꜀Ng, ᶜhò ꜀lá.$^2$ | Well good, 21. |

## CONVERSATION 43RD.—THE BOY PUT INTO AUTHORITY.

| | | |
|---|---|---|
| 1. | Ná$^2$, Sz$^2$-ᶜtsaí, ᶜngo ꜀káú-táí' ko'-$_o$ti ꜀ngan héí' kwo' ᶜnéí ᶜléí. | There, Boy I hand-over those silver articles over-to you to-attend-to. |
| 2. | ᶜYaú ᶜkéí ꜀to kín$^2$ ꜀ni ?$^3$ | Have how many articles, eh ? 53. |
| 3. | ᶜLöng $_o$tá táí$^2$ $_o$kang $_o$ch'á. Yaú$^2$ ᶜyaú yat, ꜀chí saí' $_o$ch'á shat, ᶜcho, ꜀cháng ko' yat, ꜀chí, saí' $_o$ch'á $_o$káng $_o$tò haí$^2$ táí$^2$ $_o$ch'á $_o$kang kòm' $_o$to. | Two dozen large spoons forks. Further have one [C.] small fork lost [s. of p. t.], wanting that one [C.], small forks spoons also are large forks spoons so many. |

## CONVERSATION 43RD.—THE BOY PUT INTO AUTHORITY.

| | | |
|---|---|---|
| 4. | Are there any fruit knives and forks? There are of each kind a dozen and a half, and there are fish knives and forks. | 有食菓刀叉有冇呀、每樣有一哳半、又有食魚刀叉添、 |
| 5. | There are boxes for these two kinds, I suppose. | 呢兩樣大概有箱裝啩、 |
| 6. | There are. I hand over the keys for you to hold. | 有嘅、鎖匙我交過你揸 |
| 7. | Where are the tea-spoons? | 茶羹呢、 |
| 8. | Here they are. The egg spoons, fruit spoons, salt cellars, and salt spoons are all here. | 喺呢處拿、鷄蛋羹、揔菓羹、鹽盅、鹽羹、咸𠺢唥都喺齊嚹呢處呀、 |
| 9. | And the caster is on the table. Did I not see that you had two small ones besides? | 五味架在檯上、我唔係見你另外有兩個細嘅添、 |
| 10. | Quite so. This case holds the fish slice and fork. | 冇錯、呢個盒裝住分魚大刀叉、 |
| 11. | The tea-pot, coffee-pot, sugar-bowl, and cream-jug are on the side-board. | 茶壺、架啡壺、唐兜 (or 盅)、牛奶嚶、咸𠺢唥喺西啵處、 |
| 12. | The hot-water-jug is there too. Did not you see it? | 熱水嚶都喺個處呀、你唔見咩、 |
| 13. | I saw it. Here are some sugar spoons, and some vegetable-dishes you have not mentioned. | 見咯、呢處又有啲揔糖羹、有啲菜兜、你都唔曾講到嚟、 |
| 14. | There, that is all. I want you to count them over very night, and see if there are any wanting. If there are any lost, you will have to make them good. Do you understand? | 拿、係咁多咯、我晚晚要你點過嚹睇吓齊嚹唔齊、有乜唔見咗、要你賠咯、你明白嗎、 |

## CONVERSATION 43RD.—THE BOY PUT INTO AUTHORITY.

| | | |
|---|---|---|
| 4. | ᶜYaú shik, ᶜkwo ꜀tò ˳ch'á ᶜyaú ᶜmò áᵓ? ᶜMúi yöng² ᶜyaú yat, ˳tá pún', yaú² ᶜyaú shik₂ ꜀yü* ꜀tò ˳ch'á ꜀t'ím. | Have eat fruit knives forks, have not, eh? 2. Each kind have one dozen half, also have eat fish knives forks besides. |
| 5. | ꜀Ni ᶜlöng yöng² tái²-k'oí¹* ᶜyaú ˳söng ꜀chong kwáᵓ? | These two kinds probably have case hold is-it-not-so? 18, |
| 6. | ᶜYaú keᵓ. ᶜSo-꜀shí ᶜngo ꜀káú kwoᵓ ᶜnéi ꜀chá. | Have, 15. Lock's-key I hand-over to you to-hold. |
| 7. | ꜀Ch'á-˳kang ꜀ni? | Tea-spoons, eh? 53. |
| 8. | ᶜHaí ꜀ni shüᵓ ꜀ná. ꜀Kaí-tán³*-˳kang, fat, ᶜkwo ˳kang, ꜀yím-˳chung, ꜀yím ˳kang, hám²-pá²-láng² ˳tò ᶜhaí, ꜀ts'ai sáiᵓ ꜀ni shüᵓ áᵓ. | At this place, there. Fowl's-egg-spoons, lift fruit spoons, salt-cellar, salt spoons all also at together all this place, 2. |
| 9. | ᶜNg-méi²-ká¹* tsoí² ꜀t'oi* shöng². ᶜNgo ꜀m haí² kínᵓ ᶜnéi ling²-ngoí² ᶜyaú ᶜlöng koᵓ saíᵓ keᵓ ꜀t'ím? | Five-seasonings-stand also on table surface. I not have seen you besides have two [C.] small [s. of possessing] besides? |
| 10. | ᶜMò ts'oᵓ. ꜀Ni koᵓ hòp₃* ꜀chong chü² ꜀fan ꜀yü* tái² ꜀tò ˳ch'á. | Not wrong. This [C.] case holds [s. of containing] divide fish large knife fork. |
| 11. | ꜀Ch'á-꜀wú*, ꜀ká-꜀féi-꜀wú*, ꜀t'ong-˳taú (*or* ˳chung) ꜀ngaú-ᶜnái-mak₃, hám²-pá²-láng² ᶜhaí ꜀sái-꜀pò shüᵓ. | Tea-pot, coffee-pot, sugar-basin (*or* bowl *say*), cow's-milk-mug, all at side-board place. |
| 12. | Yít₂-ᶜshöü-mak, ˳tò ᶜhaí koᵓ shüᵓ áᵓ. ᶜNéi ꜀m kínᵓ ꜀me?² | Hot-water-mug also at that place, 2. You not see, eh? 39. |
| 13. | Kínᵓ lok˳. ꜀Ni shüᵓ yaú² ᶜyaú ˳ti fat, ꜀t'ong ˳kang, ᶜyaú ˳ti ts'oíᵓ-˳taú, ᶜnéi ˳tò ꜀m ꜀ts'ang ᶜkong tòᵓ ꜀laí. | Seen, 32. This place also have some lift sugar spoons; have some vegetable-dishes, you also not yet speak reach come. |
| 14. | ꜀Ná, haí² kòmᵓ ˳to lok˳. ᶜNgo ᶜmán-ᶜmán yíúᵓ ᶜnéi ᶜtím kwoᵓ sáiᵓ ᶜt'aí ᶜhá ꜀ts'ai sáiᵓ ꜀m ꜀ts'aí. ᶜYaú mat, ꜀m kínᵓ-ᶜcho, yíúᵓ ᶜnéi ꜀p'úi lok˳. ᶜNéi ꜀ming-pák₂ máᵓ? | There, it-is-that-there-are so many, 32. I every night want you count over all see a-bit together all not together. Have anything not seen [s. of p. t.], want you make-good, 32. You understand, eh? 35. |

CONVERSATION 43RD.—THE BOY PUT INTO AUTHORITY.—*(Continued.)*

| | |
|---|---|
| 15. Quite, Sir. | 明白嗻咯先生、 |
| 16. Where are the plates, and dishes, and Chinaware? | 碗碟瓷器呢、 |
| 17. In the cupboard. I have looked them over. There are large plates and small plates, soup plates and dessert plates and meat-dishes, tea-cups and saucers, coffee-cups, egg-cups, and vegetable-dishes. | 喺(碗)櫃嚟咯、我睇過嚟咯、有大碟、有細碟、湯碟、菓碟、裝肉碟、茶盃、茶盃碟、架啡盃、鷄蛋杯、菜兜、 |
| 18. There is a soup tureen. | 有個湯兜、 |
| 19. An iron? No. | 熨斗、冇吖、 |
| 20. To put soup in. | 裝湯嘅、 |
| 21. Oh, a soup tureen; yes. | 呵、湯兜、有、 |
| 22. There is also glass ware. | 又有玻璃器添、 |
| 23. A number of the tumblers are broken and cracked. | 好多個啲玻璃杯係爛咽、裂咽、 |
| 24. I do not think so. | 唔係嘞、 |
| 25. Yes, they are, and two or three of the finger-glasses. | 係吖、兩三個手盅、又係呀、 |
| 26. You must take care and not break more of them. | 你要仔細、咪整爛多啲、 |
| 27. The two large lamps need new shades and chimney. | 個兩盞大燈、要新燈筒、燈罩至得、 |
| 28. You must cut the wicks better. The lamp did not burn well last night. Is there enough oil in it? Has any oil been put in this morning? | 你要剪個啲燈心好啲至得、昨晚個盞燈唔燒得好、够油唔够呢、今朝斟油唔曾呀、 |

## CONVERSATION 43RD.—THE BOY PUT INTO AUTHORITY.—(*Continued.*)

| | | |
|---|---|---|
| 15. | ꜁Ming-pák$_2$ sáí꜄ lok꜄, ꜀Sín-꜀sháng. | Understand all, 32, Sir. |
| 16. | ꜂Wún típ$_2$, ꜁ts'z-héí꜄ ꜀ni? $^2$ | Bowls, plates, porcelain-articles, eh ? 53. |
| 17. | ꜂Haí (꜂wún) kwaí$^5$* ꜁laí lok˳. ꜃Ngo ꜂t'aí kwo꜄ ꜁laí lok˳. ꜃Yaú táí$^2$ típ$_2$, ꜃yaú saí꜄ tip$_2$, ꜀t'ong típ$_2$, ꜂kwo tip$_2$, ꜀chong yuk$_2$ tip$_2$, ꜁ch'á-꜀púí, ꜁ch'á-꜀púi-típ$_2$, ká꜄-˳féí-˳púi, ꜀kaí-tán$^5$*-˳púí, ts'oí꜄-꜄taú. (Note 1) | In (bowl) press come-to-be, 32. I look over come, 32. Have large plates, have small plates, soup plates, fruit plates, hold meat plates, tea-cups, tea-cup plates, coffee-cups, fowl-egg-cups, vegetable-dishes. |
| 18. | ꜃Yaú ko꜄ ꜀t'ong-˳taú. | Have a soup tureen. |
| 19. | T'ong꜄-꜂taú ? ꜃Mò ꜀á.$^2$ | Iron ? No, 1. |
| 20. | ꜀Chong ꜀t'ong ke꜄. | Hold soup, 15. |
| 21. | ꜁O, ꜀t'ong-˳taú ; ꜃yaú. | Oh ! soup tureen ; have. |
| 22. | Yaú$^2$ ꜃yaú ꜀po-˳léí* héí꜄ ꜀t'ím. | Besides have glass ware also. |
| 23. | ꜂Hò ꜀to ko꜄-˳ti ꜀po-˳léí-˳púí haí$^2$ lán$^2$ ꜂cho, lít$_2$ ꜂cho. | Very many of-those glass-cups [i.e. glasses] broken (s. of p. t.], cracked [s. of p. t.] |
| 24. | ꜁M haí$^2$ kwá꜄. | Not are probable, 18. |
| 25. | Ha.$^2$ ꜀á.$^2$ ꜃Löng ꜀sám ko꜄ ꜂shaú-˳chung, yaú$^2$ haí$^2$ á꜄. | Are, 1. Two three [C.] hand-bowls also are, 2. |
| 26. | ꜃Néí yíú꜄ ꜂tsz-saí꜄ ꜃maí ꜃ching-lán$^2$ ꜀to-˳ti. | You must-be careful do-not make-break more. |
| 27. | Ko꜄ ꜃löng ꜂chán táí$^2$ ꜀tang (*or* ˳tang) yíú꜄ ꜀san ˳tang ꜁tung*, ˳tang cháú꜄ chí꜄ tak꜄. | Those two [C.] large lamps want new lamp chimneys, lamp globes before (they can) do. |
| 28. | ꜃Néí yíú꜄ ꜂tsín ko꜄-˳ti ꜀tang ꜀sam ꜂hò-˳ti chí꜄ tak꜄. Tsok$_2$ ꜃mán ko꜄ ꜂chán ꜀tang ꜁m ꜀shíú tak꜄ ꜂hò. Kaú꜄ ꜁yaú, ꜁m kaú꜄ ꜀ni ? ꜀Kam ꜀chíú ꜀cham (*or* ˳cham) ꜁yaú ꜀m ꜁ts'ang a꜄? | You must cut (with scissors) those lamp wicks better before-it will-do. Last night that [C.] lamp not burn can good. Enough oil, not enough, eh ? 53. This morning pour-in oil not yet, eh ? 2. |

[Note. 1—All these *plates* can be either as above or típ$_5$.*

## CONVERSATION 43RD.—THE BOY PUT INTO AUTHORITY.—(*Concluded.*)

| | | |
|---|---|---|
| 29. | Shall I put on the table cloth now? | 而家鋪檯布好嗎, |
| 30. | Yes, you had better. I want my dinner earlier to night. | 好呀, 我今晚要早啲食大餐, |
| 31. | There are no serviettes. | 冇檯巾, |
| 32. | Go to the wardrobe, and get some out. | 去衣櫃攞出嚟, |

## CONVERSATION 44TH.—THE OUTSIDE BARBARIAN.

| | | |
|---|---|---|
| 1. | I have heard of a place called Europe, and yet I have never seen a man from Europe. Each of you foreign devils say you are Red Haired Men, or Flowery Flag Men (Vulgar term for English and American), or people of some other place, which no one knows anything about at all. | 聽聞有笪叫做歐羅巴, 誰不知未曾見過歐羅巴人, 你哋番鬼個個都認自已係紅毛人, 或花旗, 抑或別處嘅人, 都冇人知呢啲地方在邊處嘅, |
| 2. | I thought you were a scholar. | 我估先生係讀書人, |
| 3. | So I am. Do you foreign devils read? I take it people like what you are do not have much literature to trouble yourselves about. | 冇錯, 你哋番鬼有讀書冇呀, 我睇得你哋噉嘅人冇乜書讀嘅, |
| 4. | I cannot believe that you are a scholar. | 我唔信得先生係讀書人, |
| 5. | Why? | 因何[illegible], |
| 6. | In the first place, you do not treat people politely. | 第一件, 先生不用禮貌待人, |
| 7. | Why do you say that? | 何故噉講呢, |

## CONVERSATION 43RD.—THE BOY PUT INTO AUTHORITY.—(*Concluded.*)

| | |
|---|---|
| 29. ꜁Yí-ₒká ꜀p'ò ꜁t'oí*-pò꜄ ꜂hò ꜃má ?. | Now spread table-cloth good, eh ? 35. |
| 30. ꜂Hò á꜄. ꜃Ngo ꜀kam-꜃mán yíú꜄ ꜂tsò-ₒti shik$_2$ tái$^2$-ₒts'án. | Good, 2. I to-night want earlier eat the-big-meal. |
| 31. ꜃Mò ꜁t'oí* ₒkan. | No table napkins. |
| 32. Höü꜄ ꜀yí-kwai$^2$ ꜂lo ch'ut꜆ ꜁laí. | Go clothes-press get out come. |

## CONVERSATION 44TH.—THE OUTSIDE BARBARIAN.

| | |
|---|---|
| 1. ꜃Ngo ꜀t'eng† -꜁man ꜃yaú tát₀ kíú꜄ tsò$^2$ ꜀Aú-꜁lo-꜀pá, shöü$^2$-pat꜆-꜀chí méí$^2$ ꜁ts'ang kín꜄ kwo꜄ ꜀Aú-꜁lo-꜀pá-꜁yan. ꜃Néí-téí$^2$ ꜀fán-꜃kwaí ko꜄-ko꜄ ₒtò ying$^2$ tsz$^2$-꜂kéí haí$^2$ ꜁Hung-꜁mò ꜁yan, wák$_2$ ꜀Fá-꜁k'éí, (*or* ꜀Fá-꜁k'éí*), yík꜆-wák$_2$ pít$_2$ ch'ü꜄-ke꜄ ꜁yan. ₒTò ꜃mò ꜁yan ꜀chí ꜀ni-ₒti téí$^2$-꜀fong tsoí$^2$ ₒpín ch'ü꜄ ke$^1$*. | I heard have place called to be Europe, anyone-not-knows (i.e. no one knows) not yet seen have European. You foreign devils each also acknowledge yourselves are Red-Haired Men, or Flowery-Flag or other place's men. Even no man knows these places at what place, 15. |
| 2. ꜃Ngo ꜂kwú ꜀Sín-꜀sháng† haí$^2$ tuk$_2$-꜀shü-꜁yan. | I thought (you), Sir, were read-book-man. |
| 3. ꜃Mò ts'o꜄. ꜃Néí-téí$^2$ ꜀fán-꜂kwaí ꜃yaú tuk$_2$ shü꜄ ꜃mò á꜄ ? ꜃Ngo ꜂t'aí tak꜆ ꜃néí-téí$^2$ ꜂kòm-ke꜄ ꜁yan ꜃mò mat꜆ ꜀shü tuk$_2$ ke$^1$*. | No mistake. You foreign devils have read books not eh ? 2. I see able (i.e. It appears to my sight) you such people (i.e. such people as you are) not much books read, 15. |
| 4. ꜃Ngo ꜁m sun꜄ tak꜆ ꜀Sín-꜀sháng† haí$^2$ tuk$_2$-꜀shü-꜁yan. | I not believe able (you), Sir, are read-book-man. |
| 5. ꜀Yan ꜁ho ꜀á?. | On-account-of what eh ? 1. |
| 6. Taí$^2$ yat꜆ kín$^2$, ꜀Sín-꜀sháng† pat꜆ yung$^2$ ꜃laí-máú$^2$ toí$^2$ ꜁yan. | In first instance (you), Sir, not use polite-manners towards people. |
| 7. ꜁Ho kwú꜄ ꜂kòm ꜂kong ꜀ni? ꜄ | For-what reason so speak, eh ? 53. |

## CONVERSATION 44RD.—THE OUTSIDE BARBARIAN.

| | | |
|---|---|---|
| 8. | Because Confucius, says, 'Not to do to others as you would not wish done to yourself.' | 因孔夫子有(話)己所不欲勿施於人、 |
| 9. | Halloa! Why! Do you foreign devils know the Four Books? | 唉咄、你哋番鬼都識四書嘅、 |
| 10. | If we are devils, probably we do not understand them; but if we are human, it is possible we can understand them. | 若係鬼、大槪唔識嘅：倘若係人、都怕噲識嘅、 |
| 11. | It is truly laughable. You foreigners do not like to be called devils. Is that it? | 眞正好笑咯、你哋番人唔中意人哋叫你做鬼、係唔係呢、 |
| 12. | I wish to ask you a question. | 我請問先生一句呀、 |
| 13. | Very good. What is it? | 好喇、乜野呢、 |
| 14. | If any one were to style you a devil, would you be pleased? Certainly not. If you are not pleased, do you suppose I am? I consider it a breach of politeness. | 若有人稱先生做鬼、先生願唔願呢、確實唔願咯、先生、先生估我願咩、我算失禮咯、 |
| 15. | Foreigner, there is something in what you say. | 老番、你所講嘅都有啲道理、 |
| 16. | Our code of politeness differs from yours. You do not know ours. I have gradually learnt your estimable country's politeness, and I wish to treat you in a courteous manner; but you, Sir, are rude to me. | 我哋西人嘅禮法、唔同你哋唐人禮法、你不知我嘅禮法吖、我漸漸學先生貴國禮貌、我想合禮待先生、但先生冇禮接我、 |

## CONVERSATION 44TH.—THE OUTSIDE BARBARIAN.

| | | |
|---|---|---|
| 8. | ꜀Yan ᶜHung ꜀Fú-ᶜTsz ᶝyaú wá[2], 'ᶜKéi ᶜsho pat꜆ yuk꜇, mat꜇ shíˀ ꜀yü ꜁yan.' | Because Confucius Master have said, 'Yourself what not wish, don't try-it-on to (other) men.' |
| 9. | ꜀Ai-꜀yá, (*or* ꜀ai ꜀yá, *or* ꜀ai ᶝyá) ᶝnéi-téi[2] ꜀fán-ᶜkwai ꜀tò shik꜆ 'Szˀ ꜀Shü' keˀ! | Dear me, you foreign devils also know 'Four Books,' 15. |
| 10. | Yök꜇-hai[2] ᶜkwai, taí[2]-k'oi[1]* ꜁m shik꜆ ke[1]*; ᶜt'ong-yök꜇ hai[2] ꜁yan, ꜀tò p'áˀ ᶝwúi shik꜆ ke[1]*. | If-are devils probably not know, 15. If are men, also perhaps can know, 15. |
| 11. | ꜀Chan-chingˀ ᶜhò-síúˀ lok꜀, ᶝnéi-téi[2] ꜀fán-꜁yan ꜁m ꜀chung-yíˀ ꜀yan-téi[2] kíúˀ ᶝnéi tsò[2] ᶜkwai; hai[2] ꜁m hai[2] ꜀ni? [2] | Truly very-laughable, 32, you foreigners not pleased people call you to-be devils; is not is, eh? 53. |
| 12. | ᶝNgo ᶜts'eng*† ꜁man ꜀Sín-꜀shàng† yat꜆ köüˀ áˀ. | I request-to ask (you), Sir, one sentence, 2. |
| 13. | ᶜHò ꜀lá; [2] mat꜆ ᶝye ꜁ni? [2] | Good, 21; what thing, eh? 53. |
| 14. | Yök꜇ ᶝyaú ꜁yan ꜀ch'ing ꜀Sín-꜀shàng† tsò[2] ᶜkwai, ꜀Sín-꜀shàng† yün[2] ꜁m yün[2] ꜀ni? [2] K'ok꜀ shat꜇ ꜁m yün[2] lok꜀. ꜀Sín-꜀shàng† ꜁m yün[2], ꜀Sín-꜀shàng† ᶜkwú ᶝngo yün[2] ꜀me? [2] ᶝNgo sünˀ shat꜆-ᶝlai lok. | If-it-happened there-was anyone styled (you), Sir, to-be devil (you), Sir, satisfied, not satisfied eh? 53. Certainly not satisfied 32. (You), Sir, not satisfied (you), Sir, think I satisfied, eh? 39. I consider (a) loss-of-politeness, 32. |
| 15. | ᶝLò ꜀fán ᶝnéi ᶜsho ᶜkong keˀ ꜀tò ᶝyaú ꜀ti tò[2]-ᶝléi. | Venerable Foreigner, you what say, 15, also have some principle (in it). |
| 16. | ᶝNgo-téi[2] ꜀Sai-꜁yan-keˀ ᶝlai-fát꜀ ꜁m ꜁t'ung ᶝnéi-téi[2] ꜁T'ong-꜁yan ᶝlai-fát꜀. ᶝNéi pat꜆ ꜀chi ᶝngo-keˀ ᶝlai-fát꜀ áˀ. ᶝNgo tsím[2]-tsím[5]* hok꜇ ꜀Sín-꜀shàng† kwaiˀ-kwok꜀ ᶝlai-máú[2], ᶝngo ᶜsöng hòp꜀-ᶝlai toi[2] ꜀Sín-꜀shàng†; tán[2] ꜀Sín-꜀shàng† ᶝmò ᶝlai tsíp꜆ ᶝngo. ᶝNgo, yök꜇ | We Western-men's politeness-regulations not same your Chinese politeness-rules. You not know our politeness regulations, 2. I gradually learn (your), Sir's, honourable country's good-manners. I wish in-conformity-with-politeness to-treat (you), Sir, but (you), Sir, no |

## CONVERSATION 44TH.—THE OUTSIDE BARBARIAN.—(*Continued.*)

| | | |
|---|---|---|
| | If I fail, it is through ignorance; if you fail, it is not from ignorance, as the code of politeness is your own. | 我、我若有不及、係因不盡地知呢啲禮法、若先生有不及、唔係因此緣故、因禮法係先生貴國嘅、 |
| 17. | I am in fault. | 有過；有過咯、 |
| 18. | 'If you have faults, do not fear to correct them.' | 有過則勿憚改、[1] |
| 19. | Who would ever have thought that Western men could be so intelligent! | 誰想洋人能咁聰明、 |
| 20. | I am unworthy of such praise. | 不敢當、不敢當、 |
| 21. | I must beg you to overlook what I have done: for I have offended you. | 要求老師睇開、因我得罪老師咯、 |
| 22. | You need not say anything about it. Only I hope you will never use such terms again. | 唔使講咯、但望先生下次唔用噉嘅話頭、 |
| 23. | I should have remembered that Confucius said that the people of the West have sages. | 我應要記孔子有話西方有聖人焉、 |
| 24. | You were asking about Europeans. | 你問及歐羅巴人、 |
| 25. | I was. Who are they? | 係哩、歐羅巴人係乜人呢、 |
| 26. | I am a European. | 我係歐羅巴人、 |
| 27. | You are, Sir? | 先生係歐羅巴人、 |
| 28. | I am. | 係哩、 |
| 29. | I thought you said, Sir, that you were an Englishman. | 我估先生話你係大英國人、 |
| 30. | I am that as well. | 都係吖、 |

Note 1.—It must be noted that this and the other quotations are in the book language. It is also scarcely necessary to say that some of the words, used in this lesson, are such as should never be used by natives in speaking to foreigners, amongst that number being 紅毛人、꜀hung ꜀mò ꜀yan.

Note 2.—It will be noted that the terms used for the foreigner improve as the conversation goes on. Starting with the obnoxious 番鬼、꜀fan ꜂kwai, they finally culminate with a considerable amount of politeness in 老師、꜂lò-꜀sz.

## CONVERSATION 44TH.—THE OUTSIDE BARBARIAN.—(*Concluded.*)

| | | |
|---|---|---|
| | ꜂yaú pat꜃ k'ap$_2$, hai$^2$ ꜀yan pat꜃ tsun$^2$-téi$^3$* ꜀chí ꜀ni-ti ꜂lai-fat꜀: yök$_2$ ꜀Sin-꜀sháng† ꜂yaú pat꜃ k'ap$_2$, ꜀m hai$^2$ ꜀yan ꜂ts'z yün$^2$-kwú꜃, ꜀yan ꜂lai-fát꜀ hai$^2$ ꜀Sin-꜀sháng† kwai꜃-kwok ke꜃. | politeness receive me. I, if have not reach, (it) is because not entirely know these politeness-regulations; (you), Sir, have not attain-to not is because of this reason, since (the) politeness-regulations are (your) Sir's honourable country's, 15. |
| 17. | ꜂Yaú kwo꜃: ꜂yau kwo꜃ lok. | Have overpassed (the limits of right), have transgressed, 32. |
| 18. | '꜂Yaú kwo꜃, tsak꜃ mat$_2$ tán$^2$ ꜂koí.' | 'If faults, then not but alter.' |
| 19. | ꜀Shöü ꜂söng ꜀yöng-꜀yan ꜀nang kòm꜃ ꜀ts'ung ꜀ming! | Who would-think Ocean-men could-be-so deeply intelligent! |
| 20. | Pat꜃ ꜂kòm ꜀tong; pat꜃ ꜂kòm ꜀tong. | Not dare to-consider-myself-equal-to (the praise you bestow on me). |
| 21. | Yíú꜃ ꜀k'aú ꜂Lò-꜀sz ꜂t'ai-꜀hoi, ꜀yan ꜂ngo tak꜃ ts'öü$^2$ ꜂Lò-꜀sz lok. | Must beg Old-Scholar to-overlook, because I have sinned-against Venerable-Scholar 32. |
| 22. | ꜀M ꜂shaí ꜂kong lok, tán$^2$ mong$^2$ ꜀Sín-꜀sháng† há$^2$ ts'z꜃ ꜀m yung$^2$ ꜂kòm ke꜃ wá$^2$-꜀t'aú. | Not need to-speak, 32. (I) only hope (you), Sir, after times not use such, 15, words. |
| 23. | ꜂Ngo ꜀ying-yiú꜃ kéi꜃ ꜂Hung-꜂t'sz ꜂yaú wá$^2$, '꜀Sai-꜀fong ꜂yaú Shing꜃ ꜀yan ꜀yín.' | I ought-to-have remembered Confucius has said, 'Western-regions have sages (final).' |
| 24. | ꜂Néi man$^2$-k'ap$_2$ ꜀Aú-꜀lo-꜀pá-꜀yan. | You asking concerning Europeans. |
| 25. | Hai$^2$ ꜀le.$^2$ ꜀Aú-꜀lo-꜀pá-꜀yan hai$^2$ mat꜃ ꜀yan* ꜀ni?$^2$ | Yes, 24. Europeans are what men, eh? 53. |
| 26. | ꜂Ngo hai$^2$ ꜀Aú-꜀lo-꜀pá-꜀yan | I am European. |
| 27. | ꜀Sín-꜀sháng† hai$^2$ ꜀Aú-꜀lo-꜀pá-꜀yan? | Sir, (you), are European? |
| 28. | Hai$^2$ ꜀le.$^2$ | Yes, 24. |
| 29. | ꜂Ngo ꜂kwú ꜀Sín-꜀sháng† wá$^2$ ꜂néi hai$^2$ Tái$^2$-꜀ying-kwok ꜀yan. | I thought, Sir you (said) you were Great England man. |
| 30. | ꜀Tò hai$^2$ ꜀á. | Also am, 1. |

## CONVERSATION 44TH.—THE OUTSIDE BARBARIAN.

| | |
|---|---|
| 31. How is that? | 噉點解呢、 |
| 32. England is in the continent of Europe, so is France, Spain, Portugal, Italy, Holland, Russia, and Turkey: all of these are in Europe. | 英國在歐羅巴大洲、法蘭西、大呂宋、西洋國、以大利、荷蘭國、俄羅斯國、土耳基國、喊唪呤都喺歐羅巴嘅、 |

## CONVERSATION 45TH.—GOVERNMENT.

| | |
|---|---|
| 1. Is there a queen on the throne in England? | 英國係有皇后坐位咩、 |
| 2. Not now; but during the last few hundred years there have been several queens in England. | 而家唔係、但呢幾百年間英國係幾次有皇后坐位嘅、 |
| 3. We have the six boards in Peking, and lately another has been added to them. Have you English any thing of that kind? | 我哋唐人有六部在北京、近來又加多一個添、你哋英國人有噉嘅冇呢、 |
| 4. We have, but first tell me what the names of the seven boards are. | 有、但你先頭講我聽個啲七部點叫法呢、 |
| 5. Very well, they are the Board of Civil Office, the Board of Revenue, the Board of Rites, the Board of War, the Board of Punishment, the Board of Works, besides the new board, the Admiralty. | 好喇、有吏部、戶部、禮部、兵部、刑部、工部、另外重有個新嘅、卽海軍衙門、 |

## CONVERSATION 44TH.—THE OUTSIDE BARBARIAN.—(*Continued.*)

| | |
|---|---|
| 31. ᶜKòm ᶜtím ᶜkái ꜀ni? | So how explain, eh? 53. |
| 32. ꜀Yìng kwok꜄ tsoí$^2$ ꜀Aú-꜁lo-꜀pá taí$^2$-꜀chaú. Fát꜄-꜀lán-꜄saí, Taí$^2$-ᶜlöü-sung˒, ꜀Saí-꜁yöng-kwok꜄, ꜁Yí-taí$^2$-léí$^2$, ꜁Ho-꜄lán*-kwok꜄, ꜀Ngo-꜁lo-꜄sz-kwok꜄, ᶜT'ò-ᶜyí-꜁k'éi-kwok꜄, hám$^2$-pá$^2$-láng$^2$ ꜄tò ᶜhaí ꜀Aú-꜁lo-꜀pá ke˒. | England in Europe continent. France, Spain, Portugal, Italy, Holland, Russia, Turkey, all also in Europe, 15. |

## CONVERSATION 45TH.—GOVERNMENT.

| | |
|---|---|
| 1. ꜀Ying-kwok꜄ haí$^2$ ᶜyaú ꜁Wong-Haú$^2$ ᶜts'o*† waí$^2$ (*or* wai$^5$*) ꜀me? [2] | England is have Queen sit throne eh? 39. |
| 2. ꜁Yí-꜀ká ꜁m haí$^2$; t'án$^2$ ꜀ni ᶜkéi pák꜄ ꜁nín ꜀kán ꜀Ying-kwok꜄ haí$^2$ ᶜkéi ts'z˒ ᶜyaú ꜁Wong-Haú$^2$ ᶜts'o*† waí$^2$ (*or* waí$^5$*) ke$^1$*. | Now not is; but this few years period England is several times have queens sit throne, 15. |
| 3. ᶜNgo-téí$^2$ ꜁T'ong-꜁yan ᶜyaú luk꜄ pò$^2$ tsoí$^2$ Pak꜄-꜀king, kan$^2$-꜁loi* yaú$^2$ ꜀ká ꜀to yat꜄ ko˒ ꜀t'ím. ᶜNéi-téí$^2$ ꜀Ying-Kwok꜄-꜁yan ᶜyaú ᶜkòm-ke˒ ᶜmò ꜀ni? [2] | We Chinese have six boards in Peking (*lit.* Northern capital), lately, moreover, add more one [C.] besides. You Englishmen have so's fashion not, eh? 53. |
| 4. ᶜYaú, tán$^2$ ᶜnéi ꜁sín-꜁t'aú ᶜkong ᶜngo ꜀t'eng ko˒-꜄ti ts'at꜄ pò$^2$ ᶜtím kíú˒-fát꜄ ꜀ni. [2] | Have, but you first (*lit.* before head, i.e., 'firstly heading,' what you have to say) tell me to-hear those seven boards how call-style (i.e., the style or method they are called), 53. |
| 5. ᶜHò ꜀lá, [2] ᶜyaú Léí$^2$-pò$^2$, Wú$^2$-pò$^2$, ᶜLaí-pò$^2$, ꜀Ping-pò$^2$, ꜁Ying-pò$^2$, ꜀Kung-pò$^2$, ling$^2$-ngoí$^2$ chung$^2$ ᶜyaú ko˒ ꜀san ke˒, tsik꜄ ᶜHoí ꜀Kwan ꜁Ngá-꜁Mún. | Well, 21, have Civil Office Board, Revenue Board, Rites Board, Soldiers Board, Punishment Board, Work Board, besides moreover have the new one, the Sea Forces Yamên. |

## CONVERSATION 45TH.—GOVERNMENT.

| | |
|---|---|
| 6. Well, in England there are the Treasury, the Home Office, the Colonial Office, the Foreign Office, the War Office, the Admiralty, the India Office, the Board of Trade, the Post Office, the Office of Works, besides other Government Offices. | 拿，在英國有度支院、內政衙門、外政衙門、藩政衙門、兵政衙門、水師兵政衙門、總理印度政務衙門、商政衙門、郵政衙門、工政衙門、及別個衙門、 |
| 7. The Emperor has to assist him in governing the country, the Grand Secretariat (or Imperial Chancery, or Inner Council). Does your King have any such council? | 皇帝有內閣帮佢打理國事、你個皇帝有噉嘅冇呢、 |
| 8. There is a Privy Council in England, and a number of Privy Councillors. | 英國有內閣及有好多中閣參議、 |
| 9. Besides that there is a Cabinet, which is composed of Cabinet Ministers. | 另外有樞密院、丞相做嘅、 |
| 10. Who are the Cabinet Ministers? | 邊個叫做丞相呢、 |
| 11. There are a number of Cabinet Ministers. Amongst them the First Lord of the Treasury, the Secretary of State for Foreign Affairs, The Secretary of State for the Colonies, the Chancellor of the Exchequer, and others. | 有幾十個做、其中有樞密院首相、外政大臣、理藩院、度支院使、及別個大臣、 |
| 12. In Western countries when the Sovereign dies who ascends the throne? | 在西國皇崩乜誰登位呢、 |
| 13. The heir apparent succeeds, as in China. | 都係太子呗、同中國一樣嘅、 |

CONVERSATION 45TH.—GOVERNMENT.

6. Nä, tsoi$^{2}$ Ying-kwok $^{}$yaú To$^{2}$-Chí-Yün$^{2}$, Noi$^{2}$-Ching' Ngá-Mún, Ngoi$^{2}$-Ching' Ngá-Mún, Fán-Ching' Ngá-Mún, Ping-Ching' Ngá-Mún, Shöü-Sz-Ping-Ching' Ngá-Mún, Tsung-Léí Yan'-Tò$^{2}$ Ching' Mò$^{2}$ Ngá-Mún, Shöng-Ching' Ngá-Mún, Yaú-Ching' Ngá-Mún, Kung-Ching' Ngá-Mún, k'ap$_{2}$ pít kán' Ngá-Mún.

Well-now, in England have Treasury, Home Office, Foreign Office, Colonial Office, War Office, Water-soldiers Government Office. Generally-attending-to India Office, Board of Trade, Post Office, the Office of Works, and other [C.] Government Offices. (No variants are introduced, as it is like reading a list over from a book, but in conversation it would be Sz and Mún.*)

7. Wong-Tai' yaú Noi-kuk pong k'öü tá-léí Kwok-sz$^{2}$. Néí ko' Wong-Taí' yaú kòm ke' mò ni?$^{2}$

Emperor has Inner-Council, assist him attending-to Government business. Your [C.] King has such-a-one 15, not, eh? 53.

8. Ying-kwok yaú Noi$^{2}$-kok, k'ap$_{2}$ yaú hò to Chung-kok, Ts'ám-Yí.

England have Privy Council, and have great many Privy Councillors.

9. Ling$^{2}$-ngoi$^{2}$ yaú Shü-Mat$_{2}$-Yün$^{5}$* Shing Söng' tsò$^{2}$ ke'.

Besides have Cabinet, Cabinet ministers compose, 15.

10. Pín ko' kiú' tsò$^{2}$ Shing Söng' ni?$^{2}$

Who [C.] called are Cabinet Ministers? 53.

11. Yaú kéí shap$_{2}$ ko' tsò$^{2}$. K'éí-chung yaú Shü-Mat$_{2}$-Yün$^{5}$* Shau Söng', Ngoi$^{2}$ Ching' Taí$^{2}$ Shan, Léí Fán Yün$^{2}$, Tò$^{2}$ Chí-Yün$^{5}$* Sz', k'ap$_{2}$ pit ko' Taí$^{2}$-Shan.

There-are several tens-of ones, [or C.] amongst (*lit.* their midst) there-are Treasury First Lord, Foreign Affairs Great Minister, Attend-to Foreign (Colonial) Secretary-of-State, Chancellor of Exchequer, and other [C.] Great Ministers-of-State.

12. Tsoi$^{2}$ Saí kwok Wong pang, mat-shöü* tang' waí$^{5}$* ni?

In Western countries Sovereign dying, who ascends throne, eh? 53

13. Tò haí$^{2}$ Taí' Tsz chek. T'ung Chung-kwok yat, yöng$^{2}$ ke'.

Also is Heir Apparent just, 7, Same-as Middle Kingdom one manner, 15.

## CONVERSATION 45TH.—GOVERNMENT.—(*Continued.*)

| | | |
|---|---|---|
| 14. | I do not think it is the same, because in China Princesses cannot ascend the throne; in England they can. | 我斷估唔係一樣、因爲中國公主唔坐得位嘅、英國又做得呢、 |
| 15. | What is done if the heir apparent is not of age? | 太子唔曾成人就點呢、 |
| 16. | There is a great deal of trouble if the empire falls into disorder. | 國亂、有好多事、 |
| 17. | But you have not answered my question. | 我問你個句、你又唔曾答我囉噃、 |
| 18. | Oh! Didn't I? What did you say? What did you ask me? | 呵、係咩、先生點話、問我乜呢、 |
| 19. | I asked you, supposing the Emperor died, and the Heir Apparent was not of age, who then would be Emperor? I suppose the Heir Apparent could not sit on the throne. | 我問你譬如皇崩個陣時太子又未長大、邊個做皇帝呢、太子唔坐得位卦、 |
| 20. | If such were the case, the Empress Dowager would attend to the affairs of the country until the Heir Apparent was grown up. In other words the Empress acts. | 倘若有噉事、皇太后就理國事等到太子大個陣時、皇后就垂簾聽政咯、 |
| 21. | It is said that in America there is no king. It seems very strange to me. | 人哋講話美國冇皇帝、我見得好出奇嘅、 |
| 22. | In America the people elect from their midst one as head, whom they call the President. | 在美國百姓設立其中一個人做頭人、噉樣稱呼爲大伯理璽天德、 |
| 23. | Then does the office pass on from father to son and grandson? | 噉樣佢死之後係佢子孫承繼係唔係呢、 |

易學廣東話



CONVERSATION 45TH.—GOVERNMENT.—(*Concluded.*)

| | | |
|---|---|---|
| 14. | ʿNgo tün˒-ʿkwú ꜀m hai² yat˒ yöng², ꜀yan-wai² ꜀Chung-kwok˳ ꜀Kung-ʿChü ꜀m ʿts'o*† tak˒ wai² (*or* wai⁵*) ke˒, ꜀Ying-kwok˳ yaú² tsò² tak˒ ꜀ni. | I think not is one same, because China Princesses not sit able throne, 15; England yet do can, 53. |
| 15. | T'ai˒-ʿTsz ꜀m ts'ang˒ ꜀shing-꜀yan tsaú² ʿtím ꜀ni ?² | Heir-Apparent not yet established a-man then how, eh ? 53. |
| 16. | Kwok˳ lün², ʿyaú ˳hò ꜀to sz². | Country in-confusion, have very much trouble. |
| 17. | ʿNgo man² ʿnéi ko˒ köü˒, ʿnéi yaú² ꜀m ꜀ts'ang táp˳ ʿngo lo˒ po˒. | I ask you that sentence, you also not yet answered me, 31, 60. |
| 18. | ꜀O ! Hai² ꜀me ? ꜀Sín-꜀sháng ʿtím wá²; man² ʿngo mat˒ ꜀ni ?² | Oh ! Is-it so, eh ? 39. Sir how said ; asked me what, eh ? 53. |
| 19. | ʿNgo man² ʿnéi p'éi˒-yü² ꜀Wong ꜀pang ko˒ chan² ꜀shí,* T'ái˒-ʿt'sz yaú² méi² ʿchöng tái², ˳pín ko˒ tsò² ꜀Wong-tai˒ ꜀ni ? T'ái˒-ʿtsz ꜀m ʿts'o*† tak˒ wai⁵* kwá˒. | I asked you supposing Emperor died-at that period-of time, Heir-Apparent also not raised great, who[C.] becomes Emperor, eh ? 53. Heir-Apparent not sit can throne, I-suppose, 18. |
| 20. | ʿT'ong-yök˒ ʿyaú ʿkòm sz², ꜀Wong-T'ái˒-Haú² tsaú² ʿléi kwok˳ sz². ʿtang tò˒ T'ái˒-ʿtsz tái² ko˒ chan² ꜀shí.* ꜀Wong-haú² tsaú² ꜀shöü ꜀lím t'ing˒ ching˒ lok˳. | If have such matter, Empress-Dowager then attend country's business, wait till Heir-Apparent large that period time. Empress then drops curtain listens to-matters-of-state, 32. |
| 21. | ꜀Yan-téi² ʿkong wá² ʿMéi-kwok˳ ʿmò ꜀Wong-tai˒. ʿNgo kín˒ tak˒ ʿhò ch'ut˒-꜀k'éi ke˒. | People speaking say America no Emperor, I see able very extraordinary, 15. |
| 22. | Tsoi² ʿMéi-kwok˳ pák˳-sing˒ ch'ít˳-láp˒ ꜀k'éi ꜀chung yat˒ ko˒ ꜀yan tsò² ꜀T'aú-꜀yan, ʿkòm yöng⁵* ꜀ch'ing-꜀fú wai² Tái²-Pák˳-ʿLéi-ʿSái ꜀T'ín-Tak˳. | In America hundred-surnames elect-and-set-up from-their midst one [C.] man to-be Headman, so fashion, politely-called (him) to-be President. |
| 23. | ʿKòm yöng⁵* ʿk'öü ʿsz-꜀chí haú², hai² ʿk'öü ʿtsz ꜀sün ꜀shing kai˒, hai² ꜀m hai² ꜀ni ?² | So fashion his death's afterwards, is-it his son grandson receive succession, is not is, eh ? 53. |

## CONVERSATION 45TH.—GOVERNMENT.—*(Continued.)*

24. No; that is not the way. After he has been President for four years, he gives up the position to another. If he has done very well, he is sometimes asked to remain another term in office.

唔係噉樣、佢做四年、噉就要讓俾第二個做、或者佢做得十分好、都有時請佢再做一任添、

25. What becomes of him when he ceases to be the Headman of the nation?

佢唔做國嘅頭人個時點呢、

26. He is the same as the rest of the people. He leaves the capital and goes to his own house. If he is engaged in business, he goes back, and manages his business the same as usual.

同百姓一樣呮、離開京城翻去自己屋、或有生意做、翻去打理事幹同平常一樣、

27. That is well: that is humility.

噉好咯、噉萛係謙卑咯、

28. I have heard that America is composed of a number of countries united in one, and called the United States. Is it so, or not?

我聽聞美國係有幾十國合埋爲一、叫做合衆國話、係噉唔係呢、

29. What you have heard is true. There are between forty and fifty states united together in one. Each state has its own laws and attends to its own affairs; but what relates to the whole country is attended to by the government of the whole country.

你所聽嘅係眞、有四十幾省合埋做一國、每省有自己嘅律例、及理自己嘅事、但係衆國嘅事幹係國家理嘅、

30. Has not America another name?

大美國唔係重有個名、

## CONVERSATION 45TH.—GOVERNMENT.—(*Continued.*)

| | |
|---|---|
| 24. ˓M hai$^2$ ᶜkòm yöng$^5$. ᶜK'öü tsò$^2$ szˀ ˓nín, ᶜkòm tsaú$^2$ yíúˀ yöng$^2$ ᶜpéi tai$^2$-yí$^2$ koˀ tsò$^2$. wák$_2$-ᶜche ᶜk'öü tsò$^2$ tak$_3$ shap$_2$-˓fan ᶜhò ˓tò ᶜyaú ˓shí (*or* ˓shí*) ᶜtseng† ᶜk'öü tsoiˀ tsò$^2$ yat$_3$ yam$^2$ ˓t'ím. | Not is so fashion. He is (for) four years, then just must resign-up-to give to another [C.] to-be. If he does able ten parts good, also have times invite him again be one term more. |
| 25. ᶜK'öü ˓m tsò$^2$ Kwok$_3$-keˀ ˓T'aú-˓yan koˀ ˓shí ᶜtím ˓ni ? | He not be country's Headman that time how, eh ? 53. |
| 26. ˓T'ung pák$_3$-singˀ yat$_3$ yöng$^2$ chek$_3$, ˓léi ˓hoi ˓king-˓sheng†. ˓fán höüˀ tsz$^2$-ᶜkéi nk$_3$. Wák$_2$ ᶜyaú ˓sháng-yíˀ tsò$^2$. ˓fán höüˀ ᶜtá-ᶜléi sz$^2$-kònˀ, ˓t'ung ˓p'ing-˓shöng yat$_3$ yöng$^2$. | With hundred-surnames one same only. Separates (himself) apart-from capital-city, back goes his-own house. If have business to-do, back goes attend-to business with ordinary (times) one same. |
| 27. ᶜKòm ᶜhò lok ; ᶜkòm sünˀ hai$^2$ ˓hím-˓péi lok$_3$. | So good, 32 : so consider is humble, 32. |
| 28. ᶜNgo ˓t'eng†-˓man ᶜMéi-kwok$_3$ hai$^2$ ᶜyaú ᶜkéi shap$_2$ kwok$_3$ hòp$_2$-˓mái wai$^2$ yat$_3$, kíúˀ tsò$^2$ Hòp$_2$-Chungˀ-Kwok$_3$ waˀ. Hai$^2$ ᶜkòm ˓m hai$^2$ ˓ni ?$^2$ | I heard America is have several tens countries united-together become one, called to-be United States, it-is-said. 61. Is so not is, eh ? 53. |
| 29. ᶜNéi ᶜsho ˓t'eng†-keˀ hai$^2$ ˓chan. ᶜYaú szˀ shap$_2$ ᶜkéi ᶜsháng hòp$_2$-˓mái tsò$^2$ yat$_3$ kwok$_3$. ᶜMúi ᶜsháng ᶜyaú tsz$^2$-ᶜkéi keˀ lut$_2$-lai$^2$, k'ap$_2$ ᶜléi tsz$^2$-ᶜkéi-keˀ sz$^2$, tán$^2$-hai$^2$ chungˀ-kwok$_3$-keˀ sz$^2$-kònˀ hai$^2$ Kwok$_3$-˓ká ᶜléi keˀ. | You what heard—(i.e. what you have heard) is true. Have four tens (and) several provinces (or states) united-together become one country. Each state has its-own laws and manages its-own business : but whole-country's business is Government attends, 15. |
| 30. Tái$^2$ ᶜMéi-kwok ˓m hai$^2$ chung$^2$ ᶜyau koˀ ˓meng ?*† | Great America not is besides have a [i.e. C.] name ? |

## CONVERSATION 45TH.—GOVERNMENT.—(*Concluded.*)

| | |
|---|---|
| 31. Yes; it is also called the Land of the Flowery Flag, on account of the national flag having many colours. | 係吖、又叫做花旗國、因爲個國旗有好多色水嘅、 |
| 32. That is a rather a nice name. | 噉都幾好名咯、 |

## CONVERSATION 46TH.—BUYING FURNITURE.

| | |
|---|---|
| 1. Oh! You sell furniture in this shop, do you? | 呵、你在呢間舖賣傢私什物咩、 |
| 2. Yes, Sir. What do you want to buy? | 係吖、先生、你想買乜野呢、 |
| 3. I wish to buy a great many things; but you have not got many things for sale here. I want them good, and I want them cheap. | 我想買好多野、但係你呢處冇乜野賣嘅、又要好、又要平、 |
| 4. Then it will be difficult to come to terms. Good things are dear, and cheap things are bad. But, I think, Sir, that you will be willing to pay a just price. | 噉都幾難講嘅、好傢伙係貴、唅貨係平、但先生肯俾公道價錢啩、 |
| 5. My furniture is good. The things are made by myself. I guarantee them for a year. If anything should break, I will mend it or change it for another, just as you like, without charging any more. | 我貨好吖、係自己整嘅、包你一年用嘅、如果年間有乜爛法、我同你換過、或整翻好、隨你中意、唔使錢嘅、 |

易學廣東話



## CONVERSATION 45TH.—GOVERNMENT.—(Concluded.)

31. Haí² ,á²; yaú² kíú' tsò² ,Fá-,K'éi-kwok,, ,yan-waí² ko' kwok, ,k'éi ʿyaú ʿhò ,to shik,-ʿshöü ke'. | It-has, 1; also called to-be Flowery Flag Country, because that country's flag have very many colours, 15.

32. ʿKòm ,tò ʿkéi ,hò ,meng*† lok,. | Such also rather good name, 32.

## CONVERSATION 46TH.—BUYING FURNITURE.

1. ,O! ʿNéi tsoí² ,ni ,kán p'ò' mái² ,ká-,sz-shap,-mat, ,me? | Oh! You in this [C.] shop sell furniture, eh? 39.

2. Haí² ,a², ,Sín-,sháng, ʿnéi ʿsöng ʿmái mat, ʿye ,ni?² | Yes 1, Sir, you wish to-buy what thing, eh? 53.

3. ʿNgo ʿsöng ʿmái ʿhò ,to ʿye, tán²-haí² ʿnéi ,ni shü' ʿmò mat, ʿye mái² ke'. Yaú² yíú' ʿhò, yaú² yíú' ,p'eng†. | I wish to-buy great many things, but you this place not much things for-sale, 15. Also want good, also want cheap.

4. ʿKòm ,tò ʿkéi ,nán ʿkong ke' (or ke'*). ʿHò ,ká-ʿfo haí² kwaí', ,yai fo' haí² ,p'eng†. Tán² ,Sín-,sháng† ʿhang ʿpéi ,kung-tò² ká'-,ts'ín kwá'. | So also rather hard to-speak, 15. Good furniture is dear, bad articles are cheap. But, Sir, willing to-give just price probably, 18.

5. ʿNgo fo' ʿhò ,á.² Haí² tsz²-ʿke ʿching ke'. ,Páú ʿnéi yat, ,nín yung² ke'. ,Yü-ʿkwo ,nín ,kán ʿyaú mat, lán²-fát,, ʿngo ,t'ung ʿnéi wún²-kwo', wák, ʿching-,fán ʿhò, ,ts'öü* ʿnéi ,chung-yi, ,m ʿshai ,ts'ín* ke'. | My goods good, 1. Are myself made, 15. Guarantee you one year use, 15. If year within have any breakage, I for you will-change, or make-again good, as you like, not need money, 15.

CONVERSATION 46TH.—BUYING FURNITURE.—(*Continued.*)

| | | |
|---|---|---|
| 6. | The furniture in other shops is bought at auction. It is old, and when you take it up to your house it suddenly breaks. | 第二間舖個啲傢私係喊夜冷買到嘅、係舊嘅、抬翻上你屋一陣間噲爛咯、 |
| 7. | Oh! There are good things sold at auction. It depends upon circumstances. | 嗌、喊夜冷都有好野嘅、睇嚟湊、 |
| 8. | Now, look at this dining table. It is only just newly made. Some one ordered it from me and afterwards did not want it; so I will sell it cheaply to you now. | 嗱、睇呢張大餐檯喇、就新整起嘅啫、人哋定我做嘅、收尾佢唔要、噉我家吓平啲賣俾你喇、 |
| 9. | Well, it is pretty good. What wood is it made of? How do you sell it? | 唔、都幾好吖、係乜野木整嘅、點賣呢、 |
| 10. | Pretty good, is it? It is first rate. It is made of teak. If you, Sir, buy it, I will sell it cheaply to you. I will not trouble about the price. Say thirty dollars. | 幾好咩、係第一好嘑、俾柚木整嘅、先生係買、賣平俾你喇、唔計帶咯、三十文喇、 |
| 11. | Thirty dollars? So dear! Dear me! I cannot buy that. | 三十文、咁貴嘅、唉、唔買得咯、 |
| 12. | It is not dear. | 唔係貴吖、 |
| 13. | It is too dear. How can I bargain with you when you start with such a high figure? | 貴過頭、你開得噉大價點同得你講呢、 |

## CONVERSATION 46TH.—BUYING FURNITURE.—(*Continued.*)

6. Tai$^2$-yi$^2$ ˏkán pʻoʾ koʾ-ˌti ˏkai-ˏsz hai$^2$ hámʾ-ye$^2$-ˏlán ᶜmái-tòʾ keʾ. Hai$^2$ káu$^2$ keʾ, ˏtʻoi ˏfán ᶜshöng ᶜnéi nk͵ yat͵ chan$^2$-ˏkán ᶜwúi lán$^2$ lokˏ.
Other [C.] shops that furniture is at-auction bought, 15. Is old, 15, carry again up your house one short time can break, 32.

7. ˏAi! (*or* ˏAi). Hámʾ-ye$^2$-ˏlán ˏtò ᶜyaú ᶜhò ᶜye keʾ. ᶜTʻai ˏlai tsʻaiʾ.
Oh! At auction also have good articles, 15. Depends on circumstances.

8. ˏNá, ᶜtʻai ˏni ˏchöng tai$^2$-ˏtsʻán-ˏtʻoi* ˏlá.$^2$ Tsaú$^2$ ˏsan ᶜching-ᶜhéi keʾ ˏche.$^2$ ˏYan-téi$^2$† teng$^2$† ᶜngo tsòʾ (*or* tsò$^2$) keʾ, (*or* keʾ*) ˏshaú-ˏméi (*or* ˏshaú ᶜméi*) ᶜkʻöü ˏm yiúʾ; ᶜkòm ᶜngo ˏká-ᶜhá ˏpʻeng†-ˏti mái$^2$ ᶜpéi ᶜnéi ˏlá.$^2$
There, look-at this [C.] dinner-table, 21. Just new made-finished, 15, only, 7. Some-one fixed-with me to-make, 15, finally he not want; so I now cheaper sell to you, 21.

9. ˏNg, ˏtò ᶜkéi ᶜhò ˏá.$^2$ Hai$^2$ mat͵-ᶜye muk$_2$ ᶜching keʾ? ᶜTím mái$^2$ ˏni?$^2$
Well also pretty good, 1. Is what wood make, ? 15. How sell, eh? 53.

10. ᶜKéi ᶜhò ˏme?$^2$ Hai$^2$ tai$^2$ yat͵ ᶜhò káʾ. ᶜPéi ˏyaú* muk$_2$ ᶜching keʾ. ˏSín-ˏsháng† hai$^2$ ᶜmái, mái$^2$ ˏpʻeng† ᶜpéi ᶜnéi ˏlá.$^2$ ˏM kai$^2$ tai$^2$ lokˏ. ˏSám-shap$_2$ ˏman ˏlá.$^2$
Pretty good, eh? 39. Is number one good, 14. Use teak wood to-make, 15. (If You) Sir do buy, sell cheap to you, 21. Not reckon price. 21. Thirty dollars, 21.

11. ˏSám-shap$_2$ ˏman? Kòmʾ kwaiʾ keʾ! ˏAi!$^2$ ˏM ᶜmái tak͵ lokˏ.
Thirty dollars? So dear! 15. Oh! Not buy able, 32.

12. ˏM hai$^2$ kwaiʾ ˏá.$^2$
Not is dear, 1.

13. Kwaiʾ ᶜkwoʾ* ˏtʻaú. ᶜNéi ˏhoi tak͵ kòmʾ tai$^2$ káʾ, ᶜtím ˏtʻung ˏtak͵ ᶜnéi ᶜkong ˏni?$^2$
Dear over much. You open able so great price, how with can you bargain, eh? 53.

## CONVERSATION 46TH.—BUYING FURNITURE.—(*Continued.*)

| | |
|---|---|
| 14. Well, what do you say you will give, Sir? It is not dear. It is made of teak wood. It is a first-rate article. There was a great deal of work required in it. What will you give? | 噉、先生話俾幾多呢、唔係貴吖、又用柚木整嘅、第一好傢伙吖、要好多工夫做成嚟嘅、俾幾多呢、 |
| 15. I do not want such a large one, but, if you will reduce it to a reasonable figure, perhaps I will buy it. I should say twenty dollars was enough for it. I will give you twenty dollars for it. | 我唔係要咁大嘅、但係你減到平、我或者買唔定、我話二十文够咯、我俾二十文你喇、 |
| 16. That will not do. It will not pay me. How can that do? Come now, do not stand out. I will reduce my price a little, and you raise your offer. Twenty-five dollars now. That is very cheap. I shall lose on it. Oh! It is really cheap. | 唔做得、唔够本呀、點得吖、呵、廉廉地喇、我減啲、你添啲喇、二十五文喇、好平咯、噉就我賠本咯、唉吔、眞正平咯、 |
| 17. Oh! no; it is not cheap. It cannot be considered to be very cheap. You say you will lose on it! Dear me! You will make a good profit. Say twenty-three dollars. | 都唔係平吖、唔算得十分平嘅、你話唔够本、唉、賺得好多咯、二十三文喇、 |
| 18. Raise your price a little. Say twenty-four dollars. I will varnish it for you as well. Where would you get it as cheap? | 添啲喇、二十四文喇、我同你抹過花喇時添喇、邊處有得咁平嘅呢、 |

CONVERSATION 46TH.—BUYING FURNITURE.—(*Continued.*)

14. ᶜKòm, ꜀Sín-꜀shángt wá$^{2}$ ᶜpéi ᶜkéi ˳to ꜁ni? ꜁M haí$^{2}$ kwaí' ꜀á.$^{2}$ Yaú$^{2}$ yung$^{2}$ ꜁yaú* muk$_{2}$ ᶜching ke'. Taí$^{2}$ yat, ᶜhò ꜀ká-ᶜfo ꜀á.$^{2}$ Yíú' ᶜhò ꜀to ꜀kung-꜀fú tsò$^{2}$ ꜁shengt ꜁laí ke'. ᶜPéi ᶜkéi ˳to ꜀ni?

So, Sir, say give how much, eh? 53. Not is dear, 1. Also use teak wood to-make, 15. Number one good article 1. Needed great deal work to-make complete come, 15. Give how much, eh? 53.

15. ᶝNgo ꜁m haí$^{2}$ yíú' kòm' taí$^{2}$ ke', tán$^{2}$ haí$^{2}$ ᶝnéi ᶜkám tò' ꜁p'engt, ᶝngo wák$_{2}$-ᶜche ᶝmáí ꜁m ting$^{2}$, ᶝngo wá$^{2}$ yí$^{2}$-shap$_{2}$ ˳man kaú' lok꜀. ᶝNgo ᶜpéi yí$^{2}$-shap$_{2}$ ˳man ᶝnéi ꜀lá.$^{2}$

I not do want so large, 15, but is reduced to cheapness I perhaps buy, not certain. I say twenty dollars sufficient, 32. I give twenty dollars to-you, 21.

16. ꜁M tsò$^{2}$ tak,. ꜁M kaú' ᶜpún á'. ᶜTím tak, ꜀á?$^{2}$ O$^{2}$! má$^{2}$-má$^{5}$* téi$^{5}$* ꜀lá$^{2}$. ᶝNgo ᶜkám ˳ti, ᶝnéi ꜀t'ím ˳ti ꜀lá.$^{2}$ Yí$^{2}$-shap$_{2}$ ᶝng ˳man ꜀lá. ᶜHò ꜁p'engt lok˳. ᶜKòm tsaú$^{2}$ ᶝngo shít$_{2}$-ᶜpún lok˳. ꜀Aí-꜀yá!$^{2}$ ꜀Chan-ching' ꜁p'engt lok꜀.

Not do can. Not equal original-price, 2. How can, eh? 1. Oh! let it pass, 21. I reduce a-little, you rise a-little, 21. Twenty-five dollars, 21. Very cheap, 32. So then I lose, 32. Dear me! Truly cheap. 32.

17. ꜀Tò ꜁m haí$^{2}$ ꜁p'engt ꜀á.$^{2}$ ꜁M sün' tak, shap$_{2}$ ꜀fan ꜁p'engt ke'. ᶝNéi wá$^{2}$ ꜁m kaú' ᶜpún. ꜀Aí!$^{2}$ chán$^{2}$ tak, ᶜhò ꜀to lok. Yí$^{2}$-shap$_{2}$-꜀sám ꜀man ꜀lá.$^{2}$

Also, not is cheap, 1. Not considerable ten parts cheap, 15. You say not equal-to original-price. Oh! make-profit can very much, 32. Twenty-three dollars? 21.

18. ꜀T'ím-˳ti ꜀lá.$^{2}$ Yí$^{2}$-shap$_{2}$-sz' ˳man ꜀lá. ᶝNgo ꜁t'ung ᶝnéi mát˳ kwo' ꜀fá-léi$^{2}$-꜁shí* ꜀t'ím ꜀lá.$^{2}$ ˳Pín-shü' ᶝyaú tak, kòm' ꜁p'engt ke' ꜀ni?$^{2}$

Increase a little, 21. Twenty-four dollars, 21. I for you wipe over varnish besides, 21. Where have can so cheap, 15, eh? 53.

## CONVERSATION 46TH.—BUYING FURNITURE.—(*Continued.*)

| | | |
|---|---|---|
| 19. | Oh! one of the feet is loose. That will not do, I do not want it. It is no use with one foot loose. It will not be safe. By and bye when the table is set all the things will come tumbling down. | 唉吔、有一隻檯脚鬆嘵咯、唔做得咯、唔要咯、一隻脚鬆就冇用咯、唔穩陣咯、後來擺檯成檯野都跌曬咯、 |
| 20. | One of the legs loose, is it? Dear me, so it is! How is that? Oh! the workmen have not nailed it on firmly, that is all. That does not matter much. It is easily put right. | 一隻脚鬆咩、唉吔、係咯、點解呢、呵、個啲師傅唔曾釘實呮、個啲冇乜相干、好易整翻嘅、 |
| 21. | And now it is off. I can pull it off with one hand. And that you consider a good article. | 呀、又用咯、我一隻手都搣得用咯、噉都算好傢伙咩、 |
| 22. | Sir, listen to me. The wood is not cracked. The table is new and well made. It is a good table. It is a very strong table, the only thing is that the workmen were in a hurry to bring it up. That is easily put right. I will put it right for you. | 先生呀、你聽我講吖、木又唔係裂、檯又新又好工作嘅、係好檯、係好堅固嘅檯、師傅不過想快啲搬上嚟嘅啫、個啲容易整好、我同你整好喇、 |
| 23. | Is there no fear of its giving way afterwards? I am afraid, if it gave way, there would not only be the breakage of china and dishes, but that those sitting at the table would be hurt. | 唔怕後來爛咩、我慌爛咽、唔止跌爛瓷器碗碟、又噲賫(*or* 壓)傷席上個啲人客咯、 |

## CONVERSATION 46TH.—BUYING FURNITURE.—(*Continued.*)

| | | |
|---|---|---|
| 19. | ꜀Ai-꜀yá,² ꜃yaú yat꜆ chek꜆ ꜁t'oí* kök꜆ ꜀sung-꜀híú lok꜆. ꜁M tsò² tak꜆ lok꜆, ꜁m yíú꜄ lok꜆. Yat꜆ chek꜆ kök꜆ ꜀sung, tsaú² ꜃mò yung² lok꜆, ꜁m ꜂wan-chau² lok꜆, haú²-꜁loi ꜂pái ꜁t'oi*. ꜁sheng† ꜁t'oi* ꜃ye tò tit sát꜄ lok꜆. | Dear me! have one [C.] table's foot loosened, 32. Not do can, 32, not want, 32. One [C.] foot loose, then no use, 32, not steady, 32, afterwards set table, whole table-full of-things also fall all, 32. |
| 20. | Yat꜆ chek꜆ kök꜆ ꜀sung ꜀me? ꜀Ai-꜀yá,² hai² lok꜆. ꜂Tím ꜂kái ꜀ni?² ꜁O! ko꜄-꜀ti ꜀sz-fú³* ꜁m ꜁ts'ang ꜀teng† shat꜆ chek꜆. Ko꜄-꜀ti ꜃mò mat꜆ ꜀söng-꜀kòn. ꜂Hò yí² ꜂ching-꜀fán ke꜄. | One [C.] foot loose, eh? 39. Dear me, it-is, 32. How explain, eh? 53. Oh! those workmen not yet nailed firm only, 7. That not much matter. Very easily make back-again (as it was before). 15. |
| 21. | A꜄! yaú² lat꜆ lok꜆. ꜃Ngo yat꜆ chek꜆ ꜂shaú tò ꜀mang tak꜆ lat꜆ lok꜆. ꜂Kòm, tò sün꜄ ꜂hò ꜀ká-꜂fo ꜀me?² | Oh! also come-off, 32. I one [C.] hand also pull can off, 32. So also consider good article, eh? 39. |
| 22. | ꜀Sín-꜀sháng† á꜄, ꜃néi ꜀t'eng† ꜃ngo ꜂kong ꜀á.² Muk꜆ yaú² ꜁m hai² lit꜆. ꜁T'oí* yaú² ꜀san, yaú² ꜂hò ꜀kung-tsok꜆ ke꜄. Hai² ꜂hò ꜁t'oí*. Hai² ꜂hò ꜀kín-kwú꜄ ke꜄ ꜁t'oí*. ꜀Sz-fú³* pat꜆-kwo꜄ ꜂söng fai꜄-꜀ti ꜀pún ꜃shöng ꜁lai ke꜄ ꜀che². Ko꜄-꜀ti ꜁yung-yí² ꜂ching-꜂hò. ꜃Ngo ꜁t'ung ꜃néi ꜂ching-꜂hò ꜀la.² | Sir, 2, you listen to-me speaking, 1. Wood also not is cracked. Table also new, also good workmanship, 15. Is good table. Is very strong, 15, table. Workmen only wish quickly move up come, 15, only, 7. That easily made good. I for you make good. 21. |
| 23. | ꜁M p'a꜄ haú²-꜁loi lau² ꜀me?² ꜃Ngo ꜀fong lán²-꜂cho, ꜁m ꜂chí tit꜆-lán² ꜁t'sz-hei꜄ ꜂wún-típ꜆, yaú² ꜃wúi chák (at) ꜀shöng tsik꜆ shöng² ko꜄-꜀ti ꜁yan-hák lok꜆. | No fear afterwards break, eh? 39. I afraid broke, not alone falling-break porcelain, bowls-plates, besides can press hurt feast at those guests, 32. |

CONVERSATION 46TH.—BUYING FURNITURE.—(*Continued.*)

| | | |
|---|---|---|
| 24. | There is no fear; there is no fear. There is no fear at all. I will put it all right for you. It will be safer than before. I will nail it on very carefully, and firmly, and see that the tenon fits in well. | 唔怕、唔怕、一嚫都唔怕、我同你整好嗺、重穩陣過舊時、我用心釘到好實、又整個榫頭入到好主固、 |
| 25. | All right. If it is not right, I will not have it. What did you say the price was? | 好喇、唔好、我唔要囉噃、幾多價錢話、 |
| 26. | If it is not good, of course you will not want it. I said twenty-four dollars as the lowest figure. | 若然唔好、先生自然唔要喇、我話減實二十四文、 |
| 27. | But I cannot give so much. I will not give more than twenty-three dollars. | 我唔俾得咁多吖、係二十三文呮、唔俾多咯、 |
| 28. | I cannot do it. It is too cheap—little—too little. Oh! come now, twenty-four dollars. | 唔做得吖、平過頭咯、少咯、少、少過頭咯、就噉喇、二十四文喇、 |
| 29. | No, I cannot. I will not buy it. I am going, good-bye. | 唔做得、唔買咯、我去咯、請致喇、 |
| 30. | Sir, Sir, come back. Let us split the difference. Twenty-three and a half now. | 先生呀、先生翻嚟喇、我減一半、你添一半、二十三個半喇、 |

易學廣東話



CONVERSATION 46TH.—BUYING FURNITURE.—(*Continued.*)

| | | |
|---|---|---|
| 24. | ꜀M p'a'; ꜀m p'a'. Yat˒ ti ˏtó ꜀m p'a'. ᶜNgo ꜀t'ung ᶜnéi ᶜching-ᶜhò sai'. Chung² ᶜwan-chan² kwo' kaú² ꜀shí*. ᶜNgo yung² ꜀sam ꜀teng† to' ᶜhò shat˒, yaú² ᶜching ko' ᶜsun-꜀t'aú yap˒ tò' ᶜhò ᶜchü-kwú'. | No fear; no fear. Even to-the-minutest-particle also no fear. I for you make-good all. More safe than old time, I use (my) heart and-nail-it till very firm, also make the tenon enter till very firm. |
| 25. | ᶜHò ꜀lá.² ꜀M ᶜhò, ᶜngo ꜀m yin' lo'-po'. ᶜKéi ꜀to ka'-꜀ts'in ᶜwá? | Good, 21. Not good, I not want, 31, 60. How much price you-said? 61. |
| 26. | Yök˒-꜀yín ꜀m ᶜhò, ꜀Sin-꜀shàng† tsz²-꜀yín ꜀m yin' ꜀lá.² ᶜNgo wa² ᶜkám shat˒ yí²-shap˒-sz' man. | If not good (you), Sir, of course, not want, 21. I said reduce-to fixed (price) twenty-four dollars. |
| 27. | ᶜNgo ꜀m ᶜpéi tak˒ kòm' ꜀to ꜀á. Hai² yí²-shap˒-꜀sám man chek˒, ꜀m ᶜpéi ꜀to lok. | I not give can so much, 1. Is (i.e. what I will give is) twenty-three dollars only, 7, will-not give more, 32. |
| 28. | ꜀M tsò² tak˒ ꜀á.² ꜀P'eng† kwo'*, ꜀t'aú lok˒. ᶜShíú lok˒. ᶜShíú, ᶜshíú kwo'* ꜀t'aú lok˒. Tsaú² ᶜkòm ꜀lá.² yí²-shap˒-sz' ꜀man ꜀lá. | Not do can, 7. Cheap over much, 32. Little, 32, little, little over much, 32. Just, (let it be) so, 21, twenty-four dollars, 21. |
| 29. | ꜀M tsò² tak˒. ꜀M ᶜmái lok˒. ᶜNgo höü' lok˒, ᶜtsing chí' ꜀lá.² | Not do can. Not buy. I go, 32, good-bye, 21. |
| 30. | ꜀Sin-꜀shàng† á', ꜀Sin-꜀shàng†, ꜀fán-꜀lai ꜀lá.² ᶜNgo ᶜkám yat˒ pún'; ᶜnéi ꜀t'im yat˒ pún', yí²-shap˒-꜀sám ko' pún' ꜀lá.² | Sir, 2, Sir, back come, 21. I reduce one half; you increase one half. Twenty-three [C.] half, 21. |

## CONVERSATION 46TH.—BUYING FURNITURE.—(*Concluded.*)

| | | |
|---|---|---|
| 31. | I will not raise my price any further. Twenty-three dollars. That is the most. | 我唔添多咯，廿三文咯，至多係咁多叹， |
| 32. | Very well, I will let it go. I did not want too much from you. Let it be as you say, Sir. I will give it cheaper to you. I will send it to your place to-morrow. If it is not right, you need not keep it. | 俉，都好喇．麻𠸎吔喇，都唔係要你多，先生噉話就噉喇， 就平啲俾過你喇，我聽朝使人抬上去你處，若唔好你唔要都做得嘅， |

## CONVERSATION 47TH.—A CHINAMAN'S CLOTHES.

| | | |
|---|---|---|
| 1. | Tell me the names of the clothes which a Chinaman wears. | 你講過我聽，唐人著個啲衣服叫做乜名， |
| 2. | The lower classes in hot weather only wear a pair of trousers and a jacket. | 個啲做袓嘅人、天時熱不過著一條褲，一件衫啫， |
| 3. | Yes, and in hot weather they take off the jacket. | 係呀，天時熱都除咽個件衫添， |
| 4. | Some, such as rice pounders and agricultural labourers, go even without trousers, and wear a loin cloth. | 有啲，好似舂米嘅，耕田嘅，都冇褲着，硬著條水捫， |
| 5. | Poor people do not wear shoes and stockings. Do they not feel cold? | 貧窮人冇著鞋襪，唔見冷咩， |
| 6. | It is of no consequence in summer. Probably in winter they feel cold. In winter they wear hats. | 天熱個時冇相干嘅，天時冷大概都見凍呀，天冷個時戴帽喇， |

易學廣東話



### CONVERSATION 45TH.—BUYING FURNITURE.—(*Concluded.*)

31. ˋNgo ˏm ˏt'im ˏto lok ˎ Ya²-ˏsám man lok, ˋChi ˎ ˏto hai² kòm ˎ to chek ˎ. — I not increase more, 32. Twenty-three dollars, 32. Most also is so much only. 7.

32. ˏNg, tò ˋhò ˏlá,² ma²-ma⁵*-tei⁵* ˏlá.² Tò ˏm hai² yiú ˎ ˋnéi ˏto. ˏSin-ˏsháng† ˋkòm wá², tsaú² ˋkòm ˏlá.² Tsaú² ˏp'eng†-ˏti ˋpéi kwo ˎ ˋnéi ˏlá.² ˋNgo ˏt'ing-ˏchiú ˋshai ˏyan ˏt'oi ˋshöng höü ˎ ˋnéi shü ˎ. Yök ˎ ˏm ˋhò. ˋnéi ˏm yiú ˎ ˏtò tsò² tak ˎ ke ˎ. — Well, also good, 21. Let-it-pass 21. Yet not is want you much, Sir, so say, then so (be it), 21. Then cheaper give to you, 21. I to-morrow send man carry up go your place. If not good, you not want also do em, 15.

### CONVERSATION 47TH.—A CHINAMAN'S CLOTHES.

1. ˋNéi ˋkong kwo ˎ ˋngo ˏt'eng† ˏT'ong-ˏyan chök ˳ ko ˎ-˳ti ˏyí-fuk ˎ kiú ˎ-tsò² mat ˎ ˏmeng*†. — You speak over to-me to-hear Chinese wear those clothes call what name.

2. Ko ˎ-˳ti tsò² ˏts'ò ke ˎ ˏyan ˏt'in-ˏshí-yít ˎ pat ˎ-kwo ˎ chök ˎ yat ˎ ˏt'iú fú ˎ, yat ˎ kín² shám ˏche. — Those who-are coarse, 15, men heaven's-time-hot only wear one [C.] trousers, one [C.] jacket only, 7.

3. Hai² á ˎ, ˏt'in-ˏshí yít ˎ ˏtò ˏch'öü (*or sometimes* ˏch'öü*) ˋcho ko ˎ kín² ˏshám ˏt'im. — Yes, 1, weather hot also take off that [C.] jacket also.

4. ˋYaú ˏti ˋhò-ˋts'z ˏchung-ˋmaí ke ˎ, ˏkáng ˏt'ín ke ˎ, ˏtò ˋmò fú ˎ chök ˳, ngáng² chök ˎ ˏt'iú ˋshöü-˳mún. — Have some very-similar pound-rice, 15, cultivate fields, 15, also no trousers wear, only wear [C.] water-covering.

5. ˏPan-ˏk'ung ˏyan ˋmò chök ˎ ˏhái mat ˎ. ˏM kín ˎ ˋláng ˏme?² — Poor people not put-on shoes socks. Not feel cold. eh? 30.

6. ˏT'in yít ˎ ko ˎ ˏshí ˋmò ˏsöng-ˏkón ke ˎ. ˏT'in-ˏshí ˋláng tái²-k'oi³* ˏtò kín ˎ tung ˎ á ˎ. ˏT'in ˋláng ko ˎ ˏshí tái ˎ mò⁵* ˏlá.² — Weather hot that time no matter, 15. Season cold probably also feel cold, 15. Weather cold that time wear hats, 21.

## CONVERSATION 47TH.—A CHINAMAN'S CLOTHES.—*(Concluded.)*

| | | |
|---|---|---|
| 7. | There are several kinds of hats, are there not? | 帽唔係有好幾樣嘅、 |
| 8. | There are. There are small hats, felt hats, official hats, summer hats, worn by officials, and bamboo hats and hoods. | 冇錯、有小帽、狗毛氈、大帽、涼帽、官戴嘅、竹帽、雪帽、 |
| 9. | Are there not several kinds of bamboo hats? | 唔係有幾樣竹帽、 |
| 10. | There are. There is the rain hat; that is the largest kind. The small ones, such as the Chinese policemen in Hongkong wear, are called chuk-sát. The medium size, such as boatmen and coolies wear, is called t'ung kwú. The bamboo hats worn in different localities are not the same. | 有呀、有雨帽、個停係至大嘅喇: 個啲細嘅、好似香港唐人差人戴嘅、叫做竹拆帽; 中停嘅、好似艇家咕喱戴嘅係叫做銅鼓帽; 一處處竹帽唔同樣嘅、 |
| 11. | I suppose there are a great variety of shoes as well. | 大槪都係有好多樣鞋、 |
| 12. | There are. | 有呀、 |
| 13. | Tell me what they are. | 講俾我聽喇、 |
| 14. | There are fine grass shoes, cloth shoes, cloth shoes with felt soles, cloth shoes with cloth soles, satin shoes. | 有蒲草鞋、布面鞋、布面氈底鞋、布面布底鞋、緞面鞋、 |
| 15. | Wait a bit. Are there so many kinds? | 等陣嗻、係有咁多咩、 |

易學廣東話



## CONVERSATION 47TH.—A CHINAMAN'S CLOTHES.—(*Continued.*)

| | | |
|---|---|---|
| 7. | Mò$^{5*}$, ꜁m hai$^{2}$ ꜃yaú ꜂hò ꜂ke yöng$^{2}$ ke$^{1*}$? | Hats, not being have good several kinds? 15. |
| 8. | ꜃Mò ts'o꜄, ꜃yaú ꜂shiú mò$^{5*}$, ꜂kaú-mò$^{2}$ ꜀chin, tái$^{2}$ mò$^{5*}$, ꜁löng mò$^{5*}$, ꜀kwún tái꜄ ke꜄. chuk꜆ mò$^{5*}$, süt˳ mò$^{5*}$. | No mistake, have small hats, felt hats, large hats, cool hats (which) officials wear, 15, bamboo hats, snow hats. |
| 9. | ꜁M hai$^{2}$ ꜃yaú ꜂kéi yöng$^{2}$ chuk꜆ mò$^{5*}$? | Not is have several kinds bamboo hats? |
| 10. | ꜃Yaú á꜄, ꜃yaú ꜃yü-mò,$^{2}$ ko꜄ ꜁t'ing (*or* ꜁t'ing*) hai$^{2}$ chi꜄ tái$^{2}$ ke꜄ lá꜄; ko꜄-꜀ti sai꜄ ke꜄ ꜂hò-꜃ts'z ꜀Höng-꜂kong ꜁T'ong-꜁yan ꜀ch'ái-꜁yan tái꜄ ke꜄, kiú꜄-tsò$^{2}$ chuk꜆-sát˳ mò$^{2}$. ꜀Chung ꜁t'ing* ke꜄, ꜂hò-꜃ts'z t'eng†-꜀ká, ꜀kwú-꜀léi tái꜄ ke꜄, hai$^{2}$ kiú꜄-tsò$^{2}$ ꜁t'ung-꜂kwú mò$^{2}$. Yat꜆ ch'ü$^{1*}$ ch'ü꜄ chuk꜆ mò$^{2}$ (*or* mò$^{5*}$) ꜁m ꜁t'ung yöng$^{5*}$ ke꜄. | Have, 2, have rain-hats, that variety is most large, 15, 21; those small, 15, very-like Hongkong Chinese policemen wear, 15, called-to-be chuk-sát hats. Middle quality, 15, very-like boat-people (and) coolies wear, 15, are called-to-be t'ung-kwú hats. One place place bamboo hats not same kind, 15. |
| 11. | Tái$^{2}$-k'oi$^{1*}$ ˳tò hai$^{2}$ ꜃yaú ꜂hò ꜀to yöng$^{2}$ ꜁hái. | Probably also is have good many kinds of-shoes. |
| 12. | ꜃Yaú á꜄. | There-are, 2. |
| 13. | ꜂Kong ꜂péi ꜃ngo ꜀t'eng† ꜀lá.$^{2}$ | Speak give me to-hear, 21. |
| 14. | ꜃Yaú ꜀pò ꜂ts'ò ꜁hái, pò꜄ mín$^{5*}$ ꜁hái, pò꜄ mín$^{5*}$ ꜀chin ꜂tai ꜁hái, pò꜄ mín$^{5*}$ pò꜄ ꜂tai ꜁hái, tün$^{5*}$ mín$^{5*}$ ꜁hái. | Have fine grass shoes, cloth uppers shoes, cloth uppers felt sole shoes, cloth uppers cloth soles shoes, satin uppers shoes. |
| 15. | ꜂Tang chan$^{2}$ (*or* chan$^{5*}$) ꜀chá.$^{2}$ Hai$^{2}$ ꜃yaú kòm꜄ ꜀to ꜀me?$^{2}$ | Wait a-bit only, 1. Is-it (that) there-are so many, eh? 39. |

## CONVERSATION 47TH.—A CHINAMAN'S CLOTHES.—(*Continued.*)

| | |
|---|---|
| 16. There are more. I will tell you the rest. shall I ? | 重有呀、我講埋你聽吖、 |
| 17. All right, go on, tell me them all. | 好喇、講喇、講埋晒我聽喇、 |
| 18. Paper-soled shoes, leather-soled shoes, India-rubber shoes, leather shoes, ornamented shoes, shoes in the Peking style, Foochow shoes, water shoes, Western shoes, and grass sandals. | 沙紙底鞋、皮底鞋、樹膠鞋、皮面皮底鞋、鑲鞋、京裝鞋、福州鞋、水鞋、西式鞋、又有草鞋、 |
| 19. But what do you call those grass sandals the coolies wear, and which they tie on with bits of cord ? | 你叫個啲估喱著個啲鞋、俾草整嘅俾繩綁住脚嘅呢、個啲係叫做乜野鞋呢、 |
| 20. I have just mentioned them—straw sandals ; and besides there are leather sandals with soles only : and further those called 'a thousand *li* horses.' | 個啲我就正講咽咯、即係草鞋咯、另外有個啲皮底、冇面嘅、重有啲叫做千里馬、 |
| 21. I want to return to our former topic of conversation.— | 我想翻轉頭講舊時所講嘅、 |
| 22. Very well, what do you want to talk about ? | 唔、都好吖、想講乜野呢、 |
| 23. I have seen Chinese in winter wearing some rather curious trousers. I do not know what they are called. | 天時冷個時、我見過唐人着啲幾出奇嘅褲、唔知叫做乜名呢、 |
| 24. What are they like ? | 點樣嘅呢、 |
| 25. Well, it is rather hard to say. | 都幾難講嘅、 |

## CONVERSATION 17TH.—A CHINAMAN'S CLOTHES.—(*Continued.*)

| | | |
|---|---|---|
| 16. | Chung² ꜃yaú á꜄. ꜃Ngo ꜂kong ꜁maí ꜃néi ꜀t'eng† ꜀á ?² | Besides have. 2. I speak finish-up-the-rest you to-hear ? 1. |
| 17. | ꜂Hò ꜀lá,² ꜂kong ꜀la,² ꜂kong ꜁maí saí꜄ ꜃ngo ꜀t'eng† ꜀lá.² | Good, 21. speak, 21. speak finish all to-me to-hear, 21. |
| 18. | ꜀Shá-꜂chí ꜂taí ꜁haí, ꜀peí-꜂taí ꜁haí, shü²-꜁kaú ꜁haí, ꜁p'éi mín⁵* ꜁p'éi ꜂taí ꜁haí, ꜀söng ꜁haí, ꜀king-꜀chong ꜁haí, Fuk꜆-꜀chaú ꜁haí, ꜂shöü ꜁haí, ꜀Saí shik꜆ ꜁haí, yaú² ꜃yaú ꜂ts'ò ꜁haí. | Sand-paper (Chinese not English) soled shoes, leather-soled shoes, tree-gum shoes, leather uppers leather soled shoes, ornamented shoes, metropolis fashion shoes, Fuchow shoes, water shoes, Western style shoes, (These have the soles longer than the uppers), moreover have grass shoes. |
| 19. | ꜃Néi kiú꜄ ko꜄-꜀ti ꜀kwú-꜀léí chök꜆ ko꜄-ti ꜁haí, ꜂péi ꜂ts'ò ꜂ching ke꜄, ꜂péi ꜁shing* ꜂pong-chü² kök꜆ ke꜄ ꜀ni, ko꜄-ti haí² kiú꜄-tsò² mat꜆-꜃ye ꜁haí ꜀ni ?² | You call those coolies wear those shoes give grass made. 15, give string tie to-feet, 15, 53, those are called-to-be what-thing shoe, eh ? 53. |
| 20. | Ko꜄-ti ꜃ngo tsaú²-ching꜄ (*or* cheng꜄*) ꜂kong-꜂cho lok꜆, tsik꜆ haí² ꜂ts'ò ꜁haí lok꜆ ; ling²-ngoí² ꜃yaú ko꜄-ti ꜁p'éi ꜂taí, ꜃mò mín⁵* ke꜄ : chung² ꜃yaú ꜀tí kiú꜄-tsò² '꜀ts'ín ꜃léi ꜃má.' | Those I just spoke, 32. just are grass shoes. 32 : besides have those leather soles, no uppers. 15 : besides have some called-to-be 'thousand *li* horses.' |
| 21. | ꜃Ngo ꜂söng ꜀fán-꜂chün-꜁t'aú ꜂kong kaú²-꜁shi* ꜂sho ꜂kong ke꜄. | I wish back-turn-head speak old-time (i.e. formerly) what speaking. 15. |
| 22. | ꜁Ng. to꜄ ꜂ho ꜀á. ꜂Söng ꜂kong mat꜆-꜃ye ꜀ni ?² | Well also good. 1. Wish to-talk what-thing, eh ? 53. |
| 23. | ꜀T'in-꜀shi-꜃láng ko꜄ ꜁shí, ꜃ngo kín꜄-kwo꜄ ꜁T'ong-꜁yan chök꜆ ꜀ti ꜂kéi ch'ut꜆-꜁k'éi ke꜄ fú꜄, ꜁m ꜀chí kiú꜄-tsò² mat꜆ ꜁meng*† ꜀ni. | Season cold that time, I seen Chinese wear some rather extraordinary. 15. trousers, not know called-to-be what name. 53. |
| 24. | ꜂Tím yöng⁵* ke꜄ ꜀ni ?² | What kind. 15. eh ? 53. |
| 25. | To꜄ ꜂kéi ꜁nán ꜂kong ke꜄ (*or* ke꜄ ). | Also rather hard to-speak. 15. |

## CONVERSATION 47TH.—A CHINAMAN'S CLOTHES.—*(Concluded.)*

| | |
|---|---|
| 26. Try, and see if you cannot say what they are like. | 試過睇吓講得出個樣嚟唔咋、 |
| 27. Each leg has one to itself. They are tied in with tape at the ankles in this way. They are loose at the top and tight below. | 每隻脚有一條嘅、喺脚眼上個處、俾條帶噉綁埋嘅、上高鬆嘅、下底窄嘅、 |
| 28. Are they like that? What can they be? | 噉嘅咩、乜野家伙呢、 |
| 29. Do you not know? | 你都唔知咩、 |
| 30. I do not. How can I tell from your description? If I thought for a hundred years, I would not know what they were. | 唔知咯、你係摵個樣噉嚟解法、我點想得出嚟呢、想一百年我都唔想得倒、 |
| 31. I cannot tell you any better then I have done. I have told you very plainly. | 我又唔講得明啲、我都講到好明添咯、 |
| 32. You are not speaking of leggings, are you? Perhaps they are leggings. They must be. They must certainly be leggings. | 你唔係講套褲咻、怕係都唔定咯、冇錯咯、是必係套褲咯、 |

## CONVERSATION 48TH.—EXPORTS AND IMPORTS.

| | |
|---|---|
| 1. What do the Chinese say when they come down to Hongkong and see the gas lamps in the streets? Do they say it is a good thing or not? | 唐人落嚟香港睇見街上煤氣燈話好唔好、點講呢、 |
| 2. They must certainly say it is good. | 一定話好喇、 |

易學廣東話



## CONVERSATION 47TH.—A CHINAMAN'S CLOTHES.—(*Concluded.*)

| | |
|---|---|
| 26. Shíʾ-kwoʾ, ʿt'ai-ʿhá ʿkong takˏ ch'utˏ koʾ yöng$^{5}$* ˏlaí ˏm ʿchá. | Try-over see-a-bit speak can out that kind come not, 9. |
| 27. ʿMúi chekₒ kökₒ ʿyaú yatˏ ˏt'iú keʾ. ʿHaí kökₒ-ʿngán shöng$^{2}$ koʾ shüʾ, ʿpéí ˏt'iú taíʾ ʿkòm ʿpong ˏmái keʾ. Shöng$^{2}$-ˏkò ˏsung keʾ, há$^{2}$-ʿtaí chákˏ keʾ. | Each [C.] leg had one [C.], 15. At ankle above that place give a-piece tape so tie together, 15. Up-high loose 15, down-below tight, 15. |
| 28. ʿKòm keʾ ˏme?$^{2}$ Matˏ-ʿye ˏká-ʿfo ˏni?$^{2}$ | So, 15, eh? 39. What thing, eh? 53. |
| 29. ʿNéí ₒto ˏm ˏchí ˏme?$^{2}$ | You also not know, eh? 39. |
| 30. ˏM ˏchí lokˏ. ʿNéí haí$^{2}$ ʿk'ái-koʾ yöng$^{5}$* ʿkòm ˏlaí ʿkái-fátₒ, ʿngo ʿtím ʿsöng takˏ ch'utˏ ˏlaí ˏni?$^{2}$ ʿSöng yatˏ pákₒ ˏnín ʿngo ₒtò ˏm ʿsöng takˏ ʿtò. | Not know, 32. You do take that kind so come to-explain-method I how think able out come, eh? 53, Think one hundred years I also not think able arrive-at. |
| 31. ʿNgo yaú$^{2}$ ˏm ʿkong takˏ ˏming-ₒti. ʿNgo ₒtò ʿkong tòʾ ʿhò ˏming ˏt'ím lokˏ. | I also not speak can clearer. I also speak arrive-at very clear besides, 32. |
| 32. ʿNéí ˏm haí$^{2}$ ʿkong t'òʾ-fúʾ kwáʾ. P'áʾ haí$^{2}$ ₒtò ˏm ting$^{2}$ (*or* ting$^{5}$*) lokˏ. ʿMò ts'oʾ lokˏ. Shí$^{2}$-pítˏ haí$^{2}$ t'òʾ-fúʾ lokˏ. | You not are speaking-about leggings probably? 18, Fear is also not certain, 32, No mistake, 32. Certainly are leggings, 32. |

## CONVERSATION 48TH.—EXPORTS AND IMPORTS.

| | |
|---|---|
| 1. ˏT'ong-ˏyan lokˏ ˏlai ˏHöng-ʿkong ʿt'aí-kínʾ ˏkái shöng$^{2}$ ˏmúi-héíʾ ₒtang wá$^{2}$ ʿhò ˏm ʿhò? ʿTím ʿkong ˏni?$^{2}$ | Chinese down come Hongkong look-see street upon coal-vapour lamps say good not good? How speak, eh? 53. |
| 2. Yatˏ ting$^{2}$ wá$^{2}$ ʿhò ˏlá.$^{2}$ | To-a certainty say good, 21. |

CONVERSATION 48TH.—EXPORTS AND IMPORTS.—(*Continued.*)

3. I remember when they were first introduced into Hongkong that the Chinese in the streets put their hands on the lamp-posts to see whether they were hot or not.

我記得香港新出個陣時，街上個啲唐人俾手摩埋燈柱想睇熱唔熱，

4. Oh! Did they indeed? they thought them very curious.

呵，係咩，佢哋估好出奇咯，

5. Many foreign articles are now used by the Chinese, which in former years were unknown.

現時唐人使好多洋貨嘅，舊時唔識嘅、

6. Yes: kerosene, for instance. Twenty years ago it was only used by a few foreigners in China: and now kerosene and kerosene lamps are for sale all over the city; and not only in the city, but in the country as well.

係吖，火水拿，先二十年個陣時不過有幾個西人使呗，而家拿，通城都有火水共火水燈賣，唔止城添，鄉下都有得出賣咯，

7. Yes: and it is the same with matches. Formerly when a light was wanted, tinder was used and a flint and piece of iron were struck together in this way before you got a light: now everyone has matches.

係吖，火柴都係一樣，舊時要火，就使火煤絨，俾傄火石，俾啲鐵嚟鏗致有火，呢陣時人人都有火柴咯，

8. Even the coolies have them in their pockets; and they are spread out in the streets for sale. When you wish to smoke, and ask for a light, every one has matches.

咕喱都有得袋喺袋咯，都擺在街賣，你想食烟問人哋借火，個個都有火柴咯，

## CONVERSATION 48TH.—EXPORTS AND IMPORTS.—(*Continued.*)

| | | |
|---|---|---|
| 3. | ᶜ̲Ngo kéiᵓ-tak꜄ ꜀Höng-ᶜkong ꜀san ch'ut꜄ koᵓ chan$^2$ ꜀̲shí*, ꜀kái shöng$^2$ koᵓ-꜄ti ꜀̲T'ong-꜀̲yan, ᶜpéi ᶜshaú ᶜmo mái$^2$ ꜄tang-ᶜch'ü ᶜsöng ᶜt'ai yit$_2$ ꜀̲m yit$_2$. | I remember-can Hongkong newly issue that period time, streets upon those Chinese give hands feel close-to lamp-post want see hot, not hot. |
| 4. | ꜀̲O! hai$^2$ ꜀me? ᶜ̲K'öü-téi$^2$ ᶜkwú ᶜhò ch'ut꜄-꜀̲k'éi lok˳. | Ah! Yes, eh? 39. They thought very extraordinary, 32. |
| 5. | Yín$^2$-꜀̲shí (*or* ꜀̲shí*) ꜀̲T'ong-꜀̲yan ᶜshai ᶜhò ꜀to ꜀̲yöng-foᵓ keᵓ, kaú$^2$-꜀̲shí$^2$ ꜀̲m shik꜄ keᵓ. | Present-time Chinese use very many foreign-goods, 15, olden-times not known, 15. |
| 6. | Hai$^2$ ꜀á;$^2$ ᶜfo-ᶜshöü ꜀̲ná. ꜀Sín yí$^2$-shap$_2$ ꜀̲nín koᵓ chan$^2$ ꜀̲shí* pat꜄-kwoᵓ ᶜ̲yaú ᶜkéi koᵓ ꜀Sái-꜀̲yan ᶜshai chek˳; ꜀̲yí-꜄ká ꜀̲ná, ˳t'ung ꜀̲sheng† ˳tò ᶜ̲yaú ᶜfo-ᶜshöü kung$^2$ ᶜfo-ᶜshöü ꜄tang mái$^2$; ꜀̲m ᶜchí ꜀̲sheng*† ꜀tím, ꜀höng-ᶜ̲há ˳tò ᶜ̲yaú tak꜄ ch'ut꜄ mái$^2$ lok˳. | Yes, 1: kerosene now. Before twenty years that period time only have several [C.] Western-people use only; at present now throughout city also have kerosene and kerosene lamps sell; not only city as-well, country-side also have possession (of them) to-issue in-sale, 32. |
| 7. | Hai$^2$ ꜀á;$^2$ ᶜfo-꜀̲ch'ái ˳tò hai$^2$ yat꜄ yöng$^2$. Kaú$^2$-꜀̲shí* yíúᵓ ᶜfo, tsaú$^2$ ᶜshai ᶜfo-꜀̲múi-꜀̲yung, ᶜpéi kaú$^2$ ᶜfo-shek$_2$, ᶜpéi ˳ti t'ít˳, ᶜkòm ꜀hang chíᵓ ᶜ̲yaú ᶜfo; ꜀ni chan$^2$ ꜀̲shí* ꜀̲yan-꜀̲yan ꜄to ᶜ̲yaú ᶜfo-꜀̲ch'ái lok˳. | Yes, 1: matches also is one same. Olden-time want fire, then use tinder, take lump flint, take little iron, so knock before have fire; this period of-time every-one also have matches, 32. |
| 8. | ꜀Kwú-꜄léi ˳tò ᶜ̲yaú tak꜄ toi$^2$ ᶜhai toi$^{5*}$ lok˳; ˳tò ᶜpaí tsoi$^2$ ꜀kái (*or* ꜄kái) mái$^2$. ᶜ̲Néi ᶜsöng shik$_2$ ꜀yín, man$^2$ ꜀̲yan-téi$^2$ tseᵓ ᶜfo, koᵓ-koᵓ ˳tò ᶜ̲yaú ᶜfo-꜀̲ch'ái lok˳. | Coolies also have able pocketed in pocket, 32; also spread-out in streets for-sale. You wish eat smoke, ask people lend fire, everyone also have matches, 32. |

## CONVERSATION 48TH.—EXPORTS AND IMPORTS.—(*Continued.*)

| | |
|---|---|
| 9. Even in Yun-nan there are also foreign goods for sale. In the capital of the Yun-nan province you can get condensed milk, but it is twice as dear as it is in Hongkong. Here it sells for twenty-five cents a tin, but there it is fifty cents. | 雲南亦都有洋貨賣嘅、喺雲南省城可以買得牛奶膏(即罐頭牛奶、)但係香港雙倍咁貴、喺呢嚥係賣二毫半子一罐、喺嗰嚥要五毫子致得、 |
| 10. Why is it so much dearer? | 點解貴得咁多呢、 |
| 11. It is a long distance, and the freight is high, and it is hard work to go by the mountain roads, moreover there is the li-kin tax; and so it is dear. | 路又遠、水脚又貴、山路又難行、而且又要釐金、所以貴喇、 |
| 12. And what about opium: there is a great deal of it imported, is there not? What do the Chinese say about opium; do they approve of people taking it? | 鴉片烟呢、係有好多入口唔係呢、講論鴉片烟唐人點話呢、中意人哋食唔中意呢、 |
| 13. To a man they say it is bad; but alas! a great many of them take it. | 一個都話唔好、但係可惜好多唐人都食咯、 |
| 14. Why is it bad? | 做乜唔好呢、 |
| 15. People waste their time and money, and spend all their property over it. The smoking of it weakens one. | 人哋嘥錢又要嘥時候、而且花散嘥個啲田地屋宇、食咽身子就軟弱咯、 |
| 16. I suppose there are many goods imported into China. | 大槪有好多入口貨到中國、係唔係呢、 |

## CONVERSATION 48TH.—EXPORTS AND IMPORTS.—(*Continued.*)

| | | |
|---|---|---|
| 9. | ꜀Wan-꜀nám yik꜁ ꜀tò ᶜyaú ꜀yöng-fòᵓ mái² keᵓ. ᶜHai ꜀Wan-꜀nám ᶜSháng-꜀sheng† ᶜho-ᶜyí ᶜmái-tak꜁ ꜀ngaú-ᶜnái-꜀kò (tsik꜁ kwúnᵓ-꜀t'aú* ꜀ngaú-ᶜnái); tán²-hai² ꜀Höng-ᶜkong ꜀shöng-ᶜpöü kòmᵓ kwaiᵓ. ᶜHai ꜀ni shüᵓ hai²-mái² yi²-꜀hò-púnᵓ-ᶜtsz yat꜁ kwúnᵓ. ᶜhai koᵓ shüᵓ yiúᵓ ᶜng-꜀hò-ᶜtsz chiᵓ tak꜁. | Wan-nám also moreover have foreign-goods for-sale, 15. In Wan-nám provincial-city it-is-possible to-buy-able condensed-cow's-milk (just tinned cow's-milk); but Hongkong double-fold so dear. At this place is-sold two-dimes-half one tin; at that place must five-dimes to-be able (to get it). |
| 10. | ᶜTím ᶜkái kwáiᵓ tak꜁ kòmᵓ ꜀to ꜀ni? | How explain dear-able so much, eh? 53. |
| 11. | Lò² yaú² ᶜyün: ᶜshöü-kök꜀ yaú² kwaiᵓ; ꜀shán-꜀lò yaú² ꜀nán ꜀háng; ꜀yí-ᶜche yaú² yiúᵓ ꜀léi-꜀kam. ᶜsho-ᶜyí kwaiᵓ ꜀lá. | Road also far, freight also dear, mountain-roads also difficult to-walk. Moreover also need *likin*; therefore dear, 21. |
| 12. | ꜀A-p'inᵓ-꜀yín ꜀ni? Hai² ᶜyaú ᶜhò ꜀to yap꜁-ᶜhaú ꜀m hai² ꜀ni? ᶜKong-lun² ꜀A-p'inᵓ-꜀yín ꜀T'ong-꜀yan ᶜtím wa² ꜀ni? ꜀Chung-yíᵓ ꜀yan-téi² shik꜁ ꜀m ꜀chung-yíᵓ ꜀ni? | Opium, eh? 53. Is-it (that) there-is very much imported, not is, eh? 53. Speaking-of opium Chinese how say, eh? 53. Like people to-smoke (*lit.* to-eat), not like, eh? 53. |
| 13. | Yat꜁ koᵓ ꜀tò wa² ꜀m ᶜhò; tán²-hai² ᶜho-sik꜁ ᶜhò ꜀to ꜀T'ong-꜀yan tò shik꜁ lok꜀. | To-a [C.] (man) also say not good; but it-can-be-pitied (i.e. it-is to be pitied) very many Chinese also smoke, (*lit.* eat) 32. |
| 14. | Tsò²-mat꜁ ꜀m ᶜhò ꜀ni? | Why not good, eh? 53. |
| 15. | ꜀Yan-téi² ꜀sái ꜀ts'ín*, yaú² yiúᵓ ꜀sái ꜀shí-haú², ꜀yí-ᶜche ꜀fá-sánᵓ sáiᵓ koᵓ-꜀ti ꜀t'ín-téi², uk꜁-ᶜyü. Shik꜁-ᶜcho ꜀shan-ᶜtsz tsaú² ᶜyün-yök꜁ lok꜀. | People waste money, also must waste time, besides dissipate all those fields-and-lands, houses-and-so-on. When-take (*lit.* eaten) body then weakened, 32. |
| 16. | Tái²-k'oi²* ᶜyaú ᶜhò ꜀to yap꜁-ᶜhaú-foᵓ tòᵓ ꜀Chung-kwok꜀: hai² ꜀m hai² ꜀ni? | Probably have very many imported-goods arrive-at China; is not is, eh? 53. |

## CONVERSATION 48TH.—EXPORTS AND IMPORTS.—(*Continued.*)

| | | |
|---|---|---|
| 17. | There are very many. There are agar-agar, timber, fancy cotton cambrics, chintzes, muslins, camlets, velvets, and Spanish stripes, shirtings, T-cloths, cow-bezoar, ivory, ginseng, window glass, hides, iron, zinc, and copper, quicksilver, sapan wood, and there are a great many more besides. I could not mention them all. | 入口嘅有好多咯、有海菜、木料、花布、袈裟布、花洋布、洋紗、羽紗、剪絨、哆囉呢、白色布、礪洋布、牛黃、象牙、人參、玻璃片、皮、鐵、白鉛、銅、水銀、蘇木、重有好多樣添、唔講得晒出嚟、 |
| 18. | Are there as many exports or not? | 有咁多出口貨冇呢、 |
| 19. | There are also a great many exports. There are alum, anise, arsenic, bamboo-ware, beans, joss-sticks for measuring time, camphor, li-chees, ginger, pongees, gauze, silver and gold ware, tea, ink, and others. | 出口嘅都有好多咯、有白礬、八角、信石、竹器、荳、時辰香、樟腦、荔枝、薑、綢、紗、金銀器、茶、墨、各樣、 |
| 20. | You have not spoken of birds' nests, and sharks' fins and fish-maws. Chinese eat these do they not? | 你唔曾講到燕窩、魚翅、魚肚、唐人都食呢幾樣啩、 |
| 21. | They do. Have you tasted Chinese food yet? | 係嚫、先生食過唐人餸唔曾呢、 |
| 22. | I have not. I do not know how to hold the chopsticks. | 唔曾、我唔曉揸快子、 |
| 23. | That is very easily learned. Besides to take a bowl of sharks'-fins soup you do not need chop stikes. | 個啲好容易學嘅嚧、而且食一碗魚翅、唔使用快子嘅、 |

CONVERSATION 48TH.—EXPORTS AND IMPORTS.—(*Continued.*)

| | | |
|---|---|---|
| 17. | Yap$_2$-ᶜhaú-keᵓ ᶝyaú ᶜhò ꜀to lok$_o$. ᶝYaú ᶜhoi-ts'oiᵓ, múk$_2$-líú$^2$, ꜀fá-pòᵓ, ꜀ká-꜁shá-pò, $_o$fá-꜁yöng-pòᵓ, ꜁yöng-꜀shá, ᶝyü-꜀shá, ᶜtsín-꜁yung,* ꜀to-꜀lo-꜁néí, pák$_o$-shik$_ɔ$-pòᵓ, ᶝmá-꜁yöng-pòᵓ, ꜁ngaú-꜁wong, tsöng$^2$-꜁ngá, ꜁yan-꜀sham, ꜀po-$_o$léí* p'ín$^1$*, ꜁p'éí, t'it$_o$, pák$_2$-꜁yün, ꜀t'ung, ᶜshöü-꜁ngan, ꜀sò-muk$_2$, chung$^2$ ᶝyaú ᶜhò ꜀to yöng$^2$ ꜀t'ím, ꜁m ᶜkong tak$_ɔ$ sáiᵓ ch'ut$_ɔ$ ꜁laí. | Imported-ones have very many, 32. Have agar-agar, timber, fancy-cottons, cambrics, chintzes, muslins, camlets, velvets, Spanish-stripes, shirtings, T-clothes, cow-bezoar, ivory, ginseng, glass panes, hides, iron, zinc, copper, quicksilver, sapan-wood, besides have very many kinds besides, not speak can all out come. |
| 18. | ᶝYaú kómᵓ ꜀to ch'ut$_ɔ$-ᶜhaú foᵓ ᶝmò ꜀ni? | Have as many exported goods, not, eh? 53. |
| 19. | Ch'ut$_ɔ$-ᶜhaú-keᵓ $_o$tò ᶝyaú ᶜhò ꜀to lok$_o$. ᶝYaú pák$_2$-꜁fán, pát$_o$-kok$_o$, sunᵓ-shek$_2$, chuk$_ɔ$-héíᵓ, taú$^3$*, ꜁shí-꜁shan $_o$höng, ꜀chöng-ᶝnò, (*or* ꜀chöng-ᶝlò) laí$^2$-꜀chí (*or* laí$^2$$_o$chí), ꜀köng, ꜁ch'aú*, ꜀shá, ꜀kam ꜁ngan héíᵓ, ꜁ch'á, mak$_2$, kok$_o$ yöng$^2$. | Exported-ones also have very many, 32. There-are alum, anise, arsenic, bamboo-ware, beans, time-joss-sticks, camphor, lichees, ginger, pongees, gauze, gold (and) silver ware, tea, ink, all kinds. |
| 20. | ᶝNéí ꜁m-꜁ts'ang ᶜkong-tòᵓ yínᵓ-꜀wo, ꜁yü-ch'íᵓ, ꜁yü-ᶝt'ò. ꜁T'ong-꜁yan $_o$tò shik$_2$ ꜀ni ᶜkéí yöng$^2$ kwáᵓ. | You not-yet spoken-about bird's-nests, fish-fins, fish-maws. Chinese also eat these several sorts, I-suppose. 18. |
| 21. | Hai$^2$ káᵓ. ꜀Sín-꜀sháng shik$_2$-kwoᵓ ꜁T'ong-꜁yan sungᵓ ꜁m-꜁ts'ang ꜀ni?$^2$ | Yes, 11, Sir, you-have-eaten Chinese food not-yet, eh? 53. |
| 22. | ꜁M-꜁ts'ang. ᶝNgo ꜁m ᶜhiú ꜀chá fái$^3$-ᶜtsz. | Not-yet. I not understand hold chop-sticks. |
| 23. | Ko$^2$-$_o$ti ᶜhò ꜁yung-yí$^2$ hok$_2$-keᵓ ꜀che.$^2$ ꜁Yí-ᶜch'e shik$_2$ yat$_ɔ$ ᶝwún ꜁yü-ch'íᵓ, ꜁m ᶜshai yung$^2$ fáiᵓ-ᶜtsz keᵓ. | That very easily learned, 15. Besides eat one bowl fish-fins not need use chop-sticks, 15. |

## CONVERSATION 48TH.—EXPORTS AND IMPORTS.—(*Continued.*)

| | |
|---|---|
| 24 I suppose a great deal of matting is sent to other countries. | 大概裝好多蓆去別國嘅、 |
| 25. Yes, there is, and straw as well. I have heard that foreigners take the straw for the purpose of making it into hats and bonnets. Is it so or not? | 係有、有草添呀、我聽聞西人攞嚟整帽、俾男女戴嘅、係唔係呢、 |
| 26. You are quite right; it is so. When I went to England this last time I went to a place where the straw is dyed into various colours, and made into hats and bonnets, according to the fashions of the time. Fashions differ at different times. | 冇錯係咯、我呢噸去英國、去到一處地方、在個嗰用各顏色嚟染草及整男女帽、照依時與所戴嘅、一時一時 (*or* 一時時) 時欵唔同樣嘅、 |
| 27. All goods that arrive in China in foreign ships have to pass through the Custom Houses. | 所有貨物在洋船裝嚟中國要經過海關嘅、 |
| 28. The Custom Houses, which attend to foreign vessels, have as head the Inspector General of Customs, who lives at Peking. | 個啲海關打理洋船嘅、有總稅務司管理、佢喺北京住嘅、 |
| 29. Each Custom House has a Commissioner of Customs, or Acting Commissioner, or Assistant in charge, and one, or two, Deputy Commissioners, besides Assistants of the first, second, third, or fourth classes, as well as Tide-surveyors, Assistant tide-surveyors, Examiners, and Tidewaiters, Linguists, and Chinese Clerks. | 每間海關有個稅務司、或署稅務司、抑或代理稅務司嘅、又有一個兩個副稅務司、另外有幫辦頭二三四等嘅、重有頭等總巡、二等總巡、驗貨嘅扦子手、通事、及書辦、 |

## CONVERSATION 18TH.—EXPORTS AND IMPORTS.—(*Continued.*)

| | | |
|---|---|---|
| 24. | Tái²-k'oi³* ꜀chong ᶜhò ꜀to tsek₂† höü˒ pít₀ kwok₀ ke˒. | Probably carry very much matting go other countries, 15. |
| 25. | Hai² ᶜyaú, ᶜyaú ᶜts'ò ꜀t'ím á˒. ᶜNgo ꜀t'eng†-man² ꜀Sai-꜀yan ᶜlo ꜀lai ᶜching mò⁵* ᶜpéi ꜀nám ᶜnöü tái˒ ke˒. Hai² ꜀m hai² ꜀ni ?² | Is have, have straw as-well, 2. I heard Western-people get-it-in-order-to make hats for men (and) women to-wear. 15. Is not is, eh ? 53. |
| 26. | ᶜMò ts'o˒ hai² lok₀. ᶜNgo ꜀ni chöng˒ höü˒ ꜀Ying-kwok₀, höü˒ tò˒ yat₂ ch'ü˒ téi²-꜀fong ; tsoi² ko˒ shü˒† yung² kok₀ ꜀ngán-shik₂ ꜀lai ᶜyim ᶜts'ò, k'ap₂ ᶜching ꜀nám ᶜnöü mò⁵*, chiú˒-꜀yí ꜀shí-꜀hing ᶜsho tái˒ ke˒. Yat₂ ꜀shí, yat₂ ꜀shí (*or* yat₂ ꜀shí* ꜀shí) ꜀shí-ᶜfún ꜀m ꜀t'ung yöng⁵* ke˒. | No mistake is, 32. I this time went England, went to one [C.] place ; at that place use every-kind-of colour to dye straw, and make men women's hats, according-to the-time-like what wear, 15. One time, one time, (*or* one time time) time-fashion not same fashion 15. |
| 27. | ᶜSho ᶜyaú fo˒-mat₂ tsoi² ꜀yöng ꜀shün ꜀chong ꜀lai ꜀Chung-kwok₀ yiú˒ ꜀king-kwo˒ ᶜhoi-꜀kwán ke˒. | Whatever have-of goods in foreign ships loaded come China must pass-through Customs. 15. |
| 28. | Ko˒-ti ᶜhoi-꜀kwán ᶜtá-ᶜléi ꜀yöng ꜀shün ke˒ (*or* ke³*). ᶜYaú ᶜTsung-Shöü˒-Mò²-꜀Sz ᶜkwún-ᶜléi. ᶜKöü ᶜhai Pak₂-꜀king chü˒ ke˒. | Those Customs attend-to foreign vessels. 15. Have Inspector-General rule-and-attend. He at Peking lives. 15. |
| 29. | ᶜMúi ꜀kán ᶜHoi-꜀kwán ᶜyaú ko˒ Shöü˒-Mò²-꜀Sz, wák₂ ᶜCh'ü Shöü˒-Mò²-꜀Sz, yik₂-wák₂ Toi²-ᶜléi-Shöü˒-Mò²-꜀Sz ke˒. Yau² ᶜyaú yat₂ ko˒, ᶜlöng ko˒, Fú˒-Shöü˒-Mò²-Sz, ling²-ngoi² ᶜyaú ꜀Pong-pán⁵*, ꜀t'aú, yí², ꜀sám, sz˒ ᶜtang ke˒. Chung² ᶜyaú ꜀T'aú-ᶜtang ᶜTsung-ᶜts'un*, Yí²-ᶜtang ᶜTsung-ᶜts'un*, Yim²-fo˒ ke˒, ꜀Ts'in ᶜTsz ᶜshaú, ꜀Tung-sz⁵*, k'ap₂ ꜀Shü-pán² (*or* Shü-pán⁵*). | Each [C.] Customs-house have [C.] Commissioner-of-Customs, or Acting Commissioner-of-Customs, or Assistant-in-charge. 15. Besides have one [C.], two [C.], Deputy-Commissioners, besides have Assistants, first, second, third, fourth classes. 15. Moreover have Tide-surveyors, Assistant Tide-surveyors, Examiners, Tidewaiters, Linguists, and Chinese clerks. |

## CONVERSATION 48TH.—EXPORTS AND IMPORTS.—(*Concluded.*)

30. These attend to all the business of the Customs House, collect duties and Transit duties (according to the Import and Export Tariffs) on dutiable goods, and let free goods pass. They examine the goods, ships' papers and manifests. They give Port Clearances, and Permits, to break bulk, to land, to ship, to repack, or Night Permits, and attend to many other things.

呢啲人打理海關所有嘅事幹、照依進口稅則、出口稅則、或收子口稅、內地稅、又免稅貨物、佢哋驗貨、又睇船牌、船口單、另外出紅牌、開艙准單、准到岸單、准落船單、改裝單、(*or* 改包)夜單、打理好多樣野添、

31. Then there are a great many persons carrying on the business of the Custom House.

噉、有好多人做咯、

32. Certainly.

定喇、

## CONVERSATION 49TH.—THE BAD FRIEND.

1. I did not wish to do it.

我都唔想做嘅、

2. Why did you?

做乜你做呢、

3. He told me to.

佢叫我做嘅、

4. If people tell you to do anything, must you do it?

人哋叫你做野、你是必要做嘅咩、

5. I do not say that; but he pressed me very hard.

唔係噉話嘅、但佢逼得我好緊嘕、

6. What did he say?

佢點話呢、

7. He said, could I not even lend him a few tens of dollars after such a long acquaintance?

佢話識得佢咁耐、都唔借得幾十文俾佢咩、

## CONVERSATION 48TH.—EXPORTS AND IMPORTS.—(*Concluded.*)

30. ꜀Ni-꜀ti ꜀yan ᶜtá-ᶜléí ᶜHoí-ₒkwán ᶜsho ᶜyaú-keˀ sz²-kònˀ, chiúˀ-꜀yí tsunˀ-ᶜhaú shöüˀ-tsakˏ, ch'utˏ-ᶜhaú shöüˀ-tsakˏ, wákˏ ꜀shaú ᶜtsz-ᶜhaú shöüˀ, noí²-téí² shöüˀ, yaú² ᶜmín shöüˀ foˀ-matˏ. ᶜK'öü-téí² yím² foˀ, yaú² ᶜt'ai ꜀shün ꜀p'ái, ꜀shün-ᶜhaú-ₒtán, ling²-ngoí² ch'utˏ ꜀hung-꜀p'ái, ꜀hoí-꜀ts'ong-ᶜchun-ₒtán, ᶜchun-toˀ-ngòn²-ₒtán, ᶜchun-lokˏ-꜀shün-ₒtán, ᶜkoí-꜀chong-ₒtán (*or* ᶜkoí ꜀paú), ye²-ₒtán, ᶜtá-ᶜléí ᶜhò ꜀to yöng² ᶜye ꜀t'ím. | These men attend-to Customs whatever have's business, according-to Import (and) Export tariffs, or receive Transit duties, Inland duties, moreover (pass) free (of) duties goods. They examine goods and further look-at ship's papers, and manifests, besides issue Port Clearances, Permits to break bulk, to land, to ship, to-change the-holdings (*or* change packages), night permits, attend very many kinds things also.

31. ᶜKòm, ᶜyaú ᶜhò ꜀to ꜀yan tsò² lok. | Then have very many men doing, 32.

32. Ting³* ꜀lá ² | Certainly, 21.

## CONVERSATION 49TH.—THE BAD FRIEND.

1. ᶜNgo ꜀tò ꜀m ᶜsöng tsò² keˀ. | I also not wish to-do, 15.

2. Tsò²-matˏ ᶜnéí tsò² ꜀ni ? ² | Why you do, eh ? 53.

3. ᶜK'öü kiúˀ ᶜngo tsò² keˀ. | He told me to-do, 15.

4. ꜀Yan-téí² kiúˀ ᶜnéí tsò² ᶜye, ᶜnéí ꜀shí-pitˏ yíuˀ tsò² keˀ ꜀me ? ² | Men tell you to-do things you certainly must do, eh ? 15, 39.

5. ꜀M hai² ᶜkòm wá² keˀ*: tán² ᶜk'öü pikˏ-takˏ ᶜngo ᶜhò ᶜkan káˀ. | Not do so say, 15, but he pressed me very urgently, 14.

6. ᶜK'öü ᶜtím wá² ꜀ni ? ² | He how say, eh ? 53.

7. ᶜK'öü wá² shikˏ-takˏ ᶜk'öü kòmˀ noí², ₒtò ꜀m tseˀ takˏ ᶜkéí shapˏ ₒman ᶜpéí ᶜk'öü ꜀me ? | He said know him so long, also not lend able several tens dollars give him, eh ? 39.

## CONVERSATION 49TH.—THE BAD FRIEND.—*(Continued.)*

| | | |
|---|---|---|
| 8. | Then you knew him a long time, and thought you could trust him. | 噉，你識得佢好耐、估信得佢過咯。 |
| 9. | Yes; that is just it. | 係、就噉呪。 |
| 10. | Did he have anything else to say? | 佢重有乜說話講冇呀。 |
| 11. | He had a great deal to say. | 有好多說話講嘅。 |
| 12. | Tell me what it was. | 講過我聽喇。 |
| 13. | How can I tell you all? He came to see me every day. | 點講得嗮呀。佢日日都嚟見我。 |
| 14. | Tell me something about it. | 講多少過我聽喇。 |
| 15. | He would say one day that business was dull; he had no (*or* very little) capital; if he had some, he could carry on a large business. | 今日又話生意淡，冇乜本、有啲本、可以做大盤生意。 |
| 16. | What would he say the next day? | 到聽日又點講呢。 |
| 17. | Business was not succeeding. He had no money to get on with. If he had no capital, how could he go on in business? | 生意不前．冇錢搵咯。冇本錢點做得生意吖。 |
| 18. | Then he said the same thing every day? | 日日又係噉講咯。 |
| 19. | Oh, no, he did not. | 又唔係。 |
| 20. | Why, it is about the same It is about the same with but little difference. | 都係咁上吓、差不多一樣呪。 |

## CONVERSATION 49TH.—THE BAD FRIEND.—(*Continued.*)

| | | |
|---|---|---|
| 8. | ʿKòm ˁnéi shikˎ-takˎ ˁk'öü ʿhò noí$^2$, ʿkwú sunˀ takˎ ˁk'öü kwoˀ lokˏ. | Then you knew-able him very long, thought trust able him over, 32. |
| 9. | Haí$^2$; tsaú$^2$ ʿkòm chekˎ. | Yes ; just so only, 7. |
| 10. | ˁK'öü chung$^2$ ˁyaú matˎ shütˏ-wá$^2$ ʿkong ˁmò áˀ? | He besides have what speech-words speak, not, eh? 2. |
| 11. | ˁYaú ʿhò ˏto shütˏ-wá$^2$ ʿkong keˀ. | Have very many words speak, 15. |
| 12. | ʿKong kwoˀ ˁngo ˏt'eng† ˏlá.$^2$ | Speak over me to-hear, 21. |
| 13. | ʿTím ʿkong takˎ sáiˀ áˀ? ˁK'öü yatˎ-yatˎ ˏtò ˏlai kínˀ ˁngo. | How speak able can all, eh? 2. He daily (*lit.* day day) also come see me. |
| 14. | ʿKong ˏto ʿshíú kwoˀ ˁngo ˏt'eng† ˏla.$^2$ | Speak more less for me to-hear, 21. |
| 15. | ˏKam-matˎ yaú$^2$ wá$^2$ ˏsháng-yíˀ támˀ; ˁmò matˎ ʿpún: ˁyaú ˏti ʿpún*, ʿho-ˁyí tsò$^2$ tái$^2$ ˏp'ún ˏsháng-yíˀ. | To-day moreover would-say business dull, not much (*or* any) capital; have some capital, could do large affair business. |
| 16. | Tòˀ ˏt'ing-yatˎ yaú$^2$ ʿtím ʿkong ˏni?$^2$ | Reach to-morrow again how speak, eh? 53. |
| 17. | ˏSháng-yíˀ patˎ ˏts'ín. ˁMò ˏts'ín* ˏlò lokˏ. ˁMò ʿpún-ˏts'ín, ʿtím tsò$^2$ takˎ ˏsháng-yíˀ ˏá?$^2$ | Business not advancing. No money to-handle, 32. No capital-money, how do can business, eh? 1. |
| 18. | Yatˎyatˎ yaú$^2$ haí$^2$ ʿkòm ˏkong lokˏ*? | Day (by) day also is so speak, 32? |
| 19. | Yaú$^2$ ˏm haí$^2$. | Again not is. |
| 20. | ˏTò haí$^2$ ʿkòm shöng$^2$-háˀ*. ˏCh'á-patˎ-ˏto yatˎ yöng$^2$ chekˎ. | Also is so about. Nearly one same only, 7. |

CONVERSATION 49TH.—THE BAD FRIEND.—(*Continued.*)

| | | |
|---|---|---|
| 21. | No, I have not told you all. | 唔係、我唔曾講嗮過你聽吖、 |
| 22. | What a long story. | 咁長篇嘅、 |
| 23. | You do not want to hear it then. | 噉你唔想聽咯、 |
| 24. | Yes, I do, go on. | 想呀、講喇、 |
| 25. | He came one day, and said that his accountant had embezzled a thousand dollars, which he had put by (laid by) to pay a debt. The accountant had absconded, and could not be found. His creditor was now in his shop waiting for payment, and would not be put off. There was no help for it. He would have to go to jail, and it was not his fault. What was he to do? It was very hard lines. As money matters were so pressing, he begged me to lend him a thousand dollars, and at the latest he would repay me in a month. He was receiving a remittance of three hundred dollars in two or three days' time, and a bill of exchange would be due in a fortnight. | 佢有一日嚟話、佢掌櫃虧空佢一千元、個千元佢係特登擠埋(*or* 擠定)嚟還一條債、個掌櫃走路去、搵佢唔倒、佢嚟見我個陣時、個債主坐定佢舖等攞銀、推遲佢都唔得、冇奈何咯、佢是必要坐監咯、又唔係佢過、點算好呢、好陰功咯、銀兩咁緊、佢求借住一千元過佢、至遲一個月還清㗎、遲兩三日有人附三百銀俾佢、又遲兩個禮拜有一張滙單到期嘅咯、 |
| 26. | Did you lend it to him? | 你有借俾佢冇呀、 |

## CONVERSATION 49TH.—THE BAD FRIEND.—*(Continued.)*

| | | |
|---|---|---|
| 21. | ꜁M hai²; ꜃ngo ꜁m ꜀ts'ang ꜂kong sái꜄ kwo꜄ ꜃néi ꜀t'eng† ꜀á.² | Not is; I not yet speak all for you to-hear, 1. |
| 22. | Kòm꜄ ꜁ch'öng ꜀p'in ke³*. | So long page, 15. |
| 23. | ꜂Kòm ꜃néi ꜁m ꜂söng ꜀t'eng† lok˳. | Then you not wish to-hear, 32. |
| 24. | ꜂Söng á꜄, ꜂kong ꜀lá.² | Wish, 3 speak, 21. |
| 25. | ꜃K'öü ꜃yaú yat꜆ yat꜇ ꜁laí wá² ꜃k'öü ꜂ch'öng-kwaí⁵* ꜀k'waí-꜀hung ꜃k'öü yat꜆ ꜀ts'in ꜁yün, ko꜄ ꜀ts'in ꜁yün ꜃k'öü hai² tak꜇-˳tang ꜀chai-꜁mái (*or* ꜀chai ting²) ꜁laí ꜁wán yat꜆ ꜁t'iú chái꜄, ko꜄ ꜂chong-kwaí⁵* ꜂tsaú-lò⁵*-höü꜄, ꜂wan ꜃k'öü ꜁m ꜂tò, ꜃k'öü ꜁laí kín꜄ ꜃ngo ko꜄ chan² ꜁shí (*or* ꜁shi*) ko꜄ chái꜄-꜂chü ꜃ts'o*† ting² ꜃k'öü p'ò꜄ ꜂tang ꜂lo ꜁ngan*, ꜀t'öü-꜁ch'í ꜃k'öü ꜄tò ꜁m tak꜆, ꜃mò noí²-꜁ho lok˳. ꜃K'öü ꜁shí-pit꜆ yiú꜄ ꜃ts'o*† ˳kám lok˳. Yaú² ꜁m hai² ꜃k'öü kwo꜄. ꜂Tím sün꜄ ꜂hò ꜀ni?² ꜂Hò ꜀yam-꜀kung lok˳. ꜁Ngan-꜂löng kòm꜄ ꜂kan, ꜃k'öü ꜁k'aú tse꜄-chü² yat꜆ ꜀ts'in ꜁yün kwo꜄ ꜃k'öü. Chí꜄ ꜁ch'í yat꜆ ko꜄ yüt꜇ ꜁wán ꜀ts'ing sái꜄. ꜁Ch'í ꜃löng ꜀sám yat꜇ ꜃yaú ꜁yan fú² ꜀sám pák꜆ ꜁ngan ꜂p'éi ꜃k'öü, yaú² ꜁ch'í ꜃löng ko꜄ ꜃laí-pái꜄ ꜃yaú yat꜆ ꜀chöng wúi²-˳tán tò꜄ ꜁k'éi ke꜄ lok˳. | He have one day come say his accountant embezzle him one thousand dollars. That thousand dollars he did on-purpose put-aside (*or* put-ready) in-order-to repay one item debt. That accountant ran-road-away, find him not reach. He come see me that period time, the creditor sat waiting-ready his shop wait get money. Put-off-later him also not able, no help-for-it, 3 2. He certainly must sit-in gaol, 32. Moreover not is his fault. What was-to-be-considered good, 32? Very infernal work, 32. Silver (being) so tight, he begged to-lend-for-a-while one thousand dollars to him. Most late one [C.] month repay completely all. Later-by two three days have man send three hundred dollars give him, again later-by two [C.] weeks have one [C.] bill-of-exchange reach date. 15, 32. |
| 26. | ꜃Néi ꜃yaú tse꜄ ꜂péi ꜃k'öü ꜃mò á꜄? | You have lent to him not, eh? 2. |

### CONVERSATION 49TH.—THE BAD FRIEND.—(*Continued.*)

| | |
|---|---|
| 27. I was ashamed to put him off again. I had to do it. I could not help but do it; so I lent it to him. | 又再推佢又見醜咯、不做不得、不得不做、所以借俾佢咯、 |
| 28. And how is it now? | 現時個啲事幹點呢、 |
| 29. Oh! I do not wish to say anything about it. That happened fully a year ago. He is not like what he was at all. If I stumble across him in the street, he acts as if he did not see me. | 唉、都唔想講咯、個啲事幹有成年咯、而家硬唔同舊時噉嘅、喺街上或碰親佢、佢作唔見人一樣、 |
| 30. Have you asked him for the money? | 問過佢攞銀唔曾、 |
| 31. I have, more than once; several times. The first time he said he had not any money; when he had, he would give it to me. Afterwards he put off from day to day. Then he put me off in one way and another; he said that he did not deny the debt, but asked for time to pay it in instalments. I was willing to give him time, but wished him to fix a time for payment. He said, as we were old friends, | 問咯、唔止一賬、問過佢數次咯、頭次問佢、佢就話現時冇、有就俾、後來又一日推一日、然後左推右推、又話唔係唔認、不過想同我攞時候、慢慢嘌(*or* 分)幾次還、我都肯俾時候佢、硬要佢限定幾時俾、佢話咁老朋友、 |

CONVERSATION 19TH.—THE BAD FRIEND.—(*Continued.*)

27. Yaú$^{2}$ tsoi' ꜀t'öü ᶜk'öü, yaú$^{2}$ kín' ch'aú' lok꜀. Pat' tsò$^{2}$ pat' tak' ; pat' tak' pat' tsò$^{2}$; ᶜsho-ᶜyí tse' ᶜpéí ᶜk'öü lok꜀.

Again further to-put-off him, again feel ashamed, 32. Not do not able; not able not to-do; therefore lend to him, 32.

28. Yín$^{2}$-꜀shí ko'-꜀ti sz$^{2}$-kòn' ᶜtím ꜀ni ?$^{2}$

At-present that business how, eh ? 53.

29. ꜀Ai ! (*or* ꜀aí) ꜀tò ꜀m ᶜsöng ᶜkong lok꜀. Ko'-꜀ti sz$^{2}$-kòn' ᶜyaú ꜀sheng† ꜀nín lok꜀. ꜀Yí-꜀kä ngáng$^{2}$ ꜀m ꜀t'ung kaú$^{2}$ ꜀shí * ᶜkòm ke'. ᶜHaí ꜀kái shöng$^{2}$ wák꜀ p'ung'-꜀ts'an ᶜk'öü, ᶜk'öü tsok꜀ ꜀m kín' ꜀yan yat' yöng$^{2}$.

Oh! also not wish speak, 32. That business have fully a-year, 32. Now only not same old time so, 15. In street on if knock-against him, he acts (as if) not see man one same.

30. Man$^{2}$-kwo' ᶜk'öü ᶜlo ꜀ngan* ꜀m ꜀ts'ang ?

Asked him to-get money not yet ?

31. Man$^{2}$ (*or* Man$^{5}$*) lok꜀, ꜀m ᶜchí yat' chöng'; man$^{2}$-kwo' ᶜk'öü shò' ts'z' lok꜀. ꜀T'aú ts'z' man$^{2}$ ᶜk'öü, ᶜk'öü tsaú$^{2}$ wá$^{2}$ yín$^{2}$-꜀shí ᶜmò, ᶜyaú, tsaú$^{2}$ ᶜpéí. Haú$^{2}$-꜀loi yaú$^{2}$ yat' yat' ꜀t'öü yat' yat'. Yín$^{2}$-haú$^{2}$ ᶜtso ꜀t'öü, yaú$^{2}$ ꜀t'öü; yaú$^{2}$ wá$^{2}$ ꜀m haí$^{2}$ ꜀m ying$^{2}$, pat'-kwo' ᶜsöng ꜀t'ung ᶜngo ᶜlo ꜀shí-haú$^{2}$, mán$^{2}$-mán$^{5}$* ꜀p'áng (*or* ꜀fan) ᶜkéí ts'z' ꜀wán. ᶜNgo ꜀tò ᶜhang ᶜpéí ꜀shí-haú$^{2}$ ᶜk'öü, ngáng$^{2}$ yiú' ᶜk'öü hán$^{2}$ ting$^{2}$ ᶜkéí ꜀shí*-ᶜpéí. ᶜK'öü wá$^{2}$ kòm' ᶜlò ꜀p'ang-

Asked 32, not only one time; asked-over him several times. 32. Head time asked him, he then said at-present none, have, then give. Afterwards from one day put-off (to) one day. After-that left put-off, right put-off; further said not is not acknowledge, only wish from me to-get time, by-and-by divide (*or* separate) several times repay. I also willing give time him, only want him limit certainly what time give. He said so old friends

## CONVERSATION 49TH.—THE BAD FRIEND—(*Concluded.*)

| | | |
|---|---|---|
| | why should we dispute about a few hundred dollars? He would give it me there and then if he only had it, but he had no means of livelihood. His place of business was closed. He would pay me off in full as soon as he had collected his debts. His father had assisted me; I need not be afraid of helping him a bit; and then he had the effrontery to ask me for the further loan of Five Dollars to go up to Canton to collect his debts. The last time I saw him, he said he did not know what I was talking about, that I owed him money—some scores of dollars, which he paid away on my behalf. Such a man as he is! | 使乜爭幾百銀、有、佢就個陣時、即刻俾咯、佢係冇世界、舖頭閂埋門咯、收債就還清數咯、佢老豆睇顧我、我幫吓佢到唔怕嘅、噉佢有咁大膽嚟問我借多五文、俾佢做水脚上城收賬、收尾個陣見佢、佢又話唔知我講乜野、我又爭佢銀啊、幾呀文啊、佢代我支啊、唉、噉嘅人嘅、 |
| 32. | He has no conscience. He is a bad man. What a creature! | 冇本心咯、唔好人咯、吩家伙咯、 |

## CONVERSATION 50TH THE COURTS.

| | | |
|---|---|---|
| 1. | I have been to the Hongkong Courts to-day to listen to the cases. | 我今日去香港衙門聽審案、 |
| 2. | Oh! Did you go to the Magistracy, or to the Supreme Court? | 呵、你去巡理府、抑或去按察司衙門呢、 |
| 3. | I went to both. I went in the forenoon to the Supreme Court; and in the afternoon I went for a short time to the Magistracy. | 兩間都去過咯、上晝我去按察司衙門、下晝我去巡理府一陣間(*or* 冇耐)、 |

## CONVERSATION 49TH.—THE BAD FRIEND (CONCLUDED.)

| | |
|---|---|
| ˢyaú ᶜshaí mat꜆ ꜀cháng ᶜkéi pák꜀ ꜁ngan? ˢYaú, ꜀k'öü tsaú$^2$ ᶜko chan$^2$ ꜁shí* tsik꜆-hak꜆ ᶜpéi lok꜆, tán$^2$-haí$^2$ ˢmò shaíˀ-káíˀ. Pòˀ-꜁t'aú* shán ꜀mái ꜁mún lok꜀. ꜀Shaú cháiˀ, tsaú$^2$ ꜀wán ꜀ts'ing shòˀ lok꜆. ˢK'öü ˢlò-tau$^2$ ᶜt'aí-kwüˀ ˢngo; ˢngo ꜀pong-ˢhá ˢk'öü ꜀tò ꜁m p'aˀ ke; ᶜkòm ˢk'öü ˢyaú kòmˀ tái$^2$ ᶜtám ꜀lai man$^2$ ˢngo tseˀ ꜀to ˢng꜆man, ᶜpéi ˢk'öü tsò$^2$ ᶜshöü-kök꜆ ˢshöng ꜁sheng*† ꜀shaú chöngˀ. ꜀Shaú-ᶜméi* koˀ chöngˀ kínˀ ˢk'öü, ˢk'öü yaú$^2$ wá$^2$ ꜁m ꜀chí ˢngo ᶜkong mat꜆ ˢye, ngo yaú$^2$ ꜀cháng ˢk'öü ꜁ngan* woˀ—ᶜkéi-á$^2$ ꜀man woˀ, ˢk'öü toí$^2$ ˢngo ꜀chí woˀ. ꜀Aí$^3$! ᶜkòm keˀ ꜁yan keˀ! | need why dispute several hundred of-money? Had, he then that period time immediately give, 32, but no means-of-livelihood. Shop shut to door, 32. Collect debts, then repay in-full accounts, 32. His father assisted me, I help-a-bit him also not fear, 15; then he had so great audacity to arrive- at asking me lend more five dollars give him to-be water-feet up-to city to-collect debts. Finally that time saw him, he further said not know I say what thing. I also owe him money, so-he-said—several-tens-of dollars, so-he-said, (which) he on-behalf-of me paid, so-he-said. Alas! such kind-of man, 15. |
| 32. ˢMò ᶜpún ꜀sam lok꜀. ˢM ᶜhò$^2$ ꜁yan lok꜀. ꜁Yaí ꜀ká-ᶜfo lok꜀. | No original heart, 32, Not good man, 32, Inferior article, 32. |

## CONVERSATION 50TH.—THE COURTS.

| | |
|---|---|
| 1. ˢNgo ꜀kam-mat꜆ höüˀ ꜀Höng-ᶜkong ꜁Ngá-꜁mún* ꜀t'eng† ᶜsham ònˀ. | I to-day go Hongkong Courts listen trying cases. |
| 2. ꜀O! ˢNéi höüˀ ꜀Ts'un-ˢléi-ᶜfú yik꜆-wák꜆ höüˀ Onˀ-ch'át꜆-sz ꜁Ngá-꜁mún* ꜀ni?$^3$ | Oh! You went Magistracy, or went Supreme (*lit.* Chief Justice's) Court, eh? 53. |
| 3. ˢLöng kán ꜀tò höüˀ-kwoˀ lok꜀. Shöng$^2$-chaúˀ ˢngo höüˀ Onˀ-ch'át꜀-sz ꜁Ngá-꜁mún*; há$^2$-chaúˀ ˢngo höüˀ ꜁Ts'un-ˢléi-ᶜfú yat꜆ chan$^2$ ꜀kán (*or* ˢmò noí$^2$*). | Two [C.] also went, 32. Forenoon I went Supreme Court; afternoon I went Magistracy a short time (*or* not long). |

## CONVERSATION 50TH.—THE COURTS.—(*Continued.*)

| | |
|---|---|
| 4. What cases were being tried? Were there many people in Court? People like to go in to hear the cases. | 審乜野事呢、堂中有好多人咩、人哋中意入去聽審事咯、 |
| 5. There were Criminal cases being tried in the Chief Court, and the Court was full. | 在大堂審犯案、堂中坐滿人呀、 |
| 6. If you wish to learn to speak Chinese well, the best thing you can do is to go every day to the Court and listen to the cases. | 你想學講好唐話、你至好日日去聽審案咯、 |
| 7. Yes, I think it would be; but I do not always have the time to go. I heard a number of new words to day, which I had never heard before. | 係、我估至好咯、但我唔係時時有得閒去、我今日都聽見好多新話頭、唔曾聽過嘅、 |
| 8. That is just it. If you are always in the habit of only speaking with a few people, you only get accustomed to the words which they use. There are a great many more words which you do not hear. | 就係噉咯、你若係時時不過同幾個人講說話、你獨係聽慣佢所使嘅話頭啫、重有好多話頭你唔曾聽過嘅、 |
| 9. I suppose from what you say that it is the case that some people are in the habit of using certain words, and others are in the habit of using other words; and to get a complete knowledge of the language, you must listen to many, and afterwards you will find it easy to understand. Is it not so? | 我因聽見你講斷估係噉咯、係點呢、即係有啲與講呢樣、有啲與講個樣、想曉嘥唐話、是必要聽好多人講、然後就易聽得出係唔係呢、 |

易學廣東話



CONVERSATION 50TH.—THE COURTS.—(Continued.)

| | |
|---|---|
| 4. ʿSham mat$_ˀ$-ˁye sz$^2$ ˏni? ˏT'ong ˏchung ˁyaú ʿhò ˏto ˏyan ˏme? ˏYan-téi$^2$ ˏchung-yí$^ˀ$ yap$_2$ höüʾ ˏt'eng† ʿsham-sz$^2$ lok$_o$. | Try what matters, eh? 53. Court centre [i.e. in Court) have very many people, eh? 39. People like in go listen try-cases, 32. |
| 5. Tsoi$^2$ Tái$^2$ ˏT'ong ʿsham fán$^2$-ònʾ (or fán$^3$*-ònʾ). ˏT'ong-ˏchung ˁts'o*† ˁmún ˏyan á. | In large Court try Criminal-cases. Court-centre sit full men, 2. |
| 6. ˁNéi ʿsöng hok$_2$ ʿkong ʿhò ˏT'ong-wá$^3$*, ˁnéi chíʾ-ʿhò yat$_2$-yat$_2$ höüʾ ˏt'eng† ʿsham ònʾ lok$_o$. | You wish learn talk good Chinese, you best day-by-day go hear try cases, 32. |
| 7. Hai$^2$, ˁngo ʿkwú chíʾ-ʿhò lok$_o$; tán$^2$ ˁngo ˏm hai$^2$ ˏshí-ˏshí ˁyaú tak$_ˀ$-ˏhán höüʾ. ˁNgo ˏkam-yat$_2$ $_o$tò ˏt'eng† kínʾ ʿhò ˏto ˏsan wá$^2$-ˏt'aú, ˏm ˏts'ang ˏt'eng† kwoʾ keʾ. | Yes, I think best, 32; but I not do all time (i.e. It is not, or it does not happen time after time, i.e. constantly) have leisure go. I to-day also hear perceive (i.e. by hearing, hear) very many new words, not yet heard over, 15. |
| 8. Tsaú$^2$ hai$^2$ ʿkòm lok$_o$. ˁNéi yök$_2$-hai$^2$ ˏshí-ˏshí pat$_ˀ$-kwoʾ ˏt'ung ʿkéi koʾ ˏyan ʿkong shüt$_o$-wá$^2$, ˁnéi túk$_2$-hai$^2$ $_o$t'eng† kwánʾ ˁköü ʿsho ʿshaí keʾ wá$^2$-ˏt'aú ˏche. Chung$^2$ ˁyaú ʿhó ˏto wá$^2$-ˏt'aú ˁnéi ˏm ˏts'ang ˏt'eng† kwoʾ keʾ. | Just is so, 32. You, if-do always only with several [C.] persons speak words, you only-do hear habitually (or i.e. accustomed to hear, or get familiar by hearing) they what use, 15, words only, 7. (i.e. these words which they use). Besides have very many words you not yet heard over, 15, |
| 9. ˁNgo ˏyan ˏt'eng†-kínʾ ˁnéi ʿkong, tünʾ-ʿkwú hai$^2$ ʿkòm lok$_c$. Hai$^2$ ʿtím ˏni? Tsik$_ˀ$ hai$^2$ ˁyaú $_o$ti ˏhing ʿkong ˏni yöng$^2$, ˁyaú $_o$ti ˏhing ʿkong koʾ yöng$^2$. ʿSöng ʿhiú saíʾ ˏT'ong wá$^3$*, ˏshí-pít$_ˀ$ yiúʾ ˏt'eng† ʿhò ˏto ˏyan ʿkong, ˏyín-haú$^2$ tsaú$^2$ yí$^2$ ˏt'eng† tak$_ˀ$ chut$_ˀ$, hai$^2$ ˏm hai$^2$ ˏni? | I because hear you say suppose it-is so, 32. Is how, eh? 53. Just is (what follows) have some habit-of (or like to speak) speaking this kind, have some habit-of speaking that kind. Wishing to-understand all Chinese words, certainly must hear very many men speak, afterwards then easy hear able out (this might be put, hearing able to get to hear what the words are) is not is, eh? 53. |

### CONVERSATION 50TH.—THE COURTS.—(*Continued.*)

| | | |
|---|---|---|
| 10. | I am afraid if people saw me constantly at the Courts, they would say this is a vagabond; he has nothing to do; so he is very lazy. | 我又慌人哋睇見我不歇到堂坐、佢就噲話呢個係爛仔咯、冇野做所以十分懶惰、 |
| 11. | Nonsense. If they see that you, Sir, are so respectable, how could they say you were a vagabond? There is no fear of that. Who would dare to say it? Besides if you, Sir, take some paper and a pencil with you, and if there are any words which you do not understand, put them down on the paper, and-ask your Chinese teacher what they mean, then you will understand them. | 嘆、見先生咁斯文家點叫得你做爛仔呢、唔怕嘅、邊個敢話呢、另外先生帶啲紙共筆落去、有乜話頭唔曉得嘅、俾筆上落紙噉嚟問唐先生點解就曉得咯、 |
| 12. | I put down some sentences this morning, and I intended to ask my Chinese teacher to explain the meaning to me. I am afraid I have lost the paper. I do not see it, or I would ask you to explain them. I cannot find it, though I have looked for it. | 我今朝都上住幾句、想問我唐先生解明個意思過我聽、我怕失咽個塊紙咯、唔見咯、唔係呢、我就要請你解咯、我揾嚟囉、又唔揾得翻、 |
| 13. | Well, if you will tell me all that was said, in exactly the same words that the persons used in giving their evidence, you might perhaps remember them again. | 噉、你硬照依今朝個啲人嘅口供而家一樣講出嚟俾我聽、噉就或者記起嚟唔定呀、 |

CONVERSATION 50TH.—THE COURTS.—(*Continued.*)

10. ᶜNgo yaú$^2$ ꜀fong ꜀yan-téí$^2$ ᶜt'ai kínˀ ᶜngo pat꜄-hít, tòˀ ꜀T'ong ᶜts'o*†, ᶜk'öü tsaú$^2$ ᶜwúi wá$^2$ ꜀ni-koˀ haí$^2$ lán$^3$*-ᶜtsaí lok꜀; ᶜmò ᶜye tsò$^2$, ᶜsho-ᶜyí shap꜄-꜀fan ᶜlán-to$^2$

I besides afraid people look see me without-ceasing arrive at Court sitting, they then will-be-able to-say this [C.] is vagabond, 32; nothing to-do, therefore ten-parts lazy.

11. ꜀Aí !$^2$ Kínˀ ꜀Sín-꜀sháng† kòmˀ ꜀sz-꜀man-꜀ká: ᶜtím kíúˀ tak꜄ ᶜnéi tsò$^2$ lán$^3$*-ᶜtsaí ꜀ni$^2$? ꜀M p'áˀ keˀ. ꜀Pín koˀ ᶜkòm wá$^2$ ꜀ni? Ling$^2$-ngoí$^2$ ꜀Sín-꜀sháng† taíˀ ꜀ti ᶜchí kung$^2$ pat꜄ lok꜄ höüˀ, ᶜyaú mat꜄ wá$^2$-꜀t'aú ꜀m ᶜhíú tak꜄ keˀ, ᶜpéi pat꜄ ᶜshöng-lok꜄ ᶜchí, ᶜkòm ꜀laí man$^2$ ꜀T'ong ꜀Sín-꜀sháng† ᶜtím ᶜkái, tsaú$^2$ ᶜhíú tak꜄ lok꜀.

Nonsense! See, Sir, so respectable; how call can you to-be vagabond, eh? 53. Not fear, 15. Who [C.] dare to-say, eh? 53, Besides, Sir, take some paper with pencil down go, have what words not understand able, 15, give pencil put-down paper, so come ask Chinese teacher how explain, then understand can, 32.

12. ᶜNgo ꜀kam-꜀chíú ꜀tò ᶜshöng-chü$^2$ ᶜkéí köüˀ, ᶜsöng man$^2$ ᶜngo ꜀T'ong ꜀Sín-꜀sháng† ᶜkái ꜀ming koˀ yíˀ-szˀ kwoˀ ᶜngo ꜀t'eng†. ᶜNgo p'áˀ shat꜄-ᶜcho koˀ fáiˀ ᶜchí lok꜀. ꜀M kín$^1$* lok꜀, ꜀m haí$^2$ ꜀ni, ᶜngo tsaú$^2$ yíúˀ ᶜts'eng† ᶜnéi ᶜkái lok꜀. ᶜNgo ᶜwan ꜀laí loˀ, yaú$^2$ ꜀m ᶜwan tak꜄ ꜀fán.

I this-morning also recorded several sentences, wishing to-ask my Chinese teacher explain clearly the meaning over to-me to-hear. I fear lost that piece paper, 32. Not see, 32, not is, 53, I then want invite you explain, 32. I looked come, 31, yet not find able back.

13. ᶜKòm, ᶜnéi ngáng$^2$ chíúˀ-꜀yí ꜀kam-꜀chíú koˀ-꜀ti ꜀yan* keˀ ᶜhaú-꜀kung ꜀yí-꜀ká yat꜄ yöng$^2$ ᶜkong ch'ut꜄ ꜀laí ᶜpéi ᶜngo ꜀t'eng†, ᶜkòm tsaú$^2$ wák꜄-ᶜche kéíˀ-ᶜhéí ꜀laí ꜀m ting$^2$ áˀ.

So, you just according-to this-morning those persons, 15, evidence now one same speak out come give me to-hear, so then perhaps remember-up come not certain, 2.

CONVERSATION 50TH.—THE COURTS.—(*Continued.*)

| | |
|---|---|
| 14. I am afraid I could not do that. How could I remember so much? Some of the things that were said were very unimportant. It would be of no use to repeat them. Some of them were obscene and indecent; and those I would not like to repeat. Ah! I will tell you what: I will give you a general statement of what happened, and that will do. | 我怕噉唔做得咯、點記得咁多呢、有啲說話好閒嘅啫、個啲冇用講翻出嚟嘅、有啲爛口、粗口、非禮說話、個啲我又唔想講翻出嚟、呀、我講過你聽吖、我大約講過你聽就做得咯、 |
| 15. Very good, go on. | 好喇、講喇、 |
| 16. Just as I went in they were trying a lad (who was dressed in a torn jacket and trousers, and barefooted) for stealing an old pair of trousers, which had been washed, and were hung up to dry on a bamboo pole. The wind blew them down into the street, and the thief, who was just passing at the time, picked them up and ran. The owner saw him and pursued him. Fortunately the thief met a constable, who stopped him, and took him up in arrest to the Central Police Station. | 我一筆入去個陣時、審緊一個後生仔、着爛衫褲、又脫脚、冇鞋着嘅呢、審佢因爲偷一條爛褲、個條褲係有人洗乾淨、噉就俾條竹篙晾起嚟晒乾、風吹落街、個賊啱啱經過去、執起嚟就走咯、失主見個賊執起、所以快啲追佢、好彩有個差人遇着個賊、截住佢、拉佢上大館、 |

CONVERSATION 50TH.—THE COURTS.—(*Continued.*)

14\. ᶝNgo pʻáᵓ ᶜkòm ꜁m tsò$^2$ takᵓ lok˳. ᶜTím kéiᵓ takᵓ kòmᵓ ꜀to ꜀ni?$^2$ ᶝYaú ˳ti shüt˳-wá$^2$ ᶜhò ꜁hán keᵓ ꜀che.$^2$ Koᵓ-˳ti ᶝmò yung$^2$ ᶜkong ꜀fán chʻutᵓ ꜁lai ke*. ᶝYaú ˳ti lán$^2$-ᶜhaú, ꜀tsʻò-ᶜhaú, ꜀féi-ᶝlai shüt˳-wá$^2$; koᵓ-˳ti ᶝngo yaú$^2$ ꜁m ᶜsöng ᶜkong ꜀fán chʻutᵓ ꜁lai. ꜁Á! ᶝngo ᶜkong kwoᵓ ᶝnéi ꜀tʻeng† ꜀á:$^2$ ᶝngo tái$^2$-yök˳* ᶜkong kwoᵓ ᶝnéi ꜀tʻeng,† tsaú$^2$ tsò$^2$ takᵓ lok˳.

I fear so not do can, 32. How remember able so much, eh? 53. Have some words very ordinary, 15, only, 7. Those no use speak back out come, 15. Have some broken-mouth, coarse-mouth, not-polite words; those I also not wish speak back out come. Ah! I speak to you to-hear, 1: I in-a-general-manner speak to you to-hear, then do can, 32.

15\. ᶜHò ꜀lá,$^2$ ᶜkong ꜀lá.$^2$

Well, 21, speak, 21.

16\. ᶝNgo yatᵓ patᵓ yap꜄ höüᵓ koᵓ chan$^2$ ꜁shí* ᶜsham-ᶜkan yatᵓ koᵓ haú$^2$-˳sháng†-ᶜtsai, chök˳ lán$^2$ ˳shám fúᵓ, yaú$^2$ tʻüt˳*-kök˳, ᶝmò ꜁hái chök˳ keᵓ ꜀ni. ᶜSham ᶝkʻöü ꜀yan-꜁wai ˳tʻaú yatᵓ ꜁tʻiú lán$^2$ fúᵓ; koᵓ ꜁tʻiú fúᵓ hai$^2$ ᶝyaú ꜁yan ᶜsai ꜀kòn-tseng$^2$†, ᶜkòm, tsaú$^2$ ᶜpéi ꜁tʻiú chukᵓ ꜀kò long$^2$ ᶜhéi, ꜁lai sháiᵓ ꜀kòn. ꜀Fung ꜀chʻöü lok꜄ ꜀kái (*or* ꜀kái), koᵓ tsʻák꜄ ꜀ngám (*or* ngám ꜀ngám ꜀king-kwoᵓ höüᵓ, chapᵓ ᶜhéi ꜁lai tsaú$^2$ ᶜtsaú lok˳. Shatᵓ-ᶜchü kínᵓ koᵓ tsʻák꜄ chapᵓ ᶜhéi ᶜsho-ᶝyí fáiᵓ-˳ti ꜀chöü ᶝkʻöü. ᶜHò-ᶜtsʻoi ᶝyaú koᵓ ꜀chʻái-꜁yan yü$^2$-chök꜄ koᵓ tsák꜄, tsít꜄-chü꜄ ᶝkʻöü, ꜀lái ᶝkʻöü ᶝshöngTái$^2$-ᶜkwún.

I one pencil (i.e. just) enter go that period time trying one [C.] young-lad wearing torn jacket, trousers, also take-off feet, no shoes wearing, 15, 53. Trying him because stealing one length torn trousers; That length (*English* pair) is have man wash clean, so then give piece bamboo pole hang-in-air up, in-order-to dry-in-the-sun dry. Wind blow down street, the thief just-just pass-by going, pick up come, then run, 32. Losing-owner see that thief pick up, so-therefore quickly follow him. Good-luck have a police-man meet the thief, stopped him, pull him up Great Station.

## CONVERSATION 50TH.—THE COURTS.—(*Continued.*)

| | | |
|---|---|---|
| 17. | After that there was a case of highway robbery. A woman going over the hills to Aberdeen; and several thieves robbed her of a pair of silver-gilt earrings with jadestone drops; and jadestone hairpins and bangles were all taken from her. Her husband, who was with her, was wounded by the robbers. | 審嗰件案之後又有一件打脚骨嘅、有一個女人喺山路去石排灣、有幾個賊搶佢一對鍍金耳環、連埋玉耳扣、玉簪、共鈪、一啲都搶晒佢嘅、丈夫都同埋佢行路去、個啲賊連埋佢都打傷咯、 |
| 18. | Did the prisoners not say anything? | 個啲犯冇說話講咩、 |
| 19. | They did. The thief, who stole the old trousers, said he had just come out of jail; that he had nothing to eat, and had no money; that he did not steal the trousers, but seeing them in the streets, he thought no one wanted them, and only picked them up, thinking he would pawn them to get money for his passage to the country, as he wished to go home to wait on his aged mother. He wanted to be an honest man, and he begged the Judge to have pity on him, and not send him to gaol, but banish him to his native place. | 有、偷爛褲個賊話自己正出監、冇飯食、又冇錢、佢話唔係偷個條褲、佢見個條褲喺街上、估冇人要嘅、不過執起嘅啫、想拎去當揾啲錢做水脚翻去歸鄉下、服事幾十歲嘅老母、想做好人啫、佢求大人開恩、唔好辦佢坐監、將佢解翻去原籍、 |

CONVERSATION 50TH.—THE COURTS.—(*Continued.*)

| | |
|---|---|
| 17. ʿSham ʿko kín² òn³ ꜀chí-haú² yaú² ʿyaú yat₃ kín² ʿtá-kök₀-kwat₃ ke³ (*or* ke³*). ʿYaú yat₃ ko³ ʿnöü-꜀yan* ʿhaí ꜀shán lò² höü³ Shek₂-꜀p'áí-₀wán; ʿyaú ʿkéí ko³ ts'ák₂ ʿts'öng ʿk'öü yat₃ töü³ tò²-₀kam ʿyí-꜀wán*, ꜀lín-꜀máí yuk₅* (*or* yuk₂) ʿyí-k'aú³*; yuk₂ ₀tsám, kung² ák₀₃*, yat₃ ₀ti ₀tò ʿts'öng sái³ ʿk'öü ke³. Chöng²-꜀fú ₀tò ꜀t'ung-꜀máí ʿk'öü ꜀háng lò² höü³, ko³-₀ti ts'ák₂ (*or* ts'ák₅*) ꜀lín-꜀máí ʿk'öü ₀tò ʿtá-꜀shöng lok₃. | Tried that [C.] case afterwards again have one [C.] strike-feet-bones, 15. There was one [C.] woman on mountain roads going Aberdeen; have several [C.] robbers robbed from-her one pair washed-with-gold-earrings, together-with jade (earring drops); jade hairpins, with bangles, one to-the-least (i.e., all) also snatched all hers, 15. Husband also with her walking road going. Those robbers including him also by-striking-wounded. 32. |
| 18. Ko³-₀ti fán⁵* ʿmò shüt₀-wá² ʿkong ꜀me?² | Those prisoners no words to-speak, eh? 39. |
| 19. ʿYaú. ꜀T'aú lán² fú³ ko³ ts'ák₂ wá², tsz²-ʿkéí ching³ ch'ut₃ ₀kám; ʿmò fán² shik₂, yaú² ʿmò ꜀ts'ín*, ʿk'öü wá² ꜀m haí² ꜀t'aú ko³ ꜀t'íú fú³, ʿk'öü kín³ ko³ ꜀t'íú fú³ ʿhaí ꜀káí shöng², ʿkwú ʿmò ꜀yau yíú³ ke³, pat₃-kwo³ chap₃ ʿhéí ke³ ꜀che, ʿsöng ꜀ning höü³ tong³, ʿwan ₀ti ꜀ts'ín* tsò² ʿshöü-kök₀ ꜀fán höü³ ꜀kwai꜀höng-há⁵*, fúk₂-sz² ʿkéí shap₂ söü³ ke³ ʿlò-ʿmò. ʿSöng tsò² ʿhò ꜀yan ʿwá, kʿʿöü ꜀k'aú Táí²-꜀yan ꜀hoi-꜀yan, ꜀m ʿhò pán² ʿk'öü ʿts'o*†-₀kám, ꜀tsöng ʿk'öü ʿkái-꜀fán höü³ ꜀yün-tsik₂. | Have. Stealing torn trousers that thief said, himself just out-of gaol; no rice to-eat, also no cash; he said not did steal that pair trousers, he saw that pair trousers in street on, thought no one wanted 15, only picked up, 15, 7, wished to-take away pawn, get (*lit.* find) some cash to-be water-feet back go home country-side, wait on several tens-of years, 15, mother. Wished to-become good man, he-said, 62. He begged His Lordship extend mercy, not good sentence him sit-in goal, to-deal-with him by-sending-back go native-place. |

## CONVERSATION 50TH.—THE COURTS.—(*Continued.*)

| | | |
|---|---|---|
| 20. | Were there many other cases? | 重有好多案件啩、 |
| 21. | I do not know. When I had heard so much, I went into the small court, where the Puisne Judge was trying debt cases. | 個啲我唔知咯、我聽咁多就入左堂、副臬司坐左堂審錢債案、 |
| 22. | What case was he trying? | 審乜野案呢、 |
| 23. | There was a case about a promissory note. The Plaintiff and his witness said that the Plaintiff was the managing partner in the Hop Shing stationer's shop; and that he lent nine hundred dollars with interest at the rate of one per cent, per mensem to the Defendant. | 有一件案為揭單嘅、原告同埋佢嘅証人噉話、原告係在合成紙料舖做司事人及做事頭、佢生銀俾被告、即係借九百元、利息一分[1]計嘅、 |
| 24. | They further said the money was paid over in the counting room of the Hop Shing shop; that they were all present and saw the money pass. Five hundred dollars of it was in silver (*or* Mexicans), the remainder was in four one hundred dollars bank notes. | 佢哋又話銀喺合成帳房交嘅、交銀個時各証人同埋在場見銀過手、五百元係白銀(*or* 鷹銀)、餘剩個啲係四張一百文張嘅銀紙、 |
| 25. | As soon as the dollars had been shroffed and weighed, and the notes counted, the Defendant with his accountant and shopman left. | 一睇過兌過銀、一數過銀紙被告共埋佢嘅掌櫃管店就扯咯、 |

Note 1.—The rate of interest being so commonly reckoned by the mouth in ordinary conversation the chances are that it will be taken as understood that *per mensem* is meant.

## CONVERSATION 50TH.—THE COURTS.—(*Continued.*)

| | | |
|---|---|---|
| 20. | Chung꜅ ꜃yan ꜂hò ꜀to òn꜄-kin$^{5}$* kwa꜄? | Besides have very many cases I-suppose? 18. |
| 21. | Ko꜄-꜀ti ꜃ngo ꜁m ꜀chi lok꜆. ꜃Ngo ꜀t'eng† kòm꜄ ꜁to tsaú꜅ yap꜇ ꜂Tso ꜁T'ong, Fa꜄-Yip꜇ (*or* Yit꜇) ꜀Sz ꜃ts'ò*†. ꜂Tso ꜁T'ong ꜂sham ꜁ts'am-chai꜄-òn꜄. | That I not know, 32. I heard so much then enter Left Court, Puisne Judge sitting Left Court trying Summary Cases. |
| 22. | ꜂Sham mat꜆-꜃ye òn꜄ ꜀ni? | Trying what cases, eh? 53. |
| 23. | ꜃Yaú yat꜆ ko꜅ òn꜄ wai꜅ k'it-tán ke꜄. ꜁Yün-kò꜄ ꜁t'ung-꜁mai ꜃k'öü-ke꜄ ching꜄-꜁yan ꜂kòm wa꜅. ꜁Yün-kò꜄ hai꜅ tsoi꜅ Hòp꜇-꜁Shing* ꜂Chí-lín$^{5}$* p'ò$^{1}$* tsò꜅ ꜀sz-sz꜅ ꜁yan k'áp꜇ tsò꜅ sz꜅ ꜁taú*. ꜃K'öü ꜀shàng† ꜁ngan* ꜂péi pei꜅-kò꜄, tsik꜆-hai꜅ tse꜄ ꜂kaú pák˳ ꜁yün, léi꜅-sik꜆ yat꜆ ꜀fan kai꜄ ke꜄. | Have one [C.] case on-account-of Promissory Note, 15. Plaintiff together-with his witnesses so said. Plaintiff is in Hop-Shing, Stationer's shop, being manager and is master. He lent-on-interest money to Defendant, that-is lent nine hundred dollars, interest, one candareen (i.e. one candareen to the tael, and as there are one hundred candareens to the tael that is equivalent to 1 °/o.) calculated, 15. |
| 24. | ꜃K'öü-téi꜅ yaú꜅ wá꜅ ꜁ngan* ꜂hai Hòp꜇-꜁Shing (*or* Hòp꜇-꜁Shing*) chöng꜄-꜁fong* ꜀kaú ke꜄. ꜀Kaú ꜁ngan* ko꜄ ꜁shí (*or* ꜁shi*) ꜁t'ung-꜁mái kok˳ ching꜄-꜁yan tsoi꜅-꜁ch'öng, kín꜄ ꜁ngan* kwo꜄ ꜂shaú. ꜃Ng pák˳ ꜁yün hai꜅ pák꜇ ꜁ngan* (*or* ˳ying ꜁ngan*). ꜁Yü-shing꜅ ko꜄-˳ti hai꜅ sz꜄ ꜀chöng yat꜆ pák˳ ˳man ꜀chöng ke꜄ ꜁ngan-꜂chí. | They also said money at Hop-Shing counting-room handed-over, 15. Hand money that time together-with all witnesses present, saw money pass hand. Five hundred dollars was white money (i.e. silver) (or eagle money). Balance that was four [C.] one hundred dollars each [C.], 15, money-paper (i.e. notes.) |
| 25. | Yat꜆ ꜂t'ai kwo꜄, töü꜄ kwo꜄ ꜁ngan*, yat꜆ ꜂shò kwo꜄ ꜁ngan-꜂chí, péi꜅-kò꜄ kung꜅-꜁mái ꜃k'öü-ke꜄ ꜂chöng-kwai$^{5}$*, ꜂kwún-tím$^{1}$* tsaú꜅ ꜂ch'e lok˳. | One look over, weigh over money, one count over money-paper, Defendant together-with his accountant, shop-coolie, then left, 32. |

CONVERSATION 50TH.—THE COURTS.—(*Continued.*)

| | |
|---|---|
| 26. But what about the note? | 個張揭單呢。 |
| 27. Oh! I forgot all about the note. They said that, on account of the Plaintiff and Defendant having been good friends and having known each other for many years, and having had many dealings together, no note was made out at the time; but afterwards, as the money was not repaid at due date, that is when the six months were up, the Defendant wrote out the promissory note. | 啊、我噉都唔記得個張揭單咯、佢哋話因爲兩頭原告被告舊時做好朋友、又相識好多年、兩家又好耐交手、所以個陣時冇寫揭單、但係後來到期個時、卽係六個月期滿咯、又冇還銀、所以被告寫個張揭單、 |
| 28. What did the Defendant say? Did he defend the case, or did he admit the debt and only want time to repay in instalments? | 被告點講呢、有得駁冇、抑或認係欠銀、想要攤開分幾次還呢、 |
| 29. Oh! the Defendant denied it altogether. He denied everything; he said he did not write the note, or execute it, that he did not know the Plaintiff, and that he had never seen him before; but I did not hear the Defendant's side of the case. I went up to the Magistracy. | 唉、被告硬唔認嘅、樣樣都唔認、又話佢冇寫單、又冇簽名、又話佢唔識原告、噉都唔曾見過佢添、但我冇聽審被告個頭、我就上去巡理府咯、 |

## CONVERSATION 50TH.—THE COURTS.—(*Continued.*)

| | |
|---|---|
| 26. Koᵓ ꜀chöng k'it - ꜀tán ꜀ni ?[2] | That [C.] promissory note eh ? 53. |
| 27. ꜀O ! ᶜngo hàm[2] ꜀tò ꜀m kéiᵓ-tak꜇ koᵓ ꜀chöng k'it꜇- tán lok . ᶜK'öü-téi[2] wà[2] ꜀yan-wai[2] ᶜlöng ꜀t'aù ꜀yün-koᵓ péi[2]-koᵓ kaù[2]-꜀shí* tsòᵓ ᶜhò ꜀p'ang-ᶜyaù, yaù[2] ꜀söng-shik꜇ ᶜhò ꜀to ꜀nin, ᶜlöng-꜀ká yaù[2] ᶜhò noi[2] ꜀kaù-ᶜshaú; ᶜsho-ᶜyi koᵓ chan[2] ꜀shí* ᶜmò ᶜse k'it - tán: tàn[2]-hai[2] haù[2]-꜀loí tòᵓ ꜀k'éi koᵓ ꜀shi, tsik꜇-hai[2] luk꜇ koᵓ yüt꜇ ꜀k'éi ᶜmúún lok꜇, yaù[2] ᶜmò ꜀wán ꜀ngan*, ᶜsho-ᶜyí péi[2]-koᵓ ᶜse koᵓ ꜀chöng ꜀tán lok꜇. | Oh ! I altogether also not remember that [C.] promissory note, 32. They said because both sides, Plaintiff, Defendant, old time were good friends, also mutually-acquainted great many years, two parties also very long dealt-together; therefore that period time not write promissory-note; but afterwards arrived-at date (when payment should have been made) that time, just-is six [C.] months date full 32, yet not repay money, therefore Defendant write that [C.] note, 32. |
| 28. Péi[2]-koᵓ ᶜtim ᶜkong ꜀ni ?[2] ᶜYaù tak꜇ pok ᶜmò, yik꜇-wák꜇ ying[2] hai[2] hímᵓ ꜀ngan*, ᶜsöng yíùᵓ ꜀t'án ꜀hoi, ꜀fán ᶜkéi ts'zᵓ ꜀wán ꜀ni ?[2] | Defendant how say, eh ? 53. Have can defend not, or admit does owe money, wishing want spread out, divided several times repay, eh ? 53. |
| 29. ꜀Ai ![2] Péi[2]-koᵓ ngáng[2] ꜀m ying[2] keᵓ. Yöng[2]-yöng[2] (*or* yöng[2]-yöng[5]*) ꜀tò ꜀m ying[2]; yaù[2] wà[2] ᶜk'öü ᶜmò ᶜse ꜀tán, yaù[2] ᶜmò ꜀ts'im ꜀meng*†, yaù[2] wà[2] ᶜk'öü ꜀m shik꜇ ꜀yün-koᵓ, hàm[2] ꜀tò ꜀m ꜀ts'ang kinᵓ kwoᵓ ᶜk'öü ꜀t'im; tàn[2] ᶜngo ᶜmò ꜀t'eng† ᶜsham péi[2]-koᵓ koᵓ ꜀t'aú. ᶜNgo tsaù[2] ᶜshöng höüᵓ ꜀Ts'un-ᶜLéi-ᶜFú lok꜇. | Why ! Defendant just-only not admit; 15. Everything also not admit; also he-said he not write note, again not sign name, again say he not acquainted-with Plaintiff, altogether also not yet seen over him besides; but I not hear try Defendant's that side. I then up went Magistracy, 32. |

海上絲綢之路文獻集成 科技與文化編

CONVERSATION 50TH.—THE COURTS.—(*Concluded.*)

| | |
|---|---|
| 30. There, there were a number of small cases. | 巡理府有好多小案， |
| 31. What were they? | 乜野案呢， |
| 32. Firing crackers, obstructing the road. There were no important cases, so I did not stay. | 燒爆仗，阻攔路口，冇大案件，所以我冇等咯， |

## CONVERSATION 50TH.—THE COURTS.—(*Concluded.*)

| | |
|---|---|
| 30. ꜁Ts'ün-꜃Léi-꜂Fú ꜃yaú ꜂hò ꜀to ꜂síú òn꜄. | Magistracy have very many small cases. |
| 31. Mat꜆ ꜃ye òn꜄ ꜀ni?$^2$ | What thing cases, eh? 53. |
| 32. ꜀Shíú p'áú꜄-tsöng$^5$*, ꜂cho-꜁lán lò$^2$ ꜂haú. ꜃Mò táí$^2$ òn꜄-kín$^5$*, ꜂sho-꜃yí ꜃ngo ꜃mò ꜂tang lok꜆. | Burn fire-crackers, obstruct road mouth. No great cases, therefore I not wait. |

国家出版基金项目
NATIONAL PUBLICATION FOUNDATION

# 海上絲綢之路文獻集成

總主編　陳支平　陳春聲

## 科技與文化編 98

主編　王揚宗　葉　農

海峽出版發行集團
THE STRAITS PUBLISHING & DISTRIBUTING GROUP
福建人民出版社

# 本册目次

# 拾級大成

（*Easy Lessons in Chinese or Progressive Exercises to Facilitate the Study of That Language, Especially Adapted to the Canton Dialect*）

〔美〕衛三畏（Samuel Wells Williams）編

《拾級大成》，美國衛三畏編。衛三畏（Samuel Wells Williams，一八一二—一八八四），美國公理會傳教士。生於美國由提卡，一八三三年受派至廣州負責印刷事宜，一八七七年任耶魯大學漢學教授，係美國首位漢學教授。曾編輯《中國叢報》，著有《中國總論》、《中國地志》等。此書以漢學、會話、閲讀及翻譯等統攝全書，分十章，含字部、字根、讀與寫、閲讀、會話練習、文選閲讀、量詞、漢譯英練習、英譯漢練習、篇章讀譯等，涉及聽説讀寫各項。據一八四二年澳門版影印。

道光辛丑年鐫

咪唎堅衛三畏鑒定

# 拾級大成

香山書院梓行

# EASY LESSONS IN CHINESE:

OR

## PROGRESSIVE EXERCISES

TO FACILITATE THE STUDY OF THAT LANGUAGE,

ESPECIALLY ADAPTED TO THE CANTON DIALECT.

*By S. Wells Williams.*

MACAO:

PRINTED AT THE OFFICE OF THE CHINESE REPOSITORY.

1842.

TO

D. W. C. OLYPHANT, Esq.,

OF NEW-YORK, U. S. A.

THE STEADY AND MUNIFICENT FRIEND

OF ALL EFFORTS FOR THE GOOD OF CHINA,

THIS VOLUME IS MOST RESPECTFULLY INSCRIBED

# PREFACE.

THE design of this volume is to provide a book suitable to be put into the hands of persons commencing the study of the Chinese language, not only in China itself but abroad; to be a work which can be advantageously used by the foreigner in his own country, or on his voyage hitherwards, as well as after his arrival among the people. It is introductory to larger works, yet has somewhat of completeness within itself; for while some of the lessons will require no aid from other books in order to understand them fully, for those in the two last chapters the student will probably need the help of a teacher or a dictionary to learn all their meaning. But if he has learned the previous lessons as thoroughly as he ought, he will no doubt be gratified with the degree of facility with which he can read them, and feel that he has made some progress in acquiring the language.

The first four chapters, with the VIth, VIIIth, and IXth, are as applicable to the study of any other dialect as to that of the Canton, as they contain little or nothing local or provincial. The remarks in the first three chapters should be carefully read, and it will probably be found by experience that the best way to commence learning characters will be to begin with the radicals, and make them as familiar as an alphabet is made in other languages. Their universal use in the composition of characters, their influence upon the general meaning of words, and the use made of them in arranging the imperial dictionary of Kánghí, together with the aid they afford in remembering the component parts of characters, are all strong reasons for taking them up at first. The various points briefly touched upon in the second and third chapters, regarding the construction of characters, and the rules for reading and writing Chinese, are it is hoped explained with sufficient clearness to serve the purposes of the beginner, and enable him profitably to read what other authors have said more at large upon the same subjects. Mr. Callery's Systema Phoneticum Scripturæ Sinicæ, referred to on page 47, contains nearly fourteen friend of man will rejoice to see so mighty and so ancient a race as the sons of Hán about to be made acquainted with the arts, the improvements in social life, and the knowledge of the West, together with that greatest gift, the fountain-head of all other excellencies, the religion and the hopes of the Bible. To the advancement of all these objects, and the extension of every measure to promote an honorable and Christian intercourse, is this volume contributed.

S. W. W.

# CONTENTS.

## Chapter V.

### EXERCISES IN CONVERSATION.



## Chapter VI.

### SELECTIONS FOR READING.



## Chapter VII.

### THE CLASSIFIERS.

拾級大成



## Chapter VIII.

### EXERCISES IN TRANSLATING.

## Chapter IX.

## EXERCISES IN TRANSLATING INTO CHINESE.



## Chapter X.

## LESSONS IN READING AND TRANSLATING.

(With an English Version.)



(Without an English Version.)

拾級大成

# EASY LESSONS, &c.

## Chapter First.

## OF THE RADICALS.

When commencing the study of the Chinese language, the scholar is liable to become discouraged at the apparent vastness of the work before him. He is perhaps presented with a native book containing page after page of complicated characters, which he is told must all be learned; and to not one of which is there the least clue to the sound. He attempts to write a few, and finds the labor of remembering the shape and arrangement of so many unmeaning strokes very irksome; and if, after a short interval of rest, he should endeavor to rewrite them and find himself unable to recall them, he is still more cast down. If too, after hearing them a few times, he tries to remember the sound and sense of the characters he has set himself to learn, and they too are for the most part as if he had never heard them, he is almost ready to give up his enterprise. A series of efforts somewhat like this, where the mind feels that the progress made does not equal the labor bestowed, has resulted, there can be no doubt, in more instances than one, in entire abandonment of the study, either in disgust at its insipidity, or from weakness of mind to grapple with so many things at once, ensuent upon the discouragement of repeated ill success. Now, although the Chinese language is indeed a long and hard lesson for a foreigner to learn, there is no need of making it harder than necessary by attempting to overcome all its difficulties at once. Let the scholar be content to proceed slowly at first, devoting his mind to one thing only at once, and carefully avoiding so long an application to that as to weary himself, and his progress will soon afford him satisfaction, and he be thereby encouraged to proceed. It is important, moreover, that the energy with which he commences the study of the language be directed in the most profitable paths, and that the satisfaction which is derived from mastering difficulties be one of the most encouraging reasons for proceeding in the study.

The principal labor at the commencement should be applied to learning how to write characters, both because the sense and sound are more easily remembered when the form is known, and because they attach themselves, as it were, to the character in the memory. It is not meant that the meaning should be entirely neglected, but let the form and arrangement of the strokes at first be principally attended to. There are two or three ways of learning the characters, each of which has its advantages. Chinese lads, who have spoken the language from infancy, when first sent to school, need only to learn the characters, and associate them with sounds that are already familiar. This is the plan pursued in native schools, and the tyro's daily task for the first year or two is to learn to recite and copy memoriter the books he is afterwards to learn the meaning of—a piece of drudgery which, whatever disadvantages may attend it, certainly fixes the characters very firmly in the memory. To enable the lad to acquire a good hand while learning the characters, the books he is to commit to memory are often prepared as copy-books, by printing them in white letters on a black ground, and both are learned and imitated by writing upon them through thin paper. This mode is recommended to the student for practice at first, either by having copies containing known characters written out in a large size, or by using one of these copy-slip books. After the mode of combining the characters is pretty well understood, let them be written from observation, and then from memory, always endeavoring while thus writing them to make a well proportioned character.

Another mode of learning words is to become familiar with them by constantly reading them, and seldom writing them. This is by no means a good plan at the beginning, and if the scholar trusts to mere inspection for his knowledge of characters, he will find himself continually confounding them, or else writing them so erroneously as to be unreadable. His knowledge will be more like that of an acquaintance than that of a friend, and he will constantly be obliged to turn to a dictionary to ascertain how the word he wishes is written. After a large number of characters are very familiar, the mind will readily remember the composition and form of new ones, as soon as it knows their sound and meaning, but at first this mode must not be relied on.

Another mode of learning the characters is by studying their component parts, and remembering the word by remembering the elements which compose it. This mode does not appear to be practiced by the Chinese, for they seem to recollect characters as a whole, but it is probably the easiest way of learning them, the way in fact in which every foreigner would most naturally learn them. It may be called the *orthography* of the language, and combines something of both the preceding modes. To reap the benefits of it, the elements of the characters must be made familiar, and the rules (if there are any) according to which they are formed into characters.

Chinese literati have sometimes arranged their dictionaries according to the sounds of the characters, which premises that the scholar already knows a great number, and sometimes according to their composition.

The *Luk Shü Tung*, a dictionary containing the various forms of characters ancient and modern, is arranged in the first way, and so also is the *Fan Wan*, a local vocabulary used by the people of Canton. They have also employed a number of elements, according to which all the characters containing that element or radical are placed together whatever be their sound or sense. The number of the elements chosen as keys of groups have not been the same at all times. The *Shüt Man*, a dictionary somewhat like the *Luk Shü Tung*, containing old forms of characters, has the words arranged under 540 heads or radicals. The compilers of the Imperial Dictionary of Kánghí, the one now in general use, arranged the language under 214 radicals or elements, which gives an average in the whole of little more than 200 characters under each; but it will be seen from the figures in the list hereto subjoined, that the number under each differs very much. It is recommended to the student to learn these radicals in their order, so as to be able to write them memoriter, and repeat their names and meaning. They need not be learned so as to recollect them by their number, but only according to their order, so as to facilitate finding any given character in the dictionary.

These 214 radicals, keys, clefs, or formatives, as they have been called by different authors, are nearly all of them words in common use, and the time bestowed upon learning them therefore, is by no means lost; a familiar acquaintance with them will often materially assist in remembering the meaning of words in which they occur, especially in natural groups of which they are the radical.

The first sum of the figures placed after the meaning of the radical, is the number of characters under that radical in Kánghí's Dictionary, including all the old and synonymous forms, the unusual characters, and those in common use. The second sum denotes the number of characters under the radical in common use, according to a very laborious examination of the Classics and History of the Three States, made by Mr. Dyer of Malacca. The number under some radicals is of course much smaller than it would have been had other books been chosen, but it is probably a pretty fair estimate of the number of different characters the scholar will meet in reading Chinese books. Thus, if a medical book had been examined, more characters under *nik*, disease (No. 104), would have been found; if the *Pún Tsò*, or Chinese Herbal, had been looked over, the variety under *muk*, a tree (No. 75), or *tsò*, herbs (No. 140), or under the zoölogical radicals, would have been doubled. The letter C. placed after some of the radicals, indicates that they are seldom if ever used by themselves; when placed before the small characters, it shows that those are the contracted forms used in composition.

It would appear from a general survey of the characters of the language that when the compilers of the Imperial Dictionary began to arrange them, the problem they endeavored to solve was to select such characters for keys or indices as should be easily recognized, while they also had an eye to somewhat of a natural arrangement in the groups; it was important, too, not to make the system cumbersome by having too many keys. The majority were easily assorted, but there would still be many left, that, being too unimportant to elevate to the rank of keys, must be arranged by some one of their constituent parts. So far as connection in meaning with other words went, one part might as well be taken as another; but the most prominent part of the character would naturally be first chosen. When a radical, therefore, is said to enter into combination, it means that it forms a constituent part of the character, that it is not added on; and if taken away will either leave a mutilated character, or, if perfect, the remainder will have no connection withe the meaning of the whole word. Thus *sz'* 事 is placed under *küt*, 亅 (No. 6), and that radical enters into combination with it, for if a'ken away, the remainder is not a character; so with others.

---

## List of the Tsz' Pò, 字部 or 214 Radicals,

*With their Sounds and Signification, and contracted forms; together with general remarks upon the characteristics of the words under each, and the place of the radical.*

### CHARACTERS FORMED BY ONE STROKE.

1 一 *Yat.* One, the same, similar; to make as one, to reduce to one state. 44.—16.

No uniformity of signification can be traced in the characters comprised under this radical, nor is its position uniform; this is also the case with the next seven groups. As is the case under some other radicals, such words appear to have been collected together here, as could not well be referred elsewhere; most of them are primitives.

2 丨 *Kwan.* C. To descend perpendicularly, straight; sign of the repetition of a preceding word. 22.—2.

*Kwan* passes through the middle of the other strokes in most of the characters placed under it.

3 丶 *Chü.* C. A point, a flame; a lord, headman, chief. 11.—2.

*Chü* is placed in some prominent part of the character, in the middle, or on the top.

4 丿 *Pit.* C. A left stroke, curved to the left. 24.—8.

The radical is usually placed at the top, but is so combined with the other strokes as to form a component part of the character; all the common ones are primitives.

5 乙 *Üt.* C. Curved, to mark with a crooked line; to supply; a horary character. 42.—8.

This radical is placed on the right side, very much straightened, so as to appear like a hook; in a few characters it is in the middle.

6 亅 *Küt.* C. A barb; to draw or hook up. 20.—3.

*Küt* usually passes through the middle.

FORMED BY TWO STROKES.

7 二 *I'*. Two, second, both, repetition; to divide. 31.—9.

The two strokes of the radical inclose the others in many instances; it is also found on the top, bottom and left side.

8 亠 *Tau.* C. Undefined, though some say it means the edge of a thing or place. 39.—10.

*Tau* is always placed at top, and no single radical is found below it, by which the words under it will be recognized; most of them are primitives, or old forms, and the part was selected, and made into a radical, it is said, for the purpose of grouping them.

9 人 C. 亻 *Yan.* Man, a man, a male, mankind. 800.—141.

This group, with the exception of a few primitives, is a pretty natural one; the actions, social relations, names, positions, powers, &c., of man, being the leading ideas. It is usually placed on the left in the contracted form, but in some is written astride: it is called, when describing it as a radical, 企人邊 *kí yan pín.*

10 儿 *Yan.* C. Man, a man walking; the same as the preceding. 52.—14.

This radical is always placed underneath; it is distinguished from *kí*, a stool (No. 16), by the separation of the two strokes, but characters placed here are not readily recognized, the upper part being sometimes another radical, or else *yan* combines with it.

11 入 *Yap.* To enter, to pass in, to commence; entering. 29.—5.

*Yap* is distinguished from *yan*, a man, by the right stroke overlapping the left; it is usually placed on the top, but in a few common ones, in the middle. There is no similarity of meaning among the characters under it.

12 八 *Pát.* Eight, back to back, to sèparate. 45.—12.

*Pát* is placed above or below, and looks like two diverging dots. Some practice is required to recognize the words.

13 冂 *Kwang.* C. Desert, a distant boundary. 51.—5.

Many of the characters under this radical are written with 月 *mò* on the top, which renders them difficult to be distinguished from *yat*, day (No. 72); as 杲 *chau* and 杲 *kò*; 晟 *shing* and 晟 *shing*.

14 冖 *Mít.* C. To cover or overspread, to cover, as with a napkin. 31.—2.

*Mít* lays upon the other strokes, without inclosing them as *kwang* does. There is a little uniformity of meaning among the characters, but hardly enough to render the group natural.

15 冫 *Ping*. C. An icicle, water freezing. 55.—16.

*Ping* is written on the left in almost all cases; as a radical it is called *léung tím shui*, 兩點水 double dotted water, and several words are interchanged with that radical; the characters all refer to ice, cold, wintry, freezing, severe, &c.

16 几 *Kí*. C. A bench, a stool, a stand; steady, tranquil. 40.—4.

In about half, *kí* incloses the other strokes; in the remainder, it is placed on the right or beneath. Most of the words are old forms.

17 凵 *Hóm*. C. A hollow receiver, a cavern, a receptacle. 24.—3.

Here the radical incloses and supports the other strokes, in this respect being opposite to No. 13; it, however, conveys little or nothing of its own meaning to them.

18 刀 C. 刂 *Tò*. A sword, a knife, a cutting or dividing instrument; to cut. 378.—33.

This radical, in its contracted form, occurs on the right side, and the characters have some reference in their senses to cutting, severity, scraping, dividing, &c.

19 力 *Lik*. Strength, sinewy, firm; to use force. 163.—19.

This is also placed on the right side, but without any contraction; ideas of laboring, examining, fatiguing, robust, &c., are general features of the group.

20 勹 *Páu*. C. A bundle. To envelop, to roll or pack up; to bundle. 66.—4.

This radical either completely incloses the right side and all the top of the character, or else only half of the top, thus enveloping it. There is a slight allusion to it in the meaning of many of the words.

21 匕 *Pí*. C. A ladle, a spoon; to arrange spoons. 20.—2.

The few characters grouped under *pi* have it placed in all parts of the word, and their meanings are as diverse as its position.

22 匚 *Fóng*. C. A square receiving vessel, a chest. 65.—4.

The radical incloses the strokes as if opening like a sliding chest or drawer, into which things can be shoved, which appears to be its prime meaning. The upper stroke is detached, which distinguishes it from the succeeding.

23 匸 *Hai*. C. A concealing place, a retreat. 18.—3.

Distinguished from the preceding by the longer top stroke, and like it containing all the strokes, as if concealing them, to which idea there is some allusion in most of the characters.

24 十 *Shap.* Ten, perfect, superlative. 56.—11.

This group is very heterogenous both in the situation of the radical, and in the meanings of the characters; it contains many ancient forms.

25 卜 *Puk.* To divine by the lines on a tortoise; to conjecture, to guess. 46.—4.

The meaning of the radical, in this group, modifies many of the characters under it more or less; it is usually placed on the top much shortened, as in 卣 *yau*, but it also occurs on the right side.

26 卩 C. 㔾 *Tsit.* A seal, ancient seal; to seal or stamp. 39.—7.

Here, the radical is sometimes written so as closely to resemble *kí* 巳 (No. 49); as in 卷 *kün*; it is usually placed on the right side; in a few it is on the bottom.

27 厂 *Hón.* C. An overhanging hill, a shelter. 128.—8.

Somewhat of the idea of overhanging, protecting, or sheltering, runs through many of the characters under this radical; its position is uniformly on the left side, covering all the other strokes; it is often interchanged with *ím* (No. 53).

28 厶 *Mau.* C. Perverse, base; to seduce; a certain one, such a one. 41.—2.

For the most part, the radical is found at top of the few characters here grouped, and in many of them it is repeated three times.

29 又 *Yau.* Again, further, also; the right hand. 92.—12.

*Yau* occurs on the right side or underneath; some one of the meanings of the radical enters into most of the characters, but not enough to form a natural group.

FORMED BY THREE STROKES.

30 口 *Hau.* The mouth, an opening, speech, utterance; an embouchure. 1047.—128.

This radical is usually placed on the left side, but there are many exceptions. The group is for the most part a natural one, voice, clamor, words, names, &c., or some action of the mouth, being the idea in most of the characters; many of them are attempts to express the sense of words by imitating their sounds. This radical is placed on the side of characters to denote that their sound merely is to be taken, irrespective of their signification, as when writing the sounds of a word from another language, euphonic particles, &c.

31 囗 *Ü'i.* C. An inclosure, a boundary surrounding; to encircle, to protect. 119.—16.

Here the radical incloses all the other strokes, a circumstance which will always point out the characters under it; this arrangement also gives a shade of meaning to the words, that of surrounding, inclosing, &c.

32 土 *Tò.* Earth, ground, soil: one of the 5 elements. 579.—56.

*Tò* is placed on the left or underneath, and nearly all the characters have a reference to the earth, to dykes, foundation, boundary, stability, &c ; some of them are interchanged with *fau*, a mound (No. 170), and with *kuk* a valley (No. 150).

33 士 *Sz'.* A scholar, philosopher; officers of government. 25.—4.

*Sz'* is distinguished from *tò* by the long upper stroke, and in the characters it is usually placed on top; the words under it, as well as the three next, are few and miscellaneous.

34 夂 *Chì.* C. To follow, to walk slowly and steadily. 12.—1.

The radical is usually placed astride on top of the other strokes; it is distinguished from the following by the transverse line commencing within the left hand one.

35 夊 *Shui.* C. To walk slowly. 24.—2.

The radical is placed underneath the other strokes; it is known from the preceding by the long transverse line, as well as by its position.

36 夕 *Sik.* The evening, the setting moon; inclined. 36.—6.

In this group the radical is placed without uniformity; it is doubled in most of the words, giving a sense of *tó*, many, to those into which it enters.

37 大 *Tái.* Large, great, plump, extensive, much; to enlarge, to make much of. 133—23.

This is a very miscellaneous collection of characters; the radical is placed astride of the strokes, or underneath, or it is combined.

38 女 *Nü.* Woman, a female; a daughter, a virgin; to marry out. 690.—61.

Here a marked reference is perceived in the characters to the Chinese ideas contained in the radical; they refer to women, delicate, subtle, mean, jealous, intriguing, lewd, vicious, &c. It is usually placed on the left, sometimes in combination.

39 子 *Tsz'.* A male child, a son, progeny, children; a philosopher, sage, worthy; a word of respect. 87.—17.

*Tsz'* is usually placed on the bottom; the characters under it have a reference to children, childbirth, nursing, &c.; or else to scholars.

40 宀 *Mín.* C. Covering, shelter, roof of a house, a cavern. 249.—52.

This radical is called *lam pung tau* in Canton; it covers all the other strokes, but it is difficult in some cases to tell whether the character in question is found in the dictionary under the upper or the lower radical; most of those under *mín* have some reference in their meaning to a house, shelter, protector, &c.

41 寸 *Tsun.* Tenth of a *chik* or cubit; laws, measures. 41.—11.

Here the radical is placed underneath or on the right side; the group is a very miscellaneous one.

42 小 *Siú.* Small, little, pretty; petty, contracted, mean. 32.—4.

There are but few words in this group that are common in books; the radical is frequently combined in the character, or found attached to it as part of *shíu,* 少 a few.

43 尢 C. 尤 兀 尣 *Wóng.* Lame, hunchbacked, dwarfish, crooked legs. 67.—2.

The radical supports the other strokes in most of the characters; in many of them there is some reference to walking lamely or awkwardly, to disease of the legs, &c. The first of the three contracted forms is read *yau,* with the sense of differing from, still more.

44 尸 *Shi.* C. A corpse, an effigy, lying as dead; to lay out or set in order. 149.—20.

*Shí,* a few old words excepted, is uniformly placed over all the other strokes on the left side; the characters are easily recognized, and most of them have some reference to the body, more especially to what is offensive about it.

45 屮 *Chit.* C. A sprout, a plant just rooting. 39.—1.

There are but two or three characters under this radical in use; it is usually placed at top.

46 山 *Shán.* A hill, mountain; wild, undomesticated. 637.—17.

This is a natural group, most of them having some reference to shape, aspect, name, or parts of hills and mountains. The radical is placed in all parts of the characters; it is sometimes interchanged with *tò,* earth (No. 32), and *kuk,* a valley (No. 150).

47 巛 C. 𡿨 巜 川 *Chün.* Rivulets, streams, concourse of streams. 27.—4.

Many of the characters placed here are primitives, *chün* combining with other strokes to form them, and their meanings consequently vary much.

48 工 *Kung.* Art, work, workmanship, workman; skilled in work; an officer of government. 18.—5.

Many of the words placed here are not readily recognized, for the radical enters into the character, as a component part; they are but few, however, and a little attention will enable the scholar to remember them.

49 己 *Kí.* Self, selfish, private; to record; a horary character. 21.—5.

*Kí* usually occurs underneath the other strokes; the group is small and heterogeneous; *kí* 己, *í* 已, and *sz'* 巳, must not be confounded.

50 巾 *Kan.* A napkin, kerchief, cap. 295.—19.

Considerable similarity of meaning is apparent among these characters, viz., that of cloth, sash, flag, fold, &c.; the radical is on the left side, except in a few primitives found under it.

51 干 *Kón.* A shield; to oppose, to ward off; to seek; a boundary. 18.—6.

*Kón* enters into combination with many of the words placed under it, which are few in number.

52 幺 *Yú.* C. Slender, young, small, delicate, fine. 21.—4.

The radical is found doubled in nearly all the characters placed under it.

53 广 *Ím.* C. A shed, portico, covering or shelter. 287.—29.

The characters placed here form a pretty natural group, having reference to sheltering, to buildings, protection, storing, &c. It is found covering the other strokes; this group and the 27th are similar, and many of their characters are synonymous.

54 廴 *Yan.* C. Continued walking; a long journey. 10.—5.

This radical and the 162d are often used interchangeably, but erroneously so, as *úi* 廻 for 迴; *ching* 延 for 延, &c.

55 廾 *Kung.* C. Two hands united or held up, as when bowing *à la Chinoise.* 51.—2.

*Kung* is uniformly placed underneath the other strokes; it is in many of the characters changed into *tái* 大 great, making several words under these two radicals interchangeable. The group contains several primitives, and many old forms.

56 弋 *Yik.* C. A dart, an arrow-head; to dart; to possess one's-self of. 16.—2.

*Yik* is placed on the right side, covering the other strokes; the group is small.

57 弓 *Kung.* A bow, to shoot bows; a land measure. 166.—15.

Most of the words under *kung*, except a few primitives, have some reference to the bow, either directly or figuratively; it is placed on the left.

58 彐 C. 彑 彑 *Kai.* A hog's head; a sort, genus. 26.—2.

This group is small, primitives being the only characters belonging to it in common use; the radical is placed on the top, and is liable to be overlooked, without some attention.

59 彡 *Shám.* C. Long feathers, adorning integuments of hair or feathers. 53.—7.

*Shám* is placed in all parts of the characters; the usual meaning is that of adorning or variegation, pendants, marks, &c.

60 彳 *Chik.* C. To walk, to step short; a short step. 227.—26.

This is placed on the left side, and to most of the characters conveys an idea of advancement, especially in man, motion, &c. It is called *shéung kí yan pín,* 雙企人邊, referring to the apparent doubling of the radical *yan,* and is sometimes interchanged with it; and with *chéuk,* (No. 162) to walk, characters being found under both, which are identical in meaning.

FORMED BY FOUR STROKES.

61 心 C. 忄 小 *Sam.* The heart, middle; affections, feelings; motive, origin. 1077.—142.

The contracted form of this, called *chü sam pín* 住心邊, is always used when placed on the left side, and the full form at the bottom or elsewhere. The group is tolerably natural, containing such words as express the feelings of the heart, powers of the mind, &c.

62 戈 *Kwó.* A spear, lance or halberd; weapons. 111.—15.

*Kwó* occurs on the right side, often covering the other strokes, or combined with them by lengthening the horizontal line; the group contains characters somewhat analagous to the radical, expressing the names of weapons, fighting, arsenals, prohibitions, &c.

63 戶 *U'.* An inner door, one leaved door; a hole, orifice; a family, a household or its master; to stop. 45.—5.

The radical covers the other strokes; most of the characters have some reference in their meaning to the use or parts of a door.

64 手 C. 扌 *Shau.* The arm, fore-arm, the hand; to handle. 1092.—46.

The contracted form is placed on the left, in nearly all the characters, and the full form elsewhere; it is described as 才手邊 *tsoi shau pín;* ability, beating, skill, taking, motions of the hand of all kinds, &c., are characteristics of the words in this group.

65 支 *Chí.* A branch; to branch off, to diverge, as posterity; to pay. 27.—2.

This radical is never contracted, and thereby it is distinguished from the succeeding one; there are, however, erroneous forms of the two following found under it.

66 攴 C. 攵 *Pók.* To touch; a slight stroke. 296.—21.

Those characters under this radical which are in most common use have the contracted form (called 昂文邊 *ngóng man pín,*) on the right; the others (about one half of all) have the regular form. The group contains many synonyms.

67 文 C. 攵 *Man.* Literature, letters, composition, to write lines, to paint; veins in wood. 23.—2.

The contracted form is seldom used; there is a shade of similarity in the meaning of the words, of streaks, mixed colors, variegated, &c.

68 斗 *Tau.* A dry measure; name of the constellation Ursa Major. 33.—5.

The idea of measuring, calculating, or pouring out, lading out, runs through most of the few characters placed here; the radical stands on the right.

69 斤 *Kan.* An ax; a catty or the Chinese pound. 56.—8.

To cleave, to chop, to divide, &c., is a prominent idea in most of the characters under this radical; it is placed on the right, and the left half is never (with one exception) another radical.

70 方 *Fóng.* Square, a place, the earth, a region, points of compass; two boats joined; a prescription. 83.—9.

The words placed under this radical, for the most part have some reference to flags, banners, streamers, &c. It is found on the left, and in most of the characters is a contraction of *ín*, 㫃 a flag, waving as a flag, as in *kí* 旗, *sün* 旋, &c., having no reference to *fóng*; the other characters found here have no similarity of meaning to those written in this manner, and are few in number.

71 无 C. 旡 *Mò.* Destitute of, not, wanting. 13.—2.

The few words under this radical have no uniformity of meaning.

72 日 *Yat.* The sun, day, a day, daily. 455.—51.

This group is a natural one, comprising such characters as refer to the sun, light, clear, time, &c.; the radical, when placed on the top is often written like the following, and such words also very much resemble a few under the 13th and 14th radicals. Its correct shape is nearly square, but in composition it may be either flattened or lengthened.

73 曰 *Üt.* To speak, to say, to call, to designate. 38.—13.

This radical is placed very irregularly, and sometimes combined with other strokes; a few characters found here evidently belong to the preceding.

74 月 *Üt.* The moon, a month. 70.—11.

Some reference to the moon, or to time, pervades the meaning of many of the characters under this radical. It is sometimes placed on the right side, which will distinguish all such characters from those under *yuk*, flesh (No. 130); nothing, however, but an acquaintance with the words, can enable the student to distinguish between the two in such words as have the radical on the left; those under *üt* are few in number.

拾級大成

75 木 *Muk.* Wood, a tree; one of the five elements. 1358.—17.

Names of trees, fruits, woods, posts, things made of wood, conditions of wood, or some uses of wood, characterize most of the words under this radical. It is usually placed on the left side or at bottom, rarely in combination.

76 欠 *Hím.* To owe, to be dispirited, to gape; insufficiency, want. 236.—18.

*Hím* is placed on the right, and must be distinguished from the contracted form of *puk* (No. 66), which it resembles. Most of the characters have a reference to the breath, sounds from the mouth, something proceeding from the mouth, &c.; this radical and *hau* (No. 30) are therefore interchangeably used in a few instances.

77 止 *Chí.* To stop, be still, cease, impede; to stop in an affair or at a place. 91.—9.

This radical is placed in all parts of the character, and where it is a half, usually imparts something of its meaning to the whole.

78 歹 C. 歺 *Tái.* Perverse, vicious, rebellious. 232.—12.

Whatever is putrid, offensive, murderous, dead, spoiled, &c., is expressed by most of the words found here; the radical is sometimes interchanged with *nik*, (No. 104); it is usually placed on the left, and very seldom contracted.

79 殳 *Shü.* C. To kill, to strike; a spear handle. 84.—8.

Something of the meaning of the radical is found in full one half of the words placed under it; the other half are heterogenous, many of them having it in combination. It is written on the right, the other half very seldom being a radical. There are many common characters which appear to be under this radical, as 穀 or 穀 *kuk*, 穀 *kau*, &c., but which are found under the left hand lower part, if that is a radical, the remainder of the character 㱿 or 㱿 *kuk*, being regarded as a primitive.

80 毋 *Mò.* Not, without, a prohibitory particle; an interrogative particle. 17.—5.

The radical is placed underneath the other strokes.

81 比 *Pí.* To compare, classify; to provide, prepare; equal, even; contiguous. 22.—1.

The radical is almost the only character in common use in this group; it is often placed in the middle, and in other parts of the character except the left.

82 毛 *Mò.* Hair or down on the body of animals, fur, nap, pubescence, grass. 212.—4.

*Mò* conveys something of its own meaning to almost every character under it, of hair, feathers, things made of hair, &c.; it is placed on the left, supporting all the other strokes, or else much contracted on the right side.

83 氏 *Shí.* Surname of females; a family, 15.—3.

The characters placed here have *shí* in combination; none of them have any reference to it in meaning.

84 气 *Hí.* C. Vapor, air, breath. 18.—1.

This small group is natural; *hí* covers the other strokes.

85 水 C. 氵 *Shui.* Water, tide, the tide; one of the five elements; stream. 1586.—148.

Some reference, directly or figuratively, to water, its properties and uses, collections of water, &c., characterizes nearly all the words under this radical; it is, except in a very few cases, placed on the left side in the contracted form, which is commonly called *sám tím shui* 三點水 three dotted water.

86 火 C. 灬 *Fó.* Fire, flame, heat; one of the five elements. 639.—43.

This, like the preceding, is a pretty natural group; burning, ardent, modes of cooking, vapor, &c., being the leading ideas of most of the characters. It is usually placed on the left, but also underneath, either contracted or in full.

87 爪 C. 爫 *Cháu.* Talons, nails, claws; to scratch, to tear to pieces. 37.—7.

*Cháu* is placed on the top in its contracted form in about one half of the characters; the others have it in full on the left. It is easily distinguished frou *kwá* (No. 97).

88 父 *Fú.* A father, a title of respect. 11.—2.

This radical is placed above, and all the characters refer to a father, and the different appellations he bears.

89 爻 *Ngáu.* C. To imitate, to blend, to lay across; to comply; one of the *pát kwá.* 17.—3.

This radical has but few characters, and their meanings have no reference to it.

90 爿 *Chóng.* C. Something to lean against, a couch. 50.—2.

Some of the characters under this radical have some reference to its meaning; but they are not uniform; it is placed on the left.

91 片 *Pin.* A slice, splinter, slip, fragment, petal of a flower; to snap in two. 78.—4.

These characters are distinguished from the preceding by the radical opening to the right, while that is to the left; some allusion to a plank, board, partition, &c., is found in most of them.

92 牙 *Ngá.* Tooth, tusk, eye-tooth. 9.—2.

The radical is the only character of this group usually met with.

拾級大成

93 牛 C. 牜 *Ngau.* Horned cattle, an ox; large victims. 233.—12.

In this collection, almost every character has some reference to the different sorts, purposes, ages, &c., of bovine animals.

94 犬 C. 犭 *Hün.* A dog; ravenous beasts, ferine animals. 445.—28.

Characters under this radical have *hün* on the left in the contracted form, (vulgarly called *lái kau pín*, or dog looking over his shoulder,) and most of them denote species, actions, &c., of carniverous animals, with several figurative significations of fierce, crafty, lying, &c. This radical is interchangeable with the 153d in many common characters.

FORMED BY FIVE STROKES.

95 玄 *Ün.* Sombre, color of heaven, dark, deep; to rule, control. 7.—2.

This group has the radical in combination in 率 *sut.*

96 玉 C. 王 *Yuk.* Gems, precious stones; precious, beautiful, valuable, rich (as food). 473—25.

This radical is read *yuk*, when placed on the bottom, with the dot; and *wóng* when on the side without the dot; characters under it are described by *yuk wóng pín* 玉王邊, and for the most part include the names of gems, precious things, musical instruments, &c. In many cases, this radical and *shik*, a stone, (No. 112), are interchangeable.

97 瓜 *Kwá.* Cucurbitaceous plants, a melon, cucumber. 56.—2.

This group describes varieties and parts of melons; it is distinguished from *chau*, claws, (No. 87), by the point added to the middle stroke, and is placed on the left and not on the top.

98 瓦 *Ngá.* Tiles, brick, pottery, earthen-ware vessels. 173.—2.

Tiles, pottery, jars, and things made of earth, are found under this radical; it is placed on the right or underneath the other strokes; it is sometimes interchanged with *ming*, dishes (No. 108), *tò*, earth (No. 32), and *shik*, stone (No. 112).

99 甘 *Kóm.* Sweet, pleasant, willing, delightsome, voluntary. 23.—2.

Sweetness, metaphorically or actually, is a part of the meaning of the few characters under this radical.

100 生 *Shang.* To bear, to bring forth, produce; life, living; unripe. 23.—2.

The radical conveys its meaning to all the characters under it, only two or three of which are in common use.

101 用 *Yung.* To use; use, useful; by, with; necessary expenses. 11.—2.

This group has no bond of connection; the radical combines with other parts of characters, forming primitives.

102 田 *Tín.* A field, arable land; to cultivate, to plough. 193.—26.

Characters under this radical for the most part refer to land and its divisions, cultivation, and changes made in land by tillage, &c.; a few are interchanged with *tò*, the earth, (No. 32). It is placed on the left or underneath; in the latter case, the character is usually a primitive.

103 疋 *Pat.* A numeral of pieces of cloth, the foot. Read *shú*, to record, sufficient. 16.—5.

This group mostly consists of primitives, having the radical in combination.

104 疒 *Nik.* C. Debility, ailment, sickness. 527.—25.

This group contains the names of diseases, wounds, sores, &c. The radical uniformly covers all the other strokes; it is known under the name of *tsat ping tàu* 疾病頭, i. e. the disease (radical which is) on top.

105 癶 *Pút.* C. To push aside with the feet, to stride. 16.—3.

Characters under this radical have little connection with each other; it is placed astride, covering the other strokes.

106 白 *Pák.* White, uniform, freely, clear, pure, plain, apparent; to explain or make manifest. 109.—8.

This group is tolerably natural; *pák* is placed on the left, and is easily distinguished both from *muk* the eye (No. 109) and *tsz'*, self (No. 132); in some of the words it is interchanged with *yat*, the sun (No. 72).

107 皮 *Pí.* Skin, bark, outer covering, wrapper. 95.—1.

Parts, diseases, and uses of the skin, are the most prominent of the words under this group; the radical is placed on both sides of the characters.

108 皿 *Ming.* Dishes, eating utensils of crockery. 129.—16.

Some direct or indirect reference to the radical is found in almost all of these characters. It is placed at the bottom; this and *hüt*, blood (No. 143), are easily distinguished by the stroke at top of the latter.

109 目 *Muk.* The eye, to see, to designate; index, direction. 646.—29.

Uses, forms, diseases, and references to the eye, are leading ideas in these characters. The radical is usually placed on the left; when placed beneath it is written square or nearly so, rendering it very similar to *yat* day, or *tsz'* self; in two or three common characters (as *king* 睘, *yik* 睪 &c.,) it is written like *móng*, a net (No. 122).

110 矛 *Máu.* A long barbed weapon, a halberd. 66.—3.

Reference to, or names of spears, lances, awls, &c, are the meanings of most of the characters under this radical; it is placed on the left, and must be distinguished from *wó*, grain (No. 115).

拾級大成

111 矢 *Shí.* An arrow, a dart; true to the mark, swift. 65.—8.

This radical is placed on the left in most of the characters, and conveys somewhat of its meaning to them, either directly or figuratively.

112 石 *Shik.* Stone, rocks; hard, firm. 489.—23.

This group is a pretty natural one, most of the characters meaning hard, stony, instruments or the uses of stone; some of them are interchanged with *tò*, ground (No. 32), *ngá*, tiles (No. 98), and *yuk*, a gem (No. 96). The radical is usually placed on the left.

113 示 C. 礻 *Shí.* A sign from heaven, a declaration of heaven's will; an edict; to declare, to instruct. 214.—25.

This radical is placed on the left, and in writing is often contracted; it is distinguished from *í* (No. 145), by having one dot on the right, while *í* has two, and is called *lai í pín* 礼衣邊 in allusion to this similarity. The characters refer to sacrifices, to gods, ancestors, &c., omens, blessings, cursings, and such words as are of a religious import.

114 禸 *Yau.* C. Print of a bear's foot. 13.—2.

These few characters have *yau* underneath, sometimes in combination, as in *kam* 禽, and sometimes separated; their meanings bear no resemblance to the radical.

ho 115 禾 *Wó.* Grain, growing rice; paddy; agreement, happy. 433.—31.

Appearance, age, uses, measures, &c., of grain, (especially rice,) taxes, &c., are leading ideas in these words; the radical is placed on the left. A few characters under this and *shí* (No. 113) are interchangeable, apparently from the use made of grain in sacrifices.

116 穴 *Hüt.* A cave, den, hole, orifice in the ground; to dig holes; sinus of the body. 300.—18.

This radical covers the others strokes, and it is not always easy to tell whether the character is found under the upper or lower radical; some knowledge of the meaning will, however, often decide. Hollowness, natural or artificial, emptiness, &c., are the most prominent and leading ideas.

117 立 *Lap.* Erect; to erect, establish, set up, perfect, arrange. 102.—7.

Characters into which *lap* enters are not much used; there are some primitives under it; it is usually on the left, but also occurs at top and bottom.

FORMED BY SIX STROKES.

118 竹 C. ⺮ *Chuk.* Bamboo, a reed; a thin slip of wood for writing on. 954.—45.

*Chuk*, in the contracted form, called *chuk fá tau* 竹花頭, is always placed at top; and all the common characters have some reference to the bamboo, its uses and appearance, utensils made of it, &c ; a few also refer to writing, as books were anciently carved on bamboo.

米 119 米 *Mai.* Rice, rice in the husk. 321.—16.

Characters under this radical refer to the uses of rice after it is reaped, in cooking, &c.; many are interchangeable with *wó* (No. 115).

120 糸 C. 糹 *Sz'.* Silk, silken threads, floss; small, fine. Also read *mít*, meaning the same. 821.—71.

Words placed here usually denote some kind of silk, mode and things used in raising and weaving it, and thence figures are drawn from the uses to which it is put. The radical is usually placed on the left, but is also found elsewhere; it is called *kiú sz' pín*, 絞糸邊.

121 缶 *Fau.* Crockery; large earthenware vases. 78—2.

Names of vessels, or conditions, fractures, &c., of jars, are the leading ideas in the few common characters placed here; some are interchanged with *muk*, wood, and others with *ngá* (No. 98), pottery.

122 网 C. 罒 㓁 冈 *Móng.* A net, confounded, entangled, impeded; to impose upon, to accuse falsely. 164.—15.

This radical is often recognized with difficulty; in some characters, as in *móng* 罔, it covers all the other strokes as *kwang* (No. 13) does; in others, as *hón* 罕, it is written so as to resemble *mít* (No. 14); but it is most frequently contracted to resemble *sz'*, the figure four, as in *tsúi* 罪, which is one name the contracted form bears. The characters have some reference, either directly or figuratively, to nets and their uses.

any 123 羊 *Yéung.* A sheep, goat, ovine animals. 157.—9.

This radical is written in a few cases in the ancient form 𦍌, which renders such words liable to be looked for under *tsò* (No. 140); the upright stroke is shortened in many characters, as in *kò* 羔, or else combined with other parts of the character. Sheep, their ages, kinds, uses, &c., goats and antelopes, and figures drawn from them are characteristic ideas of the group. Some of the words are interchanged with *lúk* (No. 198), a deer.

124 羽 *Yü.* Wings, feathers of the wings. 210.—9.

*Yü* is placed in all parts of the character, and conveys somewhat of its meaning to most of the words placed under it.

125 老 *Ló.* Old, aged, venerable, respected; a term of respect. 23.—5.

This radical is sometimes contracted, as in *háu* 考, *ché* 者, *tít* 耋, and others, so as not to be immediately recognized; age, and terms for certain ages, are meanings found under it.

126 而 *I'.* The soft hair on the side of the cheeks; as, and, but, yet. 23.—3.

This is a heterogenous group, and many words now found under it, which are formed of this and another radical, should, according to the usual rule of arrangement, have been placed under the other.

127 耒 *Lui.* A plough handle, a crooked share. 85—3.

An additional horizontal stroke distinguishes this radical from *wó*, grain (No. 115); the characters denote the kinds and uses of ploughs, hoes, &c.

128 耳 *I'.* The ear, ear of jars, an ear-shaped handle; an euphonic particle. 172.—16.

The ear and its uses, and figurative significations drawn therefrom, are the prominent ideas of this group. In a few it enters into combination, and its place then is usually on the left or top. It is often erroneously interchanged with *muk* the eye, from its resemblance to one mode of writing *muk;* as in 睡 *shui.*

129 聿 *Lut.* C. A pencil, a style, or writing utensil; an initial particle, forthwith, than. 20.—2.

The few characters under this radical have very little connection with it in meaning; it is combined in *suk* 肅.

130 肉 C. 月 *Yuk.* Flesh, meat, fat, soft; fleshy, dull. 675.—56.

The contracted form of *yuk* cannot be distinguished from *ut*, the moon, when the latter is placed on the left. This group is tolerably natural, including parts of the body, uses of flesh, &c. There are a considerable number of characters, written with *yuk* on the left, which do not belong to this group, but to the radical on the right; among them are *shing* 勝, *tang* 騰, *tang* 縢, and others, which are found under *lik*, *má*, *sz'*, &c.

131 臣 *Shan.* Servant of a prince, a statesman, a minister; to be subject to. 17.—4.

*Shan* is usually placed on the left; it has little or no connection with the characters under it.

132 自 *Tsz'.* Self, myself; from, originating; to use. 35.—2.

Most of these characters have some idea of putridity attached to them; the radical is sometimes erroneously written for *pák*, white (No. 106); it is placed very irregularly.

133 至 *Chi.* To, to arrive at; the limit, utmost; exceedingly, very; as to. 25.—3.

There is no bond of union among these characters, most of the common ones being primitives; the radical is often placed underneath.

134 臼 *Kau.* A mortar to hull grain in. 72.—7.

This radical must be distinguished from *pák*, white (No. 106); it is often contracted in composition, as in *sé* 寫 to write for 寫; strokes are sometimes drawn through it or in it, as in *ü* 與, *hing* 興, *ü* 臾, and others. The characters have no similarity of meaning.

135 舌 *Shít.* The tongue, taste; tongue of a bell. 35.—6.

Sucking, talking, licking, &c., are the leading ideas in those characters with which this radical is joined; there are a few others under it, in which *shé* 舍 acts as the radical, which have no reference to it.

136 舛 *Chün.* C. Uncertainty, error, wandering; to oppose, to turn the back upon. 11.—3.

This small group has no uniformity of construction, or similarity of meaning.

137 舟 *Chau.* A boat, bark, or vessel; to transport, to boat. 198.—3.

Boats, vessels, and things and parts of them, are the meanings of most of these words; the radical is in some characters interchanged with *muk*, wood, and *shui*, water, and in a few, erroneously with *yuk*, flesh, as *shing* 艖 for 賸, from the resemblance of the two. It is placed on the left.

138 艮 *Kón.* C. Opposition, fixed; read *hón*, to pull, to drag. 6.—2.

In these, the radical is placed on the right.

139 色 *Shik.* Color, quality, complexion; vice, lust. 22.—2.

*Shik* is placed on the right; almost all the characters refer to conditions of color.

140 艸 C. 艹 *Tsò.* Plants, herbage, grass. 1902.—95.

This group includes the names of small plants, flowers, grasses, &c.; the contracted form, called *tsò fá tau* 艸花頭, is found at top in nearly all cases, forming a collection of words pretty uniform in meaning and construction.

141 虍 *Fú.* C. A tiger or its skin; variegated, streaked. 115.—9.

The radical covers the other strokes; figures drawn from the nature and powers of a tiger, its kinds, age, &c., are meanings of most of the words under it.

142 虫 *Chung.* Insects, worms, reptiles, frogs. 1067.—22.

Names of insects, snakes, reptiles, and their different parts and appearances, are included under *chung;* the radical when single is on the left, but when doubled it is placed underneath; this reduplication makes a great number of synonymes.

143 血 *Hüt.* Blood, sacrificial blood. 61.—3.

This radical must be distinguished from *ming*, dishes (No. 108). It is an unimportant, though pretty natural group; vomiting, bleeding, bloody, &c., being the leading ideas.

144 行 *Hang.* To walk, to do, act; a column, a series, a row, a line of, a path. Read *hóng*, a factory, commercial house. 54.—8.

The radical always incloses the other strokes, so that the right side of the character must be examined to distinguish it from those under *chik*, a step (No. 60). The leading ideas are of going, moving, &c.

145 衣 C. 衤 *I'.* Clothes, upper garments; a rind or shell of fruit; to dress, to cover. 611.—36.

The type of this group, viz, clothes, and their parts, to dress &c., conveys somewhat of its meaning to nearly all the characters in it; the radical is always contracted when placed on the left, and often divided, containing the other strokes underneath its upper line, as in *chung* 衷, *shui* 衰, &c.; in some, as *piú* 表, it is combined, and in others placed below.

146 襾 *Há.* C. To overshadow, to invert. 30.—3.

This radical is at top, and from the common form, 西 *sai*, the west, being the most common word under it, and also the way the radical itself is almost always written, it is usually called *sai tsz' pò*.

FORMED BY SEVEN STROKES.

147 見 *Kín.* To see, to notice, to appear; seeing, finding that; aspect; to disclose, manifest. 162.—14.

Uses of the eye, and figuratively of the mind, to express emotions, are the principal ideas of this group; some of the characters interchange with *muk* (No. 109). It is placed on either side.

148 角 *Kók.* A horn, corner, jutting out, protrusion of a hill; tuft of hair. 159.—5.

Horns of animals, their uses, age, and appearance, are the meanings of these words.

149 言 *I'n.* Words, sentence, discourse; to speak, to express, to deliberate. 861.—105.

Words under this radical express operations of the mind as well as ideas pertaining to letters, conversation, words, &c. It is usually placed on the left, and interchanged with *hau*, mouth, in a few characters.

150 谷 *Kuk.* A valley, a ravine; an aqueduct, water between hills. 55.—2.

This unimportant radical has several synonymous forms under it; the kinds and appearance of vallies are the meanings of the group. It will easily be distinguished from *shít*, a tongue.

151 豆 *Tau.* Leguminous plants; an ancient sacrificial vessel. 69.—5.

Those words which have *tau* in combination uniformly refer to some kind of pulse, but there are many characters found under this radical which are in fact contractions of *kú* 鼓, a drum (No. 207), the right half of that radical being omitted; as in *tín* 鼘, *tung* 鼕, &c. The position of *tau* is not regular, but is usually on the left.

152 豕 *Chí.* C. Hog, swine; a pig. 50.—3.

This radical is placed on the left, sometimes with the addition of a stroke as in *chuk* 豩; the characters mostly refer to the hog and elephant,; this and *hün* the 94th radical are sometimes interchanged.

153 豸 *Chí.* C. Worms; insects without feet; reptiles. 141.—5.

This and *hün* the 94th radical are also often interchanged; the characters in this group denote wild beasts of some sort, or figures drawn from them, and have little connection with the radical.

154 貝 *Púi.* A pearl shell; a cowrie, formely used as a coin; precious, valuable. 278.—46.

There are many primitives under this radical, which makes the group somewhat irregular; the prevailing ideas are of property and trade, disposal of value, or honors derived from it. *Púi* occurs on the side or bottom, and is otherwise called *kü púi pín* 具貝邊.

155 赤 *Chik.* Red, carnation, color of raw cotton, naked; to tally. 32.—2.

*Chik* is placed on the left, and most of the characters convey some idea of redness.

156 走 *Tsau.* To walk, to run, to go swiftly, to escape. 236.—11.

*Tsau* supports all the other strokes, and conveys somewhat of its meaning to the characters of which it forms a part.

157 足 C. 𧾷 *Tsuk.* The human foot, full, competent, complete. 581.—30.

This group much resembles the preceding, and many characters are interchanged; but this differs from that, in referring to the form, distortion, position, &c., or uses of the foot, while that has reference to running, moving, &c.

拾級大成

158 身 *Shan.* The body, the person; trunk of a tree, hull of a ship. 98.—4.

This radical is interchanged with *yuk*, flesh (No. 130), *í*, the ear (128), *tsz'*, one's self (No. 132), *kwat*, bones (No. 188), and others. It is placed on the left.

159 車 *Ché.* A wheel. Read *kü*, a wheeled carriage; a cart, a vehicle. 362.—22.

Uses, parts, kinds, &c., of carriages are almost the only meanings of characters found under *ché*.

160 辛 *San.* Acrid, bitter, grievous, distressing, pungent; a horary character. 37.—7.

*San* is doubled in many words, the other strokes being between the two; the group is heterogenous in meaning, and the characters are irregular in construction.

161 辰 *Shan.* To excite motion; time, hours; the heavenly bodies; a horary character. 16.—3.

*Shan,* sometimes found as a radical and sometimes in combination, is generally placed above or below. It must not be confounded with *chéung*, 長 long (No. 168).

162 辵 C. 辶 *Chéuk.* Motion, swiftly going and then stopping. 382.—59.

This radical and *tsau* (No. 156), are similar in their leading ideas, and the two groups have many characters in common; it is also interchanged with *chik*, 彳 (No. 60). It is almost always used in the contracted form, supporting the other strokes, and called *cháng shün pín*, 撑船邊 'poling a boat,' from some fancied resemblance between its shape and that action.

163 邑 C. 阝 *Yap.* A city, a royal city, an inclosure. 351.—27.

*Yap* is placed on the right in its contracted form, which alone distinguishes the characters under it from those under *fau* (No. 170); with a few exceptions, they refer to land, ideas of territory, names of places, inclosures, cities, &c.

164 酉 *Yau.* Must, new wine; a horary character; matured, finished. 291.—20.

The meaning of characters under this radical generally refers to wine, spirits, pickles, &c., and to tastes, and flavor of liquids.

165 釆 *Pín.* C. To separate, to distinguish. 14.—2.

This small group is as miscellaneous in its meanings as it is irregular in its construction; the radical is very often confounded with *tsoi*, 采 variegated, the most common character under it.

166 里 *Lí.* A Chinese mile; a neighborhood of five families, a court or lane in a village; a village. 14.—5.

There is no bond of union among the few characters arranged under this; some of them are primitives, as *chung* 重, and some are old forms.

FORMED BY EIGHT STROKES.

167 金 *Kam.* Gold, metal, elegant, gilded; firm, hard. 803.—46.

Kinds of metal, things made of metal, and figures derived from metals, are ideas which characterize all the words under this radical, forming a tolerably natural group; this radical is sometimes interchanged both with *shik*, a stone, and *muk*, wood.

168 長 C. 镸 *Chéung.* Long; old, senior, aged; to grow up or grow great; remote. 56.—2.

This group contains many characters whose meanings have some reference to length, but they are not in common use; the contracted form is always used in composition.

169 門 *Mún.* A door, a gate, passage into, an entrance; a class, a profession. 249.—27.

The radical covers the other strokes, forming a very symmetrical collection of characters, which have also some ideas in common, referring to doors, gates, entrances, &c.

170 阜 C. 阝 *Fau.* A mound or hill of earth; large, great, numerous. 347.—38.

This is always placed on the left, by which it is distinguished from *yap*, a city; to designate it still further it is called *fú tau pín* 戽斗邊, referring to a water bucket. The characters have a great diversity of meaning, though still referring to names of places, hills, elevations, mounds, stairs, &c.

171 隶 *Toi.* C. To reach to, until; to approach from behind. 13.—1.

These few characters have no common idea; the radical is placed on the right.

172 隹 *Chui.* C. Gallinaceous birds, and sparrows; birds with short tails. 234.—17.

The greater portion of these characters are interchangeably used with *níú*, a bird (No. 196); a few common ones placed under this radical have figurative meanings drawn from birds. *Chui* and *kai* 佳 must not be confounded.

173 雨 *Ü.* Rain, to rain. 298.—18.

This group is a meteorological one, and, with the exception of some having figurative meanings, tolerably natural; the radical is always placed at top, and words having it at top are almost always found here.

174 青 *Tsing*. Azure, the light blue of the sky; and the light green of plants; pure, clean, clear. 18.—3.

This radical, joined to characters, gives them a shade of its meaning; it is placed on the left.

175 非 *Fi*. Not so, unpermissable; vicious, shameful; false, wrong. 26—3.

This radical imparts its name to nearly all the characters under it, but there is no similarity of meaning among them.

FORMED BY NINE STROKES.

176 面 *Min*. The human face; the surface, top, fronting to, opposite, towards. 67.—1.

The face, and the form, beauty, and aspect of the countenance, are leading ideas of these characters; the radical is usually at top.

177 革 *Kák*. Untanned hide without the hair; to reject, to degrade from office. 307.—5.

The radical is placed on the left; most of the characters refer to leather, its uses, and things made from it.

178 韋 *Wai*. C. Dressed leather, thongs; that which can bind. 101.—2.

This group does not differ much in its general features from the preceding; some of their characters are interchangeable, and nearly all of them are unusual ones.

179 韭 *Kau*. Leeks, alliaceous plants. 21.—1.

This group is incongruous, and irregular both in meaning and form, though the majority of the words refer to the radical.

180 音 *Yam*. Sound, tone, musical tone, news. 43.—3.

*Yam* imparts somewhat of its meaning to nearly all the characters placed under it.

181 頁 *Hip*. The human head; numeral of a fold, a page. 373.—30.

Forms, parts, motions, and expression of the head and face, are leading ideas of this group; the radical is almost always on the right.

182 風 *Fung*. Wind, air; manner, feeling, temper; haste; to blow, to scatter. 183.—3.

Qualities and operations of the wind are the prominent significations of the words in this group.

183 飛 *Fi*. To fly with wings; to hasten. 13.—1.

The radical is the only word in common use.

184 食 *Shik*. To eat; read *tsz'*, to feed, to be nourished by food; eclipse; to retract; to be fool. 395.—38.

Eating, cooked viands, and times for eating, appetite, &c., are ideas which characterize this group; *shik* is placed on the left.

185 首 *Shau.* The head, first, a leader; to go foremost, most prominent; the beginning, origin of. 20.—1.

This radical differs from *hip* (No. 181), in meaning the headmost, the chief, &c.; the words under it are few and unusual.

186 香 *Héung.* Fragrance, sweet smell of incense, 38.—1.

Agreeable smells, fragrances, &c., are the leading ideas of the characters under *héung*.

FORMED BY TEN STROKES.

187 馬 *Má.* A horse; anger, rage, martial. 473.—28.

The different ages, colors, kinds, and uses of the horse, with figures drawn from its temper and habits, are the meanings of these characters.

188 骨 *Kwat.* Bones, bones of bodies, fibres or hard parts of plants. 186.—4.

Names of the bones of the body are found here; some of the characters are interchanged with *hip* (No. 181), and some with *yuk*, flesh (No. 130).

189 高 *Kò.* High, exalted, eminent, noble, loud. 35.—1.

The radical is the only character of this group in common use. There are two distinct groups of characters under this radical, one of them has *kò* for the radical, and the other has *kwók* 𩫏 waste land outside of cities, (which is an original form of *kwók* 郭, and a contraction of 𩫏𨛜) as in *ún*, 𩫖 a low wall, now written 垣 *ún*. *Kò* is, in composition, sometimes contracted, as in *ting* 亭 a porch, *king* 京 a capital, &c.

190 髟 *Píú.* Hair disheveled, mane, long hair. 245.—7.

*Píú* is placed at top, and almost all the characters under it mean something connected with hair, mane, its condition, appearance, &c.

191 鬥 *Tau.* Two soldiers opposed to each other; to fight, quarrel, scuffle. 24.—1.

This radical will easily be distinguished from *mún*, a door (No. 100), by the inner strokes; the few characters have all some reference to quarreling.

192 鬯 *Chéung.* C. A fragrant plant used with black millet to ferment a liquid used for sacrificial wine. 9.—1.

*Wat* 鬱, is the only character of this group usually met with.

193 鬲 *Lik.* C. A temple vase, a tripod with crooked feet. 74.—7.

Cooked liquids, and things to cook in, are the meanings of the words under this radical; only one or two of them are in common use; *lik* is usually placed below.

194 鬼 *Kwai.* Devils, ghosts, demons; spirits of the dead. 142.—4.

Some reference to the leading idea of the radical is found in nearly all of these words; it is placed on the left, supporting the other strokes.

FORMED BY ELEVEN STROKES.

195 魚 *Yü.* A fish, the finny tribes. 572.—10.

This group also includes some reptiles, but generally speaking, it is natural; some of the characters are interchanged with *chung*, an insect (No. 110), and others with *mín*, a toad (No. 205).

196 鳥 *Niú.* A bird, the feathered tribes. 761.—21.

This is also a natural group; many of the words, especially the names of gallinaceous fowls, are interchanged with *chui*, birds (No. 180); it is placed on the right.

197 鹵 *Lú.* C. Salt land; unrefined salt, brine. 45.—1.

Salt, and ideas pertaining to it, constitute the leading ideas of these words, but, as might be supposed from such a type, very few are in use.

198 鹿 *Luk.* A deer; cervine animals. 106.—9.

Some of the characters under *luk* are interchanged with *yéung*, a sheep (No. 120); they mostly refer to deer.

199 麥 *Mak.* Wheat, bearded grain. 132.—1.

The leading idea of the type is pretty well adhered to in these characters, very few of which are in use; kinds of wheat, uses, things made of it, &c., are the common meanings.

200 麻 *Má.* Hemp, hempen; name of a musical instrument. 35.—3.

Many characters, with *má* placed at top, are found under other radicals, and more of these might also have been distributed elsewhere; part of the present group refer to hemp, and part to the other moiety of the word.

FORMED BY TWELVE STROKES.

201 黃 *Wóng.* Yellow, clay color, color of the earth. 43.—1.

Yellow, and its shades are denoted by these characters.

202 黍 *Shü.* Millet, grand millet, Sorghum. 47.—2.

The kinds, uses, and things made of millet are here denoted; the radical is divided in *lai* 黎, so that, without attention, that character will be sought for under *wó*, grain (No. 121).

203 黑 *Hak*. Black, foul, dark, wicked. 173.—4

Literal and figurative ideas of darkness, vileness, &c., are characteristic of this group; where *hak* is placed underneath as in *tóng* 黨, the character will appear as if belonging to *fó*, fire.

204 黹 *Chí*. C. Embroidered work, to embroider; variegated. 9.

Not even the radical, nor any of the characters of this group are in common use; they refer to embroidery.

205 黽 *Mín*. C. A frog or toad. 41.—2.

Many of the characters under this radical are interchanged with *kwai*, tortoise (No. 212), *chung*, an insect (No. 140), and with *yü*, a fish; it is placed underneath; the words refer to reptiles, spiders, tortoises, &c.

FORMED BY THIRTEEN STROKES.

206 鼎 *Ting*. A tripod, steady, firm; to establish or set up (as a kingdom). 15.—1.

The radical is the only word in common use.

207 鼓 *Kú*. A drum; to drum. 47.—1.

*Kú* is usually placed on top of the other strokes, and this will prevent characters of which it forms a part being confounded with *púk* (No. 62); words properly belonging to this group, but having the right half of *kú* omitted, are found under *tau* (No. 111).

208 鼠 *Shü*. A mouse, a rat; rodent animals. 103.—2.

Names of mice, squirrels, moles, weasels, &c., are placed here; a few words are interchanged with *chung*, insects (No. 111), but the group is tolerably natural.

FORMED BY FOURTEEN STROKES.

209 鼻 *Pí*. The nose, origin of; to bore the nose. 50.—1.

Words referring to the nose, and its uses and forms, are comprised in this group.

210 齊 *Tsai*. Even, regular; to even, to smooth, to adjust or arrange, to make uniform. 19.—3.

All the words placed here derive their sound from the radical, which here acts the part of a primitive, and their meaning from the other half, which is placed within the lower strokes. Many similarly formed words, having *tsai* at top, are distributed among the other radicals. The two horizontal strokes below are sometimes omitted, when their place is supplied by another character.

FORMED BY FIFTEEN STROKES.

211 齒 *Chí.* Teeth, upper teeth, the fore teeth; age; to arrange, to class. 163.—3.

Forms, uses, kinds, diseases, &c., of the teeth and gums, are the meaning of words under this radical; the group is natural, but the characters are not much used.

FORMED BY SIXTEEN STROKES.

212 龍 *Lung.* A dragon, lizard; lacertine reptiles. 25.—2.

This group has three or four words in use; the others are old forms.

213 龜 *Kwai.* The tortoise. 25.—1.

Most of the words in this group have some reference to the tortoise, though none are in common use; some of them are interchanged with *mín* (No. 201).

FORMED BY SEVENTEEN STROKES.

214 龠 *Yéuk.* A musical instrument of reed, a certain measure, 20.—1.

This small group refers to the sounds of musical instruments.

---

The sum total of characters contained in the first series of numbers in the foregoing list of radicals is 44,449; in the second series, the amount is 3232. The number of characters given by Rémusat, who has followed the *Tsz' Wai*, is 30,000, which is probably very near the actual number of different characters in the language, excluding the synonymous forms. For instance, there are 118 characters under the radical *má*, a horse, which are duplicate forms, leaving 293 distinct words; of the 204 characters under *ngau*, an ox, 39 are synonymous forms; *hün*, a dog, contains 421 characters, 65 of which are duplicates.

The characters, as they are grouped under one radical, are uniformly arranged according to the number of their strokes, exclusive of the radical. In Kánghí's Dictionary, great care has been taken to aid the scholar in finding a word, by marking the number of strokes in the characters in figures on the margin of every page. Thus, if the scholar meets with the character 鑿 in reading, he takes the volume containing the radical 金 *kam*, and turns over the pages, until he comes to the margin that is marked 19 strokes, where he finds that the character he seeks is called *tsók*, meaning a chissel.

The following sentences have been formed from the radicals, for the purpose of aiding the scholar in remembering their meanings. In some of the sentences, other words, not radicals, are added to complete the sense, the sounds of which are given in brackets.

| | |
|---|---|
| The fish leaps (*tiu*) over the dragon's gate. | 魚躍龍門 |
| The deer plays (*yau*) before the tiger's den. | 鹿遊虍穴 |
| Whatever places (*shó*) are reached by boats and carriages. | 舟車所至 |
| The sound of (*chí*) drums and pipes. | 鼓龠之音 |
| Precious valuables are (*pò*) stones and gems. | 寶貝玉石 |
| Earthen pots are utensils (*hí*) and dishes. | 器皿瓦缶 |
| Insects destroy the fragrant herbage. | 虫殳香艸 |
| The worms crawl on the dun-colored hemp. | 豸辵玄麻 |
| *Mai* and *fóng* slightly differ (*pít*). | 匸匚幺別 |
| *Shí* and *shí* are not the same (*tung*) [radical]. | 氏示非同 |
| It is necessary (*sü*) to compare *küt* and *kwan*. | 須比亅卜 |
| Do not (*yau*) confound *hóm* and *kwing*. | 休舛凵冂 |
| Four (*sz'*) quarters and eight corners. | 四方八角 |
| Two slices and one fold. | 二片一頁 |
| To fold the hands, and inquire after (*man*) one's father. | 廾手問父 |
| A malicious demon has sickened (*sui*) the man. | 歹鬼祟儿 |
| The short tailed bird (or sparrow) stops on the high mound. | 隹艮高阜 |
| With hide and bandage (*pò*) to wrap the crooked leg. | 韋布勹尢 |
| The beast's (*shau*) paw treads on the ground. | 獸疋禸地 |
| The crooked spoon takes out the broth (*tsü kang*). | 乙匕取羹 |
| The sprouts grow (*chut*) equal in the salt marsh. | 鹵出屮芽齊 |
| The statesman takes (*chí*) the seal (*fú*) of office and comes. | 臣持符卩至 |
| The wind and rain have reached a certain city. | 風雨至厶邑 |
| The sun and moon descend behind the western hills. | 日月入西山 |
| The bamboo boughs rustle upon the gate. | 竹支攴門戶 |

拾級大成

| | |
|---|---|
| With halberds and plough beams to oppose swords and axes. | 矛耒鬥刀斤 |
| To cover a peck or a mortar with a garment or a napkin. | 衣巾冖斗臼 |
| Tripods and incense pots arranged to burn perfume and worship. | 鼎鬲尸鬯示 |
| In quarrels (*chang*), there is (*yau*) always talk enough. | 爭气有口舌 |
| The debtor (*chái*) is morning (*chíú*) and evening annoyed (*fán*). | 債欠朝夕煩 |
| The slowness (*mán*) of (*chí*) traveling one after another. | 彳夊攵行之慢 |
| Traveling to a distance, striding, and reclining, are all unlike. | 廴癶几又不同 |
| The Memoirs [of *Tsó*] speaks of birds, beasts, ivory and skin. | 傳曰羽毛齒革 |
| The Ode (*shí*) speaks of using bows, arrows, darts, and spears. | 詩言弓矢干戈 |
| To shoot at birds and have them fly beneath (*ü*) the brow or eaves. | 弋鳥飛於厂广 |
| To seek cives slowly walking near (*ú*) the grotto's edge. | 釆韭彳乎宀丄 |
| *Chü* from *pít* must be discriminated (*sü fan pít*). | 丶隶丿須分別 |
| *Kai* and (*ü*) *chóng* in the memory (*kí*) must not be forgotten (*móng*). | 彐與爿記毋忘 |
| The five (*'ng*) elements are metal, wood, water, fire, and earth. | 五行金木水火土 |
| The five colors are azure, carnation, white, black, and yellow. | 五色青赤白黑黄 |
| With rice to feed pigs, sheep, cows, dogs and horses. | 米食豕羊牛犬馬 |
| The fields produce pulse, wheat, millet, rice and melons. | 田生豆麥黍禾瓜 |
| In a ten mile stream of water, two boats spread (*sát*) their nets. | 十里川二舟撒网 |
| With a three inch pencil, a scholar writes (*shü*) themes. | 三寸聿一士書文 |
| The bones, flesh, skin, blood, ears, and eyes, are all without disease. | 骨肉皮血耳目无疒 |
| The head, face, hair, teeth, hands, and nails, have no complaint. | 首面彡牙手爪毋辛 |
| Ladies who embroider in silk have small feet and long hair. | 糸黹女子足小夂髟長 |
| An old man who divines having a high nose and a large mouth. | 爻卜老人鼻高而口大 |
| From 7 o'clock A. M. to 5 P. M., do (*tsò*) your work with diligence. | 自辰至酉用力做工夫 |
| When doing (*wai*) his own affairs (*sz'*), a man goes or tarries, walks or stops, with a willing heart. | 行止走立甘心爲己事 |

## Chapter Second.

# OF THE PRIMITIVES.

---

By the term *primitive* is meant that part of characters, which is joined to the radical, to form a new one. For instance, in the words *tung* 侗, *lau*, 樓, *lin*, 憐, &c., the part of the character on the right, viz, 同, 婁, and 粦, is the primitive. The meaning of the term is also extended so as to include these characters, even when standing alone, or when they are spoken of as filling this office;—and the word is used in this sense in the preceding chapters. This part might also be called the phonetic or vocal part, inasmuch as it gives its own sound to a very great proportion of the characters; but as this rule has a multitude of exceptions, *primitive* appears to be on the whole the best term. It is not applied thus, however, on account of its original use, or for priority of any sort, but merely as a convenient term to express that part of a character which is not the radical; it is primitive solely because it was formed prior to the compound characters in which it is found. The term *derivative* has been used by Marshman to express the compound characters formed by the union of a radical and a primitive, and when speaking of them in this connection, may be used to avoid a periphrasis.

The number of primitives in the language,—that is the number of different characters, exclusive of the 214 radicals, which combine with a radical to form derivatives,—is 3867, according to Dr. Marshman from whose Clavis the following estimates are derived. They are not, however, all equally prolific in their philological progeny. More than seventeen hundred of them combine only once with a radical to form a third character; and as they are themselves for the most part compounds of radicals joined to simpler primitives (i. e. such as belong to class V.), they hardly deserve that name. For instance, one of the derivatives of *lung* 龍 is *chung* 寵, formed by joining that primitive to the radical *mín* 宀, this compound character joins once with *yan* 人, to form *chung* 𠑼, which according to Káng-hí's Dictionary means deflected, and which probably would not be met with once in a hundred volumes. For all practical purposes, therefore, these may be excluded from the list of primitives. There are also 452 others, formed, generally speaking, in the same manner, each of which produces only two philological shoots, and these may also be discarded, and for the same reason. These two sums, making 2178 characters, which, as they are the parents of only 2630 derivatives, and are themselves mostly included and defined under simpler forms, can have little or no influence on the great mass of characters, and may be considered, to borrow a term from natural history, as aberrant forms of their own primitive. There are then left 1689 primitives, out of which, by the addition of radicals, are formed about five sixths of all the characters in the language. The number of derivatives from any one of these primitives varies from three up to seventy-four, which is the highest, but the average is scarcely fifteen to each. To this number, the 214 radicals must be added, (for the majority of them also act as primitives in a greater or less degree,) making a total of 1903 primitives, from which, by the addition of 214 of their own number, at least seven eighths of all the characters in the Chinese language are formed:—a proportion, that for all practical purposes, is fully equivalent to the whole.

The primitives may, for convenience, be arranged into five classes, according to the relation they bear to the radicals. These are:

I. The 214 radicals themselves, when used as primitives.

II. Primitives formed from a radical by an addition that of itself is unmeaning.

III. Primitives formed from two radicals, or those which can be separated into two complete radicals.

IV. Primitives formed of three or four radicals.

V. Primitives formed from a derivative by the addition of another radical, or by the combination of two derivatives.

I. The extent to which the radicals act as primitives is very small compared to their more common use. When two combine side by side to form a character, that one which gives the sound is, generally speaking, the primitive; as *má* 嗎, *fóng* 坊, *kin* 涀, *shí* 視, *pák* 柏, &c. But when they are placed in an unusual manner, one above another, or different from the mass of characters under the radical, the probability is that the word is itself a primitive; as *hang* 杏, *ün* 員, *chéung* 昌, *táp* 沓, *mang* 孟, *lí* 李 &c. In cases of this kind, there will be a little difficulty at first in determining under which of the two radicals to look for the word in the Dictionary, but a few trials will fix its place in the memory. For neither of these two classes of characters, however, are these remarks of such general application as to entitle them to the name of rules; thus, out of 117 characters under *shui* (water), which are made by combining that radical with some other one, 59 follow the first remark; the other 58 are of the second sort, or follow neither. In 115 similar characters under *muk* (wood), 72 follow the first remark, and about 20 of the others are primitives. Out of 101 under *tsò* (herbs), 78 retain the sound of the primitive radical. Out of the 333 characters of this sort found under these three radicals, only one (*muk* 楇) has the sound of the radical, and that one is wrongly placed, for it means a species of bird, and *muk* is the primitive. The compilers of the Dictionary themselves appear to have had a little perplexity in deciding how such characters should be assorted, and in some instances have, according to the principles which usually guided them, placed them erroneously. For instance, they have placed *fi* 髴, fine hair, under *fi* instead of *mò*; *ngoi* 呆 is found both under *hau* and *muk*; *lung* 龍 is also repeated. No rule of uniform application can therefore be laid down with regard to finding them. Some of the characters now used as radicals, when analyzed, appear to be composed of two simpler radicals, in the same manner as those just spoken of; thus *píú* 髟 is made up of 長 and 彡, and its signification of long hair, together with its mode of combination, seem to bear out the inference, which the *Shüt Man* also corroborates, that it is thus formed; but in *héung* 香, *má* 麻, and *yam* 音, the present senses of the words and the composition of the characters, do not all correspond. And on turning to the same work, it appears that *héung* is compounded of *shü* 黍 and *kóm* 甘; *má* is from *pá* 林 and *uk* 屋 contracted; and *yam* is derived from joining *ín* 言 and *hau* 口, placing a line in the latter to represent sound. The scholar is very liable to err, therefore, if he attempts to analyze compound characters of this sort from their present forms; but compared to the derivatives from them, there is no doubt that they are, together with the radicals, among the most anciently formed characters in the language. They usually signify common things and actions,—they are extensively employed as primitives in forming derivatives (see class III.), to which they usually impart their own sound,—and their pronunciation has no resemblance to either of the two parts which form them.

II. The second class of primitives, those which are formed from a radical by an addition that of itself is unmeaning, are, as well as the radicals, for the most part contracted and modern forms of the ancient characters of the language. The compilers of the Dictionary were obliged to refer them to some one of the radicals by analyzing their component strokes, for as they are seldom or never joined with other primitives to form new characters, so they could not be classed among the radicals. It is by their radicals, also, that they are placed here, and the so called unmeaning part which remains when the radical has been taken away, is in fact an integral part of the original character, and cannot be dissevered. They are none of them, so far as their present construction is concerned, formed by the union of two distinct or simpler radicals; for if separated, the two parts convey no meaning. Thus *fat* 弗 not, is in Kánghí's Dictionary placed under the radical 弓, which if removed leaves merely two upright strokes; *chung*, 重, heavy, is found under 里, the addition at top having no meaning of itself, nor adding any idea to *lí*, which conveys the sense of heavy. Characters of this sort, then, are among the elementary words of the language. The word *í* 以, one of the most common in the language, is found under 人 *yan* in Kánghí, but it is difficult to assign any other reason for placing it there, than that its left hand stroke resembles *yan* more than any other radical, and it must go somewhere; it forms about ten derivatives. The several words, *yau* 由 from, *shan* 申 to stretch out, and *káp* 甲 scales, all appear to have been formed from 田 by variously lengthening its middle stroke; but *káp* is said by Chinese philologists to be intended as an imitation of a scale or bud, and *shan* to represent the back of a man; each of these three form between thirty or forty derivatives. *Ché* 且 moreover, *yik* 亦 also, *tai* 弟 a younger brother, *kü* 巨 great, *yéuk* 弱 weak, *wai* 爲 to be, *túi* 對 opposite, *ín* 燕 truly, *tai* 帝 an emperor, and many others, as well as the preceding, all therefore come into this class. It is estimated by Marshman to contain about one fourth of the 1689 primitives.

III. Primitives under this class, when analyzed, are found to consist of two complete radicals, although one of the two component parts, in some cases, is merely a stroke, as in *pít* 必 must, *ting* 丁 a sting or nail, *tsín* 千 a thousand, *yam* 壬 according to, &c., and others. Characters of this form, like those spoken of in class II, are among the primary words of the language. The majority of this class, however, are readily divisible into two radicals; as *séung* 相 mutual, *ü* 如 as, *kók* 各 each, *toi* 代 instead of, *mí* 尾 a tail, *kat* 吉 happiness, and numerous others. They are easily bisected, and, according to Chinese writers on the language, were originally formed from these two or from other simpler elements, now a little contracted; thus, 口 is contracted to 厶 in some words. It is however, quite sufficient for the present purpose, that they are at present thus combined, and it will greatly facilitate the remembering of them as primitives, to remember their two parts. Most of the primitives of this class occur in books as among the most common words of the language. *Yan* 因 cause, *kwan* 困 compressed, *kwan* 囷 a round granary, *ming* 名 name, *tò*, 到 at, *chuk* 畜 to domesticate, all belong to this class. Some of them are composed of a radical repeated, as *lam* 林 a forest, *pang* 朋 a friend, *tó* 多 many, *kwai* 圭 a badge of office, *tsín* or *tsán* 戔 to rob, *ím* 炎 ascending flame, &c.;—the three last do not often occur as separate words.

IV. Primitives formed of three or more radicals are few in number compared with those in the other classes. Such characters are placed here as do not, when the radical is removed, leave a complete character, but which are still further divisible into two radicals; as *king* 京 a capital, *wák* 畫 to paint, *shing* 聖 sacred, *chat* 質 substance, *lók* 樂 pleasure, *hóp* 合 to join, *tsó* 坐 to sit, *loi* 來 to come, *káp* 夾 to double, &c. A few of them are characters, where a radical is tripled; as *sò* 惢 suspicion, *níp* 聶 to whisper, *tsui* 毳 down of fur, *lui* 畾 a field laid out, &c.; but these are for the most part used in composition.

V. This class is composed of derivatives, which become primitives by being again joined to radicals. One half of the character will therefore be found in one of the preceding classes. Thus, fat 忽 suddenly, *yik* 易 to change, and *yéung* 昜 to expand, are all found under the primitive *mat* 勿 not, and are themselves all joined again to several radicals as primitives. *Shéung* 尙 still, is another instance; it combines as a primitive in *tóng* 堂 a palace, *tóng* 當 ought, *tóng* 黨 a village, *chéung* 嘗 to taste, *chang* 棠 to border, *shéung* 賞 to bestow, *chéung* 敞 open or plain, *chéung* 常 usual, and *chéung* 掌 palm of the hand, all of which combine several times with radicals to form new derivatives. Derivatives of *kók* 各 each, as *léuk* 略 a schedule, *lú* 路 a road, *lók* 洛 glare, and *hák* 客 a guest, are also primitives. *Hóp* 合 to join, among its seventy-four derivatives, has *táp* 答 to answer, *táp* 荅 to sustain, *yap* 翕 to raise, and *in* 弇 to screen from, all of which again unite more or less to form new derivatives. A few of this class are formed by repeating a derivative; as *kó* 哥 an elder brother, *king* 兢 cautious, *king* 競 violent, *kik* 棘 thorns, and *tsò* 棗 a date. Precisely similar to this description of words excepting that they do *not* again combine with radicals to form new derivatives, are several, which are formed by the combination of two primitives; of this sort are *ím* 豔 beautiful, *kwan* 䐃 round, *pí* 嚭 great, *héung* 嚮 over against (same as 向 *héung*), *yik* 鼬 a sort of mouse, &c., but they, are almost all of them, very uncommon.

It is principally in derivatives from this class, in which are found characters which combine the meanings of the two component parts, and which seem to have been put together with that intention. *Wái*, 歪 distorted, is, so far as any deductions can be drawn, evidently formed by the combination of *pat* 不 and *ching* 正 to express this sense, but in some of the other derivatives from *ching*, it is difficult to trace any shade of its own meaning of right, correct, &c. Great caution is necessary in deducing the meaning of a character from its component parts, for a person is as likely to go wrong as right, and perhaps more so: for instance, *chí* 遲 is made up of 辶 to walk and 犀 a rhinoceros, but one would be quite as likely from these two parts to say the word meant to tramp or walk heavily, as to infer its true meaning, that of slowness or walking slowly.

It may be remarked here that in this classification of the primitives, regard has been had only to the present mode of writing the characters, without any reference to their ancient form, or to their composition as described by Chinese philologists, which in many cases, is much more complicated, than it is now. As has already been observed in the radicals, so it is in the primitives—many are interchangeable, without altering the sense or sound of the word. Thus *táp* 蹋 and 蹹 to tread, are synonyms, just as *tòi* 帒 and 袋 a bag, are; in the first instance the primitive is changed, and in the second the radical. *Pán* 攀 and 扳 to drag or pull, are alike; and so are *ling* 㩕, and 拎 and 拎 to suspend; in these the apparent reason for changing the primitive is that the latter has fewer strokes. Numerous instances of this sort might be adduced. This interchanging of the primitive, however, is, in the great majority of cases referrible to a mere identity of sound, without the least reference to the meaning. Such changes are, to borrow a term from alphabetical languages, different modes of spelling the characters, rather than synonyms, as that word is usually understood.

In order to show the mode of combining the radicals and primitives, to form derivatives, and see what degree of influence they have upon the meaning of the compound character, two or three examples are given in full.

*Hó* 可 may, can, might; to have liberty or power to do, competent, able, admissable. It is formed, says the *Shüt Man*, by adding *hau* 口 a mouth, to *háu* 丂 which imparts the sound. It unites with forty-one radicals as follows:

何 *Hó*. Which, what, where, who; an interrogation, qualified by its context.

呵 *Hó*. Angry sounds, reprehending one; to ask. *Hó hó*, 呵呵 sound of laughter.

坷 *Hó*. Uneven, rugged, progressing.

奇 *Kí*. Strange, odd, remarkable, unusual; odd, an overplus, a remainder; one, a single one.

婀 *O′*. *O′ nó* 婀娜 a beautiful appearance.

岢 *Hó*. *Hó lám* 岢嵐 name of a hill in Shánsí.

岣 *Hó*. Same as the preceding.

抲 *Hó*. To carry on the shoulder, to order persons to go to their places; to screw the fingers. Read *ná* or *nik*, to lift up.

戨 *O′*. A stake to fasten the painter of a boat to, that it float not.

斨 *Hó*. To strike; to grasp hold of and raise up.

柯 *O′*. An ax-helve; name of a tree.

歌 *Hó*. To laugh, a loud laugh; noise of laughter.

肯 *Hó*. Same as *hó* 訶, to reprehend, to rail.

殉 *Kó*. Appearance of dying or death.

河 *Hó*. A river, the Yellow river, par excellence; *tín hó*, 天河 the milky way.

炣 *Hó*. Fire.

牱 *Kó*. An incorrect form of *kó*, 牁 a stake; some say, the name of a place.

牁 *Kó*. A stake to fasten a boat to; same as 戨 *ó*.

珂 *Ó.* A gem inferior to jade, white; an ornamental shell.

疴 *Ó.* Disease, sickness; read *ká*, disease or convulsions of children.

砢 *Ló.* Appearance of a multitude of small stones piled up; name of a river; same as 珂 *ó.*

祠 *Hó.* To sacrifice.

坷 *Kái.* A short, pigmy person.

笴 *Kó.* Shaft of an arrow.

絅 *Ó.* White silk.

胢 *O'.* Same as *ó* 髃 the knee-pan.

舸 *O'.* A boat, a large vessel.

苛 *Hó.* Troublesome, minute, vexatious; circumstantial; to trouble, to reprehend; quick.

蚵 *Hó.* Name of an insect.

袔 *Hó.* A sleeve, same as *hó*, 襀; read *kwá*, trowsers, a shirt next the skin.

袲 *Ó.* Appearance of garments.

褁 *Ó.* Same as the preceding.

訶 *Hó.* Some as *hó* 呵 to reprehend, to blame, to speak angrily, to scold.

跒 *Ká.* *Pá ká* 跁 跒 appearance of walking.

軻 *Ó.* Place where the wheel joins the nave; a carriage dragging heavily; *hóm ó* 轗 軻, impeded, obstructed.

阿 *O'.* Bank of stream; to lean against; a pillar; crooked. Who, which; a euphonic particle, used before names, and at the end of a dubitative assertion.

酉可 *Ká.* Bitter spirit.

鈳 *Ó.* A small boiler.

鞆 Pronunciation not known. A kind of bat or cudgel.

頙 *Hó.* To screw the neck in order to pry or look impertinently.

髃 *Ó.* The knee-pan.

魺 *Hó.* A sort of perch.

鴚 *Kó.* A sort of goose.

齣 *Ká.* To gnaw, to bite; read *kó*, appearance of the teeth.

哥 哥 *Kó.* Sound; same as 歌 to sing; *á kó*, an elder brother, a title of respect to a stranger.

哿 *Ó.* Able, can, possible; read *kó*, female ornaments. These two are instances of two derivatives uniting to form new characters.

In these forty-six derivatives, there is a remarkable uniformity of sound, but no similarity of signification can be traced running through the characters, neither when regarded as an independent group, nor when referred to their primitive. Of the whole number, *hó* 何, *hó* 河, *ó* 阿 *kó* 哥, and *ki* 奇 combine the most numerously with other radicals to form new characters.

*Ki*, 奇 strange, curious, (sometimes written 竒), one of these derivatives of *hó*, and therefore coming under class V., combines with fifty-one different radicals, as follows:

倚 *I'*. According to, to lean against, to depend on.

剞 *Kí*. A crooked sword; a crooked chissel or gouge.

埼 *Kí*. Head of a winding shore.

婍 *Kí*. An *extraordinary woman*; good.

尯 *Kí*. A hobbling, leaping, walk; to hop on one foot. Also read *hí*. Same as 踦

寄 *Kí*. To lodge, as in a tavern; to be under the protection of another; to send or forward by another.

崎 *Kí*. A mountain path that is uneven; same as 埼 *kí*.

庴 *Ai*. Appearance of leaning or sitting at ease. A storehouse for old people.

徛 *Kí*. A stone bridge; same as 碕 *kí*. To stand up; to cross a bridge.

徛 *Kí*. Parsimonious, economical, sparing; dissatisfied, uneasy.

掎 *Kí*. To entrap or drag along by one foot; to issue or educe; to bring out.

攲 *Kí*. To take up with two sticks, to nip up. *Kam kí* 钕攲 an uneven appearance.

斱 *Kí*. Same as 剞 *kí*.

椅 *I'*. A chair, a couch; the name of a tree.

欹 *I'*. *I' yü* 丨歟 an exclamation of admiration and surprise.

殑 *Kí*. To reject, to cast off; *tái kí* 大殑 to die, death.

猗 *Kí*. A distorted tiger's tooth. Depraved.

犄 *Kí*. and *I'*. Same as the following. Name of a sort of cow.

猗 *I*. An exclamation; same as 猗 *i*. Long, extended; to lean against; weak; to be near each other, as horses when pulling. A large dog. *I' i*, 丨 丨 an exclamation at seeing beautiful foliage.

琦 *Kí*. A precious stone; large appearance. *Kí wai* 丨瑋 a completed utensil of gem.

畸 *Kí*. A tabued field belonging to the emperor. A remainder in numbers. Extraordinary.

皱 *I'*. Same as *kí* 騎 to ride; same as *i* 猗 an exclamation.

痵 *I*. Weak, diseased, delicate; bedridden; to bury; as useless as if dead.

睎 *Kí*. One eyed.

碕 *Kí*. A stone bridge. A crooked bank or shore; a long coast.

矯 *I'*. A short appearance; same as *i* 痵.

禥 *Kí*. Good.

稦 *I'*. A plenteous growth of grain.

綺 *Kí*. Variegated, striped; silk used in winter, satin.

聍 *Kí*. To apply the ear to listen.

腑 *Ki.* To lay out, or to set in order the flesh for sacrifices.

螪 *Ki.* A kind of cicada; a spider with very long legs.

褘 *I.* Appearance of being well dressed; good.

觭 *Ki.* Horns on a cow, one elevated and one depressed. To obtain; single.

諦 *Ki.* To laugh or ridicule each other; read *hi*; irregular, incoherent talk.

猗 *I.* A large fierce dog; same as 猗 *i.*

踦 *Ki.* To bind the leg. To lean on one side; to stretch out the leg.

趌 *Ki.* Same as 技 *ki*; the appearance of walking; of a monkey climbing a tree.

輢 *I.* Side of a vehicle; place in a chariot where soldiers plant their spears.

躸 *Ki.* One body alone; single; unassociated.

隑 *I.* A kind of division or bank between fields. *I kui* 隑 隑 discontented, uneasy.

錡 *Ki* or *i.* A boiler to dress food; a stand for weapons; a stand or rack for bows; a surname.

雗 *Ki.* Same as *ki* 鵸, a fabulous bird.

羇 *Ki.* An ancient form of 羈 *ki.*

頎 *I.* Good.

蘬 *I.* Fragrant, odoriferous.

騎 *Ki.* To stride, to ride on the back of an animal; to ride horseback.

骑 *Ki.* Small bones.

魌 *Ki.* Ghost of a child; same as 魌 *ki.* Also garments cut out of paper and burned.

鵸 *Ki.* A fabulous bird with three heads and six tails.

齮 *I.* To bite, to gnaw.

Three out of this group again combine to form still more compound characters. *Ki* 寄 to send by one, is the parent of

徛 *Ki.* To cross or ford a creek by stepping stones; this is identical with *ki* 徛 in sense and sound.

槣 *Ki.* To take up anything with nippers, to use a pair of sticks to nip up an object; to contain in.

*Ki* 猗 long; extended, an exclamation, &c., also gives rise to two;

漪 *I.* The ripple or curl of a wave; the dashing of waves.

稿 *I.* Luxuriant grain, or grain growing plenteously.

*Ki* 羇 as it is commonly used, is itself a contraction of one of its own derivatives.

羇 *Ki.* An inn for the reception of travelers; a sojourner, a wayfarer.

羈 *Ki.* A bridle or halter; to restrain; tuft of hair on the head.

From a careful examination of this and the preceding group of characters, the scholar will immediately perceive how much more influence the radical has upon the meaning of the word than the primitive; and he will also observe how large a proportion of the characters have the same sound as the primitives. If these sounds had been written out in the court dialect, still more resemblance to the primitive would be manifest. In the first group, all, except six, have the same sound as the primitive, with simply a dialectical variation in the initial consonant, from *hó* to *ó* or *kó*—as it is sounded soft or hard. In the second group, with one exception, all the characters are either *kí* or *í*, both of which sounds are applied to the primitive. If an attempt is made to trace any similarity other than sound between the characters, or to run a thread of meaning through the whole, which, in each character, shall be modified by the radical, it will instantly be evident, that such could hardly have been the idea when first the characters were made. In the second group, the fourth word might, perhaps, be brought forward as an exception, and the conclusion drawn that it was formed by joining *extraordinary* to *woman*, to give the sense of good, or a good woman. Some one of the other significations of *kí*, as odd, alone, &c., may also be traced in the meanings of a few others of its derivatives, but in nearly all, the meaning of the primitive, either cannot be traced at all, or else only very remotely,—so remotely that it is difficult to suppose that any very great number of characters were formed on such principles.

In addition to these two examples, *lung* 龍 a dragon, will illustrate the use of a character both as a radical and a primitive. Many of the characters found in Kánghí under this, and the three words, *fi* 非, *tsai* 齊 and *tsing* 青, are homophonous with the radical, having another radical which gives the sense; perhaps one reason for this change was the few characters that would otherwise come under these radicals. The first part of this list contains such words as are found under other radicals; the remainder comprises those grouped under *lung* in *Kánghí*.

儱 *Lung*. *Lung tung* 儱侗 rude, unfinished, imperfect, incomplete.

嚨 *Lung*. The throat; *hau lung* 喉嚨 the gullet, throat, esophagus.

聾 *Lung*. A great noise; a sound.

壟 *Lung*. A barrow in a field, a mound.

壠 *Lung*. Same as the preceding.

寵 *Chung*. Affection, regard for, love, benevolence; gay.

巃 *Lung*. *Lung sung* 丨嵸 appearance of a lofty hill.

徿 *Lung*. To walk in a distorted manner; *lung tung* 徿侗 to walk straight ahead.

蘢 *Lung*. *Lung tsung* 丨悤 precipitate, hurried.

懬 *Lung*. Embarrassed, grieved, distressed.

攏 *Lung*. To grasp, to seize, to plunder.

曨 *Lung*. *Tung lung* 曈曨 the sun rising.

襱 *Lung*. A house with large open windows, or windows far apart.

櫳 *Lung*. A railing to restrain animals.

瀧 *Lung*. Appearance of a drizzling rain; name of stream.

爖 *Lung*. Fire.

瓏 *Lung*. A precious stone used in worship; same as 攏 *lung*. *Ling lung* 玲瓏 jingling of stones, bright; complete, perfect in its in kind, paragon.

礱 *Lung*. To rub, grind; same as 礲 *lung*.

礲 *Lung*. To rub, to grind; to sharpen by grinding.

穠 *Lung*. Grain corrupted, rotten.

竉 *Lung*. A den, a cavern, an aperture.

籠 *Lung*. A cage, an open workked basket to hold earth, birds, &c.; a quiver.

緟 *Chung*. Heavy, added to.

䉃 *Lung*. A cage, a basket for carrying pigs; same as 籠 *lung*.

矓 *Lung*. Same as the preceding.

聾 *Lung*. Deaf, hard of hearing.

朧 *Lung*. Fat, corpulent.

艞 *Lung*. A small boat, with a cover.

蠪 *Lung*. A fabulous quadruped.

襱 *Lung*. The two thighs of a pair of trowsers.

襲 *Tsáp*. Doubled garments; to receive, succeed to, hereditary; because; to enter; to invade; confused, suddenly.

讋 *Chíp*. Hurried enunciation as when panting, or terrified; fear; Read *Táp*, incessant talking.

贚 *Lung*. Poor, impoverished; appearance of a dragon.

躘 *Lung*. *Lung tung* 躘踵 appearance of a child walking.

蹱 *Lung*. *Lung tsung* 丨蹤 appearance of walking.

轞 *Lung*. End of an axle.

軄 *Lung*. *Lung tung* 軄躴 a deformed body.

隴 *Lung*. A dyke between fields; name of a district; a surname.

𥫽 *Chung*. Straight, correct.

靇 *Lung*. Sound of thunder; same as 靈 *ling*.

驡 *Pung*. *Pung pung* 丨丨 appearance of fullness and plenty, as a granary; same as *póng* 龐. Also read *lóng*, in the same sense.

驡 *Lung*. A wild horse. Read *chóng* in *chóng luk* 丨騄 a good horse.

鼛 *Lung*. The appearance of a broad drum. Also read *póng* in the same sense.

䵷 *Lung*. To paste up scrolls.

The couplets, analagous to dissyllables in alphabetic languages, which occur in this list, Chinese grammarians call *hín hók tsz'*, or clam-shell words; they are numerous in writing, but still more common in conversation, and would probably have become undivisible dissyllables, had it not been for the impracticable nature of the written characters.

䡁 *Hung*. An imperfectly seen dragon.

𢅵 *Kung*. Same as the following.

𢍉 *Kung*. To ascend.

龐 *Póng*. A lofty house. A confused appearance.

獵 *Lung*. Name of an animal.

龕 *Hóm*. Another form of *hóm*, 龕 a shrine.

朧 *Lung*. Another form of *lung*, 籠 a wicker-cage or basket.

龑 *I'm*. A high, bright appearance.

穠 *Lung*. Blasted, mildewed grain.

朧 *Lung*. Carnation color.

龔 *Lung*. Same as *lung* 龍.

龗 *Ling*. Same as *ling* 龗

儱 *Lung*. And, with; a cage, to drag, to draw..

龓 *Lung*. Same as the preceding.

龖 *Kín*. Backbone of a dragon. Also read *ngít*, beard of a dragon.

龖 *Kín*. Same as the preceding.

龔 *Kung*. To give, to present, to supply with; respectful; a surname.

瓏 *Lung*. A sort of gem with a dragon delineated; used in court, and in supplicating for rain. Same as *lung* 瓏.

龕 *Hóm*. To receive; many, repeated; sound, noise; to conquer; a shrine for Budha; a niche in houses where idols or tablets are placed.

龒 *Lung*. A wizard; a person dealing in supernatural arts.

靇 *Lung*. Sound of thunder.

龖 *Táp*. Flying dragon.

龗 *Ling*. A dragon, a spirit; good.

龘 *Táp*. Dragons in motion.

There is about the same proportion of homophonous words in the first part of this list, that is found in the two preceding, but still less reference to the meaning of the radical is perceptible here than in the characters under *hó* and *kí*. Six of the characters in the second part ought to have been distributed under their other radical; and in how many of the remainder, *lung* gives the meaning, and in how many it gives the sound, can easily be seen.

It is thus apparent, that a great proportion of the characters of the Chinese language have been formed by the union of idea and sound, being, in fact, partly of an ideographic, and partly of a syllabic nature. Although both of these parts, when separate, are independent and significant words, yet, when joined as has been shown above, to form new characters, one is seen to lose its sound altogether, and the other in a great majority of cases its sense. If this is the case, it is manifest why the most common characters were chosen as the phonetic part. The invention of symbols as representatives of things signified does not appear to have been carried to such an extent as to make them available for any very extensive use, the whole amount of all kinds, according to Chingtsíáu, being only 2425. It may be supposed that the plan of procedure at first was as follows. The spoken language, was already well understood, but when Ts'ongkat (or whoever else invented characters) wished to reduce it to writing, he, instead of making arbitrary marks or letters to represent sound, as has been done in other languages, endeavored to depict the thing itself, and to this hieroglyphic he applied the well understood name in the spoken language, but contrived no clue by which a person ignorant of that name could ever ascertain it from the character. But with the utmost ingenuity, it would be difficult to make a sufficient number, without, on the one hand making them so complicated as to be almost useless as media of communication, or on the other so much alike as to be undistinguishable. Hence, the plan was devised of combining existing symbols in such a way as to represent sound. This suggestion, according to Chinese philologists, arose from the imperfection of the symbolical system, 'to which,' say they, 'there are limits, but to the syllabic system, there are no limits.' From this remark, together with the examination of the lists just given, it is plainly inferred that pronunciation bears a prominent part in the Chinese written language. It has just been shown that many characters change their form without changing their sense or sound, but probably not a single character can be found which does not take another meaning if the sound or tone is changed. Thus *hò* 好 with one tone, means good; with another, it means to love: *ók* 惡 means wicked, but *ú* 惡 means to hate.

The mode of combining the ideographic and phonetic symbols in the formation of new words, appears to have been to select some common character of precisely the same sound as that by which the object in view was known, and join to it a symbol expressive of its most prominent feature. Thus, in the colloquial language, *má-nò* signified a cornelian or agate. To form a hieroglyphic symbol for this mineral was impossible; no accuracy of delineation, consistent with its use as a word, could distinguish it from any other stone, or prevent it from becoming a mere arbitrary collection of strokes. Recourse was therefore had to the syllabic system. The well understood symbol for *gem* or *stone*, joined to two symbols of exactly the same sound, forming either 瑪瑙 or 碼碯, produced characters sufficiently definite, and which briefly expressed the *má-nò gem* or *stone*. In Canton, where from intercourse with foreigners, many previously unknown articles and terms have been introduced, the number of modern characters formed on this principle is considerable; some of them, from long use, have become pretty well fixed; in others, they are changeable. Examples of this sort are *mí-sz'* 美士 for Mr.; *ká-fi* 咖啡 for coffee; *póng* 磅 for pound, &c.: *kéung pé* 薑啤 for ginger beer is partly descriptive and partly phonetic. The same plan is adopted to express the sounds of many local words, both in this and in other provincial dialects, for which no authorized characters are found. It only requires general use, and an introduction into standard works to make such characters as authorized as any others in the language. In this way, therefore, a great majority of the Chi-

拾級大成

nese characters have originated. It has been shown that the sound in many cases is only *similar* to the phonetic primitive, so that only a great degree of probability can be attained regarding the sound of the characters by mere inspection, but this probability is so great as to prove very useful in ascertaining the sound, after that of the primitive is known.

The derivatives of *ting* exhibit a few characters in which that sound is used as if imitating the sense of the word, showing an analogy in Chinese to what is found in almost every language—a similarity between the sense and sound of words. *Ting* 丁 is an ancient hieroglyphic for a sting, or a nail; its former use is lost, and it now means, a nail, bolt, pin; to nail, to fasten; a person, a member of a profession, or one of a calling; as *ping ting* 兵丁 a soldier; *nung ting* 農丁 a husbandman, &c.

亭 *Ting*. A portico, a wayside stile or porch to rest under; a high house; a dome resting on pillars; even, straight. Formed of *kò* high, and *ting*, which gives sound.

仃 *Ting*. Alone, walking alone; *ling ting* 伶仃 solitary.

冫丁 *Ting*. Icy, appearance of ice.

叮 *Ting*. *Ting ning* 叮嚀 to enjoin repeatedly, to charge upon.

圢 *Ting*. Even, level; footsteps in a field.

奵 *Ting*. A woman's name. Also read *tín*, a beautiful appearance.

宁 *Chü*. Space between the gate and screen in the palace where ministers waited.

彳丁 *Ting*. Alone; *ling ting* 彾彳丁 walking alone, same as *ting* 仃 and 趶 *ting*.

忊 *Ting*. Indignant; *ting wing* 忊憕 perturbed or moved, because not successful.

打 *Tá*. To strike, to beat, thump, fight; an auxiliary implying a doing.

朾 *Cháng*. A threshold, same as 棖 *cháng*. Also read *ting*, sound of felling timber.

汀 *Ting*. Sandy bank by a river side; a level shore.

灯 *Ting*. A strong vehement fire.

瓦丁 *Ting*. Bricks.

玎 *Ting*. Sound of gems jingling.

町 *Ting*. A path trodden in a field, a dyke used for a foot-path.

疔 *Ting*. A venereal sore, an ulcer that has a head or hard core.

矴 *Ting*. Ballast for boats.

盯 *Cháng*. To look straight a-head, to gaze.

穵 *Cháng*. A small protuberance, a small jutting out.

竹丁 *Ting*. A bamboo case or drawer.

籵 *Ting*. Rice placed on the table.

糸丁 *Cháng*. Appearance of silk or cord sticking upright.

罒丁 *Ting*. *Ting ling* 罒丁罒令 a very small net.

耓 *Ting*. A piece of wood at the bottom of a hand plough,

耵 *Ting*. *Ting ning* 耵聹 ear wax, or matter from the ear.

肘 *Ting*. Food placed for ornament; same as *ting* 飣.

芋 *Ting*. A plant resembling tea.

虰 *Cháng*. A sort of dragon-fly or libellula.

甹 *Ting*. To settle the breath.

觓 *Hang*. Same as *hang* 衡, long horns.

訂 *Ting*. To criticise, to examine; to settle, compare, collate, edit; criticism.

豨 *Ting*. Appearance of pigs and hogs.

赬 *Ching*. A carnation color. Also written 赪 *ching*.

趶 *Ting*. Walking alone. Read *cháng*, walking slowly. Read *ching*, walking crookedly.

軒 *Ting*. A carriage stopping.

邛 *Ting*. Name of a district; the name of a porch.

酊 *Ting*. To get drunk; *ming ting* 酩酊 drunk, inebriated.

釘 *Ting*. A nail, bolt, pin; to nail; to make nails; to work metal; to bind books; to fasten.

閅 *Mún*. Same as 門 *mún*.

阠 *Ting*. Name of a mound.

雩 *Cháng*. Rain.

靪 *Ting*. To mend the soles of shoes.

頂 *Ting*. The top, tip, summit, vertex, crown; summit of a hill; knob of cap; to carry on the head.

飣 *Ting*. Food placed on a table.

顁 *Ting*. Same as *ting* 頂.

骬 *Ting*. Bone of the leg.

In the old and unused character *ling* 令丁, to strike, *ting* acts the part of a radical.

Thirty-six out of the forty-seven characters in this list have the same sound as the primitive. A few of them, appear, from their meanings, to have been formed by the union of the two ideas in the radical and primitive; *ting*, an ulcer or a sore that comes to a hard head, might be adduced as an instance; *ting*, to criticise, was perhaps formed by a reference to the duties of a critic or editor, that of *nailing* or settling the text; the composition of *ting*, a dragon-fly, might also have been suggested by its nail-like body; and so of *ting*, to mend shoes, and perhaps one or two others. But in the greater part, the primitive appears to have been joined to the radical because it had the same sound as that by which the thing or action was known in the colloquial language; for instance, the sounds of the phrase *ling ting* are found under three different radicals, each having the same meaning, but no similarity can be discovered between the signification of the primitive and of the derivative. Two instances of similarity in the of sense and sound—those of *ting*, the jingling of gems, and *ting*, the sound of felling timber—occur in the group. The number of words and phrases of this sort in Chinese is not known, but probably the proportion is much the same as in other languages. They are most numerous under the radical *hau* (a mouth).

Attempts have been made by scholars to trace a leading idea running through all words containing the same primitive. Dr. Marshman, in a chapter on the primitives, in his Clavis (republished in the Chinese Repository, vol. IX., page 303), has several groups of characters, through which he endeavors to trace one leading idea; his remarks are worthy of attention, and have not been overlooked in writing these paragraphs. Mr. Lay, in an article in the Chinese Repository (vol. VII, page 255), has also several remarks on this subject; and M. Callery, a French gentleman, has published a dictionary on this plan. These writers have probably said nearly all that is worth saying on the subject. There can be no doubt that many characters can be selected from the body of the language, whose component parts do give the idea of the derivative; several have already been brought forward. They are worthy of notice because they frequently illustrate Chinese notions; but as they have been often quoted and illustrated by writers on the language, they have, perhaps more than any one thing else, tended to strengthen an idea current in the west, that the Chinese language is a wonderful collection of ideographic symbols, which are intelligible to different nations merely by presenting them to the eye, while they cannot be understood when spoken; and that in some magical way, a Chinese, a Cochinchinese, and a Japanese, who had never before seen each other, and could not understand a word of each other's conversation, as soon as a phrase in Chinese was handed to them, were able to communicate intelligibly. An anecdote is told of Scaliger, who, being visited one day by a scholar from Edinburgh, and addressed in Latin, begged his pardon, and requested an explanation, as he did not understand Gaelic. He would have understood, if his visiter had written his salutation, and this is just the case with the three Asiatics. The preceding paragraphs will tend to explain the manner in which this idea has originated, and show that, as there is no integrant sound in the character itself (as there is in an alphabetical word) which can be learned by inspection, or by observing any rules of pronunciation, its sound must be learned traditionally, while its meaning is ascertained from dictionaries, or from the context. This peculiarity has, probably been the chief cause of the dialects now existing in the empire.

## Chapter Third.

# OF READING AND WRITING.

It has been shown in the preceding chapter, that one primitive when joined to a number of radicals, gives its own sound to a large proportion of the characters thus formed. Of course, the sounds of the language were well understood in conversation, and the tones accurately distinguished long before the characters were made to which they were applied, but it appears highly probable that after the characters came into use, and when those who used them in writing endeavored also to talk in the same style, that some difficulty was found in being understood. Moreover, the words were all monosyllables, and many very common ones were sounded precisely alike, which added to the doubt of the hearer. One mode employed to reduce the difficulty has been referred to, that of combining two words of the same meaning, but having different sounds, to express one idea; and the great number of these dissyllabic combinations found in the written language, with the still greater number in use in the spoken, show how well suited it was found to remove this evil. Still, there were many cases in which doubt might arise, and to obviate it, the tones of the several characters were carefully distinguished. According to Dr. Morrison's Dictionary, which places all words with and without aspirates together, there are in the court dialect, four hundred and eleven different monysllables; in the Fukien dialect there are more than double that number; and in the Canton, according to the *Fan Wan*, there are, including aspirated sounds, four hundred and thirty-seven. In each of the three, they are increased by the application of four tones, which are still further multiplied by dividing each into a high and a low tone.

At the commencement of his studies, if he has the aid of a native teacher, the scholar should give his careful attention to the tones; but if he is without such assistance, no satisfactory progress can be made, and it is hardly worth his while to spend much time upon them. But with a teacher, let him spend an hour or more each day in simply reading Chinese, any book he has at hand, for the sole purpose of familiarizing himself with the sounds of the language. Let him follow the teacher's voice as exactly as it is possible for him to do, not content with one, two, nor half a dozen trials, but until he is satisfied that his own ear detects no difference between the teacher's enunciation and his own. Of course, no one can have any other standard of sound than this, and if this is not accurate, his pronunciation never will be. Constant practice at reading this way, (it is the Chinese mode,) imitating and following the teacher's voice, with his attention also specially directed to the same end, will sooner give the scholar a practical knowledge of the tones than any other mode. He will learn the tone as an integral part of the sound of the character, and not as if it were an addition to it.

Although it is impossible for a beginner to learn the tone of a character from barely observing any nice distinction of rules or diacritical marks, still the tones can be explained, and a few marks will materially aid the scholar who has already obtained an acquaintance with them, in recalling and remembering the proper one—just as the notes of music aid the singer after he has learned the octave. Several authors* have attempted to explain the tones, and from their remarks a few paragraphs are brought together in this place, which will afford a brief outline of the subject.

The four tones in Chinese are the *P'ing shing*, 平聲 even tone, the *Shéung shing*, 上聲 ascending tone, the *Hü shing*, 去聲 departing tone, and the *Yap shing*, 入聲 entering tone. The last three tones are collectively called *chúk shing*, 仄聲 or deflected tones, but the *p'ing shing* always retains its own name. Each is divided into an upper and lower tone, according as it is pronounced more or less elevated, making in all eight distinct intonations in two series of four each. The degree in which these two series vary from each other is not the same in all the tones; the upper and lower *p'ing shing* being distinctly marked, while there is very little perceptible difference between the upper and lower *shéung shing*.

The *p'ing shing* is precisely the musical monotone, pronounced without elevation or depression, being the natural unconstrained expression of the voice; the Chinese say, "its even path is neither high nor low." Thus in the sentences,

I am going to town;
I hope it will not rain;
You must look and see;

if the last word in each is sounded in somewhat of a dissatisfied or commanding tone, higher than the other words, the previous part of the sentence will naturally fall in the *p'ing shing*. In questions, uttered in a pleasant inviting tone, the words preceding the last naturally fall in the upper *p'ing shing*; as,

Will you let me see it?
Will you come too?

The negative answer to such questions (spoken by the same voice), would naturally fall into the lower *p'ing shing*; as,

When I asked him, 'Will you let me see it?' he said, 'No, I'll do no such thing.'

Here the different cadence of the question and reply illustrate the upper and lower *p'ing shing*. Native scholars consider this tone as the most important; one writer says respecting it, "in harmonizing the tones, the greatest attention should be given to the *p'ing shing*; there-

* See the preface to Medhurst's Dictionary of the Hokkëèn dialect, Dyer's Vocabulary of the Hokkëèn dialect, the introduction to the Chinese Chrestomathy, preface to Dr. Morrison's Dictionary, Vol. I., and the Chinese Repository, Vol. VII., page 57, and Vol. VI., page 579.

fore, the first enunciation makes that tone; raise the voice, and it makes the *shéung shing*; as it passes away, the *hü shing* is made the four tones completed, the *yap shing* is formed."

The *shéung shing* is a rising inflection of the voice ending higher than it began, such as is heard in the direct question, pronounced in somewhat of a high, shrill tone;—"it loudly calls, vehement, ardent, strong." It is also heard in exclamatory words, as *ah! Can it be!* The last word of the preceding sentences are in the *shéung shing*.

The *hü shing* is a prolonged tone, diminishing while it is uttered, just as a *diminuendo*, or an inverted swell, does in music, and sounded somewhat gruffly. The Chinese say that it "is clear, distinct, its dull, low path is long;" and they call it the *departing* tone, because it goes away like flowing water never to return. It is the converse of the *shéung shing*, ending lower than it began. The lower *hü shing* is nearer a monotone, not so gruff as the upper. The drawling tone of repressed discontent, as when one calls, but is still afraid of offending and ekes out the sound, may perhaps illustrate this tone.

The *yap shing* is on the same key as the *p'ing shing*, and might be briefly described as that tone truncated or cut off; in this dialect, it always ends in *k*, *p*, or *t*. The Chinese, having no orthography, cannot distinguish this tone as the foreigner does, by its consonantal termination; they say, "it is short, snatched, abrupt and quickly treasured up," which pretty well describes it. It is, as if a man sounding the *p'ing shing*, should be suddenly taken with a hiccup, and stop it half way; if the word *lock* be sounded, but the last two consonants omitted, it gives the *yap shing*. However the scholar will always recognize this tone by its termination.

The correct application of the tones to every word in speaking or reading is the principal difficulty with which the beginner has to contend. In English, they are all heard in conversation every day, according to the different humors of people, or their peculiar mode of enunciation; but in that language, tones of voice never affect the meaning of the speaker, except so far as they indicate his feelings; and moreover, they are applied to sentences, rather than to isolated words. In Chinese, on the contrary, the tones are applied to every word, and have nothing to do either with accent or emphasis; in asking or answering, intreating or refusing, railing or flattering, soothing or recriminating, they remain ever the same. The unlettered native knows almost nothing of the learned distinctions into four and eight tones, but he attends to them closely himself, and detects a mispronunciation as soon as the learned man, while he is much less likely to catch a foreigner's meaning.

A Chinese schoolmaster usually marks the tone of every character in the classical books which he puts into the hand of his pupil, but in printed books they are never marked, except in a few cases to prevent doubt, where the same character has two different tones and corresponding different significations. Thus, *shik* 食 means to eat; but when marked 食, it is read *tsz'*, and means to nourish or feed. *Lò* 勞 in the lower *p'ing shing* means to labor: but *lò* 勞 in the lower *hü shing*, means to reward labor. *Wó* 和 means mildness, peace; *wó* 和 is to harmonize. But even these are much oftener left unmarked than marked, for the intelligent reader is expected to learn their meaning from the context,—just as *a present* and *to present* are never accented in English. The Chinese illustrate the modulation of the tones by the following diagram, which also shows their mode of marking them at the four corners of the character. When a Chinese is asked in what tone any given character is, and doubts concerning it, he runs it through the four, until his ear catches the true sound, and many persons have a habit of aiding their ear in doing this by turning down a finger for each tone.

2. *Shéung shing*,
上聲
Rising tone.

3. *Hü shing*,
去聲
Receding tone.

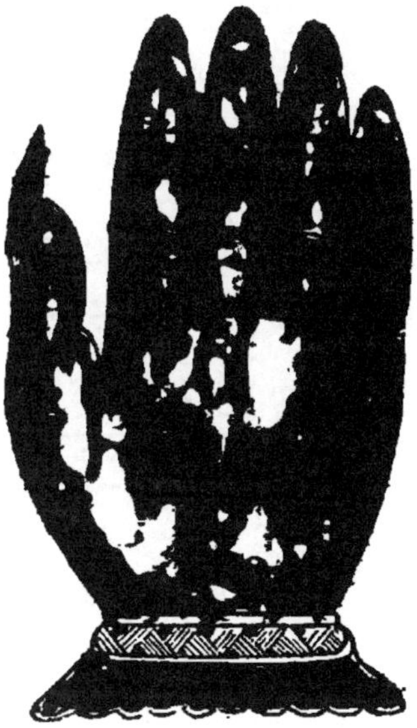

1. *P'ing shing*,
平聲
Even tone.

4. *Yap shing*,
入聲
Entering tone.

One character, employed, in connection with this diagram, to represent to the native student the mode of sounding the tones, is 厭, which has the whole four. Read ˏím (in the *p'ing shing*), it means *ease*; read 'ím (in the *shéung*), it means *to dislike*; read ím' (in the *hü*), it means *sufficient*; and read íp, (in the *yap shing*), it means *to prostrate* or *conceal*.

The authority for the tones in this dialect is the *Fan Wan* 分韻 (or divided sounds), a small Tonic Dictionary in four volumes, in which more than seven thousand of the most common characters are arranged according to their sounds. They are divided according to their termination, into thirty-three orders as shown in the following table. The first half of the table contains those characters which are considered as the standards of sound; the characters in the second half have been selected from the body of the book to illustrate the lower tones, and to aid the scholar in discriminating the two series. It will be seen that the initial sounds in the two are (except in one instance) unlike, which results from the want of a complete number of characters in the lower tones having the same initial as those in the upper.

| Ords. | FIRST SERIES, Comprising the Upper Tones. | | | | | | | |
|---|---|---|---|---|---|---|---|---|
| No. | 1 | 2 | 3 | 4 | P'ing shing. | Shéung shing. | Hü shing. | Yap shing. |
| 1 | 先 | 鮮 | 綫 | 屑 | ꜀sín | ‘sín | sín’ | sít꜄ |
| 2 | 威 | 偉 | 畏 | | ꜀wai | ‘wai | wai’ | |
| 3 | 幾 | 紀 | 記 | | ꜀kí | ‘kí | kí’ | |
| 4 | 諸 | 主 | 著 | | ꜀chü | ‘chü | chü’ | |
| 5 | 修 | 叟 | 秀 | | ꜀sau | ‘sau | sau’ | |
| 6 | 東 | 董 | 凍 | 篤 | ꜀tung | ‘tung | tung’ | tuk꜄ |
| 7 | 英 | 影 | 應 | 益 | ꜀ying | ‘ying | ying’ | yik꜄ |
| 8 | 賓 | 禀 | 嬪 | 畢 | ꜀pan | ‘pan | pan’ | pat꜄ |
| 9 | 張 | 掌 | 帳 | 着 | ꜀chéung | ‘chéung | chéung’ | chéuk꜄ |
| 10 | 剛 | 講 | 降 | 角 | ꜀kóng | ‘kóng | kóng’ | kók꜄ |
| 11 | 朝 | 沼 | 照 | | ꜀chiú | ‘chiú | chiú’ | |
| 12 | 孤 | 古 | 故 | | ꜀kú | ‘kú | kú’ | |
| 13 | 鴛 | 婉 | 怨 | 乙 | ꜀ün | ‘ün | ün’ | üt꜄ |
| 14 | 皆 | 解 | 介 | | ꜀kái | ‘kái | kái’ | |
| 15 | 登 | 等 | 発 | 德 | ꜀tang | ‘tang | tang’ | tak꜄ |
| 16 | 師 | 史 | 四 | | ꜀sz’ | ‘sz’ | sz’ | |

| Ords. | SECOND SERIES, Comprising the Lower Tones. | | | | | | | |
|---|---|---|---|---|---|---|---|---|
| No. | 1 | 2 | 3 | 4 | P'ing shing. | Shéung shing. | Hü shing. | Yap shing. |
| 1 | 連 | 璉 | 鍊 | 列 | ꜂lín | ‘lín | lín$^2$ | lit$_2$ |
| 2 | 迷 | 米 | 袂 | | ꜂mai | ‘mai | mai$^2$ | |
| 3 | 宜 | 議 | 貳 | | ꜂i | ‘i | í$^2$ | |
| 4 | 如 | 語 | 寓 | | ꜂ü | ‘ü | u$^2$ | |
| 5 | 留 | 柳 | 陋 | | ꜂lau | ‘lau | lau$^2$ | |
| 6 | 容 | 勇 | 用 | 欲 | ꜂yung | ‘yung | yung$^2$ | yuk$_2$ |
| 7 | 靈 | 領 | 令 | 力 | ꜂ling | ‘ling | ling$^2$ | lik$_2$ |
| 8 | 文 | 敏 | 問 | 勿 | ꜂man | ‘man | man$^2$ | mat$_2$ |
| 9 | 陽 | 仰 | 樣 | 藥 | ꜂yéung | ‘yéung | yéung$^2$ | yéuk$_2$ |
| 10 | 王 | 往 | 旺 | 鑊 | ꜂wóng | ‘wóng | wóng$^2$ | wók$_2$ |
| 11 | 寮 | 了 | 料 | | ꜂líú | ‘líú | líú$^2$ | |
| 12 | 無 | 母 | 務 | | ꜂mú | ‘mú | mú$^2$ | |
| 13 | 元 | 軟 | 願 | 月 | ꜂ün | ‘ün | ün$^2$ | üt$_2$ |
| 14 | 鞋 | 蟹 | 懈 | | ꜂hái | ‘hái | hái$^2$ | |
| 15 | 盟 | 猛 | 孟 | 墨 | ꜂mang | ‘mang | mang$^2$ | mak$_2$ |
| 16 | 詞 | 似 | 自 | | ꜂tsz’ | ‘tsz’ | tsz’$^2$ | |

拾級大成

| | | | | | | | | |
|---|---|---|---|---|---|---|---|---|
| 17 | 金 錦 禁 急 | ꜀kam | ʻkam | kamʼ | kap꜁ | | | |
| 18 | 交 絞 教 | ꜀káu | ʻkáu | káuʼ | | | | |
| 19 | 栽 宰 載 | ꜀tsoi | ʻtsoi | tsoiʼ | | | | |
| 20 | 兼 檢 劍 刦 | ꜀kím | ʻkím | kímʼ | kíp꜁ | | | |
| 21 | 津 贐 進 卒 | ꜀tsun | ʻtsun | tsunʼ | tsut꜁ | | | |
| 22 | 雖 髓 歲 | ꜀sui | ʻsui | suiʼ | | | | |
| 23 | 科 火 貨 | ꜀fó | ʻfó | fóʼ | | | | |
| 24 | 緘 減 鑒 甲 | ꜀kám | ʻkám | kámʼ | káp꜁ | | | |
| 25 | 翻 反 泛 發 | ꜀fán | ʻfán | fánʼ | fát꜁ | | | |
| 26 | 家 賈 嫁 | ꜀ká | ʻká | káʼ | | | | |
| 27 | 官 管 貫 括 | ꜀kún | ʻkún | kúnʼ | kút꜁ | | | |
| 28 | 魁 賄 誨 | ꜀fúi | ʻfúi | fúiʼ | | | | |
| 29 | 遮 者 蔗 | ꜀ché | ʻché | chéʼ | | | | |
| 30 | 干 趕 幹 割 | ꜀kón | ʻkón | kónʼ | kót꜁ | | | |
| 31 | 甘 敢 紺 蛤 | ꜀kʻóm | ʻkʻóm | kʻóm | kʻóp꜁ | | | |
| 32 | N. B. *In these two orders, no words occur in this series.* | | | | | | | |
| 33 | | | | | | | | |

| | | | | | |
|---|---|---|---|---|---|
| 17 | 吟 衽 任 入 | ꜂yam | ꜄yam | yam$^2$ | yap$_2$ |
| 18 | 茅 卯 貌 | ꜂máu | ꜄máu | máu$^2$ | |
| 19 | 臺 殆 代 | ꜂tʻoi | ꜄tʻoi | tʻoi$^2$ | |
| 20 | 嚴 染 驗 業 | ꜂ím | ꜄ím | ím$^2$ | íp$_2$ |
| 21 | 倫 卵 論 律 | ꜂lun | ꜄lun | lun$^2$ | lut$_2$ |
| 22 | 雷 彙 類 | ꜂lui | ꜄lui | lui$^2$ | |
| 23 | 鵝 我 臥 | ꜂ngó | ꜄ngó | ngó$^2$ | |
| 24 | 藍 覽 纜 蠟 | ꜂lám | ꜄lám | lám$^2$ | láp$_2$ |
| 25 | 闌 懶 爛 辣 | ꜂lán | ꜄lán | lán$^2$ | lát$_2$ |
| 26 | 牙 雅 迓 | ꜂ngá | ꜄ngá | ngá$^2$ | |
| 27 | 門 滿 悶 末 | ꜂mún | ꜄mún | mún$^2$ | mút$_2$ |
| 28 | 梅 每 昧 | ꜂múi | ꜄múi | múi$^2$ | |
| 29 | 蛇 社 射 | ꜂shé | ꜄shé | shé$^2$ | |
| 30 | 寒 旱 翰 褐 | ꜂hón | ꜄hón | hón$^2$ | hót$_2$ |
| 31 | 含 頷 憾 合 | ꜂hóm | ꜄hóm | hóm$^2$ | hóp$_2$ |
| 32 | 彭 棒 硬 額 | ꜂pʻáng | ꜄pʻáng | ngáng$^2$ | ngák$_2$ |
| 33 | 吾 五 悟 | ꜂ʼng | ꜄ʼng | ʼng$^2$ | |

This table of sounds should be learned thoroughly, in their proper order together with all the characters of the upper series, and it will be a good exercise for the scholar to read over with his teacher the lists of characters which are found in the index (leaves 1—13) of the *Fan Wan*, making him enunciate them very distinctly, and distinguish the two series of upper and lower tones, which are there placed together. The necessity of accurately learning the tones and the aspirates, cannot be too strongly impressed on the beginner. A great part of his usefulness will depend on his ability to converse, and people will hear him with much greater pleasure if he speaks accurately as well as fluently.

There are several deviations from the standard in pronouncing the words comprised under several of the classes, which perhaps arises from an endeavor to multiply the number of different sounds in conversation. For instance, some of the words ending in *ai* of the 2d order, in *au* of the 5th, in *an* and *at* of the 8th, in *ang* and *ap* of the 15th, and in *am* and *ap* of the 17th, have a tendency to run into the long vowel sounds of *ái*, *áu*, *án* and *át*, *áng* and *ák*, and of *ám* and *áp* of other orders; in some instances the change is complete, in others it is about half way. Many of the words ending in *ing* and *ik* of the 7th order, are usually heard sounded as *eng* and *ek*, while others, which are placed in the same order in the *Fan Wan*, are by most of the common people sounded *ang* and *ak*, differing a very little from the words in the 15th order. The termination *ú*, in *kú* of the 12th order, in more than half of the words placed in it, is exchanged for *ò*; an attempt appears to have been made by the compilers of the work to discriminate between the two; in some words the distinction is well marked between the *ú* and the *ò*, while in others, some doubt arises which way the word should be written. Further observations on these 33 orders are to be found on pages viii—x of the Introduction to the Chinese Chrestomathy.

The plan of marking the tones, when writing the sounds of the character in Roman letters, is a great assistance to the scholar in remembering them; he by degrees associates a certain mark with a certain tone, and the one aids in recalling the other. In the Fukien dialects, there are only seven tones (the upper and lower *shéung shing* being regarded as one), which are thus marked in Medhurst's Dictionary.

| | | | | | |
|---|---|---|---|---|---|
| *P'ing shing.* | 君 | *kwun.* | *Shéung shing.* | 滚 | *kwún.* |
| | 群 | *kwûn.* | | 滚 | *kwún.* |
| *Hü shing.* | 棍 | *kwùn.* | *Yap shing,* | 骨 | *kwut.* |
| | 郡 | *kwūn.* | | 滑 | *kwút.* |

In Dr. Morrison's Dictionary, the tones are not appended to the word, being written only once in brackets adjoining each character. In the Chrestomathy, Jones' system of spelling is employed, which requires accents upon some of the vowels, thus preoccupying the top

拾級大成



of the vowels, so that no marks for the tones can be placed without confusion. An attempt has been made in that work to imitate the Chinese mode, with an addition of a horizontal line underneath in order to distinguish between the upper and lower series; thus,

| | | | | |
|---|---|---|---|---|
| *P'ing shing.* | 因 ꜀*yan.* | | *Shéung shing.* | 隱 ꜂*yan.* |
| | 人 ꜁*yan.* | | | 引 ꜃*yan.* |
| *Hü shing.* | 印 *yan*꜄. | | *Yap shing.* | 一 *yat*꜆. |
| | 孕 *yan*꜅. | | | 日 *yat*꜇. |

This system of pronunciation, and this mode of marking the tones, are adopted in the following pages.

Besides the division of characters by this system of tones, there are many which are distinguished from each other by *aspirates*. This has been denoted by the French sinologues by a *t*, as *tchuene;* other writers have expressed it by the common Greek spiritus asper (ʽ) placed after the initial consonant and before an *h;* when that mark could not be obtained, an inverted comma (ʻ) has been employed. The aspirate is called *p'an hí* 噴氣, but the Chinese have no mark to denote it, leaving the scholar to learn it by the ear alone. It is a very important part of pronunciation, as much so in every respect as the tones, and should be particularly attended to. The aspirated characters are arranged by themselves in the *Fan Wan*, and reading them over with the teacher several times, will aid in remembering them. It is marked in this work by the spiritus asper; as *k'í, t'óng, &c.* It is almost wholly confined to words beginning with *k, kw, ch, t,* or *p.*

In reading Chinese books, the scholar sensibly feels the want of the various marks of punctuation, capital letters to distinguish proper names, and other grammatical additions to the bare text, which so much facilitate the understanding of books in western languages. He should therefore request his teacher to accurately punctuate the books he reads, and have him mark the names of persons and places, if they occur frequently. There are appropriate marks to indicate these, but in the most finished pieces of composition, the sentences are so framed, that the intelligent reader feels no need of any marks to show their division into sentences, and they are therefore in such writings usually omitted. The Chinese regard the characters as very elegant in themselves, and prefer a severe simplicity, destitute of the least addition. The want of a well understood system of punctuation, however, is a cause of many discrepancies in their standard works, and a fruitful source of misapprehension in reading. Sometimes, especially in school-books, and geographical and historical works, &c., it is otherwise. There is an edition of the Four Books, called *Sz' Shü, Lí kü, tsáp chü,* 四書離句集註 or "the Four Books, divided into sentences, with comments" by Chü fûtsz', which is carefully punctuated, and on this account, is better for a beginner than any other edition. The *Kóng Kám I' Chí* (or History Made Easy) is also very carefully punctuated. According to this work, "a complete proposition, where the sense also is complete, makes a period (*kü* 句), and is indicated by a small round mark placed at the side of the word [where it terminates]. A complete proposition, where the sense is not complete, makes a clause (*tau* 讀), and is indicated by a small round mark placed between the words." The former of these answers to the period in English, the latter to the comma; the first is frequently met with in common books, but the last is more seldom used.

Paragraphs are indicated by a large circle ○ placed between two sentences in the column, and called *tái hün*, but neither is this mark much used. There is a mode of emphasizing certain passages, analogous to the use of italics and capitals in English, frequently employed, which consists in marking a row of points or circles down the column, one or more opposite each character. This plan has been refined upon by the compilers of the ***Kóng Kám***, who have, by a row of white open circles given praise to the subject matter of the passage, and by a row of black circles, passed censure upon it. Names of places are sometimes designated by double lines drawn down the side of the characters, while names of persons are marked by a single line drawn in the same manner—both of which are shown in the following sentence, taken from the ***Sám Kwók Chí***. Names of books are, in Kánghí, in the ***Pún Tsò***, and in some other works, quoted by being inclosed in lines drawn around them.

登曰兒亦有計了乃
入見呂布曰徐州四
面受敵操必力攻

"Tang said, '*I also have a plan;*' then entering and seeing Lupò he said, 'Chüchow will be attacked on all sides, and Tsò will strenuously fight.'"

There is another way of marking respect, somewhat analagous to capitalizing or spacing a word in English, common in public documents, prefaces, &c., which is done by placing the word or name at the top of a new column. The rule appears to be to place the name of the reigning emperor's father or ancestors four characters above the other columns; the name or titles of the emperor himself, three characters above the rest; the palace, the capital, the laws, or whatever emanates from his majesty, are elevated two characters; the Tribunals, high officers, &c., are placed one character above the other columns. Emphatic words, honorable epithets, &c., begin a new column, but at the same elevation. When there is not space for a new column for high officers or honorable appellations, it is considered as indicating the same respect to write the same in the column, only leaving a blank space before the first word equivalent to one character. The mode of marking these various grades is not, however, always the same;—for instance, when an inferior magistrate issues an edict that has been received from his superiors, he elevates the latter's names or titles two or three characters above the other columns, according to their rank. The words to express the reigning emperor or dynasty, however, are always placed the highest in all official papers or books in which they are mentioned. There is also a mode, the opposite of this, of expressing one's-self by a kind of degradation in the position of the character, which is indicated by writing it in a smaller size to the right of the column. The most usual mode, however, is to avoid writing the name by using some well understood periphrasis.

Some further explanation of the system of pronunciation adopted will conclude the remarks on reading. The system proposed by sir William Jones, afterwards recommended by Mr. Pickering, and now adopted, with some variations, throughout almost all India, in the islands of the Pacific, and among the native tribes of North America, seems better fitted than any other to express the sounds of the Chinese language. And with very few exceptions and alterations, it is followed in this work. The system is too well-known to need here any explanations, and too generally approved to need any defense. The changes made in it are such as the peculiarities of the Chinese language necessarily require. In defining the letters, no attempt has been made to distinguish the double vowels from the true diphthongs, nor to separate the consonants into different classes. This list contains only those that are found in this dialect.

VOWELS AND DIPHTHONGS.

1. *a* pronounced as in *quota*, *America*, *agreeable*, and like short *u* in *tun*, *pun*—e. g. 近 *kan*, 肯 *hang*.
   *á* pronounced as in *calm*, *balm*, *father*—e. g. 鹹 *kám*, 横 *wáng*.

2. *e* pronounced as in *men*, *hen*, which is heard in many words under the 7th order,—e. g. 石 *shek*, 聽 *teng*.
   *é* pronounced as *a* in *may*, *lay*, and as *ei* in *neigh*—e. g. 寫 *sé*.

3. *i* pronounced short as in *pin*, *sin*—e. g. 姓 *sing*.
   *í* pronounced long as in *machine*, *marine*, *police*—e. g. 記 *kí*, 面 *mín*.

4. *ó* pronounced as in *lord*, as *aw* in *awful*, and as *a* in *all*, *tall*—e. g. 歌 *kó*, 看 *hón*.

5. *ò* pronounced as in *no*, *so*; or as *ow* in *snow*, *flow*, *glow*—e. g. 做 *tsò*, 好 *hò*.

6. *u* pronounced as in *bull, pull;* or as *oo* in *foot, book*—e. g. 工 *kung*.
*ú* pronounced as in *rule;* or *oo* in *school, fool*—e. g. 門 *mún*, 故 *kú*.
7. *ü* pronounced as in *l'une;* the French sound—e. g. 柱 *ch'ü*.
8. *ai* pronounced as in *aisle;* as *ie* in *tie;* or as *i* in *life*, but closer—e. g. 畏 *wai*.
*ái* pronounced nearly like the word *aye*—e. g. 怪 *kwái*.
9. *au* pronounced as *ou* in *plough, our;* or as *ow* in *cow, brow*, but closer—e. g. 鈕 *nau*, 救 *kau*.
*áu* pronounced like the preceding, with the *a* long—e. g. 教 *káu*.
10. *éu* pronounced with both letters distinct, resembling the colloquial contraction *say 'em*—e. g. 長 *chéung*.
11. *íú* pronounced as *ew* in *pew*, but more open or lengthened—e. g. 料 *líú*.
12. *oi* pronounced as in *oil;* or *oy* in *joy, alloy*—e. g. 內 *noi*.
13. *ui* pronounced nearly as in *fluid, ruined*, but more open—e. g. 雖 *sui*.
*úi* pronounced like the preceding, with *u* long—e. g. 灰 *fúi*.

CONSONANTS.

14. *ch* pronounced as in *chair, cheap*.
15. *f* pronounced as in *fine, fair, face*.
16. *h* pronounced as in *he, home, house*.
17. *k* pronounced as in *kite, key, king*.
18. *kw* pronounced as *qu* in *quite, quash*.
19. *l* pronounced as in *lane, lay, low, long*.
20. *m* pronounced as in *may, man, much*.
21. *n* pronounced as in *nay, new, no*.
22. *ng* pronounced as in *singing:* as an initial sound it may be represented by sounding the word *hanging*, omitting the first two letters—e. g. 我 *ngó*, 岸 *ngón*.
23. *p* pronounced as in *pay, pomp, pound*.
24. *s* pronounced asin *son, sea, say*.
25. *sh* pronounced as in *shall, she, show*.
26. *sz'* pronounced with a strong emission of breath, as if followed by *i* half suppressed—e. g. 士 *sz'*.
27. *t* pronounced as in *time, tune, tent*.
28. *ts* pronounced as in *wits, bits*.
29. *tsz'* pronounced like *sz'*, with only the addition of a *t*—e. g. 此 *ts'z'*.
30. *w* pronounced as in *wind, woe, will*.
31. *y* pronounced as in *young, your, youth*.

Some remarks on writing have already been made (see page 2), but the subject demands fuller explanations and directions. The Chinese are great admirers of calligraphy, and take unwearied pains to write their characters in a uniform, correct, and elegant manner. Correctness in writing is, indeed, regarded as more important than elegance; but to the eye of a Chinese a stiff, disproportioned character is very displeasing. After the copy-slip books mentioned above have been copied repeatedly, the teacher requires his pupil to copy by the eye upon paper ruled into squares of the proper size; this teaches him to proportion the characters, so as to write all, whether the strokes be more or less numerous, in nearly the same space. In addition to this, the scholar provides himself with a painted board, called *fan pái*, upon which, with a pencil dipped in blackened water he writes the characters repeatedly in a free and bold manner. All these modes should be more or less practiced by the foreign student; they will make the shape and composition of the character very familiar.

The usual mode of holding the pencil is shown in the subjoined figure.

At first, it will seem irksome to hold it in this manner, but a few trials, made at intervals, will soon habituate the hand to the motion. Minute rules are given for forming the different parts of characters by authors who have paid particular attention to this subject. One of the best treatises on writing is that of Wóng Yaukwan, called ***Pat Ch'an T'ò***, 筆陣圖 or Plates and Rules for the Pencil. He thus describes the mode of holding the pencil. "Let the thumb be placed with the back towards the body facing outwards; let the fore and middle fingers, with the back turned outwards, be brought near it, facing the body; thus holding fast the pencil: let the fourth and little finger, placed close together, be brought part way in [beyond the pencil], pointing towards you; so holding the pencil, with the first half open and hollow, and with the fingers close together: this is the best way of holding the pencil." He gives twelve plates to illustrate the different modes of holding the pencil for writing small and large characters, sign-boards, &c., with ample directions for each. In writing, the Chinese begin with the upper or horizontal strokes, then follow the upright ones, afterwards those on the left side, and finish the word on the right. All the elementary strokes are considered as being combined in the character *Wing*, eternal.

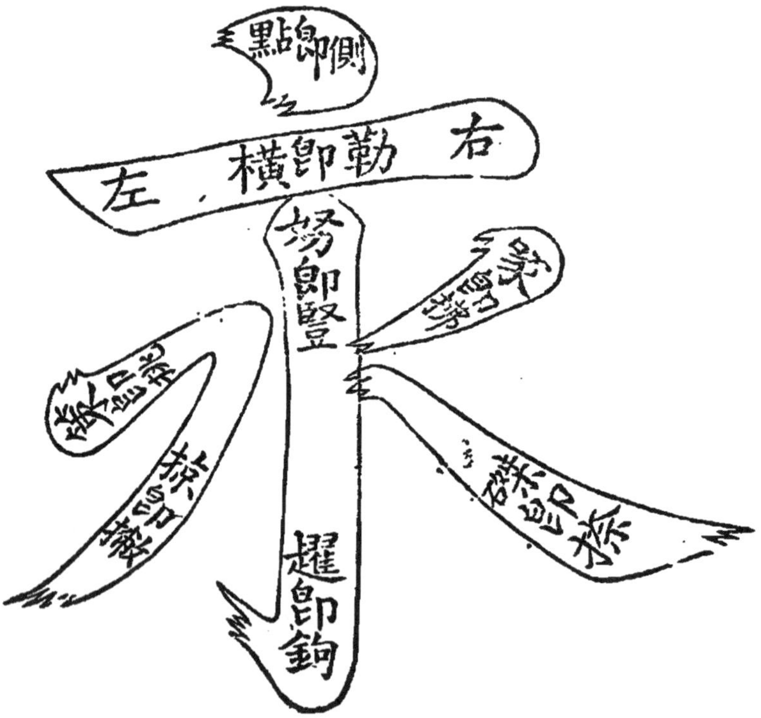


The component strokes of this character are thus named in books, but the common terms, which form the lower line of words, are different; both of them are inserted in the middle of the strokes in this diagram, and their names run as follows:

| 側 | 勒 | 努 | 趯 | 策 | 掠 | 啄 | 磔 |
|---|---|---|---|---|---|---|---|
| chak, | lak$_2$ | ʻnò | yéuk$_2$ | ch'ák, | léuk$_2$ | téuk, | chák$_2$ |
| ʻtim | ₍wáng | shü | ngau | ₍t'iú | p'ít, | fat, | nát$_2$ |
| dot. | horizontal. | perpendicular. | hook. | spike. | sweep. | dash. | stroke. |

Each of these is varied a little, which gives rise, according to Wóng, to 82 different forms; all of them are found in his work, with illustrative examples under each. In order to aid the memory, each one of the varieties has a specific name, some of them very fanciful, but illustrating the minuteness with which the Chinese have studied the

宇宙定寧至聖盂蓋勅部幼即讀蝀議續嘉吾貴去
甲平干午葡萄蜀葛向勻匀勿左在尤尨右有厷灰
木本朱東樂桀築梟十上下士才斗半井丕亚亞並
目自因固川升邦邦伊侈傪修亦赤然無三冊冉聿
雖願顧體御謝樹術鑾響需留章意素累吸呼峰峻
和知鈿細囂囂器器齒爾爽鹽此七也乜云去且旦
丈尺史又武成戓幾思息必志勉旭魁拋天父外文
鷄鳩輝頫鳥馬馮為師明既野朝故辰後樊談荼黍
耒林森樾聚迷哥乘冠覓甚空雲昔皆齊衆表萬禹
洈騰讓靖敬獻欽劉鄧辭衍仰蕃筆衝擲鸞鷲鷺鷽

風鳳飛氣先見元毛庭居尹底友及反皮参修須形
治洪流海是足走夌者耆老考馨聲繁繫繼纚纏屬
車申中巾卓犖單畢易乃毋力正主本王身目耳貝
白工曰四會合金命琴吝各谷土止山公了寸卜才
上下千小贏齋龜羅晶磊轟森燹鬱靈糜口日田由
丁芋寧亭遠邊遂逮嗔唉咲[illegible]作仰冲行匝巨於佳
[illegible]
官宮宋等虞虛屬郡下工乇口血邵郊鄭鄰阱阝陟階
登發發癸祭蔡察登氶泉衆聚家象豪豕仁儀俯休
從徐循後乳亂色包

characters of their language. It is unnecessary, however, for the foreign student to attend much to these minutiæ, further perhaps than to read them over. He will more readily learn the proper form of characters by copying them, in any or all the ways that Chinese scholars employ. The accompanying table contains four characters under each of all the varieties given by Shíú Wing, another author on calligraphy, in his copy-slip book. This book is one of those previously described, printed in white letters on a black ground, and the student cannot do better in order to learn to write well proportioned characters than to copy them until he can write them by the eye. It may, however, be considered an unnecessary outlay of time in trying to learn to write an elegant hand, for native copyists can probably always be procured when necessary. With regard to this, the scholar must determine for himself how far he will carry his lessons in writing, according to the use he intends to put his skill to. Further particulars, with a translation of Shíú Wing's directions for every variety of character, will be found in the Chinese Chrestomathy, pages 19—41.

The mode of counting the number of strokes in a character ought to be noticed. The Chinese, when searching for a word in the dictionary, always write it with their finger, counting the strokes as they write. But this is a slow way, and the scholar should learn to ascertain the number of strokes by inspection, that is, by learning to add up the number of strokes by looking at the constituent parts of the character. For instance, 樂 is composed of four parts, severally formed of 3, 5, 3, and 4 strokes, which together make 15 strokes. A little practice will make this very easy, and in the end save much time.

The scholar, while practicing with the pencil, will do well to attend also to the running-hand form of the characters; one variety is called *hang tsz'* 行字, or *hang shü* 行書; and the other *ts'ò tsz'* 草字, or plant character. Both these forms of characters are employed in common transactions of life, and to many people are more familiar than the correct and full form found in books. They occupy nearly the same place in Chinese as common writing does in English, though not so essential, since many persons always write in the full form. There are certain rules for contracting the different parts of characters, particularly in the *hang tsz'*, which can be learned from copies written by the teacher. Chinese lads learn it by practice, or from copy-slip books. The *Chik Ts'ò Ts'in Tsz' Man* 直草千字文 or Thousand Character Classic in the Correct and Running Hand, is one of the books used to teach running-hand. The text is written in both forms in parallel columns and copied by placing a sheet of thin paper upon the page.

# Chapter Fourth.

## LESSONS IN READING.

---

The following sentences are all selected from good Chinese writings, such as the *Sám Kwók Chí, Líú Chái*, &c. Each one of them forms a complete period, and is read from left to right for convenience in printing the sound, and the signification underneath. The literal translation of each word is placed underneath its sound, and the free idiomatic translation at the foot of the page. To derive all the benefit possible from the lessons, the sound and sense of every character as it here stands should be committed to memory; so that if the Chinese line be covered, every character can be written by seeing its sound; if the sounds be covered, the line of Chinese can be read off fluently; or if the line of English be exposed, the Chinese characters and sound will immediately recur to the mind.

1 呂 布 無 義 之 人 不 可 信 也
*‘Lü Pò’ ,mò i’ ,chí ,yan, pat, ‘hó sun’ ‘yá.*
Lü Pò no principle 's man, not can believe truly.

2 屈 身 守 分 以 待 天 時 不 可 與 命
*Wat, ,shan ‘shau fan’ ‘i toi’ ,t‘in ,shí, pat, ‘hó ‘ü ming’*
Succumb myself keeping place by waiting heaven's time, not can with fate

爭 也
*,chang ‘yá.*
quarrel.

3 吾 與 奉 先 無 隙 何 故 引 兵 至 此
*‘Ng ‘ü Fung’ ,sín ,mò kwik,. ,hó kú’ ‘yan ,ping chí’ ‘ts‘z’.*
I with Fungsín without altercation, what reason lead troops to this-place?

4 公 等 皆 讀 書 之 人 何 不 達 理
*,Kung ‘tang ,kái tuk, ,shü ,chí ,yan; ,hó pat, tát, ‘lí?*
Sirs all read books 's men; how not understand reason?

---

1. Lü Pò, a man of no principle, cannot be trusted.

2. By succumbing and keeping my place, I shall await heaven's time; I cannot contend with fate.

3. I have no dispute with Fungsín, and why therefore should I lead troops here?

4. You, gentlemen, are all scholars; how is it then that you do not understand what is right?

5 你年尙輕未可爲大將
'Ní ,nín shéung' ,hing, mí² 'hó ,wai tái² tséung'.
Your years still few, not-yet able to be great captain.

6 可惜當日火不大不曾燒死你這國賊
'Hó sik,! ,tóng yat, 'fó pat, tái², pat, ,ts'ang 'shíú 'sz' 'ní ché' kwók, ts'ak,.
How sad! that day fire not powerful, not yet burned dead you that state rebel.

7 宮曰汝心術不正吾故棄汝
,Kung üt,, 'ü ,sam shut, pat, ching' ,'ng kú' hí' 'ü.
Kung said, 'Your heart's designs not upright, I therefore discarded you.'

8 廟堂之上何太無禮
Miú² ,t'óng ,chí shéung², ,hó t'ái' ,mò 'lai?
Ancestral court 's within, how greatly destitute of propriety?

9 欺君罔上乃爲無禮
,Hi ,kwan 'móng shéung², 'nái ,wai ,mò 'lai.
Deceiving prince, despising superiors, is to be destitute of propriety.

10 先生此去天各一方未知相會却於何日
,Sín ,shang 'ts'z' hü', ,t'ín kók, yat, ,fóng, mí² ,chí ,séung úi² k'éuk, ,ü ,hó yat,.
Sir this departure, heaven each one place, not know mutual meeting will-be in what day.

11 其人身長七尺面黃睛赤形容古怪
,K'í ,yan ,shan 'ch'éung ts'at, ch'ik, mín² ,wóng, ,tsing ch'ik, ,ying ,yung 'kú kwái'.
This man's body length seven cubits, face yellow, pupil reddish, form appearance odd wild.

---

5. You, still young in years, are not able to act as a high general.

6. How sad, that on that day the fire was not powerful enough to have burned you to death,—you that rebel against the state!

7. Kung said, 'your designs were not upright, and I therefore cast you off.'

8. In the court of ancestors, how can you be so utterly devoid of propriety?

9. He, who deceives his prince and despises his superiors, is one who is without propriety.

10. After this departure, sir, each of us will have his own sky; we know not the day when we shall meet again.

11. This man was seven cubits tall, his face yellow, his pupil reddish, and his whole appearance very remarkable.

12 兄 長 不可去 呂布必有異 心
꜀*Hing* ‘*chéung pat*꜆ ‘*hó hü*’, ‘*Lü Pò*’ *pít*꜆ ‘*yau í*$^2$. ꜀*sam.*
Elder brother not can go: Lų Pò certainly has specioūs intentions.

13 卓 擎 杯 問 曰 青 春 幾何
*Ch‘éuk*꜆ ˏ*k‘ing* ꜀*púi man*$^2$ *üt*$_2$, ꜀*ts‘ing* ꜀*ch‘un* ‘*kí* ˏ*hó?*
Ch‘éuk, raising glass, asked, saying, ‘Green springs many how?’

14 適間所 囑不可有 悮
*Shik*꜆ ꜀*kán* ‘*shó chuk*꜆, *pat*꜆ ‘*hó* ‘*yau* ’*ng*$^2$.
Just while what ordered, not can be unfulfilled.

15 此 計 速 行 不可 遲 悮
‘*Ts‘z*’ *kai*’ *ch‘uk*꜆ ˏ*hang*, *pat*꜆ ‘*hó* ˏ*ch‘i* ’*ng*$^2$.
This plan quickly accomplished, not can tardily miss.

16 旣 子 敬 相 請 我 明 日 便 來 赴 宴
꜀*Kí* ‘*Tsz*’ *king*’ ꜀*séung* ‘*ts‘ing*, ‘*ngó* ˏ*ming yat*$_2$ *pín*$^2$ ˏ*loi fú*$^2$ *ín*’.
Already Tsz’king has invited, I to-morrow then come to feast.

17 不 必 多 言 來 日 到 府 下 公 議
*Pat*꜆ *pít*꜆ ꜀*tó* ˏ*ín*, ˏ*loi yat*$_2$ *tò*’ ‘*fú há*$^2$ ꜀*kung* ‘*í*.
Not needed much talking, coming day come-to office down publicly consult.

18 見 一 人 綸 巾 道 服 坐 在 船 頭 乃
*Kín*’ *yat*꜆ ˏ*yan* ꜀*kwán* ꜀*kan* *Tò*$^2$ *fuk*$_2$, *tsó*$^2$ *tsoi*$^2$ ˏ*shün* ˏ*t‘au*, ‘*nái*
Saw a man, silken cap, Taou dress, sitting on vessel’s head, it-was

孔 明 也
‘*Hung* ˏ*ming* ‘*yá*.
Hungming indeed.

19 向 慕 先生 才 德 未 得 拜 晤 今 幸
*Héung*’ *mò*$^2$ ꜀*sín* ꜀*shang* ꜀*ts‘oi tak*꜆ *mí*$^2$ *tak*꜆ *pái*’ ’*ng*$^2$, ꜀*kam hang*$^2$
Long esteemed your talents virtue, not-yet obtained respect meet, now happy

相 遇
꜀*séung ü*$^2$.
mutnal meeting.

---

12. My brother must not go, for Lü Pò certainly has some specious designs.

13. Ch‘éuk raising his glass, asked, ‘How old are you?’

14. That which I have just ordered you to do, must not fail to be fulfilled.

15. This scheme must be quickly acted upon and not lost by delay.

16. Tsz’king has already invited me, and to-morrow I shall come to the feast.

17. We do not want so much talking; to-morrow come down to the office for a public consultation.

18. He saw a man sitting on the vessel’s bow, dressed in a silken cap, and garb of the Taou sect, who was Hungming.

19. For a long time, I have admired your talents and virtues, but

20 見 張 飛 怒 目 橫 茅 立 馬 于 橋 上
*Kín' ‹Chéung ‹Fí, nò$^{2}$ muk$_{2}$ ‹wáng ‹mau, lap$_{2}$ ‘má ‹ü ‹k‘íú shéung$^{2}$.*
Saw Chéung Fí, menacing eyes, rested spear, standing horse on bridge top.

21 孔 明 安 在 願 求 一 見
*‘Hung ‹ming ‹ón tsoi$^{2}$? ün$^{2}$ ‹k‘au yat› kín'.*
Hungming where is? I-wish to seek an interview.

22 賢 弟 見 過 吳 侯 却 來 敘 話
*‹Ín tai$^{2}$ kín' kwò' ‹’Ng ‹hau, k‘éuk› ‹loi tsü$^{2}$ wá$^{2}$.*
Worthy brother seen have ’Ng's prince, then coming converse words.

23 何 事 在 心 寢 食 俱 廢
*‹Hó sz'$^{2}$ tsoi$^{2}$ ‹sam, ‘ts‘am shik$_{2}$ ‹k‘ü fai'?*
What affair in heart, sleeping eating both gone?

24 兩 國 相 爭 不 斬 來 使
*‘Léung kwók› ‹séung ‹chang, pat› ‘chám ‹loi sz'.*
Two states together contending, not kill coming messenger.

25 子 敬 休 問 來 日 便 見
*‘Tsz' king' ‹yau man$^{2}$, ‹loi yat$_{2}$ pín$^{2}$ kín'.*
Tsz'king cease asking, coming day then see.

26 瑜 曰 軍 中 無 戲 言
*‹U üt$_{2}$ ‹kwan ‹chung ‹mò hí' ‹ín.*
U said, army midst have-no idle words.

27 曹 操 馬 步 水 軍 約 有 一 百 五 十 餘 萬
*‹Ts‘ò ‹Ts‘ò ‘má pò$^{2}$ ‘shui ‹kwan yéuk› ‘yau yat› pák› ‘’ng shap$_{2}$ ‹ü mán$^{2}$.*
Ts‘ò Ts‘ò's cavalry, infantry, marine troops, about were one hundred fifty more myriads.

---

hitherto have had no opportunity of paying my respects; now I have the pleasure of meeting you.

20. He saw Chéung Fí, with menacing eyes and rested spear, standing his horse on the bridge.

21. Where is Hungming? I wish to seek an interview.

22. When you, worthy sir, have seen the prince of ’Ng, then return to me to talk over the matter.

23. What is there on your mind that your sleep and appetite have both failed?

24. When two states are at war, public messengers are not killed.

25. Tsz'king cease to ask, for to-morrow you will know about it.

26. U said, ‘we have no idle talk in the army.’

27. Ts‘ò Ts‘ò's cavalry, infantry, and marines, were in all about one million five hundred thousand.

28 瑜 大 驚 流 汗 滿 臂
ˏU tái² ˎking, ˏlau hón² ˊmún pí².
U much alarmed, flowed perspiration filled arms.

29 丞 相 勿 言 恐 有 泄 漏
ˏShing séung² mat₂ ˏin, ʻhung ˊyau sit₁ lau².
Your excellency, do-not speak, lest there-be leak ooze.

30 連 日 不 晤 君 顏 何 期 貴 体 不 安
ˏLín yat₂ pat₁ ʼng² ˎkwan ˏngán, ˏhó ˎkʻi kwai² ʻtʻai pat₁ ˎón!
Successive days not seen your face, why now your body not well?

31 大 霧 迷 漫 百 步 之 外 人 亦 不 見
Tái² mò² ˏmai mán₂ pák₁ pò² ˎchí ngoi², ˏyan yik₂ pat₁ kín².
Thick fog concealed covered hundred step 's beyond, man even not visible.

32 遙 望 山 清 水 秀 景 致 異 常
ˏYü móng² ˎshán ˎtsʻing ʻshui sau², ʻking chí² í² ˏshéung.
Distant seeing hills distinct, water picturesque, prospect fine unlike usual.

33 吾 自 幼 熟 讀 兵 書 深 知 奸 僞 之 道
ˏʼNg tsz'² yau² shuk₂ tuk₂ ˎping ˎshü, ˎsham ˎchí ˎkán ngai² ˎchí tʻò².
I from youth thoroughly read military works, fully know deception strategy 's rules.

34 其 船 拽 起 滿 帆 乘 順 風 去 了
ˏKʻi ˏshün yai² ʻhí ˊmún ˏfán ˏshing shun² ˎfung hü² ˊlíú.
His vessel hoisted raised full sail, improved favorable wind went away.

35 孤 意 已 决 先 生 勿 疑
ˎKú í² ˊí kʻüt₁ ˎsín ˎshang mat₂ ˏí.
Our determination already fixed, sir do-not doubt.

---

28. U was so much alarmed that the flowing perspiration covered his arms.

29. Let not your excellency (i. e. the prime minister) speak about it, lest the affair become divulged.

30. For several days I have not seen you; why now are you so ill?

31. The thick fog concealed things, so that at the distance of more than a hundred paces even a man was not visible.

32. Looking at a distance the hills were distinct, and the water picturesque,—the prospect was unusually fine.

33. From my youth, I have thoroughly read military authors, and fully know the rules of deception and strategy.

34. The sails being hoisted to their full extent, he took advantage of the fair wind, and departed.

35. My royal determination is already fixed, and you sir, need not doubt.

36 得 功 者 賞 何 計 貴 賤 乎
*Tak*, *kung* *'ché* *'shéung*, *hó* *kai'* *kwai'* *tsín* *ú!*
Obtaining meritorious persons reward, why reckon honorable mean eh?

37 詩 詞 歌 賦 妙 冠 當 時
*Shí* *ts'z'* *kó* *fú'* *miú* *kún'* *tóng* *shí.*
Poetry, songs, ballads, lays, excellent preëminent that day.

38 曹 子 建 詩 成 七 步 世 罕 其 儔
*Ts'ò* *'Tsz'* *kín'* *shí* *shing* *ts'at*, *pò*, *shai'* *'hón* *k'i* *ch'au.*
Ts'ò Tsz'kín stanza completed seven paces, age rare his class.

39 道 士 出 一 葫 盧 拔 其 塞 無
*Tò* *sz'* *ch'ut*, *yat*, *ú* *lú*, *pát*, *k'i* *sak*, *mò*
Taou priest brought-out a gourd, drew its stopper, without

限 兵 馬 殺 出
*han* *ping* *'má* *shat*, *ch'ut*.
limit war horses furiously issued.

40 廟 堂 重 地 禁 止 喧 嘩
*Miú* *t'óng* *chung* *tí*, *kam'* *'chí* *hün* *wá.*
Temple hall important place, prohibit stop boisterous talk.

41 孔 明 亦 人 耳 臣 何 畏 彼 哉
*'Hung* *ming* *yik*, *yan* *'í*, *shan* *hó* *wai'* *'pí* *tsoi!*
Hungming but man indeed, I why fear him eh?

42 街 上 大 多 光 棍 須 要 小 心
*Kái* *shéung*, *tái* *tó* *kwóng* *kwan'*, *sü* *íú'* *'síú* *sam.*
Street in great many sharpers, - must need careful attention.

43 匪 徒 太 多 隄 防 剪 綹
*'Fi* *t'ò* *t'ái'* *tó*, *t'ai* *fóng* *'tsín* *nau*.
Vagabonds great many, take care cut purses.

---

36. In rewarding the meritorious, why bring into account their honorable or low rank?

37. For poetry, songs, ballads, and lays, he was preëminent in his time.

38. Ts'ò Tsz'kín could complete a stanza while taking seven paces; the age had few such men.

39. The Taou priest, producing a gourd, drew the stopper, when innumerable war horses furiously issued.

40. In the temple's venerated spot, all boisterous talk is strictly prohibited.

41. Hungming is nothing but a man, why I should dread him?

42. In the streets are numerous sharpers, it is necessary to take great care.

43. The vagabonds are very numerous, take care lest your purse be cut.

44 兄 今 番 出 征 何 故 如 此 忙 速
꜀Hing ꜀kam ꜀fán ch'ut꜆ ꜀ching, ꜁hó kú꜄ ꜁ü 'ts'z' ꜁fóng chuk꜆.
Brother this occasion go-out rectify, what reason such this bustling haste?

45 將 在 外 君 命 有 所 不 受
꜀Tséung tsoi² ngoi² ꜀kwan ming² ꜂yau 'shó pat꜆ shau².
General is abroad, prince commands are what not obey.

46 鄭 康 成 好 學 多 才 侍 婢 俱
Ching² ꜀Hóng ꜁shing hò' hók꜇ ꜀tó ꜁ts'oi shí² ꜂pí ꜀k'ü
Ching Hóngshing loved study esteemed talents, waiting maids all
通 毛 詩
꜀t'ung ꜁mò ꜀shí.
thorough-in Ode poetry.

47 僧 繇 善 畫 嘗 畫 一 鷹 于 壁
꜀Sang ꜁Yau shín² wák꜇, ꜁shéung wák꜇ yat꜆ ꜀ying ꜀ü pik꜆,
Sang Yau expert drawer; had drawn one hawk on wall,
雀 鴿 不 敢 近
tséuk꜆ kóp꜆ pat꜆ 'kóm kan².
sparrows doves not dare approach.

48 李 思 訓 善 畫 山 水 極 窮 其
꜂Lí ꜀Sz' fan' shín² wák꜇ ꜀shán 'shui, kik꜇ ꜁k'ung ꜁k'i
Lí Sz'fan expert drawing land water, extremely like their
態 恍 聞 水 聲
tái', 'fóng ꜁man 'shui ꜀shing.
form, almost hear water dash.

49 後 主 有 畫 牛 一 軸 晝 則 噛
Hau² 'chü ꜂yau wá² ꜁ngau yat꜆ chau²; chau' tsak꜆ ít꜇
Hauchü had. painted ox one sheet; day then ate
草 欄 外 夜 則 歸 卧 欄 中
'ts'ò ꜁lán ngoi², yé² tsak꜆ ꜀kwai ngó² ꜁lán ꜀chung.
grass fence beyond, night then returned sleep fence within.

---

44. Why, sir, on this occasion of going out to restore order is there such bustle?

45. When a general is abroad there are at times orders from the prince which he does not receive.

46. Ching Hóngshing so loved study and esteemed talents that his waiting-maids were all well versed in the Book of Odes.

47. Sang Yau was skillful at drawing; he once drew a hawk on the wall, which the sparrows and doves did not dare to approach.

48. Lí Sz'fan cleverly drew landscapes, so extremely like their appearance, that one could almost hear the dashing of the water.

49. Hauchü had a painting of an ox, which by day cropped grass beyond the fence, and by night returned to sleep within it.

50 左 慈 擲 盃 空 中 化 成 一 百
‘Tsó ˏTsʻz’ chak$_2$ ˎpúi ˎhung ˎchung fá’ ˏshing yat› pák$_2$
Tsó Tsʻz’ tossed cup sky in metamorphosed into one hundred

鳩 遶 殿 而 飛
‘kau, ˁiú tʻin$^2$ ˏi ˎfi.
pigeons, encircled palace and flew.

51 久 不 相 見 今 居 何 處
‘Kau pat› ˎséung kin’, ˎkam ˎkü ˏhó chʻü’?
Long not each-other seen, now live what place?

52 孟 德 此 行 將 欲 何 往
Mang’ tak› ‘tsʻz ˏhang ˎtséung yuk$_2$ ˏhó ˁwóng’?
Mangtak this walk about wishing where go?

53 某 今 興 兵 討 賊 正 爲 國 家
ˁMau ˎkam ˎhing ˎping ‘tʻò tsʻak› ching’ wai$^2$ kwók›, ˎká
I now raise troops destroy rebel, truly for country's house

除 害 耳
ˏchʻü hoi$^2$ ˁi.
drive-off trouble.

54 至 夜 深 月 明 允 策 杖 步 入 後 園
Chí’ yé$^2$ ˎsham üt$_2$ ˏming, ˁWan chʻák› chéung$^2$ pò$^2$ yap$_2$ hau$^2$ ˏün.
At night late moon light, Wan taking cane walking entered rear garden.

55 此 等 碌 碌 小 人 何 足 挂 齒
‘Tsʻz’ ‘tang luk› luk› síú ˏyan, ˏhó tsuk› kwá’ ‘chʻi?
This sort so so small men, what worth hang-on teeth?

56 轉 盼 間 狐 忽 化 一 美 人
‘Chün pʻán’ ˎkán, ˏú fat› fá’ yat› ˁmí ˏyan,
Turning gazing whilst, fox suddenly metamorphosed a beautiful person,

光 艷 奪 目
ˎkwóng im$^2$ tüt$_2$ muk$_2$.
bright lustrous fixed eyes.

---

50. Tsó Tsʻz’, tossing the cup into the air, it was metamorphosed into a hundred pigeons, which flew around the palace.

51. We have not seen each other for a long time, where do you now live?

52. Where does Mangtak intend going in this walk?

53. I am now raising troops to destroy this rebel, simply for the purpose of averting harm from the imperial family.

54. Late at night, when it was moonlight, Wan, taking a cane, walked into the rear garden.

55. Why longer speak about such a contemptible set of fellows?

56. In the twinkling of an eye, the fox was metamorphosed into a beautiful person—her bright splendor fixed the gaze.

57 汝 無 端 獻 讒 欲 害 好 人 耶
ʿU ˏmò ˎtün hín$^2$ ˏtsʻán yuk$_2$ hoi$^2$ ʿhò ˏyan ˏyé.
You without cause offer accusations wishing injure good man eh!

58 慈 曰 我 數 十 年 不 食 亦 不
ˏTsʻz' üt$_2$, ʿngó shò' shap$_2$ ˏnín pat, shik$_2$ yik$_2$ pat,
Tsʻz' said, I several tens years not eat and not

防 日 食 千 羊 亦 能 盡
ˏfóng; yat$_2$ shik$_2$ ˎtsʻín ˏyéung yik$_2$ ˏnang tsun$^2$.
matter; day eat thousand sheep and can finish.

59 車 已 去 遠 布 緩 轡 于 土 岡
ˎKü ʿí hü' ʿün, Pò' ún$^2$ pí$^2$ ˎü ʿtʻò ˎkóng
Carriage already gone far, Pò slacked bridle on earthy hillock

之 上 眼 望 車 塵 嘆 惜 痛 恨
ˎchí shéung$^2$, ʿngán móng$^2$ ˎkü ˏchʻan tʻán' sik, tʻung' han$^2$.
's top, eyes beheld carriage's dust, sighing grieved pained exceedingly.

60 布 曰 吾 欲 殺 此 老 賊 奈 是
Pò' üt$_2$, ˏ'ng yuk$_2$ shat, ʿtsʻz' ʿlò tsʻak$_2$, noi$^2$ shí$^2$
Pò said, I wish kill this old rebel, only is

父 子 之 情 恐 惹 後 人 議 論
fú$^2$ ʿtsz' ˎchí ˏtsʻing, ʿhung ʿyé hau$^2$ ˏyan ʿí lun$^2$.
father son 's relations, fear induce after men reflect remark.

61 布 拔 帶 刀 刺 臂 出 血 爲 誓
Pò' pat$_2$ tái' ˎtò tsʻz'' pí' chʻut, hüt, ˏwai shai$^2$.
Pò drew belt sword pricked arm drew blood for oath.

62 卓 大 喜 曰 吾 夜 夢 一 龍 罩
Chʻéuk, tái$^2$ ʿhí üt$_2$, ˏ'ng yé' mung$^2$ yat, ˏlung cháu'
Chʻéuk much pleased said, I night dreamed one dragon covered

身 今 日 果 得 此 喜 信
ˎshan, ˎkam yat$_2$ ʿkwó tak, ʿtsʻz' ʿhí sun'.
me, to day truly obtained the joyful verity.

---

57. Do you thus needlessly bring in accusations, desiring to injure a good man!

58. Tsʻz' replied, 'If I should not eat for several tens of years it would be of no consequence, while, in one day, I could consume a thousand sheep.'

59. The carriage was already distant, when Pò, slacking his bridle on the top of a hillock, and following with his eyes the dust, sighed most deeply.

60. Pò said, 'I wish to kill this old rascal, but, on account of our relation of [adopted] father and son, I fear lest it will induce the criticism of future ages.

61. Pò, drawing his belt sword, pricked blood from his arm to declare his oath.

62. Chʻéuk, much pleased, said, 'In the night, I dreamed that a

拾級大成



63 卓 出 塢 上 車 前 遮 後 擁 望
*Ch'éuk, ch'ut, 'U' 'shéung ,kü ; ,ts'ín ,ché hau² 'yung, mòng²*
Ch'éuk leaving U' ascended chariot; before guarded behind protected towards

長 安 來 行 不 到 三 十 里 所
*,Ch'éung ,ón ,loi ; ,hang pat, tò' ,sám shap₂ 'lí 'shó*
Ch'éungón went; gone not to thirty *lí* that

乘 之 車 忽 折 一 輪
*,shing ,chí ,kü fat, chít, yat, ,lun.*
rode-in 's carriage suddenly broke a wheel.

64 卓 問 肅 曰 車 折 輪 馬 斷 轡
*Ch'éuk, man² Suk, üt₂, ,kü chít, ,lun, 'má 'tün pí',*
Ch'éuk asking Suk said, chariot broke wheel, horse split bridle,

其 兆 若 何
*,k'i chiú² yéuk₂ ,hó?*
these omens how what?

65 肅 曰 乃 太 師 應 詔 漢 禪 棄
*Suk, üt₂, 'nái t'ái' ,sz' ying' chiú' Hón' ,shim, hí'*
Suk replied, are great officer responding call Hán throne, discard

舊 換 新 將 乘 玉 輦 金 鞍 之 兆 也
*kau² ún² ,san, ,tséung ,shing yuk₂ 'lín ,kam ,ón ,chí chiú² 'yá.*
old change new, about mounting gemmeous chariot golden saddle 's omens indeed.

66 王 允 大 呼 曰 反 賊 至 此 武
*,Wóng 'Wan tái² ,fú üt₂, 'fán ts'ak₂ chí' 'ts'z', 'mò*
Wóng Wan loud calling said, lawless rebel to this, military

士 何 在 兩 旁 轉 出 百 餘 人
*sz'² ,hó tsoi²? 'Léung ,póng 'chün ch'ut, pák, ,ü ,yan*
officers where are? Both sides sallied out hundred more men

---

dragon covered me, and to-day, behold, I obtain the joyful verification.'

63. Ch'éuk, going out of U', got into his carriage, guarded in front and protected in rear; setting his face towards Ch'éungón, he had not proceeded thirty *lí*, when a wheel of the carriage in which he rode suddenly broke.

64. Ch'éuk, asking Suk, said, 'What do the omens of breaking the carriage wheel, and snapping the horse's bridle, prognosticate?'

65. Suk replied, 'They foreshow that a great statesman is responding to the call from the throne of Hán, who, discarding the old and changing it for new, will shortly occupy the imperial chariot and royal saddle.'

66. Wóng Wan exclaimed aloud, 'The rebellious outlaw has come, where are the officers?' From both sides, armed with halberds and maces, more than a hundred men rushed out and attacked him;

持 戟 挺 槊 刺 之 卓 裹 甲 不
ˏchʻí kikˎ ʻting shókˎ tsʻzʼ ˏchí; Chʻéukˎ ʻkwó kápˎ patˎ
grasping halberds holding maces wounded him; Chʻéuk's inner armor, not

入 傷 臂 墮 車
yap₂, ˏshéung pí ʼ chúi² ˏkü.
pierce wounded arm fell-out chariot.

67. 吾 匣 中 寶 劍 新 磨 汝 試 言
ˏʼNg háp₂ ˏchung, ʻpò kímʼ ˏsan ˏmó, ʻü shíʼ ˏín
My armory in valuable sword newly ground, you try speak

之 其 言 不 通 便 請 試 劍
ˏchí, ˏkʻí ˏín patˎ ˏtʻung pín² ʻtsʻing shíʼ kímʼ.
it, your words not intelligible then request try sword.

68 某 雖 不 才 願 去 萬 軍 中 取
ʻMau ˏsui ˏpatˎ ˏtsʻoi ün² hüʼ mán² ˏkwan ˏchung, ʻtsʻü
I although not clever wish go myriad troops among get

其 首 級 來 獻 丞 相
ˏkʻi ʻshau kʻapˎ ˏloi hínʼ ˏshing séungʼ.
his head skull bring present prime minister.

69 融 諫 操 曰 楊 公 四 世 清
ˏYung kánʼ ˏTsʻò üt₂, ˏYéung ˏkung szʼ shaiʼ ˏtsʻing
Yung remonstrating Tsʻò, said, Yéung lord four generations unsullied

德 豈 可 因 袁 氏 而 罪 之 乎
takˎ, ʻhí ʻhó ˏyan ˏUn shí² ˏí tsúi² ˏchí ˏú?
virtue, how can because Un family also criminate him eh!

70 謀 士 程 昱 說 操 曰 今 明 公 威
ˏMau sz'² ˏChʻing Yukˎ shuiʼ ˏTsʻò üt₂, ˏkam ˏming ˏkung ˏwai
Counselor Chʻing Yuk addressing Tsʻò said, now distinguished lord's awful

名 日 盛 何 不 乘 此 時 行 王 霸 之 事
ˏming yat₂ shing², ˏhó patˎ ˏshing ʻtsʻz ˏshí ˏhang ˏwóng páʼ ˏchí sz'²?
reputation daily increases, why not improve this time to do ruler tyrant's affair!

---

Chʻéuk's hauberk could not be pierced, but wounded in the arms, he fell from his carriage.

67. In my armory is a valuable sword just sharpened; you can try to speak about it (the business), but if your words are not straightforward then I shall beg to use the sword.

68. Although I am not clever, yet I wish to go into the midst of the multitude of troops, and get his head to present to your excellency.

69. Yung, remonstrating with Tsʻò, said, lord Yéung is a man whose family for four generations has maintained an unsullied virtue; why do you criminate him on account of the Messrs. Un?

70. Counselor Ching Yuk, speaking to Tsʻò, said, Your honor's reputation is now daily increasing in dignity; why do you not take advantage of this opportunity to become the ruling prince?

71 帝 曰 朕 今 欲 看 皇 叔 射 獵
*Tai' üt, cham' ˌkam yuk, hón' ˌwóng shuk, shé' lip,.*
Emperor said, we now wish see imperial uncle shoot archer-like.

玄 德 領 命 上 馬 忽 草 中 趕 起
*ˌUn tak, ˊling ming' ˊshéung ˊmá, fat, ˊts'ò ˌchung ˊkón ˊhí,*
Untak obeying order mounted horse, suddenly grass midst drove up;

一 兎 玄 德 射 之 一 箭 正 中 那 兎
*yat, t'ò'; ˌUn tak, shé' ˌchí yat, tsín' ching' chung' ˊná t'ò'.*
one hare; Untak shooting it one shot, directly hit the hare.

72 建 寧 二 年 四 月 望 日 帝 御 温 德
*Kín' ˌning, í' ˌnín, sz' üt, móng' yat, tai' ü' ˌWan Tak,*
Kinning, 2d year, 4th month, 15th day, emperor visiting Mild Virtue,

殿 方 陞 座 殿 角 狂 風 驟 起 只 見
*tín', ˌfóng ˌshing tsó', tín' kók, ˌkwóng ˌfung cháu' ˊhí, chat, kín'*
palace, just ascended throne palace corner furious blast suddenly arose, only saw

一 條 大 青 蛇 從 梁 上 飛 將 下 來
*yat, ˌt'íú tái' ˌts'ing ˌshé ˌts'ung ˌléung shéung' ˌfi ˌtséung há' ˌloi*
one single great green serpent from ridge above glided directly down coming

蟠 于 椅 上 帝 驚 倒 左 右 急 救
*ˌpún ˌü ˊi shéung'; tai' ˌking ˊtò, ˊtsó yau' kap, kau'*
wound about throne on; emperor affrighted fell, left right quickly caught-up

入 宫 百 官 俱 奔 避 須 臾 蛇 不 見
*yap, ˌkung; pák, ˌkún ˌk'ü ˌpan pí'. ˌSü ˌü ˌshé pat, kín'*
entered apartment; the officers all hastily fled. Instantly serpent not observ-

了 忽 然 大 雷 大 雨 加 以 冰 雹 落
*ˊlíú fat, ˌín tái' ˌlui tái' ˊü ˌká ˊi ˌping puk, lók,*
ed, suddenly loud thunder great rain, added to-which icy hail fell

到 半 夜 方 止 壞 却 房 屋 無 數
*tò' pún' yé' ˌfóng ˊchí, wái' k'éuk, ˌfóng uk, ˌmò shò'.*
till mid night then stopped, ruin ed buildings dwellings without number.

---

71. The emperor said, 'We now wish to see our uncle draw the bow in an archer-like manner.' Untak obeyed the order, and mounted his horse, when suddenly from among the grass a hare was started up, which was directly shot through with an arrow thrown by him.

72. In the 15th day of the 4th month, 2d year of Kínning's reign, the emperor was visiting the palace of Mild Virtue, and had just ascended the throne, when at the corner of the house a furious blast suddenly arose, and a large green serpent was seen gliding down from the ridge, which wound itself around the throne; the affrighted emperor fell to the ground, and his attendants instantly taking him up carried him into his apartment, and all the officers fled in terror. In a moment, the serpent vanished, and suddenly there was loud thunder

73 於 是 揀 選 良 馬 名 鷹 俊 犬
ˏU shí² 'kán 'sün ˏléung 'má ˏming ˏying tsun' 'hün
There upon selected chose gentle horses famous falcons apt dogs
弓 矢 俱 備 先 聚 兵 城 外 操
ˏkung 'ch'í; ˏk'ü pí², ˏsín tsü² ˏping ˏshing ngoi², ˏTs'ò
bows arrows; all. prepared, first collecting troops city without, Ts'ò
入 請 天 子 畋 獵
yap₂ 'ts'ing ˏt'ín 'tsz' ˏt'ín líp₂.
entering invited heaven's son field hunt.

74 便 縱 馬 接 戰 典 韋 畧 戰 數 合
Pín² tsung' 'má ts'íp, chín'; 'Tín ˏWai léuk₂ chín' shò' hóp₂
Then giving-reins horse joined fight; Tín Wai briefly fought several times,
便 回 馬 走 壯 士 只 顧 望 前 趕 來
pín² ˏúi 'má 'tsau, chóng' sz'² chat, kú' móng² ˏts'ín 'kón ˏloi,
then turning horse fled, brave man only intently looking before pursuing after,
不 隄 防 連 人 帶 馬 都 落 于 陷 坑 之 內
pat, ˏt'ai ˏfóng ˏlín ˏyan tái' 'má ˏtò lók₂ ˏü hám² ˏháng ˏchí noi².
not caring guarding both man and horse all fell into trap pit 's within.

75 操 忙 下 帳 叱 退 軍 士 親 解
ˏTs'ò ˏmóng há² chéung' ch'ik, t'úi' ˏkwan sz'², ˏts'an 'kái
Ts'ò hastily descending-from tent, hooted retire army officers, himself loosed
其 縛 急 取 衣 衣 之 命 坐 問 其 鄉
ˏk'í fók₂, kap, 'ts'ü ˏí í' ˏchí, ming² tsó² man² ˏk'í ˏhéung
his bonds quickly taking clothes clothed him, ordering sit asked his village
貫 姓 名
kún' sing' ˏming.
native surname name.

---

and heavy rain, together with hail, which, falling till midnight, stopped, having ruined innumerable dwellings.

73. He thereupon selected gentle horses, famous falcons, and excellent dogs, with bows and arrows; when all things were in readiness, Ts'ò, having first marshaled his troops without the city-walls, entered and invited his majesty to take a hunt.

74. Then giving reins to his horse, he joined in battle, but Tín Wai, after engaging in a few rencontres, turned his horse and fled; the brave man, only looking straight before him, pursued after him, but not heeding his steps, both he and his horse tumbled into a pit.

75. Ts'ò, hastily coming out of his tent, shouted to the officers of the army to retire, and, unloosing his bonds with his own hands, quickly disrobed himself and clothed him, bidding him to be seated, and asking his native village, his surname and name.

拾級大成



76 賊驅牛至塢外 牛皆奔走回還被
*Ts'ak, k'ü ngau chí' 'U' ngoi', ngau kái pan 'tsau úi wán, pí'*
Robbers drove oxen to U' without, oxen all quickly ran turn back, by

我雙手掣二牛尾倒行 百餘步
*'ngó shéung 'shau chai' í' ngau 'mí, 'tò hang pák, ü pò'.*
my two hands grasped two oxen tails backwards dragged hundred more paces.

77 操問曰何故見賜 承 曰 因 念
*Ts'ò man' üt, hó kú' kín' ts'z'? Shing 'üt, yan ním'*
Ts'ò asking said, what cause has conferred? Shing replied, because remembering

某舊日西都救駕之功 故 有此賜
*'mau kau' yat, Sai tò kau' ká' chí kung, kú' 'yau 'ts'z' ts'z'.*
my former day Saitò saved car 's merit, therefore have this reward.

78 他爲人沉靜寡欲不貪 名利
*T'á wai yan ch'am tsing' 'kwá yuk, pat, t'ám ming lí',*
He was man very quiet few desires not coveting reputation profit,

懶于逢迎但以詩酒自娛
*'lán ü fung ying, tán' 'í shí 'tsau tsz' ü.*
heedless in meeting receiving, but for poetry wine self delighted.

79 這白太常官又高家又富才
*Ché' Pák, t'ái' shéung kún yau' kò, ká yau' fú', ts'oi*
This Pák superior constant office also high, family also rich, talent

學 政 望 又大有聲名
*hók, ching' móng', yau' tái' 'yau shing ming.*
learning government conspicuous, besides great has fame reputation.

80 尊寓在何處尙未曾到拜候
*Tsün ü' tsoi' hó ch'ü'? shéung' mí' ts'ang tò' pái' hau'.*
Sir live in what place? still not yet come respect wait-on.

---

76. The robbers had driven the oxen to the outskirts of U', when they all turned to run back, but with my two hands grasping two of them by their tails, I dragged them backwards more than a hundred paces.

77. Ts'ò asking said, 'Why has he conferred them upon you?' Shing replied, 'Because, remembering my meritorious action on a former day when I saved his majesty at Saitò, he in consequence has bestowed this.'

78. He was a man very fond of quiet, with few desires, not coveting reputation or gain, and careless about the etiquette of society, but delighting in poetry and wine.

79. This president (of the Sacrificial Court) Pák fills a high office, his family is rich, his talents and learning are conspicuous in the government, and besides his reputation is also very high.

80. Where, sir, do you reside? I have not yet called to pay my respects.

81 良辰美景只該飲酒賦詩若
*꜀Léung ꜀shan ꜂mí ꜂king, chat꜆ ꜀koi ꜂yam ꜂tsau fú꜄ ꜀shí, yéuk꜆*
Leisure time beautiful prospect only ought quaff wine indite poetry, if

是花下談朝政頗覺不宜
*shí² ꜀fá há² ꜀tám ꜀ch'íú ching꜄, ꜂p'ó kók꜆ pat꜆ ꜀í.*
are flowers beneath converse court government, rather consider not right.

82 蘇友白須臾之間即將二詩
*꜀Sú ꜂Yau pák꜆ ꜀sü ꜀ü ꜀chí ꜀kán, tsik꜆ ꜀tséung í² ꜀shí*
Sú Yaupák moment 's interval, immediately taking two poetic

題就半行半楷寫滿花箋雙手
*꜀t'ai, tsau² pún꜄ ꜀hang pún꜄ ꜂kái, ꜂sé ꜂mún ꜀fá ꜀tsín, ꜀shéung ꜂shau*
themes, then half running half text wrote full flowery card, both hands

遞與嫣素
*tai² ꜂ü ꜀I'n sò꜄.*
passed to I'nsò.

83 小姐道涇渭自分黑白難掩
*꜂Síú ꜂tsé tò², ꜀King ꜂Wai tsz'² ꜀fan, hak꜆ pák꜆ ꜀nán ꜂ím,*
Young lady said, King Wai certainly distinguish, black white hard shade,

爹爹若遲疑不決何不聚二生
*꜀té ꜀té yéuk꜆ ꜀ch'í ꜀í pat꜆ k'üt꜆, ꜀hó pat꜆ ꜂ts'ü² í² ꜀shang*
pa pa if delaying suspect not decide, why not collect two youths

于一堂命題考試不獨誰妍誰
*꜀ü yat꜆ ꜀t'óng, ming² ꜀t'ai ꜂háu shí꜄; pat꜆ tuk꜆ ꜀shui ꜀ín ꜀shui*
in one hall, order theme examine try; not only which handsome which

媸可以立辨異日去去取取彼
*꜀ch'í ꜂hó ꜂í lap꜆ pín², í² yat꜆ hü꜄ hü꜄ ꜂ts'ü ꜂ts'ü ꜂pí*
ugly, can by-this settle selection, another day dimissing go, taking take they

亦無怨也
*yik꜆ ꜀mò ün꜄ ꜂yá.*
also without ill-will.

---

81. When at leisure and enjoying a fine prospect, it is best to do nothing but quaff wine and write poetry; while we are among the flowers, it is, in my opinion, not exactly proper to converse about the court and government.

82. Sú Yaupák, after a moment's interval, took the two themes for poetry, and half in a running hand, half in a text hand, wrote the flowered card paper full, and with both hands gave it to I'nsò.

83. The young lady replied, 'The rivers King and Wai can be distinguished, black and white are not easily blended; if papa cannot remove his doubts by delaying, why not bring the two young men together in one hall and give them a theme for trial? It will not only decide who is handsome and who is ugly, but we can in this way

84 吳翰林見黜退了蘇友白前
ˏ'Ng Hón² ˏlam kín' chut, t'úi' ˏlíú ˏSú ˏYau pák₂ ˏts'in
'Ng pencil forest had cast back already Sú Yaupák fore
程雖出了一時之氣然心下也
ˏch'ing, ˏsui ch'ut, ˏlíú, yat, ˏshí ˏchí hí', ˏín ˏsam há² ˏyá
road, although issu ed, one occasion 's anger, still heart in also
有三分不過意
ˏyau ˏsám ˏfan pat, kwó' í'.
had three parts not pass thoughts.

85 我昨日見他一時未睹其長
ˏNgó tsók₂ yat₂ kín' ˏt'á yat, ˏshí mí² 'tò ˏk'i ˏchéung,
I yesterday saw him one time not aware his capability,
心下甚是狐疑但是舍親書來
ˏsam há² sham² shí² ˏú ˏí, tán² shí² shé' ˏts'an ˏshü ˏloi
mind in very is turning doubt, but is mean relative's letter come,
不好慢他故今日邀他一敘
pat, 'hò mán² ˏt'á; kú' ˏkam yat₂ ˏíú ˏt'á yat, tsü².
not well neglect him; wherefore to day invited him an interview.

86 白公問道二兄佳作曾完否
Pák₂ ˏkung man² tò², í² ˏhing ˏkai tsók, ˏts'ang ˏün 'fau?
Pák Mr. asking said, two brothers fine writings yet done or-no?

87 白公道我兒我今日看張蘇
Pák₂ ˏkung tò² ˏngó ˏí ˏngó ˏkam yat₂ hón' ˏChéung ˏSú
Pák Mr. said, my child, I to day saw Chéung Sú
二人行徑俱大有可疑幾乎被
í² ˏyan ˏhang king', ˏk'ü tái² ˏyau 'hó ˏí, ˏkí ˏú pí²
two men acted done, they much have can suspect, many chances by
他瞞過
ˏt'á ˏmún kwó'.
them deceiv ed.

---

settle our choice; afterwards, the one who is dismissed will go, and the one who is chosen will be taken, and there will, moreover, be no dissatisfaction.'

84. Doctor 'Ng had degraded Sú Yaupák from promotion; notwithstanding this single ebullition of anger, he still had some compassion for him.

85. I saw him yesterday, but at one opportunity I could not fully observe his ability, and I had many doubts concerning him; but since he brought my relative's letter, it would not be well to neglect him, and I have therefore invited him to-day to an interview.

86. Mr. Pák asking said, 'Have you gentlemen yet finished your elegant composition?'

87. Mr. Pák replied, 'To-day, my child, I saw the performances

88 白公到次日吽人備酒伺候
*Pák₂ ꜀kung tò' ts'z' yat₂ kiú' ꜁yan pí² 'tsau tsz'² hau².*
Pák Mr. on next day called men prepare wine attend wait.

89 白公在軒後窺見二人形狀
*Pak₂ ꜀kung tsoi² ꜀hin hau² ꜀kw'ai kin' í² ꜁yan ꜁ying chóng²*
Pák Mr. in library behind furtively saw two men form aspect;

心下又氣又惱又好笑却又不
*꜀sam há² yau² hí' yau² 'nò; yau² 'hò siú', k'éuk yau² pat*
mind in partly surprised partly angry; now laughable and now not

好十分羞辱他們
*'hò shap₂ ꜀fan ꜀sau yuk₂ ꜀t'á ꜁mún.*
well ten parts shame disgrace them.

90 先生倘不嫌俚俗晚生卽當
*꜀Sin ꜀shang 'tóng pat ꜁im 'lí tsuk₂, 'mán ꜀shang tsik ꜀tóng*
First born should not displease poor vulgar, late born then ought

献笑
*hin' síú'.*
present ridiculous.

91 操拜許褚爲都尉賞勞甚厚
*꜀Ts'ò pái' 'Hü 'Chü ꜁wai ꜀tò wai', 'shéung lò² sham² hau².*
Ts'ò bowed-in Hü Chü to-be general soother, rewarded toils very liberally.

---

of these two men Chéung and Sú, and there is great cause to suspect that we have been deceived by both of them.'

88. Mr. Pák, on the following day, called his servants to set out wine, and wait to attend them.

89. Mr. Pák, from behind the library, secretly saw the actions of the two men, and was both surprised and angry; they were very laughable, but still he did not think it well to disgrace them.

90. Sir, should you not disdain my vulgar performance, then I must offer you that which is ridiculous.

91. Ts'ò conferred the office of general soother upon Hü Chü, and liberally rewarded him for his toils.

拾級大成

# Chapter Fifth.

# EXERCISES IN CONVERSATION

THESE exercises are designed principally as guides in the construction of simple sentences; from them, the scholar can learn the colloquial idiom of this dialect, and by comparison with the preceding lessons in reading, also mark the principal features of difference between the two. He should learn the sentences so thoroughly as to speak them with perfect freedom, for it will require no small degree of careful attention to avoid speaking in an English idiom; which is, to a Chinese ear as barbarous and uncouth as the English spoken at Canton by the Chinese according to their idiom is to a newly arrived Englishman. Although the spoken language is more diffuse than the written, its idioms have the same general characteristics, which are both so unlike western languages as to prove one of the greatest difficulties in acquiring the Chinese tongue. In learning to converse, it will be found to be a good plan to request the teacher to write down a few of the first conversations as they are spoken, that they may be read and reread until made familiar.

The following conversation contains such phrases and requests as the beginner will be most likely to need. The grammatical terms contained in the lesson comprise only a part of those found in writings on the language, but they are all that will be useful at first. The English translation is given in a parallel column, and the literal one omitted; but the corresponding words in both languages can, however, easily be ascertained.

### CONVERSATION WITH A TEACHER.

1. Please to be seated.
*'Ts'ing tsó*$^{2}$.
Please sit.
*'Ts'ing tsó*$^{2}$.

請坐
請坐

2. What is your surname?
*˛Kò sing' á'?*
Thank you, my mean surname is Ó.
*'Hò wá*$^{2}$*, tsin*$^{2}$ *sing' ˛Ó.*

高姓呀
好話賤姓柯

3. I trust you are very well.
*Shat*$_{2}$ *'shau ˛kung 'hí ˛lá?*
Thank you, having seen you, sir.
*'Hó wá*$^{2}$*, 't'ai ká' ˛ché.*

實首恭喜辣
好話睇駕啫

4. Bring some tea (*to a servant*).
Please take some tea.
*Kuk*$_{2}$ *˛ch'á ˛lai. 'Ts'ing ˛ch'a.*

局茶嚟請茶

Please to drink.
ʻTsʻing ˏchʻá.

請茶

5. I am now thinking of studying the provincial dialect of Canton; what is the shortest mode, sir, you would recommend to teach me?
ˏI′ ˏká ˊngó ʻséung hók₂ ʻKwóng ˏtung ʻsháng ˏshing tsuk₂ wá²; ˏsín ˏshang ʻkán ˏpín tikˎ tsit₂ kingʼ káuʼ ˊngó ˏní?

而家我想學廣東省城俗話先生揀邊的捷徑教我呢

First learn to speak the sounds accurately, and afterwards learn to read and write.
ˏSín iúʼ hók₂ ʻkóng chingʼ kóʼ tikˎ ˏyam, ˏin hau² hók₂ tuk₂ ˏshü, ʻsé tsz'².

先要學講正個的音然後學讀書寫字

6. If it is so, it will be best for you first to speak, when I will follow.
ʻKóm wá², ˏsín ˏshang ˏsín ˏhoi ʻhau, ʻtang ˊngó ˏkan chü² ˏé.

咁話先生先開口等我跟住唉

You must hear accurately, and closely follow me.
ˊNi iúʼ ˏting ˏchan ˏkan ʻkan ˊngó chingʼ ʻhò áʼ.

你要聽眞跟緊我正好呀

7. If that is the way, please distinguish the four sounds by marking them.
ʻKóm wá², ʻtsʻing ˏfan szʼʼ ˏshing ˏhün ˏló.

咁話請分四聲圈囉

The pʻing, shéung, hü and yap [shing] are here all marked.
ˏNi chʻüʼ ˏpʻing ʻshéung hüʼ yap₂ ˏtò ˏhün lókˎ.

呢處平上去入都圈咯

8. Please also distinguish the upper and lower tones, with the aspirates.
Tsoiʼ ʻtsʻing ˏfan ʻshéung há² ˏshing kʻap₂ pʻanʼ híʼ ˏó.

再請分上下聲及噴氣呵

Very well.
Tsò² takˎ.

做得

9. I would further request you to plainly mark the sentences and periods.
Chung² iúʼ ʻtsʻing ˊní ʻtím ˏming küʼ tau² ˏá.

重要請你點明句讀呀

With much pleasure; besides this, names of persons have a single stroke and names of places a double stroke, both which you need in order to remember them easily.
ˏA′ ʻhò; yik₂ ˊyau ˏyan ˏming yung² ˏtán ˊkí ti² ˏming yung² ˏshéung ˊkí, ˊni ˏtò iúʼ kiʼ ʻkan ˏá.

呀好亦有人名用單企地名用雙企你都要記緊呀

10. What character is this?
*Kó' kó' hai*$^1$ *mat› tsz'*$^2$ *‹ní?*
It is the character *shü*.
*Hai*$^2$ *‹shü tsz'*$^2$.

箇個係乜字呢
係書字

11. What tone has it?
*Hai*$^2$ *mat› ‹shing ‹ní?*
It has the *shéung p'ing*.
*Hai*$^2$ *shéung*$^2$ *‹p'ing*.

係乜聲呢
係上平

12. What is this word *shü* called in English?
*‹Ní kó' ‹shü tsz'*$^2$ *‹Ying wá*$^2$ *kiú' mat› 'yé ‹ní?*
It is called *book* in English.
*‹Ying wá*$^2$ *kiú' tsò*$^2$ *puk›.*

呢個書字英話
叫乜野呢
英話叫做卜

13. What does that character *hang* mean?
*Kó' kó' hang*$^2$ *tsz'*$^2$ *'tím 'kái?*
Not likely to obtain and yet obtaining, not able to avoid and yet avoiding, are both called *hang*.
*Pat› ‹tóng tak› ‹í tak›, 'ü pat› 'hó 'mín ‹í 'mín, ‹kái üt*$_2$ *hang*$^2$.

个个幸字點解
不當得而得與
不可免而免皆
曰幸

14. Please, sir, examine the dictionary, and see what that character means.
*Kó' kó' tsz'*$^2$ *'ts'ing ‹sín ‹shang ‹ch'á tsz'*$^2$ *'tín 't'ai 'há 'tím 'kái.*

個個字請先生
查字典睇吓點
解

15. What radical is that character *ts'ung* under? how many strokes has it?
*Kó' kó' ‹ts'ung tsz'*$^2$ *yap*$_2$ *mat› pò*$^2$*? 'kí ‹tó wák*$_2$ *‹ní?*
It is found under the radical *yau*, and has sixteen strokes.
*Yap*$_2$ *yau*$^2$ *tsz'*$^2$ *pò*$^2$*; shap*$_2$ *luk*$_2$ *wák*$_2$ *lók*$_2$.

個個叢字入乜
部幾多畫呢
入又字部十六
畫咯

16. Is there another character having the same meaning as this word *kwái?*
*Kó' kwái' tsz'*$^2$ *'yau pít*$_2$ *í*$^2$ *tsz'*$^2$ *‹t'ung 'kái 'mò ‹ní?*
In the phrase *ch'ut k'í*, the character *k'í* is of the same meaning.
*Kung*$^2$ *ch'ut› ‹k'í, kó' ‹k'í tsz'*$^2$ *yat› yéung*$^2$ *'kái.*

個怪字有别二
字同解有呢
共出奇個奇字
一樣解

17. What is the sound of that character in the court dialect? In this (Canton) dialect? In the Fukien dialect?
*Kó' kó' tsz'*$^2$ *‹kún 'wá hai*$^2$ *mat› ‹yam; pák*$_2$ *'wá hai*$^2$ *mat› ‹yam; Fuk› kín' hai*$^2$ *mat› ‹yam ‹ní?*

個個字官話係
乜音白話係乜
音福建係乜音
呢

Each place has its own local pronunciation, all places are not alike, but the court dialect is universally current.
*Kók꜀ ꜂yau kók꜀ ꜂t'ò ꜂wá, ch'ü꜄ ch'ü꜄ ꜁'m ꜁t'ung; tán꜄ ꜀kún ꜂wá ꜀t'ung ꜁hang tik꜀.*

各有各土話、處處唔同但官話通行的。

18. Please explain to me from that character *yan* to this character *yá*.
*꜁Yau kó꜄ ꜁yan tsz'꜄ chí꜄ ꜂yá tsz'꜄, ꜂ts'ing ꜂kái ꜂ngó ꜀chí.*

由個人字至也字請解我知。

Do you yet understand it by this explanation?
*꜂Kóm yéung꜄ ꜂ní ꜂hiú tak꜀ ꜁'m ꜁ts'ang ꜀ní!*

咁樣你曉得唔曾呢。

19. What does that sentence mean?
*Kó꜄ kü꜄ yau꜄ ꜂tím ꜂kái?*

個句又點解。

20. My memory is not good, please explain it again.
*꜂Ngó ꜁'m ꜂hò kí꜄ sing꜄, ꜂ts'ing ꜂ní tsoi꜄ ꜂kóng.*

我唔好記性請你再講。

21. I do not yet understand this sentence, please employ an illustration, and explain it clearly while I hear.
*꜂Ts'z' kü꜄ ꜂ngó mí꜄ ꜂hiú, ꜂ts'ing ꜂ní ꜂shai p'í꜄ ü꜄ ꜂kóng ꜁ming ꜂ngó ꜀t'ing.*

此句我未曉請你使譬喻講明我聽。

22. I must trouble you to write an explanation of this sentence.
*꜀Tó ꜁fán ꜂ní chü꜄ ꜂kái ꜀ní kü꜄.*

多煩你註解呢句。

23. *Wai hók ché, pít yau ch'ó*; please, these sir, write two sentences a in plain sentence in the colloquial dialect, so that I can easily understand the meaning.
*꜁Wai hók꜄ ꜂ché, pít꜀ ꜂yau ꜀ch'ó; í꜄ kü꜄ ꜂ts'ing ꜀sín ꜀shang ꜂sé yat꜀ kü꜄ ꜁ming pák꜄ ké꜄ tsuk꜄ ꜄wá ꜂tang ꜂ngó í꜄ ꜂hiú ꜁sá.*

爲學者必有初二句請先生寫一句明白嘅俗話等我易曉呀。

Being learning 's man, certainly must have a single beginning commencement first putting hand eh.
*꜁Wai hók꜄ ké꜄ ꜁yan, pít꜀ ting꜄ ꜂yau yat꜀ kó꜄ ꜂ch'i ꜀ch'ó ꜀sín ꜁mái ꜂shau lók꜀.*

爲學嘅人必定有一個始初先埋手咯。

24. If you do not understand the simple text, then you should examine the commentary.
*꜂Ní ꜁'m ꜂hiú pák꜄ ꜁man, tsau꜄ ꜀kói ꜂t'ai chü꜄ ꜀lá.*

你唔曉白文就該睇註嚹。

25. Please sir write several large characters for me.
*'Ts'ing ˏsín ˏshang toi² ˤngó ˤsé ˤkí kó' tái² kó' ké' tsz'².*

I must trouble you to bring me a pencil, ink, and stone, for me to write with.
*ˏTó ˏfán ˤní ˏning pat, mak, in² ˏlai ˤngó ˤsé ˏlá.*

請先生代我寫幾個大個嘅字墨多煩你揼筆硯嚟我寫啦

26. I must again request you to teach me to write.
*Tsoi² ˤts'ing ˤní káu² ˤngó ˤsé tsz'².*

再請你教我寫字

Let me write some large characters for you to copy by laying paper upon them.
*ˤTang ˤngó ˤsé ˤkí kó' tái² tsz'² ˤní yan'.*

等我寫幾個大字你印

27. It is necessary first to rule black lines to copy that edict.
*Iˊú' ˏsín kán' kó' kák, ˏch'áu kó' ˏchéung kò' ˏshí'.*

要先間個格抄個張告示

Do you wish me to write the text hand, or the running hand, or the plant character?
*ˤNí ú' ˤngó ˤsé ˏkái ˏshü, yik, wák, ˏhang ˏshü, ˤts'ò ˏshü ˏní?*

你要我寫楷書抑或行書艸書呢

28. Now in copying this sheet, you must take care and not copy it erroneously.
*ˏI ˏká ˏch'áu ˏní ˏchéung, ú' yung² ˏsam mók, ˏch'áu ts'ó.*

而家抄呢張要用心莫抄錯

29. Please, sir, read the 33 orders of sounds in the Tonic Dictionary while I follow closely to learn them.
*'Ts'ing ˏsín ˏshang tuk, ˏFan Wan² ˏsám shap, ˏsám ˏyam, ˤtang ˤngó ˏkan chü² hók,.*

請先生讀分韻三十三音等我跟住學

30. Please look in the Tonic Dictionary and see where this character is to be found.
*ˏNí kó' tsz'² tsoi² ˏFan Wan² ˏpín ˏch'ü', ˤts'ing ˤní ˏch'á yat, ˏch'á.*

呢個字在分韻邊處請你查一查

31. In which (class of) sounds is it
*Tsoi² tai² ˤkí ˏyam?*

在第幾音

32. This sheet is a rough draft of my first composition, I will trouble you to correct it.
*ˏNi ˏchéung hai² ˤngó ˏch'ó hók, tsók, tik, ˤts'ò ˤkò, ˏtó ˏfán ˤní ˤkoi ˤhá.*

呢張係我初學作的艸稿多煩你改吓

33. Written in this way, is it according to the rules of grammar?
*'Kóm yéung² tsók, hóp₂ ˏman fát, mí² ˏní?*

咁樣作合文法未呢

Yes, it is, but the idea is not perspicuous.
*Yik₂ hóp₂ lók,; tán² ˏts'z' pat, tát₂ í' ˏché.*

亦合咯但詞不達意啫

34. How are substantives divided?
*Shat₂ tsz'² 'tím yéung² ˏfan ˏní?*

實字點樣分呢

Into verbs and nouns.
*ˢYau út₂ tsz'², ˢyau 'sz' tsz'².*

有活字有死字

35. How are particles divided?
*ˏH'ü tsz'² 'tím ˏfan ˏní?*

虛字點分呢

There are initials, conjunctives, disjunctives, possessives, collectives, interjections, and finals.
*ˢYau 'hí ˢü ˏts'z', tsíp, ˢü ˏts'z', 'chün ˢü ˏts'z', ch'an' ˢü ˏts'z', ch'uk, ˢü ˏts'z', t'án' ˢü ˏts'z', hít, ˢü ˏts'z'.*

有起語辭接語辭轉語辭襯語辭束語辭嘆語辭歇語辭

36. How is poetry [arranged]?
*ˏShí hai² 'tím yéung² ké' ˏní?*

詩係點樣嘅呢

There is the pentametrical stanza of four lines which has four lines of five words each, and the stanza of the same metre of eight lines; there is the heptameter stanza of four lines, having four lines of seven words each, and the stanza of the same metre of eight lines. The double stanza has sixteen lines.
*ˢYau ˢ'ng tsüt₂ hai² ˢ'ng ˏín sz' kü', ˢ'ng lut₂ ˢ'ng ˏín pát, kü'; ts'at, tsüt₂ ts'at, ˏín sz' kü', ts'at, lut₂ ts'at, ˏín pát, kü'. ˏPái lut₂ tsak, shap₂ luk, kü' lók,.*

有五絕係五言四句五律五言八句七絕七言四句七律七言八句排律則十六句咯

37. I have made an attempt [to speak]; taking the meaning of the sentence I have spoken, please, sir, write a sentence having the same signification.
*ˢNgó shí' yat, shí', ˏtséung ˢngó í' sz' 'kóng yat, kü' 'wá 'ts'ing ˏsín ˏshang yáu² chiú' ˢngó í' sz' 'sé yat, kü' ˏá.*

我試一試將我意思講一句話請先生又照我意思寫一句呀

Do you wish it written in the court dialect or in the provincial?
*'Sé ˏkún wá² ting² 'sé pák₂ 'wá ˏní?*

寫官話定寫白話呢

38. I purchased a set of the Four Books yesterday; please mark them.
*Tsók₂ yat₂ ˢmái yat, t'ò' Sz' ˏShü, 'ts'ing ˢní hò².*

昨日買一套四書請你號

I must trouble you to give me the marking boards, which will make it much easier to mark them.
*꜀Tó ꜁fán ꜂ní ꜂pí kó꜄ káp꜆ ꜂pán ꜂tang ꜂ngó ꜂hò í$^2$ hò$^2$.*

多煩你俾個夾
板等我好易號

39. How many volumes has this set?
*꜀Ní t'ò꜄ ꜀shü ꜂kí ꜀tó pò$^2$?*

呢套書幾多簿

40. Are you able to speak English?
*꜂Ní ꜂úi ꜂kóng ꜀Ying wá$^2$ ꜁'m ꜂úi?*

你噲講暎話唔
噲

I have studied it six months, and understand it only a very little.
*꜂Ngó hók꜇ kwó꜄ luk꜇ kó꜄ üt꜇ léuk꜇ léuk꜇ ꜂híú tak꜆ tík꜆ ꜀ché.*

我學過六個月
畧畧曉得的啫

---

CONVERSATION WITH A COMPRADOR.

1 What is your name?
*꜂Ní kíú꜄ tsò$^2$ mat꜆ ꜁ming?*
It is Álai.
*꜂Ngó kíú꜄ Á꜄ ꜂lai.*

你叫做乜名
我叫阿禮

2. How old are you now?
*꜂Ní ꜀kam ꜁nín ꜂kí tái$^2$ á꜄?*
Twenty-four years.
*Í$^2$ shap꜇ sz'꜄ sui꜄.*

你今年幾大呀
二十四歲

3. Have you a father and mother?
*꜂Ní ꜂yau fú$^2$ ...*
Yes, and also one elder and two younger brothers.
*꜂Yau, ꜀kím ꜂yau yat꜆ kó꜄ á꜄ ꜀kó, ꜂léung kó꜄ sai꜄ ꜂lò ꜀tím.*

你有父母有呀
有兼有一個亞
哥兩個細佬添

4. Where does your father live?
*꜂Ní ꜂lò ꜂tsz' chü$^2$ tsoi$^2$ ꜀pín ch'ü꜄?*

你老子住在邊
處

In the country, near Caza Branca.
*Tsoi$^2$ ꜀héung há$^2$ kan$^2$ ꜁Ts'in ꜀shán.*

在鄉下近前山

5. How far distant?
*꜂Yau ꜂kí ꜂ün lò$^2$ á꜄?*
About thirty [Chinese] miles.
*꜀Sám ꜁t'óng san꜄, kóm꜄ shéung$^2$ há$^2$.*

有幾遠路呀
三唐汎咁上下

6. Are you married?
*꜂Ní ts'ü꜄ ꜀ts'an mí$^2$?*
Yes sir.
*Ts'ü꜄ lók꜇.*

你娶親未
娶咯

7. If I hire you, how much wages do you wish to have each month?

*P'í ꜂ü ꜀ní ꜂hai ꜀ngó ch'ü' kú' ꜀kung, yat꜆ üt꜆ íú' ꜂kí ꜀tó ꜀kung ꜁ngan ꜀ní?*

譬如你喺我處僱工一月要幾多工銀呢

Five dollars a month.

*꜀Ng kó' ꜁ngan ꜁ts'in yat꜆ üt꜆.*

五個銀錢一月

8. In what gentleman's house have you already lived?

*꜀Ní ꜀sín yat꜆ tsoi꜄ ꜀pín wai꜄ ꜁yan hák꜆ ꜁hóng ch'ü' ꜀ní?*

你先日在邊位人客行處呢

In Mr. P.'s hóng a long time.

*Tsoi꜄ ꜀Mí sz'꜄ ꜀Pí ꜁hóng ꜂hò noi꜄ lók꜆.*

在美士啤行好耐咯

9. What did you attend to there?

*꜀Ní tsoi꜄ kó' ch'ü' pán꜄ mat꜆ ꜀yé sz'꜄ ꜁ní?*

你在個處辦乜野事呢

I assisted the comprador to manage his affairs.

*Tsoi꜄ ꜀mái pán꜄ ch'ü' ꜀póng pán꜄.*

在買辦處幫辦

10. I think of employing you to act as my comprador, who will stand surety for you?

*꜀Ngó ꜂séung yung꜄ ꜀ní tsò꜄ ꜀mái pán꜄, mat꜆ ꜁shui ꜀tám ꜂pò ꜀ní ꜀ní.*

我想用你做買辦乜誰擔保你呢

My cousin, who acts as comprador to Mr. * * *; I think you know him, is it so?

*꜀Ngó ꜂píu ꜀hing tsoi꜄ ꜀Mí sz'꜄ ꜀mau ꜀mau ch'ü', tsò꜄ ꜀mái pán꜄; ꜀ní ꜀tò shik꜆ ꜀k'ü ꜂kú á'?*

我表兄在美士么么處做買辦你都識佢估呀

11. I have heard his name, but I have not made his acquaintance; if he has leisure ask him to come and see me.

*꜀Ngó ꜀tò ꜁man tak꜆ ꜀k'ü ꜁ming lók꜆, tán꜄ mí꜄ shik꜆ ꜀k'ü mín꜄, ꜁hán ꜁shí ꜂ts'ing ꜀k'ü ꜁loi ꜀ngó yat꜆ kín' ꜀ó.*

我都聞得佢名咯但未識佢面閒時請佢來我一見啊

Very well.

*꜁Á tsò꜄ tak꜆.*

呀做得

12. I will take you one or two months, on trial as comprador; when will you bring your things?

我試用你先做一兩個月買辦

拾級大成

ˢ*Ngó shí*ˀ *yung*² ˢ*ní* ˓*sín tsò*² *yat*ˀ ˢ*léung kó*ˀ *üt*₂ ˢ*mái pán*², ˢ*ní* ʻ*kí* ˓*shí tái*ˀ ˓*p'ò k'oi*ˀ ˓*lai* ˓*ní?*

你幾時帶鋪盖
嚟呢

I will now go back, and immediately bring them here.

˓*I* ˓*ká* ˓*fán hü*ˀ, *tsau*² ˓*ním* ˓*lai* ˓*tò tak*ˀ ˓*ché.*

而家番去就拈
嚟都得嗜

13. How many men are necessary to employ in this establishment?

ʻ*Pún* ˓*hóng iú*ˀ ʻ*kí* ˓*tó* ˓*yan* ʻ*shai* ˓*ní?*

本行要幾多人
使呢

Two coolies, one cook, one door-keeper, and four personal servants, are enough.

ˢ*Léung kó*ˀ ʻ*kún tím*ˀ, *yat*ˀ *kó*ˀ ˓*ch'ü* ʻ*tsz*ˀ, *yat*ˀ *kó*ˀ ˓*hón* ˓*mún*, *sz*ˀ *kó*ˀ *sz*² ʻ*tsai*, *tsò*² *tak*ˀ *lók*ˀ.

兩個管店一個
廚子一個看門
四個事仔做得
咯

14. All that these men are to be employed in doing is your concernment, and for whatever they may do you will be accountable.

ʻ*Shó yung*² *kó*ˀ *tik*ˀ ˓*yan yat*ˀ ˓*tí* ˓*tò hai*² ˓*kwán* ˢ*ní sz*² *pó*ˀ; *tán*² ˢ*yau mat*ˀ ˢ*yé sz*² ˓*tò* ˓*wai* ˢ*ní shí*² *man*² ʻ*hai lò*ˀ.

所用個的人一
哋都係關你事
噃但有乜野事
都爲你是問喺
嘮

Certainly; I know the dispositions of every one of them very well.

*Tsz*² ˓*ín* ˓*lé; yat*ˀ ˓*tí* ˢ*ngó* ˓*tò shik*ˀ *tak*ˀ ˢ*k'ü* ʻ*pan sing*ˀ ˓*ké* ˓*lók*ˀ.

自然哩一哋我
都識得佢品性
嘅咯

15. I want you to have breakfast ready every morning at eight o'clock.

ʻ*Ts'ò* ˓*ch'á* ˢ*múi* ˓*chíú iú*ˀ *pát*ˀ ʻ*tím* ˓*chung pín*² *lá*².

早茶每朝要八
點鐘便嚧

Very well; when do you want dinner and tea ready?

ʻ*Hò lé*ˀ; *tái*² ˓*ts'án*, ˢ*mán* ˓*ch'á* ˓*ní?*

好喇大餐晚茶
呢

16. Dinner at four o'clock, tea at such time as it is ready.

*Tái*² ˓*ts'án sz*ˀ ʻ*tím*, ˢ*mán* ˓*ch'á kó*ˀ ˓*shí pin*² *kó*ˀ ˓*shí* ʻ*yam* ʻ*hái* ˓*lá.*

大餐四點晚茶
個時便個時飲
喺嚧

How many gentlemen sit at table in this hong?
*‘Pún ˏhóng ‘kí ˌtó wai² ˏyan hák, kung² ˏmái shik, á’?*

本行幾多位人客共埋食呀

17. Usually four persons.
*ˏShéung ˏshí sz’² kó’ ˏyan.*

常時四個人

18. You must always tell the cook to sweep his kitchen clean; it is very important to have it done.
*‘Ni ˏshi ˏshi kiú’ kó’ ˏch‘ü ‘tsz’ ‘tá sò’ ˌkón tsing² kó’ ˏch‘ü ˏfóng, chí’ tsò² tak, ó’.*

你時時叫箇廚子打掃乾净個廚房致做得啲

. Yes, I know about that.
*Hai² lók, ‘ngó ˌchí tak, lók.*

係咯我知得咯

---

### Conversation with a Servant.

1. What are you doing that you come up so tardily? After this, when you hear my bell ring, come up stairs immediately.

*Tsò² mat, ‘ní ‘shéung ˏlai kóm’ ˏch‘i; ‘ts‘z’ hau² ‘ní ˌt‘ing kín’ ‘ngó ˏngò ˌchung, ‘ní tsau² ‘shéung ˏlau lá’.*

做乜你上嚟咁遲此後你聽見我撳鐘你就上樓嚟

Because I was eating at the time.

*ˌYan wai² ‘ngó kó’ chan² shik, fán².*

因為我個陣食飯

2. This morning take all my clothes, and sorting them out, write a list of them.
*‘Ní ˌkam ˌchiú ˌtséung ‘ngó kók, ˌi fuk, lit, yat, ˌchéung ˌtán ˌá.*

你今朝將我各衣服列一張單呀

I have done so; there are altogether 88 pieces.
*‘Sé lók, kung² pát, shap, pát, kín².*

寫咯共八十八件

3. Select out such clothes as are ragged, and take them to be mended.
*‘Kán ˌpín kín² ˌi fuk, hai² lán² ké’, ˌním hü’ ‘pò ˌá.*

揀邊件衣服係爛嘅拈去補呀

I have taken several pieces to be mended; besides them there are some

擰幾件去補咯

very much worn out that cannot be mended.
*꜀Ning ꜂ki kin$^{1}$ hü꜃ ꜂pò lók꜁ ; ling$^{2}$ ngoi$^{2}$ ꜂yau ꜂ki kin$^{2}$ shat$_{2}$ ꜂shau lán$^{2}$, ꜄'m ꜂pò tak꜁ kè꜃ lók꜁.*

另外有幾件實
首爛唔補得嘅
咯

4. In that basket there are some dirty clothes; take them to be washed, and write a list and give it to me.
*Kó꜃ kó꜃ lap꜁ ꜂yau tik꜁ ꜀ú ꜀tsò ꜀í fuk$_{2}$, ꜀nim hü꜃ ꜂sai, ꜂sé ꜀fán ꜄t'iú ꜀tán kwó꜃ ꜂ngó.*
I will now read the list for you to hear: six shirts, three pair of pantaloons, three pair of stockings, five jackets, one vest, two handkerchiefs, one pair of gloves, two sheets, one pillow-case, one suit of sleeping clothes, one towel, one neckcloth; in all twenty-seven pieces.
*꜄I ꜀ká tuk$_{2}$ kó꜃ ꜄t'iú ꜀tán ꜂ní ꜀t'ing lá꜃ : luk$_{2}$ kin$^{2}$ hón$^{2}$ ꜀shám, ꜀sám ꜄t'iú fú꜃, ꜀sám túi꜃ mát$_{2}$, ꜂'ng kin$^{2}$ ꜀chung ꜀shám, yat꜁ kin$^{2}$ púi꜃ ꜀sam, ꜂léung ꜄t'iú ꜂shau ꜀kan, yat꜁ túi꜃ ꜂shau lap꜁, ꜂léung ꜀chéung ꜂p'í ꜀tán, yat꜁ kó꜃ ꜂cham toi$^{2}$, yat꜁ fú꜃ shui$^{2}$ ꜀í, yat꜁ ꜄t'iú min$^{2}$ ꜀kan, yat꜁ ꜄t'iú ꜂king ꜀kan ; kung$^{2}$ yá$^{2}$ ts'at꜁ kin$^{2}$.*

個個笠有的污
漕衣服秥去洗
寫番條單過我
而家讀個條單
伱聽鏬六件汗
衫三條褲三對
襪五件中衫一
件背心兩條手
巾一對手笠兩
張被單一個枕
袋一副睡衣一
條面巾一條頸
巾共什七件

5. How much does the washerman want per hundred for washing?
*꜀I fuk$_{2}$ ꜂lò iú꜃ ꜂ki ꜀tó ꜄ngan yat꜁ pák꜁ kin$^{2}$ ꜀ní?*
He wants one tael per hundred.
*꜂K'ü iú꜃ yat꜁ ꜂léung ꜄ngan yat꜁ pák꜁.*

衣服佬要幾多
銀一百件呢
佢要一両銀一
百

6. You tell the washerman that he need not starch the sleeping-dress.
*꜂Ní ꜀fan fú꜃ kó꜃ ꜀í fuk$_{2}$ ꜂lò ꜄'m ꜂shai ꜀tséung kó꜃ tik꜁ shui$^{2}$ ꜀shám.*

伱吩咐個衣服
佬唔使槳個的
睡衫

I told him yesterday.
*Tsók$_{2}$ yat$_{2}$ wá$^{2}$ ꜂k'ü ꜀chí lók꜁.*
7. Change that bowl, and bring some clean water to wash my face.
*Wún$^{2}$ kwó꜃ ꜄p'ún ꜀kón tsing$^{2}$ ꜂shui ꜄lai ꜂sai min$^{2}$.*

昨日話佢知咯
換過盤乾净水
嚟洗面

It is changed; do you want some hot water for shaving?
*I'ún³ lók›, ‘ní iú³ ít› ‘shui t‘ai³ ‹sú ˛’m iú³?*

換咯你要熱水剃鬚唔要

8. No; brush that coat clean, that will be enough.
*˛’M ‘shai lók›, ts‘át› tsing² kó³ kín³ tái² ‹shám pá² ‹ló.*

唔使咯擦净個件大衫罷嘮

The barber has just come, have you time to have him cut your hair?
*˛I ‹ká t‘ai³ ˛t‘au ‘lò ˛lai lók›, ‘ní tak› ˛hán ‘tsín fát› mí² ‹ní?*

而家剃頭佬嚟咯你得閒剪髮未呢

9. Call him up; and at the same time call the coolie to sweep the floor.
*Kiú³ ‘k‘ü ‘shéung ˛lai ‹lé; yat› ‘hi kiú³ ‘kún tím³ sò³ ˛lau ‹lé.*

叫佢上嚟唎一起叫管店掃樓唎

The coolie is busy doing something else; he'll come directly.
*‘Kún tím³ ‘kón tsò² pít› tik› sz’², tsau² ˛lai lók›.*

管店赶做别的事就嚟咯

10. What are you doing now?
*‘Ní ˛í ‹ká tsò² mat› ‘yé?*

你而家做乜野

I am brushing your room, and arranging your bed.
*˛Ü ‹kam ‘tá sò³ ‘ní ‹kán ˛fóng, ‹kím ‹p‘ò ‘hò ‘ní kó³ ‹chéung ˛ch‘óng.*

如今打掃你間房兼鋪好你個張床

11. Which do you want?
*‘Ní oí³ ‹pín kó³?*

你愛邊個

I want the broadest.
*‘Ngó oí³ chí³ fút› ké³.*

我愛至闊嘅

12. What do you want?
*‘Ní iú³ mat› ‘yé?*

你要乜野

There is a Chinese below who calls you.
*‘Yau kó³ ˛T‘óng ˛yan ‘hai ˛lau há² kiú³ ‘ní.*

有個唐人喺樓下叫你

13. What business has he?
*Mat› ‘yé sz’² kón³ á²?*

乜野事幹呀

I do'nt know, but I think he has come to call on you.
*˛’M ‹chí ‹ní, ˛loi t‘ám³ ‘ní kwá³.*

唔知呢來探你啩

14. Request him to come up.
*‘Ts‘ing ‘shéung ˛lai ‹lá.*

請上黎啦

15. What is contained in this box?
‹Ní kó' ‹séung tsoi' mat› ʻyé á'?

呢個箱載乜野
呀

Crockery-ware is packed in it.
‹Ch'óng ‹ts'z' hí' kè'.

裝磁器嘅

16. How was this plate broken?
ʻTím yéung² lán² tak› ‹ní chik› típ₂?

點樣爛得呢隻
碟

The coolie inadvertently let a knife drop which broke it.
ʻKún tím' ‹'m kók› tút› ʻpá ‹tò lók₂ hü' ʻtá lán² kè'.

管店唔覺跌把
刀落去打爛嘅

17. Tell the comprador to go to the shop and buy a new one in his stead, to replace this.
Kíú' ʻmái pán² hü' p'ò' ‹t'au toi² ʻk'ü ʻmái kwó' chik› ‹san kè' ‹púí ‹fán kwó' ʻngó ‹lá.

叫買辦去舖頭
代佢買過隻新
嘅倍番過我啦

This sort is a foreign one, and I fear the Chinese shops have none for sale.

‹Ní kó' yéung² hai² ‹loi lò² kè' pó'; ‹T'óng ‹yan p'ò' ‹t'au p'á' ʻmò tak› mái² á'.

呢個樣係來路
嘅噃唐人舖頭
怕冇得賣呀

18. This tumbler is cracked and leaks; bring another.

‹Ní chik› ʻshui ‹púi lít₂ lá' lau² ʻshui kè' lók›; ‹ním kwó' tai² í² chik› ‹lai pá² ‹lá.

呢隻水盃裂鏬
漏水嘅咯拈過
第二隻嚟罷啦

There are none.
ʻMò lók›.

冇咯

19. Is that table done yet?

Tsò² ʻhí kó' ‹chéung ‹t'oi ‹'m ‹ts'ang á'?

做起個張枱唔
曾呀

It will certainly be finished in a few days.
Kwó' ʻkí yat₂ pít› ting² tsò² ʻhí lók›.

過幾日必定做
起咯

20. He promised to have it completed to-day; does he again put me off several days more!
ʻK'ü ‹ying ‹shing ‹kam yat₂ tsò² ʻhí, yau² ‹t'úi ʻkí yat₂ ‹t'ím.
He says his workmen have all gone

佢應承今日做
起又推幾日添
佢話夥計去睇

to see the play, and there is nobody to assist him.
*ʻK'ü wá² ʻfó kí' hü' ʻt'ai hí', ʻmò mat, ˏyan ˏpóng ʻshau tsò².*

戲冇乜人帮手
做

21. Why did you not come before?
*Tsò² mat, ʻní ˏsín ˏshí ˏʻm ˏlai ˏní?*

做乜你先時唔
來呢

Because the rain, having made the road slippery, it was difficult to walk.
*ˏYan wai² lók₂ ʻü, lò² wát₂, ók, ˏhang.*

因爲落雨路滑
惡行

22. What are you looking for?
*ʻNi ˏts'am mat, ʻyé?*

你尋乜野

Yesterday I did not see the penknife, and am now looking for it.
*Tsók₂ yat, ˏʻm kín' ʻpá ˏtò ʻtsai, ˏí ˏká ʻwan ʻhá ˏché.*

昨日唔見把刀
仔而家搵吓啫

23. Perhaps it is in my vest pocket.
*Wak₂ ʻché tsoi² ʻngó púi' ˏsam toi² ˏlai.*

或者在我背心
袋嚟

No, I have looked everywhere, and cannot find it.
*ʻMò, ʻngó ch'ü' ch'ü' ʻwan kwó' ˏtò ˏʻm kín'.*

冇我處處搵過
都唔見

24. You must have looked very carelessly, for here it is under this ink-rag.
*ʻNi ˏmá ˏmá ʻtí ˏts'am ʻhá, ʻhai lók,, ʻhai kó' fáí' ʻkíú pat, pò' ʻtai ˏlai ˏní.*

你嘛嘛哋尋吓
喺咯喺個塊繳
筆布底嚟呢

Well, I thought it was on the writing-desk after all.
*A'! ʻngó ʻkú pat, ʻking ʻhai ʻsé tsz'² ˏt'oi ˏlai ˏlé.*

哆我估畢竟喺
寫字枱嚟唎

25. Bring me a light, to seal this letter, quick!
*ˏNim kó' ʻfó ˏlai ʻtang ʻngó ˏfung ˏní ˏfung san', fáí' tik,!*

拈個火嚟等我
封呢封信快的

Where is it to be sent?
*Kí' hü' ˏpín ch'ü' á'?*

寄去邊處呀

26. Send it to Mr. T.'s hong, and bid the coolie make haste, for I fear it will be too late. Do you know where he lives?
*Kí' hü' ʻMí sz'² Tí² ˏhóng, kíú' ʻkún tím' fáí' ˏning hü' ʻngó ˏtò p'á' t'áí' ˏch'í lók,; ʻní shik, tak, kó' ˏyau ʻhai ˏpín ch'ü' chü² ˏʻm á'?*

寄去美士哋行
吽管店快擰去
我都怕太遲咯
你識得個人喺
邊處住唔呀

拾級大成

Yes sir, I know the house, No. 3 Danish hong.
*Shik, tak,, hai² ˌWóng ˌk'i ˌhóng, tai² ˏsám ˈtáp₂.*

識得係黃旗行第三啓

27. Put this table to rights, the inkstand, pens, stamps, paper folder, paper weights, ruler, bell, lead pencils, wax, wafers, paper, put them all in order.

*Ping' 'hò ˏní ˏchéung ˌt'oi; kó' tik, mak₂ 'shui ˏáng, pat,, 'fó ts'at, yan', 'chí ˏtò, 'chí át,, kái' ch'ik,, ˏchung 'tsai, ˌün pat,, 'fó ts'at,, 'shui ts'at,, 'chí, yat₂ 'tsung, ping' 'hò 'k'ü ˏló.*

柄好呢張檯個的墨水罌筆火漆印紙刀紙壓界尺鐘仔鉛筆火漆水漆紙一總柄好佢囉

Please show me how you wish it done, then I shall know.

*'Ts'ing 'ní 'ching 'hò 'ngó 't'ai kwó', 'tang 'ngó hau² ˌloi ˏchí tak, ˏá.*

請你整好我睇過等我後來知得呀

28. In this manner, and I wish you to do it in this way every morning.
*'Kóm yéung² 'ngó iú' 'ní 'múi ˏchíu chíú' yéung² 'ching 'hò.*

咁樣我要你每朝照樣整好

29. Spread out those books to air, and afterwards brush them clean of all dirt and insects.
*'Pái ˏhoi kó' tik, ˏshü ˌfung ˏch'úi 'há, ˌín hau² ts'át, tsing² kó' tik, 'kün ˏshü ˌtsan ˌch'ung.*

擺開個的書風吹吓然後擦淨個的捲書塵虫

Which book-case?
*ˏPín kó' ˏshü kwai²?*

邊個書櫃

30. That one in the hall on the side of the fire-place, having glass windows.

*Tsoi² tái² ˌlau 'fó ˌlò tsak, ˏpín ˏp'ó ˌlí ˌmún, kó' kó' ˏní.*

在大樓火爐側邊玻璃門個個呢

I have never yet done this, and do not understand how to do it.

*'Ngó ˏsín ˌshí ˌ'm ˌts'ang tsò² kwó', ˌ'm 'hiú 'tím yéung² tsò' pó'.*

我先時唔曾做過唔曉點樣做噃

31. Who broke this window?
*Mat, ˌyan 'ching lán² kó' tò² ˏp'ó ˌlí ˏch'éung ˌmún á'?*

乜人整爛個度玻璃窗門呀

A boy in the street threw a stone in and broke it.

*Kó' tik› sai' ‹man ‘tsai ‘hai ‹kái ‹p'au shik$_2$ yap$_2$ ‹lai ‘tá lán$^2$ ké'.*

個的細蚊仔喺
街抛石入嚟打
爛嘅

32. Where did this come from?
*‹Ní tik› ‹pín ch'ü' ‹ním ‹lai?*

呢的邊處拈黎

The stranger brought it last night.
*Tsók$_2$ ‘mán ‹yan hák› ‹ním ‹lai.*

昨晚人客拈黎

33. Where are you going to take this?
*‹Ní tik› ‹ním hü' ‹pín ch'ü'?*

呢的拈去邊處

Away to the boat to go aboard ship.
*‹Tám ‹hoi hü' ‹sám ‘pán lók$_2$ ‹shün.*

擔開去三板落
船

34. Which is the best of these two?
*‹Ní tik› kung' kó' tik› ‹pín tik› chí' ‘hò ‹ní?*

呢的共個的邊
的至好呢

I think the highest is the best.
*‘Ngó ‘t'ai tak› kó' tik› chí' tái$^2$ ké' chí' ‘hò.*

我睇得個的至
大嘅至好

35. When it has done raining, tell the coolie to go to Howqua's hong, and bring a lackered chair here.
*Lók$_2$ ‹ün ‘ü, kiú' ‘kún tím' hü$^2$ ‹Í ‹wó ‹hóng t'ók› kó' ‹chéung ts'at› ‘i ‹fán ‹lai.*

落完雨叫管店
去怡和行托個
張漆椅番黎

The coolie is not in; he went home early this morning.
*‘Kún tím' ‹'m ‘hai ch'ü', ‹kam ‹chíú ‘tsò hü' ‹kwai.*

管店唔喺處今
朝早去歸

36. Why did he go of his own accord, without telling me of it?
*Tsò$^2$ mat› shín$^2$ tsz'$^2$ hü' ‹tò ‹'m wá$^2$ kwó' ‘ngó ‹t'ing ‹ní?*

做乜擅自去都
唔話過我聽呢

His wife is sick, and very early in the morning a man came to call him, before you, sir, had risen; consequently he did not inform you.

*‘K'ü ‘lò ‹p'ó ‘yau ping$^2$, tsüt$_2$ ‘tsò ‘yau ‹yan ‹lai kiú' ‘k'ü, sz'$^2$ ‹t'au ‘ní yau$^2$ mí$^2$ ‘hí ‹shan; ‘shó ‘i ‘k'ü ‹'m wá$^2$ tak› kwó' ‘ní ‹chí lók›.*

佢老婆有病絕
早有人黎叫佢
事頭你又未起
身所以佢唔話
得過你知咯

37. When will he come back?
*‘K'ü ‘kí ‹shí ‹fán ‹lai á'?*

佢幾時番黎呀

拾級大成

I do not know when his wife will be well, but he will return as soon as she is well.
*ˏ'M ˏchí ˢk'ü ˢlò ˏp'ó ˢkí ˏshí ˢhò ˏní; shü² pít, ˢtang tò' ˢhò chí' ˏfán ˏlai kwá'.*

唔知佢老婆幾
時好呢是必等
到好至畨嚟啩

38. Where shall I put this?

*ˢNgó fóng' ˏní tik, tsoi² ˏpín ch'ü'?*

我放呢的在邊
處

Place it up on the shelf.
*Fóng' ˢshéung ˢkau ˢpi ká' ch'ü'.*

放上狗脾架處

39. Are you ready yet?
*ˢNí pín² ˏ'm ˏts'ang ˏní?*

你便唔曾呢

Do 'nt be so impatient, I'll come pretty soon.
*ˏ'M ˢshai kóm' ˏsam kap,, tsau² ˏlai lók,.*

唔使咁心急就
嚟咯

40. Why do you do it so?
*ˢNí wai² ˏhó ˢkóm yéung² tsò²?*

你爲何咁樣做

I thought you would like it so.

*ˢNgó ˢkú ˢní ˏchung í' ˢkóm yéung².*

我估你中意咁
樣

41. Have you not finished that job yet?
*ˢNí kó' tün² sz'² chung² mì² tsò² ˢhí?*

你個叚事重未
做起

It is very difficult to do, I cannot do it quickly.
*Shap, ˏfan ók, tsò², ˏ'm fái' tak, ké'.*

十分惡做唔快
得嘅

42. How did you tell him?

*ˢNí ˢtím wá² kwó' ˢk'ü ˏchí á'?*

你點話過佢知
呀

Just according to your words; to be ready at eight o'clock.
*Tsau² chíú' ˢní wá², pát, ˢtím ˏchung pín², ˢkóm lók,.*

就照你話八點
鐘便咁咯

43. What did he answer you?
*ˢK'ü ˢtím táp, ˢní ˏni?*

佢點答你呢

He replied, very well.
*ˢK'ü wá², tsò² tak,.*

佢話做得

44. Have you sent after chair-bearers?
*ˢNí ˢyau ˢshai ˏyan hü' kíú' ˏt'oi ˢkiú ˢlò, ˏ'm ˏts'ang á'?*

你有使人去叫
抬轎佬唔曾呀

A coolie has just now gone to call them.
*ˢKún tím' tsau² chí' hü' kíú'.*

管店就至去叫

45. Tell them, that when the lady wants them to put the chair down, to take it up, to go slow or fast, to go through this street, or stop at that house, or whatever she bids them to do, they must obey her.

*Wá$^2$ ᶜk'ü ti$^2$ ꜀chí kó’ wai$^2$ ꜀kú ꜁néung wá$^2$ iú’ lók$_2$ ᶜkiú, wák$_2$ iú’ ᶜshéung ᶜkiú, wá$^2$ ꜁hang mán$^2$ tik’, wák$_2$ fái’ tik’, wá$^2$ iú’ ꜀king kwó’ ᶜmau ꜀kái ᶜmau uk’ lók$_2$ ᶜkiú, tsau$^2$ iú’ ꜀t'ing ᶜk'ü ꜀fan fú’ lá’.*

話佢地知個位姑娘話要落轎或要上轎話行慢的或快的話要經過某街某屋落轎就要聽佢吩咐嚇

It is not necessary to tell them, for their business is to carry chairs, and they know all these things.

*Kó’ tik’ ꜁'m ᶜshai ꜀fan fú’ ᶜk'ü ti$^2$, ꜀yan wai$^2$ ᶜk'ü hai$^2$ ꜁t'oi kún’ ᶜkiú ké’, kó’ tik’ sz’$^2$ kón’ ᶜk'ü shuk$_2$ shik$_2$ ké’ lók’.*

個的唔使吩咐佢地因爲佢係抬慣轎嘅個的事幹佢熟識嘅咯

46. Ask the comprador what he is going to get for dinner to-day; there are four guests coming here to dine.

*Man$^2$ ᶜmái pán$^2$ ᶜséung hü’ ᶜmái mat’ ᶜyé tsò$^2$ ꜀kam yat$_2$ tái$^2$ ꜀ts'án; ᶜyau sz’ wai$^2$ ꜁yan hák’ ꜁lai ꜀ní ch'ü’ ꜀t'im.*

問買辦想去買乜野做今日大餐有四位人客嚟呢處添

He says he has provided crab soup, boiled garoupa, shell-fish, a roast pig, cutlet chicken, mutton chop, baked potatoes, greens and eggs, hashed turnips, onions with beefsteak, sweet potatoes, orange tarts, suet pudding, custards, cheese, biscuit, fruit of two or three kinds, wines and beer.

*ᶜK'ü wá$^2$ ü$^2$ ting$^2$ tsò$^2$ ᶜhái ꜀t'óng, sháp$_2$ shik$_2$ ꜀pán ꜁ü, kuk$_2$ ꜁hò, ꜀shíú ꜀chü ᶜtsai, kat’ lít$_2$ ꜀kai, ꜁yéung ꜁pái kwat’, kuk$_2$ ꜁shü ᶜtsai, tán$^2$ ts'oi’, ꜁ló pák$_2$ ᶜfan, t'ít’ ꜁p'á ꜀ts'ung ꜁ngau yuk$_2$, ꜁hung ꜁shü, ꜁ch'áng tát$_2$, ꜁ngau kwat’ ᶜsui pò’ ꜀tín, tun$^2$ kat’ ꜁shí, ꜁ngau ᶜnái ᶜp'ing, ᶜp'ing ꜀kón, ᶜléung ꜀sám yéung$^2$ ᶜkwó ᶜtsz’, ᶜtsau, ꜀pé ᶜtsau.*

佢話預定做蟹湯烚石斑魚局蠔燒猪仔吉烈鷄羊排骨局薯仔蛋菜蘿蔔粉鐵鈀葱牛肉紅薯燈噠牛骨髓布顛燉吉時牛奶餅餅乾兩三樣菓子酒啤酒

47. Tell him those will be enough.

*Wá$^2$ ᶜk'ü ꜀chi ᶜkóm kau’ lók’.*

話佢知咁够咯

These two conversations with a comprador and a servant, as will have already been seen, are not continuous dialogues, but are made up for the most part of such leading questions as are most likely to be needed by persons employing such domestics, and also to a great degree in intercourse with all classes. They will, it is hoped, if learned as recommended in the paragraph at the beginning of the chapter, be sufficient to guide the learner in the formation of other sentences as his wants may suggest. Those who are learning the language where they hear it used every day, should attend closely to the people as they talk among themselves, try to catch the sounds and intonation of the words, and sentences as they fall from the lips of the speakers, observe their phrases, and endeavor to preserve them in his memory. Similar conversations with tradesmen, teachers, and other classes of society on different subjects, all written in the colloquial style, are also contained in the Chinese Chrestomathy, to which the student is referred.

# Chapter Sixth.

## SELECTIONS FOR READING.

These selections are longer than the sentences in the fourth chapter, and those from the writings of Lukchau exhibit a more condensed style of writing than the preceding extracts from the History of the Three States. Like them they should be learned thoroughly.

### No. I.—Heroism of an Imperial Concubine.

(鹿洲 女學 卷一 第十章)

漢 元 帝 幸 虎 圈 鬬 獸 忽 有 熊 逸
*Hón', ˛Ün tai' hang$^{2}$ 'fú ˓hün, tau' shau'; fat˒ 'yau ˛hung yat$_{2}$*
Hon, Un emperor went tiger inclosure, fight beast; suddenly was bear bolting

出 攀 檻 欲 上 宮 人 皆 避 匿 馮
*ch'ut˒ ˓pún lám$^{2}$ yuk$_{2}$ 'shéung. ˓Kung ˛yan ˓kái pí$^{2}$ nik˒; ˛Fung*
out clambered fence trying to-ascend. Palace people all fled hid; Fung

---

The emperor Ün of the Hón dynasty once went to the Tiger menagerie to see the wild beasts fight. Suddenly, a bear bursting out clambered up on the railing, and tried to escape. The inmates of the palace all fled and hid themselves; Fung, a lady of the bedchamber, alone rushing out directly opposed the bear, and kept standing until the attendants dispatched him with

昭 儀 挺 然 直 前 當 熊 而 立 及 左
*‹chiú ‹í ‘t‘ing ‹in chik› ‹ts‘ín ‹tóng ‹hung ‹í lap›, k‘ap› ‘tsó*
refulgent rule rushed alone straight before opposed bear and stood till left

右 格 殺 熊 帝 問 昭 儀 何 獨 不
*yau' kák› shat› ‹hung. Tai' man' ‹chiú ‹í, ‹Hó tuk› pat›*
right cudgeled killed bear. Emperor asked refulgent rule, Why alone not

懼 對 曰 夫 猛 獸 得 人 而 止 妾
*küi'? Túi' üt›, ‹fú ‘mang shau' tak› ‹yan ‹í ‘chí; ts‘ip›*
terrified? Answering said, now furious beast obtain person then stop; concubine

恐 犯 御 座 故 身 當 之 帝 以 此
*‘hung fán' ü' tsó', kú' ‹shan ‹tóng ‹chí. Tai' ‘i ‘ts‘z',*
fearing desecrate imperial seat, therefore I-personally opposed it. Emperor for this

倍 加 敬 重 焉
*‘púi ‹ká king' chung' ‹in.*
redoubled added respect esteem truly.

---

No. II.—A Daughter-in-law's Obedience.

（鹿洲女學卷一第二十章）

禮 修 者 張 氏 女 趙 嵩 妻 也 姑
*‘Lai ‹sau ‘ché ‹Chéung shí' ‘nü Chíú' ‹Sung ‹ts‘ai ‘yá. ‹Kú*
Laisau one, Chéung family female Chíú Sung's wife. Mother-in-law

酷 惡 無 道 遇 之 不 以 禮 修
*huk› ók› ‹mò tò'; ü' ‹chí pat› ‘i ‘lai. ‹Sau*
hardhearted wicked without principle; meeting her not with propriety. Sau

終 無 慍 色 及 歸 寧 父 母 問 之 但
*‹ch‘ung ‹mò wan' shik›; k‘ap› ‹kwai ‹ning fú' ‘mò man' ‹chí, tán'*
ever without passion color; when home visited father mother asked her, only

引 咎 不 道 姑 卒 感 悟 更 慈
*‘yan kau' pat› tò'. ‹Kú tsut› ‘kóm 'ng' kang' ‹ts‘z'*
introduced faults, not speak. Mo.-in-law subsequently moved aroused very kind

愛 之 鄉 人 相 訓 曰 作 婦 不 當 如
*oi' ‹chí. ‹Héung ‹yan ‹séung fan' üt›, tsók› ‘fú pat› ‹tóng ‹ü*
loved her. Village men each-other taught, saying, Act wife not ought like

---

cudgels. The emperor asked her, "Why were you alone not terrified?" She replied, "If the furious beast could get a person he would then stop; I, fearing he would desecrate the imperial seat, therefore threw myself before him." The emperor, for this action, redoubled his respect and esteem for her.

Laisau, a female of the family of Chéung, was the wife of Chíú Sung. Her mother-in-law was inhumanly wicked and unreasonable, and whenever she met her could not act towards her with decorum. Sau never manifested the least discomposure, and when visiting at home and her parents asked her, she only introduced her own delinquencies, and never mentioned [her mother-in-law's]. She, subsequently wrought upon and aroused [by this conduct],

趙 伯 高 婦 乎 使 惡 姑 知 變 可
*Chiú² Pák› ‹kò ‘fú ‹ú ? ‘Sz’ ók› ‹kú ‹chí pín’ ‘hó*
Chiú Pákkò's wife ? Causing wicked mother-in-law know change can

謂 婦 師
*wai² ‘fú ‹sz’.*
called Wives' Instructor.

---

No. III.—Intrepidity of a Widow.

(鹿洲女學卷二第七十七章)

皇 甫 規 之 妻 善 屬 文 能 草 書
*‹Wóng ‘Fú ‹kw‘ai ‹chí ‹ts‘ai, shín² shuk₂ ‹man, ‹nang ‘ts‘ò ‹shü·*
Wóng Fúkw‘ai 's wife, clever compiling writings, able running-hand write·

規 卒 董 卓 聞 其 名 聘 以 輜 軿
*‹Kw‘ai tsut›, ‘Tung Ch‘éuk› ‹man ‹k‘i ‹ming, p‘ing’ ‘i ‹sz’ ‹ping*
Kw‘ai dead, Tung Ch‘éuk hearing her fame, espoused with chariots curricles

百 乘 馬 二 十 匹 奴 婢 錢 帛 充
*pák› shing², ‘má i² shap₂ p‘at›, ‹nò ‘pi ‹ts‘in pák₁, ‹ch‘ung*
hundred carriages, horses twenty animals, slaves maids, money silk, filled

路 妻 乃 輕 服 詣 卓 門 跪 自 陳
*lò². ‹Ts‘ai ‘nái ‹hing fuk₂ ngai² Ch‘éuk› ‹mún, kwai² tsz’² ‹ch‘an*
road. She in light dress repaired-to Ch‘éuk's door, kneeling herself stated

情 辭 甚 酸 愴 卓 使 奴 拔 刀
*‹ts‘ing, ‹ts‘z’ sham² ‹sün ‘ts‘óng. Ch‘éuk› ‘sz’ ‹nò pat₂ ‹tò*
feelings, speaking very bitterly affecting. Ch‘éuk, ordering slaves draw swords

圍 之 而 謂 曰 孤 之 威 教 欲 令 四 海
*‹wai ‹chí, ‹í wai² üt₂, ‹Kú ‹chí ‹wai káu’, yuk₂ ling² sz’’ ‘hoi*
surround her, and speaking said, My 's awe law about-to order four seas,

風 靡 豈 有 不 行 于 一 婦 乎 妻 知-
*‹fung ‘mí, ‘hi ‘yau pat› ‹hang ‹ü yat› ‘fú ‹ú ? ‹Ts‘ai ‹chí*
influence submit, how have not act on one women eh ? She knowing

---

became very affectionate and loving to her. The villagers taught each other, saying, "Ought not every wife to act as Chiú Pákkò's wife? For knowing how to change a wicked mother-in-law, she can be called the Instructor of Wives."

The wife of Wóng Fúkw‘ai was very clever in compiling literary works, and was able to write the running-hand. After her husband's death, Tung Ch‘éuk, hearing of her fame, sent a marriage present to her consisting of a hundred baggage and light wagons, twenty horses, with slaves and maid-servants, money and silk, filling the road with them all. She, in a sorry dress, went to Ch‘éuk's gate, and kneeling, stated her own feelings, speaking in an exceedingly touching and moving manner. Ch‘éuk, ordering his slaves to draw their swords and surround her, then called to her, saying, "My awe and my commands are about to rule the empire, and all will submit

不免厲聲罵曰君羗胡之種毒害
*pat‹ ‘mín, lai$^{2}$ ‹shing má$^{2}$ üt$_{2}$, ‹kwan ‹Këung ‹ú ‹chí ‘chung, tuk$_{2}$ hoi$^{2}$*
not loose, undaunted voice railing said, Sir barbarian 's sort, poison destroy

天下猶未足耶妾之先人清
*‹t‘ín há$^{2}$; ‹yau mí$^{2}$ tsuk‹ ‹yé? Ts‘ip‹ ‹chí ‹sín ‹yan, ‹ts‘ing*
heaven below; still not satisfied? Concubine 's former men, unsullied

德奕世皇甫氏文武上才爲漢
*tak‹ yik$_{2}$ shai’, ‹Wóng ‘fú shí$^{2}$ ‹man ‘mò shéung$^{2}$ ‹ts‘oi ‹wai Hón’*
virtue successive ages, Wóngfú family civil military high talents, were Hón's

忠臣君親非其趨使走吏乎
*‹chung ‹shan. ‹Kwan ‹ts‘an ‹fí ‹k‘i ‹ts‘ü ‘sz’ ‘tsau lí$^{2}$ ‹ú?*
faithful ministers. Your family not his bidding servants hasting clerks eh?

敢行非禮于汝君夫人耶卓乃引車
*‘Kóm ‹hang ‹fí ‘lai ‹ü ‘ü ‹kwan ‹fú ‹yan ‹yé? Ch‘éuk‹ ‘nái ‘yan ‹kü*
Dare act not proper with your lord's wife eh? Ch‘éuk then led carriage

庭中以其頸繫軛鞭朴交下妻
*‹t‘ing ‹chung, ‘í ‹k‘i ‘king hai$^{2}$ ák‹, ‹pín puk‹ ‹káu há$^{2}$. ‹Ts‘ai*
house in, on her neck bound yoke, whips cudgels together beat. She

謂杖者曰何不重乎速盡爲惠
*wai$^{2}$ chéung’ ‘ché üt$_{2}$, ‹Hó pat‹ chung$^{2}$ ‹ú? Ch‘uk‹ tsun$^{2}$ ‹wai wai$^{2}$.*
calling club men said, Why not heavier eh? Quickly finish is kind.

遂死車下後人圖畫號曰禮
*Sui$^{2}$ ‘sz’ ‹kü há$^{2}$. Hau$^{2}$ ‹yan ‹t‘ò wá$^{2}$ hò$^{2}$ üt$_{2}$ ‘Lai*
Then died carriage under. After men drew painting termed called Propriety

宗云
*‹tsung ‹wan.*
Pattern.

---

at my name; and shall I not have power over one woman!" She, knowing that he would not let her go, in an undaunted tone railed at him, saying, "Barbarian and savage, the pest and destruction of the country! Are you still unsatiated? My ancestors were of the Wóngfú family, who maintained unsullied virtue for successive generations, and held civil and military offices with high talents; they were faithful ministers of the Hón dynasty. Were not your relatives their clerks and servants, to come and go at their beck? Dare you act improperly with your lord's wife?" Ch‘éuk then led her into the carriage-house, and bound a carriage-yoke on her neck, and simultaneously beat her with whips and cudgels. She calling to the clubmen, said, "Why do you not strike heavier? Be kind and quickly finish me." She then died under the carriage. Afterwards, men made a painting of her, and named her the Pattern of Propriety.

## No. IV.—A Mother's Severity.

(鹿洲女學卷三第九十九章)

李景讓母鄭氏性嚴明早寡
*ʿLí ʿKing yéung² ʿmò Ching² shi²; sing' ˏim ˏming. ʿTsò ˏʿkwá.*
Lí Kingyéung's mother Ching family; nature stern intelligent. Early widow,

家貧子幼母自教之三子景
*ˏká ˏpan, ʿtsz' yau', ʿmò tsz'² káu' ˏchí; ˏsám ʿtsz' ʿKing*
family poor, sons young, mother herself taught them; three sons, King

讓景温景莊皆進士及第
*yéung², ʿKing ˏwan, ʿKing ˏchóng, ˏkái tsun' sz'² k'ap₂ tai².*
yéung, Kingwan, Kingchóng, each advanced scholar attained degree.

景讓在浙西有都押衙迕其意
*King' yéung² tsoi² Chít, ˏsai ʿyau ˏtò át, ˏngá ʿ'ng ˏk'i í',*
Kingyéung in Chítkóng's west had all guard office opposed his wishes,

景讓杖之而斃軍中憤怒將爲
*King' yéung² chéung² ˏchí ˏí pai². ˏKwan ˏchung ʿfan nò², ˏtséung ˏwai*
Kingyéung caned him and died. Army in displeased angry about to-be

變景讓方視事母出坐廳事
*pín'. ʿKing yéung² ˏfóng shi² sz'² ʿmò ch'ut, tsó' ˏt'ing sz'²,*
mutinous. Kingyéung, while examine business, mother went sat hear affair,

立景讓于庭責之曰天子付
*lap₂ ʿKing yéung² ˏü ˏt'ing chak, ˏchí, üt₂, ˏt'in ʿtsz' fú²*
standing Kingyéung in hall, reprimanded him saying, heaven's son conferred

汝以方面國家刑法豈得爲
*ʿü ʿí ˏfóng mín², kwók, ˏká ˏhing fát,: ʿhi tak, ˏwai*
you to region face, state family's punishment laws, how able to-be

汝喜怒之資妄殺無罪之人乎
*ʿü ʿhi nò² ˏchí ˏtsz'? Móng² shat, ˏmò tsúi² ˏchí ˏyan ˏú?*
your pleasure anger 's behest? Causelessly killed without crime 's man eh?

萬一致一方不寧豈惟上負朝
*Mán² yat, chí' yat, ˏfóng pat, ˏning, ʿhi ˏwai shéung² fú² ˏchiú*
Myriad one make this region not peace, how alone emperor despise his

---

The mother of Lí Kingyéung was of the family of Ching. Her mind was both stern and intelligent; and becoming a widow early, her family being poor, and her sons young, she taught them herself. Her three sons, Kingyéung, Kingwan and Kingchóng, all became graduates of the degree of *tsunsz'*. Kingyéung, while [in office] in the western part of Chítkóng, had a subaltern in the ranks who opposed his wishes, whom he caned so that he died. The army was exceedingly irritated and angry, and on the point of becoming mutinous, when, as Kingyéung was exercising his office, his mother came out and sat down to examine into the business, and ordered her son to stand out in the midst. Then reprimanding him, said, "The emperor has conferred upon you the duties of inspecting this region, according to the laws and

廷 使 垂 年之母 銜羞入地
*ˏt'ing;* *'sz'* *ˏshui* *ˏnín ˎchí* *ˋmò,* *ˏhóm* *ˎsau* *yap* *tí;*
government; causing descending years 's mother, covered shame enter earth;

何以見汝先人 命 左右褫其衣
*ˏhó* *ˋi* *kín'* *ˋü* *ˏsín* *ˏyan?* *Ming* *'tsó yau* *'ch'í ˏk'í* *ˎí,*
how can see your before men? Commanding left right strip his clothes,

撻其背;將佐 皆爲之 請 拜且
*tát,* *ˏk'í púi';* *tséung'* *tsó'* *ˎkái wai* *ˎchí* *'ts'ing* *pái'* *'ch'é*
whipped his back; officers assistants all for him requested, bowed moreover

泣 久乃釋之軍中由是遂 安
*yap,;* *'kau* *ˋnái shik,* *ˎchí.* *ˎKwan ˎchung* *ˏyau shí,* *sui* *ˎón.*
wept; long then loosed him. Army in from this, accordingly quieted.

---

### No. IV.—Confucius and the Boy.

(見東園雜字 小兒論)

孔子名丘字仲尼設教於魯
*'Hung 'tsz'* *ˏming* *ˎYau,* *tsz'* *Chungˏní;* *ch'ít,* *káu'* *ˎü* *ˋLú*
Confucius named Yau, styled Chungní; set-up to-teach in Lú

國之西一日率諸弟子御車出
*kwók,* *ˎchí* *ˎsai.* *Yat,* *yat,* *shut,* *ˎchü* *tai* *'tsz',* *ü* *ˎkü ch'ut,*
state 's west. One day, followed all disciples, sitting carriage went

游路逢數兒 嬉 戲 中有一兒
*ˏyau;* *lò* *ˏfung shò'* *ˏí* *ˎhí* *hí';* *ˎchung* *ˋyau* *yat,* *ˏí*
rambling; road met several children childishly playing; among was one lad

不戲孔子乃駐車問曰獨汝
*pat,* *hí'.* *'Hung* *'tsz'* *ˋnái* *chú'* *ˎkü,* *man* *üt,* *tuk,* *ˋü*
not play. Confucius then stopping carriage, asking said, only you

不戲何也小兒答曰凡戲無 益
*pat,* *hí',* *ˏhó* *ˋyá?* *'Síú* *ˏí* *táp,* *üt,* *ˏfán* *hí'* *ˏmò* *yik,,*
not play, why eh? Small boy replying said, all play without advantage,

---

penalties of the empire. How then can you, at your own pleasure, illegally kill an innocent man? Ten thousand to one that this does not disturb the peace of this region: how can you alone oppose the emperor and despise his government, and bring your poor old mother, covered with shame, down to the grave! How can I then meet your ancestors?" She then ordered the attendants to strip off his clothes and beat him on the back, till the officers and assistants all intreated her for him, bowing and weeping. After a long time she let him off, and the army by this was quieted.

The name of Confucius was Yau, and his style Chungní; he established himself as an instructor in the western part of the kingdom of Lú. One day, followed by all his disciples, riding in a carriage, he went out to ramble, and on the road, came across several children at their sports; among them was one who did not join them. Confucius, stopping his carriage, asked him, saying, "Why is it that you alone do not play?" The lad replied,

衣 破 難 縫 上 辱 父 母 下 及 門
*꜀í p'ó' ꜀nán ꜀fung; shéung' yuk꜇ fú' ꜂mò, há' k'ap꜇ ꜁mún*
clothes torn difficult mend; above disgrace father mother, below even-to door

中 必 有 鬬 爭 勞 而 無 功 豈 爲
*꜀chung, pít꜇ ꜂yau tau' ꜀chang; ꜁lò ꜁í ꜁mò ꜀kung; ꜂hí ꜁wai*
midst, certainly have fighting quarreling; labor and without gain, how is

好 事 故 乃 不 戲 遂 低 頭 以 瓦
*꜂hò sz'? kú' ꜂nái pat꜇ hí'. Sui' ꜀tai ꜁t'au ꜂í ꜂ngá*
good business? therefore is not play. Then hanging head with tile

片 作 城
*p'ín' tsók꜇ ꜁shing.*
pieces made city.

孔 子 責 之 曰 何 不 避 車 乎 小
*꜂Hung ꜂tsz' chak꜇ ꜀chí, üt꜇, ꜁hó pat꜇ pí' ꜀kü ꜁ú? ꜂Síú*
Confucius reprimanding him said, why not turn-out carriage eh? Little

兒 答 曰 自 古 及 今 爲 當 車 避
*꜁í táp꜇ üt꜇, Tsz' ꜂kú k'ap꜇ ꜀kam, ꜁wai ꜀tóng ꜀kü pí'*
boy replying said, From antiquity till now, is proper carriage turn-out

于 城 不 當 城 避 于 車 孔 子 乃
*꜀ü ꜁shing, pat꜇ ꜁tóng ꜁shing pí' ꜀ü ꜀kü. ꜂Hung ꜂tsz' ꜂nái*
for city, not proper city turn-out for carriage. Confucius then

勒 車 論 道 下 車 而 問 焉 汝 年
*lak꜇ ꜀kü, lun' tò'. Há' ꜀kü ꜁í man' ꜁ín, ꜂ü ꜁nín*
held-in carriage, discourse reason. Leaving car and asked so, your years

尙 幼 何 多 詐 乎 小 兒 答 曰 人
*shéung' yau', ꜁hó ꜀tó chá' ꜁ú? ꜂Síú ꜁í táp꜇ üt꜇, ꜁Yan*
still young, why much quickness eh? Little boy replying said, Man

生 三 歲 分 別 父 母 兔 生 三 日
*꜀shang ꜀sám sui' ꜀fan pít꜇ fú' ꜂mò; t'ò' ꜀shang ꜀sám yat꜇*
born three years distinguishes parents; hare born three days

---

"All play is without any profit: one's clothes get torn, and they are not easily mended; above me, I disgrace my father and mother; below me, even to the lowest, there is fighting and altercation: so much toil and no reward, how can it be a good business? It is for these reasons, that I do not play." Then dropping his head, he began making a city out of pieces of tile.

Confucius, reproving him, said, "Why do you not turn out for the carriage?" The boy replied, "From ancient times till now, it has always been considered proper for a carriage to turn out for a city, and not for a city to turn out for a carriage." Confucius then stopped his carriage, in order to discourse of reason. He got out of the carriage, and asked him, "You are still young in years, how is it you are so quick?" The boy replied, saying, "A human being, at the age of three years, discriminates between his father and mother; a hare, three days after it is born, runs over the ground and furrows

走地畎畝魚生三日遊于江湖天
*'tsau tí² 'ün 'mau; ‚ü ‚shang ‚sám yat‚, ‚yau ‚ü ‚kóng ‚ú; ‚t'in*
runs earth ridges fields; fish born three days, wander in rivers lakes; heaven

生自然豈謂詐乎
*‚shang tsz'² ‚ín, 'hí wai² chá' ‚ú?*
produces just so, how called brisk eh?

孔子曰汝居何鄉何里何姓
*'Hung 'tsz' üt‚, 'ü ‚kü ‚hó ‚héung, ‚hó 'lí, ‚hó sing',*
Confucius replied, You reside what village, what neighborhood, what surname,

何名何字小兒答曰吾居敝鄉
*‚hó ‚ming, ‚hó tsz'²? 'Síú ‚í táp‚ üt‚, ‚'ng ‚kü pai' ‚héung*
what name, what style? Lad replying said, I reside poor village,

賤地姓項名橐未有字也
*tsín² tí²; sing' Hóng², ‚ming T'ók‚; mí² 'yau tsz'² 'yá.*
mean land; surname Hóng, name T'ók; not have style.

孔子曰吾欲共汝同遊汝意下如何
*'Hung 'tsz' üt‚, ‚'ng yuk‚ kung² 'ü ‚t'ung ‚yau; 'ü í' há² ‚ü ‚hó?*
Confucius said, I wish with you together ramble; your thought as how?

小兒答曰家有嚴父須當事之家
*'Síú ‚í táp‚ üt‚, ‚Ká 'yau ‚ím fú², ‚sü ‚tóng sz'² ‚chí; ‚ká*
Lad answering said, Home have stern father, very proper serve him; home

有慈母須當養之家有賢兄
*'yau ‚ts'z' 'mò, ‚sü ‚tóng yéung² ‚chí; ‚ká 'yau ‚ín ‚hing,*
have indulgent mother, very proper cherish her; home have worthy eld.-brother,

須當順之家有弱弟須當教
*‚sü ‚tóng shun² ‚chí; ‚ká 'yau yéuk‚ tai² ‚sü ‚tóng káu'*
very proper obey him; home have weak younger-brother, very proper teach

之家有明師須當學之何暇
*‚chí; ‚ká 'yau ‚ming ‚sz', ‚sü ‚tóng hók‚ ‚chí: ‚hó há²*
him; home have intelligent teacher, very proper learn-of him: what leisure

同遊也
*‚t'ung ‚yau 'yá?*
together ramble?

---

of the fields; fish, three days after birth, wander in rivers and lakes, what heaven thus produces naturally, how can it be called brisk?"

Confucius added, "In what village and neighborhood do you reside, what is your surname and name, and what your style?" The boy answered, "I live in a mean village and in a poor land; my surname is Hóng, my name is T'ók, and I have yet no style."

Confucius rejoined, "I wish to have you come and ramble with me; what do you think of it?" The youth replied, "A stern father is at home, whom I am bound to serve; an affectionate mother is there, whom it is my duty to cherish; a worthy elder brother is at home whom it is proper for me to

孔 子 曰 吾 車 中 有 三 十 二 棋
'Hung 'tsz' üt2, ˏ'ng ˏkü ˏchung ˁyau ˏsám shap2 í2 ˏk'í
Confucius said, my carriage within have three tens two chess

子 與 汝 奕 博 汝 意 下 如 何 小 兒 答
'tsz', ˁü ˁü yik2 pók; ˁü í' há2 ˏü ˏhó? 'Siú ˏí táp,
men, with you play game; you think down as how? Lad answering

曰 天 子 好 博 四 海 不 理 諸 侯 好 博
üt2, ˏt'in 'tsz' hò' pók, sz' 'hoi pat ˁlí; ˏchü ˏhau hò' pók,
said, heaven's son love playing, four seas not ruled; all nobles love playing,

有 妨 政 紀 士 儒 好 博 學 問 廢 弛
ˁyau ˏfóng ching' 'kí; sz'2 ˏü hò' pók, hók2 man2 fai' 'chí;
have disorder government; scholars love playing, learning lost discarded;

小 人 好 博 輸 却 家 計 奴 婢 好 博
'siú ˏyan hò' pók ˏshü kéuk ˏká kai'; ˏnò ˁpí hò' pók
lower classes love playing, lose quite family support; domestics love playing,

必 受 鞭 朴 農 夫 好 博 耕 種 失
pít shau2 ˏpín pók; ˏnung ˏfú hò' pók ˏkang chung' shat
must get whip cudgel; husbandmen love playing, ploughing sowing lose

時 是 故 不 博 也
ˏshí; shí2 kú' pat pók ˁyá.
time; is reason not play.

孔 子 曰 吾 欲 與 汝 平 却 天 下 汝 意 下
'Hung 'tsz' üt2, ˏ'ng yuk2 ˁü ˁü ˏp'ing kéuk ˏt'in há2; ˁü í' há2
Confucius said, I wish with you equalize truly empire; you think down

如 何 小 兒 答 曰 天 下 不 可 平 也 或
ˏü ˏhó? 'Siú ˏí táp, üt2, ˏt'in há2 pat 'hó ˏp'ing ˁyá. Wák2
as how? Lad replying said, empire not can equalize. Perhaps

有 高 山 或 有 江 湖 或 有 王 侯 或 有
ˁyau ˏkò ˏshán, wák2 ˁyau ˏkóng ˏú; wák2 ˁyau ˏwóng ˏhau, wák2 ˁyau
are high hills, or are rivers lakes; perhaps are princes nobles, or are

---

obey, with a tender younger brother whom I must teach; and at home is an intelligent teacher from whom I am required to learn: where have I any leisure to go a rambling with you?"

Confucius said, "I have in my carriage thirty-two chess-men; what do you say to having a game together?" The lad answered, "If the emperor loves gaming, the empire will not be governed; if the nobles love play, the government will be impeded; if scholars love it, learning and investigation will be lost and thrown by; if the lower classes are fond of gambling, they will utterly lose the support for their families; if servants and slaves love to game, they will get a cudgeling; if farmers love it, they will miss the time for ploughing and sowing: for these reasons I shall not play with you."

Confucius rejoined, "I wish to have you go with me and fully equalize the empire; what do you think of this?" The lad replied, "The empire cannot be equalized: here are high hills; there are lakes and rivers; either there are

奴 婢 平 却 高 山 鳥 獸 無 依 塡 却
ˏnò ˋpí ; ˏp'ing kéukˎ ˏkò ˏshán, ˋníú shau' ˏmò ˏí ; ˏt'in kéukˎ
maids servants; level - ed high hills, birds beasts without resort; fill - ed

江 湖 魚 鱉 無 歸 除 却 王 侯 民 多
ˏkóng ˏú, ˏü pítˎ ˏmò ˏkwai; ˏch'ü kéukˎ ˏwóng ˏhau, ˏman ˏtó
rivers lakes, fishes turtles without home; remove king nobles, people many

是 非 絶 却 奴 婢 君 子 使 誰 天 下 蕩
shí² ˏfi; tsütˎ kéukˎ ˏnò ˋpí, ˏkwan ˋtsz' ˋshai ˏshui? ˏT'ín há² tóng²
right wrong; discard servants, prince employ whom? Empire vast

蕩 豈 可 平 乎
tóng², ˋhí ˋhó ˏp'ing ˏú?
vast, how can equalize eh?

孔 子 曰 汝 知 天 下 何 火 無 烟 何
ˋHung ˋtsz' üt₂, ˋü ˏchí ˏt'ín há² ˏhó ˋfó ˏmò ˏin? ˏHó
Confucius rejoined, You know sky under what fire without smoke, What

水 無 魚 何 山 無 石 何 樹 無 枝
ˋshui ˏmò ˏü? ˏHó ˏshán ˏmò shik₂? ˏHó shü² ˏmò ˏchí?
water has-no fish? What hill without stones? What tree has-no branches?

何 人 無 婦 何 女 無 夫 何 牛 無 犢
ˏHó ˏyan ˏmò ˋfú? ˏHó ˋnü ˏmò ˏfú? ˏHó ˏngau ˏmò tuk₂,
What man has-no wife, What woman without husband? What cow no calf,

何 馬 無 駒 何 雄 無 雌 何 雌 無
ˏHó ˋmá ˏmò ˏkau? ˏHó ˏhung ˏmò ˏtsz'? ˏHó ˏtsz' ˏmò
What horse has-no colt? What cock without hen, What hen has-no

雄 何 爲 君 子 何 爲 小 人 何
ˏhung? ˏHó ˏwai ˏkwan ˋtsz'? ˏHó ˏwai ˋsíú ˏyan? ˏHó
cock? What constitutes excellent men? What constitutes inferior men? What

爲 不 足 何 爲 有 餘 何 城 無
ˏwai patˎ tsukˎ? ˏHó ˏwai ˋyau ˏü? ˏHó ˏshing ˏmò
is-there not enough, What is-there having overplus? What city has-no

市 何 人 無 字
ˋshí? ˏHó ˏyan ˏmò tsz'²?
market, What man has-no style?

---

princes and nobles, or there are slaves and servants. If the high hills be leveled, the birds and beasts will have no resort; if the rivers and lakes be filled up, the fishes and turtles will have nowhere to go; do away with kings and nobles, and the common people will have much dispute about right and wrong; obliterate slaves and servants, and who will there be to serve the prince? If the empire be so vast and unsettled, how can it be equalized?"

Confucius again asked, "Can you tell, under the whole sky, what fire has no smoke, what water no fish; what hill has no stones, what tree no branches; what man has no wife, what woman no husband; what cow has no calf, what mare no colt; what cock has no hen, what hen no cock; what consti-

小兒答曰螢火無烟井水無

'Síú ꜁í táp꜀ üt$_2$, ꜁ying 'fó ꜁mò ꜀in, 'tsing 'shui ꜁mò

Lad answering said, glowworm's fire without smoke, well water has-no

魚土山無石枯樹無枝仙人無

꜁ü; 't'ò ꜀shán ꜁mò shik$_2$, ꜀kú shü$^2$ ꜁mò ꜀chí ꜀sin ꜁yan ꜁mò

fish; earthy hills have-no stones, rotten trees have-no branches; genii without

婦玉女無夫土牛無犢木

'fú, yuk$_2$ 'nü ꜁mò ꜀fú; 't'ò ꜁ngau ꜁mò tuk$_2$, muk$_2$

wives, gem girls without husbands; earthen cows have-no calves, wooden

馬無駒孤雄無雌孤雌無雄

'má ꜁mò ꜀kau; ꜀kú ꜁hung ꜁mò ꜀ts'z', ꜀kú ꜀ts'z' ꜁mò ꜁hung;

horses no colts; orphan cocks without hens, orphan hens without cocks;

賢爲君子愚爲小人冬日不

꜁in ꜁wai ꜀kwan 'tsz', ꜁ü ꜁wai 'síú ꜁yan; ꜀tung yat$_2$ pat꜀

worth makes excellent men, folly makes inferior men; winter's day not

足夏日有餘皇城無市小

tsuk꜀, há$^2$ yat$_2$ 'yau ꜁ü; ꜁wóng ꜁shing ꜁mò 'shí, 'síú

enough, summer's day has overplus; imperial city has-no market, little

人無字

꜁yan ꜁mò tsz'$^2$.

folks no style.

孔子問曰汝知天地之綱紀陰

'Hung 'tsz' man$^2$ üt$_2$, 'ü ꜀chí ꜀t'in ti$^2$ ꜀chí ꜀kóng 'kí, ꜀yam

Confucius asking said, You know heaven earth 's controlling union, dual

陽之終始何爲左何爲右何爲

꜁yéung ꜀chí ꜀ch'ung 'ch'í? ꜁Hó ꜁wai tsó$^2$, ꜁hó ꜁wai yau$^2$? ꜁Hó ꜁wai

power s' ending beginning? What is left, what is right, What is

表何爲裏何爲父何爲母何爲夫

'piú, ꜁hó ꜁wai 'lí? ꜁Hó ꜁wai fú$^2$, ꜁hó ꜁wai 'mò? ꜁Hó ꜁wai ꜀fú,

outside, what is inside? Who is father, who is mother, Who is husband,

---

tutes an excellent man, and what an inferior man; what is that which has not enough, and what that has an overplus; what city is without a market, and who is the man without a style?"

The boy replied, "A glowworm's fire has no smoke, and well-water no fish; a mound of earth has no stones, and a rotten tree no branches; genii have no wives, and fairies no husbands; earthen cows have no calves, nor wooden mares any colts; lonely cocks have no hens, and solitary hens no cocks; he who is worthy is an excellent man, and a fool is an inferior man; a winter's day is not long enough, and a summer's day is too long; the imperial city has no market, and little folks have no style."

Confucius inquiring said, "Do you know what are the connecting bonds between heaven and earth, and what is the beginning and ending of the dual powers? What is left, and what is right; what is out, and what in; who is father, and who is mother; who is husband and who is wife? [Do you

何 爲 婦 風 從 何 來 雨 從 何 至 雲
꜁hó ꜁wai ˁfú? ꜁Fung ꜁ts'ung ꜁hó ꜁loi, ˁü ꜁ts'ung ꜁hó chì'? ꜁Wan
who is wife? Wind from what comes, rain from what reaches? Clouds

從 何 出 霧 從 何 起 天 地 相 去 幾
꜁ts'ung ꜁hó ch'ut›, mò$^2$ ꜁ts'ung ꜁hó 'hi? ꜀T'in tí$^2$ ꜀séung hü' 'kí
from what proceed, dew from what arise? Sky earth together go how-many

千 萬 里
꜀ts'in mán$^2$ ˁlí?
thousand myriad miles?

小 兒 答 曰 九 九 還 歸 八 十 一 是 天 地
'Síú ꜁í táp› üt$_2$, 'kau 'kau ꜁wán ꜀kwai pát› shap$_2$ yat› shí$^2$ ꜀t'in tí$^2$
Lad replying said, nine nine multiplied eighty - one is heaven earth

之 綱 紀 八 九 七 十 二 是 陰 陽 之 終
꜀chí ꜀kóng 'kí; pát› 'kau ts'at› shap$_2$ í$^2$ shí$^2$ ꜀yam ꜁yéung ꜀chí ꜀ch'ung
's controlling record; eight nines seventy-two is dual power s' ending

始 天 爲 父 地 爲 母 日 爲 夫 月 爲
'ch'í. ꜀T'in ꜁wai fú$^2$, tí$^2$ ꜁wai ˁmò; yat$_2$ ꜁wai ꜀fú, üt$_2$ ꜁wai
beginning. Heaven is father, earth is mother; sun is husband, moon is

婦 東 爲 左 西 爲 右 外 爲 表 內 爲 裏
ˁfú; ꜀tung ꜁wai 'tsó, ꜀sai ꜁wai yau$^2$; ngoi$^2$ ꜁wai 'píú, noi$^2$ ꜁wai ˁlü;
wife; east is left, west is right; outside is without, inside is within;

風 從 蒼 梧 雨 從 郊 市 雲 從 山
꜀fung ꜁ts'ung ꜀Ts'óng ꜁'ng, ˁü ꜁ts'ung ꜀káu ˁshí; ꜁wan ꜀ts'ung ꜀shán
wind issues-from Ts'óng-'ng, rain from waste places; clouds from hills

出 霧 從 地 起 天 地 相 去 有 千 千
ch'ut›, mò$^2$ ꜁ts'ung tí$^2$ 'hí; ꜀t'in tí$^2$ ꜀séung hü' ˁyau ꜀ts'in ꜀ts'in
proceed, dew from ground arises; sky earth together go have thousands

萬 萬 餘 里 東 西 南 北 皆 有 寄 耳
mán$^2$ mán$^2$ ꜁ü ˁlí; ꜀tung ꜀sai ꜁nám pak› ꜀kái ˁyau kí' ˁí.
myriads more lí; east west south north each have locality.

---

know] where the wind comes from, and from whence the rain? From whence the clouds issue, and the dew arises? And for how many tens of thousands of miles the sky and earth go parallel?"

The youth answering said, "Nine multiplied nine times makes eighty-one, which is the controlling bond of heaven and earth; eight multiplied into nine makes seventy-two, the beginning and end of the dual powers. Heaven is father, and earth is mother; the sun is husband, and the moon wife; east is left, and west is right; without is out, and inside is in; the winds come from Ts'óng-'ng, and the rains proceed from wastes and wilds; the clouds issue from the hills, and the dew rises from the ground. Sky and earth go parallel for ten thousand times ten thousand miles, and the four points of compass have each their stations."

拾級大成

孔子問曰汝言父母是親夫婦是
'Hung 'tsz' mán2 üt2, 'ü ‹ín fú2 'mò shí2 ‹ts'an, ‹fú 'fú shí2
Confucius inquiring said, You say father mother are near, husband wife are

親小兒答曰父母是親夫婦不親
‹ts'an? 'Síú ‹í táp› üt2, fú2 'mò shí2 ‹ts'an, ‹fú 'fú pat› ‹ts'an.
near? Boy replying said, father mother are near, husband wife not near.

孔子曰夫婦生則同衾死則同
'Hung 'tsz' üt2, ‹fú 'fú ‹shang tsak› ‹t'ung ‹k'am, 'sz' tsak› ‹t'ung
Confucius replied, husband wife alive then same coverlet, dead then same

穴何得不親小兒答曰人生無婦
üt2; ‹hó tak2 pat› ‹ts'an? 'Síú ‹í táp› üt2, ‹yan ‹shang ‹mò 'fú,
grave; how be not near? Boy rejoining said, man alive without wife

如車無輪無輪再造必得其
‹ü ‹kü ‹mò ‹lun; ‹mò ‹lun tsoi' ts'ò2, pít› tak› ‹k'í
like carriage without wheels; have-no wheels again make, must obtain his

新婦死更索又得其新賢家之
‹san; 'fú 'sz' kang' sók›, yau2 tak› ‹k'í ‹san. ‹I'n ‹ká ‹chí
new; wife dead again seeks also obtains a new. Worthy family 's

女必配貴夫十間之室須得
'nü, pít› púi' kwai' ‹fú; shap2 ‹kán ‹chí shat›, ‹sü tak›
daughter must match honorable husband; ten room 's house, must possess

棟樑三窗六牖不如一戶之光
tung' ‹léung, ‹sám ‹ch'éung luk2 'yau pat› ‹ü yat› ú2 ‹chí ‹kwóng;
plate ridge; three windows six sky-lights not equal one door 's light;

衆星朗朗不如孤月獨明父
chung' ‹sing 'lóng 'lóng pat› ‹ü ‹kú üt2 tuk2 ‹ming. Fú2
all stars sparkling brilliance, not equal solitary moon single splendor. Father

母之恩奚可失也
'mò ‹chí ‹yan, ‹hai 'hó shat› 'yá!
mother 's affection, how can lose!

---

Confucius asking, said, "Which do you say is the nearest relation, father and mother, or husband and wife?" The boy responded, "One's parents are near; husband and wife are not [so] near."

Confucius rejoined, "While husband and wife are alive, they sleep under the same coverlet; when they are dead, they lie in the same grave. How then can you say they are not near?" The boy replied, "A man without a wife is like a carriage without a wheel: if there be no wheel, another one is made, for he can doubtless get a new one: so, if one's wife die, he seeks again, for he also can obtain a new one. The daughter of a worthy family must certainly marry an honorable husband: a house having ten rooms always has a plate and a ridge-pole: three windows and six lattices do not give the light of a single door: the whole host of stars with all their sparkling brilliance do not equal the splendor of the solitary moon: the affection of a father and mother—alas, if it be once lost!"

孔子嘆曰賢哉賢哉小兒問孔子
ʻHung ʻtszʼ tʻánʼ üt$_2$, ˏin ꜀tsoi! ˏin tsoi! ʻSíú ˏí man$^2$ ʻHung ʻtszʼ
Confucius, sighing, said, clever how! clever how! Lad asking Confucius

曰適來問橐橐一一荅之橐今
üt$_2$, shik꜆ ˏloi man$^2$ Tʻók꜆, Tʻók꜆ yat꜆ yat꜆ táp꜆ ꜀chí; Tʻók꜆ ꜀kam
said, just now asked Tʻók, Tʻók one one answered them; Tʻók now

欲求教夫子一言明以誨
yuk$_2$ ˏkau káuʼ, ꜀fú ʻtszʼ yat꜆ ˏin, ˏming ʻí fúiʼ
wishes seek instruction, teacher one sentence, plainness employ instruct

橐幸請勿棄小兒曰鳧鴨何以能
Tʻók꜆; hang$^2$ ʻtsʻing mat$_2$ híʼ. ʻSíú ˏí üt$_2$, ˏfú áp꜆ ˏhó ʻí ˏnang
Tʻók; pleased request not reject. Lad said, mallards ducks what by able

浮鴻雁何以能鳴松柏何以
ˏfau? ˏHung ngán$^2$ ˏhó ʻí ˏnang ˏming? ˏTsʻung pák꜆ ˏhó ʻí
swim? Wild-geese cranes what by able sing? Firs pines what by

冬青孔子荅曰鳧鴨能浮皆因
꜀tung ꜀tsʻing? ʻHung ʻtszʼ táp꜆ üt$_2$, ˏfú áp꜆ ˏnang ˏfau, ꜀kái ꜀yan
winter green? Confucius replied, mallards ducks can swim all because

足方鴻雁能鳴皆因頸長松
tsuk꜆ ꜀fóng; ˏhung ngán$^2$ ˏnang ˏming ꜀kái ꜀yan ʻking ˏchéung; ˏtsʻung
feet broad; wild-geese cranes can sing, all because necks long; firs

柏冬青皆因心堅小兒荅曰不
pák꜆ ꜀tung ꜀tsʻing, ꜀kái ꜀yan ꜀sam ꜀kín. ʻSíú ˏí táp꜆ üt$_2$, pat꜆
pines winter green, all because heart strong. Lad answering said, not

然魚鼈能浮豈皆足方蝦蟆能
ˏín; ˏü pít꜆ ˏnang ˏfau, ʻhí ꜀kái tsuk꜆ ꜀fóng? ꜀há ˏmá ˏnang
so; fishes turtles can swim, how all feet broad? frogs toads can

鳴豈因頸長綠竹冬青豈因
ˏming, ʻhí ꜀yan ʻking ˏchéung? luk$_2$ chuk꜆ ꜀tung ꜀tsʻing, ʻhí ꜀yan
sing, how because necks long? green bamboo winter green, how because

心堅
꜀sam ꜀kín?
heart strong?

---

Confucius sighing, said, "How clever! how worthy!" The boy asking the sage said, "You have just now been giving me questions, which I have answered one by one; I now wish to seek instruction; will the teacher in one sentence, afford me some plain instruction? I shall be much gratified, if my request be not rejected." He then said, "Why is it that mallards and ducks are able to swim; how is it that wild geese and cranes can sing; and why are firs and pines green through the winter?" Confucius replied, "Mallards and ducks can swim because their feet are broad; wild geese and cranes can sing because they have long necks; firs and pines remain

小兒又問曰天上零零有幾星
*‹Siú ‹i yau² man² üt₂, ‹t'in shéung² ‹ling ‹ling ʿyau ʿkí ‹sing?*
Lad again asking said, sky above all-together have how-many stars?

孔子答曰適來問地何必談天
*ʿHung ʿtsz' táp› üt₂, shik› ‹loi man² tí², ‹hó pít› ‹t'ám ‹t'in?*
Confucius replying said, just now ask earth, how certain converse sky?

小兒曰地下碌碌有幾屋孔子
*ʿSiú ‹i üt₂, tí² há² luk› luk› ʿyau ʿkí uk›? ʿHung ʿtsz'*
Boy rejoined, earth below every-one have how-many houses? Confucius

曰且論眼前之事何必談天
*üt₂, ʿch'é lun² ʿngán ‹ts'in ‹chí sz'², ‹hó pít› ‹t'ám ‹t'in*
said, still converse eyes before 's things, how certain converse sky

說地小兒曰若論眼前之事眉
*shüt› tí²? ʿSiú ‹i üt₂, yéuk₂ lun² ʿngán ‹ts'in ‹chí sz'², ‹mí*
discourse-of earth? Lad answered, if speak eyes before 's things, eye-

毛中有幾枝
*‹mò ‹chung ʿyau ʿkí ‹chí?*
brows among have how-many hairs?

孔子笑而不答顧謂諸弟子曰
*ʿHung ʿtsz' siú', ‹í pat› táp›, kú' wai² ‹chü tai² ʿtsz' üt₂,*
Confucius smiled but not answering, turned calling all disciples, said,

後生可畏焉知來者之不如今也
*hau² ‹shang ʿhó wai'; ‹in ‹chí ‹loi ʿché ‹chí pat› ‹ü ‹kam ʿyá.*
after born can fear; truly know future person he not as now.

於是登車而去
*‹Ü shí² ‹tang ‹kü ‹í hü'.*
On that ascended carriage and departed.

---

green throughout the winter because they have strong hearts." The youth rejoined, "Not so; fishes and turtles can swim, is it because they all have broad feet? Frogs and toads can sing, is it because their necks are long? The green bamboo keeps fresh in winter, is it on account of its strong heart?"

Again interrogating, he said, "How many stars are there altogether in the sky?" Confucius replied, "At this time inquire about the earth; how can we converse about the sky with certainty?" The boy said, "Then how many houses in all are there on the earth?" The sage answered, "Come now, speak about something that's before our eyes; why must you converse about heaven and earth." The lad resumed, "Well, speak about what's before our eyes—how many hairs are there in your eyebrows?"

Confucius smiled, but did not answer, and turning to his disciples called them and said, "This boy is to be feared; for it is easy to see that the subsequent man will not be like the child." He then got into his carriage, and rode off.

詩 曰 休 欺 年 少 聰 明 子
*Shí üt: Yau hi nín síú, ts'ung ming 'tsz';*
Ode says: Do-not despise years young, intelligent bright lad;

廣 有 英 才 智 過 人
*'Kwóng 'yau ying ts'oi, chí kwó yan;*
Extensive had great talents, wisdom beyond men;

談 論 世 間 無 限 事
*T'ám lun shai kán, mò hán sz';*
Converse discourse world in, without limit affairs;

分 明 古 聖 現 其 身
*Fan ming 'kú shing, in k'i shan.*
Perceive clearly ancient sage, expose his body.

---

No. VI.—A Wife's Constancy.

(鹿洲女學卷二六十五章)

魯 秋 胡 子 娶 妻 五 日 去 而 官 于 陳
*'Lú Ts'au U' 'tsz' ts'ü ts'ai, 'ng yat hü, í kún ü Ch'an*
Lú Ts'au U' tsz' marrying wife, five days left, and governed in Ch'an

五 年 乃 歸 將 至 家 見 採 桑 婦
*'ng nín 'nái kwai. Tséung chí ká, kín 'ts'oi sóng 'fú,*
five years then returned. About at house, saw picking mulberry woman,

而 悅 之 下 車 與 語 婦 人 採 桑 不
*í üt chí, há kü 'ü 'ü. 'Fú yan 'ts'oi sóng pat*
and fancying her, left carriage with speak. Woman picking mulberries not

顧 秋 胡 子 曰 力 田 不 如 逢 豐 年 採
*kú. Ts'au U' 'tsz' üt, lik t'in pat ü fung fung nín; 'ts'oi*
regard. Ts'au U' tsz' said, work fields not as had fertile year; pick

桑 不 如 見 國 卿 吾 有 金 願 以 與 夫 人
*sóng pat ü kín kwók hing; 'ng 'yau kam ün 'i 'ü fú yan.*
mulberries not as see state minister; I have gold wish with give lady.

---

The ode says,
Do not despise a youth, A bright intelligent lad:
Whose talents are discursive and great, In wisdom surpassing men;
While discoursing about things in general, Of affairs without a limit,
It is evident that an ancient sage, Has manifested himself in the body.

Ts'au U' tsz' of Lú married a wife, and five days afterwards, went to fill an office in [the state of] Ch'an. At the end of five years, on his return home, as he drew near his house, he saw a woman picking mulberry leaves, and being pleased with her looks descended from his carriage to converse with her, but the lady went on picking the leaves without stopping to look at him. Ts'au said, "You labor in the fields as if we had not had a year of plenty; you pick the mulberry as if you would not look upon a lord of the land. I have gold which I wish to give to you, my noble lady."

婦人曰 噫 吾不願人之金 秋胡子遂
ʻFú ˏyan üt2, ˏHí! ˏʻng pat, üin2 ˏyan ˏchí ˏkam! ˏTsʻau ˏU' ʻtsz' sui2
Woman replied, Out! I not wish man 's gold! Tsʻau U' tsz' then

至去家奉金遺母 母命呼妻
chí' hü' ˏká, fung2 ˏkam ˏwai ʻmò. ʻMò ming2 ˏfú ˏtsʻai;
reached going home, offered gold gave mother. Mother ordered call wife;

妻出乃桑 間婦也秋胡子大 慚
ˏtsʻai chʻut, ʻnái ˏsóng ˏkán ʻfú ʻyá. ˏTsʻau ˏU' ʻtsz' tái2 ˏtsʻám.
wife out was mulberries among woman. Tsʻau U' tsz' greatly chagrined.

妻責之曰見色 棄金而忘其母
ˏTsʻai chak, ˏchí üt2, kín' shik, hí' ˏkam ˏí ˏmóng ˏkʻí ʻmò:
Wife reproving him said, saw beauty discarded gold and forgot your mother:

大不孝也事 親不孝則事君不
tái2 pat, háu' ʻyá. Sz'2 ˏtsʻan pat, háu' tsak, sz'2 ˏkwan pat,
greatly not dutiful. Serving parents not dutiful, then serve prince not

忠慮家不義 則治官不理 孝義
ˏchung: lü2 ˏká pat, í2, tsak, chí2 ˏkún pat, ʻlí; háu' í2
faithful: rule house not right, then rule office not proper: duty justice

並亡禍不遠矣任君別娶妾投
ping2 ˏmóng, wó2 pat, ʻün ʻí. Yam2 ˏkwan pít2 tsʻü'. Tsʻip, ˏtʻau
together lost, misfortune not far-off. May sir another marry. She plunged

河水而死乃作詩曰郎恩葉薄妾
ˏhó ʻshui ˏí ʻsz'. ʻNái tsók, ˏshí üt2, ˏLóng ˏyan íp2 pók2, tsʻíp,
river water and died. But made verse said, Lord's affection leaf's thinness, my

氷清 郎與黃金妾不應若使偶
ˏping ˏtsʻing; ˏLóng ʻü ˏwóng ˏkam, tsʻip, pat, ˏying; Yéuk2 ʻsz' ʻngau
icy pure; Lord with yellow gold, I not consent; If make pair

然通一語半生誰信守孤燈
ˏín ˏtʻung yat, ʻü; Pún' ˏshang ˏshui sun' ʻshau ˏkú ˏtang?
sudden exchange a word; Half life who faithfully guarded lonely lamp?

---

The woman replied, "away with you! I do not wish a man's gold." Tsʻau leaving her, then went on to his home, and gave the money as a present to his mother. She ordered his wife to be called; but his wife had gone out, and was that woman [he saw] among the mulberries. Tsʻau was very much ashamed. His wife upbraiding him, said, "You saw a pretty face and threw away your gold, the while entirely forgetting your mother; this was very undutiful. If you do not honor your parents, you cannot be faithful to your prince; ordering in your family improperly, you will rule in your office unjustly, and when filial duty and justice are both neglected, trouble is not far off. You may marry another wife." She then threw herself into the river, and was drowned, but left behind her a verse, as follows:

"My lord's affection was thin as a leaf, But [my virtue] was unsullied as ice;
"My lord wished to give me yellow gold, But I would not consent!
"Now he comes suddenly upon me, And wishes to join in loose converse:
"For half her life who has faithfully trimmed the lonely lamp?"

### No. VII.—The Mother of Mencius.

（鹿洲女學卷三第九十四章）

孟子之母其舍近墓孟子之少也
*Mang$^2$ ‘tsz’ ˏchí ʿmò, ˏk‘í shé’ kan$^2$ mò$^2$; Mang$^2$ ‘tsz’ ˏchí shíú’ ʿyá,*
Mencius 's mother her cottage near graves; Mencius 's youth;

嬉戲爲墓間之事踴躍築埋孟
*ˏhí hí’ ˏwai mò$^2$ ˏkán ˏchí sz’$^2$, ‘yung yéuk$_2$ chuk, ˏmái. Mang$^2$*
childish plays were graves among 's acts, active spry piling tombs. Mencius'

母曰此非所以居子也乃去舍
*ʿmò üt$_2$, ‘ts‘z’ ˏfi ‘shó ʿí ˏkü ‘tsz’ ʿyá; ʿnái hü’ shé’*
mother said, This not what use reside son indeed; then removed house

市其嬉戲爲賈衒孟母曰此
*ʿshí. ˏK‘í ˏhí hí’ ˏwai ‘kú ˏün. Mang$^2$ ʿmò üt$_2$, ‘ts‘z’*
market. His childish plays were shopping peddling. Mencius' mother said, this

非所以居子也乃徙舍學宮
*ˏfí ‘shó ʿí ˏkü ‘tsz’ ʿyá; ʿnái ‘sái shé’ hók$_2$ ˏkung*
not what use reside son indeed; then removed cottage learning room

之旁其嬉戲乃設俎豆揖讓進
*ˏchí ˏp‘óng. ˏK‘í ˏhí hí’ ʿnái ch‘ít, ‘chó tau$^2$, yap, yéung$^2$ tsun’*
's side. His childish plays then set-up pots vases, bowing yielding entering

退孟母曰此眞可以居子矣遂
*túi’. Mang$^2$ ʿmò üt$_2$, ‘ts‘z’ ˏchan ‘hó ʿí ˏkü ‘tsz’ ʿí. Sui$^2$*
retiring. Mencius' mother said, this truly can use reside son surely. Accordingly

居之
*ˏkü ˏchí.*
resided there.

孟子幼時問東家殺猪何爲母
*Mang$^2$ ‘tsz’ yau’ ˏshí, man$^2$ ˏtung ˏká shát, ˏchü ˏhó ˏwai? ʿMò*
Mencius youth time, asked, east house killed hogs what for? Mother

曰欲啖汝旣而悔曰吾聞古有
*üt$_2$, yuk$_2$ tám$^2$ ʿü. Ki’ ˏí fúi’ üt$_2$, ˏ’ng ˏman ‘kú ʿyau*
replied, about-to feed you. Done just repented said, I heard ancients had

---

The dwelling of Mencius' mother was near the graves, and while her son was still young, his childish plays were doing such things as are done at graves, gamboling and playing at building up tombs. She said, "This place will not do for my son to reside in," and moved her house into a market. Here his boyish sports were peddling and bartering. She said, "This also is not the place for my son to reside in," and straightway moved next door to a school-house. Here, his plays were in arranging sacrificial vessels and dishes, in bowing and courteously yielding, and in entering and retiring. His mother said, "This is just the place for my son to reside in;" and accordingly she resided there.

Mencius, when a boy, asked, "For what purpose does the master slaughter hogs?" His mother replied, "He is about to feed you." But immediately

胎 教 今 適 有 知 而 欺 之 是 教
*˓t'oi káu'; ˓kam shik˒ ˓yau ˓chí ˓í ˓hí ˓chí, shí$^{2}$ káu'*
womb instruction; now just have discrimination, and deceived him, is teaching

之 不 信 也 乃 買 猪 肉 以 食 之
*˓chí pat˒ sun' ˓yá: ˓nái ˓mái ˓chü yuk$_{2}$ ˓í tsz'$^{2}$ ˓chí.*
him not truth so: then bought hog's flesh to feed him.

孟 子 既 學 而 歸 母 問 學 所 至
*Mang$^{2}$ 'tsz' ki' hók$_{2}$ ˓í ˓kwai; ˓mò man$^{2}$, hók˒ 'shó chi'?*
Mencius already learning but came-home; mother asked, learned what attained?

孟 子 曰 自 若 也 母 以 刀 斷 其 織 曰 子
*Mang$^{2}$ 'tsz' üt$_{2}$, tsz'$^{2}$ yéuk$_{2}$ ˓yá. ˓Mò ˓í ˓tò tün$^{2}$ ˓k'i shik˒ üt$_{2}$, 'tsz'*
Mencius replied, myself please. Mother with knife cutting her weaving said, son

之 廢 學 若 吾 斷 斯 織 也 夫 君 子
*˓chí fai' hók$_{2}$, yéuk$_{2}$ ˓'ng tün$^{2}$ ˓sz' shik˒ ˓yá; ˓fú ˓kwan 'tsz'*
's desist learning, like my cut this weaving so; the excellent man

學 以 立 名 問 則 廣 智 是 以
*hók$_{2}$ ˓í lap$_{2}$ ˓ming; man$^{2}$ tsak˒ 'kwóng chi'; shí$^{2}$ ˓í,*
learn to establish reputation; inquire then extensive knowledge; is by-this,

居 則 安 寧 動 則 遠 害 今 而 廢 之
*˓kü tsak˒ ˓ón ˓ning, tung$^{2}$ tsak˒ ün$^{2}$ hoi$^{2}$; ˓kam ˓í fai' ˓chí*
residing then quiet rest, moving then remove injury; now still desist it,

是 不 免 於 厮 役 而 無 以 離 於
*shí$^{2}$ pat˒ ˓mín ˓ü ˓sz' yik$_{2}$, ˓í ˓mò ˓í ˓lí ˓ü*
is not remit from serving menial, and without by-which separate from

禍 患 也 孟 子 懼 旦 夕 勤 學 不
*wó$^{2}$ wán$^{2}$ ˓yá. Mang$^{2}$ 'tsz', kü$^{2}$, tán' sik$_{2}$ ˓kan hók$_{2}$ pat˒*
misfortune misery. Mencius feared, morning evening diligently learned not

息 遂 成 大 儒
*sik˒. Sui$^{2}$ ˓shing tái$^{2}$ ˓ü.*
ceased. Therefore became great scholar.

---

repenting, she said, "I have heard that the ancients instructed in the womb; at this time he possesses discrimination, and I have deceived him, which is teaching him to lie." She thereupon bought some pork in order to feed him.

Mencius was already at school, but he returned home. His mother asked him what he had learned. Mencius replied, "I please myself." His mother, cutting her weaving with a knife, said, "My son's desisting from his studies is just like my cutting this web; the excellent man studies in order to establish a reputation; by research, he becomes extensively informed; by this means, if he resides in one place he is at peace and rest; or if moving about, he keeps at a distance all injury. If you now throw by your studies, you cannot avoid becoming a serving menial, you will have no means to keep yourself from misfortune and misery." Mencius was alarmed, and morning and evening unremittingly pursued his studies with diligence, so that he consequently became a distinguished scholar.

### No. VIII.—Remonstrance of a Mother.

### (鹿洲女學卷四二十七章)

吳夫人者孫堅妻孫策母也策以功
*ˏ'Ng ˏfú ˏyan 'ché, ˏSün ˏKín ˏts'ai, ˏSün Ch'ák˒ ˓mò ˓yá. Ch'ák˒ ˓í ˏkung*
'Ng lady the, Sün Kín's wife, Sün Ch'ák's mother. Ch'ák by merit

曹魏騰忤己意將殺之吳夫人
*ˏts'ò Ngai² ˏT'ang ˓'ng 'ki í', ˏtséung shát˒ ˏchí, ˏ'Ng ˏfú ˏyan*
clerk Ngai T'ang opposed his wishes, about killing him, 'Ng lady

倚大井謂之曰汝新造江南
*'í tái² 'tsing, wai² ˏchí üt₂, ˓ü ˏsan ts'ò² ˏKóng ˏnám,*
reclining great well, telling him said, you lately established Kóngnám,

其事未集方當優賢禮士
*ˏk'í sz'² mí² tsap₂; ˏfóng ˏtóng ˏyau ˏín, ˓lai sz'²,*
its affairs not-yet quieted; then ought indulge worthies, respect scholars,

捨過錄功魏曹在公盡規
*'shé kwó', luk₂ ˏkung. Ngai² ts'ò² tsoi² ˏkung tsun² ˏkw'ai;*
overlook offenses, reward merit. Ngai officer in public altogether regular;

汝今自殺之則明日人皆叛汝
*˓ü ˏkam tsz'² shát˒ ˏchí, tsak˒ ˏming yat₂ ˏyan ˏkái pún² ˓ü.*
you now yourself kill him, then brightened day men all desert you.

吾不忍見禍之及當先投此井中
*ˏ'Ng pat˒ ˓yan kín' wó² ˏchí k'ap₂, ˏtóng ˏsín ˏt'au 'ts'z' 'tsing ˏchung.*
I not bear see evil 's descent, shall first jump this well into.

策大驚釋之
*Ch'ák˒ tái² ˏking, shik˒ ˏchí.*
Ch'ák much alarmed, released him.

---

The lady 'Ng was the wife of Sün Kín, and the mother of Sün Ch'ák. Ch'ák, having been opposed in his wishes by an under-secretary Ngai T'ang, was about to kill him, when the lady 'Ng reclining upon the great well, called him and said, "You have only recently established yourself in Kóngnám, and its affairs are not yet in a settled state; you ought therefore to act liberally towards worthy persons, and respectfully towards literary people, overlooking offenses and rewarding merit. The officer Ngai has always acted properly in his public duties, but if you now kill him yourself, to-morrow all men will desert you. I cannot bear to see evil come upon you, and shall first jump into this well." Ch'ák was much alarmed, and released him.

## No. IX. Hardheartedness Punished.

(聊齋卷一第六篇)

有 鄉 人 貨 梨 於 市 頗 甘 芳 價 騰
ʻYau ˏhéung ˏyan fóʾ ˏlí ˏü ʻshí, ʻpʻó ˏkóm ˏfóng, káʾ ˏtʻang
Was village man peddled plums in market, rather sweet fragrant, price rise

貴 有 道 士 破 巾 絮 衣 丐 於 車 前
kwaiʾ. ʻYau Tò² sz'², pʻóʾ ˏkan ʻsü ˏí, kʻoiʾ ˏü ˏkü ˏtsʻin.
dear. Was Taou priest, ragged garments mean dress, begged at wagon before.

鄉 人 咄 之 而 不 去 鄉 人 怒 加
ˏHéung ˏyan tatˎ ˏchí, ˏí patˎ hüʾ, ˏhéung ˏyan nò², ˏká
Village man scolded him, but not going, village man irritated, added

以 叱 駡 道 士 曰 一 車 數 百
ʻí chʻikˎ má². Tò² sz'² üt₂, yatˎ ˏkü shòʾ pákˎ
with opprobrious railing. Taou priest said, one wagon several hundreds

顆 老 衲 止 丐 其 一 於 居 士 亦 無 大
ʻfó, ʻlò náp₂ ʻchí kʻoiʾ ˏkʻí yatˎ; ˏü ˏkü sz'² yik₂ ˏmò tái²
fruit, old priest only beg their one; for respected sir indeed no great

損 何 怒 爲 觀 者 勸 置 劣 者 一
ʻsün; ˏhó nò² ˏwai? ˏKún ʻché künʾ chíʾ lütˎ ʻché yatˎ
loss; what anger cause? Looking those advised give poor one single

枚 令 去 鄉 人 執 不 肯
ˏmúi, ling² hüʾ. ˏHéung ˏyan chapˎ patˎ ʻhang.
fruit, order go. Village man held not willing.

肆 中 傭 保 者 見 喋 聒 不 堪
ʻSz'ʾ ˏchung ˏyung ʻpò ʻché kinʾ típ₂ kút₂ patˎ ˏkóm,
Market in, hired assistants those seeing noise clamor not endure,

遂 出 錢 市 一 枚 付 道 士 道 士 拜
sui² chʻutˎ ˏtsʻin ʻshí yatˎ ˏmúi fú² Tò² sz'² Tò² sz'² páiʾ
then gave cash bought one fruit gave Taou priest. Taou priest bowing

---

Once there was a villager selling plums in the market, which were rather sweet and fragrant, and the price was high; and there was a Taou priest, with ragged garments and a coarse cotton dress, begging before his wagon. The villager scolded him, but he would not go off; whereupon, becoming angry, he reviled and hooted at him. The Taou priest said, "The wagon contains several hundreds of fruit, and I have only begged one of them, which for you, respected sir, would certainly be no great loss; what cause is there for so much anger?" The lookers on recommended to give him a single poor plum, and send him away, but the villager held on to them and would not consent.

The workmen in the market seeing there was a great noise and clamor, which they would not endure, then furnished cash, and buying a plum gave it to the Taou priest. He bowing thanked them, and speaking to the crowd said, "I do not practice a niggard economy, and now having a delicious plum, I request you my friends to partake of it." One of them said,

謝 謂 衆 曰 出 家 人 不 解 吝 惜
*tsé$^2$ wai$^2$ chung' üt$_2$, ch'ut, ˛ká ˛yan pat, 'kái lun' sik,;*
thanked, speaking crowd said, leave family man not practice niggard care;

我 有 佳 梨 請 出 供 客 或 曰 旣 有
*'ngó 'yau ˛kai ˛lí, 'ts'ing ch'ut, ˛kung hák,. Wák$_2$ üt$_2$, kí' 'yau*
I have delicious plum, please give feed friends. One said, already have

之 何 不 自 食 曰 吾 持 需 此 核 作 種
*˛chí, ˛hó pat, tsz'$^2$ shik$_2$? Ut$_2$, ˛'ng tak$_2$ ˛sü 'ts'z' hat$_2$ tsók, 'chung.*
it, why not yourself eat? Replied, I only need this stone make plant.

於 是 掬 梨 大 啗 且 盡 把 核 於 手
*˛U shí$^2$ kuk, ˛lí tái$^2$ tám$^2$; 'ch'é tsun$^2$, 'pá hat$_2$ ˛ü 'shau,*
Upon that taking plum large munch; when finished, taking stone in hand,

解 肩 上 鑱 坎 地 上 深 數 寸 納
*'kái ˛kín shéung$^2$ ˛ts'ám 'hóm tí$^2$ shéung$^2$ ˛sham shò' ts'ün', náp$_2$*
removing shoulder on spade dug ground upon deep several inches, inserted

之 而 覆 以 土 向 市 人 索 湯 沃
*˛chí ˛í fuk, 'i 't'ò. Héung' 'shí ˛yan sók, ˛t'óng yuk,*
it and covered with earth. Turning-to market people got broth fertilized

灌 好 事 者 於 臨 路 店 索 得 沸
*kún. Hò$^1$ sz'$^2$ 'ché ˛ü ˛lam lò$^2$ tím' sók, tak, fai'*
watered. Desired affair persons at near road shops brought got boiling

瀋 道 士 接 浸 坎 處 萬 目 攢 視
*'sham, Tò$^2$ sz'$^2$ ts'ip, tsam' 'hóm ch'ü'. Mán$^2$ muk$_2$ ˛ts'ün shí$^2$*
dregs, Taou priest reciving poured dug place. All eyes around looking

見 有 勾 萌 出 漸 大 俄 成 樹
*kín' 'yau ˛kau ˛ming ch'ut,, tsím$^2$ tái$^2$; ˛ngó ˛shing shü$^2$,*
saw was hooked sprout issuing, gradually increased; presently formed tree,

枝 葉 扶 疎 倐 而 花 倏 而 實 碩 大
*˛chí ip$_2$ ˛fú ˛shó, shuk, ˛í ˛fá, shuk, ˛í shat$_2$, shik$_2$ tái$^2$*
branches leaves abundant, presently and flowers, soon and fruit, large very

芳 馥 纍 纍 滿 樹 道 人 乃 卽 樹
*˛fóng fuk, ˛lui ˛lui 'mún shü'. Tò$^2$ ˛yan 'nái tsik, shü$^2$*
fragrant odoriferous heaped-up filled tree. Taou man then approaching tree

---

"You have one already, why do you not eat it yourself?" He replied, "All I want is this stone in order to plant it." Thereupon taking the plum in his hand, he eat it up by large mouthfuls, and when finished, holding the stone in his hand, took a spade from off his shoulder, and dug a hole in the ground several inches deep, into which he put it, and covered it up with earth. Then turning to the market people, he procured some broth with which he watered and fertilized it. Some persons, who wished to see what would come of this, also obtained boiling dregs from the shops near the roadside, which the priest receiving poured upon the spot just dug. The eyes of every one around being intently fixed, they saw a crooked sprout issuing forth, which

拾級大成

頭 摘 賜 觀 者 頃 刻 而 盡 已 乃
ˏtʻau chák$_2$ tsʻzʼ ˏkún ʻché; ʻkʻing hak› ˏí tsun$^2$, ʻkí ʻnái
trunk plucked gave behold - ers; moment's while and consumed, he then

以 鑱 伐 樹 丁 丁 良 久 乃 斷 帶
ʻí ˏtsʻám fat$_2$ shü$^2$; ˏting ˏting ˏléung ʻkau ʻnái ʻtün, táiʼ
with spade felled tree; chop chop good while then severed, carried

葉 荷 肩 頭 從 容 徐 步 而 去
ip$_2$ hó$^2$ ˏkín ˏtʻau, ˏtsung ˏyung ˏchʻü pò$^2$ ˏí hüʼ.
foliage placed shoulder head, easy gait leisure steps and departed.

初 道 士 作 法 時 鄉 人 亦 雜 衆
ˏChʻó Tò$^2$ szʼ$^2$ tsók› fát› ˏshí, ˏhéung ˏyan yik$_2$ tsáp$_2$ chungʼ
First Taou priest did magic when, village man also crowd multitude

中 引 領 注 目 竟 忘 其 業 道
ˏchung ʻyan ʻling chüʼ muk$_2$ ʻking ˏmóng ˏkʻí ip$_2$. Tò$^2$
amongst stretching neck fixed eyes completely forgot his business. Taou

士 旣 去 始 顧 車 中 則 梨 已 空 矣
szʼ$^2$ kiʼ hüʼ, ʻchʻi kúʼ ˏkü ˏchung, tsak› ˏlí ʻí ˏhung ʻí.
priest having gone, began looking wagon in, then plums were empty.

方 悟 適 所 俵 散 皆 己 物 也 又
ˏFóng ʼng$^2$ shik› ʻshó píúʼ sánʼ, ˏkái ʻkí mat$_2$ ʻyá. Yau$^2$
Then perceived just what distributed given, all his goods. Moreover

細 視 車 上 一 靶 亡 是 新 鑿 斷 者
saiʼ shí$^2$ ˏkü shéung$^2$, yat› páʼ ˏmóng, shí$^2$ ˏsan tsók$_2$ ʻtün ʻché.
closely looking wagon upon, one dash-board lost, was lately chiseled cut it.

心 大 憤 恨 急 跡 之 轉 過 牆
ˏSam tái$^2$ fanʼ han$^2$, kap› tsik› ˏchí, ʻchün kwóʼ ˏtséung
Mind much excited angered, hastily followed him, turning passed wall

隅 則 斷 靶 棄 垣 下 始 知 所 伐 梨
ˏü, tsak› ʻtün páʼ hiʼ ˏún há$^2$; ʻchʻi ˏchí ʻshó fat$_2$ ˏlí
corner, then cut board thrown wall below; first knew what felled plum

---

gradually increasing presently became a tree, with branches and leaves; soon after there were flowers, and then fruit, large and very fragrant, which covered the tree. The priest then approached the tree, plucked and gave to the beholders; in a little while all were consumed, and he then felled the tree with the coulter:—the sound *chop, chop* was heard a good while, but at last being cut, he shouldered the foliage with an easy gait, and very leisurely walked off.

When first the Taou priest began to perform his magic arts, the villager was also among the crowd, and with outstretched neck and fixed eyes, completely forgot his own business. When the priest had gone, he began to look into his wagon, and lo! it was empty of plums. He then perceived that what had just been distributed were all his goods. Moreover looking narrowly about his wagon, he saw that the dash-board was gone, having just been cut off with a chisel. Much excited and very angry, he hastily pursu-

木 卽 是 物 也 道 士 不 知 所 在 一
mukₗ, tsikˎ shi$^2$ matₗ ʻyá. Tò$^2$ sz'$^2$ patˎ ˏchí ʻshó tsoi$^2$; yatˎ
tree, just was thing. Taou priest not know where was; whole

市 粲 然
ʻshí tsʻánʼ ˏín.
market laughed truly.

---

No. X. Grave of Tsʻò Tsʻò.

(聊齋卷十三第六十二篇)

許 城 外 有 河 水 洶 湧 近 崖 深 黯
ʻHü ˏshing ngoi$^2$ ʻyau ˏhó ʻshui ʻchung ʻyung; kan$^2$ ˏngai ˏsham ʻóm.
Hü city outside was river water rapid rushing; near bank deep dark.

盛 夏 時 有 人 入 浴 忽 然 若 被 刀
Shing$^2$ há$^2$ ˏshi ʻyau ˏyan yap$_2$ yuk$_2$, fatˎ ˏin yéuk$_2$ pí$^2$ ˏtò
Full summer time, was man entered bathe, suddenly as-if by sword

斧 尸 斷 浮 出 後 一 人 亦 如 之 轉
ʻfú ˏshí ʻtün ˏfau chʻutˎ. Hau$^2$ yatˎ ˏyan yik$_2$ ˏü ˏchí, ʻchün
ax, corpse cut floated out. Afterward another person also like him, turning

相 驚 怪 邑 宰 聞 之 遣 多 人 閘
ˏséung ˏking kwáiʼ. Yapˎ ʻtsoi ˏman ˏchí, ʻhín ˏtó ˏyan cháp$_2$
mutual alarmed terrified. City magistrate hearing it, sent many men bank

斷 上 流 竭 其 水 見 崖 下 有 深 洞
ʻtün shéung$^2$ ˏlau; hót$_2$ ˏkʻi ʻshui, kínʼ ˏngai há$^2$, ʻyau ˏsham tʻung$^2$,
stop above flowing; dried the water, saw precipice below, was deep hollow,

中 置 轉 輪 上 排 利 刃 如 霜 去
ˏchung chí$^2$ ʻchün ˏlun, shéung$^2$ ˏpái lí$^2$ yan$^2$ ˏü ˏséung. Hüʼ
in fixed revolving wheel, upon spread sharp blades as hoar-frost. Removed

輪 攻 入 有 小 碑 字 皆 漢 篆
ˏlun ˏkung yap$_2$ ʻyau ʻsíú ˏpí; tsz'$^2$ ˏkái Hónʼ sün$^2$;
wheel, daring enter was small tablet; characters all Hón seal-characters

---

ed him, and as he turned the corner of the wall, there was the board thrown down beneath the hedge; he then learned that that with which the plum-tree had been felled was this thing. Nobody knew where the Taou priest was, and the whole market laughed heartily at it.

Beyond the city of Hü, there was a rapid flowing river, and near by a deep dark overhanging bank. In the midst of summer, a man entered there to bathe, when suddenly a corpse, looking as if it had been cut with a knife, floated out. Afterwards, another person met with the same; and the thing becoming noised abroad, people were alarmed at so strange an event. The magistrate of the city sent men to bank up the stream above from flowing, and having dried the water, they saw a deep hollow under the bank, in which was placed a revolving wheel, on which were spread blades sharp as hoar-frost. Having taken away the wheel, and got courage to enter, they met a

細　視　之則曹孟德墓也破棺散
*sai' shí² ‹chí, tsak› ‹Ts'ò Mung' tak› mò² 'yá. P'ó' ‹kún sán'*
carefully examined them, then Ts'ò Mangtak's grave. Broke coffin dispersed

骨　所　殉　金　寶　盡　取　之
*kwat›, 'shó ‹sun ‹kam 'pò tsun² 'ts'ü ‹chí.*
bones, what buried gold gems all seized them.

---

No. XI. A Thief Detected.

(聊齋　卷十三　第六十三篇)

邑　西　白　家　莊　居　民　某　盜　鄰
*Yap› ‹sai Pák₂ ‹ká ‹chóng, ‹kü ‹man 'mau, t'ò² ‹lun*
City west, White family hamlet lived commoner certain, stole neighbor's

鴨　烹　之　至　夜　覺　膚　癢　天　明　視　之
*áp›, ‹p'ang ‹chí. Chí' yé² kók› ‹fú 'yéung, ‹t'in ‹ming shí² ‹chí,*
duck, cooked it. At night perceived skin itching, sky bright saw it,

茸　生　鴨　毛　觸　之　則　痛　大　懼
*‹yung ‹shang áp› ‹mò. Chuk› ‹chí tsak› t'ung'; tái² kü²,*
thick growth duck's feathers. Irritating it, then painful; much alarmed,

無　術　可　醫　夜　夢　一　人　告　之
*‹mò shut₂ 'hó ‹i. Yé² mung² yat› ‹yan kò' ‹chí*
without remedy could cure. Night dreaming a man informed him

曰　汝　病　乃　天　罰　須　得　失　者
*üt₂, 'ü ping² 'nái ‹t'in fát₂; ‹sü tak› shat› 'ché*
saying, Your disease is heaven's judgment; must get losing person's

罵　毛　乃　可　落　而　鄰　翁　素
*má², ‹mò 'nái 'hó lók›. ‹I' ‹lun ‹yung sò'*
reprimand, feathers then can fall-off. But neighboring gentleman uniformly

雅　量　生　平　失　物　未　嘗　徵　於　聲　色
*'ngá léung², ‹shang ‹p'ing shat› mat₂, mi² ‹chéung ‹ching ‹ü ‹shing shik›.*
refined liberal, life whole lost things, never exhibited proof in voice color.

---

small tablet, graven with seal characters of the Hón dynasty, and closely examining found it was the grave of Ts'ò Mangtak (or Ts'o Ts'ò). They broke up the coffin, scattered the bones, and seized all the gold and gems interred with it.

On the west of the city, in the hamlet of the White family, lived a certain commoner, who stole his neighbor's duck and cooked it. At night, he felt his skin to itch, and on looking at it in the morning, saw a thick growth of duck's feathers, which, if irritated were painful. He was much alarmed, for he had no remedy to cure it with. At night dreaming, a man informed him, saying, "Your disease is a judgment from heaven; you must get the loser to reprimand you, and the feathers will fall off." Now this gentlèman, who was

某詭告翁曰鴨乃某甲所盜彼
*'Mau 'kwai kò' ,yung üt, áp, 'nái 'mau káp, 'shó t'ò', 'pí*
He craftily told gentleman saying, duck was certain man who stole, he

深畏罵罵之亦可警將來
*,sham wai' má'; má' ,chí yik, 'hó 'king ,tsëung ,loi.*
much dreads reprimand; reprimand him truly can warn about come.

翁笑曰誰有閒氣罵惡人
*,Yung síú' üt, ,shui 'yau ,hán hí' má' ók, ,yan ?*
Gentleman laughing said, who has leisure spirits reprimand wicked man?

卒不罵某益窘因實
*Tsut, pat, má'. 'Mau yik, ,kwan, ,yan shat,*
Steadfastly not reprimand. Man exceedingly embarrassed, because truly

告鄰翁翁乃罵其病良已
*kò' ,lun ,yung; ,yung 'nái má', ,k'i p'ing' ,lëung 'í.*
inform neighboring gentleman; gentleman then reprimanded, his disease well.

---

his neighbor, was always liberal and refined, nor during his whole life, whenever he lost anything, had he even manifested any displeasure in his countenance. The man craftily told this gentleman, "The fellow who stole your duck is exceedingly afraid of a reprimand, but reprove him and he will no doubt then fear in future." The gentleman laughing replied, "Who has the time and disposition to scold at wicked men," and he altogether refused to do it. The man being hardly bestead, was obliged to tell him the truth; upon which the gentleman reprimanded him, and his disorder was removed.

The lessons in this and the fourth chapter can be advantageously employed in teaching English to Chinese lads after they have already made some progress in it. Let the boy be first taught to read the sounds in Roman letters as they are written under the characters; and then let the instructor read with him the literal English until he can easily read it himself. He should then be made to con both the Chinese and English, and exercised in translating either line with the opposite one exposed: so that he can recollect the Chinese when he sees only the English, and *vice versâ*. When the text has been made familiar, let him copy the free translation at the foot of the page, and write each Chinese original word under its corresponding English word; this exercise will show him the idiom of the English, and aid in teaching him how to express himself properly.

## Chapter Seventh.

# THE CLASSIFIERS.

If the student has made himself quite familiar with the preceding lessons, so that he can readily remember and write all the characters in them, he will have learned a good proportion of the most common characters used in books. He will find that by making himself perfect master of a few lessons, so that he can easily read them, write every character in them, and give its meaning from memory, and by becoming to a good degree familiar with the construction of the sentences, he will advance the most rapidly to a thorough knowledge of Chinese. In the last three chapters, he will also have seen something of the peculiarities of the style and grammar of common sentences, and wherein the idioms of the Chinese language differ from his native tongue, and from other languages with which he may be acquainted. This chapter is designed to exercise him in his knowledge of characters, by giving their sounds and tones, and the signification of the sentence, and then requiring him to write the characters out in full.

The chapter is also intended to make him acquainted with the use of a class of words holding an important place in Chinese writing and conversation, by giving him such sentences as contain examples of them, and arranging them into sections. This class of words has been denominated *numerals*, but this term confounds them with the proper numerals, with which they have no connection; and it is otherwise inapplicable; for it is somewhat catachrestic to say, as Dr. Morrison does, that "the *numeral* has an allusion to some *quality* or circumstance of the noun." It is better to select another word than to define one well known in such an unusual manner. The term *Classitive* or *Classifier* expresses tolerably well the office which this class of words fills; for each one is used to define and designate a certain class of objects, the members of which are supposed to have some quality or circumstance in common, as size, use, material, form, &c. They are used both in reckoning a large number, and in speaking of individuals, but express the sort of thing spoken of, and not the number of them. They are similar to the English words *piece*, *sail*, *member*, *gust*, *sheet*, &c., but are applied much more extensively than those words are, being used whenever the sense requires any individuality. They are met with more frequently in spoken than in written language, and are best learned by studying phrases in which they occur. Their proper application is a point which requires particular attention, for it will sound as incongruous to a Chinese to hear the phrase 一條人 *yat t'íú yan*, or 一粒行 *yat nap hóng*, as it would to an Englishman to hear a person talk of a *gust of horses*, a *sheet of wind*, or *a herd of ships*. Some of them are interchangeably used, as *túi* 對 and *shéung* 雙; *kó* 個 and *chik* 隻, and others; and the same object, when in different positions or uses, sometimes requires two different classifiers; for instance, *yat chéung tí lí t'ò*, 一張地理圖 expresses a map in a loose sheet, and *yat fuk tí lí t'ò*, 一幅地理圖 denotes the same mounted and suspended on a wall. *Yat chik mún*, 一隻門 means the leaf of a door, and *yat tò mún*, 一度門 means a gateway or door, the passage.

This class of words is applied only to nouns, and this use of them arose probably from the necessity of removing the liability of confounding homophonous words. To avoid confusion in verbs and adjectives, whenever there is danger of being misunderstood, two synonymous and dissonant words are frequently joined together in a compound phrase, analogous to a dissyllable; as *chá chát* 查察 to examine; *kák túi* 革退 to degrade: in some cases, the same word is repeated. For the great majority of nouns or names of things, there are of course no synonymes, while the inconvenience arising from a misapprehension might sometimes be very great. To remedy this, certain words have been selected to prefix to certain nouns, and they are so uniformly applied, and have become so distinctive, as to obviate all danger of not being understood; and if this view of their origin be correct, it shows the necessity of becoming familiar with their application. Each of the words has other significations as well as this, and in most cases, their use as classifiers can be seen to be derived from an application of their meaning in an adjective sense to the nouns ranged under them.

The student must not lightly pass over the following exercises in writing characters, for he will derive benefit from the labor of looking out new words, and refreshing his memory with rewriting old ones, and fixing them all in his mind in a new connection in these common phrases. He ought to make sure that he can write every character, and give its meaning. Those words which do not occur in the preceding pages, he must get his teacher to write for him, or he can find them in a dictionary: the index to the Chinese Chrestomathy will prove a guide to nearly or quite all of them.

1. *Kó* 個 (also written 箇 and 个) is applied to human beings, and inanimate things, and to objects when spoken of individually. It corresponds to the word *thing* or *individual;* in the phrases *ché kó* 這個 this, *ná kó* 那個 that, *pít kó* 別個 another, and a few others. This very common use must not be confounded with its application as a classifier, which is more extensive than that of any other one; it is applied to periods of time, to portions of land, and to such things as are somewhat roundish or compact, as boxes; as well as to many other things made by men. It is also used interchangeably with No. 2. in denoting many things made by art.

| | |
|---|---|
| Three jars for one dollar is quite enough. | ‹Sám kó' ‹áng yat› kó' ˏngan ˏts'in ‹tò kau' lók›. |
| Gave him an inkstone. | Sung' ‹t'á yat› kó' mak› ín$^{2}$. |
| A servant girl has handed up a box. | ʿYau kó' múi$^{2}$ ʿˏsai ʿfung yat› kó' hóp$_{2}$. |
| Will you sell this bureau? | ‹Ní kó' kwai$^{2}$ mái$^{2}$ ˏ'm mái$^{2}$? |
| Pierce a hole. | ʿChing ‹ch'ün yat› kó' ‹lung. |
| I have four fish-ponds. | ʿNgó ʿyau sz' kó' ˏü ˏt'óng. |
| One catty contains eight oranges. | Yat› ‹kan kung$^{2}$ ʿyau pát› kó' ˏch'áng. |
| There is a bird's nest on the mulberry tree. | ‹Sóng shü$^{2}$ ʿyau yat› kó' tséuk› ˏch'áu. |
| I say you have several hearts (or plans). | ʿNgó wá$^{2}$ ʿní ʿyau ʿkí kó' ‹sam. |
| There are several hundred bamboo baskets on the ship's stern. | ˏShün ʿmí ʿyau ʿkíp ák› kó' chuk› ˏlám. |
| Roll a ball into the water. | Luk› yat› ko' ˏk'au lók$_{2}$ ʿshui. |
| There are ten and more bells in the temple. | Míú$^{2}$ noi$^{2}$ ʿyau shap$_{2}$ ʿkí kó' ‹chung. |
| There are several muscles on the side of the field. | ˏT'ín ˏpín ʿyau ʿkí kó' ʿp'óng. |
| One hill opposite. | Túi' mín$^{2}$ yat› kó' ‹shán. |
| Not worth a single cash. | Yat› kó' ˏts'ín ‹tò ˏ'm chik$_{2}$. |
| Made a furnace. | ʿTá kwó' yat› kó' tsò'. |
| The thieves stole two boilers. | Ts'ak$_{2}$ ‹t'au ʿléung kó' wók$_{2}$. |
| Does this watch go well or not? | ‹Ní yat› kò' ‹píú ˏhang tak› ʿchun ˏ'm ʿchun? |
| See there is a sun at the bottom of the water! | ʿShui ʿtai yik$_{2}$ ʿyau yat› kó' yat$_{2}$! |
| Put up five awnings on the parade ground. | ʿKáu ˏch'éung táp› ʿ'ng kó' ˏp'ang. |
| He promised to come back within three months. | ʿK'ü ‹ying ˏshing ‹sám kó' üt$_{2}$ noi$^{2}$ ‹fán ˏloi. |
| Fetch one mat bag here to put some rice in. | ʿPí kó' tsik$_{2}$ ‹páu ˏlai ‹chóng ʿhí tik› ʿmai. |
| Buy several basket-trays to dry the laichís. | ʿMái ʿkí kó' ‹wó ˏlám ‹fán ˏlai shái' lai$^{2}$ ‹chí. |
| Go to the shop and buy ten or more muskmelons. | Hü' p'ò' ˏt'au ʿmái shap$_{2}$ ʿkí kó' ‹héung ‹kwá. |
| These three characters are written very well. | ‹Ní ‹sám kó' tsz'$^{2}$ ʿsé tak› ʿkí ʿhò. |
| There is a man's head exposed on the beach to all people. | ʿHai ʿhoi ‹pín ʿyau kó' ˏyan ˏt'au shí$^{2}$ chung'. |
| Men have two nostrils. | ˏYan ʿyau ʿléung kó' pí$^{2}$ ‹kó ʿlung. |
| The jackets of foreigners have two pockets. | Ngoi$^{2}$ kwok› ˏyan ‹chung ‹shám ʿyau ʿléung kó' toi$^{2}$. |

*Notes.—Fung* 捧 means to hand up respectfully in both hands as to a superior.—*Ching ch'ün* 整穿 expresses present action, do perfo-

2. *Chik* 隻 (frequently but incorrectly written 只) is applied to almost if not quite all kinds of animals, birds, and insects, to single ones of such things as occur in pairs, or in sets, in a fixed number, as members of the body, plates, chess-men, and to many other things.

| | |
|---|---|
| There are ten or more sparrows on the tiled roof. | ˢNgá púiˀ ˢyau shap$_2$ ˋkí chikˀ tséukˀ. |
| A fly has drowned in that cup of congee. | Kóˀ ˋún chukˀ ˏchʻam ˋszˀ yatˀ chikˀ ˏying |
| A pilferer has stolen a shoe. | ˢYau koˀ ˋsíú ˋshau ˎtʻau ˍyatˀ chikˀ ˏhái. |
| Draw an ear on the wall to hear your words. | Wák$_2$ yatˀ chikˀ ˢí ˋhai ˏtséung ˎtʻing ˢní ˋkóng ˎlá. |
| How heavy is a single crab? | Yatˀ chikˀ ˢhái ˢyau ˋkí ˋchung ˎní? |
| Broken five cups. | ˋTá lán$^2$ ˢˋng chikˀ ˋún. |
| Newly made several finger-rings. | ˎSan ˋtá ˋkí chikˀ káiˀ ˋchí. |
| Pushed down one leaf of a door. | ˎTʻúi tʻítˀ yatˀ chikˀ ˏmún. |
| Searched for a lamp cup but there is none. | ˋWan yatˀ chikˀ ˎtang ˋchʻán ˎtò ˢmò. |
| Where did you buy these combs? | ˢNí kóˀ ˋkí chikˀ ˎshó ˎpín chʻüˀ ˢmái tikˀ? |
| Mark the name on those baskets. | Hò$^2$ kóˀ ˋkí chikˀ ˏlô. |
| I do not find a stocking. | Patˀ kínˀ yatˀ chikˀ mát$_2$. |
| Make another silver spoon. | ˋTá ˎfán yatˀ chikˀ ˏngan ˏshí. |
| Pressed upon and broke six jars. | A'tˀ lán$^2$ luk$_2$ chikˀ ˏchʻing. |
| There is still another chess-man. | Shéung$^2$ ˢyau yatˀ chikˀ ˏkʻí ˋtszˀ. |
| One hundred cash for ten hen's eggs. | Yatˀ pákˀ ˏtsʻín shap$_2$ chikˀ ˎkai tán$^2$. |

---

rate a hole.—*Chʻáu* 巢 denotes a nest in a tree above the ground; *wó* 窩 a nest on the ground.—*Luk* 摝 has a local signification, that of rolling a thing over or along.—*Chun* 準 is employed in this sentence in a local sense to mean exact, correct.—*Yik* 亦 is here employed in an exclamatory manner, meaning indeed, truly.—*Káu chʻéung* 較場 is an arena or parade ground, where stated reviews are held, and trials of skill in archery.—*Pʻang* 棚 is an awning woven of broad bamboo splints.—*Tsik páu* 蓆包 is an open mat bag, used to pack rice or other articles in.—*Shí chung* 示衆 'expose to the populace' is a term used with reference to the exposure of the heads of criminals in cages as a warning.

*Notes.*—*Síú shau* 小手 'small hand' is a term applied to pilferers, pickpockets, and light fingered gentry.—*Ún* 碗 a cup, takes the classifier *chik;* so also do plates, cups, tumblers, &c., and whatever of dishes are found in sets; other articles of crockery, as tureens, bottles,

| | |
|---|---|
| This single hog with those three hens—how many catties do they together weigh? | ‹Ní yat› chik› ‹chü ‹t'ung ‹mái kó' ‹sám chik› ‹kai, ʻts'ung kung' ‹ch'ing tak› ʻkí ‹tò ‹kan á'? |
| At present there is a steamer here. | ‹Ü ‹kam ‹ní ch'ü' ʻyau yat› chik› ʻfó ‹lun ‹shün. |
| The pictures on this tea-cup are drawn beautifully. | ‹Ní chik› ‹ch'á ‹púi tik› wá' ʻsé tak› ʻtsing chí'. |
| That man is deficient one eye. | Kó' kó' ‹yan ‹tán ʻkám yat› chik› ʻngán. |
| That hawk's foot is wanting one claw. | Kó' chik› ‹ying kéuk› hü' ʻkám yat› chik› ʻcháu. |
| This dog has shaggy hair. | ‹Ní chik› ʻkau hai' ‹sung ‹mò ké'. |
| Bring a fan here to flirt this butterfly. | Ním ʻpá shín' ‹lai pók› ʻtò ‹ní chik› ‹ú típ'. |
| He is going to kill a cow this evening. | ‹Kam ʻmán ʻk'ü ʻtséung ‹t'óng yat› chik› ‹ngau. |

3. *Túi* 對 is applied to such things as are found in pairs, as hands, eyes, shoes, bacelets, &c. Its proper meaning is opposite or to oppose, to correspond, a pair, &c., and hence its application to classify such things as occur in couplets.

| | |
|---|---|
| Light a pair of candles. | ʻTím chéuk' yat› túi' láp' chuk›. |
| A pair of hands, or two hands—both ways can be said. | Yat› túi' ʻshau, ʻléung chik› ʻshau—ʻléung yéung' ‹tò ʻkóng tak›. |
| Hang up two pair of scrolls on the wall. | ‹Tséung shéung' kwá' ʻléung túi' ʻtúi. |

---

&c., take the term *kó*.—*Tang chǎn* 燈盞 is a small shallow cup containing oil, in which are placed several wicks made of the pith of a grass.—*Hò* 號 means to mark a name on anything.—*Ch'ing* 埕 is the name of a kind of spherical water jar, in very common use, having a small mouth.—*Ts'ung kung* 總共 is an expression denoting the whole, or altogether.—*Tsing chí* 精緻 is a common term for whatever is elegant, beautiful, fine, &c.—*Tán kám* 單減 together denote 'one lost,' a single one alone.—*Sung* 鬆 is a word of extensive application, meaning loose, open, easy, to make easy, to relax or open.—*Pók* 撲 is a sudden short motion, and is applied to motions with a fan.

*Notes.*—*Cháu* 找 means to exchange money, or that which is as valuable as money, and here denotes that the article bought is weight for weight nearly as valuable as the coin paid.—*Tang lung* 燈籠 here refer to large translucent globular lanterns hung up at each side of doorways, on which are written the name of the shop, the surname

| | |
|---|---|
| Bought eight pairs of gem bracelets. | ʻCháu ʿhú pát˓ túi' yuk$_2$ ák˓. |
| On the top of the bamboo, stand a pair of cranes. | Chuk˓ shü$^2$ ʿmí ʿk'í yat˓ túi' hók$_2$. |
| This dragon-fly has two pair of wings. | ˓Ní chik˓ ˓tsing ˏt'ing ʿyau ʿléung túi' yik$_2$. |
| There is a pair of mandarin ducks near the pond. | ˏCh'í ˓pín ʿyau yat˓ túi' ˓ün ˓yéung. |
| Suspend a pair of lanterns in the gateway. | ˏMún ʻhau kwá' yat˓ túi' ˓tang ˏlung. |
| In all seven pair of stockings. | Yat˓ kung$^2$ ts'at˓ túi' mát˓. |
| He conceals a pair of knives about him. | ʿK'ü ˓shan ˏt'ó yat˓ túi' ˓tò. |
| In the doorway are several tens of pairs of flag-staffs. | ˏMún ʻhau ʿyau ʻkí shap$_2$ túi' ˏk'í ˓kón. |
| The soles of that pair of shoes are too thick. | Ko' túi' ˏhái ʻtai t'ái' hau$^2$. |

4. *Shéung* 雙 is used synonymously with *túi* in same phrases, and in others it cannot be interchanged. The difference in the meaning and uses of the two words can be best learned by observation.

| | |
|---|---|
| Bring a pair of chopsticks here. | ˓Ním yat˓ ˓shéung fái' ʻtsz' ˏlai. |
| A pair of swallows flying hither and thither. | Yat˓ ˓shéung ín' ʻtsz' ˓fí ˏloi ˓fí hü'. |
| A certain officer wearing a double eyed peacock's feather. | ʿMau tái$^2$ ʻlò ˏyé tái' ˓shéung ʿngán ˓fá ˏling. |
| Put down that pair of legs. | Fóng' lók˓ kò' ˓shéung kéuk˓. |
| Raise up that pair of hands. | ʻKü ʻhí ko' ˓shéung ʻshau. |
| There are a couple of pots of the double jasmine. | ʿYau ʿléung ˏp'ún ˓shéung t'ók˓ mút$_2$ lí$^2$. |
| Two persons playing chess. | ʿLéung ˏyan ʻtá ˓shéung luk$_2$. |
| His parents have been dead a long time. | ʿK'ü ˓shéung ˓ts'an kwó' shai' ʻhò noi$^2$. |

of the inhabitant, or some other inscription according to the owner's fancy.—*Yat túi tò*, — 對刀 refers to a kind of large knife, the blades and hilts of which are made flat on one side, so that the two lie close together, and are always put into one scabbard; to conceal a pair of such knives in the dress is called *t'ó* 馱. These *k'í kón* 旗杆 are a kind of staff used in processions to suspend small banners to, and are always carried in couples.

*Notes.*—Swallows, *ín tsz'*, 燕子 often build their nests in Chinese dwellings, under the roof, and their domestics habits caused them to be often referred to in pairs.—*Tái lò yé* 大老爺 is applied only to officers of a certain rank.—To wear things on the head, as caps, spectacles, &c., is denoted by the term *tai* 戴.—*T'ók mút li*, 托茉莉 is a 'receptacle of a jasmine'; when the receptacle con-

5. *Pa* 把 means to seize, to grasp or lift up with one hand, and as a classifier is for the most part applied to many things held in the hand by a handle when used.

| | |
|---|---|
| Twelve cash for a bundle of straw. | Shap$_2$ í$^2$ ꜁ts‘ín yat꜀ ‘pá ‘kón. |
| Light a couple of torches and go there. | ‘Tím ˢléung ‘pá ‘fó ꜀chí hü’ tak꜀ tò’. |
| One state umbrella went before. | Yat꜀ ‘pá ꜁ló sán’ ꜀sín ꜁hang. |
| Each one has concealed a girdle knife. | ˢMúi kó’ ꜁t‘ó yat꜀ ‘pá ꜀íú ꜀tò. |
| He has given an umbrella to me. | ˢK‘ü sung’ yat꜀ ‘pá ꜀ché ˢü ˢngó. |
| Find a rule. | ‘Wan yat꜀ ‘pá ch‘ik꜀ ꜁lai. |
| Carry a steelyards in the left hand. | ‘Tsó ‘shau ˢwán yat꜀ ‘pá ch‘ing’. |
| This pair of shears is not sharp. | ꜀Ní ‘pá káu’ ‘tsín ꜁’m lí$^2$. |
| Snapped open a lock. | ‘Náu chít꜀ yat꜀ ‘pá ‘só. |
| His beard is very long. | ˢK‘ü kó’ yat꜀ ‘pá ꜀sò shap$_2$ ꜀fan ꜁ch‘éung. |
| Lost a pair of tongs. | Shat꜀ ˢlíú yat꜀ ‘pá ‘fó ꜁k‘ím. |
| Buy again several brooms. | ˢMái ꜀fán ‘kí ‘pá sò’ ‘pá. |
| My place possesses two punkas. | ˢNgó ch‘ü’ ˢyau ˢléung ‘pá ꜀fung shín’. |
| Lü Pò, with one gripe, stopped him. | ˢLü Pò’ yat꜀ ‘pá ‘ch‘é chü$^2$. |
| Splice four ladders, still they will not reach. | Pók꜀ sz’ ‘pá ꜀t‘ai wáng$^2$ ꜀tò mí$^2$ tak꜀ tò’. |
| The basket contains a handful of greens. | ꜁Lám ˢyau yat꜀ ‘pá ts‘oi’. |
| He holds a knife and is scraping a bow. | ˢK‘ü ‘chá yat꜀ ‘pá ꜀tò kwát꜀ ‘kan yat꜀ ‘pá ꜀kung. |
| His whiskers look well. | ˢK‘ü ‘pá ꜁ú ꜀sò ‘hò ‘t‘ai. |
| Papa holds a rake to scratch the ground. | ꜀Pá ꜀pá ‘pá ‘pá ꜁p‘á ꜁p‘á tí$^2$. |

---

tains two flowers, it is called *shéung t‘ók;* when three, it is called *sám t‘ók*, &c.—*Shéung luk* 雙陸 is the term given a complicated game of chess played with 360 men.

5. *Notes.*—*Kón* 稈 straw, is used by the poor as a substitute for wood in cooking.—*Wán* 挽 means to carry slung on the arm or hung by the finger.—*Náu chít* 扭折 is to hold in the hands and snap asunder, or to break a thing in the middle, which joins or is fixed at the ends.—*T‘ai wáng* 梯橫 is a common ladder.—*Kwát kan* 刮緊 expresses present time, he is scraping.—*P‘á p‘á* 爬爬 is a sentence where the same character is used in one place as a verb and in the other as a noun.

6. *Chéung* 張 means to spread out, to extend, &c., and is joined to such things as are extended, whose thickness bears a very small proportion to their surfaces; also to advertisements, edicts, &c., which are to be proclaimed abroad.

| | |
|---|---|
| Give me three sheets of paper. | ‘Pí ‹sám ‹chéung ‘chí kwó’ ‘ngó. |
| In the hall are spread ten mats. | Tái$^2$ ˏlau ‹p‘ò shap$_2$ ‹chéung tsik$_2$. |
| Sun those two carpets. | Shái’ kó’ ‘léung ‹chéung tí$^2$ ‹chín. |
| Lost a quilt. | Shat› hü’ yat› ‹chéung ‘p‘í. |
| Hang up again a door-screen. | Kwá’ ‹fán yat› ‹chéung ˏmún ˏlím. |
| Copied nine maps. | ‹Ch‘áu ‘hí ‘kau ‹chéung tí$^2$ ‘lí ˏt‘ò. |
| To one man one rain cloke. | Yat› kó’ ‹kung yat› ‹chéung ‹só ‹í. |
| Go to the ironmonger's, and buy a fish cleaver. | Hü’ t‘ít› p‘ò’ ‘mái yat› ‹chéung ˏü ‹tò. |
| Standing upon it he snapped the bench. | ‘K‘í chít› yat› ‹chéung tang’. |
| He has lately received a newspaper. | ‘K‘ü kan’ yat› ‹shau yat› ‹chéung ‹san ˏman ‘chí. |
| This morning was newly issued an edict. | ‹Kam ‹chíú ‹san ch‘ut› yat› ‹chéung kò’ shí$^2$. |
| A literary advertisement is pasted up at his door. | ‘K‘ü ˏmún ‘hau t‘íp› yat› ‹chéung pò’ ˏt‘íú. |

7. *Chí* 枝 means a branch, a sprig, a twig, &c., and for the most part distinguishes things made of wood, and which like a branch, are round and slender. It is also employed in a metaphorical sense.

| | |
|---|---|
| Wear a flower on the head. | ˏT‘au tái’ yat› ‹chí ‹fá. |
| Carry a bamboo in the hand. | ‘Shau ‹ním yat› ‹chí chuk›. |
| Spoiled a hundred pencils this year in writing. | ‹Kam ˏnín ‘sé lán$^2$ yat› pák› ‹chí pat›. |
| Grasping a spear in the hand. | ‘Shau ˏt‘ai yat› ‹chí kik›. |
| As quick as an arrow. | Yat› ‹chí tsín’ kóm’ fái’. |
| In the box are four tooth-brushes. | Hóp$_2$ noi$^2$ ‘yau sz’ ‹chí ˏngá ts‘át›. |
| Looking afar I see two large flags. | ‘Ün móng$^2$ kín’ ‘léung ‹chí tái$^2$ tuk$_2$. |

---

6. *Notes.*—*Ch‘áu hí* 抄起 expresses the perfect tense.—*Kung* 公 means a person, a laborer.—*Pò t‘íú* 報條 is a paper containing the name and degree of a graduate, with all necessary particulars, and is pasted up near his door.

7. *Notes.*—The word *ním* 拈 means to carry along, to carry and give to; the word *t‘ai* 提 is to hold, to grasp, for action.—*Tái tuk* 大纛 are large flags suspended at an angle by means of a pole, and having inscriptions on them.—*Tsám* 簪 is a hair-pin made of metal or colored glass, used to restrain the tuft of hair on a woman's head.—*T‘ai* 遞

| | |
|---|---|
| Dropped a hair-pin. | Tít, ˢlíú yat, ˌchí ˌtsám. |
| Behind the ridge of the hill a line of horsemen issued out. | ˌShán púi' hau² ˈchün ch'ut, yat, ˌchí ˌping ˢmá. |
| Bring two branches of corol here. | ˌNím ˢléung ˌchí ˌshán ˌú ˌlai. |
| Taking it on a fork pass it to him. | T'ai² yat, ˌchí ˌtò ˌch'á ˈpí ˢk'ü. |
| I see there is an opium-pipe on his bed. | Kín' ˢyau yat, ˌchí ˌín ˌts'éung ˈhai ˢk'ü ˌch'óng ch'ü'. |
| The study seat has two lamps. | ˌShü wai² ˢyau ˢléung ˌchí ˌtang. |
| On the Lapa there is a lucky pagoda. | Túi' mín² ˌshán ˢyau yat,. ˌchí ˌman pat,. |
| That ship, meeting a gale, broke one mast. | Kó' chik, ˌshün ˌtsò ˌfung ˈtá chít, yat, ˌchí ˌwai. |
| At the stern of the vessel is a wind vane. | ˌShün ˢmí ˢyau yat, ˌchí ˌfung sun' ˌk'í. |
| The branch that man belongs to divided off from the same ancestor as mine. | ˢK'ü tí² kó' yat, ˌchí ˌyan ˌtò hai² ˌt'ung ˢngó tí² t'ái' ˈtsò ˌfan ch'ut, ké'. |

8. *T'iú* 條 properly means a branch like *chí*, but it is applied more extensively to such things as are long, without regard to their form or material; it is also employed to denote divisions.

| | |
|---|---|
| Seen at a distance it looks like a snake. | ˢÜn ˈt'ai ˢts'z' yat, ˌt'íú ˌshé. |
| It is exceedingly like a tail. | Tsuk, ˢts'z' yat, ˌt'íú ˢmí ˈkóm yéung². |
| That man's cue is spliced with a false one. | Kó' kó' ˌyan kó' ˌt'íú ˌpín ˌtsam ˌpín ˌpái. |
| Open another drain. | ˌHoi ˌtó yat, ˌt'íú ˌk'ü. |
| Before us one river. | Mín² ˌts'ín yat, ˌt'íú ˌhó. |
| A worm is in the flower. | ˌFá ˌsam ˢyau yat, ˌt'íú ˌch'ung. |
| I found a watch-chain this morning. | ˌKam ˌchíú chap, yat, ˌt'íú ˌpíú lín². |

means to take up and pass along anything to another person.—*Ín ts'éung* 烟鎗 is a slang term for an opium-pipe, nor is it an unapt term for so suicidal an implement.—*Man pat* 文筆 denotes the forked top on the roof of some pagodas, which are supposed to have great influence on the fortunes of the surrounding country.—*Túi mín shán* 對面山 or opposite hills, is the Chinese name of the island to the westward of Macao.—*Tsò* 遭 means to meet what is unfortunate, and *ü* 遇 what is fortunate.

8. *Notes.*—*Tsuk ts'z'* 足似 means fully like, exceedingly similar to.—*Kóm yéung* 咁樣 is literally 'so fashion.'—*Tsam pín pái* 侵辮排 false cue joined or spliced; this is very frequently done by such persons as are solicitous about their appearance.—*K'ü* 渠 is a sewer or drain, either covered or uncovered.—*Fá sam* 花心 means the centre of the corol.—*Chap* 執 means to pick up, to put things

| | |
|---|---|
| Both roads are passable. | ᶜLéung ꜀tʻíú lò² ꜀tò hü' tak꜄. |
| I cannot find that girdle. | ꜀Tsʻam ꜀'m chéuk₂ kó' yat꜄ ꜀tʻíú tái'. |
| Last evening in the east there was a rainbow. | Tsók꜄ ᶜmán ꜀tung pín'ᶜyau yat꜄ ꜀tʻíú ꜀hung. |
| Six bills have come from the tavern. | ꜀Kò ꜀lau ᶜyau luk₂ ꜀tʻíú ꜀tán pái' ꜀loi. |
| In one raft how many pine-logs? | Yat꜄ ꜀pái ᶜyau ᶜkí ꜀tʻíú chʻám'? |
| Saw him carrying a single stick. | Kín' ᶜkʻü ꜀tám yat꜄ ꜀tʻíú kwan'. |
| Lately made a pair of trowsers. | ꜀San tsʻò² yat꜄ ꜀tʻíú fú'. |
| Seventy dollars for a petticoat. | Tsʻat꜄ shap₂ kó' ꜀ngan ꜀tsʻín yat꜄ ꜀tʻíú ꜀kwʻan. |
| Give that horsewhip to me. | ᶜPí kó' yat꜄ ꜀tʻíú ᶜmá ꜀pín kwó' ᶜngó. |
| As light as a feather's down. | Yat꜄ ꜀tʻíú ꜀mò ꜀sz' kóm' ꜀hing. |
| Bought eight handkerchiefs. | ᶜMái ᶜlíú pát꜄ ꜀tʻíú ᶜshau ꜀kan. |
| That theme is extremely hard to write upon. | Kó' ꜀tʻíú ꜀tʻai muk₂ shap₂ ꜀fan ꜀nán tsók꜄. |
| Caught one garoupa. | Tíú' tak꜄ yat꜄ ꜀tʻíú shik₂ ꜀pán ꜀ü. |
| His tongue is furred. | ᶜKʻü ꜀tʻíú shít₂ ᶜyau ꜀wóng ꜀tʻoi. |

9. ***Kán*** 間, when a noun, means a crevice, an interval of space or time, the midst; when used as a verb, it commonly means to separate, to make a space between: its use as a classifier is restricted to buildings and parts of buildings, in which its application seems to refer to the space covered by them.

| | |
|---|---|
| In that place are two council chambers. | Kó' chʻü' ᶜyau ᶜléung ꜀kán ꜀kung ᶜshó. |
| It is reckoned the village contains thirteen school-houses. | Yat꜄ ꜀tsʻün kung² kai' ᶜyau shap₂ ꜀sám ꜀kán ꜀shü ᶜkún. |
| Each factory has seven divisions. | ᶜMúi ꜀kán ꜀hóng ᶜyau tsʻat꜄ táp₂. |

---

within, and here denotes finding a chain and picking it up.—*Tsʻam 'm chéuk* 尋唔着 seeking not get or receive; the last two words is a common expression for not accomplishing what the preceding verb shows had been undertaken.—*Pín* 邊 side, quarter, is joined to the points of compass.—*Pái loi* 派來 distributed sent; bills are sent to the parties receiving entertainment at eating-houses.—*Kwan* 棍 is a stick or log, large or small.—*Kwʻan* 裙 is the petticoat, the folds of which appear below the frock, and sometimes gaily embroidered.—*Mò sz'* 毛絲 hair-floss, are the minute feathers on quills.—*Tʻai muk* 題目 is the term for themes given at examination.—*Shik pán ü* 石班魚 is the name of the garoupa, so called on account of its marbled skin.—*Wóng tʻoi* 黃胎 is a common term for this state of the tongue.

9. *Notes.*—*Kung shó* 公所 'public place,' is the name given to certain public buildings where different tradespeople meet for consultation,

| | |
|---|---|
| There are only two eating-houses in Macao. | Ò꜄ ꜁mún tuk꜇ ꜃léung ꜀kán ꜂tsau ꜁lau. |
| There are several inns on the road. | Lò꜅ shéung꜅ ꜃yau ꜂kí ꜀kán hák꜆ tím꜄. |
| How many shops are there on the Praya Grande? | ꜁Nám ꜀wán ꜃yau ꜂kí ꜀kán p‘ò꜄ ꜀uí? |
| Two storehouses in Honam. | ꜃Léung ꜀kán chán꜅ ꜁fóng ꜂hai ꜀Hó ꜁nám. |
| There is a military station half-way. | Pún꜄ lò꜅ ꜃yau yat꜆ ꜀kán ꜁ying sun꜄. |
| The next door is an opium smoking shop. | Kák꜆ ꜁lí yat꜆ ꜀kán ꜀á p‘ín꜄ ꜀ín ꜂kún. |
| Obtained only one room. | Tuk꜇ tak꜆ yat꜆ ꜀kán ꜁fóng. |
| A lookout lodge is there to watch the vegetables. | Kó꜄ ch‘ü꜄ ꜃yau yat꜆ ꜀kán ꜁mau ꜁líú ꜀hón ꜀kwá ts‘oi꜄. |
| Several tens of gambling-houses. | ꜂Kí shap꜇ ꜀kán ꜀fán ꜀tán ꜂kún. |

10. *Tsó* 座 is a seat, a structure built up, a throne, a foundation or base on which something is placed; it is applied like the preceding to houses and stories, but its uses in denoting other things is different; it denotes a structure that is high and large.

| | |
|---|---|
| One row has several dwellings. | Yat꜆ ꜁p‘ái ꜂kí tsó꜅ uk꜆. |
| One story in front. | ꜁Ts‘ín mín꜅ yat꜆ tsó꜅ ꜁lau. |
| Many marriage sedans have passed to-day. | ꜀Kam yat꜇ ꜃yau ꜂kí tsó꜅ ꜀fá kíú꜅ ꜀king kwó꜄. |
| The garden contains two arbors. | ꜀Fá ꜁ün ꜃yau ꜃léung tsó꜅ ꜁t‘ing. |
| A pagoda has been lately raised. | ꜀Sun ꜂hí yat꜆ tsó꜅ t‘áp꜆. |

---

or for other purposes connected with their fraternity.—When the 行 *hóng* is formed of a number of small roofs one succeeding the other, each of these roofs or divisions is called a *táp* 沓.—*Nám wán* 南灣 or the southern beach, is the Chinese designation for the Praya at Macao.—*Chán fóng* 棧房 is the name usually given to workshops and packing-houses connected with the shop or store where the goods are sold.—*Ying sun* 營汛 is a station or guard-house, placed at different intervals, where several soldiers live and maintain a look-out.—*Mau liú* 茅寮 is a triangular shaped thatch erected upon the ground in fields, where a person remains to watch the ripening fruits. *Fán tán* 番攤 is the name of a game of chance consisting in quadrating an unknown number of cash, and from its frequency has given its own term to gambling-houses.

10. *Notes.*—The *fá kíú* 花轎 is a gay and ornamented sedan used in marriage processions.—*T‘ing* 亭 is a high arbor or summer-house erected to afford accommodations for enjoying the breeze.—*Ts‘ai* 砌 is a term applied to the construction of the artificial limestone

| | |
|---|---|
| I think of making a rockwork hill. | ʻSéung tsʻaiʼ yat˒ tsó² shik˳ ˏshán. |
| A screen inside the door. | ˳Mún noi² yat˒ tsó² ˳pʻing ˏfung. |
| One city quite overflowed by the water. | Yat˒ tsó² ˳shing ˏtò pí² ʻshui tsamʼ ˢlíú. |

11. *Tò* 度 denotes a rule, a measure, that by which anything is measured or marked off. Its application as a classifier, however, is derived from *tò* 渡 to pass over, to cross over or through a passage, for which it is often erroneously used.

| | |
|---|---|
| Went by five passes. | ˏKing kwóʼ ˢʼng tò² ˏkwán. |
| Broken down that bamboo screen. | Chʻák˒ ˢlíú kóʼ tò² chuk˒ pik˒. |
| Nine windows open toward the east. | Héungʼ ˏtung ʻkau tò² ˏchʻéung. |
| Locked both the barred gates. | ˢLéung tò² cháp˳ ˏtò ʻsó ˢlíú. |
| Raised two bridges in addition. | ʻHí ˏtó ˢléung tò² ˳kʻíú. |
| Open that door. | ʻI'm ˏhoi kóʼ yat˒ tò² ˳mún. |

12. *Fuk* 幅 is a long piece or roll of cloth, silk, or paper, the two ends of which are mounted on rollers like a map; it is applied to such things as roll up or are stretched out, &c., as maps, pictures, inscriptions.

| | |
|---|---|
| Hang up several landscapes. | Kwáʼ ʻkí fuk˒ ˏshán ʻshui wá². |
| Have you pasted the four papers yet? | ʻPíú ʻhí szʼʼ fuk˒ ˳tʻau mí²? |
| This roll of cloth is just enough to make one coat. | ˏNí fuk˒ pòʼ ʻkan ʻhó tsò² tak˒ yat˒ kínʼ ˏshám. |
| A wall has fallen down next door. | Kák˒ ˳lí tít˒ ˢlíú yat˒ fuk˒ ˳tsʻéung. |

---

rockwork, the *shik shán* 石山 or stone hill—so much esteemed by the Chinese.—*Ping fung* 屏風 is the name of the large screen standing before doorways.—*Pí* 被 means by, done by, caused by;—the city was overflowed by the water, i. e. the water overflowed the city; the first is the Chinese construction.

11. *Notes.—Kwán* 關 is a pass or gateway where toll is collected on passengers and goods.—*Chuk pik* 竹壁 is a thick bamboo screen hung in a doorway instead of a more expensive wooden door.—*Cháp* 閘 is a kind of gate made of posts in a frame, and placed across streets, where watchmen are stationed to open and shut them at certain hours. *I'm hoi* 揜開 is to open a door with the hand as one passes through it; *ím mái* 揜埋 is to close it with the hand.

12. *Notes.—Shán shui wá* 山水畫 is the general term for landscape paintings.—*Píú* 裱 originally meant a neckerchief, but its most common signification at present is to paste pictures or inscriptions on silk or paper, and fit them to a roller.—*Szʼ fuk tʻau* 四幅頭 is the

拾級大成

13. *Chan* 陣 means to arrange, to spread out, as soldiers, a case or an argument, and is applied to such things as quickly pass away, as a spell of time, a gust of wind, &c.

| | |
|---|---|
| A puff of wind blew down that sheet of paper. | Yat, chan$^2$ ˏfung ˏchʻui tít, kòʼ ˏchéung ʻchí. |
| A shower of rain fell just now. | Shik, ˌloi lòk$_2$ yat, chan$^2$ ʻü. |
| As large as a cloud of dust. | Yat, chan$^2$ ˌchʻan kómʼ tái$^2$. |
| A sudden breath of floral perfume. | Fat, ˌín yat, chan$^2$ ˏfá ˏhéung. |
| A sudden stroke of vertigo. | Sáp, ˌshí yat, chan$^2$ ˏwan ˌmai. |
| All at once I have forgotten his name. | Yat, chan$^2$ móng$^2$ kíʼ ʻkʻü kíúʼ mat, ˌming. |
| Just before a gleam of light darted out. | Tsau$^2$ ˏsín chʻut, yat, chan$^2$ yat$_2$ ˌtʻau. |
| Like a cloud of smoke. | Yat, chan$^2$ ˏín ʻkóm yéung$^2$. |
| Puff after puff of hot air ascended up. | Yat, chan$^2$ chan$^2$ ít$_2$ híʼ ˏshing ʻshéung ˌlai. |
| A cloud darkened the moon. | Yat, chan$^2$ ˌwan ˏché chü$^2$ kóʼ üt$_2$. |
| To-day we have a clear sky. | ˏKam yat$_2$ ʻhò tak, yat, chan$^2$ ˏtʻín. |
| In an instant he wrote it off. | Yat, chan$^2$ ˏkán tsau$^2$ ʻsé ʻhí lók,. |

14. *Nap* 粒 a kernel of rice, is applied to almost all small and roundish things, of whatever kind or material they may be, as buttons, small weights, seed, pockmarks, &c.

| | |
|---|---|
| As much as one bean. | Yat, nap, tau$^2$ kómʼ ˏtó. |
| As high as a dice. | Yat, nap, shik, kómʼ ˏkò. |
| Some more pieces of silver in your fob. | ˌHó ˏpáu chung$^2$ ʻyau ʻkí nap, ˌngan. |
| A grain of sand fell into the eye. | Yat, nap, ˏshá tít, yap, ʻngán. |

---

term for a uniform set of inscriptions consisting of four rolls, often hung up in sitting-rooms. A set of them is called a *fú* 副.—*Kan hó tsò* 僅可做 'barely can do,' means that the roll is just enough, there is nothing over and nothing short.—*Kák lí* 隔離 means adjoining, next door; it is also sometimes applied to dwellings two or three removes, to one's neighbors, &c.

13. *Notes.*—*Sáp shí* 霎時 is a local phrase of much the same import as *fat ín*.—*Yat chan* 一陣 means one instant, one moment's passage of time, in an instant; in this sentence and in the 9th, it is not used as a classifier.—*Tsau sín* 就先 means just before, directly before.—*Shing shéung* 陞上 is like the English phrase ascended up.

14. *Notes.*—The first expression is sometimes used in jest when ridiculing anything as being very small; the second is used when speaking contemptuously of a person, he is as high as—*yat nap shik*

| | |
|---|---|
| This orange has twenty seeds. | ꜀Ní kò' ꜀kóm ᶜyau í² shap꜀ nap꜄ hat꜀. |
| A pimple has come on his hand. | ᶜShau ꜀shang yat꜄ nap꜄ tsít꜄ ᶜtsai. |
| Like a grain of fish spawn. | Yat꜄ nap꜄ ꜁ü ꜀ch'un kòm' yéung². |
| There are two spots on the ear. | ᶜI' ꜀pín ᶜyau ᶜléung nap꜄ mak꜀. |
| Several pearls hanging from the forehead. | Ngák꜀ shéung² tíú' ᶜkí nap꜄ ꜀chan ꜀chü. |
| Fasten on a button. | ꜀Ting ꜀fán yat꜄ nap꜄ ᶜnau. |

15. *Ch'éung* 塲 is an arena, a parade-ground, a thrashing-floor, a piece of ground laid out and appropriated to some particular object; its application as a classifier intimates more duration or extent than *chan* 陣, No. 13.

| | |
|---|---|
| A heavy rain fell before. | ꜀Sín ꜁shí lòk꜀ yat꜄ ꜁ch'éung tái² ꜁ü. |
| Several years before a fire burned many shops. | ꜀Sín ᶜkí ꜁nín kó' ꜁ch'éung ꜀fó ᶜshíú ᶜhò ꜀tó p'ò'. |
| Year before last a freshet rose to the gateway. | ꜁Ts'ín ꜁nín kó' ꜁ch'éung ᶜshui ꜁sham tò' ꜁mún ᶜhau. |
| A storm of wind blowing threw down all the pears. | ᶜKwan yat꜄ ꜁ch'éung kü² ᶜtá lòk꜀ sái' kó' tik꜄ ꜀shá ꜁lí. |
| Obtained nothing but a spell of joy. | Chán² tak꜄ yat꜄ ꜁ch'éung ꜀fún ᶜhí. |
| Did it all for nothing. | Tsò² tak꜄ yat꜄ ꜁ch'éung ꜀hung. |
| I think you have a fit of vexation. | ᶜNgó ᶜkú ᶜní ᶜyau yat꜄ ꜁ch'éung ꜁fán ᶜnò. |
| I knew there would be an altercation. | ᶜTsò ꜀chí ᶜyau yat꜄ ꜁ch'éung ᶜch'áu náu². |
| I think I was very lucky. | ꜀Tò sün' yat꜄ ꜁ch'éung ᶜts'oi. |

---

一粒色 a dice.—*Hat* 核 a kernel, is sometimes also read *wat*.—*Tsít tsai* 癤仔 is a pimple or pustule coming on the skin, arising from impure blood.—*Ch'un* 橓 spawn or eggs is a general term for the ova of fish, frogs, &c.—*Mak* 癦 compounded of *ink* and *disease*, is a vulgar and local character, and appears as if intended to describe the thing it signifies, a black spot on the skin.

15. *Notes*.—*Sham* 浸 is here a verb, to deepen,—the freshet deepened to the gateway.—*Kwan* 滚 means to bubble, to boil up, and is applied to the *kü* 颶 or storm in allusion to the turmoil it causes.—*Sái* 嘥 is a provincial word for the whole.—*Chán* 賺 means to get profit; 'profited only one ebullition of joy' is a phrase used when a man's trading speculations bring him only a prospect of pleasing profit and no gain.—*Hung* 空 means empty; 'done got one spell of emptiness' is the literal rendering of the whole sentence.—*Fán nò* 煩惱 is vexatious annoyance, what discomposes a man's equanimity.—*Tsò chí* 早知 early knew is equivalent to I knew beforehand.—*Ch'áu náu* 炒鬧 is an altercation, a row.—*Tò sün* 都算 altoge-

16. *Túi* 隊 strictly means a hundred men formed into a company; also a collection of people, a group, a party. It is never applied to inanimate things.

| | |
|---|---|
| Several parties of men going to see the play. | ʻYau ʻkí túi² ˏyan hüʼ ʻtʻai híʼ. |
| A bevy of ladies in the garden. | ˓Fá ˏüen yatˀ túi² ʻnü ˏyan. |
| A flock of wild geese on the beach. | ˓Shá ˓tán yatˀ túi² ngán². |
| A school of fishes leaped out. | Yatˀ túi² ˏü ˏyau ʻhí. |

17. *Kwan* 羣 means a herd or flock, and differs but little from the preceding, and in most cases the two can be used interchangeably; it however applies rather to collections containing a large number of individuals of the same kind, while *túi* refers to a smaller group.

| | |
|---|---|
| A flock of sheep at the foot of the hill. | ˓Shán kéukˀ yatˀ ˏkwan ˏyéung. |
| A flock of wild ducks flew past. | Yatˀ ˏkwan ʻyé ápˀ ˏfí kwóʼ. |
| A great entertainment of all the ministers. | Tái² ínʼ ˏkwan ˏshan. |
| Three companies and five parties always go a hunting. | ˏShí ˏshí ˓sám ˏkwan ʻʼng túi² hüʼ ʻtá líp₂. |

18. *Tát* 笪 in the Canton dialect means a bamboo screen hung before a door, woven coarser than the *chuk pik* 竹壁 or the bamboo wall; its signification in the Imperial Dictionary differs from this local use. As a classifier it is applied to irregular pieces or spots.

| | |
|---|---|
| The sleeve of the coat has an indelible spot. | ˓Shám tsau² ʻyau yatˀ tátˀ yanʼ tsikˀ. |
| A spot of rust has come on that sword. | Kóʼ ʻpá kímʼ ˓shang yatˀ tátˀ sauʼ. |

---

ther calculate, taking all things into account.—*Tsʻoi* 彩 here is much the same as the word chance, luck. The phrase is used when a man escapes a great danger in getting a less injury; for instance, when his hand is broke instead of his neck.

16. *Notes.*—*Shá tán* 沙灘 is often applied to stony beaches where the tide-water runs over the shingle rapidly; *tán* alone means a rapid in a river.—*Yau hí* 游起 applied to fish, refers to their gamboling and leaping out of the water.

17. *Notes.*—The term *yé áp* 野鴨 is closely translated by wild duck.—*Tái in* 大宴 means literally 'great entertained,' in which *tái* refers to a noun *in* understood; the sentence in full would read 'with a great entertainment entertained all the officers.'—*Shí shí* 時時 is a common word for continually, habitually; *tá lip* 打獵 simply means to hunt, *tá* denoting action.

18. *Notes.*—*Yan tsik* 印跡 seal's traces, is applied to almost any

| | |
|---|---|
| The stone steps have produced a patch of green mold. | ‹Tʻín ‹kái ‹shang yat› tát› ‹tsʻing ˏtʻoi. |
| In the south arises a black cloud. | ˏNám pín² ʻhí yat› tát› ‹ú ˏwan. |
| The bottom of the vessel has a leak, and the water runs in. | ˏShün ʻtai ˢyau yat› tát› sham' ʻshui yap₂ ˏlai. |
| This mat has a rent. | ‹Ní ‹chéung tsik₂ ˢyau yat› tát› lán² ké'. |
| This jar certainly has a leaky crack. | ‹Ní kó' ‹áng pít› ˢyau yat› tát› lau² lá'. |
| The flesh of his hand is broken. | ˢKʻü ʻshau ˢyau yat› tát› lán² yuk₂. |

19. *Fú* 副 means a secondary, an assistant, and frequently occurs in official titles; it is employed to denote a set of things, all of which are used for one purpose, as tools, plates.

| | |
|---|---|
| Lately purchased a set of ebony tables and chairs. | ‹Sun chí' yat› fú' ‹sün ‹chí ˏtʻoi ʻí. |
| Presented a set of *kénám* beads to him. | Sung' yat› fú' ˏké ˏnám ‹chü kwó' ˢkʻü. |
| Spread out a set of writing apparatus on the study table. | ‹Shü wai² ʻpái yat› fú' ˏman ˏfóng sz'' ʻpò. |
| Hung up two sets of musical instruments in the hall. | Tái² ˏlau kwá' ˢléung fú² ˏín sók›. |
| His whole disposition is bad. | ˢKʻü kó² fú' ‹sam ˏchʻéung ˏ'm ʻhò. |
| That lad is incomparably clever. | Kó' kó' sai' ‹man ʻtsai yat› fú' ‹tʻín ‹tsʻung. |
| He at least has an excellent memory. | ˢKʻü ʻhò tsʻoi² ˢyau yat› fú' kí' sing'. |

---

kind of foul and indelible spot, such as grease, or ink, on clothes on paint, &c.—*Shang* 生 in the second and third sentences is an active verb,—'that sword bears a spot of rust.'—*Tʻin kái* 天 堦 is the name given to the stone steps in a courtyard.—*Tʻoi* 苔 is a general term for minute cryptogamous plants.—*Sham* 滲 is usually a verb, and means to leak, but here refers to the leaky plank or place.—*Ké* 嘅 is used in this sentence as a sign of the genitive, having *chʻü* 處 place, or some such word understood.—*Lá* 罅 or *lau lá* is the provincial word for a crack.

19. *Notes.*—*Chí* 置 strictly means to purchase something valuable, or an article which is intended to be durable, or to be kept permanently.—*Sün chí* 酸 枝 is a heavy black wood used in making fine furniture.—The *ké nám* 茄 南 is a porous fragrant wood used to make dress beads.—The *man fóng sz' pò* 文 房 四 寶 or four precious things of the library, are the pencil, stone, ink, and water cup.—*I'n sók* 絃 索 is a term for stringed instruments of music, as the lute, pípá, rebeck, &c.—*Sam chʻéung* 心 腸 heart and bowels

| | |
|---|---|
| Lend him that set of cups and plates for a while. | Kung² ʻkʻü tsé' kó' yat, fú' ʻún típ, ʻshai chü². |
| One half of this set of instruments is useles. | ˓Ní fú' hí' kü² yat, pún' ˏ'm ʻshai tak, ké'. |

20. *Kín* 件 means to distinguish things individually, to denote a particular subject, affair, or article. It is used in connection with articles of dress, items of business, food, goods, and many other nouns that otherwise have nothing in common.

| | |
|---|---|
| Have you sewed that robe yet? | Kó' kín² ˏpʻò ˏlün hí' mí² ˏtsʻang? |
| There has happened a truly remarkable affair. | ʻYau yat, kín² sz'² ˓chan ching' chʻut, ˏkʻí. |
| Eat ten and more cakes at tiffin. | Án' chau' shik, ʻlíú shap, ʻki kín² ʻtím ˓sam. |
| To each man was distributed eight bits of pork. | ʻMúi ˏyan pái' pát, kín² ˓chü yuk,. |
| This sort of goods is indeed difficult of sale. | ˓Ní yat, kín² fó' kók, hai² ók, mái². |
| I do not want that thing. | ˏ'M íú' kó' kín² ˓tung ˓sai. |

21. *Fái* 塊 is a clod, a segment, a piece, or portion of a larger thing having no definite or regular shape, and is applied to small pieces of such articles as are often cut or divided, as earth, paper, wood, stone, cloth, &c.

| | |
|---|---|
| As thin as a piece of paper. | Yat, fái' ʻchí kóm' pók,. |
| Boiled three slices of beef. | Sháp, ʻlíú ˓sám fái' ˏngau yuk,. |
| This piece of floss is the best. | ˓Ní yat, fái' ˏyung chí' ʻhò. |

---

denote the heart of a man, his disposition.—*Tʻín tsʻung* 天聰 is heavenly cleverness; *yat fú tʻín tsung* is the whole assortment of heaven-conferred talents.—*Hò tsʻoi* 好彩 is a good part, a good quality, and is here used in connection with something which has gone before. *Shai chü* 使住 is to use for a short time until he can get a set for himself.—*Hí kü* 器具 denotes implements of any kind, mechanical, surgical, or others.

20. *Notes.*—*Pʻò* 袍 is a long robe of ceremony used by official persons.—*Lün* 聯 is to make up a dress from fresh materials.—*Chan ching* 眞正 is a dissyllabic and common phrase for truly, really.—*Tím sam* 點心 'add heart' is the general name given to small cakes eaten at luncheon.—*Pái* 派 in this sentence has its nominative understood.—*Kók* 確 is an adverb somewhat like *chan ching* in its signification.—*Tung sai* 東西 is a common term nearly equivalent to *mat kín* 物件 or thing.

21. *Notes.*—*Yat kín chü yuk* 一件猪肉 in the preceding paragraph, is a bit of pork, such as a host would help his guest to at

| | |
|---|---|
| Sweep away that clod of dirt. | Sò' kó' yat, fái' ˌnai hü'. |
| Just like a leaf. | Tsuk, ˌmò yat, fái' íp,. |
| Several tiles are broken on the roof. | Uk, púi' 'kí fái' ˌngá lít, ˌlíú. |
| The herdboy has broken a grave-stone. | Muk, ˌt'ung 'tá lán² yat, fái' mò² ˌpí. |

22. *T'óng* 繶 is a large cord or rope, and is applied to nets, ladders, sails, &c. It is a word very seldom met with, and its use in classifying the few nouns to which it is applied is a provincial one; other characters of the same sound are sometimes used instead of this one.

| | |
|---|---|
| There is a net on the deck. | ˌShün mín² ˌyau yat, ˌt'óng 'móng. |
| Altogether ten lifting-nets on the jetty for catching fish. | Tò² ˌt'au kung² shap, ˌt'óng ˌtsang 'au ˌü. |
| A passage-boat sails with three suit of sails. | Yat, chik, tò² 'shai ˌsám ˌt'óng ˌlí. |
| He has two suits of musketoe curtains. | ˌK'ü ˌyau ˌléung ˌt'óng ˌman chéung². |
| A sun screen. | Yat, ˌt'óng ít, ˌché. |
| Four ladders. | Sz' ˌt'óng ˌt'ai wáng². |

23. *Hóng* 行 is a row, a line, a regular series, and is in most cases closely rendered by a row, as a row of men, of characters, of flowers, &c.

| | |
|---|---|
| That row of willows will soon flower. | Kó' ˌhóng ˌlau ˌtséung kan² ˌhoi ˌfá. |
| The seats are arranged into rows. | 'Tsz' ˌpáng kán' ˌhoi yat, ˌhóng ˌhóng. |

---

table; *yat fái ngau yuk* 一塊牛肉 is such a slice of beef as he would buy at market.—*Yung* 絨 is floss, or the silk used in embroidery.—*Tsuk mò* 足莫 complete [to the] pattern, is like the phrase *tsuk ts'z'* on a preceding page.—*Muk tung* 牧童 is a general name for herdboys, whatever animals they may watch.—*Mò pí* 墓碑 is a gravestone.

22. *Notes.*—*Tò t'au* 渡頭 (also sometimes erroneously called *pò t'au* 步頭) is a stone landing-place or jetty running out into the water a few feet, used either as a ferry, or for the convenience of the private owner; the term *má t'au* 馬頭 often applied to them, originally denoted that horses and vehicles were ferried.—*Tò* 渡 is to pass across, through, or over, and is here used as a noun by metonymy, to denote that by which the passage is made, viz., the passage-boat.—*Shai* 駛 means to sail.—*Ít ché* 熱遮 is a movable screen made of cloth, placed on dwelling-houses above the windows.

23. *Notes.*—*Tséung kan* 將近 is always applied to time, 'about

| | |
|---|---|
| A line of war boats is anchored near the beach. | ʻHoi ˏpin pok˒ yat˒ ˏhong chín' ˏshün. |
| Among the clouds are several lines of geese in flocks. | ˏWan ˏkán shò' ˏhóng ngán² tsz'². |

24. *Ká* 架 is a wooden frame, a stand on which things are placed, a shelf or rack for holding articles; it is applied to only a few nouns.

| | |
|---|---|
| Eight fire-engines went to put out the fire. | Pát˒ ká' ʻshui ˏch'é hü' kau' ʻfó. |
| In the doorway is hung a variegated tablet. | ˏMún ʻhau kwá' yat˒ ká' ʻts'oi ˏmún. |
| A lute is placed on the table. | Chéuk˒ shéung² fóng' yat˒ ká' k'am. |
| I have read all the books in these stands. | ˏNí ʻkí ká' ˏshü ʻngó ˏtò tuk₂ kwó'. |
| Those two pair of scales do not weigh alike. | Kó' ʻléung ká' ˏt'ín ˏp'íng túi² kwó' ˏtò ˏ'm ˏt'ung. |

25. *Tó* 朵 is a pendent branch, a twig of a cluster of flowers; it is applied to only a few nouns.

| | |
|---|---|
| In that nosegay of flowers, one branch has seven flowers, and four branches have three [each]. | Kó' yat˒ chát˒ ˏfá ʻyau yat˒ ˏchí ts'at˒ ʻtó, sz'' ˏchí ˏsám ʻtó. |
| On the hill-top [rests] a red cloud. | ˏShán ʻting yat˒ ʻtó ˏhung ˏwan. |

---

nearing,' i. e. soon.—*Tsz' páng* 子棚 is the name given to the seats, at a theatre.—*Yat hóng₂ hóng* 一行行 is a row of rows, or many rows.—The Chinese very often begin a sentence with an adjunct governed by a preposition understood, as in this phrase, where the reader is left to supply the proper one: *hoi pín* 海邊 means simply the beach, but the writer concludes that no one need be told that it is *near* the beach, where the *chín shün* 戰船 or war-vessels, are anchored.—*Ngán tsz'* 雁字 geese character, alludes to the well-known wedge form of the flock adopted by these birds in their migrations.

24. *Notes.—Kau fó* 救火 prevent the fire, or cause it cease, is the term for extinguishing a conflagration.—The *ts'oi mún* 綵門 is a kind of triangular frame, now usually painted red, but anciently made of variegated silk, which is hung at the top of the doors of all governmental offices, and of private houses during marriage festivities, for the sake of ornament. It will be seen that this sentence begins with an adjunct having the preposition governing it understood, and *kwá* 掛 is in the passive voice.—*K'am* 琴 a lute, and other stringed instruments of music are classified by *ká*, and also by *kó* 個; wind and other instruments by the latter alone.—*Túi* 兌 means to weigh.

25. *Notes.—Chát* 札 is a bunch, a sheaf.—*Ting* 頂 is the apex the top, the crown.—In the second sentence, the substantive verb is

| | |
|---|---|
| This fire is gone out. | ꜀Ní ꜂tó ꜂fò sik꜇ ꜂hú. |
| I saw a large mushroom this morning. | ꜀Kam ꜀chíú kín꜄ yat꜇ ꜂tó tái² ꜁kw'an. |

26. *F'in* 片 is a slice, a piece, a slip, a shred, and is used in these senses as well as figuratively.

| | |
|---|---|
| When eating fish, it is necessary to take some slices of ginger. | Shik₂ ꜀ü pít꜇ ú꜄ lók₂ ꜂kí p'ín꜄ ꜀kéung. |
| What he says is all a lie. | ꜁K'ü ꜂kóng ꜀ts'an ꜀tò hai² yat꜇ p'ín꜄ tái꜄ wá² ké꜄. |
| That which you told me was all false. | ꜁Ní wá² kó꜄ tün² sz'² yat꜇ p'ín꜄ ꜂ká ké꜄. |
| He gives it to you from his heart. | ꜁K'ü yat꜇ p'ín꜄ ꜀sam sz'² sung꜄ ꜂pí ꜁ní. |

27. *Tsik* 席 is a table spread, a repast or feast; it is also used to denote a few words, a conversation or discourse.

| | |
|---|---|
| He has spread a banquet and invited guests. | Pán² yat꜇ tsik₂ ꜂tsau ꜂ts'ing ꜀yan hák꜇. |
| During that conversation, Ts'ò Tsò, with closed mouth, said nothing. | Kó꜄ yat꜇ tsik₂ wá² shüt꜇ tak꜇, ꜀Ts'ò ꜀Tsò ꜂á ꜂hau ꜀mò ꜀ín. |
| The priest has spread several courses of vegetables and sent them as a present. | Tái² ꜀sz' pán² ꜂kí tsik₂ ꜀chái sung꜄ ꜀lai. |
| The geomancer says that in a certain place is a plat of lucky ground. | ꜀Fung ꜂shui ꜀sín ꜀shang wá² ꜁mau ch'ü꜄ ꜁yau yat꜇ tsik₂ ꜂hò ꜀shán tí². |

---

omitted, (which is very frequently the case when it follows an initial clause governed by a preposition,) and is here better translated in English by some word more explicit.—*Yat tó fó* 一朶火 is a roll of bamboo paper used by the Chinese as a match.—*Kw'an* 菌 is a general name for large agarics.

26. *Notes.*—*Kóng ts'an* 講親 is a local phrase for a whole narrative or relation, which is—*yat p'in tái wá* 一片大話 one piece great talk—all a lie.—*Yat p'in sam sz'* 一片心事 one slice heart's act, means with honest intentions, with the whole heart; the gift itself may be contemptible, but the motive was respectful.

27. *Notes.*—*Pán* 辦 means to regulate, put in order or get a feast ready in all respects for the guests.—*A' hau* 啞口 is dumbing his mouth.—*Tái sz'* 大師 is a respectful term for a Budhist priest.—*Chái* 齋 is a term for all vegetable food, the tenets of this sect prohibiting all flesh and fish.—The *fung shui sín shang* 風水先生 is a class of people who are always consulted in fixing the position of graves, so that the resting-place of deceased friends may be in a fortunate spot.

28. *T'un* 團 is a conglomerated mass, an united harmonious body. It is applied to only a few nouns.

| | |
|---|---|
| Buy a roll of ink for me. | Kung² ˊngó ˊmái yat, ˏt'ün mak, |
| Like a lump of dough. | Yat, ˏt'ün mín² ˋkóm yéung². |
| A harmonious spirit. | Yat, ˏt'ün ˏwó hí'. |
| A fighting couple on the ground. | ˋTá ˏmái yat, ˏt'ün. |

In order to make the list of classifiers more complete, several are here placed together which are of very limited use, being employed to denote only two or three kinds of things, the principal of which are placed under them; the classifier, or the noun classified, is put in italics in the translation. The number of nouns being so few, the characters are placed in the opposite column instead of their sounds, consequently very few notes are necessary to explain the sentences.

| | |
|---|---|
| 29. When changing the dress for the season, you must buy *a* new *cap*. | 頂一過買要季換新帽咯 |
| Call *a sedan-chair* for me. | 嚟轎頂一叫我共 |
| 30. For a thousand cash to hire *a carriage* to ramble over the hills. | 車乘一僱錢千一遊山 |
| Ask him for how many cash he will let *a sedan* to go twenty *li?* | 要路里十二佢問轎乘一僱錢多幾 |
| 31. On the hill-side is *a* small four-wheeled *carriage*. | 小輪四輛一邊山車 |

---

28. *Notes.—Kung* 共 is here used in a local sense, meaning the same as *toi* 代 instead of, for, &c.—*Mín* 麵 flour, here means unbaked or unboiled dough. This phrase is sometimes applied in ridicule to excessively corpulent people.—*Wó hí* 和氣 is an expression for the good feeling which should be found between married people or partners in trade.—*Tá mái yat t'ün* 打埋一團 fighting closed one heap, is one of those peculiar phrases in Chinese which cannot be translated otherwise than by an equivalent phrase. A couple of wrestlers on the ground are supposed to be rolled close enough together to be termed a heap or roll.

*Notes.*—29. The phrase *ún kwai* means changing for the season; the officers of government are notified when they must put on their winter or summer dresses. *Yat ting kiú* is a large sedan, such as are

32. How much postage does he want for carrying *a letter* to Canton.

要幾多水腳寄一
封信去省呢

33. I wish you to bind *one quire* of paper into three books.

一刀紙要釘兩個
簿

34. At that place there is *a play* in four acts.

個處有四本戲做

He has *a book* in his hand the whole day.

成日揸住一本書

35. That elderly man has *two mustaches*.

個個伯爺兩匹鬚

*That horse* is exceedingly fat and strong.

個一匹馬極肥壯

36. One volume is missing from *this set* of books.

呢套書失了一部

That friend has lent me *a suit* of ceremonial garments.

個位朋友借了我
一套袍褂

37. That *suit* of clothes was not washed clean.

先個一脱衣服洗
唔乾净

38. The business of this shop is divided into *eight shares*.

鋪頭分作八股生
意

That *essay* is divided into three principal heads.

個篇文章分三大
股作

39. In *one game* of chess to consume the livelong day.

以一局棋消永日

40. Plant *a thousand bamboos* about the door.

門外種千竿竹

41. At early morn reverently to arrange *a cluster* of incense sticks.

清早誠心裝一炷
香

---

used by officers of government, gentlemen, &c., having a knob or ball on the top: 30.—*Yat shing kiú* is a small chair, just large enough for a person to sit in, usually made very cheaply.—32. *Fung* is also applied to small packages of coin, sealed and stamped.—34.—*Sz' pún hí* is also usually understood to intimate that the play will last four days, as well as consist of four acts.—41. A cluster of incense sticks, *yat chü héung*, consists of three or five sticks.

42. Among the hills is *a band* of daring robbers. 山中有一夥大賊

43. Not worth *two cash*. 唔值得兩文錢

44. Men-of-war have many tens of *cannon*. 戰船有幾十門大炮

His *kind* of business is really very difficult to do. 佢個門生意確係難做

45. A *rasher* of pork can also be termed a *slice*. 一塊豬肉能話一方

*A cake* of ink has six sides. 一方墨有六面

46. Vendued ten *pieces* of red floss. 投得十疋紅絨

47. The reflection of the moon in the river is like *a pearl*. 月照江心一顆珠

Went straight into the encampment of the robbers, and cut off more than *ten heads*. 直入賊寨斬首十餘顆

48. I heard *a piece* of news yesterday. 昨日聽一段新聞

49. Still there is one *job* of work not yet done. 尚有一欵事未做

Respectfully spread out several *sorts* of trifles for you. 謹具微儀數欵

50. *A visitor* has come to visit you. 有位人客來探你

Lately arose an efficacious *deity*. 新有一位靈菩薩

51. For this kind I owe in all *a* hundred *dollars*. 此項共該銀一百圓

---

47. The first-part of the sentence, *üt chiú kóng sam*, is in opposition to the second, *yat fó chü*, the verb being omitted; in this instance, the ellipsis would be supplied by *ü* 如, or *ts'z'* 似, to resemble. *Fó* frequently occurs in books, applied to beads, kernels, fruit, or small round things, but is not often heard in conversation.—48. *Tün* is also applied to a piece of land, to an order given to a servant, and in common with the next, to an affair of business.—49. *I'* 儀 cere-

52. He lives in the third *story*.
佢住第三層樓

53. When worshiping at the tombs in the spring, you must secure several *strips* of paper on the top of the hillock.
清明拜山必壓幾頁紙錢在山頭

54. I have sent two or three *messengers* one after another to hasten him.
使過兩三道人去催佢

Specially sent down *one* imperial *command*.
特降諭旨一道

55. He has *a plaster* on his wrist.
佢手眼貼一貼膏藥

Received some *papers* of rouge.
收埋幾貼胭脂

56. There are several *officers* in the hall consulting on business.
有幾員官在花廳議事

57. Out of the window are several very brilliant *stars*.
窓外數點星甚光明

58. An old merry-andrew carrying *a load* of boxes on his shoulder.
耍戲法佬擔一擔箱

The porter has carried his *baggage* to the wrong place.
挑夫擔錯佢個擔行李

59. Passed straight through several *successive doors*.
直入經過幾重門

60. Each side has *a baluster*.
每邊有一[口棟]欄杆

Before the arbor is planted a *row* of olive flowers.
亭前植一[口棟]桂花

---

mony, propriety, is here used by metonymy for that which propriety or custom in certain cases requires to be presented to a friend, and which the donor calls *mi* 微 trifling.—53. *I'p* is sometimes applied to the folds of cloth as they lie one above another.—57. *Tím* is also applied to the strokes of the clock, drops of water, &c.; stars are also classified by *nap* (No. 14).—58. *Tám* is a pecul in weight, and being a fair load for a man to carry, the word has come to denote a load

61. That child has a *string* of cash about him. 細蚊仔馱一串錢

62. I have *one* valuable *sword* which I will give to your excellency. 某有寶劍一口送與丞相

63. Send this frame to the metropolis to glaze *a mirror* in it. 寄呢個架去省鑲番一面鏡

To stick *a* small *banner* in the lookout house on the city wall. 城樓上插一面小旗

64. It is spoken of as having been *a noble act*. 論起來也是一宗美事

His *whole disposition* is excessively bad. 佢宗品性實首惡

He has proposals to engage in many *sorts* of business. 佢有幾宗頭路

65. Only one *fish* in the basket. 籃內獨裝一尾魚

66. There are several *plays* acted here every year. 年年呢處都有幾檯戲做

67. Several tens of *processions* have gone to usher in the spring. 有幾十板春色去迎春

That monastery has at once bought a hundred and more *frames* of bean curd. 個間寺連氣買百幾板荳腐

68. He felled that *tree* at the side of the house. 倒了屋側個根樹

In Shingtò are eight hundred mulberries. 成都有桑八百株

69. Holding a *pencil* in the hand. 手拈一管筆

---

that a man can shoulder at once.—60. *Lát* is a local word, for which there is no proper character; it is locally used for a row of things with interstices between them, as a row of trees, of boats, of stakes, of men, and is frequently interchanged with *hóng* (No. 23).—61. *Ch'ün* is applied to things run upon a cord, to a line of ants, of men moving, &c.—62. *Shing séung* is the prime minister, and the title is used in

The tone of this *flute* does not equal that. 呢一管笛聽音不及佢個管

70. On the summit of the hill, *a seat* can be erected. 山頂可以起得一所屋

---

direct address.—64. "Spoken-of rise coming (afterwards) altogether is one affair fine action," is the literal rendering of this sentence.—67. Processions are got up by priests, by corporations, or by governmental people; they are partly of a civic, partly of a religious, and partly of a festive character.—68. A tree is also termed *yat pó shú*, *yat tʻiú shü*, *yat hóm shü*, and *yat pún shü*.

The number of words which might be strictly called classifiers cannot be exactly ascertained, but it is not supposed the preceding list contains all of them. A word is sometimes used to denote the individuals of a certain class of objects in one connection, which would not be understood if separated from that connection. As an instance of this, see No. IX of the lessons in the last chapter, page 117, where *fó* 顆 and *múi* 枚 are both used instead of the noun *lí* 梨, as classifying that fruit. In fact, the use of this class of words appears to be subject to no certain rules, one word being applied to an object in one part of the country, and another to the same object elsewhere. It is said that in some parts of this province, *chik* 隻 is applied to a man, as well as animals; *chéung* 張 to vessels; and other similar discrepancies. For many of the words employed by the people of Canton, (as was observed of *tát*, No. 18, and *tʻóng*, No. 22,) there are no appropriate characters, and every person uses such as come the nearest in sound. In diffuse composition, the use of the classifiers is frequently avoided by depending upon the context to particularize the noun; in higher or terse writing they seldom occur, nor in fact are they required, when the name of the thing itself is presented to the eye. To what extent the application of this class of words in other dialects of China is the same as in that of Canton, could be readily ascertained by writing the sentences out in full, and presenting the characters to a person familiar with that dialect; and if he was unused to the colloquial idiom of the sentence, he still could reärrange the nouns by such terms as he was in the habit of designating them.

# Chapter Eighth.

## EXERCISES IN TRANSLATING.

---

The literal version and sounds of the characters of the lessons contained in this chapter are only given, as the student is expected by this time to have learned enough of the idiom of the language to be able to translate them into good English without much if any assistance. In translating from Chinese into English, great care ought to be taken to avoid inversions of style from following too closely the Chinese idiom, which will often render the style of the version stiff, without adding to its perspicuity. Compound or dissyllabic terms are common in Chinese writing, and stereotyped phrases that are seldom if ever separated, but which contain only one idea; these are in some cases properly translated by a single word. Knowledge of the meaning of the characters merely is not sufficient to make a person a good translator; he must attend also to the force of the word or phrase in its connection in the original so as to select an apt expression by which to render it. Some attention should be paid to such peculiar phrases in the original as are deserving of being transfused into the version, while too close a fidelity will make it inelegant or vapid. Good taste will prove the best guide in the choice of words, and teach when to express a native phrase in its literal dress, and when to render it by an equivalent; so that while the reader is not offended by barbarisms and harsh epithets, he will feel that he is possessed of whatever in the original is witty in thought, and elegant in expression.

### No. I.—Cleverness of Hung Yung.

(見三國志 卷之六 第十一回)

北 海 孔 融 字 文 舉 魯 國 曲 阜 人 也
*Pak˒ ‘hoi, ‘Hung ˏYung, tsz’² ˏMan ‘kü, ˢLú kwók˒, Huk˒ fau² ˏyan ˢyá*
Pakhoi, Hung Yung, styled Mankü, [was a] Lú state, Hukfau man

孔 子 二 十 世 孫 泰 山 都 尉
*‘Hung ‘tsz’ í² shap₂ shai’ ˓sün. T‘ái’ ˓shán ˓tò wai’,*
Confucius twentieth generation’s descendant. T’áishán general soother’

孔 宙 之 子 自 少 聰 明 年 十 歲
*‘Hung Chau² ˓chí ‘tsz’. Tsz’² shiú’ ˓ts‘ung ˏming; ˏnín shap₂ sui’*
Hung Chau’ ’s son. From youth clever intelligent; aged ten years

時 往 謁 河 南 尹 李 膺 閽 人 難 之
*ˏshí, ˢwóng ít˒ ˏHó ˏnám ˢwan, ˢLí ˓Ying; ˓fan ˏyan ˏnán ˓chí.*
time, went visit Hónám officer, Lí Ying; door porter hindered him.

融 曰 我 係 李 相 通 家 及 入 見
*ˏYung üt₁, ‘Ngó hai² ‘Lí séung’ ‹t‘ung ‹ká; k‘ap₂ yap₂ kín’.*
Yung said, I am Lí minister allied family; and entering saw.

膺 問 曰 汝 祖 與 吾 祖 何 親
*‹Ying man² üt₂, ‘ü ‘tsò ‘ü ˏ’ng ‘tsò, ˏhó ‹ts‘an?*
Ying asked saying, Your ancestor and my ancestor, what connection?

融 曰 昔 孔 子 曾 問 禮 于 老 子
*ˏYung üt₂, Sik₁ ‘Hung ‘tsz’ ˏts‘ang man² ‘lai ‹ü ‘Lò ‘tsz’;*
Yung replied, Anciently Confucius already asked propriety of Laoutsze:

融 與 君 豈 非 累 世 通 家 膺 大
*ˏYung ‘ü ‹kwan: ‘hí ‹fi ‘lui shai’, ‹t‘ung ‹ká! ‹Ying tái²*
Yung with Lí: how not bound generation, allied family! Ying much

奇 之
*ˏk‘i ‹chí.*
surprised-at him.

少 頃 大 中 大 夫 陳 煒 至 膺 指
*‘Shiú ‘k‘ing tái² ‹chung tái² ‹fú ˏCh‘an ‘Wai chí’, ‹Ying ‘chí*
Short space, principal inner great lord Ch‘an Wai coming, Ying pointed-to

融 曰 此 奇 童 也 煒 曰 少 時 聰
*ˏYung üt₂, ‘Ts‘z’ ˏk‘i ˏt‘ung ‘yá. ‘Wai üt₂, Shiú’ ˏshí ‹ts‘ung*
Yung said, This remarkable lad. Wai replied, Young time clever

明 大 時 未 必 聰 明 融 即
*ˏming, tái² ˏshí mí² pít₁ ‹ts‘ung ˏming. ˏYung tsik₁*
intelligent, old time not certainly clever intelligent. Yung immediately

應 聲 曰 如 君 所 言 幼 時 必
*ying’ ‹shing üt₂, ˏü ‹kwan ‘shó ˏín, yau’ ˏshí pít₁*
echoing tone said, According-to honor what says, young time must

聰 明 者 煒 等 皆 笑 曰 此 子 長 成
*‹ts‘ung ˏming ‘ché. ‘Wai ‘tang ‹kái siú’ üt₂, ‘Ts‘z’ ‘tsz’ ‘chéung ˏshing,*
intelligent person. Wai others all laughing said, This child older become,

必 當 代 之 偉 器 也 自 此 得 名
*pít₁ ‹tóng toi² ‹chí ‘wai hí’ ‘yá. Tsz’² ‘ts‘z’ tak₁ ˏming.*
certainly present age ’s renowned individual. From this got reputation.

後 爲 北 海 太 守 極 好 賓 客
*Hau² ˏwai Pak₁ ‘hoi t‘ái’ shau’, kik₂. hò’ ‹pan hák₁;*
Afterwards was Pakhoi head defender, exceedingly loved entertain guests;

常 曰 座 上 客 常 滿 罇 中 酒
*ˏshéung üt₂, Tsó² shéung² hák₁ ˏshéung ‘mún, ‹tsun ‹chung ‘tsau*
usually remarking, Hall in guests always full, bottle in wine

不 空 吾 之 愿 也
*pat₁ ‹hung, ˏ’ng ‹chí ün² ‘yá.*
never empty, my ’s wish.

## No. II.—Scheme of Wóng Wan to inveigle Lü Pò.

## (見三國志卷之四第八回)

董 卓 一 日 大 會 百 官 酒 至
*Tung Ch'éuk yat yat tái úi pák kún; tsau chí*
Tung Ch'éuk one day greatly entertained all officers; wine reached

數 巡 呂 布 向 卓 耳 邊 語 卓
*shò ts'un, Lü Pò héung Ch'éuk í pín ü. Ch'éuk*
several bouts, Lü Pò turning-to Ch'éuk's ear side spoke. Ch'éuk

命 于 筵 上 揪 張 溫 下 堂 不 多
*ming ü in shéung tsau Chéung Wan há t'óng. Pat tó*
ordered from feast above carry Chéung Wan below hall. Not much

時 侍 從 將 紅 盤 托 張 溫 頭
*shí shí ts'ung, tséung hung p'ún t'ók Chéung Wan t'au,*
time, waiting follower, taking red waiter bearing Chéung Wan's head,

入 獻 百 官 魂 不 附 體 卓 笑
*yap hín. Pák kún wan pat fú t'ai. Ch'éuk siú*
entered handed-up. All officers' souls not left-in body. Ch'éuk laughing

曰 諸 公 勿 驚 張 溫 結 連 袁 術 欲
*üt, Chü kung mat king; Chéung Wan kít lín Un Shut, yuk*
said, All sirs no fear; Chéung Wan leagued joined Un Shut, about

圖 害 我 因 使 人 寄 書 來 錯
*t'ò hoi ngó; yan sz' yan kí shü loi, ts'ók*
scheming to-injure me; because messenger brought letter here, inadvertently

下 在 吾 兒 奉 先 處 故 斬 之 公 等
*há tsoi 'ng í Fung sín ch'ü, kú chám chí: kung tang*
delivered in my son Fungsín's place, therefore behead him: Sirs all

無 故 不 必 驚 畏 衆 官 唯 唯 而 散
*mò kú, pat pít king wai. Chung kún wai! wai! í sán.*
is-no cause, not need fear dread. All officers [said] Yes! Yes! and separated.

司 徒 王 允 歸 到 府 中 尋 思 今
*Sz' t'ò Wóng Wan kwai tò fú chung ts'am sz': Kam*
Chancellor Wóng Wan returning to house in deeply thought: This

日 席 間 之 事 坐 不 安 席 至 夜 深
*yat tsik kán chí sz', tsó pat ón tsik. Chí yé sham,*
day feast during 's acts, sitting not easy seat. At night deep,

月 明 策 杖 步 入 後 園 立 於
*üt ming ch'ák chéung, pò yap hau ün, lap ü*
moon bright, taking cane, walked into rear garden, standing at

荼 薇 架 側 仰 天 垂 淚 忽 聞 有
*t'ò mi ká chak, yéung t'ín shui lui, fat man yau*
small - rose frame side, looking-up heaven falling tears, suddenly heard was

入在牡丹亭畔長吁短嘆允
꜀yan tsoi$^2$ ꜂mau ꜀tán ꜀t'ing pún$^2$, ꜀ch'éung ꜀hü ꜂tün t'án꜃. ꜂Wan
person in peony arbor's side, long sighs short groans. Wan

潛步窺之乃府中歌妓貂蟬也
꜀ts'ím pò$^2$ ꜀kw'ai ꜀chí, ꜂nái ꜂fú ꜀chung ꜀kó kí$^2$ ꜀Tíú ꜀Shín ꜂yá.
carefully stepping watched person, was house in singing girl Tíú Shín.

其女自幼選入府中教以歌
꜀K'i ꜂nü tsz'$^2$ yau꜃ ꜂sün yap$_2$ ꜂fú ꜀chung, káu꜃ ꜂í ꜀kó
This girl from youth brought into house within, taught to sing

舞年方二八色伎俱佳允
꜂mò; ꜀nín ꜀fóng í$^2$ pát꜁, shik꜁ kí$^2$ ꜀k'ü ꜀kai. ꜂Wan
dance; age just twice eight, beauty accomplishments both superior. Wan

以親女待之是夜允聽良久
꜂í ꜀ts'an ꜂nü toi$^2$ ꜀chí. Shí$^2$ yé$^2$, ꜂Wan t'ing꜃ ꜀léung ꜂kau
as-if own daughter behaved her. In night, Wan listening good while

喝曰賤人將有私情耶貂蟬
hót꜁ üt$_2$, Tsín$^2$ ꜀yan ꜀tséung ꜂yau ꜀sz' ꜀ts'ing ꜂yé? ꜀Tíú ꜀Shín
exclaiming, said, Low person about having underhand designs eh? Tíú Shín

驚跪答曰賤妾安敢有私
꜀king kwai$^2$, táp꜁ üt$_2$, Tsín$^2$ ts'íp꜁ ꜀ón ꜂kóm ꜂yau ꜀sz'?
alarmed kneeled replied saying, Poor handmaid how dare have treachery?

允曰汝無所私何夜深於此長
꜂Wan üt$_2$, ꜂ü ꜀mò ꜂shó ꜀sz', ꜀hó yé$^2$ ꜀sham ꜀ü ꜂ts'z' ꜀ch'éung
Wan said, You nothing which-is secret, why night's depth in here long

嘆蟬曰容妾伸肺腑之言允曰
t'án꜃? ꜀Shín üt$_2$, ꜀Yung ts'íp꜁ ꜀shan fai꜃ ꜂fú ꜀chí ꜀ín. ꜂Wan üt$_2$,
sighs? Shín replied, Permit handmaid express inmost 's words. Wan said,

汝勿隱匿當實告我蟬曰妾蒙
꜂ü mat$_2$ ꜂yan nik꜁, ꜀tóng shat$_2$ kò꜃ ꜂ngó. ꜀Shín üt$_2$, Ts'íp꜁ ꜀mung
You not hide conceal, must truly tell me. Shín replied, I grateful

大人恩養訓習歌舞優
tái$^2$ ꜀yan ꜀yan ꜂yéung, fan꜃ tsáp$_2$ ꜀kó ꜂mò, ꜀yau
your honor's kindness care, teaching practice singing dancing, utmost

禮相待妾雖粉骨碎身莫報
꜂lai ꜀séung toi$^2$; ts'íp꜁ ꜀sui ꜂fan kwat꜁ súi꜃ ꜀shan, mók$_2$ pò꜃
propriety towards behave; I, if powder bones crush body, not recompense

萬一近見大人兩眉愁鎖必
mán$^2$ yat꜁. Kan$^2$ kín꜃ tái$^2$ ꜀yan ꜂léung ꜀mí ꜀shau ꜂só, pít꜁
myriad one. Lately seen your honor's two eyebrows anxiety knit, must

有國家大事又不敢問今晚又
꜂yau kwók꜁ ꜀ká tái$^2$ sz'$^2$; yau$^2$ pat꜁ ꜂kóm man$^2$; ꜀kam ꜂mán yau$^2$
have state family great affairs; still not presume ask; this evening also

見 行 坐 不安 因此 長嘆 不 想
*kín' ꜀hang tsó² pat꜆ ꜀ón. ꜀Yan 'ts'z', ꜀ch'éung t'án'; pat꜆ 'séung*
saw moving sitting not easy. Because this, long sighing; not thinking

爲 大 人 窺 見 倘 有 用 妾 之 處
*꜀wai tái² ꜀yan ꜀kw'ai kín'. 'T'óng 'yau yung² ts'ip꜆ ꜀chí ch'ü',*
was your honor furtively observing. If have use my 's place,

萬 死 不 辭
*mán² 'sz' pat꜆ ꜀ts'z'.*
myriad deaths not decline.

允 以 杖 擊 地 曰 誰 想 漢 天 下
*'Wan 'í chéung² kik꜆ tí², üt₂, ꜀Shui 'séung Hón' ꜀t'in há²,*
Wan with cane striking earth, said, Who thought Hón's dominion,

却 在 汝 手 中 耶 隨 我 到 畫 閣 中
*k'éuk꜆ tsoi² 'ü 'shau ꜀chung ꜀yé? ꜀Ts'ui 'ngó tò' wá² kók꜆ ꜀chung*
really in your hands' within eh? Follow me to picture gallery in

來 貂 蟬 跟 允 到 閣 中 允 盡 叱
*꜀loi. ꜀Tíú ꜀Shín ꜀kan 'Wan tò' kók꜆ ꜀chung. 'Wan tsun² ch'ik꜆*
come. Tíú Shín followed Wan to gallery in. Wan entirely ordering

出 婦 妾 納 貂 蟬 於 坐 回 頭 便 拜
*ch'ut꜆ 'fú ts'ip꜆, náp₂ ꜀Tíú ꜀Shín ꜀ü tsó², ꜀úi ꜀t'au pín² pái'.*
out wives concubines, instated Tíú Shín in chair, turning head then bowed.

貂 蟬 驚 伏 于 地 曰 大 人 何 故
*꜀Tíú ꜀Shín ꜀king, fuk꜆ ꜀ü tí², üt₂, Tái² ꜀yan ꜀hó kú'*
Tíú Shín alarmed, prostrate on ground, said, Your honor what reason

如 此 允 曰 汝 可 憐 漢 天 下 生
*꜀ü 'ts'z'? 'Wan üt₂, 'ü 'hó ꜀lín Hón' ꜀t'in há² ꜀shang*
as this? Wan replied, You able compassionate Hón's empire's living

靈 言 訖 淚 如 泉 湧
*꜀ling. ꜀I'n kat꜆, lui² ꜀ü ꜀ts'ün 'yung.*
souls. Words finished, tears like fountain's bubbling.

貂 蟬 曰 適 間 賤 妾 曾 言 但 有
*꜀Tíú ꜀Shín üt₂, Shik꜆ ꜀kán tsín² ts'ip꜆ ꜀ts'ang ꜀in, tán² 'yau*
Tíú Shín rejoined, Just now humble handmaid already said, only have

使 令 萬 死 不 辭 允 跪 而 言
*'sz' ling², màn² 'sz' pat꜆ ꜀ts'z'. 'Wan kwai² ꜀í ꜀in,*
employ command, myriad deaths not decline. Wan kneeling and speaking,

曰 百 姓 有 倒 懸 之 危 君 臣 有 纍
*üt₂, Pák꜆ sing' 'yau 'tò ꜀ün ꜀chí ꜀ngai, ꜀kwan ꜀shan 'yau 'lui*
said, The - people are-in topsy - turvy 's danger, prince lords are-in piled

卵 之 急 非 汝 不 能 救 也 賊 臣
*'lun ꜀chí kap꜆; ꜀fi 'ü pat꜆ ꜀nang kau' 'yá. Ts'ak₂ ꜀shan*
eggs 's hazard; without you not able save. Treacherous minister

董 卓 將 欲 篡 位 朝 中 文 武
*'Tung Ch'éuk꜄ ꜀tséung yuk2 'shán wai2, ꜁ch'iú ꜀chung ꜁man 'mò*
Tung Ch'éuk presently wishes supplant throne, court among civil military

無 計 可 施 董 卓 有 一 義 兒
*꜁mò kai' 'hó ꜀shí. 'Tung Ch'éuk꜄ 'yau yat꜄ í2 ꜁í,*
have-no plans available. Tung Ch'éuk has an adopted son,

姓 呂 名 布 驍 勇 異 常 我
*sing' 'Lü, ꜁ming Pò', ꜀iú 'yung, í2 ꜁shéung. 'Ngó*
surnamed Lü, named Pò, daring brave, unlike usual. I

觀 二 人 皆 好 色 之 徒 今 欲
*꜀kún í2 ꜁yan ꜀kái hò' shik꜄ ꜀chí ꜁t'ò. ꜀Kam yuk2*
have-observed two men both lustful beauty 's slaves. Now wish

用 連 環 計 先 將 汝 許 嫁 呂 布 後
*yung2 ꜁lín ꜁wán kai'; ꜀sín ꜀tséung 'ü, 'hü ká' 'Lü Pò', hau2*
employ inveigling scheme; first taking you, promise to-wed Lü Pò, then

獻 與 董 卓 汝 于 中 取 便 諜 間
*hín' 'ü 'Tung Ch'éuk꜄: 'ü ꜀ü ꜀chung 'ts'ü pín2 típ2 kán'*
offer to Tung Ch'éuk: you in betwixt seize opportunity slander sever

他 父 子 分 顏 令 布 殺 卓 以
*꜀t'á fú2 'tsz' ꜀fan ꜁ngán ling2 Pò' shát꜄ Ch'éuk꜄, 'í*
this father son sunder-faces [disagree], cause Pò kill Ch'éuk, in-order-to

絕 大 惡 重 扶 社 稷 再 立 江 山
*tsüt2 tái2 ók꜄, ꜁ch'ung ꜁fú 'shé tsik꜄, tsoi' lap2 ꜀kóng ꜀shán:*
terminate great evil, again uphold country's - gods, re - establish government:

皆 汝 之 力 也 不 知 汝 意 若 何
*꜀kái 'ü ꜀chí lik2 'yá. Pat꜄ ꜀chí 'ü í' yéuk2 ꜁hó.*
all your 's courage. Not aware your notions as how.

貂 蟬 日 妾 許 大 人 萬 死 不 辭
*꜀Tiú ꜁Shín üt2, Ts'ip꜄ 'hü tái2 ꜁yan, mán2 'sz' pat꜄ ꜁ts'z'.*
Tiú Shín replied, I promised your honor, myriad deaths not decline.

望 即 獻 妾 與 彼 妾 自 有 道 理 允
*Móng2 tsik꜄ hín' ts'ip꜄ 'ü 'pí, ts'ip꜄ tsz'2 'yau tò2 'lí. 'Wan*
Trust when offered me to them, I myself have proper plans. Wan

日 事 若 洩 漏 我 滅 門 矣 貂 蟬
*üt2, Sz'2 yéuk2 sit꜄ lau2, 'ngó mit2 ꜁mún 'í. ꜀Tiú ꜁Shín*
said, Affair if leaks out, us exterminate house truly. Tiú Shín

日 大 人 勿 憂 妾 若 不 報 大
*üt2, Tái2 ꜁yan mat2 ꜀yau; ts'ip꜄ yéuk2 pat꜄ pò' tái2*
rejoined, Your honor need-not be-anxious; I if not requite great

義 死 于 萬 刃 之 下 允 拜 謝
*í2, 'sz' ꜀ü mán2 yan2 ꜀chí há2. 'Wan pái' tsé2.*
liberality, kill in myriad sword s' under. Wan bowing thanked.

拾級大成

次日便將家藏明珠數顆
*Tsz' yat, pín' tséung ká ts'óng míng chü shò' fó,*
Next day, then taking family preserved brilliant pearls several ones,

令良匠嵌造金冠一頂使人
*ling léung tséung kám ts'ò kam kún yat, ting; sz' yan*
ordered skillful workman inlay make golden crown one piece; sent man

密送呂布布大喜親到王允
*mat sung Lü Pò. Pò tái hí, ts'an tò Wóng Wan*
secretly gave Lü Pò. Pò much pleased, himself went-to Wóng Wan's

宅致謝允預備嘉殽美饌
*chák chí tsé. Wan ü pí ká ngáu mí chán*
house render thanks. Wan had-prepared excellent meats delicious viands,

候呂布至允出門迎迓接入後
*hau Lü Pò chí. Wan ch'ut mún ying ngá, tsip yap hau*
waited Lü Pò's arrival. Wan went out to meet waited into rear

堂延之上坐布曰呂布乃相府
*t'óng, in chí shéung tsó. Pò üt, Lü Pò nái séung fú*
hall, invited him at-top sit. Pò said, I am premier's office

一將司徒是朝廷大臣何
*yat tséung; sz' t'ò shí ch'iú t'ing tái shan: hó*
a general; your excellency is imperial court high minister: what

故錯敬允曰方今天下別
*kú ts'ók king? Wan üt, Fóng kam t'in há pít*
cause mistaken respect? Wan replied, Just now empire besides

無英雄惟有將軍耳允非敬
*mò ying hung, wai yau tséung kwan í. Wan fí king*
without hero, only is you, sir. I do-not reverence

將軍之職敬將軍之才也
*tséung kwan chí chik, king tséung kwan chí ts'oi yá.*
your honor 's rank, reverence your honor 's talents.

布大喜允慇懃敬酒口稱
*Pò tái hí. Wan yan k'an king tsau, hau ch'ing*
Pò excessively pleased. Wan diligent-attentive urged wine, mouth praised

董太師並布之德不絕布大
*Tung t'ái sz' ping Pò chí tak pat tsüt. Pò tái*
Tung high statesman and Pò 's virtues un-ceasingly. Pò loud

笑暢飲允叱退左右只留
*siú ch'éung yam. Wan ch'ik t'ui tsó yau, chí lau*
laughter hilariously drank. Wan ordered retire attendants, only detained

侍妾數人勸酒酒至半酣
*shí ts'ip shò yan hün tsau. Tsau chí pún kóm,*
waiting maids several persons serve wine. Drank till half merry,

允 曰 喚 孩 兒 來 少 頃 二 青 衣
ˢWan ǖt₂, Fún' ˌhoi ˌí ˌloi. 'Shíú 'k'ing, í² ˌts'ing 'í
Wan said, Call young child come. Little while, two green-dresses

引 貂 蟬 艷 粧 而 出 布 驚 問
'yan ˌTíú ˌShín ím² ˌchóng ˌí ch'ut. Pò' ˌking man²
led Tíú Shín gorgeously dressed and came-out. Pò surprised asked,

何 人 允 曰 小 女 貂 蟬 也 允 蒙
ˌHó ˌyan? ˢWan ǖt₂, 'Síú 'nü ˌTíú ˌShín 'yá. ˢWan ˌmung
What person? Wan replied, Little daughter Tíú Shín. I grateful-for

將 軍 錯 愛 不 異 至 親 故 令
ˌtséung ˌkwan ts'ók, oi', pat, í² chí' ˌts'an, kú' ling²
your honor's mistaken kindness, not unlike nearest relatives, therefore ordered

其 與 將 軍 相 見 便 命 貂 蟬 與 呂
ˌk'i ˢü ˌtséung ˌkwan ˌséung kín'. Pín² ming² ˌTíú ˌShín ˢü ˢLü
her with your honor interview. Then bid Tíú Shín to Lü

布 把 盞 貂 蟬 送 酒 與 布 兩 下
Pò' 'pá 'chán. ˌTíú ˌShín sung' 'tsau ˢü Pò', ˢléung há²
Pò hand goblet. She presenting wine to Pò, both parties

眉 來 眼 去 允 佯 醉 曰 孩 兒
ˌmí ˌloi ˢngán hü'. ˢWan ˌyéung tsui' ǖt₂, ˌHoi ˌí
eyebrows coming eyes going. Wan feigning drunkenness said, The child

央 及 將 軍 痛 飲 幾 盃 吾 一
ˌyéung k'ap₂ ˌtséung ˌkwan t'ung' 'yam 'kí ˌpúi; ˌ'ng yat,
requests to your honor strongly to-drink several cups; my single

家 全 靠 着 將 軍 哩 布 請 貂 蟬 坐
ˌká ˌtsün k'áu' chéuk₂ ˌtséung ˌkwan ˌlé. Pò' 'ts'ing ˌTíú ˌShín tsó².
family entirely depend upon your honor. Pò requested Tíú Shín to-sit.

貂 蟬 假 意 欲 入 允 曰 將 軍
ˌTíú ˌShín 'ká í' yuk₂ yap₂, ˢWan ǖt₂, ˌTséung ˌkwan
She feigning wish about to-retire, Wan observed, The general

吾 之 至 友 孩 兒 便 坐 何 妨 貂
ˌ'ng ˌchí chí' ˢyau, ˌhoi ˌí pín² tsó²: ˌhó ˌfóng? ˌTíú
my 's intimate friend, my child then be-seated: what apprehension? Tíú

蟬 便 坐 于 允 側 呂 布 目 不 轉 睛
ˌShín pín² tsó² ˌü ˢWan chak,. ˢLü Pò' muk₂ pat, 'chün ˌts'ing
Shín then sat at Wan's side. Lü Pò's eyes not strayed pupil

的 省 又 飲 數 盃
tik, hón'; yau² 'yam shò' ˌpúi.
's gaze; also drinking many cups.

允 指 蟬 謂 布 曰 吾 欲 將 此 女 送
ˢWan 'chí ˌShín wai² Pò', ǖt₂, ˌ'Ng yuk₂ ˌtséung 'ts'z' ˢnü sung'
Wan pointing-to Shín spoke-to Pò, saying, I wish taking this girl give

與將軍爲妾還肯納否布
*ˊü ˏtséung ˏkwan ˏwai ts'ip˒, ˏwán ˋhang náp˛ ˋfau? Pò˒*
to your honor to-be concubine, but willing receive or-not? Pò

出席謝曰若得如此布當效
*ch'ut˒ tsik˛ tsé˛ üt˛, Yéuk˛ tak˒ ˏü ˋts'z', Pò˒ ˏtóng háu˛*
leaving table thanked saying, If obtain as this, I will emulate

犬馬之報允曰早晚選一
*ˋhün ˊmá ˏchí pò˒. ˊWan˒ üt˛, ˋTsò ˊmán ˋsün yat˒*
dogs horse 's requital. Wan replied, Immediately selecting a

良辰送至府中布欣喜無
*ˏléung ˏshan sung˒ chí˒ ˋfú ˏchung. Pò˒ ˏyan ˋhí ˏmò*
fortunate day send-her to house in. Pò pleased delighted im-

限頻以目視貂蟬貂蟬亦以
*hán˛, ˏp'an ˊí muk˛ shí˛ ˏTiú ˏShín. ˏTiú ˏShín yik˛ ˊí*
measurably, continually with eyes observed Tiú Shín. She also with

秋波送情少頃席散允曰
*ˏts'au ˏpó sung˒ ˏts'ing. ˋShiú ˋk'ing, tsik˛ sán˒. ˊWan üt˛*
ogling - glances exhibited passion. Little while, feast broke-up. Wan said,

本欲留將軍止宿恐太師見
*ˋPún yuk˛ ˏlau ˏtséung ˏkwan ˋchí suk˒, ˋhung t'ái˒ ˏsz' kín˒*
I would detain your honor stop sleep, fear you may-be

疑布再三拜謝而去
*ˏí. Pò˒ tsoi˒ ˏsám pái˒ tsé˛ ˏí hü˒.*
apprehensive. Pò again thrice bowing thanked and departed.

---

### No. III.—Prescience of the Birds.*

(見聊齋 卷之十 第六十八篇)

中州境有道士募食鄉村
*ˏChung ˏchau ˋking ˊyau Tò˛ sz'˛ mò˛ shik˛ ˏhéung ˏts'ün.*
[In] Chungchau borders, was Taou priest begging food country village.

食已聞鸝鳴因告主人使
*Shik˛ ˊí, ˏman ˏlí ˏming, ˏyan kò˒ ˋchü ˏyan ˋsz'*
Eaten having, heard parrot sing, therefore told head man to-order

---

* *Liú Chái* 聊齋 or Pastimes of the Study, is a collection of stories usually printed in sixteen duodecimo volumes. It was written by Pò Ts'ung-ling 蒲松齡 a distinguished scholar of Shántung province, who flourished in the reign of Kánghí; his preface is dated in 1679. It is regarded as a highly finished production, and is written in excellent style and pure Chinese.

海上絲綢之路文獻集成　科技與文化編

愼 火 問 故 答 曰 鳥 云 大 火 難
shan$^{2}$ 'fó. Man$^{2}$ kú', táp, üt$_{2}$, 'Niú ,wan, tái$^{2}$. 'fó ,nán
careful-of fire. Asking cause, replying said, Bird says, great fire difficult

救 可 怕 衆 笑 之 竟 不 備 明
kau', 'hó p'á'. Chung' síú' ,chí: 'king pat, pí$^{2}$. ,Ming
extinguish, to-be feared. All ridiculed him: at-last unprepared. Next

日 果 火 延 燒 數 家 始 驚 其
yat$_{2}$ 'kwó 'fó ,ín ,shíú shò' ,ká. 'Ch'í ,king ,k'í
day indeed fire spreading consumed several houses. Began to-wonder-at his

神 好 事 者 追 及 之 稱 爲 仙
,shan. Hò' sz'$^{2}$ 'ché ,chui k'ap$_{2}$ ,chí, ,ch'ing ,wai ,sín.
divine-powers. Liked matter persons following after him, saluted as genius.

道 士 曰 我 不 過 知 鳥 語 耳 何 仙 也
Tò$^{2}$ sz'$^{2}$ üt$_{2}$, 'Ngó pat, kwò' ,chí 'níú 'ü 'í; ,hó ,sín 'yá?
Taou priest said, I merely know bird's words indeed; how a-genius?

適 有 皂 花 雀 鳴 樹 上 衆 問 何
Shik, 'yau tsò$^{2}$ ,fá tséuk, ,ming shü' shéung$^{2}$. Chung' man$^{2}$, ,hó
Just was black-speckled bird singing tree upon. Crowd asked, what

語 曰 雀 言 初 六 養 之 初 六 養
'ü? Ut$_{2}$, Tséuk, ,ín, ,ch'ó luk$_{2}$ 'yéung ,chí; ,ch'ó luk$_{2}$ 'yéung
say? Replied, Bird says, first sixth nourish it; first sixth nourish

之 十 四 十 六 殤 之 想 此 家 孿 生
,chí; shap$_{2}$ sz' shap$_{2}$ luk$_{2}$ ,shéung ,chí. 'Séung 'ts'z' ,ká 'lün ,shang
it; fourteenth sixteenth destroy it. I-think that family twins born

矣 今 日 爲 初 十 不 出 五 六 日 當 俱
'í. ,Kam yat$_{2}$ ,wai ,ch'ó shap$_{2}$, pat, ch'ut, 'ng luk$_{2}$ yat$_{2}$, ,tóng ,k'ü
so. To-day is first tenth, not overpass five six days, will both

死 也 詢 之 果 二 子 無 何 並 死
'sz' 'yá. ,Sun ,chí 'kwó í$^{2}$ 'tsz'; ,mò ,hó ping$^{2}$ 'sz'.
die. Inquired-of him, truly two sons; not long both died.

其 日 悉 符 邑 令 聞 其 奇 招 之
,K'í yat$_{2}$ Shik, ,fú yap, ling$^{2}$ ,man ,k'í ,k'í, ,chíú ,chí
That day Shikfú's city magistrate heard this wonder, called him

延 爲 客 時 羣 鴨 過 因 問 之 對
,ín ,wai hák,. ,Shí ,kwan áp, kwò', ,yan man$^{2}$ ,chí; túi'
stay to-be guest. Once flock ducks passed, then asked him; replied

曰 明 公 內 室 必 相 爭 也 鴨 云
üt$_{2}$, ,Ming ,kung noi$^{2}$ shat, pít, ,séung ,chang 'yá: áp, ,wan,
saying, Distinguished sir inner apartment, truly altercation: ducks say,

罷 罷 偏 向 他 偏 向 他 令 大 服
Pá$^{2}$, pá$^{2}$, ,p'in héung' ,t'á; ,p'in héung' ,t'á. Ling$^{2}$ tái$^{2}$ fuk$_{2}$,
Enough, enough, dote towards her; dote towards her. Officer fully agreed,

蓋 妻 妾 反 脣 令 適 被 喧 聒 而
k'oi' ˏts'ai ts'ip˒ 'fán ˓shun, ling² shik˒ pí² ˏhün kút˒, ˓í
for wife concubine's altercation, officer then was-by clamor stunned, and

出 也 因 留 居 署 中 優 禮 之 時
ch'ut˒ 'yá. ˏYan ˓lau ˏkü 'ch'ü ˏchung, ˏyau 'lai ˏchí; ˓shí
went-out. Therefore detained live office in, treated politely him; constantly

辨 鳥 語 多 奇 中 而 道 士 樸 野
pán² 'niú 'ü ˏtó ˓k'i ˏchung, ˓í Tò² sz'² puk₂ 'yé,
discerning birds' talk many wonders amongst, and Taou priest honest rustic

肆 言 輒 無 所 忌
sz' ˓in ts'üt˒ ˓mò 'shó kí².
heedlessly talked, fully nothing which avoided.

令 最 貪 一 切 供 用 諸 物 皆 折
Ling² tsui' ˏtám; yat˒ ts'it˒ ˏkung yung² ˏchü mat₂, ˏkái chít˒
Officer very avaricious, one whole supplied use every thing, all changed

爲 錢 以 入 之 一 日 方 坐 羣 鴨 復
˓wai ˓ts'in 'í yap₂ ˏchí. Yat˒ yat₂ ˏfóng tsó², ˓kwan áp˒ fuk₂
to-be cash for giving-to him. One day just seated, flock ducks again

來 令 又 詰 之 答 曰 今 日 所 言
˓loi, ling² yau² kit˒ ˏchí: táp˒ üt₂, ˏKam yat₂ 'shó ˓in,
coming, officer again interrogated him: answering said, To-day what say,

不 與 前 同 乃 爲 明 公 會 計 耳 問
pat˒ 'ü ˓ts'in ˓t'ung; 'nái wai² ˓ming ˏkung úi² kai' 'í. Man²
not with before agree; but is noble sir confederating scheme so. Asked

何 計 曰 彼 云 蠟 燭 一 百 八
˓hó kai'? Ut₂, 'pí ˓wan, láp₂ chuk˒ yat˒ pák˒ pát˒,
what scheme? Replied, they say, waxen candles one hundred eight,

銀 硃 一 千 八 令 慚 疑 其 相
˓ngan ˏchü yat˒ ˏts'in pát˒. Ling² ˓ts'ám ˓í ˓k'i ˏséung
vermilion one thousand eight. Officer ashamed suspected him at-him

譏 道 士 求 去 令 不 許 踰 數 日
ˏkí. Tò² sz'² ˓k'au hü'; ling² pat˒ 'hü. ˓U shò' yat₂,
bantering. Taou priest begged to-leave; officer not consent. After several days,

宴 客 忽 聞 杜 宇 客 問 之 曰 鳥
ín² hák˒, fat˒ ˓man tò², 'ü: hák˒ man² ˏchí, üt₂, 'Niú
feasting guests, suddenly heard pheasant: guests asking him, replied, Bird

云 丟 官 去 衆 愕 然 失 色
˓wan, ˏtiú ˏkún hü'. Chung' ngók₂ ˓ín, shat˒ shik˒;
says, throw magistrate away. Company amazed indeed, lost countenance;

令 大 怒 立 逐之去未 幾 令
*ling*$^{2}$ *tái*$^{2}$ *nò*$^{2}$, *lap*ˌ *chuk*ˌ ˏ*chí kü*ʾ. *Mi*$^{2}$ ʿ*kí*, *ling*$^{2}$
officer highly incensed, instantly drove him off. Not many-days, officer

果 以 墨 敗 嗚 呼 此 仙 人 儆 戒 之 而
ʿ*kwó* ʿ*i* *mak*ˌ *pái*$^{2}$. ˏ*U*ʾ ˏ*fú*! ʿ*ts*ʿ*z*ʾ ˏ*sín* ˏ*yan* ʿ*king kái*ʾ ˏ*chí*, ˏ*í*
surely by mark disgraced. Alas! this magician warned him, but,

惜 乎 危 厲 熏 心 者 不 之 悟 也
*sik*ˌ ˏ*ú*, ˏ*ngai* *lai*$^{2}$, ˏ*fan* ˏ*sam* ʿ*ché*, *pat*ˌ ˏ*chí* ʾ*ng*$^{2}$ ʿ*yá*.
sad enough, endangered by-cruelty, dim minded man, not him arouse.

---

## No. IV.—The Magic Carpet.

(見聊齋 卷之十二 第六十七篇)

紅 毛 國 舊 許 與 中 國 相 貿 易
ˏ*Hung* ˏ*mò* *kwók*ˌ *kau*$^{2}$ ʿ*hü* ʿ*ü* ˏ*Chung Kwók*ˌ ˏ*séung mau*$^{2}$ *yik*ˌ.
Red haired country whilom permitted in Middle Kingdom mutual commerce.

邊 帥 見 其 人 衆 不 聽 登 岸
ˏ*Pín* *shui*ʾ *kin*ʾ ˏ*k*ʿ*í* ˏ*yan* *chung*ʾ, *pat*ˌ *t*ʿ*ing*ʾ ˏ*tang* *ngón*$^{2}$.
Frontier admiral seeing these men numerous, not hear-to coming ashore.

紅 毛 人 固 請 但 賜 一 氈 地
ˏ*Hung* ˏ*mò* ˏ*yan* *kú*ʾ ʿ*ts*ʿ*ing* *tán*$^{2}$ *ts*ʿ*z*ʾ *yat*ˌ ˏ*chín* *tí*$^{2}$
Red haired men obstinately besought only to-give a carpet's earth,

足 矣 帥 思 一 氈 所 容 無 幾 許
*tsuk*ˌ ʿ*i*. *Shui*ʾ ˏ*sz*ʾ *yat*ˌ ˏ*chín* ʿ*shó* ˏ*yung* ˏ*mò* ʿ*kí*, ʿ*hü*
enough quite. Admiral thinking a carpet what allow not much, consented-to

之 其 人 置 氈 岸 上 僅 容 二
ˏ*chí*. ˏ*K*ʿ*í* ˏ*yan* *chí*ʾ ˏ*chín* *ngón*$^{2}$ *shéung*$^{2}$, ʿ*kan* ˏ*yung* *í*$^{2}$
them. The men placing a-carpet shore upon, about accommodate two

人 扯 之 容 四 五 人 且 扯 且 登
ˏ*yan*; ʿ*ch*ʿ*é* ˏ*chí*, ˏ*yung* *sz*ʾ ʿ*ng* ˏ*yan*; ʿ*ch*ʿ*é* ʿ*ch*ʿ*é* ʿ*ch*ʿ*é* ˏ*tang*,
men; pulling it, accommodate four five men; more pulled more came,

頃 刻 氈 大 畝 許 已 數 百 人 矣
ʿ*k*ʿ*ing* *hak*ˌ ˏ*chín* *tái*$^{2}$ ʿ*mau* ʿ*hü*, ʿ*í* *shò*ʾ *pák*ˌ ˏ*yan* ʿ*i*.
short time carpet large-as acre over, already several hundred persons.

短 刀 並 發 出 於 不 意 被 掠
ʿ*Tün* ˏ*tò* *ping*$^{2}$ *fát*ˌ, *ch*ʿ*ut*ˌ ˏ*ü* *pat*ˌ *í*ʾ, *pí*$^{2}$ *léuk*ˌ
Short swords at-once drew, ending as not imagine, by-them seized

數 里 而 去
*shò*ʾ ʿ*lí* ˏ*í* *hü*ʾ.
several miles, and departed.

No. V.—Courage of a Concubine.

(見聊齋 卷之十四 第十二篇)

益都西鄙之貴家某者富有
*Yik, tò ,sai 'p'í ,chí kwai' ,ká, 'mau 'ché, fú' 'yau*
Yiktò's western border 's honorable family, certain person rich had

巨金蓄一妾頗婉麗而家
*kü² ,kam. Ch'uk, yat, ts'íp, 'p'ó 'ün lai², ,í 'ch'ung*
much money. Reared a concubine, rather charming handsome, but head

室凌折之鞭撻橫施妾
*shat, ,ling chít, ,chí. ,Pín t'át, ,wáng ,shí, ts'íp,*
wife cruelly beat her. Whipped struck causelessly, concubine

奉事之惟謹某憐之往往私
*fung² sz'² ,chí ,wai 'kan. 'Mau ,lín ,chí, 'wóng 'wóng ,sz'*
obediently served her still attentively. He pitying her, again-and-again privately

語慰撫妾殊未嘗有怨言
*'ü wai' 'fú. Ts'íp, ,shü mí² ,shéung 'yau ün' ,ín.*
spoke to-soothe comfort. She certainly not having had discontented expression.

一夜數十人踰牆入撞其屋
*Yat, yé², shò' shap, ,yan ü² ,ts'éung yap, chóng² ,k'í uk,*
One night, several tens-of men getting-over wall entered broke the house's

扉幾壞某與妻惶遽喪魄搖戰不
*,fí ,kí wái². 'Mau 'ü ,ts'ai ,wóng kü' sóng' p'ák,, ,íu chín' pat,*
doors nearly open. He and wife fearful irresolute lost courage, trembled not

知所爲妾起嘿無聲息暗
*,chí 'shó ,wai. Ts'íp, 'hí mak, ,mò ,shing sik,, óm'*
knowing what to-do. She rising secretly without noise breathing, stealthily

摸屋中得挑水木杖一拔關
*mók, uk, ,chung tak, ,t'íu 'shui muk, chéung² yat, Pat, ,kwán*
felt house in got carrying water wooden pole one. Drawing bar

遽出羣賊亂如蓬麻妾舞
*kü' ch'ut,, ,kw'an ts'ak, lün² ,ü ,pung ,má. Ts'íp, 'mò*
rushed out, gang-of robbers confused as tangled hemp. She brandishing

杖動風鳴鉤響擊四五人仆
*chéung² tung², ,fung ,ming ,kau 'héung, kik, sz'' 'ng ,yan fú'*
pole about, whirring noise hook sounding, struck four five men flat-on

地賊盡靡駭愕亂奔
*tí². Ts'ak, tsun² 'mí ,hoì ngók, lün² ,pan.*
ground. Robbers completely disconcerted, intimidated confusedly fled.

牆 高 急 不 得 上 傾 跌 咿 啞 亡 魂

*ˏTsʻéung ˏkò kapˎ patˎ takˎ ʿshéung, ˏkʻing titˎ ˏi ˏá! ˏmóng ˏwan*

Wall high quickly unable to-ascend, headlong fell [cried] alack! failed hearts

失 命 妾 拄 杖 於 地 顧 笑 曰 此

*shatˎ ming2. Tsʻipˎ ʿchü chéung2 ˏü ti2, kúˋ síúˋ ütˎ, ʿTsʻz*

lost spirits. She laying pole on ground, looking-at laughing said, These

等 物 事 不 直 下 手 插 打 得 亦 學

*ʿtang mat2 sz2, patˎ chik2 há2 ʿshau chʻápˎ ʿtá takˎ; yik2 hók2*

sort thing's business, not worth act pierce strike to; also learn

作 賊 我 不 汝 殺 殺 嫌 辱 我 悉

*tsókˎ tsʻakˎ! ʿngó patˎ ʿü sháˎ: shátˎ, ˏim yuk2 ʿngó. Shikˎ*

to-act thief! I not you kill: kill, demean disgrace myself. Straight

縱 之 逸 去 某 大 驚 問 何 自

*tsʻungˋ ˏchí yat2 hüˋ. ʿMau tái2 ˏking, man2, ˏHó tsz2*

releasing them hastened away. Man much alarmed, asked, How yourself

能 爾 則 妾 父 故 槍 棒 師 妾

*ˏnang ʿi? Tsakˎ tsʻipˎ fú2 kúˋ ˏtsʻéung ʿpʻáng ˏsz, tsʻipˎ*

able eh? For-as concubine's father formerly fencing master, she

盡 傳 其 術 殆 不 啻 百 人 敵 也

*tsün2 ˏchʻün ˏkʻi shut2, ʿtʻoi patˎ chʻiˋ pákˎ ˏyan tik2 ʿyá.*

fully acquired his art, nearly more-than hundred men oppose.

妻 尤 駭 甚 悔 向 之 迷 於 物 色

*Tsʻai ˏyau ˏhoi, sham2 fúiˋ héungˋ ˏchí ˏmai ˏü mat2 shikˎ,*

Wife more alarmed, deeply grieved former 's lusting for carnality,

由 是 善 顏 視 妾 妾 終 無 纖

*ˏyau shi2 shín2 ˏngán shi2 tsʻipˎ. Tsʻipˎ ˏchung ˏmò ˏtsʻim*

henceforth kind aspect regarded her. She to-the-last without least

毫 失 禮 鄰 婦 或 謂 妾 嫂 擊

*ˏhò shatˎ ʿlai. ˏLun ʿfú, wák2 wai2 tsʻipˎ, ʿSò kikˎ*

degree failed respect. Neighbouring women, certain spoke-to her, You beat

賊 若 豚 犬 顧 奈 何 俛 首 受 撻

*tsʻakˎ yéuk2 ˏtʻün ʿhün; kúˋ noi2 ˏhó ʿmín ʿshau shau2 tʻátˎ*

thieves like hogs-and-dogs; but cause what submissively receive castigation

楚 妾 曰 是 吾 分 耳 他 何 敢 言

*ʿchʻó? Tsʻipˎ ütˎ, Shi2 ʿng fan2 ʿi; ˏtʻá ˏhó ʿkóm ˏin!*

pains? She replied, It-is my lot indeed; otherwise how presume speak!

聞 者 益 賢 之

*ˏMan ʿché yikˎ ˏin ˏchí.*

Hearers highly praised her.

## No. VI.—The Faithful Dog.

(見聊齋 卷之十四 第五十五篇)

潞安 某甲父陷獄將死 搜
Lò$^{2}$ ˓ón, ʻmau káp˒ fú$^{2}$ hám$^{2}$ yuk$_{2}$ ˓tséung ʻsz'. Sau$^{2}$,
[In] Lò-ón, certain person's father lay-in prison ready-to die. Scarching

括囊蓄得百金將詣郡關
kút˒ ˓nóng ch'uk˒ tak˒ pák˒ ˓kum, ˓tséung ʻngai kwan$^{2}$ ˓kwán
collecting bags hoards got hundred taels, taking visit district's office

說跨 騾出則所養黑犬從
shüt˒. Kw'á' ˓lü ch'ut˒, tsak˒ ʻshó ʻyéung hak˒ ʻhün ˓ts'ung
to-speak. Mounting ass sallied, immediately which had-bred black dog followed

之呵逐便退既走則又從
˓chí. ˓Hó chuk$_{2}$ pín$^{2}$ t'üi'; kí' ʻtsau, tsak˒ yau$^{2}$ ˓ts'ung
him. Hooted away straight went-back; it-had run, then again followed

之鞭逐不返 從行數十里某
˓chí; ˓pín chuk$_{2}$ pat˒ ʻfán; ˓ts'ung ˓hang shò' shap$_{2}$ ʻlí. ʻMau
him; whipped off, not return-home; followed going several tens-of miles. Man

下騎趨路側私焉既乃以石投
há$^{2}$ ˓k'i, ˓ts'ü lò$^{2}$ chak˒ ˓sz' ˓ín. Kí', ʻnái ʻi shik˒ ˓t'au
got-off riding, hasted road side private. Done, then with stones stoned

犬 犬始奔去某既行則犬欻然
ʻhün: ʻhün ʻch'i ˓pan hü'; ʻmau kí' ˓hang, tsak˒ ʻhün hat˒ ˓ín
dog: dog began to-run away; man had gone, then dog suddenly-

復來齧騾尾足某怒鞭之犬
fuk$_{2}$ ˓loi, ngít$_{2}$ ˓lü ʻmí tsuk˒. ʻMau nò$^{2}$, ˓pín ˓chí; ʻhün
re - turning, bit ass's tail feet. Man irritated, whipped him; dog

鳴吠不已 忽躍在前 憤齕騾首
˓ming fai$^{2}$ pat˒ ʻi, fat˒ yéuk$_{2}$ tsoi$^{2}$ ˓ts'in, ʻfan ngat$_{2}$ ˓lü ʻshau,
barked unceasingly, suddenly jumping-up ahead, madly snapped-at ass's head,

似欲阻某去路某以爲不祥
ʻts'z' yuk$_{2}$ ʻchó ʻmau hü$^{2}$ lò$^{2}$. ʻMau, ʻi ˓wai pat˒ ˓ts'éung
as-if wished to-intercept his going journey. He, regarding-it as not lucky,

益怒回騎馳逐之 視犬已遠
yik˒ nò$^{2}$, ˓úi ˓k'i ˓ch'i chuk$_{2}$ ˓chí. Shí$^{2}$ ʻhün ʻi ʻün,
highly angered, turning rode swiftly drove-off him. Seeing dog already distant,

乃返轡疾馳 抵郡已暮 及捫
ʻnái ʻfán pí$^{2}$ tsat˒ ˓ch'i. ʻTai kwan$^{2}$ ʻi mò$^{2}$; k'ap$_{2}$ ˓mún
then turning bridle quickly galloped. Reached town was dusk; first feeling-for

腰橐金亡其半涔涔汗下魂魄
*꜀íú tʿók꜃, ꜀kam ꜁móng ꜁kʿi púnʾ; ꜁sham ꜁sham hón$^{2}$ há$^{2}$, ꜁wan pʿák꜃*
girdle bag, money lost its half; trick - ling sweat ran-down, spirits

都失輾轉終夜頓念犬吠
*꜀tò ꜀shat꜃; ʿchín ʿchün ꜀chung yé$^{2}$. Tun$^{2}$ nim$^{2}$ ʿhün fai$^{2}$*
all gone; tossing rolling all night. All-at-once remembered dog's barking

有因候關出城細審來途
*ʿyau ꜀yan; hau$^{2}$ ꜀kwán chʿut꜃ ꜁shing, saiʾ ʿsham ꜁loi ꜁tʿò.*
was reason; waited-at gate left town, carefully examined came road.

又自計南北衝衢行人如
*Yau$^{2}$ tsz$^{2}$ kaiʾ ꜁nám pak꜃ ꜀chʿung ꜁kʿü ꜁hang ꜁yan ꜁ü*
Also himself judged all - parts' a-traveled thoroughfare, travel - ers like

蟻遺金寧有存理逡巡至
*ʿngai, ꜁wai ꜀kam, ꜁ning ʿyau ꜁tsʿün ʿli? ꜀Sun ꜁tsʿun chíʾ*
ants, lost money, where was preserving honesty? Looking - about reaching

下騎所見犬斃草間毛汗溼如洗
*há$^{2}$ ꜁kʿi ʿshó, kínʾ ʿhün pai$^{2}$ ʿtsʿò ꜀kán, ꜁mò hón$^{2}$ shap꜃ ꜁ü ʿsai;*
got-off riding place, saw dog dead grass midst, hair sweat wet as-if washed;

提耳起視則封金儼然感
*꜁tʿai ʿi ʿhi shi$^{2}$, tsak꜃ ꜀fung ꜀kam ʿim ꜁ín. ʿKóm*
grasping ear lifting to-look-at, there-was package money safe quite. Moved-at

其義買棺葬之人以爲義
*꜁kʿi i$^{2}$, ʿmái ꜀kún tsóngʾ ꜀chí. ꜁Yan ʿi ꜁wai i$^{2}$*
his fidelity, bought coffin buried him. Men regarded-it as faithful

犬塚云
*ʿhün ʿchʿung ꜁wan.*
dog's grave so.

## No. VII.—Remarkable Earthquake.

(見聊齋卷之十四第五十八篇)

康熙七年六月十七日戌刻
*꜀Hóng ꜀hi tsʿat꜃ ꜁nín, luk꜄ üt꜄, shap꜄ tsʿat꜃ yat꜄, sut꜃ hak꜄,*
Hónghí's seventh year, sixth month, seventeenth day, evening time,

地大震余適客稷下方與表兄
*ti$^{2}$ tái$^{2}$ chanʾ. ꜁U shik꜃ hák꜃ Tsik꜃ há$^{2}$, ꜀fóng ʿü ʿpíú ꜀hing*
earth greatly quaked. I then visiting-at Tsikhá, just-was with cousin-german

李篤之對燭飲忽聞有聲如
*ʿLí Tuk꜃ ꜀chí túiʾ chuk꜃ ʿyam; fat꜃ ꜁man ʿyau ꜀shing ꜁ü*
Lí Tukchí opposite the-candle drinking; suddenly hearing was sound like

雷 自 東南 來 向 西北 去 衆
*ˏlúi, tsz'² ˏtung ˏnám ˏloi héung' ˏsai pak˒ hü'. Chung'*
thunder, from southeast came towards northwest went. Everybody

駭 異 不 解 其 故 俄 而 几 案
*ˏhoi í², pat˒ 'kái ˏk'i kú'. Ngó² ˏí ·'i ón'*
frightened terribly, not understanding the reason. Presently then chairs table

擺 簸 酒 杯 傾 覆 屋 梁 椽 柱 錯 折
*'pái p'ó', 'tsau ˏpúi ˏk'ing fuk˒, uk˒ ˏléung ˏün 'ch'ü ts'ók˒ chít˒*
vibrated shook, wine glasses turned over, house's rafters beams posts strangely burst

有 聲 相 顧 失 色 久 之 方 知
*'yau ˏshing. ˏSéung kú' shat˒ shik˒; 'káu ˏchí, ˏfóng ˏchí*
with-a noise. Mutually looking turned pale; whiling it, then aware

地 震 各 疾 趨 出 見 樓 閣 房
*tí² chan'. Kók˒ tsat˒ ˏts'ü ch'ut˒, kín' ˏlau kók˒ ˏfóng*
earthquake. Each-one hastily running out, saw story lofts dwellings

舍 仆 而 復 起 墻 傾 屋 塌 之 聲
*shé', fú² ˏí fuk₂ 'hí. ˏTs'éung ˏk'ing, uk˒ t'áp˒ ˏchí ˏshing,*
houses, bowing and again rising. Walls falling, houses crashing 's noise,

與 兒 啼 女 號 喧 如 鼎 沸 人
*'ü ˏí ˏt'ai, 'nü ˏhú, ˏhün ˏü 'ting fai'. ˏYan*
with children crying, women screaming, the-roar like caldron's bubbling. People

眩 暈 不 能 立 坐 地 上 隨 地 轉
*ˏün ˏwan pat˒ ˏnang lap₂, tsó² tí² shéung², ˏts'úi tí² 'chün*
blinded dizzy not able to-stand, sat ground upon, with earth turned

側 河 水 傾 潑 丈 餘 雞 鳴 犬 吠
*chak˒. ˏHó 'shui ˏk'ing pút˒ chéung² ˏü. ˏKai ˏming 'hün fai²,*
sided. River's water rolled surged rod more. Hens cackling dogs howling

滿 城 中 踰 一 時 許 始 稍 定 視
*'mún ˏshing ˏchung. Ü² yat˒ ˏshí 'hü 'ch'i 'cháu ting², shí²*
filled city in. After an hour more began little to-settle, looking

街 上 則 男 女 裸 聚 競 相 告
*ˏkái shéung² tsak˒ ˏnám 'nü 'ló tsü² king² ˏséung kò'*
streets in there-were men women naked collected anxiously together telling

語 並 忘 其 未 衣 也 後 聞 某
*'ü; ping² ˏmóng ˏk'i mí² ˏi 'yá. Hau² ˏman 'mau*
talking; all had-forgotten they not-yet dressed. Afterwards heard one

處 井 傾 仄 不 可 汲 某 家 樓
*ch'ü' 'tsing ˏk'ing chak˒ pat˒ 'hó k'ap˒. 'Mau ˏká ˏlau*
place, well inclined leaned un - able draw-water. One family's loft-

臺 南 北 易 向 棲 霞 山 裂 沂 水
*ˏt'oi, ˏnám pak˒ yik₂ héung'. ˏTs'ai ˏhá ˏshán lít₂; ˏI' 'shui*
terrace, south north changed direction. Ts'aihá hill riven; I' river

陷 穴 廣 數 畝 此 眞 非 常 之 奇
*hám² 'üt₂ 'kwóng shò' 'mau. 'Ts'z' ,chan ,fí ,shéung ,chí ,k'i*
deepened hole extending several acres. This truly uncommon 's extraordinary

變 也
*pín' 'yá.*
phenomenon.

---

## No. VIII.—Paraphrase of a Maxim.*

(見聖諭第一條)

敦 孝 弟 以 重 人 倫
*,Tun háu' tai², 'i chung² ,yan ,lun.*
"Zealously-practice filial fraternal-duties, thereby giving-weight-to human relations."

---

萬 歲 爺 意 思 說 我 聖 祖 仁
*Mán² sui' ,yé í' sz' shüt,: 'Ngó shing' 'tsò ,Yan*
His-imperial-majesty's intentions express: Our sacred ancestor Pious

皇 帝 坐 了 六 十 年 的 天 下 最
*,wóng tai' tsó² 'líú luk₂ shap₂ ,nín tik, ,t'ín há². Tsui'*
imperial sovereign reign - ed six - ty years 's empire. Highly

敬 重 的 祖 宗 親 自 做 成 孝
*king' chung² tik, 'tsò ,tsung; ,ts'an tsz'² tsò² ,shing Háu'*
reverenced regarded ancestors; personally himself completed Filial-Duty

經 衍 義 這 一 部 書 無 非 是 要
*,King 'I'n I'², ché' yat, pò² ,shü. ,Mò ,fi shí² íú'*
Memoir's Commentary, this one volume book. Nothing - else - than wish

普 天 下 人 都 盡 孝 道 的 意 思
*'p'ò ,t'ín há² ,yan ,tò tsun² háu² tò² tik, í' sz'.*
whole empire's people all perform filial duty 's requirements.

所 以 聖 諭 十 六 條 頭 一 件
*'Shó 'i Shing' Ü² shap₂ luk₂ ,t'íú, ,t'au yat, kín²*
Therefore Sacred Commands, sixteen maxims, at-head first one

---

* This is the first of the sixteen maxims of the emperor Kánghí, which were certain pithy sentences that he drew up, containing in his view the quintessence of good morals, and which his son, the emperor Yungching, commented upon, and one of his ministers, Wóng Yaupò, paraphrased. The whole is called the *Shing Ü* 聖諭 or Sacred Commands and is required by law to be publicly read semi-monthly, in the ears of all the people. The paraphrase of Wóng Yaupò is considered as among the best examples of writing in the colloquial style, and has been selected on that account; the idiom is that of the Peking or court dialect, and the attentive scholar will easily perceive wherein it differs from the Canton dialect, and also from the other lessons of this chapter. A translation of this extract will be found in Dr. Milne's Sacred Edict, pages 34—48.

就 說個孝弟 如今萬歲

*tsau$^2$ shüt kó' háu' tai$^2$. U kam mán$^2$ sui'*

consequently discourses-on the filial fraternal-duties. When now his imperial

爺坐了位想着聖祖教人的

*yé tsó$^2$ liú wai$^2$, séung chéuk shing' tsò káu' yan tik*

majesty sat-on throne, reflecting-on sacred ancestor teaching men 's

意思做出聖諭廣訓十六

*í' sz', tsò$^2$ ch'ut Shing' U$^2$ · Kwóng Fan', shap luk*

intentions, published Sacred Commands Universal Instruction, sixteen

篇來先把這孝弟的道理講

*p'in loi, sín pá, ché' háu' tai$^2$ tik tò$^2$ lí, kóng*

heads, first taking-up the filial fraternal 's obligations, discoursed

給你們眾百姓聽

*k'ap ní mún chung' pák sing' t'ing.*

to you all people to-hear.

怎麼是孝呢這個孝順的道理大

*Tsam mó shí$^2$ háu' ní? Ché' kó' háu' shun$^2$ tik tò$^2$ lí tái$^2$*

What is filial-duty eh? This filial duty 's obligations great

得緊上而天下而地中間的

*tak kan. Shéung$^2$ í t'ín, há$^2$ í tí$^2$, chung kán tik*

exceedingly. Above is heaven, beneath is earth, midst 's

人沒有一個離了這個理的

*yan, mút yau yat kó' lí liú ché' kó' lí tik.*

mankind, not contain one individual relieved-from this obligation.

怎麼說呢只因孝順是一團的

*Tsam mó shüt ní? Chat yan háu' shun$^2$ shí$^2$ yat t'ün tik*

What speak-of eh? Only that filial duty is one whole 's

和氣你看天地若是不和如

*wó hí'. Ní hón' t'in tí$^2$ yéuk shí$^2$ pat wó, ü*

harmony. You observe heaven earth, if are inharmonious, then

何生養得許多人物出來呢人

*hó shang yéung tak hü tó yan mat ch'ut loi ní? Yan*

how produce nurture able so many men things forth come eh? Men

若是不孝順就失了天地的和氣了

*yéuk shí$^2$ pat háu' shun$^2$, tsau$^2$ shat liú t'in tí$^2$ tik wó hí' liú;*

if are un-dutiful, then lose heaven earth 's harmony;

如何還成個人呢

*ü hó wán shing kó' yan ní?*

then how still perfect the man eh?

如今且把父母疼愛你們的

*U kam ch'é pá fú$^2$ mò t'ang oi' ní mún tik*

Now therefore taking-up parents ardently loving you 's

心 腸 說 一 說 你 們 在 懷 抱 的
*꜀sam ꜀ch'éung, shüt꜆ yat꜆ shüt꜆. ꜂Ní ꜁mún tsoi2 ꜁wái ꜂p'ò tik꜆*
affection, I-speak a word. You on breast fondled 's

時 候 餓 了 呢 自 己 不 會 吃 飯 冷 了
*꜁shí hau2: ngó2 ꜂líú ꜀ní? tsz'2 ꜂kí pat꜆ ꜂úi hat꜄ fán2. ꜂Lang ꜂líú*
time: hungered eh? yourself not able to-eat food. Cold

呢 自 己 不 會 穿 衣 服 你 的 老 子
*꜀ní? tsz'2 ꜂kí pat꜆ ꜂úi ꜀ch'ün ꜀í fuk꜄. ꜂Ní tik꜆ ꜂lò ꜂tsz'*
eh? yourself not know to-put-on clothes. Your father

娘 看 着 你 的 臉 兒 聽 着 你 的
*꜁néung hón' chéuk꜄ ꜂ní tik꜆ lím2 ꜁í, ꜀t'ing chéuk꜄ ꜂ní tik꜆*
mother observing your cheeks [face], hearing your

聲 音 兒 你 笑 呢 就 喜 歡 你 哭 呢
*꜀shing ꜀yam ꜁í;—꜂ní síú' ꜀ní? tsau2 ꜂hí ꜀fún. ꜂Ní huk꜆ ꜀ní?*
cries;— you smile eh! then gladdened pleased. You cry eh?

就 憂 愁 你 走 動 呢 就 步 步 跟
*tsau2 ꜀yau ꜁shau. ꜂Ní ꜂tsau tung2 ꜀ní? tsau2 pò2 pò2 ꜀kan*
then grieved afflicted. You walk move eh? then step-by-step attended.

着 你 若 是 略 略 的 有 點 病 兒
*chéuk꜄. ꜂Ní yéuk꜄ shí2 léuk꜄ léuk꜄ tik꜆ ꜂yau ꜂tím ping2 ꜁í,*
near. You if are very little 's have touch-of illness,

就 愁 的 了 不 得 茶 不 是 茶 飯 不 是
*tsau2 ꜁shau tik꜆ ꜂líú pat꜆ tak꜆. ꜁Ch'á pat꜆ shí2 ꜁ch'á: fán2 pat꜆ shí2*
then griev - ed exceedingly. Tea not as tea: food not as

飯 只 等 你 身 子 好 這 纔 放 下 了
*fán2; chat꜆ ꜂tang ꜂ní ꜀shan ꜂tsz' ꜂hò, ché' ꜁ts'oi fóng' há2 ꜂líú*
food: only wait your body well, just then reliev - ed

心 眼 巴 巴 的 看 着 一 年 小 兩 年
*꜀sam. ꜂Ngán ꜀pá ꜀pá tik꜆ hón' chéuk꜄ yat꜆ ꜁nín ꜂síú, ꜂léung ꜁nín*
heart. Eyes constantly seeing one year small, two years

大 不 知 受 了 多 少 辛 苦 躭
*tái2, pat꜆ ꜀chí shau2 ꜂líú ꜀tó ꜂shíú ꜀san ꜂fú; ꜀tám*
larger, un - conscious of - experiencing much little hardships; of-

了 多 少 驚 恐
*꜂líú ꜀tó ꜂shíú ꜀king ꜂hung.*
receiving much little fearful dread.

養 活 你 教 導 你 到 得 你 成
*꜂Yéung út꜄ ꜂ní, káu' tò2 ꜂ní, tò' tak꜆ ꜂ní ꜁shing*
Nurturing rearing you, teaching counseling you, till to you complete

人 長 大 替 你 娶 妻 生 子 望 你 讀
*꜁yan ꜂chéung tái2, tai' ꜂ní ts'ü' ꜀ts'ai ꜀shang ꜂tsz'. Móng2 ꜂ní tuk꜄*
man grown up, for you engage wife to-beget sons. Hopes you will-study

書成名 替你掙家立業 那<br>
‚shü ‚shing ‚ming; t'ai' 'ní ‚chang ‚ká, lap‚ ip‚. 'Ná<br>
books establish reputation; [or] for you seek property, settle inheritance. Which

一件兒不關父母的心 這個恩<br>
yat‚ kín' ‚í pat‚ ‚kwán fú' 'mò tik‚ ‚sam? Ché' kó' ‚yan<br>
one thing not concern parent 's mind? These kindnesses

是報得盡的麼 你若是不曉得<br>
shí' pò' tak‚ tsun' tik‚ ‚mó? 'Ni yéuk‚ shí' pat‚ 'hiú tak‚<br>
are requite able wholly eh? You if do not comprehend

你父母的恩 只把你待兒子的<br>
'ní fú' 'mò tik‚ ‚yan, chat‚ 'pá 'ní toi' ‚í 'tsz' tik‚<br>
your parent s' affection, just to (acc.) you towards your-children 's

心腸想一想就曉得了<br>
‚sam ‚ch'éung, 'séung yat‚ 'séung, tsau' 'hiú tak‚ 'liú.<br>
affection, [and] think a little, then will understand.

古人說的好 養兒方知父母<br>
'Kú ‚yan shüt‚ tik‚ 'hò: 'Yéung ‚í ‚fóng ‚chí fú' 'mò<br>
The ancients expressed it well: "Bring-up children then will-know parents'

恩 既然知道 父母的恩了爲<br>
‚yan. Kí' ‚in ‚chí tò' fú' 'mò tik‚ ‚yan 'liú, wai'<br>
affection." Already acquainted-with parent s' affection, is

甚麼不去 孝順他呢 這個孝順<br>
sham' ‚mó pat‚ hü' háu' shun' ‚t'á ‚ni? Ché' kó' háu' shun'<br>
why unwilling dutifully obey them eh? This filial duty

也不是做不來的事 且如古來的<br>
'yá pat‚ shí' tsò' pat‚ ‚loi tik‚ sz'. 'Ch'é ‚ü 'kú ‚loi tik‚<br>
truly not is do not come 's act. Moreover be-as ancient s'

人有臥冰的 有割股的 有埋兒<br>
‚yan: 'Yau ngó' ‚ping tik‚, 'yau kót‚ 'kú tik‚; 'yau ‚mái ‚í<br>
men: Was slept ice one, was cut thigh one; was buried child

的 這樣的事 便難學了 也不必定<br>
tik‚. Ché' yéung' tik‚ sz', pín' ‚nán hók‚ 'liú, 'yá pat‚ pít‚ ting'<br>
one. This sort of acts, is hard to-learn, still not absolutely

要這麼做 纔叫做孝 只要<br>
íú' ché' ‚mó tsò', ‚ts'oi kíú' tsò' háu'. Chat‚ íú'<br>
necessary that kind do, yet can-be-termed filial. Only require

心心念念的放在父母身上 就好<br>
‚sam ‚sam ním' ním' tik‚ fóng' tsoi' fú' 'mò ‚shan shéung' tsau' 'hò.<br>
heartily remember towards in parents' persons, will suffice.

你們果然要報恩 但凡自己力<br>
'Ni ‚mún 'kwó ‚in íú' pò' ‚yan, tán' ‚fán tsz' 'kí lik‚<br>
You really wishing requite affection, only all your own strength

量 做 將 來 的 無 所 不 至 去 奉
léung² tsò² ˏtséung ˏloi tikˎ, ˏmò ʻshó patˎ chí' hü' fung²
ability doing for-them, whatever can perform to present

承 兩 個 老 人 家 寧 可 自 已 少
ˏshing ʻléung kó' ʻlò ˏyan ˏká. ˏNing ʻhó tsz'² ʻkí ʻshiú
offer both those old persons of-house. Preferable yourself little

吃 少 用 的 儘 父 母 吃 儘 父 母 用
hatˎ, ʻshiú yung² tikˎ, ʻtsun fú² ʻmò hatˎ, ʻtsun fú² ʻmò yung²,
eat, little use, fully parents eat, fully parents use,

替 他 代 些 勞 不 可 去 賭 錢 吃
t'ai' ˏt'á toi² ˏsé ˏlò. Patˎ ʻhó hü' ʻtò ˏts'ín, hatˎ
for them instead lessen toils. Im-proper go gamble money, guzzle

酒 不 可 去 和 人 打 架 不 可 暗
ʻtsau; patˎ ʻhó hü' ˏwó ˏyan ʻtá ká'; patˎ ʻhó óm'
wine; im-proper go join men wrangle fight; im-proper secret

地 裏 私 自 積 儹 銀 子 錢 疼 自
ti² ʻlü ˏsz' tsz'² tsikˎ ʻtsán ˏngan ʻtsz' ˏts'ín, ˏt'ang tsz'²
places in privately yourself hoard up silver coin, dote your

己 的 老 婆 孩 子 不 顧 着 父 母
ʻkí tikˎ ʻlò ˏp'ó, ˏhoi ʻtsz', patˎ kú' chéukˏ fú² ʻmò.
own 's old woman (wife) little children, not regard for parents.

縱 然 外 邊 的 儀 節 做 將 不 來
Ts'ung' ˏín ngoi² ˏpín tikˎ ˏí tsítˎ, tsò² ˏtséung patˎ ˏloi,
Allowing-that the-external demeanor, acting to-[them] not effect,

都 不 妨 事 只 要 心 裏 邊 誠
ˏtò patˎ ˏfóng sz'²; chatˎ íú' ˏsam ʻlü ˏpín ˏshing
still not injure this-duty; only necessary heart in-side sincerely

實 便 好 就 是 每 日 裏 粗 菜 淡
shatˏ, pín² ʻhò. Tsau² shí² ʻmúi yatˏ ʻlü ˏts'ò ts'oi' tám²
honest, then well. Suppose it-is each day in coarse vegetables plain

飯 的 只 要 叫 他 歡 歡 喜 喜 吃
fán² tikˎ, chatˎ íú' kíú' ˏt'á ˏfún ˏfún ʻhí ʻhí hatˏ
rice, simply need to-cause them pleasurably gladly to-eat

得 下 去 這 就 是 孝 順 了 如 是
takˎ há² hü': ché' tsau² shí² háu' shun² ʻlíú. ˏU shí²,
it down; this then is filial obedience. Whereupon,

把 這 個 道 理 推 開 說 就 如
ʻpá ché' kó' tò² ʻlí, ˏt'úi ˏhoi shütˎ. Tsau² ˏü
taking-up this principle, [let us] investigate explain speak. Hence, if

舉 動 之 間 不 端 端 正 正 的 這 就
ʻkü tung² ˏchí ˏkán, patˎ ˏtün ˏtün ching' ching' tikˎ, ché' tsau²
rising moving 's midst, not perfectly-correct decorous, this then

是褻慢了父母的遺體便
*shí2 sít, mán2 ʿlíú fú2 ʿmò tik, ˏwai ʿtʻai; pín2*
is disgracing disesteeming parent s' entailed body; consequently

爲不孝了替朝廷做事不
*ˏwai pat, háu2 ʿlíú. Tʻai2 ˏchʻíú ˏtʻing tsò2, sz2, pat,*
is un - dutiful. On-behalf-of government doing business, [if] not

盡心竭力的做事君不忠
*tsun2 ˏsam kít2 lik2 tik, tsò2, sz2, ˏkwan pat, ˏchung,*
undivided mind utmost strength 's acting, [but] serve prince un - faithfully,

就如待父母不好一般就
*tsau2 ˏü toi2 fú2 ʿmò pat, ʿhò, yat, ˏpún. Tsau2*
then resembles behaving-to parents ill, same thing. This-then

是不孝了
*shí2 pat, háu2 ʿlíú.*
is un - dutifulness.

做官的若是不好惹百姓
*Tsò2 ˏkún tik,, yéuk2 shí2 pat, ʿhò, ʿyé pák, sing2*
Being a-magistrate, if act im - properly, provoking the - people

們笑駡這是把父母遺體輕
*ˏmún síú2 má2, ché2 shí2 ʿpá fú2 ʿmò ˏwai ʿtʻai ˏhing*
to-ridicule revile, this is to (acc.) parents' bestowed body despising

慢了就是不孝了在朋友前
*mán2 ʿlíú. Tsau2 shí2 pat, háu2 ʿlíú. Tsoi2 ˏpʻang ʿyau ˏtsʻín*
reproaching. This-then is un - dutifulness. In friends' presence

說話做事不着實便玷
*shüt, wá2 tsò2 sz2 pat, chéuk, shat2, pín2 ʿtím*
conversing doing things not according-to honesty, then dishonors

辱着父母也是不孝若是
*yuk2 chéuk2 fú2 ʿmò; ʿyá shí2 pat, háu2. Yéuk2 shí2*
disgraces parents; also is un - dutifulness. Supposing it-is

你們兵丁們上陣出兵的
*ʿní ˏmún ˏping ˏting ˏmún ʿshéung chʻan2 chʻut, ˏping tik,*
you soldiers' at - advance army order-out troop s'

時節不肯勇猛爭先叫人
*ˏshí tsít,, pat, ʿhang ʿyung ʿmang ˏchang ˏsín, kíú2 ˏyan*
occasion, refuse bravely valiantly fight advance, causing men

笑話你軟弱這是把父母
*síú2 wá2 ʿní ʿün yéuk2, ché2 shí2 ʿpá fú2 ʿmò*
to-sneer saying you effeminate cowardly, this is to (acc.) parent

的遺體下賤了也是不孝如今
*tik, ˏwai ʿtʻai há2 tsʻín2 ʿlíú. ʿYá shí2 pat, háu. ˏU ˏkam*
s' conferred body degrade dishonor. Also is undutifulness. Present

世上忤逆的兒子很多 父
shai$^2$ shéung$^2$ ‘’ng yik$_2$ tik, ‚í ‘tsz’ ‘han ‚tó. Fú$^2$
age in refractory disobedient 's children very numerous. To-father

母、説他句他就變臉父母駡
‘mò shüt, ‚t‘á kü’, ‚t‘á tsau$^2$ ‘pín’ lim$^2$; fú$^2$ ‘mò má’
mother telling them a-word, they forthwith alter faces; to-parents reproving

他聲他就應嘴 叫他東
‚t‘á ‚shing, ‚t‘á tsau$^2$ ying’ ‘tsúi; kiú’ ‚t‘á ‚tung,
them voice, they straight give-back lip; to-calling them this-way,

他往西還有自己的老婆
‚t‘á ‘wóng ‚sai. ‚Wán ‘yau tsz’$^2$ ‘kí tik ‘lò ‚p‘ó
they go that. Moreover they-have their own wife

娃子都飽飽煖煖的父母倒忍飢
‚wá ‘tsz’, ‚tò ‘páu ‘páu ‘nün ‘nün tik, fú$^2$ ‘mò ‘tò ‘yan ‚kí,
children, all full-fed warmly-clad, parents still bear want

受餓自己撞下禍來帶累
shau$^2$ ngó$^2$. Tsz’$^2$ ‘kí chóng$^2$ há$^2$ wó$^2$ ‚loi, tái’ lui$^2$
suffer hunger. Themselves rushing into troubles, lugs-in involves

父母受氣 自己犯了事
fú$^2$ ‘mò shau$^2$ hí’. Tsz’$^2$ ‘kí fán’ ‘liú sz’$^2$,
parents [who] suffer consequences. Their own transgressing acts,

帶累父母上官入府的
tái’ lui$^2$ fú$^2$ ‘mò ‘shéung ‚kún yap$_2$ ‘fú tik,.
involve parents before magistrates into courts.

這樣人莫説天理上不容
Chè’ yéung$^2$ ‚yan, mók$_2$ shüt, ‚t‘ín ‘lí shéung$^2$ pat, ‚yung,
This class-of persons, I-need-not say heavenly propriety in disallows,

就是自己兒子看了樣也就
tsau$^2$ shí$^2$ tsz’$^2$ ‘kí ‚í ‘tsz’ hón’ ‘liú yéung$^2$, ‘yá tsau$^2$
but is their own children seeing example, also then

跟着學了你看不孝順的人
‚kan chéuk$_2$ hók$_2$ ‘liú. ‘Ní hón’ pat, háu’ shun$^2$ tik, ‚yan,
follow to learn. Do-you observe disobedient 's persons,

那裏養得出個好兒子來你們
‘ná ‘lí ‘yéung tak, ch‘ut, kó’ ‘hò ‚í ‘tsz’ ‚loi? ‘Ní ‚mún
where nurturing can find those good children come? Do-you

想一想還不省悟麼
‘séung yat, ‘séung. ‚Wán pat, ‘sing ‘ng$^2$ ‚mó?
think a thought. Still not excited aroused eh?

除了父母就是兄弟 這弟
‚Ch‘ü ‘liú fú$^2$ ‘mò, tsau$^2$ shí$^2$ ‚hing tai$^2$. Chè’ tai$^2$
Besides father mother, then is elder younger-brothers. These

兄們 非 不是兩個人他
꜀hing ꜁mún ꜀fí pat꜆ shí2 ʿléung kó꜄ ꜁yan. ꜀T'á
brethren doubtless not are two individual men. His

身上的骨肉就是我身上的骨
꜀shan shéung2 tik꜆ kwat꜆ yuk2, tsau2 shí2 ʿngó ꜀shan shéung2 tik꜆ kwat꜆
body in 's bones flesh, truly is my body in 's bones

肉所以呌做手足你若薄
yuk2, ʿshó ʿí kíú꜄ tsò2 ʿshau tsuk꜆. ʿNí yéuk2 pók2
flesh, wherefore called to-be hands feet. You if slightingly

待了弟兄便是薄待了父母了
toi2 ʿlíú tai2 ꜀hing, pín2 shí2 pók꜆ toi2 ʿlíú fú2 ʿmò ʿlíú.
behave-to brothers, that-then is disrespectfully treating parents.

就是弟兄們不同母也是一個
Tsau2 shí2 tai2 ꜀hing ꜁mún pat꜆ ꜁t'ung ʿmò, ʿyá shí2 yat꜆ kó꜄
What-if is brother s not the-same mother, still is one

父毋的骨血不可說不是同母
fú2 ʿmò tik꜆ kwat꜆ hüt꜆; pat꜆ ʿhó shüt꜆ pat꜆ shí2 ꜁t'ung ʿmò,
father 's bones blood; cannot say not is same mother, [and]

就看做兩樣了人世最親的
tsau2 hón꜄ tsò2 ʿléung yéung2 ʿlíú. ꜁Yan shai꜄ tsui꜄ ꜀ts'an tik꜆
then regard act different manners. Nowadays men's nearest relation

是妻子死了還可以另娶得一個
shí2 ꜀ts'ai ʿtsz'; ʿsz' ʿlíú, ꜁wán ʿhó ʿí ling2 ts'ü꜄ tak꜆ yat꜆ kó꜄.
is wife; being-dead, still can by another marriage obtain one.

這兄弟若是歿了那裏還討得
Ché꜄ ꜀hing tai2, yéuk2 shí2 mút2 ʿlíú ʿná ʿlí ꜁wán ʿt'ò tak꜆
The brother, if he-is departed, where again seek get

一個來喲你們想一想還是該
yat꜆ kó꜄ ꜁loi yéuk꜆? ʿNí ꜁mún ʿséung yat꜆ ʿséung. ꜁Wán shí2 ꜀koi
one come eh? Do-you think one thought. Still is-it ought

親愛不該親愛怎麼樣個
꜀ts'an oi꜄, pat꜆ ꜀koi ꜀ts'an oi꜄? ʿTsam ꜀mó yéung2 kó꜄
attachedly love, not ought affectionately love? What manner is-this

親愛呢做兄弟的要敬重
꜀ts'an oi꜄ ꜀ní? Tsò2 ꜀hing tai2 tik꜆, íú꜄ king꜄ chung2
affectionate love eh? Being a-younger-brother, he-should respect defer-to

哥哥但凡有甚麼事或是
꜀kó ꜀kó. Tán2 ꜁fán ʿyau sham2 ꜀mó sz'2? Wák2 shí2
elder brother. But altogether are what sort-of affairs? Whether it-is

吃飯或是穿衣服或是隨
hat2 fán2; wák2 shí2 ꜀ch'ün ꜀í fuk2; wák2 shí2 ꜁ts'ui
eating food; or it-is putting-on clothes; or is waiting-on

人 禮 或是說話或是走路
ˏyan ˊlai; wák2 shí2 shüt› wá2; wák2 shí2 ˊtsau lò2;
people ceremoniously; or is conversing; or is walking-in path;

或是坐或是站 都要儘讓做
wák2 shí2 tsó2; wák2 shí2 chám2: ‹tò íú' ˊtsun yéung2 tsò2
or is sitting; or is standing: in-all must entirely yield-to he-who-is

哥哥的
‹kó ‹kó tik›.
elder brother.

古來的人就是一鄉一村兒上
ˊKú ˏloi tik› ˏyan, tsau2 shí2 yat› ‹héung yat› ‹ts'ün ˏí shéung2
Olden time 's people, if it-was same village same hamlet in

的人他若比我大十歲我
tik› ˏyan;— ‹t'á, yéuk2 ˊpí ˊngó, tái2 shap2 sui', ˊngó
's person;— he, if compared-to me, exceeded ten years, I

就尊他做哥 他若比我大
tsau2 ‹tsün ‹t'á tsò2 ‹kó. ‹T'á, yéuk2 ˊpí ˊngó tái2
then honored him to-be eld.-brother. He, if compared-to me exceeded

五歲我就挨肩隨着他就不
ˊ'ng sui', ˊngó tsau2 ‹ái ‹kin ˏts'ui chéuk2 ‹t'á, tsau2 pat›
five years, I then retiring shoulder followed near him, indeed not

敢 僭 越他了 外人比 我年紀
ˊkóm ts'im' üt2 ‹t'á ˊlíú. Ngoi2 ˏyan ˊpí ˊngó ˏnín ˊkí
presuming little precede him. A-stranger compared-with my age

大我還要這樣的敬重他何況
tái2, ˊngó ˏwán íú' ché' yéung2 tik› king' chung2 ‹t'á; ˏhó fóng'
older, I still ought in-this manner respect defer-to him; how much-more

是我的親〃哥呢
shí2 ˊngó tik› ‹ts'an ‹kó ‹kó ˏní?
[ought I] to mine own elder brother eh?

至於做哥哥的要 疼 愛著
Chí' ‹ü tsò2 ‹kó ‹kó tik›, íú' ˏt'ang oi' chéuk2
As to he-who-is an-elder brother, he-ought affectionately love younger-

兄弟. 兄弟們 凴 他多 大年紀
‹hing tai2. ‹Hing tai2 ˏmún ˏp'ang ‹t'á ‹tó tái2 ˏnín ˊkí,
brothers. Younger-brethren according-to their more [or] greater age,

我只把他當 娃兒待 比如我的
ˊngó chat› ˊpá ‹t'á tóng' ‹wá ˏí toi2. ˊPí ˏü, ˊngó tik›
I only to them ought-as own-children behave. For-instance, my-own

兒子若是不成才 我也着實
ˏí ˊtsz', yéuk2 shí2 pat› ˏshing ˏts'oi, ˊngó ˊyá chéuk› shat2
child, if does not act the-man I also verily indeed

恨他罵他打他轉過臉
*han$^{2}$ ˏt'á, má$^{2}$ ˏt'á, ‘tá ˏt'á, ‘chün kwó’ ‘lím*
displeased-at him, scold him; punish him, [then] change regain counte-

兒依舊的疼他惟獨到了兄弟
*ˏí ˏí kau$^{2}$ tik˒ ˏt'ang ˏt'á. ˏWai tuk˒ tò’ ‘liú ˏhing tai$^{2}$*
nance, as before love him. But only regarding younger-brothers,

偏只是不好再不肯慢慢兒
*ˏp'in chat˒ shí$^{2}$ pat˒ ‘hò: tsoi’ pat˒ ‘hang mán$^{2}$ mán$^{2}$ ˏí*
bent-on only what-is ill: then un - willing deliberately

勸他說他一遇兄弟有了
*hün’ ˏt'á, shüt˒ ˏt'á; yat˒ ü$^{2}$ ˏhing tai$^{2}$ ‘yau ‘liú*
admonish them, converse-with them; all-at-once observe younger-brother has had

些不是就要爭鬭起來你
*ˏsé pat˒ shí$^{2}$, tsau$^{2}$ ‘iú’ ˏchang tau’ ‘hí ˏloi. ‘Ní*
trifling offense, then straightway wrangling quarrels spring up. Do-you

想你和你兄弟都是一個老子
*‘séung ‘ní ˏwó ‘ní ˏhing tai$^{2}$ ˏtò shí$^{2}$ yat˒ kó’ ‘lò ‘tsz’*
reflect you and your younger-brothers all are one single father

娘養的你若打你兄弟就是
*ˏnéung ‘yéung tik˒; ‘ní yéuk˒ ‘tá ‘ní ˏhing tai$^{2}$ tsau$^{2}$ shí$^{2}$*
mother nurtured by; you if beat your younger-brothers, then is

自家打自家一般了
*tsz’$^{2}$ ˏká ‘tá tsz’$^{2}$ ˏká, yat˒ ˏpún ‘liú.*
own family beating own family, one - and - the - same.

做兄弟的又不知好歹見哥哥
*Tsò$^{2}$ ˏhing tai$^{2}$ tik˒, yau$^{2}$ pat˒ ˏchí ‘hò ‘tái, kín’ ˏkó ˏkó*
Being younger-brothers, still ignorant-of good evil, seeing elder-brother

打他也就還起手來比如一個
*‘tá ˏt'á, ‘yá tsau$^{2}$ ˏwán ‘hí ‘shau ˏloi. ‘Pí ˏü, yat˒ kó’*
beating him, also then return lift hand. For instance, one

人的手足假如失手打了
*ˏyan tik˒ ‘shau tsuk˒: ‘ká ˏü shat˒ ‘shau ‘tá ‘liú*
man’ s hands feet: suppose inadvertently hand pound - ed

脚難道還把脚去踢手不成
*kéuk˒, ˏnán tò$^{2}$ ˏwán ‘pá kéuk˒ hü’ t'ik˒ ‘shau pat˒ ˏshing!*
foot, it-cannot-be said forthwith with foot go-to kick hand not act!

如今弟兄們不和都是爲爭
*ˏU ˏkam, tai$^{2}$ ˏhing ˏmún pat˒ ˏwó ˏtò shí$^{2}$ wai$^{2}$ ˏchang*
At present, brethren dis - agreeing all are from contending-for

財起見都是聽老婆的話
*ˏts'oi ‘hí kín’, ˏtò shí$^{2}$ t'ing’ ‘lò ˏp'ó tik˒ wá$^{2}$.*
property arise, [or] all are from-hearing wives ’s words.

這 些 老 婆 們的 話 也 不 是 盡 情 没
*Ché˒ ˏsé ˋlò ˏp'ó ˏmún tik˒ wá², ˋyá pat˒ shí² tsun² ˏts'ing mút₂*
These wives 's talk, still not is in-all respects destitute-of

道 理 的 正 因 為 他 的 說 話 也 有 些
*tò² ˋlí tik˒; ching˒ ˏyan wai² ˏt'á tik˒ shüt˒ wá², ˋyá ˋyau ˏsé*
reason; truly because their talk, still has a-little

理 兒 便 不 知 不 覺 的 聽 進
*ˋlí ˏí; pín² pat˒ ˏchí pat˒ kók˒ tik˒ t'ing˒ tsun˒*
reason; consequently unconsciously unawares heard entered

去 就 如 做 嫂 子 的 向 哥 哥
*hü˒. Tsau² ˏü tsò² ˋsò ˋtsz˒. tik˒, héung˒ ˏkó ˏkó*
in. Suppose one-who-is sister-in-law, towards [the] elder- brother

說 小 叔 兒 怎 麼 樣 懶 怎 麼 樣 花
*shüt˒, ˋsíú shuk˒ ˏí ˋtsam ˏmó. yéung² ˋlán, ˋtsam ˏmó yéung² ˏfá*
says, our-little-uncle [is] so-and-so fashion idle, so-and-so fashion spends

錢 你 辛 辛 苦 苦 的 掙 錢 養 活 着
*ˏts'ín. ˋNí ˏsan ˏsan ˋfú ˋfú tik˒ ˏchang ˏts'ín ˋyéung út₂ chéuk₂*
money. You laboriously painfully obtain money feed support

他 還 說 長 道 短 難 道 我 們 是
*ˏt'á, ˏwán shüt˒ ˏch'éung, tò² ˋtün; ˏnán tò² ˋngó ˏmún shí²*
him, still he-calls this-long, says that-is-short; cannot say we are

他 的 兒 子 媳 婦 該 當 孝 順 他
*ˏt'á tik˒ ˏí ˋtsz˒, . sik˒ ˋfú, ˏkoi ˏtóng háu˒ shun² ˏt'á*
his son, [his] daughter-in-law, proper ought dutifully obey him

的 麼
*tik˒ ˏmò?*
eh?

那 個 兄 弟 媳 婦 也 會 向 兄 弟 說
*ˋNá kó˒ ˏhing tai² sik˒ ˋfú, ˋyá ˋúi héung˒ ˏhing tai² shüt˒:*
That younger-brother's wife, also knows towards him talk:

就 是 哥 哥 會 掙 錢 你 也 掙 過
*Tsaü² shí² ˏkó ˏkó ˋúi ˏchang ˏts'ín, ˋní ˋyá ˏchang kwó˒*
Let-it be-that elder-brother is-able collect money, you also have-collected

錢 你 在 家 裡 一 般 兒 做 長 做 短
*ˏts'ín; ˋní tsoi² ˏká ˋlü yat˒ ˏpún ˏí tsò² ˏch'éung, tsò² ˋtün;*
money; you in the-family same degree doing long, doing short;

就 是 僱 個 長 工 也 沒 有 這 般 勞
*tsau² shí² kú˒ kó˒ ˏch'éung ˏkung, ˋyá mút₂ ˋyau ché˒ ˏpún ˏlò*
if you-were hired one servant, even not have this degree toil

苦 的 偏 他 的 娃 子 就 是 娃 子
*ˋfú tik˒. ˏP'in ˏt'á tik˒ ˏwá ˋtsz˒ tsau² shí² ˏwá ˋtsz˒;*
labor. Partial-to his own children forthwith are-as children;

買這個吃 買那個吃 難道我們
*'mái ché' kó' hat2, 'mái 'ná kó' hat2: ,nán tò2 'ngó ,mún*
buy this to-eat, buy that to-eat; shall-I-not say our

的娃子 就都是該死的麽
*tik, ,wá 'tsz', tsau2 ,tò shí2 ,koi 'sz' tik, ,mó?*
own children, straightway all are ought to-die eh?

照這般的說話今日有些明日
*Chiú' ché' ,pún tik, shüt, wá2, ,kam yat2 'yau ,sé, ,ming yat2*
Such-as this kind of talk, to - day have a-little, to - morrow

有些不由做哥兒們的聽不進去
*'yau ,sé, pat, 'yau tsò2 ,kó ,í ,mún tik, t'ing' pat, tsun' hü'.*
have a-little, not let those husband s' hearing not impress.

從此便把弟兄們的心腸都冷淡
*,Ts'ung 'ts'z' pín2 'pá tai2 ,hing ,mún tik, ,sam ,ch'éung ,tò 'lang tám2*
From this then to (acc.) the brother s' affections all cool weaken

下來了一日一日的攢湊便至於
*há2 ,lai 'liú; yat, yat2 yat, yat2 tik, ,tsün ts'au'; pín2 chí' ,ü*
proceed; each day each day 's increase addition, then even to

打架廝鬧 却不知道弟兄們
*'tá ká' ,sz' náu2, K'éuk, pat, ,chí tò2 tai2 ,hing ,mún*
fighting wrangling. Really not reflect brethren

原是一個人
*,ün shí2 yat, kó' ,yan.*
originally were one individual.

就是哥哥無能些做兄弟
*Tsau2 shí2 ,kó ,kó ,mò ,nang ,sé, tsò2 ,hing tai2*
Suppose is elder brother without ability somewhat, being younger brother

的養活着他也是該當的兄
*tik, 'yéung út2 chéuk2 ,t'á, 'yá shí2 ,koi ,tóng tik, ,Hing*
nurturing supporting him, also is proper ought. Younger

弟無能些做哥哥的養活着
*tai2 ,mò ,nang ,sé, tsò2 ,kó ,kó tik, 'yéung út2 chéuk2*
brother without ability rather, being elder brother nurturing supporting

他也是該當的便是一時間有
*,t'á, 'yá shí2 ,koi ,tóng tik, Pín2 shí2 yat, ,shí ,kán 'yau*
him, also is proper ought. If is any occasion whilst there-are

些閑言閑語只當他醉了
*,sé ,hán ,ín ,hán 'ü, chat, tóng' ,t'á tsui' 'liú,*
some unseeming words unbecoming speeches, only consider him drunken,

或是說夢話便大家撒開了
*wák2 shí2 shüt, mung2 wá2, pín2 tái2 ,ká sát, ,hoi 'liú.*
or-as-if are spoken dreaming talk, then all of-them scatter-it away quite.

偏要認的眞譬如兩隻手右
*ˏP'ín iú' yan² tik˒ ˏchan, p'í' ˏü ˋléung chik˒ ˋshau; yau²*
Obstinately-bent to-regard it sincere, compare [you] to two hands; right

手極其能幹寫字也是他
*ˋshau kik₂ ˏk'í ˏnang kón', ˋsé tsz'² ˋyá shí² ˏt'á*
hand extols its ability to-perform, writing characters only is its,

打算盤也是他拿東拿西的也
*ˋtá sün' ˏp'ún ˋyá shí² ˏt'á, ˏná ˏtung ˏná ˏsai tik˒ ˋyá*
reckoning-on abacus only is its, take that take this 's only

是他這隻左手就笨的緊沒
*shí² ˏt'á: ché' chik˒ ˋtsó ˋshau tsau² pan² tik˒ ˋkan: 'mút₂*
is its: this left hand indeed stupid 's exceedingly: no-one

有聽見人拿右手去打左手的
*ˋyau t'ing' kín' ˏyan ˏná yau² ˋshau hü' ˋtá ˋtsó ˋshau tik˒.*
has heard seen man raising right hand went-about beating left hand.

一個哥兒兄弟親親的手足如
*Yat˒ kó' ˏkó ˏí ˏhing tai², ˏts'an ˏts'an tik˒ ˋshau tsuk˒, ˏü*
An elder brother younger brother, nearly related [as] hands feet, what

何爭長論短你想一想
*ˏhó ˏchang ˏch'éung lun² ˋtün? ˋNí ˋséung yat˒ ˋséung.*
reason wrangle-about long talk-about short? Do-you reflect one thought.

銀子錢是淌來之物去了還
*ˏNgan ˋtsz' ˏts'ín, shí² ˋt'óng ˏloi ˏchí mat₂; hü' ˋlíú ˏwán*
[As to] silver money, it-is circuitously coming 's thing; gone again

有來的老婆們他不和我是一個
*ˋyau ˏloi tik˒. ˋLò ˏp'ó ˏmún ˏt'á pat˒ ˏwó ˋngó shí² yat˒ kó'*
has return. Our-wives they not with us have same

老子娘他知道甚麼道理呢只
*ˋlò ˋtsz' ˏnéung, ˏt'á ˏchí tò² sham² ˏmó tò² ˋlí ˏní? Chat˒*
father mother, they understand what proper feelings eh? Only

顧弟兄們不和做父母的
*kü' tai² ˏhing ˏmün pat˒ ˏwó; tsò² fú² ˋmò tik˒,*
observe brothers disagreeing; those-who-are parents,

必然生氣你只看你兒子們打
*pit˒ ˏín ˏshang hí'. ˋNí chat˒ hón' ˋní ˏí ˋtsz' ˏmún ˋtá*
undoubtedly excites feeling. You just observe your children's fight-

架你心裏惱不惱所以做孝子的
*ká', ˋní ˏsam ˋlü ˋnò pat˒ ˋnò? ˋShó ˋí tsò² háu' ˋtsz' tik˒*
ing, your heart in angry not angry? Therefore being dutiful son 's

人再沒有不和美弟兄的
*ˏyan, tsoi' mút₂ ˋyau pat˒ ˏwó ˋmí tai² ˏhing tik˒.*
persons, still-more not are dis - cordant brothers.

俗語說的好打虎還得親兄弟
*Tsuk₂ ʿü shüt, tik, ʿhò: ʿTá ʿfú ₛwán tak, ₑtsʻan ₑhing tai²;*
Common proverbs say well: Attacking tiger still obtain own brothers;

上陣還須父子兵又說道好
*ʿShéung chan² ₛwán ₑsü fú² ʿtsz' ₑping. Yau² shüt, tò²: ʿHò*
Advancing battle still require fathers sons' soldiers. Also it-is-said: Good

殺了是他人壞殺了是自己又
*shát, ʿlíú shí² ₑtʻá ₛyan; wái² shát, ʿlíú shí² tsz² ʿkí. Yau²*
surpassingly [still] is stranger; bad surpassingly [still] is myself. Again

說道兄弟不和旁人欺只顧
*shüt, tò², ₑHing tai² pat, ₛwó ₛpʻóng ₛyan ₑhí. Chat, ₑkú*
it-is-said, Brothers disagreeing by-standers despise. Just notice

你們爭閑氣就有人來挑唆你們
*ʿní ₛmún ₑchang ₛhán hí², tsau² ʿyau ₛyan ₛloi ₑtʻíú ₑsó ʿní ₛmún,*
your quarreling trifling anger, then are men come stir-up vilify you,

搬鬬你們的是非或是鬬毆
*ₑpún tau² ʿní ₛmún tik, shí² ₑfí; wák₂ shí² tau² ʿau,*
tale-bearing your rights wrongs; either arise fightings,

或是打官司再沒有個不敗
*wák₂ shí² ʿtá ₑkún ʿsz'. Tsoi² mút₂ ʿyau kó² pat, pái²*
or are make lawsuits. Certainly none there-are of-these not ruin

家的你們若是孝順友愛呢
*ₑká tik,. ʿNí ₛmún yéuk₂ shí² háu² shun² ʿyau oi² ₑní?*
the-family. You perhaps are dutifully filial brotherly affectionate?

做民的纔是良民做兵的
*Tsò² ₛman tik, ₛtsʻoi shí² ₛléung ₛman; tsò² ₑping tik,*
Those-who-are people then will-be good people; those-who-are soldiers

纔是好漢子
*ₛtsʻoi shí² ʿhò Hón² ʿtsz'.*
then will-be brave Chinese.

但是你兵民們那一個不知道
*Tán² shí² ʿní ₑping ₛman ₛmún, ʿná yat, kó² pat, ₑchí tò²*
But he-is of-you soldiers people all, who is-one individual not know

孝順是好事弟兄們和美是好
*háu² shun² shí² ʿhò sz'², tai² ₑhing ₛmún ₛwó ʿmí shí² ʿhò*
filial obedience is good thing, brothers harmonizing is good

事既然知道說好爲甚麼不去
*sz'²? Kí² ₛín ₑchí tò² shüt, ʿhò, wai² sham² ₑmó pat, hü²*
thing? Already know speaks well, for what not go-about

實心實力的做阿必定心心
*shat₂ ₑsam, shat₂ lik₂ tik, tsò² ó²? Pít, ting² ₑsam ₑsam*
upright heart honest zeal to-do eh? Indispensible heartily

念 念 想 着 父 母 兄 弟 不 要 光
*nim' nim' ˋséung chéuk, fú² ˋmò ˏhing tai². Pat, iú' ˏkwóng*
meditate-upon remember parents brothers. Not require polite

向 外 面 的 儀 文 不 要 忽 略 了 小
*shéung² ngoi² min² tik, ˏí ˏman; pat, iú' fat, léuk, ˋliú ˋsiú*
elegant external 's gentility; not need disregard small

處 不 要 止 圖 外 人 的 虛 名
*ch'ü'; pat, iú' ˋchí ˏt'ò ngoi² ˏyan tik, ˏhü ˏming;*
matters; not need only plan-for observer s' empty reputation;

不 要 以 前 好 以 後 又 不 好 了 這
*pat, iú' ˋí ˏts'in ˋhò ˋí hau² yau² pat, ˋhò ˋliú. Ché'*
not need previously well, subsequently also not well. This

才 是 眞 眞 的 孝 子 眞 眞 的 好
*ˏts'oi shí² ˏchan ˏchan tik, háu' ˋtsz', ˏchan ˏchan tik, ˋhò*
manner is verily of-a filial son, truly of affectionate

弟 兄
*tai² ˏhing.*
brothers.

你 若 是 不 孝 或 是 弟 兄 們 不
*ˋNí yéuk, shí² pat, háu', wák, shí² tai² ˏhing ˏmún pat,*
You if are un - dutiful, or are brothers who-cannot

和 就 要 拿 刑 法 處 治 了 但
*ˏwó, tsau² iú' ˏná ˏying fát, ˋch'ü chí² ˋliú; tán²*
agree, then necessary to-arrest punish legally in-order to-correct; but-if

你 心 裏 不 明 白 處 你 也 是 枉 然
*ˋní ˏsam ˋlü pat, ˏming pák,, ˋch'ü ˋní ˋyá shí² ˋwóng ˏín.*
your heart in not understand, regard you still as-being perverse indeed.

萬 歲 爺 心 裏 不 忍 所 以 反
*Mán² suí' ˏyé ˏsam ˋlü pat, ˋyan, ˋshó ˋí ˋfán*
Ten-thousand years grandfather's heart in cannot bear-it, therefore again

反 覆 覆 的 勸 誡 你 你 們 肯 聽
*ˋfán, fuk, fuk, tik, hün' kái' ˋní. ˋNí ˏmún ˋhang t'ing'*
again this way that way exhorts admonishes you. You willing to-hear

萬 歲 爺 的 話 大 家 做 個 孝 子
*mán² suí', ˏyé. tik, wá², tái² ˏká tsò² kó' háu' ˋtsz'*
his imperial majesty 's words, altogether be those obedient children

悌 弟 不 但 一 生 不 犯 法 就
*tai², tai², pat, tán² yat, ˏshang pat, fán² fát,, tsau²*
affectionate brothers, not only one generation not transgress laws, but-then

你 的 兒 子 孫 子 也 學 個 好 樣 子
*ˋní tik, ˏí ˋtsz' ˏsün ˋtsz', ˋyá hók, kó' ˋhò yéung² ˋtsz'.*
your own children grandchildren, also learn this good example.

拾級大成



俗語說的好　孝　順還生孝順
*Tsuk₂ ʻwá shüt, tik, ʻhò: Háuʼ shun² ˏwán ˏshang háuʼ shun²*
Common proverb says well: The-dutiful obedient also bear dutiful obedient

子　忤　逆　還　養　忤　逆　兒　果
*ʻtszʼ; ʻʼng yik₂ ˏwán ʻyéung ʻʼng yik₂ ˏí. ʻKwó*
children; undutiful obstinate also bring-up undutiful obstinate children. Undoubted-

然　子　子　孫　孫　都是孝　子　悌
*ˏín ʻtszʼ ʻtszʼ ˏsün ˏsün ˏtò shí² háuʼ ʻtszʼ tai²*
ly-when children grandchildren all are filial children affectionate

弟　天　下　再　沒　有　不　太　平　的
*tai², ˏtʻin há² tsoiʼ mút₂ ʻyau pat, tʻáiʼ ˏpʻing tik,.*
brothers, the-empire will by-no-means be not profoundly peaceful.

你們都　着　實　的　做　萬　萬　不可
*ʻNí ˏmún ˏtò chéuk₂ shat₂ tik, tsò²; mán² mán² pat, ʻhó*
You all cause-it strenuously performed; on-no-account not may

看　做　常　套　辜　負　聖　祖　仁
*hónʼ tsò² ˏshéung tʻòʼ; ˏkú fú² shingʼ ʻtsò ˏYan*
regard-as being common needless; criminally oppose sacred ancestor Pious

皇　帝　一　片　盛　心　阿
*ˏwóng taiʼ yat, pʻinʼ shing² ˏsam ʻó.*
imperial sovereign's single desire overflowing heart.

---

## No. IX.—Proper Education of Children.*

(見三字經 王伯厚纂)

苟　不　教　性　乃　遷
*ʻKau pat, káuʼ, singʼ ʻnái ˏtsʻin:*
If not educate, nature then deteriorates:

教　之　道　貴　以　專
*káuʼ ˏchí tò², kwaiʼ ʻí ˏchün.*
of-education 's rules, foremost is application.

養　正　之　謂　何　謂　能　教　也　人　非
*ʻYéung chingʼ ˏchí wai² ˏhó? Wai² ˏnang káuʼ ʻyá. ˏYan ˏfi*
Train-up correctly them is-called what? Is-called ability to-teach A-man not

聖　人　豈　能　生　知　非　親　不　育
*shingʼ ˏyan, ʻhí ˏnang ˏshang ˏchí? ˏFi ˏtsʻan pat, yuk₂,*
a-sage man, how can-he-be naturally wise? Without parents not rear,

---

* This and the two next extracts are taken from the *Sám Tszʼ King* or Trimetrical Classic, a hornbook in use in Chinese schools, which is put into the hands of the lad to commit to memory as soon as he commences his

非教弗成有子而不教則
꜀fí káu' fat꜀ ꜁shing. ꜂Yau ꜂tsz' ꜁í pat꜀ káu', tsak꜀
without teaching not perfect. Having a-son but not teaching, this-then

昧其天賦之良悖理縱
múi² ꜁k'í ꜀t'ín fú' ꜀chí ꜁léung; púi' ꜂lí, ts'ung'
bedims that heaven conferred 's goodness; [by] transgressing propriety, following

欲日遷于不善矣教之何
yuk₂ yat₂ ꜀ts'ín ꜀ü pat꜀ shín² ꜂í. Káu' ꜀chí ꜁hó
passions, daily advances in wickedness truly. Instructing them what

如古者婦人有娠坐不偏卧
꜁ü? ꜂Kú ꜂ché ꜂fú ꜁yan ꜂yau ꜀shan; tsó² pat꜀ ꜀p'ín, ngó²
like? Ancient the females when-were pregnant; sat not awry, slept

不側立不跛倚行不亂步目
pat꜀ chak꜀, lap₂ pat꜀ ꜂p'ó ꜂í, ꜁hang pat꜀ lün², pò², muk₂
not on-side, stood not on-one-leg leaning, walked not mincing steps, eyes

不視惡色耳不聽淫聲不出亂
pat꜀ shí² ók꜀ shik꜀, ꜂í pat꜀ t'ing' ꜁yam ꜀shing, pat꜀ ch'ut꜀ lün²
not see wicked sights, ears not hear jarring sounds, not utter indiscreet

言不食邪味常行忠孝友
꜁ín, pat꜀ shik₂ ꜁ts'é mí², ꜁shéung ꜁hang ꜀chung hau' ꜂yau
words, not eat impure tasted-things, always performed faithful filial friendly

愛慈良之事往往生子聰
oi' ꜁ts'z' ꜁léung ꜀chí sz'²: ꜂wóng ꜂wóng ꜀shang ꜂tsz' ꜀ts'ung
affectionate merciful good 's actions: constantly bore sons clever

明才智賢德過人此未生
꜁ming ꜁ts'oi chí' ꜁ín tak꜀ kwó' ꜁yan. ꜂Ts'z' mí² ꜀shang
intelligent talented wise good virtuous surpassing men. This-was un-born

之胎教也
꜀chí ꜀t'oi káu' ꜂yá.
's uterine instruction.

子能食教以右手能言勿使
꜂Tsz' ꜁nang shik₂, káu' ꜂í yau² ꜂shau; ꜁nang ꜁ín, mat₂ ꜂sz'
Son able to-eat, was-taught to-use right hand; able to-talk, disallowed

嬌聲能行使知四方上下能
꜀kiú ꜀shing; ꜁nang ꜁hang, ꜂sz' ꜀chí sz'' ꜀fóng shéung² há²; ꜁nang
whining tone; able to-walk, caused to-know four points-zenith nadir; able

---

studies. Like the preceding extract, these consist of a text and commentary, but not in so colloquial and familiar a style; the line at the head is the text, the sentences following are the commentary of Wóng Pákhau, and afford good examples of the style and manner of Chinese scholars in amplifying and explaining their standard works.

拾級大成

揖 教 以 禮 讓 尊 親 此 阿 保

*yap, káu' ˓í ˓lai yéung$^2$ ˏtsün ˏts'un. ˓Ts'z' ˏó ˓pò*

to-bow, taught to-be polite obliging honoring parents. This-was nurse

母 氏 之 教 也 至 於 洒 掃 應

*˓mò shí$^2$ ˏchí káu' ˓yá. Chí' ˏü ˓shá sò' ying'*

woman 's tutelage. With regard-to sprinkling sweeping responding

對 進 退 之 節 禮 樂 射 御

*túi' tsun' t'úi' ˏchí tsít, ˓lai ngok$_2$ shé$^2$ ü$^2$*

replying entering retiring 's observances, etiquette music archery charioteering

書 數 之 文 此 父 師 之 教 也

*ˏshü shò' ˏchí ˏman, ˓ts'z' fú$^2$ ˏsz' ˏchí káu' ˓yá.*

writing arithmetic 's accomplishments, these-were father tutor 's instruction.

然 教 之 之 道 又 貴 在 專 而

*ˏI'n káu' ˏchí ˏchí tò$^2$, yau$^2$ kwai' tsoi$^2$ ˏchün ˏí*

Truly instructing them 's principles, verily foremost is-in application and

無 倦 蓋 不 專 則 學 難 成 就

*ˏmò kün$^2$; k'oi' pat, ˏchün tsak, hók$_2$ ˏnán ˏshing tsau$^2$.*

without weariness; for-if not diligent, then education is-hard to-complete.

倦 教 則 子 益 廢 弛 非 教

*Kün$^2$ káu$^2$, tsak, ˓tsz' yik, fai' ˏch'í; ˏfi káu'*

Listlessly instructing, then lad still-more loses opportunity, not instruction

之 善 道 也

*ˏchí shín$^2$ tò$^2$ ˓yá.*

's commendable principles.

---

## No. X.—Necessity of Instruction.

(見三字經王伯厚纂)

玉 不 琢 不 成 器

*Yuk$_2$ pat, téuk, pat, ˏshing hí';*

Gem not wrought, un-serviceable thing;

人 不 學 不 知 義

*ˏyan pat, hók$_2$, pat, ˏchí í$^2$.*

man un-taught, ignorant-of rectitude.

義 道 義 也 禮 經 學 記 曰 玉

*I$^2$, tò$^2$, í$^2$, ˓yá. ˓Lai King, Hók$_2$ Kí' üt$_2$, Yuk$_2$*

I' [means] reasonable rectitude. Rites Book-of, in-Learning Record, says, Gem

不 琢 不 成 器 人 不 學 不 知 道

*pat, téuk, pat, ˏshing hí'; ˏyan pat, hók$_2$, pat, ˏchí tò$^2$.*

un- wrought, unserviceable thing; man un-taught, ignorant-of reason.

雖 有 美 玉 不 琢 不 磨 不 成
*˛Sui ˊyau ˊmí yuk₂, pat˒ téuk˒ pat˒ ˛mó, pat˒ ˛shing*
Although have beautiful gem, not carved nor ground, in - complete

器 物 則 無 所 用 猶 人 雖 有 美
*hí˒ mat₂, tsak˒ ˛mò ˊshó yung². ˛Yau ˛yan, ˛sui ˊyau ˊmí*
utensil thing, then without any use. Likewise a-man, although has superior

材 不 勤 學 問 則 不 能 知 理 義
*˛ts'oi, pat˒ ˛k'an hók₂ man², tsak˒ pat˒ ˛nang ˛chí ˊlí í²*
parts, not diligently learn inquire, then not can know reason rectitude

道 德 終 不 可 謂 成 人 也
*tò² tak˒. ˛Chung pat˒ ˊhó wai² ˛shing ˛yan ˊyá.*
propriety virtue. To-the-last unable to-be-called accomplished man.

---

No. XI.—Instance of Filial Duty.

(見三字經 王伯厚纂)

香 九 齡 能 温 席
*˛Héung ˊkau ˛ling, ˛nang ˛wan tsik₂;*
Héung when-nine years, could warm the-mat;

孝 於 親 所 當 執
*háu˒ ˛ü ˛ts'an, ˊshó ˛tóng chap˒.*
dutifulness to parents what should-be maintained.

百 行 之 首 以 孝 爲 先 初 學 之
*Pák˒ hang² ˛chí ˊshau, ˊí ˊháu˒ ˛wai ˛sin, ˛ch'ó hók₂ ˛chí*
Of-all action s' head regard filial-duty as chief, the-beginning to-learn 's

士 不 可 不 知 也 昔 漢 時 有
*sz'², pat˒ ˊhó pat˒ ˛chí ˊyá. Sik˒, Hón˒ ˛shí, ˊyau*
scholar, not admissable ignorant-of. Anciently, Hón's time, was [in]

江 夏 黃 香 年 九 歲 卽 知 孝 於
*˛Kóng há², ˛Wóng ˛Héung, ˛nín ˊkau sui˒, tsik˒ ˛chí háu˒ ˛ü*
Kóngha, Wóng Héung, aged nine years, even knew to-be-filial to

親 每 當 夏 日 炎 熱 之 時 則
*˛ts'an. ˊMúi ˛tóng há² yat₂, ˛ím ít₂ ˛chí ˛shí, tsak˒*
parents. Whenever summer time, excessively hot 's period, then

扇 父 母 之 帷 帳 使 枕 席 清 涼
*shín˒ fú², ˊmò ˛chí ˛wai chéung˒; ˊsz˒, ˊcham tsik₂ ˛ts'ing ˛léung,*
fanned father mother 's bed-curtains; making pillows mat fresh cool,

蚊 蚋 遠 避 以 待 親 之 安 寢
*˛man yui² ˊün pí², ˊí toi² ˛ts'an ˛chí ˛ón ˊtsam.*
muskctocs gnats away flying, and-thus waited-till parent s' quietly slept.

至於冬日嚴寒則以身温煖
*Chí' ˏü ˏtung yat˳ ˏím ˏhón, tsak˳ ˊi ˏshan ˏwan ˊnün*
Coming to winter day's severe cold, then with body nicely warmed

其親之衾裯枕席以待親之
*ˏk'i ˏts'an ˏchi ˏk'am ˏch'au ˊcham tsik˳, ˊi toi² ˏts'an ˏchi*
his parent s' coverlet pillow mat, and-thus waited-till parent s'

煖卧幼而行孝如此雖云
*ˊnün ngó.² Yau' ˏi ˏhang háu' ˏü ˊts'z', ˏsui ˏwan*
warmly slept. Young and act filially like this, although called

天性然人子之道昏定
*ˏt'in sing', ˏin ˏyan ˊtsz' ˏchi tò². ˏFan ting²*
heavenly disposition, still-is man child 's principles. In-evening wish-repose,

晨省冬温夏凊禮
*ˏshan ˊsing, ˏtung ˏwan, há² tsing², ˊlai*
in-morning inquire-health, in-winter warm, in-summer cool, [are] propriety's

當然也
*ˏtóng ˏin ˊyá.*
indispensable-requirements.

---

No. XII.—Doctrines of Mencius.*

(見四書上孟首章)

孟子見梁惠王
*Mang² ˊtsz' kín' ˏLéung Wai² ˏwong:*
Mencius waited-on Léung's Wai king:

梁惠王魏侯罃也都大
*ˏLéung Wai² ˏwóng, Ngai² ˏhau ˏYing ˊyá; ˏtò Tái²*
Léung's Wai king, [was] Ngai's earl Ying; built-court-in Great

梁僭稱王謚曰惠史記
*ˏLéung, ts'im' ˏch'ing ˏwóng; shí² üt˳ Wai². ˊSz' Ki',*
Léung, assumed to-be-called a-king; deceased called Wai. Historical Record

惠王三十五年卑禮厚
*Wai² ˏwóng ˏsám shap˳ ˊ'ng ˏnín, ˏpí ˊlai hau²*
[says], Wai king's thirty - fifth year, [employed] respectful invitation valuable

幣以招賢者而孟軻至梁
*pai² ˊi ˏchíú ˏin ˊché; ˏí Mang² ˏO' chí' ˏLéung.*
presents in-order to-invite the-worthy; wherefore Mang O' went-to Léung.

---

* This is a single and continuous extract from the commencement of the *Shéung Mang* 上孟 or First part of the Discourses of Mencius; the commentary of Chú fútsz' immediately follows the text, the two being distinguished by a different size of English type.

王曰叟不遠千里而來
*Wóng üt, 'Sau pat, 'üin ts'ín 'lí í loi,*
King said, Honored-sir, not regard-far thousand miles still come,

亦將有以利吾國乎
*yik, tséung 'yau 'í lí 'ng kwók, ú?*
also presently have that-which will-benefit my country eh?

叟長老之稱王所謂利
*'Sau 'chéung 'lò chí ch'ing. Wóng 'shó wai lí,*
*Sau* [is] respectable old 's appellation. King that-which calls benefit,

蓋富國彊兵之類
*k'oi fú kwók, k'éung ping chí lui.*
is to-enrich country, inspirit soldiery 's sort.

---

孟子對曰王何必曰
*Mang 'tsz' tui üt, Wóng hó pít, üt,*
Mencius replied saying, Your-majesty why must speak-of

利亦有仁義而已矣
*lí, yik, 'yau yan í 'í 'í.*
benefit, rather-also have philanthropy justice and stop-there.

仁者心之德愛之理義者
*Yan 'ché sam chí tak, oi chí 'lí; í ché*
Philanthropy this [is] heart 's virtue, love s' principle; justice this [is]

心之制事之宜也此二句乃
*sam chí chai, sz' chí í 'yá. 'Ts'z' í kü 'nái*
heart 's regulator, business 's equity. These two sentences are

一章之大旨下文乃詳言
*yat, chéung chí tái 'chí; há man 'nái ts'éung in*
whole chapter 's leading topics; subsequent text then clearly explains

之後多倣此
*chí. Hau tó 'fóng 'ts'z'.*
them. Afterwards many imitate this.

---

王曰何以利吾國大夫
*Wóng üt, Hó 'í lí 'ng kwók, ? Tái fú*
[If]-king says, How can benefit my kingdom? [If]-high ministers

曰何以利吾家士庶人
*üt, Hó 'í lí 'ng ká? Sz' shü yan*
say, How can benefit my family? [If]-scholars common people

拾級大成

曰 何 以 利 吾 身。 上 下 交 征
*üt*, *Hó 'í lí 'ng shan? Shéung há háu ching*
say, How can benefit my self? [The]-high low reciprocally strive-for

利 而 國 危 矣 萬 乘 之 國
*lí, í kwók, ngai 'í. Mán shing chí kwók,*
benefit, and the-country endangered. Myriad chariots 's kingdom,

弑 其 君 者 必 千 乘
*shí' k'í kwan 'ché, pít, ts'in shing*
conspire-against its prince person, certainly-will-be thousand chariot

之 家 千 乘 之 國 弑 其 君
*chí ká; ts'in shing chí kwók, shí' k'í kwan*
s' head; thousand chariot s' state, conspire-against its ru-

者 必 百 乘 之 家 萬 取
*'ché, pít, pák, shing chí ká. Mán 'ts'ü*
ler, certainly-will-be hundred chariot s' head. In-myriad to-get

千 焉 千 取 百 焉 不 爲 不 多
*ts'in ín, ts'in 'ts'ü pák, ín, pat, wai pat, tó*
a-thousand, in-thousand to-get a-hundred, not is inconsiderable

矣 苟 爲 後 義 而 先 利
*'í. Kau wai hau í, í sín lí,*
indeed. If regard secondarily right, and primarily advantage,

不 奪 不 饜
*pat, tüt, pat, ím'.*
not seized [will-be] not satiated.

此 言 求 利 之 害 以 明 上
*'Ts'z' ín k'au lí chí hoi, 'í ming shéung*
This speaks-of seeking advantage 's injury, in-order-to explain preceding

文 何 必 曰 利 之 意 也 征 取 也
*man, Hó pít, üt, lí chí í 'yá. Ching 'ts'ü 'yá.*
text, "Why must [you] speak-of benefit" 's meaning. *Ching* [means] obtain.

上 取 乎 下 下 取 乎 上 故 曰
*Shéung 'ts'ü ú há; há 'ts'ü ú shéung, kú üt,*
Superiors get from inferiors, inferiors get from superiors, therefore termed

交 征 國 危 謂 將 有 弑 奪
*káu ching. Kwók, ngai wai tséung 'yau shí' tüt,*
reciprocal striving. State endangered speaks-of about having conspiring seizing

之 禍 乘 車 數 也 萬 乘 之 國 者
*chí wó. Shing kü shò' 'yá. Mán shing chí kwók, 'ché,*
's evil. *Shing* chariot classifier. Myriad chariot 's state a,

天子畿內地方千里出車
꜀tʻin ʿtsz’ ꜀ki noi², tí² ꜀fóng ꜀tsʻin ʿlí², chʻut꜄ ꜀kü
emperor's dominions in, land squares thousand miles, furnish chariots

萬乘。千乘之家者天子之公卿
mán² shing². ꜀Tsʻin shing² ꜀chí ꜀ká ʿché, ꜀tʻin ʿtsz’ ꜀chí ꜀kung ꜀hing,
myriad ones. Thousand chariot s' family a, emperor 's lordly minister

采地方百里出車千乘也
ʿtsʻoi tí² ꜀fóng pák꜄ ʿlí, chʻut꜄ ꜀kü ꜀tsʻin shing² ʿyá.
granted land squares hundred miles, furnishes chariots thousand ones.

千乘之國諸侯之國百乘之
꜀Tsʻin shing² ꜀chí kwók꜄, ꜀chü ꜁hau ꜀chí kwók꜄: pák꜄ shing² ꜀chí
Thousand chariot s' state, [is] nobleman 's country: hundred chariot s'

家諸侯之大夫也弒下殺
꜀ká, ꜀chü ꜁hau ꜀chí tái² ꜀fú ʿyá. Shí’ há² shát꜄
family, [is] nobleman 's chief man. Shí [means] inferior killing

上也饜足也言臣之於君每
shéung² ʿyá; ím’ tsuk꜄ ʿyá. ꜁I'n ꜁shan ꜀chí ꜀ü ꜀kwan, ʿmúi
superior; ím [means] enough. Speaks-of minister 's from prince, every

十分而取其一分亦已多矣
shap꜆ ꜀fun ꜁í ʿtsʻü ꜁kʻi yat꜄ ꜀fun, yik꜆ ʿí ꜀tó ʿí.
tenth part and obtains his single part, also already-has much indeed.

若又以義爲後而以利爲
Yéuk꜆ yau² ʿí í² ꜁wai hau², ꜁í ʿí lí² ꜁wai
If [he] still regards right as secondary, and regards advantage as

先則不弒其君而盡奪
꜀sín, tsak꜄ pat꜄ shí’ ꜁kʻi ꜀kwan ꜁í tsun² tüt꜆
primary, then not conspire-against his prince and completely subvert

之其心未肯以爲足也
꜀chí, ꜁kʻi ꜀sam mí² ʿhang ʿí ꜁wai tsuk꜄ ʿyá.
him, his heart unwilling to be satisfied.

---

未有仁而遺其親
Mí² ʿyau ꜁yan, ꜁í ꜁wai ꜁kʻi ꜀tsʻan
Never was-there a-philanthropist, and discarded his parents

者也未有義而後其君者也
ʿché ʿyá: mí² ʿyau í² ꜁í hau² ꜁kʻi ꜀kwan ʿché ʿyá.
person: never was-there a-just, and neglected his prince person.

此言仁義未嘗不利以
ʿTsʻz’ ꜁ín ꜁yan í² mí² ꜁shéung pat꜄ lí², ʿí
This speaks-of philanthropy rectitude never without advantage, in-order

明 上 文 亦 有 仁 義 而 已
꜀ming shéung$^2$ ꜁man yik꜇ ꜂yau ꜁yan í$^2$ ꜁í ꜂í
to-explain preceding text "also possess philanthropy rectitude and enough"

之 意 也 遺 猶 去 也 後 不 急 也
꜀chí í꜄ ꜂yá. ꜁Wai ꜁yau hü꜄ ꜂yá. Hau$^2$ pát꜆ kap꜆ ꜂yá.
's meaning. *Wai* same-as discard. *Hau* [means] not hasty.

言 仁 者 必 愛 其 親 義 者 必 急
꜁I'n ꜁yan ꜂ché pít꜆ oi$^2$ ꜁k'i ꜀ts'an, í$^2$ ꜂ché pít꜆ kap꜆
It-means philanthropist will love his parents, just man will dispatch-for

其 君 故 人 君 躬 行 仁 義 而
꜁k'i ꜀kwan, kú꜄ ꜁yan ꜀kwan ꜀kung ꜁hang ꜁yan í$^2$, ꜁í
his prince, therefore the-prince himself act benevolently justly, and

無 求 利 之 心 則 其 下 化
꜁mò ꜁k'au lí$^2$ ꜀chí ꜀sam, tsak꜆ ꜁k'i há$^2$ fá꜄
not-having seek-for advantage 's disposition, then his inferiors are-trans-

之 自 親 戴 於 已 也
꜀chí. Tsz'$^2$ ꜀ts'an táí꜄ ꜀ü ꜂kí ꜂yá.
formed-by him. From parents [they] go-on to themselves.

---

王 亦 曰 仁 義 而 已 矣
꜁Wóng yik꜇ üt꜇ ꜁yan í$^2$ ꜁í ꜂í ꜂í:
[If]-king also speaks-of philanthropy rectitude and stop-there:

何 必 曰 利
꜁hó pít꜆ üt꜇ lí$^2$?
why must [you] speak-of advantage?

重 言 之 以 結 上 文 兩 節
꜁Ch'ung ꜁in ꜀chí ꜂í kít꜆ shéung$^2$ ꜁man ꜂léung tsít꜆
Again speaks-of them in-order-to connect preceding text's two sentences

之 意 此 章 言 仁 義 根 於 人 心
꜀chí í꜄. ꜂Ts'z' ꜀chéung ꜁in ꜁yan í$^2$, ꜀kan ꜀ü ꜁yan ꜀sam
's meaning. This section speaks-of philanthropy right, rooted in human heart

之 固 有 天 理 之 公 也 利 心
꜀chí kú꜄ ꜂yau, ꜀t'ín ꜂lí ꜀chí ꜀kung ꜂yá. Lí$^2$ ꜀sam,
's fixed possessions, [are] heavenly reason 's justness. Covetous desires,

生 於 物 我 之 相 形 人 欲 之 私
꜀shang ꜀ü mat꜇ ꜂ngó ꜀chí ꜀séung ꜁ying, ꜁yan yuk꜇ ꜀chí ꜀sz'
springing from things my 's mutual attraction, [are] human desire s' selfish-

也 循 天 理 則 不 求 利 而 自
꜂yá. ꜁Ts'un ꜀t'ín ꜂lí, tsak꜆ pat꜆ ꜁k'au lí$^2$, ꜁í tsz'$^2$
ness. Following heavenly reason then not seeking advantage, still himself

無不利 循人欲則求利未得
꜀mò pat꜀ lí$^2$: ꜀ts'un ꜀yan yuk꜁, tsak꜀ ꜀k'au lí$^2$ mí$^2$ tak꜀,
without disadvantage: following human desires, then seeking advantage not obtain,

而害已隨之所謂毫釐之
꜀í hoi$^2$ ꜂i ꜀ts'ui ꜀chí; ꜂shó wai$^2$ ꜀hò ꜀lí ꜀chí
still injury already follow it; is-what may-be-called hair-breadth 's

差 千里之謬此孟子之
꜀ts'z' ꜀ts'ín ꜂lí ꜀chí máu$^2$. ꜂Ts'z' Mang$^2$ ꜂tsz' ꜀chí
difference [causing] thousand mile s' mistake. These Menciu s'

書所以造端托始之
꜀shü, ꜂shó ꜂i tsò$^2$ ꜀tün t'ók꜀ ꜀ch'i ꜀chí
writings, [are] what whereby form the-principal educe the-beginning s'

深意學者所宜精察而明
꜀sham í'; hók꜁ ꜂ché ꜂shó ꜀í ꜀tsing ch'át꜀ ꜀í ꜀ming
deep meaning; learner what ought intelligently examine and clearly

辨也
pín$^2$ ꜂yá.
discriminate.

These lessons will exhibit to some extent the idioms and the grammatical construction of sentences in the language, and if learned thoroughly will not fail to prove of material assistance in reading Chinese generally. It will be found to be a good practice for the beginner to make a literal rendering of such papers or exercises as are to be translated, somewhat in the manner of these lessons, until he has acquired very great facility in expressing the sense of the original in an English dress: this plan will show better than almost any other the force of every word in it. It will perhaps seem like slow progress to the scholar, who is impatient to advance, and to read many books; but he does not here require to be told that the quickest progress is really that which is the surest, which leaves nothing behind half learned and half understood, acquirements which are soon half forgotten, and almost wholly useless for all practical purposes of reading or writing. The practice of committing the original to memory has already been suggested (page 62), and it is attended with so many advantages, that it is deserving of trial. Prémare goes so far as to recommend the student to commit to memory the whole of the Four Books, and his attainments in Chinese give to his opinion of its advantages no small weight.

## Chapter Ninth.

# EXERCISES IN TRANSLATING INTO CHINESE.

THE design of this volume does not include many exercises in translating English into Chinese, for that part of the student's education, requires particular rules and examples, not only under the different parts of speech, but also for individual characters. It should not, however, be omitted altogether, but attempts should be made, as soon as a moderate number of characters has been learned, to form them into sentences. In this exercise, the natural way, or that in which children learn to talk, will perhaps soonest give facility to the foreigner in expressing his thoughts in Chinese; let him imitate those about him as closely as he can, copy their modes of expression, at first writing his sentences just as he would utter them; and he will soon be able to mold his thoughts to some extent in their style when he wishes to put them on paper. This practice of imitation, however, from various obstacles, partly resulting from his already fixed habit of thinking, and partly from his imperfect freedom and intimacy with the people themselves, will be but slowly acquired. But let him not be discouraged because his first attempts at speaking and writing are awkward, nor displeased because the people have so little manners and sympathy as to laugh at his ill expressed sentences: perseverance and patience will smooth the road, and those who laughed at his rudeness will soon begin to praise his proficiency in the most fulsome manner. They will not, however, often take the trouble to correct an erroneous expression, and hence the more need of the closest attention to the people when talking among themselves. In preserving and remembering such expressions and phrases as he may notice, the student had better follow his own plan, and choose that which previous habits has already made most easy.

This series of sentences is to be translated into Chinese, and care has been taken to make them all very simple, by avoiding all peculiar phrases. The two Chinese characters under a single number are in every instance antithetical, and the word in italics in the opposite English column is to be rendered by the Chinese character on its left.

| | |
|---|---|
| 1. High, 高 ꜀*kò*. | A *high* house. A *lofty* tree. |
| Low, 矮 ꜂*ái*. | A *low* fence. A *short* woman. |
| 2. Right, 右 *yau*². | My *right* hand is weak. *True* doctrines. |
| Left, 左 ꜂*tsó*. | That on the *left* side is the best. |
| 3. Unlucky, 凶 ꜀*hung*. | An *unlucky* omen. A *bad* year. |
| Lucky, 吉 *kat*꜊. | Choose a *lucky* day. A *fortunate* event. |

| | | | |
|---|---|---|---|
| 4. Good, | 善 | *shin*$^2$. | A *good* man. A *good* disposition. |
| Bad, | 惡 | *ók*,. | A *bad* heart. *Tattered* clothes. |
| 5. Black, | 黑 | *hak*,. | A *black* hog. A *dark* night. |
| White, | 白 | *pák*$_2$. | *White* paper. *Clear* daylight. |
| 6. Poor, | 貧 | ₅*p'an*. | A *poor* family. *Poor* but not covetous. |
| Rich, | 富 | *fú*'. | He is very *rich*. *Rich* and not proud. |
| 7. Cheap, | 平 | ₅*p'ing*. | This pair of shoes is poor and *cheap*. |
| Dear, | 貴 | *kwai*'. | This garment is very *dear*. Your *honorable* country. |
| 8. Beautiful, | 美 | ʿ*mí*. | A *beautiful* girl. An *elegant* scholar. |
| Ugly, | 醜 | ʿ*ch'au*. | An *ugly* countenance. A *vicious* heart. |
| 9. Straight, | 直 | *chik*$_2$. | A *straight* line. He came *direct*. |
| Crooked, | 曲 | *huk*,. | A *crooked* bow. A *curved* handle. |
| 10. True, | 眞 | ₍*chan*. | He speaks *true* words. *Honest* goods and fair prices. |
| False, | 假 | ʿ*ká*. | This is a *false* pearl. A *lying* speech. |
| 11. New, | 新 | ₍*san*. | That cap is *new*. A *lately* arrived person. |
| Old, | 舊 | *kau*$^2$. | An *old* coat. Do it the same way as *before*. |
| 12. Near, | 近 | *kan*$^2$. | He lives *near*. He died *lately*. |
| Far, | 遠 | ʿ*ün*. | Four miles *distant*. Very *far*. |
| 13. Long, | 長 | ₅*ch'éung*. | This door is too *long*. A good *length* of time. |
| Short, | 短 | ʿ*tün*. | This shoe is rather *short*. A *short* life. |
| 14. Tall, | 高 | ₍*kò*. | He is much *taller* than I. |
| Low, | 低 | ₍*tai*. | A *low* sound. A *low* price. |
| 15. Top, | 上 | *shéung*$^2$. | Put it on *top*. To be *above* the people. |
| Bottom, | 下 | *há*$^2$. | Nail it on the *bottom*. A *vulgar* man. |
| 16. Hard, | 難 | ₅*nán*. | Chinese is *hard* to learn. A *difficult* affair. |
| Easy, | 易 | *í*$^2$. | With a firm determination it will soon be *easy*. |
| 17. Clear, | 明 | ₅*ming*. | This piece of crystal is not *clear*. |
| Obscure, | 暗 | *óm*'. | An *obscure* valley. This lamp burns *dimly*. |

18. Dirty, 濁 chuk$_2$. The water of the river is *dirty*.
Clean, 清 ꜀ts'ing. My purse is *clean*. His heart is *pure* as water.

19. Disobedient, 逆 yik$_2$. *Disobedient* persons will have *disobedient* children.
Obedient, 順 shun$^2$. A filial *obedient* son. He acts *according* to my wishes.

20. Weak, 弱 yéuk$_2$. Lewchew is a *weak* country.
Strong, 強 ꜁k'éung. He is a *strong* man.

21. Brittle, 脆 ts'ui꜄ Glass is very *brittle*.
Tough, 韌 ngan$^2$. Deer's sinews are *tough*.

22. Thick, 厚 hau$^2$. This is *thicker* than that.
Thin, 薄 pók$_2$. As *thin* as a leaf.

23. Large, 大 tái$^2$. A *large* potato. A *great* man.
Small, 小 ꜂síú. A *small* cottage. A *selfish* fellow.

24. Fine, 幼 yau꜄. *Fine* cloth. *Fine* thread.
Coarse, 粗 ts'ò꜄. *Coarse* work. He is *heedless*.

25. Deep, 深 ꜀sham. The water is *deep* there. A *deep* blue.
Shallow, 淺 ꜂tsín. A *shallow* fish-pond. A *light* red.

26. Hot, 熱 ít$_2$. This tea is too *hot* to drink. *Hot* weather.
Cold, 冷 ꜃lang. This room is *cold*. A *heartless* laugh.

27. Hungry, 饑 ꜀kí. I am very *hungry* and thirsty.
Satiated, 飽 ꜂páu. He has eaten *enough*. He is *well* read.

28. Dull, 鈍 tun$^2$. This penknife is *dull*.
Sharp, 利 lí$^2$. Take the other, that is *sharp*.

29. Fresh, 淡 tám$^2$. This is a *fresh* water fish.
Salt, 鹹 ꜁hám. It is unpleasant to eat if too *salt*.

30. Old, 老 ꜃lò. Respect *old* men. He is *old* and deaf.
Young, 幼 yau꜄. He is *young* and beautiful.

31. Green, 生 ꜀shang. This is a *green* orange. A *strange* face.
Ripe, 熟 shuk$_2$. He sells *ripe* plums. I know him very *intimately*.

32. Public, 公 ꜀kung. This shop belongs to a *public* company.
Private, 私 ꜀sz'. A *private* affair. A *selfish* heart.

| | | | |
|---|---|---|---|
| 33. Full, | 滿 | ˏmún. | This cup is *full* of water. |
| Empty, | 空 | ˓hung. | Strike it and see if it is *empty*. His purse is *empty*. |
| 34. Proud, | 傲 | ngò². | He is too *proud* to speak to me. |
| Humble, | 謙 | ˓hím, | A *humble* man will go a thousand miles. |
| 35. Light, | 輕 | ˓hing. | As *light* as a feather's down. |
| Heavy, | 重 | chung². | I cannot lift so *heavy* a box. |
| 36. Stiff, | 硬 | ngáng². | As *stiff* as iron. |
| Limber, | 軟 | ˓ün. | As *limber* as flour. A *tender* heart. |
| 37. Square, | 方 | ˓fóng. | This table is *square*. |
| Round, | 圓 | ˏün. | Cut it exactly *round*. As *round* as the moon. |
| 38. In, | 內 | noi². | He is not *within*. The *interior* of China. |
| Out, | 外 | ngoi². | Tell him to leave that *out*. *Outside* barbarians. |
| 39. Before, | 先 | ˓sin. | Please walk *before*. Do this *first*. |
| After, | 後 | hau². | He stands *behind* me. |
| 40. Early, | 早 | ˓tsò. | I got up *early* this morning. |
| Late, | 晚 | ˓mán. | He repented of it too *late*. |
| 41. Hurtful, | 損 | ˓sün. | To *injure* another and benefit one's self. |
| Strengthening, | 益 | yik˒. | This medicine is beneficial and *strengthening*. |
| 42. Laughable, | 笑 | síú˒. | How *laughable!* We were talking a *pleasant* matter together. |
| Crying, | 哭 | huk˒. | The sound of *crying* shows his heart's sorrow. |
| 43. Strong, | 濃 | ˏnung. | This tea is too *strong* for me. |
| Weak, | 淡 | tám². | This wine is *weak*, try a glass. |
| 44. Tight, | 緊 | ˓kan. | This lock is very *tight*. |
| Loose, | 鬆 | ˓sung. | Plane it a little more to make it *loose*. |
| 45. Fat, | 肥 | ˏfi. | He is *fat* as a pig. A large and *gross* man. |
| Lean, | 瘦 | shau˒. | He is *lean* as a monkey. Why are you so *lean!* |
| 46. Narrow, | 窄 | chák˒. | This board is very *narrow*. |
| Broad, | 闊 | fút˒. | Make it five feet *broad*. |

拾級大成



47. Spacious, 廣 'kwóng. This house is *spacious*. He has a *liberal* mind.

Confined, 狹 háp₂. This boat is long and *narrow*.

48. Lazy, 懶 'lán. Don't be *lazy* and waste the day. An *idle* woman.

Industrious, 勤 ₍k'an. So *industrious* as to forget to eat.

49. Quick, 快 fái'. Make *haste*, and open the door. Run *quick* and catch him.

Slow, 慢 mán². Do it *slowly*, and not be too hasty.

50. Sweet, 甜 ₍t'ím. As *sweet* as honey. He uses *sweet* words and polite talk to deceive.

Bitter, 苦 'fú. The soft part of mustard is *bitter*.

52. Rotten, 枯 ₍fú. *Rotten* bones are found in graves.

Sound, 堅 ₍kín. This timber is *sound* and solid. A *hale* hearty old man.

53. Damp, 濕 shap₁. This go-down is very *damp*, and must be floored.

Dry, 乾 ₍kón. Put this in the sun to *dry*. Wet it a little, it is too *dry*.

54. Smooth, 滑 wát₂. Plane it *smooth*. A *slippery* road is difficult to travel.

Rough, 澁 sik₁. *Rough* is called ₍hái 嚡 in Canton.

55. Right, 是 shí². If it is *right*, say so.

Wrong, 非 ₍fi. If it is *wrong*, say so.

56. Good, 好 'hò. It is hard to act the *good* man. This is a *good* book.

Bad, 歹 'tái. *Bad* is called 'ch'au 醜 and also wái² 壞 in Canton.

57. Loving, 好 hò'. He is *fond* of rowing. He *loves* to eat fruit.

Hating, 惡 ú'. I *hate* him. How *detestably* he acts!

58. First, 首 'shau. What does the *first* page say? The *chief* of all actions.

Last, 尾 'mí. To the *last*, these goods are alike.

59. Fair, 順 shun². With a *fair* wind, we shall soon reach.

Foul, 逆 yik₂. With a *foul* wind and *head* current, we must anchor.

| | | | | |
|---|---|---|---|---|
| 60. | Male, | 牡 | ˓*mau.* | *Male* is called ˓*kung* 公 in Canton. |
| | Female, | 牝 | ˓*fan.* | *Female* is called ˓*ná* 乸 in Canton. |
| 61. | Cock, | 雄 | ˓*hung,* | 'Flat haired' are called *cock* and hen. |
| | Hen, | 雌 | ˓*ts'z'.* | *Hen* birds are not as handsome as cocks. |
| 62. | Text, | 文 | ˓*man.* | Mencius wrote this *text.* |
| | Commentary, | 註 | *chü'* | Chú fútsz' made this *commentary.* |
| 63. | Glad, | 樂 | *lók*˳. | When I saw you, my heart was *glad.* |
| | Sorry, | 憂 | ˓*yau.* | I am *sorry* because of my parents' age. |
| 64. | Superior, | 上 | *shéung*˳. | This piece of woolen is very *superior.* |
| | Inferior, | 下 | *há*˳. | This is *inferior* in quality. |
| 65. | Opened, | 開 | ˓*hoi.* | *Open* the window to look at the moon. |
| | Shut, | 閉 | *pai'.* | *Shut* the door and consider your faults. |
| 66. | Bought, | 買 | ˓*mái.* | *Bought* a horse yesterday for one hundred dollars. |
| | Sold, | 賣 | *mái*˳. | Rice is *sold* in the market by the pecul. |
| 67. | Add, | 添 | ˓*t'ím.* | *Add* a little milk. Please *give* a little higher price. |
| | Diminish, | 減 | ˓*kám.* | *Take off* a little. If you do not *diminish,* we cannot settle it. |
| 68. | Ascended, | 陞 | ˓*shing.* | He suddenly *ascended* three degrees of rank. |
| | Descended, | 降 | *kóng'.* | He *descended* the steps to meet the guest. |
| 69. | Received, | 收 | ˓*shau.* | Please *receive* this money into your safe keeping. |
| | Gave out, | 放 | *fóng'.* | *Gave out* money on interest. *Liberated* the thieves. |
| 70. | Extended, | 伸 | ˓*shan.* | *Stretch* off your fatigue. The snail *stretches* out its eyes to see the road. |
| | Drew in, | 縮 | *shuk*˳. | Seeing men coming it *draws* in its eyes. |
| 71. | Rose, | 長 | ˓*chéung.* | The water of the river *rose* five feet. |
| | Decreased, | 消 | ˓*síú.* | Take some medicine and *relieve* your illness. |
| 72. | Beginning, | 始 | ˓*ch'í.* | The *beginning* of the book is in Chinese. |
| | Ending, | 終 | ˓*chung.* | His life is ready to *end.* The *end* of the book is gone. |

| | | | | |
|---|---|---|---|---|
| 73. | Having, | 有 | ‘yau. | He *has* a heart to learn the Bible. |
| | Without, | 無 | ‚mò. | He is *without* a cash. He *has no* desire to seek good. |
| 74. | He, that, | 彼 | ‘pí. | *His* heart is not satisfied. *That* rich man is not proud. |
| | This, | 此 | ‘ts‘z’. | *This* day we must be diligent. *This* disease is hard to cure. |
| 75. | Misery, | 禍 | wó$^{2}$. | If a man does ill, heaven will recompense him with misery. |
| | Happiness, | 福 | fuk‚. | He is a *happy* man. *Happiness* does not come a second time. |
| 76. | Good omen, | 祥 | ‚ts‘éung. | On him who does well heaven will confer many *felicities*. |
| | Bad omen, | 殃 | ‚yéung. | He who does ill, heaven will visit him with many *ills*. |
| 77. | Preserve, | 存 | ‚ts‘ün. | Eighty out of a hundred troops *saved* their lives. |
| | Lost, | 亡 | ‚móng. | If the emperor be without reason, the country will certainly be *lost*. |
| 78. | Eternal, | 永 | ‘wing. | The wicked man will abide *eternally* in hell. |
| | Transitory, | 暫 | tsám$^{2}$. | For a *little* time, rest from reading. |
| 79. | Tired, | 倦 | kün$^{2}$. | Teach men not *idly*. I am very *tired* |
| | Vigorous, | 爽 | ‘shóng. | I am in good spirits and very *vigorous*. |
| 80. | Brilliant, | 靚 | ling’. | Rub this table till it *shines*. |
| | Dull, | 啞 | ‘á. | The silk of this piece is not good, and therefore the color is *dull*. |
| 81. | Right, | 着 | chéuk$_{2}$. | Everybody says this business is *right*. |
| | Wrong, | 錯 | ts‘ó’. | If you do it *wrong*, I fear all will laugh. |
| 82. | Cool, | 凉 | ‚léung. | The weather is *cool* to-day, and you will not want an umbrella. |
| | Warm, | 暖 | ‘nün. | The evening is *warm*, throw off your cloak. |
| 83. | Joined, | 合 | hóp$_{2}$. | These two boards do not *join*. *Agreeing* in disposition. |
| | Separated, | 離 | ‚lí. | This tenon is *separated*. That town is 5 miles *distant*. |

| | | | | |
|---|---|---|---|---|
| 84. | Conquered, | 贏 | ꜀ying. | The first *conquered* the second. His work *excels* mine a hundred fold. |
| | Beaten, | 輸 | ꜀shü. | His quail was *beaten* because it had eaten too much. |
| 85. | Victorious, | 勝 | shing꜄. | *Victorious*, he is a king. |
| | Discomfited, | 敗 | pái꜄. | *Discomfited*, he is a bandit. Completely *routed*. |
| 86. | Awake, | 醒 | ‛sing. | As soon as I *awoke*, I forgot the dream of last night. |
| | Sleep, | 睡 | shui꜄. | To *sleep* is vulgarly called *fan*꜄ 瞓 in this provincial city. |
| 87. | Born, | 生 | ꜀shang. | He was *born* on new year's day. |
| | Dead, | 死 | ‛sz'. | He has been *dead* ten years. |
| 88. | Love, | 愛 | oi꜄. | Affectionate mothers *love* their children. |
| | Hate, | 憎 | ꜀tsang. | That man certainly begs men's *hate*, I do not think of seeing him. |
| 89. | Upright, | 正 | ching꜄. | An *upright* man—his eyes will not look at vice. |
| | Vicious, | 邪 | ꜁ts'é. | *Vicious* sort of folks fear lest men will know their failings. |
| 90. | Ancient, | 古 | ‛kú. | *Ancient* men respected and esteemed the honest. |
| | Modern, | 今 | ꜀kam. | The *present* age first regards the silken dress, then respects the man. |
| 91. | True, | 正 | ching꜄. | Put that table *true*. |
| | Awry, | 歪 | ꜀wái. | This wall is a little *awry*. |
| 92. | Inflexible, | 剛 | ꜀kóng. | He is *inflexible* and will not bend. |
| | Yielding, | 柔 | ꜁yau. | A *mild* woman. A *supple* pettifogger. |
| 93. | Many, | 多 | ꜀tó. | Too *many* men have come. |
| | Few, | 少 | ‛shiú. | A *few* will be enough. |
| 94. | Without, | 表 | ‛piú. | *Without* and within are alike. |
| | Within, | 裡 | ꜂lü. | The *inside* is the same. |
| 95. | Going, | 往 | ‛wóng. | Once *gone* it will not return. |
| | Coming, | 來 | ꜁loi. | I can know that which is gone and that which has not yet *come*. |
| 96. | Gone out, | 出 | ch'ut꜀. | The robber has just *escaped* his prison. |
| | Enter in, | 入 | yap꜀. | Please *enter in* and take a seat. |

| | | | |
|---|---|---|---|
| 97. Confer, | 賞 | ‘shéung. | Better *bestow* on him a slap of the hand. |
| Forfeit, | 罰 | fat₂. | *Forfeit* to you a glass of wine. |
| 98. Clear, | 明 | ˏming. | Open the window to get a *clear* light. |
| Obscure, | 昏 | ˏwan. | The sky is *obscure* and the earth dark. |
| 99. Capital, | 本 | ‘pún. | The thief's is a business without a *capital*. |
| Profit, | 利 | li². | Everybody wishes to get *profit*. |

The student can multiply exercises similar to these to any extent he deems expedient, and he will find the practice of writing such short and easy sentences of very great utility. A good plan, which may here be mentioned, is for him to provide himself with a slate, and write a number of sentences, and then let the teacher write the corrected idiomatic sentences in parallel columns, that the difference between the two may be seen. He will see that the modes of expression, the mold in which the native casts his thought, are so unlike his own, that close attention and long practice will be necessary before anything like ease or aptitude can be attained. He will in these attempts, feel the great advantage that is derived from committing to memory portions of Chinese. And in Chinese composition, he ought to propose to himself no inferior mark, to be satisfied with nothing less than being able unaided to write Chinese so that he is sure it will be intelligible to the native reader. Perhaps he may never be able to write so that an educated native could not alter his composition for the better, but he ought to strive to attain such a knowledge of the language as to know that what he writes is understood just as he wrote it, and meant it to be understood. In submitting his compositions to his teacher, let him almost compel him to change the expressions till they are perfectly according to Chinese idioms, and not have any attachment to what he himself may deem a good sentence, lest the teacher, partly out of respect to him, and still more from mental indolence, allows him to form bad habits, and declares sentences to be well written which are far from being so. It is not, among the Chinese themselves, regarded as polite to criticise another's composition, and some little address on the part of the foreigner will be required to obtain the unbiassed corrections and criticisms of his teacher. The practice of requesting the teacher to put the same meaning into as many different forms of expression as possible, will also be useful in learning synonimous terms and modes of expression. Every care should be taken not to get into the habit of writing English idioms in a Chinese dress.

## SELECTIONS
### FROM THE HISTORY OF THE THREE STATES.

(此數句選三國志卷一第二回第十一板之後)

These are successive extracts to be retranslated into Chinese, and the reference to the original is given at the end of each sentence, by which the place can be found. The edition is the common duodecimo one, having twenty-two columns on a leaf; they are numbered from the first column on the right side.

---

1. "On that day, he having been disrespectful to Üntak (玄德), Chéung Fí (張飛) of a hasty temperament, straightway wished to kill him."—(15 *characters.*)—section 2d, leaf 11, last column.

2. "Fí said, If I do not kill that fellow, then it will be necessary, being in his clan, to obey his commands: this, indeed, would not be pleasant."—(19 *char.*)—*Ibid.*, leaf 12, column 1st.

3. "Thereupon, the three men by night and day, led their troops to Chü Tsun (朱雋); Tsun acted towards them very friendly."—(17 *char.*)—*Ibid.*, col. 4th.

4. "Chéung Pò (張寶) ordered colonel Kò Shing (副將高昇) to sally out on horseback, and provoke a combat."—(11 *char.*)—*Ibid.*, col. 7th.

5. "Üntak sent Chéung Fí to fight him; Fí giving reins to his horse and grasping his spear, joined battle with Shing; after a few onsets he pierced Shing, who fell off his horse."—(23 *char.*)—*Ibid.*, col. 8th.

6. "Chéung Pò, then on horseback, disheveling his hair and brandishing his sword, performed his magical arts; there was only to be seen a great wind and thunder, and a mass of black vapor descending from the sky; within this black vapor what resembled innumerable horsemen furiously sallied forth."—(38 *char.*)—*Ibid.*, col. 9th.

7. "Üntak, hearing the orders, directed Lord Kwán (關公) and Chéung Fí each to lead a detachment of a thousand, and hide behind the hills on a high eminence."—(22 *char.*)—*Ibid.*, col. 13th.

8. "Chéung Pò, seeing his arts all fail, hastily endeavored to withdraw his troops; but on the left Lord Kwán, on the right Chéung Fí, both detachments sallied out, and in the rear Üntak and Chü Tsun simultaneously coming up, the rebel soldiers were completely routed."—(34 *char.*)—*Ibid.*, col. 19th.

9. "Üntak, seeing afar the banner of general Lord of Earth (地公將軍) wite flying horse pursued after; Chéung Pò entered the wilds and fled, and Üntak, letting fly an arrow, hit his left arm."—(28 *char.*)—*Ibid.*, col. 20th.

10. "Opening Chéung Kok's (張角) coffin, he cut his corpse in pieces, cut off his head, and sent it to the capital; the rest of the troop all submitted."—(17 *char.*)—*Ibid.*, leaf 13th, col. 14th.

11. "Üntak, following in the rear assaulted and killed them; the robbers were routed and fled into the citadel of Ün. (完) (15 *char.*) *Ibid.*, col. 14th.

12. "Üntak said, Anciently, Kòtsò's (高祖) obtaining of the empire was because he was able to invite submissions and receive their fealty;—why do you, sir, repel Hón Chung? (韓忠)—(20 *char.*)—*Ibid.*, col. 16th.

13. "Üntak said, Not to permit the rebels to submit is correct. Now they are hemmed in on all sides like an irón tube, and the rebels beg to submit; if they cannot, they will assuredly fight to the last."—(25 *char.*)—*Ibid.*, col. 20th.

14. "Kín (堅) speaking to his father said, 'These robbers should be seized.' Then, rousing his energy and grasping his sword, he ascended the bank, lifting up a loud voice, calling and pointing to the east and west as if ordering men; the robbers, supposing them to be soldiers of government coming, all left the property and hastily fled. Kín rushing forward killed one robber."—(46 *char.*)—*Ibid.*, leaf 14th, col. 7th.

15. "After he had occupied his office, he ate at the same table and slept in the same bed, with Kwán and Chéung; whenever Üntak sat in the midst of a crowd of people, Kwán and Chéung stood behind him the whole day without being fatigued."—(31 *char.*)—*Ibid.*, leaf 15th, col. 9th.

16. "The clerk said, Tuk Yau (督郵) is acting pompously; it is nothing he wants but a douceur."—(12 *char.*)—*Ibid.*, col. 19th.

17. "Üntak replied, I have not committed the least illegality with the people; where shall I get a bonus to give him?"—(16 *char.*)—*Ibid.*, col. 19th.

18. "Chéung Fí, in great anger, rolling his eyes and grinding his teeth firmly, vaulted down from his horse, and straight entered the post-house, thrust aside the door-keeper, who there was opposing his way, and rushed directly into the back hall, where he saw Tuk Yau just sitting up in the hall, while the district clerk was lying bound on the ground. Fí cried out, 'Villainous oppressor of the people! Do you know who I am?' Tuk Yau did not have time to say a word, before his hair was firmly grasped by Chéung Fí, and he dragged out of the post-house straight to a horse-post before the magistrate's, and fast tied up to it."—(84 *char.*)—*Ibid.*, leaf 16th, col. 2d.

19. "Pulling down a branch of a willow, upon Tuk Yau's two thighs, with all his strength, he whipped him. Each time he struck, he snapped ten and more twigs of the willow."—(23 *char.*)—*Ibid.*, col. 6th.

20. "Fí said, Such a rascally oppressor of the people, for what shall I wait before beating him to death? Tuk Yau calling said, Lord Üntak save my life."—(23 *char.*)—*Ibid.*, col. 10th.

21. "Tò (陶) said, On all sides, thieves and robbers simultaneously rise up, devastating and robbing the country; these evils all spring from the ten eunuchs selling offices and oppressing the people; they despise their prince and contemn their superiors, and all upright men have left the court; evil is before your eyes."—(38 *char.*)—*Ibid.*, leaf 17th, col. 4th.

22. "The ten eunuchs all took off their caps, and knelt prostrate before the emperor, saying, 'The high minister not agreeing with us, we cannot live; we wish to beg our lives, return to our fields and villages, and employ all our possessions to aid the expenses of the army.' Their words ended, they wept bitterly."—(42 *char.*)—*Ibid.*, col. 6th.

23. "Lau Tò (劉陶) cried out, My death is unimportant! how sad that the house and empire of Hón, [enduring] four hundred years and more to this time, as in one night, should be extinct."—(24 *char.*)—*Ibid.*, col. 9th.

24. "Tám (耽) said, The people of the empire wish to eat the flesh of the ten eunuchs; your majesty respects them like a father and mother; their body has not one inch of merit, and all have been created noble earls."—(28 *char.*)—*Ibid.*, col. 12th.

25. "Lau Ü (劉虞) privately memorializing regarding Lau Pí's (劉備) great merit, the court pardoned his offense in whipping Tuk Yau."—(12 *char.*)—*Ibid.*, col. 22d.

26. "The emperor Ling (靈) being dangerously sick, called the high general Hó Tsun (何進) into the inner palace to consult upon subsequent business."—(16 *char.*)—*Ibid.*, leaf 18th, col. 3d.

27. "Now, the high general hearing Ün Shíú's (袁紹) words, wishes to exterminate all the ministers; we beg your ladyship to pity us."—(19 *char.*)—*Ibid.*, leaf 19th, col. 6th.

28. "Ün Shíú said, If you do not cut off the plant and extirpate the root, it certainly will become a tree to kill us."—(15 *char.*)—*Ibid.*, col. 11th.

29. "The empress Tung (董) summoning Chéung Yéung (張讓) and the others into the inner palace to consult, said, Hó Tsun's sister, from the first I have promoted her; now her son sits on the

拾級大成

throne as emperor, and all the ministers within and without are her bosom friends, her dignity and power is very great: what shall I do?" —(47 *char.*)—*Ibid.*, col. 13th.

---

SELECTIONS FROM THE YUK KÍÚ LÍ.

## (此數句選玉嬌梨 第一回之後)

1. "Within this village, although there were a thousand and more dwellings of the residents, if you should number the rich and honorable families, you would select that of the councillor Pák (白太常) as the first."—(25 *char.*)—Chapter 1st, leaf 1, col. 16th.

2. "He only regretted that he was past forty, and still without a son and heir."—(11 *char.*)—*Ibid.*, col. 18th.

3. "Mr. Pák (白公) sighed, and regarding it as his fate, did not thereafter again buy concubines."—(15 *char.*)—*Ibid.*, col. 20th.

4. "On the day that she was born, Mr. Pák dreamed that a divine personage bestowed upon him a single beautiful gem, the color ruddy as the sun; therefore in choosing her milk name he called her *Red-gem.*"—(30 *char.*)—*Ibid.*, col. 22d.

5. "By eight or nine years, she had learned female work and needlework, in every branch surpassing ordinary people."—(15 *char.*) —*Ibid.*, leaf 2, col. 3d.

6. "By the time she was fourteen or fifteen, she was acquainted with authors and could compose, till at last she became an accomplished female scholar."—(19 *char.*)—*Ibid.*, col. 7th.

7. "He only wished to choose a proper son-in-law, talented and handsome, to match her."—(15 *char.*)—*Ibid.*, col. 11th.

8. "He supposed that in this single village and town the men of talents were limited."—(10 *char.*)—*Ibid.*, col. 17th.

9. "Every day, when public business was over, he did nothing but quaff wine and compose verses."—(13 *char.*)—*Ibid.*, leaf 3, col. 3d.

10. "Mr. Pák, seeing that one of his clerks had given him twelve jars of chrysanthemums, arranged them at the foot of the library stairs."—(19 *char.*)—*Ibid.*, col. 5th.

11. Whenever, in the leisure from governmental duties, you are seeking for me, then I also am inquiring for you."—(17 *char.*)—*Ibid.*, col. 13th.

12. "Yesterday, I was indeed coming to visit [the flowers], but unexpectedly, just as I got out of the door, I ran against old Yéung (楊) (the loathed thing) holding a longevity address, whch he wished me to stop and correct that he might give it to general Shik (石

都督), congratulating him on his age; this let me in for a day's work."—(42 *char.*)—*Ibid.*, col. 17th.

13. "The censor Sú (蘇御史) said, For several days I have wished to come, but because there was so much business in the office, I could not help declining the pleasure of the sight."—(24 *char.*)—*Ibid.*, col. 21st.

14. "The three men speaking passed on into the hall, and having interchanged civilities, and thrown off their dress and tea being handed about, he then invited them into the library to see the chrysanthemums."—(26 *char.*)—*Ibid.*, col. 22d.

15. "Having drank several cups, doctor 'Ng (吳翰林) thereupon remarked, These flowers are neat but not gaudy, beautiful without being gairish; and although the red, yellow, carnation, and white colors are all of them fresh and lustrous, still there is so much of what is elegant and diversified in their appearance, that one is led to delight in and admire them."—(48 *char.*)—*Ibid.*, leaf 4, col. 5th.

16. "Every day, he busies himself in paying court to the powerful and great, only in hopes to get himself into office: he is one whom the flowers would ridicule."—(19 *char.*)—*Ibid.*, col. 7th.

17. "The censor Sú replied, the capital is undoubtedly the theatre for reputation and profit; and their striving for reputation and trying to get gain, truly is their right."—(23 *char.*)—*Ibid.*, col. 11th.

18. "It is that I am only one 'adviser of the path' (i. e. *a censor*), and in these times, if I wish to open my mouth, I cannot do it, or if I wish to keep silence I also cannot do it: truly it is difficult to act."—(33 *char.*)—*Ibid.*, col. 17th.

19. "Mr. Pák then bade the domestics bring out pencils and ink-stone, and with doctor 'Ng and the censor Sú they immediately there selected a rhythm for making an ode on the chrysanthemums."—(26 *char.*)—*Ibid.*, leaf 5th, col. 1st.

20. "The three persons were thus wielding their pencils, when suddenly a chairman coming in announced that the censor Yéung had come. The three men hearing this were all of them not at all pleased. Mr. Pák immediately scolded the chairman, saying, You scoundrel, knowing that I and the gentlemen 'Ng and Sú were drinking wine, you ought to have replied to him, *not at home*."—(52 *char.*)—*Ibid.*, col. 3d.

21. "The chairman stating said, I had already gone out of the gate to bow off the visitor, when Yéung's chairmen said, Mr. Yéung was in Mr. Sú's office asking for him, and was told that he was here taking wine, and he has consequently come here seeking him. Moreover, they saw the two gentlemen's chairs and horses at the door, wherefore this reply could not be made."—(57 *char.*)—*Ibid.*, col. 5th.

拾級大成

22. "Yéung the censor was a man, whose words and conversation were coarse and vulgar; externally he loved to be extensively acquaint. ed, but internally he was covetous and time-serving."—(17 *char.*)—*Ibid.*, col. 11th.

23. "Mr. Pák said, I was about to invite you, sir, to view the chrysanthemums, but was fearful the duties of your office were so great that you could not find time to attend to such trifling business."—(29 *char.*)—*Ibid.* col. 16th.

24. "When yesterday, I engaged the high attainments of you, sir, to improve the style, it might be termed touching iron and changing it to gold. This morning I gave it to general Shik, who was exceedingly delighted, and more than before he added his respects and thanks."—(33 *char.*)—*Ibid.*, leaf 6, col. 1st.

25. "Mr. Pák bade the attendants put on more cups and chopsticks, and bowed to the three men to sit down and drink wine."—(16 *char.*)—*Ibid.*, col. 7th.

26. "Recently I have learned, that distant from the city twenty *li*, there is an exceedingly fertile and rich piece of land, which, being exceedingly desirous of, he did nothing less than send one of his domestics and seize it."—(27 *char.*)—*Ibid.*, col. 19th.

27. "Whenever I spoke to him good words, he as often refused to listen."—(14 *char.*)—*Ibid.*, col. 19th.

28. "The censor Sú hearing, his mind was discomposed to a considerable degree."—(12 *char.*)—*Ibid.*, col. 22.

29. "The censor Yéung, seeing the censor Sú's words and countenance disagreeing, then sat silently without speaking."—(16 *char.*)—*Ibid.*, leaf 7, col. 3d.

30. "Mr. Pák therefore smiling said, I only supposed, that my friend Yéung simply came to delight in the flowers, but from the first he has been talking about Wóng Tsun's (汪全) affairs; you will not therefore regard it as strange that I have not yet invited you to come in and see the flovers."—(41 *char.*)—*Ibid.* col. 4th.

31. "Dr. 'Ng also laughing observed, On happy days and fine prospects, we ought only to quaff wine and compose verses; but if under the flowers, we converse about governmental affairs, I think it is a little bizarre. Our friend Yéung ought to be mulcted a large goblet, in order to atone for his outrage upen the goddess of the flowers."—(44 *char.*)—*Ibid.* col. 6th.

32. "The censor Yéung taking the wine said, I consequently here receive the forfeit; and after this he who talks about politics, I truly will not excuse him."—(29 *char.*)—*Ibid.*, col. 12th.

33. "The censor Yéung drank off the wine, and because he saw on the table pencils and ink-stone, he said, You three gentlemen have already been here with high entertainment making verses; why have I not been instructed?"—(31 *char.*)—*Ibid.*, col. 14th.

34. "Dr. 'Ng replied, We have just now thought of it, and have not yet put our pencils to paper."—(12 *char.*)—*Ibid.*, col. 16th.

35. "The censor Yéung said, If you have not yet begun to write, do not let me interrupt your pleasurable pursuits, but please to give utterance to your thoughts. I will accompany you with glasses of wine; how will this do?"—(33 *char.*)—*Ibid.*, col. 16th.

36. "Mr. Pák observed, If you wish me to forfeit wine I am quite willing, but if you wish me to make verses, I cannot do them at all." —(18 *char.*)—*Ibid.*, leaf 9, col. 15th.

---

## SHORT SENTENCES TO BE TRANSLATED.

Here follow a few miscellaneous sentences, selected for the most part from the Sám Kwók Chí, intended to exercise the student in translating. The benefit of this practice will by no means be lost if he does not express the idea of a sentence in exactly the same words as its original; for the search after new words, the mental labor of endeavoring to cast the idea in a Chinese form, and the several trials of writing the sentence in this or that way, will all prove highly beneficial, and combine to give him that readiness in writing in Chinese which is the main object of these lessons. It is intended that these short sentences should be translated after the preceding continuous extracts; for in writing them, reference should be made to the original in order to compare the two.

1. Goods are dear this year because but few ships have come.
2. What is the price of tea lately?
3. Send this letter to the provincial city this evening, and on no account forget it.
4. We can converse as we go together, and the way will not seem long.
5. As the sky is dark now and there is no sun, I fear in the evening there will be a foul wind.
6. Let us bring out the chess-board and spend the livelong day.
7. To-day gain a little, to-morrow gain a little, you will presently collect a good deal.
8. I do not fear that the way is far, but I must go there to be satisfied.

9. He is so stingy that a cash seems as big as a tray basket.

10. Explain it to him clearly one thing at a time, and no doubt he will believe.

11. You must be very careful of your purses, when walking abroad at the end of the year or near new-year.

12. Having already unsuccessfully searched, you need not go again.

13. If he works for you with all his heart and strength, it is not right to call him lazy.

14. Better to eat congee with a pleasant face than rice with wrinkled eyebrows.

15. Nobody would have thought that he would have stolen; truly it surpasses people's thoughts.

16. What news is there lately? I will trouble you to tell me.

17. For these several successive cold days I have not seen any snow fall.

18. After rain has fallen, the street is slippery and difficult to walk.

19. The lantern is dim, probably there is no oil.

20. A day has twelve hours—if it is so long, no fear it will not be finished.

21. If a man be good, heaven will certainly recompense him.

22. The poor cannot contend with the rich, the rich cannot strive with the magistrates.

23. A natural disposition is hard to change, hills and stones are hard to move.

24. Let each family sweep away the snow before its own door, and not remark upon the hoarfrost on their neighbor's roof.

25. He feared and retreated—why did you not pursue him?

26. If you do not help, for what business have you come here?

27. Sir, with such words, will not all the world laugh at you.

28. If I rely upon faithfulness and uprightness, and still die, how will it cause the world to laugh?

29. Tsun (進) exclaiming said, You set of fellows! How can you know the great affairs of government?

30. To shade your eyes and seize a swallow, is to ridicule yourself.

31. Tung Ch'éuk was a man of benignant face and wicked heart.

32. He who has many doubts is not equal to planning great affairs.

33. A good bird selects a tree and nestles in it; a virtuous statesman selects a master and serves him.

34. Tsò, leading his horse out of the minister's office, laid on the whip, and looking to the southwest, went away.

35. Tsò said, How can a swallow or sparrow know of the intentions of a swan or stork?

36. Sir, in the government, whom do you regard as the hero of the age?

37. Lü Pò is a hero unequalled by any man.

38. This man speaks immodest words—why not kill him?

39. Wanchéung (雲 長) is an upright man; he certainly will not forfeit his word.

40. I have begotten five sons, but the youngest pleases me most.

41. You are a villain, who scoffs at his prince and despises his superiors; everybody wishes to kill you.

42. Üntak said, I have already promised the man, and dare not forfeit my word.

43. Üntak said, This affair, I certainly cannot presume to promise you.

44. Sir, your appearance is quite fat, what regimen have you been adopting to become so?

45. Lü Pò is at bottom an unprincipled man; what fear if we do kill him?

46. His power is gone, and he has come to join me; if I kill him it will be dishonorable.

47. I have been away from my village many years, and we have not yet become acquainted.

48. When fellow villagers meet, how is it possible they will not talk of old affairs?

49. I have some private business; it is not easy yet to speak it fully.

50. He saw on the thatched cottage a youth cowering over a furnace, holding his knees and singing.

51. Your words have cleared up my misapprehension.

52. Küin (權) drew his side sword and cutting one corner of the office table before him said, Whoever of all the officers again speaks of submitting to Ts'ò shall be made like this table.

53. How can you presume to speak so much and disarrange my rules?

54. I have long heard your great reputation—now why do you privately dwell in this place?

55. Sir, do not so extravagantly extol me, still I hope to have your instruction.

56. I have received the emperor's orders to punish faithless ministers.

57. If you plunder the blackhaired race, azure heaven will not protect you.

58. The marines are much diseased, we must employ a skillful physician to heal them.

59. Are not my troops and officers rather brave and courageous?

60. Tung (統) said, I am neither rich nor honorable but I wish to save the people.

61. Towards evening, the moon rose above the eastern hills with great splendor like the clear day: the whole length of the river was like a band of clear white.

62. Wóng Tsò's (黃祖) disposition was overbearing, and he was unable to use men: therefore this misfortune was caused.

63. To employ one very malevolent to punish one very benevolent —how will he not fail?

64. Your words exactly coincide with my ideas.

65. A heavy mist conceals the river, and that army suddenly approaching, you must be concealed, you ought not inconsiderately to move.

66. Léung (亮) has very insignificant inferior talents; how can he have an admirable scheme?

67. Kün, observing that Üntak's deportment and bearing were not those of the commonalty, in his heart arose thoughts of fear and dread.

68. Má (馬) traded in flour for an occupation; his family was poor, and he had no wife to be miserable with his mother.

69. I abstract people's property in order to teach my son; how can I myself regard such a heart as pure?

70. Whenever Máng (猛) was full of rage, no one dared to admonish him; but he served his mother very dutifully, and when she came then he stopped.

71. There was a stranger from Chungchau (中州) lodging at the Shé Fat (蛇佛) monastery. The priests of the monastery every evening dined on delicious meat and soup, and every piece was round like a fowl's neck. Doubting, he asked the priest how many fowls he killed to get so many necks. The priest said, These are bits of snakes.

72. After drinking wine, I speak at random, but do not, sir, reprimand me.

73. It was a year of great dearth, and the common people ate dates and greens.

Any number of sentences similar to these might be given, but the preceding extracts will be sufficient for examples in this exercise of retranslating. The student will find it advantageous in writing sentences, to commence with such as are plain narrative, or with short phrases of command, (which are the simplest forms of speech,) and then proceed to more complicated sentences. The books which are used in schools for teaching the rudiments of the English language will afford abundance of easy narrative reading lessons, well fitted for rendering into Chinese. It will be better as an exercise to try a faithful translation of a selected portion than to attempt original composition at first; for the mind will be too much divided between the idea and the characters to express it, to do either well. Fables, parables, the narrative portions of the Scriptures, descriptions in natural history, stories, &c., are subjects which are easily understood in all languages, and which the student can explain the meaning of to his teacher, without much risk of misapprehension. It will be necessary, however, whatever is the theme, to use some caution in this latter particular, for many of those subjects and those ideas which to the foreigner are of the simplest and most familiar kind, are new to the native, and when he hears them expressed in broken sentences by the beginner, he may not in all cases rightly understand them.

This part of the student's Chinese education—that of translating into, and writing in, Chinese—cannot be too much or too carefully attended to; for when he has attained that facility of expression, aptness of illustration, clearness of diction, that natural style of writing, and ability to express his thoughts in good Chinese, which a native scholar has, he has a power at his command that may and ought to be exerted to the great good of this people. If their literature soon becomes uninteresting and jejune, and he finds it wearisome and distasteful toil to plod through their books, he should remember the treasures of knowledge and truth in the English language, which he has at his command, and whose diffusion will elevate them to their proper place among the nations. If foreigners have but comparatively little to learn from the Chinese, they have much to teach them; and it should act as no mean incitement to learn their language in order to convey to them that knowledge.

# Chapter Tenth.

## LESSONS IN READING AND TRANSLATING.

In this chapter, forms of various kinds of writing, as letters, edicts, memorials, imperial commands, selections, &c., are collected, which are intended to exercise the student in reading the characters, and in translating them literally, in the same manner as has been done on preceding pages. The version at the bottom of the page will enable him to punctuate the original, and to give to each character its proper meaning. In printing these papers, the Chinese forms have been followed closely, such as placing some characters higher than others, and making certain of a smaller size, so that they will serve in a small degree to show the styles used in writing such papers.

No. I.—A FATHER TO HIS SON AT SCHOOL.

父字示阿富知之聞汝在家讀
書惟虛應故事全不以汝
祖叮囑之語爲念寄來會課文字
並無可取比從前大不如也然
文字日漸進步方爲有用似汝
有退無進何若不讀之爲妙免
至徒負虛名也見字卽當痛改
勿蹈前轍爲囑此與
阿富看

父天爵字

內平安信煩
駕帶至北山村交小兒阿富收啟
天爵付寄

Your father writes commanding A'fú to be acquainted with it. I have heard that you are studying your books at home, but doing it in a very inefficient useless manner; not at all remembering your grandfather's admonitory words. The themes and compositions sent to me I cannot at all receive, they are by no means as good as those formerly sent. Truly, in composition daily to advance a step, there is advantage to be obtained: but, as you are doing, to retrograde and make no advances, by far the best way will be to study no more, and not so very uselessly bear an empty reputation. On seeing this letter, my orders are that you must immediately earnestly reform, and do not walk in your former ways. This is sent to A'fú for his perusal.

Your father T'íntséuk's letter.

(*Outside address.*)

The within complimentary letter I will trouble you, Sir, to take to the village of Pakshán, and give it to my son A'fú to receive and open. T'íntséuk sends it.

No. II.—A SON TO HIS PARENTS FROM ABROAD.

字稟
二位大人知之昨伏讀 手諭知玉
體安泰家中俱獲康寧皆蒼天
福祐也男自別 親客外沾利
無幾貨物雖云易售賬目總屬
難歸是以久欲思回奈被賬頭
牽阻非兒故戀棲異地以取不
孝之罪惟願 二親茹養天和
益增遐算兒遙居異地心亦歡
樂也男在外平安無庸遠慮謹
此叩請
金安
男亞用敬稟

A writing requesting the two distinguished persons to be acquainted with it. Yesterday, I received and read the command from your hands, and learned that your honored persons were well and happy, and that the family were all in tranquil health, every one being blessed by azure heaven. Your son, himself, separated from his parents, dwells abroad; I have yet but a little gain, for goods although it may be said they are easily sold, still the accounts are all collected with difficulty, and for these reasons I have long had thoughts of returning; but have been hindered and detained by these accounts. It is not that I have any attachment to residing (*lit.* nestling) in a foreign land, by which I get the imputation of being unfilial, but wishing both my parents to have all the support and ease of heavenly peace, and to add still more to the number of your days, I live away in a foreign land, and my heart is also glad and happy. While I am away in peace, it is unnecessary for you to be anxious about me. Respectfully [writing] this, prostrate I wish you golden enjoyment.

Your son Ayung respectfully states.

## No. III.—A HUSBAND TO HIS WIFE FROM ABROAD.

自別賢妻忽經半載每想家中
心神如醉常夜夢魂千里清晨
思念悲傷　老親在堂幼子在
抱皆賴賢妻調護不致老親
有不孝之怨子女失教誨之方
賢妻之恩德大矣卑人客外風
霜因家用浩繁經商覓利皆爲
飢寒二字情出無奈孰甘上拋
父母下撇妻兒遠離客地也將
來倘得如意我卽歸家決不久
羈他方今某人歸托帶銀物若
干聊資家用書不盡言言不盡
意此致
王氏賢妻粧次
愚夫楊逢春謹書

While away from my worthy wife, suddenly has passed away half a year. Every time I think of those in my family, my heart is like that of a drunken man; every night my spirit in dreams goes thousands of miles, and in the morning my thoughts afflict and grieve me. My aged parents in the hall, my tender children at the breast, all depend upon my worthy wife to look after and cherish them, thus causing that my aged parents do not repine for my unfilial conduct, nor my children lose my rules of careful instruction. Great is my worthy wife's kindness and merit. I am a stranger abroad, [exposed] to the weather on account of the numerous necessities of my family, doing business and seeking gain solely on account of those two particulars—hunger and cold; my circumstances allow no other course. How could I willingly on the one hand leave father and mother, and on the other separate from wife and children, dwelling abroad in a strange land! When I have obtained according to my wishes, I shall immediately return, by no means remaining long in another land. Now, a certain person returning home, I have engaged him to carry home a sum of money for the household expenses. I cannot write all my words, cannot speak all my thoughts. This is sent to Mrs. Wóng my worthy wife, in her own apartment.

Your humble husband Yéung Fungch'un's attentive letter.

No. IV.—A WIFE TO HER HUSBAND ABROAD.

夫君別後芙蓉兩度開矣行時
萬縷千言妾惓惓在念不敢有
違　高堂中饋妾自任之弱女
幼子妾自撫之家務一切妾自
理之毋勞遠慮但我　夫君客
外風霜舉家念切倘有盈餘之
利即當返駕奉侍雙親教誨子
女骨肉完聚笑語一堂庶免
老親有倚閭之望賤妾有白頭
之嘆也室邇人遙寸心千里惟
加餐自愛爲禱此達
瑞廷夫君大人座右
妾王氏敬禀

Since my honored husband's departure, the Hibiscus has twice opened itself. The multiplied words and innumerable injunctions you gave when you left, your handmaid has remembered with the greatest care, not presuming to contravene them. Those in the high hall have been nourished, I myself waiting on them; the tender daughters and youthful sons, I have myself taken care of; everything in the house I have myself looked after. Do not make yourself anxious about those at a distance, but while my honored husband is [suffering] the weather abroad, we who are at home do all ardently remember him. If you procure a little overplus of gain, then you ought straightway to bring yourself back, respectfully to wait upon your parents, and carefully to teach your children. Your kindred will then all collect together, and laughing converse [fill] the hall. Then will those venerable parents not have the longing of those who lean at the village gate, nor your humble handmaid have the sighing of a grayhaired person. The house is near, but its lord is far;—my little heart [flies] a thousand miles. But my wishes are that you take good care of yourself, and regard your own comfort. This is to inform Suiting my honored husband, placed on the right of his seat.

Your handmaid Wóng respectfully states.

No. V.—A PERSON TO HIS FRIEND AND THE REPLY.

敬啟者前所云京都之行未審嚴程
有期否弟擬定於三日後發軫意欲
邀
兄促裝同往俾弟得藉光教幸
何如也耑此并候
近
佳不一
上
文臺兄台大人如晤
愚弟陳一桂字頓

答
承諭京都偕行得爲執鞭實所欣慕
俗務煩冗一時未能整頓行裝恐難
定日登途
仁兄先請榮行俟弟諸
事轉暇亦即趨步行塵也肅此仍候
近
安不宜
上
一桂兄台大人座右
愚弟梁文臺謹覆

I would respectfully state. With regard to what you before stated about going to the capital, I did not ascertain whether you was going soon, or had not fixed on a time? I have decided to leave on the third day following, and I am much inclined to invite you sir to get ready quickly to accompany me. Thus shall I be able to engage your clear instruction, which will be exceedingly pleasant. For this I write, also wishing you present hapiness in no small degree.

To Mantoi, worthy and respected sir, as if present.

Your stupid younger brother Chan Yatkwai
writes with compliments.

*(Reply.)*

I have received your commands regarding accompanying you to the capital, to be your traveling attendant (*lit.* whip-holder), for which I am very deeply grateful. But my little affairs are exceedingly hurried and troublesome, and at once I cannot arrange them so as to pack up and be off, and fear I cannot start with you on the appointed day. Will you, respected sir, please to precede with your equipage, and when my affairs allow me leisure, I will immediately follow after you as fast as possible. I respectfully return this answer, and wish you much present peace, without ceremonious trouble.

To Yatkwai, worthy and respected sir, on the left of his seat.

His stupid younger brother Leung Mantoi
respectfully replies.

No. VI.—LETTER TO A DISTANT FRIEND.

敬啟者弟自與
台翁別後不覺韶光易邁兩經梅花
自矣念闊別已久無日不神馳
左右曩日正思慕間琅函忽降
過荷獎諭然世事如棋心已久
灰敗鼓之皮豈堪藥用承 仁
兄下問弟實無志觀光矣謹此
佈復并請
近好不一
上
三畏仁兄大人足下
弟林英徐字頓

I would respectfully state. From the time when I left you, honored sir, imperceptibly the time has slipped away; twice has the plum flower blossomed. I constantly remember that we have been already far separated for a long time, there is not a day in which my heart does not glance to your place. The other day, just while I was thinking of you, your valued favor suddenly came to me,—I am most deeply indebted for your gracious favor. Truly the affairs of life are like the moves of chess:—My heart has for a long time been like ashes, or as the rent head of a drum: How can it be remedied by medicine? You, worthy sir, have condescended to ask after me, but indeed I have no inclination to look after any serious business. I respectfully send this answer to inform you, and also wish you present good in every particular.

To Sámwai my worthy and respected brother at his feet.

His junior Lam Yingtsü
writes with compliments.

No. VII.—Note accompanying a Present of Ink, and the Reply.

松君數筋綠烟浮處或可以稱龍賔
也玆敬達座右聊助右軍揮灑錦繡
之文雲烟之藻須從此出祈莞存是
幸謹此順候
文祺不一
上
香園二兄大人史右
愚弟李雲英頓首

答
承貺烏玉玦雖臨池有資然弟非
善藻不能一噴成章以光 寵贈惟
滴露研之而雲烟靄靄從池中起也
敬珍之豹囊謹領容謝兼候
日佳不宣
上
雲英大兄先生文几
愚弟陳香園敬復

Several cakes from the noble fir, [produced by] the sombre smoke floating about, or which might also be called 'dragon-guests;'—are herewith respectfully presented on the right of your seat, that they may aid a little in wielding Yaukwan's sprinkling [pencil]. Elegant and tasteful composition, and characters like the cloudy smoke; will of course from them proceed. I beg you will place this trifle by you, and I shall be highly favored. Respectfully sending this, I wish you full success in all your studies.

To Héungün, the second brother, respected sir on the right of his table,

His unworthy junior Lí Wanying, humbly compliments.

*(Reply.)*

I have received your valued gift of the black gemmeous cakes; although when they come on the pool they are of great value, still I am by no means skillful at composing, and cannot off-hand complete an essay, to illuminate (i. e. equal) your bounteous gift. But with drops of dew to rub on the stone, characters like cloudy smoke in curling wreaths will from the pool arise. Your respected present, [which is placed] in a pard-skin bag, I thankfully accept, and if you will excuse me for a short time, I will come and thank you for it; at the same time wishing you pleasant days in all respects.

To Wanying, respected sir, on his writing-table,

His unworthy junior Chan Héungün respectfully replies.

No. VIII.—Note of Congratulation on becoming a Graduate (*küyan*).

足下角藝文場榮膺鶚薦不特榜
慶得人亦信蛟龍終非池中物
也便擬來春傳臚首唱攀蟾宮
桂蕚一枝其藉光更何如也謹
具不腆之儀聊助金樽一敬謹
此順請
文祺不一
上
天德先生大人座右
硯弟陸國龍頓首

內函煩
駕帶至省城太平門外十三行
天和洋貨店送與
黎先生印天德高發
沙尾陸國龍拜干
信到奉梹資錢叁拾文
謹 *or* 吉 *or* 護
封

My friend has been competing on the arena for literary honors, and with honor receiving high advancement; but you will not only have the happiness of being entered in the graduate roll, for I also believe the water dragon will not long be found in the pool (i. e. he will go on to higher honors). Therefore I conjecture that on the coming year you will, at the regular presentation [of Hánlin], be the first one called out, thus plucking a sprig of the fragrant Olea from the palace of the moon, and then how much distinction will I not borrow! Respectfully presenting you with an insignificant trifle, to assist you somewhat in draining the golden goblet, I carefully send this, humbly wishing you all literary success.

To T'íntak, learned and respected sir, at the right of his seat.

His young schoolmate, Luk Kwóklung humbly bows.

(*Outside address.*)

The inclosed letter I will trouble you, sir, to take to the provincial city outside of the Great Peace gate near the Thirteen Factories, to the foreign merchandize shop T'ínwó, and present it to Mr. Lai, surnam-T'íntak, with high respect. Luk Kwóklung of Shámí's compliments.

On the letter reaching, you will receive for postage 30 cash.

Carefully (*On the back is written*) Sealed.
[*or* happily, *or* defensively]

No. IX.—Reply to the preceding.

答
謭劣之材每慚玷立宮墻毛羽
未滿何敢冀望雲飛逐隊而行
不過三年一應點耳偶爾僥倖
得捷秋闈夙志雖酬榜花深辱
仁臺其何以洗滌我厚顏哉過荷
鼎貺敬即拜嘉佝容躬謝肅此
并候
起居佳勝
上
國龍長兄大人史右
硯弟黎天德謹覆

斯信懇携至省城聯興街
成利寶店求代交
陸國龍先生大人安啟
天德由永唐街封寄

*(Reply.)*

I, who possess the poorest and shallowest talents, always disgraced the seat of learning when in it; my wings are not yet full grown, and how can I presume to hope of rising to the clouds. I merely followed in the common order, for it is only once in three years that we can answer to our names, when unexpectedly I was lucky enough to enter into the autumn gate (i. e. become a graduate). Although my early anticipations are realized, I am deeply ashamed at seeing my name in the list,—how will you, my worthy friend, be able to cleanse my shameless face! I am exceedingly obliged for your valued gift, and do now respectfully thank you for your goodness, and if you will excuse me a little while, I will come in person and thank you. I humbly send this, at the same time wishing you, rising or sitting, abundant delights.

To Kwóklung, honored and respected sir, at the left of his table,

His junior schoolmate Lai T'íntak respectfully replies.

*(Outside address.)*

I beg you to take this letter to Lünhing street in the provincial city, to the shop Shinglí, and in my stead give it Mr. Luk Kwóklung, &c., to be quietly opened. T'íntak, from Wingt'óng street, seals and sends it.

No. X.—Request to borrow Money, and the Reply.

屢次承情銘感五內刻下弟偶値急
需無從告貸知
台翁賙濟有素必憫涸轍而激以西江
之水故不揣汗色懇借白金壹百両
得以救急歲內子母一併歸還斷不
延爽仰望俯允以便叩階趨領謹
此並候
日安
其彥四兄先生如面
弟郭尚文字頓

答
相好朋友奚云賙濟　仁兄旣有急
需弟敢不應命惟是近日囊空如
洗轉乞于鄰但不能如數只可集腋
成裘耳祈收入是幸耑此佈覆并請
福安
尚文仁兄大人座右　愚弟黃其彥頓首

The many times I have received kindness from you is inscribed upon and affects my five inwards (i. e. my whole man). Just now I have suddenly met with a most pressing emergency, and am without any source from whence to request a loan. Knowing that you, honored sir, uniformly bestow charity, and will undoubtedly commiserate [me in] the dry rut [into which I am fallen], and overflow it with the water of the western river, I therefore [as if] not perceiving my sweaty face (i. e. putting a great constraint on myself), beg you to lend me one hundred taels silver, by which I shall be relieved from my embarrassment; I will repay you the principal and interest within the year, nor on any account will I delay or fail in so doing. Looking up I hope you will condescend to accede to my request, and I will then bowing upon your steps hasten to receive it. I respectfully send this, at the same time wishing you daily peace.

To K'ingán, the fourth brother and honored sir, as if before him,

His junior Kók Shéungman writes with respects.

*(Reply.)*

My very good friend, why do you talk of 'bestowing charity?' If my worthy brother is now in an embarrassed situation, how shall I presume not to accede to his request? But indeed recently my purse is as clean as if it had been washed, and I have been among my neighbors to borrow, yet am unable to get the whole amount; I can only collect what will [be like a patch] under the armpit to complete the fur jacket. I beg you will receive it, and I shall be satisfied. For this I return an answer, also wishing you happiness and quiet.

To Shéungman, worthy and respected sir, at the right of his seat,

His humble junior Wóng K'ingán sends compliments.

No. XI.—Edict from the magistrates of Héungshán district.

署廣州澳門軍民府加十級紀錄十次蔣
香山縣正堂加十級紀錄十次三爲
署香山縣左堂加十級紀錄十次彭
出示曉諭事照得前因嘆咭唎國
夷人桀驁不馴諸事違抗以致
欽差大臣督憲親臨香城扎飭嚴斷接
濟大震聲威疊經出示曉諭在案
玆查所有住澳之嘆夷俱以知畏
之懼先後紛紛全數出澳除要隘
各海口現仍派撥兵役梭織往來
嚴密巡查不准稍有偷漏外所有
海口以內澳門各村市日用米石
業經 本分府等稟准各

Tséung, the acting sub-prefect of Macao in Kwángchau, raised ten steps and recorded ten times;
Sám, the principal district magistrate of Héungshán, raised ten steps and recorded ten times; and
P'áng, the acting assistant magistrate of Héungshán, raised ten steps and recorded ten times, Hereby issue a clear proclamation.

*Whereas*, because, formerly, the English foreigners were exceedingly overbearing and disobedient, in all things rebelliously opposing, therefore their excellencies, the imperial commissioner great minister, and the governor, in person came to the town of Héungshán, with great state and sound of pompous dignity, and issued an order to us strictly to forbid supplying them with food. On this point we have already repeatedly issued plain commands, as is on record. Now it appears, that all the English foreigners who lived in Macao, being thereby filled with dreadful fear, have, at one time and another, one and all left Macao. Besides stationing soldiers now at every important port of entrance to sift and examine in the strictest manner whoever passes and repasses, not permitting that there be any clandestine leaking out, we the sub-prefect, &c., have also, in order that there be a daily supply of rice for the places within the seaboard, Macao and all the villages and mar-

CONCLUSION OF THE SAME.

大

憲飛催前途源源運米接濟此外
一切食物俱准照通流貿易並無
阻滯是因前各物俱不致有缺乏
惟查澳門各處物價尚未平減是
有囤積居奇之事殊屬有妨民食
合再示諭禁爲此示諭澳門及附
近各村市鋪戶人等知悉爾等售
賣善民及西洋並各夷人一切米
麵食物務須按照時價平買平賣
毋得藉端高擡價值利已損人倘
敢不遵定將該鋪查封拘拿鋪主
究懲不貸各宜凜遵毋違特示

道光十九年七月十九日示

kets, already petitioned and obtained the permission of the high authorities, to quickly urge it in all directions that food be freely furnished. Moreover, all kinds of provisions are permitted to be bought and sold without any let or hindrance, nor as was the case before, should there be on any articles deficiency or want. But we have ascertained that in Macao and other places the prices of articles are not yet cheapened, and moreover that some are hoarding it up to sell, which is indeed obstructing the food of the people, and which we do again by this command prohibit.

Wherefore this command is issued, that all the shopkeepers and inhabitants of Macao, and the adjacent villages and hamlets, may be fully acquainted with it. You may all traffic with the peaceable inhabitants, with the Portuguese and all other foreigners in rice, flour, &c. It should be according to the current price, both buying cheap and selling cheap, and do not on account of the demand raise the price, in order to benefit yourselves at the expense of others; if any one presume not to regard this, that shop shall be straightway sealed up, and the shopkeeper seized, and strictly examined without leniency. Let every one reverently obey, without opposition. A special edict.

Promulgated on the 19th year, 7th month, and 19th day of Tòkwóng.

No. XII.—Proclamation and rules regarding the Capture of Grasshoppers.

特調南海番禺縣正堂加十級紀錄十次徐黃為
申明捕蝗要法俾知預防以弭
災害事　道光十三年八月初
七日奉　本府札開轉奉
督撫各憲札開本年五月內廣西柳潯
桂梧各屬有飛蝗入境已據報
捕除凈盡聞高州府屬毗連廣
西地方有蝗蝻入境滋生最易
當此晚造長發之時殊為民害
應即按屬捕除會營上緊撲滅
惟粵東向無此患恐官民不曉
捕法合將捕蝗緊要各條開列
飛勘　督屬會營照法捕捉并

Tsü and Wóng, by special appointment magistrates of the districts of Námhoi and Púnyü, raised ten steps and recorded ten times, Hereby distinctly publish important rules for the capture of grasshoppers, that it may be known how to guard against them, in order to ward off injury and calamity. On the 7th day of the 8th month in the 13th year of Tòkwóng (Sept. 20th, 1833), we received a communication from the prefect of this [department of Kwóngchau], transmitting a dispatch from their excellencies the governor and lieut.-governor, as follows:

" During the fifth month of the present year, flights of grasshoppers appeared in the limits of Kwóngsai, in [the departments of] Liú, Ts'am, Kwai, and 'Ng, and their vicinage; which have already, according to report, been clean destroyed and driven off. We have heard that in the department of Kòchau and its neighborhood, conterminous to Kwóngsai, grasshoppers have appeared which multiply with extreme rapidity. At this time, the second crop is in the blade, (which if destroyed will endamage the people,) and it is proper therefore immediately wherever they are found to capture and drive them off, marshaling the troops to advance and wholly exterminate them. But Kwóngtung heretofore has never experienced this calamity, and we apprehend the officers and people do understand the mode of capture, wherefore we now exhibit in order the most important rules for catching grasshoppers. Let the governor's combined forces be immediately instructed

CONTINUATION OF THE SAME.

示諭鄉農齊集捕捉官爲設局收買務期掃除净盡倘捕蝗不力處分决重慎無匿延貽患致干法紀仍將遵辦緣由通報查核等因計粘抄捕蝗各條一紙由院行司札府轉札到縣奉此除咨呈廣州協臺飛報所屬各營及行各巡撿一體留心隨時查察如有蝗蝻潛生立卽合力捕滅免貽民害所有奉行捕蝗各條要法合就臚列于左

一 蝗之初起見于大澤之涯及驟盈滿寬闊之處生子于黑土高

to capture them *secundum artem*, at the same time let orders be issued for the villagers and farmers at once to assemble and take them, and for the magistrates to establish storehouses for their reception and purchase, thus without fail sweeping them clean away. If you do not exert yourselves to catch the grasshoppers, your guilt will be very great; let it be done carefully, not clandestinely delaying, thus causing this misfortune to come upon yourselves, transgressing the laws, and causing us again according to the exigencies of the case to promulge general orders, and make thorough examinations, &c., &c. Appended hereto are copies of these rules for catching grasshoppers, which from the lieut.-governor must be sent to the treasurer, who will enjoin it upon the magistrates of the departments, and he again enjoin it upon the district magistrates."

Having received the preceding, besides respectfully transmitting it to the colonel of the department to be straightway forwarded to all the troops under his authority, and also to all the district justices, that they all with united purpose bend their energies to observe at the proper time, that whenever the grasshoppers become numerous they join their forces and extirpate them, thus removing calamity from the people, we also enjoin upon whoever receives this that they catch the grasshoppers according to these several directions, which are therefore here arranged in order as follows:

1. When the grasshoppers first issue forth, they are to be seen on the borders of large morasses, from whence they quickly multiply and fill large

CONTINUATION OF THE SAME.

亢之地用尾裁入土中深不及寸
仍留孔竅狀如蜂窩一蝗所下十
餘粒其形如豆一粒中即有細子
百餘蓋蝗之生也羣飛羣食其子
之下也必同時同地形若蜂房最
易尋覓
一蝗在麥田禾稼深草中每日清晨
盡聚草梢含露體重不能飛躍日
午蝗始交飛日昏蝗聚一日止有
三時可捕民夫亦得休息捕之之
法宜掘坑于前長闊爲佳兩傍用
板或門扇等類接連八字擺列集
衆發喊手執木板驅而逐之入于

tracts of land; they produce their young in little hillocks of black earth, using the tail to bore into the ground, not quite an inch in depth, which still remain as open holes, the whole somewhat resembling a bee's nest. One grasshopper drops ten or more pellets, in form like a pea, each one containing a hundred or more young. For the young grasshoppers fly and eat in swarms, and this laying of their young is done all at once and in the same spot; the place resembles a hive of bees, and therefore it is very easily sought and found.

2. When the grasshoppers are in the fields of wheat and tender rice and the thick grass, every day at early dawn they all alight on the leaves of the grass, and their bodies being covered with dew are heavy and they cannot fly or hop; at noon, they begin to assemble for flight, and at evening they collect in one spot. Thus each day there are three periods when they can be caught, and the people and gentry will also have a short respite. The mode of catching them is to dig a trench before them, the broader and longer the better, on each side placing boards, or doors, screens and such like things, one stretched on after another, and spreading open each side. The whole multitude then must cry aloud, and holding boards in their hands, drive them all into the trench; meanwhile those on the opposite side, provided with brooms and

CONTINUATION OF THE SAME.

坑內又于對坑用數掃把見其躍跳往上者盡行掃入覆以乾草用火燒之先燃火于坑內然後驅而逐之若只掩埋隔宿多能穴地而出

一 飛蝗見樹木成行或旌旗森列每翔而下農家多用長竿掛紅白衣裙或紅綠紙旗然太驟亦不下也又畏金鼓銃炮之聲聞之遠而飛去若蔽空而來宜發炮鳴鑼或放炮竹擊其前行驚奮後面隨之而退

一 蝗若去其翅足曝乾味若蝦米且可久貯而不壞加以旱蝗飼鴨易

rakes, on seeing any leaping or crawling out, must sweep them back; then covering them with dry grass, burn them all up. Let the fire be first kindled in the trench, and then drive them into it; for if they are only buried up, then many of them will crawl out of the openings and so escape.

3. When the swarms of grasshoppers see a row of trees, or a close line of flags and streamers, they usually hover over and settle; and the farmers frequently suspend red and white clothes and petticoats on long poles, or make red and green paper flags, but they do not always settle with great rapidity. Moreover, they dread the noise of gongs, matchlocks, and guns, hearing which they fly away. If they come so as to obscure the heavens, you must let off the guns and clang the gongs, or fire the crackers; it will strike the front ranks with dread, and flying away, the rest will follow them and depart.

4. When the wings and legs of the grasshoppers are taken off and [their bodies] dried in the sun, the taste is like dried prawns, and moreover they can be kept a long time without spoiling. Ducks can also be reared upon the dried grasshoppers, and soon become large and fat. Moreover, the hill people catch them to feed pigs: these pigs, weighing at first only twenty catties

CONCLUSION OF THE SAME.

大且肥又山人中捕蝗飼猪其猪
初重二十餘斤旬日間即重至五
十餘斤以之食畜皆爲有用有產
者出力擒捉或錢或米俱可量給
既去禾稼之害何憚不爲以上各
捕蝗蝻之法屢著成效合行抄錄
示諭閤屬軍民人等知悉爾等即
便遵照隨時查察鳴鑼如見蝗蝻
潛生立即一面捕捉一面報官會
營合力齊捕務期迅速撲滅免貽
民害即將首先查出報官之農民
獎賞各宜凜遵特示
道光十三年八月十五日示

or so, in ten days' time grow to weigh more than fifty catties; and in rearing all domestic animals they are of use. Let all farmers exert themselves, and catch them alive, giving rice or money according to the number taken. In order to remove this calamity from your grain, what fear is there that you will not perform this? Let all these rules for catching the grasshoppers be diligently carried into full effect.

Wherefore these commands are transcribed that all you soldiers and people may be fully acquainted with them. Do you all then immediately in obedience to them, when you see the proper time has come, sound the gong; and when you see the grasshoppers and their young increasing, straightway get ready, on the one hand seizing them, and on the other announcing to the officers that they collect the troops, that with united strength you may at once catch them, without fail making an utter extermination of them, by which calamity will be removed from the people. We will also then confer rewards upon those of the farmers and people who first announce to the magistrates their approach. Let every one implicitly obey. A special command.

Promulgated Tòkwóng, 13th year, 8th month, and 15th day.

(Sept. 28th, 1834.)

No. XIII.—Proclamation from Yikshán to the People.

太子少保兵部尚書兩廣總督部堂祁
參贊大臣湖南提督軍門果勇侯楊
欽
命靖逆將軍御前大臣領侍衛奕　爲遵
內大臣正紅旗漢軍都統宗室
參贊大臣四川提督軍門齊
兵部侍郎廣東巡撫部院怡
旨曉諭事照得我
朝統馭寰區撫綏中外深仁厚澤二
百年於茲屬在荒服不遠數萬里
而來貿遷有無奔赴宇下者舳艫
相接歷來酌定章程無非厚往薄
來優加體恤此中外商民所共聞
共見者也即如𠸄咭唎國自互市
以來相安已久因爲奸民煽惑竟
啟兵端我

Yik, by imperial commission the rebel-quelling general, high minister in the imperial presence, charged with the command of the palace body guard, a principal general in the Red [Mantchou] standard division, and in the Chinese army, and one of the imperial kindred;

Yéung, an imperial councillor and great minister, major-general of the forces in U'kwóng, and a marquis of distinguished bravery;

Ts'ai, an imperial councillor and great minister, and major-general of the forces in Sz'ch'ün;

Kí, secondary guardian of the heir-apparent, president of the Board of War, and duly appointed governor of the two Kwóng; and

Í, vice-president of the Board of War, and lieutenant-governor of Kwóngtung:

Hereby, in obedience to the imperial will, issue a plain proclamation.

*Whereas*, our dynasty, widely ruling over all countries, soothes and tranquillizes both at home and abroad with deep benevolence and large bounty, and for two hundred years even to this time has swayed over those from afar, who not regarding many myriads of miles as distant have still come to engage in commerce and reciprocal barter; and for those who have sped their way here from other lands, their ships following one another in succession, there have been stated regulations at different times established, so that all who came poor went away rich through our abundant favor and compassion: this is what every trader, native

CONTINUATION OF THE SAME.

皇上軫念民依又慮他國夷商致阻生
計故特
命將出師相機剿撫本將軍陛辭之
日
天語煌煌首以不妄殺爲戒凡有血氣
者宜如何同聲感激欽仰
皇仁耶惟念省垣接仗數日礮火相持
人心惶懼而匪徒又乘勢燒燬房
屋城內百姓紛紛稟求息兵本將
軍等目擊情形恐違
聖主好生之心復憫商民流離之苦是
以連銜籲請現奉
諭旨准其凜遵前定條例照常與英吉
利貿易所被燒房屋並令查明妥
爲撫卹仰見我

and foreign, have all heard and seen. Now, it appears that from the time the English first came to this market, there was mutual quiet for a long time; but by reason of traitorous natives inciting and deluding them, at last war has arisen. Our august emperor, fondly thinking on the people dependent upon him, and moreover compassionating the merchants from other lands whose trade has been stopped, has specially commissioned us to lead on troops, and according to circumstances to exterminate or to make peace. On the day, when I the general had audience of leave, the most urgent of his majesty's commands was not to rashly kill—whoever has blood and breath (i. e. all men) will with united voice express their grateful feelings, and reverently look up to his imperial majesty's benevolence.

But reflecting that for several days there had been fighting upon the walls of the city, and that the cannonading having been very sharp, the hearts of people were terrified; and also, banditti improving the opportunity, set fire to dwelling-houses, so that the people within the city tumultuously come and besought me to quiet the troops; I, the general, and my colleagues have been exceedingly affected with all these circumstances and appearances, and afraid of opposing his sacred majesty's kind feelings, have again pitied the unhappiness of the people in fleeing and leaving their homes; and have therefore unitedly besought the favor, and have now received the imperial commands permitting us with reverent obedience to the former fixed regulations to carry on trade with the English as usual, and at the same time to make full investigations as to all those whose dwellings have been

CONCLUSION OF THE SAME.

皇上仁育義正曲賜矜全予以自新宥
其既往柔遠人正所以子庶民格
外之
恩同于覆載中外商民均當傾心
感戴矣為此通行曉諭爾商民人
等知悉自示之後惟當奉公守法
與各國通商一切照舊章程恪遵
定例並不得夾帶違禁之物致干
功
令現在各省大兵陸續凱撤從此
永息干戈虞詐兩忘猜疑盡釋
各安本業共享太平本將軍叅贊叅贊暨本部院堂
有厚望焉特示
道光二十一年五月廿八日示

consumed, that every one may be properly compassionated and cared for. Looking up we perceive our imperial sovereign's benevolence and care to be liberal and correct, lenient to those out of the way and pitying all, granting that from this time shall be an amnesty, and forgiving all that has past. He shows kindness to far-traveled men, and regards the blackhaired people as his own children, exhibiting favor even beyond bounds, protecting and upholding them like [the heaven and earth]; trading people, both natives and foreigners, ought alike with humble hearts gratefully to receive his compassion.

Wherefore this explicit proclamation is everywhere published that you trading people and others may be fully acquainted therewith. After its publication, you must, respectfully regarding public interests, keep the laws, trading with the merchants of all countries, in all respects observing the old regulations and carefully obeying the fixed rules, while at the same time you are not allowed to clandestinely introduce any prohibited articles, and transgress the strict commands. The soldiers of the different provinces at present here, will in succession return victorious to their homes, for, from this time spears and shields will for ever be at rest; all deception and hypocrisy will on both sides cease, and suspicion be entirely removed. That every one may quietly follow his own business, and all enjoy complete peace, we, the general [Yik], and the councillors [Yéung and Ts'ai], together with the governor and lieut.-governor, do most earnestly hope. A special command.

Promulgated Tọkwóng, 21st year, 5th month, and 28th day. (July 6th, 1841.)

## No. XIV.—Memorial from Yikshán to the Emperor.

靖逆將軍奕山參贊大臣隆文楊
芳等
奏爲𠸄夷船隻攻擊省城督兵竭力
保護幸尚無虞而體察局勢欲期
久守惟有權宜辦理謹將實在情
形恭摺會奏仰祈
聖鑒事切臣等於本月初六日將連日
接仗緣由馳報在案查廣東省會
城垣枕于觀音山之麓前臨大河
西北韶肇南連等府州之水由花
地匯流入海客商行旅即從此道
入省城溯自夷船駛入省河排列
多艘咽喉已爲所扼東西兩路由
獵德大王滘達黃埔而至虎門海

Yikshán, the rebel quelling general, with Lungman and Yéung Fóng, imperial councillors, memorialize respecting the ships of the English foreigners making an attack upon the provincial city, and that leading on the troops we exerted our utmost strength to save it, and happily it still remains unharmed; and also that carefully considering all the advantages of the place, we hope and expect to be able to defend it for a long time, but have been obliged to adopt temporary measures in the management of the business:—carefully taking all these important particulars, we herewith reverently embody them in an united memorial, and looking up intreat the sacred glance upon it. Your ministers, on the sixth day of this moon, most carefully detailing all the causes and circumstances of several successive days of fighting, have already dispatched them by courier, as is recorded.

We find that the walls of the city of Canton rest on the acclivity of Kún-yam hill, on the front extending down to the river; and that the streams from the departments of Shíúchau, Shíúhing, Námhung and Línchau all join and flow down from Fátí into the sea, and that the merchants all come by this road to the provincial city. Since the foreigners sailed their ships into the river [leading to] the city, they have distributed many vessels in different places, so that the throats [of the river] are already completely in their possession; and in both the eastern and western channels, from Líptak (near Howqua's Folly) and from Táiwóngkáu

CONTINUATION OF THE SAME.

道分岐徑路叢集瀰漫平衍并無要隘可守且田塍山狹不能紮營駐兵此路各山皆可俯瞰城中時有夷人潛往窺伺戒備未易前者備辦火攻各具皆於離城之十五里泥城用廣西解到木排稻草從三水縣金山寺前以下地方分頭委員偏札該逆探知二項木排將成自初一日開仗以後該逆即密遣三板船前往探水經看守弁兵開放鎗炮擊退迨初五日夷船三十八隻全數駛入攻城另駕火輪船駛至泥城河面開炮漢奸扮作水手混入我草船左右縱火將後

(in the Macao passage), quite through to Whampoa, and thence on to the Bocca Tigris, where the outlets of the river to sea divide into branches, and the side passages are exceedingly numerous, and the shallows and sands level and expansive, there are in all of these places no important positions which we can defend. Moreover, the embankments of the fields near the hills are narrow, so that we cannot pitch a camp or intrench the troops; and from all the hills on the north, one can look down into the city; where foreigners have been at all times secretly going about, spying, and examining, for it has been no easy matter to prevent them.

When, on the former occasion, we had completely prepared all our materials for an attack by fire at a place called Naishing, (distant from the city fifteen *lí*,) employing rafts and paddy straw, which had been sent on from Kwóngsai by way of the town of Sámshui, and had placed them in the country opposite the monastery at Kamshán and below, appointing a head deputy to have them all in readiness; the said rebels, having made inquiries and ascertained that both kinds of our rafts were about ready, on the first day of the moon and afterwards opened the attack. They soon secretly sent their ships' boats to sound the depth of the water, but the troops who were then on the lookout guarding opened upon them a fire of cannon and musketry, and compelled them to retire. However, on the fifth of the moon, thirty-eight sail of foreign vessels sailed into the river to attack the city, and others

CONTINUATION OF THE SAME.

軍裝柴草焚燒過半其漢奸梟水
登岸自陸路抄赴我兵之後遂至
三面受敵泥城不能拒守此時河
道梗塞文報難通趕辦攻具一切
無從前往督催亦無從運送來省
至兵糧尙有倉儲可碾而民間食
米向皆來自鄉間茲已堅守城池
則商販不來尤於民食有礙兼之
火砲不絕新城居民相率移入老
城以內相持日久卽不能無匱乏
之虞民氣搖動不堪設想省城重
地爲全省關係稍有疎失各府州
縣匪徒必致乘機蜂起況大兵聚
集亦復在在可虞使在郊野行兵

[of the enemy] on board of steamers went up to Naishing and attacked it by water; while Chinese traitors, dressed as sailors, in a body got into our vessels filled with straw, and set fire to them in all directions, so that the greater part of the faggots and straw stored in the rear of the army was quite destroyed. These Chinese traitors, then taking to the water like ducks went ashore, and taking a circuit by land came upon our force in the rear, which was thus attacked on three sides, and Naishing could no longer be maintained.

At this time the communications by water were quite stopped, and it was also difficult to report by letter; those who were hastening to direct implements of attack, on the one hand could not get there quickly to oversee them, and on the other could not expeditiously forward them to the city. Moreover, although there were provisions for the troops in store which could at any time be ground, still the food of the people all comes in from the villages; and if we had at this time made a stout defence of the city, then no supply of rice could have been brought to the trader,—and still worse, food for the people would have been hard to procure. Added to this, the cannonading was unintermitting, and the inhabitants of the New city moved in a mass into the Old city. Now, in the event of a long struggle, there would undoubtedly be a serious impediment from want of provisions, and the wrath of the people would be aroused, which we could not think of being able to sustain. And the provincial city is a most important spot, being of the greatest

CONTINUATION OF THE SAME.

倘可層層擇險誘敵而省城萬無
棄理城全與全本係奴才等一身
之責而城亡與亡實非成地方萬
全之計奴才等日夜焦思萬分無
術先是勘得省城北面原有砲臺
製甚狹隘不能多駐兵丁祇得於
北城挑選精兵安砲固守迨夷船
由泥城登岸直逼北城城上開砲
轟擊攻斃逆夷十餘名漢奸百餘
名該夷退守土山而炮臺已爲所
踞天已昏黑官兵暫收入城迨初
七日城內居民紛紛遞稟籲懇保
全合城民命又據守垛口兵丁稱
報城外夷人向城上招手似有所

consequence to the whole province, and if it is lost by any remissness, marauding banditti will take advantage thereof, and in every department, district, and town, rise up like wasps. Moreover, the grand army is now assembled, and we are under continual apprehension for them while here; but if we should lead the troops into the open country, we could there select numerous localities into which to entice [the enemy] and give them battle; but there is not the least reason why the provincial capital should be abandoned. If it is saved and we with it, the responsibility wholly rests with us, your slaves; but to lose both it and us, truly does not by any means seem to be the plan for preserving the country;—we your slaves have most anxiously reflected upon the matter for days and nights, and in truth there is no other plan.

When we examined the northern side of the city on arriving, the forts which were there originally, were made exceedingly contracted and small, insufficient to contain large garrisons, and we could only select the bravest of our troops for the northern city, and place guns there to maintain it strictly. Thus it was, when the foreigners, on landing from their ships at Naishing came straight to the northern city, the cannon on the walls opened a thundering fire, and killed ten or more of the rebels, and more than a hundred native traitors. The foreigners then retired to maintain themselves on the hills, they having already taken possession of the forts there; and it being now dark, our officers and troops for the time drew

拾級大成



CONTINUATION OF THE SAME.

言當即差參將熊瑞升登堺看視
見有夷目數人以手指天指地熊
瑞升不解何語即喚通事詢之據
云要請大將軍有苦情上訴總兵
段永福喝以
天朝大將軍豈肯見爾奉
命而來惟知有戰該夷目即免冠作
禮屏其左右將兵仗投地向城作
禮段永福向奴才稟請詢問即差
通事下城問以抗拒中華屢肆猖
獗有何冤抑據稱英夷不准貿易
貨物不能通流資本折耗負欠無
償因新城之外兩邊砲火轟擊不
能傳話是以來此求大將軍轉懇

off and retired within the city. Further, on the seventh of the moon, the inhabitants of the city came in great numbers and presented a petition begging the favor that we would save the lives of all the citizens. Also the soldiers stationed to guard the embrasures, verbally announced that the foreigners without the city were beckoning towards the walls as if they had somewhat to say; whereupon I immediately dispatched colonel Hung Suishing to mount the wall and reconnoitre. He saw several foreign eyes (leaders) pointing to the heaven, and then to the earth, but he (Hung Suiching) not understanding what they said, thereupon called a linguist to ask them what they wanted. It appears that they said, 'we wish to request the high general [to come out], as we have some grievances to state to him.' Major-general Tün Wingfuk angrily replied, 'This high general of the celestial dynasty, how can he come and see you! He has come here by order, and knows only to fight you.' These foreign leaders upon this took off their hats and made a bow, sent away their attendants, laid down their arms upon the ground, and performed an obeisance towards the wall.'

Tün Wingfuk, having requested and obtained permission of us, your slaves, then sent a linguist down from the walls to ask 'why they so rebelliously resisted the [forces of the] Central-flowery land, and had been unruly and contumacious so frequently, and what it was that oppressed them!' It appears that they replied, 'The English foreigners are not allowed to trade, and cannot dispose of their goods; their capital is altogether wasted, and they have nothing

CONTINUATION OF THE SAME.

大皇帝開恩追完商欠俯准通商立即
退出虎門繳還砲臺不敢滋事等
語旋據衆洋商禀稱該夷商等轉
求照前通商並將歷年商欠清還
伊即將兵船全數撤去虎門之外
等情奴才等通盤籌畫虎門藩籬
既失內外無所憑依與其以全城
百萬生靈與之爭不可必得之數
似不若依允輿情以保危城以甦
民困竊計廣東一省關權賦稅每
歲不下二百萬兩祗須夷務清釐
數歲後元氣可復若堅持日久或
致意外之虞不特攻復大費周章
而民爲根本或遭荼毒關係非輕

to pay their debts; that because the cannonading on the side of the New city was so terrible they were unable to communicate, and had come this side to intreat the high general to beg the mighty emperor to compassionate them, and condescend to permit them to carry on their commerce: they would then immediately withdraw out of the Bocca Tigris, restore all the forts, and not presume to make any more such disturbance, &c., &c.' At the same time, the whole body of hong-merchants stated, saying, 'That all the said foreign merchants had begged of them to get the trade carried on as before, and also to have the debts due them for many years cleared off, when they would immediately withdraw all their men-of-war outside of the Bocca Tigris, &c., &c.'

Your slaves, having considered all the circumstances of the case, that the defences of the Bocca Tigris are already lost, and that neither within nor without was there a place which could be depended upon;—also considering the hundreds of thousands of living souls within the city, and that we could not successfully contend with the foreigners, there was no better plan than to accede to the request of the people, by which we should preserve the city from danger, and reanimate the drooping spirits of the people. On carefully estimating the duties and revenues of this province of Kwóngtung, they do not fall under two millions of taels; and if we can only quite clear off these foreign claims, after a few years the resources [of the province] will recover; whereas, if we long maintain the contest, perhaps it will give rise to some unforeseen evil,

CONCLUSION OF THE SAME.

是以公同商議酌派委廣州府知
府余保純妥爲查辦姑念商人所
請暫准其與各國一體貿易先甦
民困該逆以通商爲命脉該夷船
退出漢奸解散之後先從省河以
及虎門各處要隘磊塞河道增築
砲臺添鑄砲位門戶旣固阻守足
據卽扼其吭如再敢鴟張立杜通
商庶辦理有所措手所有近日省
河攻拒實在情形並權宜辦理緣
由謹合詞瀝陳伏乞
皇上聖鑒訓示謹
奏

which not only will be exceedingly difficult to remedy or recover from, but also the common people, who are the support and foundation of the state, if they should experience so grievous a calamity, the consequences would be very serious. Therefore, having publicly deliberated together, we concluded specially to depute Yü Pòshun, the prefect of Kwóngchau fú, to investigate and temporarily allow them to trade alike with all countries—it being of the first importance to reanimate the people. These said rebels regard a mutual trade as their very life blood. And when the foreign ships have withdrawn, and the native traitors are all dispersed, then, beginning from the river at the city down to the Bocca Tigris, we will at every important pass block up the channel with stones, and build new forts, at the same time casting cannon for the embrasures. Thus when the door of entrance is firmly secured, and our means of defence such as can be depended upon, we shall, as it were, have our gripe on their throat. Then, if they again presume to act outrageously, we can instantly cut off their trade, so that we have the means in our hands of managing them.

All these true particulars which have taken place in this recent attack on and defence of the city, together with the causes of the temporary expedients we have adopted, being carefully brought together and arranged in their minutest points, we do humbly beg his majesty's holy glance upon, and that we may be instructed thereupon by edict. A careful memorial.

No. XV.—Imperial Rescript to the Preceding.

道光二十一年四月二十九日奉
上諭
奕山等奏英夷船隻攻擊省城督
兵保護無虞權宜辦理一摺覽奏
均悉𠸄夷自我兵兩次擊退之後
計窮勢蹙併力進攻該夷性等犬
羊不值與之計較況既經懲創以
示兵威現經城廂內外居民紛紛
遞稟又據奏稱該夷免冠作禮欲
求轉奏乞恩朕諒爾不得已之苦
衷准令通商該將軍等惟當嚴諭
該夷目立即將各兵船退出外洋
繳還砲臺仍須凜遵前定條例只
准照舊貿易不准夾帶違禁烟土

On the 29th day of the 4th moon, in the 21st year of Tòkwóng, we received [the following] high mandate: The memorial of Yikshán and his colleagues respecting the attack of the ships of the English foreigners upon the provincial capital, and that marshaling the troops they have preserved it without loss, and of the temporary expedients they have adopted, has been examined and its contents fully ascertained. Since the time our troops attacked and twice drove out the English foreigners, their schemes being exhausted and their strength reduced, they have joined their forces and [again] entered to join battle; their disposition resembles that of the dog or sheep, with whom it is not worth while to enter into arrangements. Moreover, they have already been reprimanded, by which was manifested the terror of our arms. It seems that the inhabitants of the city both within and without tumultuously came presenting a petition; and also it appears from the memorial that the said barbarians taking off their hats made obeisance, and requested that a memorial might be prepared begging favor on their behalf. We sincerely believe that they could not but thus give utterance to the griefs of their hearts, and we permit that you give them liberty to trade. It was exceedingly proper that the said general and his colleagues should most peremptorily instruct the aforesaid leaders of the foreigners instantly to withdraw all their troops and ships to the outer ocean, and render back all the forts. It is necessary too that they do, as before, tremblingly obey the former fixed regulations; they can

CONCLUSION OF THE IMPERIAL RESCRIPT.

倘敢故違斷不寬恕並著將軍等
會同該督撫悉心籌議妥定章程
夷性叵測乃當嚴密防範不得稍
有疎懈該夷船退後迅將各炮臺
及防守要隘等處趕緊修築堅固
如暎夷露有桀驁情形仍當督兵
勦滅不得因已施恩遂諸事任其
需索另片奏城廂內外居民房屋
多被其焚燒著祁𡊮怡良即派委
員查明妥爲撫卹所有借撥貯庫
銀二百八十萬兩著即着落該商
分年歸補不得延宕餘著照所議
辦理將此由六百里加緊諭令知
之欽此

only trade as of old, nor is it allowable to oppose the prohibitions, and clandestinely bring in the smoking earth (opium). If they dare again to rebel, they can on no account be forgiven. We at the same time require the general and his colleagues in connection with the governor and lieut.-governor to deliberate with their whole hearts, and carefully settle the regulations. The disposition of the foreigners is hard to calculate upon, and consequently it is necessary closely to guard against their wiles, not permitting the least remissness or oversight. After the ships of the said foreigners have retired, let all the forts and such important passes as are to be guarded, be straightway carefully repaired and built up in a strong and firm manner; and then if the English foreigners exhibit their obstinate overbearing disposition, let the troops be marshaled as before, and they at once exterminated. It may not be, that because favor has already been granted them, that all their avaricious demands should therefore be complied with.

With reference to the other memorial respecting the dwellings of the inhabitants within and without the city having many of them been burned by the fire, let Kí, Kung and Ileung immediately send a deputy to examine fully regarding what is proper to be done to re-assure and help them. And with reference to the 2,800,000 taels of silver borrowed from the treasury, let [the same officers] immediately instruct the said merchants to return it in a given number of years; not the least remissness or delay can be allowed. Whatever else there is let it be managed according to the established mode. Let this be hastened at the rate of 600 *li* a day, and command them to be made acquainted with it. Respect this.

### No. XVI.—A Petition to the Prefect of Canton.

具稟美理哥國商人某某等稟
爲河道艱險懇
請酌量挑挖免碍商船進口事
縁商等來粤貿易貨船進埔者
不少從無內河遭破之弊茲于
本年十月中旬吶拿船進埔不
料駛至內河港口被石撞破船
底斯時救護不及艙內棉花已
濕一半雖有引水帶行無奈河
道狹窄砂石壅塞以致窒碍難
行深為遠客之害不敢
請酌量疏通商等不勝感激之
致謹稟赴
府尊大老爺臺前察奪施行
道光二十年十一月初三日具稟

A duly prepared petition of the American merchants X. X., Y. Y. and others. They petition, that whereas the channel of the river being seriously obstructed, they beg that deliberation may be held respecting clearing it out, and removing the danger to merchantmen entering the port. Since we have come to Canton to trade, the merchantmen which have entered the port have not been few, and heretofore there has been no risk of encountering any damage within the river; but it happened in the middle decade of the tenth month of this year that [the Eos, captain] Turner's ship, not being carefully sailed into the inner anchorage, the bottom of the vessel was stove in by the stones; and at present she cannot be saved or got off, while one half of the cotton in her hold is already wet. Although she had a pilot, yet this happened wholly from the narrowness of the channel, the sand and stones stopping it up, and causing a very serious impediment that made it difficult to pass. This is to the deep injury of the foreign merchants, and we take the liberty of requesting a consultation as to opening [the channel], and making it passable, for which we will be exceedingly obliged.

A respectful petition presented to his excellency the prefect, requesting him to examine and decide upon, it and grant us this request.

Tòkwóng, 20th year, 11th month, 3d day.

No. XVII.—Reply to a Petition.

天朝廣州澳門軍民府蔣　諭美理哥國
夷商士荔卑等知悉本月初六日據
該夷商等稟稱竊因英國領事義律
通諭各國貨船限以本月初十日之
後不得進埔等語惟思商等所爲生
意是圖何敢滋事與之抗拒但願趨
避其宄爲幸但本國有貨船數隻邇
日將到想到之日卽要在澳通稟查
明復行帶引進埔恐有擔擱日子延
阻後船惟患過其限期留泊外洋難
進卽防牽累不淺矣特此懇恩卽准
船直到虎門鍊關之內停泊查明後
行帶引進埔等情據此查暎夷領事
律義種種刁抗不法已極今復欲挾

Tséung, sub-prefect of Macao in the department of Kwóngchau, attached to the celestial dynasty, commands the American foreign merchants Sz', Lai, and Pí, to become fully acquainted with the following. On the sixth of the present month, it appears that the said foreign merchants petitioned, [in substance] saying: "That the English superintendent Elliot has promulgated an order that after the tenth day of this month, the merchantmen of all countries shall not be allowed to enter the port, &c., &c.: but since we merchants are only engaged about matters of trade, we cannot think of opposing him, and shall consider ourselves fortunate in soon avoiding his machinations. Now the merchantmen of our country which will presently arrive are numerous, and we think that if, on their arrival, they are required to be examined at Macao, and then take a pilot to go up the river, there will be a delay of some days, which will retard those ships just arriving: and moreover, the injury accruing from overpassing the limited time by remaining at anchor outside, will not be trifling. Therefore, on this account, we request that the ships may be allowed to proceed directly to the Bocca Tigris and anchor within the chain, there to be examined, and then get a pilot to go up the river, &c., &c." From this it appears that the English superintendent Elliot, perversely unruly in all possible ways, and setting the laws at defiance, now wishes again to exercise authority over the merchantmen of all countries and prohibit their enter-

CONCLUSION OF REPLY TO A PETITION.

制各國貨船不准進埔尤爲謬妄茲既據該夷商等不肯幫同附和稟請將後到各貨船直駛到虎門停泊聽候查明再行帶引進埔前來雖屬有違定例惟當此嚴辦英夷之際姑允稍爲變通以示體恤各國良夷正經貿易之心除現已據情轉稟
大憲批示飭遵外合行諭飭諭到該夷商等卽便遵照准令暫將後到各國貨船直駛至虎門查驗帶引進埔一俟查辦英夷事畢仍令照常在澳稟明查驗帶引可也速速特諭
道光十九年八月初七日

ing the port, which is still more audacious; and these foreign merchants, unwilling to aid or side with him, have petitioned that the merchantmen about to arrive may be allowed to sail directly to the Bocca Tigris and there anchor; and after waiting to be examined, take a pilot and sail up the river.

This coming before me, although it will be against the fixed regulations, yet on account of the present difficulties with the English foreigners, a little indulgent favor may be shown, in order to compassionate those peaceable foreigners of other countries who carry on a legal trade. While, therefore, I now lay all these circumstances before their excellencies (the governor and lieut.-governor), and petition for an answer to be sent down regarding it, I also issue these commands. When they reach the said foreign merchants, they are, according the tenor thereof, permitted to carry such merchantmen as shall soon arrive directly up to the Bocca Tigris, and after examination then to take a pilot and proceed up the river. However, let this mode be acted on only till affairs with the English are brought to a conclusion, when they are commanded, as is the regular custom, to petition to be examined at Macao, and there take in a pilot. Hasten, hasten! A special command.

Tòkwóng, 19th year, 8th month, and 7th day. (Sept. 14th, 1839.)

No. XVIII.—Letter from Commissioner Lin to the Queen of England

欽差大臣兵部尚書兩湖總督林
兵部尚書兩廣總督鄧
兵部侍郎廣東巡撫怡　會同照會
暎咭唎國王爲令禁鴉片烟事照
得天道無私不容害人以利已人
情不遠孰非惡殺而好生
貴國雖在重洋二萬里外而同此天
道同此人情未有不明於死生利
害者也我
天朝四海爲家
大皇帝如天之仁無所不覆而遐荒絕
域亦在並生並育之中廣東自開
海禁以來流通貿易凡內地民人
與外來番船相安於樂利者有數

Lam, high imperial commissioner, a president of the Board of War, and governor of the two Ú;

Tang, a president of the Board of War, and governor of the two Kwóng;

I, a vice-president of the Board of War, and lieut.-governor of Kwóngtung,—conjointly address this communication to the sovereign of the English nation, for the purpose of requiring the interdiction of opium.

*Whereas*, the ways of heaven are without partiality, and no sanction is allowed to injure others in order to benefit one's self, and that men's natural feelings are not very diverse; (for where is he who does not abhor death and love life?)—therefore your honorable nation, though beyond the wide ocean, at a distance of twenty thousand miles, also acknowledges the same ways of heaven, the same human nature, and has the like perception of the distinctions between life and death, benefit and injury. Our heavenly court has for its family all that is within the four seas; and as to the great emperor's heaven-like benevolence—there is none whom it does not overshadow; even regions remote, desert, and disconnected, have a part in his general care of life and wellbeing.

In Kwóngtung, since the removal of the interdicts upon maritime communication, there has been a constantly flowing stream of commercial intercourse. The people of the land, and those who come from abroad in foreign ships, have reposed together in the enjoyment of its advantages, for tens of years past, even until this

### CONTINUATION OF COMMISSIONER LIN'S LETTER.

十年於茲矣且於大黃茶葉湖絲
等類皆中國寶貴之產外國若不
得此卽無以爲命而
天朝
一視同仁許其販賣出洋絕不靳
惜無非推恩外服以天地之心爲
心也乃有一種奸夷製爲鴉片夾
帶販賣誘惑愚民以害其身而謀
其利前吸食者尚少近則互相傳
染流毒日深在中原富庶蕃昌雖
在此等愚民貪口腹而戕其生亦
屬孽由自取何必爲愛惜也然以
大清
一統之天下務在端風俗以正人
心豈肯使海內生靈甘心鴆毒是
以現將內地販賣鴉片並吸食之

time. And as regards the rhubarb, teas, raw silk, and similar rich and valuable products of China, should foreign nations be deprived of them, they would be without the means of continuing life. So that the heavenly court, by granting, in the universality of its common benevolence, permission for their sale and exportation, without the least stint or grudge, has indeed extended its favors to the utmost circuit [of the nations], making its heart one with that of heaven and earth. But there is a tribe of depraved and barbarous people, who, having manufactured opium for smoking, surreptitiously bring it hither for sale, seducing and leading astray the simple folk, in order to destroy their bodies and drain their resources. Formerly the smokers thereof were few; but of late, from each to other the practice has spread its contagion, and daily do its baneful effects more deeply pervade the central source—its rich, fruitful, and flourishing population. It is not to be denied that the simple folk, inasmuch as they indulge their appetite at the expense of their lives, are indeed themselves the authors of their miseries: and why then should they be pitied? Yet, in the universal empire of the great Pure dynasty, it is of essential import, for the right direction of men's hearts, that their customs and manners should be correct. How can it be borne that the living souls who dwell within these seas, should be left at will to take a deadly poison? Hence it is, that those who deal in opium, or who inhale its fumes, within this land, are all alike now to be subjected to severest punishment, and that a perpetual interdict is to be placed on this prevailing practice.

CONTINUATION OF COMMISSIONER LIN'S LETTER.

人一體嚴行治罪永禁流傳惟思
此等毒物係
貴國所屬各部轄內鬼蜮奸人私行
造作自非
貴國王令其製賣但各國之中亦只
數國製造此物並非諸國皆然又
聞
貴國亦不准民人吸食犯者必懲自
係知其害人故特爲之厲禁然禁
其吸食何如禁其販賣並禁其製
造乃爲淸源之道若自不食而仍
敢製造販賣引誘內地愚民則是
欲己之生而陷人之死欲己之利
而貽人以害此皆人情之所痛恨
天道之所不容以

We have reflected, that this poisonous commodity is the clandestine manufacture of malicious schemers and depraved people of various tribes under the dominion of your honorable nation; for it cannot be, that you, the honorable sovereign of that nation, have commanded the manufacture and sale of it. But amid the various nations there are a few only that make this article: it is by no means the case that all the nations are herein alike. And we have also heard that in your honorable nation, the people are not permitted to inhale the drug, and that offenders in this particular expose themselves to sure punishment. It is clearly from a knowledge of its injurious effects on man, that you have directed this severe prohibition against it. But what is prohibiting its use, in comparison with prohibiting its sale, or its manufacture,—as a means of thoroughly purifying the source? Though not making use of it one's self, to venture nevertheless to manufacture and sell it, and with it to seduce the simple folk of this land, is to seek one's own livelihood by exposing others to death—to pursue one's own advantage by other men's injury. Now all such acts are bitterly abhorrent to the nature of man, and utterly opposed to the ways of heaven. To the vigorous sway exercised by the celestial court over both the civilized and the barbarous, what difficulty can there be to hinder immediately taking their lives? But as we contemplate and give substantial being to the fullness and vastness of the sacred intelligence, it befits us to adopt first the course of admonition. Moreover, as we have not yet sent any

CONTINUATION OF COMMISSIONER LIN'S LETTER.

天朝力振華夷何難立制其命而仰體
聖明寬大自宜告誡於先且從前未用
公文移會
貴國王一旦嚴禁則猶得諉為不知
今與
貴國王約將此害人之鴉片永遠斷
絕我內地禁人吸食亦屬國禁人
製造其從前已經造作者
貴國立即須令行搜盡投之海底斷
不許天地間更有毒物非獨內地
民人不受其害即
貴國民人既有造作安知其不吸食
果並造作倘禁之則該國亦不受
其害豈不各享太平之福益昭
貴國恭順之忱如此則明於天理而

public communication to your majesty,—should these severe interdicts be all at once enforced, you might say, in excuse, that you had no previous knowledge of them. We would now, then, concert with your majesty means to bring to a perpetual end this opium, so hurtful to mankind: we in this land forbidding the use of it, and you, in the nations under your dominion, forbidding its manufacture. As regards what has already been made, we would have your honorable nation immediately issue a mandate for its entire collection, that the whole may be cast into the depths of the sea. We would thus prevent the longer existence between heaven and earth of any portion of the baneful thing. Not only then will the people of this land be relieved from its pernicious influence; but the people of your honorable nation too (for as they make, how know we that they do not also smoke it?) will, when the manufacture is indeed forbidden, be likewise relieved from the danger of its use. Will not each then enjoy the happiness of a general peace, for your honorable nation's sense of duty being thus devout shows a clear apprehension of celestial principles, and the supreme heavens will ward off from you all calamities. It is also in perfect accordance with human nature, and must surely meet the approbation of sages.

Furthermore, the opium is now so severely prohibited in this land that none will be found to smoke it; should your nation continue its manufacture, it will be discovered after all that no place will afford opportunity for selling it, and that no

CONCLUSION OF COMMISSIONER LIN'S LETTER.

上天不致降災協乎人情而
聖人亦必嘉許況內地既經嚴禁無使
吸食卽使該國製造終亦無處可
賣無利可圖與其虧本徒勞何不
改圖別業況內地搜出鴉片盡行
付火油燒燬再有夷船夾帶鴉片
前來不能不一體燒燬恐內所載
他貨難免玉石俱焚是利不得而
害已形欲害人而先害已也
天朝之所以平服萬國者正有不測之
神威毋謂言之不早也貴國王接
到此文卽將各海口斷絕緣由速
行移覆幸勿諉飾支延盼切盼切
道光十九年二月日移會英國王知照

profits are attainable. Is it not far better to turn and seek other occupations, than vainly to labor in the pursuit of a losing employment? And again, whatever opium can be discovered in this land is entirely committed to the flames, to be consumed. If any be again privily introduced in foreign vessels, it too must be subjected to a like process of destruction. It may well be feared, lest other commodities imported in such vessels should meet a common fate—the gem and the pebble not being distinguished. Thus it will be, that gain being no longer acquirable, while hurt has assumed a visible form, such as desire to injure others will find that they themselves are the first to be injured. The instrumentality whereby the celestial court holds in subjection all nations is truly divine and awe-inspiring beyond the power of computation. Let it not be said that early warning of this has not been given.

When your majesty receives this document, let a speedy reply be returned [informing] us of the measures you adopt for entirely eradicating it from every seaport. Do not, on any account, by false embellishments evade or procrastinate. Earnestly reflect hereon. Earnestly observe these things.

Tòkwóng, 19th year, 2d month,——day. Communication sent to the sovereign of the English antion.

The preceding specimens of state papers, all of which, with one exception, are genuine, exhibit the most common forms of those documents; and although they do not, by any means, contain all the technical terms and phrases which the student will meet with in this kind of writing, they will show him their general structure, and assist him in a measure to translate others. Notwithstanding the general uniformity of the legal style among the Chinese, it still allows great scope in which to exhibit the talents and learning of the writer, and some of the proclamations and memorials of high officers are finished pieces of composition. In translating a document of this nature, care must be taken to express whatever commands from a superior to an inferior officer are contained in it, or the injunction of the officer who issues it to those to whom it is directed, in the imperative form, by a *let it be so*, or *let them do thus and thus, &c.*; the form *do you do* is not according to the spirit of an order from a Chinese magistrate. This is especially the case in all imperial rescripts and commands, his majesty very rarely employing phraseology that approaches in the least to a personal address to his ministers. It may here be added also, that as in translating from Chinese into English, cases will constantly occur in which one, two, or more words must be added to convey the full meaning of the original, it is well to distinguish them from any explanatory parenthetical clauses the translator may wish to add, by placing them between brackets and not parentheses.

The exercises which follow are extracts from good authors, consisting of short and easy sentences, and are to be translated into English; which, the learner, by this time can no doubt perform unaided without much difficulty, if he has thoroughly learned the characters in the preceding chapters. The columns are printed so as to read from left to right, and not from right to left, as they are in the letters and edicts. The independent extracts are separated by a large circle.

## 此數句見三國志

俱降。○玄德從背後掩殺。賊衆大敗。奔入宛城。○玄德
箭中其左臂。○發張角之棺。戮尸梟首。送往京師。餘衆
望見地公將軍旗號。飛馬趕來。張寶落荒而走。玄德發
兩軍都出背後。玄德朱雋一齊趕上。賊兵大敗。○玄德
高崗之上。○張寶見解了法。急欲退軍。左關公右張飛
殺來。○玄德聽令。撥關公張飛各引軍一千。伏于山後
風雷大作。一股黑氣從天而降。黑氣中似有無限人馬
合刺昇落馬。○張寶就馬上披髮仗劍。作起妖法。只見
搦戰。○玄德使張飛擊之。飛縱馬挺矛與昇交戰。不數
引軍來投朱雋。雋待之甚厚。○張寶遣副將高昇出馬
這厮。反要在他部下聽令。其實不甘。○於是三人連夜
當日怠慢了玄德。張飛性發。便欲殺之。○飛曰。若不殺

## 此數句見三國志

驛直到縣前馬椽上縛住。○攀下柳條去督郵兩腿上
認得我麽。督郵未及開言早被張飛揪住頭髮扯出館
堂見督郵正坐廳上將縣吏綁倒在地飛大喝害民賊
牙滾鞍下馬逕入館驛把門人那裏阻擋得住直奔後
毫無犯那得財物與他。○張飛大怒睜圓環眼咬啐鋼
○吏曰督郵作威無非要賄賂耳。○玄德曰我與民秋
桌寢則同牀如玄德在稠人廣坐關張侍立終日不倦。
財物奔走。堅趕上殺一賊。○到任之後與關張食則同
岸揚聲大叫東西指揮如喚人狀賊以爲官兵至盡棄
得必然死戰。○堅謂父曰此賊可擒也。遂奮力提刀上
○玄德曰。不容寇降是也今四面圍如鐵桶賊乞降不
曰昔高祖之得天下蓋爲能招降納順公何拒韓忠耶。

拾級大成

## 此數句見三國志

曰。若不斬。草除根。必爲喪身之本。○董太后宣張讓等
大將軍聽袁紹之言。欲盡誅臣等。乞娘娘憐憫。○袁紹
之罪。○靈帝病篤。召大將軍何進入宮商議後事。○今
功皆封列侯。○劉虞表奏劉備太功。朝廷赦免鞭督郵
天下人民欲食十常侍之肉。陛下敬之如父母。身無寸
不惜。可憐漢室天下四百餘年。到此一旦休矣。○躭曰。
田里盡將家產以助軍資。言罷痛哭。○劉陶大呼。臣死
伏於帝前曰。大臣不相容。臣等不能活矣。願乞性命歸
罔上。朝廷正人皆去。禍在目前矣。○十常侍皆免冠跪
盜賊並起。侵掠州郡。其禍皆由十常侍賣官害民。欺君
不打死等甚。督郵告曰。玄德公救我性命。○陶曰。四方
着力鞭打。一連打折柳條十數枝。○飛曰。此等害民賊

## 此數句見玉嬌梨

盆菊花。擺在書房堦下。○每每于政事之暇。不是你尋事完了。便只是飲酒賦詩。○白公因一門公送了廿二貌的佳壻配他。○料此一鄉一邑。人才有限。○每日公書能文。竟已成一個女學士。○只要選擇一個有才有歲。便學得女工針指。件件過人。○到得十四五時。便知玉一塊。顏色紅赤如日。因取乳名叫做紅玉。○到八九以為有命。以後遂不復買妾。○白公夢一神人。賜他美常為第一。○但只恨年過四十。却無子嗣。○白公嘆息。這村中。雖有千餘戶居民。若要數富貴人家。當推白太

（一）由此而下四篇見玉嬌梨。○

皇帝位。內外臣僚皆其心腹。威權太重。我將如何。入宮商議曰。何進之妹。始初我擡舉他。今日他孩兒即

## 此數句見玉嬌梨

韻作賞菊詩。○三人纔待揮毫。忽長班來報。楊御史老白公便叫左右取過筆硯來。與吳翰林蘇御史卽席分務。要開口又開不得。要閉口又閉不得。實是難爲矣。○奪利。正其宜也。○只是小弟做了這一個言路。當此時而敬之。○蘇御史道。這京師原是個名利塲。他們爭名白顏色種種鮮妍。却終帶幾分疎野瀟酒氣味。使人愛杯。吳翰林因說道。此花秀而不艷。美而不妖。雖紅黃紫相見過。更了衣。待了茶。遂邀入書房中看菊。○飲了數衙門中多事。未免辜負芳辰。○三人說着話。走到堂上又悞了一日工夫。○蘇御史道。小弟連日也要來。只因楊厭物。拿一篇壽文。立等要改了。與石都督夫人上壽。我。就是我訪你。○昨日正要來賞。不期剛出門。撞見老

## 此數句見玉嬌梨

好話。他再不肯聽。○蘇御史聽了。心下有幾分不快。○
分膏腴。彼甚欲之。竟叫家人奪了。○小弟每每與他說
人坐下飲酒。○近日聞知離城二十里有一所民田十
歡喜。比往日倍加敬重。○白公叫左右添了盅筯。讓三
先生大才潤色。可謂點鐵成金。今早送與石都督。十分
年兄貴衙門事冗。不得工夫幹此寂寞之事。○昨賴老
外好濫交。內多貪忌○白公道本該邀年兄來賞。但恐
轎馬在門前。因此回不得了。○楊御史爲人言語粗鄙。
門裡問來。說蘇爺在此喫酒。故此尋來。又看見二位爺
小的已回出門拜客。楊爺的長斑說道。楊爺在蘇爺衙
得我與吳爺蘇爺飲酒。就該回不在家了。○長斑稟道。
爺來了。三人聽了。都不歡喜。白公便罵長斑道。蠢才。曉

拾級大成

## 此数句見玉嬌梨

何如。○白公道。要罰酒。小弟情願。若要做詩。決做不成。不可因小弟打斷了興頭請傾珠玉。待小弟飲酒奉陪林道。纔有此意。尚未下筆。○楊御史道。既未下筆。三兄硯。便說道。原來三兄在此高興做詩。何不見教。○吳翰小弟却也不饒他。○楊御史喫乾酒。因看見席上有筆御史拿着酒說道。小弟便受罰了。倘後有談及朝政者。不宜。楊老先生該罰一巨觴。以謝唐突花神之罪。○楊笑道。良辰美景只該飲酒賦詩。若是花下談朝政頗覺情。這等便怪不得小弟不來邀兄賞菊了。○吳翰林也道。小弟只道楊年兄特來賞菊。却原來是為汪全說人楊御史見蘇御史詞色不順。便默默不語。○白公因笑

## 雜句

日十二個時辰咁長。唔怕做唔起。○人若爲善。天必報
雪落。○落了雨街滑。實難行。○燈暗大概係有油。○一
日有乜新聞。多煩你講我聽。○連冷幾日。都重未見有
食愁眉飯。○世不估到佢會偷野。眞係出人意外。○近
○盡心盡力同你做。就唔好話佢懶。○寧食開眉粥。唔
歲晚行路要謹愼荷包。○如果找唔倒。唔使去第二回。
筒籃咁大。○逐一逐二解明佢聽。唔怕佢唔信。○年近
起嚟。⊙唔怕路遠。定要去到爲止。○慳到睇個錢好似
同你捉盆棋消吓永日。○今日睇的明日睇的就唅多
話唔覺路遠。○而家天陰有日頭。晚吓就怕番風。○我
○今晚寄個封信止省。千祈莫忘記。○同一齊去有講
今年貨貴。因爲船嚟得少。○近來茶葉價錢點上下呢。

# 雜句

備已許人。不敢失信。○玄德曰。此事决不敢應命。○公
吾意。○汝乃欺君罔上之賊。天下皆欲殺汝。○玄德曰。
之。○雲長義士。必不失信。○吾生五子。惟最幼者極快
英雄。○呂布英雄。無人可敵。○此人出言不遜。何不殺
操曰。燕雀安知鴻鵠志哉。○兄在朝廷。觀何人爲世之
賢臣擇主而事。○操牽馬出相府。加鞭望東南而去。○
爲人。面善心惡。○多疑不足謀大事。○良禽擇木而棲。
輩。安知朝廷大事。○掩目而捕燕雀。是自欺也。○董卓
笑乎。○吾仗忠義而死。安得爲天下笑。○進叱曰。汝小
不追之。○既不相助。來此何幹。○兄此言。豈不爲天下
○各家打掃門前雪。莫管他人瓦上霜。○彼懼而退。何
之。○貧不與富敵。富不與官爭。○情性難改。山石難移。

## 雜句

不仁伐至仁。安得不敗乎。○吾之軍士頗雄壯否。○先
帶如橫素練。○黃祖性暴不能用人。故致此禍。○以至
欲救萬民耳。○向脫東山月上皎皎如同白日。長江一
祐。○我軍多疾。須用良醫治之。○統曰。某非爲富貴。但
望指教。○予奉天子詔以討不臣。○刼掠黎民。蒼天不
法度。○久聞大名。今何僻居此地。○先生勿得過譽。倘
諸官將有再言降曹者。與此案同。○汝何敢多言亂吾
先生之言頓開茅塞。○權拔佩劍砍面前奏案一角曰。吾
事。未易明言。○見草堂之上一少年。擁爐抱膝而歌。○
年。不曾相識。○鄉人相遇。安得不敘舊情耶。○吾有心
何礙。○他勢窮而來投我。若殺之亦是不義。○離鄉多
尊顏充腴。以何調理而至此。○呂布本無義之人。殺之

## 雜句

已罄。其人愁苦無策。烏云何不售我。送我王邸。當得善與之俱。相將數年矣。一日將過絳州去家尚遠而資斧王汾濱言。其鄉有養八哥者。教以語言。甚狎習。出游必

### 雛鴿

劣弟酒後狂言。兄勿見責。○是歲大荒。百姓皆食棗菜。類鷄項。疑問僧殺鷄幾何。遂得多頸。僧曰。此蛇段耳。○州者。寄宿蛇佛寺。寺僧具晚餐。肉湯甚美。而段段皆圓。猛每盛怒。無敢勸者。惟事母至孝。母至則解。○有客中母共作苦。○我耗人之財以教己子。此心何以自明。○非凡。心中有畏懼之意。○馬以貨麵爲業。家貧無婦。與可輕動。○亮乃碌碌庸才。安有妙計。○權觀玄德儀表生之言甚合予意。○重霧迷江。彼軍忽至。必有埋伏不

## 聊齋雜選

價。不愁歸路無貲也。其人云。我安忍。鳥言不妨。主人得價疾行。待我城西二十里大樹下。其人從之。攜至城相問答。觀者漸衆。有中貴見之。聞諸王。王召入。欲買之。其人曰。小人相依爲命。不願賣。王問鳥。汝願住否。答言願住。王喜。鳥又言給價十金。勿多予。王益喜。立畀十金。其人故作懊恨狀而出。王與鳥語。應對便捷。呼肉啖之。食已。鳥曰。臣要浴。王命金盆貯水。開籠令浴。浴已。飛簷間。梳翎抖羽。尙與王喋喋不休。頃之羽燥。蹁躚而起。操晉聲曰。臣去呀。顧盼已失所在。王及內侍仰面咨嗟。急覓其人。已渺矣。後有往秦中者。見其人攜鳥在西安市上。

### 黑獸

聞李太公敬一言。某公在瀋陽。宴集山顛。俯瞰山下。有

拾級大成

## 聊齋雜選

虎銜物來。以爪穴地。瘞之而去。使人探所瘞。得死鹿。乃取鹿而虛掩其穴。少間。虎導一黑獸至。毛長數寸。虎前驅。若邀尊客。既至穴。獸眈眈蹲伺。虎探穴失鹿。戰伏不敢少動。獸怒其誑。以爪擊虎額。虎立斃。獸亦逕去。

### 牛飛

邑人某購一牛頗健。夜夢牛生兩翼飛去。以爲不祥疑有喪失。牽市口損價售之。以巾裹金纏臂上。歸至半途。見有鷹食殘兔。近之甚馴。遂以巾頭縶股臂之。鷹屢擺撲。把捉稍懈。帶金騰去。某每謂定數不可逃。而不知不疑夢。不貪拾遺。走者何遽能飛哉。

### 橘樹

陝西劉公爲興化令。有道士來獻盆樹。視之則小橘。細裁如

# 聊齋雜選

楊天一言。見二鼠出。其一爲蛇所吞。其一瞪目如椒。似甚恨

## 義鼠

曰。君任此不久矣。至秋果解任。

結也。更奇之。莊任三年。繁實不改。第四年。憔悴無少華。夫人纍以千計。問之故役。皆云。劉公去後。橘甚茂而不實。此其初令。夫人大喜。竊意十餘年橘不復存。及至。則樹已十圍。實纍移栽墀下乃行。女歸。受莊氏聘。莊丙戌登進士。釋褐爲興化將。復來。女信之。涕始止。又恐爲大力者負之而去。立視家人裝將行。以橘重贅。謀棄去。女抱樹嬌啼。家人紿之曰。暫去且諸閨闥。朝夕護之。唯恐傷。劉任滿。橘盈把矣。是年初結實。簡大人清玩。聊祝女公子福壽耳。乃受之。女一見。不勝愛悅。寘指。擯弗受。劉有幼女。時六七歲。適值初度。道士云。此不足供

## 聊齋雜選

怒。然遙望不敢前。蛇果腹。蜿蜒入穴。方將過半。鼠奔來。力嚙其尾。蛇怒。退身出。鼠故便捷。歘然遁去。蛇追不及而返。及入穴。鼠又來。嚙如前狀。蛇入則來。蛇出則往。如是者久。蛇出吐死鼠於地上。鼠來嗅之。啾啾如悼息。銜之而去。

### 象

廣中有獵獸者。挾矢入山。偶臥憩息。不覺沉眠。被象來。鼻攝而去。自分必遭殘害。未幾。釋置大樹下。頓首一鳴。羣象紛至。四面旋繞。若有所求。前象伏樹下。仰視樹而俯視人。似欲其登。獵者會意。卽以足踏象背。攀援而升。雖至樹巔。亦不知其意向所存。少間。有狻猊來。衆象皆伏。狻猊擇一肥者意將搏噬。象戰慄。無敢逃者。惟共仰樹上。似求憐拯。獵者因望狻猊發一弩。狻猊立殪。諸象瞻空。意若拜舞。其人乃下。象復伏以鼻牽。衣似欲其乘。獵者遂跨身其上。象乃行至一處。以蹄穴地。得脫牙無算。獵人下。束治已。象乃負送出山。乃始返。

## 趙城虎

趙城嫗。年七十餘。止一子。一日入山。爲虎所噬。嫗悲痛。幾不欲活。號啼而訴於宰。宰笑曰。虎何可以官法制之乎。嫗愈號咷。不能制止。宰叱之。亦不畏懼。又憐其老。不忍加威怒。遂諾爲捉虎。嫗伏不去。必待勾牒出。乃肯行。宰無奈之。即問諸役誰能往者。一隸名李能。醺醉詣坐下。自言能之。持牒下。嫗始去。隸醒而悔之。猶謂宰之僞局。姑以解嫗擾耳。因亦不甚爲意。持牒報繳。宰怒曰。固言能之。何容復悔。隸窘甚。請牒拘獵戶。宰從之。隸集諸獵人。日夜伏山谷。冀得一虎。庶可塞責。月餘。受杖數百。寃苦罔控。遂詣東郭嶽廟。跪而祝之。哭失聲。無

# 聊齋雜選

何。一虎自外來。隸錯愕。恐被咥噬。虎入。殊不他顧。蹲立門中。隸祝曰。如殺某子爾也。其俯聽吾縛。遂出縲索縶虎頸。虎帖耳受縛。牽達縣署。宰問虎曰。某子爾噬之耶。虎頷之。宰曰。殺人者死。古之定律。且嫗止一子。而爾殺之。彼殘年垂盡。何以生活。倘爾能爲若子也。我將赦之。虎又頷之。乃釋縛令去。嫗方怨宰不殺虎以償子也。遲旦啟扉。則有死鹿。嫗貨其肉革。用以資度。自是以爲常。時銜金帛擲庭中。嫗由此致豐裕。奉養過於其子。心竊德虎。虎來時臥簷下。竟日不去。人畜相安。各無猜忌。數年嫗死。虎來吼於堂中。嫗素所積。綽可營葬。族人共瘞之。墳壘方成。虎驟奔來。賓客盡逃。虎直赴冢前。嗥鳴雷動。移時始去。土人立義虎祠於東郊。至今猶存。

## 鴻

## 聊齋雜選

天津弋人得一鴻。其雄者隨至其家。哀鳴翱翔。抵暮始去。次日弋人早出。則鴻已至。飛號從之。既而集其足下。弋人將並捉之。見其伸頸俛仰吐出黃金半鋌。弋人悟其意。乃曰是將以贖婦也。遂釋雌。兩鴻徘徊。若有悲喜。遂雙飛而去。弋人稱金。得二兩六錢。强噫。禽鳥何知。而鍾情若此。悲莫悲於生別離。物亦然耶。

### 牧豎

兩牧豎入山。至狼穴。穴有小狼二。謀分捉之。各登一樹。相去數十步。少選。大狼至。入穴失子。意甚倉皇。豎於樹上扭小狼蹄耳。故令嗥。大狼聞聲仰視。怒奔樹下。號且爬抓。其一豎又在彼樹致小狼鳴急。狼聞四顧。始望見之。乃舍此趨彼。跑號如前狀。前樹又鳴。又轉。口無停聲。足無停趾。數十往復。奔漸

拾級大成

# 子不語雜選

吾欲知鬼神之情狀。請與子俱。令沮之。客不可。亦縛而墜焉。
縋縛而墜焉。衆持留之。令不可。其幕客李詵豪士也。謂令曰。
人敢往。令毅然曰。爲民請命。死何惜。吾當自行。命左右取長
能與鬼神言明。乃可。令曰。鬼神何在。曰。井底即鬼神所居。無
初。知縣劉綱到任。聞而禁之。衆論譁然。令持之頗堅。衆曰。公
鏹投之。約費三千金。名納陰司錢糧。或吝惜。必生瘟疫。國
四川酆都縣。俗傳人鬼交界之處。縣中有井。每歲焚紙錢帛

## 酆都知縣。

以爲戲耳。
聲嘶更。無敵者。豈不暢然自雄。不知此禽獸之威。人故弄之
有豪强子。怒目按劍。若將搏噬。爲所怒者。乃闔扉去。豪力盡
遲。聲漸弱。既而奄奄僵臥。久之不動。竪下視之氣已絕矣。今

# 子不語雜選

此誰敢相違。今更寵臨。具徵仁勇。語未竟。紅光自天而下。包
幽明道隔。不能家喻戶曉破其誣罔。明公爲民除弊。雖不來
惡道。借鬼神爲口實。誘人修齋打醮。傾家者不下千萬。鬼神
再作租戶哉。知縣冒死而來。爲民請命。包公笑曰。世有妖僧
旱頻年。民力竭矣。朝廷國課尙苦不輸。豈能爲陰司納帛鏹。
迎。揖以上坐。曰。陰陽道隔。公來何爲。令起立拱手曰。酆都水
而坐者年七十餘。容貌方嚴。羣鬼傳呼曰。某縣令至。公下堦
之。令曰。包公何在。曰。在殿上。引至一處宮室巍峩上。有冕旒
免陰司錢糧。衆鬼嘖嘖稱賢。手加額。曰。此事須與包閻羅商
也。見縣令皆羅拜曰。公陽官來何爲。令曰。吾爲陽間。百姓請
世。其人民藐小。映日無影。蹈空而行。自言在此者不知有地
入井五丈許。地黑復明。燦然有天光。所見城郭宮室悉如陽

# 子不語雜選

蘇友白奉叔父命往江口路遇楊科

背問有印處不壞。李竟中風而亡。未幾暴雷震電繞其棺椁衣服焚燒殆盡惟李袍背印之。令與幕客李拜謝畢仍縋而出甫至酆都南門爲乞哀。包公曰但令速死免致焚屍取匣中玉印方尺許解救汝矣。此事何可問也況于臣子之前呼其君之字乎。令代帽髮盡指。即辭去包公大驚謂李曰汝必爲雷擊死吾不能不及幽明之事李素謇遽問曰玄德公何在關不答色不懌。之令與幕客李惶恐出拜關賜坐顏色甚温問世事甚悉惟有生人氣何也包公具道所以關曰若然則賢令也我願見長髯冉冉而下與包公行賓主禮語多不可辨關神曰公處公起曰伏魔大帝至矣公少避劉退至後堂少傾關神綠袍

## 見玉嬌梨第五回

蘇友白看完了書。心下暗想道。家中已是貧乏。一個秀才又黜退了。親事又都回絕。只管住在此處。亦覺無味。莫若隨了叔父上京。一時雖不貪他的富貴。倘或因此訪得一個佳人。也可完我心願。主意已定。隨對衆人說道。既是老爺來接。至親骨肉。豈可不去。但此處到江口路甚遙遠。恐怕今日到不得了。衆人道。老爺性急。立候開船。這裡到江口。有八十里路。有馬在此。若肯就行。去到那裡。還甚早。蘇友白道。既如此。列位可先行。回復老爺。我一面打發行李。一面隨後就來。隨卽封了一兩銀子。送與衆人道。匆匆起程。不及留飲。作代一飯。衆人推辭道。大相公是老爺一家人。怎敢受賞。蘇友白道。到從直些。不要躭閣工夫。衆人受了先去。因留下一匹好馬。蘇友白隨卽吩咐個老家人。叫做蘇壽。留他在家中。看守房屋。

## 見玉嬌梨第五回

因自想道。吳家這頭親事。早是有主意辭脫了。若是沾了手。此時春風正暖。一路上柳明花媚。蘇友白在馬上觀之不盡笑道。這畜生不打。便不肯走。可見人生處世。一日不可無權。裡。照馬屁股儘力連打了幾下。那馬負痛。只得前行。蘇友白不怕他不走了。蘇友白道。正是我到忘了。叫人取出拿在手打。如何肯走。舊時老相公。有一條珊瑚鞭。何不取了帶去。便蘇友白心中焦燥。似這般走。幾時得到。家人蘇壽說道。馬不亂扯。那馬往前走不得一步。把屁股一掀。到往後退了兩步。慣騎馬的。又無鞭子打他。便立定不走。蘇友白忙忙將繮繩當。隨即上馬要行。爭奈那匹馬最是狡猾。見蘇友白不是久家人送到江口。自家只帶一個小廝。叫做小喜。當下吩咐停又打點些衣服鋪陳之類。結束做兩扣。叫人挑了。先着一個

## 見玉嬌梨第五回

要打。那人慌忘道。相公不要打。小人的妻子不見了。都在相只道好了。有下落了。蘇友白見那人說話胡塗。便担起鞭子麼人。爲何扯住我的轡繩。那人跑得氣吁吁。一時答應不淸。腿蒲鞋。走得塵土亂迸。滿身上汗如雨溫。慌忙問道。你是甚帽。歪在半邊。身披一領短靑布夾襖。懷都開了。脚穿一雙綁可裡吃了一驚。忘將那人一看。只看那人頭帶一頂破尖氈便雙手把轡繩扯住。蘇友白因心下胡思亂想。不曾防備。猛跑出一個人來。將蘇友白上下一看。口裡道一聲。果然有了。個纔罷。心中自言自語。不覺來到一個十字路口。忽岔路裡是京中沒有。便辭了叔子出來。隨你天涯海角。定要尋他一得一個便好。若是撞不着。可不辜負我一片念頭。又想道。若那得便容你自由自在。到京中去尋訪。又自想道。若有分撞

# 玉嬌梨第五回

何賴我過路的。那人道。小人怎敢圖賴相公。只求相公把這
上來看。蘇友白亂嚷道。天下有這等奇事。你不見了妻子。如
路的。及村中住的人。見他兩個有些古怪。不知爲何。便都圍
是小人。口裡雖然叫苦。那兩手扯住轡繩。死也不放。此時過
一發說不清。只是亂叫相公住手罷。可憐我有苦情。我實不
夾頭夾面亂打。小喜赶上氣不過。也來亂打。那人被打慌了。不
我是蘇巡撫老爺的公子。你不要錯尋了對頭。就提起鞭子
上見明白。你敢是短路小人。怎敢青天白日攔住我的去路。
白道。你這等一發胡說。我又過路的。你的妻子如何在我身
公拐我妻子。只是我的妻子要在相公身上見個明白。蘇友
我何干。我與你無相識。難道我拐了你的。那人道不說是相
公身上。蘇友白大怒道。你這人好胡說。你的妻子不見了。與

# 玉嬌梨第五回

身穿柳黃衣服。騎一匹點子馬來。你只扯着他。求了他手中去尋。他說向東北方。四十里上。十字路口。有一位少年官人他許我只在今日申時三刻便見。小人又問他該向那一方日清晨。在句容鎮上遇着個起課先生。小人求他起了一課。城中贖當。不知去路上被甚人拐去。日日追尋。並無消息。今的。是單陽縣陽家村人。小人叫做楊科。數日前曾叫妻子到便問那人道。你是那裡人。有甚緣故。可細細說明。那人道。小的說個明白。衆人勸道。相公且息怒。待問個明白再打不遲。你。氣不過提起鞭來又要打。那人叫起來道。相公慢打。容小蘇友白說道。我這根馬鞭子是珊瑚的。值幾兩銀子。如何與笑起來道。這人敢是個風子。如何不見妻子。一根馬鞭便有。根鞭子賞了小人。小人的妻子就有了。看的人聽見。都一齊

## 玉嬌梨第五回

能知。他如何曉得。便有幾分信他。因說道。便把這鞭子與你。了半晌。心下暗想道。這件事乃肺腑隱情。便是鬼神亦未必是。相公心下便明白了。蘇友白聽見說出求婚姻三字。便呆不由人不信。也還說相公此行。是爲求婚姻的。不知是也不道。小人怎敢。小人也自知說來不信。只因那先生件件說着。馬顏色。希圖騙我鞭子。便駕此一篇說謊。我如何信得。楊科你這人一味胡說。世間那有這樣靈先生。你分明看見我衣了小人。使小人夫妻相見。便是相公萬代陰德。蘇友白笑道。衣服顏色相對。豈不是實。只求相公施仁心。把這馬鞭子賞喫。直趕了四十里路。到此十字路。恰恰遇着相公騎馬而來。此後便再不能勾見了。小人聽了。一口氣赶來。連飯也不敢那條馬鞭子。你妻子便有了。只要快赶。遲了一步。放過他去。

## 玉嬌梨第五回

上去扒到樹上。纔要折柳。忽聽得廟中有人啼哭。他分開柳破廟。旁邊有三四株大柳樹。高出墻頭。楊科看見。慌忙扒將是柔弱枝條。折來折馬不動。只東南角上。一條冷巷中。一所身來。東張西望。去尋柳條。此時是三月中旬。路旁小柳樹。都鞭子。千恩萬謝道。多謝相公。若尋着妻子定然送還。便立起許了你。豈肯失信。可快折一枝柳條來。我好趕路。楊科接了肯放手。蘇友白曉得他的意思。便將鞭子先遞與他說道既公權用。楊科欲待去折柳條。又恐怕蘇友白去了。猶扯住不掇道。既是這相公肯賞你的鞭子。何不快去折柳條來與相如何尋妻子。又見蘇友白口鬆。有個肯與他意思。便替他攛肯行。却何處。旁看的人。見說得有此奇異。都要看拿了鞭子。也是小事。只是我今日還要趕到江口。若無鞭子。這馬決不

拾級大成

# 玉嬌梨第五回

多謝相公。不要了。蘇友白道。天下有這等奇事。險些兒錯怪
子去折柳條。便今生也不能見了。便將鞭子遞還蘇友白道•
見蘇友白進來。便對他妻子訴說。若不得這位相公這條鞭
甚是驚訝。也下了馬。叫小喜看着。自步進廟中來看。楊科看
驚駭。方信楊科說得俱是眞情。此時蘇友白聽見尋着妻子。
一人。兩人相見。不勝大喜。轉扯着哭將起來。衆人看見。都各
到廟後。時那三個拐子已往墻闕裡逃去多時。止剩下妻子
頂倒。楊科也不顧好歹。一頓脚將轉軸登折。擠了進去。忙跑
人聽見叫在這裡。便一齊擁了來看•楊科到廟前。廟門已被
賊奴拐人妻子。却躲在這裡。慌忙跳下樹來。竟撲廟門。看的
行淫。妻子不從。故此啼哭。楊科看見了。便忍不住叫起來。好
棻。往內一張。又見有三個男子。將他妻子圍在中間。要逼勒

海上絲綢之路文獻集成　科技與文化編

# 玉嬌梨第五回

不是多情愛狂蕩。因春無賴聽春吹。
樹頭風絮亂依依。空裡遊絲無定飛。

堆裡轉出個佳人。生死場中拾回個才子。正是馬頭。向西南楊科去的路上趕來。只因此一去。有分教。是非神仙。問明婚姻。再到叔父船上未爲遲也。主意定了。遂勒轉去尋覔。何其愚也。今天色尚早。不如趕到句容鎮上。見了賽我婚姻在何處。我放着現消息不去訪問。却向無蹤無影處爲尋訪佳人。這賽神仙他旣曉得我爲婚姻出門。必然曉得頭想道。我蘇友白。聰明一世。懞懂一時。我此行雖因叔命。原原從舊路上揚揚去了。蘇友白走出廟來。上了馬。一頭走。一喚他做賽神仙。說罷便再三謝了。蘇友白并衆人。領着妻子他的姓名。只因他挂着一面牌。上寫賽神仙三字。人就順口了你。我今問你那起課的先生叫甚姓名。楊科道。人都不知

拾級大成

# 聖諭廣訓第七條

## 黜異端以崇正學

朕惟欲厚風俗。先正人心。欲正人心。先端學術。夫人受天地之中以生。惟此倫常日用之道。爲智愚之所共由。索隱行怪。聖賢不取。易言蒙以養正。聖功以之。書言無偏無頗。無反無側。王道以之。聖功王道。悉本正學。至於非聖之書。不經之典。驚世駭俗。紛紛藉藉。起而爲民物之蠹者。皆爲異端。所宜屏絕。凡爾兵民。愿謹淳樸者固多。間或迷於他岐。以無知而罹罪戾。朕甚憫之。自古三教流傳。儒宗而外。厥有仙釋。朱子曰。釋氏之教。都不管天地四方。只是理會一箇心。老氏之教。只是要存得一箇神氣。此朱子持平之言。可知釋道之本指矣。自游食無藉之輩。陰竊其名。以壞其術。大率假災祥禍福之事。以售其誕幻無稽之談。始則誘取貲財。以圖肥己。漸至男

# 聖諭廣訓第七條

世道人心計者。至深遠矣。爾兵民等宜仰體

聖祖仁皇帝漸民以仁。摩民以義。藝極陳常。煌煌大訓。所以爲

哉。我

無憂。而顧昧恒性。而即匪彝。犯王章而干國憲。不亦愚之甚

就安。爾兵民以父母之身。生太平無事之日。衣食有賴。俯仰

刑。朝廷立法之意。無非禁民爲非。導民爲善。黜邪崇正。去危

爾等不可不知也。夫左道惑衆。律所不宥。師巫邪術。邦有常

如西洋教宗天主。亦屬不經。因其人通曉歷數。故國家用之。

爲罪魁。福緣且爲禍本。如白蓮聞香等教。皆前車之鑒也。又

世誣民。及一旦發覺。徵捕株連。身陷囹圄。累及妻子。教主已

甚者。奸回邪慝。竄伏其中。樹黨結盟。夜聚曉散。干名犯義。惑

女混淆。聚處爲燒香之會。農工廢業。相逢多語怪之人。又其

# 勸世良言

世。傳授教誨世上之人。凡誠心敬信者。必得救寶貝靈魂之
此乃保羅所說救世福音之道。是由神天命救世主耶穌降
之乎。又未聞之。何能信之。併未傳道。何能聽道乎。
聖保羅曰。但凡告禱主名者。必得救也。然未信之。何能求
論眞道福音宣到該處衆人應該敬信求福免禍。

遵蕩平正直之化。則異端不待驅而自息矣。
業者。即可以迓神慶。爾服爾耕爾講爾武。安布帛菽粟之常。
事君忠。盡人事者。即足以集天休。不求非分。不作非爲。敦本
品行端方。諸邪不能勝正。家庭和順。遇難可以成祥。事親孝。
害。害及人心。心之本體有正無邪。苟有主持自然不惑。將見
聖教擯斥異端。直如盜賊水火。且水火盜賊。害止及身。異端之
聖心祗遵

# 勸世良言

能救也。此救世福音眞道。由神天令救世主傳諭世上之人。寶貝靈魂之罪。不知自罪。而咈逆之者。其寶貝之靈魂亦弗在於人心。但肯悔罪敬信。呼求救世主耶穌之名者。必得救然傳到之處。不論富貴貧賤之人。凡得知斯道者。信與不信。倍矣。夫救世福音眞道。定必佈散傳揚於普天下萬國之中。固無由而信。罪有可容。且已聽知之後。猶不肯信者。罪則加惡念。陷害自己寶貝靈魂之至。蓋未知未聞福音眞道之時。肯棄除舊惡。偏要貼從風俗。跟隨衆人私意如此。即是愈增寶貝之靈魂。亦可望救矣。若只聽福音眞道。明知其義。而不耶穌代贖罪之功。呼求救世主耶穌之名。必得赦免諸罪。而時。即傾心敬信。立改前非。遵着福音眞道而行。藉賴救世主罪。夫如是。凡欲求救寶貝靈魂者。若得知救世福音眞道之

拾級大成

# 勸世良言

此耶哥伯言云。人生血氣之怒不可有。理義之怒不可無。因絶餘剩之惡。温心必承所種之道。救爾靈矣。

聖耶哥伯曰。蓋人發怒。不遵上帝行。義矣故棄諸濁之弊。論人謙心納受福道可能得靈魂之救。

罪。但死後之苦禍。豈能逃脫哉。自召禍矣。蓋有等人偏執不肯敬信者。雖生前或者不罰其尤反違逆之。豈無罪乎。故我們世人敬信者則爲福。咈逆者。之皇。降下福音聖諭。令世人敬信遵守而行。乃不肯遵信之。諭。尚要遵守而不敢犯。何況神天上帝。乃係萬國之主各皇內。人人俱要遵守而行。若有犯之者。必懲治其罪。夫皇上聖者。罪不姑寬。正如皇上降下聖諭一般。須行於天下各省之是以世上萬國之人。凡得知者。皆當敬信凜遵而行。如違之

# 勸世良言

並進。善義日新。滋養靈魂。自有至樂之美。則實守而勿失之而理傳。從此生枝放蕊。結實成功。只待獲收其果。正如道德內外範圍固守。則救世眞道福音之義。恒常根固於心。根固而存養於心。守而謹行於外。日累月積。行之不厭。樂之不倦。涵養靈魂之志。則可以納接駁言生救世眞道福音之義。拘游之語。異端誕幻無根之談。務懷謙虛遜順潔淨之心。和緩邪淫褻瀆之氣。戲謔巧弄奸猾之心。與夫一切虛言狂妄浮乎。是以欲恒守神天眞道之義而行者。固當棄除諸般汚穢眞道之義哉。蓋眞道不能存。而惡逆必生。豈能行神天道義志氣必不順。志氣有不順。則胸中乖戾。齷齪悖逆。焉能恆存遷而增其怒也。蓋怒於甲者。不可怒於乙。夫若藏怒於心。則紛紜於俗務。此去彼來。互相交往。豈無反目瞋怒。然怒不可

# 新遺詔書選

是謂能救靈魂之基。固結長生之業。苟能恒心遵守救世眞道福音。竭力而爲善義者。則靈魂必得救。而來生永遠眞福亦在其中矣。豈謂徒然不遵者。可望得救靈魂哉。

## 無度浪子

或人有二子。其仲語父云。請父賜我該得之家業也。父遂分業給予矣。後無幾日。仲子收拾家物。遠遊異方。在彼浪費無度。散盡家業也。錢財消化。忽該地有饑荒。自覺缺乏矣。遂投本地居民。其打發之往田牧猪。且猪所食之粗糠。彼貪充飢益無人供食矣。畢竟醒悟。暗想道。吾父所僱許多傭人。得食有餘。惟吾在此。幾乎饑死矣。吾必起身。回見家父。求云。老爹吾獲罪天。並虧尊顏。故稱父子所不敢當。乃以兒爲傭人足矣。隨卽起身。回見家父。惟子尙遠。父遙見之。遂感慈悲。行走

# 新遺詔書選

忽然有教法之師立起。想試耶穌。卽謂之曰。師也。吾當何行

## 行客施善証

復生。失而再遇。故應當爲之喜樂也。

犢也。曰兒常待膝下。吾所有者。皆兒所得也。惟此爾弟死而使可與朋友快樂也。惟此爾子。宿娼費業。旣歸家來。隨宰肥語父曰。歷年以來。吾常事父。總無違命。倘且未嘗賜兒小羊。宰肥犢慶賀矣。長子遂怒。不肯進來。及父自出邀之也。長子舞之音。故召僕來。問有何事。曰貴弟歸來。令尊遇之無恙。故而再遇也。故舉快樂矣。且其長子在田。歸來近屋。聽作樂跳鞋履。又牽肥犢屠之。大家食歓得樂。蓋此吾兒死又復生。失所不敢當。然父諭僕曰。頂好之袍。取出衣之。給之指環。賜之抱頸。而親嘴之。子曰。老爹。吾得罪天。併虧尊顏。今後稱父子。

拾級大成

# 新遺詔書選

可享永生。曰。載法何錄。念經如何。曰。當以盡心。專意。竭力。盡志。敬愛上主。爾所崇之上帝。又當愛憐如己焉。耶穌曰。所答甚是。斯行可生矣。教法之師。倘要自推有義。曰。鄰者誰耶。耶穌應道。或人由耶路撒冷往耶哩砢。遭賊奪衣。打傷半死。賊遂走去。偶有祭司。行由彼路。既見之。則過去他邊矣。再有利未族人。既適彼處。來看一看。又過去他邊矣。畢竟有撒馬哩亞人。行路之間。近至。既見其人。則憐憫之。趨來用藥酒油膏抹傷縛之。又扶上畜背。帶入歇店。好照顧之。次早起程。取出二錢銀交店主。曰。小心照顧此人。再有費者。吾復來時將清還也。請問三者之中。誰爲遇賊者之憐耶。曰。矜憐之者是也。耶穌曰。爾且往去。效此而爲也。

拾級大成終

# 上海方言教程

（*Lessons in the Shanghai Dialect*）

〔美〕卜舫濟（Francis Lister Hawks Pott）編

《上海方言教程》，美國卜舫濟編。卜舫濟（Francis Lister Hawks Pott，一八六四—一九四七），美國聖公會傳教士。生於美國紐約，一八八六年來華。一八八七年接掌約翰書院（後改爲聖約翰大學），任職達六十年。此書設三十課，依據西方語言學理論，詳述量詞、代詞、數字、形容詞、疑問詞與否定詞、副詞、動詞、複合動詞、各類習語成語、問答、語氣、時間、度量衡、家庭關係、意思相反之對仗詞、敬語等，每課均有標題、英文解説、詞彙、中譯英與英譯中練習等。據一九〇七年上海版影印。

# LESSONS

—IN THE—

# SHANGHAI DIALECT

BY

Rev. F. L. HAWKS POTT, D.D.

Shanghai:
PRINTED AT THE AMERICAN PRESBYTERIAN MISSION PRESS
1907

# PREFACE.

AT a time when there is much discussion in China as to the desirability and possibility of the adoption of a uniform language all over the Empire, it may seem strange to put forth a book on the Shanghai Dialect.

The writer sympathizes fully with the aims of those who would make Mandarin the Medium of Communication throughout China, but at the same time feels very strongly that a great many years must pass before this can be accomplished.

Local Dialects die hard, as witness the still existing varieties of speech found in Great Britain. Even more perfect means of communication binding the parts of a country closely together, and even the introduction of a common language into the School System, are not able of themselves to do away with the speaking of the old local dialect. Men cling persistently to the speech of their forefathers.

When we reflect that the so-called Shanghai Dialect is in reality the ancient language of the Wu Kingdom, and is perhaps more closely akin to the original language of the Chinese people than Mandarin, we can understand why it will last for many years.

Further, it has a very wide range. Although local varieties occur every few miles, yet in the main the Shanghai Dialect is understood by at least 20,000,000 of people.

For the Missionary working in the Kiangsu Province a knowledge of the local dialect is indispensable, and the acquisition of it would be most useful for all those whose lot is cast in this part of China. Foreigners living in Shanghai would find it a great advantage to speak the native language, and in their business relations with the Chinese would be greatly helped if they could converse in something better than the jargon known as "Pidgin" English.

It is for the purpose of making the attainment of a speaking knowledge of the language somewhat less difficult that the writing of this book has been undertaken.

It has seemed to the writer that the acquisition of a knowledge of the written characters, and of the spoken language are two distinct things. It is possible for one to learn to speak the language without being able to read the characters.

By the use of the clear and simple System of Romanization, adopted by missionaries in Shanghai, it is possible to represent approximately all the sounds employed in the dialect.

In these lessons this system is adopted, and the student is urged to master it thoroughly. If he will do so, he can use these lessons and learn to speak the language even without knowing the characters.

The characters of all the words and sentences employed are given, but they are put in the book for the benefit of the Chinese teacher. It would be unwise to trust entirely to the Romanization. The student in using the book should have a teacher by his side, who by reading the Chinese corresponding to the romanized sounds can give him a clearer idea of the pronounciation.

Although in a sense the book is a short cut to learning the spoken language, of course it is not meant to discourage the student from mastering the written language. This is, however, a distinct study, and should be undertaken in a different way. The best method for this will be to use the primer in vernacular containing the most familiar characters, and then to advance from it to the reading of the New Testament or other books in the vernacular. Vernacular books should be read first, for the reading of them will be a great assistance in learning the spoken language. After the first year, books in the literary style (Wên-li) should be begun.

In using this book, the first thing to be mastered thoroughly is the introductory matter. The student must get this first, for it is the key to the rest of the book. He must also learn to distinguish the tones, and the inflections of the voice which they imply. Then he will be ready to go on with the lessons.

Although the book is divided into thirty lessons, it is not expected that the student will be able to master a lesson a day. Some of the lessons will require three or four days' work.

In putting the English sentences into Chinese, the best plan would be to write out in the Romanization what the student thinks the proper way of translating them would be. Then these sentences may be read to the teacher, who will correct them, and from the Chinese text will be able to tell the right way to say them.

At present only thirty lessons are published. The writer hopes, however, if the method proves to be useful to extend these lessons still further in the future.

In preparing these lessons, many books have been consulted, especially the lessons by Dr. Yates, which contain a most useful collection of words and sentences, and has long been the Standard book for learning the Dialect, the Grammar by Dr. Edkins which contains a mass of useful information in regard to the structure of the language, and the Mandarin Lessons by Dr. Mateer, a most exhaustive work on spoken Chinese.

The writer's thanks are due especially to Rev. J. A. Silsby for the permission to make use of his clear statement of the Shanghai System of Romanization, and to Prof. F. C. Cooper for many suggestions and the trouble he has taken in reading the proofs.

The unfailing courtesy of Rev. G. F. Fitch, D.D., and Mr. Gilbert McIntosh has been much appreciated, in the care they have taken in seeing the book through the Press.

F. L. H. P.

January 1st, 1907.

# Description of the Shanghai Romanized System.

Nearly all the syllables are represented by the combination of an initial and a final, a system which has been found to be well adapted to the Chinese language.

## Initials.

Chinese sounds are divided into upper and lower series. The initials to represent the UPPER SERIES are—*p, 'm, 'v, t, ts, s, 'l, 'n, 'ny, 'ng, k, ky, kw, i* and *'w*. These initials are pronounced in most cases much the same as in English, but without aspiration, higher in pitch and with very little vibration of the larynx. The apostrophe before a letter indicates that the letter belongs to the "higher series." Pure vowel initials also belong to this series.

*'ny* has a sound similar to that of *ni* in span*i*el.

*ky*=*ch* in *ch*uk with all aspiration eliminated.

*i* as an initial has the sound of *i* in dahlia.

The ASPIRATES are—*ph, f, th, tsh, kh, ch, khw, h, hy*, and *hw* (*th* as in *Th*omson—not as in *th*ing).

*ch*=*ch* in *ch*urch.

*hy* is nearly like *ti* in Por*tia*.

The other aspirates are like the corresponding initials of the higher series with the addition of a strong aspiration (indicated by *h*).

The initials to represent the LOWER SERIES are—*b, m, v, d, dz, z, l, n, ny, ng, g, j, gw, y*, and *w*. Their pronunciation is much the same as in English. They are lower in pitch than corresponding initials of the "higher series," and have more "voice," being pronounced with more decided vibration of the larynx. The lower vowel initials, indicated by an inverted comma (') and attended with a slight aspiration, belong to this series. It will be noted that this sign differs from that employed to indicate that a consonant initial belongs to the upper series, an apostrophe being used to denote the "upper initial." This inverted comma is used only before vowels, and if, by mistake, this sign is used before a consonant instead of the apostrophe, this need not confuse the reader, for the sign of the upper series is properly used only before the initial consonants *m, v, l, n, ny, ng, w*, and *r*.

It should be noted well that the difference between the corresponding initials of the upper and lower series is not so much a difference in consonantal quality as a difference in pitch, but there is a real consonantal difference. The higher series may be classified as *surd* and the lower as *sonant*.

## Finals.

1. The VOWEL ENDINGS are—*a, e, i, au, o, oo, oe, eu, u, ui, ia, iau, ieu,* and *ie*.

2. The NASAL ENDINGS are—(*a*) *an, en, ien* and *oen*, in which the *n* is not sounded, but lengthens out and imparts a nasal quality to the preceding vowel; (*b*) *ang, aung, oong, ung* and *iang*, in which *ng* has the value of *ng* in *song*; (*c*) *uin*, in which *n* is sonant and has a value varying between *n* and *ng*.

3. The ABRUPT VOWEL ENDINGS are—*ak, ah, eh, ih, auh, ok, oeh, uh,* and *iak*, in which *h* and *k* are the signs of the *zeh-sung* (入聲), and the vowel is pronounced in a short, abrupt manner.

The sounds of the vowels are—

*a* as in f*a*r, except when followed by *n* or *h*, when it has the sound of *a* in m*a*n or m*a*t.

*e* as in pr*ey*; before *h* it has the sound of *e* as in m*e*t.

*i* ,, capr*i*ce; before *h* or *ng* it is shortened to *i* as in m*i*t or s*i*ng.

*au* ,, *Au*gust.

*o* ,, s*o*.

*oo* as *ou* in t*oo*.

*oe* as in G*oe*the (German ö).

*eu* ,, French Mons*ieu*r.

*u* ,, *oo* in f*oo*t (always preceded by an *s* sound).

*ui* ,, in fr*ui*t (or rather, French ü).

In *ia, iau, ieu* and *ie*, we have short *i* followed closely by *a, au, eu,* and *e*, as described above.

Of course it is understood that the Chinese sounds in a majority of cases vary somewhat from the English sounds which are given as the nearest equivalent. The true pronunciation of Chinese sounds should be learned from a Chinese Teacher, and the student should always bear it in mind that *any Romanization used does not represent English sounds, but Chinese sounds*. This fact can not be too strongly emphasized.

The DOK-YOONG Z-MOO—"Initials *used alone*," i.e., without vowels, are—*ts, tsh, dz, s, z, m, ng,* and *r*. The first five are followed by the vowel sound in the second syllable of *able*—prolonged. Mateer and Baller use ï for this sound and the new Mandarin Romanized uses ı̤. It is not written, but understood in the Shanghai system. *m* has the sound of *m* in chas*m* and *ng* the sound of *ng* in ha*ng*er. *r* is a sound between final *r* and *l*.

## Tones.

The tones are four in number, each occuring in the upper and lower series. As has been stated, the upper and lower series can be distinguished by the initials. Sounds in the upper series are of higher pitch and those in the lower series of a lower pitch.

## DESCRIPTION OF THE SHANGHAI ROMANIZED SYSTEM.

The names of the tones are:—

Bing sung = Even sound 平聲.
Zang sung = Rising sound 上聲.
Chui-sung = Going sound 去聲.
Zeh-sung = Entering sound 入聲.

### Tone Signs.

° to the left of a word indicates the tone to be °*zang-sung*.

° to the right indicates the *chui-sung*. Final *h* or *k* indicate the *zeh-sung*. All other words are in the *bing-sung*.

### Sounds of the Tones.

The sounds of the tones of course can only be learnt from the Chinese Teacher.

The Bing-sung is an even tone, the voice being kept on the level, neither rising or falling. It is the same in both the upper or lower series.

The Zang-sung in the upper series is a twanging sound, and sounds something like the vibration of a string of a musical instrument.

In the lower series it has a wave sound which can be symbolized to the eye by the curve ∿ ; the voice first falls and then rises.

The Chui-sung has the same sound in both the upper and lower series. The voice rises much as it does when we ask a question.

The student should practise with the teacher on the following table of sounds, and in time will be able to distinguish the tones clearly and to make the proper inflection himself. Foreigners are seldom able to perfect themselves in the use of tones, but this is due not so much to inability as to the lack of attention paid to the matter at the beginning of the study of the language.

Complete List of Initials and Finals used in the Shanghai Dialect.

# ZAUNG-HE LOO-MO Z.

## Z-MOO.

| | | | |
|---|---|---|---|
| P | p | 不 | 杯 |
| Ph | ph | 潑 | 坏 |
| B | b | 孛 | 賠 |
| 'M | 'm | 每 | 螟 |
| M | m | 末 | 明 |
| 'V | 'v | 勿 | |
| F | f | 拂 | °粉 |
| V | v | 物 | °忿 |
| T | t | 縋 | 堆 |
| Th | h | 脫 | 推 |
| D | d | 疊 | 臺 |
| Ts | ts | 鐵 | 遮 |
| Tsh | tsh | 出 | 父 |
| Dz | Dz | 絰 | 荼 |
| S | s | 失 | 衰 |
| Z | z | 十 | 裁 |
| 'L | 'l | 拎 | °擄 |
| L | l | 垃 | °櫓 |
| 'N | 'n | 乃 | 懦° |
| N | n | 納 | 怒° |

| | | | |
|---|---|---|---|
| 'Ny | 'ny | 拈 | °撚 |
| Ny | ny | 業 | °染 |
| 'Ng | 'ng | '顔 | 一顔 |
| Ng | ng | 兀 | 呆 |
| K | k | 鴿 | 加 |
| Kh | kh | 磕 | 揩 |
| G | g | 狢 | 茄 |
| Ky | ky | 吉 | 鳩 |
| Ch | ch | 怯 | 邱 |
| J | j | 及 | 求 |
| Kw | kw | 骨 | 規 |
| Khw | khw | 闊 | 奎 |
| Gw | gw | 掇 | 葵 |
| I | i | 一 | 腰 |
| Y | y | 葉 | 姚 |
| 'W | 'w | 威 | 彎 |
| W | w | 活 | 還 |
| H | h | 黑 | 亨 |
| Hy | hy | 歇 | 興 |
| Hw | hw | 忽 | 昏 |
| ' | ' | 合 | 恒 |

## IUNG-YUIN.

| | | | |
|---|---|---|---|
| A | a | 挨 | 篩 |
| Ang | ang | 櫻 | 生 |
| Ak | ak | 矮 | 柵 |
| An | an | 俺 | 三 |
| Ah | ah | 押 | 殺 |
| E | e | 哀 | 衰 |
| En | en | 菴 | 攙 |
| Eh | eh | 盒 | 失 |
| I | i | 衣 | 西 |
| Ien | ien | 煙 | 先 |
| Ing | ing | 喑 | 心 |
| Ih | ih | 一 | 雪 |
| Au | au | 凹 | 燒 |
| Aung | aung | 盎 | 霜 |
| Auh | auh | 惡 | 朔 |
| O | o | 喔 | 沙 |
| Ok | ok | 屋 | 束 |

| | | | |
|---|---|---|---|
| Oo | oo | 烏 | 梭 |
| Oong | oong | 翁 | 松 |
| Oe | oe | 隨 | 雖 |
| Oen | oen | 安 | 酸 |
| Oeh | oeh | 曷 | 率 |
| Eu | eu | 謳 | 收 |
| Ung | ung | 恩 | 深 |
| Uh | uh | 厄 | 色 |
| U | u | 如 | 書 |
| Ui | ui | 餘 | 須 |
| Uin | uin | 雲 | 熏 |
| Ia | ia | 雅 | 斜 |
| Iang | iang | 央 | 廂 |
| Iak | iak | 約 | 削 |
| Iau | iau | 夭 | 小 |
| Ieu | ieu | 要 | 修 |

## DOK YOONG Z-MOO.

| | | | |
|---|---|---|---|
| M | m | 嘸 | 姆 |
| Ts | ts | 之 | 貲 |
| Tsh | tsh | 雌 | 痴 |
| Dz | dz | 池 | 遲 |

| | | | |
|---|---|---|---|
| S | s | 思 | 施 |
| Z | z | 時 | 鰣 |
| 'R | 'r | °耳 | |
| R | r | 而 | 兒 |
| Ng | ng | 魚 | 吳 |

The student should practise repeating after the teacher the pronunciation of the characters in which these sounds occur.

## Exercise in Tones.

| | | | | | | | |
|---|---|---|---|---|---|---|---|
| 上平聲 | Upper Bing-sung. | Tau, | 刀 | Pa, | 叭 | Si, | 犀 |
| 下平聲 | Lower Bing-sung. | Dau, | 桃 | Ba, | 排 | Zi, | 徐 |
| 上上聲 | Upper Zang-sung. | °Tau, | 禱 | °Pa, | 擺 | °Si | 死 |
| 下上聲 | Lower Zang-sung. | °Dau, | 道 | °Ba, | 罷 | °Zi | 薺 |
| 上去聲 | Upper Chui-sung. | Tau°, | 倒 | Paʿ, | 拜 | Siʿ | 壻 |
| 下去聲 | Lower Chui-sung. | Dau°, | 導 | Ba°, | 敗 | Ziaʿ | 謝 |
| 上入聲 | Upper Zeh-sung. | Tauh, | 沰 | Pah, | 八 | Sih | 息 |
| 下入聲 | Lower Zeh-sung. | Dauh, | 度 | Bah, | 拔 | Zih | 蓆 |

The student should practise upon the sounds illustrating the different tones. The columns should be read from the top down. The teacher can guide him by first pronouncing the Chinese characters.

# LESSONS IN THE SHANGHAI DIALECT.

## LESSON I.

### The Classifier.

A or an is translated into Chinese by the numeral *ih* (一) one, and a classifier placed between the numeral and the noun. There are over forty classifiers, different nouns taking different ones, according to the class to which they belong. Nouns being generally used with classifiers accounts for the fact that in Pidgin English we have the oft recurring expression, "one piecee."

Most concrete nouns take classifiers, but not all. Exceptions will be pointed out later on. Sometimes when the object spoken of is quite definitely known, the noun is used without the classifier.

In this lesson, the two most common classifiers will be introduced, and in succeeding lessons the others will appear gradually.

It must be remarked that some nouns may take more than one classifier, sometimes one being used and sometimes another.

The most common classifier is ***kuh*** (个). "It is applied to such nouns as have no special classifier, and *may* upon occasion be applied to almost any noun as a substitute for the special classifier" (Mateer).

The classifier ***tsak*** (隻) is used with animals, birds, fowls, insects, also with articles of furniture having legs or resting on a base; also with vessels, boats, etc.

VOCABULARY.

A man, **ih kuh nyung** 一个人.
A woman, **ih kuh °nyui-nyung** (lit. female human being) 一个女人.
A teacher, **ih kuh sien-sang** (lit. born before) 一个先生.
A child, **ih kuh °siau-noen** 一个小囝.
An egg, **ih kuh dan°** 一个蛋.
A cash, **ih kuh doong-dien** 一个銅錢.
A dollar, **ih kuh yang-dien** 一个洋錢.
A servant, **ih kuh yoong°-nyung** 一个用人.
A table, **ih tsak de-°ts** 一隻枱子.
A chair, **ih tsak iui°-°ts** 一隻椅子.
An orange, **ih tsak kyoeh-°ts** 一隻橘子.
A pupil, **ih kuh 'anh-sang-°ts** 一个學生子.
To want, to wish, **iau°** 要. Also used in forming the future tense of verbs, as will be explained later.

## EXERCISES.

(Translate into English.)

(1). Ih kuh nyung iau° ih tsak de-°ts. (2). Ih kuh °nyui-nyung iau° ih tsak iui°-°ts. (3). Ih kuh °siau-noen iau° ih kuh doong-dien. (4). Ih kuh ‘auh-sang-°ts iau° ih kuh sien-sang. (5). Ih kuh yoong°-nyung iau° ih kuh dan.° (6). Ih kuh yoong°-nyung iau° ih kuh yang-dien. (7). Ih kuh °siau-noen iau° ih tsak kyoeh-°ts.

(一) 一个人要一隻檯子　　(二) 一个女人要一隻椅子
(三) 一个小囝要一个銅錢　　(四) 一个學生子要一个先生
(五) 一个用人要一个蛋　　(六) 一个用人要一个洋錢
(七) 一个小囝要一隻橘子

(Translate into Chinese.)

(1). A pupil wants an orange. (2). A woman wants a dollar. (3). A servant wants a cash. (4). A teacher wants a table. (5). A man wants an egg. (6). A pupil wants a chair. (7). A teacher wants a pupil.

(一) 一个學生子要一隻橘子　　(二) 一个女人要一个洋錢
(三) 一个用人要一个銅錢　　(四) 一个先生要一隻檯子
(五) 一个人要一个蛋　　(六) 一个學生子要一隻椅子
(七) 一个先生要一个學生子

NOTES. (1). It is difficult to form idiomatic sentences in Chinese until a larger vocabulary has been given.
(2). With *yang-dien* (洋錢) the classifier generally used is *kwhe*° (塊), a piece or slice.
(3). It will be noticed how many words are formed from the combination of two or more words. This is a characteristic of the Chinese language; for instance the word *yoong°-nyung* (用人) is composed of the verb *yoong*° (用) use, and the word *nyung* (人) man, and means the man whom you use or employ.
(4). With *sien-sang* (先生), the classifier *we*° (位) is generally used.
(5). Nouns take no change in form for the plural, but the classifier is omitted.

# LESSON II.

## Demonstrative, and Personal Pronouns.

The definite article *the* is not expressed directly in Chinese, but the demonstrative pronoun takes its place.

The demonstrative pronouns are

| | |
|---|---|
| This or these, **°di kuh** 第个. | That or those, **i kuh** 伊个. |

The demonstrative pronouns change their forms with different nouns, being formed by the ***°di*** (第) or ***i*** (伊) and the classifier belonging to the noun. Thus "this table" is not ***°di-kuh de-°ts*** but ***°di-tsak de-°ts*** (第隻檯子).

When the demonstrative is used with a numeral it retains the form ***°di-kuh*** (第个) or ***i-kuh*** (伊个) and the classifier of the noun comes between the numeral and the noun. Thus "this one table" is ***°di-kuh ih tsak de-°ts*** (第个一隻檯子).

The personal pronouns are as follows:

SINGULAR NUMBER.

| *Nominative and Objective.* | *Possessive.* |
|---|---|
| I. Person, I, or me, **°ngoo** 我. | I. Person, My or mine, **°ngoo-kuh** 我个. |
| II. Person, Thou, Thee or you, **noong°** 儂. | II. Person, Thy, thine or yours, **noong°-kuh** 儂个. |
| III. Person, He, she, it, him, her, **yi** 伊. | III. Person, His, hers, its, **yi-kuh** 伊个. |

PLURAL NUMBER.

| *Nominative and Objective.* | *Possessive.* |
|---|---|
| I. Person, We or us, **nyi°** or **°ngoo-nyi°** 我伲. | I. Person, Ours, **nyi°-kuh** or **°ngoo-nyi°-kuh** 伲个, 我伲个. |
| II. Person, You or ye, **na°** 㑚. | II. Person, Your or yours, **na°-kuh** 㑚个. |
| III. Person, They or them, **yi-la** 伊拉. | III. Person, Their or theirs, **yi-la-kuh** 伊拉个. |

The use of ***kuh*** (个) in the possessive case must be noted. ***Kuh*** (个) serves to form the possessive case of nouns as it does of pronouns. Thus to say "a man's table" would be ***ih kuh nyung kuh de-°ts*** (一个人个檯子). Exercise in possessive case formation will be found in this lesson.

VOCABULARY.

A son, **ih kuh 'eu-°ts** or **ih kuh nyi-°ts** 一个兒子.
A daughter, **ih kuh noen°** 一个囡.
A friend, **ih kuh bang-°yeu** 一个朋友.
A sheep, **ih tsak yang** 一隻羊.
A bird, **ih tsak °tiau** 一隻鳥.
A bed, **ih tsak zaung** 一隻牀.

***°Po*** (把) is the classifier used with tools, instruments or articles grasped in the hand.

A knife or sword, **ih °po tau** 一把刀.
A fork, **ih °po tsho** 一把叉.
A spoon, **ih °po tshau** 一把抄.
An umbrella, **ih °po san°** 一把傘.
To have, or has, **°yeu** 有.

EXERCISES.

(Translate into English).

(1). °Ngoo iau° ih °po tau. (2). °Di-kuh nyung °yeu ih kuh yang-dien. (3). Noong° kuh bang-°yeu kuh 'eu-°ts °yeu ih tsak yang. (4). I-kuh °nyui-nyung kuk noen° iau° ih tsak °tiau. (5). Yi iau° ih °po san°. (6). °Ngoo iau° ih °po tsho. (7). Nyi° iau° ih tsak zaung. (8). Na° °yeu ih kwhe° yang-dien. (9). °Di-kuh sien-sang °yeu ih tsak kyoeh-°ts. (10). Yi-kuh yoong°-nyung °yeu ih kuh dan°.

(一) 我要一把刀
(二) 第个人有一个洋錢
(三) 儂个朋友个兒子有一隻羊
(四) 伊个女人个囡要一隻鳥
(五) 伊要一把傘
(六) 我要一把叉
(七) 伲要一隻牀
(八) 倻有一塊洋錢
(九) 第个先生有一隻橘子
(十) 伊个用人有一个蛋

(Translate into Chinese.)

(1). Your teacher has a table. (2). My friend has a son. (3). Their daughter has an umbrella. (4). They want a bed. (5). That servant wants a knife. (6). This pupil's teacher has a chair. (7). My son wants a dollar. (8). He wants a fork. (9). She wants a spoon. (10). The woman's daughter has an orange. (11). This is mine. (12). That is yours.

(一) 儂个先生有一隻檯子

(二) 我个朋友有一个兒子

(三) 伊拉个囡有一把傘

(四) 伊拉要一隻牀

(五) 伊个用人要一把刀

(六) 第个學生子个先生有一隻椅子

(七) 我个兒子要一塊洋錢

(八) 伊要一把义

(九) 伊要一把抄

(十) 一个女人个囡有一隻櫥子

(十一) 第个是我个

(十二) 伊个是儂个

NOTES. (1). Verbs undergo no change in form for the singular and plural number. Tense formation will be explained later.

(2). The verb °*yeu* is often used for the expression "there is." Thus °*yeu ih kuh nyung iau*° *doong-dien* (有一个人要銅錢) means, "There is a man who wants cash."

(3). °*yeu kuh* (有个) means "some." Thus °*yeu kuh nyung* (有个人) is "some men."

(4). Sometimes the *kuh* is omitted and we have °*yeu nyung*. Thus °*yeu nyung iau*° *yang-dien* (有人要洋錢) means, "some man want dollars."

---

## LESSON III.

### The Numerals up to one Hundred.

One, **ih** 一.
Two, **nyi**° or °**liang** 二, 兩.
Three, **san** 三.
Four, **s**° 四.
Five, °**ng** 五.

Six, **lok** 六.
Seven, **tshih** 七.
Eight, **pah** 八.
Nine, °**kyeu** 九.
Ten, **zeh** 十.

From ten to twenty the numerals are formed by adding the digits after ten.

Eleven, **zeh-ih** 十一.
Twelve, **zeh-nyi**° 十二, etc.
Fifteen, **zeh-°ng**, pronounced °**so-°ng** 十五.
Twenty, **nyan**°. (In speaking of the day of the month **nyi°-seh** is used) 念, 二十.
Thirty, **san-seh** 三十. (Lit. three tens. The Z sound in zeh becomes S when preceded by another word.)

Forty, **s°-seh** 四十.
Fifty, °**ng-seh** 五十.
Sixty, **lok-seh** 六十.
Seventy, **tshih-seh** 七十.
Eighty, **pah-seh** 八十.
Ninety, °**kyeu-seh** 九十
One Hundred, **ih pak** 一百.

The intervening numbers between twenty and thirty, etc., are formed regularly by adding the digits to the decimals. Thus Twenty-one is ***nyan°-ih.*** Thirty-one, is ***san-seh-ih***, etc.

Thirty-five is pronounced ***san-°so-°ng.***

In using the numeral with the noun, the classifier of the noun is introduced between the numeral and the noun. Thus "Four men" is ***s°-kuh nyung*** (四个人) not ***s° nyung.*** "Six chairs" is ***lok tsak iui°-°ts*** (六隻椅子) not ***lok iui°-°ts.***

In speaking of a thing well understood the noun is often omitted, and we have simply the numeral with the classifier, as ***lok kuh, tshih tsak,*** etc.

## VOCABULARY.

A cow, **ih tsak nyeu** 一隻牛.

A native, **ih kuh °pung-di°-nyung** 一个本地人.

A foreigner, **ih kuh °nga-kok-nyung,** 一个外國人. (Literally, outside kingdom man).

A large box or trunk, **ih tsak siang-°ts** 一隻箱子.

A small box, **ih tsak ‘ah-°ts** 一隻匣子.

A fan, **ih °po sen°-°ts** 一把扇子.

A broom, **ih °po °sau-°tseu** 一把掃帚.

A tea pot, **ih °po dzo-‘oo** 一把茶壺.

To be, is, are, **°z** 是.

## EXERCISES.

(Translate into English.)

(1). °Ngoo iau° san tsak siang-°ts. (2). °Di °po sen°-°ts °z noong°-kuh. (3). Yi kuh ‘eu-°ts °yeu ih tsak ‘ah-°ts. (4). °Ngoo kuh sien-sang iau° ih °po dzo-‘oo. (5). San-seh-ih tsak yang °z yi kuh. (6). Nyan°-tshih tsak nyeu °z yi kuh. (7). I-kuh °nga-kok-nyung °yeu °liang tsak iui°-°ts. (8). San-seh, °z san kuh zeh. (9). Ih pak, °z zeh kuh zeh. (10). °So-°ng kuh nyung °yeu °so-°ng tsak de-°ts. (11). Sien-sang °z °pung-di°-nyung, °ngoo °z °nga-kok-nyung. (12). Yoong°-nyung iau° ih °po °sau-°tseu.

(一) 我要三隻箱子
(二) 第把扇子是儂个
(三) 伊个兒子有一隻匣子
(四) 我个先生要一把茶壺
(五) 三十一隻羊是伊个
(六) 念七隻牛是伊个
(七) 伊个外國人有兩隻椅子
(八) 三十是三个十
(九) 一百是十个十
(十) 十五个人有十五隻檯子
(十一) 先生是本地人我是外國人
(十二) 用人要一把掃箒

(Translate into Chinese).

(1). He wants three tea pots. (2). Four pupils want four fans. (3). This large box is my friend's. (4). He has thirty knives. (5). These five dollars are the pupils'. (6). The teacher has twenty-five pupils. (7).

These two fans are his. (8). That small box is the foreigner's. (9). Six tens are sixty. (10). My friend has five children, three sons and two daughters.

(一) 伊要三把茶壺　(二) 四个學生子要四把扇子
(三) 第隻箱子是我个朋友个　(四) 伊有三十把刀
(五) 第个五塊洋錢是學生子个　(六) 先生有念五个學生子
(七) 第个兩把扇子是伊个　(八) 伊隻匣子是外國人个
(九) 六个十是六十　(十) 我个朋友有五个小囝三个兒子兩个囡

NOTE. *'Ah-°ts* is a small box in distinction for *Siang-°ts*, a large box, but as will be seen later the adjectives for large and small may also be used with both of these words.

## LESSON IV.

### Adjectives.

Certain words in Chinese are distinctly used as adjectives, but many other words, such as nouns, verbs and adverbs may be used to qualify nouns. In the expression ***dok su-nyung*** (讀書人), meaning "a scholar," we have the verb ***dok*** (讀), "to read," and the noun ***su*** (書), "book," qualifying ***nyung*** (人) "man;" the whole expression being literally "the reading-book-man."

Adjectives may be compared as follows: ***°tien*** (點) is added after the adjective to make the comparative degree, and ***°ting*** (頂) is placed before the adjective to form the superlative degree. Thus, Positive Degree, "Good," is ***°hau*** (好). Comparative Degree, "Better," is ***°hau °tien*** (好點). Superlative Degree, "Best," is ***°ting °hau*** (頂好).

There are, however, many other ways of expressing the Superlative. Thus we may have ***°hau-le-°si*** (好來死), which is literally "good-come death," that is, "good to the death." This is a very frequent expression.

We have also ***tsoe °hau*** (最好) or ***juh °hau*** (極好). Very good is usually ***'man °hau*** (蠻好).

The adjective ***°hau*** (好) has a very wide use. Everything that is good, suitable, correct or proper may be said to be ***°hau*** (好).

VOCABULARY.

Good, **°hau** 好.
Bad, **cheu** (𣜿). More often **veh °hau** (勿好). **Veh** means not.
Cold, **°lang** 冷.
Hot, **nyih** 熱.
White, **bak** 白.
Black, **huh** 黑.
Large, **doo°** 大.

Small, °siau 小.

A scholar, **ih kuh dok-su-nyung** 一个讀書人.

A dog, **ih tsak °keu** 一隻狗.

Water. °s 水. (Generally used without a classifier).

A horse, **ih tsak °mo** (一隻馬). (匹) **phih** is sometimes used as the classifier of horse.

***°Pung*** (本) is the classifier for book.

A book, **ih °pung su** 一本書.

***Diau*** (條) is the classifier used with long, winding or limber objects.

A bridge, **ih diau jau** 一條橋.

A street, **ih diau ka** 一條街.

A road, **ih diau loo°** 一條路.

To read, to study, **dok** 讀.

To come, **le** 來.

To go, **chi°** 去

## EXERCISES.

(Translate into English).

(1). °Di-tsak °keu °z ‘hau kuh. (2) °Ngoo iau° dok su. (3). °Ngoo iau ‘lang ‘s. (4) °Di-tsak yang °z huh kuh. (5). I-tsak nyeu °z bak kuh. (6). I-kuh °pung-di°-nyung °yeu ‘liang tsak huh kuh °mo. (7). °Ngoo ‘yeu ih kuh bang-°yeu iau° le. (8). Yi kuh sien-sang iau° chi°. (9). °Di-kuh °s °z nyih kuh. (10). °Di-diau jau °z doo° kuh. (11) °Di-kuh ih diau ka °z ‘siau kuh. (12). °Di-kuh ih diau loo° °z veh ‘hau. (13). I-‘pung su °z sien-sang kuh, °di-‘pung su °z °ngoo kuh. (14). °Di-tsak de-°ts °z °siau ‘tien. (15). °Di-tsak zaung °z °ting doo°.

(一) 第隻狗是好个

(二) 我要讀書

(三) 我要冷水

(四) 第隻羊是黑个

(五) 伊隻牛是白个

(六) 伊个本地人有兩隻黑个馬

(七) 我有一个朋友要來

(八) 伊个先生要去

(九) 第个水是熱个

(十) 第條橋是大个

(十一) 第个一條街是小个

(十二) 第个一條路是勿好

(十三) 伊本書是先生个第本書是我个

(十四) 第隻檯子是小點

(十五) 第隻牀是頂大

(Translate into Chinese.)

(1) These five oranges are bad. (2). The teacher wishes me to study (3). The native's cows are good. (4). I have a white bird. (5). I want warm water. (6). The dog is very black. (7). That bed is smaller. (8).

This box is larger. (9). The tea pot is very white. (10). My teacher will come. (11). The foreigner will go. (12). I want a large dog.

(一) 第个五隻橘子是勿好　　(二) 先生要我讀書
(三) 本地人个牛是好个　　(四) 我有一隻白个鳥
(五) 我要熱水　　(六) 一隻狗是黑得極
(七) 一隻牀是小點　　(八) 第隻箱子是大點
(九) 一把茶壺是蠻白　　(十) 我个先生要來
(十一) 一个外國人要去　　(十二) 我要大个一隻狗

NOTES. (1). Adjectives generally take *kuh* after them; the kuh 个 standing between the adjective and the noun. In some cases the kuh is omitted, as in the expression °*lang* °*s* (冷水), "cold water." We do not say °*lang kuh* °*s*.

(2). *Dok-su* (讀書) is the common expression for "to study."

(3). In such a sentence as "I want warm water" the °*ngoo* (我) may be omitted. In speaking to a servant one would say *iau*° *nyih* °*s* (要熱水), "I want hot water."

## LESSON V.

### Interrogatives, and Negatives.

***Va***° (呀) is used as the sign of a direct question, expecting the answer "yes" or "no." It is added at the end of the sentence. Thus ***°di-kuh °z noong° kuh va°?*** (第个是儂个呀) means, "is this yours?" ***°Di kuh °hau va°?*** (第个好呀) means, "is this good?" (the verb °*z* being omitted). The Chinese do not use a rising inflection of the voice to indicate that a question is being asked.

***Meh*** is used for asking a question when the action is presumed to have been completed. Thus ***van° chuh meh?*** (飯喫沒) means, "have you eaten your rice?" or "have you dined?" ***Sien-sang chi° meh?*** (先生去沒) means, "has the teacher gone?"

***Nyi*** (呢) is used for asking a question implying the alternative. Thus ***noong° chi° nyi veh chi°?*** (儂去呢勿去) means, "are you going or not going?" ***Noong° le nyi veh le?*** (儂來呢勿來) means, "are you coming or not coming?"

***Nyi*** (呢) is also used in a question expecting a negative answer, but the explanation of this must be reserved until later.

"Who" is ***sa°*** (啥). In this sense it is always joined to the noun ***nyung*** (人). Thus ***sa° nyung?*** (啥人) means, "who?" Pidgin English, "who man?"

***Sa°*** (啥) is also used in the sense of "what." It sometimes precedes the noun as ***sa° sang-i°?*** (啥生意). "what business?" In a sentence like "what do you want," it follows the verb. Thus ***noong° iau° sa°?*** (儂要啥). Literally, "you want what?"

***Sa°*** is also used with ***va°*** in the sense of "any," in asking a question. Thus ***noong° iau° sa° va°?*** (儂要啥陌) means, "do you want anything?" ***°Yeu sa° nyung iau° chi° va°?*** (有啥人要去陌 means, "does any one wish to go?" ***Noong° °yeu sa° doong dien va°?*** (儂有啥銅錢陌) means, "have you any cash?"

Which is ***°a-°li*** (那裡). It is always used with numeral and classifier. Thus ***°a-°li ih kuh nyung?*** (那裡一个人) means, "which man?" ***°A-°li ih diau loo°?*** (那裡一條路) means, "which road?" ***°A-°li ih °pung su?*** (那裡一本書) means, "which book?" ***°A-°li °liang °po tau?*** (那裡兩把刀) means, "which two knives?" When the subject is understood about which you are conversing, the noun may be omitted, and ***°a-°li*** with the numeral and the classifier are sufficient. Thus in speaking of roads ***°a-°li ih diau?*** would be enough.

"No" or "not" is expressed by ***'veh*** (勿). Thus ***yi 'veh iau° chi°*** (伊勿要去) means, "he does not wish to go."

***M-meh*** (嘸沒) is used in the sense of "not any" in answering a question asking whether you have any, thus ***noong° °yeu sa° yang-dien va°?*** (儂有啥洋錢陌) "have you any dollars?", the answer might be ***m-meh.***

Sometimes ***m-sa°*** (嘸啥) is used in answering questions in the negative. Thus ***noong° °yeu sa° tsoo° va°?*** (儂有啥做陌) "have you anything to do?" (Have you any employment?) The answer might be ***m-sa° tsoo°*** (嘸啥做) "not anything to do."

No one is ***m-sa°-nyung*** (嘸啥人). Thus ***°yeu sa° nyung le va°?*** (有啥人來陌), "has any one come?" The answer might be ***m-sa°-nyung*** (嘸啥人).

## VOCABULARY.

Rice (cooked), **van°** 飯.

A hat, cap or bonnet, **ih °ting mau°-°ts** 一頂帽子 or **ih tsak mau°-°ts** 一隻帽子.

A carpenter, **ih kuh mok-ziang°** 一个木匠. Lit. Wood worker.

A hand, **ih tsak °seu** 一隻手.

A foot, **ih tsak kyak** 一隻脚

***Kung*** (根) is the classifier denoting objects long and generally stiff.

A cane or stick, **ih kung °baung** 一根棒.

***Zoo°*** (座) is the classifier for hills and buildings.

A house, **ih zoo° vaung-°ts** 一座房子. (Sometimes **ih zak vaung-°ts** 一宅).

***Sen°*** is the classifier for broad objects.

A door, **ih sen° mung** 一扇門.

To eat, eats, eat, **chuh** 吃.

To invite, invites, invite, **°tshing** 請. (Also used in the sense of please, when making a request of any one).

To take, **tan** (担) or **nau** (拿).

To call, calls, call, **kyau°** 叫.

To open, opens, open, **khe** 開.

To shut, shuts, shut, **kwan** 關

To do, does, perform, make, **tsoo°** 做.

To enter, enters, come in, **tsing°** 進.

## EXERCISES.

(To be translated into English).

(1). I-kuh sien-sang van° chuh meh? (2). °Ngoo iau° °tshing ih we° sien-sang. (3). Khe khe mung. (4). °Di-kuh kyau° sa°? (5). Kwan mung. (6). °Di-°pung su sa° nyung tan le kuh? (7). °'A-°li ih kung °baung °z noong° kuh? (8). °'A-°li ih zoo° vaung-°ts °z yi-kuh? (9). Sa° nyung tan chi° kuh? (10). Nyung °yeu °liang tsak °seu, °liang tsak kyak. (11). Noong° °yeu sa° sang-i° tsoo° va°? (12). Ngoo m-sa° sang-i° tsoo°. (13). Noong° kyau° sa°? (14). °Yeu sa° nyung tsing° le va°? m-sa° nyung. (15). Noong° mau°-°ts °yeu va°? m-meh.

(一) 伊个先生飯喫末
(二) 我要請一位先生
(三) 開開門
(四) 第个叫啥
(五) 關門
(六) 第本書啥人担來个
(七) 那裡一根棒是儂个
(八) 那裡一座房子是伊个
(九) 啥人担去个
(十) 人有兩隻手兩隻脚
(十一) 儂有啥生意做陌
(十二) 我嘸啥生意做
(十三) 儂叫啥
(十四) 有啥人進來陌，嘸啥人
(十五) 儂帽子有陌，嘸沒

(To be translated into Chinese).

(1). Have the children eaten their rice? (2). Which cow is yours? (3). Which bird is black? (4). Bring the hot water. (5). Bring the boiling water. (6) Please come in. (7). Who did it? (8). Who brought it? (9). Who took it away? (10). Who wants it? (11). Who entered? (12). Who opened the door? (13). Who shut the door? (14). Which table is yours? (15). What do you want? (16). Have you anything to eat? (17). I have nothing to eat. (18). Have you any oranges? (19). I have. (20). I have none.

(一) 小囡飯喫沒
(二) 那裡一隻牛是儂个
(三) 那裡一隻鳥是黑个
(四) 担熱水來
(五) 担開水來
(六) 請進來

(七) 啥人做个　　(八) 啥人担來个

(九) 啥人担去个　　(十) 啥人要个

(十一) 啥人進來个　　(十二) 啥人開門

(十三) 啥人關門　　(十四) 那裡一隻櫈子是儂个

(十五) 儂要啥　　(十六) 儂有啥喫陌

(十七) 嘸啥喫　　(十八) 儂有啥橘子陌

(十九) 有个　　(二十) 嘸沒

NOTES. (1). Note the difference between °*tshing* (請), *kyau*° (叫) and *han*° (喊). °*Tshing* is used in speaking to an equal or to a superior. *Kyau*° in speaking to a servant. *Han*° is even more curt than *kyau*°. Thus °*tshing yi le* (請伊來) means, "invite him to come," and is the polite form of speech if you wish an equal to come to you. *Kyau*° *yi le* (叫伊來) or °*han yi le* (喊伊來) would be used if you tell some one to call your servant or a workman to you.

(2). Notice the repetition of the *khe* (開) in the third sentence of the first exercise. This makes it more emphatic.

(3). The verbs *tan* (担) "take" and *le* (來) "come" are often used together in the sense of "bring." Literally "take-come." So also with *tan* (担) and *chi*° (去), this means, "Take away." Literally "Take-go." Sometimes the *tan* and the *le*, and the *tan* and the *chi*° are separated from one another by other words in the sentence. Thus *tan su le* (担書來) means "Bring the books." The above remarks also hold true of *nau*.

(4). In the sixth sentence of the first exercise the words °*di*-°*pung su* stand first. This is because they are emphatic. It is difficult to give any hard and fast rule in regard to the order of words in a Chinese sentence, but generally speaking, we may say that the most emphatic word is placed first. In this sentence it is the *book* which is being talked about, and so it occurs first.

(5). The words in the fifth sentence of the first exercise would only be addressed to a servant or to a child. "What are you called?" means, "what is your name?" not "what is your surname?" In polite phraseology, in speaking to a person the pronoun *no ng*° is never employed. The third person is used instead of the second. To ask your teacher his name, you would say *Tsung sing*°*?* (尊姓), which means, "what is your honorable name?" (surname). If you wish to inquire further as to his other name, you would say °*tshing kyau*° *da*° *'au ?* (請叫大號), which means, "please tell me your great official name?" The requirements of etiquette as to the use of words will be explained later somewhat fully.

(6). In the fifth sentence of the second exercise, the expression boiling water is used. For this the words *khe* (開) "open," and °*s* (水) "water" are used. It signifies that boiling water is *open water* on account of the bubbles which proceed from it.

# LESSON VI.

## Some remarks on the Verb.

In a monosyllabic language like the Chinese the words themselves are never inflected, and therefore the Moods and Tenses of the Verbs are formed by the addition of auxiliary words to mark the change of meaning.

We will take the verb ***chuh*** (吃) to illustrate.

INDICATIVE MOOD.

*Present Tense, Simple Form*, I eat, **°ngoo chuh 我吃.**

*Present Tense. Continuous*, I am eating, **°ngoo leh-°li chuh 我垃裏吃, °ngoo la° chuh 我拉吃.**

*Past Tense, Simple Form*, I ate, **°ngoo chuh kuh 我吃个.**

*Past Tense, Continuous*, I was eating, **°ngoo leh-la° chuh 我垃拉吃.**

*Past Tense, Emphatic Form*, I did eat, **°ngoo °z chuh kuh 我是吃个.**

*Perfect Tense*, I have eaten, **°ngoo chuh tse 我吃哉. °ngoo chuh la° tse 我吃拉哉, °ngoo chuh koo° tse 我吃過哉.**

*Past Perfect*, I had eaten, **ngoo °i kyung chuh tse 我已經吃哉, °ngoo °i-kyung chuh la° tse 我已經吃拉哉, °ngoo °i-kyung chuh koo° hyih tse 我已經吃過歇哉.**

*Future Tense*, I will or shall eat, **°ngoo iau° chuh 我要吃.**

The *Future Perfect Tense* cannot be expressed directly.

The only change for the different persons in the above will be in the use of the pronouns of the different persons.

IMPERATIVE MOOD.

Eat, **chuh** (吃), **chuh meh tse** 吃末哉).

PARTICIPLES.

Present, Eating, **chuh** (吃), Past, Having eaten, **chuh-°ts** (吃仔).

A few words of explanation are necessary. The use of ***leh-°li*** and ***leh-la°*** are a little difficult to understand at first. As stated ***°ngoo leh-°li chuh*** (我垃裏吃) means, "I am eating." If, however, a third person asked your servant ***Sien-sang van° chuh meh?*** (先生飯吃末), "Has the Teacher eaten his rice?" the servant would answer, if you were still eating, ***yi leh-la° chuh*** (伊垃拉吃) meaning "he is eating." If you yourself said ***ngoo leh-la° chuh***, it would mean, "I was eating." In the Perfect Tense the word ***koo°*** (過) means literally to pass over. In the Past Perfect the words ***°i-kyung*** 已經 mean "already."

The real force of ***leh-°li*** (垃裏) is "here," and the real force of ***leh-la°*** (垃拉) is "there."

There are a great many ways of expressing completed action in Chinese. These will be explained later. In this lesson one of the most common will be explained. It is by the use of the adjective °***hau*** after the verb. Thus ***chuh °hau tse*** (吃好哉) means, "I have finished eating." ***Dok °hau tse*** (讀好哉) means, "I have finished reading."

°***Hau*** (好), "good," is also used before the verb to qualify it. Thus we have the expressions °***hau chuh kuh*** (好吃个) meaning "good to eat." °***Hau dok kuh*** (好讀个), "Easy to read." °***Hau tsoo° kuh*** (好做个) "Easy to do," etc.

VOCABULARY.

To arrive, **tau°** 到.
To give by hand, **peh** 撥.
To buy, **°ma** 買.
To speak, **wo°** 話.
To burn or cook, **sau** 燒.
To learn, **'auh** 學
A table boy, **ih kuh si°-tse°** 一个細崽.
A horse boy or coachman, **ih kuh °mo-foo** 一个馬夫.
A pear, **ih tsak sang-li** 一隻生梨.
A peach, **ih tsak dau-°ts** 一隻桃子.
A tailor, **ih kuh ze-voong** 一个裁縫.
China or Chinese, **Tsoong-kok** (中國), Lit. Middle Kingdom.
Shanghai, **°Zaung-°he** 上海.

***Jien°*** is the classifier denoting garments, pieces of baggage and merchandize, and also an affair.

A garment, **ih jien° i-zaung** 一件衣裳.

***Saung*** (雙) is the classifier denoting pairs.

A pair of shoes, **ih saung 'a-°ts** 一雙鞋子.
A pair of socks or stockings, **ih saung mah** 一雙襪.
New, **sing** 新.
Old, **°jeu** 舊, or **°lau** 老. (Of persons, only **°lau** is used.) **°Lau** is old as to time. **°Jeu** generally means worn out, in bad condition. (**°Lau** is often used as a title of respect, meaning venerable).

EXERCISES.

(Translate into English.)

(1). °Ngoo iau° 'auh wo° tsoong-kok wo°. (2). °Ngoo iau° 'auh dok tsoong-kok su. (3). Noong° iau° dok su va°? (4). °I-tsak siang-°ts tan chi° meh? (5). Kyau° yi chi° meh tse. (6). °I-kuh °mo-foo iau° °ma san tsak °mo. (7). °Ngoo peh yi °ng kwhe° yang-dien kyau° yi chi° °ma ih tsak yang. (8). °Ngoo °i-kyung wo° koo° tse. (9). °Zaung-°he tau° koo° hyih meh? (10). Tau° koo° hyih tse. (11). °Ngoo kuh i-zaung ze-voong tsoo° °hau meh? (12). Yi leh-la° tsoo°. (13). Noong° chuh °hau-°ts van° iau° tsoo° sa°? (14). Chuh ᶜhau-°ts van° iau° dok su. (15). °Ngoo iau° chi° °ma ih saung sing kuh °a-°ts. (16). Van° sau °hau meh? (17). Sau ᶜhau tse. (18). °Lau sien-sang kyauᵓ siᵓ-tseᶜ chi° °ma sang-li. (19). Kyau° yi le tsooᵓ meh tse. (20). °Di-kuh tsooᵓ koo° hyih meh ? Tsoo° koo hyih tse.

(一) 我要學話中國話
(二) 我要學讀中國書
(三) 儂要讀書㖸
(四) 伊隻箱子担去末
(五) 叫伊去末哉
(六) 伊个馬夫要買三隻馬
(七) 我撥伊五塊洋錢叫伊去買一隻羊
(八) 我已經話過哉
(九) 上海到過歇末
(十) 到過歇哉
(十一) 我个衣裳裁縫做好末
(十二) 伊垃拉做
(十三) 儂喫好仔飯要做啥
(十四) 喫好仔飯要讀書
(十五) 我要去買一雙新个鞋子
(十六) 飯燒好末
(十七) 燒好哉
(十八) 老先生叫西崽去買生梨
(十九) 叫伊來做末哉
(二十) 第个做過歇末,做過歇哉

(Translate into Chinese).

(1). I have already read this book. (2). Do you want to buy a dog? (3). When I arrive at Shanghai I wish to buy an umbrella. (4). Has my friend come? (5). I gave him four dollars and told him to buy a table. (6). The teacher is eating his dinner. (7). I have already given him ten dollars. (8). Come along. (9). When the Teacher has come, call me. (10). Have you ever eaten Chinese peaches? (11). I have eaten them. (12). Those pupils are studying Chinese. (13). The foreign teacher is learning to speak Chinese.

(一) 第本書我已經讀過哉
(二) 一隻狗要買㖸
(三) 到仔上海我要買一把傘
(四) 我个朋友來末
(五) 我撥伊四塊洋錢叫伊去買一隻檯子
(六) 先生垃拉吃飯
(七) 我已經撥伊十塊洋錢
(八) 來末哉
(九) 先生來仔來叫我
(十) 中國桃子儂喫過歇末
(十一) 喫過歇哉
(十二) 伊个學生子垃拉讀中國書
(十三) 外國先生垃拉學中國話

NOTES. (1). China is known by many different names. The most common is *Tsoong-kok* (中國). We also have *Da° tshing kok* (大清國), "the great pure kingdom." *Tsoong-wo* (中華), "the middle civilized kingdom," and *Zeh pah °sang* (十八省) "the eighteen provinces" (used of China Proper, without its dependencies). A modern name, now much in vogue is *Ts-na* (支那). It represents the sound of China, and is much used by the reform party.

(2). In the ninth sentence of the first exercise the force of the *Tau°* (到) is visiting the place for the first time.

(3). In the twentieth sentence of the first exercise the meaning, is "Have you ever done this before?"

(4). In the ninth sentence of the second exercise, you use the past participle, *le ts* (來仔). After it *meh* (末) is often used for euphony, thus the sentence would be *Sien-sang le ts meh, le kyau° °ngoo* 先生來仔末來叫我.

(5). In the twelfth sentence of the second exercise *su* (書) is added after *tsoong-kok* (中國). The meaning is "The pupils are studying Chinese books."

(6). In the thirteenth sentence of the second exercise, the foreign teacher would be *nga°-kok sien sang* (外國先生). *Nga°-kok* is used as an adjective.

---

# LESSON VII.

## Prepositions and Postpositions, and Common Connectives.

The words expressing the relations of nouns to one another are placed, some of them before and some of them after the governed substantive. 'At' or 'to' is expressed by ***la°*** **(拉)**. Thus ***°ngoo peh la° yi*** **(我撥拉伊)**, "I gave it to him."

'To' or 'towards' in the sense of direction is expressed by ***tau°*** (到). Thus: ***°ngoo iau° tau° °Zaung-°he chi°*** **(我要到上海去)**, "I wish to go to Shanghai." 'To' or 'towards' is also expressed by ***te°*** **對**, as in the expression to speak to a person. Thus ***°ngoo te° yi wo°*** **(我對伊話)**, "I said to him." 'From' is expressed by ***dzoong*** **(從)**. Thus: ***°ngoo dzoong °Zaung-°he le*** **(我從上海來)**, "I came from Shanghai."

'With' is expressed by ***tah*** **搭** or ***doong*** **同**. Thus: ***°ngoo tah yi bak wo°*** **(我搭伊白話)** or ***°ngoo doong yi bak wo°*** **(我同伊白話)**, "I talked with him."

'Instead of' is ***thi°*** **(替)** or ***°de thi°*** (代替). Thus: ***°ngoo °de thi° yi tsoo°*** **(我代替伊做)**, "I do it instead of him." The idea of doing it for a person is expressed by ***theh*** (忒) Thus: ***°ngoo theh yi tsoo°*** **(我忒伊做)**, "I will do it for him."

'In' is expressed by placing ***la°*** (拉) or ***leh-la°*** **(垃拉)** before the noun and ***°li*** **(裏)** or ***°li-hyang°*** **(裏向)** after the noun. Thus: ***la° vaung-°ts °li*** **(拉房子裏)** means, "In the house." ***La° siang-°ts °li*** **(拉箱子裏)** means "In the box."

'On' is expressed by placing ***la°*** or ***leh-la°*** before the noun and ***laung°*** **(上)** after it. Thus: ***la° loo° laung°*** **(拉路上)** means, "On the road." ***La° de-°ts laung°*** **(拉檯子上)** means, "On the table."

***Nga°*** **(外)** means "out." The usual expression is ***nga°-deu*** **(外頭)** "outside." It follows the noun.

Other prepositions will be introduced later.

The most common connective is °*lau* (咾) and corresponds quite closely to our use of "and." Thus °*ngoo iau*° °*ma* ‘*a*-°*ts* °*lau mah* (我要買鞋子咾韈) means, "I wish to buy shoes and stockings." Nouns are often placed beside one another without any connective between them.

'Also' is °‘*a-z* (也是) or ‘*a* (也). Thus: *di-kuh* °‘*a-z hau kuh* (第个也是好个) means, "This also is good." °*Ngoo* °‘*a iau*° °*ma* (我也要買) means, "I also wish to buy." °*Ngoo wan iau*° °*ma* (我還要買) means, "I still wish to buy."

VOCABULARY.

A city, **ih zoo° dzung 一座城.**
A school, **ih kuh ‘auh-daung 一个學堂.**
A hat, **ih °ting mau°-°ts 一頂帽子.**
A head, **ih kuh deu 一个頭.**
A foot, **ih tsak kyak 一隻脚.**
A hand, **ih tsak seu 一隻手.**
A heart, **ih kuh sing 一个心.**
Father, **ya 爺.**
Mother, **nyang 娘**
A body, **ih kuh sung-°thi 一个身體.**
Home, **ok-°li 屋裏.**
To sit, **°zoo 坐.**
To live, dwell, **dzu° 住.**
To wear, **tsak 着.**
To place, **faung° (放), °pa (擺).**
To use, **yoong° 用.**
To wear on the head, **ta° 戴.**

EXERCISES.

(Translate into English.)

(1). Sa° nyung peh la° yi kuh. (2). Yi kuh ya peh la yi kuh. (3). °Di-kuh iau° tan tau° ok-°li chi°. (4). Mau°-°ts iau° ta° la deu laung°. (5). °A-°ts iau° tsak la° kyak laung°. (6). I-zaung iau° tsak la° sung laung°. (7). Sien-sang dzu° la° dzung° li° va? (8). ‘Auh sang-ts iau° tau° ‘auh-daung °li chi°. (9). °Ngoo kyau° si-tse° °pa °ngoo kuh i-zaung la° siang-°ts °li. (10). Sien-sang dzoong nga°-kok tau° Tsoong-kok le. (11). Sien-sang kyau° °siau-noen yoong° sing dok su. (12). Veh iau° °zoo la° zaung laung°, iau° °zoo la° iui°-°ts laung°. (13). Su faung° la° de-°ts laung°. (14). Bang-°yeu °i-kyung le koo° ts °lau chi° tse. (15). Sang-li °z °hau chuh kuh, dau-ts °‘a-°z °hau chuh kuh. (16). °Di-kuh °siau-noen ‘m ya nyang kuh. (17). Sa° nyung la° ‘auh-daung °li? Sien-sang tah-ts ‘auh-sang-°ts. (18). Noong° wan iau° °ma sa° va°? ’Veh iau°.

(一) 啥人搿拉伊个
(二) 伊个爺搿拉伊个
(三) 第个要担到屋裏去
(四) 帽子要戴拉頭上
(五) 鞋子要着拉脚上
(六) 衣裳要着拉身上
(七) 先生住拉城裏陌
(八) 學生子要到學堂裏去

(九) 我叫細崽擺我个衣裳拉箱子裏

(十) 先生從外國到中國來

(十一) 先生叫小囡用心讀書

(十二) 勿要坐拉牀上要坐拉椅子上

(十三) 書放拉檯子上

(十四) 朋友已經來過仔咾去哉

(十五) 生梨是好吃个桃子也是好吃个

(十六) 第个小囡嘸爺娘个

(十七) 啥人拉學堂裏，先生搭仔學生子

(十八) 儂還要買啥陌，勿要

(Translate into Chinese.)

(1). I placed the knives and the forks on the table. (2). Who lives in this house? Mr. Tsang. (3). The father and mother wish the child to study. (4). Do you live in the city or out of the city? (5). The cat is on the table. (6). Take it in your hand. (7). Keep it in mind (place it on your heart). (8) The heart is in the body. (9). That child has no shoes on his feet. (10). That man has no hat on his head. (11). To whom do the cows and sheep belong? (12). When you have put on your clothes, come and eat. (13). The horse boy wishes to feed the horse also. (14). You and I are friends. (15). Have you ever been to foreign countries?

(一) 刀叉我放拉檯子上

(二) 啥人住拉第个房子裏，張先生

(三) 爺娘要第个小囡讀書

(四) 儂住拉城裏呢城外

(五) 貓拉檯子上

(六) 担拉手裏

(七) 放拉心上

(八) 心垃拉身體裏

(九) 伊个小囡脚上嘸沒鞋子

(十) 伊个人頭上嘸沒帽子

(十一) 牛咾羊是啥人个

(十二) 着好仔衣裳咾來吃

(十三) 馬夫也要撥馬吃

(十四) 儂搭仔我是朋友

(十五) 外國去過歇末

NOTES. (1). There are many different ways of saying father and mother, but these will have to be explained later.

(2). *Laung°* is really the character *°Zaung*. It has the latter sound when used in the adverb "above," which is *°Zaung-deu*, 上頭.

(3). The seventh sentence of the first exercise is correct grammatically, but would not be used in polite speech. The usual way of asking a gentleman where he lives is to say *Sien-sang °foo laung° la° °'a-°li*, 先生府上拉哪裏.

(4). In the eleventh sentence of the first exercise the expression *yoong° sing* means to be diligent, or to pay attention.

NOTES. (5). In the second sentence of the second exercise Mr. Tsang is translated *Tsang Sien-sang*. *Tsang* is a common surname in Chinese. The *Sien-sang* follows the surname.

(6). Doong (同) is generally used with *ih-dau* (一淘). *Doong* coming before the noun, and *ih-dau* after it. Thus °*Ngoo doong* °*ngoo kuh bung-yeu ih-dau tau*° °*Zaung-*°*he chi*°.

# LESSON VIII.

## Potential and Subjunctive Moods, and some Interrogative Adverbs.

"May" or "can" is expressed by ***°khau-°i*** **(可以)**. Thus "I may or can eat" is ***°ngoo °khau-°i chuh*** **(我可以吃)**. When physical ability is implied ***nung-keu°*** **(能彀)** is frequently used. Thus "I have the physical ability to do," is ***°ngoo nung-keu° tsoo°*** **(我能彀做)**. When acquired ability is to be expressed ***we°*** **(會)** is generally used. Thus: "I have the ability to speak Chinese" is ***°ngoo we° wo° Tsoong-kok wo°*** **(我會話中國話)**.

The Subjunctive Mood is expressed exactly like the Indicative Mood except that some word meaning "If" is placed at the beginning of the clause, and that the particle ***meh*** **(末)** is generally placed at the end of the clause.

"If" is ***zak*** **(若)**, ***zak-s°*** **(若使)**, ***zak-zen*** **(若然)**, ***°thaung-zen*** **(倘然)**, ***°thaung-s°*** **(倘使)**. Thus "If I go, I will call you," is expressed ***zak zen° °ngoo chi° meh, °ngoo iau° kyau° noong°*** **(若然我去末我要叫儂)**.

Very often the word implying "If" is omitted at the beginning of the clause, and the condition is implied simply by the use of the ***meh*** **(末)** at the end of the clause. Thus: "When he has finished it, come and tell me" is ***yi tsoo° °hau meh, le te° °ngoo wo°*** **(伊做好末來對我話)**.

"How" is ***°na-nung*** **(那能)**. Thus "How do you know?" is ***°noong °na-nung °hyau-tuk?*** **(儂那能曉得)**.

"When" is ***°kyi-z*** **(幾時)** Thus "When did you come?" is ***noong° °kyi-z le kuh?*** **(儂幾時來个)**. "When did you arrive?" is ***noong° °kyi-z tau°?*** **(儂幾時到)**. Beginners in Chinese often make the mistake of using ***°kyi-z*** as the ordinary adverb of time. To express such a sentence as "When I come he will go," we say ***°ngoo le-ts meh yi iau° chi°*** **(我來仔末伊要去)**, the past participle being used, and ***meh*** implying that it is conditional. It is very bad to say ***°ngoo °kyi-z le, yi iau° chi°***. Let it be remembered that ***°kyi-z*** is only used in asking a question.

We have the ***°kyi-z*** used after the verb in such a sentence as ***noong° tau°-°ts °kyi-z tse?*** **(儂到仔幾時哉)** meaning, "How long since you arrived?" or ***yi chi°-°ts °kyi-z tse?*** **(伊去仔幾時哉)** meaning, "How long since he went?"

海上絲綢之路文獻集成 科技與文化編



## VOCABULARY.

To sell, **ma°** (**賣**) or **ma°-theh** (**賣脫**).

To see, **khoen°** (**看**) or **khoen°-kyien°** (seen) (**看見**).

To walk, **°tseu 走**.

To run, **bau 跑**.

To know, **°hyau-tuk 曉得**.

To know a person, **nyung°-tuk 認得**.

To understand, **°toong** (**懂**) or **ming-bak** (**明白**).

A pagoda, **ih zoo° thah 一座塔**.

A sedan chair, **ih °ting jau°-°ts 一頂轎子**.

A visitor or guest, **ih we° khak-nyung 一位客人**.

A doctor, **ih we° laung tsoong** (**一位郎中**) or **ih we i-sung** (**一位醫生**).

A grave mound, **ih kuh vung-san 一个墳山**.

A mouth, **ih kuh °kheu** (**一个口**) or **ih tsang °ts** (**一張嘴**).

A doorway, **ih kuh mung-°kheu** (Mouth of the door) (**一个門口**) or **mung-°kheu-deu** (**一个門口頭**).

An ear, **ih tsak °nyi-°too 一隻耳朶**.

A nose, **ih kuh bih-deu 一个鼻頭**.

An eye, **ih tsak °ngan-tsing 一隻眼睛**.

A face, **ih kuh mien°-khoong 一个面孔**.

***Boo*** (**部**) is the classifier used with carriages, and vehicles on wheels.

A carriage, **ih boo °mo-tsho 一部馬車**.

A Ric-sha, **ih boo toong-yang-tsho 一部東洋車**. (Lit. East of the Ocean carriage.) Japan is known as the land East of the Ocean, and ric-shas were first used there.

A wheelbarrow, **ih boo tsho-°ts** (**一部車子**) or **°siau-tsho** (**小車**).

Short, **°toen 短**.

Long, **dzang 長**.

Fast, **kwha° 快**.

Slow, **man° 慢**.

To-morrow, **ming-tsau 明朝**.

## EXERCISES.

(Translate into English).

(1). Noong° ming-bak va°? ‘Veh ming-bak. (2). Tsoong-kok wo°, noong° we° wo° va°? °Ngoo ‘veh we° wo°. (3). Tsoong-kok su noong° we° dok° va°? °Ngoo ‘veh we° dok. (4). °Tshing sien-sang ming-tsau le. (5). Noong° °kyi-z° khau-°i chi°? °Ngoo ming-tsau° khau-°i chi°. (6). Di tsak °mo veh nung-keu° bau le kwha°. (7). Zak-zen sien-sang le meh, noong° te° yi wo° °ngoo °Zaung-°he chi° tse. (8). Chi° kyau° ih boo toong-yang-tsho. (9). °Di zoo° thah noong° khoen°-kyien° hyih meh? (10). Mok-ziang° °zoo-°ts °siau tsho-°ts tau °Zaung-°he chi° tse. (11). °Di kuh nyung noong° nyung-°tuk °va? ‘Veh nyung-tuk. (12). Noong° °na-nung chi° kuh? °Ngoo °zoo °mo-tsho chi° kuh. (13). Iau° noong° chi° °tshing i-sung le. (14). °Tshing sien-sang wo° le man° tien. (15). Zah-zen sien-sang wo° le kwha° meh °ngoo ‘veh °toong.

(16). °Di kung °baung °z dzang kuh, °di °po tau °z °toen kuh. (17). Khak-nyung tau°-°ts mung-°kheu-deu iau° °tshing yi °li-hyang °zoo. (18). °I-kuh °siau-noen kuh mien°-khoong man °hau khoen°. (19). Nyung °yeu °liang tsak °nyi-°too, °liang tsak °ngan-tsing, ih kuh bih-deu, °lau ih tsang °ts. (20). °Di zoo° vaung-°ts °i-kyung ma° theh tse.

(一) 儂明白陌，勿明白 (二) 中國話儂會話陌，我勿會話
(三) 中國書儂會讀陌，我勿會讀 (四) 請先生明朝來
(五) 儂幾時可以去，我明朝可以去 (六) 箇隻馬勿能彀跑來快
(七) 若然先生來末儂對伊話我上海去哉 (八) 去叫一部東洋車
(九) 箇座塔儂看見歇末
(十) 木匠坐仔小車子到上海去哉 (十一) 箇个人儂認得陌，勿認得
(十二) 儂那能去个，我坐馬車去个 (十三) 要儂去請醫生來
(十四) 請先生話來慢點 (十五) 若然先生話來快末我勿懂
(十六) 箇根棒是長个，箇把刀是短个 (十七) 客人到仔門口頭要請伊裏向坐
(十八) 伊个小囝个面孔蠻好看
(十九) 人有兩隻耳朶，兩隻眼睛，一个鼻頭咾一張嘴 (二十) 箇座房子已經賣脫哉

(Translate into Chinese.)

(1). Please take a seat. (2). When will that teacher come? (3). He said he will come to-morrow. (4). Have you seen my dog? (5). Ask the visitor to come in. (6). The sheep is on the grave mound. (7). I wish to ride in a sedan chair, and go into the city. (8). When the doctor comes, come and call me. (9). Call two ric-shas. (10). How long have you been in China? (11). If men had no eyes they would not be able to see. (12). If the pupil is not diligent he will not be able to learn Chinese. (13). I do not know how to say this. (14). When will the doctor come? (15). To-morrow he will come. (16). The road to Shanghai is very long. (17). If you do not understand you can ask the teacher to speak more slowly. (18). The ears of that dog are very long. (19). The child runs very fast. (20). Do you know my friend? I do not.

(一) 請坐

(二) 伊个先生幾時要來

(三) 伊話伊明朝要來

(四) 我个一隻狗儂看見歇末

(五) 請客人進來

(六) 第隻羊拉墳山上

(七) 我要坐轎子到城裏去

(八) 醫生來仔末來叫我

(九) 去叫兩部東洋車

(十) 儂到仔中國幾時哉

(十一) 若然人嘸沒眼睛伊拉勿能彀看見

(十二) 若然學生子勿用心伊勿會學中國話

(十三) 第个我勿曉得那能話个

(十四) 醫生幾時要來

(十五) 伊明朝要來

(十六) 到上海路是蠻長

(十七) 若然儂勿懂末儂可以請先生話來慢點

(十八) 伊隻狗个耳朵是蠻長

(十九) 第个小囝跑來蠻快

(二十) 我个朋友儂認得陌，勿認得

NOTES. (1). In the sixth sentence of the first exercise, notice that the adjective *kwha°* is turned into an adverb by the *le* coming before it. Adjectives are often used with verbs in this way.

(2). In the twelfth sentence of the first exercise, notice the expression for travelling in a carriage. In Chinese you "sit a carriage."

(3). In the first sentence of the second exercise we have the usual polite expression for asking one to be seated *°Tshing °zoo*. This should be said as soon as a guest or stranger enters the room, but of course is not used in speaking to inferiors. In such cases it is enough to say *°zoo-°zoo* (坐坐).

(4). Notice the difference between *°ma* (買) to buy, and *ma°* (賣) to sell. To our ears the sounds are hard to distinguish. The only difference is in the tones.

---

## LESSON IX.

### The Use of Dzak, Reduplication of Verbs, Reflexive Pronouns.

In expressing the carrying of the action of the verb into effect ***dzak*** (着) is often used after it. Thus: ***zing-dzak*** (尋着) means that a thing has been actually found. ***Zing*** means to find. There are a great many active verbs which can take the ***dzak*** after them. For example we have ***tuh-dzak*** (得着), meaning a thing has been obtained. ***Tuh*** means to get. ***Bang°-dzak***(撞着) means a person or thing has been met. ***Bang°*** (撞) means to strike against.

Verbs are often repeated for emphasis. We have had an example of this in the expression ***°zoo °zoo***, meaning "sit down." Thus ***khoen° khoen°*** (看看) means "Look, look."

In many cases *ih* (一) is inserted between the verbs as ***khoen° ih khoen°***. In such cases the last verb is changed into a verbal noun. Literally it would be "Look a look."

The Reflexive Personal Pronouns hardly require any explanation. They are formed by adding ***z'-ka*** (自家) after the Personal Pronouns. Thus "I myself" would be ***°ngoo z°-ka*** (我自家). "You yourself" would be ***noong° z°-ka*** (儂自家) and so on for the rest.

## VOCABULARY.

To teach, **kau°** 教.
To write, **°sia** 寫.
To ask, **mung°** 問.
To pay, **foo°** 付.
To build, **°zau** 造.
To look for, **zing** 尋.
To hear, **thing** 聽 or **thing kyien°** (heard) 聽見.
To know a Chinese character, **suh** 識.
To strike against, **bang°** 搒.
To get, **tuh** 得.
A mason, **ih kuh nyi-°s ziang°** 一个泥水匠.
A water buffalo, **ih tsak °s-nyeu** 一隻水牛.
A dining table, **ih tsak chuh-van°-de-°ts** 一隻喫飯檯子.
An office desk, **ih tsak °sia-z°-de-°ts** 一隻寫字檯子, **ih tsak °sia-z'-de.**
A Chinese character, **ih kuh z°** 一个字.
A drawer of a table, **ih tsak tsheu-thi** 一隻抽屜.
An unmarried woman, **ih kuh °siau-tsia** 一个小姐.
Tea, **dzo** 茶
Now, **yien°-°dze** 現在.
Not yet, **'veh zung** 勿曾.
Still not yet, **wan 'veh zung** 還勿曾.
Why? **we° sa°** 爲啥 or **we° sa°-°lau** 爲啥咾.
Because, **iung-we°** 因爲 or **we°-ts** 爲之.

In using ***iung-we°*** the particle ***°lau*** (咾) is generally added at the end of the clause. Thus: "Why did you not go? Because I did not want to go" is ***noong° we°-°sa 'veh chi°? Iung we° °ngoo 'veh iau° chi° °lau*** 儂爲啥勿去,因爲我勿要去咾.

## EXERCISES.

(Translate into English.)

(1). °Tshing sien-sang kau° °ngoo dok Tsoong-kok su. (2). Yien°-°dze °ngoo iau° 'auh °sia Tsoong-kok z°. (3). Noong° °ma-°ts ih tsak °sia-z°-de, doong-dien foo° meh? 'Veh zung. (4). °Di kuh z°, °ngoo 'veh suh. (5). Zak-zen noong° 'veh suh meh °khau-°i mung° sien-sang. (6). Vaung-°ts °zau °hau meh? Wan 'veh zung. (7). °Ngoo kuh sen-°ts °tshing noong° theh °ngoo zing zing-khoen°. (8). Sen°-°ts °i-kyung zing-dzak tse. (9). Noong° we°-sa°-°lau 'veh zung chi°? Iung we° °ngoo iau° dok su °lau. (10). °Tshing sien-sang chuh dzo.

(11). °Tshing sien-sang yoong° dzo. (12). Zak-zen nyung m-meh nyi°-°too, yi-la ‘veh nung-keu° thing. (13). °Ngoo ‘veh zung tau° Tsoong-kok le, °s-nyeu ‘veh zung khoen°-kyieu° hyih. (14). Nyi-°s-ziang° bang°-dzak hyih meh ? ‘Veh zung. (15). °Sia-°z-de-°ts laung° kuh su °z sa° nyung kuh ? °Z °ngoo-z°-ka kuh. (16). °Ngoo kyau° noong° faung° °ngoo kuh i-zaung la tsheu-thi °li, noong° we°-sa° ‘veh zung faung° kuh ? (17). Chi° khoen° khoen° sien-sang le meh. (18). °Ngoo kuh san° noong° zing-dzak meh ? Zing ‘veh dzak. (19). Zak-zen m-meh sien-sang meh, noong° z°-ka °khau-°i dok su. (20). Iau° °ngoo foo° doong dien-meh, kyau° yi-la z°-ka le nau.

(一) 請先生教我讀中國書

(二) 現在我要學寫中國字

(三) 儂買仔一隻寫字檯銅錢付末，勿曾

(四) 第个字我勿識

(五) 若然儂勿識末可以問先生

(六) 房子造好末，還勿曾

(七) 我个扇子請儂忒我尋尋看

(八) 扇子已經尋着哉

(九) 儂爲啥咾勿曾去，因爲我要讀書咾

(十) 請先生吃茶

(十一) 請先生用茶

(十二) 若然人嘸沒耳朶，伊拉勿能殼聽

(十三) 我勿曾到中國來，水牛勿曾看見歇

(十四) 泥水匠搥着歇末，勿曾

(十五) 寫字檯子上个書是啥人个，是我自家个

(十六) 我叫儂放我个衣裳拉抽屜裏，儂爲啥勿曾放个

(十七) 去看看先生來末

(十八) 我个傘儂尋着末，尋勿着

(十九) 若然嘸沒先生末，儂自家可以讀書

(二十) 要我付銅錢末，叫伊拉自家來拿

(Translate into Chinese.)

(1). Why don't you pay it ? (2). Why do you do this ? (3). When will you do it ? (4). I don't want it now. (5). When did you go ? (6). I do not want to go now, but I will go to-morrow. (7). Does the teacher teach well ? (8). Does the pupil write well ? (9). Why do you not look for my fan ? Because I have already found it. (10). This carpenter can make a dining table. (11). Go, see if the Doctor has come. (12). They themselves said they wished to build a new house. (13). I told the table boy to go to the city and buy me four chairs, a trunk, a bed, and an office desk. (14). When the teacher comes, ask him please to be seated and to take some tea. (15). If one does not study he is unable to know characters. (16). My office desk has three drawers. (17). This unmarried girl also wishes to study. (18). Have you bought the apples? They cannot be obtained. (19). Do you know whether the guest has already arrived? I do not know. (20). Can you obtain these? They are unobtainable.

(一) 儂爲啥勿付个

(二) 第个儂爲啥做个

(三) 儂幾時要做个

(四) 現在勿要

(五) 儂幾時去个

(六) 現在勿要去，明朝要去

(七) 先生教來好陌

(八) 學生子寫來好陌

(九) 儂爲啥咾勿尋我个扇子，因爲已經尋着哉

(十) 第个木匠可以做一隻吃飯檯

(十一) 去看看醫生來末

(十二) 伊拉自家話，伊拉要造新个房子

(十三) 我叫細崽到城裏去，買四把椅子，一隻箱子，一隻牀咾一隻寫字檯

(十四) 先生來仔末請伊坐坐咾吃茶

(十五) 若然一个人勿讀書，伊勿會識字

(十六) 我个寫字檯有三隻抽屜

(十七) 第个小姐也要讀書

(十八) 苹果買好末，買勿着

(十九) 客人已經到儂曉得陌，我勿曉得

(二十) 第个儂可以得着陌，得勿着

NOTES. In the seventh sentence of the first exercise notice the *khoen°* after the reduplicated verb *zing*. This gives the force of try to look for it. "Look, look, see." *Khoen°* is used after many verbs in this way. Thus: *T'soo° tsoo° khoen°* 做做看 means "try to do it." *°Sia °sia khoen°* 寫寫看 means "try to write it." *Wo° wo° khoen°* 話話看 means, "try to say it."

(2). In the tenth and eleventh sentences of the first exercise we have two ways of asking a person to drink tea. The second is the polite form. Literally it means that you ask a person "to use tea."

(3). In the nineteenth sentence of the first exercise, notice the use of *meh* for euphony after sien-saung, and so also in the twentieth after *doong-dien*.

(4). In the eighteenth sentence of the first exercise, notice the way in which *'veh* comes between the *zing* and the *dzak*. This means "seek not find" or "it can not be found." So also in the second exercise in the eighteenth sentence "They cannot be obtained" should be translated *°ma-'veh dzak?* and in the twentieth sentence "They are unobtainable" should be *Tuh 'veh dzak.*

# LESSON X.

## Divisions of Time. More Adverbs.

"An hour" in Chinese is ***ih °tien tsoong*** (一點鐘). Literally "one point of the clock." This is a foreign division of time. The Chinese divide the day into twelve periods of two hours each, known as ***z-zung*** (時辰). Now, the divisions into hours has become very familiar.

***Ih °tien tsoong*** may also mean "one o'clock," and the other hours are indicated in the same way by the change of the numeral. Thus "Two o'clock" is ***°liang °tien tsoong*** (兩點鐘). "Three o'clock" is ***san °tien tsoong*** (三點鐘), etc.

"A day" is usually ***ih nyih*** 一日. The character ***nyih*** literally means "sun." In speaking of the Heavenly body, in the colloquial, ***deu*** is added to the ***nyih***, making the expression ***nyih-deu*** (日頭). Sometimes the word ***thien*** (天). meaning "Heaven," is used for "day." Thus ***san thien*** means "three days." No classifier is introduced between the numeral and the ***nyih*** or the ***thien***. Thus we have for "four days" ***s° nyih*** (四日) or ***s° thien*** (四天).

"A week" is ***ih kuh °li-pa°*** (一个禮拜) or ***ih °li-pa°*** (一禮拜). This of course is a foreign division of time which has been adopted into Chinese. It takes its name from the name of Sunday, which is usually ***°li-pa°-nyih*** (禮拜日). Lit. "the day of ceremonial worship." ***°Li*** means ceremony, ***pa°*** is to worship. The other days of the week are formed with the addition of the numerals as follows: Monday is ***°li-pa°-ih*** (禮拜一). Tuesday is ***°li-pa°-nyi°***. Wednesday is ***°li-pa°-san***. Thursday ***°li-pa°-s°***. Friday ***°li-pa°-°ng*** and Saturday ***°li-pa°-lok***.

"A month" is ***ih kuh nyoeh*** (一个月). Lit. "a moon." The Chinese year is made up of twelve lunar months. The first month is called ***tsung nyoeh*** (正月), the second, ***nyi° nyoeh*** (二月), the third, ***san nyoeh*** (三月) and so forth.

"A year" is ***ih nyien*** (一年). No classifier is used between the numeral and the word "year," ***nyien***.

"How many?" or "How much?" is ***°kyi-hau°?*** (幾化). Thus ***°kyi-hau° nyung le?*** (幾化人來) means "How many men came?" ***°Kyi-hau° °s?*** (幾化水) means "How much water?"

***°Kyi*** is often used without the ***hau°***. In such cases it is followed by the classifier of the noun. Thus "How many men came?" might be ***°kyi kuh nyung le?*** (幾个人來). "How many horses have you?" ***noong° °yeu °kyi tsak °mo?*** (儂有幾隻馬).

"Where?" is ***°°a-°li*** (那裏). Thus "Where are you going?" is ***noong° tau° °°a-°li chi°?*** (儂到那裏去). "Where are you?" is ***noong° la°-°°a-°li?*** (儂拉那裏).

***Sa°*** meaning "what" with ***di°-faung*** meaning "place" also expresses "Where?" Thus ***sa° di°-faung?*** (啥地方). We also have ***sa° dzang-hau°?*** (啥場化) meaning

"What place?" or "Where?" but this refers to a more circumscribed area than ***di°-faung***. We also have ***sa° °'oo-daung°*** (啥戶蕩) used much in the same way as ***sa° dzang-hau°***.

VOCABULARY.

To return, **°tsen-le** (轉來). Lit. To come back, **°tsen-chi°** (轉去). Lit. To go back.

To come out or forth, **tsheh-le** 出來.

To go out, **tsheh chi°** 出去.

To thank, **zia°** 謝.

Near, **°jung** 近.

To-day, **kyung-tsau** 今朝.

Yesterday, **zau-nyih** 昨日.

Thus, **zeh-ke°** (實蓋) or **zeh-ke°-nung** (實蓋能).

Then (used as a conjunction), **nan-meh** (難末).

Only, **pih-koo°** 必過.

South, **nen** 南.

Immediately, **zieu°** 就.

Time, **z-'eu°** 時候, **zung-kwaung** 辰光 or **koong-foo** 工夫.

But, **dan°-°z** 但是, **dok-°z** 獨是.

EXERCISES.

(Translate into English).

(1). °Tshing sien-sang ming-tsau °kyeu °tien-tsoong le. (2). Kyung-tsau °z °li-pa° ih, ming-tsau °z °li-pa° nyi°. (3). °Di-kuk nyoeh °yeu san-seh nyih. (4). Ih °li-pa° °yeu tshih nyih. (5). Noong° kuh bang-°yeu dzu° la° sa° di°-faung? La° dzung-°li. La° dzung °li, sa° dzang-hau°? °Jung nen mung. (6). °Ngoo kuh tau noong° faung° la°-°'a-°li? (7). Zau-nyih °ngoo dok-ts °ng °tien-tsoong su, nan-meh tsheh-chi° °tseu loo°. (8). °Kyi °pung su °z noong° kuh °lau °kyi °pung °z yi-kuh? (9). °I-kuh nyung °yeu °kyi-kuh 'eu-°ts? Yi pih-koo° °yeu ih kuh. (10). Noong° tau°-°ts Tsoong-kok °kyi-kuh nyoeh tse? °Ngoo le-ts san kuh nyoeh. (11). Noong° °kyi-z iau° °tsen-chi°? °Li-pa°-san iau° °tsen-chi°. (12). °Zaung-°he °kyi-z °tsen-le kuh? Zau-nyih °tsen-le kuh. (13). Noong° we°-sa°-°lau 'veh tsheh-chi° °tseu °tseu? °Iung-we° m-meh koong-foo °lau. (14). Zia° zia° noong° chi° °tshing i-sung le. (15). °Ngoo dok °hau-ts su zieu° iau° chuh van. (16). °Z zeh-ke° va°? °Z zeh-ke° kuh.

**(一) 請先生明朝九點鐘來**

**(二) 今朝是禮拜一,明朝是禮拜二**

**(三) 第个月有三十日**

**(四) 一禮拜有七日**

**(五) 儂个朋友住拉啥地方,拉城裏,拉城裏啥場化,近南門**

**(六) 我个刀儂放拉那裏**

**(七) 昨日我讀仔五點鐘書,難末出去走路**

**(八) 幾本書是儂个咾幾本是伊个**

(九) 伊个人有幾个兒子，伊必過有一个

(十) 儂到仔中國幾个月哉，我來仔三个月

(十一) 儂幾時要轉去，禮拜三要轉去

(十二) 上海幾時轉來个，昨日轉來个

(十三) 儂爲啥咾勿出去走走，因爲嘸沒工夫咾

(十四) 謝謝儂去請醫生來

(十五) 我讀好仔書就要吃飯

(十六) 是實蓋陌，是實蓋个

(Translate into Chinese).

(1). Where have you put my shoes? (2). I put them in the box. (3). I do not want to study on Sunday, but I will study on Monday. (4). How many weeks are there in a month? (5). How many peaches have you eaten. (6). How many dollars did you give your servant? (7). What time is it now? (8). Where do you live? (9). When you have bought the fish, return immediately. (10). The guest will stay here four months, and then will return. (11). Please tell the painter to come. (12). The teacher having taught for three hours, left immediately. (13). Why do you do it this way? because the teacher told me to do it thus. (14). I wish to do it, but I have no time to do it. (15). Go see what time it is now.

(一) 我个鞋子儂放拉那裏

(二) 我放拉箱子裏

(三) 禮拜日勿要讀書，禮拜一咾讀个

(四) 一个月有幾个禮拜

(五) 儂吃仔幾隻桃子

(六) 儂撥仔儂个用人幾塊洋錢

(七) 現在是幾點鐘

(八) 儂住拉啥地方

(九) 買好仔魚就轉來

(十) 客人要住四个月，難末轉去哉

(十一) 謝謝儂叫漆匠來

(十二) 先生教仔三點鐘工夫，就轉去

(十三) 儂爲啥實蓋做，因爲先生教我實蓋做

(十四) 我要做个，但是嘸沒工夫

(十五) 去看現在幾點鐘

NOTES. (1). "Thank you" is expressed by repeating the *Zia°*. Thus "Thank you" is *Zia°-zia° noong°*. In speaking to an equal or superior, the *Noong°* would be dropped. Often in Chinese when you ask a person to do a thing for you, you preface the request by thanking the person. Thus *Zia° zia° noong chi° tan °ngoo kuh san° le* (謝謝儂去担我个傘來) means "Thank you, go bring my umbrella."

(2). *Koong-foo* has the double sense of "work" or "time." Thus *Tsoo° koong-foo* means to do work. But *Meh koong-foo* means "I have no time." You never say *Sa° koong-foo* meaning "What time?" but *Sa z-'en°?* or *Sa° zung-kwaung?* In asking what time it is by the clock the usual expression is *°Kyi °tien-tsoong?*

(3). The force of the question in the third sentence of the First Exercise is due to the fact that some Chinese months have thirty days and some have twenty-nine. A month of thirty days is called *Doo° nyoeh* (大月) "a large month," and one with twenty-nine days is called a small month *°Siau nyoeh* (小月). In order to make the seasons come right, an intercalary month is put in about every three years. This in Chinese is called *Nyung° nyoeh* (閏月).

(4). Notice the elliptical form of expression in the seventh sentence of the First Exercise. Literally it means "Yesterday I read five hours' book."

(5). In the third sentence of the Second Exercise the Chinese idiom is peculiar. You say *°Li-pa° nyih 'veh iau° dok su, °li-pa°-ih° lau dok kuh.* Literally "Sunday not want to study, Monday and study."

(6). In the eleventh sentence of the Second Exercise, the "please" should be translated *Zia°-zia° noong°*.

## LESSON XI.

### The Passive Voice, and Adverbs of Place and Time.

***Peh*** (撥) (Mandarin 被) is used to form the Passive, and is the regular and proper form of the Passive. Thus: the verb ***°tang*** (打) means to "Strike." ***°Ngoo °tang yi*** (我打伊) means "I strike him." To put this into the Passive we would say ***°ngoo peh yi °tang*** (我撥伊打). Literally "I gave him strike," or "I was struck by him."

"Here" is expressed by ***leh-li°*** or ***°tsh-di°*** (垃裏, 此地) or ***di°-deu*** (第頭). ***°Tsh-di°*** means literally "this place."

"There" is ***leh-la°*** (垃拉) or ***i-deu*** (伊頭) or ***i-kwhe°*** (伊塊). "I am here" is ***°ngoo leh-li°*** (我垃裏). "I am there" is ***°ngoo leh-la°*** (我垃拉).

These adverbs are often used as adverbial nouns and may take prepositions before them. Thus ***Tau° °di-deu le*** (到第頭來) means "Come here." Lit. "To here come." ***Tau° i-deu chi°*** (到伊頭去) means "Go there." Lit. "To there go." ***°Pa la °tsh-di°*** (擺拉此地) means "Place it here." Lit. "Place it at here." ***°Pa la i-kwhe°*** (擺拉伊塊) means "Place it there." Lit. "Place it at there."

#### VOCABULARY.

Half an hour, **pen° °tien-tsoong** 半點鐘, (**pen°** means half.)

Quarter of an hour, **ih khuh** 一刻.

A minute, **ih fung** 一分.

In the morning, **°zaung-pen°-nyih** 上半日. Lit. Above half day.

In the afternoon, **°au-pen°-nyih** 下半日 Lit. Lower half day.

Night, **ya°** 夜.
At night, **ya°-deu** 夜頭 or **ya° °li** 夜裏.
Day before yesterday, **koo°-nyih-°ts** 過日子, **zien-nyih-°ts** 前日子, **i-nyih-°ts** 伊日子.
Day after to-morrow, **°eu nyih** 後日.
Early in the morning, **°tsau zung-deu** 早晨頭. **°Tsau** is early.
In the evening, **ya°-kwha°** 夜快. Lit. Night coming fast.
In the middle of the day or noon, **nyih-tsoong** 日中.
To cook, **sau** 燒.
To strike, **°tang** 打.
To wait, **°tung** 等. **°Tung-ih-°tung** means "Wait a little."
To rest, **hyih** 歇. **Hyih-ih-hyih** means "Wait a little." We also have **°tung-ih-hyih.**
To remember, **kyi°** 記 or **kyi°-tuh** 記得.
To forget, **maung°-kyi°** 忘記.
An affair (abstract), **ih °jien z°-°thi** or **ih tsaung z°-°thi** 一樁事體.
A thing or object (concrete), **ih kuh meh-z°** 一个物事.
Wind, **foong** 風.
A loaf of bread, **ih kuh men-deu** 一个饅頭.
A mosquito, **ih tsak mung-°ts** 一个蚊子 or **ih kuh mung-°ts.**
A boat, **ih tsak zen** 一隻船.
Many, much, **too hau°** 多化, or **too** 多.
To sting, **ting** 叮
To bite, **°ngau** 咬.
To spoil, **wa°** 壞, or **wa°-theh** 壞脫 (completely spoil).
A snake, **ih diau zo** 一條蛇.

## EXERCISES.

(Translate into English.)

(1). Van° sau °hau meh? Sau °hau tse. (2). °Ngoo kuh i-zaung tan tau° °tsh-di° le. (3). I-zaung tsoo° °hau meh? 'Veh zung iau° hyih °liang nyih tsoo° °hau. (4). °Tshing sien-sang ming-tsau °zaung-pen°-nyih zeh °tien-tsoong le. (5). Van° sau °hau-ts meh zieu° iau° chuh. (6). °Ngoo nyih °li dok tsoong-kok su, ya° °li dok nga°-kok su. (7). I-tsak °mo we°-ts °tseu le man° °lau peh la °mo-foo °tang. (8). Zien-nyih-ts °ngoo la° °Zaung-°he °ma-ts too-hau° meh-z°. (9). °Di tsaung z°-°thi °ngoo theh noong° wo°, dan°-z° 'veh iau° peh i-kuh nyung °hyau-tuh. (10). °Tsau-zung-deu °z °ting °hau dok su kuh zung-kwaung. (11). Tung-ih-hyih °ngoo zieu° iau° le. (12). Noong° dok koo° hyih° kuh su kyi°-tuh va? (13). Ih pen° kyi°-tuh, ih pen° maung°-kyi. (14). °Ngoo peh la mung-°ts °ting. (15). Men-deu peh la °siau-noen chuh theh tse. (16). °Ngoo kuh kyak peh la zo °ngau-ts ih °kheu. (17). Zen peh la doo° foong °tang wa°. (18). Tshing sien-sang °di-deu °zoo.

(一) 飯燒好末,燒好哉　(二) 我个衣裳担到此地來
(三) 衣裳做好末,勿曾要歇兩日做好　(四) 請先生明朝上半日十點鐘來

(五) 飯燒好仔末就要吃
(六) 我日裏讀中國書，夜裏讀外國書
(七) 伊隻馬爲之走來慢咾撥拉馬夫打．
(八) 前日子我拉上海買之多化物事
(九) 第椿事體我對儂話，但是勿要撥伊个人曉得
(十) 早晨頭是頂好讀書个辰光
(十一) 等一歇我就要來
(十二) 儂讀過歇个書記得陌
(十三) 一半記得，一半忘記
(十四) 我撥拉蚊子叮
(十五) 饅頭撥拉小囝吃脫哉
(十六) 我个脚撥拉蛇咬仔一口
(十七) 船撥拉大風打壞
(十八) 請先生第頭坐

(Translate into Chinese).

(1). When will you come, in the morning or in the afternoon? (2). I do not know, if I have no affairs to attend to, I will come in the morning. (3). Has the carpenter finished making the table? If so, I will come and look at it. (4). Place the bed here and the table there. (5). These fish are cooked badly. (6). The day after to-morrow I have invited some guests to dinner. (7). It is already twenty minutes past ten, and my teacher has not yet come. (8). Do you remember what I told you yesterday? I have forgotten it. (9). In studying Chinese, you must not forget what you have already learnt. (10). Please sit down a little while; there are many things I want to say to you. (11). How did you come? I came in a carriage. (12). My child was struck by your child. (13). My face and hands were bitten by mosquitoes.

(一) 儂幾時要來，上半日呢下半日
(二) 我勿曉得若然嘸沒事體，要上半日來
(三) 檯子木匠做好末，若然做好之末，我要來看看
(四) 牀排拉第頭，檯子擺拉伊頭
(五) 魚燒來勿好
(六) 後日我請幾个客人來吃飯
(七) 已經十點過廿分哉，先生還勿曾來
(八) 我昨日對儂話个儂記得陌，我忘記脫哉
(九) 讀中國書已經學過拉个，勿要忘記
(十) 請坐一歇，有多化事體要對儂話
(十一) 儂那能來个，我坐馬車來个
(十二) 我个小囝撥儂个小囝打
(十三) 我个面孔咾手撥拉蚊子叮

NOTES. (1). It will have been noticed that in Lesson VI. *Leh-li°* was used in the Present Tense Continuous of the Verb, and that *Leh-la°* was used for the Past Continuous. It was pointed out then that these words really signify "Here" and "There." The literal sense would be "I am here eating," and "I was there eating."

(2). It is very important that beginners should distinguish clearly between *meh-z°* and *z°-°thi.* Any concrete object may be called a *meh-z°*. But an abstract action or affair is always *z°-°thi.*

In mandarin-speaking districts *toong-si* 東 西 (Lit. "East-West") is often used for *meh-z°*, and sometimes it is heard in the Shanghai District.

(3). In the fifth sentence of the First Exercise, notice how the *°ts* is tacked on to the *°hau*, and not to the *sau*.

(4). In the tenth sentence of First Exercise notice how the *dok su* has become a verbal adjective. Lit. "Reading book time."

(5). In the fifteenth sentence of the First Exercise the force of the *theh* after *chuh* is that it has been entirely eaten up. *Theh* often comes after verbs to express completed action.

(6). In the sixteenth sentence of the First Exercise, *°Ngau-ts ih °kheu* means literally "Bitten a mouthful."

(7). In the seventeenth sentence we have two verbs used together—*°tang* and *wa°*. Literally "Beat" or "strike spoil."

(8). In the seventh sentence of the Second Exercise twenty minutes past ten is expressed *zeh °tien koo° nyan° fung.* *°Tien* is a shortened form for *°tien-tsoong.* *Koo°* means "passed over" or "beyond."

(9). In the twelfth sentence of the First Exercise notice the use of *kuh.* It has the force of the relative pronoun, and the translation would be "the books which you have read."

---

# LESSON XII.

## Some Verbal Idioms.

We have already explained the use of ***°khau-°i, nung-keu°***, and ***we°***. There are other ways of expressing the possibility and impossibility of doing things in Chinese. For instance one way is by the addition of ***tuh le*** or ***'veh le*** after the verb. Thus: ***Dok-tuh-le*** (讀 得 來) means "Able to read." ***Dok-'veh-le*** (讀 勿 來) means "Unable to read it." Many verbs of one character admit of this construction. Thus: ***Wo°-tuh-le*** means "Able to speak." ***Wo-'veh-le*** means "Unable to speak." ***Tsoo°-tuh-le*** (做 得 來), "Able to do." ***Tsoo°-'veh-le*** (做 勿 來), "Unable to do."

Verbs made up of two characters do not take the ***tuh-le*** and ***'veh-le*** after them. Thus we do not hear ***°hyau-tuh 'veh le*** for "Unable to know," but ***'veh we° °hyau-tuh*** (勿 會 曉 得).

The literal meaning of ***tuh-le*** is "Obtain, come," and the literal meaning of ***'veh-le*** is "Not come."

We also have the use of ***tuh-kuh*** after verbs, expressing possibility, and ***'veh-tuh***, expressing impossibility. Thus we have ***tsoo°-tuh-kuh*** (做 得 个), meaning "it is possible to do a thing," and ***tsoo°-'veh-tuh*** (做 勿 得), meaning "it is impossible to do a thing." With verbs of physical action, we have ***tuh-°doong*** (得 動) and ***'veh-°doong*** (勿 動) used after the verb implying possibility and impossibility. Thus we have ***°tseu-tuh-°doong*** (走 得 動), meaning "I have the physical ability to walk," and ***°tseu-'veh-°doong*** (走 勿 動), meaning "I have not the physical ability to walk." In the same way we have ***tsoo°-tuh-°doong*** (做得動) and ***tsoo°-‘veh-°doong*** (做勿動). ***‘Veh-°doong*** literally means "Not move."

Strange to say we have ***°zoo-‘veh-°doong*** (坐勿動), meaning "I have not the physical ability to sit up," and ***°zoo-tuh-°doong***, (坐得動), meaning "I have the physical ability to sit up."

***°Ma-tuh-°doong*** (買得動) means "Possible to buy." ***°Ma-‘veh-°doong*** (買勿動) means "Impossible to buy."

With verbs of hearing and seeing impossibility is expressed in still another way. Thus we have ***khoen°-tuh-kyien°*** (看得見), meaning "It is possible to see," and ***khoen°-‘veh-kyien°*** (看勿見) meaning "It is impossible to see it." Literally translated these expressions are "See, obtain, behold," and "See, not behold." We also have ***khoen°-tuh-tsheh*** (看得出), meaning to see a thing clearly. Literally "See, obtain, come forth," and ***khoen° ‘veh-tsheh*** (看勿出), meaning not to be able to see, or literally "See, not come forth."

In the same way we have ***thing tuh-tsheh*** (聽得出) and ***thing-‘veh-tsheh*** (聽勿出) in regard to hearing. Instead of ***thing-tuh-kyien°*** and ***thing-‘veh-kyien°*** we have ***thing-tuh-dzak*** (聽得着) and ***thing-‘veh-dzak*** (聽勿着). Literally "Hear, obtain" and "Hear, not obtain."

We have already explained the use of ***°hau*** after verbs expressing completed action. We also have other words used much in the same way. Thus ***dok-°hau-tse*** (讀好哉), ***dok-wen-tse*** (讀完哉) or ***dok-°ba-tse*** (讀罷哉) all mean the same thing. The verb ***wen*** means "to finish." Accordingly in asking a question ***tsoo°-°hau-meh*** (做好末), ***tsoo°-wen-meh*** (做完末) and ***tsoo°-°ba-meh*** (做罷末), all mean "Have you finished it?"

Verbal nouns are often formed by the addition of ***deu*** (頭) or ***fah*** (法) after the verb. Thus ***tsoo°-deu*** (做頭) or ***tsoo°-fah*** (做法) means the manner of doing a thing.

## VOCABULARY.

To move, to excite, **°doong 動**.

To hear, **thing** (聽). Heard, **thing-kyien° 聽見**.

To knock, to strike, **khau 考**.

To finish, **wen 完**.

***Kan*** (間) is the classifier used with rooms.

A room, **ih kan 一間**.

A bed room, **ih kan vaung-kan 一間房間**.

A guest room, **ih kan khak-daung-kan 一間客堂間**.

An office, **ih kan sia°-z°-kan 一間寫字間**.

A shroff's room, **ih kan tsang°-vaung-kan 一間帳房間**.

A study, **ih kan su-vaung 一間書房**.

A dining room, **ih kan chuh-van°-kan 一間喫飯間**.

A kitchen, **ih kan sau-van°-kan 一間燒飯間** or **dzu-vaung 廚房** or **tsau°-kan 灶間**.

All, °loong-°tsoong 攏總 or koong°-°tsoong 共總.
All in general, most, da-ke 大概.
Few, °sau 少.
Each, °me 每.
Every, kauh 各.
Other, bih 別.
High, kau 高.
Low, ti 低.
Broad, kwheh 闊.
Narrow, ‘ah 狹.
Deep, sung 深.
Shallow, °tshien 淺.
Too (denoting excess), thuh 忒.
Above, °zaung-deu 上頭
Below, °‘au-deu (下頭). °‘au-ti-deu (下底頭), °‘au-ti (下底).
Under, beneath, ti-°‘au 底下.
Outside, nga°-deu 外頭.
After, °‘eu 後.
Behind, °‘eu-°ti (後底), °‘eu-ti-deu, (後底頭) °‘eu-deu (後頭).
Before, zien (前) zien-deu 前頭.
Earth, di° 地 or di°-jeu.

EXERCISES.

(Translate into English.)

(1). °Zaung-deu °yeu thien, °‘au-deu °yeu di°. (2). °Yeu too-hau° z° °ngoo °sia-‘veh-le. (3). Noong° we°-sa°-°lau °tseu le man° le °si, iung-we° °ngoo °tseu ‘veh °doong °lau. (4). Tsoong-kok wo°, zak-zen nyung wo° le kwha° meh, °ngoo thing ‘veh tsheh. (5). °Yeu-kuh su °ngoo dok ‘veh le. (6). °Di zak vaung-ts °kyi-hau° kau, °kyi-hau° kwheh. (7). °Di zak vaung-ts °yeu °kyi kan? (8). °Yeu ih kan khak-daung, ih kan °sia-z°-kan, ih kan chuh-van° kan, °lau s° kan vaung-kan. (9). °Di kuh meh-z° °yeu sa° yoong°-deu va? ‘M-sa° yoong°-deu. (10). Sa° nyung la° khau mung? °Ngoo ‘veh zung thing-kyien° °yeu sa° nyung la° khau mung. (11). °Di diau loo° thuh ‘ah, °ting °hau noong° °tseu la° zien-deu, °ngoo °tseu la° °‘eu-deu. (12). °Tshing khak nyung khak-daung °li °zoo. (13). Dzoong °Zaung-°he tau° °ts-di° °yeu °kyi-hau° loo°? (14). Vaung-°ts nga°-deu °z °lang-tien, vaung-°ts °li-hyang° °z nyih-tien. (15). °Di diau ‘oo °yeu-kuh di°-faung °z sung-tien, °yeu-kuh di°-faung °z °tshien-tien. (16). Noong° na°-nung °hyau-tuh °di tsaung z°-thi, iung-we° °ngoo thing tuh °yeu nyung wo° °lau. (17). Ze-voong tsoo° le ‘veh °hau, °loong °tsoong kuh i-zaung thuh doo°. (18). Kauh nyung °yeu kauh nyung kuh z°-°thi.

(一) 上頭有天, 下頭有地 (二) 有多化字我寫勿來 (三) 儂爲啥咾走來慢來死, 因爲我走勿動咾 (四) 中國話若然人話來快末, 我聽勿出 (五) 有个書我讀勿來 (六) 第宅房子幾化高, 幾化闊 (七) 第宅房子有幾間 (八) 有一間客堂, 一間寫字間, 一間吃飯間, 咾四間房間 (九) 第个物

事有啥用頭陑,嘸啥用頭　(十) 啥人拉敲門,我勿曾聽見有啥人拉敲門　(十一) 第條路忒狹,頂好儂走拉前頭,我走拉後頭　(十二) 請客人客堂裏坐　(十三) 從上海到此地有幾化路　(十四) 房子外頭是冷點,房子裏向是熱點　(十五) 第條河有个地方是深點,有个地方是淺點　(十六) 儂那能曉得第椿事體,因為我聽得有人話咾　(十七) 裁縫做來勿好,攏總个衣裳忒大　(十八) 各人有各人个事體

(Translate into Chinese.)

(1). Where is your teacher? He is in the study writing. (2). Did you tell the table boy to bring the tea? (3). If the carpenter does not make it well, I shall call another man. (4). This manner of doing it is bad; I want you to do it better. (5). I walked to Shanghai, and then I could walk no further. (6). Then what did you do? I called a ric-sha and came back. (7). Is the Master in? He has gone out. (8). Three days ago I went to see the pagoda. (9). There is water beneath the earth. (10). The cat is under the chair. (11). When I have finished reading the book, I want to learn to write characters. (12). Tell him to come inside. (13). This table is too low; I cannot write characters on it. (14). May I come in? Come right in.

(一) 儂个先生拉啥地方,拉寫字間裏寫字　(二) 担茶來,儂對西崽話陑　(三) 若然木匠做來勿好,我要叫別人來做　(四) 實蓋做頭是勿好,我要儂做來好點　(五) 我走到上海難末走勿動哉　(六) 難末儂那能做頭,我叫之東洋車咾轉來　(七) 先生垃拉陑,出去拉　(八) 三日前頭我去看一座塔　(九) 地底下有水　(十) 貓拉椅子底下　(十一) 我讀罷之書要學寫字　(十二) 叫伊到裏向來　(十三) 第隻檯子忒低,勿好寫字　(十四) 我可以進來陑,進來末哉

NOTES. (1). In regard to °*sau*, meaning few, it should be noted that it never occurs before a noun. If you wish to say a few men the idiomatic expression would be °*yeu* ‘*veh too* °*kyi-kuh nyung* (有勿多幾个人) or *m-meh* °*kyi-hau*° *nyung* (嘸沒幾化人). The men are few would be *nyung* °*sau* (人少). °*Sau* is often used to qualify verbs. Thus we have °*sau dok kuh*, meaning "to read less."

(2). As already pointed out in a previous lesson what correspond to prepositions in English are really postpositions in Chinese, as they come after the nouns instead of before them. When used with verbs, however, they generally precede them. Thus we have °*li-hyang*° °*zoo* for "Sit inside," °*zaung-deu* °*zoo* (上頭坐) for "take a higher seat." This is the usual polite phrase said to a guest when he enters your guest room. He will take a seat near the door, and you ask him "to be seated higher."

(3). The first sentence of the First Exercise is really an oath, and is used when one is calling Heaven and Earth to witness that his words are true.

(4). Note the impersonal use of °*yeu* in the second sentence of the First Exercise. Literally it is "There are many characters."

(5). In the seventh sentence of the Second Exercise you have the usual form of inquiring whether the gentleman you wish to see is at home. You say *Sien-sang leh-la*° *va*°? "is the master there?" The answer is *leh-la*°, if he is at home, meaning "He is there." If he is not at home, the answer may be *tsheh chi*° *la*°, "he has gone out," or '*veh leh-la*°, "he is not there."

---

# LESSON XIII.

## Auxiliary Verbs.

The verb °*chi* (起) is often used as an auxiliary verb after the principal verb to express the idea of inception. Thus *doh*-°*chi* (讀起) means "Begin to read." °*Chi* also expresses the idea of erectness, but when used in this sense, *le* follows the °*chi* (來). Thus *Lih* °*chi-le* (立起來) means "Stand up." *Loh*-°*chi-le* (踍起來) means "Get up." It also has a progressive meaning, as when you say *Doh*-°*chi-le* (讀起來) it means "read on," "go on reading."

We have the °*chi*, used also in combination with *tuh* (得). Thus *Loh-tuh*-°*chi* (踍得起) means "Able to get up." *Loh-veh*-°*chi* (踍勿起) means "Unable to get up." °*Ma-tuh* °*chi* (買得起) means "Can afford to buy it." °*Ma-veh* °*chi* (買勿起) means "Cannot afford to buy it." *Kwhung* °*veh* °*chi* (睏勿起) means "unable to sleep." *Khoen*° *veh* °*chi* (看勿起) means "to look down upon," "to disdain."

°*Zaung* (上) and °'*Au* (下) are used both as principal verbs and as auxiliaries. Thus we have the expressions °*Zaung san* (上山), meaning "to go up hill." °'*Au san* (下山), "to go down hill." °'*Au zen* (下船), "to go on board a boat," °*Zaung su* (上書), "to take an advanced lesson in a book," etc. In these cases they are used as principal verbs.

As auxiliary verbs, they express motion upwards and motion downwards.

They are not confined to verbs of motion, but are used freely with other verbs. To both of them *le* (來) and *chi*° (去) are frequently added.

Thus we have *doh*-°'*au-chi*° (讀下去), meaning "Read on down." *Tsoo*°-°'*au-chi*° (做下去), meaning "Go on doing it." *Thiau*°-°*au le* (跳下來), meaning "Jump down." *Thiau*°-°*zaung-chi*° (跳上去), meaning "Jump up to that place." *Thiau*° *zaung le* (跳上來) "Jump up to this place."

Although the Chinese language is, strictly speaking, a monosyllabic language, yet as has already been probably noticed there is a strong tendency to use two or more words together, forming as it were disyllables or trisyllables. In this lesson some verbs are used, composed of two characters occurring together.

上海方言教程



VOCABULARY.

To like, to enjoy, **hwen-°hyi** 歡喜.
To play, take recreation, **beh-siang°** 勃相.
To converse, **bak-wo°** or **dan-dan** 白話, 談談.
To believe, **siang-sing°** 相信.
To fall, **lauh** or **tih** 落, 跌.
To stand up, **lih** 立.
To get up, **lok** 睩.
To be willing, **°khung** 肯.
To back the book, **pe°** 背.
To think, **°siang** 想.
To sleep, **kwhung°** 睏.
To wipe, **kha** 揩.
To fly, **fi** 飛.
To reckon, **soen°** 算.
To build, **°zau** 造.
A stove, **ih kuh °hoo-loo** 一个火爐, or **ih tsak °hoo-loo.**
A rat, **ih tsak °lau-°ts** or **ih tsak °lau dzoong** 一隻老鼠, 一隻老蟲.
A washstand, **ih tsak kha mien° de-°ts** 一隻揩面檯子.
A temple, **ih zoo° miau°** 一座廟.
A window, **ih sen° tshaung** 一扇窗.

***Ban*** (爿) is the Classifier for firms, shops, etc.

A tea shop, **ih ban dzo-kwen°** 一爿茶館.
A pair of chop-sticks, **ih saung kwhan** 一雙筷.
Words, **seh-wo°** or **wo°-deu** 說話 or 話頭.
A sentence, **ih kyui° seh-wo°** 一句說話.
Only, **pih-koo°** or **dok-°z** or **tsuh-tuh,** 必過, 獨自, 只得.
Not only, **'veh-dan°-°z** or **'veh-dan°** or **'veh-ba** 勿但, 勿但是, 勿罷.
Heavy, **°dzoong** 重.
Light (in weight), **chung** 輕.
Cheap, **jang** 强
Dear (in price), **kyui°** 貴.
Happy, **kha°-weh** 快活.
Clear or distinct, **tshing-°saung** 清爽.
Soo-chow, **Soo-tseu** 蘇州.
Therefore, **°soo-°i** 所以 or **keh-°lau** 葛咾.
First, **sien** 先.

EXERCISES.

(Translate into English).

(1). °Di-kuh °liang we° bang-yeu hwen-°hyi ih dau bah-wo°. (2). °Ngoo dok ba°-ts su iau° tsheh chi° beh-siang°. (3). Zak-zen yi °khung ma° meh, noong° °ma-meh-tse. (4). °Di zoo° vaung-°ts °zau-°chi-le 'man kwha°. (5). °Ngoo kyau° °i-kuh °siau-noen lih-°chi-le pe° su. (6). °Ngoo °siang °di-kuh 'auh-sang-°ts kyung-tsau 'veh zung kha mien°. (7). Tsoong-kok nyung chuh van° yoong° ih saung kwhan, nga°-kok-nyung yoong° tau °lau tsho. (8). Zauh ya°-deu la° vaung-kan °li °ngoo thing-tuh ih tsak °lau-°ts leh-la° kyau°. (9). Zak-zen yi wo° yi veh zung tan meh, yi-kuh seh-wo° °ngoo °khung siang-sing°. (10). Thien °hau meh °ngoo iau° tau° dzo-kwen° °li chi° °zoo-°zoo dan-dan chuh dzo. (11). °Yeu bih saung °a-°ts va°? °Ngoo pih-koo° °yeu °di saung. (12). Zauh-ya°-deu °ngoo kwhung° veh dzak, °soo-°i kyung-tsau lok-veh-°chi. (13). Thien nyih kuh zung-kwaung iau° khe tshaung °lau mung, °lang meh °iau° kwan. (14). Tsoong-kok-wo° wo° le veh tshing-°saung meh bih nyung veh °toong kuh. (15). °Di tsak kha-mien°-de-°ts noong° °ma le jang va°? ‘Veh hau soen° jang, °ngoo °siang ‘man kyui°. (16). Noong° °kyi kwhe° yang-dien °ma le kuh? Zeh kwhe° yang-dien la. (17). Noong° we°-sa°-°lau °ma le zeh-ke° kyui°? Iung-we° tsuk-tuh °di-kuh ih tsak. (18). °Ngoo tsheh chi° bau loo° ‘veh dan° khoen°-kyien° ih zoo° miau°, miau° mung zien ‘a °yeu ih zoo° thah. (19). °Di tsak °hoo-loo °z °dzoong kuh nyi chung kuh? °Z ‘man °dzoong kuh. (20). °Tshing sien-sang °zoo °zaung chi°. (21). Sien-sang kyau° ‘auh-sang-°ts dok °‘au chi°. (22). °I °pung su dzoong de-°ts laung° lauh °‘au le. (23). °Siau-noen dzoong iui-°ts laung° tih °‘au le. (24). °Ngoo khoen°-kyien° ih tsak °tiau dzoong thien laung° fi °‘au le. (25). °Ngoo ming-tsau iau° °‘au zen tau° Soo-tseu chi°.

(一) 第个兩位朋友歡喜一淘白話　(二) 我讀罷之書要出去勃相　(三) 若然伊肯賣末儂買末哉　(四) 第座房子造起來蠻快　(五) 我叫伊个小囝立起來背書　(六) 我想第个學生子今朝勿曾揩面　(七) 中國人吃飯用一雙筷外國人用刀咾叉　(八) 昨夜頭拉房間裏我聽得一隻老鼠垃拉叫　(九) 若然伊話伊勿曾担末伊个說話我肯相信　(十) 天好末我要到茶館裏去坐坐談談吃茶　(十一) 有別雙鞋子陌,我必過有第雙　(十二) 昨夜頭我睏勿着所以今朝踈勿起　(十三) 天熱个辰光要開窗咾門冷末要關　(十四) 中國話話來勿清爽末別人勿懂个　(十五) 第隻揩面檯子儂買來强陌,勿好算强我想蠻貴　(十六) 儂幾塊洋錢買來个,十塊洋錢拉　(十七) 儂爲啥咾買來實蓋貴,因爲只得第个一隻　(十八) 我出去跑路勿但看見一座廟廟門前也有一座塔　(十九) 第隻火爐是重个呢輕个,是蠻重个　(二十) 請先生坐上去　(二十一) 先生叫學生子讀下去　(二十二) 伊本書從檯子上落下來　(二十三) 小兒從椅子上跌下來　(二十四) 我看見一隻鳥從天上飛下來　(二十五) 我明朝要下船到蘇州去

**(Translate into Chinese).**

(1). Do you like to eat this? (2). In the day time men work, in the night time they sleep. (3). The cat came in by the window and the rat ran out by the door. (4). I conversed with him, and he taught me many words in Chinese. (5). I want you to wipe the windows. (6). Last night I only slept four hours. (7). I not only bought a washstand, I also bought a stove and three chairs. (8). Children like to play, men like to study. (9). Why do you go to the tea shop? Because there I can hear many men conversing, and so learn many Chinese words. (10). Are you willing to go with me to see the temple? (11). To-day I am very happy, because I have finished the book. (12). The child jumped down from the table. (13). Please write on down. (14). When will you go up the hill with me to take a look? (15). The teacher first hears the scholars back the book, and then gives them an advanced lesson.

(一) 第樣物事儂歡喜吃陌 (二) 日裏个辰光人做工夫拉夜裏末睏 (三) 貓是從窗裏進來老鼠從門裏跑出去 (四) 我對伊白話咾伊教我多化中國話 (五) 要儂去揩揩窗 (六) 昨夜頭我必過睏之四點鐘工夫 (七) 我勿但買之一隻揩面檯子也買之一隻火爐咾三把椅子 (八) 小囝歡喜孛相大人歡喜讀書 (九) 儂爲啥咾到茶館裏去,因爲伊頭我可以聽得多化人白話咾學多化中國話 (十) 儂肯搭我一淘到廟裏去看看陌 (十一) 今朝我蠻快活因爲一本書讀完哉 (十二) 小囝從檯子上跳下來 (十三) 請寫下去 (十四) 儂幾時搭我一淘上山去看看 (十五) 先生先聽學生子背書難末對伊拉上書

NOTES. (1). Note that *siang-sing°* means to like as well as to believe. °*Ngoo siang-sing° ih kuh nyung* (我相信一个人) means, "I like him."

(2). The expression "to back the book" arises from the old Chinese custom of the pupil turning his back upon the teacher when he recites his lesson.

(3). Notice the order of the words in the eleventh sentence of the First Exercise. The verb '*Yeu* comes first in the sentence.

(4). The word *la* is added at the end of the sixteenth sentence of the First Exercise merely for euphony.

(5). In the twentieth sentence of the First Exercise we have another polite way of asking a person to take a higher seat in the guest room.

(6). In sentences twenty-two and twenty-three of the First Exercise we have the use of *lauh* and *tih* for fall. It is difficult to distinguish between the two, but *Tih* is used always when we speak of a person falling down.

(7). The correct way of translating the first sentence of the Second Exercise is °*Di yang meh-z*° *noong*° *hwen*°-*hyi chuh va*°. °*Di yang* means "this sort."

(8). The thirteenth sentence of the Second Exercise of course refers to the fact that the Chinese write from the top down and not across the page.

(9). The last clause of the fifteenth sentence of the Second Exercise should be *nan-meh theh yi-la* °*zaung su*. "Then for them, advances in the book."

---

## LESSON XIV.

### Causality, and Necessity.

The idea of causality, in the sense of causing a person to do a thing, is expressed in Chinese by the use of the auxiliary verbs ***kau*** (教) and ***tsha*** (差). Thus "I caused him to do it," would be ***ngoo kau yi tsoo*** (我教伊做). "I caused him to go," would be ***ngoo tsha yi chi*** (我差伊去). The word ***tsha*** literally means "to send." The word ***kau*** is the same as ***kyau°***, but used with different pronunciation and different tone. When one of higher rank causes a person of lower rank to do a thing the word ***s°*** (使) is used. Thus ***S°*** °***ngoo ieu-mung***, "Caused me to sorrow."

"Must" is expressed by the expressions ***tsoong-iau°*** (總要), ***pih-ding° iau°*** (必定要), ***ih-ding° iau°*** (一定要).

"It must be" is ***tsoong*** °***z*** (總是). Thus "It must be so" is ***tsoong*** °***z zeh-ke°*** (總是實蓋).

"Ought," implying obligation, is expressed by ***iung-ke*** (應該). Thus "You ought to do it" is ***noong° iung-ke tsoo° kuh*** (儂應該做个).

#### VOCABULARY.

Perhaps, **°khoong-p'o°** 恐怕.

Just now, a little while ago, **khan khan** or **'veh too °kyi-z** 纔纔, 勿多幾時.

Quickly, **'au-sau°** or **kwha°-kwha°** 豪燥, 快快.

Moreover, **°ping-°tshia** or **r-°tshia** or **hwaung-°tshia** 并且, 而且, 況且.

Although, **soe-zen** or **soe-°z** 雖然, 雖是.

Yet, **zen-r** 然而.

Still (in the sense of in addition), **wan** or **wanau°** 還, 還要. **°ngoo wan iau° °ma** (我還要買), "I still wish to buy more."

On the contrary, or on the other hand, **°tau** 倒.

To complete, **dzung-koong** 成功.

To light (a lamp or candle), **°tien** 點.

To light (a fire), **sang** 生.

To take with you, **ta° chi'** 帶去.

To bring with you, **ta° le** 帶來.

To kill, **sah** or **sah-theh** 殺脫.

To kill with a blow, **tang sah** 打殺.

To die, **°si** or **°si-theh** 死.

To live, **weh** 活.

A lamp, **ih °tsan tung** 一盞燈.

***Foong*** **(封)** is the classifier used for letters and other sealed parcels.

A letter, **ih foong sing° 一封信.**
An envelope, **ih foong sing° khauh** or **ih foong sing° foong 一封信殼, 一封信封.**
A candle, **ih kung lah tsok 一根蠟燭.**
Fire, **°hoo 火.**

***Tsang*** **(張)** is the classifier denoting sheets.

A sheet of paper, **ih tsang °ts** or **ih tsang °ts-deu 一張紙頭.**
A fowl, **ih tsak kyi 一隻雞.**

**EXERCISES.**

**(Translate into English).**

(1). °Ngoo nyi° iung-ke tsoo° kuh z°-°thi, °tau ‘veh tsoo°. (2). Thien °lang-°ts meh pih-ding° iau° sang °hoo. (3). Ya°-deu iau° dok su meh, tsoong-iau° °tien tung. (4). °Ngoo ‘veh °hyau-tuh na°-nung tsoo° deu, °ngoo kuh bang-yeu °i-kyung °si-theh tse. (5). Tan ih tsang °ts-deu le, °ngoo iau° °sia ih foong sing°. (6). °Ngoo la° su-vaung °li zing °ngoo kuh mau-°ts, soe-zen °tien-ts lah-tsok ‘a zing veh dzak kuh. (7). °Ngoo iau° ‘auh dok tsoong-kok z° °ping-°tshia iau° ‘auh °sia tsoong-kok z°. (8). Soe-zen noong° wo° ‘veh zung tan tsheh chi° zen-r °ngoo ‘veh °khung siang-sing°. (9). Kwha° tien chi° kyau° i-sung le, °khoong pho° yi iau° °si tse. (10). Sien-sang leh-la° va°? Yi khan khan leh-°li, yien°-°dze ‘veh °hyau-tuh °a-°li chi° tse. (11) Zak-zen yi wan ‘veh zung le, °ngoo °tung yi ‘veh tuh. (12). °Ngoo kyau° yoong-nyung sah ih tsak kyi, la° chuh van° kuh zung-kwaung iau° chuh kuh. (13). °Di tsak de-°ts moh-ziang° tsoo° le wan °hau. (14). °Ngoo man kha° weh thing tuh noong° wo° °ngoo yeu ih foong sing° le, °khoong-pho° °z °ngoo kuh bang-yeu °sia le kuh. (15). Nyung iau° sien tsoo° dzung-koong ih tsaung z°-°thi nan-meh °khau-°i tsoo° bih yang°. (16). M-meh ih kuh nyung hwen-°hyi °si.

**(一) 我伲應該做个事體倒勿做 (二) 天冷之末必定要生火 (三) 夜頭要讀書末總要點燈 (四) 我勿曉得那能做頭我个朋友已經死脫哉 (五) 担一張紙頭來我要寫一封信 (六) 我拉書房裏尋我个帽子雖然點之蠟燭也尋勿着个 (七) 我要學讀中國字幷且要學寫中國字 (八) 雖然儂話勿曾担出去然而我勿肯相信 (九) 快點去叫醫生來恐怕伊要死哉 (十)**

先生垃拉陌伊幾幾垃裏現在勿曉得那裏去哉　(十一) 若然伊還勿曾來我等伊勿得　(十二) 我叫用人殺一隻雞拉吃飯个辰光要吃个，(十三) 第隻檯子木匠做來還好　(十四) 我蠻快活聽得儂話我有一封信來恐怕是我个朋友寫來个　(十五) 人要先做成功一樁事體難末可以做別樣 (十六) 嘸沒一个人歡喜死

(Translate into Chinese.)

(1). I told you a little while ago that I did not want you to open the window; why do you not listen to me? (2). Light the lamp and put it on the table in the study. (3). If a guest comes, I want you to light the fire in the reception room. (4). Do not strike the dog; perhaps you will kill him. (5). You must study diligently, and then you can learn to speak Chinese. (6). How many hours a day ought I to study? I think you should study at least four hours a day: two in the morning and two in the afternoon. (7). If your letter has been written, I will send the servant to take it. (8). Early in the morning I want you to sweep the floor and wipe the table and chairs. (9). Although the carpenter works quickly, he cannot finish it in a week. (10). When you have finished this do not think there is nothing more to do, but come and tell me. (11). I did not tell you to take it away, but on the contrary told you to put it in the office. (12). If the doctor does not come immediately, this man cannot live. (13). Who caused you to do it? He caused me to do it.

(一) 幾幾我叫儂勿要開窗儂爲啥勿聽說話　(二) 要點燈拉書房裏擺拉檯子上　(三) 客人來末拉客堂間裏要儂生火　(四) 勿要打狗恐怕要打殺哉　(五) 儂總要用心讀書難末可以學讀中國話　(六) 一日我應該讀幾點鐘工夫，我想須少要讀四點鐘工夫拉上半日兩點鐘咾下半日兩點鐘　(七) 信寫好之末我差用人担去个　(八) 早晨頭要儂掃掃地揩揩檯子咾椅子　(九) 木匠雖然做來快一禮拜工夫勿能做好　(十) 第个做好之來告訴我勿要想嘸啥做　(十一) 我勿曾叫儂帶出去倒叫儂放拉寫字間裏　(十二) 醫生勿就來末第个人勿能殼活　(十三) 啥人敎儂做个，伊敎我做个

NOTES. (1). Wan is sometimes used to qualify adjectives. Thus *Wan °hau* (還好) means "fairly good" or "pretty good."

(2). *Soe-zen* and *Zen-r* are generally used together; the first introducing the first clause, and the second, the second clause.

(3). In the first sentence of the First Exercise notice the formation of the verbal noun, "the things which we ought to do."

(4). In the ninth sentence of the First Exercise notice that *kwha° °tien* does not mean "faster," but is used for "quickly."

(5). In the eleventh sentence of the First Exercise *°Tung yi 'veh tuh* means lit. "Wait him not get," that is, "I cannot wait for him."

(6). In the fifteenth sentence of the First Exercise notice the use of *le*. *Le* and *chi* are frequently used with other verbs to make the direction of the action clear. Thus *°Sia le* is, "write come to me" *°Sia chi°* is, "Write send away," or "write go."

(7). In the fifth sentence of the Second Exercise, Diligently can be expressed by *Yoong° sing*, "Use heart or mind."

(8). In this Lesson frequent use has been made of the verb *°Si* 死. In speaking of a person dying the more euphonious expression is *Koo°-s°* 故世.

---

# LESSON XV.

## Further Remarks on Numerals, the Relative Pronoun.

Numbers above one hundred are expressed as follows: One hundred and one, is ***ih pak ling ih***, and so on to ***ih pak ling °kyeu;*** then the ***ling*** is dropped, and we have ***ih pah zeh*** (一百十), ***ih pah zeh ih, ih pah zeh nyi°, ih pah zeh san,*** etc. ***Ling*** really means "in addition."

The hundreds are expressed simply by ***nyi pak*** (二百), "two hundred," ***san pak*** (三百), "three hundred," etc. "One thousand" is ***ih ts'ien*** (一千). In expressing "one hundred and one," we say ***ih pak ling ih*** (一百零一). In expressing "one thousand and one," we say ***ih tshien ling ling ih.***

"Ten thousand" is ***ih man°*** (一萬). "One million" is ***ih pak man°*** (一百萬). The ordinal numerals are expressed in Chinese by prefixing ***°di*** (第) before the cardinal. Thus "the first" is ***°di ih*** (第一), "the second" ***di nyi°*** (第二), and so forth.

***°Soo*** 所 (lit. a place) is often used as a relative pronoun. It translates the English "who," "which," "what," "that," and "the things which." The clause it introduces usually comes before the subject of the sentence. Thus "All which you do, I am able to do also," would be ***noong soo tsoo kuh z-thi ngoo a nung-keu tsoo kuh.*** As has already been pointed out ***kuh*** often has the force of the relative.

VOCABULARY.

To tell, narrate, **kau°-soo°** 告訴.
To wonder, be surprised, **hyi-ji** 希奇.
To wear, **tsak** 着.
To take off, **thoeh** or **thoeh-theh** 脫脫.
To wear a hat, **ta°** 戴.
To take off a hat, **dzu** 除.

To laugh, **siau°** 笑.
To ridicule, **°lang-siau°** (Lit. Cold laugh) (冷笑). **Hyi°-siau°** 戲笑.
Laughable, **°hau-siau°** 好笑.
Very laughable, **siau°-sah-tse** 笑殺哉.
By the side of, **pien-deu** or **baung-pien** 邊頭, 傍邊.
Place, **han deu** 場頭.
My place, **°ngoo han-deu** 我場頭.
Right (Direction), **yeu°** 右.
Right hand, **yeu° °seu** 右手.
Left, **tsoo°**. (Sometimes pronounced **tsi°**), 左.
Left hand, **tsi° °seu** 左手.
Right side, **yeu°** pien (右邊), **yeu° pan-pan** (右板爿).
Early, **°tsau** 早.
Late, **an°** 晚.
Sharp, **kwha°**. (Same character as that used for fast), 快.
Dull, **dung°** 鈍.
Sweet, **dien** 甜.
Bitter, **°khoo** 苦.
Ugly, **pho°**. (Same character as that used for fear), 怕.
Pretty, **tshui°** 趣.
A shop, **ih ban tien°** 一爿店.
Take care, **°taung sing** or **°siau sing** 當心, 小心.
Take great care, **too° °taung sing** 多當心.
Tools, implements, **ka-sang** 傢生.
Furniture, **ka-°hoo** 傢伙.
A tea pot, **ih °po dzo-oo** 一把茶壺.
A class (in a school), **ih pan** 一班

EXERCISES.

(Translate into English.)

(1). °Ngoo tau° tien° °li chi° khoen°-kyien° too-hau° meh-z°, dan°-°z °ma ‘veh °chi kuh. (2). °Taung sing °tseu °hau. (3). °Taung sing °di-kuh yang-dien, faung° °hau la° siang-°ts °li. (4). Zung-kwaung an° tse, zieu° chi° kwhung°. (5). Kyung-tsau °ngoo ‘m-sa° °hau, lok veh °chi. (6). °Ngoo °soo kau°-soo° noong° kuh ih tsaung z°-°thi ‘veh iau° te bih nyung wo°. (7). Yoong-nyung wan ‘veh zung le °z peh °ngoo hyi-ji. (8). °Taung sing° di po tau °z °man kwha° kuh. (9). Yi te °ngoo wo° kuh z°-°thi °z °hau siau° kuh. (10). °Ngoo loo° °laung bang yi ‘veh dzak, ‘veh °hyau-tuh tau° ‘°a-°li chi° tse. (11). °Di °po dzo-oo tan tau° sien-sang han-deu chi°. (12). °I-kuh nyung tsi° °seu °sia z°, da°-ke nyung yeu° °seu °sia kuh. (13). Nyih °li °soo tsak kuh i-zaung, ya°-°li kwhung° kuh z-eu° iau° thoeh theh kuh. (14). °Nga-kok sien-sang tsing° mung kheu thoeh theh mau°-°ts, tsoong-kok nyung ‘veh thoeh-theh kuh. (15). °I-tsak mau man °hau khoen°, dan°-°z °i tsak °keu °z pho°-le-°si. (16). Too-hau° nyung hwen-°hyi chuh dien kuh meh-z°, ‘m-nyung hwen-°hyi chuh °khoo kuh. (17). Dzung °li °yeu °kyi-hau° nyung? Khoong pho° °yeu zeh man. (18). °Di-kuh ‘auh-sang-ts, man yoong° sing dok su, la° ih pan °li °z deu ih. (19). Ih kuh nyung tan le ih pak ling san kuh doong-dien.

(一) 我到店裡去看見多化物事但是買勿起个 (二) 當心走好 (三) 當心第个洋錢放好拉箱子裡 (四) 辰光晚哉就去睏 (五) 今朝我嘸啥好跦勿起 (六) 我所告訴儂个一庄事體勿要對別人話 (七) 用人還勿曾來是擬我希奇 (八) 當心第把刀是蠻快个 (九) 伊對我話个事體是好笑个 (十) 我路上撞伊勿着勿曉得到那裡去哉 (十一) 第把茶壺担到先生墻頭去 (十二) 伊个人左手寫字大槩人右手寫个 (十三) 日裡所著个衣裳夜裡睏个時候要脫脫个 (十四) 外國先生進門口脫脫帽子中國人勿脫脫个 (十五) 一隻猫蠻好看但是一隻狗是怕來死 (十六) 多化人歡喜吃甜个物事,嘸人歡喜吃苦个 (十七) 城裡有幾化人恐怕有十萬 (十八) 第个學生子蠻用心讀書拉一班裡是頭一 (十九) 一个人担來一百另三个銅錢

(Translate into Chinese).

(1). When I was in the carriage, I told the coachman to take care. (2). The clothes which that maiden wears are very pretty. (3). The boat is by the side of the river. (4). Yesterday I met a man who told me that he saw a carpenter kill a man with a sharp knife. (5). Although I do not speak Chinese well, please do not laugh at me. (6). I asked a man which road to take; he told me to go to the right. (7). I did not meet a single person on the road. (8). This bird is very beautiful; can it sing? (9). When it is warm you do not want to wear many clothes. (10). This tea is bitter and not good to drink. (11). Yesterday I walked very far, and so could not get up to-day. (12). Take this letter to the teacher.

(一) 我拉馬車裡个辰光叫馬夫當心 (二) 伊个小姐着个衣裳蠻趣 (三) 一隻船拉河邊上 (四) 昨日我撞着一个人告訴我話伊看見一个木匠担之快个刀殺一个人 (五) 我雖然中國話話來勿好請儂勿要笑我 (六) 我問一个人走那裡一條路伊話右手一條 (七) 我路上一个人也撞勿着 (八) 第隻鳥蠻趣會唱陌 (九) 天熱末儂勿要着多化衣裳 (十) 第个茶苦个勿好吃个 (十一) 昨日我走之多化路所以今朝跦勿起哉 (十二) 第封信担到先生墻頭去

NOTES. (1). *Han-deu* is very frequently used with persons and personal pronouns. Thus you do not say *Tan tau° yi* for take it to him, but *Tan tau° yi han-deu chi°*. "Leave it with me" would be *°Pa la° °ngoo han-deu.*

(2). The second sentence of the First Exercise is often used in speaking to a guest when he is departing. When he is about to go, he announces the fact by saying *Chi° tse* (去哉), meaning "I am going." You say *Man° chi°* (慢去), meaning "Go slowly," and then when he is walking away, *°Taung sing °tseu °hau* 當心走好.

(3). In the fifth sentence of the First Exercise *M-sa° °hau* means "not at all well."

(4). In the tenth sentence of the First Exercise notice how the object *yi* splits up the verb into two parts.

(5). In the sixth sentence of the Second Exercise "to the right" is expressed by *yeu° °seu* 右手.

---

# LESSON XVI.

## Verbal Idioms.

The idea of there being time to accomplish a thing is expressed by adding the words ***tuh-ji°*** (得及) after the principal verb. If there is not sufficient time to do a thing you add ***'veh-ji°*** (勿及) after the principal verb. Thus, ***Tsoo° tuh ji°*** (做得及) means "there is time to do a thing." ***Tsoo° 'veh ji°*** (做勿及) means "there is not time."

This expression is used most frequently with the verb ***le*** (來). ***Le tuh ji*** means "there is time," and ***le-veh-ji*** means "there is not time."

The idea of a thing being important is expressed by the words ***iau° °kyung kuh*** 要緊个. "Not being important," by the words ***'veh iau° °kyung*** (勿要緊), or ***'veh nge° sa°*** (勿礙啥). "Is it important?" or "Does it make any difference?" would be ***nge° sa° va°*** (礙啥陌).

***'Veh lauh*** is often used after verbs giving the idea of inability to do a thing. Thus ***Chuh 'veh lauh*** (吃勿落) means "unable to eat." ***°Zoo 'veh lauh*** (坐勿落) "Unable to sit because of lack of room." We also have the affirmative forms ***°zoo tuh lauh*** and ***chuh tuh lauh*** (坐得落, 吃得落).

### VOCABULARY.

Lest, **°sang-ts** 省之.

Either, or, **ok-°z** (或是), **ok-tse** 或者.

Difficult, **van-nan** (煩難), **Nan** 難

Easy, **yoong-yi°** 容易.

Slowly, gently, **man°-man°-nung** 慢慢能.

Walk slowly, **man°-man°-ts °tseu** 慢慢之走.

Besides, in addition, **ling°-nga°** (另外), **dze-nga°** (在外), **wan** 還.

How much more, **oo-°hwaung** (with **nyi** at the end of the clause), 何況.

Still more, **kung°-'ka 更加, yoeh-ka 越加.**
To start (on a journey), **°doong-sung 動身.** Lit. to move the body.
To become ill, **sang bing° 生病.**
To heal, **i-°hau 醫好,** or **khoen°-°hau 看好.**
To welcome (a guest), **nyung-tsih 迎接.**
To return (a debt or thing borrowed), **wan 還.**
To cry, **khok 哭.**
To lead, **°ling 領.**
To borrow or to lend, **tsia° 借.** (See Note).
To wash, **zing° 淨.**
Illness, **mau-bing° 毛病.**
A sedan coolie, **ih kuh jau°-pan 一个轎班,** or **ih kuh jau°-foo 一个轎夫.**
A star, **ih kuh sing 一个星.**
A grave mound, **ih kuh vung-san 一个墳山.**
A goat, **ih tsak san-yang 一隻山羊.**
A hog or pig, **ih tsak ts-loo 一隻豬玀.**
A stool, **ih tsak ngeh-°ts 一隻杌子.**
A chest of drawers, **ih tsak tsheu-deu 一隻抽頭.**
A drawer, **ih tsak tsheu-thi 一隻抽屜.**
A wash bowl, **ih tsak mien°-bung 一隻面盆.**
A plate, **ih tsak bung-°ts 一隻盆子.**
A Chinese eating bowl, **ih tsak °wen 一隻碗.**

***°Kwen*** **(管)** is the classifier for tubular things.

A Chinese or foreign pen, **ih °kwen pih 一管筆.**
A Chinese ink tablet, **ih kuh nyien°-°ts 一个硯子. Nyien°-de 硯台.**
A piece of ink, **ih khwe° muh 一塊墨.**
Foreign ink, **muh-°s 墨水.**
Clean, **koen-zing° 乾淨.**
Stop, **ding 停.**
Moon, **nyoeh-liang° 月亮.**
Precious, **°pau-pe° 寶貝.**

**EXERCISES.**

**(Translate into English.)**

(1). °Di-kuh °z iau° °kyung kuh, °tshing noong° 'veh iau° maung-kyi°. (2). °Di-kuh °siau-noen van° chuh 'veh lauh, °koong-p'o° °yeu mau-bing°. (3). Kyung-tsau le-'veh-ji°, ming-tsau °lau tsoo°. (4). °Liang kuh nyung ih tsak iui°-°ts laung° °zoo 'veh lauh. (5). 'Auh-sang-°ts mung° sien-sang °'a-°li-deu dok °chi °lau °'a-°li-deu ding. (6). Tshau zing° °hau-°ts meh, faung°-la° tsheu-thi °li. (7). Tsoong°-dien-nyung °i-kyung °ma-°ts san tsak san-yang, °i-kuh bang-yeu ling°-nga° wan iau° °ma s° tsak. (8). Noong° iung-ke te loong-tsoong nyung °hau, °oo-°hwaung te z°-ka nyung °hau nyi. (9). Bung-°ts lau °wen iau° kung°-ka koen-zing°. (10). Noong° iung-ke °tsau-zung-deu °doong-sung, °'au-pen°-nyih °doong-sung le-veh-ji° tau° kuh. (11). Noong° °kyi-z wan peh la° °ngoo? Ok-tse kyung-tsau °'au-pen°-nyih, ok-tse ming-tsau °tsau-zung-deu. (12). °Ngoo kuh bang-yeu sang bing° °soo-°i iau° °tshing i-sung khoen° khoen°. (13). Ya° °li la° thien laung° °khau-°i khoen° too °hau sing °lau nyoeh-liang°, nyih °li pih-koo° khoen° kyien° nyih-deu. (14). °Di-kuh °siau-noen nyih °li ‘veh khok, dan°-°z ya°-deu doo° khok. (15). °Ngoo tsia°-peh yi san-seh kwhe° yang-dien, ‘veh hyau°-tuh yi °kyi-z wan. (16). Kyau° jauᶜ-foo man°-man°-ts °tseu iung-we° °di-diau ka ‘ah °lau. (17). Iung-we° loo° ‘veh nyung-tuh °soo-°i °ngoo °tshing bih nyung °ling loo°. (18). °Ngoo la° bang-yeu han-deu tsia°-ᶜts nyanᵓ kwhe° yang-dien iung-we° iau° ma° ih tsak kha-mien°-de °lau s° tsak ngeh-°ts. (19). Kha °hau-ts mien°, mien°-bung iau° faung° °hau. (20). °Ngoo °tseu tau° mung-°kheu-deu nyung-tsih khak-nyung. (21). °Ngoo mung° i-sung °di-kuh mau-bing° i-tuh-°hau va°, yi wo° man°-man°-nung we° °hau kuh. (22). °Ts-deu, muh, pih, nyien°-de, tsoong-kok nyung soen° dok-su-nyung kuh s° yang °pau-pe°.

(一) 第个是要緊个請儂勿要忘記 (二) 第个小囝飯吃勿落恐怕有毛病 (三) 今朝來勿及明朝咾做 (四) 兩个人一隻椅子上坐勿落 (五) 學生子間先生那裏頭讀起咾那裏頭停 (六) 抄淨好之末放拉抽屜裏 (七) 種田人已經買之三隻山羊伊个朋友另外還要買四隻 (八) 儂應該待攏總人好何況待自家人好呢 (九) 盆子咾碗要更加乾淨 (十) 儂應該早晨頭動身下半日動身來勿及到个 (十一) 儂幾時還撥拉我,或者今朝下半日或者明朝早晨頭 (十二) 我个朋友生病所以要請醫生看看 (十三) 夜裏拉天上可以看多化星咾月亮日裏必過看見日頭 (十四) 第个小囝日裏勿哭但是夜頭大哭 (十五) 我借撥伊三十塊洋錢勿曉得伊幾時還 (十六) 叫轎夫慢慢之走因為第條街狹咾 (十七) 因為路勿認得所以我請別人領路 (十八) 我拉朋友壗頭借之廿塊洋錢因為要買一隻揩面檯咾四隻杌子 (十九) 揩好之面面盆要放好 (廿) 我走到門口頭迎接客人 (廿一) 我間醫生第个毛病醫得好陌伊話慢慢能會好个 (廿二) 紙頭,墨,筆,硯台,中國人算讀書人个四樣寶貝

(Translate into Chinese.)

(1). Which is easier, to learn to read Chinese or to learn to write Chinese? (2). I told you there was not time to do it; why do you still want to do it? (3). Why do you cry? Because I have heard that my friend is dead. (4). We will go early to-morrow morning to meet our friends, who have come from abroad. (5). Goats like to stand on the tops of the grave mounds. (6). You say that this temple is so fine to see, that I want to go more than ever to see it. (7). Please, teacher, do not speak so fast. If you will speak more slowly, I can understand. (8). If you do not return it immediately, no matter, I can wait two or three days. (9). Why did not the pupil come to school? Because he was sick. (10). I told the servant to put my clothes in the drawer. (11). The Chinese when they eat, use bowls; the foreigners use plates. (12). This fan belongs either to the teacher or to the pupil. (13). If you want to learn to write you must buy a pen, a piece of ink, and an ink tablet. (14). If you borrow money from another person, and do not return it, he will be unhappy. (15). I told the driver to stop the carriage at my friend's house.

(一) 那裏一様容易點學讀中國書呢還是學寫中國字 (二) 我對儂話來勿及做儂爲啥咾仍舊要做 (三) 儂爲啥咾哭，因爲我聽得我个朋友已經過世哉 (四) 明朝早晨頭我伲要去迎接外國來个朋友 (五) 山羊歡喜立拉坟山上 (六) 儂話第座廟是實蓋好看所以我更加要去看 (七) 請先生勿要話來實蓋快，若然先生話來慢點我可以聽得出 (八) 若然儂勿是就還勿礙啥，我可以等兩三日 (九) 學生子爲啥咾勿到學堂裏來，因爲伊生病咾 (十) 我叫用人放我个衣裳拉抽屜裏 (十一) 中國人吃飯个辰光用碗外國人用盆子 (十二) 第把扇子或者是先生个或者是學生子个 (十三) 若然儂要學寫字儂總要買一管筆一塊墨咾一个硯台 (十四) 若然儂拉別人壗頭借銅錢咾勿還个伊要勿快活 (十五) 我叫馬夫停馬車拉我个朋友屋裏

NOTES. (1). The word for "to borrow" and "to lend" is exactly the same in Chinese. The only way you can distinguish between them is by auxiliary words used in connection with them. Thus *Tsia*° *peh* (借撥) means "to lend." *Tsia*° *le* (借來) means "to borrow." Again *Tsia*° *chi*° (借去) means "to lend." But we have such constructions as °*Ngoo tsia*° *la*° *yi* (我借拉伊), meaning "I lend to him," and °*Ngoo la*° *yi han-deu tsia*° *kuh* (我拉伊壗頭借个), meaning "I borrowed it from him."

(2). In the fifth sentence of the First Exercise *Dok* °*chi* means "read begin," and *ding* means "stop." This is an ordinary form for asking where to begin the lesson and where to end it.

(3). In the fourteenth sentence of the First Exercise notice how *too* qualifies the verb *khok*.

(4). The twenty-second sentence of the First Exercise is a paraphrase of a Chinese proverb.

## LESSON XVII.

### More Verbal Idioms.

In asking questions °*yeu tuh?* (有得) sometimes precedes a verb with the sense, "is there to be had?" Thus °*Yeu-tuh °ma va°?* (有得買陌) means, "Is there to be bought?" °*Yeu tuh chuh va°?* (有得吃陌) means, "Is there anything to eat?" The answers to these questions would be °*yeu-tuh °ma kuh* (有得買个), °*yeu tuh chuh kuh* (有得吃个), "It can be bought." "There is something to eat."

*'Veh pih* (勿必) means "It is not necessary." Thus *'Veh pih khok* (勿必哭), "It is not necessary to cry." *'Veh pih chi°* (勿必去), "It is not necessary to go."

*Ih ngan 'veh* (一顏勿) before verbs means, "Not at all." Thus °*Ngoo ih ngan 'veh hyau°-tuh* (我一顏勿曉得) means, "I do not know at all." *Ih ngan 'veh zung khoen°-kyien° hyih* (一顏勿曾看見歇) means, "I have not seen it at all." *Ih ngan 'veh iau° khoen°* (一顏勿要看) means, "I do not want to see it at all."

VOCABULARY.

To visit, to pay respects to, **maung°** (望), **pa° maung°** 拜望.
To worship, **pa°** 拜.
To pay a ceremonial visit, **pa° khak** 拜客.
To bathe, **zing° yok** 淨浴.
To catch, seize, arrest, **tsauh** 捉.
To prepare, to provide, **yui°-be°** 預備.
To move a thing, **°doong** 動.
Loose, unstable, **°doong °lau °doong** 動咾動.
Immovable, **°doong-°'a veh-°doong** 動也勿動.
To remove (a residence), **pen** 搬, **pen-dzang** 搬場.
To commence work, **°doong °seu** 動手, **khe koong** 開工.
To open school, **khe 'auh** 開學.
To dismiss school, **faung° 'auh** 放學.
A finger, **ih tsak tsih-deu** 一隻指頭.
A toe, **ih tsak kyak-tsih-deu** 一隻脚指頭.
A cup, **ih tsak pe-°ts** 一隻杯子.
A clock, **ih tsak z°-ming-tsoong** 一隻自鳴鐘.
A watch, **ih tsak piau** 一隻錶.
A well, **ih tsak °tsing** 一隻井.
A basket, **ih tsak lan** 一隻籃.
An apple, **ih tsak bing-°koo** 一隻平菓.
A crab apple, **ih tsak hwo-'oong** 一隻花紅.
A towel, **ih diau °seu-kyung** 一條手巾.
A life, **ih diau sing°-ming°** 一條性命.
A hill, mountain, **ih zoo° san** 一座山.
A board, **ih kwhe° °pan** 一塊板.

*Fok* (幅) is the classifier of paintings or engravings.

A painting, **ih fok wo°** 一幅畫.
A chart or map, **ih fok doo** 一幅圖. **ih fok di°-°li-doo** 一幅地理圖
One time, **ih we** (一回), **ih thaung°** 一盪.
Two times, twice, **°liang we** (兩回), **°liang thaung°** 兩盪.

Whosoever, **van-i°** 凡係.

No matter who, **'veh lung° sa° nyung** 勿論啥人.

Whatsoever, no matter what, **'veh lung° sa°** 勿論啥, **dzoe-bien°-sa°** 隨便啥, **'veh kyui-sa°** 勿拘啥.

Whichever, **dzoe-bien°** 隨便.

Whatever time you please, **dzoe-bien° °kyi-z** 隨便幾時.

Wet, **sak** 濕.

Dry, **koen** 乾.

Always, **dzang-tsaung** 常庄, **dzang-dzang** 常常.

EXERCISES.

(Translate into English.)

(1). Z°-ming-tsoong kuh yoong°-deu °z peh nyung hyau°-tuh zung-kwaung. (2). I-tsak mau 'm-sa° yoong°-deu, ih ngan 'veh we° tsauh lau-°ts. (3). Ming-tsau °ngoo iau° tsheh chi° maung° bang-°yeu. (4). °Ngoo thing-tuh sien-sang m-sa° °hau °soo-°i le maung° maung°. (5). °Ngoo mung° mok-ziang° °zau vaung-°ts °kyi-z iau° °doong-°seu. (6). °Liang tsak °seu °yeu zeh tsak tsih-deu, °liang tsak kyak °yeu zeh tsak kyak-tsih-deu. (7). Sang bing° meh tsoong iau° °tshing i-sung we°-ts nyung kuh sing°-ming° °z iau° °kyung kuh. (8). °Zaung san °z van-nan, '°au san °z yoong-yi°. (9). °Di foong sing° iau° sa° nyung tan chi°? Veh lung° sa° nyung °khau-i tan chi°. (10). Kyung-ya°-deu iau° yui°-be° °hau, we°-ts ming-tsau °tsau-zung-deu iau° °doong-sung. (11). Yien°-°dze chi° ok-tse ming-tsau chi°, dzoe-bien° noong° meh tse. (12). °Tsing °li °s °i-kyung koen tse, veh hyau°-tuh na°-nung tsoo°-deu. (13). Zing°-ts yok iau° yoong° °seu kyung kha koen sung-°thi. (14). Khan-khan °ngoo faung° nyan tsak ping-°koo la° lan °li, yien°-°dze pih-koo° °yeu °so-°ng tsak, 'veh hyau°-tuh sa° nyung tan theh kuh. (15). °Ths di° piau °yeu tuh °ma va°? °Tsh-di° yang° yang° °yeu tuh °ma kuh. (16). °Loong-°tsoong kuh z°-°thi °ngoo °i-kyung hyau°-tuh, noong° 'veh pih te° °ngoo wo°. (17). °Di °pung su ih ngan m-meh wo°-doo. (18). °I-tsak pe-°ts °li °yeu sa° meh-z°? Pih-koo° °lang °s. (19). Tsoo° °di tsak de-°ts iau° yoong° °kyi kwhe° °pan? (20). °Di sen tshaung tsoo° le ih ngan 'veh °hau, dzang-tsaung °doong-°lau °doong. (21). Chi° koo° hyih meh? Chi° koo°-ts °liang we. (22). Sien-sang wo° ming-tsau 'veh °hau le, we°-ts iau° pen dzang °lau. (23). Van-i° nyung yoong° sing meh °khau-°i dzung-koong z°-°thi.

(一) 自鳴鐘个用頭是撥人曉得辰光 (二) 伊隻貓嘸啥用頭一顆勿會捉老鼠 (三) 明朝我要出去望朋友 (四) 我聽得先生嘸啥好所以來望望 (五) 我問木匠造房子幾時要動手 (六) 兩隻手有十隻指頭兩隻脚有十

隻脚指頭 (七) 生病末總要請醫生爲之人个性命是要緊个 (八) 上山是煩難下山是容易 (九) 第封信要啥人担去,勿論啥人可以担去 (十) 今夜頭要預備好爲之明朝早辰頭要動身 (十一) 現在去或者明朝去隨便儂末哉 (十二) 井裏水已經乾哉勿曉得那能做頭 (十三) 淨之浴要用手巾揩乾身體 (十四) 纔纔我放廿隻平菓拉籃裏現在不過有十五隻勿曉得啥人担脫个 (十五) 此地𨱏有得賣陌,此地様様有得賣个 (十六) 攏總个事體我已經曉得儂勿必對我話 (十七) 第本書一顏𠶒沒畫圖 (十八) 伊隻杯子裏有啥物事,必過冷水 (十九) 做第隻檯子要用幾塊板 (二十) 第扇窗做來一顏勿好常庄動咾動 (廿一) 去過歇末,去過之兩回 (廿二) 先生話明朝勿好來爲之要搬場咾 (廿三) 凡係人用心末可以成功事體

(Translate into Chinese.)

(1). When I have finished studying, I shall go to visit my friends. (2). No matter who comes; tell him I am busy (have affairs). (3). When the weather is wet I cannot go out to walk. (4). The pupils should not eat apples in the school room. (5). Children like to play the game of catching men. (6). The pupils read badly to-day; I think they did not prepare. (7). At what time does the school open, and at what time does it close? (8). I shall be pleased to have a conversation with you whenever you come. (9). This child does not want to study a bit; I think it would be best for him to go and do business. (10). I have already told you two or three times; do not forget. (11). Next month we shall remove our residence. (12). Near Shanghai there are no high hills, only grave mounds. (13). I cannot open this window; it is immovable. (14). Has the clock already struck? (15). How many eggs are there in the basket?

(一) 我讀罷之書要出去望朋友 (二) 勿論啥人來對伊話我有事體 (三) 天濕末我勿能彀出去跑路 (四) 拉學堂間裏學生子勿應該吃平菓 (五) 小囝歡喜做捉人个勃相 (六) 今朝學生子讀來勿好我想伊拉勿曾預備 (七) 啥辰光開學,啥辰光放學 (八) 儂隨便幾時來我𢡟歡喜

對儂白話 （九）第个小囝一顆勿歡喜讀書我想頂好伊出去做生意 （十）我已經對儂話兩三回勿要忘記 （十一）下个月我伲要搬場 （十二）近上海嘸沒高山必過坟山 （十三）第扇窗開勿來个動也勿動 （十四）鐘已經敲過末 （十五）籃裏有幾个蛋

NOTES. (1). In the fourth sentence of the First Exercise *'m-sa° °hau* means "not at all well."

(2). In the eleventh sentence of the First Exercise the expression *Dzoe-bien° noong° meh tse* is one very frequently used. It implies, "do it whenever and however you please."

(3). In the fourteenth sentence of the First Exercise *T'an theh* means "take away." We have already had the use of *Theh* after verbs, as *Thoeh-theh*, "to take off clothes." It can be used with almost any verb of motion. We have *Peh theh*, "to give away." *Chuh theh*, "to eat up." *Chi° theh*, "to cast off, disown." *Ma° theh*, "to sell away, etc."

(4). In the fifteenth sentence of the First Exercise *Yang° yang°* repeated means, "Things of every sort."

(5). Note that the usual expression in Chinese to say you are busy is *°Ngoo °yeu z°.°thi*. It is never very polite to tell any one that you are busy. A person asking whether you were busy would say *maung va*? "Are you busy?"

(6). In the fifth sentence of the Second Exercise the game *Tsauh nyung*, frequently played by Chinese children, is referred to.

(7). In the eighth sentence of the Second Exercise the clauses should be reversed. *Noong° dzoe-bien° °kyi-z-le* should come first.

(8). In the ninth sentence of the Second Exercise "to go and do business" is *Chi° tsoo° sang-i°*.

(9). In the fourteenth sentence of the Second Exercise *Tsoong k'au koo° meh* is the usual way of asking the question. *Tsoong* is shortened form of *Z°-ming tsoong*.

---

## LESSON XVIII.

### More Verbal Idioms.

***Siang*** (相) is often placed before transitive verbs and usually gives the idea of mutual or reciprocal. In some cases it is reflexive. As instances of reciprocal action we have ***siang °tang*** (相 打), to fight with one another. ***Siang mo°*** (相 罵), to revile one another. ***Siang lien*** (相 聯) to be connected together. ***Siang paung*** (相 幫), to help one another. In ***siang-sing°*** (相 信) the ***siang*** seems "to be used merely for emphasis."

***Khe*** (開) or ***khe-le*** (開 來) is used with many verbs to give the idea of spreading wide open. Thus ***Than-khe-le*** (攤 開 來) means "to unroll a bundle." ***Hyih-khe-le*** (揭 開 來) means "to open a box." ***Fung-khe*** (分 開) to divide, ***san°-khe*** (散 開), to scatter wide cast. ***Tshih-khe*** (切 開) or ***tshih-khe-le*** (切 開 來) means "To cut open, etc."

Not inclined to do a thing is expressed by the phrase ***'veh kau-hyung°*** (勿 高 興). Thus ***'Veh kau-hyung° chi°*** (勿 高 興 去) means "not inclined to go."

VOCABULARY.

To follow, **kung** 跟.
To tie, **vok** 縛.
To tie firmly, **vok-lau** 縛牢, or **vok lau-dzu°** 縛牢住.
To desire, to expect, **maung°** 望, or **po-maung°** 把望.
To bite or bark, **°ngau** 咬.
To blow, **tsh** 吹.
To blow out, to extinguish, **tsh °iung** 吹隱.
To blow into a blaze or flame, **tsh yaung°** 吹旺.
To fly, **fi** 飛.
To explain, **°ka-seh** 解釋.
To forsake, desert, depart from, **li-khe** 離開.
To permit, **°hyui** 許.
To allow, **nyang°** 讓.
Colour, **ngan-suh** 顏色.
Variegated colours, **°ng-ngan-loh-suh** 五顏六色.
Thought or meaning, **i°-s°** 意思.
A thief, **ih kuh zuk** 一个賊.

***Mien°*** (面) is used as the classifier for flat objects.

A drum, **ih mien° °koo** 一面鼓.
Hope, **maung°-deu** 望頭.
Wind, **foong** 風.
Wine, **°tsieu** 酒.
Rope, **ih diau zung** 一條繩, or **ih kung zung** 一根繩.

***Tsung*** (尊) is the classifier denoting idols or cannon.

A Buddhist idol, **ih tsung Veh** 一尊佛, or **ih tsung boo-sah** 一尊菩薩.
A Taoist god or idol, **ih tsung zung-dau°** 一尊神道.
A piece of bread, **ih kwhe° men-deu** 一塊饅頭.

***Khoo*** (顆) is the classifier used with plants, trees and flowers.

A tree, **ih khoo zu°** 一顆樹.
A flowering plant, **ih khoo hwo** 一顆花.
Cotton seed, **hwo-°ts** 花子.
A Chinese mile, **ih °li** 一里, or **ih °li-loo°** 一里路.
To regret, to be placed in an embarrassing position, **nan-we-dzing** 難爲情.

EXERCISES.

(Translate into English).

(1). **°Di-kuh °liang kuh ‘auh-sang-°ts °ngoo ’veh °hyui tsheh chi° beh-siang° we°-ts la° ‘auh-daung °li siang mo° °lau. (2). °Di kyui° sch wo° kuh i°-s° °ngoo ’veh °toong °tshing sien-sang °ka-seh. (3). °Di-tsak °tiau fi le kau-le-°si. (4). Tsauh-dzak-ts i-kuh zuk iau° yoong° ih kung zung vok-lau-ts. (5) °Di khoo hwo kuh ngan suh man tshui°. (6). Ya° °li kwhung° kuh z-‘eu° tung iau° tsh °iung. (7). °Ngoo faung° la° tshaung-°keu laung° kuh ih tsang °ts-deu peh foong tsh** thch tse. (8). Zak-zen °tshing khak °lau m meh °tsieu °z nan-we-dzing kuh. (9). 'Veh iau° pho°, °di tsak °keu 'veh °ngau kuh. (10). °Ngoo tau° miau° °li khoen°-kyien° ih tsung veh °lau too-°hau boo-sah. (11). °Ngoo thing-tuh °yeu nyung la° khau °koo. (12). °Di-deu tau° Zaung°-°he °yeu °so-°ng °li-loo°. (13). Soe-zen °di khoo zu° man °hau khoen°, zeu-r 'veh khe hwo kuh. (14). Zak-zen noong° iau° tau° san laung°, nyang° °ngoo kung noong° chi°. (15) Men-deu °tshing noong° tshih khe-le peh ih kwhe° la°·°ngoo chuh. (16) Bing° saug le man °dzoong, yieu°-°dze i-sung m meh maung°-deu. (17) Tsoong°-dien-nyung nau hwo-°ts san°-khe-le. (18). 'Auh-sang-°ts beh-siang° man kau-hyung°, dok su 'veh da° kau-hyung°. (19). Li-khe-ts Zaung°-°he nan meh °ngoo tau° Soo-tseu chi° tse. (20). °Ngoo po-maung° yi le, 'veh hyau°-tuh yi na°-nung wan 'veh zung le.

(一) 第个兩个學生子我勿許出去勃相爲之拉學堂裏相罵咾 (二) 第句說話个意思我勿懂請先生解釋 (三) 第隻鳥飛來高來死 (四) 捉着之一个賊要用一根繩縛牢之 (五) 第顆花个顏色蠻趣 (六) 夜裏睏个時候燈要吹隱 (七) 我放拉窗口上个一張紙頭撥風吹脫哉 (八) 若然請客咾嘸沒酒是難爲情个 (九) 勿要怕第隻狗勿咬个 (十) 我到廟裏看見一尊佛咾多化菩薩 (十一) 我聽得有人拉敲鼓 (十二) 第頭到上海有十五里路 (十三) 雖然第顆樹蠻好看然而勿開花个 (十四) 若然儂要到山上讓我跟儂去 (十五) 饅頭請儂切開來撥一塊拉我吃 (十六) 病生來蠻重現在醫生嘸沒望頭 (十七) 種田人拿花子散開來 (十八) 學生子勃相蠻高興讀書勿大高興 (十九) 離開之上海難末我到蘇州去哉 (二十) 我把望伊來勿曉得伊那能還勿曾來

(Translate into Chinese).

(1). The dog bit the sheep two or three times; it will probably die. (2). To-day there is no wind, and so it is not cold. (3). Men ought not to drink too much wine. (4). I have eaten a slice of meat and drunk a cup of tea, and now am able to walk. (5). Men can walk, only birds can fly. (6). There are many trees and flowers on the hill. (7). Many Chinese worship Buddhist and Taoist idols. (8). I wanted to follow you, but the teacher would not permit me. (9). Let me go and tell him that you have already returned. (10). I will use my knife and cut open the pear. (11). I heard the dogs barking in the night and so could not sleep. (12). Children like to play at beating the drum. (13). These flowers are of many different colours. (14). How many miles is it to Soochow? (15). When the pupils take an advanced lesson, the teacher should first explain it to them.

(一) 狗咬之羊兩三回恐怕要死脫 (二) 今朝𠲎沒風所以勿冷 (三) 人勿應該多吃酒 (四) 我已經吃之一塊肉咾一碗茶咾現在走得動哉 (五) 人會走必過鳥會飛 (六) 山上有多化樹咾花 (七) 多化中國人拜菩薩咾神道 (八) 我要跟儂但是先生勿許我去 (九) 讓我去告訴伊儂已經轉來哉 (十) 我要用我个刀切開第隻生梨 (十一) 夜裏我聽得狗垃拉叫所以睏勿着 (十二) 小兒歡喜敲鼓做勃相 (十三) 第顆花是五顏六色个 (十四) 到蘇州有幾化里路 (十五) 學生子要上書先生應該先對伊拉解釋

NOTES. (1). In the Buddhist religion in China a Buddha or one of his manifestations is known as a *veh*, the bodhisattvas are known as *Boo-sah*.

(2). A Chinese mile is about one-third of an English mile.

(3). In the sixteenth sentence of the First Exercise notice the expression *man °dzoong*, very heavy. This is the way the Chinese speak of a serious illness. They also speak of a disease being light, *chung*, just as we do.

(4). In the eighteenth sentence of the First Exercise *Veh da°* means "not very." This is a very frequent expression.

---

# LESSON XIX.

## Asking Questions, Expecting Negative and Affirmative Answers.

In addition to the interrogative forms already given there are ways of asking questions when a negative, or when an affirmative answer is expected.

Thus when the negative answer is expected, the clause begins with ***°chi*** (豈) and ends with ***nyi*** (呢). Thus ***°Chi °yeu sa° yoong°-deu nyi*** (豈有啥用頭呢). "Is it of any use?" It implies that it is not of any use and expects the negative answer. ***°Chi*** (豈) corresponds to the Latin ***num***, and implies No, or a negative of the proposition conveyed.

When the affirmative answer is expected the clause begins with ***°chi ‘veh*** (豈吥) and ends with the usual interrogative ***va°*** (𠲎).

Thus °*Chi* '*veh iung-ke tsoo*° *va*° (豈吥應該做㕵), "Ought you not to do it?" Implies that you ought to do it and expects the affirmative answer.

It will be seen that in this case also the °*chi* (豈) expects the negative of the proposition conveyed, that is, the negative of a negative proposition which is an affirmative. In other words the answer is, "That you ought not not to do it," or "You ought to do it."

## VOCABULARY.

Every place or everywhere, **kauh tshu°** 各處, or **kauh tau° lauh tshu°** 各到落處.

Of course, **z°-zen** 自然.

Afterwards, hereafter, **°'eu-°seu** 後首, **°'eu-le** 後來, **°i-°'eu** 以後.

Until, **dzuk-tau°** 直到, **°tung-tau°** 等到.

Daily, **nyih nyih** 日日, or **nyih-dzok** 日逐.

About, **iak-kwe** 約規, **iak-tsak** 約酌.

About the same (not much difference) **tsho-'veh-too** 差吥多.

Secretly, **'en°-'en°-°li** 暗暗裡.

True, **tsung** 眞.

False, **°ka** 假

Secure, **°'wung-taung°** 穩當.

A long time, **dzang-°yoen** 長遠, **dzang-°yoen-tse** 長遠哉, **ta-z-tse** 多時哉.

***Phih*** (疋) is the classifier denoting whole pieces of dry goods.

A piece of cloth, **ih phih poo°** 一疋布.

A piece of shirting, **ih phih yang poo°** 一疋洋布.

A piece of silk, **ih phih dzeu** 一疋綢.

A piece of satin, **ih phih doen°-°ts** 一疋緞子.

Grass, **°tshau** 草.

Vegetation in general, **hwo-°tshau-zu°-mok** 花草樹木.

Coal, **me** 煤.

To add, **ka** 加.

To add a little, **ka-°thien** 加點.

Honest, **lau-zeh** 牢實.

To pawn, **taung°** 當, **taung°-theh** 當脫.

To mortgage, **ah** 押, **ah-theh** 押脫.

To change a dollar into cash, **de°** 兌.

A ten cent piece, **ih kauh** 一角.

One cent, **ih fung** 一分.

Twenty cents, **°liang kauh** 兩角, 四開.

A half a dollar, **pen° kwhe° yang-dien** 半塊洋錢.

Small money, **°siau kauh-°ts** 小子角, **°siau yang-dien** 小洋錢.

Change, **°tsau-deu** 找頭.

Ricsha coolie, **tsho-foo** 車夫.

A great many, **kyau-kwan** 交關.

## EXERCISES.

(Translate into English.)

(1). We°-ts °lang °lau °hoo-loo °li iau° ka-°thien me. (2). °Ma °hau-ts, °tsau-deu iau °peh °ngoo. (3). 'Veh zung °zoo toong-yang-tsho iung-ke tah tsho-foo sien °kaung ding° peh yi °kyi kauh. (4). °I-kuh nyung °i-kyung taung°-theh-ts yi-kuh i-zaung. (5). °Ngoo iau° °ma °i-kwhe° di°-be dan°-°z °ngoo thing-tuk °i-kyung ah-theh tse. (6). °Mo man hwen-°hyi chuh °tshau. (7). °Ngoo pih-koo° °yeu pen° kwhe° yang-dien °soo-°i °ma-veh-°chi. (8). Yi ʻveh °khung lau-zeh wo° °soo-°i °ngoo ʻveh °hau siang-sing°. (9). Noong° °chi ʻveh iung-ke tsoo° dzuk tau° tsoo° °hau va°. (10). °Ngoo soe-zen kauh-tau° lauh tshu° zing °ʻa zing-veh dzak. (11). Noong° wo° lau-zeh wo°, nyung z°-zen siang-sing° kuh. (12). Nyih nyih dok su z°-zen °khau-°i ʻauh kuh. (13). °Tung tau° noong° dok wen ts °di °pung su nan-meh noong° we° wo° tsoong-kok wo°. (14). °Di-kuh °liang phih poo° kuh ngan-suh tsho-ʻveh-too ih yang° kuh. (15). ʻEn°-ʻen°-°li tsoo° z°-°thi °chi °yeu sa° yoong°-deu nyi. (16). °Di-deu tau° Soo-tseu °yeu °kyi-hau° °li soo? Iak-kwhe °yeu san pak °li-loo°. (17). °Di-kwhe° zak-deu iau° °pa le °ʻwung-taung° °tien. (18). Yi chi°-ts dzang-°yoen-tse wan veh zung °tsen le. (19). °Ngoo sien iau° ʻauh dok su °ʻeu-le ʻauh °sia z°. (20). Hwo-°tshau-zu°-mok nyung nyung hwen-°hyi khoen°. (21). Doo° yang-dien de°-ts °siau yang-dien iau° taung sing iung-we° °yeu too-hau° °siau kauh-°ts °z °ka kuh. (22). Tsung lau °ka van-nan khoen°-tuh tsheh. (23). °Di °pung su °yeu kyau-kwan z° °ngoo suh-veh-tsheh kuh.

(一) 爲之冷咾火爐裡要加點煤 (二) 買好之找頭要撥我 (三) 勿曾坐東洋車應該搭車夫先講定撥伊幾角 (四) 伊个人已經當脫之伊个衣裳 (五) 我要買伊塊地皮但是我聽得已經押脫哉 (六) 馬蠻歡喜吃草 (七) 我不過有半塊洋錢所以買勿起 (八) 伊勿肯牢實話所以我勿好相信 (九) 儂豈勿應該做直到做好陌 (十) 我雖然各到落處尋也尋勿着 (十一) 儂話牢實話人自然相信个 (十二) 日日讀書自然可以學个 (十三) 等到儂讀完之第本書難末儂會話中國話 (十四) 第个兩疋布个顏色差勿多一樣个 (十五) 暗暗裡做事體豈有啥用頭呢 (十六) 第頭到蘇州有幾化里數約規有三百里路 (十七) 第塊石頭要擺來穩當點 (十八) 伊去之長遠哉還勿曾轉來 (十九) 我先要學讀書後來學寫字 (二十) 花草樹木人人歡喜看 (廿一) 大洋錢兌之小洋錢要當心因爲有多化小角子是假个 (廿二) 眞咾假煩難看得出 (廿三) 第本書有交關字我識勿出个

(1). I do not know where the child has gone to; I have looked for him everywhere and do not know where to find him. (2). Call the servant to come and add some coal. (3). I told the pupil to sit here until the teacher returned. (4). I was almost beaten to death by him. (5). Take the dollar and change it into cash. (6). An honest man speaks true words. (7). I thought he was coming, but afterwards he wrote a letter to me and told me he could not come. (8). The children have played for a long time and now they should go to sleep. (9). Can you say that you did not know this? (10). Is it not good to do things so as to please others? (11). I had to walk here because I had no small money and so could not call a ricsha. (12). If he said he would do it, of course he will do it. (13). How many cash can you get for a dollar? (14). That man is not at all honest, and he has already pawned a lot of clothes which were not his own. (15). This man wears silk and satin; he must have a lot of money.

**(一) 小囝到那裡去我勿曉得,我各到落處去尋伊尋勿着 (二) 叫用人來加點煤 (三) 我叫學生子坐拉第頭等到先生轉來 (四) 我差勿多撥伊打殺哉 (五) 拿第塊洋錢兌銅錢 (六) 牢實个人話眞个說話 (七) 我想伊要來但是後來伊寫一封信來話伊勿好來 (八) 小囝勃相之長遠哉現在應該去睏 (九) 儂豈可以話第个是儂勿曉得陌 (十) 做事體撥別人快活豈阫是好陌 (十一) 因爲我嘸沒小洋錢勿能彀叫東洋車所以我只好走 (十二) 若然伊話要做个難末自然要做个 (十三) 一塊洋錢可以兌幾化銅錢 (十四) 伊个人一顚勿牢實已經當脫之多化勿是伊自家个衣裳 (十五) 第个人着之綢哫緞子个衣裳伊一定有多化洋錢**

NOTES. (1). In the third sentence of the First Exercise the expression °*kaung ding*° (講定) means "to settle the price." Literally it signifies declaiming to a fixed point.

(2) In the sixteenth sentence of the First Exercise °*Soo* (數) is added after °*li* (里) for the sake of euphony.

(3). In the twenty-second sentence of the First Exercise *suh* (識) is used. This is always used of knowing characters in the Chinese language. Sometimes it is used in the expression *Suh hoo*° *kuh* (識貨个), meaning to understand affairs. A man who does not *suh hoo* is a stupid fellow.

# LESSON XX.

## More Verbal Idioms.

***Tuk dzu°*** (得 住) and ***'veh dzu°*** (勿 住) are often used after the verb ***Lih*** (立) to stand, and give the sense of "able to stand," or "unable to stand." Thus ***Lih tuk dzu°*** (立 得 住) means "able to stand," and ***Lih 'veh dzu°*** (立 勿 住) unable to stand. The same words are used after other verbs also. Thus we have ***Khau° tuk dzu°*** (靠 得 住), meaning "Worthy to be trusted" and ***Khau° 'veh dzu°*** (靠 勿 住), meaning "unworthy to be trusted."

***Tuk koo°*** (得 過) is also used after verbs, and ***'Veh koo°*** (勿 過). Thus we have ***°Tang tuk koo°*** (打 得 過), meaning "Can be beaten." Literally "Beat, obtain surpass." ***°Tang 'veh koo°*** (打 勿 過) means "Can not be beaten." Literally "Beat, not surpass."

The expressions ***I°-tuk-koo°*** (意 得 過) and ***I°-'veh koo°*** (意 勿 過) are also idiomatic. The former means, "Within the range of pity;" the latter "Beyond the range of pity," or "greatly to be commiserated.

VOCABULARY.

To steal, **theu** 偷.
To beg, **°thau** 討.
A beggar, **°thau van° kuh** 討 飯 个 Lit. "To beg rice," or **kau° hwo°-°ts** 告化子.
To marry a wife, **°thau nyang-°ts** 討 娘 子. Lit. To beg for a wife. See note.
To tie (as a small parcel), **tsah** 紮.
To bind with a cord, **°paung** 綁.
To command, **fung-foo°** 分 付.
Price, **ka°-dien** (價 錢) or **'Aung-dzing**. (Most frequently used in the market) 行 情.
How much is it, or what is the price? **Sa° ka°-dien** 啥 價 錢. **sa° 'aung-dzing**.
A thief, **ih kuh zuk** 一 个 賊.
A robber, **ih kuh °jang-°dau** 一 个 强 盜.
A magistrate or mandarin, **ih kuh kwen-°foo**, or **ih kuh kwen** 一 个 官 府. Often **ih we°** (一 位) is used as the classifier.
Mandarin dialect, **kwen wo°** 官 話.
Shanghai dialect, **°Zaung-°he °thoo bak** 上 海 土 白.
A buddhist priest, **ih kuh oo-zaung°** 一 个 和 尚.
A taoist priest, **ih kuh dau°-z°** 一 个 道 士.
A nun, **ih kuh nyi-koo** 一 个 尼 姑.

***Tsang*** (張) is the classifier used for sheets of things.

A newspaper, **ih tsang sing-vung-°ts** 一 張 新 聞 紙.
A proclamation, **ih tsang kau°-z°** 一張告示.
A sheet of paper, **ih tsang°ts-deu** 一 張 紙 頭.

***Pau*** (包) is the classifier used for bales of things.

A bale of merchandize, **ih pau hoo°-suh 一包貨色.**

***Te*** (堆) is the classifier used for piles of things.

A pile of timber, **ih te mok-deu 一堆木頭.**

A pile of bricks, **ih te lok-tsen 一堆碌磚.**

***°Kwen*** (管) is the classifier for tubular things.

A flute, **ih °kwen dih 一管笛.**
A pen, **ih °kwen pih 一管筆.**
A pencil, **ih °kwen khan-pih 一管鉛筆.**
Green, **lok 綠.**
Red, **‘oong 紅.**
Blue, **lan 藍.**
Yellow, **waung 黃.**
Black, **huh 黑.**
Few, **°sau 少.**
Truly, **zeh-°dze 實在.**
More than, **’veh °ba (勿罷).** More than a hundred men is **‘veh °ba ih pak nyung 勿罷一百人.**
Less than, **’veh siau, ’veh °men 勿消, 勿滿.**
A small quantity of, **°tien** (used after the verb) **點.**
The whole of a thing, **ih tshih 一切.**
A man or two, **koen-°po-nyung 干把人.**
About (used with a number), **°po 把.**
About a hundred, **pak °po 百把.**
Nearly, **mau 毛.**
Nearly three miles, **mau san °li-loo° 毛三里路.**
A queue, **ih kuh °bien-°ts 一條辮子.**
Hair on the head, **deu-fah 頭髮.**
News, **sing°-sih 信息.**
To take things by force, **°tsiang**, or **°tsiang doeh 搶, 搶奪.**
To tie up, **°paung 綁.**
To put forth a proclamation, **tsheh kau°-z° 出告示.**

## EXERCISES.

(Translate into English).

(1). °I-kuh zuk dzang-tsaung lè theu meh-z°, tsauh dzak-ts meh iau° °paung yi °chi-le. (2). °Ngoo khoen°-kyien° sing-vung-°ts laung° wo° kwen-°foo °i-kyung tsheh kau°-z° tsha ping-ting chi° tsauh °jang-dau°. (3). Noong° na°-nung °lau peh yi °tang, iung-we° °ngoo °tang ’veh koo° yi °lau. (4). °Ngoo la° miau° °li khoen°-kyien° too-hau° ‘oo-zaung° la° pa° boo-sah. (5). Noong° iau° ‘auh kwen-wo° nyi ‘auh °Zaung-°he °thoo bak. (6). ‘Oo-zaung° tah-ts dau°-z° °z °liang yang° kuh, ‘oo-zaung° m-meh deu-fah, dau°-z° °yeu °bien-°ts kuh. (7). °Ngoo dzang-°yoen ’veh khoen° sing-vung-°ts tse, kyung-tsau °yeu sa° sing°-sih va°? (8). °Di-kuh ih pau hoo°-suh sa°-ka°-dien? (9). °I-kuh °siau-noen °kyi soe° tse? Lok soe°. (10). Nyi-°s-ziang° °i-kyung °ma-ts ih te lok-tsen yui°-be° °zau vaung-°ts. (11). Ya°-°li °yeu nyoeh-liang°, nyung hwen-°hyi tsh dih.

(12). °Di-kuh ih pau °li-hyang° °yeu °kyi °kwen pih? °Yeu ih pak °kwen. (13). Yi we°-sa°-ᶜlau 'veh °thau nyang-°ts? Iung we° yien°-°dze °thau 'veh °chi °lau. (14). San laung° ‘Ngoo khoen° too-hau° hwo, °yeu ‘oong °lau waung °lau bak, zeh-°dze °khau-°i wo° °ng-ngan-loh-suh kuh. (15). Nga°-kok nyung hwen-°hyi yoong° khan-pih °sia z°. (16). Tau° °Zaung-°he 'veh °men nyan° °li-loo°, °lau 'veh °ba zeh-nyi° °li-loo°. (17). Iung-we° °ngoo khoen° kyienᶜ °i-kuh °thau-van°-kuh dzang-°yoen 'veh chuh sa°, kuh-°lau kyau° yoong° nyung peh °tien meh-z° yi chuh. (18). °Di kuh pau iau° tsah °hau tan tau° tien° °li chi°. (19). °Lau-zeh kau°-soo° °ngoo °z zeh-ke° ka°-dien va°? (20). S° °lau tshih °lau bah °z sa° kuh soo°-mak? °z zeh °kyieu. (21). Nyi-koo °z ‘veh tsheh ka° kuh °siau-°tsia.

(一) 伊个賊常庒來偷物事捉着之末要綁伊起來 (二) 我看見新聞紙上話官府已經出告示差兵丁去捉强盜 (三) 儂那能咾撥伊打因爲我打勿過伊咾 (四) 我拉廟裡看見多化和尚拉拜菩薩 (五) 儂要學官話呢學上海土白 (六) 和尚搭之道士是兩樣个和尚無沒頭髮道士有辮子个 (七) 我常遠勿看新聞紙哉今朝有啥信息陌 (八) 第个一包貨色啥價錢 (九) 伊个小囝幾歲哉,六歲 (十) 泥水匠已經買之一堆磜磚預備造房子 (十一) 夜裡有月亮,人歡喜吹笛 (十二) 第个一包裡向有幾管筆,有一百管 (十三) 伊爲啥咾勿討娘子因爲現在討勿起咾 (十四) 山上我看多化花有紅咾黃咾白實在可以話五顏六色个 (十五) 外國人歡喜用鉛筆寫字 (十六) 到上海勿滿念里路咾勿罷十二里路 (十七) 因爲我看見伊个討飯个長遠勿吃啥蓋咾𠯗用人撥點物事伊吃 (十八) 第个包要紮好拿到店裡去 (十九) 牢實告訴我是實蓋價錢陌 (二十) 四咾七咾八是啥个數目,是十九 (廿一) 尼姑是勿出嫁个小姐

(Translate into Chinese.)

(1). If you do not read the newspaper, you will not know the news, and then when you converse with others, you will have nothing to say. (2). When a man dies many of the Chinese invite Buddhist and Taoist priests to the house to perform funeral ceremonies (3). I put my pen and pencil on my writing table, but now I cannot find them; has any one been in and taken them? (4). Which do you think is the pleasanter to listen to, mandarin or the Shanghai dialect? (5). When I was young I very much liked to play the flute. (6). A thief enters secretly and steals things, a robber kills men and enters and takes things by force. (7). Chinese are called yellow men, foreigners white men. (8). When you go to the shop, ask the price of the boots, and come and tell me. (9). I caught the thief and bound him to the tree. (10). If you use a foreign pen to write Chinese characters, they do not look well, you must learn to use a Chinese pen. (11). The Chinese beggars in the city are numberless. (12). When the Mandarin has important things to announce to the people, he puts forth a proclamation. (13). I saw more than a thousand soldiers. (14). The merchant bought more than five hundred chests of tea. (15). Are three hundred dollars sufficient to buy the house? Less than three hundred will do.

(一) 若然儂勿看新聞紙信息儂勿會曉得難沒儂搭別人白話儂嘸啥好話 (二) 人死之末中國人請和尚咾道士到屋裡來念經 (三) 我个筆咾鉛筆擺拉寫字檯上但是現在尋勿着，有啥人進來拿脫陌 (四) 儂想官話咾上海土白那裡一樣好聽點 (五) 年紀輕个時候我蠻歡喜吹笛 (六) 賊末偷伴之進來偷物事强盜末打殺之人咾進來搶物事 (七) 中國人是叫黃人外國人是叫白人 (八) 儂到店裡去問鞋子个價錢來告訴我 (九) 我捉之伊个賊咾綁伊拉樹上 (十) 若然用外國筆咾寫中國字是勿好看个儂終要學用中國筆 (十一) 城裡个告化子嘸數目拉 (十二) 官府有要緊个事體對百姓話啥伊要出告示 (十三) 我看見勿罷一千兵丁 (十四) 生意人買之勿罷五百箱个茶葉 (十五) 買房子三百塊洋錢有末，勿消三百塊个

NOTES. (1). To marry a wife is expressed by °*Than nyang-°ts*. When we speak of a woman being married we use the expression *Tsheh ka°* (出嫁), literally to go forth from the house or family. The woman leaves her own family entirely and joins the family of the husband whom she marries.

(2). The words '*Veh-°ba* (勿罷), more than, and '*Veh siau* (勿消), less than, are used in answer to questions. The words '*Veh °men* (勿滿) are often used for less than, meaning literally "Not full."

(3). In the second sentence of the Second Exercise "to perform funeral ceremonies" should be translated *Tsoo° koong-tuh* (做功德), or *Nyan°-kyung* (念經). It means to say masses for the soul of the departed.

(4). In the thirteenth sentence of the Second Exercise, "More than a thousand soldiers" can be expressed *Ih tshien too* (一千多) and in the fourteenth sentence "More than five hundred chests of tea" °*Ng pak too* (五百多).

(5). In the fifteenth sentence of the Second Exercise the answer would be '*Veh siau san pak kwhe°*.

## LESSON XXI.

### Verbal Idioms, Ordinals, and Remarks on the Expression of Time.

To express the idea of "about to do a thing" in Chinese you can use the words ***tsiang-iau°*** (將要). Thus ***Tsiang-iau°-chi°*** (將要去) means "about to go." ***Tsiang iau° °si*** (將要死) means "about to die." Another way of expressing the same idea is by adding ***kwha° tse*** after the verb. ***Kwha°*** means "fast." ***Chi° kwha° tse*** (去快哉) means "I will go fast," that is, in a moment. ***Le kwha° tse*** (來快哉) means "will come fast," that is, in a few minutes. ***Thih-°tsung*** is often used, meaning "just on the point of doing a thing." Thus ***°Ngoo thih-°tsung iau° chi°*** (我貼準要去) means "I was just going."

The expression "According to," or "as it seems to me," is expressed in Chinese by the words ***tsau° °ngoo khoen°*** (照我看). ***Tsau° °ngoo*** (照我) used alone would mean "Follow me." "Follow my example."

The Ordinals are formed from the Numerals in a very simple way. The word ***deu*** (頭) is prefixed before the first numeral and ***di°*** (第) before all the others. Thus "the first" is ***deu ih*** (頭一), the second is ***di° nyi°*** (第二), the third is ***di° san*** (第三), and so on. When first is used with the verb in the sense of the action being prior to some other action the word ***sien*** (先) is used. Thus we have ***noong° veh zung tsheh chi° kuh zien-deu °ngoo sien iau° kau°-soo° noong° ih tsaung z°-°thi*** (儂勿曾出去个前頭我先要告訴儂一庄事體), meaning, "Before you go I first want to tell you something." Again ***sien tsoo° °di yang° nan-meh tsoo° °i-yang°***, (先做第樣難末做伊樣) means "First do this and then do that." Again we have for the same expression ***sien tsoo° °di kuh, man° tsoo° i-kuh***, "First do this, slowly do that."

#### REMARKS ON TIME.

About midnight, **pen° ya° °po** 半夜把.

Just before daylight, **thien-liang°-kwha°** 天亮快.

In the evening, **waung-hwung-deu** 黃昏頭, **waung-hwung-°doong** 黃昏動.

Last month, **zien nyoeh** 前月, **zien kuh nyoeh** 前个月.

Next month, **°'au-nyoeh** 下月, **°'au kuh nyoeh** 下个月.

First part of the month, **nyoeh deu** 月頭, **nyoeh-deu-laung°** 月頭上.

The end of the month, **nyoeh °ti** 月底.

The middle of the month, **nyoeh pen°** 月半.

Every month, **nyoeh-nyoeh** 月月, **nyoeh-too** 月多, **°'me-nyoeh** 每月.

First day of the month, **tshoo-ih** 初一; second day of the month, **tshoo nyi°** 初二, and so on up to the tenth day of the month, which is **tshoo zeh**. After that **di°** 第 is used instead of **tshoo**. Thus the thirteenth of the month would be **di° seh-san** 第十三.

A year, **ih-nyien** 一年.

Half a year, **pen° nyien** 半年.

This year, **kyung nyien** 今年.

Last year, **jeu° nyien** 舊年.

Next year, **khe nyien** 開年, **le nyien** 來年, **ming nyien** 明年.

Every year, **nyien nyien** 年年, **°'me-nyien** 每年. (See note).

The new year, **sing nyien** 新年.

New year's day, **nyien tshoo ih** 年初一.

The end of the year, **nyien ya°** 年夜, literally "the night of the year." Also we have **nyien °ti** 年底.

At the beginning of the year, **nyien deu laung°** 年頭上.

To pass from the old year to the new, **koo° nyien** 過年.

**°Zaung pen°** and **°'au-pen°** are used with year, month, and night, just as they are used with day to denote the first half and the second half. Thus we have **°zaung pen° nyien** 上半年 for the first half of the year, and **°'au-pen° nyien** 下半年 for the second half.

Rice (bought in the shop), **°mi** 米.

**EXERCISES.**

**(Translate into English.)**

**(1). Leh-la° nyoeh-pen°, nyoeh-liang° °ting °hau khoen°. (2). °Hoo-loo iau° °iung kwha° tse °soo-°i iau° ka °tien me. (3). Tsau° °ngoo khoen°, °di kuh nyung °z khau°-veh-dzu° kuh. (4). °Tsau-zung-deu nyih-deu tsheh, le ya°-kwha° lok san. (5). °Di-kuh °z °ngoo °di nyi° kuh nyi-°ts, deu ih kuh °i-kyung tsheh mung tse. (6). Nyien tshoo ih too hau° nyung chi° pa° nyien. (7). Jeu° nyien °mi kyui° le °si, kyung nyien jang tse. (8). Noong° °'a-°li-deu koo° nyien? °Ngoo °siang la° ok-°li-koo° nyien. (9). Noong° su dok-ts °kyi-z tse? Pih-koo° pen° nyien. (10). Nyien ya° nyung nyung °yeu z°-°thi, sing nyien °li °loong-°tsoong nyung beh-siang°. (11). Yi tsiang iau° chi° kuh z-'eu° °yeu nyung le kyau° yi 'veh iau° chi°. (12). °Tshing °zoo ih hyih, sien-sang iau° le kwha° tse. (13). Thien liang° kwha° °z °ting °lang kuh z-'eu°. (14). °'Au kuh nyoeh °ngoo iau° tsheh mung, tau° Soo-tseu chi°. (15). Jeu°-nyien sang-i° ih ngan 'veh °hau kyung nyien po-maung° yi °hau-°tien. (16). °Zaung pen° nyien °di kuh 'auh-sang-°ts su dok le man °hau, °au pen° nyien ih ngan 'veh °hau. (17). °I-zak vaung-°ts °kyi-z °khau-°i °zau °hau? °Ngoo °siang khe nyien °khau-°i °zau °hau. (18). Lok nyoeh tshoo san °ngoo °sia ih foong sing° peh la° yi, yien°-°dze °z tshih nyoeh tshoo ih dan°-°z wan 'veh zung °yeu we sing° le. (19). Noong° 'veh zung tsheh chi°, sang-weh iau° sien tsoo° °hau. (20). Nyoeh-deu laung° peh doong-dien, yien°-°dze 'veh °hau peh kuh.**

(一) 垃拉月半月亮頂好看 (二) 火爐要隱快哉所以要加點煤 (三) 照我看第个人是靠勿住个 (四) 早晨頭日頭出來夜快落山 (五) 第个是我第二个兒子頭一个已經出門哉 (六) 年初一多化人去拜年 (七) 舊年米貴來死今年强哉 (八) 儂那裡頭過年,我想拉屋裡過年 (九) 儂書讀之幾時哉,必過半年 (十) 年夜人人有事體新年裡攏總人勃相 (十一) 伊將要去个時候有人來叫伊勿要去 (十二) 請坐一歇先生要來快哉 (十三) 天亮快是頂冷个時候 (十四) 下半月我要出門到蘇州去 (十五) 舊年生意一顏勿好今年把望伊好點 (十六) 上半年第个學生子書讀來蠻好下半年一顏勿好 (十七) 伊宅房子幾時可以造好,我想開年可以造好 (十八) 六月初三我寫一封信撥拉伊現在是七月初一但是還勿曾有回信來 (十九) 儂勿曾出去生活要先做好 (二十) 月頭上撥銅錢現在勿好撥个

(Translate into Chinese.)

(1). We will close the school on the fifth of next month. (2). For how many weeks will you close the school? For about six weeks. (3). Sometimes in the evening as the sun is sinking there are many beautiful colours in the sky. (4). As it appears to me you can finish this book in six months. (5). Just as I was about to go to sleep, I heard some one call out that the house was on fire. (6). The thief enters about midnight. (7). Before you go to school you should first wash your face and hands. (8). On the first day of the year all the shops close their doors. (9). When will you begin to study Chinese again? I think next year. (10). A year has twelve months, a month has thirty days or twenty-nine days. If it has thirty days, it is called a large month; if it has twenty-nine days, it is called a small month. (11). Last month I was sick, but now I am better. (12). Where were you yesterday afternoon? I had gone out to pay New Year's calls. (13). At New Year's time every one wears their best clothes. (14). Now I have no money; I will pay you at the end of the month.

(一) 下个月初五伲要放學 (二) 放之幾个禮拜,約酌六个禮拜 (三) 拉夜快日頭落山个時候常時拉天上有多化趣个顏色 (四) 照我看第本書儂六个月功夫可以讀完 (五) 我貼準要睏个時候我聽見人喊房子火着

哉 (六) 賊進來是半夜把个時候 (七) 儂勿曾到學堂裡先要揩面咾淨手 (八) 拉年初一攏總个店全關門个 (九) 儂幾時再起頭讀中國書,我想開年起頭 (十) 一年有十二个月一个月或者有三十日或者有念九日,若然三十日是叫大月若然念九日是叫小月 (十一) 前个月我生病哉但是現在我好點 (十二) 昨日下半日儂拉那裡頭,我出去拜年哉 (十三) 垃拉新年裡各人着頂好看个衣裳 (十四) 現在無沒銅錢垃拉月底撥儂

NOTES. (1). In regard to the expressions *Nyien-nyien* and *Nyoeh-nyoeh* it may be remarked that a very common way of forming the plural in Chinese is by the repetition of the noun. Thus *Nyung-nyung* means men in general.

(2). In the sixth sentence of the First Exercise the expression *Pa° nyien* means to pay respects at New Year's time." *Pa°*, to worship, is used of worshipping deities, and also of worshipping or paying respect to men.

(3). In the fifth sentence of the Second Exercise the expression for a house to be on fire is *°Hoo-dzak tse*, 火着哉.

---

# LESSON XXII.

## On Comparison.

The usual way of forming the Comparative Degree of Adjectives has already been stated.

When two things are compared with one another in Chinese the words ***°pi*** (比) or ***°Pi-ts*** (比之) are used between them. Thus ***°Mo °pi-ts °keu doo°*** (馬比之狗大) means, "the horse is larger than the dog." ***Yi °pi noong° °hau*** (伊比儂好), "He is better than you."

There are a good many other ways of expressing comparison. Thus ***'Veh jih*** (勿及) means, "not equal to." Also we have ***'Veh zu*** (勿如), meaning, "not equal to, or not up to."

### VOCABULARY.

To present or send, to escort a person on the way, **soong°** 送.
To count, **°soo** 數.
To reckon, **soen°** 算.
To send (a person), **tsha** 差.
To send a letter, **kyi°** 寄.
To deport oneself, to treat others, **°de** 待.
To treat rudely, **°de man°** 怠慢.
To keep, observe, **°seu** 守.
To knock the head on the ground, to kow-tow, **kheh-deu** 磕頭.
A loaf, **ih kuh men-deu** 一个饅頭.

A stone mason, **ih kuh zak-ziang°** 一个石匠.
A hammer, **ih kuh laung-deu** 一个榔頭, or **ih °po** 一把.

A wine shop, **ih ban °tsieu tien°** 一爿酒店.

***Te°*** (一對) is the classifier denoting a pair or a brace.

A pair of fowls, **ih te° kyi** 一對雞.
A pair of candles, **ih te° lah-tsok** 一對蠟燭.

A husband and wife, **ih te° foo-tshi** 一對夫妻.

***°Kheu*** (口) is the classifier for some articles of furniture, and for a well.

A book case, **ih °kheu su-dzu** 一口書櫥.
Convenient, **bien°-taung°** 便當.
Clever, wise, **tshoong-ming** 聰明.
Propriety, custom, **kwe-°kyui** 規矩.

Sometimes, **dzang-z** 常時.
As if, like, **°hau-°ziang** 好像.
To compare, **°pi** 比.
An account, **tsang°** 賬.

## EXERCISES.

(Translate into English.)

(1). La° nyien ya° kauh nyung iau° soen° tsang°. (2). Noong° we°-sa°-°lau iau° chi°? iung-we° yi tsha °ngoo chi° °lau. (3). Sing° kyi°-tsheh chi° meh? Veh zung zieu° iau° kyi° chi°. (4). Zak-ziang° iau° yoong° °kyi kwhe° zak-deu? °Ngoo 'veh hyau°-tuh veh zung soen° koo° hyih. (5). Yi dzang-tsaung °de °ngoo man °hau, °soo-°i °ngoo iau° soong° °tien meh-z° la° yi. (6). Su-dzu °li noong° °pa-ts °kyi °pung su? 'Veh °hyau-tuh we°-°ts 'veh zung° °soo °lau. (7). Khak nyung tsheh chi° meh iung-ke soong° yi tau° mung-°kheu. (8). °Di-°kheu kwen-ze sa° nyung tsoo° kuh? Mok-ziang° tsoo° kuh. (9). Noong° kuh °mo °pi °ngoo kuh kwha° too-hau°. (10). °Di-kuh 'auh-sang-°ts °pi-ts °i-kuh tshoong-ming °tien. (11). °Di-kuh ih te° lah-tsok °khau-°i °pi °pi khoen°, ih ngan meh doo° °siau. (12). °I-kuh °liang kuh nyung siang-mo° kuh yoen-koo° °z we°-ts la° °tsieu tien° °li too-chuh-ts °tsieu °lau. (13). Yien°-°dze foo° tsang° 'veh bien°-taung°, °tung tau° °'au kuh nyoeh. (14). °Di-kuh ih te° foo-tshi man° °hau ih ngan 'veh siang-mo°. (15). °Di-kuh nyung tsoo° z°-°thi 'veh jih °i-kuh nyung °hau. (16). Pa° nyien kuh z-'eu° °siau-noen iung-ke te doo° nyung kheh-deu. (17). °Nga-kok nyung chuh van° kuh zung-kwaung hwen-°hyi chuh men-deu. (18) °Di-kuh nyung ih ngan veh °toong sa°, °z °hau-°ziang 'veh zung dok hyih su. (19). Sien-sang dzang-tsaung kyau° 'auh-sang-ts° seu kwe-°kyui. (20). 'Veh iau° °de man° bih nyung.

(一) 拉年夜各人要算帳 (二) 儂爲啥咾要去,因爲伊差我去咾 (三) 信寄出去末,勿曾就要寄去 (四) 石匠要用幾塊石頭,我勿曉得勿曾算過歇 (五) 伊常庄待我蠻好所以我要送點物事拉伊 (六) 書橱裡儂擺之幾本書,我勿曉得爲之勿曾數咾 (七) 客人出去末應該送伊到門口 (八) 第口棺材啥人做个,木匠做个 (九) 儂个馬比我个快多化 (十) 第个學生子比之伊个聰明點 (十一) 第个一對臘燭可以比比看一顛無末大小 (十二) 伊个兩个人相駡个緣故是爲之拉酒店裡多吃之酒咾 (十三) 現在付帳勿便當等到下个月 (十四) 第个一對夫妻蠻好一顛勿相駡 (十五) 第个人做事體勿及伊个人好 (十六) 拜年个時候小囝應該搭大人磕頭 (十七) 外國人吃飯个晨光歡喜吃饅頭 (十八) 第个人一顛勿懂啥好像勿曾讀歇書 (十九) 先生常庄叫學生子守規矩 (二十) 勿要待慢別人

(Translate into Chinese).

(1). The Chinese use rice to make wine. (2). This man treats his servants very well. (3). According to Chinese custom before a man dies his coffin is made. (4) If I wish you to come, I will send you a letter. (5). To take the child along with us will not be convenient. (6). He is older than you. (7). The stone mason uses stones, the carpenter uses wood. (8). I pay my bills at the end of the month. (9). He and I have had a quarrel because he treated me rudely. (10). I wish the carpenter to come and make a book case. (11). Because I have forgotten so many characters, it is as if I had not read this book before. (12). A scholar is wiser than a farmer. (13). If a man takes too much wine he can not do his work. (14). My friend came to visit me, and then I escorted him to his home. (15). This book I will present to you, do not return it.

(一) 中國人用米做酒 (二) 第个人待伊个用人蠻好 (三) 照中國規矩一个人勿曾死先要做棺材 (四) 若然要儂來末我寄一封信來 (五) 帶小囝去是勿便當 (六) 伊比之儂年紀大點 (七) 石匠用石頭木匠用木頭 (八) 我个帳是拉月底付个 (九) 因爲伊待慢我所以我對伊相駡 (十) 我要木匠來做一口書橱 (十一) 因爲我忘記脫之多化字所以好像

我勿曾讀歇第本書 (十二) 讀書人比之種田人聰明點 (十三) 若然一个人多吃之酒伊勿會做生活 (十四) 我个朋友來望望我後來我送伊到伊屋裡去 (十五) 第本書我送撥儂勿要還个

NOTES. (1). In the fifth sentence of the First Exercise notice the use of *Soong*° °*tien*. °*Tien* means "a few things."

(2). In the ninth sentence of the First Exercise *kwha*° *too-hau*° means very much faster.

(3). In the sixteenth sentence of the First Exercise the expression *Kheh-deu* refers to the most formal salute of the Chinese. It is used by an inferior before a superior. The usual polite salutation is to clasp the hands together and move them from the feet to the forehead. This is called *Tshaung*° *zo*° (唱喏) or *Tsauh-ih* 作揖.

(4). In the nineteenth sentence of the First Exercise we have the expression °*Seu kwe*-°*kyui* 守規矩. This is very frequently used. It means to act according to the laws of propriety. It is a command frequently given to children.

---

## LESSON XXIII.

### The Points of the Compass.

The four cardinal points of the compass in Chinese are expressed as follows: ***Toong, nen, si, pok*** (東、南、西、北), East, South, West, North. Thus it will be seen that they do not follow the same order as we. North East is ***Toong-pok*** (東北). Lit. East North. North West is ***Si-pok*** (西北). Lit. West North. South East is ***Toong-nen***, and South West is ***Si-nen*** 西南.

The word ***pien*** (邊) is generally added when direction or place is indicated. Thus we have for the North ***Pok-pien***, for the West ***Si-pien***. ***Pien*** literally means "side," and is a shortened form of ***pien-deu*** (邊頭).

In giving directions as to locality, the Chinese make very frequent use of the points of the compass.

### VOCABULARY.

To break, smash, **se°** or **°tang-se°** or **khau-se°** 碎, 打碎, 敲碎.

To beget, to nourish, **°yang** or **sang °yang** 養, 生養.

To lose, to forfeit, **seh**, or **seh-theh** 失, 失脫.

To arrange, to attend to matters, to direct, **ban°** 辦.

A Compradore, **°ma-ban°** 買辦.

To consult, **saung-liang**, **tsung-tsak** 商量, 斟酌.

To point with the hand, **°tien** or **°ts-°tien** 點, 指點.

To separate, **fung** or **fung-khe** 分, 分開.

To hinder, oppose, **°tsoo** or **°tsoo-taung°** 阻, 阻擋.

To answer, **we-deu** or **we-tah** 回頭, 回答.

To exchange, to barter, **wen°** or **diau°** 換, 調.

To attend to a thing to make it right, **loong** or **loong °hau** 弄, 弄好.

To distinguish, **fung-pih** 分别.
A difference, **ih kuh fung-pih** 一个分别.
Wages. **koong-dien** 工錢.
Salary, **sok-sieu**, or **sing-foong°**, or **sing-°soe** 束脩, 薪俸, 薪水.
Misery, **°khoo-nau°** 苦惱.
Rain, **°yui** 雨.
To rain, **lauh °yui** 落雨.
Coolie, **tsheh-tien°** 出店.
A duck, **ih tsak ah** 一隻鴨.
A broom, **ih °po °sau-°tseu** 一把掃帚.
A snake, **ih diau zo** 一條蛇.
A stick of bamboo, **ih kung tsok-deu** 一根竹頭.
Glass, **poo-li** 玻璃.
A glass (for the table), **ih tsak poo-li pe-°ts** 一隻玻璃杯子.

***Doong*** (桶) is the classifier for casks, tubs and buckets.

A bucket of water, **ih doong °s** 一桶水.

***Bing*** (瓶) is the classifier for bottles.

A bottle of medicine, **ih bing yak** 一瓶藥.

***Siang*** (箱) is the classifier for boxes of things.

A box of dollars, **ih siang yang-dien** 一箱洋錢.
A box of tea, **ih siang dzo-yih** 一箱茶葉.
Tired, **sa-doo** 弛潳.
Square, **faung** 方.
Round, **yoen** 圓.
Thick, **°'eu** 厚.
Thin, **bok** 薄.
Instead of, **°de-thi°** 代替.
Sufficient, **keu-z°** or **keu-z°-tse** or **°yeu-tse** 彀事, 彀事哉, 有哉.
Together with (two persons doing a thing), **da ka** 大家.

**EXERCISES.**

**(Translate into English.)**

(1). Tsoong-kok tsok-deu doo° °yeu yoong°-deu, °khau-°i tsoo° lau °lau de-°ts °lau iui-°ts °lau too-hau° meh-z°. (2). °Ngoo mung°-ts yi san we, dan°-°z yi ih kyui° 'veh we-deu. (3). Tsoong°-dien nyung °yang too-hau° kyi °lau ah. (4). °Hau-la-va°? Hau-la zia°-zia°. (5). Kyung-tsau °hau-°tien va°? Zauh-ya°-deu chuh-ts yak °lau kyung-tsau sau-we °hau-°tien. (6). Nyih-deu toong-pien tsheh °lau si-pien lauh. (7). Pok-pien °lang °lau nen pien °noen. (8). °Ngoo-nyi iau° da-ka saung-liang na°-nung tsoo°-deu. (9). Di-kuh poo-li 'man bok kuh, yoong-yi° 'taug-se°. (10). Khoen°-kyieu° nyung iau° tsoo° 'veh °hau kuh z°-°thi meh, iung-ke °tsoo-taung° yi. (11). Khoen°-yang-nyung seh-theh-ts ih tsak yang °lau iau chi° zing yi. (12). Sien-sang iau° °kyi-hau° sok-sieu? Iau° zeh kwhe° yang-dien ih nyoeh. (13). Noong° kuh yoong°-nyung °kyi-hau° koong-dien ih nyoeh?

Lok kwhe° yang-dien ih nyoeh. (14). Toong-pok foong iau° lauh °yui. (15). Yien°-°dze la lauh °yui, tsoong-iau° tan ih °ting san° sang-ts ling sak. (16). Zauh-nyih °ngoo °tseu-ts san-seh °li-loo°, °soo-°i kyung-tsau 'man sa-doo. (17). °Ngoo °tien peh yi khoen° ih diau zo. (18). °Di-kuh kwen-°foo 'veh we° ban° z°-°thi. (19). Noong° °tau le-tse, °ngoo thih-tsung iau° tau noong° han-deu chi°. (20). °Di kuh nyung seh-theh-ts yi-kuh sang-i °lau saug-ts dzang-°yoen kuh bing° zeh°-dze °khoo-nau tuh-juk. (21). °Di tsak siang-°ts °z faung kuh, °di tsak °doong °z yoen-kuh. (22). Tsheh-tien° le wo° iau° doong-dien we°-ts iau° chi° °ma ih °po °sau-°tseu °lau. (23). °Di kuh °ts-deu thuk bok iau° noong° chi° weu° °‘cu-tien kuh. (24). Noong° thuh sa-doo, °ngoo le °de noong° tsoo°. (25). °Di sen° mung 'veh °hau khe, chi° kyau° mok-ziang loong °hau. (26). Yi-kuh seh-wo° tah-ts noong° kuh seh-wo° °yeu fung-pih. (27). °Di-kuh °liang kuh nyung° dzang-tsaung siang-mo°, fung-khe meh °hau.

(一) 中國竹頭大有用頭可以做籃咾檯子咾椅子咾多化物事 (二) 我問之伊三回但是伊一句勿回頭 (三) 種田人養多化雞咾鴨 (四) 好拉陌,好拉謝謝 (五) 今朝好點陌,昨夜頭吃之藥咾今朝稍爲好點 (六) 日頭東邊出咾西邊落 (七) 北邊冷咾南邊煖 (八) 我伲要大家商量那能做頭 (九) 第个玻璃蠻薄个容易打碎 (十) 看見人要做勿好个事體末應該阻擋伊 (十一) 看羊人失脫之一隻羊咾要去尋伊 (十二) 先生要幾化束脩,要十塊洋錢一月 (十三) 儂个用人幾化工錢一月,六塊洋錢一月 (十四) 東北風要落雨 (十五) 現在拉落雨終要担一頂傘省之淋濕 (十六) 昨日我走之三十里路所以今朝我蠻弛瘏 (十七) 我點撥伊看一條蛇 (十八) 第个官府勿會辦事體 (十九) 儂倒來哉我貼準要到儂壗頭去 (二十) 第个人失脫之伊个生意咾生之長遠个病實在苦惱得極 (廿一) 第隻箱子是方个第隻桶是圓个 (廿二) 出店來話要銅錢爲之要去買一把掃帚咾 (廿三) 第个紙頭忒薄要儂去換厚點个 (廿四) 儂忒弛瘏我來代儂做 (廿五) 第扇門勿好開去叫木匠弄好 (廿六) 伊个說話搭之儂个說話有分別 (廿七) 第个兩个人常庄相罵分開末好

(Translate into Chinese.)

(1). Is there any answer? Yes, please wait until I write it. (2). The cold wind blows from the North; you ought to wear more clothes. (3). The scholar was unable to answer what the teacher asked him. (4). I want to consult with you on an important matter. (5). When it rains the children cannot go out to play. (6). I have a fan, you have a knife, I want a knife you want a fan, let us exchange. (7). I killed the snake with a stick. (8). Tell the compradore what you want to buy and he can buy it for you. (9). I have lost my watch and am willing to give five dollars to the man who finds it and returns it to me. (10). My salary is not sufficient; I must ask you to increase it. (11). This coolie wipes and sweeps very clean. (12). I pointed out the river to him on the map. (13). I cannot go away until I have arranged this matter. (14). I could not study diligently to-day because I was too tired. (15). How many bottles of medicine have you taken? I have already finished three.

(一) 有啥回信陌,有个,請等一歇等我寫好仔 (二) 冷風從北邊吹來儂應該多着點衣裳 (三) 先生問个,學生子回頭勿出 (四) 我要搭儂商量要緊个事體 (五) 落之雨小囝勿好出去勃相 (六) 我有一把扇子儂有一把刀我要一把刀儂要一把扇子讓我伲調一調 (七) 我用之一根棒打殺之一條蛇 (八) 儂對買辦話儂要買啥伊可以對儂買个 (九) 我失脫之我个表情願撥拾着之咾還撥我个人五塊洋錢 (十) 我个薪水勿彀事我終要請儂加點 (十一) 第个出店揩咾掃瓚瀏漉 (十二) 地圖上我點撥伊看一條河 (十三) 我勿曾辦好第庄事體我勿能彀出去 (十四) 今朝我勿能彀用心讀書因爲我忒弛瘏 (十五) 儂吃之幾瓶藥,我已經吃完之三瓶

NOTES. (1). Those learning to speak Chinese must be careful never to refer to the remuneration given to their teachers as *koong-dien* (工錢). but to use the polite form of speech, *sok-sieu* or *sing-foong* 束脩, 薪俸. *Sok-sieu* means literally "dried meat," and comes from the ancient custom of paying a teacher in kind. The teacher himself could refer to remuneration as *sing-soe* 薪水.

(2). °*Eu* 厚 and *Bok* 薄 refer to things. In speaking of a person being thin we use the word *seu*° 瘦, and of being fat, the word *Tsaung*° 壯.

(3). The fourth sentence of the First Exercise is the usual salutation meaning, "How do you do?" "Does it go well with you?" The answer is also the usual one.

(4). In the seventh sentence of the First Exercise °*Noen* means "warm" 煖.

(5). In the eleventh sentence of the First Exercise *Khoen°-yang-nyung* means "shepherd." Literally "Look-sheep-man."

(6). In the twenty-fifth sentence of the First Exercise the word *Loong* has a very wide meaning. There is hardly anything in China that you cannot *Loong °hau*, that is, "put to rights."

---

# LESSON XXIV.

## Some Remarks on Gender.

As already remarked words in Chinese do not change their form to indicate gender. Sometimes, however, words indicating gender are placed before them. ***Nen*** **(男)**, "Male" and **°*Nyui*** **(女)**, "female," are used with human beings in this way. Thus we have ***Nen nyung*** **(男 人)** for "man," and **°*Nyui nyung*** **(女 人)** for "woman." ***Nen noen*** (男 囝) means "a male child," and **°*Nyui noen*** (女 囝) "a female child."

When speaking of the male and female of animals ***Yoong*** (雄) and ***Tsh*** (雌) are used. Thus we have ***Yoong Kyi*** **(雄 雞)** for "cock," and ***Tsh kyi*** **(雌 雞)** for "hen," ***Yoong s-°ts*** **(雄 獅 子)** for "lion," and ***Tsh s-°ts*** (雌 獅 子) for "lioness."

VOCABULARY.

To crow, **di** 啼.
To offend, **tuh-°dzoe** 得 罪.
To hide oneself, **ben°-°loong** 背 攏.
To hide a thing, **khaung°-°loong** (囥 攏), or **khaung°** 囥.
To gain or make a profit, **dzan°** 賺.
Profits in business, **dzan°-deu** 賺 頭.
To lose in business, **zeh** 折, **zeh-theh** 折 脫, **zeh-°pung** 折 本.
To congratulate a person, **koong-°hyi** 恭 喜.
To become rich, **fah-dze** 發 財.
To lock, **°soo** 鎖.
To bar or bolt the door, **sen** 閂.
The bar, or bolt of the door, **sak** 栅.
To examine carefully, **dzo** 查, **dzo-°khau** 查 考.
To examine a class, **°khau-su** 考 書.
To fall, **tih** 跌.
To save, **kyeu°** 救.
To stop, **ding** 停.
Stop a minute, **ding-ih-ding** 停 一 停.
Garden, **hwo-yoen** 花 園.
College, **su-yoen°** 書 院.
A lock, **ih °po °soo** 一 把 鎖.
A key, **ih °po yak-dz** 一 把 鑰 匙.
A creek or canal, **ih diau pang** 一 條 浜.
A two story house, **ih zoo° leu** or **leu-vaung** 一 座 樓, 樓 房.

***Dzung*** **(層)** is the classifier for a story of a house or for anything like a ladder.

A three-storied house, **san dzung leu** 三 層 樓.
A ladder, **ih dzung voo-thi** 一 層 扶 梯.

***Dzaung°*** (幢) is the classifier denoting things piled one on top of the other.

A pile of clothes, **ih dzaung° i-zaung 一幢衣裳.**

***Da°*** (埭) is the classifier for rows of things.

A row of trees, **ih da° zu 一埭樹.**
Spring (the first of the seasons), **tshung 春.**
Summer, **'au° 夏.**
Autumn, **tshieu 秋.**
Winter, **toong 冬.**
A season, **kyi° 季.**
The four seasons, **s°-kyi° 四季.**
Politeness, **khak-chi° 客氣.**
Happiness, **fok-chi° 福氣.**
Slippery, **wah 滑.**
Hard, **ngang° 硬.**
Soft, **°nyoen 軟.**
Smooth, **kwaung 光.**
Rough, **mau 毛.**
Good (moral), **°zen 善.**
Wicked, **auh 惡.**
Fierce, **hyoong 凶.**
Precious, **°pau-pe° 寶貝.**
Clear, **tshing 清.**
Muddy, **wung 渾.**
Level, **bing 平.**
Light (opposite of dark), **liang° 亮.**
Dark, **en° 暗.**

EXERCISES.

(Translate into English.)

(1). Di°-laung° wah lau, taung-sing °tien °tseu. (2). S°-kyi° kyau° tshung 'au° tshieu toong. (3). °Ngoo baug°-dzak-°ts ih kuh nyung °lau iau° yi nyang° loo°, °soo-°i te yi wo° tuh-°dzoe, tuh °dzoe. Yi wo° 'veh iau° khak-chi°. (4). Noong° tsoo° °di-kuh sang-i, ih nyien iau° dzan° °kyi-hau°? m-sa° dzan°-deu °tau zeh-°pung. (5). Nyien tshoo ih, bang°-dzak-ts nyung tsau° kwe-°kyui iung-ke te° yi wo° koong-°hyi, fah-dze. (6). Nyung tsoo° auh kuh z°-°thi, °z la° en°-°li tsoo° kuh. (7). We°-ts pho° bih nyung iau° dzo-dzak °lau, °i-kuh nyung chi° ben°-°loong. (8). Ya°-°li tsoong-iau° °soo mung°, °khoong-pho° zuk tsing° le theu meh-z°. (9). Tsoong-kok mung yoong° sak °le sen kuh, nga°-kok mung yoong° yak-dz le °soo kuh. (10). °Siau-noen la° beh-siang° kuh z-'eu° tih la° pang °li, kwha°-°tien chi° kyeu° yi. (11). Yoong tiau we° kyau°, tsh tiau 'veh we° kyau°. (12). Tsh s-°ts °pi-ts yoong s-°ts kung°-ka hyoong. (13). °Di-kuh nyung °yeu san kuh neu-noen, lau ih kuh °nyui-noen, 'zeh-dze °yeu fok-chi°. (14). °Di-kuh meh-z° °z °pau-pe° kuh, iau° khaung° °hau. (15). °'Au-°li-pa°, su-yoen° °li iau° °khau su. (16). °Di-kuh ih da° vaung-°ts kau-le-°si, °loong-°tsoong °z s° dzung leu. (17). Di-diau loo° 'veh bing, van-nan °tseu kuh. (18). Tshing °s °hau chuh kuh, wung °s 'veh °hau chuh. (19). Zak-deu °z ngang° kuh, men-deu °z °nyoen kuh. (20). Tau°-°ti meh °zen nyung ih ding° iau° tuh-dzak fok-chi°.

(一) 地上滑咾當心點走　(二) 四季叫春夏秋冬　(三) 我碰着之一个人要伊讓路所以對伊話得罪得罪, 伊話勿要客氣　(四) 儂做第个生意一年要賺幾化, 無啥賺頭倒析本　(五) 年初一碰着之人照規矩應該對伊話恭喜發財　(六) 人做惡个事體是拉暗裡做个　(七) 爲之怕別人要查着咾, 伊个人去背攏　(八) 夜裡終要鎖門, 恐怕賊進來偷物事　(九) 中國門用栅來閂个, 外國門用鑰匙來鎖个　(十) 小囝拉勃相个時候跌拉浜裡, 快點去救伊　(十一) 雄𪇰會叫, 雌𪇰勿會叫　(十二) 雌獅子比之雄獅子更加凶　(十三) 第个人有三个男囝咾一个女囝, 實在有福氣　(十四) 第个物事是寶貝个, 要囥好　(十五) 下禮拜, 書院裡要考書　(十六) 第个一埭房子高來死, 攏總是四層樓　(十七) 第條路勿平, 煩難走个　(十八) 清水好吃个, 渾水勿好吃　(十九) 石頭是硬个, 饅頭是軟个　(二十) 到底末善人一定要得着福氣

(Translate into Chinese.)

(1). In the garden the gardeners have planted three rows of apple trees. (2). After the cock crows in the morning I am unable to sleep any more. (3). This man is very polite, and so every one likes him. (4). In the winter we close all the doors and windows and light a fire, in the summer we open all the doors and windows. (5). The water in the creek is muddy and not fit to drink. (6). Some men become rich in business, and some lose money. (7). Lock the door and do not let the cat come in. (8). The child fell off the chair and therefore cries. (9). Yesterday I went to see a seven storied pagoda. (10). This account is not right; it is not reckoned clearly. (11). I cannot find out that this man has done anything wicked. (12). When I met the robber I cried out to others to come and save my life. (13). This man is very fierce; he is always fighting. (14). At the end of the year, all the scholars in the College must be examined. (15). I have lost my key and cannot open my box. (16). I think you have not lost it, but you have hidden it away somewhere, and have forgotten where you put it; let me go and look for it.

(一) 拉花園裡種花園个種三埭蘋菓樹　(二) 早晨頭雞啼个以後我勿能再睏　(三) 第个人是蠻客氣所以攏總人歡喜伊　(四) 冬天个時候我伲

關攏總个門咾窗咾生火夏天个時候我伲開攏總个門咾窗 （五）浜裡水是渾咾勿好吃个 （六）有人做生意是發財有人末折本 （七）鎖門咾勿要讓貓進來 （八）小囝從椅子上跌下來所以拉哭 （九）昨日我去看七層樓个塔 （十）第个帳勿對个算來勿清爽 （十一）我查勿出第个人做啥惡事 （十二）我碰着之强盜我喊人來救命 （十三）第个人凶來死所以常庄相打 （十四）拉年底書院裡攏總个學生子要考書 （十五）我失脫之我个鑰匙咾勿好開我个箱子 （十六）我想儂勿曾失脫恐怕儂已經囥好咾忘記擺拉啥地方,讓我去尋尋看

NOTES. (1) *Tuh-°dzoe, tuh °dzoe* is the usual expression for making an apology in Chinese. It literally means, "I have sinned against you" 得罪.

(2). A two storied house is generally called *leu vaung* 樓房.

(3). In the fifth sentence of the First Exercise we have the formal salutation used on New Year's Day *Koong-°hyi, fah-dze*, meaning, "may you be happy and grow rich" 恭喜發財.

(4). In the twelfth sentence of the Second Exercise the expression to save life should be *Kyeu° ming°* 救命.

---

# LESSON XXV.

## Weights and Measures.

The following three Tables are very commonly used in China, and the speaker of the language should be familiar with them.

### MEASURE OF WEIGHT.

One ounce, ***ih °liang*** 一兩.
One catty (16 ounces), ***ih kyung*** 一斤.
One picul (100 catties), ***ih tan°*** 一担.

### MEASURE OF DISTANCE.

1/10th of an inch, ***ih fung*** 一分.
One inch, ***ih tshung°*** 一寸.
One foot (ten inches in Chinese measure), ***ih tshak*** 一尺.
Ten feet, ***ih °dzang*** 一丈.

### MEASURE OF AREA.

One square foot, ***ih faung tshak*** 一方尺.
Ten square feet, ***ih faung*** 一方.
A mow, ***ih °m*** 一畝 (one sixth of an acre.)

## CURRENCY.

Until recently, aside from copper cash, the Chinese had no regular system of currency. An ounce of silver was taken as a standard. The following Table is based upon that:—

An ounce of silver, *ih °liang nyung-°ts* 一兩銀子.
1/10th of an ounce, *ih dzien* 一錢.
1/10th of a dzien, *ih fung* 一分.
1/10th of a fung, *ih li* 一釐.
1/10th of a li, *ih 'au* 一毫.

## VOCABULARY.

To expound, explain, **°kaung** 講.
To preach, **°kaung-su** 講書.
To exhort, **choen°, choen°-mien, choen°-'oo** 勸,勸勉,勸和.
To gather, as fruit or flowers, **°tshe** 採.
To boil **zah**, (used in regard to water), **°kwung** 煠,滾.
To weigh, **tshung** 稱.
To measure, **liang** 量, **°ien** 演.
To carry in arms like a child, **°bau** 抱.
To carry a load (one man, with load suspended on two ends of a bamboo), **thiau** 挑.
To carry a load (load suspended between two men on a bamboo pole), **kaung** 扛.
To carry a load on the back, **pe°** 背.
To carry a load on the shoulder, **jien** 掮.
To carry a load in one hand, **ling** 拎.
A tiger, **ih tsak °lau-°hoo** 一隻老虎.
A dish, **ih tsak dzang bung-°ts** 一隻長盆子.
A saucer, **ih tsak dzo bung-°ts** 一隻茶盆子.
A wine glass, **ih tsak °tsieu pe** 一隻酒杯.
A cooking stove, **ih tsak thih-tsau°** (Foreign), 鐵灶 **tsau°-deu** (Chinese), 灶頭.
Gold, **kyung-°ts** 金子.
Silver, **nyung-°ts** 銀子.
Iron, **thih** 鐵.
Tin, **sih** 錫.
Brass, **doong** 銅.
Lead, **khan** 鉛.
A railroad carriage, **ih boo °hoo-lung-tsho** 一部火輪車.
A steam boat, **ih tsak °hoo-lung-zen** 一隻火輪船.
A pair of spectacles, **ih foo° °ngan-kyung°** 一副眼鏡.
A set of tools or instruments, **ih foo° ka-sang** 一副傢生.
A cannon, **ih tsung phau°** 一尊砲.
Cotton, **hwo** 花.
Cotton stalks, **hwo-ji** 花萁.
Cotton (already ginned), **mien-hwo** 棉花.
A plant of wheat, **ih khoo mak** 一棵麥.
A plant of rice, **ih khoo dau°** 一棵稻.
Vegetables, **tshe°** 菜.
Dishes of vegetables and meat placed on the table for meals, **°siau-tshe°** 小菜.

***°Kwhung*** (梱) is the classifier denoting bundles of things.

A bundle of fuel, **ih °kwhung za** 一梱柴, **ih °kwung dau-za** 一梱稻柴.
Still, yet, **dzung-jeu°** 仍舊.
Among, **taung-tsoong** 當中.
All (collective), **zen** 全.

### EXERCISES.

(Translate into English).

(1). Noong° choen°-choen° yi 'veh iau° °doong-chi°. (2). Khoen°-kyien° °liang-kuh nyung siang-°tang meh iung-ke choen°-'oo yi-la. (3). °Di tsak siang-°ts °ngoo °i-kyung liang-koo°-hyih-tse °z san tshak dzang °lau nyi° tshak s° tshung kwheh. (4). La° hwo-yoen °li, °tshe hwo °z 'man °hau beh-siang°. (5). °Di-kuh °liang tsak siang-°ts ih kuh nyung thiau 'veh °chi °z iung-ke kaung kuh. (6). Kyung, nyung, doong, thih, sih, Tsoong-kok nyung kyau° °ng kyung. (7). Tsoong° dien-nyung la° toong °li tsoong° mak, la° tshung laung° tsoong° hwo. (8). La° °ng kyung taung-tsoong thih °z °ting °yeu yoong°-deu, doo° °lau °siau kuh meh-z° zen °khau-°i tsoo° kuh. (9). °Ngoo kuh bang-yeu °z °jung-z°-°ngan °soo-°i iau° ta° °ngan-kyung°. (10). °S faung° la° thih-tsau° laung°, °kwung-ih-°kwung. (11). Dze-°tsu-nyung tsak dzeu-doen °lau joong nyung tsak poo°. (12). °Di-kuh nyung °kaung su °kaung le 'man °hau thing. (13). Dih la kuh °mi tshung-tshung khoen° kyung-liang te va°. (14). °Di-kwhe° di-be °yeu °kyi °m? iak-tsak °yeu lok °m. (15). La° °ya-seu° taung-tsoong Tsoong-kok nyung ting pho° kuh °z °lau-°hoo. (16). We°-ts °siau-noen la° khok °lau, °nyui-nyung °bau la° seu °li. (17). Nyok °lau tshe° ih dau° kyau° °siau tshe°. (18). Lok-tsen °z lan°-nyi tsoo° la kuh, °zau vaung-°ts ting °yeu yoong°-deu. (19). °Di-kuh yang-dien 'veh °hau, 'veh-°z nyung-ts, °z khan kuh. (20). °Ngoo wan iau° °ma dzang-bung-°ts, dzo-bung-°ts, °lau °tsieu-pe. (21). Tung-loong °khau-°i ling la° °seu °li, ih kung mok-deu °khau-°i jien la kyien-ka laung°, de meh pe° la pe° laung°. (22). °Ng-seh nyien zien-deu, Tsoong-kok m-meh °hoo-lung tsho °lau °hoo-lung zen, yieu°-°dze zen °yeu-kuh. (23). Tsau-zung-deu °ngoo thing-tuk ping-ting faung° phau°. (24). Yieu°-°dze m-meh za, 'veh °hau sang °hoo, iau° noong° chi° °ma °liang san °kwhung. (25). Nyeu °lau °mo la° dieu °li chuh °tshau.

(一) 儂勸勸伊勿要動氣 (二) 看見兩个人相打末應該勸和伊拉 (三) 第隻箱子我已經量過歇哉,是三尺長咾二尺四寸闊 (四) 拉花園裡探花是蠻好勃相 (五) 第个兩隻箱子一个人挑勿起是應該扛个 (六) 金銀銅鐵錫中國人叫五金 (七) 種田人拉冬裡種麥拉春上種花 (八) 拉五金當中鐵是頂有用頭,大咾小个物事全可以做个 (九) 我个朋友是近視眼所以要帶眼鏡 (十) 水放拉鐵灶上滾一滾 (十一) 財主人着綢緞咾

窮人着布 (十二) 第个人講書講來蠻好聽 (十三) 糶拉个米稱稱看勿兩對陌 (十四) 第塊地皮有幾畝,約酌有六畝 (十五) 拉野獸當中,中國人頂怕个是老虎 (十六) 爲之小囝拉哭咾,女人抱拉手裡 (十七) 肉咾菜一淘叫小菜 (十八) 磚是爛泥做拉个,造房子頂有用頭 (十九) 第个洋錢勿好,勿是銀子是鉛个 (二十) 我還要買長盆子茶盆子咾酒杯 (廿一) 燈籠可以拎拉手裡,一根木頭可以掮拉肩胛上,袋末背拉背上 (廿二) 五十年前頭中國無沒火輪車咾火輪船,現在全有个 (廿三) 早晨頭我聽得兵丁放砲 (廿四) 現在無沒柴勿好生火,要儂去買兩三捆 (廿五) 牛咾馬拉田裡吃草

(Translate into Chinese).

(1). The Chinese make most of their clothing out of cotton. (2). Among the pupils this one is the brightest. (3). I will tell you a wonderful thing: two men were fighting, and a woman came and exhorted them to peace. (4). Among the metals, gold is the most precious. (5). The dollars used in China are made of silver. (6). How many men will it take to carry the stove? (7). I think four men can carry it. (8). How much ought I to give the ric-sha coolie? (9). I think thirty cents is sufficient. (10). There are still many men in Shanghai who have never been in a railway carriage. (11). Most of the Chinese scholars wear spectacles. (12). I have been gathering apples and peaches in the garden. (13). The carpenter has not brought his tools; and so can do no work. (14). A Chinese foot has ten inches, a foreign foot has twelve. (15). In China wood, and rice and cotton stalks are used as fuel.

(一) 中國人做衣裳用棉花布个是頂多 (二) 拉學生子當中第个是頂聰明个 (三) 我要告訴儂一庄希奇个事體,兩个人拉相打一个女人來勸和 (四) 拉五金當中金子是頂寶貝个 (五) 中國个洋錢是銀子做拉个 (六) 第隻火爐幾个人好扛 (七) 我想四个人好扛个 (八) 拖東洋車个人我應該撥伊幾錢 (九) 我想三角有哉 (十) 拉上海還有多化人勿曾坐過歇火輪車个 (十一) 中國讀書人大一半末是帶眼鏡 (十二) 我拉花園



海上絲綢之路文獻集成 科技與文化编

裡拉探蘋果咾桃子 （十三）木匠勿曾帶傢生來所以勿好做生活 （十四）中國尺是十寸外國尺有十二寸 （十五）中國人用木頭咾稻咾花萁做柴

NOTES. (1). In the fifth sentence of the First Exercise *Thiau 'veh-°chi* 挑 勿 起 means "unable to carry."

(2). In the sixth sentence of the First Exercise *°Ng kyung* 五 金 is generally pronounced as *°oo kyung*, as it is a *vung-li* expression.

(3). In the ninth sentence of the First Exercise *°Jung-z°-°ngan* 近 視 眼 means "near-sighted."

(4). In the thirteenth sentence of the First Exercise notice that "to buy rice" is *dih mi* not *°ma mi*.

(5) In the ninth sentence of the Second Exercise "sufficient" may be translated *°yeu-tse* 有 餘.

---

# LESSON XXVI.

## Family Relations.

The relations in Chinese are exceedingly complex. Here only the simplest will be given. To be able to understand the complicated ramifications will take a long time, and can only be learnt by long experience.

It must be noted that different words are used when one speaks of his own relations from what are used when another person is referring to them. In the latter case more polite language is employed.

Thus the following words for "father" are used: If you yourself are speaking of your father, you might call him ***Ya*** (爺), or ***°Lau-nyang-ka*** (老 娘 家), or ***Kya-°voo*** (家 父), or ***°Voo-tshing*** (父 親), or ***Kya-nyien*** (家 嚴). Other people would refer to your father if they were polite as ***Tsung-da°-zung*** (尊 大 人) Lit. "The honorable great man." ***Kya*** or ***Ling°-tsung*** (令 尊). Children often call their father ***Tia-tia*** (爹 爹), or ***Ya-ya*** (爺 爺), or ***Pak-pak*** (伯 伯).

So in regard to mother. If you speak of her you say ***Nyang*** (娘), or ***Kya-°moo*** (家 母), or ***°Moo-tshing*** (母 親), or ***Kya-dz*** (家 慈). If you speak of the mother of another person you may say ***Ling°-daung*** (令 堂).

Brother is different as to whether you refer to an older or a younger one. An older brother is ***Ak-koo*** (阿 哥). A younger brother is ***Hyoong-°di*** (兄 弟). Brothers (plural) is ***°Di-hyoong*** or ***Hyoong-°di*** (弟 兄). A familiar term for a younger brother is ***°Di-°di*** (弟 弟). An older sister is ***Ah-°tsi*** (阿 姊). A younger sister is ***°Tsi-me°*** (姊 妹) or ***Me°-me°*** (妹 妹).

In referring to a son a father would call him ***Nyi-°ts*** (兒 子) or ***°Siau-noen*** (小 囝); others would refer to your son by saying ***Ling°-laung*** (令 郎) or (公 郎) ***Koong-laung.*** In speaking of one's own daughter you would say ***°Siau-°nyui*** (小 女); others would refer to her as ***Tshien-kyung*** (千 金) Lit. "A thousand catties of gold," or ***Ling°-e°*** (令 嬡).

## VOCABULARY.

To love, e° **愛**.
To love reciprocally, **siang-e° 相愛**.
To injure, **'e° 害**.
To be injured, **°zeu-'e° 受害**.
To begin, **°chi 起**.
A beginning, **°chi-deu 起頭**, **khe-dzang 開場**.
To repair, **sieu 修**. **seu-tsauh 收作**.
Repairs, **sieu-°li 修理**.
To take hold of, to grasp, **nyah 捏**.
To receive or accept, **°zeu 受**.
To suffer, **°zeu-°khoo 受苦**, or **°zeu-nan° 受難**.
To hand, to deliver in person, **dzeu° 授**.
To save, be economical, **°sang 省**, **tsoo° nyung-ka 做人家**.
To save time, **°sang koong-foo 省功夫**.
To waste, to be extravagant, **saung 傷**.
To seal officially, or to seal an envelope; to deify; to exalt to a high station, **foong 封**.
To rely upon, to entrust, **khau° 靠**, **khau°-thauh 靠托**, **thauh 托**.
A battery or a fort, **ih kuh phau°-de 一個砲台**.
A deer, **ih tsak lok 一隻鹿**.
To hunt, **°tang-lah 打獵**.
A hare, **ih tsak thoo°-°ts 一隻兎子**
A fox, **ih tsak 'oo-li 一隻狐狸**.
A wolf, **ih tsak za-laung 一隻豺狼**.
A squirrel, **ih tsak soong-°su 一隻松鼠**.
A weasel, **ih tsak waung-laung 一隻黃狼**.
A pheasant, **ih tsak °ya-kyi 一隻野雞**.
A goose, **ih tsak ngoo 一隻鵝**.
A set of dice, **ih foo° deu°-°ts 一副骰子**.
To gamble with dice, **zak deu°-°ts 擲骰子**.
A set of dominoes, **ih foo° ba 一副牌**.
To gamble with dominoes, **teu° ba 鬥牌**.
Again, **tse° 再**.
Medicine, **yak 藥**.
Tobacco, **ien 烟**.
A gun, **ih °kwen yang-tshiang 一桿洋槍**.
Powder, **°hoo-yak 火藥**. Lit. Fiery medicine.
Tide flowing out, **lauh-°s 落水**.
Tide coming in, **tsang°-°s 漲水**.

## EXERCISES.

(Translate into English.)

(1). Zau°-nyih °ngoo tan-ts yang-tshiang tau° san laung° chi° °tang-lih, °tang-dzak-ts san tsak lok° lau s° tsak thoo°-°ts °lau ih tsak soong-°su. (2). °Ngoo °bang-dzak-ts ih kuh nyung la °tang °tiau, yi °i-kyung °tang-dzak-ts s° tsak °ya-kyi °lau ih tsak °ya-ngoo. (3). Teu° ba °lau zak deu°-°ts thok °z 'veh °hau. (4). °Di-kuh phau°-de °yeu °ng tsung phau° °lau too-°hau °hoo-yak. (5). Zau°-ya°-deu °yeu waung-laung theu kyi, 'veh hyau°-tuh °z waung-laung nyi wan-°z 'oo-li, kyung-ya°-deu °ting °hau °tung yi le °lau yoong° yang-tshiang °tang-sah yi. (6). °Ngoo la° yi han-deu °zeu-°ts too-hau° meh-z°, iau° soong°-°tien sa° la° yi.

(7). °Di-foong sing° iau° foong-°hau dzeu° peh la° i-sung. (8). Seu-tsauh vaung-°ts zieu° iau° °chi-deu, iung-we° °yeu too-hau° di°-faung iau° sieu-°li, zak-zen °tse an° meh °khoong-pho° le-'veh ji°. (9). Too chuh °tsieu °lau too chuh ien z saung sung-°thi. (10). °Di-kuh bing° °dzoong tuh-juh, chuh yak '°a m-yoong°-deu. (11). Tsoo° nyung-ka meh, °khau-°i nyih-nyih °sang doong-dien. (12). °Di-kuh si-°tse hwen-°hyi °too doong-dieu °lau chuh °tsieu, 'zeh-dze khau°-'veh-dzu° kuh. (13). °Ngoo thauh noong° tsoo° ih tsaung z°-thi, noong° we°-sa° 'veh zung tsoo°? (14). Zeh-°ke tsoo°-deu saung koong-foo, iau° tsau° °ngoo wo° meh °hau. (15). Di°-hyoong iung-ke da°-ka siang-e°, 'veh iau° siang-mo° °lau siang-°tang. (16). Tsung-da°-zung °hau-la°-va? Zia°-zia°, °lau-nyang-ka °hau-la°. (17). Ya-nyang °i-kyung tsheh mung, pih-koo° ak-koo la° ok-°li. (18). °Ngoo °yeu ih kuh ah-°tsi °lau °liang-kuk me°-me°. (19). °Kyi-z iau° khe zen? Lauh °s zieu° khe. (20). Za-laung °z 'man hyoong kuh °ya-seu°, hwen-°hyi chuh yang. (21). °Di-kuh ih pe yak iau° peh la° bing° nyung chuh. (22). Noong° °yeu °kyi we° °ling-laung? °Yeu °liang-kuh °siau-noen.

(一) 昨日我担之洋槍到山上去打獵打着之三隻鹿咾四隻兎子咾一隻松鼠 (二) 我撞着之一个人拉打獵伊已經打着之四隻野雞咾一隻野鵝 (三) 門牌咾瓣骰子秃是勿好 (四) 第个砲台有五尊砲咾多化火藥 (五) 昨夜頭有黄狼偷雞勿曉得是黄狼呢還是狐狸今夜頭頂好等伊來咾用洋槍打殺伊 (六) 我拉伊壗頭受之多化物事要送點啥拉伊 (七) 第封信要封好授撥拉醫生 (八) 收作房子就要起頭因爲有多化地方要修理若然再晚末恐怕來勿及 (九) 多吃酒咾多吃烟是傷身體 (十) 第个病重得極吃藥也無用頭 (十一) 做人家末可以日日省銅錢 (十二) 第个西崽歡喜賭銅錢咾吃酒實在靠勿住个 (十三) 我托儂做一庄事體爲啥勿曾做 (十四) 實蓋做頭傷工夫要照我話末好 (十五) 弟兄應該大家相愛勿要相罵咾相打 (十六) 尊大人好拉陌,謝謝老娘家好拉 (十七) 爺娘已經出門必過阿哥拉屋裡 (十八) 我有一个阿姊咾兩个妹妹 (十九) 幾時要開船,落水就開 (二十) 豺狼是蠻凶个野獸歡喜吃羊 (廿一) 第个一杯藥要撥拉病人吃 (廿二) 儂有幾位令郞,有兩个小囝

(Translate into Chinese).

(1). You should do to others as you would they should do to you. (2). If we do not call the carpenter and mason to repair this house, we shall not be able to live in it. (3). When I began I considered the study of Chinese very difficult; now I consider it easier. (4). The younger brother should listen to the older brother's words. (5). You should love others as yourself. (6). On the other side of the river there are many forts. (7). This man wastes his money in drinking wine. (8). Where did you get the money to buy these clothes? I saved it from my wages. (9). The deer can run faster than the dog, but gets tired sooner. (10). The father is head of the house. (11). Hand this bowl of tea to the guest. (12). I trust to you to help me do the work. (13). The fox comes at night to steal chickens. (14). Pheasants are fine birds to look at and are very good to eat. (15). Geese and ducks like to remain in the water. (16). The older sister takes care of her little sister. (17). Take hold of it firmly in your hand and do not let it fall on the ground. (18). According to what Chinese say, to become a good man you must repair your heart.

(一) 儂要人那能待儂儂也應該那能待別人 (二) 若然伲勿叫木匠咾泥水匠來修房子我伲勿好住垃化 (三) 我起頭讀个辰光我算中國書是煩難讀个現在算是容易點 (四) 兄弟應該聽阿哥个說話 (五) 儂應該愛別人像愛自家 (六) 垃拉河過邊有多化砲台 (七) 第个人吃酒咾傷脫伊个銅錢 (八) 買第个衣裳儂那裡頭來个銅錢,我工錢上省下來个 (九) 鹿比之狗可以跑來快點但是鹿先要弛瘏 (十) 爺末是一家个主 (十一) 第个一碗茶授撥拉客人 (十二) 我托儂相幫我做第庄事體 (十三) 狐狸是夜頭來偷雞 (十四) 野雞是蠻好看个篤也是蠻好吃个 (十五) 鵝咾鴨歡喜登拉水裡向 (十六) 阿姊是當心伊个小妹妹 (十七) 揸牢拉手裡勿要放伊落拉地上 (十八) 照中國人話成功好个人終要修儂个心

NOTES. (1). In the sixth sentence of the First Exercise notice the expression *Soong°-°tien-sa°* 送點啥, meaning "to make a small present."

(2). In the eighth sentence of the First Exercise notice the expression °*Tse an*° (再晏), Lit. "again late;" the idea is "if we wait any longer."

(3). In the fourteenth sentence of the First Exercise notice the expression *Tsau° °ngoo wo° meh °hau* (照我話末好). Lit. "Follow my saying then good."

(4). In the first sentence of the Second Exercise the sentence would be turned round in Chinese, and we would say, *Noong° iau° nyung na°-nung °de noong°, noong° °a iung-ke na°-nung °de bih nyung* (儂要人那能待儂,儂也應該那能待別人).

---

# LESSON XXVII.

## Compound Verbs.

By compound verbs we mean those made up of more than one verb. As we have already seen, Chinese words having a distinct meaning when used by themselves also form part of larger compound words. This is true especially of verbs. A good example is the verb ***°Tang*** (打), to strike. It enters into combination with many other words to form compound verbs.

Thus. To fight a battle, ***°tang-tsang°*** 打仗.
To attack an enemy, ***koong-°tang*** 攻打.
To gain a victory, ***°tang-yung*** (打贏), ***°tang-sung°-tsang°*** 打勝仗.
To suffer a defeat, ***°tang-su*** (打輸), ***°tang-ba°*** (打敗), ***°tang-ba°-tsang°*** 打敗仗.
To wound, ***°tang-saung*** 打傷.
To make inquiries, ***°tang-thing*** 打聽.
To fool with one another, ***°tang-bang°*** 打棚.
To injure by striking, ***°tang-wa°*** 打壞.
To consider, ***°tang-soen°*** 打算.
To dress in a showy manner, ***°tang-pan°*** 打扮.

### VOCABULARY.

To collect, to receive payment, **seu** 收.
To collect accounts, **seu-tsang°** 收帳.
To receive payment for a lease, **seu-tsoo** 收租.
To be imprisoned, **seu-kan** 收監.
To build a wall, **tshi°** (砌), **tshi° ziang** 砌墻.
To build a partition, **tshi° pih** 砌壁.
To mend a path, **tshi° ka** 砌街.
To be wounded, **°zeu-saung** 受傷.
To prosecute at law, **°tang-kwen-s** 打官司.
To cut with a sharp knife, **koeh** 割.
To cut in two, **koeh-°doen** 割斷.
To cut with sword, or heavy knife or axe, **tsan** 斬.
To split, **phih** 劈.
To saw, **zih** 鋸 or **ka°** 解.
To boil, **zah** 煠.
To grill, to broil, **tsien** 煎.
To smoke (meat), **hyuin** 燻.
To bake, **hoong** 烘.

To sew, to stitch, **ling** 鈴.
To take a stitch, **ling-ih tsung** 鈴一針, (**tsung** means needle).
To iron, to burn, to scald, **thaung°** 燙.
To brush, **seh** 刷.
To rise (as the tide), **tsang°** 漲.
To fall, **lauh** 落.
Duty, **ming-vung°** 名分.
Rumours, **yau-yien** 謠言.
Receipt, **seu-phiau°** 收票, **seu-diau** 收條.
A bell, **tsoong** 鐘.
Piles (such as are driven into the ground), **tsaung** 樁.
Tide, **dzau** 潮, **dzau-°s** 潮水.
A cake, **ih kuh kyi dan°-kau** 一个雞蛋糕.
Japanese, **Toong-yang nyung** 東洋人, **Zeh-°pung-nyung** 日本人.
Russians, **Ngoo-kok-nyung** 俄國人.
A biscuit, **ih kuh thah-°ping** 一个餲餅.
A grate, **ih kuh °hoo-khaung** 一个火匟.
A sparrow, **ih tsak mo-tshiak** 一隻麻雀, **mo-tsiang** 麻將.
A swallow, **ih tsak ien°-°ts** 一隻燕子.
A pigeon, **ih tsak keh-°ts** 一隻鴿子.
An ax, **ih po °foo-deu** 一把斧頭.
A saw, **ih po ke°-°ts** 一把鋸子.
A file, **ih po tshoo°-tau** 一把銼刀.
A plane, **ih tsak bau°** 一隻刨.
A quilt or blanket, **ih diau °bi-deu** 一條被頭.
A sheet, **ih diau tan-°bi** 一條單被.
Unripe or raw, **sang** 生.
Ripe, **zok** 熟. Also used in the sense of being thoroughly cooked.
Shameful, **than-tshoong** 坍銃.
Face (cheek), **nyi-kwaung** 耳光.

## EXERCISES.

(Translate into English.)

(1). Kyau° tsoong°-hwo-yoen-kuh la° hwo-yoen °li tsan-theh i-kuh °liang khoo zu°. (2). °Di-diau ka ih ngan 'veh bing, iau° tse° tshi°. (3). Sing-vung-°ts laung° °ngoo khoen° °tang-tsang° kuh zung-kwaung, Toong-yang-nyung dzang-tsaung °tang sung°-tsang°, °lau Ngoo-kok nyung dzang-tsaung °tang-ba°. (4). °Di °po tau kwha°-le-°si, °khoong-pho° °siau-noen iau° koeh thoong° °seu. (5). °Nyui-nyung kuh ming-vung° la° ok-°li sau vau°, tsoo° i-zaung, taung-sing °siau-noen; nen-nyung kuh ming-vung° la° °nga-deu tsoo° sang-i°. (6). I-zaung koen-°ts meh nan-meh iau° thaung°-ih-thaung°. (7). La° ka laung° yi-la° tsauh-°ts° ih kuh zuk, yien°-°dze soong° tau° kwen hau-deu seu-kan. (8). °Di-saung 'a-°ts noong° seh le 'veh °hau, ih ngan 'veh liang°. (9). Khau-°ts tsoong °loong-°tsoong kuh 'auh-sang-°ts zieu° iau° tsing° chi° dok su, 'auh-daung-°li iau° °zoo ding°, °tung sien-sang le, 'veh iau° da°-°ka °tang-bang°. (10). Iau° tshi° ziang meh sieu iau° °tang tsaung. (11). Dzau tsang° meh zieu° iau° khe zen, 'ang tau° bing °s °lau ding. (12). °Di-kuh mok-za iau° yoong° °foo-deu °lau phih-khe-le. (13). Noong° foo°-°ts yang-dien meh, °ngoo peh seu-diau noong°. (14). °Di-kuh dan° zah le thuh sang, iau° zok-°tien. (15). Kyung-tsau °yeu khak-nyung le, iau° noong°

tsoo° kyi-dan°-kau °lau thah-°ping. (16). Peh bih nyung °tang nyi°-kwaung meh soen° °ting than-°tshoong kuh z°-°thi. (17). Dien-°li kuh mak seu °hau meh? Wan 'veh zung we°-ts dzang-tsaung lauh °yui °lau. (18). Iau° noong° chi° °tang-thing °tang-thing sa° nyung °zau °di-kuh yau-yien. (19). °Di-kuh men-deu tan tau° °hoo-khaung° pien-deu chi° hoong-hoong. (20). Kyau° mok-ziang° le yoong° ke°-°ts °ka-khe °di-kuh mok-deu. (21). Tau° mok-ziang° han-deu chi° tsia° ih °po tshoo-tau °lau ih tsak bau°. (22). Mo-tshiak °lau ien°-°ts °z °siau kuh °tiau, 'veh °hau chuh, keh-°ts meh °hau chuh kuh. (23). Tan-°bi °lau °bi-deu than °hau la° zaung laung°. (24). Ng hyuin °hau meh tan le peh °ngoo chuh chuh khoen. (25). I-kuh nyung koong-°tang le, °ngoo dih-'veh-dzu° yi, peh yi °tang-saung. (26). Tsheh-chi` pa° khak kuh z-eu° sien iau° °tang-pan°.

(一) 叫種花園个人拉花園裡斬脫伊个兩棵樹 (二) 第條街一頭勿平要再砌 (三) 新聞紙上我看打仗个辰光東洋人常庄打勝仗咾俄國人常庄打敗 (四) 第把刀快來死恐怕小囝要割痛手 (五) 女人个名分拉屋裡燒飯做衣裳當心小囝,男人个名分拉外頭做生意 (六) 衣裳乾之末難末要燙一燙 (七) 拉街上伊拉捉之一个賊,現在送到官壚頭收監 (八) 第雙鞋子儂刷來勿好一顚勿亮 (九) 敲之鐘㯐總學生子全要進去讀書學堂裡要坐定等先生來勿要大家打棚 (十) 要砌牆末先要打樁 (十一) 潮漲末就要開船行到平水咾停 (十二) 第个木柴要用斧頭來劈開來 (十三) 儂付之洋錢末我撥收條儂 (十四) 第个蛋煠來脫生要熟點 (十五) 今朝有客人來要儂做雞蛋糕咾餳餅 (十六) 撥別人打耳光末算頂坍銃个事體 (十七) 田裡个麥收好末,還勿曾爲之常庄落雨咾 (十八) 要儂去打聽打聽啥人造第个謠言 (十九) 第个饅頭担到火匠邊頭去烘烘 (二十) 叫木匠來用鋸子解開第个木頭 (廿一) 到木匠壚頭去借一把銼刀咾一隻刨 (廿二) 麻雀咾燕子是小个鳥勿好吃,鴿子末好吃个 (廿三) 單被咾被頭攤好拉床上 (廿四) 魚𤇍好末担來撥我吃吃看 (廿五) 伊个人攻打來,我敵勿住伊,撥伊打傷 (廿六) 出去拜客个時候先要打扮

(Translate into Chinese.)

(1). In cold countries the swallows fly away in the winter and return in the spring. (2). To have a lawsuit is a miserable affair, for you must use up much money. (3). My clothes were very dirty, so I told my servant to brush them well. (4). In the summer when it is warm you do not need a quilt, but in the winter you do. (5). The mandarin gave orders to cut off the robber's head. (6). Some wicked people do not fear shame. (7). Has the school bell rung? If so I am late. (8). What is the matter with your foot? It was scalded by hot water. (9). When the tide rises the boat can travel very fast. (10). In front of my house I want to erect a fence. (11). Put some coal in the grate; probably to-night I will want to light a fire. (12). When you have split the fuel tie it up in a bundle. (13). At the beginning the boys were only fooling, but afterwards they began to fight, and one of them was hurt. (14). A hammer, a saw, a plane, and a file are useful implements. (15). These pears and apples are unripe; if you eat them you will become ill. (16). At the end of the month the man goes out to collect his accounts. (17). Every one should do his duty.

**(一) 拉冷个地方到之冬天燕子飛出去到之春上末轉來 (二) 打官司是苦腦个事體因爲儂總要用多化銅錢 (三) 我个衣裳齷齪來死所以我叫我个用人刷刷好 (四) 夏天熱个辰光儂勿要用被頭到之冬天末要个 (五) 官府分付殺脫第个强盜个頭 (六) 有个惡人勿怕坍銃 (七) 鐘敲好末,若然已經敲好之我末晚哉 (八) 儂个脚那能,是撥滾水燙之咾 (九) 潮漲末船可以行來快來死 (十) 拉我个房子个門前我要打笆 (十一) 火匠裡要擺煤,今夜頭恐怕我要生火 (十二) 柴劈好之末要紮之一梱一梱 (十三) 起頭个辰光小囝必過拉打棚但是後來末就相打一个末受傷 (十四) 一个榔頭一把鋸子一个刨一把銼刀是有用頭个傢生 (十五) 第个生梨咾蘋果是生个,吃之要生病 (十六) 拉月底一个人要去收帳 (十七) 各人應該盡伊个名分**

NOTES. (1). In the ninth sentence of the First Exercise, notice the expression °*zoo-ding*° 坐定, "to sit quiet."

(2). In the eleventh sentence of the First Exercise *Khe zen* 開船 means "to start the boat." Literally it is "to open the boat." In the same sentence *bing* °*s* 平水 means "slack water."

(3). In the eighteenth sentence of the First Exercise *zau yau yien* 造謠言 means "to start a rumor."

(4). In the twenty-fifth sentence of the First Exercise *dih-'veh-dzu*° 敵勿住 means "unable to oppose."

(5). In the fifth sentence of the Second Exercise, "to cut off the robber's head," is *sah theh* °*di kuh* °*jang-dau*° *kuh deu* 殺脫伊个頭.

(6). In the ninth sentence of the Second Exercise "to travel" is *'ang* 行.

(7). In the tenth sentence of the Second Exercise "to erect a fence," is °*tang-po* 打笆.

上海方言教程



# LESSON XXVIII.

## Abstract Nouns formed from two Adjectives of opposite meaning.

Very often two adjectives of opposite meaning are joined together to form an abstract noun of quality. Naturally the Chinese language is defective in abstract nouns, and their lack is partially supplied in this way. Thus ***Too-°sau*** (多少), Much-little, means "quantity."

***Dzang-°toen*** (長短), "Long-short," means "length." ***°Yoen-°jung*** (遠近), "Far-near," means "distance." ***Kau-ti°*** (高低), "High-low," means "height." ***°'Eu-bok*** (厚薄), "Thick-thin," means "thickness." ***Kwheh-'ah*** (闊狹), "Broad-narrow," means "breadth." ***°Lang-nyih*** (冷熱), "Cold-hot," means "temperature." ***Sung-°tshien*** (深淺), "Deep-shallow," means "depth." ***Chung-°dzoong*** (輕重), "Light-heavy," means "weight." ***Tshoo-si°*** (粗細), "Coarse-fine," means "texture" (of cloth.).

Verbs are also used in much the same way. Thus we have ***Le-°waung*** (來往). "Come-go," meaning "intercourse," or ***Le-chi°*** (來去), "Come-go," "meaning," "going back and forth." It generally occurs as ***Le-le-chi°-chi°***, ***°Ma-ma°*** (買賣), "Buy-sell," means "business."

### VOCABULARY.

To kneel, **°jui** 跪.

To forgive, **nyau-°so** 饒赦, **kwhen-°an** 寬限 **nyoen-liang°** 原諒 **kwhen-yoong** 寬容.

To comfort, **oen-we°** 安慰.

To sharpen, **moo** 磨.

To drive away, **°koen** 赶 **°koen-theh** 赶脫.

To criticize, **phi-bing** 批評, **phi-thah** 批撻.

To roll, **°kwung** 滾, **°kwung 'au° chi°** 滾下去.

To plaster, **°fung** 粉. To plaster a partition, **°fung pih** 粉壁.

To string, (as cash), **tshen** 串.

To thread a needle, **tshen °yung-sien°** 穿引線.

To slander, **wo°-°liau** 話料, **hwe°-°paung** 毀謗, **wo-wa°** 話壞.

To accompany, or stay with a person, **be** 陪.

To nurse, **su-°tsang** 輸帳.

To crawl, **ban** 蹩.

To climb, **bo** 爬.

To jump, to leap, **thiau°** 跳.

To reject, **the** 推, **the-theh** 推脫.

To feel, to touch, **mok** 摸.

To hoist (as a sail or flag), **tsha** 扯.

To run, as water, **lieu** 流.

To turn over, **fan** 翻, **fan-°tsen-le** 翻轉來.

To upset (as water), **°tang-fan** 打翻.

To turn round, **zien** 旋, **zien-°tsen-le** 旋轉來.

To manage, **kyung-°seu** 經手.

To pray, **jeu** 求.
To offer prayer, **tau°-kau°** 禱告.
To repent, **hwe°-°ke** 悔改.
To regret, **au-lau°** 懊憦.
A crow, **ih tsak lau°-au** 一隻老鴉.
A hawk, **ih tsak iung** 一隻鷹. **°lau-iung** 老鷹.
A butterfly, **ih tsak 'oo-dih** 一隻蝴蝶.
A pair of scissors, **ih °po °tsien-tau** 一把剪刀.

So that, **i-ts** 以致.
A screen, **ih sen° bing-foong** 一扇屏風.
A sail, **ih sen° boong** 一扇篷.
Scales, **thien-bing** 天秤.
A gong, **ih mien° kyung-loo** 一面金鑼.
Flour, **koen-mien°** 乾麵.
Butter, **°na-yeu** 乳油.
Milk, **nyeu-°na** 牛乳.
Sugar, **daung** 糖.

**EXERCISES.**

**(Translate into English.)**

**(1). °Di sen° bing-foong °kyi-hau° kwheh-'ah? (2). °Di tsak siang-°ts iau° liang-liang-khoen° dzang-°toen, kau-ti °lau kwheh-'ah. (3). Iau° noong° chi° ma ih tsang °ts-deu theh di tsang ih yang° °'eu-bok. (4). Thien-bing °z iau°-°kyung kuh ka-sang, °khau-i tshung meh-z° kuh chung-°dzoong. (5). °Ngoo °jui la° yi mien°-zien jeu yi nyau-°so. (6). °Siau-noen sang bing° meh, nyang 'veh li-khe yi, °soo la° zaung pien-deu su-°tsang yi. (7). 'Veh phi-bing bih nyung, keh-meh 'veh °zeu bih nyung kuh phi-bing. (8). We°-ts °khoong-pho° loo° 'veh zok, °soo-i °tshing bih nyung be °ngoo chi°. (9). °Di °po °tsien-tau ih ngan 'veh kwha°, iau° chi° moo-moo. (10). Kyau° sau-van°-kuh nau °tien koen-mien°, dan°, nyeu-°na, °lau daung, tsoo° kyi-dan°-kau. (11). Thah °tien nyeu-°na la° men-deu laung°, keh-meh °hau chuh-°tien. (12). 'Auh-sang-°ts la° khok we°-°ts bih nyung wo°-°liau yi, sien-sang kyau° yi 'veh iau° khok, °lau oen-we° yi. (13). °Ngoo kyau°-°ts yi meh, yi zieu° zien-°tsen-deu le khoen°. (14). °Di kuh ih tsaung z°-°thi sa° nyung kyung-°seu kuh. (15). Bo zu° meh 'veh da° °wung-taung°, °khoong-pho° iau° dih thoong° °lau dih saung. (16). Iung-ke °koen-theh i-tsak °keu, °khoong-pho° iau° °ngau °siau-noen. (17). Tsha boong meh, zeu 'ang le kwha°. (18). Tsoong°-dien-nyung 'veh hwen-°hyi °lau-au, we°-°ts yi-la° chuh-theh yi-la° san° la°-kuh °ts. (19). Dzang-z °lau-iung dzoong thien laung° fi-'au°-le chuh-theh-°ts °siau kyi. (20). Tshen-°hau °di-kuh doong-dien, °lau soen°-soen° khoen° °yeu °kyi-hau°. (21). Ping-ting tsheh-chi° °tang-tsang°, khau koo °lau kyung-loo. (22). °Di-kuh zak-deu dzoong san °ting laung° °kwung 'au°-le.**

海上絲綢之路文獻集成　科技與文化編

(一) 第扇屏風幾化闊狹 (二) 第隻箱子要量量看長短高低咾闊狹 (三) 要儂去買一張紙頭對第張一樣厚薄 (四) 天秤是要緊个傢生可以稱物事个輕重 (五) 我跪拉伊面前求伊饒赦 (六) 小囝生病末娘勿離開伊坐拉床邊頭輪幮伊 (七) 勿批評別人蓋末勿受別人个批評 (八) 爲之恐怕路勿熟所以請別人陪我去 (九) 第把剪刀一顏勿快要去磨磨 (十) 叫燒飯个拿點乾麵蛋牛乳咾糖做雞蛋糕 (十一) 搨點牛乳拉饅頭上蓋末好吃點 (十二) 學生子拉哭爲之別人話料伊先生叫伊勿要哭咾安慰伊 (十三) 我叫之伊末伊就旋轉頭來看 (十四) 第个一樁事體啥人經手个 (十五) 爬樹末勿大穩當恐怕要跌痛咾跌傷 (十六) 應該赶脫伊隻狗恐怕要咬小囝 (十七) 扯篷末船行來快 (十八) 種田人勿歡喜老鴉爲之伊拉吃脫伊拉散拉个子 (十九) 常時老鷹從天上飛下來吃脫之小雞 (二十) 串好第个銅錢咾算算看有幾化 (廿一) 兵丁出去打仗敲鼓咾金鑼 (廿二) 第个石頭從山頂上滾下來

(Translate into Chinese.)

(1). These two men constantly have intercourse with one another. (2). The servant did not take care, and so upset a bucket of water. (3). Butterflies are very pretty, and children like to catch them. (4). Children before they learn to walk can first crawl on the ground. (5). If a man wants to be forgiven he should first repent. (6). What is the depth of this creek? (7). If you wish to know the texture of the cloth, you must feel it with your hand. (8). If you do not wear spectacles when you are old, you will be unable to thread your needle. (9). I drove away the beggar, because he followed after me calling out. (10). What is the distance between the sun and the earth? About ninety-two millions of miles. (11). The cat climbed up the tree and the dog could not catch it. (12). The little girl has no time to study, because her mother is sick, and she must stay at home and nurse her. (13). The water flows down from the top of the hill. (14). I regret that I told him, because he went and told everyone, and now every one knows it. (15). When you pray you should kneel down.

(一) 第个兩个人常庄大家來往 (二) 用人勿當心所以打翻之一桶水 (三) 蝴蝶是蠻好看所以小囝歡喜捉个 (四) 小囝勿曾學會走先會得蹱拉地上 (五) 一个人要得着饒赦先應該悔改 (六) 第條浜有幾化深淺 (七) 若然儂要曉得第塊布个粗細儂終要用手摸摸看 (八) 年紀老之咾勿帶眼鏡恐怕勿能彀穿引綫眼 (九) 我赶脫之伊个告化子因為伊跟拉後頭咾喊 (十) 地球離開日頭有幾化遠近,約酌有九千二百萬里 (十一) 貓爬到樹上所以狗捉伊勿着 (十二) 小囝無沒工夫讀書因為伊个娘生病伊終要登拉屋裡輪帳伊 (十三) 水從山頂上流下來 (十四) 我懊憦我告訴伊因為伊去對攏總人話以致攏總人全曉得个 (十五) 儂聽告个時候應該跪下來

NOTES. (1). In the seventh sentence of the First Exercise notice how *phi-bing* is used both as a noun and as a verb.

(2). In the eighth sentence of the First Exercise *Zok* (熟), which means "ripe" of fruit, also means "well-known." It also has the meaning of "thorough" as in the expression *dok-zok* (讀熟), meaning to read thoroughly.

(3). In the thirteenth sentence of the First Exercise notice the position of the *deu* (頭), "head" between the °*Tsen* (轉) and the *le* (來)." This is usual in Chinese. Verbs are often broken up in this way.

(4). In the fifteenth sentence of the First Exercise °*wung-taung*° (穩當) means safe.

## LESSON XXIX.

### Some useful Phrases.

As will be seen from the lessons already gone over Chinese is very largely composed of idiomatic phrases. The only way to become acquainted with these phrases is by the constant hearing of the spoken language. We shall introduce in this lesson a few useful phrases and show how they occur in sentences.

"All one's life," ***ih sang-ih-s°*** "一生一世." Lit. "One life, one world." "To run about," ***Bau-le-bau-chi°*** (跑來跑去). Lit. "Run come, run go." "To decide,' ***Lih-ding-°tsu-i°*** (立定主意). "Lit. To stand still the will."

Good-bye (French, au-revoir), ***An°-hyih-we°*** (晏歇會). Lit. "We will meet later," or ***Tse°-we°*** (再會). Lit. "I will see you again."

The ordinary way of saying "good-bye" when you have been to call on a person is to say ***Chi°-tse*** (去哉). Lit. "I am going." Your host will say ***Man°-chi°*** (慢去), meaning "Go slowly."

The expression ***Kan-nyih-we°*** (間日會) would mean "I will see you in a day or two."

"Universal" ***°Phoo-thien-'au°*** (普天下), or ***'Eh-thien-°ti-'au°*** (合天底下). Lit. "Beneath the whole of heaven."

"Useless, in vain," is ***Bak-bak-°li*** (白白裡). "Indispensable" is ***°Ba-'veh-tuk*** (罷勿得).

## VOCABULARY.

If it be so, **kyi°-zen zeh-ke** 既然實蓋.
By chance, **°ngeu-zen** 偶然.
Purposely, **°yeu-i°** 有意, **koo°-i°** 故意.
At the point of, **°kyi-oo** 幾乎.
For the most part, generally, **da°-liak** 大畧.
Suddenly, **hweh-zen** 忽然.
Instantaneous, **lih-khuh** 立刻.
Advantage, profit, **iuh-tshu°** 益處, **°hau-tshu°** 好處.
Lord, **°Tsu** 主.
Master, **°tsu-nyung** 主人, **toong-ka** 東家.
Heavenly Lord (a term used for God) **thien-°Tsu** 天主.
God, **Zung** 神.
Omnipotent, **voo-°soo-peh-nung** 無所不能.
Omnipresent, **voo-°soo-peh-°dze** 無所不在.
Omniscient, **voo-°soo-peh-ts** 無所不知.
Life, **sing°-ming°** 性命.
A dragon, **ih diau loong** 一條龍.
An account book, **ih °pung tsang°-°boo** 一本賬簿.
A small blank book, **ih °pung boo°-ts** 一本簿子.
Carefully, **ts-si°** 仔細.
To waste, **fi°-theh** 廢脫.
A carpet, **ih diau mau-°than**

***°Boo*** (部) is the classifier for sets of books.

A set of books, **ih °boo su** 一部書.
A flag, **ih mien° ji** 一面旗.
A mirror, **ih mien° kyung°-°ts** 一面鏡子.

## EXERCISES.

(Translate into English.)

(1). Noong° zeh-ke° tsoo° meh, °khoong-pho° ih-sang-ih-s° iau° au-lau° tse. (2). °Ngoo bak-bak-°li te° yi wo°, yi dzung-jeu° 'veh thing. (3). Sien-sang tsiang iau° chi° yi te° °ngoo wo°, chi°-tse°, lau °ngoo te° yi wo°, mau°-chi°. (4). Noong° iung-ke lih-ding-°tsu-i° 'veh tsoo° zeh-ke° thau-°tshoong kuh z°-°thi. (5). Thien-°tsu °z voo-°soo-peh nung, voo-°soo-peh-dze, °lau voo-°soo-peh-ts. (6). Nyung iau° khoen° z°-ka mien-khoong meh, ih mien° kyung°-°ts °z °ba-veh-tuk-kuh. (7). Tuh-dzak° phoo-thien-'au° °lau seh-theh-ts z°-ka-kuh sing°-ming° meh °yeu sa° iuh-tshu° nyi? (8). °Di-tsak °mo la° dien °li bau-le-bau-chi°, van-nau tsauh-dzak kuh. (9). °Di °boo su °yeu °kyi °pung? °Yeu nyan° °pung. (10). Kyi°-zen zeh-ke°-nung, nau-meh °ngoo 'veh °hau wo° sa°. (11). 'Auh-sang-°ts °tang-se° poo-li °z °yeu-i° nyi wan-z °ngeu-zen kuh z°-°thi? (12). °I-kuh nyung dih la pang-°li, °kyi-‘oo dzung-sah, dan°-°z °yeu ih kuh nyung le thoo yi chi°-le. (13). ‘°Au-pen-°nyih hweh-zen fah-°chi doo° foong le. (14). ‘Auh-daung-li °loong-°tsoong °yeu °kyi-kuh ‘auh-sang-°ts? Da°-iak °yeu san pak kuh. (15). °Ngoo kyau° yi lih-khuh °doong-sung. (16). Tsoong-kok ji-‘au° °z loong. (17). °Di-kuh nyung °pung-le °z auh nyung, yien°-°dze hwe°-°ke-tse. (18). °Ngoo au-lau° °ma-ts °di-diau mau-°than, we°-ts °than la° khak-daung-°li thuh °siau. (19). Noong° seu-tsing°-le °lau foo-°tsheh-chi°-kuh °loong-°tsoong iau° kyi la° tsang°-°boo laung°. (20). °Di kuh ‘auh-sang-ts iau° the-°theh, iung-we° su dok-veh °zaung.

(一) 儂實蓋做末恐怕一生一世要懊憦哉 (二) 我白白裡對伊話伊仍舊勿聽 (三) 先生將要去伊對我話去哉我對伊話慢去 (四) 儂應該立定主意勿做實蓋坍銃个事體 (五) 天主是無所不能無所不在咾無所不知 (六) 人要看自家面孔末一面鏡子是罷勿得个 (七) 得着普天下咾失脫之自家个性命末有啥益處呢 (八) 第隻馬拉田裡跑來跑去煩難捉着个 (九) 第部書有幾本, 有念本 (十) 旣然實蓋能難末我勿好話啥 (十一) 學生子打碎玻璃是有意呢還是偶然个事體 (十二) 伊个人跌拉浜裡幾乎沉殺但是有一个人來拖伊起來 (十三) 下半日忽然發起大風來 (十四) 學堂裡攏總有幾个學生子, 大約有三百个 (十五) 我叫伊立刻動身 (十六) 中國旗號是龍 (十七) 第个人本來是惡人現在悔改哉 (十八) 我懊憦買之第條毛毯爲之攤拉客堂裡忒小 (十九) 儂收進來咾付出去个攏總要記拉帳簿上 (二十) 第个學生子要退脫因爲書讀勿上

(Translate into Chinese.)

(1). The man is very sick, even at the point of death. (2). One should not only think how to get profit for oneself, but how to give advantage to others. (3). In the evening the master gave the servants their wages. (4). I think that he offended me purposely, and therefore I am angry. (5). A student should not only learn while in school, but should be learning all his life. (6). I saw a dragon come up suddenly out of the water. (7 . Truly all men under heaven are brethren, and ought to love one another. (8). A business man can see from his account book how much he has gained in his business or how much he has lost. (9). If you really ran very fast, how is it that you did not arrive sooner? (10). I have looked over this book in a general way, but I have not read it carefully. (11). If you wish to repent and become a good man, the first thing is to make up your own mind. (12). I knew the boat was a Chinese one, because they hoisted the Chinese flag. (13). A man's life is most precious, so he ought to take care of his body. (14). When I had finished the work I found he had already done the same thing, and so I had wasted my time to no purpose. (15). The children like to run about and play in the garden.

**(一) 第个人毛病鬱重幾乎要死 (二) 人勿但要想到自家个益處也要想到別人个益處 (三) 拉夜快主人發工錢拉伊个用人 (四) 我想伊有意得罪我所以我動氣 (五) 學生子勿但拉學堂裡要學,一生一世應該學个 (六) 我看見一條龍從水裡忽然上來 (七) 普天下人實在是弟兄應該大家相愛 (八) 生意人從帳簿上可以看伊賺之幾化或者折脫之幾化 (九) 既然儂跑來快爲啥咾勿早點到 (十) 我大略看過第本書但是勿曾仔細看 (十一) 若然儂要悔改成功好个人,頭一要自家立定主意 (十二) 我曉得第隻船是中國船因爲伊扯拉个是中國旗 (十三) 人个性命是頂寶貝个所以應該當心自家个身體 (十四) 我做好之第个生活我看別人搭我一樣个所以我白白裡廢脫第个工夫 (十五) 小囝拉花園裡歡喜跑來跑去勃相**

NOTES. (1). *Thien-°tsu* is the term used for God by the Romanists and by some Protestants. The other terms used for God are *Zung* (神). Lit. "a Spirit" and °*Zang-ti*° (上帝). Lit. "The Celestial Ruler."

(2). In the fourteenth sentence of the Second Exercise for "to no purpose," one can say *Bak-bak-li-fi°-theh*, or the *bak* (白) can be used with the verb. Thus we can say *Bak fi°-theh* (白廢脫). *Bak* is often used in this way with verbs. Thus *Bak-tsoo°* (白做), "to do in vain." *Bak °siang* (白想), "to think in vain, to no purpose," etc.

# LESSON XXX.

## Polite Language.

In the Chinese language there are a great many polite phrases used in conversation. The ability to use these is a sign of education. Every student of the language should become acquainted with the most common ones, for he will have occasion to use them constantly. Some of these phrases have been introduced and explained in these lessons already, but here an attempt will be made to gather together all those that would be ordinarily used in conversation.

When you meet any one for the first time, according to Chinese etiquette you are at liberty to ask him what his honorable name may be. The expression for this is ***Tsung sing°*** (尊姓). or ***Kwe°-sing°*** (貴姓). In answer he will tell you his surname, but in doing so he will refer to it as his humble name. Thus he will say ***Bi°-sing° Tsang*** (敝姓張) (if his surname is Tsang).

Next you might proceed to inquire what his other name was, that is, his private name in distinction from his surname. This you would ask by saying ***°Tshing kyau° da° 'au°*** (請叫大號). "Please teach me your great appellation" or ***The °foo*** (台甫). In answer he might say ***°Tshau-z° Kya-foo*** (草字嘉甫), meaning "the grass characters are ***Kya-foo,"*** or he might say ***°Siau-ming*** (小名). (***Kya-foo*** is taken as an example of a name).

Then you might proceed to ask his age. This you would do by saying ***Too-sau kwe°-kang*** (多少貴庚). The answer would be ***°Ngoo hyui doo° san seh soe°*** (我虛度三十歲). Lit. "I have vainly passed thirty years." If you ask an old gentleman his age you would say ***°Kyi-hau° kau-zeu°*** (幾化高壽). Lit. "What is your high longevity?"

If you ask a person how he is, as has been already intimated, you would say ***°Hau-la°-va°*** (好拉陌). The answer might be ***Khau° fok*** (靠福), meaning "I depend upon you for my happiness."

If a person asked you how many years you had been in China, he would say ***Tau°-ts bi°-kok °kyi z-tse*** (到之敝國幾時哉). You would answer ***°Ngoo tau°-ts kwe°-kok nyan nyien*** (我到之貴國念年), "I arrived in your honorable country twenty years ago." (or any length of time you had been in the country).

When you are asking a guest to take a seat, if he is at all an honorable guest, you must request him to take an honorable seat. This you do by saying ***Tshing °zaung-deu °zoo*** (請上頭坐), meaning "Please sit up higher."

In asking how many children you have your guest would say ***°Kyi-we °sau-kyuin*** (幾位少君). "How many little princes have you." "Your answer is ***San kuh °siau-koen*** (三个小干), or ***°siau-nwen*** (三个小囝), or ***san kuh °siau-°choen*** (三个小犬).

上海方言教程



At table, if you finish before others, you raise your chop-sticks and say to the others ***Man°-yoong°*** (慢用), "use slowly." Then place the chop-sticks on top of the bowl. Your host could answer ***Yoong°-°pau*** 用飽, meaning, "Take plenty."

When a guest is leaving, in addition to saying ***Chi°-tse,*** he may say ***Kyung-tshau*** (驚吵), meaning, "I have troubled you." Your answer may be ***De-man de-man*** (待慢), meaning, "I have treated you without proper respect." You should say to a guest as he is walking away ***°Tshing lieu kyung-boo°*** (請留經步), meaning, "Please restrain your orderly footsteps," or simply ***Lieu-boo°.*** It you have to excuse yourself after a short stay, you should say ***Sau-be*** 少陪.

## VOCABULARY.

England, **Iung-kok 英國.**
America, **°Me-kok 美國, Hwo-ji-kok 花旗國.** Lit. Kingdom of the flowery flag.
France, **Fah-kok 法國.**
Germany, **Tuk-kok 德國.**
Russia, **Ngoo-kok 俄國.**
Antiquity, Anciently, **°koo-z-kan 古時間.**
Neighbor, **ling-°so 鄰舍.**
Post Office, **Yeu-tsung°-jok 郵政局.**
A godown, **°dzan-vaung 棧房.**
Inconceivable, **°siang-'veh-tau 想勿到.**
Lazy, **°lan-phok 懶朴.** **°Lau-doo° 懶惰.**
Tricky, **diau°-bi 掉皮.**
Matches, **z°-le-°hoo 自來火.**
Next (juxtaposition), **kah-pih 隔壁**
Promise, **iung°-°hyui 應許.**
Recently, **°jung-le 近來.**
Originally, **°pung-le 本來.**
To meet with misfortune, **chuh °khoo 吃苦.** Literally "Eat bitterness."
Comfortable, **suh-i° 適意.**
The earlier, the better, **yoeh °tsau yoeh °hau 越早越好.**
To relax the mind, **san° sing 散心.**
Soap, **bi-zau° 肥皂.**
To strike a match, **wak 劃.**

## EXERCISES.

**(Translate into English).**

(1). °Di-foong sing° iau° noong° tan tau° Yeu-tsung°-jok °li chi°. (2). °Koo-z-kan Tsoong-kok tah-ts bih-kuh kok-doo° ih ngan 'veh le-°waung. (3). °Jung-le Ngoo-kok tah-ts Toong-yang da°-ka °tang-tsang°. (4). Dzu° la° kah-pih kuh nyung °z kyau° ling-°so. (5). °Di-kuh nyung 'veh ba° °z °lan-phok, yi° 'a-z diau°-bi. (6). Sang-i° nyung la° °dzan-vaung °li tsaung too-hau hoo°-suh. (7). °Tshing °zoo la° bih kuh iui°-°ts laung°, °i-tsak 'veh da° suh-i°. (8). °Ngoo iung°-°hyui °ngoo kuh si-tse, zak-zen tsoo° le °hau meh iau° ka yi-kuh koong-dien. (9). °I-kuh nyung we°-ts chuh °tsieu, °too doong-dien, °lau 'veh °lau-zeh °i-kyung chuh-ts too-hau° khoo. (10). Tsoong-kok tah °Me-kok tsho-'veh-too ih yang° doo°-°siau. (11). °Pung-le °Me-kok nyung °z dzoong Iung-kok le kuh. (12). °Di-foong sing° °kyi-z iau° °ngoo °sia kuh? Yoeh-°tsau yoeh-°hau. (13). °I-kuh nyung zeh-ke° diau°-bị zeh-dze °siang-veh-tau^-kuh. (14). °Seu °lau mieu°-khoong iau° kha le koen-zing meh tsoong iau° yoong° bi-zau°. (15). Iau° wak z°-le-°hoo tsoong iau° wak la° ‘ah-°ts laung°, ’veh zen meh ’veh we° yaung.

(一) 第封信要儂担到郵政局裏去 (二) 古時間中國搭之別个國度一頸勿來往 (三) 近來俄國搭之東洋大家打仗 (四) 住拉隔壁个人是叫鄰舍 (五) 第个人勿罷是懶朴也是掉皮 (六) 生意人拉棧房裡裝之多化貨色 (七) 請坐拉別个椅子上伊隻勿大適意 (八) 我應許我个西崽若然做來好末要加伊个工錢 (九) 伊个人爲之吃酒賭銅錢咾勿牢實已經吃之多化苦 (十) 中國搭美國差勿多一樣大小 (十一) 本來美國人是從英國來个 (十二) 第封信幾時要我寫个,越早越好 (十三) 伊个人實蓋掉皮實在想勿到个 (十四) 手咾面孔要揩來乾淨末終要用肥皂 (十五) 要劃自來火終要劃拉匣子上勿然末勿會旺

(Translate into Chinese).

(1). You should love your neighbor as yourself. (2). All over China now there are post offices, and you can send a letter to any part of China for two cents. (3). America is called the Kingdom of the Flowery Flag, because its flag is very beautiful. (4). A lazy man likes to get up late in the day, and during the day he likes to go to sleep. (5). Germany and France are next to one another on the map. (6). The fox is one of the most tricky of all the animals. (7). How long have you been in my humble country? I arrived in your honorable country only about one year ago. (8). Since I have promised it, I will certainly do as I said. (9). In ancient times most men were unable to read and write; now a large portion of the people can do so. (10). Children should not play with matches, because they might set the house on fire (11). Men can not always be using their minds; they must at times relax their minds. (12) Yesterday I felt very wretched, and was in bed all day; to-day I am more comfortable.

(一) 儂應該愛鄰舍像愛自家 (二) 垃拉中國各處地方有郵政局二分洋錢可以送一封信到隨便那裡頭 (三) 美國是叫花旗國因爲伊个旗是變

好看 (四) 懶朴个人是歡喜晚𥑮起來日裡也要睏 (五) 德國搭之法國𡍲拉地理圖上是隔壁 (六) 拉中牲當中狐狸蠻棹皮个 (七) 到之敝國幾時哉，到之貴國不過年把 (八) 我既然應許个一定要照我話个𠰌做 (九) 拉古時間攏總人勿會讀書𠰌寫字現在大一半人可以个 (十) 小囡勿應該拿自來火來弄勃相恐怕要弄開火來 (十一) 人勿可以常庄用心有常時末終要散心 (十二) 昨日我一顏勿好一日睏拉床上今朝稍爲適意點

NOTES. (1). In the third sentence of the First Exercise *da-ka* (大家) means "together."

(2). In the fifteenth sentence notice the '*Veh zen meh* (勿然末), meaning, "If not so."

(3). In the tenth sentence of the Second Exercise "to set the house on fire," may be translated *Loong khe °hoo le* 弄開火來.

(4). In the twelfth sentence of the Second Exercise *Yoong°-sing* (用心) and *San°-sing* (散心) are just the opposite of one another.

国家出版基金项目
NATIONAL PUBLICATION FOUNDATION

# 海上絲綢之路文獻集成

總主編　陳支平　陳春聲

## 科技與文化編 100

主編　王揚宗　葉　農

海峽出版發行集團
THE STRAITS PUBLISHING & DISTRIBUTING GROUP
福建人民出版社

# 本册目次

# 新關文件録［二］

（*Hsin-kuan Wên-chien-lu: Text Book of Documentary Chinese, with a Vocabulary, for the Special Use of the Chinese Customs Service*）

〔美〕夏德（Friedrich Hirth）編

# PART II.

## VOCABULARY, ALPHABETICALLY ARRANGED.

16

# VOCABULARY.

## II. ALPHABETICALLY ARRANGED.

### A.

*a* 阿 (or 亞) inferior; often forms the first part of a proper name, chiefly among the lower classes, *e.g.*, *A-ming;* used in representing the sound *a* or *o* in foreign names.

阿拉比國 *(a-la-pi-kuo)* Arabia.

阿爾敦布爾額 *(a-êrh-tun-pu-êrh-ngo)* Oldenburg.

阿魏 asafœtida.

*ai* 挨 to receive; to suffer.

挨打 to be beaten.

挨及國 *(ai-chi-kuo)* Egypt.

*ai* 哀 grief; pain.

哀號 to scream from pain or grief.

哀叩 to pray for urgently.

哀悃 the sentiments of grief.

哀思 thoughts of grief.

*ai* 涯 a shore; a limit.

*ai* 碍 (or 礙) to endanger; danger; difficulty; to cause difficulties to; to obstruct; to interfere with.

碍處 obstructions; difficulties.

*ai* 隘 a pass; straits.

*an* 安 peaceful; contented with; to make easy; to place; to lay down.

安分 peaceful and contented; orderly.

安天命 contented with Heaven's decree; to submit to fate.

安心 to make one's heart easy.

安商業 to make the merchant's business easy.

安家之費 payments for the benefit of one's family.

安設 to erect; to lay down (as a buoy).

安息香 gum benjamin.

安息油 oil of gum benjamin.

安徽省 the province of Anhwei.

安南國 *(an-nan-kuo)* Annam; Annamese.

安平 An-p'ing, near T'ai-wan, Formosa.

安慶 *(an-ch'ing)* Ank'ing (capital of the Anhwei province, and a port of call on the Yangtze).

*an* 按 according to; to examine.

按察使 a provincial judge.

按照 according to.

按照辦理 to act accordingly.

按…………計 calculated at…………

按貨科稅 to calculate duties on the goods carried.

按限 within the limit (of time).

按日 according to date.

按七日 weekly; by the week.

按月 by the month; monthly.

按年 annually.

按年計月 yearly or monthly.

按期定數 at regular (fixed) dates.

按股分 according to share.

按類 according to category; according to denomination.

按律 according to law.

按羅經方向 magnetic bearings.

按時 at the proper time; punctually.

按此卽知 it may be known therefrom.

*an* 案 a court; a case; (= 案查) whereas; according to.

案查 whereas.

案內 in the case.

案內情形 the particular circumstances of the case.

案情 the details of a case.

案情抄錄 a copy of the minutes of a case.

案由 cases and their details.

*an* 暗 dark; secret; hidden.

暗沙 a sandbank or shoal below water.

暗輪船 a steamer driven by an unseen or hidden wheel; *i.e.*, a screw steamer.

*an* 諳 to know about.

*an* 岸 a shore; the coast.

*ang* 昂 high; to raise.

*ang* 昂稅 to raise the duty.

昂布爾 *(ang-pu-êrh)* the city of Hamburg.

*ao* 熬 to boil.

熬作糖觔 to boil, or refine, sugar.

*ao* 凹 a cavity; concave.

凹鏡 a concave lens, or a reflector.

凹鏡迴射鐙光 a concave and reflecting light; a catoptric light.

*ao* 奧 mysterious; obscure.

奧斯底里雅 *(ao-ssŭ-ti-li-ya)* Australia.

*ao* 澳 a bay.

澳門 Macao.

## C.

*cha* 札 a despatch from a superior. See *cha* 劄.

*cha* 紮 [also written 劄, 劄, 札, and 扎] to be stationed at.

*cha* 劄 [also written 札] a despatch from a superior to an inferior; to be stationed at.

劄行 to address a despatch to an inferior.

劄令 to order, in a despatch.

劄飭 to instruct.

劄委 to write officially to an inferior.

劄文 a despatch to an inferior; instructions.

*cha* 乍 suddenly; abruptly.

乍明乍滅 lighting up suddenly and eclipsing suddenly; occulting (as a navigation light).

*cha* 炸 to blow up; to explode.

炸火藥 dynamite.

*ch'a* 查 to examine; to look into; whereas; often denotes merely what we should express by a new paragraph.

查照 to take official notice; for official information; placed after the name of the recipient in addresses, etc.; used for *an chao* (按照), according to.

查照施行 to note and act accordingly.

查照遵辦 to act according to instructions received.

查照辦理 to act accordingly.

查抄 to seize for confiscation.

查究 to examine; to try.

查出 it comes out; it is brought home to one; to find out; to discover.

查獲 to seize (as smuggled goods).

查銷 to cancel.

查看 to inspect.

*ch'a* 查管 to examine and control; to be charged with the inspection of.

查明 to inspect (as a document); to ascertain; to recognise on examination; to find to be.

查明聲復 to examine and report in reply.

查拏 to search and seize; to seize.

查辦 to investigate.

查收 to receive officially; to take delivery of.

查對 to check; to examine.

查艙 to search the hold of a ship.

查驗 to examine; examination.

查閱 to note; to examine and take note of; to peruse.

查有 there was found to be.

*ch'a* 差 mistaken; erroneous. See *ch'ai* and *tz'ŭ*.

差遠 very different; quite mistaken.

*ch'a* 察 to examine; to search.

察看 to examine.

察奪 to examine and judge; to decide.

*ch'a* 擦 to scatter; to rub.

擦損 to destroy by rubbing or scratching; to efface.

*ch'a* 茶 tea.

茶末 tea dust.

茶師 a tea taster or tea inspector.

茶碗 a tea-bowl.

茶葉 tea (as merchandise).

*ch'a* 搽 to rub on; to besmear.

*ch'a* 詧 to inquire into.

詧核 to inquire into; to examine.

*ch'a* 詫 to deceive by brag and talk.

詫異 strange; incredible.

*chai* 側 oblique; to lie on one side.

*chai* 摘 to pluck; to pick.

摘列 to give an extract from; an extract from (as from a document or a book).

摘頂 to take off the button of an official by way of punishment.

*chai* 債 to owe; to be in debt.

債主 a creditor.

債項 a debt; debts.

*chai* 宅 a private residence; a house.

*chai* 窄 narrow.

*chai* 寨 an encampment; a fort.

*ch'ai* 差 to send; a messenger. See *ch'a* and *tz'ŭ*.
差遣 to send; to depute.
差拘 to seize; to arrest.
差使 to be sent (as an envoy); to depute.
差委 to depute.
差役 official messengers.

*ch'ai* 拆 to break open.
拆壞 to break up; to demolish.
拆毀 to break up.
拆信 to open a letter.
拆動 to tamper with; to open (as packages under bond).

*ch'ai* 柴 firewood.
柴薪 firewood.
柴魚 stock-fish.

*chan* 佔 to usurp; to encroach on.
佔艙 to trespass upon the space of a ship's hold (by not taking delivery of cargo).

*chan* 沾 to moisten; to be affected by; to receive favour.
沾恩 to receive favour.
沾染 saturated with; infected by.
沾仁 to receive humane treatment.
沾益 to participate in profit; to receive profit.

*chan* 霑 (=沾) to moisten; to receive favours.

*chan* 粘 to paste on. See *nien* 粘.

*chan* 氈 felt; rugs; carpets; carpeting; blankets.
氈帽 felt caps.
氈碎 felt cuttings.
氈毯 carpets and druggets.

*chan* 展 to expand; to extend.
展轉 repeatedly; again and again.
展限 to extend a limit.
展緩 to postpone; to extend (as a limit of time).

*chan* 棧 a warehouse; a godown; to store in a godown.
棧房 a warehouse; a godown.

*chan* 斬 to cut in two; to behead.
斬絞 to behead and strangle.
斬罪 capital punishment.

*chan* 暫 temporarily; a short time.
暫且 temporarily.
暫先 beforehand; for the time being.
暫存 to keep on deposit; on deposit.

*chan* 暫時 temporarily; for the time being.

*chan* 戰 to fight; a battle; war.
戰船 a war junk; a man-of-war; a gunboat.

*ch'an* 攙 to mix (as good metal with an inferior metal); to make up; to repair.
攙錄器 plated ware.

*ch'an* 產 to give birth to; to produce; produce.
產製 to manufacture.
產業 a business to make a living from; a living; a property.

*chang* 章 regulations.
章程 regulations.

*chang* 彰 to promulgate.
彰明 to promulgate; to make known to the public.

*chang* 樟 (or 漳) camphor.
樟腦 camphor.
漳州府 the prefecture of Chang-chou, near Amoy.

*chang* 長 to grow; to extend. Cf. *ch'ang* 長, long.
長進 to make progress.
長落 to grow and fall; increase and decrease; fluctuation.

*chang* 帳 an account; curtains. See *chang* 賬.
帳子 curtains.
帳務 accounts business.
帳房 an office where accounts are settled; a counting-house; a shroff's or compradore's office; an accountant; a shroff.

*chang* 賬 (=帳) an account.
賬本 } an account book.
賬簿 }
賬尾 the balance of an account.
賬目 accounts.

*chang* 張 a sheet; classifier of mats, bed sheets, mattresses, etc., and of lottery tickets; to stretch.
張掛 to hoist, or fly, a flag.

*chang* 漲 water rising; to overflow.
漲潮 a rising tide.

*chang* 掌 to control.
掌管 to manage; to control.

*chang* 丈 a *chang* (=141 inches, or 11¾ feet, English).
丈尺 *chang* and *ch'ih*; *i.e.*, length or measurement (as of piece goods).
丈量 a measure of length.

*chang* 仗 to fight.

*chang* 杖 to beat with the bamboo.

*ch'ang* 倡 a leader.

*ch'ang* 娼 a singing woman; a prostitute.

*ch'ang* 常 constantly; usually; commonly.

常川 uninterruptedly; continuously; regularly (*lit.*, an uninterrupted stream).

常川照辦 to manage matters permanently in this manner.

常明鐙 a fixed light.

常用 in constant use; constantly occurring.

常用雜費 ordinary expenditure.

常鎮通海 the four departments of Ch'ang-chou-fu (常 *ch'ang*), Chên-chiang-fu (鎮 *chên*), T'ung-chou (通 *t'ung*), and Hai-mên-t'ing (海 *hai*), forming the circuit in charge of the Taot'ai at Chinkiang.

*ch'ang* 廠 a shed; a yard; a tax office.

*ch'ang* 償 to indemnify.

償還 to pay a debt; to repay; to refund.

*ch'ang* 嘗 to taste; a sign of the past: have, has.

*ch'ang* 長 long; length. Cf. *chang* 長 to grow.

長江 the Yangtze river.

長江六處 the six landing stages on the Yangtze (opened to trade by the Chefoo Convention).

長江統共章程 the Revised Yangtze Trade Regulations.

長方式 diamond shaped.

長工 constant work; long contract work.

長短 length.

長承 to receive for a long time.

長岐山 Chang-ch'i Peak, near Foochow.

*ch'ang* 塲 an enclosure; barracks (as at an emigration agency); an arena; saltflats; salt factories.

塲價 the official price of salt.

*chao* 召 to summon.

召見 to call to court; to assemble at court.

*chao* 招 to invite; to encourage; to beckon; to call.

招搖 to entice by showing oneself off; to put on false airs.

招募 to enlist; to engage.

招商 to invite merchants; to promote commerce.

招商局 / 招商船局 } the China Merchants' Steam Navigation Company.

招商分局 a branch office of the China Merchants' Company.

*chao* 招帖 a hand-bill; an advertisement.

招租 to be let (as a house).

招致華民 to seek for Chinamen (as for coolie emigration).

招工 to seek work; to emigrate; emigrant; emigration.

招工章程 regulations for the emigration of coolies.

招主 (= 招工主) a coolie employer.

*chao* 詔 to proclaim.

詔旨 an imperial decree.

*chao* 昭 to make known; to display; bright; intelligent.

昭豫 intelligent and contented (of a well-balanced mind).

昭和 bright and accordant.

*chao* 照 to reflect; a document; a certificate; a pass; to certify; according to; as.

照面鏡 mirrors.

照貨相符 certificate and goods agreeing; if the goods are found to agree with the certificate covering them.

照案 according to precedent.

照章 according to regulations.

照例 according to rule; in accordance with, *i.e.*, not contrary to, regulations.

照銅錢一律 in conformity with [the rule regarding] copper cash.

照值百抽五例 according to the five per cent. *ad valorem* principle.

照舊 as heretofore; as before.

照常 as usual.

照依 according to.

照尋常式樣 in customary form.

照呈 (= 照數呈送) to hand over an amount as per account.

照數查收 to receive an amount as per account.

照塡 to fill in (as in a document).

照知 to inform in a despatch.

照會 an official communication; a despatch; to address in a despatch.

照復 / 照覆 } to reply in a despatch.

照送 to forward officially.

照詳施行 to report [in order to solicit instructions] for one's guidance.

照辦 to act accordingly.

*chao* 照所請 as requested.
照得 whereas.
照稱 an official despatch stating; to state in an official document.
照料 to superintend; to manage.
照完 to pay in accordance with (viz., the proper rate).
照登底簿 to enter in a book.

*chao* 朝 the morning. Cf. *ch'ao* 朝, court.
朝夕 morning and evening; between morning and evening; in the course of a day.

*chao* 著(=着) certain; true; to manifest.

*chao* 找 to seek.
找錢 to change money.
找還 to repay.
找尋 to seek.

*ch'ao* 吵 to wrangle.
吵鬧 to altercate; to scold.

*ch'ao* 抄 to seize; to confiscate; to copy.
抄粘 to annex, or enclose, a copy.
抄書 a copy book.
抄莊 a wholesale establishment.

*ch'ao* 鈔 money orders; tonnage dues; to copy.
鈔項, 鈔課, 鈔銀 } tonnage dues.
鈔票 Government notes.
鈔單 a copy of a document.
鈔存備查 to file a copy in the archives; to take a record of.

*ch'ao* 朝 the court; the dynasty. Cf. *chao* 朝, morning.
朝服 court dress.
朝考 the grand examination at Peking.
朝廷 the court.

*ch'ao* 潮 the flood tide; damp.
潮漲 the flood rising.
潮漲時 at high-water time; the flood rising.
潮滿時 at high-water time; when the tide is full.
潮落時 at low-water time.
潮濕 damp.
潮州 the prefecture of Ch'ao-chou, near Swatow.
潮海關 the Swatow Customs.
潮陽縣 the district of Ch'ao-yang, near Swatow.

*ch'ao* 巢 a nest; a nest of robbers; a den of thieves.

*chê* 遮 to screen; to conceal; an umbrella.
遮蔽 to obscure; to render invisible.
遮滅 to eclipse.
遮掩不見 to be shaded off and become invisible.

*chê* 者 that which; gives the verb preceding it the force of a participle or a relative clause. *Shou-mai* (售賣) to sell; *shou-mai-chê* (售賣者), the selling ones, or, those who sell. Such a phrase may be preceded by a noun, *e.g.*, *shang-jên shou-mai-chê* (商人售賣者), which means "those of the merchants who sell," or "such merchants as may sell." For other uses of this particle, *see* WILLIAMS' "Syllabic Dictionary," p. 38, and the several works existing upon Chinese grammar.

*chê* 折 to break off; to deduct; to calculate a proportion.
折毀 to break up; to demolish.
折增 to add to (in calculating).
折合 to calculate.
折交 to pay in proportion to......
折抽 to levy a proportionate tax.
折抽膏釐 a tax levied on boiled opium; the *kao-li* tax.
折中 to strike an average; average.
折收 to receive in proportion; to receive...... per cent.
折銀 to calculate an amount of money.

*chê* 浙(=浙江) the province of Chêkiang.
浙海關 the Ningpo Customs.

*chê* 摺 to fold up; a paper folded up; a report; an account; a memorial to the Throne.
摺奏 to memorialise the Emperor.

*chê* 輙 then (denoting sequence). Cf. *chi* 卽.
輙卽 then (denoting sequence); at once.

*ch'ê* 車 a cart; a carriage.
車輛 carts; carriages.

*ch'ê* 扯 to pull apart; to tear away; to haul up; to hoist.
扯挂 to hoist (as a flag).
扯旗望臺 a signal station.
扯上扯下 to hoist and lower (as a signal flag or lantern on board ship).
扯平 to strike an average.

*ch'ê* 撤 to remove; to withdraw; to set aside; to recall (as troops).
撤銷 to cancel; to expire.
撤去不用 to remove and cease using; to discontinue.

ch'ê 撤回 to turn back; to send back.

撤究(=撤任究辦) to remove from office and punish.

撤退 to resign, to withdraw (as from an office); to remove; to dismiss (as an employé).

ch'ê 澈 to search thoroughly.

澈查 to search out; to sift to the bottom.

ch'ê 轍 the track of a wheel; a precedent.

ch'ê 掣 to drag; to pull.

掣肘 *lit.*, "to pull elbows," *i.e.*, to hinder; to embarrass.

掣取 to take delivery of; to receive.

chên 眞 true; real.

眞參 real ginseng.

眞金線 real gold thread.

眞銀線 real silver thread.

眞正 real; regular; in the proper sense of the word; *bonâ fide*.

眞實 true; really.

chên 鎭 a regiment; a brigade; (=鎭台) a brigadier-general; a town.

鎭協各營 the battalions of a regiment.

鎭守 to guard; to have charge of (as a general).

鎭鄉 towns and villages.

鎭(=鎭江 *chên-chiang*) Chinkiang.

鎭江關 the Chinkiang Customs.

chên 珍 precious (as a gem).

珍愛 to be fond of (as a curiosity, jewel, etc.).

珍珠 real pearls.

珍寶 precious things; valuable.

chên 診 to examine.

診視 to see and examine a patient (as a physician does).

chên 臻 to collect; many.

chên 針 (or 鍼) a needle; needles.

chên 斟 to deliberate.

斟酒 to consult; to deliberate.

斟酌適中之論 to consult about a middle course; to strike an average.

chên 朕 I, the Emperor; We.

朕心 Our Imperial heart.

chên 賑 to relieve; to aid the distressed.

chên 震 to shake; to alarm.

震悼 to be shocked with grief.

ch'ên 臣 a Minister of State.

臣衙門 my, the Minister's, yamên or office.

ch'ên 沉 to sink; deep.

沉有 there is sunk (as a wreck).

沉香 garoo-wood.

沉思 to think deeply.

沉船 a sunken ship; a wreck.

沉船木料 materials from vessels wrecked.

ch'ên 辰 the Chinese hour from 7 to 9 A.M.

ch'ên 陳 to state to; old; stale.

陳說 to explain; to state; to set forth.

陳明 to state.

陳皮 dried orange peel.

chêng 正 exactly; only; the first; the principal; full (as full duty, full rank); added to numeral expressions in order to prevent unauthorised additions being made, and corresponding to "*only*," as in "one hundred taels *only*"; just; just at the time when; as applied to colours, deep.

正直 regular; straight.

正西 due west.

正稅 full duty; *i.e.*, full import duty.

正稅單(=土貨出口正稅單) an export duty-paid certificate.

正稅憑單 a full duty proof.

正半兩稅 the full and half duty.

正半稅單 a full and half duty-paid certificate (for Yangtze ports).

正數 the full amount.

正副 the principal and second; chief and assistant.

正堂 the chief magistrate (whether prefect or district magistrate, as opposed to the assistant magistrates).

正品 full rank; the first or *A* division of each of the nine grades of official rank, as opposed to 從品, the second or *B* division.

正工 regular work, *i.e.*, work done during working hours; contract work.

正賊 the ringleaders of a band of robbers.

正法 capital punishment.

正月 the first month of the year.

正在 just at (local or temporal).

正在前面 directly in front of.

正在籌辦間 just at the time when matters were arranged.

正在核辦間 when just engaged in managing [a case].

*chêng* 正黃色 a deep yellow colour.

正白旗 one of the eight banners of Imperial troops; the "Plain White Banner."

*chêng* 征 to levy duty.

征稅 to levy duty.

征鈔 to levy tonnage dues.

征收 to collect (as duties).

*chêng* 政 Government administration; to regulate.

*chêng* 症 sickness.

*chêng* 証 to bear witness; to verify.

証人 a witness.

証據 testimony; evidence; a protest lodged in order to serve afterwards as evidence.

*chêng* 整 to adjust; to repair; (= 正) after numbers, "only."

整理 to adjust; to repair; to keep in order; to arrange for.

整潔 in proper order and clean; in good condition.

整頓 to set in order; to arrange; to repair.

*chêng* 禛 lucky; auspicious; being a forbidden character, should be written 禎 *(chêng)*.

*chêng* 爭 to quarrel.

爭論 to quarrel; to discuss.

*chêng* 徵 to levy; evidence; to prove.

徵收 to levy; to collect.

徵免船鈔章程 the Tonnage Dues Regulations.

*chêng* 證 to substantiate; evidence; a witness.

證質 cross-examination.

證據 proof; evidence.

*ch'êng* 稱 to weigh; to correspond to; to be adequate; to state; to style.

稱職 to be adequate to one's post; to perform one's duties as an official in proper form.

*ch'êng* 呈 to state to a superior; to address a superior; to hand to a superior.

呈明 to state clearly.

呈照 to deliver a certificate.

呈請 to apply for; to request to.

呈乞 to present a request.

呈報 to report.

呈稟 to present a petition.

呈具 to draw up and hand in (as a bond).

呈具報單 to make a written declaration; to send in a declaration.

*ch'êng* 呈繳 to present (as a document at an office); to hand up.

呈交 to tender; to present; to pay (as duties).

呈交備寄 to deliver for filing in the archives.

呈出 to produce (as a certificate).

呈驗 to present for examination.

呈送 to send in; to transmit to [a superior].

呈遞 to hand in; to present.

呈准 to apply for and receive permission; by authority.

呈存 to deliver for safe custody.

*ch'êng* 程 regulations; a pattern; to travel; a road.

*ch'êng* 丞 literary designation of a sub-prefect; an assistant.

丞相 a Prime Minister.

*ch'êng* 承 to receive; to undertake; a sign of the passive.

承大人派 I have been deputed by you, the Ta-jên.

承遣 to be sent; an emissary.

承囑 to receive instructions to; to be commissioned with.

承認 to acknowledge.

承任 to fill a post; to take charge of an office.

承充 to be entrusted with the duties of; to act as.

承工 to undertake work; to do coolie labour; a coolie.

承人招工 to engage a man for coolie labour.

承辦 to undertake the management of; to take in hand business (such as law suits, etc.).

承買 to contract for purchase.

承約 to make an agreement.

承當 to become liable; to be bound to.

承准 to receive.

承函 to receive, or to have received, a letter.

承歡 to receive pleasure.

承襲 to enter upon hereditary rank; to inherit.

*ch'êng* 成 complete; full; fulness; ready; to become; to make; made of; a tenth; tenths.

成案 a precedent; *lit.*, a ready case.

成直線 a straight line.

成疾 to contract a disease.

成本 to make into a book or pamphlet.

成色 per-centage or proportion of pure metal in an alloy.

成色若干 the touch (of silver).

*ch'êng* 城 a city; a city wall.
城外 outside the city; in the suburbs.

*ch'êng* 誠 really; sincerely; honest.
誠恐 there is real fear that.
誠懇 sincere and earnest.

*ch'êng* 乘 to avail oneself of.
乘機 to embrace an opportunity.
乘勢 to make use of the circumstances.

*ch'êng* 懲 (or 懲) to correct; to punish.
懲辦 to try and punish an offender.
懲治 to punish.

*ch'êng* 秤 to weigh.
秤計 to calculate the weight; to weigh.
秤準 to adjust the weight; to weigh.
秤碼 scales and weights; weights and measures.
秤頭 a balance; scales.

*chi* 幾 how many? a certain number (as in 第幾號 = "No. so-and-so;" "what number?"); several; nearly; almost.
幾名 how many persons? so many persons; several persons.
幾次 how many times? several times.
幾……幾…… so many…… as…… (*e.g.*, to pay *so many* times the Likin duty *as* there are barriers on the road).
幾倍 so many times.
幾致成災 almost amounting to a calamity.
幾不欲生 almost not to desire to live; I might have wished to die.

*chi* 機 a mechanical contrivance; to seize an opportunity; to watch the right moment for.
機宜 to consider *à propos*; to judge proper.
機器 machinery.
機器局 a manufactory for machinery; an arsenal.
機會 an opportunity.
機密 secretly; with discretion; a secret motive.

*chi* 譏 to ridicule.
譏誚 to ridicule.

*chi* 饑 famine; starvation.
饑寒 hunger and cold.

*chi* 寄 to send.
寄信 to send letters; to send messages.
寄信館 a post-office.
寄信旗 signalling flags; code signals.
寄賣 to commission one to sell; to make a consignment of goods.
寄帶 to forward (as in a letter).
寄頓 to send for storage.

*chi* 濟 succour; assistance.

*chi* 積 to collect.
積年 for many years.
積久 for a long time.
積勞 to amass labour; accumulation of toilsome work.
積勞成疾 to fall sick from overwork.
積德累仁 to accumulate merit and humanity.

*chi* 績 merit; business.

*chi* 賫 (or 齎) to give; to send.
賫回 to send back.

*chi* 及 to extend to; to concern; and; or.

*chi* 汲 to draw forth (as water out of a well).
汲水 to draw water.

*chi* 級 a step; a degree.

*chi* 基 foundation; base.
基業 family estates; property inherited; a patrimony.
基羅 (in imitation of the sound "kilo.") a kilogram.

*chi* 亟 haste; prompt; urgent.
亟速 urgently.

*chi* 極 extremely; the utmost point; a limit.
極美 most excellent.
極妙 most admirable.
極力 to the utmost of one's strength.
極欲 to desire very much.
極為明透 } to be extremely clear; to be very explicit.
極為明晰 }

*chi* 妓 a prostitute.

*chi* 擊 to strike.
擊殺 to strike to death; to kill with blows.

*chi* 繫 to bind; to connect.

*chi* 訖 to finish; to clear off (as an account); after a verb it often has the force of a sign of the past; also used for 迄 (*hsi*), till.

新關文件録



*chi* 卽 then; thereupon; marks sequence, and is therefore used in introducing the apodosis after the protasis in a conditional, temporal, etc., clause; *e.g.*, if it rains, [*then*] he goes; when it rained, [*then*] he went. In either sentence *chi* may appear in the place of the English *then*. But this particle is also used after single nouns and single verbs, as if we were to say: rain, *then* he goes; rain falling, *then* he goes; *e.g.*, *nien-t'ieh chi ch'ê* (粘貼卽扯) "pasting on then it is torn off," which means "placards will be removed," an inscription often seen on the walls at street corners. The following particles are similarly used: *tsê* (則), *tsai* (再), *fang* (方), *pien* (便), *jêng* (仍), *ch'ê* (輙), and *chiu* (就); the last word is colloquial.

卽係 that is; *i.e.*; that means; namely; is equal to.

卽時 / 卽日 } forthwith; at once (denoting immediateness of action).

*chi* 稽 to examine into; to delay.

稽察 to examine.

稽查弁兵勇丁數目 to muster officers and privates; a general muster.

稽考 to examine; to inquire into.

稽延 / 稽時 } to detain; to delay.

*chi* 激 to set back (as by water).

激刷 to wash away.

*chi* 跡 traces; definite grounds for.

*chi* 急 hurried; anxious; urgent.

急需 necessary.

急叩伏乞 to urgently request; to pray for.

急切 exaggeration.

*chi* 籍 to be registered as a native of......; lists; books.

籍貫 the origin (or parentage) and birthplace of a person.

*chi* 集 to collect; to assemble.

集衆 a multitude.

集會 to assemble.

集資 to collect money (as capital for trade in a company).

集腋 to collect small bits of fur [and thus make a coat]; to make use of many trifles in order to obtain great results; "every little helps;" cf. the Scotch phrase "mony a little mak's a muckle."

*chi* 吉 happy; lucky.

吉席 "the happy mat;" wedlock; marriage.

吉祺 I wish you good luck (a concluding phrase in letters).

*chi* 疾 sickness.

疾病 disease; sickness.

*chi* 己 self; oneself; one's own.

己見 one's own view.

*chi* 紀 to write down; to record.

紀錄 to record.

紀錄十次 recorded ten times for merit at the Board of Civil Office.

紀事 to record, or make a note of, facts.

*chi* 記 to remember; to record; a mark; a sign; a seal (of a private person or a petty official); a chop.

記清 to distinctly remember; to recollect.

記事簿 a log-book.

記功 to record merit.

記賬 to put down to one's account.

記名 to make a list of names.

記載 to place on record.

記號 a trade mark; a mark on packages of merchandise.

*chi* 給 to give; to grant; to address to (as a despatch).

給照 to grant a certificate.

給護 (=給發護照) to grant a passport.

給票 to issue a chop or certificate.

給單 to issue a certificate, bill, memo., etc.

給假 to grant leave of absence.

給假日 a holiday; holidays.

給發 to issue.

給領 to issue (as a document).

給還 to hand back; to return.

給與 to issue; to grant.

給予 to give; to grant.

給以存票 to grant drawback.

給以免單 to grant an exemption certificate.

給事中 a supervising censor.

*chi* 際 a time; a juncture; an occasion; at the time when; on the occasion of; while.

*chi* 冀 to hope.

*chi* 計 to calculate; calculated to make; calculated at; to take into account; contrivances; tricks.

計核 to calculate.

計算 to calculate; to count.

計量 to calculate and measure; to measure.

計噸科鈔 to calculate the tonnage dues from the tonnage.

*chi* 計開 namely; to wit (before an enumeration of things).

計本 representing capital, or an investment.

計抄單壹件 copy of one document is annexed hereto.

計送 forwarded herewith (as an amount of money, etc., with a despatch).

*chi* 季 a season of three months; a quarter.

*chi* 旣 after; if; as soon as; since; a sign of the past.

旣然 since.

旣經 from the time that; since......has, having, etc.; from the time that......shall have, *i.e.*, as soon as......

旣銷 used up.

*chi* 暨 together with; at the same time; as well.

*chi* 覬 to covet.

覬覦 to wish for ardently; to covet profit.

*chi* 棘 thorny; prompt.

棘手 a difficulty; hard to manage.

*chi* 繼 to connect; to follow.

繼又 "it follows that also."

*ch'i* 妻 a wife.

妻子 wife, or wives, and children.

*ch'i* 悽 pain; grief.

悽慘 sorrowful; melancholy; sad.

*ch'i* 棲 a dwelling-place.

棲止 to stop; to rest.

*ch'i* 奇 strange; rare things; curiosities.

*ch'i* 騎 to ride a horse.

騎都尉 a *Ch'i-tu-wei*, of the 7th degree of hereditary nobility.

*ch'i* 七 (or 柒) seven.

七二番銀 *lit.*, a seven [mace] two [candareen] foreign silver [coin]; a Mexican dollar, of which 100 are equal to 72 taels.

七星礁 Pagoda Rock (Pagoda Anchorage, Foochow).

七里礁 Min Reef, near Foochow.

*ch'i* 祈 to state one's case to a god; to pray; to request.

祈請示祗遵 to solicit instructions to be respectfully obeyed, *i.e.*, "for one's guidance."

祈賜 to ask for the giving of; to beg for a gift.

*ch'i* 戚 sorry; relatives.

戚屬 relatives.

*ch'i* 漆 paints; varnish; crude lacquer.

漆器 lacquerware.

*ch'i* 漆綠 green paint.

*ch'i* 其 of it; he, she, it; his, its, etc.; the; as to the......

其中 in this; therein.

其內 therein; in it.

其間 amongst them.

其餘 the remainder; the remaining.

其實 the truth of it; the matter of fact.

其次 the following; the next.

其權屬在該關 the authority or power to do so rests with the said Custom House.

其外另有他商 besides him there are other merchants.

*ch'i* 期 a limit of time; a fixed period; to expect; to hope for.

期候 a limit of time; time.

期滿 a term expires.

期頤 very old age; a centenarian.

期望 to look forward; to expect.

*ch'i* 祺 fortunate; lucky.

*ch'i* 旗 (or 旂) a flag.

旗用羽布 bunting.

旗號 a signal flag; a distinguishing flag (as the national ensign).

旗幟 flags and pennants.

旗杆 a flagstaff.

*ch'i* 欺 to deceive.

欺哄 to be false to; to belie.

欺淩 to insult.

欺侮 to deceive; to insult.

欺騙 to belie one; to delude; to cheat.

*ch'i* 契 a bond; an agreement.

*ch'i* 乞 to beg; to request.

乞恩 to request favour; to ask as a favour.

*ch'i*, *hsi* } 汽 (or 滊) an unauthorised character used for "steam," or *shui-ch'i* 水氣.

汽螺 a steam fog horn.

*ch'i* 氣 vapour; air; breath.

氣塞 the stopping of the breath.

*ch'i* 起 to start from; to commence; to raise; to land; to discharge (as cargo).

起蓋 to commence building.

起行 to start (as on a journey).

起程 to start on a journey.

起造 to commence making or building.

*ch'i* 起算 to commence reckoning (as from a given time).

起錨鍊 to lift anchors; to clear chain.

起見 to conceive the idea of; the motive of.

起色 a rise; an improvement (as in one's prospects).

起卸 } to land or discharge goods.
起卸貨物 }

起艙 to land goods.

起出 to unload goods.

起岸 to land goods; "to be landed."

起貨[准]單 a permit to land.

起淸 completely discharged (as a cargo).

*ch'i* 齊 completely; all.

齊集 to assemble completely; to have a successful, or complete, meeting; a quorum.

齊整 well arranged; in order.

齊全 complete; in order.

齊楚 to arrange well; to systematise.

*ch'i* 豈 how? not.

豈敢 how could I dare? *i.e.*, I could not dare.

*ch'i* 緝 to arrest; to seize.

緝私 to seize smuggled goods.

緝盜 to capture a thief.

緝捕 to arrest.

緝獲 to seize (as thieves, or smuggled goods).

*ch'i* 戢 to lay aside (as arms in time of peace).

*ch'i* 詰 to investigate; to ask with authority.

詰問 to cross-examine.

*ch'i* 耆 old; elders; seniors.

耆老 an elder; elders.

*ch'i* 技 skill.

技能 talent; ability.

技藝 professional competency.

*ch'i* 歧 diverging; discrepancy.

歧異 difference; divergence.

*ch'i* 啟 (or 啓) to begin; to inform; a notice.

啟知 to inform.

啟者 a communication; an opening phrase in letters: "you are hereby informed that;" "I beg to inform you."

啟程 to start on a journey.

*ch'i* 棄 to throw away.

棄靡 to waste by throwing away.

*ch'i* 隙 a gap; an interval.

*ch'i* 器 utensils; goods; ware.

器具 utensils; furniture.

器械 weapons; arms.

器皿 household utensils, as dishes, cups, etc.

*chia* 夾 double; the lining of clothes.

夾帶 to carry secretly; to smuggle.

夾雜 to mix; to confuse.

夾板船隻 sailing vessels.

*chia* 家 a family; one's home.

家書 (or 家信) a home letter.

家中 in my family; at home.

家產 family property.

家主 the head of a household.

家眷 one's family; relatives and members of a household.

家屬 one's family or household.

家父 my father.

家室 husband and wife.

家丁 domestic servants.

家用 for domestic use.

家用雜物 household stores; *articles de ménage.*

*chia* 傢 household furniture.

傢伙 furniture; utensils.

*chia* 嫁 to marry (said of the bride).

*chia* 稼 to sow grain; farming; cereals.

*chia* 加 to add to; to grant.

加增 to add; to increase.

加減 to increase and diminish; to fluctuate.

加倍 to add; to double.

加封 to enclose in an official (sealed) envelope.

加蓋印信 to affix a seal.

加恩 to confer favour.

加工 extra work.

加意 to take special care.

加水 to charge a discount on coin or bullion on account of difference in the value of sycee. Cf. *wên* 紋水.

加稅 to charge additional duty.

加餉 to increase a tax.

加囑 to give additional orders; to specially enjoin upon.

加官 to rise in office.

chia 加級 to increase in rank.

加三級 granted three steps of merit.

加刑 to inflict punishment.

加以重罰 to inflict a heavy punishment; to punish severely.

加沙 (= 袈裟) muslins.

chia 枷 the cangue worn by criminals.

枷號 the sentence written on the cangue.

枷責 the punishment of wearing the cangue.

chia 袈 representing the sound *ka* in Sanskrit *kashaya*, from which the modern term for "cambrics" (*ka-sha-pu*) is derived.

袈裟布 cambrics; muslins.

chia 駕 a chariot; he who sits in a chariot; hence, as a term of respect, "you"; to sit (as in a carriage).

駕駛 to sail.

駕臨 your arrival.

chia 架 a frame; a scaffolding.

chia 嘉 excellent.

嘉意 an excellent idea; your valuable opinion.

chia 假 false; imitated; leave of absence; if; supposing.

假造 to counterfeit.

假報 to make a false report; to fraudulently report.

假參 imitation ginseng.

假金綫 imitation gold thread.

假銀綫 imitation silver thread.

假珊瑚 false corals.

假珍珠 false pearls.

假單 a false document (as a "false manifest").

假道 the indirect road; making a *détour* for some reason or other.

假借 to be the wrong one; to be a substitute (and not the proper person); to personate another; to borrow on false grounds (as a certificate made out in the name of another).

假冒借名 to personate another.

假若 / 假如 / 假使 } if; supposing.

假手於人 to commit to a person's care.

chia 甲 a ward, or beat, for keeping watch over a sub-division of the community; the first of the "ten stem" characters, hence the first; the finger nails.

甲長 a village elder; the head constable of a ward.

甲乙 the one and the other; so and so; first and second.

chia 佳 excellent; superior.

佳節 holidays; a festival.

佳妙 excellent; clever work.

佳音 good news.

chia 價 price; value.

價式 the standard value of an article.

價低減 the price is falling; to deteriorate in value.

價值 / 價錢 } value; price.

價銀 price; proceeds of sale.

ch'ia 卡 a barrier. Also read *k'a*.

卡隘 / 卡子 } Customs barriers.

ch'ia 恰 fitly; properly.

恰克圖 (*k'ia-k'o-t'u*) Kiakhta.

chiang 江 a river; abbreviated name of the provinces of Kiangnan (江南) or Kiangsu (江蘇).

江水 river water.

江漲 the river overflowing.

江南岸 the southern shore of the river.

江南 (*chiang-nan*) the province of Kiangnan, consisting of the two provinces of Anhwei and Kiangsu, each under a Governor, the two being under the control of the Governor-General of Kiangnan.

江南海關 / 江海北關 / 江海關 } the Customs of Kiangnan; the Shanghai Custom House.

江漢關 the Hankow Customs.

江蘇 the province of Kiangsu.

江西 the province of Kiangsi.

江甯 the city of Chiang-ning-fu, commonly called Nanking.

江甯定約 the Treaty of Nanking.

江平銀 common sycee, at Ningpo; the Ningpo local tael, 1.0583 of which make 1 Haikwan tael.

chiang 將 to take; places the words between this character and the principal verb of the sentence in the accusative case; before a verb, a sign of the future: "about to."

將到 about to arrive.

將開船時刻 the time when a ship will start; the hour appointed for a ship's departure.

將次……之日 when the day for……has nearly arrived; about the time of……

將來 afterwards.

*chiang* 將軍 a Tartar General; also a military Governor in Manchuria, Mongolia, or Turkestan. The Tartar General of Foochow is *ex officio* Superintendent of Customs at the Treaty Ports in Fukien (Foochow, Amoy, Takow, and Tamsui), and one of his adjutants, generally with the rank of a *Hsieh-chên*, is deputed by him to act as Superintendent at each of the several Custom Houses.

將軍憲 His Excellency the Tartar General.

*chiang* 奬 to encourage.

奬勵 to encourage by praise.

奬賞 to encourage by rewards.

*chiang* 醬 }
醬油 } soy; bean sauce.

*chiang* 薑 (or 薑) ginger.

薑黃 turmeric.

*chiang* 彊 a boundary.

彊界 a boundary.

*chiang* 講 to converse; to expound (as the Classics).

講官 an Imperial expositor of the Classics.

講究 fastidious.

講和 to mediate.

*chiang* 港 a harbour; an anchorage.

港口 ports; harbours.

港內 in port.

*chiang* 匠 a mechanic.

匠人 a workman; a manufacturer (as a watch-maker, etc.).

*chiang* 降 to descend; to come from above.

降級 to degrade in rank.

降旨 to have received an Imperial edict; an edict has been issued.

降臨 to condescend.

降香 laka-wood.

*ch'iang* 搶 to take by force; to rush against; to rob; to plunder.

搶奪 to plunder.

*ch'iang* 槍 (used for *ch'iang* 鎗) a musket; a lance; a spear.

槍子 cartridges.

*ch'iang* 鎗 (also 槍) a spear; a musket; firearms; rifles.

鎗藥 gunpowder.

*ch'iang* 羗 elegant; used for 薑 or 薑 *(chiang)*, ginger.

*ch'iang* 强 to force.

强輸官稅 to be forced to pay Government duties in a certain coin; to be obligatory as a legal tender in payment of duties.

*ch'iang* 强制 to enforce a rule; to force a rule upon.

强借 to violently ask for.

强辯 a one-sided view; an *ex parte* argument.

强盜 banditti.

*chiao* 交 to give; to hand; intercourse; intimacy; conterminous; just at the time of.

交納 to pay (as duties).

交付 to give to; to hand over to.

交回 to hand back.

交價 to pay the price of a purchase.

交印 to hand over seals, as to a successor in office.

交客 to deliver to the merchant (as goods to a purchaser).

交清 to pay an amount in full.

交好 to be on terms of friendship with.

交易 barter; trade.

交涉 to be connected with; relating to.

交碍 to interfere with each other.

交界 a frontier.

交夏後 just after the summer.

*chiao* 校 to compare.

校閱 to compare; to examine (as the courts of two countries examine the credentials of each other's envoys).

*chiao* 狡 artful; crafty.

狡猾 cunning.

*chiao* 絞 to strangle.

絞罪 the punishment of strangulation.

絞縊 to strangle oneself.

絞監候 to await death by strangulation in prison.

*chiao* 較 to compare; rather more than; than (comparative).

較重 to be comparatively heavy; too heavy in comparison with.

較多 rather much; more than.

較多幾至一元有半 an overplus of up to \$1½ against......(the object compared preceding with *yü* 與).

較少 rather little; less than usual.

較對 to compare.

較兌 to tally; to agree (as the balance of a set of scales).

較準 to adjust; properly adjusted.

較準砝碼 standard weights.

*chiao* 焦 burned; scorched.

焦炭 coke.

*chiao* 礁 }
礁 石 } a rock; rocks.

礁 淺 to ground (as a vessel); to touch a rock.

*chiao* 蕉 plantains.

*chiao* 轎 a sedan chair.

*chiao* 膠 glue.

*chiao* 轇 confused.

轇 轕 confusion; a muddle.

*chiao* 椒 pepper.

*chiao* 敎 to teach; instruction.

敎 士 a teacher; a teacher of religion; a missionary.

敎 練 to drill troops.

敎 育 to supply spiritual and bodily food.

*chiao* }
*chüo* } 角 a horn; horns; a pointed corner; the end of a rock, spit, etc.

角 器 hornware.

*chiao* 勦 to attack; to destroy and scatter the force of an enemy.

勦 賊 to destroy rebels.

勦 捕 to make a clean sweep (as of a band of banditti).

*chiao* 脚 the leg; workmen; labourers; porters.

脚 價 }
脚 力 } coolie hire (for goods carried).

*chiao* 繳 to hand over; to pay.

繳 案 to pay into court (as a fine).

繳 庫 to pay into a treasury.

繳 存 to pay as a deposit.

繳 回 to return; to hand back.

繳 銷 to deliver (a document) for cancelling.

*chiao* 覺. See *ch'üo*.

*ch'iao* 橋 a bridge.

*ch'iao* 巧 clever; crafty.

巧 妙 ingenious; clever.

*ch'iao* 撬 to prise; to force with a lever.

撬 門 to prise a door.

*chieh* 街 a street.

街 道 public roads.

街 市 the market; on the market.

*chieh* 皆 all; giving a preceding noun plural force.

*chieh* 竭 to exhaust; to try the utmost.

竭 力 to exert one's strength; to do one's utmost.

竭 盡 to the utmost.

*chieh* 結 a knot; a tie; to tie; to close; to give a bond for; to guarantee; a bond; to end; a fixed period or term for settling accounts; a Customs (financial) quarter of three months; fixed; firm.

結 案 to close a case (of law, etc.).

結 賬 to close an account.

結 實 durable; secure; material.

結 實 信 據 a material guarantee.

結 底 at the end of the quarter.

*chieh* 節 a period of time; a feast day; a section in a composition; the paragraphs of an account; a statement; an article, a paragraph (in a set of regulations); also, the rules contained therein; to abridge.

節 期 a festival; a periodical feast day; a holiday.

節 畧 一 紙 a statement of particulars.

*chieh* 接 to receive; to connect; contiguous; to be connected with; to bound on.

接 來 }
接 准 } to receive.
接 收 }

接 得 to have received.

接 領 to receive; to take over; to take charge of.

接 儎 to receive goods for shipment (as a shipping broker).

接 辦 to take over charge of an office; to take in hand the management of.

接 印 to take over the seal of office.

接 連 to connect; joined.

接 續 to connect; in continuation of; supplementary.

接 懸 to suspend one above the other, in a contiguous line.

*chieh* 捷 to overcome; prompt; quick.

捷 報 a quick message; an express.

*chieh* 潔 pure; clear; clean.

潔 淨 pure and clean.

*chieh* 刦 to rob; to take by force.

刦 搶 to rob; highway robbers.

刦 奪 to rob; to plunder.

刦 盜 robbers.

*chieh* 截 to cut off; to cut asunder; exactly (as applied to a limit of time).

截 而 爲 樑 to cut into beams.

*chieh* 解 to forward; to explain; to understand.

解 交 to hand over to; to send to (as a destitute to his authorities).

新關文件録



*chieh* 解省 to send to the provincial capital.

解釋 to explain; to interpret.

解法 meaning; explanation.

*chieh* 介 a guest; respectful.

介意 careful; attentive.

*chieh* 界 a limit; a boundary.

界址 boundaries.

界限 a limit.

*chieh* 戒 to ward off; to discontinue; to wean.

戒酒 to leave off drinking wine.

戒烟 to leave off smoking opium.

戒險螺 a fog horn.

*chieh* 誡 to enjoin; orders.

*chieh* 借 to lend; to borrow; to make a pretext of.

借用 to borrow for use.

借貸 to borrow; a loan.

借詞 to make a pretext of sophistical arguments.

借名 to pretend; to make a pretext of; to use another's name or card.

借端滋弊 to make a pretext of a matter for creating trouble.

借墊 to advance money; a deed; a proof.

*chieh* 藉 to avail oneself of; to make a pretext of.

藉口 to make a pretext of; under the pretext.

藉生口舌 to make use of a matter as a pretext to create altercations or quarrels.

藉稱 to allege.

藉圖 to make use of an opportunity for illegal plots; to seize an occasion for plotting.

藉邀 to avail oneself of an invitation.

藉聆 to avail oneself of listening to; to listen to (as to the conversation of one's host).

藉足以 by means of which; the availing oneself [of which] is apt to.

藉以均濟 to help in effecting equal succour.

*chieh* 屆 a limit; a set time; "the time has come for" or "this is the time of."

屆滿 to complete (as a term).

屆期 on the day fixed; punctually.

屆時 at the time fixed for.

*ch'ieh* 切 urgent; very; to cut.

切實 true and sincere; trustworthy; most accurate.

切要 very important.

切赴 to go quickly; "an urgent letter;" "immediate."

*ch'ieh* 切切 very urgent; very important.

切切上稟 an urgent petition (concluding phrase in petitions).

切不可 cannot under any circumstances; cannot at all.

切勿 not by any means.

切水面 at the water-line.

*ch'ieh* 竊 (or 窃) a thief; a term of modesty denoting the writer of a document addressed to a superior, as "my humble self"; it is frequently followed by the personal name *(ming)* of the petitioner, or by some other term of modesty, written in smaller characters.

竊職 as a term of modesty, "I," if the speaker be an official of any grade, even though he may hold his rank by purchase. Non-official writers will say 竊身. Merchants say 竊商; a woman of low rank says, 竊氏; the wife of an official, 竊職婦; a common man of the people, 竊小的, etc. When addressing the Emperor, Ministers of Chinese parentage say 竊臣, whereas Manchu Ministers say 竊奴才.

竊職商 we (being a body consisting of persons of official rank and merchants).

竊查 it is my humble opinion that.

竊念 I respectfully think or thought.

竊閲 my humble self learns; I respectfully beg to refer to......

竊盜 to steal; a thief.

*ch'ieh* 且 moreover; and; also; (= 然 *jan*) gives an adjective adverbial force.

*chien* 牋 note paper ruled, or containing ornamental designs or water marks; a note; a document.

*chien* 餞 comfits; salted provisions.

*chien* 賤 cheap; low; of little value.

*chien* 建 to establish; to construct; to build.

建築 to build.

建造塔鐙 to build lighthouses.

建立 to establish.

建修費 expenditure on account of construction and purchase (購) and maintenance in repair (修).

建 (=福建) the province of Fukien.

*chien* 健 vigorous; robust.

健壯 robust; strong; able-bodied.

*chien* 間 to separate; an interval; in the place of; at the time of; *e.g.*, 夜間 at night-time.

*chien* 簡 to abridge; to make short; to select.

簡畧 a *résumé*.

*chien* 簡牒 a memorandum.
簡捷 short; concise.
簡練 to try by experiment.
簡札 an official document.
簡便 convenient; clean; plain.
簡任 to choose for a post.
簡缺 a post of little work; an easy post, said of magistracies as opposed to important offices of the same class.

*chien* 減 to decrease; to diminish.
減稅 to reduce the duty.
減少 to diminish.
減半 to reduce to one-half.
減成 to diminish the per-centage or the rate of.
減色 to decrease in quality; to deteriorate.
減價 a cheap price; a reduced price.

*chien* 碱 (磏, 鹼, or 鹻) soap.

*chien* 剪 scissors; to cut with scissors.
剪絨 velvet (both of silk and cotton).
剪裁 to cut out; to plan; to arrange.

*chien* 堅 stable; immovable.
堅固 durable; firm.
堅意 a firm intention.
堅欲 to immovably wish; to persevere in wishing.
堅執 obstinate; to obstinately maintain.

*chien* 尖 pointed.
尖圓 conical.
尖圓式 conical shaped.
尖石 a pinnacle rock.
尖 (= 錢?) locally (at Amoy), a cent; $\frac{1}{100}$ dollar.

*chien* 奸 villainous.
奸詐 fraudulent; deceitful.
奸巧 cunning; villainous.
奸拐 to deceive and kidnap.
奸商 corrupt merchants; dishonest traders.

*chien* 漸 gradually; by degrees.
漸明漸滅 lighting up gradually and eclipsing gradually (said of a navigation light); revolving.
漸長暗沙 a shoal gradually forming.

*chien* 兼 to connect; and; also; together with.
兼轄 to have joint charge of several offices.

*chien* 歉 insufficient (as a crop).

*chien* 歉薄 insufficient and short of the full amount (as a crop).

*chien* 艱 difficult.
艱難 difficulty.

*chien* 監 to superintend; to inspect; a jail; a prison.
監理 to superintend.
監察 to inspect; to examine.
監視 to personally superintend.
監同 to take part in the superintendence of.
監督 to superintend; the Superintendent (of Customs).
監獄 } a prison.
監牢 }

*chien* 鑒 a mirror; to survey; to view; to examine; to trace a matter to its source.
鑒核 to examine for approval.
鑒核賜教為禱 I shall be thankful if you will consider the matter and let me know your opinion.

*chien* 鐫 to engrave.
鐫刻 to engrave (as a block for printing).

*chien* 儉 moderate; saving; economical.
儉節 economical.

*chien* 撿 to restrict; to bind.
撿束 to bind.

*chien* 檢 to examine; to arrange; to collate.
檢查 to examine; to look up the records.
檢閱 to examine.

*chien* 繭 cocoons.
繭殼 pierced cocoons.
繭綢 Shantung silk piece goods; silk pongees.

*chien* 揀 to choose; to select.
揀選 to select.
揀淨 to sort; to clarify.
揀出 to select from; to pick out.

*chien* 諫 to remonstrate; to censure.

*chien* 見 to see; to be of opinion; to maintain; the view one takes of a matter; sometimes a sign of the passive; *e.g.*, 見痊, to be cured, to recover; 見復, to be replied to, to receive a reply; 見示, to be instructed; 見允, to be permitted; 見殺, to be killed.
見召 to be called; to be invited.
見更改 to be altered.
見商於有約各國 to be considered by the Treaty Powers.

新關文件録



*chien* 見諒 to be trusted; to be excused; excuse me.
見長 to make progress.
見面 an interview; to interview.
見識 knowledge; experience.
見有 to see that there is; to discover.
見證 a witness.

*chien* 件 a package; packages; a classifier of documents and of 案 (*an*), cases.
件數 the number of packages.
件色 number of packages and description of goods.

*chien* 薦 / 薦舉 } to recommend.

*ch'ien* 鈐 an official stamp.
鈐蓋關防 to affix one's seal.

*ch'ien* 黔 the Kweichow province.

*ch'ien* 牽 to connect; to drag; to implicate.
牽涉 to be implicated in.
牽混 to create confusion.

*ch'ien* 遷 to remove; to shift; to alter.
遷移 to move away; to change one's residence.

*ch'ien* 僉 all; unanimously.

*ch'ien* 籤 to draw a lot; to subscribe; to sign one's name.
籤掣 to select by lot.
籤名 to sign by writing one's name.
籤押 to affix one's signature.

*ch'ien* 愆 fault; crime; failure; to fail; to miss.

*ch'ien* 謙 respectful; humble.

*ch'ien* 千 thousand.
千里鏡 telescopes.

*ch'ien* 扦 (or 攙) to graft into; to put in.
扦子 an iron rod ending in a spoon bowl with a sharp point, used by tidewaiters for thrusting into packages when examining goods.
扦子手 / 扦手 } a tidewaiter.

*ch'ien* 鉛 lead.
鉛塊 lead, in pigs.
鉛片 lead, in sheets.
鉛粉 white lead; ceruse.
鉛筆 a lead pencil.

*ch'ien* 淺 (the opposite of 滿, *man*, full) not full; empty (as a ship in ballast); shallow; also faint, said of colours.

*ch'ien* 淺水 shallow water; a shoal.
淺沙灘 a bar (as the Woosung Bar).

*ch'ien* 錢 a mace (the 10th part of a tael); copper cash.
錢文 money; cash.
錢局 a mint.
錢鈔 / 錢票 } bank notes.
錢貨 copper cash (as cargo).
錢莊 a cash shop; a money-changer's.
錢糧 money and grain; rations.

*ch'ien* 前 before; to advance; the before-mentioned.
前因 the afore-mentioned.
前項 of the afore-mentioned description; the before-mentioned.
前纜 the forestay of a ship.
前次 on a former occasion; on former occasions.
前日 the other day; on a former day.
前稅 the duty [paid] previously.
前稅司 the former Commissioner of Customs.
前年 the year before last.
前面 in the front of.
前後 before and after; nearly; about; in front and behind.
前途 on the road; ahead on one's road.
前輩 former generations; seniors; predecessors.
前赴 to proceed to.
前來 to have come forward; to have come to hand (as a despatch, a report, etc.). These two words frequently follow the mention of a document received or its tenor.

*ch'ien* 潛 to abscond.

*ch'ien* 乾 heaven; the north-west.
乾隆 the Emperor KIEN LUNG.

*ch'ien* 虔 sincere; respectful.
虔肅 respectful; reverential.

*ch'ien* 遣 to send.
遣員代往 to send an officer on one's behalf; to be represented by deputy.
遣丁 to send servants.
遣派 to send for business (as workmen).

*ch'ien* 欠 to owe money; to be in arrear; to be short of; to deduct; less.
欠債 to be in debt.
欠主 a debtor.

*ch'ien* 欠單 a promissory note; a debit note.

欠款 debts.

*ch'ien* 荐 (used for *chien* 薦) to set forth; to bring to the front (as a meritorious official for promotion).

*chih* 知 to know; to inform; to be known.

知悉 to be thoroughly aware of.

知閱 to take notice of.

知照 } to inform.
知會 }

知情 to be aware of the circumstances.

知府 a prefect.

知縣 a district magistrate.

知道了 "I know it"; the formula used by the Emperor to show that he has taken note of the contents of a document submitted to him.

*chih* 智 wise; wisdom; ability.

*chih* 之 originally a personal pronoun: he, him, it, etc.; marks the genitive case, which is otherwise expressed by anteposition; after a verb or a verbal expression it may impart to the verb the force of a passive participle; corresponds to *ti* (的) of the colloquial language. The relation of grammatical dependence which in Western languages is often expressed by placing the noun upon which something else depends in the genitive case is in Chinese expressed by anteposition. This "something else" depending upon a noun may be another noun, or a verb, or even a complete sentence; *e.g.*, 各[1]關[2]監[3]督[4],—[3]*chien*-[4]*tu*, the Superintendents, OF [1]*ko*-[2]*kuan*, all the Custom Houses; 存[1]留[2]餘[3]銀[4],—[3]*yü*-[4]*yin*, the balance, OF [1]*ts'un*-[2]*liu*, keeping; *i.e.*, the balance which is or has been kept. This shows how in Chinese the genitive of a verb or of a complete sentence may come to have the force of a relative clause. In either case the force of anteposition may be increased by adding the character 之 *(chih)*; *e.g.*, 各關之監督 *ko-kuan chih chien-tu*, "the Superintendents of Customs," or 存留之餘銀, *ts'un-liu chih yü-yin*, "the balance which is kept." Such relative clauses, whether formed by anteposition merely, or by anteposition with 之 *(chih)*, may be further enforced by adding the relative pronoun proper, 所 *(so)*; *e.g.*, 所存之餘銀 *so ts'un chih yü-yin*, "the balance which is kept." If this relative clause has its own logical subject, the word denoting it stands before *so*; *e.g.*, 銀[1]號[2]所[3]存[4]之[5]餘[6]銀[7],—[6]*yü*-[7]*yin*, the balance, [3]*so* [5]*chih* (in connexion with anteposition), which, [1]*yin*-[2]*hao*, the Bank, [4]*ts'un*, keeps or kept: "the balance kept by the Bank." (See *so* 所.)

*chih* 芝 a sort of grass.

芝麻 sesamum seed.

芝麻油 sesamum seed oil.

*chih* 旨 an Imperial rescript; His Majesty's commands.

*chih* 脂 grease; fat.

脂粉 cosmetics.

*chih* 指 to point out.

指揮 to give directions; directions; to point out.

指定 to point out; to state clearly; to destine for (as a certificate for a certain vessel).

指名 to nominate.

指明 to point out, or to report, a person (as an offender); to mention; to refer to; to mark (as a buoy marks a place).

指謫 to point out.

指證 to point out the evidence; to conduct a case on behalf of the prosecution.

指薦 to point out and recommend; to suggest a nomination.

指示 } to point out; to assign (as a berth to a ship).
指引 }

指泊人 a berthing officer.

*chih* 執 to grasp; to hold; to retain.

執照 a certificate; a passport.

執據 a license (as a pilot's).

執意 to stick to one's view; a firm purpose.

執已見 to stick to one's own view.

執掌 to superintend.

執政 a Government official.

執政大臣 Ministers of State.

*chih* 織 to weave.

織機 a loom.

*chih* 職 to direct; to manage; "office," as opposed to rank (*p'in* 品) and official employ (*jên* 任); used for "I" in connexion with an official title.

職分 official rank.

職銜 brevet rank.

職名 a visiting card.

職道 I, the Taot'ai.

職守 official guard; to be on duty (as a guard).

*chih* 識 to know. Cf. *shih*.

*chih* 至 very; extremely; to arrive at; to go to; to; till; up to; as regards.

至多 very many; very frequently; at the most; not more than.

至少 the least; not less than.

至遲 at the latest; not later than.

海上絲綢之路文獻集成 科技與文化編

*chih* 至便 most convenient.

至懇 to wish for ardently.

至囑至囑 stringent injunctions; be careful not to overlook.

至完稅一節 as regards the question of paying duty.

至於 with regard to.

*chih* 致 to arrive at; to reach to; to address (as a letter); so as to. The opposite of 不致, "so as not to."

致有 so that there is; so as to; resulting in.

致干 so as to become guilty of.

致意 to convey one's desires; to express one's wish.

*chih* 窒 to obstruct; to hamper.

窒礙 difficulty; to hinder.

窒礙之處 difficult points; difficulties.

窒礙難行 difficult to be carried out.

*chih* 止 to stop; ending; only.

*chih* 址 the limits of a lot of land.

*chih* 祉 happiness.

*chih* 治 to heal; to cure; to regulate; to govern; the jurisdiction of an officer; "under your jurisdiction;" to punish.

治病 to cure a disease.

治國 to govern a country.

治辦 to put in order; to deal with.

治罪 to try and punish an offender.

治理 to regulate; to keep in order.

*chih* 直 straight; direct.

直線 a straight line.

直紗 the horizontal threads of a texture; the warp.

直捷 promptly.

直隸 the province of Chihli, *lit.*, under direct government.

直隸州 an inferior department subject to no prefectural control, but under provincial government; the magistrate of such a department.

*chih* 値 price; value; cost; to buy; to bear an expense.

値班 to take one's turn on duty.

値事 the president of a society.

値百抽五 to value at a hundred and levy five, *i.e.*, to charge a five per cent. *ad valorem* duty.

*chih* 植 plants; trees.

*chih* 置 to establish; to fix; to place; to arrange; to purchase.

*chih* 置辦 to arrange; to settle; to buy.

置買 to buy.

置用 to purchase and use; to buy for one's own use.

*chih* 擲 to throw down; by way of civility, a person of exalted rank, or the person addressed in a despatch, not of rank inferior to that of the writer, is requested to "throw down" an object, in lieu of "presenting it by hand," the writer thereby placing himself in the position of one not worthy to receive it direct from the hands of the addressee.

擲交 to give by throwing down, *i.e.*, to favour one with supplying; to be pleased to give.

擲下 to throw down; to give to.

擲回 to reject a petition.

擲還 to give back.

*chih* 只 only.

只可 one need only.

*chih* 隻 single; alone; a classifier of boxes, ships, etc.

隻身 a single body; alone; by oneself.

*chih* 支 a twig; a branch; to pay; to attend to; to manage; to pay out; to rig out, as the swinging-boom of a ship; a classifier of tobacco-pipes, etc.

支發 to pay for; to defray.

支款 payments; credit; Cr.

支借各項 advances.

支持 *lit.*, twig-grasping, *i.e.*, having to strive hard in order to succeed.

支出 to rig out, as the swinging-boom or jib-boom of a ship.

支吾 to make excuses.

*chih* 枝 a branch; to branch off.

枝節 affairs branching off; many small troubles arising out of one case; one expense being followed by many others.

*chih* 肢 the limbs.

肢體 the limbs and body.

*chih* 祇 only; but; however.

*chih* 祗 to respect; respectfully; as a conjunction, only, but.

祗遵 to respectfully obey; for one's respectful guidance.

祗候 to respectfully await.

*chih* 紙 paper; a document; a sheet; classifier of documents and certificates.

紙傘 }
紙遮 } paper umbrellas; kittysols.

*chih* 紙花 artificial flowers.
紙扇 paper fans.
紙張 paper.
紙張筆墨 writing materials; stationery.

*chih* 質 to substantiate; proof; to pawn; a pawnshop.
質對 to check; to compare.

*chih* 滯 to obstruct; to hinder.
滯礙 to impede; difficulty.

*chih* 制 to limit; to make; to regulate; rules.
制宜 to do what is proper.
制度 to make rules; direction; management.
制造 to make; to create.

*chih* 製 to make.
製造 to make; to manufacture.

*chih* 志 will; resolution.
志意 will; intention; purpose.

*chih* 誌 to record; statistical or historical records; the official gazetteer of a province, prefecture, etc.

*ch'ih* 侈 extravagant.

*ch'ih* 飭 to order; to instruct.
飭令 to order; to instruct.
飭知 to inform subordinates.
飭屬遵照 to instruct one's subordinates for their guidance.
飭賜 to order the bestowal of; to cause to be given.
飭撥 to have transferred (as moneys).

*ch'ih* 勅 Imperial orders.

*ch'ih* 吃 to stammer; used for *ch'ih* 喫, to eat, to swallow.

*ch'ih* 喫 to eat; to swallow; to bear.
喫虧 to suffer a loss.
喫苦 to suffer distress.
喫烟 to smoke (tobacco or opium).

*ch'ih* 斥 } to expel.
斥逐 }
斥革 to deprive of rank; to dismiss; to withdraw the license of a pilot.

*ch'ih* 幟 a streamer; a pennant.

*ch'ih* 赤 carnation colour; naked.
赤金 gold.
赤糖 brown sugar.
赤沙澳 (*ch'ih-sha-ao*) Breaker Point, near Swatow.

*ch'ih* 持 to hold; to grasp.
持意 to hold to one's opinion.
持赴 to proceed to......, holding, or with [a document].
持照 provided with a passport.
持躬 to preserve one's integrity.

*ch'ih* 池 a tank; a reservoir.

*ch'ih* 馳 speedily; promptly; to hasten; to proceed to.
馳赴 to proceed to.

*ch'ih* 遲 to delay.
遲悞 delay; to neglect.
遲留 to postpone; to put off.
遲延 to defer.
遲疑 to delay and doubt; to raise obstructive doubts.

*ch'ih* 齒 the teeth; one's age.

*ch'ih* 尺 a *ch'ih;* the Chinese foot (= $14\frac{1}{10}$ inches, English).
尺寸 feet and inches; *i.e.*, measurement.
尺牘 a book containing forms for letters, etc.

*ch'ih* 翅 wings; fins.

*ch'ih* 掣 to select; to draw a lot.

*ch'ih* 恥 to be ashamed; to be disgraced.
恥辱 disgrace; shame.
恥笑 to get laughed at.

*chin* 斤 (or 觔) a catty; catties.
斤兩 catties and taels; *i.e.*, weight.

*chin* 近 near; lately.
近聞 it has lately been rumoured; I have recently heard.

*chin* 勁 strong; violent.

*chin* 筋 sinews.

*chin* 今 now.
今朝 the present dynasty.
今年 this year.

*chin* 金 gold.
金銀 gold and silver; bullion.
金銀珍寶等器 } jewellery.
金銀首飾 }
金銀器 gold and silver ware.
金葉 gold leaf.
金箔 gold leaf or foil; tinsel.
金線 gold thread.
金礦 gold mines.

*chin* 金剛石 the diamond.
金針菜 dried lily flowers.
金利源 *(chin-li-yüan)* the Kin-lee-yuen Wharf, Godowns, etc., on the French Bund at Shanghai.
金陵 *(chin-ling)* book name of the city of Nanking.
金門島 the island of Quemoy.
金牌門 the Kimpai Pass, near Foochow.
金山 California.

*chin* 禁 to restrict; to prohibit; restriction; prohibition.
禁制 prohibitory measures.
禁止 to prohibit.
禁貨 contraband goods.
禁止逃越 to restrict evasion of the law.

*chin* 巾 a napkin.
巾帕 handkerchiefs.

*chin* 僅 only; barely.
僅及一年 a year having scarcely elapsed.

*chin* 謹 respectfully; carefully.
謹稟 respectfully petitioning, or a respectful petition (concluding phrase in petitions).
謹呈 to state respectfully.
謹慎 careful.

*chin* } *ching* } 津 a ford; a ferry; (=天津) Tientsin.
津海關 the Tientsin Customs.

*chin* 盡 to exhaust; all; wholly.
盡用 used by all; in general use.
盡善 in complete order.
盡責 to be equal to all one's responsibilities.
盡述 to narrate the whole.
盡守 to closely observe.
盡力 to exert one's strength; to the best of one's ability.
盡心 to exhaust one's heart; to take the greatest trouble about.

*chin* 藎 faithful.
藎臣 a loyal, faithful officer.

*chin* 緊 important; urgent; quickly.
緊要 important.
緊急 urgent; pressing.
緊妥 fast and tight (as a package is bound).
緊密 secret.

*chin* 錦 brocaded silk.

*chin* 晉 to go to; to enter; to increase.
晉省 to proceed to the provincial capital.
晉贈 to bestow increased rank.

*chin* 進 to enter; to come in; incoming.
進口 to enter port; to import; import.
進口稅 import duties.
進口貨單 an import manifest.
進泊 to enter [a port] and anchor.
進售內地 to import for sale in the interior.
進院 to enter a court-yard.
進退維谷 whether I advance or retreat, there is difficulty; a dilemma.
進工 to join work; to enter on employment.
進士 the *Chin-shih* literary degree.

*chin* 浸 to soak (as in water).

*ch'in* 親 a relative; self, in person; one's own.
親屬 relatives.
親王 an Imperial prince of the 1st order.
親自 oneself; in person.
親身 in person.
親詣 to go in person.
親視 to inspect in person.
親筆 one's own signature; to sign in person.
親手畫押 to sign with one's own hand; to affix one's signature.
親供 one's own deposit; the protocol of what one has said oneself.
親兵 body-soldiers; a body-guard.

*ch'in* 侵 to encroach.

*ch'in* 寢 to sleep.

*ch'in* 勤 diligent.
勤工 to work diligently.
勤慎 careful.
勤政 attentive to Government work.

*ch'in* 禽 birds.

*ch'in* 擒 to seize; to arrest.
擒獲 to arrest.
擒拿 to seize; to apprehend.

*ch'in* 衾 bedding.

*ch'in* 欽 Imperial; (=欽差) an Ambassador.
欽差 sent by the Emperor; an Imperial Ambassador; an Envoy.
欽命 by Imperial command.

*ch'in* 欽加 granted by the Emperor.

欽派 deputed by the Emperor.

欽賜 bestowed by the Emperor.

欽此 "The above is Imperial" or "such is His Majesty's pleasure," a concluding phrase added to Imperial edicts by the ministers promulgating them.

*ching* 徑 a diameter; a straight line across; a by-road; a short cut; direct; directly; quickly.

徑入 to pass into.

*ching* 經 the warp of a texture; a degree of longitude; to cross; to pass over; to pass; *vid;* regular; standing; a classic; classical books; a canon; religious books; Buddhist prayers; to manage; places the verb in the perfect tense, in which case the verb may either follow this particle immediately, or be separated from it by several characters representing other parts of the sentence.

經絲 thrown silk.

經度 longitudinal degrees; longitude.

經度英國中線東 longitude east of Greenwich.

經過 to pass; to come across *(en route).*

經摺子 a banker's pass-book; a pass-book.

經過之事 the events that have happened (such as are stated in a log-book).

經費 standing expenditure; office expenditure (=Customs Account *A*).

經書 the classical books.

經筵 the Hall of Classics; the hall where the Emperor meets academicians.

經筵講官 an Imperial expositor of the Classics.

經治 to manage.

經歷 a secretary.

經手 a broker; an agent; to manage.

經紀 an agent; a consignee; a broker.

經租帳房 a house agent; a rent collector.

經報 to have reported; having reported.

*ching* 逕 to pass by; straight; directly.

逕曲 straight and crooked.

逕啟者 I beg to inform you (an opening phrase in letters).

*ching* 靖 peaceful; to establish peace; to tranquillise.

*ching* 精神 healthy; in good physical condition.

精潔 clean; pure.

精詳謀國 to be a clear-headed politician and patriot.

精明 clear-headed; intelligent.

*ching* 精妙 admirable.

精巧 clever.

*ching* 京 the capital; Peking.

京師 the capital; the residence.

京都 the capital; Peking, as the capital of China (also, the city of Kioto in Japan).

京報 the "Peking Gazette."

京官 metropolitan officers.

京堂 a director of a court in the Imperial Household.

*ching* 景 view; prospect; scenery.

景泰藍 "Ching-t'ai-lan," a celebrated mark for old copperware; cloisonné of the Ching T'ai period (A.D. 1450–57).

*ching* 敬 respectful; to venerate; sedate.

敬啟者 I respectfully inform you (an introductory phrase in letters).

敬覆者 a respectful reply; I beg to reply.

敬稟者 a respectful petition.

敬請台安 with respectful kind inquiries (a concluding phrase in letters).

敬遵 to respectfully obey.

敬重 to respect; to treat with consideration.

敬謹 respectfully and carefully.

敬謹管理 to superintend with due reverence and care.

*ching* 儆 (= 警) to warn; to urge to reform.

儆戒 to warn; to caution.

儆將來 to be a warning for the future.

*ching* 警 to rouse; to warn; to alarm.

警船浮 a buoy.

*ching* 驚 to alarm; to astonish.

驚懼 to frighten.

*ching* 井 a well.

*ching* 矜 to commiserate.

*ching* 竟 really; indeed; then.

竟不 not at all; even not. Cf. *ping* 並未.

*ching* 境 a boundary; a place for living; a site.

*ching* 鏡 a mirror; mirrors; looking-glasses; the lens of a telescope, microscope, etc.

*ching* 競 to wrangle; to quarrel.

*ching* 兢 uneasy; cautious; anxious.

*ching* 凈 (or 淨) to clean; clean; clarified; net (as opposed to gross).

*ching* 淨數 the net figures; the net amount.
淨重 the net weight.
淨貨輕重 the net weight of goods.
淨魚翅 clarified sharks' fins.

*ching* 靜 calm; silent; repose.
靜密 silent; secret.

*ch'ing* 輕 light; not heavy; to treat lightly.
輕重 weight; light and heavy.
輕木板 soft-wood planks.
輕木樑 soft-wood beams.
輕重木桅 hard-wood and soft-wood spars.
輕耗 loss in weight; under-weight.

*ch'ing* 青 blue; green.
青蓮 a kind of dye-stuff.
青麻 green hemp.
青礬 green alum; copperas.
青荳 green peas.
青嶼 Tsingseu Island, near Amoy.

*ch'ing* 情 the feelings; disposition; circumstances.
情狀 appearance.
情義 disinterestedness.
情理 reason; sense.
情深 the depth of affection.
情願 to be willing; to wish; to bind oneself to.
情甘 voluntarily; willingness.
情形 circumstances; particulars.
情節 particulars; circumstances; details.
情寔難已 matters really difficult to bring about.
情難推却 according to the circumstances, or as matters happened to be, it was difficult to decline.

*ch'ing* 晴 clear.
晴時 in clear weather.

*ch'ing* 清 clear; accurate; correct (as an account).
清冊 an accurate list or table.
清摺 a correct account or report; an official periodical account rendered to the Government.
清摺一扣 a fair copy of a document.
清單 a ship's manifest.
清妥 clear and safe (as the anchor chains of a ship).
清楚 clear; distinct; to settle; to clear an account.
清款項 to clear (settle concerning certain) items; to close accounts.

*ch'ing* 清正 pure and upright.
清正持躬 to maintain one's person pure and upright; to lead a spotless life.
清潔 pure; clean.
清文 Manchu writing.
清朝 the Ch'ing dynasty.

*ch'ing* 請 to request; to apply for; you are requested to; please; to invite.
請假 to apply for leave.
請飭 to ask for instructions; be pleased to instruct.
請命 to ask for orders; to ask for permission.
請旨飭下 to ask for the Emperor's orders to his subordinate officers.
請領 to receive on application (as a document); to receive.
請起貨單 an application to land.
請下貨單 an application to ship.
請改 to apply for permission to correct.
請索賠償 to claim an indemnity.
請予 please grant.
請煩查核 please trouble to examine and decide.
請煩查收賜覆 please trouble to receive and reply to (as a despatch).
請安 to inquire after a person's health.

*ch'ing* 頃 presently; careful; a *king* (= 100 *mou* or Chinese acres).
頃接 I have just received.
頃接來函 I have just received your note.

*ch'ing* 傾 to assay; to smelt.
傾鎔 to melt.
傾鎔之費 expenses of melting; melting fees.
傾化 to assay.

*ch'ing* 卿 a dignitary; the director of one of the minor courts in the Imperial household.
卿貳 a second director in an Imperial Court.
卿相 a Minister of State.

*ch'ing* 擎 to lift; to raise; to salute.

*ch'ing* 慶 to congratulate; congratulatory; beneficial; happy.
慶慰 to feel consoled.

*ch'ing* 檾 a kind of hemp; jute.
檾麻 jute.

*chio* 角. See *chiao*.

*chio* 爵. See *chüeh*.

*chio* 脚. See *chiao*.

*ch'io* 確. See *ch'üeh*.

*ch'io* 却. See *ch'üeh*.

*chiu* 酒 distilled liquors; wine; samshu.

酒醉 drunk; drunkenness.

*chiu* 九 (or 玖) nine.

九江 Kiukiang.

九江關 the Kiukiang Customs.

九段 (or 九團) Kiutoan; the site of the Kiutoan Lighthouse, near Shanghai.

*chiu* 究 to examine; to try; at last; finally; thereafter; after all; in the end; at the utmost.

究察 to investigate.

究辦 to investigate and punish; to deal with a case (as a judge).

究審 to try a cause.

究竟 really; indeed; after all; even then.

*chiu* 久 a long time.

久延 to delay.

*chiu* 柩 a corpse in a coffin.

*chiu* 救 to save; to rescue.

救護 to save; salvage.

救護章程 salvage regulations.

救濟 to help; to relieve; to rescue.

救援 to rescue.

救起之貨 goods saved from wrecks; salvage.

救出 to save (as property not destroyed).

救火 to extinguish fire.

救命 to save human life.

*chiu* 就 to follow; according to; immediately; forthwith.

就貨價每百抽二 to levy 2 per cent. *ad valorem.*

就近 neighbouring; near; the nearest.

*chiu* 臼 a mortar.

*chiu* 桕 the tallow tree.

桕油 vegetable tallow.

*chiu* 舊 old.

舊銅 old copper.

舊銅片 old copper sheathing.

舊棉絮 cotton rags.

舊年 last year; in former years.

舊案 old cases.

*chiu* 咎 evil; criminal; a fault; guilt.

咎無可辭 an undeniable offence; the guilt cannot be gainsaid.

咎實難辭 the mistake can hardly be denied.

咎罪 a crime; criminal.

*ch'iu* 秋 the autumn.

秋季 the autumn season.

秋冬颶東北風 the north-east monsoon.

*ch'iu* 求 to beg; to ask for; to pray.

求恩 to request a favour.

*ch'iu* 球 a globe; a ball.

球式 spherical.

球式籃帽 a ball-shaped basket top; a spherical cage.

*ch'iu* 囚 to imprison; a prison; a criminal.

*chiung* 窘 straitened; pressed.

*ch'iung* 窮 exhaust; poor.

*ch'iung* 瓊 a kind of jade.

瓊州府 the prefecture of Kiungchow in Hainan.

瓊海關 the Kiungchow Customs.

*ch'iung* 迥 remote; in a high degree (used to emphasise negation). Cf. *ping* 並未.

迥不相同 widely different.

迥不相符 in entire disagreement with.

*cho* 桌 (or 棹) a table.

*cho* 着 (or 著) to wear (as clothes, shoes, etc.); I, the Emperor, command that; let (in Imperial edicts); to order; to instruct; "the instructions are that."

著充 I, the Emperor, command......to fill the post of; We hereby appoint......as.

*cho* 拙 stupid; unskilful.

*cho* 捉 to grasp; to seize.

捉拿 to arrest.

*cho* 鐲 a bracelet.

*cho* 擢 to select (as for Government employ); to promote.

*cho* 酌 to deliberate upon; to consider; to arrange for.

酌量 to consider.

酌奪 }
酌議 } to consult; to deliberate.

酌體 to meet the wishes of another; to treat with consideration.

酌視 to consult about and look after.

酌改 to alter (as regulations).

酌減 to decide upon diminishing.

*cho* 酌記 to decide upon recording (as an officer's name for a reward).

酌復 to reply on being consulted.

酌數 the authorised amount; In certain quantities.

酌帶銀洋若干 to carry with oneself an amount of dollars sufficient for intended purchases.

*cho* 醊 (= 餟) to offer libations.

*ch'o* 擉 to strike.

擉撞 to rush against; to collide (as two ships).

*ch'o* 戳 to stamp; a stamp.

戳記 to affix a seal; an official seal; a chop.

*chou* 州 an inferior department; a *chou* district.

州同 } first and second class assistant department
州判 } magistrates.

*chou* 洲 an island.

*chou* 舟 a boat.

舟山 the Chusan Islands.

*chou* 周 to surround; complete; to provide for.

周圍 to surround; circumference.

周妥 complete; satisfactory; quite correct.

周知 to inform all.

周章 much trouble (with comparatively small result); useless toil.

周備 well prepared; well arranged.

周濟 to assist.

周密 well arranged; satisfactory; secret.

*chou* 粥 rice-water; congee.

*chou* 縐 a kind of crape.

縐紗 silk crape.

*chou* 肘 the elbow.

*chou* 晝 daylight; in the daytime.

晝夜 day and night.

*chou* 咒 to curse; to imprecate.

咒誦 to chant the liturgy.

*ch'ou* 紬 woven silk. Used for *ch'ou* (綢).

*ch'ou* 抽 to take out with the hand; to take out (as silk from a cocoon, *i.e.*, to reel); to levy (as duties).

抽查 to select and examine one article out of a lot.

抽出 to select; to pick out.

抽絲 to reel silk; reeled silk.

抽換 to take out and change (as goods from original packages).

抽派 to send on special duty; to take out of one's routine for special duty.

*ch'ou* 抽分 to take a per-centage.

抽撥 to divide in per-centages; to allot in proportion to.

抽身 to take oneself off; to stay away; to retire.

抽稅 to levy duty.

抽課 to levy taxes or duties.

抽釐 to collect likin taxes.

抽不敷解 to levy an amount insufficient for remittance (said of a tax farmer who does not collect the amount contracted for).

*ch'ou* 儔 a company; companions.

儔伴 companions.

*ch'ou* 籌 to calculate; to reckon.

籌計 to calculate.

籌畫 to devise schemes; to consider.

籌辦 to arrange; to plan.

籌議 to consider; to deliberate.

*ch'ou* 躊 irresolute.

*ch'ou* 愁 mournful; melancholy.

*ch'ou* 綢 silk cloth; thin silks.

綢緞 silk piece goods; silk damask and satin.

綢綾 manufactured silks.

綢衣服 silk clothing.

綢帽 silk caps.

*ch'ou* 酬 to reward.

酬謝 to reward; to return thanks.

酬勞 to reward merit.

酬值 a gratuity.

*ch'ou* 讐 to fight; an enemy.

讐應 revenge.

讐怨 hatred; enmity.

*ch'ou* 仇 an enemy; hatred; animosity.

仇敵 enemies.

*ch'ou* 丑 an horary character (1 to 3 A.M.).

*ch'ou* 臭 an unpleasant odour; stinking.

臭腥 rancid.

*chu* 主 a master; the owner (as of goods).

主治 to govern; to regulate.

主意 decision; will.

主事 an assistant secretary of a Government Board.

主旗 "the ruling flag;" a national ensign.

chu 住 to dwell; to live at.

住宅 a private residence of a non-official personage.

住宿 to stop; to lodge.

chu 註 to sign; to endorse; a commentary; to explain.

註明 to enter in a document; to state by way of explanation; to make clear.

註銷 to cancel an entry in a book; to write off.

註冊 to enter on a list.

註記 to enter (as in a register).

chu 駐 to reside at; to halt and rest.

駐京大臣 the Foreign Ministers residing at Peking.

駐紮 to be stationed at.

駐寓 to reside at.

chu 注 to record; to comment upon.

注記 to record.

注明 to comment upon; to state.

chu 朱 vermilion colour; rouge; red.

chu 株 (= 誅) to punish; to reprove; to involve in another's crime.

株連 to involve in punishment.

chu 珠 a pearl; beads.

珠邊時辰表 watches *émaillées à perles.*

珠蘭 the chloranthus (used in scenting tea).

珠蘭茶 scented teas; "scented caper."

chu 硃 vermilion.

硃砂 cinnabar.

硃筆 the vermilion, *i.e.*, the Imperial, pencil; an Imperial order; Imperial sanction; the Imperial handwriting.

硃批 the vermilion orders; an Imperial rescript.

chu 誅 to put to death.

chu 猪 a pig.

猪鬃 pigs' bristles.

chu 諸 all; as a sign of the plural, *the.*

諸弊 all the malpractices; *the* malpractices.

諸外洋 all the foreign seas; foreign countries.

諸多 very many; all the many......

chu 築 to build.

築立 to build; to erect.

chu 燭 a candle.

chu 囑 to enjoin upon; to order; to request.

chu 逐 to expel; to drive away; according to; one by one; in detail.

chu 逐款 according to kinds; item by item; by paragraphs; each considered by itself.

逐一 one by one; item by item.

chu 助 to assist.

chu 詝 knowledge; being a forbidden character, should be written 詝 (*chu*), the last stroke of the full character being omitted.

chu 貯 } 貯存 } to store up.

chu 鑄 to cast; to coin (as money).

chu 竹 the bamboo.

竹竿 bamboo canes; canes.

竹笋 bamboo shoots.

竹器 bambooware.

竹布 bamboo cloth (a cotton texture of Chinese manufacture).

竹籠 a bamboo cage or basket.

ch'u 出 to go out; to give out; to produce; to pay; the credit side of an account; to advance an offer; to bid (as a price at an auction).

出入 to go out and in; outward and inward; to make a difference by causing an increase or a decrease.

出入多寡 the amount received (入) after deducting expenses (出); the net amount.

出口 to export; to leave port; to clear from a port.

出口稅 export duty.

出口單 a port clearance.

出口貨單 an export manifest.

出口海關 the exporting Custom House, *i.e.*, the Custom House where outward transit goods are to pay export duty.

出口海關設卡 the barrier established at the port where [transit] goods are exported.

出內地 transit outwards.

出島 to leave the island.

出關 to cross the provincial boundary, or the Great Wall, at Shan-hai-kuan.

出外 to go out; to go abroad.

出洋 to export abroad; for export to foreign countries; also, to go to sea; to emigrate.

出洋輪船 an ocean steamer (as opposed to a "river steamer").

出水 to come out of the water; to be landed from the sea; to be exported across the sea.

出水面 to stand out from the water; to be dry (not being covered by water).

出首 to come out first; to be the first to reveal a fact.

新關文件録



*ch'u* 出首人 one who lays the earliest information; an informer.

出使 to be sent abroad (as an envoy).

出身 official advancement; official employ.

出示 / 出示曉諭 } to issue a public notice; to issue a proclamation.

出具切結 / 出具甘結 } to sign a bond.

出資 to provide means; to pay for.

出船資 to pay travelling expenses.

出賣 / 出售 } to sell; for sale.

出糶 to sell grain.

出力 to exert oneself.

出格 out of rule.

出行 to proceed on a journey.

出缺 a vacancy.

*ch'u* 絀 an impediment, a hindrance (especially in trade and finance).

*ch'u* 初 first; placed before the first 10 dates of the month (as 初捌日, the eighth).

初原 from the outset; at first.

初旬 the first decade; *i.e.*, the first 10 days of a month.

初末 beginning and end; the whole of.

初次 the first time.

*ch'u* 除 to do away with; to subtract; to deduct; to divide.

除根 to eradicate.

除此 besides this.

除……外 deducting……; besides…… Very lengthy and complicated passages are sometimes included between these two characters, the literal meaning of which is: besides (doing all that is said between *ch'u* and *wai*).

除以一百 to divide by 100.

除皮核算之 to calculate [the net weight] by deducting the *emballage*; to tare.

*ch'u* 儲 to collect; to accumulate; to put by; to store.

儲庫 to store in an armoury.

*ch'u* 處 a place; a public office; the different points of an *exposé*; circumstances; to punish.

處所 a place.

處分 fines and other punishments imposed upon an official.

*ch'u* 處制 to regulate.

處治 to set to rights.

*ch'u* 楚 distinct; well defined; properly finished.

*ch'u* 畜 domestic animals; cattle.

*ch'uai* 揣 to ascertain; to detect; to feel; to try.

*chuan* 專 specially; solely; singly.

專一 very particularly; to be devoted to one thing.

專謂 / 專指 } to specially refer to.

專指藥料而言 to refer to medicines.

專照 a special certificate.

專單 a special permit.

專單費 the fee for a special permit.

專章 / 專條 } special rules; special regulations.

專屬 to belong to especially; to specially refer to.

專此 I specially write this note (a concluding phrase in letters).

專此奉布 I specially inform you of this.

專此布覆 I specially inform you of this in reply.

專寄 to forward.

專人 to send a special messenger; to summon witnesses.

*chuan* 傳 a record; a chronicle. See *ch'uan*.

*chuan* 磚 bricks; tiles; flags; slabs (as of copper, etc.).

磚瓦 bricks and tiles.

磚茶 brick tea.

*chuan* 轉 to revolve; to convey; to bring on (as loss); to transmit.

轉咨 to further write to another what has been communicated to oneself; to transmit in a despatch a communication received.

轉報 to further report to another what has been reported to oneself; to communicate a report received.

轉詳 to communicate a report received.

轉呈 to transmit a report to a superior.

轉稟 to communicate a report received from an inferior.

轉飭 to give instructions for transmission (to subordinates).

轉准 to receive a document for further transmission.

*chuan* 轉請 to forward a request; to further request.

轉達 to forward; to send on.

轉運 to carry on to some further place; to re-transport.

轉賣 to re-sell; to further sell to other parties.

轉售 for sale; to further sell to others.

轉行………遵照辦理 to transmit for the guidance of………

轉付 to be transferred to the hands of; change hands (as property).

*chuan* 撰 to arrange; to compose (as a letter).

*ch'uan* 川 a mountain stream; to flow; to travel; stands for 四川 (*ssŭ-ch'uan*), the province of Szechwan.

川流不息 an uninterrupted stream; incessantly; constantly.

川資 travelling expenses.

川羌 *lit.*, Szechwan ginger (a kind of medicine).

川土 Szechwan opium.

川綢 Szechwan silk piece goods; Szechwan crape.

川省 the province of Szechwan.

*ch'uan* 穿 to put on garments.

穿孝 to put on the garment of filial piety, *i.e.*, white mourning clothes (as worn for the first hundred days after the death of a parent); to mourn for a parent.

穿貫 to string; to connect.

*ch'uan* 傳 to forward (as letters); to send for; to summon; to transfer; to interpret.

傳案 to summon to court; to impeach; to prosecute.

傳究 to summon for investigation.

傳集人證 to summon witnesses.

傳話 to interpret; an interpreter.

傳問 to address questions to; to interrogate.

傳驛 a mounted courier.

傳旨 to publish an Imperial decree.

傳教 to propagate religion; a missionary.

傳染症 a contagious disease.

*ch'uan* 船 a ship.

船隻 vessels.

船艇 a boat.

船戶 the people on board a ship; the shipowner; a ship's employé; a boatman.

船家 a ship's crew.

船行 a ship's agents; a shipping firm.

*ch'uan* 船主 a ship's captain.

船東 a shipowner; a ship's captain.

船夥 a mate; a ship's officer.

船手 } boatmen; sailors.
船夫 }

船式 the type of a ship; the rig of a ship.

船艙 a ship's hold.

船身 a ship's hull.

船首 } the bow of a ship.
船頭 }

船頭支出之桅 a jib-boom.

船尾 the stern of a vessel.

船欄 a ship's rail.

船旁 a ship's side; on the side of a ship.

船桅 a ship's mast, or masts.

船舵 a ship's rudder.

船篷 sails.

船燈 a ship's light; a lightship.

船廠 a dock.

船澳 a dockyard.

船政局 a Government dockyard; an arsenal.

船政大臣 the Imperial Commissioner for the Foochow Arsenal.

船名之旗 a signal flag denoting the name of a ship.

船用雜物 ship's stores.

船用洋煤 foreign coal for ship's use.

船貨 the cargo of a vessel; the vessel *and* her cargo.

船鈔 tonnage dues; the "Tonnage Dues Account" (=Customs Account *C*).

船鈔執照 a tonnage dues certificate.

船料 port dues (paid by Chinese junks at native Custom Houses).

船課 boat taxes; tonnage dues.

船牌 a ship's register.

船契 a ship's certificate of sale.

船路 the ships' channel (as in a river).

船行正路 the fairway channel (for ships in a river or near the coast).

*ch'uan* 舛 an error.

舛錯之誤 a mistake.

舛駁 contradictory.

*ch‘uan* 串 to connect; to string together.

串通 to combine (as for an illegal act).

串謀 to intrigue.

*chuang* 庄 a cottage. Cf. *chuang* 莊.

*chuang* 粧 to dress; rouge; ornamental.

粧飾 to ornament.

*chuang* 狀 appearance; shape; form; to accuse.

狀師 an attorney.

狀子 an accusation; a plaint.

狀元 the best scholar at the metropolitan examination; a senior wrangler.

*chuang* 壯 strong; able-bodied.

壯勇 irregular troops; braves.

*chuang* 裝 to load; to be laden with; to contain.

裝載 to carry; to be laden with (as a ship); to contain.

裝載于撥船 to be placed on board a cargo-boat.

裝運 to be laden with and to transport to; to take to (as a ship takes cargo).

裝船 to put on board a ship (as goods); to ship.

裝船處 the place of shipment.

裝上 to put into; to take in.

裝卸 to ship and discharge goods; to "work" (as a vessel in port).

裝貨逾限 loading goods beyond a limit of time contracted for.

裝滿貨物 full of cargo (as a vessel).

裝免 to carry cargo exempted from duty.

裝免數目 the "exemption account," showing exemption from duties on account of *tribute* rice carried.

*chuang* 莊 sedate; serious; (= *chuang* 庄) a cottage; a shop.

莊田 a farm; farm labourers.

莊寮 a country establishment; a farm.

莊稼 the crops.

莊敬 serious and respectful.

莊誠 serious and truthful.

*chuang* 樁 a beacon; beacons.

*chuang* 撞 to rush against; to collide.

撞騙 to swindle; to defraud.

*ch‘uang* 創 to invent.

創始 to commence.

創造 to make as the first; to invent.

*ch‘uang* 創設 to establish, to build, etc. (as a lighthouse).

*ch‘uang* 床 a bed; a couch.

床氈 blankets.

床帳 bed curtains.

*chui* 追 to pursue; to prosecute.

追出 to trace out; to find out on sifting matters.

追究 to investigate (a case).

追拏 to pursue and seize.

追取 to be pressed to furnish; to be bound to pay.

追繳 to sue for payment.

追還 to press for recovery.

*ch‘ui* 吹 to blow (as a horn).

吹戒險汽螺 to blow a steam fog horn.

吹哨 to whistle; a whistle.

*ch‘ui* 垂 to drop down; to condescend.

垂詢 to condescend to inquire; [the Emperor] inquiring after a subject's health.

垂憐豁免 to have pity and magnanimously disregard.

垂恩 condescending kindness.

*chun* 准 to permit; to approve.

准單 a permit.

准行 to sanction.

准予免稅 to grant exemption from duty.

准令 to allow that.

准往憑單 a parents' certificate of emigration given to minors.

*chun* 準 to equalise; to adjust; to approve.

準秤 adjusted scales.

準對 to be equal; to agree (as two balances properly adjusted).

準情酌理 to consider the circumstances of.

準則 a standard; a rule.

*ch‘un* 春 spring.

春夏颶西南風 the south-west monsoon.

*ch‘un* 純 pure; genuine; honest.

*chung* 中 middle; placed after a noun, in, within, among; the second quality out of three, when *shang* (上) means first and *hsia* (下) third; to obtain a literary degree; to succeed; China; Chinese.

中間 in the middle of.

中途 on the road; *en route*.

中旬 the middle decade; *i.e.*, from the 10th to the 20th day of a month.

*chung* 中桅 the middle mast; the main mast of a ship.
中線 the middle thread, *i.e.*, the meridian (of Greenwich, Peking, etc.) from which longitude is reckoned.
中堂 a *Chung-t'ang* (title of a Grand Secretary or Minister of State).
中人 a go-between.
中保 a surety; a mediator.
中燕窩 birds' nests, 2nd quality.
中國, 中華 China; Chinese.
中外, 中西 Chinese and foreign.

*chung* 忠 honest.
忠臣 a loyal minister.
忠信 faithful.
忠純 honest and solid.

*chung* 衷 heart or mind; equity; the true feeling of.

*chung* 重 heavy; weight; weighing; to give weight to; to secure respect for. Cf. *ch'ung* 重.
重輕 heavy and light; either heavy or light; whereas *ch'ing-chung* (輕重) usually means "weight" as a neutral term; high and low (as prices).
重木樑料, 重木方樑 hard-wood beams.
重木板 hard-wood planks.
重究 to inquire into strictly; to deal severely with (as an offender).
重究不貸 to be severely dealt with (as an offender).
重稅餉 to maintain due regard for revenue interests.
重釐餉 to give due weight to likin tax interests.
重以 to consider of importance the fact that; considering the fact that.

*chung* 種 to plant; kind; sort.
種類 kind; category.
種式 pattern; kind.

*chung* 鐘 a clock; a bell.
鐘表 clocks and watches.
鐘時 clock time; *i.e.*, time by the foreign division.

*chung* 終 finally; in the end; whole.
終日 a whole day.
終始 beginning and end; always.

*chung* 衆 all; many; the whole of.
衆商 all the merchants; the mercantile community.
衆洋商 the foreign merchants as a body; the foreign mercantile world.
衆洋商情 the interests of foreign commerce.

*ch'ung* 冲 (or 沖) to strike against; to collide; imitation; spurious; standing for 充 (*chung*), to act as.
冲羽紗 imitation camlets.
冲小羽綾 imitation lastings.
冲銷 to sell clandestinely while evading payment of taxes.

*ch'ung* 重 a second time; again; twice; to be distinguished from *chung* (重), heavy.
重錄 to enter twice.
重複 again; repeatedly; to repeat.
重新 to renew.
重新商訂 to negotiate, or deliberate upon, for the second time.
重修 to revise.
重稅 a second duty; further charges (on goods).
重洋 to cross the sea twice; to cross two or several seas; to make a long sea journey.

*ch'ung* 衝 to rush against; a thoroughfare.
衝移 to carry away (as a buoy is carried away in a gale).

*ch'ung* 充 to fill; to act as; to become.
充滿 to fill; filled; full.
充補 to fill a vacancy.
充艄工 to act as master of a ship.
充引水 to perform the duties of a pilot; to be eligible as a pilot.
充當 to fill the duties of an office; to be eligible for an office; to serve as.
充當水手 to act as a sailor.
充賞 to serve as a reward; as, or in lieu of, a reward.
充公 to become public property; to be confiscated.
充足 sufficient; ample.

*ch'ung* 銃 a blunderbuss; a pistol; a gun.

*ch'ung* 崇 lofty; eminent; honourable.

*ch'ung* 虫 (or 蟲) insects or reptiles.

*ch'ung* 寵 a favourite; affection.

*chü* 句 a sentence; a phrase.
句段 sentences and paragraphs.

*chü* 拘 to grasp; to seize; to arrest.

*chü* 局 a public company; a commission; an administrative board; an establishment working under such a board; all.

局董 a manager in a public company.

局員 the employés, or clerks, of a public company.

局卡 Likin barriers.

*chü* 居 to dwell; to live.

居民 } the inhabitants.
居民人等 }

居住 to dwell; to live at or in; to reside.

居心 the heart dwells on; to set one's heart on.

*chü* 鋸 a saw; to saw.

*chü* 巨 great; vast; numerous.

*chü* 拒 to oppose; to resist.

*chü* 矩 rule; usage.

矩模 a pattern.

*chü* 詎 how; in what manner.

詎料 "how could I expect?" *i.e.*, to my surprise; unexpectedly; however.

*chü* 距 the distance between; distant from.

距水面 above the water-level.

距岸約一里 about 1 *li* distant from the shore.

*chü* 具 to arrange; to prepare; to furnish; to state; to present to.

具稟人 the petitioner.

具保結 to sign a bond.

具呈 to prepare and hand up; to present (as a document).

具呈保單 to sign a guarantee.

具奏 to present a memorial to the Throne.

具文 a written despatch; an official paper; an empty form.

具有天良者 frank-hearted, honest people.

*chü* 俱 all; equally; gives a preceding noun plural force.

*chü* 橘 an orange.

橘子 oranges.

橘皮 orange peel.

*chü* 桔 (otherwise *chieh*, a water-wheel) contracted from 橘, an orange.

桔子 oranges.

*chü* 舉 to raise; to recommend a matter proposed; a proposition; a matter; an affair; to commence.

舉人 the *chü-jên* literary degree.

舉世 the whole world.

舉行 to commence; to put into operation.

*chü* 據 in accordance with; whereas; documentary proof; an official record; a protest noted.

據此 on the ground of this (statement, application, etc.); accordingly.

據云 as it is said; as to the remark that.

據情 according to the circumstances.

據情面稟 to submit the facts in a personal address.

據實稟明 to make an accurate report.

*chü* 遽 hurried; hasty; suddenly.

遽議 to decide hastily.

遽予免征 to grant exemption from duty in a hurry.

*chü* 覷 to spy; to watch for.

覷機會 to watch for an opportunity.

*chü* 懼 to be afraid; to fear.

*chü* 聚 to assemble.

聚集 to assemble; to collect.

聚衆 to assemble in numbers.

聚儎 to pack together with.

*ch'ü* 曲 crooked; bent; yielding.

曲直 crooked and straight.

曲加矜恤 to have pity on; to feel compassion for.

曲斜 to go obliquely; to trend away from the straight course.

*ch'ü* 去 to go away; past; gone.

去官 to leave the public service.

去年 last year; in former years.

去世 to depart from this world; to die.

去文 an outgoing despatch.

去後 (= 以後) (after a verb) on having......; after.

*ch'ü* 趨 to run; to follow quickly; to hasten.

趨赴 to hasten to; to readily follow an invitation.

趨利 to run after gain.

*ch'ü* 屈 to bend down; grievance; wrong.

屈枉 injustice; wrong.

屈從 to submit; to consent.

*ch'ü* 區 a store-room; to sort; petty; trifling.

區別 to distinguish; distinction.

*ch'ü* 軀 the human body.

*ch'ü* 驅 to expel.

驅除 to expel; to send away.

*ch'ü* 驅逐 to expel.

*ch'ü* 取 to fetch; to get; to select.

取具 to produce (as a certificate); to furnish.

取去 to take away.

取回 to fetch back; to take back.

取鬧 to create altercation; to commence a row.

取巧 to exact an undue advantage.

取巧販賣 deceitful traffic in goods.

*ch'ü* 娶 to marry.

*ch'ü* 趣 pleasure; enjoyment; a jest.

*chüan* 捐 to subscribe (as in a subscription list); to pay a Government special tax; special taxes; likin, etc.

捐輸 to purchase official rank.

捐錄 to subscribe money.

捐貲 to subscribe; a subscription.

捐官 to purchase office.

*chüan* 絹 a thin silk texture; silk taffeta; pongees.

*chüan* 蠲 to put aside; to remit (as taxes).

*chüan* 眷 the relatives and members of one's household; affectionate.

眷口 / 眷屬人口 } the members of a family or household.

眷族 relatives.

眷念 to think of with affection.

*chüan* 卷 a roll; a scroll; a record; a document.

*chüan* 捲 to roll up; to receive.

*chüan* 倦 tired; fatigued.

*ch'üan* 券 a deed; a contract.

券契 an agreement.

券約 a bond; a deed.

*ch'üan* 圈 a circle; to encircle; an enclosure; to punctuate.

圈銷 to erase by drawing a ring; to cancel.

*ch'üan* 全 complete.

全數 the whole amount; completely.

全貨之數 the complete amount of goods; the whole lot.

全權 having full powers; plenipotentiary.

全案 the complete [records of a] case.

全卷照錄 to make a copy of all the documents of a case.

全敍云云 "as quoted before;" "*see* above;" *lit.*, the complete quotation as stated. Cf. *yün* 云云.

*ch'üan* 痊 to cure; to recover.

*ch'üan* 泉 a spring.

泉州府 the prefecture of Ch'üan-chou (Chinchew), near Amoy.

*ch'üan* 勸 to advise.

勸戒 to caution; to warn.

勸慰 to console.

*ch'üan* 權 authority; power; circumstances.

權屬在該關 the power of......rests with the said Custom House.

權勢 influence; authority.

權辦 to manage a matter, or act, temporarily, under the pressure of circumstances; to adopt an exceptional course owing to special circumstances.

權宜 a temporary measure; a measure one cannot help adopting.

權宜之舉 a temporary arrangement to meet pressing circumstances.

*ch'üan* 犬 a dog.

犬牙交錯 interlocked like dog's teeth.

*chüeh* 絕 to cut off; to break; to interrupt; extremely; very.

*chüeh* 譎 to impose on.

*chüeh* 決 (or 决) to flow; to decide; decidedly.

決不 by no means. Cf. *ping* 並未.

決不姑寬 on no account will leniency be shown.

*chüeh* 角. See *chiao*.

*chüeh* 覺. See *chüo*.

*chüeh* 脚. See *chiao*.

*chüeh* / *chio* } 爵 a rank of nobility.

*ch'üeh* 缺 empty; a deficiency; a vacancy.

缺虧 deficient; a deficit.

缺額 short of the stipulated amount.

缺出 a vacancy occurring (as from resignation).

缺本 to lose capital.

缺防 insufficiently guarded against; to fail to take protective measures.

缺處 an empty place; an open spot.

*ch'üeh* 却 but; nevertheless; then; really; to refuse; to decline.

*ch'üeh* / *ch'io* } 確 true; accurate.

確實 the true facts; no mistake.

確知 to know properly.

確當 correct and in order.

*ch'üeh* / *ch'io* } 確鑿 true; really.

確據 proved by fact; criminative evidence; criminative.

確切 with the utmost accuracy.

*chün* 君 a sovereign; a king; a gentleman; after a surname, and followed by the personal name (*ming*), corresponding to our "Mr." before surnames, *e.g.*, 陶君詠常 Mr. T'AO YUNG-CH'ANG.

君長 superiors; the chiefs of a tribe.

君民 the sovereign and the people.

君主 a king; a queen; a sovereign.

*chün* 郡 a principality; an earldom.

郡王 a prince of the 2nd order.

*chün* 軍 a regiment; military; the army.

軍需 military equipments.

軍器 implements of war.

軍火 munitions of war.

軍民 the soldiery and the people.

軍門 honorary title of a *T'i-tu* (high military official) (employed in correspondence only).

軍裝所 a depository for arms, etc.; an armoury.

軍前要物 munitions of war.

軍機 a council of war.

軍機處 the Grand Council.

軍機大臣 a Minister of the Grand Council.

軍牌 a medal awarded for military services.

*chün* 竣 to complete; to finish.

竣事 to complete an affair.

*chün* 均 all; equally; gives a preceding noun plural force.

均齊 even and regular; well adjusted.

均平 impartial.

*chün* 鈞 important; just; politely, that which belongs to the person addressed: your.

鈞劄 your respected orders (as alluding to an official letter from a superior).

鈞諭 your instructions.

鈞安不一 with many kind inquiries (a concluding phrase in letters).

鈞裁 to consider in justness; to duly weigh the arguments.

*ch'ün* 羣 a flock; all; they all.

*chüo* 爵. See *chüeh*.

*chüo* / *chiao* } 覺 to perceive; to be aware of; to understand; to arouse.

覺察 to be aware of and examine.

## Ê.

*ê.* See *o.*

*ên* 恩 favour; kindness.

恩准 to kindly grant.

恩情 kindness; affection.

恩義 kindness and justice.

恩眷 Imperial favour.

恩便 a favour; a kindness.

恩恤商艱 to have sympathy with the merchant's hardships.

恩賜 the bestowal of favour; bestowed by favour.

恩慈 kindness and mercy.

恩公兩便 both a matter of favour and of justice.

*êrh* 兒 a child.

兒茶 cutch.

*êrh* 耳 ear; at least; only (restrictive particle at the close of sentences).

耳環 ear-rings.

耳目 "ears and eyes;" *i.e.*, spies.

耳聞 to hear (as a rumour).

*êrh* 而 and; but; and yet; yet. After verbs it often has the force of the Latin gerund; *e.g.*, 煮海水而作鹽 *chu hai-shui êrh tso yen*, "to make salt by boiling sea water"; 輪船拖帶而入 *ju*, to enter (port), *êrh*, by, *lun-ch'uan t'o-tai*, being steamer-towed, *i.e.*, "to be towed into port by a steamer." It is frequently used in introducing the apodosis in a concessive clause, no matter whether the protasis be opened by *sui* (雖), "although," or not; *e.g.*,......, 而......, or 雖......, 而......, "although......, yet......" Cf. *sui* 雖.

而已 and no more (a final phrase); only; merely.

*êrh* 爾 you; it often has the force of making an adverb of the word preceding it.

爾等 you (plural).

*êrh* 邇 / 邇近 } near to; close at hand.

邇來 recently; hitherto.

*êrh* 二 (or 貳) two; both.

二價 two prices; no fixed prices.

二心 double-minded.

二套口 Êrh-t'ao-kow (a Likin station on the Yangtze).

## F.

fa 法 law; rule; method; French.
法網 netted by the law; caught and punished.
法度 regulations; ways.
法碼 standard weights.
法蘭呢 (*fa-lan-ni*) flannel.
法國 (=法蘭西, *fa-lan-hsi*; also 佛蘭西, *fo-lan-hsi*, or 法郎西, *fa-lang-hsi*) France; French.
法文 the French text.

fa 伐 to strike; to cut down; to reduce.
伐國 to subdue a country.
伐木 to cut down timber.

fa 發 to send; to issue.
發縣 to send to the District Magistrate (as a criminal for punishment).
發貨 to send goods.
發寄 to send (as a letter or a despatch).
發給 to issue.
發給收執 to issue and place in the hands of.
發回 to issue back; to return (as documents deposited).
發還 to return (as moneys).
發還存票 to issue drawback in exchange (for duty paid).
發單 to issue a bill, permit, etc.
發單起貨 to issue a permit to land.
發潮 to become damp or mouldy.
發怒 to get angry.
發財 to grow rich.
發賣 to sell; to expose for sale.

fa 乏 to be in want of; exhausted.

fa 罰 to fine; to punish.
罰罪 to punish.
罰錢 to fine pecuniarily.
罰俸 to have one's salary reduced by way of fine.
罰商銀兩 proceeds of fines [collected] from merchants.
罰貨物入官變價 proceeds of confiscated goods sold.
罰充入官 to be punished by confiscation; to be confiscated.
罰辦 to decide a case by fine or confiscation.
罰款 fines [and confiscations] items; account of fines and confiscations (= Customs Account *B*).

fa 罰款案由清摺 a confiscation report.
罰款清冊 a report of fines and confiscations.
罰項 moneys received on account of fines.
罰繳 to be fined and pay; to pay as a fine.

fan 番 foreign; (= 次) time; times.
番人 a foreigner.
番邦 foreign kingdoms.
番紀 flannel.

fan 繙 to translate.
繙譯官 an official interpreter.

fan 翻 to turn over; to revise (as a case).
翻播 to mix up; to muddle.

fan 藩 a boundary; a frontier.
藩司 the Provincial Treasurer; the same as *Fan-t'ai* (藩臺) or *Pu-chêng-shih* (布政使).
藩臬兩司 the Provincial Treasurer and the Provincial Judge; the two chief commissioners of provincial government.

fan 凡 every; whenever; if.
凡………者 all………who (or which)………
凡遇 whenever.
凡例 the introductory explanations in a book.

fan 帆 a sail; to sail.
帆船 sailing vessels.
帆蓬 sails.
帆杠 a yard (of a ship's mast).
帆布 canvas.

fan 繁 numerous; many.
繁多 very many.

fan 樊 a railing; an enclosed place.
樊口 Fankow (a Likin station on the Yangtze).

fan 礬 alum.

fan 煩 to trouble; please; I shall be obliged if you will.

fan 反 to turn; but; on the contrary.
反昂 very high; exorbitant (as in price).
反案 to go contrary to a case.
反坐 on the contrary, to be guilty [oneself]; to bring a charge back on one's own head (as a false accuser does).
反復 } backwards and forwards; coming and going;
反覆 } again and again; to repeat.
反口 to deny one's own words.

*fan* 販 to trade; to buy and sell; to deal in.

販賣 to trade; to deal in.

販運 to traffic; to forward (goods).

販運圖利 to traffic for the sake of profit.

販戶 dealers (in salt, etc.).

*fan* 返 to return; to revert to.

*fan* 飯 boiled rice; food; meals.

*fan* 泛 to float; vague.

泛言 vague language.

*fan* 犯 a criminal; to be guilty; to offend against.

犯法 to offend against the law.

犯例 to break the regulations.

犯罪 to offend; offence; to commit a crime; criminal.

*fan* 範 a rule; a pattern.

*fang* 方 square; a place; direction; a recipe; then (*i.q.*, *chi* 卽); just then; at the same time.

方式 square

方格 chequers; chequered.

方格式 a chequered muster.

方圓 square and round; size (of timber).

方徑 the measurement of a square body (as square beams).

方向 the direction [of the compass].

方便 a convenience; an advantage.

方法 means; plans.

方伯 epistolary designation of a *Fan-t'ai* or Provincial Treasurer.

方始 then; but then; then, and not sooner.

方冀 at the same time wishing.

*fang* 仿 (or 倣) like; as; to imitate.

仿照 like; as; analogous with; to follow; to conform to (as to a set of regulations); conformably with.

仿造 to imitate a pattern; to construct according to a pattern.

*fang* 妨 to hinder; an impediment.

*fang* 彷 like (= 仿).

彷彿 like; for instance, if.

*fang* 房 a house; a building; a room.

房間 rooms; houses.

房科 an office.

*fang* 訪 to inquire.

訪察 }
訪問 } to inquire into.

*fang* 訪確 to ascertain.

*fang* 防 to protect; to guard against.

防碍 a hindrance; a difficulty to be provided against.

防患 to guard against calamities.

防範 to take protective measures.

防險號 signals made to avoid danger; fog signals.

防不勝防 to take protective measures against what cannot be protected (said if there is no help against running risks).

*fang* 放 to release.

放行 to release; to let go.

放行單 a release permit.

放出 to release; to let out.

放鎗 to fire a musket.

放礮 to fire cannon; to fire a gun.

放花 to let off fireworks.

放汽 to let off steam; to blow the steam whistle.

放藍光 to burn a blue light.

放斂 to give off and concentrate again (as a fixed and flashing light).

放手 to release one's hands, *i.e.*, to stay one's hand; to leave off work.

放心 to make one's mind easy; also, to lose heart.

*fei* 非 not; not to be, the opposite of *shih* (是) to be: wrong.

非但……亦……not only……but also……

非止 not only.

非常 uncommonly.

非是 it is not so; not real; hollow. Cf. *shih* 是非.

非分 what is not in harmony with one's duties; irregular; improper.

非通商口岸華船 a Chinese vessel not [registered at] a Treaty port.

*fei* 扉 a door.

*fei* 誹 to calumniate; to slander.

*fei* 匪 banditti; enemies; not.

匪類 robbers; banditti.

*fei* 飛 to fly; quick, as if flying.

飛速 post haste; speedily.

飛報 to send immediate notice to; to send a flying message.

飛送 to send by courier.

飛筆 quick writing.

*fei* 肥 fat; to fatten; to enrich [oneself].

肥巳 to enrich oneself.

*fei* 肥土 rich soil.

肥皂 Chinese soap.

*fei* 廢 to waste; to annul.

廢棄 to abandon.

廢紙 waste paper; documents cancelled.

廢燈塔 an abandoned lighthouse.

*fei* 費 expenditure; a fee; fees.

費錢 expenses; a fee.

費項 fees; expenses; charges.

費一番枝節 an expense once made being followed by many others.

費事 vexation; trouble.

費解 not intelligible.

費心 to cause trouble.

費時 to waste one's time.

*fên* 分 to divide; fractional (as in 三分之一, one third); to separate; separately; respectively; to distribute. Before a verb it means that the action of the verb is to be applied at different places, to different objects, etc., *respectively;* a candareen (the 100th part of a tael); also, a tenth part of anything; a set (as of printed regulations); a copy of a book, or of a document, of which several copies have been made; one's duty.

分而爲二 to distinguish two kinds of.

分鋸爲板 to saw into planks.

分開 to distinguish; to enumerate in detail.

分明 to distinguish; clearly.

分別 to distinguish; to separate.

分別輕重 light or heavy, as the case may be (said of punishment).

分別飭挂號記 to exhibit distinguishing flags.

分辨 to discriminate.

分撥 to detach; to keep separate.

分派 to detail; to detach (as for special duty).

分派兩處 to send to two different places.

分散 to disperse; to distribute.

分布 to distribute over; to spread over (as over the country).

分次序 in order; in rotation.

分成 to distribute in portions.

分晰清楚 to clearly distinguish.

分款 according to categories.

分類 to class; classified; classed.

*fên* 分守 to have the control of several administrative districts respectively.

分巡 to inspect several districts respectively (used in the title of a Taot'ai).

分巡道 an inspector of circuit; a Taot'ai.

分章 branch rules; byelaws; local rules.

分府 title of a sub-prefect.

分縣 a sub-magistrate.

分身 to absent oneself; to stay away.

分肥 to divert undue advantages to oneself.

*fên* 份 a portion; a share.

*fên* 吩 / 吩咐 } to order.

*fên* 忿 anger; hatred.

*fên* 粉 flour; powder; cosmetics in powders.

粉絲 vermicelli; macaroni.

粉飾 the "get-up" in packing goods; ornamental packing.

*fên* 紛 confused; ill-assorted; mottled; the bustle of a crowd.

紛雜 mixed; confused.

紛繁 manifold; endless.

紛紛效尤 many others will follow; others will claim what is allowed to a few.

*fên* 焚 to burn.

*fên* 墳 a grave.

墳墓 a grave; a tomb.

*fên* 憤 zeal; ardour; anger.

*fên* 奮 impetuous; to shake.

*fên* 糞 manure.

*fêng* 風 wind; the spirit of; the habits of; usage; custom.

風浪 / 風濤 } wind and waves; a heavy sea; bad weather at sea.

風笙 a whistle.

風雨表 a barometer.

風順 the wind being favourable.

風俗 local custom; usage.

風聲 rumour; news.

風聞 it is rumoured; hearsay.

*fêng* 瘋 insane; insanity; paralysis.

*fêng* 丰 fine; pleasing.

*fêng* 蜂 a bee.

蜂蜜 honey.

*fêng* 峯 a peak.

*fêng* 蜂 a bee.

蜂蜜 honey.

*fêng* 鋒 the point of a weapon; the van of an army.

*fêng* 逢 to meet; to happen; to come across; whenever.

逢迎 to go out to meet one, as in receiving a guest.

逢關 to pass a Customs station.

逢關納稅遇卡抽釐 to pay duty at Custom Houses and likin taxes at Likin stations met on the road, *i.e.*, to pay all inland taxes due *en route*.

*fêng* 縫 to sew; to mend.

*fêng* 奉 to offer to; to receive (especially, to receive from a superior); before the title of a high Government authority, denotes the doer of the action implied in the verb following; to pay obedience to.

奉勸 to offer one's advice to; to warn.

奉旨 to have received an Imperial edict.

奉達 to receive instructions.

奉行 to receive orders from a superior; to act in compliance [with instructions].

奉求 to request.

奉到 to receive (as from a high authority); to have come to hand.

奉到憲劄 to have received instructions from the authorities.

奉家主之命 to receive orders from one's master.

奉公 to be careful of Government interests.

奉養 to respectfully nurse; *i.e.*, to bestow filial care on one's parent.

奉天府 the prefecture of Fêng-t'ien; Manchuria.

奉錦山海關 the territorial divisions of Fêng-t'ien-fu (*fêng* 奉), Chin-chou-fu (*chin* 錦), and the Custom House at Shan-hai-kuan (山海關, at the eastern terminus of the Great Wall), constituting the administrative district of the Tao-t'ai of Newchwang.

*fêng* 俸 Government salaries.

俸祿 salary.

*fêng* 捧 to hold in both hands or claws (as the eagle on Mexican dollars, holding a snake in one claw and a twig of cactus in the other).

*fêng* 豐 rich; affluent; abundance.

豐年 a year of plenty; a good harvest.

*fêng* 封 to seal; to envelop; to close up; to confer.

封好 duly sealed; after being sealed.

封存 to keep under bond.

*fêng* 封關 to close the Custom House.

封艙 to seal a boat by closing its hold with sealed strips of paper pasted over the hatches.

封舖 to seal a shop in bankruptcy.

封皮 paper labels for sealing.

封書 to seal a letter.

封套 an envelope.

封印 to close the office during holidays.

*fou* 否 not; whether or not; if not.

*fou* 浮 to float; to be light like pumice-stone; light; idle; frivolous; a buoy; buoys.

浮石 pumice-stone.

*fou* 埠 a port; an anchorage.

*fu* 夫 a workman; a coolie; a husband.

夫船 workmen and boats.

夫役 porters; coolies.

夫婦 husband and wife.

*fu* 扶 to shield; to accompany (as a coffin); to assist.

扶助 to assist.

*fu* 甫 to begin; first; at first.

甫臨近口 first just approaching a port; when arriving off a port.

*fu* 輔 to aid; to assist.

輔助 to assist.

輔弼 to assist (the Throne); a Minister of State.

*fu* 傅 to lay on; an instructor.

傅油 to apply oil.

*fu* 縛 to bind; to tie.

縛緊 to fasten by binding.

*fu* 敷 to be sufficient for.

敷解 to remit the full amount contracted for (as a tax farmer remits to Government).

*fu* 俘 a prisoner of war; to capture.

*fu* 弗 not; it should not be.

*fu* 佛 like; for example.

*fu* 拂 to oppose; to thwart.

拂逆 perverse; obstinate.

*fu* 付 to give; to deliver to; to send; to engage.

付給 to hand over to; to place in one's hands; to tender (as payment).

付搭便船 to charter a convenient ship; to make use (for cargo or passage) of a ship which happens to be on the berth.

*fu* 咐 to order.

*fu* 府 a house; a store; a palace; a prefecture, or department, of the first order; a *fu*.

府城 prefectural cities.

府丞 a Vice-Director in the Imperial Clan Court.

*fu* 俯 to stoop down; to condescend.

俯伏 to fall prostrate.

俯念 to condescend to think of; to take into consideration.

俯念商艱 to kindly take into consideration our (the merchants') difficulties.

俯賜照會 to favour one with a despatch (said of a superior, or an equal by way of civility).

俯賜咨商 be pleased to write to and consult with.

俯恤商情 to look down with a pitiful heart on mercantile interests.

俯准 to graciously permit; to grant.

*fu* 腐 to spoil; to rot; rotten.

*fu* 符 to agree; to tally.

*fu* 附 to append; to enclose; a supplement; near.

附給 to issue [a document] in an enclosure.

附有 there is enclosed (as in a letter or postal bag).

附呈抄案清摺 to append a fair copy of the correspondence in a case.

附送 to forward as an enclosure (in a letter or despatch).

附續 to append; a supplement.

附編 an appendix.

附閱 to learn from an enclosure (in a letter).

附搭 to take passage (in a ship).

附近 near; neighbouring; the nearest.

*fu* 伏 to fall prostrate; humble; humbly; to submit; respectfully.

伏希 to respectfully hope.

伏祈 to humbly request.

伏乞 to humbly pray or petition; to respectfully request.

伏思 I humbly consider; in my humble opinion.

伏候 to respectfully wait.

伏查 it is my humble opinion that; in my humble opinion.

*fu* 副 to assist; assistant (in titles); deputy; a set; sets.

副都統 a Lieutenant-General.

副領事官 a Vice-Consul.

副稅務司 a Deputy Commissioner of Customs.

*fu* 副本 a duplicate copy.

*fu* 幅 a strip of cloth; a roll of silk.

幅寬 the breadth of a flag.

幅地 (*fu-ti*, in imitation of the English sound "foot") a foot; feet.

*fu* 福 happiness; prosperity.

福建 (*fu-chien*) the province of Fukien.

福州府 the prefecture of Foochow.

*fu* 富 rich; riches; to enrich.

富貴 rich and influential; wealthy.

*fu*, *p'u* } 匐 to fall prostrate.

*fu* 腹 the bowels; the stomach.

*fu* 複 to double; lined (as cloth).

*fu* 復 again; to reply; to write in reply to a letter previously received.

復行 to go again; to continue a journey (after having put into a port).

復行下船 to re-ship; to re-export.

復[運]進口 to import again; to re-import, as native goods from another Treaty port.

復進口半稅 coast trade duty.

復入內地 to be taken on to the interior.

復查 to re-examine.

復啓者 I beg to inform you (said in reply to a letter received).

復者 a reply; in reply to your note I beg to say.

復核可行 to reply that a matter may be carried out; to reply in the affirmative.

復淨洋參 re-clarified foreign ginseng.

*fu* 覆 again; to and fro; to examine.

覆奏 to memorialise again; to refer (a matter) back to the Throne; to memorialise the Throne in reply.

覆審 to re-investigate.

*fu* 服 to swallow; to submit to; to agree; to be willing; clothes; mourning clothes.

服藥 to take medicine.

服制 regulations for wearing mourning.

*fu* 撫 to pacify.

撫慰 to soothe; to pacify.

撫臺 }
撫院 } the Governor of a province.
撫部院 }

撫憲 His Excellency the Governor.

*fu* 父 a father.

*fu* 父母 father and mother; one's parents.

*fu* 斧 an axe; a hatchet.

*fu* 釜 a cooking-pan.

*fu* 訃 to announce the death of a friend.

*fu* 赴 to proceed to.

赴銀號 to go to the bank.

赴考 to proceed to an examination.

赴命 to obey a call; to follow an invitation.

*fu* 負 to bear; to carry on the back; to turn the back on; to disregard.

負咎 to be in debt.

負債 to turn the back on; to carry on the back.

負違 to oppose.

負恩 to be ungrateful.

負咎 to bear [the consequences of] an offence; to be blamed for.

負約 to disregard or break a Convention.

*fu* 賦 to exact; to receive taxes.

賦稅 taxes; impost.

*fu* 婦 a wife; a married woman.

婦女 women.

婦子 wife and children.

## H.

*ha* 哈 to laugh.

哈喇呢 (*ha-la-ni*, also read *ka-la-ni*) Russian cloth.

哈外意國 (*ha-wai-i-kuo*) Hawaii; Hawaiian.

*hai* 孩 a child.

*hai* 海 the sea; maritime.

海菜 agar-agar; seaweed.

海帶 seaweed.

海參 bêche de mer. (Fr) bicho de mar (Port.)

海馬 the sea-horse; the seal; the Hippocampus.

海馬牙 sea-horse teeth.

海騾 the beaver.

海騾皮 beaver skins.

海龍 the sea-otter.

海龍皮 sea-otter skins.

海濱 the sea-coast.

海口 a seaport.

海島 an island.

海關 a maritime Custom House.

海關紋銀 pure silver in which the Customs duties are to be paid; Haikwan sycee.

*hai* 海關監督 a Superintendent of Customs.

海關馬頭 the Customs Jetty.

海道圖 a sea chart; Chinese charts published by the Kiangnan Arsenal.

海道圖說 sailing directions; text explanatory of sea charts.

海防 the protection of the sea-coast; pertaining to maritime matters.

海防兵備道 a Taot'ai with military authority and charged with coast defence; title of the Tao-t'ai at Shanghai.

海防廳 a *hai-fang-t'ing*, *i.e.*, a magistrate in certain maritime districts, *e.g.*, at Amoy.

海防同知 a maritime sub-prefect.

海防支應局 the "Coast Defence Office" at Tientsin.

海防經費 the current expenses for the maintenance of coast defences; a tax levied to defray such expenses; the *hai-fang* tax.

海防膏釐商人 a mercantile firm to whom the *hai-fang* (coast defence) and *kao-li* (opium boiling) taxes in Kwangtung were farmed out in 1880.

海防水利驛鹽事務 matters pertaining to coast defence, fisheries, post and salt administration.

海澄縣 the district of Hai-ch'êng, near Amoy.

海珠礮臺 Dutch Folly (a fort in the Canton river).

*hai* 害 to injure; injury.

*han* 罕 rare; few.

*han* 旱 dry; a drought.

旱傘 parasols.

*han* 函 a cover; a letter.

函件 }
函信 } a letter; letters.

函稱 to state in a letter.

函達 to inform by letter.

函致 to write to; to give notice to in writing.

函詢 to inquire by letter.

函請核示 to apply for instructions by letter.

函商核奪 to consider by correspondence and decide.

*han* 含 to cherish; to hold in the mouth.

含混 to encourage confusion; to be negligent about matters.

*han* 寒 cold; poor.

寒暑表 a thermometer.

*han* 韓 name of an ancient feudal state.

*han* 韓江 the Han river, near Swatow.

*han* 翰 a quill; a pencil; something written; a letter.

翰林院 the Hanlin College.

*han* 喊 to vociferate; to call.

喊追 to call out and pursue (as in chasing a thief).

*han* 撼 to move; to shake.

*han* 漢 Chinese; the Han river, near Hankow; Hankow.

漢人 a Chinese.

漢文 Chinese writing; in Chinese.

漢洋兩文 in Chinese and foreign writing.

漢軍 the Chinese portion of the army called banner troops.

漢口 Hankow.

漢號 a Hankow firm.

漢黃德 the three departments of Han-yang-fu (漢 *han*), Huang-chou-fu (黃 *huang*), and Tê-an-fu (德 *tê*), forming the circuit in charge of the Taot'ai at Hankow.

漢諾威 *(han-no-wei)* Hanover; Hanoverian.

漢謝城 *(han-hsieh ch'êng)* the Hanse towns in Germany.

*hang* 杭 / 杭州 } Hang-chou-fu in Chêkiang.

*hang* 行 a hong; a firm; a row; a series. Cf. *hsing* 行, to go.

行名 the name of a firm.

行商 a foreign merchant; a resident merchant.

行主 the head of a firm.

行家 the hong people; merchants; firms.

行棧 hong and godowns; a mercantile establishment; warehouses.

*hao* 毫 a hair; a trifle.

毫無疑議 there is not the slightest doubt. Cf. *ping* 並未.

毫無異議 not to differ in the least in one's opinion; to agree in every respect.

毫無更改 not to make the slightest change.

毫釐 a hair's breadth; the least portion of.

*hao* 豪 brave; martial.

*hao* 壕 a ditch.

*hao* 耗 waste; to waste; to diminish; to lose.

耗輕銀 waste silver.

耗費 the cost of the waste silver or of the under-weight found when extracting pure from impure silver; to waste.

*hao* 號 a number; a firm; a bank; registered mark or sign; to scream; to call; to style.

號數 a registered number.

號記 signals.

號船 registered boats; boats used as navigation marks; lightships.

號照 a certificate of registry.

號商 a licensed merchant.

號衣 a livery; a soldier's uniform.

號收 a bank receipt (for payment of duty).

*hao* 鶴 a stork; a crane.

*hao* 好 good. After verbs, denotes that the action of the verb is finished; hence, a sign of the past. To like; to be addicted to.

好處 advantages; benefit.

*hei* 黑 black.

黑胡椒 black pepper.

黑棗 black dates.

黑海參 black bicho de mar.

黑魚翅 black sharks' fins.

黑鉛塊 plumbago.

黑龍江 *(hei-lung-chiang)* the Amoor river.

*hên* 很 very; extremely.

*hên* 恨 anger; resentment; to hate.

*hêng* 亨 to persevere; persevering.

*hêng* 衡 a balance; to weigh; to judge.

衡平 a pair of scales.

衡情 to judge of the circumstances.

*hêng* 橫 cross-wise; horizontal.

橫木 a cross-beam; a boom.

橫徑 the warp of a texture.

橫線 horizontal stripes (painted on the outer surface of navigation marks).

橫線相間 / 橫間 } horizontal bands.

橫樑 cross-beams.

橫逆 perverse; obstinate.

*hêng* 恒 constantly.

恒產 a patrimony; property; income.

*ho* 曷 why; wherefore; what.

曷故 for what reason?

曷其有極 why should it come to this? why should he come to his death?

曷勝 (= 不勝) how could it equal? *i.e.*, not equal to; inexpressibly; highly.

新關文件錄



*ho* 曷勝欣躍 I shall be extremely delighted.

曷勝感戴 I am deeply indebted for.

*ho* 河 a river.

河岸 a river's bank.

河口 the mouth of a river.

河面 the river surface; on the river.

河泊所 an inspector of river police.

河南 the province of Honan.

河間府 the prefecture of Ho-chien, in Chihli.

*ho* 何 what; which; (=何以) why; how.

何處 at which place? where; whether at any place.

何時 at what time? at which time? at that time; *e.g.*, 何[1]時[2]起[3]貨[4]卽[5]何[6]時[7]照[8]納[9], [1]*ho* [2]*shih*, at which time, [3]*ch'i* [4]*huo*, the goods are landed, [5]*chi*, then, [6]*ho* [7]*shih*, at that time, [8]*chao* [9]*na*, the duty is paid; *i.e.*, "the duties (or dues) are due at the time when goods are landed."

何日 on what date?

何故 for what reason? why.

何事 what matter? what business?

何國人 of what nationality?

何姓名 of what name?

何敢冒瀆 how could I dare to be disrespectful?

何得又更估價 how can the value be changed again?

何至如此 why should we go so far?

何以 what by? by what means? wherefore. Cf. *shih i* 是以 thereby; therefore.

*ho* 荷 the lotus or water-lily; to be obliged for.

荷蘭國 } (*ho-lan-kuo*) Holland; the Netherlands; Dutch.
荷蘭 }

*ho* 禾 grain; crops.

禾米 paddy.

禾黍 millet.

*ho* 和 harmony; to harmonise.

和好 to conclude friendship; peace and friendship.

和睦 friendly; friendship.

和誼 friendly feelings.

和尙 a Buddhist priest.

和碩親王 a prince of the 1st order.

*ho* 合 to unite; duly; to accord with; to unite; in all; total.

合宜 justifiable; fit; proper.

合亟 promptly; duly; with the proper despatch.

*ho* 合併 to duly expose; duly; properly.

合併聲明 to duly state; the above is hereby officially stated.

合再聲明 it is duly further stated (if an additional statement is made).

合就 duly.

合就照知 to duly inform.

合就照送 to forward in due course.

合行備文 to duly write a despatch.

合式 according to pattern; in proper shape.

合規矩 according to usage.

合意 according to one's opinion.

合同 to make a contract; a contract.

合局 partnership in trade.

合會 to form a society or guild.

合共 a grand total; the total of several totals united.

合算 to add up.

合衆 all present; public (as a public examination); all united.

合衆國 the United States.

合一國 the United Principalities.

*ho* 盒 a small box; a box (as of matches); a canister.

*ho* 闔 all; the whole.

闔家 the whole family.

*ho* 核 a kernel; a walnut; to examine; often preceding verbs involving the meaning of a mental exertion.

核仁 a fruit kernel.

核桃 the walnut.

核計 } to examine and add up; to calculate.
核算 }

核算淸單 a table for calculation or conversion.

核加 to add; to calculate the additional......

核明 to examine carefully.

核査 to examine; to recall facts.

核議 to consider; to consult.

核示 to give a decision.

核定 to decide upon; to ascertain.

核奪 to examine and decide; to ascertain.

核斷 to decide a case; to finish a calculation.

核准 to examine into and allow; *i.e.*, to take a petition into favourable consideration; to permit.

核對 to examine and compare; to pass (as an account).

*ho* 核知 to know; to be satisfied as to the correctness of.

核估 to estimate; to assess.

核估時價 to calculate the market value of an article.

核辦 to transact business.

核錯 to discover a mistake.

*ho* 覈 to verify.

覈查 to investigate.

覈驗 to verify.

覈對 to compare.

覈定 to ascertain.

*ho* 赫 blazing; luminous; bright; great reputation.

*ho* 貉 a badger.

貉獾皮 racoon skins.

*ho* 賀 to congratulate.

賀勞 to reward merit.

賀壽 birthday congratulation.

*hou* 侯 / 侯爺 } a marquis.

*hou* 喉 the throat; a narrow passage.

*hou* 候 to wait; to wait upon; to expect; time.

候驗 to await examination.

候訊 / 候質 } to await examination or trial.

候結 to await the termination of a trial.

候示 to await a reply or a decision.

候駕 I await you.

候缺 to wait for a vacancy.

候補 to wait to fill a vacancy; "expectant" (as an Expectant Taot'ai).

候補道 an Expectant Taot'ai.

*hou* 厚 thick; thickness; liberal.

厚薄 thickness (as a relative term).

厚祿 a liberal salary.

厚恩 great kindness.

厚待 to treat liberally.

*hou* 後 after; behind.

後日 on a future day; the day after to-morrow.

後來 hereafter.

後輩 after generations; posterity; successors.

後續 supplementary.

後悔 to repent.

後面 behind; astern (of a ship).

後開 enumerated hereafter; under-mentioned.

後據 an extended protest.

*hou* 后 a ruler; a sovereign; a queen.

*hsi* 西 west; western.

西人 a European.

西歷 western calendar; according to the foreign calendar.

西洋 the western sea; European; foreign.

西洋國 Portugal.

西藏 Thibet.

*hsi* 息 interest (on money); to stop.

息業 to put a stop to one's business.

*hsi* 晰 explicit; clear; to distinguish.

*hsi* 希 to hope; few; rare.

希冀 to desire.

希請 to request; to beg to request.

希卽酌量情形 please consider the circumstances and decide.

希卽轉移 I shall be obliged by your communicating the contents of my letter to......

希望 to look forward to; to hope.

希圖 to hope; to anticipate; hoping that.

希圖偷漏 to intend a fraud on the revenue

希國 Greece; Greek.

*hsi* 稀 few; rare.

稀少 very little; very rare.

稀罕 rare.

稀製紮布 muslins.

*hsi* 係 to be; it is that; this is; (= 關係) to be connected with; to be the essence of; consequences.

*hsi* 奚 how; why; what.

*hsi* 繫 to bind up; to fasten.

*hsi* 喜 pleasure; joy; glad.

*hsi* 習 to practise; expert.

*hsi* 戲 theatricals; to play.

*hsi* 昔 formerly.

昔年 in former years.

昔日 in former days; formerly.

*hsi* 惜 to pity; to spare.

*hsi* 夕 the evening; in the evening.

*hsi* 攜 to lead.

*hsi* 攜帶 to take along with one.
攜同 to carry with one; to be accompanied by.
攜去 to take away.
*hsi* 徙 to shift; to remove.
*hsi* 犀 the rhinoceros.
犀角 rhinoceros horns.
犀皮 rhinoceros hides.
*hsi* 席 a mat; a repast.
*hsi* 蓆 } a mat; mats.
蓆子 }
*hsi* 悉 to know; all; fully.
悉心 with one's whole heart; attentively.
*hsi* 襲 to inherit; hereditary.
襲爵 hereditary rank; nobility.
襲恩 to receive favour.
*hsi* 洗 to wash; to cleanse.
*hsi* 迄 till; to reach.
迄今 till the present; up to the present.
迄未 (= 迄今未) not as yet.
*hsi* 錫 tin.
錫磚條 tin, in slabs.
錫器 tinware.
錫箔 tin-foil.
*hsi* } 檄 to address an inferior; to issue a summons.
*chi* }
*hsi* 細 fine; detailed.
細驗 to examine in detail.
細數 detailed figures.
細磁器 fine chinaware.
細夏布 fine grasscloth.
細斜紋布 jeans.
細葵扇 trimmed palm-leaf fans.
細蔴布 linen goods; fine linen; Irish or Scotch linen.
細絲 sycee silver.
*hsia* 暇 disengaged; leisure.
*hsia* 蝦 crabs.
蝦米 dried shrimps; dried prawns.
*hsia* 遐 distant; advanced in years.
遐齡 to become very old; old age.
*hsia* 瞎 blind; ignorant; false.
*hsia* 轄 to rule over; to govern; to be under the rule or government of.

*hsia* 匣 a chest; a box.
*hsia* 夏 summer.
夏間 during the summer time.
夏季 the summer season.
夏布 grasscloth.
夏灣拏 (*hsia-wan-na; in Cantonese, ha-wan-na*) Havana.
*hsia* 廈 (=廈門 *hsia-mên*) Amoy.
廈門關 the Amoy Customs.
廈防分府 the Magistrate of Amoy.
*hsia* 下 below; inferior; the lowest of two or three qualities; a modest term for "I," "me," "my," etc.; to descend; after a verb it may correspond to colloquial 了 (*liao*) or 過 (*kuo*), denoting the past tense; to ship; to export.
下旬 the last (third) decade of a month; *i.e.*, the days from the 20th to the 30th.
下等絨 inferior Spanish stripes.
下燕窩 birds' nests, 3rd quality.
下冰片 refuse camphor baroos.
下等參 crude ginseng.
下錨 to lower the anchors; to anchor.
下錨鍊 to pay out [anchor] chain.
下霧 mist falling.
下艙 to ship; to disembark.
下入 to ship (by such and such a vessel).
下入艙 to ship.
下載 to ship; to export.
下齊貨物 to have shipped all the goods; to have completed loading.
下貨單 a shipping order.
下貨[准]單 a permit to ship.
下段 the lower limit (as of a harbour).
下游 down the river.
下午 in the afternoon.
下情 the facts stated by me, the inferior.
*hsia* 洽 to harmonise with.
*hsiang* 相 mutual; each other; reciprocal; with; to assist; to watch the time for; to look at.
相離 to take the one away from the other.
相待 to treat each other; mutual treatment; to treat.
相度 to consider the steps to be taken; to adopt the proper means.
相商 to consult about a matter.

*hsiang* 相見 an interview.
相交 to mutually give; to associate.
相近 near.
相符 to agree; to tally; to correspond.
相左 not to suit; to disagree.
相邀 to invite.
相幫 to assist.
相公 a minister of state.
相國 a prime minister.
相遇 to happen to one (as an accident).
相機 to seize an opportunity; according to circumstances; according to requirements.
相應 duly.
相宜 what is proper; right; in order.
相間 painted in stripes or bands.
相若 similar; alike.
相同 identical; the same as; analogous with.
相距 distant from.
相對 opposite; *vis-à-vis*.
相隔一日 a difference in time of one day.

*hsiang* 想 to think; to consider.
想念 }
想思 } to consider; to reflect; to think.
想望 to expect.

*hsiang* 箱 a box.
箱隻 boxes.
箱包 cases and packages.

*hsiang* 香 incense; aromatic drugs; fragrant.
香水 fragrant water; perfumery.
香菌 mushrooms.
香柴 }
香木 } fragrant-wood.
香料 perfumery.
香油 scented oil; sweet oil.
香牛皮 Russia leather.
香港 Hongkong.

*hsiang* 鄉 a village; a community consisting of a number of villages.
鄉村 a village.
鄉長 a village elder.
鄉紳 a country gentleman.
鄉試 the triennial, or provincial, examinations.

*hsiang* 曏 a little while; formerly; recently.

*hsiang* 響 sound; noise; rumour.

*hsiang* 嚮 to lead to; towards.

*hsiang* 鑲 to inlay; to enclose; to border (as a figure on a flag).
鑲藍旗 one of the eight banners of Imperial troops; the "Bordered Blue Banner."

*hsiang* 庠 a school; a provincial graduate.

*hsiang* 祥 an auspicious omen; happiness.

*hsiang* 詳 to state in detail; to report carefully.
詳稟 to report to a superior.
詳錄 to state in detail.
詳細 to report in detail; to state particulars in detail.
詳細載明 to give an accurate, detailed account.
詳細查覆 to reply in detail.
詳察 to examine in detail.
詳文 an official report.
詳咨 to report details.
詳數 to state; to enumerate.
詳明 to explain.
詳記 to take careful notice.
詳分 to distinguish.
詳訂 to clearly define.
詳問 to ask the real facts; to inquire about details.
詳閱 to take careful notice of; to read carefully.
詳悉 to know clearly; a clear account.
詳知 to inform minutely.
詳請 to request respectfully.
詳慎 very carefully.
詳加核對 to compare carefully.

*hsiang* 降 to submit; to cause to submit. Cf. *chiang* 降, to descend.
降服 }
降伏 } to submit.

*hsiang* 向 hitherto; towards; to proceed to; a preposition placed before nouns denoting the object of verbs meaning to ask, to say, to give, etc., *e.g.*, 向[1]子[2]口[3]呈[4]單[5], [4]*ch'êng* [5]*tan*, to hand a document. *hsiang*[1], TO, [2]*tzŭ*-[3]*k'ou*, the barrier office.
向來 heretofore; hitherto.
向常 according to the routine hitherto observed; in the ordinary way; ordinarily.
向例 according to the rule hitherto in force.

*hsiang* 向南 facing the south; in a southerly direction.
向南二十度西 S. 20° W.
向海外面 towards the sea; seaward.
向上 turned upwards; upwards.

*hsiang* 餉 taxes; duties.
餉單 a receipt for taxes; a duty receipt.
餉銀 taxes; commissariat funds.
餉平 a standard weight of sycee silver used in paying duties at Pakhoi.

*hsiang* 享 to enjoy.

*hsiang* 象 an elephant.
象牙 elephants' teeth; ivory.
象牙碎 broken elephants' teeth.
象牙器 ivoryware.

*hsiang* 像 resembling; like; to imitate.

*hsiang* 項 kind; item; funds; moneys; the neck.

*hsiang* 巷 a lane; a street.

*hsiao* 小 small.
小山 a hillock; a mound.
小船 a small boat; a gig; a sampan.
小輪船 a steam-launch; a tug-boat.
小哨 guard-boats.
小官 petty officers!
小民 the common people.
小夥計 a writer; a clerk (as in a bank).
小鐙 a lantern.
小寫 small writing; small text.
小心 to take care.
小行 "the small firm;" a modest term for "I" or "we," used by merchants in petitions.
小絨 flannel.
小呢 cassimeres; narrow cloth.
小羽綾 imitation orleans.
小原布 *T*-cloths (the smaller size).
小洋藥
小土 } Malwa opium.
小麥 wheat.
小呂宋 the Philippines.

*hsiao* 宵 night; at night.

*hsiao* 消 to melt; to thaw.
消化 to dissolve; to melt.
消貨 to sell, or distribute, goods.

*hsiao* 硝 saltpetre.

*hsiao* 硝磺 saltpetre; sulphur and brimstone.

*hsiao* 銷 (=消) to melt; to sell out; to cancel.
銷售 to sell off; to sell.
銷路 circulation of goods; the range of sale.
銷燬 to destroy by fire; to cancel by burning.

*hsiao* 削 to cut; to pare.
削職 to degrade; to dismiss from office.
削字 to engrave characters.
削地 to seize territory.

*hsiao* 曉 to make known; light; clear.
曉諭 for the information of everybody; to inform by proclamation.
曉布 to make known by proclamation.

*hsiao* 蕭 poor; indigent.

*hsiao* 梟 an owl; to expose the head of a decapitated criminal.

*hsiao* 孝 filial piety; the period of mourning for a parent.
孝服 mourning clothes.
孝滿 the expiration of the period of mourning for a parent.

*hsiao* 學 to learn.
學生 an apprentice; an unpaid assistant (as in a firm or bank).
學徒 an apprentice.

*hsiao* 笑 to laugh; to ridicule.

*hsiao* 効
効力 } to exert oneself.
効勞 to exert one's strength; to work for.
効功 to work for merit; meritorious exertion.

*hsiao* 效 to imitate; to do as others do.
效尤 to excel the pattern (as in doing evil) (WILLIAMS); to imitate a bad example; to do what others do.

*hsieh* 歇 to desist; to leave off.
歇工 to stop work.

*hsieh* 屑 trifling; troublesome.

*hsieh* 斜 oblique; sloping.
斜長 diagonal length.
斜紋布 drills; jeans.

*hsieh* 鞋 shoes.

*hsieh* 協 harmony; to assist; a subdivision of a *chên* (鎮) or brigade; a regiment under the command of *hsieh-t'ai* or colonel.
協鎮 the commandant of a garrison; an assistant *chên-t'ai* or brigadier-general; a colonel.
協領 a military title (colonel).

*hsieh* 協領銜 having the rank of a *hsieh-ling* (colonel).

協辦 to assist; an assistant (as an Assistant Grand Secretary).

協同 to assist in; to act conjointly.

*hsieh* 脅 (=協) to aid; to yield; to submit.

脅從 to submit to following.

*hsieh* 邪 bad; vicious; illegal; obscene.

*hsieh* 攜. See *hsi*.

*hsieh* 寫 to write.

寫立憑單 to draw up a certificate.

寫立賣契 to draw up a deed of sale.

*hsieh* 洩 to ooze out; to leak.

洩露 to leak out, as a secret; to reveal; to disclose.

*hsieh* 謝 to thank.

謝恩 to be thankful for favours.

*hsieh* 卸 to unload; to lay down (as an office).

卸賣 to land [goods] for sale.

卸載貨物 to discharge and take in cargo.

卸事 to give up an affair; to resign office.

卸印 to resign office.

*hsien* 先 first; beforehand; before.

先發 to issue beforehand.

先行知照 to give official notice beforehand.

先期聲明 to make a declaration beforehand; to give due notice.

先期 at an early time; in good time.

先期報明 to give timely notice.

先行試辦 to put into operation as a provisional measure.

先妣 a deceased mother.

先考 a deceased father.

先後 before and after; about; repeatedly.

先世 former generations.

*hsien* 仙 genii; fairies.

仙馭 the fairy ride, *i.e.*, death; to die.

*hsien* 掀 to lift; to raise up.

*hsien* 險 danger; risk; dangerous.

險處 a dangerous place; a difficulty.

險阻 an obstacle.

險船 a vessel in distress.

*hsien* 鮮 fresh, as opposed to preserved.

鮮魚 fresh fish.

*hsien* 鮮菜 fresh vegetables.

鮮鹹雜貨店 a shop in which fresh and preserved victuals and sundries are sold.

*hsien* 嫌 dislike; to reject.

*hsien* 暹 Siam.

暹羅國 *(hsien-lo-kuo)* Siam; Siamese.

*hsien* 閒 leisure; idle.

閒人 idle people; vagrants.

*hsien* 閑 to guard against; to bar; without occupation.

閑人 (= 閒人) idlers.

*hsien* 嫻 accomplished; skilled in.

*hsien* 咸 all; the whole of; gives a preceding noun plural force.

咸豐 the period of the reign Hsien Fêng (A.D. 1851–62).

*hsien* 鹹 saltish; salted.

鹹魚 salt fish.

*hsien* 銜 rank; brevet rank; to control.

*hsien* 賢 virtuous; wise.

賢良祠 the Temple of Wisdom and Goodness.

*hsien* 顯 obvious; conspicuous; illustrious (as a deceased hero whose example is always conspicuous amongst the living generation).

顯明 conspicuous.

*hsien* 陷 to fall into.

陷坑 to fall into a pit.

陷罪 to be involved in crime.

*hsien* 獻 to offer up (as tribute); to present to.

*hsien* 線 thread; wire; a line drawn.

*hsien* 現 now; ready; apparent.

現經 } now having; now being; sign of the perfect
現已 } tense.

現已撤銷 having been cancelled; cancelled.

現時 the present time; present.

現今 }
現在 } now.
現下 }

現往 about to proceed to.

現成 ready-made; ready.

現銀 ready money; cash.

*hsien* 縣 a magistracy; a district.

縣署 a district magistrate's office.

縣丞 an assistant magistrate.

*hsien* 羨 to covet; to admire.

*hsien* 憲 an official above the 4th rank; official authorities.

憲台 } (honorary title given to high officials) Your
憲臺 } Excellency; Your Honour; you.

憲札 a despatch or instructions from the authorities.

憲恩 Your Honour's favour.

憲禁 prohibited by the authorities.

憲書 an official calendar.

*hsien* 啣 to hold in the mouth.

啣怨 to harbour resentment.

啣結 an allusion to an old saying, 啣環結草, "to carry in one's mouth the ring and the straw of bondage," as a sign of being never ungrateful; to be bound to; to be in bondage.

*hsien* 限 a limit; to limit; to regard as a limit; hence, as a preposition, "on (such and such a day), as a limit."

限期 a limit; limited.

限度 a restriction.

限制 restriction; restraint.

限內 within the limit.

限到口日 on the date of arrival in port; *i.e.*, neither sooner nor later than on date of arrival.

限以三日 within three days' time.

*hsien* 綫 (= 線) thread; wire.

*hsin* 心 the heart; intention; mind; the centre.

心性 one's disposition; temper.

心領 to be indebted for; *lit.*, received and kept by one's heart.

*hsin* 辛 bitter; acrid; grievous.

辛苦 bitterness; grief; affliction.

*hsin* 昕 morning; day.

昕宵 day and night; at all times.

*hsin* 欣 (or 忻) delighted; happy; joy; pleasure.

欣躍 to be delighted.

欣悅 to rejoice.

欣聞 I am glad to hear that.

*hsin* 新 new; newly; lately; fresh.

新關 the new, *i.e.*, the Foreign, Customs, as opposed to *ch'ang kuan* (常關) or *ch'ao kuan* (鈔關), the Native Customs.

新鈔兩關 the Foreign and Native Customs.

新月 the new moon.

新洋藥 Benares opium.

新式 new pattern; new style.

*hsin* 新式洋錢 a new pattern foreign coin.

新節 the new year; the feast of lanterns.

新年 the new year.

新造 } newly made.
新製 }

新出 newly issued.

新近 recently.

新到 newly arrived; just imported.

新聞 news; tidings.

新聞紙 a newspaper.

新派 to appoint.

新授 having lately received (as a post).

新定 newly fixed; lately settled upon.

新定稅則 the new Tariff.

新爲領換之執照 a new certificate exchanged for an old one.

新金山 Australia; *lit.*, new California.

新加坡 *(hsin-kia-po)* Singapore.

*hsin* 薪 fuel; firewood.

薪水 } a salary; salaries; official emoluments.
薪俸 }

*hsin* 信 a letter; to trust; to believe; true; reliable; a seal (as a sign of belief or trust).

信差 a letter-carrier; a courier.

信袋 a letter-bag.

信封 an envelope.

信局 a postal agency.

信據 a guarantee.

信實 authenticity; sincere.

信息 news.

信石 arsenic.

*hsing* 幸 fortunately; to rejoice at; to hope for; please; you are requested to.

幸勿 please do not; you are requested not to.

幸勿有稽 I hope there will be no delay; "at your earliest convenience."

*hsing* 倖 servile.

*hsing* 姓 a surname; a family name.

姓名 the surname and personal name; the full name of a person.

*hsing* 性 nature; character; disposition.

性理 natural disposition.

性情 personal conduct.

22

*hsing* 星 a star; a spark.
星宿 the stars; the constellations.
星臺 an observatory.
星羅 scattered about like stars.

*hsing* 腥 stench; rancid; raw meat.

*hsing* 興 to arise; to raise; flourishing.
興工 to commence work.
興辦 to put into operation.
興盛 to flourish (as trade).
興旺 to prosper.
興泉永 the three departments of Hsing-hua-fu (興 *hsing*), Ch'üan-chou-fu (泉 *ch'üan*), and Yung-ch'un-chou (永 *yung*), forming the circuit in charge of the Taot'ai at Amoy.

*hsing* 形 shape; form; to describe; description.
形似 to purport; to amount to (in sense).

*hsing* 刑 punishment; to punish.
刑罰 to punish.
刑問 to examine by torture.
刑部 the Board of Punishments.

*hsing* 行 to go; to cause to; to do; placed before verbs to denote action; to work (as to load and unload). Cf. *hang* 行, a hong.
行走 to walk; pedestrians; to go (in and out); one who goes in and out at an office in order to learn its routine, without being an actual member; an associate; a supernumerary; to act in another function in addition to one's own duties; to officiate; to do duty as.
行寓 a temporary residence while on a journey.
行人 a traveller.
行商 a travelling merchant.
行市 commercial usage.
行李 luggage; baggage.
行船正路 the ships' channel (in a river or near the coast).
行知 to inform (an inferior) in a despatch.
行文 to write to.
行文知照 to inform officially; to inform in a despatch.
行駛 to sail.
行准 to receive (as a despatch).

*hsing* 杏 almonds; plums.
杏仁 almonds; apricot seeds.

*hsiu* 休 to stop; to cease.
休息 to stop (for rest after work).

*hsiu* 羞 to be ashamed; shame.
羞恥 to be ashamed.

*hsiu* 修 to repair; to regulate.
修造 to repair.
修整 to repair; to mend.
修改 to repair; to alter; to amend; to revise.
修改稅則 to revise a Customs Tariff.
修補 to amend.
修船雜物 dock stores.
修廠 a dock.
修書 to compose a letter carefully.
修志局 a commission for preparing a new edition of the provincial, etc., archives (*chih* 志).
修鐙 to trim a light.

*hsiu* 宿 a night; to rest; formerly; old.
宿怨 an old resentment.

*hsiu* 朽 to rot; rotten.

*hsiu* 秀 elegant; beautiful.
秀才 the *Hsiu-ts'ai* literary degree.

*hsiu* 繡 to embroider; embroideries.
繡貨 embroidered goods; *articles de tapisserie.*

*hsiu* 袖 a sleeve.

*hsiung* 兄 an elder brother; as a term of respect, "you."
兄台 an elder brother; "you."
兄弟 a younger brother; "I."

*hsiung* 凶 adversity; inauspicious.

*hsiung* 兇 a murderer; a criminal; cruel.
兇犯 a criminal guilty of a capital crime; a murderer.
兇要各犯 murderers and [other] important criminals.

*hsiung* 洶 a great rush of water; a heavy sea.
洶湧 the rushing of waves in a heavy sea.

*hsiung* 胸 the breast; *fig.*, the mind.

*hsü* 胥 inferior clerks; all; altogether.
胥吏 yamên writers; *shupan.*
胥役 yamên underlings; writers.
胥皆 all; equally.

*hsü* 虛 empty.
虛揑 to make a fictitious report.
虛懸 *lit.*, to suspend in the empty space; "to pay over the left shoulder."

*hsü* 須 must; necessary.

新關文件録



*hsü* 須至總單者 "a cargo certificate which must be despatched" (至 = *ta* 達, to send?), a concluding phrase used to prevent unauthorised additions, but, owing to its antiquated form, it is difficult to explain.

須至照會者 "a necessary despatch."

須用 necessaries.

*hsü* 鬚 a beard; fine (hairy) ginseng.

*hsü* 卹 (or 恤) rewards bestowed on the families of deceased high officials; to pity; to commiserate; to sympathise with; to befriend.

卹典 regulations for bestowing posthumous honours.

卹商 to facilitate trade.

*hsü* 需 it is required; to use.

需用經費 current expenses for one's maintenance.

*hsü* 戌 the eleventh of the twelve branches; applied to time, the eleventh Chinese hour of the day, *i.e.*, about 7 to 9 P.M.

*hsü* / *ch'u* } 畜 to feed; to nourish. Cf. *ch'u* 畜, domestic animals.

畜養 to nourish; to support.

*hsü* 許 to allow; to be allowed; it is allowed to; to promise.

*hsü* 嶼 a small rocky island.

*hsü* 敘 to converse.

*hsü* 序 to follow in order; series.

*hsü* 緒 a thread; a clue; the commencement.

*hsü* 續 to continue to; continuous; additional; supplementary; to renew.

續增 to accumulate.

續假 extension of leave.

續添 supplementary; additional.

續議 additionally agreed upon.

續修 to revise; revised; supplementary.

續修條約 / 續約 } a Supplementary Convention.

續購書籍 to buy additional books.

續領之費 the expenses of issuing again; a fee for renewing a license.

續油 to supply oil to a light.

*hsü* 絮 refuse cotton or silk.

*hsü* / *yü* / *yeh* } 燁 brilliant; being a forbidden character, should be written 燁 (*hsü*, *yü*, or *yeh*), the last stroke of the full character being omitted.

*hsüan* 旋 to revolve; to come back to; then; forthwith.

旋轉 to revolve.

*hsüan* 旋里 to return to one's home.

旋即 at once; then; thereon.

*hsüan* 玄 black; sombre; a prohibited character, which ought to be avoided in documents. In certain combinations the last stroke is omitted, *e.g.*, 眩 *(hsüan)*; it appears, however, in 畜 *(hsü* or *ch'u)* and its compounds. Otherwise, 元 *(yüan)* is used as a substitute.

*hsüan* 衒 to display for sale; to seek praise.

衒奇院 an exhibition court.

*hsüan* 宣 to proclaim.

宣示 to proclaim; to inform by circular.

宣布 to proclaim; to make generally known.

宣詔 to proclaim an Imperial edict.

*hsüan* 懸 to be suspended; to hang down; to suspend; to hang up; unlike; different.

懸掛 to suspend; to hang up.

懸牌 to exhibit a tablet; a list.

懸望 to be in suspense; to await anxiously.

懸案不結 a pending and unfinished case.

懸殊 / 懸絕 } very unlike; quite different.

*hsüan* 選 / 選中 } to choose; to select.

*hsüeh* 靴 boots.

靴鞋 boots and shoes.

*hsüeh* 穴 a hole; a den; a cave.

*hsüeh* 雪 snow.

*hsüeh* 血 blood; money; property.

血竭 dragon's blood gum.

血本 capital in trade.

*hsün* 熏 steam; evaporation.

*hsün* 勳 merit; meritorious; patriotic distinction.

勳銜 rank conferred for merit.

勳勞 honours bestowed for good service.

*hsün* 循 to comply with; to follow.

循法 to obey the law.

循良 docile; conscientious.

循照 (= 按照) in accordance with.

循理 to follow reason; reasonable.

*hsün* 旬 a decade; one of three divisions into which a month may be divided: 上旬, the first decade, *i.e.*, the 1st to the 10th of a month; 中旬, the 11th to the 20th; 下旬, the 21st to the 30th.

*hsün* 旬日 a decade; ten days.

*hsün* 殉 (=徇) to follow; to connive at; also, to die; to be killed.

*hsün* 洵 really.

*hsün* 徇 to connive at; to follow; to be greedy of.

徇私 to follow one's private ends; selfishness; favouritism.

徇縱 to connive at.

*hsün* 詢 to inquire.

詢問 to ask particulars; to inquire.

詢商 to inquire into; to ask.

詢請 to inquire about and request (that a matter be done).

*hsün* 訓 to teach; instruction; to exhort.

*hsün* 巡 to cruise; a tidewaiter; an executive employé.

巡查 to cruise about (as a revenue cruiser); to inspect (as ports).

巡歷 to inspect (as a district, a port).

巡防 to cruise and guard; to cruise about.

巡船 [Customs] boats; cruisers.

巡捕 a constable; a policeman.

巡撫 to go about and console; a provincial Governor.

巡撫部院 a provincial Governor.

*hsün* 尋 common; usual; to seek; to investigate.

尋常 ordinary; as usual.

尋常日行事件 the current daily business.

尋常日用物件 articles of daily use.

尋查 to investigate; to search.

*hsün* 汛 a guard house; a military station; to guard.

汛官 officers in charge of a military station.

*hsün* 訊 to investigate; to examine judicially.

訊訪 to inquire into.

訊究 to investigate.

訊斷 to try, and give judgment in, a case.

訊結 to inquire into and settle [a case].

*hsün* 迅 / 迅速 } quickly; promptly.

迅行措辦 to put into operation at once.

迅賜賞給 to kindly give as soon as possible.

迅賜給領 to promptly allow to be given up.

*hsün* 勛 (=勳) merit; patriotic distinction.

勛安 [I wish you] merit and peace (a concluding phrase in letters).

*hu* 呼 to call out for; to name; to call.

呼搶 (=呼天搶地) to call to Heaven and hit the ground with the head; *i.e.*, to feel pangs of grief.

*hu* 虎 a tiger.

虎骨 tigers' bones.

虎皮 tigers' skins.

*hu* 琥 / 琥珀 } amber.

*hu* 忽 to forget; to disregard; unexpectedly; suddenly.

忽畧 careless.

忽畧不論 to carelessly refuse discussing; to take no notice of (as a matter one need not care about).

*hu* 惚 doubt; uncertainty.

*hu* 胡 why; what; how; Tartars or Turks; Central Asiatic; reckless.

胡椒 pepper.

胡麻 foreign hemp; linseed.

胡人 Central Asiatics.

*hu* 湖 a lake; the prefecture of Hu-chou, near Shanghai and Ningpo; (=湖廣) the provinces of Hupei and Hunan (= Hukwang).

湖絲 Shanghai fine raw silk (silk of Hu-chou).

湖北 *(hu-pei)* the province of Hupeh.

湖南 *(hu-nan)* the province of Hunan.

湖廣 *(hu-kuang)* the two provinces of Hupeh and Hunan.

湖口 Hukow (a port of call on the Yangtze).

*hu* 瑚 coral.

*hu* 糊 to paste; (=餬) gruel; food; subsistence.

糊口 sustenance; a livelihood.

*hu* 壺 a pot.

*hu* 狐 a fox; suspicious.

狐狸 a fox.

狐狸皮 foxes' skins.

*hu* 戶 a family; population; a door; an orifice.

戶部 the Board of Revenue.

戶部稅則 the Customs Tariff issued by the Board of Revenue (in force at the Native Custom Houses).

戶口 population.

戶冊 a register of population.

*hu* 滬 Shanghai.

滬關 the Shanghai Customs.

*hu* **互** mutually; each other.
**互相** mutual; each other.
**互撥貨物** to tranship goods from one vessel to another.
**互較** to confront with each other.
**互換** to exchange.
**互異** different from each other; to disagree.

*hu* **獲** to take in hunting; to catch (as a thief).
**獲益** to reap benefit.

*hu* **護** to protect; to assist.
**護照** a passport.
**護送** to accompany; to escort.
**護衛** an officer of the Imperial body-guard.
**護書** a sealed letter.

*hua* **化** to change; to reform.
**化消** to melt.
**化寶** a compound of silver in current use at Tientsin.
**化民** to reform the people.

*hua* **花** flowers; painted or carved ornaments; fancy [articles]; to spend.
**花梨木** rose-wood.
**花生** ground-nuts.
**花生餅** ground-nut cake.
**花板** ornamented boards.
**花洋布** printed cottons; chintzes.
**花布** fancy cotton cloth; figured calicoes.
**花素棉絨布** fancy woollens.
**花剪絨** velvets; velveteens; fustians.
**花名冊** a muster roll; a list of names.
**花色** description; denomination.
**花紅** a reward.
**花費** to spend; expenditure.
**花錢** to spend money.
**花旗** the American flag, *lit.*, the flowery banner; the United States; American.
**花旗布** American drills; domestics.
**花押** (＝**畫押**) to sign; signature.

*hua* **華** Chinese; China; flowery.
**華人** a Chinese; a native (of China).
**華商** Chinese merchants.
**華客** a Chinese passenger.
**華官** Chinese officials; native authorities.
**華式** native (Chinese) type.

*hua* **華翰** your flowery epistle; your note.
**華陽** Hwayang (a Likin station on the Yangtze).

*hua* **划** a pinnace; a scow; a small boat.
**划船** an open boat; a sampan.

*hua* **畫** to draw; to paint.
**畫一** uniform.
**畫一款式** } uniform; of a uniform pattern.
**畫一式樣** }
**畫押** to affix one's signature; to sign.
**畫定界址** to determine a site (as for a settlement).

*hua* **劃** to cut; to mark; to divide.
**劃分** to divide; to distinguish between.

*hua* **話** language.

*hua* **滑** smooth; slippery.
**滑石** soapstone.
**滑利** deceitful.

*huai* **壞** to spoil; to be lost.
**壞船** a wreck; a vessel damaged in distress.
**壞船拆毀木料** materials from vessels broken up.
**壞爛** to spoil (as fruit).

*huai* **懷** the bosom; to cherish.
**懷想** to cherish thoughts of; to think.

*huai* **淮** the river Huai.
**淮南** (*huai-nan*) *lit.*, south of the Huai river; *i.e.*, the city of Huai-an-fu, in Kiangsu.

*huan* **還** to return; to repay.
**還債** to repay a debt.
**還價** to abate in price.
**還拜** to return a visit.

*huan* **歡** to be pleased; delight.
**歡欣** to delight in; to rejoice.

*huan* **緩** to be lax; to remit (as taxes); to postpone; slowly; to delay; to exchange.
**緩駛** to slacken speed; to stop (as a ship); to slow down.

*huan* **換** to change; to substitute one for another.
**換船** to tranship; to be transhipped.
**換取現銀** to exchange for cash (as a drawback).
**換領新牌** to exchange against a new certificate.
**換發** to issue in exchange for.
**換易** to exchange.
**換約** to exchange (*i.e.*, to ratify) a Treaty.

*huan* 宦 a Government officer.

*huan* 患 a calamity; to be afflicted with.

患病 to fall sick.

患傳染症 afflicted with a contagious disease.

*huang* 荒 wild; barren; dearth; draught.

*huang* 謊 falsehood; lies; to lie.

*huang* 皇 the Emperor; Imperial.

皇帝 the Emperor.

皇上 His Majesty the Emperor.

皇上聖鑒訓示 the instructions from His Imperial Majesty's sacred glance.

皇后 the Empress.

皇太后 the Empress Dowager.

皇朝 the present dynasty.

皇清 the Imperial Ch'ing dynasty; Imperial Chinese.

*huang* 惶 fear; to fear.

*huang* 黃 yellow.

黃銅 yellow copper; brass.

黃銅器 brassware.

黃銅皮 copper sheathing; yellow metal.

黃蠟 yellow wax.

黃丹 yellow lead; massicot.

黃旗 a yellow flag; the quarantine flag; the Danish flag.

黃馬褂 the "yellow jacket" (as a distinction of merit).

黃連 (=黃蓮) a kind of dye-stuff; gentian.

黃薑 turmeric.

黃河 the Yellow River.

黃州府 the prefecture of Huang-chou.

黃岡縣 the district of Huang-kang.

黃浦河 the river Whangpoo, at Shanghai.

*huang* 磺 sulphur; brimstone.

*huang* 況 more; moreover; how much more.

*hui* 揮 to direct; to point out.

*hui* 灰 ashes.

灰色 ash colour; grey.

灰鼠 the squirrel.

灰鼠皮 squirrel skins.

*hui* 回 (or 囘) to come back; to send back; back; Mahomedan.

回歸<br>回家 } to return [home].

*hui* 回駛 to sail back.

回國 to return, or to be sent back, to one's country.

回文 an official reply.

回書 to reply to a letter.

回絨 *lit.*, Mahomedan wool; fustian.

回回 a Turk; a Mahomedan.

*hui* 迴 (or 廻) to return; to turn round.

迴避 to withdraw from office, because a senior relative holds office in the same province; to avoid a superior officer in passing him on a public road.

*hui* 悔 to regret; to repent.

*hui* 誨 to advise; to admonish; to instruct.

*hui* 會 to communicate with; together with; conjointly; to meet together; to make an agreement; an association; a club; a guild.

會晤 to confer; to meet to discuss a question.

會議 to discuss conjointly; to have an interview; to agree upon.

會商 to consult with.

會驗<br>會同驗明 } to examine conjointly.

會訊 to investigate conjointly; joint investigation.

會訊章程 the Joint Investigation Rules.

會集<br>會合 } to assemble.

會同 to meet together; conjointly.

會同四譯館 an office under the Board of Ceremonies; an office where meetings of Foreign Envoys take place (?); "the residence for Tributary Envoys."

會銜 conjointly (said of two officials issuing a joint proclamation).

會咨 to make a joint communication.

會理 to manage conjointly.

會館 a guild; a public company.

會主 the president of a public company, guild, etc.

會齊考試 a competitive examination.

*hui* 繪 to sketch; to draw; to paint.

繪圖 to draw a sketch, plan, or map.

*hui* 賄<br>賄賂 } to bribe.

賄買 to bribe; to purchase by bribing.

*hui* 滙 (or 匯) to exchange [money].

滙費 expenses of remitting money.

新關文件録



*hui* 匯兌費 expenses of exchanging and weighing (money); loss by exchange.

匯豐銀行 the Hongkong and Shanghai Banking Corporation.

*hui* 慧 intelligent.

*hui* 毀 to break; to destroy.

毀謗 to slander.

*hui* 燬 to burn.

*hui* 惠 kindness; liberality.

惠臨 to kindly descend; to honour with a visit.

惠來縣 the district of Hui-lai, near Swatow.

*hui* 穢 dirt; filth.

*hui* 彙 to sort; to classify; to collect.

彙集 to collect.

彙報 to make a collective report to.

彙解 to forward collectively; to collect and remit.

彙訂 to arrange; to classify.

*hui* 諱 to shun; to avoid.

*hun* 昏 dark; obscure.

*hun* 婚 to marry.

婚姻 bride and bridegroom; to marry.

*hun* 惛 confused; forgetful.

*hun* 混 confused; confusion; mixed; ill-assorted.

混雜 to mix together.

混行上船 to board a ship promiscuously and without permission.

*hung* 洪 great; vast.

洪恩 a great favour.

*hung* 哄 to cheat.

*hung* 鴻 great; vast; a kind of wild goose, being a symbol of swiftness.

鴻慈 immense kindness.

鴻便 an opportunity of sending a letter.

鴻啟 an envelope.

*hung* 紅 red.

紅花 safflower; fine chinaware (at Kiukiang, *lit.*, porcelain with red patterns).

紅丹 red lead; minium.

紅棗 red dates.

紅糧 millet.

紅木 red-wood.

紅茶 black tea.

紅毛 red haired; red-haired foreigners, originally the Dutch, afterwards the English, and now all foreigners. It is not considered a respectful term by foreigners.

*hung* 紅單 a port clearance. The port clearance of earlier days was a formidable-looking document of yellow paper, and ornamented with curling dragons. Its large vermilion seals obtained for it the name of *hung p'ai* (紅牌), or red permit; *Anglicè*, "grand chop" (WILLIAMS). The present name, *hung tan*, may apparently be similarly explained.

*hung* 弘 large; vast; being a forbidden character, was changed into 弘 (*hung*); later, 宏 (*hung*). In certain combinations 強 (*chiang*) is used for 彊 (*chiang*).

*hung* 轟 to blast.

轟爆之物 explosive matter or articles.

*huo* 禍 calamity; evil.

*huo* 豁 liberal; magnanimous.

豁免 kindly to exempt from [punishment]; to pardon.

*huo* 或 or; if; if perhaps; either.

或……或 either……or ……; whether……or….

或致 or even.

或曰 one may say; some say that.

*huo* 惑 to doubt; to suspect.

*huo* 活 lively; alive; movable; cheerful.

活機之木 a movable beam on board a ship; a swinging-boom.

活字 movable type.

*huo* 火 fire; fiery.

火夫 a fireman (as one who tends the engines of steamers).

火食 cooked meals; provisions; stores.

火腿 hams.

火石 flint stones.

火絨 tinder.

火油 kerosene oil.

火輪船 a steamer.

火藥 gunpowder.

火藥開花彈子 shell loaded with gunpowder.

火票 a *huo-p'iao* (a despatch of great importance, forwarded, through the Board of War, by special fast couriers).

火牌 an urgent despatch.

*huo* 伙 household furniture.

伙長 (= 夥長) a ship's mate.

*huo* 夥 a clerk in a firm; a partner; a company; many.

夥長 a chief mate; a senior partner.

*huo* 貨 goods; merchandise.

*huo* 貨物 goods; merchandise; articles of trade.
貨物清單 a ship's manifest; an invoice.
貨單 an invoice.
貨主 the owner [of goods].
貨船 a merchant vessel.
貨價 the value of goods; the price.
貨樣 samples.
貨色 description of goods.
貨財 goods and [other] property; movables.

### I.

*i* 伊 he, his; she, her, etc.
伊等 they; their.
*i* 一 (or 壹) one; (= 一切) all; throughout; to be one with; to be the same as; at the same time; together; as soon as; if once...... Before a noun and preceded by a genitive, or a clause corresponding to a genitive, may be said to represent the definite article: 末尾一關, "*the* Custom House at the end," "*the* last Custom House," not "*a* Custom House at the end," etc.
一一 one by one.
一則......二則 first......, second......
一案 with regard to (such and such) a case; *re.*
一......卽......; 一屆......卽...... } as soon as......, then......
一經 as soon as.
一經.........卽 as soon as........., then.........
一經查出 as soon as discovered; when caught (as in an illegal act).
一家 the whole family.
一體, 一切, 一律, 一併, 一概, 一同, 一齊, 一節, 一總 } all; equally; uniformly; all at once; often merely denoting plurality of nouns preceding.
一番 once; in one instance.
一項 the item of.
一開 if once opened; if once we commence [acting like this].
一覽而知 to see and notice a matter at a glance; synoptical.

*i* 一面 at the same time.
一面......一面......on the one hand,......on the other, ......; partly......, partly......
一力 with the whole strength; by one's own exertion.
一心 in the same spirit; with one heart; with the whole heart.
一樣 of the same kind; the same; not different.
一名 another name is; also called.
一半爲斷 to divide into two halves.
一帶 in the neighbourhood of; all along.
一壇 one altar; one spread (as of sacrifices to be offered).
一直 straight.
一共 all; the whole of; total.
一時 at the same time; sometimes; at one time; inadvertently.
一等 (= 頭等) of the first class.
一定 certainly; at all events; positively; fixed; not changeable.
一定不易 fixed; not changeable.
一次 once.
一次之課 a tax paid once for all; a single charge (compounding for several charges, as the transit duty).
一味 of the same taste; in the same style.
*i* 宜 must; suitable; to suit; to make fit; that which is proper; that which must necessarily be done in connexion with; business; affair.
宜廣開來路 to encourage (or develop) the import trade.
宜昌關 the Ichang Customs.
*i* 誼 a disinterested friend; goodness.
*i* 倚 to depend on; to lean against.
倚畀 an important trust.
倚靠 to depend on; to rely on.
*i* 椅 a chair.
*i* 意 to think; intention; meaning; purpose.
意思 meaning; thought; intention.
意外 unexpected; unforeseen.
意外之虞 unexpected dangers.
意見 one's opinion.
意見不同 to be of a different opinion.
意有不洽 to disagree; not to fall in with one's ideas; to have fault to find with.
意圖 to intend; to plan.
意薩貝勒寶星 the Royal Order of Isabel the Catholic.

i 憶 to think; to reflect.

i 薏 a kind of lotus seed.

薏仁米 pearl barley.

i 醫 to cure; a physician.

醫生 a doctor.

醫治 medical attendance; to cure.

醫藥 medicines.

醫院 a hospital.

i 衣 clothes.

衣服 }
衣物 } clothing.

衣箱 boxes containing clothes; a clothes chest.

i 依 to rely on; as; according to; to accede to.

依議 "let it be as it was recommended" (in Imperial edicts).

依允 to consent to; to comply with.

依律 according to law.

依限 within a prescribed limit of time.

依舊 as before.

i 亦 also.

亦可 will also do; may also.

i 夷 barbarian; foreign. By Article LI of the British Treaty of Tientsin (1858) it was agreed that this character should not be applied, in Chinese official documents, to the British Government or to British subjects; it is therefore no longer used in international correspondence.

i 胰 fat over the stomach; soap.

胰子 soap.

i 怡 harmonious; to please; pleasure.

怡養 healthy; well nourished.

i 貽 to bring on; to cause; to leave; to bequeath; to involve in; to cease to.

貽悞 to cause an error or a wrong impression; to mislead.

i 移 to forward to; to change; a despatch; to write officially.

移縣 to send to the magistrate (for trial or punishment).

移送 to forward.

移交 to send to.

移換 to change.

移遷 to remove.

移泊 to shift anchorage; to remove from one berth to another.

i 移去 to remove.

移動 to move; to be carried away.

移離 to move away.

移咨 to inform in a despatch.

移飭 to instruct in a despatch.

i 頤 the chin; the 27th diagram, denoting "to feed;" hence, a man so old that he has to be fed.

i 疑 to suppose; to suspect; to be in doubt about.

疑惑 to doubt; to suspect.

疑難事件 matters doubtful and difficult to decide upon.

i 擬 to propose; to design; to decide (as in a criminal case).

擬辦 to give judgment; to sentence; to propose managing.

擬辦試行 about to put into operation provisionally.

擬度 to estimate.

擬議 to decide; decision.

擬定 to decide.

擬定辦法 to propose a fixed mode of procedure.

i 遺 to leave; to bequeath (as when dying); to lose.

遺失 to lose; loss.

遺悞 to make a mistake.

遺誥 }
遺命 } the last words of a dying person; the dying commands.

遺書 a will.

i 義 meaning; principle; righteous; justice.

義國 (=意大利 *i-ta-li*) Italy; Italian.

i 儀 rite; ceremony; rule; pattern.

i 蟻 an ant; as a term of modesty, "I, the petitioner."

蟻等 "we, the petitioners."

i 議 to deliberate; to discuss; to decide; it is agreed that; to deliberate in council; to recommend to the Emperor; (=義 or 文義) the meaning of a passage.

議明 to agree upon.

議定 to decide.

議酬 to award a gratuity; to pay for.

議事廳 an office for the discussion of public matters; a Chancellor's office; a ministry.

議事廳事務大臣 the Chancellor of the [German] Empire; the *Bundeskanzler*.

23

*i* 以

1. as a verb: to use; to have; to possess.

2. using; with; and therefore denoting the instrumental or ablative case of a noun.

以官濟私 to further one's private ends by means of official resources.

以假攙眞 to mix up truth with falsehood; to adulterate.

以畫一辦理 to treat a matter in a uniform manner.

以概論 to take the broad view of a matter.

以內 inside of; within; less than. Similarly, *i wai* (以外), outside; more than; *i ch'ien* (以前), before; *i hou* (以後), after; *i shang* (以上), above; *i hsia* (以下), below; *i pei* (以北), to the north of, etc.

以東 to the east of......; *e.g.*, 大通以東, to the east of Tat'ung.

以代 to serve for something else; in lieu of.

3. it is sometimes employed, like *chiang* (將), in marking the object of a verb, when the verb follows, as in the classical example *i t'ien-hsia yü jên* (以天下與人), "to give the empire to man;" but in the business style such accusatives more frequently follow the verb, *e.g.*, *chiao i han-shu* (教以漢書), "to teach Chinese literature;" *chia i hsing-ho* (加以刑嚇), "to inflict torture." It most frequently occurs in connexion with a second object, as in 以[1]多[2]報[3]少[4] [3]*pao*, to declare, [1]*i* [2]*to*, much, or a large quantity, as [4]*shao*, little, or a small quantity, "to make a false declaration of quantity;" especially so in the phrase *i*......*wei*......(以......爲......), to consider......as......, "to treat......as," etc.; *e.g.*, *i ch'i wei ch'ieh* (以妻爲妾), "to treat a wife as a concubine."

以遠報近 to report far as near; to make a false declaration as to the number of Likin stations passed by certain goods.

以細報粗 to declare a superior as an inferior quality; to make a false declaration of quality.

以貴價報賤價 to declare a higher as a lower value; to make a false declaration of value.

以......爲......to consider......as......

以......爲是 to consider (a matter) to be so; to consider as correct.

以......爲度 to consider......as a limit.

以......爲準 to take......as a standard.

以此爲例 this is to be regarded as the rule.

以國事爲重 to keep Government matters in due regard.

以四個月爲期 to consider four months as a limit; *i.e.*, within four months.

*i*

以不應納子稅爲詞 to write (or maintain) that transit dues are not payable.

以價値爲率 to declare the value as the principle to go by.

以壹百分爲算 to divide into 100 parts or shares.

4. with 爲 forms the verb 以爲, to consider; in which sense it is also employed above.

以爲然 to consider that it be so; to accede to a request.

以爲公當 to consider as fair.

以(=以爲)全始終之美 to consider the advantages from beginning to end.

5. by reason of; because of; because. *Cf.* the phrases *shih-i* (是以), therefore; *ho-i* (何以), by what? wherefore? why? *so-i* (所以), by which; therefore; *wu-i* (無以), to have nothing by which; there is no reason for.

6. that; to the effect that; especially after terms involving a communication like *ch'êng* (稱), to state, or *han* (函), a letter: "to the effect that."

7. 以 (=自 *tzŭ*) from.

以此口運至彼口 to move from one port to another.

以是日起 to date from this, or that, day.

8. 以 gives a verb the force of the second supine (*facile dictu*) after terms meaning "difficult," "easy," "capable," or "sufficient," such as *nan* (難), *i* (易), *k'an* (堪), *tsu* (足), etc., *e.g.*, *tsu i ai* (足以礙), "sufficient or capable to hinder;" *nan i ch'êng-kung* (難以成功), "difficult to bring about." In all these cases *yü* (於) may take the place of *i* (以). We may add here phrases like 自開海以來, "since the sea, or navigation, was opened," though here, as in most other cases, the real force of the Chinese will scarcely admit of comparison with any foreign grammatical term.

9. 以及 and; or.

10. In order to; "and hereby." In this sense it often occurs in a sort of stereotyped phrase the pattern of which is contained in the 16 maxims forming the Emperor K'ANG-HSI's Sacred Edict, *e.g.*, 重農桑以足衣食, "give importance to agriculture and the mulberry, *and so* provide enough food and raiment" (BRIDGMAN); or "*in order to* provide enough food and raiment." A similar phrase is often added to longer periods as a mere stylistic ornament, to round off the sentence as it were; it is therefore often suppressed in the English version, though some means will usually be found to express its sense without placing the natural run of the English version under any constraint, as has been well shown in Sir THOMAS WADE's translations. The following examples may occur in documents:—

以安善良 in order to tranquillise good subjects.

以昭誠衷 in order to show sincere feelings; out of sincere sympathy.

以昭周備 for the sake of greater clearness and completeness.

以昭劃一 for the sake of uniformity.

以昭核實 in order to show the fact to be true; in order to furnish a correct statement (as of value); for the sake of accuracy.

以昭激勸 for the sake of encouragement.

以昭信實 in order to manifest authenticity; "in witness thereof."

以昭信守 in order to exhibit the guard of trust; "in witness thereof."

以昭公允 }
以昭平允 } in order to show justice; for the sake of justice; for the sake of fairness.

以期相安 so that mutual peace may be hoped for.

以期曉然 in order that it may be thus known.

以期得實 in order to arrive at the truth.

以期妥善 in order that matters may be properly managed.

以致錯漏 so as to result in an erroneous evasion (as of duty).

以靖地方 in order to tranquillise the place.

以清界限 in order to have a clearly defined limit.

以清欠款 in order to clear debts.

以清款項 in order to clear (settle account concerning these) items; in order to close accounts.

以儆效尤 in order to warn against bad examples.

以救蟻命 in order to save poor peoples' lives.

以救微生 in order to save an unimportant life.

以專責成 in order to impose responsibility.

以全蟻命 in order to render complete a poor man's life; in order to restore a poor man to life.

以重稅課 in order to show due respect to revenue interests.

以防弊混 in order to guard against irregularities.

以符舊制 in order to agree with the old rule.

以符原案 in accordance with the original arrangement.

以息浮議 in order to stop idle discussions.

以弭後患 in order to forestall calamities.

以備稽查 in order to provide for examination; for future identification (said of documents containing particulars as to goods, and filed in archives); for future reference.

以便查明 in order to facilitate examination.

以便照辦 in order to act accordingly.

以便征稅 in order to levy the duty (properly).

以便商民 }
以便商旅 } in order to accommodate merchants.

以便商艱 in order to be of help in commercial difficulties.

以便輸餉 in order to facilitate the payment of duties.

以憑徵稅 in order to furnish the documentary proof for charging duty.

以憑核辦 in order to have proof for acting.

以憑查驗 in order to furnish vouchers for the examination [of goods]; on the ground of which examination may be made.

以憑轉復 in order to have a basis for making a reply.

以示求救 in order to show that rescue is required; to make signals of distress.

以示區別 in order to show the distinction.

以示限制 in order to draw a limit; as a restrictive measure.

以示優獎 in order to show, or mark, special merit.

以順商情 in order to meet commercial requirements.

以肅鹺政 in order to inspire respect for the Salt Gabel.

以杜假冒 in order to prevent fraud.

以杜勾串 in order to prevent fraudulent combinations.

以杜弊端 in order to restrict malpractices.

以杜偏累 in order to prevent partiality.

以杜隱漏 in order to prevent evading (as payment of duties).

以資勸戒 in order to warn; in order to caution (as a warning).

以資稽查 for examination; for inspection.

以資鼓勵 for the sake of encouragement.

以資覽觀 in order to avail myself of the spectacle.

以完此案 in order to close this case.

以為卹商 in order to facilitate trade.

i 以免周章 in order to avoid useless trouble.

以免重輸 in order to avoid [too] heavy payment; in order to avoid over-taxation.

以免舛悞 in order to avoid mistakes.

以免紛歧 in order to avoid divergency (inconsistency in acting).

以免紛更 in order to avoid perplexing changes.

以免饒舌 in order to avoid altercation.

以免曠悞 in order to avoid delay.

以免疎虞 in order to avoid danger.

以免參差 in order to avoid discrepancy or want of uniformity.

以免貽誤 in order to avoid mistakes.

以免推諉 in order to avoid the shifting of responsibility.

---

以冀裕課恤商 in order that revenue and commercial interests may be benefited.

以期無碍稅餉 in order that no difficulties may arise to the revenue.

以防觸礁之患 in order to guard against collisions.

以補應完之釐 in order to make up for the likin taxes due.

以示鐙塔所在 in order to indicate the position of the light.

以示沉船所在 in order to indicate the position of the wreck.

以示儆 in order to show warning; "as a warning."

以杜避重就輕之弊 to prevent shirking the heavy and taking to the light, *i.e.*, substituting the easy for the onerous.

---

以免觸沙之患 in order to avoid grounding on the shoal.

以免辦理兩歧 to avoid divergency (inconsistency) of action.

以免參差爭論 in order to prevent misunderstanding.

---

以防 in order to guard against.

以冀 in order to hope; to thereby hope.

以期 (=以望) so that it may be hoped; so as not to interfere with.

以致 so that; so as to; so as to result in, or lead to.

以免 in order to avoid; so as not to; the opposite of i *pien* (以便), in order to.

i 以憑 by means of which supported; on the ground of which; provided with which.

以示 in order to make known that.

以資........in order to afford.........; by means of which one may......

以便 in order to; so that.

---

i 已 a sign of the past; it precedes the verb, and, like *ching* (經), is often separated from it by other parts of the sentence; having (the opposite of 未 *(wei)*, not having).

已經 a sign of the past; "having already;" already.

已滿 filled up; already full; loaded full (as a ship); having expired (as a limit of time).

已極 having reached the extreme; extremely; to the utmost.

已開 having been opened; opened; open (as the Treaty ports).

已用 having been used; old; second-hand.

已完稅 having paid duty; duty paid.

已完正稅 to have paid, or having paid, full duty.

已完正稅憑單 a certificate (proof) showing that full duty has been paid; a duty proof.

已下船 having been shipped.

已離原泊方向 to have left the original anchorage (as a ship).

已有地方官給領船照 the local authorities *having* issued a ship's certificate.

已在內地買貨 to have bought goods in the interior.

已一年 after the lapse of a year.

已兩載之久 after the lapse of two years.

已逾兩年 having exceeded [the time] of two years.

已逾十有餘年之久 more than 10 years since.

已甚 very excessive.

i 矣 a final particle, denoting the close of a sentence.

i 邑 a town; a city.

i 益 advantages or concessions (granted to certain nations in Treaties); to add; to increase.

益處 advantage.

益算 to add.

益矢 to increase in speed; with increased energy.

益臻 to multiply and accumulate.

*i* 益於實濟 to be conducive to real advantage; to be of benefit to.

益加 to increase.

*i* 縊 to strangle; to hang oneself.

*i* 譯 to translate; to interpret; an interpreter; an official interpreter.

譯名 a name translated or transliterated.

譯漢 to translate into Chinese.

*i* 驛 post; postal; a courier.

*i* 易 easy; change; to exchange.

易知 to easily understand; to easily learn.

易剖別 }
易爲分別 } easy to distinguish.

易於 (or 易以) easy to; to find no difficulty in......

易於相符 easy to agree; handy for calculation.

易於核算 easy to calculate.

易於傷損之貨 damageable goods.

易破碎 easy to break; breakable.

易換 to exchange (as a bank note against cash).

*i* 異 different from; the opposite of *t'ung* (同), the same; strange; unusual.

異邦 a foreign country.

異違 to oppose.

異鄉 to be separated from one's home.

異詞 different language; dissent; difference of opinion.

異議 a different arrangement.

*i* 藝 skill; ability in working; profession.

*i* 役 a low employé; a servant; an officer.

*i* 疫 an epidemic; a plague.

*i* 毅 stern; resolute.

*i* 抑 else; if; or; or whether; to repress.

抑或 or else; or.

抑制 to restrain; restraint.

*i* 逸 to set free; to abscond; idle.

*i* 詣 to go to.

詣關 to go to the Custom House.

## J.

*jan* 然 yet; however.

然否 whether or not so.

然後 thereafter; then.

*jan* 染 to dye; to infect (as with a disease).

染病 to communicate a disease to another.

*jang* 嚷 altercation.

嚷鬧 to quarrel.

*jang* 攘 to throw away; to reject.

*jang* 讓 complaisant; to invite.

*jao* 繞 (or 遶) to wind round; to make a *détour.*

繞避 to avoid (as a rock in sailing).

繞越 to evade the law.

繞途 }
繞路 } to make a *détour;* to travel on a route not being the direct one.

*jao* 饒 to indulge; to be liberal; an overplus.

饒舌 to indulge one's tongue; to wrangle; to dispute.

*jao* 擾 to trouble; to infest.

擾累 to involve in trouble; to interfere with.

*jê* 惹 to provoke.

*jê* 熱 hot.

*jên* 忍 to endure; to bear.

*jên* 認 to recognise; to confess.

認付 to be responsible for (payment); to have to submit to.

認明 to acknowledge.

認爲 to recognise as; to accept as.

認繳 to bind oneself in paying (as a tax farmer pays a fixed sum to his Government).

認理 to be responsible for.

認保無訛 to professedly guarantee that there is no mistake; *i.e.*, to be responsible for correctness.

認餉接辦 to bind oneself to remit a certain sum out of taxes collected; to take over the collection of a tax, on the farming system; to guarantee the revenue.

認粗爲細 to recognise coarse as fine.

認眞 careful; diligently; to acknowledge.

*jên* 壬 an astronomical character; north.

壬午 *(jên wu)* the 19th year of a cycle; *e.g.*, the year 1882.

*jên* 任 to bear; to sustain; it is incumbent on; it is a duty to; an incumbent; a post; an office; relying on.

任內 belonging to one's office; during the time of one's holding an office.

任便 freely; at liberty; to be at liberty to; at one's own discretion.

*jên* 任便隨時 at one's own discretion and at any time.

任意 as one thinks fit; arbitrarily.

任聽 to be at liberty to.

任從英商 at the pleasure of British merchants.

任憑 allowed to depend on; it is in the free will of.

*jên* 人 a man.

人人 everybody; all men.

人客 passengers; a visitor.

人數 a number of men.

人所共知 it is known to everybody; the public are aware of it.

人口 individuals.

人丁 a man; a male adult.

人參 ginseng.

*jên* 仁 humane; humanity; a kernel; seed.

仁憲 (in petitions, an honorary title given to officials) your kindness.

*jên* 芢 name of a plant.

芢米 a kind of rice; pearl barley (=薏仁米 *i-jên-mi*).

*jêng* 仍 still; again; yet; then (=卽 *chi*).

仍舊 as of old; as before.

仍照舊章 still according to the old rule.

仍前 as heretofore.

仍復 yet again; again.

*jêng* 擲. See *chih*.

*jih* 日 the sun; a day; a date; in the daytime (as opposed to night-time).

日日 every day; daily.

日間 during the daytime.

日後 afterwards; in the course of time.

日久 a long time; after a long time.

日形 fluctuations.

日行事宜 the daily business.

日行通用 in daily and general use.

日用 the daily needs.

日用常事 services attending the necessities of daily life.

日甚一日 more intense from day to day; growing worse and worse.

日記簿 a log-book.

日期 fixed days; terms; a limit; a period of time.

日增 to increase (day by day).

*jih* 日旺 to prosper (as trade).

日落 (or 日入) the sun setting; sunset.

日落以後 after sunset.

日出 the sun rising; sunrise.

日出以前 before sunrise.

日斯巴尼亞國 } (*jih-ssŭ-pa-ni-a*, España) Spain; Spanish.
日國 }

日本國 (*jih-pên-kuo*) Japan; Japanese.

日本參 Japanese ginseng.

日本蠟 Japan wax.

*jo* 若 if; as.

若干 an indefinite amount; the amount of; so and so much; so many.

*jo* 弱 weak.

*jou* 柔 soft; yielding.

柔毛 sheeps' wool.

*jou* 肉 meat; fleshy.

肉菓荳蔲 nutmegs.

肉翅 clarified sharks' fins.

肉桂 cinnamon.

*ju* 汝 you; your.

汝等 you (plural).

*ju* 如 if; as; like.

如何 how? in what manner? the manner in which.

如何征稅 the manner in which duties are levied; the mode of levying duties.

如是 } like this; thus.
如此 }

如今 now.

如遇 if there be; if.

如果 if; in the case of.

如故 as of old; as formerly.

如約 as by Treaty bound; as agreed to.

如所擬 as suggested.

如所稟辦理 to act as has been reported.

*ju* 儒 a scholar; literati.

*ju* 辱 to disgrace; to insult.

辱承 *lit.*, I have disgraced you in receiving; *i.e.*, you have honoured me without my deserving.

辱承見召 I have been honoured with an invitation.

*ju* 褥 a mattress; bedding.

*ju* 入 to enter; to receive; the debit side of an account.

入華 to come, or to be sent, to China.

入選 to receive an appointment.

入款 receipts; debit; Dr.

入內地 to enter the interior; transit inwards.

入祀 to sacrifice before an ancestral tablet.

入官 to enter the official exchequer; to be confiscated.

入承大統 to take charge of the empire.

入出數目 "figures showing the debit and credit," *i.e.*, a properly balanced account; an account.

*ju* 乳 milk; to suck; nipple-shaped.

乳香 gum olibanum; frankincense.

*juan* 軟 (or 輭) soft; yielding.

*jui* 瑞 a good omen.

瑞嗔國 (*jui-tien-kuo*)
瑞敦國 (*jui-tun-kuo*)
瑞國 (*jui-kuo*)
} Sweden; Swedish.

*jun* 閏 intercalary.

閏十月 the tenth intercalary month.

*jun* 潤 to moisten; moist; to benefit.

*jung* 茸 soft; downy; deer horns.

*jung* 榮 honour; glory.

榮歸 to return with glory; *i.e.*, to retire from public life.

*jung* 絨 silk floss; woollen.

絨毛 wool.

絨毛布 woollen piece goods.

絨線 woollen yarn.

絨棉布 woollen and cotton mixtures.

*jung* 容 to endure; to tolerate.

*jung* 鎔 to fuse metals.

鎔化
鎔銷
} to melt.

鎔兌 to melt and weigh; to ascertain the touch (of silver).

*jung* 冗 affairs; duties; scattered.

冗雜 confused; scattered.

冗費 extra expenditure.

## K.

*k'a* 卡 a barrier. See *ch'ia*.

*kai* 該 the said; the respective; that; the; to owe.

該管之官 the authorities to whom one is amenable.

該欠 to owe.

該當 ought to; should.

*kai* 賅 to give; uncommon; rare.

賅載 to be given; to be contained in (as in a book or in a document); written down.

賅備 to be contained in; to be provided for.

*kai* 改
改變
} to alter.

改為 to alter into (as one reading of a document to another).

改註底簿 to change an entry in the original books.

改包
改裝
} to repack (as goods for re-exportation).

改泊 to shift berth (as a vessel in harbour).

改運別口售賣 to change the destination [of goods] to another port of sale.

改正 to correct (as a mistake in a document).

*k'ai* 葢 (蓋 or 盖) to build; a cover (as the cover of a boat); a roof; to roof; bedding; to over-top; to affix (as a seal); for; because of.

葢戳 to affix a seal; to stamp.

葢印加封 to seal a document and enclose it in an envelope.

葢用關防 to affix one's official seal.

葢有……印信 to contain the seal of……

葢因 the reason, generally, is that……

*kai* 概 all; equally; then.

概行免稅 all must be exempted from duty.

*k'ai* 開 to open (a book, a port, etc.); introducing the tenor of a document quoted: to state; stating; "to the effect that."

開關 to open the Custom House.

開行 to open a firm.

開舖 to open a shop.

開市 to open the market.

開印 to re-open an office (as after holidays).

開艙 to open hatches; to break bulk.

開艙准單 a permit to break bulk.

開驗 to open (packages) for examination.

開驗復綑 to open (packages) for examination and close again.

開張 to open business; to keep an account.

開船廠 to open a dock; to have a dock.

開采煤鑛 to work coal and iron mines.

*k'ai* 開各商覬覦之漸 to stimulate the appetite (for illegal privileges) amongst merchants; *lit.*, to open the gradual development (*ch'ien* 漸) of merchants' [illegal] desires.

開明 to state; to enumerate; to write out clearly.

開載 to state; to enter (as in a document).

開錄 to record.

開具 to state.

開單 to make out a document, bill, memorandum, etc.

開列 to enumerate; to state (as in a list).

開列清單 to enter in a list; to make a list of.

開列於左 to mention hereafter; enumerated below.

開具清單 to draw up an official statement of particulars.

開辦 to put into operation.

開船 the departure of a ship; the lifting of anchors; to start on a sea journey.

開行 to start on a journey; to lift anchors.

開行最速 to start in a great hurry (as a ship).

開出 to proceed to (as a ship on having lifted anchors); also, to state in particular.

開駛 to proceed on a journey (as a ship).

開價 to declare the value (of an article).

開設 to establish; to be established.

開缺 to open a vacancy; to quit one's post.

開放 to release (*e.g.*, goods detained).

開放大砲 to fire off cannon.

開釋 to release.

開來 to come from (as a ship).

開復 to recover; to restore.

開化 K'ai-hua-fu (in the province of Yünnan).

開平 K'ai-p'ing (a coal-producing place in Chihli).

*kan* 乾 dry; dried.

乾魚 dried fish; stock-fish.

乾花 dried flowers.

*kan* 幹 skilful; to attend to business; affairs.

幹事 to manage an affair.

幹阿達 (*kan-a-ta*) Canada.

*kan* 干 to concern; concerning; to offend against.

干涉 to be connected with.

干預 to meddle with.

干例 to offend against the law.

*kan* 干例禁 to offend against what is prohibited by law.

干犯 to offend against.

干咎 to be guilty; to become guilty of.

*kan* 杆 a stick; a post; a flagstaff.

*kan* 肝 the liver; anger; irritation.

*kan* 桿 a pole; a post; a flagstaff.

*kan* 趕 to hasten; to hurry; to pursue.

趕緊 to pursue closely; as quickly as possible.

*kan* 竿 sticks.

*kan* 甘 sweet; agreeable; willing.

甘心 voluntarily.

甘願 free will; voluntarily.

甘結 a bond of good faith; a voluntary agreement.

甘草 liquorice.

*kan* 柑 the mandarin orange.

柑皮 orange peel.

*kan* 敢 to dare; can; also in the interrogative, and hence negative, sense, can I? should I? *i.e.*, I cannot, I dare not (= 豈敢, how can I? I dare not).

敢不敬遵 how could I dare not to respectfully obey?

*kan* 橄 the Chinese olive.

橄欖 olives (Chinese).

*kan* 感 to be grateful.

感激 to thank; grateful.

感荷 to be obliged.

感恩 to feel obliged.

感鴻恩 to be greatly obliged.

*k'an* 看 to see; to look; to inspect.

看守 to watch (a ship); a watcher; a tidewaiter.

*k'an* 堪 to be able.

堪以 to be fit for.

堪克 adequate to; competent to.

堪虞 fraught with danger.

*k'an* 勘 to inspect.

勘度 to measure; to survey (as land for a site to build upon).

勘量 to survey (as a ship).

*k'an* 刊 to cut; to cut blocks for printing; to engrave; to print.

刊刻 to cut blocks for printing; to print.

刊刻成本 } to print (on blocks) in pamphlet or book form.
刊本 }

*kang* 杠 (also written 扛) a yard on a mast; a pole.

*kang* 槓 a trunk; a box; a carrying-pole.

*kang* 剛 hard; firm.

剛石 granite.

*kang* 綱 to control.

*kang* 鋼 steel.

*k'ang* 康 the feeling of vigour; ease; repose.

康慶 healthy-minded and joyful.

康頤 enjoying robust health in old age.

康强 robust; strong; vigorous.

康熙 the Emperor K'ANG HSI.

*k'ang* 抗 } to oppose; to resist.
抗敵 }

抗價 to keep up the price.

*kao* 高 high; lofty.

高下 high and low; the rate of; higher or lower; differently adjusted.

高估 a high valuation; to assess at a high value.

高升 to be promoted to a high post.

高掛 to suspend high up.

高粱 millet.

高麗 *(kao-li)* Corea; Corean.

高麗參 Corean ginseng.

*kao* 稿 the draft of a document; an original copy.

*kao* 膏 fat; greasy; a preparation of greasy appearance, like ointment, etc.; prepared opium.

膏釐 the likin tax on prepared opium; the boiling tax; the *kao-li* tax.

膏粱 rich; wealthy; well off.

*kao* 羔 a lamb; standing for 膏 *(kao)*, fat, greasy, etc.

*kao* 告 to inform; to tell; to announce; to ask for; to accuse.

告假 to ask for leave of absence; leave.

告病 to report oneself sick; to ask for sick leave.

告白 a notice; a placard.

告知 to inform.

告狀 an indictment; to prosecute; to accuse.

告示 a public notice; a proclamation.

告罪 to apologise.

*kao* 誥 to enjoin upon; to proclaim.

*k'ao* 靠 to lean against; by the side of; to rely on.

*k'ao* 考 to examine; aged; deceased parents.

考試 to examine; to take one's degree.

考驗 to examine (as a candidate).

考選局 a board of examination.

考究 to examine; to investigate.

*k'ao* 栲 the mangrove tree.

栲皮 mangrove bark.

*kei* 給. See *chi*.

*kên* 根 classifier of needles, muskets, wood beams, etc.; the root; thoroughly.

根本 root; origin.

根末 beginning and end; the whole of.

根究 to investigate thoroughly.

*k'ên* 肯 willing; to wish.

*k'ên* 懇 to beg; truly; earnest.

懇請 }
懇求 } to beg; to petition; to beseech; to entreat.
懇祈 }

懇恩 to pray for favour.

*kêng* 更 a watch (of the night = two hours); to alter; still more; moreover; again.

更改 }
更變 } to change.
更換 }

更正 to correct.

更張 to overrule; to change existing ways.

更加 to make alterations and additions.

更訂 to alter; to amend (as rules).

更定條約 an amended or revised Treaty.

更不 still less; much less.

*kêng* 梗 straight.

*kêng* 耕 to plough; to till.

*k'êng* 坑 a pit.

坑砂 manure-cake; poudrette.

*ko* 各 each; every; all; sign of the plural.

各款 all kinds; the various kinds.

各項 all kinds; all descriptions.

各樣 all sorts.

各樣傘 all sorts of umbrellas.

各種 of all kinds; of every class.

各色 of all kinds; of all descriptions.

*ko* 各名 of all denominations.

各國 foreign countries; the Treaty Powers.

各國大臣 the Treaty Power Ministers.

各國領事官 the Treaty Power Consuls.

各路 at all places; in all directions.

各省 the provinces.

各口 the ports; the Treaty ports.

各口分章 local rules (at the various ports).

各行 the shops (of a place); the firms.

各商 the merchants; all the merchants.

各稅 duties (of various classes).

各貨 *the* goods.

各事人等 individuals connected with the several functions of; those who are charged with the duties of.

各等因 *i.q.*, 等因 *(têng yin)*; "such arguments;" "etc.," after the enumeration of a number of arguments.

各該關 all the said Custom Houses.

各適其用者 each accords with (or is adapted to) the use (to which it is put).

各羅斯 *(ko-lo-ssŭ)* a gross.

*ko* 格 a rule.

格式 a pattern.

格外 outside the rule; extraordinary.

格外施恩 to grant a special favour.

*ko* 閣 an upper room; a council chamber.

閣下 Sir; you (as a term of respect in letters, etc.).

*ko* 擱 to obstruct; to put down at a place.

擱淺 to run ashore; to strand.

*ko* 哥 an elder brother.

*ko* 歌 to sing; to praise.

*ko* 割 to cut off; to injure; to ruin.

割斷 to cut asunder.

*ko* 隔 to divide off; to occupy the middle between two localities.

*ko* 噶拉 *(ko-la)* the city of Galatz.

*ko* 轇 chariots and spears; mixed; confused.

*ko* 革 to deprive of rank and office; to dismiss from office.

革職 to degrade an official.

革退 to dismiss from office.

革換 to remove from office; to suspend.

*ko* 個 (箇 or 个) a piece (a general classifier).

*k'o* 可 can; may; will do.

*k'o* 可也 "this will do" (a final phrase which need not be translated).

可以 can; may.

可行 may be done; allowable.

可惡 detestable; hateful.

可惜 it is a pity; to be regretted.

可見 one may see; it is evident that.

可否 whether or not it is possible to.

可不必 need not be......; ......may be dispensed with.

可無慮 one need not fear this.

可期漸旺 one may hope for a gradual rise.

*k'o* 科 to calculate from; practice; profession; medical art; the examination for the two highest degrees; series; rank.

科征 to tax at a certain rate; to assess a tax; to fix the rate of a tax; taxation.

科稅 extra duty; additional duty; to exact a tax.

科試 the triennial examination.

*k'o* 課 taxes; revenue; a task; a job; to examine; to counsel.

課稅 duties; charges on goods.

課館 a revenue office.

*k'o* 錁 a silver ingot; bullion.

*k'o* 刻 to engrave; the eighth part of a Chinese hour, or 15 minutes; a set time.

刻明 to engrave legibly.

刻下 at present.

刻日 a fixed day.

*k'o* 殼 shell; skin; husk.

*k'o* 溘 (used for 䆟 *k'o*) to comply with; to die.

溘逝 to depart for a better life; to die (said of the death of high officials).

*k'o* 磕 to knock.

磕頭 to knock the head (on the floor); to perform the *k'o-t'ou*.

*k'o* 克 able to; competent to; to subdue.

克享 to be able to enjoy life; to enjoy good health.

克堪 adequate to; competent to.

*k'o* 剋 to overcome; to injure; to kill.

*k'o* 恪守 to carefully maintain (as rules and regulations).

恪遵 to respectfully obey; to recognise as binding.

*k'o* 客 a guest; a stranger; a travelling merchant; a passenger.

客商 a merchant; a commercial traveller.

*k'o* 客家 a customer.
客貨 merchandise.
客寓 travellers' lodgings; (on board ship) cabins.

*k'o* 闊 broad; breadth.

*k'o* 廓 wide; spacious.
廓清 spacious and clear.

*kou* 勾 to be connected with; a hook.
勾通 } in connexion with; in collusion with.
勾串 }
勾引 to entice.

*kou* 抅 to hook; to adhere to; to grasp.

*kou* 鈎 a hook; a spear.

*kou* 搆 to pull; to scheme; to plot.

*kou* 購 } to buy.
購買 }
購用 to buy for one's own use.
購運 to buy and forward.

*kou* 彀 enough.

*k'ou* 口 the mouth; by word of mouth; the mouth of a river, creek, street, road, etc.; a port; a classifier of persons, cannon balls, bags, coffins, etc.
口供 depositions; oral statements; testimony.
口詞 a verbal communication.
口奏 a verbal statement to the Emperor.
口難分剖 difficult to explain.
口舌 altercation.
口岸 a port; ports.
口內口外 in port and outside a port.
口外引費 pilotage fees; pilotage charges.

*k'ou* 叩 to knock; to pray for.
叩頭 to knock the head (on the floor); to perform the *k'o-t'ou.*
叩乞 to implore; to beg.
叩恩豁免 to ask to be magnanimously exempted from punishment.

*k'ou* 扣 to knock off; to discount; a classifier of documents; standing for 釦, a button.
扣算 }
扣計 } to deduct.
扣除 }
扣除核算 to deduct in calculating (as the number of days spent in repair in calculating the term of tonnage dues certificates).
扣布 *T*-cloths.

*k'ou* 釦 a button.

*k'ou* 寇 } robbers; banditti.
寇賊 }

*k'ou* 蔻 cardamom seeds.

*ku* 古 old; ancient.
古今 ancient and modern; of all periods.
古年 in ancient years.
古窰 old porcelain.
古董 } curiosities; antiques.
古玩 }
古銅器 old copperware.
古巴 *(ku-pa)* Cuba.

*ku* 估 value; to value.
估價 value; to estimate value.
估徵 to charge duty *ad valorem.*

*ku* 故 a cause; a reason; causing; to cause; therefore; on purpose; old.
故意 on purpose.
故犯 to offend wilfully.
故違 to wilfully offend against the law.
故蹈前轍 to purposely follow in the old track; to resume one's former malpractices.

*ku* 沽 to buy; to sell.

*ku* 辜 fault; crime.
辜負 to be ungrateful for.

*ku* 固 assuredly; decidedly; firmly; (=本來) originally; in itself.
固屬堪虞 to be in itself fraught with danger; to constitute a danger in itself (not to speak of other dangers).

*ku* 姑 to tolerate; lenient; a girl.
姑寬 to show indulgence.
姑息 indulgent.

*ku* 孤 an orphan; single; solitary.
孤寡婦女 orphans and widows.

*ku* 股 the thigh of a leg; a share in a concern; a lot.
股肱 the legs and arms [of the monarch]; *i.e.,* his highest officers, "his right hand."
股肱心膂 the right hand and backbone [of Imperial power].
股分 a share in a concern.
股分票 a share certificate.

*ku* 穀 grain; substantial; wealthy.

*ku* 箍 a hoop.

*ku* 骨 a bone.

*ku* 谷 a valley; a ravine; difficulty; embarrassment.

*ku* 鼓 a drum; to drum; to stimulate.

鼓勵 to "drum to exertion;" to encourage.

鼓動 to rouse; to stimulate.

鼓浪嶼 the island of Kulangsu (Amoy).

*ku* 賈 to buy; to sell; a resident merchant, as opposed to 商 *(shang)*, a travelling merchant; a shop-keeper; price.

賈買 to buy.

賈售 to sell.

賈市 a market; a bazaar.

*ku* 僱 (or 雇) to hire.

僱覓 to seek to hire; to engage the services of.

僱船 to charter a vessel.

僱用 to hire; to charter (as a vessel).

僱工 to hire labourers.

僱定 to settle about an engagement; to hire; to engage (as an employé).

僱主 the employer of a labourer, vessel, etc.

*ku* 顧 to attend to; to be a customer; to visit; to look; to consider; to care for.

顧慮 to consider.

顧復 to remember kindly; to take protective care.

顧全大局 to look out for the best interests of a matter.

*k'u* 枯 decayed; rotten.

*k'u* 苦 bitter; distress.

苦不堪言 ineffable distress.

*k'u* 哭 to weep.

*k'u* 窟 a cave; a cavern.

*k'u* 庫 a depôt; a treasury; an armoury.

庫聽 an assistant treasurer in the Provincial Treasury, *i.q. ying* 盈庫大使 (*q.v.*), of which it is the abreviated official form.

庫吏 a treasury clerk.

*kua* 瓜 cucumbers, melons, etc.

瓜子 melon seeds.

瓜哇 (*kua-wa*) Java; corrupted from 爪哇 (*chao-wa*).

*kua* 刮 to scrape; to pare off.

*kua* 括 to include.

*kua* 寡 few; little; single; alone; a widow.

寡人 "I, the Emperor."

寡婦 a widow.

*kua* 卦 a prognostic.

*kua* 卦命 to tell fortunes.

*kua* 掛 to hang up; to suspend.

掛燈 lanterns.

掛號 to provide with a number; to register.

掛旗望臺 a signal station.

掛心 suspense; anxiety.

掛念 to anxiously think of; to be in a state of suspense.

*k'ua* 誇 to boast; to brag.

*kuai* 乖 eccentric; strange.

乖巧 clever; artful.

*kuai* 拐 to swindle; to kidnap.

拐騙 to swindle; to beguile.

*kuai* 怪 strange; singular.

*k'uai* 快 glad; cheerful; quick.

快慰 pleased; glad.

快活 cheerful; lively.

*k'uai* 塊 a piece; a lump; classifier of wooden planks.

*kuan* 官 a Government officer; a mandarin; official; superior.

官員 Government officers.

官商 officials and merchants.

官民 officials and private people.

官守 to hold office; to have jurisdiction.

官欵 official moneys.

官設銀號 an official bank; a banker authorised by the Government to receive official moneys.

官用 for official use.

官差 official servants.

官銜 brevet rank; official rank.

官碼頭 a Government jetty; an authorised jetty (for the shipment of goods).

官書局 a provincial government printing office.

官監 an official jail.

官結 to be guaranteed by the authorities; to possess a certificate of character issued by a public office.

官天平砝碼 an official or standard set of scales and weights.

官燕窩 superior birds' nests.

*kuan* 棺 } a coffin.
棺材 }

*kuan* 管 to control; a tube.

管轄 to regulate; to govern.

*kuan* 管理 to manage; to govern.

管下 under one's jurisdiction.

管束 to exercise supervision over; to restrain.

管押 to keep custody (as of a ship).

管事 a manager (as of a bank).

管銀房 a treasurer; an accountant.

管銅務 in charge of coinage matters.

管輪 an engineer of a steamer.

管船夥長 the first mate of a ship.

*kuan* 館 (or 舘) an inn; a lodge.

*kuan* 灌 to pour into; to drink; to assemble.

灌藥槍彈 cartridges.

*kuan* 觀 to look at; to see; to inspect.

觀望 to look on; remiss; negligent.

觀光 to view the glory; politely for "to meet you" (as in accepting an invitation).

*kuan* 關 to lock (as a gate); a Custom House; the Customs; to concern.

關閉 to close.

關口 a Custom House; a pass.

關汛 a post or guard station.

關吏 }
關役 } Custom House officers.

關大使 an examiner or an accountant in the Native Customs.

關哨 a Customs officer; tidewaiters; watchers.

關船 a Customs cruiser; Customs property: ships.

關房 Customs houses; Customs property: houses.

關憲 honorary title used in addressing a high Customs official; the Customs authorities.

關部 official designation of the Hoppo at Canton.

關卡 barriers.

關津 guard houses at fords.

關棧 bonded warehouses.

關板 printed by the Customs.

關照 to come to an understanding with each other; a sailing letter (for junks); a passport.

關照船 a registered junk.

關剝船 a registered cargo-boat.

關防 an official seal; concerns; consequences.

關防圖記 State seals and private seals; to affix one's seal or seals.

關章 a Customs regulation; Customs regulations.

關費 Customs fees.

*kuan* 關平銀 *lit.*, silver as per Customs weight; Customs money; Haikwan tael money.

關涉 to concern; to affect; to be implicated.

關係 }
關繫 } to concern; to be connected with; to result in; consequences.

關乎 to be connected with; to be the result of.

關東 Kuantung, or Manchuria.

關東人蔘 native (Manchurian) ginseng.

*kuan* 冠 a cap; the cap as a symbol of majority; the chief.

*kuan* 貫 a string (as of cash); to string; to connect.

貫串 to string; to connect.

*kuan* 慣 accustomed to.

慣習 to have routine in.

*k'uan* 寬 to extend; broad; wide; breadth; width; forgiving; leniency; to relax; to mitigate.

寬厚 breadth and thickness.

寬長 broad and long; dimensions; size.

寬窄 broad and narrow; breadth.

寬闊若干噸數若干 a ship's measurement and tonnage.

寬恩 to extend favour; benevolence.

寬緩 liberal; slowly.

寬免 to kindly exempt; to forgive.

寬貸 to let off leniently; to remit punishment; to show leniency.

寬予假期 to liberally grant a term of leave.

寬釋 to indulgently release.

*k'uan* 款 (or 欵) an item; a kind; a sort; also, a paragraph; an article (as in a Treaty); a section; items of money; means of existence; funds.

款項 items; expenditure.

款式 a pattern; a kind; a specimen.

*kuang* 光 brilliant; to shine; to give off light; bright; brightness; to illumine.

光臨 to honour one with a visit.

光緒 the period of reign of the Emperor KUANG HSÜ.

*kuang* 廣 broad; to make broad; to extend; (= 廣東) the province of Kwangtung; Canton; Cantonese.

廣曉諭 to give wide circulation; to make proclamation everywhere.

廣儲司 the Treasury of the Privy Purse.

廣糧廳 a departmental grain-collector at Canton.

廣貨 Cantonese goods.

廣東 the Kwangtung province; Cantonese.

*kuang* 廣東索 Canton hemp twine.
廣州省城 the city of Canton.
廣西 the Kwangsi province.
廣濟 Kuang-ch'i-hsien (a coal-producing district in Hupeh).
*k'uang* 筐 a basket.
*k'uang* 誆 to lie; to deceive.
*k'uang* 狂 mad; madness.
狂風 a gale of wind.
*k'uang* 況 more; moreover; still more.
*k'uang* 曠 to waste (as time); clear; bright.
*kuei* 歸 to revert to; to belong to; to be under the control of.
歸於 to come within the category of.
歸於至當 to attain to the highest degree of suitableness.
歸伍 to return to one's regiment or division.
歸併承辦 to revert to the conjoint management of.
歸另議 to become the subject of special negotiation.
歸中國入官 to become liable to confiscation by the Chinese Government.
歸官 to be confiscated.
歸畫一 to make uniform; to obtain uniformity.
歸償 to make compensation for; to indemnify; to pay back.
歸某人 to belong to such and such a person.
*kuei* 規 rule; usage; custom; customary.
規費 customary fees; gratuities.
規矩 custom; usage.
規模 a pattern; a rule.
規條 regulations; byelaws.
規平銀 / 規銀 } the local tael currency at Shanghai; the Shanghai tael.
*kuei* 桂 cassia; Kuei-lin-fu, the capital of Kwangsi.
桂皮 cassia lignea.
桂皮油 cassia oil.
桂子 cassia buds.
桂枝 cassia twigs.
桂圓 dried lung-ngans.
桂圓肉 lung-ngans without the stone; lung-ngan pulp.
桂帶 silk ribbons.
*kuei* 詭 to deceive; to blame.
詭譎 treacherous.

*kuei* 跪 to kneel down.
跪奏 to make a respectful representation to the Throne.
跪稟 to make an humble petition.
*kuei* 貴 dear; esteemed; "you," or that which pertains to the person addressed.
貴價 a high price.
貴客 esteemed merchants; "you" (when addressing merchants).
貴國 your country.
貴恙 your disease.
貴庚 your age.
貴業 your profession; your trade.
貴處 your office; you.
貴道 you, the Taot'ai.
貴稅務司 you, the Commissioner of Customs.
貴王 Your Highness.
貴王大臣 Your Highness (*i.e.*, Prince KUNG) and the other Ministers [of the Tsungli Yamên].
貴州 the Kweichow province.
*kuei* 櫃 a box; a counter.
*k'uei* 虧 to lose; to fail; a defect.
虧空 a deficit; failure in payment.
虧缺 a deficiency.
虧累 to involve in losses.
虧折 to suffer loss.
*k'uei* 揆 to surmise.
*k'uei* 葵 the sun-flower; the tree furnishing palm-leaf fans.
葵扇 palm-leaf fans.
*k'uei* 窺 to peep; to spy.
*k'uei* 傀 strange; extraordinary.
*k'uei* 愧 to be ashamed.
*k'uei* 魁 great; eminent; the head.
魁首 a head; a chief.
*k'uei* 饋 food; victuals; to present to.
*kun* 棍 a stick; a knave.
棍徒 sharpers; villains; *mauvais sujets.*
*k'un* 困 fatigued; weak; poor.
*k'un* 悃 real feelings or sentiments.
*k'un* 捆 to bind; to tie.
捆押 to bind and lock up; to put in irons.
*k'un* 綑 to bind; to cord up; to weave.
*kung* 工 work; to work; workmen.

*kung* 工人 a workman; a coolie.
工食 rations; food provided for a labourer.
工值 } the price of work; wages.
工俸 }
工作 to do work; coolie labour; the work done (as at a dock).
工期 a period or term for doing labour (as entered upon by a coolie workman).
工課 job work; jobs.
工夫 work; labour; business.
工部 the Board of Works.
工部局 the Municipal Council (at Shanghai).

*kung* 功 merit.
功勞 merit; meritorious service.
功牌 a badge of merit; a medal awarded to soldiers.
功賜 to bestow on account of merit.

*kung* 攻 to attack; to assault.

*kung* 貢 tribute; superior in quality.
貢品 articles of tribute.
貢茶 tribute tea; superior tea.

*kung* 弓 a bow.

*kung* 躬 the body; one's person.

*kung* 公 just; correct (as standard weights); fair; public; a duke.
公正 public spirited and upright in character.
公允 just; fair.
公明 just and intelligent.
公署 a public office; a yamên.
公所 a public office; an agency; a trade union; a guild.
公館 the residence of an official or a literary man.
公會 a confederation; a union; a national assembly; a universal exhibition.
公欵 Government moneys.
公欵購辦 to buy from Government funds.
公用之物 articles for Government use.
公用之欵 moneys for Government use.
公項 public moneys.
公估 an assay office.
公估店 a silver appraiser's shop.
公費 public expenditure.
公事 } public affairs; official business; office work.
公務 }

*kung* 公司 a public company; a mail steamer company.
公司輪船 a mail steamer.
公洋藥 }
公班土 } Patna opium.
公烟 }
公冗 public business; official duties.
公立 to publicly draw up (as a protocol); to sign a public......(as a protest).
公議 to discuss in public; a public meeting.
公同 conjointly; on joint account; in company.
公同商定 to conjointly agree upon.
公同商定准行 conjointly discussed and approved of (as by a body of officials).
公私 official and private.
公便 just and expedient.
公道 just; fair.
公侯 duke and marquess; *fig.*, high rank.

*kung* 共 all; in all.
共計 calculated to make in all; total.
共合 all united; grand total.
共同 all together; total.

*kung* 供 to deposit; the deposition (of a witness); to supply; to give.
供詞 to give evidence; to depose.
供養 to support; to nourish; to supply.

*kung* 恭 courteous; respectful.
恭敬 most respectfully.
恭叩 to respectfully pray; a respectful petition.
恭請 to respectfully request or invite.
恭錄 to respectfully copy or record.
恭摺 to respectfully memorialise.
恭賀 to congratulate.

*kung* 宮 a palace.
宮保 Guardian of the Heir Apparent (a title).

*kung* 肱 the arm; a support to the Throne; the right hand of.

*kung* 礦 a mine.

*kung* 鑛 ore; a mine.
鑛銅 copper ore.

*k'ung* 空 empty.
空瓶 empty bottles.
空船 an empty vessel; a vessel in ballast.

*k'ung* 空白 blank (as a form not filled up); a blank form.
空白式樣 blank forms.

*k'ung* 控 to strike; to accuse.
控告 to accuse.

*k'ung* 恐 to fear; to apprehend.
恐有未合 it is to be feared that it is not in order.

*k'ung* 孔 a hole; hollow; excellent.
孔雀 a peacock.
孔雀翎 the peacock's feather as a decoration of merit.

*kuo* 國 (or 国) a country.
國家 the Government.
國法 the laws of the country.
國費 Government expenditure.
國課 the Imperial revenue.
國計 Government plans; politics; finances of a country.
國會 a parliament; a national assembly.

*kuo* 鍋 a pan.

*kuo* 過 to pass; to exceed; too; after a verb, a sign of the past: have, has, having.
過關 to pass a Custom House.
過卡 to cross a Customs barrier.
過攔江沙 to cross the bar.
過秤 to pass the scales; to be weighed.
過載 to transfer cargo from one ship to another; to tranship.
過載輪船 to tranship to a steamer.
過船之准單 a permit to tranship.
過年 } the new year.
過節 }
過期 } to exceed a limit.
過限期 }
過時 beyond the stipulated time.
過帳 the Kwochang system, a speciality of banking business at Ningpo and other places.
過長 excessively long; too long.
過重 excess; too heavy.
過寬 too lenient; to go too far in being lenient.
過衆 too many; an excessively large crowd.
過慮 to care too much about; to trouble about.

*kuo* 果 fruit; really; truly; indeed.
果品 fruit.

*kuo* 菓 fruit.

*kuo* 裹 to wrap up; to fetter; a bundle.
裹足 to impede; to fetter.

*k'uo* 闊 open; wide.

*k'uo* 擴 to enlarge; to expand.
擴充 to carry out to the utmost.

## L.

*la* 喇 to talk fast.
喇庄土 Benares opium.

*la* 拉 to pull; to drag.
拉司 (in imitation of the English sound "last") a last (English weight or measure).

*la* 臘 the winter month.
臘月 the twelfth moon of the year.

*la* 蠟 wax.
蠟燭 candles.

*lai* 來 to come.
來往 to come and go; to traffic; intercourse.
來家 to come to one's house.
來省 to come to the provincial capital.
來控 to lodge a complaint.
來信 an incoming letter.
來文 an incoming despatch; an official letter received.
來路 to come by a road; brought from abroad, like foreign goods; *provenance;* source; origin.
來年 next year.

*lai* 賚 to give; to bestow.

*lai* 賴 to rely on; to depend on.

*lan* 攔 }
攔擋 } to stop; to obstruct; to intercept.
攔阻 }
攔江沙 a bank or shoal barring the river; a bar; the Woosung Bar.

*lan* 欄 a railing.
欄杆 silk ribbons.

*lan* 爛 to break; to tear; over-ripe (as fruit); rotten.

*lan* 濫 to encroach; to intrude.
濫膺赴考 to become a candidate for examination without the necessary qualification.

*lan* 籃 a basket.
籃帽 a cage (top of a beacon made of basket-work).

*lan* 籃心 the centre of a cage or basket.

*lan* 藍 blue; (=法藍 *fa-lan* or 琺琅 *fa-lang*) cloisonné or enamelled ware.

藍翎 the "Blue Feather" as a distinction of merit.

藍靛 indigo.

藍白色旂 a blue and white flag; the rendezvous flag (MARRYAT'S Code).

藍光 a blue light.

藍花 coarse chinaware (at Kiukiang); *lit.*, "blue pattern."

*lan* 覽 to inspect; to behold from a distance.

覽觀 to take a view; to witness a spectacle.

*lan* 攬 to grasp; to seize; to hoard up.

*lan* 欖 olives (Chinese).

欖仁 olive seeds.

*lan* 纜 a rope; a cable.

*lan* 婪 covetous; greedy; extortion.

*lan* 懶 idle; lazy.

*lang* 浪 waves; unsettled; dissipated.

*lang* 郎 a term of respect for officers and persons; clear; lofty.

郎中 a secretary in a metropolitan board.

*lang* 榔 betel-nuts.

*lao* 老 old; venerable; hard; dark in colour.

老鹿茸 old deer horns.

老爺 a term of respect: the Honourable; Mr., when applied to officials.

老幼 old and young; all; everybody.

老鈍無準 used up and inaccurate (as an old set of scales).

老實 honest; free from vice; genuine.

*lao* 勞 toil; exertion; merit; to exert oneself.

勞績 merit.

勞賚 to encourage by rewards.

*lao* 牢 } a prison.
牢監 }

*lao* }
*lo* } 烙 to burn; to brand.

烙印 to emboss; to brand.

*lê* 勒 to coerce; to bind; to force.

勒索 to extort; to "squeeze."

勒死 to strangle.

*lê* 泐 to write.

泐此奉覆 I write this in reply.

*lê* 泐覆 to reply.

*lê* 樂 to be glad; joyous.

樂用 to gladly use; to like using.

*lei* 累 to involve; to implicate; trouble; troublesome repetition.

累次 repeatedly; again and again.

*lei* 儡 to injure; to destroy.

*lei* 壘 to pile up; reiterated; repeatedly.

*lei* 儽 idle; lazy; sickly.

*lei* 類 a category.

*lêng* 冷 cold; frigid; indifferent.

*li* 里 a hamlet; a village; one's native village; a Chinese measure of length equal to about a third of an English mile.

*li* 理 a theory; a rule; ought to; duly; to manage; to regulate.

理論 to discuss; to reason.

理應 } duly; as in duty bound.
理合 }

理合備文 to duly write a despatch.

理當 must; it is right (or proper) to; proper.

理船廳 a harbour master.

理船廳章程 Harbour Regulations.

*li* 裏 (or 裡) inside; within.

*li* 李 a plum; to prepare for a journey.

*li* 利 profit; interest; sharp; edged.

利息 interest (on money); profit on trade.

利益 advantage; profit.

利病 advantage and disease; *i.e.*, good and evil.

利器 edged tools; knives; cutlery.

*li* 梨 a pear tree.

*li* 璃 strass; glass.

*li* 離 to take away; to part; to leave; away from.

離開 to leave (a place); to start from; to be apart from.

離馬頭 to leave the jetty.

離家 to leave home.

離父母 to be separated from one's parents.

離卡不遠 not far from the barrier.

*li* 麗 elegant; graceful.

*li* 曆 astronomical calculation; a calendar; being a forbidden character, should be written 厯 or 歴 (*li*).

*li* 歴 (or 厯) a calendar (=曆); a succession of; to pass by; up to the present.

*li* 歷書 an almanac; a calendar.
歷經 to have [done] up to the present.
歷來 hitherto.
歷今年久 up to the present year.
歷年 for a number of years; in the lapse of years.
歷陳 to state events one by one, in order.
歷情 to narrate facts one by one, in order.

*li* 釐 (or 厘) a cash (the 1,000th part of a tael); the likin tax.
釐金 } the likin tax.
釐捐 }
釐稅 the likin tax; also, likin taxes *(li)* and ordinary duties *(shui)*. Cf. *shui* 稅釐.
釐務總局 a head Likin office.

*li* 禮 rites; ceremony.
禮儀 the ceremonial; politeness.
禮部 the Board of Ceremonies.
禮貌 polite; politeness.
禮物 presents.
禮單 a list of presents sent.
禮拜 a week; to worship.
禮拜日 Sunday; on Sundays.
禮拜五 Friday.
禮體 one's moral and physical condition.

*li* 履 to walk; to tread in the path of.
履德 to tread in the path of virtue.

*li* 立 to erect; to settle; to conclude (as a Treaty); to draft; to set up; (=立刻) immediately; at once; thereupon.
立定 to introduce (as an arrangement); to put into operation; to settle.
立定合同 to fix by contract.
立業 to establish in business; to work for a living.
立生意 to set up in business.
立案 to enter a plaint in court.
立據 to draw up a certificate, or a record, which is to have legal force; to place on official record; to lodge a protest; a protest.
立憑單 to draw up a certificate.
立此專條 to draw up this special rule.
立約 to conclude a Treaty; to make an agreement.
立傳 to send for at once; to summon one without delay.
立刻 immediately; instantly.

*li* 粒 a grain of rice; a classifier of bullets, cartridges, shells, etc.

*li* 勵 to animate; to encourage; to exert one's strength.

*li* 蠣 oysters.
蠣殼 oyster shells; sea shells.

*li* 栗 } the chestnut; chestnuts.
栗子 }

*li* 慄 fear; to fear.

*li* 力 strength; to be able to.
力量 vigour; ability; solvency.
力衰 weak; worn out (as by age).
力能 to be strong enough to.

*li* 荔 } the lichee fruit; lichees.
荔枝 }

*li* 戾 a crime; a fault; to stoop.

*li* 吏 a magistrate; a Government officer; a deputy.
吏部 the Board of Civil Office.

*li* 隸 official servants; attached to; belonging to.
隸卒 attendants in public offices.

*li* 例 rule; law; according to regulation.
例准 permitted by the regulations.
例不納稅之物 articles not subject to duty.
例應完稅之貨 merchandise subject to duty.

*liang* 兩 a tael; taels; two; both.
兩宮 the two Empresses.
兩歧 diverging; ambiguous; a double mode of dealing with a question.
兩歧辦法 two different methods of acting.
兩廣 the Two Kwang provinces (Kwangtung and Kwangsi).
兩江 the Two Kiang,—a viceregal district comprising the three provinces of Kiangsu, Anhwei, and Kiangsi. The two first named being formerly considered as one, under the name of Kiangnan, is the cause of only two divisions being named in the expression.
兩旁 on both sides.
兩造 } plaintiff and defendant; the two parties in a suit.
兩造之處 }
兩有裨益 to be of advantage in both respects.

*liang* 輛 a classifier of carts or carriages.

*liang* 量 to measure; to calculate; to consider.
量地 to measure land.
量船執照 a certificate of measurement (for a ship).
量加 to consider and add; to negotiate for additional stipulations in a Treaty.

*liang* 量減 to diminish; to lower.

*liang* 糧 (or 粮) grain paid to Government in lieu of taxes; grain; rations.
糧食 grain.
糧道 a grain collector.
糧臺 an army paymaster.

*liang* 良 good; goodness; very; in a high degree.
良辰 a lucky hour; a lucky time.
良法 a good method; a practical scheme.
良民 good, loyal subjects.
良深 very much; deeply.
良薑 galangal.

*liang* 梁 (or 樑) a beam; beams; piles; joists.
梁木 beams (timber).

*liang* 掠 to rob; to plunder.

*liang* 諒 to believe; to think.

*liang* 亮 clear; light; bright.
亮直 clear-headed and straightforward.

*liao* 僚 a colleague; a companion.

*liao* 寮 a stall; a country house; a fellow-officer; a comrade.

*liao* 撩 to grasp; to manage.
撩理 to manage.

*liao* 燎 a signal light; to illuminate.

*liao* 遼 remote; distant.
遼東 the province of Liaotung; Manchuria.
遼河 the river Liao, near Newchwang.

*liao* 料 to dispose properly; to consider; to think; materials; stuff; strass; coloured glass.
料理 to manage.
料器 glass, or vitrified ware.
料珠 glass beads.
料手鐲 glass bangles or armlets.

*liao* 聊 careless; dissolute.

*liao* 了 to finish.
了結 to settle (as a case); to finish; to bring to an end.

*lieh* 列 to enumerate; to class; a sign of the plural.
列下 enumerated below.
列稅則 enumerated in the Tariff.
列名冊報 to report names entered on a list.
列島 islands; the islands.

*lieh* 烈 ardent; fiery; impetuous.

*lieh* 裂 to split; to crack; to tear.

*lien* 連 to connect; to take all together; together with; with; and; *plus;* to be connected with; inseparable from.
連皮 the *emballage* connected with the goods.
連縛 to make fast to.
連號 a connected series of numbers; a series.
連日 for a number of days; on successive days.
連江縣 the district of Lien-chiang (Foochow).

*lien* 蓮 the water lily; the lotus.
蓮子 lily flower seeds; lotus-nuts.

*lien* 鏈 a chain; to lock together.

*lien* 聯 to join; to connect.
聯貫 to join; to bring into line (as several objects seen at a distance).
聯名 to sign conjointly (as several names signed by way of surety).

*lien* 臉 the face; the countenance; reputation.

*lien* 斂 (sometimes wrongly written 歛) to amass; to collect; to accumulate.

*lien* 煉 to separate dross by fire; to melt.
煉成 to burn; to make by burning (as coke by burning coal).

*lien* 練 to practise; to drill; to experiment.
練軍 to drill troops.

*lien* 鍊 a chain; to smelt; to refine metals.

*lien* 憐 to pity.

*lin* 林 a forest; a clump of trees.

*lin* 臨 at the point of; about to; whilst; to descend.
臨行 about to start.
臨……時 just at the time of; when about to……
臨御 to occupy the Throne.

*lin* 遴 to select; to walk; to desire.
遴派 to appoint; to select.

*lin* 鄰 near; neighbouring.
鄰國 the neighbouring countries.

*lin* 凜 (interchanged with 懍 *lin*, to fear) to tremble.
凜遵 to obey strictly.
凜之遵之 / 凜之慎之 "tremble and obey;" "be careful to observe these injunctions,"—a concluding phrase in proclamations.

*lin* 廩 a Government granary.
廩生 a literary title: an expectant *chü-jên.*

*lin* 檁 a cross-beam; hatch-combings (of a ship).

*lin* 吝 mean; niggardly.

吝嗇 stingy; sparing; frugal.

*lin* 賃 to rent; to hire.

*ling* 令 to order; to let; to call upon......to......; your.

*ling* 伶 clever.

伶巧 clever; ingenious.

伶便 convenient.

*ling* 翎 a pendent tail feather; the plume worn as a decoration of merit.

*ling* 聆 to hear; to listen; to obey.

聆教 to listen to one's teaching; "I shall be glad to listen to your conversation" (said in accepting the announcement of a visit).

*ling* 零 fractional; denotes a break in the decimal notation (corresponding to zero in a series of numbers).

零星 }
零星小件 } miscellaneous things; odds and ends.
零物 }

*ling* 齡 the front teeth; one's age.

*ling* 領 to receive; to issue (as a document); to govern; a collar.

領繳 to hand to; to issue to.

領回 to issue back; to hand back (as a document deposited); to re-issue; to renew, as a license handed in for cancelling.

領照 to issue a certificate.

領獲 to have received; to get issued (as arms from the Government).

領事官 a consul.

領港 to pilot; a pilot.

*ling* 靈 a spirit; spiritual; a soul; a coffin.

靈妙 ingenious; clever.

靈柩 a coffin with corpse.

*ling* 綾 thin silk cloth; damask.

*ling* 陵 Imperial tombs; high; eminent.

*ling* 另 extra; apart; separately; besides; again.

另外 besides.

另項 a different kind of......; other.

另款 separate items; the "Special Account" (= Customs Account *D*).

另款之賬目 an account of extra receipts [= Customs Account *D*].

另照 having a separate certificate.

另冊 a list, or table, is separately given.

另日 another day.

另換 to exchange; to change for another.

*ling* 另換船隻 to transfer [cargo] to another vessel.

另立合同 to renew a contract.

*lio* 畧 (or 略) to abridge; an abridged statement; a little; some.

畧同 about the same; alike.

*liu* 琉 strass; glaze; vitreous.

琉璃 glass; opaque glass; glazed.

琉璃瓦 glazed tiles.

琉球 (*liu-ch'iu*) the Lu-chu Islands.

*liu* 硫 sulphur; brimstone.

硫黃 sulphur and brimstone.

硫黃强水 sulphuric acid.

*liu* 流 to flow.

流通 to flow freely; to expand (as trade).

流弊 a standing nuisance.

*liu* 柳 the willow; striped.

柳條 stripes; striped.

柳條布 striped cottons; dimities; quiltings.

*liu* 留 to keep; to detain.

留難 to raise difficulties by detention; to delay and obstruct; obstruction.

留滯 to detain.

留住 to remain in a place; to detain.

留空 to keep open or unoccupied (as a berth for a ship).

留心 to be careful; carefully.

*liu* 六 (or 陸) six.

六部 the six Boards of Government.

*lo* 擄 to seize; to plunder.

*lo* 螺 a conch.

螺絲 a screw.

*lo* 羅 a net; a lace-like texture; thin silk; to arrange in order.

羅經 a compass.

羅經變差 the variation of the compass.

*lo* 鑼 a gong.

*lo* 駱 }
駱駝 } a camel.

駱駝毛 camel's hair.

駱駝絨 camel's wool.

*lo* 落 to fall; to drop; to go down (as the setting sun); to ship goods; to export.

落貨 to ship goods.

*lou* 樓 an upper story; a two-storied house; a tower.

*lou* 簍 a basket.

*lou* 漏 to leak; to evade (as payment of duty); to smuggle.

漏網 to escape (as out of a net).

漏稅滋弊 all the vicious modes of defrauding the revenue.

漏射 to flash through (as a ray of light through a gap in hills).

*lu* 路 a road; on the way; *en route.*

路上 }
路過 } on the road; *en route.*

路費 travelling expenses.

*lu* 露 dew; to disclose; to divulge; to show through.

露出 to be exposed; to be visible (as a sunken mast sticking out of the water); to disclose.

*lu* 錄 a record; to record; to enter.

錄摺咨呈 to submit a copy of.

*lu* 陸 dry land; (=六) six.

陸路 an overland road; dry land roads (as opposed to sea routes); land troops (as opposed to the navy).

陸路提督 a provincial Commander-in-Chief of Land Forces.

陸運 to forward by land.

陸續 successively (as a land road not interrupted by water); one by one.

陸溪口 *(lu-ch'i-k'ou)* Lu-k'i-k'ow (a port of call on the Yangtze).

*lu* 鹿 a deer.

鹿角 }
鹿茸 } deer horns.

鹿皮 deer skins.

鹿嶼 *(Lu-hsü)* Sugar Loaf Island, near Swatow.

*luan* 亂 to disarrange; confused; in confusion.

亂絲頭 silk refuse; waste silk.

亂礁 a number of reefs; extensive reefs.

*lun* 倫 relation; right; in order.

倫敦 *(lun-tun)* London.

*lun* 掄 to choose.

掄擇 to select.

*lun* 淪 lost, as in a whirl of water.

淪落 to be lost or ruined (morally).

*lun* 綸 to twist silk; to classify.

綸扉 the silken gate; the Imperial Palace; the Court.

*lun* 論 to discuss; to reason.

論及 to discuss.

論定 to settle by discussion; to decide about.

*lun* 輪 a wheel; round; rotatory; alternately.

輪船 a steamer; steamers.

輪派 to send on duty in rotation.

輪角稍圓 having rounded corners and rather broad surfaces.

*lung* 龍 a dragon; Imperial.

龍眼 lung-ngan.

龍眼肉 lung-ngan pulp.

龍旗 the "dragon" flag; the Chinese national ensign.

龍位 the Imperial Throne.

龍筆 the Imperial pencil; the Emperor's signature.

*lung* 隴 a dyke; to monopolise.

隴貨 to monopolise goods.

隴斷 to monopolise.

*lung* 隆 exalted; abundant; intense (as summer heat or winter cold); Imperial.

隆冬 the extreme of winter; very cold weather.

*lü* 屢 }
屢次 } repeatedly; often.

*lü* 縷 the threads of a texture; silk threads.

*lü* 呂 the spine.

呂宋 *(lü-sung)* originally, the island of Luzon; the Philippine Islands; Manila.

呂宋繩 Manila cordage.

呂宋票 a Manila lottery ticket.

*lü* 閭 a small village.

*lü* 慮 to think.

*lü* 旅 }
旅客 } a stranger; a traveller; a guest.

*lü* 膂 the backbone.

*lü* }
*lu* } 綠 green.

綠茶 green tea.

綠膠 lü-kiao (a green vegetable dye).

綠皮 green leather.

*lü* 律 laws; statutes.

律師 a barrister-at-law; a lawyer.

律例 statutes; the law.

律條 statutes; laws.

律伯克 *(lü-po-k'o)* the city of Lübeck.

## M.

*ma* 馬 a horse.

馬路 a road for riding or driving; used in Shanghai to express the roads suitable for general carriage traffic.

馬撥 an overland courier.

馬賊 mounted robbers.

馬口鐵 tinplates.

馬巷廳 the Magistrate of Ma-hsiang (Mahang).

*ma* 瑪 the agate.

瑪瑙 cornelians.

瑪瑙珠 cornelian beads.

*ma* 碼 weights; a yard; yards; figures or numbers written in the running hand style.

碼頭 a jetty; a wharf.

碼號 a number, or a distinguishing number added to the mark on packages of merchandise; No.

*ma* 駡 (or 嗎) to scold; to abuse.

*ma* 麻 (or 蔴) hemp.

麻袋 hemp bags.

麻繩索 hemp cordage.

麻栗木 teak-wood.

麻栗樹板 teak-wood planks.

麻蓮布 hemp sacking.

麻布 linen.

麻棉帆布 canvas and cotton duck.

麻子 hemp seed.

*mai* 麥 wheat.

*mai* 嘜 (pronounced *mák* in Cantonese) an unauthorised character used to represent the sound of the English word "mark."

嘜什貨 marked "Sundries."

*mai* 埋 to bury; to conceal.

埋藏 to conceal; to store up.

*mai* 買 to buy.

買賣 to trade; commerce.

買到 to have imported.

買土貨報單 a transit memorandum (authorising the purchase of goods in the interior).

買船准單 a license for buying a ship.

買船契 a certificate of purchase of a ship.

買主 the purchaser. Cf. *mai* 賣主.

買客 the purchaser.

買貨之人 purchasers of goods.

*mai* 買辦 a comprador.

買保險 to take out an insurance policy.

*mai* 賣, 賣出 to sell.

賣售 to sell off.

賣主 the seller. Cf. *mai* 買主.

賣與華人 to sell (or for sale) to Chinese.

賣契 a bill of sale.

*mai* 邁 to go; to walk; to disregard.

邁當 (*mai-tang*, in imitation of the French sound "mètre") a mètre; mètres.

*man* 滿 full; complete; Manchurian.

滿年 a whole year.

滿十年 at the end of 10 years; the limit of 10 years having expired.

滿漢 Manchu and Chinese.

滿洲 *(man-chou)* Manchu; Manchurian.

*man* 慢 slow; slowly.

*man* 漫 reckless; vague.

*mang* 忙 busy; hurried.

*mao* 貓 a cat.

*mao* 錨 an anchor.

錨鍊 anchor chains.

*mao* 毛 feathers; hair; wool; rough.

毛布 ginghams.

毛柿 camagon-wood.

毛病 a flaw; a blemish.

*mao* 冒 to make bold; blindly; rashly.

冒瀆 to venture troubling (as a superior with a petition).

冒充 to fraudulently take the place of; to falsely substitute.

冒昧 ignorant; headstrong.

冒犯 to offend inconsiderately.

冒告 to accuse falsely.

*mao* 帽 a hat; a cap.

帽頂 the top of a thing; the top of a beacon; a cap button.

*mei* 每 every; each.

每日 every day; daily.

每一分鐘時 every minute.

每次 each time; in each separate case.

每逢 whenever; when; at the time of.

每逢四個月 every four months.

*mei* 每啟對仗之時 whenever fighting takes place.

*mei* 梅 a plum.

*mei* 沒. See *mo*.

*mei* 煤 coal.

煤炭 coal and charcoal.

煤灰 coal ashes.

煤礦 a coal-mine; coal mining.

煤窰 a coal-pit.

煤艙 the space allowed for coal on board a steamer; coal bunkers.

*mei* 美 beautiful; beauties; advantages.

美國 America; American.

美國揀淨參鬚參 American clarified ginseng.

美國參下 crude American ginseng.

*mei* 昧 dark; obscure in mind.

*mên* 門 a door; a gate; a classifier of guns, rifles, etc.

門面 the front side of a gate.

門牌 a census ticket.

門上 a gatekeeper; a private secretary in a yamên; a factotum.

*mêng* 蒙 to receive (from a superior); sign of the passive.

蒙恩 to receive favours.

蒙大人面允 to receive the Ta-jên's (*i.e.*, your) verbal promise; I have been promised by Your Excellency.

蒙古 Mongolia; Mongolian.

*mêng* 朦 to deceive; dull; obscure.

朦混 a misunderstanding.

*mêng* 盟 an oath; to swear; to vow.

盟誓 to swear; an oath.

盟約 a solemn agreement.

*mi* 米 rice.

米袋 rice bags.

米穀 } rice and other grain.
米粮 }

米麥雜糧 grain of all kinds.

*mi* 迷 to deceive; stupid; to lose.

迷失 to lose.

*mi* 靡 not; without.

靡涯 without limit; endless.

*mi* 弭 to stop; to put down.

*mi* 覓 to search; to seek for.

覓承工 to seek emigrants for coolie labour.

*mi* 覓醫生 to send for a doctor; to seek medical attendance.

*mi* 蜜 honey; sweet.

蜜餞 preserves; confectionery.

蜜餞糖菓 preserves; comfits; sweetmeats.

蜜蠟 beeswax.

蜜理邁當 (*mi-li-mai-tang*, in imitation of the French sound "millimètre") a millimètre; millimètres.

*mi* 密 secret; silent; close.

密札 to give confidential instructions to.

密力 (*mi-li*) a mille.

*miao* 妙 perfect; excellent.

*miao* 秒 a second.

*miao* 廟 a temple.

*mieh* 滅 to extinguish; to be dark; to eclipse.

*mien* 棉 (interchanged with 綿 (*mien*), downy) the cotton plant; cotton.

棉花 raw cotton.

棉絮 waste cotton; cotton rags.

棉紗 cotton yarn.

棉線 cotton thread.

棉布 cotton cloth; cotton piece goods.

棉被胎 cotton bed quilts; palampores.

棉帆布 cotton duck.

棉絨布 woollen and cotton mixtures.

棉羊褥 cotton and woollen mattresses.

棉洋毛 wool.

棉衣服 cotton clothes.

棉子 cotton seed.

*mien* 面 the face; a surface; personally; in person; verbally.

面前 in front of.

面諭 to give verbal instructions.

面見 to see personally; to interview.

面議 to discuss personally.

面爲商定 to consult in person.

面告 to inform in person.

面稟 to report to a superior in person; to speak to a superior (on business).

面拍 to bid at an auction.

*mien* 麪 (or 麵) wheat flour.

麪粉 flour.

麪餅 cakes; biscuits.

*mien* 免 to avoid; to be exempt; to exempt; duty free.

免稅 to exempt from duty; duty free.

免稅執照 an exemption certificate.

免鈔 to be exempted from payment of tonnage dues.

免照 an exemption certificate; a duty-free certificate for rice in times of famine and short crops.

免其議罰 to remit a fine.

免拆驗 to exempt [packages] from opening for examination [of goods].

免傷損之累 to avoid damage.

免重徵執照 a certificate exempting from levying duty a second time; an exemption certificate.

免致 (the opposite of 以致 *i-chih*) so as not to; so that there may not be.

免致收稅不公 to avoid the duty being collected in an unjust manner.

免致滋生弊端 in order that it may not result in confusion and abuse.

免致後難更易 so that afterwards there may be no difficulty in altering.

*mien* 勉 to urge; to make an effort.

勉節 to endeavour to abridge.

勉加 to make an effort.

勉勵 to exert oneself; to urge.

勉强 to be forced against one's own will; to coerce.

勉强脅從 to follow against one's own will.

*min* 民 the people (not being officials or soldiers); people; subjects.

民人 one of the people; a subject.

民間 among the people; the people.

民食 the people's food.

民生 life, or maintenance, of the people.

民船 a "native boat" (as opposed to "foreign boats"); a "private or merchant junk" (as opposed to "Government vessels"); also, a registered junk plying between the ports of call on the Yangtze.

*min* 旻 melancholy; being a forbidden character, should be written 旼 (*min*) or 綿 (*mien*).

*min* 閩 / 閩省 } the Fukien province.

閩海關 the Foochow Customs.

閩浙總督 the Governor-General of Fukien and Chêkiang.

閩江 the Min river.

*min* 敏 acute; grave; serious.

*min* 皿 porcelain or glass vessels (as cups, etc.); crockery.

*ming* 名 a personal name; a name; to name; named.

名號 a designation; a name; a title.

名單 a muster roll.

名目 denomination; description of kind.

名另具 "the name is separately furnished" (a concluding phrase in letters, meaning that one's card is enclosed).

*ming* 茗 the tender leaves of tea; superior tea.

*ming* 銘 to engrave.

*ming* 明 clear; bright; shining; it is clear that; this shows that; often added to verbs meaning to state, to inform, etc.; to light up (as a revolving or occulting light, which lights up and eclipses at intervals); to-morrow.

明沙 a sand bank or shoal above water.

明晰 clearly; to inform; to communicate.

明知 to clearly know; to be clearly known to......

明訂 to clearly define.

明示 to give explicit instructions to.

明敘 to state.

明文 an unmistakable written passage; a stipulation in writing; there being a written understanding about.

明滅 to light up and eclipse.

明日 to-morrow.

*ming* 鳴 the cry of a bird; to cry; to sound.

鳴鑼 to sound a gong.

鳴鐘 to strike a bell.

鳴鼓 to beat a drum.

*ming* 命 to order; to cause to; human life.

命案 a case in which human life is concerned; a case of murder.

命駕 to order one's carriage; to get ready for a visit.

*mo* 莫 do not; not.

莫非 cannot but; bound to.

莫若 (=不如 *pu ju*) it is better to; we had better......; *lit.*, not like.

*mo* 模 a mould; a pattern; a model.

模樣 pattern; style.

模令布爾額 (*mo-ling-pu-êrh-ngo*) Mecklenburg.

*mo* 末 the end; ends; leavings; dust.

末後 at the end; the last; finally; when all is finished.

末尾 the last; at the last.

*mo* 末尾一關 that Custom House which is at the end; the last Custom House [passed].

*mo* / *mei* / *mu* 沒 to sink in the water; to die; not; without.

沒藥 myrrh.

*mo* 默 silent; to think; thoughtful.

*mo* 墨 ink (in cakes); Chinese, or Indian, ink.

墨魚 cuttle-fish.

墨西哥國 *(mo-hsi-ko)* Mexico.

*mou* 某 certain (as in "a *certain* person"); so-and-so.

某某 so-and-so; such-and-such.

某國 a certain country; some [foreign] country.

*mou* 謀 to plan; to plot; to devise.

謀殺 to plot a murder.

謀生 to carry on trade.

謀國 to make plans for one's country.

*mou* 貿 trade; to trade.

貿易 trade.

貿易行市 commercial usage.

*mu* 募 to invite; to enlist.

*mu* 墓 a grave; a tomb.

*mu* 幕 / 幕友 a private secretary.

*mu* 慕 to respect.

*mu* 暮 evening.

*mu* 母 a mother; female.

母丁香 mother cloves.

*mu* 牧 to pasture; a shepherd.

牧畜 to tend cattle.

*mu* 畝 a *mu* or *mou*; a Chinese land measure varying in dimensions, according to locality, but averaging about the sixth of an English acre.

*mu* 木 wood; wooden; a tree.

木浮 a wooden buoy.

木料 wooden materials (as of a ship); timber.

木器 woodware.

木植 timber.

木桅 a mast; a spar.

木板 a board; a plank (classifier, *kuai* 塊).

木杆 a spar.

木杆樁 a spar beacon.

木樁梁舵柱 piles, poles, and joists.

木牌 a wooden board.

*mu* 木鞋 wooden shoes; clogs.

木匠 / 木工 a carpenter.

木架 a wooden frame or stand.

木耳 fungus; agaric.

木香 putchuck.

*mu* 沐 to wash; to receive favours.

沐恩 to receive favours.

*mu* 目 the eye; numbers.

目今 now.

目覩 to see; to observe.

目錄 a table of contents; an index; an inventory.

*mu* 穆 majestic.

穆宗毅 Mu Tsung I (the dynastic title of the late Emperor T'UNG CHIH).

*mu* 睦 friendly.

睦和 friendly relation; being on cordial terms.

## N.

*na* 那 how; where.

那有差錯之理 where is the reason for our having been at fault? *i.e.*, there is nothing to show that we were in the wrong.

*na* 拏 (or 拿) to take; to seize (as smuggled goods).

拏獲 to seize.

*na* 納 to pay (as taxes, duties, etc.).

納稅 to pay duty.

*nai* 乃 (or 迺) that is; to wit; also; and; but.

乃指……而言 that is to say; that is.

*nai* 奶 milk.

*nai* 奈 a remedy; a resource.

奈何 what resource? no resource; no help; no alternative (*i.q.*, 無奈, *wu nai*).

*nai* 耐 to endure; to bear; patient.

*nan* 南 south; southern.

南洋大臣 the Superintendent of Southern Trade.

南北洋通商大臣 the High Commissioners of Northern and Southern Trade.

南美國 South America.

南京 the city of Nanking.

南海 the district of Nan-hai (Canton).

南滙縣 the district of Nan-hui (province of Kiangsu).

*nan* 南臺口 the port of Nan-tai, *i.e.*, the foreign settlement at Foochow; the foreign community there.

*nan* 難 difficult; to make difficulties.

難易 hard or easy; the relative difficulty of a matter.

難甘 difficult to submit to cheerfully.

難安 difficult to appease.

難保 difficult to secure.

難辦 difficult to manage.

難行之處 questions difficult to settle; practical difficulties.

難容 inexcusable; unendurable; incompatible.

難以成功 }
難於成功 } difficult to bring about.

*nang* 囊 a bag.

*nao* 撓 to pervert; to vex.

*nao* 惱 vexation; anger; annoyance.

*nao* 瑙 the cornelian stone.

瑙威國 (*nao-wei-kuo*) Norway; Norwegian.

*nao* 腦 brain; camphor.

*nao* 鬧 noise; to scold.

鬧事 a noisy disturbance; a quarrel.

*nei* 內 placed after a noun: in; within; inside; near to (as near to a matter or having a close knowledge of a matter).

內稱 }
內載 }
內開 } it is stated or said therein; in which it is stated or said that.
內云 }

內地 the interior (of a country); all that pertains to transit from or to the interior; native, as "native opium" or "native salt."

內地湖河各口 inland lake and river ports.

內地貨物 goods carried to (入) or from (出) the interior; goods under transit.

內地稅項 transit dues.

內地稅單 a transit certificate (inward).

內地洋藥 opium grown in the interior; native opium.

內地商船 native merchant vessels; merchant junks.

內江輪船 a river steamer (as opposed to an "ocean steamer").

內外 inside and outside; native and foreign.

內外土產 native and foreign produce.

*nei* 內港 ports in the interior; ports not open to trade; inland waters.

內閣 the Grand Secretariat, or Imperial Cabinet; the Court Archives.

內輪器具 the engines (on board a steamer).

*nêng* 能 to be able; capable.

能出海堪用之船 a seaworthy ship.

能引火之油 inflammable oil (as kerosene, etc.).

能否 whether or not it is possible.

*ni* 呢 woollen cloth of foreign manufacture.

呢廓來業福斯克 (*ni-k'uo-lai-yeh-fu-ssŭ-k'o*) Nicolaievsk.

*ni* 溺 foolish; to drown.

*ni* 匿 }
匿藏 } to conceal; to hide away.

匿單少報 to conceal the document and report less [than the proper quantity]; to make a false declaration while withholding the document.

匿過紅單 fraudulently omitted in the clearance document (as goods not declared at the Custom House).

*ni* 逆 rebellious; to oppose.

*niang* 釀 to ferment; fermented.

*niao* 鳥 birds.

鳥鎗 fowling-pieces.

*nieh* 揑 to work up; to feign.

揑報 a false report; to make a false report.

揑造 to counterfeit.

揑告 to accuse falsely.

*nieh* 湼 (=涅) to blacken; to dye.

*nieh* 臬 rule; law; to judge; a target.

臬司 }
臬台 } a provincial judge.

*nien* 粘 to paste on.

粘貼 to paste up (as a public notice).

粘送 to forward (as an enclosure).

粘開款目 the items pasted on or annexed.

*nien* 年 a year.

年歲 a year; years; the age of a man.

年底 at the end of the year.

年限 a period; a term of years; a limit of time.

年節 New Year's day.

年號 the year (in dates, as such and such a year of an Emperor).

*nien* 念 to think of; thought; idea; to read aloud; to read; sometimes used to denote the number "twenty," and hence read *êrh-shih* (二十).

*ning* 寧 being a forbidden character, should be written 寗 or 甯 *(ning)*; to prefer; it is better to......than ......(in which case *than* is expressed by a negation, as in "better die and not be disgraced"); repose; quiet; (=甯波) Ningpo.

甯死不辱 it is *better* to die *than* be disgraced.

甯缺而毋用 it is *better* to keep a vacancy open *than* to employ [a bad man].

甯幫 the Ningpo men (as a class).

甯紹台 the three departments of Ning-po-fu (*ning* 甯), Shao-hsing-fu (*shao* 紹), and T'ai-chou-fu (*t'ai* 台), forming the circuit in charge of the Taot'ai at Ningpo.

甯國府 the prefecture of Ning-kuo-fu (in Anhwei).

*niu* 牛 cows; oxen; buffaloes.

牛皮 cow hides.

牛角 cow horns; buffalo horns.

牛角器 hornware.

牛骨 cows' bones.

牛骨器 boneware.

牛鹿筋 buffalo and deer sinews.

牛油 butter; also, animal tallow.

牛奶 cows' milk.

牛奶酥 }
牛奶餅 } cheese.

牛奶油 butter.

牛黃 cow bezoar.

牛莊 Newchwang.

*niu* 扭 to twist; to wrench.

扭摔 to wrench; to wrestle and throw down.

扭解 to arrest.

*niu* 鈕 buttons.

鈕扣 brass buttons.

鈕西蘭 *(niu-hsi-lan)* New Zealand.

*niu* 謬 erroneous; mistaken.

謬誤 an error.

*no* 挪 to shift; to transfer.

挪撥 to misappropriate funds.

挪爾威國 *(no-êrh-wei-kuo)* Norway.

*nu* 奴 a slave.

奴才 a slave; Manchu officials use it for "I" when addressing the Emperor.

*nun* 嫩 young; soft; delicate; light, or pale (as colour); the opposite of *lao* (老), old, hard, dark in colour.

嫩鹿茸 young deer horns.

嫩藍 light blue.

*nü* 女 a woman.

## O.

*o* 俄 hasty; Russian.

俄國 Russia; Russian.

俄呢 Russian cloth.

*o* 訛 wrong; a mistake.

訛誤 a mistake.

*o* 額 a fixed number; the forehead.

額外 outside the fixed number; supernumerary.

額設船隻 a fixed number of vessels.

*o* / *wu* } 惡 to hate; to dislike; vicious; bad.

*ou* 歐 to vomit.

歐羅巴 *(ou-lo-pa)* Europe.

*ou* 甌 a bowl; the book name of Wênchow.

甌海關 the Wênchow Customs.

甌河 the river Ou, near Wênchow.

*ou* 偶 accidentally; unforeseen; an image.

偶爾 accidentally.

## P.

*pa* 八 (or 捌) eight.

八角 *lit.*, eight horns or corners; star aniseed.

八角渣 broken aniseed.

八角油 aniseed oil.

八角形 octangular.

八音琴 musical boxes.

*pa* 巴 to adhere.

巴圖魯 a *baturu* (military title of honour).

巴理京城 the capital city of *pa-li*, *i.e.*, Paris.

*pa* 把 a classifier of fans and other objects having a handle; to grasp.

*pa* 芭 a fence.

芭蕉 the plantain.

芭蕉山 *(pa-chiao-shan)* Sharp Peak, near Foochow.

*pa* 拔 to pull out; to raise; to excel.

*pa* 罷 to stop.

*p'a* 帕 a kerchief.

p'a 怕 to fear.

pai 白 white.

白糖 white sugar.

白胡椒 white pepper.

白海參 white bicho de mar.

白酒 white wine; sherry.

白色布 white plain shirtings.

白提花布 white figured, brocaded, etc., shirtings; cotton brocades.

白點布 white spotted shirtings.

白鉛 spelter; zinc.

白丹 white lead.

白魚翅 white sharks' fins.

白礬 alum.

白蠟 white wax; insect wax.

白荳蔻 superior cardamoms.

白寶 "white bullion;" Tientsin white sycee.

白皮土 }
白洋藥 } Malwa opium.

白晝之間 during daytime.

白字 a wrong character in a printed text.

pai 百 (or 佰) a hundred.

百貨 goods of every description.

pai 擺 to expose; to arrange (as articles for sale).

擺設 to arrange; to set up.

pai 敗 to break; to spoil.

pai 拜 to worship; to visit; to salute.

拜候 to wait upon; to visit.

拜貼 a visiting card.

p'ai 牌 a board; a certificate (especially a ship's register); a despatch to an inferior; a Government notification; an official permit.

牌照 a ship's certificate of registry; the ship's papers.

牌票 a warrant.

牌示 a notification.

p'ai 排 to arrange in order.

排字 to set up type for printing; to "compose."

p'ai 派 to depute.

派役 to depute officers.

派丁 to depute servants; to get servants to.

派去 to depute.

派委員弁 to depute officers.

p'ai 派辦之人 a deputy.

派定 to allot; to decide (as on the site of a buoy to be laid down).

p'ai 擗 to break off.

擗拉 (*p'ai-la*) the city of Braila.

pan 板 a board; boards; planks; bars (as of iron, etc.); to print on wooden blocks.

板木 planks (timber).

pan 般 manner; class; sort.

pan 搬 to move; to transfer; to tranship.

搬取 to move away; to shift.

pan 班 class; rank; to make known.

班貓 (or 斑蝥) cantharides.

pan 頒 to publish abroad.

頒發 to promulgate; to publish.

頒下 to send or issue to a subordinate (for his use or guidance).

頒賜 to confer.

pan 半 a half; "and a half."

半稅 half duty, *i.e.*, coast trade duty; also, transit dues.

半稅單 (=土貨出口半稅單) a coast trade duty [deposit] certificate.

半稅單照 a half-duty certificate; a transit certificate (inwards).

半絲綿 silk and cotton mixtures.

pan 伴 an associate; a partner.

pan 辦 }
辦理 } to manage; to buy.

辦貨 to buy goods.

辦外國機器 to buy foreign machinery.

辦妥 to manage satisfactorily; to settle.

辦賑 to manage the distribution of relief funds (in distressed districts).

辦公事 to do official work.

辦公房屋 office buildings; a public office.

辦事 to do official work; to be on duty; to work for the public.

p'an 盤 to move; to travel; a dish.

盤運各費 expenditure on account of transport.

盤川 travelling expenses.

p'an 番 }
番禺 } the district of P'an-yü (Canton). See *fan* (番).

p'an 判 to divide; to decide.

判定口界 to define the port limits.

*p'an* 判斷 to decide a case.

*pang* 邦 a kingdom; a state; a country.

*pang* 幫 (or 幇) to assist; a guild; a union of people.

幫助 to assist.

幫辦 an assistant.

幫買辦 a comprador's assistant.

幫錢 to assist with money.

*pang* 榜 a list of graduates; to publish a list.

榜示 to issue a public notice.

*pang* 艕 to board a vessel.

*pang* 謗 to slander.

*p'ang* 旁 the sides; by the side of; close to.

旁邊 by the side of.

*p'ang* 傍 by the side of; near; to depend on.

*p'ang* 磅 (in imitation of the English sound "pound") a pound; pounds.

*pao* 豹 a leopard.

豹皮 leopard skins.

*pao* 包 a bundle; a package; to wrap up.

包括 to bundle up; to contain; to be comprised in.

包封 to put into a sealed envelope; a sealed enclosure.

包皮 *emballage*; packing.

包皮鐵 metal trusses for binding bales of goods.

包攬 to manage; to mediate in business (as a broker).

包辦 to undertake the transaction of.

包藏 to store up; to conceal.

*pao* 胞 the womb.

胞弟 a uterine brother.

*pao* 鮑 pickled fish.

鮑魚 awabi; shell-fish.

*pao* 抱 to grasp; to feel; to have in the heart; to cherish.

抱歉 to feel uncomfortable about a matter; to feel regret.

抱歉之處希爲原恕爲禱 I pray that you will regard my regret as a proof of my original good intention.

*pao* 保 to protect; a ward; a guardian; to guarantee; to be surety for.

保衛 }
保護 } to protect.

保險 to protect against danger; to insure against (as fire, marine accident, etc.); insurance.

*pao* 保舉 to recommend; to recommend for promotion; to be security for.

保結 }
保單 } a bond; a guarantee.

保單執照 a bond certificate (for rice).

保人 a guarantee; a security.

保定 the department of Pao-ting-fu (in Chihli).

*pao* 薄 thin; poor; few.

*pao* 寶 valuable; precious; treasure; sycee; the Imperial Seal; in letters, "your," "your valuable."

寶砂 emery powder.

寶星 an order; the Chinese order of the *Pao-hsing*.

寶號 your signature.

寶山正頂 Paoshan Point (a locality in Shanghai Harbour).

*pao* 暴 fierce; passionate.

*pao* 爆 fire-bursting; fireworks.

爆竹 fire-crackers.

*pao* 報 to announce; to requite.

報知 to give notice to; to bring to the knowledge of; to report.

報卸 to declare goods as having to be landed.

報驗 to declare for examination.

報稅 to declare [goods] for payment of duty.

報餉人 a taxpayer; a payer of duties.

報單 an application for permission to land or ship goods; a report.

報卡 to report [goods] at a barrier.

報函 a written report; to report in writing.

報信之人 messengers; informers; reporters.

報警 to sound an alarm.

報應 to recompense.

報讎 to revenge.

報償 to repay; to requite.

報恩 to return favours; to show oneself thankful for favours received.

*p'ao* 炮 (used for 爆 *pao*) to crackle.

*p'ao* 砲 (or 礮) }
砲位 } cannon.

砲手 a gunner.

砲台 a fort; a battery.

*p'ao* 跑 to run; to race.

跑報 a courier; to announce by courier.

*p'ao* 拋 to throw away; to put down.

*p'ao* 拋棄 to throw away.
拋擲 to throw down.
拋費 to squander.

*pei* 卑 low; inferior; mean; as a term of modesty, "my."
卑職 my office; "I."

*pei* 俾 so that; so as to; to enable; to follow.
俾得 so that I may; so as to enable; so that; so as to.
俾得交還失主 so that it may be returned to the loser.
俾裕課恤商 so as to benefit the revenue and promote commerce.
俾免沿途阻滯 in order to avoid obstruction *en route*.
俾免漫無限制 in order to avoid abuse.
俾歸有著 so that it may serve as a pledge; as a substantial proof.

*pei* 裨 beneficial; to assist.
裨補 to assist.
裨益 advantage; profit; to benefit.

*pei* 被 a bed cover; to cover; to suffer; sign of the passive, when the word denoting the doer of an action stands between *pei* and the verb following.
被胎 a cotton bed quilt; a palampore.
被本關查拏 is, was, etc., seized by this office.
被......拏 to be seized; to be apprehended.
被殺 to be killed.
被傷 to be wounded.
被毀 to be broken to pieces (as a vessel by plunderers).
被搶 to be plundered.
被焚 to be burned; to be on fire.
被匪竊去 to be robbed of......by outlaws.
被告 to be accused; the accused; the defendant.
被告案件 cases of accusation; charges against.
被山遮蔽 to be kept out of view, or obscured by hills (as a light).
被風浪衝移 to be driven away by a storm (as a vessel from its moorings).
被水激刷 to be washed away by the water.
被風......收口 to put into a port for shelter.

*pei* 北 north; northern.
北闈 the northern side door of an examination hall; *fig.*, the examination for *chü-jên*.
北船 a northern vessel; *i.e.*, a vessel trading to the north of China.
北洋大臣 the Superintendent of Northern Trade.
北首 the northern end.
北京 Peking.
北海關 the Pakhoi Customs.
北河口 Pei-ho-k'ow (a Likin station on the Yangtze).
北椗 Dodd Island (near Amoy).
北德意志公會 the North-German Confederation.

*pei* 背 the back; behind the back; on the back (as of a document); to oppose.
背負 ungrateful; to carry on the back.
背約 to disregard an agreement.

*pei* 輩 generation; kind; people; when appended to a noun, expressing plurality, *e.g.*, *wo pei* 我輩, people of my kind, *i.e.*, we.

*pei* 倍......fold, as 五倍 fivefold or five times; to double.

*pei* 貝 pearls; valuable.
貝勒 a *bei-lê*, or prince of the 3rd order.

*pei* 備 to prepare; to provide; ready.
備辦 to prepare for managing a matter.
備試 to prepare for examination.
備考者 one who prepares for examination; a candidate for examination.
備呈 to submit; to supply (as copies of a document asked for).
備查 to file in the archives; to keep for reference; for inspection; for reference.
備全 to provide for the whole of.
備由 to provide for details; to prepare a statement.
備情 the complete details; "these are the facts."
備嘗辛苦 to experience hard times.

*p'ei* 棓 a flail; to strike.
棓子 nutgalls.

*p'ei* 賠 to indemnify.
賠補 to make up for; to compensate.
賠還 to repay.
賠禮 to return a call.
賠償 to compensate for; to indemnify.
賠墊 to make up (as a deficiency).
賠累 to involve in indemnification; to cause one to make up for a deficit.

*p'ei* 陪 to bear company; to assist.
陪助 to assist.

*p'ei* 披 to spread; to cover. See *p'i*.

*p'ei* 佩 a girdle; to respect.

佩帶 carried on the girdle; worn on the ribbon or the collar (as a decoration).

*p'ei* 配 to mate; to pair.

配合 to unite; to join together.

配鉛 to mix with lead.

*pên* 奔 to run; to hurry.

奔走 to run away.

奔波 to flee like billows; to run at great speed; to be in trouble about; to hurry.

*pên* 本 this, as in "*this* office"; the possessive pronoun of the person speaking or writing, as in *pên shui-wu-ssŭ* (本稅務司) = I, the Commissioner; root; source; original fund; capital.

本身 I; myself.

本處 this place.

本關 this Custom House.

本行 this firm; our firm.

本號 this bank.

本業 one's profession; my trade.

本國 my (the writer's) country; also his (another's own) country.

本地 native.

本年 this year; the present year.

本月 this month.

本結 this quarter.

本部堂 I, the Governor-General.

本部院 I, the Governor.

本道 I, the Taot'ai.

本屬商民 the merchants under one's jurisdiction.

本商 the merchant concerned (in a matter).

本人 the person concerned; oneself; in person.

本當 properly speaking, I ought to; ought; should.

本領 (=*pên-shih* 本事) able; competent.

本分 the duties of a man's occupation; one's business.

本事 ability.

本始 the beginning.

本末 beginning and end; the whole of; the essence of.

本來 originally.

本錢 capital; funds.

本利 the interest on capital; profit in trade.

*pên* 本利之盈虧 increase and decrease in profit.

*pêng* 浜 a side creek; a canal.

*p'êng* 朋 } a friend.
朋友 }

*p'êng* 棚 a shed.

*p'êng* 篷 a sail.

篷船 a sailing vessel.

*p'êng* 烹 to boil (as tea).

烹茗 to prepare good tea; to prepare for receiving a visitor.

*p'êng* 碰 to run against; to collide.

碰撞 to collide; collision.

碰壞 to wreck from collision; to damage by collision.

*pi* 逼 to press; to urge.

逼迫 to compel; to urge.

*pi* 鼻 the nose.

鼻烟 snuff.

*pi* 必 must; bound to.

必欲 to want; to wish.

必用 to be obliged to use; to be bound to use.

*pi* 比 to compare; than; to correspond; to accord with.

比例 to follow the rule; to refer to a rule by way of analogy; to treat analogously.

比較 to compare with; when compared with; may be compared with.

比照 according to; analogous to.

比如 for instance; if, for instance.

比擬 to compare; to treat analogously.

比體 of equal rank; on equal terms.

比國 (=比利時國, *pi-li-shih*), Belgium; Belgian.

*pi* 陛 the steps leading to the Throne.

陛下 Your Majesty.

陛見 to have an audience with the Emperor.

*pi* 妣 a deceased mother.

*pi* 璧 a princely gem.

璧斯瑪 *pi-ssŭ-ma* (the name of Prince BISMARCK).

*pi* 避 to flee from; to escape; to avoid; to shun.

避稅 to evade [payment of] duty.

避就 to shirk [one thing] and take [to another].

避匿 to abscond.

避諱 to avoid; to conceal.

*pi* 避諱之字 characters to be avoided in correspondence; forbidden characters, because they occur in the personal name or *shêng-hui* (聖諱) of one of the Emperors of the present dynasty, and are therefore avoided in official correspondence. According to Chinese ideas, it would show want of respect towards the sacred person of an Emperor if a character occurring in his personal name were used in its profane meaning, and it has become customary either to substitute another character of the same meaning or to slightly alter the shape of the character prohibited, unless special orders to the contrary are on record.

According to an Imperial Edict of 1846, the first character in an Emperor's personal name is to remain unaltered, and merely the second character is to be slightly altered (*see* "Translation of the Peking Gazette for 1875," p. 9). Authorities seem to disagree on some of the details regarding this question.

The following characters are considered to be forbidden:—

| Characters prohibited. | Characters substituted. |
|---|---|
| 玄 *hsüan* ...... | In certain combinations the last stroke is omitted, *e.g.*, 眩 (*hsüan*); it appears, however, in 畜 (*ch'u*) and its compounds. Otherwise, 元 (*yüan*) is used as a substitute. |
| 燁 *hsü* ........ | 燁 (*hsü*), the last stroke of the full character being omitted. |
| 胤 *ying* ........ | 胤 (*ying*), the first stroke being omitted, or 允 (*yün*). |
| 禛 *chêng* ...... | 禎 (*chêng*). |
| 弘 *hung* ....... | 弘 (*hung*); later, 宏 (*hung*). In certain combinations 强 (*chiang*) is used for 強 (*chiang*). |
| 曆 *li* .......... | 歷 or 厤 (*li*). |
| 顒 *yung* ....... | 顒 (*yung*), the two last strokes of the full character being omitted. |
| 琰 *yen* ........ | 琰 (*yen*). |
| 旻 *min* ........ | 旻 (*min*); later, 綿 (*mien*). |
| 寧 *ning* ....... | 寕 or 甯 (*ning*). |
| 詝 *chu* ......... | 詝 (*chu*), the last stroke of the full character being omitted. |
| 淳 *shun* ...... | 湻 (*shun*). |
| 湉 *tien* ......... | 湉 (*tien*), the last stroke of the full character being omitted. |

*pi* 彼 that (as opposed to *tz'ŭ* 此, this); another; there.

彼時 at that time.

彼此 there and here; *i.e.*, on either side.

*pi* 敝 mean; poor; hence, as a term of modesty, "my."

敝署 my office or yamên; *i.e.*, I (if the writer be at the head of the yamên).

敝公館 my residence; my house.

*pi* 敝前任 my predecessor.

敝國 my country.

敝官 I, the officer.

*pi* 弊 a malpractice.

弊混 irregularities; smuggling.

弊竇 a mistake; a malpractice.

弊端 malpractices.

*pi* 蔽 to keep out of view.

*pi* 筆 a pen; a pencil.

筆跡 hand-writing.

筆墨 pen and ink; composition; to compose or write a letter.

筆墨紙張 writing materials; stationery.

筆誤 a slip of the pen; a clerical error.

*pi* 畀 to confer on; to give.

*pi* 蓖 a medicinal plant.

蓖麻草 the castor oil plant.

蓖麻油 castor oil.

*pi* 閉 to close the doors; to close.

*pi* 畢 to finish; the end; at last.

畢幾 (or 嗶嘰 *pi-chi*) long ells.

*pi* 弼 to assist (as a statesman assists his monarch).

*p'i* 譬 to compare; if.

譬如 if, for instance.

*p'i* 皮 skins; hides; leather; *emballage.*

皮貨 skins of all kinds.

皮器 leather articles (as pouches, purses, etc.).

皮箱 } leather trunks.
皮櫃 }

皮膠 glue.

皮毯 hair or skin rugs.

皮蛋 preserved eggs.

皮包 *emballage;* packing.

*p'i* 披 to open; to unroll a scroll.

披閱 to open and read; to note the contents of.

*p'i* 疲 fatigue; loss of strength.

疲敝 weakness.

*p'i* 批 to write in reply to a petition; to endorse a petition.

批示 } to reply officially to an inferior; an official reply.
批迴 }

批明 to endorse (as a certificate is endorsed by an official).

新關文件録



*p'i* 批註 to endorse; to comment upon.

批准 to be sanctioned; to sanction.

*p'i* 疋 a piece; a classifier of piece goods.

疋數 the number of pieces (as of piece goods).

*piao* 標 a signal; a mark; a brigade; a naval division; a squadron.

標記 marks; navigation marks.

標桿 a beacon pole (classifier, 根 *kên*).

標明 to endorse.

標布 *T*-cloths.

*piao* 表 to make known; a guide; a signal; a watch.

表角 *(piao-chio)* Cape of Good Hope, near Swatow.

*p'iao* 票 a money order; a warrant; a ticket (as a pawn ticket, a lottery ticket); *e.g., fa-ts'ai p'iao* (發財票), a lottery ticket; *Lü-sung p'iao* (呂宋票), a Manila [lottery] ticket.

*p'iao* 飄 a whirlwind; to be driven about by a storm.

*p'iao* 漂 to toss about.

漂移無定 to drift away (as a ship from its moorings).

漂流水面 to drift about on the water; to be adrift.

漂撞 to be shipwrecked.

*pieh* 別 another; otherwise; to distinguish; to separate.

別口 another port.

別項 other kinds of.........

別項貨物 other goods; goods of a description not covered by a document.

別項華商 another Chinese merchant.

別力 (*pieh-li*, in imitation of the English sound "penny") a penny; pence.

*pien* 扁 flat; a tablet.

*pien* 匾 a signboard; a tablet.

匾額 a laudatory tablet.

*pien* 編 to arrange in order; registered under No. .......; to plait; to weave; to compile.

編列字號 to register (as a cargo-boat).

編冊 a register.

*pien* 遍 (or 徧) everywhere; to go round; small.

遍喩 to inform all; to notify the public.

遍處懸掛 to hang up, or exhibit, everywhere (as a proclamation).

遍運天下 to convey everywhere in the empire.

*pien* 便 convenient; convenience; to accommodate; to facilitate; cheap; (=卽 *chi*) then; thereupon.

*pien* 便於 to meet with no difficulty in; to be expedient to; to facilitate; to be given facilities in.

便商 to accommodate merchants; to show due consideration to the convenience of trade.

便船 a convenient ship; a ship which happens to be on the berth, with destination to a port one may wish to send passengers or cargo to, but not chartered for the purpose.

便用 to use as one sees fit; for convenient use.

便附 to enclose in a letter.

便宜 advantageous; to be of advantage to; cheap; having full power to act without reference to a superior; to do as one pleases.

便宜行事大臣 a Minister having discretionary power to act according to the requirements of his office; a Minister Plenipotentiary.

便當 comfortable; convenient.

*pien* 緶 to plait.

*pien* 邊 a side; a border; an edge; the frontier.

邊沿 in the margin (of a document).

邊疆 the frontier.

*pien* 貶 to censure; to discharge (as an officer).

貶退 to discharge; to dismiss.

*pien* 弁 officers of an inferior grade; military officers.

*pien* 辨 to cut asunder; to divide; to distinguish.

辨明 }<br>辨認 } to distinguish.

*pien* 辯 to dispute; to argue; to discriminate.

辯駁 to contradict; to dispute; contradictory.

辯論 to argue; to discuss; to controvert.

*pien* 變 to change.

變通 to change; to make a change by way of accommodation or of compromise; for convenience sake; to accommodate.

變約 to change one's mind after having made a contract.

變價 to dispose of by sale; to sell.

變天風浪較大 bad weather at sea.

*p'ien* 片 a flat piece of something; a strip; a sheet.

片函 a note; a card.

片子 a visiting card.

*p'ien* 偏 inclined to one side; partial; to incline to a certain direction of the compass, *e.g.*, 西北偏北, north-north-west.

偏見 a one-sided view; partiality.

偏私 }<br>偏枯 } selfish; partial; partiality.<br>偏累 }

*pien* 偏重 to make a one-sided charge; to impose difficulty by partiality.

*p'ien* 篇 a section; a page; a leaf.

*p'ien* 諞 to boast; to impose upon.

*p'ien* 騙 to defraud; to delude; to inveigle.

騙往魁强脅從 to kidnap.

*pin* 殯 a funeral; funeral rites.

*pin* 賓 a guest; a stranger.

*p'in* 貧 poor; poverty.

*p'in* 品 degree; rank; the nine degrees of Chinese official rank; to arrange; delicacies.

品銜 rank.

*ping* 氷 ice; crystallised.

氷河時 when the river is covered with ice.

氷糖 sugar candy.

氷片 Baroos camphor.

*ping* 兵 a soldier; military.

兵船 a man-of-war; a gun-boat.

兵船廠 a naval yard.

兵勇 soldiers.

兵役 soldiers and runners.

兵營 a camp; a garrison.

兵械 arms; military stores.

兵部 the Board of War.

兵備道 a Taot'ai.

*ping* / *pin* } 梹 (or 檳) / 梹榔 } the betel-nut; betel-nuts.

梹榔衣 betel-nut husk.

梹榔膏 gambier.

*ping* 並 (竝 or 幷) and; or; also; at the same time; together with.

並未 not by any means. All negative particles—*pu* (不), *wu* (無), *wei* (未), etc.—may be reinforced by the addition of certain words, which need not be translated except where it seems necessary to emphasise negation, *e.g.*, when they correspond to the English "by no means," "not at all," etc. The following words and expressions are often so employed: *ping* (並), *tuan* (斷), *ch'ien* (千), *wan* (萬), *ch'ien wan* (千萬), *hao* (毫), *ssŭ hao* (絲毫), *chüeh* (決), *chüeh* (絕), *ch'ieh* (切), *tsung* (總), *chung* (終), *ch'iung* (迥), *ching* (竟).

並非 not at all; not. Cf. *ping* 並未.

並無 not by any means. Cf. *ping wei* 並未.

並無不合 by no means unjust; quite approvable.

*ping* 並經 having at the same time.

*ping* 併 (used for 並 *ping*) and; both; with; altogether; together with.

*ping* 餅 cakes; paste; pastry.

*ping* 病 sick; sickness.

病勢 the state of a disease.

病故 to die of disease.

*ping* 稟 a communication from an inferior to a superior; a petition; to petition.

稟詞 / 稟帖 / 稟書 } a petition; a statement.

稟明 to inform in a petition; to apply to; to represent.

稟知 to inform (a superior).

稟報 to report (to a superior).

稟稱 to state in a petition; to report (to a superior).

稟訴 to petition the court in reply to an accusation; a counter-statement.

稟見 to wait upon a superior.

稟告 to inform in a petition; to accuse in writing.

稟控 to accuse; to make a written charge.

稟求 / 稟請 } to apply for.

稟請賠補 to claim compensation.

稟假 to apply for leave of absence.

稟命 to apply for orders.

稟批 to decide in reply to a petition.

*ping* 秉 to uphold (as a principle).

秉公 upholding justice; impartially; to act fairly.

秉權 holding powers; plenipotentiary.

*p'ing* 平 even; level; weight; standard weight (as of sycee silver, *e.g.*, 關平, the Customs standard weight of the Haikwan tael); to weigh (as silver); cheap; tranquil; peaceful.

平等 of equal standing.

平行 of equal rank; on the same footing.

平允 just; fair.

平定 to arrive at a just settlement; to agree upon.

平常 common; usual.

平時 in ordinary times; ordinarily.

平準 to adjust.

*p'ing* 平兌 to weigh.

平糶 to sell grain at even (*i.e.*, fair) and reasonable prices; to sell cheaply (as grain bought up by Government for cheap sale in a famine-stricken district).

平安 peace.

*p'ing* 評 to discuss.

*p'ing* 瓶 a bottle; a vase.

*p'ing* 憑 to lean on; on the ground of; according to.

憑商人報明 to rely on (*i.e.*, to accept) the merchant's declaration.

憑碼均行 to ascertain the value (as of silver) according to weight.

憑單 "leaning [on this] bill;" "as per memo.;" also, a "duty proof;" a voucher; a certificate.

憑據 a written guarantee; evidence; proof.

憑證 proof; evidence.

*po* 玻 glass.

玻璃 glass; window glass.

玻璃片 window glass.

玻璃球 glass balls (used as paper weights).

玻璃器皿 glass vessels; glassware; crystal-ware.

*po* 波 a wave.

波斯 Persia; Persian.

波斯洋藥 / 波斯金花土 } Persian opium.

波羅蜜 pineapples.

*po* 伯 / 伯爵 } an earl.

伯磊們 (*po-lei-mên*) the city of Bremen.

*po* 迫 to urge; to embarrass.

*po* 鉑 (for which 箔 and 薄 are used) metal leaf; foil.

*po* 泊 to moor; to anchor.

泊船 to anchor a ship.

泊設 to moor (as a new lightship).

泊界 the harbour limits.

泊船章程 regulations for the mooring of ships.

*po* 剝 to peel; to scrape off; to extort; used for 駁 *po*, to tranship.

剝船 (=駁船) a cargo-boat.

*po* 撥 to transfer; to send; to set aside for; used for 駁 *po*, to tranship.

撥交 to set aside and hand over; to appropriate.

撥給 to set aside for; to appropriate for.

撥用 to appropriate (as funds).

*po* 撥還 to re-appropriate; to recover [funds defrayed].

*po* 播 to disperse; to scatter; to winnow.

播棄 to reject.

*po* 薄 thin; thinness.

薄荷油 peppermint oil.

薄荷冰 peppermint ice; *i.e.*, peppermint oil crystallised.

薄荷葉 peppermint leaf.

*po* 跋 to walk through the grass; to travel.

跋涉 to travel far; far-travelled.

*po* 駁 to tranship; to dispute; to argue.

駁船 a cargo-boat.

駁貨 to tranship goods.

駁貨船隻 cargo-boats.

駁過別船 to tranship to another vessel.

駁運 to tranship; to carry goods (as in a cargo-boat).

駁復 to argue against; counter-argument.

*p'o* 坡 a slope; the side of a hill; a bluff.

*p'o* 破 to break; to tear.

破爛 torn; broken.

破爛鷹捧番銀 broken-dollar money.

破眼 to be broken and having holes.

破損 breakage; *i.e.*, the loss caused by breaking.

*p'o* 頗 rather; very; extremely.

頗願 to eagerly wish for.

*p'o* 拍 to beat; to slap a table; to bid; used for *po* 泊, to anchor.

拍賣 to sell by auction.

拍定 to settle a purchase at auction.

*p'o* 珀 amber.

*p'ou* 剖 to split asunder; to lay open.

剖別 to distinguish.

剖判 to decide a case.

*pu* 不 not.

不諳 not knowing; ignorant.

不成 incomplete; impracticable.

不卽 not immediately; forthwith not.

不卽………而 forthwith not to ……, but to ……; instead of …… (doing this), …… (doing that).

不及 not to reach; not to come up to; to be less than.

不及候聽 cannot wait.

不計 not counting; excepting.

*pu* 不識 ignorant; not knowing.
不識姓名 unknown by name.
不致 so as not to; so that there may not be; the opposite of 致 (*chih*) or 以致 (*i chih*), so that.
不久 within a short time.
不出情願 without uttering a wish; not of one's own accord.
不揣冒昧 not able to detect signs of rash stupidity.
不准 not allowed; forbidden.
不准停輪之處 a place where steamers are not allowed to stop; a place not authorised as a landing-stage (on the Yangtze).
不拘 no matter whether.
不法 unruly.
不妨 there is no difficulty in.
不分 making no distinction between.
不分何處進口 without distinguishing the place of importation.
不符 to disagree.
不敷 not sufficient for; not to cover.
不合 it is not convenient.
不合銷 not all sold (as goods).
不洽 to disagree.
不休 not to stop or cease; unceasingly.
不一 not the same; different; more than one; several; not a few; many; many times; also, a very common concluding phrase in letters, which, like the corresponding phrases, 不宣, 不備, 不盡, and others, are mere expletives, but serve to show that a letter is finished.
不一而足 not confined to one; more than one.
不宜 must not; should not.
不然 not so; if not so.
不日 shortly.
不若 / 不如 } it is better to; we had better.
不入等 unclassed.
不堪之實在情形 it is really impossible to bear this; the state of matters is indeed more than we can bear.
不肯 not willing.
不克 not able to.
不顧 not to care for.
不顧大局 not to care for the public interest; to have no regard for society.
不公 not just; incorrect (as the weights of a balance).

*pu* 不過 not exceeding; only.
不過……而已 only……and nothing more.
不樂於使用 to dislike using.
不領 not having been issued (as a certificate, etc.); *i.e.*, without (a certificate, etc.).
不論粗細 irrespective of quality.
不能不 bound to; cannot help being.
不便 inconvenient.
不便於民 inconvenient to the public.
不必 must not; need not.
不善 bad.
不稍 not in the least.
不稍寬貸 not the slightest leniency will be shown.
不勝詫異 very strange; quite incredible.
不勝感激 to be greatly obliged.
不勝其煩 it is attended with endless trouble.
不貸 without leniency; strictly.
不但……且…… not only……, but also……
不得 cannot; should not.
不得已 there is no help; inevitable.
不等 after two expressions, "and," "or," "or so"; *e.g.*, 輕重不等 light or heavy; light ones and heavy ones; 二三不等 two or three.
不妥之處 unsafe places; passages not quite in order and requiring correction.
不在列 unclassed; unenumerated.
不在此例 not covered by this rule.
不足 not enough; insufficient; incapable.
不足以礙其來路 not capable of discouraging importation.
不遵 to disobey; to disregard.
不端 improper; incapable.
不爲無見 to consider a matter to be reasonable enough.
不惟不……反…… not only not ……, but even……
不問自用出售 no matter whether for own use or for sale.
不無 to be bound to. (Note that two negatives combined make a strong affirmative.)
不無窒碍 cannot avoid difficulties; bound to be attended by difficulties.
不易 not easy to; difficult to; unchanged; unchangeable.
不易之規 an unchangeable rule.
不應爲之事 improprieties; misconduct.

*pu* 捕 to seize; to pursue.

捕獲 } to seize; to arrest.
捕拿 }

捕役 police runners.

*pu* 補 to assist; to supplement; to mend; to do afterwards what ought to have been done before.

補助 to assist.

補缺 to fill a vacancy.

補發之欵 a supplementary grant.

補領 to issue anew (as a document lost).

補請牌照 to apply for a new certificate of registry (to replace one lost).

補增 to add by way of supplement; to make a supplementary payment.

補交 to pay afterwards (what should have been paid before).

補具退稟 to send in a supplementary statement regarding one's resignation.

補用 employed as a supernumerary; supernumerary.

補水 (=補交紋水) when making a payment in dollars, to pay a premium on account of the difference in the price of pure sycee silver. See *wên* 紋水.

補足 to pay for difference in standard of silver.

*pu* 簿 a register; a ledger; an account book.

*pu* 僕 a vassal; a servant; your servant; "I."

*pu* 布 cloth; cotton, linen, etc., cloth; to spread; to diffuse; to inform.

布疋 cotton piece goods.

布衣服 cotton clothing.

布置 to place in order; to arrange.

布達 to inform.

布政使 a provincial treasurer or Fant'ai.

布國 (=布路斯國 *pu-lu-ssŭ*) Prussia; Prussian.

*pu* 佈 to extend; a public notice.

佈覆 to reply to a letter.

*pu* 部 tribe; class; one of the *liu pu* (六部) or Boards of Government.

部曹 member of one of the six Boards.

部堂 official designation of a President of a Board (as such the title of a Governor-General).

部院 official designation of a Vice-President of a Board (as such the title of a Provincial Governor).

部頒 issued by the Board [of Revenue] (as standard weights and measures).

*pu* 步 a pace; to pace; to move up and down.

步位 space.

*p'u* 鋪 bedding; a shop.

鋪蓋 bedding.

鋪田 factories and farms.

鋪戶 factory workmen; shop people.

*p'u* 匍 } to be prostrate; to prostrate.
匍匐 }

*p'u* 浦 a river; the Hwangpu at Shanghai.

浦東岸 the shore of the river opposite Shanghai; the Pootung shore.

*p'u* 舖 a shop.

舖商人 traders; merchants.

## S.

*sa* 撒 to scatter; to let go.

*sai* 塞 to stop (as a hole); to hinder.

*sai* 賽 to emulate; to try who can make the best show.

賽奇公會 an industrial exhibition.

賽奇物件 exhibits (at an industrial exhibition).

賽馬 horse-racing.

賽馬之期 a race meeting.

*san* 三 (or 叁) three; thrice.

三角 three cornered; triangular.

三桅鐙船 a three-masted lightship.

三口通商大臣 the Minister Superintendent of the Three Ports (formerly the only ones open to trade).

三單 } a triplicate transit memorandum.
三連單 (or 三聯單) }

三抬頭 the raising of the column in a text by the space of three characters in the case of terms relating to a deceased Sovereign.

三思 to think three times; *i.e.*, to carefully consider.

三四月間新月後之禮拜五, the Friday following after the new moon in the third or fourth Chinese month; *i.e.*, Good Friday.

三奈 } capoor cutchery.
三賴 }

*san* 散 to scatter; to let go; to dismiss.

*san* 傘 an umbrella.

*sang* 喪 to mourn; a funeral; to die.

喪服 mourning clothes; to wear mourning.

喪禮 funeral rites.

*sang* 桑 the mulberry tree.

*sao* 掃 to brush; to sweep; to clear off.

掃門 to sweep before the door; *i.e.*, to keep one's house ready to receive a visitor.

掃數 to clear off an account.

*sê* 色 colour; to colour; to dye.

色樣 colour.

色布 dyed cloth.

色花點布 dyed, figured, brocaded, etc., shirtings.

*sha* 砂 gravel; sand; gritty, like sand.

砂仁 inferior cardamoms or grains of paradise.

砂穀米 sago.

*sha* 紗 gauze; untwisted thread; yarn; thin silk.

*sha* 沙 sand; a sand or mud bank.

沙尾 a sandspit.

沙灘 a sand or mud bank; a shoal; a bar (as the Woosung Bar).

沙籐 rattans.

沙市 Shashih (a port of call on the Yangtze).

*sha* 裟 representing the Indian sound *sha* in 袈裟 *kasha*, the robe of a Buddhist priest; gauze.

*sha* 鯊 (or 魦) the shark.

鯊魚皮 sharks' skins.

*sha* 殺 to kill; to murder.

*shan* 山 a hill; a mountain; an island; a promontory.

山羊 a goat.

山羊毛 goats' hair.

山羊皮 goats' skins.

山東 the Shantung province.

山西 the Shansi province.

山海關 the Newchwang Customs.

*shan* 汕 a spit of land.

汕頭 Swatow.

汕埠 the port of Swatow.

*shan* 訕 to slander.

*shan* 舢 (an unauthorised character) a small boat.

舢板 a sampan. Cf. *shan* 杉板.

*shan* 扇 fans.

*shan* 擅 arbitrarily; on one's own authority and without permission; without authority; to venture.

擅行...... to......[*verb*] without authority.

擅便 to act on one's own authority.

擅加 to make unauthorised additions.

*shan* 杉 a kind of pine.

杉板 a sampan; a cargo-boat.

*shan* 衫 a shirt.

*shan* 刪 to cut out; to cancel; to revise and correct.

刪除 to expunge; to remove a name from a list.

刪改 to revise and correct.

*shan* 珊 } coral.
珊瑚 }

*shan* 閃 a flash; to shun; to peep.

*shan* 陝 } the province of Shensi.
陝西 }

*shan* 善 good; to make good.

善法 a good measure or method.

善後 to make good what comes after; to make rules supplementary to a set of rules originally not complete.

善後條約 } the Supplementary Rules appended to the Tariff; the "Tariff Rules" or "Trade Regulations."
善後條款 }
善後章程 }

善後總局 a special commission for the revision of regulations; a provincial administrative board.

*shan* 繕 to write out; to copy.

繕立 to make out a document; to place on record; to note (as a protest).

繕立預據 to note a protest.

繕書 writers; copyists.

*shang* 上 above; superior; first quality; to go up; to ascend; to land.

上下 superior and inferior; first and second quality; clean and refuse; up and down; to land and ship; to communicate with the shore (as from on board a ship).

上中下 superior, middling, and inferior; first, second, and third quality.

上燕窩 first quality birds' nests.

上冰片 clean Baroos camphor.

上面 above; on it (as on a surface).

上司 superiors.

上憲 one's superior authorities; high Government officers.

上官 high officials.

上次 a first and a second time; of the first and second class; the last, *i.e.*, previous, time.

上大下小 broad above and narrow below.

上寬下窄 broad above and narrow below; (if round) an inverted frustum.

*shang* 上段 the upper limit (as of a harbour).

上旬 the first decade; the first to the tenth day of a month.

上堂 to proceed to the court-room; to come into court.

上船 to board a ship; to embark; to ship.

上岸 to land.

上水 to go up river.

上游 up the river.

上下游 up and down the river.

上駛 to sail, or steam, up the river.

上諭 an Imperial edict.

上稟 to hand up a petition (a concluding phrase in petitions).

上控 to appeal.

上稅 to pay duty.

上年 last year.

上結 the preceding quarter.

上午 the forenoon.

上屆 the last time; the last occasion.

上海 Shanghai.

上洋 *(shang-yang)* used locally for Shanghai (上海).

*shang* 尚 yet; still; to control; to esteem; to be fond of; to be inclined to.

尚有 there is still.

尚未 not yet.

尚爲周到 all is yet quite in order.

尚屬平允 it is yet fair.

尚詳洽 clear and satisfactory enough.

尚屬 it might be; I daresay it is.

尚書 the President of a Board; a Minister of State.

*shang* 裳 clothes.

*shang* 賞 to bestow; to confer (as a reward); to rejoice; to take pleasure in.

賞給 to give; to award; to make a present of.

賞賜 to bestow.

賞功 to distinguish merit; public rewards of merit, such as feathers, badges, or titles.

賞罰 rewards and punishments; to reward and fine.

賞還 to kindly return.

賞需之用 to give for one's use; to present; to give as a premium.

賞戴藍翎 wearing the blue plume or crow's feather.

*shang* 賞鑒 to enjoy a view or spectacle.

*shang* 商 trade; a merchant; to consider; to consult; to devise.

商販 to buy and sell; trade; traders; merchants.

商人 a merchant.

商戶 merchants.

商賈 merchants; travelling and resident merchants.

商旅 travelling merchants.

商夥 a partner in a firm; an agent.

商局 the "Merchants' Company"; *i.e.*, the China Merchants' Company.

商本 capital in trade.

商情 commercial interests.

商貨全書 the entire books regarding trade; *i.e.*, the Customs statistical publications.

商辦 to consider and act.

商量 } to consider; to deliberate; to consult.
商酌 }

商定 to decide upon.

*shang* 傷 to wound; to injure.

傷損 to damage; to be damaged.

*shao* 少 little; in the least; the least amount; short of; young; junior (as opposed to *ta* 大 or *t'ai* 太, senior).

少於單 [a quantity of goods] less than [is stated in] the document.

少報 to declare short; to understate.

少保 a junior guardian of the Imperial Heir Apparent.

*shao* 哨 to whistle; a whistle.

哨船 a revenue cruiser.

*shao* 艄 the stern of a vessel.

艄工 the commanding officer on board a ship; a ship-master.

*shao* 梢 the top of a staff.

*shao* 稍 slightly; gradually; rather.

稍寬其禁 to slightly relax a restriction; to grant a facility.

稍有誤會 there is a slight misapprehension.

稍有不同 it is not exactly the same; there are slight differences in.

稍申 to explain somewhat; to show to a certain extent.

稍戢 to gradually lay aside.

*shao* 燒 to burn; to roast; to boil.

燒完 burnt off; consumed and finished (as coal on board a steamer).

*shê* 賒 to credit; to give credit.

賒賬 to credit.

*shê* 奢 extravagant; wasteful.

*shê* 涉 to ford; to wade; to concern; to be connected with; to be implicated in.

*shê* 舌 the tongue.

*shê* 舍 a cottage; as a term of modesty, "my."

*shê* 捨 to reject; to part with.

*shê* 射 to shoot out; to project (as a shadow).

射光 to shine; luminous.

*shê* 麝 the musk deer.

麝香 musk.

*shê* 設 to arrange for; if; supposing that.

設序 to arrange in order.

設傳文信 to arrange for the transmission of official documents and private letters; to undertake the forwarding of correspondence.

設立 to erect; to establish.

設浮椿 to lay down buoys and beacons.

設計 to contrive; to plan.

設法 to devise a plan; to see that.

設法籌辦 to adopt measures for.

設新章 to introduce new regulations.

設席 to prepare a banquet.

設使 } 設若 } if; supposing that.

*shê* 赦 to remit; to release.

赦免 to forgive.

*shên* 身 the body; in petitions, a modest term for "I."

身家 one's person and family.

身故 to die.

*shên* 申 to explain; to state to a superior; the book name of the city of Shanghai.

申文 a despatch to a superior; a report.

申稱 } 申詳 } 申報 } to report (to a superior).

申報咨行札委 to inform superiors, equals, and inferiors in rank.

申信 to convey news.

申明 to explain clearly; to state clearly (as to a superior).

*shên* 申覆 to reply (to a superior).

申請 to apply for (as for instructions).

申請查照施行 to request (a superior) to receive a document for action to be taken.

申請酌核示遵 } 申請核奪示覆 } to apply for instructions (in a despatch to a superior).

申江 Shanghai.

*shên* 伸 equal to; worth; to extend to; (= 申) to explain.

伸謝 to present one's thanks.

伸得 to be equal to; to be worth.

伸訴 to make a statement; to complain.

*shên* 紳 a sash; a girdle; the gentry.

紳士 a scholar.

紳耆 the gentry and elders.

紳商 the gentry and merchants; the community.

*shên* 深 deep; deeply; extremely; very.

深淺 deep and shallow; depth.

深沾 } 深荷 } deeply obliged; deeply indebted (as for benefits received).

深願 to wish sincerely.

深資 to be a great help.

*shên* 參 ginseng. Cf. *ts'an* and *ts'ên*.

*shên* 甚 very; extremely.

甚大 very large.

甚稀 very rarely.

甚屬公允 } 甚為公允 } it is very fair; it is very just.

甚願 to wish ardently.

*shên* 慎 careful; to be careful.

慎勤 careful; diligent; diligence.

慎重 to carefully observe; to treat as important.

慎重之人 a careful and serious man.

慎選 to select with care.

*shên* 審 to examine; to try (as a legal case); to investigate.

審案 } 審訊 } to try a case.

審究 to investigate thoroughly.

審明 to investigate; to try (as a case).

審辦 to settle judicial cases.

審斷 to give judgment; to decide a case.

*shên* 審結 (or 審理) to decide and settle legal cases.

審判 to decide legal cases; to have jurisdiction.

*shêng* 生 raw; unmanufactured; unripe; to be born; to come into existence; to create.

生熟 raw and cooked; crude and prepared; unmanufactured and manufactured.

生菓 fresh fruit; unripe fruit.

生絲 raw silk.

生鐵 unmanufactured iron.

生鐵磚 pig iron.

生銅 unmanufactured copper; copper ore.

生牛皮 cow or buffalo hides.

生質 natural disposition.

生疏 raw; coarse; incomplete.

生生世世 one's offspring for many generations.

生計 to get a living; a livelihood.

生理 occupation; business.

生意 } trade; business.
生涯 }

生事 to make trouble.

生弊竇 to create malpractices; to commit an offence.

生流弊 to result in a standing nuisance.

*shêng* 笙 a pipe (for whistling).

*shêng* 勝 to be able to; adequate to; worthy of; to be superior to; to conquer.

勝防 to be able to ward off; to protect.

勝選 eligible; competent for election.

勝選憑照 a certificate of competency; a document certifying to the eligibility of a person for a certain post.

勝意 superior thoughts; *i.e.*, "your valuable opinion."

*shêng* 升 to rise; to raise; to hoist (as a flag); to rise in office; a Chinese grain measure, of which 10 are equal to a *tou* (斗) and 100 are equal to a picul (石).

升祉 [I wish you] promotion and happiness (a concluding phrase in letters).

升安 [I wish you] promotion and peace (a concluding phrase in letters).

升遐 to rise to the distant land; *i.e.*, to die.

*shêng* 陞 to rise; to be promoted.

陞官 to be promoted.

陞啓 *lit.*, to ascend [the steps of your door] to be opened; written after the name on the address of a letter, it means, "to be delivered into the hands of.....," in which sense it is more polite than 查收 *(ch'a-shou)*, otherwise similarly employed.

*shêng* 聲 to make known; to report; to state; a sound.

聲明 to report.

聲稱 to state; to declare.

聲候 to make a personal statement.

聲聞 it is rumoured; report; to report.

*shêng* 繩 a cord; a string; to restrain.

繩索 cordage; the rigging of a ship.

*shêng* 省 a province; also, the provincial capital; to save; to diminish.

省城 } the provincial capital.
省會 }

省河 the river at the provincial capital.

省力 to spare one's strength.

*shêng* 盛 abundant; great; plenteous; to thrive.

盛恩 great kindness; your favour.

盛多 plenty.

盛業 prosperity; thriving trade.

盛情 kind feelings; kindness.

盛京 the Liaotung province; Shêngking; Moukden.

*shêng* 乘 to avail oneself; to multiply.

乘坐 to make use of a boat or carriage.

乘以一百 to multiply by 100.

*shêng* 剩 to remain (after deduction); a remainder; an overplus.

剩貨 remnants of goods.

*shêng* 聖 holy; sacred.

聖旨 an Imperial mandate.

聖覽 the sacred glance; an Imperial order.

聖鑒 the sacred glance; the Emperor's approval.

*shih* 駛 to hasten; to sail; quick.

駛赴 to sail to; to be bound for.

*shih* 使 if; supposing that; in the event of; to cause to; to let; so that; to send; a messenger.

使然 to cause to be thus; to bring about.

使令 to order; to cause.

使費 to lay out; to incur an expense for another; expenses; charges.

使用 to employ; to be employed; to lend one's services; an outlay; expenses.

使人 to send someone; a messenger.

使臣 an envoy.

使役 a servant.

*shih* 市 a market; a fair; exchange of produce; to trade.

*shih* 市價 the market price.

*shih* 柿 the persimmon fruit; persimmons.

*shih* 飾 to adorn; ornaments; to paint; to pretend; to make believe.

飾以紅色 to paint red; to be painted red.

飾詞偷漏 a pretext for evading payment of duties.

*shih* 師 an expert; a master; a patron; a brigade; military; naval.

師船 a naval boat; a man-of-war.

*shih* 侍 to accompany; to follow (as an attendant).

侍郎 a Vice-President of a Board.

侍衛 Imperial guards.

*shih* 時 time; at the time; then; thereupon; each time; at any time; an hour, both in the Chinese sense (*i.e.*, the twelfth part of a day, corresponding to two hours of our time) and in the foreign sense.

時分 time; hour.

時屆 at the time; at the proper time; punctually.

時刻 time.

時刻簿 a time-book; a [postal] delivery-book.

時辰 a Chinese hour.

時辰表 a watch; watches.

時辰香 joss-sticks.

時常 at any time; always.

時價 the market value.

*shih* 識 to know. Cf. *chih*.

*shih* 弛 to relax; to abrogate.

弛禁 to abrogate a prohibition; to rescind a law.

*shih* 施 to bestow; to relieve; to rescue.

施恩 to bestow a favour.

施及 to bestow on; to extend to (as a privilege).

施行 to grant that it be so; to comply with a petition; to carry out a scheme; to put into operation.

*shih* 濕 damp; wet.

*shih* 是 this; that; to be; this means that; the above amounts to this, that, etc.; that is; correct; satisfactory (as an explanation).

是非 to be and not to be; yes and no; positive and negative; right and wrong.

是否 whether or not.

是否可行 whether or not it may be done.

是否有當 whether or not it ought to be thus; whether it is the proper course to adopt.

是以 therefore; hence; thereby.

是日 that day; on the same date.

*shih* 是所至禱 this is what I very much pray for; I would urgently ask for this.

是為至荷 I shall be much obliged thereby.

是為至要 this is very important.

是荷 I shall thank you for; to be obliged.

是幸 I shall be pleased if you will; I shall thank you for.

是寔 the very truth; to be really true; really genuine.

*shih* 實 (or 寔) real; really; truly; indeed; true; the truth.

實情 } 實事 } the real facts; the matter of fact.

實在 really.

實係 to be in reality; to prove to be.

實屬 it really is; is indeed.

實存 the real balance; the net total.

實重 the real weight.

實心 sincerely; with the *bonâ fide* intention.

實據 documentary proof.

實估之價 the true value.

實則有損 in reality there is a loss.

實為德便 it will be a real kindness or benefit.

實為公便 } 實於公便 } it is really in the public interest; it will really be conducive to fairness.

*shih* 矢 an arrow; swift; to resolve.

*shih* 失 to lose; to miss; to fail.

失去 to lose; to have lost.

失落 to drop and lose (as goods dropping into the sea); to lose.

失事 to miss one's aim; to be shipwrecked.

失機 to miss an opportunity.

失信 to break one's promise.

失火 to catch fire; fire breaking out.

失主 the loser; the person whose property is lost, stolen, etc.

失防 to neglect guarding against; to fail to take precautions.

*shih* 示 to make known; to inform; a proclamation.

示知 to inform by proclamation; to make known; to inform.

示諭 a public notice.

示仰 to issue a proclamation with a view to......

示禁 prohibited by proclamation; forbidden by Government.

新關文件録



*shih* 示路警船浮 a fairway buoy.

示覆 to give instructions in reply to an application.

示復飭遵施行 to issue instructions for one's guidance (in reply to a despatch).

示求救 to make signals of distress.

*shih* 視 to see; to take the bearing.

視爲 to look [at a matter] as; to consider as.

視爲具文 to regard as a mere document (said of rules which exist on paper only).

*shih* 嗜 to relish; to be fond of; to indulge in.

*shih* 十 (or 拾) ten.

十分 all; complete; completely; very.

*shih* 什 ten; sundry; miscellaneous.

什物 / 什貨 } miscellaneous goods; sundries.

*shih* 拾 to pick up; to collect; (= 十 ten).

*shih* 石 a stone; a rock; mineral; a picul (in this sense also read *tan* (担), when it is often written 石).

石礁 rocks.

石樁 a stone beacon.

石羔 ground gypsum; plaster of Paris.

石黄 hartall; orpiment; yellow lead.

石灰 lime.

石綠 malachite; copper ore; a kind of green paint.

石花菜 agar-agar.

石碑山 (*shih-p'ai-shan*) Breaker Point, near Swatow.

*shih* 碩 great; eminent.

*shih* 世 a generation; an age; hereditary.

世職 hereditary office.

世襲 a hereditary nobleman; an earl; hereditary.

世爵 hereditary nobility.

世世公侯 may your generation rise to the ranks of duke and marquess.

*shih* 食 to eat; eatables; food; provisions; to drink; to smoke.

食鹽 salt (ready for use); kitchen salt.

食物 provisions; eatables.

食言 to eat one's words, *i.e.*, not to keep one's word; to break one's promise.

*shih* 室 a house; a room.

*shih* 氏 after a name, denotes that the person is a woman; in petitions, "I," said by a woman; a clan; a clan or family name.

*shih* 始 first; the first time; then; not till then; the beginning.

始終 the beginning and end; a period taken altogether; the entire period.

*shih* 釋 to release; to explain; Buddhist.

釋放 to release.

釋義 to explain the meaning.

*shih* 式 pattern; type.

式樣 a pattern.

式類 class; category.

*shih* 試 to examine; examination; to try.

試驗 to examine; to test.

試用 to be employed on trial; to serve on probation; probationary.

試辦 to work as an experiment; provisional.

試辦再議 to work by way of experiment and then decide, *i.e.*, experimental and open to revision (as a regulation); provisional.

*shih* 事 a matter; a subject; business; a law case; trouble; service; to serve.

事情 an affair; a matter.

事由 circumstances; particulars.

事體 an affair; a concern.

事主 the prosecutor in a law suit; a master; an employer.

事務 business matters; affairs.

事務大臣 a Minister in charge of affairs.

事宜 that which properly pertains to the business of ......; affairs; matters; business.

事勢 the state of matters; circumstances.

事實 the matter of fact; the truth of a matter.

事權 authority; power.

事前 before matters [go wrong]; before something happens.

事如屬實 if the fact be true.

事出權宜 a course adopted as being dictated by circumstances.

事關約則 a matter concerning the Treaty and the Tariff.

*shih* 勢 power; condition; circumstances.

勢力 strength; prowess; influence.

勢難 under the circumstances it is hard to.

*shih* 士 a scholar; the literati; an able-bodied man; a soldier; a gentleman.

*shih* 誓 an oath; to swear; a vow.

*shih* 逝 to depart; to die.

*shih* 適 to suit; to accord with; just; just now; then.
適得其平 to obtain just one's equal share.

*shih* 諡 a posthumous title.

*shou* 收 to receive; a receipt; to take in; to rig in (as the swinging-boom of a ship).
收割 / 收成 } to get in the crop; to reap the harvest.
收買 to take over on sale; to buy from another.
收賬 to collect bills.
收規 to collect fees.
收單 a receipt.
收稅 to collect duties.
收稅單 a duty-paid certificate.
收稅免照 an exemption certificate.
收釐單 a Likin receipt.
收據 a proof of receipt; a certificate of the reception of goods on board; a bill of lading.
收訖 having received; having been received; payments being cleared; to receive in full.
收訖紅單 a certificate showing that [duties] have been received; a clearance certificate.
收畢 to have received in full; all received; received.
收執 to receive and hold (as a document); to be placed in one's hands.
收領 to receive; [to deliver] into the hands of.
收納 to collect (as duties); to receive; to accept.
收到 "arrived, or come to hand, by receiving," *i.e.*, received; "received from" (in receipts).
收到字樣 the word "received"; the endorsement of a receipt.
收留 to receive and keep; to harbour (as a fugitive).
收存 to keep; to retain.
收取 / 收集 } to collect together.
收辦 to receive; to appropriate.
收口 to put into a port (as a vessel in distress).
收口躲避 to seek shelter in a port.
收工 to quit work.
收藏 to store up; to lay by.
收拾 to repair; to gather up; to store up for keeping.
收進 to rig in (as a jib-boom).

*shou* 熟 ripe; cooked; tanned; manufactured; the opposite of *shêng* (生), raw or unmanufactured.
熟肉 preserved meats.

*shou* 熟菜 preserved vegetables.
熟膏 boiled or prepared opium.
熟鐵 manufactured iron.
熟銅 manufactured copper.
熟牛皮 leather.
熟驢皮條 ass leather in strips.
熟悉 to ripely know; to be well acquainted with.
熟思 to consider maturely.
熟諳船隻之人 experts in nautical matters.

*shou* 手 the arm; the hand; a "hand"; a working man.
手中 in hand.
手執 to hold in the hand.
手槍 pistols.
手巾 a napkin; a towel.
手帕 handkerchiefs.

*shou* 守 to observe (as a rule); to guard.
守候 to wait; to attend to.
守法 to observe the law.
守分 to attend to one's duties.
守業 to attend to one's trade.
守鐙人 lightkeepers.

*shou* 首 the head; what is or ought to be done first; in the first instance; a direction towards which a thing lies.
首飾 head ornaments; jewellery.
首事 the leading man; the chairman of a company.
首尾 head and tail; beginning and end; the bow and stern of a ship; the two ends of a vessel.
首先 first; the first.
首告 an informer.
首功 first-class merit.
首報 to report first, or in the first instance.
首經之子口 the barrier first crossed *en route*.
首從 the principal and accomplices.

*shou* 受 to receive; to become; to suffer; sometimes a sign of the passive.
受雇 to be hired, engaged, etc. (as an employé).
受恩 to receive favour; to be favoured.
受辱 to be disgraced.
受難 to suffer distress.
受罰 to be fined; to be punished.
受損 to sustain damage.
受暑受瘴 to suffer heat and malaria.
受潮濕 to become damp (as goods on board ship).

*shou* 授 to deliver to; to grant.

授受 to give and receive.

*shou* 壽 old age; long life; longevity.

壽器 a coffin.

*shou* 售 to sell.

售價 proceeds of sale.

售賣 to sell off; to sell.

*shu* 書 to write; documents; books.

書寫 to write; to copy.

書明 to write legibly.

書吏 }<br>書辦 } a copyist; a clerk; a book-keeper.

書院 a school; a college.

書籍 books.

書價開單 a list in which the price of books is stated; a list of books purchased; an invoice of books.

書箱 books in boxes. Cf. *i-hsiang* 衣箱, clothes in boxes.

書信 letters; postal matter.

*shu* 輸 to send in tribute; to tender (as taxes).

輸納 to pay (as duties).

輸稅 to pay duties.

輸稅期候 the term at which duties are payable.

*shu* 殊 distinction; difference; differing; unlike; very.

殊異 very different.

殊於華商生計窒礙 to materially interfere with the "bread and butter" of Chinese merchants.

殊屬費解 this is really not to be understood.

殊屬不成事體 this is most unsatisfactory.

*shu* 舒 open; to open; ease; comfort.

*shu* 孰 who.

*shu* 熟. See *shou*.

*shu* 述 to narrate; to state.

*shu* 屬 (屬, or 属) to be; to belong to; all that belongs to the jurisdiction of; subordinates.

屬國 a tributary state.

屬官 a subordinate officer.

*shu* 贖 to redeem; to re-buy.

贖回 to re-buy; to buy back.

*shu* 暑 heat.

*shu* 署 a yamên; a public office; to act for another; acting.

*shu* 署內 in the yamên; in the office.

署中緊要公事 important office matters.

署任 to hold office provisionally; an acting, or officiating, appointment.

署理 to act for another; acting; officiating.

署公使 an acting envoy.

署大臣 an acting Minister of State.

*shu* 數 number; amount; several; a few.

數目 number; numbers; amounts.

*shu* 恕 benevolent; loyal; to forgive.

*shu* 庶 all; many; so that; so that there be hope for; with a view to; about; nearly.

庶幾 nearly; almost; about; probably.

庶民 all people; the people; the subjects.

庶屬允當 so that it may be fair; for the sake of fairness.

庶不致於轇轕 so as to avoid confusion.

庶乎 almost; about; nearly.

*shu* 豎 vertical; upright; perpendicular.

豎線相間 vertical stripes (painted on a buoy or beacon); vertically striped.

*shu* 樹 }<br>樹木 } a tree; trees.

*shua* 刷 to brush; to wipe away; to strike off a copy (as in printing).

*shua* 耍 to trifle; to gamble; to fence.

*shuai* 衰 weak; to decay.

*shuai* 率 to lead; to guide; the leading principle; generally.

率師 to lead an army.

率由舊章 to be guided by the old rule; to act according to precedent.

*shuai* 帥 a leader; a commander-in-chief.

帥旗 the flag of a commander-in-chief; an admiral's flag.

*shuan* 拴 to bind up; to fasten.

拴紮 to tie up; to fasten.

*shuang* 雙 a pair; double.

雙數 an even number.

雙眼鏡 opera-glasses.

雙眼花翎 the double-eyed peacock's feather (as a distinction of merit).

*shui* 水 water; liquid.

水烟袋 a water pipe; a hubble-bubble.

水脚 fare by water; freight (by ship).

*shui* **水脚費用等項** freight (or passage money) and other expenses.

**水道** water road; sea road; the fairway channel for ships.

**水路** by water; a water route (by sea or by river, as opposed to overland carriage).

**水闊之處** a position with plenty of water or room [for sailing].

**水師** belonging to the navy; naval; marine.

**水師提督** / **水提台** } a naval commander-in-chief; an admiral.

**水師部** the Admiralty.

**水巡捕** the river police (at Shanghai).

**水手** a sailor.

**水利** taxes on water industries (as fisheries).

**水靛** liquid indigo.

**水晶** crystal.

**水銀** quicksilver; money paid on account of the difference or fluctuation in the price of sycee silver. See *wên* **紋水**.

*shui* **誰** who; whose; whom.

**誰是誰非** who is in the right and who is in the wrong?

*shui* **稅** duty; duties (on merchandise).

**稅項** a duty class; duties.

**稅款** kinds of duties; duties.

**稅餉** duties; the revenue.

**稅課** the duty taxation; the rates of the Tariff; duties; the revenue.

**稅課司大使** an examiner in the Native Customs.

**稅額** a fixed amount of revenue to be collected.

**稅單** a duty-paid certificate.

**稅則** a Customs Tariff; the Tariff.

**稅則半稅** half the Tariff duty; *i.e.*, the coast trade duty or the transit dues.

**稅鈔** duties on merchandise and tonnage dues; dues and duties.

**稅鈔清摺** a return of dues and duties; a Customs revenue return.

**稅務** duty matters; Customs matters.

**稅務司** / **稅司** } one who manages Customs matters; a Commissioner of Customs.

**稅局** / **稅館** } a revenue office; a Customs station.

**稅釐** ordinary duties and Likin taxes.

*shui* **稅釐局** a native revenue office for likin taxes, etc.

**稅捐** duties and other taxes; regular duties and extraordinary taxes; maritime duties and inland taxes.

*shun* **淳** pure; being a forbidden character, should be written **湻** *(shun)*.

*shun* **順** to obey; going with, not against; to suit; to agree.

**順潮** with the tide.

**順流** flowing with the tide or current.

**順風** with the wind; a fair wind.

**順從** to comply with.

**順輿情** to please public opinion; to act in accordance with public interests.

**順候** / **順頌** / **順請** } "I avail myself of this opportunity to present my kind regards," "with kind wishes," "accept my best wishes" (concluding phrases in letters).

**順天府** the metropolitan department of Shun-t'ien, in Chihli; Peking.

*shuo* **說** to speak; to say.

*shuo* **朔** the new moon; the first day of a month; to commence.

**朔望** new moon and full moon; the 1st and 15th of a [Chinese] month.

**朔望潮落時** when the tide is low with the new moon and the full moon, *i.e.*, at low water spring tides.

*shuo* **溯** (or **遡**) to trace up to a source; to carry one's thoughts back to. See *su*.

*so* **索** to bind; string; cord; twine; to ask for; to extort.

**索結** connected.

**索討** to demand; to extort.

**索看** to be desirous to see; to ask for a copy of......for inspection; to ask to be shown.

**索賠** to claim compensation for.

**索賠甚急** to ask for damages very urgently.

**索賠延擱貿易銀兩** to claim damages for delay in business; to claim demurrage.

*so* **擦** to select; to infer.

*so* **唆** to make mischief.

*so* **瑣** petty; troublesome.

**瑣屑** trifling (or vexatious) business.

*so* **鎖** a lock; to lock.

**鎖禁** to lock up; to put in irons.

*so* 所 a place; (=公 所) an office; an agency; the relative pronoun *who* or *which*; its use differs from that of our relative pronoun, *e.g.*, 船$^1$ 所$^2$ 載$^3$ 貨$^4$ = *huo*$^4$, the goods, *so*$^2$, which *ch'uan*$^1$, the ship, *tsai*$^3$, contains; and not "the ship which contains the goods."

所 在 the place where; the position of.

所 載 the passage quoted; this quotation.

所 致 that which is the cause; that causes it.

所 自 } 所 從 } that from which it comes; the source; the cause.

所 有. If an individual or individuals are distinguished from others of the same class by some attribute (adjective, participle, relative clause, etc.), the phrase *so yu* 所有 (properly, a short relative clause meaning "the so-and-so that there is" or "that there are") often serves to express the English definite article; *e.g.*, 所$^1$有$^2$現$^3$約$^4$五$^5$條$^6$, $^1$*so yu*$^2$, THE, $^5$*wu*, five, $^6$*t'iao*, articles of, $^3$*hsien*, the present $^4$*yüeh*, treaty; 所$^1$ 有$^2$ 商$^3$ 人$^4$ 採$^5$ 買$^6$ 米$^7$ 石$^8$, $^1$*so* $^2$*yu*, THE, $^7$*mi*-$^8$*tan*, rice, $^3$*shang*-$^4$*jên* $^5$*ts'ai* $^6$*mai*, bought up by the merchants.

所 以 in order to thereby; by which means it is intended to; therefore; thereby.

所 關 [all] that pertains to.

*sou* 搜 to search.

搜 驗 to search; to examine.

搜 拏 to search and seize (as smuggled goods).

*ssŭ* 司 to manage; to control; a controller; a Commissioner.

司 官 a secretary at a board; a police magistrate at Peking.

司 馬 literary designation for a sub-prefect.

司 事 a manager; to manage an affair.

司 事 之 人 an officer on duty; a managing man.

司 簿 a book-keeper.

司 理 to manage; to superintend.

司 理 筆 札 writers or clerks (as in a bank).

司 獄 a jailer.

司 巡 人 等 managing and executive officers.

司 平 the local scale for Haikwan tael money at Canton.

司 道 the *ssŭ* and the *tao*. By the former the high provincial officials whose titles end in *ssŭ* (viz., the *Pu-chêng-shih-ssŭ* or Provincial Treasurer, the *An-ch'a-shih-ssŭ* or Provincial Judge, and the *Yen-yün-ssŭ* or Inspector of Salt Gabel) are understood; by the latter, the *Liang-tao* (糧道) or Grain Collector, and sometimes also territorial and other Taot'ais. These officials together form an administrative board which is sometimes shortly called the *ssŭ-tao*.

*ssŭ* 飼 to feed; to nourish.

*ssŭ* 嗣 hereafter; afterwards; to succeed; posterity.

嗣 後 hereafter.

*ssŭ* 絲 silk; the hairy appearance of anything cut fine like silk, *e.g.*, Chinese prepared tobacco, vermicelli, wire.

絲 經 thrown silk.

絲 線 silk thread; sewing silk.

絲 線 帽 頂 cap buttons of twisted silk thread.

絲 帶 silk sashes; silk ribbons.

絲 棉 雜 貨 silk and cotton mixtures.

絲 斤 silk (as cargo); *lit.*, "silk catties." Cf. *yen chin* (鹽 斤), salt; *t'ung-chin* (銅 斤), copper; *yu-chin* (油 斤), oil; *mei-chin* (煤 斤), coal. The classifier placed immediately after the noun to which it usually belongs has the force of what in French grammar is called the "article partitif," *e.g.*, *ch'uan san chih* (船 三 隻), three ships, but *ch'uan-chih* (船 隻), "*des* vaisseaux," ships; *yin ssŭ-liang* (銀 四 兩), four taels of money, but *yin-liang* (銀 兩), "*de l'*argent," money. Similarly, *mi-tan* (米 石), rice; *pu-p'i* (布 疋) cotton piece goods, cloth (as cargo); *ma-p'i* (馬 匹), horses.

絲 毫 the least; in the least; used to enforce negations; "not in the least."

*ssŭ* 斯 this; that; these.

*ssŭ* 厮 a servant; a menial.

*ssŭ* 思 to think.

思 慮 } 思 維 } to think; to consider.

思 維 再 四 to consider very carefully.

*ssŭ* 死 to die.

*ssŭ* 俟 to wait till; not until; when.

俟 候 to wait.

俟......卽 } 俟......方 } 俟......再 } as soon as........, then........; wait till......, and then; not until.

俟 十 年 再 行 更 改 to alter after the lapse of 10 years.

俟 船 造 畢 waiting till the vessel is finished being built; *i.e.*, *after* the vessel has, or shall have, been built.

*ssŭ* 祀 to offer sacrifices.

*ssŭ* 似 like; it seems that; it looks as if; as; as if.

似 此 like this; thus.

似 可 照 議 辦 理 it seems one may manage the matter as proposed.

*ssŭ* 似覺 it seems as if it may be considered; it might be thought.

似覺合宜 it looks reasonable enough.

*ssŭ* 四 (or 肆) four.

四結 the fourth quarter (of a financial year); the four quarters; the year.

四品銜 of the fourth class of rank.

四面 in all directions of the compass; all round.

四方 square; the four points of the compass; all round.

四方之式 square; rectangular.

四方若干 the circumference (in timber measurement).

四海 the four seas; everywhere.

四項清摺 a report to Government on "the four kinds" of account, *i.e.*, the Customs Quarterly Abstract Accounts *A*, *B*, *C*, and *D*.

四川 the Szechwan province.

四川黃絲 Szechwan yellow silk.

四川寶 Szechwan sycee.

*ssŭ* 肆 reckless; dissolute; 四

肆擾 to infest [a place] with robbers.

*ssŭ* 私 private; oneself; one's own; selfish; clandestinely; to smuggle; smugglers; smuggled goods.

私心 one's own heart; my heart; partial.

私受 to receive secretly.

私帶 to carry clandestinely.

私下 / 私行下貨 } to ship [goods] clandestinely; to ship without a permit.

私起 / 私行起動 } to land clandestinely.

私行互撥 to clandestinely tranship goods from one vessel to another.

私運進口 to import clandestinely.

私赴別口 to clandestinely resort to another port.

私赴沿海別口 to clandestinely resort to another port (viz., a non-Treaty port) on the coast.

私鑄 to clandestinely cast; to make counterfeit coin.

私自 clandestinely and on one's own authority; privately.

私自藏匿 to conceal fraudulently.

私自過卡 to cross a barrier clandestinely.

*su* 俗 common; vulgar; manners and customs.

*su* 酥 curd; cheese.

*su* 蘇 plentiful; (=蘇州府) Su-chou-fu.

蘇木 sapanwood.

蘇合油 rose maloes; liquid storax.

蘇州索 Soochow hemp twine.

蘇松太 the three departments of Su-chou-fu (蘇 *su*), Sung-chiang-fu (松 *sung*), and T'ai-ts'ang-chou (太 *t'ai*), forming the circuit in charge of the Taot'ai at Shanghai.

*su* 疏 to discard; coarse; careless; distant; far.

疏忽 to forget; careless.

疏縱 laxity.

*su* 速 hasty; speedy; quick; at once.

速爲辦理 to manage with despatch.

速議具奏 to speedily deliberate and report to the Throne [upon a matter].

*su* 粟 maize; Indian corn.

粟米粉 Indian meal; oatmeal.

*su* 肅 respectful; to inspire awe; respect; reverence.

肅敬 respectful; respect.

肅復 to respectfully reply.

肅泐 to write respectfully; I respectfully inform you [of the above] (a concluding phrase in letters).

*su* 素 plain; formerly; usually; contented.

素色布 dyed plain shirtings.

素紅布 Turkey red cloths.

素守本分 to pursue one's business peacefully.

素服 ordinary mourning clothes (as worn after the term of strict mourning is over); half-mourning.

*su* 訴 to tell; to inform; to accuse.

訴狀 to accuse; to bring a charge against.

訴冤 to tell one's grievance; to complain.

訴病 to report sick; to complain of illness.

*su* 溯 to look back (as to a period of time); to trace up to a source.

溯查 considering the origin of a matter; [on going back to the beginning of the matter] I find that.

溯自通商征稅以來 ever since duties have been levied upon foreign trade.

*suan* 酸 sour; grieved; distressed.

*suan* 算 to calculate; to consider as.

算除 to deduct.

算清 to calculate the proper amount of.

算書 a calculator; a clerk.

*suan* 蒜 / 蒜頭 } garlic.

*sui* 歲 a year.

*sui* 雖 although (the "yet" following may be expressed by *jan* 然 or *êrh* 而).

*sui* 綏 to tranquillise; steady; quiet.

綏 靖 to tranquillise; to restore peace.

*sui* 隨 to follow; to accompany; enclosed in (as in a despatch); together with; (=隨 時) instantly; at the same time; in the sequel, etc.

隨 從 to follow; to accompany.

隨 帶 to carry with one's person; to accompany.

隨 帶 加 三 級 granted three steps of merit, and so recorded in the Board of Civil Office, which distinction attaches to the person of the promoted official (*sui-tai* 隨 帶, "taken along with him"), whereas steps granted as not *sui-tai* are lost when the official is transferred to another office, because they are attached to the *post* and not to the *person*.

隨 意 } 隨 便 } as one thinks fit; according to pleasure; as one pleases.

隨 勢 } 隨 事 } according to circumstances.

隨 事 酌 情 to decide according to circumstances.

隨 之 日 起 to increase day by day.

隨 時 in future; hereafter; at the same time; suiting one's time; in due course; at once; forthwith.

隨 卽 forthwith.

*sui* 遂 afterwards; to follow; to accompany.

*sui* 碎 fragments; broken pieces or bits.

碎 銀 broken bits of silver; broken dollars.

碎 白 銀 broken sycee (so called in Chefoo).

*sun* 孫 a grandchild.

*sun* 損 to lose; to injure; to spoil.

損 害 } 損 傷 } to injure; to be damaged; damage.

損 壞 to be spoilt; to be out of order; to wreck.

損 壞 船 隻 vessels wrecked.

損 益 loss and gain; the relative advantages of.

*sung* 訟 to tell; to report; to accuse.

訟 師 a lawyer.

訟 告 to accuse.

*sung* 頌 to praise; homage.

*sung* 松 a fir tree; a pine tree.

松 香 resin.

松 香 油 turpentine.

*sung* 松 江 府 the prefecture of Sung-chiang, near Shanghai.

*sung* 鬆 loose; lax; dishevelled.

鬆 緩 to slacken.

*sung* 誦 to read in a murmuring tone (as prayers); to read (as a letter).

*sung* 送 to send; to accompany; to present.

送 去 to send away.

送 交 to send to; to hand over to.

送 貨 之 人 the person accompanying goods; a supercargo.

送 禮 to present; presents.

## T.

*ta* 大 great; high (as in rank); first; principal; very; as pertaining to the person addressed, "your."

大 小 large and small; of all sizes; the size of a thing.

大 小 扣 布 *T*-cloths (all sizes).

大 原 布 *T*-cloth (the larger size).

大 呢 broadcloth; medium cloth.

大 黃 rhubarb.

大 洋 藥 } 大 土 } Patna opium.

大 頭 菜 salted turnips.

大 風 子 lucraban seed.

大 青 smalt.

大 麥 barley.

大 員 a high officer.

大 憲 the High Authorities.

大 學 士 a Grand Secretary.

大 使 a sub-commissioner (*e.g.*, in the Provincial Treasurer's or the Salt Commissioner's yamên).

大 關 the [Native] Custom House (at Chefoo).

大 臣 a Minister of State.

大 人 a *ta-jên* (honorary title used in addressing officials from the third rank upwards and members of the Censorate or of the *Han-lin* College).

大 老 爺 a *ta lao-yeh* (honorary title used in addressing officials of the fourth, fifth, or sixth grades).

大 風 a storm.

大 書 in large characters; large writing.

大 寫 a chief clerk; large writing; the *ta-hsieh* style of writing numerals.

大 半 the greater half; mostly.

*ta* 大行 the great journey; having gone the great journey; defunct (applied to an Emperor or an Empress).

大統 the great whole, *i.e.*, the charge of Empire; the Throne.

大喪 general mourning; the funeral of an Emperor.

大局 the great aims of society; public interest.

大會 a general meeting.

大副 a mate of a ship; the first mate.

大項 principal kinds.

大宗 a principal, or staple, article (as amongst goods).

大概 generally speaking; the general features of......; chiefly.

大抵 on the whole; generally speaking.

大約 } generally speaking; on the whole; about; probably.
大略 }

大略相符 to agree in the main.

大移 your communication; your letter.

大教 the great instruction (politely for "your instructive conversation").

大才 the great talent; a polite phrase for "you."

大相懸殊 very different.

大不相同 very unlike each other.

大漸 to increase considerably.

大淸 the Ch'ing dynasty, now ruling in China; the Chinese Empire; Imperial Chinese.

大淸律例 the Chinese Penal Code.

大皇帝 the Emperor.

大英國 Great Britain; British.

大呂宋國 the kingdom of Spain.

大浪山嘴 South Africa (Cape Colony).

大沽 Taku (near Tientsin).

大通 Ta-t'ung (a port of call on the Yangtze).

*ta* 達 to inform; intelligent.

*ta* 答 to reply.

*ta* 搭 to add to; to engage (as a ship or a passage); to charter; to take passage in a ship; to ship.

搭解 to hand over or to pay in addition.

搭船 a passenger ship.

搭客 passengers.

搭客行李 passengers' luggage.

*ta* 打 to strike; to beat; (= 打臣) a dozen.

打臣 (*ta-ch'ên*, in Cantonese *ta-sun*) a dozen; dozens.

打開備查 to open for examination (as packages at the Custom House).

*t'a* 他 another; other; heterogeneous.

他貨 other goods.

他國 other countries; foreign countries.

他項 other kinds.

他故 other reasons.

他往 to proceed to another place.

他用 to use for other purposes.

*t'a* 塌 to fall down, or break away, as the banks of river.

*t'a* 塔 a pagoda; a tower; a lighthouse.

塔表 a light tower; lighthouses.

塔燈 (= 燈塔) a lighthouse.

*t'a* 獺 the otter.

獺皮 land-otter skins.

*tai* 歹 bad; vicious.

*tai* 呆 (or 獃) silly; foolish; idiotic.

*tai* 代 a generation; in place of another; for; acting for.

代其 on his behalf; for him (them, etc.).

代客 on behalf of a mercantile friend; a commission agent; a broker.

代理 to act for another.

代理領事 } an acting Consul.
代領事 }

代用 to use instead; to substitute.

代收 to receive for another; to collect (fees, etc.) on account of another.

代呈 to state on behalf of another.

代權 to hold authority for another; delegated authority.

代辦 to manage for another; to act as deputy.

代爲辦理 to act for another; to take action in a matter which another has not taken up.

代拆代行 to open letters and act for another; to do all the business of a post on behalf of another.

*tai* 玳 (or 瑇) } tortoiseshell.
玳瑁 }

玳瑁碎 broken tortoiseshell.

玳瑁殼器 tortoiseshellware.

*tai* 袋 a bag.

*tai* 貸 to lend on interest; to borrow; to give; to release; to let off.

*tai* 帶 a sash; a girdle; to carry; to take along with one; together with; to lead; to be in charge of troops.

帶有 to carry; to be provided with.

帶同 to take with one.

*tai* 帶回 to take back; to lead back (as troops).
帶縣 to take [a man] to the magistrate; to arrest.
帶赴領事官 to take [a man] to the Consul.
帶兵 to lead an army, or troops.
帶領 to conduct; to escort.
帶抽 to collect a tax conjointly with some other tax the collection of which is one's regular business.

*tai* 殆 to begin; nearly; about to.

*tai* 迨 till; until; to reach to.
迨今 till now.
迨至其時 up to that time.

*tai* 戴 to wear on the head; to uphold.
戴德 to uphold virtue, *i.e.*, to do a matter conscientiously; imbued with goodness.
戴頂 to wear the button.

*tai* 待 to treat; to wait.
待價 to wait for prices [to rise]; to watch the market.

*t'ai* 太 large; too; excessive; in certain titles, denotes respect.
太遠 too far.
太嚴 too strict; over-strict.
太后 the Emperor's mother.
太子 the Imperial Prince; heir to the Throne.
太子少保 a junior guardian of the Imperial Prince.
太子太保 / 太保 } a senior guardian of the Imperial Prince.
太守 a prefect.
太傅 a Grand Tutor.
太倉州 the prefecture of T'ai-ts'ang (Kiangsu).

*t'ai* 臺 (or 台) eminent; exalted; a terrace; a term of respect entering into combination with certain titles and much used in petitions.
臺巡 Your Honour's searching officer.
臺鑒 in petitions, a respectful compliment alluding to the addressee's clearness of mind; "Your Honour's superior intellect."
臺端 / 臺下 / 臺前 } in petitions, honorary titles given to officials; "Your Honour."
臺函 Your Honour's letter.
臺示 Your Honour's instructions; your letter.
臺命 Your Honour's orders.
臺灣府 the prefecture of Taiwan, Formosa.

*t'ai* 臺灣關 the Taiwan Customs.
臺北府 the prefecture of Tai-pei (North Formosa).

*t'ai* 擡 (or 抬) to carry; to lift; to raise.
擡頭 to raise the head; to raise a column by the space of one, two, or three characters above the line, as a means of indicating respect.
擡雙頭 to raise a column by the space of two characters.
擡價 to raise the price.

*t'ai* 泰 great.
泰西 the great West; Western (as in "the Western calendar").

*tan* 單 single; a document consisting of a single sheet; a bill; a certificate; a memo.; a permit.
單身 a single body; alone; by oneself.
單桅 single-masted; one-masted.
單眼花翎 the single-eyed peacock feather (as a distinction of merit).
單擡 to raise a column by the space of a single character as a means of indicating respect.
單雙 odd and even; single and double.
單數 an odd number.
單式 a *pro formâ* document; a form.
單照 a certificate.
單據 a permit; a documentary proof.
單契牌照 permits (or licenses), bonds, and [ship's] certificates.
單貨不得相離 "this document is to accompany the goods which it covers;" the document is not to be separated from the goods.

*tan* 彈 a bullet; a shot; a shell.
彈子 shot.
彈壓 to suppress; to keep in order.

*tan* 躭 to prevent; to obstruct; to delay.
躭悞 / 躭擱 / 躭延 } to delay.
躭延時日 to procrastinate; to delay.

*tan* 丹 cinnabar; red; carnation.
丹砂 cinnabar.
丹國 Denmark; Danish.

*tan* 但 only; merely; however.

*tan* 擔 (for which 担 is used) a load; a picul; to bear; a pole. Cf. *shih* 石.

*tan* 膽 (or 胆) the gall; courage; bold.

*tan* 膽玩 to play a bold game; to trifle with the law in an impudent manner.
膽大 courageous; bold.
膽大已極 the extreme of effrontery.
膽小 cowardly.
膽敢 to possess the boldness to; to dare to.

*tan* 淡 insipid; flat; dull (as trade); poor and deficient (as receipts of profit).
淡菜 dried mussels.
淡收 deficient receipts; a deficit.
淡水縣 the district of Tan-shui (Tamsui).
淡水關 the Tamsui Customs.

*tan* 蛋 an egg; eggs.

*t'an* 炭 charcoal.
炭碎 }
炭灰 } charcoal ashes.

*t'an* 毯 rugs; druggets; druggetting; carpets.

*t'an* 痰 phlegm.
痰湧 to cough up phlegm.

*t'an* 談 to converse.
談論 to converse; to discuss.

*t'an* 探 to spy; to explore; to examine.
探詢 to inquire.

*t'an* 貪 to covet; covetous.
貪圖 to covet; to be greedy of.

*t'an* 攤 to contribute to; to subscribe (as money); to unfold; to spread out.

*t'an* 灘 rapids in a stream; an obstruction arising from rocks or sand-banks; a shoal; a beach.

*t'an* 坍 a bank breaking down; ruined.
坍塌 banks breaking down; to wash away (said of a river bank, etc.); to fall to ruin.

*t'an* 壇 an altar for sacrificing.

*t'an* 檀 }
檀香 } sandalwood.
檀香器 sandalwoodware.
檀香山 the Sandwich Islands.

*tang* 當 to suit; right; proper; to act as; at the time; then; in due course; in the presence of; to pawn; to pledge.
當……之時 during the time when……; when.
當倘未……之時 before the time of……; previous to……
當今 at present.
當即 thereupon; at once.
當經 I have thereupon, or with reference thereto (denoting past tense and immediateness of action).
當已 (=當經 *tang-ching*) at the time; then; in due course.
當時 at the time; at that time.
當日 to-day; on the same day.
當中 in the middle.
當面 in one's presence.
當堂 before the magistrate; at the Consulate; in court.
當堂畫押 to sign before a magistrate, or before the Consul.
當舖 a pawn-shop.
當票 a pawn-ticket.
當手 a manager (of a bank, a firm, etc.).

*tang* 擋 to oppose; to impede; to stop.

*tang* 檔 a set of shelves; pigeon-holes for filing records.
檔卷 archives; documents pigeon-holed.

*tang* 黨 a band; an association; to club together.

*t'ang* 湯 broth; soup.
湯藥 broth and medicines.

*t'ang* 倘 (for which 儻 is used) if; suppose.
倘或 if perchance; in case of.
倘遇 if there is; in case of.

*t'ang* 堂 a hall; a court; a magistrate; a shop; a firm.

*t'ang* 儻 accidental; used for *t'ang* (倘), if.

*t'ang* 糖 sugar.
糖菓 preserved fruits; preserves.
糖薑 preserved ginger.

*tao* 道 a road; a circuit; an officer in charge of a circuit; a Taot'ai; principle; reason; idea; to speak; to say.
道路 a road; a route; the distance of a journey.
道台 a Taot'ai; an inspector of circuit.
道理 reason; principle.
道謝 to express one's thanks.

*tao* 導 to guide; to lead.

*tao* 刀 a knife; knives; a sword.

*tao* 島 an island.
島嶼 islands.

*tao* 到 to arrive; to go to; to come to.
到此 to arrive here; to arrive at this port; up to this time.

*tao* 到口 to arrive in port; to enter port.

到關 to come to the Custom House; to attend at the Customs Office.

到旗 to arrive at one's banner or at one's home (said of a Manchu soldier).

到道 it has come to my, the Taot'ai's, hands.

*tao* 倒 to upset; to pour out.

*tao* 禱 to pray; to entreat.

*tao* 稻 unhusked rice; paddy.

稻米 paddy and rice.

稻糧 grain.

*tao* 蹈 to tread on.

*tao* 悼 afflicted; to grieve for.

*tao* 盜 to rob; to steal; thieves; robbers.

盜賊 thieves; robbers.

盜風 the habit of robbing; thievish propensities (amongst the population).

*t'ao* 逃 to run away; to abscond.

逃人 fugitives; runaways.

逃犯 an escaped prisoner.

*t'ao* 濤 billows; a heavy sea.

*t'ao* 討 to demand; to ask for.

*t'ao* 套 an envelope; a book cover; a set (of books, clothes, etc.); a snare.

*tê* 得 must; to receive; to get; to obtain.

得手 to manage satisfactorily.

得確數 to ascertain the exact amount of.

得悉 to be informed of; to note the contents of (as of a note).

*tê* 德 virtue; kindness; benefit; favour.

德便 advantages granted; benefit.

德意志 (*tê-i-chih* = Deutsch) German.

德意志人 German subjects.

德意志各國 the States of the North-German Confederation; the German States.

德國 Germany; German.

德商 German merchants.

*t'ê* 特 special; especially; on purpose.

特旨 a special decree from the Emperor.

特劄 a special order (a concluding phrase in despatches from superiors).

特諭 }
特示 } a special order; a special proclamation.

特達 special intelligence.

特意 on purpose; intentional.

*t'ê* 特發准單 }
特准單據 } a special permit.

特撥之項 moneys specially set aside; special grants.

特辦之工費 expenditure on account of special works.

特用各費 expenses for special use; extraordinary expenditure.

特奉准買 to be licensed for the purchase [of exceptional goods].

特此懇祈 I make this special petition.

特揀 }
特簡 } to select; to appoint; specially selected.

*têng* 登 to ascend; to enter (as in a book).

登山 to ascend a hill.

登舟 to get on board ship; to embark.

登岸 to go on shore; to land.

登簿 to enter in a ledger; to register.

登記 to enter (as in a register); to record.

登撰 to insert or to enter (as in a book).

登州 Têng-chow-fu, in Shantung.

登萊青 the three departments of Têng-chow-fu (登 *têng*), Lai-chow-fu (萊 *lai*), and Ch'ing-chou-fu (青 *ch'ing*), forming the circuit in charge of the Taot'ai at Chefoo.

*têng* 澄 clear; limpid.

澄茄 cubebs.

*têng* 鐙 a stirrup, now commonly used for *têng* (燈), a lamp; a light; lights (coast and river).

鐙塔 a lighthouse (tower-shaped); a light-tower.

鐙房 a lighthouse (house-shaped).

鐙樓 a lighthouse (being a house of several stories).

鐙亭 a lighthouse (pavilion-shaped).

鐙船 a lightship.

鐙架 a beacon with a light.

鐙火 the flame or centre of a light.

鐙籠 a lantern.

鐙草 lampwicks.

*têng* 等 to wait; class; rank; sign of the plural; after a single proper name it has a generalising force, as "and others," "etc.," "and the like," "such as"; after a series of names it simply denotes plurality, when it should be left untranslated.

等級 rank; degree.

等候 to wait.

*têng* 等因 such arguments; "and the like arguments;" "etc.," closing a quotation, when from a document written by a superior or an equal, but not used when quoting an inferior. The following expressions are similarly used: 等由 *(têng yu)*; 等情 *(têng ch'ing)*, "such circumstances" (should only be used when quoting an inferior); 等事 *(têng shih)*, "such matters." When the words used by another writer (or speaker) are quoted, the quotation may be closed by adding the words 等語 *(têng yü)*, "such words"; if an accusation is the subject of the quotation, by adding the words 等詞 *(têng tz'ŭ)*, "such charges"; after an enumeration of malpractices or nuisances we often find the words 等弊 *(têng pi)*, "such malpractices." Such concluding phrases need not be translated; they simply show that a quotation or an enumeration of arguments, circumstances, facts, charges, malpractices, etc., is concluded, and correspond to what in English writing is expressed by inverted commas. The phrase 等因 *(têng-yin)* is sometimes inserted in copies of documents when the tenor of another document, which in the original appears at full length, is omitted for the sake of convenience. Cf. *yün yün* 云云.

等類 such articles; "etc., etc."

*t'êng* 謄 to copy.

謄錄 to copy; a copyist.

謄清 to make a fair copy.

*t'êng* 籐 (or 藤) cane; rattan.

籐竿 rattans.

籐器 rattanware.

籐肉 split rattans.

籐黃 gamboge.

*t'êng* 騰 to ascend; to inform.

*t'êng* 疼 pain; painfully; sorely; intensely.

*ti* 低 low; to lower.

低昂 low or high (as price); a fluctuation in the rate of.

低處 a low place.

低稅 to lower the duty.

*ti* 底 the bottom; at the bottom of; end; at the end of; a rough draft.

底長 the length at the base.

底稿 a draft.

底簿 to enter in a book; a book entry; a book of drafts.

*ti* 抵 to act as; to perform the service of; to consider as equivalent; to substitute; to oppose; to arrive at.

抵充 to act as; to perform the service of.

抵換 to exchange; to substitute.

*ti* 抵賬 to settle an account.

抵押未清 pawned and not redeemed.

抵卡 to arrive at a barrier.

抵埠 to arrive in port.

抵滬 to arrive at Shanghai.

*ti* 隄 (used for *ti* 堤, a dyke) to guard against; an embankment; the bank of a river.

隄防 dykes; coast defences; to guard against.

*ti* 敵 an enemy; to compete with; to oppose.

敵私 to compete with smuggling.

*ti* 糴 to buy grain.

糴糶 to buy and sell grain.

*ti* 帝 an Emperor.

*ti* 弟 a younger brother; a junior; as a term of modesty, "I," "my."

*ti* 第 number; No.; but; however; merely.

第..........號 No. ..........; Registered No. ..........

第一子口 the first barrier.

*ti* 地 earth; ground; land; bottom.

地基 a foundation.

地方 a place. This noun is frequently added to local names, and need not then be translated.

地方官 the local authorities; *i.e.*, the prefect, sub-prefect, magistrate, etc., of a place.

地方公事 local business.

地勢 the particulars regarding a lot of land; the nature of a place.

地主 a land-owner.

地丁 the land tax.

地圖 a map.

地位 a situation; a site.

地甲 the tithing system, by which one man is made responsible for the behaviour of his district; an elder.

地保 a tithing-man; a *ti-pao*.

地蓆 matting.

*ti* 遞 to give; to hand to; to present (as a document).

遞貨單 to hand in a cargo list; to present a ship's manifest.

遞加 to add *pro ratâ*; to add a fraction of a certain amount.

遞奏 to address the Throne.

*ti* 的 true; certain.

的保 a true guarantee.

的筆 an autograph.

新關文件録



*t'i* 提 to raise; to bring forward; to mention; to send; to submit; to remit (as moneys).

提淨 to extract the pure metal from an alloy.

提及 to mention; to refer to.

提關 to send to the Custom House (as an offender for examination).

提案 to bring up a case in court.

提究 to try a case; to examine into; to prosecute (for legal punishment).

提項 remittances.

提歸 to remit for.........

提成分賞 to allot rewards.

提台 / 提督 } a provincial general-in-chief or admiral-in-chief.

提布 brocades.

*t'i* 題 to discuss; to bring forward.

題升 to recommend for promotion.

*t'i* 蹄 hoofs.

*t'i* 替 to abolish; to substitute.

*t'i* 體 the human body; also the body as opposed to the extremities (as "the body of a structure"); to receive courteously; substantial; decent.

體較輭弱 the frame or body is weak and shaky.

體恤 to befriend.

體察情形 to investigate the circumstances.

體面 respectable.

*tiao* 貂 the marten or sable.

貂皮 sable skins; marten skins.

*tiao* 調 to remove to another post; to transfer; read *t'iao:* to harmonise; to restore harmony; to regulate; to mix or compound.

調遷 to remove or transfer to another port or station.

調閩黔軍 a Kweichow regiment transferred to Fukien.

調治 a cure; to cure.

調理 to nurse one's health.

*tiao* 雕 (雕, or 彫) to engrave; to carve.

雕刻 to engrave; to cut in wood.

*tiao* 吊 (or 弔) to condole; to hang; a quantity of copper cash varying in number, according to locality, but generally representing about a thousand.

*t'iao* 挑 to carry.

挑夫 a porter; a carrier.

*t'iao* 條 twigs; a paragraph; an article (as of a Treaty); strips (as of leather); a classifier of long, slender things, also of bags, roads, etc., and of rods (of iron, copper, etc.).

*t'iao* 條編 twisted, or plaited, like basket-work.

條約 an agreement containing a number of articles; a Treaty.

條款 Treaty paragraphs; a Convention; articles; regulations.

條規 regulations; byelaws.

條例 rules for procedure; regulations.

條理 reasonable; logical; well founded in detail; regulations; rules. Cf. 條條有理 every section has its rules (WILLIAMS).

*t'iao* 糶 to sell grain.

糶米 to sell rice.

*tieh* 迭 alternate; satisfactory.

迭次 repeatedly.

*tieh* 牒 an official document; a despatch; a warrant; a genealogical table.

*tieh* 疊 to reiterate; repeatedly.

疊次 repeatedly.

*t'ieh* 帖 a card; a billet; a document.

*t'ieh* 貼 to paste up (as a public notice); to make up for; to supply a deficiency.

貼水 to pay the difference in price of sycee; *i.q.*, *pu* 補水.

*t'ieh* 鐵 (鉄, or 銕) iron.

鐵條 nail-rod iron.

鐵板 bar iron; sheet iron.

鐵磚 pig iron.

鐵片 an iron plate.

鐵片條 hoop iron.

鐵絲 iron wire.

鐵釘 iron nails.

鐵器 ironware.

鐵刀利器 cutlery.

鐵鍊 iron chains.

鐵箍 iron hoops.

鐵樁 an iron beacon.

*tien* 點 (or 点) a point; a dot; a stroke; to dot; to tick off; to punctuate; spotted; to light (as a lamp).

點名 / 點明 } to tick off (as the names of soldiers when mustered, or of emigrants when shipped); to muster.

點驗 to dot and examine; to tick off while examining; to check (as a list of articles).

點鐘 an hour; hours; o'clock.

點燈 to light a lamp.

點照 to light (as a lamp); to exhibit a light.

*tien* 店 a commercial establishment; a shop.

店主 the owner of a shop.

店堂 in the shop.

店夥 a mercantile assistant; a partner.

*tien* 典 a standard; a law; a rule; authentic documents; statutes.

典當 to mortgage; a pawn-shop.

典賣 to mortgage; to pledge.

典主 a mortgagee.

典田 to mortgage land.

典史 an inspector of jails.

*tien* 佃 to work in the fields; a field labourer.

佃戶 agricultural population.

*tien* 靛 indigo.

*tien* 電 lightning; electric; glance; to glance at (said of a superior who investigates a matter); hence, in composition with various verbs, "may Your Honour be pleased to......"

電氣 electricity.

電線 an electric wire; a telegraph; telegraphic.

電線行 a telegraph company.

電報 a telegram.

電鑒 (an honorary style of addressing officials) "your enlightened mind."

電察 be pleased to investigate.

*tien* 殿 a palace; the Imperial Palace.

殿下 the Imperial prince.

*tien* 墊 to advance money; to fill up; to add to.

墊款 advances (in accounts).

*tien* 奠 to offer libations to a god.

奠醊 to sacrifice to the gods.

*t'ien* 天 heaven; the sky.

天命 Heaven's decree; fate; destiny.

天眞 Heaven's goodness; the good nature inherent in man.

天主 the Lord of Heaven, *i.e.*, God (so called by Roman Catholics).

天主教 the Roman Catholic creed.

天主堂 a Roman Catholic church.

天下 the empire; China; the world.

天下各國 all the countries in the world.

天平 a balance; a scale.

天津 Tientsin.

天津條約 the Treaty of Tientsin; the British Treaty concluded in 1858.

*t'ien* 天后宮橋 a bridge at the Quai de la Pagode, in the French Concession at Shanghai.

*t'ien* 添 to add; to increase; additional.

添改 to make additions and alterations (as in a document).

添註 to fill in.

添錨 to moor (a vessel).

*t'ien* 甜 sweet.

甜言 sweet words; flattering language.

*t'ien* 湉 tranquil; being a forbidden character, should be written 湉 (*t'ien*), the last stroke of the full character being omitted.

*t'ien* 塡 to fill up; to write up (as the blank spaces in a printed form).

塡築 to fill up (for building).

塡還 to return (as borrowed money); to pay a debt; to make up for a deficiency.

塡補 to make up for (as a deficiency).

塡簿 to insert in a book or register.

塡寫 to fill in by writing.

塡註英文 to fill in the English [version].

塡發 to fill up and issue; to make out (as a document).

*t'ien* 田 a field; land.

田庄 a farm house.

田地 landed property; land.

田賦 a tax on land; ground rent.

*ting* 定 to fix; to stipulate; it is stipulated; it is agreed that; it shall be the rule that.

定額 } a fixed amount; a fixed number.
定數 }

定期 to name a day; to fix a time for; at fixed times; regularly.

定限 a fixed limit of time.

定制 a fixed routine; fixed rules.

定規 a fixed rule; to fix; fixed; to decide.

定式 having a fixed pattern; uniform; standard.

定地段 to divide the country into sections.

定爲 to fix as; to fix at (as at a certain rate).

定明 to settle; to decide.

定局 a fixed arrangement; to settle; to decide.

定立 to frame (as a rule); to settle.

定擬 to decide upon (as upon rules); to give judgment.

定斷 } to decide a case.
定案 }

新關文件録



*ting* 定評 to decide; to have a casting vote.
定單 a contract.
定銀 earnest money; bargain money.
定海廳 the inferior department of Ting-hai.

*ting* 錠 an ingot of silver.

*ting* 丁 a nail; an adult male.
丁香 cloves.
丁役 official attendants; runners.
丁憂 to mourn for parents during the customary period.

*ting* 訂 to fix; to settle; to arrange; to adjust; to settle terms.
訂局 to decide.
訂定日期 to appoint a day.
訂問 to examine.

*ting* 釘 a nail; to nail; to bind (as books).

*ting* 頂 the crown of the head; the top; the vane (of a light tower); an official button; the top of anything.
頂戴 to wear a button; the wearer of a button.
頂德 imbued with virtue; "please your goodness."
頂替 a substitute.

*t'ing* 亭 a pavilion; a dome.
亭式 pavilion-shaped; dome-like.

*t'ing* 停 to stop; to delay; to anchor.
停輪 to stop a steamer.
停止 to stop; to abolish (as a practice).
停留 to delay.
停工 to stop work.
停辦公事 to close a public office; to stop work (as on a holiday).
停泊處所 a place for anchoring; a berth.
停船界 the harbour limits.

*t'ing* 廷 the Court.

*t'ing* 庭 a hall of audience; a house; a room.

*t'ing* 艇 a boat.
艇隻 boats.

*t'ing* 聽 to hear; to obey; to wait for; to yield to; to permit.
聽聞 to hear.
聽制 to be subordinate to; under the control of.
聽憑 to depend on; will depend on.
聽從 to yield; to give way; to comply with.
聽審 to abide by the decision of a court.

*t'ing* 聽任 to allow.
聽其便 at his, or their, option.
聽船主自便 at the option of the shipmaster.
聽商自便 at the merchant's option.
聽候 to wait; to await (as a decision).
聽稟 to entertain a petition; to consider a report (from an inferior).

*t'ing* 廳 an inferior department; a *t'ing*; a court of justice; a hall; a reception-room.
廳縣 territorial magistrates; *t'ing* and *hsien* districts.

*tiu* 丟 to lose; to throw away.
丟失 to lose.

*to* 多 much; many; several; too much; (after a number) more than.
多寡 quantity; how much.
多時 a long time.
多定 to fix upon a great number (as of holidays to be kept).
多有小暗沙 there are numerous patches of shoals.
多有價值漸減 the prices of various articles have gradually declined.
多傳各字號洋行 to summon a number of native and foreign firms.
多徵稅銀 the duty overcharged; an excess of duty.
多於單 more than [is stated in] the document.
多報 to overstate.
多報之數 an amount or quantity overstated; an excess.
多收 to receive too much (as a set of scales not properly balanced).
多出寬長若干 the excess in width or length.
多至 up to [so much] in quantity; at the most up to; not exceeding.

*to* 哆 representing the sound *to* in foreign words.
哆囉呢 *(to-lo-ni)* Spanish stripes.

*to* 度 to calculate; to consider; to think. Cf. *tu* 度.
度量 to measure (as a vessel).

*to* 奪 to criticise; to settle.

*to* 朶 a head of flowers; flowery; as a term of respect, "your."
朶翰 your flowery epistle; your note.

*to* 躲 to hide away; to escape from.
躲避 to seek shelter; to escape from.

*to* 垛 to pile up; a heap; a target.

*to* 舵 a ship's rudder.

30

*to* 舵工 a helmsman.
舵柱 wood poles used for ships' rudders; poles.
*to* 惰 lazy.
*to* 馱 to carry a burden; a beast's load.
*t'o* 妥 safe; proper; settled; steady.
妥員 a reliable officer.
妥當 safe; satisfactory.
妥便 safe and comfortable.
妥善 safe and good; properly managed.
妥協 in proper order; safely done.
妥速 safely and promptly; without delay.
妥定 to settle satisfactorily; well settled.
妥理 to safely arrange; to regulate; to manage.
妥辦 to manage safely; to take the proper measures in carrying out business.
妥議 to devise or draw up (as rules and regulations).
妥商 to consult; to negotiate about.
妥派巡船 to send out cruisers.
妥為商辦 to deliberate upon.
妥設良法 to adopt the safest measures for.
*t'o* 陀 steep; dangerous; representing the sound *to*, or *dha*, in foreign [Sanskrit] names.
陀羅 (*t'o-lo* = 陀羅呢, *t'o-lo-ni*) the Sanskrit *dharani*, a Buddhist prayer.
陀羅經被 a pall with Buddhist prayers embroidered on it.
*t'o* 駝 a camel; to carry burdens.
駝毛 camel's wool.
*t'o* 托 (or 拓) to take up with the hand; the distance one can measure with the hands, *i.e.*, a fathom.
托付 to entrust to the care of.
*t'o* 託 to commission.
託買 to commission one to buy.
託帶 to ask one to bring.
*t'o* 脫 to take away; to retire; to escape.
脫身 to retire; to withdraw; to stay away.
脫免 to avoid.
脫除 to remove.
脫卸 to unload.
*t'o* 拖 to drag; to pull.
拖帶 to tow (as a ship).
拖帶船隻之輪船 a tug steamer.
*t'o* 拖船 a tug-boat.
拖船簿 a register of licensed steam tugs.
拖延 to cause delay.
*tou* 荳 beans; peas; pulse.
荳子 beans.
荳石 pulse. Cf. *ssŭ* 絲斤.
荳餅 beancake.
荳腐 beancurd.
荳油 bean oil.
荳蔻 cardamoms; nutmegs.
荳蔻花 mace.
荳規銀 Shanghai tael silver (so called at the Yangtze ports).
*tou* 鬥 (or 鬭) to fight.
*tou* 斗 a Chinese grain measure, 10 of which are equal to a picul.
*tou* 陡 suddenly; to stop; to desist.
陡重 to aggravate suddenly (as a disease).
*tou* 竇 a hole; a mistake.
*t'ou* 頭 the head; the end, or an end, whether upper or lower (as the upper and lower points of a buoy); first; foremost.
頭等 of the first class.
頭尾 head and tail; first and last; beginning and end; both ends.
頭目 an overseer; a chief.
頭桅 the foremast.
頭白寶 pure sycee of the first class.
*t'ou* 偷 to steal; to pilfer.
偷漏 to fraudulently evade (payment of duty); to smuggle; thieves and smugglers.
偷漏稅課 to defraud the revenue.
偷稅 to rob the revenue; to smuggle.
偷竊 } to rob; to steal; thieves.
偷盜 }
*t'ou* 投 to deliver; to present to; to send in; to give up to (by sale or as a gift).
投報 to send in an application; to report (as for payment of duty).
投文 to present a despatch.
投帖 to send in one's card.
*t'ou* 透 to penetrate; transparent.
透鏡 dioptric.
透澈 to be thoroughly acquainted with.
*tsa* 雜 miscellaneous; to mix.

新關文件録



*tsa* 雜樣 miscellaneous sorts.
雜貨 sundries; miscellaneous goods.
雜藥 miscellaneous drugs.
雜糧 miscellaneous sorts of grain.
雜費 miscellaneous expenses.
雜亂 confused; confusion.
雜混 to get mixed up.

*tsai* 在 to be; in; at; in the written language, generally a preposition of place.
在江甯 at Nanking.
在關 in Customs employ; at the Custom House.
在地 on land (as opposed to the sea).
在置貨時 at the time of buying goods.
在事 to do service as; to be on duty; on service.
在事者 the members of a service or of an office; connected with business.
在案 "it is on record;" "as records show;" a concluding phrase showing that the facts stated are on official record; it need not be translated.
在逃 to have run away; to have absconded.
在坐 being seated; occupying a seat on the bench (in court).
在內 inside; included; inclusive of.
在外 outside; not including; exclusive of.
在卽 speedily; quickly.

*tsai* 哉 an interrogative particle expressing doubt, or conviction, placed at the end of sentences.

*tsai* 載 to contain; as a vessel *contains* cargo, or as a document *contains* a statement; to be laden with; to contain; a year; years.
載客 to carry passengers (as a passenger boat).
載貨 to carry goods (said of a vessel).
載貨憑單 a bill of lading.
載運 to convey.
載在撥船 to be placed on board a cargo-boat.
載入總單 to enter on the cargo certificate.
載明 it is stated in......
載回 to carry back; to provide a home passage.

*tsai* 儎 to stow cargo.
儎赴 to send by boat to.

*tsai* 灾 (or 災) a calamity; calamitous.

*tsai* 宰 to rule; a ruler; a governor; to kill cattle.
宰相 a Prime Minister; a Grand Secretary.

*tsai* 再 still; again; farther; besides; in addition to what has been stated before; often merely opens a new sentence.

*tsai* 再者 further; besides; in addition to this, it has to be stated that.
再三 }
再四 } again and again.
再四熟思 }
再四思維 } to consider over and over again; to consider ripely.

*ts'ai* 才 mental capacity; power; talent.
才拙 inability; incompetency.

*ts'ai* 材 }
材料 } materials.

*ts'ai* 財 riches; funds.

*ts'ai* 裁 to cut (as clothes).
裁撤 to cut away; to do away with; to remove.
裁剪 to cut out (as cloth); to plan; to arrange.
裁酌 }
裁奪 } to decide.
裁奪示遵 to decide and notify for guidance.

*ts'ai* 采 to pluck; to gather.

*ts'ai* 彩 bright colours; to adorn with colours.

*ts'ai* 採 to gather; to choose.
採買 to buy up.
採辦 to buy.

*ts'ai* 綵 coloured silk.
綵緞 coloured satin.

*ts'ai* 菜 vegetables.

*ts'ai* 猜 to guess; to suspect.

*tsan* 贊 to counsel; to assist; a counsellor.

*tsan* 讚 to commend; used for 贊 *(tsan)*, to counsel, etc.

*ts'an* 參 (or 叅) to counsel; to impeach. Cf. *shên* and *ts'ên.*
參贊 a Secretary of Legation; a Military Assistant Governor in Turkestan.
參奏 to memorialise the Throne.
參謀 a State Counsellor.
參軍 a military secretary.
參將 a colonel.
參酌 to consult.
參劾 to impeach; to denounce for dismissal.
參究 to impeach; impeachment.
參懲 to punish by impeachment.
參革 to deprive of office; to dismiss.
參拜 to visit a superior.

*ts'an* 讒 to slander; to criticise.

*ts'an* 殘 to injure; to destroy; deficient; cruel.

*ts'an* 蠶 the silkworm.

蠶子 silkworms' eggs.

蠶繭 }
蠶絲 } cocoons.

*tsang* 賍 (or 贓) to bribe; to loot.

賍物 plunder; the spoil carried away by robbers.

賍賊 a plunderer; a thief.

*ts'ang* 倉 a granary.

倉庫 granaries and treasuries.

*ts'ang* 艙 the hold of a ship.

艙口單 a ship's manifest.

艙底 at the bottom of a ship's hold.

艙房 cabins.

*ts'ang* 藏 }
藏匿 } to conceal.

*tsao* 早 morning; in the morning; early.

早晚 between morning and night; within short intervals (as daily fluctuations).

早晚不同 to change between morning and night (as the price of goods subject to frequent fluctuations).

*tsao* 皂 black; police runners.

*tsao* 糟 rotten; decayed.

*tsao* 遭 to meet.

遭遇 to meet with; to happen.

遭風 to meet with a storm; to be in distress.

*tsao* 棗 dates.

*tsao* 造 to make; to build; a party in a cause.

造册 to prepare a list or table; to make statistics.

造册處 the Statistical Department of the Inspectorate General of Customs.

造屋物料 building materials.

造船 to build vessels.

造船局 a Government dock; the Foochow Arsenal.

造船准單 a permit or license for building a ship.

造具 to prepare.

造具清册 to prepare statistics.

*ts'ao* 草 plants; grass; straw.

草帽 straw hats.

草帽緶 straw braid.

草字 running-hand characters; rough writing.

草稿 a rough draft.

草鞋 straw shoes.

*ts'ao* 曹 an official; order; class; a sign of plurality.

曹平銀 common sycee; the *Ts'ao-p'ing* or market tael.

*ts'ao* 漕 to transport by water.

漕糧 Government grain; tribute rice.

漕運 to convey by water.

漕船 a vessel carrying tribute grain.

漕河 the Grand Canal.

*ts'ao* 操 to take in hand; to manage; to drill.

操作 to do manual work.

操兵 }
操練 } to drill soldiers; to exercise troops.

*tsê* 則 a list; a tariff; then; a particle of inference, marking the apodosis of a sentence (see *chi* 即).

則例 regulations; a tariff.

*tsê* 責 to charge; to be responsible for; to punish.

責納 to charge a fee.

責罰 to punish.

責問 to interrogate; to hold responsible for.

責令 to charge with; to order; to let.

*tsê* 擇 to select; to choose.

擇選 to select.

擇吉日 to select a lucky day.

擇訂 to assign (as a berth to a ship).

擇取 to make a selection of.

*tsê* 澤 kindness; favour; a marsh.

*ts'ê* 策 a scheme; a proposition; a means of; to urge.

*ts'ê* 拆 to break open. *See* also *ch'ai* 拆.

拆開 to open (as packages for examination).

拆驗 to open for examination.

拆賣 to break up for sale.

拆賣船料 materials from vessels broken up for sale.

拆湊一處 to remove (as hoops from packages), and collect in one place.

*ts'ê* 測 to fathom; to measure.

測量 to survey (as a river).

*ts'ê* 册 statistical, etc., tables; a list; an inventory.

册簿 a list; a book for registry.

*tsei* 賊 robbers; to plunder; in warfare, the enemy.

賊類 }
賊匪 } robbers; thieves; banditti.

*ts'ên* 參 mixed; confused. Cf. *ts'an* and *shên*.

新關文件録



*ts'ên* 參差 *(ts'ên-tz'ŭ)* incongruous; to disagree; irregular; uneven; to make distinction between; to make a difference.

參差爭論 to disagree and quarrel.

*tsêng* 增 to add to.

增長 to increase.

增添 / 增益 } to add to; to increase.

增改新例 additional and modified rules; revised rules.

*tsêng* 贈 to give; to bestow.

*ts'êng* 曾 a sign of the past.

曾經 a sign of the past: have, has, had.

曾立 having been set up; drawn up.

*ts'êng* 層 a story; a tier; an item; a paragraph; a question or subject matter.

*tso* 作 to make; to do; before verbs, like *hsing* (行), gives a verb active force, *e.g.*, in the sentence 可作考選之人 (*i.e.*, "the persons who may examine, or may be members of the Board of Examination"), *tso* (作) has the effect of preventing the sentence being misconstrued as "the persons who may be examined, or may be admitted to examination;" (= 爲) to consider as; *i.q.*, *tso* 做.

作工 to work; to do coolie labour.

作成 to make ready; to complete.

作保 to be surety; to guarantee.

作証 to act as witness; in witness [thereof].

作速 to hurry; speedily.

作官 to be an official; a mandarin.

作一家糊口 to constitute the living or food for the whole family.

作抵 to substitute; to tender in lieu of (as duties of one kind for those of another kind).

作事 to transact business.

作文章 to compose essays.

作爲 to make; to manufacture; to act as; to consider as; to treat as.

*tso* 昨 / 昨日 } yesterday; the other day.

昨夜 last night; the other night.

*tso* 鑿 to bore; to dig; to sift a matter; to furnish evidence.

*tso* 左 the left side; the senior of two deputies where only two are employed; not agreeing.

左邊 the left side; the starboard side.

*tso* 左右 right and/or left; on either side of; more or less; about.

左堂 an Assistant Magistrate.

*tso* 佐 to assist; assistant.

佐領府 a military title (colonel or major).

*tso* 坐 to sit; to sit on the bench in a court.

坐視 to sit and see; *i.e.*, to look on without acting.

坐船 to go in a vessel; by ship.

坐艙 to sit in the ship's hold; to be in charge of the ship's hold.

坐艙司事 an employé in charge of a ship's hold.

坐堂 to sit in court.

*tso* 座 a classifier of houses, beacons, lighthouses, etc.; a seat; a throne.

*tso* 做 to do; to act; *i.q.*, *tso* 作.

做工 to do work; to be employed.

*ts'o* 措 to employ; to use; to publish; to give out.

措辦 to put into operation (as a Tariff).

*ts'o* 錯 confused; mixed; wrong; an error.

錯誤 a mistake.

錯雜 to mix up by mistake.

*ts'o* 鹺 brine; salt.

鹺政 / 鹺綱 } the Salt Administration; the Salt Gabel.

*ts'o* 撮 to bring together; to gather up.

撮要 to collect the important points; to make an abstract; a *résumé*.

撮合 to unite; to make a match; to reconciliate.

*tsou* 走 to walk; to go; to depart; to run.

走私 to smuggle.

走私漏稅 to evade payment of duty by smuggling; to smuggle.

*tsou* 奏 to address the Emperor.

奏請 to petition the Throne.

奏明 / 奏稱 } to state in a petition to the Throne.

奏書 / 奏摺 / 奏本 } a memorial to the Throne.

奏定 decided by the Emperor in reply to a memorial.

奏奉諭旨 to receive a reply from the Throne.

*ts'ou* 湊 to collect; to assemble.

*tsu* 助 to co-operate.

助救 to assist in rescuing; to come to the rescue.

*tsu* 祖 / 祖宗 } ancestors.

祖廟 an ancestral temple.

*tsu* 租 rent; to rent; to hire.

租銀 rent.

租費 expenditure on account of rent.

租契 a lease.

租雇 to hire; to charter (as a ship).

租界 land on which ground rent is paid; a concession: a settlement (as the British Settlement at Shanghai).

*tsu* 阻 to impede.

阻滯 to obstruct; to stop; obstruction; stoppage.

阻撓 to be vexatious.

*tsu* 卒 lictors; police runners; soldiers; suddenly.

*tsu* 足 enough; sufficient; the foot.

足數 enough; sufficient; the complete amount.

足色 sufficient colour; full standard silver; pure sycee.

足色紋銀 / 足紋 } full standard silver; pure sycee.

*tsu* 族 a clan; a family; a class; a sort.

*ts'u* 粗 (or 麤) coarse.

粗細 coarse and fine; the quality.

粗磁器 coarse chinaware.

粗夏布 coarse grasscloth.

粗麻布 coarse linen.

粗斜紋布 drills.

粗葵扇 untrimmed palm-leaf fans.

*tsui* 嘴 the lips; the mouth; a beak.

*tsui* 最 very; extremely; most; sign of the superlative.

最西之處 in the extreme west; the westernmost point.

最後子口 the last barrier; the barrier nearest a Treaty port.

最優之禮 the most courteous treatment (such as is granted to the representatives of the most favoured nation).

最關緊要 most important in connexion with [this subject].

*tsui* 罪 crime; punishment; to punish.

罪犯 a criminal.

*tsui* 醉 intoxicated.

*ts'ui* 催 to urge.

*ts'ui* 翠 / 翠毛 } kingfishers' feathers.

*tsun* 尊 honoured; honourable; to honour; as a term of civility, "your."

*tsun* 遵 to obey; to comply with; to follow.

遵照 in compliance with; in obedience to; to be guided by; for the guidance of.

遵依 to comply with; to obey.

遵行 to comply with orders; to be guided by; for one's guidance.

遵守 to observe; to be guided by.

遵悉 to be apprised of for one's guidance.

遵斷 to abide by the decision in a case.

遵繳 to submit to paying (as a fine).

遵奉 to obey; to observe.

遵奉之日 days to be kept as holidays.

*tsun* 竣. See *chün*.

*ts'un* 寸 an inch, the tenth part of a *ch'ih* or foot.

*ts'un* 忖 to consider; to conjecture.

*ts'un* 村 a village.

*ts'un* 存 to keep; to keep as a balance.

存行 to keep in one's hong or store (as for sale).

存棧 to store goods in a godown; to keep in store.

存庫 to keep on deposit (as funds paid into a treasury).

存查 / 存案 } to file in the archives; to keep on record.

存根 a butt; a counterfoil.

存關 to file in the Customs archives.

存票 a drawback.

存留 to keep; to detain.

存款 a balance.

*tsung* 宗 kind; description; class.

宗廟 an ancestral temple.

宗室 the Imperial family.

宗人府 the Imperial Clan Court.

*tsung* 綜 to arrange threads in weaving; to collect.

綜算 to estimate; to calculate.

綜紛緒 to collect the confused threads of a texture; to arrange in order.

*tsung* 棕 coir.

棕色 brown.

棕繩 coir rope.

*tsung* 鬃 (interchanged with 騣 *tsung*, dishevelled hair); bristles; a wig; a cue.

新關文件録



*tsung* 縱 to loosen; to allow; making allowance for; although.

縱不知情亦應革換 although they did not know the circumstances, yet they are to be removed from office.

*tsung* 總 all; general; central; chief; collective.

總須 all must; must on any account.

總口 a central Customs station.

總卡 a principal barrier; a head barrier office.

總署 a head office.

總單 a cargo certificate.

總旋單 a cargo certificate issued by the Likin office at one of the Yangtze ports of call, for delivery at a Foreign Custom House.

總名 a general designation; a term.

總目 a synoptic table; a table of contents.

總冊 a general list; a general table; a statistical summary.

總數 totals.

總簿 a book for general entries; a ledger.

總例 a general rule.

總管 to have the general control of; a general manager.

總辦 to superintend; a chief manager.

總理 to have the general management of.

總理各國事務衙門 the Yamên having the general control of matters connected with foreign countries; the Tsungli Yamên.

總理委員 a deputy in general charge of matters.

總督 a Governor-General.

總兵 a brigadier-general; a *chên-t'ai*.

總稅務司 an Inspector General of Customs.

總營造司 an engineer-in-chief.

總信差 a chief letter-carrier.

總不 not on any account. Cf. *ping* 並未.

總不能 not at all able to; in no case shall......

總是 after all; finally it is; generally speaking.

總期 it is expected to be; hoping that; with the general aim of.

*ts'ung* 從 to follow; liable; to agree with; to yield; (=自) from (local and temporal); since; (=從來) hitherto; so far; read *tsung*, a clan; to be attached to, as one of secondary rank.

從便 to follow one's convenience.

從繁 to follow, or to cause to follow, many (as many restrictive rules); to impose a great many (as holidays to be kept).

*ts'ung* 從旁 to be present at.

從重 severe; strict (as punishment).

從重議罰 liable to be severely punished.

從重治罪 to be severely punished.

從輕 yielding and light, *i.e.*, lenient (as with punishment); to mitigate.

從輕減罰 to mitigate a fine.

從優 liberal; considerate.

從豐 liberal; plenteous.

從寬 to remit (as punishment); to treat with leniency; to mitigate.

從給照之日起 to date from date of issue (of a certificate).

從此以後 after this; from henceforth.

從前 formerly.

從衆爲定 the [absolute] majority decides.

從新另議 to negotiate anew and separately; to renew negotiations.

從品 (*tsung-p'in*) the second or *B* division of any of the nine degrees of Chinese rank.

*tu* 杜 to restrict; to prohibit; to stop; to prevent.

杜私運 to stop secret traffic.

*tu* 肚 the belly; the stomach.

*tu* 覩 to look; to see.

*tu* 賭 to gamble; to play; to bet.

賭博 to gamble.

*tu* 都 a metropolis; all.

都統 a lieutenant-general.

都察院 the Court of Censors; the Censorate.

都御史 a President of the Censorate.

*tu* 督 to superintend; a superintendent; a Governor-General.

督管 to have control over.

督率 to superintend; to direct; to have under one's orders; to lead (as soldiers); to place oneself at the head of; to direct (as a body of workmen).

督理 to superintend; to govern.

督辦 to manage.

督憲 the Governor-General or Viceroy.

督撫 Viceroy and Governor.

督撫司道 the provincial authorities, viz., Viceroy, Governor, Treasurer, Judge, Salt Commissioner, and Grain Collector (or Tao-t'ais). Cf. *ssŭ* 司道.

督糧道 a provincial Grain Collector.

*tu* 瀆 to trouble another (as with a petition).

*tu* 牘 documents; archives; registers.

*tu* 讀 to read; to study.

讀書 to read books; to study; a literary man.

*tu* 篤 very much; highly; true; real.

篤念 to keep in high memory.

*tu* 獨 single; alone; only; on one's own account.

獨樹 a single tree.

獨身一人 a single person; alone.

*tu* 度 degrees of a circle or a sphere; degrees of latitude or longitude; to pass over; a rule; a limit. Cf. *to* 度.

度數 degrees.

*tu* 渡 to cross; to ferry over; to make a passage by water.

渡船 a ferry-boat; a passage-boat.

*tu* 鍍 / 鍍金 } to plate; to gild.

鍍銀 to wash with silver; to plate.

*t'u* 土 earth; raw opium, so called owing to its earthy appearance; land; native; local.

土產 native produce.

土貨 native goods; local produce.

土煤 native coal.

土布 native cotton cloth; nankeens.

土染洋布 native-dyed foreign cottons.

土絲 silk from the Canton district; fine raw silk.

土靛 dried indigo; a kind of Prussian blue made in China.

土茯苓 china-root.

土人 the natives; aborigines.

土妓 a local prostitute.

土匪 local robbers.

土耳基國 (*t'u-êrh-chi-kuo*) / 土耳國 (*t'u-êrh-kuo*) } Turkey; Turkish.

土耳基洋藥 / 土耳基金花土 } Turkish opium.

*t'u* 途 a road.

途間 / 途中 } on the way; *en route*.

*t'u* 塗 mud; dirty; to besmear.

塗朱搽粉 to besmear one's face with cosmetics; to paint faces with rouge and chalk.

*t'u* 突 abruptly; unexpectedly.

*t'u* 兎 a hare; a rabbit.

*t'u* 兎皮 hare skins; rabbit skins.

*t'u* 徒 a foot-soldier; a follower; a rowdy; a pupil; a disciple; to banish.

*t'u* 圖 to plan; to covet; a map; an illustration; a seal.

圖記 a private seal.

圖書 a seal; an illustrated book.

圖利 to be covetous of profit.

圖免 to try to evade (as payment of duties).

圖們江 (*t'u-mên chiang*) the River Tumen, near Vladivostock, on the Corean and Russian boundary.

*tuan* 短 short; not sufficient.

短少 to be curtailed; to decrease.

短絀 a deficit; deficient.

*tuan* 端 upright; correct; serious; also, matters; affairs; a paragraph; a passage; the head; the end; a terminus; a spot.

端正 upright; correct.

端莊 modest; grave; serious.

端裕 upright and generous.

端裕康慶昭和莊敬 (*Tuan-yü K'ang-ch'ing Chao-ho Chuang-ching*) the honorary name (*hui-hao*, 徽號) of the Empress Dowager Tz'ŭ-an.

端佑 an upright help; a true help.

端佑康頤昭豫莊誠 (*Tuan-yu K'ang-i Chao-yü Chuang-ch'êng*) the honorary name (*hui-hao*, 徽號) of the Empress Dowager Tz'ŭ-hsi.

端陽節期 the dragon-boat festival.

端陽 (or 端午) the dragon-boat festival (5th day of 5th moon).

*tuan* 段 a lot; a section; a paragraph; a band; a limit; a section of the coast line, comprising a distance of 10 *li*; a classifier of rocks, shoals, etc.

*tuan* 緞 silk cloth; satin; thick silk.

緞布 cotton damasks.

*tuan* 斷 to break asunder; to cut off; to decide; very (used to enforce negative particles).

斷半 to halve a thing.

斷令交出 to decide that payment is to be made; to order, by way of decision in a case, that payment be made.

斷難 very difficult; decidedly difficult; impossible.

斷不 not at all; by no means. Cf. *ping* 並未.

斷而不連 by no means connected with.

*t'uan* 團 to collect together; a ball; a lump.

團聚 to accumulate; to collect together; to keep order among a crowd.

*t'uan* 團練 to drill soldiers.

*tui* 對 to compare; to check; to agree; a pair; opposite.

對徑 opposite.

對面 opposite to; off......

*tui* 堆 a heap; to heap up; to accumulate.

堆積 to heap up.

*tui* 兌 to weigh; to weigh silver; to pay in silver or sycee.

兌收 to receive weighing (sycee); *i.e.*, to receive cash or bullion.

兌換 to exchange (as sycee).

*tui* 隊 an army; a company.

隊伍 rank and file.

*t'ui* 退 to retire; to refuse.

退去 to withdraw; to retire.

退還 to return.

退回 to shut out goods (from a ship); to retire.

退辦 to throw up the management of.

*t'ui* 腿 a leg; a thigh.

*t'ui* 推 to shirk responsibility; to refuse; (=推算) to reckon.

推辭 } to decline; to refuse.
推却 }

推諉 to retract what one had agreed to; to shirk responsibility; to back out.

*tun* 敦 sound; generous; honest.

敦崇和誼 to be pervaded by the honest feeling of peace and friendship.

*tun* 墩 a hillock; a beacon mound.

*tun* 鈍 dull; blunt.

*tun* 頓 to lay down; to store; to part with; to injure; a ton.

*tun* 噸 a ton (weight or cubic measure).

噸數 tonnage (amount of).

噸鈔 tonnage dues.

*tun* 躉 a storehouse; to store.

躉船 a receiving ship; a hulk.

躉關 stored under bond, as in a bonded hulk or godown; "bonded."

*t'un* 呑 to swallow; to usurp.

呑佔 to usurp.

*tung* 冬 winter; the end.

*tung* 東 east; eastern; (=東家) the master of a household; a ship-owner, etc.

*tung* 東西 east and west; eastern and western.

東西洋各國 the countries of the eastern and western seas; foreign countries.

東北首 towards the north-east.

東家 a master; a host.

東洋 the eastern sea; Japan; Japanese.

東洋車 a Japanese carriage; *i.e.*, a jinricsha.

東閣大學士 one of the four Chinese Grand Secretaries.

東門小河 the East Gate Creek (Shanghai).

東海關 the Chefoo Customs.

*tung* 動 to move; to work; to carry out work; to change; to meddle with; to appropriate (as funds); to use.

動工 to commence work.

動手 to move hands; to go to work.

動身 to get up; to start.

動展 to move about.

動撥 to tranship goods.

*tung* 董 to manage; (=董事) a senior employé; an expert.

董事 a senior in a firm; a manager.

*tung* 懂 to understand.

*t'ung* 同 with; the same as.

同此 the same as this; to the same effect.

同前由 } particulars being the same as the former; "to the same effect as the former."
同前因 }

同時 at the same time.

同意 of the same opinion.

同重 an equal weight; the same weight.

同樣 of the same kind.

同樣三紙 triplicate copies (of a document).

同列 }
同等 } belonging to the same category; of the same class.
同類 }

同類之貨 goods of the same denomination.

同坐 to occupy the bench with another.

同行 to do together; to co-operate; to go together.

同霑 to participate in favours, or privileges, granted to others.

同鄉 a countryman; a fellow-townsman.

同商 a mercantile friend; a fellow-merchant.

同一 in conformity with; in every respect the same.

*t'ung* 同是一貨 it is the same cargo.

同功絲 silk reeled from dupions.

同知 a sub-prefect.

同治 the period of reign of the Emperor T'UNG CHIH (1862 to 1875).

同安 T'ung-an-hsien (near Amoy).

*t'ung* 銅 copper; brass.

銅板 bar copper.

銅條 copper rods.

銅磚 copper, in slabs.

銅片 sheet copper; copper sheathing.

銅箔 brass-foil.

銅釘 copper nails.

銅帽 percussion caps.

銅絲 copper wire; brass wire.

銅器 copperware; brassware.

銅料器 copper material and articles; unmanufactured copper and copperware.

銅鈕釦 brass buttons.

銅錢 copper cash.

銅盆 a copper basin.

銅務 copper business, *i.e.*, mint matters; business connected with the coining of copper cash.

*t'ung* 桶 a cask; a barrel.

*t'ung* 通 all; to communicate with; to bring about; a classifier of documents.

通知 to inform through another; to notify.

通報 to report, through the channel of an inferior, to a higher officer; to announce.

通悉 to make generally known; to inform by circular or proclamation.

通達 to inform; well versed in a matter.

通明 clear; intelligible; perspicuous.

通曉 to inform the public; to make generally known.

通行 for general circulation; general; current.

通行曉諭 to make known to the public.

通行出口入口 to traffic inwards and outwards at a port.

通劄 to issue circular instructions to.

通用 in, or for, general use; used by all; in common use.

通用旗號 the Commercial Code signals.

通寶 currency; copper cash.

通書 a calendar.

*t'ung* 通事 an interpreter; a linguist.

通判 a deputy sub-prefect.

通商 to communicate by trade; to traffic; foreign trade.

通商後 after the opening up of trade.

通商和約 a Commercial Treaty.

通商稅則 the Customs Tariff (according to Foreign Treaties).

通商章程 Trade Regulations under Foreign Treaties; the Rules appended to the Tariff.

通商各款 the articles regarding trade.

通商各口 the Treaty ports.

通商別口 another Treaty port.

通商各關 the foreign Custom Houses.

通商事務 foreign trade matters.

通商大臣 a Minister Superintendent of Trade.

通商總局 the Board of Foreign Trade (at Foochow); a Chamber of Commerce.

通商稅務公會 the German Zollverein.

通志 a local (provincial, etc.) gazetteer.

通共 total; complete.

通共章程 complete regulations; in particular, the Revised Yangtze Trade Regulations; also, the Five Rules regarding Transit Trade, called 通商各口通共章程.

通同 to be connected with.

通同舞弊 to take part in the commission of an irregularity.

通融 to befriend; to accommodate; by way of accommodation or compromise.

通融辦理 to make an arrangement by way of accommodation or compromise.

*t'ung* 蓪 / 蓪草 } the pith-paper plant; the *Aralia papyrifera.*

蓪紙 pith-paper; rice-paper.

蓪紙畫 pictures on pith or rice paper.

*t'ung* 統 all; uniformly; total; the beginning.

統共 / 統計 } total; a grand total.

統轄 to be in general charge of.

統帶 to bring with oneself (as witnesses to court).

統帥 a commander-in-chief.

*tzŭ* 子 a child; a son; affiliated; added to nouns as an ending, as it were, which usage is generally borrowed from the colloquial language; children; seed.

tzŭ 子口 a small port affiliated to a larger port; a Customs barrier.

子口稅 transit dues.

子棉花 seed cotton.

tzŭ 字 a written character; a number, inasmuch as it is expressed by a character.

字樣 style; phrase; "the words" ............ in a document.

字號 a mark (as on a package of merchandise).

字據 a license.

字據費銀 a license fee (as paid by pilots).

tzŭ 紫 purple; brown.

紫黃銅器 copperware and pewterware.

紫梗 sticklac.

紫竹林 *(Tzŭ-chu-lin)* the local name for the site of the Foreign settlement at Tientsin.

tzŭ 資 (for which *tzŭ* 貲 is used) commodities; necessaries; capital in trade; to assist in.

資貨 goods; stock.

資送 to assist in forwarding; to send with presents of money, etc. (as a destitute to his home).

資給 to provide by way of assistance (as a destitute with means of support).

tzŭ 咨 a despatch; to address in a despatch (used among Chinese correspondents and equals).

咨文 a despatch; an official document.

咨明 to inform in a despatch.

咨請 to request in a despatch.

咨請核復 to ask in a despatch for a reply.

咨稟 to petition; to address a superior in writing.

咨行 to address in a despatch; to address an equal.

咨覆 to reply in a despatch.

咨商 to deliberate; to consult by correspondence.

tzŭ 玆 this; these; now.

玆者 now.

tzŭ 滋 numerous; great; much; very; to increase.

滋深 very deeply; severely.

tzŭ 自 self; spontaneous; of course; must; from.

自巳 oneself.

自備 to prepare oneself; self-made; self-owned (as foreign ships owned by Chinese); to provide oneself; to furnish.

自用 to use oneself; for own use.

自着 to wear oneself; for own wear.

自報 one's own declaration; to declare oneself.

自赴 to proceed in person to.

tzŭ 自造 / 自作 } self made; own manufacture.

自辦之事 matters to be managed by oneself.

自願 by one's own wish; with one's own consent.

自行出洋 to emigrate from one's own free will.

自行赴卡 to go to the barrier office of one's own accord.

自鳴鐘 a striking clock; clocks.

自鳴風笙 an automatic whistling apparatus.

自能爆開 inflammable; explosive.

自來火 lucifer matches; also, gaslight; gas.

自來水 water from the waterworks.

自存 to support oneself; to be able to do without help.

自盡 to commit suicide.

自應 / 自必 / 自宜 / 自當 } must; must of course; bound to.

自然 of course; spontaneous; natural.

自然銅 native copper.

自…起至…止 from *(such a date)* to *(such a date)*.

自日落起至日出止 from sunset till sunrise.

自古以來 from ancient times up to now.

自……之後 from after ......

自接函之時 from the date of notice being given; from the date when the letter was received.

自通商征稅以來 ever since duties have been levied on foreign trade.

自外觀之 to look at from outside; from a superficial point of view.

自沙市以至大通 between Shashih and Tat'ung.

tz'ŭ 次 second; the next in order; a time.

次日 on the following day.

次序 to arrange in order; *seriatim*.

tz'ŭ 此 this; here.

此照 "this is [hereby] certified."

此佈 "this is a public notice;" for general information; "I beg to inform you of this" (of the above).

此致 "this is what I wanted to address you with" (a concluding phrase in letters).

此致順頌升祉 "while communicating to you the above, allow me to express my best wishes," etc. (a concluding phrase in letters).

*tz'ŭ* 此頌升祺 "with best wishes;" "with kind regards" (a concluding phrase in letters).
此項 this kind of; such; this.
此項貨物 this class of goods; such goods.
此項公文 this document.
此等 of this class; *i.e.*, such.
此等案件 such cases.
此誠關乎事勢使然 this has really become thus through the influence of circumstances.
此端 this affair.
此時 during such time; at this time; now.
此日 the same day; this day.
此次 this time.
此外 besides this.
此去 from here; from this (place).
此後 after this; hereafter.
此八月十九日 on this, the 19th day of the 8th moon.

*tz'ŭ* 差 irregular; uneven. Cf. *ch'a* and *ch'ai*.

*tz'ŭ* 祠 an ancestral hall; to offer sacrifice to ancestors.

*tz'ŭ* 詞 to write; to declare in writing; to accuse; a rhyme; a rhythmical sentence; tales; empty phrases.

*tz'ŭ* 辭 to decline; to refuse; to deny; to use as a plea for not complying.
辭退 to refuse.
辭官 to resign office.
辭工 to leave one's work; to come off duty.

*tz'ŭ* 慈 kindness; mercy; the standing epithet for mothers; just as *yen* (嚴), stern, is the epithet for fathers; hence, 慈母, "my mother;" 嚴父, "my father."
慈躬 my mother's body.
慈愉 kind and joyful.
慈安 the late Empress Dowager Tz'ŭ-AN.
慈禧 the Empress Dowager Tz'ŭ-HSI.

*tz'ŭ* 磁 porcelain.
磁器 chinaware.
磁商 a trader in chinaware.

*tz'ŭ* 賜 to confer; to bestow.
賜予 to grant; to bestow.
賜覆 to bestow an answer; to favour one with a reply.
賜祭 to bestow sacrifices (so as to honour the spirit of a deceased).
賜教 to bestow instruction; to communicate one's opinion.

*tz'ŭ* 賜恩 to bestow favour.
賜邺 to grant special rewards [to the family of a deceased official].

## W.

*wa* 瓦 tiles; earthen.
瓦甎 tiles and bricks.
瓦器 earthenware.

*wa* 凹. See *ao*.

*wa* 挖 to dig; to scrape out.
挖補 to erase and cover with a new patch of paper on which the amended reading is written; to correct by erasure.

*wai* 外 outside; besides; extraordinary; in correlation with *ch'u* 除 (which see), besides.
外國 a foreign country; foreign.
外國人 a foreigner; foreigners.
外國煤 foreign coal.
外國酒 foreign wines or spirits.
外國烟 foreign tobacco.
外國月分 the foreign calendar; the month according to the foreign calendar.
外邦 foreign countries.
外洋口 a port across the sea; a seaport; a foreign port; the port of destination (for a ship about to leave).
外洋別地 other countries abroad.
外需情事 extraordinary requirements; under exceptional circumstances.
外獎 an exceptional reward; *i.e.*, a reward not granted by the Emperor, but by the provincial authorities.

*wan* 玩 trifles; to trifle; to play with.
玩物 playthings; toys; curios.

*wan* 頑 thick-headed; obstinate; stupid.

*wan* 完 to end; to finish; to settle (as an account, a payment, or a case).
完工 to finish work.
完結 } 完竣 } to complete an affair or a job; to wind up; to settle.
完稅 to pay duties.
完清 to pay the full amount; to settle an account.
完過 has paid; having paid (duty).
完娶 } 完婚 } 完姻 } to marry.

*wan*
*yüan* } 宛 to yield; to give in; accommodating.

宛轉 yielding to circumstances.

*wan* 碗 a bowl; a basin.

*wan* 灣 a bay; a gulf.

*wan* 挽 to revert to the former state; to restore; to pull; to draw.

*wan* 晚 evening.

*wan* 萬 ten thousand; a very large number; all; used to enforce negation. Cf. *ping* 並未.

萬一 one in ten thousand; perhaps; probably.

萬壽 *lit.*, the "Ten Thousand Ages"; the Emperor's birthday.

萬代 ten thousand generations; "your offspring."

萬國 all nations; international.

萬國公法 international law.

*wan* 丸 anything round; a pill; pills.

*wang* 王 a prince; a King.

*wang* 旺 much; in a high degree; prosperous.

*wang* 枉 a wrong; a grievance; to force; *e.g.*, 枉駕, to force oneself (as to pay a visit to an inferior); in vain.

枉顧 to honour one with a visit.

*wang* 往 to go to; towards; to; formerly.

往來 to come and go; traffic; correspondence.

往來信件 correspondence exchanged.

往日 constantly; usually; on a former day.

往常 constantly; usually.

往年 in former years.

往世 formerly; former generations.

往往 always; constantly; repeatedly.

*wang* 亡 to perish.

亡故 dead; deceased.

*wang* 妄 irregular; what is not in order; falsely.

妄告 to accuse falsely.

*wang* 忘 to forget; to disregard.

*wang* 望 to look to; to see; to hope; full moon; the 15th day of a Chinese month.

望見 to see; to observe; to be within sight.

望準 to take the bearing of.

望臺
望樓 } a look-out; a signal station; a light-station; a beacon or house visible at a long distance.

望示 to look forward to [the receipt of] instructions.

*wang* 望切望速 hoping for strict and speedy attention [to the matter].

望日 the 15th day of a Chinese month.

*wang* 罔 not; without.

罔極 limitless; illimitable.

*wang* 網 a net; to catch (as in a net).

*wei* 爲 (read in the *shang-p'ing* tone): to make; to consider; to hold that.........; (read in the *ch'ü-shêng* tone): because of; on behalf of; in matters of.

爲善 is good; recommendable.

爲證 in witness thereof; as a voucher.

爲業 as my business.

爲憑 as a voucher.

爲此 on account of this [matter]; therefore.

爲此照會 this despatch is written, or addressed, to......

爲此移請查照 writing a despatch on this account, please take official notice; "I shall be obliged by your noting the subject of my despatch."

爲此叩稟 on this account I make a petition.

爲何 on what account? for what reason? why.

爲............事 in the matter of............

爲照覆事 in the matter of a reply.

爲咨請事 in the matter of an official request (introductory phrase to a despatch).

*wei* 僞 to counterfeit; false; fictitious.

僞造 to counterfeit.

僞錢 counterfeit money.

*wei* 圍 to surround; stands for 闈 (*wei*), "the side doors of the palace where candidates once underwent their examination" (WILLIAMS); the public literary examinations.

圍姓票 Wei-sing lottery tickets. The *Wei-hsing*, or "literary examination surnames," lottery is a kind of betting on the surnames of successful candidates. Being regarded as a form of gambling, it was until lately forbidden by law, and the tickets were liable to seizure.

*wei* 幃 curtains.

*wei* 緯 the woof of a texture; parallel lines; to weave; fringes; tassels.

緯度北 northern latitude.

緯線 silk tassels.

*wei* 違 to offend against; to oppose.

違避 to abscond; to avoid.

違命 to disobey an order.

違章 to offend against regulations; to break the rule.

*wei* 違此例 to offend against this rule.

違禁 offending against prohibitory rules; prohibited.

違禁貨物 prohibited goods; contraband.

違犯 to offend against.

違背 to disobey orders; to disregard a rule; to break a contract.

違背合同耽擱船事 demurrage payable under charter party.

違和 to become unwell; to fall sick.

*wei* 闈 the door of an examination hall; hence, examination for a degree generally. See *wei* 圍.

*wei* 衛 to escort; to guard; the country of Wei, an ancient feudal state comprising parts of Honan and Chihli; stands for "Tientsin."

衛閭閻 to guard the villages and hamlets; to keep peace within the country.

衛護 to guard; to escort.

*wei* 畏 }
畏懼 } to fear; to dread; to be alarmed.

畏途 to fear the road; to avoid the transport of goods from fear of difficulties.

*wei* 委 to depute; really; indeed; to bend down; to do injustice; a grievance.

委員 to depute officers; a deputy; a delegate.

委員代辦 to depute an officer as one's agent.

委實 truly; in reality.

委屈 an injustice; wrongful oppression.

*wei* 諉 to shirk one's duty; to back out.

*wei* 謂 to speak of; to mean.

*wei* 威 majestic; dignified; stern.

*wei* 微 small; trifling.

微物 a small matter; a trifle.

微利 small profit.

微碍之處 obstructions of small extent.

微細之事 the details (as opposed to the general features of an affair).

*wei* 危 }
危險 } dangerous; danger.

危險之處 an obstruction.

危險防碍之物 articles of a dangerous nature; *e.g.*, gunpowder and other explosives.

*wei* 桅 masts; spars.

桅木 masts or spars (timber).

桅梢 on the top of a mast.

*wei* 唯 excepting; but.

*wei* 帷 }
帷帳 } a curtain; curtains.

帷屏 a screen.

*wei* 惟 to consider; to hold that; only; but; except.

惟某人自行認理 }
惟某人是問 } So-and-so will be held responsible.

惟照 "direct your thoughts to this note" (a concluding phrase in letters).

*wei* 維 to tie; to help; (= 惟) to consider, etc.

*wei* 尾 a tail; a spit of land; any pointed shore, if quite flat; what is left behind; a balance.

尾隨 to follow close after.

尾隨其後 to follow close after one.

尾數 unsettled items; moneys to be recovered; recoveries.

*wei* 未 not; not having; not being; the opposite of 已 (*i*), having (sign of the past).

未善 not good; not properly.

未便 inconvenient.

未能 cannot; impossible.

未獲 cannot; cannot manage to.

未蒙緝獲 I have not yet been favoured with the capture [of the robbers who stole my property].

未免 cannot avoid; is bound to.

未完 not settled; unsettled; outstanding.

未然 not so; that which has not occurred yet, *e.g.*, 防患於未然, to take steps against calamities before they occur.

未盡事宜 matters not exhausted, *i.e.*, not completely settled.

未列 not enumerated.

未領執照 without a license; without a bond certificate.

未經 have not; has not; not yet; not having.

未經完稅 not having paid the duty.

未曾 have not; has not; not having; without having.

未撤之先 before being removed.

未領紅單之先 before the issue of the port clearance.

未士 in Cantonese pronounced Mi-sze; the pidgin-English word for Mister, Mr.

*wei* 味 taste; flavour; style.

*wei* 位 position; place; a throne; a gentleman.

*wei* 慰 to soothe; to console.

*wei* 骫 to crook; to bend.

骫法 to pervert the law.

*wên* 文 a despatch; an official letter; a text; a passage in a text; a cash; a copper cash.
文內 in the despatch.
文件 despatches; documents.
文書 an official letter; a document.
文憑 a documentary proof; a protocol.
文武地方官 civil and military local authorities.
文宗顯 Wên Tsung Hsien (the dynastic title of the late Emperor Hsien Fêng).
文安縣 the district of Wên-an, in Shun-t'ien-fu.
*wên* 紋 streaks.
紋銀 silver with streaks (refers to the corrugated appearance common to the outside of a shoe of pure sycee, as contrasted with the smoother surface of an impure shoe); pure sycee.
紋水 the difference or fluctuation in the price of sycee silver.
*wên* 溫 warm.
溫州府 the prefecture of Wênchow.
*wên* 瘟 } 瘟病 } an infectious disease; an epidemic.
*wên* 問 to ask; to hold responsible.
*wên* 聞 to hear; it is rumoured.
聞報 to receive a report.
*wên* 穩 firm; safe; steady.
*wo* 我 our; we; I; me.
*wo* 倭 Japan; Japanese.
*wo* 窩 a nest; birds' nests.
*wu* 五 (or 伍) five.
五棓子 nutgalls (so called in the Customs Tariff); gallnuts.
*wu* 伍 a body of soldiers; a military division.
*wu* 吾 I; my; we; our.
吾兄 my elder brother; *i.e.*, "you," when addressing a senior.
吾弟 my younger brother; *i.e.*, "you," when addressing a junior.
吾友 my friend.
*wu* 晤 to see face to face; to meet in person.
晤會 to meet in person.
*wu* 汚 filthy.
*wu* 烏 black.
烏木 ebony-wood.
烏煙 opium.

*wu* 槝 } 槝木 } ebony-wood.
*wu* 誣 to deceive; to lie.
誣揑 to accuse falsely; to forge an account.
誣告 to accuse falsely.
誣證 false evidence.
*wu* 屋 a room; a house.
*wu* 握 to grasp; to hold tight; to have proper control of, as in *pa-wu* (把握), to have sway over.
*wu* 武 military.
武官 a military officer.
武備院 the Imperial Armoury.
武穴 *(wu-hsüeh)* Wusüeh (a port of call on th Yangtze).
*wu* 吳 the ancient state of Wu, comprising the country about Soochow.
吳淞 Woosung (an out-station at the mouth of the Shanghai river).
*wu* 悞 delay.
*wu* 誤 wrong; a mistake; to delay; to neglect.
誤會 to misapprehend; a mistake.
誤認 to erroneously take as; to mistake for.
誤疑 to erroneously suspect.
誤罰 to punish in error.
誤犯 to unintentionally break the law.
誤入險途 to enter a dangerous road by mistake; to run into danger.
*wu* 無 not; the opposite of *yu* (有), having; not having; without; *nil*.
無非 cannot but; bound to; by all means.
無不合 bound to agree; certainly not at variance with.
無論 no matter whether.
無論遠近 no matter whether far or near; irrespective of distance.
無論多寡 irrespective of quantity.
無論貴賤 irrespective of price or value.
無事 no business to; not necessary to; no trouble; peace.
無虞 there is no cause to fear; without danger.
無虧 there is no loss arising from.
無照 without a certificate.
無花 having no ornament; plain.
無花布 drills and jeans.
無旗 without flag (as a vessel).
無旣 } 無極 } without end; infinitely; endless.

*wu* 無訛 without mistake; correct.

無力 not having the power of; being unable to; incapable.

無欵 having no funds; insolvent.

無準可憑 there is no reliable standard; inaccurate and unreliable.

無理 unreasonable.

無見 without experience; unreasonable.

無奈 there is no help for; no alternative.

無從 not able to follow; not able to.........; there is no way to.........; there is no opportunity to.........; there is no help for.

無干 }
無涉 } not affecting; not concerned in; not connected with; to have nothing to do with.

無足重輕之舉 a matter of insufficient importance.

無足爲示引之處 not apt to show the course a ship ought to steer; to be of no use as a guide to shipping.

無大用處 not of much use.

無異言 of the same opinion; expressing oneself to the same effect.

無異議 to be of the same opinion.

無出入 it causes no increase or decrease; it makes no difference.

無恥之輩 shameless people.

無約各國 non-Treaty Powers.

無慮影射 not to fear false statements.

無所適從 there is no means to follow [a rule].

*wu* 蕪 }
蕪湖 } Wuhu.

蕪湖關 the Wuhu Customs.

*wu* 舞 to dance; to fence; to play tricks.

舞弊 to wink at a malpractice; hoodwinking; secret malpractices; irregularities.

*wu* 毋 do not; not.

毋違此諭 do not disobey this order.

毋違特札 special instructions not to be disobeyed.

毋違特示 a special order not to be offended against; a proclamation to be obeyed strictly.

毋令一名漏網 do not let one man escape.

毋任違背 do not stand opposition.

毋須遽議訂章 you must not make regulations in a hurry.

毋庸 need not; not necessary to.

*wu* 毋庸議 need not take into account; to except.

*wu* 午 a horary character; noon; the time from 11 A.M. to 1 P.M.

午刻 before noon, say between 11 A.M. and noon.

午後 afternoon.

*wu* 勿 not; do not.

勿論 no matter whether.

勿須 must not.

勿忘 be not forgetful; keep well in mind.

勿忽 do not disregard; be very careful about.

*wu* 物 things; articles.

物件 packages.

*wu* 惡 to hate; to dislike. See *o*.

*wu* 務 must; business; matters.

務須 must.

務希 it is much to be desired that.

*wu* 霧 mist; fog.

## Y.

*ya* 牙 a tooth; ivory.

*ya* 呀 to wrangle.

呀囒治木 kranjee-wood.

呀囒米 cochineal.

*ya* 鴉 a raven; a crow.

鴉片煙 opium.

*ya* 押 to sign; to affix a seal; a seal; in copies of documents, represents the place where the seal appears in the original: "L.S."; to keep under supervision; to guard (as a ship or goods); to escort; to pawn; to mortgage; a pawn-shop; stands for 壓 *(ya)*, to press down.

押註 to seal and sign; to endorse.

押解 }
押送 } to escort prisoners.

押案追比 to arrest one for criminal prosecution.

押封 to place under seal, as a godown, a boat, etc.

押載之物 ballast.

押載噸數 the tonnage of a vessel which is used for cargo; the registered tonnage; the net tonnage.

*ya* 壓 to press down; to impress.

壓載 }
壓載重物 } ballast.

壓載鐵 kentledge iron.

壓載沙土石塊 ballast of sand, mud, and stones.

壓印戳記 to impress a seal or mark.

*ya* / *yai* } 涯 a limit; a shore.
涯涘 the banks of a river; limits; limited.
*ya* 衙 / 衙門 / 衙署 } a *yamên;* a Government office; a public court.
衙役 yamên runners; the lower employés in Government offices.
*yang* 羊 a sheep.
羊毛 sheep's wool; woollen.
*yang* 恙 sickness; grief; sorrow.
*yang* 洋 the sea; the ocean; foreign; foreign coins.
洋面 on the open sea; the sea; waters.
洋人 a foreigner.
洋行 a foreign firm.
洋商 a foreign merchant.
洋商船隻 foreign merchant vessels.
洋船 a foreign vessel.
洋式 foreign type.
洋式船隻 foreign-type vessels.
洋藥 opium; *lit.*, the foreign drug.
洋藥土 raw opium.
洋藥膏 / 洋藥熟膏 } boiled or prepared opium.
洋藥釐局 a tax office for likin on opium.
洋米 foreign rice.
洋酒 foreign wine.
洋鎗 foreign guns.
洋鐵箍 foreign iron hoops.
洋標 *T*-cloths.
洋紗 muslins.
洋布 foreign cloths.
洋燭 foreign candles.
洋貨 foreign goods.
洋土各貨 foreign and native goods.
洋錢 / 洋銀 } foreign coins; foreign currency; foreign silver (as Mexican dollars).
洋例銀 the local currency at Hankow (1 Haikwan tael = local tael 1.0875).
洋番 foreign; foreign dollars.
洋法 the foreign method.
洋文 a document, or a despatch, written in a foreign language; foreign writing.
洋信 foreign letters.

*yang* 洋正月初 the beginning of January.
洋稅新關 the foreign Customs.
*yang* 樣 a sort; a kind; a pattern.
樣式 a pattern.
*yang* 養 to nourish.
養生 to support oneself or one's family; to support life.
養家之費 expenses for the maintenance of one's family.
*yang* 央 to invite; to entreat.
央求 to solicit; to urgently ask for.
*yang* 陽 the male principle; the sun.
*yang* 仰 to look up to; to rely on; to expect.
仰稟 to receive respectfully.
仰懇 to respectfully pray for.
仰求 to respectfully ask; *lit.*, looking up, to ask.
仰祈 to humbly pray for.
仰沐 to look forward to receiving kindness.
仰望 to hope for; to expect.
仰卽遵照辦理 you will be guided by these instructions.
*yao* 要 must; must be; important.
要務 important business.
要故 an urgent reason.
要緊 important.
要端 important matters; essential points.
要隘各口 the important approaches (of traffic).
*yao* 腰 the loins; the waist.
腰牌 a belt ticket; a ticket worn by soldiers a their sides as an authority.
*yao* 邀 to invite.
邀請 to invite; to engage for service.
*yao* 搖 to shake; to wave to and fro.
*yao* 窰 a kiln; a pottery.
窰貨 / 窰器 } pottery; earthenware.
*yao* 謠 rumour; lies; falsehood.
*yao* 遙 remote; distant; distance.
*yao* 藥 / 藥材 / 藥料 } medicines; drugs.
藥局 a dispensary.
*yao* 鑰 a key; a lock.
*yeh* 夜 the night; at night.

*yeh* 夜晚 in the evening; at night.
夜中 at night; "after hours."
夜間 during night-time; at night.

*yeh* 腋 the armpits; pieces of fur taken from under a fox's legs (such as are sewn together into coats and jackets).

*yeh* 爺 a father; a term of respect: a gentleman.

*yeh* 頁 the leaf of a book; a folio; the head.

*yeh* 也 a final particle; also.

*yeh* 野 wild; savage; uncultivated.
野粗絲 wild and coarse silk.
野蠶絲 wild raw silk.
野蜂釀蜜 wild uncleaned honey.

*yeh* 業 land; property; trade; occupation; "my trade or business;" hence a modest term for "I," used by trades-people; a sign of the past: have, has.
業等 a modest term for "we," used by trades-people in petitions.
業經 } 業已 } a sign of the past: has, have; already.

*yeh* 葉 a leaf.

*yen* 言 to say; words; what is said.
言明 to state distinctly.
言狀 to describe; to state.
言及 to say with regard to; to mention.

*yen* 咽 to swallow; the throat; a narrow pass.
咽喉 the throat; an important pass; a thoroughfare of traffic.

*yen* 烟 (煙, or 菸) tobacco; smoke; opium.
烟葉 leaf tobacco.
烟絲 prepared tobacco.
烟捲 cigars.
烟台 Yen-t'ai (=Chefoo).
烟台條款 } 烟台會議條款 } the Chefoo Convention of 1876.

*yen* 胭 the throat; rouge.
胭脂 rouge.

*yen* 厭 to reject; to dislike.

*yen* 焉 an interrogative particle: how.
焉敢 how could I dare? (=I dare not).

*yen* 燕 a swallow.
燕窩 swallows' nests; [edible] birds' nests.

*yen* 掩 to screen; to conceal.
掩蔽 to shelter.

*yen* 琰 a gem; being a forbidden character, should be written 琂 *(yen)*.

*yen* 沿 to go along; along.
沿海江巡查 to cruise along the coast and the river; "coast" service.
沿海各處 the places on the sea-coast.
沿江 along the river; on the river; on the Yangtze.
沿途 on the road.
沿途子口 the barriers *en route*.
沿途私賣 to sell clandestinely on the road; unauthorised sale [of goods] *in transitu*.
沿途情形 [a record of] occurrences on the road; the log of a ship.

*yen* 延 to invite; to protract; to delay; dilatory.
延請 to invite; to engage the services of (as of a lawyer).
延未繳銀 to delay payment.
延擱 to delay.
延抗 to be renitent.
延祺 a long period of happiness.

*yen* 筵 a mat; a feast; a banquet; a dining-hall.

*yen* 嚴 strict; stern; to respect; the standing epithet for fathers, just as *tz'ŭ* (慈), kind, is the epithet for mothers; hence 嚴父, "my father."
嚴密 strictly secret; confidential.
嚴拿 to seize strictly; to arrest.
嚴拿偷漏 [to have authority for] arresting thieves and smugglers.
嚴傳 to summon.
嚴加告誡 to add strict warnings.
嚴加逐察 to subject to strict and detailed examination.
嚴防偷漏 } 嚴查漏稅 } to prevent the revenue from suffering by fraud or smuggling; to prevent smuggling.
嚴令 to give strict orders to.
嚴禁 to strictly prohibit.
嚴察 to examine strictly.
嚴比捕役 to deal strictly with the police runners (in order to ensure the proper discharge of their duties).
嚴肅 solemn; grave; dignified.

*yen* 顏 colours; the countenance.
顏色 colour.
顏料 dyeing materials; dye-stuff.

新關文件錄



*yen* 鹽 salt; to salt; salted.
鹽池 salt-cellars.
鹽魚 salt fish.
鹽廠 a salt manufactory.
鹽商 a salt merchant.
鹽運使司 an inspector of salt gabel; a Salt Commissioner.
鹽大使 a sub-inspector in the Salt Commissioner's yamên.

*yen* 宴 repose; a banquet.

*yen* 眼 the eye.
眼前 before one's eyes.
眼同 together with another (so that both parties may see); conjointly and before one's eyes.
眼同閱看 to participate in the inspection of.
眼目 the eyes.
眼科 an ophthalmist.
眼鏡 spectacles.

*yen* 演 to practise; to exercise; to drill.

*yen* 黤 pitchy; black.
黤滅 to extinguish (as a light).

*yen* 騐 (or 驗) to examine.
騐單 a duty memo. (debit note for duties to be paid, issued after the examination of goods and hence called "examination bill").
騐明 to examine; to ascertain (by examining).
騐收 to examine and receive; to accept (as a document); to take delivery of.
騐看 to examine; to inspect.
騐估核稅 to assess duties according to value; to charge *ad valorem* duty.
騐貨 to examine goods.
騐貨廠 a Customs examination shed.
騐貨手 an examiner.
騐貨人役 officers charged with the examination of goods; examiners.
騐訖 examination being finished; "examined."
騐訖完餉 to pay duties after examination.
騐試事由 the particulars or results of an examination.

*yen* 讞 to decide in judicial cases.
讞局 a court of justice.

*yen* 贋 spurious.
贋製 to imitate; to counterfeit.

*yen* 閻 a hamlet.

*yi.* See *i.*

*yin* 音 sound.
音語 language.
音聞 report; rumour.

*yin* 因 on account of; to cause.
因爲 because of; on account of.
因而 therefore; on which account he......
因事故而斥革 to be dismissed from office for some reason or other.
因何 the reason why; on what account?
因此 thereby; therefore.
因公 on public business.
因風收口 to put into a port in distress.
因時 on account of the time; at the proper time.
因時制宜 to take the necessary steps, as circumstances may require.
因別故 for some other reason.
因循 remissness; delay.
因制 (in imitation of the English sound "inch") an inch; inches.

*yin* 姻 (or 婣) to marry; a bride.

*yin* 殷 abundance.
殷實 having ample means; to be solvent.

*yin* 霪 continuous rain.

*yin* 銀 silver; money; treasure.
銀礦 a silver mine.
銀硃 vermilion.
銀線 } silver thread; silver wire.
銀絲 }
銀兩 silver in taels; money.
銀箔 silver leaf.
銀錢 silver coins.
銀員 dollars; Mexican dollars.
銀洋 foreign coins; Mexican dollars.
銀單 } a money order; a bank note; a cheque.
銀票 }
銀局 a mint; a bank.
銀匠 experts in melting silver.
銀號 a bank; *the* Bank; the Customs Bank.
銀數 a sum of money.
銀鼠 the ermine; also, the squirrel.
銀鼠皮 ermine skins; squirrel skins.

*yin* 引 to lead.

引水 a pilot; pilotage.

引水董事 a senior pilot.

引水船 a pilot boat.

引水章程 the Pilotage Regulations.

引水字據 a pilot's license.

引費 pilotage fees.

引務 pilotage business.

引見 to introduce; to have an audience with the Emperor.

引誘 to entice.

引火 to strike fire; to inflame.

*yin* 飲 to drink.

飲食之銀 maintenance expenses.

*yin* 隱 dark; to avoid; to conceal; to keep out of view.

隱漏 to avoid, to evade (as payment of duties); to defraud the revenue by concealment of facts.

隱匿干咎 to be guilty of concealing (*e.g.*, a document to be delivered).

*yin* 印 to print; a seal; to stamp.

印信 a seal; credentials.

印官 an official holding a seal, *i.e.*, an official appointed by Government direct, and not a deputy or *wei-yüan* (委員).

印照 a sealed certificate; a passport; a bond certificate.

印牒 a sealed document; a license.

印發 to seal and issue; to hand back (as a petition is sealed and handed back with sealed endorsement).

印簿 books to be sealed; books containing duplicates of documents sealed (as a "Protest Book").

印務 the affairs of an office so far as they concern the sealing of documents; responsible affairs.

印花布 printed cotton cloth; chintzes; chintzes, furnitures, and cotton prints.

印花袈裟布 jaconets, cambrics, lawns, and muslins.

印字 to print characters; to print.

印字之役 a printing-office employé.

印書 to print books.

印度國 (*yin-tu-kuo*) India; Indian.

印度牛黃 Indian cow bezoar.

*yin* 胤 posterity; generations; being a forbidden character, should be written 胤 (*yin*), the first stroke being omitted, or 允 (*yün*).

*ying* 迎 to meet; to welcome.

*ying* 盈 to be full; overflowing; increase; gain.

盈餘 an overplus.

盈虧 abundant and deficient; profit and loss.

盈庫大使 an assistant treasurer; a treasury keeper.

*ying* 應 (read in the *hsia-p'ing* tone) must; (read in the *ch'ü-shêng* tone) to answer; to respond to.

應該
應當
應須 } must; ought to.

應稅
應征
應徵
應完 } having to pay duty; dutiable.

應完正稅 the full duty due.

應完稅之貨 dutiable goods.

應免
應行免稅 } liable to exemption from duty; duty free.

應值 liable to be valued at ......

應照 ought to reflect or shine; to be visible (as a light).

應如何酌量 in what manner it is to be settled.

應否 whether or not it is necessary to.

應否免稅 whether duty free or not.

應允 to consent to.

應試 to respond to the call for examination; o report for examination.

*ying* 膺 to undertake.

*ying* 鷹 an eagle; a falcon; a hawk.

鷹銀
鷹洋
鷹捧番銀 } eagle money; Mexican dollars.

*ying* 營 military; a camp; a subdivision of a *hsieh* (協) or regiment; a battalion commanded by a *yu-chi* or major, or an officer of similar rank; to do; to make; to devise mechanical plans.

營汛 a guard house; a military station.

營造 engineering; public works.

營造尺量 the official measure of the Board of Works.

營造司 the "Office of Works," a sub-department of the Imperial household; an engineer (for light-houses, etc.).

營造處 an engineer's office.

營哨 a patrol; a division of a battalion.

*ying* 營私 to practise smuggling.

營口 } 營子 } Yingtzŭ; the port of Newchwang.

*ying* 英 excellent; brave; English; British.

英吉利 (*ying-ki-li* = English) English; British.

英國 England; Great Britain; British.

英船 a British ship.

英民 British subjects.

英文 English writing; in English.

英德兩商 both British and German merchants.

英捧 wrongly for *ying* 鷹捧 [番銀], *q.v.*

*ying* 鸚 a parrot.

鸚鵡洲 Ying-wu-chou (a Likin station on the Yangtze).

*ying* 影 a shadow; a delusion.

影射 a shadow projecting; false statements; false declarations.

影射之弊 the malpractice of spreading lies; false statements.

*ying* 硬 hard.

硬木 hard-wood.

*yo* 籲 to pray; to implore.

籲懇 to entreat; to invoke.

*yo* 躍 to leap (as for joy); to exult.

*yu* 有 to have; to be; there is.

有無 whether there is; whether there was.

有之 there is; there are.

有花 having ornaments; figured (as piece goods).

有花無花色布 dyed figured and plain cotton piece goods.

有賞 to be rewarded.

有罰 to be attended with punishment.

有功 meritorious; there is merit in......

有益 to benefit; there is an advantage in.

有碍 to obstruct.

有所窒碍 there are difficulties; to be fraught with difficulties.

有條約各國 the Treaty Powers.

有船被焚之旗 a fire-alarm; a signal flag hoisted when a ship is on fire.

有便商情無虧稅課 to serve commercial interests while causing no loss to the revenue.

有礙收稅 to interfere with the collection of the revenue.

*yu* 有干未便 to be guilty of some disorder.

有涉 to be connected with.

有理 there is reason in; sensible.

有當 there is necessity for.

有異 } 有別 } there is a difference; to be different.

有虧 to entail loss.

有餘 more than; there is a surplus.

有限 there is a limit; limited; few.

有零 and a fraction; and odd.

有年 a number of years.

有日 some day; there is a day or term fixed for it.

有時 sometimes; at any time.

*yu* 宥 to forgive; to assist.

宥罪 to forgive an offence; to remit punishment.

*yu* 憂 sorrow; sadness.

憂愁 to be full of sorrow.

*yu* 優 to excel; excellent; competent; excessive; complaisant; tranquil; gentle; fully.

優待 to treat with consideration; to treat civilly.

*yu* 攸 a relative pronoun, *i.q.*, *so* (所); commonly used in phrases like *yu-chi* (攸繫) or *yu-kuan* (攸關), "that which concerns."

*yu* 幼 young.

幼弟 a young brother.

幼兒 young children.

*yu* 猶 more; further; if; like; still.

*yu* 由 circumstances; details; from; by way of. It is frequently used to denote the doer of an action, or the logical subject of a sentence if it is not inanimate; *e.g.*, 由[1]領[2]事[3]官[4]飭[5]該[6]商[7], [1]*yu* (expressing that the term following is the subject of the sentence) [2]*ling*-[3]*shih*-[4]*kuan*, the Consul, [5]*ch'ih*, orders, instructs, [6]*kai*, the said, THE, [7]*shang*, merchant; 先[1]由[2]委[3]員[4]申[5]報[6]司[7]道[8], [2]*yu* [3]*wei*-[4]*yüan*, the Deputy, [must] [1]*hsien*, before, first, [5]*shên*-[6]*pao*, report to, [7]*ssŭ*, the high provincial authorities and, [8]*tao*, the Taot'ais.

由水道 by sea.

由陸路 by land.

由驛 by post; by courier.

由是 from there.

由廈至漢 from Amoy to Hankow.

*yu* 柚 the pumelo.

柚皮 pumelo peel.

柚子 pumeloes.

yu 油 oil.

油斤 oil (as merchandise). Cf. *ssŭ* 絲斤.

油漆 oil paint; paints.

油漆畫 oil paintings.

油紙 oiled paper.

yu 尤 furthermore; still more; more; particularly.

尤爲緊要 it is still more important; it is of special importance.

yu 游 (or 遊) to wander about; wandering; to travel; to float; to swim.

游歷 to wander about; to travel; to cruise about.

游擊 } a major.
游府 }

yu 又 further; moreover; and; often answering to *ditto* or *idem*.

yu 友 a friend; friendly.

友邦 a friendly state.

yu 誘 } to entice; to induce.
誘令 }

yu 右 right; that which is on the right; after a document: the above; the junior of two deputies where only two are employed.

右邊 the right side; the port side.

右照 the above certificate.

右照會 the above despatch.

右貨 the goods (enumerated) on the right hand, *i.e.*, the above goods.

右堂 an assistant magistrate.

yu 佑 to assist.

yung 用 to use.

用示 by means of a proclamation; to show, or express, thereby.

用人 employés.

用功 to make an effort.

用心 to be attentive.

用寶 provided with the Imperial Seal.

yung 勇 brave; a brave; a soldier.

yung 踴 to leap; to exult.

踴躍 to leap for joy; to gladly fall in with an idea.

yung 湧 to bubble; to rise.

yung 庸 to use; to have use for.

yung 傭 to hire (as a workman).

傭役 a coolie hired for work.

yung 鎔 to melt.

yung 顒 being a forbidden character, should be written 禺 *(yung)*, the two last strokes of the full character being omitted.

yung 融 clear; intelligent; harmony.

yung 永 everlasting; eternal.

永爲定式 to regard as a permanent standard.

永無相左之處 never any disagreements.

永行弗替 to be always so and not be changed; so it shall always be.

永遠 everlasting; for ever.

永嘉縣 the district of Yung-chia.

yü 魚 fish.

魚網 a fishing-net.

魚肚 fish maws.

魚皮 fish skins.

魚翅 sharks' fins.

魚膠 isinglass.

yü 漁 to fish; fishermen.

漁戶 fishermen.

yü 於 (or 于) in; at; on; through; by; after an adjective, than.

於是 after this; thereupon.

於是日 on the same day.

於此 here.

於後 in the sequel; as follows.

於商人有便 it is a convenience to merchants.

於稅餉無甚出入 it makes no great difference in the revenue.

於貿易有損 to be detrimental to trade.

yü 與 with; to; or; and; to give.

與否 whether......or not; ......or not.

與......同 the same as; equal to.

與平日不同 not as usual.

與國課有關 to concern the Imperial revenue.

與......無關 to have nothing to do with; not to be one's business.

與德國無涉 it has nothing to do with Germany.

與商情攸關 to be connected with commercial interests.

yü 輿 the earth; mankind; the public.

yü 寓 a dwelling; to lodge.

寓居 to reside; residence (at a place).

yü 愚 stupid; simple minded; "I;" "my."

*yü* **愚民** the stupid people; the common people; the ignorant; the masses.

**愚人** the common people.

**愚見** I am of opinion; my humble view.

*yü* **遇** to meet; to happen; happening; whenever.

**遇見** to meet (as a person in the street).

**遇卡** to pass a Customs barrier.

**遇有缺出** when a vacancy occurs.

**遇大霧時** during foggy or thick weather.

**遇……之時** at the time when; when the time for……has arrived.

*yü* **喻** (interchanged with *yü* **諭**) to manifest; to proclaim.

*yü* **愈** to get the better of; to recover; more; the more (as in the phrase "the more the better").

**愈……愈……** the more…… the more……

**愈多愈好** the more the better.

**愈甚** still more; much more.

*yü* **覦** to desire; to covet.

*yü* **諭** an order; to order; to proclaim; a proclamation.

**諭示** to proclaim; a proclamation.

**諭令** to order.

**諭旨** an Imperial rescript.

**諭飭遵辦** to give orders for the guidance [of those concerned].

**諭知** to inform by proclamation.

**諭止** to proclaim the stoppage of; to order a subordinate to discontinue a certain mode of action.

**諭阻** to decree prevention; to interfere.

*yü* **逾** (or **踰**) / **逾過** } to exceed (as a limit); to pass over; beyond.

**逾限** to exceed a limit.

**逾於五年** to exceed five years; more than five years.

*yü* **虞** apprehension; danger; accident.

*yü* **餘** a surplus; the remainder; the remaining ones; profits in trade.

**餘銀** a balance; surplus money.

**餘財** surplus funds; savings.

*yü* **羽** wings; feathers; wool.

**羽翼** wings; helps; to assist.

**羽扇** feather fans.

**羽布** alpaca; bunting.

**羽紗** English camlets; crape, *lit.*, woollen gauze.

**羽緞** Dutch camlets; lastings.

*yü* **羽綾** woollen lastings.

**羽縐** crape lastings.

**羽綢** imitation camlets; bombazettes.

*yü* **雨** rain.

**雨霪** rain without end.

**雨遮** kittysols; umbrellas.

**雨傘** umbrellas.

*yü* **語** words; language; statements.

*yü* **玉** jade; precious; Imperial; "your."

**玉石** jadestone.

**玉器** jadestoneware.

*yü* **獄** / **獄牢** } a prison; a jail.

*yü* **裕** to enrich; abundance; liberal.

**裕課** to benefit the revenue.

*yü* **欲** to wish; about to; also a sign of the future tense.

**欲要** to want to.

*yü* **慾** to desire; to covet.

*yü* **御** Imperial.

**御醫** an Imperial physician.

**御覽** the Emperor's view; for His Majesty's inspection.

**御前** in the Imperial presence.

**御前大臣** a Grand Chamberlain.

**御筆** the Imperial Pencil; *i.e.*, the Emperor's endorsement.

**御筆批准** to be sanctioned by the Emperor.

**御批** a reply from the Emperor.

**御河** the Imperial Canal; the Grand Canal.

*yü* **禦** to oppose; to stop.

*yü* **尉** to soothe; to tranquilise.

*yü* **育** to rear; to maintain; to bear.

**育嬰堂** a foundling hospital.

*yü* **予** to give; to bestow; to grant.

**予假** to grant leave.

**予免稅** to grant exemption from duty; to pass [goods] duty free.

**予謚** to confer a posthumous title.

**予正法** to apply capital punishment.

**予以** to grant (**以** *i*, introducing the object of the verb **予** *yü*).

*yü* **預** (or **豫**) to prepare; beforehand.

**預據** to note a protest.

*yü* 預爲錄示 to prepare and publish a list.
預爲詳訂 to provide for a clear understanding.
預爲籌計 to calculate beforehand.
預爲言明 to declare clearly beforehand.
預行知會 to give official notice.
預定 to fix beforehand; to settle (as by contract).
預支 payments made beforehand; advances.
預料 to foresee.
預先 beforehand.
預先備辦 to keep ready (as documents for issue).
預備 to prepare.

*yü* 馭 to drive a horse; to rule over.

*yüan* 原 original; origin; source; really.
原報 originally declared.
原訂 originally fixed upon; drafted.
原勘地方 the site originally inspected; the original site.
原恕 originally sympathising.
原所以杜......by which means it was originally intended to prohibit............
原包 original packages.
原貨 the original goods.
原價 the original price; the prime cost.
原照 the original certificate.
原稿 an original copy; a draft.
原委 the original grievance; the details of an accusation.
原本 original; the original value; origin; root.
原告 he who originally accuses; the plaintiff.
原布 plain cotton cloth; shirtings.
原色布 grey shirtings; unbleached and undyed cotton piece goods.
原粗布 sheetings.
原細斜紋布 jeans and twills.
原由 circumstances; particulars.

*yüan* 願 to wish; to be willing.
願望 to hope; to desire.
願從 to be willing.

*yüan* 怨 ill-will; resentment; hatred.

*yüan* 冤 to oppress; injustice.
冤苦 a grievance; an injustice.
冤枉 an injustice; a grievance; to accuse falsely; to ill-use.

*yüan* 員 a classifier of officers; an officer; wrongly used for 圓 *(yüan)*, a dollar.
員弁 officers (of low rank, both civil and military).
員外郎 Second Class Secretary of a Board.

*yüan* 圓 round; a globe; a ball; a circle; a round coin; a dollar.
圓形 round.
圓球 a ball.
圓頂 a ball-shaped top (as a wicker ball on the top of a beacon pole).
圓徑 the diameter (of a circle).
圓徑作爲方徑 to convert round measure into square measure (as of timber).
圓樑木 round beams; beams other than square.

*yüan* 緣 as; because; cause; origin; circumstances.
緣故 a cause; a reason.
緣由 circumstances; particulars.
緣簿 a register.

*yüan* 遠 far.
遠近 distance; far and near.
遠見 to see from afar.
遠涉 to come from afar; far-travelled.

*yüan* 元 the beginning; the first; No. 1; commonly used for 圓 *(yüan)*, a dollar.
元旦 New Year's day.
元年 the first year of a reign.
元寶 round ingot sycee.

*yüan* 院 a court; a hall; a college.

*yüan* 援 to assist; to rescue; to put forward; to quote by way of analogy; to claim (as privileges granted to others).
援救 to rescue.
援引 to quote.
援照 on the ground of (as a Treaty paragraph); according to.
援照成案 according to precedent.
援免 to apply (an exceptional rule) to the exemption (of goods from payment of duty); to claim exemption.
援以爲例 to quote [a fact] as a precedent so as to constitute a rule.

*yüeh* 月 the moon; a month.
月滿時 at full moon (*i.q.*, *wang* 望).
月初生時 at new moon (*i.q.*, *shuo* 朔).
月初 at the beginning of the month.
月底 at the end of the month.

*yüeh* 曰 to say; says; it is said.

*yüeh* 悅 to rejoice; pleased; delighted; gladly.

悅從 to gladly comply with.

*yüeh* 閱 to inspect; to peruse; to read.

閱看 to inspect; to review.

閱核 to inspect and examine.

*yüeh* 越 to exceed; to transgress; to encroach on.

越過 to pass over; to cross (as a barrier).

越獄 to break out of prison.

越南 Annam.

*yüeh* / *yo* } 約 to agree; an Agreement; a Treaty.

約與 / 約同 } to consult with; to agree upon a matter with.

約束 to restrain; to keep in order; to exercise a proper control over.

約國 (or 有約國) a Treaty Power.

約外 not in the Treaty; not provided for by the Treaty.

約章 Treaty regulations.

約條 the paragraphs of a Treaty; a Treaty; an Agreement.

*yüeh* 粵 Kwangtung and Kwangsi; Canton.

粵東 Kwangtung.

粵西 Kwangsi.

粵省 the Canton province.

粵海關 the Canton Customs.

粵海關部 official designation of the Haikwan or Hoppo of Canton.

粵南 Annam.

*yün* 云 to say.

云云 used in quotations when, for the sake of brevity, the tenor of a document is either wholly or partially omitted; "etc., etc." Cf. *têng* 等因.

*yün* 雲 a cloud.

雲母石 talc.

雲母殼 mother-of-pearl.

*yün* 雲母殼器 mother-of-pearlware.

雲石 marble slabs; marble.

雲集 to assemble in great numbers.

雲南 the Yünnan province.

*yün* 運 to transport.

運來 to move inwards; brought from; imported.

運往 carried outwards; exported.

運入 to transport into (the river or the interior).

運出 to transport out of the interior.

運到 to have imported; to be consignee for.

運抵 to arrive (as goods at the place of destination).

運回 to send back; to remove.

運動 to move about; to circulate (as goods in the country).

運帶 to convey (as a boat conveys passengers).

運照 a transit pass.

運粮 to transport grain.

運粮船 a grain or rice junk.

運河 the Grand Canal.

運米執照 a special certificate for the transport of rice.

運貨之人 a person attending the transport of goods.

運脚 the cost of transporting goods; freight.

運臺 / 運司 } an inspector of salt gabel; a Salt Commissioner.

*yün* 允 to agree; to promise; to allow; sincere; what is proper.

允定 it is agreed.

允服 to agree to; to be willing.

允從 to agree with; to permit; to consent.

允許 to promise.

允准 to sanction; to grant; to consent.

允行 to give authority to.

允當 just; fair.

允協 harmonious; perfect; effective.

# APPENDIX.

## SELECTED TRANSLATIONS.

# APPENDIX.

## SELECTED TRANSLATIONS.

### 1.

**Shanghai Customs Duty Memo.**

Now whereas the German merchants ***Shên-ch'ên hang*** [*i.e.*, Messrs. SIEMSSEN & Co.] report that the British ship No. 18,468, named *Yangtsze*, carries import cargo—

| | | | *Piculs.* | *Tls.m.c.c.* |
|---|---|---|---|---|
| 2 packages | Bicho de Mar, Black | . . . . . . . . | 3.24 | 4.8.6.0 |
| 1 „ | Birds' Nests, 2nd Quality | . . . . . | 0.67 | 0.3.0.1 |
| 2 „ | Cloves | . . . . . . . . . . . . . . | 1.52 | 0.7.6.0 |
| 1 „ | Fish Maws | . . . . . . . . . . . | 1.35 | 1.3.5.0 |
| 1 „ | Elephants' Teeth | . . . . . . . . . . | 0.48 | 1.9.2.0 |
| 3 „ | Cow Hides | . . . . . . . . . . . | 2.42 | 1.2.1.0 |
| | TOTAL IMPORT DUTY | . . . . . | *Hk.Tls.* | 10.4.0.1 |

The holder of this Memo. may proceed to the [Customs] Bank to hand in the amount in pure sycee silver and take delivery of a Bank Receipt. This is hereby certified.

Issued on the 13th day of the 6th month of the 8th year of KUANG HSÜ.

---

### 2.

**Shanghai Customs Import [Duty] Bank Receipt.**

Received from Messrs. SIEMSSEN & Co. on the following goods [*same as in above Duty Memo.*], which have been reported as for the British ship No. 18,468, named *Yangtsze*, the full duty payable, ten taels four mace and one cash only.

This Bank, having weighed and received the amount of money as specified in the Customs Duty Memo., duly issues this receipt, which the said merchants may deliver to the Customs Authorities for examination. This is hereby certified.

Issued by the Shanghai Customs Bank on the 13th day of the 6th month of the 8th year.

---

## 3.

### Shanghai Customs Duty Memo.

Now whereas the Chinese merchants *Chao-shang-chü* [*i.e.*, the China Merchants' Steam Navigation Company] report that the Chinese ship, Shanghai Series, No. 4,283, named *Kiang-piao*, carries export cargo—

| | | | *Piculs.* | *Tls.m.c.c.* |
|---|---|---|---|---|
| 4 | packages | Chinaware, Fine | 3.64 | 3.2.7.6 |
| 3 | „ | Cotton, Raw | 2.42 | 0.8.4.7 |
| 5 | „ | Dates, Black | 4.84 | 0.7.2.6 |
| 2 | „ | Tobacco, Prepared | 1.65 | 0.7.4.2 |
| 4 | „ | Paper, 1st Quality | 2.28 | 1.5.9.6 |
| 3 | „ | Curios, *value* Tls. 240 | — | 12.0.0.0 |
| 6 | „ | Beancake | 4.68 | 0.1.6.4 |
| | | TOTAL EXPORT DUTY | Tls. | 19.3.5.1 |

The holder, etc. [*as in Document No. 1,* mutatis mutandis].

## 4.

### Shanghai Customs Export [Duty] Bank Receipt.

Received from the C. M. S. N. Co. on the following goods [*same as in above Duty Memo.*], which have been reported as for the [Chinese] ship, Shanghai Series, No. 4,283, named *Kiang-piao*, the full duty payable, nineteen taels three mace five candareens and one cash.

This Bank, etc. [*as in Document No. 2,* mutatis mutandis].

## 5.

**Shanghai Customs Duty Memo. for Coast Trade Duty.***

Now whereas the American merchants *Ch'i-ch'ang hang* [*i.e.*, Messrs. RUSSELL & Co.], [on account of ship] Registered No. 10,213, report [their] having brought from the port of Foochow the following goods, being Native produce, viz.:—

| | | Piculs. | Tls.m.c.c. |
|---|---|---|---|
| 4 packages | Olives | 3.42 | 0.3.0.8 |
| 5 „ | Oranges (value, Tls. 5.2.0.0) | 4.32 | 0.1.3.0 |
| 3 „ | Indigo, Liquid | 3.60 | 0.3.2.4 |
| 2 „ | Lung-ngans, Dried | 1.54 | 0.1.9.2 |
| 1 „ | Lotus Seed | 1.20 | 0.3.0.0 |
| 4 „ | Dates, Red | 4.65 | 0.2.0.9 |
| | TOTAL COAST TRADE DUTY PAYABLE . Tls. | | 1.4.6.3 |

The holder, etc. [*as in Document No. 1*].

* *Lit.*, half duty for Native produce again moved for import.

## 6.

**Shanghai Customs Bank Receipt for Coast Trade Duty collected.**

Received from the American merchants Messrs. RUSSELL & Co., [on account of ship] Registered No. 10,213, on goods, being Native produce, imported, viz., [*same as in above Duty Memo.*] the Coast Trade Duty payable, one tael four mace six candareens and three cash.

This Bank, etc. [*as in Document No. 2*].

## 7.

**Shanghai Customs Duty Memo. issued for Coast Trade Duty on Native Goods carried into the Yangtze River.**

Now whereas the British merchants *T'ai-ku hang* [*i.e.*, Messrs. BUTTERFIELD & SWIRE], [on account of ship] Registered No. 23,684, report [their] carrying into the Yangtze River the following Native goods, viz.:—

| | | | *Piculs.* | *Tls.m.c.c.* |
|---|---|---|---|---|
| 2 | packages | Ground-nuts | 1.84 | 0.0.9.2 |
| 1 | " | Glassware | 0.86 | 0.2.1.5 |
| 4 | " | Hams | 2.38 | 0.6.5.4 |
| 2 | " | Lead, Red | 1.92 | 0.3.3.6 |
| 5 | " | Iron, Manufactured | 4.28 | 0.2.6.7 |
| 6 | " | Sugar, White | 3.52 | 0.3.5.2 |
| | | TOTAL HALF DUTY payable for re-importation at Kiukiang, over and above the full Export Duty to be charged | Tls. | 1.9.1.6 |

The holder, etc. [*as in Document No. 1*].

---

## 8.

**Shanghai Customs Bank Receipt for Coast Trade Duty collected on Native Goods carried into the Yangtze River.**

Received from the British merchants Messrs. BUTTERFIELD & SWIRE, [on account of ship] Registered No. 23,684, on Native goods carried into the Yangtze River, viz., [*same as in above Duty Memo.*] the Coast Trade Duty for re-importation at Kiukiang, payable over and above the full Export Duty to be charged, viz., one tael nine mace one candareen and six cash.

This Bank, etc. [*as in Document No. 2*].

---

## 9.

### Shanghai Customs Duty Memo. for Goods under Transit.

Now whereas the British merchants *I-ho hang* [*i.e.*, Messrs. JARDINE, MATHESON, & Co.] report [their] sending to the interior [the following] goods, viz.:—

| | *Pieces.* | *Tls.m.c.c.* |
|---|---|---|
| Shirtings, Grey | 15 | 0.6.0.0 |
| *T*-Cloths, 34 ins. × 48 yds. | 21 | 0.8.4.0 |
| „ 34 ins. × 24 yds. | 23 | 0.4.6.0 |
| Drills, 30 ins. × 30 yds. | 25 | 0.9.3.7 |
| Shirtings, Dyed | 24 | 1.8.0.0 |
| Damasks | 40 | 4.0.0.0 |
| Chintzes | 22 | 0.7.7.0 |
| TOTAL DUES | Tls. | 9.4.0.7 |

The holder, etc. [*as in Document No. 1*].

## 10.

### Shanghai Customs Bank Receipt for Goods under Transit Inwards.

Received from the British merchants Messrs. JARDINE, MATHESON, & Co., for [goods] sent to the interior, viz., [*same as in above Duty Memo.*] the duty payable, nine taels four candareens and seven cash.

This Bank, etc. [*as in Document No. 2*].

## 11.

### Shanghai Customs Duty Memo. for Goods under Transit.

Now whereas the British merchants *I-ho hang* [*i.e.*, Messrs. JARDINE, MATHESON, & Co.] report [their] transporting from the interior [the following] goods, viz.:—

| | *Piculs.* | *Tls.m.c.c.* |
|---|---|---|
| Silk, Fine Raw | 4.80 | 24.0.0.0 |
| „ Refuse | 2.60 | 1.3.0.0 |
| „ Cocoons | 1.40 | 2.1.0.0 |
| Lily Flowers, Dried | 31.00 | 4.1.8.5 |
| TOTAL DUES | | Tls. 31.5.8.5 |

The holder, etc. [*as in Document No. 1*].

---

## 12.

### Shanghai Customs Bank Receipt for Goods under Transit Outwards.

Received from the British merchants Messrs. JARDINE, MATHESON, & Co., for [goods] transported from the interior, viz., [*same as in above Duty Memo.*] the duty payable, thirty-one taels five mace eight candareens and five cash.

This Bank, etc. [*as in Document No. 2*].

---

## 13.

### Quarterly Revenue Return.

*Hankow Customs: 87th or December Quarter, 1882.*

| | Foreign Flags. | Native Flag. |
|---|---|---|
| | *Hk.Tls m.c.c.* | *Hk.Tls m.c.c.* |
| 1. Import Duties | 21.0.7.0 | *Nil.* |
| 2. Export " | 147,528.9.3.1 | 84,125.2.1.8 |
| 3. Coast Trade " | 1,885.6.8.3 | 76.3.2.6 |
| 4. Opium " : Foreign and Native Drug, Crude and Prepared:— | | |

| | Foreign Flags. | Native Flag. |
|---|---|---|
| | *Hk.Tls m.c.c.* | *Hk.Tls m.c.c.* |
| Import | *Nil.* | *Nil.* |
| Export | 3,469.3.5.0 | 3,677.7.0.0 |
| Coast Trade | *Nil.* | *Nil.* |
| Total amounts collected on *Native Drug*, included in above, are:— | 3,469.3.5.0 | 3,677.7.0.0 |

| | Foreign Flags. | Native Flag. |
|---|---|---|
| Total | 3,469.3.5.0 | 3,677.7.0.0 |
| 5. Tonnage Dues | 797.3.0.3 | 275.2.0.0 |
| 6. Yangtze River Steamer Coast Trade Duty Deposits:— | | |

| | Foreign Flags. | Native Flag. |
|---|---|---|
| | *Hk.Tls m.c.c.* | *Hk.Tls m.c.c.* |
| Deposited 1st January to date | 91,036.0.5.8 | 52,793.6.6.9 |
| Refunded " " | 64,326.4.0.3 | 28,678.8.4.2 |

| | Foreign Flags. | Native Flag. |
|---|---|---|
| Balance on 31st December | 26,709.6.5.5 | 24,114.8.2.7 |

| | |
|---|---|
| | *Hk.Tls m.c.c.* |
| Total Foreign Flag Collection | 180,411.9.9.2 |
| " Native " " | 112,269.2.7.1 |
| 7. Transit Dues:— Inwards, *Hk.Tls* 24,487.0.1.6; Outwards, " 2,206.1.3.1 | 26,693.1.4.7 |
| Total Collection: Foreign, Native, and Transit * | 319,374.4.1.0 |

* Drawbacks marked for cash payment during quarter, to be deducted from total collection ... *Hk.Tls* *Nil.*

8. NATIVE FLAG: *Special Exemption Account:—*

| | | |
|---|---|---|
| Government Grain carried ........: | 140 catty *shih*........ | *Nil.* |
| Merchandise exempted from........duty: | 120 catty *shih*........ | *Nil.* |
| Amount of........duty remitted: | *Hk.Tls.*........ | *Nil.* |

Chinese version prepared by

T. W. L.,
*Deputy Commissioner.*

Submitted by

P. S. C.,
*Commissioner.*

HANKOW CUSTOM HOUSE, *8th January* 1883.

Forwarded in Despatch No. 1.

Examined and passed.

T.,
*Commissioner* [*Statistical Secretary*].

Forwarded [to Inspector General] in Despatch No........

Submitted [to Tsungli Yamên] by the Inspector General *H. T.* on [*date*].

---

## 14.

### Canton Customs (Export) Cargo Certificate.

CH'UNG, by His Imperial Majesty's commands Superintendent of Customs [Haikwan or Hoppo] at Canton, issues [the following] Export Cargo Certificate.

Whereas the British merchant ship No. 181 has reported for examination and exportation to Shanghai [the under-mentioned goods], this Cargo Certificate is duly issued for the Foreign and Native goods which are contained in the said ship, in order that it may be taken to the Customs at Shanghai and presented for examination. A necessary Cargo Certificate.

| No. of Application. | SHIPPERS. | GOODS. | Packages. | Weight (Pieces, etc.). | Value. | Document granted. |
|---|---|---|---|---|---|---|
| | | | | *Taels.* | | |
| ... | Government Paymaster HUANG........ | Treasure [Silver]........ | 41 | 122,300 | ... | Free. |
| | | Clothing, Boxes........ | 22 | ... | ... | " |
| | | Books........ | 14 | ... | ... | " |
| | | Luggage........ | 1 | ... | ... | " |
| | | Coffin and Corpse........ | 1 | ... | ... | " |
| ... | SSŬ MEI........ | Foreign Spirits........ | 1 | ... | ... | " |

The remaining goods not enumerated in this Certificate have been entered in due order on the special Certificates herewith enclosed, viz., 25 Exemption Certificates, 12 Duty Paid Certificates, and 23 Full Duty Proofs, [for which reason] a detailed description of goods and number of packages need not be repeated in this Cargo Certificate. The above is duly stated.

[*Date.*]

---

## 15.

### Tientsin [Foreign] Customs (Export) Cargo Certificate.

The Superintendent of the Tientsin Foreign and Native Custom Houses, in charge of Foreign trade matters in the province of Chihli and Taot'ai with Coast Defence and Military Authority, issues [the following] Export Cargo Certificate.

Whereas the Chinese merchant ship No. 94 has reported for examination and exportation to Shanghai [the under-mentioned goods], this Cargo Certificate is duly issued for the Foreign and Native goods which are contained in the said ship, in order that it may be taken to the Customs at Shanghai and presented for examination. A necessary Cargo Certificate.

| No. of Application. | Shippers. | Goods. | Packages. | Weight (Pieces, etc.). | Value. | Document granted. |
|---|---|---|---|---|---|---|
| | | | | | *Tls* | |
| ... | China Merchants' Steam Navigation Company's Manager | Rice Bags | 200 | ... | ... | Free. |
| | | Coffins with Corpses | 2 | ... | ... | " |
| 33 | Wan Shun | Ch'ing-lien [Dye-stuff] | 1 | *Pls.* 0.37½ | 50 | To pay. |
| ... | Kao Lin | Empty Bottles | 18 | ... | ... | Free. |
| ... | Pao Ch'ang | Hemp Bags | 10 | *Pcs.* 1,000 | ... | " |
| ... | Kao Lin | Empty Bottles | 10 | ... | ... | " |

The remaining goods not enumerated in this Certificate have been entered in due order on the special Certificates herewith enclosed, viz., 1 Exemption Certificate, 27 Duty Paid Certificates, and 5 Full Duty Proofs, [for which reason] a detailed description of goods and number of packages need not be repeated in this Cargo Certificate. The above is duly stated.

[*Date.*]

---

## 16.

### Value of the Trade carried on between the Chinese Treaty Ports and each of the Foreign Countries.

| COUNTRY. | 1882. *Hk.Tls.* | 1882. *Total, Hk.Tls.* |
|---|---|---|
| Great Britain:— | | |
| Imports from | 18,755,582 | |
| Exports to | 22,309,071 | 41,064,653 |
| Hongkong (including Trade with Foreign Countries *viâ* Hongkong):— | | |
| Imports from | 29,063,006 | |
| Exports to | 16,487,573 | 45,550,579 |
| India:— | | |
| Imports from | 18,264,372 | |
| Exports to | 477,114 | 18,741,486 |
| Singapore and Straits (British Settlements):— | | |
| Imports from | 1,565,387 | |
| Exports to | 1,027,730 | 2,593,117 |
| Australia (British Colony):— | | |
| Imports from | 530,072 | |
| Exports to | 2,044,967 | 2,575,039 |
| New Zealand (British Colony to the east of Australia):— | | |
| Imports from | ... | |
| Exports to | 177,924 | 177,924 |
| South Africa (Cape of Good Hope, British Colony):— | | |
| Imports from | ... | |
| Exports to | 111,246 | 111,246 |
| Canada (British Colony adjoining and to the north of the United States):— | | |
| Imports from | 218,779 | |
| Exports to | 57,946 | 276,725 |
| America (United States):— | | |
| Imports from | 3,276,728 | |
| Exports to | 8,420,130 | 11,696,858 |
| South America:— | | |
| Imports from | ... | |
| Exports to | ... | ... |
| Europe (Great Britain and Russia excepted):— | | |
| Imports from | 2,484,429 | |
| Exports to | 8,751,847 | 11,236,276 |
| Russia (by sea):— | | |
| Imports from | 9,127 | |
| Exports to | 946,324 | 955,451 |
| Russia (overland from Tientsin *viâ* Kiakhta):— | | |
| Imports from | ... | |
| Exports to | 3,286,345 | 3,286,345 |
| Russia (north of Tumên River [Russian Manchuria]):— | | |
| Imports from | 152,034 | |
| Exports to | 568,767 | 720,801 |
| Japan:— | | |
| Imports from | 4,442,241 | |
| Exports to | 1,766,858 | 6,209,099 |
| Philippine Islands:— | | |
| Imports from | 18,891 | |
| Exports to | 249,449 | 268,340 |
| Annam:— | | |
| Imports from | 487,002 | |
| Exports to | 65,472 | 552,474 |
| Siam:— | | |
| Imports from | 197,416 | |
| Exports to | 267,534 | 464,950 |
| Java (Netherlands' Colony):— | | |
| Imports from | 38,808 | |
| Exports to | 266,007 | 304,815 |
| Egypt (Arabia, etc.):— | | |
| Imports from | 369 | |
| Exports to | 54,542 | 54,911 |
| Sandwich Islands:— | | |
| Imports from | ... | |
| Exports to | ... | ... |
| Total Imports | 79,504,243 | |
| Less Re-exports to Foreign Countries | 1,789,015 | |
| TOTAL Net Imports | 77,715,228 | |
| TOTAL Exports | 67,336,846 | 145,052,074 |

## 17.

### Special Section: Articles of Trade.

I.—IMPORT (Nett, *i.e.*, deducting Re-exports abroad) at the CHINESE TREATY PORTS of FOREIGN GOODS [from FOREIGN COUNTRIES].

| DESCRIPTION OF GOODS. | Classifier of Quantity. | 1882 | |
|---|---|---|---|
| | | Quantity. | Value. |
| OPIUM:— | | | *Hk.Tls* |
| Malwa | *Piculs* | 29,335.88 | 13,089,647 |
| Patna | „ | 15,379.24 | 5,957,915 |
| Benares | „ | 15,017.17 | 5,499,118 |
| Other kinds | „ | 5,977.31 | 2,199,617 |
| OPIUM, TOTAL | *Piculs* | 65,709.60 | 26,746,297 |
| COTTON GOODS:— | | | |
| Shirtings, Grey, Plain | *Pieces* | 5,270,875 | 7,013,938 |
| „ White, Plain | „ | 1,608,191 | 2,731,831 |
| „ „ Figured, Brocaded, Spotted, etc. | „ | 3,977 | 6,839 |
| „ Dyed, Plain | „ | 100,949 | 208,339 |
| „ „ Figured, Brocaded, Spotted, etc. | „ | 63,257 | 134,508 |
| *T*-Cloths | „ | 2,174,383 | 2,140,051 |
| Drills, English, American, Dutch | „ | 903,411 | 2,017,987 |
| Sheetings | „ | 869,078 | 2,048,462 |
| Jeans and Twills | „ | 242,040 | 406,335 |
| Chintzes, Furnitures, and Cotton Prints | „ | 223,443 | 252,510 |
| Turkey Red Cloths | „ | 380,273 | 446,025 |
| Damasks [Dyed] | „ | 6,990 | 24,903 |
| Velvets, Velveteens, and Fustians | „ | 52,083 | 197,294 |
| Jaconets, Cambrics, Lawns, and Muslins | „ | 39,116 | 28,859 |
| Handkerchiefs | *Dozens* | 240,265 | 89,661 |
| Cotton Goods, Unclassed | *Pieces* | 220,696 | 453,851 |
| „ Yarn and Thread | *Piculs* | 184,939.97 | 4,505,391 |
| COTTON GOODS, TOTAL | *Value* | ... | 22,706,784 |
| WOOLLEN GOODS:— | | | |
| Alpaca | *Pieces* | 39 | 538 |
| Blankets | *Pairs* | 20,288 | 58,417 |
| Bombazettes | *Pieces* | 298 | 1,218 |
| Bunting | „ | 866 | 3,545 |
| Camlets, English | „ | 112,599 | 994,908 |
| „ Dutch | „ | 1,004 | 16,582 |
| „ Imitation, Camleteens, Japanese Cords | „ | 5 | 50 |
| Cloth, Broad, Medium, and Habit | „ | 32,607 | 682,214 |
| Spanish Stripes | „ | 64,001 | 551,170 |
| Russian Cloth | „ | 22,049 | 617,372 |
| Flannels | „ | 11,128 | 90,414 |
| Lastings | „ | 85,014 | 629,918 |
| „ Crape | „ | 2,339 | 11,731 |
| „ Imitation | „ | 21 | 126 |
| Long Ells | „ | 101,413 | 476,933 |
| Lustres and Orleans, Plain and Figured | „ | 81,872 | 201,040 |
| Woollen Goods, Unclassed | „ | 21,970 | 160,087 |
| WOOLLEN GOODS, TOTAL | *Value* | ... | 4,496,263 |

| Description of Goods. | Classifier of Quantity. | 1882. | |
|---|---|---|---|
| | | Quantity. | Value. |
| **Miscellaneous Piece Goods:—** | | | *Hk.Tls* |
| Woollen and Cotton Mixtures | *Pieces* | 10,669 | 55,323 |
| Cotton and Silk Mixtures | *Piculs* | 15.30 | 1,530 |
| Linen Goods | *Pieces* | 33,288 | 197,824 |
| Canvas | *Bolts* | 5,859 | 32,208 |
| Miscellaneous Piece Goods, Total | *Value* | ... | 286,885 |
| **Metals:—** | | | |
| Copper, Bar and Rod | *Piculs* | 9,648.48 | 144,727 |
| „ Sheet and Nails | „ | 11,325.92 | 180,378 |
| „ Old | „ | 433 | 6,318 |
| „ Ore and Unmanufactured | „ | 1,128.05 | 17,025 |
| „ Wire | „ | 290.23 | 7,244 |
| „ Manufactured and Ware, Unclassed | „ | 986.11 | 14,324 |
| Iron, Nail-rod | „ | 226,646.75 | 398,513 |
| „ Bar | „ | 71,016.21 | 142,383 |
| „ Hoop | „ | 7,770.17 | 17,181 |
| „ Wire | „ | 15,977.32 | 64,220 |
| „ Pig and Kentledge | „ | 9,574.58 | 9,578 |
| „ Ware and Manufactured, Unclassed | „ | 97,506.29 | 236,389 |
| „ Unmanufactured, Unclassed | „ | 318,132.27 | 415,807 |
| Lead, in Pigs | „ | 248,856.21 | 986,261 |
| „ in Sheets | „ | 3,652.32 | 23,741 |
| Quicksilver | „ | 2,155.81 | 88,731 |
| Spelter [and Zinc] | „ | 4,230.50 | 20,101 |
| Steel | „ | 23,606.11 | 73,553 |
| Tin, in Slabs | „ | 67,431.07 | 1,439.681 |
| Tinplates | „ | 5,242.19 | 21,572 |
| Metals, Manufactured, Unclassed, as Steelware, Brassware, Tinware, Cutlery | *Value* | ... | 392,806 |
| Metals, Total | *Value* | ... | 4,700,533 |
| **Sundries:—** | | | |
| Sugar, Brown | *Piculs* | 50,957.76 | 187,392 |
| „ White | „ | 25,953.17 | 182,138 |
| Betel-nuts | „ | 15,015.07 | 75,994 |
| Birds' Nests | „ | 816.94 | 553,116 |
| Bicho de Mar | „ | 26,179.92 | 635,055 |
| Cloves, of all kinds | „ | 6,350.82 | 180,537 |
| Coal | *Tons* | 253,099 | 1,219,685 |
| Cotton, Raw | *Piculs* | 178,478.37 | 1,916,734 |
| Fish, Dried and Salt | „ | 82,108.85 | 490,094 |
| Flint Stones | „ | 77,464.77 | 29,099 |
| Ginseng, of all kinds | „ | 4,731.47 | 763,065 |
| Grain and Pulse | „ | 8,363.32 | 13,541 |
| Indigo, Dried and Liquid | „ | 7,036.47 | 28,431 |
| Isinglass | „ | 5,879.48 | 91,413 |
| Matches | *Gross* | 1,904,629 | 852,596 |
| Mangrove Bark | *Piculs* | 97,694.84 | 88,266 |
| Needles | *Mille* | 1,853,637 | 285,682 |
| Oil, of all kinds | *Value* | ... | 963,657 |
| Paints | *Piculs* | 8,560.03 | 57,185 |
| Pepper, Black and White | „ | 37,691.57 | 297,882 |
| Rattans | „ | 46,173.30 | 150,490 |

| Description of Goods. | Classifier of Quantity. | 1882. | |
|---|---|---|---|
| | | Quantity. | Value. |
| Sundries—*continued*:— | | | *Hk.Tls* |
| Rice | *Piculs* | 233,149.49 | 288,002 |
| Seaweed and Agar-agar | " | 400,106.27 | 1,344,159 |
| Sandalwood | " | 103,302.26 | 612,217 |
| Sapanwood | " | 163,483.28 | 373,685 |
| Wood, Hard and Fragrant, of all kinds | *Value* | ... | 221,366 |
| Shell-fish, Awabi, Shrimps, etc. | *Piculs* | 48,545.66 | 476,577 |
| Silk, Raw, Japan | " | 54.65 | 5,448 |
| " Piece Goods | " | 12.89 | 6,725 |
| Tea, Japan | " | 17,574.39 | 87,095 |
| Timber, of all kinds | *Value* | ... | 974,142 |
| Wax, Vegetable, and Tallow, of all kinds | *Piculs* | 134.16 | 2,658 |
| Window Glass | *Boxes* | 43,928 | 96,563 |
| Sundries, Unenumerated | *Value* | ... | 5,227,777 |
| Sundries, Total | *Value* | ... | 18,778,466 |
| Grand Total | *Value* | ... | 77,715,228 |

## 18.

### Export of Native Goods to Foreign Countries.

| Description of Goods. | Classifier of Quantity. | 1882. | |
|---|---|---|---|
| | | Quantity. | Value. |
| | | | *Hk.Tls* |
| Silk, Raw and Thrown | *Piculs* | 60,419.74 | 16,989,881 |
| " Refuse | " | 28,657.77 | 1,356,826 |
| " Coarse and Wild | " | 4,089.38 | 344,720 |
| " Cocoons | " | 3,847 | 207,523 |
| " Piece Goods | " | 6,598.26 | 3,396,374 |
| " Thread, Sashes, etc. [Silk Manufactured Goods, Unclassed] | " | 2,701.73 | 541,928 |
| Silkworms' Eggs | " | 0.19 | 48 |
| Tea, Black | " | 1,611,916.82 | 25,878,238 |
| " Green | " | 178,839.52 | 4,090,900 |
| " Brick | " | 219,026.60 | 1,303,964 |
| " Dust | " | 7,367.90 | 59,105 |
| Bags, of all kinds | *Pieces* | 697,895 | 22,751 |
| Bamboo, of all kinds, and Ware | *Value* | ... | 107,282 |
| Beans and Beancake | *Piculs* | 179,427.30 | 184,591 |
| Cassia Lignea | " | 58,170.61 | 271,566 |
| Camphor | " | 5,162.02 | 42,466 |
| Chinaware, Earthenware, and Pottery | " | 98,243.98 | 471,388 |
| Coal | " | 10,436.50 | 1,204 |
| Clothing, Boots and Shoes [Chinese] | *Value* | ... | 388,758 |
| Cotton, Raw | *Piculs* | 41,690.09 | 404,405 |
| " Seed | " | 3.51 | 41 |
| " Waste | " | 689.62 | 830 |

| Description of Goods. | Classifier of Quantity. | 1882. Quantity. | 1882. Value. |
|---|---|---|---|
| | | | *Hk.Tls* |
| Curios | *Value* | ... | 37,238 |
| Dyes, Colours, and Paints | *Piculs* | 198.77 | 873 |
| Fans, of all kinds | *Pieces* | 2,571,512 | 25,780 |
| Fish, " " | *Piculs* | 9,699.41 | 91,901 |
| Fire-crackers | " | 40,616.81 | 376,863 |
| Flour | " | 23,328.47 | 36,103 |
| Fruits, of all kinds | " | 109,962.57 | 152,038 |
| Fungus | " | 27.37 | 614 |
| Grain and Pulse | " | 18,819.53 | 19,735 |
| Glassware, of all kinds | " | 12,171.80 | 234,761 |
| Grasscloth | " | 1,685.53 | 144,679 |
| Hair, of all kinds | " | 7,244.19 | 109,129 |
| Hemp and Cordage | " | 24,824.51 | 192,026 |
| Hides, of all kinds | " | 34,945.81 | 386,148 |
| Hoofs, " " | " | 97.97 | 345 |
| Horns, " " | *Value* | ... | 60,840[*] |
| Indigo, Dried and Liquid | *Piculs* | 1,872.62 | 7,382 |
| Lung-ngans | " | 12,066.34 | 55,394 |
| Mats and Matting | *Pieces* | 498,078 | 486,365 |
| Medicines | *Piculs* | 34,082.13 | 207,050 |
| Metals, Manufactured, as Copperware, Ironware, Tinware, and Pewterware | " | 14,251.52 | 133,066 |
| Metals, Unmanufactured | " | 2.68 | 19 |
| Musk | " | 20.24 | 162,414 |
| Nankeens | " | 2,602 | 110,213 |
| Nutgalls | " | 8,803.70 | 87,179 |
| Oil, of all kinds | " | 9,232.26 | 74,284 |
| Paper, Books, Tin-foil, Brass-foil | " | 57,853.55 | 623,432 |
| Preserves | " | 19,905.97 | 158,965 |
| Provisions | " | 95,940.56 | 78,499 |
| Rattans and Rattanware | " | 3,912.21 | 17,739 |
| Rhubarb | " | 6,861.31 | 183,699 |
| Safflower | " | 1,267.68 | 73,013 |
| Skins, of all kinds | *Pieces* | 573,321 | 471,948 |
| Straw Braid | *Piculs* | 55,498.26 | 1,498,596 |
| Sugar, White | " | 274,709.81 | 1,099,711 |
| " Brown | " | 757,125.42 | 1,821,993 |
| " Candy | " | 29,926.40 | 181,673 |
| Tobacco, Leaf and Prepared, of all kinds | " | 7,003.56 | 81,563 |
| Vermicelli and Macaroni | " | 44,829.40 | 167,173 |
| Wax | " | 72.71 | 2,584 |
| Wool | " | 22,755.39 | 199,029 |
| Sundries, Unenumerated | *Value* | ... | 1,420,001 |
| Total | *Value* | ... | 67,336,846 |

[* In the Chinese text (Vol. I, p. 30, col. 8), "90,840" appears wrongly for "60,840."]

## 19.

**Number and Tonnage of Vessels Entered and Cleared at the Chinese Treaty Ports.**

| FLAG. | 1882. | |
|---|---|---|
| | No. | Tons. |
| British | 14,337 | 10,814,779 |
| American | 762 | 167,801 |
| German | 1,864 | 882,856 |
| French | 192 | 172,381 |
| Dutch | 38 | 23,226 |
| Danish | 270 | 126,003 |
| Spanish | 320 | 61,123 |
| Swedish and Norwegian | 124 | 70,245 |
| Russian | 82 | 74,751 |
| Belgian | ... | ... |
| Italian | 2 | 1,762 |
| Japanese | 250 | 194,584 |
| Siamese | 56 | 22,636 |
| Hawaiian (*i.e.*, Sandwich Islands) | ... | ... |
| Chinese: Foreign-type vessels | 5,105 | 4,667,753 |
| " Native-type vessels [Junks] | 1,324 | 108,216 |
| Annamese | 3 | 736 |
| None | ... | ... |
| TOTAL | 24,729 | 17,388,852 |

The Shipping has been divided between STEAMERS and SAILING VESSELS in the following proportions:—

| YEAR. | STEAMERS entered and cleared. | | SAILING VESSELS (including Chinese type [*i.e.*, Junks]) entered and cleared. | | TOTAL entered and cleared. | |
|---|---|---|---|---|---|---|
| | No. | Tons. | No. | Tons. | No. | Tons. |
| 1880 | 17,300 | 14,572,718 | 5,670 | 1,301,634 | 22,970 | 15,874,352 |
| 1881 | 18,170 | 15,350,954 | 5,017 | 1,289,324 | 23,187 | 16,640,278 |
| 1882 | 19,607 | 16,102,574 | 5,122 | 1,286,278 | 24,729 | 17,388,852 |

## 20.

.................................................................Customs.

ACCOUNT of RECEIPTS and PAYMENTS under the four Heads: *A.* (Office Expenditure), *C.* (Tonnage Dues), *B.* (Fines and Confiscations), and *D.* (Separate Items) for the 89th or December Quarter (1st October to 31st December) 1882.

### [A.] Office Expenditure.

| | |
|---|---|
| [*a.*] RECEIPTS:— | *Hk.Tls.* |
| 1. Balance taken over from last Quarter's Account . . | 5,267.28 |
| 2. Office Expenditure [Customs Allowance] for current Quarter, from Superintendent . . . . . . . . . | 40,000.00 |
| 3. Supplementary Grant from Inspector General . . . | *Nil.* |
| [*b.*] PAYMENTS:— | |
| 1. Balance due on last Quarter's Account . . . . . . | *Nil.* |
| 2. Salaries, Foreigners and Natives . . . . . . . . | 31,747.94 |
| 3. Transport . . . . . . . . . . . . . . . . . . | 815.33 |
| 4. Rent . . . . . . . . . . . . . . . . . . | 2,764.62 |
| 5. Houses: Construction and Purchase; Maintenance in Repair . . . . . . . . . . . . . . . . . . | 503.86 |
| 6. Ships, Boats, etc.: Construction and Purchase; Maintenance in Repair . . . . . . . . . . . . . . | 148.11 |
| 7. Coast (Sea and River) Guard Expenses . . . . . | 742.90 |
| 8. Ordinary Miscellaneous [*i.e.*, Expenses made on standing authority] . . . . . . . . . . . . . . . | 2,867.17 |
| 9. Extraordinary: special Expenses for which special authority has been applied for and granted . . . | 1,537.17 |
| 10. Loss by Exchange . . . . . . . . . . . . . | *Nil.* |
| 11. Remittances to Inspector General's Account . . . . | *Nil.* |
| [*c.*] BALANCE [to be accounted for]:— | |
| Receipts as per above Account . . . . . . . . . . | 45,267.28 |
| Payments „ „ . . . . . . . . . . . | 41,127.10 |
| BALANCE . . . . . . . . . *Hk.Tls.* | 4,140.18 |

### [C.] Tonnage Dues.

| | |
|---|---|
| [*a*.] RECEIPTS :— | *Hk.Tls.* |
| 1. Balance taken over from last Quarter's Account . . | 20,433.75 |
| 2. Tonnage Dues : $\frac{7}{10}$ths [of Collection], from Superintendent, for current Quarter . . . . . . . . . . | 17,810.00 |
| 3. Special Grant from Superintendent for current Quarter . . . . . . . . . . . . . . . . | *Nil.* |
| 4. Supplementary Grant from Inspector General . . . | *Nil.* |
| [*b*.] PAYMENTS :— | |
| 1. Balance due on last Quarter's Account . . . . . . | *Nil.* |
| 2. Salaries, Foreigners and Natives . . . . . . . | 6,103.89 |
| 3. Transport . . . . . . . . . . . . . . . . . | 104.27 |
| 4. Rent . . . . . . . . . . . . . . . . . . . | 698.26 |
| 5. Plant (Lights, Buoys, and Beacons): Construction and Purchase; Maintenance in Repair . . . . . . . | 747.72 |
| 6. Property (Houses and Boats): Construction and Purchase; Maintenance in Repair . . . . . . . . | 202.35 |
| 7. Works (all classes of work undertaken on special authority) . . . . . . . . . . . . . . . . | 100.62 |
| 8. Ordinary Miscellaneous [*i.e.*, Expenses made on standing authority] . . . . . . . . . . . . . . . | 1,145.57 |
| 9. Extraordinary: special Expenses for which special authority has been applied for and granted . . . | 1,200.00 |
| 10. Loss by Exchange . . . . . . . . . . . . . | *Nil.* |
| 11. Remittances to Inspector General's Account . . . . | *Nil.* |
| [*c*.] BALANCE [to be accounted for] :— | |
| Receipts as per above Account . . . . . . . . . . . | 38,243.75 |
| Payments " " . . . . . . . . . . . | 10,302.68 |
| BALANCE . . . . . . . . *Hk.Tls.* | 27,941.07 |

### [B.] Fines and Confiscations.

| | |
|---|---|
| [*a.*] RECEIPTS:— | *Hk.Tls.* |
| 1. Balance taken over from last Quarter's Account . . . | 1,285.60 |
| 2. Fines levied during current Quarter. . . . . . . . | 100.00 |
| 3. Proceeds from sale of Confiscated Goods . . . . . | 911.80 |
| 4. Supplementary Grant from Inspector General . . . | *Nil.* |
| [*b.*] PAYMENTS:— | |
| 1. Balance due on last Quarter's Account . . . . . . | *Nil.* |
| 2. Ordinary miscellaneous Expenses of Seizures . . . | 171.73 |
| 3. Remitted to Tsungli Yamên, $\frac{3}{10}$ths of net proceeds . . | 252.02 |
| 4. Remitted to Superintendent, $\frac{3}{10}$ths of net proceeds . | 252.02 |
| 5. Special Payments, for which authority has been applied for and granted, made from $\frac{4}{10}$ths of net proceeds to be remitted to Inspector General . . . . . . . | *Nil.* |
| 6. Loss by Exchange . . . . . . . . . . . . . . | *Nil.* |
| 7. Remittances to Inspector General's Account . . . . | 1,285.60 |
| [*c.*] BALANCE [to be accounted for]:— | |
| Receipts as per above Account . . . . . . . . . . | 2,297.40 |
| Payments „ „ . . . . . . . . . . | 1,961.37 |
| BALANCE . . . . . . . . . *Hk.Tls.* | 336.03 |

### [D.] Separate Items [Fees and Special Moneys].

| | |
|---|---|
| [*a.*] RECEIPTS:— | *Hk.Tls.* |
| 1. Balance taken over from last Quarter's Account . . . | 3,629.50 |
| 2. Moneys appropriated by order of Tsungli Yamên . . | *Nil.* |
| 3. Fees for Chinese Ships' Registers . . . . . . . . . | 300.00 |
| 4. Fees for Junks' Sailing Letters . . . . . . . . . | 100.00 |
| 5. Pilotage Account Moneys . . . . . . . . . . . . | 420.70 |
| 6. Emigration Account Moneys . . . . . . . . . . | *Nil.* |
| 7. Special Permit Moneys . . . . . . . . . . . . . | 2,500.00 |
| 8. Proceeds of sale of Customs Publications . . . . . | 1,027.00 |
| 9. Salvage and Charter Account Moneys . . . . . . | *Nil.* |
| 10. Interest on Bank Deposits . . . . . . . . . . . | 236.80 |
| 11. Fines levied on Staff for breach of Rules . . . . . | 2.75 |
| 12. Moneys of all descriptions, not provided for [*i.e.*, unclassed] . . . . . . . . . . . . . . . . . | 15.42 |
| 13. Recoveries from the four Accounts *A*, *B*, *C*, and *D* . | *Nil.* |
| 14. Supplementary Grant from Inspector General . . . | *Nil.* |

| [*b.*] Payments:— | *Hk.Tls.* |
| --- | --- |
| 1. Balance due on last Quarter's Account . . . . . . | *Nil.* |
| 2. Payments made from Moneys appropriated by order of Tsungli Yamên . . . . . . . . . . . . . . . | *Nil.* |
| 3. Tsungli Yamên's share, $\frac{1}{3}$rd of Fees for Chinese Ships' Registers . . . . . . . . . . . . . . . . . | 100.00 |
| 4. Superintendent's share, $\frac{1}{3}$rd of Fees for Chinese Ships' Registers, and $\frac{5}{10}$ths of Fees for Junks' Sailing Letters | 150.00 |
| 5. Pilotage Service Account Moneys . . . . . . . . | *Nil.* |
| 6. Emigration Account Moneys . . . . . . . . . | *Nil.* |
| 7. Salvage and Charter Account Moneys . . . . . . | *Nil.* |
| 8. Unclassed Payments . . . . . . . . . . . . . | *Nil.* |
| 9. Disbursements supplementary to Accounts *A*, *C*, and *B* | *Nil.* |
| 10. Remittances to Inspector General's Account . . . . | 3,629.05 |

| [*c.*] Balance [to be accounted for]:— | |
| --- | --- |
| Receipts as per above Account . . . . . . . . . . . | 8,232.17 |
| Payments „ „ . . . . . . . . . . | 3,879.05 |
| Balance . . . . . . . . . | *Hk.Tls.* 4,353.12 |

Chinese version prepared by

C. D.,
*First Class Assistant.*

Approved and certified correct.

A. B.,
*Commissioner.*

.................................. Custom House, 3rd *February* 1883.

Forwarded in Despatch No. 8.

Examined and passed by

..................................................

Submitted [to Tsungli Yamên] by the Inspector General *H. T.* on [*date*].

## 21.

## Quarterly Confiscation Report.

*SHANGHAI CUSTOMS: 87th or June Quarter, 1882.*

I. OLD CASES SETTLED: Or cases remaining over from preceding, and settled during this Quarter; in all, 1 case.

II. NEW CASES: Or cases occurring during the Quarter; in all [settled and unsettled], 20 cases.

III. OUTSTANDING CASES: Or cases still unsettled [and to be dealt with hereafter]; in all, old and new, 1 case.

| Case No. | Date and Place of Offence or Seizure. | Name of Offender: Hong, Individual, or Vessel; and Nationality. | Denomination and Quantity of Goods. | Offence committed or Rule broken. | Decision: Date and Nature. | Amount of Fine. | Amount realised by sale of Goods confiscated. |
|---|---|---|---|---|---|---|---|
| | I.—OLD CASES SETTLED. | | | | | | |
| | 1882. | | | | | Hk.Tls. | Hk.Tls. |
| 745 | March 15 [*], Customs Jetty. | * * * * British firm, for Chinese. | Application stated:— [Medicine] Ch'uan-ch'iang pls. 9.12<br>Examination proved:— [Medicine] Ch'uan-ch'iang ,, 5.48 | False declaration of quantity of re-exports for drawback. | 29 April. Fined.. | 10.00 | ... |
| | II.—NEW CASES. | | | | | | |
| | 1882. | | | | | | |
| 751 | April 3, Customs Jetty. | Chên Hsing, Chinese firm. | Application stated:— Japanese Seaweed..........pls. 2,061<br>Examination proved:— Japanese Seaweed.......... ,, 2,213.46 | False declaration of quantity of imports. | 4 April. Fined five times duty on difference short declared. | 114.34 | ... |
| 752 | April 8, Customs Jetty. | * * * * British firm, for Chinese. | Application stated:— American Ginseng, Crude.pls. 1.70<br>Examination proved:— American Ginseng, Clarified ,, 1.98 | False declaration of quantity and quality of imports. | 10 April. Fined | 15.00 | ... |
| 753 | April 14, Examination Shed. | Ming Chi, Chinese merchant. | Application stated:— Dried Flowers..............pls. 2.17<br>Value.....................Tls. 4<br>Examination proved value to be..................... ,, 17.36 | False declaration of value of exports. | 15 April. Fined ten times full duty on difference short declared. | 6.68 | ... |
| 754 | April 25, Examination Shed. | Tung Li, Chinese merchant. | Application stated:— Jadestone....................pls. 1.23<br>Value.....................Tls. 553<br>Examination proved value to be..................... ,, 857 | ,, ,, | 27 April. Bought by Customs at owner's valuation, Tls. 553, plus 20 per cent.; in all, Tls. 663. Resold to him for Tls. 857. | ... | 194.00 |
| 755 | April 27, British s.s. *Pekin*. | Ch'ien Yüan, Chinese merchant. | Application stated:— Fungus.....................pls. 2.61<br>Cargo certificate stated.... ,, 2.11<br>Examination proved...... ,, 2.65 | Quantity of imports not in agreement with Hankow cargo certificate. | 29 April. Fined five times full and half duty on total import. | 11.93 | ... |

[* In the Chinese text (Vol. I, p. 45, col. 8), 正月 should be read for 貳月.]

| Case No. | Date and Place of Offence or Seizure. | Name of Offender: Hong, Individual, or Vessel; and Nationality. | Denomination and Quantity of Goods. | Offence committed or Rule broken. | Decision: Date and Nature. | Amount of Fine. | Amount realised by sale of Goods confiscated. |
|---|---|---|---|---|---|---|---|
| | | | | | | *Hk.Tls.* | *Hk.Tls.* |
| 756 | May 1, Chinese s.s. *Hwaiyuen*. | China Merchants' Steam Navigation Company, for Chinese. | Application stated:— Satin.............pls. 0.42—a re-export. Examination proved:— Silk Piece Goods pls. 0.42—an original shipment. | Declaring an export to be a duty-paid re-export. | 30 June. Confiscated. | ... | 148.64 |
| 757 | May 5, British s.s. *Nestor*. | Ho Ch'ang, Chinese merchant. | Lung-ngans...................pls. 3.55 | Shipping clandestinely | 5 May. Fined. Goods spoilt whilst awaiting payment of fine. | ... | ... |
| 758 | May 6, Chinese s.s. *Chiyuen*. | Chang Yüan-fu, Chinese passenger. | Applied for and examined:— Nankeens....................pls. 0.40 Shipped:— Nankeens.................... ,, 0.64 | Substituting upon shipment other goods than those examined. | 15 May. Confiscated. | ... | 11.00 |
| 759 | May 15, Registered Ningpo boat *No. 70*. | T'ung Shui-chih, Chinese, and Chinese master of boat. | Examined and shipped:— 10 cases Japan Ginseng, 2nd Quality..............pls. 5.87 Substituted on board:— 10 bales Ginseng Beard...pls. 7 | Unauthorised substitution of goods after shipment. | 23 May. Ginseng and Ginseng Beard confiscated. Boat master fined. | 100.00 | 344.57 |
| 760 | May 20, on the River. | Ch'ang Shun-i, Chinese merchant. | Ginseng, Corean..............pls. 2 | Removing examined re-exports to merchant's godowns instead of to re-exporting vessel, with view to substitution of other goods. | 25 May. Confiscated. Resold to owner. | ... | 500.00 |
| 761 | May 25, British s.s. *Kiungchow*. | Chinese crew of vessel. | Cartridges.....................pcs. 710 Gunpowder.................boxes 500 | Concealing contraband imports on board vessel. | 15 June. Confiscated. Gunpowder sent to Superintendent. 250 Cartridges bought and retained for Customs use; remainder sold in Hongkong. | ... | 5.57 |
| 762 | May 27, Customs Jetty. | Chou Ting, owner of cargo-boats. | ... ... ... ... | Employing two cargo-boats the licenses of which had been cancelled. | (Unsettled)......... | ... | ... |
| 763 | May 31, China Merchants' Steam Navigation Company's s.s. *Kiang-teen*. | Chinese passenger, name unknown. | Spurious Cash.................pls. 0.55 | Concealing contraband imports in luggage. | 1 June. Confiscated. Melted down and sold. | ... | 2.40 |
| 764 | June 3, China Merchants' Steam Navigation Company's s.s. *Kiang-teen*. | T'ung T'ai, Chinese bankers. | Copper Cash........................ 350,000 | Importing clandestinely goods covered by special regulations. | 3 June. Confiscated. | ... | 185.00 |
| 765 | June 9 [Office]. | T'ai Ch'ang, Chinese firm. | Rice...........................pls. 900 | Fraudulently altering amount stated in certificate issued by Hankow Superintendent from pls. 300 to pls. 900. | 15 June. Fined.. | 200.00 | ... |
| 766 | June 12, Danish s.s. *Activ*. | Chinese assistant compradore on board. | Weising Lottery Tickets.....pcs. 109 | Landing a specially prohibited article clandestinely, and offering a bribe to officer on duty of $15. | 13 June. Dollars and Lottery Tickets confiscated, the latter handed to Superintendent for destruction. | ... | 10.00 |

| Case No. | Date and Place of Offence or Seizure. | Name of Offender: Hong, Individual, or Vessel; and Nationality. | Denomination and Quantity of Goods. | Offence committed or Rule broken. | Decision: Date and Nature. | Amount of Fine. | Amount realised by sale of Goods confiscated. |
|---|---|---|---|---|---|---|---|
| | | | | | | *Hk.Tls.* | *Hk.Tls.* |
| 767 | June 19, British s.s. *Hardwick*. | Master of vessel, British. | Sundry packages containing dynamite.... | Discharging outside of Harbour limits and before receipt of permit. | 26 June. Fined.. | 25.00 | ... |
| 768 | June 19, alongside British s.s. *Pakhoi*. | Chinese boatwomen. | One Sampan.................................. | Boarding steamer previous to its anchoring. | 20 June. Fined. Sampan confiscated. | 1.00 | 2.00 |
| 769 | June 26, British s.s. *Pekin*. | Chinese, name unknown, carrier of Hsieh Hsing Ch'ang Post Office. | Silk Cap Buttons............pcs. 1,000<br>Silk Piece Goods...........pls. 0.04 | Concealing dutiable imports in letter-bag. | 29 June. Confiscated. Goods sold to Post Office at nominal value. | ... | 10.00 |
| 770 | June 28, British s.s. *Hankow*. | Chinese servants of vessel. | Salt............................pls. 5.50 | Concealing contraband imports on board vessel. | 30 June. Confiscated. Sold through Superintendent. | ... | 11.00 |

III.—Outstanding Cases.

| | | | | | | | |
|---|---|---|---|---|---|---|---|
| 762 | 87th/June Quarter. | | | | | | |

Chinese version prepared by

C. D.,

*Acting Deputy Commissioner* [*General Office*].

Submitted by

A. B.,

*Commissioner.*

Shanghai Custom House, 15*th July* 1882.

Forwarded in Despatch No. 156.

Copies compared and passed.

.............................................................

[*Chinese Secretary.*]

Submitted [to Tsungli Yamên] by the Inspector General *H. T.* on [*date*] in Despatch No......................

## 22.

### A Shupan's Application for Leave.

*To*

*The Commissioner of Customs,*

SHANGHAI.

The undersigned most respectfully applies for twenty days' leave, dating from the 3rd to the 22nd August 1882, for the purpose of getting married, and humbly wishes that his application may be granted. He farther states, as he is required to do, that his former leaves extended from the 13th to the 27th December 1879, in all fifteen days, and that during the present year he has not attended at the office for two days.

Most respectfully,

WU TÊ-HÊNG.

[*Date.*]

---

## 23.

### A Compositor's Application for Leave.

*To*

*The Commissioner of Customs* [*Statistical Secretary,*

STATISTICAL DEPARTMENT,

*Inspectorate General of Customs*].

MAO TA-YU most respectfully begs to state that, having served as a Compositor in the Statistical Department without applying for home leave ever since he first joined in February 1866, the arrival of a letter from his family urging him to come home, in order to get married, now causes him to venture troubling Your Honour with his most respectful request to kindly grant him two months' leave, in order that he may get married and settle other important matters; for granting which he will be ever grateful. He has asked Mr. *Pa-la-mao-tan* to kindly speak to Your Honour on his behalf.

Most respectfully,

MAO TA-YU.

[*Date.*]

---

## 24.

### Shanghai Customs Port Clearance.

The Superintendent of Customs and Territorial Taot'ai at Shanghai, in the matter of the collection of Duties and Tonnage Dues.

Whereas an application for a Port Clearance Certificate has come forward after due exhibition of Bank Receipts showing that all dues and duties have been paid in conformity with the Treaty Regulation by which "all goods declared at the Custom House by any British merchant ship shall at once be charged Tonnage Dues and ordinary duties thereafter to be paid by the merchant at the Customs Bank as per Duty Memo.," this Port Clearance Certificate is herewith duly issued into the hands of the master of the said ship. A necessary Port Clearance.

PARTICULARS.

Nationality: British.
Vessel's name: *Po-wei Ka-sha-êrh* [*Bothwell Castle*].
Registered No.: 23,836.
Destination: Japan.
Tonnage Dues paid on 1,654 registered tons, for which a separate Certificate is issued.

| | | |
|---|---|---|
| Import Duties paid | Tls. | 16.1.5.9 |
| Export " " | " | 666.1.5.9 |
| TOTAL | Tls. | 682.3.1.8 |

Issued this, etc. [*date*].

## 25.

### Tientsin Customs Duty Paid Certificate.

CHOU, by His Imperial Majesty's commands holding brevet rank of the second class, Superintendent of both the Foreign and Native Custom Houses at Tientsin, in charge of Foreign trade matters in the province of Chihli, and Taot'ai with Coast Defence and Military Authority, in the matter of issuing a [Duty] Paid Certificate.

Whereas the British merchants *Fêng-ch'ang* [Messrs. MACLAY & Co.] report their having bought in the interior the under-mentioned goods, in all 44 packages, weighing.......... piculs, and, the Export Duty being paid, their forwarding the said goods for sale to Shanghai by the British merchant ship No. 91 called *Nanzing*, a Certificate showing that the Export Duty has been paid at the Tientsin Customs is hereby duly issued, for delivery at the port of destination, in order to pay the Import [*i.e.*, Coast Trade] Duty accordingly. It is not allowed to be tendered for payment of duties at another port [but that named above, *i.e.*, Shanghai]. A necessary Duty Paid Certificate.

PARTICULARS.

1 package Cow Hides . . . . . . . . piculs 9.90.
10 packages Pigs' Bristles . . . . . . . „ 14.29, value Tls. 342.91.
33 bundles Cotton and Woollen Mattresses, pieces 5,600, „ „ 3,920.
Duty paid: Tls. 218.0.9.8.

The above Certificate is issued for the British merchant ship No. 91.

[*Date.*]

To be delivered on date of arrival in port.

---

## 26.

### Full and Half Duty [Paid] Certificate for Native Goods Exported.

The Superintendent of the Hankow Customs, in the province of Hupeh, and Taot'ai of the Hankow Circuit, in the matter of issuing a Full Duty Receipt on Native goods.

Whereas it is stated in the Revised Yangtze Trade Regulations that "Native Produce exported from the River when exported from [the regulation quoted says 'imported at,' 進口] any of the three Custom Houses on the Yangtze-kiang shall alike be examined and charged duty at such port itself just as at any of the ports opened to trade by the Treaty," and as now a Bank Receipt has come forward showing that the British merchants *T'ai-ku* [Messrs. BUTTERFIELD & SWIRE], ship *Pekin*, have purchased at Hankow Native goods for exportation, which have been examined and granted a Duty Memo. by this Custom House, ordering them to proceed to the Bank to pay [the duty], this Full Duty Paid Certificate is herewith duly issued, in order that its holder may deliver it at the port of discharge for examination. This Certificate is to accompany the goods which it covers. A necessary Duty Paid Certificate.

PARTICULARS.

5 packages Medicines, piculs 8.20, original [value] Tls. 96.
4 „ Vermiçelli, „ 6.

The $\frac{\text{full}}{\text{half}}$ duty on the above has been paid with Tls.* $\frac{\text{. . . 5.8.8.0}}{\text{. . . 2.9.4.0}}$.

[*Date.*]

The above Certificate is handed to the British merchants Messrs. BUTTERFIELD & SWIRE.

If a mistake be discovered, application to have it altered should be made.

Certificate No. .......................90.

To be delivered on date of arrival at Shanghai.

* In the Chinese text (Vol. I, p. 55, col. 10) the characters 百 and 拾, standing for "hundred" and "ten" respectively, should each be preceded by a blank space. They originally appear on a printed form, and the hundreds and tens are merely filled in if required. In this case they are not.

---

## 27.

### Duty Proof.

The Superintendent of Customs and Taot'ai at Ningpo, in the matter of issuing a Duty Proof.

Whereas a despatch is on record from the Tsungli Yamên enjoining that "apart from the three Yangtze Ports where the Coast Trade Duty has to be paid beforehand at the port of exportation, the Half Duty payable on the importation of Native goods at all other ports is to be paid at the port of importation, and that the issue of Coast Trade Duty Paid Certificates is no longer permitted;" and as now a representation has come forward from the.................................. [*nationality*] merchant HSÜ FÊNG to the effect that "he has brought [the under-mentioned] Native goods from Shanghai by the Chinese ship No. 135; that these goods were accompanied by a Shanghai Duty Paid Certificate, on the production of which Coast Trade Duty has been paid; and that, since it is no longer convenient to sell these goods on the spot, he will now re-ship them to the port of Shanghai by the British ship No. 100;" this Custom House, having examined the goods and found them to correspond, now (while returning drawback for the Coast Trade Duty received by this Custom House) duly issues proof that a Full Duty Paid Certificate received from the Shanghai Customs has been produced for the said goods. Issued into the hands of the said merchant, that it may be taken to Shanghai for examination. A necessary Proof.

PARTICULARS.

1 package Huang-lien [Dye-stuff], piculs 1.05, value Tls. 73.50.

[*Date.*]

---

## 28.

### Shanghai Customs Exemption Certificate.

The Superintendent of Customs and Taot'ai of Shanghai, in the matter of issuing an Exemption Certificate.

When a merchant, on having paid all the duties due on certain goods brought by him [into port], wishes to change the destination of such goods to another port of sale, a special Certificate shall be issued to him for the amount of goods so exported, on their being ascertained to be the identical goods in their original packages and to agree with the books without having in the least been tampered with or exchanged for other goods, and he shall be allowed to proceed to the said port and there produce the Certificate so issued, in order that they may be exempted from a further charge of duty. Now whereas the German merchants *Mei-tsui-shih* [Messrs. MELCHERS & Co.] report that, having previously paid the duties on the under-mentioned goods, they will ship the same goods by the British merchant ship No. 23,902, called the *Chungking*, to be forwarded to the port of Tientsin for sale, and the goods having been examined and found to agree, an Exemption Certificate is duly issued to them. The document being issued on this ground, they shall be allowed to forward the under-mentioned goods to the said port, where, on this Certificate being produced and found to agree with the goods, they shall be allowed to land the same for sale without any further charge of duty being made. A necessary Exemption Certificate.

PARTICULARS.

5 packages Brass Buttons = 500 gross.

These goods had been imported by the northern ship, Registered No. 1,217, and paid duty Tls. 27.5.0.0.

The above Certificate is issued into the hands of the British merchants *I-ho* [Messrs. JARDINE, MATHESON, & Co.].

[*Date.*]

To be delivered on date of arrival at the Tientsin Customs.

---

## 29.

### Shanghai Customs Tonnage Dues Certificate.

The Superintendent of Customs and Taot'ai of Shanghai, in the matter of issuing a Tonnage Dues Certificate.

According to the British Treaty, "any merchant vessel wishing to proceed to any of the Treaty ports or to Hongkong shall be entitled, on application of the master, to a special Certificate from the Customs, [on exhibition of which] she shall be exempted from all further payment of Tonnage Dues for a four-monthly term, dating from the date of issue, if the limit of four months has not been exceeded." Now whereas an application for a Tonnage Dues Certificate has come forward from the .......................... merchants .........................., after the production of the Bank Receipt showing that Tonnage Dues have been paid, this document is duly issued into the hands of the said merchants, who are hereby granted exemption from further payment of Tonnage Dues for a term of four months. A necessary Tonnage Dues Certificate.

PARTICULARS.

Applicants: the Danish merchants "Telegraph Company."

Vessel: the Danish merchant ship *Ssŭ-ta-no-ti* [*Store Nordiske*].

Registered No.: 622.

Registered tonnage: 596 tons.

Tonnage Dues paid: Tls. 238.40 (two hundred and thirty-eight taels and four mace only).

Date of expiry: 17th of the 9th month.

[*Date.*]

---

## 30.

### Huchao.

SHÊN, by His Imperial Majesty's commands Taot'ai, with the brevet rank of a Provincial Treasurer, and Superintendent of Customs at Chinkiang, in the matter of issuing a Huchao.

An official letter has been received from the Chief Manager of the China Merchants' Steam Navigation Company to the effect "that an official letter has come to his hands from the 'Commission for the new edition of the Provincial Archives' at Pao-ting-fu, through the medium of the 'Coast Defence Office' at Tientsin, forwarding a list of books for additional library purchases, and writing to the Company to send a special messenger to the Provincial Government Printing Offices at Nanking and Huai-an to effect purchases as per list, to forward them from Chinkiang to Shanghai, for further transmission to Tientsin, and apply for exemption from duty and release on examination." This letter having come to hand, and whereas an application for a passport has come forward from the Company's employé WU LUAN for twenty-three cases of books bought in the first instance from the Provincial Printing Office at Nanking, weighing in all thirty-five piculs, inclusive of package, which are to be forwarded by China Merchants' Company's steamer from Chinkiang to Shanghai and further on to Tientsin, this Huchao is therefore duly issued. When produced at any of the Custom Houses or Barriers they may pass *en route*, the goods covered by it are to be released on examination without let or hindrance. A necessary Huchao.

The above Document is issued into the hands of the China Merchants' Steam Navigation Company.

[*Date.*]

To be delivered on arrival for cancellation.

---

## 31.

### Huchao.

JUI, Superintendent of Customs and Taot'ai at Ningpo, in the matter of issuing a Huchao.

A despatch is on record from the Tsungli Yamên to the effect that "whenever any Government officers pass a Custom House carrying with them effects and goods on which no duty is chargeable by law, they may go to the Custom House and apply to the Superintendent for the issue of a sealed Certificate, and after in this sealed Certificate the number of boxes and packages are clearly entered, then they shall be allowed to be exempted from examination." Now whereas the expectant *chü-jên* CHI P'EI, a native of the Wên-an district, in the prefecture of Shun-t'ien, states in an application that "this being the time for the 1882 triennial examination, he is on his way to the examination hall, and carrying with him a number of packages by way of luggage and clothing, applies for a free pass;" this application having come forward, I duly issue this Huchao accordingly. The Custom Houses, Barriers, and Guard Houses on the road to which the holder of this document will proceed are requested not to raise difficulties by detention, which is to be kept in view as an urgent enjoinment. A necessary Huchao.

PARTICULARS.

Two boxes Books.
Four boxes Clothing.
One set Carved Boards.
Four packages Sundries.

The above Certificate is to be exhibited at all the Guard Houses and Customs Barriers *en route*.

[*Date*.]

To be delivered for cancellation within............................days.

---

## 32.

### Duty Free Certificate.

SHAO, holding rank, granted by His Imperial Majesty, of the second class, Superintendent of Customs and Territorial Taot'ai at Shanghai, and Inspector of Mints, with three steps of merit granted to his person, in the matter of issuing a Certificate.

The records of this office show that the following documents have been received from the Provincial Treasurer at Soochow, viz., on the 1st July 1867, an official letter, which says:—

"I am in receipt of a despatch from His Excellency the Provincial Governor to the effect that a letter was addressed to him by the Board of Revenue advising the issue of an Imperial Edict sanctioning the proposal made in the Supervising Censor HUNG CH'ANG-YEN's Memorial to the Throne, according to which exemption from Likin taxes as well as Customs duties should be granted alike on the export and import of such cargoes of paddy, rice, and other grain as merchants were called upon to buy up for transportation to Tientsin and for sale at that port."

Further, later on, in 1870, an official letter which says:—

"I am in receipt of a despatch from the Board of Revenue to this effect: the Prefect of Shun-t'ien-fu had written in reply [to an inquiry from the Board] that, 'since the crops in the country about Peking had fallen short of the full amount, and since commercial enterprise had again to be looked to as a means of forwarding rice and grain in support of the people's maintenance, it would be necessary to grant the temporary remission of Customs duties and Likin taxes,' and the Board now writes to say that matters are to be treated as in the case referred to the Throne in 1867."

Records also show that on receipt of this letter proclamations [to that effect] have been issued to the public.

Now whereas the licensed merchant YUNG CHI, having purchased one hundred packages of Rice, weighing one hundred and fifty piculs, to be carried to Tientsin by the vessel *Shunho* [*El Dorado*], and having signed a Bond [to this effect], applies for a Certificate which will exempt his cargo from Likin taxes and Customs duties at the various Customs and Likin stations; the Bond referred to is filed in the archives and reported in due form, and this Certificate is duly issued.

The Certificate issued on these grounds is placed into the hands of the said merchant, in order that he may produce it at the various Customs and Likin stations he may meet on the road, and apply for their examination and release. If goods not covered by this Pass be contained in his cargo, they will have to pay all the inland taxes and duties required by regulation. As soon as he returns to Shanghai the merchant will deliver this Certificate to be cancelled, which is to be kept in view as an urgent enjoinment. A necessary Certificate.

The above Certificate is issued to the licensed merchant YUNG CHI.

[*Date.*]

Shanghai Customs.

To be delivered within six months.

---

## 33.

### Special Certificate.

LIU, holding rank, granted by His Imperial Majesty, as Provincial Treasurer, Territorial Taot'ai at Shanghai, Inspector of the Coast Defence, Post, Fisheries, and Salt Administration, with ten steps of merit and recorded ten times at the Board, in the matter of issuing a Special Certificate.

On the 4th September 1880 a despatch was received [at this office] from His Excellency LIU, Governor General of the Two Kiang Provinces, who states that he has been addressed by the Governor of the Fukien Province LÊ to the following effect:—

"Incessant rains at the close of this last summer season having caused the rivers of the province of Fukien to overflow to an almost calamitous extent, the year's crop of grain could not but be deficient; and since measures were taken to induce merchants to import this commodity with a view to assist the population, the Throne has been applied to for the extension, by rule of precedent, of exemption from payment of duties."

And a despatch to the same effect was received from His Excellency Governor WU.

The above having come to the Taot'ai, the matter is, on the one hand, brought to the knowledge of the public and the Commissioner of Customs is written to for his guidance, and, on the other hand, cargoes of Rice bought up by merchants here to be sent to Foochow for sale will be provided with Certificates in analogy with the precedent by which the carrying of Rice to Foochow was exempted from payment of duty on the last occasion.

Now whereas the merchant Ho CH'ANG CH'ÊNG has purchased one hundred packages of Rice, weighing one hundred and fifty piculs, to be shipped by the steamer *Appin* to Foochow for sale, and whereas a Bond signed by him has come forward, this Certificate is duly issued, while replying [to the applicant's petition]. Being issued on this ground, this Certificate entitles its holder to have the goods covered by it released without payment of duty on awaiting the Commissioner's examination at the Custom House. A necessary Special Certificate.

The above Certificate is issued to the merchant Ho CH'ANG CH'ÊNG.

[*Date.*]

[*Taot'ai's endorsement.*]

To be delivered for concellation within six months.

---

## 34.

### Duty Receipt for the carrying of Goods into the Interior [*i.e.*, Transit Pass Inward].

SHAO, Superintendent of Customs and Taot'ai at Shanghai, in the matter of issuing a Transit Pass.

Whereas it is stipulated in the Rules appended to the Tariff that—

"Notice being given [at the port of entry] from which the imports are to be forwarded inland, of the nature and quantity of the goods and the place inland to which they are bound, the Collector of Customs will, on due inspection made, and on receipt of the Transit Duty due, issue a Transit Duty Certificate; this must be produced at every Barrier Station, *viséd.* No further duty will be leviable upon imports so certificated, no matter how distant the place of their destination:"

And whereas, further, it is stipulated in Article I of the [Yangtze] Transit Regulations that—

"Foreign merchants carrying Foreign imports up the Yangtze-kiang must, after having arrived at any of the Yangtze Ports, and as soon as they have left port, proceed themselves to the interior for the sale of their goods, pay all the Native inland charges at the various Customs and Likin stations, unless they be provided with a Transit Pass from any of the Custom Houses on the Yangtze,"—a final paragraph stating that at the northern and southern coast ports matters are to be treated in the same manner as at the Yangtze Ports:

And whereas, further, it is stipulated in the Chefoo Convention that—

"As regards Foreign goods sent to the interior under Transit Pass, the Tsungli Yamên is to devise a uniform system to be followed, according to which Foreigners and Natives, without distinction, shall be at liberty to take out Passes:"

And whereas, apart from the practice in the case of Foreign goods carried to the interior *without* a Transit Pass, still following the [Yangtze] Transit Regulations, the German / Chinese merchant *Mei-chi* [MÜLLER & Co.] reports to the Customs his intention to transport the under-mentioned Foreign goods to Ning-kuo-hsien / chou, in the prefecture of Ning-kuo, province of Anhwei, and applies for the issue of a Transit Pass:

I therefore issue, as in duty bound, this Transit Pass, in order that it may be examined and stamped on the road; and that the goods may be released. A necessary Transit Pass.

PARTICULARS.

1 package Palm-leaf Fans, Trimmed = 2,200 pieces.

The Transit Duty on these goods has been paid.

This Pass is handed to the German / Chinese merchant MÜLLER & Co.

[*Date.*]

To be delivered for cancellation within ............ days.

---

## 35.

### Certificate of Declaration for Native Goods to be purchased [*i.e.*, Transit Memorandum].

LIU, Superintendent of Customs and Taot'ai at Shanghai, in the matter of issuing a blank Certificate of Declaration.

Whereas a despatch has come to hand from the British Consul to the effect that the British merchant *Hsiang-mao* [A. R. BURKILL] has represented that since the under-mentioned goods have arrived at the first Barrier, he has to pay the Transit Duty at the port of exportation, in accordance with the Customs Tariff, and now applies for the provisional issue of a blank Certificate of Declaration [or Transit Memorandum]:

This Custom House duly issues three identical copies of this blank Certificate of Declaration [*i.e.*, this triplicate Transit Memorandum]. The Consul is to call upon the said merchant to sign this Certificate at the Consulate before issue; and at the first Barrier met with on coming from the authorised place of purchase, either the said merchant or his representative will present this triplicate Certificate, in order that he may, together with the Barrier authorities, inspect the said goods. The number of packages and the weight of the goods and the name of the exporting Custom House are to be entered on the Certificate by the merchant himself. After this triplicate Certificate has been received at the Barrier, one copy is to be sealed and, duly enclosed in an envelope, sent by the quickest post to the Custom House where the said merchant says in his declaration the goods are to be exported; a second copy is to be sealed and sent at the end of the month to the Tsungli Yamên, for the Yamên's archives; the third copy remaining is to be kept at the Barrier, where a Transit Pass [運照] will be made out from the particulars contained in this Certificate. This Pass will be issued to the said merchant, who will present it at the various Barriers along the road, where the goods will be released on the Pass being stamped. On arrival at the locality where the Barrier of the exporting Custom House is established, [the officers of] the Barrier will accompany the person in charge of the goods to the Custom House and apply for a Certificate showing that the Transit Duty has been paid at the Customs, on the ground of which the goods will then be allowed to pass the Barrier. If anyone should offend against this rule or should clandestinely sell *en route* goods which have been declared as destined for such and such a port, or defraud the revenue in any other manner, the goods will be confiscated, besides which the said merchant will be held to pay at the sea-port half the Tariff Duty on the goods as described at the time of passing the first Barrier. False declaration of goods effected by suppressing the Certificate will be punished by the confiscation of all the goods belonging to the same denomination [as those fraudulently under-stated]. A necessary Certificate of Declaration.

The following is a list of the Native goods and the quantities purchased:—

Destinations: *Nan-hsün, Ling-hu, Chên-tsê, Hsin-shih, Wu-chên, Shuang-lin.*

Twenty-six packages Silk Refuse . . . Weighing twenty-six piculs.

Thirty-one packages Pierced Cocoons . . „ twelve piculs and forty catties.

Stowed in two boats.

The above goods arrived at the first Barrier, *i.e.*, the .................... Custom House, on the [*date*], and, being examined, are now destined for the .................... Customs for exportation.

Issued by the Shanghai Customs on [*date of Certificate*].

To be forwarded by immediate post from the Barrier to the .................... Customs, declared as the port of exportation by the said merchant, to serve as a voucher in payment of duty.

---

## 36.

### Bond Certificate.

The Superintendent of the Newchwang Native Customs and Territorial and Customs Taot'ai at Newchwang, in the matter of issuing a sealed Certificate.

Whereas by the regulations newly agreed upon the restriction formerly prohibiting the exportation of copper cash, rice, and other grain has been relaxed, inasmuch as a Foreign merchant shall be free to ship these commodities from one of the open ports of China to another, under the condition that the said merchant shall bind himself, either by Bond or by depositing some other material guarantee, to return for cancellation within six months from the date of issue the Certificate issued to that effect, with the sealed endorsement of the Superintendent of Customs at the port of discharge, showing that the goods have been there received; and a freight or part freight of any of these commodities will render the vessel carrying them liable to pay Tonnage Dues:

And whereas the Foreign merchant *K'o Ch'ih-shun* represents that, being about to ship the under-mentioned goods by the Chinese merchant vessel Registered No. 1 for Shanghai, he has signed a Bond in accordance with the regulations, and applies for the issue of an official Certificate:

The details having been found to agree, and the Bond having been filed in the archives, this Certificate is now duly issued. The Certificate so issued will entitle the said merchant to forward the goods enumerated therein to Shanghai. As soon as the vessel arrives in port, this Certificate will have to be presented to the Shanghai Customs for examination, and on having been there endorsed and sealed, it will have to be returned to the Newchwang Customs for cancellation within six months, reckoned from the date of issue. If after the expiration of the said six months it is not delivered, the sum stipulated in the Bond shall be forfeited as a fine to the Chinese Government. A necessary Bond Certificate.

PARTICULARS.

*Jên* (壬) Rice . . . . . . . . 144 *bags*=*Piculs* 184.32.

The above Certificate is handed to the Foreign merchant *K'o Ch'ih.*

Issued by the Newchwang Customs this [*date*].

To be returned within six months.

---

## 37.

### Customs Regulations for the Port of Shanghai, for (Foreign) Shipping.

I.—The port for Foreign shipping is limited by a line drawn from Paoshan Point to the Battery on the right bank of the river below Woosung; vessels having crossed that line are held to have entered the port of Shanghai.

II.—Customs officers will board ships entering the port, and examine them after clearance outwards.

III.—The limits of the anchorage for Foreign vessels and the discharge and taking in of cargo is between the East Gate Creek and the Creek below the British Naval Yard.

IV.—Masters must deposit their ship's papers and Manifest with their Consul (if they have no Consul, with the Customs) within 24 hours after entering the port. For failing to do this within 48 hours, they are liable, under Treaty, to fine.

V.—The master is responsible for the correctness of the Manifest, which should contain a full and true account [marks and number of packages] of the cargo on board. For presenting a false Manifest he subjects himself, under Treaty, to a fine of $500; but he will be allowed to correct, within 24 hours after delivery of it to the Customs officers, any clerical mistake he may discover in his Manifest, without incurring this penalty. If any portion of the cargo be for re-exportation, it should be so entered on the Manifest.

VI.—Except under special permission, the place for shipping and unshipping cargo and ballast shall be confined to the limits of the anchorage, and the time—excluding Sundays and holidays—to between sunrise and sunset.

VII.—When a vessel is entered and her Manifest received, the consignees of her cargo hand in to the Customs their Applications to Land. These must give the number of packages, with their marks, weight, value, and other such-like particulars, and be accompanied by their Delivery Orders. The Delivery Orders will be stamped and returned to the consignees, who may then land their consignments. If cargo be unshipped without such Delivery Order duly stamped, it is liable to confiscation, and the master to fine.

VIII.—When the whole of the inward cargo is discharged, the vessel is examined by a Customs officer. Shippers may then hand in to the Customs their Applications to Ship, which must, as in the case of the Applications to Land, give full particulars, and be accompanied by their Shipping Orders. The Shipping Order will be stamped by the Customs and returned to the shippers, who may then ship their goods. Goods shipped or placed on board a cargo-boat without such Shipping Order duly stamped are liable to confiscation.

IX.—Cargo which, after the issue of a Permit, cannot be received on board, because the vessel is full, must not be re-landed without being brought to the Customs Jetty for examination.

X.—When the loading of a vessel is completed, a Manifest of her outward cargo must be handed in to the Customs. It must contain an account of the particulars—marks, numbers, and contents—of every package on board. For exhibiting a false Manifest the master is liable to fine.

XI.—Goods transhipped without special permission are liable to confiscation.

XII.—Tonnage Dues are payable when the ship has been 48 hours in port, or as soon before then as any cargo has been [shipped or] unshipped.

XIII.—When a vessel's Clearance is applied for, her stamped Delivery and Shipping Orders are examined on board; and if they are found in order, and the Customs are satisfied of the correctness of the inward and outward Manifests, and that the whole of the dues and duties have been paid, the Clearance is issued, and the vessel is entitled to receive back her papers and to leave the port.

XIV.—The Custom House is open from 10 A.M. to 4 P.M. on all days, Sundays and holidays excepted.

Special applications regarding business connected with the foregoing Regulations should be addressed to "The Commissioner of Customs."

---

## 38.

### Harbour Regulations for the Port of Shanghai.

The following Regulations have been agreed to and sanctioned by the Treaty Power Consuls at this port.

I.—The anchorage for Foreign vessels is between the East Gate Creek (Upper Reach) and the Creek below the British Naval Yard (Lower Reach).

II.—Vessels entering the anchorage will, when they come abreast of the Harbour Master's Office at the Lower Reach [British Naval Yard], be boarded by the Assistant Harbour Master, who will direct them to proper berths. In the case of a vessel being towed, the tug steamer must stop, before passing the Harbour Master's Lower Station at Pootung, to be boarded.

III.—Vessels running regularly [*i.e.*, river, coast, and mail steamers] having determined berths are allowed on arrival to proceed to them without stoppage, unless they have dangerous or explosive cargo on board, in which case they are to be governed by Clauses XI, XII, and XIV of these Regulations.

IV.—Four berths in the Upper Reach of the harbour will be kept open for the use of men-of-war.

V.—Vessels are to moor in accordance with the orders received from the Harbour Master, and not to shift their berths or remove from the anchorage without a special Permit.

VI.—Applications for permission to shift berths must be made to the Harbour Master's Office at the Custom House, Upper Reach, or to the Lower Station by the shipmaster, the first officer, or pilot in charge.

VII.—All vessels are required to keep a light burning bright and clear at the starboard yard-arm, or starboard fore-rigging when vessels have no yards, from dark until daylight.

VIII.—No vessels except men-of-war may use swinging booms. The swinging booms of men-of-war shall be rigged in from sunset until sunrise.

IX.—Vessels are required to keep their chains clear, especially towards the full and change of the moon, and not to have lines out from one vessel to another any longer time than necessary. Boats towing astern are to have short lines, in order not to block up the passage.

X.—Merchant vessels shall not fire off cannon or small arms within the limits of the port without written permits from the Harbour Master.

XI.—Vessels arriving at this port and having on board as cargo any number of loaded shell, or as much as 100 pounds of gunpowder, or as many as 20,000 rounds of [rifle, sporting, gatling, mitrailleuse, pistol, or revolver] cartridges, shall anchor not less than one mile below the lower limit of the harbour, and fly a red flag [No. 5 MARRYAT'S, or *B* Commercial Code] at the fore during the daytime, and shall abide by the instructions received from the Customs concerning the discharge of the same.

XII.—Vessels arriving at this port and having on board as cargo any explosive substances, in whatever quantity, shall be subject to the same conditions as are laid down in Clause XI of these Regulations.

XIII.—Vessels shall not be allowed to take on board as cargo any of the articles mentioned in Clauses XI and XII of these Regulations without first proceeding to an anchorage not less than one mile below the lower limit of the harbour, from which, while having such cargo on board, they shall only depart for the purpose of proceeding outside [of Woosung].

XIV.—Vessels arriving with inflammable oils [kerosene or petroleum] on board as cargo shall be berthed on the Pootung side of the 9th section of the harbour, and must remain there until all such cargo has been discharged.

XV.—A vessel arriving with a contagious disease on board shall not come nearer the lower limit of the harbour than one mile, shall fly at the fore a yellow flag, and shall not allow anyone to disembark or come on board without permission from the Harbour Master's Office.

XVI.—Masters of vessels shall not permit ballast or ashes to be thrown into the river.

XVII.—All vessels in port must keep on board a sufficient number of hands to clear and pay out chain, etc., when required.

XVIII.—Vessels on arriving in port must, as soon as possible, rig in their jib-booms, and must not subsequently rig them out [while within the harbour limits] without permission from the Harbour Master.

XIX.—No buoy may be laid down without the sanction of the Harbour Master and his approval of the moorings by which it is to be held in position. Unoccupied buoys must be lighted at night.

XX.—Buoys that are already laid down are subject to the control of the Harbour Master, and where they are so placed as to obstruct the passage of vessels through the harbour, or for any other reason, the Harbour Master will be at liberty to order them to be shifted. In case of refusal or neglect on the part of the owners of a buoy to shift its position as directed by the Harbour Master, the latter may cause it to be removed at the expense of the owners thereof.

XXI.—In case of fire occurring on board a vessel in port, the bell must be rung [immediately by that vessel and] by those above and below her, and the signal [2109 MARRYAT'S, or *B T F* Commercial Code] "Ship on fire" hoisted [by the burning vessel, if possible, and] by those above and below her during the day, or the yard-arm light lowered and hoisted continually during the night. Notice should be sent immediately to the River Police Hulk, Harbour Master's Station, or Pootung Signal Tower, and to the nearest municipal police station.

XXII.—Vessels infringing Clauses XI and XII of these Regulations by coming within the harbour limits with dangerous or explosive cargo on board in excess of the quantity therein allowed will be notified by the Harbour Master to proceed to an anchorage not less than one mile below the lower limit of the harbour, and their working and clearance will be stopped by the Customs until this notice is complied with. All other vessels not occupying the berth assigned to them as required by Clauses II, V, and VI of the above Regulations are likewise liable to have their working and clearance stopped by the Customs until the Harbour Master reports them as berthed in accordance with his directions. Masters of vessels committing breaches of the other Regulations will be dealt with by the Consular Authorities.

## SUPPLEMENTARY NOTICE.

I.—On entering the anchorage vessels should show their numbers, in order that the same may be signalled from the Harbour Master's signal stations.

II.—On having entered port, masters of vessels are requested to furnish the Harbour Master or harbour pilot with any information they may possess relative to discoveries of rocks, shoals, or wrecks, or vessels signalled on the way as coming from a certain port to Shanghai, and their positions, the state of weather and storms experienced during voyage, the time of leaving last port, and the time of arrival. They are also requested to report if any change has taken place in the position of buoys, or if any of the lights are out of order.

III.—Masters of vessels having fault to find with pilots, whether as regards professional competency or personal conduct, are especially requested to report the same, as soon as they arrive in port, to the Harbour Master, from whom such cases will receive immediate attention.

IV.—At the Harbour Master's Office (Custom House) will be found a board, on which all notices [pertaining to the Department] will be exhibited, also any information of interest to shipmasters; it will also show the names of pilots, etc.

V.—Vessels are recommended not to sail or steam through the shipping with the tide, it being highly dangerous to do so in respect of collision with other vessels. Vessels so doing will incur responsibility for all damages.

VI.—The master of a vessel may refuse to pay inward pilotage until a certificate is produced from the Harbour Master or his deputies that the vessel is properly moored.

## Harbour Regulations for Woosung.

The following Regulations have been agreed to and sanctioned by the Treaty Power Consuls at this port.

I.—The anchorage for Foreign vessels at Woosung is between the Woosung Creek and the White Cottage above the Chinese Camp.

II.—Inward-bound vessels having to anchor at Woosung must hoist the rendezvous flag [Marryat's Code] when passing the Woosung Spit Buoy, and they will then be boarded, between the Woosung Creek and the Harbour Master's Station, by the Berthing Officer, who will direct them where to anchor. The pilot or officer in charge of every such vessel shall see that proper facilities are afforded the Berthing Officer to enable him to come on board.

38

III.—No vessel will be allowed to anchor in the line of the fairway marks (consisting of three beacon poles to be seen in a line) across the Bar, or within 300 feet above or below said line.

IV.—The officer in charge of the Harbour Master's Station at Woosung is authorised to keep a clear channel from the Inner Bar as far out as Woosung Harbour, and to notify any vessel which may be anchored in such a position as to obstruct or endanger the navigation of this channel, to remove to such berth as he may point out.

V.—Should the commanding officer of a vessel refuse to move her after the Berthing Officer has called upon him to do so, such vessel will be held responsible for all damage done to his own or other vessels which may be caused by collision.

VI.—No vessel will be allowed to discharge or take on board cargo at Woosung until she is moored in a berth approved by the Berthing Officer, except in very urgent cases, when special permission has to be obtained from the Commissioner of Customs.

VII.—The management of vessels when taking up the berths to which they are directed will in all cases be left in the hands of the pilot or commanding officer.

VIII.—The officer in charge of the Harbour Master's Station at Woosung will board all inward-bound sailing vessels between the Woosung Creek and the Station, for the purpose of receiving their reports, and in case of a vessel being towed, the tug must slow down or stop while the vessel is being boarded.

Masters of vessels committing breaches of the foregoing Regulations will be dealt with by the Consular Authorities.

---

## 39.

### Shanghai Customs Notification.

Whereas the 5th day of the 5th moon is the day of the Dragon Boat festival, [the staff of] this Custom House will, in compliance with regulations, be granted one day's leave and not attend to public business. A special Notification.

[*Date.*]

---

## 40.

### Proclamation.

P'AN, Superintendent of Customs and Territorial Taot'ai at Chefoo, with rank as Provincial Judge granted by His Imperial Majesty, in the matter of instructions for the guidance of the public.

Whereas in landing imports from Foreign steamers and sailing vessels it has been an old-established rule for Native merchants to report their goods at the Foreign Custom House, and on receipt of the customary Permit present the same at the Native Custom House, where goods are examined, and, if found to agree, receive permission to be landed: And whereas this arrangement was made for the purpose of checking all the infractions committed by false declaration of goods and smuggling, but it has lately come to the Taot'ai's knowledge that of the goods declared to be landed from Foreign vessels, some have been landed before presentation of the Permit at the Native Custom House, and some, on being taken on shore clandestinely, while suppressing the Permit altogether, were not even reported at the Native Custom House at all: And whereas such disorderly manœuvres are utterly incompatible with the restriction of the above-mentioned irregularities: It [now] becomes necessary, in order to check these malpractices and to show that the Imperial revenue is not to be looked at as an unimportant institution, to clearly state the rule as it has been of old, for the information and guidance of all whom it may concern.

The Taot'ai, therefore, in due form issues this Proclamation, with a view to its being duly noted by the merchants of all districts that, after the issue of this public notice, "[the consignees of] all goods to be discharged from steamers or sailing vessels, on having paid the duty and being furnished with a Permit, on application to the Foreign Customs, will have to proceed *with* such Permit to the Native Custom House for examination, and if there the goods be found to agree with those entered on the Permit, the latter being endorsed with a stamp showing that re-examination at the Native Customs has taken place, then the goods will be allowed to be discharged and taken on shore. Anyone who may be proved to have taken his goods on shore previous to having tendered the Permit, or to have taken his goods on shore clandestinely without exhibiting any Permit at all, will be sent to the Custom House for trial and punishment. If the goods discharged do not agree with those enumerated in the Permit, such irregularity will be visited with severe punishment, and no leniency will be shown. A special Proclamation to be strictly obeyed!"

## 41.

### Notice from the Superintendent of Customs.

The wharf built for this Custom House is destined for the examination of goods; it was not intended to serve as a stage for merchants coming on shore or going on board ships, and pedestrians generally. I hear that prostitutes and singing women also mix with the company [making use of] this wharf, who, with the arts of the toilet, entice the passers-by, which is indeed a bold game to be played with the law. Now police runners have been sent to seize and arrest any such shameless folks, who, if they again dare to come to this wharf, will be sent to the Magistrate to be punished severely and without mercy.

The above public notice is suspended at the wharf in front of the Customs gate.

## 42.

### Notice from the Superintendent of Customs.

[This office has authority to] arrest [revenue] thieves and smugglers, and restrict evasion of the [revenue] law; wilful offenders will be punished severely and without mercy.

The above public notice in four rhymes is identical with one that is suspended at the wharf in front of the Customs gate.

---

## 43.

### Shanghai Customs Notice.

Notice is hereby given that a number of confiscated goods, comprising Silk Piece Goods, Szechwan Opium, Japanese Ginseng, English Camlets, Shoes, Fans, and Sundries, will be sold for this office by public auction at 2 P.M. on the 26th instant by *Lu-i-shih-mo* [LOUIS MOORE] at the Customs Godown. Intending purchasers are requested to attend punctually to offer their bids. It will be necessary for purchasers to carry with them a certain amount of Foreign money, in order that, when the sale is settled, the goods may be delivered; they must not back out after the sale has been settled, on the plea of having brought no money with them, which should be well kept in mind.

[*Date.*]

---

## 109.

### Despatch from the Tsungli Yamên to the Inspector General of Customs.

The Imperial Chinese Board of Foreign Affairs, in the matter of official instructions to ROBERT HART, Inspector General of Customs, with rank as Provincial Treasurer.

The following Imperial Decree was received on the 27th May 1876:—

"The Grand Secretary WÊN HSIANG, a man of spotless integrity, a clear-headed politician, and a patriot, ever candid in his views and straightforward, sincere, and earnest in his actions, just and intelligent in his advice; rising from the position of a member in one of the Metropolitan Boards, he had to thank the fact of being known to the discriminating intelligence of His late Majesty the Emperor WÊN TSUNG HSIEN (HSIEN FÊNG) for being promoted to the position of a Director in Our Imperial Court and being commanded to visit, as an associate member, the sessions of the Grand Council; and, again, he had repeatedly important trusts confided to him by Their Majesties the two Empresses Regent and His late Majesty the Emperor MU TSUNG I (T'UNG CHIH). When, in the year 1865, he was selected to proceed across the

Great Wall at the head of a body of troops, in order to subdue the hordes of mounted robbers who then infested the country about Fêng-t'ien, it was he who by destroying the force of the enemy made a thorough clean sweep of this pest throughout that extensive territory. When promoted in his turn to a position connected with Our Court, he became an invaluable help, and by devoting his best energies to all questions where the good or evil of politics as well as the welfare of the people was concerned, and to the settlement of any complications that would arise between China and Foreign countries, he deserves indeed to be considered THE Officer who was at the same time Our right hand and the backbone of Our Imperial Power. It was solely by the fact that the accumulation of toilsome work had thrown him on the sick bed that he could be got to apply on different occasions for permission to quit his post; the Court had granted him a liberal term of leave, an Imperial physician was sent to him for consultation, and presents of ginseng were bestowed on him to render his heart easy and promote his recovery. At the meetings of the Grand Council We have repeatedly inquired after his health, expressing Our wishes for his recovery, that he might live to enjoy Our Imperial favour for a long term of years. The news which is now brought to Us of his having departed for a better life fills Our heart with shocking grief. We therefore hereby command that a *to-lo* pall be provided for his funeral; that TSAI CHÊNG, a *Beilé*, with rank of a Prince of the second order, be deputed to at once set out with an escort of ten officers of Our Imperial Guards to offer the customary libations. We further bestow on the deceased as a favour the posthumous title of a Grand Tutor, and command that, in accordance with the law regulating the relations of Grand Secretaries, honorary gratifications be granted to his family, and that sacrifices be offered up in his memory at the Temple of Wisdom and Goodness; that a donation of *Tls.* 3,000 be issued by the Treasury of Our Privy Purse; that hereditary nobility with the rank of *Ch'i-tu-wei* be given to his son HSI-CHIH, to take effect after the expiration of the latter's term of a hundred days' mourning; and that all the fines which may have become due during his tenure of office be restored. As to the posthumous honours due to him, the proper Yamên is to look up the regulations and make the necessary application to Us. When the body of the deceased is taken back to his home, the local officials stationed on the road will make the necessary preparations, and when the *cortége* has arrived at the station of his Banner, We hereby command TS'UNG SHIH to proceed thither to make all the necessary arrangements for the sacrifices there. We wish hereby to express Our anxious desire to honour the memory of a faithful servant."

The above Decree having been received from His Majesty the Emperor, communication is duly made thereof to the Inspector General of Customs. A special Despatch.

29th May 1876.

No. 744.
General.

## 110.

### Despatch from the Tsungli Yamên to the Inspector General of Customs.

The Imperial Chinese Board of Foreign Affairs, in the matter of official instructions.

The following Imperial Decree was received by the Grand Secretariat on the 9th April 1881:—

"Ever since We took charge of the Empire We have respectfully received the illimitable proofs of the depth of motherly affection of Her Majesty the now defunct Empress TZ'Ŭ-AN *Tuan-yü K'ang-ch'ing Chao-ho Chuang-ching* [the last expression being the Empress' *hui-hao* (徽號), or special honorary title]; ever since We ascended the Throne these last seven years We have been deeply indebted to Her loving delight for the pleasure We received in bestowing upon Her Our filial care. Being a constant witness to Her agility and physical strength and Her restless attention to Government work, Our heart felt consoled in the hope We cherished that protracted happiness might add to the number of Her days, so that She might live to reach the acme of human life. There, on the seventh of April Our beloved Mother was attacked by an accidental indisposition, when all medical care was at once applied, which it was hoped would result in speedy relief. On the eighth of April, however, a sudden aggravation took place, contrary to all expectation; the patient would cough up phlegm, the breath stopped; and when, in the sequel, these symptoms recurred with increased pressure, at 8 o'clock in the evening She suddenly closed Her eyes to awake no more. Under pangs of grief We burst into tears, crying aloud: 'Alas! why must it come to this?' We have received Her dying commands, which were to the effect that mourning clothes should be worn for twenty-seven days, and then no more; but such a course would indeed not easily appease Our Imperial heart, and we shall give a faint idea of Our sadness by nevertheless wearing full mourning for a hundred days, and half mourning for the full term of twenty-seven months. With regard to Her last words, uttered by way of consolation to the motherly heart of the Empress TZ'Ŭ-HSI *Tuan-yu K'ang-i Chao-yü Chuang-ch'êng* [the last being the honorary title of the Empress TZ'Ŭ-HSI], namely, that 'restraining Our mournful thoughts would be as much as keeping Government interests in due regard,' We could not but respectfully obey the commands thus bequeathed to Us by making every effort to restrain Our grief.

"As to the funeral ceremonies, We hereby command that I TSUNG, Prince of Tun; I HSIN, Prince of Kung; the *Beilê* I K'UANG; the Grand Chamberlain CHING SHOU; the Grand Secretary PAO YÜN; the Assistant Grand Secretary and President LING KUEI; and the Presidents ÊN CH'ÊNG and WÊNG T'UNG-HO be deputed to superintend them with due reverence and care."

The above Decree, received from His Majesty the Emperor, is now duly and respectfully placed on record for the guidance of the Inspector General of Customs. A necessary Despatch.

11th April 1881.

No. 1,917.
General.

# CORRIGENDA.

## VOLUME I.

Page vi (Index of Subjects). Under "CERTIFICATES:" insert "Port Clearance; No. 24, p. 53."

Page 30, col. 8. For 九萬 read 六萬.

Page 45, col. 8. For 貳月 read 正月.

Page 55, col. 10. The characters 百 and 拾 should each be preceded by a blank space. *See* note on p. 280, Volume II.

Page 82, col. 6, *infra*. For 英商 read 通商.

Page 95, col. 11, *infra*. For 仰或 read 抑或.

Page 195, col. 11, *supra*. For 待 read 侍; and for 醱 read 醱.

Page 204, col. 15. For 扁額 read 匾額.

Page 211, col. 3. For 阢法 read 骫法.

Page 265, col. 12. For 竭立 read 竭力.

## VOLUME II.

Page 18$^{a}$. For *chih* 職 read *shih* 識.

Page 21$^{b}$, after *t'ung* 通商別口. For "a non-Treaty port" read "another Treaty port."

Page 27$^{b}$, line 10. Before 籍 insert *chieh*.

Page 53$^{b}$. For *shi* 計 read *chi* 計.

Page 72$^{a}$. For *tsê* 特 read *t'ê* 特.

Page 87$^{a}$, after *chiao* 交碍. For "not to interfere with each other" read "to interfere with each other."

Page 122$^{a}$. Under "*ch'ang* 常 constantly; usually; commonly," insert "常關, the Native Customs, as opposed to 新關 (*hsin-kuan*), the Foreign Customs."

Page 123$^{a}$. Under "*ch'ao* 鈔 money orders; tonnage dues; to copy," insert "鈔關, the Native Customs, as opposed to 新關 (*hsin-kuan*), the Foreign Customs."

Page 143$^{b}$, under *ch'ou* 讐. For 讐怨 read 讐怨.

Page 213$^{a}$, under *shêng* 陞. For 陞啓 read 陞啓.

For transliteration of sounds in this Volume, Part II should be referred to in preference to Part I.

# 文件自邇集七卷

（*Wên-chien Tzŭ-erh Chi: A Series of Papers Selected as Specimens of Documentary Chinese Designed to Assist Students of the Language as Written by the Officials of China*）

〔英〕威妥瑪（Thomas Francis Wade）編

《文件自邇集》七卷，英國威妥瑪編。威妥瑪（Thomas Francis Wade，一八一八—一八九五），英國漢學家。生於英國倫敦，一八四二年來華，一八八八年任劍橋大學首任漢學教授。著有《漢字習寫法》、《語言自邇集》等，與翟理斯合創之北京官話拼音系統「翟理斯-威妥瑪拼音」影響甚深。此書係爲在華外交官學習漢語書面語「文件體」所編之教材，可與北京官話口語教材《語言自邇集》互爲補充。全書録文七十五篇，分爲平行公文、往來信函、小民稟稿、欵貼法程、移詳公牘、陳公檄文、韓公奏疏七卷。初版於一八六七年，一九〇五年再版，較初版有所修訂。據一九〇五年上海版影印。

# 文件自邇集

WÊN-CHIEN TZŬ-ERH CHI

## A SERIES OF PAPERS

SELECTED AS SPECIMENS OF

# DOCUMENTARY CHINESE

DESIGNED TO ASSIST STUDENTS OF THE LANGUAGE AS WRITTEN
BY THE OFFICIALS OF CHINA

IN SEVEN PARTS

**WITH KEY**

BY

THOMAS FRANCIS WADE, C.B.
Secretary to H.B.M. Legation at Peking

SECOND EDITION

SHANGHAI HONGKONG-SINGAPORE-YOKOHAMA
KELLY AND WALSH, LIMITED
1905

# TABLE OF CONTENTS.

## PART I.

### Despatches.

# WÊN-CHIEN TZŬ-ERH CHI.

## PART II.

### Semi-Official Notes, 1864–5.



## PART III.

### Petitions presented at Hongkong, 1845–9.



## PART IV.

### Forms.

## TABLE OF CONTENTS

### PART V

**Documents taken from the Printed Correspondence of K'uei-lien, Prefect of Pao-ching Fu in 'Hu Nan, at the commencement of the T'ai P'ing Insurrection, 1852.**



### PART VI.

**Documents taken from the Printed Correspondence of Ch'en 'Hung-mou, an official of the reign Ch'ien Lung, 1735 1796.**



### PART VII.

**Memorials taken from the Printed Correspondence of 'Han Wen-chi, an official of the reigns Chia Ch'ing and Tao Kuang, 1797 1836.**

# TZŬ ERH CHI.

## DOCUMENTARY SERIES.

### PART I. DESPATCHES.

PAPERS 1—20.

# 文件自邇集卷之一

第一件

欽差大臣太子少保廣州將軍宗室者
欽命乍浦都統前閣部堂紅帶子伊　爲

照會事。六月二十七日接到來文。以本大臣無全權字樣。碍難公議通商之事。查本朝向無全權大臣官名。凡有

欽差大臣字樣。卽與

貴國全權二字相同。至通商一事。欽奉

大皇帝簡派本大臣都統前來會議。是以疊次咨明在案。今若實心願通舊好。卽按兵不動。揀派人員。會同公議。以期早定全局。覆書告知。尙望

貴大臣熟思之。須至照會者。

右　照　會

欽奉全權公使大臣世爵璞

道光二十二年六月二十七日

第二件

大清欽差大臣太子少保兵部尚書兩江總督部堂宗室耆　爲

照會事。前准

貴大臣照會內稱。寧波口領事官。須俟調回郭施

拉。再令羅伯聃前往在案。茲查郭施拉回粤在即。

應給文羅伯聃。於到寧之日。親交查照。除經本大

臣由五百里飛咨

浙江撫部院查照外。所有劄飭管理口岸之寧紹

4

台道。公文一角。相應照送
貴大臣查收。轉給賚投。可也。須至照會者。
右　照　會
大英欽差大臣佩帶頭等寶星世爵璞
道光二十三年九月十六日

第三件

大淸太子少保兵部尙書兩廣總督部堂祁　爲
照會事。案據潮州府具禀。樟林地方。有英人一名。
現飭海陽縣移明前途各縣。小心護解。赴臬司衙
門投收。聽候飭傳通事。譯訊辦理。等由。當經飭司
俟該英人護解到日。立傳通事譯訊供詞。禀覆核

辦在案。茲據廣州府具稟。遞到英人一名。當即發縣轉發洋商。妥為安頓。已飭通事譯訊。據該英人供名㖗呿。年二十八歲。係英吉利。孟丫剌人。受雇在本國的英人。威厘船上。充當水手。通船水手。共有二十人。那船主載有貨物。記不得日子。在本國開行。來廣東售賣。因風飄到不識洋面寄椗。船主威厘叫我們共三人。坐駕三板。上岸探取淡水。同行二人先已回船。我想起常被船主打罵。受苦難當。乘間逃走。並無別故。如今原船駛往何處。我不知道。求把我交本國在省英商收領。附搭便船回國等語。錄供稟報前來。除批飭將該英人。即交在省英商收領。俟有便船附搭回國。以免失所外。相

6

應照會

貴大臣查照。須至照會者。

右　照　會

大英欽差大臣佩帶頭等寶星世爵璞

道光二十三年十月十九日

第四件

太子少保兵部尚書兩廣總督部堂祁

大清欽差大臣太子少保兵部尚書兩江總督部堂宗室耆　爲

督理粵海關稅務文

照會事。照得通商案內。應用大秤砝碼丈尺。業經

照式成造。鐫刻監造官姓名花押。比較均屬準確。

惟砝碼係屬銅外鉛裡。恐未能經久。已由本關部

另造純銅砝碼備用外。現距廣州開市。僅止一日。
只可將銅外鉛裡者。暫時行用。茲將大秤砝碼丈
尺各一副。先行交廣州領事官查收。統俟純銅砝
碼鑄就。再行照會
貴大臣互換。其福州等四口。亦俟純銅砝碼鑄就。
一併送去可也。須至照會者。

右　照　會

大英欽差大臣佩帶頭等寶星世爵璞

道光二十三年六月二十九日

8

## 第五件

大清欽命太子少保兵部尚書兩廣總督部堂祁
欽差大臣太子少保兩江總督部堂宗室耆
欽命督理粵海關稅務文　爲

照會事。照得通商案內。應用大秤砝碼丈尺。業經照式成造。因砝碼一項。係屬銅外鉛裡。恐未能經久。已由本關部另造純銅砝碼備用外。一面先將秤碼丈尺一副。發交廣州領事官。暫時行用。俟純銅砝碼鑄就。再行互換在案。茲純銅砝碼現已鑄成。相應照會

貴大臣查收。飭發廣州領事官存貯備用。一面將前發外銅內鉛砝碼一副。送回查銷。並將附去福州廈門甯波上海四口。應用秤碼丈尺四副。希爲

分發各口領事官。查收應用。可也。須至照會者。

計送大秤丈尺砝碼各五副

右　照　會

大英欽差大臣佩帶頭等寶星世爵璞

道光二十三年七月初三日

第六件

大清欽差大臣太子少保協辦大學士兵部尚書兩廣總督部堂宗室耆　為

照復事。現接

貴大臣來文。據石商金天賜禀稱。於本月初旬雇船。裝有石塊。由赤灣洋面經過。被新安縣福永司巡船捉拏。解司勒索銀兩。至今未放。惟煩嚴辦。並着立行釋放所捕之人。等因。查香港石船。前於本年七月內。在佛山被拿。卽經本大臣嚴飭放行在案。茲該福永司巡船。輙復妄拿勒索。殊屬不合。已劄行新安縣。將妄拿之巡船。從嚴究辦。並將被拿之人。立卽釋放矣。合先照復

貴大臣查照。順候

蕃祉榮增。須至照復者。

右　　照　　會

大英欽　差　大　臣　世　爵　德

道光二十五年十二月二十一日

預用空白

第七件

大清欽差大臣太子少保協辦大學士兵部尚書兩廣總督部堂宗室耆　爲

照復事。現接

貴大臣來文內稱。厦門口瓦器之稅。前經會商議

定。瓦器僅照估價。每百兩抽稅五兩。已飭該領事

官遵行辦理等因。均已閱悉。擬卽咨行閩省。嗣後

細磁器及粗磁盤碗。仍照磁器秤觔完餉。其極粗

瓦器僅照估價。每百兩抽稅五兩。以符稅則而昭

畫一。是否如斯。尚祈明晰

見覆。以便備咨

福州將軍。轉飭厦門口知照。合再照復。順候

蕃祉駢增。須至照復者。

右　照　會

大英欽　差　大　臣　世　爵　德

道光二十六年正月二十五日

第八件

大淸欽差大臣太子少保協辦大學士兵部尙書兩廣總督部堂宗室耆　爲

照復事。昨接

貴大臣二月初八日來文。均已閱悉。送還前次公

文二件。另繕附達。即請

詧照。至

來文屢稱懷存友誼。具見

貴大臣善體我兩國

君上。講信修睦。萬年和好之至意。與本大臣實有同心。
不勝欣悅之至。爲此照覆。順候
履祉延庥。須至照復者。
計附送公文二件
右　照　會
大英欽　差　大　臣　世　爵　德
道光二十六年二月十四日
第九件
大淸欽差大臣協辦大學士兵部尚書兩廣總督部堂宗室耆　爲
照復事。現接
貴大臣二月二十九日來文。訂於三月初八日。在

虎門寨會晤。業已閱悉。本大臣自當如期前往該
處。以便會商一切藉伸渴想之忱。至
來文所稱。約內各條必總准施行。斷不可獨取幾
條而准如議。是以今將約式繕修英漢兩稿。以便彼
此畫押蓋印。等因。查約內各條大意。俱可商議准
行。惟字句之間。於文義尚有未盡明顯之處。必須
會面後公同商定。酌加修飾。以歸妥當。且查各國
歷次定立條約。均係公同商酌。從無尚未商明。即
自行定約之事。所有現約五條。應俟晤面後。彼此
議定。再行飭繕。畫押蓋印。語句無多。臨時不難定
辦也。爲此照復。順候
履祺綏吉。須至照復者。

右照會

大英欽差大臣世爵德

道光二十六年三月初四日

第十件

大淸欽差大臣協辦大學士兵部尚書兩廣總督部堂宗室耆爲

照復事。現接

貴大臣四月十二日來文所言火輪船裝貨之事。均已閱悉。此事本大臣前接馬領事官申陳。欲以個爾寫兒火輪船。往來裝貨。並因該船裝載茶葉一單運往香港被海關阻止等情。本大臣當經劄復該領事官。並遣委員甯通判。向領事官告知。如該船必須將茶葉裝回香港。則此次姑准裝回。所有應完鈔餉。本大臣當爲全行代墊。俟酌議再行定奪。領事官不肯依允。本大臣實未嘗於該火輪船有所稽留也。至咪國止有小火輪船一隻。曾帶零碎貨物。赴關輸稅二次。彼時本大臣實不知有此事。且

貴國有火輪船多隻。與咪國不同。若紛紛裝貨。誠恐屢有碰沉慘事。是以前次照復。未便率准。但我兩國結約和好。友誼正殷。不可因此等細事。屢有爭論。所有帶送書信之火輪船捎帶貨物。既與咪國嘖吋吐船無異。自可准其輸納稅鈔。通融辦理。仍當嚴飭該火輪船。務須小心行駛。若碰壞內地

船隻。損傷貨物人口。均須按公議賠補。不得推諉
不認。有傷雅誼。福州之事。
來文亦已閱悉。閩省民情。與粤省民情同一獷悍。
本大臣因
貴國商人在彼。每爲懸系。遇有與該省地方官。書
信往來。無不以彈壓地方爲囑。上冬因
貴大臣來文。有福州民情甚是相安之說。本大臣
稍覺放心。不料復有搶貨之事。深爲隱憂。近接
閩浙督部堂來信。云有廣東人陳通事。迭次挑唆
水手人等。強買食物。以致起衅滋鬧。地方官極力
彈壓。並拏獲滋事民人三十餘名。始各相安。未知
即此事否。已轉咨閩省查明。按照條約妥辦矣。順

德縣逃犯。知承出示懸賞購拏。友誼關情。深爲銘
感。統此照復。順候
吉祉日崇。須至照復者。
右　照　會
大英欽差大臣世爵德
道光二十六年四月十七日

第十一件

大清欽差大臣協辦大學士兵部尚書兩廣總督部堂宗室耆
欽命兵部侍郎廣東巡撫部院黃　爲
照會事。現准
兩江督部堂暨
江蘇撫部院來咨內稱。據蘇松太道稟稱。五月二

十三日。據程增齡沙船水手潘六順稟報。本月十六日。在大沙頭洋面。被一三桅外國船駛攏。有一白面人過船。先仲手索銀。後又寫給字條一紙。舵工高鳳元回覆無銀。卽被砍死。又有黑面人二十餘個過船。各用刀槍。將各水手盡行殺傷。搬去布匹九十五捆。將船鑿沉。伊被漁船救回等情。當將字條交與巴領事辨認。云係英字。間有湖絲沒有字樣。又云。英國亦有盜船。去歲英國貨船。曾有在外洋被刼之事。此時卽令兵船駛去追拏。求給公文。令水手潘六順作線同去。告以大沙頭洋面係在佘山東北。數百里之外。前議章程。外國兵船不可前往。巴領事總以既係英船。若不令英國兵船追回。則管理通商之領事。實無以對中華。卽於二十九日寅刻。自派英國兵船出口而去。等情。到本部堂。相應咨會。等因。到本大臣部院准此。查該領事官。一聞英船在洋行刦。卽派兵船前往追捕。實屬認眞公事。惟前定條約。五口之外。沿海各口。兵船不便往來。茲佘山東北一帶。係兵船未便駛往之處。應請

貴大臣飭令該兵船。卽行回帆。幸勿駛往北洋。致與成約不符。其行刦盜船。應由中國該管各營。派船追捕。務獲按約辦理。爲此照會。順候

暑祺茂集。須至照會者。

右　照　會

大英欽差大臣世爵德

道光二十六年六月初八日

第十二件

大淸

前任浙江甯紹台道鹿
欽命江蘇常鎮通海道咸
欽命浙江甯紹台道麟
前任浙江甯紹台道陳

爲照會事。案准

貴總兵照會舟山所屯官兵。業經於道光二十六年閏五月二十八日未刻飭令全數登舟。其所遣兵棧等房以及養病院等處均遵守和約。盡行交與中華收管。昨經本總兵於中刻面請驗收在案。理合備文照會等因准此查此案先准貴總兵來文。定於本月二十八日。交還城外房屋。囑本道等前往接收等因，本道等遵於是日前抵寓所。同往各處。兵棧各房。及養病院等處。逐一點交。本道等。均已接收各屋俱屬整齊。門牕墻垣。並無拆動。具見

貴總兵恪遵和約。惇崇信義之意。本道等不勝欽佩。茲准前因。合行照覆。爲此照會

貴總兵。煩爲查照。並候

萬福雲臻。須至照會者。

右　　照　　會

大英御前侍衛駐劄舟山總理軍務總兵懇

道光二十六年閏五月二十九日

第十三件

大清欽命兵部侍郎廣東巡撫部院黃　爲

照復事。昨接

貴大臣轉交領事官送來

欽差大臣者　公文一件地圖一封。本部院當卽拆閱。

均已備悉。緣

者大臣閱兵。前赴廣西。距廣東較遠。是以各國交

涉尋常公事。均由本部院代辦代行。以歸捷便。今

貴大臣此次來文事關初創。本部院未便擅專。已

差弁將

來文地圖各件。馳送廣西。賫投

者大臣行轅。查收酌辦。俟辦理如何。自當由
者大臣另備公文照復。合先照會。順候
福祉日增。須至照會者。
右　照　會
大英欽　差　大　臣　世　爵　德
道光二十六年十月初六日

第十四件

大淸欽差大臣協辦大學士兵部尚書兩廣總督部堂宗室耆
欽　命　兵　部　侍　郞　廣　東　巡　撫　部　院　黃　爲
照復事。現接
貴大臣來文。接前上海領事官巴。照會該處道臺
公文一稿。望以辦事功績奏聞是幸等因。並粘文

稿一紙。均已閱悉。查上海道宮。在彼辦理一切交涉事件。諸臻妥協。俱係分所應爲之事。過承貴大臣稱譽有加。益見友誼殷肫。本大臣部院同深欣慰。特此照復。順候

時祺佳勝。須至照復者。

右照會

大英欽差大臣世爵德

道光二十六年九月十九日

第十五件

大清欽差大臣協辦大學士兵部尚書兩廣總督部堂宗室耆
欽命兵部侍郎廣東巡撫部院黃　爲

照復事。前接

貴大臣來文。內言省渡新永泰等。控番禺縣工書。設立渡船。需索銀兩。並將懷吉。洪泰。兩渡。封鎖一事。當經備文照復。並劄飭番禺縣查復去後。茲據該縣覆稱。遵查近來香港地方。往來商民客貨。較前加增。本年五六月間。據舖戶聯、德、店等。公舉呂、順、陳廣銓、萬順泰等。承充餉渡共三隻。業經先後取結。詳請給照開擺。嗣於九月內。據差役獲解私渡胡宇隆一名。續又獲解黃亞隆。黎亞成二名。訊據供認。用懷吉洪泰招牌。由天字馬頭開往香港。私渡屬實。情愿具限請照承餉。因尙未據遞具供結。交差暫行管帶。復提工書陳榮查訊。據供香港省渡。應行取結承餉。係循照向章辦理。該書並無

4　27

私設省渡、及需索銀兩情事。查承充渡船。必須取具鋪戶保隣甘結。查明實係殷實良民。方准詳請給照開攏。係屬百餘年來之定章。本爲稽察奸民私渡攬載。侵吞客貨等弊。而設。況香港地處外洋。而渡船俱係內地民人。以中國人攬載外國人貨物。良莠難分。尤未便漫無稽察。致滋流弊。今新永泰等。願充香港餉渡。並不照呂順等公舉保充之案。輙行違例私設、近因胡宇隆等。私渡被獲。慮被併究。復以工書設立渡船。需索銀兩等情。赴英國巡理處瞞稟。希免查驗給照。實屬狡詐。必非安分良民。不可不查詢明確。以防弊混。今據該縣查復前情。如新永泰等。現在香港。應請貴大臣飭令循照舊章。備具舖戶保隣各結。赴縣聽候查驗。詳請給照往來開擺。由縣約束工書。不准絲毫需索使費。儻無人具保。應卽禁止私設。庶地方官有所稽查。該渡船等亦不敢攬載侵呑。爲害商旅。實於內地香港商民。兩有裨益。爲此照復。順候

履祺集茂。須至照復者。

右　照　會

大英欽　差　大　臣　世　爵　德

道光二十六年十一月初一日

第十六件

大清欽差大臣協辦大學士兵部尚書兩廣總督部堂宗室耆 為

照復事。現接

貴軍門來文。欣諗

德公使。前往南向。所有香港公務。悉係

貴軍門辦理。並承友誼殷肫。逾情獎飾。良切心篆。

貴軍門和平處事。敦睦為懷。本大臣素所深知亦

素相傾洽。遇有事件。定必彼此和衷商辦。利益兩

國商民。何幸如之。英國梳了林船三板被劫一案。

於上月二十六日。接據馬領事官申陳。本大臣以

該匪等。膽敢在內河駕艇肆劫。拒傷事主。大干法

紀。實堪痛恨。當經劄飭該管營縣。嚴緝去後。隨於

本月初三日。據該管營縣獲到案犯吳亞六等九名。並起出贓物木箱一個。內洋布十疋。訊據吳亞六供認。起意行刦梳了林船三板。得贓拒傷事主不諱。其餘各犯。或認過船搜刦拒捕。或認扳船接贓。並供出未獲夥黨。現將該犯等發委確審。並一面飭緝各逸犯。務獲併究。一俟訊明定案。當再備文照知也。爲此照復。順候

蓍釐茂介。須至照會者。

右　照　會

大英署總理香港地方軍務陸路提督戴

道光二十七年　九月　日

第十七件

湖廣總督盧　　爲

移咨事。照得本部堂於四月二十八日行抵平頭鋪途次。有瀏陽縣民婦鄒江氏。呈控地棍袁宏趾劉才等。誆將伊夫洋玉幪作夫兄艮玉鎖拏。並搶去許多衣物。解府看押致斃。及伊子三束領尸。又覊佀自刎。尸尚未見。雖經該府兩次委員審辦。亦未擬結等情一案。復據江西廬陵縣民人劉朝陽。呈控開染店之蕭蘭皋。伊兄劉秧陽在伊店內染匠傭工。身死不見屍骨。疊經在各衙門控告。終未提案審辦等情。呈控一案。又據長沙縣民婦郭賀

32

氏。呈控秦勗卿借銀多年不償。該氏故夫拖欠鄭鴻來銀兩。催偪甚緊。無項抵還。曾經屢控追要。秦勗卿借欠之銀。以便抵還欠債。未能擬辦完結等情。呈控一案。查該三案。屢經在各衙門呈控。均未擬辦完結。一係勒偪人命。尸骨無蹤。一係匿尸不現。一係銀兩細故。本部堂馳驛查辦軍營緊要事件。礙難提訊。相應將原呈三紙。並借契抄錄各原呈單張。連鄒江氏。劉朝陽。郭賀氏三名口。一併移咨

貴撫部院。煩爲查照辦理。仍希見覆可也。

咨 南撫

第十八件

湖廣總督盧　爲

移咨事。照得本部堂於四月二十九日行抵湖南省城、據茶陵州民人蕭啟龍、呈控在伊染店傭工病故之劉秧陽之妻。劉羅氏。弟劉朝陽。屢控劉秧陽死後未見尸骨。疑有傷痕、被屈拖累多年、等情、呈控一案。又據酃邑民人鄧德欽。呈控羅姓田地、業已出賣、今羅文亮等、復以遠年墳墓碑記爲憑、誣控墾佔騎葬、以前有案據可憑。今經半載有餘、並未擬斷完結、等情、呈控一案。查劉朝陽前控蕭啟龍之父。蕭蘭皋。開設染店。伊兄在內傭工。身死。

尸骨不見。曾經具呈。當經據情移咨在案。今蕭啓龍。又以劉羅氏。劉朝陽。誣控拖累等情。互相呈控。但人命關係綦重。而誣控亦非輕舉。究係原被兩造。各執一詞。再查鄧德欽所控。先人置買羅姓田地。今羅文亮等以遠年碑記爲憑。誣控壟佔騎葬。此係田土細故。本部堂行程急迫。均難提辦。相應將原呈二紙。並各粘單。連蕭啓龍鄧德欽二名。仍

一併移咨

貴撫部院。煩爲查照辦理。仍希見覆可也。

咨　南撫

第十九件

湖廣總督盧　爲

移咨事。據衡陽縣民。劉劍閣。呈控該府縣。聽信胥役。酷虐病民。等情一案。又衡陽縣民。蕭泰山。呈控該縣浮收漕糧。聽訟需索使費。等情一案。先後呈控前來。案關控訐本管府縣。虛實均應究辦。相應將各原呈。移咨

貴督部堂。請煩查照。另委賢員。秉公辦理。至原告劉劍閣。蕭泰山二名。希一併飭傳備質。仍希見覆可也。

咨　湖廣總督

36

第二十件

湖廣總督盧　爲

移咨事。據衡山縣民婦譚羅氏。呈控糧臺尹國賢等。勾通該縣門丁富二等。勒索漕規。聳縣將伊夫譚開儒。州同職銜斥革。管押致斃一案。又衡山縣民曾廷舉。呈控被曾華翰等。搶掠多贓。殺斃妻命。現在贓賊並未全獲一案。又衡陽人王惟初。呈控戶書朱景雲等。勒索浮徵銀兩。朦縣押追一案。又湘潭縣民彭長齡。呈控郭成文等。掘毀糧田。案懸七載。未經審結一案。又清泉縣民婦李楊氏。呈控伊子李嘉言。經管錢糧。該縣勒索盈餘。酷刑比追一案。又清泉縣戶書蔣經緯。呈控監生甯偉人等。

恃衿把持錢漕。捉伊關禁。勒寫收餉分據一案。又
貴州天柱縣客民楊茂昌。呈控在龍陽縣地方被
搶。該縣輕估失贓。延不究追一案。又清泉縣民婦
唐林氏。呈控唐清奇等。侵蝕家產銀兩一案。又衡
山縣民丁迪德遣抱控告。縣總譚國棟。浮徵勒折。
發縣鎖押一案。先後呈控前來。　查譚羅氏控案。
關係詐贓斃命。曾廷舉以已結之案。復行翻控。戶
書蔣經緯。所控衿棍把持漕務。關禁欺辱。及楊茂
昌控告。被匪肆行搶掠等共四案。控情較重。相應
將各原呈。移咨
貴撫部院。請煩查照辦理。共原告譚羅氏。曾廷舉。
蔣經緯。楊茂昌四名口。希一併飭傳備質。至王惟

初。丁迪德。李楊氏。以浮徵勒索。及彭長齡。以田土被佔。案久不結。唐林氏以家產被侵等詞具控。查此五案。並未控經該管司道。已分別劄飭衡永郴桂道。及長沙府知府。就近訊辦詳結。仍希見覆可也。

咨　南撫　劄　衡永郴桂道　長沙府

# TZŬ ERH CHI.

## DOCUMENTARY SERIES.

### PART II. OFFICIAL NOTES.

PAPERS 21—30.

# 文件自邇集卷之二

第二十一件

復啟者。昨接

來函。知

貴大臣不日榮旋。今日枉

駕來館。本大臣屆時拱候可也。專此布復。順頌

日祉。

名另具十一月初十日

第二十二件

復啟者。接讀

來函。備悉

貴大臣抱恙。尚未大痊。並勞專函致候。銘泐殊深。
現在天氣漸寒。諸惟
珍攝。至來往過從。儘可不拘形迹。切勿
介意。再本大臣前患微痾。兹已大愈。因承
齒及。並用附陳。此覆順頌
勛祉。
名另具十一月十四日

第二十三件

逕復者。接誦
來函。備承
雅意送行。足徵

雲誼殷拳。曷勝欣感。惟本大臣。業於十一日請
訓。起程在邇。諸務煩冗。未暇細談。不敢動勞
玉趾。俟明春假滿回京。再行趨赴
貴館。暢談一切也。泐此布謝。順頌
日祉。
名另具十一月十二日

第二十四件
敬啓者。昨閱邸抄。欣知
貴大臣榮遷
總憲。曷勝歡悅。容明日相晤時。敬當面賀。專此佈
達。用賀

44

升禧。順頌
日祉不盡。
名另具十一月十三日

第二十五件

敬覆者。昨接
來函。備承
吉詞致賀。盥誦之下。慚歉交縈。用特布函。先行致
謝。餘容晤罄。此覆順頌
日祉。
名另具十一月十四日

第二十六件

啟者。日昨。聞得

令正夫人玉體違和。勢甚沉重。不勝懸系之至。未

悉是否願服外國醫藥。如有欲延醫用藥之處。本

大臣深可代爲效勞。中懷挂念。希即

玉復是望。此達。順頌

日祉。並候

令正夫人金安。

名另具　閏五月十四日

第二十七件

頃接

來函。備悉
雅意諄諄。銘泐無似。惟病者勢已垂危。現在僅存
呼吸。恐非藥餌所能見效。茲承
美意。惟有感謝而已。泐此佈覆。順頌
日祉。
名另具 閏五月十四日

第二十八件
啓者。茲據東便門城門領慶玉。東河沿汛守備寶
珍。東便汛守備王世英。稟呈。僉稱本年九月初三
日。有
英國公館需用物件。計裝箱三隻。轎車三輛。車夫

白大。拉運來京。並無執照。立即派兵。將箱隻車輛。

押送至

英國公館查收等語。查是日

貴館有無車夫白大。拉運箱子三隻。轎車三輛。進

館。即希

示知爲荷。順頌

日祉。

名另具　九月初七日

第二十九件

啓者。昨據廣渠汛官面稟。有外國人三名。隨帶跟

人箱隻。進廣渠門。並不呈驗執照。該門向其查問。

詎該外國人不服攔阻。竟向門官揮鞭毆打。硬行闖進。該門派人跟追。該外國人至正陽門又欲闖進城去。復經正陽門查無執照。向其攔阻。始將車輛折回。等語。本大臣等當卽派員。邀同貴國繙譯官阿。前往查驗。至前門外觀音寺鴻興店內。該外國人三名。並跟役人三名。隨帶箱隻等物。在該店住歇。查驗有無執照。始據該三人交出天津領事官畢。所給游歷執照三紙。係貴國人。錫。底。三名。現將執照帶回本衙門。查該洋人等進城。門官兵役。原因不肯交出執照。是以不敢擅自放行。乃錫底等。不將執照取出給看。公然闖進。實出情理之外。其如何教戒之處。應由

貴大臣自行酌奪。並希

飭知天津領事官。嗣後遇發給執照。須告以經過

之處。務將執照呈驗。不得故意藏匿不交。以符條

約。至游歷執照。應在原領執照之處繳銷。茲特送

去原執照三紙。並將該門未加戳記之故一併註

明。卽希

轉交錫底等收執。俟回天津後繳銷。可也。專此佈

泐。順頌

日祉。

名另具　初四日

第三十件

啓者。昨送來蓋印之護照一張內。已將阿畢一名添入。其照內八員。亦改爲九員。并查出繙譯官錫威綵照內。誤書錫威靈。明知不過筆誤。但恐該處地方官見之。致生疑惑。亦宜代爲挖補更正。一律加蓋順天府印信。送上。卽望查收。此布。卽頌日祉。

名另具 三十日

外天津給阿畢執照一張附還。并望查收。又及



7

51

# TZŬ ERH CHI.

## DOCUMENTARY SERIES.

### PART III. PETITIONS.

PAPERS 31—38.

# 文件自迩集卷之三

## 第三十一件

具稟人盧怡記厰。鄧亞蘇 陳亞光 等。爲血本無歸。乞
恩勒限追還。以免延累事。竊蟻等被英民某姓。騙去
洋銀一萬零八百一十二員。業經
大人高懸明鑑。洞悉民寃。將某姓監禁嚴追在案。乃延
累日久。未蒙勒令淸還。似此歸款無期。延宕胡底。
蟻自被騙而後。飢寒切身。債帳火迫。萬種艱難。慘
遭莫極。故迫再叩
鴻恩。乞勒作速。如數塡還。俾免延累。則感
大德於無涯矣。沾恩切赴
大人臺前。作主施行。

第三十二件

具稟人。曹安江隆店珠盛店等。

稟爲懇請免改原議。庶能擔保無誤事。緣有匠人梁三。承接英商某行一座。包辦工料建造。按照工夫成數多少。陸續收取銀兩。現在除收之外。尙存下洋銀一千九百元。因梁三本銀不敷。某行恐其有誤日期。是以招約蟻等擔保。當經面議。限六箇禮拜竣工。卽將未收之洋銀。一千九百元。照數支給等情。蟻等方肯簽字擔保。刻日買備材料興工。

今因忽奉

明諭。又要罰減梁三所存之銀九百元。只續給銀一千元。云云。如此不惟與原議不符。而且銀少工多。實係不敷竣工之用。恐將來梁三辦理不前。必致逾限。未免累及保人。蟻等亦不敢擔保。只得懇請大憲。另飭別人作保。以免貽累。實爲恩便。特此具稟。

第三十三件

具稟人歐陽意等稟。爲叩乞准給牌票。以得貿易事。竊民等欲在石塘嘴山邊孤零屋宇。製造火藥。照例計地距鎮相離六里。又不附近大路。以及民居房屋。俱已遠離。並無相連。

至於發賣火藥。仍不敢在內地貯屯。似此製賣處所。一切與例無礙。只得稟叩
台前。陳明情實。是否有當。伏乞
俯批。給領牌票。俾民等貿易有賴。則感
恩無旣矣。切赴
大老爺台前。准給施行。

第三十四件

具稟人中環各街坊子民等稟。爲失業無倚懇
恩按鋪給銀。庶搬遷有藉事。民等前蒙
司憲勘給地方。建造鋪戶屋宇。曾經發與執照。在民等

以爲永遠基業。世守無失。不料
貴國竟將地段取回。民等 自當惟命是聽。但思從前
血本建造。本期久遠棲身。或藉租度活。今不數年
而盡行拆去。從前血本虧空。後來棲身無地。苦上
加苦。命何以堪。惟是
大人奉天行道。公如平衡。明如清鏡。民間困苦。罔不周
知。且有戶書某姓。於 民等 建造事情。一一洞悉可
質可據。茲者闔街聯呈稟叩。伏乞按鋪補銀。庶幾
得些貲財。稍助搬遷費用。並求寬限日期。不致匆
忙無措。則永沐
鴻恩不戩矣。切赴
大人台前。作主施行。

第三十五件

具禀新安縣工房典吏鄭棟

禀。爲人船被拏。乞

恩釋放事。緣𨐌房奉　本縣主。給發

藩憲頒發漁照。出海轉發各漁戶。執持採捕。於前月二十五日。派伴坐船。攜帶路照出海。情因本月初十日。船在香港海面。遇有熟識鄭全興小料船。在此灣泊領照。適有

貴國巡船一隻駛攏。見有防盜礮火器械。疑係匪船。將伴連船。並船上銀錢各物。及將領照之鄭全興等。一併捉解到案。忖思船上。現有漁照告示爲憑。

共非歹船可知。只得瀝情叩乞
仁臺。伏乞迅將人船。并船上銀物。連領照之人。一概
釋放。以免誤公。則感
恩靡既矣。切赴
臺前。伏乞
恩准施行。

第三十六件

具稟淡民蘇福。年四十八歲。番禺縣人。郭貫年三
十歲。番禺縣人
稟爲懇給旗照。巡洋緝捕。以靖海疆事。緣民奉
新安縣福永司。召充部設巡船頭領。自僱殷實民

船。置備外洋捕盜器械。管募妥當水手。駕駛船隻。
不分晝夜。巡察洋面。緝捕盜賊。護衛來往商船。惟
福永司屬。洋面遼闊。港汊紛歧。且與
貴港洋面相接。民慮盜船。常在外洋各處。刼掠客貨。
突見向捕。定必東擊西竄。非仗
霜威旗照。風行雷厲。凡遇盜警。不分畛域。越境窮追。
嚴拏解辦。海氛莫靖。理合鈔諭。粘叩
台堦。仰懇
俯准給領旗照。俾民船遵照。在於
貴轄洋面。停泊往來。不分疆界。實力巡緝。獲賊報効。
庶商船安業。洋面肅清。實為
公便。頂祝切赴

台前。
恩准施行。
計粘鈔福永司諭一紙。

第三十七件
具稟人李福有
稟。爲風聞來歸。乞給田土。以便安身事。切思
貴港開創。歷已數年。法律森嚴。規條盡美。商賈來歸。
咸歌樂國。蟻等聞風向慕。襁褓歸來。暫在黃茅角。
未得安居。但見徐保所遺之田屋。未曾領給耕耤。
欲叩
恩給。仰覩

仁憲愛民如子。保民若赤。斷不忍坐視無依。故特匍

叩

台堦。伏望垂憐。

恩恤無依。懇將徐保之屋宇田園。給予蟻等居住耕

種。俾得安身樂業。即

國課自應需納。庶幾躬親治化。永沐

鴻麻矣。切赴

台前。

恩給施行。

第三十八件

具稟孀婦杜唐氏

稟。爲夫死鋪存乞
恩准給氏與各子收管事。竊氏夫。杜英生。有四子。長
亞根。次亞閏。次亞金。次亞榮。俱在省城居住。茲因
氏夫前用銀置有
貴港上環十七號鋪一間。又太平山二百四十六號
鋪一間。每年收租。除納稅外。所賸得爲氏家中使
用。不料氏夫去年回省。因病身故。迨至
鈞諭。飭傳氏子亞根赴案。着令氏子備具使費。按例
攏同妥保立單。准以洋銀二千五百元擔保。始能
管業。如有不遵。則歸官用。但氏夫該鋪所値銀不
過幾百。而氏子在港。朋友熟識無多。既未能如命。
只得即懇速備使費。覓保二名。竟諭不准。忖思氏

64

夫生前所置各鋪。原爲氏與各子日後贍養。今若

將氏夫各鋪歸入官用。則氏舉家絕食。況氏子亞

根。委係氏夫長子。闔港周知。而子承父業。天下皆

然。氏迫得瀝情哀訴

崇轅。伏乞矜憐婦老子幼。准將氏夫各鋪。給氏與各

子收管。俾日食有賴。歿存均感。沾

恩萬代。切赴

大人爵前。

恩准施行。

# TZŬ ERH CHI.

## DOCUMENTARY SERIES.

### PART IV. FORMS.

PAPERS 39—57.

9

# 文件自邇集卷之四

## 第三十九件

原告呈狀

如係生員監生。自稱爲生。有功名人。自稱爲職。有功名人暨生員監生。稱縣官爲父臺大人。府道以上爲公祖大人。餘俱相同。

具呈卜世仁年六十八歲。係大興縣人。住安定門外五里村。

呈爲恃強賴債。喝衆毆傷。懇

恩作主。以伸寃抑事。竊身於同治三年。三月初一日。

憑中人管賢士。借給宛平縣吳家莊民人吳良紋銀一百兩。當面言明每月按三分行息。定於五年三月初一日。本利全還。立有借約爲憑。吳良自用銀之後。當年六七兩月。交過利銀。嗣後利限到日。

卽行支吾。身向管賢士理論。令其代爲催討。伊尙以好言搪塞。不料管賢士。於四年夏間。因事赴陜未回。身只得自行討要。至今年三月初一日。約限已到。本利共欠銀二百零二兩。始終未見分文。身至吳家莊。連找數次。吳艮藏匿不見。本月二十七日清早。身又赴該莊。吳艮在門外站立。身卽向其討要欠款。乃伊視身老朽無能。不但不以理論。竟爾出言混賴。身情急氣忿。與伊爭辯。伊卽喝令伊弟吳成。及子吳克用。吳克昌等。幷不識姓名三四人。將身摔倒在地。一齊踢打。身骽打傷四處。腰間打傷二處。頭項破傷二處。昏暈在地。幸未致命。該處地保與身家送信。始行擡回。伏思有心抗債。已屬不情。猶復恃強抵賴。喝衆羣毆。實爲目無法紀。
身冤抑難伸。情出無奈。爲此叩懇
仁天大老爺作主。傳案訊究。則感
鴻慈無旣矣。上
呈。
同治　年　月　日具呈人卜世仁　花押

第四十件
被告訴呈
具訴呈吳良。年四十三歲。係宛平縣人。住德勝門
外吳家莊。
呈爲恃強凌弱。誣告善良。懇

恩提審。以明寃抑事。竊身於同治三年。三月初一日。憑中人管賢士。借用大興縣五里村民人卜世仁。紋銀一百兩。當面言明。每月按三分行息。定於五年三月初一日。本利全還。立有借約爲據。當卽將三四五三月利銀交過。嗣又交過六七兩月利銀。後因連年災歉。田地不收。度日甚難。屢向中人管賢士哀告。求其向卜世仁說合。暫緩索討。不料四年夏間。管賢士因事赴陝未回。卜世仁卽持票往身家討要。身因耕種事忙。未曾在家。卜世仁在身門首辱罵數次。本月二十七日清早。身在門口站立。卜世仁來到。向身討要欠款。身因一時難以措辦。向其央緩。卜世仁卽說身係賴賬。肆口大罵。身

與伊理論。伊卽扭住身衣衿。用拳毆傷身左右眼
胞並用磚塊打傷身肐膊胸膛。現有傷痕可証。身
被毆情急。喊叫救命。經身弟吳成。子吳克用吳克
昌等。攏前解勸。卜世仁仍復嚷罵。身弟吳成等。將
其勸解。送回伊家。孰意次日午刻。
憲差趙大馬升。手執傳票。到身家內。聲言卜世仁已
將身喊稟。並誣身聚衆羣毆。傳身赴案聽審。等語。
伏思身借用卜世仁銀兩。按月行息。雖因年荒未
曾清結。見卜世仁時。實係用好言哀懇。卜世仁既
將身辱罵毆傷。身仍令弟吳成等。將其送回。何以
卜世仁反行誣告。爲此情急。具呈申訴。叩求
仁天大老爺。俯賜公斷。則感

鴻慈無旣矣。上

呈。

同治 年 月 日具訴呈人吳長 花押

第四十一件 拏人票

差票

特授順天府大興縣正堂加三級紀錄五次王 爲

嚴拏事。案照順治門內石駙馬大街。事主蔡芳田呈控。二十八日夜間。被賊明火執仗。搶去銀錢衣物一案。據前次拏獲之夥犯于七。供出在逃首犯郞大毛三。暨韋升、衞九、蔡三、鄭六、任七、十兒。均應嚴拏究辦。照例治罪。爲此票仰捕役黃太、關升。務須嚴密購線。迅將郞大等。全數弋獲。不准一名漏網。如有延誤。重責不貸。懍之愼之。特票。

同治 年 月 日差捕役黃太 關升

第四十二件 傳人票

# 差票

特授順天府宛平縣正堂加一級紀錄二次孫 爲

傳訊事。案照張四呈控。余九因變賣地畝拖欠銀兩一案。據

張四供稱。向日買地。係中人王九齡周春魁二人作保。立有

字據爲憑。合行傳案審訊。爲 此票仰差役。陸喜江鴻。卽將

張四案內。王九齡。周春魁。傳集到案。聽候審訊。不得延誤。切

切。特票。

同治 年 月 日差役 陸喜 江鴻

計傳 王九齡 周春魁

# 第四十三件

保告狀人甘結。

具甘結王三。係大興縣民人。年二十七歲。向在大柵欄開設文古齋。玉器鋪生理。現因張大控告李七。賴帳不還。反行毆打一案。蒙

憲差將李七傳案禁押。身向與李七交好。情願出具保結。將李七保出。聽候傳訊。如有逃走抗傳等弊。

身情甘重罰。所具保結是實。

同治　年　月　日具甘結人王三　花押

第四十四件

保人甘結。

具保結王子英。係順天府昌平州生員。現因

敬祥厚洋貨寶號。聘請趙實齋。管理帳目。兼司銀錢

出入事件。例須親友代爲作保。今趙實齋係生至

親。情願出具保結。如有偷漏虛耗虧空等弊。均惟

保人是問。所結是實。

同治　年　月　日具保結生員王子英　花押

第四十五件

京官印結 保同鄉人考試用。如係捐官。即於印上。塡寫捐職二字。

76'

具印結官。刑部郎中沈士蘭。今於
與印結事。依奉結
得。同鄉張連第。
同治（鄉會試）年　月　日

第四十六件
候選官互保結
具互結楊瑞庭。今於
與互結事。依奉結得。同選官
張曉先。係順天通州進士。由捐納知府赴

大部投供。並無假冒違礙等弊。所具互結是實。

同治　年　月　日

第四十七件

轉寄收單

江蘇上海。日興蔚銀號。今收到

上海候補縣正堂王　公館銀壹百兩。匯至京都

前門外。東珠市口。

寶興布店收下。即付回條。交哈達門外木廠胡同。日

興蔚本號。轉寄不誤此照。

同治　年　月　日日興蔚記　花押圖章

第四十八件

收單

立收單公源銀號。今收到

廣生藥行。紋銀壹千伍百兩。俱已眼同來人。一併兌

清。特立此收單爲據。

同治　年　月　日立收單公源銀號　花押

第四十九件

借票

立借票人余自修。現因手乏。借到

張卜仁大兄。紋銀壹百兩整。當與中人何憬。三面言

明。每月按三分行息。準於三年期內。本利淸還。如

有拖欠。惟保人何憬是問。恐後無憑。立此借票爲

據。

同治　年　月　日立借票人余自修　花押

中人何　憬　花押

第五十件

匯兌單

立匯兌單人杜芷軒。今因 . .

寶生金店。櫃存敝處銀陸百兩。現有急需。務懇
兌銀〈壹百兩〉面交
王志和老爺收領。恐後無憑。特立此單爲據。

同治　年　月　日立匯兌單人杜芷軒　花押

第五十一件

包工字據

立字據人。木匠左志淸。今因
阿老爺買定台吉廠坐南朝北住房一所。共五十六
間。所有門牕戶壁一概收拾見新。議立工料銀伍
百兩整。身情願包辦。以後如有偷工減料。或房屋

滲漏。磚瓦不整。等弊。情甘重罰。恐事後無憑。特立字據爲證。

同治　年　月　日立字據人木匠左志清　花押

保人乾泰昌錢舖　花押

第五十二件

賣房契

立賣房契人王松菴。現因手乏。將自身祖遺坐落順治門內。刑部後身旗手衛。住房一所。共計六十八間。門牕隔扇。簾架影壁俱全。憑中人胡厚齋。賣與。

美國施老爺爲業。當下三面言明。房價銀壹千貳百兩整。俱已眼同兌清收訖。共付上紅白契九張。恐後無憑。特立賣契爲據。

同治　年　月　日立賣契人王松菴　花押

中人胡厚齋　花押

第五十三件

賣人契

立賣契人吳鳳鳴。今因貧苦。將本身親生女吳月珍。年十七歲。憑中人杜二。賣與余老爺爲妾。當下三面言明。身價銀六百兩整。俱已

眼同兌清收訖。自賣之後。任憑將親女吳月珍領
去。身與身妻丁氏。永無異言。並議定永無來往看
視。等情。如身女干犯
余宅家規。任憑家主處治。身不能干預。至疾病夭亡。
各聽天命。若有勾串欺騙情弊。惟中人杜二是問。
恐後無憑。立此賣契爲據。

同治　年　月　日立賣契人吳鳳鳴 丁氏　花押 手印 手印

中人杜二　花押

第五十四件

賣地契

立賣地契人王七。今因手乏。將自 身 祖遺坐落通州八里莊。田地壹百畝。憑中人卜世眞。賣與李九老爺永遠爲業。三面言明。地價銀五百兩整。俱已眼同兌淸收訖。當付上紅契一張。白契三張。自賣之後。如有同族人。及本 身 找價訛詐等事。任憑李宅告官處治。並惟保人卜世眞是問。恐後無憑。立此賣契爲據。

同治　年　月　日立賣契人王七　花押

中　人卜世眞　花押

第五十五件

書吏衙役履歷簿

書吏〇名

吏房

王　喜

年〇〇歲〇〇府〇〇縣人

同治元年五月二十日招充

同治三年五月二十日役滿

吳贊廷

年〇〇歲〇〇府〇〇縣人

咸豐十年十月招充

同治三年八月革退

丁　升

年〇〇歲〇〇府〇〇縣人

同治二年八月招充

同治三年九月病故

戶房

某人同上

某人同上

某人同上

禮房

某人同上

某人同上

某人同上

兵房

某人同上

某人同上

某人同上

刑房

某人同上

某人同上

某人同上

工房

某人同上

某人同上

某人同上

衙役○名

捕役

王升 年○○歲○○府○○縣人 同治元年正月投充 同治三年正月役滿

艾德 年○○歲○○府○○縣人 同治二年二月投充 同治四年正月革退

孟大鴻 年〇〇歲〇〇府〇〇縣人 同治二年八月投充 同治三年九月病故

皁役

某人同上

某人同上

某人同上

頭役

某人同上

某人同上

某人同上

散役

某人同上

某人同上
某人同上
門役
某人同上
某人同上
某人同上
茶役
某人同上
某人同上
某人同上
牢頭
某人同上

某人同上

某人同上

禁子

某人同上

某人同上

某人同上

第五十六件

書吏衙役花名册每逢卯期。到者。名上加紅點。不到者。不點。

書吏〇名

吏房某人

某人

戶房某人
某人
禮房某人
某人
兵房某人
某人
刑房某人
某人
工房某人
某人
捕役〇名
某人

某人

某人

皁隸〇名

某人

某人

某人

某人

頭役〇名

某人

某人

某人

散役〇名

某人

某人

茶役〇名

某人

某人

某人

門役〇名

某人

某人

牢頭〇名

某人

某人

禁子〇名

某人

某人

第五十七件

匯票

山東歷城縣裕泰銀號。今收到

候補府正堂宮　紋銀壹千兩。特此出具匯票。送交京都

翰林院余子明老爺收下。請煩卽至彰儀門內騾馬市大

街裕泰本號。當面將前銀如數交清。不悞。此據

同治　年　月　日出匯票裕泰銀號

# TZŬ ERH CHI.

## DOCUMENTARY SERIES.

### PART V. K'UEILIEN.

PAPERS 58—61.

# 文件自邇集卷之五

## 第五十八件

寶慶守魁聯移署武岡遊府張 壬子三月二十四日

爲

飛移事。本月二十三日。奉

督部堂程 批敝府稟團練壯勇各事宜。奉批。查金雞鋪蓬崗隘口。共有九處。昨本部堂已劄調。永順。永綏、綏靖。保靖。等處官兵。赴永補防。仰卽飛飭武岡州知照。毋論何處之兵、必由該州行走者、可卽速截留二三百名。該守仍會同張遊擊查明、城步要隘。酌量添派防兵若干。以昭愼重。至匪徒窺伺武新之謠。自屬無稽。處以鎭靜。加以嚴防。仍隨時確探賊情。馳稟查核。等因。奉此。查金雞鋪蓬嵩一帶。

貴府既稱防兵單薄。自應酌量添派。除飛飭武岡州葆牧。侯永順。永綏。綏靖。保靖。官兵。毋論何處到境。立卽截留一百名。先令馳赴金雞鋪蓬嵩。聽候

貴府酌派。幷飭葆牧查看武岡地方。如須添兵協防。亦卽截留稟報外。合亟移知。爲此飛移

貴府。一俟武岡州葆牧截留兵到日。立卽查明要隘。酌量分派。協同認眞巡防。務期嚴益加嚴。密益加密。勿使一匪竄入。是爲至要。仍祈將如何添派。及截留各兵到防日期。逕稟

督部堂查核。幷賜詳細移覆。竚切竚切。須至移者。

第五十九件

魁聯移武岡遊擊張　壬子五月

爲

移催確查解審事。案查敝府風聞。派防武岡州練勇。有與

貴營兵丁爭毆情事。當經飛札武岡州。將玩法練勇。先行鎖拏解審。一面移請

貴府。確查示覆在案。迄今未准移到。該兵勇等互毆。究係因何起衅。如何爭鬬情形。必須逐一查實。澈底究辦。方足以彰

國法而服衆心。除飛催武岡州。先將練勇鎖解外。所

100

有滋事各兵。亟應移提。幷請將此等兵丁。係何弁
管轄。因何任其滋事。逐一實覆。以憑核辦。當此邊
防喫緊之際。敝府祇知爲
國爲民。一秉至公。於兵於勇。一視同仁。均不能絲毫
姑息瞻徇。況平日逞兇滋事之人。有警斷不能守
城殺賊。所謂不能知方。安能有勇。兵勇皆食
朝廷錢糧。輒敢同室操戈。置
國家法紀於何地。此案敝府立等審明詳辦。合亟移
催
貴府。希即查明。此等滋事兵丁。係何弁管轄。先行
移覆。一面查明滋事兵丁姓名。飛速移解。以憑提
同練勇嚴審澈辦。竚切竚切。再敝府訪聞武岡兵

役。多有勾串土娼。混雜民情事。是否屬實。敝府練勇。有無串同兵役。在外雜詐情事。亦即一併確查具覆。現在辦理邊防。以保固民心爲第一義。兵役練勇。如有前項情事。立即治以軍法。萬勿稍有姑息。切切。須至移者。

第六十件

寶慶守魁聯札各營盤詰奸細 壬子九月二十二日

爲

飛飭嚴查事。探聞粵逆經省門攻剿。勢已窮蹙。其前陷興安裹脅各土匪。現在紛紛薙髮。或三五人一隊。或七八人一隊。假冒歸家楚勇潛逃。惟內有甘心從逆怙惡不悛之土匪等。意在爲賊窺探。各處情形。勾結五排一帶匪類。其人多肩高脚擔子。行李中藏有小紅綉鞵。髮際眉叢。每有火印。幷暗藏太平聖兵腰牌。於夾衣褲内等語。本府查近日各卡盤查。多有游手之徒。假稱楚勇。往來三五成羣。幷無腰牌護照。誠恐逆匪溷跡其中。難以辨認。不可不嚴加盤詰。除移明統帶楚勇。陝西卽補府江行營。嗣後如有遣歸之勇。務須由行營發給護照。塡注姓名。以便各卡查驗放行。如無印照。許沿途州縣營汛一體截拏。或係逃勇。或係匪類假冒。立卽訊明。分別辦理。幷飭新寗縣。嗣後如赴營投効。必須有紳士禀報。由縣發給腰牌護照。一面示諭本地壯丁。如無腰牌印照。不得擅自成羣結隊。遊者。即行截拏究辦。并通行邵陽。武岡。新化。城步。及長沙府屬之湘鄉。寧鄉。湘潭。益陽。安化。各州縣。一體查照外。合亟札飭。札到該縣。即便會督兵勇。加意盤查。毋使匪徒溷入。是爲至要。切切此札。

## 第六十一件

魁聯道稟刋發保甲積穀各章程示稿 庚戌九月初四日

敬稟者。竊編查保甲團練村莊。勸捐義穀。皆爲今日之急務。於寶屬情形。尤爲切要。前蒙飭委永順府夏升道來郡。卑府 當經會同遵照奏案。督飭印委各員實心查辦勸捐。均經稟復在案。惟是自來良法美意。無不委曲繁重。其事可歷久不徹者。其功斷非旦夕可程。況愚民易於圖終。難於慮始。是以由各牧令。粗辦大槩。先行取結。卑府一面採訪輿論。與牧令教雜各官。暨公正紳士。因地因時。酌定章程。刊刻示諭。不委多員。不立期限。不假書差之手。使士民自爲稽查。互相激勸。以實心行實事。一村辦畢。再辦一村。但得三四村行之有效。則各村自聞風興起。果能一律妥辦。則匪類自無所容身。而歉歲亦有所藉手。除業經刊成飭發。卑府仍隨時督飭牧令教雜各官。切實認眞辦理外。理合將劄示各稿錄呈。伏乞

俯賜察核。再保甲果能周密。則團練卽在其中。是以

皋府示內、將團練一府。附於保甲章程之內。以省
繁牘、合併陳明。
爲劄飭編查保甲章程事。照得保甲爲弭盜安
良之善政。現奉
上憲飭委各員會同牧令教雜各官編查。業經劄
飭遵辦在案。該州縣會同各委員。實心查辦。毫
不擾累民家。深堪嘉尚。第日期迫促。而地方遼
闊。或不無遺漏。且未立條規。恐美意不能持久。
而良法易成具文。茲本府酌定章程。刋刻示諭。
除俟刋成飭發外。合先抄稿行知。爲此劄仰該
州縣。查照章程。會督教雜各官。分往各鄉。妥爲
辦理。再辦理此等事件。固宜遵守成法。尤須因

地制宜。卽如邵陽地方保正。十年輪流一次。恒與烟戶生疏。五十六都。大者五六十里。小者三四十里。而洪仁一十四都。四分五裂。一甲之戶。往往相隔數十里不等。都各十里。茫無界限。往往有一戶之糧。分寄數甲者。編甲甚非易易。豈數句所能畢事。惟是本府再四籌畫。都甲憑錢糧。雖無一定之界限。而丁口憑居址。自有一定之方隅。查社廟爲祈賽之所。訪聞鄉民議事。有曰會十廟。會五廟者。一廟不過二三里。而老幼男婦人口。年年開載明晰。賽社時交付廟中。號爲時運簿。又謂之祀商紙。賽社完畢。交値年首事收貯。地方雖闊。無一丁一家不受轄於社廟

者。邵陽風土如此。各縣諒不甚相遠。果飭各保
正協同催差。查明本都社廟若干。無許疏漏。取
各廟首事所藏時運簿。無許僞造。則烟戶瞭然
在目。從此辦理保甲。則姦宄既無所潛藏。而荒
歉賑䘏事宜。亦有所藉手。府縣須求地方實有
裨益。爲民卽所以爲己。願與賢牧令。教職佐貳
各官共勉之。當不僅如奉委銷差。虛了故事也。
如本府章程。有不便於民之處。許牧令教雜各
官。隨時據實稟商。但求有益於地方。斷不固執
乎己見。共各勉之。切切。此劄。

爲曉諭力行保甲以除匪類而安善良事。照得
寶慶所屬。近年盜賊叢生。爲害閭里。逆匪肆擾。

屢動大兵。茲當辦理善後事宜。欽奉
上諭。嚴飭整頓保甲團練章程。業經會同委員督飭
查辦在案。第查保甲者。所以排比跟查。使宵小
無從潛藏。聯絡守望。雖單弱不被強壓。誠古今
安民之良法也。無如歷年奉行。往往虛應故事。
烟冊門牌。所載戶口。十漏六七。夫戶口尚多遺
漏。善惡何由稽查。家懸一牌。行此何益。訪查其
故。一由訛傳。恐有事時。按冊抽丁。故先漏載。以
防多抽。不知果欲抽丁。豈容減免。試思自爾祖
父以來。耳聞目見。曾有抽丁事否。一由編查時。
書役串同地保。按丁派錢。故各減丁。以圖省費。
又有按牌科費。故合數戶。省爲一牌。本屬安民

之良法。轉爲擾民之弊政。言之殊堪痛恨。若不立定章程。臚列示諭。誠恐仍屬有名無實。今特與爾士民約。革除從前科派。務期實力奉行。盜匪雖多。不如士民善良之衆。蹤跡雖秘。難瞞隣近耳目之眞。現經本府訓練壯勇。委員管帶。會同各地方文武員弁。認眞嚴密訪拏。更得爾等如法挨查。何難根株淨盡。除札飭所屬牧令教雜等官。切實辦理外。爲此剴切曉諭爾士民等。其各懍遵。勿違。所有章程列後。

一愼擇團總。　南省團練章程。向有團總。本府俯順輿情。亦不裁革。但後團總。須公正明白。有身家之人。不得以單寒及愚不識字者充數。專掌園內册結。以備查核。一切錢糧命件之事。不許干預。册結殘缺。則責罰之。有盜賊窩匪會匪。率園衆禀官拘治。或自捆送。如敢誣良生事。加等反坐。徇情隱匿。別經發覺。照例治罪。

一賓載戶口。　一戶一小牌。十戶一大牌。由官籌款購發。園總分給戶口。照依牌式填載。委官不時抽查。如有省一戶漏一口者。責罰更換。

一造具册結。　每十戶合訂一册。挨次各照門牌填載。丁口姓名年歲。田宅生理。册後一頁。各具互結。結書某某等。實結得册內各戶口。並無作賊窩賊。吃齋拜會等事。如有犯者。九家甘願連坐。末書年月。各畫押於其名下。此册長短寬窄。團內一律。不得參差不齊。送團總收掌。

一酌量戶數。十家一牌。此定式也。亦有不足十家者。亦有十餘家者。任其量地。通融辦理。總以易於互相覺察爲要。惟總牌及册面。須載明共戶數。

一論換册結。戶口有生沒遷徙、分晰之不一。且有善惡改轍。前後如兩人者。故册結不可不換、准於每歲正月。向團總取出改造。限日仍送團總收掌。有可仍舊不須改者聽。

一開自新之路。十家中如有一家爲匪者。准開具實跡。告團總禀官究治。如祇風聲不好。形跡可疑。九家共告團總。不敢互結。而其人尙愛體面。或自愧悔。許其獨具册結。送交團總。以開自新之路。惟既無互結。又不自具結者。團總率衆稟究。

一行團練之法。　團練之法。除例禁火器不准私置外。此外禦賊器械。准其各備。共立守望條規。市場公修柵欄。村落各葺牆垣。某處要隘可守。某處路徑宜防。俱在平日互相警察。一家被盜。九家聞聲幫助。一團有警。鄰團聞聲幫助。或傳梆。或鳴鑼。無故不至者。團衆查點記過。再蹈前轍。稟官責懲。如此聲勢聯絡。雖有強暴。不敢入其境矣。其平日面生之人。宜隨時稽察。強丐扒竊。以及左道邪術。俱宜隨時驅逐。果能力行。

自有實效。盜匪可絕。風俗可淳。本府實有厚望焉。

爲札發勸捐積穀章程事。照得本府遵奉
各憲札飭。業將保甲團練事宜。採訪輿論。因時因地。妥立章程。刊刻示諭。抄稿行知在案。至勸捐義穀一層。尤爲目前善後最切最要之急務。前奉
各憲。飭委永順府夏。會同本府剴切曉諭。並該牧令教雜各官。會同各委員。分往各鄉勸捐。除新甯典史黎永清。首倡捐穀二千石。士民鄭南屏倡捐穀一千石。李元楨捐穀三百石。李輔朝等各捐穀二百石。均經本府會同永順府夏。稟請

從優分別獎叙外。此外各州縣紳庶。踴躍樂輸。急公好義者。當不乏人。何日來捐數。尙屬寥寥。此雖邊氓瘠苦。慳吝成風。抑由未經明立規條。不免逡巡觀望。今本府酌定規條。與保甲章程。一併飭匠刋刷。業已刋齊。合併劄發。劄到該州縣。卽將發來保甲積穀示諭。挨照城鄉村莊。遍爲張貼。其有應交教雜各員。帶往分貼曉諭之處。亦卽相機隨時妥辦。務使窮鄉僻壤。咸知圖匱於豐。使荒歉之年。有備無患。庶幾痞棍無可藉口。阻米惡習。從此永除。是爲至要。至保甲各事宜。已於前劄內備詳言之。惟在實心實政。行之以漸。持之以恒。均毋因循泛視。切切。此劄。

爲曉諭勸捐積穀。以裕籌備。而靖閭里事。照得寶慶所屬本產穀之鄉。乃訪聞近年偶逢歉薄。遂形飢荒。痞棍乘機結黨。遏糶強糴。鄉城騷然。且有歛費設卡。詐索客商。擄掠錢物。種種不法。肆爲民害。本府蒞任以來。訪緝究辦。大加懲創。此風指日可除。然不可不思善其後也。年歲之豐歉無常。地方之貯備宜早。在樂歲餘糧棲畝。捐升斗於公亦何傷。至荒年積穀在倉。雖青黃不接而無恐。聚少乃能成多。所望綢繆於未雨。濟貧即以安富。庶幾親睦之可風。爲此示諭士民人等。其各通盤籌畫。踴躍勸捐。所有章程列後。

一按畝攤捐。十畝之家。每畝出穀一升。以次遞增。二十畝二升。三十畝三升。至百畝每畝一斗而止。其田逾百畝者。每畝一斗以上。不爲限制。聽其樂輸。

一照例議叙。田多則捐穀亦多。亦有不按田數。慨然多捐者。總以捐至二百石。則照例詳請議叙。品級職銜。捐穀愈多。議叙加優。既以利濟鄉里。又邀

朝廷褒寵。尙何顧惜不爲。

一愼擇首事領管。每都所捐之穀。分作二十起。擇公正殷實首事二十人。分領分管。一年一換。稟請官給印簿。載明所領穀數。憑衆車颺淨

盡。斗量多少實數。每年冬月約日。憑衆算量移交。不得戀充。初捐時寄貯私倉。三年後將息穀變價。擇地起倉。一切出納。不准書差干預。

一嚴定收放程規。　每年夏至前後。分三期分借。每石二分收息。借者照烟戶牌册所載家口。需穀若干。邀鄰里殷戶的保。親書借劵。秋分前後三期。用原斗量還歸倉。不得以私賬抵賴。其逋者保人賠還。否則鳴官追究。

一預限積穀定數。　積穀太多。難於收管。且易起侵蝕之弊。今通計一都上中下貧戶大歉之年。約需穀若干。俟積滿其數後。每歲算明。除留存此數。仍舊收放。將所贏餘變價。置本都義學義塚。及造橋修路。視所當爲之舉。憑衆估算動用。另存起息。歸下年估用。但不得以與僧道寺觀。一遇荒歉。將所貯本穀。按上中下貧戶。照牌册所載家口。或概行賑貸。或酌量賑邮。所存無幾。下年仍照前次。按畝攤捐。如法積貯收放。

一推廣各項公積。　查所屬氏族。有祭田墓田。都甲有文昌會。有團總田。又有燈會。醮會。茶亭田。其類不一。皆屬義舉。然其動用。或亦不無過費。今特勸諭。其各節省。妥爲掌管。遇荒歲。一族所貯。可濟族中之貧。一團所貯。可濟團內之貧。此與前項積穀。可並行不悖。又足以濟其所不及者。尙願推廣行之。總在得人得法耳。

右六條。最簡最要。與保甲法。皆爲今日急務。或有書差。從中需索。或有痞棍。藉端生事。准首事指名禀拏。必爲爾輩痛懲。使不得有阻撓也。總期爲爾百姓。長治久安之計。尚望各體此意。相率勸行毋忽。

# TZŬ ERH CHI.

## DOCUMENTARY SERIES.

### PART VI. CH'ÊN 'HUNG-MOU.

PAPERS 62—64.

# 文件自遡集卷之六

## 第六十二件

天津道陳宏謀宣洩積水以廣種植檄（乾隆三年八月）

今歲伏秋二汛。連有大雨。水勢潑發。異於常年。雖運河淀河兩岸。幸無衝決之虞。而各屬低窪之地。有因積水難消而被淹者。有因堤埝漫溢而被淹者。現在白露已過。河水已退。而境內仍多積水。一派汪洋。田地廬舍。半在水中。若不設法宣洩。有誤冬春種麥之期。案查乾隆二年。嵩福條奏。印汛各官。因係官堤。不便詳請開放。一任屯聚。坐視成災。經工部議覆。積潦之水。無路歸河。原有開堤洩放之例。應令於秋汛後。相度形勢開放。等因。奉旨准行。通飭遵照在案。備查各屬情形。大概一境之水。俱會聚於低窪之處。從此泝流測量。自必各有去路。如青縣之興濟減水河。則原有涵洞二座。可以疏通宣洩。如滄州捷地之減水河。原詳明於艮口莊。閻家莊。呂家橋。等處。建設涵洞。繼因下流建閘一案。尚未定議。是以未經建設。而此處原可相機開放。以資宣洩。如天津縣南境。則尚有南北二閘數道溝渠。可以洩水歸入河海。又文安境內。積水更深。查陶官營以下。勢漸低窪。逼近淀河。淀河水退。亦可相機開放。如大城境內河南四十八村之水。亦有朱家村。小流漂。小店村等處涵洞。現在開放亦可再加疏濬。如任邱獻縣。可以宣洩之處。現在已據詳明開放。儻水落堤高。亦可並爲開濬。以上皆可以宣洩之處。其餘四境類此可以宣洩者。自必尙多。至靜海。交河。肅甯。故城。霸州。均在積水被淹之中。亦自有可以相度宣洩之法。夫汛前之築堤防護者。有備斯可以無患也。汛後之開堤宣洩者。除害卽所以興利也。因地相時。原可相濟爲用。況當此異漲之後。四境皆水。層層堤岸。有如重圍。水來甚易。水去甚難。得早消去一寸。民卽得一寸之土田。得早退去一日。民得安一日之棲止。高者可望趕種秋麥。低者亦可以趕種春麥。明歲資生之計。全關乎此。相提而論。目下之宣洩。較之汛前之防護。似更難緩。似更有益。誠恐各廳印汛等官。以爲汛期已過。可弛防汛之責。不肯留心民瘼。切爲經理。除行四廳外。仰府官吏。卽轉飭被淹各屬徧查境內積水之處。如有涵洞者。再爲疏濬。使其暢流。無涵洞而河水已落。水可外流者。亦卽開堤宣洩。無論官民堤岸。卽將所開丈尺。並如何勒限責成。堵築完固之處。詳明立案。如事關隣境者。彼此會同勘明定議。但不許將渾水擅放偷淤。遺害下流。亦不得將積水放於原未被淹之村莊。敢有不禀報官府。而統衆強挖。私自偷挖者。立卽嚴拏。照盜決河防之律治罪。地方廳印汛防等官。各宜悉心體察。實力辦理。務期有益無害。上下相安。仍將有無積水被淹。及如何宣洩。或實在並無可以宜洩各情形、據實回覆、愼勿泛視。

## 第六十三件

### 天津道陳宏謀飭修車路檄 乾隆三年十一月

天河二府所屬地方。均與東省接壤。犬牙相錯。境內均各有兩省經由之大路。目今南河阻凍。往來行人。均仗車輛絡繹不絕、難容稍有阻滯者也。其中偶有積水淤泥。或崎嶇不平之處。地方官即應查明修補。以便行人、今聞沿途地方。尚有積水結凍。崎嶇難行之處。層層阻隔。以致車輛到彼。或繞道遠行。或僻道取便、而附近村莊有種刁民。將小路刨挖。專圖車輛到彼、勒索錢文。方肯擡車護送、

又沿河兩岸。亦有通行大路。而守堤河兵。更動借

欽堤名目。索取錢文。商旅車夫。均各視爲畏途。實堪痛

恨。合亟飛飭該州縣官吏。立將該屬境內凡係通行

之大路。逐加查驗。如阻水淤泥。崎嶇難行之處。星

速修墊平穩。以便車輛行走。橋梁單薄者。亦卽補

架。其餘繞道便路。凡有刁民刨挖溝濠。立卽押令

鄉地墊平。並嚴禁河兵。凡河岸車道聽人行走。不

得借端勒索。致干革究。仍出示沿途地方市店。曉

諭通知。如有前項不法。阻滯勒索情事。隨卽喊稟

究處。并將遵行緣由。及修過處所。具文報查。

# 第六十四件

福建巡撫陳宏謀曉諭出洋貿易各民攜眷回籍檄 乾隆十九年六月

閩省沿海各屬。多藉出洋貿易。以資生計。從前禁止南洋例前入洋者。勒限三年回籍。例後入洋者。不准回籍。自雍正五年奏開洋禁。內地商賈。往番貿易者。源源不絕。惟遠隔重洋。亦有不能如期回棹者。前

郝督部堂。先後

奏准。聽其回籍。嗣因乾隆十四年。有龍溪縣民陳怡老。由粵東私往噶喇叭充當甲必丹。爲番邦經管貨稅。既非貿易良民。難免藉端滋事。曾經查出番

擬發遣。自此貿易商民。稽留在番者。各懷疑畏。不敢回籍。此輩陷於異域。拋離家室。情殊可憫。日久人多。亦恐滋事。伏思我

皇上中外一體。外番貿易。絡繹不絕。柔遠惠商。體恤周至。本部院奏明。仍准一體回籍。荷蒙

聖恩俞允。欽遵通行文武各衙門在案。爲此示仰閩省商民船戶人等知悉。凡在番邦貿易良民。無論例前例後。果因貨帳未清。不能依限回籍者。一概准其回籍。所攜貲財貨物。地方文武各官。不得藉端索擾。在番所娶妻妾子女。准其隨帶回籍。如本身已故。留遺妻妾子女。有在番親屬。或素相熟識之人。准其搭船回籍。族屬人口。寫單交船戶帶回。交

本屬保領。如無人保領。或頂冒揑混。及如陳怡老
之充當甲必丹。供其役使者。均照例嚴加治罪。在
洋逾限之船。仍照舊例。舵水人等。不許再行出洋。
無籍游惰之人。本無挾貲貿易。私渡外洋。招搖誘
騙者。嚴行查察。不許回籍。凡回籍之人。均令船戶
出具實係良民。如虛甘罪保結。事犯一體治罪。本
部院與督部堂。念爾等在番貿易良民。出洋年久。
孰無故土之思。茲荷
聖主格外鴻慈。准令回籍。爾等感戴
天恩。各宜及早均歸故土。不得仍復觀望延捱。以致終
淪異域。亦不得夾帶違禁貨物。及異色之人。入閩。
以致自干罪戾。庶年年貿易往來。各安生計。以仰

酬我

皇上懷柔外番。愛養黎元之至意。各宜懍遵。

# TZŬ ERH CHI.

## DOCUMENTARY SERIES.

### PART VII. HAN WÊN-CH'I

### PAPERS 65—75.

# 文件自遹集卷之七

第六十五件

審擬阜甯縣民吳超宗京控疏

奏爲遵

旨審明定擬具

奏事。竊前准步軍統領衙門咨。據阜甯縣民吳超宗。呈控左亦衢左芹。父子隱匿高地錢糧縣書裴瓚等。侵吞賑濟。等情一案。奏奉

諭旨。此案著交孫玉庭魏元煜。親提人證卷宗。秉公研審。定擬具奏。原告吳超宗。該部照例解往備質。欽此。遵卽飭行江甯藩司。委提人卷。訊錄供詞。詳解親勘。隨據查覈卷宗。吳超宗。屢次赴京控

告。總以左亦衢。將高地揑報低窪。冒減糧地爲詞。牽及書差。串呑賑銀。節經前督撫臣、審明治罪。發配及徒滿釋回復控。審擬枷杖。玆又砌控前情。查得被告左亦衢已故。非委員押同吳超宗左芹。再詣該地確切勘明。定其應否陞復賦額。不足以折服其心。先委淮安通判。詣勘情形。未得切實。復委江甯府北浦通判羅心源、會同該縣王錫蒲。勘明吳超宗。所控左芹減地。在昔實係低窪應減、近因築堰加培。堪可種植陞賦。並查明所借籽種口糧。實經發領。各有借領在卷。並無書差串呑不法情事。繪具圖結稟覆。並據藩司張志緒、督同加道銜江甯府知府余霈

元等。審解前來。隨同衆案情。卽由臣孫玉庭。就
近親提研鞫。如所控卑甯窪地。奏准減免糧額。
高地仍舊交糧。左亦衢賄通經書鞠履台。揑報
窪地二十九頃。將糧減去。屢控委勘。仍令完糧。
左亦衢已故。其子左芹。仍揑報窪地。總不完糧
一節。覆覈原案審明。卑邑低窪。積水無收之區。
於嘉慶二年奉文查辦減則。吳超宗左亦衢。各
自赴縣呈報。委員勘明。左亦衢地內。准減二十
九頃九十二畝零。吳超宗地俱高阜。不准減則。
吳超宗因地未准減。心疑書差作弊。且聞左亦
衢將報減地五頃四十餘畝。賣與夏全管業。仍
載大糧字樣。不知立契在未奉准減部覆之前。

不能即註減則。而吳超宗誤執不服。以致旣結屢翻。及審慮擬徒。年滿釋回。復見左芹報減地內。布種有收。因而復控。茲委員勘明。左芹故父左亦衢。報減地畝。坐落該縣。夏梁河西岸。東南一帶。偪近河涯。實屬低窪。惟廸西較高。現種二麥。臨河築有長堰。訊據附近居民供稱。此堰實係左亦衢在日。挑築保護田疇。昔日地本低窪應減。今越二十餘載。節年加培。漸形淤阜。訊據左芹供稱。報減窪地。因築堰培護。始漸有收。今被吳超宗疊控不休。情願一律復賦。質之吳超宗亦稱。左亦衢地畝。在昔低窪應減。經左芹父子培護成熟。可以復賦。乃仍照舊減糧。是以控告。今蒙勘實。斷令陞復賦額。情已輸服。不敢再控。至詞內牽列委員勘訊勒結。及左芹賄賂司書。弊捏收管等詞。均無憑據可指。實屬懷疑誣告。又如所控嘉慶二十五年。籽種口糧。書吏並未散給災民。道光元年口糧。未給一半。籽種亦未散給。是冬加給一月。延至今春始放。每戶一二三口。每口關領一百五十五文。蠹書戴鶴年等。任意剋扣舞弊。或賣票。或詭名。現有李春臺一戶。給票九百十七張。蘇克明控案。係河里實戶二千零。書吏報縣四千七百零一節。控關書吏弊吞賑卹。尤應徹底查究。覆覈嘉慶二十五年。及道光元年。該縣因災。請借籽種口糧。均經詳明借領。貧戶田在十畝以下者。籽種口糧並借。二十畝以下。但借口糧。不給籽種。每戶以三口爲率。總以有無借領爲憑。不能憑空散放。元年冬賞口糧。經知縣賀雲舉。按照摺報銀價。每庫平一兩。易錢一千零三十文。每大口給銀一錢五分。合錢一百五十四文半。該縣捐足尾零散給。是呈內所指。每口關領一百五十五文。並未短扣。又元年春間計叅知縣周右。分別災田熟田。復請酌給籽種口糧。於五月內委員解銀到縣。維時成熟村莊。因二麥登場。諮詢鄉農。不願領借。將銀繳還司庫。並非書吏侵吞不給。今吳超宗或稱全未散給。或稱未給一半之處。必須指出憑據。方可徹底究追。隨先提吳超宗詰訊。卽據供明。伊此次京控。總因左芹減糧地畝。漸次成熟。尚未復賦。是以始終不甘。必求勘明辦理。至伊牽控縣書裴瓚等。侵吞籽種口糧不散。實因伊往裴橋里。連年涉訟。田已賣盡。家僅五人。伊父子常不在家。故節年籽種口糧。均未借領。所有本縣續請借項。因鄉農不願再領。仍將銀兩解還司庫。是以未散。伊未悉情由。誤疑書吏弊吞。牽連控及。至承領各戶。曾否全數領得。抑止領一半。只求弔驗縣中。各戶領狀自明。又所控蠹書戴鶴年等。任意舞弊。剋扣賣票詭名。係因鬪李春臺一戶。給九百十七張。蘇克明郎舒克明。在縣具控。條河里實戶二千。浮報四千七百零。是以如此砌告。希圖聳聽。今蒙諭知李春臺。已因京控另案。審出恃強勒索實情。從重究辦。蘇克明條河里。郎調和里。有上下兩圖。經委員帶同戶書戴聯芳等。查明。兩圖貧民。共四千五百九十一戶。並冊造報。蘇克明只知所注上圖。止有二千貧戶。誤控浮報。已經淮安府訊明詳覆。此是伊誤聽人言牽告。並非有心等語。覆核吳超宗。於道光元年六月。赴京翻控。揑報減糧案內。牽及縣書裴瓚等。侵吞口糧賑濟。先經前撫臣。魏元煜提蘇。委員審明。誤控屬實。擬以枷杖。並無籽種口糧未放。斷令全結之事質訊書差裴瓚、唐文杰、戴鶴年等僉供並無朦混使吞。且伊等被吳超宗控提在省。直至道光二年春間。始得回縣。元年冬間。所請口糧。其時尚在蘇省。並未承辦。何能使吞。只求詳察等供。並據被控之縣差楊元等。亦各供。並未差辦賑務。實被牽累。調發放過籽種口糧。各鄉里領狀。均發與詳報散放銀數相符。以上各情。反覆質詰。矢口不移。似無遁飾。查吳超宗因左芹承父遺業。減糧地畝。加培漸熟。屢控冒減。復以近年該縣被災。頻邀賑貸。該原告常因涉訟在外。未得借領籽種口糧。誤聽蘇克明浮報。貧戶傳言。牽連砌告。雖究非憑空誣指。實屬健訟為能。惟

現在委勘地畝。應行陞科復賦。情稍可原。應請
免其枷號。仍照不應重律。杖八十折責發落。李
春臺勒給賑票。已另案從重擬軍。蘇克明在本
省控告浮報戶口。訊由誤疑所致。其誤執妄控。
亦應擬以重杖發落。左芹訊非欺隱地畝錢糧。
應與本案訊無侵口之書吏裴瓚等。均免置議。
所有勘明復賦地畝、飭縣查明原額科則。造具
頃畝册結。專案詳請。照額徵解。至牽涉災民。與
戶書戴鶴年等。因查災毆鬧。現據竈戶劉爲封
赴京控告。該書等因災索費。經提督衙門奏、交
臣韓文綺。督同臬司審辦。業已飭提人卷。俟解
審究明另結。除備錄全案咨部外。合將會覈審

擬緣由。恭摺具
奏。伏乞
皇上聖鑒。勅部議覆施行。奉
硃批刑部議奏。

第六十六件

請將尋常遣軍流徒人犯由道審勘疏

奏爲淮徐海三府州屬。尋常遣軍流犯。及秋審人
犯。請歸巡道審勘。以恤罪囚。而省拖累。恭摺仰
祈
聖鑒事。竊查臬司衙門爲刑名總滙。一切命盜雜案，
應擬斬絞軍流。及命案擬徒人犯。向俱解司勘

轉。江蘇省幅幀遼闊。案件繁多。各府州屬。解省人犯。程途遠近不同。應行酌量變通。以期恤囚免累。據江蘇按察使林則徐詳稱。江北之淮安。徐州。海州。三府州所屬地方。與蘇州省城相距寫遠。有在一千數百里之外者。中間經過黃河揚子江。每當伏秋水勢盛漲。風汛靡常。難於涉渡。所有斬絞重囚。及關係人命。罪干軍流各犯。尤宜加意詳愼。自應解司提審。詳解巡撫衙門。分別覆勘。

題奏。其尋常遣軍流徒人犯。應行咨結之案。巡撫例不提審。如概行解司。則道里迢遙。江河險阻。恐致疏失耽延。且江北民風刁悍。復有訟棍爲之播唆。每遇人犯解省。倚恃對簿無人。畏罪狡翻。甚或挾讎扳累。勢不能不摘提要證。到案質審。而無辜良民。長途跋涉。廢時失業。苦累不可勝言。或遇應質人證。患病外出。及畏累潛逃。往往提解不前。因而詳咨展限。經年累月。案牘每致拖延。辦理徒滋煩擾。且該府州所屬。濱臨湖海。地屬疲瘠。類多食力貧民。遠道就質。一切舟車飯食。及到省旅費。無不仰藉有司支給。在有司不勝賠累。或至化大爲小。將就完結。而鄰證慮恐貽害。又必遇事調停。私和匿報。刁風日長。民困難蘇。殊非刑期無刑之道。查江西省之南贛甯三府州。廣東省之雷瓊高廉潮五府。皆因

離省較遠。奏奉
諭旨。將尋常案犯。罪止發遣軍流。及命案徒罪人犯。統由各該道。於覆審後。將犯發回。徑行詳轉。一面移咨臬司備案。免其解省在案。茲查淮徐海三府情形。與江西之南贛。廣東之雷潮等府州相仿。請將淮徐海三府州屬。尋常遣軍流徒等犯。援照成例。就近解赴該管巡道。提審詳辦。移明臬司備案。毋庸解省。或犯供翻異。亦卽就近由道提證質審。不致遂其狡延拖累之計。於清理庶獄。似爲便益。再查例載。距省窵遠之秋審人犯。均免其解省。責成巡道親鞫。造册移報院司彙覈。儻有鳴寃翻異者。將本犯解省覆審。等

語。各省俱經遵行。該三府州屬。秋審人犯。亦請
照例由各道勘辦。免其解省等情。詳請會
奏前來。臣等伏查江蘇省。各府州屬。一切命盜雜
案。應擬斬絞軍流。及命案擬徒人犯。向俱解由
臬司勘轉。分別
題咨。今據該臬司。以淮徐海三府州屬。地方離省
窵遠。江河險阻。請將尋常遣軍流徒。各項人犯。
援照江西南贛。廣東雷潮等府州之例。由道勘
轉。毋庸解省。如徐州一府。即歸徐州道。海州一
屬。歸淮海道。淮安一府。則按河工分管縣分。山
陽鹽城清河桃源。歸淮揚道。阜甯安東。歸淮海
道。將審勘之案。徑詳督撫衙門。分別覈辦。仍將

審轉緣由。移明臬司備案。毋庸解犯至省。以避江河之險。並免拖延之累。設或犯供翻異。亦卽由道提證質審。案獄更可速結。相應會摺具

奏請

旨。如蒙

俞允。所有各該道。審轉限期。及一切處分。請卽照臬司之例辦理。該三府州屬。秋審人犯。亦請由各該道審勘。詳移巡撫臬司會覈辦理。如有鳴冤翻異者。再行解省覆審。臣等仍隨時察覈。如該巡道審斷不公。亦卽據實劾叅。不敢稍有狥隱。是否有當。臣等謹合詞。恭摺具

奏。伏乞

皇上聖鑒訓示。

第六十七件

審擬安東縣監生宋康年京控疏

奏爲遵
旨審明定擬。恭摺仰祈
聖鑒事。竊照安東縣監生宋康年。赴京呈控。孟思鑑等。占管地畝。並原問官。熬訊強斷等情一案。經
都察院奏奉
諭旨。此案著交魏元煜。督同按察司誠端。親提人證卷宗。秉公嚴審。定擬具奏。原告宋康年。該部照例解往備質。欽此。欽遵。並准刑部咨開。此案前經朱

名魁。呈控宋康年。占地割草等情。咨交兩江總
督。審擬報部。茲宋康年復來京翻控。奏交嚴審。
所有該督咨稿。應行扣存。毋庸聚覆。各等因。移
咨到前撫臣魏元煜。行司飭提人卷解省。因此
案控爭地畝起釁。提訊兩造。供詞各執。非勘不
明。當經咨部展限。一面飭委候補知縣。楊桂。李
鴻鈞。押帶原被人等。往控爭處所。會同海州安
東二州縣。確勘繪圖稟覆。將人卷押解來省。復
因海州安東二州縣界址。尙未逐細丈明。劄飭
海州知州孫源潮。安東縣知縣杜禮。確勘詳報。
去後。前撫臣魏元煜。旋奉
命調任鉚事。臣抵任後。催據該州縣。將海州安東界

址。查勘明確。詳覆前來。隨卽查覈各卷。親提人
證。督同臬司林則徐。逐一研鞫。緣宋康年籍隸
安東。伊父宋克明。與族伯宋克敏。有祖遺八間
房地畝。坐落魚溝河。南岸爲安東所轄。其北岸
地屬海州。前於雍正二年。經淮安府勘定分界。
又孟思鑑。有祖業魚溝河北岸。長拐短拐地畝。
與葛姓管業之程圩毘連。向在海州鐵牛鎮完
糧。先經孟思鑑祖父。賣與趙姓三十六頃。尙自
留地十四頃零。乾隆三十六年間。孟思鑑之祖
孟悳從。買汪潤益卽汪雲安地契載四十頃。與
前留祖遺之地相連。將糧過立。孟泰康等四戶。
在湖坊鎮完納。又汪潤益南界。有孟又坡地九

頃零。亦在魚溝河之北。因地土瘠薄。孟又坡家。久已無人承管。孟惠從。因與伊地毘連。一並占管。嘉慶十三年間。孟思鑑將祖遺賣賸。長拐短拐餘地。並所買汪潤益地內。割出十二頃零。賣與葛漢三。又十二頃零。賣與湯維坤。又三頃六十畝。賣與李雲龍。各自過戶辦糧。十六年五月。孟思鑑。又將所占孟又坡地。九頃零。連已業餘地。共湊十頃零。賣與朱名魁。得價五百十九千四百十文。未經過戶。宋克敏先於十五年六月。藉有八間房地畝。欲圖侵占。赴安東縣控告孟思鑑等。占地未結。十六年六月。減壩漫溢。魚溝河淤成車路。海安界址不清。宋克明更欲藉此圖占。割去禾草。經朱名魁赴海州具控。十九年閏二月間。宋克明雇人至葛漢三地內搶割菜籽。佃戶劉宗玉。石萬林。攔阻。劉宗玉被宋克明放鎗。轟傷倒地。又被用刀砍傷。石萬林亦被刀砍倒地。當有昔存今故之黃立祥。聞喊趕護。放鎗轟傷宋克明佃戶齊艮。將鎗遺棄。宋克明拾鎗。並與葛漢三控驗。經海州孫源潮。會同前任安東縣封藩。親詣勘丈。葛漢三地畝。並無侵占。飭令照舊管業。朱名魁所買地畝。因查驗孟思鑑老契。四至不符。且價值過廉。斷令朱名魁將地劃出六頃。歸與安東。給宋克明管業。朱名魁不甘。赴都察院呈控。咨交督臣孫玉庭。委護理

淮海道袁培等審明。將地畝仍斷歸朱名魁執業。議擬詳咨。宋康年復牽砌熬訊強斷。偪結朦詳等詞。赴京翻控。經都察院

奏明。交審。臣督司。提集人證。訊悉前情。查宋康年管業。八間房地畝。係在魚溝河南岸。其控爭之地。係在河北。久經斷定。以魚溝河南北。爲安東海州分界。今宋康年等。執有安東縣糧串。止應管安東地畝。海州卽有界址不明之地。非宋康年等所當過問。乃伊父宋克明。藉圖侵占地畝。搶割葛漢三荣籽。復鳥鎗傷人。本應按例擬軍。現與涉訟肇釁之宋克敏。及鎗傷齊艮之黃立祥。俱已病故。應毋庸議。宋康年控詞失實。究由

伊父伯宋克明等。控爭圖占在先。惟於朱名魁
前控提審時。伊伯宋克敏並未到案。輒以問官
然審虛詞。赴京混控。殊屬不合。宋康年照申訴
不實律。杖一百折責發落。仍照原案斥革監生。
追照繳銷。朱名魁先曾赴京牽扯已結舊案呈
控。應照原擬不應重律。杖八十。係武生。杖不滿
百。照例收贖。孟思鑑賣給葛漢三等地畝。皆係
已產。應聽照舊管業。朱名魁所買孟思鑑之地。
係屬孟又坡家無人承管之產。本不應孟思鑑
出賣。應歸海州查丈。葛漢三南界除孟思鑑業
地四十二弓外。其餘釘界充公。召變。著令孟思
鑑將原得地價。照數交還朱名魁收領。以斷葛

藤至從前所得花息因地土本極瘠薄即有所
收亦零星無幾且在節奉
恩詔以前應請從寬免其著追孟思鑑將無主承管
之産混行價賣殊有不合姑念伊祖父流傳已
久事在歷次
赦前免其置議宋克敏訊因患病未經到案止遞親
供原問官並無煞審情事亦毋庸議被控詐錢
之清河縣差役陳亮飭縣緝獲另行究結烏鎗
案結銷毀再宋康年之父宋克明等因海安界
址混淆是以隔河圖占訟擾多年無干之人受
其拖累應請於定案後飭令海州安東二州縣
於八間房莊後清出魚溝河舊址豎立界碑河

以南歸於安東。河以北歸於海州。使兩州縣地界分明。永遠遵守。不惟田土無從控爭。並可杜命盜案件彼此推諉之弊。所有充公田畝。應飭海州丈清頃畝確數。詳明歸於海州書院。以充生童肄業膏火經費。除全案供招送部外。臣謹恭摺具奏。伏乞皇上聖鑒。勅部核覆施行。奉硃批刑部議奏。

第六十八件

快丁貧疲酌籌調劑疏

奏爲江甯等縣。快丁貧疲。追徵運造兩費。極形苦
累。酌籌調劑。以甦積困。仰祈
聖鑒事。竊查江淮興武二衛。十八幫額設漕船。九百
六十一隻。所隸各丁。有運快之分。快丁在前明。
爲食糧操軍。撥駕黃快船隻。專供貢舫之差。故
名爲快。因不諳水性。每丁出銀三錢。雇人代駕。
我
朝革除軍糧。仍徵丁銀。康熙雍正年間。爲運丁扳
擾訐訟。曾禁僉運。迨乾隆二十四年。因運丁疲
乏。句僉難於足額。經漕臣楊錫紱
奏准。運快各半分僉。待運丁缺。陸續掣補。繼以快
不諳運。到幫數年。卽累。復經督臣高晉

奏准。快丁不諳駕運者。仍委運伍代運。酌定每船
每年。追解貼費銀。一百三十兩。十年輪造。協貼
造費銀三百兩。按年應攤派三十兩。共徵銀一
百六十兩。准共銀當人差。有願自運者聽。嗣丁
力不齊。往往延欠。復定縣官追徵。完解期限。照
地丁錢糧例考覈。比至嘉慶五年。因丁情貧疲。
徵解不易。奏
旨查辦。復經督漕二臣會議。請於上江耗米變價。及
存公籌備息款內撥給快丁每船銀三十兩。只
追徵運費銀一百兩。造費如舊。共在例後僉換
之船。無款可撥。運造兩費。仍照原額徵解。並因
衙幫。每藉提快自運。移縣擾累。又經糧道詳定。

快不欠貼。不准提攪。此分僉徵費。委伍代運之
原委也。各快籍中。惟上元江甯江浦等三縣丁
多般少。上元縣額僉快船。三十三隻內。自運十
三船。未及輪僉一船。徵貼代運者十九船。江甯
縣額僉快船。二十七隻。按額均已僉足。內自運
者七船。徵貼代運者二十船。江浦縣額僉快船。
四十九隻。內自運十三船。未及僉換者八隻半。
徵貼代運者二十七隻半。因歷年徵費維艱。江
甯縣有前陞守許兆椿捐墾官洲。及救生局紳
士。捐買洲地。招租撥貼者。有快船自行集資繳
官。發典生息完費。以免催追。上元縣亦有官爲
節省公費。及快丁捐資生息。濟運之船。其無濟

貼之丁。竭資湊費。日益苦累。而江浦已僉快船、
向無籌貼。積欠尤多。經徵官每屆追徵限滿。顧
慮考成。於追比不足之數、不得不挪湊墊解。完
至五分以上。幸免目前降革處分。而代運之丁。
貼費不能全收。不免於賠累。故在衛請提快丁
自運之案、仍復不少。快丁情急無措。非輾轉躲
匿。即不免影射扳民。更有刁劣之丁。從中串擾。
吏胥貪緣爲奸。其弊百出。丁民積困。漕公掣肘。
已非一日。臣等屢思剔弊調劑。未得善全之策。
茲據江甯紳士伍光瑜等。赴臣孫玉庭衙門具
呈。以江邑快丁。類多貿易營生。或傭工力佃。非
如他屬州縣丁籍。有自置田產。或族衆自買之

業。歸船贍運。可以歷久勷辦。是以數十年奉僉
各丁。多因追呼運造貼費。積至破產傾家。甚有
賣男鬻女完費。以及流亡死徙者。且有實係民
籍。該快追比無措。或藉同姓。或指親故。不免妄
報自寬。更有姦猾吏胥。勾串報殷。每僉一丁。卽
纏訟無休。雖僉案未定。而株累已多。故一快僉
名。闔族驚惶。伊等皆屬民籍。現無干累。惟誼屬
桑梓。目擊心傷。急思補救。惟有代籌。每年應出
貼費。使漕公有濟。永免追呼。庶可保全快丁生
命。上元快丁。同隸省城。除已有幫貼外。尚有數
船。亦資調劑。一體議邺。則扳擾之累。方可永杜。
伊等公同募捐。及快丁自將瘠田變賣。共湊得

銀八千兩。發典生息。可得息銀九百六十兩。惟
統覈歲需。尚多不敷。懇乞暫借庫款二萬兩。湊
發生息。歲有積餘。十年之內。卽可將借款全歸。
在庫項並無虧耗。而窮丁悉資救濟。呈乞轉籲
恩施。又據江浦縣知縣。王頫詳稱。浦邑快丁。除自運
十三船外。共徵貼代運者。共船二十七隻半。每
逢僉追。按產派貼。田產逐漸典賣。殷變爲疲。疲
極徙亡。卽隻身傭趁之丁。亦無不在朋勷什貼
之中。差役畏比催輸。窮丁輾轉扳擾。身在快籍。
安息無時。撫察丁情。殊堪憐憫。屆當
奏銷緊迫。勢不能不籌款墊解。明知無可追比。而
漕運關要。亦不能不違心比責。從前尚有書差。

僉貧賣富之弊。今則不但無富可賣。抑且無貧可僉。據該邑行店職員馬德潾等公呈。各因念切桑梓親誼。情願抽捐釐頭濟郵。並據各衛正丁船頭。通力合作。公議捐銀二萬三千兩。請於本年八月內繳齊。又自運各丁。亦公議積貲一萬五千兩。均請發典生息。分別抵貼贍運。尚有未僉船八隻半。將來照案僉派。丁力更不易支。必須豫行籌款生息。以爲續僉公費。庶不至遺後累。擬將行商所捐釐頭。按年底完積欠運造二費。再請公款銀二萬兩。同各丁湊捐銀兩。分發典商。營運繳息。完解每年運造二費。俾窮丁積困頓甦。永免僉運派貼之累。其籌借公項。請以十年拔本歸款。於郵丁𠛬運。實資兩益等情。
當經臣等。察覈稟詳。各該縣快丁疲累。追貼維
艱。僉報扳擾。勢所難免。第請於紳民各丁捐本
之外。籌借庫款、湊發生息、有無可撥之項。是否
不至懸欠。批令藩司。會同糧道衙門詳查妥議
去後。茲據江甯布政司張志緒。會同江安督糧
道湯藩。查議詳請覈
奏前來。臣等伏查江甯等屬快丁。自並僉以來。歷
今六十餘年。在僉管之初。力尚可支。今則積累
成疲。其間多有蕩產傾家。逃亡遷徙。以致僉丁
追貼。掣肘難名。此項銀兩。又係代丁捐款辦運、
歲所必需。較之正項錢糧、遇災可蠲緩者。尤爲

緊要。凡有未完、例應計考列叅。經徵印官。勢不能不嚴加比追、窮丁計無所出。從此扳民入快。串同書役。表裏爲奸、設法詐擾。害民殆無虛日。該紳士等所稱。一快僉名。闔族驚惶、實非虛語。經徵之員。非不知此中情弊。無如貼費無完。例干嚴議。卽如前任江甯縣于會堂、於復叅限內。積欠快貼無完。一年三罹叅處。此其明證。似此官丁交累。若不設法補救。將來誤運累民。所關匪細。查江甯縣額僉快船。二十七隻內。除快丁自行捐本生息船三隻。運造有資。不計外。仍該船二十四隻。其間雖有自運船七隻。並無贍運之資。亦應照徵貼額數。籌項撥濟。共計歲需運造費銀。三千四百六十六兩六錢六分零。除有捐墾中屯營。及烈山營各官洲租息。連快丁胡友仁之妻。出慈塘招佃繳租。合計共有銀。一千八百兩。仍不敷銀。一千六百六十六兩有零。又上元縣極疲快船四隻。每年需籌給運造費銀。五百二十兩。共應再籌餘息銀。二千一百八十餘兩。方敷歲貼之需。據紳士等捐湊市平本銀。八千兩。折實庫平紋銀七千二百九十兩有奇。又請借庫項銀。二萬兩。共合銀。二萬七千二百九十一兩二錢。又江浦縣額僉快船。四十九隻內。有已僉自運船十三隻。據稱各丁。現在議捐銀。一萬五千兩。發商生息。永爲贍運之資。毋庸另議調劑。並各行商所捐釐銀。撥抵各快舊欠。
運造二費。俟完足停捐不計外。其已僉捐貼。並
現在查僉。及待僉各船三十六隻。歲需運造費
銀。五千一百六十兩。經該縣各快丁。認捐本銀
二萬三千兩。又請借庫項銀二萬兩。共銀四萬
三千兩。江甯縣籌款銀。二萬七千二百九十一
兩零。均請分發江甯揚州二府屬典商。按月一
分起息。分給各快。爲額徵歲貼之需。所借庫款。
各請扣至十年期滿。拔本歸還。卽將餘息捐款。
作本存典。永資生息。完解運造。經該司道。以現
奉部咨。條奏各直省。務當力節經費。不得例外
請支。不應爲之瀆請。惟該縣等官紳。所請係暫

時請借生息濟公。仍籌積項歸還原款。與例外
支銷。無可還本者不同。自可俯如所請。俾資劑
郵。所有該二縣各請借庫項銀二萬兩。查道庫
減存項下現有候撥銀五萬一千餘兩。堪以動
借。自發典生息之日起。先按年於典息項下。各
提還銀一千兩。俟積至十年期滿。計每歲連閏
餘息。又可存典作本。卽於原發本銀內。各掣回
銀一萬兩。連逐年提還之一千兩。共合銀四萬
兩。如數歸還原借庫款。並無虧短。其紳士及快
丁自捐本銀。同歷年積欠餘息。仍照案交典生
息。永爲該丁運造之費。如此辦理。毋須另爲比
追。丁民皆可相安。官無經徵之累。丁無缺運之

虞。而於庫款。又不至久懸。洵於漕務。大有裨益。
各快子子孫孫。永賴
皇仁無旣。至該二縣丁費。雖有息銀貼給。如遇編審
之年。仍應照例查造。以免脫漏。而別軍民。其以
典息代完貼費。仍按年由縣。照原僉丁名。應完
額數。造報戶部查考。其未經籌款以前。舊欠貼
費。分別由道。照數催提。完繳銷結。臣等察覈所
議。爲調劑窮丁。裨益漕運起見。非此不能濟公
紓困。合無仰懇
皇上天恩。俯准在於道庫減存項下。照數撥借。分發
典商。領運生息。以資救濟。如蒙
允准。另飭司道。議立章程。咨部備覈。並令扣滿年限。

提本歸還原借庫款。臣等往返劄商。意見相同。
謹合同漕運總督臣魏元煜。安徽撫臣陶澍。合
詞恭摺具
奏。伏乞
皇上聖鑒。訓示施行

第六十九件
低田被水情形疏
奏爲江蘇各府州屬低田被水。委員查辦情形。恭
摺仰祈
聖鑒事。竊照江蘇省。本年五月初旬。陰雨連綿。自十
一日起。至二十一二三四五等日。大雨如注。並

兼江河水漲。臣等接據江甯。蘇州。松江。常州。鎮江。揚州。太倉。各府州屬。先後稟報。高田均已栽插齊全。長發青葱。惟沿近江河低窪之區。積水二三尺。至六七尺不等。已蒔者禾棉根蒂腐爛。未蒔者趕緊車戽補種。驛路間段被淹。兼有圩堤衝破之處。又常鎮道稟報。江潮異漲。瓜州城外江岸。亦有漫塌處所。等情前來。臣等均卽批飭兩藩司。委員會同各該地方官。逐一親勘。諭令農佃人等。設法疏消積水。趕緊補種。務期一律普收。至瓜州江岸。業經河臣黎世序。委員會同常鎮道王賡言。督率廳營。互相防護。臣等亦嚴飭加意防守。務保無虞。並飭該州縣。將漫淹

驛路。及護田圩堤。分別趕修。如有極窪處所。實
在無法疏消。不能補種者。查明被水輕重情形
迅速彙詳具
奏。分別緩徵接濟。以期仰副
皇上軫念民瘼。不使一夫失所之至意。再淮徐二府
屬高阜田畝。間有缺雨之處。臣等亦已飭令該
管道府。確查詳辦。所有通省糧價。微有增減。不
致昂貴。民情均屬安貼。謹將江蘇各府州屬低
田被水情形。先行據實恭摺奏
聞。伏乞
皇上聖鑒。

第七十件

審擬泰州民彭德州京控疏

奏爲遵

旨審明定擬恭摺奏請

聖鑒事。竊照江蘇泰州民。彭德州以父寃不伸。具結

請檢等詞。赴京呈控。經都察院奏奉

諭旨。此案著交韓文綺親提人證卷宗。秉公嚴審。按

律定擬具奏。原告彭德州。該部照例解往備質。欽

此。並准兵部將原告遞解前來。臣遵卽飭提人

卷至省。逐一親加研鞫。緣彭德州。籍隷泰州。伊

父彭恆義在日。憑韋百萬石遐廣作中。佃種李

進柏田十三畝。並租住草屋一間。道光元年四

月初一日晚間。彭恆義因失雞一隻。疑走入李進柏家藏匿。在門首混罵。李進柏爭論。被彭恆義推跌。擦傷額顱。李進柏之子李廣生幫護。彭恆義拳毆其左眼胞。又用木棒毆傷其左肩甲。李廣生奪棒回毆彭恆義左肩甲。經趙文忠勸散。初二日早。李廣生因伊父李進柏年老。被推跌傷。臥牀不起。欲行控究。並囑韋百萬石遐廣。令彭恆義退佃出屋。彭恆義恐到官治罪。又慮退佃出屋後。難以度活。愁急莫釋。即於是日下午。從戶樞旁牆洞伸手出外。將門反鎖。在屋內自縊身死。經韋百萬等。從門縫窺見。掇門入內。解救無及。時彭德州同妻韋氏。駕船在外捕魚。

屍弟彭恆年。又不在家。經鄉保周正和等。報明泰州知州趙鉞。驗訊通詳。嗣彭恆年回歸。聞伊兄彭恆義。曾與李廣生爭毆。心疑毆斃。央母舅黃爾恭。轉倩孫惟鑾代作呈詞。赴揚州府並臬司衙門具控。委經江都縣知縣陳文述。會同該州趙鉞。訊明彭恆義。實以失雞叫罵。與李進柏等口角爭毆。慮恐控官退佃。情急自縊。將李廣生。彭恆年。分別問擬枷杖。詳結有案。三年正月間。彭德州與孫惟鑾會遇。述及伊父命案。業已審結。孫惟鑾稔知李廣生。同族李祥李恒等。家道豐裕。起意藉案訛詐。當令彭德州向李祥借用錢文。並稱如不應允。卽以京控拖累嚇制。彭

德州聽從。往懇李祥母舅黃春年轉借。黃春年
不允。彭德州向孫惟鑾回復。孫惟鑾遂捏彭恆
義被李祥等佃討租錢。喝令李恒等毆斃。串同
黃春年等。假裝自縊。賄囑鄉保周正和。仵作梁
魁。匿傷朦報。並書差私押佃結各情。寫就呈詞。
備帶盤費。領同彭德州進京。在都察院衙門呈
告。奉
諭旨交臣審辦。飭提人卷來省。據彭德州供出。孫惟
鑾藉端圖詐。作詞唆訟各情。飭拏孫惟鑾。潛逃
無獲。臣就現到人證。逐加質訊。供悉前情。嚴詰
實無喝毆致斃。裝縊匿傷情弊。臣以彭恆義縊
在屋內。何以門鎖在外。恐有別情。復向見證韋

百萬究問。據供草屋一間。門旁土牆有洞一箇。
緊靠戶樞側邊。可以伸手出外。想那日彭恆義
起意自縊。恐被人經見。伸手出外。將門反鎖。並
無別故。究詰不移。案無遁飾。查孫惟鑾。圖詐唆
訟。衆供確鑿。現在弋獲無期。自應先行擬結。查
例載驀越赴京。告重事不實。並全誣十人以上
者。發邊遠充軍。又教唆詞訟。如原告並未起意
誣告。係教唆之人起意主令者。以主唆之人爲
首。聽從控告之人爲從。各等語。此案彭德州之
父彭恆義。因失雞叫罵。將李進柏李廣生推毆
致傷。旋聞李廣生欲控退佃。情急自縊。業經訊
明詳結。乃孫惟鑾藉案圖詐。輒揑寫李祥等毆

斃裝縊。賄囑匿傷。等詞。羅織多人。領同彭德州誣控。實屬起意唆訟。將來拏獲到日。自應照主唆誣控爲首例擬軍。彭德州赴京誣控。係孫惟鑾主唆。應照爲從科斷。彭德州合依蓦越赴京。告重事不實。並全誣十人以上者。發邊遠充軍。爲從減一等。例杖一百。徒三年。到配折責充徒。黃爾恭既知彭恆義死由自縊。乃於伊甥彭恆年控府控司時。並不阻止。轉代慫孫惟鑾作詞。實屬不合。應照不應重律。杖八十。折責發落。李廣生傴迫彭恆義。致令自縊。業已照威傴人致死律擬杖發落。追給埋銀。例免重科。李祥訊未喝令。李恒等均未向毆。黃春年亦無串通裝縊

180

情事應與訊非朦報匿傷徧結私押之鄉保周
正和趙鼎仵作梁魁書役黃泰等及並未阻驗
之韋百萬均毋庸議餘屬無干概予省釋未到
人證並免提質彭恆義實係自縊毋庸開檢屍
棺飭屬領埋主唆之孫惟鑾罪應擬軍該犯查
係從九品職銜應先斥革嚴拏務獲另行究結
除供册送部外臣謹恭摺具
奏伏乞
皇上聖鑒訓示奉
硃批刑部議奏

## 第七十一件

審擬桃源縣民人孔毓慶京控疏

奏爲遵
旨審明定擬。恭摺仰祈
聖鑒事。竊照桃源縣寄居民人孔毓慶、赴京呈控。史
福新串謀。誆娶伊女。後令爲妾。淩偪自縊。等情
一案。經都察院奏奉
諭旨。此案著交韓文綺親提人證卷宗。秉公審訊定
擬具奏。原告孔毓慶。該部照例。解往備質。欽此。旋
准兵部將原告孔毓慶。遞解前來。遵即飭提人
卷至省。臣親提逐一研訊。緣孔毓慶、原籍山東
曲阜。寄居桃源縣。民人史福新。係史亶馨之子。

因伊叔史克家病故無嗣。經族議立。史福新一子雙繼。史亶馨先爲史福新聚妻張氏。生子夭亡。史克家之妻喬氏。復與聘妻鄒氏爲次房之媳。鄒氏素有心痛病症。時發時愈。嘉慶二十四年二月初九日。史福新探親外出。鄒氏因心痛發。叫苦難忍。私自服滷身死。史亶馨投同地保報縣。經鄒氏之父鄒汝苞。查無別故。具結禀縣免驗。本年三月喬氏欲爲史福新續娶。央陳陞高。袁蔚若。爲媒。求聘孔毓慶之女孔氏爲繼室。並將史福新。先經長房娶妻張氏情由實告。嗣陳陞高等。向孔毓慶說媒。因恐不允。止稱史福新前妻鄒氏病故。欲求伊女爲室。並未將史福新。先在長房娶有張氏實情轉述。孔毓慶應允。史福新於道光元年十二月。迎娶過門成婚。迨孔氏向伊父孔毓慶。將史福新有妻張氏現依長房緣由訴知。業已彼此相安。亦不置議。二年閏三月初二日。史福新之本生父史亶馨患病。令孔氏煎藥。孔氏失於照管。將藥煎乾。史福新向其斥責。惟時史亶馨病已沉重。是夜身故。孔氏愧悔交加。於初三日午間。乘間在房。投繯殞命。經史福新瞥見。解救無及。報縣驗訊。孔毓慶因陳陞高等說媒時。未將史福新先娶張氏之言道破。且因伊女死於非命。痛女情切。即以史福新串謀誆娶。後令爲妾。淩偪自縊。等情。先赴淮安府呈控未准。隨進京在都察院衙門控告。

奏奉

諭旨。交臣審辦。提集人證。訊悉前情。臣以所控鄒氏。死由服滷。孔氏又係縊斃。恐實有壓良爲賤。淩逼致死別故。嚴加究詰。據史福新堅供。鄉間俗例。一子雙祧。兩房各娶正妻。無分嫡庶。孔氏成婚以後。與張氏素相和睦。實因伊父病重時。孔氏將藥煎乾。被斥愧悔。乘隙自盡。前妻鄒氏實因心痛病發。輕生。均無淩逼情事。質之陳陞高等。供無異詞。查核各卷內屍親等俱經具有輸服甘結。復訊孔毓慶。亦自認圖准架詞不諱。其非淩逼致死。似無疑義。查獨子雙祧。前於嘉慶十八年。經禮部議定。通行各省。凡獨子承祧兩房。只應娶嫡妻一人。不得兩門均爲娶妻。有違定例。等因。此案史福新以一身兼祧兩房。既經本生父史亶馨爲娶張氏。則業已有嫡妻。乃嗣母喬氏。又娶孔氏、作爲次房之媳。雖鄉愚婦女無知。究屬違例。史喬氏應依有妻更娶妻者杖九十。律杖九十。媒人陳陞高。不將史福新先已有妻張氏。向孔傭慶言明。殊屬不合。應照不應重律杖八十。事在嘉慶二十五年八月二十七日。恭逢

大赦以前。各犯杖罪。均予援免。史喬氏並免收贖。其與陳陞高一同媒合之袁蔚若。於提省後。在寓

病故。驗明並無別情。應毋庸議。孔毓慶所控史福新。以妻爲妾。淩逼致死。因媒人陳陞高等。先未據實告知。且因痛女情切。尚非平空誣告。今到案卽行供明。被告史福新。又係緦麻卑幼。應予免議。史福新訊無淩妻致死情事。應與並未揑稟之地保韓金聲周玉。刑書徐文光。均毋庸議。無干省釋。案已訊明。未到人證。並免提質。以省拖累。再獨子雙祧。不得兩門均爲娶妻。恐鄉愚未諳例禁。應再出示曉諭。咸使週知。除供招送部外。臣謹恭摺具

奏。伏乞

皇上聖鑒訓示。奉

硃批刑部議奏。

第七十二件

審擬阜甯縣民蘇萬全京控疏

奏爲遵

旨秉公嚴審定擬。奏祈

聖鑒事。竊照阜甯縣民。蘇萬全。赴京呈控岳可維等。

殺害伊弟蘇萬有身死。賄買洪萬淋項兇一案。

經都察院奏奉

諭旨。此案着交韓文綺。親提人證卷宗。秉公研審。按

律定擬具奏。原告蘇萬全。該部照例解往備質。欽

此。並准兵部將原告蘇萬全遞解到蘇。遵即飭

提人卷至省。臣查此案控鬬謀命頂兇罪名出
入綦重。訊辦倍宜詳慎。隨率同署臬司王賡言。
蘇州府知府額騰伊等。臣親督提集犯證。逐一
隔別研審。緣洪萬淋。籍隸安東。蘇萬全。梁萬和。
均籍隸阜甯。梁萬和。同弟梁萬興。梁萬昌。向在
阜境黃河南岸。合開魚行。蘇萬全另在北灘。王
姓魚行幫夥。彼此素有訟嫌。道光元年七月十
八日。梁萬和弟兄三人。雇船至黃河北灘。收買
魚鰾。將錢先給漁戶陸珍侯定買。嗣嫌魚鰾潮
溼。欲令還錢爭鬧。經陳大學勸將魚鰾十一觔。
折作十觔。合錢完事。陸珍侯受虧不甘。向蘇萬
全告知。蘇萬全因與梁萬和弟兄。本有讐隙。並

風聞梁家欲在北灘開張魚行。爭奪生意。更抱
不平。許爲陸珍侯出氣。二十二日蘇萬全糾同
陸珍侯並馬芳等。坐船前往梁萬和等船邊。當
卽過船。梁萬昌攔阻。蘇萬全用刀劃傷其右臂
膊。右胳膊。又同將梁萬和等弟兄用繩綑縛在
船。惟時蘇萬有未經同往。比有賈正宏勸解。蘇
萬全告以梁萬和等平日多收漁戶行用錢文。
欲令立票還錢。並另寫永不許至北灘收取用
錢筆據。梁萬和等無奈應允。蘇萬全將梁萬和
船內魚鰾錢文。約共作錢十五千。因數不敷。勸
寫錢票。又不信梁家弟兄。經賈正宏出名。代寫
一百三十五千之票。始將梁萬和兄弟釋放。蘇

萬全將票分給漁戶而散。梁萬和等畏兇。不敢
指告。旋據梁萬昌將賈正宏控縣。揑稱被刼。冀
俟賈正宏到官。供出蘇萬全等。差拏究辦。經代
理縣姚廷臣驗傷。會勘提訊勒緝。九月十一日。
蘇萬全之兄蘇萬百。弟蘇萬有。同在堂母舅沈
成璧家。修理農具。蘇萬全並未同往。梁萬和詭
聞。蘇萬全弟兄一同在彼。起意捉拏送官。即糾
允洪萬淋。並屠正祖。秦鳴鳳。及已故之周履泰。
一共五人。分拏刀鎗鞭棍往捉。其時賈正宏。因
錢票係伊出名代寫。趕往該處。欲爲說和。梁萬
和不允。並令同行。十二日偕抵沈成璧家。一齊
進內。屠正祖與周履泰。將草屋北間隔扇撥落。

蘇萬百走出。周殿泰用鎗戳其右膝。受傷躲避。
洪萬淋見草屋南間笆門關閉。心疑有人躲在
裏面。用刀向笆門戳進。因刀長勢猛。深透入門。
卽聞哼聲。洪萬淋拔刀見有血汙。當與梁萬和
等逃散。緣蘇萬有在內聞嚷窺探。甫至笆門邊
斜立。猝値刀戳傷。由右肋橫透左肋。卽時身死。
蘇萬百報縣驗緝。旋據縣差訪獲洪萬淋訊認。
將蘇萬有用刀戳死。迨經覆訊。洪萬淋畏罪圖
翻。因岳可維曾談論伊等行兇生事。卽揑供梁
萬和先向岳可維商議。岳可維主令同去捉拏。
復因屠正祖在逃。推賴屠正祖之子屠殿元戳
死。屠正祖囑其權認正兇等語。該前縣賀雲舉。

詳經飭委山陽縣會訊。一面差拏屠正祖等未到。二年二月二十六日。蘇萬全探知屠正祖屠殿元父子。在龔家集躲避。糾同馬芳等前往捉拏。適屠正祖父子。與獵戶汪六在彼閒談。見而幫助。卽將打獵鳥鎗點放。轟傷馬芳左胳膊左手指。汪六當時逃逸。屠正祖。屠殿元。被蘇萬全等。及在該處放賑委員孫逢瑞。連鎗獲解。該縣提訊。屠殿元先不承認。及被洪萬淋堅質。年輕畏刑。含糊招服。迨經會訊。屠殿元極口呼冤。洪萬淋亦卽據實供明。蘇萬有委係該犯隔笆戳傷致斃不諱。蘇萬全因洪萬淋。曾供岳可維主令糾毆。屠殿元亦供認行兇。疑有賄買頂兇情獘赴。臣衙門呈控。批司飭審。因犯供支離閃爍。
尙未成招。蘇萬全赴都察院呈控。奏奉
諭旨交。臣審辦。屢提人證。督同司府。訊悉前情。臣恐
洪萬淋。實係受賄頂凶。疊加研詰。堅供如前。復
訊屠殿元供稱。先因被洪萬淋堅質。且恐受刑。
隨口混認。其實當時並未同至洸成壁家。衆目
共覩。質之在場要證。各供僉同。蘇萬全亦自認
懷疑妄控。矢口不移。似無遁飾。查洪萬淋。聽從
梁萬和。往捉蘇萬全等未見。輒疑笆門內有人
藏躲。用刀猛戳。致在內之蘇萬有被傷身死。核
與同謀共毆有間。而蘇萬全毆綑梁萬和等。並
取其船上錢物。蘇萬有未經同往。亦非有罪之

人。今洪萬淋將其傷斃。自應仍以鬬殺科斷。洪萬淋合依鬬毆殺人者。不問手足他物金刃並絞律。擬絞監候。秋後處決。據供親老丁單。是否屬實。應俟秋審時。照例查辦。梁萬和因伊弟兄被蘇萬全綑毆勒票。並不據實告官。輒糾衆持械捉拏。以致洪萬淋將蘇萬有戳死。實屬肇衅釀命。梁萬和應革去監生。比依原謀杖流律。杖一百。流三千里。屠正祖秦鳴鳳聽從持械同行。並未下手。應比照餘人律。各杖一百。屠正祖所供。馬芳鎗傷係獵戶汪六點放。汪六現係在逃。恐狡供避就。應將屠正祖監禁。勒拘汪六到案。質明辦理。蘇萬全京控岳可維主謀。並屠正祖賄買頂兇各情皆。由洪萬淋供扳在先。照供牽控。尚非平空誣陷。惟糾衆將梁萬和等綑毆勒寫票據。並將梁萬昌砍傷。情同擾害。姑念該犯之弟。已死非命。不無一線可原。蘇萬全應於兇惡棍徒。生事擾害擬軍例上。量減一等。杖一百。徒三年。梁萬和。蘇萬全。均發配折責安置。賈正宏先曾出名立票。繼復被邀同往。應與在場並不理阻之陸珍俟。均照不應重律。杖八十。岳可維訊未主謀。惟談論行兇案情。致洪萬淋妄供牽訟。亦屬多事。應照不應輕律。笞四十。賈正宏係監生。照例納贖。陸珍俟等分別折責發落。梁萬和捐監實收。追出繳銷。梁萬昌原報被刼。措詞失實。亦屬非是。第事出有因。且畏懼蘇萬全。不敢指告。情尙可原。應與訊未同行之屠殿元。均與免議。差役于相等。究無賄囑情弊。應毋庸議。票據塗銷。蘇萬全京詞牽敘岳可維。包誣訟搶之案。久已訊結。無庸再議。其蘇萬全牛車踐踏梁萬和麥地爭控。及梁萬和糾搶陳高氏未結等案。現在人證未齊。應發回該縣就近訊明詳結。以免提省拖累。兇器刀鎗等件。隨招解驗。案結飭銷。魚鰾錢文。已經分散各漁戶。且爲數無多。免其追繳。除將供册咨部外。所有審明定擬緣由。理合恭摺具

奏。奉

硃批刑部議奏

第七十三件

審擬誤傷出母人犯疏

奏為審明殺死姦占出母之姦夫。誤傷出母致斃之犯。按律定擬。恭摺仰祈
聖訓事。竊據上元縣知縣陳道坦。詳報民人張世昌。殺死姦占出母之張磻文。並誤傷出母應氏身死之案。臣因案情重大。批飭將犯解省。飭委蘇州府知府額騰伊。候補通判劉文澈。嚴審究辦去後。茲據該委員等審明定擬。由臬司林則徐覆審。招解前來。臣親提犯證。悉心研鞫。緣張世

昌籍隸上元。已死應氏。係該犯親母。張馨文係無服族姪。張馨文平素兇橫。不務正業。嘉慶十三年間。張馨文與應氏通姦。時該犯張世昌。年甫四歲。伊父張餘祥控縣提訊。因張餘祥帶子張世昌旋赴安徽亳州生理。張馨文輒冒稱王姓。出名騙買應氏。公然姦占在該縣陶家邊地方租房居住。迨張世昌長大。張餘祥告知伊母因姦嫁賣情由。道光三年十二月。張世昌回家祭掃。聽聞張馨文冒娶姦占。向伊叔張開淋查問。並親至張馨文家。與伊母應氏見面後。在祖祠復聞族衆談及張馨文兇惡異常。姦占伊母。因伊父張餘祥懦弱。屢被欺侮之言。張世昌羞

忿交集。旋回亳州。向張餘祥告述。張餘祥因此
忿激成病。臥床不起。張世昌目覩心傷。益加懷
恨。起意殺死張馨文報讎。即向父捏稱回家掃
墓。在不識姓名攤上買得腰刀一把。藏帶身邊。
由亳州起身。本年四月十六日晚。始抵陶家遊
地方。恐人撞見。潛躲張馨文屋後草堆過夜。次
早張馨文姦生之子張又幅。開門走出。張世昌
即拔刀闖進臥房。張馨文瞥見。赤身下床。張世
昌上前用刀砍傷其左腮頰。並劃斷門額顱。應
氏驚醒。下床喊救。時値張馨文上前奪刀。張世
昌恐被奪獲。又用刀向戳。不料張馨文側身閃
避。適應氏趕攏攔護。張世昌一時收手不及。致

200

誤戳伊母應氏左乳。並帶傷左腕倒地。張馨文喊叫欲逃。張世昌又用刀砍傷張馨文左肐膊。並連戳傷其右肋。張馨文應氏旋各因傷身死。經張又幅聞聲轉回。喊知隣人。趕往看明。張世昌先已攜刀跑出。赴縣投首。經上元縣驗訊通詳。行提犯證至省。委審供悉前情。臣恐張世昌因伊母與張馨文通姦。或竟設意一並殺死。復加嚴詰。據供實止起意將張馨文殺死報讎。不意張馨文閃避。伊母趕攏攔護。收手不及。倉猝誤傷適斃。委非逞兇干犯。伊父張餘祥。實不知情。等語。再三究詰。矢口不移。查律載子毆父母殺者。淩遲處死。又查嘉慶十八年三月。刑部議覆山西省白鵬鶴。誤傷伊母白王氏身死一案。

奉

旨。此案。白鵬鶴。因向伊嫂白葛氏。借取燈油不給。出街嚷罵。白葛氏趕出門首理論。白鵬鶴拾取土坯。向白葛氏擲毆。不期伊母白王氏出勸。以致誤傷殞命。刑部引子毆父母殺者。淩遲處死律。又引鬬毆誤殺旁人。以鬬殺論律。比擬問以淩遲處死。核其情節。白鵬鶴遙擲土坯。誤殺其母。非其思慮所及。與鬬毆誤殺者。究屬有間。白鵬鶴着改爲斬立決。嗣後有案情似此者。卽照此問擬。餘依議。欽此。

欽遵在案。此案張世昌起意將姦占出母之張謦文。殺死洩忿。殺姦既在姦所登時。罪不應抵。

惟並將出母誤傷斃命。應氏雖自絕於夫。該犯係其所生之子。究無義絕之理。仍應照律定擬。惟該犯因母被姦占。伊父復忿激成病。目擊心傷。意在復讎。不虞將母誤傷適斃。實非有心逞兇干犯。揆其情節。似較白鵬鶴之案。尤爲可憫。張世昌除姦所獲姦。登時殺死姦占伊母之姦夫。輕罪不議外。合依子毆父母殺者。淩遲處死。律淩遲處死。仍援照白鵬鶴成案。聲明。可否

恩予酌情量減之處。恭候

欽定。照例先行刺字。犯父張餘祥。訊不知情。應毋庸議。兇刀發回貯庫。張馨文揑姓冒買姦婦爲妻。有無媒證知情騙買。姦夫姦婦已死。無從根究。

請免置議。屍棺飭縣。給領埋瘞。無干省釋。除將
全案供招咨部外。所有審明定擬緣由。理合恭
摺具
奏。伏乞
皇上聖鑒訓示。奉
硃批刑部妥速議奏。

第七十四件

拏獲會匪首要各犯疏
奏爲會匪案內首要各犯。均已就獲。遵
旨嚴訊。按律定擬。恭摺仰祈
聖鑒事。竊臣前與藩臬兩司。風聞贛州道府。訪獲會

匪。未據禀報。派員前往會督查拏。旋據禀獲要
犯。黄百幅等。並起獲木印等件。因贛郡距省較
遠。犯證衆多。飭令臬司輿科。前往查辦。
奏奉
上諭。務將在逃夥黨。購線密拏。並嚴訊該犯等木印。
作何行用。黄百幅因何有安遠公名號。是否係該
犯自稱。抑有首犯給與。其餘夥黨。有無稱號。及聚
衆滋事等情。務令水落石出。查拏淨盡。早絕根株。
毋許一名漏網。等因。欽此。遵卽恭錄轉行。欽遵辦
理。並先准督臣蔣攸銛。訪聞咨會。飭拏。續據禀
獲。張貴等先後共獲犯八十二名。於各犯家內
逐一搜查。並無違悖字跡。惟於張貴家牆穴內。

起出張貴守備職銜。劄付一張。首列安遠公。前威勝將軍黃。中營副總府鍾僞銜。劄尾有周四年字樣。經臬司會督該道府等。提犯研訊。究出安遠公。卽係黃百幅。將軍係黃沅瀧。副總府係鍾心瀧。均係自稱名號。並無另有首犯給與。因該犯等已故之師毛元奇。有師祖流傳符書一本。交黃百幅收存。內載劄付式樣。有招集人才等句。並周四年等字。註明順天天運年號。屢經查禁。改用周字。取天運周流之意。不知四年係在何時。亦不知毛元奇師祖。係何姓名。黃百幅起意。與黃沅瀧。鍾心瀧。商允雇黃明佳。照刊劄付。刷印塡給。張貴守備職銜一張。因奉訪拏。卽將刊板並符書本等件燒燬。至長方木戳一顆。刻萬大哥行令五字。三角木戳一顆。刻同心協力四字。均在花帖上蓋用。嚴究並無聚衆滋事別情。該臬司於取供後回省。並將緊要各犯。分起解省。飭委署南昌府經額布等。先提黃百幅。令將劄付照寫。與所填筆跡相符。及試以文義。未能講解。訊供解審前來。臣查各木戳及花帖所載。均核與歷辦會匪各案相同。惟填用劄付。恐該犯等另有不法重情。必須澈底跟究。盡絕根株。隨提各犯。督同藩司繼昌。臬司興科。逐一隔別研鞫。緣黃百幅籍隸信豐縣。係在安遠地方生育。小名安遠仔。測字度日。先於道光二年九月。與同縣已獲之黄沅瀧。鍾心瀧。張北斗。及在逃之黄二狗。於南康地方會遇素識已故之上猶縣人毛元奇。告知係添弟會。即三點會內人。誘令拜師入會。可免外人欺侮。如肯多給錢文。領受花帖。即可自行傳徒。黄百幅等允從。初九日毛元奇買備香燭。設立從前傳會之萬提喜。即洪二和尚牌位。用布搭橋。令黄百幅等鑽過。毛元奇口念。有忠有義橋下過。無忠無義劍下亡。俚語。宰鷄取血。滴酒同飲。傳授開口不離本。出手不離三。並三八二十一。暗藏洪字口訣。黄百幅。鍾心瀧。各送給錢八百文。均給有花帖。餘因錢少未給花帖。旋因毛元奇。另傳徒弟王貞才犯案緝拏。毛元奇當將傳徒長方三角木戳二顆。同符書一本。交黃百幅收存。黃百幅曾向毛元奇問知。係伊師祖流傳。當同花帖等件密藏。與毛元奇等各自逃避。嗣於七年五月事冷潛回。黃百幅貧苦難度。起意傳徒。五月十三日。在信豐地方。誘令黃翔罄等十八人入會。拜伊爲師。仍照前式。鑽橋飲酒。傳授口訣。黃翔罄。黃觀受。及在逃之黃書汶。黃二生。四人領受花帖。黃纍組保。葉二罄孜。黃泰傑。黃閏狗。黃喭孜。黃冠陰孜。葉艮鼁。黃創成。黃閏妹。黃泰貴。及在逃之陳狗孜。鍾觀瀧。黃炳孜。十三人。均未領受花帖。黃罄受。僅傳口訣。各給錢二三百至八九百文不等鍾心瀧。亦於五月十三日。在信豐地方誘張貴等七人。入會拜伊爲師。張貴領受花帖。胡光孜、鍾堤孜。廖石幅。曾華幗。黃言洪。及在逃之鄧細孜。均鑽橋傳訣。未曾飲酒。亦未領受花帖。張貴旋於五月二十日。在信豐地方。轉誘黃地辛保。盧五仔。羅丙瀧。入會。鑽橋飲酒。拜伊爲師。黃地辛保。領受花帖。餘因錢少。未給花帖。六月內黃百幅因傳徒無多。會內花帖習見難以哄誘。憶及毛元奇。交存符書本內。戳有札付式樣。可以惑衆。起意照刋。塡給假官名號。多騙錢文。與黃沅瀧。鍾心瀧。商允。三人合夥。騙錢均分。黃百幅小名安遠仔。卽稱爲安遠公。黃沅瀧小名威勝。總理會事。稱爲威勝將軍。鍾心瀧副理會事。稱爲中營副總府。黃百幅。當照符書本所載札付錄出。塡寫僞銜。屢不諳文義之黃明佳來家刻板。並刋僞銜戳記。蓋於札尾。當經鍾心瀧向張貴告知。引誘買札。張貴給錢三千五百文。塡給守備職銜札付一張。黃纍組保。亦欲向買。因措錢不出。尙未塡給。卽經文武各官訪拏。黃百幅畏懼。將刋板戳記。符書本等件。概行燒燬。花帖木戳。先藏鍾心瀧家。張貴札付。藏於牆穴。均不及燬丟。各自逃匿。此黃百幅等。始則結會傳徒。繼復刋刷札付。妄稱名號。冀圖騙錢之實在情形也。又籍隸信豐縣之陳土養。與原籍安遠縣寄居定南廳之郭文瀾。並信豐縣人葉沅胡。劉泰霄。定南廳人練賤妹。及在逃之張書太。與黄百幅等。並非同夥。均於道光六年七月十九日。在定南廳地方。拜三點會內已故之溫塊老爲師。鑽橋飲酒。傳授口訣。陳土養。郭文瀾。各給錢八百文。均受花帖。餘未領帖。陳土養旋於七年六月十八日。在龍南與信豐交界之龍口地方。轉誘郭中魁等三十三人入會。拜伊爲師。郭中魁。劉瀧標。張維城。及在逃之曹三珠。郭洪吉。郭汶沛。六人。均得花帖。邱亨翔。劉猴孜。二人鑽橋飲酒。劉紹旦。劉年狗孜。賴老滿。劉汶學。張奇芳。劉斗孜。劉新牯孜。季保魁。李見德。劉

炳瀧。謝貴米仔。郭經銘。李癸瀧孜。劉東升。及在
逃之呂成仔。十五人俱各鑽橋。並未飲酒。領帖。
謝乙受孜。黃二孜。王以廷。劉巳受孜。黃普翔保。
鍾土燌生。黃冠陰保。黃辛年保。張朝陽。謝學誠。
十人。僅傳口訣。各給錢二三百至八九百文不
等。郭文瀾亦於七年六月十三日。在信豐地方。
誘令郭汶奇等二十六人入會。拜伊爲師。郭汶
奇。郭經理。郭崇輝。陳老七。朱茂貴。及在逃之黃
明勝。胡義賢七人。鑽橋飲酒。傳授口訣。練長閏。
郭汶江。郭物貴。郭言瀧。王重懷。練千長。袁萬太。
袁幗盛。曾半邊蘇。劉西佐。及在逃之余登仕。余
節軒。戴井仔。十三人。鑽橋傳訣。並未飲酒。郭沅

吉。顧崇秀。余已受孜。許長受孜。余四十一。練滿瀧。六人。止傳口訣。均未領有花帖。各給錢二三百至八九百文不等。此陳土養。郭文瀾。各自結會傳徒之原委也。旋經地方文武各官。派委員弁兵役。並曉諭紳士。探引緝拏。將首要各犯。先後獲解。審悉前情。臣復提黃百幅。再三嚴詰。堅供實止圖騙多錢。照流傳符書本內。所載札付式樣。刊刷塡給職銜。妄自稱爲安遠公等名號。如果另有首犯給與。豈有不於札內列入。至札付實止塡給張貴一紙。正在誆騙。卽被訪拏。委無聚衆。謀爲不法別情。加以刑嚇。矢曰不移。檢查該道府稟報。黃百幅與黃沅瀧等。係先後獲案各供如一。並據傳訊各該犯族隣人等僉供，並無悖逆情事，似無遁飾。查律載謀叛已行，但共謀者，不分首從皆斬。知已行而不首者，杖一百，流三千里。又律載左道異端，煽惑人民爲首者，絞監候。又例載傳習白陽等邪教，習念荒誕不經咒語，拜師傳徒惑衆者，爲首擬絞立決。爲從發回城給大小伯克，及力能管束之回子爲奴各等語。此案黃百幅本係傳徒會匪，膽敢自稱爲公，刋刷札付，填給張貴守備職銜，實屬不法。雖札付底稿年號得自流傳，該犯僅圖騙錢，並無謀爲不軌情事，但既妄稱名號，填用札付，形同謀叛，自應比例問擬。訊係黃百幅起意，黃百幅應比照謀。叛已行斬律。擬斬立決。仍梟首傳示犯事地方。以昭炯戒。黄沅瀧。鍾心瀧。妄稱將軍副總府。於札付內。聽從列名。郎屬爲首。黄沅瀧。鍾心瀧。均請比照謀叛已行。不分首從皆斬律。擬斬立決。俱已監斃。應毋庸議。案係比照問擬。照例免其緣坐。張貴得受札付。先未預謀、由於鍾心瀧引誘所致。與實在爲從有間。其傳徒已給花帖。應與各自給帖傳徒之陳士養。各照傳習白陽等邪教。習念荒誕不經咒語。拜師傳徒惑衆者。爲首絞決例。均擬絞立決。郭文瀾傳徒。未給花帖。應照左道異端。煽惑人民爲首律。擬絞監候。陳士養。郭文瀾。均已監斃。應毋庸

議。張北斗。葉沅胡劉泰霄。練賤妹。黃翔罄。黃觀
受。黃鼎組保。葉二罄孜。黃泰傑。黃閏狗。黃嵺孜。
黃冠陰孜。葉艮竈。黃創成。黃閏妹。黃泰貴。黃地
辛保。盧五仔。羅丙瀧。郭中魁。劉瀧標。張維城。邱
亨翔。劉猴子。郭汶奇。郭經理。郭崇輝。陳老七。朱
茂貴。二十九名。均係鑽橋飲酒。或領有花帖。尙
未傳徒。均照邪教爲從。例發回城給大小伯克。
及力能管束之回子爲奴。練賤妹。黃觀受。黃閏
妹。黃泰貴。黃地辛保。張維城。邱亨翔。郭汶奇。已
在監在途病故。應毋庸議。黃明佳。因不諳文義。
誤爲刋刻札付。應比照謀叛知情不首律。杖一
百。流三千里。胡光孜。鍾提孜。廖石幅。曾華幗。黃

言洪。劉紹旦。劉年狗孜。賴老滿。劉汶學。張奇芳。
劉斗孜。劉新牯孜。季保魁。李見德。劉炳瀧。謝貫
米孜。郭經銘。李癸瀧孜。劉東升。練長閏。郭汶江。
郭物貴。郭言瀧。王重懷。練千長。袁萬太。袁幗盛。
曾半遜蘇。劉西佐二十九名。均僅止鑽橋傳訣。
未飲血酒。亦未領帖。若照邪教爲從罪上減一
等擬徒。與僅受口訣者。漫無區別。應與徒罪上
加一等。各擬杖一百。流二千里。黃明佳。黃言洪。
練長閏。郭汶江。郭物貴。郭言瀧。王重懷。練千長。
已在監在途病斃。應毋庸議。黃簪受。謝乙受孜。
黃二孜。王以廷。劉已受孜。黃晋翔保。鍾土熿生。
黃冠陰保。黃辛年保。張朝陽。謝學誠。郭沅吉。顧

崇秀。余已受孜。許長受孜。余四十一。練滿瀧。十七名。均止傳授口訣。且係逼脅入會。情節較輕。應各擬杖一百。徒三年。謝學誠。練滿瀧。業已提禁身故。應毋庸議。餘各到配折責。分別安置。札付底稿。傳自何人。無從追究。起獲木戳花帖札付。案結銷燬。毛元奇溫塊老。傳徒給帖。均罪應絞決。查明均已身故。應毋庸議。逸犯黃二狗等。飭緝務獲另結。除將全案供招咨部外。謹會同大學士兩江總督臣蔣攸銛。合詞恭摺具

奏。伏乞

皇上聖鑒。勅部核覆施行。奉

硃批另有旨。

附片

再定例姦民倡設邪教。惑衆斂錢。該管各官。如能訪出迅速查辦。功過相抵。免其從前失察處分。等因。今會匪黃百幅等一案。該地方文武均有失察處分。惟於臣等未經訪聞之先。業經獲犯多名。後又懸立重賞。分派督拏。將案內首要各犯。全行弋獲。尚知愧奮。功過似足相抵。可否

仰懇

聖恩。俯准將歷任文武各官應得處分。一並寬免之處。出自

逾格鴻施。又臣派委南昌府同知候補知府陳煦。同知銜。臨江府通判徐瀓。南昌城守營守備李步

月。前往查辦。該員等會督地方文武。不辭勞瘁。
不動聲色。於一月之內。續獲匪犯六十餘名。辦
理尚爲妥速。查陳煦係候補知府。徐瀓係同知
銜。通判。職分較大。不敢仰邀議敘。守備李步月。
本係應陞之員。亦無庸再予鼓勵。此外尚有隨
同查辦之文武員弁。及探引緝拏之地方紳士。
現已行令兩司。確加查核。將員弁分別超委記
功。紳士給匾示獎。合並附片
奏
聞。奉
硃批另有旨。內閣奉
上諭。韓文綺奏。審擬會匪案內首要各犯一摺。着刑

部速議具奏。此案黃沅瀧鍾心瀧。均罪應斬決。此等要犯。自應明正刑誅。因何俱令其監斃。是否該犯等畏罪自盡。抑係地方官諱避處分。縱令禁役人等淩虐致斃。此時姑免其深究。嗣後各直省督撫。遇有此等要犯。務須飭屬。嚴行羈禁。小心防守。毋得鬆放刑具。致有疎虞。重干咎戾。將此通諭知之。又另片奏。此案失察各員。例有處分。惟現將首要各犯全獲。功過尙足相抵。着加恩將歷任文武各官。應得處分。一並寬免。餘着照所奏辦理。

第七十五件

審明毒斃母命照例定擬疏

奏爲被逼取砒。致母服毒斃命。審明照例定擬。恭

摺具

奏。仰祈

聖鑒事。竊照南城縣民。饒錦盛。以伊母劉氏。被族人

饒錦玉。毆傷額顱等處身死。報經該縣張玕驗

明。劉氏額顱左眼胞。各有磕傷。牙根青色。口開

用銀針探入。取出青黑色。兩手心等處。均青色。

係受傷後服毒身死。核與報呈不符。拘集人證。

究出劉氏。因向饒錦玉借欠該族公項錢文未

還。被索爭鬧。失跌磕傷。該氏抱忿。起意服毒圖

詐。逼令伊子饒錦盛取砒。自行吞服身死。等情。

由府審明。因案情重大。將犯證卷宗押解來省。

委據南昌府督審定擬。由臬司解勘前來。臣親提犯證研鞫。緣饒錦盛係劉氏次子。其父早故。與兄饒錦幅分居。劉氏向同饒錦盛居住。與族人饒錦玉毘隣。本年七月間。饒錦玉等。因合族祖墳坍塌。商議將公存祭田一段。賣錢五十二千文。擇日修墳。劉氏因貧苦難度。向饒錦玉於公項內暫借錢十二千文應用。屢討未還。八月十二日上午。饒錦盛出外工作。劉氏赴饒錦玉家閑坐。饒錦玉索討前欠。劉氏以錢係公項。不應佰索。饒錦玉斥責賴債。稱欲稟官究追。劉氏吵鬧趕毆。失跌磕傷額顱。左眼胞。經饒錦成勸散。劉氏哭泣走回。忿恨莫釋。迨饒錦盛回家。告知前情。並稱藏有毒鼠砒末一包。伊已年老無用。不如服毒。往饒錦玉家自盡圖詐。可以得錢棺殮。免還欠項。逼令饒錦盛尋取砒末。饒錦盛向勸。劉氏聲言。如不允從。卽行撞死。饒錦盛被逼無奈。尋出砒末交給。冀圖暫順母意。再行勸阻。詎劉氏接砒開看。當卽吞入口內。順取桌上冷茶送服。饒錦盛攔阻不及。劉氏卽趕往饒錦玉家。維時饒錦玉與妻。鎖門外出探親。不能進去。經饒錦盛勸回。劉氏毒發。嘔吐不止。適饒錦盛之嫂鄢氏。路過進看查問。劉氏告知自行起意服毒。逼令取砒緣由。經饒錦盛與鄢氏。將劉氏扶至床上。一同灌救無效。至十三日早殞命。

鄧氏哭泣。饒錦盛因伊母原欲向饒錦玉賴欠。
詭詐服毒身死。嚇禁鄧氏不許聲張。即揑稱伊
母被饒錦玉毆死。投保報縣。經縣驗明。究出前
情。解省審供不諱。詰無從旁聳恿。調藥加功情
事。查饒錦盛因母劉氏借欠不還。被饒錦玉斥
責失跌。抱忿起意服毒詐賴。該犯向勸不允。被
逼無奈。取砒交給。原冀暫順母意。再行勸阻。不
期劉氏即時呑服。以致毒發斃命。尚非有心致
死其母。惟倫紀攸關。自應照律問擬。饒錦盛合
依謀殺母已死者。凌遲處死律。凌遲處死。請
旨定奪。饒錦玉並無毆打情事。第索欠口角致釀人
命。地保李顯失於查察。隨同混報。均照不應重

律。杖八十。各折責發落。饒錦幅先期外出。並不知伊母毒斃情事。後經查知。卽行赴縣供明。應與灌救不及。後被嚇禁聲張之鄢氏。均免置議。劉氏所借田價。身死勿徵。除供招咨部外。合將審擬緣由恭摺具
奏。伏乞
皇上聖鑒勅部議覆施行。奉
硃批刑部速議具奏

**圖書在版編目（CIP）數據**

海上絲綢之路文獻集成.科技與文化編.第十二輯/
王揚宗，葉農主編.－－福州：福建人民出版社，
2024.7.－－ISBN 978-7-211-09495-0

Ⅰ.K203

中國國家版本館CIP數據核字第2024NQ4980號

**海上絲綢之路文獻集成·科技與文化編（第十二輯）**

主　　編　王揚宗　葉　農
文化卷主編　葉　農
責任編輯　張煜傑
美術編輯　白　玫
出版發行　福建人民出版社
電　　話　0591-87533169（發行部）
電子郵箱　fjpph7221@126.com
地　　址　福建省福州市東水路76號
經　　銷　福建新華發行（集團）有限責任公司
印刷裝訂　上海中華印刷有限公司
地　　址　上海市青浦區匯金路889號
電　　話　021-69213456
開　　本　787毫米×1092毫米　1/16
印　　張　259.75
版　　次　2024年7月第1版第1次印刷
書　　號　ISBN 978-7-211-09495-0
定　　價　3200.00元（共8册）

国家出版基金项目
NATIONAL PUBLICATION FOUNDATION

# 海上絲綢之路文獻集成

總主編　陳支平　陳春聲

## 科技與文化編

99

主編　王揚宗　葉　農

海峽出版發行集團
THE STRAITS PUBLISHING & DISTRIBUTING GROUP
福建人民出版社

# 本册目次

# 新關文件録［一］

（*Hsin-kuan Wên-chien-lu: Text Book of Documentary Chinese, with a Vocabulary, for the Special Use of the Chinese Customs Service*）

〔美〕夏德（Friedrich Hirth）編

《新關文件録》，美國夏德編。夏德（Friedrich Hirth，一八四五——一九二七），美籍德裔漢學家。生於德國，一八七〇年來華，此後於中國各地海關任職，精研漢語及中國史。著有《中國古代的海上交通》、《中國藝術史》、《中國古代歷史》等，曾與柔克義合譯宋代趙汝适《諸蕃志》。是書分兩卷：卷一輯録海關公文一百四十三篇，於一八八五年出版；卷二含單課生詞表、音序生詞表、選譯附録及勘誤表，於一八八八年出版。一八九一年英國籍海關職員鄧羅（Charles Henry Brewitt-Taylor）加以修訂改編，成爲其後數十年洋員晉級考試之指定用書。據一八八五年及一八八八年上海版影印。

# TEXT BOOK

OF

# DOCUMENTARY CHINESE,

## WITH A VOCABULARY.

EDITED BY

F. HIRTH, Ph.D.,

*Deputy Commissioner and Assistant Statistical Secretary, Inspectorate General of Customs, Shanghai.*

IN TWO VOLUMES.

VOL. I.

Published by Order of the Inspector General of Customs.

SHANGHAI:

STATISTICAL DEPARTMENT OF THE INSPECTORATE GENERAL OF CUSTOMS.

1885.

# 新關文件録

HSIN - KUAN WÊN - CHIEN - LU.

# TEXT BOOK

OF

# DOCUMENTARY CHINESE,

WITH A VOCABULARY,

FOR THE SPECIAL USE OF THE CHINESE CUSTOMS SERVICE.

EDITED BY

F. HIRTH, Ph.D.,

*Deputy Commissioner and Assistant Statistical Secretary, Inspectorate General of Customs, Shanghai.*

IN TWO VOLUMES.

VOL. I.

Published by Order of the Inspector General of Customs.

SHANGHAI:

PUBLISHED AT THE STATISTICAL DEPARTMENT OF THE INSPECTORATE GENERAL OF CUSTOMS,

AND SOLD BY

MESSRS. KELLY & WALSH, SHANGHAI, YOKOHAMA, AND HONGKONG.

LONDON: P. S. KING & SON, CANADA BUILDING, KING STREET, WESTMINSTER, S.W.

1885.

# TABLE OF CONTENTS.

# INDEX OF SUBJECTS.

I.

# 江海關驗單

今據德國商人禪臣行投報
第一萬八千四百六十八號英船名央思
裝載進口貨物

| | | | |
|---|---|---|---|
| 黑海参 | 二件 | 三百二十四觔 | 計四兩八錢六分 |
| 中燕窩 | 一件 | 六十七觔 | 計三錢零一厘 |
| 丁香 | 二件 | 一百五十二觔 | 計七錢六分 |
| 魚肚 | 一件 | 一百三十五觔 | 計一兩三錢五分 |
| 象牙 | 一件 | 四十八觔 | 計一兩九錢二分 |
| 生牛皮 | 三件 | 二百四十二觔 | 計一兩二錢一分 |

共計進口稅關平銀拾兩肆錢壹厘
憑單持赴銀號交納足色銀兩掣取號收可也此照
光緒　八年　六月　十三日給單

1

## 2.

### 江海關進口號收

今收到禪臣經報英國一萬八千四百六十八號 船名央思

| | | | |
|---|---|---|---|
| 黑海參 | 二件 | 三百二十四觔 | 計四兩八錢六分 |
| 中燕窩 | 一件 | 六十七觔 | 計三錢零一厘 |
| 丁香 | 二件 | 一百五十二觔 | 計七錢六分 |
| 魚肚 | 一件 | 一百三十五觔 | 計一兩三錢五分 |
| 象牙 | 一件 | 四十八觔 | 計一兩九錢二分 |
| 生牛皮 | 三件 | 二百四十二觔 | 計一兩二錢一分 |

應完正稅銀拾兩肆錢壹厘正

本號按照海關驗單所載銀數兌收合給號收以憑該商持赴

關憲呈請驗收可也此照

光緒八年六月十三日江海關銀號給單

# 3.

## 江海關驗單

今據中國商人招商局投報

滬字第四千二百八十三號華船名江表

裝載出口貨物

| | | | |
|---|---|---|---|
| 細磁器 | 四件 | 三百六十四觔 | 計三兩二錢七分六厘 |
| 棉花 | 三件 | 二百四十二觔 | 計八錢四分七厘 |
| 黑棗 | 五件 | 四百八十四觔 | 計七錢二分六厘 |
| 烟絲 | 二件 | 一百六十五觔 | 計七錢四分二厘 |
| 上紙 | 四件 | 二百二十八觔 | 計一兩五錢九分六厘 |
| 古玩 | 三件 | 估價銀二百四十兩 | 計十二兩 |
| 荳餅 | 六件 | 四百六十八觔 | 計一錢六分四厘 |

共計出口稅銀拾玖兩叁錢伍分壹厘

憑單持赴銀號交納足色銀兩掣取號收可也此照

光緒 八年 六月 十三日給單

# 4.

## 江海關出口號收

今收到招商局經報中國滬字四千二百八十三號 船名江表

| | | | |
|---|---|---|---|
| 細磁器 | 四件 | 三百六十四觔 | 計三兩二錢七分六厘 |
| 棉花 | 三件 | 二百四十二觔 | 計八錢四分七厘 |
| 黑棗 | 五件 | 四百八十四觔 | 計七錢二分六厘 |
| 烟絲 | 二件 | 一百六十五觔 | 計七錢四分二厘 |
| 上紙 | 四件 | 二百二十八觔 | 計一兩五錢九分六厘 |
| 古玩 | 三件 | 估價銀二百四十兩 | 計十二兩 |
| 荳餅 | 六件 | 四百六十八觔 | 計一錢六分四厘 |

應完正稅銀拾玖兩叁錢伍分壹厘

本號按照海關驗單所載銀數兌收合給號收以憑該商持赴

關憲呈請驗收可也此照

光緒八年六月十三日江海關銀號給單

## 5.

### 江海關復運進口土產半稅驗單

今據美國一萬二百十三號商人其昌行投報福州口運來土產貨物

計開

橄欖 四件 三百四十二觔 計三錢零八厘

桔子 五件 四百三十二觔 估銀五兩二錢 計一錢三分

水靛 三件 三百六十觔 計三錢二分四厘

桂圓 二件 一百五十四觔 計一錢九分二厘

蓮子 一件 一百二十觔 計三錢

紅棗 四件 四百六十五觔 計二錢零九厘

共計應完復進口半稅銀壹兩肆錢陸分叁厘

憑單持赴銀號交納足色銀兩掣取號收可也

光緒八年六月十三日給單

## 6.

# 江海關征收復進口土產半稅號收

今收到美國商人其昌行第一萬二百十三號運來土產貨物

計開

橄欖　四件　三百四十二觔　計三錢零八厘

桔子　五件　四百三十二觔　估銀五兩二錢　計一錢三分

水靛　三件　三百六十觔　計三錢二分四厘

桂圓　二件　一百五十四觔　計一錢九分二厘

蓮子　一件　一百二十觔　計三錢

紅棗　四件　四百六十五觔　計二錢零九厘

應完復進口半稅銀壹兩肆錢陸分叁厘

本號按照海關半稅驗單所載銀數兑收合給號收以憑該商持赴

關憲呈請驗收可也此照

光緒八年六月十三日江海關銀號給單

# 7.

## 江海關給發運入長江土貨半稅驗單

今據英國第二萬三千六百八十四號商人太古行投報運入長江土貨

計開

| | | | |
|---|---|---|---|
| 花生 | 二件 | 一百八十四觔 | 計九分二厘 |
| 料器 | 一件 | 八十六觔 | 計二錢一分五厘 |
| 火腿 | 四件 | 二百三十八觔 | 計六錢五分四厘 |
| 紅丹 | 二件 | 一百九十二觔 | 計三錢三分六厘 |
| 熟鐵 | 五件 | 四百二十八觔 | 計二錢六分七厘 |
| 白糖 | 六件 | 三百五十二觔 | 計三錢五分二厘 |

除另征出口正稅外計應完復進九江半稅銀壹兩九錢壹分陸厘

憑單持赴銀號交納足色銀兩掣取號收可也

光緒八年六月十三日給單

## 8.

### 江海關征收運入長江土貨半稅號收

今收到英國商人太古行第二萬三千六百八十四號運入長江土貨

計開

| | | | |
|---|---|---|---|
| 花生 | 二件 | 一百八十四觔 | 計九分二厘 |
| 料器 | 一件 | 八十六觔 | 計二錢一分五厘 |
| 火腿 | 四件 | 二百三十八觔 | 計六錢五分四厘 |
| 紅丹 | 二件 | 一百九十二觔 | 計三錢三分六厘 |
| 熟鐵 | 五件 | 四百二十八觔 | 計二錢六分七厘 |
| 白糖 | 六件 | 三百五十二觔 | 計三錢五分二厘 |

除另征出口正稅外計應完復進九江半稅銀壹兩玖錢壹分陸厘

本號按照海關發給運入長江土貨半稅驗單所載銀數兌收合給號

收以憑該商持赴

關憲呈請驗收可也此照

光緒八年六月十三日江海關銀號給單

## 9.

# 江海關內地貨稅驗單

今據英國商人怡和行投報運入內地貨物

計開

原色布　十五疋　計六錢

大原布　二十一疋　計八錢四分

小原布　二十三疋　計四錢六分

斜紋布　二十五疋　計九錢三分七厘

色布　二十四疋　計一兩八錢

緞布　四十疋　計四兩

印花布　二十二疋　計七錢七分

共計稅銀玖兩肆錢柒厘

憑單持赴銀號交納足色紋銀掣取號收可也　此照

光緒八年六月十三日給單

2

10.

## 江海關運入內地貨稅號收

今收到英國商人怡和運入內地

計開

原色布 十五疋 計六錢

大原布 二十一疋 計八錢四分

小原布 二十三疋 計四錢六分

斜紋布 二十五疋 計九錢三分七厘

色布 二十四疋 計一兩八錢

縐布 四十疋 計四兩

印花布 二十二疋 計七錢七分

應完稅銀玖兩肆錢柒厘

本號按照海關驗單所載銀數兌收合給號收以憑該商持赴

關憲呈請驗收可也此照

光緒 八年 六月 十三日江海關銀號給單

## 11.

# 江海關內地貨稅驗單

今據英國商人怡和行投報運出內地貨物

計開

湖絲　四百八十觔　計二十四兩

亂絲頭　二百六十觔　計一兩三錢

蠶繭　一百四十觔　計二兩一錢

金針菜　三十一担　計四兩一錢八分五厘

共計稅銀叁拾壹兩五錢捌分五厘

憑單持赴銀號交納足色銀兩掣取號收可也　此照

光緒八年六月十三日給單

12.

江海關運出內地貨稅號收

今收到英國怡和運出內地

計開

湖絲　四百八十觔　計二十四兩

亂絲頭　二百六十觔　計一兩三錢

繭　一百四十觔　計二兩一錢

金針菜　三十一担　計四兩一錢八分五厘

應完稅銀叁拾壹兩五錢八分五厘

本號按照海關驗單所載銀數兌收合給號收以憑該商持赴

關盡呈請驗收可也此照

光緒八年六月十三日江海關銀號給單

## 13.

江漢關

自光緒捌年捌月貳拾日起

第捌拾玖結華洋商船各款稅鈔數目清摺

至光緒捌年拾壹月貳拾貳日止

# 洋商船隻各稅款

一收洋貨進口正稅　共關平銀貳拾壹兩柒分

一收土貨出口正稅　共關平銀拾肆萬柒千伍百貳拾捌兩玖錢叁分壹厘

一收土貨復進口稅　共關平銀壹千捌百捌拾伍兩陸錢捌分叁厘

一收洋藥土膏各稅　進口正稅銀無　出口正稅銀叁千肆百陸拾玖兩叁錢伍分　復進口稅銀無　共關平銀叁千肆百陸拾玖兩叁錢伍分

其中有內地洋藥各稅共關平銀叁千肆百陸拾玖兩叁錢伍分合併聲明

一收船鈔　共關平銀柒百玖拾柒兩叁錢叁厘

一本年代收發還暫存復進口稅銀續增核計共玖萬壹千叁拾陸兩伍分捌厘陸萬肆千叁百貳拾陸兩肆錢叁厘除發還外本年四結底仍存關平銀貳萬陸千柒百玖兩陸錢伍分伍厘

以上本結收洋商稅鈔共關平銀拾捌萬肆百拾壹兩玖錢玖分貳厘

# 華商船隻各稅款

一收洋貨進口正稅　共關平銀無

一收土貨出口正稅　共關平銀捌萬肆千壹百貳拾伍兩貳錢壹分捌厘

一收土貨復進口稅　共關平銀柒拾陸兩叁錢貳分陸厘

一收洋藥土膏各稅　進口正稅銀無　出口正稅銀叁千陸百柒拾柒兩柒錢　復進口稅銀無　共關平銀叁千陸百柒拾柒兩柒錢

其中有內地洋藥各稅共關平銀叁千陸百柒拾柒兩柒錢合併聲明

一收船鈔　共關平銀貳百柒拾伍兩貳錢

一本年代收／發還暫存復進口稅銀續增核計共伍萬貳千柒百玖拾叁兩陸錢陸分玖厘／貳萬捌千陸百柒拾捌兩捌錢肆分貳厘　除發還外本年四結底仍存關平銀貳萬肆千壹百拾肆兩捌錢貳分柒厘

以上本結收華商稅鈔共關平銀拾壹萬貳千貳百陸拾玖兩貳錢柒分壹厘

## 裝免數目

再漕糧口　共裝無　石　斗　升　每石按一百四十斤計

一免稅貨物　共裝無　石　斗　升　每石按一百二十斤計

一貨物免稅　共免關平銀無

合併聲明

# 華洋子口稅款

一收洋貨入內地子口稅　共關平銀貳萬肆千肆百捌拾柒兩壹分陸厘

一收土貨出內地子口稅　共關平銀貳千貳百陸兩壹錢叁分壹厘

以上本結收華洋子口稅共關平銀貳萬陸千陸百玖拾叁兩壹錢肆分柒厘

統計三款共收關平銀叁拾壹萬玖千叁百柒拾肆兩肆錢壹分

查第捌拾玖結內本關並無押註之現銀存票合併聲明

光緒捌年拾壹月叁拾日　三品銜江漢關稅務司裴式楷　呈報

四品銜副稅務司屠邁倫譯漢

隨申文第壹號

光緒〇年〇月〇日　總稅務司赫德轉呈

杜稅務司　核對

隨申文第〇〇號

14.

# 粵海關出口貨總單

欽命督理粵海關稅務崇　爲給發出口貨物總單事茲據　英國
第一百八十一號商船報驗出口前赴上海合將該船內所裝洋土
各貨給發總單以憑持赴
上海海關呈請查驗須至總單者

計開

| 報單號數 | 商名 | 貨色 | 件數 | 斤兩或疋數丈尺 | 估價 | 單照 |
| --- | --- | --- | --- | --- | --- | --- |
| | 糧臺 | 銀 | 四十一件 | 十二萬二千三百兩 | | 免 |
| | 黃 | 衣箱 | 二十二件 | | | 免 |
| | | 書 | 十四件 | | | 免 |
| | | 行李 | 一件 | | | 免 |
| | | 靈柩 | 一件 | | | 免 |
| | 四美 | 洋酒 | 一件 | | | 免 |

其餘未列此單之各貨均已按類逐款開明分別附給免稅執照二
十五紙收稅單十二紙正稅憑單二十三紙總單毋庸重録詳細件
色合並聲明

光緒　八年　五月　二十三　日給

3

## 15.

# 津海新關出口貨總單

監督天津新鈔兩關辦理直隸通商事務兼管海防兵備道　爲給發出口貨物總單事茲據中國第九十四號商船報驗出口前赴上海合將該船內所裝洋土各貨給發總單以憑持赴上海海關呈請查驗須至總單者

計開

| 報單號數 | 商名 | 貨色 | 件數 | 觔兩或疋數丈尺 | 估價 | 單照 |
|---|---|---|---|---|---|---|
| | 招商局 | 米袋 | 二百件 | | | 免 |
| | 董 | 靈柩 | 二具 | | | 免 |
| 三十三 | 萬順 | 青蓮 | 一件 | 三十七斤半 | 五十兩 | 應征 |
| | 高林 | 空瓶 | 十八件 | | | 免 |
| | 保昌 | 麻袋 | 十件 | 一千條 | | 免 |
| | 高林 | 空瓶 | 十件 | | | 免 |

其餘未列此單之各貨均已按類逐欵開明分別附給免稅執照一紙收稅單二十七紙正稅總單五紙總單內毋庸重錄合並聲明

光緒　八年　五月　二十三　日給

16.

## 通商各關與東西洋各國往來貿易貨價總數

| 一千八百八十二年 | 洋貨運來 | 土貨運往 | 共計 |
|---|---|---|---|
| 英國 | 一千八百七十五萬五千五百八十二兩 | 二千二百三十萬九千七十一兩 | 四千一百六萬四千六百五十三兩 |
| 香港轉運來往各國 | 二千九百六萬三千六兩 | 一千六百四十八萬七千五百七十三兩 | 四千五百五十五萬五百七十九兩 |
| 印度國 | 一千八百二十六萬四千三百七十二兩 | 四十七萬七千一百十四兩 | 一千八百七十四萬一千四百八十六兩 |
| 新加坡等處屬英國 | 一百五十六萬五千三百八十七兩 | 一百二萬七千七百三十兩 | 二百五十九萬三千一百十七兩 |
| 新金山屬英國 | 五十三萬七十二兩 | 二百四萬四千九百六十七兩 | 二百五十七萬五千三十九兩 |
| 鈕西蘭在新金山之東屬英國 | 無 | 十七萬七千九百二十四兩 | 十七萬七千九百二十四兩 |
| 大浪山嘴屬英國 | 無 | 十一萬一千二百四十六兩 | 十一萬一千二百四十六兩 |
| 幹阿達接美國北界屬英國 | 二十一萬八千七百七十九兩 | 五萬七千九百四十六兩 | 二十七萬六千七百二十五兩 |
| 美國卽合衆國 | 三百二十七萬六千七百二十八兩 | 八百四十二萬一百三十兩 | 一千一百六十九萬六千八百五十八兩 |
| 南美國 | 無 | 無 | 無 |
| 歐羅巴除英俄兩國之外 | 二百四十八萬四千四百二十九兩 | 八百七十五萬一千八百四十七兩 | 一千一百二十三萬六千二百七十六兩 |

| | | | |
|---|---|---|---|
| 俄國由水道 | 九千一百二十七兩 | 九十四萬六千三百二十四兩 | 九十五萬五千四百五十一兩 |
| 俄國由天津陸路經恰克圖 | 無 | 三百二十八萬六千三百四十五兩 | 三百二十八萬六千三百四十五兩 |
| 俄國圖們江北 | 十五萬二千三十四兩 | 五十六萬八千七百六十七兩 | 七十二萬八百一兩 |
| 日本國 | 四百四十四萬二千二百四十一兩 | 一百七十六萬六千八百五十八兩 | 六百二十萬九千九十九兩 |
| 小呂宋 | 一萬八千八百九十一兩 | 二十四萬九千四百四十九兩 | 二十六萬八千三百四十兩 |
| 安南國 | 四十八萬七千二兩 | 六萬五千四百七十二兩 | 五十五萬二千四百七十四兩 |
| 暹羅國 | 十九萬七千四百十六兩 | 二十六萬七千五百三十四兩 | 四十六萬四千九百五十兩 |
| 瓜哇屬荷蘭國 | 三萬八千八百八兩 | 二十六萬六千七兩 | 三十萬四千八百十五兩 |
| 埃及國阿拉比國等處 | 三百六十九兩 | 五萬四千五百四十二兩 | 五萬四千九百十一兩 |
| 檀香山 | 無 | 無 | 無 |
| 統共 | 七千九百五十萬四千二百四十三兩 | 六千七百三十三萬六千八百四十六兩 | 一萬四千六百八十四萬一千八十九兩 |
| 除洋貨轉運出洋 | 一百七十八萬九千十五兩 | | 一百七十八萬九千十五兩 |
| 洋貨實存 | 七千七百七十一萬五千二百二十八兩 | | |
| 淨數 | | | 一萬四千五百五萬二千七十四兩 |
| 土貨出洋 | | 六千七百三十三萬六千八百四十六兩 | |

# 貨物花色專欵

## 第一欵 通商各關洋貨進口除轉運出洋外花色總數

| 一千八百八十二年 | 洋貨共運進口 | 洋貨運進價值 |
| --- | --- | --- |
| **洋藥類** | | |
| 小洋藥 | 二萬九千三百三十五担八十八斤 | 一千三百八萬九千六百四十七兩 |
| 大洋藥 | 一萬五千三百七十九担二十四斤 | 五百九十五萬七千九百十五兩 |
| 新洋藥 | 一萬五千十七担十七斤 | 五百四十九萬九千一百十八兩 |
| 雜樣洋藥 | 五千九百七十七担三十一斤 | 二百十九萬九千六百十七兩 |
| 共計洋藥 | 六萬五千七百九担六十斤 | 二千六百七十四萬六千二百九十七兩 |
| **棉布類** | | |
| 原色布 | 五百二十七萬八百七十五疋 | 七百一萬三千九百三十八兩 |
| 白色布 | 一百六十萬八千一百九十一疋 | 二百七十三萬一千八百三十一兩 |
| 白提花布 | 三千九百七十七疋 | 六千八百三十九兩 |

| | | |
|---|---|---|
| 素色布 | 十萬九百四十九疋 | 二十萬八千三百三十九兩 |
| 色花點布 | 六萬三千二百五十七疋 | 十三萬四千五百八兩 |
| 大小扣布 印洋標 | 二百十七萬四千三百八十三疋 | 二百十四萬五十一兩 |
| 斜紋布 英美荷國 | 九十萬三千四百十一疋 | 二百一萬七千九百八十七兩 |
| 原粗布 | 八十六萬九千七十八疋 | 二百四萬八千四百六十二兩 |
| 原細斜紋布 | 二十四萬二千四十疋 | 四十萬六千三百三十五兩 |
| 印花布 | 二十二萬三千四百四十三疋 | 二十五萬二千五百十兩 |
| 素紅布 | 三十八萬二百七十三疋 | 四十四萬六千二十五兩 |
| 緞布 | 六千九百九十疋 | 二萬四千九百三兩 |
| 花剪絨 | 五萬二千八十三疋 | 十九萬七千二百九十四兩 |
| 印花袈裟布 | 三萬九千一百十六疋 | 二萬八千八百五十九兩 |
| 手帕 | 二十四萬二百六十五打臣 每打臣即十二條 | 八萬九千六百六十一兩 |
| 棉布 不在列 | 二十二萬六百九十六疋 | 四十五萬三千八百五十一兩 |
| 棉紗棉綫 | 十八萬四千九百三十九担九十七斤 | 四百五十萬五千三百九十一兩 |
| 共計棉布 | | 二千二百七十萬六千七百八十四兩 |

絨毛布類

| | | |
|---|---|---|
| 羽布 | 三十九疋 | 五百三十八兩 |
| 床氈 | 二萬二百八十八雙 | 五萬八千四百十七兩 |
| 羽綢 | 二百九十八疋 | 一千二百十八兩 |
| 羽布作旗用 | 八百六十六疋 | 三千五百四十五兩 |
| 羽紗 | 十一萬二千五百九十九疋 | 九十九萬四千九百八兩 |
| 羽緞 | 一千四疋 | 一萬六千五百八十二兩 |
| 冲羽紗 | 五疋 | 五十兩 |
| 大呢 | 三萬二千六百七疋 | 六十八萬二千二百十四兩 |
| 粗哆囉呢 | 六萬四千一疋 | 五十五萬一千一百七十兩 |
| 哈喇呢 | 二萬二千四十九疋 | 六十一萬七千三百七十二兩 |
| 法蘭呢 | 一萬一千一百二十八疋 | 九萬四百十四兩 |
| 羽綾 | 八萬五千十四疋 | 六十二萬九千九百十八兩 |
| 羽縐 | 二千三百三十九疋 | 一萬一千七百三十一兩 |
| 冲小羽綾 | 二十一疋 | 一百二十六兩 |
| 嗶嘰 | 十萬一千四百十三疋 | 四十七萬六千九百三十三兩 |
| 花素棉絨布 | 八萬一千八百七十二疋 | 二十萬一千四十兩 |
| 絨類不在列 | 二萬一千九百七十疋 | 十六萬八十七兩 |
| 共計絨毛布 | | 四百四十九萬六千二百六十三兩 |

| | | |
|---|---|---|
| **雜樣布類** | | |
| 棉絨布 | 一萬六百六十九疋 | 五萬五千三百二十三兩 |
| 半絲棉布 | 十五担三十斤 | 一千五百三十兩 |
| 細蘇布 | 三萬三千二百八十八疋 | 十九萬七千八百二十四兩 |
| 帆布 | 五千八百五十九疋 | 三萬二千二百八兩 |
| 共計雜樣布 | | 二十八萬六千八百八十五兩 |
| **銅鐵雜貨類** | | |
| 銅板銅條 | 九千六百四十八担四十八斤 | 十四萬四千七百二十七兩 |
| 銅片銅釘 | 一萬一千三百二十五担九十二斤 | 十八萬三百七十八兩 |
| 舊銅 | 四百三十三担 | 六千三百十八兩 |
| 鑄銅生銅 | 一千一百二十八担五斤 | 一萬七千二十五兩 |
| 銅絲 | 二百九十担二十三斤 | 七千二百四十四兩 |
| 熟銅及銅器不在列 | 九百八十六担十一斤 | 一萬四千三百二十四兩 |
| 鐵條 | 二十二萬六千六百四十六担七十五斤 | 三十九萬八千五百十三兩 |

| | | |
|---|---|---|
| 鐵板 | 七萬一千十六担二十一斤 | 十四萬二千三百八十三兩 |
| 鐵片條 | 七千七百七十担十七斤 | 一萬七千一百八十一兩 |
| 鐵絲 | 一萬五千九百七十七担三十二斤 | 六萬四千二百二十兩 |
| 生鐵磚及壓載鐵 | 九千五百七十四担五十八斤 | 九千五百七十八兩 |
| 熟鐵及鐵器不在列 | 九萬七千五百六担二十九斤 | 二十三萬六千三百八十九兩 |
| 生鐵不在列 | 三十一萬八千一百三十二担二十七斤 | 四十一萬五千八百七兩 |
| 鉛塊 | 二十四萬八千八百五十六担二十一斤 | 九十八萬六千二百六十一兩 |
| 鉛片 | 三千六百五十二担三十二斤 | 二萬三千七百四十一兩 |
| 水銀 | 二千一百五十五担八十一斤 | 八萬八千七百三十一兩 |
| 白鉛 | 四千二百三十担五十斤 | 二萬一百一兩 |
| 鋼 | 二萬三千六百六担十一斤 | 七萬三千五百五十三兩 |
| 錫磚條 | 六萬七千四百三十一担七斤 | 一百四十三萬九千六百八十一兩 |
| 馬口鐵 | 五千二百四十二担十九斤 | 二萬一千五百七十二兩 |
| 鋼銅錫熟鐵器等不在列 | | 三十九萬二千八百六兩 |
| 共計銅鐵 | | 四百七十萬五百三十三兩 |

各色洋貨

| | | |
|---|---|---|
| 赤糖 | 五萬九百五十七担七十六斤 | 十八萬七千三百九十二兩 |
| 白糖 | 二萬五千九百五十三担十七斤 | 十八萬二千一百三十八兩 |
| 梹榔 | 一萬五千十五担七斤 | 七萬五千九百九十四兩 |
| 燕窩 | 八百十六担九十四斤 | 五十五萬三千一百十六兩 |
| 海參 | 二萬六千一百七十九担九十二斤 | 六十三萬五千五十五兩 |
| 丁香各樣 | 六千三百五十担八十二斤 | 十八萬五百三十七兩 |
| 煤 | 二十五萬三千九十九噸 | 一百二十一萬九千六百八十五兩 |
| 棉花 | 十七萬八千四百七十八担三十七斤 | 一百九十一萬六千七百三十四兩 |
| 魚乾鹽 | 八萬二千一百八担八十五斤 | 四十九萬九十四兩 |
| 火石 | 七萬七千四百六十四担七十七斤 | 二萬九千九十九兩 |
| 人參各樣 | 四千七百三十一担四十七斤 | 七十六萬三千六十五兩 |
| 粮食 | 八千三百六十三担三十二斤 | 一萬三千五百四十一兩 |
| 靛土水 | 七千三十六担四十七斤 | 二萬八千四百三十一兩 |
| 魚膠 | 五千八百七十九担四十八斤 | 九萬一千四百十三兩 |
| 自來火 | 一百九十萬四千六百二十九各羅斯每各羅斯卽一百四十四盒 | 八十五萬二千五百九十六兩 |
| 栲皮 | 九萬七千六百九十四担八十四斤 | 八萬八千二百六十六兩 |
| 針 | 一百八十五萬三千六百三十七密力每密力卽一千根 | 二十八萬五千六百八十二兩 |
| 油各樣 | | 九十六萬三千六百五十七兩 |
| 漆 | 八千五百六十担三斤 | 五萬七千一百八十五兩 |

| | | |
|---|---|---|
| 椒黑白 | 三萬七千六百九十一担五十七斤 | 二十九萬七千八百八十二兩 |
| 沙藤 | 四萬六千一百七十三担三十斤 | 十五萬四百九十兩 |
| 米 | 二十三萬三千一百四十九担四十九斤 | 二十八萬八千二兩 |
| 海菜海帶 | 四十萬一百六担二十七斤 | 一百三十四萬四千一百五十九兩 |
| 檀香 | 十萬三千三百二担二十六斤 | 六十一萬二千二百十七兩 |
| 蘇木 | 十六萬三千四百八十三担二十八斤 | 三十七萬三千六百八十五兩 |
| 硬木香木各樣 | | 二十二萬一千三百六十六兩 |
| 鮑魚蝦米等 | 四萬八千五百四十五担六十六斤 | 四十七萬六千五百七十七兩 |
| 絲日本 | 五十四担六十五斤 | 五千四百四十八兩 |
| 綢縐 | 十二担八十九斤 | 六千七百二十五兩 |
| 茶葉日本 | 一萬七千五百七十四担三十九斤 | 八萬七千九十五兩 |
| 木桅木板 | | 九十七萬四千一百四十二兩 |
| 蠟桕油各樣 | 一百三十四担十六斤 | 二千六百五十八兩 |
| 玻璃 | 四萬三千九百二十八箱 | 九萬六千五百六十三兩 |
| 雜貨不在列 | | 五百二十二萬七千七百七十七兩 |
| 共計雜貨價值 | | 一千八百七十七萬八千四百六十六兩 |
| 統共進口洋貨價值 | | 七千七百七十一萬五千二百二十八兩 |

18.

# 通商各關土貨出洋花色總數

| 一千八百八十二年 | 土貨共運出洋 | 土貨出洋價值 |
|---|---|---|
| 湖土生經絲斤 | 六萬四百十九担七十四斤 | 一千六百九十八萬九千八百八十一兩 |
| 亂絲頭 | 二萬八千六百五十七担七十七斤 | 一百三十五萬六千八百二十六兩 |
| 野粗絲 | 四千八十九担三十八斤 | 三十四萬四千七百二十兩 |
| 蠶繭 | 三千八百四十七担 | 二十萬七千五百二十三兩 |
| 綢緞 | 六千五百九十八担二十六斤 | 三百三十九萬六千三百七十四兩 |
| 絲線絲帶等 | 二千七百一担七十三斤 | 五十四萬一千九百二十八兩 |
| 蠶子 | 十九斤 | 四十八兩 |
| 紅茶 | 一百六十一萬一千九百十六担八十二斤 | 二千五百八十七萬八千二百三十八兩 |
| 綠茶 | 十七萬八千八百三十九担五十二斤 | 四百九萬九百兩 |
| 磚茶 | 二十一萬九千二十六担六十斤 | 一百三十萬三千九百六十四兩 |
| 茶末 | 七千三百六十七担九十斤 | 五萬九千一百五兩 |
| 袋各樣 | 六十九萬七千八百九十五個 | 二萬二千七百五十一兩 |
| 竹竿竹器各樣 | | 十萬七千二百八十二兩 |

| | | |
|---|---|---|
| 荳子荳餅 | 十七萬九千四百二十七担三十斤 | 十八萬四千五百九十一兩 |
| 桂皮 | 五萬八千一百七十担六十一斤 | 二十七萬一千五百六十六兩 |
| 漳腦 | 五千一百六十二担二斤 | 四萬二千四百六十六兩 |
| 磁器窰器 | 九萬八千二百四十三担九十八斤 | 四十七萬一千三百八十八兩 |
| 煤 | 十萬四百三十六担五十斤 | 一千二百四兩 |
| 衣服靴鞋 | | 三十八萬八千七百五十八兩 |
| 棉花 | 四萬一千六百九十担九斤 | 四十萬四千四百五兩 |
| 子棉花 | 三担五十一斤 | 四十一兩 |
| 棉絮 | 六百八十九担六十二斤 | 八百三十兩 |
| 古玩 | | 三萬七千二百三十八兩 |
| 顏料各樣 | 一百九十八担七十七斤 | 八百七十三兩 |
| 扇各樣 | 二百五十七萬一千五百十二把 | 二萬五千七百八十兩 |
| 魚各樣 | 九千六百九十九担四十一斤 | 九萬一千九百一兩 |
| 炮竹 | 四萬六百十六担八十一斤 | 三十七萬六千八百六十三兩 |
| 麪粉 | 二萬三千三百二十八担四十七斤 | 三萬六千一百三兩 |
| 果品 | 十萬九千九百六十二担五十七斤 | 十五萬二千三十八兩 |
| 木耳 | 二十七担三十七斤 | 六百十四兩 |

| | | |
|---|---|---|
| 粮食 | 一萬八千八百十九担五十三斤 | 一萬九千七百三十五兩 |
| 料器各樣 | 一萬二千一百七十一担八十斤 | 二十三萬四千七百六十一兩 |
| 夏布 | 一千六百八十五担五十三斤 | 十四萬四千六百七十九兩 |
| 毛各樣 | 七千二百四十四担十九斤 | 十萬九千一百二十九兩 |
| 蔴繩索 | 二萬四千八百二十四担五十一斤 | 十九萬二千二十六兩 |
| 皮各樣 | 三萬四千九百四十五担八十一斤 | 三十八萬六千一百四十八兩 |
| 蹄各樣 | 九十七担九十七斤 | 三百四十五兩 |
| 角各樣 | | 九萬八百四十兩 |
| 靛土水 | 一千八百七十二担六十二斤 | 七千三百八十二兩 |
| 桂圓 | 一萬二千六十六担三十四斤 | 五萬五千三百九十四兩 |
| 蔴子地蔴 | 四十九萬八千七十八條 | 四十八萬六千三百六十五兩 |
| 藥材 | 三萬四千八十二担十三斤 | 二十萬七千五十兩 |
| 銅鐵錫鉛等器 | 一萬四千二百五十一担五十二斤 | 十三萬三千六十六兩 |
| 生銅鐵錫鉛 | 二担六十八斤 | 十九兩 |
| 麝香 | 二十担二十四斤 | 十六萬二千四百十四兩 |
| 土布 | 二千六百二担 | 十一萬二百十三兩 |
| 棓子 | 八千八百三担七十斤 | 八萬七千一百七十九兩 |
| 油各樣 | 九千二百三十二担二十六斤 | 七萬四千二百八十四兩 |

| | | |
|---|---|---|
| 紙書銅錫箔 | 五萬七千八百五十三担五十五斤 | 六十二萬三千四百三十二兩 |
| 蜜餞 | 一萬九千九百五担九十七斤 | 十五萬八千九百六十五兩 |
| 食物各樣 | 九萬五千九百四十担五十六斤 | 七萬八千四百九十九兩 |
| 籐竿籐器 | 三千九百十二担二十一斤 | 一萬七千七百三十九兩 |
| 大黃 | 六千八百六十一担三十一斤 | 十八萬三千六百九十九兩 |
| 紅花 | 一千二百六十七担六十八斤 | 七萬三千十三兩 |
| 皮貨 | 五十七萬三千三百二十一件 | 四十七萬一千九百四十八兩 |
| 草帽緶 | 五萬五千四百九十八担二十六斤 | 一百四十九萬八千五百九十六兩 |
| 白糖 | 二十七萬四千七百九担八十一斤 | 一百九萬九千七百十一兩 |
| 赤糖 | 七十五萬七千一百二十五担四十二斤 | 一百八十二萬一千九百九十三兩 |
| 氷糖 | 二萬九千九百二十六担四十斤 | 十八萬一千六百七十三兩 |
| 烟葉烟絲各樣 | 七千三担五十六斤 | 八萬一千五百六十三兩 |
| 粉絲 | 四萬四千八百二十九担四十斤 | 十六萬七千一百七十三兩 |
| 蠟 | 七十二担七十一斤 | 二千五百八十四兩 |
| 駝羊毛 | 二萬二千七百五十五担三十九斤 | 十九萬九千二十九兩 |
| 雜貨不在列 | | 一百四十二萬一兩 |
| 統共出洋土貨價值 | | 六千七百三十三萬六千八百四十六兩 |

19.

## 通商各關來往各船隻噸總數

一千八百八十二年

| | 船隻進出 | 共用噸數 |
|---|---|---|
| 英國 | 一萬四千三百三十七隻 | 一千八十一萬四千七百七十九噸 |
| 美國 | 七百六十二隻 | 十六萬七千八百一噸 |
| 德國 | 一千八百六十四隻 | 八十八萬二千八百五十六噸 |
| 法國 | 一百九十二隻 | 十七萬二千三百八十一噸 |
| 荷國 | 三十八隻 | 二萬三千二百二十六噸 |
| 丹國 | 二百七十隻 | 十二萬六千三噸 |
| 日國 | 三百二十隻 | 六萬一千一百二十三噸 |
| 瑙威瑞敦國 | 一百二十四隻 | 七萬二百四十五噸 |
| 俄國 | 八十二隻 | 七萬四千七百五十一噸 |
| 比國 | 無 | 無 |
| 義國 | 二隻 | 一千七百六十二噸 |
| 日本國 | 二百五十隻 | 十九萬四千五百八十四噸 |
| 暹羅國 | 五十六隻 | 二萬二千六百三十六噸 |
| 哈外意國卽檀香山 | 無 | 無 |
| 中國洋式船隻 | 五千一百五隻 | 四百六十六萬七千七百五十三噸 |
| 中國華式船隻 | 一千三百二十四隻 | 十萬八千二百十六噸 |
| 安南國 | 三隻 | 七百三十六噸 |
| 無旗 | 無 | 無 |
| 統共 | 二萬四千七百二十九隻 | 一千七百三十八萬八千八百五十二噸 |

兹另將以上進出船隻噸數按年劃分輪船篷船各數列下

| | 一千八百八十年 | 一千八百八十一年 | 一千八百八十二年 |
|---|---|---|---|
| 輪船 | 一萬七千三百隻 | 一萬八千一百七十隻 | 一萬九千六百七隻 |
| 噸數 | 一千四百五十七萬二千七百十八噸 | 一千五百三十五萬九百五十四噸 | 一千六百十萬二千五百七十四噸 |
| 篷船華船之數在內 | 五千六百七十隻 | 五千十七隻 | 五千一百二十二隻 |
| 噸數 | 一百三十萬一千六百三十四噸 | 一百二十八萬九千三百二十四噸 | 一百二十八萬六千二百七十八噸 |
| 共計各船 | 二萬二千九百七十隻 | 二萬三千一百八十七隻 | 二萬四千七百二十九隻 |
| 共計噸數 | 一千五百八十七萬四千三百五十二噸 | 一千六百六十四萬二百七十八噸 | 一千七百三十八萬八千八百五十二噸 |

## 20.

某某關

自光緒捌年捌月貳拾日起

第捌拾玖結

罰欵　經費　船鈔　另欵

四項入出數目清摺

至光緒捌年拾壹月貳拾貳日止

# 經費

## 入款

| | |
|---|---|
| 入上結所存之餘銀 | 共關平銀伍仟貳伯陸拾柒兩貳錢捌分 |
| 入本結監督撥交之經費 | 共關平銀肆萬兩 |
| 入總稅務司補發之款 | 共關平銀無 |

## 支款

| | |
|---|---|
| 出還上結未入之墊欵 | 共關平銀無 |
| 出華洋人各項薪水 | 共關平銀叁萬壹仟柒伯肆拾柒兩玖錢肆分 |
| 出盤運各費 | 共關平銀捌伯拾伍兩叁錢叁分 |
| 出租費 | 共關平銀貳仟柒伯陸拾肆兩陸錢貳分 |
| 出各項關房建修費 | 共關平銀伍伯叁兩捌錢陸分 |
| 出各項關船建修費 | 共關平銀壹伯肆拾捌兩壹錢壹分 |

出沿海江巡查經費　共關平銀柒百肆拾貳兩玖錢

出常用雜費　共關平銀貳千捌百陸拾柒兩壹錢柒分

出呈准特用各費　共關平銀壹千伍百叁拾柒兩壹錢柒分

出滙兌費　共關平銀無

出總稅務司提項　共關平銀無

存款

以上共入關平銀肆萬伍千貳百陸拾柒兩貳錢捌分

共出關平銀肆萬壹千壹百貳拾柒兩壹錢

共存關平銀肆千壹百肆拾兩壹錢捌分

# 船鈔

## 入款

| | |
|---|---|
| 入上結所存之餘銀 | 共關平銀貳萬肆百叁拾叁兩柒錢伍分 |
| 入本結監督撥交船鈔七成 | 共關平銀壹萬柒千捌百拾兩 |
| 入本結監督特撥之項 | 共關平銀無 |
| 入總稅務司補發之項 | 共關平銀無 |

## 支款

| | |
|---|---|
| 出還上結末入之墊款 | 共關平銀無 |
| 出華洋人各項薪水 | 共關平銀陸千壹百叁兩捌錢玖分 |
| 出盤運各費 | 共關平銀壹百肆兩貳錢柒分 |
| 出租費 | 共關平銀陸百玖拾捌兩貳錢陸分 |
| 出浮燈塔樁各項建修費 | 共關平銀柒百肆拾柒兩柒錢貳分 |

出各項關房船建修費　共關平銀貳百貳兩叁錢伍分

出各項特動之工費　共關平銀壹百兩陸錢貳分

出常用雜費　共關平銀壹千壹百肆拾伍兩伍錢柒分

出呈准特用各費　共關平銀壹千貳百兩

出滙兌費　共關平銀無

出總稅務司提項　共關平銀無

存款

以上共入關平銀叁萬捌千貳百肆拾叁兩柒錢伍分

共出關平銀壹萬叁百貳兩陸錢捌分

共存關平銀貳萬柒千玖百肆拾壹兩柒分

## 罰款

### 入欵

| | |
|---|---|
| 入上結所存之餘銀 | 共關平銀壹千貳百捌拾伍兩陸錢 |
| 入本結罰商銀兩 | 共關平銀壹百兩 |
| 入本結罰貨物入官變價 | 共關平銀玖百拾壹兩捌錢 |
| 入總稅務司補發之項 | 共關平銀無 |

### 支欵

| | |
|---|---|
| 出還上結末入之墊款 | 共關平銀無 |
| 出緝私常用雜費 | 共關平銀壹百柒拾壹兩柒錢叁分 |
| 出提歸總理衙門三成 | 共關平銀貳百伍拾貳兩貳分 |
| 出提歸監督三成 | 共關平銀貳百伍拾貳兩貳分 |
| 出應提總稅務司四成項下呈准特用各費 | 共關平銀無 |

出滙兌費　共關平銀無

出總稅務司提項　共關平銀壹千貳百捌拾伍兩陸錢

存款

以上共入關平銀貳千貳百玖拾柒兩肆錢

共出關平銀壹千玖百陸拾壹兩叁錢柒分

共存關平銀叁百叁拾陸兩叁分

## 另款

### 入欵

| | |
|---|---|
| 入上結所存之餘銀 | 共關平銀叁千陸百貳拾玖兩伍錢 |
| 入奉總理衙門飭撥之欵 | 共關平銀無 |
| 入華商船牌費 | 共關平銀叁百兩 |
| 入華商船關照費 | 共關平銀壹百兩 |
| 入引水帳各銀兩 | 共關平銀肆百貳拾兩柒錢 |
| 入招工帳各銀兩 | 共關平銀無 |
| 入責納專單費 | 共關平銀貳千伍百兩 |
| 入關板商貨全書售價銀 | 共關平銀壹千貳拾柒兩 |
| 入酬謝關船救護銀 | 共關平銀無 |
| 入暫存銀號銀兩之利息 | 共關平銀貳百叁拾陸兩捌錢 |

| | |
|---|---|
| 入本關人等違章罰項 | 共關平銀貳兩柒錢伍分 |
| 入未能預先列各名項銀 | 共關平銀拾伍兩肆錢貳分 |
| 入經費罰款船鈔另款各尾數 | 共關平銀無 |
| 入總稅務司補發之項 | 共關平銀無 |

## 支款

| | |
|---|---|
| 出還上結末入之墊款 | 共關平銀無 |
| 出奉總理衙門飭撥銀兩之支項 | 共關平銀無 |
| 出華商船牌費歸總理衙門三分之一 | 共關平銀壹百兩 |
| 出華商船牌關照費歸監督三分之一五成 | 共關平銀壹百伍拾兩 |
| 出引水帳各銀兩 | 共關平銀無 |
| 出招工帳各銀兩 | 共關平銀無 |
| 出關船救護得酬謝銀之支項 | 共關平銀無 |

出未能預先列名之項　共關平銀無

出船鈔經費罰款各尾數　共關平銀無

出總稅務司提項　共關平銀叁千陸百貳拾玖兩伍分

存欵

以上共入關平銀捌千貳百叁拾貳兩壹錢柒分

共出關平銀叁千捌百柒拾玖兩伍分

共存關平銀肆千叁百伍拾叁兩壹錢貳分

光緒捌年拾貳月貳拾陸日　三品銜某某關稅務司某某呈報

頭等幇辦某某譯漢

隨申文第捌號

核對

光緒　年　月　日　總稅務司赫德轉呈

隨申文第　號

21.

江海關

自光緒捌年貳月拾肆日起

第捌拾柒結罰款案由清摺

至光緒捌年伍月拾伍日止

茲將本關本結罰款內之罰辦各案由開具於後

一本結以前各舊案至本結始完之案　共壹件

一本結各新案　共貳拾件

一本結底未完新舊各案　共壹件

計開

一本結以前各舊案至本結始完之案

第柒百肆拾伍案　光緒捌年貳月貳拾陸日在本關碼頭查有英商　洋行代華人將川羌重玖百拾貳斤報運復出口經本關查明該貨實重伍百肆拾捌斤該商係假報復出口貨物斤兩希圖照多報之數請領存票於叁月拾貳日罰繳關平銀拾兩

# 一本結各新案

第柒百伍拾壹案 光緒捌年貳月拾陸日在本關碼頭查有華商鎮興號將應稅之東洋海菜重貳拾萬陸千壹百斤報運進口經本關查明該貨實重貳拾貳萬壹千叁百肆拾陸斤該商係假報進口貨物斤兩卽於次日按少報之數罰繳應完正稅伍倍得關平銀壹百拾肆兩叁錢肆分

第柒百伍拾貳案 光緒捌年貳月貳拾壹日在本關碼頭查有英商　洋行代華商將應稅之美國下等參重壹百柒拾斤報運進口經本關查明實係美國揀凈參鬚參重壹百玖拾捌斤該商係假報進口貨色斤兩於貳拾叁日罰繳關平銀拾伍兩

第柒百伍拾叁案 光緒捌年貳月貳拾柒日在驗貨廠查有華商明記號將應稅之乾花重貳百拾柒斤估值關平銀肆兩報運出口經本關查明該貨應值關平銀拾柒兩叁錢陸分該商係假報出口貨物價值卽於次日按少報價值之數罰繳應完正稅拾倍得關平銀陸兩陸錢捌分

第柒百伍拾肆案　光緒捌年叁月初捌日在驗貨廠查有華商東利號將應稅之玉石壹百貳拾叁斤估值關平銀伍百伍拾叁兩報運出口經本關查明該貨應值關平銀捌百伍拾柒兩該商係假報出口貨物價值於初拾日照原報之價加增貳成合銀陸百陸拾叁兩購買復准該商按照實估之價贖回得關平銀壹百玖拾肆兩

第柒百伍拾伍案　光緒捌年叁月初拾日在英國北京輪船查有華商乾元號將木耳貳百陸拾壹斤報運進口江漢關總單內載木耳貳百拾壹斤本關查驗實係貳百陸拾伍斤係進口貨物斤兩與總單不符於拾貳日按全貨之數罰繳正半兩稅伍倍得關平銀拾壹兩玖錢叁分

第柒百伍拾陸案　光緒捌年叁月拾肆日在招商局懷遠輪船查有招商局代華人將緞肆拾貳斤報運復出口經本關查明實係綢肆拾貳斤未經完稅該商係揑報已完稅之復出口貨物於肆月拾伍日罰充入官變價得關平銀壹百肆拾捌兩陸錢肆分

第柒百伍拾柒案　光緒捌年叄月拾捌日在英國呢斯得輪船查有華商何昌號私下應稅之桂圓叄百伍拾伍斤被本關查拏卽於是日議繳罰項該商延未繳銀桂圓日久壞爛無從變價

第柒百伍拾捌案　光緒捌年叄月拾玖日在招商局致遠輪船查有華客張元甫將土布肆拾斤報運出口呈驗後經本關查出下船之貨實係土布陸拾肆斤該商係不將呈驗之原貨下船於貳拾捌日罰充入官變價得關平銀拾壹兩

第柒百伍拾玖案　光緒捌年叄月貳拾捌日在關照船第柒拾號查有華人名童水芝勾通船主華人私將已下船之日本下等參拾箱重伍百捌拾柒斤抵換參鬚拾簍重柒百斤經本關查出於肆月初柒日將貨全數罰充入官變價得關平銀叄百肆拾肆兩伍錢柒分並罰船主關平銀壹百兩

第柒百陸拾案　光緒捌年肆月初肆日在黃浦河面查有華商昌順怡將高麗參貳百斤報復運出口查驗後不卽將貨下船而私運回棧意圖抵換他貨經本關查出於初玖日罰充入官准貨主照關訂減價買回得關平銀伍百兩

第柒百陸拾壹案 光緒捌年肆月初玖日在英國瓊州輪船查有該船水手華人等將違禁之槍子柒百拾個火藥伍百盒藏匿船內進口被本關查拏於叁拾日罰充入官火藥送交監督儲庫槍子本關購用貳百伍拾個其餘寄往香港變價共得關平銀伍兩伍錢柒分

第柒百陸拾貳案 光緒捌年肆月拾壹日在本關碼頭查有駁船行主華人周鼎擅用現已撤銷執照之駁船貳隻撥運貨物此案尚未了結

第柒百陸拾叁案 光緒捌年肆月拾伍日在招商局江天輪船查有不識姓名華客將違禁之私鑄小銅錢伍拾伍斤藏匿行李內進口被本關查拏即於次日罰充入官領銘變價得關平銀貳兩肆錢

第柒百陸拾肆案 光緒捌年肆月拾捌日在招商局江天輪船查有華商通泰錢莊未領執照將銅錢叁百伍拾千文私運進口被本關查拏即於是日罰充入官變價得關平銀壹百捌拾伍兩

第柒百陸拾伍案　光緒捌年肆月貳拾肆日查有華商泰昌號將米玖百擔報運進口並呈交　江漢關監督發給運米執照壹紙經本關查出原照內載叁百擔該商係私自改爲玖百擔字樣於叁拾日罰繳關平銀貳百兩

第柒百陸拾陸案　光緒捌年肆月貳拾柒日在丹國益德輪船查有該船幫買辦華人私起示禁之闈姓票壹百玖張並將拾伍元之銀票壹紙呈交司事之人意圖賄買放行經本關查出卽於次日一倂入官闈姓票送由　監督銷燬銀票易換得關平銀拾兩

第柒百陸拾柒案　光緒捌年伍月初肆日在英國厚華輪船查有該船主英國人在停船界外未領特發准單將違禁之炸火藥數件擅行起入躉船經本關查出於拾壹日罰繳關平銀貳拾伍兩

第柒百陸拾捌案　光緒捌年伍月初肆日英國北海輪船到口尚未下錨查有舢板華女等擅行上船經本關查出於次日罰繳關平銀壹兩並將該舢板入官變價得關平銀貳兩

第柒百陸拾玖案 光緒捌年伍月拾壹日在英國北京輪船查有協興昌信局不識姓名華人將應稅之絲線帽頂壹千個綢緞肆斤藏匿信袋內進口被本關查拏於拾肆日罰充入官准該局照關訂減價買回得關平銀拾兩

第柒百柒拾案 光緒捌年伍月拾叁日在英國漢口輪船查有該船傭役華人等將違禁之食鹽伍百伍拾斤藏匿船內進口被本關查拏於拾伍日罰充入官送由監督變價得關平銀拾壹兩

一本結底未完新舊各案

第柒百陸拾貳案 詳在本結清摺

光緒捌年陸月初壹日一等寶星三品銜江海關稅務司阿貝呈報

署理江海關左副稅務司頭等幫辦席笛譯漢

隨申文第壹百伍拾陸號

光緒　年　月　日　總稅務司赫德轉呈

核對

隨申文第　號

## 22.

謹稟

稅務司大人台下茲因完姻

請假二十日計自光緒八年六月二十日起至七月初九（西歷一千八百八十二年八月初三日起至八月二十二）

日止伏希

核准施行再者前次係於光緒五年十一月初一日起至十一（西歷一千八百七十九年十二月十三日起至十二）

月十五（二十七）日止請假十五日又本年共有兩日未經到關合並聲明

光緒八年六月十八日　吳德衡呈

## 23.

具稟人茅大有為懇請給假事竊大有在本造冊處充當印字之役計自英

一千八百六十六年二月進工迄今已歷年所未曾告假旋里茲因接來家

書催速回家完娶故敢冒瀆

臺前求為恩准給假兩個月俾得完婚及妥理要務則戴德靡涯矣故特懇求

末士拔拉茂旦代呈

稅務司大人台電

光緒元年九月　日　茅大有字稟

## 24.

# 江海關紅單

監督江南海關蘇松太兵備道　爲徵收稅鈔事據英國商船投報貨物當經遵照條約章程計噸科鈔按貨科稅即令本商自赴銀號按照驗單完納稅鈔茲已照完清楚呈驗號收稟請發給紅單前來合行塡發收訖紅單給該船主收執須至紅單者

計開

英國商船名波威卡沙耳編第二萬三千八百三十六號前往東洋完納船一千六百五十四噸鈔銀另照

完納進口稅銀十六兩一錢五分九厘

完納出口稅銀六百六十六兩一錢五分九厘

通共完銀六百八十二兩三錢一分八厘

光緒　八年　六月　二十二　日給

## 25.

# 天津海關收稅單

欽命二品銜監督天津新鈔兩關辦理直隸通商事務兼管海防兵備道周　為

給發收單事茲據英國商人豐昌稟報置買內地後開貨物共計

四十四件石已經完納出口稅餉今將該貨裝載英國第九十一

號商船名南升運往上海口銷售合行發給已完天津海關出口

稅項單持赴外洋口呈驗照完進口稅銀不准作抵別口稅課須

至收單者

計開

生牛皮　一件　九百九十斤

猪鬃　十件　十四担二十九斤　估銀三百四十二兩九錢一分

棉羊褥　三十三包　五千六百張　估銀三千九百二十兩

完稅銀二百十八兩九分八厘

右照給英國第九十一號商船收執

光緒　八年　六月　十七　日給

限到口日呈繳

## 26.

# 土貨出口正半稅單

監督湖北江漢關漢黃德道　爲給發出口土貨正稅單事案查長江
統共章程內開長江出口土貨在長江三關出口均由各該關查驗
自行征收稅餉按照條約已開通商各口辦理等因今據　英國太
古商北京船在漢置辦出口土貨由本關查驗給予驗單令該商自
赴銀號交納呈繳號收前來合給正稅單收執以憑持往起貨之關
呈驗單貨不得相離須至稅單者

計開

藥材　五件　八担二十斤本九十六兩

粉絲　四件　六担

其正半稅銀業已完清　計百拾五二兩八九錢八四分　厘

光緒　八年　六月　十七日給

右單給英國商人太古收執

如有核錯即請更正此單係第　萬

千　百玖拾　號限到上海關呈繳

## 27.

# 已完正稅憑單

監督浙江海關分巡甯紹台兵備道　爲給發憑單事案奉行准
總理衙門咨查土貨復進口半稅除長江三口應在所出之口預
行呈交外其餘各口均應於所進之口呈交不准再發已收土貨
復進口半稅執照等因奉遵在案今據某國商人敘豐稟有前由
中國第一百三十五號船由上海口運來土貨曾經帶有江海關
征收出口正稅收單呈驗當已照完復進口半稅茲因仍不合銷
現將原貨下入英國第一百號船轉運上海口等情前來本關查
貨相符除將本關所收復進口半稅發還存票外合行塡發該貨
業已呈過江海關已收出口正稅收稅單之憑據給該商持赴上
海口查驗可也須至憑單者

計開

黃連　一件　一百五斤　估銀七十三兩五錢

光緒　八年　六月　二十　日給

# 28.

## 江海關發給免重徵執照

監督江南海關分巡蘇松太兵備道　爲給發免重征執照事查商人運貨完清稅課復欲改運別口售賣者驗明寔係原包原貨查與底薄相符並未拆動抽換即照數塡給執照准其前赴該口呈驗俾免重征茲據德國商人美最時照報後開貨物前經完納稅課今將原貨裝載英國第二萬三千九百零二號商船名重慶運往天津口售賣當經查驗貨物相符合行發給免重征執照爲此給照准將後開貨物運赴該口呈照驗明照貨相符准其起貨售賣免其重征須至免重征執照者

計開

鈕扣　五件　五百各羅斯

此貨前由一千二百十七號北船進口完過稅銀二十七兩五錢

分　厘

右照給英商怡和收執

光緒　八年　六月　十四　日給

限至天津關日繳

8

29.

# 江海關船鈔執照

監督江南海關蘇松太兵備道　爲給船鈔執照事案查英國條約凡商船欲往通商各口並香港地方該船主稟明海關發給專照自是日起以四個月爲期如未逾四個月之限毋庸另納船鈔茲據商　完納船鈔呈驗號收請給專照前來合行給照該商收執准其四個月以內免重納鈔須至執照者

計開

丹商電線行報到丹國商船名斯打諾的編列第六百二十二號該船計五百九十六噸完納鈔銀二百三十八兩四錢正

九月十七日起限

光緒　七年　十月　初三　日給

## 30.

護照

欽命布政使銜江蘇分巡常鎮通海兵備道監督鎮江關沈　爲
給發護照事准
總辦輪船招商局咨准
天津海防支應局轉准
保定修志局咨解書價開單續購書籍咨局專人赴
金陵淮南官書局照購由鎮運滬轉津咨請免稅驗放等因准此並據局
董吳鑾稟先購到
金陵局書籍裝貳拾叁箱連箱共重叁拾伍担由鎮局輪船運滬轉
津稟請給照前來合行給護爲此照給收執經過沿途
關卡呈請查驗放行以免阻滯須至護照者
右照給招商輪船局收執
光緒　八年　六月　二十二　日給
關　限到日繳銷

# 31.

## 護照

監督浙江海關分巡甯紹台海防兵備道瑞　爲
給發護照事前奉
總理衙門文開凡遇官員人等過關如係照例隨帶各物並無應行
納稅之貨赴關報明監督發給印照並於印照內註明箱隻物件數
目方准免驗等因在案茲據順天府文安縣廩生紀培稟稱茲届壬
午科鄉試馳赴北闈應試隨帶行李衣箱等件請給護照前來合行
給護爲此照給持赴沿途關卡營汛查驗放行幸勿留難阻滯切切
須至護照者

計開

書箱 貳隻　衣箱 肆隻　花板 壹副　零星什物 肆件

右照給持赴前途關津卡隘准此

光緒 八年 六月 日給

關

限 日繳銷

## 32.

# 免照

欽加二品銜監督江南海關分巡蘇松太兵備道兼管銅務隨帶加三級邵　爲
給照事案於同治六年五月三十日准　蘇藩司移奉
撫憲札准
戸部咨議復給事中洪昌燕奏請招商採買稻米雜糧赴津銷售其
出口進口概免厘稅一摺奉
旨依議欽此嗣於同治九年又奉札准
戸部咨順天府查復近京一帶收成歉薄仍賴商販米糧接濟民食
應准暫緩納稅抽厘移咨查照六年奏案辦理等因奉經出示曉諭
在案茲據號商永記採買米一百包重一百五十担由順和船裝運
赴津取具保結禀求給照持赴關津局卡驗免厘稅等情據此除將
保結存案並詳咨外合行給照爲此照給該商收執前往沿途如遇
關津局卡即將此照呈請驗放倘帶別項貨物仍照例逢關納稅遇
卡抽厘一俟回滬即將此照繳銷切切須至執照者

右照給號商　永記　收執

光緒　八年　五月　二十九　日給

江南海關

限六個月日繳

## 33.

### 執照

欽加布政使銜江南分巡蘇松太兵備道兼管海防水利驛鹽事務加十級紀錄十次劉　爲

給發執照事光緒六年七月三十日奉

兩江督憲劉　札准

福建撫部院勒　咨閩省本年交夏後雨霪江漲幾致成灾稻糧不

無減色現在設法招商購運藉以均濟

奏請照案概行免稅等因並奉

撫憲吳　札同前由各到道奉此除出示曉諭並函致

新關稅務司照辦外所有商人採買米石運赴福州省城銷售應即

查照上屆運閩免稅成案給照辦理今據商人和昌成採米壹百包

重壹百伍拾担裝恰便輪船運往福州省城銷售呈具保結前來除

批示外合行給照爲此照給收執持赴新關聽候

稅務司驗明免稅放行可也須至執照者

右照給商人和昌成收執

光緒　八年　肆月　十九　日給

兵備道　限六個月繳銷

## 34.

# 運洋貨入內地之稅單

監督江南海關分巡蘇松太兵備道邵　爲
給發稅單事照得通商章程內載運入內地洋貨該商應將該貨名
目若干往內地何處報關查驗照納內地稅項該關發給內地稅單
該商應向沿途各子口呈單照驗蓋戳放行無論遠近俱不重徵又
通商各口通共章程第一欵載明洋商由上海運洋貨進長江俟到
長江各口後一經離口自入內地販運如無長江各關稅單者進關
納稅遇卡抽釐末後聲明南北各海口均照長江一律辦理又烟台
會議條款載明洋貨運入內地請領半稅單照應由總理衙門核定
畫一款式不分華洋商人均可請領各等因除運入內地不領稅單
之洋貨仍照通共章程辦理外茲據 德國商人美記 華商 報關欲將後開
洋貨販運前往安徽省寧國府 甯國縣 州 請給發內地稅單等情據此
合應發給稅單以便沿途查驗蓋戳放行須至單照者

計開

細葵扇　一件　二千二百把

其內地稅業已完清

右照給 德國商人美記 華商 收執

光緒八年六月二十六日

限　日繳銷

35.

# 買土貨之報單

監督江南海關分巡蘇松太兵備道劉　爲
給發空白報單事據英國領事官來文內開茲有英國商人祥茂稟
明後開之貨既祇第一子口該商自必在海口照通商稅則完納半
稅茲請先發空白報單等因據此本關合給空白報單同樣三紙由
領事官飭該商在單上當堂畫押給領准往買貨所經第一子口或
該商或商夥呈此三單眼同子口驗看該貨件數斤兩並現往何海
關出口商人均自行註明單內子口收下三單即將一單蓋印加封
飛速由驛移送該商所報出口海關查照又將一單蓋印按月呈送
總理各國事務衙門備查其餘一單存留子口即照單填發該貨運
照給該商前往路上各子口呈驗蓋戳放行俟將到出口海關設卡
之處則由卡帶同運貨之人赴海關請領已在海關完納半稅單據
方准過卡若有違此例及業經報明指赴何口沿途私賣者或別有
隱漏之弊除將各貨均罰入官外仍令該商在海口照第一子口所
註明之貨數完納稅則半稅如有匿單少報等情應將單內同類之
貨全數入官須至報單者
所買土貨數目開列於後

赴 南潯 菱湖 震澤 新市 烏鎮 雙林 辦 亂絲頭 念陸包 繭殼 叁拾壹包 計重 念陸担 壹千貳百肆拾斤
計裝船兩隻

右貨於　年　月　日祇第一子口即　關查驗現在運往　海關出口

光緒　八年　正月　十七日　由江南海關發給

此紙應由子口飛送該商所報出口之　海關查收以憑徵稅

## 36.

# 保單執照

監督山海鈔關分巡奉錦山海關兵備道　爲

給發印照事案照銅錢米穀等物向例不准出口現照新定章程稍寬其禁准令洋商於中國通商口岸以此口運至彼口或由該商呈具保單或另交結實信據方准給照別口監督於印照上註明收到字樣從給照之日起限六個月繳回驗銷船載無論淺滿均納船鈔等因在案茲據洋商可熾順稟有後開貨物下入中國第元號商船運上海照章呈具保結請發印照前來除經核驗相符並將保結存查外合行給照爲此照給該商准將照內貨數運往上海一經到口即行呈請

江海關驗明批註加蓋印信從給照之日起限六個月回山海關驗銷倘逾限不繳即按保結所載銀數罰繳入官須至印照者

計開

芒米　一百四十四袋　一百八十四担三十二斤

右照給洋商可熾收執

光緒　八年　二月　初六日

山海關給照

限六個月繳回

## 37. 江海關各國商船進出起下貨物條款

第一欵凡商船赴上海者行至寶山正頂與砲台對徑之界過此卽爲進上海口

第二欵凡商船進口本關派役管押領紅單出口之時復由本關一體查驗

第三欵凡商船進口停泊船隻及起下貨物之界限南自東門小河口起北至英國兵船廠止

第四欵凡商船進口該船主須在二十四點鐘內將船牌及艙口單呈交本國領事官如本國現無領事卽由該船主自行呈關倘過四十八點鐘尚未呈送卽將船主按照條約議罰

第五欵凡商船進口之艙口單須由該船主認保無訛該單內應將艙內所有一切貨物何字號何件數詳細載明倘查有呈遞假單者該船主應照條約罰洋銀五百元如係但有錯誤在遞單後二十四點鐘內請改者免其議罰再所載之貨如有不在此口起岸者亦應於單內註明

第六欵凡商船只許在例准起貨下貨之界限內起貨下貨以及裝上押載之物均須日間不得在日出以前日落以後禮拜日給假日均不准行

第七欵凡商船呈交船牌進口貨單欲起貨者由該商自備起貨單一紙詳細開載某字號某貨件數斤兩及估價數目等情呈關請領起貨單卽照單起貨如無本關蓋戳之起貨單私行起動者該貨入官該船主照罰

第八欵凡商船應起貨物已經起清本關派役查艙之後方准下貨亦照起貨之例由該商自備請下貨單一紙詳載某字號某貨件數斤兩及估價數目等情呈關請領下貨單即許照單下貨如無本關蓋戳之下貨單私行下貨或下入剝船者該貨入官

第九欵凡商人領單下貨因船載已滿復行退回者須帶貨赴本關碼頭查驗方准上岸

第十欵凡商船下齊貨物須呈出口貨單應將艙內出口一切貨物何字號何件數均須詳細開載呈關如遞假單船主照罰

第十一欵凡兩船欲行互撥貨物必先請領本關特准單據方准互撥不領單據私行互撥者所撥之貨入官

第十二欵凡商船進口應納之船鈔銀兩如在四十八點鐘內何時起貨即何時照納如過四十八點鐘後即不起貨亦應照納鈔銀

第十三欵凡商船欲請紅單先由本關派人到船將起貨下貨各單通行查對俟本關核知進出艙口單皆無訛誤各項稅鈔均已完清即准給發紅單領回船牌出口

第十四欵本關每日十點鐘開關四點鐘封關禮拜日給假日停辦公事

以上各欵如商人有應特請之事須隨時聲候　稅務司酌行

## 38. 上海口理船廳章程

此章係經在口各國領事官公同商定准行

第一欵凡洋船停泊界限以東門外小河口起爲上段至英國兵船廠之中止爲下段

第二欵凡洋船進口駛至英國兵船廠之處理船廳之幫辦應須上船指引妥當之處停泊倘有船隻係用小輪船拖帶而入者將到泊界下段理船廳所設辦公房屋之處該拖船應當暫行緩駛以便理船廳幫辦到船指引停泊

第三欵凡有常川來往船隻向經理船廳指有停泊之處者到口後可以徑入泊界至該處停泊不必等候理船廳帮辦到船倘船內載有危險防碍之物則應按照章程內第十一十二十四等欵辦理

第四欵凡泊界上段之內常應留空四船步位以備兵船到口停泊之用

第五欵凡船隻停泊之處須聽理船廳指示倘未奉有理船廳特發准單不得擅行移動

第六欵凡船隻泊定後欲由此處移往彼處須由該船主或頭等船夥或引水人前

赴泊界上段新關署理船廳公所內通報或赴下段內理船廳辦公房屋內通報亦可

第七欵凡船在口內停泊每逢日落以後日出以前須在頭桅第一層帆杠右邊懸掛白色明燈如無帆杠即於右邊繩索上懸掛

第八欵凡船旁外邊拴繫小船之橫木如係商船不准用可收可支活機之木惟兵船可用活機但白晝之間須將該木支出至夜晚時方始收回

第九欵凡船上所用錨鍊必須時常整理淸妥惟至月滿及月初生時尤爲緊要亦不准牽用繩索由此船至彼船至於船隻後面若帶有小船其繫船繩索要短不能過長以期便於船隻來往

第十欵凡商船未領理船廳特准單據不可在泊界內開放大砲及小槍

第十一欵凡商船進口載有裝火藥開花彈子數粒或火藥至一百磅灌藥槍彈至二萬粒必須在泊界三里路以外先行停泊頭桅上扯挂紅旗專候海關派人到船邊照指示之法辦理

第十二款凡商船進口載有自能爆開各項物料無論多寡必須按照第十一欵辦理

第十三欵凡船隻欲裝第十一十二兩欵內各項物件出口須先開出泊界三里外停泊以便裝載俟裝齊後只准向外開駛

第十四款凡商船進口載有各項能引火之油須在泊界第九段靠浦東岸邊停泊等候起清

第十五欵凡船隻進口內有瘟病之事須在泊界三里外先行停泊頭桅上扯挂黃旗若未領有理船廳特准單據不准有人私行上下

第十六欵凡各船船主不得准船上之人將船內壓載重物及煤灰炭碎抛棄浦中

第十七欵凡商船停泊界內船上水手人等欲要登岸必須酌留人數以數起下錨鍊之用

第十八欵凡商船進口必須將船頭支出之桅收進及收進之後如非理船廳所准不得再行支出

第十九欵凡商人欲設浮樁未先報准理船廳查看錨鍊及地方是否妥當不准自行安設至准設之浮樁如係無船拴繫之時每夜晚間必設一燈於上

第二十欵凡有派定准設之浮樁皆歸理船廳管理倘日後理船廳查出該浮樁或於行船不便或有他故可由理船廳諭令該浮主移換地方如理船廳業已諭令移換而浮主不即遵行理船廳可以代爲辦理一切使費應由浮主認付

第二十一款凡界內有船失火則在該船前後所泊之兩船應當鳴鑼報警並應照例扯挂有船被焚之旗如係夜間即將頭桅右邊所挂之燈扯上扯下再應飛報水巡捕理船廳及浦東挂旗望臺工部局等處知照

第二十二款凡商船進口載有可以轟爆之物於十一十二兩款如不按照辦理理船廳必令該船回駛出至泊界三里外停泊如未回至界外三里海關不准該船上下貨物亦不給發紅單所有商船如不按照第二第五第六等款不泊於理船廳所指之處海關亦是不准起下貨物不發紅單如後經理船廳報明該船業已照章辦理本關亦即照例准其所行至於船主如犯則款係由該本國領事查辦

# 續議告白

第一款商船進口後應掛該船船名之旗以便浦東扯旗望臺可以遠見

第二款商船進口後應請船主報知理船廳或引水人該船於路在何處見有礁石何處見有淺水何處見有壞船並於某處與某船相遇該船係由某口開來上海途間有無大風何日出口何日到此各等情形倘見有浮樁移動或船燈塔燈有踣滅損壞等情亦請報知理船廳知照

第三款船主凡於引水人意有不洽或引水人技藝生疎或性情不善該船一經到口即請船主趕緊通知理船廳即爲趕緊查辦

第四欵新關署理船廳公所大門內懸掛木板一塊隨時粘貼告白在上均係各船主所應知閱又各引水人姓名亦在上面可以一覽而知

第五款理船廳奉勸各船主切勿順潮進出誠恐碰壞別船或已船亦有損傷均惟該船主自行認理

第六款引水進口之價該船主可俟見有理船廳或派辦之人所給該船已在妥當之處停泊之據後再行付給

# 上海口吳淞泊船章程

此章係經在口各國領事官公同商定准行

第一款凡洋船至吳淞口其停泊之處係從口內小河口起至兵營傍白色房屋面前爲止

第二款凡洋船進口要在吳淞停泊者行至吳淞口外浮樁之處須掛藍白色旂相報行至吳淞內小河口所有理船廳派駐吳淞指泊人可以上船指示停泊之處該船主或引水人應當設法使指泊人便於上船

第三欵凡洋船進吳淞後欲過口內之淺沙灘須望準南岸所設標桿三根而行所有三桿聯貫對直線內及線左右各三百幅地內之處均不准停泊船隻

第四欵凡理船廳派去之指泊人應於沙灘起至吳淞口留出妥便之路一條以便船隻往來如見有在此路中停泊者恐其有碍則船可以令其移泊

第五欵凡有指泊人已經令其移船而未遵行銷因此故碰壞別船或已船亦有損傷均惟該船主自行認理

第六欵凡洋船進吳淞口如未按照指泊人所指之處停泊不准在吳淞起貨下貨再各船如有要故須在吳淞口起下貨物者必先特請海關稅務司查核允行方可照辦

第七欵凡指泊人指令拍定後所有船內之事仍歸引水人或船主自行料理

第八欵凡有夾板船進口行至吳淞內小河口指泊人必須上船接收該船所繼沿途情形之報函如該船係用小輪船拖帶者該拖船應當緩行以便指泊人易於上船

以上各欵如有船主違犯係由該本國領事官查辦

10

39.

# 江海關諭

照得五月初五日爲端陽節期本關例應給假一日停辦公事特諭

光緒　十年　五月　初二日

40.

欽加按察使銜東海關監督分守登萊靑兵備道潘　爲諭飭遵辦事案查外國火輪夾
板等船進口貨物卸地前經定章赴新關
稅務司處報稅給發紅單之後由該舖商人持紅單赴大關呈驗貨物相符准其上
岸原所以杜影射夾帶諸弊近聞有報卸外國等船貨物有先將貨物上岸後赴大
關呈驗紅單者有將貨物私卸上岸匿過紅單竟不赴大關呈驗者似此含混取巧
難保無影射夾帶各情弊自應申明舊章諭飭一體遵辦以杜弊端而重
國課合亟出示曉諭爲此示仰各路舖商人等知悉自此次出示之後凡有報卸火輪
夾板等船貨物在新關投稅請發紅單即將紅單持赴大關呈驗查明貨物與紅單

相符即蓋印大關覆驗訖戳記方准將貨物起卸上岸如有先將貨物上岸後投紅單者以及有私自上岸匿不呈驗紅單者一經查出定行提關查究倘所卸貨物與紅單所關不符從重議罰不稍寬貸各宜凜遵毋違特示

## 41.

### 本監督示

本關建築碼頭　專為查驗貨物　商人上岸登舟　行走原所不計
聞有土妓游娼　也在碼頭混雜　塗朱搽粉招搖　實屬膽玩已極
現經派差巡查　嚴拿無恥之輩　敢有再到碼頭　發縣重究不貸

以上告示懸掛海關門前碼頭

## 42.

### 本監督示

嚴拿偷漏　禁止逾越
如敢故違　重究不貸

以上告示四詞本關門前碼頭懸掛相同

43.

# 江海關啓

啟者本關現有充公綢緞川土東洋參羽紗鞋子扇子及零星等貨於本月二十六日二點鐘時由督意師摩洋行在本關棧房代爲拍賣　貴客有欲購買者即屆時赴關面拍可也再者買貨之人必須酌帶銀洋若干以便拍定時隨即交付不得於拍定後以未帶銀洋借詞推諉至囑至囑此佈

光緒　十年　四月　二十二日

44.

欽加按察使銜東海關監督分守登萊青兵備道潘　爲曉諭事照得烟台海關爲中外商船雲集之所向來各路船隻進口隨意停泊漫無定處倘有碰撞彼此皆有損傷現經本監督與

本關稅務司商定凡外國火輪夾板等船均停泊在東北首鼻烟台山一帶不得逾滋大碼頭其內地商船均停泊在西南大關之前一帶亦以滋大碼頭爲界庶中外商船各有停泊定處不致有互相碰撞損壞之虞除照會

稅務司查照外合亟出示曉諭爲此示仰各路商船知悉凡到烟台海口船隻務照所定界限停泊毋違特示

右仰知悉

同治　六年　正月　二十二日

告示押　　實貼新關

45.

欽加按察使銜東海關監督分守登萊青兵備道潘　爲曉諭事照得各路商船進烟台海口不得將壓載沙土石塊抛擲海口致礙船行前經示令中外一切商船凡有壓載沙土石塊即用杉板運至新關前堆積如有不遵照章議罰在案兹查新關業已築立碼頭未便再行堆積現與本關稅務司議定於大關前設立木樁凡有壓載沙土石塊仍用杉板運至木樁界內堆積不得在別處抛擲合亟出示曉諭爲此示仰各路商船知悉嗣後凡外國火輪夾板以及內地江浙建廣湖衞關東並本省一切商船進口內有壓載沙土石塊即用杉板運至大關前木樁界內堆積倘有在海口別處任意抛棄以致有礙船行如外國船由稅務司查明照章議罰內地船由本監督查明一律照章議罰不稍寬貸各宜凜遵毋違特示

右仰知悉

同治　六年　正月　二十二日

告示　押　實貼新關

46.

謹按天津條約原訂在上海兩國各派委員酌議各口及內地稅則現今面爲商
定彼此分送

大清
欽差大臣東閣大學士正白旗滿洲都統總理刑部事務桂
欽差大臣經筵講官吏部尚書鑲藍旗漢軍都統稽察會同四譯館花
欽差大臣太子少保兵部尚書都察院右都御史江南江西總督何
欽差大臣二品頂戴武備院卿明
欽差大臣五品卿銜軍機處行走刑部員外郎段
大英
欽差世襲額羅金並金喀爾田二郡伯爵額
逐欵核定並另行酌定章程俾得申明條約更爲周備所有稅則及後開各章程
兩國官民與條約一同遵守爲此本大臣等親筆畫押蓋用關防以昭信實合將
新定稅則開列於左

通商章程善後條約

第一欵

一此次新定稅則凡有貨物僅載進口稅則未載出口稅則者遇有出口皆應照進口
稅則納稅或有僅載出口稅則未載進口稅則者遇有進口亦皆照出口稅則納稅

倘有貨物名目進出口稅則均未賅載又不在免稅之列者應核估時價照值百抽五例征稅

第二款

一凡有金銀外國各等銀錢麵粟米粉砂穀米麵餅熟肉熟菜牛奶酥牛油蜜餞外國衣服金銀首飾攙銀器香水碱炭柴薪外國蠟燭外國烟絲烟葉外國酒家用雜物船用雜物行李紙張筆墨氈毯繡貨鐵刀利器外國自用藥料玻璃器皿以上各物進出口通商各口皆准免稅除金銀外國銀錢行李毋庸議外其餘該船裝載無論淺滿雖無別貨亦應完納船鈔倘運往內地除前三項仍無庸議外其餘各貨皆每百兩之物完納稅銀貳兩伍錢

第三款

一凡有違禁貨物如火藥大小彈子砲位大小鳥鎗幷一切軍器等類及內地食鹽以上各物概屬違禁不准販運進出口

第四欵

一凡有稅則內所算輕重長短中國壹担卽係壹百觔者以英國壹百叁拾叁磅零叁分之壹爲準中國壹丈卽拾尺者以英國壹百肆拾壹因制爲準中國壹尺卽英國拾肆因制又拾分因制之壹英國拾貳因制爲壹幅地叁幅地爲壹碼肆碼欠三因制卽合中國壹丈均以此爲例

第五欵

一向來洋藥銅錢米穀荳石硝磺白鉛等物例皆不准通商現定稍寬其禁聽商遵行納稅貿易洋藥准其進口議定每百觔納稅銀叁拾兩惟該商止准在口銷賣一經離口即屬中國貨物祇准華商運入內地外國商人不得護送即天津條約第九條所載英民持照前往內地通商并二十八條所載內地關稅之例與洋藥無涉其如何征稅聽憑中國辦理嗣後遇修改稅則仍不得按照別貨定稅又銅錢不准運出外國惟通商中國各口准其以此口運至彼口照現定章程遵行該商赴關報明數目若干運往何口或令本商及同商二人聯名具呈報單抑或聽監督飭令另交結實信據方准給照別口監督於執照上註明收到字樣加蓋印信從給照之日起限六個月繳回驗銷若過期不繳銷執照即按其錢貨原本照數罰繳入官其進出口均免納稅至船載無論淺滿均納船鈔　又凡米穀等糧不拘內外土產不分何處進口者皆不准運出外國惟英商欲運往中國通商別口則照銅錢一律辦理出口時照依稅則納稅其進口毋庸納稅至船載無論淺滿均遵納船鈔　又荳石荳餅在登州牛莊兩口者英國商船不准裝載出口其餘各口該商照稅則納稅仍可帶運出口及外國俱可　又硝磺白鉛均為軍前要物應由華官自行採辦進口或由華商特奉准買明文方准進口該關未能查明該商實奉准買定不發單起貨此三項止准英國商人於通商海口銷售不准帶入長江並各內港亦不准代華商護送

除在各海口外卽係華民貨物與英商無涉以上洋藥銅錢米穀荳石荳餅硝磺白鉛等項止准照新章買賣敢違此例所運貨物全罰入官

第六欵

一天津條約英國第三十七條所載英船進口限壹日報領事官知照並照第三十條所載英國貨船進口並未開艙欲行他往限貳日之內出口卽不征收船鈔以上二條無論先後總以該船進口界限時刻起算以免參差爭論至各口界限並上下貨物之地均由海關妥爲定界旣要便商更不得有礙收稅知會領事官曉諭本國商民遵辦

第七欵

一天津條約第二十八條所載內地稅餉之議現定出入稅則總以照例一半爲斷惟第二欵所載免稅各貨除金銀外國銀錢行李三項毋庸議外其餘海口免稅各物若進內地仍照每値百兩完稅銀貳兩伍錢此外運入內地各貨該商應將該貨名目若干原裝何船進口應往內地何處各緣由報關查驗確實照納內地稅項該關給發內地稅單該商應向沿途各子口呈單照驗蓋戳放行無論遠近均不重征至運貨出口之例凡英商在內地置貨到第一子口驗貨由送貨之人開單註明貨物若干應在何口卸貨呈交該子口存留發給執照准其前往路上各子口查驗蓋戳至最後子口先赴出口海關報完內地稅項方許過卡俟下船出口時再完出口之稅若進出有違此例及業經報明指赴何口沿途私賣者各貨均罰入官倘有匿單

少報等情將單內同類之貨全數入官所運各貨如無內地納稅實據應由海關飭令完清內地關稅始行發單下貨出口以杜隱漏內地稅則經此次議定既准一次納稅概不重征所有英國第二十八欵所載經過處所應納銀實數明晰照復彼此出示曉布華英商民均得通悉一節可毋庸議

第八欵

一天津條約英國第九條所載英民持照前往內地通商一欵現議京都不在英商之列

第九欵

一向例英商完納稅餉每百兩另交銀壹兩貳錢作爲傾鎔之費嗣後裁撤英商毋庸另交傾鎔銀兩

第十欵

一通商各口收稅如何嚴防偷漏自應由中國設法辦理條約業已載明然現已議明各口畫一辦理是由總理外國通商事宜大臣或隨時親詣巡歷或委員代辦任憑總理大臣邀請英人幫辦稅務並嚴查漏稅判定口界派人指泊船隻及分設浮樁號船塔表望樓等經費事毋庸英官指薦干預其浮樁號船塔表望樓等經費在於船鈔項下撥用至長江如何嚴防偷漏之處俟通商後察看情形任憑中國設法籌辦

## 47. 鐘表稅章

凡鐘表進口完稅現准一體照值百抽五例辦理各商報關請驗單納稅時除件數價值外須將其運進口之鐘表註明匠人行名鐘表號數開列清單存關以備稽查由關按件壓印戳記作爲此鐘表完稅之據倘有假作此戳記者除將此鐘表入官充公外華商則照例從重治罪洋商則由領事官從重懲辦日後凡已有號數存關之鐘表復運出口回國者給以存票復進口者給以免單倘有商人將未經挂號之鐘表存行發賣或復運出口一經查出則准該關照各口貨物違章漏稅應行查拏之總例查獲入官凡有以細報粗以貴報賤價者准該關隨事酌情照該商自開之價收買至各行現存之鐘表自係已經納稅之物應限商人以六個月爲期將行內鐘表按匠人號數開列清單赴關報明備查六個月已滿違者不准發給存票免單等件並隨時將未經挂號之物查拏入官

## 48.

大清欽命總理各國事務衙門　爲

劄行事同治九年閏十月初五日據總稅務司申稱竊查洋商船隻完納鈔課原應畫一辦理始爲允協惟其間應徵應免各事非但各國條約本有不同即善後

所添章程亦多零星未能齊楚且有隨時更改因時制宜修補文件以致條欵重複章程紛雜擬議不一其勢實難一律遵行茲將條約章程善後條欵並往來文件詳加核對復以各口情形各關辦法細爲比較綜紛緒各條核存備各欵作成各關徵免洋商船鈔章程十一條彙訂清單即煩核奪轉飭遵行以免紛歧而歸畫一等因前來當經本衙門將章程十一條詳加查核尙屬周妥除將章程開明咨行南北洋通商大臣轉飭各關遵照並照會

各國大臣查照外相應將章程十一條劄行總稅務司轉行各口一體遵照辦理可也須至劄者 計章程十一條

右劄布政使銜總稅務司赫　准此

同治玖年拾壹月　日

各關徵免洋商船鈔章程十一條

一洋商船隻應納鈔課壹百伍拾噸以上每噸納鈔銀四錢一百五十噸正及一百五十噸以下每噸納鈔銀一錢惟各國噸數拉司數大小多寡不同而各關以英噸爲準則應照泰西一千八百六十五年在嚋拉所立之核算清單辦理

嚋拉所立核算清單列後

皇國噸數　乘以捌拾貳　除以壹百　其數爲英噸

法國噸數　乘以壹百　除以壹百　與英噸同

| | | | |
|---|---|---|---|
| 意國噸數 | 乘以捌拾玖 | 除以壹百 | 其數爲英噸 |
| 土耳國噸數 | 乘以壹百 | 除以陸千壹百伍拾叁 | 其數爲英噸 |
| 布國拉司 | 乘以壹百伍拾 | 除以壹百 | 其數爲英噸 |
| 俄國噸數 拉司 | 乘以壹百零捌 壹百捌拾玖 | 除以壹百 | 其數爲英噸 |
| 美國噸數 | 乘以壹百 | 除以壹百 | 與英噸同 |
| 比國噸數 拉司 | 乘以玖拾伍 壹百捌拾壹 | 除以壹百 | 其數爲英噸 |
| 伯磊們拉司 | 乘以壹百捌拾玖 | 除以壹百 | 其數爲英噸 |
| 丹國噸數 拉司 | 乘以壹百零貳 壹百玖拾陸 | 除以壹百 | 其數爲英噸 |
| 日國噸數 | 乘以壹百 | 除以壹百 | 與英噸同 |
| 希國噸數 | 乘以柒拾陸 | 除以壹百 | 其數爲英噸 |
| 昂布爾拉司 | 乘以貳百貳拾伍 | 除以壹百 | 其數爲英噸 |
| 漢諾威噸數 拉司 | 乘以玖拾捌 貳百貳拾伍 | 除以壹百 | 其數爲英噸 |
| 荷蘭國噸數 拉司 | 乘以捌拾玖 壹百叅拾伍 | 除以壹百 | 其數爲英噸 |
| 律伯克拉司 | 乘以壹百捌拾玖 | 除以壹百 | 其數爲英噸 |
| 模令布爾額噸數 拉司 | 乘以壹百零玖 貳百肆拾肆 | 除以壹百 | 其數爲英噸 |

挪爾爲國噸數拉司　乘以玖拾捌貳百零捌　除以壹百　其數爲英噸

阿爾敵布爾額拉司　乘以壹百伍拾　除以壹百　其數爲英噸

合一國噸數　乘以壹百　除以壹百與英噸同若係噶拉基羅乘以壹百除以肆百捌拾貳若蹡拉基羅乘以壹百除以叁百零壹

瑞國噸數拉司　乘以壹百零貳壹百玖拾捌　除以壹百　其數爲英噸

一各國商船進口尚未開艙欲行他往者限二日之內赴關報明則出口時不徵船鈔倘逾二日之限始領開艙准單即須當時輸納船鈔

一各國商船出口欲往通商他口並香港呂宋安南日本呢廓來業福斯克等處該船主赴關報明由關發給專照自領紅單之日起以四個月爲期如係往以上所指各口者其復進通商口岸時如在限內仍勿庸另行納鈔

一各國商船准赴各關請由該關派人度量其船再照所算之噸數納鈔由關發給量船執照爲憑此等船出口時無論赴何地何處均准自領紅單之日起以四個月爲期復在通商口岸往來毋庸另納船鈔凡遇進口時應將量船執照呈關查驗以便各關征鈔之事得以畫一辦理試辦再議

一凡通商口岸洋商自用艇隻運帶客人行李書信食物及例不納稅之物勿庸完鈔倘帶例應完稅之貨其船在一百五十噸以上下者則每四個月納鈔一次每噸

銀一四錢惟由他國所來之船進口時雖係搭客未裝貨物仍應納鈔其執有四個月專照者倘係向常運貨來往若遇專照應銷之日雖係祇搭客進口仍應照四個月之例納鈔辦理

一凡有公司輪船其由某國立定合同設傳文信按期定數由外國來往外國去者各關所給之四個月專照即可勿用指定某船收執緣此項船隻有時抵充來往既係公司按期出口之船即按其已納一次之鈔免四個月之鈔計算凡有該公司另項輪船進口並非抵額設等船之用者不在此例仍應按某船進口某船完鈔辦理試辦再議

一凡有商船收口躲避者其進口時須由領事官行文知照海關並將其末後出口單送關查閱以資稽查該船須遵守該口一切章程由關擇訂停泊處所不致與另項貿易船隻日行事宜有所窒碍並隨時派差看守倘係從外國來者則應按約免征船鈔放行倘係來自通商別口執有四個月專照者則計在口內躲避日期應扣除核算由該關註明專照放行惟該船除應修理方准照章起貨暫時存棧外其餘各船若係空船進口仍須空船出口若係裝貨進口仍須原船原貨出口凡有收口後在本口起卸貨物或零裝貨物販運出口者自應照約完納船鈔仍由該關查明有無專照進口按躲避日期核算辦理

一凡有往他口之輪船因煤炭燒完進此口買煤炭而復行者該船實非搭客進口在口內並無起貨下貨等事自應按照避收口例免征其鈔放行至納鈔者其牌內註明煤輪及內輪器具各處之噸數均應免納

一凡有洋商僱用內地船隻在長江一帶運貨者該船到關仍照內地船隻完納船料若在沿海各口來往者其船在一百五十噸以上下者即應每四個月納鈔一次每噸銀四一錢

一通商各口凡有拖帶船隻之輪船均應每逢四個月按其噸數納鈔一次

一凡引水之船自與商船有別准照引水章程免納船鈔來往

## 49. 引水章程專條

第一欵各口分章宜定擬也

一凡各口應定之分章及定明引水之界限並應用引水者若干名其引水各費一切事宜均應由理船廳準情酌理約與各國領事官並通商總局妥爲擬定

一引水界限各口應將本口界限自行註明

一口外引費各口應將本口引費自行註明

第二欵引水者宜寬其招募也

一凡華民及有條約各國之民有欲充引水者均准其一體充當惟遇有缺出即應由考選局按照現定之章程並本口之分章揀選充補

第三欵各口宜立有考選局也

一凡通商口岸每年應由理船廳約同各領事官並通商局將其可作考選之姓名預爲錄示以資幫辦考選之事俟有引水缺出即由理船廳於所錄之人中簽掣二人督同引水董事辦理考選之事

第四欵考選引水之人宜愼也

一凡有缺出應由理船廳榜示招募引水以八日後由考選局會齊考試

一備考者其中儻有曾充引水因事故而斥革者或未充引水而無本國官結者此二項人均不准濫膺赴考

一凡備試者勿庸納有規費等項考選局應合衆秉公考試於衆人中擇其最優者以爲入選然在備試中雖爲最優使其於引水之事仍非有實在本領亦甯缺而毋用以免貽誤

一備考者其國領事官或本人或派員均可在局從旁監同考試

一局內在事各人同有事權選中與否從衆爲定如領事委員均不在局其有各執已見者則以理船廳爲定評

12

第五欵充引水者宜發給執據也

一凡考選局派充引水者應赴稅務司由稅司代地方官發給引水字據請領字據者如非華民應令該引水赴本國之官處將字據呈驗挂號

一每年夏季引水各人應赴關將所領字據呈驗後續行領回並繳呈續領之費關平銀拾兩

一凡領有引水字據者發給引水章程並該口專條一分收執遇有索看者卽應並字據隨時呈出

第六欵引水學徒者宜有定制也

一凡已領字據之引水應准其各帶學徒一名須先赴理船廳報明並願保其學徒之人請領學徒之專照方准攜帶

一凡學徒領有考選局勝選憑照者如遇外需情事由理船廳於此項人內揀派數人准其在當時特定之界限暫行引水

第七欵引水宜聽制於理船廳也

一凡領有引水字據者或係獨作引船之事或係公同作引船之事均屬可行惟俱歸理船廳管理諭示一切皆須一體遵守奉行儻有違背者或暫撤執據或將執據撤銷皆由理船廳辦理惟仍准該引水限三日內赴領事官處稟訴撤據原委

一凡引水者若犯關章或另有違犯由領事官懲辦亦可由理船廳暫撤執據或撤銷執據引水者仍可在三日內赴領事官處稟訴撤銷執據之原委

一凡查出引船而無引水字據者或係假借他人字據應由理船廳知會其該國官照其本國例治罪凡領有字據者而借與他人除由理船廳將其字據撤銷辦理外亦應知會該國官照例治罪

一凡船主艄工若私以無字據之人引水者由該領事官罰銀壹百兩

## 第八欵引水船隻宜有定章也

一凡引水之船應由該引水將其船名船式大小及該船水手姓名開具清單一併呈報由理船廳發給號照後須將引水船字樣第幾號書明於船尾及篷上其旗須挂四方之式上半黃色下半綠色該船原有之本國牌照或存於領事署內或存稅司處皆可該引水果遵照各節方准該船在本口及引水界限內任便往來並免完納船鈔儻稅司理船廳派人在其界限內往來或號船及望樓運取應用物件一有理船廳吩咐其引水船即應任為使用

一引水船隻每年應交出字據費銀貳拾兩

一凡引水遇有緊急引務乘坐未經挂號船隻准將引水旗號暫時懸挂若平時未奉有理船廳特允不得擅行常用此無字據之船隻

一凡遇有未經掛號船艇並無領據引水人在上擅行懸掛引水旗號應將船戶
或僱用此船之人知會該管之官照例查辦
一凡引水船艇並無引水人在上或亦無學徒在上此時不得懸掛引水旗號

第九欵船隻進口宜有分別也

一凡船將至泊船界限時應由引水人分別飭掛號記
一如從通商口岸及香港東洋等處前來者應懸紅白旗（即英寄信旗第三號）
一如從外洋口岸前來者應懸藍白旗（即第二號）
一如並未裝載貨物應懸黃藍旗（即第十號）
一如載火藥或別樣引火之物應懸三角紅旗（即第五號）

第十欵口內停泊宜有定制也

一凡遇船隻駛至停泊地界應由口內引水前赴接領按照理船廳所指之處將
船停泊其或應行改泊及進出修廠來去馬頭並復行出口一切事宜均應由
口內之引水照料
一凡理船廳料理停泊事務宜酌體艄工經紀之便如有船不遵指定處所擅自

移泊他處則可由稅司將該船開艙起貨下貨各准單並出口紅單暫停准發俟其遵照改泊後再爲辦理

一凡停泊之處宜聽理船廳指示未經奉有特發准單不得擅行移離

一凡口內引費由理船廳照後開之例代收凡引至停泊之處及由停泊之處引至界外等事輪船及輪船拖帶之篷船每尺繳費銀　篷船每尺繳費銀

凡引帶出入修廠及添錨等事輪船及輪船拖帶之篷船每尺繳費銀　篷船每尺繳費銀

凡更移停泊輪船及輪船拖帶之篷船每尺繳費銀　篷船每尺繳費銀

凡引船來去馬頭輪船及輪船拖帶之篷船每尺繳費銀　篷船每尺繳費銀（其所空之銀數應各按各口情形自行擬訂塡寫）

以上十欵仍係試辦之章若猶有未能妥協之處亦可隨時酌擬更訂

同治　七年　九月　十五日

50.

一凡有商船進口搭船之人客應俟扦子手上船方准將行李起岸倘有未遵應將該船艄工議罰以專責成若扦子手疑所起行李內有違禁漏稅物件該客人如願自行打開備查如不願查即由扦子手將該件扣留送該關稅務司限該客三日內赴關眼同開看如逾限不到徑由關上開驗倘查有或違禁或漏稅之物除將扣留之件全行入官另將該客議罰

一凡有船進口除客人行李外倘裝有善後章程第二欵所載免稅各物須俟該關發給開艙准單方准起出倘有未領准單之先自行起卸或已入駁船或已起上岸一經查出除將所起之件入官外另照條約明文罰該船艄工銀五百兩至各種免稅物件該船艙口單均須註明貨主亦須照納稅物件章程先請起貨下貨各准單並將該貨赴關遵驗方准分別入棧下船

一通商各口凡有拖帶船隻之輪船應將船牌存領事官署內由領事行文報明係拖帶之輪船並無裝貨來往等事由該關將船名登簿後該船平常拖帶進出毋庸赴關稟明亦毋庸請領出口紅單倘欲赴通商別口仍須照條約定章赴關請領紅單赴領事官署內取回船牌若有此等拖帶輪船私赴別口未在原口領有紅單應將

該船罰銀五百兩該船每四個月完納船鈔一次如有私帶貨物或偷漏稅餉一經查出除將貨物入官外應由關於拖帶簿內將其船名刪除嗣後須照條約明定洋船之例時行報關請領紅單辦理

## 51. 會訊章程

一凡各口有干涉稅務案件領事官應先與稅務司彼此關照或面見會議或移文往來定案時仍照後開數條辦理

一凡有洋商或船或貨各在通商海口被關屬吏扣留立宜稟明監督監督聽稟以爲罰辦合宜即委稅務司函致該商所犯何法是以扣留限自接函之時以五日爲期准商稟報領事官知悉倘至第六日午刻領事官尚未來文咨請公同查核該船該貨即可入官該商接函後於期內仍見自無犯法任便先向稅務司陳明轉報監督監督若以該商之言爲是即行釋放船貨設該商不願赴關具稟仰或先稟監督不以爲然均准稟知領事官據其所稟轉咨監督請其定期公同查辦

一凡監督接到領事官來文照覆定期何日到關當堂晤會領事官諭飭該商是日統帶見證各人等赴關是時領事官親身來關上堂監督請其同坐該稅務司亦當在

坐相幫監督監督先令海關原拏船貨人役將如何扣留情節禀明監督監督按照情節隨時詰問凡如該商倘有辯駁情節准其當堂禀明領事官領事官即代爲逐一詰問以期得實而杜偏累設若監督領事官欲不親赴海關亦可遣員代往所有辦法一律相同

一詢問之間所有關役商證人等口供隨時抄錄監督領事各爲畫押蓋印時令全案人證退去監督面告領事官可否如何辦理或該船貨領事以爲應放而監督不以爲然又准該商任意上控具禀領事官行知監督均即各將案情抄錄蓋印申請
總理衙門與
駐京大臣查核定奪倘監督不肯釋放船貨領事官以爲然該商不准上控禀請轉詳再該船貨或經海關當堂詢明或經兩國
總理衙門
駐京大憲核定應行釋放均不能以原被扣留請索賠償

一案情既各詳請大憲定斷准該商按估價出具日後情願遵斷繳案切結由領事官蓋印交存該關即由監督將該船貨先行發還俟大憲斷定後或罰銀多少或全數入官再行飭商遵照倘該商不肯具結即將船貨扣留無論大憲定准誰是誰非不准該商禀請賠補

一凡各口指謂商人犯章其所犯之係並非船貨入官係按約按章應罰銀兩者稅務司一面知照監督一面遣人在領事官署內立案由領事官定期訊斷定期後應先知照稅司屆期傳集人證或稅司本人或委員即在坐指證如訊明該商實有應罰之處如係約章程內載有銀兩之數目即由領事官按其數斷令交出或可從寬辦理則其權屬在該關即由監督會同稅司自定可也倘查明該商實無應罰之處稅司亦無異言如有船貨因此案留滯者可一同開放仍將案情知照監督不得就延時日致該商稍有費用該商不得索賠延擱貿易銀兩亦不得索賠一切水脚費用等項若稅司與領事官意見不合即行知會監督一面抄錄全案各詳

總理衙門駐京大憲查核當尙未定案之時貨主亦應一律將擬罰銀數出具日後情願遵斷繳案切結送交領事官由領事官行文知照監督始准該商船貨先行開放

一如有監督領事官不能自定應徵應免之事均須援照本章程第五欵所載亦令該商出具日後情願遵斷繳案切結由領事官蓋印送交監督存案即由監督先將該商貨物暫時免稅放行一面將此案情形各詳

總理衙門駐京大憲倘日後斷定實係應免之稅該監督即將原結發還領事官查銷如斷定實係應納若干稅項之物該領事官即飭該商赴關按數完稅銷結

一凡有洋商或船或貨應入官者或船貨均應入官者監督與領事官意見未合案情既各詳
總理衙門
駐京大憲核斷當尚未定案之時該商應援照本章程第五款估價具結由領事官蓋印交存監督惟所估數目恐多寡不符即按該商自稱定價爲准由該關酌核情形亦可按價收買倘經收買後日後斷定船貨實應入官即飭該商將關上收買原銀如數呈繳銷結若斷定船貨實應釋放該關即將原結送還領事官發商完案所有收買原銀即作爲船貨賣價該商不得再持收買原銀赴關收贖以昭核實

## 52. 長江六處章程

案查烟臺條款第三款內載至沿江安徽之大通安慶江西之湖口湖廣之武穴陸溪口沙市等處均係內地處所並非通商口岸按長江統共章程應不准洋商私自起下貨物今議通融辦理輪船准暫停泊上下客商貨物皆用民船起卸仿照內地定章辦理除洋貨半稅單照章查驗免釐其有報單之土貨只准上船不准卸賣外其餘應完稅釐由地方官自行一律妥辦外國商民不准在該處居住開設行棧等語

所載不過是大槪辦法現將詳細章程開列於後

## 計關

一條款所載輪船字樣並非出洋輪船乃指內江輪船而言

一條款所載民船字樣並非各項船隻乃指該六處由卡掛號准作撥船編列字號而言

一六處除領有稅單之洋貨並領有報單運照之土貨驗明單貨相符洋貨即准其裝船或起岸放行土貨即准其裝船前赴所報出口海關該六處均不另征稅釐外其餘無單照各貨均照後開章程辦理

一由六處裝船運往六處起岸之貨先完裝船處釐金報明由此處運往彼處並不過關者如自大通赴安慶自陸溪赴沙市無庸完稅其須過一關者如自大通安慶至武穴自武穴至陸溪沙市俟到該關照完正稅此兩項均應將此去途中所經釐卡由裝船處釐局核明共有幾卡即照所完釐數令其再完幾倍以補應完之釐其須過兩關者俟到第一關照完正半兩稅應由裝船處釐局將此去所經第一關以前第二關以後共有釐卡幾所即照所完釐數令其再完幾倍以補應完之釐如由大通安慶運至沙市陸溪口起岸由沙市陸溪口運至大通安慶之貨中間一關以後二關以前釐卡准其免補若祇過一關及不過關者不得援免

一由六處裝船運往長江各關暨上海關起岸之貨先完裝船處釐金報明運赴何關俟到第一關照完正半兩稅應由裝船處將此去所經第一關以前共有釐卡幾所

卽照所完釐數令其再完幾倍以補應完之釐如所報起岸之關卽係第一關如自大通安慶至九江關自武穴至江漢關自陸溪沙市至宜昌關到關只完正稅不完半稅

一由上海關暨長江各關裝船運往六處起岸之貨除先在該關照完正半兩稅或只完正稅如自蕪湖關報運大通是僅經一關只完正稅如在鎮江關報運大通是所經兩關應完正半兩稅其經三四關者亦只完正半兩稅一次而止以上正半各稅均在裝船之關照完報裝輪船指赴某處並領收稅單到起岸處呈驗外應於起岸處照完該處釐金並由該釐局核明所經末尾一關以後共有釐卡幾所卽照所完釐數令其再完幾倍以補應完之釐如所經僅止裝船一關卽以該關爲末尾之關

一凡裝船處收釐均須塡發收釐單交該商於到關及起岸處呈驗如該貨須到關完稅該裝船處釐局仍應另寫總釐單封好交與船主送到所經第一關稅務司查收一面由該商持收釐單赴關呈驗完稅該關另給收稅單並將所呈收釐單加戳給還俾到起岸處再行呈驗倘六處裝船之貨到關及起岸處該商竟無完釐完稅各單呈驗者該貨入官其有以遠報近希圖偷漏者查出罰辦倘有在不准停輪之處私行上下貨物者該貨入官該輪船照章查辦

一六處內湖口一處應行另立完稅專章惟因湖口情形現在尚未查明其餘五處應

照現議之章先行試辦湖口一處須俟查明再議

一六處抽收釐金本與稅則無涉向就貨價每百抽二各按本處時價核收其收銀驗貨秤碼應與各關一律均不得稍有高下

一六處自沙市以至大通沿江抽收往來貨船釐卡查有沙市北河口鸚鵡洲樊口武穴（以上湖北五卡）二套口（以上江西一卡）華陽安慶大通（以上安徽三卡）共爲九卡該六處應各將沿江釐卡按上下游遠近次序懸牌寫明備查其應補釐金卽在六處之間不逾大通以東沙市以西並使各商知悉

一六處裝船之貨必須聽候查驗完清釐金將貨由官碼頭上掛號發船送上輪船六處起岸之貨應由掛號發船向輪船發出送到官碼頭聽候查驗辦理倘有私用未曾掛號之民船送貨發貨者該貨入官船戶提究

一六處所收釐金應分別各還各卡定期彙解以清款項所有釐金細數及貨色斤件應由各該處委員按七日造具清册並按外國月分造具總册分別呈送本省稅關及駐紮江漢關巡查六處關稅務司查核以便按結詳報

以上各欵均擬試辦一年如有未盡事宜及或有窒碍之處隨後相機酌改以期妥善查本年五月二十一日係泰西七月初一日卽爲第六十八結之始若此章可以暫爲試行擬卽從此日開辦

53. 稅務司諭

現下藥材進口無論正稅半稅開驗單時必須逐款開出名目觔數并估價照登底簿以免原貨出口有舛錯之悮毋違此諭

光緒元年六月二十一日諭

54. 稅務司諭 現牽

總稅務司諭日本參一項稅則內載上等日本參每重一觔征稅五錢下等參每重一觔征稅三錢五分現將上下之分酌定章程以便征稅

一日本參每觔價值五兩及五兩以外者作爲上等每觔征稅五錢

一日本參每觔價值一兩以外五兩以內者作爲下等每觔征稅三錢五分

一日本參每觔價值一兩以內者作爲不入等每觔征稅五分

所有價值一兩以內作爲不入等之日本參如有不願遵照此例完稅者則須按下等日本參之例每觔征稅三錢五分緣稅則所定原不過上下兩等也各海關一體

遵照以歸劃一[illegible]合[illegible]　　[illegible]進口須

用報單專報不得與他貨錯雜同列一單並須將該參所值價銀分類逐一開明是

爲至要特諭

光緒　柒年　拾貳月　初七　日

## 55.

## 稅務司諭　現奉

總稅務司諭夏布一項稅則內載細夏布每重百觔征稅二兩五錢粗夏布每重百觔征稅七錢五分現將粗細之分酌定章程以便征稅係將夏布量其橫徑每闊一因制之中核其直紗有若干縷其不過四十縷者作爲粗夏布征稅若過四十縷以外概作細夏布征收稅餉各海關一體遵照以歸劃一等因合即諭知各商遵照嗣後凡有夏布報關完稅必先自行核明該夏布橫徑每一因制之中其直紗在四十縷以內者作爲粗夏布其直紗在四十縷以外者作爲細夏布分別報關以免貽誤是爲至要特諭

光緒　柒年　肆月　初一　日

# 56. 第八十七結各口稅務司遇有疑難事件申請總稅務司核示辦法案由

一野蜂釀蜜徵稅辦法

據瓊海關稅務司本年第四十七號申文內稱本口森寶洋行將未凈野蜂釀蜜報運出口本關卽經按稅則所載蜂蜜一項徵稅嗣該商以若按稅則納稅其稅銀係按估價値百抽收十六之數未免過重請按稅則未載各貨照値百抽五之例徵收等情究應如何徵稅之處申請核示遵行等語

當經發寄該口第一百三十九號劄文內飭以出口稅則旣載蜂蜜一項野蜂釀蜜卽在其內自應一律徵稅不得有所歧異等因

一船鈔執照按德國新約展限辦法

據粵海關稅務司本年第四十一號申文內稱查德國續修條約第二款內載中國允德國夾板船隻在中國口岸停泊十四日以外者則自第十五日起卽於應交正數船鈔減半又第五款內載中國允尻德國船隻或在通商各口內口外受損應行修理者准由該口海關查明日期扣算該船應交之鈔項各等因現有德國夾板船

名韓墨尼亞於光緒七年九月二十六日進口旋於十月初六日卸貨後因該船受有損壞始行修理至十六日修理完竣請領紅單出口共計在口二十一日內有十一日係因受損修理自應按照第五款將船鈔執照展限十一日核算除展限十一日外計該船在口不過十日之期其第二欵所載應無庸議如此辦理是否與德國續約以上兩款相符申請核奪示覆遵行等語

當經發寄該口第七百五十四號劄文內飭以此案該關辦理並無不合茲按所指續約以上兩款解釋數端以期曉然開錄於後

一設若該船在口內停泊二十一日並無修船情事則應照續約第二欵自第十五日起至二十一日止共七日減半係三日半亦可通融將船鈔執照作四日

扣算展限

一設若該船於修理完竣後未於是日請領紅單至十月二十九日始行請領紅單出口因領單後去留係聽船主自便故領單之日不應計算共計該船在口三十三日除修船十一日外尚有二十二日則自第十五日起至二十二日止共有八日減半係四日應將船鈔執照連修船日期共扣算展限十五日

一設若該船進口或無船鈔執照或有執照因何故展限而在出口之先應行繳

銷者此船於出口之日自應完納船鈔惟不得於新爲領換之執照內將展限
日期接續扣算

一拆賣船料免稅辦法

據粤海關稅務司本年第六十號申文內稱查德國續修條約第六欵內載中國允凡德國損壞船隻有在中國通商各口內拆賣該船各料者准其不另徵進口稅銀惟起岸時仍須照各貨一律赴關請領起貨准單爲憑等語倘係無約各國或係華商船隻進口拆賣是否應一律免稅或該船無船牌者是否應按該船未拆賣之先所挂旗號爲憑登入某國册簿或該船有船牌而在口無領事官者該船拆賣後船牌應呈繳何處存銷相應一併申請核示等語

當經發寄該口第七百五十五號劄文內飭以按照德國續約第六款凡有洋式船隻進口拆賣該船各料者俱應一律免徵稅銀若該船係由華商在香港購買駛赴廣東拆毀該船牌已在香港理船廳衙門繳銷是以進口無船牌者應按該船未拆賣之先所挂旗號爲憑登入某國册簿如該船有船牌無領事官者則應於該船拆賣後由該口稅務司將拆賣情形申呈總稅務司查照並將船牌一併呈交備寄等因

一輕木板徵稅辦法

據粵海關稅務司本年第六十二號申文內稱本口華商廣記號將輕木板一百三十塊每塊厚四因制十分之六報運出口查稅則雖載輕木板一項並未指明厚薄按外國貿易行市向係以四因制及四因制以下爲一板是以本關歷來俱以四因制上下作一板計算然稅則載明重木板厚三因制爲一板嗣後是否應按稅則所載重木板一項俱以厚三因制計算仰或應按歷來所辦以厚四因制爲一板並四因制以上應行如何徵稅之處申請酌核示遵等語

當經發寄該口第七百五十六號劄文內飭以稅則既載有重木板厚三因制之語不若比例將一切木板俱一律按照厚三因制爲一板計算其三因制以上至六因制者即按二板計加倍科稅其六因制以上者爲輕木樑應按稅則未載各貨照値百抽五之例徵稅等因

一假金綫徵稅辦法

據粵海關稅務司本年第九十九號申文內稱本口現有洋商欲將黃銅攙銀鍍金之金綫報運進口請按稅則所載假金綫徵稅等情本關查稅則載有假金綫一項所有本處產製之假金線向亦按照稅則徵稅惟其價値每斤不過五六錢而該商欲運進口之假金綫每斤約値銀十兩其價大相懸殊若一律徵稅恐有未合究應如何徵收之處申請核示遵行等語

當經發寄該口第七百五十七號劄文內飭以進口稅則既載有假金線名目則凡各項假金線無論貴賤均在其內自應一律徵稅不得歧異等因

一續添修船雜物免稅辦法

據江海關稅務司本年第一百四十五號申文內稱查德國續修條約第七款內載中國允凡德商船廠應用雜物准其免稅由總稅務司將應行免稅進口各物名目須發清冊曉諭等語旋由貴總稅司將船廠免稅各物須發清冊劄飭遵照前來查原劄內開如有清冊未載各物按照善後章程第八款該物實係船廠修船所用者須將應完稅銀暫行繳存卽申請總稅務司核示遵辦等語現有祥生船廠將鐵錬琉璃瓦黑鉛塊寶砂油斤松香油等物報運進口並聲明專爲本廠修船之用呈請按照免稅各物一律辦理本稅務司當將稅銀暫令繳存惟查該廠報運進口各物實係修船應用物件似應援照准免稅銀並將所報各物添入免稅清冊之內庶臻允當申請核示遵行等語

當經發寄該口第二千四十七號劄文內飭以該廠此次報運之琉璃瓦鐵錬黑鉛塊寶砂油斤松香油各物既經查明實係修船應用之物件自應援免稅銀並將所報各物添入免稅清冊之內以便嗣後遵辦等因

## 57.

督理廈門總口通商稅務協鎮成　爲
照送銅帽價銀事案准
貴稅務司照送緝獲南澳輪船有人私帶銅帽一包計四十盒到關當經敝前任
佐領府延稟奉
將軍憲札飭解交廈門稅釐局驗收解省軍裝所點驗核價移由廈門稅釐局撥
價去後幷經照知各在案玆准
廈門稅釐局移送銅帽價銀五兩六錢到關合就照送爲此照會
貴稅務司請煩查收賜覆須至照會者
計送銅帽價銀五兩六錢
右　照　會
欽加三品銜辦理廈門關通商稅務司吳
光緒　七年　正月　二十八　日

58.

大清欽命總理各國事務衙門　為

劄行事同治十二年九月二十一日准德國和署公使照稱本國新派之福州克領事官本署大臣暫令其將福建省以及台灣島遇有德意志人被告案件或犯罪情事統歸該領事審判其本國駐紮厦門台灣府淡水領事官亦均令該領事督率此乃本署大臣暫且自行擬辦試行尙應俟本國執政大臣允准方可立定施行再德意志人在廣東省以及海南島如有被告犯罪案件均歸本國駐紮廣州領事官審斷其駐紮汕頭領事官亦令廣州領事官督管嗣後如派領事官赴海南島亦應歸廣州領事官督管至於德意志人在江蘇安徽湖北江西浙江等省遇有被告犯罪等情統歸本國駐紮上海領事官審結其本國駐紮甯波領事官亦係上海領事官督率若直隸山東以及

盛京等省德意志人如有被告犯罪者統歸本國駐紮天津領事官所辦案件之內審理本國駐紮牛莊烟台二處副領事官亦係聽天津領事官督率等因前來相應劄行總稅務司查照可也須至劄者

右劄布政使銜總稅務司赫　准此

同治拾貳年玖月　叁拾　日

稅字肆百柒拾貳號

59.

欽加協領銜督理厦門總口通商稅務佐領府黃　　　　爲

照會事玆准

厦防分府劉　移開敝署派丁扶柩一口隨帶箱簍椅棹鋪蓋等物共十六件欲

搭鎭東輪船由上海回歸漢口並無帶有違禁貨物請予免驗爲此移請查照希

即轉移　洋稅司發給由厦至漢經過各關一概免驗單付該家丁收執俾免沿

途阻滯等因准此合就照知爲此照會

貴稅務司請煩照驗給單放行須至照會者

右　　照　　　會

署理厦門關通商稅務司韓

光緒　捌年　陸月　初十　日

60.

欽命二品銜福建分巡興泉永海防兵備道孫　爲

照覆事光緒七年三月十三日准

貴稅務司照會建造塔燈本年擬在北碇興工不日會同副管造司畢詩禮前往原勘地方酌定起卸物料處所並勘度地勢先行遣派工人填築地基此後材料可於三四個月間備便送往該處動工起蓋燈樓約年底卽可竣事點用玆與前定之案毫無更改毋庸再行履勘照請札飭馬巷廳示諭居民不得阻撓生事等因除報明並照章札飭馬巷廳卽先出示曉諭外合就照覆爲此照會

貴稅務司請煩查照仍請將興工完工日期隨時照知須至照會者

右　照　會

欽加三品銜辦理厦門關通商稅務司吳

光緒　柒年　叁月　拾肆　日

## 61.

督理厦門總口通商稅務協鎭成　爲

照會事本年九月初三日准

貴稅務司照會淡水茶葉准具保結免完暫存半稅一案若本口竟照上海辦法可

期愼重不須過慮各等因准此查此案旣奉

軍憲札飭自應查照遵辦第准

貴稅務司來文陳說俱有條理自應據爲轉詳但所稱上海關辦法如何尚未明叙

相應照會

貴稅務司請煩查照卽將上海關如何辦法一切章程詳錄照知以便轉稟

軍憲察奪寔爲公便須至照會者

右　照　會

署理厦門關通商稅務司勞

光緒　柒年　玖月　初六　日

62.

賞戴藍翎協領銜督理厦門總口通商稅務佐領府黃　爲

照送食鹽價銀事前准

貴稅務司照送緝獲食鹽一案當經移飭厦課館同安帮販戶照數收領核價充

賞去後併經照知在案玆於本月十七日據該販戶遣丁具稟到關請領所獲食

鹽十三包計重六百四十九斤鹽即按照現時場價每七二番銀購鹽二百十五

斤核計關獲食鹽六百四十九斤共應値價銀二兩一錢六分照呈到關合就照

送爲此照會

貴稅務司請煩照數查收賜覆施行須至照會者

計送食鹽價銀二兩一錢六分

右　照　會

署理厦門關通商稅務司勞

光緒　捌年　貳月　十八　日

63.

大清欽命福建省會通商總局司道　爲
照會事奉
宮保巡撫部院岑　牌開照得本部院奏奉
諭旨將調閩黔軍先撤一半交
新授雲南開化鎮蔡　統帶回黔歸伍所有該黔軍前由貴州領獲洋鎗四百八
十門應仍帶回黔省呈繳並咨明
貴州撫部院查照外合行檄局遵照即便移知各洋關查照辦理毋違等因奉此
合就照會
貴稅司查照如遇黔軍到關照驗施行須至照會者
右　照　會
署廈海洋稅新關事宜稅務司勞
大清　光緒　捌年　伍月　十二　日照會

64.

欽命二品銜福建分巡興泉永海防兵備道 爲

照知事照得本道現在因公晉省面稟地方公事定於本月二十五日由厦附搭輪船啟程所有署中緊要公事包封寄至行寓自行核辦其餘一切尋常日行事件暫委署厦防同知劉丞代拆代行以免曠悞除分別申報咨行札委外合就照知爲此照會

貴稅務司請煩查照施行須至照會者

右 照 會

欽賜一等寶星三品銜厦門關稅務司柏

光緒 捌年 捌月 貳拾伍 日

65.

大清欽命總理各國事務衙門 爲

劄行事案查前據兩江總督沈 等奏稱湖北開采煤鐵現用洋法煤產必旺勢須酌減煤稅銷路乃可流通請將土煤出口每噸減爲稅銀一錢援照臺灣成案

辦理等語當經本衙門覆奏以湖北廣濟用洋法開煤卽據該督等奏稱與臺灣情事相同應准其援照成案每噸減爲稅銀一錢此外出煤處所旣不加增其出口稅銀應仍照舊徵收以示限制等因於光緒三年三月十七日奉
旨依議欽此相應劄行總稅務司遵照可也須至劄者

右劄布政使銜總稅務司赫 准此

光緒 叄年 陸月 貳拾叄 日

總字第捌百叄拾陸號

## 66.

總理衙門劄行總稅務司

爲劄行事光緒八年三月初三日准
北洋大臣咨開據津海關道詳稱焦炭一項新開進出口稅則未載照章應核估時價照値百抽五例征稅惟光緒七年四月奏定開平煤出口稅每噸銀一錢現查焦炭須煤一噸四五始能煉成焦炭一噸照煤斤加五收稅合銀壹錢伍分似亦公允因函知津海關稅務司核議據稅務司法來格函復開平煤礦所出之土煤每噸値

銀伍兩焦煤每噸值銀七八兩每噸焦炭定稅銀壹錢伍分甚爲公允等情據此查焦炭每噸定出口稅銀壹錢伍分既經該道函詢稅務司復稱公允似應照此定案爲此咨明核復等因前來本衙門查所定焦炭出口稅銀尚屬公允自應照准征收除咨復北洋大臣外相應劄行總稅務司飭知可也須至劄者光緒捌年叁月初拾日

總字第壹千壹百柒拾伍號

## 67.

總理衙門劄行總稅務司

爲劄行事所有日本商人烟酒進口請免征稅一案本衙門前據總稅務司申陳咨行

南洋大臣核議辦理並照復

日本鄭署大臣在案茲准

南洋大臣咨稱據江海關道詳稱奉到憲劄遵即函致新關稅務司查辦茲據復稱日本烟酒進口本關向係遵照總稅務司通劄征收稅銀若爲數無多實係日本商人自用者查照劄內鈔單事理酌量免征餘皆照舊征收等由伏查日本烟酒抵滬如係日本官商自用者前議烟數十斤酒一二百斤開單送關查驗免稅原係格外

優待之意既經總稅務司復核可行現在滬關赫稅務司亦照前議酌量免稅應請此後日本官商自用烟酒滬關查驗免稅者烟以三四十斤爲度酒以一二百斤爲度由新關稅務司隨時詳愼查驗辦理現在上海有日本官商駐紮者是以將所用日本烟酒酌數免稅係屬權宜之舉此外中國通商口岸幷無日本官商駐紮者遇有日本烟酒到口則係賣與華人可知無論多寡仍應一律征稅以示區別而昭公允詳祈核咨等情咨請核復前來除咨復

南洋大臣外相應劄行總稅務司查照可也須至劄者 光緒伍年伍月拾叁日

總字第玖百捌拾叁號

## 68.

大清欽命總理各國事務衙門 爲

劄復事光緒四年正月初三日據赫總稅務司申稱汕頭現有洋商裝運外國機器進口在汕頭本行內熬作糖觔又烟台另有洋商運外國機器進口在烟台本行內作爲抽絲之用又上海有洋商擬辦外國機器在上海本行內製造棉布以上三行洋商均請以所辦機器准予免稅進口據稱所辦機器請免稅因係本行自用並非出售於人等語惟查應稅之百貨其終無非歸於自用而機器與善後

章程第二欵所載之尋常日用物件迥不相同又據云請免稅因外國機器宜廣開來路等語惟查凡有益於實濟之機器按其原價每百兩徵稅五兩不足以礙其來路又據云機器局造船局所用之機器皆准免稅進口惟查此局內之物乃官用之件不得比擬此事再四思維擬嗣後凡有機器進口無論官民運來均令按原價每值百兩徵稅五兩爲例伏思官用機器係動公款購辦若於進口時復令完稅不過在原價外每百兩加銀五兩其物爲公用之物其價爲公用之款其所納之稅係本自公項其所收之稅亦歸於公項是有徵收得稅之事而無輸納喫虧之人如此則凡機器進口即不致有兩歧辦法所有機器之稅應徵應免請酌核示復等因前來本衙門查約章內外國機器既無免稅之條若遽予免徵恐將來紛紛效尤適以開各商覬覦之漸自應按照值百抽五之例無論官運商運均令一律照章完納以昭公允而重稅餉除咨行

南北洋船政局大臣轉飭遵照外相應劄行總稅務司查照可也須至劄者

右劄布政使銜總稅務司赫　准此

光緒　肆年　正月　初九　日

總字第捌百捌拾肆號

## 69.

大清欽命總理各國事務衙門　　爲

劄覆事光緒三年十月初六日准

德國巴大臣函稱天津本國洋行以縈麻出口該處海關欲照稅則征稅本國領事以縈麻係稅則未載之物應照值百抽五之例征收查天下各國稅則俱以麻與縈麻分而爲二總以值百抽五之例征收爲是等因經本衙門於十月十六日劄交總稅務司查覆去後茲於十一月十九日據總稅務司申稱奉到鈞劄當經抄錄轉飭津海關稅務司詳細查覆現據代理稅務司克黎詳稱天津出口之麻各商常報爲縈麻亦報青麻皆係洋商運送外國之物其餘各種麻斤俱係由南省運津現查縈麻價值每担約銀三兩至進口麻斤種類甚多價亦不一每担值銀自七兩五錢至十兩之數縈麻與別項麻斤式樣大不相同查驗易爲分別並將麻斤數種樣式呈送前來據此總稅務司查縈麻與他項麻斤有異體較輭鬆扭之則斷溼之則腐按天津市價尋常麻斤價值較縈麻大至二三倍稅則內載麻斤稅餉每百斤完三錢五分現若以縈麻之稅每百斤訂爲二錢則與值百抽五之例大略相符除苧麻川麻白麻等類麻斤仍照則征稅三錢五分外所有縈麻一項應請貴衙門酌奪可否每百斤征稅二錢縈麻與他項麻斤驗貨手易爲

16

分別則影射之弊似可無慮除將麻斤樣式呈送外理合備文申覆即請裁奪示
遵等因前來本衙門查各國稅則所載出口麻斤每百斤納稅三錢五分並未將
綮麻一項分別開載
德國大臣以麻與綮麻應分爲二照值百抽五之例征收既據總稅務司查明申
覆尋常麻斤每百斤值銀自七兩至十兩不等而綮麻僅值三四兩之數且生質
與他項麻斤有異驗貨手易爲分別無慮影射等因自應量減稅銀以順商情除
他項麻斤仍照稅則原數征稅外其綮麻一項即照總稅務司所擬每百斤納稅
銀二錢自第柒拾結起各關一體開辦除咨行南北洋大臣轉行外相應劄覆總
稅務司轉飭各關稅務司知照可也須至劄者

右劄布政使銜總稅務司赫　准此

光緒　叁年　拾壹月　貳拾柒　日

總字第捌百柒拾肆號

70.

大清
欽命總理各國事務衙門　爲
劄行事案查洋煤進口稅銀請給存票一事本年五月間准南洋大臣咨據江海
關道稟報各情本衙門以此事未據赫總稅司申呈並未核准有案先行咨復並

劄令總稅務司查明聲復據稱凡已完正稅之洋煤復行下船不問自用出售一概發給存票等因本衙門旋卽轉行
南北洋大臣飭查核復現准復稱據江海關道稟稱向來洋貨進口完稅後復將該貨運往外國准將前完進口稅銀給還存票其改運中國通商別口者或請免照或請存票聽商自便倘未請免照之貨運抵通商他口則須在他口照則完納則此口請領存票者他口仍行納稅查船用洋煤向准免稅各洋煤進口完稅後復於限內裝船出口運往外國則前完進口稅銀准給存票倘運往通商別口未在進口之關請領免照則別關亦必照則收稅是出售之煤無虞漏稅滋弊赫總稅務司所議不問自用出售一經裝船轉運概准給還存票尙與稅課無虧似可照議辦理惟須飭令總稅務司通飭各口稅務司如遇洋煤到口起岸並無中國通商各關收稅免照呈驗者一律收稅以昭核實等因本衙門查核江海關道所稱係照約章辦理尙爲周到除咨行
南北洋大臣轉飭遵辦外相應劄行總稅務司轉飭各關稅務司遵照辦理可也須至劄者

右劄布政使銜總稅務司赫　准此

光緒　叁年　拾貳月　貳拾伍　日

總字第捌百柒拾捌號

71.

大清欽命總理各國事務衙門　爲

劄行事同治十一年十二月二十一日據總稅務司申稱據江海關狄稅務司申報洋貨進口時箱包原用之洋鉄箍拆湊一處復運通商別口與監督函商准照估價徵稅如有願領免照出口其稅自然照徵倘願至別口納稅本關將該貨載入英文總單令在別口完稅等語查此兩項辦法若出口時令補納進口稅則有多發免照之累不如在總單內註明俟其復進口時再完進口稅爲善等因申請酌復前來查鉄箍一項載在進口貨物稅則洋貨箱包所用鉄箍既有破眼自與專運進口之新鉄箍不同該稅務司所擬按照估價徵稅辦法尙屬平允至完稅一節總稅務司請專收復進口稅較爲簡便應如所稱辦理爲此劄行總稅務司轉飭通商各口一體查照辦理可也須至劄者

右劄布政使銜總稅務司赫　准此

同治　拾貳年　正月　初伍　日

總字第伍百伍拾壹號

72.

大清欽命總理各國事務衙門　爲

劄復事同治十一年十二月二十五日據總稅務司申稱九月初八日鈞劄內開
八月二十三日准
署南洋大臣咨據江南海關道稟稱案據新關稅務司狄妥瑪來函以進口稅則
哆囉呢一款註明寬五十一因制至六十四因制每丈稅銀一錢二分茲有德全
旗昌等行進口俄呢計寬至七十二因制仿照原布過於稅則所載核加稅數該
商未服其應如何徵稅函請核示當查稅司核加稅數其法甚善應即按照辦理
嗣據德國領事官函請給還多徵稅銀又經職道照案駁覆現在德全廣豐加增
之稅雖完終未允服再另有商人運進印花布各種按照法國增改新例酌增稅
數之案錄摺咨呈查核前來查哆囉呢印花布兩項既與稅則因制不符狄稅司
加增稅銀辦理甚屬公允查從前咸豐十一年法國哥大臣曾以印花布比英美
兩國較爲寬長請中國加稅當經改爲每疋共納稅銀一錢二分並照此次所議
寬長永爲定式等因照辦十餘年均無異議此次德全廣豐哆囉呢一項既是因
制與稅則有增自宜比照法國所定印花布稅數加稅一律辦理海關未便兩歧
寔恐於稅務有碍爲此劄行總稅務司查復等因前來查此案已據江海關狄稅
司申報並抄錄與監督往來信件申請核辦前來據此查哆囉呢進口每疋計寬

五十一至六十四因制自應按照稅則明文每丈完納稅銀一錢二分若寬過六十四因制即應按照多出寬長若干折增丈數徵收稅銀是將此寬出之因制折合丈數按丈徵稅辦理其不過稅則所載之數仍係按稅則計量丈數之明文納稅也惟日後倘有復出口之事該關應照此核算分別發給免照存票等件庶不致於轇轕矣合行備文申請查照施行等因前來除咨行

南北洋大臣轉飭各海關道遵照外相應劄行總稅務司轉飭各關稅務司遵照辦理可也須至劄者

右劄布政使銜總稅務司赫　准此

同治　拾貳年　正月　拾玖　日

總字第伍百伍拾肆號

73.

大清欽命總理各國事務衙門　爲

劄行事同治十三年五月十九日准

北洋大臣咨據津海關道詳稱二月初四日准

德國章代領事函稱信遠洋行運到玻璃球一項未能確知應否免稅函商核奪

並於五月間函稱業經申報

德國駐京公使會同總理衙門商辦等因查善後章程第二款所載免稅各物並無自用字樣唯藥料玻璃器皿二項獨加自用二字明其非自用即係不能免稅茲准

北洋大臣咨信遠行玻璃球一項自應按照該關道所擬辦理現在本衙門並未准德國公使知照有案相應鈔錄

北洋大臣咨文一件清摺一扣劄行總稅務司轉行天津稅務司查照可也須至

劄者

右劄布政使銜總稅務司赫 准此

同治 拾叁年 陸月 拾壹 日

總字第陸百貳拾陸號

照錄代理德國章領事來函

啟者准信遠洋行報稱該商現有玻璃球一項因未能確知應否免稅故照章出具甘結稟請核辦等因本代理領事查會訊章程內載如有不能自定應徵應免之事均須援照本章程第五條所載亦令該商出具日後情願遵斷繳案切結由領事官送交監督存案即由監督先將該商貨物暫時免稅放行等語又案查前年三月二十一日阿領事曾准

來函以世昌行鹽池掛鐙洋燭䏰子白酒等件接奉
總理衙門行知凡善後章程第二欵註明免稅之物無論自用轉售均予免稅凡
未註明免稅又不在進口稅則者均照値百抽五之例辦理等因今信遠行所報
玻璃器應作何辦理之處理合函商
貴道核奪茲特將該行所具甘結送去即希
貴道查照見復可也此致順頌
升祺　　二月初四日
具甘結人德國信遠洋行商人今有玻璃球二十打
未能定其稅之應征應免爲此本行出具甘結俟本國
領事官與本處
監督大人定明或本國
駐京欽差與
總理衙門定明由領事官飭本行完納本行即行完納並請　領事官轉請
監督大人暫時免稅放行所具甘結是寔
大清同治十三年二月初三日　天津信遠洋行
大德一千八百七十四年三月二十日

照錄復代理德國韋領事函

復者頃接

來函以信遠洋行運到玻璃球照章出具甘結禀請核辦等情函商核奪等因查玻璃球並非善後章程第二欵載明免稅之物自應照從前

總理衙門行知按値百抽五例辦理爲此函復

貴代理領事查照即希

轉飭該行商報請新關驗估核稅可也此頌

升祺　　二月初四日

照錄北洋大臣來文

爲咨請事同治十三年五月十三日據津海關道陳欽詳稱二月初四日准德國韋代領事函稱信遠洋行運到玻璃球一項因未能確知應否免稅照章出具甘結應作何辦理函商核奪等因當經職道覆以玻璃球並非第二欵載明免稅之物應按値百抽五例估價徵稅等因日久未接韋代領事來信玆於五月初九日復准來函內稱信遠洋行進口玻璃球一項稅銀應否免徵之處已申報德國駐

京公使會同

總理衙門商辦等因查前年因德國世昌行進口鹽池掛燈白酒等件曾奉憲札
准
總理衙門行知凡善後章程第二欵註明免稅之物無論自用轉售均予免稅凡
未註明免稅又不在進口稅則者均照値百抽五例辦理等因在案職道復查善
後章程第二款所載免稅各物如銀錢麪粟及外國衣服蠟燭煙酒等類雖有免
稅明文並無自用字樣自應不論自用出賣一槪免稅至藥料玻璃器皿二項獨
加自用二字明其非自用即不能免稅也緣藥料玻璃器二項各色甚多若非實
係自用斷難槪予免稅所以當日定立約章時即加自用字樣以示與外國蠟燭
煙酒等類有別現在玻璃球一項天津街市賣者甚多前次章代領事來函並未
聲明自用是以仍令納稅究竟可否免徵之處章領事並未再行函商輒即申報
駐京公使未免瑣屑玆准前因理合將前與章代領事來往信函照錄清摺具文
詳請查核轉咨謹呈清摺一扣等情到本大臣據此相應咨請爲此合咨
貴衙門請煩查核示覆飭遵施行須至咨者

隨總字第陸百貳拾陸號

74.

大清欽命總理各國事務衙門　爲

劄行事光緒二年閏五月初八日准總稅務司申稱

德國巴大臣文內稱玻璃器皿係免稅之物復爲詳閱法文自用二字係專指藥料而言與玻璃器皿四字斷而不連按照德約法文而論雖係售賣與人之物而仍係免稅之物再善後條約內註明凡有玻璃器皿進出口皆准免稅而進口稅則又註有玻璃片千里鏡照面鏡各應完稅銀若干出口稅則又註有各色料珠料器每百觔完稅銀若干之文是玻璃一類除中國料珠料器應照出口稅則納稅並外國玻璃片千里鏡照面鏡應照進口稅則納稅外其餘各玻璃器皿進出口皆准免稅爲是等因前來本衙門查玻璃器皿免稅旣准總稅務司詳查申復與稅項大數實無出入自應如所擬辦理除照復

德國巴大臣並咨行

北洋南洋大臣轉飭照辦外相應劄行總稅務司轉飭各口知照可也須至劄者

右劄布政使銜總稅務司赫　准此

光緒　貳年　閏伍月　拾捌日

總字第柒百伍拾肆號

## 75.

總稅務司致　北洋大臣函

敬啓者昨接得九江一信係唐廷樞所致者內稱九江招商分局局董函告該口出口貨以磁器爲大宗近年轉運數目較少大抵以磁器之粗細不易區別開驗復細恐其傷損就延客商多畏而陸運等事幷另具近年出口數目節略一紙欲請將磁器不論粗細計每百觔收正稅六錢七分五釐收半稅三錢三分七釐餘或於紅花藍花分別粗細探詢能否變通辦理以爲邮商裕課兩有裨益等語前來查磁器有粗細之別價値有貴賤之殊磁細而價貴者則稅數較多磁粗而價賤者則稅數較少按稅則自無不合故原訂細磁每百斤收正稅九錢粗磁正稅四錢五分以其物値之貴賤訂其稅數之多寡似覺合宜惟稅數既有參差則在收稅者不能不認眞嚴察以定其粗細而認眞嚴察雖自外觀之似屬於稅有益而內實則有損緣加意開驗則已經細縛緊妥之器須逐一翻播重復再裝既不能如初則中途傷損虧累生涯或息業或繞途則稅課之不能日旺亦卽可想矣故此種易於傷損之貨可不必別其粗細於花色應以概論無事詳分自於商情

稅務兩有益也至該招商分局所擬請者勿論粗細每百觔正稅按六錢七分五釐收之總稅務司則不以爲然也蓋如此辦理雖細貴者已低其稅而粗賤者則反昂其稅事關約則不能不見商於有約各國能否訂局亦不可知不如以粗磁之稅每百觔四錢五分統爲各項磁之稅數此不過減稅之舉係中國自辦之事勿須見商於約國者此減稅辦法外尙有一法祇不改稅則所定而已細者仍九錢粗者仍四錢五分惟磁器報關時無事嚴加逐察但憑該磁商報單辦理若以此明訂爲關章在磁商既免傷損之累則生意日旺而稅餉自亦隨之日起矣雖商人藉此或有以細報粗之弊而具有天良者亦不致盡以粗賤報關也竊維此事既與國課有關與商情攸繫幷係民生所用亦屬關稅訂章

中堂辦理通商自有裁奪總稅務司特將其原函抄錄呈閱即希

鑒核賜教爲禱此佈即請

鈞安不一

名另具光緒六年四月初五日

釐字第陸拾柒號

北洋大臣劄行總稅務司

爲劄行事五月十四日准

署南洋大臣兩江總督江蘇撫部院吳　咨開四月二十六日准

總理衙門函開九江關出口磁器日形短少因該關須將原包開驗分別粗細收稅既屬稽時又易破碎且或認粗爲細加以重罰故各商視爲畏途玆特鈔錄北洋函件附閱應如何酌量變通俾裕課恤商兩有裨益即由台端察奪等因前來查九江關磁器稅既因拆驗太嚴衆商裹足稅收減色自應相機變通以冀裕課恤商查核鈔件招商局董擬將粗細磁器兩稅扯平北洋大臣以爲粗磁之稅反昂且須諭商各國諸多窒碍洵爲確論赫總稅司所擬辦法兩層一係細磁亦照粗磁完稅一係稅則仍舊但憑商人報明粗磁細磁均免拆驗北洋大臣以第一層未免過寬不若第二層辦法稅項可期漸旺自是斟酌適中之論照此辦理則該磁器到關向來稽延破損誤罰之弊可以悉除各商自必樂於報運而稅數當可日增應由該關示諭嗣後凡有商人報運磁器該關但須查明是否以防夾帶別項重稅之貨至該磁器粗細悉聽該商自報不必仍前拆開細驗致羣視爲畏途並須聲明此項辦法專屬磁器一宗別項土貨均不得援以爲例且係先行試辦一年如一年內磁稅果增以後即可常川照辦倘一年內竟因磁器停止拆驗

致有意外流弊轉於稅項有虧即由該道據實稟明另候咨商核辦除分咨並札飭九江關遵照核明辦理具報外相應咨請查照等因到本大臣准此合亟劄行該總稅務司即便轉飭該關稅務司查照辦理須至劄行者 光緒六年五月十六日

傳字第壹百伍拾號

## 76.

大清欽命總理各國事務衙門 爲

劄行事光緒元年七月二十七日准福州將軍咨據厦門口委員佐領黃恩錄稟竊照本年六月十一日准康稅務司照會內開案上年據英商怡記稟稱該行同治十二年四五閏六等月由格林乃因各輪船自外國運來米石若干因不合銷售存棧待價嗣於十二年閏六月及十三年四月間以該米四十四萬六千七百六十二觔下入雅素廣東甯波楷那各輪船復往福州粵東照章出具保單存關惟該米於出口時在本關納過稅銀四千四百四十六兩七錢六分二釐伏思條約載明之義係中國土產運往通商則口照則納出口稅與外國運來無涉稟請前稅司代其申呈總稅務司察核批示遵行當經據情申請候示玆據該行稟稱

昨奉總稅務司批示內云酌核案內情形凡外國米穀進口後復運往他口尤如驗貨船隻相同自應免稅辦理等因奉此稟請核奪前來查英國通商章程善後條約第五款第五條內載凡米穀等糧不拘內外土產不分何處進口者皆不准運出外國惟英商欲運往中華通商別口則照銅錢一律辦理出口時照依稅則納稅其進口毋庸納稅云云等語按此卽知內中有別一照銅錢一律辦理不拘內外土產一出口時照依稅則納稅專謂各口土產出運別口有涉與凡米穀等糧不分何處進口者復出運別口無干及檢閱總稅務司來劄內云比照驗船辦理及與英國條約第四十五款所載亦爲符合爲此照會查照核奪發給存票照復來關等因併粘單一紙執照四張到關職查此項洋米因不合銷售報明轉運別口當時係照章程飭完出口稅銀始有執照給予隨運指往銷售之口起卸應由是口監督標明蓋印依限賫回繳銷方符條約按其所報出口日期計今已逾兩年始行將照繳回且未蓋有彼口監督印信遽請給還前稅其中恐有別故是否總稅務司稟准有案應俟請 示遵行當復照查去後旋准照復前來惟將粘開款目及續復照會鈔錄清摺同繳回執照一併具稟呈繳可否給與存票之處伏

乞察核批示祇遵等情並送清摺一扣執照四張前來查通商善後條約第五款內載銅錢不准運出外國惟通商中國各口准其以此口運至彼口照現定章程遵行該商赴關報明數目若干運往何口或令本商及同商二人聯名具呈保單抑或聽監督飭令另交結實信據方准給照則口監督於執照上註明收到字樣加蓋印信從給照之日起限六個月繳回驗明若過期不繳銷執照即按其錢貨原本罰繳入官其進口均免納稅又凡米穀等糧不拘內外土產不分何處進口者皆不准運出外國唯英商欲運往中華通商別口則照銅錢一律辦理出口時照依稅則納稅其進口毋庸納稅各等語此案英商怡記運米赴廈不合銷售復運出口當時該口照此第五款章程按則徵收出口稅銀並照銅錢之例核給執照載明從給照之日起限六個月回廈繳銷倘逾限不繳即按貨價照數罰繳入官等字樣是該口當時均照通商條約辦理毫無疑議乃英商怡記於同治十二年閏六月及十三年四月完稅領照之後迄今或已一年或已兩載之久忽請給發存票殊與條約未符且查第五款內既有載明米穀等糧不拘內外土產不分何處進口之語而康稅司以為出口納稅專謂各口土產出運別口有涉與不分

何處進口者復運出別口無干殊屬費解況運米出口當時厦口稅司委員既有給發執照定限繳銷而該商怡記所領執照均逾定限多時自當按照條約辦理今該口並不扣計限期查辦反以可否給發存票具稟請示是與當時徵稅給照之案前後懸殊通商稅務自應查照條約辦理難容互異除稟批令該口委員黃恩錄迅將此案確核條約妥速完結具報外相應咨請察照酌核辦理等因前來查米穀等糧英商欲運往中華通商別口其應如何辦理載在英國善後條約第五款極為明悉此次英商怡記行運米復往通商別口自應按照約內第五款辦理該商於厦口稅司所發執照均逾定限多時且未蓋有彼口監督印信顯與約內所載別口監督於執照上註明收到字樣加蓋印信從給照之日起限六個月繳回驗銷等語迥不相符福州將軍咨按條約辦理自係正辦相應劄行總稅務司轉飭查核條約遵照辦理可也須至劄者

右劄布政使銜總稅務司赫　准此

稅字五百四十四號

光緒　元年　八月　初七　日

總字第柒百陸號

77.

大清欽命總理各國事務衙門　爲

劄行事光緒元年五月二十一日據總稅務司申覆內稱前奉劄開德國署公使函稱德國稅則內載梁木應無論其木之方圓均列稅則等因此案粵海關監督照估價值百抽五收稅該商不願照此納稅者蓋因各項貨物有時價之不同商情頗願稅數有一定不易之規以便置貨時預爲籌計其本利之盈虧即在關務亦必有一定不易之稅數可免互相饒舌此案圓梁木其圓徑與稅則之方徑堪以比例應按每根壹錢伍分之例辦理其外另有他商願估價納稅者則值百抽五其願照稅則納稅者則每根壹錢伍分等因前來本衙門查總稅務司申覆各情既於商人有便而於稅餉無甚出入即照所請自第六十一結起開辦其六十一結以前仍照舊章辦理以清界限除照會　德國並咨行　南北洋大臣暨劄粵海關監督外相應抄錄本衙門照會一件劄行總稅務司查照辦理可也須至劄者

右劄布政使銜總稅務司赫　准此

光緒元年陸月貳拾肆日

總字第陸百玖拾肆號

照錄給　德國照會

爲照覆事上年十一月間准

和署大臣函稱本國加羅威治洋行僱用華船裝木來省一事已由呂領事官與粵海關公同辦理完竣無庸再行提及惟恐嗣後無定例可憑不如將稅則案內梁木一節預爲詳訂查稅則內載梁重木長不過七邁當零九百八十五釐理邁當四方不到三百零五釐理邁當等語請貴衙門明示粵海關無論其木之方圓均列入稅則等因本年三月間復准貴大臣函詢請速爲辦理均經本衙門前後劄飭粵海關監督暨總稅務司酌復在案茲據赫總稅務司申稱查木植按稅則內載應分三大項一曰桅木一曰梁木一曰板木儻木値進口有未能按照此三項木植比例納稅者祇可按照監督意見以雜木論照雜木估價納稅緣板木一項既不能作梁亦不能作桅是以稅則按其長若干寬厚若干訂其稅餉若干至梁木一項可以作梁亦可以分鋸爲板而究不可以作桅是以稅則按其長若干四方若干訂其稅餉若干至桅木一項可以分鋸爲板可以截而爲梁然祇此桅木始可以作桅是以稅則按其長短若干以訂其稅餉若干木植雖難區別惟以板梁桅三大項分晰清楚各適其用者自各有定規既易剖別亦無牽混而梁木一項稅則並無四方梁木之名目不過僅注明梁木每根應照其長若干四方若干納稅若干四方之梁木比較圓梁木輪角稍闊而運圓木者願將圓徑作爲方

徑納稅似於稅則三項之分易於相符卽徵收稅數亦覺易於核算至稅則所載貨物名目其應納之稅數起初原無非按值百抽五之義而核定納數故於所未賅者復增一値百抽五之例其意不過因此外有未賅備者之名目亦歸劃一耳此案粵海關監督照雜木估價値百抽五之例收稅在該商其不願照此輪納者何故蓋因各項貨物各有時價之不同溯自通商征稅以來迄今已逾十有餘年之久各貨色先後時價懸殊卽早晚時價亦各有重輕不能相若故在商情願稅數有一定不易之規以便在置貨時預爲籌計其本利之盈虧卽在關務亦必各有一定不易之稅數亦可免互相饒舌之事此案德商加羅威治行圓梁木係可以作梁可以作板而不可以作桅者之木且其圓徑與稅則之方徑堪以比例似應按稅則中之梁木每根壹錢伍分之例辦理餉其外另有他商不願照此輪納者卽將鐘表之例比擬納稅亦可其願估價納稅者則値百抽五其願照稅則納稅者則每根壹錢伍分如此辦理各商既無可藉口卽於稅餉之無甚出入等因前來本衙門復查無異擬照所請自六十一結起開辦其六十一結以前仍照舊章辦理以淸界限除咨行南北洋大臣並劄粵海關監督暨總稅務司外相應照會

貴大臣查照可也

隨總字第陸百玖拾肆號

## 78.

大清欽命總理各國事務衙門　爲

劄行事同治十三年正月二十六日據粵海關監督呈稱准英國羅領事照會本
國人徐士買到舊兵船一隻轉賣與中國人周姓將船送到省河康稅務司令該
船照估價抽稅因此徐士來控等因當經照會康稅務司查復令該商將稅銀繳
關存庫咨呈總理衙門及總稅務司批示遵行續查同治八年英船麻吉麻各里
恩敉風在汕頭收口壞船拆毀木料在該處售賣經總理衙門核定按值百抽伍
例抽稅一案核與此案拆料銷售情節相同又經函致羅領事照辦據復已呈本
國

欽差大臣核奪只有聽候劄知辦理等因抄錄全案呈請核復前來查同治八年間准
英國阿大臣照會英商船名麻吉麻各里恩敉風在汕頭收口貨物另換船載壞
船拆毀木料在該處售賣該處監督必欲商人完納船鈔此船並非前往該口貿
易希飭退還船鈔當經本衙門查據兩廣總督咨復據康稅務司查復此船由新
加波前往上海路過因風收口船主查看船身損壞斷難駕駛將貨物全撤剩船
裝載該船即在本口拆毀售賣共得價洋銀叁千壹百伍拾元該船并無貿易其
時收納船鈔稍有誤會若按拆賣價值數目抽稅似覺平允旋經本衙門劄據總
稅務司申復此船拆賣按值百抽伍例抽稅應完稅銀即在應退船鈔銀內算除
以完此案等因行文兩廣總督轉飭照辦并照復

英國阿大臣在案此案徐士舊船賣與周姓拆料銷售該稅務司按照值百抽伍之例估價抽稅核與麻吉麻各里恩之船成案相符自應准其查照辦理除由本衙門行令該監督遵照外相應劄行總稅務司轉飭該稅務司循照辦理嗣後遇有此等案件務須均照成案核辦以免歧異而重稅課可也須至札者

右劄布政使銜總稅務司赫　准此

同治　拾叁年　貳月　初六　日

總字第陸百拾叁號

# 79.

大清欽命總理各國事務衙門　爲

劄行事同治十年十二月二十八日准總稅務司申稱據東海關署稅司好博遜申呈現有貨船未領紅單之先遭風稅銀可否給還并錄呈商人大成行禀一件查潮州前有洋船裝滿貨物未曾出口失火奉札毋庸發給稅銀自應按照前札示知查約內進口稅卸貨時完納出口稅下貨時完納所謂卸貨時者應以貨物何時離關運進口之原船爲卸貨之時下貨時應以貨物何時離碼頭前往出口船爲下貨之時是出口貨物一經離關碼頭或暫時載在駁船或已經入于洋船

遇有貨物失落之事已完之出口正稅毋庸發還凡進口貨物已離原運進口之船或裝載于駁船或從碼頭赴棧房遇有失落之事已完進口稅毋庸發還等語查英約第四十四款內載英國貨物如受潮濕致價抵減者應行按價減稅等語是進口貨物受潮減稅立此專條原爲體恤商人而設此外並無進出口貨物失落准還稅銀明文同治八年五月間潮海關有布國商船科爾千裝載貨物在未領紅單出口之先船隻失火貨物被焚請還稅銀一案稅司康發達擬定辦法無論已買保險與不買保險均毋庸發給存票當經本衙門札知總稅務司進出貨物既經完稅後其意外之虞甚多防不勝防全在商人自已加意防範即存留棧房以及未經入船貨物亦難免有意外各事分則保險與否諸多轇轕應照康稅司所擬辦法等因在案除由本衙門咨行北洋大臣并札行東海關道大成棧洋船遭風一案查照潮海關成案以免辦理兩歧外爲此札行總稅務司即飭各稅司嗣後凡進出口貨物倘有意外之虞無論貨物離口與未離口一切均照本衙門前札辦理毋須遽議訂章可也須至札者

右劄布政使銜總稅務司赫　准此

同治　拾壹年　正月　初陸　日

總字第肆百捌拾叁號

80.

大清欽命總理各國事務衙門　爲

劄行事同治十二年七月初一日准北洋大臣咨稱據津海關道詳前因各洋商販運古銅器出口並無完過內地稅項憑據詢據鈔關委員面稱古玩一項未載戶部稅則職道當經函商稅務司凡洋商販運古玩出口於估徵出口正稅後令再補交子口稅方准放行近來洋商販運古銅器串通華商代赴鈔關報稅比照銅料器折中完納每百斤按伍錢伍分徵收較新關估價徵稅輕重大相懸殊覆查該商等所運古銅器均係贋製景泰藍內地銷售甚稀聞各西國頗皆珍愛天津出口貨向來稀少此貨現在出口甚多職道擬請嗣後無論華洋各商凡販運古銅器均歸新關令一律按估價報納子稅以杜勾串避就是否有當理合將上年函商稅司洋商販運古玩估徵子稅全卷照錄清摺具文詳請查核立案附呈抄案清摺一扣等情到本大臣據此除批據詳並摺均悉嗣後遇有華洋各商販運古銅器卽歸新關按照估價令其一律完納子稅以杜避重就輕之弊應准立案等因抄錄函件咨明前來查稅則內出口雜貨類內開古玩每值百兩抽稅伍兩此項古銅器係古玩之物應照稅則抽稅洋商入內地置買應照條約完納子

口半稅俟出口時再完出口正稅倘該商將此項銅器復運進通商別口並應完
復進口半稅以符舊制除咨行南北洋大臣轉飭遵照外相應札行總稅務司轉
飭各口稅務司遵照辦理可也須至札者

右劄布政使銜總稅務司赫　准此

同治　拾貳年　柒月　拾玖日

總字第伍百捌拾陸號

81.

大清欽命總理各國事務衙門　為
劄行事同治十一年十二月初六日准總稅務司申稱軍火過載輪船開行最速
至多不過限以三日一節查軍火進口過載之事甚少並非常有進口者大半係
前往東洋餘則從東洋來滬付搭便船回外國輪船開行雖速而三日之內却不
常有開行者若以三日之期定限即遇請准過船之時萬一於定限掣肘案情有
應准之勢而章內又有碍難奉行之明文再四熟思現擬凡洋商運軍火等物不
准販運進出各口善後條約本有明文惟軍火由此外邦運彼外國不過假道暫
進中華港口並非在此售賣亦無請准登岸之情販運者擬准過船[illegible]進口
時由船商赴關報明載有過船之軍火其貨主請領過船之准載時具結按限過

載復運出口倘限內未經過運按估價若干受罰三倍此結於未請過船單之先應請由領事官當堂畫押爲憑至定限應由該關稅務司按情酌訂惟究不得過十五日此等過載之單火均不准登岸其過船時須由關查明係原包原貨派差押送俟原貨如數復出口方准將結撤銷倘有擬由原船復運出口者在未領關艙准單之先須由船商按過載之例一體具結方准放行以上所擬似不致另生流弊是否可行應請酌奪示復分別行文以便照辦等因前來本衙門查閱總稅務司所擬各節均尚詳洽應如所稱辦理至定限一層最關緊要總稅務司聲稱由該關稅務司按情酌訂究不得過十五日等語查十五日係兩禮拜之期軍火過船是否須候兩期禮拜應令該關稅務司即行體察情形核實妥定但至遲總以十五日期限爲斷從前軍火等物不准販運進出口條約本有明文現因商人由此外邦運彼外國必須假道中華港口是以暫議約外通融辦法特爲格外恤商起見倘或過船商人因此夾帶影射借端滋弊本衙門惟有照約一概禁止應併由該關稅務司曉諭商人知悉除由本衙門咨行南洋大臣外爲此劄行總稅務司轉飭查照可也須至劄者

右劄布政使銜總稅務司赫　准此

同治　拾壹年　拾貳月　拾捌日

總字第伍百肆拾玖號

82.

大清欽命總理各國事務衙門　爲

劄行事同治十一年三月二十九日准

威大臣照會內稱墨西哥國新造銀錢近在廣州經

兩廣總督暨領事官等各派委員會同驗明成色寫立憑單等因旋於四月初八

日准

兩廣總督咨同前因查英國條約第三十三款有按照道光二十三年在廣東所

定各樣成色交納明文法國條約第二十一款內載海關與領事官嚴其市價情

形將洋銀比較紋銀應補稅銀若干照數補足美國條約第二十二款內載以洋

銀按時價折交各等語同治五年間准

阿大臣照稱香港新製洋銀經中英國官員在廣州會驗成色每百兩合足紋九十

兩之數寫立憑單等因當經本衙門行文查復屬實即經照復准令補交紋水輸

納稅餉在案此次墨西哥新造銀錢既經兩國官員公同會驗成色足數九成自

應准其補交紋水輸納稅餉惟此項鷹銀日後成色倘有不足商民或不樂用以

及銀局舞弊以官濟私以假攙眞不便於民即未便准其強輸官稅以期無碍稅

餉而順輿情除由本衙門咨行

南北洋大臣查照復
威大臣外相應抄錄往來照會各一件札行總稅務司查照辦理可也須至札者
右劄布政使銜總稅務司赫　准此
同治　十一年　四月　十二　日
總字第伍百拾貳號

照錄　英國照會

爲照會事案查前因墨西哥國擬鑄新式洋錢本大臣希請
貴親王轉飭各口海關監督查照收納於同治十年四月二十五日備文知照嗣
於五月初五日接准
貴親王來文內開將來墨西哥國所造新錢按照紋銀實在能得成色若干以便
輸納稅餉之處應由本衙門咨行南北洋通商大臣轉飭各海關監督察看情形
查照成案一律核明辦理等因各在案玆據駐札廣州領事官羅詳報內稱同治
十一年二月初五日在省城經
兩廣總督部堂
粵海關監督　暨敝領事官各派委屬官一員會同監視令將新式洋銀鎔兌傾
化覈定成色寫立憑單爲據以憑單核算計新式洋銀壹百圓知與舊式洋銀百

圖成色較多幾至一元有半等因附送憑單前來本大臣據此相應抄錄憑單備
文粘送
貴親王查閱並祈
轉飭各口海關監督遵照天津條約第三十三款嗣後凡有英商將新式洋錢呈
交稅課者遵即核計實在成色一律收納可也須至照會者

大清補用知府署廣糧廳方
粵海關部代辦粵盈庫大使葉　爲
大英特揀繙譯官璧
會同言明驗得新出鷹銀成色事照得本分府庫廳繙譯官於同治十一年二月初五日在
關部銀號恆茂店經將新出銀員當面試驗核定成色玆將會驗事由詳細開列

一新出銀員貳拾捌員先行平兌約重貳拾兩零貳錢伍分

一嗣將該銀貳拾捌員配鉛同重鎔銷提淨平兌共得海關紋銀壹拾捌兩壹錢伍分

一所得海關紋銀較未鎔化之原銀共輕貳兩壹錢

玆將新出鷹銀覈對海關紋銀查以上驗試事由核定成色聲明於後

一照上算以新銀壹百員重柒拾貳兩叁錢貳分

一新出鷹銀壹百兩即伸海關銀捌拾玖兩陸錢叁分

另鍋底約耗輕銀叁錢柒分合共玖拾兩正
連輕耗計伸得呈色紋銀玖成正
現得關部銀號高恆茂等五家字號所立憑單粘附爲證
計核新出鷹銀壹百壹拾壹兩壹錢壹分可抵足色紋銀壹百兩正憑碼均行爲
此會立約據立明一切用英漢文各書一通共立五張分別呈據
本日在廣州省城
英國領事官署內會同畫押
同治十一年二月初五日

照錄覆英國照會

爲照復事同治十一年三月二十九日准
貴大臣照會內稱墨西哥國新造銀錢近在廣州經兩廣總督暨領事官等各派
委員會同驗明成色寫立憑單等因當經本衙門以未據粵省咨報有案抄單行
查去後兹於四月初八日准兩廣總督咨稱正月十四日接駐劄廣州領事官羅
申陳內稱香港銀局製造新鷹銀成圓請照同治五年成案委員會同試驗以便
輪餉通用等情當經本部堂派委候補知府方功惠並咨商粵海關監督派委庫

大使葉滋鈞會同璧緇譯官眼同銀匠將此項新鷹銀傾鎔試驗據報與海關紋銀比較成數計足九成以此次新鷹銀一百十一兩一錢一分抵海關紋銀一百兩立有憑單爲據此項新鷹銀既經傾驗成色與紋銀比較計足九成與現在通用鷹錢相同其輪納稅餉向按紋銀計算補交紋水自應准其輪納並日行通用以便商民等因前來查兩廣總督所報前項鷹銀計足九成與

貴大臣來文內粘憑單所開之數相符自應准各商民補交紋水輪納稅餉業經兩廣總督等出示嚴禁棍徒假造影射本衙門應卽咨行南北洋大臣並札總稅務司查照成案辦理倘日後成色不足商民或不樂於使用或銀局中有舞弊等事以官濟私以假攙眞彼時不便於民用者卽不能强輪官稅蓋中國官員僅能禁止內地棍徒揑造而不能禁銀局另有他故並不能强制商民以必用也本衙門顧慮及此不得不預爲言明至現在既經兩廣總督核明自應卽照來文辦理相應照覆

貴大臣查照可也

隨總字伍百拾貳號

83.

大清欽命總理各國事務衙門　為
劄行事同治六年九月初六日准上海通商大臣曾　來文以通商各口華商如
有租雇外國火輪夾板等船或購買或仿造以便裝載現已核定章程通行各口
試辦如有於商情滯礙之處准由商戶呈明酌辦等情並將刊本章程咨送前來
相應將原章程四款抄錄劄行總稅務司查照可也切切特劄　計抄單壹件
右劄按察使銜總稅務司赫　准此
同治　陸年　玖月　貳拾肆　日

華商置用火輪夾板等項船隻章程

第一欵 領繳單契牌照

一凡有華商欲買夾板等船應赴本口監督衙門稟明由監督詳查本人實屬華民
並無假借等弊即發買船准單內將華商姓名籍貫註明發該商執領前赴新關
由稅務司挂號在准單空白內照塡英文發還該商承買倘買船後復經查出假
借等情即將該船入官

一凡領准單者遇有合式船隻先應由稅務司派人前赴查明實係能出海堪用之
船俟議明價值帶同賣主赴該國領事官衙門將准單呈驗由該領事官查明並

20

無假冒借名等弊卽准立據將船契畫押蓋印發交華商收領其原領外國船牌由領事官立卽查銷

一凡領船契者應赴新關由稅務司查驗挂號將該船寬闊若干噸數若干及本船式樣詳細開單請由監督將船牌照填註送回照填英文發給華商收執一面飭繳牌費銀叁百兩

一凡領牌照船隻其船名須在船尾大書並將牌照之號數用漢洋文字書明船頭兩旁日後不得私自更改

一領牌後若有遺失該商卽赴關報明補領倘非在原口遺失仍須按情稟報並請先發暫用憑據俟回原口將暫用之據赴關呈繳補請牌照如遇有遭風失火等情均應赴關報明或止將牌照救出亦須呈繳不得隱匿干咎

一凡領牌照之船須將噸數若干並牌照號數於船中樑上刻明

一凡買船契應填價值倘船內有抵押未清之項乃客商平常私事與官無涉

一日後擬將該船改樣式應由該商將所改之處開單赴關稟明請於原牌內添註由原口改註底簿

一凡船應以壹百分爲算以一人之船船牌註明壹百分歸某人若數人有分卽按股分計算

一凡船倘係會館置買請領准單船牌等件應由會館首事料理

一凡華商日後欲將船隻轉賣倘係賣與外國人須赴關報明將船牌呈繳由原領之關查銷倘賣與別華商應帶同買主赴監督衙門稟明核准寫立賣契一面將原牌繳回換領新牌仍用原繳原名赴新關掛號請由稅務司塡註英文

一凡華商如有情願自造夾板等項船隻亦應一律先赴監督衙門請發造船准單赴關塡註英文俟船造畢由稅務司派人勘量開具清單照請發給牌照

第二欵來往進出輸納稅鈔

一凡有華商夾板等船請領牌照者准赴外國貿易並准在中國通商各口來往不得私赴沿海別口亦不得任意進泊內地湖河各口致有礙壞船隻事

一凡船進口時須將船牌等件呈存稅務司出口時領回至何處泊船如何起下貨物請領准單呈具報單一切事宜均照洋船定例辦理

一凡船所裝貨物均照洋商稅則納稅其船鈔照納

一凡結底應由各口稅務司將此等船隻完稅若干分欵開列由總稅務司轉報

第三欵雇用工人

一華商買用此等船隻所用管船夥長應用華人以期易知中國各項法度方可爲一船之主

一凡有外國人受雇充艄工者須先將本國考驗可充艄工之據呈由稅務司驗明俟雇定後即由稅務司將該艄工係何國人何姓名並受雇月日註明船牌如日後更換宜將辭工之日添註

一凡艄工須照洋船規矩在船記事簿內按日註明經過之事

一凡華商夾板等船須立水手名單內將各水手姓名籍貫年歲工銀註明倘雇有外國人充當水手須帶赴領事官或稅務司畫押受雇

一船出口之後如水手人等有不法者即由艄工將其捆押俟進口交稅務司轉送監督或領事官分別辦理

第四欵違章罰辦

一凡有華商買用夾板等船未遵以上各章應由監督會同稅務司先將船扣留按情罰辦

一凡華商夾板等船違犯洋商船隻應遵條約載明各章即由監督會同稅務司酌量將此船一體罰辦

一凡有起下貨物違犯該關章程即由監督會同稅務司酌定或將貨入官或將該商議罰

84.

大清欽命總理各國事務衙門　爲

劄行事前據總稅務司申呈英德兩商運貨進口均用華船裝貨一願常關完稅
一願新關完稅彼此互異並稱華船有涉於通商者有四項歸新關完稅一係洋
商洋船一係洋商雇用華船一係華商來往外國如香港澳門等處華船一係通
商各口新添華商火輪夾板等項洋船凡非通商口岸華船不准前往外國凡通
商口岸准往外國華船均須請領新關牌照至華船應完船鈔德國商人加羅威
治並未照納德國領事以完鈔章程係法國之事與德國無涉等語申請酌復前
來本衙門當經咨行
南北洋大臣轉飭各關監督核議並劄復總稅務司在案茲准
南北洋大臣將各關監督核議各條由先後咨送本衙門查核等因查通商各口
各項船隻內洋商洋船本係照約歸新關完稅新添華商火輪夾板等項洋船現
在招商船局已定章程歸新關完稅以上兩項船隻來往通商各口自應均歸新
關完稅其華商來往外國如香港澳門等處華船一項現據
南洋大臣咨稱江浙閩粵各海關此項船隻已有地方官給領船照若必令赴新
關請領牌照不無窒礙

北洋大臣咨稱南洋沿海各處華船赴香港安南琉球暹羅新加坡小呂宋等處貿易者領有地方官牌照應准通行出口入口常關納稅總稅務司申呈等語殊於華商生計常關稅額俱多窒礙是總稅務司所稱華商來往外國華船應歸新關完稅並由新關請領牌照一節旣經

南北洋大臣查明窒礙難行應毋庸議所有華商前往外國貿易華船無論是否通商口岸之船但有地方官給領牌照卽准前往貿易應完稅項統歸常關完納其洋商雇用華船一項查英約第十四款往來卸貨下貨任從英商雇船剝運不論各項船隻倘有走私漏稅查出照例懲辦又第三十一款英商在各口自用艇隻倘帶例應完稅之貨每四個月一次納鈔又長江通商統共章程第六條洋商雇用內地船隻按照條約納稅各等語總稅務司以此項船隻沿海祇有納鈔明文沿江本有納稅明文可引長江之章作証

南洋大臣咨稱洋商雇用華船通商各口無論暨暫雇常雇所用何船均應歸新關完稅以昭劃一

北洋大臣咨稱洋商雇用華船有請單不請單之分請單者照新關定章完稅不請單者照華商例逢關納稅遇卡抽釐查洋商運洋貨進通商各口完正稅後運入內地完過子口半稅者領有新關稅單爲憑洋商在通商各口報明入內地置

買運回外國之土貨領有新關報單爲憑回至最後子口先赴新關完納子口半稅方准過卡其未領有稅單報單者均照華商沿途逢關納稅遇卡抽釐今洋商雇用華船運貨納稅除長江通商三口仍照統共章程條欵辦理外洋商如在通商各口雇用華船運洋貨入內地及入內地置買回國土貨無論雇用何項華船亦無論常雇暫雇自應以有無稅單報單爲憑分別完納稅釐其領有稅單報單雇用之華船該船倘有走私偷漏情事一經查出應令該監督照例懲辦以杜弊端除由本衙門咨行

南北洋大臣轉飭各關監督遵照外相應劄行總稅務司即飭各關稅務司一體遵照辦理至洋商雇用華船運貨英國條約本有四個月一次納鈔明文法國更定條約第二十二款本衙門亦已通行各關遵辦且德國條約第四十欵載明日後如將噸稅無論何國施行改變一經通行德意志通商稅務公會各國商民等一體遵照毋庸再議條欵茲德國領事以完鈔章程與德國無涉未免强辯應由

南洋大臣轉飭粵海關監督照會該領事照約辦理毋任違背可也特劄

右劄布政使銜總稅務司赫　准此

同治　拾叁年　叁月　初捌日

總字第陸百拾捌號

85.

大清欽命總理各國事務衙門 爲

劄行事同治十二年二月十五日准北洋大臣咨稱准本衙門咨赫總稅司申各關大小巡船掛用新式龍旗式樣稍有不同恐失畫一請於各項旗幟發一定式以便轉示各口稅務司遵掛等語當將現定龍旗畫一式樣照繪一分咨送前來相應將現定旗式繪圖劄行總稅司轉飭各口稅務司一體遵照掛用可也特劄

附現繪旗圖一紙

右劄布政使銜總稅務司赫 准此

同治 拾貳年 貳月 貳拾 日

總字第伍百伍拾玖號

此三角旗用正黃色上鑲龍形龍頭向上常掛桅梢作主旗凡船身長二十丈以內者其旗斜長八尺幅寬四尺底長六尺九寸三分船身長二十丈以外者其旗斜長一丈二尺幅寬六尺五寸底長一丈一寸均用中國工部營造尺量製

隨總字第伍百伍拾玖號

## 86.

具稟人莊吉年二十一歲原籍廣東潮州現住英租界稟爲求

恩給領事竊身素在申江謀生有年安分守業緣因胞弟莊有年在汕頭搭牛莊輪船於本月十一日下午至申帶來已用色布五段計本紋銀柒兩本應赴 關報驗奈因胞弟初次來申不識章程所有失慎叩求

關憲大人俯念零星小件乞 恩飭賜具領深沾

德便上稟

計 開

色布五疋 估本銀柒兩正

光緒 八年 五月 日叩呈

87.

具稟政大信局稟爲寄帶貨樣被

關扣留籲懇

憲恩豁免給領事竊業在英租界九江路開設長江信局有年素守本分玆緣客商

便附貨樣情難推却是於初二日有寄鎭江貨樣壹包有寄安慶貨樣壹包由初

二日江表輪船出口適值臺下貴巡搜驗在案竊念貨樣微物並非販運圖利

現下客家說是業等遺悞索賠甚急有口難分剖爲此瀝情伏乞

稅務司關憲大人垂憐豁免微物給領施行世世公侯項

德上稟

計開

鎭江寄紅丹　壹包陸匣　計重二觔四兩　估銀一兩五錢

安慶寄銀硃　壹包　計重一百兩　估銀一兩七錢

光緒　八年　五月　初八　日政大源信局稟呈

## 88.

具稟老沙遜經租帳房

爲漢號託買自着木鞋叩　恩豁免迅賜給領事竊身在　治英租界老旗昌地

方老沙遜房租帳房爲業於本月十一日由江孚輪船出口帶去木鞋三十雙計

三包送船時經　臺巡查驗在案緣身等集資在漢口開張同椿號鮮鹹雜貨店

夥友數十人皆用甯幫之人而鮮鹹貨生涯店堂難免潮濕所以各友向着木鞋

爲便此次帶去實係店夥自用並非取巧販賣仰沐

憲臺鑒原下情念身無知不諳憲章應完稅課願照補納求　恩賞給實爲德便

備情急叩伏乞

稅務憲大人電鑒　恩賜豁免給領施行沾仁上稟

計開

漢口同椿號收　木鞋三包計三十雙　計買價錢六千文

光緒八年四月　日稟

89.

具稟商人恒茂行

稟爲求　恩賞給事竊於六月初三日海晏輪船進口由天津載得翟客X鞋子

五包經小行報關驗訖完餉因於初八晚九點半鐘經該客出去行至金利源北

首天后宮橋下被西人由東洋車上携去X鞋子九十六雙該客與其理論惟因

中西音語彼此不懂由是該客祗得尾隨其後目覩西人將貨携進江海北關方

知係　貴關查私西人扦子手誤疑私貨因而携去伏思此貨屬實由海晏輪船

進口並無舛錯迺今　貴關扦子手誤認私貨爲此不得不瀝陳下情叩乞

稅務司大人　恩賜賞還俾得給領而安商業戴德上稟

光緒　八年　六月　日呈

# 90.

具稟福興信局

爲客號託帶水烟袋叩 恩豁免迅賜賞給事竊身在治二馬路地方開設長江信局于本月十一日由江寬輪船進口有漢號寄牛庄大興利收水烟袋四支船抵埠時經 臺巡查驗在案念身代客寄信附有自用水烟袋實非取巧販賣之物仰沐

仁憲鑒原下情求恩賞給實爲德便備情急叩

稅務憲大人電鑒 恩賜豁免給領施行沾德上稟

計開

牛庄大興利收 水烟袋四支不知買價

光緒 八年 四月 日稟

91.

具稟民人陳瑞麟
爲家用帳子夏布叩 恩豁免迅賜給領事竊身在治二馬路地方全昌仁信局
爲業于本月二十七日北京輪船進口有漢口胞弟陳鞠堂帶來帳子夏布一包
蒙 臺巡查驗在案念身係秋季家中吉席做大床帳之用並非取巧販賣求
恩賞給實爲德便爲此備情急叩
稅務憲大人電鑒 恩賜豁免給領施行沾仁上稟

計 開

藍粗夏布 一段 十二丈二尺半做大床帳用
藍夏布 一段 一丈九尺做女布衫用
共計買價錢五千四百另

光緒 八年 四月 日稟

92.

具稟戴起祥天津紫竹林人爲懇恩事身幼弟在上洋做工與豐順輪船陳姓交好手中畧有餘財煩陳姓帶來小雨傘一百三十二把旱傘十八把囑身賣出作一家糊口於六月二十五日到天津被關取去身一家老幼十餘口賴此微物養生伏祈

大人格外施恩將雨傘一百三十二把旱傘十八把賜下身一家老幼得生均感鴻

恩矣爲此叩稟

93.

具稟算書黃瑞墀爲懇

恩事竊算書在關十一年多前於光緒四年夏間承

大人派同法馬大老爺親往河間府辦賑受暑受瘟備嘗辛苦回津後即患病月餘

當蒙

大人面允必給好處今已三年未敢言及現聞法馬大老爺俱已高升辦賑各員皆

得保舉而

大人不日榮歸爲此不揣冒昧仰求

格外施恩可否將薪俸酌增之處伏候

鈞裁感激之至謹稟

94.

具稟商人普源公稟爲雜貨漏報祈
恩寬釋事竊小號向在宮北街開設代客接儎生意於二月初二日由廣東甯波船
運申轉裝保大船來津於本月十六日進口嚟什貨十一件承
貴差查驗內一件中有氷片雜藥等未經報稅當被扣留緣該客貨色繁多開單時
悞漏一色自粵出口偶未開驗故彼此尚未知但小號照原來花色報稅以致錯漏
咎實難辭惟念該客跋涉重洋祇求微利血本無歸苦不堪言伏祈
稅務司大人俯恤商情准將該貨照例完稅卽飭領回實爲
恩便不勝感激之至切赴

95.

具稟粵東廣州帮商人公和號稟爲估價無定受罰難甘懇
恩秉公照估完稅放行以便商旅事竊於本月初六日由夾板船運入口花梨木板
九塊報關請驗共估價銀七十兩當蒙查驗放行隨於次日由德治蘭夾板船運入
口花梨木板二十三塊卽照前價呈報詎料

貴關大寫不照前估實以每塊估銀十三兩並議罰三倍商以此板同是一貨相隔
一日何得價估兩歧因此木急須變客未便久延只得呈請照稅惟求免罰旬日
央求未蒙允准伏思關設罰條原爲奸商偷漏罰以示儆今估價貨物竟以任意
高估而議罰實令無從遵辦不得不叩乞
大人台前恩恤商艱迅賜照估上稅免罰放行則感
恩無旣矣切切上稟

## 96.

具稟張于氏年七十歲
爲懸案不結懇再提究事竊氏被劉張氏扭摔一案業已屢控迄今半年尙未訊結
而該氏仍復來家吵鬧不休並强借錢文不得已再求
本縣正堂嚴傳劉張氏到案訊究俾免無理取鬧則感荷
鴻慈實無涯涘謹稟

97.

具禀鄒旺係山東登州府寧海州人為再懇

恩速賜追究以救蟻命事竊身因於四月十三日在新南陞輪船被匪竊去銀五百兩當已具禀在案所失之銀盡係為人携帶具禀之後守候多日未蒙緝獲進退維谷幾不欲生幸有同鄉帮助川資回家告明失主而失主不允向身要銀無奈只得匍匐來津復懇

大人究追以救微生且聞天津縣已獲屢竊輪船客物之匪董三即董祥已押案追比身銀亦係輪船被竊現經拏獲該匪不難究追哀叩

大人俯賜恩准飭縣嚴追該匪究出原銀俾得交還失主則

大人公侯萬代積德累仁身啣結之報生生世世於無極矣頂德上禀

98.

具禀粵東廣州帮商人粵豐隆禀為貨有定稅突更估價懇

恩飭照定則完稅放行以便商賈事竊商由巴拿士夾板船運入口重木樑料陸續詣關報稅查此貨稅則內載長不過二十六幅地四方不到十二因制每根稅銀一錢五分即間有長短大小不一均照此例尺寸核計各商均皆遵照報稅商連日照例呈報均已按例尺寸核計完稅突於月之十八日請驗時

貴關以此貨議估價銀七十兩之多不准按例尺寸核計飭令照估完稅伏思估價一節原屬稅無定例始行議估況今此貨經有照例核稅何得又更估價未免貨同稅異寔令商無所適從思維再四情寔難已不得不叩乞

大人恩准仍照稅則內載重木樑料尺寸核計完稅放行寔爲

恩公兩便除稟 津海關道憲外切切上稟

## 99.

具稟華民林柔福建人爲稟明懇恩事竊柔於去年六月間隨家主陳自新到京鄉試本年二月間家主起行回籍路過天津寓河北福來店適有人携高麗參來賣家主向買二十斤轉託寶通泰投稅帶回福州銷售不料該貨只有四斤零是眞參其餘十五斤零皆係假參家主以被人欺騙將原參十五斤零交柔附塔怡興行夾板船帶到天津找尋原經手退還於本月初九日進口柔耳聞原貨帶回似可無庸再報當將行李聚儎經 台差摟拿而去竊思柔奉家主之命數千里奔波爲送換假參而來今被拿入官柔無以復家主之命勢必淪落異鄉憂愁不可言狀且參產北地本無由南運北之理如非退換實情何敢冒瀆不得已急懇

稅務司大人驗明該參曲加矜恤俯准給還以全蟻命頂德切稟

100.
具稟張德年四十歲爲
呈請緝捕以靖地方事竊身居紫竹林昨夜忽有賊匪數人於三更時分進院撬門
竊去銅盆衣服茶碗等物當卽喊追不及誠恐時屆隆冬迫於饑寒不免屢來偷竊
爲此稟懇
恩准嚴比捕役務緝正賊贓物究辦以安善良而衛閭閻實爲德便上稟

101.
具稟本關總信差胡永安稱在京津及王秦莊楊村河西務張家灣設立馬撥多年
專寄
總稅務司公署及 各海關並
北洋大臣
各國公使等署文函所有楊村信差馬撥設立在楊村街永源義洋貨小店內不料
本年五月初六日十二點鐘後被賊由門面撬開失去海關寄中外文函時刻簿一
本信差號衣一件並零物當卽報明該村文武地方官並通知地保王允明而地保
不惟不管反向總信差言此後洋信不准在楊村街裏來往特此懇祈
大人恩准函致
海關道札飭武清縣務獲贓賊嚴懲地保庶免信差來往中途漸有意外之虞實爲
公便上稟

102.

# 海江警船示

稅務營造處總營造司韓　爲
通行曉諭事照得本總營造司前奉
總稅務司赫　憲劄行以沿海沿江建造鐙塔浮樁等事或係創
設或宜改移或有增添或須裁撤營造旣有變更務卽隨時彰
明出示通曉各處俾得行江海船隻周知徧喻等因茲本總營
造司查江海關稅務司所屬界內吳淞江口停泊小船一隻以
示沉船所在合將其情形開列於左

計開

一長江太倉州寶山縣進吳淞江口船行正路於該處鐙塔及警船浮兩端之間沉
有甯波華船一隻恐沉船漂移無定現用小船一隻連縛沉船停泊日挂紅旗夜
懸紅鐙爲號以示沉船所在

爲此合卽遵行出示通曉各處船隻其務宜留心詳記以免疎
虞勿忘勿忽切切特示

同治　十二年　十一月　十七日　第三十號示

103. **閩海關**

一福州府連江縣閩江口內烏礁上向設之警船石樁一座前約於本月十七日先後被水激刷損毀不日卽行興工修造仍置原處

光緒七年閏七月二十九日　第一百三十八號示

104. **通商各關**

一凡各處所設之警船浮爲指明船隻由海進口時應行於浮之左邊（卽在水道之右）各浮一律飾以紅色

一凡各處所設之警船浮爲指明船隻由海進口時應行於浮之右邊（卽在水道之左）各浮一律飾以黑色

一凡往來船隻應傍浮行駛（卽在水道中間）所有示路警船各浮一律飾以紅黑橫線相間色樣

一凡沙尾之角即係兩傍有水道而中間隔有明暗沙以及亂礁之處其內外角所設之警船浮一律飾以紅黑豎線相間色樣

一凡指明洋面有石礁以及行船正路中間遇有微碍之處所設警船浮一律飾以紅黑方格色樣其水道中間指明碍處之浮均設於向海外面

一凡進口船隻遇危險之處於兩傍設有方格警船浮其飾以紅白二色方格者爲指明水道之右該船隻應行於浮之左邊其黑白方格者爲指明水道之左該船隻應行於浮之右邊

一凡指明沉船之浮一律飾以綠色浮上以白色書有洋文WRECK即係沉船字樣該沉船或在洋面或在港內船易行駛於兩傍有水闊之處該浮一律設於向海之外面並無別項標記凡指明沉船有碍水道必須繞避之處即於該浮所有沉船字樣之上加以白色書有洋文第幾號字樣其係雙數者均爲指明由海進口船隻應行正路之右邊其單數者均爲指明由海進口船隻應行正路之左邊

其餘以上未經詳載各項情形均於本關每年所發燈塔燈船燈杆警船浮樁總册內一律開列

每警船浮於切水面以上易以縛繫之處縛有鐵片一塊上烙印漢洋兩文照册內所載註明某關某處該浮倘遇風浪衝移漂流水面但須驗明鐵片字樣即知爲何處何關所屬

一凡各處所設之警船樁爲指明船隻由海進口時應行於樁之左邊（即在水道之右）各樁
一律飾以紅色

一凡各處所設之警船樁爲指明船隻由海進口時應行於樁之右邊（即在水道之左）各樁
一律飾以黑色

一凡沙尾之角即係兩傍有水道而中間隔有（明晴）沙以及亂礁之處其內外角所設
之警船樁一律飾以紅黑竪線相間色樣

一凡指明洋面有石礁以及港內正路之小礁兩傍有水道處所設警船樁一律飾
以紅黑方格色樣

一凡有危險處之兩傍設有繪方格式警船樁其飾以紅白二色方格者爲指明水
道之右該進口船隻應行於樁之左邊其黑白方格者爲指明水道之左該進口
船隻應行於樁之右邊

凡以上所言警船樁之色樣係專指樁體而言其樁體飾以一色或係黑色或
係紅色之類若上有帽頂者則該帽頂或專飾與樁體同色或飾用樁體之色
間以白色者或係全飾以白色不等

其樁體若飾以兩色該帽頂所飾亦不出此兩色之外凡樁上所有帽頂各項
情形均於本關所發册內一律開列

一海江各岸上所有警船樁一律飾用顯明色樣惟用紅黑白三色以便行船易於辨明度勢又過攔江沙以及上江進口等方向此項警船樁各等情形均於冊內註明

光緒八年六月二十一日第一百五十一號示

105.

## 廈門關

一泉州府同安縣金門島大沙尾對面現據大英國水師部所製海道圖於西歷本年七月新發第一千七百六十七號內載該處漸長暗沙一段現已於該沙之南邊設有紅色尖圓形警船浮一個上置黑色球式鑑帽浮切水面處徑五尺一寸往來船隻不宜行於該浮及金門島岸之中間以免觸沙之患

光緒九年八月初一日第一百七十三號示

## 106. 江海關

一長江口外九段鐙塔附近一帶地方於本年九月間經　大英國巡船名弗來音非是之官員測量該處將所測得情形申報其本國上憲查此事現接有總理大英國遊歷大清國等洋面各巡船二等水師提督軍門魏　來文據此合行抄錄原文詳示於後

長江松江府南滙縣自黃家灣九段地方所設警船小鐙架下遊相距約六里之處至九段鐙塔下遊相距約三里之處於船行正路將近中間之處查有新長之暗沙一段於該沙以及江南岸之間另有船隻可行之水道寬二里餘朔望潮落時該處之水常深有二丈

自該暗沙西北尾水深十四尺餘之處

視九段小架爲北八十八度五十五分西相距九里餘

視九段廢鐙塔爲南十六度四十五分東相距十一里餘

視九段鐙船爲南五十度五十五分東相距十二里半

視干沙（光緒七年所出沿海圖說作高沙）望臺爲南六十六度十五分東相距二十四里餘

自該暗沙東南尾水深十五尺餘之處

覩九段廢鐙塔爲北八十八度五十五分西相距六里餘

覩該處獨樹英語所爲更得利者爲南五十三度四十五分西相距九里

覩九段鐙船爲北四度四十五分東相距三里

覩干沙望臺爲北八十五度東相距十二里半

其西北東南兩沙尾成直線處多有小暗沙沙上水深一丈二尺餘至一丈四五尺餘不等自西北水深一丈四尺餘之沙段起該沙尾曲斜向西北偏北之方向附近該處所有之暗河沙島

凡以上所開度數均按羅經方向羅經變差二度十五分西按該沙查本國水師部所發海道圖之第一千一百九十九及一千六百二等號均未詳載合並聲明

等因

查此項公文前於十月十六日所出之第一百七十七號示諭事無少異惟較此示簡畧所有前示應毋庸議可也

光緒　九年　十一月　初四日　第一百七十八號示

107.

茲將通商各關警船鐙浮樁總册所載各事擇取欵式列下（光緒十年即西歷一千八百八十四年總册）

第一鐙第二鐙

廣州府南海番禺兩縣交界海珠礮臺在船路北之地方於大浪三浪兩石上各設紅色圓形剛石鐙塔一座自基至頂高二丈二尺各置紅光常明小鐙鐙火距水面一丈三尺晴時應照六里咸豐九年設此鐙與本册所列之第一第二樁同

第七鐙

潮州府惠來縣石碑山（又名赤沙澳）地方設有黑白二色橫線相間圓形塔一座自基至頂高十丈二尺上置有頭等透鏡紅白二光乍明乍滅鐙每明八秒即滅二秒鐙火距水面十三丈晴時應照五十七里自南五十五度西起經正西至北五十三度東止俱見白光其餘向岸之處俱見紅光塔在緯度北二十二度五十六分三十秒經度中國中線西三十八秒英國中線東一百十六度二十八分十秒遇大霧時該守鐙人等若聞船隻有用防險號者如鳴鐘吹戒險螺放汽等即放礮二次每次間時十秒該船續用防險號者即俟十分時再行放砲以示鐙塔所在光緒六年設

第八鐙

潮州府潮陽縣表角（一名東鄉頭一名廣澳）地方設有白色圓形塔一座自基至頂高一丈九

尺上置有四等透鏡紅白二光一面常明一面乍明乍滅鐙鐙火距水面十四丈五尺晴時白光應照四十五里紅光應照二十四里自南三十二度東起至南十度東止俱見常明紅光自南十度東起經正南正西至北八度三十分東止俱見白光該白光鐙每一分鐘時即遮滅約三秒又自北八度三十分東起至南交表角遮掩不見鐙光之處即西音所謂馬兒角地方止仍見紅光鐙每一分鐘時亦遮滅約三秒塔在緯度北二十三度十四分三十五秒經度中國中線東十九分四十三秒英國中線東一百十六度四十八分三十一秒遇大霧時該守鐙人等若聞船隻有用防險號者如鳴鐘吹戒險螺放汽等即放砲二次每次間時一分該船續用防險號者即俟十五分時再行放砲以示鐙塔所在光緒六年設

第九鐙

潮州府潮陽縣汕頭口鹿嶼即德洲頂之東角地方設有紅色圓形塔一座自基至頂高一丈八尺上置有六等透鏡四面白光常明放歛鐙每半分鐘時即放紅光一閃鐙火距水面十七丈晴時應照二十四里塔在緯度北二十三度十九分五十四秒經度中國中線東十六分四十四秒英國中線東一百十六度四十五分三十二秒光緒六年設

第十三鐙

漳州府海澄縣青嶼北坡上設有紅白二色豎線八角形塔一座自基至頂高二丈

八尺上置四等透鏡紅白二光常明鐙鐙火距水面十一丈晴時白光應照四十五里紅光應照二十四里自北一度東起經正北至北五十七度西止俱見紅光自北五十七度西起經正西正南至南五十度東止俱見白光自南五十度東起至南八十九度東止又見紅光塔在緯度北二十四度二十二分八秒經度中國中線東一度三十八分二十三秒英國中線東一百十八度七分十一秒守鐙房垣俱白色光緒元年設

第十八鐙

臺灣府臺灣縣安平老砲台距該砲台中小山頂上所有樹木正在前面向海洋約二十五丈之處設有木桅一杆上置六等透鏡白光常明鐙鐙火距水面五丈一尺晴時應照三十里自東南起經正西正北至正東止俱見鐙光塔在緯度北二十三度二十秒經度中國中線東三度四十一分十二秒英國中線東一百二十度十分秋冬颷東北風時往來該處之船隻視該鐙自北六十二度東起至北七十三度東止凡測有四拓半至五拓水深之地方俱可停泊無虞其春夏颷西南風時視該鐙約在東北方如測有六七拓不等水深之處停泊最宜光緒七年設

第二十六鐙

定海廳小龜山頂上設有黑色圓形塔一座自基至頂高四丈上置三等透鏡漸明漸滅鐙每半分時明滅一次鐙火距水面高二十丈餘晴時應照六十六里該鐙自

北二十度五十四分東起至北四十一度十七分東止爲該處鼎足島所蔽其外東霍與小龜等山東邊及東南邊自北八十八度三十九分西起至北五十七度四十一分西止亦不見鐙光又該處（海道圖說所載之）何勒以及休爲得等島之西邊以及西北邊自南八十二度十三分東起至南六十三度三十五分東止被山遮蔽惟自南六十五度五十三分東起至南六十四度三十九分東止此一方向適於山缺處漏射鐙光一隊塔約在緯度北三十度十二分二十七秒經度中國中線東六度七分二十五秒英國中線東一百二十二度三十六分十三秒遇大霧時該守鐙人等若聞船隻有用防險號者如鳴鐘吹戒險螺放汽等卽放砲三次每次間時三分該船續用防險號者卽俟十分時再行放砲以示鐙塔所在

第六十八鐙

長江黃州府黃岡縣戴家洲及廣濟縣大藥山西角兩處按時每設單桅鐙船一隻桅上有條編圓球懸挂六等透鏡四面白光常明鐙鐙火距水面二丈七尺晴時應照二十一里自洋正月初至六月底船泊在大藥山西角自洋七月初至十二月底泊在戴家洲南角同治十年原設十二年修改

第七十七鐙

奉天府遼河口外在攔江沙外向西南偏西距約十一里於水深二丈五尺之處設有三桅鐙船一隻船身紅色兩旁書有洋文 NEWCHWANG 卽係牛莊字樣中桅上有黑色

圓球上置凹鏡逼射白光常明鐙鐙火距水面三丈四尺晴時應照三十三里船在緯度北四十度三十五分經度中國中線東五度三十一分十二秒英國中線東一百二十二度該守船人等見來往船隻誤入險途即放砲一次並升通用旗號以示應行之路遇大霧時每十秒吹戒險汽螺一次修鐙續油時另懸白光小鐙以代並放藍光爲號自日落至日出時於桅之前纜距船欄高五尺挂白光小鐙一個以示船首方向該船自洋四月初至十一月中旬停泊該處其氷河時船則移去該鐙船倘被風浪衝移已離原泊方向至無足爲示引之處即將舊照之鐙撤去於船之首尾代用紅光常明小鐙各一個並將桅上圓頂不日撤去於未撤之先在桅上挂一紅旗爲號以免舛悞同治六年原設十年修改

粵海關第一浮

廣州府番禺縣海珠礮臺地方瀑口礁設有紅色尖圓式警船木浮一個浮下水深七尺爲指明船行由亂石中間正路北邊最西之處自日落起至日出止浮上點照紅光鐙朔望潮落時礁上水深三尺

潮海關第一浮

潮州府潮陽縣韓江口外相距烏礁耳即下烏礁之尖石約一百二十三丈於水深二丈三尺之處設有紅黑二色方格自鳴風笙警船浮一個爲指明該礁之東南角浮切水面處徑八尺五寸

潮海關第二浮

潮州府澄海縣汕頭口內在礜盤角卽距海關碼頭向東微偏北二里餘地方設有紅色尖圓形警船浮一個切水面處徑五尺一寸上有黑色球式籃帽浮下水深一丈爲指明該處沙灘之南角

潮海關第三浮

潮州府潮陽縣汕頭口內附近宮鞋砵之地方設有黑色尖圓形警船浮一個切水面處徑五尺一寸上有黑色上寬下窄圓形籃帽浮下水深三丈五尺浮在礁之西北約距十丈

潮海關第四浮

潮州府潮陽縣汕頭口內距前英公司輪船名嗎的拉司所碰之虎口砵向北少東約十丈地方設有黑色尖圓形警船浮一個切水面處徑五尺一寸上有黑色球式籃帽每朔望潮落時浮下水深一丈八尺該礁上水深只有六尺八寸

厦門關第三浮

泉州府同安縣厦門內港南路內戶椗向東附近地方設有黑白方格尖圓形警船浮一個切水面處徑五尺一寸上有黑色條編圓球徑一尺七寸浮下水深六丈往來船隻不宜行於此浮及該礁西邊之浮兩浮之間以防觸礁之患

淡水關第一浮

臺北府淡水縣淡水口進口船隻將過攔江沙正路之北設有黑色尖圓形警船浮一個切水面處徑五尺一寸浮下水深二丈六尺自浮視該處土人所設之黑樁爲北五十六度東又視白樁爲南八十六度東

閩海關第一浮

福州府連江縣閩江口外七星礁北角對面之處設有紅黑方格自鳴風笙警船浮一個切水面處徑八尺五寸上以白色書有洋文MIN即係閩字樣浮下水深五丈六尺自浮視長岐山爲北四十九度東視芭蕉山爲北七十三度西

閩海關第二浮

福州府連江縣閩江口外馬祖裡半洋洲（即光緒三年美國蓬船名本嗟民哎瑪爾所觸之礁）地方距該礁向東約一里設有紅黑方格警船浮一個上有黑色長方式係編帽浮切水面處徑五尺一寸浮下水深五丈六尺浮上以白色書有洋文AYMAR即係哎瑪爾字樣自浮視長岐山爲北六十六度三十分東視東犬山鐙塔爲南三十五度十五分東視海狗石（即老泉）頂爲南五十五度三十分東

**第四五六等椿**

廣州府番禺縣新造水大石杉北所有大石闆地方之北設有警船木椿（東中西）三座於潮漲時距水面高二丈四尺其東西椿二座各繪紅白紅三色相間上各有圓形木架自日落至日出各置紅光常明鐙其中間一椿飾以紅白二色

第九椿

泉州府同安縣厦門口內鼓浪嶼北角之東北於棺柴礁之頂上設有黑色四方上尖形警船石椿一座距該礁之頂高一丈九尺潮落時礁出水面

第二十六椿

福州府連江縣金牌門破甑礴地方設有紅色警船木杆椿一座於朔望潮滿時距水面高一丈二尺上有方式上大下小籃帽上方三尺三寸下方二尺一寸帽上以白色書有洋文ORIENTAL ROCK字樣於朔望潮滿時礁上水深三尺餘船行該處南邊不宜距該椿近至九丈之內

第三十椿

温州府永嘉縣甌河內雙門對面孤嶼（即江心寺）東角向東南約距五十丈之小尖石名象巖（即東釘）上設有紅色警船鐵椿一座徑二尺五寸上罝兩頭紅色中段白色竹籃徑五尺一寸椿頂距朔望潮滿時之水面高一丈三尺其籃心距水面高八尺於朔望潮滿時礁上水深六尺八寸

第四十三椿

松江府南匯縣長江口南岸九段（海道圖說作九圖墩）地方設有黑色圓形塔一座高六丈塔上前設有警船鐙一個於光緒四年三月泊設九段鐙船（即本冊第三十三鐙）之後遂將塔上之鐙撤去不用該塔距岸約一里半於不熟悉該處水道之人無大用處

## 108.

摘列天津所立英國條約自二十四至四十九等款

第二十四欵

一英商起卸貨物納稅俱照稅則爲額總不能較他國有彼免此輸之別以昭平允而免偏枯

第二十五欵

一輸稅期候進口貨於起載時出口貨於落貨時各行按納

第二十六款

一前在江甯立約第十條內定進出口各貨稅彼時欲綜算稅餉多寡均以價值爲率每價百兩征稅伍兩大概核計以爲公當旋因條內載列各貨種式多有價值漸減而稅餉定額不改以致原定公平稅則今已較重擬將舊則重修允定此次立約加用印信之後奏明

欽派戶部大員卽日前赴上海會同英員迅速商奪俾俟本約奉到
硃批卽可按照新章迅行措辦

第二十七款

一此次新定稅則並通商各款日後彼此兩國再欲重修以十年爲限期滿須於六個月之前先行知照酌量更改若彼此未曾先期聲明更改則稅課仍照前章完納復俟十年再行更改以後均照此限此式辦理永行弗替

第二十八款

一前據江甯定約第十條內載各貨納稅後卽准由中國商人遍運天下而路所經過稅關不得加重稅則只可按估價則例若干每兩加稅不過　分等語在案迄今子口課稅實爲若干未得確數英國每稱貨物或自某內地赴某口或自某口進某內地不等各子口恒設新章任其征稅名爲抽課實於貿易有損現定立約之後或在現通商各口或在日後新開口岸限四個月爲期各領事官備文移各關監督務以路所經處應納稅銀實數明晰照復彼此出示曉布漢英商民均得通悉惟有英商已在內地買貨欲運赴口下載或在口有洋貨欲進售內地倘願一次納稅免各子口征收紛繁則准照行此一次之課其內地貨則在路上首經之子口輸交洋貨則在海口完納給票爲他子口毫不另征之據所征若干綜算貨

價爲率每百兩征銀二兩五錢俟在上海彼此派員商酌重修稅則時亦可將各貨分別種式應納之數議定此僅免各子口零星抽課之法海口關稅仍照例完納兩例並無交碍

第二十九欵

一英國商船應納鈔課一百五十噸以上每噸納鈔銀四錢一百五十噸正及一百五十噸以下每噸納鈔銀一錢凡船隻出口欲往通商他口並香港地方該船主稟明海關監督發給專照自是日起以四個月爲期如係前赴通商各口俱無庸另納船鈔以免重輸

第三十欵

一英國貨船進口並未開艙欲行他往者限二日之內出口卽不征收船鈔倘逾二日之限卽須全數輸納此外船隻出進口時並無應支費項

第三十一款

一英商在各口自用艇隻運帶客人行李書信食物及例不納稅之物毋庸完鈔倘帶例應完稅之貨則四個月一次納鈔每噸一錢

第三十二款

一通商各口分設浮樁號船塔表望樓由領事官與地方官會同酌視建造

第三十三欵

一稅課銀兩由英商交官設銀號或紋銀或洋錢按照道光二十三年在廣東所定各樣成色交納

第三十四款

一秤碼丈尺均按照粵海關部頒定式由各監督在各口送交領事官以昭畫一

第三十五款

一英國船隻欲進各口聽其僱覔引水之人完清稅務之後亦可僱覔引水之人帶其出口

第三十六欵

一英國船隻甫臨近口監督官派委員弁丁役看守或在英船或在本艇隨便居住其需用經費由關支發惟於船主並該管船商處不得私受毫釐倘有收受查出分別所取之數多寡懲治

第三十七欵

一英國船隻進口限一日該船主將船牌艙口單各件交領事官即於次日通知監督官並將船名及押載噸數裝何貨物之處照會監督官以憑查驗如過限期該船主並未報明領事官每日罰銀五十兩惟所罰之數總不能逾二百兩以外至其艙口單內須將所載貨物詳細開明如有漏報者船主應罰銀五百兩倘係筆誤即在遞貨單之日改正者可不罰銀

第三十八欵

一監督官接到領事官詳細照會後即發開艙單倘船主未領開艙單擅行下貨即罰銀五百兩並將所下貨物全行入官

第三十九欵

一英商上貨下貨總須先領監督官准單如違即將貨物一併入官

第四十欵

一各船不准私行撥貨如有互相撥貨者必須先由監督官處發給准單方准動撥違者即將該貨全行入官

第四十一欵

一各船完清稅餉之後方准發給紅單領事官接到紅單始行發回船牌等件准其出口

第四十二欵

一至稅則所載按價若干抽稅若干倘海關驗貨人役與英商不能平定其價即須各邀客商二三人前來驗貨客商內有願出價銀若干買此貨者即以所出最高之價爲此貨之價式免致收稅不公

第四十三欵

一凡納稅實按觔兩秤計先除皮包粉飾等料以淨貨輕重爲準至有連皮過秤除皮核算之貨即若茶葉一項倘海關人役與英商意見不同即於每百箱內聽關役揀出若干箱英商亦揀出若干箱先以一箱連皮過秤得若干觔每秤其皮得若干觔除皮算之即可得每箱實在觔數其餘貨物凡係有包皮者均可准此類推倘再理論不明英商赴領事官報知情節由領事官通知監督官商量酌辦惟必於此日稟報遲則不爲辦理此項尚未論定之貨監督官暫緩塡簿免致後難更易須俟秉公核斷明晰再爲登塡

第四十四欵

一英國貨物如因受潮濕以致價低減者應行按價減稅倘英商與關吏理論價值未定則照按價抽稅條內之法置辦

第四十五欵

一英國民人運貨進口既經納清稅課者凡欲改運別口售賣須稟明領事官轉報監督官委員驗明寔係原包原貨查與底簿相符並未拆動抽換即照數塡入牌照發給該商收執一面行文別口海關查照仍俟該船進口查驗符合即准開艙

出售免其重納稅課如查有影射夾帶情事貨罰入官至或欲將該貨運出外國
亦應一律聲稟海關監督驗明發給存票一紙他日不論進口出口之貨均可持
作已納稅餉之據至於外國所產糧食英船裝載進口未經起卸仍欲運赴他處
概無禁阻

第四十六款

一中國各口收稅官員凡有嚴防偷漏之法均准其相度機宜隨時便宜設法辦理
以杜弊端

第四十七款

一英商船隻獨在約內准開通商各口貿易如到別處沿海地方私做買賣即將船
貨一併入官

第四十八款

一英國商船查有涉走私該貨無論式類價值全數查抄入官外俟該商船賬目清
後亦可嚴行驅除不准在口貿易

第四十九款

一約內所指英民罰款及船貨入官皆應歸中國收辦

109. 大清欽命總理各國事務衙門　爲
劄行事光緒二年五月初五日奉
上諭大學士文祥清正持躬精詳謀國忠純亮直誠懇公明由部曹荷
文宗顯皇帝特達之知荐升卿貳並令在軍機大臣上行走復蒙兩宮
皇太后
穆宗毅皇帝重加倚畀同治四年間因奉天馬賊肆擾特派帶兵出關勦捕地方賴以廓清旋經簡任綸扉深資輔弼於國計民生利病所關及辦理中外交涉事務無不盡心籌畫實爲股肱心膂之臣祇以積勞成疾屢請開缺朝廷寛予假期曾遣
御醫診視賞給人參俾得安心調理並於召見軍機大臣時迭次垂詢方冀克享遐齡長承恩眷茲聞溘逝震悼良深著賞給陀羅經被派郡王銜貝勒載澂帶領侍衛十員即日前往奠醊加恩予諡晉贈太傅照大學士例賜䘏入祀賢良祠賞銀三千兩由廣儲司給發賞給騎都尉世職即令伊子熙治於百日孝滿後承襲任內一切處分悉予開復應得䘏典該衙門查例具奏靈柩回籍時沿途地方官妥爲照料到旗後著崇實前往賜祭一壇用示篤念藎臣至意欽此相應劄行總稅務司查照可也特劄

右劄布政使銜總稅務司赫　准此

光緒　貳年　伍月　初七日

總字第柒百肆拾肆號

## 110.

總理衙門劄行總稅務司
爲劄行事光緒七年三月十一日內閣奉
上諭朕入承大統仰蒙
大行慈安端裕康慶昭和莊敬皇太后顧復恩慈情深罔極臨御以來於玆七載承
歡奉養深荷
慈愉常見
勤履康强旰宵勤政私心慶慰方冀延祺錫算克享期頤初九日
慈躬偶爾違和當進湯藥調治以爲卽可就安不意初十日病勢陡重痰湧氣塞遂至
大漸遽於戌時
仙馭升遐呼搶哀號曷其有極欽奉
遺誥喪服二十七日而除朕心實所難安仍穿孝百日並素服滿二十七月稍申哀悃
至
諭以勉節哀思一以國事爲重用慰
慈禧端佑康頤昭豫莊誠皇太后教育之心敢不敬遵
遺命勉加抑制所有
大喪禮儀著派惇親王奕誴恭親王奕訢貝勒奕劻御前大臣景壽大學士寶鋆協辦
大學士尙書靈桂尙書恩承翁同龢敬謹管理等因欽此相應恭錄
諭旨劄行總稅務司可也須至劄者 光緒七年三月十三日
總字第壹千玖拾柒號

III.

大清欽命總理各國事務衙門　爲
劄行事光緒元年七月二十八日奉
上諭候補侍郎郭嵩燾直隷候補道許鈐身著充出使
大英國欽差大臣許鈐身並著賞給二品頂戴欽此相應恭錄
諭旨劄行總稅務司遵照可也須至劄者
光緒　元年　拾壹月　拾柒日
右劄布政使銜總稅務司赫　准此
總字第柒百拾玖號

大清欽命總理各國事務衙門　爲
劄行事光緒元年十一月十四日奉
上諭二品頂戴候補三四品京堂陳蘭彬三品銜同知容閎著充出使
大美國
大日國
大秘國欽差大臣容閎並著以道員用賞給二品頂戴欽此相應恭錄
諭旨劄行總稅務司遵照可也須至劄者
光緒　元年　拾壹月　拾柒日
右劄布政使銜總稅務司赫　准此
總字第柒百貳拾號

112.

大清欽命總理各國事務衙門　爲

劄行事光緒二年八月十七日准法國白公使照會內稱茲據本國總理衙門咨文令轉達貴國執政請派員詳查會議整理衙奇院事查二年後在本國巴里京城整理各國衙奇院查爲日不多應請貴親王遴派切實妥員前往本國會同總理商辦整理一切事宜並分指各國應用地方至各國送來各物所用之項均應議明分別官給自給之規矩其收來各物應接收者擺設之院內一切章程幷徵細之事均應妥爲商辦俟本國總理委員定准章程應俟本大臣接到本國來文再行照會察照可也等因前來查從前奧國所立公會美國所立賽奇公會均曾由總稅務司斟酌辦理在案茲准法國白公使照稱前因相應劄行總稅務司查照聲復本衙門再行核辦可也須至劄者

右劄布政使銜總稅務司赫　准此

光緒　貳年　捌月　貳拾壹　日

總字第柒百陸拾捌號

## 113.

總理衙門劄行總稅務司

爲劄行事　等因前來除由本衙門照復

威大臣並咨行

南北洋大臣查照外相應劄行總稅務司轉飭各關稅務司諭知各口華商如願助

送賽奇物件其出口時准免納稅可也須至劄者

光緒伍年捌月貳拾叁日

總字第玖百玖拾捌號

## 114.

總稅務司申呈　總理衙門

爲申呈事竊查各關章程除禮拜暨年節等日應行放假外每日係自早十點鐘起至午後四點鐘止在關辦公而各船裝卸係自日出至日入爲限如欲於夜中暨禮拜年節應行放假之日上下貨物亦可惟須特請專單幷遵繳專單費各口歷經照辦在案查所謂禮拜之日人所共知並無異詞惟於所謂年節暨應行放假日期各關辦法不一以致藉生口舌因思外國商民船隻既係遠涉重洋前來

貿易未便耽延其事則雖放假之日不應從繁多定然中國所遵奉之日亦不可忽畧不論查外國除禮拜之日外則以正月初一日并三四月間新月後之禮拜五暨十二月二十五日共三日爲應行放假之期而中國以正月初一二三日五月初五日八月十五日暨

皇上萬壽均應放假新關向守此規如

貴衙門視爲妥善應請咨行通飭各口卽將以上日期作爲新關放假之日此外不得放假以歸畫一而免饒舌是否可行應請

酌核示遵可也須至申呈者

光緒　　三年　　十二月　　初五日

京字第玖百柒拾捌號

總理衙門劄復總稅務司

爲劄復事光緒三年十二月初九日據赫總稅務司申呈以各關放假日期請咨行通飭各口以歸畫一等因查所呈放假日期業經本衙門抄錄原文咨行南北洋大臣轉飭查照相應劄復總稅務司轉飭各口稅務司遵照可也須至劄者

光緒　　三年　　十二月　　十六日

總字第捌百柒拾陸號

115.

大清欽命總理各國事務衙門　爲

劄行事本衙門前因各省洋面時有中外船隻遭風遇險已將福建巡撫所擬救護章程奏請通行在案惟海面危險情形不一而足風礁固屬堪虞盜匪尤須防範所有各省沿海地方亟應於事前妥派巡船分布要隘各口認眞查緝如有中外船隻遇盜刦搶卽行趕緊追拏按律懲辦毋令一名漏網庶盜風稍戢藉足以綏靖洋面保衛商船除咨南北洋大臣及沿海各督撫飭屬設法嚴防加意緝捕外相應札行總稅務司轉飭各口知照可也須至劄者

右劄布政使銜總稅務司赫　准此

光緒　貳年　伍月　貳拾玖日

總字第柒百伍拾壹號

116

大清欽命總理各國事務衙門　為
劄行事所有德國安納船遭風被搶一案業經閩浙總督等會咨拏獲兇要各犯
審明擬辦在案並准福建巡撫將示諭福建各屬辦理保護中外船隻遭風遇險
章程五條鈔送前來查此項章程係為救護中外船隻防患未然起見沿海各省
均應請
旨飭令通行查照辦理本衙門於五月初四日具
奏本日奉
旨依議欽此相應恭錄
諭旨鈔錄原奏劄行總稅務司遵照可也須至劄者
右劄布政使銜總稅務司赫　准此
光緒　二年　五月　初十日
總字第柒百肆拾伍號
謹
奏為閩省現擬舉行保護中外船隻遭風遇險章程請
飭各省通行查照辦理恭摺仰祈

聖鑒事竊查德國安綸船主在閩省洋面被殺並搶奪貨物拆毀船隻一案上年臣衙
門據德國駐京使臣巴蘭德照會當即咨行閩省督撫等查辦並迭次行催本年
四月間據福州將軍臣文煜等以拏獲此案兇要各犯審明擬辦等因奏奉
諭旨刑部速議具奏欽此並據福建撫臣丁日昌函稱此案據閩省德國領事官克勞
申陳該船被毀被搶各件共三萬七千七百八十圓零二尖奉駐京使臣飭總
須如數收訖現經追出贓物共估價折銀一萬三千八百八十圓已交領事查收
又稱從前在江蘇時定有救護中外船隻遭風遇險章程俟此案辦妥後曉諭閩
省倣照舉行以弭後患並將章程五條抄送底稿前來臣等伏查各省沿海地方
中外船隻遭風遇險事所常有該處居民人等認真保護者有之乘機搶奪者亦
有之該撫臣所定救護章程五條不獨福建一省當即照行即沿海各省亦應一
律查照辦理庶中外船隻往來洋面可免搶奪之虞而海濱人民皆知勸戒除該
省審明安綸船一案各犯舉名應由刑部定擬覆奏及此案未經追出贓物應由
臣衙門咨行閩省再行設法盡力追繳外相應抄錄該撫臣所定章程五條恭呈
御覽請
旨飭下南北洋大臣及各省將軍督撫曉諭所屬沿海地方文武官民人等一體實力
遵行以期相安無事是否有當伏乞

皇太后

皇上聖鑒訓示謹

奏

照錄救護船隻條規

一定地段以專責成也查沿海島嶼星羅犬牙交錯非明定界址必致彼此推諉茲責成沿海廳縣會同營汎定明所轄界限每十里爲一段飭令就近公正紳耆保舉地甲一人其島嶼則保舉耆老頭目一名列名册報以專責成凡遇中外船隻漂撞礁淺一切危險本船日則高掛白旗夜則接懸兩鐙以示求救在地之居民漁戶人等見有此等旗鐙卽時首報地甲頭目一面飛報文武汎官一面酌量夫船數目集舨助救其文武汎官聞報後亦卽督率兵役親往勘驗救護不得稍有遲悞其往來報信之人一切費用均由失事船主給還惟官役不得勒索使費

一明賞罰以免推諉也查沿海文武汎官如有救護船貨至一萬兩以上中外人等救至十名以上者一經該管上司查明申報及領事官照會關道有案藩司立卽註册記功三功以上者文武汎官詳請酌記外獎五功以上者分別詳請

題升以示優獎其地甲頭目亦分別上次勞績隨時賞給頂戴扁額以昭鼓勵倘文武汎官不肯認眞辦理照例叅懲地甲頭目若有救援不力甚至希冀分肥者分

別輕重嚴究至於望見船隻危險首先報知地甲頭目及文武汛官者以初報之人爲首功由失事船主給予花紅大船多至三十兩中小船以十兩爲度

一定章程以免混亂也凡遇險船隻其力尚可自存船主並不顧他人上船者則救援之人自不得混行上船倘船主須人援救或係應先救船或係應先救貨或係應先救人均聽船主指揮不得自行動手救起貨物應寄頓何處亦由船主作主其有擅行撤取或私自藏匿者一經船主及地甲頭目指明查有確據者卽行由官追究治罪倘有人出首確鑿者亦賞以應賞之款誣揑者不准幷行反坐

一定酬勞以資鼓勸也凡救起之貨須候文武汛官驗報如係外國船貨則幷報明附近領事官會同查核將貨估價按照出入多寡難易抽撥充賞多至三分之一以賞救援之人若有貨無人則須稟明就近地方官及領事官秉公將貨酌賞倘無貨有人則須將人救護無論中國外國之人均先行給以衣食就近送交地方官領事官妥給船夫分別資送回籍倘係外國人無領事可交者卽報明通商局資給盤川俾令自行回國其小船出力救護者倘本人無力可以酬謝者卽就近稟報地方官小船每救人一名賞給洋銀十元就近由地方官先行核給按月彙報通商局撥還虛揑者嚴究至遇風濤洶湧人力難施或在大洋爲救援所不及者均宜各安天命不得任意株連

一廣曉諭以資勸戒也凡海濱愚民皆緣不知救援之有賞不救船之有罰是以坐視不救或致乘機搶奪此後所有沿海文武各官均宜將以上告示條規分別札行各汛嚴加告誡並將告示條規書寫木牌遍處懸掛使一切漁戶愚人皆知遇險之船救護爲有功不救護爲有罪庶人人有救船之念在其胸中不致視爲無足重輕之舉矣

隨總字第柒百肆拾伍號

## 117.

大清欽命總理各國事務衙門　爲

劄行事本衙門現與

德國巴大臣面議洋商出售洋貨在上海租界內免其抽釐及發給存票准其以三十六個月爲限各開辦日期准巴大臣面稱曾經會商

各國大臣在案應將開辦日期開列於後

一上海租界內不再抽釐

查新舊各口岸除尚未定有各國租界應俟會商畫定再行將洋貨免釐一事定期開辦外其上海一口已定有洋商租界凡有洋商進口貨正洋貨無論賣與華商洋商自光緒三年正月初一日起上海租界內不再抽收釐金

二存票定限

査凡有貨正洋貨已完進口正稅後如欲運往外國實係原包原貨並無拆動抽換自光緒三年正月初一日起核計該貨進口之日到該貨出口船之日在三十六個月限內准其請領存票或將存票換取現銀聽商自便其光緒三年正月初一日以前發給存票不拘限期准抵稅鈔不換現銀

以上兩條除由本衙門照會

各國大臣並通行南北洋大臣飭關遵照辦理外相應劄行總稅務司查照可也

須至劄者

右劄布政使銜總稅務司赫　准此

光緒　貳年　拾月　貳拾柒日

總字第柒百捌拾貳號

## 118.

欽差大臣曾　札

爲咨行事同治七年九月十一日准

兵部火票遞到

總理各國事務衙門咨案查布國條約第十三款內未將船主漏報揑報罰辦章程詳細載明本衙門曾於上年十二月間照會布國公使酌辦並咨行貴大臣暨

三口通商大臣及札知總稅務司各在案茲准布國李使照復內稱貴王大臣所擬漏報揑報之船主應罰銀若干兩業經詳文本國請爲按照所擬辦理茲已奉本國回文德意志各國嗣後皆願按照所擬罰條辦理並將此作爲章程今將德意志文法郞西文漢文三分文底特送貴衙門查閱等因前來除由本衙門咨行三口通商大臣並札知總稅務司一體照辦外相應抄錄布國照會一件並照會內漢文罰條文底一紙咨行貴大臣查照轉飭各口遵照辦理可也等因並抄單到本署大臣准此合行抄粘札飭札關即便遵照辦理毋違特札

計抄粘

同治七年九月十六日

照錄布國照會

爲照會事溯查同治六年十二月二十九日本大臣已將

貴王大臣所擬漏報揑報之船主應罰銀若干兩業經詳文本國請爲按照所擬辦理等因照復

貴王大臣在案茲本大臣已奉本國回文內稱此事係北德意志公會所應管者是以本國令北德意志公會各該管官商議妥定今本國總管北德意志公會議事廳事務大臣璧斯瑪來文行知本大臣令爲聲明所有北德意志國公會暨不屬北德意志國出會之德意志通商稅務公會各國嗣後皆願按照

貴王大臣所擬罰條辦理並將此作爲章程因此本大臣今將德意志文法郎西
文漢文三分文底特送
貴衙門查閱本大臣諒
貴王大臣見此章程不能不知德意志各國凡遇
貴國循理之事端無不深願遵行也爲此照會
貴王大臣查照須至照會者　七月十六日
照錄漏報揑報罰條
爲聲明遵照罰條事查本大臣前接
大清欽命總理各國事務王大臣來文內稱咸豐十一年七月二十八日卽
大布一千八百六十一年九月初二日
大清國
大布路斯國暨德意志通商稅務公會各國並模令布而額水林模令布而額錫特利
子兩邦　律百克伯磊門　昂布尓三漢謝城所立和好貿易船隻事宜和約章
程第十三款內有不妥之處特爲指明漏報揑報等弊應照
中國與各國所立和約內罰銀之數辦理等因前來彼時本大臣卽將此事詳文
本國今奉本國回文命本大臣聲明所有北德意志公會暨不屬北德意志公會
之德意志通商稅務公會各國皆准概行按照

27

中國所擬罰係將漏報揑報之船主罰銀若干兩但須知每遇此等事件必按其所犯之事輕重定其所罰之數多寡惟所罰最重者亦不可過五百兩之數再者該商貨單內舛錯之處如於一日內即外國二十四時之內改正者即不應罰至有漏報揑報之時應如何查明之處須該口海關所派委員與該口本國領事官所派委員當堂公同會訊確查如該二委員同意擬罰銀兩若干該商即應將銀兩按數交清此事即算完結倘該二委員意見不同即應將此事詳送駐京之總稅務司與管理北德意志公會事務大臣公同查核定奪可也爲此聲明本大臣

並親手畫押鈐蓋關防

大清同治七年七月十六日

大布一千八百六十八年九月初二日

119.

南洋大臣札行招商局委員

爲札飭事據蕪湖關道恭鍹稟稱五月十二日據本關稅務司班謨函稱本日午刻招商局江靖輪船上水本關扦手赴船查出食鹽多包又見本地划船裝載食鹽想係該輪船水手等私帶此項違禁貨物藏匿艙底希圖偷漏既經查獲船貨均應充

公等因鹽斤六十八包計一千七百二十斤送交職道處照例變價除俟變價後將價銀送由稅務司照章提成分賞並分成辦理外竊思鹽斤由輪船夾帶私運最干例禁招商係屬官局該輪船司事水手人等何竟似此玩法營私亟應澈查究辦以肅鹾政而儆將來職道未敢擅便理合稟請示遵等情到本大臣據此除批查招商局江靖輪船前於光緒三年經鎮江關查獲私鹽九十餘担六年六月又經鎮江關查獲私鹽七十餘包當經念該局領有官款未便驅逐出江不准貿易僅將私鹽充公仍嚴飭該局員將該船船主人等嚴查懲究在案近據江漢九江等關呈送罰款清冊商局江靖等船仍屢有夾帶私鹽及各項貨物之事正在籌辦間茲核來稟江靖輪船又帶私鹽六十八包寔屬胆大已極該局員於各該船船主人等先既不能慎選繼又不能約束及至屢被拏獲私鹽仍復一味疎縱聽其玩法營私不遵定章不顧大局不慮外人恥笑直不知其是何居心嗣後若但將所帶私鹽充公殊不足以儆將來而杜私運查洋商輪船船主未領開艙單擅行下貨罰銀五百兩所下貨物全行入官載在英約同治十二年英艇謙渡夾帶私鹽被獲從寬免其驅除仍罰繳銀四百兩有案此後招商局船如再有夾帶私鹽及一切走私情事即照此章除將走私貨物入官外仍將該船主罰銀五百兩倘該船主不能遵繳即責令該局員代繳該局員仍不得延抗不遵及以該局公款挪繳致干叅究仰即遵照辦理繳印發鹽呑明

總理衙門查照外合行札飭札到該局即便遵照辦理此札光緒七年五月二十二日

招商局委員稟覆　南洋大臣

敬稟者竊職道等於本年五月二十八日奉

憲台札據蕪湖關道恭鍹稟稱全敘云云遵照辦理等因奉此伏查江靖輪船於六年六月二十日經鎮江關沈道申詳於查獲各輪船私鹽案內有該船夾帶七十一包零當經職局遵飭傳究實係水手等藉稱食鹽矇混坐艙司事並非通同作弊惟毫不覺察咎無可辭即將坐艙司事等撤退水手等移縣懲辦在案乃僅及一年該船水手等又生弊竇深爲可惡職局前接蕪局來信於未奉

憲札之先業於本月十九日咨請江海關劉道瑞芬密札上海縣將全船水手火夫等三十名差拘帶縣嚴行審辦重懲坐艙司事暫留候質縱不知情亦應革換竊念職局辦公恰無官守不便責人是以咨由地方嚴加懲治以儆效尤仍一面傳諭各輪船坐艙司事人等凜遵查禁謹將咨諭兩稿錄呈

憲鑒職道等未能事先約束負咎滋深嗣後惟有益矢慎勤格外認眞查察並加囑各船主一體恪遵以副

憲台整頓鹺綱之至意奉札前因理合稟覆恭叩云云

120.

## 辦理商人運貨私越過卡章程

一凡有商人將土產貨物自內地運赴海口到該海口總卡之時若已過卡而載貨之船隻車輛並帶貨之挑夫雖入海口界內然在彼離卡不遠候驗其貨主在該卡未經查出拏獲之先自行赴卡請驗則其尚未有意走漏然過卡不聽查驗自行過去亦屬不合議將其貨罰稅餉五倍方准放行如運貨入內地者亦照一律辦理

一凡有商人將土產貨物自內地運赴海口到該海口總卡之時若私自過卡而載貨之船隻車輛並帶貨之挑夫已入海口界內未曾報卡經該卡拏獲即將所拏之貨照數充公如運貨入內地者亦照一律辦理

一凡有商人運貨抵卡遵驗如不肯完納子稅者應由關卡將該貨全數扣留立刻將情形禀明海關監督以便查明是否應納如若查明不應納者立即放行倘或監督之見查明應納者而該商仍不肯照納應將其貨依舊扣留俟該國領事官行文詢問該監督即將因何扣留之處詳細照覆若該領事以應納子稅為然當亦無難徵收倘該領事以不應納子稅為詞而監督之意仍應行納稅即應由監督並領事官將此案詳細情事申明

總理衙門及駐京公使聽候酌議查辦並應由監督將扣留之貨算清應納之稅數
知會領事官由領事官即令該商照數出結聽候
大憲定斷隨將此結單送交監督收存則准該貨放行俟
大憲斷後再行照辦

121.

致　總署總辦大人
敬啓者招商局輪船現在不但於通商各口販運往來且有前往日本呂宋諸處去者其由日本呂宋諸外洋運回之貨若入內地有應納子口稅一節是否按照洋商稅則畫一辦理抑另照華商船隻常徵辦理若照洋商稅則辦之則與洋商一律似不致偏重但內地關卡未知能允從否若另照華商船隻則須逢關納稅過卡抽厘又較洋商未免吃虧多多究應如何飭辦之處統望
示悉以便遵行專此順候
吉祺

名另具　十二月十九日

稅字第伍拾柒號

大清欽命總理各國事務衙門　爲

劄行事前據總稅務司函稱招商局輪船現在不但於通商各口販運往來且有前往日本呂宋去者其由日本呂宋諸外洋運回之貨若入內地有應納子口稅一節是否照洋商稅則畫一辦理抑另照華商船隻常徵辦理統望示悉以便遵行等因當經本衙門行查

南北洋大臣幷函復總稅務司俟該大臣核復再行札飭查照在案茲准

南洋大臣復稱洋商運洋貨入內地准其只完半稅沿途概不重徵商局輪船運來洋貨自應照辦同此一貨由洋船運來則復入內地只完半稅由局船運來則復入內地仍須逢關納稅遇卡抽釐是使洋商獨得便宜似非擴充商局輪船之道現在局船報關裝貨均照洋船辦法則運來洋貨復入內地應照洋商運來之洋貨一律辦理庶局船與洋船適得其平等語此項招商局輪船運洋貨入內地既據南洋大臣查復按照洋商運貨進口已完正稅後運入內地完納子口半稅之例以歸一律應如所稱辦理除咨行

南北洋大臣轉飭遵辦外爲此札行總稅務司轉飭各關稅務司遵照辦理可也須至劄者

右劄布政使銜總稅務司赫　准此

同治　拾叁年　貳月　初三日

122.

總理衙門劄行總稅務司

爲劄行事案查煙台會議條款內載洋貨稅單應由總理衙門核定劃一款式不分華洋商人均可請領等語本年七月間准

英國威大臣面請通行各省按照條款辦理以免參差當經本衙門行知

南北洋大臣查照在案兹准酌擬稅單式樣及加蓋戳式送請核定等因前來查所擬單式戳式甚屬周妥自應通飭各關一體照辦除由本衙門行知

南北洋大臣轉飭遵辦外相應照錄單式戳式各一件劄行總稅務司查照希即轉行各關稅務司遵照辦理可也須至劄者 光緒六年玖月叁拾日

總字第壹千柒拾肆號

單式

兹據 國商人 華商 稟報現有後開之洋貨欲運往內地 省 府 州縣 銷售

計開

其內地稅業已完清

年 月 日

字第 號

關道衙　　爲

給發稅單事照得通商章程內載運入內地洋貨該商應將該貨名目若干往內地
何處報關查驗照納內地稅項該關發給內地稅單該商應向沿途各子口呈單照
驗蓋戳放行無論遠近俱不重征又通商各口通共章程第一欵載明洋商由上海
運洋貨進長江俟到長江各口後一經離口自入內地販運如無長江各關稅單者
逢關納稅遇卡抽釐末後聲明南北各海口均照長江一律辦理又煙台會議條欵
載明洋貨運入內地請領半稅單照應由總理衙門核定畫一欵式不分華洋商人
均可請領各等因除運入內地不領稅單之洋貨仍照通共章程辦理外茲據華商/國商人
報關欲將後開洋貨販運前往　省　府　州/縣　請給發內地稅單等情
據此合應發給稅單以便沿途查驗蓋戳放行須至單照者

計開

其內地稅業已完清

右照給華商/國商人　收執

年　月　日

限　日繳銷

28

戳式
眞正洋貨華洋商人均准請領稅單照完半稅運入內地不得出入海口沿途關卡
倘查出貨少於單卽註明單內仍蓋戳放行一面行文給單原關查辦查出貨多於
單卽係漏完半稅夾帶私運應將所多之洋貨扣留一面知照原關辦理倘查有土
貨冒充洋貨及將單內所塡貨名及數目字樣添改挖補均將單貨扣留行查原關
分別辦理此單應於運貨已到所指地方卽赴地方官衙門或釐局繳銷

123.

照錄詳欽督撫憲八月初七日發
爲詳請事竊于本年五月二十三日准浙海關代理稅務司馬照稱本年五月十八
日有美國拖帶船隻之輪船一隻譯名福里駛進本口詢其來自何口據稱在外海
遇有中國人令其送至甯波等語查該船雖未裝有貨物惟並無原出口之關所給
紅單係屬私赴別口按照同治六年間
總理衙門議定通商各口應辦各事之章程第三條應罰該船銀五百兩當經本稅
務司將該船扣留一面知照美國領事旋准司領事來文請將該輪船先釋放出口
願作保聽候查辦由本稅務司核准該輪船卽于是日出口除將此案緣由申報總
稅務司察核照會查照以便俟有上憲公文與美國領事會商辦理等因准此當查
同治六年七月間奉

前通商大臣曾　札行續發引水章程三條案內第三條內載凡拖帶船隻之輪船欲赴通商別口仍須按照條約定章赴關請領紅單赴領事官署內取回船牌若有此等拖帶輪船私赴別口未在原口領有紅單應將該船罰銀五百兩等語此次美國福里拖帶輪船並未領有原出口紅單私行來甯現經查明自當照章罰辦即經職道照會駐甯美國領事司提文俟馬稅務司奉到總稅務司公文請即會商辦理去後旋准司領事照復以此案與稅務司不相關涉祇須領事暨關道會商了結等因其意蓋以此事擬欲從輕罰辦所罰之款不必照章罰銀五百兩其時適馬稅務司奉到此案總稅務司札文內開應如所擬罰該輪船銀五百兩等因函知到道即經職道照會司領事請即轉飭該福里輪船照章遵繳罰銀五百兩即日送關等因旋于六月十七日准司領事照復以此案論及罰欵彼此不合則各須申詳上憲同行裁奪欲先會晤談論等因業經職道訂期於六月二十一日在美國領事公館會晤互相辯論司領事之意以此案雖屬違章固應罰辦而罰款應無定限之數未能照章罰銀五百兩等云職道答以此項章程載明罰銀五百兩極爲明晰不比別項罰款並無一定數目可以隨時會商酌辦所請有關更改章程未能應允而司領事堅欲職道查案從輕減罰又經職道函詢江海關並檢查檔卷均無從輕減成罰辦之成案復經函致領事仍應照引水章程罰辦去後而屢次議商領事之意總須減

罰置原定數目於不顧迄未議定完案七月二十六日接司領事來函以此案現卽
申詳本國欽差並將詳文照抄譯送前來職道遵查會訊船貨入官章程第六款內
載該商寔有應罰之處如係約章程內載有銀兩之數目卽由領事按其數斷令交
出或可從寬辦理則其權屬在該關卽由監督會同稅務司自定等語今查此案禍
里拖帶輪船因無原出口之紅單私進甯口有違條約定章照引水章程第三條應
罰該船銀五百兩且引水章程係前經
總理衙門照准美國公使照復行知各口領事官宣示遵照辦理之章司領事理當
遵照飭繳應無異言迺堅執以此事與稅務司無關欲減成罰辦僅肯認罰洋二百
元數既懸殊各關又向無似此從寬罰繳之成案竊以此端一開則以後條約定章
所載之罰欵恐皆視爲具文職道寔未敢擅便現在司領事既已申詳
駐京公使職道理合抄錄全案具文詳請仰祈
憲臺詧核俯賜咨商
總理衙門查核作何辦理飭知遵辦並祈
訓示祗遵寔爲公便除詳
督欽撫憲外爲此備由另冊呈乞
照詳施行

124.

# 德商船廠修船物件免稅章程

一凡有德商開船廠修船者其廠內實用修船之物件均應按照新約條欵免稅辦理

一凡德商開廠者須赴該關稅務司處請領空白甘結後赴領事官署塡明畫押由領事官蓋印後呈交該關存案此項甘結內有兩項要端一本商承當凡有免稅物件進廠不得私賣於他人亦不得私作他用一該關如已査出有私賣於他人私做他用者本商即認罰銀伍百兩

一凡德商開廠者除進口時照章赴關報明請領放行單外廠內須立修船免稅物件之册簿凡有免稅物件進廠均須詳細按日按類註記並須將其如何使用修理何船按日按類登記註銷

一凡德商開廠者其免稅物件進廠後倘擬將其物件做爲他用該商須先行赴關報明一切請領船廠補稅驗單完納進口稅方准起其物件出廠一面一律登記註銷

一凡德商開廠者須准由該關任便派人入廠親視工作並其册簿等件亦可隨時索看倘有攔阻不許親視工作與不給册簿閱看以及不將免稅之物按日登記

註銷等事該關即將所存之甘結註銷移交該領事官發還一面不准該廠物件
此後免稅
以上各章係試辦之章應俟照辦兩年之後或增或減或改或留再行會同核訂
以期歸於至當可也

## 125.

總理衙門劄行總稅務司
爲劄行事查光緒六年二月二十一日本衙門與
德國巴大臣公同畫押續修條約第七欵內載德商船廠應用雜物准其免稅由
總稅務司將應行免稅進口各物名目須發清冊曉諭等語茲於光緒七年二月
二十七日接准
巴大臣照會以前項條約一經兩國
御筆批准即宜彼此遵行茲接電報內稱本國國會業經齊集則批准有日不久即當
換約備文照請查照轉知總稅務司先將德商船廠免稅各物辦妥清冊以免貽
誤並將所具清冊擬交一分等因前來相應劄行總稅務司查照前項續修條約
第七欵所載德商船廠應用雜物實係修理船隻應行免稅進口各物名目先行
造具清冊數本申送本衙門以憑轉復可也須至劄者光緒七年三月初一日
總字第壹千玖拾號

126.

總理衙門劄行總稅務司

爲劄行事光緒八年正月十三日准總稅務司申稱查德國續修條約內載船廠雜物免稅一節前經遵照劄文將應行免稅各物並各口擬辦之章程開具清册申覆在案查册內章程第二條內載凡德商開廠者須赴該關稅務司處請領空白甘結後赴領事官處塡明畫押由領事官蓋印呈交該關存案等語當經特劄江海關稅務司代擬一空白甘結並換發之准單式現據該關稅務司將此結單兩式擬就均尚妥協除通行各關稅務司一律遵照外合行備呈送請查照並將結單式樣各三分附送前來查結內所擬各條均尚明晰除將原件存留本衙門并分咨

南北洋大臣備查外相應劄行總稅務司轉飭各關稅務司遵照辦理可也須至劄者光緒八年正月拾捌日

總字第壹千壹百陸拾柒號

127.

總理衙門劄行總稅務司

爲劄行事光緒六年本衙門與德國巴大臣會同商定續修條約十欵章程九款於二月二十一日在本衙門蓋印畫押以昭信守其有未盡事宜另用照會聲明當經彼此奏明欽奉

諭旨允准嗣因一年未能如期互換旋又公立憑單展緩期限茲於光緒七年七月二十八日本衙門奏奉

諭旨批准用

寶頒發漢文條款巴大臣亦奉

大德國

大皇帝御筆批准德文條欵於閏七月二十三日在本衙門同時互換現將欽奉

諭旨條欵刊刻成本相應劄行總稅務司轉飭各口稅務司一體遵照辦理可也須至劄者　附條約十五本　光緒柒年閏柒月貳拾肆日

總字第壹千壹百叁拾捌號

續修條約

大清國
大皇帝
大德國
大皇帝兼
布國
大君主今欲將咸豐十一年七月二十八日所定通商和約章程益臻恪守因案查前定條約第四十一款內載日後德國若於現議章程條款內有欲行變通之處應俟自章程互換之日起至滿十年爲止方可再行籌議等語玆彼此循照前約量加修增是以
大清國
大皇帝特派總理各國事務協辦大學士兵部尚書沈
總理各國事務戶部尚書景
大德國
大皇帝兼
布國
大君主特派欽差駐劄中華便宜行事大臣巴　各將所奉全權大臣便宜行事之
上諭互相校閱俱屬妥當現將會議修增各款開列於後

第一款

一中國允除在湖北宜昌安徽蕪湖浙江温州廣東北海前已派開通商口岸並沿江安徽之大同安慶江西之湖口湖廣之武穴陸溪口沙市等處前已作爲上下客貨之處外現又允江蘇吳淞口一處德國船隻暫准停泊上下客商貨物一切由江海關道等自行妥議章程辦理

一德國允中國如有與他國之益彼此立有如何施行專章德國既欲援他國之益使其人民同霑亦允於所議專章一體遵守其咸豐十一年七月二十八日所立條約內第四十款特爲言明仍遵其舊嗣後中國所有施於他國及他國人民各益德國人民如欲照第四十款之意一體均霑則亦應於彼此訂明專章一律遵守

第二款

一中國允德國船隻已在中國完納船鈔者如往中國通商各口或往各國口岸在四個月限內均不重征再德國夾板在中國口岸停泊十四日以外者則自第十五日起即於應交正數船鈔減半

一德國允凡德國各處准各國領事官駐紮者中國亦可派員駐紮按照待各國官員最優之禮相待

第三款

一中國允凡中國通商各口由該監督等酌量情形如係衆洋商情願無碍地方者該監督等妥議章程自行設立關棧

一德國允德國船隻進中國通商各口其貨物清單須將貨色件數開明內有舛錯處准於十二時限內改正（禮拜節期不計）倘有漏報揑報之事除將該貨物充公外仍應罰該船主惟所罰之數不得過五百兩

第四款

一中國允凡德國商人裝運中國土煤出通商各口者應完出口正稅銀兩定爲每噸三錢並允如有某口前定不及三錢者將來仍照不及三錢之數征收

一德國允凡無照冒充各項船隻引水者即應議罰惟所罰之數每次不得過一百兩並允妥速會定約束水手章程

第五款

一中國允凡德國船隻或在通商各口內口外受損應行修理者准由該口海關查明日期扣算該船應完之鈔項

一德國允中國商民自備各項船隻不准張掛德國旗號德國船隻亦不准張掛中國旗號

第六款

一中國允凡德國損壞船隻有在中國通商各口內拆賣該船各料者准其不另徵進口稅銀惟起岸時仍須照各貨一律赴關請領起貨准單爲憑

一德國允德國人等如有未領領事所發中國地方官蓋印執照赴中國內地游歷者准該地方官將其人解交附近領事官管束外仍應議罰惟所罰之數不得過三百兩

第七款

一中國允凡德商船廠應用雜物准其免稅由總稅務司將應行免稅進口各物名目頒發清册曉諭

一德國允凡德國人等運洋貨入內地及入內地游歷所領單照自發給之日起均以十三個月爲限均照中國月日計算

第八欵

一中外官員審辦交涉案件以及商人運洋貨入內地及洋商入內地買土貨如何科征又中外官員如何往來一切事宜此三節應歸另議今兩國暫先訂明彼此均允妥商

第九欵

一咸豐十一年七月二十八日兩國前定條約除現修條款未改舊章者均經特爲言明仍舊恪遵外其有變通舊章者均照現修各款辦理

第十款

一現修增各款恭候兩國
御筆批准仍自畫押之日起限一年內在
大清京師互換並經言明所有各款自互換之日起卽行遵辦現兩國
欽差大臣將漢文德文條約章程各四分校對無訛先爲親筆畫押蓋用關防圖記以昭信守光
緒七年七月二十八日奉
旨依議欽此

續修條約善後章程

現將續修條約再行酌定章程俾得申明以昭周備所有後開各章程兩國官民應與條約一同遵守爲此兩國大臣蓋印畫押以昭信實

第一款

一江蘇吳淞口一處議准通融辦法如有德國船隻欲在該處載卸客商貨物或由他處運來上海或由上海運往他處均聽其便由江海關道等自行設法嚴定偷漏稅課及防各項弊端章程中外商民一體遵守仍不准德國商民在該處起造馬頭設立行棧

第二款

一中國通商口岸如何設立關棧先由上海試辦卽由該監督會同總稅務司酌量情形妥議章程由該監督等自行設立

第三款

一凡德國船隻有應領海關准單方准起下之貨物而清單未開明者無論船主有無畫押收據在先均為漏報

第四款

一德國船隻或在中國通商各口內口外受損應行修理者其修理日期扣算在免鈔期內准中國官前往查明辦理如查係飾詞偷漏者即照該船圖免噸鈔之數加倍議罰

第五款

一中國人等自備各項船隻不准張掛德國旗號如有可疑之跡中國該管官知照德國領事官查明實係不應掛德國旗號之船當將該船及船上華商之貨即行解交中國地方官辦理倘有德國人等知情通同舞弊者即將船內所有該德國人貨物全行入官仍將其人按例懲辦德國船隻如張掛中國旗號即將其事由中國地方官查明如實係不應張掛中國旗號之船當將其船並船上德商貨物即行解交德國領事官辦理並將舞弊之人由領事官照例懲辦倘查明有德國貨主人等知情通同舞弊者即將其人船上貨物交中國全行入官其船上華人貨物可由中國地方官即行入官

第六款
一凡德國損壞船隻有在中國通商各口內拆賣該船各料者如有將船內裝運各項貨物影射偷漏者除將漏報貨物入官外仍照應完進口稅銀加倍議罰

第七款
一德國人等運洋貨入內地或入內地游歷所領單照均係自發給之日起以十三個月爲限均照中國月日計算逾限作爲廢紙仍呈本關繳銷如游歷道路太遠不能一年爲限者發照時即將此節照內由地方官會商領事官批明倘未繳銷在補繳之前不准再行請領倘或遺失單照無論限內限外即向就近中國官員據實報明由該官員設法查辦以杜假冒如查係揑報運貨者貨物入官游歷者解交附近領事官懲辦

第八款
一德商船廠應用雜物實係修理船隻者方准免稅進通商口岸一面由關派員進廠將其如何使用各物之處眼同閱看如係製造新船其進出口稅則內所載之貨照稅則辦理其未載明之物均照値百抽五例徵稅令該商赴關補納至開船廠者必先赴關領照此照並無關費並具保結結內所註明各節悉由該關妥議酌辦

第九款

一所有續修條約內各國款仍照咸豐十一年七月二十八日所定條約第二十九款辦理

光緒七年七月二十八日奉

旨依議欽此

大清光緒六年二月二十一日

大德一千八百八十年三月三十一日

署刑部左侍郎內閣學士兼禮部侍郎銜崇
吏部左侍郎麟
軍機大臣戶部尚書景
軍機大臣協辦大學士兵部尚書沈
和碩恭親王
軍機大臣大學士管理吏部事務寶
軍機大臣署吏部尚書李
戶部尚書董
軍機大臣戶部左侍郎王
二品頂戴宗人府府丞夏

大清欽命總理各國事務　為

照會事查此次修約第二欵內稱德國夾板在中國口岸停泊十四日以外者則自第十五日起即於應交正數船鈔減半等語此節現經兩國大臣訂明先行試辦如有窒礙難行之處可由兩國從新另議特此聲明須至照會者

光緒　六年　二月　二十一日

大德欽差入華便宜行事大臣巴　爲
照復事頃接
來文內開此次修約第二款內稱德國夾板在中國口岸停泊十四日以外者則
自第十五日起即於應交正數船鈔減半等語此節現經兩國大臣訂明先行試
辦如有窒礙難行之處可由兩國從新另議等語披閱之餘本大臣均無異議嗣
後彼此即應遵照施行特此備文聲明可也須至照會者
大清光緒六年二月二十一日
大德一千八百八十年三月三十一日
照錄憑單
大清國總理各國事務衙門大臣王麟沈景崇　爲
大德國欽差入華便宜行事大臣巴
公立文憑事案照兩國特派
欽差大臣於光緒六年二月二十一日（一千八百八十年三月三十一日）續修條約末後第十款內所載自畫押之日
起限一年內互換一條現議將期限改在光緒七年十月初十日（一千八百八十一年十二月初一日）互換除此
款其餘以上議定各款概不更改現經

30

兩國
欽差大臣將漢德文約章各二分校對無訛先爲親筆畫押蓋用關防圖記以昭信守須至文
憑者
大清光緒六年七月十六日
大德一千八百八十年八月二十一日

128.

總理衙門劄行總稅務司

爲劄行事光緒五年八月初一日美國何參贊來署面稱本國旗昌行商船裝載鴉片煙在上海換船前經該處稅務司發過執照兩次惟該稅司曾說嗣後不得照辦恐將來再有此船不免費事該貨係往新金山舊金山奧斯底里雅地方去並不在中國售賣不過在上海換船而已緣鴉片煙由外國運至香港該處向來收稅交由行家辦理每年約有數百萬稅則最重商人爲避稅起見此貨係由澳門轉運到上海總稅務司亦經說過此事原不要緊等語查此案未經總稅務司申報有案究應如何辦理以防弊混之處相應劄行總稅務司查明申復以憑核辦可也須至劄者

光緒伍年捌月初肆日

總字第玖百玖拾陸號

總稅務司申覆　總理衙門

爲申覆事奉到光緒五年八月初四日

鈞劄內開美國何參贊面稱旗昌行商船裝載鴉片煙在上海換船往新舊金山等處去並不在中國售賣前經上海稅務司發給執照兩次曾說嗣後不得照辦等語飭查此案如何辦理以防弊混查明申覆以憑核辦等因奉此總稅務司查美國旗昌洋行以鴉片煙在上海換船赴新舊金山等處一案竊閱美國條約第二十三款內載大合衆國船隻停泊口內如有貨物必須剝過別船者應先呈明領事官轉報海關委員查驗確當方准剝運倘不稟明候驗批准輒行剝運者即將所剝之貨歸中國入官等因至他國條約內亦有過載之欵與此欵之意相同總稅務司擬如嗣後遇有商人將鴉片煙運到上海過載別船以赴外國新舊金山等處者經由海關照他貨之例驗明確當准其過載則與稅餉並無虧損之處似此商人所請准將鴉片煙過載亦屬寔無不可理合備文申覆卽請

貴衙門核奪示復可也須至申復者光緒伍年捌月拾玖日

京字第壹千壹百貳拾陸號

總理衙門劄覆總稅務司

為劄復事光緒五年八月十九日據總稅務司申稱查美國旗昌洋行以鴉片煙在上海換船赴新舊金山等處一案竊閱美國條約第二十三款內載大合衆國船隻停泊口內如有貨物必須剝過別船者應先呈明領事官轉報海關委員查驗確當方准剝運倘不稟明候驗批准輒行剝運者即將所剝之貨歸中國入官至他國條約內亦有過載之款與此欵之意相同擬如嗣後遇有商人將鴉片煙運到上海過載別船以赴外國新舊金山等處者經由海關照他貨之例驗明確當准其過載則與稅餉並無虧損之處似此商人所請准將鴉片煙過載亦無不可等因除由本衙門函復美國西大臣並咨行南洋大臣江蘇巡撫轉飭江海關道查照辦理外相應劄復總稅務司查照可也須至劄者 光緒伍年捌月貳拾伍日

總字第玖百玖拾玖號

129.

續定招工章程條約

議將咸豐庚申年九月十一十二等日中外各國
欽差大臣在京先後續立增約內指華民出口在外洋別地承工俱宜酌情會定章程
以期保其身家禮體今中國移行按約行辦爲此
大清欽命總理各國事務和碩恭親王
大英欽差特簡駐劄中華便宜行事大臣功賜佩帶二等寶星阿
大法署理欽差全權大臣駐劄中國京都總理本國事務伯同在總理各國事務衙門
議定招工章程開列於左

第一欵一中國通商口岸凡有商民欲請准設公所開辦招工既擬與該工人何以立約所內華工何以治理各等節應將合同底稿並在公所治理工人章程各紙稟請領事官查閱又因各國搭船之例不同必有該商已經按例遵辦實據領事官始能查明

第二欵一該商稟請前來領事官查其實屬殷實妥當之人即將所呈合同章程各紙查核酌情删改方可轉移該管地方官查閱俱屬妥協立給印牒准設招工公所領事官即將印牒及合同等件一併在本署鈔錄存案

第三欵一印牒既出不能無故註銷其有故者必須地方官與領事官會議如果意見相同該所方可關閉罷招該商自不准追請賠償

第四欵一合同章程等件該商須於招工公所門外房中書寫懸掛以便工人均可知其詳細合同章程等件及經地方官暨領事官查明准辦該商嗣欲删改均可稟明施行惟各該官尚未批准不可專自擅行至於該商或欲遣人代覓承工准將合同章程各件鈔單稟請領事官及地方官用印發給收執方准遣人分赴該省鎭鄉等處代爲宣布

第五欵一招工各商既立合同與該華工定議務須按期逐款盡守凡有負約之處惟該商是問俱按伊國之例傳案究審

第六欵一招工各商欲遣華民代覓承工此項承遣者必由地方官先給蓋印准單方可前往後或干例無論故違誤犯惟本人是問俱歸地方官傳案究審

第七欵一凡有招工事務中國專派委員協同監理華民有欲承工任便赴所該商眼同委員註寫姓名於簿註畢該工任聽回家或在公所候搭便船出洋

第八欵一華民承工出洋或係獨身一人或係攜同家眷所立合同字樣必須逐欵開載〇一指定何國何處承工年限多寡一限滿回國計其人口給保水脚路費若干〇一在彼作工預定日期時刻〇一在彼承工應受衣物工食鹽各等利益

○一遇有疾病醫治醫藥不用該人工值○一隻身出洋或有眷口留在中華意欲按年計月撥給養家之費應扣若干○一所有今定章程第八九十以及十四二十二等欵盡須開列以上七節之外不准更加形似工人容免全行之條倘有擅加理應置勿庸議

第九欵一合同所定承工年限不准逾於五年期滿如欲回國彼處必將合同所註水脚路費若干按數備全交付便船送回中華如或限滿不欲回國其法有二一則聽憑該處官憲准否留住准時即將合同原定路費一項全數付給便用一則聽其復行承工另立合同即將原約所定銀數付給一半聽其自用而此次合同仍不過五年為期期滿仍照前次合同原數付船送回設若華工到彼處後患病不能作工該處不俟限滿先行按數給錢送回否則准其赴官稟請伸訴

第十欵一承工工作日期時刻定准七日之內必得休息一日一日之內作工不過四時六刻（即外國九點鐘零二刻也）如足所定日時之數不准強其工作過時至於休息時日之間如果正工之外該工力能則有操作抑或另承工課准向本主酌定酬值惟牧畜以及日用常事仍屬正工不必因係休息時日格外議酬

第十一欵一華民年不及二十歲者或欲承工出洋必須取具本身父母准往憑單蓋用地方官印信方准承招如或無從取其父母確據亦應取具地方官蓋印憑單如無此單不准前往

第十二欵一所有華工姓名既已註簿自是日起至少扣至四日方准在監理委員面前將合同念與該工聽明問其是否願往伊實願去立卽令其畫押

第十三欵一合同既已畫押該工自應總由招工商人准否離所不能擅自出入將次下船之日監理委員親至公所各該華工當面認明畫押合同是實領事官卽將合同鈔存備查該船未出口之前一日海關監督暨領事官或行親往或派委員赴船將該華工按數點明核對淸楚將單繳到監督領事官各署分別畫押鈔錄存案點明以後華工內有變約不肯前往卽准查明住居公所之日每日追取飲食之銀一錢如該工無欵歸償應交該管官按例治罪

第十四欵一華工未走之先該商如有預支銀錢皆應以爲承招賞需之用不准追還惟因支用安家之費准商預支每月扣還一元以淸欠款其數亦不准過六月工値此項銀兩該領事官必須設法實令安家不得別用其餘支借各項一槪不准又以華工或在船上之時或在彼處之後曾借銀錢等物約明期滿後作工抵還一併嚴禁如至期滿將欲回國之時或有債主伸訴藉此情節請爲扣留華工亦必不准因此攔阻

第十五款一所有招工公所其中如何辦理領事官與地方官既經會議定章華民承工居住總須遵照奉行

第十六款一華工居住公所或有滋事各等情弊立即鎖禁俟地方官委員查收按例審辦所中商夥人等不准擅行治辦

第十七款一所有該口招工公所俱准兩國委員隨時任便出入傳問華工所中房間均歸該員等查管以期分撥華工眷屬人口得以團聚免其雜混又以各房必須治理精潔方足怡養精神華工畫押合同以及下船之時該委員等亦當在塲監視如見所下之船似不妥協恐碍於人准令華工暫免下船俟覓醫生抑或熟識船隻之人勘明裁奪船內華工內有現患傳染症人即刻令其離船上岸

第十八款一華工下船委員點名開單該商按照所招之工每名出銀三元交付海關銀號收存以備監理委員經費

第十九款一犯法華民或在逃或越獄承工地方官查出照會領事官交出領事官立飭移付地方官計期該犯居住所中之日除將每日償銀一錢以補該商虧欠外所有所中簿上註明付給該犯銀錢衣物等項亦應一體償還

第二十款一各國運載客民之船所有布置客寓艙房預備火食保其整潔俱有定例招工之商欲將華工運往外洋先須稟明領事官查核實有符於定例方准運往惟於領事官既經批准或有委員以該船尚有不妥情節稟明地方官以爲不宜出口海關暫准不給紅牌俟能確切詳查轉報該國

欽差大臣會議定奪

第二十一欵一華工下船點名開單應備兩本分別存留帶往船到前指定某國口岸該船主先將剛本邊沿註明華工在途或已生死疾病各等情節呈上伊國領事官並該處地方官等請爲分別畫押以備送回俟該單至中華之時招工商人必呈領事官即合轉移地方官查核

第二十二欵一華工出洋到彼夫婦不能分派兩處作工幼兒不及十五歲者不准令離父母至於華民在彼承人招工不分鋪戶莊田其後鋪田轉付他人該工亦當奉爲招主如或原主仍在鋪田或因別故欲使另投他主該工自願方可否則不准强行更換

以上各欵公同酌定之外又經言明除華民不待承招自行出洋中國官盡毫不攔阻外若有意圖招工不遵章程另行設法招致華民承約出洋作工此爲例所嚴禁查出另行重辦更有華民不肯離國有人膽敢私行騙往勉强脅從即照刑部奏定新章立予正法且以招工事務既經明定章程通商各口均准設所仍須地方官與領事官會議監理方爲按例與辦設若某口內外各官無從會理該商理應不准開所招工等語以上三節核定存案中外官民應與前項二十二條同一遵守奉行今於同治五年正月十九日將章程等件各繕三分蓋印畫押以昭信守

130.

茲
大清國大皇帝
大日國大君主
甚願將中國人民前往古巴寓居之事重新商訂妥協以期永無相左
之處爲此
大清國大皇帝特派
總理各國事
務衙門大臣
成毛沈董夏
作爲全權大臣
大日國大君主特派
駐劄中國欽差兼駐劄粤
南暹羅欽差御賜頭等
意薩貝勒等寶星大臣
伊作爲全權大臣
妥議其事所有議定各條開
列於後
第一欵
所有同治三年九月初十日
大清國
大日國
在天津定立條約內載立約爲憑招華人承工各節嗣後既不招人出洋承工
自無庸立約爲憑惟前約第十款內有不得收留中國逃人之語仍遵其舊
第二款
前約承工出洋未能盡善之情既經今已除去自應將前者議及賠償一層

兩國互相罷論

第三欵

兩國定准嗣後彼此庶民出口前往無論單身或携帶家屬皆以出於情甘自願爲要總不准或在中國各口或在他處妄用勉强之法及施詭譎之計誘令華民人等不出情願而往如有

兩國人民船主人等違背此約者則

兩國必將其人從嚴查辦均照本國律例從重定擬罪名

大日國又允所有待各大國同類之人最優之處中國人民或已在古巴者或嗣後前往者亦應一體均霑

第四欵

中國所開之通商各口如有中國男女人等自願備川資往古巴居住者

大清國自此聽其自便并無禁阻之意並令通商各口關道及地方等官如有遵照此次之約願載該民前往者通商各口關道及地方等官自聽各國之船在該口內自備應用之物以便載客出口所有該船之船東船行及經手各事人等如果能遵守此約通商各口關道及地方等官亦不攔阻

第五欵

所有華民出口前往一切情事是否果遵此約各章之處各該口關道地方等官

自可自行詳細查明以昭愼重如有華人自願出洋者應先赴關道處報明掛號請領蓋印執照（此項執照各關道預先備辦）送交日國領事官畫押蓋印由關道發給該華人上船出洋俟船到古巴後由該處該管官將關道原給蓋印執照送交中國領事官查驗其通商各口載客出洋之船該關道仍可派中國委員

大日國領事官亦派委員同往該船親爲訪察如查出華人內有並未領關道所給蓋印執照者立將此等華人撤回倘到古巴後有未領關道所給蓋印執照之華人卽由該處日國官員會同中國領事官商辦至船欲何時出口該船主船東務將開船時刻先期報明以期委員於應查各節詳細驗明不致因循貽悞如該船主不遵此章輙以開船在卽不及候驗爲辭則照會日國領事官先將船牌等件存署不發並准將該船扣留照日國律例辦理俟各章遵辦後方可放行

第六欵

大清國卽派總領事官前往古巴夏灣拏地方駐劄此外所有日國准各國領事官等員駐劄之各處地方中國亦可一律派員前往駐紮惟所有中國派總領事等官一節均照互相訂明辦法辦理日國允待中國各員與待各國駐紮古巴各官一樣

大清國所派之總領事領事副領事等員

大日國古巴各官自應盡力照料令其易於稱職妥爲保護在彼本國之民

第七欵

所有在古巴中國人等均准隨便出島他往唯其中倘有罪犯應行候訊者不在此例至華民在島隨便來往立業自應設法以與第三款所言之利益相符以上或應由日國執政大臣會同中國駐劄日國

欽差大臣抑或由日國夏灣拏地方官會同中國總領事官妥設良法俾令中國人等均能獲此約內所言之益與各大國在彼同類之人一例相待唯所設之法既應與該處防範滋事之章均宜相符即以後在島再立防範滋事之章亦皆包括又應由日國地方官每人予以隨便往來之准單一紙至此准單自應與各國人所執之單式樣相符

第八款

一中國人等或自被告赴署分辯者或爲原告赴署理論者所有該處日國讞局優待各國兩造之處該讞局應令中國人等一律均霑

一中國人等在讞局有事之時准其延請律師及傳話之人無論他國日國均准請去且或自覓其人或請中國總領事領事等員代覓均可惟其人必須按照日國律例能在日國讞局承辦此事者方可延請

一至現今在古巴島之華民人等內有未行互換此次條約之前自言曾受委屈

者均可前往該處日國讞局訴其冤枉該處讞局即將各案次序確查秉公斷結
與優待各國人所能得者一樣
第九款
大清國所派夏灣拏之總領事官急與該島各該管官妥訂章程令現今在古巴之華
民人等以及嗣後再來之華民均皆報名掛號立花名册其册存於中國總領事
等官署內每人由領事官發給執照一紙以爲業經報名之據此等執照應呈各
府城莊寮等所查驗
一古巴地方官急將該島各處現有華人多寡之數並其姓名知會中國總領事
等官並設良法令中國總領事等官易於前往該島莊寮等處以便將中國在彼
承工之人實在情形親自詳察
第十款
各國之船願載華民出洋除此約各條自應一體遵照外尚宜遵守其本國載客
之章以免船上或乏應用之物或缺防客染病之法各等情形是各國之船若不
遵守此二項規矩即不准載客出洋
第十一款
一現今在古巴承工之華人內恐有從前在中國或讀書或作官及此項人之親
圖

大日斯巴呢啞國敦崇和誼願將此項人等由日國自出船貲載回中國以昭誠衷俟此次條約互換後卽行開辦惟應由中國總領事領事等員先將實在情形查明知會日國該處地方官俟該處地方官將各情詳細核明如果屬實卽將其人放行載回

一現今在古巴之華工內所有年老力衰以致不能作工之人並中國孤寡婦女玆

大日國允將此二項內自願出島回國之人亦由日國出貲送回

第十二欵

一現今在古巴之華工合同期滿原合同內如有僱主人等應送回國等語

大日國自應督令該僱主人等按照合同而行

一現今在古巴之華工人等內亦有工期已滿而原合同未載送回本國之語者至此項內誠恐有無力自備船貲回國之人應由古巴地方官與中國總領事等官詳商設法以便送回

一所有現今在古巴合同之期已滿之華工俟此次條約互換之後卽應一體予以期滿之執照一紙所有以上第七欵所言之利益其人自應一體均霑其人或願仍在該島居住或願出島他往均聽其便

第十三欵
古巴島各處地方官倘察某處當時情形其處若聚人過衆恐滋事端以致地方不靖該地方官一面禁止中國人民一面知照領事官不准前往居住與待各國人一律辦理若果有此情形卽不得以第七款有隨便來往之語爲辭

第十四欵
一現今在古巴工期未滿之華人仍應按合同之期將工作滿其餘如執照准單等一切事宜新到之華人與期滿之華人所獲利益亦應一律同霑
一現今在古巴所有拘於各處工所之華人俟此次條約互換之後一體放出並將應立之章內所定各項執照亦皆發給摠將其人與在彼處各項華人一律相待至於犯罪已未定案之人仍送官監候結

第十五欵
在此次所立各條內日後如有願行删改之意則應至少於一年之前預行知會以備日後詳商
大清國 大日國
大清國如於華民出洋一事內以後若將此次條約未載之利益施及他國則日國卽應一體均霑

第十六欵

現今所立各條應由

兩國

御筆批准於八個月限內在

大淸國都中互換或能先互換均可

右載條約

今已將日文法文漢文各二分校對無訛在

大淸國光緒三年十月十三日

大日國一千八百七十七年十一月十七日由

兩國所派秉權之大臣在京師親各畫押鈐用關防以昭信守

十月十二日收日國伊使照會

爲照會事照得中國人前往古巴居住一事經

貴衙門各大臣與本大臣屢次商議定立條欵而現今所定條約第六款內載所有派中國總領事等官一節均照互相訂明辦法辦理等因查嗣後

貴國派此等官員前往該處自爲保定各節謹照條款辦理起見若非慎重之人
難盡其責本大臣前已將該處較他處尤難之情形在
貴大臣前屢次述明幷請如派總領事領事副領事官務希專派中國本國之人
爲此現請
貴衙門將
貴國允否此節照此辦理之處妥爲示覆可也爲此照會須至照會者

十月十三日給日國伊使照覆

爲照復事本月十二日接准
貴大臣照會內稱中國人前往古巴居住一事經貴衙門各大臣與本大臣屢次
商議定立條約第六款內載所有派中國總領事等官一節均照互相訂明辦法
辦理等因查嗣後貴國派此等官員前往該處自爲保定各節謹照條款辦理起
見若非慎重之人難盡其責本大臣前已將該處較他處尤難之情形在貴大臣
前屢次述明幷請如派總領事領事副領事等官務希專派中國本國之人爲此
現請貴衙門將貴國允否此節照此辦理之處妥爲示復等因前來查條款第六
款內中國派總領事等官一節本王大臣等與貴大臣屢行籌議已極詳明茲准
前因自當查照辦理相應照復
貴大臣查照可也須至照會者

十月十三日給日國伊使照會

爲照會事照得古巴華工章程各款本大臣等已與
貴大臣逐款當面訂定一俟彼此畫押蓋印後本衙門應即奏明飭令南北洋大臣轉飭通商各口關道及該地方官等一體遵照辦理此後倘有自願出洋之華人已經前赴該關道衙門報名掛號領有該關道蓋印執照下船時忽又不願出洋者如該船船東船主有借墊該華人銀錢若干該關道及該地方官應令該華人將親立劵約呈驗相符後即行勒令如數繳還倘有未能繳還情事應由該關道及該地方官取具的保俾歸有著可也相應照會
貴大臣轉飭領事官一切查照辦理並希　先行照復爲要須至照會者

十月十三日收日國伊使照覆

爲照覆事本日接到
來文內開俟彼此畫押蓋印後本衙門應即奏明飭令南北洋大臣轉飭通商各口關道等官此後倘有自願出洋之華人已經領有該關道執照下船時忽又不願出洋者如該船船東船主有借墊該華人銀錢若干該關道等應令該華人將親立劵約呈驗相符後即行勒令如數繳還倘有未能繳還情事應由該關道等取具的保俾歸有着等因前來查如此辦理寔於今已畫押之條款易於得手自應由本大臣即行轉飭各口本國領事官查照一切辦理可也爲此照覆須至照會者

131\. 謹將保險事宜應赴稅務司處繕立各據擬定專章開呈

鑒核

計開

第一欵

凡通商口岸華民船商以及無約或無領事官之商倘有應行畫押立據一切事宜均准任便隨時親赴稅務司處繕立（指示各關辦理稅務之人勿論正任署任及代理人員於據內均稱本關稅務司）

第二欵

凡商船進口應准由該船主於進口次日限內親赴稅務司處繕立預據

第三欵

凡船主立預據後出口之先倘有應立後據之故應准帶同本船大副人等復行親赴稅務司處繕立後據此後據應將其船行海時按照日記簿所錄並按照船主大副管輪水手人等所見所聞記清之事如何遇見變天風浪如何遇見一切未能預料未能防範之險一一詳細繕寫並應將該船主人等遇險之時如何設法防範如何設法救援一律註明畫押立據

第四欵

凡船主倘有應繕立後開各項証據亦准一律赴稅務司處繕立

一船碰船之據

一裝貨逾限之據

一卸貨佔船之據

一違背合同躭擱船事之據

一各項應行畫押爲據之件

第五欵

凡商人若以爲某船船主有爲不應爲之事或有酒醉不端或有躭悞不按時開船以及載貨憑單未肯照尋常式樣給還各情事亦准一律親赴稅務司處繕立各據

第六欵

凡赴稅務司處畫押爲憑以及繕立各項証據應繳立據之稅銀壹兩整惟後據一項應繳伍兩至請抄錄備查各件在一百字以內應繳銀壹兩一百字以上應繳銀貳兩二百字以上應繳銀叁兩(以此遞加)

第七欵

凡立各據應照功牌式樣繕寫或用漢文或用英文均可

第八欵

凡無約以及無領事官之商民倘有應行畫押立據之事亦可任便隨時親赴稅務司處繕立

第九欵

凡商民立據繳稅之銀兩應由各該稅務司在稅務司另款之帳目按結核報

第十款

凡立各項証據之印簿應存税務司處由税務司按結將所立之各據以及所繳之銀數知會本關監督查照倘其內有應轉申之件即由該税務司照錄備呈

隨京字第壹千貳百捌拾柒號

132. 摘錄烟台條約事件

第三端 通商事務

一所有現在通商各口岸按前定各條約有不應抽收洋貨釐金之界茲由威大臣議請本國准以各口租界作爲免收洋貨釐金之處俾免漫無限制隨由中國議准在於湖北宜昌安徽蕪湖浙江温州廣東北海四處添開通商口岸作爲領事官駐紥處所又四川重慶府可由英國派員駐寓查看川省英商事宜輪船未抵重慶以前英國商民不得在彼居住開設行棧俟輪船能上駛後再行議辦至沿江安徽之大通安慶江西之湖口湖廣之武穴陸溪口沙市等處均係內地處所並非通商口岸按長江統共章程應不准洋商私自起下貨物今議通融辦法輪船准暫停泊上下客商貨物皆用民船起卸仍照內地定章辦理除洋貨半税單照章查驗免釐其有報單之土貨只准上船不准卸賣外其餘應完税釐由地方官自行一律妥辦外國商民不准在該處居住開設行棧

一新舊各口岸除已定有各國租界應無庸議其租界未定各處應由英國領事官會商各國領事官與地方官商議將洋人居住處所畫定界址

一洋藥一宗威大臣議請本國准爲另定辦法與他項洋貨有別令英商販運洋藥入口時由新關派人稽查封存棧房或躉船俟售賣時洋商照則完稅並令買客一併在新關輸納釐稅以免偷漏其應抽收釐稅若干由各省察看情形酌辦

一洋貨運入內地請領半稅單照各國條約內原已訂明自當遵辦嗣後各關發給單照應由總理衙門核定畫一款式不分華洋商人均可請領並無參差洋商將土貨由內地運往口岸上船條約內亦有定章英商完納子口半稅請領單照卽可運往海口若非英商民買土貨該貨若非實在運往海關出口不得援照辦理所有應定章程免致滋生弊端之處威大臣卽願會同總理衙門設法商辦至通商善後章程第七款載明洋貨運入內地及內地置買土貨等語係指沿海沿江沿河及陸路各處不通商口岸皆屬內地應由中國自行設法防弊

一咸豐八年所定條約第四十五款內載英商若將已經完納稅項洋貨復運外國稟明海關監督發給存票他日均可持作已納稅餉之據等語原約並未定有年限今訂明三年爲期限滿不得將此項存票持作完納稅項之據

一香港洋面粵海關向設巡船稽查收稅事宜屢由香港官憲聲稱此項巡船有擾累華民商船情事現在議定卽由英國選派領事官一員由中國選派平等官一員由香港選派英官一員會同查明核議定章遵辦總期於中國課餉有益於香港地方事宜無損

133.

照錄　總理衙門劄復　署總稅務司費

爲劄復事同治五年七月二十六日據署總稅務司申稱轉據福州稅司來文內稱本口洋商完納稅課及買賣稅物幾於盡用破爛鷹棒番銀以致此處紋銀甚少而紋銀價值竟致由該商等任憑定價是以刻下與其議增十兩不如遵依條約按照道光二十三年廣東所定各成色畫一辦理庶免日後再有辯論等因前來查此案先於七月初二二十等日准閩浙總督咨稱據南臺口稟准駐紮福州買領事照會內稱本月初九日中外官僚會議洋商納稅補水本應遵照和約第三十三款辦理未便更張特因海關納稅每百兩補水陸兩不敷耗費洋銀時價早晚不同不若暫先定一準則嗣後洋商凡用洋銀納稅者每百兩補水拾兩即於本年六月二十一日開辦惟事出權宜應詳

駐京大臣察核須奉到批廻方能定準本司道復查該領事所議係爲體恤商人起見應請暫准照辦嗣後再有長落仍遵和約隨時商酌等因本衙門正在核辦間接准署總稅務司來文擬照廣東所定各番銀成色定規辦理所議尤爲周密惟閩浙總督擬每百兩加銀拾兩係爲一時權宜起見將來銀價再有長落亦仍照廣東所

定各成色畫一辦理相應劄行署總稅務司劄飭福州稅司商同地方監督及領事
官酌量情形詳細核辦或暫加拾兩水銀或照廣東所定成色總期有便商情無虧
稅課是爲至要仍候查復可也須至劄者
同治　五年　捌月　拾叁日

譯閩字申文第柒拾柒號一千八百七十八年

福州將軍英　札稅務司布
鎮守福州等處將軍統轄福建陸路鎮協各營事務兼管閩海關印務英　爲
札行事案承准
總理各國事務衙門咨洋商納稅以鷹棒番銀易換紋銀自應另加補水今因閩省
紋銀稀少以洋銀易銀其貼水由六兩增至十兩是鷹棒銀色實短紋銀一成業經
各口委員與領事等商定於六月二十一日暫行開辦此事本應由閩省酌定無須
本衙門照會駐京公使唯費總稅司擬照廣東所定各番銀成色定規辦理以免日
後再有辯論所請不爲無見現在福州口業已開辦希即酌量情形可否按照總稅
務司之議辦理抑或照十兩之議權辦將來銀價或再增長仍照廣東所定各成色

畫一辦理庶於稅務商情兩無窒碍均由貴處酌定相應抄錄費總稅務司申陳咨覆查照可也等因承准此隨即飭令通商局司道督同各委員悉心妥議辦理茲據通商局司道呈覆督同通商局員暨移會海關委員長協領照會各國領事官訂期妥議去後茲據局員以會議前向英國星領事暨各國領事官悉心核議該領事等僉云此次定議十兩補水與現時市價不相上下各洋商亦皆允願儘可照辦若照道光二十三年廣東所定成色按照時價高下貼水不但洋商不勝其煩且閩海關納稅英棒並用官銀號勢難逐一辦認未免多費周章莫若查照前議仍將番銀一律搭解十兩貼水完納關稅較爲妥協嗣後銀價如有低昂不妨隨時另請核議等語據情面稟前來本司道查前項洋稅既據局員與各國領事商定仍照前議貼水十兩自應准予照辦以免紛更等由前來除呈覆

總理衙門暨咨明

通商大臣李　察照外爲此札行布稅司知照此札

同治　五年　十二月　初二日

隨閩字申文第柒拾柒號一千八百七十八年

謹將英商怡記洋行稟官銀號加增兌收照會厦門關委員諭止及厦門關委員
黄照請訂期比較砝碼往來照會錄呈
電鑒

計開

爲照會事照得本月十六日英商怡記洋行到關稟稱完稅餉時官銀號每千元
均要加增一元譬如本行秤準一千元到彼該銀號均止認爲九百九十九元之
數但此銀並非本行自已秤準且經英商滙豐銀行秤過亦有差錯之理懇請稅
務司諭阻等因當經敝稅司隨時喊其來關面諭嗣後斷不可故蹈前轍而該銀
號亦踴躍聽從去後於二十二日接到
英國駐厦領事官　公文內開據怡記洋行稟稱該銀號原是照前多秤請貴稅
務司要設法不可再准其如是行爲寔於公便等因並附一信內云若該銀號不
改原秤本領事定必申請
駐京大臣查辦彼時就不請本處
地方官辦理等語本稅司現擬此節務祈
貴佐領府卽速查明嚴行諭止該銀號原秤必須改換不然後來總多枝節爲此
照會

貴佐領府請煩查照施行須至照會者

右　照　會

賞戴藍翎督理厦門稅務佐領府黃

同治　十三年　八月　二十三　日

爲據情照請訂期比較砝碼事本年八月二十三日准

貴稅務司照會內開據英商怡記洋行稟稱完稅餉時官銀號每千元均要加增一元請即諭止等因准此當經立傳該銀號到關諭飭旋據稟稱竊來等承充厦門口洋稅官銀號征收洋華各商稅課向照驗單塡載銀兩遵章加增十兩水銀照關發較準砝碼秤收按日將原平櫃數繳庫歷辦無異突於本月二十三日蒙

面諭本日接到稅務司照會前來內云怡記稟稱完餉時銀號每千元均要加增一元譬如本行秤準一千元到銀號只有九百九十九元之數且經英商滙豐秤過那有差錯之理事如屬寔有干未便等因奉諭之下不勝詫異伏思來等按日征收稅餉均照驗單塡註銀兩加水與報餉人等眼同秤收奉公守法不敢稍涉非分之事且洋番內有輕重不等向無計元兌收之例各商報餉非止怡記一家即怡記報納稅課亦非一日來等經辦銀號兩載於玆洋華各行尊無異議茲蒙

傳諭怡記洋行具稟等因理合瀝情叩懇電察寔在情形俯賜照會

稅務司立傳怡記洋行到關訂日將銀號征收砝碼會仝
稅務司當堂比較以息浮議等因據此合就據情照請爲此照會
貴稅務司請煩查照來文希即飭傳怡記洋行訂期到關會同比較砝碼並新訂
定日期先行照覆敝關幸勿有緩須至照會者
右　照　會
辦理厦門洋稅事務稅務司休
同治　十三年　八月　二十七　日
爲照會事照得本月十一日接准
英國領事官來洋文內開銀號秤頭砝碼委實多收本領事到關親見秤頭旣鈍
砝碼不公業經多日未見更改仍前多收殊屬不成事體其中尚有別弊暫停後
日再題但查同治八年間曾立會訊章程凡各口有干涉稅務案件領事官應先
與稅務司彼此關照或面見會議或移文往來定案時仍照後開數條辦理貴稅
務司似應作速設法重新較準以便商艱以免照章抄錄全案各詳
總理衙門駐京大憲查核且銀一被收受其勒索諸多藉口將來發還又費一番枝節即現
怡記所完稅銀俱在本署立案將來想要照數給還似此公事實多掣肘等因復
又於十三日

英國領事官親自來關會商怡記洋行完納稅銀一事惟因官銀號之天平砝碼
老銹無準可憑而怡記之天平與滙豐銀行之天平皆相符合以
英國領事官見先行按照會訊章程第七欵辦理本稅務司以爲不便嗣擇其第
七欵內開有令該商出具日後情願遵斷繳案切結由領事官蓋印存案等語茲
令怡記出具切結仍行照常完稅但於完稅銀時用其本行天平秤準兩數如一
千銀元該銀號不得扣其一元惟俟
軍憲須下官天平砝碼到關比時較其輕重如怡記之天平與官天平砝碼不符
應行每千元補增一元即令該怡記按其所出切結補繳等由本稅司緣據
英國領事官若此意見合行據情照會
貴佐領府請煩
查照允其所議即希轉飭官銀號先行遵辦一俟官天平砝碼到日再定其應繳
與否可也爲此照會須至照會者

右　照　會

賞戴藍翎督理廈門稅務佐領府黃

同治　十三年　九月　十九　日

爲遵批照請覆驗砝碼切寔較準事照得官銀號與怡記洋行較對砝碼一案前
准
貴稅務司照會到關當經敝府轉稟
軍憲察奪並請另給砝碼去後玆於本年九月二十四日接奉
批示內開據稟官銀號砝碼與怡記洋行比較輕重不能準對稟請另給等情查
厦門口砝碼自洋稅開關以來歷今年久從無更換何以不能準對仰即會仝稅
務司再提銀號砝碼覆驗如果寔有不符應即由口將砝碼切實修整較準符合
以期公平較兌不准多收等因奉此查本月十九日接准
貴稅務司照錄
英國領事官照會內開有銀號之天秤砝碼老鈍無準可憑等語其與怡記之秤
不能符合似即老鈍之故玆奉
批示前因合就照請覆驗爲此照會
貴稅務司請煩查照
憲批飭傳怡記洋行並多傳各字號洋行齊集到關將官銀號及各洋行天秤砝
碼公同切實較對如果不符應即遵批當堂修整以期平準實爲公便並祈訂期
照知以便飭傳該銀號集候較對望切望速施行須至照會者
右　照　會
辦理厦門洋稅事務稅務司休
同治　十三年　九月　二十五　日

134\. 謹將廣東善後總局以汕埠海防膏釐商人退辦後由洋藥釐局暫爲照章帶抽告
示抄呈
電鑒
計開
廣東善後總局兼辦海防事務
廣東布政使司姚
廣東釐務總局　爲
出示曉諭事案照洋藥海防經費折抽膏釐兩項前據效忠堂商人虞齊政即李玉
衡呈請加餉歸併承辦每年共認繳餉銀九十萬元當經本司局等會同核明詳奉
批准給諭開辦並分別移行遵照各在案現據該商虞齊政禀稱竊職商承辦洋藥
海防經費膏釐自開辦計至上年十一月初九日止一年之內業經鈌本一十八萬
元有零然猶竭立支持以冀後有起色不料收數短絀日甚一日前兩月六廠較前
收數雖屬有長而獨汕頭一口稅釐未減致被福建厦門仍舊冲銷以目下所抽計
該廠不及往日三分之一故自去年十一月起計至本年三月又復鈌本銀數萬元
此乃商本先後賠墊虧鈌不堪之實在情形也復思商等承辦之始認繳餉數係六

年以前各廠所收照計認餉故敢每年認至九十萬元之多不料自加膏釐一款之後前後情形大相懸殊近來所收竟不及昔日之半況商等自開辦以來均未照章收過足數俱由隨時變通酌減或九成七成折收或減至六成不等無非減價敵私以挽冲銷起見無奈極力變通設法籌辦仍屬淡收如故抽不敷解此誠關乎事勢使然抑亦商等才拙無能辦理未善所致也然既案經稟明試辦倘得稍可支持之策即使商廠毫不沾益但求日後不至如前賠累之甚商等亦當顧全大局辦滿五年之期以全始終之美惟是商本虧折業已二十餘萬若再照舊賠累實有力量不能再支再四思維惟有遵章先三月稟明退辦業經職商稟由商局總辦雷委員轉代稟明在案茲奉鈞諭著由商等再行補具退稟等因奉此職商復查此案係於本年四月十六日由商局委員轉稟遞到憲局應請仍以是日起扣至本年七月十六日止即准商等退辦此三月內餉項自當遵章按照解繳不敢少欠惟有仰懇憲恩俯念商艱照准退辦以免貽誤而重釐餉除經委員先代轉稟外合再瀝情具稟察核俯准施行實爲德便等情據此本司局等伏查商人虞齊政稟承洋藥海防經費歸併折抽膏釐原稟聲明試辦五年如五年內或有疲敝准予預先三月稟明退辦等情茲據該商具稟情愿退辦並據聲明此三月內餉項不敢短欠似應照准以符原案惟該商自四月十六日具稟退辦之日起扣足三月截至七月十六日止所有

以前餉項仍由該商核算明確照數清繳其七月十六日以後經費膏釐兩款不能盧懸應查照光緒六年舊商黃進源撤退之後新商虞齊政未經接辦之先各廠帶抽章程由洋藥各廠暫爲帶抽另欵彙解仍一面另招殷實商人認餉接辦以重釐務除分別具詳批飭移行查照並分劄洋藥各廠遵照辦理外合行出示曉諭爲此示仰各商販軍民人等知悉現在洋藥海防經費膏釐兩欵自商人虞齊政七月十六日退辦後暫由洋藥各廠照商人現在抽收章程一律帶抽爾等嗣後販運洋藥務須據實完納毋得遲疑觀望倘各廠司巡人等敢有留難勒索許即指名稟控或扭解到官定必從嚴究辦決不姑寬爾商販人等亦不得偷漏走私致干重咎各宜凜遵毋違特示　光緒捌年陸月拾捌日示

135.

稅務司柏　致興泉永道孫

巡啓者頃承

函訂二十八日四點鐘

惠臨敝公館幸得聆

教快慰之至屆期自當掃門候

駕也泐此奉覆順請

勛安

名另具十一月二十七日

136.

稅務司柏　致海關委員得提督道台仝此

敬啟者本年十一月三十十二月初一初二等日爲西國紳商賽馬之期玆本稅務司承各紳商囑代恭請

貴協鎮屆期於午刻

命駕光臨藉邀

賞鑒咼勝欣躍肅泐順請

升安

名另具十一月二十八日

137.

水師提督軍門彭　致稅務司柏

敬覆者頃奉

來翰以本年十一月三十日十二月初一初二等日爲西國紳商賽馬之期辱承

見召本富如約緣昨日已示練軍各營三十日點名稽查弁兵勇丁數目十二月初

一日是閱核本衙門辦過案件之期初二日核算各營本年錢糧帳務均須親自
督率眼同核閱未能抽身不及赴
命藉聆
大教抱歉之處希爲
原恕爲禱肅復伸謝敬請
台安惟
照不一

名另具二十九日

## 138.

與泉永道孫　致稅務司柏
逕啓者昨准
來函以西國紳商賽馬相邀前往本擬趨赴以資覽觀廼近日署中俱有緊要公事
届時不克分身
盛情心領併希轉爲道謝是荷專此布覆順頌
升祺維
照不一

名另具十一月二十九日

139.

海關委員得　致稅務司柏

敬覆者昨准

台函得悉十一月三十十二月初一初二等日爲

貴紳商賽馬大會極欲恭赴觀

光緣此數日適有公冗未獲放手前往尙祈

貴稅務司代爲告罪是幸肅泐敬請

升安唯

照不一

名另具十一月二十九日

140.

海關委員得　致稅務司柏

敬啓者現奉

將軍憲札開此八月十九日止屆滿第八十八結飭卽預先知會

貴稅務司屆期迅將結內所有徵收各項洋稅數目照送來關趕卽造册稟報等因

奉此相應函達

貴稅務司請煩查照一屆本結期滿卽將各項數目照送來關以便轉報幸勿有綏

是所至禱專此布請

升安惟

照不一

名另具八月十九日

141.

海關委員得　致稅務司柏

敬覆者頃准

台示昨夜關哨扣留藥料各件係醫院備用可否准予放行即希酌覆等因查出水貨件無論何項均應來關聲明該船戶明知故犯寔屬有違關章第重以

貴稅務司函示旣係醫院備用自未便執意辦理除飭令放行外特此泐覆布

達卽祈

轉囑該教士嗣後如有儀赴醫院應用各物務須先令來關聲明俾免該船戶藉圖

弊混是爲至荷專此復請

升安不一

名另具九月初八日

142.

興泉永道孫　致稅務司柏

逕啓者前准

來函看守呂宋來船須有住宿可否借用營哨小艇等因當卽佈覆一面轉致

水提台商辦茲准覆稱本標師船皆分派各處巡防各有職守碍難抽派且小哨
有底無蓋不能住宿用特馳達即請
貴稅務司查照應否另僱或將本關渡船如何酌量輪派備用之處務望
大才裁酌辦理是荷專此奉布順頌
升祺維
照不一

名另具八月二十一日

## 143.

與泉永道孫　致稅務司柏
巡啟者昨誦
華翰並准
大移暨附送章程一紙已備覆會銜曉示矣承
示於明後日
枉顧先訂時刻請於初三日下午三點鐘
惠臨當恴茗祇候也先此布覆順頌
升祺

名另具八月初二日

# 新關文件録

# TEXT BOOK

OF

# DOCUMENTARY CHINESE,

## WITH A VOCABULARY.

EDITED BY

F. HIRTH, PH. D.,

*Deputy Commissioner and Assistant Statistical Secretary, Inspectorate General of Customs, Shanghai.*

IN TWO VOLUMES.

VOL. II.

Published by Order of the Inspector General of Customs.

SHANGHAI:

STATISTICAL DEPARTMENT OF THE INSPECTORATE GENERAL OF CUSTOMS.

1888.

# 新關文件録

## HSIN - KUAN WÊN - CHIEN - LU.

# TEXT BOOK

OF

# DOCUMENTARY CHINESE,

## WITH A VOCABULARY,

FOR THE SPECIAL USE OF THE CHINESE CUSTOMS SERVICE.

EDITED BY

F. HIRTH, PH.D.,

*Deputy Commissioner and Assistant Statistical Secretary, Inspectorate General of Customs, Shanghai.*

IN TWO VOLUMES.

VOL. II.

Published by Order of the Inspector General of Customs.

SHANGHAI:
PUBLISHED AT THE STATISTICAL DEPARTMENT OF THE INSPECTORATE GENERAL OF CUSTOMS,
AND SOLD BY
KELLY & WALSH, LIMITED: SHANGHAI, HONGKONG, YOKOHAMA, AND SINGAPORE.
LONDON: P. S. KING & SON, CANADA BUILDING, KING STREET, WESTMINSTER, S.W.
1888.

# TABLE OF CONTENTS.



The reference pages given in Part I of this Volume are intended to refer to the pages of the Chinese text (Volume I).

# PART I.

## VOCABULARY, ANALYTICALLY ARRANGED.

# VOCABULARY.

## I. ANALYTICALLY ARRANGED.

**Document No. 1.** [p. 1]

*chiang* 江 a river; abbreviated name of the province of Kiang-nan (江南).

江海關 the Customs of Kiang-nan; the Shanghai Custom House.

*hai* 海 the sea.

海關 a maritime Custom House.

*kuan* 關 to lock (as a gate); a custom house; the Customs.

*yen* 驗 to examine.

驗單 a duty memo. (debit note for duties to be paid, issued after the examination of goods and hence called "examination bill").

*tan* 單 single; a document consisting of a single sheet; a bill; a certificate; a memo.; a permit.

*chin* 今 now.

*chü* 據 in accordance with; whereas.

*tê* 德 virtue.

德意志 (*tê-i-chih*=Deutsch) German.

德國 Germany; German.

*kuo* 國 a country.

*shang* 商 trade; a merchant.

商人 a merchant.

*jên* 人 a man.

*hang* 行 a hong; a firm.

*t'ou* 投 to send in; to present.

投報 to send in an application; to report (for payment of duty).

*pao* 報 to report.

*ti* 第 number; No.

第..................號 No..................; Registered No...............

*hao* 號 a number; a firm.

*i* 一 or 壹 one.

*êrh* 二 or 貳 two.

*san* 三 or 叁 three.

*ssŭ* 四 or 肆 four.

*wu* 五 or 伍 five.

*liu* 六 or 陸 six.

*ch'i* 七 or 柒 seven.

*pa* 八 or 捌 eight.

*chiu* 九 or 玖 nine.

*shih* 十 or 拾 ten.

*pai* 百 or 佰 hundred.
(The first or smaller style of writing the above numerals is that ordinarily used; the second or larger style is employed in expressing money items or other figures of importance, in order to prevent unauthorised changes.)

*ch'ien* 千 thousand.

*wan* 萬 ten thousand.

*ying* 英 excellent; brave; English; British.

英吉利 (*ying-ki-li*=English) English; British.

英國 England; Great Britain; British.

英船 a British ship.

*ch'uan* 船 a ship.

*ming* 名 a name; to name; named.

*chuang* 裝 to load; to be laden with; to contain.

裝載 to carry; to be laden with (as a ship).

*tsai* 載 to be laden with; to contain.

*chin* 進 to enter; to come in; incoming.

進口 to enter port; to import.

*k'ou* 口 a port.

*huo* 貨 goods; merchandise.

貨物 goods; merchandise; articles of trade.

*wu* 物 things; articles.

*hei* 黑 black.

*hai* 海參 bicho de mar.

*shên* 參 ginseng.

*chien* 件 a package; packages.

*chin* 觔 or 斤 a catty; catties.

*chi* 計 to calculate; calculated to make; calculated at.

*liang* 兩 a tael; taels.

*ch'ien* 錢 a mace (the 10th part of a tael).

*fên* 分 a candareen (the 100th part of a tael).

*li* 釐 or 厘 a cash (the 1,oooth part of a tael).

*chung* 中 middle; the second quality out of three, when *shang* (上) means first and *hsia* (下) third.

*yen* 燕 a swallow.

燕窩 swallows' nests; birds' nests.

*wo* 窩 a nest.

*ling* 零 denotes a break in the decimal notation.

*ting* 丁 a nail.

丁香 cloves.

*hsiang* 香 incense; aromatic drugs.

*yü* 魚 fish.

魚肚 fish maws.

*tu* 肚 the belly; the stomach.

*hsiang* 象 an elephant.

象牙 elephants' teeth; ivory.

*ya* 牙 a tooth.

*shêng* 生 raw; unmanufactured.

*niu* 牛 cows; oxen.

牛皮 cow hides.

*p'i* 皮 skins; hides.

*kung* 共 all; in all.

共計 calculated to make in all; total.

*chin* 進口稅 import duties.

*shui* 稅 duty; duties (on merchandise).

*kuan* 關平銀 *lit.*, silver as per Customs weight; Customs money; Haikwan tael money.

*p'ing* 平 even; level; weight; standard weight.

*yin* 銀 silver; money; treasure.

*p'ing* 憑 to lean on; on the ground of.

憑單 "leaning [on this] bill;" "as per memo.;" also, a "duty proof."

*ch'ih* 持 to hold.

持赴 to proceed to......holding, or with, [a document].

*fu* 赴 to proceed to.

*yin* 銀號 a bank; *the* Bank; the Customs Bank.

*chiao* 交 to give; to hand.

交納 to pay (as duties).

*na* 納 to pay (as taxes, duties, etc.).

*tsu* 足 enough; sufficient.

足色 sufficient colour; full standard silver; pure sycee.

*sê* 色 colour; to colour; to dye.

*ch'ê* 掣 to pull; to hold.

掣取 to take delivery of; to receive.

*ch'ü* 取 to fetch; to get.

*hao* 號收 a bank receipt (for payment of duty).

*shou* 收 to receive; a receipt.

*k'o* 可 can; may; will do.

可也 "this will do" (a final phrase which need not be translated).

*yeh* 也 a final particle; also.

*tz'ŭ* 此 this.

此照 "this is (hereby) certified."

*chao* 照 a document; a certificate; a pass; to certify; according to.

*kuang* 光 bright; brightness; to illumine.

光緒 the period of reign of the Emperor Kuang Hsü.

*hsü* 緒 the commencement.

*nien* 年 a year.

*yüeh* 月 the moon; a month.

*jih* 日 day; date.

*chi* 給 to give; to issue.

給單 to issue a certificate, a bill, a memo., etc.

### Document No. 2. [p. 2]

*shou* 收到 "arrived, or come to hand, by receiving," *i.e.*, received, received from (in receipts).

*tao* 到 to arrive.

*ching* 經 places the verb in the perfect tense; the verb may either follow this particle immediately, or be separated from it by several characters representing other parts of the sentence.

經報 to have reported; having reported.

*ying* 應 must.

應完 having to pay duty; dutiable.

*chêng* 正 full; as full duty, full rank. Added to numeral expressions in order to prevent unauthorised additions being made, and corresponding to "*only*," as in "one hundred taels *only*."

正稅 full duty; *i.e.*, full import duty.

*pên* 本 this, as in "*this* office"; the possessive pronoun of the person speaking or writing; *pên shui-wu-ssŭ* (本稅務司)=I, the Commissioner.

本號 this bank.

*an* 按 according to.

按照 according to.

*so* 所 the relative pronoun *who* or *which*; its use differs from that of our relative pronoun, *e.g.*, 船$^{1}$ 所$^{2}$ 載$^{3}$ 貨$^{4}$ = *huo*$^{4}$, the goods, *so*$^{2}$, which, *chʻuan*$^{1}$, the ship, *tsai*$^{3}$, contains; and not the ship which contains the goods.

*tsai* 載 to contain; as a vessel *contains* cargo, or as a document *contains* a statement.

*yin* 銀數 a sum of money.

*shu* 數 number; amount; several.

*tui* 兌 to weigh.

兌收 to receive weighing (sycee); *i.e.*, to receive cash or bullion.

*ho* 合 duly.

*i* 以 to use; using which; by means of which.

以憑 by means of which supported; on the ground of which; provided with which.

*kai* 該 the said; the respective; that; the.

*kuan* 關憲 the Customs authorities.

*hsien* 憲 an official above the 4th rank; authorities.

*chʻêng* 呈 to state to a superior.

呈請 to apply for; to request to.

*chʻing* 請 to request; to apply for.

*yen* 驗收 to examine and receive; to accept (as a document).

**Document No. 3.** [p. 3]

*chung* 中 middle.

中國 China; Chinese.

*chao* 招 to invite.

招商局 the "China Merchants' Steam Navigation Company."

招商 to invite merchants; to promote commerce.

*chü* 局 a board of management; a public company.

*hu* 滬 Shanghai.

*tzŭ* 字 a character; a number, inasmuch as it is expressed by a character.

*hua* 華 Chinese.

*chʻu* 出 to go out; to take out; outgoing.

出口 to export; to leave port; to clear from a port.

*hsi* 細 fine.

*tzʻŭ* 磁 porcelain.

磁器 chinaware.

*chʻi* 器 utensils; goods; ware.

*mien* 棉 the cotton plant.

棉花 cotton.

*hua* 花 flowers.

*tsao* 棗 dates.

*yen* 烟 tobacco.

烟絲 prepared tobacco.

*ssŭ* 絲 silk; the hairy appearance of anything cut fine like silk, *e.g.*, Chinese prepared tobacco, vermicelli, wire.

*shang* 上 above; superior; first quality.

*chih* 紙 paper.

*ku* 古 old.

古玩 curiosities.

*wan* 玩 to play; trifles.

*ku* 估 value; to value.

估價 value.

*chia* 價 price; value.

*tou* 荳 beans.

荳餅 beancake.

*ping* 餅 cakes; pastry.

*chʻu* 出口稅 export duty.

**Document No. 4.** [p. 4]

**Document No. 5.** [p. 5]

*fu* 復 again.

復[運]進口 to again import; to re-import, as native goods from another treaty port.

*tʻu* 土 earth; land; native; local.

土產 native produce.

*chʻan* 產 to give birth to; to produce; produce.

*pan* 半 half.

半稅 half duty, *i.e.*, coast trade duty; also, transit dues.

*mei* 美 beautiful.

美國 America; American.

*fu* 福州 Foochow.

*yün* 運 to transport.

運來 to move inwards; brought from.

*chi* 計開 namely; to wit (before an enumeration of things).

*kan* 橄欖 olives (Chinese).

*lan* 欖 olives (Chinese).

*chü* 桔 contracted from 橘, the orange.

桔子 oranges.

*tzŭ* 子 a child; a son; added to nouns as an ending, as it were, which usage is generally borrowed from the colloquial language.

*shui* 水 water.
水靛 liquid indigo.
*tien* 靛 indigo.
*kuei* 桂 cassia; Kuei-lin-fu, the capital of Kwangsi.
桂圓 dried lung-ngan (perhaps balls of Kuei, *i.e.*, of Kuei-lin-fu in Kwangsi).
*yüan* 圓 round; a globe; a ball.
*lien* 蓮 the water lily; the lotus.
蓮子 lotus seeds.
*hung* 紅 red.
*fu* 復進口半稅 coast trade duty.

**Document No. 6.** [p. 6]

*chêng* 征 to levy.
征收 to collect (as duty).

**Document No. 7.** [p. 7]

*chi* 給發 to issue.
*fa* 發 to issue.
*yün* 運入 to transport into (the river or the interior).
*ch'ang* 長 long.
長江 the Yangtze river.
*t'u* 土貨 native goods.
*hua* 花生 ground-nuts.
*liao* 料 glass.
料器 glass or vitrified ware.
*huo* 火 fire.
火腿 hams.
*t'ui* 腿 a leg; a thigh.
*hung* 紅丹 red lead.
*tan* 丹 cinnabar.
*shou* 熟 ripe; cooked; tanned; manufactured; the opposite of *shêng* (生), raw or unmanufactured.
熟鐵 manufactured iron.
*t'ieh* 鐵, 銕, or 鐵 iron.
*pai* 白 white.
白糖 white sugar.
*t'ang* 糖 sugar.
*ch'u* 除 to deduct.
除……外 deducting ……; besides ……
*wai* 外 outside; besides.
*ling* 另 extra; apart; separately.
*chiu* 九江 Kiukiang.

**Document No. 8.** [p. 8]

*fa* 發給 to issue.

**Document No. 9.** [p. 9]

*nei* 內 within; inside.
內地 the interior (of a country).
內地貨物 goods carried to (入) or from (出) the interior.
*ti* 地 earth; ground; land.
*ju* 入內地 to enter the interior; transit inwards.
*yüan* 原 original.
原色布 grey shirtings.
*pu* 布 cloth; cotton, linen, etc., cloth.
*p'i* 疋 a piece; classifier of piece goods.
*ta* 大 great.
大原布 *T*-cloth (the larger size).
*hsiao* 小 small.
小原布 *T*-cloth (the smaller size).
*hsieh* 斜 oblique.
斜紋布 drills.
*wên* 紋 streaks.
*sê* 色布 dyed cloth.
*tuan* 緞 satin.
緞布 damasks.
*yin* 印 to print; a seal.
印花布 printed cotton cloth; chintzes.
*tsu* 足色紋銀 full standard sycee.
*wên* 紋銀 silver with streaks (refers to the corrugated appearance common to the outside of a shoe of pure sycee, as contrasted with the smoother surface of an impure shoe); pure sycee.

**Document No. 10.** [p. 10]

**Document No. 11.** [p. 11]

*ch'u* 出內地 transit outwards.
*hu* 湖 a lake; the prefecture of Hu-chou, near Shanghai and Ningpo.
湖絲 Shanghai fine raw silk.
*luan* 亂 to disarrange; in confusion.
亂絲頭 silk refuse.
*t'ou* 頭 head; added to nouns, like *tzŭ* (子) (*see* Document No. 5).
*ts'an* 蠶 the silkworm.
蠶繭 cocoons.

*chien* 繭 cocoons.

*chin* 金 gold.

金針菜 dried lily flowers.

*chên* 針 or 鍼 a needle.

*ts'ai* 菜 vegetables.

*tan* 担 a picul.

**Document No. 12.** [p. 12]

**Document No. 13.** [p. 13]

*chiang* 江漢關 the Hankow Customs.

*han* 漢 Chinese; the Han river.

*tzŭ* 自 from.

自...起至...止 from *(such a date)* to *(such a date)*.

*ch'i* 起 to start from; commencing.

*chih* 至 to; till.

*chih* 止 to stop; ending.

*chieh* 結 a bond; to end; a fixed period or term for settling accounts; a Customs (financial) quarter of three months.

*yang* 洋 the sea; the ocean; foreign.

*ko* 各 each; all; sign of the plural.

各款 all kinds; the various kinds.

*k'uan* 款 or 欵 an item; a kind; a sort; also, a paragraph; an article (as in a Treaty); a section.

*shui* 稅鈔 duties on merchandise and tonnage dues; dues and duties.

*ch'ao* 鈔 tonnage dues.

*shu* 數目 number; numbers; amounts.

*mu* 目 the eye; numbers.

*ch'ing* 清 clear; accurate; correct, as an account.

清摺 a correct account or report; an official periodical account rendered to the Government.

*chê* 摺 to fold up; a paper folded up; a report; an account.

*shui* 稅鈔清摺 a Customs revenue return.

*yang* 洋商船隻 foreign merchant vessels. [p. 14]

*shui* 稅款 kinds of duties; duties.

*yang* 洋貨 foreign goods.

洋藥 opium; *lit.*, the foreign drug.

洋藥土 raw opium.

洋藥膏 prepared opium.

*yao* 藥 medicines; drugs.

*t'u* 土 earth; raw opium, so called owing to its earthy appearance.

*kao* 膏 fat; greasy; a preparation of greasy appearance, like ointment, etc.

*ko* 各稅 duties.

*wu* 無 not; not having; *nil.*

*ch'i* 其 of it; the; as to the......

其中 in this; therein.

*chung* 中 middle; placed after a noun, in, within.

*nei* 內地洋藥 opium grown in the interior; native opium.

*ho* 合 to unite; duly.

合併 duly exposed.

*ping* 併 or 幷 together with; to expose.

*shêng* 聲 to report; to state.

聲明 to report.

*ming* 明 clear; often added to verbs meaning to state, to inform, etc.

*ch'uan* 船鈔 tonnage dues.

*pên* 本年 this year; the present year.

*tai* 代 in place of another.

代收 to receive; to collect on account of another.

*fa* 發還 to return (as moneys).

*huan* 還 to return.

*chan* 暫 temporarily.

暫存 kept temporarily, *i.e.*, on deposit.

*ts'un* 存 to keep.

*hsü* 續 to continue to; continuous.

續增 to accumulate.

*tsêng* 增 to add to.

*ho* 核 to examine.

核計 to examine and add up; to calculate.

*ssŭ* 四結 the fourth quarter (of a financial year).

*ti* 底 bottom; end; at the end of.

*chieh* 結底 at the end of the quarter.

*yüeh* 月底 at the end of the month.

*nien* 年底 at the end of the year.

*jêng* 仍 still.

*i* 以 to use; with; because.

以上 the above.

*pên* 本結 this quarter.

*hua* 華商 Chinese merchants. [p. 15]

*chuang* 裝免 to carry cargo exempted from duty.

裝免數目 exemption account.

*mien* 免 to be exempt; duty free.

*tsai* 再 besides; in addition to what has been stated before.

*ts'ao* 漕 to transport by water.

漕糧 Government grain; tribute rice.

*liang* 糧 grain paid to Government in lieu of taxes.

*shih* 石 a stone; a picul (in this sense also read *tan* (担), when it is often written 石).

*tou* 斗 a *tou*, a measure of grain, of which 10 go to a picul.

*mei* 每 each.

*an* 按............計 calculated at............

*shêng* 升 a *shêng*, a measure of grain, of which 10 go to a *tou* (斗), or 100 to a picul.

*tzŭ* 子 a child; a son; affiliated. [p. 16]

子口 a small port affiliated to a larger port; a Customs barrier.

子口稅 transit dues.

*t'ung* 統 total.

統計 total; grand total.

*ch'a* 查 to examine; to look into; whereas; often denotes merely what we should express by a new paragraph.

*pên* 本關 this Custom House.

*ping* 並 and; used to emphasise negation.

並無 there are no............

*ya* 押 to seal.

押註 to seal and sign; to endorse.

*chu* 註 to sign; to endorse.

*hsien* 現 now; ready.

現銀 ready money; cash.

*ts'un* 存票 a drawback.

*p'iao* 票 a money order.

*ssŭ* 四品銜 of the 4th class of rank.

*p'in* 品 rank; class.

品銜 rank.

*hsien* 銜 rank.

*fu* 副 to assist; assistant; deputy.

副稅務司 a Deputy Commissioner of Customs.

*shui* 稅務 duty matters; Customs matters.

稅務司 one who manages Customs matters; a Commissioner of Customs.

*wu* 務 business; matters.

*ssŭ* 司 to manage; to control; a controller; a Commissioner.

*yi* 譯 to translate.

譯漢 translated into Chinese.

*ch'êng* 呈報 to report.

*sui* 隨 to follow; to accompany; enclosed in (as in a despatch).

*shên* 申 to state to a superior.

申文 a despatch (to a superior).

*ho* 核對 to examine and compare; to pass (as an account).

*tui* 對 to compare; to agree; a pair; opposite.

*tsung* 總 general.

總稅務司 the Inspector General of Customs.

*chuan* 轉 to transmit.

轉呈 to transmit a report to a superior.

**Document No. 14.** [p. 17]

*yüeh* 粵 Kwangtung, Canton.

粵海關 the Canton Customs.

*tsung* 總單 a cargo certificate.

*ch'in* 欽 Imperial.

欽命 by Imperial command.

*tu* 督 to superintend.

督理 to superintend.

*li* 理 to manage.

*wei* 爲 to make; on behalf of; in matters of.

爲..............事 in the matter of..............

*shih* 事 a matter; a subject.

*tzŭ* 茲 now.

*pao* 報驗 to declare for examination.

*ch'ien* 前 before; to advance.

前赴 to proceed to.

*shang* 上海 Shanghai.

*chiang* 將 to take; places the words between this character and the principal verb of the sentence in the accusative case.

*nei* 內 placed after a noun, in; within.

*yang* 洋土各貨 foreign and native goods.

*ch'êng* 呈請 to apply for.

*ch'a* 查驗 to examine; examination.

*hsü* 須 must; necessary.

須至總單者 "a cargo certificate which must be despatched" (至 = *ta* 達, to send?), a concluding phrase used to prevent unauthorised additions, which, owing to its antiquated form, is difficult to explain.

*chê* 者 that which; gives the verb preceding it the force of a participle or a relative clause.

*pao* 報單 an application for permission to land or to ship goods.

*hao* 號數 a registered number.

*huo* 貨色 description of goods.

*chien* 件數 number of packages.

*chin* 斤兩 catties or taels; *i.e.*, weight.

*huo* 或 or.

*p'i* 疋數 number of pieces (as of piece goods).

*chang* 丈 a *chang* (=141 inches, or 11¾ feet, English).

丈尺 *chang* and *ch'ih*; *i.e.*, length or measurement (as of piece goods).

*ch'ih* 尺 a *ch'ih* (=14 1/10 inches, English).

*tan* 單照 a certificate.

*liang* 糧臺 an army paymaster (*see* MAYERS' "The Chinese Government," No. 566).

*t'ai* 臺 or 台 eminent; exalted; a term of respect; enters into combination with certain titles.

*i* 衣 clothes.

衣箱 boxes containing clothes.

*hsiang* 箱 a box.

*shu* 書 books.

*hsing* 行 to go; to cause to.

行李 luggage.

*li* 李 a plum; to prepare for a journey.

*ling* 靈 a spirit; a soul; a coffin.

靈柩 a coffin with corpse.

*chiu* 柩 a corpse in a coffin.

*yang* 洋酒 foreign wine.

*chiu* 酒 distilled liquors; wine.

*ch'i* 其餘 the remainder; the remaining.

*yü* 餘 the remainder.

*wei* 未 not; not having; not being; the opposite of *i* (已), having (sign of the past).

未列 not enumerated.

*lieh* 列 to enumerate.

*chih* 之 marks the genitive case, which is otherwise expressed by anteposition; after a verb or a verbal expression it may impart to the verb the force of a passive participle; corresponds to *ti* (的) of the colloquial language.

*ko* 各貨 *the* goods.

*chün* 均 all; marking plurality.

*i* 已 sign of the past; precedes verb, and, like *ching* (經), is often separated from it by other parts of the sentence.

*an* 按類 according to category; according to denomination.

*lei* 類 category.

*chu* 逐 according to; one by one.

逐款 according to kinds; item by item.

*k'ai* 開 to state.

開明 to state; to enumerate.

*fên* 分 to divide; separately; respectively.

分別 to distinguish; to separate.

*fu* 附 to append; to enclose.

附給 to issue [a document] in an enclosure.

*mien* 免稅 to exempt from duty; duty free.

免稅執照 an exemption certificate.

*chih* 紙 paper; a document; a sheet; classifier of documents and certificates.

*shou* 收稅單 a duty-paid certificate.

*chêng* 正稅憑單 a full duty proof.

*p'ing* 憑單 a duty proof.

*chêng* 正稅單 (= 土貨出口正稅單) an export duty-paid certificate.

*pan* 半稅單 (= 土貨出口半稅單) a coast trade duty (deposit) certificate.

*wu* 毋 do not; not.

毋庸 need not.

*yung* 庸 to use; to have use for.

*ch'ung* 重 a second time; again; to be distinguished from *chung* (重), heavy.

重錄 to enter twice.

*lu* 錄 a record; to record; to enter.

*hsiang* 詳 to detail.

詳細 to state particulars in detail.

*chien* 件色 No. of packages and description of goods.

**Document No. 15.** [p. 18]

*chien* 監 to superintend.

監督 to superintend; the Superintendent (of Customs).

*t'ien* 天津 Tientsin.

*hsin* 新 new.

新關 the new, *i.e.*, the Foreign, Customs, as opposed to *ch'ang kuan* (常關) or *ch'ao kuan* (鈔關), the Native Customs.

新鈔兩關 the Foreign and Native Customs.

*pan* 辦 to manage.

辦理 to manage.

*chih* 直隸 the province of Chihli.

*t'ung* 通 to communicate with.

通商 to communicate by trade; to traffic.

通商各口 the treaty ports.

通商各關 the Foreign Custom houses.

通商事務 foreign trade matters.

*chien* 兼 to connect; and.

*kuan* 管 to control.

*hai* 海防 the protection of the sea coast; pertaining to maritime matters.

海防兵備道 a Taot'ai with military authority and charged with coast defence; title of the Taot'ai at Shanghai.

海防廳 a *hai-fang t'ing*, *i.e.*, a magistrate in certain maritime districts, *e.g.*, at Amoy.

海防同知 a maritime sub-prefect (*see* MAYERS' "The Chinese Government," No. 282).

*fang* 防 to protect; to guard against.

*ping* 兵備道 a Taot'ai.

兵 a soldier; military.

*pei* 備 to prepare; to provide.

*tao* 道 a road; a circuit; an officer in charge of a circuit; a Taot'ai.

*mi* 米 rice.

米袋 rice bags.

*tai* 袋 a bag.

*ch'ing* 青 blue.

青蓮 a kind of dye-stuff.

*lien* 蓮 the lotus; the water lily.

*pan* 半 a half; "and a half."

*ying* 應 must.

應征 "must levy;" liable to pay duty; "to pay."

*chêng* 征 to levy duty.

*k'ung* 空 empty.

空瓶 empty bottles.

*p'ing* 瓶 a bottle.

*ma* 麻 hemp.

麻袋 hemp bags.

*t'iao* 條 classifier of long, slender things; also of bags.

**Document No. 16.** [p. 19]

*tung* 東 east; eastern.

東西 east and west; eastern and western.

東西洋各國 the countries of the eastern and western seas; foreign countries.

*hsi* 西 west; western.

*wang* 往 to go to.

往來 to come and go; traffic.

*mou* / *mao* } 貿 trade; to trade.

貿易 trade.

*i* 易 change; to exchange; easy.

*huo* 貨價 the value of goods.

*tsung* 總數 totals.

*yang* 洋貨 foreign goods.

*yün* 運來 carried inwards; imported.

運往 carried outward; exported.

*hsiang* 香港 Hongkong.

*chiang* 港 a harbour; an anchorage.

*chuan* 轉運 to carry on to some further place; to re-transport.

*ko* 各國 foreign countries.

*yin* 印度國 (*yin-tu-kuo*) India; Indian.

*hsin* 新加坡 (*hsin-kia-po*) Singapore.

*têng* 等 sign of the plural; after a single proper name it has a generalising force, as "and others," "etc.," "and the like," "such as"; after a series of names it simply denotes plurality, when it should be left untranslated.

*shu* 屬 to belong to.

*hsin* 新金山 Australia; *lit.*, new California.

*shan* 山 a hill; a mountain; an island.

*chin* 金山 California.

*niu* 紐西蘭 (*niu-hsi-lan*) New Zealand.

*ta* 大浪山嘴 South Africa (Cape Colony).

*lang* 浪 waves.

*tsui* 嘴 the lips; the mouth; a beak.

*kan* 幹阿達 (*kan-a-ta*) Canada.

*chieh* 接 to be connected with; to bound on.

*pei* 北 north; northern.

*chieh* 界 boundary.

新關文件録



*chi* 卽 or ; then (*see* p. 46).

*ho* 合衆國 the United States.

*chung* 衆 all ; many.

*nan* 南 south.

南美國 South America.

*ou* 歐羅巴 (*ou-lo-pa*) Europe.

*ngo* 俄國 Russia ; Russian. [p. 20]

*yu* 由 by way of ; from ; when placed before the name or title of a person, often expresses the doer of an action.

由水道 by sea.

由陸路 by land.

*shui* 水 water.

水道 water road ; sea road.

*lu* 陸 dry land.

陸路 an overland road.

*lu* 路 a road.

*ching* 經 to pass ; *viâ*.

*ch'ia* 恰克圖 (*k'ia-k'o-t'u*) Kiakhta.

*t'u* 圖們江 (*t'u-mên-chiang*) the River Tumen near Vladivostock, on the Corean and Russian boundary.

*pei* 北 north.

*jih* 日 the sun ; a day.

日本國 (*jih-pên-kuo*) Japan ; Japanese.

*hsiao* 小呂宋 the Philippines.

*ta* 大呂宋 the kingdom of Spain.

*lü* 呂宋 (*lü-sung*) originally, the island of Luzon ; the Philippine Islands ; Manila.

*an* 安南國 (*an-nan-kuo*) Annam ; Annamese.

*hsien* 暹羅國 (*hsien-lo-kuo*) Siam ; Siamese.

*kua* 瓜哇 (*kua-wa*) Java.

*ho* 荷蘭國 (*ho-lan-kuo*) Holland ; the Netherlands ; Dutch.

*ai* 埃及國 (*ai-chi-kuo*) Egypt.

*a* 阿拉比國 (*a-la-pi-kuo*) Arabia.

*t'an* 檀香山 the Sandwich Islands.

*t'ung* 統共 total ; a grand total.

*ch'u* 出洋 to export abroad ; export to foreign countries ; also, to go to sea ; to emigrate.

*shih* 實 real.

實存 real balance ; net total.

*ching* 淨 clean ; net (as opposed to gross).

淨數 net figures ; net amount.

淨重 net weight.

**Document No. 17.** [p. 21]

*hua* 花色 description ; denomination.

*chuan* 專 special.

*chia* 價值 value ; price.

*chih* 值 price ; value.

*hsiao* 小洋藥 Malwa opium.

*ta* 大洋藥 Patna opium.

*hsin* 新洋藥 Benares opium.

*tsa* 雜 miscellaneous.

雜樣 miscellaneous sorts.

*yang* 樣 sort ; kind ; pattern.

*mien* 棉布 cotton cloth ; cotton piece goods.

*pai* 白色布 white plain shirtings.

白提花布 white figured, brocaded, etc., shirtings.

*t'i* 提 to raise ; to bring forward.

*su* 素 plain. [p. 22]

素色布 dyed plain shirtings.

*sê* 色花點布 dyed, figured, brocaded, etc., shirtings.

*tien* 點 a point ; to punctuate ; spotted.

*k'ou* 扣布 *T*-cloths.

*ta* 大小扣布 *T*-cloths, all sizes.

*yang* 洋標 *T*-cloths.

*piao* 標 a signal ; a mark.

*yüan* 原粗布 sheetings.

原細斜紋布 jeans and twills.

*ts'u* 粗 coarse.

*yin* 印花布 chintzes, furnitures, and cotton prints.

*su* 素紅布 Turkey red cloths.

*hua* 花剪絨 velvets, velveteens, and fustians.

*chien* 剪 scissors ; to cut with scissors.

*yin* 印花袈裟布 jaconets, cambrics, lawns, and muslins.

*chia* 袈裟布 cambrics and muslins.

*sha* 裟 representing the Indian sound *sha* or *shaya* in 袈裟 *kashaya*, the robe of a Buddhist priest.

*shou* 手 the arm ; the hand.

手帕 handkerchiefs.

*p'a* 帕 a kerchief.

*ta* 打臣 (*ta-ch'ên*, in Cantonese *ta-sun*) dozen.

*pu* 不在列 unclassed ; unenumerated.

*tsai* 在 to be.

2

mien 棉紗 cotton yarn.
棉線 cotton thread.
sha 紗 gauze; untwisted thread.
hsien 線 thread.
jung 絨 silk floss; woollen. [p. 23]
絨毛 wool.
絨毛布 woollen piece goods.
mao 毛 feathers; hair; wool.
yü 羽 feathers; wool.
羽布 alpaca.
ch'uang 床 a bed.
床氈 blankets.
chan 氈 felt; rugs; blankets.
shuang 雙 a pair.
yü 羽綢 bombazettes.
ch'ou 綢 silk cloth; thin silks.
ch'i 旗 a flag.
旗用羽布 bunting.
yung 用 to use.
yü 羽紗 camlets, English; *lit.*, woollen gauze.
羽緞 camlets, Dutch.
tuan 緞 silk cloth; satin; thick silk.
ch'ung 沖 imitated, not genuine; standing for 充 (*ch'ung*), to act as.
沖羽紗 imitation camlets.
ta 大呢 broadcloth; medium cloth.
to 哆囉呢 *(to-lo-ni)* Spanish stripes.
ha 哈喇呢 *(ha-la-ni)* Russian cloth.
fa 法蘭呢 *(fa-lan-ni)* flannel.
ni 呢 woollen cloth.
yü 羽綾 lastings.
ling 綾 thin silk cloth; damask.
yü 羽縐 crape lastings.
chou 縐 a kind of crape.
ch'ung 沖小羽綾 imitation lastings.
pi 嗶嘰 *(pi-chi)* long ells.
hua 花素棉絨布 fancy woollens.
mien 棉絨布 woollen and cotton mixtures. [p. 24]
pan 半絲棉 silk and cotton mixtures.
hsi 細蔴布 linen goods.
fan 帆 a sail; to sail.
帆布 canvas.

t'ung 銅 copper.
t'ieh 鐵 iron.
tsa 雜貨 sundries.
t'ung 銅板 bar copper.
pan 板 a board; boards; planks; bars.
t'ung 銅條 copper rods.
銅片 sheet copper.
p'ien 片 a flat piece of something; a strip; a sheet.
t'ung 銅釘 copper nails.
ting 釘 a nail.
chiu 舊 old.
舊銅 old copper.
kung 鑛 ore; a mine.
鑛銅 copper ore.
shêng 生銅 unmanufactured copper.
t'ung 銅絲 copper wire.
shou 熟銅 manufactured copper.
chi 及 and.
t'ung 銅器 copperware.
t'ieh 鐵條 nail-rod iron.
鐵板 bar iron. [p. 25
鐵片條 hoop iron.
鐵絲 iron wire.
shêng 生鐵磚 pig iron.
chuan 磚 bricks; tiles; flags.
ya 壓 to press.
壓載 ballast.
壓載鐵 kentledge iron.
t'ieh 鐵器 ironware.
shêng 生鐵 unmanufactured iron.
ch'ien 鉛 lead.
鉛塊 lead, in pigs.
k'uai 塊 a piece; a lump.
ch'ien 鉛片 lead, in sheets.
shui 水銀 quicksilver.
pai 白鉛 spelter; zinc.
kang 鋼 steel.
hsi 錫 tin.
錫磚條 tin, in slabs.
ma 馬口鐵 tinplates.
ko 各色 of all kinds. [p. 26
ch'ih 赤糖 brown sugar.

*ping* 梹 the betel-nut; betel-nuts.

梹榔 betel-nuts.

*lang* 榔 betel-nuts.

*mei* 煤 coal.

*tun* 噸 a ton (weight or cubic measure).

*kan* 乾 dry; dried.

乾魚 dried fish.

*yen* 鹽 salt.

鹽魚 salt fish.

*huo* 火 fire.

火石 flint stones.

*shih* 石 a stone.

*jên* 人參 ginseng.

*liang* 粮 grain.

粮食 grain.

*shih* 食 to eat; eatables.

*t'u* 土靛 dried indigo.

*yü* 魚膠 isinglass.

*chiao* 膠 glue.

*tzŭ* 自 self; spontaneous.

自來火 matches; also gaslight.

自來水 water from the waterworks.

*ko* 各羅斯 (*ko-lo-ssŭ*) a gross.

*ho* 盒 a box (as of matches).

*k'ao* 栲 the mangrove tree.

栲皮 mangrove bark.

*chên* 針 needles.

*mi* 宻力 (*mi-li*) a mille.

*kên* 根 classifier of needles, muskets, etc.

*yu* 油 oil.

*huo* 火油 kerosene oil.

*ch'i* 漆 paints.

*hei* 黑椒 black pepper. [p. 27]

*pai* 白椒 white pepper.

*chiao* 椒 pepper.

*sha* 沙 sand.

沙藤 rattans.

*t'êng* 藤 cane; rattan.

*hai* 海菜 agar-agar.

海帶 seaweed.

*tai* 帶 a sash; a girdle.

*t'an* 檀 sandalwood.

檀香 sandalwood.

*su* 蘇 plentiful.

蘇木 sapanwood.

*mu* 木 wood; wooden.

*ying* 硬 hard.

硬木 hard-wood.

*hsiang* 香木 fragrant-wood.

*pao* 鮑 pickled fish.

鮑魚 awabi; shell-fish.

*hsia* 蝦 crabs.

蝦米 shrimps.

*ch'ou* 綢縐 manufactured silks.

*ch'a* 茶 tea.

茶葉 tea (as merchandise).

*yeh* 葉 a leaf.

*wei* 桅 masts; spars.

*la* 蠟 wax.

*chiu* 桕 the tallow tree.

桕油 vegetable tallow.

*po* 玻璃 glass; window glass.

**Document No. 18.** [p. 28

*t'u* 土絲 silk from the Canton district.

*shêng* 生絲 raw silk.

*ching* 經 the warp of a web.

經絲 thrown silk.

*ssŭ* 絲斤 silk (as cargo); *lit.*, "silk catties." Cf. *yen-chin* (鹽斤), salt; *t'ung-chin* (銅斤), copper; *yu-chin* (油斤), oil; *mei-chin* (煤斤), coal. The classifier placed immediately after the noun to which it usually belongs has the force of what in French grammar is called the "article partitif," *e.g.*, *ch'uan san chih* (船三隻), three ships, but *ch'uan-chih* (船隻), "*des* vaisseaux," ships (*see* Document No. 19); *yin ssŭ-liang* (銀四兩), four taels of money, but *yin-liang* (銀兩), "*de l'*argent," money. Similarly, *mi-tan* (米石), rice; *pu-p'i* (布疋), cotton piece goods, cloth (as cargo); *ma-p'i* (馬匹), horses.

*yeh* 野 wild.

野粗絲 wild and coarse silk.

*ch'ou* 綢緞 silk piece goods.

*ssŭ* 絲綫 silk thread.

絲帶 silk sashes; silk ribbons.

*ts'an* 蠶子 silkworms' eggs.
*hung* 紅茶 black tea.
*lü* } *lu* } 綠 green.
綠茶 green tea.
*chuan* 磚茶 brick tea.
*ch'a* 茶末 tea dust.
*mo* 末 the end; ends; leavings; dust.
*ko* 個 a piece (a general classifier).
*chu* 竹 bamboo.
竹竿 bamboo canes.
竹器 bambooware.
*kan* 竿 sticks.
*tou* 荳子 beans. [p. 29]
*kuei* 桂皮 cassia lignea.
*chang* 潭 or 樟 camphor.
樟腦 camphor.
*nao* 腦 brain; camphor.
*yao* 窰 a kiln.
窰器 pottery; earthenware.
*i* 衣 clothes.
衣服 clothing.
*fu* 服 clothes.
*hsüeh* 靴 boots.
靴鞋 boots and shoes.
*hsieh* 鞋 shoes.
*tzŭ* 子 children; seed.
子棉花 seed cotton.
*mien* 棉絮 waste cotton.
*hsü* 絮 refuse cotton or silk.
*yen* 顏 colours.
顏料 dying materials; dye-stuff.
*liao* 料 materials; stuff.
*shan* 扇 fans.
*pa* 把 a classifier of fans and other objects held in the hand.
*p'ao* 炮 used for 爆 *(pao)*, to crackle.
*pao* 爆竹 fire crackers.
*mien* 麪 wheat flour.
麪粉 flour.
*fên* 粉 flour; powder.

*kuo* 果 fruit.
果品 fruit.
*p'in* 品 rank; class; delicacies.
*mu* 木 wood; a tree.
木耳 fungus.
*êrh* 耳 ear.
*hsia* 夏 summer. [p. 30]
夏布 grasscloth.
*mao* 毛 hair.
*ma* 蔴繩索 hemp cordage.
*shêng* 繩 string; cord.
繩索 cordage.
*so* 索 to bind; string; cord.
*p'i* 皮 skins; hides.
*t'i* 蹄 hoofs.
*chiao* 角 horns.
*hsi* 蓆 mats.
蓆子 mats.
*ti* 地 ground.
地蓆 matting.
*yao* 藥材 medicines.
*ts'ai* 材 materials.
*shê* 麝 the musk deer.
麝香 musk.
*t'u* 土布 native cloth; nankeens.
*p'ei* 棓子 nutgalls.
*wu* 五棓子 nutgalls (so called in Tariff).
*t'ung* 銅箔 brass-foil. [p. 31]
*hsi* 錫箔 tin-foil.
*po* 箔 or 鉑 metal leaf; foil.
*chin* 金箔 gold leaf.
*yin* 銀箔 silver leaf.
*mi* 蜜 honey; sweet.
蜜餞 preserves.
*chien* 餞 comfits.
*shih* 食物 provisions; eatables.
*t'êng* 籐竿 rattans.
籐器 rattanware.
*ta* 大黃 rhubarb.
*huang* 黃 yellow.

*hung* 紅花 safflower.

*p'i* 皮貨 skins of all kinds.

*ts'ao* 草 straw.

草帽 straw hats.

草帽辮 straw braid.

*mao* 帽 hats; caps.

*pien* 辮 to plait.

*ping* 氷 ice; crystallised.

氷糖 sugar candy.

*yen* 烟 tobacco; smoke.

烟葉 leaf tobacco.

烟絲 prepared tobacco.

*fên* 粉絲 vermicelli; maccaroni.

*t'o* 駝 a camel.

駝毛 camel's wool.

*yang* 羊 a sheep.

羊毛 sheep's wool.

**Document No. 19.** [p. 32]

*ch'uan* 船隻 vessels.

*chih* 隻 a classifier of ships.

*tun* 噸數 tonnage (amount of).

*fa* 法 law; rule.

法國 (=法蘭西, *fa-lan-hsi*; also 佛蘭西, *fo-lan-hsi*), France; French.

*ho* 荷國 (=荷蘭, *ho-lan*) Holland; the Netherlands; Dutch.

*tan* 丹國 Denmark; Danish.

*jih* 日國 (=日斯巴尼亞, *jih-ssŭ-pa-ni-a*, España), Spain; Spanish.

*nao* 瑙威國 (*nao-wei-kuo*) Norway; Norwegian.

*jui* 瑞敦國 (*jui-tun-kuo*) Sweden; Swedish.

*pi* 比國 (=比利時, *pi-li-shih*), Belgium; Belgian.

*i* 義國 (=意大利, *i-ta-li*), Italy; Italian.

*ha* 哈外意國 (*ha-wai-i-kuo*) Hawaii; Hawaiian.

*chung* 中國 China; Chinese.

*yang* 洋式 foreign type.

*hua* 華式 native (Chinese) type.

*shih* 式 pattern; type.

*wu* 無旗 without flag (as a vessel).

*an* 按年 annually.

*hua* 劃 to cut; to mark; to divide.

劃分 to divide; to distinguish between.

*lun* 輪 a wheel.

輪船 a steamer; steamers.

*p'êng* 篷 a sail.

篷船 a sailing vessel.

*lieh* 列下 enumerated below.

*hsia* 下 below.

**Document No. 20.** [p. 34]

*mou* 某 certain; so-and-so.

某某 so-and-so; such-and-such.

*ching* 經 regular; standing.

經費 standing expenditure; office expenditure (= Customs Account *A*).

*fei* 費 expenditure; a fee; fees.

*ch'uan* 船鈔 tonnage dues; the "Tonnage Dues Account" (=Customs Account *C*).

*fa* 罰 to fine.

罰款 fines [and confiscations] items; account of fines and confiscations (= Customs Account *B*).

*ling* 另款 separate items; "Special Account" (=Customs Account *D*).

[*Note.*—If a series of names, titles, or items of any kind are written side by side, the middle is commonly read before the sides, and the right side before the left side, *e.g.*:

‖ 3 | 1 | 2 ‖; or

‖ 4 | 2 | 1 | 3 ‖; or

‖ 6 | 4 | 2 | 1 | 3 | 5 ‖.]

*ssŭ* 四項清摺 report to Government on "the four kinds" of account, *i.e.*, the Customs Quarterly Abstract Accounts *A*, *B*, *C*, and *D*.

*hsiang* 項 kind; item.

*ju* 入 to enter; to receive; the debit side of an account.

入出數目 "figures showing the debit and credit," *i.e.*, a properly balanced account; an account.

*ch'u* 出 to go out; to give out; to pay; the credit side of an account.

*ju* 入款 receipts; debit; Dr. [p. 35]

*shang* 上結 the preceding quarter.

*ts'un* 存 to keep as a balance.

*chih* 之 a sign of the genitive case. The relation of grammatical dependence which in Western languages is often expressed by placing the noun upon which something else depends in the genitive case is in Chinese expressed by anteposition. This "something else" depending upon a noun may be another noun, or a verb, or even a complete sentence; *e.g.*, 各[1]關[2]監[3]督[4],—[3]*chien*-[4]*tu*, the Superintendents, or [1]*ko*-[2]*kuan*, all the Custom Houses; 存[1]留[2]餘[3]銀[4],—[3]*yü*-[4]*yin*, the balance,

OF ¹tsun-²liu, keeping; i.e., the balance which is or has been kept. This shows how in Chinese the genitive of a verb or of a complete sentence may come to have the force of a relative clause. In either case the force of anteposition may be increased by adding the character 之 (chih); e.g., 各關之監督 ko-kuan chih chien-tu, "the Superintendents of Customs," or 存留之餘銀, tsun-liu chih yü-yin, "the balance which is kept." Such relative clauses, whether formed by anteposition merely, or by anteposition with 之 (chih), may be further enforced by adding the relative pronoun proper, 所 (so); e.g., 所存之餘銀 so tsun chih yü-yin, "the balance which is kept." If this relative clause has its own logical subject, the word denoting it stands before so; e.g., 銀¹ 號² 所³ 存⁴ 之⁵ 餘⁶ 銀⁷,—⁶yü-⁷yin, the balance, ³so ⁵chih (in connexion with anteposition), which, ¹yin-²hao, the Bank, ⁴tsun, keeps or kept: "the balance kept by the Bank." (See so (所), Document No. 2.)

*yü* 餘銀 a balance.

*po* 撥 to set aside for.

撥交 to set aside and hand over; to appropriate.

*pu* 補 to assist.

補發之款 a supplementary grant.

*chih* 支 to pay.

支款 payments; credit; Cr.

*huan* 還 to return; to repay.

*tien* 墊 to advance money.

墊款 advances (in accounts).

*yang* 洋人 a foreigner.

*hua* 華人 a Chinese; a native.

*ko* 各項 all kinds.

*hsin* 薪 fuel.

薪水 a salary; salaries.

*p'an* 盤 to move.

盤運各費 expenditure on account of transport.

*tsu* 租 rent; to rent.

租費 expenditure on account of rent.

*kuan* 關房 Customs property; houses.

*chien* 建 to establish; to construct.

建修費 expenditure on account of construction and purchase (建), and maintenance in repair (修).

*hsiu* 修 to repair.

*kuan* 關船 Customs property; ships.

*yen* 沿 to go along; along. [p. 36]

沿海江巡查 to cruise along the coast and the river; "coast" service.

*hsün* 巡 to cruise.

巡查 to cruise about (as a revenue cruiser).

*ch'ang* 常 constant; ordinary.

常用 in constant use; constantly occurring.

常用雜費 ordinary expenditure.

*tsa* 雜費 miscellaneous expenses.

*ch'êng* 呈准 to apply for and receive permission; by authority.

*chun* 准 to permit.

*t'ê* 特 special; especially.

特用各費 expenses for special use; extraordinary expenditure.

*yung* 用 to use.

*hui* 滙 to exchange (money).

滙兌費 expenses of exchanging and weighing (money); loss by exchange.

*t'i* 提 to submit; to remit (as moneys to I.G.'s account).

提項 remittances (to I.G.), etc.

*ts'un* 存款 a balance.

*ch'êng* 成 a tenth. [p. 37]

*t'ê* 特撥之項 moneys specially set aside; special grants.

*têng* 鐙 a lamp; a light; lights (coast and river).

*fou* 浮 a buoy; buoys.

*chuang* 樁 a beacon; beacons.

*t'a* 塔 a tower; a lighthouse.

*t'ê* 特動之工費 expenditure on account of special works. [p. 38]

*tung* 動 to move; to work; to carry out work.

*kung* 工 work; to work.

*fa* 罰商銀兩 proceeds of fines (collected) from merchants. [p. 39]

罰貨物入官變價 proceeds of confiscated goods sold.

*ju* 入官 to enter the official exchequer; to be confiscated.

*pien* 變 to change.

變價 to dispose of by sale.

*ch'i* 緝 to arrest; to seize.

緝私 to seize smuggled goods.

*ssŭ* 私 clandestinely; to smuggle; smugglers; smuggled goods.

t'i 提歸 to remit for .........

kuei 歸 to revert to; to belong to.

fêng 奉 to receive (from a superior); before the title of a high Government authority denotes the doer of the action implied in the verb following. [p. 41]

ch'ih 飭 to order.

飭撥 to have transferred (as moneys).

ch'uan 船牌 a ship's register.

p'ai 牌 a Government notification; an official permit.

kuan 關照 a sailing letter (for junks).

yin 引 to lead.

引水 a pilot; pilotage.

chang 帳 an account.

chao 招 to seek.

招工 to seek work; to emigrate; emigrant; emigration.

tsê 責 to charge.

責納 to charge a fee.

chuan 專單 a special permit.

kuan 關板 printed by the Customs

pan 板 a board; to print.

shang 商貨全書 the entire books regarding trade (used for "Customs publications").

ch'üan 全 complete.

shou 售 to sell.

售價 proceeds of sale.

ch'ou 酬 to reward.

酬謝 to reward.

hsieh 謝 to thank.

kuan 關船 a Customs cruiser.

chiu 救 to save.

救護 to save; salvage.

hu 護 to protect.

li 利 profit.

利息 interest (on money).

hsi 息 interest (on money).

wei 違 to offend against. [p. 42]

違章 to offend against regulations.

chang 章 regulations.

fa 罰項 moneys received on account of fines.

wei 未能 cannot; impossible.

nêng 能 to be able; capable.

yü 預 to prepare.

預先 beforehand.

hsien 先 before.

lieh 列 to enumerate; to class.

ko 各名 of all denominations.

wei 尾 a tail; what is left behind.

尾數 unsettled items; moneys to be recovered; recoveries.

fên 分 to divide; fractional (as in 三分之一, one third).

tê 得 must; to receive; to obtain.

t'ou 頭 the head; first. [p. 43]

頭等 of the first class.

pang 幫 to assist.

幫辦 an assistant.

### Document No. 21. [p. 44]

fa 罰款案由清摺 a confiscation report.

an 案 a case.

案由 cases and their details.

yu 由 circumstances; details.

fa 罰辦 to decide a case by fine or confiscation. [p. 45]

k'ai 開具 to state.

chü 具 to arrange; to state; to present to.

yü 於後 in the sequel; as follows.

i 以前 before.

以後 after.

chiu 舊 old.

舊案 old cases.

shih 始 first; the first time; then; but until; the beginning.

wan 完 to end; to settle (as an account, a payment, or a case).

chien 件 classifier of 案 (*an*), cases.

wei 未完 not settled; unsettled; outstanding.

tsai 在 in; at; in the written language, generally a preposition of place.

ma 碼 weights; a yard.

碼頭 a jetty; a wharf.

ch'a 查有 there was found to be.

yang 洋行 a foreign firm.

tai 代 for; acting for.

*ch'uan* 川 stands for 四川 (*ssŭ-ch'uan*); from the province of Szechwan.

川羌 *lit.*, Szechwan ginger (a kind of medicine).

川土 Szechwan opium.

川綢 Szechwan silk piece goods.

*ch'iang* 羌 used for 薑=薑 (*chiang*), ginger.

*chung* 重 heavy; weight; weighing.

*ch'a* 查明 to recognise on examination; to find to be.

*shih* 實重 real weight.

*hsi* 係 to be; it is that; this is.

*chia* 假 false.

假報 to make a false report; to fraudulently report.

*hsi* 希 to hope.

希圖 to hope; to anticipate; hoping that.

*t'u* 圖 to plan; to covet.

*to* 多報 to overstate.

多報之數 an amount or quantity overstated; an excess.

*ch'ing* 請領 to receive on application (as a document); to receive.

*ling* 領 to receive.

*fa* 罰繳 to be fined and pay; to pay as a fine.

*chiao* 繳 to hand over; to pay.

*ying* 應稅 liable to duty; dutiable. [p. 46]

*tung* 東 east; eastern.

東洋 the eastern sea; Japan; Japanese.

*chi* 即 then; thereupon; marks sequence, and is therefore used in introducing the apodosis after the protasis in a conditional, temporal, etc., clause; *e.g.*, if it rains, [*then*] he goes; when it rained, [*then*] he went. In either sentence *chi* may appear in the place of the English *then*. But this particle is also used after single nouns and single verbs, as if we were to say: rain, *then* he goes; rain falling, *then* he goes; *e.g.*, *nien-t'ieh chi ch'ê* (粘貼即扯) "pasting on then it is torn off," which means "placards will be removed," an inscription often seen on the walls at street corners. The following particles are similarly used: *tsê* (則), *tsai* (再), *fang* (方), *pien* (便), *jêng* (仍), *ch'ê* (輒), and *chiu* (就); the last word is colloquial.

*tz'ŭ* 次 second.

次日 the following day.

*shao* 少報 to declare short; to understate.

*ying* 應完正稅 the full duty due.

*pei* 倍 ...... fold, as 五倍 fivefold or five times.

*hsia* 下等參 crude ginseng.

*shih* 實係 to be in reality; to prove to be.

*chien* 揀 to select.

揀淨 to sort; to clarify.

*ching* 淨 to clean.

*hsü* 鬚 a beard; fine (hairy) ginseng.

*mei* 美國揀淨參鬚 American clarified ginseng.

*yen* 驗貨廠 a Customs examination shed.

*ch'ang* 廠 an open shed; a yard.

*kan* 乾花 dried flowers.

*ying* 應值 liable to be valued at ......

*ch'u* 初 first; placed before the first 10 dates of the month (as 初捌日, the eighth). [p. 47]

*yü* 玉 jade.

玉石 jadestone.

*yüan* 原 original.

原報 originally declared.

*chia* 加 to add.

加增 to add.

*tsêng* 增 to add.

*ho* 合 to unite; in all; total.

*kou* 購 to buy.

購買 to buy.

*mai* 買 to buy.

*fu* 復 again.

*an* 按照 according to; at.

*shih* 實估之價 the true value.

*shu* 贖 to redeem; to re-buy.

贖回 to re-buy; to buy back.

*hui* 回 to return; back.

*mu* 木耳 fungus; agaric.

*yü* 與 with; to.

*pu* 不符 to disagree.

*fu* 符 to agree, to tally.

*ch'üan* 全貨之數 the complete amount of goods; the whole lot.

*chêng* 正半兩稅 the full and half duty.

*tuan* 緞 satin.

*ch'ou* 綢 silk piece goods.

*wei* 未經 not yet; not having.

未經完稅 not having paid the duty.

*nieh* 揑 to work up; to feign.

揑報 a false report; to make a false report.

*i* 已 sign of the past; having (the opposite of 未 *(wei)*, not having).

已完稅 having paid duty; duty paid.

*fa* 罰充入官 to be punished by confiscation; to be confiscated.

*ch'ung* 充 to fill; to act; to become.

充公 to become public property; to be confiscated.

*ssŭ* 私下 to ship (goods) clandestinely; to ship without a permit. [p. 48]

*hsia* 下 to ship.

*pei* 被 to suffer; sign of the passive, when the word denoting the doer of an action stands between *pei* and the verb following.

被本關查拏 is, was, etc., seized by this office.

被 … 拏 to be seized.

*ch'a* 查拏 to search and seize; to seize.

*na* 拏 to take; to seize (as smuggled goods).

*shih* 寔 this; that.

寔日 that day; the same date.

*i* 議 to decide.

*yen* 延 to delay; to protract.

延未繳銀 to delay payment.

*jih* 日久 a long time; after a long time.

*chiu* 久 a long time.

*huai* 壞 to spoil.

壞爛 to spoil (as fruit).

*lan* 爛 over-ripe (as fruit); rotten.

*wu* 無從 there is no way to ..........; there is no opportunity to ........

*hua* 華客 a Chinese passenger.

*k'o* 客 a stranger; a travelling merchant; a passenger.

*ch'a* 查出 to find out; to discover.

*hsia* 下船 to ship.

*kuan* 關照船 a registered junk.

關剝船 a registered cargo-boat.

*kou* 勾 to be connected with.

勾通 in connexion with; in collusion with.

*ch'uan* 船主 a ship's captain.

*chu* 主 a master; the owner (as of goods).

*i* 已下船 having been shipped.

*ti* 抵 to substitute.

抵換 to exchange.

*huan* 換 to exchange.

*lou* 簍 a basket.

*ch'üan* 全數 completely.

*huang* 黃浦河 the river Whangpoo, at Shanghai.

*ho* 河 a river.

河面 the river surface; on the river.

*kao* 高麗 *(kao-li)* Corea; Corean.

*pu* 不即 ..... 而 forthwith not to ....., but to .....; instead of ..... (doing this), ..... (doing that).

*êrh* 而 and; but; yet. Cf. *êrh* 而 in Document No. 38, p. 68.

*yün* 運回 to send back; to remove.

*chan* 棧 a godown.

*i* 意 to think; intention.

意圖 to intend; to plan.

*t'a* 他 another; other.

他貨 other goods.

*huo* 貨主 the owner (of goods).

*ting* 訂 to fix; to settle.

*chien* 減 to diminish.

減價 a cheap price; a reduced price.

*shui* 水手 a sailor. [p. 49]

*shou* 手 hand; arm; a "hand"; a working man.

*wei* 違禁 offending against prohibitory rules; prohibited.

違禁貨物 prohibited goods; contraband.

*chin* 禁 to prohibit.

*ch'iang* 槍 used for 鎗 *(ch'iang)*, a musket.

槍子 cartridges.

*huo* 火 fire.

火藥 gunpowder.

*ho* 盒 a box; a canister.

*ts'ang* 藏 to conceal.

藏匿 to conceal.

*ni* 匿 to conceal.

*sung* 送 to send.

送交 to send to; to hand over to.

*ch'u* 儲 to lay up for need; to store.

儲庫 to store up in an armoury.

*k'u* 庫 a depôt; a treasury; an armoury.

*kou* 購 to buy.
購用 to buy for one's own use.
*chi* 寄 to send.
*po* 駁 to tranship.
駁船 a cargo-boat.
*hang* 行主 the head of a firm.
*hsien* 現 now.
現已 now having; now being; sign of the perfect tense.
現已撤銷 having been cancelled; cancelled.
*ch'ê* 撤 to remove; to set aside.
撤銷 to cancel; to expire.
*hsiao* 銷 to melt; to cancel.
*po* 撥運 to tranship; to carry goods (as in a cargo-boat).
*shang* 尚 still; yet.
尚未 not yet.
*liao* 了 to finish.
了結 to settle (as a case).
*pu* 不識姓名 unknown by name.
*chih* 識 to know.
*hsing* 姓 a surname.
姓名 the surname and personal name; the full name of a person.
*ming* 名 a personal name.
*ssŭ* 私鑄 to clandestinely cast; to make counterfeit coin.
*chu* 鑄 to cast (as coin).
*t'ung* 銅錢 copper cash.
*ch'ing* 傾 to melt.
傾鎔 to melt.
*yung* 鎔 to melt.
*ch'ien* 錢莊 a cash shop; a money-changer's.
*chuang* 莊 a cottage; a shop.
*wei* 未領執照 without a license; without a bond certificate.
*wên* 文 a cash; a copper cash.
*ssŭ* 私運進口 to import clandestinely.
*tan* 擔 a picul. [p. 50]
*ch'êng* 呈交 to hand in at an office; to present (as a document).
*yün* 運米執照 a special certificate for the transport of rice.
*yüan* 原照 the original certificate.

*ssŭ* 私自 clandestinely and without authority.
*kai* 改 to alter.
改爲 to alter into (as one reading of a document to another).
*tzŭ* 字 a written character.
字樣 style; phrase; "the words" ............ in a document.
*pang* 幫買辦 a comprador's assistant.
*mai* 買辦 a comprador.
*ssŭ* 私起 to land clandestinely.
*ch'i* 起 to land; to discharge (as cargo).
*shih* 示 to make known; a proclamation.
示禁 prohibited by proclamation; forbidden by Government.
*wei* 圍 to surround; here standing for 闈 *(wei)*, "the side doors of the palace where candidates once underwent their examination" (WILLIAMS); the public literary examinations.
圍姓票 Wei-sing lottery tickets. The *Wei-hsing*, or "literary examination surnames," lottery is a kind of gambling or betting on the surnames of successful candidates. Like all gambling, it is forbidden by law, and when the prohibition is enforced, its tickets are liable to seizure.
*p'iao* 票 a ticket; a lottery ticket; a pawn ticket, etc.; *e.g.*, *fa-ts'ai p'iao* (發財票), a lottery ticket; *lü-sung p'iao* (呂宋票), a Manila (lottery) ticket.
*chang* 張 a sheet; a classifier of lottery tickets.
*yüan* 元 (=圓) a dollar.
*yin* 銀票 a money order; a bank note.
*ssŭ* 司事之人 an officer on duty; a managing man.
*hui* 賄 to bribe.
賄買 to bribe; to purchase by bribing.
*fang* 放 to release.
放行 to release; to let go.
*i* 一 one; the same; at the same time; together.
一併 altogether; the whole.
*ping* 併 (=並) and; both; with; altogether.
*hsiao* 銷燬 to destroy by fire; to cancel by burning.
*hui* 燬 to burn.
*yi* 易換 to exchange (as a bank note against cash).
*t'ing* 停 to stop; to anchor.
停船界 the harbour limits.
*chieh* 界 a limit; a boundary.
*t'ê* 特發准單 a special permit.

*cha* 炸 to blow up; to explode.

炸火藥 dynamite.

*shu* 數 several.

*shan* 擅 without authority.

擅行 ...... to [*verb*] without authority.

*hsing* 行 to do; placed before verbs to denote action.

*tao* 到 to arrive.

到口 to arrive in port; to enter port.

*hsia* 下錨 to lower the anchors; to anchor.

*mao* 錨 an anchor.

*shan* 舢 a small boat.

舢板 a sampan.

*nü* 女 a woman.

*shang* 上船 to board a ship.

*hsin* 信 a letter. [p. 51]

信局 a postal agency.

*ssŭ* 絲線帽頂 cap buttons of twisted silk thread.

*mao* 帽 a hat; a cap.

帽頂 the top of a thing; a cap button.

*ting* 頂 the crown of the head; the top.

*hsin* 信袋 a letter-bag.

*yung* 傭 to hire (as a workman).

傭役 a coolie hired for work.

*yi* 役 a low employé; a servant.

*shih* 食 to eat.

食鹽 salt (ready for use).

*yen* 鹽 salt.

*hsiang* 詳 to state in detail.

*shu* 署 a public office; to act for another; acting.

署理 to act for another; acting; officiating.

*tso* 左 the left side; the senior of two deputies where only two are employed.

*yu* 右 the right side; the junior of two deputies where only two are employed.

*i* 一等 (= 頭等) of the first class.

*pao* 寶 precious.

寶星 an order; the Chinese order of the *Pao-hsing*.

*hsing* 星 a star.

### Document No. 22. [p. 52]

*chin* 謹 respectful.

謹稟 respectfully petitioning.

*ping* 稟 a communication from an inferior to a superior; a petition; to petition.

*ta* 大人 an honorary title given to officials of, and above, the third class of rank.

*t'ai* 臺下 a title of respect; your honour.

*yin* 因 on account of; to cause.

*wan* 完婣 to marry.

*yin* 婣 (= 姻) a bride.

*ch'ing* 請假 to apply for leave.

*chia* 假 leave of absence.

*hsi* 西歷 western calendar; according to the foreign calendar.

*li* 歷 a calendar.

This character stands for 曆 (*li*)—a calendar, a succession of years,—which occurs in the personal name (*shêng hui* 聖諱) of one of the Emperors of the present dynasty, and is therefore avoided in official correspondence. According to Chinese ideas, it would show want of respect towards the sacred person of an Emperor if a character occurring in his personal name were used in its profane meaning, and it has become customary to substitute either another character of the same meaning or to slightly alter the shape of the character prohibited, unless special orders to the contrary are on record. The characters belonging to imperial names of the present dynasty, and therefore to be avoided in documents, are given below, together with the equivalents usually substituted for them:—

| Characters prohibited. | Characters substituted. |
|---|---|
| 玄 *hsüan*..... | In certain combinations the last stroke is omitted, *e.g.*, 眩 (*hsüan*); it appears, however, in 畜 (*ch'u*) and its compounds. Otherwise, 元 (*yüan*) is used as a substitute. |
| 燁 *hsü* ....... | 燁 (*hsü*), the last stroke of the full character being omitted. |
| 胤 *ying*...... | 亂 (*ying*), the first stroke being omitted, or 允 (*yün*). |
| 禛 *chêng*..... | 禎 (*chêng*). |
| 弘 *hung* ..... | 弘 (*hung*); later, 宏 (*hung*). In certain combinations 强 (*chiang*) is used for 強 (*chiang*). |
| 曆 *li* ......... | 歷 or 厯 (*li*). |
| 顒 *yung*...... | 顒 (*yung*), the two last strokes of the full character being omitted. |
| 琰 *yen* ....... | 琰 (*yen*). |
| 旻 *min* ...... | 旻 (*min*); later, 緜 (*mien*). |
| 寧 *ning*...... | 寍 or 甯 (*ning*). |
| 詝 *chu*........ | 詝 (*chu*), the last stroke of the full character being omitted. |
| 淳 *shun*...... | 湻 (*shun*). |
| 湉 *tien*....... | 湉 (*tien*), the last stroke of the full character being omitted. |

According to an Imperial Edict of 1846, the first character in an Emperor's personal name is to remain unaltered, and merely the second character is to be slightly altered (*see*

"Translation of the Peking Gazette for 1875," p. 9). Authorities seem to disagree on some of the details regarding this question.

*fu* 伏 to submit; respectfully.
伏希 to respectfully hope.

*ho* 核准 to examine into and allow; *i.e.*, to take a petition into favourable consideration.

*shih* 施 to bestow.
施行 to grant that it be so; to comply with a petition.

*tsai* 再 again.
再者 further; in addition to this, it has to be stated that.

*ch'ien* 前次 on a former occasion; on former occasions.

*yu* 又 moreover; and.

*wei* 未經 have not; has not.

*tao* 到關 to come to the Custom House; to attend at the (Customs) Office.

### Document No. 23. [p. 52]

*chü* 具 to prepare; to present.
具稟人 petitioner.

*k'ên* 懇 to beg.
懇請 to beg; to petition.

*chi* 給假 to grant leave of absence.

*ch'ieh* 竊 a thief; a term of modesty denoting the writer of a document addressed to a superior, as "my humble self"; it is frequently followed by the personal name *(ming)* of the petitioner, or by some other term of modesty, written in smaller characters.

*tsao* 造 to make.
造冊處 the Statistical Department of the Inspectorate General of Customs.

*ts'ê* 冊 statistical, etc., tables.

*ch'u* 處 a place; a public office.

*ch'ung* 充當 to fill the post of.

*tang* 當 to suit; right; proper; to act as.

*yin* 印字 to print characters; to print.
印字之役 a printing-office employé.

*chin* 進工 to join work; to enter an employment.

*hsi* 迄 till.
迄今 till the present.

*li* 歷 a succession of.
歷年 for a number of years; in the lapse of years.

*wei* 未曾 have not; has not.

*tsêng* 曾 a sign of the past.

*kao* 告 to tell; to announce; to ask for.
告假 to ask for leave of absence.

*hsüan* 旋 to revolve; to come back to.
旋里 to return to one's home.

*li* 里 a hamlet; a village; one's native village; a Chinese mile.

*chieh* 接 to receive.
接來 to receive.

*chia* 家 a family; one's home.
家書 or 家信 a home letter.

*ts'ui* 催 to urge.

*su* 速 quick; at once.

*hui* 回家 to return home.

*wan* 完娶 to marry.

*ch'ü* 娶 to marry.

*ku* 故 to cause; therefore.

*kan* 敢 to dare; to venture.

*mao* 冒 to make bold.
冒瀆 to venture troubling (as a superior with a petition).

*tu* 瀆 to trouble another (as with a petition).

*t'ai* 臺前 a title of respect; your honour.

*ch'iu* 求 to ask; to pray.

*ên* 恩 favour; kindness.
恩准 to kindly grant.

*pei* 俾 so that.
俾得 so that I may; so as to enable.

*wan* 完婚 to marry.

*hun* 婚 to marry.

*t'o* 妥 safe; proper.
妥理 to safely arrange; to regulate; to manage.

*yao* 要 must; important.
要務 important business.

*tsê* 則 then; a particle of inference, marking the apodosis of a sentence (see *chi* 即, Document No. 21, p. 46).

*tai* 戴 to wear on the head; to uphold.
戴德 to uphold virtue; *i.e.*, to do a matter conscientiously.

*mi* 靡 not; without.
靡涯 without limit; endless.

*ai* 涯 a shore; a limit.

*i* 矣 a final particle, denoting the close of a sentence.

新關文件録



*wei* 未士 in Cantonese pronounced Mi-sze; the pidgin-English word for Mister, Mr.

*tai* 代呈 to state on behalf of another.

*t'ai* 臺電 a term of respect; your honour.

*tien* 電 lightning; electric; glance (used in certain terms of respect).

**Document No. 24.** [p. 53]

*hung* 紅單 a port clearance. The port clearance of earlier days was a formidable-looking document of yellow paper, and ornamented with curling dragons. Its large vermilion seals obtained for it the name of *hung p'ai* (紅牌), or red permit; *Anglicè*, "grand chop" (WILLIAMS). The present name, *hung tan*, may apparently be similarly explained.

*chiang* 江南海關 the Shanghai Customs (see *chiang* 江 in Document No. 1, p. 1).

*su* 蘇松太 the three departments of Su-chou-fu (蘇 *su*), Sung-chiang-fu (松 *sung*), and T'ai-ts'ang-chou (太 *t'ai*), forming the circuit in charge of the Taot'ai at Shanghai.

*chêng* 徵 to levy.

徵收 to levy; to collect.

*tang* 當 (= 當時), at the time; at that time.

*ts'un* 遵 to obey; to comply with.

遵照 in compliance with.

*t'iao* 條 a paragraph; an article (as of a Treaty).

條約 an agreement containing a number of articles; a Treaty.

*yüeh* } *yo* } 約 to agree; a Treaty.

*chang* 章程 regulations.

*ch'êng* 程 regulations; a pattern.

*chi* 計噸科鈔 to calculate the tonnage dues from the tonnage.

*k'o* 科 to calculate from.

*an* 按貨科稅 to calculate duties on the goods carried.

*ling* 令 to order; to let.

*tzŭ* 自赴 to proceed in person to.

*ch'ing* 清楚 to clear an account.

*ch'u* 楚 properly finished.

*ch'êng* 呈驗 to present for examination.

*ping* 稟請 to apply for.

*ch'ien* 前來 to have come forward; to have come to hand (as a despatch, a report, etc.) These two words frequently follow the mention of a document received, or its tenor.

*t'ien* 填 to fill up (as the blank spaces in a printed form).

填發 to fill up and issue; to make out (as a document).

*chi* 訖 to finish; to clear off (as an account); after a verb it often has the force of a sign of the past; also used for 迄 (*hsi*), till.

*shou* 收訖 having received; having been received; payments being cleared.

收訖紅單 a certificate showing that [duties] have been received; a clearance certificate.

收執 to receive and hold (as a document); to be placed in one's hands.

*pien* 編 to arrange in order; registered under No............

*ch'ao* 鈔餉 tonnage dues.

*ling* 另照 having a separate certificate.

*t'ung* 通共 total.

**Document No. 25.** [p. 54]

*shou* 收稅單 a duty-paid certificate.

*chih* 置買 to buy.

*hou* 後開 enumerated hereafter; under-mentioned.

*i* 已經 a sign of the past; "having already."

*shui* 稅餉 duty.

*hsiang* 餉 a duty.

*chuang* 裝載 to load (as a ship); to contain.

*hsiao* 銷售 to sell off; to sell.

*shui* 稅項 a duty class; duties.

*wai* 外洋口 a port across the sea; a seaport; here, at the port of destination (Shanghai).

*pu* 不准 not allowed; forbidden.

*tso* 作 before verbs, like *hsing* (行), denoting action.

作抵 to substitute; to tender in lieu of (as duties of one kind for those of another kind).

*ti* 抵 to substitute; to oppose.

*pieh* 別 another.

別口 another port.

*t'ung* 通商別口 a non-Treaty port.

*shui* 稅課 duties.

*k'o* 課 taxes; duties.

*shêng* 生牛皮 cow hides.

*chu* 猪 a pig.

猪鬃 pigs' bristles.

*tsung* 鬃 (= 騣 *tsung*) bristles.

*mien* 棉羊褥 cotton and woollen mattresses.

*ju* 褥 a mattress; bedding.

*pao* 包 a bundle; a package.

*chang* 張 a sheet; classifier of mats, bed sheets, mattresses, etc.

*yu* 右 the right; after a document; the above.

右照 the above certificate.

*hsien* 限 a limit; to limit; to regard as a limit; hence, as a preposition, "on (such and such a day) as a limit."

限到口日 on the date of arrival in port; *i.e.*, neither sooner nor later than on date of arrival.

**Document No. 26.** **[p. 55]**

*chêng* 正半稅單 a full and half duty-paid certificate (for River ports).

*hu* 湖 a lake.

湖北 (*hu-pei*) the province of Hu-peh.

*han* 漢黃德 the three departments of Han-yang-fu (漢 *han*), Huang-chou-fu (黃 *huang*), and Tê-an-fu (德 *tê*), forming the circuit in charge of the Taot'ai at Hankow.

*an* 案查 whereas.

*ch'ang* 長江 the Yangtze river.

長江續共章程 the Revised Yangtze Trade Regulations.

*nei* 內開 it is stated in......

*chün* 均 all; equally.

*ko* 各該關 all the said Custom Houses.

*chêng* 征收 to collect (as duties).

*i* 已開 having been opened; opened; open (as the Treaty ports).

*k'ai* 開 to open (as a port).

*têng* 等因 such arguments; "and the like arguments;" "etc.," closing a quotation. The following expressions are similarly used: 等由 *(têng yu)*; 等情 *(têng ch'ing)*, "such circumstances"; 等事 *(têng shih)*, "such matters." When the words used by another writer (or speaker) are quoted, the quotation is closed by adding the words 等語 *(têng yü)*, "such words"; if an accusation is the subject of the quotation, by adding the words 等詞 *(têng tz'ŭ)*, "such charges"; after an enumeration of malpractices or nuisances we often find the words 等弊 *(têng pi)*, "such malpractices." Such concluding phrases need not be translated; they simply show that a quotation or an enumeration of arguments, circumstances, facts, charges, malpractices, etc., is concluded, and correspond to what in English writing is expressed by inverted commas.

*han* 漢 Hankow.

*chih* 置辦 to buy.

*chi* 給予 to give; to grant.

*yü* 予 to give; to grant.

*ch'êng* 呈繳 to present (as a document at an office).

*shou* 收執 to receive and hold.

*tan* 單貨不得相離 "this document is to accompany the goods which it covers;" the document is not to be separated from the goods.

*hsiang* 相 mutually; each other.

相離 to take the one away from the other.

*li* 離 to take away; to part.

*yeh* 業 a sign of the past: have, has.

業已 a sign of the past: have, has.

*pai* 百拾 hundreds and tens. These characters, as well as 萬 *(wan)* and 千 *(ch'ien)* (*see* the two last columns on p. 55), are sometimes printed in forms, in order to have the space before them filled up when necessary. In the present case there were no figures to be filled in, so that the two characters are here without meaning. Note that the figures following on the right side and corresponding to *chêng* (正), above, denote the full, *i.e.*, the Export, Duty; those on the left side, corresponding to *pan* (半), the half, *i.e.*, the Coast Trade, Duty.

*ju* 如 if.

*ho* 核錯 to discover a mistake.

*ts'o* 錯 wrong; an error.

*ch'ing* 請 to request; you are requested to; please.

*kêng* 更 to alter.

更正 to correct.

**Document No. 27.** **[p. 56]**

*i* 已完正稅憑單 a "certificate (proof) showing that full duty has been paid."

*p'ing* 憑單 a duty proof.

*chê* 浙江 (*chê-chiang*) the province of Chêkiang.

*fên* 分巡 to inspect several districts respectively (used in the title of a Taot'ai; *see* MAYERS' "The Chinese Government," No. 280.)

*ning* 甯紹台 the three departments of Ning-po-fu (*ning* 甯), Shao-hsing-fu (*shao* 紹), and T'ai-chou-fu (*t'ai* 台), forming the circuit in charge of the Taot'ai at Ningpo.

*hsing* 行准 to receive (as a despatch).

*tzŭ* 咨 a despatch; to address in a despatch.

*yü* 預 to prepare; beforehand.

*ch'êng* 呈交 to tender; to present; to pay (as duties).

*tsai* 再 again.

*fêng* 奉遵 to receive instructions.

*tsai* 在案 "it is on record;" "as records show;" a concluding phrase showing that the facts stated are on official record; it need not be translated.

*tsêng* 曾經 a sign of the past: have, has, had.

*tai* 帶 to carry.

帶有 to carry; to be provided with.

*tang* 當 at the time; then; in due course.

當已 (=當經 *tang ching*) at the time; then; in due course.

*chao* 照完 to pay in accordance with (viz., the proper rate; as Coast Trade Duties, which represent half the full rate).

*jêng* 仍 again; still; yet.

*pu* 不合銷 not all sold (as goods).

*hsia* 下入船 to ship.

*têng* 等情 such matters; "etc.;" marking the end of a quotation. Cf. *têng yin* 等因 in Document No. 26, p. 55.

*hsiang* 相符 to agree; to tally.

*fa* 發還存票 to issue drawback in exchange (for duty paid).

*kuo* 過 after a verb, a sign of the past: have, has, having.

*p'ing* 憑據 a written guarantee; evidence; proof.

*huang* 黃連(=黃蓮) a kind of dye-stuff.

**Document No. 28.** [p. 57]

*mien* 免重徵執照 a certificate exempting from levying duty a second time; an exemption certificate.

*chih* 執照 a certificate.

*yü* 欲 to wish; about to; also a sign of the future tense.

*kai* 改運別口售賣 to change the destination [of goods] to another port of sale.

*chê* 者 after a verb, has the force of a participle or a relative pronoun (cf. Document No. 14, p. 17); *shou mai* (售賣), to sell; *shou-mai-chê* (售賣者), the selling ones, or, those who sell. Such a phrase may be preceded by a noun, *e.g.*, *shang-jên shou-mai-chê* (商人售賣者), which means "those of the merchants who sell," or "such merchants as may sell." In the present case translate "such merchants who, having paid all duties on their goods (imported), may wish to send the same for sale to another port."

*yen* 驗明 to ascertain (by examining).

*yüan* 原包 original package.

原貨 original goods.

*ti* 底簿 to enter in a book; a book entry.

*pu* 簿 a register; a ledger; an account book.

*ping* 並未 not by any means. All negative particles—*pu* (不), *wu* (無), *wei* (未), etc.—may be reinforced by the addition of certain words, which need not be translated except where it seems necessary to emphasise negation, *e.g.*, when they correspond to English "by no means," "not at all," etc. The following words and expressions are often so employed: *ping* (並), *tuan* (斷), *ch'ien* (千), *wan* (萬), *ch'ien wan* (千萬), *hao* (毫), *ssŭ hao* (絲毫), *chüeh* (決), *chüeh* (絕), *ch'ieh* (切), *tsung* (總), *chung* (終), *ch'iung* (迥), *ching* (竟).

*ch'ai* 拆 to break open.

拆動 to tamper with; to open (as packages under bond).

*tung* 動 to move; to change; to meddle with.

*ch'ou* 抽 to take out; to levy (as duties).

抽換 to take out and change (as goods from original packages).

*huan* 換 to change; to substitute one for another.

*wei* 為此 on account of this [matter].

*chi* 給照 to issue a certificate.

*ch'êng* 呈照 to deliver a certificate.

*chao* 照貨相符 certificate and goods agreeing; if the goods are found to agree with the certificate covering them.

*niu* 鈕 buttons.

鈕扣 brass buttons.

*k'ou* 扣 standing for 釦, a round or chased button.

*pei* 北船 a northern vessel; *i.e.*, a vessel trading to the North of China.

*wan* 完過 has paid; having paid (duty).

**Document No. 29.** [p. 58]

*ch'uan* 船鈔執照 a tonnage dues certificate.

*fan* 凡 every; whenever; if.

*ping* 並 and; or.

*ti* 地方 a place. This noun is frequently added to local names, and it need not then be translated.

*ping* 稟明 to inform in a petition; to apply to.

*chuan* 專照 a special certificate.

*i* 以, *lit.*, to use; it is sometimes employed like *chiang* (將), in marking the object of a verb, when the verb follows, as in the classical example *i-t'ien-hsia yü jên* (以天下與人), "to give the empire to man;" but in the business style such accusatives more frequently follow the verb, *e.g.*, *chiao i han shu* (教以漢書), "to teach Chinese literature," *chia i hsing-ho* (加以刑嚇), "to inflict torture." It most frequently occurs in connexion with a second object, as in 以[1]多[2]報[3]少[4] [3]*pao*, to declare, [1]*i* [2]*to*, much, or a large quantity, as [4]*shao*, little, or a small quantity; especially so in the phrase *i* ...... *wei* ...... (以 ...... 爲 ......), to consider ...... as ......, "to treat ...... as," etc.; *e.g.*, *i ch'i wei ch'ieh* (以妻爲妾), "to treat a wife as a concubine."

以 ...... 爲 ...... to consider ...... as ......

以四個月爲期 to consider four months as a limit; *i.e.*, within the limit of four months.

*ch'i* 期 a limit of time; a fixed period.

*yü* 逾 to exceed (as a limit).

*ling* 另 separately; besides; again.

*i* 以內 inside of; within. Similarly, *i wai* (以外), outside; *i ch'ien* (以前), before; *i hou* (以後), after; *i shang* (以上), above; *i hsia* (以下), below; *i pei* (以北), to the north of, etc.

*tien* 電線 an electric wire; a telegraph; telegraphic.

電線行 a telegraph company.

### Document No. 30. [p. 59]

*hu* 護 to protect.

護照 a passport.

*pu* 布政使 a provincial treasurer or Fant'ai.

*ch'ang* 常鎮通海 the four departments of Ch'ang-chou-fu (常 *ch'ang*), Chên-chiang-fu (鎮 *chên*), T'ung-chou (通 *t'ung*), and Hai-mên-t'ing (海 *hai*), forming the circuit in charge of the Taot'ai at Chinkiang.

*chên* 鎮江 (*chên-chiang*) Chinkiang.

*tsung* 總辦 to superintend; a chief manager.

*hai* 海防支應局 the "Coast Defence Office" at Tientsin.

*chuan* 轉 to transmit.

轉准 to receive a document for further transmission.

*pao* 保定 the department of Pao-ting-fu, in Chihli.

*hsiu* 修志局 a commission for preparing a new edition of the provincial, etc., archives (*chih* 志).

*chieh* 解 to forward.

*shu* 書價開單 a list in which the price of books is stated; a list of books purchased; an invoice of books.

*hsü* 續 additional.

續購書籍 to buy additional books.

*shu* 書籍 books.

*chi* 籍 lists; books.

*chuan* 專人 to send a special messenger.

*chin* 金陵 (*chin-ling*) book name of the city of Nanking.

*ling* 陵 imperial tombs.

*huai* 淮 the river Huai.

淮南 (*huai-nan*), *lit.*, south of the Huai River; *i.e.*, the city of Huai-an-fu, in Kiangsu.

*kuan* 官書局 a provincial government printing office.

*chên* 鎮 (=鎮江) Chinkiang.

*hu* 滬 Shanghai.

*ching* 津 (=天津) Tientsin.

*tzŭ* 咨請 to request in a despatch.

*fang* 放 to release.

*tung* 董 (=董事) a senior employé; an expert.

*lien* 連 to connect; to take all together; with.

*chi* 給護 to grant a passport.

*ching* 經過 to pass; to come across (*en route*).

*yen* 沿途 on the road.

*t'u* 途 a road.

*kuan* 關卡 barriers.

*ch'ia* / *ka* } 卡 a barrier.

*i* 以免 in order to avoid; so as not to; the opposite of *i pien* (以便), in order to.

*tsu* 阻 to impede.

阻滯 to obstruct; to stop; obstruction; stoppage.

*chih* 滯 to obstruct.

### Document No. 31. [p. 60]

*wên* 文 a despatch; an official letter.

*k'ai* 開 to state; stating; "to the effect that."

*fan* 凡遇 whenever.

*yü* 遇 to meet; to happen; happening; whenever.

*kuan* 官員 Government officers.

*yüan* 員 a classifier of officers; an officer.

*kuo* 過關 to pass a Custom House.

*chao* 照例 according to rule; in accordance with, *i.e.*, not contrary to, regulations.

*sui* 隨 to follow; together with.

隨帶 to carry with one's person.

*ping* 並無 not by any means. Cf. *ping wei* 並未, p. 57.

*yin* 印照 a sealed certificate; a passport; a bond certificate.

*chu* 註 a commentary; to explain.

註明 to enter in a document; to state by way of explanation.

*hsiang* 箱隻 boxes. Cf. *ssŭ chin* 絲斤, p. 28.

*chih* 隻 a classifier of boxes.

*wu* 物件 packages.

*fang* 方 then. Cf. *chi* 卽, p. 46.

*shun* 順天府 the department of Shun-t'ien-fu, in Chihli.

*wên* 文安縣 the district of Wên-an-hsien, in Shun-t'ien-fu.

*lin* 廩 a government granary.

廩生 a literary title: an expectant *chü-jên* (*see* MAYERS' "The Chinese Government," No. 470).

*ping* 稟稱 to state in a petition.

*ch'êng* 稱 to state.

*chieh* 屆 a limit; a set time; "the time has come for" or "this is the time of."

*jên* 壬午 (*jên wu*) the 19th year of a cycle, *e.g.*, the year 1882 (*see* MAYERS' "Chinese Reader's Manual," pp. 362, 363).

*k'o* 科 the examination for the two highest degrees.

科鄉試 the triennial examination.

*hsiang* 鄉 a village; a community consisting of a number of villages.

鄉試 the triennial examination.

*shih* 試 to examine; examination; to try.

*shih* 馳 to hasten; to proceed to.

馳赴 to proceed to.

*pei* 北闈 the northern side door of an examination hall; *fig.*, the examination for *chü-jên*.

*wei* 闈 the door of an examination hall; hence, examination for a degree generally (see *wei* 圍, Document No. 21, p. 50).

*ying⁴* 應 to answer; to respond to.

應試 to respond to the call for examination; to report for examination.

*ying* 營 military; a camp.

營汛 a guard house.

*hsün* 汛 a guard house.

*hsing* 幸 please; you are requested to.

幸勿 please do not; you are requested not to.

*liu* 留 to detain.

留難 to raise difficulties by detention.

*nan* 難 difficult; to make difficulties.

*ch'ieh* 切 urgent.

切切 very urgent.

*shu* 書箱 books in boxes. Cf. *i-hsiang* 衣箱, clothes in boxes, p. 17.

*hua* 花 flowers; painted or carved ornaments.

花板 ornamented boards.

*fu* 副 a set; sets.

*ling* 零星 odds and ends.

*shih* 什 ten; sundry; miscellaneous.

什物 sundries.

*ch'ien* 前途 on the road; ahead on one's road.

*kuan* 關津 guard houses at fords.

*chin* / *ching* } 津 a ford; a ferry.

*ch'ia* / *k'a* } 卡隘 Customs barriers.

*ai* 隘 a pass; straits.

### Document No. 32. [p. 61]

*mien* 免照 an exemption certificate (see also *mien ch'ung-chêng chih-chao* 免重徵執照 in Document No. 28, p. 57); here, a duty-free certificate for rice in times of famine and short crops.

*ch'in* 欽加 granted by the Emperor.

*chia* 加 to add to; to grant.

*chien* 兼 and; also.

*kuan* 管銅務 in charge of coinage matters.

*t'ung* 銅務 copper business, *i.e.*, mint matters; business connected with the coining of copper cash.

*sui* 隨帶加三級 granted three steps of merit, and so recorded in the Board of Civil Office, which distinction attaches to the person of the promoted official (*sui tai* 隨帶, "taken along with him"), whereas steps granted as not *sui tai* are lost when the official is transferred to another office, because they are attached to the *post* and not to the *person*.

*chia* 加三級 granted three steps of merit.

*chi* 級 a step; a degree.

*an* 案 (=案查) whereas; according to.

*t'ung* 同治 the period of reign of the Emperor T'ung Chih (1862 to 1875).

*su* 蘇 (=蘇州府) Su-chou-fu.

*fan* 藩 a boundary; a frontier.

藩司 the provincial treasurer; the same as *Fan-t'ai* (藩臺) or *Pu-chêng-shih* (布政使).

*i* 移 to change; a despatch.

*fu* 撫憲 the provincial governor.

*cha* 札 a despatch from a superior.

*hu* 戶 a family; population.

戶部 the Board of Revenue.

*pu* 部 tribe; class; one of the *liu pu* (六部), or Boards of Government.

*i* 議 to deliberate in council; to recommend to the Emperor.

*fu* 復 to reply.

*chi* 給事中 a supervising censor.

*tsou* 奏 to address the Emperor.

奏請 to petition the Throne.

*chao* 招商 to encourage trade; to induce merchants.

*ts'ai* 採 to gather.

採買 to buy up.

*tao* 稻 unhusked rice; paddy.

稻米 paddy and rice.

*tsa* 雜糧 miscellaneous sorts of grain.

*kai* 概 all; equally.

*li* 厘 (=釐) the thousandth part of a tael; the Likin tax.

厘金 the Likin tax.

厘稅 Likin taxes *(li)* and ordinary duties *(shui)*.

*chê* 摺 a memorial to the Throne.

*fêng* 奉旨 to have received an Imperial edict.

*chih* 旨 an Imperial edict.

*i* 依 to accede to; as.

依議 "let it be as it was recommended" (in Imperial edicts).

*ch'in* 欽此 "The above is Imperial," or "such is his Majesty's pleasure," a concluding phrase added to Imperial orders by the ministers promulgating them.

*ssŭ* 嗣 afterwards.

*fu* 復 to reply; to write in reply to a letter previously received.

*chin* 近 near.

*ching* 京 the capital; Peking.

*i* 一帶 in the neighbourhood of.

*shou* 收成 to get in the crop.

*ch'êng* 成 complete; full; fulness; ready; to become.

*chien* 歉 insufficient (as a crop).

歉薄 insufficient and short of the full amount (as a crop).

*pao* 薄 thin.

*lai* 賴 to rely on; to depend on.

*shang* 商販 to buy and sell; trade.

*fan* 販 to trade; to buy and sell.

*mi* 米糧 rice and other grain.

*chieh* 接 to receive.

*chi* 濟 succour; assistance.

*min* 民 the people.

民食 the people's food.

*chan* 暫 temporarily.

*huan* 緩 to be lax; to remit (as taxes).

*ch'ou* 抽厘 to collect Likin taxes.

*i* 移咨 to inform in a despatch.

*ch'a* 查照 to take official notice (as of the contents of a despatch. Cf. *ch'a shou* 查收, to receive officially); here (=*an chao* 按照), according to.

*ch'u* 出示 to issue a proclamation.

*hsiao* 曉 to make known.

曉諭 for the information of everybody.

*yü* 諭 to proclaim; a proclamation.

*hao* 號商 a licensed merchant.

*ch'ü* 取 to fetch.

取具 to furnish.

*chü* 具 to arrange; to prepare; to furnish.

*pao* 保 to guarantee.

保結 a bond.

*chieh* 結 a knot; a tie; a bond.

*ping* 稟求 to apply for.

*ch'iu* 求 to beg; to ask for.

*chü* 局卡 Likin barriers.

*ts'un* 存案 to file in the archives; to keep on record.

*hsiang* 詳 to state in detail.

詳咨 to report details.

*t'ang* 倘 if.

*pieh* 別項貨物 other goods; goods of a description not covered by a document.

新關文件録



*fêng* 逢 to meet; to come across.

逢關 to pass a Customs station.

逢關納稅遇卡抽釐 to pay duty at Custom Houses and Likin taxes at Likin stations met on the road, *i.e.*, to pay all inland taxes due *en route*.

*yü* 遇卡 to pass a Customs barrier.

*ssŭ* 俟 to wait till; till; not until; when.

俟……… 即………as soon as………, then………

Document No. 33. [p. 62]

*shui* 水利 taxes on water industries (fisheries).

*i* 驛 post; postal.

*yen* 鹽 salt.

*hai* 海防水利驛鹽事務 matters pertaining to coast defence, fisheries, post and salt administration.

*chi* 紀 to write down; to record.

紀錄十次 recorded ten times for merit at the Board of Civil Office.

*liang* 兩江 the Two Kiang,—a viceregal district comprising the three provinces of Kiangsu, Anhwei, and Kiangsi. The two first named being formerly called or considered as one, under the name of Kiangnan, is the cause of merely two divisions being named in the expression.

*tu* 督憲 the Governor-General or Viceroy.

*fu* 福建 (*fu-chien*) the province of Fukien.

*fu* 撫部院 the Governor of a province.

*pu* 部院 title of a Provincial Governor.

*yüan* 院 a court; a hall.

*min* 閩省 the province of Fukien.

*shêng* 省 a province.

*chiao* 交 conterminous; just at the time of.

交夏後 just after the summer.

*hsia* 夏 summer.

*yü* 雨 rain.

雨霪 rain without end.

*yin* 霪 continuous rain.

*chiang* 江漲 the river overflowing.

*chang* 漲 to overflow.

*chi* 幾 nearly; almost.

幾致成災 almost amounting to a calamity.

*chih* 致 to arrive at; to reach to.

*tsai* 災 a calamity.

*tao* 稻糧 grain.

*pu* 不無 to be bound to. Note that two negatives combined make a strong affirmative.

*chien* 減 to decrease; to diminish.

減色 to decrease in quality; to deteriorate.

*hsien* 現在 now.

*shê* 設法 to devise plans.

*kou* 購運 to buy and forward.

藉以均濟 to help in effecting equal succour.

*chao* 照案 according to precedent.

*kai* 概行免稅 all be exempted from duty.

*t'ung* 同 with; the same as.

同前由 particulars being the same as the former; "to the same effect as the former."

*tao* 到道 has come to my, the Taot'ai's, hands.

*han* 函 a cover; a letter.

函致 to send a letter to.

*chao* 照辦 to act accordingly.

*so* 所有. If an individual or individuals are distinguished from others of the same class by some attribute (adjective, participle, relative clause, etc.), the phrase *so yu* 所有 (properly, a short relative clause meaning "the so-and-so that there is" or "that there are") often serves to express the English definite article; *e.g.*, 所[1]有[2]現[3]約[4]五[5]條[6], [1]*so* [2]*yu*, THE, [5]*wu*, five, [6]*t'iao*, articles of, [3]*hsien*, the present, [4]*yüeh*, treaty; 所[1]有[2]商[3]人[4]採[5]買[6]米[7]石[8], [1]*so* [2]*yu*, THE, [7]*mi*-[8]*tan*, rice, [3]*shang*-[4]*jên* [5]*ts'ai* [6]*mai*, bought up by the merchants.

*shang* 上屆 the last time; the last occasion.

*ch'êng* 成案 a precedent; *lit.*, a ready case.

*p'i* 批示 to reply officially to an inferior.

*shih* 示 to make known.

*t'ing* 聽 to hear; to wait; to obey.

聽候 to wait; to await.

*hou* 候 to wait.

Document No. 34. [p. 63]

*shui* 稅單 a duty-paid certificate.

*t'ung* 通商章程 Trade Regulations under Foreign Treaties; the Rules appended to the Tariff.

*ming* 名目 denomination; description of kind.

*jo* 若 if.

若干 an indefinite amount; the amount of; so and so much; so many.

*kan* 干 to concern; concerning.

*ho* 何 what; which.

何處 at which place; where.

*nei* 內地稅項 transit dues.

內地稅單 a transit certificate (inward).

*hsiang* 向 towards; to proceed to; a preposition placed before nouns denoting the object of verbs meaning to ask, to say, to give, etc.; *e.g.*, 向[1]子[2]口[3]呈[4]單[5], [4]*ch'êng* [5]*tan*, to hand a document, *hsiang*[1], TO, [2]*tzŭ*-[3]*k'ou*, the barrier office.

*yen* 沿途子口 the barriers *en route*.

*kai* 蓋 a cover; to over-top.

蓋戳 to affix a seal; to stamp.

*ch'o* 戳 a stamp; to stamp.

*wu* 無論 no matter whether.

無論遠近 no matter whether far or near; irrespective of distance.

*lun* 論 to discuss.

*yüan* 遠 far.

遠近 distance.

*chü* 俱 all; equally.

*t'ung* 通共章程 complete regulations; *e.g.*, the Revised Yangtze Trade Regulations; also, the Five Rules regarding Transit Trade, called 通商各口通共章程.

*fan* 販運 to convey.

*mo* 末 the end.

末後 finally; when all is finished.

*shêng* 聲 to make known; to report.

聲明 to report.

*hai* 海口 a seaport.

*i* 一律 uniformly.

*yen* 烟台 Yen-t'ai (=Chefoo).

*hui* 會 conjointly; to meet together; to make an agreement.

會議 to agree upon.

*i* 議 to deliberate; to discuss.

*t'iao* 條款 treaty paragraphs; a convention.

*yen* 烟台會議條款 the Chefoo Convention of 1876.

*pan* 半稅單照 a transit certificate (inwards).

*ho* 核定 to decide upon.

*hua* 畫 to draw; to paint.

畫一 uniform.

畫一款式 uniform; of a uniform pattern.

*k'uan* 款式 a pattern; a kind; a specimen.

*pu* 不分 making no distinction between.

*ko* 各等因; *i.q.*, *têng yin* 等因, p. 55, *q.v.*

*pu* 不領 not having been issued (a certificate, etc.), *i.e.*, without (a certificate, etc.).

*an* 安徽省 the province of Anhwei.

*ning* 甯國府 the prefecture of Ning-kuo-fu, in Anhwei.

*chü* 據此 on the ground of this (statement, application, etc.); accordingly.

*i* 以便 in order to; so that.

*hsi* 細葵扇 trimmed palm-leaf fans.

*k'uei* 葵 the sun-flower; the tree furnishing palm-leaf fans.

葵扇 palm-leaf fans.

### Document No. 35. [p. 64]

*mai* 買土貨報單 a transit memorandum (authorising the purchase of goods in the interior).

*k'ung* 空 empty.

空白 blank (as a form not filled up).

*ling* 領事官 a consul.

*lai* 來文 an incoming despatch; an official letter received.

*chi* 既 after; if; as soon as.

*ti* 抵 to arrive.

*ti* 第一子口 the first barrier.

*tzŭ* 自 of course; must.

自必 must.

*pi* 必 must.

*t'ung* 通商稅則 the Customs Tariff (according to Foreign Treaties).

*shui* 稅則 a Customs Tariff; the Tariff.

*tsê* 則 a list; a tariff.

*hsien* 先發 to issue beforehand.

*t'ung* 同樣 of the same kind.

同樣三紙 triplicate copies (of a document).

*yu* 由. This particle, otherwise meaning "from," "by way of," is frequently used to denote the doer of an action, or the logical subject of a sentence if it is not inanimate; *e.g.*, 由[1]領[2]事[3]官[4]飭[5]該[6]商[7], [1]*yu* (expressing that the term following is the subject of the sentence) [2]*ling*-[3]*shih*-[4]*kuan*, the Consul, [5]*ch'ih*, orders, instructs, [6]*kai*, the said, THE, [7]*shang*, merchant; 先[1]由[2]委[3]員[4]申[5]報[6]司[7]道[8], [2]*yu* [3]*wei*-[4]*yüan*, the Deputy, [must] [1]*hsien*, before, first, [5]*shên*-[6]*pao*, report to, [7]*ssŭ*, the high provincial authorities and, [8]*tao*, the Taot'ais. Cf. *yu* 由, Document No. 16, p. 20.

*ch'ih* 飭 to order; to instruct.

*tang* 當 right; proper; at the time of; in the presence of.

當堂 before the magistrate; at the Consulate.

當堂畫押 to sign before a magistrate, or before the Consul.

*t'ang* 堂 a hall; a court; a magistrate.

*hua* 畫押 to affix one's signature; to sign.

*ya* 押 to sign; to affix a seal.

*chi* 給領 to issue (as a document).

*huo* 或 or.

或……或 either……… or ……..; whether……… or……

*shang* 商夥 a partner in a firm; an agent.

*huo* 夥 a partner.

*san* 三單 (= 三連單 or 三聯單 *san lien tan*) a triplicate transit memorandum.

*yen* 眼 the eye.

眼同 together with another (so that both parties may see).

*yen* 驗看 to examine.

*k'an* 看 to see; to look.

*hsien* 現往 about to proceed to.

*hsia* 下 below; after a verb it may correspond to colloquial 了 (*liao*) or 過 (*kuo*), denoting the past tense.

*kai* 盖印加封 to seal a document and enclose it in an envelope.

*chia* 加封 to enclose in an official (sealed) envelope.

*fei* 飛 to fly.

飛速 post haste; speedily.

*su* 速 hasty; speedy.

*yu* 由驛 by post; by courier.

*i* 驛 the post; a courier.

*i* 移 to change; to forward to.

移送 to forward.

*sung* 送 to send.

*ch'u* 出口海關 the exporting Custom House, *i.e.*, the Custom House where outward transit goods are to pay Export Duty.

*ch'a* 查照 to take official notice of, as of a letter; placed after the name of the recipient in addresses, etc. Cf. *ch'a* 查照 in Document No. 32, p. 61.

*an* 按月 by the month; monthly.

*ch'êng* 呈送 to send in; to transmit to [a superior].

*tsung* 總理 to have the general management of.

總理各國事務衙門 the Yamên having the general control of matters connected with foreign countries; the Tsungli Yamên.

*pei* 備查 to file in the archives; to keep for reference.

*ts'un* 存留 to keep.

*liu* 留 to keep; to detain.

*yün* 運照 a transit pass.

*lu* 路上 on the road.

*chiang* 將 to take; before a verb, a sign of the future: "about to." Cf. Document No. 14, p. 17.

*ch'u* 出口海關設卡 the barrier established at the port where [transit] goods are exported.

*tai* 帶同 to take with one.

*yün* 運貨之人 a person attending a transport of goods.

*tan* 單據 a documentary proof.

*kuo* 過卡 to cross a Customs barrier.

*wei* 違此例 to offend against this rule.

*yeh* 業經 a sign of the past; already.

*chih* 指 to point out.

*pieh* 別 another; otherwise.

*yin* 隱 to keep out of view.

隱漏 to defraud the revenue by concealment of facts.

*lou* 漏 to evade [payment of duty]; to smuggle.

*pi* 弊 a malpractice.

*shui* 稅則半稅 half the Tariff Duty.

*ni* 匿單少報 to conceal the document and report less (than the proper quantity); to make a false declaration while withholding the document.

*têng* 等情 "such circumstances and the like actions." Cf. *têng yin* 等因, Document No. 26, p. 55.

*t'ung* 同類之貨 goods of the same denomination.

*chien* 繭殼 pierced cocoons.

*k'o* 殼 shell; skin; husk.

*nien* 念 to think. Used locally to denote the number "twenty," and hence read *êrh-shih* (二十).

*yu* 右貨 the goods (enumerated) on the right hand, *i.e.*, the above goods.

*fei* 飛送 to send by courier.

*ch'a* 查收 to receive officially; to take delivery of. Cf. Document No. 32, p. 61.

*i* 以憑徵稅 in order to furnish the documentary proof for charging duty.

海上絲綢之路文獻集成　科技與文化编

### Document No. 36. [p. 65]

*pao* 保單執照 a bond certificate (for rice).
*shan* 山海關 the Newchwang Customs.
*fêng* 奉錦山海關 the territorial divisions of Fêng-t'ien-fu (*fêng* 奉), Chin-chou-fu (*chin* 錦), and the Custom House at Shan-hai-kuan (山海關) (at the eastern terminus of the Great Wall), constituting the administrative district of the Tao-t'ai of Newchwang.
*mi* 米穀 rice and grain.
*hsiang* 向 hitherto.
*li* 例 according to regulation.
*pu* 不准 not allowed; forbidden.
*hsin* 新定 newly decided upon.
*shao* 稍 slightly.
稍寬其禁 to slightly relax a restriction; to grant a facility.
*k'uan* 寬 to relax; to mitigate.
*chin* 禁 to restrict; to prohibit; restriction; prohibition.
*chun* 准令 to allow that.
*k'ou* 口岸 a port; ports.
*an* 岸 a shore; the coast.
*i* 以 from (= 從 *ts'ung*).
以此口運至彼口 to transport from one port to another.
*pi* 彼 that (as opposed to *tz'ŭ* 此, this); another; there.
彼此 there and here, *i.e.*, on either side.
*ch'êng* 呈具 to draw up and hand in (as a bond).
*pao* 保單 a bond.
*chieh* 結 to tie; a knot; fixed; firm.
結實 durable; secure; material.
結實信據 a material guarantee.
*hsin* 信 a letter; to trust; to believe; true; reliable.
信據 a guarantee.
*shou* 收到字樣 the word "received"; the endorsement of a receipt.
*ts'ung* 從 (= 自) from (local and temporal); since.
*ch'ien* 淺 (the opposite of 滿 (*man*), full) not full; empty (as a ship in ballast).
*yüan* 元 the beginning; the first; No. I.
*ts'un* 存查 to keep on record; to file in the archives.
*i* 一經.........即 as soon as........., then.........
*p'i* 批註 to endorse.
*chia* 加蓋印信 to affix a seal.
*hui* 回 to come back; to send back.
*yü* 逾限 to exceed a limit.
*jên* 苡米 a kind of rice; pearl barley (=薏仁米 *i-jên mi*).

### Document No. 37. [p. 66]

*t'iao* 條款 articles; regulations.
*fan* 凡.........者 all.........who [or which].........
*pao* 寶山正頂 Paoshan Point (a locality in Shanghai Harbour).
*p'ao* 砲台 a fort; a battery.
*tui* 對 opposite.
對徑 opposite.
*ching* 徑 a bye-road; a short cut; direct.
*chieh* 界 a boundary; a limit.
*wei* 爲 to consider; to hold that.........
*p'ai* 派役 to depute officers.
*kuan* 管押 to keep custody (as of a ship).
*ya* 押 to put a seal on; to keep under supervision; to guard (as a ship or goods).
*i* 一體 all; uniformly.
*chieh* 界限 a limit.
*tung* 東門小河 the East Gate Creek (Shanghai).
*k'ou* 口 the mouth of a river, creek, street, road, etc.
*ping* 兵船 a man-of-war.
兵船廠 a naval yard.
*tien* 點 a point; a dot; a stroke.
點鐘 an hour; hours; o'clock.
*chung* 鐘 a bell; a clock.
*ts'ang* 艙 the hold of a ship.
艙口單 a ship's manifest.
*pên* 本國 my (the writer's) country; also his (another's own) country.
*kuo* 過 to exceed.
*jên* 認 to recognise; to confess.
認保無訛 to professedly guarantee there being no mistake, *i.e.*, to be responsible for correctness.
*wu* 無訛 without mistake.
*ngo* 訛 wrong; a mistake.
*i* 一切 all.

新關文件録



*tzŭ* 字號 a mark (as on a package of merchandise).
*hsiang* 詳細載明 to give an accurate detailed account.
*ch'êng* 呈遞 to hand in; to present.
*ti* 遞 to hand to; to present (as a document).
*chia* 假 false.
假單 a false document (as a false manifest).
*tan* 但 only; merely.
*ts'o* 錯 wrong.
錯誤 a mistake.
*wu* 誤 mistake.
*ch'ing* 請改 to apply for permission to correct.
*mien* 免其議罰 to remit a fine.
*tsai* 再 again; further; often merely opens a new sentence.
*ch'i* 起岸 to land (as goods from a ship).
*yi* 亦 also.
*chih* 只 only.
*hsü* 許 to allow; to be allowed.
*li* 例准 permitted by the regulations.
*i* 以及 and; or.
*chuang* 裝上 to put into; to take in.
*ya* 押載之物 ballast.
*jih* 日間 during the daytime.
*chien* 間 at the time of; in the place of.
*jih* 日出以前 before sunrise.
日落以後 after sunset.
*lo* 落 to fall; to drop; to go down.
*li* 禮 rites; ceremony.
禮拜日 Sunday; on Sundays.
*pai* 拜 to worship; to visit.
*chi* 給假日 a holiday; holidays.
*hsing* 行 to work (as to load and unload).
*chin* 進口貨單 an import manifest.
*tzŭ* 自備 to provide oneself; to furnish.
*ch'i* 起貨單 a delivery order (for goods to be landed).
*ch'i* 起貨[准]單 a permit to land.
*ssŭ* 私行起動 to land clandestinely.
*ch'i* 起清 completely discharged (as a cargo). [p. 67]
*ch'a* 查艙 to search the hold of a ship.
*ch'ing* 請起貨單 an application to land.
請下貨單 an application to ship.

*hsia* 下貨單 a shipping order.
下貨[准]單 a permit to ship.
*hsü* 許 to permit; to be permitted.
*ssŭ* 私行下貨 to ship clandestinely.
*po* 剝船 (＝撥船) a cargo-boat.
*i* 已滿 filled up; already full; loaded full (as a ship).
*t'ui* 退回 to shut out goods (from a ship).
*shang* 上岸 to land.
*hsia* 下齊貨物 to have shipped all the goods; to have completed loading.
*ch'i* 齊 completely; all.
*ch'u* 出口貨單 an export manifest.
*k'ai* 開載 to state; to enter (as in a document).
*chia* 假單 a false document (as a "false manifest").
*hu* 互 mutually; each other.
互撥貨物 to tranship goods from one vessel to another.
*po* 撥貨 to tranship goods.
*t'ê* 特准單據 a special permit.
*chun* 准單 a permit.
*tan* 單據 a permit.
*ssŭ* 私行互撥 to clandestinely tranship goods from one vessel to another.
*ho* 何時 at what time; at which time; at that time; *e.g.*, 何[1]時[2]起[3]貨[4]卽[5]何[6]時[7]照[8]納[9], [1]*ho* [2]*shih*, at which time, [3]*ch'i* [4]*huo*, the goods are landed, [5]*chi*, then, [6]*ho* [7]*shih*, at that time, [8]*chao* [9]*na*, the duty is paid; *i.e.*, "the duties (or dues) are due at the time when goods are landed."
*t'ung* 通 all.
*ch'a* 查對 to check; to examine.
*tui* 對 to compare; to check; to agree.
*ho* 核知 to know; to be satisfied as to the correctness of.
*chieh* 皆 all.
*ngo* 訛誤 a mistake.
*wu* 誤 wrong; a mistake.
*ling* 領回 to issue back; to hand back (as a document deposited).
*mei* 每 every; each.
每日 every day; daily.
*k'ai* 開關 to open the Custom House.
*fêng* 封關 to close the Custom House.

*t'ing* 停辦公事 to stop work (as when closing an office).

*sui* 隨時 suiting one's time; in due course.

*shêng* 聲候 to make a personal statement.

*hou* 候 to wait; to wait upon.

*cho* / *chê* } 酌 to deliberate upon.

### Document No. 38. [p. 68]

*li* 理船廳 a harbour master.

理船廳章程 Harbour Regulations.

*ko* 各國領事官 the Treaty-power Consuls.

*kung* 公同商定 to conjointly agree upon.

*shang* 商 to consult; to devise.

*chun* 准行 to sanction.

*tuan* 段 a section; a limit.

*shang* 上段 the upper limit (as of a harbour).

*hsia* 下段 the lower limit (as of a harbour).

*ying* 應須 must.

*chih* 指引 to point out; to assign (as a berth to a ship).

*t'o* 妥 safe.

妥當 safe.

*hsiao* 小輪船 a steam-launch; a tug-boat.

*t'o* 拖 to drag; to pull.

拖帶 to tow (as a ship).

*êrh* 而 and; and yet. After verbs it often has the force of the Latin gerund; *e.g.*, 煮海水而作鹽 *chu hai-shui êrh tso yen*, "to make salt by boiling sea water"; 輪船拖帶而入 *ju*, to enter (port), *êrh*, by, *lun-ch'uan t'o-tai*, being steamer-towed; *i.e.*, "to be towed into port by a steamer."

*chiang* 將到 about to arrive. Cf. *chiang* 將, Document No. 35, p. 64.

*po* 泊界 the harbour limits.

*pan* 辦公房屋 office buildings; a public office.

*fang* 房 a house; a building.

*wu* 屋 a room.

*t'o* 拖船 a tug-boat.

*ying* 應當 must.

*huan* 緩 slowly; to delay.

緩駛 to slacken speed; to stop (as a ship); to slow down.

*ch'ang* 常 constantly; usually; commonly.

常川 uninterruptedly; continuously; regularly (*lit.*, an uninterrupted stream).

*ch'uan* 川 a mountain stream.

*ching* 徑入 to pass into.

*pu* 不必 must not; need not.

*têng* 等 to wait.

等候 to wait.

*wei* 危 danger.

危險 dangerous.

*hsien* 險 danger; dangerous.

*fang* 防碍 a hindrance; a difficulty to be provided against.

*ai* 碍 to obstruct; to interfere with.

*wei* 危險防碍之物 articles of a dangerous nature, *e.g.*, gunpowder and other explosives.

*liu* 留空 to keep open or unoccupied (as a berth for a ship).

*pu* 步 a pace; to pace; to move up and down.

步位 space.

*wei* 位 position; place.

*chih* 指示 to assign (as a berth to a ship).

*i* 移動 to move.

*ch'uan* 船夥 a mate; a ship's officer.

*kung* 公 just; fair; public. [p. 69]

公所 a public office.

*so* 所 a place.

*t'ung* 通報 to report, through the channel of an inferior, to a higher officer.

*yi* 亦可 will also do; may also.

*mei* 每逢 whenever; when; at the time of.

*fêng* 逢 to meet; to happen; whenever.

*t'ou* 頭桅 the foremast.

*ts'êng* 層 a story; a tier.

*fan* 帆 a sail; to sail.

帆扛 a yard (of a ship's mast).

*kang* 扛 (standing for 杠 *kang*); a yard on a mast; a pole.

*yu* 右邊 on the right side.

*pien* 邊 a side; a border; an edge.

*hsüan* 懸 to be suspended; to hang down; to suspend; to hang up.

懸掛 to suspend; to hang up.

*kua* 掛 to hang up.

*ming* 明 clear; bright; shining.

*têng* 燈 a lamp; a light.

*shêng* 繩 a cord; a string.
繩索 cordage; the rigging of a ship.
*so* 索 to bind; a cord; twine.
*shuan* 拴 to bind up; to fasten.
拴繫 to tie up; to fasten.
*hsi* 繫 to bind up; to fasten.
*ch'uan* 船旁 a ship's side; on the side of a ship.
*hsiao* 小船 a small boat; a gig; a sampan.
*hêng* 橫 cross.
橫木 a cross-beam; a boom.
*shou* 收 to receive; to take in; to rig in, as the swinging-boom of a ship.
*chih* 支 to pay out; to rig out, as the swinging-boom of a ship.
*huo* 活 lively; alive; movable.
活機之木 a movable beam on board a ship; a swinging-boom.
*chi* 機 a mechanical contrivance.
*wei* 惟 but; except.
*pai* 白晝之間 during daytime.
*chou* 晝 daylight; in the daytime.
*chih* 支出 to rig out, as the swinging-boom or jib-boom of a ship.
*yeh* 夜 the night; at night.
夜晚 in the evening; at night.
*wan* 晚 evening.
*fang* 方始 then; but then; then, and not sooner.
*mao* 錨鍊 anchor chains.
*lien* 鍊 a chain.
*shih* 時常 at any time; always.
*chêng* 整 to adjust; to repair.
整理 to adjust; to keep in order.
*ch'ing* 清妥 clear and safe (as the anchor chains of a ship).
*yüeh* 月滿時 at full moon (*i.q.*, *wang* 望).
月初生時 at new moon (*i.q.*, *shuo* 朔).
*shêng* 生 to be born; to come into existence.
*yu* 尤 more; still more; particularly.
尤爲緊要 it is still more important; it is of special importance.
*chin* 緊 important.
緊要 important.
*ch'ien* 牽 to connect.
*chih* 至 as regards.

*hou* 後面 behind; astern (of a ship).
*yao* 要 must; must be.
*tuan* 短 short.
*kuo* 過長 excessively long; too long.
*i* 以期 (= 以望) so that it may be hoped; so as not to interfere with.
*pien* 便 convenient.
便於 to be expedient to; to facilitate.
*k'ai* 開放大砲 to fire off cannon.
*p'ao* 砲 cannon.
*ch'iang* 槍 a gun.
*huo* 火 fire.
火藥 gunpowder.
火藥開花彈子 shell loaded with gunpowder.
*tan* 彈 a bullet; a shot; a shell.
*li* 粒 a grain of rice; a classifier of bullets, cartridges, shells, etc.
*chih* 至 up to.
*p'ang* 磅 (in imitation of the English sound "pound") a pound; pounds.
*kuan* 灌 to pour into.
灌藥槍彈 cartridges.
*san* 三里路 a distance of three *li*, or one English mile.
*lu* 路 a road.
*ch'ê* 扯 to haul up; to hoist.
扯挂 to hoist (as a flag).
*tzŭ* 自能爆開 inflammable; explosive.
*pao* 爆 to burn; to burst into flame.
*to* 多寡 quantity; how much.
*kua* 寡 little.
*k'ai* 開出 to proceed to (as a ship on having lifted anchors). [p. 70]
開駛 to proceed on a journey (as a ship).
*nêng* 能引火之油 inflammable oil (as kerosene oil, etc.).
*yin* 引火 to strike fire; to inflame.
*k'ao* 靠 to lean on; to rely on; by the side of.
*p'u* 浦東岸 the shore of the river opposite Shanghai; the Pootung shore.
*wên* 瘟 an infectious disease; an epidemic.
瘟病 an infectious disease.
*ping* 病 sick; sickness.
*huang* 黃旗 a yellow flag; the quarantine flag.
*shang* 上下 up and down; to land and ship; to communicate with the shore (as from on board a ship).

5

*ya* 壓載重物 ballast.

*mei* 煤灰 coal ashes.

*hui* 灰 ashes.

*t'an* 炭 charcoal.

炭碎 charcoal ashes.

*sui* 碎 fragments; broken pieces or bits.

*p'ao* 拋 to throw away.

拋棄 to throw away.

*ch'i* 棄 to throw away.

*p'u* 浦 a river; the Hwangpu at Shanghai.

*yü* 欲要 to want to.

*têng* 登 to ascend; to enter (as in a book).

登岸 to go on shore.

*cho* 酌 to consider; to arrange for.

*jên* 人數 a number of men.

*fu* 敷 to be sufficient for.

*ch'i* 起錨鍊 to lift anchors; to clear chain.

*hsia* 下錨鍊 to pay out [anchor] chain.

*ch'uan* 船頭 the bow of a ship.

船頭支出之桅 a jib-boom.

*shou* 收進 to rig in (as a jib-boom).

*shê* 設浮樁 to lay down buoys and beacons.

*ch'a* 查看 to inspect.

*shih* 是否 whether or not.

*fou* 否 not; whether or not; if not.

*an* 安 to place; to lay down.

安設 to erect; to lay down (as a buoy).

*p'ai* 派定 to allot; to decide (as on the site of a buoy to be laid down).

*kuei* 歸 to revert to; to be under the control of.

*jih* 日後 afterwards; in the course of time.

*pu* 不便 inconvenient.

*ku* 故 a cause; a reason; causing.

*yü* 諭令 to order.

*chu* 主 the owner of an object.

*i* 移換 to change.

*ti* 地方 a place.

*êrh* 而 and; but; yet; and yet.

*pu* 不即 not immediately; forthwith not.

*tsun* 遵行 to comply with orders.

*tai* 代爲辦理 to act for another; to take action in a matter which another has not taken up.

*shih* 使 to cause to.

使費 to lay out; to incur an expense for another; expenses.

*jên* 認付 to be responsible for (payment); to have to submit to.

*fu* 付 to give to.

*shih* 失 to lose; to miss; to fail. [p. 71]

失火 to catch fire; fire breaking out.

*ch'ien* 前後 in front and behind.

*ming* 鳴 the cry of a bird; to cry; to sound.

鳴鑼 to sound a gong.

*lo* 鑼 a gong.

*pao* 報警 to beat alarm.

*ching* 警 to rouse; to warn; to alarm.

*yu* 有船被焚之旗 a fire-alarm; a signal flag hoisted when a ship is on fire.

被焚 to be burned; to be on fire.

*fên* 焚 to burn.

*ch'ê* 扯上扯下 to hoist and lower (as a signal flag or lantern on board ship).

*fei* 飛報 to send immediate notice to; to send a flying message.

*shui* 水巡捕 the river police (at Shanghai).

*kua* 挂旗望臺 a signal station.

*wang* 望 to look to; to see; to hope.

望臺 a look out; a signal station; a tower beacon.

*kung* 工部局 the Municipal Council (at Shanghai).

*chih* 知照 to inform.

*hung* 轟 to blast.

轟爆之物 explosive matter or articles.

*pao* 爆 fire bursting; fireworks.

*hui* 回駛 to sail back.

*hsü* 續 to continue; additional; supplementary.

續議 additionally agreed upon.

*kao* 告白 a notice.

*ch'uan* 船名之旗 a signal flag denoting the name of a ship.

*ch'ê* 扯旗望臺 a signal station.

*yüan* 遠見 to see from afar.

*pao* 報知 to give notice to.

*ho* 何處 at what place; whether at any place.

*chien* 見有 to see that there is; to discover.

*chiao* 礁 a rock.

礁石 a rock.

新關文件錄



*ch'ien* 淺 shallow.
淺水 shallow water; a shoal.
*huai* 壞 to spoil; to be lost.
壞船 a wreck.
*hsiang* 相遇 to happen to one (as an accident).
*k'ai* 開來 to come from (as a ship).
*t'u* 途間 on the way; *en route*.
*yu* 有無 whether there is; whether there was.
*ta* 大風 a storm.
*ho* 何日 on what date.
*tao* 到此 to arrive here; to arrive at this port.
*ch'ing* 情形 circumstances.
*hsing* 形 shape; form; to describe; description.
*i* 移動 to move; to be carried away.
*ch'uan* 船燈 a ship's light; a lightship.
*t'a* 塔 a tower; a lighthouse.
塔燈=(燈塔) a lighthouse.
*yen* 黯 pitchy; black.
黯滅 to extinguish (as a light).
*mieh* 滅 to extinguish.
*sun* 損 to lose.
損壞 to be spoilt; to be out of order; to wreck.
*i* 意有不洽 to disagree; not to fall in with one's ideas; to have fault to find with. [p. 72]
*pu* 不洽 to disagree.
*hsia* 洽 to harmonise with.
*ch'i* 技 skill.
技藝 professional competency.
*i* 藝 skill; ability in working.
*shêng* 生疏 raw; coarse; incomplete.
*su* 疏 coarse; careless.
*hsing* 性 nature; character.
性情 personal conduct.
*pu* 不善 bad.
*shan* 善 good.
*kan* 趕 quickly.
趕緊 as quickly as possible.
*chin* 緊 important; quickly.
*t'ung* 通知 to inform through another.
*ch'a* 查辦 to investigate.
*mu* 木板 a board (classifier, *kuai* 塊).

*nien* 粘 to paste on.
粘貼 to paste up (as a public notice).
*t'ieh* 貼 to paste up (as a public notice).
*chih* 知閱 to take notice of.
*yüeh* 閱 to peruse.
*shang* 上面 above; on it (as on a surface).
*i* 一覽而知 to see and notice a matter at a glance; synoptical.
*lan* 覽 to inspect; to behold from a distance.
*fêng* 奉 to offer to; to receive.
奉勸 to offer one's advice to; to warn.
*ch'üan* 勸 to advise.
*ch'ieh* 切勿 not by any means. Cf. *ping* 並未, Document No. 28, p. 57.
*wu* 勿 not; do not.
*shun* 順 to obey; going with, not against.
順潮 with the tide.
*ch'ao* 潮 the flood tide.
*ch'êng* 誠 really; sincerely.
誠恐 there is real fear that.
*k'ung* 恐 to fear.
*p'êng* 碰 to collide.
碰壞 to wreck from collision; to damage by collision.
*chi* 己 self; oneself; one's own.
*sun* 損傷 to be damaged; damage.
*jên* 認理 to be responsible for.
*wei* 惟 to consider; to hold that; only.
*p'ai* 派辦之人 a deputy.
*fu* 付給 to tender (as payment).
*wu* 吳淞 Woosung (an out-station at the mouth of the Shanghai river).
*po* 泊船章程 regulations for the mooring of ships.
*kung* 公同商定准行 conjointly discussed and approved of (as by a body of officials).
*ping* 兵營 a camp.
*ying* 營 a camp.
*mien* 面前 in front of.
*lan* 藍白色旂 a blue and white flag; the rendezvous flag (MARRYAT's Code).
*ch'i* 旂 (=旗) a flag.
*chu* 駐 to reside.
*chih* 指泊人 a berthing officer.

*k'o* 可以 can; may.
*chih* 指示 to point out; to assign (as a berth to a ship).
*shê* 設法 to devise a plan; to see that.
*shih* 使 to cause to; so that.
*pien* 便 to facilitate.
便於 to meet with no difficulty in; to facilitate; to be given facilities in.
*ch'ien* 淺沙灘 a bar (as the Woosung Bar). [p. 73]
*sha* 沙 sand; a sand or mud bank.
沙灘 a bar (as the Woosung Bar).
*t'an* 灘 rapids in a stream; an obstruction arising from rocks or sand-banks.
*wang* 望準 to take the bearing of.
*chun* 準 to equalise; to adjust.
*piao* 標桿 a beacon pole (classifier, *kên* 根).
*kan* 桿 a pole.
*lien* 聯 to join; to connect.
聯貫 to join (as several objects seen in a line).
*kuan* 貫 a string (as of cash); to string; to connect.
*chih* 直線 a straight line.
*hsien* 線 thread; wire; a line drawn.
*tso* 左右 right $\frac{\text{and}}{\text{or}}$ left; on either side of; more or less; about.
*fu* 幅地 (*fu-ti*, in imitation of the English sound "foot") a foot; feet.
*p'ai* 派去 to depute.
*t'o* 妥便 safe and comfortable.
*t'iao* 條 a classifier of roads, etc.
*ai* 碍 to endanger; danger; difficulty.
*i* 移泊 to shift anchorage; to remove from one berth to another.
*yin* 因此 thereby; therefore.
*wei* 惟某人自行認理 or 惟某人是問 So-and-so will be held responsible.
*yao* 要故 an urgent reason.
*yün* 允 to permit.
允行 to give authority to.
*p'o* 拍 here standing for *po* 泊, to anchor.
*liao* 料 to consider.
料理 to manage.
*chieh* 接收 to receive.
*shan* 繕 to write out; to copy.
*yen* 沿途情形 [a record of] occurrences on the road; the log of a ship.

*pao* 報函 a written report.
*i* 易於 or 易以 easy to; to find no difficulty in ......
*wei* 違犯 to offend against.
*fan* 犯 to be guilty; to offend against.

## Document No. 39. [p. 74]

*yü* 諭 an order.
*tuan* 端 upright; correct; also, matters; affairs.
端陽節期 the dragon-boat festival.
端陽 or 端午 the dragon-boat festival (5th day of 5th moon).
*yang* 陽 the male principle; the sun.
*chieh* 節 a period of time; a feast day.
節期 a festival; a periodical feast day.
*t'ing* 停 to stop.
停辦公事 to close a public office; to stop work (as on a holiday).
*t'ê* 特諭 a special order.

## Document No. 40.

*an* 按察使 a provincial judge.
*tung* 東海關 the Chefoo Customs.
*fên* 分守 to have the control of several administrative districts respectively.
*têng* 登萊青 the three departments of Têng-chou-fu (登 *têng*), Lai-chou-fu (萊 *lai*), and Ch'ing-chou-fu (青 *ch'ing*), forming the circuit in charge of the Taot'ai at Chefoo.
*yü* 諭飭遵辦 orders for the guidance [of those concerned].
*hsieh* 卸 to unload.
*pao* 報稅 to declare [goods] for payment of duty.
*p'u* 舖 a shop.
舖商人 traders; merchants.
*ta* 大關 the [Native] Custom House (at Chefoo).
*so* 所以 in order to thereby; by which means it is intended to.
*yüan* 原所以杜......by which means it was originally intended to prohibit...........
*tu* 杜 to restrict; to prohibit.
*ying* 影 a shadow; a delusion.
影射 a shadow projecting; false statements; false declarations.
*shê* 射 to shoot out; to project (as a shadow).

*chia* 夾 double; the lining of clothes.
夾帶 to carry secretly; to smuggle.
*chu* 諸 all; as a sign of the plural, *the*.
諸弊 all the malpractices; *the* malpractices.
*chin* 近 near; lately.
近聞 it has lately been rumoured; I have recently heard.
*wên* 聞 to hear; it is rumoured.
*pao* 報卸 to declare goods as having to be landed.
*ni* 匿過紅單 fraudulently omitted in the clearance document (as goods not declared at the Custom House).
*ching* 竟 really; indeed.
竟不 not at all; even not. Cf. *ping* 並未, Document No. 28, p. 57.
*ssŭ* 似 like.
似此 like this; thus.
*han* 含 to cherish.
含混 to cherish confusion; to be negligent about matters.
*hun* 混 confused; confusion; mixed; ill-assorted.
*ch'ü* 取巧 to exact an undue advantage.
*ch'iao* 巧 clever; crafty.
*nan* 難保 difficult to secure.
*shên* 申明 to explain clearly; to state clearly.
*chiu* 舊 old.
*i* 一體 all; uniformly.
*i* 以 in order to.
以杜弊端 in order to restrict malpractices.
*pi* 弊端 malpractices.
*chung* 重 to give weight to; to secure respect for.
*kuo* 國課 the Imperial revenue.
*ko* 課 taxes; revenue.
*chi* 亟 promptly; quickly.
*ch'u* 出示曉諭 to issue a proclamation.
*wei* 爲此 on this account; therefore.
*shih* 示仰 to issue a proclamation with a view to......
*ko* 各路 at all places; in all directions.
*chih* 知悉 to be thoroughly aware of.
*hsi* 悉 to know.
*tzŭ* 自......之後 from after ......
*tz'ŭ* 此次 this time.
*fu* 覆 again; to and fro. [p. 75.]

*chi* 訖 to finish; after a verb, a sign of the past tense, like *kuo* 過.
*ch'o* 戳 to stamp; a stamp.
戳記 to affix a seal.
*chi* 記 to remember; to record; a mark; a sign; a seal.
*ch'i* 起卸 to discharge goods.
*ssŭ* 私自 clandestinely and on one's own authority; privately.
*t'i* 提關 to send to the Custom House (as an offender for examination).
*ch'a* 查究 to examine; to try.
*chiu* 究 to examine; to try.
*ts'ung* 從 to follow; to be attached to; liable.
從重議罰 liable to be severely punished.
*pu* 不稍 not in the least.
不稍寬貸 not the slightest leniency will be shown.
*k'uan* 寬 broad; forgiving; leniency.
寬貸 to let off leniently; to remit punishment; to show leniency.
*tai* 貸 to lend on interest; to give; to release; to let off.
*i* 宜 must.
*lin* 凜 to tremble.
凜遵 to obey strictly.
*wu* 毋違特示 a special order not to be offended against; a proclamation to be obeyed strictly.

## Document No. 41.

*chien* 建 to establish; to build.
建築 to build.
*chu* 築 to build.
*chuan* 專 specially.
*têng* 登 to ascend.
登舟 to get on board ship; to embark.
*chou* 舟 a boat.
*hsing* 行走 to walk; pedestrians.
*tsou* 走 to walk.
*chi* 計 to take into account.
*t'u* 土妓 a local prostitute.
*chi* 妓 a prostitute.
*yu* 游 to wander about; wandering; to travel.
*ch'ang* 娼 a singing woman; a prostitute.
*hun* 混雜 to mix together.

*t'u* 塗 mud; dirty; to besmear.

塗朱搽粉 to besmear one's face with cosmetics; to paint faces with rouge and chalk.

*chu* 朱 vermilion; rouge.

*ch'a* 搽 to rub on; to besmear.

*fên* 粉 flour; powder; cosmetics in powders.

*chao* 招 to beckon; to call.

招搖 to entice by showing oneself off.

*yao* 搖 to shake; to wave to and fro.

*shih* 實屬 it really is.

*shu* 屬 to be.

*tan* 膽 the gall; courage; bold.

膽玩 to play a bold game; to trifle with the law in a cheeky manner.

*wan* 玩 trifles; to trifle; to play with.

*i* 已極 to the utmost; extremely.

*chi* 極 extremely; the utmost point.

*hsien* 現經 has; have; also a sign of the perfect tense.

*yen* 嚴 strict.

嚴拿 to seize strictly; to arrest.

*wu* 無恥之輩 shameless people.

*ch'ih* 恥 to be ashamed.

*pei* 輩 generation; kind; people; when appended to a noun, expressing plurality, *e.g.*, *wo pei* 我輩, people of my kind, *i.e.*, we.

*kan* 敢 to dare; to venture.

*fa* 發 to send.

發縣 to send to the district magistrate (as a criminal for punishment).

*chung* 重究 to inquire into strictly; to deal severely (with an offender).

重究不貸 to be severely dealt with (as an offender).

*pu* 不貸 without leniency; strictly.

### Document No. 42.

*yen* 嚴拿偷漏 [to have authority for] arresting thieves and smugglers.

*t'ou* 偷 to steal; to pilfer.

偷漏 thieves and smugglers.

*lou* 漏 to leak; to evade [payment of duty]; to smuggle.

*chin* 禁止遶越 to restrict evasion of the law.

*jao* 遶 to wind around; to make a *détour*.

遶越 to evade the law.

*yüeh* 越 to exceed; to transgress.

*ku* 故 on purpose.

故違 to wilfully offend against the law.

*tz'ŭ* 詞 a rhyme; a rythmical sentence; tales; empty phrases.

*hsiang* 相同 identical; the same.

### Document No. 43. [p. 76]

*ch'i* 啓 to inform; a notice.

啟者 a communication; an opening phrase in letters: "you are hereby informed that;" "I beg to inform you."

*chan* 棧 a warehouse; a godown.

棧房 a warehouse; a godown.

*p'o* 拍 to beat; to slap a table; to bid.

拍賣 to sell by auction.

*kuei* 貴 esteemed; "you," or that which pertains to the person addressed.

貴客 esteemed merchants; "you" (when addressing merchants).

貴國 your country.

貴恙 your disease.

*chieh* 屆時 at the time fixed for.

*mien* 面 the face; personally; in person; verbally.

面拍 to bid at an auction.

*tsai* 再者 further; besides.

*mai* 買貨之人 purchasers (of goods).

*cho* 酌帶銀洋若干 to carry with oneself an amount of dollars sufficient for intended purchases.

*yin* 銀洋 foreign coins; Mexican dollars.

*p'o* 拍定 to settle a purchase at auction.

*chiao* 交付 to hand (as payment).

*fu* 付 to give; to deliver to.

*i* 以 because; on account of.

*chieh* 借 to lend; to borrow; to make a pretext of.

借詞 to make a pretext of sophistical arguments.

*t'ui* 推 to shirk responsibility; to refuse.

推諉 to retract what one had agreed to; to shirk responsibility; to back out.

*wei* 諉 to shirk one's duty; to back out.

*chih* 至 very; extremely.

至囑至囑 very urgent to tell you; be careful not to overlook.

*chu* 囑 to enjoin upon.

*tz'ŭ* 此佈 this is a public notice; for general information.

*pu* 佈 to extend; a public notice.

### Document No. 44.

*yen* 烟台 (*Yen-t'ai*) Chefoo.

*chung* 中外 Chinese and foreign.

*yün* 雲 a cloud.

雲集 to assemble in great numbers.

*chi* 集 to collect; to assemble.

*so* 所 a place.

*sui* 隨意 as one thinks fit; according to pleasure.

*man* 漫 reckless; vague.

*p'êng* 碰 to run against; to collide.

碰撞 to collide; collision.

*chuang* 撞 to rush against; to collide.

*shang* 商定 to decide upon.

*tung* 東北首 towards the north-east.

*shou* 首 a head; a direction towards which a thing lies.

*k'ao* 靠 to lean against; by the side of.

*tzŭ* 滋大 name of a firm in Chefoo, Messrs. Fergusson & Co.

*nei* 內地商船 native merchant vessels; merchant junks.

*shu* 庶 so that.

*pu* 不致 so as not to; so that there may not be; the opposite of *chih* 致 or *i chih* 以致, so that.

*yü* 虞 danger; accident.

*chao* 照會 an official communication; a despatch; to address in a despatch.

*hui* 會 to communicate with.

*ch'a* 查照 to take official notice; for official information.

*ho* 合亟 promptly; duly.

*chi* 亟 haste; prompt; urgent.

*wu* 務 must.

*ya* 押 to seal; a seal; in copies of documents, representing the place where the seal appears in the original: "L.S."

### Document No. 45. [p. 77]

*ya* 壓載沙土石塊 ballast of sand, mud, and stones.

*p'ao* 拋擲 to throw down.

*chih* 擲 to throw down.

*chih* 致 so as to. See *pu* 不致, Document No. 44, p. 76.

*ai* 礙 to cause difficulties to.

*shan* 杉 a kind of pine.

杉板 a sampan; a cargo-boat.

*tui* 堆 a heap; to heap up.

堆積 to heap up.

*chi* 積 to collect.

*pu* 不遵 to disobey; to disregard.

*chu* 築立 to build; to erect.

*li* 立 to erect.

*wei* 未便 inconvenient.

*tsai* 再 still; again; farther.

*i* 議定 to decide.

*shê* 設立 to erect; to establish.

*chiang* 江 (=江蘇) the province of Kiangsu.

*chê* 浙 (=浙江) the province of Chêkiang.

*chien* 建 (=福建) the province of Fukien.

*kuang* 廣 (=廣東) the province of Kwangtung.

*hu* 湖 (=湖廣) the provinces of Hupei and Hunan (=Hukuang).

*wei* 衛 the country of Wei, an ancient feudal state comprising parts of Honan and Chihli; here standing for "Tientsin."

*kuan* 關東 Kuantung, or Manchuria.

*jên* 任 a post; an office; relying on.

任意 as one thinks fit; arbitrarily.

*i* 一律 uniformly; all.

*lü* 律 laws; statutes.

### Document No. 46. [p. 78]

*chin* 謹 respectfully; carefully.

*t'ien* 天津條約 the Treaty of Tientsin; here the British Treaty concluded in A.D. 1858.

*ting* 訂 to settle terms.

*cho* 酌議 to consult about.

*shui* 稅則 the Customs tariff.

*mien* 面爲商定 to consult in person.

*ta* 大淸 the Ch'ing dynasty now ruling in China; the Chinese Empire; Imperial Chinese.

*ch'in* 欽差 sent by the Emperor; an Imperial Ambassador.

*ta* 大臣 a Minister of State.

*chên* 臣 a minister.

*tung* 東閣大學士 one of the four Chinese Grand Secretaries (*see* MAYERS' "The Chinese Government," No. 135).

*ta* 大學士 a Grand Secretary.

*chêng* 正白旗 one of the eight banners of Imperial troops; the "Plain White Banner."

*man* 滿洲 *(man-chou)* Manchu; Manchurian.

*tu* 都統 a lieutenant-general.

*hsing* 刑 punishment; to punish.

刑部 the Board of Punishments.

*shih* 事務 business matters; affairs.

*ching* 經 a classic; classical books.

經筵 the hall of classics; the hall where the Emperor meets academicians.

經筵講官 an Imperial expositor of the Classics.

*yen* 筵 a mat; a dining-hall.

*chiang* 講 to converse; to expound (as the Classics).

講官 an Imperial expositor of the Classics.

*li* 吏 a magistrate; a Government officer.

吏部 the Board of Civil Office.

*shang* 尙 yet; still; to control.

尙書 the President of a Board; a Minister of State.

*hsiang* 鑲 bordered (as a banner).

鑲藍旗 one of the eight banners of Imperial troops; the "Bordered Blue Banner."

*han* 漢軍 the Chinese portion of the army called banner troops.

*chi* 稽 to examine into.

稽察 to examine.

*ch'a* 察 to examime.

*hui* 會同 to meet together; conjointly.

會同四譯館 an office under the Board of Ceremonies; an office where meetings of Foreign Envoys take place (?); "residence for Tributary Envoys" (*see* MAYERS' "The Chinese Government," No. 179).

*i* 譯 to translate; to interpret; an interpreter.

*t'ai* 太 large.

太子 the Imperial Prince; heir to the throne.

太子少保 a junior guardian of the Imperial Prince.

*shao* 少 little; young; junior (as opposed to *t'ai* 太, senior).

*pao* 保 to protect; a ward; a guardian.

*ping* 兵部 the Board of War.

*tu* 都察院 a censor.

都御史 a President of the Censorate.

*chiang* 江南 *(chiang-nan)* the province of Kiangnan, consisting of the two provinces of Anhwei and Kiangsu, each under a Governor, the two being under the control of the Governor-General of Kiangnan.

江西 *(chiang-hsi)* the province of Kiangsi.

*ting* 頂 an official button; the top of anything.

頂戴 to wear a button; the wearer of a button.

*tai* 戴 to wear on the head.

*wu* 武 military.

武備院 the Imperial Armoury.

*ch'ing* 卿 a dignitary; the director of one of the minor courts in the Imperial household (*see* MAYERS' "The Chinese Government," No. 232).

*chün* 軍機處 the Grand Council (*see* MAYERS' "The Chinese Government," No. 133).

*hsing* 行走 to act in another function in addition to one's own duties; to officiate.

*yüan* 員外郎 Second Class Secretary of a Board (*see* MAYERS' "The Chinese Government," No. 164).

*lang* 郎 a term of respect for officers and persons.

*ta* 大英 Great Britain; British.

*shih* 世 a generation; an age.

世襲 a hereditary nobleman; an earl.

*hsi* 襲 to inherit; hereditary.

*chün* 郡 a principality; an earldom.

*po* 伯 an earl.

伯爵 an earl.

*chüeh* } *chio* } 爵 a rank of nobility.

*chu* 逐 to take up in order one by one.

逐欵 by paragraphs; each considered by itself.

*chou* 周 to provide for.

周備 well prepared; well arranged.

*kuan* 官民 the officials and the people.

*min* 民 the people (not being officials or soldiers).

*i* 一同 the same as; uniformly.

*tsun* 遵守 to observe; to be guided by.

*ch'in* 親 a relative; self, in person.

親筆 with one's own hand (as to sign a document).

*kai* 蓋用關防 to affix one's official seal.

*kuan* 關防 an official seal.

*i* 以昭信實 in order to manifest authenticity; "in witness thereof."

*hsin* 信實 authenticity.

*hsin* 新定 newly fixed; lately settled upon.

*t'ung* 通商章程 the Trade Regulations appended to the Tariff.

*shan* 善 good; to make good.

善後 to make good what comes after; to make rules supplementary to a set of rules originally not complete.

善後條約 the Supplementary Rules appended to the Tariff; the "Tariff Rules" or "Trade Regulations."

*chin* 僅 only.

*kai* 賅 to give; uncommon; rare. [p. 79]

賅載 to be given; to be contained in (as in a book or in a document); written down.

*ho* 核估 to estimate; to assess.

核估時價 to calculate the market value of an article.

*shih* 時價 the market value.

*chao* 照值百抽五例 according to the five per cent. *ad valorem* principle.

*chih* 值百抽五 to value at a hundred and levy five, *i.e.*, to charge a five per cent. *ad valorem* duty.

*chêng* 征稅 to levy duty.

*yin* 銀錢 coins.

*su* 粟 maize; Indian corn.

粟米粉 Indian meal.

*sha* 砂穀米 sago.

*mien* 麵餅 cakes; biscuits.

*shou* 熟 ripe; cooked; preserved.

熟肉 preserved meats.

*jou* 肉 meat.

*shou* 熟菜 preserved vegetables.

*niu* 牛奶酥 cheese.

*nai* 奶 milk.

*su* 酥 curd; cheese.

*niu* 牛油 butter; also, animal tallow.

*shou* 首飾 head ornaments; jewellery.

*shih* 飾 ornaments; to ornament; to paint.

*ch'an* 攙 to mix (as good metal with an inferior metal).

攙銀器 plated ware.

*hsiang* 香水 fragrant water; perfumery.

*chien* 碱 (礆 or 鹻) soap.

*t'an* 炭 charcoal.

*ch'ai* 柴 firewood.

柴薪 firewood.

*la* 蠟燭 candles.

*chu* 燭 a candle.

*chia* 家用雜物 household stores.

*ch'uan* 船用雜物 ship's stores.

*chih* 紙張 paper. Cf. *ssŭ* 絲斤, Document No. 18, p. 28.

紙張筆墨 stationery.

*pi* 筆 a pen; a pencil.

*mo* 墨 ink (in cakes).

*chan* 氈毯 carpeting and druggeting.

*t'an* 毯 rugs; druggets.

*hsiu* 繡 to embroider; embroideries.

繡貨 *articles de tapisserie.*

*t'ieh* 鐵刀利器 cutlery.

*tao* 刀 a knife; knives.

*li* 利 sharp; edged.

利器 edged tools; knives; cutlery.

*tzŭ* 自用 for own use.

*yao* 藥料 medicines.

*p'o* 玻璃器皿 glassware.

*min* 皿 vessels (as cups, etc.)

*wu* 毋庸 need not; not necessary to.

毋庸議 need not take into account; to except.

*sui* 雖 although (the "yet" following may be expressed by *yeh* 亦, *jan* 然, or *êrh* 而).

*ch'ien* 前 the before-mentioned.

*nei* 內地 native, as "native opium" (cf. Document No. 13, p. 14) or "native salt."

*fan* 販運 to traffic in (goods).

*suan* 算 to calculate.

*ch'ing* 輕 light.

輕重 weight.

*chang* 長短 length.

*chi* 即係 that is; namely; is equal to.

*fên* 分 to divide; used to denote a fraction, *e.g.*, 三分之一, one third.

*i* 以……為準 to consider……as a standard.

*yin* 因制 (in imitation of the English sound "inch") an inch; inches.

*ma* 碼 a yard; yards.

*ch'ien* 欠 to owe; to be short of; to deduct; less.

*i* 以此爲例 this is to be regarded as the rule.

*tou* 荳石 pulse. Cf. *ssŭ* 絲斤, Document No. 18, p. 28. [p. 80]

*hsiao* 硝 saltpetre.

硝磺 saltpetre; sulphur and brimstone.

*huang* 磺 sulphur.

*chih* 止 to stop; only.

*chih* 祇 only; but.

*hu* 護送 to accompany.

*ying* 英民 British subjects.

*ch'ih* 持照 provided with a passport.

*wu* 無涉 to have nothing to do with.

*shê* 涉 to concern; to be connected with.

*ju* 如何 in what manner; the manner in which.

如何征稅 the manner in which duties are levied; the mode of levying duties.

*t'ing* 聽憑 to depend on; will depend on.

*hsiu* 修改 to amend; to revise.

修改稅則 to revise a Customs tariff.

*jêng* 仍 again; then. Cf. *chi* 即, Document No. 21, p. 46.

*t'ung* 同商 a mercantile friend; a fellow merchant.

*lien* 聯名 to sign conjointly (as a surety).

*i* 抑 else; or.

抑或 or else.

*ch'ih* 飭令 to order.

*kuo* 過期 to exceed a limit.

*ch'ien* 錢貨 copper cash as cargo.

*yüan* 原本 original; the original value.

*pu* 不拘 no matter whether.

*nei* 內外土產 native or foreign produce.

*t'u* 土產 produce.

*t'ung* 通商別口 another Treaty port.

*chao* 照依 according to.

*i* 依 to rely on; as; according to.

*niu* 牛莊 Newchwang.

*têng* 登州 Têng-chow-fu.

*chün* 軍前要物 munitions of war.

*hua* 華官 Chinese officials; native authorities.

*ts'ai* 採辦 to buy.

*t'ê* 特奉准買 to be licensed for the purchase [of exceptional goods].

*ming* 明文 an unmistakable written passage; a stipulation in writing; there being a written understanding about.

*ch'a* 查明 to inspect (as a document).

*ting* 定 it is agreed that; it shall be the rule that.

*fa* 發單起貨 to issue a permit to land.

*nei* 內港 ports in the interior; ports not open to trade; inland waters.

*k'ai* 開艙 to open hatches. [p. 81]

*t'a* 他往 to proceed to another place.

*tsung* 總 all.

*shih* 時刻 time.

*ch'i* 起算 to commence reckoning (as from a given time).

*i* 以免參差爭論 in order to prevent misunderstanding.

*ts'an* 參 mixed; confused.

參差 incongruous; to disagree.

參差爭論 to disagree and quarrel.

*chêng* 爭 to quarrel.

爭論 to quarrel; to discuss.

*chi* 旣 since.

*pien* 便商 to accommodate merchants; to show due consideration to the convenience of trade.

*kêng* 更 still more; moreover; again.

更不 still less; much less.

*yu* 有礙收稅 to interfere with the collection of the revenue.

*pên* 本屬商民 the merchants under one's jurisdiction.

*i* 議 (= 義 or 文義) the meaning of a passage.

*i* 一半爲斷 to divide into two halves.

*tuan* 斷 to break asunder.

斷半 to halve a thing.

*yüan* 緣 cause; origin; circumstances.

緣由 circumstances; particulars.

*ch'io* / *ch'üeh* } 確 true.

確實 the true facts; no mistake.

*sung* 送 to accompany.

送貨之人 the person accompanying goods; a supercargo.

*k'ai* 開單 to make out a bill, a memorandum, etc.

*lu* 路上 on the road.

*tsui* 最後子口 the last barrier; the barrier nearest a Treaty port.

*hsü* 許 to allow; to be allowed.

*yen* 沿途私賣 to sell clandestinely on the road; unauthorised sale (of goods) *in transitu*.

*shih* 實據 documentary proof. [p. 82]

*wan* 完淸 to pay the full amount.

*shih* 始 then first; not till then.

*i* 以杜隱漏 in order to prevent evading (as payment of duties).

*tu* 杜 to stop; to prevent.

*yin* 隱 dark; to avoid; to conceal.

隱漏 to avoid, to evade (as payment of duties).

*ming* 明晰 clearly.

*hsi* 晰 clear; to distinguish.

*hsiao* 曉布 to make known by proclamation.

*t'ung* 通悉 to make generally known; to inform by circular or proclamation.

*i* 一節 all; equally.

*i* 議 it is agreed that.

*ching* 京都 the capital; Peking, as the capital of China (also, the city of Kioto in Japan).

*hsiang* 向例 according to the rule hitherto in force.

*ch'ing* 傾 to assay; to smelt.

傾鎔之費 expenses of melting; meltage fees.

*jung* 鎔 to fuse metals.

*ts'ai* 裁 to cut (as clothes).

裁撤 to cut away; to do away with.

*ch'ê* 撤 to remove; to take away.

*yen* 嚴防偷漏 to protect the revenue; to prevent smuggling.

*jan* 然 yet; however.

*i* 議明 to agree upon.

*ko* 各口 the ports; the Treaty ports.

*shih* 是 this means that; the above amounts to this, that, etc.

*shih* 事宜 that which properly pertains to the business of ……; affairs; matters.

*i* 宜 that which is proper; that which must necessarily be done in connexion with.

*ch'in* 親詣 to go in person.

*i* 詣 to go to.

*hsün* 巡歷 to inspect (a district, a port).

*wei* 委員代辦 to depute an officer as one's agent.

*jên* 任 to bear; to sustain.

*jên* 任憑 allowed to depend on; it is in the free will of ……

*yao* 邀 to invite.

邀請 to invite; to engage for service.

*yen* 嚴查漏稅 to protect the revenue; to prevent smuggling.

*p'an* 判 to divide; to decide.

判定口界 to define the port limits.

*fên* 分 respectively. Before a verb it means that the action of the verb is to be applied at different places, to different objects, etc., *respectively*; similarly before nouns, *e.g.*, 三分文, *i.e.*, "the three versions respectively."

*hao* 號船 a lightship.

*t'a* 塔表 a light tower.

*piao* 表 to make known; a guide; a signal; a watch.

*wang* 望樓 a beacon.

*lou* 樓 an upper story; a tower.

*chih* 指薦 to point out and recommend; to suggest a nomination.

*chien* 薦 to recommend.

*kan* 干預 to meddle with.

*po* 撥用 to appropriate (as funds).

*t'ung* 通商後 after the opening up of trade.

*ch'a* 察看 to examine.

*shê* 設法籌辦 to adopt measures for.

*chou* 籌 to calculate.

籌辦 to arrange.

### Document No. 47. [p. 83]

*chung* 鐘 a clock; a bell.

鐘表 clocks and watches.

*chiang* 匠 a mechanic.

匠人 a workman; a manufacturer (as a watchmaker, etc.)

*hang* 行名 the name of a firm.

*i* 以備稽查 in order to provide for examination; for future identification (said of documents containing particulars as to goods, and filed in archives); for future reference.

*ya* 壓印戳記 to impress a seal or mark.

*ch'uo* 戳記 an official seal.

*chi* 記 a seal (of a private person or a petty official); a chop.

*tso* 作爲 to consider as.

*ts'ung* 從重治罪 to be severely punished.

*chih* 治 to regulate; to punish.

治罪 to try and punish an offender.

*ch'êng* 懲辦 to try and punish an offender.

*hui* 回國 to return, or to be sent back, to one's country.

*chi* 給以存票 to grant drawback. Cf. *i* 以, Document No. 29, p. 58.

給以免單 to grant an exemption certificate.

*kua* 挂號 to provide with a number; to register.

*ts'un* 存行 to keep in one's hong or store (as for sale).

*fa* 發賣 to sell; to expose for sale.

*i* 一經查出 as soon as discovered; when caught (as in an illegal act).

*wei* 違章 to break the regulations.

*tsung* 總例 a general rule.

*ch'a* 查獲 to seize (as smuggled goods).

*i* 以細報粗 to declare a superior as an inferior quality; false declaration of quality. Cf. *i* 以, Document No. 29, p. 58.

以貴價報賤價 to declare a lower as the real value; false declaration of value.

*sui* 隨事酌情 to decide according to circumstances.

*k'ai* 開價 to declare the value (of an article).

*shou* 收買 to take over on sale; to buy from another.

*ko* 各行 the shops (of a place); the firms.

*tzŭ* 自 of course.

*k'ai* 開列清單 to enter in a list; to make a list of.

*i* 已滿 being full; having expired (as a limit of time).

*sui* 隨時 in future; hereafter.

**Document No. 48.**

*cha* 劄 a despatch from a superior to on inferior.

劄行 to address a despatch to an inferior.

*jun* 閏 intercalary.

閏十月 the tenth intercalary month.

*shên* 申 to report.

申稱 to report (to a superior).

*ch'ieh* 竊查 it is my humble opinion that.

*ch'ao* 鈔課 tonnage dues.

*yün* 允協 harmonious; perfect; effective.

*ch'i* 其間 amongst them.

*ying* 應徵 liable to payment of duty.

應免 to be exempted (from duty); free.

*fei* 非 not; the opposite of *shih* (是).

非但……亦……not only……but also……

*t'ien* 添 to add. [p. 84]

*ch'i* 齊楚 to arrange well; to systematise.

*ch'ieh* 且 moreover.

*yin* 因時制宜 to take the necessary steps, as circumstances may require.

因時 on account of the time; at the proper time.

*chih* 制 to make.

制宜 to do what is proper.

*hsiu* 修補 to amend.

*wên* 文件 despatches; documents.

*i* 以致 so that; so as to.

*ch'ung* 重複 again; repeated.

*fu* 複 to double.

*fên* 紛 to mix; to confuse.

紛雜 mixed; confused.

*i* 擬議 to decide; decision.

*pu* 不一 not the same; different; more than one; several.

*shih* 勢 power; condition.

*shan* 善後條款 the Rules appended to the Tariff.

*hsiang* 詳加核對 to compare carefully.

*pi* 比較 to compare.

*tsung* 綜 to hold the threads (in weaving); to collect.

綜紛緒 to collect the confused threads of a texture; to arrange in order.

*fên* 紛 confused; ill-assorted.

*hsü* 緒 a thread; a clue.

*tso* 作成 to make ready; to complete.

*hui* 彙 to sort; to classify.

彙訂 to arrange; to classify.

*ting* 訂 to arrange; to adjust.

*fan* 煩 to trouble; please; I shall be obliged if you will.

*ho* 核奪 to examine and decide.

*to* 奪 to criticise; to settle.

*chuan* 轉 to transmit.

轉飭 to give instructions for transmission (to subordinates).

*i* 以免紛歧 in order to avoid divergency (in acting).

*ch'i* 歧 diverging; discrepancy.

*kuei* 歸畫一 to make uniform; to obtain uniformity.

*shang* 倘屬 it might be; I daresay it is.

*chou* 周妥 quite correct.

*k'ai* 開明 to write out clearly.

*tz'ŭ* 咨行 to address in a despatch.

*nan* 南北洋通商大臣 the High Commissioners of Northern and Southern Trade.

*ko* 各國大臣 the Treaty Power Ministers.

*hsiang* 相應 duly.

*chuan* 轉行……遵照辦理 to transmit for the guidance of.......

*chêng* 徵免船鈔章程 the Tonnage Dues Regulations.

*chêng* 正 exactly; only. After figures, cf. Document No. 2, p. 2.

*la* 拉司 (in imitation of the English sound "last") a last (English weight or measure).

*i* 以……爲準 to take......as a standard.

*t'ai* 泰 great.

泰西 the great West; Western (as in "the Western calendar").

*ko* 嗝拉 *(ko-la)* the city of Galatz.

*li* 立 to erect; to draft; to set up.

*ho* 核算清單 a table for calculation or conversion.

*shêng* 乘 to avail oneself; to multiply.

乘以一百 to multiply by 100.

*ch'u* 除 to subtract; to divide.

除以一百 to divide by 100.

*yü* 與……同 the same as; equal to.

*t'u* 土耳國 *(tu-êrh-kuo)* Turkey; Turkish. [p. 85]

*pu* 布國 (=布路斯 *pu-lu-ssŭ*) Prussia; Prussian.

*po* 伯磊們 *(po-lei-mên)* the city of Bremen.

*hsi* 希國 Greece; Greek.

*ang* 昂布爾 *(ang-pu-êrh)* the city of Hamburg.

*han* 漢諾威 *(han-no-wei)* Hanover; Hanoverian.

*lü* 律伯克 *(lü-po-k'o)* the city of Lübeck.

*mo* 模令布爾額 *(mo-ling-pu-êrh-ngo)* Mecklenburg.

*no* 挪爾爲國 *(no-êrh-wei-kuo)* Norway. Cf. Document No. 19, p. 32. [p. 86]

*a* 阿爾敦布爾額 *(a-êrh-tun-pu-êrh-ngo)* Oldenburg.

*ho* 合一國 the United Principalities.

*chi* 基羅 (in imitation of the sound "kilo.") a kilogram.

*p'ai* 掰拉 *(p'ai-la)* the city of Braïla.

*jui* 瑞國 (=瑞嗔 *jui-tien*) Sweden; Swedish. Cf. Document No. 19, p. 32.

*shu* 輸納 to pay (as duties).

*ni* 呢廓來業福斯克 *(ni-k'uo-lai-yeh-fu-ssŭ-k'o)* Nicolaievsk.

*to* 度 to calculate.

度量 to measure (as a vessel).

*liang* 量 to measure.

量船執照 a certificate of measurement.

*tz'ŭ* 此等 of this class; *i.e.*, such.

*chêng* 征鈔 to levy tonnage dues.

*i* 以畫一辦理 to treat a matter in a uniform manner.

*shih* 試辦再議 to work by way of experiment and then decide, *i.e.*, experimental and open to revision (as a regulation); provisional.

*t'ing* 艇 a boat.

*shu* 書信 letters.

*shih* 食物 eatables; articles of provision.

*li* 例不納稅之物 articles not subject to duty.

例應完稅之貨 merchandise subject to duty.

*i* 一次 once.

*t'a* 他國 other countries; foreign countries. [p. 87]

*ta* 搭 to engage (as a ship or a passage).

搭客 passengers.

*hsiang* 向常 according to the routine hitherto observed; in the ordinary way; ordinarily.

*yü* 遇……之時 at the time when; when the time for......has arrived.

*chih* 祇 only.

*kung* 公司 a public company; a mail steamer company.

公司輪船 a mail steamer.

*mou* 某國 a certain country; some foreign country.

*li* 立定合同 to fix by contract.

*ho* 合同 to make a contract.

*shê* 設 if; to arrange for.

設傳文信 to arrange for the transmission of official documents and private letters; to undertake the forwarding of correspondence.

*ch'uan* 傳 to forward (as letters).

*an* 按期定數 at regular (fixed) dates.

*chih* 指定 to destine for (as a certificate for a certain vessel).

*yüan* 緣 because.

*yu* 有時 sometimes; at any time.

*ti* 抵 to act as; to perform the service of.

抵充 to act as; to perform the service of.

*ling* 另項 a different kind of ......; other.

*ngo* 額 a fixed number.

額設船隻 a fixed number of vessels.

*pu* 不在此例 not covered by this rule.

*shou* 收口躲避 to seek shelter in a port.

*to* 躲 to hide away; to escape from.

躲避 to seek shelter; to escape from.

*pi* 避 to flee from; to escape.

*hsing* 行文知照 to inform officially.

*mo* 末 the end.

末後 at the end; the last.

*ch'u* 出口單 a port clearance.

*ch'a* 查閱 to examine (as a document); to peruse.

*i* 以資稽查 for examination; for inspection.

*tsun* 遵守 to observe (as regulations).

*tsê* 擇 to select; to choose.

擇訂 to assign (as a berth to a ship).

*t'ing* 停泊處所 a place for anchoring; a berth.

*pu* 不致 so as not to; so that there may not be.

*jih* 日行事宜 the daily business.

*yu* 有所窒碍 there are difficulties; to be fraught with difficulties.

*chih* 窒 to impede; to hamper.

窒碍 difficulties.

*k'an* 看守 to watch (a ship); a watcher; a tidewaiter.

*k'ou* 扣除核算 to deduct in calculating (as the number of days spent in repair in calculating term of tonnage dues certificates).

*ts'un* 存棧 to store goods in a godown.

*k'ung* 空船 an empty vessel; a vessel in ballast.

*shou* 收口 to enter port (as for shelter).

*shao* 燒 to burn. [p. 88]

燒完 burnt off; consumed and finished (as coal on board a steamer).

*fu* 復行 to go again; to continue a journey (after having put into a port).

*p'ai* 牌 a board; a certificate (especially a ship's register).

*mei* 煤艙 the space allowed for coal on board a steamer; coal bunkers.

*nei* 內輪器具 the engines (on board a steamer).

*ku* 僱用 to hire; to charter (as a vessel).

*ch'uan* 船料 port dues (paid by Chinese junks at native Custom Houses).

*mei* 每逢四個月 every four months.

*yu* 有別 to be different from.

**Document No. 49.**

*yin* 引水章程 the Pilotage Regulations.

*chuan* 專條 special rules.

*ko* 各口分章 local rules (at the various ports).

*fên* 分章 branch rules; local rules.

*ting* 定擬 to decide upon (as upon rules).

*chun* 準情酌理 to consider the circumstances of.

*yüeh yo* } 約與 to consult with; to agree upon a matter with.

*t'ung* 通商總局 a Chamber of Commerce.

*k'ou* 口外引費 pilotage fees; pilotage charges.

*k'uan* 寬 to extend. [p. 89]

*chao* 招募 to enlist; to engage.

*mu* 募 to invite; to enlist.

*yu* 有條約各國 the Treaty Powers.

*min* 民 people; subjects.

*ch'ung* 充引水 to perform the duties of a pilot; to be eligible as a pilot.

充當 to fill the duties of an office; to be eligible for an office.

*yü* 遇有缺出 when a vacancy occurs.

*ch'üeh* 缺 a vacancy.

缺出 a vacancy occurring (as from resignation).

*k'ao* 考 to examine.

考選局 a board of examination.

*hsüan* 選 to choose; to select.

*chien* 揀 to choose.

揀選 to select.

*ch'ung* 充補 to fill a vacancy.

*yüeh yo* } 約同 to consult with......

*tso* 作 to make; to do; gives a verb active force, *e.g.*, in the sentence 可作考選之人, *i.e.*, "the persons who may examine, or may be members of the Board of Examination," *tso* (作) has the effect of preventing the sentence being misconstrued as "the persons who may be examined, or may be admitted to examination."

*yü* 預爲錄示 o prepare and publish a list.

*i* 以資......in order to afford...... ; by means of which one may......

*lu* 錄 a record; to record.

*chien* 籤 to draw a lot.

籤掣 to select by lot.

*ch'ih* 掣 to select; to draw a lot.

*tung* 董 to manage.

董事 a senior in a firm; a manager.

*yin* 引水董事 a senior pilot.

*shên* 愼 careful; to be careful.

*pang* 榜 a list of graduates.

榜示 to issue a public notice.

*hui* 會齊考試 a competitive examination.

*k'ao* 考試 to examine.

*pei* 備考者 one who prepares for examination; a candidate for examination.

*t'ang* 儻 (used for *t'ang* 倘) if.

*yin* 因事故而斥革 to be dismissed from office for some reason or other.

*ch'ih* 斥 to expel.

斥革 to deprive of rank; to dismiss; to withdraw the license of a pilot.

*ko* 革 to deprive of rank and office; to dismiss from office.

*chieh* 結 to give a bond for; to guarantee.

*kuan* 官結 to be guaranteed by the authorities; to possess a certificate of character issued by a public office.

*lan* 濫 to encroach; to intrude.

濫膺赴考 to become a candidate for examination without the necessary qualification.

*ying* 膺 to undertake.

*fu* 赴考 to proceed to an examination.

*pei* 備試 to prepare for examination.

*kuei* 規 rule; usage; custom; customary.

規費 customary fees; gratuities.

*ho* 合衆 all present; public (as a public examination).

*ping* 秉 to uphold (as a principle).

秉公 upholding justice; impartially.

*tsê* 擇 to select.

*yu* 優 to excel; excellent; competent.

*ju* 入選 to receive an appointment.

*shih* 使 if; supposing that; in the event of.

*shih* 實在 really.

*pên* 本領 (=*pên-shih* 本事) able; competent.

*ning* 甯 to prefer; it is better to......than......(in which case *than* is expressed by a negation, as in "better die and not be disgraced," which means "it is better to die *than* be disgraced").

甯死不辱 it is *better* to die *than* be disgraced.

甯缺而毋用 it is *better* to keep a vacancy open *than* to use (a bad man).

*i* 以免貽誤 to avoid the occurrence of errors.

*i* 貽 to bring on; to cause.

*pên* 本人 oneself; in person.

*ts'ung* 從 to follow.

從旁 to be present at.

*chien* 監同 to take part in the superintendence of.

*tsai* 在事 to do service as; to be on duty; on service.

在事者 the members of a service, or of an office; connected with business.

*shih* 事權 authority; power.

*hsüan* 選中 to choose; to select.

*yü* 與 and; or.

與否 whether.........or not.

*ts'ung* 從衆爲定 the [absolute] majority decides.

*chih* 執己見 to stick to one's own view.

*chi* 己見 one's own view.

*chien* 見 to be of opinion; to maintain; the view one takes of a matter.

*ting* 定評 to decide; to have a casting vote if votes are divided.

*p'ing* 評 to discuss.

*chih* 執據 a license (as a pilot's). [p. 90]

*yin* 引水字據 a pilot's license.

*tzŭ* 字據 a license.

*hsia* 夏季 the summer season.

*chi* 季 a season of three months.

*hsü* 續 to continue; to renew.

*ling* 領回 to re-issue; to renew, as a license handed in for cancelling.

*hsü* 續領之費 the expenses of issuing again; a fee for renewing a license.

*fên* 分 a set (as of printed regulations).

*so* 索 to ask for.

索看 to be desirous to see; to ask for a copy of......for inspection; to ask to be shown.

*ping* 並 together with.

*ch'êng* 呈出 to produce (as a certificate).

*hsiao* 學 to learn.

學徒 an apprentice.

*t'u* 徒 a pupil; a disciple.

*ting* 定制 a fixed routine; fixed rules.

*yüan* 願 to wish; to be willing.

*pao* 保 to guarantee; to be surety for.

*hsi* 攜 to lead.

攜帶 to take along with oneself.

*shêng* 勝 adequate to; worthy of.

勝選 eligible; competent for election.

勝選憑照 a certificate of competency; a document certifying to the eligibility of a person for a certain post.

*hsü* 需 it is required.

*wai* 外需情事 extraordinary requirements; under exceptional circumstances.

*t'ing* 聽制 to be subordinate to; under the control of.

*tu* 獨 alone; on one's own account.

*kung* 公同 on joint account; in company.

*k'o* 可行 may be done; allowable.

*fêng* 奉行 to receive orders from a superior.

*wei* 違背 to disobey orders.

*pei* 背 the back; behind the back; to oppose.

*ch'ê* 撤銷 to take away and cancel.

*ping* 稟訴 to make a petition; a counter-statement.

*su* 訴 to tell; to inform; to accuse.

*yüan* 原委 the original grievance; the details of an accusation.

*wei* 委 a grievance.

*chia* 假借 to borrow on false grounds (as a certificate made out in the name of another). [p. 91]

*chieh* 借 to lend to another; to borrow from another.

*chih* 治罪 to punish.

*shao* 艄 the stern of a vessel.

艄工 the commanding officer on board a ship; a ship-master.

*ch'uan* 船式 the type of a ship; the rig of a ship.

*ta* 大小 the size of a thing.

*hao* 號照 a certificate of registry.

*yin* 引水船 a pilot boat.

*chi* 幾 how many; a certain number, as in 第幾號 = "No. so-and-so;" "what number?"

*shu* 書明 to write legibly.

*ch'uan* 船尾 the stern of a vessel.

*p'êng* 篷 a sail.

*ssŭ* 四方之式 square; rectangular.

*p'ai* 牌照 the ship's papers.

*shui* 稅司 (=稅務司) a Commissioner of Customs.

*kuo* 果 really.

*chieh* 節 an article, a paragraph (in a set of regulations); also, the rules contained therein.

*jên* 任便 freely; at liberty.

*wang* 望樓 a light-station.

*i* 一……卽…… as soon as ……, ……

*fên* 吩 to order.

吩附 to order.

*fu* 附 to order.

*jên* 任 it is incumbent on; it is a duty to.

*shih* 使用 to employ; to be employed; to lend one's services.

*tzŭ* 字據費銀 a license fee (paid by pilots).

*chin* 緊急 urgent.

*yin* 引務 pilotage business.

*ch'êng* 乘 to avail oneself.

乘坐 to make use of a boat or a carriage.

*p'ing* 平時 in ordinary times; ordinarily.

*ch'uan* 船艇 a boat. [p. 92]

船戶 the people on board a ship; the shipowner.

*kai* 該管之官 the authorities to whom one is amenable

*tz'ŭ* 此時 during such time.

*fên* 分別飭挂號記 to exhibit distinguishing flags.

*hao* 號記 signals.

*chi* 寄信旗 signalling flags; code signals.

*chiao* 角 a horn; a corner.

*chieh* 接領 to receive; to take over; to take charge of.

*kai* 改泊 to shift berth (as a vessel in harbour).

*hsiu* 修廠 a dock.

*chao* 照料 to superintend; to manage.

*liao* 料 to dispose properly.

料理 to manage.

*cho* 酌體 to meet the wishes of another; to treat with consideration.

*t'i* 體 the body; to receive courteously.

體恤 to befriend.

*ching* 經紀 an agent; a consignee; a broker.
*pien* 便 convenience.
*i* 移離 to move away. [p. 93]
*yin* 引費 pilotage fees.
*tai* 代收 to receive for another; to collect (fees, etc.).
*t'ien* 添 to add.
添錨 to moor (a vessel).
*tien* 塡寫 to fill in by writing.
*shih* 試辦 provisional.
*yu* 猶 more; further; if; like.
*kêng* 更訂 to alter; to amend (as rules).

### Document No. 50. [p. 94]

*ta* 搭船 a passenger ship.
*jên* 人客 passengers.
*ch'ien* 扦 (=插) to graft into; to put in.
扦子 an iron rod ending in a spoon bowl with a sharp point, used by tidewaiters for thrusting into packages when examining goods.
扦子手 a tidewaiter.
*i* 以專責成 in order to mark responsibility.
*i* 疑 to suppose; to suspect.
*ta* 打開備查 to open for examination (as packages at the Custom House).
*ching* 徑 directly; quickly.
*kuan* 關上 the Customs.
*ch'i* 起出 to unload goods.
起卸 to unload goods.
*ko* 各種 of all kinds.
*têng* 登簿 to enter in a ledger; to register.
*ch'ü* 取回 to fetch back; to take back.
*t'o* 拖帶簿 a register of licensed steam tugs. [p. 95]
*shan* 删 to expunge.
删除 to expunge; to remove a name from a list.
*shih* 時 each time; at any time.

### Document No. 51.

*hui* 會訊 to investigate conjointly; joint investigation.
會訊章程 the Joint Investigation Rules.
*kan* 干 to concern.
干涉 to be connected with.
*kuan* 關照 to come to an understanding with each other.
*mien* 面見 to see personally; to interview.
*hui* 會議 to discuss conjointly; to have an interview.
*li* 吏 an officer.
*li* 立 at once; without delay.
*t'ing* 聽稟 to entertain a petition; to consider a report (from an inferior).
*ho* 合宜 justifiable.
*han* 函致 to write to; to give notice to in writing.
*shih* 是以 therefore.
*tzŭ* 自接函之時 from the date of notice being given; from the date when the letter was received.
*i* 以五日爲期 within five days.
*wu* 午刻 before noon, say between 11 A.M. and noon.
*k'o* 刻 the eighth part of a Chinese hour, or 15 minutes; a set time.
*jên* 任便 to be at liberty to.
*ch'ên* 陳明 to state.
*chuan* 轉報 to further report to another what has been reported to oneself; to communicate a report received.
*i* 以……爲是 to consider (a matter) to be so; to consider as correct.
*shih* 是 correct; satisfactory (as an explanation).
*shih* 釋放 to release.
*shê* 設 if; supposing that.
*i* 以爲然 to consider that it be so; to accede to a request.
*ping* 稟知 to inform (a superior).
*chuan* 轉咨 to further write to another what has been communicated to oneself; to transmit in a despatch a communication received.
*ting* 定期 to name a day; to fix a time for.
*wu* 晤 to see face to face; to meet in person.
晤會 to meet in person.
*t'ung* 統帶 to bring with oneself (as witnesses to court).
*chien* 見證 a witness.
*chêng* 證 to substantiate; evidence; a witness.
*ch'in* 親身 in person.
*shang* 上堂 to proceed to the court-room; to come into court.
*t'ung* 同坐 to occupy the bench with another.
*tso* 坐 to sit; to sit on the bench in a court.
*hsiang* 相幫 to assist. [p. 96]
*ling* 令 to call upon......to......

*ch'ing* 情節 particulars; circumstances.

*chieh* / *ch'i* } 詰 to investigate; to ask with authority.

詰問 to cross-examine.

*pien* 辯 to dispute; to argue against.

辯駁 to contradict; to dispute; contradictory.

*po* 駁 to dispute; to argue against.

*chu* 逐 one by one; in detail.

*i* 以期得實 in order to arrive at the truth.

以杜偏累 in order to avoid partiality.

*p'ien* 偏 inclined to one side; partial.

偏累 partiality.

*lei* 累 to involve; to implicate.

*shê* 設若 if; supposing that.

*ch'ien* 遣 to send.

遣員代往 to send an officer on one's behalf; to be represented by deputy.

*hsün* 詢 to inquire.

詢問 to ask particulars; to inquire.

*chien* 間 at the time of; *e.g.*, 夜間 at night-time.

*kuan* 關役 Customs officers.

*k'ou* 口供 depositions; oral statements; testimony.

*kung* 供 to deposit; the deposition (of a witness).

*shih* 時 at the time; then; thereupon.

*an* 案 a court.

*t'ui* 退 to retire.

退去 to withdraw; to retire.

*mien* 面告 to inform in person.

*k'o* 可否 whether or not it is possible to.

*shang* 上控 to appeal.

*an* 案情 the details of a case.

案情抄錄 a copy of the minutes of a case.

*chu* 駐 to reside at.

駐京大臣(憲) the Foreign Ministers residing at Peking.

*pu* 不肯 not willing.

*k'ên* 肯 willing.

*ch'ing* 請索賠償 to claim an indemnity.

*p'ei* 賠 to indemnify.

賠償 to compensate for; to indemnify.

*ch'ang* 償 to indemnify.

*ta* 大憲 the High Authorities.

*ting* 定斷 to decide a case.

*ch'u* 出具切結 to give a bond.

*ch'ing* 情願 to be willing; to bind oneself in.

*tsun* 遵斷 to abide by the decision in a case.

*chiao* 繳案 to pay into court (as a fine).

*shui* 誰 who; whose; whom.

誰是誰非 who is in the right and who is in the wrong.

*shih* 是非 to be and not to be; yes and no; positive and negative; right and wrong.

*ping* 稟請賠補 to claim compensation.

*chih* 指明 to point out. [p. 97]

*i* 一面......一面...... on the one hand,......on the other,......

*li* 立案 to enter a plaint in court.

*hsün* 訊 to investigate.

訊斷 to try, and give judgment in, a case.

*chuan* 傳集人證 to summon witnesses.

*tsai* 在坐 being seated; occupying a seat on the bench (in court).

*chih* 指證 to point out the evidence; to conduct a case on behalf of the prosecution.

*tuan* 斷令交出 to give judgment that (a fine) shall be paid.

*ts'ung* 從寬 to mitigate a sentence.

*wu* 無異言 of the same opinion.

*chüan* 權屬在該關 the power of......rests with the said Custom House.

*liu* 留滯 to detain.

*chih* 滯 to obstruct; to hinder.

*i* 一同 at the same time with; at once.

*k'ai* 開放 to release.

*tan* 躭 to prevent; to obstruct; to delay.

躭延時日 to procrastinate; to delay.

*yen* 延 to protract; to delay.

*so* 索賠 to claim compensation for.

索賠延擱貿易銀兩 to claim damages for delay in business; to claim demurrage.

*yen* 延擱 to delay.

*ko* 擱 to obstruct; to put down at a place.

*shui* 水脚 fare by water; freight (by ship).

水脚費用等項 freight (or passage money) and other expenses.

*chiao* 脚 the leg; workmen; labourers; porters.

*i* 意見 one's opinion.

*tang* 當……之時 during the time when......

當尙未……之時 before the time of......; previous to......

*hsing* 行文知照 to inform in a despatch.

*yüan* 援 to put forward; to quote.

援照 on the ground of (as a Treaty paragraph); according to.

*i* 一面 at the same time.

*ho* 核斷 to decide a case. [p. 98]

*i* 以昭核實 to ascertain a correct statement (as of value).

### Document No. 52.

*ch'ang* 長江六處 the six landing stages on the Yangtze (opened to trade by the Chefoo Convention).

*yen* 烟臺條款 the Chefoo Convention.

*yen* 沿江 on the Yangtze.

*an* 安徽 *(an-hui)* the province of Anhwei.

*ta* 大通 Ta-t'ung (a port of call on the Yangtze).

*an* 安慶 *(an-ch'ing)* Ank'ing (capital of the Anhwei province, and a port of call on the Yangtze).

*chiang* 江西 *(chiang-hsi)* the province of Kiangsi.

*hu* 湖口 Huk'ow (a port of call on the Yangtze).

湖廣 *(hu-kuang)* the two provinces of Hupeh and Hunan.

*wu* 武穴 *(wu-hsüeh)* Wusüeh (a port of call on the Yangtze).

*lu* 陸溪口 *(lu-ch'i-k'ou)* Lu-k'i-k'ow (a port of call on the Yangtze).

*sha* 沙市 Shashih (a port of call on the Yangtze).

*t'ung* 通融 to befriend; to accommodate; by way of accommodation or compromise.

通融辦理 to make an arrangement by way of accommodation or of compromise.

*yung* 融 clear; intelligent; harmony.

*fang* 仿 (=倣) to imitate.

仿照 to follow; to conform to (as to a set of regulations); conformably with.

*hsieh* 卸賣 to land (goods) for sale.

*t'o* 妥辦 to manage safely; to take the proper measures in carrying out business.

*chü* 居住 to reside at.

*hang* 行棧 hong and godowns; a mercantile establishment.

*so* 所載 the passage quoted; this quotation.

*ta* 大概 generally speaking; the general features of......

*ch'u* 出洋輪船 an ocean steamer (as opposed to a "river steamer"). [p. 99]

*nai* 乃指……而言 that is to say; that is.

*nei* 內江輪船 a river steamer (as opposed to an "ocean steamer").

*min* 民船 a "native boat" (as opposed to "foreign boats"); a "private or merchant junk" (as opposed to "Government vessels"); here, a registered junk plying between the ports of call on the Yangtze.

*pien* 編列字號 to register (as a cargo-boat).

*chuang* 裝船 to put on board a ship (as goods); to ship.

裝船處 the place of shipment.

*tz'ŭ* 此去 from here; from this (place).

*chi* 幾……幾…… so many...... as...... (*e.g.*, to pay *so many* times the Likin duty *as* there are barriers on the road).

幾倍 so many times.

*i* 以補應完之釐 to make up for the Likin taxes due.

*yüan* 援免 to apply (an exceptional rule) to the exemption (of goods from payment of duty); to claim exemption.

*mo* 末尾 the last; at the last. [p. 100]

末尾一關 that Custom House which is at the end; the last Custom House (passed).

*i* 一 before a noun and preceded by a genitive, or a clause corresponding to a genitive, may be said to represent the definite article: 末尾一關, "*the* Custom House at the end," "*the* last Custom House," not "*a* Custom House at the end," etc.

*t'ien* 填發 to fill out and issue; to issue (as a certificate).

*shou* 收釐單 a Likin receipt.

*tsung* 總釐單 a cargo certificate issued by the Likin office at one of the Yangtze ports of call, for delivery at a Foreign Custom House.

*fêng* 封好 duly sealed; after being sealed.

*hao* 好 good. After verbs, denotes that the action of the verb is finished; hence, a sign of the past.

*chi* 給還 to hand back; to return.

*i* 以遠報近 to report far as near; to make a false declaration as to the number of Likin stations passed by certain goods.

*hsi* 希圖偷漏 to intend a fraud on the revenue.

*pu* 不准停輪之處 a place where steamers are not allowed to stop; a place not authorised as a landing stage (on the Yangtze).

*t'ing* 停輪 to stop a steamer.

*chuan* 專章 a special rule.

*chiu* 就 to follow; according to. [p. 101]

就貨價每百抽二 to levy 2 per cent. *ad valorem*.

*ch'êng* 秤碼 scales and weights; weights and measures.
*ma* 碼 weights; a yard.
*kao* 高下 higher or lower; differently adjusted.
*tzŭ* 自沙市以至大通 between Shashih and Tat'ung.
*pei* 北河口 Pei-ho-k'ow (a Likin station on the Yangtze).
*ying* 鸚鵡洲 Ying-wu-chou (a Likin station on the Yangtze).
*fan* 樊口 Fankow (a Likin station on the Yangtze).
*êrh* 二套口 Êrh-t'ao-kow (a Likin station on the Yangtze).
*hua* 華陽 Hwayang (a Likin station on the Yangtze).
*shang* 上下游 up and down the river.
上游 up the river.
*hsia* 下游 down the river.
*yu* 游 to float; to swim.
*tz'ŭ* 次序 to arrange in order; *seriatim*.
*hsü* 序 to follow in order; series.
*hsüan* 懸牌 to exhibit a tablet; a list.
*pei* 備查 for inspection; for reference.
*i* 以東 to the east of......; *e.g.*, 大通以東, to the east of Tat'ung. Cf. *i* 以內, Document No. 29, p. 58.
*shih* 使 to cause to; to let.
*kuan* 官碼頭 a Government jetty; an authorised jetty (for the shipment of goods).
*t'i* 提究 to prosecute (for legal punishment).
*ting* 定期 at a fixed time; regularly.
*hui* 彙解 to collect and forward.
*i* 以清款項 in order to clear (settle account concerning these) items; in order to close accounts.
*ch'ing* 清款項 to clear (settle account concerning certain) items; to close accounts.
*hsi* 細數 detailed figures.
*an* 按七日 weekly; by the week.
*tsao* 造具 to prepare.
造具清冊 to prepare statistics.
*an* 按月 monthly.
*wai* 外國月分 the foreign calendar; the month according to the foreign calendar.
*tsung* 總冊 a general table; a statistical summary.
*chu* 駐紮 to be stationed at.
*cha* 紮, also written 劄 or 扎, to be stationed at.
*hsün* 巡查 to inspect (as ports).

*chin* 盡 to exhaust; exhaustive.
*shih* 事宜 matters.
*chih* 窒 to obstruct.
窒碍之處 difficult points; difficulties.
*hsiang* 相機 according to circumstances; according to requirements.
*cho* 酌改 to alter (as regulations).
*i* 以期妥善 in order that matters may be properly managed.
*k'ai* 開辦 to put into operation.

**Document No. 53.** [p. 102]

*yü* 諭 an order.
*hsien* 現下 now.
*k'ai* 開單 to make out a document.
開出 to state in particular.
*chao* 照登底簿 to enter in a book.
*yüan* 原貨 the original goods.
*ch'uan* 舛 an error.
舛錯之誤 a mistake.
*wu* 毋違此諭 do not disobey this order.

**Document No. 54.**

*i* 以便征稅 in order to levy the duty (properly).
以外 outside; more than.
*tso* 作爲 to consider as; to treat as.
*i* 以內 inside; less than.
*pu* 不入等 unclassed.
*tsun* 遵照 to be guided by; for the guidance of.
*pu* 不過 only.
*shang* 上下 superior and inferior.
*yü* 諭知 to inform by proclamation. [p. 103]
*ts'o* 錯雜 to mix up by mistake.
*t'ung* 同列 belonging to the same category.
*fên* 分類 to class; classified; classed.
*chu* 逐一 one by one; item for item.
*shih* 是爲至要 this is very important.

**Document No. 55.**

*liang* 量 to measure.
*hêng* 橫徑 the warp of a texture.
*k'o* 闊 broad; breadth.

*chih* 直紗 the horizontal threads of a texture; the warp.

*lü* 縷 the threads of a texture.

*kai* 概 (=皆 *chieh*) all.

*ho* 核明 to examine carefully.

*i* 以免貽誤 in order to avoid mistakes.

*i* 貽 to leave; to bequeath; to involve in; to cease to.

**Document No. 56.** [p. 104]

*i* 疑難事件 matters doubtful and difficult to decide upon.

*shên* 申請 to apply for (as for instructions).

*ho* 核示 to give a decision.

*yeh* 野蜂釀蜜 wild uncleaned honey.

*fêng* 蜂 a bee.

蜂蜜 honey.

*niang* 釀 to ferment; fermented.

*shên* 申文 a despatch to a superior; a report.

*i* 以 because; to consider that.

*wei* 未免 cannot avoid; is bound to.

*kuo* 過重 excess; too heavy.

*chiu* 究 thereafter; finally.

*tsun* 遵行 to be guided by; for one's guidance.

*tang* 當經 I have, with reference thereto (denoting past tense and immediateness of action).

*fa* 發寄 to send (as a letter or a despatch).

*cha* 劄文 a despatch to an inferior; instructions.

*chi* 既 since; because.

*ch'i* 歧 diverging.

歧異 difference; divergence.

*chan* 展 to expand.

展限 to extend a limit.

*hsü* 續修 revised; supplementary.

*yün* 允 to agree; to allow; sincere; what is proper.

*chia* 夾 double.

夾板船隻 sailing vessels.

*chêng* 正數 the full amount.

*chien* 減 to diminish; to reduce.

減半 to reduce by one-half.

*t'ung* 通商各口 the Treaty ports.

*k'ou* 口內口外 in port and outside a port.

*shou* 受損 to receive damage; to be damaged.

*jih* 日期 a limit; a period of time.

*k'ou* 扣算 to deduct.

*ch'ao* 鈔項 tonnage dues.

*hsüan* 旋 forthwith. [p. 105]

*sun* 損壞 to be damaged; to be wrecked.

*wan* 完竣 to complete (as a job).

*chün* 竣 to finish.

*ho* 核算 to calculate.

*hsü* 續約 a supplementary Convention.

*hsiang* 相符 to agree.

*shên* 申請核奪示覆 to apply for instructions (in a despatch to a superior).

*shih* 示覆 to give instructions in reply to an application.

*ping* 並無不合 by no means unjust; quite approvable.

*chieh* 解釋 to explain; to interpret.

*shu* 數 several; a few.

*i* 以期曉然 in order that it may be thus known.

*k'ai* 開錄 to record.

*t'ing* 聽船主自便 at the option of the shipmaster.

*chi* 計算 to calculate.

*shang* 尙有 there is still.

*lien* 連 and; *plus*.

*chiao* 繳銷 to deliver (a document) for cancelling. [p. 106]

*hsin* 新爲領換之執照 a new certificate exchanged for an old one.

*chieh* 接續 in continuation of.

*ts'ê* 拆賣 to break up for sale.

拆賣船料 materials from vessels broken up for sale.

*liao* 料 materials.

*nei* 內稱 it is stated therein; in which it is stated that.

內載 it is said therein; in which it is said that.

*tuan* 端 a paragraph; a passage.

*sun* 損壞船隻 vessels wrecked.

*ch'i* 起岸 to be landed; to land goods.

*jêng* 仍 again; still.

*wu* 無約各國 non-Treaty Powers.

*ts'ê* 冊簿 a list; a book for registry.

*yang* 洋式船隻 foreign-type vessels.

*shih* 駛赴 to sail to; to be bound for.
*ts'ê* 拆毀 to be broken up (as a ship).
*ch'êng* 呈交備寄 to deliver for filing in the archives.
*ch'ing* 輕 light; not heavy. [p. 107]
輕木板 soft-wood planks.
*k'uai* 塊 classifier of wooden planks.
*hou* 厚 thick; thickness.
*sui* 雖 although.
*chih* 指明 to point out; to mention; to refer to.
*hou* 厚薄 thickness (as a relative term).
*po* 薄 thin; thinness.
*mou* 貿易行市 commercial usage.
*li* 歷來 hitherto.
*tso* 作 (=為) to consider as.
*tsai* 載明 it is stated in......
*i* 抑 perhaps; or; if.
抑或 or.
*shên* 申請酌核示遵 to apply for instructions in a despatch.
*pu* 不若 it is better to.
*pi* 比例 to follow the rule.
*chia* 加倍 to add; to double.
*k'o* 科稅 extra duty; additional duty.
*chia* 假 false; imitated.
假金綫 imitation gold thread.
*hsien* 綫 (=線) thread; wire.
*huang* 黃銅 yellow copper; brass.
*ch'an* 攙 to mix up; to foist in.
攙銀 silver plated.
*tu* 鍍 to plate; to gild.
鍍金 to gild.
*ch'an* 產製 to manufacture.
*chih* 製 to make.
*ta* 大 very.
大相懸殊 very different.
*hsüan* 懸 to suspend; separate; different.
懸殊 different.
*shu* 殊 differing; unlike.
*k'ung* 恐有未合 it is to be feared that it is not in order.
*ch'u* 處 place; places; the different points of an *exposé*. [p. 108]
*wu* 無論貴賤 irrespective of price or value.

*ch'i* 其內 therein; in it.
*tzŭ* 自應 must; of course.
*hsü* 續添 supplementary; additional.
*hsiu* 修船雜物 dock stores.
*ch'uan* 船廠 a dock.
*ying* 應行免稅 liable to exemption from duty; duty free.
*pan* 頒 to publish abroad.
頒發 to promulgate; to publish.
*hsüan* 旋 then; forthwith.
*chiao* 繳存 to pay as a deposit.
*ssŭ* 似 it seems that.
*t'ieh* 鐵鍊 iron chains.
*shu* 庶 so that there may be; about; nearly.
庶屬允當 so that it may be fair; for the sake of fairness.
*yün* 允當 just; fair.
*liu* 琉 strass; glaze.
琉璃 glass.
琉璃瓦 glazed tiles.
*li* 璃 strass.
*hei* 黑鉛塊 plumbago.
*pao* 寶 valuable; precious.
寶砂 emery powder.
*sha* 砂 gravel; sand; gritty, like sand.
*yu* 油斤 oil (as merchandise). Cf. *ssŭ* 絲斤, p. 28.
*sung* 松 a fir; a pine.
松香油 turpentine.
*chi* 既經 since it has; as soon as it shall have.

**Document No. 57.** [p. 109]

*tsung* 總口 a central Customs station.
*hsieh* 協 to assist.
協鎮 the commandant of a garrison; an assistant *chên-t'ai* or brigadier-general; a colonel.
*chên* 鎮 a regiment; a brigade; (=鎮台) a brigadier-general.
*chao* 照送 to forward officially.
*t'ung* 銅帽 percussion caps.
*chia* 價銀 price; proceeds of sale.
*ch'i* 緝 to seize.
緝獲 to seize (as thieves, or smuggled goods).
*ssŭ* 私帶 to carry clandestinely.

*pao* 包 a bundle; a package.

*ho* 盒 a small box.

*pi* 敝 mean; common; an epithet used by the speaker or writer; hence, my.

敝前任 my predecessor.

*jên* 任 a post; an incumbent.

*tso* 佐領府 a military title (colonel).

*chiang* 將軍憲 His Excellency the Tartar General.

*chieh* 解交 to forward to.

*shui* 稅釐局 (a native revenue office).

*yen* 驗收 to examine and receive; to take delivery of.

*chieh* 解省 to send to the provincial capital.

*shêng* 省 a province; also the provincial capital.

*chün* 軍裝所 a depository for arms, etc.; an armoury.

*tien* 點 to dot; to tick off.

點驗 to dot and examine; to tick off while examining; to check (as a list of articles).

*i* 移 to write officially.

*ch'ü* 去後 (= 以後) (after a verb) on having......; after.

*ping* 幷經 having at the same time.

*chao* 照知 to inform in a despatch.

*tsai* 在案 it is on record; as records show.

*ho* 合就照送 to forward in due course.

*wei* 爲此照會 this despatch is written, or addressed, to......

*kuei* 貴稅務司 you, the Commissioner of Customs.

*ch'ing* 請煩查收賜覆 please trouble to receive and reply to (as a despatch).

*fan* 煩 to trouble about.

*tz'ŭ* 賜 to confer; to bestow.

賜覆 to bestow an answer; to favour one with a reply.

*chi* 計送 forwarded herewith (as an amount of money, etc., with a despatch).

*yu* 右 right; that which is on the right; in documents, the above.

右照會 the above despatch.

**Document No. 58.** [p. 110]

*shu* 署公使 an acting envoy.

*chao* 照稱 an official despatch stating; to state in an official document.

*hsin* 新派 to appoint.

*shu* 署大臣 an acting Minister of State.

*i* 以及 and; or.

*t'ai* 台灣島 the island of Formosa.

*tê* 德意志人 German subjects.

*pei* 被告 to be accused; the accused; the defendant.

被告案件 cases of accusation; charges against.

*fan* 犯罪 to offend; offence; crime; criminal.

*t'ung* 統 all.

*shên* 審 to examine; to try (as a legal case).

審判 to decide legal cases; to have jurisdiction.

*tu* 督率 to have under one's orders.

*chan* 暫且 temporarily.

*ch'ieh* 且 (= 然 *jan*) (gives an adjective adverbial force).

*i* 擬辦試行 about to put into operation provisionally.

*ssŭ* 俟......方...... wait till......, and then; not until.

*chih* 執政大臣 Ministers of State.

*yün* 允准 to sanction.

*fang* 方 then.

*li* 立定 to introduce (as an arrangement); to put into operation.

*shih* 施行 to carry out a scheme; to put into operation.

*shên* 審斷 to give judgment; to decide a case.

*tu* 督管 to have control over.

*shên* 審結 (or 審理) to decide and settle legal cases.

**Document No. 59.** [p. 111]

*hsieh* 協領 a military title (colonel).

協領銜 having the rank of a *hsieh-ling*.

*hsia* 廈 (= 廈門 *hsia-mên*) Amoy.

廈防分府 the Magistrate of Amoy.

*fên* 分府 title of a sub-prefect.

*pi* 敝署 my office or yamên; *i.e.*, I (if the writer be at the head of a yamên).

*p'ai* 派丁 to depute servants; to get servants to.

*fu* 扶 to shield; to accompany (as a coffin).

*k'ou* 口 a classifier of coffins.

*sui* 隨帶 to accompany.

*lou* 簍 a basket.

*i* 椅 a chair.

*cho* 棹 a table.

*p'u* 鋪 bedding.

鋪蓋 bedding.

*kai* 蓋 a cover; bedding.
*ta* 搭 to charter; to take passage in a ship; to ship.
*hui* 回歸 to return (home).
*ch'ing* 請予 please grant.
*yü* 予 to give.
*wei* 爲此移請查照 writing a despatch on this account, please take official notice; I shall be obliged by your noting the subject of my despatch.
*hsi* 希即轉移 I shall be obliged by your communicating the contents of my letter to……
*yu* 由厦至漢 from Amoy to Hankow.
*chia* 家丁 domestic servants.
*pei* 俾免沿途阻滯 in order to avoid obstruction *en route*.
*ho* 合就照知 to duly inform.

**Document No. 60.** [p. 112]

*hsing* 興泉永 the three departments of Hsing-hua-fu (興 *hsing*), Ch'üan-chou-fu (泉 *ch'üan*), and Yung-ch'un-chou (永 *yung*), forming the circuit in charge of the Taot'ai at Amoy.
*chao* 照覆 to reply in a despatch.
*chien* 建造塔鐙 to build lighthouses.
*pei* 北椗 Dodd Island (near Amoy).
*hsing* 興 to arise; to raise.
興工 to commence work.
*pu* 不日 shortly.
*hui* 會同 conjointly with.
*fu* 副 to assist; assistant (in titles).
*ying* 營造司 an engineer (for lighthouses, etc.).
*yüan* 原勘地方 the site originally inspected; the original site.
*k'an* 勘 to inspect.
*ch'i* 起卸 to land goods from a ship.
*ch'u* 處所 a place.
*k'an* 勘度 to measure; to survey (as land for a site to build upon).
*ti* 地勢 the particulars regarding a lot of land.
*ch'ien* 遣派 to send for business (as workmen).
*kung* 工人 workmen.
*t'ien* 填築 to fill up (for building).
*ti* 地基 a foundation.
*tz'ŭ* 此後 after this.
*ts'ai* 材料 material.
*pei* 備便 to make ready; to complete.
*tung* 動工 to commence work.
*ch'i* 起蓋 to commence building.
*kai* 蓋 to build.
*têng* 燈樓 a lighthouse.
*nien* 年底 at the end of the year.
*tsün* 竣 to finish.
竣事 to complete an affair.
*hao* 毫無更改 not to make the slightest change.
*kêng* 更 to alter.
更改 to change.
*cha* 札飭 to instruct.
*ma* 馬巷廳 the Magistrate of Ma-hsiang (Mahang).
*chü* 居 to dwell; to live.
居民 the inhabitants.
*pu* 不得 cannot; should not.
*tsu* 阻撓 to be vexatious.
*nao* 撓 to pervert; to vex.
*shêng* 生事 to make trouble.
*wan* 完工 to finish work.

**Document No. 61.** [p. 113]

*chü* 具保結 to sign a bond.
*chan* 暫存 to keep on deposit; on deposit.
*ching* 竟 indeed; then.
*ch'i* 期 to expect; to hope for.
*shên* 愼重 to carefully observe; to treat as important.
*kuo* 過慮 to care too much about; to trouble about.
*ch'a* 查照遵辦 to act according to instructions received.
*ti* 第 but.
*ch'ên* 陳說 to explain; to state; to set forth.
*t'iao* 條理 reasonable; logical; well founded in detail. Cf. 條條有理 every section has its rules (WILLIAMS).
*chuan* 轉詳 to communicate a report received.
*tan* 但 however.
*shang* 尚未 not yet.
*ming* 明敘 to state.
*hsü* 敘 to converse.
*i* 一切 all.
*hsiang* 詳錄 to state in detail.

*chuan* 轉稟 to communicate a report received from an inferior.

*ch'a* 察奪 to examine and judge.

*shih* 寔爲公便 it is really in the public interest.

### Document No. 62. [p. 114]

*shang* 賞 to bestow; to confer (as a reward).

賞戴藍翎 wearing the blue plume or crow's feather.

*lan* 藍 blue.

*ling* 翎 a pendent tail feather; the plume worn as a decoration of merit.

*shih* 食鹽 salt; kitchen salt.

*i* 移飭 to instruct in a despatch.

*k'o* 課館 a revenue office.

*t'ung* 同安 T'ung-an-hsien (near Amoy).

*pang* 幇 a guild; a union of people.

*fan* 販戶 dealers (in salt, etc.).

*ch'ung* 充賞 to give a reward.

*ch'ien* 遣丁 to send servants.

*sui* 隨(=隨時) instantly; at the same time.

*hsien* 現時 the present time; present.

*ch'ang* 塲 an arena; saltflats; salt factories.

塲價 the official price of salt.

*ch'i* 七二番銀 *lit*, a seven [mace] two [candareen] foreign silver [coin]; a Mexican dollar, of which 100 are equal to 72 taels.

*fan* 番 foreign.

*chao* 照呈(=照數呈送) to hand over an amount as per account.

照數查收 to receive an amount as per account.

### Document No. 63. [p. 115]

*fu* 福建 *(fu-chien)* the province of Fukien.

*shêng* 省會 the provincial capital.

*t'ung* 通商總局 the Board of Foreign Trade (at Foochow).

*ssŭ* 司道 the high provincial officials (Fant'ai, Nieh-t'ai, Yünt'ai, and the Taot'ais).

*kung* 宮保 Guardian of the Heir Apparent (a title).

*hsün* 巡撫部院 a provincial Governor.

*p'ai* 牌 a despatch to an inferior.

*k'ai* 開 to open (a book, etc.); introducing the tenor of a document quoted: to the effect that.

*chao* 照得 whereas.

*pên* 本部院 I, the Governor.

*tsou* 奏 to address the Throne.

奏奉諭旨 to receive a reply from the Throne.

*yü* 諭旨 an Imperial rescript.

*chih* 旨 an Imperial rescript; His Majesty's commands.

*tiao* 調 to remove to another post; to transfer.

調閩黔軍 the Kweichow regiment transferred to Fukien.

*min* 閩 the Fukien province.

*ch'ien* 黔 the Kweichow province.

*chün* 軍 a regiment; military.

*hsien* 先 first; beforehand.

*ch'ê* 撤 to remove; to withdraw; to recall (as troops).

*hsin* 新 new; newly; lately.

新授 having lately received (as a post).

*yün* 雲 a cloud.

雲南 the Yünnan province.

*k'ai* 開化 K'ai-hua-fu (in the province of Yünnan).

*tai* 帶 to lead; to be in charge of troops.

*kuei* 歸伍 to return to one's regiment or division.

*wu* 伍 a body of soldiers; a military division.

*ling* 領獲 to have received; to get issued (as arms from the Government).

*yang* 洋鎗 foreign guns.

*mên* 門 (a classifier of guns, rifles, etc.).

*tai* 帶回 to take back; to lead back (as troops).

*ch'êng* 呈繳 to hand up.

*tzŭ* 咨明 to inform in a despatch.

*chi* 檄 to address an inferior; to issue a summons.

*ho* 合就 duly.

*ju* 如遇 if there be; if.

*yang* 洋稅新關 the Foreign Customs.

*shih* 事宜 affairs; business.

### Document No. 64. [p. 116]

*pên* 本道 I, the Taot'ai.

*hsien* 現在 now.

*yin* 因公 on public business.

*chin* 晉 to go to; to enter.

晉省 to proceed to the provincial capital.

*mien* 面稟 to report to a superior in person; to speak to a superior (on business).

8

*ti* 地方公事 local business.
*fu* 附搭 to take passage (in a ship).
*ch'i* 啟 to begin.
啟程 to start on a journey.
*shu* 署中緊要公事 important office matters.
*chin* 緊 urgent.
緊要 important.
*pao* 包 to wrap up.
包封 to put into a sealed envelope.
*hsing* 行寓 a temporary residence while on a journey.
*yü* 寓 a dwelling.
*ho* 核辦 to transact business.
*hsün* 尋 common; usual.
尋常 ordinary; as usual.
尋常日行事件 the current daily business.
*t'ung* 同知 a magistrate (*see* Mayers' "The Chinese Government," No. 282).
*ch'êng* 丞 literary designation of a sub-prefect.
*tai* 代拆代行 to open letters and act for another.
*i* 以免曠悞 in order to avoid delay.
*k'uang* 曠 to waste (as time).
*wu* 悞 delay.
*shên* 申報 to report to a superior.
申報咨行札委 to inform superiors, equals, and inferiors in rank.
*tzŭ* 咨行 to address an equal.
*cha* 札委 to write officially to an inferior.
*ch'a* 查照施行 to note and act accordingly.
*ch'in* 欽賜 bestowed by the Emperor.

### Document No. 65.

*liang* 兩江 the two Kiang provinces, *i.e.*, Kiangnan (now Kiangsu and Anhwei) and Kiangsi.
*têng* 等 (after the name or title of a single person) and others. Cf. *têng* 等 sign of the plural, p. 19.
*tsou* 奏稱 to state in a memorial to the Throne.
*hu* 湖北 the Hupeh province.
*k'ai* 開采煤鐵 to work coal and iron mines.
*ts'ai* 采 to pluck; to gather.
*yang* 洋法 foreign method.
*wang* 旺 much; in a high degree.
*shih* 勢 circumstances.
*hsiao* 銷路 circulation of goods; the range of sale.

*liu* 流通 to flow freely; to expand (as trade).
*yüan* 援照成案 according to precedent.
*ch'êng* 成 to complete; completed; ready.
成案 a precedent.
*fu* 覆奏 to memorialise again; to refer (a matter) to the Throne; to memorialise the Throne in reply. [p. 117]
*kuang* 廣濟 Kuang-ch'i-hsien (a coal-producing district in Hupeh).
*hsiang* 相同 the same as.
*chia* 加增 to increase; to add to.
*chao* 照舊 as heretofore; as before.
*i* 以示限制 in order to draw a limit; as a restrictive measure.

### Document No. 66.

*pei* 北洋大臣 the Superintendent of Northern Trade.
*hsiang* 詳稱 to report to a superior.
*chiao* 焦 burned; scorched.
焦炭 coke.
*ho* 核估時價 to ascertain the market value.
*tsou* 奏定 decided by the Emperor in reply to a memorial.
*k'ai* 開平 K'ai-p'ing (a coal-producing place).
*lien* 煉 to separate dross by fire.
煉成 to burn; to make by burning (as coke by burning coal).
*kung* 公允 just; fair.
*ho* 核議 to consider; to consult.
*mei* 煤礦 a coal-mine.
*t'u* 土煤 native coal.
*shên* 甚爲公允 it is very fair. [p. 118]
*chi* 旣經 from the time that; since......has, having, etc.; from the time that......shall have, *i.e.*, as soon as......
*han* 函詢 to inquire in a letter.
*tzŭ* 咨覆 to reply in a despatch.
*ch'ih* 飭知 to inform subordinates.

### Document No. 67.

*nan* 南洋大臣 the Superintendent of Southern Trade.
*fêng* 奉到憲劄 to have received instructions from the authorities.
*tsun* 遵照 in obedience to.

*t'ung* 通劄 to issue circular instructions to.

*tzŭ* 自用 to use oneself; for own use.

*ch'ao* 鈔單 a copy of a document.

*cho* 酌量 to consider.

*têng* 等由 and the like matters; etc. Cf. *têng* 等因, p. 55.

*fu* 伏 to fall prostrate; humble; humbly.

伏查 it is my humble opinion that; in my humble opinion.

*ti* 抵 to arrive at.

抵滬 to arrive at Shanghai.

*kuan* 官商 officials and merchants.

*ko* 格 a rule.

格外 outside the rule; extraordinary.

*yu* 優 tranquil; gentle; fully; to excel. [p. 119]

優待 to treat with consideration.

*i* 意 meaning; intention.

*fu* 復核可行 to reply that a matter may be carried out; to reply in the affirmative.

*hu* 滬關 the Shanghai Customs.

*i* 以……爲度 to consider……as a limit.

*hsiang* 詳愼 very carefully.

*cho* 酌數 the authorised amount; in certain quantities.

*ch'üan* 權宜之舉 a temporary arrangement to meet pressing circumstances.

*tz'ŭ* 此外 besides this.

*mai* 賣與華人 to sell (or for sale) to Chinese.

*wu* 無論多寡 irrespective of quantity.

*i* 以示區別 in order to show the distinction.

*ch'ü* 區 a store-room; to sort.

區別 to distinguish; distinction.

*chao* 昭 to make known; to display.

*hsiang* 詳祈 to request respectfully.

*ch'i* 祈 to state one's case to a god; to pray.

*tzŭ* 咨請核復 to ask in a despatch for a reply.

### Document No. 68.

*shan* 汕頭 Swatow.

*chi* 機器 machinery.

*pên* 本行 this firm; our firm.

*ao* 熬 to boil.

熬作糖觔 to boil, or refine, sugar.

*ling* 另 besides.

*tso* 作爲 to make; to manufacture.

*ch'ou* 抽 to take out with the hand; to take out (as silk from a cocoon, *i.e.*, to reel).

抽絲 to reel silk; reeled silk.

*pan* 辦 to buy.

辦外國機器 to buy foreign machinery.

*chih* 製造 to make; to manufacture.

*i* 以 (= 將 *chiang*) denotes the object.

*chun* 准予免稅 to grant exemption from duty.

*ping* 並非 not at all; not. Cf. *ping* 並未, Document No. 28, p. 57.

*ch'u* 出售 to sell; for sale.

*pai* 百貨 goods of every description.

*chung* 終 finally; in the end.

*wu* 無非 is bound to; by all means.

*êrh* 而 is frequently used in introducing the apodosis in a concessive clause, no matter whether the protasis be opened by *sui* (雖), "although," or not; *e.g.*, ……, 而……, or 雖……, 而……, "although……, yet……" Cf. *sui* 雖, p. 79. In the present case *sui* (雖) does not appear. The sense is: "although in the end all kinds of dutiable goods will come to be 'for own use,' yet the article 'machinery' is quite different from 'the articles of daily use' mentioned in the Tariff Rules."

*kuei* 歸於 to come within the category of.

*hsün* 尋常日用物件 articles of daily use. [p. 120]

*ch'iung* 迥 remote; in a high degree (used to emphasise negation). Cf. *ping* 並未, Document No. 28, p. 57.

迥不相同 widely different.

*yu* 又 further; moreover.

*chü* 據云 as it is said; as to the remark that.

*i* 宜 to suit; to make fit.

宜廣開來路 to encourage (or develop) import trade.

*kuang* 廣 broad; to make broad; to extend.

*i* 益於實濟 to be conducive to real advantage; to be of benefit to.

*pu* 不足以礙其來路 not capable of discouraging importation.

*i* 以 gives a verb the force of the second supine (*facile dictu*) after terms meaning "difficult," "easy," "capable," or "sufficient," such as *nan* (難), *i* (易), *k'an* (堪), *tsu* (足), etc.; *e.g.*, *tsu i ai* (足以礙), "sufficient or capable to hinder;" *nan i ch'êng-kung* (難以成功), "difficult to bring about." In all these cases *yü* (於) may take the place of *i* (以).

*chi* 機器局 a manufactory for machinery; an arsenal.

*tsao* 造船局 a Government dock; the Foochow arsenal.

*chü* 局 a commission; an administrative board; an establishment working under such a board.

*nai* 乃 that is; is.

*kuan* 官用 for official use.

*pi* 比擬 to compare; to treat analogously.

*tsai* 再四 again and again.

*ssŭ* 思 to think.

思維 to think.

*wei* 維 to think; to consider.

*kuan* 官民 officials and private people.

*fu* 伏思 I humbly consider; in my humble opinion.

*tung* 動 to appropriate (as funds); to use.

*kung* 公欵 Government moneys.

公欵購辦 to buy from Government funds.

公用之物 articles for Government use.

公用之欵 moneys for Government use.

公項 public moneys.

*ch'ih* 喫 to eat; to swallow; to bear.

喫虧 to suffer a loss.

*pu* 不致 so that not; not to result in.

*liang* 兩歧辦法 two different methods of acting.

*ch'i* 歧 diverging.

*yüeh* 約章 Treaty regulations.

*chü* 遽 hurried.

遽予免征 to grant exemption from duty in a hurry.

*chiang* 將來 afterwards.

*fên* 紛 mottled; confused; the bustle of a crowd.

紛紛效尤 many others will follow; others will claim what is allowed to a few.

*hsiao* 效 to imitate; to do as others do.

效尤 to excel the pattern, as in doing evil (WILLIAMS).

*k'ai* 開各商覬覦之漸 to stimulate the appetite (for illegal privileges) amongst merchants; *lit.*, to open the gradual development (*ch'ien* 漸) of merchants' [illegal] desires.

*chi* 覬 to covet.

覬覦 to wish for ardently.

*yü* 覦 to desire.

*i* 以昭公允 for the sake of fairness.

*chung* 重稅餉 to maintain due regard for revenue interests.

*ch'uan* 船政局 a Government dockyard; an arsenal.

**Document No. 69.** [p. 121]

*ch'ing* 檾 a kind of hemp; jute.

檾麻 jute.

*t'ien* 天下各國 all the countries in the world.

*fên* 分而爲二 to distinguish two kinds of.

*tsung* 總 all.

*chün* 鈞 important; just; that which belongs to the person addressed: your.

鈞劄 your respected orders (as alluding to an official letter from a superior).

*hsiang* 詳細查覆 to reply in detail.

*pao* 報爲 to report as.

*ch'ing* 青麻 green hemp.

*chung* 種類 kind; category.

*shih* 式樣 a pattern.

*ta* 大不相同 very unlike each other.

*i* 易爲分別 easy to distinguish.

*yang* 樣式 a pattern.

*t'a* 他項 other kinds.

*yu* 有異 different from; there is a difference.

*t'i* 體較輭鬆 the frame or body is weak and shaky.

*niu* 扭 to twist; to wrench.

*nieh* 涅(=湼) to blacken; to dye.

*fu* 腐 to spoil; to rot; rotten.

*ta* 大略相符 to agree in the main.

*yen* 驗貨手 an examiner.

*ying* 影射之弊 the malpractice of spreading lies; false statements. [p. 122]

*k'o* 可無慮 one need not fear this.

*li* 理合備文 to duly write a despatch.

*ts'ai* 裁奪示遵 to consider and decide and notify for guidance.

*shêng* 生質 natural disposition.

*wu* 無慮影射 not to fear false statements.

*liang* 量減 to diminish; to lower.

*i* 以順商情 in order to meet commercial requirements.

### Document No. 70. [p. 123]

*cha* 劄令 to order in a despatch.
*ch'a* 查明聲復 to examine and report in reply.
*i* 已完正稅 to have paid, or having paid, full duty.
*fu* 復行下船 to re-ship; to re-export.
*pu* 不問自用出售 no matter whether for own use or for sale.
*wên* 問 to ask.
*hsüan* 旋即 at once; then; thereon.
*t'ing* 聽商自便 according to merchants' option.
*yün* 運抵 to arrive (as goods at the place of destination).
*ch'uan* 船用洋煤 foreign coal for ship's use.
*hsien* 限內 within the limit.
*shih* 是 this means that......; that is.
*wu* 無虞 there is no cause to fear.
*lou* 漏稅滋弊 all the vicious modes of defrauding the revenue.
*i* 一經 as soon as.
*kai* 概 all; then.
*wu* 無虧 there is no loss arising from.
*ssŭ* 似可照議辦理 it seems one may manage the matter as proposed.
*ju* 如遇 if there be.
*shou* 收稅免照 an exemption certificate.
*i* 以昭核實 in order to show the fact to be true.
*shang* 尚爲周到 all is yet quite in order.

### Document No. 71. [p. 124]

*hsiang* 箱包 cases and packages.
*yang* 洋鐵箍 foreign iron hoops.
*t'ieh* 鉄箍 iron hoops.
*ku* 箍 a hoop.
*ts'ê* 拆湊一處 to remove (as hoops from packages), and collect in one place.
*shang* 商 to consider.
*tzŭ* 自然 of course.
*tsai* 載入總單 to enter on the cargo certificate.
*lei* 累 trouble; troublesome repetition.
*pu* 不如 it is better that; we had better.
*wei* 爲善 is good; recommendable.
*i* 一項 the item of.
*p'o* 破 to break.
破眼 to be broken and having holes.
*shang* 尚屬平允 it is yet fair.
*p'ing* 平允 fair.
*chih* 至完稅一節 as regards the question of paying duty.
*chiao* 較 to compare; rather more than; than (comparative).
*chien* 簡 to abridge; to make short.
簡便 convenient.
*ju* 如所稱辦理 to act as has been reported.

### Document No. 72. [p. 125]

*chu* 註明 to explain as; to state clearly.
*k'uan* 寬 broad; wide; breadth; width.
*ngo* 俄呢 Russian cloth.
*fang* 仿 like; as; to imitate.
仿照 like; as; analogous with.
*yüan* 原布 plain cotton cloth; shirtings.
*ho* 核加 to add; to calculate the additional......
*fu* 服 to agree; to be willing.
*han* 函請核示 to apply for instructions by letter.
*an* 按照辦理 to act accordingly.
*ssŭ* 嗣 hereafter; afterwards.
*to* 多徵稅銀 the duty overcharged; an excess of duty.
*chih* 職 office; used for "I" in connexion with an official title.
職道 I, the Taot'ai.
*po* 駁復 to argue against; counter-argument.
*chia* 加增 to add; to increase.
*yün* 允服 to agree to; to be willing.
*tsêng* 增改新例 additional and modified rules; revised rules.
*lu* 錄摺咨呈 to submit a copy of.
*shên* 甚屬公允 it is very fair; it is very just.
*ts'ung* 從前 formerly.
*hsien* 咸豐 the period of the reign HSIEN FÊNG (A.D. 1851-62).
*k'uan* 寬長 broad and long; dimensions; size.
*kai* 改爲 to change into.
*yung* 永 everlasting.
永爲定式 to regard as a permanent standard.
*i* 異議 a different arrangement.
*tzŭ* 自宜 must of course.

*pi* 比照 according to; analogous to.

*wei* 未便 inconvenient.

*liang* 兩歧 diverging; ambiguous; a double mode of dealing with a question.

*wang* 往來信件 correspondence exchanged.

*to* 多出寬長若干 the excess in width or length. [p. 126]

*chê* 折 to deduct; to calculate.

折增 to add to (in calculating).

折合 to calculate.

*chi* 計量 to calculate and measure.

*shu* 庶不致於轇轕 so as to avoid confusion.

*chiao* 轇 confused.

轇轕 confusion; a muddle.

*ko* 轕 chariots and spears; mixed; confused.

*ho* 合行備文 to duly write a despatch.

*shên* 申請查照施行 to request (a superior) to receive a document for action to be taken.

**Document No. 73.**

*hsiang* 詳稱 to report.

*tai* 代領事 an acting Consul.

代理領事 an acting Consul.

*yün* 運到 to have imported; to be consignee for.

*po* 玻璃球 glass balls (used as paper weights).

*ch'iu* 球 a globe; a ball.

*ch'io* / *ch'üeh* } 確知 to know properly.

*ying* 應否 whether or not it is necessary to.

應否免稅 whether duty free or not.

*shang* 商辦 to consider and act. [p. 127]

*tzŭ* 字樣 a phrase; an expression; the words "........"

*wei* 唯 but.

*yao* 藥料 drugs; medicines.

*po* 玻璃器皿 glass vessels.

*min* 皿 porcelain or glass vessels (as cups, etc.).

*tu* 獨 alone; only.

*ming* 明 it is clear that; this shows that.

*chien* 件 a classifier of documents.

*ch'ing* 清摺一扣 a fair copy of a document.

*k'ou* 扣 a classifier of documents.

*chao* 照章 according to regulations.

*ch'u* 出具甘結 to sign a bond.

*yen* 鹽池 salt-cellars. [p. 128]

*ch'ih* 池 a tank; a reservoir.

*kua* 掛鐙 lanterns.

*yang* 洋燭 foreign candles.

*i* 胰 fat over the stomach; soap.

胰子 soap.

*pai* 白酒 white wine; sherry.

*hsing* 行知 to inform (an inferior) in a despatch.

*chuan* 轉售 for sale; to further sell to others.

*yü* 予免稅 to grant exemption from duty; to pass (goods) duty free.

*li* 理合 duly.

*kuei* 貴道 you, the Taot'ai.

*sung* 送去 to send away.

*tz'ŭ* 此致 this is what I wanted to address you with (a concluding phrase in letters).

此致順頌升祉 while communicating to you the above, allow me to express my best wishes, etc. (a concluding phrase in letters).

*shun* 順頌 accept my best wishes (a concluding phrase in letters).

*sung* 頌 to praise; homage.

*shêng* 升 to rise in office.

升祉 [I wish you] promotion and happiness (a concluding phrase in letters).

*chih* 祉 happiness.

*ta* 打 (=打臣) a dozen (*see* Document No. 17, p. 22).

*pên* 本處 this place.

*ting* 定明 to settle; to decide.

*chuan* 轉請 to forward a request; to further request.

*shih* 是寔 the very truth; to be really true; really genuine.

*fu* 復者 a reply; in reply to your note I beg to say. [p. 129]

*ch'ing* 頃 presently.

頃接來函 I have just received your note.

*yen* 驗估核稅 to assess duties according to value; to charge *ad valorem* duty.

*tz'ŭ* 此頌升祺 with best wishes; with kind regards (a concluding phrase in letters).

*wei* 爲咨請事 in the matter of an official request (introductory phrase to a despatch).

*han* 函商核奪 to consider by correspondence and decide.

*jih* 日久 a long time since.

*lai* 來信 an incoming letter.

*ch'ien* 前年 the year before last. [p. 130]

*hsien* 憲札 a despatch or instructions from the high authorities.

*fu* 復查 to re-examine.

*têng* 等類 such articles; etc.

*ch'u* 出賣 for sale.

*yüan* 緣 as; because.

*tuan* 斷難 very difficult; decidedly difficult.

*so* 所以 therefore.

*ting* 定立 to frame (as a rule); to settle.

*i* 以示 in order to make known that.

*yu* 有別 there is a difference; to be different.

*chieh* 街 a street.

街市 the market; on the market.

*chiu* 究 after all; finally.

究竟 really; indeed; after all; even then.

*ch'ê* 輙 then (denoting sequence). Cf. *chi* 卽, Document No. 21, p. 46.

輙卽 then (denoting sequence); at once.

*so* 瑣 petty; troublesome.

瑣屑 trifling (or vexatious) business.

*hsieh* 屑 trifling; troublesome.

*chin* 謹呈 to state respectfully.

*ch'ing* 請煩查核 please trouble to examine and decide.

*shih* 示復飭遵施行 to issue instructions in reply to a despatch.

## Document No. 74. [p. 131]

*wên* 文 a despatch; a text; a passage in a text.

文內 in the despatch.

*hsiang* 詳閱 to take careful notice of; to read carefully.

*yüeh* 閱 to inspect; to peruse.

*fa* 法文 the French text.

*chuan* 專指 to specially refer to.

專指藥料而言 to refer to medicines.

*tuan* 斷而不連 by no means connected with.

*po* 玻璃片 window glass.

*ch'ien* 千里鏡 telescopes.

*ching* 鏡 a mirror; the lens of a telescope, microscope, etc.

*chao* 照面鏡 mirrors.

*liao* 料 strass; coloured glass.

料珠 glass beads.

料器 glassware.

*wu* 無出入 it causes no increase or decrease; it makes no difference.

*ch'u* 出入 to make a difference by causing an increase or a decrease.

*ju* 如所擬 as suggested.

*chao* 照復 to reply in a despatch.

## Document No. 75. [p. 132]

*ching* 敬 respectful.

敬啓者 I respectfully inform you (introductory phrase in letters).

*tso* 昨 yesterday; the other day.

*chieh* 接得 to have received.

*tê* 得 to get; to obtain.

*chih* 致 to address (as a letter).

*chü* 局董 a manager in a public company.

*kao* 告 to inform.

*ta* 大宗 a principal article (as amongst goods).

*chiao* 較少 rather little; less than usual.

*ta* 大抵 on the whole; generally speaking.

*pu* 不易 not easy to; difficult to.

*k'ai* 開驗 to open (packages) for examination.

開驗復綑 to open (packages) for examination and close again.

*k'un* 綑 to bind; to cord up.

*shang* 傷損 to damage.

*tan* 躭延 to delay.

*wei* 畏 to fear.

*lu* 陸運 to forward by land.

*chieh* 節 a section in a composition; the paragraphs of an account; a statement.

節畧一紙 a statement of particulars.

*lio* 畧 to abridge; an abridged statement.

*pu* 不論粗細 irrespective of quality.

*hung* 紅花 fine chinaware (at Kiukiang, *lit.*, porcelain with red patterns).

*lan* 藍花 coarse chinaware (at Kiukiang, *lit.*, porcelain with blue patterns).

*t'an* 探 to spy; to explore.

探詢 to inquire.

*hsün* 詢 to inquire.

*nêng* 能否 whether or not it is possible.

*pien* 變 to change.

變通 for convenience sake; to accommodate.

*t'ung* 通 to bring about.

*i* 以爲卹商 in order to facilitate trade.

*hsü* 卹商 to facilitate trade.

*yü* 裕 to enrich; abundance.

裕課 to benefit the revenue.

*pei* 裨 beneficial; to assist.

裨益 advantage; profit.

*shu* 殊 distinction; difference.

*chiao* 較多 rather much; more than.

*wu* 無不合 bound to agree; certainly not at variance with.

*yüan* 原訂 originally fixed upon; drafted.

*to* 多寡 quantity.

*kua* 寡 few; little.

*ssŭ* 似覺合宜 it looks reasonable enough.

*chiao* 覺 to understand; to be aware of.

*pu* 不能不 bound to; cannot help being.

*jên* 認眞 careful.

*yen* 嚴察 to examine strictly.

*tzŭ* 自外觀之 to look at from outside; from a superficial point of view.

*nei* 內 inside; near to (as near to a matter or having a close knowledge of a matter).

*shih* 實則有損 in reality there is a loss.

*chia* 加意 to be careful.

*fu* 縛 to bind.

*chin* 緊妥 fast and tight (as a package is bound).

*fan* 翻播 to mix up; to muddle.

*po* 播 to disperse; to scatter.

*ch'ung* 重複 again; repeatedly.

*chung* 中途 on the road; *en route.*

*shang* 傷損 to be damaged.

*k'uei* 虧累 to involve in losses.

*shêng* 生涯 trade; business.

*ya* 涯 a limit; a shore.

*hsi* 息業 to put a stop to one's business.

*jao* 繞途 to make a *détour*; to depart from the proper road.

*jih* 日旺 to prosper (as trade).

*wang* 旺 prosperous.

*i* 易於傷損之貨 damageable goods. Cf. *i* 以, Document No. 68, p. 120.

*k'o* 可不必 need not be......; ......may be dispensed with.

*pieh* 別 to distinguish.

*i* 以概論 to take the broad view of a matter.

*hsiang* 詳分 to distinguish.

*shang* 商情 commercial interests.

*yu* 有益 to benefit; there is an advantage in. [p. 133]

*chao* 招商分局 a branch office of the China Merchants' Company.

*wu* 勿論 no matter whether.

*kai* 蓋 for; because of.

*ti* 低 low; to lower.

低稅 to lower the duty.

*fan* 反 on the contrary.

*ang* 昂 high; to raise.

昂稅 to raise the duty.

*shih* 事關約則 a matter concerning the Treaty and the Tariff.

*chien* 見 to see; sometimes a sign of the passive; *e.g.*, 見痊, to be cured, to recover; 見復, to be replied to, to receive a reply; 見示, to be instructed; 見允, to be permitted.

見商於有約各國 to be considered by the Treaty Powers.

*yüeh* 約國 or 有約國 a Treaty Power.

*ting* 訂局 to decide.

*t'ung* 統 all; uniformly.

*chü* 擧 a matter; an affair.

*tzŭ* 自辦之事 matters to be managed by oneself.

*wu* 勿須 must not.

*chien* 減稅 to reduce the duty.

*chih* 祇 but; however.

*êrh* 而已 and no more (a final phrase); only; merely.

*wu* 無事 no business to; not necessary to.

*yen* 嚴加逐察 to subject to strict and detailed examination.

*tz'ŭ* 磁商 a trader in chinaware.

*ming* 明訂 to clearly define.

*kuan* 關章 a Customs regulation; Customs regulations.

*mien* 免傷損之累 to avoid damage.

*shêng* 生意 trade.

*shui* 稅餉 duties; the revenue.

*hsiang* 餉 taxes; duties.

*sui* 隨之日起 to increase day by day.

*chieh* 藉 to avail oneself of; to make a pretext of.

新關文件録



*chü* 具有天眞者 frank-hearted, honest people.

*t'ien* 天眞 heaven's goodness; the good nature inherent in man.

*liang* 眞 good; goodness.

*chin* 盡 to exhaust; all; wholly.

*wei* 維 to think; to consider.

*yü* 與國課有關 to concern the Imperial revenue.

*kuan* 關 to concern.

*yü* 與商情攸繫 to be connected with commercial interests.

*yu* 攸 a relative pronoun, *i.q.*, *so* (所); commonly used in phrases like *yu-chi* (攸繫) or *yu-kuan* (攸關), "that which concerns."

*hsi* 係 (=關係) to be connected with; to be the essence of.

*min* 民生 life, or maintenance, of the people.

*chung* 中堂 a *Chung-t'ang* (title of a Minister of State).

*ts'ai* 裁奪 to decide.

*chien* 鑒核賜敎爲禱 I shall be thankful if you will consider the matter and let me know your opinion.

*tz'ŭ* 賜敎 to bestow instruction; to communicate one's opinion.

*chiao* 敎 to teach; instruction.

*tao* 禱 to pray.

*tz'ŭ* 此佈 I beg to inform you (of the above).

*chün* 鈞安不一 with many kind inquiries (a concluding phrase in letters).

*ming* 名另具 "the name is separately furnished" (a concluding phrase in letters, meaning that one's card is enclosed).

*chiang* 江蘇 the province of Kiangsu. [p. 134]

*jih* 日形 fluctuations.

*tuan* 短少 to be curtailed; to decrease.

*yüan* 原包 original package.

*chi* 稽時 to detain; to delay.

*i* 易破碎 easy to break; breakable.

*jên* 認粗爲細 to recognise coarse as fine.

*chia* 加以重罰 to inflict a heavy punishment; to punish severely. Cf. *i* 以 Document No. 29, p. 58.

*ku* 故 causing; therefore.

*ko* 各商 the merchants; all the merchants.

*wei* 畏途 to fear the road; to avoid the transport of goods from fear of difficulties.

*han* 函件 a letter; letters. Cf. *ssŭ* 絲斤, Document No. 18, p. 28.

*fu* 附閱 to learn from an enclosure (in a letter).

*ying* 應如何酌量 in what manner it is to be settled.

*ju* 如何 how? in what manner?

*pien* 變通 to alter.

*pei* 俾 so that; so as to.

俾裕課恤商 so as to benefit the revenue and promote commerce.

*liang* 兩有裨益 to be of advantage in both respects.

*t'ai* 台端 a term of respect: you.

*ts'ê* 拆驗 to open for examination.

*t'ai* 太嚴 too strict; over-strict.

*chung* 衆商 all the merchants; the mercantile community.

*kuo* 裹 to wrap up; to fetter.

裹足 to impede; to fetter.

*chien* 減色 to diminish; to decrease.

*hsiang* 相 mutual; to assist; to watch the time for.

相機 to seize an opportunity.

*i* 以冀裕課恤商 in order that revenue and commercial interests may be benefited.

*chi* 冀 to hope.

*ch'ê* 扯 to pull apart; to tear away.

扯平 to strike an average.

*fan* 反昂 very high; exorbitant (as in price).

*hsün* 詢商 to inquire into; to ask.

*chu* 諸多 very many; all the many......

*chih* 窒礙 difficulty.

*hsün* 洵 really.

*ch'üeh* 確論 true; really.

*ts'êng* 層 an item; a paragraph.

*jêng* 仍舊 as before; as of old.

*p'ing* 憑商人報明 to rely on (*i.e.*, to accept) the merchant's declaration.

*mien* 免拆驗 to exempt (packages) from opening for examination (of goods).

*kuo* 過寬 too lenient; to go too far in being lenient.

*k'o* 可期漸旺 one may hope for a gradual rise.

*chên* 斟酌適中之論 to consult about a middle course; to strike an average.

*chi* 稽延 to delay.

*p'o* 破損 breakage; *i.e.*, the loss caused by breaking.

*wu* 誤罰 to punish in error.

*ch'u* 除 to do away with.

*tzŭ* 自必 must of course; bound to.

*lô* 樂 to be glad; joyous.

*jih* 日增 to increase (day by day).

*i* 以防...... in order to guard against......

*chia* 夾帶 to carry clandestinely; to smuggle.

*tzŭ* 自報 one's own declaration; to declare oneself.

*jêng* 仍前 as heretofore.

*ts'ê* 拆開 to open (as packages for examination).

*hsi* 細驗 to examine in detail.

*ch'ün* 羣 all; they all.

*chuan* 專屬 to belong to especially; to specially refer to.

*tsung* 宗 kind; description; class.

*yüan* 援以爲例 to quote [a fact] as a precedent so as to constitute a rule.

*hsien* 先行試辦 to put into operation as a provisional measure.

*ch'ang* 常川照辦 to manage matters permanently in this manner.

*t'ing* 停止 to stop; to abolish (as a practice).

*i* 意外 unexpected; unforeseen. [p. 135]

*liu* 流弊 a standing nuisance.

*chuan* 轉 to convey; to bring on (as loss).

*yu* 有虧 to entail loss.

*chü* 據實稟明 to make an accurate report.

*tzŭ* 咨商 to consult by correspondence.

*ho* 合亟 with the proper despatch.

### Document No. 76.

*ping* 稟稱 to report (to a superior).

*pu* 不合 it is not convenient.

*ts'un* 存棧 to keep in store.

*tai* 待 to wait.

待價 to wait for prices [to rise]; to watch the market.

*hsia* 下入 to ship (by such and such a vessel).

*ts'un* 存關 to file in the Customs archives.

*wu* 無涉 not connected with; to have nothing to do with.

*ch'ien* 前稅司 the former Commissioner of Customs.

*tai* 代其 on his behalf; for him (them, etc.).

*chü* 據情 according to the circumstances.

*hou* 候示 to await a reply or a decision. [p. 136]

*nei* 內云 it is said therein; in which it is said.

*yün* 云 to say.

*an* 案內情形 the particular circumstances of the case.

*mi* 米穀 grain.

*yu* 尤 furthermore; still more.

*po* 撥貨船隻 cargo-boats.

*hsiang* 相同 the same as; analogous with.

*nei* 內外土產 native and foreign produce.

*pu* 不分何處進口 without distinguishing the place of importation.

*i* 一律 uniformly.

*chao* 照依 according to.

*yün* 云云 used in quotations when, for the sake of brevity, the tenor of a document is either wholly or partially omitted; "etc., etc." Cf. *têng* 等因, Document No. 26, p. 55.

*an* 按此卽知 it may be known therefrom.

*chao* 照銅錢一律 in conformity with [the rule regarding] copper cash.

*chuan* 專謂 to specially refer to.

*yu* 有涉 to be connected with.

*wu* 無干 not affecting; to have nothing to do with.

*chien* 檢閱 to examine.

*yang* 洋米 foreign rice.

*piao* 標明 to endorse.

*i* 依限 within a prescribed limit of time.

*chi* 賫 to give; to send.

賫回 to send back.

*i* 已逾兩年 having exceeded [the time] of two years.

*yin* 印信 a seal.

*hsin* 信 a seal (as a sign of belief or trust).

*ch'ien* 前稅 the duty [paid] previously.

*chan* 粘 to paste on.

粘開款目 the items pasted on or annexed.

*i* 一併 at the same time.

*chi* 給與 to issue; to grant.

*fu* 伏乞 to respectfully request. [p. 137]

*ch'i* 乞 to beg; to request.

*chih* 祗 to respect; respectfully; as a conjunction, only, but.

祗遵 to respectfully obey; for one's respectful guidance.

*i* 以(=自) from.

以此口運至彼口 to move from one port to another.

*pên* 本商 the merchant concerned (in a matter).

*t'ung* 同商 a fellow-merchant.
*lien* 聯 to connect.
聯名 to conjointly sign.
*chü* 具呈保單 to sign a guarantee.
*pao* 保單 a guarantee; a bond.
*chieh* 結實 firm; durable; lasting.
結實信據 a material guarantee.
*ts'ung* 從給照之日起 to date from date of issue (of a certificate).
*chi* 給照 to grant a certificate.
*wei* 唯 excepting; but.
*hao* 毫 a hair; a trifle.
毫無疑議 there is not the slightest doubt. Cf. *ping* 並未, Document No. 28, p. 57.
*ling* 領照 to issue a certificate.
*hsi* 迄今 up to the present.
*i* 已一年 after the lapse of a year.
已兩載之久 after the lapse of two years.
*hu* 忽 unexpectedly; suddenly.

[p. 138]

*shu* 殊屬費解 this is really not to be understood.
*fei* 費解 not intelligible.
*chieh* 解 to explain; to understand.
*to* 多時 a long time.
*tzŭ* 自當 must of course.
*k'ou* 扣計 to deduct.
*fan* 反 but; on the contrary.
*ch'ien* 前後 before and after.
*hsüan* 懸 to suspend; unlike.
懸殊 very unlike; quite different.
*nan* 難容 inexcusable; unendurable; incompatible.
*jung* 容 to endure; to tolerate.
*hu* 互異 to disagree.
*ping* 稟批 to decide in reply to a petition.
*hsün* 迅 speedily.
*t'o* 妥速 safely and expeditiously.
*wan* 完結 to finish; to conclude.
*chi* 極爲明悉 it is extremely clear.
*kai* 蓋有......印信 to contain the seal of......
*hsien* 顯 obviously.
*chia* 加蓋印信 to seal and enclose in an envelope.
*ch'iung* 迥不相符 in entire disagreement with. Cf. *ch'iung* 迥, Document No. 68, p. 120.

### Document No. 77. [p. 139]

*shên* 申覆 to reply (to a superior).
*liang* 梁 a beam.
梁木 beams (timber).
*fang* 方 square.
方圓 square and round; size (of timber).
*yüan* 圓 round.
*lieh* 列稅則 enumerated in the Tariff.
*shang* 商情 commercial interests.
*p'o* 頗 rather; very; extremely.
頗願 to eagerly wish for.
*i* 一定 certainly; at all events.
*pu* 不易 unchanged; unchangeable.
不易之規 an unchangeable rule.
*kuei* 規 rule; usage.
*yü* 預 to prepare; beforehand.
預爲籌計 to calculate beforehand.
*ch'ou* 籌 to calculate.
籌計 to calculate.
*pên* 本 original fund; capital.
本利 the interest on capital; profit in trade.
本利之盈虧 increase and decrease in profit.
*ying* 盈 to be full; overflowing; increase; gain.
*jao* 饒 to indulge; to be liberal.
饒舌 to indulge one's tongue; to wrangle; to dispute.
*shê* 舌 the tongue.
*yüan* 圓梁木 round beams.
圓徑 the diameter (of a circle).
*ching* 徑 a diameter; a straight line across.
*fang* 方徑 the measurement of a square body (as square beams).
*k'an* 堪 to be able.
堪以 to be fit for. Cf. *i* 以, Document No. 68, p. 120.
*pi* 比例 to refer to a rule by way of analogy; to treat analogously.
*kên* 根 a classifier of wood beams, etc.
*ch'i* 其外另有他商 besides him there are other merchants.
*yü* 於商人有便 it is a convenience to merchants.
於稅餉無甚出入 it makes no great difference in the revenue.
*chao* 照所請 as requested.

*jêng* 仍照舊章 still according to the old rule.

*i* 以清界限 in order to have a clearly defined limit.

*chi* 給 to address to (as a despatch). [p. 140]

*wei* 爲照覆事 in the matter of a reply.

*ku* 僱 to hire.

僱用 to hire; to charter (as a ship).

*lai* 來省 to come to the provincial capital.

*kung* 公同 conjointly.

*wan* 完竣 to complete; to bring to an end.

*chün* 竣 to complete; to finish.

*t'i* 提 to bring forward; to mention.

提及 to mention; to refer to.

*chi* 及 to extend to; to concern.

*an* 案內 in the case.

*yü* 預爲詳訂 to provide for a clear understanding.

*hsiang* 詳訂 to clearly define.

*mai* 邁當 (in imitation of the French sound "mètre") a mètre; mètres.

*mi* 蜜理邁當 (in imitation of the French sound "millimètre") a millimètre; millimètres.

*ming* 明示 to give clear instructions to.

*hsün* 詢請 to inquire about and request (that a matter be done).

*su* 速爲辦理 to manage with despatch.

*cho* 酌復 to reply on being consulted.

*mu* 木植 timber.

*chih* 植 plants; trees.

*ta* 大項 principal kinds.

*wei* 桅木 masts or spars (timber).

*pan* 板木 planks (timber).

*k'uan* 寬厚 breadth and thickness.

*fên* 分鋸爲板 to saw into planks.

*chü* 鋸 a saw; to saw.

*chiu* 究 at last; finally.

*ssŭ* 四方若干 the circumference (in timber measurement).

*chieh* 截 to cut asunder.

截而爲樑 to cut into beams.

*fên* 分晰淸楚 to clearly distinguish.

*hsi* 晰 explicit; clear.

*ch'ing* 淸楚 clear; distinct.

*ch'u* 楚 distinct; well defined.

*shih* 適 to suit; to accord with.

*ko* 各適其用者 each accords with (or is adapted to) the use (to which it is put).

*ting* 定規 a fixed rule.

*i* 易剖別 easy to distinguish.

*p'ou* 剖 to split asunder; to lay open.

剖別 to distinguish.

*ch'ien* 牽 to drag; to implicate.

牽混 to create confusion.

*chin* 僅 only; barely.

*chu* 注 to record; to comment on.

注明 to comment upon; to state.

*pi* 比較 to compare with; when compared with; may be compared with.

*yüan* 圓樑木 round beams; beams other than square.

*lun* 輪 a wheel; round.

輪角稍闊 having rounded corners and rather broad surfaces.

*yüan* 圓徑作爲方徑 to convert round measure into square measure (as of timber).

[p. 141]

*i* 易於相符 easy to agree; handy for calculation.

易於核算 easy to calculate.

*ch'u* 初原 from the outset; at first.

*wu* 無非 cannot but; bound to.

*i* 義 meaning; principle.

*kai* 賅備 to be contained in; to be provided for.

*êrh* 耳 at least; only (restrictive particle at the close of sentences).

*ho* 何故 for what reason? why?

*kai* 蓋因 the reason, generally, is that......

*su* 溯 to look back (as to a period of time).

*tzŭ* 自通商征稅以來 ever since duties have been levied on foreign trade.

*i* 已逾十有餘年之久 more than 10 years since.

*yu* 有餘 more than.

*tsao* 早晚 between morning and night; within short intervals (as daily fluctuations).

*chung* 重輕 heavy and light; either heavy or light; whereas *ch'ing-chung* (輕重) usually means "weight" as a neutral term.

*hsiang* 相若 similar; alike.

*tsai* 在置貨時 at the time of buying goods.

*i* 一定不易 fixed; not changeable.

*pi* 比擬 to treat analogously.

*chih* 值百抽五 five per cent. *ad valorem*.

*chieh* 藉口 to make a pretext.

### Document No. 78. [p. 142]

*chêng* 正月 the first month of the year.

*mai* 買到 to have imported.

*chuan* 轉賣 to re-sell; to further sell to other parties.

*shêng* 省河 the river at the provincial capital.

*lai* 來控 to lodge a complaint.

*ts'un* 存庫 to keep on deposit (as funds paid into a treasury).

*pei* 被風……收口 to put into a port for shelter.

*shou* 收口 to put into a port (as a vessel in distress).

*huai* 壞船 a wreck; a vessel damaged in distress.

*ts'ê* 拆毀 to break up (as a vessel).

*mu* 木料 materials (as of a ship).

*i* 一案 with regard to (such and such) a case; *re*.

*ch'ing* 情節 particulars, details.

*han* 函致 to send a letter to.

*t'ing* 聽候 to await (as a decision).

*ch'üan* 全案 the complete (records of a) case.

*ling* 另換船載 to transfer (cargo) to another vessel.

*pi* 必欲 to want.

*t'ui* 退還 to return.

*lu* 路過 on the road; *en route*.

*yin* 因風收口 to put into a port in distress.

*ch'uan* 船身 a ship's hull.

*tuan* 斷難 decidedly difficult; impossible.

*chia* 駕 to sit (as in a carriage).

駕駛 to sail.

*pan* 搬 to move; to transfer; to tranship.

*shou* 收納 to collect (as duties).

*shao* 稍有誤會 there is a slight misapprehension.

*wu* 誤會 to misapprehend; a mistake.

*ssŭ* 似覺 it seems as if it may be considered; it might be thought.

*p'ing* 平允 just; fair.

*suan* 算除 to deduct in an account.

*i* 以完此案 in order to close this case.

*hsing* 行文 to write to.

*ch'a* 查照辦理 to act accordingly. [p. 143]

*hsün* 循照 (=按照) in accordance with.

*tz'ŭ* 此等案件 such cases.

*wu* 務須 must.

*i* 以重稅課 in order to show due respect to revenue interests.

### Document No. 79.

*huo* 貨船 a merchant vessel.

*wei* 未領紅單之先 before the issue of the port clearance. Note the use of the negation *wei* (未).

*ts'ao* 遭 to meet.

遭風 to meet with a storm; to be in distress.

*ch'ao* 潮州 the prefecture of Ch'ao-chou, near Swatow.

*chuang* 裝滿貨物 full of cargo (as a vessel).

*wei* 未曾 not having; without having.

*li* 離 to go from; to part; to leave.

離開 to leave (a place); to start from.

離馬頭 to leave the jetty.

*tsai* 載在撥船 to be placed on board a cargo-boat.

*yü* 于 in; at.

*shih* 失落 to drop and lose (as goods dropping into the sea). [p. 144]

*chuang* 裝載于撥船 to be placed on board a cargo-boat.

*shou* 受潮濕 to become damp (as goods on board ship).

*ch'ao* 潮濕 damp.

*shih* 濕 damp; wet.

*chia* 價低減 the price is falling.

*li* 立此專條 to draw up this special rule.

*i* 擬定辦法 to propose a fixed mode of procedure.

*mai* 買保險 to take out an insurance policy.

*pao* 保 to protect.

保險 to protect against danger; to insure against (as fire, marine accident, etc.); insurance.

*hsien* 險 danger; risk.

*i* 意外 unexpected.

意外之虞 unexpected dangers.

*fang* 防不勝防 to take protective measures against what cannot be protected; said if there is no help against running risks.

*shêng* 勝 to be able to; adequate to.

勝防 to be able to ward off; to protect.

*chia* 加意 to take special care.

*fang* 防範 to take protective measures.

*fan* 範 a rule; a pattern.

*yü* 與否......or not.

*chu* 諸多 very many.

*i* 以免辦理兩歧 to avoid divergency (inconsistency) of action.

*wu* 毋須遽議訂章 you must not make regulations in a hurry.

*chü* 遽 hurried; hasty.

遽議 to decide hastily.

**Document No. 80.** [p. 145]

*fan* 販運 to traffic; to forward (goods).

*ku* 古銅器 old copperware.

古玩 curiosities.

*hu* 戶部稅則 the Customs Tariff issued by the Board of Revenue, in force at the Native Custom Houses.

戶 household; population.

戶部 the Board of Revenue.

*ku* 估 value; to value.

*pu* 補交 to pay afterwards (what should have been paid before).

*ch'uan* 串 to connect; to string together.

串通 to combine (as for an illegal act).

*t'ung* 銅料器 copper material and articles; unmanufactured copper and copperware.

*chê* 折中 to strike an average; average.

*yen* 贗 spurious.

贗製 to imitate; to counterfeit.

*ching* 景泰藍 "Ching-t'ai-lan," a celebrated mark for old copperware; cloisonné of the Ching-t'ai period (A.D. 1450–57).

*lan* 藍 (=法藍 *fa-lan* or 琺琅 *fa-lang*) cloisonné or enamelled ware.

*shên* 甚稀 very rarely.

*hsi* 稀 few; rare.

*chên* 珍愛 to be fond of (as a curiosity, jewel, etc.).

*hsi* 稀少 very little; very rare.

*i* 以杜勾串 in order to prevent fraudulent combinations.

*pi* 避就 to shirk [one thing] and take [to another].

*yu* 有當 there is necessity for.

*li* 理合 duly.

*ku* 估徵 to charge duty *ad valorem*.

*ch'üan* 全卷照錄 to make a copy of all the documents of a case.

*chüan* 卷 a record; a document.

*fu* 附 to append; to enclose.

附呈抄案清摺 to append a fair copy of the correspondence in a case.

*i* 以杜避重就輕之弊 to prevent shirking the heavy and taking to the light, *i.e.*, substituting the easy for the onerous.

[p. 146]

*ssŭ* 俟......再...... to wait till...... and then......

*i* 以符舊制 in order to agree with the old rule.

**Document No. 81.**

*kuo* 過載 to tranship.

過載輪船 to tranship to a steamer.

*k'ai* 開行最速 to start in a great hurry (as a ship).

*chih* 至多 very many; very frequently.

*hsien* 限以三日 within three days' time.

*ta* 大半 the greater half; mostly.

*fu* 付搭便船 to charter a convenient ship.

*ch'üeh* 却 but.

*wan* 萬一 one in ten thousand; perhaps.

*ting* 定限 a fixed limit of time.

*ch'ê* 掣 to drag; to pull.

掣肘 *lit.*, "to pull elbows," *i.e.*, to hinder; to embarrass.

*chou* 肘 the elbow.

*tsai* 再四熟思 to consider ripely; to think twice before acting.

*shu* 熟思 to consider ripely.

*wai* 外邦 foreign countries.

*pang* 邦 a kingdom.

*chia* 假道 the indirect road; making a *détour* for some reason or other.

*chung* 中華 China; Chinese.

*chiang* 港口 ports; harbours.

*têng* 登岸 to come on shore; to land.

*kuo* 過船之准單 a permit to tranship.

*an* 按限 within the limit (of time).

*shou* 受罰 to be fined; to be punished. [p. 147]

*chiu* 究 in the end; at the utmost.

*k'ai* 開艙准單 a permit to break bulk.

*shêng* 生流弊 to result in a standing nuisance.

*i* 以便照辦 in order to act accordingly.

*ch'a* 查閱 to note; to examine and take note of.

*shang* 尙詳洽 clear and satisfactory enough.

*ts'êng* 層 an item; a question or subject matter.

*tsui* 最關緊要 most important in connexion with (this subject).

*li* 禮拜 a week.

*t'i* 體察情形 to investigate the circumstances.

*t'o* 妥定 to settle satisfactorily.

*chih* 至遲 at the latest; not later than.

*yüeh* 約外 not in the Treaty; not provided for by the Treaty.

*ch'i* 起見 to conceive an opinion.

*chieh* 借端滋弊 to make a pretext of a matter for creating trouble.

### Document No. 82. [p. 148]

*mo* 墨西哥國 *(mo-hsi-ko)* Mexico.

*hsin* 新造 newly made.

*hui* 會同驗明 to examine conjointly.

*yen* 驗明 to examine.

*ch'êng* 成色 per-centage or proportion of pure metal in an alloy.

*hsieh* 寫 to write.

寫立憑單 to draw up a certificate.

*t'ung* 同前因 to the former effect; to the same effect.

*ho* 覈 to verify.

*yang* 洋銀 foreign silver (as Mexican dollars).

*pu* 補足 to pay for difference in standard of silver.

*chê* 折交 to pay in proportion with......

*hsin* 新製 newly made.

*hui* 會驗 to examine conjointly.

*tsu* 足紋 (=足色紋銀) full standard silver; pure sycee.

*wên* 紋水 the difference or fluctuation in the price of sycee silver.

*tsu* 足數 enough; sufficient.

*ch'êng* 成 a tenth; tenths.

*ying* 鷹 an eagle.

鷹銀 eagle money; Mexican dollars.

*pu* 不足 not enough; insufficient.

*lê* 樂用 to gladly use; to like using.

*yin* 銀局 a Bank.

*wu* 舞 to dance; to fence.

舞弊 to wink at a malpractice.

*i* 以 to use; with; by means of.

以官濟私 to further one's private ends by means of official resources.

以假攙眞 to mix up truth with falsehood; to adulterate.

*pu* 不便於民 inconvenient to the public.

*ch'iang* 强 to force.

强輸官稅 to be forced to pay Government duties in a certain coin; to be obligatory as a legal tender in payment of duties.

*i* 以期無碍稅餉 in order that no difficulties may arise to the revenue.

*shun* 順輿情 to please public opinion; to act in accordance with public interests.

*yü* 輿 the earth; the public.

*ch'ien* 前因 the afore-mentioned. [p. 149]

*chu* 鑄 to cast (as coins).

*hsin* 新式洋錢 a new pattern foreign coin.

*hsi* 希請 to request; to beg to request.

*ch'in* 親 a relative.

親王 an Imperial prince of the 1st order.

*chieh* 接准 to receive.

*shih* 實在 real; really.

*ch'êng* 成色若干 the touch (of silver).

*shêng* 省城 the provincial capital.

*pu* 部堂 official designation of a President of a Board; as such the title of a Governor General.

*pi* 敝 mean; poor; a respectful term for my, mine, our, ours.

*shu* 屬官 a subordinate officer.

*chien* 監 inspect.

監視 to superintend an act in one's own presence.

*shih* 視 to see.

*jung* 鎔兌 to melt and weigh; to ascertain the touch (of silver).

*ch'ing* 傾化 to assay.

*hua* 化 to change.

*ho* 覈定 to ascertain.

*chiao* 較多幾至一元有半 an overplus of up to \$1½ against......(the object compared preceding with *yü* 與). [p. 150] *fu* 附送 to forward as an enclosure (in a letter or despatch).

*chan nien* } 粘送 to forward as an enclosure.

*ch'i* 祈 to request.

*pu* 補用 employed as a supernumerary.

*chih* 知府 a prefect.

*kuang* 廣糧廳 a departmental grain-collector at Canton.

*yüeh* 粵海關部 official designation of the Haikwan or Hoppo of Canton.

*ying* 盈庫大使 an assistant treasurer; a treasury keeper (*see* MAYERS' "The Chinese Government," No. 297).

*ta* 大使 a sub-commissioner (*e.g.*, in the Provincial Treasurer's, or the Salt Commissioner's yamên).

*tsê* 特 specially.

特揀 to select; to appoint.

*fan* 繙 to translate.

繙譯官 an official interpreter.

*k'u* 庫廳 an assistant treasurer in the Provincial Treasury, *i.q.*, *ying* 盈庫大使 (*q.v.*), of which it is the abreviated official form.

*kuan* 關部 official designation of the Hoppo at Canton.

*tien* 店 a commercial establishment; a shop.

*hsin* 新出 newly issued.

*yin* 銀員 dollars.

*tang* 當面 in one's presence.

*shih* 試驗 to examine; to test.

*ho* 核定 to ascertain.

*shih* 事由 circumstances; particulars.

*hsiang* 詳細 to report in detail.

*p'ing* 平兌 to weigh.

*p'ei* 配 to mate; to pair.

配鉛 to mix with lead.

*t'ung* 同重 an equal weight; the same weight.

*jung* 鎔銷 to melt.

*t'i* 提淨 to extract the pure metal from an alloy.

*hai* 海關紋銀 Haikwan sycee.

*jung* 鎔化 to melt.

*ho* 覈對 to compare.

*yen* 驗試事由 the results of an examination.

*shên* 伸 equal to; worth.

*kuo* 鍋 a pan. [p. 151]

*ti* 底 the bottom; at the bottom of.

*hao* 耗 waste.

耗輕銀 waste silver.

*lien* 連 to connect; together with; and.

*ch'ing* 輕耗 loss in weight; under-weight.

*shên* 伸得 to be equal to; to be worth.

*li* 立憑單 to draw up a certificate.

*wei* 爲證 in witness thereof; as a voucher.

*chi* 計核 to calculate.

*ti* 抵 to consider as equivalent.

*p'ing* 憑碼均行 to ascertain the value (as of silver) according to weight.

*han* 漢文 Chinese writing; in Chinese.

*ying* 英文 English writing; in English.

*t'ung* 通 a classifier of documents.

*kuang* 廣州省城 the city of Canton.

*shu* 署內 in the yamên; in the office.

*liang* 兩廣 the Two Kwang provinces (Kwangtung and Kwangsi).

*yüeh* 粵省 the Canton province.

*yin* 銀局 a mint.

*ch'êng* 成 to make; made of.

*wei* 委員 to depute officers; a deputy.

*i* 以便輸餉 in order to facilitate the payment of duties.

*t'ung* 通用 in, or for, general use; used by all.

*pên* 本部堂 I, the Governor General.

*hou* 候補 "expectant" (as an *Expectant* Taot'ai).

*tzŭ* 咨商 to deliberate; to consult by letter.

*yen* 眼同 conjointly and before one's eyes. [p. 152]

*yin* 銀匠 experts in melting silver.

*jih* 日行通用 in daily and general use.

*i* 以便商民 in order to accommodate merchants.

*yeh* 業經 a sign of the past: has, have.

*kun* 棍 a stick; a knave.

棍徒 sharpers; villains; *mauvais sujets*.

*t'u* 徒 a foot-soldier; a follower; a rowdy.

*chia* 假造 to counterfeit.

*pu* 不樂於使用 to dislike using.

*nieh* 揑造 to counterfeit.

*t'a* 他故 other reasons.

*ch'iang* 強制 to enforce a rule; to force a rule upon.

*pi* 必用 to be obliged to use; to be bound to use.

新關文件録



*ku* 顧 to look; to consider; to care for.

顧慮 to consider.

*yü* 預爲言明 to declare clearly beforehand.

Document No. 83. [p. 153]

*tsu* 租雇 to hire; to charter (as a ship).

*fang* 仿造 to imitate a pattern; to construct according to a pattern.

*hsien* 現已 (sign of the perfect tense) now have, has, etc.

*chih* 滯礙 to impede; difficulty.

*shang* 商戶 merchants.

*k'an* 刋 to cut; to cut blocks for printing; to print.

刋本 to print (on blocks) in pamphlet or book shape.

*chi* 計抄單壹件 copy of one document is annexed hereto.

*chih* 置用 to purchase and use; to buy for one's own use.

*ling* 領繳 to hand to; to issue to.

*tan* 單契牌照 permits (or licenses), bonds, and (ship's) certificates.

*p'ai* 牌照 a ship's certificate of registry.

*pên* 本人 the person concerned.

*chia* 假借 to be the wrong one; to be a substitute (and not the proper person); to personate another.

*mai* 買船准單 a license for buying a ship.

*chi* 籍貫 the origin (or parentage) and birthplace of a person.

*ch'êng* 承買 to contract for purchase.

*ho* 合式 according to pattern; in due shape.

*nêng* 能出海堪用之船 a seaworthy ship.

*mai* 賣主 the seller. Cf. *mai* 買主, p. 155.

*chia* 假冒借名 to personate another. [p. 154]

*li* 立據 to draw up a certificate.

*ch'uan* 船契 a ship's certificate of sale.

*shou* 收領 to receive; [to deliver] into the hands of.

*ch'a* 查銷 to cancel.

*k'uan* 寬闊若干噸數若干 a ship's measurement and tonnage.

*chao* 照塡 to fill in (as in a document).

*shou* 收執 to receive and keep (as a certificate).

*fei* 費銀 expenses; a fee.

*ta* 大書 in large characters; large writing.

*liang* 兩旁 on both sides.

*i* 遺失 to lose.

*pu* 補領 to issue anew (as a document lost).

補請牌照 to apply for a new certificate of registry (to replace one lost).

*chiu* 救出 to save (out of other property destroyed).

*yin* 隱匿干咎 to be guilty of concealing (*e.g.*, a document to be delivered).

*kan* 干 to offend.

干咎 to be guilty.

*chiu* 咎 evil; criminal.

*lin* 檁 a cross-beam; hatch-combings (of a ship).

*k'o* 刻 to engrave.

刻明 to engrave legibly.

*mai* 買船契 a certificate of purchase of a ship.

*ti* 抵押未淸 pawned and not redeemed.

*k'o* 客商 a merchant.

*wu* 無涉 not concerned in.

*shê* 涉 to be concerned in; to be implicated in.

*t'ien* 添註 to fill in.

*kai* 改註底簿 to change an entry in the original books.

*i* 以壹百分爲算 to divide into 100 parts or shares.

*kuei* 歸某人 to belong to such and such a person.

*an* 按股分 according to share.

*ku* 股 a share in a concern; a lot.

*hui* 會館 a guild; a public company. [p. 155]

*shou* 首事 the leading man; the chairman of a company.

*liao* 料理 to manage.

*pieh* 別華商 another Chinese merchant.

*tai* 帶同 to take with oneself.

*mai* 買主 the purchaser. Cf. *mai* 賣主, p. 153.

*ho* 核准 to consider the permittance; to permit.

*hsieh* 寫立賣契 to draw up a deed of sale.

*huan* 換領新牌 to exchange against a new certificate.

*t'ien* 塡註英文 to fill in the English (version).

*tsao* 造船准單 a permit or license for building a ship.

*pi* 畢 to finish.

*k'an* 勘量 to survey (as a ship).

*k'ai* 開具淸單 to draw up an official statement of particulars.

*ssŭ* 私赴沿海別口 to clandestinely resort to another port (viz., a non-Treaty port) on the coast.

*chin* 進泊 to enter (a port) and anchor.

10

*nei* 內地湖河各口 inland lake and river ports.

*chih* 致有 so that there is; so as to; resulting in.

*p'êng* 碰壞 collision and damage; to receive damage from collision.

*ch'êng* 呈存 to deliver for safe custody.

*ho* 何處 at what place?

*po* 泊船 to anchor a ship.

*ch'êng* 呈具報單 to make a written declaration; to send in a declaration.

*fên* 分款 according to categories.

*kuan* 管船夥長 the first mate of a ship.

*huo* 夥長 a chief mate; a senior partner.

*i* 易知 to easily understand; to easily learn.

*fa* 法度 regulations; ways. [p. 156]

*shou* 受 to receive; sometimes a sign of the passive.

受雇 to be hired, engaged, etc. (as an employé).

*ch'ung* 充艙工 to act as master of a ship.

*k'ao* 考驗 to examine (as a candidate).

*ku* 雇定 to settle about an engagement; to hire; to engage (as an employé).

*ho* 何國人 of what nationality?

何姓名 of what name?

*tz'ŭ* 辭 to decline; to refuse.

辭工 to leave one's work; to come off duty.

*kuei* 規矩 custom; usage.

*chü* 矩 rule; usage.

*chi* 記 to record.

記事簿 a log-book.

*ching* 經過之事 the events that have happened.

*ming* 名單 a muster roll.

*nien* 年歲 the age of a man.

*kung* 工銀 wages.

*ch'ung* 充當水手 to act as a sailor.

*tai* 帶赴領事官 to take [a man] to the Consul.

*pu* 不法 unruly.

*k'un* 捆押 to bind and lock up; to put in irons.

*wei* 違犯 to offend against.

**Document No. 84.** [p. 157]

*ying* 英德兩商 both British and German merchants.

*hu* 互異 different from each other.

*ao* 澳 a bay.

澳門 Macao.

*fei* 非通商口岸華船 a Chinese vessel not [registered at] a Treaty port.

*yü* 與德國無涉 it has nothing to do with Germany.

*chao* 招商船局 the China Merchants' Steam Navigation Company.

*i* 已有地方官給領船照 the local authorities *having* issued a ship's certificate.

*pu* 不無窒碍 cannot avoid difficulties; bound to be attended by difficulties.

*yen* 沿海各處 the places on the sea-coast. [p. 158]

*liu* 琉球 (*liu-ch'iu*) the Lu-chu Islands.

*t'ung* 通行出口入口 to traffic inwards and outwards at a port.

*shu* 殊於華商生計窒碍 to materially interfere with the "bread and butter" of Chinese merchants.

*shêng* 生計 to get a living; a livelihood.

*shui* 稅額 a fixed amount of revenue to be collected.

*chih* 窒碍難行 difficult to be carried out.

*jên* 任從英商 at the pleasure of British merchants.

*ch'a* 查出 it comes out; it is brought home to one.

*tsou* 走私漏稅 to smuggle.

*t'ing* 艇 a small boat.

*yen* 沿江 along the river; on the river.

*tso* 作証 to act as witness; in witness (thereof).

*chi* 暨 together with; at the same time; as well.

*i* 以昭劃一 for the sake of uniformity.

*i* 一經查出 as soon as proved or brought home to. [p. 159]

*i* 以杜弊端 in order to prevent malpractices.

*kêng* 更定條約 an amended or revised Treaty.

*kai* 改變 to alter.

*t'ung* 通商稅務公會 the German Zollverein.

*ch'iang* 强辯 a one-sided view; an *ex parte* argument.

*wu* 毋任違背 do not stand opposition.

*t'ê* 特劄 a special order (a concluding phrase in despatches from superiors).

**Document No. 85.** [p. 160]

*hsün* 巡船 [Customs] boats; cruisers.

*hsin* 新式 new pattern; new style.

*lung* 龍 a dragon.

龍旗 the "dragon" flag; the Chinese national ensign.

新關文件録



*shih* 失畫一 to lose sight of uniformity; not to be uniform.

*ch'i* 旗幟 flags and pennants.

*ch'ih* 幟 a streamer; a pennant.

*hua* 畫一式樣 a uniform pattern.

*hui* 繪 to sketch; to draw; to paint.

繪圖 to draw a sketch, plan, or map.

*hsieh* 斜 oblique.

斜長 diagonal length.

*ti* 底長 length at the base.

*fu* 幅 a strip of cloth.

幅寬 the breadth of a flag.

*san* 三角 three cornered; triangular. [p. 161]

*chêng* 正 as applied to colours, deep.

正黃色 a deep yellow colour.

*hsiang* 鑲 to inlay; to enclose; to border (as a figure on a flag).

*hsiang* 向上 turned upwards; upwards.

*wei* 桅梢 on the top of a mast.

*shao* 梢 the top of a staff.

*chu* 主旗 "the ruling flag;" a national ensign.

*kung* 工部 the Board of Works.

*ying* 營 to devise mechanical plans; a battalion.

營造 engineering; public works.

營造尺量 the official measure of the Board of Works.

### Document No. 86.

*chü* 具稟人 the petitioner.

*chi* 籍 to be registered as a native of......

*tsu* 租界 land on which ground rent is paid; a concession; a settlement (as the British Settlement at Shanghai).

*ch'iu* 求恩 to request a favour.

*ch'ieh* 竊身 I, the petitioner. Note that 身 *shên*, standing for "I," is written smaller, like all modest terms denoting the person of the writer.

*shên* 身 in petitions, a modest term for "I."

*su* 素 formerly; usually; contented.

*shên* 申江 Shanghai.

*mou* 謀 to plan; to plot.

謀生 to carry on trade.

*yu* 有年 a number of years.

*an* 安分 peaceful and contented; orderly.

*shou* 守業 to attend to one's trade.

*pao* 胞 the womb.

胞弟 a uterine brother.

*hsia* 下午 in the afternoon.

*i* 已用 having been used; old; second-hand.

*tuan* 段 a lot.

*chi* 計本 representing capital, or an investment.

*pu* 不識 ignorant; not knowing.

*kuan* 關憲 honorary title used in addressing a high Customs official.

*ta* 大人 a *ta-jên* (honorary title used in addressing officials from the third rank upwards).

*fu* 俯念 to condescend to think of; to take into consideration.

*ling* 零星 miscellaneous things; odds and ends.

零星小件 odds and ends; miscellaneous trifles.

*ch'i* 乞恩 to ask as a favour.

*ch'ih* 飭賜 to order the bestowal of; to cause to be given.

*shên* 深沾 deeply indebted (as for benefits received).

*chan* 沾 to moisten; to be affected by; to receive favour.

*tê* 德便 advantages granted; benefit.

### Document No. 87. [p. 162]

*chi* 寄帶 to forward (as in a letter).

*huo* 貨樣 samples.

*yo* 籲 to pray; to implore.

籲懇 to entreat; to invoke.

*hsien* 憲恩 Your Honour's favour.

*huo* 豁 liberal; magnanimous.

豁免 kindly to exempt from [punishment].

*yeh* 業 trade; occupation; "my trade or business;" hence a modest term for "I," used by trades-people.

*k'ai* 開設 to establish; to be established.

*su* 素守本分 to pursue one's business peacefully.

*pên* 本分 the duties of a man's occupation; one's business.

*pien* 便附 to enclose in a letter.

*ch'ing* 情難推却 according to the circumstances, or as matters happened to be, it was difficult to decline.

*t'ui* 推却 to decline; to refuse.

*t'ai* 臺下 in petitions, an honorary title given to officials.

*hsün* 巡 a tidewaiter; an executive employé.

*sou* 搜 to search.
搜驗 to search; to examine.
*ch'ieh* 竊念 I respectfully think or thought.
*wei* 微 small; trifling.
微物 a small matter; a trifle.
*fan* 販運圖利 to traffic for the sake of profit.
*k'o* 客家 a customer.
*yeh* 業等 a modest term for "we," used by trades-people in petitions.
*i* 遺悞 to make a mistake.
*so* 索賠甚急 to ask for damages very urgently.
*k'ou* 口難分剖 difficult to explain.
*li* 瀝情 to state facts one by one in order.
*fu* 伏乞 to humbly pray or petition.
*ch'ui* 垂憐豁免 to have pity and magnanimously to disregard.
*shih* 世世公侯 may your generation rise to the ranks of duke and marquess.
*ting* 頂德 imbued with virtue; please your goodness.
*shang* 上稟 to hand up a petition (concluding phrase in petitions).
*hsia* 匣 a chest.

**Document No. 88.** [p. 163]

*ching* 經租帳房 a house agent; a rent collector.
*chang* 帳房 an office where accounts are settled; a counting-house; a shroff's or comprador's office; an accountant; a shroff.
*han* 漢號 a Hankow firm.
*t'o* 託 to commission.
託買 to commission one to buy.
*tzŭ* 自着 to wear oneself; for own wear.
*cho* 着 to wear (as clothes, shoes, etc.).
*mu* 木鞋 wooden shoes; clogs.
*k'ou* 叩恩豁免 to ask to be magnanimously exempted from punishment.
*hsün* 迅賜給領 to promptly allow to be given up.
*chih* 治 the jurisdiction of an officer; "under your jurisdiction."
*wei* 爲業 as my business.
*t'ai* 臺巡 Your Honour's searching officer.
*chi* 集貲 to collect money (as capital for trade in a company).
*k'ai* 開張 to open business.

*hsien* 鮮鹹雜貨店 a shop in which fresh and preserved victuals and sundries are sold.
*ning* 甯幫 the Ningpo men (as a class).
*tien* 店堂 in the shop.
店夥 a mercantile assistant; a partner.
*fan* 販賣 to trade.
*yang* 仰沐 to look forward to receiving kindness.
*mu* 沐 to wash; to receive favours.
*hsien* 憲臺 (honorary title given to high officials) Your Honour; you.
*chien* 鑒原 to examine; to trace a matter to its source.
*hsia* 下 below; inferior; a modest term for "I," "me," "my," etc.
下情 the facts stated by me, the inferior.
*pu* 不諳 ignorant; not knowing.
*an* 諳 to know about.
*shang* 賞給 to give; to award.
*pei* 備情 the complete details; "these are the facts."
*chi* 急叩伏乞 to urgently request; to pray for.
*tien* 電鑒 (an honorary style of addressing officials) "your enlightened mind."
*ên* 恩賜 the bestowal of favour.
*chan* 沾仁 to receive humane treatment.

**Document No. 89.** [p. 164]

*hsiao* 小行 "the small firm;" a modest term for "I" or "we," used by merchants in petitions.
*yen* 驗訖完餉 to pay duties after examination.
*chi* 訖 to finish; after a verb, may assume the force of a sign of the past: after, having.
*chin* 金利源 *(chin-li-yüan)* the Kin-lee-yuen Wharf, Godowns, etc., on the French Bund at Shanghai.
*pei* 北首 the northern end.
*t'ien* 天后宮橋 a bridge at the Quai de la Pagode, in the French Concession at Shanghai.
*hsi* 西人 a European.
*tung* 東洋車 a Japanese carriage, *i.e.*, a jinricsha.
*hsi* 攜去 to take away.
*li* 理論 to discuss.
*chung* 中西 Chinese and foreign.
*yin* 音 sound.
音語 language.
*tung* 懂 to understand.
*yu* 由是 from there.

*wei* 尾隨 to follow close after.
尾隨其後 to follow close after one.
*mu* 目覩 to see; to observe.
*tu* 覩 to look; to see.
*chiang* 江海北關 the Shanghai Custom House.
*wu* 誤疑 to erroneously suspect.
*yin* 因而 therefore; on which account he......
*nai* 迺 (or 乃) that is; to wit; also; and; but.
*wu* 誤認 to erroneously take as; to mistake for.
*li* 瀝陳 to state events one by one, in order.
*shang* 賞還 to kindly return.
*an* 安商業 to make the merchant's business easy.

Document No. 90. [p. 165]

*t'o* 託帶 to ask one to bring.
*shui* 水烟袋 a water pipe; a hubble-bubble.
*hsün* 迅賜賞給 to kindly give as soon as possible.
*ch'ieh* 竊 (=竊) a thief; "I."
*ma* 馬路 a road for riding or driving; used in Shanghai to express the roads suitable for general carriage traffic.
*chih* 支 a classifier of tobacco-pipes.
*ti* 抵埠 to arrive in port.
*tai* 代客 on behalf of a mercantile friend.
*fu* 附有 there is enclosed (as in a letter or postal bag).
*ch'ü* 取巧販賣 deceitful traffic in goods.
*jên* 仁憲 (in petitions, an honorary title given to officials) your kindness.
*shih* 實爲德便 it will be a real kindness or benefit.

Document No. 91. [p. 166]

*min* 民人 one of the people; a subject.
*chia* 家用 for domestic use.
*chang* 帳子 curtains.
*mêng* 蒙 to receive (from a superior); sign of the passive.
*ch'iu* 秋季 the autumn season.
*chia* 家中 in my family; at home.
*chi* 吉 happy; lucky.
吉席 "the happy mat;" wedlock; marriage.
*ch'uang* 床帳 bed curtains.
*shan* 衫 a shirt.

Document No. 92. [p. 167]

*tzŭ* 紫竹林 (*Tzŭ-chu-lin*) the local name for the site of the Foreign settlement at Tientsin.
*k'ên* 懇恩 to pray for favour.
*yu* 幼 young.
幼弟 a young brother.
*tso* 做工 to do work; to be employed.
*chiao* 交 intercourse; intimacy; to give.
交好 to be on terms of friendship with.
*shou* 手中 in hand.
*liao* / *lio* / *lüeh* } 畧 a little; some.
*yü* 餘財 surplus funds; savings.
*ts'ai* 財 riches; funds.
*fan* 煩 to trouble; to request.
*yü* 雨傘 umbrellas.
*han* 旱 dry.
旱傘 parasols.
*chu* 囑 to order; to request.
*mai* 賣出 to sell.
*tso* 作一家糊口 to constitute the living or food for the whole family.
*i* 一家 the whole family.
*hu* 糊 (for 餬) gruel; food; subsistence.
糊口 sustenance; a livelihood.
*ch'ü* 取去 to take away.
*lao* 老幼 old and young; all.
*lai* 賴 to rely on.
*yang* 養 to nourish.
養生 to support oneself or one's family.
*fu* 伏祈 to humbly request.
*ko* 格外施恩 to grant a special favour.
*kan* 感 to be grateful.
感鴻恩 to be greatly obliged.
*hung* 鴻 great; vast.
*wei* 爲此叩稟 on this account I make a petition.

Document No. 93.

*suan* 算書 a calculator; a clerk.
*tsai* 在關 in Customs employ; at the Custom House.
*to* 多 (after a number) more than.

*hsia* 夏間 during the summer time.

*ch'êng* 承 to receive; a sign of the passive.

承大人派 I have been deputed by you, the Ta-jên.

*ta* 大老爺 a *ta-lao-yeh* (title of an official of the fourth or a lower grade).

*ho* 河間府 the prefecture of Ho-chien, in Chihli.

*pan* 辦賑 to manage the distribution of relief funds (in distressed districts).

*chên* 賑 to relieve; to aid the distressed.

*shou* 受暑受瘟 to suffer heat and malaria.

*shu* 暑 heat.

*pei* 備嘗辛苦 to experience hard times.

*ch'ang* 嘗 to taste.

*hsin* 辛 bitter.

辛苦 bitterness; grief.

*k'u* 苦 bitter; distress.

*huan* 患 calamity; to be afflicted.

患病 to fall sick.

*mêng* 蒙大人面允 to receive the Ta-jên's (*i.e.*, your) verbal promise; I have been promised by Your Excellency.

*hao* 好處 advantages; benefit.

*yen* 言及 to say with regard to; to mention.

*kao* 高升 to be promoted to a high post.

*pao* 保舉 to recommend for promotion.

*chü* 舉 to recommend.

*jung* 榮 honour; glory.

榮歸 to return with glory; *i.e.*, to retire from public life.

*pu* 不揣冒昧 not able to detect signs of rash stupidity.

*ch'uai* 揣 to ascertain; to detect.

*mao* 冒昧 ignorant; headstrong.

*mei* 昧 dark; obscure in mind.

*yang* 仰求 to respectfully ask; to look up to ask.

*hsin* 薪俸 a salary; official emoluments.

*ch'u* 處 circumstances; points of a matter.

*fu* 伏候 to respectfully wait.

*chün* 鈞裁 to consider in justness; to duly weigh the arguments.

*kan* 感激 to thank.

*chin* 謹稟 a respectful petition (concluding phrase in petitions).

## Document No. 94. [p. 168]

*k'uan* 寬釋 to indulgently release.

*shih* 釋 to release.

*chieh* 接載 to receive goods for shipment (as a shipping broker).

*mai* 嘜 (pronounced *mák* in Cantonese) an unauthorised character used to represent the sound of the English word "mark." Note that in Canton characters representing foreign sounds are commonly preceded by the radical 口.

嘜什貨 marked "Sundries."

*shih* 什貨 miscellaneous goods; sundries.

*ping* 氷片 Baroos camphor.

*tsa* 雜藥 miscellaneous drugs.

*fan* 繁 numerous; many.

繁多 very many.

*ou* 偶 accidentally; unforeseen.

*i* 以致錯漏 so as to result in an erroneous evasion (as of duty).

*chiu* 咎實難辭 the mistake can hardly be denied.

*po* 跋 to walk through the grass; to travel.

跋涉 to travel far; far-travelled.

*shê* 涉 to ford; to wade.

*ch'ung* 重洋 to cross the sea twice; to cross two or several seas; to make a long sea journey.

*wei* 微利 small profit.

*hsüeh* 血 blood; money; property.

血本 capital in trade.

*k'u* 苦不堪言 ineffable distress.

*fu* 俯恤商情 to look down with a pitiful heart on mercantile interests.

*ên* 恩便 a favour; a kindness.

*pu* 不勝感激 to be greatly obliged.

*ch'ieh* 切赴 to go quickly; "an urgent letter;" "immediate."

## Document No. 95.

*nan* 難甘 difficult to submit to cheerfully.

*ping* 秉 to hold up.

秉公 holding up justice; to act fairly.

*i* 以便商族 in order to accommodate merchants.

*hua* 花梨木 rose-wood.

*li* 梨 a pear tree.

*chü* 詎 how; in what manner.

詎料 "how could I expect?" *i.e.*, to my surprise; unexpectedly; however.

*t'u* 突 abruptly; unexpectedly. [p. 169]

*t'ung* 同是一貨 it is the same cargo.

*hsiang* 相隔一日 a difference in time of one day.

*chiao* 交客 to deliver to the merchant (as goods to a purchaser).

*chiu* 久延 to delay.

*hsün* 旬 a decade.

旬日 a decade; ten days.

*yang* 央 to invite; to entreat.

央求 to solicit; to urgently ask for.

*chien* 奸 villainous.

奸商 corrupt merchants; dishonest traders.

*i* 以示儆 in order to show warning; "as a warning."

*ching* 儆 to warn.

*kao* 高估 a high valuation; to assess at a high value.

*wu* 無從 not able to follow; not able to......

*k'ou* 叩乞 to implore; to beg.

*ên* 恩恤商艱 to have sympathy with the merchant's hardships.

*shang* 上稅 to pay duty.

*wu* 無旣 without end; infinitely.

*ch'ieh* 切切上稟 an urgent petition (concluding phrase in petitions).

## Document No. 96.

*hsüan* 懸案不結 a pending and unfinished case.

*t'i* 提究 to try a case; to examine into.

*shih* 氏 after a name denoting that the person is a woman; in petitions "I," said by a woman.

*niu* 扭摔 to wrench; to wrestle and throw down.

*lü* 屢 repeatedly; often.

*hsün* 訊結 to inquire into and settle [a case].

*jêng* 仍復 yet again; again.

*lai* 來家 to come to one's house.

*ch'ao* 吵 to wrangle.

吵鬧 to altercate; to scold.

*pu* 不休 not to stop or cease; unceasingly.

*ch'iang* 强借 to violently ask for.

*ch'ien* 錢文 money; cash.

*pu* 不得巳 there is no help; inevitable.

*chêng* 正堂 the chief magistrate (as opposed to the assistant magistrates).

*yen* 嚴傳 to summon.

*wu* 無理 unreasonable.

*ch'ü* 取鬧 to create altercation; to commence a row.

*kan* 感荷 to be obliged.

*ho* 荷 to be obliged for.

*hung* 鴻慈 immense kindness.

*ya* 涯涘 the banks of a river; limits; limited.

## Document No. 97. [p. 170]

*chui* 追究 to investigate (a case).

*i* 以救蟻命 in order to save poor peoples' lives.

*pei* 被匪竊去 to be robbed of...... by outlaws.

*shou* 守候 to wait.

*wei* 未蒙緝獲 I have not yet been favoured with [their] capture.

*ch'i* 緝獲 to pursue and seize.

*chin* 進退維谷 whether I advance or retreat, there is difficulty; a dilemma.

*ku* 谷 a ravine; difficulty; embarrassment.

*chi* 幾不欲生 almost not to desire to live; I might have wished to die.

*hsing* 幸 fortunately; to rejoice at; to hope for.

*t'ung* 同鄉 a countryman; a fellow-townsman.

*pang* 幫助 to assist.

*ch'uan* 川資 travelling expenses.

*hui* 回家 to return home.

*shih* 失主 the loser; the person whose property is lost, stolen, etc.

*wu* 無奈 there is no help for; no alternative.

*nai* 奈 a remedy; a resource.

*p'u* 匍 to be prostrate.

匍匐 to prostrate.

*fu* 匐 to fall prostrate.

*i* 以救微生 in order to save an unimportant life.

*ya* 押案追比 to arrest one for criminal prosecution.

*ai* 哀叩 to pray for urgently.

*pei* 俾得交還失主 so that it may be returned to the loser.

*kung* 公侯 duke and marquess; *fig.*, high rank.

*wan* 萬代 ten thousand generations; "your offspring."

*chi* 積德累仁 to accumulate merit and humanity.

*hsien* 啣 to hold in the mouth.

啣結 an allusion to an old saying, 啣環結草, "to carry in one's mouth the ring and the straw of bondage," as a sign of being never ungrateful; to be bound to; to be in bondage.

*shêng* 生生世世 one's offspring for many generations.

*wu* 無極 endless.

### Document No. 98.

*ch'ieh* 竊商 I, the merchant (in petitions).

*chung* 重木樑料 hard-wood beams.

*lu* 陸續 successively (as a land road not interrupted by water); one by one.

*i* 詣 to go to.

詣關 to go to the Custom House.

*lien* 連日 for a number of days; on successive days.

*ho* 何得又更估價 how can the value be changed again? [p. 171]

*wu* 無所適從 there is no means to follow [a rule].

*ssŭ* 思維再四 to consider very ripely.

*ch'ing* 情實難已 matters really difficult to bring about.

*ên* 恩公兩便 both a matter of favour and of justice.

### Document No. 99.

*chia* 家主 the head of a household.

*ch'i* 起行 to start (as on a journey).

*t'ou* 投 to deliver; to present to.

*chên* 眞參 real ginseng.

*chia* 假參 imitation ginseng.

*ch'i* 欺 to deceive.

欺騙 to belie one; to delude.

*p'ien* 騙 to defraud.

*chao* 找尋 to seek.

*ching* 經手 a broker; an agent.

*êrh* 耳聞 to hear (as a rumour).

*chü* 聚 to assemble.

聚儹 to pack together with.

*fêng* 奉家主之命 to receive orders from one's master.

*p'ên* 奔 to run; to hurry.

奔波 to flee like billows; to run at great speed; to be in trouble about; to hurry.

*shih* 勢 condition; circumstances.

*lun* 淪 lost, as in a whirl of water.

淪落 to be lost or ruined (morally).

*i* 異鄉 to be separated from one's home.

*yu* 憂愁 to be full of sorrow.

*ch'ou* 愁 mournful.

*yen* 言狀 to describe; to state.

*li* 理 a theory; a rule.

*ho* 何敢冒瀆 how could I dare to be disrespectful?

*ch'ü* 曲 crooked; bent; yielding.

曲加矜恤 to have pity for; to feel compassion for.

*ching* 矜 to commiserate.

*fu* 俯准 to graciously permit; to grant.

*i* 以全蟻命 in order to render complete a poor man's life; in order to restore a poor man to life.

### Document No. 100. [p. 172]

*i* 以靖地方 in order to tranquillise the place.

*tso* 昨夜 last night; the other night.

*tsei* 賊匪 robbers.

*kêng* 更 a watch (of the night = two hours).

*shih* 時分 time; hour.

*chin* 進院 to enter a court-yard.

*ch'iao* 撬 to prise; to force with a lever.

撬門 to prise a door.

*t'ung* 銅盆 a copper basin.

*ch'a* 茶碗 a tea-bowl.

*wan* 碗 a bowl.

*tang* 當即 thereupon; at once.

*han* 喊 to vociferate; to call.

喊追 to call out and pursue (as in chasing a thief).

*pu* 不及 not to reach.

*shih* 時屆 at the time.

*lung* 隆 exalted; abundant; a very high state (as of summer heat or winter cold).

隆冬 the extreme of winter; very cold weather.

*po* 迫 to urge; to embarrass.

*chi* 饑 famine; starvation.

饑寒 hunger and cold.

*t'ou* 偷竊 to rob; to steal.

*yen* 嚴比捕役 to deal strictly with the police runners; (in order to ensure the proper discharge of their duties).

*pu* 捕役 police runners.

*chêng* 正賊 the ringleaders of a band of robbers.

*tsang* 賍(＝贜) to bribe; to loot.

賍物 plunder; the spoil carried away by robbers.

*i* 以安善良 in order to tranquillise good subjects.

*wei* 衛閭閻 to guard the villages and hamlets; to keep peace within the country.

*lü* 閭 a small village.

*yen* 閻 a hamlet.

## Document No. 101.

*tsung* 總信差 a chief letter-carrier.

*ma* 馬撥 an overland courier.

*po* 撥 to transfer; to send.

*chuan* 專寄 to forward.

*kung* 公署 a public office; a yamên.

*shu* 署 a yamên; a public office.

*hsin* 信差 a letter-carrier; a courier.

*mên* 門面 the front side of a gate.

*shih* 失去 to lose; to have lost.

*shih* 時刻簿 a time-book; a [postal] delivery-book.

*hao* 號衣 a livery.

*wên* 文武地方官 civil and military local authorities.

*ti* 地保 a *ti-pao* (police officer).

*pu* 不惟不……反…… not only not……, but even……

*hsiang* 向 towards (denotes the object in the case of verbs implying a real or verbal communication).

*yen* 言 to say.

*yang* 洋信 foreign letters.

*t'ê* 特此懇祈 [I make] this special petition.

*hu* 獲 to take in hunting; to catch (as a thief).

*tsang* 賍賊 a plunderer; a thief.

## Document No. 102. [p. 173]

*ying* 營造處 an engineer's office.

*tsung* 總營造司 an engineer-in-chief.

*t'ung* 通行曉諭 to make known to the public.

*ch'uang* 創設 to establish, build, etc. (as a lighthouse).

*ts'ai* 裁撤 to remove.

*chang* 彰明 to promulgate; to make known to the public.

*ch'u* 出示 to issue a public notice.

*t'ung* 通曉 to inform the public.

*pei* 俾得 so that; so as to.

*chou* 周知 to inform all.

*pien* 徧 everywhere; to go around.

徧喻 to inform all; to notify the public.

*ch'ên* 沉船 a wreck.

*so* 所在 the place where; the position of.

*k'ai* 開列於左 to mention hereafter; enumerated below.

*t'ai* 太倉州 the prefecture of T'ai-tsang.

*ch'uan* 船行正路 the fairway channel (for ships in a river or near the coast).

*ching* 警船浮 a buoy.

*tuan* 端 the head; the end; a terminus; a spot.

*ch'ên* 沉有 there is sunk.

*p'iao* 漂 to toss about.

漂移無定 to drift away (as a ship from its moorings).

*lien* 連縛 to make fast to.

*i* 以示沉船所在 in order to indicate the position of the wreck.

*liu* 留心 to be careful.

*hsiang* 詳記 to take careful notice.

*i* 以免確虞 in order to avoid danger.

*wu* 勿忘 be not forgetful; keep well in mind.

勿忽 do not disregard; be very careful about.

*hu* 忽 to forget; to disregard.

## Document No. 103. [p. 174]

*fu* 福州府 the prefecture of Foochow.

*lien* 連江縣 the district of Lien-chiang (Foochow).

*min* 閩江 the Min river.

*shih* 石樁 a stone beacon.

*tso* 座 a classifier of beacons, lighthouses, etc.

*pei* 被水激刷 to be washed away by the water.

*chi* 激 to set back (as by water).

激刷 to wash away.

*shua* 刷 to brush; to wipe away.

*hsing* 興工 to start work.

*hsiu* 修造 to repair.

11

### Document No. 104.

*chih* 指明 to mark (as a buoy marks a place).
*shui* 水道 the fairway channel for ships.
*shih* 飾以紅色 to paint red; to be painted red.
*p'ang* 傍 by the side of.
*hsing* 行駛 to sail.
*chung* 中間 in the middle of.
*shih* 示路警船浮 a fairway buoy.
*hêng* 横線相間 horizontal bands (painted on a buoy or beacon).
*sê* 色樣 colour.
*sha* 沙 sand; a sand or mud bank. [p. 175]
沙尾 a sandspit.
*wei* 尾 a tail; a spit of land; any pointed shore, if quite flat.
*chiao* 角 a pointed corner; the end of a rock, spit, etc.
*ko* 隔 to divide off; to occupy the middle between two localities.
*ming* 明沙 a sand bank or shoal above water.
*an* 暗 dark; secret; hidden.
暗沙 a sand bank or shoal below water.
*luan* 亂 confused.
亂礁 a number of reefs; extensive reefs.
*shu* 竪線相間 vertical stripes (painted on a buoy or beacon).
*yang* 洋面 on the open sea; the sea; waters.
*shih* 石礁 rocks.
*hsing* 行船正路 the ships' channel (in a river or near the coast).
*wei* 微碍之處 obstructions of small extent.
*fang* 方格 chequers; chequered.
*ai* 碍處 obstructions.
*hsiang* 向海外面 towards the sea; seaward.
*wei* 危險之處 an obstruction.
*tso* 左邊 the left side; the starboard side.
*yu* 右邊 the right side; the port side.
*chi* 卽係 that is; *i.e.*; that means.
*chiang* 港內 in port.
*shui* 水闊之處 a position with plenty of water or room [for sailing].
*pieh* 別項 other kinds of......
*piao* 標記 marks; navigation marks.
*yu* 有碍 to obstruct.
*jao* 繞 to wind round.
繞避 to avoid (as a rock in sailing).
*pi* 避 to avoid; to shun.
*shuang* 雙數 an even number.
*tan* 單數 an odd number.
*hsiang* 詳載 to state; to enumerate.
*tsung* 總冊 a general list.
*fu* 縛繫 to fasten by binding.
*t'ieh* 鐵片 an iron plate.
*lao* / *lo* } 烙 to burn; to brand.
烙印 to emboss.
*han* 漢洋兩文 in Chinese and foreign writing.
*t'ang* 倘遇 if there is; in the case of.
*fêng* 風浪 wind and waves; a heavy sea.
*ch'ung* 衝 to rush against.
衝移 to carry away (as a buoy is carried away in a gale).
*p'iao* 漂流水面 to drift about on the water; to be adrift.
*fang* 方格式 a chequered muster. [p. 176]
*t'i* 體 the body, as opposed to the extremities (as "the body of a structure").
*mao* 帽頂 the top (of a beacon).
*hsien* 顯明 conspicuous. [p. 177]
*pien* 辨明 to distinguish.
*fang* 方向 the direction [of the compass].

### Document No. 105.

*ch'üan* 泉州府 the prefecture of Ch'üan-chou (Chinchew).
*chin* 金門島 the island of Quemoy.
*tui* 對面 opposite to; off......
*shui* 水師部 the Admiralty.
*hai* 海道圖 a sea chart.
*chien* 漸長暗沙 a shoal gradually forming.
*chang* 長 to grow; to extend. Cf. *ch'ang* 長 long, Document No. 7, p. 7.
*tuan* 段 a classifier of rocks, shoals, etc.
*chien* 尖圓 conical.
*ch'iu* 球式 spherical.
*lan* 籃帽 a cage (top of a beacon made of basket-work).
*ch'ieh* 切水面 at the water-line.
*i* 以免觸沙之患 in order to avoid grounding on the shoal.

### Document No. 106. [p. 178]

*i* 一帶 in the neighbourhood of.

*yu* 遊歷 to travel; to cruise about.

*shui* 水師提督 an Admiral.

*chün* 軍門 honorary title of a *t‘i-tu* (high military official; employed in correspondence only). *See* MAYERS' "The Chinese Government," No. 440.

*sung* 松江府 the prefecture of Sung-chiang, near Shanghai.

*nan* 南滙縣 the district of Nan-hui (province of Kiangsu).

*chiu* 九段 Kiutoan, the site of Kiutoan Lighthouse, near Shanghai.

*têng* 燈架 a beacon with a light.

*hsiang* 相距 distant from.

*chiang* 江南岸 the southern shore of the river.

*shuo* 朔 new moon; the first day of a month.

朔望 new moon and full moon; the 1st and 15th of a [Chinese] month.

朔望潮落時 when the tide is low with the new moon and the full moon, *i.e.*, at low water spring tides.

*wang* 望 full moon; the 15th day of a month.

*ch‘ao* 潮落時 at low-water time.

*lo* 落 to fall; to drop.

*shih* 視 to see; to take the bearing.

*fei* 廢燈塔 an abandoned lighthouse.

*wang* 望臺 a look-out; a beacon or house visible at a long distance.

*tu* 獨 single; alone. [p. 179]

獨樹 a single tree.

*ch‘êng* 成直線 a straight line.

*to* 多有小暗沙 there are numerous patches of shoals.

*ch‘ü* 曲斜 to go obliquely; to trend away from the straight course.

*p‘ien* 偏 to incline to a certain direction of the compass; *e.g.*, 西北偏北, north-north-west.

*tu* 度 degrees of a circle or a sphere; degrees of latitude or longitude.

度數 degrees.

*an* 按羅經方向 magnetic bearings.

*lo* 羅經變差 the variation of the compass.

*ts‘ŭ* 此項公文 this document.

*shih* 示諭 a public notice.

*chien* 簡 to abridge.

簡畧 a *résumé*.

### Document No. 107. [p. 180]

*tsê* 擇取 to make a selection of.

*k‘uan* 欵式 a pattern; a muster.

*nan* 南海 the district of Nan-hai (Canton).

*p‘an* 番禺 the district of P‘an-yü (Canton).

*chiao* 交界 a frontier.

*hai* 海珠礮臺 Dutch Folly (a fort in the Canton river).

*ch‘uan* 船路 the ships' channel (as in a river).

*yüan* 圓形 round.

*kang* 剛 hard; firm.

剛石 granite.

*chi* 基 foundation; base.

*ting* 頂 top; vane (of a light tower).

*chih* 置 to establish; to fix; to place.

*ch‘ang* 常明 fixed (as a light).

*hsiao* 小燈 a lantern.

*têng* 燈火 the flame or centre of a light.

*chü* 距水面 above the water-level.

*ch‘ing* 晴 clear.

晴時 in clear weather.

*ying* 應照 ought to reflect or shine; to be visible.

*hui* 惠來縣 the district of Hui-lai, near Swatow.

*shih* 石碑山 (*shih-p‘ai-shan*) } Breaker Point, near
*ch‘ih* 赤沙澳 (*ch‘ih-sha-ao*) } Swatow.

*t‘ou* 透 to penetrate; transparent.

透鏡 dioptric.

*kuang* 光 brilliant; to shine; to give off light.

*cha* 乍 suddenly; abruptly.

乍明乍滅 lighting up suddenly and eclipsing suddenly; occulting (as a navigation light).

*ming* 明 to light up (as a revolving or occulting light).

*mieh* 滅 to extinguish; to be dark; to eclipse.

*miao* 秒 a second.

*ching* 經 to cross; to pass over.

*chêng* 正西 due west.

*wei* 緯 the woof of a texture.

緯度北 northern latitude.

*ching* 經 the warp of a texture.

經度 longitude.

經度英國中線東 longitude east of Greenwich.

*chung* 中線 the middle thread, *i.e.*, the meridian (of Greenwich, Peking, etc.) from which longitude is reckoned.

*yü* 遇大霧時 during foggy or thick weather.

*shou* 守鐙人 lightkeepers.

*fang* 防險號 signals made to avoid danger; fog signals.

*ming* 鳴鐘 to strike a bell.

*ch'ui* 吹 to blow (as a horn).

*chieh* 戒 to ward off.

戒險螺 a fog horn.

*lo* 螺 a conch.

*fang* 放汽 to let off steam; to blow the steam whistle.

*ch'i* 汽 or 滊 an unauthorised character used for "steam," or *shui-ch'i* 水滊

*fang* 放礮 to fire a gun.

*i* 以示鐙塔所在 in order to indicate the position of the light.

*ch'ao* 潮陽縣 the district of Ch'ao-yang, near Swatow.

*piao* 表角 *(Piao-chio)* Cape of Good Hope, near Swatow.

*i* 一名 also called.

一面……一面……partly……, partly……[p. 181]

*mei* 每一分鐘時 every minute.

*chung* 鐘時 clock time; *i.e.*, time by the foreign division.

*chê* 遮滅 to eclipse.

遮掩不見 to be shaded off and become invisible.

*lu* 鹿嶼 *(Lu-hsü)* Sugar Loaf Island, near Swatow.

*ssŭ* 四面 in all directions of the compass; all round.

*fang* 放斂 to give off and concentrate again (as a fixed and flashing light).

*lien* 歛 (wrongly for 斂) to collect; to concentrate.

*shan* 閃 a flash.

*chang* 漳州府 the prefecture of Chang-chou, near Amoy.

*hai* 海澄縣 the district of Hai-ch'êng, near Amoy.

*ch'ing* 青嶼 Tsingseu Island, near Amoy.

*p'o* 坡 a slope; the side of a hill.

*pa* 八角形 octangular.

[p. 182]

*t'ai* 臺灣府 the prefecture of T'ai-wan, Formosa.

*an* 安平 An-p'ing, near T'ai-wan, Formosa.

*hsiao* 小山 a hillock; a mound.

*shu* 樹木 a tree.

*chêng* 正在前面 directly in front of.

*mu* 木桅一杆 a mast.

*ch'iu* 秋冬颳東北風 the north-east monsoon.

*wu* 無虞 without danger.

*ch'un* 春夏颳西南風 the south-west monsoon.

*i* 宜 suitable.

*ting* 定海廳 the inferior department of Ting-hai.

*chien* 漸明漸滅 lighting up gradually and eclipsing gradually (said of a navigation light); revolving.

*ming* 明滅 to light up and eclipse.

*hai* 海道圖說 sailing directions; the *Hai-tao-t'u-shuo* (title of a Chinese work on that subject).

[p. 183]

*pei* 被山遮蔽 to be kept out of view, or obscured, by hills (as a light).

*chê* 遮蔽 to obscure; to render invisible.

*pi* 蔽 to keep out of view.

*ch'üeh* 缺處 an empty place; an open spot.

*lou* 漏射 to flash through (as a ray of light through a gap in hills).

*hsi* 隙 a gap.

*huang* 黃州府 the prefecture of Huang-chou.

黃岡縣 the district of Huang-kang.

*kuang* 廣濟縣 the district of Kuang-chi.

*tan* 單桅 single-masted; one-masted.

*t'iao* 條 twigs.

條編 twisted, or plaited, like basket-work.

*yüan* 圓球 a ball.

*yang* 洋正月初 the 1st of January.

*hsiu* 修改 to repair; to alter.

*fêng* 奉天府 the prefecture of Fêng-t'ien.

*liao* 遼河 the river Liao, near Newchwang.

*san* 三桅鐙船 a three-masted lightship.

*niu* 牛莊 Newchwang.

*chung* 中桅 the middle mast; the main-mast of a ship.

*ao* / *wa* } 凹 a cavity; concave. [p. 184]

凹鏡 a concave lens, or a reflector.

凹鏡逼射 a concave and reflecting light; catoptric.

*wu* 誤入險途 to enter a dangerous road by mistake; to run into danger.

*shêng* 升 to rise; to raise; to hoist (as a flag).

*t'ung* 通用旗號 Commercial Code signals.

*ch'ui* 吹戒險汽螺 to blow a steam fog horn.

*ch'i* 汽螺 a steam fog horn.

*hsiu* 修鐙 to trim a light.

*hsü* 續油 to supply oil to a light.

*i* 以代 to serve for something else; in lieu of.

*fang* 放藍光 to burn a blue light.

*lan* 藍光 a blue light.

*ch'ien* 前纜 the forestay of a ship.

*lan* 纜 a rope; a cable.

*ch'uan* 船欄 a ship's rail.

*lan* 欄 a railing.

*ch'uan* 船首 the bow of a vessel.

*hsün* 旬 a decade; one of three divisions into which a month may be divided: 中旬, the middle decade, *i.e.*, the 11th to the 20th of a month; similarly 上旬, the 1st to the 10th; 下旬, the 21st to the 30th.

*ping* 氷河時 when the river is covered with ice.

*i* 移去 to remove.

*pei* 被風浪衝移 to be driven away by a storm (as a vessel from its moorings).

*i* 已離原泊方向 to have left the original anchorage (as a ship).

*wu* 無足爲示引之處 not apt to show the course a ship ought to steer; to be of no use as a guide to shipping.

*shou* 首尾 the bow and stern of a ship; the two ends of a vessel.

*tai* 代用 to use instead; to substitute.

*yüan* 圓頂 a top ball.

*wei* 未撤之先 before being removed. (Note the use of *wei* 未.)

*i* 以免舛悞 in order to avoid mistakes.

*chien* 尖 pointed.

尖圓式 conical shaped.

*mu* 木浮 a wooden buoy.

*tsui* 最西之處 in the extreme west; the westernmost point.

*tzŭ* 自日落起至日出止 from sunset till sunrise.

*tien* 點照 to light (as a lamp); to exhibit a light.

*han* 韓江 the river Han, near Swatow.

*chien* 尖石 a pinnacle rock.

*tzŭ* 自鳴風笙 an automatic whistling [apparatus].

*fêng* 風笙 a whistle.

*shêng* 笙 a pipe (for whistling).

*ch'iu* 球式籃帽 a ball-shaped basket top; a spherical cage. [p. 185]

*sha* 沙灘 a sand or mud bank; a shoal.

*t'an* 灘 a rapid; a shoal.

*shang* 上寬下窄 broad above and narrow below; (if round) an inverted frustum.

*kung* 公司輪船 a company's steamer; *i.e.*, a mail steamer.

*pu* 不宜 must not; should not.

*i* 以防觸礁之患 in order to guard against collisions.

*t'ai* 臺北府 the prefecture of T'ai-pei (North Formosa). [p. 186]

*tan* 淡水縣 the district of Tan-shui (Tamsui).

*kuo* 過攔江沙 to cross the bar.

*lan* 攔江沙 a bank or shoal barring the river; a bar; the Woosung Bar.

*t'u* 土人 the natives.

*lien* 連江縣 the district of Lien-chiang, near Foochow.

*ch'i* 七星礁 Pagoda Rock (Pagoda Anchorage, Foochow).

七里礁 Min Reef, near Foochow.

*ch'ang* 長歧山 Chang-ch'i Peak, near Foochow.

*pa* 芭蕉山 *(pa-chiao-shan)*, Sharp Peak, near Foochow.

*ch'ang* 長方式 diamond shaped.

*ch'ao* 潮漲時 at high-water time; the flood rising. [p. 187]

潮漲 the flood rising.

*chang* 漲 water rising; to overflow.

*hsiang* 相間 painted in stripes or bands.

*mu* 木架 a wooden frame or stand.

*ku* 鼓浪嶼 the island of Kulangsu (Amoy).

*ch'u* 出水面 to stand out from the water; to be dry (not being covered by water).

*chin* 金牌門 the Kimpai Pass, near Foochow.

*mu* 木杆 a spar.

木杆樁 a spar beacon.

*ch'ao* 潮滿時 at high-water time; when the tide is full.

*fang* 方式 square.

*shang* 上大下小 broad above and narrow below.

*wên* 温州府 the prefecture of Wênchow.

*yung* 永嘉縣 the district of Yung-chia.

*ou* 甌河 the river Ou, near Wênchow.

*t'ieh* 鐵樁 an iron beacon.

*t'ou* 頭 the head; the end, or an end, whether upper or lower (as the upper and lower points of a buoy).

*tuan* 段 a section; a band.

*chu* 竹籃 a bamboo cage or basket.
*lan* 籃心 the centre of a cage or basket.
*hsin* 心 the centre.
*po* 泊設 to moor (as a new lightship). [p. 188]
*sui* 遂 afterwards.
*ch'ê* 撤去不用 to remove and discontinue.
*chü* 距岸約一里 about 1 *li* distant from the shore.
*shu* 熟悉 to ripely know; to be well acquainted with.
*wu* 無大用處 not of much use.

**Document No. 108.**

*chai* / *tsê* } 摘 to pluck; to pick.
摘列 to give an extract from; an extract from (as from a document or a book).
*li* 立 to erect; to settle; to conclude (as a Treaty).
*ch'i* 起卸貨物 to land and discharge goods.
*tsung* 總不能 not at all able to; in no case shall......
*i* 以昭平允 in order to show justice; for the sake of justice.
*p'ien* 偏枯 partiality.
*k'u* 枯 decayed; rotten.
*shu* 輸稅期候 the term at which duties are payable.
*ch'i* 期候 a limit of time; time.
*hou* 候 time.
*ch'i* 起載 to land goods.
*lo* 落 to fall; to drop; to ship goods; to export.
落貨 to ship goods.
*tsai* 在江甯 at Nanking.
*chiang* 江甯 the city of Chiang-ning-fu, commonly called Nanking.
*li* 立約 to conclude a Treaty.
*ting* 定 to stipulate; it is stipulated.
*tsung* 綜 to arrange threads in weaving; to collect.
綜算 to estimate; to calculate.
*i* 以價值爲準 to declare the value as the principle to go by.
*shuai* 率 to lead; to guide; the leading principle.
*i* 以爲公當 to consider as fair.
*chung* 種式 pattern; kind.
*to* 多有價值漸減 the prices of various articles have gradually declined.
*ting* 定額 a fixed amount.
*chiao* 較重 to be comparatively heavy; too heavy in comparison with.

*ch'ung* 重修 to revise again.
*yün* 允定 it is agreed.
*tsou* 奏明 to petition the Throne.
*ch'in* 欽派 deputed by the Emperor. [p. 189]
*ta* 大員 a high officer.
*chi* 卽日 then at once (denoting immediateness of action).
*fêng* 奉到 to receive (as from a high authority); to have come to hand.
*chu* 硃批 the vermilion orders; an Imperial rescript.
*hsün* 迅行措辦 to put at once into operation.
*ts'o* 措 to employ; to use; to publish; to give out.
措辦 to put into operation (as a Tariff).
*hsin* 新定稅則 the new Tariff.
*t'ung* 通商各款 the articles regarding trade.
*ch'i* 期滿 a term expires.
*hsien* 先行知照 to give official notice beforehand.
先期聲明 to make a declaration beforehand; to give due notice.
*shui* 稅課 the duty taxation; the rates of the Tariff.
*ssŭ* 俟十年再行更改 to alter after the lapse of 10 years.
*yung* 永行弗替 to be always so and not be changed; so it shall always be.
*fu* 弗 not; it should not be.
*t'i* 替 to abolish.
*chiang* 江甯定約 the Treaty of Nanking.
*pien* 遍 everywhere.
遍運天下 to convey everywhere in the empire.
*t'ien* 天下 the empire; China; the world.
*lu* 路 on the way; *en route*.
*ch'ung* 重稅 a second duty; further charges (on goods).
*chia* 加稅 to charge additional duty.
*k'o* 課稅 duties; charges on goods.
*tê* 得確數 to ascertain the exact amount of.
*hêng* 恒 constantly.
*shê* 設新章 to introduce new regulations.
*ch'ou* 抽課 to levy taxes or duties.
*yü* 於貿易有損 to be detrimental to trade.
*ming* 明晰 to inform; to communicate.
*i* 巳在內地買貨 to have bought goods in the interior.
*hsia* 下載 to ship; to export.
*chin* 進售內地 to import for sale in the interior.

*fên* 紛繁 manifold; endless.

*fan* 繁 numerous.

*i* 一次之課 a tax paid once for all; a single charge (compounding for several charges, as the transit duty).

*shou* 首經之子口 the barrier first crossed *en route*.

*chi* 給票 to issue a chop or certificate.

*chiao* 交碍 not to interfere with each other. [p. 190]

*ch'ao* 鈔課 tonnage dues.

鈔銀 amount of tonnage dues.

*i* 以免重輸 in order to avoid [too] heavy payment.

*k'ai* 開艙 to open hatches; to break bulk.

*t'a* 他往 to proceed to another place.

*ch'üan* 全數 the whole amount.

*ts'ŭ* 此外 besides this.

*fei* 費項 fees; expenses; charges.

*t'ing* 艇隻 boats.

*yün* 運帶 to convey (as a boat conveys passengers).

*shu* 書信 letters; postal matter.

*li* 例 according to rule.

*ying* 應完稅之貨 dutiable goods.

*hao* 號船 registered boats; boats used as navigation marks; lightships.

*t'a* 塔表 lighthouses.

*piao* 表 a signal.

*cho* 酌視 to consult about and look after.

*kuan* 官設銀號 an official bank; a banker authorised by the Government to receive official moneys. [p. 191]

*pu* 部頒 issued by the Board [of Revenue], as standard weights and measures.

*ting* 定式 having a fixed pattern; standard.

*ku* 僱覓 to seek to hire; to engage the services of.

*fu* 甫 to begin; first; at first.

甫臨近口 first just approaching a port; when arriving off a port.

*lin* 臨 at the point of; about to; whilst.

*p'ai* 派委員弁 to depute officers.

*pien* 弁 officers of an inferior grade.

*ting* 丁役 official attendants; runners.

*k'an* 看守 to guard (as a ship).

*chü* 居住 to dwell; to live at or in.

*hsü* 需用經費 current expenses for one's maintenance.

*chih* 支發 to pay for; to defray.

*ssŭ* 私受 to receive secretly.

*hao* 毫釐 a hair's breadth; the least portion of.

*ch'êng* 懲 to correct; to punish.

懲治 to punish.

*tz'ŭ* 次日 on the following day.

*ya* 押載噸數 the tonnage of a vessel which is used for cargo; the registered tonnage; the net tonnage.

*i* 以憑查驗 in order to furnish vouchers for the examination [of goods]; on the ground of which examination may be made.

*kuo* 過限期 to exceed a limit.

*tsung* 總不 not on any account. Cf. *ping* 並未, Document No. 28, p. 57.

*pi* 筆誤 a slip of the pen; a clerical error.

*ti* 遞貨單 to hand in a cargo list; to present a ship's manifest.

*kai* 改正 to correct (as a mistake in a document).

*shan* 擅 arbitrarily; on one's own authority and without permission. [p. 192]

*tsung* 總須 all must; must on any account.

*tung* 動撥 to tranship goods.

*fa* 發回 to issue back; to return (as documents deposited).

*yen* 驗貨人役 officers charged with the examination of goods; examiners.

*p'ing* 平定 to arrive at a just settlement; to agree about.

*yao* 邀 to invite.

*ch'u* 出 to advance an offer; to bid (as a price at an auction).

*chia* 價式 the standard value of an article.

*mien* 免致 (the opposite of *i-chih* 以致) so as not to; so that there may not be.

免致收稅不公 to avoid the duty being collected in an unjust manner.

*ch'êng* 秤計 to calculate the weight; to weigh. [p. 193]

*p'i* 皮 leather; skin; *emballage*.

皮包 *emballage*.

*fên* 粉飾 the "get-up" in packing goods; ornamental packing.

*liao* 料 materials.

*ching* 淨貨輕重 the net weight of goods.

*lien* 連 together with; to be connected with or inseparable from.

連皮 the *emballage* connected with the goods.

*kuo* 過秤 to pass the scales; to be weighed.

*ch'u* 除皮核算之 to calculate [the net weight] by deducting the *emballage*; to tare.

*chien* 揀出 to select from; to pick out.

*pao* 包皮 *emballage*.

*t'ui* 推(=推算) to reckon.

*ts'ŭ* 此日 the same day.

*lun* 論定 to settle by discussion; to decide about.

*huan* 緩 to postpone.

*t'ien* 填簿 to insert in a book or register.

*mien* 免致後難更易 so that afterwards there may be no difficulty in altering.

*ho* 核斷 to finish a calculation.

*têng* 登填 to insert or to enter (as in a book).

*chia* 價低減 to deteriorate in value.

*kuan* 關吏 Custom House officers.

*li* 吏 an officer; a deputy.

*chih* 置 to arrange.

置辦 to arrange; to settle.

*yen* 嚴防偷漏 to prevent the revenue from suffering by fraud or smuggling. [p. 194]

*hsiang* 相 to look at.

相度 to consider the steps to be taken; to adopt the proper means.

*to* 度 to consider.

*chi* 機 to use an opportunity; to watch the right moment for.

機宜 to consider *à propos*; to judge proper.

*pien* 便宜 having full power to act without reference to a superior; to do as one pleases; cheap; advantageous.

*i* 以杜弊端 in order to restrict malpractices.

*shih* 式類 class; category.

*ch'a* 查抄 to seize for confiscation.

*ch'ao* 抄 to seize; to confiscate.

*chang* 賬目 accounts.

*ch'ü* 驅 to expel.

驅除 to expel; to send away.

*shou* 收辦 to receive; to appropriate.

**Document No. 109.** [p. 195]

*ch'ing* 清正 pure and upright.

清正持躬 to maintain one's person pure and upright; to lead a spotless life.

*ch'ih* 持躬 to preserve one's integrity.

*kung* 躬 the body; one's person.

*ching* 精詳謀國 to be a clear-headed politician and patriot.

*mou* 謀國 to make plans for one's country.

*chung* 忠純 honest and solid.

*liang* 亮 clear; light.

亮直 clear-headed and straightforward.

*ch'êng* 誠懇 sincere and earnest.

*k'ên* 懇 to beg; truly; earnest.

*kung* 公明 just and intelligent.

*pu* 部曹 member of one of the six Boards.

*ts'ao* 曹 an official.

*wên* 文宗顯 Wên Tsung Hsien (the dynastic title of the late Emperor Hsien Fêng).

*hsien* 顯 conspicuous; illustrious (as a deceased hero whose example is always conspicuous amongst the living generation).

*t'ê* 特達 special intelligence.

*chih* 知 to be known.

*chien* 荐 (used for *chien* 薦) to set forth; to bring to the front (as a meritorious official for promotion).

*ch'ing* 卿貳 a second director in an Imperial Court. Cf. *ch'ing* 卿, Document No. 46, p. 78.

*chün* 軍機大臣 a Minister of the Grand Council. Cf. *chün* 軍機處, Document No. 46, p. 78.

*hsing* 行走 to go (in and out); one who goes in and out at an office in order to learn its routine, without being a real member; an associate; a supernumerary.

*liang* 兩宮 the two Empresses (*see* Mayers' "The Chinese Government," No. 2, p. 1).

*huang* 皇太后 an Empress Dowager.

*mu* 穆 majestic.

穆宗毅 Mu Tsung I (the dynastic title of the late Emperor T'ung Chih).

*i* 毅 stern; resolute.

*i* 倚 to depend on.

倚畀 an important trust.

*pi* 畀 to confer on; to give.

*ma* 馬賊 mounted robbers.

*ssŭ* 肆 reckless; dissolute.

肆擾 to infest [a place] with robbers.

*jao* 擾 to trouble; to infest.

*tai* 帶兵 to lead an army, or troops.

*ch'u* 出關 to cross the provincial boundary, or the Great Wall at Shan-hai-kuan.

*chiao* 勦 to attack; to destroy and scatter the force of an enemy.

勦捕 to make a clean sweep (as of a band of banditti).

*lai* 賴 to depend upon.

*k'o* 廓 wide; spacious.

廓清 spacious and clear.

*hsüan* 旋 forthwith.

*chien* 簡 to select.

簡任 to choose for a post.

*lun* 綸 to twist silk.

綸扉 the silken gate; the Imperial Palace; the Court.

*fei* 扉 a door.

*shên* 深資 to be a great help.

*fu* 輔 to aid; to assist.

輔弼 to assist (the Throne).

*pi* 弼 to assist (as a statesman assists his monarch).

*kuo* 國計 government plans; politics.

*min* 民生 the people's maintenance.

*li* 利病 advantage and disease; *i.e.*, good and evil.

*so* 所關 [all] that pertains to.

*chin* 盡心 to exhaust one's heart; to take the greatest trouble about.

*ch'ou* 籌畫 to devise schemes.

*ku* 股 the thigh of a leg.

股肱 the legs and arms [of the monarch]; *i.e.*, his highest officers, "his right hand."

*kung* 肱 the arm.

*ku* 股肱心膂 the right hand and back bone of Imperial power.

*lü* 膂 the back bone.

*chi* 積勞 to amass labour; accumulation of toilsome work.

*lao* 勞 toil; exertion; merit.

*ch'êng* 成疾 to contract a disease.

*chi* 疾 sickness.

*k'ai* 開缺 to open a vacancy; to quit one's post.

*k'uan* 寬予假期 to liberally grant a term of leave.

*yü* 予假 to grant leave.

*yü* 御醫 an Imperial physician.

*chên* 診 to examine.

診視 to see and examine a patient (as a physician does).

*shang* 賞給 to make a present of.

*an* 安心 to make one's heart easy.

*t'iao* 調 to regulate; to mix or compound.

調理 to nurse one's health.

*chao* 召 to summon.

召見 to call to court; to assemble at court.

*tieh* 迭 alternate.

迭次 repeatedly.

*ch'ui* 垂 to drop down; to condescend.

垂詢 to condescend to inquire; [the Emperor] inquiring after a subject's health.

*fang* 方 just then; at the same time.

方冀 at the same time wishing.

*k'o* 克 able to.

克享 to be able to enjoy life; to enjoy good health.

*hsiang* 享 to enjoy.

*hsia* 遐 distant; advanced in years.

遐齡 to become very old; old age.

*ling* 齡 the front teeth; one's age.

*ch'ang* 長承 to receive for a long time.

*ên* 恩眷 Imperial favour.

*k'o* 溘 (used for 㱁 *k'o*) to comply with; to die.

溘逝 to depart for a better life; to die (said of the death of high officials).

*shih* 逝 to depart; to die.

*chên* 震 to shake; to alarm.

震悼 to be shocked with grief.

*tao* 悼 afflicted; to grieve for.

*liang* 良 good; very; in a high degree.

良深 very much; deeply.

*cho* 着 (or 著) I, the Emperor, command that; let (in Imperial edicts).

*t'o* 陀羅經被 a pall with Buddhist prayers embroidered on it.

陀羅 (*t'o-lo* = 陀羅尼, *t'o-lo-ni*) the Sanskrit *dharani*, a Buddhist prayer.

*ching* 經 a canon; religious books; Buddhist prayers.

*pei* 被 a bed cover; to cover.

*chün* 郡王 a prince of the 2nd order.

*pei* 貝勒 a *bei-lê*, or prince of the 3rd order.

*tai* 帶領 to conduct; to escort.

*shih* 侍 to accompany; to follow (as an attendant).

侍衛 Imperial guards.

12

*tien* 奠 to offer libations to a god.

奠醊 to sacrifice to the gods.

*cho* 餟 (= 醊) to offer libations.

*yü* 予諡 to confer a posthumous title.

*shih* 諡 a posthumous title.

*chin* 晉 to increase.

晉贈 to bestow increased rank.

*tsêng* 贈 to give; to bestow.

*t'ai* 太傅 a Grand Tutor (*see* MAYERS' "The Chinese Government," No. 138).

*tz'ŭ* 賜卹 to grant special rewards [to the family of a deceased official].

*hsü* 卹 rewards bestowed on the families of deceased high officials.

*ju* 入祀 to sacrifice before an ancestral tablet.

*ssŭ* 祀 to offer sacrifices.

*hsien* 賢良祠 the Temple of Wisdom and Goodness.

*tz'ŭ* 祠 an ancestral hall; to offer sacrifice to ancestors.

*kuang* 廣儲司 the Treasury of the Privy Purse (*see* MAYERS' "The Chinese Government," No. 67).

*ch'u* 儲 to collect; to accumulate.

*ch'i* 騎都尉 a *Ch'i-tu-wei*, of the 7th degree of hereditary nobility (*see* MAYERS' "The Chinese Government," No. 455).

*shih* 世 a generation; hereditary.

世職 hereditary office.

*i* 伊 he; his.

*hsiao* 孝 filial piety; the period of mourning for a parent.

孝滿 the expiration of the period of mourning for a parent.

*ch'êng* 承襲 to enter upon hereditary rank.

*hsi* 襲 hereditary; to inherit.

*jên* 任內 belonging to one's office; during the time of one's holding an office.

*ch'u* 處分 fines and other punishments imposed upon an official.

*k'ai* 開復 to recover; to restore.

*hsü* 卹典 regulations for bestowing posthumous honours.

*chao* 照料 to superintend; to manage.

*tao* 到期 to arrive at one's banner or at one's home (said of a Manchu soldier).

*tz'ŭ* 賜祭 to bestow sacrifices (so as to honour the spirit of a deceased).

*i* 一壇 one altar; one spread (as of sacrifices to be offered).

*t'an* 壇 an altar for sacrificing.

*yung* 用示 by means of a proclamation; to show, or express, thereby.

*tu* 篤 very much; highly.

篤念 to keep in high memory.

*chin* 藎 faithful.

藎臣 a loyal, faithful officer.

*chih* 至意 to wish for ardently.

### Document No. 110. [p. 196]

*chên* 朕 I, the Emperor; We.

*ju* 入承大統 to take charge of the Empire.

*ta* 大統 the great whole, *i.e.*, the charge of Empire; the Throne.

*yang* 仰蒙 to receive respectfully.

*ta* 大行 the great journey; having gone the great journey; defunct (applied to an Emperor or an Empress).

*tz'ŭ* 慈安 the late Empress Dowager TZ'Ŭ-AN.

*tuan* 端裕 upright and generous.

端裕康慶昭和莊敬 *Tuan-yü K'ang-ch'ing Chao-ho Chuang-ching*; the honorary name (*hui-hao*, 徽號) of the Empress Dowager TZ'Ŭ-AN.

*k'ang* 康 the feeling of vigour.

康慶 healthy-minded and joyful.

*chao* 昭和 bright and accordant.

*chuang* 莊 sedate; serious.

莊敬 serious and respectful.

*ku* 顧復 to remember kindly; to take protective care.

*ên* 恩慈 kindness and mercy.

*ch'ing* 情深 the depth of affection.

*wang* 罔 not; without.

罔極 limitless; illimitable.

*chi* 極 the utmost point; a limit.

*lin* 臨御 to occupy the Throne.

*tzŭ* 玆 this; these.

*tsai* 載 a year; years.

*ch'êng* 承歡 to receive pleasure.

*fêng* 奉養 to respectfully nurse; *i.e.*, to bestow filial care on one's parent.

*shên* 深荷 deeply obliged.

*tz'ŭ* 慈愉 kind and joyful.

*tung* 動履 to move about.

*li* 履 to walk.

*k'ang* 康强 robust; strong.

*hsin* 昕 morning; day.

昕宵 day and night; at all times.

*hsiao* 宵 night; at night.

*ch'in* 勤 diligent.

勤政 attentive to Government work.

*ssŭ* 私 private; oneself; one's own.

私心 one's own heart; my heart; partial.

*ch'ing* 慶慰 to feel consoled.

*wei* 慰 to soothe; to console.

*yen* 延祺 a long period of happiness.

*ch'i* 祺 fortunate; lucky.

*i* 益算 to add.

*ch'i* 期頤 very old age; a centenarian.

*i* 頤 the chin; the 27th diagram, denoting "to feed;" hence, a man so old that he has to be fed.

*tz'ŭ* 慈 kindness; mercy; the standing epithet for mothers; just as *yen* (嚴), stern, is the epithet for fathers; hence, 慈母, "my mother;" 嚴父, "my father."

慈躬 my mother's body.

*ou* 偶爾 accidentally.

*êrh* 爾 you (often has the force of making an adverb of the word preceding it).

*wei* 違和 to become unwell; to fall sick.

*t'ang* 湯藥 broth and medicines.

*t'iao* 調 to harmonise; to restore harmony.

調治 a cure; to cure.

*chih* 治 to govern; to heal; to cure.

*chiu* 就 to follow; immediately; forthwith.

*ping* 病勢 the state of a disease.

*tou* 陡 suddenly.

陡重 to aggravate suddenly (as a disease).

*t'an* 痰 phlegm.

痰湧 to cough up phlegm.

*yung* 湧 to bubble; to rise.

*ch'i* 氣塞 the stopping of the breath.

*sai* 塞 to stop (as a hole); to hinder.

*ta* 大漸 to increase considerably.

*chü* 遽 suddenly.

*hsü* 戌 the eleventh of the twelve branches; applied to time, the eleventh Chinese hour of the day, *i.e.*, about 7 to 9 P.M.

*hsien* 仙馭 the fairy ride, *i.e.*, death; to die.

*yü* 馭 to drive a horse.

*shêng* 升遐 to rise to the distant land; *i.e.*, to die.

*hsia* 遐 distant.

*hu* 呼 to call out for.

呼搶 (= 呼天搶地) to call to heaven and hit the ground with the head; *i.e.*, to feel pangs of grief.

*ch'iang* 搶 to take by force; to rush against.

*ai* 哀 grief; pain.

哀號 to scream from pain or grief.

*hao* 號 to scream.

*ho* 曷 why.

曷其有極 why should it come to this? why should she come to her death? Cf. "Shih-king," I, X, 8, 2, where LEGGE translates "when shall [our service] have an end?"

*i* 遺 to leave; to bequeath (as when dying).

遺誥 the dying commands.

*kao* 誥 to enjoin upon.

*sang* 喪 to mourn.

喪服 mourning clothes; to wear mourning.

*chên* 朕心 Our Imperial heart.

*nan* 難安 difficult to appease.

*ch'uan* 穿 to put on garments.

穿孝 to put on the garment of filial piety, *i.e.*, white mourning clothes (as worn for the first hundred days after the death of a parent); to mourn for a parent.

*su* 素服 ordinary mourning clothes (as worn after the term of strict mourning is over); half-mourning.

*shao* 稍申 to explain somewhat; to show to a certain extent.

*shên* 申 (= 申明) to explain.

*ai* 哀悃 the sentiments of grief.

*k'un* 悃 real feelings or sentiments.

*mien* 勉 to urge; to use effort.

勉節 to use effort in abridging.

*chieh* 節 to abridge.

*ai* 哀思 thoughts of grief.

*i* 一 (= 一切) all; throughout; to be one with; to be the same as.

*i* 以國事爲重 to keep Government matters in due regard.

*tz'ŭ* 慈禧 the Empress Dowager Tz'ŭ-HSI.

*tuan* 端佑 an upright help; a true help.

端佑康頤昭豫莊誠 *Tuan-yu K'ang-i Chao-yü Chuang-ch'êng;* the honorary name (*hui-hao,* 徽號) of the Empress Dowager Tz'ŭ-HSI. Note the parallelism in the sets of names given to the two Empresses Tz'ŭ-AN and Tz'ŭ-HSI, each of which contains, with the principal name, ten characters in five dissyllables, the first character in each pair being common to both Empresses.

*yu* 佑 to assist.

*k'ang* 康頤 enjoying robust age.

*chao* 昭 bright; intelligent.

昭豫 intelligent and contented (of a well-balanced mind).

*yü* 豫 contented; to be comfortable.

*chuang* 莊誠 serious and truthful.

*chiao* 教育 to supply spiritual and bodily food.

*yü* 育 to rear; to maintain.

*kan* 敢 to dare; can; also in the interrogative, and hence negative, sense, can I? should I? *i.e.,* I cannot, I dare not (=豈敢, how can I? I dare not).

敢不敬遵 how could I dare not to respectfully obey?

*ching* 敬遵 to respectfully obey.

*i* 遺命 the dying commands.

*mien* 勉加 to make an effort.

*i* 抑 to repress.

抑制 to restrain; restraint.

*chih* 制 to limit.

*ta* 大喪 general mourning; the funeral of an Emperor.

*sang* 喪 to mourn; a funeral.

*li* 禮儀 the ceremonial.

*yü* 御前大臣 a Grand Chamberlain (*see* MAYERS' "The Chinese Government," No. 103).

*hsieh* 協辦 to assist; an assistant (as an Assistant Grand Secretary).

*ching* 敬謹管理 to superintend with due reverence and care.

*kung* 恭錄 to respectfully copy or record.

**Document No. 111.** **[p. 197]**

*shih* 侍郎 Vice-President of a Board (*see* MAYERS' "The Chinese Government," No. 161).

*hou* 候補道 an Expectant Taot'ai.

*cho* 著充 I, the Emperor, command...... to fill the post of; We hereby appoint......as.

*ch'u* 出使 to be sent abroad (as an envoy).

*ping* 並 and; also; at the same time.

*ching* 京堂 a director of a court in the Imperial Household (*see* MAYERS' "The Chinese Government," No. 232).

*t'ung* 同知 a Sub-Prefect (*see* MAYERS' "The Chinese Government," No. 282).

*tsun* 遵悉 to be apprised of for one's guidance.

**Document No. 112.** **[p. 198]**

*chuan* 轉達 to forward; to send on.

*chih* 執政 a Government official.

*chêng* 政 Government administration.

*hui* 會議 to conjointly discuss.

*chêng* 整 to repair; to arrange.

整理 to arrange for; to manage.

*hsüan* 衒 to display for sale; to seek praise.

衒奇院 an exhibition court.

*ch'i* 奇 strange; rare things; curiosities.

*pa* 巴理京城 the capital city of *pa-li, i.e.,* Paris.

*jih* 日不多 in a short time.

*lin* 遴 to select.

遴派 to appoint.

*ch'ieh* 切實 true and sincere; trustworthy.

*t'o* 妥員 a reliable officer.

*pai* 擺 to expose; to arrange (as articles for sale).

擺設 to arrange; to set up.

*wei* 微細之事 the details (as opposed to the general features of an affair).

*t'o* 妥爲商辦 to deliberate upon.

*tsung* 總理委員 a deputy in general charge of matters.

*kung* 公會 a national assembly; a universal exhibition.

*sai* 賽 to emulate; to try who can make the best show.

賽奇公會 an industrial exhibition.

**Document No. 113.** **[p. 199]**

*têng* 等因 (*see* Document No. 26, p. 55). This phrase is sometimes inserted in copies of documents when the tenor of another document, which in the original appears at full length, is omitted for the sake of convenience. Cf. *Yün-yün* (云云), Document No. 76, p. 136.

*tsu* 助 to co-operate.

*sai* 賽奇物件 exhibits (at an industrial exhibition).

### Document No. 114.

*nien* 年節 New Year's day.

*tsao* 早 morning; in the morning; early.

*wu* 午後 afternoon.

*pan* 辦夜 to do official work; to be on duty; to work for the public.

*chuang* 裝卸 to ship and discharge goods; to "work" (as a vessel in port).

*yeh* 夜中 at night; "after hours."

*tsun* 遵繳 to submit to the payment of.

*chuan* 專單費 the fee for a special permit.

*li* 歷經 to have [done] up to the present.

*jên* 人所共知 it is known to everybody; the public are aware of it.

*i* 異詞 different language; dissent; difference of opinion.

*jih* 日期 fixed days; terms.

*chieh* 藉生口舌 to make use of a matter as a pretext to create altercations or quarrels.

*k'ou* 口舌 altercation.

*yüan* 遠涉 to come from afar; far-travelled.

*tsung* 從繁 to follow, or to cause to follow, many (as many restrictive rules); to impose a great many (as holidays to be kept). [p. 200]

*to* 多定 to fix upon a great number.

*tsun* 遵奉之日 days to be kept as holidays.

*hu* 忽畧不論 to carelessly refuse discussing; to take no notice of (as a matter one need not care about).

忽畧 careless.

*san* 三四月間新月後之禮拜五, the Friday following after the new moon in the third or fourth Chinese month; *i.e.*, Good Friday.

*hsin* 新月 the new moon.

*li* 禮拜五 Friday.

*huang* 皇上 His Majesty the Emperor.

*wan* 萬壽 *lit.*, the "Ten Thousand Ages"; the Emperor's birthday.

*shou* 守 to observe (as a rule).

*t'o* 妥善 safe and good; properly managed.

*i* 以免饒舌 in order to avoid altercation.

*shih* 是否可行 whether or not it may be done.

### Document No. 115. [p. 201]

*ko* 各省 the Provinces.

*chiu* 救護章程 salvage regulations.

*pu* 不一而足 not confined to one; more than one.

*ku* 固 (= 本來) originally; in itself.

固屬堪虞 to be in itself fraught with danger; to constitute a danger itself (not to speak of other dangers).

*k'an* 堪虞 able to be dangerous; fraught with danger.

*chi* 亟 promptly; urgently.

*shih* 事前 before matters [go wrong]; before something happens.

*t'o* 妥派巡船 to send out cruisers.

*fên* 分布 to distribute over; to spread over (as over the country).

*yao* 要隘各口 the important approaches (of traffic).

*ai* 隘 a pass.

*chieh* 刦 to rob; to take by force.

刦搶 to rob; highway robbers.

*ch'iang* 搶 to rob; to plunder.

*kan* 趕 to pursue.

趕緊 to pursue closely.

*chui* 追拏 to pursue and seize.

*an* 按律 according to law.

*wu* 毋令一名漏網 do not let one man escape.

*lou* 漏網 to escape (as out of a net).

*wang* 網 a net.

*shu* 庶 so that there be hope for; with a view to.

*tao* 盜風 the habit of robbing; thievish propensities (amongst the population).

*fêng* 風 wind; the spirit of; the habits of.

*shao* 稍戢 to gradually lay aside.

*ch'i* 戢 to lay aside (as arms in time of peace).

*chieh* 藉足以 by means of which; the availing oneself [of which] is apt to.

*sui* 綏 to tranquillise.

綏靖 to tranquillise; to restore peace.

*ching* 靖 peaceful; to establish peace; to tranquillise.

*pao* 保衛 to protect.

### Document No. 116. [p. 202]

*pei* 被搶 to be plundered.

*min* 閩浙總督 the Governor-General of Fukien and Chêkiang.

*têng* 等 after a single name or title, "and others." Cf. *têng* 等, Document No. 16, p. 19.

*hui* 會咨 to make a joint communication.

*hsiung* 兇 a murderer; a criminal.

兇要各犯 murderers and [other] important criminals.

*fan* 犯 a criminal.

*shên* 審 to investigate (as a criminal case).

審明 to investigate; to try (as a case).

*i* 擬 to decide (as in a criminal case).

擬辦 to give judgment; to sentence.

*shu* 屬 all that belongs to the jurisdiction of; subordinates.

*fang* 防患 to guard against calamities.

*wei* 未然 not so; that which has not occurred yet; *e.g.*, 防患於未然 to take steps against calamities before they occur.

*chü* 具奏 to present a memorial to the Throne.

*chü* 舉行 to commence; to put into operation.

*ch'ing* 請飭 to ask for instructions; be pleased to instruct.

*kung* 恭摺 to respectfully memorialise.

*yang* 仰祈 to humbly pray for.

*shêng* 聖 holy; sacred. [p. 203]

聖鑒 the sacred glance; the Emperor's approval.

*pei* 被殺 to be killed.

*ch'iang* 搶奪 to plunder.

*shang* 上年 last year.

*tu* 督撫 Viceroy and Governor.

*tieh* 迭次 repeatedly.

*ts'ui* 催 to urge.

*chiang* 將軍 a Tartar General (*see* MAYERS' "The Chinese Government," No. 426).

*hsing* 刑部 the Board of Punishments.

*su* 速議具奏 to speedily deliberate and report to the Throne [upon a matter].

*han* 函稱 to state in a letter.

*pei* 被毀 to be broken to pieces (as a vessel by plunderers).

*chien* 尖 (= 錢?) locally (at Amoy), a cent; $\frac{1}{100}$ dollar.

*tsung* 總須 must all; must on any account.

*shou* 收訖 to receive all, or in full.

*chui* 追出 to trace out; to find out on sifting matters.

*tsang* 賍 (= 贜) to bribe; booty; boot.

賍物 spoil; plunder.

*chê* 折銀 to calculate an amount of money.

*pan* 辦妥 to manage satisfactorily; to settle.

*i* 以弭後患 in order to forestall calamities.

*mi* 弭 to stop; to put down.

*ti* 底稿 a draft.

*kao* 稿 the draft of a document; an original copy.

*chü* 居民人等 the inhabitants.

*yu* 有之 there is; there are.

*pêng* 浜 a side creek; a canal.

*ch'üan* 勸戒 to caution.

*ting* 定擬 to decide; to give judgment.

*fu* 覆奏 to report back to the Throne; to memorialise again.

*ch'ên* 臣衙門 my, the Minister's, yamên or office.

*chin* 盡力 to exert one's strength; to the best of one's ability.

*chui* 追繳 to sue for payment.

*yü* 御覽 the Emperor's view; for His Majesty's inspection.

*ch'ing* 請旨飭下 to ask for the Emperor's orders to his subordinate officers.

*i* 以期相安 so that mutual peace may be hoped for.

*wu* 無事 no trouble; peace.

*shih* 是否有當 whether or not it ought to be thus; whether it is the proper course to adopt.

*fu* 伏乞 to humbly pray for.

*huang* 皇上聖鑒訓示 the instructions from His Imperial Majesty's sacred glance. [p. 204]

*t'iao* 條規 regulations.

*ting* 定地段 to divide the country into sections.

*i* 以專責成 in order to impose responsibility.

*tao* 島嶼 islands.

*hsing* 星羅 scattered about like stars.

*ch'üan* 犬 a dog.

犬牙交錯 interlocked like dogs' teeth.

*ts'o* 錯 confused; mixed.

*chieh* 界址 boundaries.

*chih* 址 the limits of a lot of land.

*t'ing* 廳縣 territorial magistrates.

*ying* 營汛 military stations.

*tuan* 段 a section of the coast line, comprising a distance of 10 *li*.

*ch'ih* 飭令 to order; to instruct.

*chiu* 就近 neighbouring; near; the nearest.
*kung* 公正 public spirited and upright in character.
*shên* 紳 a sash; a girdle; the gentry.
紳耆 the gentry and elders.
*ch'i* 耆 old; elders; seniors.
*pao* 保舉 to recommend.
*ti* 地甲 the tithing system by which one man is made responsible for the behaviour of his district; an elder.
*chia* 甲 a ward, or beat, for keeping watch over a subdivision of the community.
*ch'i* 耆老 an elder.
*t'ou* 頭目 an overseer; a chief.
*lieh* 列名冊報 to report names entered on a list.
*p'iao* 漂擱 to shipwreck.
*chiao* 礁淺 to ground (as a vessel); to touch a rock.
*jih* 日 in the daytime (as opposed to nighttime).
*kao* 高掛 to suspend high up.
*chieh* 接 to connect; contiguous.
接懸 to suspend one above the other, in a contiguous line.
*i* 以示求救 in order to show that rescue is required; to make signals of distress.
*shih* 示求救 to make signals of distress.
*tsai* 在地 on land (as opposed to the sea).
*chü* 居民 the inhabitants.
*yü* 漁戶 fishermen.
*chi* 卽時 forthwith; at once.
*shou* 首 the head; what is or ought to be done first; in the first instance.
首報 to report first, or in the first instance.
*fei* 飛報 a flying message.
*hsün* 汛官 officers in charge of military stations.
*fu* 夫 a workman; a coolie.
夫船 workmen and boats.
*chi* 集腋 to collect small bits of fur [and thus make a coat]; to make use of many trifles in order to obtain great results; "every little helps;" cf. the Scotch phrase "mony a little maks a muckle."
*yeh* 腋 the armpits; pieces of fur taken from under a fox's legs (such as are sewn together into coats and jackets).
*tsu* 助救 to assist in rescuing; to come to the rescue.
*wên* 聞報 to receive a report.
*tu* 督率 to lead (as soldiers); to place oneself at the head of; to direct (as a body of workmen).
*ping* 兵役 soldiers and runners.
*ch'ih* 遲悞 delay.
*pao* 報信之人 messengers.
*shih* 失事 to miss one's aim; to shipwreck.
*lê* 勒 to coerce.
勒索 to extort; to "squeeze."
*shih* 使費 expenses; charges.
*shang* 賞罰 rewards and punishments.
*i* 以免推諉 in order to avoid the shifting of responsibility.
*shang* 上司 superiors.
*fan* 藩司 the Fant'ai or Provincial Treasurer.
*chu* 註冊 to enter on a list.
*chi* 記功 to record merit.
*cho* 酌記 to decide upon recording (as an officer's name for a reward).
*wai* 外獎 an exceptional reward; *i.e.*, a reward not granted by the Emperor, but by the provincial authorities.
*t'i* 題升 to recommend for promotion.
*i* 以示優獎 in order to show, or mark, special merit.
*shang* 上次 a first and a second time; of the first and second class.
*lao* 勞 to exert oneself.
勞績 merit.
*chi* 績 merit.
*pien* 匾 a signboard; a tablet.
匾額 a laudatory tablet.
*i* 以昭激勸 for the sake of encouragement.
*ts'an* 叅懲 to punish by impeachment.
*chiu* 救援 to rescue.
*yüan* 援 to assist; to rescue.
*hsi* 希冀 to desire.
*fên* 分肥 to divert undue advantages to oneself.
*fei* 肥 fat; to fatten; rich; to enrich [oneself].
*fên* 分別輕重 light or heavy, as the case may be (said of punishment). [p. 205]
*wang* 望見 to see; to observe.
*shou* 首先 first.
*pao* 報知 to bring to the knowledge of; to report.
*shou* 首功 first-class merit.
*hua* 花紅 a reward.

*to* 多至 up to [so much] in quantity; at the most up to; not exceeding.

*hsien* 險船 a vessel in distress.

*li* 力 strength; to be able to.

*tzŭ* 自存 to support oneself; to be able to do without help.

*hun* 混行上船 to board a ship promiscuously and without permission.

*yüan* 援救 to rescue.

*chih* 指揮 to give directions; directions.

*hui* 揮 to direct.

*tung* 動手 to move hands; to go to work.

*chi* 寄頓 to send for storage.

*tun* 頓 to lay down; to store.

*pan* 搬 to shift; to move.

搬取 to move away; to shift.

*ssŭ* 私自藏匿 to conceal fraudulently.

*ch'üeh* 確據 proved by fact; criminative evidence; criminative.

*ch'u* 出首 to come out first; to be the first to reveal a fact.

*tso* 鑿 to bore; to dig; to sift a matter; to furnish evidence.

*wu* 誣 to deceive; to lie.

誣揑 to accuse falsely.

*fan* 反坐 on the contrary, to be guilty [oneself]; to bring a charge back on one's own head (as a false accuser does).

*ch'ou* 酬 to requite.

酬勞 to reward merit.

*i* 以資鼓勵 for the sake of encouragement.

*ku* 鼓 a drum; to drum; to stimulate.

鼓勵 to "drum to exertion;" to encourage.

*li* 勵 to animate; to encourage.

*chiu* 救起之貨 goods saved from wrecks; salvage.

*ch'u* 出入多寡 the amount received (入) after deducting expenses (出); the net amount.

*nan* 難易 hard or easy; the relative difficulty of a matter.

*ch'ou* 抽撥 to divide in per-centages; to allot in proportion to.

*ch'ung* 充賞 to serve as a reward; as, or in lieu of, a reward.

*shih* 食 food; provisions.

*ch'uan* 船夫 boatmen; sailors.

*tzŭ* 資送 to assist in forwarding; to send with presents of money, etc. (as a destitute to his home).

資給 to provide with means of support by way of assistance (as a destitute).

*p'an* 盤 to move; to travel.

盤川 travelling expenses.

*hui* 回國 to return to one's country.

*wu* 無力 not having the power of; being unable to; incapable.

*hui* 彙報 to make a collective report to.

*po* 撥還 to re-appropriate; to recover [funds defrayed].

*hsü* 虛 empty.

虛揑 to make a fictitious report.

*fêng* 風濤 wind and waves; bad weather at sea.

*t'ao* 濤 billows; a heavy sea.

*hsiung* 洶 a great rush of water; a heavy sea.

洶湧 the rushing of waves in heavy sea.

*shih* 施 to bestow; to relieve; to rescue.

*pu* 不及 not able to reach; not within reach.

*an* 安 peaceful; contented with.

安天命 contented with Heaven's decree; to submit to fate.

*t'ien* 天命 Heaven's decree; fate; destiny.

*chu* 株 (=誅) to punish; to reprove; to involve for another's crime.

株連 to involve in punishment.

*kuang* 廣曉諭 to give wide circulation; to make proclamation everywhere. [p. 206]

*i* 以資勸戒 in order to warn; in order to caution (as a warning).

*hai* 海濱 the sea-coast.

*yü* 愚 stupid.

愚民 the stupid people; the common people; the ignorant.

*yu* 有賞 to be rewarded.

有罰 to be attended with punishment.

*tso* 坐視 to sit and see; *i.e.*, to look on without acting.

*huo* 或致 or even.

*yen* 嚴加告誡 to add strict warnings.

*shu* 書寫 to write; to copy.

*mu* 木牌 a wooden board.

*pien* 遍 everywhere.

遍處懸掛 to hang up, or exhibit, everywhere (as a proclamation).

*yü* 愚人 the common people.

新關文件録



*yu* 有功 meritorious.

*jên* 人人 everybody; all men.

*nien* 念 to think of; thought; idea.

*hsiung* 胸 the breast; *fig.*, the mind.

*shih* 視爲 to look [at a matter] as; to consider as.

*wu* 無足重輕之舉 a matter of insufficient importance.

*chü* 舉 a matter proposed; a proposition.

### Document No. 117.

*mien* 面議 to discuss personally.

*hui* 會商 to consult with.

*chên* 眞正 real; regular; in the proper sense of the word; *bonâ fide*.

*huan* 換取現銀 to exchange for cash. [p. 207]

*hsien* 現銀 ready money; cash.

*t'ing* 聽商自便 at the merchant's option.

*ch'ih* 飭屬遵照 to instruct one's subordinates for their guidance.

### Document No. 118.

*ping* 兵部 the Board of War.

*huo* 火票 a *huo-p'iao* (a despatch of great importance, forwarded, through the Board of War, by special fast couriers).

*ti* 遞 to give; to hand to.

*san* 三口通商大臣 the Minister Superintendent of the Three Ports (formerly the only ones open to trade). [p. 208]

*tê* 德意志各國 the States of the North-German Confederation; the German States.

*fa* 法郎西 *(fa-lang-hsi)* France; French.

*ch'ao* 抄粘 to annex, or enclose, a copy.

*wu* 毋違特札 special instructions not to be disobeyed.

*su* 溯 to trace up to a source.

溯查 considering the origin of a matter; [on going back to the beginning of the matter] I find that.

*kuei* 貴王 Your Highness.

貴王大臣 Your Highness (*i.e.*, Prince KUNG) and the other Ministers [of the Tsungli Yamên].

*hui* 回文 an official reply.

*pei* 北德意志公會 the North-German Confederation.

*tsung* 總管 to have the general control of.

*i* 議事廳 an office for the discussion of public matters; a Chancellor's office; a ministry.

議事廳事務大臣 the Chancellor of the [German] Empire; the *Bundeskanzler*.

*shih* 事務大臣 a Minister in charge of affairs.

*pi* 璧斯瑪 *pi-ssŭ-ma* (the name of Prince BISMARCK).

*kung* 公會 a confederation; a union.

*liang* 諒 to believe; to think. [p. 209]

*hsün* 循理 to follow reason; reasonable.

*shên* 深願 to wish sincerely.

*han* 漢謝城 *(han-hsieh ch'êng)* the Hanse towns in Germany.

*ho* 和好 to conclude friendship; peace and friendship.

*pu* 不妥之處 passages not quite in order and requiring correction.

*tsai* 再者 further. [p. 210]

*kai* 改正 to correct (as a document).

*t'ung* 同意 of the same opinion.

*chiao* 交清 to pay an amount in full.

*suan* 算 to consider as.

*i* 意見不同 to be of a different opinion.

*ch'in* 親手畫押 to sign with one's own hand; to affix one's signature.

*ch'ien* 鈐 an official stamp.

鈐蓋關防 to affix one's seal.

### Document No. 119.

*wu* 午刻 at noon.

*shang* 上水 to go up river.

*ch'ien* 扦手 a tidewaiter (= 扦子手, *see* Document No. 50, p. 94).

*hua* 划 a pinnace; a scow.

划船 an open boat; a sampan.

*ts'ang* 艙底 at the bottom of a ship's hold.

*t'i* 提成分賞 to allot rewards. [p. 211]

*fên* 分成 to distribute in portions.

*kan* 干例禁 to offend against what is prohibited by law.

*ssŭ* 司事 a manager.

*ho* 何 (= 何以) why? how?

*wei* 骫 to crook; to bend.

骫法 to pervert the law.

*ying* 營 to do; to make.

營私 to practise smuggling.

*ch'ê* 徹 to search thoroughly.

徹查 to search out; to sift to the bottom.

*i* 以肅鹺政 in order to inspire respect for the Salt Gabel.

*su* 肅 respectful; to inspire awe.

*ts'o* 鹺 brine; salt.

鹺政 the Salt Administration; the Salt Gabel.

*ching* 儆 (= 警) to warn; to urge to reform.

儆將來 to be a warning for the future.

*shan* 擅便 to act on one's own authority.

*ch'u* 除 in column 4 of p. 211, in correlation with and including the 393 characters down to 外 *(wai)* in column 1 of p. 212: besides (doing all that is said between *ch'u* and *wai*).

*ch'a* 查獲私鹽 to seize smuggled salt.

*kuan* 官款 official moneys.

*ch'ü* 驅逐 to expel.

*ch'ê* 撤究 (= 撤任究辦) to remove from office and punish.

*fa* 罰款清冊 a report of fines and confiscations.

*shang* 商局 the "Merchants' Company"; *i.e.*, the China Merchants' Company.

*chêng* 正 just; just at the time when.

正在籌辦間 just at the time when matters were arranged.

*ch'ou* 籌辦 to arrange; to plan.

*tan* 胆 (= 膽) the gall.

胆大 courageous; bold.

胆大已極 the extreme of effrontery.

*i* 已極 having reached the extreme; extremely.

*shên* 慎選 to select with care.

*chi* 繼 to connect; to follow.

繼又 it follows that also.

*yüeh* 約束 to restrain.

*i* 一味 of the same style.

*wei* 味 taste; flavour; style.

*su* 疎 to discard.

疎縱 laxity.

*pu* 不顧 not to care for.

不顧大局 not to care for the public interest; to have no regard for society.

*ta* 大局 the great aims of society; public interest.

*ch'ih* 恥 to be ashamed; to be disgraced.

恥笑 to get laughed at.

*hsiao* 笑 to laugh.

*chü* 居心 the heart dwells on; to set one's heart on.

*tu* 杜私運 to stop secret traffic.

*ts'ung* 從寬 to remit; to treat with leniency; to mitigate.

*tsun* 遵繳 to submit to paying (as a fine).

*tsê* 責令 to charge with; to order; to let.

*chü* 局員 the employés, or clerks, of a public company.

*yen* 延抗 to be renitent.

*k'ang* 抗 to oppose; to resist.

*kung* 公款 public moneys.

*no* 挪繳 to misappropriate funds.

*chih* 致干 so as to become guilty of.

*ts'an* 參究 to impeach; impeachment.

*yang* 仰即遵照辦理 you will be guided by these instructions.

*yin* 印發 to seal and issue, or hand back (as a petition is sealed and handed back with sealed endorsement).

*ching* 敬稟者 a respectful petition. **[p. 212]**

*hsien* 憲台 (a term of honour) you; Your Excellency.

*ch'üan* 全敘云云 "as quoted before;" "*see* above;" *lit.*, the complete quotation as stated. Cf. *yün* 云云, Document No. 76, p. 136.

*ch'uan* 傳 to send for; to summon.

傳究 to summon for investigation.

*chieh* 藉稱 to allege.

*mêng* 朦 to deceive.

朦混 a misunderstanding.

*tso* 坐艙 to sit in the ship's hold; to be in charge of the ship's hold.

坐艙司事 an employé in charge of a ship's hold.

*t'ung* 通同 to be connected with.

*chüo* } *chiao* } 覺 to perceive; to be aware of.

覺察 to be aware of and examine.

*chiu* 咎無可辭 an undeniable offence; the guilt cannot be gainsaid.

*tz'ŭ* 辭 to refuse; to deny.

*ch'ê* 撤退 to remove; to dismiss (as an employé).

*i* 移縣 to send to the magistrate (for trial or punishment).

*chin* 僅及一年 a year having scarcely elapsed.

*shêng* 生弊竇 to create malpractices; to commit an offence.

*pi* 弊竇 a mistake; a malpractice.

*tou* 竇 a hole; a mistake.

*k'o* 可惡 detestable; hateful.

*ngo* / *wu* } 惡 to hate.

*wu* 蕪 (=蕪湖) Wuhu.

*mi* 密札 to give confidential instructions to.

*huo* 火夫 a fireman (as one who tends the engines of steamers).

*ch'ai* 差拘 to seize; to arrest.

*chü* 拘 to grasp; to seize.

*tai* 帶縣 to take to the magistrate; to arrest.

*hou* 候質 to await trial.

*tsung* 縱 making allowance for; although.

縱不知情亦應革換 although they did not know the circumstances, yet they are to be removed from office.

*ko* 革換 to remove from office; to suspend.

*ch'ia* 恰 fitly; properly.

*kuan* 官守 to hold office; to have jurisdiction.

*i* 以儆效尤 in order to warn against bad examples.

*fu* 負 to bear; to carry on the back.

負咎 to bear [the consequences of] an offence; to be blamed for.

*tzŭ* 滋 numerous; great; much; very.

滋深 very deeply; severely.

*i* 益矢 to increase in speed; with increased energy.

*shih* 矢 an arrow; swift; to resolve.

*shên* 慎勤 careful; diligent; diligence.

*chia* 加囑 to give additional orders; to specially enjoin upon.

*k'o* 恪遵 to respectfully obey; to recognise as binding.

*chêng* 整頓 to set in order; to arrange; to repair.

*ts'o* 鹺綱 the control of salt matters; the Salt Gabel.

*kung* 恭叩 to respectfully pray; a respectful petition.

## Document No. 120. [p. 213]

*yüeh* 越過 to pass over; to cross (as a barrier).

*tsung* 總卡 a principal barrier; a head barrier office.

*ch'ê* 車輛 carts; carriages.

*liang* 輛 a classifier of carts or carriages.

*t'iao* 挑 to carry.

挑夫 a porter; a carrier.

*li* 離卡不遠 not far from the barrier.

*tzŭ* 自行赴卡 to go to the barrier office of one's own accord.

*ssŭ* 私自過卡 to cross a barrier clandestinely.

*pao* 報卡 to report [goods] at a barrier.

*ti* 抵卡 to arrive at a barrier.

*i* 以便查明 in order to facilitate examination.

*t'ang* 倘或 if perchance; in case of.

*i* 依舊 as before.

*yin* 因何 the reason why; on what account?

*i* 以不應納子稅爲詞 to write (or maintain) that transit dues are not payable.

*tz'ŭ* 詞 to write; to declare in writing.

*suan* 算清 to calculate the proper amount of. [p. 214]

## Document No. 121.

*tsung* 總署 a head office.

總辦 a chief manager.

*fan* 販運 to traffic.

*chu* 諸外洋 all the foreign seas; foreign countries.

*i* 抑 or; or whether.

*p'ien* 偏重 to make a one-sided charge; to impose difficulty by partiality.

*yün* 允從 to agree with; to permit.

*ts'ung* 從 to agree with.

*wang* 望示 to look forward to [the receipt of] instructions.

*chuan* 專此 I specially write this note (a concluding phrase in letters).

*shun* 順候 I avail myself of this opportunity to present my kind regards (a concluding phrase in letters).

*chi* 吉祺 I wish you good luck (a concluding phrase in letters).

*pien* 便宜 advantageous; to be of advantage to; cheap. Cf. Document No. 127, p. 225. [p. 215]

*k'uo* 擴 to enlarge; to expand.

擴充 to carry out to the utmost.

*tao* 道 principle; idea.

*fu* 復入內地 to be taken on to the interior.

*shih* 適得其平 to obtain just one's equal share.

### Document No. 122. [p. 216]

*i* 以免參差 in order to avoid discrepancy or want of uniformity.

*ts'ěn* 參差 irregular; uneven.

*ts'ŭ* 差 irregular.

*chou* 周 to surround; complete.

周妥 complete; satisfactory.

*tan* 單式 a *pro formâ* document; a form.

*hou* 後開 hereafter mentioned. [p. 217] [p. 218]

*shao* 少於單 less than [is stated in] the document.

*to* 多於單 more than [is stated in] the document.

*mao* 冒充 to fraudulently take the place of; to falsely substitute.

*t'ien* 添改 to make additions and alterations (as in a document).

*wa* 挖 to dig; to scrape out.

挖補 to erase and cover with a new patch of paper on which the amended reading is written; to correct by erasure.

### Document No. 123.

*ch'in* 欽 (= 欽差) an ambassador.

*chao* 照稱 a despatch stating; to state in a despatch.

*t'o* 拖帶船隻之輪船 a tug steamer.

*i* 譯名 a name translated or transliterated.

*ssŭ* 私赴別口 to clandestinely resort to another port.

*shih* 釋放 to release.

*tso* 作保 to be surety; to guarantee.

*yü* 于是日 on the same day.

*ch'ü* 取回 to fetch back. [p. 219]

*liao* 了 to finish.

了結 to finish; to bring to an end.

*ts'ung* 從輕 yielding and light, *i.e.*, lenient (as with punishment); to mitigate.

*lun* 論及 to discuss.

*hui* 會晤 to confer; to meet to discuss a question.

*t'an* 談 to converse.

談論 to converse; to discuss.

*pien* 辯論 to argue; to discuss; to controvert.

*ku* 固 assuredly; decidedly; firmly.

*ta* 答 to reply.

*chi* 極為明晰 to be extremely clear; to be very explicit.

*chien* 堅 stable; immovable.

堅欲 to immovably wish; to persevere in wishing.

*ts'ung* 從輕減罰 to mitigate a fine.

*chien* 檢 to examine; to arrange; to collate.

檢查 to examine; to look up the records.

*tang* 檔 a set of shelves; pigeon-holes for filing records.

檔卷 archives; documents pigeon-holed.

*chien* 減成 to diminish the per-centage or the rate of.

*hsi* 迄未 (= 迄今未) not as yet. [p. 220]

*tuan* 斷令交出 to decide that payment is to be made; to order, by way of decision in a case, that payment be made.

*ch'i* 其權屬在該關 the authority or power to do so rests with the said Custom House.

*ch'üan* 權 authority; power.

*hsüan* 宣 to proclaim.

宣示 to proclaim; to inform by circular.

*li* 理當 must; it is right (or proper) to.

*chien* 堅執 obstinate; to obstinately maintain.

*yü* 與……無關 to have nothing to do with; not to be one's business.

*hsüan* 懸殊 very unlike; quite different.

*tz'ŭ* 此端 this affair.

*i* 一 as soon as; if once......

一開 if once opened; if once we commence [acting like this].

*shih* 視為具文 to regard as a mere document (said of rules which exist on paper only).

*chü* 具文 a written despatch; an official paper; an empty form.

*ch'a* 督 to inquire into.

督核 to inquire into; to examine.

*fu* 俯賜咨商 be pleased to write to and consult with.

*ch'i* 祈訓示祇遵 to solicit instructions to be respectfully obeyed, *i.e.*, for one's guidance.

*pei* 備由 to provide for details; to prepare a statement.

*ling* 另冊 a list, or table, is separately given.

*ch'êng* 呈乞 to present a request.

*chao* 照詳施行 to report [in order to solicit instructions] for one's guidance.

### Document No. 124. [p. 221]

*tê* 德商 German merchants.

*k'ai* 開船廠 to open a dock; to have a dock.

*yao* 要端 important matters; essential points.

*ch'êng* 承當 to become liable; to be bound to.

*t'a* 他用 to use for other purposes.

*ts'ê* 冊簿 a register.

*an* 按日 according to date.

按類 according to class or description.

*chu* 註記 to enter (as in a register).

*têng* 登記 to enter (as in a register).

*chu* 註銷 to cancel an entry in a book; to write off.

*jên* 任便 at one's own discretion.

*ch'in* 親視 to inspect in person.

*kung* 工作 the work done (as at a dock).

*so* 索看 to demand for inspection.

*lan* 攔阻 to obstruct.

*yü* 與 or; and.

*yüeh* 閱看 to inspect.

*i* 移交 to send to. [p. 222]

*kuei* 歸於至當 to attain to the highest degree of suitableness.

### Document No. 125.

*pan* 頒發 to issue; to publish.

*ch'ing* 清冊 an accurate list or table.

*chieh* 接准 to receive.

*ch'ien* 前項 of the afore-mentioned description; the before mentioned.

*i* 一經……卽 as soon as ……, then ……

*yü* 御筆 the Imperial Pencil; *i.e.*, the Emperor's endorsement.

御筆批准 to be sanctioned by the Emperor.

*p'i* 批准 to be sanctioned; to sanction.

*tien* 電報 a telegram.

*kuo* 國會 a parliament; a national assembly.

*ch'i* 齊集 to assemble completely; to have a successful, or complete, meeting; a quorum.

*yu* 有日 some day; there is a day or term fixed for it.

*pu* 不久 within a short time.

*huan* 換約 to exchange (*i.e.*, to ratify) a Treaty.

*chih* 擲 to throw down; by way of civility, a person of exalted rank, or the person addressed in a despatch, not of rank inferior to that of the writer, is requested to "throw down" an object, in lieu of "presenting it by hand," the writer thereby placing himself in the position of one not worthy to receive it direct from the hands of the addressee.

擲交 to give by throwing down, *i.e.*, to favour one with supplying; to be pleased to give.

*fên* 分 a set; a copy of a book, or of a document, of which several copies have been made.

*hsü* 續修條約 a Supplementary Convention.

*tsao* 造具 to prepare.

*i* 以憑轉復 in order to have a basis for making a reply.

### Document No. 126. [p. 223]

*i* 擬 to propose; to design.

*huan* 換發 to issue in exchange for.

*t'o* 妥協 in proper order.

### Document No. 127. [p. 224]

*i* 以昭信守 in order to exhibit the guard of trust; in witness thereof.

*wei* 未盡事宜 matters not exhausted, *i.e.*, not completely settled.

*kung* 公立 to publicly draw up (as a protocol); to sign a public……

*p'ing* 憑單 a voucher; a certificate.

*chan* 展 to expand.

展緩 to postpone; to extend (as a limit of time).

*yung* 用寶 provided with the Imperial Seal.

*pao* 寶 precious; the Imperial Seal.

*t'ung* 同時 at the same time.

*k'an* 刊刻 to cut blocks for printing; to print.

刊刻成本 to print in pamphlet shape.

*ch'êng* 成本 to make into a book or pamphlet.

*chün* 君主 a king or a queen. Cf. Mayers' "The Chinese Government," p. 129 *seqq.* [p. 225]

*t'ung* 通商和約 a Commercial Treaty.

*i* 益臻 to multiply and accumulate.

*chên* 臻 to collect; many.

*k'o* 恪守 to carefully maintain (as rules and regulations).

*pien* 變通 to alter.

*hu* 互換 to exchange.

*man* 滿十年 at the end of 10 years; the limit of 10 years having expired.

*ch'ou* 籌議 to consider; to deliberate.

*liang* 量加 to consider and add; to negotiate for additional stipulations in a Treaty.

*pien* 便宜行事大臣 a Minister having discretionary power to act according to the requirements of his office; a Minister Plenipotentiary.

*ch'üan* 全權 having full powers; plenipotentiary.

*chiao* 校 to compare.

校閱 to compare; to examine (as the courts of two countries examine the credentials of each other's envoys).

*k'o* 客貨 merchandise. [p. 226]

*t'o* 妥議 to devise or draw up (as rules and regulations).

*i* 益 advantages or concessions (granted to certain nations in Treaties).

*chuan* 專章 special regulations.

*chi* 既 if; as soon as.

*yüan* 援 to quote by way of analogy; to claim (as privileges granted to others).

*t'ung* 同霑 to participate in favours, or privileges, granted to others.

*chan* 霑 (=沾) to moisten; to receive favours.

*chien* 減半 to reduce to one-half.

*tai* 待 to treat.

*tsui* 最優之禮 the most courteous treatment (such as is granted to the representatives of the most favoured nation).

*yu* 優 excessive; excellent; complaisant.

*hsiang* 相待 to treat each other; mutual treatment.

*chung* 衆洋商 the foreign merchants as a body; the foreign mercantile world. [p. 227]

衆洋商情 the interests of foreign commerce.

*kuan* 關棧 bonded warehouses.

*huo* 貨物清單 a ship's manifest.

*shih* 時 an hour, both in the Chinese sense (*i.e.*, the twelfth part of a day, corresponding to two hours of our time) and in the foreign sense.

*chieh* 節期 holidays.

*pu* 不計 not counting; excepting.

*ting* 定爲 to fix as; to fix at (as the rate of).

*pu* 不及 not to reach; not to come up to; to be less than.

*wu* 無照 without a certificate.

*mei* 每次 each time; in each separate case.

*t'o* 妥速 safely and promptly; without delay.

*yüeh* 約束 to restrain; to keep in order; to exercise a proper control over.

*shou* 受損 to sustain damage.

*tzŭ* 自備 to prepare oneself; self-made; self-owned (as foreign ships owned by Chinese).

*chang* 張掛 to hoist, or fly, a flag.

*ch'i* 旗號 a signal flag; a distinguishing flag (as the national ensign).

*wei* 爲憑 as a voucher. [p. 228]

*yu* 游歷 to wander about; to travel.

*chieh* 解交 to hand over to; to send to (as a destitute to his authorities).

*kuan* 管束 to exercise supervision over.

*shên* 審辦 to settle judicial cases.

*chiao* 交涉 to be connected with; relating to.

*k'o* 科征 to tax at a certain rate; to assess a tax; to fix the rate of a tax; taxation.

*kuei* 歸另議 to become the subject of special negotiation.

*chan* 暫先 beforehand; for the time being.

*t'o* 妥商 to consult; to negotiate about.

*ch'in* 親筆 one's own signature; to sign in person. [p. 229]

*kuan* 關防圖記 State seals and private seals; to affix one's seal or seals.

*t'u* 圖記 a private seal.

*shan* 善後章程 special stipulations appended to a Treaty. Cf. 善後條約 (*shan-hou-t'iao-yüeh*), Document No. 46, p. 78.

*i* 以昭周備 for the sake of greater clearness and completeness.

以昭信實 in proof thereof.

*t'ing* 聽其便 at his, or their, option.

*t'ou* 偷漏稅課 to defraud the revenue.

*ch'i* 起造 to commence making or building.

*hang* 行棧 warehouses.

*shih* 試辦 to work as an experiment.

*ch'ing* 清單 a ship's manifest. [p. 230]

*shou* 收據 a proof of receipt; a certificate of the reception of goods on board; a bill of lading.

*mien* 免鈔 to be exempted from payment of tonnage dues.

*shih* 飾 to adorn; to pretend; to make believe.

飾詞偷漏 a pretext for evading payment of duties.

*t'u* 圖免 to try to evade (as payment of duties).

*tun* 噸鈔 tonnage dues.

*chia* 加倍 to double.

*i* 疑 to suspect.

*chi* 跡 traces; definite grounds for.

*chih* 知情 to be aware of the circumstances.

*t'ung* 通同舞弊 to take part in the commission of an irregularity.

*wu* 舞弊 hoodwinking; secret malpractices; irregularities.

*fei* 廢紙 waste paper; documents cancelled. [p. 231]

*tao* 道路 a road; a route; the distance of a journey.

*t'ai* 太遠 too far.

*p'i* 批明 to endorse (as a certificate is endorsed by an official).

*i* 以杜假冒 in order to prevent fraud.

*yen* 眼同閱看 to participate in the inspection of.

*kuan* 關費 Customs fees.

*ho* 和碩親王 a prince of the 1st order (*see* MAYERS' "The Chinese Government," No. 17). [p. 232]

*shih* 碩 great; eminent.

*tsung* 宗人府 the Imperial Clan Court (*see* MAYERS' "The Chinese Government," No. 55).

*fu* 府丞 a Vice-Director in the Imperial Clan Court (*see* MAYERS' "The Chinese Government," No. 56).

*nan* 難行之處 questions difficult to be settled; practical difficulties.

*ts'ung* 從新另議 to negotiate anew and separately; to renew negotiations.

*ju* 入華 to come, or to be sent, to China. [p. 233]

*ch'ing* 頃接 I have just received.

*p'i* 披 to open; to unroll a scroll.

披閱 to open and read; to note the contents of.

*wu* 無異議 to be of the same opinion.

*wên* 文憑 a documentary proof; a protocol.

*mo* 末後 at the end.

### Document No. 128. [p. 234]

*ts'an* 參 to counsel.

參贊 a Secretary of Legation (*see* MAYERS' "The Chinese Government," p. 133); a Military Assistant Governor in Turkestan (*ibid.*, pp. 93, 95).

*tsan* 贊 to counsel; to assist.

*ya* 鴉片煙 opium.

*huan* 換船 to tranship; to be transhipped.

*fei* 費事 vexation; trouble.

*ao* 奧斯底里雅 (*ao-ssŭ-ti-li-ya*) Australia.

*pu* 不過……而已 only……and nothing more.

*hang* 行家 the *hong* people; merchants; firms.

*pi* 避稅 to evade [payment of] duty.

*ch'i* 起見 to conceive the idea of; the motive of.

*i* 以防弊混 in order to guard against irregularities.

以憑核辦 in order to have proof for acting.

*ch'ieh* 竊聞 my humble self learns; I respectfully beg to refer to…… [p. 235]

*po* 剝過別船 to tranship to another vessel.

*ch'üeh* 確當 correct and in order.

*po* 剝運 to tranship.

*hou* 候驗 to await examination.

*kuei* 歸中國入官 to become liable to confiscation by the Chinese Government.

*kuo* 過載 to transfer cargo from one ship to another; to tranship.

### Document No. 129. [p. 237]

*chao* 招工章程 regulations for the emigration of coolies.

*wai* 外洋別地 other countries abroad.

*ch'êng* 承工 to undertake work; to do coolie labour; a coolie.

*shên* 身家 one's person and family.

*li* 禮體 one's moral and physical condition.

*t'ê* 特簡 specially selected.

*kung* 功賜 to bestow on account of merit.

*p'ei* 佩 a girdle.

佩帶 carried on the girdle; worn on the ribbon, or the collar (as a decoration).

*kung* 公所 a public office; an agency.

*kung* 工人 a workman; a coolie.

*chih* 治理 to regulate.

*ho* 合同 a contract.

*yin* 殷 abundance.

殷實 having ample means; to be solvent.

*shan* 删 to cut out; to cancel; to revise and correct.

删改 to revise and correct.

*yin* 印牒 a sealed document; a license.

*tieh* 牒 an official document.

*chu* 註銷 to cancel. [p. 238]

*ju* 如果 if; in the case of.

*kuo* 果 really; truly; indeed.

*so* 所 (=公所) an office; an agency.

*kuan* 關閉 to close.

*pi* 閉 to close doors.

*mi* 覓承工 to seek emigrants for coolie labour.

*fa* 發給收執 to issue and place in the hands of.

*shou* 收執 to receive in one's hands.

*chên* 鎮鄉 towns and villages.

*hsüan* 宣布 to proclaim; to make generally known.

*chin* 盡守 to closely observe.

*fu* 負約 to disregard or break a convention.

*ch'uan* 傳案 to summon to court; to impeach; to prosecute.

*chiu* 究審 to try a cause.

*ch'êng* 承遣 to be sent; an emissary.

*kan* 干例 to offend against the law.

*ku* 故違 to purposely offend against.

*wu* 誤犯 to unintentionally break the law.

*hsieh* 協同 to assist in; to act conjointly.

*chien* 監理 to superintend.

*jên* 任聽 to be at liberty to.

*pien* 便船 a convenient ship to take passage in.

*ch'u* 出洋 to go to sea; to embark; to emigrate.

*tu* 獨身一人 a single person; alone.

*hsi* 攜同 to carry with oneself; to be accompanied by.

*chia* 家眷 one's family; relatives and members of a household.

*chüan* 眷 the relatives and members of one's household.

*chih* 指定 to point out; to state clearly.

*nien* 年限 a period; a term of years; a limit of time.

*lu* 路費 travelling expenses.

*tso* 作工 to work; to do coolie labour.

*yü* 預定 to fix beforehand; to settle (as by contract).

*i* 衣物 clothing.

*kung* 工食 rations; food provided for a labourer.

*li* 利益 advantage.

*chi* 疾病 disease; sickness. [p. 239]

*i* 醫治 medical attendance.

醫藥 medicines.

*chih* 值 to buy; to bear an expense.

*chih* 隻身 a single body; alone; by oneself.

*chüan* 眷口 the members of one's household.

*an* 按年計月 yearly or monthly.

*po* 撥給 to set aside for; to appropriate for.

*yang* 養家之費 expenses for the maintenance of one's family.

*kêng* 更加 to make alterations and additions.

*hsing* 形似 to purport; to amount to (in sense).

*jung* 容 to endure; to bear.

*shan* 擅加 to make unauthorised additions.

*yü* 逾於五年 to exceed five years.

*pei* 備全 to provide for the whole of.

*chiao* 交付 to give to; to hand over to.

*liu* 留住 to remain in a place.

*fu* 付給 to hand over to; to place in one's hands.

*pien* 便用 to use as one sees fit; for convenient use.

*ling* 另立合同 to renew a contract.

*huan* 患病 to be afflicted with sickness; to contract a disease.

*shên* 伸訴 to make a statement; to complain.

*kung* 工作 to do work; coolie labour.

*hsiu* 休息 to stop (for rest after work).

*k'o* 刻 the eighth part of a Chinese hour (時 *shih*); *i.e.*, 15 minutes of Western time.

*kuo* 過時 beyond the stipulated time.

*chêng* 正工 regular work, *i.e.*, work done during working hours; contract work.

*li* 力能 to be strong enough to.

*ts'ao* 操 to take in hand; to manage; to drill.

操作 to do manual work.

*kung* 工課 job work; jobs.

*k'o* 課 a task; a job.

*ch'ou* 酬值 a gratuity.

*mu* 牧 to pasture; a shepherd.

牧畜 to tend cattle.

*ch'u* 畜 domestic animals; cattle.

*jih* 日用常事 services attending the necessities of daily life.

*i* 議酬 to award a gratuity; to pay for.

*ch'ü* 取具 to produce (as a certificate).

*chun* 准往憑單 a parents' certificate of emigration given to minors.

*chih* 至少 the least; not less than. [p. 240]

*k'ou* 扣 to knock off; to discount.

*nien* 念 to read aloud.

*chiang* 將次……之日 when the day for……has nearly arrived; about the time of……

*jên* 認明 to acknowledge.

*ch'ao* 鈔存備查 to file a copy in the archives; to take a record of.

*tien* 點明 (or 點名) to tick off (as the names of soldiers when mustered, or of emigrants when shipped); to muster.

*ch'ing* 清楚 clear; distinct; to settle.

*pien* 變約 to change one's mind after having made a contract.

*chui* 追取 to be pressed to furnish; to be bound to pay.

*yin* 飲食之銀 maintenance expenses.

*wu* 無款 having no funds; insolvent.

*k'uan* 款 items of money; means of existence; funds.

*kuei* 歸償 to make compensation for; to indemnify; to pay back.

*tsou* 走 to go; to depart.

*yü* 預支 payments made beforehand; advances.

*shang* 賞需之用 to give for one's use; to present; to give as a premium.

*chui* 追還 to press for recovery.

*an* 安家之費 payments for the benefit of one's family.

*i* 以清欠款 in order to clear debts.

*ch'ien* 欠 to owe money; to be in arrear.

欠款 debts.

*kung* 工值 the price of work; wages.

*chih* 支借各項 advances.

*chai* 債 to owe; to be in debt.

債主 a creditor.

*so* 鎖禁 to lock up; to put in irons. [p. 241]

*ch'uan* 傳問 to address questions to; to interrogate.

*fang* 房間 rooms; houses.

*ch'a* 查管 to examine and control; to be charged with the inspection of.

*fên* 分撥 to detach; to keep separate.

*chüan* 眷屬人口 the members of a family or household.

*jên* 人口 individuals.

*t'uan* 團 to collect together.

團聚 to accumulate; to collect together; to keep order among a crowd.

*tsa* 雜混 to get mixed up.

*chih* 治理 to regulate; to keep in order.

*ching* 精潔 clean; pure.

*i* 怡 harmonious.

怡養 healthy; well nourished.

*ching* 精神 healthy; in good physical condition.

*ch'ang* 塲 an enclosure; barracks (as at an emigration agency).

*mi* 覓醫生 to send for a doctor; to seek medical attendance.

*shu* 熟識船隻之人 experts in nautical matters.

*huan* 患傳染症 afflicted with a contagious disease.

*ch'uan* 傳染症 a contagious disease.

*chêng* 症 sickness.

*tsai* 在逃 to have run away; to have absconded.

*t'ao* 逃 to run away; to abscond.

*yüeh* 越獄 to break out of prison.

*pu* 布置 to place in order; to arrange.

*k'o* 客寓 travellers' lodgings; (on board ship) cabins.

*ts'ang* 艙房 cabins.

*huo* 火食 cooked meals; provisions; stores.

*chêng* 整潔 in proper order and clean; in good condition.

*ch'üeh* 確切 with the utmost accuracy.

*fu* 副本 a duplicate copy. [p. 242]

*pien* 邊沿 in the margin (of a document).

*fu* 夫 a husband.

夫婦 husband and wife.

*fên* 分派兩處 to send to different places.

*yu* 幼兒 young children.

*li* 離父母 to be separated from one's parents.

*ch'êng* 承人招工 to engage a man for coolie labour.

*p'u* 鋪戶 factory workmen.

*chuang* 莊田 a farm; farm labourers.

*p'u* 鋪田 factories and farms.

*ch'uan* 轉付 to be transferred to the hands of; to change hands (as property).

*fêng* 奉 to receive respectfully; to pay obedience to.

*chao* 招主 a coolie employer.

*yin* 因別故 for some other reason.

*t'ou* 投 to give up to (by sale or as a gift).

14

*tzŭ* 自願 by one's own wish; with one's own consent.
自行出洋 to emigrate from one's own free will.
*chao* 招致華民 to seek for Chinamen (as for coolie emigration).
*ch'êng* 承約 to make an agreement.
*kêng* 更 more; moreover.
*tan* 胆敢 to possess the boldness to; to dare to.
*p'ien* 騙 to defraud; to delude; to inveigle.
騙往勉强脅從 to kidnap.
*mien* 勉强 to be forced against one's own will.
勉强脅從 to follow against one's own will.
*hsieh* 脅 (=協) to aid; to yield; to submit.
脅從 to submit to following.
*li* 立 (=立刻) immediately; at once; thereupon.
*yü* 予正法 to apply capital punishment.
*chêng* 正法 capital punishment.
*hsing* 興辦 to put into operation.
*wu* 無從 there is no help for.
*hui* 會理 to manage conjointly.
*t'ung* 同一 in conformity with; in every respect the same.
*fêng* 奉行 to act in compliance [with instructions].

**Document No. 130.** [p. 243]

*shên* 甚願 to wish ardently.
*ku* 古巴 (*ku-pa*) Cuba.
*yü* 寓居 to reside; residence (at a place).
*ch'ung* 重新商訂 to negotiate, or deliberate upon, for the second time.
*yung* 永無相左之處 no disagreements for ever.
*hsiang* 相左 not to suit; to disagree.
*tso* 左 left; not agreeing.
*tso* 作爲 to act as.
*yüeh* 粤南 Annam.
*i* 意薩貝勒寶星 the Royal Order of Isabel the Catholic.
*shou* 收留 to receive and keep; to harbour (as a fugitive).
*t'ao* 逃人 fugitives; runaways.
*chin* 盡善 in complete order.
*shu* 庶民 all people; the people; the subjects. [p. 244]
*tan* 單身 a single body; alone; by oneself.
*chia* 家屬 one's family or household.
*ch'ing* 情甘 voluntary; willingness.

*wang* 妄 irregular; what is not in order; falsely.
*kuei* 詭 to deceive.
詭譎 treacherous.
*chüeh* 譎 to impose on.
*chi* 計 contrivances; tricks.
*yu* 誘令 to entice; to induce.
*pu* 不出情願 without uttering a wish; not of one's own accord.
*tsai* 載客 to carry passengers (as a passenger boat).
*ch'uan* 船東 a shipowner; a ship's captain.
*tung* 東 (=東家) the master of a household; a shipowner, etc.
*ch'uan* 船行 a ship's agents; a shipping firm.
*ko* 各事人等 individuals connected with the several functions of; those who are charged with the duties of.
*yü* 預先備辦 to keep ready (as documents for issue). [p. 245]
*fang* 訪察 to inquire into.
*ch'ê* 撤回 to turn back; to send back.
*chiang* 將開船時刻 the time when a ship will start; the hour appointed for a ship's departure.
*k'ai* 開船 the departure of a ship; the lifting of anchors; to start on a sea journey.
*hsien* 先期 at an early time; in good time.
先期報明 to give timely notice.
*yin* 因循 remissness; delay.
*i* 貽悞 to leave an error or a wrong impression; to mislead.
*tsai* 在卽 speedily; quickly.
*pu* 不及候驗 cannot wait.
*tz'ŭ* 辭 to refuse; to use as a plea for not complying.
*hsia* 夏灣拏 (*hsia-wan-na*; in Cantonese, *ha-wan-na*) Havana.
*ch'êng* 稱 to weigh; to correspond to; to be adequate. [p. 246]
稱職 to be adequate to one's post; to perform one's duties as an official in proper form.
*ch'u* 出島 to leave the island.
*hou* 候訊 to await examination or trial.
*li* 立業 to establish business; to work for a living.
*chih* 執政大臣 Ministers of State.
*t'o* 妥設頁法 to adopt the safest measures for.
*hu* 獲益 to reap benefit.
*pao* 包括 to bundle up; to contain; to be comprised in.
*kua* 括 to include.

*yü* 予以 to grant (以 *i*, introducing the object of the verb 予 *yü*).
*yen* 讞 to decide in judicial cases.
讞局 a court of justice.
*yu* 優待 to treat civilly.
*liang* 兩造之處 both parties; the plaintiff and defendant.
*tsao* 造 a party in a cause.
*yen* 延 to invite.
延請 to invite; to engage the services of (as of a lawyer).
*lü* 律師 a barrister-at-law; a lawyer.
*shih* 師 an expert; a master; a patron.
*ch'uan* 傳話 to interpret; an interpreter.
*hua* 話 language.
*ch'êng* 承辦 to undertake the management of; to take in hand business (such as law suits, etc.).
*wei* 委 to bend down; to do injustice.
委屈 an injustice; wrongful oppression.
*ch'ü* 屈 to bend down; grievance; wrong.
*yüan* 寃 to oppress; injustice. [p. 247]
寃枉 an injustice; a grievance.
*wang* 枉 a wrong; a grievance.
*hua* 花名册 a muster roll; a list of names.
*fu* 府城 prefectural cities.
*chuang* 莊寮 a country establishment; a farm.
*liao* 寮 a stall; a country house.
*fa* 乏 to be in want of; exhausted.
*ch'üeh* 缺防 insufficiently guarded against; to fail to take protective measures.
*tu* 讀書 to read books; to study; a literary man.
*tso* 作官 to be an official; a mandarin.
*tun* 敦崇和誼 to be pervaded by the honest feeling of peace and friendship. [p. 248]
*ho* 和誼 friendly feelings.
*ch'u* 出資 to provide means; to pay for.
出船資 to pay travelling expenses.
*tsai* 載回 to carry back; to provide a home passage.
*i* 以昭誠衷 in order to show sincere feelings; out of sincere sympathy.
*ch'êng* 誠 sincere; honest.
*chung* 衷 heart or mind; equity; the true feeling of.
*li* 力衰 weak; worn out (as by age).
*shuai* 衰 weak.

*ku* 孤寡婦女 orphans and widows.
*ku* 僱主 the employer of a labourer.
*kung* 工期 a period or term for doing labour (as entered upon by a coolie workman).
*kuo* 過衆 too many; an excessively large crowd. [p. 249]
*chü* 拘 to seize; to arrest.
*fang* 放出 to release.
*kuan* 官監 an official jail.
*chien* 監 a jail.
*hou* 候結 to await the termination of a trial.
*chih* 至少 at least.
*yü* 預行知會 to give official notice.
*shih* 施及 to bestow on; to extend to (as a privilege).
*ping* 秉權 holding powers; plenipotentiary. [p. 250]
*shên* 愼重之人 a careful and serious man. [p. 251]
*chin* 盡責 to be equal to all one's responsibilities.
*wu* 務希 it is much to be desired that.
*chieh* 借墊 to advance money; a deed; a proof. [p. 252]
*tien* 墊 to advance money.
*ch'üan* 劵約 a bond; a deed.
*lê* 勒 to coerce; to bind; to force.
*ti* 的 true; certain.
的保 a true guarantee.
*pei* 俾歸有著 so that it may serve as a pledge; as a substantial proof.
*chao* 著 (= 着) certain; true.
*tê* 得手 to manage satisfactorily.

### Document No. 131. [p. 253]

*shan* 繕立 to make out a document; to place on record; to note (as a protest).
*chü* 據 documentary proof; an official record; a protest noted.
*chien* 鑒核 to examine for approval.
*li* 立據 to draw up a record which is to have legal force; to place on official record; a protest.
*jên* 任便隨時 at one's own discretion and at any time.
*shan* 繕立預據 to note a protest.
*yü* 預據 to note a protest.
*hou* 後據 an extended protest.
*ta* 大副 a mate of a ship.
*jih* 日記簿 a log-book.

*kuan* 管輪 an engineer of a steamer.

*chi* 記清 to distinctly remember; to recollect.

*pien* 變天風浪 bad weather at sea.

*yü* 預料 to foresee.

*chêng* 証據 testimony; evidence; a protest lodged in order to serve afterwards as evidence.

*chuang* 裝貨逾限 loading goods beyond a limit of time contracted for. [p. 254]

*chan* 佔 to usurp.

佔艙 to trespass upon the space of a ship's hold (by not taking delivery of cargo).

*wei* 違背合同躭擱船事 demurrage payable under charter party.

*pu* 不應爲之事 improprieties; misconduct.

*chiu* 酒醉 drunk; drunkenness.

*tsui* 醉 intoxicated.

*pu* 不端 improper; incapable.

*an* 按時 at the proper time; punctually.

*tsai* 載貨憑單 a bill of lading.

*chao* 照尋常式樣 in customary form.

*chêng* 整 (= 正) after numbers, "only." See *chêng* 正, Document No. 2, p. 2.

*ti* 遞加 to add *pro rata;* to add a fraction of a certain amount.

*kung* 功牌式樣 (wrongly for 空白式樣) blank forms.

*ling* 另欵之賬目 an account of extra receipts [= Customs Account *D*].

*yin* 印簿 books to be sealed; books containing duplicates of documents sealed (as a "Protest Book"). [p. 255]

*pei* 備呈 to submit; to supply (as copies of a document asked for).

### Document No. 132.

*pei* 俾免漫無限制 in order to avoid abuse.

*man* 漫 recklessness.

*hsien* 限制 restriction; restraint.

*chu* 駐寓 to reside at.

*ch'uan* 川省 the province of Szechwan.

*shang* 上駛 to sail, or steam, up the river.

*hua* 畫定界址 to determine a site (as for a settlement).

*fêng* 封存 to keep under bond. [p. 256]

*tun* 躉 a storehouse.

躉船 a receiving ship; a hulk.

*mai* 買客 the purchaser.

*li* 釐稅 the Likin tax.

*pan* 半稅單照 a half-duty certificate.

*ts'ên* 參差 to make distinction between; to make a difference.

*mien* 免致滋生弊端 in order that it may not result in confusion and abuse.

*nien* 年限 a limit of years.

*jao* 擾累 to involve in trouble; to interfere with.

*p'ing* 平等 of equal standing.

*tsung* 總期 it is expected to be; hoping that; with the general aim of.

### Document No. 133. [p. 257]

*chin* 盡用 used by all; in general use.

*p'o* 破爛 torn; broken.

破爛鷹捧番銀 broken-dollar money.

*lan* 爛 to break; to tear.

*ying* 鷹捧番銀 Mexican eagle dollars.

*fêng* 捧 to hold in both hands or claws (as the eagle on Mexican dollars, holding a snake in one claw and a twig of cactus in the other).

*k'o* 刻下 at present.

*tsun* 遵依 to comply with; to obey.

*nan* 南臺口 the port of Nan-tai, *i.e.*, the foreign settlement at Foochow; the foreign community there.

*pu* 補水 (= 補交紋水) when making a payment in dollars, to pay a premium on account of the difference in the price of pure sycee silver. See *wên* 紋水, Document No. 82, p. 148.

*kêng* 更張 to overrule; to change existing regulations.

*pu* 不敷 not sufficient for; not to cover.

*hao* 耗費 the cost of the waste silver or of the underweight found when extracting pure from impure silver.

*tsao* 早晚不同 to change between morning and night (as the price of goods subject to frequent fluctuations).

*chun* 準則 a standard; a rule.

*shih* 事出權宜 a course adopted as being dictated by circumstances.

*ch'üan* 權宜 a temporary measure; a measure one cannot help adopting.

*p'i* 批迴 an official reply.

*hui* 迴 (or 回) to return.

*ssŭ* 司道 the *ssŭ* and the *tao*. By the former the high provincial officials whose titles end in *ssŭ* (viz., the *Pu-chêng-shih-ssŭ* or Provincial Treasurer, the *An-ch'a-shih-ssŭ* or Provincial Judge, and the *Yen-yün-ssŭ* or Inspector of Salt Gabel) are understood; by the latter, the *Liang-tao* (糧道) or Grain Collector, and sometimes also territorial and other Taot'ais. These officials together form an administrative board which is sometimes shortly called the *ssŭ-tao*. Cf. MAYERS' "The Chinese Government," Nos. 275 to 279.

*chang* 長落 to grow and fall; increase and decrease; fluctuation.

*chêng* 正在核辦間 when just engaged in managing [a case]. Cf. Document No. 119, p. 211.

*chou* 周密 well arranged; satisfactory.

*yu* 有便商情無虧稅課 to serve commercial interests while causing no loss to the revenue. [p. 258]

*chiang* 將軍 a Tartar General; also a military Governor in Manchuria, Mongolia, or Turkestan (*see* MAYERS' "The Chinese Government," Nos. 367, 426, etc.). The Tartar General of Foochow is *ex officio* Superintendent of Customs at the Treaty Ports in Fukien (Foochow, Amoy, Takow, and Tamsui), and one of his adjutants, generally with the rank of a *Hsieh-chên*, is deputed by him to act as Superintendent at each of the several Custom Houses.

*chên* 鎮守 to guard; to have charge of (as a general).

*t'ung* 統轄 to be in general charge of.

*hsia* 轄 to rule over; to govern.

*lu* 陸路 dry land roads (as opposed to sea routes); land troops (as opposed to the navy).

*chên* 鎮 (=鎮標) a brigade under the command of a *chên-t'ai* or brigadier-general.

鎮協各營 the battalions of a regiment.

*hsieh* 協 a subdivision of a *chên* (鎮) or brigade; a regiment under the command of a *hsieh-t'ai* or colonel.

*ying* 營 a subdivision of a *hsieh* (協) or regiment; a battalion commanded by a *yu-chi* or major, or an officer of similar rank.

*yin* 印務 the affairs of an office inasmuch as they concern the sealing of documents; responsible affairs.

*ch'êng* 承准 to receive.

*i* 易 to exchange for.

易換 to exchange for.

*t'ieh* 貼 to make up for; to supply a deficiency.

貼水 to pay the difference in price of sycee; *i.q.*, *pu* 補水, p. 257.

*tuan* 短 short; not sufficient.

*pu* 不爲無見 to consider a matter to be reasonable enough.

*wu* 無見 without experience; unreasonable.

*hsi* 希即酌量情形 please consider the circumstances and decide.

*ch'üan* 權辦 to manage a matter, or act, temporarily, under the pressure of circumstances; to adopt an exceptional course owing to special circumstances.

*tsêng* 增長 to increase.

*kuei* 貴處 your office; you. [p. 259]

*sui* 隨即 forthwith.

*hsi* 悉心 with one's whole heart; attentively.

*ch'ien* 僉 all; unanimously.

*kao* 高下 high and low; the rate of.

*pu* 不但......且......not only......, but also......

不勝其煩 it is attended with endless trouble.

*ying* 英捧 wrongly for 鷹捧番銀, *q.v.*, on p. 257.

*shih* 勢難 under the circumstances it is hard to.

*pien* 辨認 to distinguish.

*chou* 周章 much trouble (with comparatively small result); useless toil.

*mo* 莫若 (=不如 *pu ju*) it is better to; we had better......; *lit.*, not like.

*ta* 搭 to add to.

搭解 to hand over or to pay in addition.

*ti* 低昂 low or high (as price); a fluctuation in the rate of.

*pu* 不妨 there is no difficulty in.

*fang* 妨 to hinder; an impediment.

*chü* 據情面禀 to submit the facts in a personal address.

*i* 以免紛更 in order to avoid perplexing changes.

*yü* 諭止 to proclaim the stoppage of; to order a subordinate to discontinue a certain mode of action. [p. 260]

*p'i* 譬 to compare; if.

譬如 if, for instance.

*ch'êng* 秤準 to weigh.

*jên* 認爲 to recognise as; to accept as.

*hui* 滙豐銀行 the Hongkong and Shanghai Banking Corporation.

*na* 那 how; where.

那有差錯之理 where is the reason for our having been at fault? *i.e.*, there is no reason showing that we were wrong.

*yü* 諭阻 to decree prevention; to interfere.

*mien* 面諭 to give verbal instructions.

*ku* 故蹈前轍 to purposely follow in the old track; to resume one's former malpractices.

*tao* 蹈 to tread on.

*ch'ê* 轍 the track of a wheel; a precedent.

*yung* 踴 to leap; to exult.

踴躍 to leap for joy; to gladly fall in with an idea.

*yo* 躍 to leap (as for joy).

*t'ing* 聽從 to yield; to give way.

*ju* 如是 like this; thus.

*shih* 寔於公便 it will really be conducive to fairness.

*pu* 不然 not so; if not so.

*chih* 枝 a branch; to branch off.

枝節 affairs branching off; many small troubles arising out of one case; one expense being followed by many others.

*li* 立傳 to send for at once; to summon one without delay. [p. 261]

*ch'êng* 承充 to be entrusted with the duties of; to act as.

*shui* 水銀 money paid on account of the difference or fluctuation in the price of sycee silver. See *wên* 紋水, Document No. 82, p. 148.

*chiao* 較準 to adjust; properly adjusted.

較準砝碼 standard weights.

*p'ing* 平 to weigh (as silver).

*sao* 掃 to brush; to sweep; to clear off.

掃數 to clear off an account.

*chiao* 繳庫 to pay into a treasury.

*shih* 事如屬實 if the fact be true.

*yu* 有干未便 to be guilty of some disorder.

*pu* 不勝詫異 very strange; quite incredible.

*ch'a* 詫 to deceive by brag and talk.

詫異 strange; incredible.

*chia* 加水 to charge a discount on coin or bullion on account of difference in the value of sycee. Cf. *wên* 紋水, Document No. 82, p. 148.

*pao* 報餉人 a taxpayer; a payer of duties.

*fêng* 奉公 to be careful of Government interests.

*shou* 守法 to observe the law.

*fei* 非分 what is not in harmony with one's duties; irregular; improper.

*yang* 洋番 foreign; foreign dollars.

*pu* 不等 after two expressions, "and," "or," "or so"; *e.g.*, 輕重不等 light or heavy; light ones and heavy ones; 二三不等 two or three.

*fei* 非止 not only.

*hao* 毫無異議 not to differ in the least in one's opinion; to agree in every respect.

*tien* 電 lightning; to glance at (said of a superior who investigates a matter); hence, in composition with various verbs, "may Your Honour be pleased to......"

電察 be pleased to investigate.

*fu* 俯賜照會 to favour one with a despatch (said of a superior). [p. 262]

*i* 以息浮議 in order to stop idle discussions.

*fou* 浮 to float; to be light like pumice-stone; light; idle; frivolous.

*ting* 訂定日期 to appoint a day.

*hsing* 幸勿有稽 I hope there will be no delay; "at your earliest convenience."

*yang* 洋文 a document, or a despatch, written in a foreign language.

*ch'êng* 秤頭 a balance; scales.

*wei* 委 really; indeed.

委實 truly; in reality.

*to* 多收 to receive too much (as a set of scales not properly balanced).

*chi* 旣鈍 used up.

*tun* 鈍 dull; blunt.

*pu* 不公 not just; incorrect (as the weights of a balance).

*kung* 公 just; correct (as standard weights).

*chien* 見更改 to be altered.

*shu* 殊屬不成事體 this is most unsatisfactory.

*pu* 不成 incomplete; impracticable.

*shih* 事體 an affair.

*t'i* 題 to discuss; to bring forward.

*ts'êng* 曾立 having been set up; drawn up.

*tso* 作速 speedily.

*ch'ung* 重新 to renew.

*i* 以便商艱 in order to be of help in commercial difficulties.

以免照章 probably wrongly for 以免周章, in order to avoid useless trouble. Cf. *chou* 周章, p. 259.

*chieh* 藉口 to make a pretext of; under the pretext.

*fei* 費一番枝節 an expense once made being followed by many others.

*i* 一番 once; in one instance.

*fan* 番 (=次) time; times.

*ch'in* 親自 oneself; in person. [p. 263]

*t'ien* 天平 a pair of balances.

*lao* 老鈍無準 used up and inaccurate (as an old set of scales).

*pan* 頒下 to send or issue to a subordinate (for his use or guidance).

*kuan* 官天平砝碼 an official or standard set of scales and weights.

*pu* 補增 to add by way of supplement; to make a supplementary payment.

*ch'ieh* 切實 most accurate. [p. 264]

*chiao* 較對 to compare.

*chun* 準對 to be equal; to agree (as two balances properly adjusted).

*li* 歷今年久 up to the present year.

*ts'ung* 從 (=從來) hitherto; so far.

*chiao* 較兌 to tally; to agree (as the balance of a set of scales).

*wu* 無準可憑 there is no reliable standard; inaccurate and unreliable.

*to* 多傳各字號洋行 to summon a number of native and foreign firms.

*ch'i* 齊集 to assemble together.

*p'ing* 平準 to adjust.

*wang* 望切望速 hoping for strict and speedy attention [to the matter].

### Document No. 134. [p. 265]

*shan* 善後總局 a special commission for the revision of regulations; a provincial administrative board (*see* MAYERS' "The Chinese Government," No. 279).

*shan* 汕埠 the port of Swatow.

*hai* 海防膏釐商人 a mercantile firm to whom the *hai-fang* (coast defence) and *kao-li* (opium boiling) taxes in Kwangtung were farmed out in 1880. Regarding these taxes, *see* Swatow Trade Report for 1881, p. 3, *seqq*.

*kao* 膏 prepared opium.

膏釐 the Likin tax on prepared opium; the boiling tax; the *kao-li* tax.

*t'ui* 退辦 to throw up the management of.

*yang* 洋藥釐局 a tax office for Likin on opium.

*tai* 帶 to take along with one; together with.

帶抽 to collect a tax together with some other tax the collection of which is one's regular business.

*li* 釐務總局 a head Likin office.

*hai* 海防經費 the current expenses for the maintenance of coast defences; a tax levied to defray such expenses; the *hai-fang* tax.

*ché* 折抽 to levy a proportionate tax.

折抽膏釐 a tax levied on boiled opium; the *kao-li* tax.

*t'ang* 堂 a shop; a firm.

*chia* 加餉 to increase a tax.

*kuei* 歸併承辦 to revert to the conjoint management of.

*jén* 認繳 to bind oneself in paying (as a tax farmer pays a fixed sum to his Government).

*ch'ieh* 竊職 as a term of modesty, "I," if the speaker be an official of any grade, even though he may hold his rank by purchase. Non-official writers will say 竊身. Merchants say 竊商; a woman of low rank 竊氏; the wife of an official 竊職婦; a common man of the people 竊小的, etc. When addressing the Emperor, Ministers of Chinese parentage say 竊臣, whereas Manchu Ministers say 竊奴才.

竊職商 we (being a commission consisting of persons of official rank and merchants).

*ch'üeh* 缺本 to lose capital.

*yu* 有零 and a fraction; and odd.

*yu* 猶 still.

*chieh* 竭 to exhaust.

竭立 (wrongly for 竭力) to exert one's strength; to do one's utmost.

*chih* 支持 *lit.*, twig-grasping, *i.e.*, having to strive hard in order to succeed.

*i* 以冀 in order to hope; to thereby hope.

*ch'i* 起色 a rise; an improvement (as in one's prospects).

*tuan* 短絀 a deficit; deficient.

*ch'u* 絀 an impediment, a hindrance (especially in trade and finance).

*jih* 日甚一日 more intense from day to day; growing worse and worse.

*ch'ang* 廠 a tax office.

*ch'ung* 沖 to strike against; to collide; imitation; spurious.

沖銷 to sell clandestinely while evading payment of taxes.

*hsiao* 銷 (=消) to melt; to sell out.

*wang* 往日 constantly; usually.

*shang* 商本 capital in trade.

*p'ei* 賠墊 to make up (as a deficiency).

*k'uei* 虧缺 a deficiency.

*pu* 不堪之實在情形 it is really impossible to bear this; the state of matters is more than we can bear.

*hsi* 昔日 former days. [p. 266]

*tsu* 足數 the complete amount.

*pien* 變通 to change; to make a change by way of accommodation or of compromise.

*cho* 酌減 to decide upon diminishing.

*chê* 折收 to receive in proportion; to receive...... per cent.

*ti* 敵 an enemy; to compete with.

敵私 to compete with smuggling.

*wan* 挽 to revert to the former state; to restore.

*ch'i* 起見 to start the idea of; the motive for.

*chi* 極力 with the utmost of one's strength.

*tan* 淡 insipid; flat; dull (as trade); poor and deficient (as receipts of money).

淡收 deficient receipts; a deficit.

*ju* 如故 as of old; as formerly.

*ch'ou* 抽不敷解 to levy an amount insufficient for remittance (said of a tax farmer who does not collect the amount contracted for).

*fu* 敷解 to remit the full amount contracted for (as a tax farmer remits to Government).

*tz'ŭ* 此誠關乎事勢使然 this has really become thus through the influence of circumstances.

*kuan* 關乎 to be connected with; to be the result of.

*shih* 事勢 the state of matters; circumstances.

*shih* 使然 to cause it to be thus; to bring about.

*ts'ai* 才 mental capacity; power; talent.

才拙 inability; incompetency.

*cho* 拙 stupid; unskilful.

*wei* 未善 not good; not properly.

*so* 所致 that which is the cause; that causes it.

*ts'ê* 策 a scheme; a proposition; a means of.

*chan* 沾益 to participate in profit; to receive profit.

*p'ei* 賠累 to involve in indemnification; to cause one to make up for a deficit.

*ku* 顧全大局 to look out for the best interests of a matter.

*i* 以全始終之美 to consider the advantages from beginning to end.

*shih* 始終 the beginning and end; a period taken altogether.

*mei* 美 advantages.

*k'uei* 虧折 to suffer loss.

*li* 力量 vigour; ability; solvency.

*chih* 支 to attend to; to manage.

*tsai* 再四思維 to consider over and over again; to consider ripely.

*ssŭ* 思維 to consider.

*chün* 鈞諭 your instructions.

*cho* 著 to order; to instruct; "the instructions are that."

*pu* 補具退禀 to send in a supplementary statement regarding one's resignation.

*i* 以是日起 to date from this, or that, day.

*shao* 少 little; in the least; the least amount.

*yang* 仰懇 to respectfully pray for.

*fu* 俯念商艱 to kindly take into consideration our (the merchants') difficulties.

*chung* 重釐餉 to give due weight to Likin tax interests.

*p'i* 疲 fatigue; loss of strength.

疲敝 weakness.

*i* 以符原案 in accordance with the original arrangement.

*chieh* 截 to cut off; exactly (as applied to a limit of time).

*hsü* 虛懸 *lit.*, to suspend in the empty space; "to pay over the left shoulder." [p. 267]

*ch'ê* 撤退 to resign, to withdraw (as from an office).

*ch'ieh* 接辦 to take over charge of an office; to take in hand the management of.

*hui* 彙解 to forward collectively; to collect and remit.

*jên* 認餉接辦 to bind oneself in remitting a certain sum out of taxes collected; to take over the collection of a tax, on the farming system; to guarantee the revenue.

*shang* 商販 traders.

*chün* 軍民 military people; the soldiery.

*ch'ih* 遲疑 to delay and doubt; to raise obstructive doubts.

*kuan* 觀望 to look on; remiss; negligent.

*ssŭ* 司巡人等 managing and executive officers.

*liu* 留難 to delay and obstruct; obstruction.

*hsü* 許 to allow; it is allowed to.

*chih* 指明 to point out, or to report, a person (as an offender).

*ping* 禀控 to accuse.

*niu* 扭解 to arrest.

*chüeh* 決不姑寬 on no account will leniency be shown.

*ku* 姑 to tolerate; lenient.

姑寬 to show indulgence.

### Document No. 135.

*ching* 逕 to pass by; directly.

逕啓者 I beg to inform you (an opening phrase in letters).

*ch'êng* 承函 to receive, or to have received, a letter.

*hui* 惠臨 to kindly descend; to honour with a visit.

*pi* 敝 mean; poor; hence, as a term of modesty, "my."

敝公館 my residence; my house.

*kung* 公館 the residence of an official or a literary man.

*kuan* 館 an inn; a lodge.

*ling* 聆 to hear; to listen; to obey.

聆教 to listen to one's teaching; "I shall be glad to listen to your conversation" (said in accepting the announcement of a visit).

*k'uai* 快 glad; cheerful; quick.

快慰 pleased; glad.

*sao* 掃門 to sweep before the door; *i.e.*, to keep one's house ready to receive a visitor.

*hou* 候駕 I await you.

*chia* 駕 a chariot; he who sits in a chariot; hence, as a term of respect, "you."

*lê* 泐 to write.

泐此奉覆 I write this in reply.

*shun* 順請 "with kind wishes" (a concluding phrase in letters).

*hsün* 勛 (or 勳) merit; patriotic distinction.

勛安 [I wish you] merit and peace (a concluding phrase in letters).

### Document No. 136. [p. 268]

*t'i* 提督 a general-in-chief or admiral-in-chief (*see* MAYERS' "The Chinese Government," No. 440).

*tao* 道台 a Taot'ai.

*t'ung* 同此 the same as this; to the same effect.

*shên* 紳商 the gentry and merchants; the community.

*sai* 賽馬之期 a race meeting.

*ch'êng* 承囑 to receive instructions to; to be commissioned with.

*kung* 恭請 to respectfully request or invite.

*ming* 命駕 to order one's carriage; to get ready for a visit.

*kuang* 光臨 to honour one with a visit.

*chieh* 藉邀 to avail oneself of an invitation.

*shang* 賞 to rejoice; to take pleasure in.

賞鑒 to enjoy a view or a spectacle.

*chien* 鑒 to survey; to view.

*ho* 曷勝 (= 不勝) how could it equal? *i.e.*, not equal to; inexpressibly; highly.

曷勝欣躍 I shall be extremely delighted.

*hsin* 欣 delighted; happy.

欣躍 to be delighted.

*su* 肅泐 to write respectfully; I respectfully inform you [of the above] (a concluding phrase in letters).

*shêng* 升安 [I wish you] promotion and peace (a concluding phrase in letters).

### Document No. 137.

*ching* 敬覆者 a respectful reply; I beg to reply.

*to* 朶 a head of flowers; flowery; as a term of respect, "your."

朶翰 your flowery epistle; your note.

*han* 翰 a quill; a pencil; something written; a letter.

*i* 以 that; to the effect that.

*ju* 辱 to disgrace.

辱承 *lit.*, I have disgraced you in receiving, *i.e.*, you have honoured me without my deserving.

辱承見召 I have been honoured by you with an invitation.

*chien* 見召 to be called; to be invited.

*pên* 本當 properly speaking, I ought to.

*ju* 如約 as by Treaty bound; as agreed to.

*lien* 練 to practise; to drill.

練軍 to drill troops.

*chi* 稽查弁兵勇丁數目 to muster officers and privates; a general muster.

*yüeh* 閱核 to inspect. [p. 269]

*ch'ien* 錢糧 money and grain; rations.

*chang* 帳務 accounts business.

*tu* 督率 to superintend; to direct.

*ch'ou* 抽身 to take oneself off; to stay away.

*fu* 赴命 to obey a call; to follow an invitation.

*chieh* 藉聆 to avail oneself of listening to; to listen to (as to the conversation of one's host).

*ta* 大教 the great instruction (politely for "your instructive conversation").

*pao* 抱 to grasp; to feel; to have in the heart.

抱歉 to feel uncomfortable about a matter; to feel regret.

抱歉之處希爲原恕爲禱 I pray that you will regard my regret as a proof of my original good intention.

*yüan* 原恕 originally sympathising.

*shu* 恕 benevolent; loyal.

*su* 肅復 to respectfully reply.

*shên* 伸謝 to present one's thanks.

*ching* 敬請台安 with respectful kind inquiries (a concluding phrase in letters).

*wei* 惟照 direct your thoughts to this note (a concluding phrase in letters).

*pu* 不一 not a few; many; many times; also, a very common concluding phrase in letters, which, like the corresponding phrases 不宣, 不備, 不盡, and others, are mere expletives, but serve to show that a letter is finished.

**Document No. 138.**

*hsiang* 相邀 to invite.

*ch'ü* 趨 to run; to follow quickly; to hasten.

趨赴 to hasten to; to readily follow an invitation.

*i* 以資覽觀 in order to avail myself of the spectacle.

*lan* 覽觀 to take a view; to witness a spectacle.

*pu* 不克 not able to.

*fên* 分身 to absent oneself; to stay away.

*shêng* 盛情 kind feelings; kindness.

*hsin* 心領 to be indebted for; *lit.*, received and kept by one's heart.

*tao* 道 to speak; to say.

道謝 to express one's thanks.

*shih* 是荷 I shall thank you for; to be obliged.

*chuan* 專此布覆 I specially inform you of this in reply.

**Document No. 139.** [p. 270]

*t'ai* 台函 your letter.

*tê* 得悉 to be informed of; to note the contents of (as of a note).

*ta* 大會 a general meeting.

*chi* 極欲 to desire very much.

*kuan* 觀光 to view the glory; politely for "to meet you" (as in accepting an invitation).

*kung* 公冗 public business; official duties.

*jung* 冗 affairs; duties.

*wei* 未獲 cannot; cannot manage to.

*fang* 放手 to release one's hands, *i.e.*, to stay one's hand; to leave off work.

*kao* 告罪 to apologise.

*shih* 是幸 I shall be pleased if you will; I will thank you to.

**Document No. 140.**

*tz'ŭ* 此八月十九日 on this, the 19th day of the 8th moon.

*chieh* 屆滿 to complete (as a term).

屆期 on the day fixed; punctually.

*hsün* 迅 quickly; promptly.

*kan* 趕 to hasten; to hurry.

*han* 函達 to inform by letter.

*ta* 達 to inform.

*i* 一屆……卽……as soon as……, then.

*shih* 是所至禱 this is what I very much pray for; I would urgently ask for this.

**Document No. 141.** [p. 271]

*t'ai* 台示 your instructions; your letter.

*tso* 昨夜 last night.

*kuan* 關哨 a Customs officer; tidewaiters; watchers.

*i* 醫院 a hospital.

*ch'u* 出水 to come out of the water; to be landed from the sea, or to be exported across the sea.

*ch'uan* 船戶 a ship's employé; a boatman.

*ming* 明知 to clearly know; to be clearly known to……

*ti* 第 but; however; merely.

*chung* 重以 to consider of importance the fact that; considering the fact that.

*chih* 執意 to stick to one's view.

*li* 勵覆 to reply.

*pu* 布達 to inform.

*chiao* 教士 a teacher; a teacher of religion; a missionary.

*tsai* 儎 to stow cargo.

儎赴 to send by boat to.

*chieh* 藉圖 to make use of an opportunity for illegal plots; to seize an occasion for plotting.

*pi* 弊混 irregularities; smuggling.

*shih* 是爲至荷 I shall be much obliged thereby.

### Document No. 142.

*chu* 住宿 to stop; to lodge.

*chieh* 借用 to borrow for use.

*ying* 營哨 a patrol; a division of a battalion (*see* MAYERS' "The Chinese Government," No. 439).

*pu* 佈覆 to reply.

*shui* 水提台(＝水師提督) an admiral. [p. 272]

*piao* 標 a brigade; a naval division; a squadron.

*shih* 師船 a naval boat.

*fên* 分派 to detail.

*hsün* 巡防 to cruise and guard; to cruise about.

*chih* 職守 official guard; to be on duty (as a guard).

*ch'ou* 抽派 to send on special duty; to take out of one's routine for special duty.

*hsiao* 小哨 guard-boats.

*ti* 底 a bottom (as of a boat).

*kai* 蓋 a cover (as the cover of a boat).

*ch'ih* 馳 speedily; promptly.

*tu* 渡船 a ferry-boat; a passage-boat.

*lun* 輪派 to send on duty in rotation.

*ta* 大才 the great talent; a polite phrase for "you."

*ts'ai* 裁酌 to decide.

*chuan* 專此奉布 I specially inform you of this.

### Document No. 143.

*sung* 誦 to read in a murmuring tone (as prayers); to read (as a letter).

*hua* 華翰 your flowery epistle; your note.

*ta* 大移 your communication; your letter.

*hui* 會銜 conjointly (said of two officials issuing a joint proclamation).

*wang* 枉 to force; *e.g.*, 枉駕, to force oneself (as to pay a visit to an inferior).

枉顧 to honour one with a visit.

*ku* 顧 to attend to; to be a customer; to visit.

*p'êng* 烹 to boil (as tea).

烹茗 to prepare good tea; to prepare for receiving a visitor.

*ming* 茗 the tender leaves of tea; superior tea.

*chih* 祗候 to respectfully await.